Insights into IFRS

KPMG's practical guide to IFRS Standards

15th Edition 2018/19

Volume 1

The KPMG International Standards Group

SWEET & MAXWELL

THOMSON REUTERS

ISBN 978-0-414-06957-2

Printed and bound by L.E.G.O. S.p.A., Lavis (TN), Italy

EMBEDDING AND EXPLAINING THE CHANGES

After many years of deliberation and preparation, the new standards on revenue recognition and financial instruments are finally effective! Companies across the globe have worked hard to implement their requirements – now it's time to fully embed the changes and clearly explain their effects to investors and other stakeholders.

Under the new revenue standard, IFRS 15, companies will find that the analysis that needs to be performed and the disclosures required are very different – even if the numbers in their financial statements don't change significantly as a consequence of implementing the new requirements.

As for the new financial instruments standard, IFRS 9… The impairment requirements for banks may steal the limelight, but for corporates more broadly it brings opportunities for more effective hedge accounting, which could produce a more stable earnings environment – no small prize.

As you apply these new standards in your 2018 annual financial statements, I would encourage you to embrace the opportunity to think through how best to explain the changes. Remember that the quality and clarity of explanations of changes in accounting policies and their impacts are key. And that investors will be keenly interested in disclosures of key judgements and estimates.

At the same time, keep an eye on IFRS 16. The new leasing standard will be effective before we know it. And although many companies are well advanced with their preparations, no one can afford to become complacent.

And finally, let's not forget insurers, who face a major task in preparing for IFRS 17. For many, this will involve an overhaul of their business processes, with many taking advantage of the opportunity to streamline and achieve efficiencies.

With so many moving parts, *Insights into IFRS* provides in-depth guidance across the complete set of standards, including detailed information on existing standards as well as analysis of the new ones. Whether you read it in hard copy or e-book – or both – I hope it will prove a valuable companion as you embed and explain the changes.

Reinhard Dotzlaw, Global IFRS Leader
KPMG International Standards Group

OVERVIEW OF CONTENTS

ABOUT THIS PUBLICATION

Insights into IFRS, now in its 15th edition, emphasises the application of IFRS in practice and explains the conclusions that we have reached on many interpretative issues. Based on actual questions that have arisen in practice around the world, *Insights into IFRS* includes many illustrative examples to elaborate or clarify the practical application of IFRS.

Insights into IFRS is an interpretative guide to IFRS that builds on those standards and should be read alongside them.

ORGANISATION OF THE TEXT

This publication is organised into topics and is presented in two volumes.

Volume 1 includes separate sections dealing with:
- general issues such as business combinations and fair value measurement;
- specific items in the statement of financial position and statement of profit or loss and OCI;
- special topics such as leases; and
- issues relevant to those making the transition to IFRS.

Volume 2 includes separate sections dealing with:
- financial instruments;
- insurance contracts; and
- fair value measurement (the guidance included in Volume 1 is reproduced in Volume 2).

Both volumes include the following Appendices.
- Appendix I: List of standards and interpretations that comprise the currently effective requirements and the forthcoming requirements.
- Appendix II: Table of concordance showing how the guidance that was included in the 14th edition has moved.
- Appendix III: List of examples.

Paragraphs dealing with **separate financial statements** are indicated by an Ⓢ in the outer margin.

STANDARDS AND INTERPRETATIONS

This 15th edition of *Insights into IFRS* reflects IFRS in issue at 1 August 2018. The guidance differentiates between **currently effective requirements, forthcoming requirements** and **possible future developments**.

Currently effective requirements

The main text is based on those standards that are required to be applied by an entity with an annual reporting period beginning on 1 January 2018 – i.e. an entity with an annual reporting date of 31 December 2018. These requirements are referred to as the **currently effective requirements**.

IFRS 15 *Revenue from Contracts with Customers* has come into force, so this edition of *Insights into IFRS* no longer contains the guidance on the superseded standards; chapter 4.2 now focuses on the newly effective requirements of IFRS 15.

This edition also contains detailed guidance on both the newly effective and predecessor financial instruments standards.
- *Section 7:* Provides guidance on IFRS 9 *Financial Instruments*, issued in 2014 and amended in 2017, and the related standards, including consequential amendments introduced by IFRS 9.
- *Section 7I:* Provides guidance on the predecessor standard – IAS 39 *Financial Instruments: Recognition and Measurement* – and the related standards, excluding any amendments introduced by IFRS 9.

An introduction to Sections 7 and 7I explains when an entity can continue to apply some or all of the requirements in the predecessor standard.

This publication does not consider the requirements of IAS 26 *Accounting and Reporting by Retirement Benefit Plans*. In addition, this publication does not address the requirements included in the *IFRS for Small and Medium-sized Entities* (IFRS for SMEs), which was published in July 2009, other than in a brief overview of the IFRS for SMEs in chapter 1.1.

Forthcoming requirements

A currently effective requirement may be subject to change by a new requirement that has been issued at 1 August 2018, but is not yet effective for an annual reporting period ending on 31 December 2018. These new requirements are referred to as **forthcoming requirements**.

In addition, the following chapters relate entirely to forthcoming requirements.

5.1A	IFRS 16 *Leases*
8.1A	IFRS 17 *Insurance Contracts*

Future developments

For some topics, we anticipate changes to IFRS in issue at 1 August 2018 – typically as a result of an IASB project. These changes are referred to as **future developments**.

REFERENCES

Currently effective requirements	Our discussion of the current requirements of IFRS and our related interpretations are referenced to the 2018 *IFRS Standards required 1 January 2018* ('Blue Book').
	References in square brackets after the text identify the relevant paragraphs of the standards or other literature – e.g. *IFRS 1.7* is paragraph 7 of IFRS 1; *IFRIC 12.IE27–IE28* is paragraphs 27 to 28 of the IFRIC 12 illustrative examples; and *IFRS 13.EM.02-13.13* is paragraph 13 of the educational material on fair value measurement (IFRS 13) issued in February 2013.
	Currently effective requirements also refer to the IFRS Practice Statements – e.g. *IPS 2.70* is paragraph 70 of *IFRS Practice Statement 2: Making Materiality Judgements*.
Forthcoming requirements	The forthcoming requirements are referenced to the 2018 *IFRS Standards issued at 1 January 2018* ('Red Book'), except for *Plan Amendment, Curtailment or Settlement – Amendments to IAS 19* that were issued after the Red Book 2018 was published.
IFRS Interpretations Committee decisions and IASB tentative decisions	References to IFRS Interpretations Committee decisions and IASB tentative decisions, addressed in their publications *IFRIC Update* and *IASB Update*, respectively, are also referenced – e.g. *IU 03-11* is *IFRIC Update* March 2011; and *IASBU 05-09* is *IASB Update* May 2009.

E-BOOK EDITION

Insights into IFRS is also now available as an e-book on ProView™. It makes your most complex searches efficient, lets you make notes, highlight text, bookmark text, share content (via email or PDF) and review your browsing history. But perhaps best of all is that your annotations will be automatically transferred to subsequent editions of *Insights*.

For more information on accessing your personal e-book, speak to your usual KPMG contact.

KEEPING IN TOUCH

For the latest on IFRS, visit kpmg.com/ifrs. To join the conversation, follow KPMG IFRS on LinkedIn.

Whether you are new to IFRS or a current user, you can find digestible summaries of recent developments, detailed guidance on complex requirements, and practical tools such as illustrative disclosures and checklists.

IFRS news	The latest need-to-know information on IFRS
IFRS toolkit	Insights into IFRS Guides to financial statements: • Illustrative IFRS disclosures • Disclosure checklist Newly effective standards Fair value measurement: Questions and Answers IFRS compared to US GAAP Combined and/or carve-out financial statements
Major new standards	Financial instruments Revenue from contracts with customers Leases Insurance contracts
Amendments to existing standards	Business combinations and consolidation Presentation and disclosure
Sectors	IFRS for banks IFRS 15: Are you good to go? • Aerospace and defence • Airlines • Automotive suppliers • Banks • Construction • Food, drink and consumer goods • Insurers • Investment management • Media • Pharma • Real estate • Retail • Technology IFRS 16 for: • Consumer markets and retail • Oil and gas • Telcos

For access to an extensive range of accounting, auditing and financial reporting guidance and literature, visit KPMG's Accounting Research Online. This web-based subscription service can be a valuable tool for anyone who wants to stay informed in today's dynamic environment. For a free 30-day trial, go to aro.kpmg.com and register today.

ABBREVIATIONS

The following abbreviations are used often within this publication.

CDO	Collateralised debt obligation
CDS	Credit default swap
CEO	Chief Executive Officer
CGU	Cash-generating unit
CODM	Chief operating decision maker
COO	Chief Operating Officer
CPI	Consumer price index
DPF	Discretionary participation feature
E&E	Exploration and evaluation
EBIT	Earnings before interest and taxes
EBITDA	Earnings before interest, taxes, depreciation and amortisation
EPS	Earnings per share
ESPP	Employee share purchase plan
EU	European Union
FASB	US Financial Accounting Standards Board
FIFO	First-in, first-out
GAAP	Generally accepted accounting principles/practices
IAS	International Accounting Standards
IASB	International Accounting Standards Board
IFRS	International Financial Reporting Standards
IPO	Initial public offering
IT	Information technology
LIBOR	London interbank offered rate
LIFO	Last-in, first-out
NCI	Non-controlling interests
Newco	New entity
NRV	Net realisable value
OCI	Other comprehensive income
R&D	Research and development
REACH	Regulation for the *Registration, Evaluation and Authorisation of CHemicals* in the European Union
SIC	Standing Interpretations Committee
SPPI	Solely payments of principal and interest
WACC	Weighted-average cost of capital

ACKNOWLEDGEMENTS

This publication was made possible by the invaluable input of many people working in KPMG member firms worldwide. The overview of the requirements of IFRS and the interpretative positions described reflect the work of both current and former members of the KPMG International Standards Group, for which the authors and editors are grateful.

Current members of the International Standards Group and a panel of reviewers from KPMG member firms around the world generously contributed their time for exhaustive and challenging reviews of this edition. A list of contributors to this edition who we would like to thank is included below.

KPMG MEMBER FIRMS' CONTRIBUTORS
Principal editors

Suzanne Arnold	United Kingdom
Stacy Brown	United Kingdom
Irina Ipatova	United Kingdom

Authors and principal contributors

Angie Ah Kun	South Africa
Kimber Bascom	United States
Ewa Bialkowska	United Kingdom
Jim Calvert	Ireland
Peter Carlson	Australia
Albert Chai	Hong Kong
Jessica Cheong	Hong Kong
Matthew Cook	United Kingdom
Gina Desai	United Kingdom
Bryce Ehrhardt	United States
Otilia Gheaus	Romania
Alan Goad	United States
Audrey Hamm	Switzerland
Hakob Harutyunyan	Canada
Kim Heng	Australia
Martijn Huiskers	The Netherlands
Irina Ipatova	United Kingdom
Ramon Jubels	Brazil
Prabhakar Kalavacherla	United States

Manish Kaushik	India
Gabriela Kegalj	Canada
Hagit Keren	United Kingdom
Sarah Kindzerske	United States
Joachim Kölschbach	Germany
Kirill Kulakov	Russia
Julia LaPointe	United States
Wolfgang Laubach	Germany
Jee Won Lee	Korea (Republic of)
Sylvie Leger	Canada
David Littleford	United Kingdom
Colin Martin	United Kingdom
Hirotaka Matsuo	Japan
Mike Metcalf	United Kingdom
Mark Northan	United States
Brian O'Donovan	United Kingdom
Andrea Schriber	United Kingdom
Anne Schurbohm	Germany
Agnieszka Sekita	United Kingdom
Marina Shu	Australia
Chris Spall	United Kingdom
Shunya Uchida	Japan
Anisa Vallee	South Africa
Fred Versteeg	The Netherlands
Ido Vexelbaum	United Kingdom
Avi Victor	Romania
Nicolas Vigneron	France
Anthony Voigt	United Kingdom
Guy Zmora	Israel

PANEL OF REVIEWERS

IFRS Panel

Archana Bhutani	India
Reinhard Dotzlaw (Global IFRS Leader)	Canada
Ramon Jubels	Brazil
Prabhakar Kalavacherla	United States
Dick Korf	The Netherlands
Michael Sten Larsen	Denmark
Wolfgang Laubach	Germany
Andrew Marshall	United Kingdom
Reyaz Mihular	Sri Lanka
Catherine Morley	Hong Kong
Brad Owen	Canada

xiv

Emmanuel Paret	France
Tara Smith	South Africa
Patricia Stebbens	Australia
Hirotaka Tanaka	Japan

Business Combinations and Consolidation Topic Team

Mahesh Balasubramanian	Bahrain
Nicholas Beggs	Czech Republic
Hanne Böckem	Germany
Peter Carlson (Deputy leader)	Australia
Heather de Jongh	South Africa
Ralph Menschel	Mexico
Mike Metcalf (Leader)	United Kingdom
Paul Munter	United States
Emmanuel Paret	France
Andrea Schriber	United Kingdom
Marilyn Stitt	Canada
Hirotaka Tanaka	Japan
Jim Tang	Hong Kong
Michael Voogt	Australia

Employee Benefits Topic Team

Kees Bergwerff	The Netherlands
Zola Beseti	South Africa
Rodrigo Corominas	Mexico
Regina Croucher	United States
Barbara Griessner	United Kingdom
Kim Heng (Leader)	Australia
Sarah Inglis	Australia
Gale Kelly	Canada
Ko Sin	China
Michael Sten Larsen	Denmark
Takanobu Miwa	Japan
Balasubramanian Sundaresan	India
Anthony Voigt	United Kingdom

Financial Instruments Topic Team

Aram Asatryan	Russia
Ewa Bialkowska	United Kingdom
Jean-François Dandé	France
Simon Fishley	Brazil
Erik Hoogcarspel	The Netherlands
Gale Kelly	Canada
Colin Martin (Deputy leader)	United Kingdom

Mark Northan (Deputy leader)	United States
Toshihiro Ozawa	Japan
Tara Smith	South Africa
Chris Spall (Leader)	United Kingdom
Patricia Stebbens	Australia
Venkataramanan Vishwanath	India
Danny Vitan	Israel
Andreas Wolsiffer	Germany
Ella Zhang	China

Income Taxes Topic Team

Syed Anjum	Pakistan
Yen San Chan	Singapore
Kayreen Handley	United States
Yuki Hayashi	Japan
Irina Ipatova	United Kingdom
Tomasz Książek	Poland
Benoit Lebrun	France
Jesus Luna	Mexico
Agnes Lutukai	Nigeria
Zuzana Paulech	Australia
Cheryl Robinson	Canada
Anne Schurbohm	Germany
Fred Versteeg (Leader)	The Netherlands

Insurance Contracts Topic Team

Jennifer Austin	United States
Erik Bleekrode	Hong Kong
Dana Chaput	Canada
Danny Clark	United Kingdom
Paolo Colciago	Italy
Frank Dubois	Singapore
Bhavesh Gandhi	Kuwait
Alan Goad (Deputy leader)	United States
Hagit Keren	United Kingdom
Joachim Kölschbach (Leader)	Germany
Viviane Leflaive	France
Csilla Leposa	Hungary
Ian Moyser	Australia
Esther Pieterse	South Africa
Chris Spall	United Kingdom
Danielle Torres	Brazil
Mary Trussell (Deputy leader)	Germany

Leases Topic Team

Kimber Bascom (Leader)	United States
Zola Beseti	South Africa
Archana Bhutani	India
Judit Boros	Hungary
Úna Curtis	Ireland
Karine Dupré	France
Ramon Jubels	Brazil
Wolfgang Laubach	Germany
Sylvie Leger	Canada
Andrew Marshall	United Kingdom
Brian O'Donovan (Deputy leader)	United Kingdom
Yen San Chan	Singapore
Julie Santoro	United States
Patricia Stebbens	Australia
Mag Stewart	Canada
Beth Zhang	China

Presentation Topic Team

Holger Erchinger	United States
Yoshiaki Hasegawa	Japan
Se Bong Hur	Korea (Republic of)
Gabriela Kegalj (Deputy leader)	Canada
Wietse Koster	The Netherlands
David Littleford (Leader)	United Kingdom
Esther Pieterse	South Africa
Luis Preciado	Mexico
Ruchi Rastogi	India
Edith Schwager	France
Agnieszka Sekita	United Kingdom
Sanel Tomlinson	Hong Kong

Revenue Recognition and Provisions Topic Team

Brian Allen	United States
Eric Damotte	Spain
Lise du Randt	South Africa
Yusuf Hassan	United Arab Emirates
Kim Heng	Australia
Ramon Jubels	Brazil
Prabhakar Kalavacherla (Leader)	United States
Reinhard Klemmer	Singapore
David Littleford	United Kingdom
Vijay Mathur	India

Thanks to Camila Benedetti and Christopher Czarnecki from Babson College (United States) for their assistance.

1.   BACKGROUND

1.1   Introduction

1. BACKGROUND

1.1 Introduction

CURRENTLY EFFECTIVE REQUIREMENTS

This publication reflects IFRS in issue at 1 August 2018, and the currently effective requirements cover annual periods beginning on 1 January 2018.

The requirements related to this topic are mainly derived from the following.

STANDARD/ REFERENCE	TITLE
Constitution	IFRS Foundation Constitution
Due Process Handbook	IASB and IFRS Interpretations Committee Due Process Handbook
Preface	Preface to International Financial Reporting Standards
IAS 1	Presentation of Financial Statements

FORTHCOMING REQUIREMENTS

For this topic, there are no forthcoming requirements.

FUTURE DEVELOPMENTS

The currently effective requirements that may be affected by future developments are highlighted with a * and are briefly discussed in 1.1.220.

1.1.10   **IFRS FOUNDATION**

1.1.10.10   The objectives of the IFRS Foundation), as stated in its constitution, are to:

- develop, in the public interest, a single set of high-quality, understandable, enforceable and glob-ally accepted financial reporting standards based on clearly articulated principles. These standards require high quality, transparent and comparable information in financial statements and other financial reporting to help investors, other participants in the world's capital markets and other users of financial information to make economic decisions;
- promote the use and rigorous application of those standards;
- consider the needs of a range of sizes and types of entities operating in diverse economic set-tings; and
- promote and facilitate the adoption of IFRS by convergence of national accounting standards with IFRS. [*Constitution 2*]

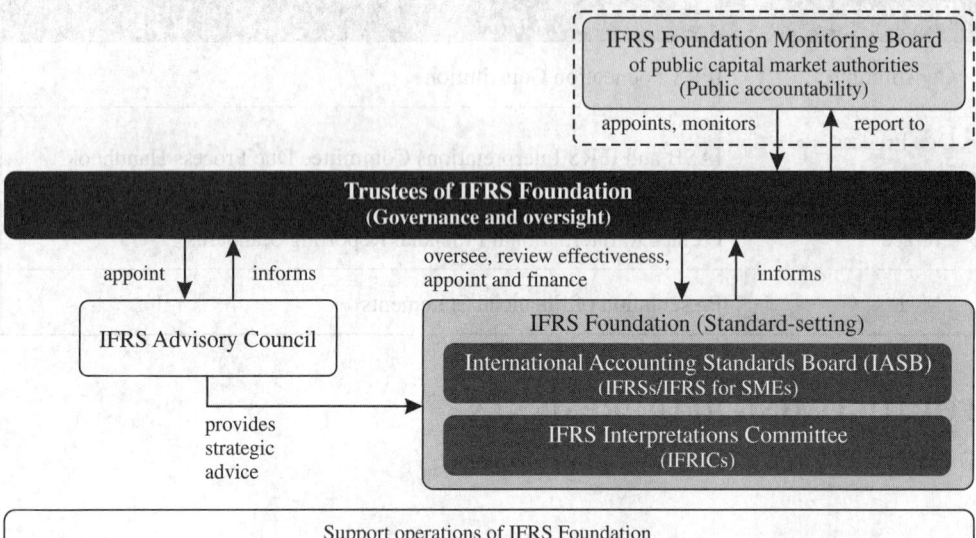

1.1.10.20   The Trustees of the IFRS Foundation (Trustees) are responsible for the governance of the IFRS Foundation. The Trustees are required to act in the public interest in all matters. The 22 Trustees comprise:

- six Trustees appointed from the Asia/Oceania region;
- six Trustees appointed from Europe;
- six Trustees appointed from the Americas;
- one Trustee appointed from Africa; and
- three Trustees appointed from any area, subject to maintaining the overall geographic balance. [*Constitution 3–4, 6*]

1.1.10.30   The responsibilities of the Trustees, among others, include:

- appointing the members of the IASB (see 1.1.30), the IFRS Interpretations Committee (see 1.1.60) and the IFRS Advisory Council (see 1.1.70);

- funding the IFRS Foundation and the IASB;
- approving the budget of the IFRS Foundation;
- reviewing compliance with the operating procedures, consultative arrangements and due process;
- approving amendments to the IFRS Foundation Constitution after a due process, including consultation with the IFRS Advisory Council and publication of an exposure draft for public comment; and
- fostering and reviewing the development of educational programmes and materials that are consistent with the IFRS Foundation's objectives. [*Constitution 15*]

1.1.10.40   The Trustees' Due Process Oversight Committee (DPOC) is responsible for overseeing the due process procedures of the IASB and the IFRS Interpretations Committee. The DPOC meets regularly with the IASB, the IFRS Interpretations Committee and the IFRS Foundation staff. [*Due Process Handbook 2.2, 2.9*]

1.1.20   MONITORING BOARD

1.1.20.10   The Monitoring Board, comprising capital market authorities with responsibility for setting reporting requirements for listed entities, is a formal link between the Trustees and public authorities. The objective of the Monitoring Board is to enhance the public accountability of the IFRS Foundation, while at the same time maintaining the operational independence of the IFRS Foundation and the IASB. [*Constitution 18*]

1.1.20.20   The Monitoring Board is responsible for overseeing the Trustees' fulfilment of their constitutional duties. Specific responsibilities of the Monitoring Board include:
- participating in the nomination process for Trustees of the IFRS Foundation and approving the appointment of Trustees; and
- meeting with the Trustees, or a subgroup of the Trustees, at least once annually. [*Constitution 19*]

1.1.20.30   The membership of the Monitoring Board is institutional and comprises representatives of the:
- European Commission;
- Growth and Emerging Markets Committee of the International Organization of Securities Commissions (IOSCO);
- Board of the IOSCO;
- Japanese Financial Services Agency;
- US Securities and Exchange Commission;
- Brazilian Securities and Exchange Commission;
- Korean Financial Services Commission;
- Ministry of Finance of the People's Republic of China; and
- as an observer, the Basel Committee on Banking Supervision. [*Constitution 21*]

1.1.20.40   The Monitoring Board reconsiders its composition from time to time relative to its objectives. From 2013, membership of the Monitoring Board requires the domestic use of IFRS in the relevant jurisdiction and a financial contribution by the jurisdiction to the setting of IFRS. At the same time, membership was expanded to include a maximum of four additional permanent members chosen from major emerging markets. Also, two rotating seats for members from all other markets will be created and filled following a selection process to be initiated by the Monitoring Board in consultation with IOSCO. [*Constitution 22*]

1.1.30   INTERNATIONAL ACCOUNTING STANDARDS BOARD

1.1.40   Formation

1.1.40.10   The IASB started operations in April 2001 as the successor to the International Accounting Standards Committee (IASC). The IASB is the standard-setting body of the IFRS Foundation.

1.1.50   Composition

1.1.50.10   The IASB normally has 14 members comprising professionals from a range of functional backgrounds, up to three of whom can be part-time. The geographic composition guidelines for IASB membership are:

- four members from Europe;
- four members from the Americas;
- four members from the Asia/Oceania region;
- one member from Africa; and
- one member from any area, subject to maintaining the overall geographic balance. [*Constitution 24, 26*]

1.1.50.20   Members who were appointed before 2 July 2009 were appointed for a term of five years, which is renewable once for an additional five years. Members who were appointed after 2 July 2009 were appointed for a term of five years, which may be renewable for an additional three years, with the possibility of renewal up to a maximum of five years, in line with procedures developed by the Trustees for such renewals. The terms may not exceed 10 years in total length of service as a member of the Board. [*Constitution 30*]

1.1.60   IFRS INTERPRETATIONS COMMITTEE

1.1.60.10   The IFRS Interpretations Committee (formerly the International Financial Reporting Interpretations Committee or IFRIC), was reconstituted in December 2001 as the successor to the Standing Interpretations Committee (SIC) and comprises 14 voting members, appointed for a renewable period of three years. The Committee comprises a group of people representing a combination of technical expertise and diversity of international business and market experience in the practical application of IFRS. [*Constitution 38–42*]

1.1.60.20   The Committee interprets the application of IFRS and provides guidance on financial reporting issues not specifically addressed in IFRS. It also undertakes other tasks at the request of the IASB (see 1.1.120–150). [*Constitution 42*]

1.1.70   IFRS ADVISORY COUNCIL

1.1.70.10   The IFRS Advisory Council (formerly the Standards Advisory Council) advises the IASB on agenda priorities and current projects. The Council has 30 or more members, with a diversity of geographic and professional backgrounds, appointed for a renewable term of three years. It meets at least twice a year. [*Constitution 43–45*]

1.1.80   **OTHER ADVISORY GROUPS**

1.1.80.10   The IASB has a number of other advisory committees and bodies that it works with in order to obtain input from parties representing a wide range of backgrounds and geographic regions.

GROUP	BODY
Advisory bodies	Accounting Standards Advisory Forum (national accounting standard setters and regional bodies associated with accounting standard setting)
	IFRS Advisory Council
Standing consultative groups	Capital Markets Advisory Committee (users of financial statements)
	Emerging Economies Group
	Global Preparers Forum
	Islamic Finance Consultative Group
	IFRS Taxonomy Consultative Group
	SME Implementation Group
	World Standard-setters conferences
Transition resource groups (TRGs)	Impairment of Financial Instruments (see section 7)
	IFRS 17 *Insurance Contracts* (see chapter 8.1A)
	Revenue Recognition (see chapter 4.2)
Project consultative groups	Consultative Group for Rate Regulation
	Management Commentary Consultative Group

1.1.90   **IFRS STANDARDS**

1.1.100   **Definition**

1.1.100.10   'IFRS Standards' is the term used to indicate the whole body of IASB authoritative literature, and includes:
- IFRS issued by the IASB;
- International Accounting Standards (IAS) issued by the IASC, or revisions thereof issued by the IASB;
- Interpretations of IFRS and IAS developed by the IFRS Interpretations Committee and approved for issue by the IASB; and
- Interpretations of IAS developed by the SIC and approved for issue by the IASB or IASC. [*IAS 1.7, Preface 5*]

1.1.100.20   IFRS is designed for use by profit-oriented entities. The International Public Sector Accounting Standards issued by the International Public Sector Accounting Standards Board are developed for use by public sector entities. Notwithstanding this, entities engaged in not-for-profit activities may find IFRS useful, and may follow it if doing so is considered appropriate. [*Preface 9*]

1.1.100.30   IFRS is not limited to a particular legal framework. Therefore, financial statements prepared under IFRS often contain supplementary information required by local statute or listing requirements.

1.1.100.40   IFRS comprises a series of bold-type and plain-type paragraphs. Generally, the bold-type paragraphs outline the main principle and the plain-type paragraphs provide further explanation. Bold and plain-type paragraphs have equal authority. [*Preface 13*]

1.1.100.50   Many IFRSs contain appendices. A statement at the top of each appendix clarifies its status. If an appendix is illustrative only and not an integral part of the standard, then it does not have the same status as the standard itself. However, in our view the guidance in an appendix should generally be followed unless it conflicts with the requirements of an IFRS, or when such guidance merely represents an illustrative example and it is clear that a standard or requirement can be complied with in different ways. For example, Appendix A of IAS 7 presents interest paid as part of operating activities, whereas the standard itself states that interest paid may be classified as part of either operating or financing activities (see 2.3.50.20).

1.1.110   New standards and amendments

1.1.110.10   An IASB project usually goes through two phases described in the diagram below:
- research; and
- standard development.

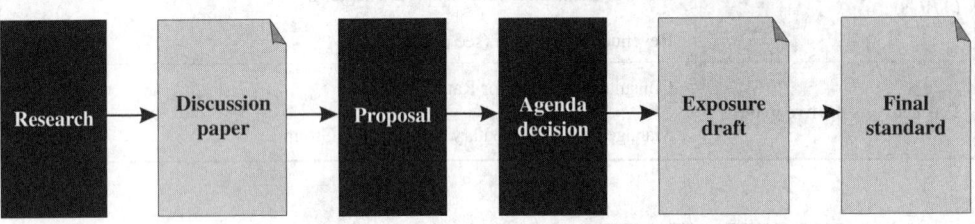

1.1.110.20   The research focuses on defining more clearly the problems that a new project is seeking to resolve and on understanding the root causes for any issues identified. The results of the research phase are published in a discussion paper, which is open for public comment for at least 120 days. During the research phase, the IASB can also issue research papers prepared by the IASB staff or other standard setters, and requests for information to seek views from constituents. [*Due Process Handbook 4.6–4.19, 5.5*]

1.1.110.30   The decision to take a project to the standard-development phase is made only after considering the results of the research phase. Therefore, not every research project will lead to a standard-level project. To make this decision, the IASB considers the following criteria:
- whether there is a deficiency that needs to be resolved;
- the importance of the issue to users;
- entities to be affected; and
- how pervasive the issue is for entities. [*Due Process Handbook 5.1–5.4*]

1.1.110.40   Minor or narrow-scope amendments to standards do not require a research phase before being added to the standard-development agenda. [*Due Process Handbook 5.8*]

1.1.110.50   Once a project has reached the standard-development phase, the IASB issues for public comment an exposure draft, which sets out a specific proposal in the form of a proposed IFRS (or amendment to an IFRS). The IASB normally allows a minimum period of 120 days for comment on an exposure draft, although a shorter period of no less than 30 days may be set for some narrow and urgent matters with approval of the Trustees' Due Process Oversight Committee. [*Due Process Handbook 6.1–6.7*]

1.1.110.60   The IASB analyses responses, including input from outreach and/or roundtables, and redeliberates its proposals. Final standards (amendments) are accompanied by a project summary and a feedback statement. Issuing an exposure draft or final standard (amendment) requires a positive vote by 9 out of 14 IASB members. [*Due Process Handbook 3.14–3.15, 6.19–6.23, 6.38*]

1.1.110.70   The IASB consults with the Trustees and the IFRS Advisory Council in developing and pursuing its technical agenda. In addition, the IASB carries out a public consultation every five years from the date of the most recent agenda consultation. The most recent public agenda consultation was launched in August 2015 and the feedback statement was published in November 2016. [*Constitution 36(d)*]

1.1.120   Implementation and maintenance

1.1.120.10   The IASB and the IFRS Interpretations Committee are responsible for the maintenance of IFRS. If an issue arises in relation to the application of IFRS – e.g. diverging interpretations or practices – then a party with an interest in financial reporting generally refers this issue to the Committee.

1.1.120.20   The Committee addresses issues:
- that are widespread and have a material effect on those affected;
- that indicate divergence in practice;
- that can be resolved efficiently within the confines of existing IFRS and the *Conceptual Framework for Financial Reporting* (Conceptual Framework); and
- that are sufficiently narrow in scope that they can be addressed in an efficient manner, but not so narrow that it is not cost effective. [*Due Process Handbook 5.14, 5.16–5.17*]

1.1.120.30   To address an issue referred to it, the Committee may issue an interpretation or propose to the IASB amending a standard. If the Committee decides not add the issue to its work programme, then it publishes a rejection notice (see 1.1.150). [*Due Process Handbook 5.19, 5.22*]

1.1.130   Interpretations

1.1.130.10   The development of a draft interpretation takes place in public meetings. A draft interpretation is issued if no more than four IFRS Interpretations Committee members and no more than three IASB members object. Draft interpretations are usually exposed for public comment for no less than 90 days. The matter is then redeliberated by the Committee. A final interpretation is issued if no more than four Committee members object and the IASB approves it, subject to the normal IASB voting requirements for an IFRS. The Committee addresses effective dates and transitional requirements of interpretations on an interpretation-by-interpretation basis. [*Due Process Handbook 7*]

1.1.140   **Annual improvements process**

1.1.140.10   Some proposed amendments to standards or interpretations that are sufficiently minor or narrow in scope can be packaged together and exposed in one document even though the amendments are unrelated. Such amendments are called 'annual improvements'. [*Due Process Handbook 6.10*]

1.1.140.20   The IASB involves the IFRS Interpretations Committee in the process for exposing annual improvements. [*Due Process Handbook 5.19*]

1.1.140.30   Amendments made in the annual improvements process typically clarify IFRS or correct a relatively minor unintended consequence – e.g. a conflict in existing standards. Annual improvements are not intended to introduce new principles or make changes to existing ones. [*Due Process Handbook 6.11–6.14*]

1.1.140.40   An exposure draft of proposed improvements is usually published by the IASB for comment in the second half of each year, with a minimum comment period of 90 days. The Board addresses effective dates, early application and transitional requirements on an amendment-by-amendment basis. [*Due Process Handbook 6.15*]

1.1.150   **Rejection notices***

1.1.150.10   If the IFRS Interpretations Committee decides not to add an item to its agenda, then it publishes a tentative rejection notice with a comment period of normally no less than 60 days. Rejection notices are non-authoritative but are generally seen as additional guidance. The IASB does not ratify rejection notices. [*Due Process Handbook 5.22*]

1.1.160   **Post-implementation review**

1.1.160.10   The IASB is required to conduct a post-implementation review of each new standard or major amendment. A post-implementation review normally takes place after a new standard or major amendment has been applied internationally for two years. The IASB may also decide to conduct a post-implementation review in response to changes in the financial reporting environment and regulatory requirements, or in response to concerns about the quality of an IFRS that have been expressed by the IFRS Advisory Council, the IFRS Interpretations Committee, standard setters or interested parties. [*Due Process Handbook 6.52–6.53*]

1.1.160.20   Each review is performed in two phases. The first phase involves an initial identification and assessment of the matters to be examined, and includes a public consultation in the form of a request for information. In the second phase, the IASB considers information gathered through consultation activities, including comments in response to the request for information. Based on the results of the review, the IASB presents its findings and sets out the steps it plans to take. [*Due Process Handbook 6.54*]

1.1.170   **COMPLIANCE WITH IFRS**

1.1.180   **General**

1.1.180.10   Any entity claiming that a set of financial statements is in compliance with IFRS complies with all such standards and related interpretations. An entity is not allowed to claim that its financial statements are, for example, 'materially' in compliance with IFRS, or that it has complied with 'substantially all' requirements of IFRS. Compliance with IFRS encompasses disclosure as well as recognition and measurement requirements. [*IAS 1.16*]

1.1.180.20   The IASB does not carry out any inquiry or enforcement role regarding the application of its standards. This is often undertaken by local regulators and/or stock exchanges.

1.1.190   Fair presentation

1.1.190.10   The overriding requirement of IFRS is for the financial statements to give a fair presentation (often referred to as a 'true and fair view'). [*IAS 1.15*]

1.1.190.20   'Fair presentation' is the faithful representation of the effects of transactions, other events and conditions in accordance with the definitions and recognition criteria for assets, liabilities, income and expenses as set out in the *Conceptual Framework for Financial Reporting* (see chapter 1.2). Compliance with IFRS, including additional disclosure when necessary, is presumed to result in a fair presentation. [*IAS 1.15*]

1.1.190.30   If compliance with a requirement of an IFRS would be so misleading that it would conflict with the objective of financial reporting set out in the Conceptual Framework (see 1.2.20.10), then an entity departs from the required treatment to give a fair presentation, unless the relevant regulator prohibits such an override. If an override cannot be used because it is prohibited by the regulator, then additional disclosure is required in the notes to the financial statements to reduce the perceived misleading impact of compliance to the maximum extent possible. [*IAS 1.19–24*]

1.1.190.40   The use of a true and fair override is very rare under IFRS. In the extremely rare case of an override, extensive disclosures are required, including the particulars of the departure, the reasons for the departure and its effect. [*IAS 1.19–21*]

1.1.200   PRIVATE ENTITIES

1.1.200.10   An entity that claims compliance with IFRS applies all IFRSs (see 1.1.90 and 170). However, as an alternative, a private entity without public accountability (see 1.1.210.30) may consider applying the *IFRS for Small and Medium-sized Entities* (the IFRS for SMEs).

1.1.210   IFRS FOR SMALL AND MEDIUM-SIZED ENTITIES

1.1.210.10   In July 2009, the IASB published the IFRS for SMEs. The standard is intended to facilitate financial reporting by private entities that want to use international standards. In 2015, the IASB published amendments to the IFRS for SMEs, which is effective for annual periods beginning on or after 1 January 2017. The amendments align the IFRS for SMEs with IFRS developments since the standard was issued in 2009, but without adding complexity.

1.1.210.20   The IFRS for SMEs is a stand-alone document organised by topic. It does not follow the numbering of full IFRS; it also does not contain cross-references to full IFRS, except for IAS 39. The IFRS for SMEs contains reduced guidance as compared with full IFRS; therefore, even when the general principles in the IFRS for SMEs appear to be the same as full IFRS, differences in application may result. Financial statements prepared under the IFRS for SMEs cannot claim compliance with IFRS.

1.1.210.30   The IFRS for SMEs is applicable for entities that publish general purpose financial statements for external users and that do not have public accountability. An entity has public accountability if it files (or is in the process of filing) financial statements with a securities commission or other regulatory organisation for the purpose of issuing any class of instruments in a public market, or if it holds assets in a fiduciary capacity for a broad group of outsiders – e.g. a bank or insurance company. There are no quantitative thresholds to qualify as an SME.

1.1.220   FUTURE DEVELOPMENTS

1.1.220.10   In May 2018, the IASB published Exposure Draft *Accounting Policy Changes – Proposed Amendments to IAS 8*, which proposed a relief from retrospectively applying changes in accounting policies resulting from agenda decisions published by the IFRS Interpretations Committee. Under the proposal, an entity would consider the expected benefits to users of financial statements from applying the new accounting policy retrospectively and the cost to the entity of determining the effects of retrospective application. The comment period closes in July 2018.

1.2 Conceptual Framework

1.2   Conceptual Framework

CURRENTLY EFFECTIVE REQUIREMENTS

This publication reflects IFRS in issue at 1 August 2018, and the currently effective requirements cover annual periods beginning on 1 January 2018.

The requirements related to this topic are mainly derived from the following.

REFERENCE	TITLE
CF	Conceptual Framework for Financial Reporting

The currently effective requirements include newly effective requirements arising from the revised *Conceptual Framework for Financial Reporting*, which was issued in March 2018. There is no transition period for the IASB and the IFRS Interpretations Committee – i.e. they use the revised Conceptual Framework once it has been released. However, amendments to references to the Conceptual Framework in IFRS standards are effective for annual periods beginning on or after 1 January 2020. These transition provisions impact entities that use the Conceptual Framework to develop an accounting policy in the absence of specific IFRS guidance under the hierarchy in IAS 8 *Accounting Policies, Changes in Accounting Estimates and Errors* (see 2.8.20.30).

FORTHCOMING REQUIREMENTS

For this topic, there are no forthcoming requirements.

FUTURE DEVELOPMENTS

The currently effective requirements that may be affected by future developments are highlighted with a * and are briefly discussed in 1.2.200.

1.2.10 INTRODUCTION

1.2.10.10   The Conceptual Framework provides a broad discussion of the concepts that underlie the preparation and presentation of financial statements. It discusses the objective of general purpose financial reporting; the qualitative characteristics of useful financial information; the concept of the reporting entity; and, perhaps more important, the elements of financial statements, including assets, liabilities, equity, income and expenses. The Conceptual Framework also sets the general guiding principles for the recognition, derecognition, measurement, presentation and disclosure of the elements of financial statements and discusses the concepts of capital and capital maintenance.

1.2.10.20   The IASB and the IFRS Interpretations Committee use the Conceptual Framework when developing new or revised IFRSs and interpretations or amending existing IFRSs. The Conceptual Framework also provides a point of reference for preparers of financial statements in the absence of specific guidance in IFRS on a particular subject (see 2.8.20). The purpose of this chapter is to highlight some of the Conceptual Framework's key principles. [*CF SP1.1, IAS 8.11*]

1.2.20 OBJECTIVE OF GENERAL PURPOSE FINANCIAL REPORTING

1.2.20.10   The objective of general purpose financial reporting is to provide financial information about the reporting entity that is useful to existing and potential investors, lenders and other creditors in making decisions about providing resources to the entity. [*CF 1.2*]

1.2.30 QUALITATIVE CHARACTERISTICS OF USEFUL FINANCIAL INFORMATION

1.2.30.10   The purpose of the qualitative characteristics of financial information outlined in the Conceptual Framework is to identify the types of information that are likely to be most useful to existing and potential investors, lenders and other creditors for making decisions about the reporting entity on the basis of information in its financial report. [*CF 2.1*]

1.2.30.20   The qualitative characteristics are categorised as follows.

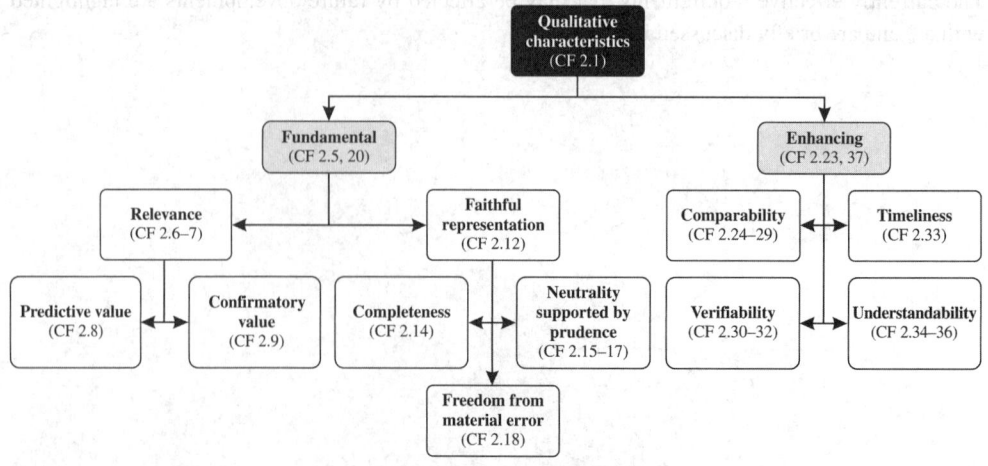

1.2.30.30   Relevance and faithful representation are fundamental qualitative characteristics that underpin the usefulness of financial information. The usefulness of financial information is enhanced if it is comparable, verifiable, timely and understandable. [*CF 2.4*]

1.2.30.40   Cost is a pervasive constraint on the information that can be provided. Therefore, it is important that costs incurred in providing information are justified by the benefits of reporting that information. [*CF 2.39*]

1.2.40   **Materiality***

1.2.40.10   IFRS does not apply to items that are 'immaterial'. The Conceptual Framework refers to materiality as an entity-specific aspect of relevance. Information is material if omitting it or misstating it could influence decisions that primary users make on the basis of financial information about a specific reporting entity. Materiality depends on the size and nature of the omission or misstatement judged in the surrounding circumstances. Either the size or the nature of the item, or a combination of both, could be the determining factor. Consideration of materiality is relevant to judgements regarding both the selection and application of accounting policies, and to the omission or disclosure of information in the financial statements. [*CF 2.11, IAS 1.7, 31, 8.5, 8*]

1.2.40.20   Materiality is a factor when making judgements about disclosure. For example, materiality affects when items may be aggregated, and the use of additional line items, headings and subtotals (see 3.1.10.30–50). If an IFRS does not explicitly specify the positioning of a disclosure, then materiality is relevant: an item may be sufficiently material to warrant disclosure on the face of the financial statements, or may only require disclosure in the notes to the financial statements. Materiality may mean that a specific disclosure requirement in a standard or an interpretation is not provided if the information resulting from that disclosure is not material. This is the case even if the IFRS contains a list of specific requirements or describes them as minimum requirements. In our view, the materiality of a disclosure item should not be determined solely by the materiality of the related financial statement line item. When making judgements about the materiality of disclosure, an entity considers the objectives of the disclosure and its relevance to the users together with the surrounding circumstances, including the consideration of qualitative factors. [*IAS 1.30–31, 86*]

1.2.40.30   An entity cannot aggregate material items that have different natures or functions and it is not permitted to obscure material information with immaterial information because this reduces the understandability of its financial statements. [*IAS 1.29, 30A–31*]

1.2.40.40   Accounting policies in accordance with IFRS do not need to be applied when their effect is immaterial. [*IAS 8.8*]

1.2.40.50   Financial statements do not comply with IFRS if they contain either material errors, or immaterial errors that are made intentionally to achieve a particular presentation of an entity's financial position, financial performance or cash flows. [*IAS 8.8, 41*]

1.2.50 **FINANCIAL STATEMENTS AND THE REPORTING ENTITY**

1.2.60 **Financial statements**

1.2.60.10   The objective of financial statements is to provide users with useful financial information about a reporting entity's assets, liabilities, equity, income and expenses. This information should enable users to assess:
- the prospects for future net cash inflows to the reporting entity; and
- management's stewardship of the reporting entity's economic resources. [*CF 3.2*]

1.2.60.20   Financial statements are prepared for a reporting period – i.e. a specified period of time – and give information about the reporting entity's:
- assets and liabilities – including its unrecognised assets and liabilities – at the reporting date;
- income and expenses for the reporting period; and
- equity that existed at the reporting date or during the reporting period. [*CF 3.4*]

1.2.60.30   To meet their objective (see 1.2.30.10), financial statements may also need to include information about transactions and other events that have occurred after the reporting date. The reporting entity provides this information only from its perspective as a whole: any of its existing or potential investors', lenders' or other creditors' perspectives are ignored. [*CF 3.7, 8*]

1.2.70 *Going concern*

1.2.70.10   Financial statements are prepared on a going concern basis, unless management intends or has no realistic alternative other than to liquidate the entity or to stop trading. If the going concern assumption is not appropriate, then IFRS is applied in a manner appropriate to the circumstances. [*CF 3.9, IAS 1.25*]

1.2.70.20   In assessing whether the going concern assumption is appropriate, management assesses all available information about the future for at least, but not limited to, 12 months from the reporting date. In our view, there is no general dispensation from the measurement, recognition and disclosure requirements of IFRS even if an entity is not expected to continue as a going concern. We believe that even if the going concern assumption is not appropriate, IFRS should be applied accordingly, with particular attention paid to the requirements of IFRS 5 (to the extent that assets are being held for sale and not abandoned), IAS 32 (with respect to the classification of the entity's debt and equity instruments), IAS 36 and IAS 37. [*IAS 1.26*]

1.2.70.30   In the case of an entity in liquidation, all liabilities continue to be recognised and measured in accordance with the applicable IFRS until the obligations are discharged, cancelled or expire.

EXAMPLE 1 – GOING CONCERN – LIABILITIES ON LIQUIDATION

1.2.70.40   Company C is in liquidation. If C has a financial liability in the scope of IFRS 9, then this financial liability cannot be derecognised until the relevant criteria in IFRS 9 are met – i.e. the obligation specified in the related contract is discharged, cancelled or expires (see 7.6.360).

1.2.70.50   If an entity ceases to be a going concern after the reporting date but before its financial statements are authorised for issue, then it is not permitted to prepare its financial statements on a going concern basis. [*IAS 10.14, 1.25–26*]

1.2.70.60   If a subsidiary is expected to be liquidated and its financial statements are prepared on a non-going concern basis, but the parent is expected to continue as a going concern, then in our view the consolidated financial statements should be prepared on a going concern basis. The subsidiary should continue to be consolidated until it is liquidated or otherwise disposed of.

1.2.80   *Disclosure related to going concern*

1.2.80.10   An entity discloses material uncertainties related to events or conditions that may cast significant doubt on its ability to continue as a going concern. In addition to the disclosure of material uncertainties, disclosures are required when management concludes that there are no material uncertainties but reaching that conclusion involved significant judgement (a 'close call' scenario). [*IAS 1.25, 122, IU 07-14*]

1.2.90   **Reporting entity**

1.2.90.10   A 'reporting entity' is one that is required, or chooses, to prepare financial statements. It need not be a legal entity but can comprise a single entity, multiple entities or a portion of an entity. [*CF 3.10*]

1.2.90.20   In the case of multiple entities, if a reporting entity comprises two or more entities that are not all linked by a parent-subsidiary relationship, then its financial statements are known as 'combined financial statements'. [*CF 3.12*]

1.2.90.30   Sometimes, determining what comprises the reporting entity can be challenging – e.g. if it is not a legal entity or it comprises multiple entities that are not linked by a parent-subsidiary relationship. In these cases, the reporting entity's boundary is determined by assessing the information needs of the primary users of its financial statements – i.e. they need information that is relevant and that faithfully represents what it claims to represent. [*CF 3.14*]

1.2.90.40   'Faithful representation' requires that:
- a reporting entity does not comprise an arbitrary or incomplete set of economic activities;
- including that set of economic activities within the boundary of the reporting entity results in neutral information; and
- the reporting entity describes how its boundary was determined and how it is comprised – i.e. what constitutes the reporting entity. [*CF 3.14*]

1.2.100   **Types of financial statements**

1.2.100.10   Financial statements (see 1.2.60) may provide information about the assets, liabilities, equity, income and expenses of:
- both the parent and its subsidiaries as a single reporting entity – i.e. consolidated financial statements;
- the parent only – i.e. unconsolidated financial statements; or

- two or more entities that are not all linked by a parent-subsidiary relationship – i.e. combined financial statements. [*CF 3.12, 15, 17*]

1.2.100.20   Because unconsolidated financial statements typically provide insufficient information to meet the needs of existing and potential investors, lenders and other creditors of a parent entity, consolidated financial statements are prepared when they are required. Unconsolidated financial statements may be provided as well as consolidated financial statements, but they cannot replace them. [*CF 3.18*]

1.2.110   THE ELEMENTS OF FINANCIAL STATEMENTS

1.2.120   Definitions

1.2.120.10   In developing new standards and interpretations, the IASB and the IFRS Interpretations Committee rely on the following definitions of assets and liabilities, which are key elements of the financial statements.
- An 'asset' is a present economic resource controlled by the entity as a result of past events.
- A 'liability' is a present obligation of the entity to transfer an economic resource as a result of past events. An 'obligation' is a duty or responsibility that an entity has no practical ability to avoid. If it is conditional on an entity's future action, then an obligation exists if the entity has no practical ability to avoid taking that action. [*CF 4.2, 29, 32*]

1.2.120.20   An 'economic resource' is a right or a set of rights that has the potential to produce economic benefits. The probability of economic benefits is not relevant for determining whether an asset or a liability exists; however, a low probability of economic benefits may affect the recognition and measurement analysis. [*CF 4.4, 14–15, 37–38*]

1.2.120.30   The definitions of equity, income and expenses are derived from the definitions of assets and liabilities. However, this does not suggest that information about equity, income and expenses is less important.
- 'Equity' is the residual interest in the assets of the entity after deducting all of its liabilities.
- 'Income' is increases in assets or decreases in liabilities that result in increases in equity, other than those relating to contributions from holders of equity claims.
- 'Expenses' are decreases in assets or increases in liabilities that result in decreases in equity, other than those relating to distributions to holders of equity claims. [*CF 4.2*]

1.2.120.40   When considering how to apply the recognition criteria or measurement concepts to an asset or liability, an entity selects a unit of account. A 'unit of account' is the right(s), the obligation(s) or the group of rights and obligations to which the recognition criteria and/or measurement concepts are applied. In some circumstances, the unit of account for recognition may differ from that for measurement – e.g. a contract may be recognised individually but measured as part of a portfolio of contracts. [*CF 4.48–49*]

1.2.120.50   An entity selects a unit of account that provides relevant information about the asset or liability and a faithful representation of the substance of the transaction that has given rise to the asset or liability. [*CF 4.54*]

1.2.130   **Executory contracts and substance of contractual rights and obligations**

1.2.130.10   An 'executory contract' is one in which neither party has performed any of its obligations or both parties have partially performed their obligations to an equal extent. If the terms of the exchange under the contract are currently favourable for the entity, then it has an asset. Conversely, if the terms are currently unfavourable for the entity, then it has a liability. The asset or liability is reflected in the financial statements depending on the recognition criteria and the selected measurement basis, including a consideration of whether a contract is onerous. [*CF 4.56–57*]

EXAMPLE 2 – EXECUTORY CONTRACT

> 1.2.130.20   Company C enters into a contract to buy equipment in six months and agrees to pay 100 at that time. Initially this is an executory contract because the seller has the obligation to deliver the equipment and the buyer has the right to receive the equipment, but also has an obligation to pay 100, and neither party has performed its obligations. [*IAS 37.3*]

1.2.130.30   An entity represents its contractual rights and obligations faithfully – i.e. its financial statements report the substance of these rights and obligations. If their substance is unclear from the contract's legal form, then the entity undertakes further analysis. The entity ignores contract terms with no substance – e.g. those that bind neither party or those that the holder has no practical ability to exercise. [*CF 4.59, 61*]

1.2.140   **RECOGNITION AND DERECOGNITION**

1.2.150   **Recognition**

1.2.150.10   An entity recognises any item meeting the definition of an asset, a liability, equity, income or expenses in the financial statements unless it affects the relevance or the faithful representation of the information provided. [*CF 5.6–5.7*]

1.2.150.20   The relevance of the information provided may be affected if there is uncertainty about the existence of an asset or liability or the probability of an inflow or outflow of economic benefits from the asset or liability is low. [*CF 5.12*]

1.2.150.30   Faithful representation may be affected by high measurement uncertainty – e.g. when an asset or lability can be measured only by using cash-flow-based measurement techniques and:
- the possible outcomes are difficult to estimate and exceptionally wide-ranging;
- the measure is very sensitive to small changes in the estimates of the probability of different outcomes; or
- the cash flows do not relate solely to the asset or liability being measured and their allocation is exceptionally subjective. [*CF 5.18, 20*]

1.2.150.40   Regardless of whether an asset or a liability is recognised, if there is uncertainty about its existence or measurement, or the probability of economic benefits is low, then an entity may need to provide explanatory information in the notes to the financial statements. [*CF 5.14, 16, 23*]

1.2.160   **Derecognition**

1.2.160.10   When an item no longer meets the definition of an asset or a liability, it is derecognised from the financial statements. This is accompanied by appropriate presentation and disclosure. This occurs when the entity loses control of all or part of a recognised asset and/or when it no longer has a present obligation for all or part of a liability. [*CF 5.26*]

1.2.160.20   Sometimes, an entity may continue to recognise a transferred asset or liability (or component thereof) – e.g. if it has entered into a transaction to reacquire the asset. In this case, derecognition would not faithfully represent the transaction and the entity would continue to recognise the transferred asset or liability (or component thereof) in its financial statements with appropriate presentation and disclosure. [*CF 5.29*]

1.2.170   **MEASUREMENT**

1.2.170.10   The Conceptual Framework describes two measurement bases and the factors to consider when selecting a measurement basis.
- *Historical cost:* Under the historical cost basis, an asset or liability is measured using information derived from the transaction price and that measurement is not changed unless it relates to impairment of an asset or a liability becoming onerous.
- *Current value:* Under the current value basis, an asset or liability is measured using information that reflects current conditions at the measurement date. [*CF 6.4, 10*]

1.2.170.20   Current value measurement bases include the following.
- Fair value – i.e. the price received to sell an asset or the price paid to transfer a liability in an orderly transaction between market participants at the measurement date.
- Value in use and fulfilment value that are based on present values of cash flows – i.e. entity-specific expectations about the amount, timing and uncertainty of those future cash flows.
- Current cost – i.e. the current amount that an entity would pay to acquire an asset or would receive to take on a liability. [*CF 6.11–12, 17, 21*]

1.2.170.25   The measurement basis selected needs to provide useful information to users of financial statements – i.e. information that is relevant and that faithfully represents what it purports to represent. The table below indicates the factors to consider when selecting a measurement basis and how the relevance and faithful representation of information are affected by each factor. [*CF 6.45*]

FACTOR	RELEVANCE	FAITHFUL REPRESENTATION
Asset/liability characteristics	• Variability of cash flows • Sensitivity of the value to market factors or other risks	
Contribution to future cash flows	• Whether cash flows are produced directly or indirectly • The nature of an entity's business activities	

FACTOR	RELEVANCE	FAITHFUL REPRESENTATION
Measurement inconsistency		• Financial statements may not faithfully represent an entity's financial position or performance if they contain measurement inconsistencies (accounting mismatch)
Measurement uncertainty		• Does not prevent use of a measurement basis that provides relevant information, but if the uncertainty is too high, then it might prompt selection of an alternative measurement basis

1.2.170.30   In some cases, the IASB may use more than one measurement basis. [*CF 6.83*]

1.2.180   PRESENTATION AND DISCLOSURE

1.2.180.10   The Conceptual Framework includes high-level concepts that describe how information is presented and disclosed in financial statements – in particular, how information is:
- classified such that similar items are grouped together and dissimilar items are separated; and
- aggregated such that information is not obscured either by unnecessary detail or by excessive aggregation. [*CF 7.7, 21*]

1.2.180.20   Classification is applied at the unit of account level but may be appropriate at the component level – e.g. separating an asset or liability into current and non-current components. It takes into account shared characteristics of elements of financial statements – e.g. their nature or role within the business and how they are measured. Classifying dissimilar items together can obscure relevant information and may not provide a faithful representation of an entity's financial information. For example, offsetting of assets and liabilities classifies dissimilar items together and is generally inappropriate. [*CF 7.9*]

1.2.180.30   The Conceptual Framework also outlines principles that the IASB applies when deciding when an item of income or expense should be:
- included in profit or loss vs in OCI; and
- reclassified from OCI to profit or loss. [*CF 7.15*]

1.2.180.40   In principle, all items of income and expense are included in the statement of profit or loss. In exceptional circumstances, the IASB may decide that including an item of income or expense in OCI provides more relevant information or a more faithful representation. In these cases, the presentation and disclosure requirements in the relevant standard will make this clear. Unlike the IASB, in the absence of specific requirements an entity cannot choose an accounting policy to present an item of income or expense outside profit or loss. [*CF 7.16, BC7.25*]

1.2.180.50   If an item of income or expense is included in OCI, then it is normally reclassified ('recycled') to income and expenses in a future period when doing so results in the statement of profit or loss providing more relevant information or a more faithful representation of the entity's financial performance during that future period. However, in developing a standard the IASB may decide that some items recognised in OCI should not be subsequently reclassified to profit or loss. An entity cannot make such a decision in developing its accounting policy in the absence of specific requirements. [*CF 7.19, BC7.25*]

1.2.190   TRANSACTIONS WITH SHAREHOLDERS

1.2.190.10   The definitions of income and expense exclude capital transactions with equity partici-pants. Accordingly, such transactions – e.g. capital contributions from shareholders – are recognised directly in equity, in the same way as the distributions made to shareholders. However, the position is less clear when the transaction with the shareholder equally could have been with a third party. [*CF 4.1,70*]

EXAMPLE 3 – TRANSACTIONS WITH SHAREHOLDERS

1.2.190.20   Company B sells inventory at fair value to a shareholder. In this case, the transaction is recognised in profit or loss because it is on market terms (i.e. fair value), which indicate that the shareholder is not acting in its capacity as a shareholder; rather, it is transacting with B in the same way as any other third party. [*CF 6.82*]

1.2.190.30   Alternatively, if B gives the inventory to a shareholder without con-sideration, then it may be argued that the shareholder has received a benefit from B in its capacity as a shareholder because an independent third party would not have been given the inventory for free. We believe that, in the absence of any other relevant facts, this transaction should be recognised directly in equity as a distribu-tion to shareholders (see 7.3.680). [*CF 6.82*]

1.2.190.40   Changing the facts further, suppose that the shareholder pays consid-erably more than fair value for the inventory. In such cases, it may be appropriate to split the transaction into a capital transaction and a revenue transaction. Pro-ceeds equal to the fair value of the inventory would be recognised in profit or loss, with the remaining proceeds being recognised directly in equity as a contribution from shareholders. [*CF 6.82*]

1.2.190.50   Generally, IFRS does not discuss the circumstances in which it would be appropriate for a transaction entered into by a shareholder on behalf of the entity to be recognised in the financial statements of the entity (i.e. attribution). However, IFRS 2 does require the attribution of expense for certain share-based payment transactions (see 4.5.80.10). In other instances, judgement is used in determining whether attribution is appropriate. IAS 24 requires attribution for disclosure purposes in certain circumstances (see 5.5.110).

1.2.190.60   The key point is that transactions with shareholders, or any transactions that are made on behalf of the entity, are considered carefully, having regard to all of the facts and circumstances, in determining the appropriate accounting.

1.2.200   **FUTURE DEVELOPMENTS**

1.2.200.10   In September 2017, the IASB published Exposure Draft *Definition of Material – Proposed amendments to IAS 1 and IAS 8*. The exposure draft is aimed at refining the definition of material and clarifying its application. The comment period closed in January 2018 and the Board is considering the feedback received.

2.   GENERAL ISSUES

2.1   Form and components of financial statements

2.   GENERAL ISSUES

2.1   Form and components of financial statements

CURRENTLY EFFECTIVE REQUIREMENTS

This publication reflects IFRS in issue at 1 August 2018, and the currently effective requirements cover annual periods beginning on 1 January 2018.

The requirements related to this topic are mainly derived from the following.

STANDARD	TITLE
IFRS 10	Consolidated Financial Statements
IFRS 11	Joint Arrangements
IAS 1	Presentation of Financial Statements
IAS 27	Separate Financial Statements
IAS 28	Investments in Associates and Joint Ventures

FORTHCOMING REQUIREMENTS

For this topic, there are no forthcoming requirements.

FUTURE DEVELOPMENTS

This topic is subject to future developments that may affect several aspects of the presentation and disclosure of information in financial statements. See 2.1.140.

2.1.10 COMPONENTS OF FINANCIAL STATEMENTS

2.1.10.10   The following comprise a complete set of financial statements:
- a statement of financial position (see chapter 3.1);
- a statement of profit or loss and OCI, presented either:
  - in a single statement that includes all components of profit or loss and OCI in two separate sections; or
  - in the form of two separate statements, one displaying components of profit or loss immediately preceding another statement beginning with profit or loss and displaying components of OCI (see chapter 4.1);
- a statement of changes in equity (see chapter 2.2);
- a statement of cash flows (see chapter 2.3);
- notes, comprising significant accounting policies and other explanatory information;
- a statement of financial position as at the beginning of the preceding period when an entity restates comparative information following:
  - a change in accounting policy;
  - a correction of an error; or
  - a reclassification of items in the financial statements (see 2.1.20); and
- comparative information in respect of the preceding period (see 2.1.50). [*IAS 1.10–10A*]

2.1.10.20   The statements presented outside the notes to the financial statements are generally referred to as 'financial statements' in IAS 1. In this chapter, those financial statements are described when necessary as 'primary financial statements' to distinguish them from the financial statements as a whole. Although IAS 1 provides the titles for the primary financial statements as outlined in 2.1.10.10, which we use throughout this publication, those titles are not mandatory. [*IAS 1.10, BC21*]

2.1.10.25   All financial statements within a complete set of financial statements are presented with equal prominence. [*IAS 1.11*]

2.1.10.30   IFRS specifies disclosures to be made in the financial statements (see 2.1.10.80). However, it does not prescribe specific formats to be followed. In our experience, entities often consider the presentation adopted by other entities in the same industry or country.

2.1.10.40   Although a number of disclosures are made in the primary financial statements, IFRS generally allows flexibility in presenting additional line items and subtotals when they are necessary to ensure a fair presentation (see 3.1.10 and 4.1.10). In addition to the information required to be disclosed in the financial statements, many entities provide additional information outside the financial statements, either voluntarily or because of local regulations or securities exchange requirements (see chapter 5.8). [*IAS 1.13, 54–55A, 82–85B*]

2.1.10.50   Notes to the financial statements are presented, to the extent practicable, in a systematic manner but not necessarily in a prescribed order and are cross-referenced from items in the primary financial statements. [*IAS 1.113*]

2.1.10.60   In determining a systematic manner of presentation, an entity considers the effect on the understandability and comparability of the financial statements. For example, notes to the financial statements may be presented or grouped in the following ways:

- giving prominence to the areas of the entity's activities that it considers to be most relevant to an understanding of its financial performance and financial position, such as grouping together information about particular operating activities;
- grouping together information about items measured similarly, such as assets measured at fair value; or
- following the order of the line items in the primary financial statements (see 2.1.10.70). [*IAS 1.113–114*]

2.1.10.70   If an entity follows the order of the line items in the primary financial statements, then the notes are generally presented in the following order:
- a statement of compliance with IFRS;
- the basis of preparation;
- other significant accounting policies applied;
- supporting information for items presented in the primary statements, in the order in which each statement and each line item is presented; and
- other disclosures, including contingencies, commitments and non-financial disclosures. [*IAS 1.112–117*]

2.1.10.80   Disclosures that are not material need not be provided in a set of financial statements, even if IFRS contains a list of specific requirements or describes them as minimum requirements (see 1.2.18). [*IAS 1.31, BC30H–BC30I*]

2.1.20   Third statement of financial position and related notes

2.1.20.10   A third statement of financial position is presented as at the beginning of the preceding period following a retrospective change in accounting policy, the correction of an error or a reclassification that has a material effect on the information in that statement of financial position. [*IAS 1.10(f), 40A*]

2.1.30   *Materiality considerations*

2.1.30.10   When interpreting the requirement to present a third statement of financial position, in our view an entity should consider materiality based on its particular facts and circumstances. An assessment of materiality requires consideration of the effect of retrospective application of the relevant accounting policy, retrospective restatement or reclassification on the information in the statement of financial position as at the beginning of the preceding period. For example, an entity may have previously presented its obligation for post-employment benefits entirely as non-current as allowed by IAS 19 (see 4.4.1090). If the entity subsequently decides to split the amount into current and non-current components in the statement of financial position, then it restates the comparatives. In this case, to the extent that the effect of the retrospective application of the accounting policy is material to the statement of financial position as at the beginning of the preceding period, a third statement of financial position would be required. [*IAS 1.40A, 19.133*]

2.1.40   *Presentation*

2.1.40.10   The third statement of financial position relates to the beginning of the preceding period. Therefore, as a minimum, a statement of financial position will be presented for the following dates:
- the end of the current reporting period;

- the end of the preceding reporting period; and
- the beginning of the preceding reporting period. [*IAS 1.40B*]

2.1.40.20   The third statement of financial position is not required in condensed interim financial statements (see 5.9.30.22). [*IAS 1.BC33*]

2.1.40.30   When an entity presents additional comparative information (see 2.1.70), the date of the third statement of financial position is required to be the beginning of the preceding period regardless of the earlier periods covered by the additional comparative information. [*IAS 1.40D*]

2.1.40.40   If an entity presents an additional comparative statement of financial position identical to the third statement of financial position that would otherwise be required, then it does not need to present the same statement of financial position twice. However, this fact is disclosed.

EXAMPLE 1 – THIRD STATEMENT OF FINANCIAL POSITION – ADDITIONAL COMPARATIVE INFORMATION

2.1.40.50   Company C usually includes an additional comparative statement of financial position and statement of profit or loss and OCI in its annual financial statements. During the reporting period ended 31 December 2018, C discovers a material error in respect of the depreciation of property, plant and equipment. The correction of the error will have a material effect on the statement of financial position at 1 January 2017. C's financial statements for 2018 will therefore include:
- a statement of financial position at 31 December 2018; and
- comparative statements of financial position at 31 December 2017 and 31 December 2016.

2.1.40.60   Because the statement of financial position at 31 December 2016 would be identical to the statement of financial position at 1 January 2017, C need not present the same statement of financial position twice. This fact could be indicated in various ways; for example, C could provide a note or specifically label the additional comparative statement of financial position – i.e. 31 December 2016/1 January 2017.

2.1.40.70   When an entity presents a third statement of financial position, it is not required to present the related notes. However, it includes the explanatory disclosures required by paragraphs 41–44 of IAS 1 and IAS 8. [*IAS 1.40C*]

2.1.40.80   For a discussion of the requirement to present a third statement of financial position and related notes for first-time adopters of IFRS, see 6.1.1550.40.

2.1.50   Comparative information

2.1.60   *Minimum comparative information*

2.1.60.10   Comparative information is required for the immediately preceding period. Unless there is a specific exemption provided in a standard, an entity presents comparative information in respect of the preceding period for all amounts reported in the current period's financial statements. The preceding period's related narrative and descriptive information is generally required only if it is relevant to understanding the current period's financial statements and regardless of whether it was provided in the prior period. For example, comparative segment information would be disclosed. [*IAS 1.38, IPS 2.70*]

2.1.60.20   No particular format is required for the presentation of comparatives. In our experience, most entities reporting under IFRS provide comparative information about the immediately preceding period alongside that for the current period.

2.1.60.30   When an entity is adopting IFRS for the first time, the required comparatives are prepared in accordance with IFRS (see 6.1.20.30–40). [*IFRS 1.7, 21*]

2.1.70   *Additional comparative information*

2.1.70.10   More extensive comparatives may be presented voluntarily or to meet regulatory – e.g. securities exchange – requirements. Such additional comparative information and related notes need to comply with IFRS. However, it need not comprise a complete set of financial statements. [*IAS 1.38C–38D*]

2.1.70.20   When an entity is adopting IFRS for the first time, any additional comparatives included in the financial statements need not comply with IFRS provided that those comparatives are labelled clearly and explanatory disclosures are included (see 6.1.1520.10). [*IFRS 1.22*]

2.1.80   **REPORTING PERIOD**

2.1.80.05   A number of terms are used, either in the literature or in practice, to describe the end of an entity's financial year, including 'reporting date', 'end of the reporting period', 'statement of financial position date', 'year end' and 'financial year end'. Generally, these terms are used interchangeably and have the same meaning. This publication consistently uses the term 'reporting date' throughout, which refers to the end of the reporting period and does not refer to the date on which the financial statements are prepared, authorised for issue, made public or filed.

2.1.80.10   The annual reporting date may change in certain circumstances – e.g. following a change of major shareholder or because of regulatory or taxation requirements. If the annual reporting date does change, then the financial statements for that period will cover either more or less than 12 months. In this case, the entity discloses the reasons for using a longer or shorter period and the fact that information in the financial statements is not fully comparable. In addition, pro forma information for the comparable preceding reporting period might be presented (see 2.1.130). [*IAS 1.36*]

2.1.80.20   IFRS is silent on the approach to take when a subsidiary changes its annual reporting date to align it with that of the parent. In our view, the consolidated financial statements should include the results of the subsidiary from its last reporting date to its new reporting date. Therefore, the subsidiary's results included in the consolidated financial statements might cover a period of either more or less than 12 months (see 2.5.440).

(S) 2.1.90 **TYPES OF FINANCIAL STATEMENTS**

2.1.90.10   IFRS sets out the requirements that apply to three distinct types of financial statements: consolidated financial statements, individual financial statements and separate financial statements. Most, but not all, recognition, measurement, presentation and disclosure requirements apply to all three types of financial statements.

2.1.90.20   It is the reporting entity's interests in subsidiaries, associates and joint ventures that determine which type of financial statements the entity is required to prepare. Certain exemptions may provide relief from those requirements.

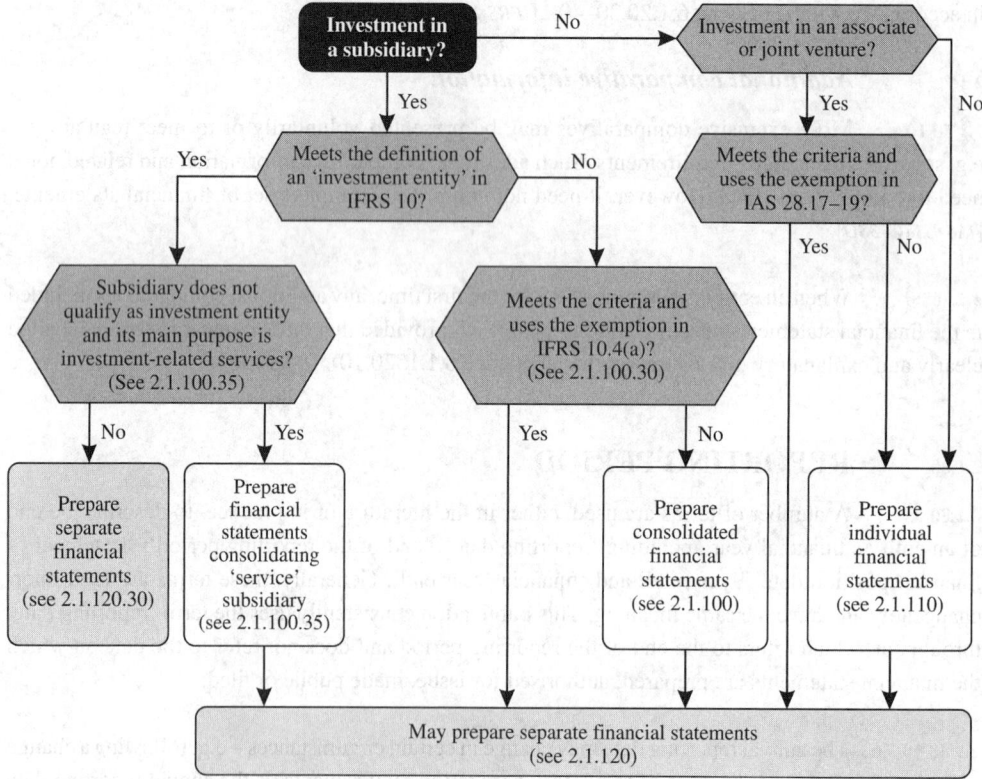

2.1.100   **Consolidated financial statements**

2.1.100.10   Consolidated financial statements are financial statements of a group in which the assets, liabilities, equity, income, expenses and cash flows of the parent and its subsidiaries are presented as those of a single economic entity. [*IFRS 10.A, IAS 27.4*]

2.1.100.20   In consolidated financial statements, subsidiaries are consolidated unless a consolidation exception applies (see 2.5.10.20). Investments in associates and joint ventures are equity accounted, unless they are held for sale (see 5.4.30.65 and 5.4.100) or an entity is exempted from applying the equity method in accordance with IAS 28 (see 3.5.90). [*IFRS 10.4, IAS 28.17–19*]

2.1.100.30   An entity with an investment in a subsidiary is exempt from preparing consolidated financial statements only if it is an investment entity that is required to measure all of its subsidiaries at fair value through profit or loss (see 2.1.100.35) or all of the following criteria are met:

- the parent is a wholly owned subsidiary, or is a partially owned subsidiary and its other owners (including those not otherwise entitled to vote) have been informed about, and do not object to, the parent not presenting consolidated financial statements;
- the parent's debt or equity instruments are not traded in a public market (a domestic or foreign stock exchange or an over-the-counter market, including local and regional markets); for further discussion of what is considered to be 'traded in a public market', see 5.2.10.12;
- the parent has not filed, nor is it in the process of filing, its financial statements with a securities commission or other regulatory organisation for the purpose of issuing any class of instruments in a public market; and
- the ultimate or any intermediate parent of the parent produces financial statements that are available for public use and comply with IFRS, such that subsidiaries are either consolidated or measured at fair value through profit or loss in accordance with IFRS 10. [*IFRS 10.4(a), 4B*]

2.1.100.35   An investment entity does not consolidate its subsidiaries, but instead measures them at fair value through profit or loss in accordance with IFRS 9. As an exception, if a subsidiary does not itself qualify as an investment entity and its main purpose and activities are providing investment-related services, then that subsidiary is consolidated (see 5.6.100.15). In addition, a parent of an investment entity that is not itself an investment entity consolidates all of its subsidiaries in the usual way – i.e. the fair value accounting is reversed at the level of the non-investment entity parent. For a detailed discussion of group structures involving investment entities, see 5.6.190. [*IFRS 10.31–33, A*]

2.1.100.40   An entity that prepares consolidated financial statements – i.e. it does not meet and use the exemption criteria in 2.1.100.30 – may elect to prepare separate financial statements in addition to its consolidated financial statements (see 2.1.120).

2.1.100.50   In our view, if an entity meets and uses the criteria for exemption from preparing consolidated financial statements and is not an investment entity (see 2.1.100.35), then there is no requirement under IFRS to prepare financial statements. However, it may elect to prepare separate financial statements as its only set of IFRS financial statements (see 2.1.120). [*IAS 27.8–8A*]

2.1.100.60   If an entity is exempt from preparing consolidated financial statements, but chooses to do so in any event, then in our view the entity is required to apply all of the requirements of IFRS that relate to consolidated financial statements. For example, the entity would be required to apply equity accounting to investments in associates and joint ventures unless exemptions from the equity method apply (see 3.5.90).

2.1.100.70   If an entity does not qualify for the exemption in 2.1.100.30, but nonetheless decides to present only separate financial statements, then in our view these separate financial statements cannot be regarded as complying with IFRS (see 1.1.170). Our view is based on the fact that the preparation of consolidated financial statements is fundamental to compliance with IFRS and pervades every aspect of the financial statements.

EXAMPLE 2 – EXEMPTION FROM PREPARING CONSOLIDATED FINANCIAL STATEMENTS

2.1.100.80   Company B is an intermediate parent of Company C, and B is owned by Company P, the ultimate parent. C has subsidiaries.

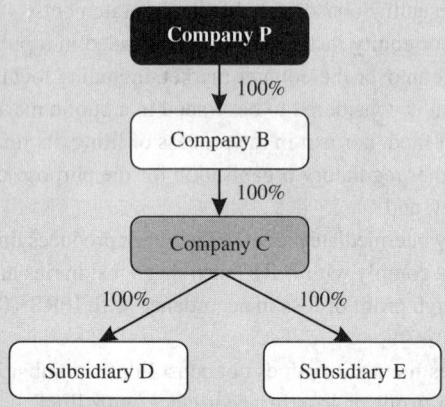

2.1.100.90   C is not required to prepare consolidated financial statements if the following conditions are met:

- either P or B prepares consolidated financial statements in accordance with IFRS and those consolidated financial statements are available to the users of the financial statements of C;
- C's debt or equity instruments are not traded in a public market, including stock exchanges and over-the-counter markets; and
- C has not filed, and is not in the process of filing, its financial statements with a regulatory organisation for the purpose of issuing any class of instruments in a public market. [*IFRS 10.4(a)*]

2.1.100.100   In our view, if an entity disposes of its last subsidiary during the current reporting period, then consolidated financial statements are not required to be prepared because the entity is no longer a parent at the reporting date. In such cases, we believe that the financial statements, including comparatives, should be presented as unconsolidated financial statements – i.e. individual or separate financial statements as appropriate (see 2.1.110 and 120, respectively) – unless the consolidated financial statements are required by a regulator. However, the entity may wish to present supplementary information on a consolidated basis (see chapter 5.8).

2.1.110   Individual financial statements

2.1.110.10   Although the term is not formally defined in IFRS, individual financial statements are those of an entity that has no subsidiaries and either:

- has investments in associates and/or joint ventures that are equity accounted – i.e. the entity does not use any exemption from equity accounting (see 2.1.110.20); or
- has neither an investment in an associate nor a joint venturer's interest in a joint venture. [*IFRS 11.24, IAS 27.7, 28.3, 16*]

2.1.110.20   An interest in an associate or joint venture is accounted for using the equity method unless one of the following criteria is met.

- The interest (or a portion thereof) is classified as held-for-sale in accordance with IFRS 5 (see 3.5.160).
- All of the following criteria are satisfied:
  - the entity is a wholly owned subsidiary, or is a partially owned subsidiary and its other owners (including those not otherwise entitled to vote) have been informed about, and do not object to, the entity not applying the equity method;
  - the entity's debt or equity instruments are not traded in a public market (see 5.2.10.12), including stock exchanges and over-the-counter markets;
  - the entity did not file, and is not in the process of filing, its financial statements with a regulatory organisation for the purpose of issuing any class of instruments in a public market; and
  - the ultimate or any intermediate parent of the entity produces financial statements that are available for public use and comply with IFRS, such that subsidiaries are either consolidated or measured at fair value through profit or loss in accordance with IFRS 10.
- The entity is a venture capital or similar organisation and elects to measure the interest at fair value through profit or loss in accordance with IFRS 9 (see 3.5.100). [*IAS 28.17–20*]

2.1.110.30   An entity that has a subsidiary cannot prepare individual financial statements.

2.1.110.40   In our view, an entity may label its individual financial statements as such, or use alternative titles that may be more understandable to readers – e.g. 'financial statements of the entity and investees'. Whatever label is used to identify individual financial statements, we believe that the notes to the financial statements should explain clearly the basis used in preparing those financial statements.

2.1.110.50   An entity that prepares individual financial statements may elect to prepare separate financial statements in addition to the individual financial statements.

2.1.110.60   In our view, if an entity meets and uses the exemption from preparing individual financial statements, then IFRS does not require it to prepare financial statements. However, such an entity may elect to prepare separate financial statements as its only set of IFRS financial statements (see 2.1.120).

2.1.120   Separate financial statements

2.1.120.10   A parent or an investor in an associate or joint venture that is not required to prepare consolidated financial statements (see 2.1.100.30) or individual financial statements (see 2.1.110) may prepare separate financial statements (see 3.5.640). Alternatively, separate financial statements may be prepared in addition to consolidated or individual financial statements. [*IAS 27.6, 8–8A*]

2.1.120.15   In separate financial statements, investments in subsidiaries, associates and joint ventures, unless they are classified as held-for-sale (see 3.5.640.20), are accounted for either:

- at cost;
- in accordance with IFRS 9 (see 7.4.20.10); or

- using the equity method as described in IAS 28 (see 3.5.640.10–30). [*IAS 27.10, 28.44, IFRS 9.2.1(a), 11.26*]

2.1.120.20   The entity applies the same accounting for each category of investments. For a further discussion, see 3.5.640.40. [*IAS 27.10*]

2.1.120.25   IAS 27 states that the financial statements of an entity that does not have an investment in a subsidiary, associate or joint venture are not separate financial statements. However, in all material respects, the requirements that will apply to those financial statements will be identical to individual financial statements. [*IAS 27.7*]

2.1.120.30   Entities may elect, or be required by local regulations, to prepare separate financial statements. However, an investment entity that in accordance with IFRS 10 does not consolidate its subsidiaries (see 2.1.100.35) is required to prepare separate financial statements. [*IAS 27.8A*]

2.1.120.40   IFRS does not preclude an entity from including both consolidated and separate financial statements within the same report. If an entity chooses to do so, then there is no required format or order in which the financial statements are presented. However, the information presented needs to be identified clearly as related to either the separate or the consolidated financial statements.

2.1.120.50   If an entity prepares separate financial statements in accordance with IFRS, then all relevant IFRSs apply equally to those separate financial statements (see 1.1.170).

2.1.120.60   All separate financial statements disclose:
- the fact that the financial statements are separate financial statements;
- a list of significant investments in subsidiaries, joint ventures and associates, including the name, principal place of business and, if it is different, country of incorporation, proportion of ownership interest and, if it is different, the proportion of voting rights; and
- a description of the method used to account for these investments. [*IAS 27.16–17*]

2.1.120.70   In addition, separate financial statements of a parent that meets the criteria and uses the criteria for exemption from preparing consolidated financial statements disclose:
- the fact that the exemption from consolidation has been used;
- the name and principal place of business and, if it is different, the country of incorporation of the entity whose consolidated financial statements that comply with IFRS have been produced for public use; and
- the address at which those consolidated financial statements are obtainable. [*IAS 27.16*]

2.1.120.80   The separate financial statements of an entity that is not exempt from preparing consolidated or individual financial statements disclose the reason for preparing them if it is not required by law and identify the related consolidated or individual financial statements. [*IAS 27.17*]

2.1.130   PRESENTATION OF PRO FORMA INFORMATION

2.1.130.10   IFRS is generally silent on the presentation of pro forma information within the financial statements, with the exception of the requirement in IFRS 3 to present, following a business combination, revenue and profit or loss of the combined entity determined as if the acquisition had been effected at the beginning of the period. [*IFRS 3.B64(q)(ii)*]

2.1.130.20   In some cases, an entity may wish to present pro forma information that is not required by IFRS – e.g. pro forma comparative financial statements following a change in the reporting date (see 2.1.80.10) or a pro forma statement of profit or loss and OCI following significant changes in the composition of the entity. In our view, such additional information is generally acceptable to the extent that it is allowed by local regulations and relevant stock exchange rules and provided that:
- the information is labelled clearly to distinguish it from the financial statements prepared in accordance with IFRS and is marked clearly as unaudited if that is the case;
- the entity discloses the transaction or event that is reflected in the pro forma financial information, the source of the financial information on which it is based, the significant assumptions used in developing the pro forma adjustments and any significant uncertainties about those adjustments; and
- the presentation indicates that the pro forma financial information should be read in conjunction with the financial statements and that the pro forma financial information is not necessarily indicative of the results that would have been attained if, for example, the transaction or event had taken place on a different date.

2.1.140   FUTURE DEVELOPMENTS

2.1.150   Disclosure initiative

2.1.150.10   The IASB is working on a broad initiative aimed at improving disclosures in the financial statements. The disclosure initiative covers various areas and includes the following projects.
- *Definition of Material – Amendments to IAS 1 and IAS 8:* In September 2017, the IASB published an exposure draft, which is aimed at refining the definition of material and clarifying its application. The comment period closed in January 2018 and the Board is considering the feedback received.
- *Principles of disclosure (including standard-level review of disclosures):* This research project is aimed at developing a set of principles for disclosure in IFRS to assist the IASB in setting better disclosure requirements and help preparers communicate information more effectively to the users of financial statements. A discussion paper was published in March 2017.

2.1.160   Primary financial statements

2.1.160.10   The IASB is working on a research project on primary financial statements. This project considers potential targeted improvements to the structure and content of the primary financial statements focusing primarily on the statements of financial performance and cash flows. A consultation document is expected in the first half of 2019.

2.2   Changes in equity

2.2   Changes in equity

CURRENTLY EFFECTIVE REQUIREMENTS

This publication reflects IFRS in issue at 1 August 2018, and the currently effective requirements cover annual periods beginning on 1 January 2018.

The requirements related to this topic are mainly derived from the following.

STANDARD	TITLE
IAS 1	Presentation of Financial Statements

FORTHCOMING REQUIREMENTS AND FUTURE DEVELOPMENTS

For this topic, there are no forthcoming requirements or future developments.

2.2.10   **STATEMENT OF CHANGES IN EQUITY**

2.2.10.10   A statement of changes in equity includes:

- total comprehensive income for the period, separately showing the total amounts attributable to owners of the parent and to NCI;
- for each component of equity, the effects of retrospective application or retrospective restatement recognised in accordance with IAS 8; and
- for each component of equity, a reconciliation between the carrying amount at the beginning and at the end of the period, separately (as a minimum) disclosing changes resulting from:
  - profit or loss;
  - OCI; and
  - transactions with owners in their capacity as owners, showing separately contributions by and distributions to owners and changes in ownership interests in subsidiaries that do not result in a loss of control. [*IAS 1.106*]

2.2.10.20   An analysis of OCI by item – for each component of equity – is presented either in the statement of changes in equity or in the notes. [*IAS 1.106A*]

2.2.10.30   All owner-related changes in equity are presented in the statement of changes in equity, separately from non-owner changes in equity. As such, dividends and the related per-share amounts are disclosed either in the statement of changes in equity or in the notes to the financial statements. Such disclosures are not included in the statement of profit or loss and OCI. [*IAS 1.107*]

2.2.20   **Entities with no equity**

2.2.20.10   Entities that have share capital that is not equity (e.g. some co-operative entities) and entities that do not have equity as defined in IAS 32 (e.g. some mutual funds) may need to adapt the financial statement presentation of members' or unit holders' interests. Because a statement of changes in equity is not relevant for such entities, a statement of changes in net assets attributable to members or unit holders may be presented. Although IFRS does not require presentation of this statement, it may provide useful information with respect to the components underlying the movements in the net assets of the entity attributable to the members or unit holders during the year. [*IAS 1.6*]

2.2.30   **Changes in accounting policies and errors**

2.2.30.10   A change in accounting policy or the correction of a material prior-period error is generally presented by adjusting the opening balance of each affected component of equity of the earliest period presented and the other comparative amounts disclosed for each prior period presented (see chapter 2.8). The adjustments for each prior period and the beginning of the period are disclosed in the statement of changes in equity. [*IAS 1.106(b), 110, 8.22*]

2.2.30.20   The total adjustment to each component of equity resulting from changes in accounting policies is presented separately from the total adjustment resulting from the correction of errors. [*IAS 1.110*]

2.2.30.30   In addition, a third statement of financial position as at the beginning of the preceding period is presented following a change in accounting policy, the correction of an error or a reclassification if those changes have a material effect on the information in the statement of financial position at the beginning of that period (see 2.1.20 and 2.8.140). [*IAS 1.10(f), 40A–40D*]

2.3   Statement of cash flows

2.3 Statement of cash flows

CURRENTLY EFFECTIVE REQUIREMENTS

This publication reflects IFRS in issue at 1 August 2018, and the currently effective requirements cover annual periods beginning on 1 January 2018.

The requirements related to this topic are mainly derived from the following.

STANDARD	TITLE
IAS 7	Statement of Cash Flows

FORTHCOMING REQUIREMENTS

For this topic, there are no forthcoming requirements.

FUTURE DEVELOPMENTS

This topic is subject to future developments that may affect several aspects of the statement of cash flows. See 2.3.130.

2.3.10   CASH AND CASH EQUIVALENTS

2.3.10.10   Cash comprises cash on hand and demand deposits. Cash equivalents are short-term highly liquid investments that are readily convertible to known amounts of cash and that are subject to an insignificant risk of changes in value. [*IAS 7.6*]

2.3.10.20   Demand deposits are not defined in IFRS, but in our view they should have the same level of liquidity as cash and therefore should be able to be withdrawn at any time without penalty. In addition, in our view demand deposits need not be held with a financial institution – e.g. monies held by solicitors for clients in separate and designated accounts could be considered demand deposits if they are not restricted. Even if a deposit fails to be classified as cash it may still meet the definition of cash equivalents.

2.3.10.30   Because the investments comprising cash equivalents are required to be readily convertible to known amounts of cash, only debt securities and deposits can generally qualify for inclusion, subject to the other criteria being met. Equity investments may also qualify if they are, in substance, cash equivalents – e.g. preference shares acquired within a short period of their maturity and with a specified redemption date.

2.3.10.35   An overriding test is that cash equivalents are held for the purpose of meeting short-term cash commitments rather than for investment or other purposes. For example, an entity gives a three-month loan to a customer to help the customer in managing its short-term liquidity position. In our view, the investment in this loan is not a cash equivalent because it was given for a purpose other than for the entity to manage its own short-term cash commitments. [*IAS 7.7*]

2.3.10.40   'Short-term' is not defined in IAS 7, but the standard encourages a cut-off of three months' maturity from the date of acquisition. In our view, three months is a presumption that may be rebutted only in rare cases when facts and circumstances indicate that the investment is held for the purpose of meeting short-term cash commitments (see 2.3.10.35) and when the instrument otherwise meets the definition of a cash equivalent (see 2.3.10.10). Cash flows related to an investment that is not a cash equivalent – e.g. those with a longer maturity for which the presumption is not rebutted – may be investing activities. [*IAS 7.7, IU 05-13*]

2.3.10.45   An investment that is redeemable at any time is a cash equivalent only if the amount of cash that would be received is known at the time of the initial investment, is subject to an insignificant risk of changes in value, and the other IAS 7 criteria for cash equivalents are met (see 2.3.10.10). The IFRS Interpretations Committee discussed this issue and noted that the fact that an investment can be converted at the market price at any time does not mean that the 'readily convertible to known amounts of cash' criterion has been met. [*IAS 7.6–7, IU 07-09*]

2.3.10.50   An investment that does not meet the definition of a cash equivalent on acquisition does not become a cash equivalent as it nears maturity. [*IAS 7.7, IU 05-13*]

2.3.10.55   An entity discloses the policy that it adopts in determining the composition of cash and cash equivalents. The effect of any change in the policy for determining components of cash and cash equivalents is then reported in accordance with IAS 8. [*IAS 7.46–47*]

2.3.10.60   Bank overdrafts repayable on demand are included as cash and cash equivalents to the extent that they form an integral part of the entity's cash management. However, even though a bank overdraft might be netted against cash and cash equivalents in the statement of cash flows, this is not permitted in the statement of financial position unless the offsetting criteria are met (see 3.1.50 and 7.10.110). [*IAS 7.8, 32.42*]

2.3.10.65   The IFRS Interpretations Committee discussed whether certain types of short-term borrowing arrangements – such as short-term loans and credit facilities with a short contractual notice period (e.g. 14 days) – may be included as a component of cash and cash equivalents in an entity's statement of cash flows. The Committee noted that the entity does not include these short-term arrangements as components of cash and cash equivalents because, unlike bank overdrafts – which are repayable on demand and form an integral part of the entity's cash management (see 2.3.10.60) – such short-term arrangements are not repayable on demand. The Committee observed that assessing whether a banking arrangement is an integral part of the entity's cash management is a matter of facts and circumstances. It also observed that if the balance of a banking arrangement does not often fluctuate from being negative to positive, then this indicates that the arrangement does not form an integral part of the entity's cash management but represents a form of financing. [*IU 06-18*]

2.3.10.70   The components of cash and cash equivalents and a reconciliation of cash and cash equivalents in the statement of cash flows to the equivalent amount presented in the statement of financial position are disclosed and may be included in the notes to the financial statements. For example, if an entity has cash balances in a disposal group that is classified as held-for-sale in the statement of financial position, then this would be a reconciling item between cash and cash equivalents in the statement of cash flows and the equivalent amount presented in the statement of financial position. [*IAS 7.45*]

2.3.20   OPERATING, INVESTING AND FINANCING ACTIVITIES

2.3.20.10   The statement of cash flows presents cash flows during the period classified by operating, investing and financing activities.
- 'Operating activities' are the principal revenue-producing activities of the entity and other activities that are not investing or financing activities.
- 'Investing activities' relate to the acquisition and disposal of long-term assets and other investments not included in cash equivalents.
- 'Financing activities' relate to shareholders' equity and borrowings of the entity. [*IAS 7.6, 10*]

2.3.20.11   The wording of the definitions means that operating activities is the default classification when a cash flow does not meet the definition of either investing or financing cash flows. There is perceived inconsistency between the primary classification principle in IAS 7 and certain specific guidance in the standard. The primary principle is that cash flows are classified based on the nature of the activity to which they relate. Such classification is done in a manner that is most appropriate to the business of the entity. However, certain guidance in IAS 7 may not lead to a consistent application of this principle. [*IAS 7.10–11*]

2.3.20.13   For example, IFRS 6 allows entities in the extractive industries to choose an accounting policy, to be applied consistently, in respect of qualifying exploration and evaluation (E&E)

expenditure. Such expenditure may be either capitalised as an asset or expensed as it is incurred (see 5.11.30). The nature of the activity to which the cash flows relate is the same regardless of the accounting policy chosen. However, IAS 7 requires the related cash flows to be classified as investing activities only if the expenditure is capitalised, because only expenditure that results in the recognition of an asset can be classified as investing activities. If such expenditure is expensed, then the related cash flows are classified as operating activities in the statement of cash flows. As a result, cash flows related to the identical activities of two entities with different accounting policies are classified differently because of the accounting policy chosen by each entity. [*IFRS 6.6, 9, 24, IAS 7.11, 16*]

2.3.20.14   Although aggregate cash flows arising from obtaining or losing control of subsidiaries or other businesses are presented separately and classified as investing activities, only expenditure that results in the recognition of an asset can be classified as investing activities. In some cases, significant judgement may be needed to classify certain cash flows that relate to business combinations. In particular, consideration may be needed of whether the cash flow relates to obtaining control and whether the expenditure results in a recognised asset in the statement of financial position. [*IAS 7.16, 39*]

2.3.20.15   In our view, in the consolidated financial statements transaction costs associated with a business combination, although they are ancillary to the assets acquired, should be classified as operating activities because the transaction costs are not capitalised.

2.3.20.16   If deferred consideration arising from a business combination is settled in cash, then the payment will reflect both the initial fair value and amounts recognised in profit or loss as a finance expense. The cash flow classification of the cash paid may require judgement, taking into account the nature of the activity to which the cash outflow relates (see 2.3.20.11). To the extent that the amount paid reflects the finance expense, classification consistent with interest paid may be appropriate. Depending on the accounting policy adopted for classification of interest paid, this may be classified as either financing or operating activities (see 2.3.50.20).

2.3.20.17   To the extent that the amount paid reflects the settlement of the fair value of the consideration recognised on initial recognition (see 2.6.270), classification of the cash flow as a financing activity would be consistent with the settlement of other financial liabilities – e.g. a loan or a finance lease obligation. However, classification as an investing activity may also be appropriate. IAS 7 is not clear whether the settlement of a financial liability is always classified as a financing activity. For example, the settlement of trade payables is often classified in line with the nature of the underlying expenditure, including as an investing activity if the payment is for an item of property, plant and equipment. Accordingly, judgement will be needed to determine whether the cash settlement arises from obtaining control or the settlement of financing provided by the seller. Factors that may be relevant to this judgement include the length of the period between initial recognition of the liability and settlement, whether the period reflects a normal credit period and whether the liability is discounted to reflect its deferred settlement; the latter would suggest that there is a financing element to the arrangement.

2.3.20.18   Similar judgements to those described in 2.3.20.16–17 apply in respect of the classification of cash outflows for contingent consideration in a business combination (see 2.6.280). Further judgement is needed if the cash payment is greater than the amount recognised on initial recognition as a result of the resolution of uncertainties – e.g. the better-than-expected operating performance of the acquired business. In this case, classification as an operating activity, or classification consistent with interest paid (see 2.3.50.20), may be appropriate.

2.3.20.20   The separate components of a single transaction are each classified as operating, investing or financing; IFRS does not allow a transaction to be classified based on its predominant characteristic. For example, a loan repayment comprises interest (which may be classified as operating or financing (see 2.3.50.20)) and principal repayment (which is classified as financing). [*IAS 7.12*]

2.3.20.30   However, the aggregate net cash flows from obtaining or losing control of subsidiaries and other businesses are presented separately as a single line item as part of investing activities. For example, when a subsidiary is acquired, a single line item equal to the consideration paid by cash and cash equivalents, less any cash and cash equivalents held by the subsidiary at the time of acquisition, is shown as an investing cash outflow, rather than as separate cash outflows and inflows for the various net assets and liabilities acquired. [*IAS 7.39–42*]

2.3.20.35   A subsequent purchase of an additional interest or a sale by a parent of a subsidiary's equity instruments that does not result in a loss of control is classified as cash flows from financing activities because such changes in ownership interests are accounted for as transactions with equity holders (see 2.3.20.10 and 2.5.570.20). [*IAS 7.42A*]

2.3.20.40   Non-cash investing or financing transactions – e.g. shares issued as consideration in a business combination, or acquisition of assets via a finance lease – are not included in the statement of cash flows, but are disclosed to provide relevant information about investing and financing activities. [*IAS 7.43–44*]

2.3.30   DIRECT VS INDIRECT METHOD

2.3.30.10   Cash flows from operating activities may be presented either under the direct method (receipts from customers, payments to suppliers etc) or under the indirect method (profit or loss for the period reconciled to the total net cash flow from operating activities). Although the standard encourages use of the direct method, in our experience the indirect method is usually used. [*IAS 7.18–20*]

2.3.30.20   For an entity that elects to present operating cash flows under the indirect method, there is often confusion about the correct starting point: should it be profit or loss or can a different figure, such as profit before income tax, be used? The standard itself refers to profit or loss, but the example provided in the appendix to the standard starts with a different figure (profit before taxation). Because the appendix is illustrative only and therefore does not have the same status as the standard, it would be more appropriate to follow the standard (see 1.1.100.50). [*IAS 7.18, 20, IEA*]

2.3.30.30   Alternatively, an entity using the indirect method may choose to present its operating cash flows by showing revenues and expenses before working capital changes as the starting point, followed by changes during the period in inventories, and operating receivables and payables. However, in our experience this approach is less common. [*IAS 7.20, IEA*]

2.3.40   **CLASSIFICATION ISSUES**

2.3.50   **Interest, dividends and taxes**

2.3.50.10   IFRS requires cash flows from interest and dividends received and paid, and income taxes paid, to be disclosed separately. In our view, this means that disclosure is required in the statement of cash flows rather than in the notes. [*IAS 7.31–36*]

2.3.50.20   The standard does not, however, specify the classification of cash flows from interest and dividends received and paid, and an entity is required to choose its own policy for classifying each of interest and dividends paid as operating or financing activities and each of interest and dividends received as operating or investing activities. An entity chooses a presentation method that will present these cash flows in the most appropriate manner for the business or industry (e.g. banking), if applicable, and the method selected is applied consistently. Taxes paid are classified as operating activities unless it is practicable to identify them with, and therefore classify them as, financing or investing activities. [*IAS 7.31–36*]

2.3.50.30   Even if it is practicable for an entity to classify certain taxes as investing or financing activities, the standard is not clear on whether:

- to allocate *all* taxes paid among the three categories of cash flows; or
- to allocate only certain taxes paid because they relate to transactions classified as investing or financing, leaving the balance in operating activities.

2.3.50.35   In our view, it is acceptable to allocate only certain material tax cash flows, while leaving the balance in operating activities, as long as the approach taken is applied consistently and disclosed appropriately. We believe that allocating, for example, 60 percent of the tax cash flows as it represents the material tax cash flows known to be from investing or financing activities, with appropriate disclosure, provides better information than not allocating any.

2.3.50.37   When borrowing costs are capitalised in accordance with IAS 23 (see 4.6.10), interest expenditure forms part of the cost of a recognised asset. Although paragraph 33 of IAS 7 specifies that interest paid may be classified as a cash flow from operating or financing activities, paragraph 16 of IAS 7 permits expenditure that results in a recognised asset to be classified as investing activities. [*IAS 7.16, 33*]

2.3.50.38   Given these inconsistencies, in our view an entity should choose an accounting policy, to be applied consistently, to classify cash flows related to capitalised interest as follows:

- as cash flows from investing activities if the other cash payments to acquire the qualifying asset are reflected as investing activities; or
- consistently with interest cash flows that are not capitalised (see 2.3.50.20).

EXAMPLE 1 – CAPITALISED INTEREST – PRESENTATION

2.3.50.40   Company C builds a plant and pays cash of 1,000, which includes 50 of capitalised interest. C should choose an accounting policy, to be applied consistently, to present the interest paid of 50 as cash flows from operating, financing

> or investing activities (see 2.3.50.38). The remaining 950 is included in investing activities. This is consistent with the requirement to classify separately the different components of a single transaction (see 2.3.20.20).

2.3.50.50   The total amount of interest paid is disclosed in the statement of cash flows, regardless of whether the related expense has been recognised in profit or loss or capitalised as borrowing costs. [*IAS 7.32*]

2.3.55   Assets held for rental and subsequently held for sale

2.3.55.10   Cash flows related to the acquisition of an asset recognised in accordance with IAS 16 are generally cash flows from investing activities (see 2.3.20.10). However, cash payments to manufacture or acquire assets held for rental that subsequently become held-for-sale (i.e. are transferred to inventory) are cash flows from operating activities (see 3.2.380.40). Cash flows from rental payments and subsequent sales of these assets are also classified as operating. [*IAS 7.14, 16.68A*]

2.3.60   Hedging

2.3.60.10   If a hedging instrument is accounted for as a hedge of an identifiable position (see chapter 7.9), then the cash flows of the hedging instrument are classified in the same manner as the cash flows of the position being hedged. For a discussion of the presentation of hedging instruments, see 7.10.150. [*IAS 7.16*]

2.3.70   Factoring arrangements

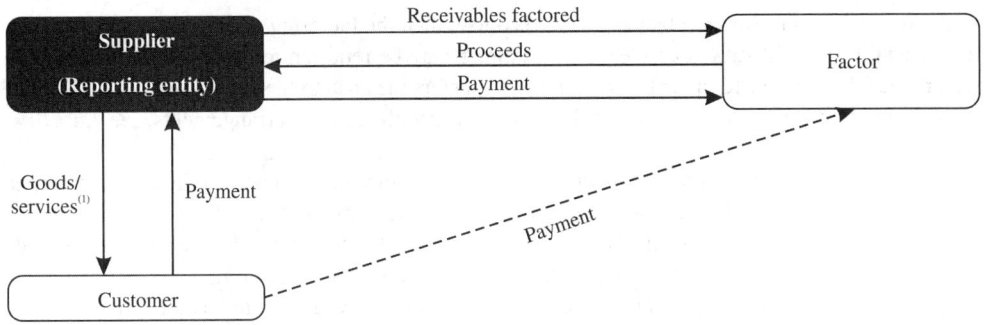

Note
1.   Goods/services – Guidance in this section focuses on factoring arrangements related to goods or services that are operating in nature (e.g. inventory) rather than, for example, the sale of property, plant and equipment.

2.3.70.10   In a traditional factoring arrangement, an entity that is a supplier of goods or services (the entity) obtains cash from a bank or other financial institution (i.e. the factor) against receivables due from the entity's customers. The arrangement might take different legal forms – e.g. the receivables might be sold to the factor or pledged as security for a loan from the factor and the factor may or may not have recourse to the entity in the event that the customer does not settle. A traditional factoring arrangement is initiated by the entity and the factor, rather than the customer. In many cases, the customer might be unaware of the arrangement.

2.3.70.20   There is no specific guidance in IFRS on the classification of cash flows from traditional factoring arrangements – e.g. whether the entity should classify the cash inflows from the factor as operating or financing in the statement of cash flows. Presenting a single *financing* cash inflow may significantly affect the statement of cash flows – e.g. in an extreme case, if the entity factored all of its receivables, then there may be no operating cash inflows presented for the sale of goods or services. The primary consideration for the classification of cash flows is the nature of the activity to which they relate (see 2.3.20.11) and judgement may be needed to apply this to factoring arrangements. For a discussion of cash flow classification of factoring of receivables without recourse, see 2.3.72, and with recourse, see 2.3.73. For a discussion of derecognition of financial assets and securitisations, see 7.6.60–330.

2.3.72   *Factoring of trade receivables without recourse*

2.3.72.10   If the receivables are factored without recourse, then in our view the proceeds from the factor should be classified as part of operating activities even if the entity does not enter into such transactions regularly. This is because the proceeds do not generally fit clearly into the definitions of either investing or financing activities (see 2.3.20). In addition, factoring of receivables without recourse can be likened to the early collection of amounts due from customers and as such the related cash inflow is considered operating in nature.

2.3.72.20   In some cases, an entity may continue to collect cash from customers on behalf of the factor even if the receivables are factored without recourse. In these circumstances, the entity may collect the cash and transfer it onwards to the factor, and it may be appropriate to either exclude these cash flows from the cash flow statement or to present the relevant cash inflow and outflows net (similar to 2.3.73.30).

2.3.73   *Factoring of trade receivables with recourse*

2.3.73.10   If receivables are factored with recourse, then the factoring arrangement may take different legal forms and structures – e.g. the customer may be required to remit cash directly to the factor (see 2.3.73.20) or to the entity, which then transfers the cash to the factor (see 2.3.73.30). For a discussion of derecognition of receivables in factoring with recourse arrangements, see 7.6.270.

2.3.73.20   If the customer remits cash directly to the factor, then in our view the following approaches to presenting cash flows are acceptable and should be applied consistently.

- *Approach 1:* Present a single financing cash inflow or a single operating cash inflow for the proceeds received from the factor against receivables due from the entity's customers. An entity applies judgement in determining whether to classify proceeds received from the factor as financing or operating cash inflows, giving consideration to the nature of the activity to which the cash inflow relates (see 2.3.70.20). Although the nature of the arrangement may be viewed as collateralised borrowing (see 7.6.270) and as such be classified as a financing cash inflow based on the guidance in paragraph 17(c) of IAS 7, we believe that it may also be acceptable to classify the proceeds from the factor as part of operating activities on the basis that the principal nature of cash flows related to the provision of goods and services will often be operating (see 2.3.20.10). Approach 1 considers the settlement of the liability to the factor by the customer as a non-cash transaction for the entity – i.e. the entity presents only a single cash flow receipt from the factor – therefore it needs to provide disclosure of non-cash transactions (see 2.3.74.20).
- *Approach 2:* Present gross cash flows. Under this approach, the entity would present a financing cash inflow for the proceeds received from the factor, followed by an operating cash inflow when

the factor collects the amounts from the customer in respect of goods or services sold by the entity and a financing cash outflow for settlement of amounts due to the factor. Approach 2 reflects that, in substance, the factor is collecting receivables on behalf of the entity and retains the proceeds in settlement of the entity's liability to the factor.

2.3.73.30   If the customer remits cash directly to the entity, then this arrangement involves multiple actual cash flows for the entity – i.e. proceeds from the factor on factoring of the receivables, receipts from the customer and payment to the factor. In this case, the entity presents a financing cash inflow for the proceeds received from the factor, followed by an operating cash inflow for the proceeds received from the customer and a financing cash outflow to settle the liability due to the factor. We do not believe that the entity could report a single operating cash flow in this case. However, the entity may be able to report the proceeds received from, and the settlement of the liability due to, the factor on a net basis if the relevant criteria are met (see 2.3.110). [*IAS 7.22, 23A(c)*]

2.3.74   *Disclosures*

2.3.74.10   In addition to the appropriate classification in the statement of cash flows, an entity that is a supplier of goods and services in a factoring arrangement is required to disclose information about those arrangements that is relevant to an understanding of its cash flows. This disclosure may include an explanation of the nature of the arrangement and how it is reflected in the financial statements. Relevant IFRS disclosure requirements include:
- disclosure of significant accounting policies; and
- disclosure of significant judgements that management has made in the process of applying the accounting policies and that have the most significant effect on the amounts recognised in the financial statements. [*IAS 1.117–122*]

2.3.74.20   The additional disclosure requirements that may be relevant to these arrangements include:
- reporting separately major classes of gross cash receipts and gross cash payments arising from investing and financing activities;
- disclosure of non-cash transactions; and
- additional information that may be relevant to users in understanding the financial position and liquidity of the entity. [*IAS 7.21, 43, 50*]

2.3.75   **Reverse factoring arrangements**

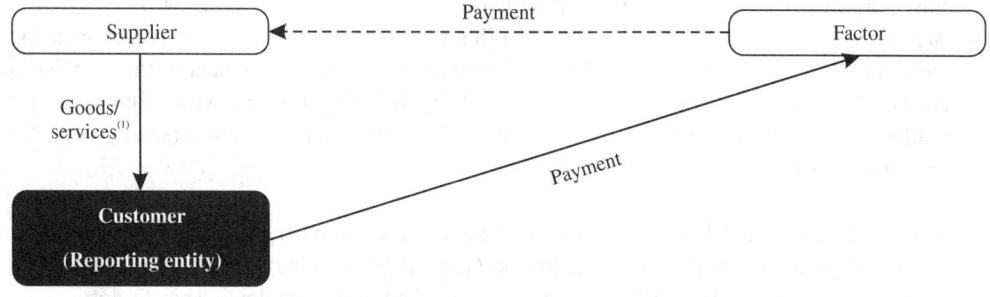

Note
1.   Goods/services – Guidance in this section focuses on arrangements related to goods or services received from the supplier that are operating in nature (e.g. inventory) rather than, for example, the acquisition of property, plant and equipment.

2.3.75.10   Under a reverse factoring arrangement (see 7.6.465 and 7.10.35), a factor agrees to pay amounts to a supplier in respect of invoices owed by the supplier's customer and receives settlement from that customer (the entity) at a later date. A reverse factoring arrangement is often initiated by the customer and the factor.

2.3.75.20   There is no specific guidance in IFRS on the classification of cash flows for an entity that is the customer in a reverse factoring arrangement – i.e. whether it should classify the cash outflows to settle amounts owed to the factor as operating or financing in the statement of cash flows. Presenting a single *financing* cash outflow may significantly affect the statement of cash flows – e.g. in an extreme case, if all of the entity's payables were reverse factored, then there may be no operating cash outflows presented for its purchases.

2.3.75.30   The appropriate presentation in the statement of financial position and disclosure about liabilities related to reverse factoring arrangements are discussed in 7.10.35.70–90, 315 and 655. However, in our view it is the nature of the activity, rather than the classification of the related item in the statement of financial position, that determines the appropriate classification of the cash outflow. [*IAS 7.10–11, IU 03-12, 07-12, 03-13*]

2.3.75.40   Reverse factoring arrangements may take different legal forms and structures. In our view, the following approaches to presenting cash flows are acceptable and should be applied consistently.
- *Approach 1:* Present a single operating cash outflow or a single financing cash outflow for the payments made to the factor: Under this approach, an entity applies judgement in determining whether to classify payments made to the factor as an operating or financing cash outflow, giving consideration to the primary principle that cash flows are classified according to the nature of the activity to which they relate (see 2.3.20.11), taking into account the specific facts and circumstances. For example, an entity needs to consider if the principal business purpose of the reverse factoring arrangement is to provide funding to the supplier or to facilitate efficient payment processing, and whether the reverse factoring arrangement significantly extends payment terms beyond the normal terms agreed with other suppliers (see 7.10.35.80). In our experience, the principal nature of cash payments related to the purchase of goods and services will often be operating. This approach considers the payment to a supplier by the factor not to be a cash transaction of the customer– i.e. the entity presents a single cash flow for cash payments made to the factor. If an entity follows this approach, then it provides disclosure of non-cash transactions (see 2.3.75.60).
- *Approach 2:* Present gross cash flows. Under this approach, the entity would present financing cash inflows and operating cash outflows when the factor makes a payment to the supplier in respect of the purchase of goods or services made by the entity, together with a financing cash outflow for settlement of amounts due to the factor. This approach presents payments by the factor to suppliers as payments made on behalf of the entity.

2.3.75.50   In addition to the appropriate classification in the statement of cash flows, an entity that is the customer in a reverse factoring arrangement (see 7.10.35) is required to disclose information about those arrangements that is relevant to an understanding of its cash flows. This disclosure may include an explanation of the nature of the arrangement and how it is reflected in the financial statements. Relevant IFRS disclosure requirements include:

- disclosure of significant accounting policies; and
- disclosure of significant judgements that management has made in the process of applying the accounting policies and that have the most significant effect on the amounts recognised in the financial statements. [*IAS 1.117–122*]

2.3.75.60   The additional disclosure requirements that may be relevant to these arrangements include:

- reporting separately major classes of gross cash receipts and gross cash payments arising from investing and financing activities;
- disclosure of non-cash transactions; and
- additional information that may be relevant to users in understanding the financial position and liquidity of the entity. [*IAS 7.21, 43, 50*]

2.3.80   FOREIGN EXCHANGE DIFFERENCES

2.3.80.10   Cash flows arising from an entity's foreign currency transactions are translated into the entity's functional currency (see 2.7.30) at the exchange rates at the dates of the cash flows; when exchange rates have been relatively stable, an appropriate average can be used. When the presentation currency is different from the functional currency, the functional currency cash flows are translated into the presentation currency at the rates at the dates of the cash flows (or appropriate averages). For example, the functional currency cash flows of a foreign operation will need to be translated into the group presentation currency when preparing consolidated financial statements. The effect of exchange rate changes on the balances of cash and cash equivalents is presented as part of the reconciliation of movements therein. [*IAS 7.25–28*]

2.3.90   Cash held in foreign currency

EXAMPLE 2 – EFFECT OF EXCHANGE RATE CHANGES – CALCULATION AND PRESENTATION

2.3.90.10   This example illustrates the calculation of the effect of exchange rate changes on the balances of an individual entity's cash and cash equivalents and its presentation in the statement of cash flows.

	FOREIGN CURRENCY	RATE	FUNCTIONAL CURRENCY
Balance of cash held in foreign currency on 1 January 2018	100	1:1	100
Receipts from customers	100	1.5:1	150
Payments to suppliers	(50)	1.6:1	(80)
Balance of cash held in foreign currency on 31 December 2018	150		170
Translated cash at the reporting date	150	2:1	300
Gain on cash held in foreign currency			130

59

Statement of financial position

	FUNCTIONAL CURRENCY 2018	FUNCTIONAL CURRENCY 2017
Share capital	100	100
Retained earnings	200[1]	-
Cash	300	100

Note
1. Calculated as (150 - 80 + 130).

Statement of cash flows extract – Direct method

	2018
Receipts from customers[1]	150
Payments to suppliers[2]	(80)
Net increase in cash	70
Cash and cash equivalents at 1 January 2018	100
Effect of exchange rate fluctuations on cash held	130
Cash and cash equivalents at 31 December 2018	300

Notes
1. All receivables collected by the reporting date.
2. All invoices paid by the reporting date.

Statement of cash flows extract – Indirect method

	2018
Net profit	200
Unrealised foreign currency gain	(130)
Net increase in cash	70
Cash and cash equivalents at 1 January 2018	100
Effect of exchange rate fluctuations on cash held	130
Cash and cash equivalents at 31 December 2018	300

2.3.100   **Other foreign exchange differences**

2.3.100.10   Assets and liabilities denominated in a foreign currency generally include an element of unrealised exchange differences at the reporting date. When applying the indirect method, it is generally more transparent for the unrealised exchange difference to be presented as a single non-cash item within operating activities, rather than left embedded in the asset or liability.

EXAMPLE 3 – UNREALISED EXCHANGE DIFFERENCES – PRESENTATION

2.3.100.20   Company Z obtains a loan in a foreign currency on 15 May 2018. The cash proceeds from the loan are exchanged into Z's functional currency on the same day. There are no other transactions in 2018. Z presents cash flows from operating activities applying the indirect method. The following facts are also relevant for this example.

	FOREIGN CURRENCY	RATE	FC[(1)]
Loan in FC[(1)] on 15 May 2018	250	1.5:1	375
Loan in FC on 31 December 2018	250	2:1	500

Balances of cash and loan in FC

	31 DECEMBER 2018	31 DECEMBER 2017
Cash	675	300
Loan	(500)	-

Note
1.   FC = Functional currency.

2.3.100.30   In the statement of cash flows for 2018, Z presents the unrealised exchange difference related to the loan in a foreign currency as a single non-cash item within operating activities as follows.

Statement of cash flows extract – Indirect method

	2018
Cash flows from operating activities	
Net loss	(125)
Unrealised foreign currency loss	125
Net cash from operating activities	–[(1)]
Cash flows from financing activities	
Loan obtained	375
Net cash increase	375
Cash at 1 January 2018	300
Cash at 31 December 2018	675

> **Note**
> 1. Because there are no receipts from customers or payments to suppliers, net cash from operating activities would also be zero under the direct method.

2.3.110   OFFSETTING

2.3.110.10   Financing and investing cash flows are generally reported gross. [*IAS 7.21*]

EXAMPLE 4 – GROSS PRESENTATION OF CASH FLOWS

> **2.3.110.20**   Company M obtains a loan of 2,000 during the reporting period and uses the proceeds to repay another loan of 2,000. M presents the following as financing activities:
> - proceeds from borrowings: 2,000; and
> - separately, repayment of borrowings: 2,000.

2.3.110.25   Receipts and payments may be netted only when the items concerned – e.g. sale and purchase of investments – turn over quickly, the amounts are large and the maturities are short; or when they are on behalf of customers and the cash flows reflect the activities of the customers. [*IAS 7.22–23A*]

2.3.110.30   In addition, a financial institution may report on a net basis certain advances, deposits and repayments thereof that form part of its operating activities. However, not all borrowings of a financial institution are part of operating activities; therefore, Example 4 in relation to financing activities applies equally to a financial institution. [*IAS 7.24*]

2.3.110.40   In our view, if a group comprises a combination of financial institution and non-financial institution subsidiaries, then the offsetting requirements would apply separately to each subsidiary's cash flows as presented in the consolidated statement of cash flows.

2.3.120   TAXES COLLECTED ON BEHALF OF THIRD PARTIES

2.3.120.10   IAS 7 is silent on the classification of cash flows from taxes that are collected on behalf of third parties when the direct method is used to present cash flows from operating activities; examples include value added tax (VAT) and goods and services tax (GST).

2.3.120.20   In our view, taxes collected on behalf of third parties, when the direct method is used, may be either:
- included as separate line items to show the impact on cash flows of such taxes separately; or
- included in receipts from customers and payments to suppliers.

2.3.120.30   In our experience, these indirect taxes are generally included in receipts from customers and payments to suppliers.

2.3.120.40 The example below illustrates alternative approaches to the presentation of taxes collected on behalf of third parties in the statement of cash flows.

EXAMPLE 5 – INDIRECT TAX CASH FLOWS – PRESENTATION

Services rendered for cash during 2018 (excluding GST of 20%)	100	
GST paid to tax authorities	10	
GST payable to tax authorities	10[(1)]	

Statement of financial position

	2018	2017
Share capital	100	100
Retained earnings	100	-
	200	100
Cash	210	100
GST payable	(10)	-
	200	100

Statement of cash flows extract – Direct method option 1

	2018
Receipts from customers[(2)]	100
Indirect taxes collected	20
Indirect taxes paid	(10)
Net cash increase	110
Cash at 1 January 2018	100
Cash at 31 December 2018	210

Statement of cash flows extract – Direct method option 2

	2018
Receipts from customers[(3)]	120
Payments to tax authorities[(3)]	(10)
Net cash increase	110
Cash at 1 January 2018	100
Cash at 31 December 2018	210

Statement of cash flows extract – Indirect method

	2018
Net profit	100
Increase in accounts payable	10
Net cash increase	110
Cash at 1 January 2018	100
Cash at 31 December 2018	210

Notes
1. Calculated as GST collected from customers less tax paid – i.e. (100 x 20%) - 10.
2. All receivables collected by the reporting date, net of GST.
3. All receivables collected, including GST, and all taxes paid by the reporting date.

2.3.123 CHANGES IN LIABILITIES ARISING FROM FINANCING ACTIVITIES

2.3.123.10   An entity discloses information that enables users of financial statements to evaluate changes in liabilities arising from financing activities, including changes from cash flows and non-cash changes. Liabilities arising from financing activities are liabilities for which cash flows were, or future cash flows will be, classified as cash flows from financing activities in the statement of cash flows (see 2.3.20.10). [*IAS 7.44A, 44C*]

2.3.123.20   One way to meet the requirement in 2.3.123.10 is to provide a reconciliation between the opening and closing balances in the statement of financial position for liabilities arising from financing activities, including:
- changes from financing cash flows;
- changes from obtaining or losing control of subsidiaries or other businesses;
- the effect of changes in foreign exchange rates;
- changes in fair values; and
- other changes. [*IAS 7.44B–44D*]

2.3.123.30   The disclosure requirement in 2.3.123.10 also applies to changes in financial assets. For example, it applies to assets that hedge liabilities arising from financing activities if cash flows from those financial assets were, or future cash flows will be, included in cash flows from financing activities. [*IAS 7.44C*]

2.3.123.40   When an entity provides the reconciliation described in 2.3.123.10, it is required to disclose sufficient information to enable users to link items included in the reconciliation to the statement of financial position and the statement of cash flows. [*IAS 7.44D*]

2.3.123.50   Although the disclosure of changes in other assets and liabilities is possible, such supplementary disclosure is provided separately from changes in liabilities arising from financing activities. [*IAS 7.44E*]

2.3.125 **CASH FLOW DISCLOSURE REQUIREMENTS OF OTHER STANDARDS**

2.3.125.10   Other standards have certain cash flow disclosure requirements – e.g. cash flows of discontinued operations (see 5.4.220.50–60) and cash flows arising from the exploration and evaluation of mineral resources (see 5.11.165).

2.3.130   **FUTURE DEVELOPMENTS**

2.3.130.10   The IASB is working on a research project on primary financial statements. This project considers potential targeted improvements to the structure and content of the primary financial statements focusing primarily on the statements of financial performance and cash flows (see 2.1.160). A consultation document is expected in the first half of 2019.

2.3.130.20   The project will be informed by the feedback received on the UK Financial Reporting Council's Discussion Paper *Improving the Statement of Cash Flows*, which was issued in October 2016.

2.4 Fair value measurement

2.4   Fair value measurement

CURRENTLY EFFECTIVE REQUIREMENTS

This publication reflects IFRS in issue at 1 August 2018, and the currently effective requirements cover annual periods beginning on 1 January 2018.

The requirements related to this topic are mainly derived from the following.

STANDARD	TITLE
IFRS 13	Fair Value Measurement

KPMG's publication *Fair Value Measurement: Questions and Answers* is an additional resource that provides guidance on fair value measurement under both US GAAP and IFRS.

FORTHCOMING REQUIREMENTS

The currently effective requirements are affected by the following forthcoming requirements. They are highlighted with a # and the impact is explained in the accompanying boxed text at the references indicated.

In May 2017, the IASB issued IFRS 17 *Insurance Contracts*, which is effective for annual periods beginning on or after 1 January 2021. See 2.4.423. IFRS 17 is the subject of chapter 8.1A.

FUTURE DEVELOPMENTS

The currently effective requirements that may be affected by future developments are highlighted with a * and are briefly discussed in 2.4.1090.

2.4.10   INTRODUCTION TO FAIR VALUE MEASUREMENT

2.4.10.10   This section provides a brief introduction to some of the key terms used in fair value measurement, as well as a diagram that shows the flow of this chapter in relation to the process of measuring fair value and determining the appropriate disclosures.

2.4.20   Overview

2.4.20.10   The key term that drives the measurement process is 'fair value': the price that would be received to sell an asset or paid to transfer a liability in an orderly transaction between market participants at the measurement date. Fair value is an 'exit price' – e.g. the price to sell an asset rather than the price to buy that asset. An exit price embodies expectations about the future cash inflows and cash outflows associated with an asset or liability from the perspective of a 'market participant' – i.e. based on buyers and sellers who have certain characteristics, such as being independent and knowledgeable about the asset or liability.

2.4.20.20   Fair value is a market-based measurement, rather than an entity-specific measurement, and is measured using assumptions that market participants would use in pricing the asset or liability, including assumptions about risk. As a result, an entity's intention to hold an asset or to settle or otherwise fulfil a liability is not relevant in measuring fair value.

2.4.20.30   Fair value is measured assuming a transaction in the 'principal market' for the asset or liability – i.e. the market with the highest volume and level of activity. In the absence of a principal market, it is assumed that the transaction would occur in the 'most advantageous market'. This is the market that would maximise the amount that would be received to sell an asset or minimise the amount that would be paid to transfer a liability, taking into account transaction and transport costs. In either case, the entity needs to have access to that market, although it does not necessarily have to be able to transact in that market on the measurement date.

2.4.20.40   A fair value measurement is made up of one or more 'inputs', which are the assumptions that market participants would make in valuing the asset or liability. The most reliable evidence of fair value is a quoted price in an active market. When this is not available, entities use another valuation technique to measure fair value, maximising the use of relevant observable inputs and minimising the use of unobservable inputs.

2.4.20.50   These inputs also form the basis of the 'fair value hierarchy', which is used to categorise a fair value measurement (in its entirety) into one of three levels. This categorisation is relevant for disclosure purposes. The disclosures about fair value measurements are extensive, with more disclosures being required for measurements in the lowest category (Level 3) in the hierarchy.

2.4.30   Steps in fair value measurement

2.4.30.10   The following flowchart sets out key points in applying IFRS 13, with references to the relevant sections in this chapter.

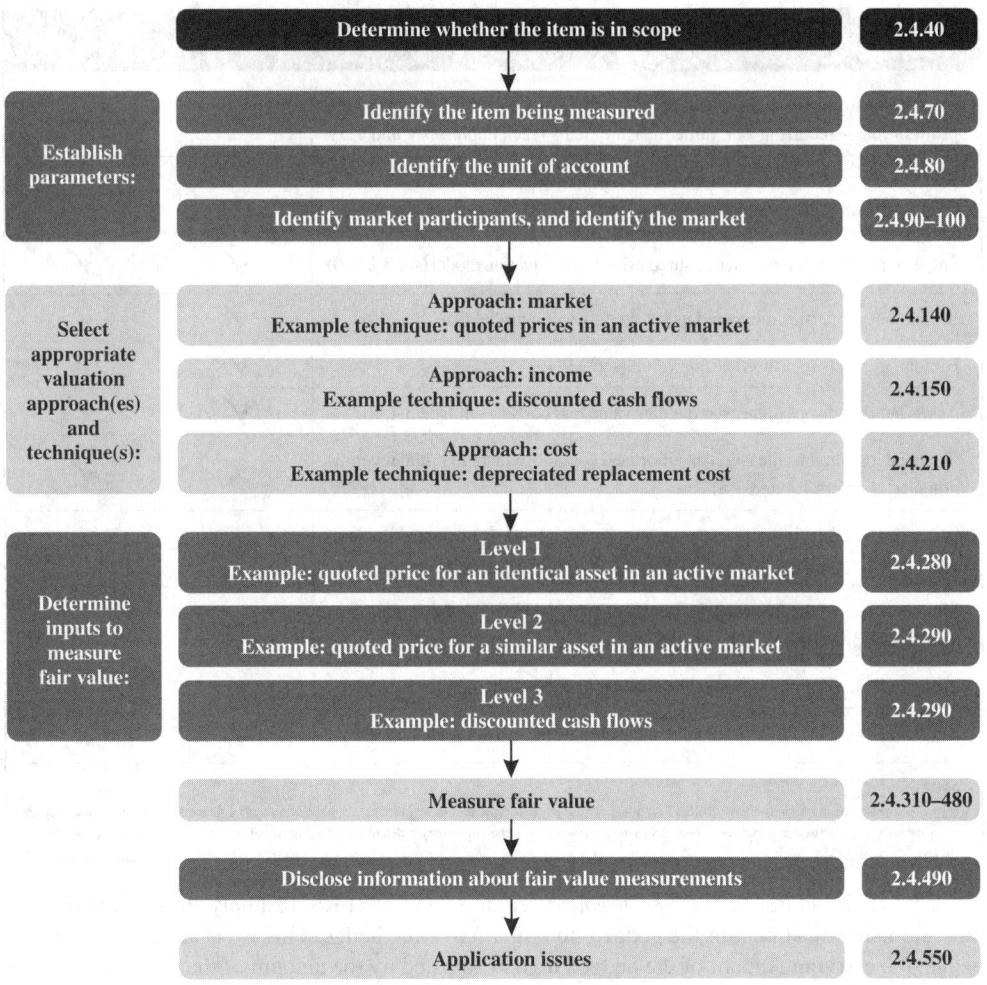

2.4.40 SCOPE

2.4.40.10   Subject to certain exceptions (see 2.4.50), IFRS 13 applies to the following:

• fair value measurements (both initial and subsequent) that are required or permitted by other standards;

• fair value measurements that are required or permitted to be disclosed by other standards, but which are not included in the statement of financial position; and

• measurements that are based on fair value, or disclosures of such measurements. [*IFRS 13.5–8, BC25*]

2.4.40.20   The following are some examples of assets and liabilities that fall in the scope of IFRS 13 for the purposes of measurement and/or disclosure. For a more in-depth discussion of the scope of the disclosure requirements, including the distinction between recurring and non-recurring fair value measurements, see 2.4.490. [*IFRS 13.5, 7*]

Topic	Measurement	Disclosure
Financial instruments measured at fair value through OCI or fair value through profit or loss – recurring fair value measurements (see chapters 7.4 and 7.5)	✓	✓
Fair value used as deemed cost by a first-time adopter of IFRS – e.g. for property, plant and equipment (see 6.1.300)	✓	✓
Property, plant and equipment measured using the revaluation model (see 3.2.300)	✓	✓
Investment properties measured using the fair value model (see 3.4.140)	✓	✓
Biological assets measured at fair value (see 3.9.40)	✓	✓
Assets held for disposal, measured at fair value less costs to sell (see 5.4.40)	✓	✓
Financial instruments measured at amortised cost subsequent to initial recognition (see chapters 7.4 and 7.5)	✗ [1]	✓
Fair value used to initially measure non-financial assets and non-financial liabilities in a business combination (see 2.4.510.10 and 2.6.600)	✓	✗
Measurements of the fair value less costs of disposal of CGUs for impairment testing (see 3.10.190)	✓	✗
Plan assets in a defined benefit scheme (see 4.4.620)	✓	✗
Retirement benefit plan investments measured at fair value under IAS 26	✓	✗

Note
1. The measurement requirements of IFRS 13 do not apply to the measurement of these investments in the statement of financial position because they are measured at amortised cost. However, the IFRS 13 measurement requirements do apply in determining the fair value for disclosure purposes (see 2.4.540.20).

2.4.40.30   In addition, the *measurement* requirements of IFRS 13 apply in determining the measurement adjustment to the hedged item in a fair value hedge. This is because in a fair value hedge, the carrying amount of the hedged item is adjusted by the amount of the fair value change attributable to the hedged risks (see 7.9.170).

2.4.40.40   However, the *disclosure* requirements of IFRS 13 relating to assets and liabilities that are measured at fair value only apply to the measurement of the hedged item in a fair value hedge if the measurement basis in the statement of financial position is or is based on fair value, independent of hedge accounting – e.g. the hedged item is a financial asset measured at fair value through OCI. In other cases, if the hedged item in a fair value hedge is measured neither at cost nor at fair value (see 7.9.170.50), then only the disclosures in paragraph 97 of IFRS 13 are required (see 2.4.540). [*IFRS 13.97*]

EXAMPLE 1 – SCOPE – HEDGING

2.4.40.50   Company B has a fixed interest liability denominated in its functional currency and measured at amortised cost. B enters into a pay-LIBOR receive-fixed interest rate swap to hedge 50% of the notional amount of the liability in respect of its benchmark interest rate exposure. The swap qualifies for hedge accounting (see 7.9.370.20–30).

2.4.40.60   Half of the liability – i.e. the proportion that is hedged – will be remeasured by B with respect to changes in fair value arising from changes in the benchmark interest rate from the beginning of the hedging relationship (see 7.9.170). B does not remeasure the liability for any changes in fair value arising from changes in credit spread, liquidity spread or other factors.

2.4.40.70   The fair value related to changes in the benchmark interest rate is measured in accordance with IFRS 13. However, the fair value disclosures for assets and liabilities measured at fair value do not apply because the hedged item, the liability, is measured on a hybrid basis (adjusted amortised cost) that is not fair value or based on fair value. Therefore, B provides only the disclosures required by paragraph 97 of IFRS 13 (see 2.4.540).

2.4.50   **Not in scope**

2.4.50.10   IFRS 13 does not apply to the following:
- share-based payment transactions in the scope of IFRS 2 (see chapter 4.5);
- leasing transactions in the scope of IAS 17 (see chapter 5.1); or
- measurements that are similar to fair value but that are not fair value – e.g. net realisable value in IAS 2 (see chapter 3.8), or value in use in IAS 36 (see chapter 3.10). [*IFRS 13.6*]

2.4.50.20   In addition, provisions measured at the best estimate of the expenditure required to settle the present obligation under IAS 37 are outside the scope of IFRS 13 (see 3.12.110).

2.4.60   **FAIR VALUE PRINCIPLES**

2.4.60.10   'Fair value' is the price that would be received to sell an asset or paid to transfer a liability in an orderly transaction between market participants at the measurement date. [*IFRS 13.9, A*]

2.4.60.20   Fair value is an exit price – e.g. the price to sell the asset rather than to buy the asset. An exit price embodies expectations about the future cash inflows and outflows associated with the asset or liability from the perspective of a market participant (see 2.4.90) that holds the asset or owes the liability at the measurement date. [*IFRS 13.A, BC39*]

2.4.60.30   Fair value is a market-based measurement, rather than an entity-specific measurement, and is measured using assumptions that market participants (see 2.4.90) would use in pricing the asset or liability, including assumptions about risk. As a result, an entity's intention to hold an asset or to settle or otherwise fulfil a liability is not relevant in measuring fair value, which is always the exit price. For example, the fact that an entity asserts that prices in orderly transactions are too low relative to its own value expectations, and accordingly that it would be unwilling to sell at such prices, is not relevant. [*IFRS 13.2–3*]

2.4.60.40   An 'orderly' transaction assumes that sufficient time to market the asset or liability in the usual and customary manner has occurred before the measurement date. For certain types of assets, such as liquid financial instruments (e.g. actively traded stock), the usual and customary market exposure may be short. In other situations (e.g. real estate assets), a longer market exposure would be required to generate interest, contact potential buyers, conduct negotiations, complete due diligence and complete legal agreements. [*IFRS 13.A, B43(a)*]

2.4.70   The item being measured

2.4.70.10   An entity takes into account characteristics of the asset or liability that market participants would take into account in a transaction for the asset or liability at the measurement date. In the case of an asset, these characteristics may include, for example:

- the condition and location of the asset (see 2.4.110); and
- restrictions, if any, on the sale or use of the asset. [*IFRS 13.11*]

2.4.70.20   It is important to distinguish a characteristic of an asset or liability from a characteristic arising from an entity's holding of the asset or liability, which is an entity-specific characteristic.

2.4.70.30   Factors used to evaluate whether a restriction on an asset is a characteristic of the asset or entity-specific may include whether the restriction is:

- transferred to a (potential) buyer;
- imposed on a holder by regulations;
- part of the contractual terms of the asset; or
- attached to the asset through a purchase contract or another commitment.

EXAMPLE 2 – RESTRICTIONS ON USE OF AN ASSET

2.4.70.40   Company B acquired a plot of land currently used as storage space for its factory in a business combination. As a condition of the acquisition, B is not allowed to change the use of the land for five years. However, the area in which the property is located has recently been re-zoned, and other land nearby has been redeveloped as residential property.

2.4.70.50   B has received legal advice that although it is restricted under the terms of the acquisition from changing the current use of the land, the land could be sold to a third party who would not be bound by the restriction. For this reason, B concludes that the restriction is a characteristic of the current holder rather than of the asset itself, and would not be considered in measuring the fair value of the land.

2.4.70.60   In measuring the fair value of a security held as an asset with a restriction on its sale or transfer, judgement is required to determine whether and in what amount an adjustment is required to the price of a similar unrestricted security to reflect the restriction.

- For security-specific restrictions – i.e. the restriction is an attribute of the instrument – the price used in the fair value measurement reflects the effect of the restriction if this would be considered by a market participant in pricing the security; this may require an adjustment to the quoted price of otherwise similar but unrestricted securities. For additional guidance, see 2.4.245.

- For entity-specific restrictions – i.e. the restriction is an attribute of the holder – the price used in the fair value measurement is not adjusted to reflect the restriction because it would not be considered by a market participant in pricing the security. [*IFRS 13.11, IE28*]

2.4.70.70   Securities that are subject to an entity-specific restriction are considered identical to those that are not subject to entity-specific restrictions. Consequently, a quoted price in an active market is a Level 1 input for a security that is subject to an entity-specific restriction (see 2.4.245.10). This is the case even if the entity is not able to sell the particular security on the measurement date because of an entity-specific restriction; an entity needs to be able to access the market but it does not need to be able to transact in the market at the measurement date to be able to measure the fair value on the basis of the price in that market (see 2.4.100). [*IFRS 13.19–20, 76*]

EXAMPLE 3 – SECURITIES SUBJECT TO LOCK-UP PROVISION

2.4.70.80   Company D offers securities in a public offering and enters into an underwriting agreement with Company E. The underwriting agreement between D and E contains a lock-up provision that prohibits D and its founders, directors and executive officers from selling their securities for a period of 180 days.

2.4.70.90   In this example, the lock-up provision arises from the underwriting agreement – i.e. a contract separate from the security – and applies only to D and its affiliates. Therefore, the restriction is entity-specific and is not considered in measuring the fair value of the securities.

2.4.70.100   In some borrowing arrangements, securities held by an investor are pledged as collateral supporting debt, or other commitments, of the investor. In these situations, the investor is restricted from selling the securities pledged during the period that the debt or other commitment is outstanding. Restrictions on securities resulting from the securities being pledged as collateral represent entity-specific restrictions that are not considered in measuring the fair value of the securities.

EXAMPLE 4 – SECURITIES SOLD UNDER REPURCHASE AGREEMENT

2.4.70.110   Bank F enters into a sale-and-repurchase agreement with Bank B in which F sells a security to B and agrees to repurchase an identical security at a future date at a fixed price. Under IFRS 9, F does not derecognise the security, and the agreement is accounted for as a secured borrowing (see 7.6.340). During the term of the sale-and-repurchase agreement, F does not own the security and so is unable to sell it or otherwise use it.

2.4.70.120   In this example, the restriction on F's ability to sell or use the security represents an entity-specific restriction. Therefore, the restriction is not considered in measuring the fair value of the security.

2.4.70.130   For a discussion of security-specific restrictions when the fair value of a liability or own equity instrument is measured with reference to the identical instrument held as an asset by a market participant, see 2.4.410.

2.4.80   **Unit of account**

2.4.80.10   The 'unit of account' is the level at which an asset or a liability is aggregated or disaggregated in an IFRS for recognition purposes. It also drives the level at which an asset or a liability is aggregated or disaggregated for the purpose of measuring fair value, although in practice the term 'unit of valuation' may be used especially when the unit of account for recognition and measurement are different. In this chapter, we refer to the unit of account in the context of both recognition and measurement. [*IFRS 13.14, A*]

2.4.80.20   IFRS 13 does not specify the unit of account; instead, it depends on the relevant standard that establishes the recognition of the item. For example, the unit of account under IAS 36 is typically the CGU and the unit of account under IFRS 9 is typically the individual financial instrument (e.g. a share). [*IFRS 13.14, BC47*]

2.4.80.30   Although the unit of account is usually key to determining the level at which fair value is measured, it is not a concept that has been used explicitly in IFRS, and there is uncertainty regarding the unit of account for investments in subsidiaries, associates and joint ventures. The unit of account for such investments is not clear because the investment held by the entity comprises a number of individual shares. The following are examples of situations in which the unit of account for such an investment needs to be determined in order to measure fair value.

- (S) • An investment in a subsidiary, associate or joint venture accounted for in accordance with IFRS 9 in separate financial statements (see 2.1.120).
- An investment in a subsidiary, associate or joint venture held by an investment entity (see chapter 5.6).
- Investments in associates and joint ventures that are accounted for in accordance with IFRS 9 by a venture capital or similar organisation (see 3.5.100).
- Shares in a subsidiary, associate or joint venture distributed to owners (see 7.3.690).
- A previously held equity interest in an acquiree in accounting for a business combination achieved in stages (see 2.6.1140).
- A retained interest following a loss of control, joint control or significant influence (see 2.5.760 and 3.5.560).

2.4.80.40   In our view, an entity may choose an accounting policy, to be applied consistently, to identify the unit of account of an investment in a subsidiary, associate or joint venture as:
- the investment as a whole; or
- the individual share making up the investment.

2.4.80.50   In applying a consistent accounting policy in accordance with IAS 8 (see 2.8.30), an entity should choose the same policy for similar items. The choice of accounting policy is important, because the value of an aggregate holding may be different from the sum of the values of the components measured on an individual basis.

2.4.80.60   In certain circumstances, when measuring fair value based on the unit of account, an entity may use a valuation technique that determines the fair value by considering the fair values of the component parts of the unit of account. This may be appropriate if market participants would consider these separate fair values when pricing the item in its entirety. [*IFRS 13.22*]

EXAMPLE 5 – MEASURING FAIR VALUE BASED ON COMPONENT PARTS OF THE UNIT OF ACCOUNT

2.4.80.70 Investment Fund D holds an investment in Company B that is accounted for at fair value. B is a private holding company with two subsidiaries operating each in a different line of business. Both subsidiaries have issued public debt and publish their financial statements.

2.4.80.80 D values its investment in B by valuing the two subsidiaries separately and includes any potential holding company value effects. Because the subsidiaries have different characteristics – i.e. growth prospects, risk profiles, investment requirements etc – this approach allows separate consideration of each of the subsidiaries' facts and circumstances and is consistent with the approach that a market participant would consider in valuing an investment in B.

2.4.80.90 For further discussion of the unit of account in the context of premiums and discounts, see 2.4.240, and for a discussion of how the unit of account interacts with the portfolio measurement exception, see 2.4.430.

2.4.90 **Market participants**

2.4.90.10 'Market participants' are buyers and sellers in the principal or most advantageous market (see 2.4.100) for the asset or liability that have all the following characteristics.
- They are independent of each other – i.e. they are not related parties as defined in IAS 24 (see chapter 5.5), although the price in a related party transaction may be used as an input to a fair value measurement (see 2.4.220) if the entity has evidence that the transaction was entered into on market terms.
- They are knowledgeable, having a reasonable understanding about the asset or liability and the transaction using all available information, including information that might be obtained through due diligence efforts that are usual and customary.
- They are able to enter into a transaction for the asset or liability.
- They are willing to enter into a transaction for the asset or liability – i.e. they are motivated but not forced or otherwise compelled to do so. [*IFRS 13.A*]

2.4.90.20 An entity considers the perspective of market participants and measures fair value based on the assumptions that would be made by market participants acting in their economic best interests. An entity does not need to identify specific market participants; instead, it identifies the characteristics that distinguish market participants, considering:
- the asset or liability;
- the principal (or most advantageous) market for the asset or liability; and
- market participants with whom the entity would enter into a transaction in that market. [*IFRS 13.22–23*]

2.4.90.30 Market participants are assumed to be knowledgeable about the asset or liability, using all available information, including information that would be expected to become available in customary and usual due diligence. To the extent that additional uncertainty exists, it is factored into the fair value measurement. [*IFRS 13.A, BC58–BC59*]

2.4.100   **Principal and most advantageous markets**

2.4.100.10   The 'principal market' is the market with the greatest volume and level of activity for the asset or liability. A fair value measurement assumes that the transaction to sell the asset or to transfer the liability takes place in the principal market for the asset or liability. [*IFRS 13.16, A*]

2.4.100.20   In the absence of a principal market, the transaction is assumed to take place in the most advantageous market for the asset or liability. This is the market that either maximises the amount that would be received to sell the asset or minimises the amount that would be paid to transfer the liability, after taking into account transaction costs and transport costs (see 2.4.110). [*IFRS 13.16, A*]

2.4.100.30   In many cases, the principal market and the most advantageous market will be the same. [*IFRS 13.BC48*]

2.4.100.40   For a market to be considered the principal or most advantageous market, the entity needs to be able to access that market at the measurement date. However, the identification of a principal market is not limited to those markets in which the entity would actually sell the asset or transfer the liability. Furthermore, although the entity has to be able to access the market, the entity does not need to be able to buy or sell the particular asset (or transfer the particular liability) on the measurement date in that market. [*IFRS 13.19–20*]

2.4.100.50   Because the entity has to have access to the principal (or most advantageous) market in order to use a price from that market, the identification of the relevant market is considered from the perspective of the entity. This may give rise to different principal or most advantageous markets for entities with different activities and for different businesses within an entity. For example, if a swap transaction takes place between an investment bank and a commercial entity, then the former may have access to wholesale and retail markets whereas the latter may only have access to retail markets. See also Example 13. [*IFRS 13.19, IE24–IE26*]

2.4.100.60   In addition, in some cases different entities within a consolidated group (and businesses within those entities) may have different principal markets for the same asset or liability. For example, a parent company may trade a particular asset in its principal market for that asset. However, because of regulatory restrictions, its overseas subsidiary is prohibited from transacting in that market. As a result, the overseas subsidiary has a different principal market for the same asset. [*IFRS 13.19*]

2.4.100.70   An entity is not required to undertake an exhaustive search of all possible markets to identify the principal market, or in the absence of a principal market, the most advantageous market; however, it takes account of all information that is reasonably available. For example, if reliable information about volumes transacted is available in trade magazines, then it may be appropriate to consider this information in determining the principal market. [*IFRS 13.17, BC53*]

2.4.100.80   In the absence of evidence to the contrary, the principal (or most advantageous) market is presumed to be the market in which an entity normally enters into transactions to sell the asset or transfer the liability. IFRS 13 contains this practical expedient because the IASB concluded that entities normally enter into transactions in the principal market for the asset or liability – i.e. the most liquid market that the entity can access. [*IFRS 13.17, BC53*]

2.4.100.90   IFRS 13 does not provide detailed guidance on:
- how an entity should identify the principal market;
- over what period the entity should analyse transactions in the asset or liability to make the determination; or
- how often the entity should update its analysis.

2.4.100.100   In our view, an entity should update its analysis to the extent that events have occurred or activities have changed in a manner that could change the entity's determination of the principal (or most advantageous) market for the asset or liability.

2.4.100.110   The concept of a market does not mean that there needs to be a structured, formal or organised market – e.g. a dealer network or an organised exchange. If such a market does not exist, then an entity needs to focus on identifying market participants to which it would sell the asset or transfer the liability in a hypothetical transaction. It also needs to consider the assumptions that those market participants would use in pricing the asset or liability, assuming that they act in their economic best interest. [*IFRS 13.22–23*]

2.4.110   *Transaction and transport costs*

2.4.110.10   'Transaction costs' are directly attributable costs that an entity would incur in selling an asset or transferring a liability. [*IFRS 13.A*]

2.4.110.20   'Transport costs' are not included in transaction costs. They are the costs that an entity would incur to transport an asset from its current location to the principal or most advantageous market. [*IFRS 13.A, 26*]

2.4.110.30   Whether transaction and transport costs are taken into account in identifying the principal and most advantageous market, and in measuring fair value, can be summarised as follows.

	TRANSACTION COSTS	TRANSPORT COSTS
Identifying the principal market	✘	✘
Identifying the most advantageous market	✔	✔
Measuring fair value	✘	✔

2.4.110.40   Transaction and transport costs are not considered in identifying the principal market, because such a market is identified based only on the volume and level of activity. However, such costs are considered in identifying the most advantageous market, because such a market is identified based on the net proceeds from the assumed transaction. [*IFRS 13.A, 25–26, BC62*]

2.4.110.50   Once the market for the transaction has been identified, the measurement of fair value is an independent, different calculation.

- Fair value is not adjusted for transaction costs; instead, they are accounted for in accordance with other applicable standards. This is because transaction costs are a characteristic of the transaction, and not a characteristic of the asset or liability.
- Fair value is adjusted for transport costs, if location is a characteristic of the asset. For example, the fair value of crude oil held in the Arctic Circle would be adjusted for the cost of transporting the oil from the Arctic Circle to the appropriate market. [*IFRS 13.25–26*]

2.4.110.60   An identified basis differential cannot generally be used as a proxy for transport costs. This is because an identified basis differential between the price at the location of the asset and at the principal (or most advantageous) market generally also includes other factors besides location. Basis differentials reflect multiple factors, such as timing, quality and location, and can be volatile because they capture the passage of time (a financing element), changes in the relative value of different qualities or grades of commodities, and changes in the attractiveness of locations from the central pricing hub relative to each other factor. Supply and demand is a critical factor in influencing the changes in basis because of quality and location. A basis differential is therefore not a simple fixed transport charge, but rather a complex and volatile variable in and of itself. [*IFRS 13.A, 26*]

EXAMPLE 6 – PRINCIPAL AND MOST ADVANTAGEOUS MARKETS

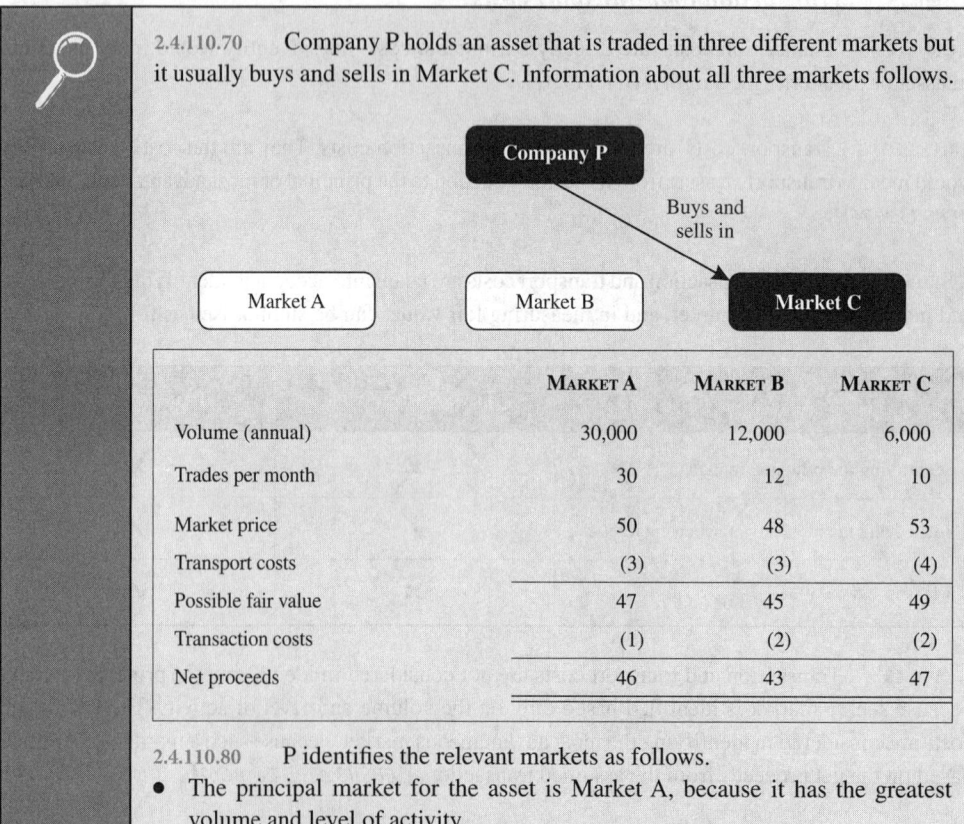

2.4.110.70   Company P holds an asset that is traded in three different markets but it usually buys and sells in Market C. Information about all three markets follows.

Company P

Buys and sells in

Market A   Market B   **Market C**

	MARKET A	MARKET B	MARKET C
Volume (annual)	30,000	12,000	6,000
Trades per month	30	12	10
Market price	50	48	53
Transport costs	(3)	(3)	(4)
Possible fair value	47	45	49
Transaction costs	(1)	(2)	(2)
Net proceeds	46	43	47

2.4.110.80   P identifies the relevant markets as follows.
- The principal market for the asset is Market A, because it has the greatest volume and level of activity.
- The most advantageous market is Market C, because it has the highest net proceeds.

> 2.4.110.90   P bases its measurement of fair value on prices in Market A, even though it does not normally transact in that market and it is not the most advantageous market. Therefore, fair value is 47, considering transport costs but not transaction costs, even though P normally transacts in Market C and could maximise its net proceeds in that market.
>
> 2.4.110.100   If P is unable to access Markets A and B, then it would use Market C as the most advantageous market. In that case, fair value would be 49 (market price less transport costs).

2.4.110.110   Example 6 highlights that it is not always appropriate to assume that the principal market is the market in which the entity usually transacts. In that example, P has information about Market A that it cannot ignore, which results in P identifying Market A as the principal market.

2.4.110.120   In sourcing market prices to value an asset or liability, spot prices on the measurement date rather than forward prices are used. A spot price is a price for almost immediate delivery on the measurement date, whereas a forward or futures price is a price to exchange the item at a future date.

2.4.110.130   In our view, an asset for which location is a characteristic, and that is not located in the principal market, should not be valued using the forward or futures price. This is because we believe that the asset should be assumed to be available in the principal market at the measurement date. The price in the principal market is adjusted for transport costs to that market from where the asset is located to measure the fair value (see 2.4.110.50).

EXAMPLE 7 – SPOT VS FORWARD PRICE TO VALUE INVENTORY

>
>
> 2.4.110.140   Company X is a commodity broker that measures physical inventory at fair value less costs to sell (see 3.8.70). At the measurement date (31 December 2018), X has physical inventory located in India and it would take two months to deliver the inventory from India to the principal market in New York.
>
> 2.4.110.150   In measuring the fair value of the inventory, X uses the spot price in New York on 31 December 2018, adjusted for appropriate transport costs. It does not use the two-month forward price that is quoted on 31 December 2018.
>
> 2.4.110.160   In addition, we believe that the fair value of the inventory on 31 December 2018, which is based on the spot price, should also be discounted to reflect:
> - the fact that it would take two months to deliver the inventory to the principal market and so it cannot be converted to cash immediately; and
> - other risks involved in such a transfer – e.g. damage to the inventory during shipment.

2.4.110.170   As noted in 2.4.110.50, transaction costs are not subtracted from a fair value measurement because they are a characteristic of the transaction and not of the asset or liability. However, it may be appropriate for future transaction costs – i.e. in subsequent sales transactions – to be deducted in a discounted cash flow analysis. For example, if discounted cash flows are used to determine the fair value of real estate, and the analysis includes an assumption that a market participant would sell the property in the future, then it may be appropriate to subtract transaction costs – e.g. selling costs – expected to be incurred at the time of that future disposition (see Example 26). [*IFRS 13.25*]

2.4.110.180   In contrast, it would not generally be appropriate to consider future transaction costs in a discounted cash flow analysis when valuing a business enterprise; this is because it is assumed that a market participant would maximise economic benefit by continuing to operate the business indefinitely. In our experience, market participants entering into a transaction for a business would not generally consider transaction costs associated with a sale in the future. A terminal value within a discounted cash flow analysis generally reflects the value of future cash flows at the end of a discrete cash flow period but does not imply that a market participant would sell the business at that point in time. For further discussion of a discounted cash flow analysis, see 2.4.160.

2.4.120   VALUATION APPROACHES AND TECHNIQUES

2.4.130   General principles

2.4.130.10   In measuring the fair value of an asset or a liability, an entity selects those valuation approaches and techniques that are appropriate in the circumstances and for which sufficient data is available to measure fair value. The technique chosen should maximise the use of relevant observable inputs and minimise the use of unobservable inputs (see 2.4.220). [*IFRS 13.61*]

2.4.130.20   IFRS 13 refers to a 'valuation approach' as a broad category of techniques, whereas a 'valuation technique' refers to a specific technique such as a particular option pricing model. Valuation techniques used to measure fair value fall under three approaches:
- market approach (see 2.4.140);
- income approach (see 2.4.150); and
- cost approach (see 2.4.210). [*IFRS 13.62*]

2.4.130.30   With one exception related to quoted prices in an active market for an identical asset or liability (see 2.4.280), IFRS 13 does not establish requirements for specific valuation technique(s) to be used. In some cases, only a single valuation technique will be appropriate; in other cases, however, using more than one valuation technique will be more appropriate. [*IFRS 13.63*]

2.4.130.40   Any, or a combination, of the three approaches could be used to measure fair value if the techniques are appropriate in the circumstances. Judgement is required in selecting the valuation technique(s), including consideration of the information available. For example, an investor in unquoted equity instruments is likely to place more emphasis on the market approach if there are sufficiently comparable entity peers. However, the investor is likely to place more emphasis on the income approach based on a present value technique if, for example, there are no close comparable entities and reliable cash flows estimates can be made. [*IFRS 13.EM.02-13.13*]

2.4.130.50   If multiple valuation techniques are used in measuring fair value, then the entity evaluates the results and weighs them based on the reasonableness of the range of values indicated by those results. The objective is to find the point within the range that is most representative of fair value in the circumstances. [*IFRS 13.63*]

2.4.130.60   This determination is a matter of judgement; it is not appropriate to simply average the outcomes of the various valuation techniques. An entity considers, among other things, the reliability of the valuation techniques and the inputs that are used in those techniques. If a particular valuation technique falling under the market approach relies on higher-level inputs (e.g. observable market prices) than a valuation technique falling under the income approach that relies heavily on projections of income, then the entity may conclude that it is appropriate to apply greater weight to the measurement of fair value generated by the valuation technique falling under the market approach, because it relies on higher-level inputs. Higher-level inputs (e.g. Level 1 or Level 2 inputs) that are available and relevant cannot be ignored. [*IFRS 13.61, BC142*]

2.4.130.70   In some cases, a secondary method is used only to corroborate the reasonableness of the most appropriate valuation technique.

2.4.140   Market approach

2.4.140.10   Valuation techniques that fall under the market approach often derive market multiples from a set of comparable assets. A market multiple expresses the value of a business or other asset in terms of its ratio to a financial, operating or physical metric. For example, a price to earnings ratio expresses an entity's per-share value in terms of its earnings per share. The multiple can then be applied to the metric of an entity with similar characteristics but different scale, subject to adjustment for differences between the entity and the selected comparable. [*IFRS 13.B5–B6*]

2.4.140.20   If multiples are derived from a number of comparable entities, then there will typically be a range of multiples calculated. Selection within the range is based on market participants' expectations. For example, in estimating the fair value of a CGU in impairment testing (see chapter 3.10), the point in the range of multiples that is selected considers differences between the CGU and comparable entities in terms of size, growth, profitability, risk, investment requirements etc. [*IFRS 13.B5–B6*]

2.4.140.30   In using quoted prices for similar assets or liabilities, adjustments are often necessary for differences between the subject asset and the comparable assets. If there is a high degree of subjectivity in estimating the adjustment – e.g. because the asset differs in important respects from the closest comparable assets – then the resulting value indication may be less reliable than when the range of possible adjustments is narrower, because the subject asset is very similar to the comparable assets.

2.4.140.40   Matrix pricing is a valuation technique that falls under the market approach. Matrix pricing is a mathematical technique mainly used to value debt securities without relying exclusively on quoted prices for the specific securities, but rather by relying on the securities' relationship to other benchmark quoted securities. Therefore, matrix prices are based on quoted prices for securities with similar coupons, ratings and maturities, rather than on actual prices for the asset being measured. For a discussion of the use of matrix pricing if an entity holds a large number of similar assets or liabilities that are measured at fair value, for which quoted prices in active markets are available but not readily accessible, see 2.4.280.100. [*IFRS 13.B7*]

2.4.150   Income approach

2.4.150.10   The valuation techniques that fall under the income approach convert future amounts such as cash flows or income streams to a current amount on the measurement date. The fair value measurement reflects current market expectations about those future amounts, discounted to their present value. The concept behind the income approach is that an asset is worth what it is expected to earn, discounted for the time value of money and associated risks. [*IFRS 13.B10*]

2.4.150.20   Common valuation techniques falling under the income approach include:
- present value techniques (see 2.4.160);
- option pricing models (see 2.4.190); and
- the multi-period excess earnings method (see 2.4.200.10). [*IFRS 13.B11*]

2.4.160   *Present value techniques*

2.4.160.10   The application guidance in IFRS 13 describes two approaches to applying a present value technique:
- the discount rate adjustment technique; and
- the expected present value technique. [*IFRS 13.B12*]

2.4.160.20   IFRS 13 does not prescribe a specific method; instead, the present value technique used to measure fair value depends on facts and circumstances specific to the asset or liability being measured and the availability of sufficient data – e.g. cash flow estimates, risk premiums, discount rates – and other factors that would be considered by market participants. [*IFRS 13.B12*]

2.4.160.30   Present value techniques differ in how they capture these elements; however, there are some commonalities in determining the inputs into the valuation techniques. [*IFRS 13.B14*]

2.4.160.40   The assumptions used for the cash flows and discount rates reflect market participants' views. In addition, the assumptions consider only the factors attributable to the asset or the liability being measured. [*IFRS 13.B14*]

2.4.160.50   The fair value of a financial instrument reflects the effect of discounting expected future cash flows. However, an entity is permitted to initially measure short-term receivables and payables with no stated interest rate at their invoiced amounts without discounting, if the effect of discounting is immaterial. Therefore, in our view receivables and payables with maturities of up to six months are not generally required to be discounted. However, in high-interest environments the impact of discounting may be significant even for maturities of less than six months. Notwithstanding the above, trade receivables resulting from contracts with customers in the scope of IFRS 15 are required or permitted to be measured initially at the transaction price as defined in IFRS 15 (rather than at fair value) if certain criteria are met – see 7.7.20. [*IFRS 9.5.1.3, 13.BC138A*]

2.4.170   *Risk and uncertainty*

2.4.170.10   A valuation using present value techniques is based on assumptions that are inherently uncertain, because they reflect estimates of the future rather than known amounts. Even contractual cash flows that may appear certain at first glance contain risk because of uncertainty about the ability of the counterparty to meet its contractual obligations. For example, contractual cash flows on a loan are subject to a risk of default. A risk premium is therefore included in the fair value measurement to reflect the amount that risk-averse market participants would demand to be compensated for the uncertainty of the cash flows. [*IFRS 13.B15–B16, BC144*]

2.4.170.20   Different options are available for making adjustments for risk in present value techniques. The discount rate adjustment technique uses a single estimate of cash flows – contractual, promised or most likely cash flows – and adjusts for risk in the discount rate. In addition, IFRS 13 notes two possible methods to incorporate risk in an expected present value technique, which is based on probability-weighted cash flows.
- Method 1 adjusts for risk in the expected cash flows, which are then discounted at the risk-free rate.
- Method 2 uses a risk-adjusted discount rate with expected cash flows. [*IFRS 13.B17*]

2.4.170.30   There is no preferred method for making adjustments for risk in a present value technique; it depends on facts and circumstances specific to the asset or liability being measured. The risk adjustment may need to be considered in both cash flows and the discount rate. However, rates used to discount cash flows do not reflect risks for which the estimated cash flows have been adjusted (and vice versa) because otherwise the effect would be double counted. [*IFRS 13.B14*]

2.4.170.40   To use a risk-free rate in valuing an asset (Method 1 in 2.4.170.20), the expected cash flows need to be adjusted to represent certainty-equivalent cash flows. This means that a market participant would be indifferent between investing in the risky asset and investing in a risk-free investment that generated those cash flows. In our experience, although it is theoretically possible that expected cash flows from an asset could be adjusted to incorporate all relevant risks so that the investor was indifferent, the practical application of this approach is very difficult outside of option pricing and certain derivative modelling. This is because expected cash flows include both positive as well as negative possible outcomes; therefore, before risk adjustment, they represent only the probability-weighted-average outcome. [*IFRS 13.B17, B25*]

2.4.180   *Discount rates*

2.4.180.10   Discount rates reflect assumptions that are consistent with those inherent in the cash flows to avoid double counting or omitting the effects of certain risk factors. [*IFRS 13.B14*]

2.4.180.20   Assumptions about cash flows and discount rates should be internally consistent. For example, if the cash flows include the effect of expected inflation, then the discount rate also incorporates inflation expectations. [*IFRS 13.B14*]

2.4.180.30   In our experience, for some assets and liabilities it is rare that a discount rate can be observed directly from the market. For example, the cost of equity of a business, which is often used as an input into a weighted-average cost of capital calculation in valuing a CGU based on discounted cash flows, cannot be observed. In such circumstances, it will generally be necessary to build up a market participant discount rate that appropriately reflects the risks associated with the cash flows of the asset or liability being measured at fair value. Other standards that deal with discount rates, such as IAS 36, refer to an entity's weighted-average cost of capital as the starting point in determining a possible appropriate discount rate (see 3.10.300).

2.4.190   *Option pricing models*

2.4.190.10   Option pricing models such as the Black-Scholes-Merton formula or a binomial model can be used to calculate the fair value of options. Option valuation models implicitly or explicitly use mathematical techniques such as closed-form solutions or numerical methods to identify a range of future scenarios. From these possible scenarios, the payoff of an option can be calculated. These intrinsic values at future exercise are then probability-weighted and discounted to their present value to estimate the fair value of the option at the measurement date. [*IFRS 13.B11(b)*]

2.4.200 *Other techniques*

2.4.200.10   The multi-period excess earnings method is commonly used to measure the fair value of intangible assets, such as customer relationships and technology assets, acquired in a business combination. The method is based on a discounted cash flow analysis that measures the fair value of an asset by taking into account not only operating costs but also charges for contributory assets; this isolates the value related to the asset to be measured and excludes any value related to contributory assets. [*IFRS 13.B11(c)*]

2.4.200.20   The with-versus-without method is useful for measuring the fair value of acquired intangible assets that market participants would be expected to use defensively (see Example 11). It measures the incremental cash flows that would be achieved by market participants arising from their ownership of an existing intangible asset by locking up the competing acquired intangible asset. Fair value is measured as the difference between the fair value of the group of assets of the market participant:

- assuming that the acquired intangible asset were to be actively used by others in the market; and
- assuming that the acquired intangible asset was withdrawn from the market.

2.4.200.30   The relief-from-royalty method measures the fair value of intangible assets using assumptions about what it would cost a market participant to use the acquired intangible asset if another entity owned it. This technique is appropriate only if the highest and best use of the asset (see 2.4.330) is to use it actively in the market. As a result of owning the asset, a market participant is relieved from making royalty payments that might otherwise be required. This method includes assumptions about the stream of payments that would be required, usually in the form of royalties, to another party for the right to use the asset. The fair value of the intangible asset is measured as the discounted stream of payments from which the acquiring entity is relieved because it owns the asset.

2.4.210 **Cost approach**

2.4.210.10   The cost approach comprises valuation techniques that reflect the amount that would be required to replace the service capacity of an asset. The concept behind the cost approach is that an investor will pay no more for an asset than the cost to buy or construct a substitute asset of comparable utility, adjusted for obsolescence. [*IFRS 13.B8–B9*]

2.4.210.20   The primary method used to measure fair value under the cost approach is the depreciated replacement cost (DRC) method. This method is sometimes used to measure the fair value of plant and equipment. A DRC valuation considers how much it would cost to reproduce an asset of equivalent utility taking into account physical, functional and economic obsolescence. It estimates the replacement cost of the required capacity rather than the actual asset. Because the cost approach is based on service capacity, it is not relevant for measuring the fair value of financial assets.

2.4.210.30   For further discussion about the DRC method in the context of valuing plant and equipment, see 2.4.600.

2.4.220   **INPUTS TO VALUATION TECHNIQUES**

2.4.230   **General principles**

2.4.230.10   Inputs to valuation techniques are the assumptions that market participants would use in pricing the asset or liability. These inputs include assumptions about risk, such as the risk inherent in a particular valuation technique used to measure fair value and the risk inherent in the inputs to the valuation technique. [*IFRS 13.A*]

2.4.230.20   An entity selects the valuation techniques:
- that are appropriate in the circumstances;
- for which sufficient data is available; and
- that maximise the use of relevant observable inputs and minimise the use of unobservable inputs. [*IFRS 13.61*]

2.4.230.30   Exchange markets, dealer markets, brokered markets and principal-to-principal markets are examples of markets that might provide observable inputs for valuation techniques. [*IFRS 13.68*]

2.4.230.40   In some cases, an entity may need to adjust the available observable inputs significantly, because of the different characteristics of the asset or liability being measured or market conditions at the measurement date. Unobservable inputs are a part of a fair value measurement if they are required inputs in order to arrive at a fair value measurement and if they relate to factors that market participants would consider.

2.4.230.50   For example, the fair value of an unquoted security held as an asset may be based primarily on observable market multiples. However, to the extent that market participants would be expected to apply a discount because the shares valued are not publicly traded, a discount for lack of marketability needs to be considered, even though this is not directly observable. For further discussion of unquoted equity instruments, see 2.4.860.

2.4.230.60   It would not be appropriate to adjust the results of a valuation technique for entity-specific factors such as the entity's perspective on uncertainty in estimated cash flows and administration costs that it expects to incur. Such factors are incorporated into a valuation technique based on the amounts that market participants would consider in setting a price. [*IFRS 13.22, 89*]

2.4.240   **Premiums, discounts and blockage factors**

2.4.240.10   An entity selects inputs that are consistent with the characteristics of the asset or liability that market participants would take into account in pricing the asset or liability. In some cases, an initial value indication may not reflect a characteristic of the asset or liability that market participants would take into account. As a result, it may be appropriate to make an adjustment – e.g. a control premium, a marketability or liquidity discount or a non-controlling interest discount – to a preliminary value indication in measuring fair value. [*IFRS 13.69*]

2.4.240.20   An entity does not apply a premium or discount if:
- it is inconsistent with the item's unit of account (see 2.4.240.30);

- it reflects size as a characteristic of the entity's holding – e.g. a blockage factor (see 2.4.240.40–70);
- the characteristic is already reflected in the preliminary value indication (see 2.4.240.110); or
- there is a quoted price in an active market for an identical asset or liability – i.e. a Level 1 input (see 2.4.280). [*IFRS 13.69*]

2.4.240.25   A liquidity adjustment may be appropriate in measuring fair value if:
- the instrument being valued is categorised in Level 2 or Level 3 of the fair value hierarchy;
- the other inputs in the valuation have not factored in the liquidity of the instrument; and
- market participants would include an adjustment when buying or selling the instrument. [*IFRS 13.69, 79–80*]

2.4.240.30   The unit of account determines the extent to which an asset or liability is aggregated or disaggregated for the purpose of measuring fair value. For example, if the unit of account is an individual financial instrument (e.g. a share), then it would not be appropriate to include a premium based on holding multiple units in measuring fair value. For a discussion of the unit of account, see 2.4.80.

2.4.240.40   As noted in 2.4.80.30–50, the unit of account in respect of investments in subsidiaries, associates and joint ventures is unclear, and in our view an entity may choose an accounting policy, to be applied consistently, in identifying the unit of account. For example, if the unit of account is the investment as a whole, then it may be appropriate to include a control premium in measuring the fair value of investments in subsidiaries even if Level 1 prices exist for an individual share (see 2.4.840).

2.4.240.50   An entity may hold a large number of identical financial instruments, but the market for the instrument does not have sufficient trading volume to absorb the quantity held by the entity without affecting the price. A 'blockage factor' is a discount that adjusts the quoted price of an asset or a liability because the market's normal trading volume is not sufficient to absorb the quantity held by the entity. IFRS 13 clarifies that a blockage factor is not a characteristic of an asset or a liability but a characteristic of the size of the entity's holding. As a result, the standard expressly prohibits application of a blockage factor. [*IFRS 13.69, 80, BC156*]

2.4.240.60   However, size may in some cases be a characteristic of an asset or liability (see 2.4.70). In these cases, adjustments may be required because of the size of the asset or liability. [*IFRS 13.11, BC156*]

2.4.240.70   Therefore, in our view if it is appropriate to make a liquidity adjustment (see 2.4.240.25), then the amount of the adjustment should be determined based on the liquidity of the specific asset's or liability's unit of account in the entity's principal (or most advantageous) market and not on the size of the entity's holding relative to the market's daily trading volume.

EXAMPLE 8 – OPTION TO BUY CONTROLLING INTERESTS

2.4.240.80   Company T purchases an option to buy 51% of the shares in Company S, a listed company, which if exercised would result in T owning a controlling interest in S. A Level 1 price is available for the underlying shares of S, but not for the option to buy 51%, which is the unit of account under IFRS 9.

> 2.4.240.90   The fair value of the option would therefore take into account adjustments to the share price if they are necessary to reflect the value of the option, such as including a control premium.

2.4.240.100   For a discussion of the implications of the guidance in 2.4.240.40–90 on specific items, see 2.4.550.

2.4.240.110   If a characteristic of an asset or a liability is not reflected in a preliminary value indication, then a separate adjustment may be required to measure the fair value of the asset or liability. If the assets being measured are non-controlling shares in a private entity and the preliminary value indication was arrived at using market multiples derived from the share prices of comparable public entities, then the resulting preliminary value indication is on a marketable, minority interest basis, because the publicly traded shares are marketable and represent the price of non-controlling holdings. To use such multiples to measure the fair values of non-marketable, non-controlling shares in a private entity, an adjustment would not generally be required to reflect the fact that the shares are non-controlling, because this is already reflected in the comparable entity share prices used to calculate the market multiples. However, an adjustment would generally be required to reflect the non-marketable nature of the assets relative to the publicly traded shares.

2.4.245   Restrictions on the sale of a security

2.4.245.10   If an entity measures the fair value of an asset such as a security that is subject to a restriction on its sale or transfer, then it determines whether it is appropriate to apply an adjustment to the price of a similar unrestricted security to reflect the restriction. To make that determination, the entity first analyses whether the restriction is security-specific or entity-specific. For entity-specific restrictions, the price used in the fair value measurement is not adjusted to reflect the restriction (see 2.4.70.70). Although an entity may not be able to sell a particular security on the measurement date because of an entity-specific restriction, it is still considered to have access to the market.

2.4.245.20   For security-specific restrictions, the price used in the fair value measurement reflects the effect of the restriction if it would be considered by a market participant in pricing the security. This may require an adjustment to the quoted price of otherwise identical but unrestricted securities. In determining the appropriate discount, an entity needs to evaluate all of the relevant drivers of the discount. These include the length of the restriction, the risk of the underlying security (e.g. volatility), expected dividends, the float and market capitalisation of the issuer, the liquidity of the market and other qualitative and quantitative factors specific to the security. [*IFRS 13.11, IE28*]

2.4.245.30   Generally, it is not appropriate to apply a discount that is a fixed percentage of the unrestricted price over the entire life of the restriction period in measuring fair value. For example, if at the measurement date the period of the security-specific restriction is two years and the discount is estimated to be 10 percent, then assuming no changes other than the passage of time the following year's discount would be less than 10 percent because the restriction period is reduced to one year.

2.4.245.40   In our experience, measuring the discount is often based on quantitative approaches (e.g. an option pricing model) that explicitly incorporate the duration of the restriction and the characteristics of the underlying security – e.g. risk, dividends, rights and preferences etc. When using these models to derive the discount, an entity needs to consider the ability of the model to appropriately quantify the liquidity adjustment under the specific facts and circumstances. For example, some option pricing models may not appropriately measure the discount that a market participant would apply. [*IFRS 13.IE28, EM.02-13.67*]

2.4.250 Inputs based on bid and ask prices

2.4.250.10   If assets or liabilities have a bid and an ask price, then an entity uses the price within the bid-ask spread that is most representative of fair value in the circumstances. Although it is not required, the use of bid prices for long positions, and ask prices for short positions, is permitted. [*IFRS 13.70*]

2.4.250.20   The bid-ask spread includes transaction costs, and may include other components. The price in the principal or most advantageous market is not adjusted for transaction costs (see 2.4.110). Therefore, an entity makes an assessment of what the bid-ask spread represents in determining the price that is most representative of fair value within the bid-ask spread in the circumstances. [*IFRS 13.BC164*]

2.4.250.30   The standard does not prohibit using mid-market prices or other pricing conventions generally used by market participants as a practical expedient for fair value measurements within a bid-ask spread. However, in our view the use of mid-market prices is subject to the condition that the mid-market price provides a reasonable approximation of an exit price. We believe that use of the practical expedient does not override the general fair value measurement guidance, and should not be used if it leads to a measurement that is not representative of fair value. Therefore, an entity should not ignore available evidence that a mid-market price does not result in a price that is representative of fair value. For example, if the bid-ask spread is particularly wide, or if the applicable bid-ask spread has widened significantly for a specific asset or liability, then a mid-market price may not be representative of fair value. [*IFRS 13.71*]

2.4.260 FAIR VALUE HIERARCHY

2.4.260.10   To increase consistency and comparability, IFRS 13 establishes a fair value hierarchy based on the inputs to valuation techniques used to measure fair value. The inputs are categorised into three levels – the highest priority is given to unadjusted quoted prices in active markets for identical assets or liabilities, and the lowest priority is given to unobservable inputs. [*IFRS 13.72*]

2.4.260.20   The fair value hierarchy is made up of three levels, with Level 1 being the highest level.
- *Level 1 inputs:* Unadjusted quoted prices in active markets for identical assets or liabilities that the entity can access at the measurement date.
- *Level 2 inputs:* Inputs other than quoted prices included within Level 1 that are observable for the asset or liability, either directly (i.e. as prices) or indirectly (i.e. derived from prices).
- *Level 3 inputs:* Unobservable inputs for the asset or liability. [*IFRS 13.76, 81, 86, A*]

2.4.270 Categorisation of fair value measurements

2.4.270.10   Fair value measurements are categorised in their entirety based on the lowest level input that is significant to the entire measurement; this is outlined in the flowchart below. [*IFRS 13.73*]

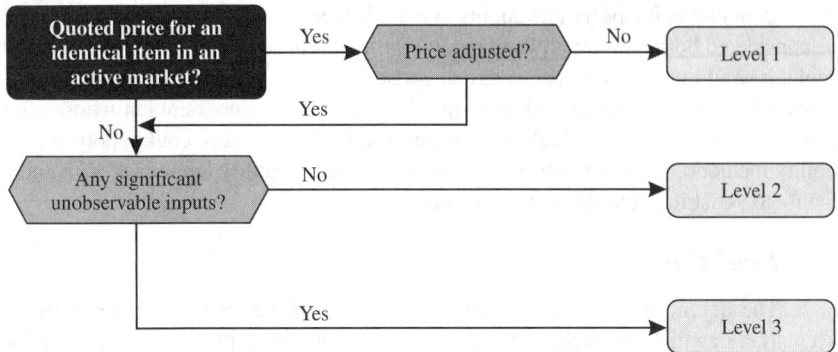

2.4.270.20   The level into which a fair value measurement is categorised in its entirety is determined with reference to the observability and significance of the inputs used in the valuation technique. Categorisation into Level 1 can only be achieved through the market approach using quoted prices in an active market for an identical asset or liability, without adjustments (see 2.4.140 and 280). [*IFRS 13.73–74, 76, 81, 86, A, IU 01-15*]

2.4.270.25   In our view, a valuation technique that uses only unadjusted quoted prices in an active market at the measurement date for an identical instrument may be categorised in its entirety within Level 1 if it uses more than one Level 1 input and the valuation technique does not include adjustments to those Level 1 inputs. This is because there could be more than one Level 1 price for an identical instrument – even in the same market and at the same time – e.g. a bid price and an ask price (see 2.4.250). Therefore, we believe that a fair value measurement that is based on a valuation technique that uses a simple average of current Level 1 prices at the measurement date to produce a value from those inputs may be considered a Level 1 measurement – e.g. a mid-market price that is an average of a Level 1 bid price and a Level 1 ask price. Similarly, we believe that the price within the bid-ask spread that is most representative of fair value may also be classified as Level 1, if the bid and ask prices are Level 1 prices.

2.4.270.27   However, we believe that a fair value measurement that is based on a model that uses complex algorithms or quoted prices in an active market from different points in time before the measurement date cannot be considered a Level 1 measurement. Similarly, a fair value measurement that is based on a model that uses only quoted prices in an active market as inputs, but not all of those inputs relate to the identical instrument being measured cannot be considered a Level 1 measurement. For further discussion on dealing with pricing services and broker quotes, see 2.4.300.

2.4.270.30   Valuation techniques often incorporate both observable and unobservable inputs. If fair value is measured using inputs from multiple levels of the fair value hierarchy, then the inclusion of a lower-level input (Level 3 is lower than Level 2) in an entity's measurement may indicate that the input is significant. This is because the entity's decision to include the lower-level input provides evidence that the entity considers the input to be significant to the overall fair value measurement. However, the final determination of whether inputs are significant is a matter of judgement that requires an entity to consider:
- factors specific to the asset or liability; and
- the effect of the input on the overall fair value measurement, including possible alternative assumptions for the input. [*IFRS 13.73–74*]

2.4.270.40   If multiple unobservable inputs are used, then in our view the unobservable inputs should be considered both individually and in total for the purpose of determining their significance. For example, it would not be appropriate to categorise in Level 2 a fair value measurement that has multiple Level 3 inputs that are individually significant to that measurement but whose effects happen to offset. If factors such as volatility inputs are used, then an entity could apply some form of comparability methodology – e.g. a stress test on an option's volatility input or a 'with and without' comparison – to assist in determining significance.

2.4.280   *Level 1 inputs*

2.4.280.10   The definition of Level 1 inputs (see 2.4.260.20) refers to the term 'active market', which is a market in which transactions for the asset or liability take place with sufficient frequency and volume for pricing information to be provided on an ongoing basis. [*IFRS 13.76, A*]

2.4.280.20   Whether transactions take place with sufficient frequency and volume is a matter of judgement, and depends on the specific facts and circumstances of the market for the asset or liability. Even if a market is considered inactive – i.e. the price for the asset or liability is not a Level 1 input – it may still provide relevant pricing information (see 2.4.290 and 480). [*IFRS 13.B44*]

2.4.280.30   In our view, it is not necessary for there to be a large number of dealers or brokers in order for an active market to exist. In some cases, information about pricing and volumes traded may be available from only one independent source – e.g. a broker. In determining whether that one source is providing an active market in the instrument, in our view an entity should take into account its past experience, knowledge of the local market and professional judgement.

2.4.280.40   In our view, the determination of whether a market is active should not be based on the size of the entity's holding. For example, a market that trades 100,000 shares of Company X ordinary shares per day may be considered active, even if the entity holds 20,000,000 shares of X.

2.4.280.50   Even if the volume or level of activity for an asset or a liability has significantly decreased, the market for that asset or liability may still be active. In such circumstances, the quoted price for the asset or liability in that market would still be categorised within Level 1. For a discussion of measuring fair value if the volume or level of activity has significantly decreased, see 2.4.480.

2.4.280.60   To be categorised as Level 1, the measurement needs to be the quoted price of an identical instrument. It is not a measurement based on a quoted rate or index to be used as an input into a valuation model to calculate the fair value of the instrument. For example, over-the-counter derivative contracts are individual agreements between specific counterparties. Therefore, they are not usually categorised as a Level 1 measurement, because there is unlikely to be an active market for an identical instrument. [*IFRS 13.76*]

2.4.280.65   In our view, certain types of executable prices – e.g. third party quotes that represent binding offers – can be considered 'quoted' prices even though they do not represent the price of an actual transaction. For example, in many markets – in particular when market makers or similar intermediaries are involved – the market price is determined on the basis of bid and ask prices (see 2.4.250), which are binding offers but do not represent the price of an actual transaction unless and until the offer is accepted and a trade occurs. We believe that these prices may represent quoted prices in the market and therefore be considered Level 1 prices when the market is active. This is because current quoted bid and ask prices (or similar binding offers to trade) from market makers or exchanges may be more representative of the price at which a market participant could sell an asset at the measurement date than the prices of actual transactions that occurred at an earlier point in time. If such a price is considered a 'quoted' price but the market is not active, then the price will be categorised in Level 2 (see 2.4.290.30).

2.4.280.67   We believe that determining whether a binding offer is considered a 'quoted' price in the market and whether a market that is subject to the binding offer is considered 'active' requires judgement and depends on the specific facts and circumstances. In particular, it would be unusual for binding offers to be available at widely different price levels if the market is active. Similarly, a wide bid-ask spread may be associated with a market not being active.

2.4.280.70   Generally, an entity is not allowed to adjust Level 1 prices. However, in the following limited circumstances, which are explained below, an adjustment may be appropriate:
● as a practical expedient;
● the quoted price in an active market does not represent fair value at the measurement date; or
● the fair value of a liability or own equity instruments is measured using the quoted price of an identical instrument traded as an asset. [*IFRS 13.77, 79*]

2.4.280.80   As a practical expedient, an entity may measure the fair value of certain assets and liabilities under an alternative method that does not rely exclusively on quoted prices. Such a practical expedient is appropriate only if:
● the entity holds a large number of similar assets or liabilities that are measured at fair value; and
● a quoted price in an active market is available but not readily accessible for each of these assets or liabilities individually. [*IFRS 13.79(a)*]

2.4.280.90   In our view, the use of such an alternative method as a practical expedient is also subject to the condition that it results in a price that is representative of fair value. We believe that application of a practical expedient is not appropriate if it would lead to a measurement that is not representative of an exit price at the measurement date.

2.4.280.100   An example of an alternative pricing method as described in 2.4.280.80–90 is matrix pricing. This pricing method involves using a selection of data points (usually quoted prices) or yield curves to calculate prices for separate financial instruments that share characteristics similar to the data points. Matrix pricing using observable market-based data points will usually result in a Level 2 fair value measurement. [*IFRS 13.79(a)*]

2.4.280.110   In practice, an entity generally uses the closing price from the principal (or most advantageous) market on its reporting date. Some entities use prices that reflect after-hours trading, which in practice is most common for instruments that trade in foreign markets that close before similar markets in other time zones. Consideration should be given to the circumstances in which adjustments to Level 1 prices may be appropriate. [*IFRS 13.B34(a)*]

2.4.280.120   If the closing price is used, then the entity considers whether that price represents the fair value at the measurement date. In an exchange market, closing prices are both readily available and generally representative of fair value. However, the definition of a closing price may represent different things on different exchanges for different types of financial instruments. For example, a closing price may range from the last transaction price for the day to a price derived from a complicated calculation or process. If an asset or a liability is subject to a bid-ask spread (see 2.4.250), then an entity needs to assess the nature of the closing price. [*IFRS 13.B34(a)*]

2.4.280.130   In some cases, the quoted price in an active market may not represent fair value at the measurement date – e.g. if a significant event takes place after the close of a market but before the measurement date, such as the announcement of a business combination. In that case, an entity chooses an accounting policy, to be applied consistently, for identifying those events that may affect fair value measurements. This exception is limited to situations in which the significant event takes place after the close of the market but before the measurement date. It does not apply to situations in which the event takes place after the measurement date. [*IFRS 13.79(b)*]

EXAMPLE 9 – ADJUSTMENT TO LEVEL 1 INPUTS – AFTERMARKET TRANSACTIONS

2.4.280.140   Company P invests in shares of Company T that are listed on the London Stock Exchange (LSE). On the reporting date, P obtains the closing price of the shares from the LSE. After the closing time of the LSE but still on the reporting date, T makes a public announcement that affects the fair value of its shares; this is evidenced by prices for a small number of aftermarket transactions in depository receipts on the shares of T that are traded on the New York Stock Exchange.

2.4.280.150   In this example, P uses the aftermarket prices to make appropriate adjustments to the closing price from the LSE, in order to measure the fair value of the shares at the measurement date. Because the adjustment is derived from observed market prices, the resulting fair value measurement is a Level 2 measurement.

2.4.280.160   In our experience, pricing data from aftermarket trades or trades for identical or similar assets or liabilities in another market may be useful to determine the existence of a significant event that affects the fair value measurement of an asset or liability. Pricing data may also be used to determine the amount of the adjustment to be made to the last quoted price sourced from the entity's principal (or most advantageous) market.

2.4.280.170   If an entity uses pricing data from aftermarket trades or trades for identical or similar assets or liabilities in another market to determine the amount of the adjustment, then it should support that adjustment through an analysis of how the pricing data or their underlying factors affect the fair value of the asset or liability.

2.4.280.180   This analysis may be based on quantitative and qualitative factors to assess whether the pricing data is relevant to the fair value measurement of the asset or liability being measured. For example, if an entity uses a statistical method in its analysis, then to the extent that the analysis supports a correlation coefficient that is other than 1:1, that factor may need to be applied to pricing data from aftermarket trades or trades for identical or similar assets or liabilities in another market to develop the adjustment to be applied to the last quoted price in the entity's principal (or most advantageous) market.

2.4.280.190   This analysis may also include a comparison between the pricing data from aftermarket trades or trades for identical or similar assets or liabilities in another market and the subsequent price in the entity's principal (or most advantageous) market. To the extent that a difference is found through this analysis, an adjustment to the last quoted price from the entity's principal (or most advantageous) market may need to reflect this difference.

EXAMPLE 10 – ADJUSTMENT TO LEVEL 1 INPUTS – OIL FUTURES CONTRACTS

2.4.280.200   Company G holds oil futures contracts at the New York Mercantile Exchange (NYMEX). On the reporting date, G obtains the closing price of the oil futures from NYMEX. On the reporting date, but subsequent to the closing time of NYMEX, there is a public announcement that affects oil prices and related financial instruments. This is evidenced by prices of oil forward contracts transacted in the over-the-counter market on the reporting date.

2.4.280.210   G needs to evaluate the futures prices with forward contracts to factor how correlated the futures and forward markets are. If this analysis supports a correlation, and the correlation coefficient is other than 1:1, then that factor may need to be applied to the aftermarket forward prices to determine the appropriate adjustments to the price quoted on NYMEX.

2.4.280.220   Because of the adjustment to the price obtained from the principal market, the resulting fair value measurement would generally be expected to be a Level 2 measurement. However, if an adjustment using unobservable inputs is significant, then a Level 3 designation would be appropriate. [*IFRS 13.75*]

2.4.280.230   An entity may measure the fair value of a liability or its own equity instruments using the quoted price of an identical instrument traded as an asset. However, there may be specific differences between the item being measured and the asset. This may happen, for example, if the identical instrument traded as an asset includes a credit enhancement that is excluded from the liability's unit of account (see 2.4.80 and 380). [*IFRS 13.39(b), 79(c)*]

2.4.280.240   Any adjustment to a quoted price in an active market will result in the fair value measurement being categorised into a lower level of the fair value hierarchy. Although a price that is adjusted based on one of the limited circumstances in 2.4.280.70 is no longer a Level 1 measurement, in our view an entity should not make other adjustments to that measurement (e.g. for market or other risks), except if the criteria to make one of the other adjustments to Level 1 prices in 2.4.280.70 are met. We believe that the circumstances that allow an entity to exceptionally adjust Level 1 inputs only allow for adjustments related to those circumstances. [*IFRS 13.79*]

2.4.280.250   Positions in a single asset or liability (including a group of identical assets or liabilities) that are traded in an active market are measured at fair value within Level 1 as the product of the quoted price for the individual asset or liability and the quantity held. This is the case even if:
• the market's normal daily trading volume is insufficient to absorb the quantity held; or
• placing orders to sell the position in a single transaction might affect the quoted price (see 2.4.240).
   [*IFRS 13.80*]

2.4.290   *Level 2 and Level 3 inputs*

2.4.290.10   The determination of whether a fair value measurement is categorised into Level 2 or Level 3 depends on:

- the observability of the inputs that are used in the valuation technique(s); and
- the significance of the inputs to the fair value measurement. [*IFRS 13.73, 81, 84, 86, A*]

2.4.290.20   'Observable inputs' are inputs that are developed using market data, such as publicly available information about actual events or transactions and that reflect the assumptions that market participants would use in pricing the asset or liability. [*IFRS 13.A*]

2.4.290.30   Level 2 inputs include:
- quoted prices (see also 2.4.280.65–67) for similar assets or liabilities in active markets;
- quoted prices for identical or similar assets and liabilities in markets that are not active; and
- other inputs that are observable for the asset or liability – e.g. interest rates, implied volatilities, credit spreads or yield curves that are observed in the market. [*IFRS 13.82*]

2.4.290.40   'Market-corroborated inputs' that are derived principally from or corroborated by observable market data (by correlation or other means) are also Level 2 inputs. For example, the variable leg of an interest rate swap is based on a specific bank's prime rate. If the bank's prime rate is derived through extrapolation and the extrapolated values are corroborated by observable market data through correlation with an interest rate that is observable over substantially the full term of the swap, then the bank's prime rate is a market-corroborated input that is categorised as a Level 2 input. [*IFRS 13.82(d), A, B35(c)*]

2.4.290.50   Correlation is a statistical concept, indicating the strength and direction of a linear relationship between two variables. In our view, for an input to be considered a Level 2 input by using correlation, the correlation between the input and relevant observable market data should be high. In using correlation or other statistical means to support Level 2 inputs, an entity may apply similar statistical considerations that are used to analyse the possible behaviour of a hedging relationship during its term to ascertain whether it can be expected to meet the risk management objective (see 7.9.830.60).

2.4.290.60   In establishing the level in the hierarchy of an input corroborated using correlation analyses, an entity considers factors including the R-squared confidence level of the statistical analysis and the number of data points.

2.4.290.70   An input to a fair value measurement of an asset or a liability with a specified term is a Level 2 input only if it is observable for substantially the full term of the asset or liability. If this is not the case, then the input is a Level 3 input. Whether the resulting fair value measurement would be categorised as Level 2 or Level 3 depends on the significance of that input to the measurement in its entirety. [*IFRS 13.73, 82, A*]

EXAMPLE 11 – LEVEL 2 INPUT NOT AVAILABLE FOR SUBSTANTIALLY THE FULL TERM

2.4.290.80   Company E has an over-the-counter contract to buy natural gas every month for the next 30 months. E accounts for the contract as a derivative instrument, measured at fair value in the statement of financial position. Natural gas prices that are quoted in an active market are available for 24 months after the reporting date. For the remaining 6 months of the term, E uses internally developed estimates of future natural gas prices. Therefore, in this example, market prices are not available for substantially the entire term of the contract, and the impact of the unobservable inputs is significant.

> 2.4.290.90   As a result, E categorises the fair value measurement of this contract as a Level 3 measurement. In the following year, if quoted natural gas prices continue to be available for the following 24 months, then the fair value measurement might be categorised as a Level 2 measurement.

2.4.290.100   As noted in 2.4.130.10 and 230.20, an entity minimises the use of unobservable inputs in measuring fair value. However, situations may occur in which relevant inputs are not observable. In such situations, unobservable inputs are used based on the best information available about the assumptions that market participants would make in pricing the asset or liability, including assumptions about risk. Adjustments to Level 2 inputs based on unobservable inputs may be necessary depending on the characteristics of the asset or liability being measured. In that case, an entity assesses whether the effects of these adjustments are significant to the entire measurement (see 2.4.270). If so, then the fair value measurement is categorised as Level 3. [*IFRS 13.61, 75, 83–84, 86–87, 89*]

2.4.290.110   Examples of unobservable inputs include:
- foreign currency interest rates that:
  – are not observable; and
  – cannot be corroborated by observable market data for the term of the financial instrument being valued;
- volatility for a share option derived from the share's historical prices, because it does not generally represent market participants' current expectations about future volatility;
- a current estimate using the entity's own data about the future cash outflow to be paid to fulfil a decommissioning obligation assumed in a business combination; and
- a financial forecast of cash flows or profit or loss developed using the entity's own data and used as an input to measure the fair value of a CGU. [*IFRS 13.B36*]

2.4.290.120   Instruments may be transferred into or out of Level 3 for a number of reasons – for example:
- changes in the inputs used in a valuation;
- refinements in modelling techniques;
- the initiation or cessation of market transactions in similar instruments; or
- the passage of time (see Example 11).

2.4.290.130   In developing unobservable inputs because of the unavailability of relevant observable inputs, an entity is not precluded from using its own data. However, an entity adjusts its own data if reasonably available information indicates that other market participants would use different information. An example of a possible adjustment would be buyer-specific synergies – i.e. synergies available to a specific acquirer in a business combination that would not be available to market participants and therefore are excluded from the valuation. [*IFRS 13.89*]

2.4.300   Pricing services and broker quotes

2.4.300.10   Using a pricing service does not change the way that inputs are categorised in the fair value hierarchy. Prices obtained from a pricing service are not considered observable simply because they were obtained from a third party.

2.4.300.20   The IFRS Interpretations Committee discussed the classification of prices provided by third parties within the fair value hierarchy. The Committee noted that when assets or liabilities are measured on the basis of prices provided by third parties, the classification of those measurements within the fair value hierarchy depends on the evaluation of the inputs used by the third party to derive those prices; it is not based on the pricing methodology used. Therefore, the Committee noted that a fair value measurement that is based on prices provided by third parties may be categorised within Level 1 only if the measurement relies solely on unadjusted quoted prices in an active market for an identical instrument that the entity can access at the measurement date (see 2.4.270). [*IU 01-15*]

2.4.300.30   An entity using a pricing service needs to understand the source of the inputs used by the pricing service in order to properly categorise any fair value measurements based on those inputs. For example, if a pricing service provides an unadjusted quoted price from an active market for an identical instrument, then a fair value measurement based only on that price would be a Level 1 measurement. Alternatively, if the pricing service provides prices based on in-house models, then any resulting fair value measurement would be a Level 2 or Level 3 measurement, depending on the observability and significance of the inputs used in the model for the measurement and for adjusting other inputs. [*IFRS 13.73, 75–76, A*]

EXAMPLE 12 – PRICE PROVIDED BY A THIRD PARTY PRICING SERVICE – FAIR VALUE HIERARCHY

2.4.300.40   Company H is a party to an interest rate swap transaction in an over-the-counter (OTC) market. There are no quoted prices in the OTC market for interest rate swaps that are identical to H's swap. H obtains rates from Company R, which provides pricing services, to use in the measurement of the fair value of the swap. To provide H with the rates, R uses transaction rates for similar swaps in the OTC market.

2.4.300.50   Although similar swaps may have been transacted in the OTC market, these swaps have different counterparties as well as different fixed coupons and residual maturities, and therefore are not identical to H's interest rate swap. The price at which H would be able to sell its interest rate swap would result from a negotiated transaction taking into account the credit ratings of the two parties to the swap and the terms of the specific swap.

2.4.300.60   Because H's swap is not identical to similar swaps for which there are transactions in the OTC market, the price cannot be categorised as a Level 1 measurement, but as Level 2 or Level 3 depending on whether significant unobservable inputs are used to produce the price.

2.4.300.70   In some cases, pricing services may provide Level 2 inputs determined using a matrix pricing methodology, even though Level 1 inputs are available to both the entity and the pricing service (see 2.4.280.100). Using Level 2 inputs in these situations is not appropriate unless the entity meets the criteria in 2.4.280.70–90. If these criteria are not met, then the entity obtains quoted prices in active markets (Level 1 inputs) either from the pricing service or from other sources. [*IFRS 13.79(a)*]

2.4.300.80   Consensus pricing services obtain information from multiple subscribers who each submit prices to the pricing service. The pricing service returns consensus prices to each subscriber based on the data received. In assessing consensus data, it is important to understand what the prices submitted represent. If the estimates provided to the service do not represent executable quotes or are not based on observable prices, then a fair value measurement derived from the consensus price will be a Level 3 measurement. However, if the inputs to the price received from the pricing service are Level 1 or Level 2 inputs, then the use of those prices will generally result in a Level 2 measurement. [*IFRS 13.73*]

2.4.300.90   Similar considerations apply to prices obtained from brokers. A broker quote is not generally a binding offer. Even if it is, it may not represent the price at which an orderly transaction would take place between market participants. If a broker quote reflects actual current market transactions in an identical instrument, then it may be a Level 1 or Level 2 input. However, if a broker quote is an indicative price based on the broker's valuation models, then it is a Level 2 or Level 3 input, depending on the significance and observability of the inputs to the model – i.e. as with a price from a pricing service, an indicative price from a broker is not automatically considered to be an observable input merely because it has been obtained from a third party. See also 2.4.480.110. [*IFRS 13.73, A, B34(c)*]

2.4.300.100   In the case of centrally cleared derivatives, the central clearing organisation provides a daily value mark that is used to calculate the variation margin – i.e. the daily amount that is paid by or to a clearing member reflecting the change in the value of the collateral (for collateralised-to-market derivatives) or the daily settlement amount (for settled-to-market derivatives). For a discussion of the recognition and derecognition of variation margin payments and receipts, see 7.6.490.

2.4.300.110   The valuation technique used by the central clearing organisation for both collateralised and settled-to-market derivatives might not be consistent with IFRS 13. This is because each clearing organisation may calculate variation margins differently and the margin may reflect assumptions specific to the clearing organisation rather than being consistent with those that a market participant would make. The daily settlement amount is not a quoted transaction price or an exit price in an active market. This amount may not represent a price at which an entity would be able to sell or assign its derivative exposure to another market participant. Although for derivative contracts cleared under a settled-to-market model, the value provided by a central clearing organisation may be used for daily settlements, the marking of a daily settlement payment does not extinguish the transaction and future payments and receipts will arise in accordance with its terms and conditions. For these reasons, an entity cannot generally rely solely on the central clearing organisation's value when measuring the fair value of the derivative. [*IFRS 13.22*]

2.4.300.120   Although the clearing organisation is not a market maker, the inputs to its calculation of value for variation margin purposes will generally reflect a selection of market data and may be close to but not necessarily the same as a fair value calculated by market participants. Therefore, the value mark may be a meaningful data point and may serve as a starting point for measuring fair value. An entity using a central clearing organisation needs to understand the source of the information used by the clearing organisation in order to properly categorise any fair value measurements based on those inputs.

2.4.300.130   When the daily variation payments on a settled-to-market derivative are considered settlements on the underlying trade (and therefore give rise to a partial derecognition of the derivative asset or liability), the derivative continues to exist but generally has a current fair value of zero (or close to zero) immediately following the daily settlement payment (see 7.6.490.120–140).

2.4.310   MEASURING FAIR VALUE

2.4.320   Fair value on initial recognition

2.4.320.10   If an asset is acquired (or a liability assumed), then the transaction price paid for the asset (or received to assume the liability) normally reflects an entry price. However, IFRS 13 requires fair value measurements to be based on an exit price (see 2.4.60). Although conceptually different, in many cases the exit and entry price are equal and therefore fair value on initial recognition generally equals the transaction price. [*IFRS 13.57–58*]

2.4.320.20   However, entities are required to take into account factors specific to the transaction and the asset or liability that might indicate that the transaction price and initial fair value measurement may differ. These may include:
- the transaction being between related parties;
- the transaction taking place under duress – e.g. if the seller is experiencing financial difficulty;
- the unit of account represented by the transaction price differing from the unit of account of the asset or liability measured at fair value – e.g. if the transaction price represents the purchase of multiple items;
- the transaction price (i.e. entry or purchase price) is not the price within the bid-offer spread that is most representative of fair value (i.e. an exit or selling price) – this may apply when an entity uses bid prices for asset positions and ask prices for liabilities; and/or
- the market in which the transaction takes place being different from the principal (or most advantageous) market. [*IFRS 13.70, B4*]

2.4.320.30   The presence of one or more of these factors does not automatically result in a fair value measurement that differs from the transaction price. For example, the price in a related party transaction may be used as an input into a fair value measurement if the entity has evidence that the transaction was entered into on market terms. [*IFRS 13.B4(a)*]

EXAMPLE 13 – DIFFERENCE BETWEEN TRANSACTION PRICE AND FAIR VALUE ON INITIAL RECOGNITION

2.4.320.40   Company R, a retail counterparty, enters into an interest rate swap in a retail market with Company D, a dealer, for no initial consideration – i.e. the transaction price is zero.
- D can access both the retail market (i.e. with retail counterparties) and the dealer market (i.e. with dealer counterparties).
- R can only access the retail market.

2.4.320.50   From the perspective of D, the dealer market is the principal market for the swap, which is different from the market in which it initially entered into the swap transaction (the retail market). Therefore, for D the transaction price of zero may not necessarily represent the fair value of the swap on initial recognition.

2.4.320.60   Conversely, R cannot access the dealer market, and the retail market is the principal market from its perspective. If R were to transfer its rights and obligations under the swap, then it would do so with a dealer counterparty in that retail market. Therefore, the transaction price of zero represents the fair value of the swap to R on initial recognition (ignoring the potential effect of the bid-ask spread). [*IFRS 13.IE24–IE26*]

2.4.320.70   In another example, it may be appropriate to measure the fair value of a hybrid instrument based on the separate fair value measurements of its individual components – i.e. the host contract and one or more embedded derivatives – if that is how market participants would price the instrument in the principal (or most advantageous) market for the hybrid instrument. If the resulting measurement on initial recognition is different from the transaction price, then the entity considers these factors in order to conclude whether it is an appropriate measure of fair value.

2.4.320.80   A day one gain or loss arises if the transaction price for an asset and/or liability differs from the fair value used to measure it on initial recognition. IFRS 13 requires day one gains or losses to be recognised in profit or loss, unless the IFRS that requires or permits fair value measurement specifies otherwise. For a discussion of this issue in the context of financial instruments, see 7.7.40. [*IFRS 13.60, BC135*]

2.4.320.90   Because transaction costs are not a component of a fair value measurement, they do not represent a difference between an exit price and an entry price (see 2.4.110). [*IFRS 13.BC33*]

EXAMPLE 14 – EFFECT OF TRANSACTION COSTS

2.4.320.100   In the following chart, a seller sells an asset in an orderly transaction at a price of 100. The seller pays broker commission of 5% out of the proceeds of the sale, and the buyer incurs transaction costs of 2.

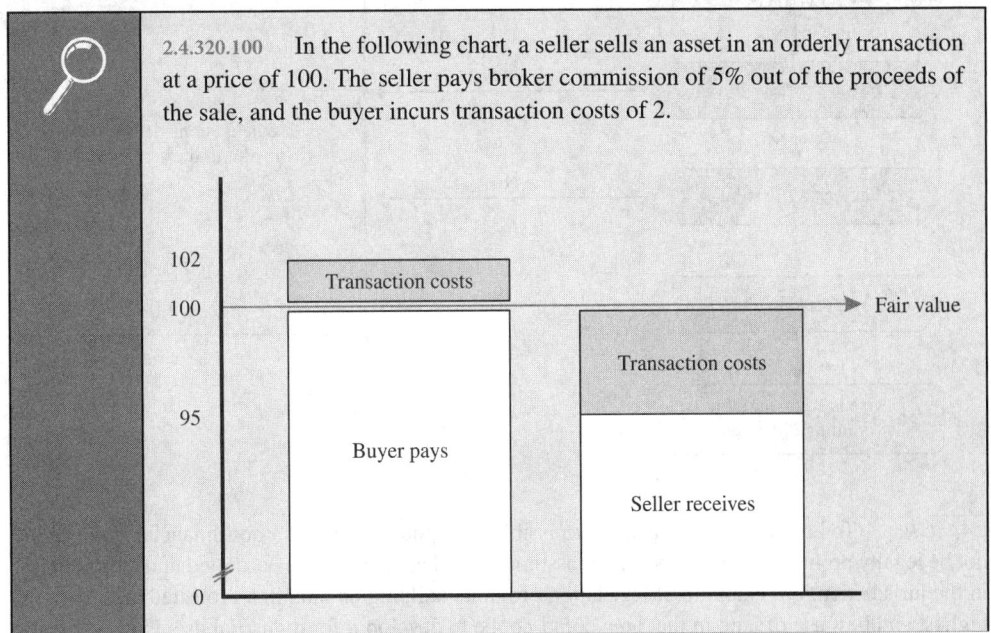

2.4.320.110   In this example, fair value is 100 and not 95 (100 exit price less 5 transaction costs). From the buyer's perspective, the fair value is the same – i.e. 100. The buyer's transaction costs of 2 are also not part of the fair value measurement.

2.4.320.120   Bid-ask spreads may represent a difference between an entry and exit price in markets for financial instruments, or if an intermediary is needed to bring together a buyer and a seller (see 2.4.250). [*IFRS 13.BC165*]

2.4.330   Highest and best use

2.4.340   *General principles*

2.4.340.10   'Highest and best use' is a valuation concept that represents the use of a non-financial asset by market participants that would maximise the value of the asset or the group of assets and liabilities (e.g. a business) within which the asset would be used. This concept does not apply to financial assets or liabilities or own equity instruments because they do not have alternative uses. [*IFRS 13.A, BC63, BC65*]

2.4.340.20   A fair value measurement of a non-financial asset considers a market participant's ability to generate economic benefits by using the asset at its highest and best use or by selling it to another market participant who would use the asset in its highest and best use; it is most often relevant in measuring the fair value of real estate. The following flowchart illustrates the factors to be considered in identifying the highest and best use. [*IFRS 13.27–28*]

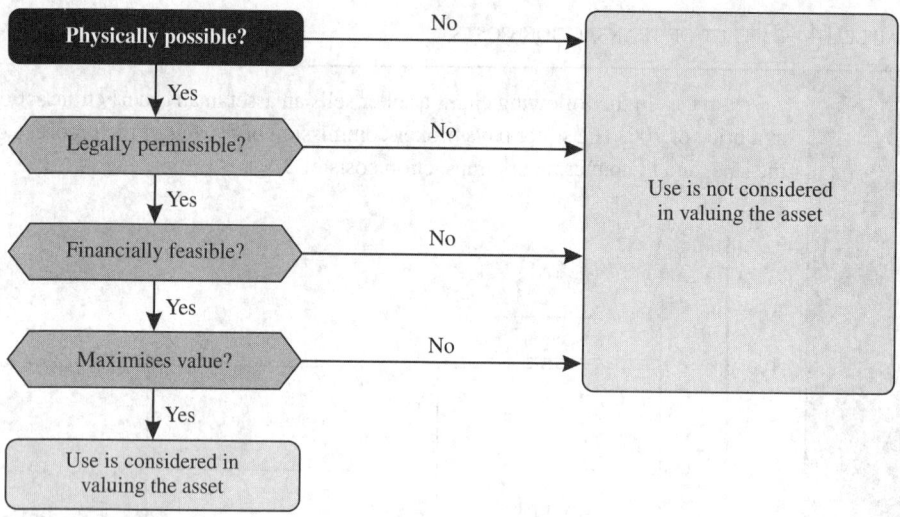

2.4.340.30   To be considered 'legally permissible', the potential use of a non-financial asset should not be legally prohibited. An entity cannot assume a use that could not be permitted under current law in the jurisdiction. For example, if legislation prohibits building on land in a protected area, then the highest and best use of land in that area could not be to develop it for industrial use. However, a use of an asset does not need to be legal at the measurement date. For example, a fair value measurement of land and buildings assumes zoning different from the current zoning if market participants would assume such a change in zoning. In such circumstances, the fair value measurement would incorporate the cost to convert the asset and obtain a different zoning permission, including the risk and uncertainty that such permission would not be granted. [*IFRS 13.BC69*]

EXAMPLE 15 – HIGHEST AND BEST USE – VALUE OF LAND

2.4.340.40   Company X acquired a brewery that is located in an area that has recently been re-zoned to allow both residential and industrial use. X determines that market participants would take into account the potential to develop the brewery site for residential use in pricing the land on which the brewery is currently located.

2.4.340.50   Therefore, X measures the fair value of the land based on the higher of:
- the value of the land as currently developed as a brewery; and
- the value of the land as a vacant site for residential use, taking into account the costs of demolishing the brewery and other costs necessary to convert the land to a vacant site. [*IFRS 13.IE7–IE8*]

2.4.340.60   In the absence of evidence to the contrary, the entity's current use of an asset is assumed to be its highest and best use. This means that an entity is not required to engage in exhaustive efforts to identify other potential highest and best uses. However, if readily available market information or other factors suggest that a different use by a market participant would maximise the value of the asset, then such information should not be ignored. The basis for conclusions to IFRS 13 notes the IASB's expectation that, after considering the cost to convert an asset to an alternative use, the entity's current use would generally be its highest and best use. [*IFRS 13.29, BC71*]

2.4.340.70   An entity may not intend to actively use a non-financial asset for reasons such as:
- the existence of an overlap with existing assets; or
- an intention to protect its competitive position. [*IFRS 13.30*]

2.4.340.80   Notwithstanding its actual use by an entity, the fair value of a non-financial asset is measured assuming that it is used by market participants in its highest and best use. This use will depend on the characteristics of market participants (see 2.4.90). [*IFRS 13.30*]

2.4.340.90   In evaluating the highest and best use to market participants, the possible perspectives of financial and strategic buyers may be considered to determine the asset's highest and best use. In general, the key difference between the two categories of potential market participants is that strategic buyers have existing operations and may have complementary assets with which an intangible asset, for example, may be used either actively or defensively, whereas financial buyers do not. There are exceptions, such as when financial buyers have existing investments in a specific market with which acquired assets may be used or when financial buyers may be pursuing a roll-up strategy. [*IFRS 13.27, 29–30*]

2.4.340.100   The highest and best use of an intangible asset to market participants may be to actively use the intangible asset with other assets, including potentially other assets already owned by the market participants. This use could apply to both financial and strategic buyers. Alternatively, the highest and best use may be to use the intangible asset defensively in a manner that results in a highest and best use of a group of complementary assets. This may be the highest and best use for strategic buyers, but would be less likely to apply to financial buyers who are more likely to use the intangible asset actively. [*IFRS 13.27, 29–31*]

EXAMPLE 16 – HIGHEST AND BEST USE – VALUE OF A BRAND

2.4.340.110   Company B acquires a brand in a business combination. B decides not to use the brand on the assumption that its removal from the market will generate greater incremental value as a result of increased revenues from its existing brands. However, a market participant would choose to continue to use the brand, because it would not hold the other brands that B does.

2.4.340.120   In this example, the fair value of the brand would be based on its continued use, because a market participant would choose to continue actively using the brand. This is despite the fact that B's decision not to use the brand results in higher benefits to B.

2.4.350   *In combination vs stand-alone*

2.4.350.10   A fair value measurement of a non-financial asset is based on its use either:
- in combination with other assets as a group or in combination with other assets and liabilities; or
- on a stand-alone basis. [*IFRS 13.31*]

2.4.350.20   The valuation premise depends on the use that is consistent with the perspective of market participants of the non-financial asset's highest and best use. [*IFRS 13.31*]

2.4.350.30   If the highest and best use would be to use a non-financial asset in combination with other assets, then it is assumed that the other assets would also be available to market participants, and that this would be considered in pricing the asset. However, the fair value measurement assumes that the asset is sold consistent with the unit of account specified in other standards (see 2.4.80). [*IFRS 13.31(a)(i), 32*]

2.4.350.40   If the highest and best use is to use the asset in combination with other assets, then the same valuation premise is used for the other non-financial assets with which it would be used. [*IFRS 13.31(a)(iii)*]

EXAMPLE 17 – CUSTOMER RELATIONSHIP

2.4.350.50   Company B acquired contractual customer relationships and technology assets as part of a business combination. B considers the following in determining whether the highest and best use of the customer relationships would be on a stand-alone basis or in combination with complementary assets.

- The relationships with customers arose in the context of the sale of a product incorporating the technology. A market participant without complementary technology would probably realise lower value from the customer relationships, because of the probability of lower expected sales.
- However, a market participant with access to complementary technology would probably realise higher sales and profits than on a stand-alone basis and would consider this in valuing the customer relationships.

2.4.350.60   In this example, the valuation premise for the customer relationships would therefore be in combination with the technology – i.e. an in-combination valuation premise. Similarly, the same analysis would apply to the technology – i.e. the technology would be more valuable as a result of its use with customer relationships.

2.4.360   Liabilities and own equity instruments

2.4.360.10   IFRS 13 contains specific requirements for applying the fair value measurement framework to liabilities (including financial liabilities) and an entity's own equity instruments. The following flowchart illustrates the process that an entity uses in measuring the fair value of such items. [*IFRS 13.37–41, 79(c)*]

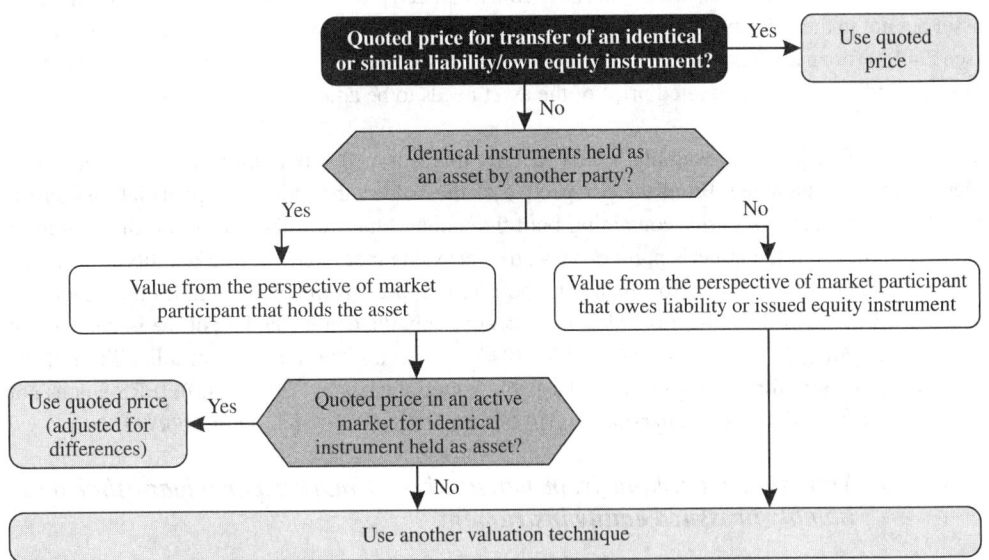

2.4.370   *Quoted price for transfer of liability or own equity instrument*

2.4.370.10   In measuring the fair value of a liability or an entity's own equity instrument, it is assumed that the item is transferred to a market participant at the measurement date – e.g. the liability remains outstanding and the market participant transferee would be required to fulfil it. It is also assumed that the non-performance risk related to a liability is the same before and after the transfer. For a discussion of non-performance risk, see 2.4.400. [*IFRS 13.34, 42*]

2.4 Fair value measurement

2.4.370.20   The transfer notion is conceptually consistent with the exit price concept (see 2.4.60). In our experience, there are many cases in which there is no observable market to provide pricing information about the transfer of a liability or an entity's own equity instruments. Also, in many cases an entity may not be able to transfer its liability to a third party. However, there may be an observable market for such items if they are held by other parties as assets. Therefore, the fair values of most financial liabilities and own equity instruments are measured from the perspective of a market participant that holds the identical instrument as an asset (see 2.4.380). [*IFRS 13.35, 37, BC81*]

2.4.370.30   Furthermore, the transfer notion reflects the fact that fair value is a market-based and not an entity-specific measurement. For example, the expected costs to an entity to fulfil an obligation may be lower than the price to transfer it to a market participant, because the entity has advantages relative to the market. However, even in such cases an entity is required to measure fair value based on the price that would be paid to transfer the liability. [*IFRS 13.BC81*]

2.4.380   *Measurement from perspective of market participant that holds identical asset*

2.4.380.10   If there is no quoted price for the transfer of an identical or a similar liability or an entity's own equity instruments, and another market participant holds the identical item as an asset, then the entity measures the item's fair value from the perspective of such a market participant. [*IFRS 13.37*]

2.4.380.20   In these circumstances, an entity adjusts quoted prices for features that are present in the asset but not in the liability or the entity's own equity instrument, or vice versa. If the unit of account (see 2.4.80) for an asset is not the same as for the liability or the entity's own equity instrument, then this also indicates that the quoted price of the asset needs to be adjusted. [*IFRS 13.39, 79(c)*]

2.4.380.30   Consider, for example, a debt security that is issued with a third party credit enhancement such as a guarantee. From the perspective of the holder, the individual financial instrument may be the combined security containing both the amount due from the issuer and the guarantee (see 7.1.130). From the issuer's point of view, the fair value measurement of a liability follows the unit of account of the liability for financial reporting purposes. If that unit excludes the guarantee, then the fair value of the obligation takes into account only the credit standing of the issuer and not the credit standing of the guarantor (see 2.4.80). Consequently, the fair value of a liability reflects the effect of non-performance risk on the basis of its unit of account (see 2.4.400). IFRS 9 does not state explicitly whether such a guarantee is part of the liability's unit of account. [*IFRS 13.39(b), BC98*]

2.4.390   *Valuation technique from perspective of market participant that owes liability or issued equity instrument*

2.4.390.10   There may be liabilities or an entity's own equity instruments that are not held by another party as an asset and for which there is no quoted price for the transfer of an identical or similar liability or own equity instrument – e.g. for some decommissioning liabilities assumed in a business combination. In such cases, an entity uses a valuation technique to measure the fair value of the item from the perspective of a market participant that owes the liability or that issued the equity instrument. In using a present value technique, an entity estimates the future cash outflows that market participants would expect to incur in fulfilling the obligation. This would include any compensation for risk and the profit margin that a market participant would require to undertake the activity. [*IFRS 13.40–41(a), B31–B33*]

2.4.390.20   The risk adjustment is often the most difficult factor to quantify in a fair value measurement of a non-financial liability. Estimating the risk adjustment, as well as other inputs, may be especially difficult if an entity has an obligation with a unique or unusual risk – as opposed to situations in which there are several obligations with similar risks. In the latter case, the entity may have experience from previous outcomes that enables it to estimate the range of possible results. Also, the price that a market participant might require to assume an obligation may reflect possible portfolio diversification effects. For example, if outcomes are not perfectly correlated, then negative outcomes may be (partially) offset by positive outcomes. In that case, a market participant may demand a lower risk premium. A greater risk adjustment would be likely if the inputs to a fair value measurement were more uncertain.

2.4.390.30   An entity may estimate future cash outflows that market participants would expect to incur in fulfilling the obligation by taking the following steps:
- estimate the cash flows that the entity would incur in fulfilling the obligation;
- exclude the cash flows that other market participants would not incur;
- include the cash flows that other market participants would incur but that the entity would not incur; and
- estimate the profit margin that a market participant would require to assume the obligation. [*IFRS 13.41(a), B31*]

2.4.400   *Non-performance risk, including credit risk*

2.4.400.10   The fair value of a liability reflects the effect of 'non-performance risk', which is the risk that an entity will not fulfil an obligation. Non-performance risk is assumed to be the same before and after the transfer of the liability. Non-performance risk includes, but may not be limited to, an entity's own credit risk. 'Credit risk' is defined as the risk that one party to a financial instrument will cause a financial loss for the other party by failing to discharge an obligation. See also 2.4.460 and 7.10.520. [*IFRS 13.42, A, 7.A*]

2.4.400.20   The effect of non-performance risk may differ depending on:
- the nature of the liability – e.g. whether the liability is an obligation to deliver cash (a financial liability) or an obligation to deliver goods or services (a non-financial liability); and
- the terms of credit enhancements related to the liability, if there are any – e.g. a pledge of assets against default. [*IFRS 13.43*]

2.4.400.30   The fair value of a liability reflects the effect of non-performance risk on the basis of its unit of account. Therefore, the issuer of a liability that is issued with an inseparable third party credit enhancement does not include the effect of that credit enhancement in the liability's fair value measurement if it accounts separately for the liability and the credit enhancement. Consequently, if the liability is a separate unit of account from the perspective of the issuing entity, then the fair value of that liability reflects the issuer's own non-performance risk and not that of the guarantor. See also 2.4.80 and 380.20–30. [*IFRS 13.43–44*]

2.4.400.35   Generally, an expected present value technique is used to measure the fair value of a decommissioning liability. An entity is not precluded from using a discount rate adjustment technique or a technique based on a market approach. However, applying these techniques is rare because observable market prices, including market interest rates for decommissioning liabilities, generally do not exist. [*IFRS 13.B31–B33*]

EXAMPLE 18 – FAIR VALUE OF A STAND-ALONE DECOMMISSIONING LIABILITY

2.4.400.40   On 1 November 2018, Company B assumes a decommissioning liability in a business combination and is therefore required to measure the liability at fair value in the acquisition accounting. B is legally required to remediate a mine pit at the end of its useful life, which is estimated to be in 10 years. B uses a present value technique to measure the fair value of the decommissioning liability.

2.4.400.50   If B were allowed to transfer its decommissioning liability to a market participant, then B concludes that a market participant would use all of the following inputs in estimating the price.

Labour costs	100
Allocated overhead and equipment costs – 60% of labour costs	60
Third party contractor margin of 20%, based on margins that contractors in the industry generally receive for similar activities – 160 x 20%	32
Annual inflation rate of 4%, based on market data for the applicable jurisdiction – 192 x 4% compounded for 10 years	92
5% risk adjustment that reflects the compensation that an external party would require in order to accept the risk that the cash flows might differ from those expected given the uncertainty in locking in today's price for a project that will not occur for 10 years – 284 x 5%	14
A risk-free rate based on 10-year government bonds in the applicable jurisdiction	5%
An adjustment to the discount rate to reflect B's non-performance risk, including its credit risk	3%

2.4.400.60   The following chart shows the make-up of these costs to give a fair value of the decommissioning liability of 138: present value at 8% of 298 (100 + 60 + 32 + 92 + 14) in 10 years.

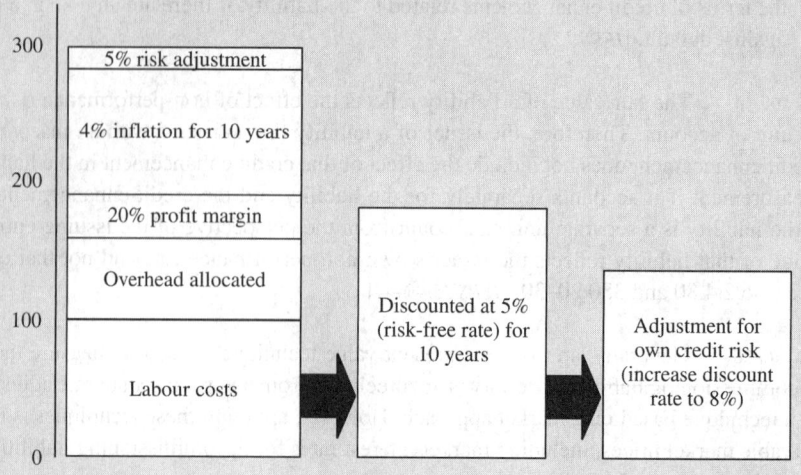

> 2.4.400.70   The adjustment for the time value of money is shown separately from the credit risk adjustment, to illustrate the direction of the adjustment. However, in our experience only one discount rate calculation would be undertaken. [*IFRS 13.IE35–IE39*]

2.4.400.80   As Example 18 shows, the adjustment for the entity's own non-performance risk has reduced the fair value of the liability – just as higher credit risk reduces the fair value of a financial asset.

2.4.410   *Restrictions on transfer of liabilities or own equity instruments, or on sale of related asset*

2.4.410.10   Separate inputs to reflect restrictions on the transfer of a liability or an entity's own equity instruments are not included in the fair value of a liability or an entity's own equity instruments. Such a restriction is assumed to be reflected implicitly or explicitly in the other inputs used by market participants to price such instruments. Therefore, if the effect of a restriction is already included in the other inputs, then an additional input or adjustment to reflect a restriction on transferability results in double counting. [*IFRS 13.45–46, BC99*]

2.4.410.20   Consequently, in measuring a liability or an entity's own equity instruments from the perspective of a market participant that holds the item as an asset, an entity ensures that the price of the asset does not reflect the effect of a restriction preventing the sale of that asset. It is assumed that restrictions on the sale of an asset relate to the marketability of that asset, whereas restrictions on the corresponding liability relate to performance of the obligation (see 2.4.70 and 240). [*IFRS 13.39, BC100*]

2.4.420   *Financial liabilities with demand feature#*

2.4.420.10   The fair value of a financial liability with a demand feature cannot be less than the amount payable on demand, discounted from the first date on which the amount could be required to be paid. [*IFRS 13.47*]

EXAMPLE 19 – FINANCIAL LIABILITY WITH DEMAND FEATURE

> 2.4.420.20   Bank B offers a fixed rate savings deposit product whereby individuals deposit an amount of 1,000 on 1 January 2018 for a period of two years. This product provides a fixed return of 5% per annum, giving a return of 103 after two years. The individuals are able to withdraw their money after one year, but in this case the total amount paid would only be 1,040. Assume that the market interest rate is 8% one year after inception of the deposit.
>
> 2.4.420.30   In this example, B calculates the present value of its liability at 31 December 2018, considering the remainder of the original period of two years, at an amount of 1,021 (1,103 discounted for one year by 8%). However, the fair value of the financial liability at 31 December 2018 is not less than the amount payable on demand, which is 1,040. Therefore, the fair value of the liability is measured at 1,040.

2.4.423   **FORTHCOMING REQUIREMENTS**

2.4.423.10   Under IFRS 17, if an entity accounts for an insurance contract acquired in a business combination or follows the fair value approach to transition to this standard, then the requirement that the fair value for a financial liability cannot be less than the amount payable on demand (see 2.4.420.10) does not apply. [*IFRS 17.B94, C20*]

2.4.425   *Fair value less costs of disposal of a CGU containing a decommissioning liability*

2.4.425.10   Under IAS 36, recognised liabilities are considered in determining the recoverable amount of a CGU when the disposal of the CGU would require the buyer to assume the liability. For example, a decommissioning liability is generally considered in determining the recoverable amount of a CGU that is tested for impairment (see 3.10.240.120). In this case, the fair value less costs of disposal (or the estimated cash flow from ultimate disposal) is the price to sell the assets of the CGU together with the decommissioning liability. [*IAS 36.78*]

2.4.425.20   When the fair value less costs of disposal of a CGU containing a decommissioning liability is calculated using discounted cash flows, a question arises about how the liability should be factored into the fair value measurement. The approach used needs to be consistent with how a market participant would determine fair value. The approach to measuring the decommissioning liability, including the discount rate applied, may vary over the life of a project. In our experience, there are two approaches used in practice.
- *Approach 1:* The CGU's assets and the decommissioning liability are treated as one unit of valuation.
- *Approach 2:* The CGU's assets and the decommissioning liability are treated as two separate units of valuation.

2.4.425.30   In our experience, Approach 1 in 2.4.425.20 is the more commonly used approach when decommissioning is expected to occur very far in the future. Under this approach, a market participant considers the risk and return profile of the assets and the liability of the CGU as one unit of valuation and considers the liability's cash flows as part of the overall project's cash flows, rather than valuing the liability on a stand-alone basis. Therefore, an entity applies a single discount rate – such as the weighted-average cost of capital (WACC) – to all cash flows, including the cash outflows for a decommissioning liability. When developing the cost of equity as an input into the determination of the WACC, the selected beta is often derived from comparable publicly traded businesses that have decommissioning liabilities.

2.4.425.40   Later in a CGU's life, the cash inflows from the CGU's assets may become insignificant compared with the cash outflows to cover the liability. As a result, a market participant is more likely to apply Approach 2 in 2.4.425.20, which allows separate consideration of the remaining cash inflows and the decommissioning outflows. Under this approach, an entity measures the fair value of the CGU excluding the decommissioning liability and then deducts from it the stand-alone fair value of the liability. The underlying assumption in this approach is that a market participant would consider the risk and return profile of the assets of the CGU and the related decommissioning liability separately as two units of valuation. In such cases, the fair value of the CGU excluding the decommissioning liability is determined using a relevant market participant rate specific to the assets only and the fair value of the decommissioning liability is determined as the amount that would be paid to a third party to assume the liability (see 2.4.400.35–70).

2.4.425.50   The discount rate applied to the cash flows generated by the CGU in Approach 1 differs from that applied to the cash flows excluding the liability in Approach 2. This is because excluding the decommissioning liability under Approach 2 changes the riskiness of the cash flows.

2.4.430   Portfolio measurement

2.4.430.10   An entity that holds a group of financial assets and financial liabilities is exposed to market risks – i.e. interest rate risk, currency risk and other price risk – and to the credit risk of each of the counterparties. If certain conditions are met, then IFRS 13 permits an entity to measure the fair value of a group of financial assets and financial liabilities with offsetting risk positions on the basis of its net exposure. [*IFRS 13.48*]

2.4.430.20   Under the exception, the fair value of the group is measured on the basis of the price that would be received to sell a net long position (or paid to transfer a net short position) for a particular risk exposure in an orderly transaction between market participants at the measurement date. Therefore, application of the portfolio measurement exception is considered to be consistent with the way in which market participants would price the net risk position at the measurement date. [*IFRS 13.BC119*]

2.4.430.30   In our view, application of the portfolio measurement exception changes the unit of account from the individual financial asset or financial liability to the net position for a particular risk exposure (see 2.4.80). Accordingly, we believe that the size of the net risk exposure is a characteristic to be considered in measuring the fair value of the net risk exposure (see 2.4.240). [*IFRS 13.14, 48, 53, 56, 69*]

2.4.430.40   An entity is permitted to apply the portfolio measurement exception to a group of financial assets, financial liabilities and other contracts that are in the scope of IFRS 9 – i.e. the portfolio may include contracts to buy or sell a non-financial item that are accounted for in accordance with IFRS 9 (see 7.1.200) – if the answer to all of the questions in the following flowchart is 'yes'. [*IFRS 13.48–49, 52, BC47(b), BC119A–BC119B*]

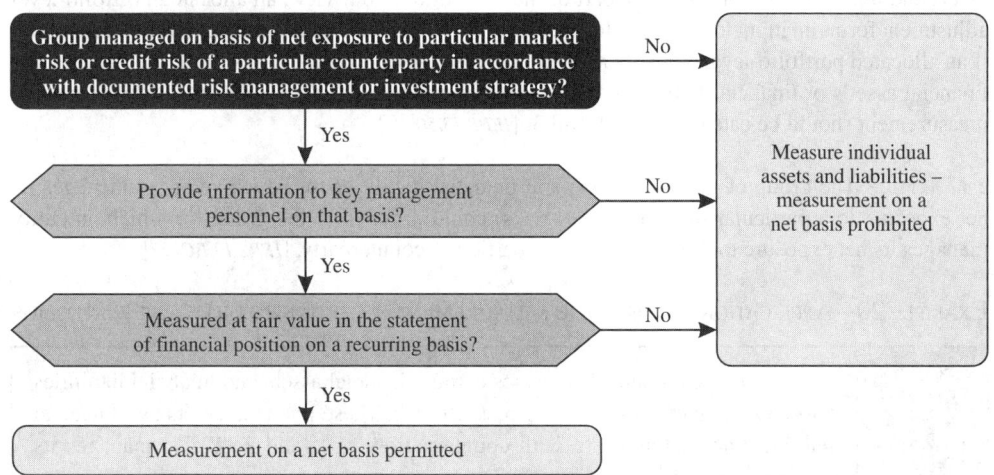

2.4.430.50   Judgement may be required to evaluate whether, based on the specific facts and circumstances, it is appropriate to apply the exception.

2.4.430.60   If the entity is permitted to use the exception, then it chooses an accounting policy, to be applied consistently, for a particular portfolio. However, an entity is not required to maintain a static portfolio. [*IFRS 13.51, BC121*]

2.4.430.70   The exception does not apply to financial statement presentation. Therefore, if an entity applies the exception, then the basis of measurement of a group of financial instruments might differ from the basis of presentation. For example, a portfolio of derivative financial instruments might be measured based on the price of the entity's net exposure to a particular market risk (or the credit risk of a particular counterparty). If the entity presents those derivative assets and derivative liabilities separately in its statement of financial position (see 7.10.110), then the portfolio-level adjustments – e.g. bid-ask adjustment or credit risk adjustments – are allocated to the individual assets and liabilities on a reasonable and consistent basis. [*IFRS 13.50*]

2.4.430.80   The exception also does not apply to hedge accounting. Therefore, for assessing hedge effectiveness and measuring ineffectiveness, an entity needs to determine the individual risk adjustments (in particular, credit risk adjustments) to arrive at the fair values of the individual hedging derivatives or the appropriate credit risk adjustment for a group of derivatives that have been designated together as the hedging instrument in a single hedging relationship. In our view, the entity should adopt a reasonable and consistently applied methodology for allocating credit risk adjustments determined at a portfolio level to individual derivative instruments for the purpose of measuring the fair values of individual hedging instruments that are used in assessing effectiveness and measuring hedge ineffectiveness (see 7.9.850.50). [*IFRS 13.50*]

2.4.430.90   For a discussion of potential bases of allocating portfolio-level adjustments related to credit risk, see 2.4.450.20–40.

2.4.430.100   If an entity applies the exception, then the portfolio-level adjustments are considered in categorising, in the fair value hierarchy, the fair value measurements of the individual financial assets and financial liabilities that are part of that portfolio. In our view, an allocated portfolio-level adjustment forms an input to the fair value measurement of the individual asset or liability. Therefore, if an allocated portfolio-level adjustment is an unobservable input and has a significant effect on the financial asset's or financial liability's fair value measurement, then we believe that this fair value measurement should be categorised as Level 3. [*IFRS 13.50, 73*]

2.4.430.110   The group of financial assets and financial liabilities for which an entity manages its net exposure to a particular market risk (or risks) could differ from the group for which an entity manages its net exposure to the credit risk of a particular counterparty. [*IFRS 13.BC127*]

EXAMPLE 20 – APPLICATION OF PORTFOLIO MEASUREMENT EXCEPTION TO DIFFERENT PORTFOLIOS

2.4.430.120   Company T manages certain financial assets and financial liabilities based on its net exposure to interest rate risk. These financial assets and financial liabilities are entered into with counterparties X, Y and Z. T also manages its

financial assets and financial liabilities with counterparty X, regardless of market risk exposure, based on the net exposure to X's credit risk.

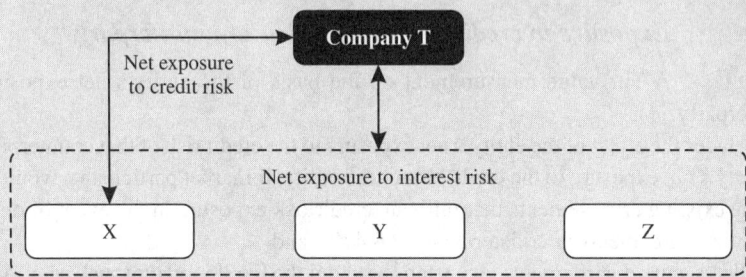

2.4.430.130   Therefore, assuming that all other criteria are met, a financial asset or a financial liability of T that is subject to interest rate risk and that is entered into with counterparty X, is both part of one group that may be measured based on the price for the net exposure to interest rate risk and of another group that may be measured based on the price for the net exposure to X's credit risk.

2.4.440   ***Exposure to market risk***

2.4.440.10   An entity that measures fair value on the basis of its net exposure to a particular market risk (or risks):
- applies the price within the bid-ask spread that is most representative of fair value (see 2.4.250); and
- ensures that the nature and duration of the risk(s) to which the exception is applied are substantially the same. [*IFRS 13.53–55*]

2.4.440.20   Any basis risk resulting from market risk parameters that are not identical is reflected in the fair value of the net position. For example, if an entity manages its interest rate risk on a net portfolio basis, then it may include financial instruments with different interest rate bases in one portfolio. However, any difference in the interest rate bases – e.g. GBP LIBOR vs UK treasury yields – is reflected in the fair value measurement. [*IFRS 13.54, BC123*]

EXAMPLE 21A – NATURE OF MARKET RISKS

2.4.440.30   Company B cannot combine interest rate risk associated with a financial asset with the commodity price risk associated with a financial liability. The nature of these risks is not substantially the same; therefore, based on these risks, these financial instruments do not qualify for the portfolio measurement exception. [*IFRS 13.54, BC123*]

EXAMPLE 21B – DURATION OF MARKET RISKS

2.4.440.40   Company C has a 12-month futures contract to offset 12 months' worth of interest rate risk exposure on a five-year financial instrument. C may be allowed to measure the exposure to 12-month interest rate risk on a net basis. However,

> it measures the interest rate risk exposure from year 2 to year 5 on a gross basis. [*IFRS 13.55, BC123*]

2.4.450 *Exposure to credit risk of a particular counterparty*

2.4.450.10   A fair value measurement on the basis of the entity's net exposure to a particular counterparty:

- includes the effect of the entity's net exposure to the credit risk of that counterparty or the counterparty's net exposure to the credit risk of the entity, if market participants would take into account any existing arrangements that mitigate credit risk exposure in the event of default – e.g. master netting agreements or collateral (see 2.4.470); and
- reflects market participants' expectations about the likelihood that such an arrangement would be legally enforceable in the event of default. [*IFRS 13.56*]

2.4.450.20   As discussed in 2.4.430.70–80, when an entity applies the portfolio measurement exception to measure the fair value of a group of financial assets and financial liabilities entered into with a particular counterparty, it may need to allocate the portfolio-level credit risk adjustment to the individual instruments within the portfolio. This allocation is required to be done on a reasonable and consistent basis, although there are no specific examples in IFRS 13. [*IFRS 13.50*]

2.4.450.30   In our experience, the following allocation methods are generally used for allocating credit risk adjustments.

- *Relative fair value approach:* Under this approach, the portfolio-level credit risk adjustment is allocated to the individual instruments in the portfolio based on their relative fair values. There are two methods that are used in practice:
  - allocate the adjustment to all instruments in the portfolio based on their relative fair values; or
  - allocate the adjustment only to those instruments that are in the same position (asset or liability) as the net position with the counterparty, based on their relative fair values; if for example the net position is an asset, then the portfolio-level credit risk adjustment is allocated only to the financial *assets* in the portfolio based on their relative fair values.
- *Relative credit adjustment approach:* Under this approach, the portfolio-level credit risk adjustment is allocated to the individual instruments in the portfolio based on their relative stand-alone credit risk adjustment. The application of this approach requires the entity to calculate the credit risk adjustment both on a gross basis – assuming that the portfolio measurement exception is not applied – and on a net basis.

2.4.450.40   If an entity applies the portfolio measurement exception and the portfolio includes multiple counterparties (see Example 20), then the credit risk adjustment will be considered separately for each individual counterparty. Therefore, the allocation will need to be performed separately for the individual financial assets and financial liabilities with each counterparty.

2.4.460 Derivatives: Own and counterparty credit risk

2.4.460.10   A fair value measurement for a liability is based on the price at which it would be transferred to a market participant – assuming that the non-performance risk, including the effect of the entity's own credit risk, remains the same before and after the transfer (see 2.4.370 and 400).

In addition, in the absence of a quoted market price for the transfer of a liability, the liability's fair value is measured from the perspective of a market participant that holds the liability as an asset (see 2.4.380). This would imply consistency between the calculation of own credit risk adjustments and counterparty credit risk adjustments in measuring derivative assets and liabilities. In principle, and assuming no differences in the unit of account, the credit risk adjustments made in the fair value measurement by both counterparties to the financial instrument should be the same. [*IFRS 13.9, 34, 37*]

2.4.460.20   Some derivatives might change from being an asset to a liability or vice versa – e.g. an interest rate swap or a forward contract – because:
- there may be a mixture of expected net cash inflows and expected net cash outflows for different settlement dates; and
- the amounts and direction of cash flows may change as a result of changes in market underlyings.

2.4.460.30   For such derivatives, an entity considers both its own and the counterparty's credit risk if market participants would do so in measuring the fair value of these instruments. Therefore, an entity should design and implement a method for appropriately considering credit risk adjustments in valuing these derivatives. If market participants would consider both counterparty and the entity's own credit risk, but the entity calculates the credit risk adjustment based on a method that considers only the current classification of the derivative (as either an asset or liability), then the entity determines whether additional credit risk adjustments are necessary based on all the expected cash flows of the derivative and the potential for the other classification. [*IFRS 13.11, 42*]

2.4.460.40   In practice, entities often determine an explicit credit valuation adjustment (CVA) to incorporate counterparty credit risk and an explicit debit valuation adjustment (DVA) to incorporate own non-performance risk, as necessary, into the fair value measurement of derivatives. Determining CVAs/DVAs can be complex. In our experience, multiple approaches are used in practice and tailored to an entity's particular facts and circumstances.

2.4.460.50   A CVA adjusts a derivative valuation to reflect the expected losses due to counterparty credit risk. Expected losses are affected by the probability of default, the credit exposure at the time of default and the loss given default. A DVA adjusts a derivative valuation to reflect the counterparty's expected losses due to the entity's own credit risk. A DVA can be thought of as a CVA from the counterparty's perspective.

2.4.460.60   First, an entity assesses whether a CVA/DVA is necessary for measuring the fair value of a derivative. For some derivatives that are valued using a market approach (e.g. exchange-traded futures contracts), the market value already incorporates non-performance risk so determining a separate CVA/DVA is not necessary. In our experience, centrally cleared OTC derivatives (e.g. centrally cleared interest rate swaps) frequently do not have significant CVA/DVA because the margin requirements of the exchange or clearing house minimise the credit risk of those contracts. However, for non-centrally cleared OTC derivatives incorporation of CVA/DVA is often significant (see 2.4.465). [*IFRS 13.42, BC92*]

2.4.460.70   The inclusion of counterparty credit risk and the entity's own credit risk in the fair value measurements of derivative instruments may affect hedging relationships. A change in the fair value of the hedging derivative instrument arising from the counterparty or the entity's own credit risk may affect the hedge effectiveness assessment and hedge ineffectiveness measurement (see 7.9.810 and 850.40).

2.4.465   **Uncollateralised and partially collateralised derivatives: Discount rate**

2.4.465.10   In our experience, there is no consensus over the most appropriate discount rate to apply in a valuation model used for measuring the fair value of uncollateralised derivatives. Recently, more banks have moved to incorporating funding valuation adjustments (FVA) in their valuations to reflect the cost (or benefit) of funding hedges of these transactions. In our experience, the biggest international over-the-counter derivatives dealers now include FVA, and for this type of business, while methodologies continue to evolve, including this type of adjustment is market practice for these participants.

2.4.465.20   However, considerable debate remains regarding the nature of inputs used to determine and calibrate FVA and therefore there is diversity in practice in how entities calculate FVA when it is incorporated in their valuations. Particular complexities include transactions that are partially collateralised, including those subject to one-way collateral requirements (i.e. only one counterparty is required to post collateral) or to collateral thresholds (i.e. collateral amounts are adjusted only when the net exposure exceeds a specified amount), and restrictions on the rehypothecation of collateral.

2.4.465.30   In our experience, in determining whether an adjustment for FVA is needed, and if so how to calculate it, an entity considers the pricing practices that would be used by market participants if derivatives were sold at the measurement date. In doing so, an entity considers the funding cost and benefit that market participants would take into account in pricing the instrument, which may differ from the entity's estimate of its own funding cost or benefit (see 2.4.90).

2.4.465.40   One challenge for calculating FVA is the potential for overlap in a valuation model between an adjustment for a funding rate that a market participant would consider and the adjustments for the counterparty's credit risk and the entity's own credit risk (see 2.4.460) – i.e. an overlap of FVA with a CVA and a DVA. This potential overlap occurs because funding cost discounting techniques usually incorporate both liquidity and credit components, and they may be difficult to separate.

2.4.465.50   Therefore, when incorporating FVA in the fair value measurement, an entity needs to ensure that the valuation appropriately eliminates any overlap of FVA with DVA and CVA, and that a symmetrical approach is applied to the measurement of derivative assets and liabilities. A symmetrical approach to measurement is consistent with the requirement for the measurement of a liability with no quoted price for the transfer of an identical or a similar liability to be made from the perspective of a market participant that holds the identical item as an asset (see 2.4.380).

2.4.470   **Collateral, master netting and credit support agreements**

2.4.470.10   The effect of a requirement to provide collateral that is part of the contractual terms of an individual financial instrument is a characteristic of the financial instrument. Therefore, this effect is included in the fair value measurement of that financial instrument – e.g. a typical residential mortgage. In this case, the requirement to provide collateral may affect the discount rate or any other credit risk adjustments that are used in measuring fair value. [*IFRS 13.11, 69, B19*]

2.4.470.15   In our experience, in valuing fully collateralised derivatives, the majority of derivative market participants agree that the estimated cash flows should be discounted at the rate agreed for cash collateral posted under the derivative's credit support annex (CSA), which is typically an overnight benchmark rate in the respective currency (e.g. sterling overnight index average (SONIA), euro overnight index average (EONIA) or federal funds rate). The overnight index swap (OIS) market reflects assumptions by market participants about the overnight rate. For a discussion of issues potentially relevant to partially collateralised derivatives and more complex collateral arrangements, see 2.4.465.

2.4.470.20   If the unit of account is the individual financial instrument, then a separate arrangement that mitigates credit risk exposure in the event of default – e.g. a master netting agreement or a credit support agreement that requires the exchange of collateral on the basis of each party's net exposure to the credit risk of a group of financial instruments – is not reflected in the fair value of the individual financial instrument. [*IFRS 13.14*]

2.4.470.30   However, if an entity applies the portfolio measurement exception to a group of financial assets and financial liabilities entered into with a particular counterparty, then the effect of such an agreement would be included in measuring the fair value of the group of financial assets and financial liabilities if market participants would do so (see 2.4.450). [*IFRS 13.56, 69*]

2.4.470.40   In our experience, for individual instruments that are actively traded on an exchange, the actual counterparty to the trade transaction is, in many instances, the exchange entity – e.g. the clearing house for the exchange. For these exchange transactions, we understand that even when there is no master netting agreement between the exchange and the entity, credit risk is usually deemed to be minimal because the operating procedures of the exchanges require the daily posting of collateral, which is, in effect, an arrangement that mitigates credit risk exposure in the event of default.

2.4.475   Assets subject to executory contracts

2.4.475.10   Some assets recorded in an entity's financial statements are the subject of executory contracts that directly affect the use of, and cash flows from, those assets. For example, a leasing company might have several aircraft recorded as property, plant and equipment that are leased to third parties under operating leases.

2.4.475.20   If the unit of account is the underlying asset on a stand-alone basis (see 2.4.80), then the effects of executory contracts, including any contractual cash flows, are not included in measuring the fair value of the underlying asset. This is because in these cases the executory contracts are entity-specific (see 2.4.70). In these cases, the fair value of the asset is measured using the price that would be received from a market participant to sell the asset at the measurement date. Alternatively, if the unit of account is determined to be an aggregation of the contract with the underlying asset, then the effects of the executory contract would be considered. [*IFRS 13.14, 31*]

2.4.475.30   If the unit of account is determined to be the underlying asset on a stand-alone basis but the entity has evidence that suggests that a market participant would sell both the executory contract and the underlying asset as a group, then it may be appropriate to measure the fair value of the entire group. The group fair value would then be allocated to the assets in the group, although IFRS 13 does not provide any guidance in this regard. [*IFRS 13.31*]

2.4.480   MEASURING FAIR VALUE IF VOLUME OR LEVEL OF ACTIVITY SIGNIFICANTLY DECREASED

2.4.480.10   A fair value measurement may be affected if there has been a significant decrease in the volume or level of activity for that item compared with normal market activity for that item. Judgement may be required in determining whether, based on the evidence available, there has been such a significant decrease. An entity assesses the significance and relevance of all facts and circumstances. [*IFRS 13.B37, B42*]

2.4.480.20   Factors that might be taken into account include the following.
- There are few recent transactions.
- Price quotations are not based on current information.
- Price quotations vary substantially over time or between market makers.
- Indices that were highly correlated with the fair value of the item at previous measurement dates are demonstrably uncorrelated with recent indications of fair value for that item.
- There is a significant increase in implied liquidity risk premiums, yields or performance indicators for transactions observed in the market or quoted prices compared with the entity's estimate of expected cash flows.
- There is a wide or significantly increased bid-ask spread.
- There is a significant decline in primary market activity for similar assets or liabilities.
- Little information is publicly available. [*IFRS 13.B37*]

2.4.480.30   If an entity concludes that the volume or level of activity for an asset or liability has significantly decreased, then further analysis of the transactions or quoted prices is required. A decrease in the volume or level of activity on its own might not indicate that a transaction or a quoted price is not representative of fair value, or that a transaction in that market is not orderly. It is not appropriate to conclude that all transactions in a market in which there has been a decrease in the volume or level of activity are not orderly. [*IFRS 13.B38, B43*]

2.4.480.40   However, determining whether a transaction is orderly is more difficult if there has been a significant decrease in the volume or level of activity in relation to normal market activity for the asset or liability (or similar assets or liabilities). To evaluate the circumstances, and to determine whether a transaction is orderly, judgement may be required. If an entity determines that a transaction or quoted price does not represent fair value, then an adjustment to that price is necessary if it is used as a basis for determining fair value. [*IFRS 13.B38, B43*]

2.4.480.50   If the volume or level of activity has significantly decreased and the entity concludes that the market for that asset or liability is not active, then it may be appropriate for an entity to change the valuation technique used or to use multiple valuation techniques to measure the fair value of an item. If multiple valuation techniques are used, then the entity considers the reasonableness of the range of the different fair value indications. The objective of the weighting process is to determine the point within the range that is most representative of fair value under current market conditions. A wide range of fair value estimates may be an indication that further analysis is needed. [*IFRS 13.B40*]

2.4.480.60   A fair value measurement reflects an orderly transaction between market participants (see 2.4.60.40). Therefore, regardless of the valuation techniques used, a fair value measurement includes appropriate risk adjustments that are reflective of an orderly transaction between market participants under current market conditions; this includes a risk premium reflecting the amount that market participants would demand as compensation for the uncertainty inherent in the future cash flows of an asset or liability. [*IFRS 13.9, B39*]

2.4.480.70 It is generally reasonable to assume that the transaction in which an asset or liability was exchanged between market participants is an orderly transaction. However, there are circumstances in which an entity needs to assess whether a transaction is orderly. Circumstances that may indicate that a transaction is not orderly include the following.

- There was inadequate exposure to the market to allow usual and customary marketing activities.
- The seller marketed the asset or liability to a single market participant.
- The seller is in distress.
- The seller was forced to sell to meet regulatory or legal requirements.
- The transaction price is an outlier compared with other recent transactions for identical or similar items. [*IFRS 13.B43*]

2.4.480.80 However, even if the seller was forced to sell, this would not necessarily indicate that the transaction is not orderly. For example, if an entity sells assets to market participants to meet regulatory requirements but the regulator does not establish the transaction price and the entity has a reasonable amount of time to market the assets, then the transaction price provides evidence of fair value.

2.4.480.90 If the evidence indicates that a transaction was not orderly, then the entity places little (if any) weight on the transaction price in measuring fair value. However, if the evidence indicates that the transaction was orderly, then the entity considers the transaction price in estimating the fair value of the asset or liability. The weight placed on that transaction price depends on the circumstances – such as the volume and timing of the transaction and the comparability of the transaction to the asset or liability being measured. If an entity does not have sufficient information to conclude whether a transaction was orderly, then it takes the transaction price into account, but places less weight on it compared with transactions that are known to be orderly. [*IFRS 13.B44*]

2.4.480.100 Although an entity need not undertake exhaustive efforts to determine whether a transaction is orderly, it does not ignore information that is reasonably available. If an entity is party to a transaction, then it is presumed to have sufficient information to conclude whether the transaction is orderly. [*IFRS 13.B44*]

2.4.480.110 An entity is allowed to use quoted prices that are provided by third parties (such as brokers or pricing services) if these quoted prices are determined in accordance with the fair value measurement requirements. If there has been a significant decrease in the volume or level of activity for an item, then an entity evaluates whether third party prices are developed using current market information that reflects orderly transactions and market participant assumptions. If an entity obtains prices from a third party pricing service or broker as inputs to a fair value measurement, then it places less weight on quotes that do not reflect the result of such transactions. Furthermore, the entity takes into account the nature of the quotes and gives a higher weight to quotes representing binding offers than to those representing indicative bids. Whether third party prices represent observable or unobservable inputs depends on their nature and source (see 2.4.300). [*IFRS 13.B45–B47*]

2.4.490   DISCLOSURES

2.4.490.10 The disclosures required by IFRS 13 are split into two categories.

- Disclosures for assets and liabilities measured at fair value in the statement of financial position after initial recognition (see 2.4.500). These disclosures are more extensive.

- Disclosures in relation to fair value measurements that are required or permitted to be disclosed by other IFRSs, but which are *not* included in the statement of financial position (see 2.4.540).

2.4.490.20   For a discussion of items to which the measurement requirements of IFRS 13 apply, but to which the disclosure requirements do not apply because of an exemption in IFRS 13, see 2.4.40.20–70.

2.4.490.30   In addition, the IFRS 13 disclosures do not apply to revenue that is measured at fair value in the case of non-cash consideration (see 4.2.150). This is because revenue is not an asset or liability recognised in the statement of financial position.

2.4.500   Assets and liabilities measured at fair value

2.4.500.10   IFRS 13 contains a comprehensive disclosure framework that combines the fair value measurement disclosures previously required by other standards and certain additional disclosures. The objectives of the disclosures for assets and liabilities that are measured at fair value are:
- to provide information that enables users of financial statements to assess the methods and inputs used to develop those measurements; and
- to assess the effect of the measurements on profit or loss or OCI of recurring fair value measurements that are based on significant unobservable inputs – i.e. recurring Level 3 measurements. [*IFRS 13.91*]

2.4.500.20   To determine whether the disclosures provided meet the disclosure objectives of the standard, an entity considers the following factors:
- the level of detail necessary to satisfy the disclosure requirements;
- how much emphasis to place on each of the various requirements;
- how much aggregation or disaggregation to undertake; and
- whether additional information to evaluate the quantitative information disclosed is needed. [*IFRS 13.92*]

2.4.500.30   These disclosures also apply to assets and liabilities measured at a value based on fair value and in the scope of IFRS 13 – e.g. biological assets measured at fair value less costs to sell (see 3.9.40). [*IFRS 13.93*]

2.4.510   *Classes of assets and liabilities*

2.4.510.10   The disclosure requirements are based on 'classes' of assets and liabilities, but do not apply to classes of assets and liabilities that are measured at fair value only on initial recognition. For example, the disclosure requirements do not apply to the fair values of assets acquired in a business combination and subsequently measured under the cost model. [*IFRS 13.93, BC184*]

2.4.510.15   Determining the appropriate classes of assets and liabilities requires judgement. A class of assets and liabilities could be more disaggregated than a single line item in the statement of financial position, and an entity needs to provide information sufficient to allow reconciliation to the statement of financial position. However, if a particular standard specifies the class for an asset or a liability – e.g. IAS 16 for property, plant and equipment (see 3.2.320) – then an entity may use that class in providing the disclosures if it meets the criteria in 2.4.510.20. [*IFRS 13.93–94*]

2.4.510.20   A class of assets or liabilities is determined based on:
- the nature, characteristics and risks of the asset or liability (e.g. shared activities or business sectors, vintage, geographic concentration, credit quality or other economic characteristics); and
- the level into which it is categorised in the fair value hierarchy. [*IFRS 13.94*]

2.4.510.25   In our view, other relevant factors to consider include:
- the extent of homogeneous or shared risks within the class of assets or liabilities;
- differences in valuation inputs and techniques used to determine the fair value measurements;
- the ranges in values of significant unobservable inputs. For example, if the range of values for an unobservable input used in measuring the fair value of a class of assets is very wide, then this may indicate that the information is not sufficiently disaggregated;
- the sensitivity of measurements to changes in unobservable inputs;
- whether other disclosures in the financial statements provide sufficient information about the classes of assets and liabilities (e.g. a schedule of investments for investment companies); and
- the significance of the class of assets or liabilities relative to the context of a particular disclosure.

2.4.510.30   The number of classes for assets and liabilities categorised as Level 3 of the fair value hierarchy may need to be greater than those categorised within other levels, given the greater degree of uncertainty and subjectivity of fair value measurements within Level 3. [*IFRS 13.94*]

2.4.520   *Recurring vs non-recurring measurements*

2.4.520.10   There are different disclosure requirements depending on whether a fair value measurement in the statement of financial position after initial recognition is recurring or non-recurring.
- Recurring fair value measurements arise from assets and liabilities that are measured on a fair value basis at each reporting date – e.g. biological assets under IAS 41. Assets accounted for under a revaluation model – e.g. a class of property, plant and equipment under IAS 16 – are also recurring fair value measurements, even though a revaluation is not necessarily performed at each reporting date (see 3.2.300).
- Non-recurring fair value measurements are fair value measurements that are triggered by particular circumstances – e.g. an asset classified as held-for-sale under IFRS 5. [*IFRS 13.93(a)*]

2.4.530   *Summary of disclosures*

2.4.530.10   The disclosure requirements, which are most extensive for recurring Level 3 measurements, are summarised in the following table.

| | | FAIR VALUE MEASUREMENT | | | | | | FAIR VALUE ONLY DISCLOSED | | |
| | | RECURRING | | | NON-RECURRING | | | | | |
IFRS 13.93:	REQUIREMENT	L1	L2	L3	L1	L2	L3	L1	L2	L3
(a)	Fair value at the reporting date									
(a)	Reasons for the measurement									
(b)	Level within hierarchy									

IFRS 13.93:	REQUIREMENT	FAIR VALUE MEASUREMENT						FAIR VALUE ONLY DISCLOSED		
		RECURRING			NON-RECURRING					
		L1	L2	L3	L1	L2	L3	L1	L2	L3
(c)	Transfers within hierarchy, including the policy for the timing of transfers	▨	▨	▨						
(d)	Description of valuation technique and inputs used		▨	▨		▨	▨		▨	▨
(d)	Any changes to valuation technique and the reasons why		▨	▨		▨	▨			
(d)	Quantitative information about significant unobservable inputs			▨			▨			▨
(e)	Reconciliation of opening and closing balances (including information on transfers in or out)			▨						
(f)	Unrealised gains/losses from remeasurement			▨						
(g)	Description of valuation processes and policies			▨			▨			▨
(h)(i)	Narrative sensitivity to changes in unobservable inputs			▨						▨
(h)(ii)	Quantitative sensitivity to changes in unobservable inputs (for financial assets and financial liabilities only)			▨						▨
(i)	If highest and best use differs from actual, then the reasons why	▨	▨	▨	▨	▨	▨			
IFRS 13.98	For a liability measured at fair value, the existence of an inseparable third party credit enhancement	▨	▨	▨	▨	▨	▨			

▨ Disclosure required – in tabular format unless another format is more appropriate. [*IFRS 13.99*]

This table does not refer to disclosures in relation to fair value measurements that are required or permitted to be disclosed by other standards (e.g. IFRS 7 for financial instruments).

2.4.530.20   In our view, the fair value measurement disclosures (for both recurring and non-recurring fair value measurements) should be based on the fair value at which the item is measured at the reporting date, even if that fair value was determined as of an earlier date. For example, if a class of property, plant and equipment is revalued at 31 October and the entity's year end is 31 December, then the disclosures apply to the fair value determined at 31 October.

2.4.530.30   An entity discloses its accounting policy choices in relation to:

- the timing of transfers between levels in the hierarchy – e.g. the date of the event or the change in circumstances that caused the transfer, the beginning of the reporting period, or the reporting date for items (c) and (e) in the table in 2.4.530.10; and

- a decision to apply the portfolio measurement exception (see 2.4.430). [*IFRS 13.95–96*]

2.4.530.40   In relation to the requirement to provide quantitative information about the significant unobservable inputs used in the fair value measurement – included in item (d) in the table in 2.4.530.10 – the extent and level of aggregation of these disclosures will depend on the specific facts and circumstances. For example, if the range of values for an unobservable input used for measuring the fair value for a class of assets or liabilities is very wide, then this may indicate that the information is not sufficiently disaggregated to meet the disclosure objectives (see 2.4.500). [*IFRS 13.91–92, 93(d)*]

2.4.530.50   The standard does not specify how to summarise this information for each class of assets or liabilities – e.g. whether to include information about the range of values or a weighted average for each unobservable input used for each class. An entity considers the level of detail that is necessary to meet the disclosure objectives. For example, if the range of values for an unobservable input that the entity uses is wide, then this may indicate that the entity should disclose both the range and the weighted average of the values. This is because disclosing information about a range without an average provides no information about how the inputs are distributed within that range or whether or to what extent inputs within that range have actually been used. Similarly, disclosing information about a weighted average without a range provides no information about the dispersion of the inputs used around that average. [*IFRS 13.91–92, 93(d), IE63*]

Example 22 – Disclosure of sensitivity to changes in unobservable inputs for financial assets

2.4.530.60   Company Z discloses quantitative information about unobservable volatility inputs used to measure the fair values of a class of equity derivatives. This class includes 100 derivatives, 90 of which are valued using a volatility of 20% per annum and the remaining 10 are valued using a volatility of 50% per annum.

2.4.530.70   Z considers whether this difference means that its disclosure of unobservable inputs should be disaggregated to a level of two smaller classes, one with 90 derivatives and one with 10. If Z determines that disclosure at the level of the class that includes all 100 derivatives is appropriate and it proposes to disclose the range of values of the volatilities used (i.e. 20–50%), then it should also consider disclosing the weighted average of the inputs (assumed to be 23%); otherwise, its disclosures would not indicate that the significant majority of the inputs used are at the low end of the range and therefore the disclosure objectives of the standard may not be met.

2.4.530.75   Disclosure of quantitative information about significant unobservable inputs is not required if the inputs to the valuation were not developed by the entity itself but were externally developed (e.g. when an entity uses prices from prior transactions or broker quotes without adjustment). However, an entity cannot ignore other quantitative information that is reasonably available. For example, if an entity develops an adjustment to a broker quote that is significant to the measurement in its entirety, then the inputs used to determine the adjustment are included in the quantitative input disclosures, even if the entity excludes the unadjusted portion of the broker quote from the disclosure.

2.4.530.77   In some circumstances, an entity might use a third party valuation specialist to measure the fair values of certain assets or liabilities. In this case, management of the entity might provide the specialist with inputs and assumptions that are significant to the valuation (e.g. projected financial information prepared by an investee). Significant unobservable valuation inputs provided to third party valuation specialists by the entity cannot be omitted from the quantitative disclosures. [*IFRS 13.93(d), BC195*]

2.4.530.80   Meeting the requirement to disclose the amount of the unrealised gains or losses included in profit or loss for the period relating to those assets and liabilities held at the reporting date – item (f) in the table in 2.4.530.10 – may be straightforward for some types of instruments; however, identifying the change in unrealised gains or losses included in profit or loss for the period may be difficult for those instruments that are subject to periodic cash settlements. In many situations, periodic cash settlements constitute both a realisation of gains or losses arising in prior periods – i.e. settlement of the initial carrying amount – and a realisation of gains or losses arising in the current period. [*IFRS 13.93(f)*]

2.4.530.85   In our view, an entity may define the change in unrealised gains or losses as those gains or losses included in profit or loss for the current period relating to assets and liabilities held at the reporting date *exclusive* of settlements received or paid in the current period for movements in fair value that occurred in the period. In that case, an entity will need to develop a reasonable method to allocate cash settlements received or paid during the period to:
- the unrealised gain or loss as of the beginning of the period or the initial carrying amount, which would not affect the realised gains or losses in the period; and
- the change in fair value during the period, which would constitute realisation of gains or losses in the period.

2.4.530.90   In relation to item (h)(ii) in the table in 2.4.530.10 for financial assets and financial liabilities, if changing one or more of the unobservable inputs to reflect reasonably possible alternative assumptions would significantly affect fair value, then an entity discloses the effect on fair value, including how the effect was calculated. For this purpose, significance is judged with respect to profit or loss, total assets or total liabilities or, if changes in fair value are recognised in OCI, then total equity. [*IFRS 13.93(h)(ii)*]

2.4.530.100   In our view, 'reasonably possible alternative' assumptions are assumptions that could reasonably have been included in the valuation model at the reporting date based on the circumstances at that date. A quantitative sensitivity analysis for financial instruments provides information about the sensitivity of the fair value measurement to changes to reasonably possible alternative unobservable inputs at the measurement date. Therefore, we do not believe that this disclosure is intended to be a forward-looking sensitivity analysis about an entity's exposure to future changes in market variables. [*IFRS 13.BC209*]

2.4.530.110   For a liability measured at fair value and issued with an inseparable third party credit enhancement (see 2.4.380.30), an entity discloses:
● the existence of the credit enhancement; and
● whether that credit enhancement is reflected in the fair value measurement of the liability. [*IFRS 13.98*]

2.4.533   *Application by investment entities*

2.4.533.10   An investment entity parent that measures an investment in an investment entity subsidiary at fair value through profit or loss needs to consider which disclosures in its financial statements are required to meet the disclosure objectives of IFRS 13 and of IFRS 7. These objectives are to enable users of the parent's financial statements to understand the valuation techniques and inputs used to develop fair value measurements in those financial statements and to evaluate the significance of the financial instruments held by the parent and the nature and extent of the related risks. This might include providing some or all of the disclosures in IFRS 13 for the subsidiary's investments. This may apply particularly for a feeder fund that invests in a master fund. See also 5.10.290.50 and 7.10.675. [*IFRS 7.7, 31, 13.91–92*]

2.4.533.20   For example, a feeder fund might disclose the categorisation of the underlying investments of the master fund in the fair value hierarchy and a description of the valuation techniques and inputs used to measure the fair values of those underlying investments. This may be particularly relevant if:
● the fair values of the master fund's investments are an input into the fair value measurement of the feeder fund's investment in the master fund (e.g. the investment in the master fund is valued based on the master fund's net asset value); or
● the feeder fund's financial statements otherwise disclose the fair values of the master fund's investments or related risk information. [*IFRS 7.7, 31, 13.91–92*]

2.4.535   *Additional information*

2.4.535.10   Entities may disclose additional information if they consider it helpful to users of the financial statements (see 2.4.500). For example, an entity may:
● separate the Level 3 fair value gains and losses into amounts arising from changes in observable inputs and amounts arising from changes in unobservable inputs; or
● for a Level 3 instrument that is economically hedged by an instrument with a fair value measurement in Level 1 or Level 2, disclose the extent to which the fair value movements offset or correlate.

2.4.540   **Assets and liabilities not measured at fair value but fair value disclosed**

2.4.540.10   The disclosure requirements in relation to fair value measurements that are required or permitted to be disclosed by other standards, but which are *not* included in the statement of financial position, are limited to items (b), (d) and (i) in the table in 2.4.530.10. In respect of item (d), disclosure of quantitative information about significant unobservable inputs is not required. [*IFRS 13.97*]

2.4.540.20   For example, the IFRS 13 disclosures apply to financial instruments that are not measured at fair value in the statement of financial position but for which fair value is disclosed in accordance with IFRS 7 – e.g. financial assets and financial liabilities measured at amortised cost (see 2.4.40.20). However, IFRS 13 disclosures are not required for such an instrument if an entity does not disclose the fair value of that instrument because it applies one of the fair value disclosure exceptions in IFRS 7 – e.g. when the carrying amount is a reasonable approximation of fair value (see 7.10.460.10). [*IFRS 7.25, 29*]

2.4.550 **APPLICATION TO SPECIFIC ITEMS**

2.4.560 **Property, plant and equipment**

2.4.560.10   IAS 16 deals with the accounting for property, plant and equipment and is the subject of chapter 3.2. However, the principles in IFRS 13 provide general guidance in measuring the fair value of any class of property, plant and equipment that is accounted for using the revaluation model. In measuring fair value, the general guidance in 2.4.10–540 applies. This section discusses specific points of interest in relation to property, plant and equipment.

2.4.570 *The item being measured*

2.4.570.10   In some cases, an item of property, plant and equipment will provide maximum value to market participants through its use in combination with other assets or with other assets and liabilities (see 2.4.350). In that case, if the asset requires installation in a particular location before it can be used, then such installation costs are generally considered an attribute of the asset in measuring fair value. Therefore, all costs (excluding transaction costs) that are necessary to transport and install an asset for future use are included in the measurement of fair value. [*IFRS 13.B3, IE11–IE12*]

2.4.570.20   Examples include delivery and other costs necessary to install an asset for its intended use. For an asset which is already installed and configured for use, installation costs are added to the estimated uninstalled value indication (e.g. replacement cost) for the asset, which results in measurement of fair value on an installed basis. [*IFRS 13.B3, IE12*]

2.4.570.30   The fair value measurements of many assets that require installation will use Level 3 inputs other than installation costs. However, for some common machinery that is traded in industrial markets, Level 2 inputs may be available. In this situation, the inclusion of installation costs in the measurement of fair value may result in a Level 3 categorisation of the measurement if those costs are significant (see 2.4.270). [*IFRS 13.73, 81, 86*]

2.4.580 *Unit of account*

2.4.580.10   The unit of account (discussed generally in 2.4.80) of property, plant and equipment is determined under IAS 16, although the standard itself is unclear. As discussed in 3.2.10.25, in our view an item that is separately identifiable and individually significant will generally constitute a unit of account under IAS 16.

2.4.580.20   A market may only exist for a group of assets as a whole, even though the component parts (e.g. land and building) are separate units of account. In that case, it will be necessary to measure the fair value of the group as a whole and then to allocate the valuation to the individual components. IFRS 13 does not provide any guidance on the appropriate method of allocation.

2.4.590 *Valuation approaches and techniques*

2.4.590.10   The fair value of property, plant and equipment is typically measured using techniques that fall under the market approach. However, the cost approach is also used for specialised plant and equipment, and this section discusses specific points of interest in respect of applying the DRC method. For a general discussion of valuation approaches and techniques, including the use of multiple approaches/techniques, see 2.4.120.

2.4.600   *DRC method*

2.4.600.10   As noted in 2.4.210.20, a DRC valuation considers how much it would cost to reproduce an asset of equivalent utility and includes an optimisation adjustment to take into account physical, functional and economic obsolescence. It estimates the cost to replace the required capacity of the asset rather than the actual asset.

2.4.600.20   In a DRC valuation, the adjustment for depreciation takes into account the age of the asset in relation to its useful life and its residual value. The adjustment for optimisation takes into account situations in which the asset is obsolete, over-engineered or has capacity greater than that required by a market participant.

EXAMPLE 23A – PROPERTY, PLANT AND EQUIPMENT – DRC ADJUSTMENT FOR OPTIMISATION

> 2.4.600.30   Company T operates a network of water pipes. The diameter of the pipes is greater than that required currently – and greater than is expected to be required – even for necessary stand-by or safety purposes. Therefore, the DRC valuation is optimised to eliminate the cost of replacing the surplus capacity in T's network.

2.4.600.40   If an asset has surplus capacity, then in our view the optimisation adjustment for the DRC valuation should consider whether the surplus capacity has an alternative use. If there is no alternative use, then no replacement cost should be included for this surplus capacity. However, if there is an alternative use that is physically possible and financially feasible, then in our view the surplus capacity should be included in the valuation. However, surplus capacity is unlikely to have an alternative use unless it is physically and operationally separable from the required capacity.

EXAMPLE 23B – PROPERTY, PLANT AND EQUIPMENT – DRC METHOD AND SURPLUS CAPACITY

> 2.4.600.50   Continuing Example 23A, in addition to the surplus diameter of the pipes, Company T's network includes an additional discrete segment of pipes that is surplus to requirements, but which could be closed off and used for other purposes such as a liquid storage facility. Although the surplus diameter would be excluded (as explained in Example 23A), we believe that the surplus segment should be included in the valuation.

2.4.600.60   If an asset is obsolete, then the DRC valuation is optimised by reducing the replacement cost of the entity's specific asset so that it is not greater than the cost of a modern equivalent asset that provides an equivalent standard of performance or service capacity.

2.4.600.70   A DRC valuation, before application of appropriate adjustments for economic obsolescence, provides an estimate of the costs to re-create an asset, but a market participant would not pay that amount for an asset if it would generate a below-market return. As a result, the determination of economic obsolescence may involve taking into account future cash flow projections – i.e. the use of techniques associated more frequently with an income approach (see 2.4.150). A measure of DRC that does not consider economic obsolescence, if applicable, would be incomplete.

2.4.610   **Investment property**

2.4.610.10   IAS 40 deals with the accounting for investment property and is the subject of chapter 3.4. However, the principles in IFRS 13 provide general guidance, supplemented by aspects of IAS 40, in measuring the fair value of investment property – either if the fair value model is applied or if fair value is disclosed. In measuring fair value, the general guidance in 2.4.10–540 applies. This section discusses specific points of interest in relation to investment property.

2.4.620   *The item being measured*

2.4.620.10   In measuring fair value, an entity takes into account characteristics of the investment property that market participants would take into account in a transaction at the measurement date. For investment property, key characteristics include the condition and location of the asset (see 2.4.70.10) and any restrictions on the sale or use of the asset. For further discussion of the item being measured, see 2.4.70 and Example 2, which deals with a restriction on the sale of land.

2.4.630   *Unit of account*

2.4.630.10   The unit of account (discussed generally in 2.4.80) of investment property is determined under IAS 40, and is discussed in 3.4.20–30. For example, the unit of account could comprise land, a building or part of a building, or both. If investment property is leased on a furnished basis, then the unit of account generally includes the related movable furniture.

2.4.630.20   The valuation of investment property will typically include all related assets and liabilities – e.g. prepaid rentals. In that case, the entity chooses an accounting policy, to be applied consistently, about how any related assets and liabilities are presented in the statement of financial position (see 2.4.720). [*IAS 40.50(b)*]

2.4.640   *Market participant assumptions*

2.4.640.10   As explained in 2.4.90, an entity considers the perspective of market participants and measures fair value based on the assumptions that would be made by market participants acting in their economic best interests. Therefore, in measuring the fair value of investment property, an entity takes into consideration future cash flows arising from planned improvements to the extent that they reflect the assumptions of market participants.

EXAMPLE 24 – INVESTMENT PROPERTY – MARKET PARTICIPANT ASSUMPTIONS

2.4.640.20   Company D acquires land for which planning permission is granted for the development of a large commercial and residential complex. The principal reason that a market participant would acquire the land is to undertake this development project. Therefore, D takes into account the expected cash inflows and outflows arising from the project in measuring the fair value of the land using an income approach.

2.4.650   *Transaction costs*

2.4.650.10   The initial measurement of an investment property is at cost. The cost of investment property includes transaction costs and other directly attributable expenditure for preparing the asset for its intended use (see 3.4.120.20).

2.4.650.20　　An entity does not consider transaction costs in subsequently measuring fair value (see 2.4.110). This means that if the property market remains flat or declines between the date of acquisition and the date of revaluation, then the capitalised transaction costs included in the initial carrying amount of a property measured at fair value will be recognised as a loss in profit or loss.

EXAMPLE 25 – INVESTMENT PROPERTY – TRANSACTION COSTS

> 2.4.650.30　　Company R acquires an investment property for 300 and incurs transaction costs of 5. Therefore, the initial carrying amount of the property is 305.
>
> 2.4.650.40　　R elects to measure its investment property using the fair value model. At the reporting date, there has been no movement in the market and the fair value of the property is 300. The loss of 5, which is equivalent to the transaction costs on acquisition, is recognised in profit or loss.
>
> 2.4.650.50　　Conversely, if the fair value of the property at the reporting date is 310, then the gain recognised in profit or loss is 5 – i.e. the difference between the initial carrying amount of 305 and the fair value.

2.4.660　　*Valuation approaches and techniques*

2.4.660.10　　The fair value of investment property is typically measured using techniques that fall under the market approach and/or the income approach; this section discusses specific points of interest in respect of measuring the fair value of investment property. For a general discussion of valuation approaches and techniques, including the use of multiple approaches/techniques, see 2.4.120.

2.4.660.20　　Under the market approach, fair value is generally measured as a product of metrics, such as price per square foot or per square metre, and the area of the investment property. The two commonly used valuation techniques under the income approach are the yield method and the discounted cash flow technique.

2.4.660.30　　The fair value of an investment property takes into account, among other things, future income from current lease contracts even if the rental payments under the contracts are above or below current market terms. [*IAS 40.40*]

2.4.670　　*Income approach: Yield method*

2.4.670.10　　Under the yield method, the yield on a property is generally calculated as the current or market rental income on a property divided by the property's value. This method is most relevant if:
- there are sufficient market transactions from which yield information may be identified;
- sufficient information is available to identify and adjust for differences between the property being valued and comparable properties; and
- the pattern and risk of the subject and comparable properties' cash flows are similar.

2.4.670.20　　The yield method is less reliable if comparable transactions cannot be readily identified. This might be the case if there are reduced transaction volumes or if significant subjective adjustments to yields are required because of differences between the subject property and comparable properties in terms of physical characteristics, age, location, leases in place etc. In addition, if the cash flows on the subject property are expected to change in the future at a rate that is different from the rate of change of the cash flows of comparable properties, then the yield method may not be appropriate.

2.4.670.30   If properties have complex arrangements or changing income flows, then a discounted cash flow method may be more appropriate (see 2.4.680).

2.4.680   *Income approach: Discounted cash flow method*

2.4.680.10   Using the present value technique, fair value is measured by discounting expected cash inflows and outflows arising from the investment property at the rate of return that investors (market participants) in the property would require.

2.4.680.20   In our experience, the forecasted cash flows may be based on an evaluation of the property on a lease-by-lease basis or on a more aggregated basis. In general, a lease-by-lease analysis allows a comprehensive incorporation of the specific facts and circumstances of individual leases; these include actual rental rates, rent-free periods, the dates of lease renewals, vacancy rates, future rental rates and leasehold improvement costs.

2.4.680.30   An estimate of future market rents is required for periods not covered by current contractual agreements or for scenarios that incorporate the probability of contractual rents not continuing into the future – e.g. because the tenant fails to pay.

2.4.680.40   Estimates of future rental income consider both the level of rents and estimates of void and rent-free periods; the latter factors are especially important in difficult market conditions. Some entities may use current rents as a proxy for future market trends. Others look to recent trends in rent levels to estimate how rents may change in the future. Care is required in any approach that assumes a simple extrapolation of recent trends. Consideration is also given to the potential for rents to go back to the mean level – e.g. if recent rents are very high relative to historical levels, then consideration is given to a potential cyclical change in rent levels.

2.4.680.50   All cash flows are discounted in a discounted cash flow analysis. This includes owner costs such as the costs of exterior maintenance, insurance, taxes, technical replacements and property management costs.

2.4.680.60   Physically similar investment properties can have significantly different values because of leases in place; differences in location are also a reason for value differences. For example, a fully let building with above-market rents and financially strong tenants will have a significantly higher value than a building that is similar in physical respects but that is vacant.

2.4.680.70   In evaluating the sustainability of a rental cash flow, the credit quality of a tenant is considered. The credit quality of an existing tenant is especially important if the remaining term of a lease is longer, or if a lease renewal is expected. Credit risk may be less of an issue if rental rates under the lease are 'at-market'. In such circumstances, if the lessee does not continue to pay under the lease, then the lessor should theoretically be able to secure a new tenant at the same lease rate. However, the lessor in such circumstances might be expected to incur costs to remove a defaulting tenant, or to experience a period with no lease revenue because of vacancy as well as potentially incurring marketing, incentive and leasehold improvement costs.

2.4.680.80   Particular care is required in evaluating the reasonableness of assumptions used in relation to vacant (void) periods and incentive costs such as rent-free periods or landlord-borne fit-out costs. The longer the period that a property is expected to be unlet and the higher the incentive costs required to secure new tenants, the lower the property's value.

2.4.690   *Discounted cash flow method: Transaction costs*

2.4.690.10   As noted in 2.4.110.170, it may be appropriate for future transaction costs – i.e. in subsequent sales transactions – to be deducted in a discounted cash flow analysis. For example, if discounted cash flows are used to determine the fair value of real estate, and the analysis includes an assumption that a market participant would sell the property in the future, then it may be appropriate to subtract transaction costs (e.g. selling costs) expected to be incurred at the time of that future disposition.

EXAMPLE 26 – INVESTMENT PROPERTY – FUTURE TRANSACTION COSTS

2.4.690.20   Company E measures the fair value of its investment real estate. A discounted cash flow analysis resulting in an estimated value of 100 for the real estate at the measurement date includes a cash inflow (discounted) of 80 for future sale proceeds and a cash outflow (discounted) of 5 for selling costs associated with the future sale at the end of an assumed five-year holding period. The remaining cash flows (discounted) of 25 are from net operating cash inflows during the five-year holding period. If the real estate were sold at the measurement date, then selling costs of 4 would be incurred by the existing investor.

2.4.690.30   E measures the fair value at 100 – i.e. including the assumed cash outflow for transaction costs at the end of the five-year holding period – on the basis that the discounted cash flow analysis is prepared from the perspective of a market participant buyer who would consider future transaction costs in determining the price that it would be willing to pay for the asset.

2.4.690.40   However, it would not be appropriate for E to measure the asset at a value of 96 – i.e. estimated value of 100 less transaction costs of 4 that would be incurred if the asset were sold at the measurement date – because market participants would transact at 100 on the measurement date. [*IFRS 13.25*]

2.4.700   *Investment property under construction*

2.4.700.10   In our experience, valuers typically measure the fair value of investment property under construction by estimating the fair value of the completed investment property and then deducting from that amount the estimated costs to complete construction, financing costs and a reasonable profit margin.

2.4.700.20   Although the cumulative cost of construction may be an appropriate input to consider in measuring the fair value of investment property under construction, particularly in very early stages of development, it would generally not be expected to equal the property's fair value. In the absence of observable and comparable transactions, in our experience the property's fair value is generally based on a discounted cash flow method where cash inflows and outflows are discounted at a risk-adjusted rate of return required by market participants.

2.4.700.30   In practice, as development progresses, the probability of completion increases and certain risks associated with the asset decrease, thereby increasing the fair value. Those risks include failure to secure necessary planning and other permissions on a timely basis, construction cost over-runs, changes in market conditions during construction that could lead to delays in leasing/sales and/or reduced lease rates or selling prices, and higher than projected operating expenses. In addition, there is an element of developer's profit that would be expected to increase the fair value of the property.

2.4.700.40   In our view, market participant assumptions used in a discounted cash flow method should include estimates of cash outflows needed to complete the project – which should consider the developer's profit for the remaining work to be completed – as well as cash inflows and outflows from operating the property and ultimately selling it at some point in the future. We believe that a market participant would also be expected to consider the likelihood of achieving those estimated cash inflows based on the risks associated with completion of development and ultimate operations of the property.

2.4.700.50   If a situation arises in which it is determined that the cumulative cost of construction is a reasonable proxy for fair value – e.g. in the very early stages of development – then it would not be appropriate to include third party costs associated with the acquisition of an investment in the determination of cost. Such costs typically relate to direct incremental costs incurred for due diligence and closing the transaction and would be excluded from a fair value measurement following the general principle that the fair value of an asset or liability is not adjusted for transaction costs (see 2.4.110).

2.4.700.60   The change in the carrying amount of investment property under construction in any given period will include additions recognised at cost as well as changes in the property's fair value. Generally, the amount recorded in profit or loss is the change in carrying amount after accounting for additions at cost.

EXAMPLE 27 – INVESTMENT PROPERTY UNDER CONSTRUCTION

2.4.700.70   Company D is constructing a property for future use as investment property. D uses the fair value model and capitalises attributable borrowing costs (see chapter 4.6). The following information is relevant for this example.

Carrying amount of property at 1 March 2018 (fair value)	1,000
During the period ended 30 June 2018:	
• Construction costs capitalised	400
• Borrowing costs capitalised	100
Fair value of property at 30 June 2018	1,700

2.4.700.80   In this example, D records a fair value gain of 200 in profit or loss (1,700 - 1,000 - 400 - 100).

2.4.710   *Use of independent valuer*

2.4.710.10   An entity is encouraged, but is not required, to have valuations carried out by an independent valuer who holds a recognised and relevant professional qualification and who has recent experience in the location and category of investment property being valued. In our experience, entities take into account the following factors in deciding whether to engage an independent valuer:

- the materiality of the assets to the statement of financial position;
- the degree of fluctuation in the market;
- the ease with which a non-expert can make a reasonable estimate of fair value from publicly available information – e.g. information on recent transactions involving comparable properties; and
- whether the entity has its own staff with relevant qualifications. [*IAS 40.32*]

2.4.710.20   If the property market is reasonably stable and there are frequent transactions in comparable properties for which information is readily available, then an entity may, for example, adopt a practice of engaging independent property experts only every three years and estimating changes in fair value by other methods in the intervening periods. Such an approach is not, in itself, an accounting policy but rather an estimation method. If, for example, the market has been unusually volatile in the past accounting period, or has become less active, then the estimation method may not be appropriate and it may be necessary to obtain additional valuation information from professional valuers.

2.4.720   *Presentation of separate assets and liabilities*

2.4.720.10   Once the fair value of investment property has been measured, an entity ensures that it does not double count assets or liabilities that are recognised separately. [*IAS 40.50*]

2.4.720.20   In our view, an entity should choose an accounting policy, to be applied consistently, to present investment property and any related assets or liabilities included in the valuation as follows in the statement of financial position.

- *Investment property only:* Under this approach, only investment property is presented, measured at the amount determined in the valuation.
- *Separate assets and liabilities:* Under this approach, investment property and the related assets and liabilities are each presented separately; investment property is recognised at the amount determined in the valuation minus (plus) amounts allocated to other assets (liabilities).

EXAMPLE 28 – INVESTMENT PROPERTY – MULTIPLE ASSETS INCLUDED IN VALUATION

2.4.720.30   Company S owns an investment property that it is leasing to Company B for five years under an operating lease. No rent is payable in year 1 and the rent for years 2 to 5 equals 100 per annum.

2.4.720.40   At the end of year 1, S has accrued rental income of 80 (see 5.1.310.110) and the fair value of the investment property is 1,000. The future cash flows of 400 from the lease are included in measuring fair value.

2.4.720.50   To avoid double counting, S decides to present two assets in its statement of financial position:
- accrued rental income of 80 ((100 x 4) / 5); and
- investment property of 920 (1,000 - 80).

2.4.720.60   For a discussion of investment property measured at fair value for which a government grant has been received, see 4.3.70.

2.4.730   Biological assets

2.4.730.10   IAS 41 deals with the accounting for biological assets and is the subject of chapter 3.9. However, the principles in IFRS 13 provide general guidance in measuring the fair value element of fair value less costs to sell of both biological assets and agricultural produce at the point of harvest, supported by aspects of IAS 41. In measuring fair value, the general guidance in 2.4.10–540 applies. This section discusses specific points of interest in relation to biological assets, which in general will also apply to agricultural produce.

2.4.740   *The item being measured*

2.4.740.10   In measuring fair value, an entity takes into account characteristics of the biological assets that market participants would take into account in a transaction at the measurement date. For biological assets, key characteristics include the age, weight, condition and location of the assets. For a general discussion of the item being measured, see 2.4.70.

2.4.750   *Unit of account*

2.4.750.10   The unit of account (discussed generally in 2.4.80) for biological assets could be either a single asset or a group of assets. For assets that are unique – e.g. horses held for breeding – each asset will be a separate unit of account.

2.4.750.20   IAS 41 allows assets to be grouped according to their significant attributes. For example, livestock or fish may be grouped according to age or weight, crops may be grouped according to quality, and trees in a forest may be grouped according to age and type. [*IAS 41.15*]

2.4.750.30   Agricultural produce (e.g. fruit) growing on a bearer plant (e.g. a fruit tree) is a biological asset in the scope of IAS 41. Bearer plants, however, are in the scope of IAS 16. Therefore, the bearer plant and the produce growing on it are two separate units of account. [*IAS 41.1, 2(b), 5C*]

2.4.750.40   In many cases, biological assets are physically attached to the land, and an active market only exists for the combined package of the biological assets, land and land improvements. In that case, it may be necessary to measure the fair value of the combined package and then to deduce the fair value of the biological assets – e.g. by deducting the fair value of just the land and the land improvements (see Example 29). [*IAS 41.25*]

2.4.760   *Principal (or most advantageous) market*

2.4.760.10   As explained in 2.4.100, fair value is measured with reference to the principal (or most advantageous) market to which the entity has access. This means that an entity cannot simply assume that its local market is the appropriate reference market for the purpose of applying IFRS 13. An entity is required to consider all information that is reasonably available in determining the principal (or most advantageous) market to which it has access at the measurement date.

2.4.760.20   Owners of biological assets may enter into contracts to sell forward the assets or related produce. These contracts may not provide evidence of current fair value, because fair value should reflect the current market in which a willing buyer and seller would enter into a spot transaction to sell the assets. If there is such a contract, then the asset to be sold is still measured at fair value less costs to sell (see 2.4.110–140 and 475.20). However, the forward contract itself may be relevant for the accounting under other standards – e.g. the contract might need to be recognised as an asset or a liability under IFRS 9 (see 7.1.200), or an onerous contract provision might be required under IAS 37 (see 3.12.630). [*IAS 41.16*]

2.4.770   *Valuation approaches and techniques*

2.4.770.10   The fair value of biological assets is typically measured using techniques that fall under the market approach and/or the income approach; this section discusses specific points of interest in respect of measuring the fair value of biological assets. For a general discussion of valuation approaches and techniques, including the use of multiple approaches/techniques, see 2.4.120.

2.4.780   *Market approach*

2.4.780.10   If there is no active market, then an entity could measure fair value using techniques such as prices of recent market transactions, market prices for similar assets or sector benchmarks etc. In using such prices, an entity makes adjustments to reflect differences in characteristics and/or stages of growth of the assets. These methods would be appropriate if there are recent transactions or if markets exist for similar assets.

EXAMPLE 29 – BIOLOGICAL ASSETS – RECENT MARKET TRANSACTIONS

2.4.780.20   Company V owns a timber plantation in the northern region of the country. There have been no recent transactions for plantations in that part of the country. However, a similar timber plantation was recently sold in another region.

2.4.780.30   In measuring fair value, V uses the price of the transaction, adjusted for significant differences in the characteristics of the timber plantations. The price of the transaction is also allocated between the biological asset (the trees) and any other assets (e.g. land, irrigation equipment etc) to measure the fair value of the biological asset itself.

2.4.790   *Income approach**

2.4.790.10   The fair value of a biological asset is likely to include not only the asset's harvest value, but also a value for potential additional biological transformation that a market participant would include in the valuation. This requires a number of factors to be considered, such as:
- risks associated with the asset – e.g. weather and disease;
- estimated yields; and
- estimated costs of bringing the asset to its intended condition.

2.4.790.20   These risks address the uncertainty related to future cash flows – i.e. the possibility of variations in cash flows – and are reflected in either the discount rate and/or the estimate of expected cash flows.

2.4.790.30   In estimating future selling prices for the purpose of discounting expected net cash flows, the assumptions used should be consistent with those of market participants. These will depend on the characteristics of the biological assets, including their stage of development, the markets in which they are sold and the sources of possible pricing information. The assumptions that market participants would make about future selling prices will depend on a number of factors, including the following.

- The expected time to sell the asset – i.e. the time to the asset's maturity or harvest. For example, some biological assets such as poultry have a short period to maturity whereas others such as timber have a long growing cycle.
- Possible events or changes in circumstances between the measurement date and the expected date of sale. For example, expected regulatory changes may affect the demand for or supply of a biological asset and its price. The longer the period from the measurement date to the assumed sale date, the greater the number and magnitude of possible events and changes in circumstances that may occur. To some extent, possible future events or changes in circumstances may already be reflected in current prices.
- The effects of seasonal changes in pricing. For example, prices may be lower at principal harvest times when supply is greatest.

2.4.790.40   Considering these factors and depending on the specific facts and circumstances, an entity could estimate the future selling price using:
- current prices, especially if the time from the measurement date to the assumed sale date is short;
- prices in futures markets, which may be correlated with expected future selling prices;
- reliable statistical models used to forecast expected future selling prices; or
- prices for future periods or annual price increases established in regulated markets.

2.4.790.50   If an entity uses present value techniques to measure fair value, then the calculations generally include a contributory asset charge for assets that are owned by the entity and used in agricultural activity. For example, if an entity owns the land on which its agricultural activities are carried out, then in measuring the fair value of its biological assets, the entity deducts an amount (contributory asset charge) that reflects a charge for use of the land in the agricultural activities. This charge may be consistent with the rent on land without the biological asset.

2.4.790.60   IAS 41 continues to include a general caveat that the fair value measurement does not include cash flows related to financing the assets, taxation, or re-establishing biological assets after harvest – e.g. replanting trees. [*IAS 41.22*]

2.4.800   *Cost as an approximation of fair value*

2.4.800.10   IAS 41 acknowledges that in some cases cost may approximate fair value, and provides the following examples:
- little biological transformation has taken place since initial recognition – e.g. spruce seedlings planted just before the measurement date; or
- the impact of biological transformation is not material – e.g. the initial growth in a 30-year pine plantation production cycle. [*IAS 41.24*]

2.4.800.20   Whether cost does approximate fair value will depend on the specific facts and circumstances of the biological assets being valued.

2.4.810   *Use of independent valuer*

2.4.810.10   In measuring fair value, there is no requirement under IAS 41 to involve an independent valuer. [*IAS 41.B33*]

2.4.820   Impairment of non-financial assets

2.4.820.10   IAS 36 provides guidance on the impairment testing of non-financial assets and is the subject of chapter 3.10. However, the principles in IFRS 13 provide general guidance in measuring the fair value element of fair value less costs of disposal for the purposes of impairment testing. In measuring fair value, the general guidance in 2.4.10–540 applies.

2.4.820.20   The unit of account (discussed generally in 2.4.80) of non-financial assets subject to impairment testing is determined under IAS 36, and depends on the level at which assets are tested for impairment. The unit of account could comprise a single asset, a CGU or a group of CGUs (see 3.10.40).

2.4.820.30   For a CGU that corresponds to an investment in a subsidiary, associate or joint venture, see 2.4.830 for a discussion of determining the unit of account for fair value measurement.

2.4.830   Investments in subsidiaries, associates and joint ventures

2.4.830.10   As discussed in 2.4.80, the unit of account may be an investment in a subsidiary, associate or joint venture. In that case, in our view an entity may choose an accounting policy, to be applied consistently, to identify the unit of account of an investment in a subsidiary, associate or joint venture as:
- the investment as a whole; or
- each individual share making up the investment.

2.4.830.20   If the unit of account is each individual share making up the investment, then a premium related to the whole investment cannot be added in measuring the fair value of the investment. However, if the unit of account is the investment as a whole, then it may be appropriate to add such a premium in measuring the fair value of the investment – even if Level 1 prices exist for individual shares.

2.4.830.30   For a discussion of the valuation of unquoted equity securities, see 2.4.860.

2.4.840   *Control premiums*

2.4.840.10   In respect of an investment in a subsidiary, an acquirer (market participant) may be willing to pay a price that reflects a control premium, if it believes that it can create value by increasing cash flows and/or reducing risk. There are three broad ways in which this may be achieved.
- An acquirer may believe that it can change the stand-alone cash flows of the business through better management. In our experience, it is uncommon to assert that a new owner would be able to better manage the stand-alone operations of the business.
- An acquirer may believe that as a controlling shareholder it would have a lower risk, and therefore a lower required rate of return, than a minority shareholder in a public company. In our experience, this is likely to be less important in markets with strong corporate governance and minority shareholder protections.

- An acquirer may expect to create synergies through combining the acquired business with existing operations to increase the aggregate cash flow of the combining units. In our experience, this is typically the most significant factor contributing to the existence of a control premium.

2.4.840.20   The amount of a control premium is best corroborated by specific, comparable and current transactions in the investee's industry. The factors giving rise to such premiums in industry transactions are considered, and their potential existence in a hypothetical acquisition is assessed. For example, control premiums in industry transactions may reflect specific synergies that were expected to be available to the combining entities. Such synergies may arise from the nature of the entities' operations, including the degree of overlap therein, anticipated tax benefits from the transaction etc. These benefits might not be available to a market participant acquirer of the investee, and therefore would not be included in measuring fair value.

2.4.840.30   If there is no (or limited) current market activity to support the amount of the control premium, then historical transactions may need to be considered. However, a control premium based on arbitrary 'rule of thumb' percentages, or on an amount selected to avoid an impairment loss, for example, are not appropriate. Changes in control premiums from prior periods should be supported by objective evidence.

2.4.850   *Premiums other than control premiums*

2.4.850.10   An analysis of whether a shareholding that conveys joint control or significant influence might be valued in excess of its pro rata share of an entity's market capitalisation would consider similar factors to those outlined in 2.4.840.10 – i.e. based on an evaluation of the potential of such a shareholder to increase cash flows or reduce risk. However, a non-controlling influential shareholder generally receives the same pro rata cash flows as other minority shareholders. Therefore, in our experience it may be difficult to support a fair value significantly in excess of the quoted share price.

2.4.860   Unquoted equity securities

2.4.860.05   Investments in unquoted equity securities (and contracts on those instruments) are required to be measured at fair value. Cost may be an appropriate estimate of fair value in limited circumstances (see 2.4.920). [*IFRS 9.B5.2.3, BC5.13*]

2.4.860.10   There are a number of sources of guidance that entities can refer to in valuing unquoted equity securities, including the IASB's educational material (referenced in this section), a practice aid issued by the American Institute of Certified Public Accountants, and valuation guidelines issued by the International Private Equity and Venture Capital Association. Although such guidance may be useful, care is required because such guidance is not necessarily consistent with IFRS 13.

2.4.860.20   Under IFRS 9, investments in equity securities are measured at fair value with changes in fair value recognised either in profit or loss or in OCI (see chapter 7.7). In measuring fair value, the general guidance in 2.4.10–540 applies. This section discusses specific points of interest in respect of the valuation approaches and techniques used to measure the fair value of unquoted equity securities.

2.4.860.30   As noted in 2.4.130.10, in measuring the fair value of an asset or a liability, an entity selects those valuation approaches and techniques that are appropriate in the circumstances and for which sufficient data is available to measure fair value. The technique chosen should maximise the use of relevant observable inputs and minimise the use of unobservable inputs. Factors relevant to measuring the fair value of unquoted equity securities include the following:

- the information that is reasonably available to an investor;
- market conditions;
- the investment horizon and investment type;
- the stage in the investee's life cycle;
- the nature of an investee's business – e.g. volatile or cyclical business; and
- the industry in which an investee operates. [*IFRS 13.EM.02-13.18*]

2.4.860.40   It is likely that greater weight will be placed on market multiples based on comparable entities (a technique under the market approach – see 2.4.870) if there are sufficiently comparable peers or if a significant amount of information is available regarding recent observed transactions involving similar entities. Similarly, it is likely that greater weight will be placed on a discounted cash flows method (a technique under the income approach – see 2.4.880) if the investee has unique characteristics that cause its cash flow profile to differ significantly from those of otherwise comparable businesses. [*IFRS 13.EM.02-13.13*]

2.4.870   *Market approach*

2.4.870.10   The following inputs are most commonly used in applying valuation techniques under the market approach:

- transaction prices paid for an identical or a similar instrument of the investee; and
- comparable entity valuation multiples derived from quoted prices in exchange markets or from prices paid in transactions. [*IFRS 13.EM.02-13.26–27*]

2.4.870.20   The transaction price of an investment in an unquoted equity instrument, which is identical to the investment being valued and made close to the measurement date, might be a reasonable starting point for measuring fair value at the measurement date. However, all information about the performance and operations of the investee and the pricing of comparable entities from the transaction date up to the measurement date is taken into account. [*IFRS 13.EM.02-13.28*]

2.4.870.30   Similarly, the transaction price of an investment in an equity instrument of an investee which is similar, rather than identical, to the investment being valued, and made close to the measurement date might be a reasonable starting point for measuring the fair value of the investment. Examples of such transactions include:

- the issue of new classes of shares to other investors; and
- transactions in such shares between other investors. [*IFRS 13.EM.02-13.32*]

2.4.870.40   In such cases, as noted in 2.4.140.30, valuation techniques are usually applied to determine the value of the subject asset (e.g. an ordinary share) taking into account the value of the comparable asset (e.g. preferred share). For example, in the case of an investee that had issued ordinary shares and preferred shares, a recent round of equity financing relating to Series C preferred shares is considered in measuring the fair value of an investment in ordinary shares, which have different liquidation preferences. It may be difficult to estimate the value effect of such differences on a per-share basis and an overall enterprise value analysis may be necessary. An equity value allocation method, such as an option pricing method, could be applied to reflect such differences. Alternatively, the recent price may be an input to a valuation technique – e.g. calibrating the valuation model to value the instrument using the recent price of a similar instrument. For a discussion of multiple valuation techniques, see 2.4.130. [*IFRS 13.EM.02-13.33*]

2.4.870.45   The following factors need to be considered when determining the nature and level of the adjustment:

- the rights and preferences associated with the instruments issued in the recent investment round (e.g. liquidation preferences, conversion ratios, dividends and anti-dilution provisions) compared with those of the instrument that is being valued;
- the proximity of the transaction to the measurement date and any events occurring between the recent investment round and the measurement date;
- the size of the recent investment round; and
- whether the recent investment round was made up of existing investors participating pro-rata. [*IFRS 13.B44(b), EM.02-13.33*]

2.4.870.50   In measuring fair value using market multiples derived from transactions, the investor considers whether the associated transactions represent the sale of a controlling interest. Any control premium is excluded in measuring the fair value of unquoted equity securities that represent a non-controlling interest or if the unit of account is the individual equity instrument (see 2.4.80 and 240). However, in using market multiples derived from quoted prices of public entities, such a non-controlling interest discount is not generally necessary because those multiples usually reflect non-controlling interest transactions. [*IFRS 13.EM.02-13.36–37*]

2.4.870.60   An investor also considers the non-marketable nature of the unquoted equity instruments being measured and the effect on fair value, as compared with equity instruments of comparable entity peers that are publicly traded and, therefore, likely to be more liquid. An adjustment to reflect the non-marketable nature of the investment might be required in those cases (see 2.4.240). [*IFRS 13.EM.02-13.64*]

2.4.870.70   Even when an IPO is a likely event for a private entity, the expected IPO price is not generally representative of the fair value of the entity's shares at the measurement date. This is because the ultimate IPO price is not finalised until the registration date and the market price will not be determinable until trading takes place. Furthermore, the expected IPO price reflects the value of the entity's shares under the assumption that they are publicly traded (i.e. a liquid instrument), whereas they are not in fact publicly traded at the measurement date. Nonetheless, the expected IPO price is a meaningful data point that needs to be considered in measuring the fair value of the entity's shares. In our experience, it is usual for management to obtain an understanding of differences between the expected IPO price and the measurement of fair value. This review can help support the reasonableness of assumptions underpinning the valuation.

2.4.880   *Income approach*

2.4.880.10   A common technique under the income approach that is used to measure the fair value of unquoted equity securities is the discounted cash flow method (see 2.4.890). Other methods used under this approach are:

- the dividend discount model (see 2.4.900.10);

- the constant-growth dividend discount model (see 2.4.900.20–30 and 50); and
- the capitalisation model (see 2.4.900.40–50). [*IFRS 13.EM.02-13.70*]

2.4.890 *Discounted cash flow method*

2.4.890.10 Under the discounted cash flow method, fair value is measured by discounting the estimated future cash flows of an investee using a rate of return that comprises the time value of money and the risks of the investment (see 2.4.160). [*IFRS 13.B13–B30, EM.02-13.71–72*]

2.4.890.20 If an investee is expected to have an indefinite life, then for practical reasons most models estimate cash flows for a discrete period and then either:
- use a constant growth model – e.g. the Gordon growth model;
- apply a capitalisation rate to the cash flows immediately following the end of the discrete period; or
- use an exit multiple to estimate a terminal value. [*IFRS 13.EM.02-13.71*]

2.4.890.30 Generally, there are two possible ways to value equity instruments using the discounted cash flow method: using either equity value or enterprise value.

2.4.890.40 Under the equity value approach, the fair value of the equity of the investee is measured directly. The cash flows used for the calculation are the cash flows available for distribution to all equity capital providers, which are the cash flows from the assets after debt payments and after making reinvestments that are needed for future growth. Accordingly, the discount rate used for the equity value reflects only the cost of equity. [*IFRS 13.EM.02-13.73*]

2.4.890.50 Under the enterprise value approach, the fair value of the equity of the investee is measured indirectly by measuring the enterprise value (which comprises the fair value of both the equity and the debt instruments of the investee) and then subtracting the value of the investee's debt. The cash flows used for the calculation are the cash flows available to all capital providers (equity and debt holders), which are the cash flows from the assets before any debt payments but after making reinvestments that are needed for future growth. Accordingly, the discount rate used for the enterprise value reflects the cost of debt and equity finance, in proportion to their use – i.e. the WACC; for further discussion of the weighted-average cost of capital, see 3.10.300. [*IFRS 13.EM.02-13.73*]

2.4.890.60 Regardless of the approach used, the assumptions about cash flows and discount rates need to be consistent. For example, post-tax (pre-tax) cash flows are discounted using a post-tax (pre-tax) discount rate. Similarly, the currency of the cash flows and the discount rate need to be the same. [*IFRS 13.EM.02-13.74*]

2.4.890.70 In measuring fair value using the discounted cash flow method, an investor considers any necessary adjustments (e.g. non-controlling or marketability discount) that market participants would incorporate in pricing the equity instruments at the measurement date and which are consistent with the investment's unit of account (see 2.4.80 and 240). [*IFRS 13.EM.02-13.76*]

2.4.900 *Other income approach methods*

2.4.900.10 Under the dividend discount model, the fair value of an equity instrument is measured as the present value of all of its expected future dividends in perpetuity. This model is often used in measuring the fair value of equity instruments for which the investee consistently pays dividends. [*IFRS 13.EM.02-13.115–116*]

2.4.900.20   The constant-growth dividend discount model is used as a simplified shortcut to the dividend discount model, which requires the estimation of dividend payments for every period into the indefinite future. [*IFRS 13.EM.02-13.117*]

2.4.900.30   The constant-growth dividend discount model assumes that dividends grow at a constant growth rate. Therefore, this model might be used for entities growing at a rate equal to, or lower than, the nominal growth in the economy with well-established dividend payment policies that they intend to continue into the future. Under this model, fair value is measured by discounting the initial dividend payment (after one period) using a rate that is calculated by deducting the constant percentage of growth from the discount rate. [*IFRS 13.EM.02-13.117–121*]

2.4.900.40   The capitalisation model assumes that the annual income stream is constant in perpetuity or that it grows at a constant annualised rate of growth (or decline). Accordingly under this model, similar to the constant-growth dividend discount model, fair value is measured by discounting the annual income using the capitalisation rate, which is calculated by deducting the constant percentage of growth from the discount rate. [*IFRS 13.EM.02-13.122–124*]

2.4.900.50   The assumptions associated with the capitalisation model and the constant-growth dividend discount model would generally not be met and therefore these models are generally not used as the primary source for fair value measurement. However, they might be used in some cases as cross-checking models. [*IFRS 13.EM.02-13.124*]

2.4.910   *Adjusted net asset method*

2.4.910.10   Under the adjusted net asset method (a technique generally considered to be under the cost approach), the fair value of unquoted equity securities is measured based on the fair value of the investee's assets and liabilities (both recognised in the statement of financial position and unrecognised). This method might be appropriate for an investee whose value is mainly derived from the holding of assets rather than from deploying those assets as part of a broader business. Examples of such investees are property-holding companies and investment entities; for a discussion of when it may be appropriate to use net asset value method for measuring the fair value of investment funds, see 2.4.970. [*IFRS 13.EM.02-13.125*]

2.4.910.20   In addition, this method might be appropriate for an investee that is not making an adequate return on assets or that is making only marginal levels of profits because it is in the very early stages of its development – e.g. an investee that has virtually no financial history or no developed product. [*IFRS 13.EM.02-13.126*]

2.4.910.30   The application of this method may require the use of many different valuation approaches and/or techniques simultaneously, to measure the fair value of the investee's assets and liabilities. [*IFRS 13.EM.02-13.20*]

2.4.910.40   If the investee has significant intangible assets (including goodwill), then it is generally not appropriate to use the adjusted net asset method for measuring fair value. This is because the measurement of the fair value of intangible assets that are significant to an investee or of a significant amount of goodwill is usually based on the same inputs that are used for measuring the fair value of the equity instruments of the investee in their entirety using an alternative valuation technique such as the discounted cash flow method. [*IFRS 13.EM.02-13.127*]

2.4.910.50   The adjusted net asset method measures a controlling interest. Therefore, the entity considers an adjustment for a non-controlling discount (see 2.4.80 and 240). In addition, in using this method, adjustments might be required under other conditions – for example:

- for a lack of liquidity or marketability – e.g. if the investee's associated assets and liabilities are publicly traded;
- for a significant time gap between the investee's reporting date and the measurement date – e.g. if the measurement of the fair values of the investee's associated assets and liabilities was made at the investee's reporting date and during the period until the investor's measurement date, the investee has made additional investments, incurred additional liabilities or the fair values of the associated assets and liabilities have changed; and
- for fund's fees or similar agreements that are not captured in the net asset valuation (see 2.4.940). [*IFRS 13.EM.02-13.128*]

2.4.920   *Cost as approximation of fair value*

2.4.920.10   All investments in equity instruments and contracts on those instruments are measured at fair value. For investments in *quoted* equity instruments, cost is never the best estimate of fair value. In limited circumstances, cost may be used as an approximation of fair value for:

- unquoted equity instruments; and
- contracts linked to them that are settled by delivery of such instruments. [*IFRS 9.B5.2.3, BC5.13–BC5.19*]

2.4.920.20   This may be the case if:

- the most recent available information is not sufficient to determine fair value; or
- there is a wide range of possible fair value measurements and cost represents the best estimate of fair value within that range. [*IFRS 9.B5.2.3*]

2.4.920.25   The basis for conclusions to IFRS 9 notes that the circumstances in 2.4.920.20 never apply to equity investments held by entities such as financial institutions and investment funds (see 2.4.930). [*IFRS 9.BC5.18*]

2.4.920.30   Examples of indicators of the circumstances in which cost may not be representative of fair value include:

- a significant change in the performance of the investee compared with budgets, plans or milestones;
- changes in expectation that the investee's technical product milestones will be achieved or the timing thereof;
- a significant change in the market for the investee's equity or its products or potential products;
- a significant change in the global economy or the economic environment in which the investee operates;
- a significant change in the performance of comparable entities, or in the valuations implied by the overall market;
- internal matters of the investee such as fraud, commercial disputes, litigation, changes in management or strategy; and

- evidence from external transactions in the investee's equity, either by the investee (such as a fresh issue of equity), or by transfers of equity instruments between third parties. [*IFRS 9.B5.2.4, 13.EM.02-13.28*]

2.4.920.40   The list of indicators in 2.4.920.30 is not exhaustive. An investor considers all information about the performance and operations of the investee that becomes available after the date of initial recognition, including whether the environment in which the investee operates is dynamic and whether there have been changes in market conditions and the passage of time. [*IFRS 9.B5.2.5, 13.EM.02-13.29*]

2.4.920.50   To determine if cost can be used as an approximation of fair value, the investor needs to carefully consider all facts and circumstances. In some cases – e.g. start-up companies – performance in accordance with original plans or the launch of a new product as expected, may lead to a significant increase in the fair value of the investment. This is because uncertainty over those events is removed. This may mean that even if there are no significant changes in performance against plans, cost may not be an appropriate estimate of fair value. In addition, all else being equal, an investment is usually expected to increase over time at a rate equal to the cost of equity less the dividend yield, before consideration of any changes associated with changes in the entity or markets.

2.4.920.60   In our experience, cost may be an appropriate estimate of fair value at the measurement date for a pre-revenue entity, when there is no catalyst for a change in fair value and the transaction date is relatively close to the measurement date.

2.4.925   *Fair value hierarchy*

2.4.925.10   Usually, there are no current observable prices for shares in private companies and accordingly the measurement of fair value is based on valuation techniques that use unobservable inputs. As a result, the fair value measurement is generally classified as Level 3 in the fair value hierarchy. [*IFRS 13.73*]

2.4.930   **Investment funds and similar investment vehicles**

2.4.930.10   In measuring fair value, the general guidance in 2.4.10–540 applies. This section discusses specific points of interest in relation to investments in investment funds and similar investment vehicles.

2.4.930.20   Although IFRS 9 includes guidance on circumstances in which cost might be representative of fair value (see 2.4.920 and 7.7.250), those circumstances would never apply to equity investments held by particular entities, such as financial institutions and investment funds. [*IFRS 9.BC5.18*]

2.4.930.30   In some cases, a fund invests in another fund. In our view, in this case the same principles apply. Therefore, if a fair value is not available for the investment in the fund directly, then an attempt should be made to value the underlying investments in the underlying fund.

2.4.940   *The item being measured*

2.4.940.10   Because the instrument held by the entity is an ownership interest in the fund and not an interest in the underlying assets of the fund, the measurement of fair value takes into account the rights and obligations inherent in that ownership interest – e.g. an obligation by the entity to meet future cash calls made by the fund. The entity considers any such obligations inherent in the ownership interest in its measurement of fair value.

2.4.940.20   This principle applies equally if fair value is measured with reference to net asset value (see 2.4.970). An entity considers any rights or obligations not reflected in the net asset value measurement for the fund (e.g. fees or similar agreements) and makes adjustments to arrive at fair value.

2.4.940.30   When an investment entity holds an investment through an intermediate entity that is accounted for at fair value through profit or loss, the direct investment in the intermediate entity represents the unit of account being measured at fair value. [*IFRS 13.14*]

EXAMPLE 30 – INVESTMENT HELD THROUGH AN INTERMEDIATE COMPANY

2.4.940.40   Company F, an investment entity, has a 100% direct investment in Company B, whose only purpose is investment in the ordinary shares of Public Company C. Therefore, F has an indirect equity investment in C. F accounts for its investment in B at fair value through profit or loss.

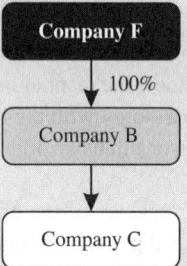

2.4.940.50   The direct investment in B represents the unit of account being measured at fair value by F. The indirect investment in the ordinary shares of C is not considered to be a separate unit of account by F. Although the market price of C's shares may be used as a valuation input in measuring the fair value of the investment in B, F considers whether there are other characteristics that a market participant would take into account (e.g. liquidity risk) when valuing its investment in B as the unit of account (see 2.4.910.50). For guidance on categorisation of the investment in B in the hierarchy level, see 2.4.990.70.

2.4.950   *Valuation approaches and techniques*

2.4.950.10   The fair value of an investment in a fund is often measured using the net asset value of the fund – either as fair value or as a key input. This section discusses specific points of interest in respect of measuring the fair value of an investment in a fund. For a general discussion of valuation approaches and techniques, including the use of multiple approaches/techniques, see 2.4.120.

2.4.960   *General considerations*

2.4.960.10   In our view, if the valuation reported by the fund – e.g. based on net asset value (see 2.4.970) – represents the amount at which an orderly transaction between market participants would occur at the measurement date, then this value should be used in measuring fair value.

2.4.960.20   If the valuation reported by the fund does not represent the amount at which an orderly transaction between market participants would occur at the measurement date, then the value of the investment in the fund is determined by applying another valuation technique, including consideration of the fund's underlying investments.

2.4.970   *Net asset value as representative of fair value*

2.4.970.05   If there is a quoted price in an active market (i.e. Level 1 price – see 2.4.280) for an investment in the fund, then the fair value of the investment is determined using the quoted price, whether or not it is equal to the net asset value. If there is no quoted price in an active market, then the entity needs to assess whether the net asset value is otherwise representative of the fair value of the investment in the fund. For a discussion of when the prices of units in a fund represent Level 1 prices, see 2.4.990.

2.4.970.10   If net asset value is used as an input in an entity's measurement of fair value (with or without further adjustments), then the entity needs to understand how net asset value is calculated, including the key inputs and valuation techniques used by the fund to value the underlying assets and liabilities.

2.4.970.20   To assess whether the net asset value or another price is representative of a quoted price in an active market, an entity considers the manner in which an investment in the fund is traded. Units in open-ended funds are often traded only with the fund or its agent at a published price – either net asset value, or net asset value plus or minus an adjustment.

2.4.970.30   Depending on the frequency of the updating of published unit prices and the trading volume at these prices, the published prices may represent a quoted price in an active market. However, in some circumstances, units in open-ended funds may be traded both with the fund at net asset value and in a secondary market – e.g. for exchange-traded funds. Also, in some circumstances, an open-ended fund may suspend redemptions, in which case the published net asset value would not represent a quoted price in an active market.

2.4.970.40   Units or shares in a fund may trade at a premium or discount to net asset value, because of supply and demand or other factors specific to the fund. For example, units or shares may trade at a discount because a market participant may consider an investment in the fund less attractive than a direct investment in the underlying assets of the fund because of the risk of future investment management changes and the loss of control over portfolio management decisions or because of a lack of liquidity or marketability of the investment. Conversely, market participants may be willing to pay a premium to invest in a fund managed by a specific investment manager.

2.4.970.50   Therefore, the existence of a discount between the net asset value reported by a fund and an entity's transaction price to sell or buy the investment does not, in and of itself, result in the transaction being considered not orderly. For example, if the transaction occurred with adequate exposure to the market, with a customary marketing period, and did not occur under duress, then it is likely that the transaction would be considered orderly. For a general discussion of this issue, see 2.4.480, which is written in the context of a significant decrease in the volume or level of activity in a market.

2.4.970.60   Although secondary market trading may not be sufficient to constitute an active market, it is still important to consider any secondary market transactions and transaction prices because, regardless of the level of market activity and trading volume, transaction prices that represent transactions that are orderly should not be ignored in measuring fair value. [*IFRS 13.B44(b)*]

2.4.970.70   To assess whether net asset value is otherwise representative of the fair value, an entity considers the following situations in which net asset value may not be representative of fair value.
- The net asset value is not dated as at the entity's measurement date.
- The net asset value is not calculated in a manner consistent with the fair value measurement principles of IFRS 13.
- The investment cannot currently be redeemed at net asset value – e.g. some open-ended funds may suspend redemptions.
- There is a significant decrease in the volume and level of activity of subscriptions or redemptions compared with normal market activity.
- The investment is traded in a secondary market at a significant discount or premium to net asset value.
- There are other uncertainties that increase the risk of the investment (e.g. deteriorated financial condition of the investment manager, allegations of fraud or non-compliance with laws and regulations).
- There are other terms attached to the investment – e.g. a commitment to make future investments.

2.4.970.80   If an open-ended redeemable fund does not allow daily redemptions at net asset value but allows, and actually has, periodic subscriptions and redemptions at net asset value, then their existence may provide evidence that net asset value approximates fair value.

2.4.970.90   In our experience, net asset value would usually be representative of the fair value of investments in open-ended investment funds that are open to new investors and allow redemptions at net asset value.

2.4.970.100   In addition, new subscriptions to a fund at its reported net asset value on or near the measurement date may provide evidence that market participants are not currently requiring a discount to net asset value or paying a premium above net asset value. Similarly, redemptions from the fund at its reported net asset value on or near the measurement date may provide evidence that market participants are currently not demanding a premium over net asset value or selling at a discount to net asset value. If both subscriptions and redemptions have occurred at net asset value near the entity's measurement date for its investment in the fund, then evidence may exist that net asset value approximates fair value.

2.4.970.110   In determining whether net asset value approximates fair value, the weight placed on the evidence provided by transactions with the fund (i.e. subscriptions and redemptions) depends on:
- market changes since the transaction activity occurred;
- the volume of both redemptions and subscriptions;
- the extent to which subscriptions were received from new investors; and
- limitations or expected limitations on the entity's ability to redeem in the future.

2.4.970.120   However, if no subscriptions and redemptions have occurred close to the reporting date, then an assertion that fair value approximates net asset value may be more difficult to support.

2.4.980   *Effect of bid-ask spread on financial information reported by investment funds*

2.4.980.10   An entity may not depart from the requirements of IFRS 13 to comply with regulatory requirements. For example, some investment funds are required to report their net asset values to investors using mid-market prices; under IFRS 13, we believe that an entity may use mid-market pricing as a practical expedient only if it provides a reasonable approximation of an exit price (see 2.4.250). [*IFRS 13.70–71*]

2.4.980.20   Problems may arise in the reporting by investment funds that offer linked investment products – i.e. the fund's obligation to unit holders is linked to the value of the underlying investments. The investments held by the fund and the liability to unit holders are not necessarily valued using the same price within the bid-ask spread (e.g. mid-market price) because different prices within the bid-ask spread may represent the exit price for the assets and liabilities (see 2.4.250). Owing to differences in the valuation bases of the investments and the unit liability, a mismatch results in the statement of financial position.

2.4.980.30   This in turn causes a presentation issue. In our view, one solution may be to present the unit liability in a two-line format. The first line would be the amount of the net assets attributable to holders of redeemable shares measured in accordance with the prospectus, which reflects the actual redemption amount at which the redeemable shares would be redeemed at the reporting date; the next line would include an adjustment for the difference between this and the amount recognised in the statement of financial position. This reflects the fact that, for a fund with no equity, all recognised income and expense is attributed to unit holders, which also means that a dilution levy of such amount would be required if all units were redeemed.

2.4.980.40   The problem in 2.4.980.20 may also be encountered by other entities, such as insurance companies offering linked investment products. We believe that the approach discussed in 2.4.980.30 could also be applied in these circumstances.

2.4.990   *Fair value hierarchy*

2.4.990.10   For funds in which ownership interests in the fund are publicly traded in an active market, the fair value measurement is based on the quoted price – i.e. a Level 1 input.

2.4.990.20   An entity may hold units in an open-ended unlisted investment fund. The units in the fund are often bought and sold but only by or to the fund or fund manager – i.e. the units are not traded on a stock exchange and cannot be sold to third parties. Because the fund is not listed, the fund calculates the price of the units only at a specific time each day to enable units to be bought and sold. The transactions take place only at this time on each day, and at the price so determined by the fund manager. The fair value of the units is determined to be the price calculated by the fund manager. Whether this is a Level 1 measurement will depend on the number and frequency of trades that occur in the units (see 2.4.280).

2.4.990.30   Daily pricing is likely to constitute evidence that trades take place with sufficient frequency. If the number of trades occurring is sufficient for the market in these units to be considered an active market then, notwithstanding that the units are being bought and sold by the fund and are not being traded between unrelated third party market participants, a fair value measurement of the units using the unadjusted daily price for the reporting date would be a Level 1 measurement.

2.4.990.40   However, if there is a quoted price but the number of trades occurring is not sufficient for the market in these units to be considered active, then a fair value measurement of the units using the unadjusted price for the reporting date would not be categorised as Level 1 in the fair value hierarchy.

2.4.990.50   If net asset value does not represent a quoted price, then it may continue to be used as an appropriate input for fair value measurement purposes (see 2.4.220 and 970). The appropriate categorisation of the resulting fair value measurement within the fair value hierarchy will be as Level 2 or Level 3 (see 2.4.290) based on the observability and significance of:
- the fair values of the underlying investments; and
- any adjustments for rights and obligations inherent within the ownership interest held by the entity (see 2.4.940).

2.4.990.60   Because many of the net asset value adjustments mentioned above will be based on unobservable inputs, the resulting fair value measurements that are subject to such adjustments are generally Level 3 measurements, unless those inputs are not significant to the measurement as a whole.

2.4.990.70   If the sole purpose of an intermediate entity is to hold publicly traded equity investments, then the fair value of the investment in the intermediate entity may be determined by adjusting the fair value of the publicly traded equity investments for the effects of risks (e.g. liquidity risk) of the intermediate entity (see 2.4.940.40–50). The investment in the intermediate entity is not an identical asset to the publicly traded equity investments that it holds, regardless of whether adjustments were applied to the fair value of the publicly traded equity investments. Therefore, assuming that the intermediate entity is not listed and actively traded, it would not be appropriate to categorise the investment in Level 1 of the hierarchy level.

2.4.995   Loans to customers measured at amortised cost

2.4.995.10   Loans are classified following the requirements of IFRS 9 (see chapter 7.4) and are usually measured at amortised cost subsequent to initial recognition, with fair value being disclosed (see 7.4.30 and 7.10.460). As a result, the fair value of such loans needs to be measured for disclosure purposes. In measuring fair value, the general guidance in 2.4.10–540 applies. This section discusses specific points of interest in relation to loans to customers measured at amortised cost.

2.4.996   *Unit of account*

2.4.996.10   The unit of account for loans is generally the individual loan (see 2.4.80.20) unless the portfolio measurement exception applies (see 2.4.430). [*IFRS 13.48, BC47*]

2.4.996.20   In some cases, observed sales transactions may relate to portfolios of loans. Therefore, an entity needs to determine the relevance of the price for the sale of a portfolio of similar loans for the purpose of valuing an individual loan. In doing that, the entity needs to consider whether a different liquidity discount or similar adjustment is implied in the portfolio price compared with that which would apply to the sale of an individual loan – e.g. a sale of a large portfolio of loans may include a blockage factor (discount) that would not be applicable to a sale of a smaller individual loan. [*IFRS 13.69*]

2.4.997   **Valuation approaches and techniques**

2.4.997.10   Some loans might be valued using a market approach – e.g. if there are secondary market transactions and prices for identical or similar loans. In our experience, most loans are not traded in secondary markets and they are often valued using the income approach. This is because the valuation technique applied needs to maximise the use of relevant observable inputs and minimise the use of unobservable inputs; and when there is not a secondary market for the sale of a loan, in some cases more relevant inputs might be derived from rates or prices in the origination market. [*IFRS 13.61, 67*]

2.4.997.20   When loans are valued using origination rates or prices, the entity needs to consider whether a sale to a market participant would reflect a premium or discount from the price in the origination market. For example, the entity could calibrate its valuation models against prices for any actual sales of similar loans. If there is not a secondary market for loans but they are valued using inputs from markets for more liquid traded instruments, then the entity also needs to consider whether a liquidity adjustment is required.

2.4.997.30   Income approaches need to be consistent with the assumptions that market participants would make with respect to future cash flows and to discount rates. Estimates of future cash flows used might, depending on the circumstances, reflect either:
- contractual cash flows, gross of expected credit losses; or
- expected cash flows, net of expected credit losses (i.e. risk-adjusted cash flows).

2.4.997.40   The discount rates used in each case need to be consistent with the cash flow estimates used. In using contractual cash flows, the discount rate would include a premium representing compensation for expected and unexpected credit losses. In using expected cash flows, the discount rate would not include an adjustment for *expected* credit losses because this is already reflected in the expected cash flows. However, the discount rate would include a premium for *unexpected* credit losses – i.e. to reflect the cost of bearing the risk that credit losses will be different from expected.

2.4.997.50   Factors that impact the estimates of expected cash flows and discount rates include the following:
- the time value of money – i.e. the risk-free rate;
- the currency of the instrument;
- the credit risk of the instrument – i.e. the credit spread over the risk-free interest rate – considering both the credit standing of the issuer and the specific terms of the instrument, such as collateral and other credit risk enhancements, seniority, subordination or non-recourse features;
- prepayment risk;
- liquidity risk;
- legal concerns – e.g. deficiencies in the security documents between the borrower and lender or in title documents of the borrower to secured assets or legislative provisions that provide priority to other creditors, such as tax authorities or employees; and
- other risks and uncertainties inherent in the cash flows that relate to specific contractual terms of the loan (not including credit risk) – e.g. terms that link cash flows to inflation or to variables specific to the borrower such as revenues or EBITDA.

2.4.997.60   An entity needs to consider all available information and to use judgement to determine, for particular loans, whether any adjustments are required to reflect differences between the characteristics of instruments from which inputs are derived and the loans being valued. For example, adjustments may be required to reflect differences in liquidity, underwriting criteria, collateral, maturity, vintage, customer type, geographic location, prepayment options or rates or other differences in credit risk.

2.4.997.70   In some cases, the par amount of a loan may be a reasonable approximation of the fair value of a loan if the interest rate is set at the discretion of the lender and the borrower is able to prepay at any time without penalty. However, before reaching such a conclusion, the entity needs to consider whether there are any factors that indicate that a market participant would price the loan at an amount different from par – e.g. based on any recent secondary market transaction data or because the loan is impaired or the loan has otherwise elevated credit risk.

2.4.997.80   For other types of floating interest rate loans – e.g. where the lender does not have full discretion to change interest rates and only the benchmark component is floating – the factors leading to differences between par and fair value will generally be stronger because:
- of the effect of interest rate changes since the last reset date; and
- the contractual spread above the benchmark rate is not usually repriced to reflect changes in market participants' views of credit and liquidity risks to the measurement date.

2.4.997.90   An entity may sell its loans to market participants that securitise them. The securitisation market cannot be the principal market for the loans because what is being sold or transferred in the securitisation market are the securities issued by the vehicle that securitised the loans. [*IFRS 13.11, 16*]

2.4.997.100   However, in measuring the fair value of loans, it may be appropriate to consider prices for securities that would be issued by a market participant that securitises the loans as an input into the valuation technique if market participants would consider this pricing. This is because a valuation technique needs to maximise observable inputs and minimise unobservable inputs. This would be the case particularly if a reliable observable price for the loans is not available. If the valuation technique uses these inputs, then the fair value of the loans would generally be obtained by adjusting the securitisation prices (including the value of retained interests) for the costs that would be incurred and the estimated profit margin that would be required by a market participant to securitise the loans. [*IFRS 13.67*]

2.4.998   *Fair value hierarchy*

2.4.998.10   In our experience, loans to customers are mostly classified as Level 3 in the fair value hierarchy because of a lack of secondary market transactions. In particular, credit-impaired loans generally fall into Level 3 because the valuation is driven by estimates of expected cash flows, which are in most cases not observable. The same may be true for loans that are credit-impaired at acquisition or origination or for other loans with elevated credit risk, even if they are not credit-impaired under IFRS 9. However, in our experience loans to banks are less likely to be classified as Level 3 because more information about the pricing of debt instruments issued by the bank is usually available.

2.4.999   *Low-interest and interest-free loans*

2.4.999.10   Sometimes interest-free or low-interest loans are provided – e.g. by a shareholder or government – to attract customers or as a means of passing on tax benefits. For specific considerations regarding the measurement of fair value of such loans, see 7.7.80 and 120.

2.4.1000   **Business combinations**

2.4.1000.10   Fair value measurements are pervasive in applying acquisition accounting under IFRS 3, which is the subject of chapter 2.6. The following are examples of areas in which fair value measurements are applied in the context of acquisition accounting:

- measuring consideration transferred, including deferred consideration (see 2.6.270) and contingent consideration (see 2.6.280);
- measuring the gain or loss on the effective settlement of a non-contractual pre-existing relationship (see 2.6.360);
- measuring assets acquired and liabilities assumed (see 2.6.600);
- measuring 'ordinary' NCI that the acquirer chooses to measure at fair value (see 2.6.940) and 'other' NCI (see 2.6.950); and
- measuring the non-controlling equity interest in the acquiree before obtaining control in a business combination achieved in stages (see 2.6.1140).

2.4.1000.20   The principles in IFRS 13 provide general guidance in measuring fair values in the context of acquisition accounting. In measuring fair value, the general guidance in 2.4.10–540 applies, as well the specific application guidance in 2.4.550–995 to the extent relevant. This section discusses specific points of interest in relation to certain assets and liabilities.

2.4.1010   *Intangible assets*

2.4.1010.10   Given the specialised nature of most intangible assets, measuring fair value using the market approach may not always be possible. In our experience, intangible assets are usually measured using a technique that falls under the income approach – present value technique (see 2.4.160), the multi-period excess earnings method (see 2.4.200.10), the with-versus-without method (see 2.4.200.20), and/or the relief-from-royalty method (see 2.4.200.30).

2.4.1010.20   In our experience, the cost approach is rarely appropriate in practice for determining the fair value of intangible assets other than internal-use software.

2.4.1010.30   One of the most important aspects of valuing an intangible asset that will not be used actively to generate direct cash flows, but which is expected to be used defensively to increase the value of other assets, is determining the characteristics of market participants. The entity's decision not to actively use the asset is not determinative in concluding who the appropriate market participants are or the highest and best use of the intangible asset to market participants (see 2.4.340.70–120). [*IFRS 13.30*]

2.4.1010.40   As for other non-financial assets, the fair value of an intangible asset to be retired or whose active use will be discontinued should be based on its highest and best use by market participants (see 2.4.330). One common methodology is the with-versus-without method. This method is useful for intangible assets that market participants would be expected to use defensively. It measures the incremental cash flows that would be achieved by market participants arising from their ownership of an existing intangible asset by locking up the competing acquired intangible asset. Fair value is measured as the difference between the fair value of the group of assets – i.e. the acquired and the existing assets – of the market participant:

- assuming that the acquired intangible asset were to be actively used by others in the market; and
- assuming that the acquired intangible asset was withdrawn from the market. [*IFRS 13.27, 30*]

2.4.1020 **Inventories**

2.4.1020.10   In our experience, the technique used to measure the fair value of inventories acquired depends on the stage of development in the production cycle. The fair value of manufactured finished goods and work in progress is typically measured based on the estimated selling price, less certain costs (and a margin thereon), that would be realised by a market participant.

2.4.1020.20   In our experience, the fair value of finished goods inventory is most frequently estimated under the market approach or income approach – i.e. at the estimated selling price less the sum of the costs to sell and a reasonable profit allowance for the selling effort (selling profit), both of which are estimated from the perspective of a market participant.

2.4.1020.30   Judgement is required in determining a reasonable amount of profit attributable to the effort incurred by the acquiree pre-acquisition, and the profit attributable to the effort that is likely to be incurred post-acquisition. In our view, the analysis should take into account the current profitability of the product at the date of acquisition, even if conditions were different when the inventory was manufactured.

EXAMPLE 31 – BUSINESS COMBINATION – FAIR VALUE OF FINISHED GOODS

2.4.1020.40   The acquiree in a business combination has finished goods measured at a cost of 100; the expected selling price is 150. The inventory is specialised and there are very few potential customers; this inventory has already been earmarked for one of those customers. Distribution costs are estimated at 20.

2.4.1020.50   In the absence of any additional factors indicating that market participants would arrive at a different estimate of the fair value of the inventory, we believe that the fair value of the inventory would be close to 130 (150 - 20), because the selling effort to be incurred is minimal.

2.4.1020.60   In our experience, work in progress of the acquiree is typically valued in a similar manner as finished goods inventory, most frequently under the market approach or income approach – i.e. at the estimated selling price of the work in progress, as if it were finished, less the sum of costs to complete, costs to sell and a reasonable profit allowance for the completion and selling effort of the acquirer, all of which are estimated from the perspective of a market participant.

2.4.1020.70   In our experience, the valuation approach used for recognising the fair value of raw materials is usually a market approach using observable market prices (if any are available) or a cost approach, both of which are estimated from the perspective of a market participant.

2.4.1030 **Unquoted financial liabilities**

2.4.1030.10   When an unquoted financial liability is assumed in a business combination, the general valuation principles outlined in 2.4.360 apply. However, a specific question arises about whether the assumptions underlying the fair value measurement – in particular, credit risk – should take into account the position of the combined entity.

2.4.1030.20   Following general principles, the assumptions should be consistent with those that a market participant would make in valuing the financial liability at the time of the business combination.

- If as a result of the business combination the acquirer becomes a legal obligor of the liability – e.g. by providing a guarantee – then in our experience market participants would value the liability on that basis. For example, non-performance risk, including credit risk, would be based on the risk that the combined entity will not fulfil the obligation.
- If only the acquiree remains the legal obligor after the acquisition, then judgement is required in assessing whether a market participant's view of non-performance risk changes as a result of the acquisition. For example, an acquiree in financial difficulty may be acquired by a group with a good credit rating such that a market participant may consider that the acquirer might support the acquiree in fulfilling its obligations even though the acquirer may have no legal obligation to do so.

2.4.1040   Financial guarantee contracts

2.4.1040.10   Depending on the circumstances, IFRS 4 or IFRS 9 may deal with the accounting for a financial guarantee contract. For a further discussion of the accounting by the issuer and the holder of a financial guarantee contract, see 7.1.60–130. Under IFRS 9, an issued financial guarantee contract is usually measured initially at fair value. In measuring fair value, the general guidance in this chapter applies. This section discusses specific fair value considerations in relation to financial guarantee contracts. [*IFRS 9.B2.5(a)*]

2.4.1050   *Valuation approaches and techniques*

2.4.1050.10   If a financial guarantee contract is issued in a stand-alone arm's length transaction to an unrelated party, then its fair value at inception is likely to equal the premium received unless there is evidence to the contrary. If there is no up-front payment – i.e. premiums will be paid at a later date – then the fair value of a financial guarantee contract between unrelated parties at inception is likely to be zero under IFRS. For a further discussion, see 7.1.120. [*IFRS 13.58–59, B4*]

2.4.1050.20   The following are examples of valuation techniques used to determine the fair value of a financial guarantee contract in other cases:
- market prices of comparable instruments;
- discounted cash flow models; and
- interest rate differentials.

2.4.1060   *Market prices of comparable instruments*

2.4.1060.10   Under the market price of comparable instruments technique, the issuer identifies a market price for financial guarantees that are similar to those that either it or a member of the group has issued or received in exchange for consideration. It might also be possible to identify market prices for similar guarantees, credit default swaps or credit insurance products. These prices could be adjusted to estimate the fair value of the financial guarantee. In our experience, this may be the easiest technique to apply.

2.4.1070   *Discounted cash flow models*

2.4.1070.10   There are different discounted cash flow models that can be applied to estimate the fair value of a financial guarantee. One method is to use a probability-weighted discounted cash flow analysis that incorporates the expected default rate of the borrower and expected recoveries in the event of default. As a starting point, the default rate can be estimated, for example, using historical default and recovery rates among entities with the same credit rating as the borrower. An entity needs to consider whether the historical default and recovery rates should be adjusted to reflect current and forecasted economic conditions.

2.4.1080 *Interest rate differentials*

2.4.1080.10   Under the interest rate differentials technique, the fair value of a guarantee provided to a lender in connection with a loan made to another entity for no consideration is estimated at inception as the difference, in present value terms, between the interest charged on the guaranteed loan and the interest that would have been charged to the borrower had the loan not been guaranteed. This difference is presumed to reflect the price that the lender is willing to pay for the guarantee. This technique requires the issuer of the guarantee to estimate the interest rate that would have been charged to the borrower without the financial guarantee based on an evaluation of the borrower's credit standing on a stand-alone basis.

2.4.1090 **FUTURE DEVELOPMENTS**

2.4.1090.10   The IFRS Interpretations Committee discussed a request to remove the current requirement in IAS 41 to exclude taxation cash flows (i.e. use pre-tax cash flows) when measuring the fair value of biological assets using a present value technique. The Committee recommended and the IASB agreed to amend IAS 41 as part of the next *Annual Improvements to IFRSs Cycle*. The proposals would enable fair value measurement of biological assets on a post-tax basis.

2.5 Consolidation

2.5   Consolidation

CURRENTLY EFFECTIVE REQUIREMENTS

This publication reflects IFRS in issue at 1 August 2018, and the currently effective requirements cover annual periods beginning on 1 January 2018.

The disclosures related to interests in subsidiaries are discussed in chapter 5.10.

The requirements related to this topic are mainly derived from the following.

STANDARD	TITLE
IFRS 10	Consolidated Financial Statements

The currently effective requirements include newly effective requirements arising from IFRS 9 *Financial Instruments*, which is effective for annual periods beginning on or after 1 January 2018. Transition requirements for IFRS 9 are the subject of chapter 7.11. The impact of the new requirements on consolidation is reflected in 2.5.760.

FORTHCOMING REQUIREMENTS

The currently effective requirements are affected by the following forthcoming requirements. They are highlighted with a # and the impact is explained in the accompanying boxed text at the references indicated.
- In September 2014, the IASB issued *Sale or Contribution of Assets between an Investor and its Associate or Joint Venture – Amendments to IFRS 10 and IAS 28*. The effective date for these amendments has been deferred indefinitely. Associates and the equity method are the subject of chapter 3.5.
- In May 2017, the IASB issued IFRS 17 *Insurance Contracts*, which is effective for annual periods beginning on or after 1 January 2021. See 2.5.445. IFRS 17 is the subject of chapter 8.1A.

FUTURE DEVELOPMENTS

For this topic, there are no future developments.

2.5.10 **ENTITIES INCLUDED IN CONSOLIDATED FINANCIAL STATEMENTS**

2.5.10.10   A 'subsidiary' is an entity that is controlled by another entity. [*IFRS 10.A*]

2.5.10.20   If an entity (parent) is required to prepare consolidated financial statements (see 2.1.100), then those consolidated financial statements include all subsidiaries of the parent – i.e. there is no exception from consolidation – except as follows.

- An investment entity (as defined) is required to account for its investments in subsidiaries at fair value through profit or loss in accordance with IFRS 9, with limited exceptions. Investment entities are the subject of chapter 5.6.
- An entity does not consolidate post-employment benefit plans or other long-term employee benefit plans in the scope of IAS 19 (see 4.4.1490). However, other employee benefit vehicles are in the scope of IFRS 10 – see, for example, Example 14. [*IFRS 10.4A, 31–32*]

2.5.10.30   Therefore, for example, there is no exception on the basis of dissimilar activities, severe long-term restrictions or the planned disposal of a subsidiary in the near future.

2.5.10.40   Venture capital organisations, investment funds, mutual funds, unit trusts and similar entities that do not qualify as investment entities are *not* exempt from the requirements of IFRS 10 and therefore their subsidiaries are required to be consolidated.

2.5.10.50   An entity is required to consolidate a subsidiary even if it is acquired exclusively with a view to its subsequent disposal. However, the disposal group – comprising the assets that are to be disposed of and directly related liabilities – is presented in the consolidated financial statements as held-for-sale or held-for-distribution on acquisition if certain criteria are met (see 5.4.20 and 35). [*IFRS 5.6, 11, 38–39*]

2.5.10.60   In our view, subsidiaries do not need to be consolidated if, both alone and in aggregate, they are *immaterial* (see 1.2.40) to the financial position, performance and cash flows of the group. Materiality depends on both the size and the nature of the omission or misstatement, or a combination of the two, judged in the surrounding circumstances. In considering materiality, the nature of a subsidiary may be important – e.g. if it is a structured entity (see 5.10.190). In our view, the non-consolidation of a subsidiary should be reconsidered in preparing financial statements at each reporting date. [*IAS 1.7, 29–31*]

2.5.10.70   An entity consolidates an investee from the date on which it obtains control over the investee until the date on which it loses control over the investee. [*IFRS 10.20, B88*]

2.5.20 **OVERVIEW OF CONTROL MODEL**

2.5.20.10   The discussion in this chapter refers to 'investor' as the entity undertaking the consolidation analysis, and 'investee' as the entity being assessed for consolidation. This is consistent with the use of the terms in IFRS 10, but is not meant to imply that the investor holds debt or equity securities in the investee.

2.5.20.20   An investor *controls* an investee when the investor is exposed to (has rights to) variable returns from its involvement with the investee, and has the ability to affect those returns through its power over the investee. Control requires power, exposure to variability of returns and a linkage between the two. [*IFRS 10.6–7, A, B2*]

2.5.20.30   To have power, the investor needs to have existing rights that give it the current ability to direct the activities that significantly affect the investee's returns – i.e. the relevant activities. An investor can have power over an investee even if other parties have existing rights to participate in the direction of the relevant activities – e.g. significant influence over the investee. [*IFRS 10.10, 14, B9, B14*]

2.5.20.40   The definition of power is based on *ability*, and therefore power does not need to be exercised. As such, evidence that the investor has been directing the relevant activities is not in itself conclusive in determining that the investor has power over the investee. Also, in the absence of other rights, economic dependence of an investee on the investor does not result in the investor concluding that it has control over the investee. [*IFRS 10.11–12, B40*]

2.5.20.50   The following diagram summarises the steps in the control analysis, which are explained in the rest of this chapter. [*IFRS 10.B2–B3*]

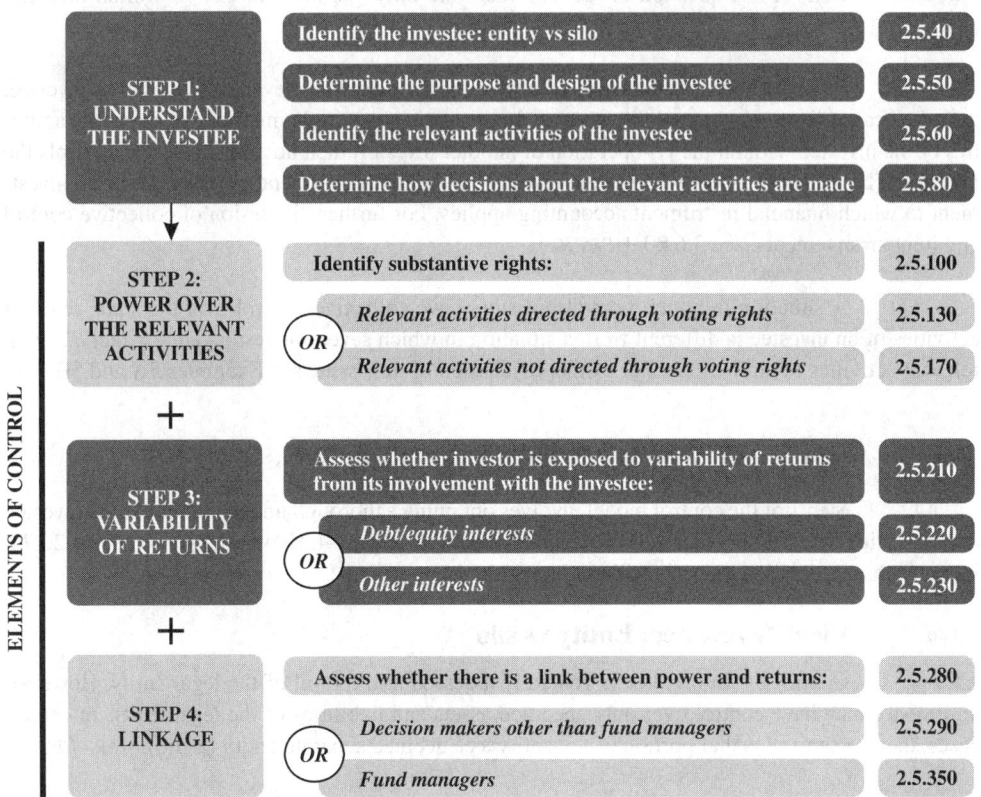

2.5.20.60   IFRS 10 refers to the three elements of control, which correspond to Steps 2–4 in the diagram. We have also included a preliminary step, *Step 1 Understand the investee*, because there may be a considerable amount of preparatory analysis required before testing the three elements of control. [*IFRS 10.8*]

2.5.20.70   Although the control model in IFRS 10 is complex and includes numerous indicators to consider, in many cases a detailed analysis will not be required. For example, a majority shareholder in a conventional operating company will consolidate that company as long as no other parties have rights that require further analysis – e.g. a third party holding a call option allowing it to purchase shares in the company.

2.5.20.80   When an in-depth analysis is required, the investor considers all relevant facts and circumstances in assessing whether it controls an investee. The standard identifies a number of indicators of control, which are discussed throughout this chapter, but no hierarchy is provided. Therefore, it requires the investor to analyse all facts and circumstances, and to apply judgement in reaching a conclusion. [*IFRS 10.8*]

2.5.20.90   The three elements of control (Steps 2–4) are cumulative. If any of the steps is failed, then the investor does not control the investee.

2.5.20.100   Control is a question of fact and therefore only one investor can control an investee. [*IFRS 10.16*]

2.5.20.110   If two or more investors need to act together to direct the relevant activities of an investee, then they can collectively control the investee. In this case, if no single investor can direct the activities of the investee without the co-operation of another investor, then no single investor controls the investee. The investors assess whether the investee is a joint arrangement, an associate or an investment to which financial instrument accounting applies. For further discussion of collective control and joint arrangements, see 3.6.20. [*IFRS 10.9*]

2.5.20.120   A situation in which several investors have collective control over the *same* relevant activities of an investee is different from a situation in which several investors *each* direct *different* relevant activities of an investee. For further discussion of this issue, see Examples 5A and 5B.

2.5.30 STEP 1: UNDERSTAND INVESTEE

2.5.30.10   Step 1 of the control model involves obtaining a thorough understanding of the investee as preparation for assessing the three elements of control in Steps 2–4. However, as noted in 2.5.20.70, in many cases a detailed analysis will not be required.

2.5.40 Identify investee: Entity vs silo

2.5.40.10   Control by an investor is generally assessed at the level of the legal entity. However, an investor may have control over only specified assets and liabilities of the legal entity. In certain cases, the investor treats that portion of the entity as a deemed separate entity (a silo). [*IFRS 10.B76*]

2.5.40.20   In effect, a silo is a ring-fenced group of assets, liabilities and equity within an entity. A silo exists only if:
- specified assets of an investee are the only source of payment for specified liabilities of, or specified other interests in, an investee; and
- parties other than those with the specified liability have no rights or obligations in respect of the assets related to that liability (specified assets) or to residual cash flows from those assets. [*IFRS 10.B76–B77*]

2.5.40.30   If these circumstances exist, then the assets, liabilities and equity of the silo are separate from the overall entity such that:
- none of those assets can be used to pay other obligations of the entity; and
- those assets are the only source of payment for specified liabilities of the silo. [*IFRS 10.B77*]

2.5.40.40   The silo criteria in 2.5.40.20 form a legally based test and there is no provision in the standard for the criteria to be met based on the probability of claims being made against the specified assets. This means, for example, that an entity could not argue that a silo exists on the basis that bankruptcy is remote and therefore that the criteria are unlikely to be relevant in practice.

EXAMPLE 1 – INVESTEE – UMBRELLA FUND

2.5.40.50   Umbrella Fund F is an open-ended investment fund with two sub-funds that are cells within the legal entity.

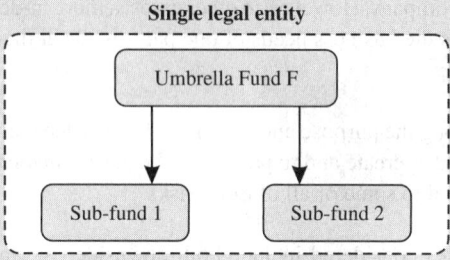

Single legal entity

Umbrella Fund F

Sub-fund 1   Sub-fund 2

2.5.40.60   The following facts are relevant to the set-up of the sub-funds.
- The structure is a protected-cell regime such that the assets of each sub-fund are not available to meet the liabilities of the other sub-fund, including in the event of insolvency.
- Any contract entered into by Sub-fund 1 contains an implied term that the counterparty does not have access to the assets of Sub-fund 2, and vice versa for contracts entered into by Sub-fund 2.
- No liquidity assistance is available from F.

2.5.40.70   In this example, each of the sub-funds is a silo for which control is assessed separately.

2.5.40.80   Example 1 is simplistic, because it ignores the fact that the governing body of the umbrella fund would typically have the discretion to allocate costs that are not directly attributable to a particular sub-fund – e.g. asset manager's fees, custodian's fees, administrator's fees and audit fees. An issue arises over whether such allocations cause the structure to fail the silo test outlined in 2.5.40.20; this is because the standard refers to 'none' of the silo's assets being used to pay other obligations of the entity. [*IFRS 10.B77*]

2.5.40.90   However, in our view such an arrangement to allocate insignificant operating costs would not cause the silo test to fail for the following reasons.

- The specified liabilities of a silo are not restricted to those that are *directly* attributable to the silo – i.e. they could include liabilities that are attributed to the silo by management. In the context of Example 1, the attribution of management costs would be made by the board of Umbrella Fund F.
- If the phrase 'specified' were interpreted literally, then it is likely that silos would be very uncommon, and there is no indication that this was the IASB's intention; this is because we expect that most potential silos will have management expenses of some sort.

2.5.40.100   In our view, there can be NCI in a silo. This is because there is nothing in the standard to suggest that only the controlling party (parent) can have an interest in the net assets of the silo after specified obligations. For a discussion of the accounting for NCI, see 2.5.450.

2.5.50   Determine purpose and design of investee

2.5.50.10   Understanding the purpose and design of the investee is important, because it can play a role in the judgement applied by the investor in all areas of the control model. In many cases, the purpose and design will be straightforward and will not require any specific analysis – e.g. for a conventional operating company. However, in other cases, a more in-depth analysis will be required – e.g. a structure that meets the business needs of one party while at the same time providing financing to another party.

2.5.50.20   Assessing the purpose and design of the investee includes considering the risks that the investee was designed to create and to pass on to the parties involved in the transaction, and whether the investor is exposed to some or all of those risks.

2.5.50.30   The risks considered include both downside risk and the potential for upside return. Other items to consider may include:
- involvement and decisions made at the investee's inception;
- contractual arrangements such as call rights, put rights or liquidation rights established at the investee's inception;
- circumstances in which the relevant activities occur – e.g. only when particular circumstances arise or events occur (see Examples 4A, 4B, 5A and 5B); and
- the investor's commitment to ensuring that the investee continues to operate as designed. [*IFRS 10.B51–B54*]

2.5.50.40   Purpose and design is relevant in all areas of the control model, with the following specific references in this chapter and in chapter 5.10. [*IFRS 10.B5*]

AREA OF THE CONTROL MODEL	REFERENCE
Step 1: Understand the investee	
Identifying the relevant activities of the investee	2.5.70.50, 180, Examples 4A–4B
Determining how decisions about the relevant activities are made	2.5.80.40
Step 2: Power over the relevant activities	
Identifying substantive rights	2.5.100.60

Area of the control model	Reference
Potential voting rights	2.5.140.70
Relevant activities not directed through voting rights	2.5.170.10, Example 14
Step 3: Variability of returns	
Analysing risks to which the investee was designed to be exposed	2.5.240
Step 4: Linkage	
Application to decision makers other than fund managers	2.5.290.30
Application to fund managers – strength of kick-out rights	2.5.370.110
Assessment on a continuous basis	2.5.410.10
Disclosure	
General	5.10.50.20
Characteristics of a structured entity	5.10.210.60
Interests in unconsolidated structured entities	5.10.250.30, 50, Example 4

EXAMPLE 2 – PURPOSE AND DESIGN

2.5.50.50   Company X and Bank B collaborate to set up a structure that facilitates the securitisation of X's trade receivables. B holds the residual equity units in the entity. Under the arrangement, X will continue to manage the collection of the receivables.

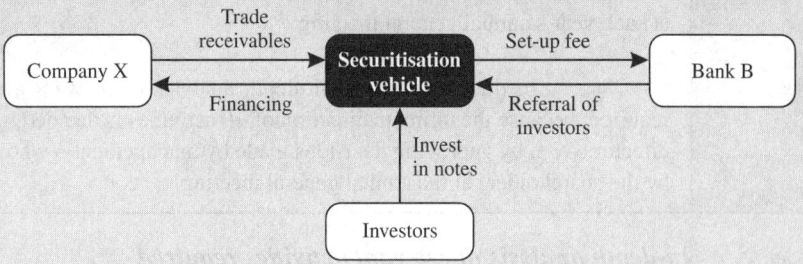

2.5.50.60   The structure is considered to be beneficial to both parties.
- X will obtain financing for its operations, thereby improving its cash flows and operational performance indicators.
- B will receive a set-up fee and can market the investment vehicle to investors.

2.5.50.70   In this example, and after considering all facts and circumstances, X concludes that overall the purpose and design of the vehicle is to give it greater access to liquidity as a financing vehicle for its operations. This conclusion is used in the analysis of control – e.g. for the identification of the relevant activities and to determine which party holds power.

2.5.60 Identify relevant activities of investee

2.5.60.10   The 'relevant activities' of the investee are the activities of the investee that *significantly* affect the investee's returns. [*IFRS 10.10, A*]

2.5.60.20   In many investees, a range of operating and financing activities significantly affect returns. For example:
- sales of goods;
- management of financial assets;
- acquisitions and disposals of operating assets;
- management of research and development activities; and
- determination of the funding structure. [*IFRS 10.B11*]

2.5.60.30   In such cases, the decisions affecting returns may be linked to decisions such as establishing operating and capital decisions (e.g. budgets) and appointing, remunerating and terminating key management personnel or other service providers. These are generally the relevant activities of conventional operating companies and further analysis would not normally be necessary. [*IFRS 10.B12, B16*]

EXAMPLE 3 – RELEVANT ACTIVITIES – CONVENTIONAL OPERATING COMPANY

2.5.60.40   Company X is a furniture manufacturer and retailer that is listed on a securities exchange, where its shares are widely traded. X has a full range of activities that significantly affect its returns, including: decisions about capital additions to production facilities, decisions on financing agreements, decisions on the product range, selection of suppliers and production schedules, and decisions on pricing. The overall decision making is done by key management personnel, who are appointed by the board of directors. The board is appointed by the shareholders at each year's annual general meeting.

2.5.60.50   In this example, an in-depth analysis of relevant activities is not required, because the ultimate direction of *all* activities is decided by the board of directors – i.e. by approving decisions made by management – who are appointed by the shareholders at the annual general meeting.

2.5.70 *In-depth analysis of relevant activities required*

2.5.70.10   In some cases, identifying the relevant activity or activities of an investee may not be as straightforward as the discussion in 2.5.60. The following scenarios may make the analysis more complex:
- the relevant activities take place outside the investee (see 2.5.70.110 and 75.80);
- the relevant activities occur at different times (see 2.5.75);
- there appear to be no relevant activities; or
- there are multiple relevant activities managed by different parties, but it is unclear which relevant activity (activities) most significantly affects the investee's returns.

2.5.70.20   For example, investees with multiple parties being associated with different relevant activities can arise:

- if the assets are managed by one party and the funding is managed by another party; or
- in the case of multi-seller conduits or multi-seller securitisations. [*IFRS 10.BC86*]

2.5.70.30   In our experience, an in-depth analysis of relevant activities is more likely to be required if the investee is directed by rights other than voting rights (see 2.5.170). Although it is theoretically possible to have an investee with no relevant activities, we expect it to be rare in practice.

2.5.70.40   The following flowchart outlines the steps that an investor may consider in an in-depth analysis of relevant activities.

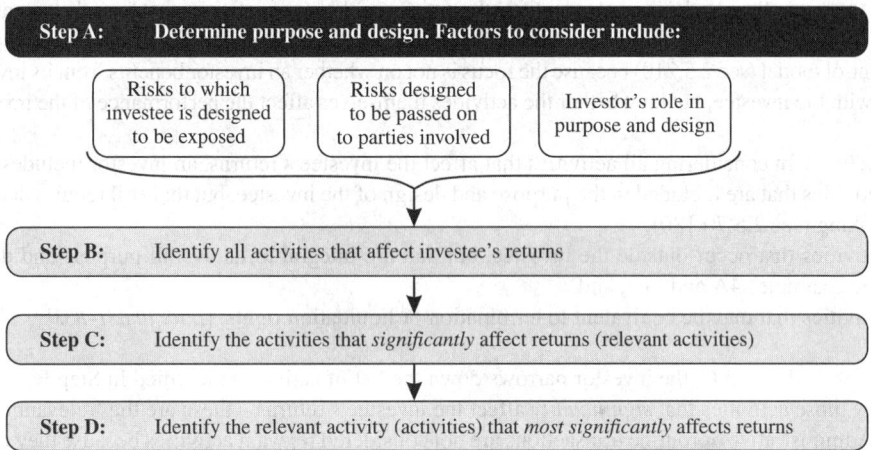

2.5.70.50   Step A in the flowchart relates to all steps in the control model; it is discussed in more detail in 2.5.50. In particular, although the investee's purpose and design is not itself a relevant activity, it forms a lens through which the analysis of relevant activities can be carried out. [*IFRS 10.B5, BC79*]

2.5.70.60   The analysis of risks to which the investee is designed to be exposed focuses on the specific risks that are key to the design of the investee, and not every risk to which it has exposure (see also 2.5.240.10). Examples of risks may include, but are not limited to, the following.
- *Credit risk* – i.e. the risk that the investee's debtors will default on all or part of their obligations to the investee.
- *Interest rate risk* – i.e. the risk that the interest payments on a floating rate financial instrument will vary or that the fair value of a fixed rate financial instrument will change based on interest rate fluctuations.

2.5.70.70   The analysis of how these risks are passed on to parties involved with the investee is based on the specific facts and circumstances, including but not limited to the following factors:
- the investee's activities;
- the terms of its contracts;
- the nature of the involvement;
- how the instruments issued by the investee were marketed to and negotiated with potential investors; and
- which parties participated significantly in the investee's design or redesign.

2.5.70.80   In addition, the analysis considers the investor's role in the purpose and design. As the investor becomes more involved, it may have more incentive to ensure that it has power over the investee's relevant activities.

2.5.70.90   The progression through Steps B to D acts as a filter and assists in carrying out the analysis of relevant activities in a structured manner. In many cases, Step C will determine the final outcome of the analysis. However, Step D is required if different investors have the ability to direct different relevant activities that occur at the same time, or different relevant activities that occur at different times (see Examples 5A and 5B). [*IFRS 10.13, B13*]

2.5.70.100   In Step B, the investor identifies the entire population of activities that have the potential to affect the investee's returns or performance. This is different from the variability of returns in Step 3 of the control model (see 2.5.210) because the focus is not on whether an investor benefits from its involvement with the investee, but on whether the activities themselves affect the performance of the investee.

2.5.70.110   In considering all activities that affect the investee's returns, an investor includes:
- activities that are included in the purpose and design of the investee, but that still require decision making (see 2.5.70.180);
- activities that occur outside the investee, but that are integral to its overall purpose and design (see Examples 4A and 5B); and
- activities that may be equivalent to termination or liquidation rights. [*IFRS 10.B51–B53*]

2.5.70.120   In Step C, the investor narrows down the list of activities identified in Step B to focus on only those activities that *significantly* affect the investee's returns – these are the 'relevant activities'. Administrative or routine transactions are not considered relevant activities because they do not significantly affect the returns of the investee. In many cases, only a single party directs all relevant activities, in which case no further analysis is required. [*IFRS 10.A*]

2.5.70.130   In Step D, the investor identifies the relevant activity (activities) that *most significantly* affects the returns of the investee. It is this activity (activities) that is key to the power analysis in Step 2 of the control model (see 2.5.90) if different relevant activities are directed by different parties.

EXAMPLE 4A – RELEVANT ACTIVITIES – SECURITISATION VEHICLE

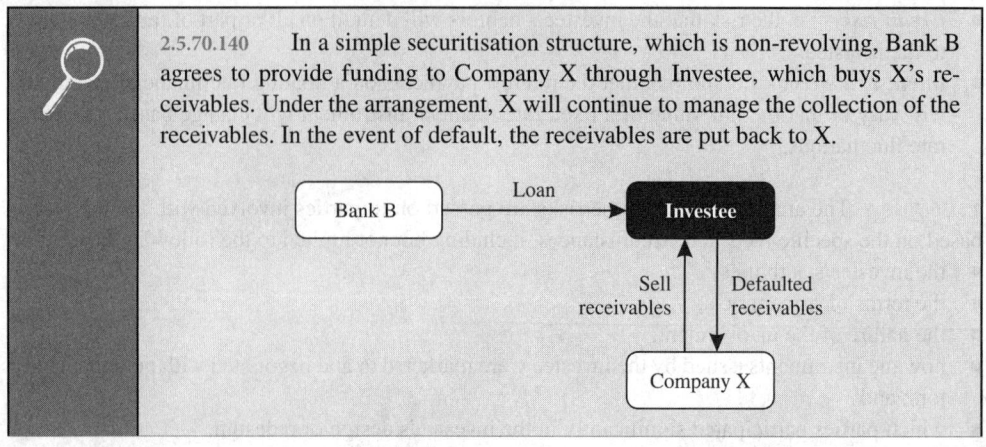

2.5.70.140   In a simple securitisation structure, which is non-revolving, Bank B agrees to provide funding to Company X through Investee, which buys X's receivables. Under the arrangement, X will continue to manage the collection of the receivables. In the event of default, the receivables are put back to X.

2.5.70.150   In this example, and after considering all facts and circumstances, X carries out its analysis of relevant activities as follows.

- *Step A:* X concludes that the overall purpose and design of Investee is to provide it with liquidity as a financing vehicle for its operations. In reaching its conclusion, X considered the following.
  - The risk to which Investee is designed to be exposed is credit risk.
  - Through the put of receivables in default, Investee is designed to transfer that credit risk back to X.
  - Although X relied on B's expertise in setting up the securitisation structure, this was done at X's request and X approved the structure.
- *Step B:* Following initial set-up, Investee has two activities.
  - Routine servicing of receivables.
  - Managing receivables in default.
- *Step C:* Of the two activities identified in Step B, the one that significantly affects the investee's returns is managing receivables in default.
- *Step D:* No analysis is required in Step D because only one activity has been identified in Step C – i.e. the activity that most significantly affects Investee's returns is managing receivables in default.

2.5.70.160   In this example, the terms of the put for receivables in default are integral to the overall arrangement and the establishment of Investee, notwithstanding that managing receivables in default occurs outside Investee. Therefore, the agreement was considered together with the founding documents of Investee in concluding that the relevant activity was managing receivables in default. [*IFRS 10.B.Ex11*]

2.5.70.170   In addition, in determining that managing receivables in default is the relevant activity, the probability of default is not considered in the analysis, because this is the *only* decision that can significantly affect the returns of Investee. [*IFRS 10.B.Ex12*]

2.5.70.180   Activities that are predetermined as part of the investee's design are not relevant activities because they do not have the potential to affect returns. However, careful analysis is required before concluding that relevant activities are predetermined. Predetermined activities are implemented at the outset of the investee with no chance of changing. Conversely, activities might be predefined – i.e. set within some parameters at the outset but requiring decision making within those parameters during the life of the investee.

EXAMPLE 4B – RELEVANT ACTIVITIES – SECURITISATION VEHICLE – PREDETERMINED ACTIVITIES

2.5.70.190   Continuing Example 4A, the decision made at inception of the structure to transfer the receivables is not considered in the assessment of relevant activities because it was predetermined at the outset. The portfolio transferred to Investee cannot affect Investee's returns because its operations only begin once the portfolio is transferred and no subsequent decision making is required.

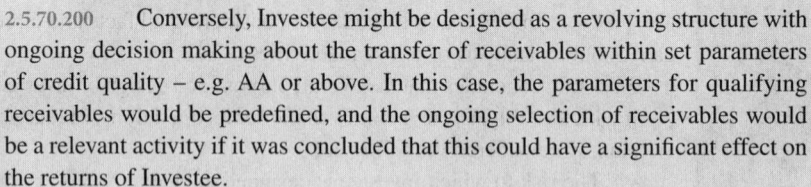

> 2.5.70.200   Conversely, Investee might be designed as a revolving structure with ongoing decision making about the transfer of receivables within set parameters of credit quality – e.g. AA or above. In this case, the parameters for qualifying receivables would be predefined, and the ongoing selection of receivables would be a relevant activity if it was concluded that this could have a significant effect on the returns of Investee.

2.5.73   *Single-asset, single-lessee lease vehicles*

2.5.73.10   The IFRS Interpretations Committee discussed whether a lessee's right to use the leased asset during the lease period gives the lessee decision-making rights over the relevant activities of a single asset leasing vehicle that is a structured entity (see 5.10.190). The Committee decided that it does not. [*IU 05-15*]

2.5.73.20   The Committee noted that as a result of entering into a lease, regardless of whether it is a finance lease or an operating lease, the leasing vehicle (the lessor) has two rights: a right to receive lease payments, and a right to the residual value of the leased asset at the end of the lease. Therefore, the activities that affect the vehicle's returns relate to managing the returns derived from these rights (e.g. managing the credit risk on rentals and/or managing the leased asset at the end of the lease term). The Committee was of the view that the lessee's right to use the leased asset for a period of time would not, in isolation, typically give the lessee decision-making rights over these activities. However, this does not mean that the lessee can never control the lessor vehicle. [*IU 05-15*]

2.5.73.30   The Committee was of the view that the relevant activities of the vehicle are those that relate to managing the right to receive lease payments and the residual value of the leased asset at the end of the lease. Therefore, in addition to the lessee, parties involved in the vehicle – e.g. lenders and/or a leasing company – need to assess whether they have power over these relevant activities, and therefore meet the power test for consolidation.

2.5.75   *Different relevant activities at different times*

2.5.75.10   For some investees, different existing investors may have decision-making rights over different relevant activities, and those relevant activities occur at different times. In such cases, consistent with the general principles in 2.5.70, it is necessary to identify the relevant activity that most significantly affects the investee's returns. [*IFRS 10.B13*]

EXAMPLE 5A – ASSESSING RELEVANT ACTIVITIES – DIFFERENT ACTIVITIES WITHIN THE INVESTEE AT DIFFERENT TIMES

> 2.5.75.20   Two investors, B and C, form an investee that is engaged in the development of a medical product (which will be registered in the name of the investee), and its subsequent manufacture and marketing. B has the unilateral ability to make decisions related to development, and C has the unilateral ability to make decisions about manufacturing and marketing. All of these activities are relevant activities that take place within the investee.

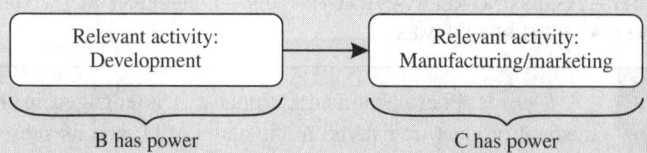

B has power   C has power

2.5.75.30 On formation, B and C each need to determine the activity that most significantly affects the investee's returns, considering:
- the factors that determine the profit margin, revenue and value of the investee, as well as the value of the medical product;
- the effect of each investor's decision-making authority on the investee's returns;
- the uncertainty of, and effort required to obtain, regulatory approval; and
- which investor controls the medical product if the development phase is successful. [*IFRS 10.B13*]

Scenario 1

2.5.75.40 At the formation date, both parties conclude that the activity that most significantly affects the returns of the investee is development up to the point of receiving regulatory approval. Accordingly, B and C both conclude that B has power over the relevant activities of the investee.

2.5.75.50 B and C would subsequently reassess control if and when regulatory approval is received, because the only decisions left to be made after that time would be manufacturing and marketing decisions, and these are made by C. B would no longer have any ongoing decision-making rights over the investee – i.e. the facts and circumstances would indicate that there have been changes to one of the three elements of control (see 2.5.410).

Scenario 2

2.5.75.60 B and C both conclude that the activity that most significantly affects the returns of the investee is the manufacturing and marketing. In this case, B and C both conclude that C has power from the outset – i.e. from the outset, C has power to make the most significant decisions, taking all future time periods together.

2.5.75.70 The analysis in Example 5A does not apply to scenarios in which there is only one existing investor – i.e. it cannot be argued that an existing investor does not consolidate an entity because it intends to divest its interest before a more relevant activity starts. [*IFRS 10.B13*]

2.5.75.80 In other scenarios, investees may have relevant activities that occur outside the investee. In our view, it does not matter whether relevant activities occurring at different times are within or outside the investee (see 2.5.70.110). We believe that the same analysis applies in both cases (see Example 5B).

EXAMPLE 5B – ASSESSING RELEVANT ACTIVITIES – DIFFERENT ACTIVITIES WITHIN AND OUTSIDE
THE INVESTEE AT DIFFERENT TIMES

2.5.75.90   Pharmaceutical Company D is engaged in the development of a medical product (registered in the name of D) and its subsequent manufacturing and marketing. D has completed all development activities, except for a series of clinical trials that need to be conducted to obtain market approval for the medical product. To do this, D approaches Company E, which specialises in managing such clinical trials.

2.5.75.100   D and E enter into the following agreement to conduct the required clinical trials.
- Company F is set up to conduct the clinical trials.
- E provides all of the financing to F.
- For the duration of the clinical trials, D grants F a right to the intellectual property relating to the medical product free of charge. D retains the ownership of all intellectual property related to the medical product and any new intellectual property created by F is automatically transferred to D.
- Subject to the trial design set out in the agreement and regulatory requirements, E has the unilateral ability to make decisions about the clinical trials.
- D has the unilateral ability to make decisions about manufacturing and marketing, which will be conducted by D.
- If market approval for the medical product is not obtained, then D has no payment obligations towards E or F.
- If market approval for the medical product is obtained, then F will receive royalties based on the sales.

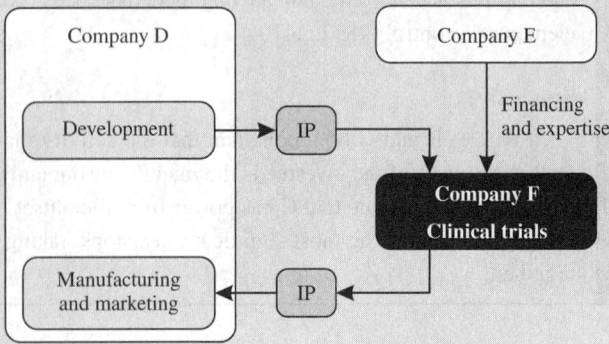

2.5.75.110   We believe that in this example, manufacturing and marketing are relevant activities to be considered in the assessment of who has the power over F because these activities affect F's returns through the royalty. Furthermore, we believe that these activities are closely related to the investee and so are, in substance, an integral part of the investee's overall activities, even though they occur outside the legal boundaries of the investee. Accordingly, manufacturing and marketing, for which decisions are made by D, are relevant activities of F. [*IFRS 10.B52–B53*]

2.5.75.120   Similar to Example 5A, companies D and E need to determine which activity (activities) most significantly affects the investee's returns in order to determine who has power over F (see 2.5.70.40 for the steps to analyse the relevant activities). In this example, D and E conclude that the relevant activities that most significantly affect F's returns are manufacturing and marketing. Therefore, D has control over F in this example. [*IFRS 10.B13*]

2.5.80   Determine how decisions about relevant activities are made

2.5.80.10   Determining how decisions about the relevant activities are made is key, and represents a 'gating' question that is relevant in Step 2 of the control analysis (assessing power – see 2.5.90). This gating question seeks to determine whether:
- voting rights are relevant in assessing whether the investor has power over the investee – i.e. the investee is controlled by voting instruments; or
- voting rights are not relevant in assessing whether the investor has power over the investee – i.e. the investee is controlled by means of other rights. [*IFRS 10.B6, B8*]

2.5.80.20   When the investee is controlled by equity instruments, with associated and proportionate voting rights, the assessment of power focuses on which investor, if any, has sufficient voting rights to direct the investee's relevant activities; this is in the absence of any additional arrangements that alter the decision making. In the most straightforward cases, the investor holding the majority of the voting rights has power over (and controls) the investee. [*IFRS 10.11, B6*]

2.5.80.30   Some investees are designed so that voting rights are not relevant to the determination of power, but instead other rights are relevant (see 2.5.170). These entities generally meet the structured entity definition of IFRS 12 (see 5.10.190). [*IFRS 10.B8*]

2.5.80.40   For more complex cases, a number of factors are relevant in determining how decisions over relevant activities are made – i.e. by voting or other rights. This involves an analysis of the following factors, which require the investor to look forward to the elements of the control model for the purpose of concluding under Step 1 (understanding the investee):
- what the purpose and design of the investee is (see 2.5.50);
- what the relevant activities are (see 2.5.60);
- whether the investor is exposed to variable returns from its involvement with the investee (Step 3 of the control model – see 2.5.210); and
- whether the investor has the ability to use its power over the investee to affect the amount of its returns (Step 4 of the control model – see 2.5.270). [*IFRS 10.B3, B7*]

2.5.85   *Governance structures*

2.5.85.10   Relevant activities of conventional operating companies are generally the decisions over the range of operating and financing activities (see 2.5.60.20–30). If these decisions are made by the investee's board members, then voting rights are generally relevant because the board members are appointed or removed by the shareholders. [*IFRS 10.B11–B12*]

2.5.85.20   In certain jurisdictions, some or all members of the governing board are independent and/or are required by law to 'act in the best interest of the entity'. Nevertheless, in our view a shareholder with the power to appoint or remove the majority of the investee's board members generally has power over the relevant activities in that situation, even though the shareholder may by law be precluded from directing the decisions of the management of the other entity.

2.5.85.30   When determining how decisions about relevant activities are made, a clear understanding of the investee's governance structure may be required. In many countries, the governing body is the board of directors; however, in some countries there may be layers of governance. Although the law may provide for different bodies to have certain rights and obligations, in assessing how the decisions about relevant activities are made, an entity considers any shareholders' agreements that amend these 'typical' rights and obligations (see 2.5.150).

EXAMPLE 6A – LAYERS OF GOVERNANCE STRUCTURE (1)

2.5.85.40   Company A has two governing bodies – i.e. a supervisory board and an executive board. The executive board determines the detailed operating and financing activities, whereas the supervisory board has a more detached role in overseeing the actions of management on behalf of shareholders and employees.

2.5.85.50   Under these circumstances, the executive board is generally the governing body that makes the decisions about relevant activities.

2.5.85.60   In some cases, the role of the supervisory board may be altered to give it much more authority over the entity's operating and financing activities. This is becoming increasingly common as the focus on corporate governance increases.

EXAMPLE 6B – LAYERS OF GOVERNANCE STRUCTURE (2)

2.5.85.70   Modifying Example 6A, investors' returns are significantly affected by the decisions of the supervisory board, such as approval of annual budgets, operational planning and appointing and terminating members of the executive board.

2.5.85.80   In this case, it might be appropriate to conclude that the supervisory board is the key governing body for the purpose of determining how decisions about relevant activities are made. Judgement is required based on facts and circumstances.

2.5.90   STEP 2: POWER OVER RELEVANT ACTIVITIES

2.5.90.10   Step 2 of the control model uses the results of Step 1 (see 2.5.30) and is the first of the three elements of control. However, as noted in 2.5.20.70, in many cases a detailed analysis will not be required.

2.5.90.20   The following flowchart summarises the analysis required under Step 2.

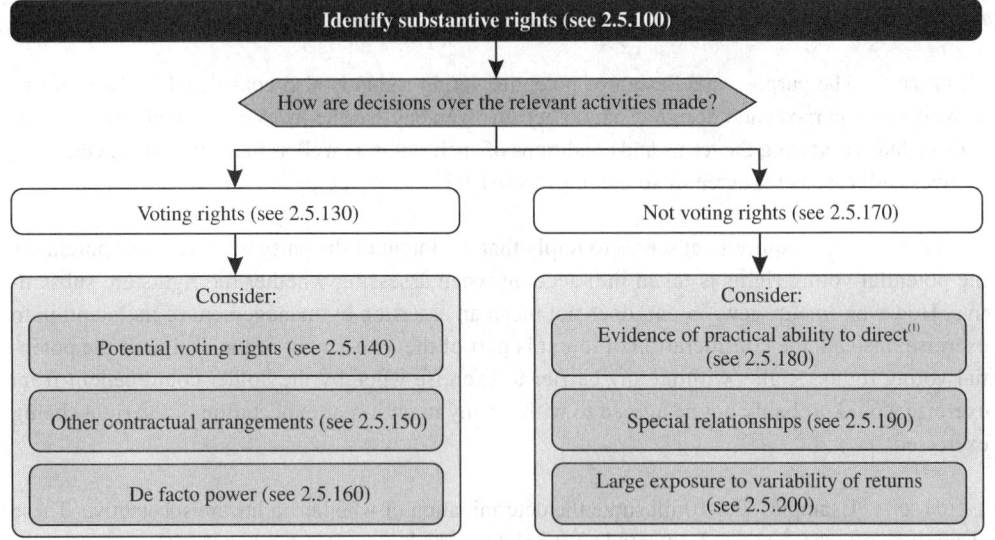

Note
1. Greatest weighting placed on this factor.

2.5.100   Identify substantive rights

2.5.100.10   An investor considers both substantive rights that it holds and substantive rights held by others; voting rights held by an investor and potential voting rights – e.g. a call option over shares of the investee – are common forms of substantive rights (see 2.5.140). [*IFRS 10.B22*]

2.5.100.20   To be substantive, rights need to be exercisable when decisions about the relevant activities are required to be made, and the holder needs to have a practical ability to exercise those rights. [*IFRS 10.B24*]

2.5.100.30   Substantive rights exercisable by other parties, if they are not merely protective (see 2.5.110), can prevent an investor from controlling the investee, even if they only give their holders the ability to approve or block decisions that relate to the investee's relevant activities. This can also apply when other parties hold potential voting rights, kick-out rights or similar rights. [*IFRS 10.B25, BC106*]

2.5.100.40   Determining whether rights are substantive requires judgement, taking into account all available facts and circumstances. Factors to consider include:
- whether there are barriers that prevent the holder from exercising the rights;
- how many parties need to agree for the rights to become exercisable or operational; and
- whether the party holding the rights would benefit from their exercise – e.g. because the rights are in the money. [*IFRS 10.B23*]

2.5.100.50   It may be that a number of parties need to agree for the rights to become exercisable or operational. In this case, the more parties needed to agree to exercise the rights, the less likely it is that the rights are substantive. However, there might be a mechanism (such as the board of directors) providing those parties with the ability to exercise their rights collectively. The absence of such a mechanism is an indicator that the rights might not be substantive. [*IFRS 10.B23*]

2.5.100.60   The purpose and design of potential voting rights is also considered in the analysis, as well as the purpose and design of any other involvement that the investor has with the investee. This includes assessing the terms and conditions of such rights as well as the apparent expectations, motives and reasons for agreeing to them. [*IFRS 10.B48*]

2.5.100.70   This requirement seems to imply that the intent of the party who writes or purchases the potential voting rights is taken into account when assessing whether the rights are substantive. However, in our view 'intent' does not mean an assertion by management of its intention to exercise; instead, the consideration of intent is part of the assessment of the design of the potential voting rights. Rights without any barrier to exercise whereby the holder could benefit from exercise would probably not be agreed to without any intention or expectation of the rights being exercised.

2.5.100.80   Examples 7 to 10 illustrate the determination of whether rights are substantive. These examples are in the context of potential voting rights, which are relevant when the relevant activities of the investee are directed through voting rights.

2.5.110   *Protective rights*

2.5.110.10   Protective rights are related to fundamental changes in the activities of an investee, or are rights that apply only in exceptional circumstances. As such, they cannot give the holder power or prevent other parties from having power and therefore control over an investee. Not all rights contingent on future events are protective. [*IFRS 10.14, A, B26–B27*]

2.5.110.20   Rights related to the following are likely to be protective rights, because they relate to fundamental changes of the investee:
- amendments to the entity's constitution;
- the liquidation of the entity or commencement of bankruptcy proceedings;
- share issues or repurchases; or
- the sale of a significant portion of the entity's operating assets. [*IFRS 10.B28*]

2.5.110.30   In some cases, protective rights may become exercisable when certain events or conditions arise – e.g. if an entity breaches a covenant attached to a borrowing arrangement – which may require a reassessment of the control conclusion. For further discussion, see 2.5.410.

2.5.120   *Franchise agreements*

2.5.120.10   Franchisor rights do not necessarily prevent parties other than the franchisor from having power over the franchisee. In many cases, the franchisor's rights are likely to be protective rights (see 2.5.110), because they are designed to protect the franchise brand. In that case, the relevant activities of the franchisee may be directed by the franchisee owner rather than by the franchisor. [*IFRS 10.B29–B32*]

2.5.120.20 The less the direct financial support provided by the franchisor and the lower the franchisor's exposure to variability of returns from the franchisee under Step 3 (variability of returns – see 2.5.210), the more likely it is that the franchisor has only protective rights. [*IFRS 10.B33*]

2.5.130 Relevant activities directed through voting rights

2.5.130.10 An investor can have power over an investee when the investee's relevant activities are directed through voting rights if the investor:
- holds the majority of the voting rights (see 2.5.130.20); or
- holds less than a majority of the voting rights but:
  - holds substantive potential voting rights (see 2.5.140);
  - holds rights arising from other contractual arrangements, including an agreement with other vote holders (see 2.5.150); and/or
  - holds voting rights sufficient to unilaterally direct the relevant activities of the investee (see 2.5.160) – i.e. de facto power. [*IFRS 10.B34–B50*]

2.5.130.20 The investor who holds the majority of the voting rights has power over the relevant activities of the investee, unless:
- the voting rights are not substantive;
- the voting rights do not provide the investor with the current ability to direct the relevant activities of the investee; or
- another party has existing rights to direct the relevant activities of the investee and that party is not an agent of the investor (see 2.5.270). [*IFRS 10.B35–B37*]

2.5.130.30 For example, an investor does not control an investee whose relevant activities are directed by a liquidator or regulator (see Example 22). Additionally, the investor holding a majority of the voting rights might not have control if another investor holds substantive rights sufficient to give it control over the investee.

2.5.130.40 In the context of an acquisition, a contractual agreement may prevent the seller from making certain decisions over the investee without consultation with the acquirer. For the impact of such terms on the assessment of power, see 2.6.240.

2.5.140 *Potential voting rights*

2.5.140.10 Potential voting rights – e.g. a call option over shares of the investee – are a common form of rights that may be substantive. Examples 7 to 10 explore whether potential voting rights are substantive in different circumstances.

EXAMPLE 7 – POTENTIAL VOTING RIGHTS – TIME TO EXERCISE CALL OPTION VS TIMING OF DECISIONS

 2.5.140.20 Company X holds an option to acquire the majority of voting shares in Company Z that is exercisable in 25 days and is in the money. Z has annual shareholders' meetings at which decisions to direct the relevant activities are made.

2.5.140.30   Although the next shareholders' meeting is scheduled for 8 months' time, shareholders can call a special meeting to change the existing policies over relevant activities. However, a requirement to give notice to the other shareholders means that such a meeting cannot be held for at least 30 days.

2.5.140.40   X has rights that are essentially equivalent to those of the ordinary shareholders in Z, because it can exercise its call option before a special shareholder meeting can be held; the call option is also in the money. Based on these factors, X concludes that its call option is substantive, and therefore is considered in its control assessment of Z. [*IFRS 10.B24*]

EXAMPLE 8 – POTENTIAL VOTING RIGHTS – NO BENEFIT FROM EXERCISING CALL OPTION

2.5.140.50   Company X holds an option to acquire Company Y's shares in Company Z. The option is in the money and can be exercised at any time.

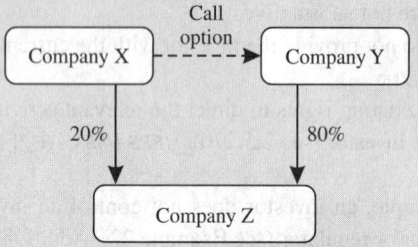

2.5.140.60   If X exercises the option, then the business would be seriously damaged, because Y is the only source of vital know-how, and could lawfully leave the arrangement taking the know-how with it. As a result, X would not benefit from exercising the option and concludes that the call option is not substantive.

2.5.140.70   An investor may have the ability to make a decision unilaterally through a call option over the shares of the investee that becomes exercisable in the event of deadlock. Although the call option cannot be exercised until a deadlock actually arises, this contingency does not limit the power associated with the option; this is because the contingency relates to decision making and the call option is exercisable when it is actually needed. However, determining whether the call option is substantive still requires judgement, taking into account all available facts and circumstances, including the purpose and design of the call option (see 2.5.50). [*IFRS 10.B24*]

EXAMPLE 9 – POTENTIAL VOTING RIGHTS – CALL OPTION EXERCISABLE IN DEADLOCK

2.5.140.80   Company B is owned by Companies X, Y and Z in the ratio of 55:40:5.
• The management and operations of B are governed by a shareholders' agreement that requires the consent of both X and Y.

- X holds a call option over the shares of Y, which is exercisable at fair value in the event of deadlock between the parties.

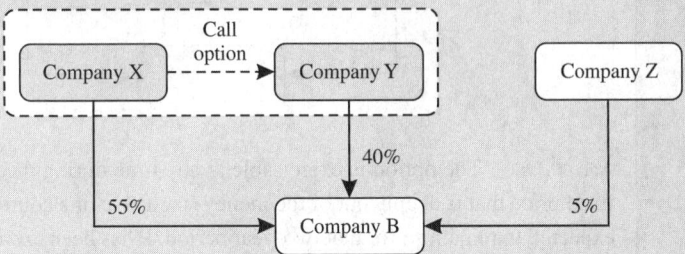

2.5.140.90   If X and Y fail to agree, then the shareholders' agreement includes various non-binding mechanisms designed to help the parties to reach agreement. However, if X and Y ultimately do not reach an agreement, then X is able to exercise its call option to acquire the shares in B held by Y. There are no barriers that would prevent X from exercising the option.

2.5.140.100   X concludes that the call option is substantive, because:
- it is exercisable when it is needed in order to make a relevant decision – i.e. in the event of deadlock; and
- there are no barriers that would prevent X from exercising the option.

2.5.140.110   A change in market conditions alone will not typically cause potential voting rights to become substantive or cease to be substantive. This is because determining whether potential voting rights are substantive is a holistic analysis that takes into account a variety of factors, including market conditions (see 2.5.100.40). However, there could be circumstances in which changes in market conditions, coupled with other factors, result in a different conclusion about whether potential voting rights are substantive. These circumstances could trigger a reassessment of the control conclusion (see 2.5.410). [*IFRS 10.BC124*]

2.5.140.120   Determining whether potential voting rights are in or out of the money may not always be straightforward. For example, potential voting rights could be out of the money when the exercise price is compared with the current market price. However, because the exercise price includes an embedded control premium, the potential voting rights are at or in the money when evaluated on a controlling-interest basis.

EXAMPLE 10 – POTENTIAL VOTING RIGHTS – CALL OPTION DEEPLY OUT OF THE MONEY

2.5.140.130   Company P holds 70% of the voting rights of Company C. Company B holds the remaining 30% of C's voting rights, as well as an option to acquire half of P's voting rights.

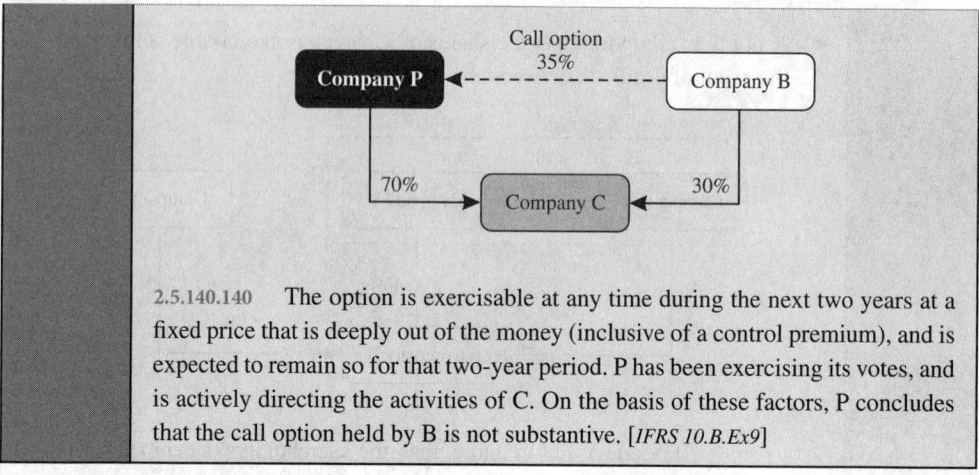

2.5.140.140   The option is exercisable at any time during the next two years at a fixed price that is deeply out of the money (inclusive of a control premium), and is expected to remain so for that two-year period. P has been exercising its votes, and is actively directing the activities of C. On the basis of these factors, P concludes that the call option held by B is not substantive. [*IFRS 10.B.Ex9*]

2.5.150   ***Rights arising from other contractual arrangements***

2.5.150.10   An agreement with other vote holders can give the investor the right to exercise voting rights or to direct enough other vote holders on how to vote, sufficient to give it power. [*IFRS 10.B39*]

EXAMPLE 11A – POWER – SHAREHOLDER AGREEMENT (1)

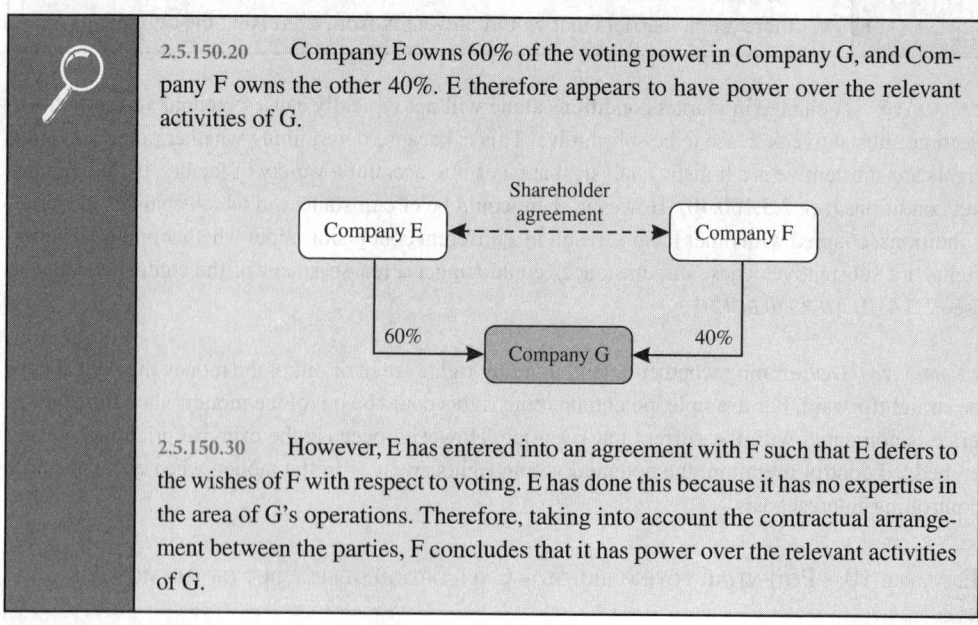

2.5.150.20   Company E owns 60% of the voting power in Company G, and Company F owns the other 40%. E therefore appears to have power over the relevant activities of G.

2.5.150.30   However, E has entered into an agreement with F such that E defers to the wishes of F with respect to voting. E has done this because it has no expertise in the area of G's operations. Therefore, taking into account the contractual arrangement between the parties, F concludes that it has power over the relevant activities of G.

2.5.150.40   However, before concluding that a shareholders' agreement confers power on a particular party, the investor should consider the break-up (termination) terms in the agreement as well as its duration.

EXAMPLE 11B – POWER – SHAREHOLDER AGREEMENT (2)

2.5.150.50 Continuing Example 11A, assume that Company E can discontinue the agreement at any time without penalty. In that case, E concludes that it has power over the relevant activities of Company G, because it can step in and exercise its rights at any time.

2.5.150.60 If a shareholders' agreement has a fixed duration, then depending on the facts and circumstances, it might be appropriate to conclude that the agreement covers too short a period to have any real impact on the power to direct the relevant activities. Although a shareholders' agreement will generally be in writing, this is not a requirement of IFRS. An oral shareholders' agreement may be as important as a written agreement in assessing control.

2.5.150.70 The rights within the arrangement, in combination with the investor's voting rights, can give it the current ability to direct some of the activities of an investee that significantly affect the investee's returns. These factors together might give the investor power over the relevant activities of the investee. [*IFRS 10.B40*]

EXAMPLE 12 – POWER – CONTRACTUAL ARRANGEMENTS

2.5.150.80 Company Z manufactures widgets and Company Y has specialist know-how in that area. As a result, Y and Z have entered into a non-cancellable 10-year contract that outsources all production and pricing decisions to Y.

2.5.150.90 Company X has a 30% voting interest in Z; other voting interests are widely dispersed. During the year, X acquires all of the shares in Y.

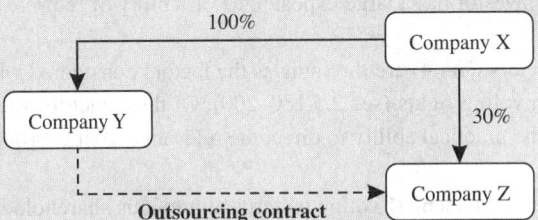

2.5.150.100 Before the acquisition of Y, X concluded that it did not control Z. However, based on the combination of its 30% voting interest in Z and control over the outsourcing contract (via its control of Y), X now concludes that it has power over the relevant activities of Z. The parties will reassess control if and when facts and circumstances change – e.g. on termination of the outsourcing contract (see 2.5.410).

2.5.160 *De facto power*

2.5.160.10 Even without potential voting rights or other contractual rights, when the investor holds significantly more voting rights than any other vote holder or organised group of vote holders, this may be sufficient evidence of power. For example, if a single investor holds 48 percent of the voting rights and the remainder are held by thousands of shareholders, then the investor may determine that it has a sufficiently dominant voting interest to give it power without considering other evidence of power. In other situations, the size of the investor's holding of voting rights relative to the size and dispersion of the holdings of other vote holders may provide sufficient evidence that the investor does not have power – e.g. when there is a concentration of other voting interests among a small group of vote holders. [*IFRS 10.B43–B44, B.Ex4*]

2.5.160.20   Determining whether an investor has de facto power over an investee is usually highly judgemental; it includes assessing the point at which an investor's shareholding in an investee is *sufficient* and the point at which other shareholdings' interests are *sufficiently dispersed*. It could also be difficult for a dominant shareholder to know whether a voting agreement amongst other shareholders exists.

2.5.160.30   In our experience, there may be situations in which the dominant shareholder does not know whether arrangements exist among other shareholders, or whether it is easy for other shareholders to consult with each other. To facilitate the analysis, the investor needs processes in place to allow it to capture publicly available information about other shareholder concentrations and agreements.

2.5.160.40   The smaller the size of the investor's holding of voting rights and the less the dispersion of the holding of other vote holders, the greater the need for additional analysis. In such cases, the standard requires the following additional factors to be considered:
1. voting patterns at previous shareholders' meetings (see 2.5.160.60);
2. evidence of the practical ability to direct the relevant activities;
3. indications of special relationships with the investee; and
4. whether the investor has a large exposure to variability of returns. [*IFRS 10.B45*]

2.5.160.50   Factors (2)–(4) are the same as the factors considered when relevant activities are not directed through voting rights (see 2.5.180–200). Of these factors, the greatest weighting is placed on evidence of the practical ability to direct the relevant activities. [*IFRS 10.B45*]

2.5.160.60   An assessment of voting patterns at previous shareholders' meetings requires consideration of the number of shareholders that typically come to the meetings to vote and *not* how the other shareholders vote – i.e. whether they usually vote the same way as the investor. [*IFRS 10.B45, B.Ex8*]

EXAMPLE 13 – DE FACTO POWER – VOTING PATTERNS

2.5.160.70   Company P holds 35% of the voting rights in Company Z, and three other shareholders (Companies B, C and D) hold 5% each. Numerous other shareholders hold the remaining 50% of voting rights, with none individually holding more than 1%.

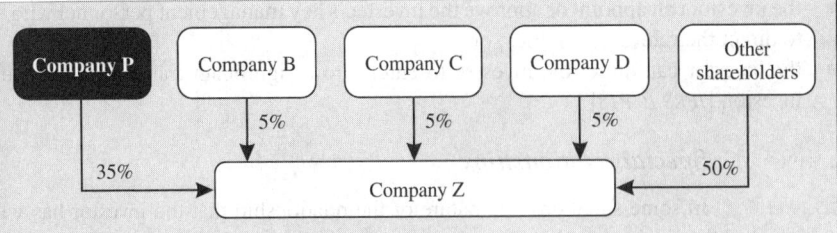

2.5.160.80 The following facts are also relevant for this example.
- Representation of 75% of the voting rights is required for a quorum.
- Once a quorum is established, decisions about relevant activities require majority approval.
- There are no arrangements between other shareholders to consult any of the others or to make collective decisions.
- 80% of voting rights have been cast at all recent shareholders' meetings.

2.5.160.90 Based on the active participation of the other shareholders at shareholders' meetings – 80% of voting rights have been voted at recent meetings – P concludes that it does not have the ability to direct the relevant activities of Z. This is based on the fact that P does not have a majority of the voting rights necessary to pass a resolution unilaterally (35 / 80).

2.5.160.100 Determining the date on which an investor has de facto power over an investee may in practice be a challenging issue. In some situations, it may lead to a conclusion that control is obtained at some point after the initial acquisition of voting interests. At the date on which an investor initially acquires less than a majority of voting rights in an investee, the investor might conclude that it does not have de facto power over the investee if it does not know how other shareholders are likely to behave. As time passes, the investor obtains more information about other shareholders, gains experience from shareholders' meetings and might ultimately conclude that it does have de facto power over the investee. Determining the point at which this happens may require significant judgement. For further discussion of the acquisition accounting in such cases, see 2.6.1140.

2.5.170 Relevant activities not directed through voting rights

2.5.170.10 If voting rights are not relevant to the analysis, then the investor considers the purpose and design of the investee (see 2.5.50) and the following factors:
- evidence of the practical ability to direct the relevant activities (see 2.5.180);
- indications of special relationships with the investee (see 2.5.190); and
- whether the investor has a large exposure to variability of returns (see 2.5.200). [*IFRS 10.B17*]

2.5.170.20 When these three factors are considered, the greatest weighting is placed on evidence of the practical ability to direct the relevant activities. [*IFRS 10.B21*]

2.5.180 *Evidence of practical ability to direct relevant activities*

2.5.180.10 In some circumstances, it may be difficult to determine whether an investor's rights are sufficient to give it power over an investee. In those circumstances, an investor considers any evidence that it has the practical ability to direct the relevant activities. Examples of such circumstances are when:

- the investor can appoint or approve the investee's key management personnel who have the ability to direct the relevant activities; or
- the investor can direct the investee to enter into a significant transaction for the benefit of the investor. [*IFRS 10.B18*]

2.5.190   *Special relationships*

2.5.190.10   In some situations, the nature of the relationship that the investor has with the investee may suggest that the investor has more than a passive interest in the investee. This could indicate that the investor has other related rights or provide evidence of existing power over the investee. [*IFRS 10.B19*]

2.5.190.20   The following suggest that the investor has more than a passive interest in the investee and, in combination with other rights, may indicate power:
- the investee's key management personnel who direct the relevant activities are current or previous employees of the investor;
- the investee's operations are dependent on the investor – e.g. for funding, critical technology or intellectual property; for additional considerations for franchisors, see 2.5.120;
- a significant portion of the investee's activities either involve or are conducted on behalf of the investor; and/or
- the investor's exposure to the returns from its involvement with the investee are disproportionately greater than its voting rights. [*IFRS 10.B19*]

2.5.190.30   Reputational risk is *not* an indicator of power in its own right. However, it may be a factor to consider together with other facts and circumstances. It may create an incentive for the investor to secure its rights in the investee, which may give it power over the investee. [*IFRS 10.BC37–BC39*]

2.5.190.40   Employees and key management personnel are not defined in IFRS 10. As such, we expect the definitions provided in IFRS 2 (see 4.5.490) and IAS 24 (see 5.5.40) to apply. [*IFRS 2.A, IAS 24.9*]

2.5.190.50   Economic dependence in itself does not lead to consolidation. Therefore, consolidation does not arise simply on the basis of a large or even a single customer whose needs dominate the decisions made by a supplier in order to protect its customer base. However, a combination of voting rights and, for example, a shareholders' agreement that provides a party with rights to direct the relevant activities of the investee could lead to consolidation. [*IFRS 10.B40*]

2.5.200   *Large exposure to variability of returns*

2.5.200.10   As part of assessing whether an investor controls an investee, the investor determines whether it is exposed to variable returns from its involvement with the investee (Step 3 of the control model – see 2.5.210). A large exposure to variability of returns is likely to mean that the investor has power over the investee; however, a large exposure to variability of returns is not, on its own, determinative. [*IFRS 10.B20*]

EXAMPLE 14 – POWER – EMPLOYEE BENEFIT VEHICLE

2.5.200.20   Company C grants share options to its employees, subject to a service condition (see 4.5.380). C establishes Trust T for the purpose of acquiring and holding the shares that will be used to settle C's obligation under the share-based payment scheme (see 4.5.2390).

2.5.200.30   The following facts are also relevant for this example.

- T has five trustees, two appointed by C, two appointed by the employees, and one independent trustee. By law, the trustees are responsible for making decisions for the benefit of the employees.
- In practice, T only buys, holds and disposes of shares to suit the wishes of C in relation to its share-based payment scheme.
- T has no significant equity and the acquisition of shares is funded by a loan from C. The proceeds from the exercise price paid by the employees are required to be used to repay the loan.
- Any residual in T reverts to C on winding up.

2.5.200.40   In this example, C concludes that it has power over the relevant activities of T because it has some rights, a special relationship, and evidence of the practical ability to direct, as follows.

- C can make and/or withdraw T's funding.
- In practice, T's relevant activities are carried out to suit C. This is indirect evidence of the practical ability to direct.
- T depends on the loan from C to acquire the shares and therefore to fund its operations; T's activities are conducted on behalf of C to settle its obligation under the share-based payment scheme; and C's exposure to returns from the loan and the residual – in fact, all of the variability of T – is greater than its voting or similar rights. [*IFRS 10.B18(b), B19(b)(i), B19(c)–B20*]

2.5.210   STEP 3: VARIABILITY OF RETURNS

2.5.210.10   To have control over an investee, an investor needs to be exposed to (have rights to) variable returns from its involvement with an investee.

2.5.210.20   An investor is exposed to variable returns from its involvement with an investee when the investor's returns from its involvement with the investee have the potential to vary based on the investee's performance. [*IFRS 10.15*]

2.5.210.30   The returns of the investee might be only positive, only negative, or either positive or negative. Sources of returns include the following, which illustrate that the definition of returns is very broad:

- dividends or other economic benefits, such as interest from debt securities and changes in the value of the investor's investment in the investee;
- remuneration for servicing an investee's assets or liabilities, fees and exposure to loss from providing credit or liquidity support;
- tax benefits;
- residual interests in the investee's assets and liabilities on liquidation; and/or
- returns that are not available to other interest holders, such as the investor's ability to use the investee's assets in combination with its own to achieve economies of scale, cost savings or other synergies. [*IFRS 10.15, B56–B57*]

2.5.210.40   For the purposes of this analysis, *variable* returns are not limited to returns that might vary in their calculation – e.g. dividends or fees that vary based on performance. Instead, variable returns include returns that are otherwise fixed but that expose the investor to variability because they are subject to the risk that the investee will default on payment – e.g. fixed interest payments on a bond. [*IFRS 10.B56*]

2.5.210.50   The variability analysis is relevant in the following circumstances.
- It has already been concluded in Step 2 of the control model (see 2.5.90) that the investor has power, in which case the objective of Step 3 is to assess whether the investor is exposed to variability of returns from its involvement with the investee. There is no requirement for the investor to be exposed to all or a majority of that variability; rather, the test is whether the investor has *some* exposure.
- The power assessment in Step 2 of the control model is inconclusive. In such circumstances, having a large exposure to variability is an indicator that the investor may have power over the investee. This scenario may arise when the investee is an entity for which voting rights are not the dominant factor in determining control (see 2.5.170).
- The linkage assessment in Step 4 of the control model partly depends on the magnitude of, and variability associated with, the investor's economic interests relative to the total variability of returns of the investee (see 2.5.270). [*IFRS 10.A, B20*]

2.5.210.60   In addition, if it is concluded that the investor is exposed to variability of returns from its involvement with the investee, then this qualifies as an 'interest' in the investee; consequently, the investor needs to consider what disclosures are required under IFRS 12 (see chapter 5.10). The disclosures are relevant even if it is concluded that the investor does not control the investee (see 5.10.240). [*IFRS 12.A*]

2.5.210.70   The remainder of this section (see 2.5.220–260) discusses what types of interest comprise a variable return and how an investor determines whether it is exposed to variable returns. It does not consider how an investor measures its variable returns.

2.5.210.80   In some cases, the variability assessment is straightforward and requires no specific analysis – e.g. when the investor holds debt or equity instruments in the investee (see 2.5.220). However, in other cases the analysis may be more complex – e.g. when the investor is a counterparty to a derivative instrument issued by the investee. The guidance in 2.5.230–260 provides a more detailed discussion of derivative instruments, which are likely to be common in analysing investees such as securitisation vehicles.

2.5.220   Involvement via debt or equity instruments

2.5.220.10   When the investor's interest in the investee is via debt or equity instruments, IFRS 10 is clear that the investor is exposed to variability of returns from its involvement with the investee. [*IFRS 10.B57(a)*]

2.5.220.20   Therefore, for example, it will be rare that an in-depth variability analysis will be required for a conventional operating company, because the equity instruments held by the investor that has power over the relevant activities of the investee in all cases expose that investor to variability of returns of the investee.

2.5.230   Involvement not via debt or equity instruments

2.5.230.10   IFRS 10 sets out a number of other types of involvement which, like debt or equity instruments, result in its investors having variable returns – e.g. a fee exposes the investor to variability of returns of the investee. [*IFRS 10.B56–B57*]

2.5.230.20   In many cases, it will therefore be clear that an investor is exposed to variability of returns from its involvement with the investee. However, it can be difficult to determine whether some types of involvement expose an investor to variability. This is particularly true when the investor is the counterparty to a derivative instrument.

2.5.230.30   In our view, the following is one approach that may be used to determine whether the counterparty to a derivative contract is exposed to variability of returns from its involvement with an investee, derived from the application guidance in IFRS 10. Steps A and B focus on the analysis of risks that are created in the investee, and Step C then considers the risks from the investor's perspective.
- *Step A:* Analyse the risks to which the investee was designed to be exposed.
- *Step B:* Analyse how the risks identified in Step A are passed on to parties involved with the investee.
- *Step C:* Assess the investor's exposure to those risks. [*IFRS 10.B8*]

2.5.230.40   Consideration of the risks includes not only the downside risk, but also the potential for upside. [*IFRS 10.B8*]

2.5.240   *Step A: Analyse risks to which investee designed to be exposed*

2.5.240.10   The objective of Step A is to analyse the risks to which the investee was designed to be exposed – i.e. those specific risks that are key to the design of the investee and not every risk to which it has an exposure.

2.5.240.20   Examples of risks may include, but are not limited to the following.
- *Credit risk* – i.e. the risk that the investee's debtors will default on all or part of their obligations to the investee.
- *Interest rate risk* – i.e. the risk that the interest payments on a floating rate financial instrument will vary or that the fair value of a fixed rate financial instrument will change based on interest rate fluctuations.

2.5.240.30   Examples 15A and 15B illustrate Step A.

2.5.250   *Step B: Analyse how risks identified in Step A are passed on*

2.5.250.10   The objective of Step B is to analyse how the risks identified in Step A are passed on to parties involved with the investee. All relevant facts and circumstances, including but not limited to the following factors, are considered when performing Step B:

- the investee's activities;
- the terms of its contracts;
- the nature of the involvement;
- how the instruments issued by the investee were marketed to and negotiated with potential investors; and
- which parties participated significantly in the investee's design or redesign.

2.5.250.20   Examples 15A and 15B illustrate Step B.

2.5.260   *Step C: Assess investor's exposure to risks identified in Step B*

2.5.260.10   The objective of Step C is to determine whether the investor has exposure to the risks identified in Step B.

- If the investor is exposed to the risks to which the investee was designed to be exposed, then it 'absorbs' variability created by the investee. As a consequence, the investor is exposed to variable returns of the investee.
- If, however, the investor has an involvement with the investee that 'creates' variability in the investee, then its involvement does not expose it to variability of returns of the investee.

2.5.260.20   The concept of absorbing vs creating variability is derived from the US GAAP guidance on variable interest entities, and was part of the IASB's thinking in developing the approach in IFRS 10 to variability. [*IFRS 10.BC66*]

2.5.260.30   The analysis is performed on a contract-by-contract basis and for each investor (contract counterparty) separately.

2.5.260.40   In some cases, the counterparty to a derivative instrument may appear to both absorb variability from the investee and create variability for the investee; this is illustrated in Example 15C with an interest rate swap. As a result, applying Step C without any limiting tests may result in a derivative counterparty being identified as having an exposure to variability simply by being the counterparty to a derivative.

2.5.260.50   In our view, if all of the following characteristics are present, then generally a derivative does not cause the investor to absorb variability – i.e. the investor is *not* exposed to variability of returns from its involvement with the investee:

- its underlying is an observable market rate, price, index of prices or rates, or other market observable variable, or the occurrence or non-occurrence of a specified market observable event;
- the derivative counterparty is not subordinate relative to any other parties that have involvement with the entity – i.e. the counterparty ranks at least pari passu with the investee's most senior instrument(s); and
- the derivative instrument does not offset substantially all of the risk in the investee.

2.5.260.60   Example 15C illustrates Step C.

Example 15A – Variability – Credit risk transferred to counterparty

2.5.260.70   A credit default swap (CDS) counterparty is assessing whether it is exposed to variability of returns from its involvement with Structured Entity SE.

2.5.260.80   SE was designed to hold a loan portfolio:
- with investors in SE earning a return on their investment linked to the returns on a loan portfolio, excluding credit risk; and
- a CDS transferring credit risk away from SE and the investors to the CDS counterparty.

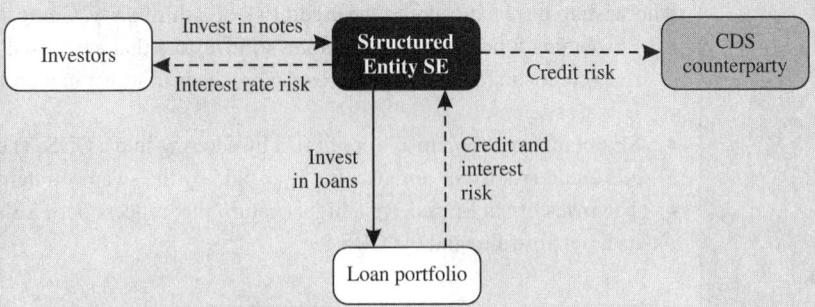

2.5.260.90   The following analysis determines whether the CDS counterparty is exposed to variability of returns from the performance of SE.
- *Step A:* The risks to which SE was designed to be exposed are interest rate risk and credit risk, through its investment in the loan portfolio.
- *Step B:* SE was designed to pass on the interest rate risk to investors, and the credit risk to a counterparty through the CDS.
- *Step C:* By entering into the CDS, the counterparty is taking on the credit risk of the loan portfolio – i.e. the counterparty absorbs variability through the CDS.

2.5.260.100   As a result of the above analysis, the CDS counterparty concludes that it is exposed to variability of returns of SE. [*IFRS 10.BC66*]

2.5.260.110   This conclusion has the following implications.
- If the CDS counterparty previously concluded that it had power over the investee in Step 2 of the control model (see 2.5.90), then Step 3 in the control model is also met and the investor moves to Step 4 (see 2.5.270).
- If the CDS counterparty's power analysis was inconclusive without an analysis of whether it has a large exposure to variability in the returns of the investee,

> then the CDS counterparty next considers the size of its exposure relative to that of other investors.
> • The CDS counterparty considers the disclosure implications of its exposure to variability (see chapter 5.10).

EXAMPLE 15B – VARIABILITY – CREDIT RISK TRANSFERRED FROM COUNTERPARTY

2.5.260.120   Similar to Example 15A, a credit default swap (CDS) counterparty is assessing whether it is exposed to variability of returns from its involvement with Structured Entity SE.

2.5.260.130   SE was designed to provide investment opportunities for investors who wish to have exposure to the credit risk of a third party, Company X.
• SE obtains funding by issuing notes to investors that are linked to X's credit risk (credit-linked notes) and uses the proceeds to invest in a portfolio of risk-free assets.
• SE obtains exposure to X's credit risk by entering into a CDS. The CDS passes X's credit risk to SE in return for a fee paid by the swap counterparty.
• The investors in SE receive a higher return that reflects both SE's return from its asset portfolio and the CDS fee.

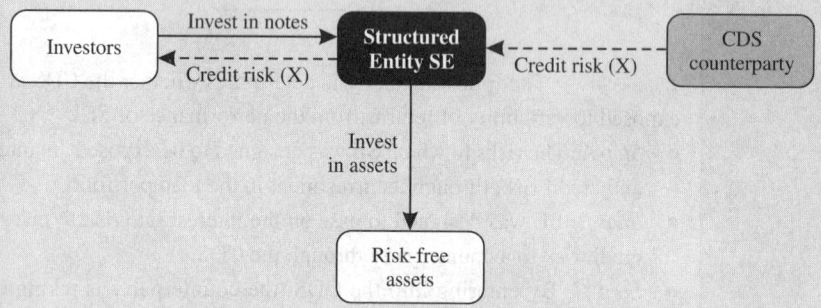

2.5.260.140   The following analysis determines whether the CDS counterparty is exposed to variability of returns from the performance of SE.
• *Step A:* SE was designed to be exposed to X's credit risk through the CDS.
• *Step B:* SE was designed to pass on X's credit risk to investors.
• *Step C:* By entering into the CDS, the counterparty is transferring the credit risk of X to SE – it is creating and not absorbing that credit risk.

2.5.260.150   As a result of the above analysis, the CDS counterparty concludes that it is *not* exposed to variability of returns from its involvement with SE. Therefore, the analysis under the control model stops and there are no disclosure implications.
[*IFRS 10.BC66*]

EXAMPLE 15C – VARIABILITY – INTEREST RATE SWAP

2.5.260.160   An interest rate swap (IRS) counterparty is assessing whether it is exposed to variability of returns from its involvement with Structured Entity SE.

2.5.260.170   SE was designed to provide investors with a fixed rate return.
- SE obtains funding by issuing notes to investors, and invests it in a loan portfolio that pays a floating rate of interest.
- SE enters into an IRS, in terms of which SE pays floating and receives a fixed rate of interest. The IRS counterparty is senior in priority relative to the investors.
- Investors are also exposed to credit risk arising from the loan portfolio.

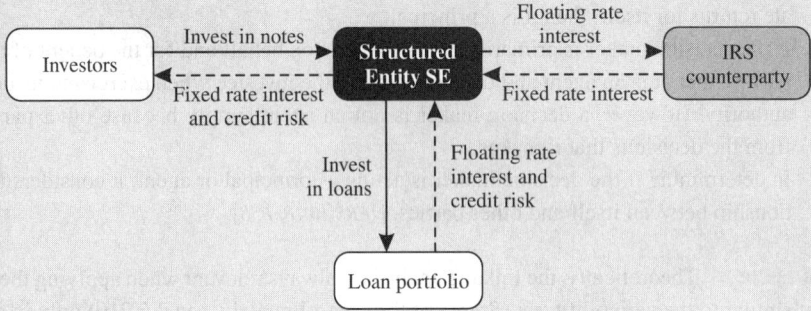

2.5.260.180   The following analysis determines whether the IRS counterparty is exposed to variability of returns from the performance of SE.
- *Step A:* The risks to which SE was designed to be exposed are interest rate risk and credit risk, through its investment in the loan portfolio.
- *Step B:* SE was designed to pass on interest rate risk (cash flow risk arising from floating rates) from the loan portfolio to the IRS counterparty, while at the same time accepting interest rate risk (fair value risk arising from fixed rates) from the IRS counterparty, and to pass on the interest rate risk (fair value risk) and credit risk to investors.
- *Step C:* By entering into the IRS, the counterparty is now taking on interest rate risk (cash flow risk) of the loan portfolio – i.e. it might therefore appear to be absorbing variability. However:
  – the underlying is an observable market rate of interest;
  – the IRS counterparty is senior in priority relative to the investors; and
  – the IRS does not offset substantially all of the risk in an investee, because credit risk arising from the loan portfolio is not transferred to the counterparty.

2.5.260.190   As a result of the above analysis, the IRS counterparty concludes that it is *not* exposed to variability of returns from its involvement with SE. Therefore, the analysis under the control model stops and there are no disclosure implications.

2.5.270 **STEP 4: LINKAGE**

2.5.280 **Link between power and returns**

2.5.280.10 To have control, in addition to power and exposure to variable returns from its involvement with the investee, an investor needs the ability to use its power over the investee to affect its returns. If the investor is an agent, then the linkage element is missing. [*IFRS 10.17*]

2.5.280.20 In this section, we refer to the investor who is the subject of the linkage analysis as the 'decision maker' (or fund manager in 2.5.350). This is to avoid confusion in distinguishing between different investors.

2.5.280.30 The following is a summary.
- If the decision maker has the power to direct the activities of the investee that it manages to generate returns for itself, then it is a principal.
- If the decision maker is primarily engaged to act on behalf and for the benefit of another party or parties, then it is an agent and does not control the investee when exercising its decision-making authority. However, a decision maker is not an agent simply because other parties can benefit from the decisions that it makes.
- In determining if the decision maker is acting as principal or agent, it considers the overall relationship between itself and other parties. [*IFRS 10.18, B58*]

2.5.280.40 Theoretically, the linkage analysis is always relevant when applying the control model, but similar to the variability test (Step 3 of the control model – see 2.5.210) only in some cases will any detailed analysis be required.

2.5.280.50 The linkage analysis will require more in-depth consideration:
- in assessing whether a fund manager has control (see 2.5.350); and
- if there is otherwise explicit delegation of power (see 2.5.290).

2.5.280.60 Outside of these circumstances, the default presumption is that the linkage test is met. For example, when an investee is controlled by voting rights, the decision maker's exposure to variability of returns will generally be correlated with its power over the investee. [*IFRS 10.BC142*]

2.5.280.70 However, there may be certain other circumstances in which the linkage analysis requires more detailed consideration. For example, because of local laws, equity interests in some investees in a country need to be held by an entity domiciled in the same country. In this case, a foreign investor willing to invest in this country may enter into an agreement with the holding entity, whereby the local holding entity agrees to act solely for the benefit and interest of, and on behalf of, the foreign investor. This local holding entity may be an agent of the foreign investor and therefore fail the linkage test. For a discussion of special relationships in the context of the control model as a whole, see 2.5.400.

2.5.280.80 When more in-depth consideration is necessary (see 2.5.280.50), the following flowchart illustrates the steps that a decision maker follows in analysing whether it is acting as a principal or an agent, which is explained throughout this section. [*IFRS 10.B58–B72*]

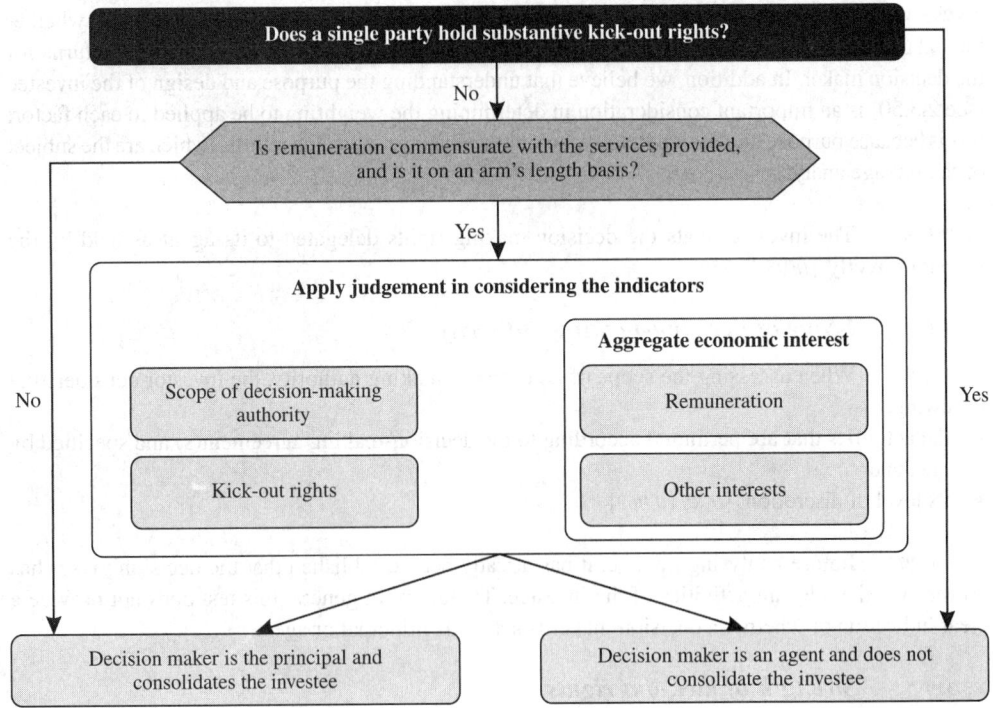

2.5.280.90   As indicated in the flowchart, two tests are determinative regardless of other indicators.

● If a single party holds substantive kick-out rights – i.e. the decision maker can be removed without cause – then the decision maker is an agent. In that case, the linkage test is failed and the decision maker does not consolidate the investee. This is regardless of the level of remuneration.

● If the decision maker's remuneration is not commensurate with the services provided, or the terms and conditions are not on an arm's length basis, then the decision maker is the principal. In that case, the linkage test is met and the decision maker consolidates the investee. [*IFRS 10.B65, B69–B70*]

2.5.290   Application to decision makers other than fund managers

2.5.290.10   In applying the linkage test, the decision maker considers the overall relationship between itself and other parties, including the following factors:

● the scope of its decision-making authority over the investee (see 2.5.300);
● kick-out rights (see 2.5.310); and
● its aggregate economic interest, comprising (see 2.5.320):
  – its remuneration for the services provided; and
  – its exposure to variability of returns because of other interests that it holds in the investee.
    [*IFRS 10.B60*]

2.5.290.20   The objective of the linkage test is to determine whether the decision maker (who has already met the power and variability tests in the control model) can use its power to affect its returns. In making the assessment, different weightings are applied to each of the factors depending on particular facts and circumstances. [*IFRS 10.B60*]

2.5.290.30   Therefore, in our view the practical objective of the linkage test is to assess whether the balance of evidence is sufficient to conclude that there is a link between power and returns for the decision maker. In addition, we believe that understanding the purpose and design of the investee (see 2.5.50) is an important consideration in determining the weighting to be applied to each factor; this is because purpose and design is a key factor in analysing power and returns, which are the subject of the linkage analysis.

2.5.290.40   The investor treats the decision-making rights delegated to its agent as held by the investor directly. [*IFRS 10.B59*]

2.5.300   *Scope of decision-making authority*

2.5.300.10   When assessing the scope of its decision-making authority, the investor considers the following:

- the activities that are permitted according to the decision-making agreement(s) and specified by law; and
- its level of discretion. [*IFRS 10.B62*]

2.5.300.20   Before analysing linkage, it has already been established that the decision maker has power over the relevant activities of the investee. Therefore, in general this test does not provide a clear indication of whether a decision maker is acting as principal or agent.

2.5.310   *Strength of kick-out rights*

2.5.310.10   As noted in 2.5.280.90, if a single party holds substantive rights to remove the decision maker without cause, then this is sufficient to conclude that the decision maker is an agent. However, if more than one party needs to act together to remove the decision maker, then this fact alone is not sufficient to conclude that the decision maker is an agent or that the removal rights are not substantive. Such rights are considered in the overall evaluation of whether the decision maker is acting as a principal. The more parties that need to agree to remove the decision maker, the less weighting that is placed on that factor – i.e. the rights are assessed on a sliding scale if not held by a single party. [*IFRS 10.B64–B65*]

2.5.310.20   For example, if the decision maker can be removed without cause by simple majority and there are only two other investors (i.e. only two votes are needed to remove the decision maker), then the removal rights are much more likely to be substantive and carry more weight than if there are 30,000 other investors (i.e. 15,001 votes are needed to remove the decision maker). [*IFRS 10.B64–B65*]

2.5.310.30   Rights that restrict the decision maker's discretion are considered in a manner similar to kick-out rights. Consequently, if the decision maker needs to obtain approval from a small number of parties to make its decisions, then it is generally an agent. [*IFRS 10.B66*]

2.5.310.40   The greater the number of parties required to act together to exercise removal or similar rights, and the greater the magnitude and variability associated with the decision maker's economic interests, the less weighting is placed on this factor. [*IFRS 10.B65*]

2.5.310.50   Consideration of the rights held by other parties includes rights exercisable by the investee's board of directors or other governing body and their effect on the decision-making authority. For example, when the board of directors is independent of the decision maker, it may in effect act as a central mechanism through which investors act collectively. Such a mechanism is more likely to be substantive and, if so, would overcome any presumption that the rights of a large number of parties required to act together is not substantive. [*IFRS 10.B23(b), B67*]

2.5.310.60   When assessing whether removal rights are substantive, the guidance in 2.5.100 is relevant. Questions may arise in respect of removal rights that are exercisable for only a limited period of time. In assessing whether such removal rights are substantive, an entity would need to consider the time period for which the rights are exercisable – especially in respect of when relevant decisions are to be made.

2.5.310.70   For further discussion of kick-out rights, see 2.5.370. Although this discussion is in the context of fund managers, the points made are generally applicable in other circumstances.

2.5.320   *Aggregate economic interest*

2.5.320.10   The decision maker's aggregate economic interest in an investee comprises any remuneration for services rendered plus any exposure to variability through other interests. The greater the magnitude of, and variability associated with, the decision maker's aggregate economic interest, the greater the likelihood that the decision maker is acting as principal. [*IFRS 10.B72(a)*]

2.5.320.20   Remuneration and other interests held may be considered in aggregate because, if the level of remuneration/other interests alone resulted in a principal conclusion, then the same conclusion would be reached when assessed in aggregate; conversely, if the assessment did not result in a principal assessment on a stand-alone basis, then the remuneration/other interests would still be required to be tested as part of a larger aggregate.

2.5.320.30   Outside of the funds sector, which is the basis for the examples in IFRS 10, the assessment of the decision maker's aggregate economic interest is more likely to require significant judgement. For example, returns may be more difficult to identify and evaluate because of their nature – e.g. synergies.

2.5.320.40   For further discussion of the 'aggregate economic interest', see 2.5.360.

2.5.330   *Remuneration*

2.5.330.10   As indicated in 2.5.280.90, for the decision maker to be an agent, its remuneration needs to be 'at market'. This means that the remuneration needs to:
- be commensurate with the services provided; and
- include only terms, conditions or amounts customarily present in arrangements for similar services and level of skill negotiated on an arm's length basis. [*IFRS 10.B69–B70*]

2.5.330.20   If the remuneration meets these two criteria, then the decision maker can be, but is not necessarily, an agent. This is because the other factors also need to be considered. [*IFRS 10.B70*]

2.5.330.30   For decision makers other than fund managers, significant judgement could be required in determining whether remuneration is at market – e.g. if the parties are related parties.

2.5.340   *Exposure to variability of returns through other interests*

2.5.340.10   A decision maker may hold other interests in the investee. 'Other interests' are any involvement that gives rise to a variable return for the decision maker as defined by IFRS 10 (see 2.5.210.30). This is because the linkage test is about determining whether the decision maker is using its power to affect its returns from its involvement with the investee – e.g. synergies achieved by the decision maker through its involvement in the investee – which is a wider concept than just the returns of the investee itself. The standard itself also gives the example of a guarantee provided by the decision maker in respect of the performance of the investee. [*IFRS 10.B56–B57, B71*]

2.5.340.20   As a result, the assessment of returns cannot be undertaken solely on a quantitative basis. Instead, in many cases a qualitative assessment will be required, with all sources of returns included in the assessment. This analysis is also consistent with the IASB's rejection of developing a model that would specify a particular level of returns that would result in an agency relationship. This decision was made to avoid encouraging structuring to achieve a particular accounting outcome. [*IFRS 10.BC141–BC142*]

2.5.340.30   As part of the assessment, the decision maker also considers whether its exposure to variability of returns is different from that of the other investors and, if so, whether this might influence its actions. [*IFRS 10.B72(b)*]

2.5.350   **Application to fund managers**

2.5.350.10   KPMG's publication *IFRS Practice Issues: Applying the consolidation model to fund managers* provides a more in-depth discussion of the application of IFRS 10 to fund managers than this chapter. This chapter summarises the key points included in that publication, and expands the discussion in 2.5.280–340 in the context of investment funds.

2.5.350.20   Fund managers generally have power over the relevant activities of the funds that they manage through their exercise of delegated power (see 2.5.90), and exposure to variability of returns through incentive fees and/or co-investment (see 2.5.210). Therefore, the link between power and returns is usually key for fund managers in assessing whether a fund manager has control over the fund.

2.5.350.30   Of the steps set out in 2.5.280.80, in our view the linkage analysis for fund managers will come down to a combined assessment of just two indicators: aggregate economic interests and kick-out rights.

2.5.350.40   This is because:
- single party kick-out rights are rarely present in the funds sector;
- a fund manager's remuneration is generally at market if there is sufficient investment from independent investors;
- the scope of decision-making authority is not a distinguishing factor because the fund manager has all of the discretion within the designed activities of the fund; and
- as noted in 2.5.320.20, remuneration and other interests do not need to be tested separately.

2.5.350.50   The two indicators (aggregate economic interests and kick-out rights) are required to be considered together. Therefore, the stronger the kick-out rights, the more aggregate economic interest can be accepted while still being an agent. Conversely, the weaker the kick-out rights, the less aggregate economic interest can be accepted while still being an agent.

2.5.350.60   The chart below provides a way of visualising a general scheme for the result of combining different strengths of each indicator.

- In the grey zone, the combination of strong kick-out rights and low aggregate economic interest suggests that the fund manager is an agent.
- In the black zone, the combination of weak kick-out rights and high aggregate economic interest suggests that the fund manager is a principal.
- In the marginal zone, the combination does not give a clear outcome.

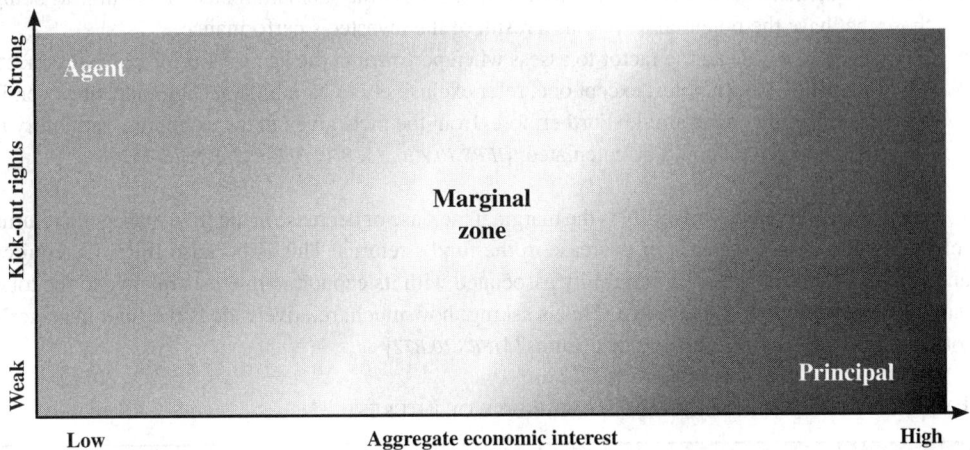

2.5.350.70   For those cases that fall into the marginal zone, the fund manager will need to consider certain other aspects of these indicators to determine if it is an agent or a principal. The question of where the central, marginal zone starts and finishes is not clear; there are no 'bright lines'.

2.5.350.80   The rest of this section summarises the key steps in the linkage analysis for a fund manager.

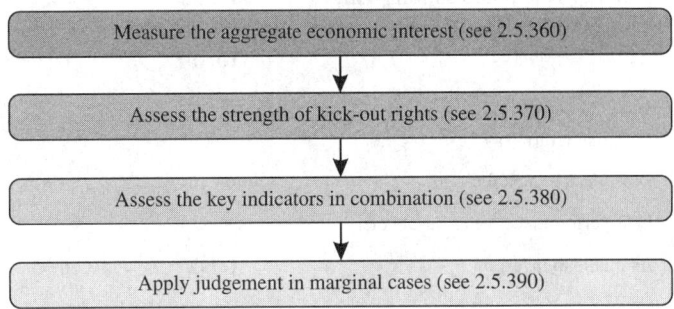

2.5.360   *Aggregate economic interest*

2.5.360.10   The first key indicator is the aggregate economic interest, comprising remuneration and other interests in aggregate. In our view, this amount is simply the sum of remuneration and other interests. [*IFRS 10.B72(a)*]

2.5.360.20   IFRS 10 requires an evaluation of the magnitude of, and variability associated with, its economic interests relative to the total variability of returns of the investee. This evaluation is made primarily on the basis of returns *expected* from the activities of the investee but should not ignore the decision maker's *maximum* exposure to variability of returns. [*IFRS 10.B72*]

2.5.360.30   On this basis, in our view the key measure is the 'variability of expected returns', for the following reasons.
- It is a key element of the definition of returns in IFRS 10; the standard focuses on returns as being those that have the potential to vary as a result of the investee's performance.
- It is identified as a headline factor to assess when performing the agent-vs-principal assessment.
- All of the IFRS 10 examples, except one, refer exclusively to variability; magnitude, however, is mentioned in only one example. Furthermore, from the facts given in the examples, variability is the only measure that could be calculated. [*IFRS 10.7(b), 15, B60, B71–B72, B.Ex13–Ex16*]

2.5.360.40   In our view, variability is the marginal increase or decrease in the fund manager's returns relative to a marginal increase or decrease in the fund's returns. This is because IFRS 10 requires an assessment of the investor's variability associated with its economic interests relative to the total variability of returns of the investee. This is asking: how much, relatively, does the fund manager's total income vary as fund performance varies? [*IFRS 10.B72*]

EXAMPLE 16 – FUND MANAGER – VARIABILITY OF INTEREST

2.5.360.50   Investment Manager M has the following interests in a fund:
- 1% management fee calculated on net asset value (NAV);
- a performance fee paying 20% of additional profits after management fees, once an 8% (profits after management fee) hurdle is reached; and
- a 10% investment.

2.5.360.60   The variability at any level of return at which a performance fee is due can be calculated as follows.

	TOTAL		MANAGER SHARE
Marginal return, say 1	1.000		
Less management fee	(0.010)[1]		0.010
Less performance fee as hurdle met	(0.198)[2]		0.198
Available to investors	0.792	At 10%	0.079
			0.287
Variability		0.287 / 1	28.7%

Notes
1.   Calculated as 1% x 1.
2.   Calculated as 20% x (1 - 0.010).

2.5.360.70   The table illustrates that for every 1 more or less of fund performance, the fund manager receives 0.287 more or less. Variability is therefore 28.7%. The

> calculation can be done in a shortcut way as follows: 1% + (20% x 99%) + (10% x (80% x 99%)) = 28.7%.

2.5.360.80 There may be different rates of remuneration at different levels of performance; usually, there is a hurdle return above which a performance fee is paid. In our view, variability should be measured at the expected level of fund returns and the level should be at a level that includes a performance fee for the following reasons.

- Performance fees are set with the intention of being achievable.
- The fees incentivise the fund manager to behave so as to obtain this return.
- The IFRS 10 examples ignore the hurdle.

2.5.360.90 Focusing on the level at which performance fees arise is also a practical approach. The calculation is simple and is not sensitive to the precise level of performance above the hurdle, assuming that the fee has only one rate/hurdle. Once the fee has become payable, the fund manager's share of further changes in the fund performance is always the same. If there is more than one performance fee level, then the decision, over which performance fee band to build into the quantitative measure will need to be more precise – i.e. determine which hurdle level is expected and build that into the initial calculation. The existence of higher bands may still need to be taken into account later as a qualitative feature of the aggregate economic interest (see 2.5.390).

2.5.360.100 In determining a fund manager's aggregate economic interest in a fund, the most common item to include after its remuneration is an investment in the fund. In some cases, the fund manager's investment model may mean that it holds investments in the underlying investments of the fund in a structure that is similar to holding a direct investment in the fund itself. In such cases, these direct investments in the investees of the fund are included when calculating the fund manager's aggregate economic interest. [*IFRS 10.B71*]

EXAMPLE 17 – FUND MANAGER – INVESTMENT MODEL

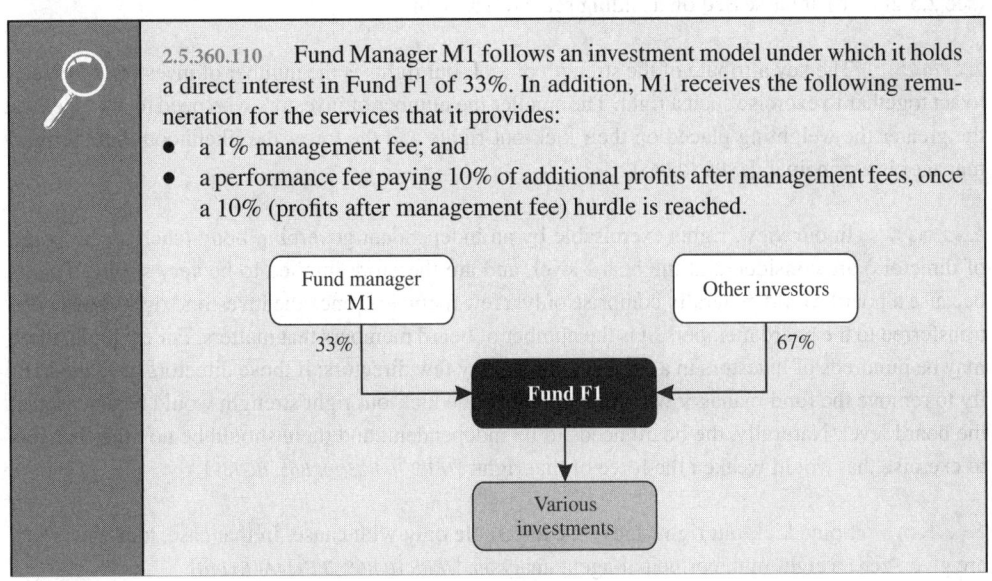

2.5.360.110 Fund Manager M1 follows an investment model under which it holds a direct interest in Fund F1 of 33%. In addition, M1 receives the following remuneration for the services that it provides:

- a 1% management fee; and
- a performance fee paying 10% of additional profits after management fees, once a 10% (profits after management fee) hurdle is reached.

2.5.360.120   In contrast, Fund Manager M2's investment model is to hold a 33% equity interest in each of the investments held by Fund F2. In addition, M2 receives the following remuneration for the services that it provides:
- a 1% management fee; and
- a performance fee paying 10% of additional profits after management fees, once a 10% (profits after management fee) hurdle is reached.

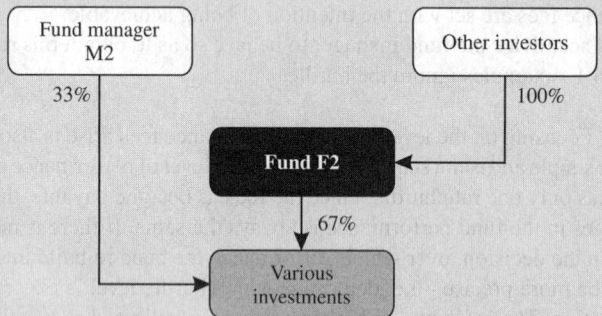

2.5.360.130   In this example, we believe that the two structures are the same in substance, and that the calculation of M2's aggregate economic interest in F2 should include the return on its direct equity investments in the various investments held by F2; these are 'other interests' under IFRS 10.

2.5.370   *Strength of kick-out rights*

2.5.370.10   The second key indicator is kick-out rights, which unless they are held by a single party (see 2.5.280.90) are assessed on a sliding scale of strength.

2.5.370.20   The key attribute of the strength of kick-out rights is the number of investors who need to act together to exercise such a right. The smaller the number of investors who need to act together, the greater the weighting placed on their kick-out rights and the lower the likelihood that the fund manager is a principal. [*IFRS 10.B65*]

2.5.370.30   In our view, rights exercisable by an independent governing body (such as the board of directors) are considered at the board level, and are therefore implied to be very strong. This is because a board would generally comprise only a few members; once the investors' rights have been transferred to the board members, it is the number of board members that matters. For example, there may be hundreds of investors in a fund but only a very few directors; if those directors have the ability to remove the fund manager without cause, then the kick-out right strength would be assessed at the board level. Naturally, the board needs to be independent, and there should be no other barriers to exercise that would weaken the force of that right. [*IFRS 10.B23(b), B65, BC139*]

2.5.370.40   Some kick-out rights may be exercisable only with cause. In that case, kick-out rights are given zero weight in the principal-agent analysis. [*IFRS 10.B65, B.Ex14A–Ex14B*]

2.5.370.50   There may be barriers to exercising kick-out rights, which affect their strength, such as:
- financial penalties;
- conditions narrowly limiting the timing of exercise;
- the absence of a mechanism allowing exercise; or
- the inability to obtain the information necessary for exercise. [*IFRS 10.B23–B24*]

2.5.370.60   In our view, the lack of an annual general meeting (AGM) may be seen as weakening the investors' practical ability to exercise kick-out rights, unless there is another mechanism in place.

2.5.370.70   Private equity investment funds might have no AGM, but usually have alternative mechanisms that give investors the practical ability to exercise kick-out rights. For example:
- there may be quarterly calls and annual meetings at which the investors are provided with information;
- an investor will usually necessarily know who the other investors are – e.g. they will be named in the partnership documents available to all investors; or
- there could be a right to call an extraordinary meeting – often requiring just five percent investment – to vote on removal of the fund manager. The ability to call such a meeting and exercise a right may even be stronger than awaiting an AGM in order to exercise a right.

2.5.370.80   As a result, the lack of an annual voting opportunity does not necessarily require zero weight to be accorded to kick-out rights.

2.5.370.90   Notice periods can also represent barriers to exercising kick-out rights. In our view, a notice period covering the whole of the life of a limited life fund (or penalties equivalent to total fees for the life of the fund) would result in zero weighting of the kick-out rights; however, other cases may not be so clear-cut.

2.5.370.100   For example, a typical arrangement in the private equity sector is to give six months' notice plus payment of a further six months' fees – in effect a combined one-year notice/fees period. However, at the outset the fund life will be five or seven years. In our view, the effect on the strength of the kick-out right is material, but not so great that the kick-out right has no weight.

2.5.370.110   Questions may arise about whether rights to terminate a fund are evaluated in the same way as removal rights. Although this may be the case in certain situations, the decision maker would need to consider:
- the specific facts and circumstances under which such rights are exercisable; and
- the purpose and design of those rights. [*IFRS 10.B66*]

2.5.380   *Combining the two indicators*

2.5.380.10   When combining the two indicators – aggregate economic interest and kick-out rights – it may be appropriate to use a matrix, grouping together categories of kick-out right strength. For each category, the fund manager could identify a level of aggregate economic interest for which the entity is clearly an agent and another for which it is clearly a principal. A marginal zone would then appear between these points (see chart in 2.5.350.60).

2.5.380.20   The standard as well as the IASB's related Effect Analysis (updated in July 2013) provides examples of combinations of kick-out rights and aggregate economic interest.

IASB EXAMPLE	VARIABILITY	KICK-OUT RIGHTS	AGENT/PRINCIPAL
13	11%	Zero	Agent
14A	22%	Zero	Agent
14B	37%	Zero	Principal
14C	37%	Without-cause	Agent
15	42%	Widely dispersed	Principal
Effect Analysis	45%	Zero	Principal

2.5.380.30   When no kick-out rights exist, and deriving returns from the IFRS 10 examples, the changeover from agent to principal occurs between approximately 22 and 37 percent (the marginal zone between the IFRS 10 Examples 14A and 14B).

2.5.380.40   When stronger kick-out rights exist, a higher variability might still support an agent outcome. For instance, IFRS 10 Example 14C has without-cause, board-level, kick-out rights (a very strong case) and can withstand 37 percent aggregate economic interest, while still being deemed an agent. In IFRS 10 Example 14B, which has the same variability but no kick-out rights, the manager is deemed a principal.

2.5.390   *Analysing marginal cases*

2.5.390.10   If a combined assessment of the key indicators falls into the marginal zone (see chart in 2.5.350.60), then other features of aggregate economic interest and kick-out rights need to be taken into account.

2.5.390.20   The other features to consider include expected magnitude, a second tier of performance fee, the proportion of investors required to vote together and the nature of variability compared with that of other investors.

2.5.390.30   Magnitude appears to be the fund manager's total return as a percentage of the fund's total return measured at the expected performance level, and is a feature of the aggregate economic interest that can help decide a marginal case. This is because it has to be different from variability, yet still be a measure of fund manager returns relative to fund returns – i.e. whereas variability is the marginal share of return, magnitude is the absolute share of return. If magnitude is low, then it may tip the scales for a marginal case to be an agent, and vice versa.

EXAMPLE 18 – FUND MANAGER – MAGNITUDE OF INTEREST IN THE FUND

2.5.390.40   Continuing Example 16, Investment Manager M now calculates the magnitude of its interest in the fund. The following additional information is relevant:
- 100 start value of the fund; and
- 10% expected performance level.

2.5.390.50   The magnitude of M's interest can be calculated as follows.

	TOTAL		MANAGER SHARE
Return	10.00		
Less management fee	$(1.10)^{(1)}$		1.10
Less performance fee	$(0.18)^{(2)}$		0.18
Available to investors	8.72	At 10%	0.87
			2.15
Magnitude		2.15 / 10.00	21.5%

Notes
1.   Calculated as 1% x 110: i.e. 1% of fund's net assets value.
2.   Calculated as 20% x (10 - 1.1 - 8): i.e. 20% of additional profits after management fees, once an 8% (profits after management fee) hurdle is reached.

2.5.390.60   In assessing magnitude as opposed to variability, the table in 2.5.390.50 illustrates that M receives 21.5% of the expected fund performance.

2.5.390.70   In some fund structures, the performance fee is cumulative over the whole life of the fund – e.g. in private equity. In other cases, the fee is determined and paid based on annual performance with no claw-back in subsequent years if cumulative performance falls. In our view, the possibility of the fee not being due would be taken into account in deciding marginal cases. If a fee has been designed to be due only occasionally then this may, in marginal cases, weight the scales towards being an agent.

2.5.400   SPECIAL RELATIONSHIPS

2.5.400.10   When assessing control over an investee, the investor considers the nature of its relationships with other parties and whether those other parties act on the investor's behalf (see also 2.5.190). This determination requires judgement in assessing the consequence of how those parties interact with each other and with the investor. [*IFRS 10.B4, B73*]

2.5.400.20   A contractual arrangement is not required in a principal-agent relationship. A party is a de facto agent if the investor or those who control the investor have the ability to direct that party to act on the investor's behalf. [*IFRS 10.B74*]

2.5.400.30   The following are examples of parties that, by the nature of their relationship, might act as de facto agents for the investor:
• related parties of the investor;
• a party that received its interest in the investee as a contribution or loan from the investor;
• a party that has agreed not to sell, transfer or encumber its interest in the investee without the investor's prior approval;
• a party that cannot finance its operations without subordinated support from the investor;
• a party for which a majority of the members of the governing body or key management personnel is the same as that of the investor; and/or
• a party that has a close business relationship with the investor. [*IFRS 10.B75*]

2.5.400.40   However, the existence of such a relationship does not automatically mean that the party is acting as a de facto agent of the investor. Instead, the investor evaluates the specific facts and circumstances, including consideration of the nature of the relationship and the way in which the parties interact with each other, and then applies judgement to determine whether the party is its de facto agent. For example, if a sister entity or director (key management personnel) of the investor also holds an interest in an investee, then they are not automatically assumed to be acting as a de facto agent of the investor. [*IFRS 10.BC146*]

EXAMPLE 19 – DE FACTO AGENT

2.5.400.50   Company P holds 35% of the voting rights in Company L, and two other shareholders (Companies T and S) hold 5% each. Numerous other shareholders hold the remaining 55% of voting rights, with none individually holding more than 1%.

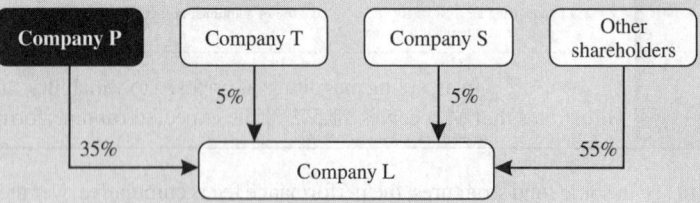

2.5.400.60   The following additional information is relevant for this example.
• There is no contractual arrangement between P, T and S on how to vote when decisions relating to L are taken. However, T and S have always voted in the same way as P in the past.
• T and S both have significant business relationships with P.
• Voting rights are relevant when assessing which investor has power over L.

2.5.400.70   In this example, P considers whether T and S are acting as its de facto agents as far as the investment in L is concerned.
• If this is the case, then it would be as if P held a 45% voting interest in L, and P would consider whether it has de facto power over L (see 2.5.160).
• If P concludes that T and S are not de facto agents on behalf of P, then P would still need to assess whether it has de facto power over L; however, that assessment would be based on P's 35% voting rights rather than on 45% voting rights.

2.5.400.80   We understand that the guidance on de facto agents was not intended to have an impact on the assessment of control for sub-holding entities in their stand-alone financial statements.

EXAMPLE 20 – LINKAGE – SUB-CONSOLIDATION

2.5.400.90   Company UP controls Company P, which controls Company S.

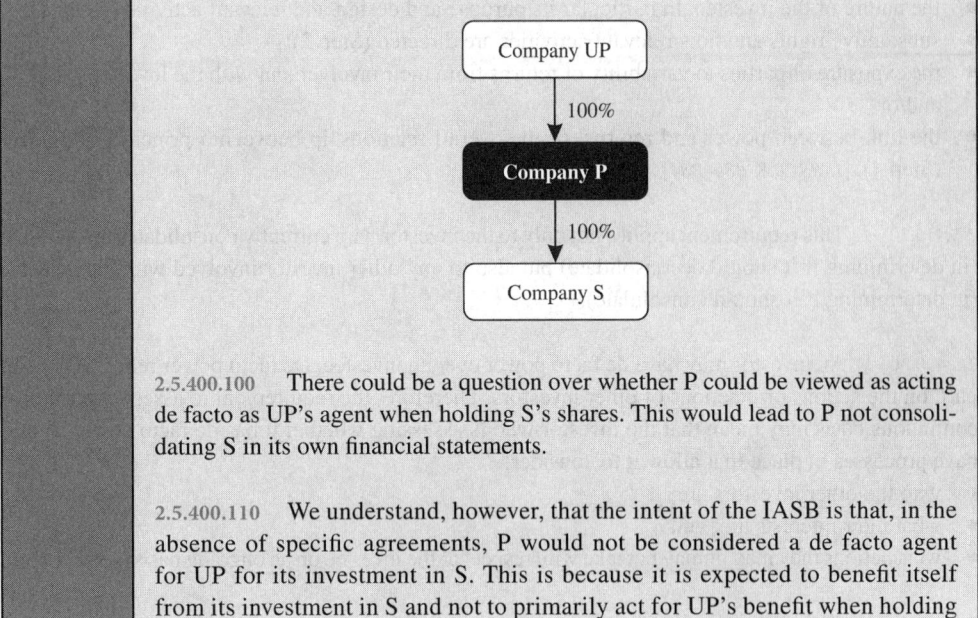

2.5.400.100   There could be a question over whether P could be viewed as acting de facto as UP's agent when holding S's shares. This would lead to P not consolidating S in its own financial statements.

2.5.400.110   We understand, however, that the intent of the IASB is that, in the absence of specific agreements, P would not be considered a de facto agent for UP for its investment in S. This is because it is expected to benefit itself from its investment in S and not to primarily act for UP's benefit when holding S's shares.

2.5.405   STRUCTURED TRANSACTIONS

2.5.405.10   There is no formal definition of a structured transaction. However, a structured transaction typically arises when parties undertake a series of actions to achieve a desired outcome. For example, an entity obtains control of an investee with a view to increasing its shareholding at a later date.

2.5.405.20   The control analysis of a vehicle that arises from a structured transaction takes into account all of the factors described in 2.5.20–400. Such transactions often have characteristics that require careful consideration – e.g. the use of derivatives, including potential voting rights, is much more common in structured transactions. If the complete transaction comprises a series of smaller transactions that would be accounted for differently if each one were viewed in isolation, then it is important to bear in mind the substance of the transaction as a whole.

2.5.405.30   In the context of losing control of a subsidiary, IFRS 10 contains specific requirements for determining whether two or more transactions should be accounted for as a single transaction – i.e. linked (see 2.5.770). [*IFRS 10.B97*]

2.5.410   ASSESSMENT ON CONTINUOUS BASIS

2.5.410.10   The assessment of control is performed on a continuous basis and an investor reassesses whether it controls an investee if facts and circumstances indicate that there are changes to one or more of the elements of the control model:

- the nature of the investee, in particular its purpose and design and relevant activities (Step 1);
- substantive rights and how relevant activities are directed (Step 2);
- the exposure of parties to variability of returns from their involvement with the investee (Step 3); and/or
- the link between power and returns, or the overall relationship between a principal and agent (Step 4). [*IFRS 10.8, B80–B84*]

2.5.410.20   This requirement applies not only to the investor who currently consolidates the investee (in determining if it should deconsolidate) but also to any other investor involved with the investee (in determining if it should consolidate).

2.5.410.30   An investor may have de facto power over an investee. De facto power relies, at least in part, on the actions or inactions of other investors. Therefore, the requirement to assess control on a continuous basis may mean that the investor who is assessing whether it has de facto power should have processes in place that allow it to consider:

- who the other investors are;
- what their interests are; and
- what actions they may or may not take with respect to the investee on an ongoing basis (see 2.5.160).

2.5.410.40   A change in market conditions does not trigger a reassessment of the control conclusion unless it changes one or more of the elements of control, or the overall relationship between a principal and an agent. [*IFRS 10.B85*]

2.5.420   Troubled debt

2.5.420.10   As noted in 2.5.110, protective rights are excluded in assessing whether an investor has power over an investee. However, protective rights may become exercisable when certain events or conditions arise – e.g. when a lender breaches a loan covenant. The IFRS Interpretations Committee noted that in this case a reassessment of control is required, because there has been a change in the factors that are considered in assessing whether an investor has power over the relevant activities of the investee. [*IU 09-13*]

2.5.420.20   IFRS 10 is structured such that protective rights are a form of substantive rights, except that protective rights are related to fundamental changes in the activities of an investee, or are rights that apply only in exceptional circumstances. As such, they cannot give the holder power or prevent other parties from having power and therefore control over an investee. However, in practice, rights are generally referred to as being either substantive (i.e. relevant in the control analysis) *or* protective (i.e. not relevant in the control analysis). Consistent with the common usage of these terms, the key issue in reassessing control in troubled debt scenarios is whether the previously protective rights are now substantive and could therefore potentially lead to power. [*IFRS 10.14, A, B26–B28*]

2.5.420.30   The guidance in this section is written from the point of view of protective rights becoming activated (exercisable), but applies equally if new rights are agreed – e.g. following debt renegotiations. In addition, in some cases the borrower is the investee itself, and in other cases the borrower is the parent of the investee that has used its shares in the investee as collateral. For a discussion of investees in bankruptcy proceedings, see 2.5.430. [*IFRS 10.14*]

EXAMPLE 21A – REASSESSMENT OF CONTROL ON BREACH OF COVENANT

2.5.420.40   Company S is a wholly owned subsidiary of Company P. S enters into a loan arrangement with Bank B, which contains several covenants. If a covenant is breached, then B can call the loan and effectively force S into liquidation.

2.5.420.50   At the outset of the loan, P concludes that B's rights are protective, because they are designed to protect the interests of B without giving it power over S. Therefore, P consolidates S.

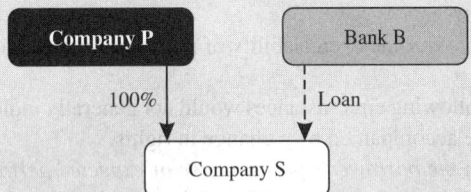

2.5.420.60   After a period of time, because of its deteriorating financial position, S breaches a covenant of the loan. B does not call the loan, although it retains the right to do so.

2.5.420.70   When the covenant is breached and B's rights become exercisable, P reassesses its relationship with S to determine whether it still has control and should continue to consolidate. At the same time, B assesses whether its relationship with S is now a control relationship.

2.5.420.80   Not all troubled debt scenarios will be as obvious as the fact pattern presented in Example 21A, and it will not always be clear whether control should be reassessed or which factors should be considered in carrying out that reassessment. In our experience, single-asset vehicles are usually the most 'at risk' for a potential change in the power conclusion because of the breadth of the lender's rights in relation to the vehicle's limited activities and assets.

2.5.420.90   The following flowchart illustrates the considerations that may be most relevant in troubled debt scenarios.

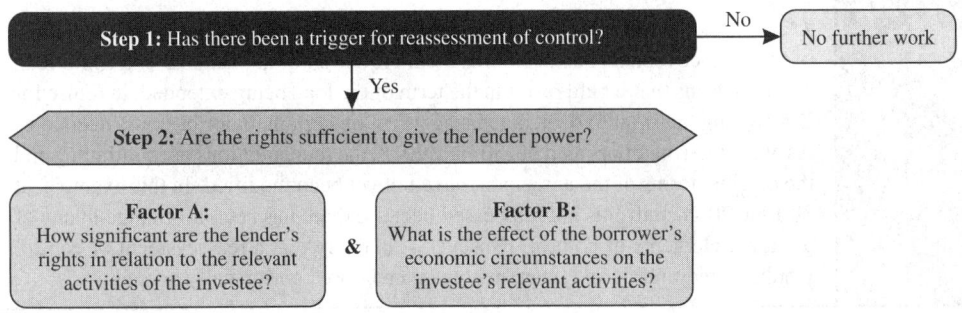

2.5.422 *Step 1: Has there been a trigger for reassessment of control?*

2.5.422.10   A reassessment of control is required when facts and circumstances indicate that one of the three elements of control may have changed (see 2.5.410.10). [*IFRS 10.B80–B82*]

2.5.422.20   The ongoing relationship between a borrower and a lender would not typically lead to a reassessment of control unless there is a change in decision-making rights. Changes to these rights arise, for example:
- when rights become exercisable on the occurrence of a particular circumstance – e.g. when the borrower breaches a covenant;
- when rights are obtained, changed or lost on the modification of the terms of an agreement or a change in law; or
- when restrictions over the exercisability of rights lapse. [*IFRS 10.11, B26, B53, B82*]

2.5.422.30   The following circumstances would not generally indicate that a reassessment is necessary, unless they are accompanied by a change in rights.
- *Deterioration in the borrower's performance or expected performance:* In considering whether an investor is a principal or agent, IFRS 10 is explicit that a change in market conditions alone does not change that initial determination (see 2.5.410.40). Similarly, in our view a change in the borrower's performance or expected performance is not enough on its own to trigger the need to reassess control – i.e. when a borrower is loss-making but still meeting all conditions of the loan agreement and is expected to continue to do so.
- *Debt renegotiations:* Borrowers will often enter into negotiations with a lender in anticipation of a breach of terms and conditions that could activate protective rights held by the lender. However, in our view during negotiations the rights have not yet been activated and would therefore not typically provide the lender with any practical ability to direct the borrower's relevant activities. Only once renegotiations have been completed and new terms and conditions agreed would the facts and circumstances usually have changed such that a reassessment would be required. [*IFRS 10.10, B80, B85, BC152*]

EXAMPLE 21B – POTENTIAL TRIGGERS FOR REASSESSMENT OF CONTROL

2.5.422.40   Changing the facts of Example 21A, in the year ended 31 December 2017 Company S records its first operating loss as a result of difficult trading conditions. None of the loan covenants has been breached, although S's management believes that this is a possibility in 2018. At 31 December 2017, control is not reassessed because there has been no change in any of the three elements of control.

2.5.422.50   During 2018, S's financial position deteriorates, although still none of the loan covenants has been breached. However, S and Bank B enter into loan renegotiations that would result in the term of the loan being extended, in return for B receiving the right to override management on certain major business decisions. As at S's interim reporting date, 30 June 2018, the renegotiations are continuing and the original terms of the agreement have not yet been modified. In this example, at 30 June 2018 control is not reassessed because there has been no change in any of the three elements of control. However, it is likely that a reassessment of control would be required if and when new loan terms are contractually agreed.

2.5.424   *Step 2: Are rights sufficient to give lender power?*

2.5.424.10   Once a triggering event in Step 1 has been identified, a new assessment of control is required. Although all steps in the control analysis are relevant in the reassessment (see 2.5.20), the key analysis in a lender-borrower relationship will typically involve determining whether the lender now has substantive rights sufficient to give it power over the relevant activities of the investee (see 2.5.100).

2.5.424.20   In applying IFRS 10, in our view the assessment of whether the lender's rights are sufficient to give it power should focus on a combination of the following.
- *Factor A:* How significant are the lender's rights in relation to the relevant activities of the investee?
- *Factor B:* What is the effect of the borrower's economic circumstances on the investee's relevant activities? [*IFRS 10.B22, B26, B80*]

2.5.424.30   As illustrated in the following diagram, we believe that these factors should be considered together in reaching a determination, making a judgement based on the facts and circumstances of the specific case. As the lender's rights become more significant and the effect of the borrower's economic circumstances on the investee's relevant activities becomes more significant, the likelihood increases that the lender now has power over the relevant activities of the investee.

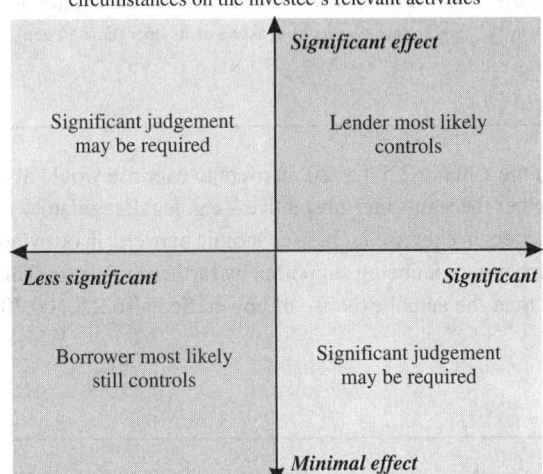

Factor B: Effect of the borrower's economic circumstances on the investee's relevant activities

Significant effect

Significant judgement may be required

Lender most likely controls

Less significant

Significant

Factor A: Significance of the lender's rights in relation to the relevant activities of the investee

Borrower most likely still controls

Significant judgement may be required

Minimal effect

2.5.426   *Factor A: Significance of lender's rights in relation to relevant activities of investee*

2.5.426.10   In considering Factor A, the parties evaluate the rights obtained by the lender in terms of how pervasive they are in the context of the investee and whether they are mitigated by other factors. Not every right will have the same significance and the lender may also obtain a combination of rights.

2.5.426.20   The following are some typical rights that a lender could obtain and examples of considerations that may be relevant. [*IFRS 10.B23*]

Type of right	Relevant considerations
1. Borrower pledges shares of the investee as collateral.	• Are there restrictions that limit the voting power associated with the shares?
2. Borrower pledges assets of the investee as collateral in a non-recourse loan; legal ownership of the assets would be transferred to the lender.	• How significant are the assets to the investee in relation to its total assets or its operations in general? See 2.5.426.90–100.
3. Lender has the right to appoint/replace members of the investee's governing body – e.g. directors.	• Can the lender appoint/replace a majority of the governing body members or key management personnel? • Are the lender's rights restricted in any way?
4. Lender has the right to approve budgets or capital decisions.	• How limited or wide-ranging are the lender's rights? • How important are these decisions to the investee's operations?
5. Lender has the right to force the auction of the pledged assets in a non-recourse loan; legal ownership of the assets would not be transferred to the lender.	• How significant are the assets to the investee in relation to its total assets or its operations in general? See 2.5.426.90–100.

2.5.426.30   When considering the rights in the table in 2.5.426.20, barriers to exercise would also be a relevant consideration to determine whether the rights are substantive – e.g. legal, regulatory or jurisdictional barriers. However, although barriers to exercise include economic barriers, in our view mere intent is not sufficient to qualify as a barrier without being supported by further indicators. This is because control is based on *ability* rather than the actual exercise of power. See also 2.5.100.70. [*IFRS 10.12, B23*]

EXAMPLE 21C – BARRIERS TO EXERCISE

2.5.426.40   Changing the facts of Example 21A, if a covenant is breached, then Bank B has the right to take ownership of substantially all of the operating assets of Company S. In 2018, a covenant is breached and B's rights become exercisable.

2.5.426.50   There are no restrictions that prevent B from exercising its rights, but in meetings between S and B, B has indicated in general that it has no intention of exercising its rights in the coming months. This is to allow some time to see if trading conditions for S improve.

2.5.426.60   In this example, we believe that B has significant rights in relation to the relevant activities of the investee for the following reasons:

- B has the right to take ownership of substantially all of S's operating assets, which would have a pervasive effect on the operations of S; and
- although B has indicated in general discussion that it does not intend to exercise its rights in the coming months, this is not a barrier to exercising the rights.

2.5.426.70   Because B's rights are significant in relation to S (Factor A in 2.5.424.20), B is positioned to the extreme right of the chart in 2.5.424.30. The next step is for the parties to consider the extent to which S's relevant activities are affected by its economic circumstances (Factor B in 2.5.424.20). This is discussed in Example 21E.

2.5.426.80   In addition, in our view barriers or penalties should be incremental or relative to external factors. It should not be concluded that a barrier exists simply because the lender makes an active decision not to change the current operating arrangements of the borrower – i.e. letting the borrower continue as a going concern; this point is illustrated in Example 21D.

2.5.426.90   Examples 2 and 5 in the table in 2.5.426.20 refer to assessing the significance of the assets over which the lender holds a pledge. In our view, relevant factors to consider include the proportion of assets subject to the pledge and whether the assets could be easily replaced. See also Example 21F.

2.5.426.100   Examples 2 and 5 in the table in 2.5.426.20 also refer to legal ownership of the underlying assets. Although the transfer of legal ownership provides clear evidence that the lender has power over the assets, this is not required in order to establish control under IFRS 10.

2.5.426.110   In some cases, a lender may enter into a 'standstill' agreement whereby it agrees not to exercise its rights for a period of time. In such cases, the timing and length of the waiver will be relevant in determining whether the rights obtained by the lender are significant. For example, a six-month standstill agreement in the case of a wind park may not significantly impair the lender's rights because the existing underlying contracts for the supply of energy by the wind park will typically be for a much longer period – e.g. 20 years – and few operational decisions will need to be made in the short term. However, a six-month standstill agreement in the technology sector, in which operational decisions are being made on a more short-term basis, may significantly impair the lender's rights such that they are not substantive. [*IFRS 10.B22, B24*]

2.5.428   *Factor B: Effect of borrower's economic circumstances on investee's relevant activities*

2.5.428.10   The financial health of the borrower provides a better context in which to understand and analyse the rights obtained by the lender. For example, the borrower may be in such financial difficulty that its existing equity holders have no reasonable prospect of a return and it is clear that the activities of the investee are now primarily being executed to ensure that the lender maximises the recovery of its investment. Conversely, the borrower may have breached a covenant because of an event that is consistent with the risks associated with its business model, which is expected to be rectified in the ordinary course of business. For example, a single-property investee loses a major tenant but is expected to replace it within a relatively short period.

EXAMPLE 21D – INVESTEE IN SIGNIFICANT FINANCIAL DIFFICULTY – SHARE PLEDGE

2.5.428.20   Company S, a wind park, is a wholly owned subsidiary of Company P. S's only substantive assets are wind turbines, and long-term contracts are in place for the sale of the electricity generated to customers. S has appointed a third party operator under a long-term contract to manage the day-to-day operations of the wind park.

2.5.428.30   S has minimal equity and is fully financed by Bank B. The loan agreement gives B the right to take ownership of the shares in S in the event of default– i.e. a zero-price call option. At the outset of the loan, P concludes that B's rights are protective, because they are designed to protect the interests of B without giving it power over S. Therefore, P consolidates S.

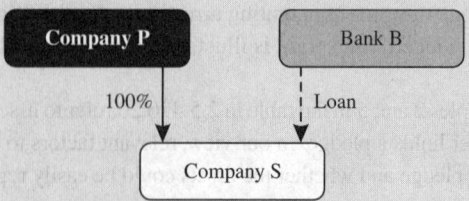

2.5.428.40   Because of unfavourable wind patterns, S has not been profitable since the start of its operations and in the past two years its financial position has deteriorated to the extent that a buyer is being sought for the assets; P has no expectation that operations can be returned to profit. As a result of its trading position, S defaults on the loan to B, which now has the right to call the shares in S.

2.5.428.50   B concludes that it should reassess its relationship with S (under Step 1 in 2.5.422) and carries out the following analysis under Step 2.
- *Factor A:* B's rights are significant because it has the right to call the shares (at an exercise price of zero) and therefore make all decisions related to the operations of S on a unilateral basis – even if it has currently chosen not to exercise these rights. There are no barriers that would prevent or deter B from exercising its rights.
- *Factor B:* S's economic circumstances are such that there is no expectation that operations can be returned to profit. Although S's relevant activities were originally focused on generating a return for investors (in the form of profits and tax credits), they have narrowed to making decisions that will best minimise the loss to B.

2.5.428.60   As a result of its analysis, B concludes that it has power over the relevant activities of S. It also determines that it is exposed to variable returns from its involvement with S by virtue of the loan (see 2.5.220), and that there is a link between power and returns (see 2.5.270–290). Accordingly, B concludes that it should consolidate S. Conversely, P concludes that it no longer controls S and should therefore deconsolidate (see 2.5.760).

2.5.428.70   As demonstrated by Example 21D, the economic circumstances of the borrower provide the context in which an evaluation can be made regarding the lender's rights. Situations in which a borrower is in significant financial difficulty would indicate a position at the top of the chart in 2.5.424.30 and may be further evidence that the lender's rights are no longer protective. [*IFRS 10.B26–B27*]

EXAMPLE 21E – BORROWER'S ECONOMIC CIRCUMSTANCES

2.5.428.80   Continuing Example 21C, Bank B now considers the extent to which Company S's relevant activities are affected by its economic circumstances.

Scenario 1: Contracts in place to facilitate turnaround

2.5.428.90   Although S has been loss-making for the past 18 months, management has newly signed contracts that indicate that the company should return to profitability within 12 months. S is expected to be in breach of the loan covenants for about the next three months, but is not expected to be in breach after that. As a result, S continues to operate as usual.

2.5.428.100   This positions B to the extreme right of the chart in 2.5.424.30 (the conclusion in Example 21C), but at the extreme bottom of the chart – i.e. the lender's rights are significant but there is minimal effect on S's relevant activities. In this example, on the basis that management has signed contracts in place, B concludes that it does not have power over the relevant activities of S and therefore that it should not consolidate S. Conversely, P concludes that it continues to control S.

Scenario 2: Long-term deterioration of financial position and capital investment required

2.5.428.110   S's financial position has been deteriorating for some time and the company is threatened by a new technology that has been introduced by a competitor. S requires significant investment if it hopes to return to profitability, but lacks the necessary resources or investors. As a result, S is no longer operating according to its original relevant activities; instead, it has narrowed its focus to efforts to repay the loan to the bank.

2.5.428.120   This positions B to the extreme right of the chart in 2.5.424.30 (the conclusion in Example 21C), and towards the top of the chart – i.e. the lender's rights are significant and there is a significant effect on S's relevant activities. In this example, B concludes that it has power over the relevant activities of S and should therefore consolidate S because the other tests in the control analysis are met. Conversely, P concludes that it no longer controls S and should therefore deconsolidate (see 2.5.760).

2.5.428.130   The borrower's ability to settle the loan is another factor that is relevant in assessing the borrower's economic circumstances and their effect on the investee's relevant activities. In considering this factor, in our view an entity should also take into account a related party's ability to settle the loan on behalf of the borrower. For example, how likely is it that the borrower's parent will be able to provide the funds for the loan to be repaid?

EXAMPLE 21F – ABILITY TO SETTLE LOAN – ASSET PLEDGE

2.5.428.140   Assume the same facts as in Example 21D except for the following.
- Bank B has the right to take ownership of the wind turbines – i.e. an asset pledge – and not the shares in Company S. If the proceeds from the sale of the wind turbines are less than the amount owing under the loan, then S is not required to pay the difference.
- S has significant accumulated tax losses that can be used in the future – e.g. by bringing new activities into the company. Company P is actively seeking ways in which the tax losses can be utilised.
- P has the ability to settle the loan on behalf of S, which would be beneficial in any future relationship with B, but it has not yet decided whether to do so.

2.5.428.150   B concludes that it should reassess its relationship with S (under Step 1 in 2.5.422) and carries out the following analysis under Step 2.
- *Factor A:* Although B has significant rights in relation to the wind turbines as assets, B has no rights in relation to the tax losses that P is seeking to utilise.
- *Factor B:* S's economic circumstances are such that there is no expectation that operations can be returned to profit. However, there is value in S by virtue of the tax losses, and P also has the ability to repay the loan should it decide to do so.

2.5.428.160   This analysis positions B slightly to the right side of the chart in 2.5.424.30, but below the horizontal line. In this example, B concludes that it does not have power over the relevant activities of S and therefore that it should not consolidate S. Conversely, P concludes that it continues to control S.

2.5.430   Bankruptcy proceedings

2.5.430.10   Another example of circumstances that result in a reassessment of control is when an investee files for bankruptcy or enters receivership or liquidation. The rights of the parent when such circumstances arise vary from jurisdiction to jurisdiction, including whether any receiver is appointed over some or all of the assets of the investee, or over the shares in the investee. Therefore, a careful assessment of whether the parent's rights still give it power over the investee's relevant activities is required.

EXAMPLE 22 – REASSESSMENT OF CONTROL ON APPOINTMENT OF RECEIVER

2.5.430.20   Company S is a wholly owned subsidiary of Company P. S has significant creditors, including Bank B, and is in financial difficulty; P has not guaranteed any of the obligations of S.

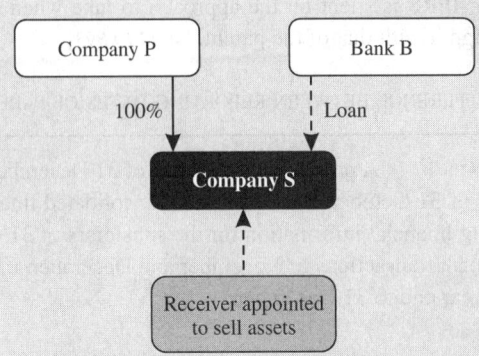

2.5.430.30   A receiver is appointed to sell the assets of S on a break-up basis. No attempt will be made to revive S's operations and there is no expectation that surplus monies will be available after settling with creditors.

2.5.430.40   The laws in the relevant jurisdiction include the following about the rights and obligations of a receiver:
- the receiver is acting on behalf of the interests of the creditors of S; and
- the usual powers of S and of the directors of S are suspended and can only be exercised with the consent of the receiver.

2.5.430.50   Although the management of S remains in place and the day-to-day operations of S continue, this is under the mandate of the receiver while a plan to dispose of the assets is formulated.

2.5.430.60   In this example, P concludes that it no longer controls S, because the rights that gave it power have been suspended. The substantive rights are now held by the receiver, because it approves all decisions over the relevant activities of S.

2.5.430.70   In addition, the change in rights causes the receiver and B to undertake control assessments to determine if they now control S.

2.5.440   SUBSIDIARIES' ACCOUNTING PERIODS AND POLICIES#

2.5.440.10   The financial statements of the parent and its subsidiary are prepared for the same reporting period. To achieve this, if the entities have different reporting periods, then additional financial statements of the subsidiary are prepared as at the parent's reporting date unless it is impracticable to do so. In any case, the difference between the year end of the parent and subsidiary cannot be greater than three months and adjustments are required to be made for the effects of significant transactions and events in that period. [*IFRS 10.B92–B93*]

2.5.440.20   If there is a difference between the reporting date of the parent and a subsidiary, then the length of the reporting periods and the gap between them is required to be consistent from period

217

to period. However, IFRS is silent on the approach to take when a subsidiary changes its annual reporting date to align it with that of the parent. [*IFRS 10.B93*]

EXAMPLE 23 – DIFFERENCE BETWEEN REPORTING DATES OF PARENT AND SUBSIDIARY

2.5.440.30   A parent has a year end of 31 December and its subsidiary has a year end of 31 October. Each year, the consolidated financial statements are prepared using financial information for the subsidiary at 31 October, adjusted for any significant transactions in November and December. In 2018, the subsidiary changes its year end to 31 December.

2.5.440.40   In our view, the 2018 consolidated financial statements should include the results of the parent for the 12 months to 31 December 2018, and the results of the subsidiary for the 14 months to 31 December 2018, unless the parent has already included the subsidiary's transactions in that time as adjustments made for significant transactions.

2.5.440.50   We believe that this is more appropriate than adjusting the group's opening retained earnings as at 1 January 2018 for the results of the subsidiary for the two months to 31 December 2017, an approach that would be necessary to limit the consolidated financial statements in the current period to 12 months of the subsidiary's results.

2.5.440.60   For the purposes of consolidation, the financial information of all subsidiaries is prepared on the basis of IFRS. Uniform accounting policies for like transactions and events are used throughout the group. Therefore, if a subsidiary uses different accounting policies from those applied in the consolidated financial statements, then appropriate consolidation adjustments to align accounting policies are made when preparing those consolidated financial statements. However, for an exception in relation to insurance contracts, see 8.1.60. [*IFRS 10.B87*]

2.5.445   FORTHCOMING REQUIREMENTS

2.5.445.10   There is no exception for insurance contracts under IFRS 17 – i.e. a group applies uniform accounting policies to all insurance contracts.

2.5.450   NON-CONTROLLING INTERESTS

2.5.450.10   NCI represent the equity in a subsidiary that is not attributable directly or indirectly to the parent. For example, if a parent owns 80 percent of a subsidiary directly and the remaining 20 percent is owned by a third party, then in the parent's consolidated financial statements the 20 percent interest held by the third party is the NCI in that subsidiary. [*IFRS 10.A, 22*]

2.5.460   Initial measurement of NCI

2.5.460.10   NCI can be categorised as:

- present ownership interests that entitle their holders to a proportionate share of the entity's net assets in liquidation (ordinary NCI – see 2.6.940); and
- all other NCI (other NCI – see 2.6.950). [*IFRS 3.19*]

2.5.460.20   When less than 100 percent of a subsidiary is acquired, the acquirer can elect on a transaction-by-transaction basis to measure ordinary NCI on initial recognition either at:
- fair value at the date of acquisition, which means that goodwill, or the gain on a bargain purchase, includes a portion attributable to ordinary NCI; or
- the holders' proportionate interest in the recognised amount of the identifiable net assets of the acquiree, which means that goodwill, or the gain on a bargain purchase, relates only to the controlling interest acquired. [*IFRS 3.19*]

2.5.460.30   This accounting policy choice relates only to the initial measurement of ordinary NCI. After initial recognition, the option of measuring ordinary NCI at fair value is not available (see 2.6.940.20).

2.5.460.40   The accounting policy choice in 2.5.460.20 does not apply to other NCI, such as equity components of convertible bonds or options under share-based payment arrangements. Such instruments are initially measured at fair value or in accordance with other relevant IFRSs – e.g. share-based payments that give rise to NCI are measured using the market-based measure in accordance with IFRS 2 (see 2.6.950). [*IFRS 3.19*]

2.5.470   Percentage attributable to NCI

2.5.470.10   NCI are the equity in a subsidiary that is not attributable directly or indirectly to the parent (see 2.5.450.10). [*IFRS 10.A*]

2.5.470.20   A parent may hold an indirect interest in a subsidiary through other entities. If a parent owns a controlling interest in a subsidiary through another subsidiary, then it includes that indirectly held interest in its share when calculating the percentage attributable to NCI. However, IFRS is silent on cases in which a parent owns a controlling interest in a subsidiary a portion of which is through an equity-accounted investee. It is not clear whether the interest held by the equity-accounted investee should be included in the parent's share when calculating the percentage attributable to NCI. In our view, the parent should choose an accounting policy, to be applied consistently, to use one of the following approaches for calculating its share in a subsidiary held indirectly through an equity-accounted investee.
- *Look-through approach:* Under this approach, the interest is included in the parent's share when calculating the percentage attributable to NCI.
- *Black-box approach:* Under this approach, the interest is not included in the parent's share when calculating the percentage attributable to NCI and only the direct holdings and indirect interest held through a subsidiary are taken into account.

2.5.470.30   When an interest in a subsidiary is partially held indirectly through equity-accounted investees, the profits of that subsidiary may be double counted. In our view, the accounting for the profit share of the subsidiary so far as it is held indirectly through an equity-accounted investee should be consistent with the accounting policy elected in 2.5.470.20 – i.e.:
- under the look-through approach, an entity should eliminate the equity-accounted earnings associated with the indirectly held subsidiary in its consolidated financial statements; and

- under the black-box approach, an entity should not eliminate equity-accounted earnings in its consolidated financial statements because this income is considered to have been earned from non-group entities.

EXAMPLE 24A – NCI AND INDIRECT HOLDINGS IN SUBSIDIARY – LOOK-THROUGH APPROACH

2.5.470.40 Company P prepares consolidated financial statements that include its two subsidiaries, Company S1 and Company S2, and the group's interest in an associate, Company Q. P's interests in the respective companies are shown in the following diagram.

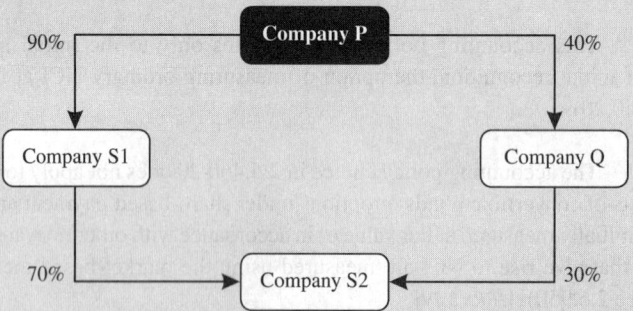

2.5.470.50 P applies the look-though approach for calculating its share in S2 that is held indirectly through Q. S2's profit for the reporting period is 1,000. P performs the following analysis to allocate S2's profit to the owners of the parent and the NCI.

2.5.470.60 P owns 63% of S2 indirectly through S1 (90% x 70%). Because P applies the look-through approach, it also includes its 12% interest in S2 held indirectly through Q (40% x 30%). Therefore, P's total interest in S2 is 75% and the NCI are 25%. P recognises in its consolidated financial statements 100% of the results of S2 allocated to the owners of the parent and the NCI as follows:
- profit attributable to the owners of the parent – 750 (1,000 x 75%); and
- profit attributable to NCI – 250 (1,000 x 25%).

2.5.470.70 When accounting for Q under the equity method, P would not recognise 120 (1,000 x 40% x 30%) of S2's profit in the consolidated financial statements to avoid the double counting.

EXAMPLE 24B – NCI AND INDIRECT HOLDINGS IN SUBSIDIARY – BLACK-BOX APPROACH

2.5.470.80 Modifying Example 24A, Company P applies the black-box approach for calculating its share in Company S2 that is held indirectly through Company Q.

2.5.470.90 Under the black-box approach, P does not consider its indirect holding in S2 through Q. Therefore, P's total interest in S2 is 63% and the NCI are 37%.

P recognises in its consolidated financial statements 100% of the results of S2 allocated to the owners of the parent and the NCI as follows:

- profit attributable to the owners of the parent – 630 (1,000 x 63%); and
- profit attributable to NCI – 370 (1,000 x 37%).

2.5.470.100   Unlike the look-through approach in Example 24A, under the black-box approach P does not eliminate 120 of its equity pick-up of Q in respect of S2's profit in its consolidated financial statements. Therefore, the total amount of S2's profit attributable to the owners of P is 750 (630 + 120) – i.e. the look-through and the black-box approaches result in the same amount of profit attributable to the owners of the parent, but in a different amount of consolidated net income and a different amount attributable to the NCI.

2.5.470.110   In some cases, the economic interests of investors will not equal their shareholding. For example, an entity may control 60 percent of the voting power in a subsidiary, but own only a 55 percent economic interest in the profits and net assets. In this case, the NCI are measured based on economic interest – i.e. 45 percent. [*IFRS 10.B89*]

2.5.480   *Transfer of interests in a subsidiary to defined benefit plans*

2.5.480.10   An entity may transfer interests in a subsidiary to a defined benefit plan and the interests may then qualify as plan assets under IAS 19 (see 4.4.600). If the contributing entity retains control over the subsidiary but a plan asset nevertheless arises under IAS 19, then in our view the entity should recognise NCI for the interests held by the defined benefit plan. If no plan asset arises – e.g. because the interests are not transferable – then no accounting entries result; the defined benefit plan has no asset and therefore the entity continues to account for the interests in the subsidiary.

2.5.480.20   We believe that after a contribution that qualifies as a plan asset, the returns associated with the shareholdings (see 2.5.210.30) accrue to the pension plan rather than to the contributing entity. It might be argued that the contributing entity continues to have these returns indirectly because, given that it is the sponsor of the plan, the benefits help reduce its obligation in respect of any deficit in the plan. However, we believe that it is only the initial contribution of the equity interests that reduces the net obligation and that, once the contribution has been made, any benefits arising from those interests thereafter – either through a change in value of the asset or a distribution – accrue directly to the plan as a return on its plan asset and are accounted for by the sponsor in accordance with the requirements of IAS 19, including the accounting for remeasurements of the net defined benefit asset or liability; they do not represent further benefits accruing to the parent entity, which then contributes them to the plan on an annual basis. Furthermore, the pension plan is a separate entity that is not in the scope of IFRS 10 (see 2.5.10.20 and 4.4.1490.30), which is the basis on which the NCI are recognised on the contribution of the shares to the plan.

2.5.480.30   Changes in a parent's ownership interest in a subsidiary that do not result in the loss of control are accounted for as equity transactions and no gain or loss is recognised (see 2.5.570). We believe that the transfer of interests in a subsidiary to become plan assets constitutes such a change in ownership interest. Therefore, net assets have to be reallocated to NCI to reflect such a change. As set out in 4.4.620, plan assets are measured at fair value on contribution, which is the consideration received in accounting for the reduction in ownership of the subsidiary. Any resulting difference between the measurement of NCI and the fair value of the interest transferred is recognised directly in equity. [*IFRS 10.23, B96*]

EXAMPLE 25 – PARTIAL DISPOSAL OF SHARES IN SUBSIDIARY TO PENSION PLAN

2.5.480.40   Company P has held 100% of the shares in Subsidiary S since its formation. The carrying amount of the net assets of S is 1,000. P transfers 20% of its interest in S to its pension plan, which qualifies as a plan asset under IAS 19. At the time of the transfer, the fair value of that interest transferred is 300.

2.5.480.50   P records the following entry.

	DEBIT	CREDIT
Net defined benefit liability (plan assets)	300	
NCI (1,000 x 20%)		200
Parent equity		100
To recognise transfer of shares and resulting NCI		

2.5.490   *Potential voting rights and the NCI proportion*

2.5.490.10   Even though the determination of control of an entity takes into account potential voting rights that are substantive (see 2.5.140), the calculation of NCI is based on current ownership interests because this corresponds to the economic interests of the parties. [*IFRS 10.B89*]

2.5.490.20   This includes in-substance current ownership interests – i.e. as a result of a transaction that gives access to the returns associated with an ownership interest. In these cases, the proportion allocated to the parent and NCI is determined by taking into account the eventual exercise of those potential voting rights and other derivatives that currently give the entity access to the returns associated with an ownership interest. [*IFRS 10.B90*]

2.5.490.30   In our view, 'the returns associated with the underlying ownership interest' are distributions of the subsidiary, and both positive and negative changes in the fair value of the underlying ownership interest. Therefore, we believe that the wider concept of returns that is used under IFRS 10 for the consolidation test – e.g. synergistic benefits due to economies of scale, cost savings and tax benefits – does not apply. This is on the basis that IFRS 10 did not intend to change the consolidation procedures that existed under the guidance in IAS 27 before its revision by IFRS 10, and the allocation of NCI with reference to, for example, synergies would be very difficult to achieve. [*IFRS 10.BC154*]

2.5.490.40   For a discussion of 'present access to the returns associated with the ownership interest' in the accounting for written put option or forward with NCI, see 2.5.690.

2.5.500   **Attribution of profits and losses**

2.5.500.10   Profit or loss and each component of OCI are generally attributed to the owners of the parent and to ordinary NCI in proportion to their ownership interests in the subsidiary. For example, if Company P owns 80 percent of Company S, then 80 percent of the earnings is allocated to the owners of the parent and 20 percent to the NCI in S. [*IFRS 10.B94*]

2.5.500.15   If there is a change in ownership interests while control is retained (see 2.5.560), then earnings are not simply allocated based on the closing proportion of the parent. In these cases, the allocation takes into account the change of ownership that has occurred during the period. [*IFRS 10.BCZ175*]

2.5.500.20   Losses applicable to the NCI in a subsidiary (including components of OCI) are allocated to the NCI even if this causes the NCI to have a deficit balance. [*IFRS 10.B94*]

2.5.510   *Profit-sharing arrangement or parent obligation to cover NCI losses*

2.5.510.10   A parent and the NCI in a subsidiary may enter into an arrangement to share profits (losses) in a manner other than in proportion to their ownership interests – i.e. a profit-sharing arrangement – or to place the parent under an obligation to absorb losses attributable to NCI. In our view, in its consolidated financial statements the parent should choose an accounting policy, to be applied consistently, for accounting for such a profit-sharing arrangement or guarantee. It can:
- take the profit-sharing arrangement/guarantee into account when doing the original attribution in the statement of profit or loss and OCI; or
- use the following two-step approach:
  1. attribute to the NCI its portion of the profits/losses in the statement of profit or loss and OCI in proportion to its present ownership interests in the subsidiary – i.e. unaffected by the existence of the profit-sharing arrangement/guarantee; and
  2. account for the profit-sharing arrangement/guarantee separately in the statement of changes in equity by attributing any additional profits/losses to the controlling interest or NCI based on the terms of the agreement. [*IFRS 10.BCZ162*]

2.5.510.20   For a discussion of the related effect on the calculation of EPS, see 5.3.60.50–60.

2.5.510.30   A guarantee issued by the parent to absorb losses does not result in a liability from the point of view of the consolidated financial statements – i.e. the transaction is between the parent and the subsidiary, and no entries are recorded in the consolidated financial statements.

2.5.520   Non-reciprocal capital contributions

2.5.520.10   In our view, non-reciprocal capital contributions (see 7.3.450) made by a parent to a non-wholly owned subsidiary should be allocated proportionately to NCI – i.e. they should be accounted for as transactions between shareholders, which have a direct impact on equity. [*IFRS 10.B96*]

EXAMPLE 26 – NON-RECIPROCAL CAPITAL CONTRIBUTION BY PARENT

2.5.520.20   Company X makes a non-reciprocal capital contribution of 100 to its subsidiary, Y, in which it holds a 75% interest. The NCI in Y make no capital contribution.

2.5.520.30   In this example, an amount of 25 is allocated to NCI and 75 is allocated to parent equity directly in equity in the consolidated financial statements of X.

2.5.530   Presentation of NCI

2.5.530.10   In the parent's consolidated statement of financial position, NCI are presented within equity, separately from the equity of the owners of the parent. If there are NCI in more than one subsidiary, then those interests are presented in aggregate in the consolidated financial statements. In the parent's consolidated statement of profit or loss and OCI, the amount of profit or loss and total comprehensive income attributable to owners of the parent and NCI are shown separately; they are not presented as an item of income or expense. [*IAS 1.54(q), 81B, IFRS 10.22*]

2.5.530.20   Income, expenses, assets and liabilities are reported in the parent's consolidated financial statements at the consolidated amounts, which include the amounts attributable to the owners of the parent and NCI. In addition, the amounts of intra-group income, expenses and balances to be eliminated in the parent's consolidated financial statements are not affected by the existence of NCI (see 2.5.550). [*IFRS 10.B86(c)*]

2.5.530.30   In our view, the presentation of NCI does not change if part of the NCI is associated with a disposal group classified as held-for-sale or held-for-distribution and/or a discontinued operation (see 5.4.20, 35 and 120).

EXAMPLE 27 – SUBSIDIARY IS DISCONTINUED OPERATION

2.5.530.40   Group P has an 80% interest in Subsidiary S, which is classified as held-for-sale and is a discontinued operation. The following additional information related to S is relevant for this example.

Net profit for the year (discontinued operation)	200
Carrying amount of assets (disposal group)	1,200
Carrying amount of liabilities (disposal group)	500
Carrying amount of NCI (disposal group)	140

2.5.530.50   In the statement of profit or loss and OCI, the result of the discontinued operation is 200. The result is not presented net of NCI of 40 (200 x 20%) because NCI are not an item of income or expense; instead, NCI are presented as an allocation of the group's profit or loss.

2.5.530.60   In the statement of financial position, the assets of the disposal group of 1,200 are presented as a separate line item. Likewise, the liabilities of the disposal group of 500 are presented as a separate line item. The NCI of 140 continue to be presented as a component of equity.

2.5.530.70   An entity should consider whether the NCI related to a disposal group and/or a discontinued operation should be disclosed separately from the NCI related to the continuing operations of the entity.

2.5.540   Non-controlling shareholders holding put options

2.5.540.10   Sometimes non-controlling shareholders of an entity's subsidiary are granted put options that convey to those shareholders the right to sell their shares in that subsidiary for an exercise price (fixed or variable) specified in the option agreement. From the perspective of the entity, such written put options meet the definition of a financial liability in IAS 32 if the entity has an obligation to settle in cash or in another financial asset, and are therefore recognised as such. For a discussion of the accounting for put options written to non-controlling shareholders, see 2.5.680.

2.5.550 INTRA-GROUP TRANSACTIONS

2.5.550.10   Intra-group balances and transactions, and resulting profits, are eliminated in full regardless of whether the unearned profit is in the parent or the subsidiary. In addition, cash flows from the parent are combined with those of its subsidiaries and intra-group cash flows are eliminated. Intra-group losses are eliminated in full except to the extent that the underlying asset is impaired. [*IFRS 10.B86(c)*]

EXAMPLE 28A – DOWNSTREAM SALE TO PARTIALLY OWNED SUBSIDIARY

2.5.550.20   This example illustrates the elimination in a 'downstream' sale of inventory from the parent to an 80% subsidiary.

	PARENT	SUBSIDIARY
Cost of inventory	700	1,000
Selling price of inventory	1,000	Not yet sold
Net profit before elimination	15,000	8,000
Net assets before elimination	125,000	65,000

Elimination entry on consolidation	DEBIT	CREDIT
Revenue	1,000	
Cost of sales		700
Inventory		300
To eliminate downstream transaction		
NCI share of profit		1,600 = 8,000 x 20%

2.5.550.30   Example 28A shows that the NCI are calculated without regard to the elimination entry because the unearned profit is in the parent's result. This is notwithstanding the fact that the unearned profit is included in the carrying amount of the inventory in the subsidiary's own financial statements.

EXAMPLE 28B – UPSTREAM SALE BY PARTIALLY OWNED SUBSIDIARY

2.5.550.40   This example is the same as Example 28A except that the 80% subsidiary makes an 'upstream' sale of inventory to the parent.

	PARENT	SUBSIDIARY
Cost of inventory	1,000	700
Selling price of inventory	Not yet sold	1,000
Net profit before elimination	15,000	8,000
Net assets before elimination	125,000	65,000

Elimination entry on consolidation	DEBIT	CREDIT
Revenue	1,000	
Cost of sales		700
Inventory		300
To eliminate upstream transaction		
NCI share of profit		1,540 = (8,000 - 300) x 20%

2.5.550.50   Example 28B shows that NCI are calculated after eliminating the unearned profit that is included in the subsidiary's results. In addition, the NCI share of net assets is also calculated after the elimination even though the inventory that was overstated from the group's perspective is in the parent's separate statement of financial position.

2.5.550.60   For a discussion of the deferred tax implications of intra-group transactions, see 3.13.1160.

2.5.560   CHANGES IN OWNERSHIP INTERESTS WHILE RETAINING CONTROL

2.5.570   General principles

2.5.570.10   After a parent has obtained control of a subsidiary, it may change its ownership interest in that subsidiary without losing control. This can happen, for example, through the parent buying shares from, or selling shares to, the NCI or through the subsidiary issuing new shares or reacquiring its shares. It can also occur when 'other' NCI are converted to 'ordinary' NCI (see 2.5.460.10).

2.5.570.20   Transactions that result in changes in ownership interests while retaining control are accounted for as transactions with equity holders in their capacity as equity holders. As a result, no gain or loss on such changes is recognised in profit or loss; instead, it is recognised in equity. Also, no change in the carrying amounts of assets (including goodwill) or liabilities is recognised as a result of such transactions. This approach is consistent with NCI being a component of equity. [*IFRS 10.23, B96*]

2.5.570.25   The accounting for the current and deferred tax effects of a transaction or other event is consistent with the accounting for the transaction or event itself (see 3.13.530.10). Therefore, in our view the direct tax effects relating to a change in a parent's ownership interest in a subsidiary while retaining control, which is accounted for as an equity transaction, should be recognised directly in equity. In our view, the amounts regarded as direct tax effects will generally be limited and do not necessarily include the full current tax crystallised by the transaction. For further discussion, see 3.13.1140. [*IAS 12.57*]

2.5.570.30   The interests of the parent and NCI in the subsidiary are adjusted to reflect the relative change in their interests in the subsidiary's equity. The IFRS Interpretations Committee has confirmed that any difference between the amount by which NCI are adjusted and the fair value of the consideration paid or received is recognised directly in equity and attributed to the owners of the parent. [*IFRS 10.B96, IU 01-13*]

2.5.570.40   These principles also apply when a subsidiary issues new shares and the ownership interests change as a result.

EXAMPLE 29 – SUBSIDIARY ISSUES ADDITIONAL SHARES

2.5.570.50   Company S has 100 ordinary shares outstanding and the carrying amount of its equity (net assets) is 300. Company P owns 90% of S – i.e. 90 shares. S has no OCI.

2.5.570.60   S issues 20 new ordinary shares to a third party for 120 in cash, as a result of which:
- S's net assets increase to 420;
- P's ownership interest in S reduces from 90% to 75% (P now owns 90 shares out of 120 issued); and
- NCI in S increase from 30 (300 x 10%) to 105 (420 x 25%).

2.5.570.70   P records the following entry in its consolidated financial statements to recognise the increase in NCI in S arising from the issue of shares.

	DEBIT	CREDIT
Cash	120	
NCI (equity)		75
Other equity (or retained earnings)		45
To recognise overall change in equity as a result of partial disposal to NCI		

2.5.570.80   IFRS does not provide guidance on the presentation of the resulting gain or loss within equity. Alternative approaches include establishing a separate category of equity (other equity) in which such amounts are recognised or recognising those amounts in retained earnings. In our view, either treatment is acceptable.

2.5.570.90   If there is a change in the ownership interest in a subsidiary without the loss of control, then the parent discloses in its consolidated financial statements a schedule showing the effects of such changes on the equity attributable to the parent. [*IFRS 12.18*]

2.5.570.100   If an entity acquires an interest in a non-wholly owned subsidiary that is not a business, then the requirements of IFRS 10 apply because the scope of the standard is not limited to subsidiaries that are businesses. In our view, IFRS 10 applies even if the subsidiary holds only a single asset. On that basis, we believe that NCI should generally be recognised in the consolidated financial statements of the parent in such cases.

2.5.580   Accounting for NCI

2.5.580.10   IFRS does not provide guidance on the treatment of goodwill when the interests of the parent and NCI are adjusted to reflect the change in interests. Depending on the initial measurement of NCI, there are different approaches possible, as discussed in 2.5.590–630.

2.5.590   *NCI initially measured at proportionate interest in identifiable net assets of acquiree*

2.5.590.10   If NCI were initially measured at their proportionate interest in the identifiable net assets of a subsidiary, because no goodwill was initially attributed to NCI, then several approaches to determining the adjustment to NCI are acceptable for purchases and sales of NCI when retaining control.

2.5.590.20   In our view, each of the following approaches is acceptable (see Examples 30A and 30B).
- *Approach 1:* Attribute a proportionate amount of all the net assets of the subsidiary, including recognised goodwill. This view interprets interests in a subsidiary as related to all net assets, including goodwill, recognised in the parent's consolidated financial statements. Under this approach, recognised goodwill is treated in the same way as any other asset.
- *Approach 2:* Attribute a proportionate amount of the net assets of the subsidiary; however, in doing so there are two separate asset pools: one asset pool is in respect of the parent's interest (net assets including goodwill) and the other asset pool is in respect of the NCI (identifiable net assets but no goodwill). Under this approach, a purchase of equity interests from the non-controlling shareholders results in adjusting NCI for the proportionate amount of the NCI asset pool because the parent is buying a portion of that pool of assets. Conversely, a sale of equity interests to the non-controlling shareholders results in adjusting NCI for a proportionate amount of the parent's assets-plus-goodwill pool because the parent is selling a portion of that asset pool to the NCI. In Example 30A, we illustrate the first transaction with NCI after obtaining control of a subsidiary; the calculations would be more complicated if there were several transactions with NCI – e.g. a purchase of NCI and a subsequent sale of NCI.
- *Approach 3:* Attribute a proportionate amount of only the identifiable net assets of the subsidiary. This view interprets interests in a subsidiary as related to identifiable assets only because NCI have been initially recognised only in respect of identifiable assets.

2.5.590.30   We believe that other approaches may also be acceptable depending on the circumstances. An entity should choose an accounting policy, to be applied consistently to both sales and purchases of equity interests in subsidiaries when control exists before and after the transaction and NCI are initially measured at their proportionate interest in the identifiable net assets of the acquiree.

2.5.600   *NCI initially measured at fair value*

2.5.600.10   In our view, if NCI were initially measured at fair value, then the adjustment of NCI on purchases or sales of equity interests in the subsidiary when control of the subsidiary by the parent exists before and after the transaction should include a portion of goodwill (see Examples 30A and 30B). This view interprets interests in a subsidiary as relating to all net assets, including goodwill, because goodwill is attributed to NCI when NCI were initially measured at fair value.

2.5.600.20   Likewise, if an entity initially acquires 100 percent of a subsidiary, then the same approach would be taken for subsequent sales or purchases of NCI because full goodwill was recognised in the acquisition accounting, just as is the case when NCI are initially measured at fair value.

2.5.610   *Impact of control premium*

2.5.610.10   If NCI are initially measured at fair value and there is a control premium in the consideration paid to obtain control of the acquiree, then a question arises about the determination of the adjustment to NCI when the parent sells equity interests to the non-controlling shareholders. In this case, we believe that a rational method should be used, based for example on a proportionate amount of the goodwill recognised in the financial statements (similar to Approach 1 in 2.5.590.20) or on a proportionate amount of the goodwill attributable to NCI (similar to Approach 2 in 2.5.590.20).

2.5.620   *Purchase of equity interests from NCI*

2.5.620.10   The following example illustrates the adjustment to NCI in the context of the purchase of equity interests from NCI.

EXAMPLE 30A – PURCHASE OF EQUITY INTERESTS FROM NCI

2.5.620.20   Company P acquired 80% of Company S in a business combination several years ago. P subsequently purchases an additional 10% interest in S.

2.5.620.30   The contribution of S to P's consolidated financial statements before the purchase of NCI is as follows.

	NCI INITIALLY MEASURED AT FAIR VALUE	NCI MEASURED AT PROPORTIONATE INTEREST IN IDENTIFIABLE NET ASSETS
Goodwill	100	80
Identifiable net assets	1,000	1,000
Total net assets	1,100	1,080
Equity (parent)	880	880
Equity (NCI)	220[1]	200
Total shareholders' equity	1,100	1,080

Note
1.   Assuming no control premium.

2.5.620.40   The contribution of S to P's consolidated financial statements after the purchase of the additional 10% interest (exclusive of the consideration paid) is as follows.

	NCI INITIALLY MEASURED AT FAIR VALUE	NCI MEASURED AT PROPORTIONATE INTEREST IN IDENTIFIABLE NET ASSETS		
		APPROACH 1	APPROACH 2	APPROACH 3
Identifiable net assets	1,000	1,000	1,000	1,000
Total net assets	1,100	1,080	1,080	1,080
Equity (parent)	990[1]	988[2]	980[3]	980[4]
Equity (NCI)	110[1]	92[2]	100[3]	100[4]
Total shareholders' equity	1,100	1,080	1,080	1,080

Notes
1.   Calculated as 880 plus 110 and 220 minus 110, where 110 = 10% x 1,100 (total net assets including goodwill) when NCI are initially measured at fair value.
2.   Calculated as 880 plus 108 and 200 minus 108, where 108 = 10% x 1,080 (total net assets including goodwill) under Approach 1.
3.   Calculated as 880 plus 100 and 200 minus 100, where 100 = (10% / 20%) x 200 (NCI) under Approach 2.
4.   Calculated as 880 plus 100 and 200 minus 100, where 100 = 10% x 1,000 (total identifiable net assets) under Approach 3.

2.5.630   *Sale of equity interests to NCI*

2.5.630.10   The following example illustrates the adjustment to NCI in the context of the sale of equity interests to NCI.

EXAMPLE 30B – SALE OF EQUITY INTERESTS TO NCI

2.5.630.20   Company P acquired 80% of Company S in a business combination several years ago. P subsequently sells a 20% interest in S but retains control of S.

2.5.630.30   The contribution of S to P's consolidated financial statements before the sale of NCI is as follows.

	NCI INITIALLY MEASURED AT FAIR VALUE	NCI MEASURED AT PROPORTIONATE INTEREST IN IDENTIFIABLE NET ASSETS
Goodwill	100	80
Identifiable net assets	1,000	1,000
Total net assets	1,100	1,080

	NCI INITIALLY MEASURED AT FAIR VALUE	NCI MEASURED AT PROPORTIONATE INTEREST IN IDENTIFIABLE NET ASSETS
Equity (parent)	880	880
Equity (NCI)	220[1]	200
Total shareholders' equity	1,100	1,080

Note
1. Assuming no control premium.

2.5.630.40   The contribution of S to P's consolidated financial statements after the sale of equity interests to NCI (exclusive of the consideration received) is as follows.

	NCI INITIALLY MEASURED AT FAIR VALUE	NCI MEASURED AT PROPORTIONATE INTEREST IN IDENTIFIABLE NET ASSETS		
		APPROACH 1	APPROACH 2	APPROACH 3
Goodwill	100	80	80	80
Identifiable net assets	1,000	1,000	1,000	1,000
Total net assets	1,100	1,080	1,080	1,080
Equity (parent)	660[1]	664[2]	660[3]	680[4]
Equity (NCI)	440[1]	416[2]	420[3]	400[4]
Total shareholders' equity	1,100	1,080	1,080	1,080

Notes
1. Calculated as 880 minus 220 and 220 plus 220, where 220 = 20% x 1,100 (total net assets including goodwill) when NCI are initially measured at fair value.
2. Calculated as 880 minus 216 and 200 plus 216, where 216 = 20% x 1,080 (total net assets including goodwill) under Approach 1.
3. Calculated as 880 minus 220 and 200 plus 220, where 220 = (20% / 80%) x 880 (parent equity) under Approach 2.
4. Calculated as 880 minus 200 and 200 plus 200, where 200 = 20% x 1,000 (total identifiable net assets) under Approach 3.

2.5.640   Changes in ownership interests in subsidiary that has OCI

2.5.640.10   When the relative interests of the parent and NCI change, in our view the balance of components of OCI should be reallocated between the parent and the NCI to reflect the new interests. For any foreign currency translation reserve, such reallocation is explicitly required following a partial disposal (see 2.7.340). [*IAS 21.48C*]

EXAMPLE 31 – REALLOCATION OF OCI

2.5.640.20   Company P owns 80% of the shares in Company S. On 1 January 2018, P acquires an additional 10% of S for cash of 30.

2.5.640.30   The carrying amount of the NCI in S before the acquisition is 48, which includes 4 for the NCI's portion of gains recognised in OCI for foreign exchange movements on translation of that subsidiary.

2.5.640.40   P records the following entries in its consolidated financial statements to recognise the decrease in NCI in S.

	DEBIT	CREDIT
NCI (equity)	24	
Other equity (or retained earnings)	6	
Cash		30
To reflect change in equity following acquisition of NCI		
Other equity (or retained earnings)	2	
Foreign currency translation reserve (4 x 10 / 20)		2
To recognise change in attribution of OCI following acquisition of NCI		

2.5.650   Transaction costs

2.5.650.10   The IFRS Interpretations Committee discussed whether an entity should recognise transaction costs for transactions with NCI while retaining control directly in equity or in profit or loss. The Committee noted that transaction costs should be recognised directly in equity. This approach is consistent with treating transactions with NCI as equity transactions and the requirement in IAS 32 that transaction costs of an equity transaction are accounted for as a deduction from equity (see 7.3.570). [*IAS 1.106(d)(iii), 109, 32.35, IU 07-09*]

2.5.660   Contingent consideration

2.5.660.10   In our view, contingent consideration payable for an acquisition of NCI should be accounted for similarly to contingent consideration payable in a business combination (see 2.6.280 and 1120). An obligation to pay contingent consideration is classified either as equity or as a financial liability based on the definitions in IAS 32 (see 7.3.270). Such an obligation is initially recognised at fair value as part of the transaction, with NCI recognised in equity. If the obligation is classified as a financial liability, then subsequent changes in the value of the liability are recognised in profit or loss in accordance with IFRS 9. [*IFRS 3.58(b)*]

2.5.670   Impairment considerations

2.5.670.10   When the parent's ownership interest in a subsidiary changes but control is retained, the change in ownership does not result in any adjustment to the carrying amount of the subsidiary's assets or liabilities, including goodwill. However, in our view if the price paid to acquire NCI is less than the carrying amount of those interests in the consolidated financial statements, then this might be an indication that certain assets of the subsidiary are impaired. In such cases, we believe that the entity should consider whether any of the underlying assets are impaired before accounting for the change in ownership interests (see 3.10.120.40).

2.5.680   Written put option or forward

2.5.680.10   An entity may write a put option or enter into a forward purchase agreement with the non-controlling shareholders in an existing subsidiary on their equity interests in that subsidiary. If the put option or forward granted to the non-controlling shareholders provides for settlement in cash or in another financial asset by the entity (see 7.3.50), then IAS 32 requires the entity to recognise a liability for the present value of the exercise price of the option or of the forward price. [*IAS 32.23*]

2.5.680.20   Recognition of a liability for the written put exercise price is required because the entity has an obligation to deliver cash or another financial asset if the non-controlling shareholders exercise the option. In our view, the likelihood of a written put option being exercised is relevant only in assessing whether the terms of the put are genuine. If the terms affecting the exercisability of the option are genuine, then we believe that a liability for the put option exercise price should be recognised. This is the case even if the put option is exercisable only on the occurrence of uncertain future events that are outside the control of both parties to the contract (see 7.3.40).

EXAMPLE 32 – NCI PUT OPTION CONTINGENT ON FUTURE EVENT

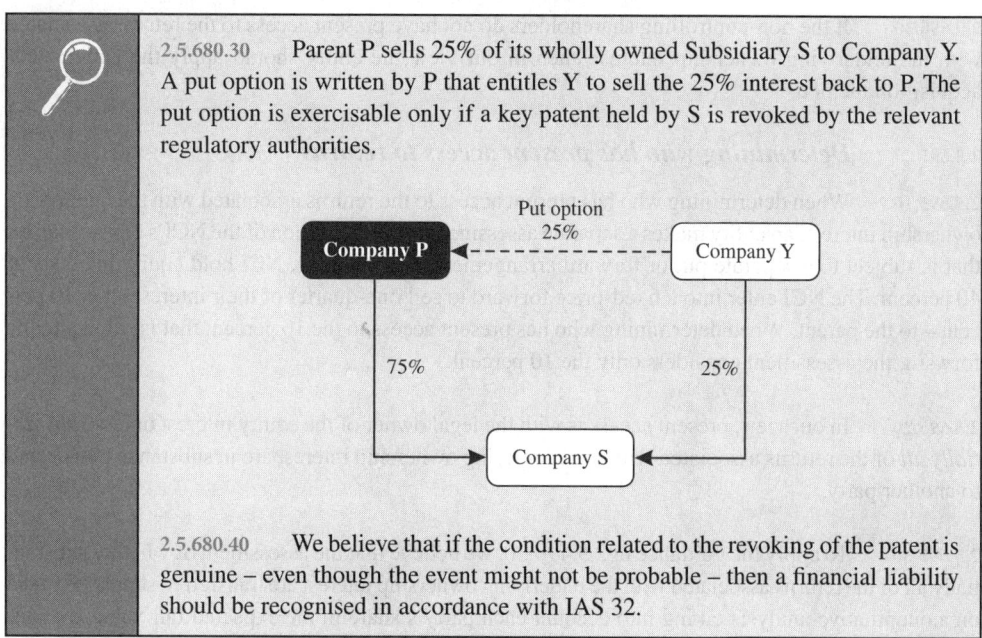

2.5.680.30   Parent P sells 25% of its wholly owned Subsidiary S to Company Y. A put option is written by P that entitles Y to sell the 25% interest back to P. The put option is exercisable only if a key patent held by S is revoked by the relevant regulatory authorities.

2.5.680.40   We believe that if the condition related to the revoking of the patent is genuine – even though the event might not be probable – then a financial liability should be recognised in accordance with IAS 32.

2.5.680.50   For a discussion of put options or forwards granted to the non-controlling shareholders that do not provide for settlement in cash or in another financial asset by the entity, see 7.3.250–260.

2.5.680.60   For a discussion of a put option written or a forward entered into as part of the acquisition of a subsidiary, see 2.5.730.

2.5.680.70   For a discussion of the presentation of discretionary dividends on NCI shares subject to a put option written by the entity, see 7.3.290.80–100.

2.5.690   *Accounting treatment driven by present access to returns*

2.5.690.10   For a written put or forward with the non-controlling shareholders in an existing subsidiary on their equity interests in that subsidiary, 2.5.680 discusses the credit side of the transaction. However, the accounting for the debit side of the transaction, as well as the subsequent accounting, is unclear under IFRS.

2.5.690.20   If the NCI still have present access to the returns associated with the underlying ownership interest, then in our view the entity could choose an accounting policy, to be applied consistently, to use one of the following methods.
- *The anticipated-acquisition method:* The contract is accounted for as an anticipated acquisition of the underlying NCI – i.e. as if the put option had been exercised already or the forward had been satisfied by the non-controlling shareholders. This is independent of how the exercise price is determined (e.g. fixed or variable) and how likely it is that the option will be exercised.
- *The present-access method:* Under this method, NCI continue to be recognised because the non-controlling shareholders still have present access to the returns associated with the underlying ownership interests; therefore, the debit entry is to 'other' equity.

2.5.690.30   If the non-controlling shareholders do not have present access to the returns associated with the underlying ownership interest, then in our view the entity should apply the anticipated-acquisition method.

2.5.695   *Determining who has present access to returns*

2.5.695.10   When determining who has present access to the returns associated with the underlying ownership interest, an entity makes a separate assessment for each portion of the NCI's equity interest that is subject to a separate put or forward arrangement. For example, NCI hold equity interests of 40 percent. The NCI enter into a fixed-price forward to sell one-quarter of their interest – i.e. 10 percent – to the parent. When determining who has present access to the 10 percent that is subject to the forward, the assessment considers only the 10 percent.

2.5.695.20   In our view, present access is with the legal owner of the equity interest unless *substantially all* of the returns associated with the underlying ownership interest are in substance transferred to another party.

2.5.695.30   To apply the guidance in 2.5.490.30, we believe that the assessment of whether substantially all of the returns associated with the underlying ownership interest are transferred should be based on a quantitative analysis taking into account each party's share in the expected fair value changes and distributions. However, in our experience distributions do not require a *separate* assessment in many cases. This is because the parent, through its control, is usually able to prevent distributions to the NCI, and therefore the value retained in the subsidiary becomes part of the change in fair value of the interest. In addition, even if distributions are paid (e.g. because there is a shareholders' agreement to do so), the exercise price formula often adjusts for them (e.g. a fixed price reduces as a result of dividends paid to the NCI or a variable price increases because value is retained rather than distributed). Therefore, dividends are often neutral to the analysis. Paragraphs 2.5.695.40–80 describe the assessment of returns from changes in fair value.

2.5.695.40   We believe that substantially all of the returns associated with the underlying ownership interest are transferred to the parent only if both of the following tests are met.
● *Test 1:* From an economic perspective, the instrument will be exercised in substantially all cases.
● *Test 2:* The sensitivity of the exercise price to the variations in the fair value of the ownership interest is sufficiently low that substantially all of that variation accrues to the parent.

2.5.695.50   Test 1 in 2.5.695.40 is automatically met for a forward. For other instruments – e.g. a put option – it is a matter of comparison of the exercise price across the range of likely variations in fair value of the shares in question. For example, if the fixed exercise price of a put option is *not* above fair value across substantially all of that range, then we believe that from an economic perspective the option will not be exercised in substantially all cases. Therefore, Test 1 is not met.

2.5.695.60   Test 2 in 2.5.695.40 is performed by considering the extent of correlation between variations in the exercise price and variations in the fair value. If there is a high correlation – i.e. variations in the exercise price are close to variations in the fair value – then the NCI will still be exposed to substantial changes in the fair value by the changes in the exercise price. For example, if the exercise price closely tracks the fair value, then the parent is not exposed to the downside risk or upside potential – i.e. not substantially all of the returns are transferred to the parent, and therefore the NCI retain present access. Test 2 is automatically met by a fixed-price instrument.

2.5.695.70   The table below shows how the two tests apply to certain instruments that ultimately aim to transfer ownership interests from NCI to the parent.

TRANSFER INSTRUMENT	TEST 1 (SEE **2.5.695.50**)	TEST 2 (SEE **2.5.695.60**)	PRESENT ACCESS – I.E. SUBSTANTIALLY ALL FAIR VALUE CHANGES
Fair value priced forward	✓	✗	Remains with NCI
Fair value priced put option	N/A [(1)]	✗	Remains with NCI
Fixed-price forward	✓	✓	Transfers to the parent
Total return swap over subsidiary shares (see 2.5.740)	✓	Depends on whether the swap is at a fixed or variable price: ● if the swap is at a fixed price, then Test 2 is met; and	Transfers to the parent if Test 2 is met. Remains with NCI if Test 2 is not met.

TRANSFER INSTRUMENT	TEST 1 (SEE 2.5.695.50)	TEST 2 (SEE 2.5.695.60)	PRESENT ACCESS – I.E. SUBSTANTIALLY ALL FAIR VALUE CHANGES
		• if the swap is at a variable price, then Test 2 is met if the degree of correlation is sufficiently low that substantially all of the variations in the fair value accrue to the parent.	
Fixed-price put option	Test 1 is met if the exercise price of the written put is high enough to be above substantially all of the likely variations in the fair value.	✓	Transfers to the parent if Test 1 is met. Remains with NCI if Test 1 is not met.
Variable priced forward	✓	Test 2 is met if the degree of correlation is sufficiently low that substantially all of the variations in the fair value accrue to the parent.	Transfers to the parent if Test 2 is met. Remains with NCI if Test 2 is not met.
Variable priced put option	Test 1 is met if the exercise price of the written put is high enough to be above substantially all of the likely variations in the fair value.	Test 2 is met if the degree of correlation is sufficiently low that substantially all of the variations in the fair value accrue to the parent.	Transfers to the parent if Test 1 and Test 2 are met. Remains with NCI if either Test 1 or Test 2 is not met.

Note
1. Both Test 1 and Test 2 need to be met for the present access to be transferred to the parent (see 2.5.695.40). Because Test 2 is not met, Test 1 does not need to be assessed.

2.5.695.80   Careful consideration is required for the analysis of combinations of call options and written put options. In our view, for the purpose of determining who has present access to returns, the assessment of call and put options that are symmetrical – i.e. call and put options that have the same fixed price or variable exercise price formula and the same or overlapping exercise time windows – is similar to the assessment of a forward since one or both parties will have an economic incentive to exercise because either the call option or the put option is in the money.

2.5.700 *Anticipated-acquisition method*

2.5.700.10   Under the anticipated-acquisition method, the interests of the non-controlling share-holders that hold the written put options or forwards are derecognised when the financial liability is recognised. This is because the recognition of the financial liability implies that the interests subject to the put options or forwards are deemed to have been acquired already. Therefore, the underlying interests are presented as already owned by the entity, both in the statement of financial position and in the statement of profit or loss and OCI, even though legally they are still NCI. In other words, profits and losses attributable to the holder of the NCI subject to the put or forward are presented as attributable to the owners of the parent and not as attributable to those non-controlling shareholders. [*IAS 1.81B, 32.DO1*]

EXAMPLE 33A – WRITTEN PUT OPTION – ANTICIPATED-ACQUISITION METHOD

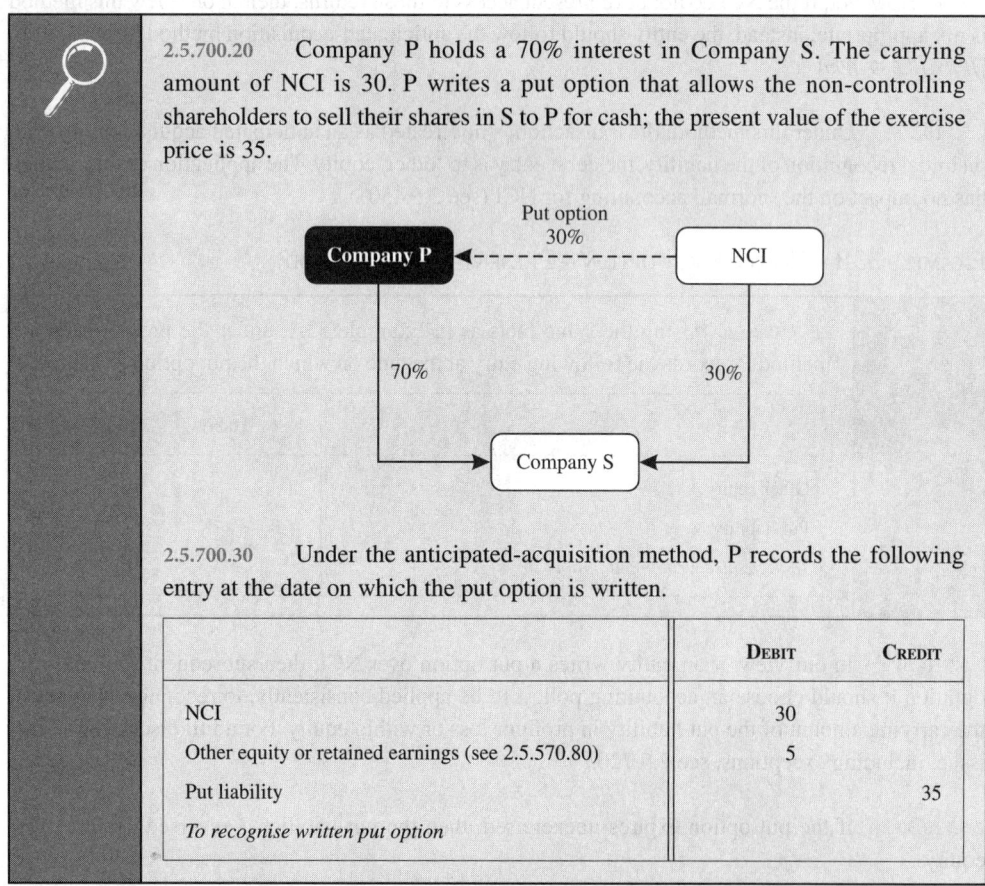

2.5.700.20   Company P holds a 70% interest in Company S. The carrying amount of NCI is 30. P writes a put option that allows the non-controlling shareholders to sell their shares in S to P for cash; the present value of the exercise price is 35.

2.5.700.30   Under the anticipated-acquisition method, P records the following entry at the date on which the put option is written.

	DEBIT	CREDIT
NCI	30	
Other equity or retained earnings (see 2.5.570.80)	5	
Put liability		35
To recognise written put option		

2.5.700.40   In our view, if an entity writes a put option over NCI, then subsequent to initial recognition it should choose an accounting policy, to be applied consistently, to recognise changes in the carrying amount of the put liability in profit or loss or within equity. For a full discussion of this issue, including exceptions, see 2.5.720.

2.5.700.50   If the put option expires unexercised, then the put liability is derecognised and NCI are recognised. In our view, this should be treated as a disposal of the 'anticipated interests' and should be treated consistently with a decrease in ownership interests in a subsidiary while retaining control (see 2.5.630).

2.5.700.60   For a discussion of the presentation of discretionary payments under the anticipated-acquisition method, see 7.3.290.80–90.

2.5.710   *Present-access method*

2.5.710.10   Under the present-access method, the non-controlling interest that is subject to the written put option or forward is not derecognised when the financial liability is recognised. This is because the NCI have present access to the returns that are the subject of the put options or forwards. However, if the NCI do not have present access to those returns, then in our view this method is not appropriate; instead, the entity should follow the anticipated-acquisition method (see 2.5.700). [*IFRS 10.B89–B90*]

2.5.710.20   Under this method, the transaction is not treated as an anticipated acquisition; instead, on initial recognition of the liability, the debit entry is to 'other' equity. The application of this method has no impact on the 'normal' accounting for NCI (see 2.5.450).

EXAMPLE 33B – WRITTEN PUT OPTION – PRESENT-ACCESS METHOD

2.5.710.30   Using the same facts as in Example 33A, under the present-access method P records the following entry at the date on which the put option is written.

	DEBIT	CREDIT
Other equity	35	
Put liability		35
To recognise written put option		

2.5.710.40   In our view, if an entity writes a put option over NCI, then subsequent to initial recognition it should choose an accounting policy, to be applied consistently, to recognise changes in the carrying amount of the put liability in profit or loss or within equity. For a full discussion of this issue, including exceptions, see 2.5.720.

2.5.710.50   If the put option expires unexercised, then the put liability is reversed against other equity.

2.5.720   *Recognising changes in put liability in equity*

2.5.720.10   As noted in 2.5.700.40 and 710.40, in our view if an entity writes a put option over NCI, then subsequent to initial recognition it should choose an accounting policy, to be applied consistently, to recognise changes in the carrying amount of the put liability in profit or loss or within equity.

2.5.720.20   Recognising changes in the carrying amount of the put liability in profit or loss is consistent with the requirement in IFRS 9 to remeasure financial liabilities through profit or loss (see 7.7.140). However, the IFRS Interpretations Committee has acknowledged diversity in practice, citing a perceived conflict between IAS 27 (2008) (carried forward into IFRS 10) and IAS 39 (carried forward into IFRS 9); therefore, we believe that recognition of the changes in equity is also acceptable. [*IU 01-11*]

2.5.720.30   In our view, the accounting policy choice described in 2.5.720.10 is not available for:
- forwards or total return swaps over NCI, because the Committee's discussion was limited to puts. In accordance with IFRS 9, changes in the carrying amount of the liability for forward contracts or total return swaps are recognised in profit or loss (see 7.7.140); or
- puttable instruments that are classified as equity by a subsidiary only by virtue of the specific presentation requirements of paragraphs 16A to 16D of IAS 32 (see 7.3.70). [*IAS 32.AG29A*]

2.5.720.40   If an entity chooses an accounting policy to recognise changes in the carrying amount of an NCI put liability in equity, then in our view this generally includes all changes in the carrying amount of the liability, including the accretion of interest.

2.5.720.50   A potential conflict similar to that between the guidance in IAS 27 (2008)/IFRS 10 and IAS 39 (carried forward into IFRS 9) discussed by the Committee may be identified between the guidance in IAS 21 and IFRS 10 on changes in the carrying amount of the put liability arising from foreign currency translation. Under IAS 21, gains or losses on the foreign currency translation of monetary items are recognised in profit or loss. In our view, an entity can choose to recognise changes arising from foreign currency translation in equity if the equity option is applied for changes in the carrying amount of NCI put liabilities. [*IAS 21.28*]

2.5.730   *Written put option or forward in business combination*

2.5.730.10   An entity may write a put option or enter into a forward with the non-controlling shareholders in an acquiree as part of the acquisition of a subsidiary. In that case, in our view there is a rebuttable presumption that the transactions are linked and that the guidance in 2.5.680–720 applies.

2.5.730.20   If the NCI still have present access to the returns associated with the underlying ownership interest, then goodwill will vary as a function of two decisions.
- *Decision 1:* Application of the anticipated-acquisition method or the present-access method (see 2.5.690.20).
- *Decision 2:* If the present-access method is applied (see Decision 1), then measurement of ordinary NCI on initial recognition at either fair value or their proportionate interest in the net assets of the acquiree.

2.5.730.30   This is because the deemed acquired interest and the consideration transferred are different under each method.
- Under the anticipated-acquisition method, the interest subject to the put option or forward is deemed to have been acquired at the date of acquisition. Accordingly, the financial liability arising from the put option or forward is included in the consideration transferred.

- Under the present-access method, the interest subject to the put option or forward is *not* deemed to have been acquired at the date of acquisition. Accordingly, the financial liability arising from the put option or forward is not included in the consideration transferred; instead, it is accounted for separately.

EXAMPLE 34 – WRITTEN PUT OPTION IN A BUSINESS COMBINATION

2.5.730.40   Company P acquires control over Company S by purchasing an 80% interest in exchange for cash of 120. The fair value of S's identifiable net assets is 100 and P elects to measure NCI at their proportionate interest in the identifiable net assets of S.

2.5.730.50   At the same time, P writes a put option that allows the non-controlling shareholders to sell their shares in S to P for cash; the present value of the exercise price is 25.

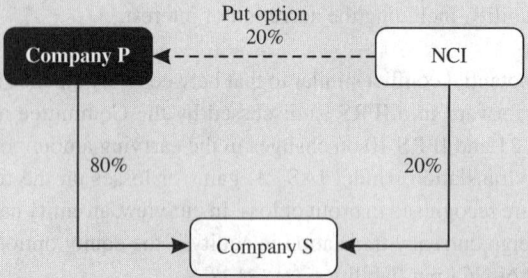

2.5.730.60   Under the anticipated-acquisition method, P records the following entry in its consolidated financial statements at the date of acquisition.

	DEBIT	CREDIT
Net assets	100	
Goodwill[1]	45	
Cash		120
Put liability		25
To recognise acquisition of S		

Note
1.   Goodwill is calculated as follows.

Consideration transferred (120 + 25)	145
Less fair value of identifiable net assets acquired	(100)
Goodwill	45

2.5.730.70   Under the present-access method and using proportionate NCI, P records the following entry in its consolidated financial statements at the date of acquisition.

	DEBIT	CREDIT
Net assets	100	
Goodwill[(1)]	40	
Cash		120
NCI (100 x 20%)		20
To recognise acquisition of S		
Other equity	25	
Put liability		25
To recognise written put option		

Note
1. Goodwill is calculated as follows.

Consideration transferred	120
Plus NCI	20
Less fair value of identifiable net assets acquired	(100)
Goodwill	40

2.5.740 Total return swap over subsidiary shares

2.5.740.10   A parent may enter into a total return swap with the non-controlling shareholders in an existing subsidiary. Under such a swap, the NCI agree to remit to the parent all of the cash flows on the equity interest (distributions and sale proceeds) in exchange for either a stream of fixed cash payments or a one-off fixed payment on sale or settlement of the total return swap. In these circumstances, the parent is exposed to all changes in fair value of the underlying interests and receives all distributions being made.

2.5.740.20   In our view, an instrument does not need to transfer legal ownership on settlement to provide present access. In addition, we believe that present access to the returns associated with the NCI's equity interest should be determined by considering the duration of the total return swap. Periods after the settlement of the total return swap should be disregarded because they would constitute *future* access to returns. Therefore, we believe that such total return swaps should be assessed similar to a fixed-price forward (see 2.5.695.70) – i.e. Test 1 in 2.5.695.40 is automatically met by a forward and Test 2 is automatically met by a fixed-price instrument. As a result, they transfer substantially all of the returns associated with the underlying ownership interest to the parent and therefore provide the parent with present access to the returns of the underlying interests.

EXAMPLE 35 – TOTAL RETURN SWAP OVER NCI

2.5.740.30   Company P holds a 70% interest in Company S. The carrying amount of NCI is 30. P and the NCI enter into a total return swap with the following terms:

- the NCI agree for a period of five years not to dispose of the shares and to remit all cash flows on their interest in S (including the fair value of the shareholding at the end of the five-year period) to P; and
- P agrees to a one-off payment to the NCI at the end of the five-year period with a present value of 35.

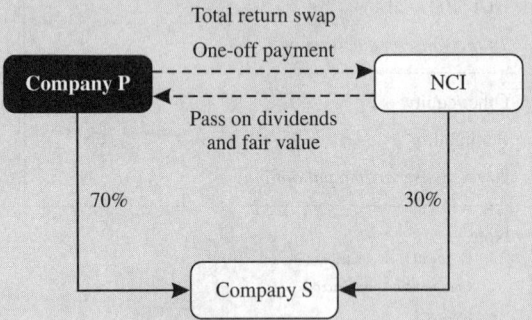

2.5.740.40   We believe that this total return swap transfers present access to the returns of the 30% interest to P for the five-year duration of the total return swap, and therefore P should apply the anticipated-acquisition method for this period (see 2.5.690.30).

2.5.740.50   P records the following entry at the date on which the total return swap is written.

	DEBIT	CREDIT
NCI	30	
Other equity or retained earnings (see 2.5.570.80)	5	
Total return swap liability		35
To recognise total return swap providing present access		

2.5.740.60   At the end of the five-year period:
- the total return swap liability with the corresponding accrued interest is extinguished by a payment from P to the NCI – i.e. the initial purchase of the 30% interest in S for a deferred consideration is now paid; and
- P receives a payment from the NCI for the fair value of the 30% shareholding in S. This is treated consistently with a decrease in ownership interests in a subsidiary while retaining control (see 2.5.630).

2.5.740.70   In our view, subsequent to initial recognition changes in the carrying amount of the total return swap liability should be recognised in profit or loss (see 2.5.720).

2.5.750   **Presentation of call options over subsidiary shares**

2.5.750.10   A parent may purchase a call option written by a third party over shares in a subsidiary. In our view, the premium paid for the call option should be debited to parent equity in the consolidated financial statements of the parent and not to NCI if the following conditions are met.

- The call does not in substance give the parent present access to the returns associated with the shareholding that is the subject of the option.
- The call meets the fixed-for-fixed criterion and is therefore classified as an equity instrument in the parent's consolidated financial statements (see 7.3.10).

2.5.750.20   We believe that the purchased call option is an equity instrument in its own right – i.e. it is part of the group's equity – that is held by the parent when these conditions are met.

2.5.760   **LOSS OF CONTROL**

2.5.760.10   A parent can lose control of a subsidiary in a variety of ways. The loss of control can happen without a change in absolute or relative ownership levels or in the absence of a transaction. There may be a loss of control if, for example:

- a parent sells all or part of its ownership interest in its subsidiary such that it loses control;
- a contractual agreement that gave control of the subsidiary to the parent expires;
- the subsidiary issues shares to third parties, thereby reducing the parent's ownership interest in the subsidiary so that it no longer has control of the subsidiary;
- substantive participating rights are granted to other parties;
- the parent distributes its ownership interest in the subsidiary; or
- the subsidiary becomes subject to the control of a government, court, administrator or regulator.

2.5.760.20   When a parent loses control of a subsidiary, it:

- stops consolidating the subsidiary by derecognising the assets (including goodwill) and liabilities of the subsidiary and NCI in the subsidiary, including any components of OCI attributable to them;
- recognises the fair value of the consideration received, if any;
- recognises the distribution of shares to the new owners of the subsidiary – i.e. the owners of the former parent – if the loss of control involves such a distribution (see also 2.5.780);
- recognises any non-controlling investment retained at fair value; and
- reclassifies to profit or loss, or transfers directly to retained earnings, amounts recognised in OCI in relation to the subsidiary on the same basis as would be required if the parent had directly disposed of the related assets or liabilities. [*IFRS 10.25, B98–B99*]

2.5.760.30   As a consequence, the amount recognised in profit or loss on the loss of control of a subsidiary is measured as the difference between (a) and (b), together with any profit or loss reclassifications.

a. The sum of:
  - the fair value of the consideration received, if any;
  - the recognised amount of the distribution of shares, if applicable;
  - the fair value of any retained non-controlling investment; and
  - the carrying amount of the NCI in the former subsidiary, including the accumulated balance of each class of OCI attributable to the NCI (see 2.5.760.50).
b. The carrying amount of the former subsidiary's net assets. [*IFRS 10.25(c), B98(d)*]

2.5.760.40   From the group's perspective, the loss of control of a subsidiary results in derecognition of the individual assets and liabilities of the subsidiary. On disposal, components of OCI related to the subsidiary's assets and liabilities are accounted for on the same basis as would be required if the individual assets and liabilities had been disposed of directly. As a result, the following amounts are reclassified to profit or loss:

- exchange differences that were recognised in OCI in accordance with IAS 21;
- changes in the fair value of debt instruments measured at fair value through OCI previously recognised in OCI in accordance with IFRS 9;
- the effective portion of gains and losses on hedging instruments in a cash flow hedge previously recognised in OCI in accordance with IFRS 9; and
- cost of hedging reserve previously recognised in OCI in accordance with IFRS 9. [*IFRS 10.B99*]

2.5.760.50   In our view, on loss of control of a non-wholly owned subsidiary, the reserve to be reclassified to profit or loss or transferred to retained earnings, as the case may be, is the net amount – i.e. excluding the amount of reserve allocated to NCI. For amounts reclassified to profit or loss, no amount of the reclassification is allocated to NCI because the reclassification of the reserve happens as a consequence of the loss of control of the subsidiary, which results in the derecognition of the NCI through profit or loss at the same time (see 2.5.760.30). [*IFRS 10.B99*]

2.5.760.60   There is some ambiguity in IFRS about how the gain or loss on the loss of control is calculated when a parent loses control of a subsidiary by contributing it to an associate or joint venture (see 2.5.810). If the entity applies the IFRS 10 approach and recognises the gain or loss in full in profit or loss, then the components of OCI of the former subsidiary are also reclassified in full as described in 2.5.760.40. If the entity applies the IAS 28 approach and eliminates a part of the gain or loss in respect of the continuing interest in the assets and liabilities contributed, then in our view the components of OCI of the former subsidiary should not be reclassified in full, but instead are reclassified on a proportionate basis. For further discussion, see 3.5.470. [*IFRS 10.B99, 21.48C*]

2.5.760.70   The NCI's share of the carrying amount of the net assets of the former subsidiary immediately before control is lost, which includes the share of all profit or loss and OCI that was attributed to the NCI, is derecognised. [*IFRS 10.B98(a)(ii)*]

2.5.760.80   Any retained non-controlling equity investment in the former subsidiary is generally remeasured to its fair value at the date on which control is lost; for a potential exception, see 2.5.810. The gain or loss on such remeasurement is included in determining the gain or loss on the loss of control. From the date on which control is lost, any remaining investment is accounted for in accordance with IFRS 9 or IAS 28, as appropriate. [*IFRS 10.B98(b)(iii), B98(d)*]

EXAMPLE 36 – PARTIAL DISPOSAL RESULTING IN LOSS OF CONTROL

2.5.760.90   Company P owns 60% of the shares in Company S. On 1 November 2018, P disposes of a 20% interest in S for cash of 400 and loses control over S.

2.5.760.100   At that date, the fair value of the remaining 40% investment is determined to be 800, and the carrying amount of the net assets of S is 1,750. OCI includes the following related to the subsidiary, which are net of amounts that were allocated to NCI:

- foreign currency translation reserve of 60; and
- fair value reserves (debt instruments) of 120.

2.5.760.110   The amount of NCI in the consolidated financial statements of P on 1 November 2018 is 700. The carrying amount of NCI includes the following amounts that were recognised in OCI before being allocated to NCI:
- foreign currency translation reserve of 40 (60 / 60% x 40%); and
- fair value reserves (debt instruments) of 80 (120 / 60% x 40%).

2.5.760.120   P records the following entry to reflect its loss of control over S at 1 November 2018.

	DEBIT	CREDIT
Cash	400	
Equity (NCI)	700	
Foreign currency translation reserve	60	
Fair value reserves (debt instruments)	120	
Investment in S	800	
Net assets of S (including goodwill)		1,750
Profit or loss		330
To recognise loss of control over S		

2.5.760.130   The 330 recognised in profit or loss represents the increase in the fair value of the retained 40% investment of 100 (800 - (1,750 x 40%)), plus the gain on the disposal of the 20% interest of 50 (400 - (1,750 x 20%)), plus the reclassification adjustments of 180 (60 + 120). Assuming that the remaining interest of 40% represents an associate, the fair value of 800 represents the cost on initial recognition and IAS 28 applies going forward (see 3.5.170).

2.5.760.140   The standard contemplates cases in which control of a subsidiary is lost and the subsidiary becomes an associate or joint venture. However, it does not currently contemplate the parent losing control of an entity and obtaining joint control of this entity, when the joint arrangement is a joint operation rather than a joint venture. [*IFRS 10.25(b)*]

2.5.770   Linking transactions

2.5.770.10   Because different accounting treatments apply depending on whether control is lost, the structure of transactions could affect the accounting result. As a consequence, IFRS 10 contains provisions for determining whether two or more transactions or arrangements that result in the loss of control of a subsidiary are treated as a single transaction. [*IFRS 10.B97*]

2.5.770.20   In some instances, it will be clear that a series of transactions are linked and should be accounted for as a single transaction. However, in other instances a careful analysis of the facts and circumstances and the exercise of judgement will be required in making the determination. If one or

more of the following indicators is present, then this may indicate that the transactions or arrangements that result in a loss of control should be accounted for as a single transaction or arrangement:
- they are entered into at the same time or in contemplation of one another;
- they form a single arrangement that achieves, or is designed to achieve, an overall commercial effect;
- the occurrence of one transaction or arrangement is dependent on the other transaction(s) or arrangement(s) happening; or
- one or more of the transactions or arrangements considered on their own is not economically justified, but they are economically justified when considered together – e.g. when one disposal is priced below market, compensated by a subsequent disposal priced above market. [*IFRS 10.B97*]

EXAMPLE 37A – LOSS OF CONTROL – LINKAGE (1)

2.5.770.30   Company P owns 70% of the shares in Subsidiary S. P intends to sell all of its 70% interest in S and is considering the following structures to effect the sale:
- sell all of its 70% interest in one transaction; or
- initially sell 19% of its interest in S without the loss of control and then afterwards sell the remaining 51% and lose control.

2.5.770.40   In the first case, the full amount of the gain or loss on the sale of the 70% interest would be recognised in profit or loss.

2.5.770.50   In the second case, if the transactions are determined not to be linked, then the gain or loss on the sale of the 19% interest would be recognised in equity, whereas the gain or loss from the sale of the remaining 51% interest would be recognised in profit or loss. However, if the transactions are determined to be linked, then the treatment would be the same as in the first case.

EXAMPLE 37B – LOSS OF CONTROL – LINKAGE (2)

2.5.770.60   Company P sells Subsidiary S to Company Q. The purchase and sale agreement includes a manufacturing and supply agreement. According to the manufacturing and supply agreement, P agrees to supply specific products to Q. The selling price of the products covers all of P's manufacturing costs (direct and indirect), transportation costs, duties and other taxes, and insurance costs, but includes no profit margin to P. The manufacturing and supply agreement starts on completion of the purchase and sale agreement and ends five years later.

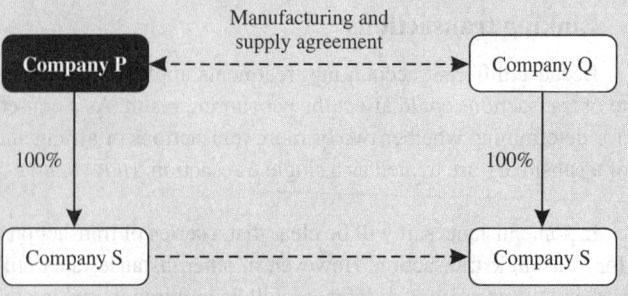

2.5.770.70   The following additional information is relevant for the example.

- P has no similar manufacturing and supply agreement with other customers.
- It is believed that P would not have received the same price for the sale of the subsidiary if the purchase and sale agreement had not been entered into simultaneously with the manufacturing and supply agreement.
- Each year, Q provides P with a two-year non-binding forecast of the expected order quantities, and a 12-month rolling forecast is provided on a monthly basis.

2.5.770.80   In this example, the agreement includes two transactions: the disposal of a subsidiary, and a manufacturing and supply agreement for goods. In our view, the transactions are linked and should be analysed together. We believe that a portion of the proceeds on the sale of the subsidiary should be deferred and recognised as revenue as the goods are delivered. Any subsequent changes in the estimate of goods to be delivered are changes in estimates and would be accounted for as such in accordance with IAS 8 (see 2.8.110).

2.5.780   Demergers/spin-offs

2.5.780.10   If a parent distributes its ownership interest in a subsidiary and loses control as a result (a demerger or spin-off), then it should consider whether the distribution is in the scope of IFRIC 17.

2.5.780.20   IFRIC 17 applies to non-reciprocal distributions of non-cash assets to owners acting in their capacity as owners, in which all owners of the same class of equity instruments are treated equally. It also applies to distributions in which each owner may elect to receive either their share of the non-cash asset or a cash alternative. IFRIC 17 excludes from its scope:

- common control transactions; and
- distributions of part of the ownership interests in a subsidiary when control is retained. [*IFRIC 17.3–4, 6–7*]

2.5.780.30   A common control transaction in this context is a distribution in which the asset being distributed is ultimately controlled by the same party (or parties) both before and after the distribution (see 5.13.10). [*IFRIC 17.6*]

2.5.780.40   For a demerger that is in the scope of IFRIC 17, the distribution is measured at the fair value of the assets to be distributed and any gain or loss on the distribution is recognised in profit or loss (see 7.3.690). [*IFRIC 17.11–14*]

2.5.780.50   The accounting for demergers that are not in the scope of IFRIC 17 is not addressed specifically in IFRS. Therefore, an entity should choose an accounting policy, to be applied consistently, for such demergers using the hierarchy for the selection of accounting policies in IAS 8. In our view, for a demerger that is not in the scope of IFRIC 17, the distribution can be measured using either book values or fair value. For a discussion in the context of common control transactions, see 5.13.90.

2.5.790   **Non-current assets held for sale**

2.5.790.10   When an entity is committed to a sale plan involving the loss of control of a subsidiary, it classifies all of the assets and liabilities of that subsidiary as held-for-sale when the IFRS 5 criteria for such classification are met (see 5.4.20). This is regardless of whether the entity will retain a non-controlling interest in its former subsidiary. [*IFRS 5.6–8A*]

2.5.790.20   If the subsidiary being sold meets the definition of a discontinued operation, then it is presented as such. For a discussion of the presentation of NCI related to a discontinued operation, see 2.5.530. [*IFRS 5.30–36A*]

2.5.800   **Amount owed to/from former subsidiary that remains outstanding after control lost**

2.5.800.10   Sometimes, an amount owed to or from a former subsidiary before losing control will remain payable after control of that subsidiary is lost. In such cases, a question arises about how to account for that amount in the consolidated financial statements on the loss of control. Because the receivable or payable is no longer eliminated at the point of loss of control, it is shown in the consolidated financial statements at the same amount as under IFRS 9 in the underlying separate financial statements. [*IFRS 10.B98*]

EXAMPLE 38 – LOSS OF CONTROL – RECEIVABLE FROM SUBSIDIARY

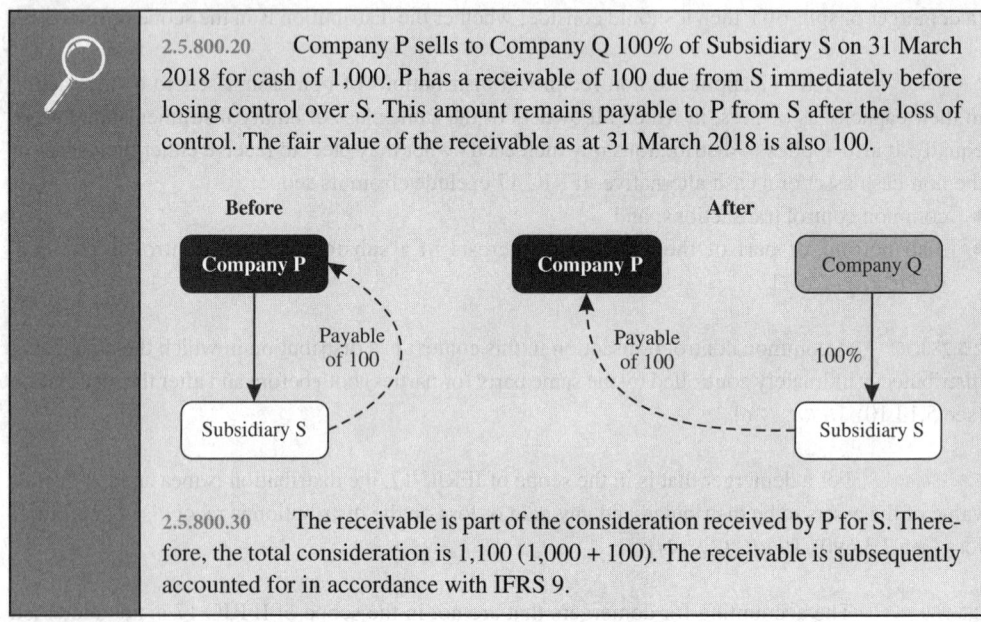

2.5.800.20   Company P sells to Company Q 100% of Subsidiary S on 31 March 2018 for cash of 1,000. P has a receivable of 100 due from S immediately before losing control over S. This amount remains payable to P from S after the loss of control. The fair value of the receivable as at 31 March 2018 is also 100.

2.5.800.30   The receivable is part of the consideration received by P for S. Therefore, the total consideration is 1,100 (1,000 + 100). The receivable is subsequently accounted for in accordance with IFRS 9.

2.5.810   **Contribution of subsidiary to associate or joint venture**

2.5.810.10   A parent may contribute a subsidiary to an associate or joint venture. A question arises about how to calculate the gain or loss because there appears to be some ambiguity in IFRS in this regard. IFRS 10 requires any resulting gain or loss to be recognised in full in profit or loss when control of a subsidiary is lost (see 2.5.750) – i.e. no elimination is made for a continuing interest in the assets and liabilities contributed. However, IAS 28 requires an elimination to be made for a continuing interest in the assets and liabilities contributed. [*IFRS 10.25, IAS 28.28, 30*]

2.5.810.20   In our view, this conflict means that the entity should choose an accounting policy, to be applied consistently, to apply either the IFRS 10 approach or the IAS 28 approach.
- *The IFRS 10 approach:* Under this approach, no elimination of the gain or loss is performed and the fair value of the retained investment is its deemed cost for the purposes of subsequent accounting.
- *The IAS 28 approach:* Under this approach, the gain or loss is eliminated to the extent of the retained interest in the former subsidiary.

2.5.810.30   For further discussion, see 2.5.760.60 (allocation of reserves) and 3.5.470 (equity-accounted investees).

2.5.810.40   The above guidance does not apply to joint operations, which are accounted for under IFRS 11. For a discussion of the sale, contribution or purchase of assets between a joint operator and its joint operation, see 3.6.270; and for the acquisition of a joint operation, see 3.6.317.

2.5.820   Written call option to sell shares in subsidiary

2.5.820.10   In some cases, an entity will sell a portion of its shares in a subsidiary and at the same time write a call option for the potential sale of additional shares. In our view, the proceeds should be split between the call option and the shares by determining the fair value of the call option at inception, required to be recognised by IFRS 9, and attributing the remaining proceeds to the sale of shares.

2.5.830   Agreement to sell ownership interests in subsidiary at later date

2.5.830.10   In some cases, an entity may enter into an agreement to sell some of its ownership inter-est in a subsidiary at a later date. If the entity retains control of the subsidiary, then the entity does not recognise NCI unless *substantially all* of the returns associated with the underlying ownership interest are transferred to the NCI (see 2.5.695).

EXAMPLE 39 – AGREEMENT TO SELL OWNERSHIP INTERESTS IN THE FUTURE

2.5.830.20   Company P owns 100% of Company S. P enters into an agreement with Company Q to sell 40% of its shares in S at the reporting date. The price of the shares to be sold is based on a fixed price determined at the agreement date. The fixed price will be reduced by any distributions made on the shares.

2.5.830.30   If P retains control of S, then P considers whether substantially all of the returns associated with the underlying ownership interest are transferred to Q. Because this is a fixed-price forward and any distributions made will be deducted from the forward price, Q is already exposed to all positive and negative changes in the fair value of the underlying shares. Therefore, substantially all of the returns associated with the underlying ownership interest subject to the forward

> have already been transferred to Q and P recognises NCI on a 40% interest at
> the reporting date.

2.5.840   Contingent consideration in seller's financial statements

2.5.840.10   A receivable relating to contingent consideration in the seller's financial statements is
accounted for under IFRS 9 if the receivable meets the definition of a financial instrument. [*IAS 32.AG8*]

2.5.840.20   Contingent consideration receivable is accounted for as a contingent asset in accordance
with IAS 37 if it is a non-financial asset – e.g. property (see 3.12.876). [*IAS 37.31–35*]

2.6 Business combinations

2.6   Business combinations

CURRENTLY EFFECTIVE REQUIREMENTS

This publication reflects IFRS in issue at 1 August 2018, and the currently effective requirements cover annual periods beginning on 1 January 2018.

The requirements related to this topic are mainly derived from the following.

Standard	Title
IFRS 3	Business Combinations
IFRS 13	Fair Value Measurement

FORTHCOMING REQUIREMENTS

The currently effective requirements are affected by the following forthcoming requirements. They are highlighted with a # and the impact is explained in the accompanying boxed text at the references indicated.

- In January 2016, the IASB issued IFRS 16 *Leases*, which is effective for annual periods beginning on or after 1 January 2019. See 2.6.585, 646 and 915. IFRS 16 is the subject of chapter 5.1A.
- In May 2017, the IASB issued IFRS 17 *Insurance Contracts*, which is effective for annual periods beginning on or after 1 January 2021. See 2.6.587 and 647. IFRS 17 is the subject of chapter 8.1A.
- In December 2017, the IASB issued *Annual Improvements to IFRSs 2015–2017 Cycle – Amendments to IFRS 3*, which are effective for annual periods beginning on or after 1 January 2019. See 2.6.1145.

FUTURE DEVELOPMENTS

The currently effective requirements that may be affected by future developments are highlighted with a * and are briefly discussed in 2.6.1170.

<table>
<tr><td>2.6.10</td><td># SCOPE</td></tr>
</table>

2.6.10 **SCOPE**

2.6.10.10   IFRS 3 does not apply to the formation of a joint arrangement; the acquisition of an asset (group of assets) that does not meet the definition of a business; or a combination of entities or businesses under common control. [*IFRS 3.2*]

2.6.10.20   Transactions that give rise to the formation of a joint arrangement – i.e. joint venture or joint operation – are outside the scope of IFRS 3 (see 3.6.350–360). However, this exemption applies only in the financial statements of the joint arrangement itself, and IFRS 3 is applied to a business combination entered into by a joint arrangement after its formation. [*IFRS 3.2(a)*]

2.6.10.30   If an entity acquires an asset or a group of assets (including any liabilities assumed) that does not constitute a business, then the transaction is outside the scope of IFRS 3 because it cannot meet the definition of a business combination. Such transactions are accounted for as asset acquisitions in which the cost of acquisition is allocated between the individual identifiable assets and liabilities in the group based on their relative fair values at the date of acquisition. For a discussion of the acquisition of tax losses other than in a business combination, see 3.13.1210. For a discussion of the accounting when the investor obtains control over an existing associate or joint venture that does not meet the definition of a business, see 3.5.580.30. [*IFRS 3.2(b)*]

2.6.10.35   In some cases, when an entity acquires a group of assets that does not constitute a business the sum of the individual fair values of the identifiable assets and liabilities differs from the transaction price. In these cases, the group may include identifiable assets and liabilities initially measured both at cost and at an amount other than cost. The IFRS Interpretations Committee discussed such scenarios and noted that to account for such an acquisition an entity first reviews the procedures used to determine those individual fair values to assess whether a difference truly exists, before choosing an accounting policy, to be applied consistently, based on one of the following approaches.
- *Approach 1:* Allocate the cost of the group of assets between the individual identifiable assets and liabilities based on their relative fair values at the date of acquisition, and then apply the initial measurement requirements in applicable standards to each identifiable asset acquired and liability assumed.
- *Approach 2:* Measure any identifiable asset or liability initially measured at an amount other than cost in accordance with the applicable standards, deduct from the cost of the group of assets the amounts allocated to these assets and liabilities, and then allocate the residual cost of acquisition to the remaining identifiable assets and liabilities based on their relative fair values at the date of acquisition. [*IFRS 3.2(b), IU 11-17*]

2.6.10.40   A business combination in which all of the combining entities or businesses are ultimately controlled by the same party or parties both before and after the combination, and that control is not transitory, is outside the scope of IFRS 3. For a detailed discussion of common control transactions, see chapter 5.13. [*IFRS 3.2(c)*]

2.6.10.50   In addition, IFRS 3 does not apply to acquisitions by an investment entity. However, this exemption applies only to investments that are not consolidated, but required to be measured at fair value through profit or loss. For a discussion of investment entities, see chapter 5.6. [*IFRS 3.2A*]

2.6.20   IDENTIFYING A BUSINESS COMBINATION*

2.6.20.10   A 'business combination' is a transaction or other event in which an acquirer obtains control of one or more businesses. An acquirer may obtain control in a number of ways including, for example, by transferring cash or other assets, incurring liabilities, issuing equity instruments or without transferring consideration. The structure of a transaction or event does not affect the determination of whether it is a business combination; whether an acquirer obtains control of one or more businesses is the determining factor. [*IFRS 3.A, B5*]

2.6.20.20   A 'business' is an integrated set of activities and assets that is capable of being conducted and managed to provide a return to investors (or other owners, members or participants) by way of dividends, lower costs or other economic benefits. A business generally consists of inputs, processes applied to those inputs and the ability to create outputs. [*IFRS 3.A, B7*]

2.6.20.30   For a transaction or event to be a business combination, the assets acquired and liabilities assumed over which the acquirer has obtained control are required to constitute a business. [*IFRS 3.3*]

2.6.30   Inputs, processes and outputs

2.6.30.10   For an integrated set of activities and assets to be considered a business, the set needs to contain both inputs and processes. Outputs are not required to qualify as a business as long as there is the ability to create outputs. If the acquired set includes only inputs, then it is accounted for as an asset acquisition rather than as a business combination (see 2.6.10.30–35). The key terms are defined as follows. [*IFRS 3.B7*]

	DESCRIPTION	EXAMPLES
Inputs	Economic resources that create (or have the ability to create) outputs when one or more processes are applied to them.	Non-current assets (including intangible assets or rights to use non-current assets), intellectual property, the ability to obtain access to necessary materials or rights, and employees.
Processes	Systems, standards, protocols, conventions or rules that create (or have the ability to create) outputs when they are applied to inputs.	Strategic management processes, operational processes and resource management processes. These processes are typically documented, but an organised workforce with the necessary skills and experience following rules and conventions may provide the necessary processes that are capable of being applied to inputs to create outputs. Accounting, billing, payroll and other administrative systems are not typically processes used to create outputs.

	DESCRIPTION	EXAMPLES
Outputs	The result of inputs and processes applied to those inputs that provide, or have the ability to provide, a return in the form of economic benefits.	Goods and services.

2.6.30.20   The acquisition of all of the inputs and processes used by the seller in operating a business is not necessary for the activities and assets acquired to meet the definition of a business. What is important is that a market participant (see 2.4.90 in the context of fair value) would be capable of producing outputs by integrating what was acquired either with its own inputs and processes or with inputs and processes that it could obtain. Therefore, it is not relevant whether the seller operated the set as a business or whether the acquirer intends to operate it as a business. [*IFRS 3.B8, B11*]

2.6.30.30   In our view, a significant characteristic of a business is that the underlying activities and assets are integrated. A group of assets without connecting activities is unlikely to represent a business.

2.6.30.40   If the acquiree has employees and the related employment contracts are transferred to the acquirer, then this may indicate that a business has been acquired. However, in our view a group of assets acquired could still be a business even if some (or all) of the staff employed formerly by the acquiree are replaced by the acquirer's own staff; and those staff will carry out the acquiree's existing activities necessary to generate economic benefits. Not taking over all of the employees might be a major part of the synergies that the acquirer is seeking to achieve by the acquisition. The acquirer's decision not to retain all employees does not mean that the acquired activities and assets do not comprise a business.

2.6.30.50   If some of the acquiree's processes and activities were outsourced before the acquisition and the related contracts are taken over by the acquirer, then this could indicate that the processes and activities necessary to create outputs are in place, and therefore that the group of assets acquired is a business. Conversely, if none of the processes or activities are in place at the date of acquisition, but instead would be designed and established by a market participant (or a market participant would already have similar processes), then this could indicate that what was acquired is not a business.

2.6.30.60   The exclusion of some components of a business does not preclude classification of an acquisition as a business combination if a market participant could operate the remaining activities and assets as a business. However, judgement is required in making this determination. [*IFRS 3.B8*]

EXAMPLE 1A – IDENTIFYING A BUSINESS – ADMINISTRATIVE PROCESSES EXCLUDED

2.6.30.70   Company P owns and operates restaurant groups in various metropolitan areas.
- P acquires from Company S a group of 10 restaurants located in a major city.

- The acquired group of assets includes land, buildings, leased assets and lease-hold improvements, equipment and the rights to the trade name used by the restaurant group.
- P also offers employment to the restaurants' employees, including management-level employees, service staff and chefs.
- P acquires S's procurement system used to purchase the food, drinks and other supplies necessary to operate the restaurants.
- P plans to integrate the 10 restaurants into its existing accounting and human resource systems.

2.6.30.80   The elements in the acquired set include the following.

Inputs	Non-current assets (land, buildings, leased assets, leasehold improvements, equipment, rights to the trade name); employees; and access to food, drinks and other supplies. If subjected to processes, then these inputs will create outputs.
Processes	Management and operational processes necessary to create outputs through the retention of management and staff; the procurement system.
Outputs	The intended outputs include food, drinks and service.

2.6.30.90   The acquired set of restaurants is a business because it contains all of the inputs and processes necessary for it to be capable of creating outputs to provide a return to P. Although the administrative systems (accounting and human resources) of S are not acquired by P, the acquired restaurants will be integrated into P's existing accounting and human resources systems. Because the acquired group of assets is a business, the acquisition is accounted for as a business combination.

EXAMPLE 1B – IDENTIFYING A BUSINESS – PROCUREMENT SYSTEM EXCLUDED

2.6.30.100   Assume the same facts as in Example 1A except that P does not acquire S's procurement system. The elements in the acquired set include the following.

Inputs	Non-current assets (land, buildings, leased assets, leasehold improvements, equipment, rights to the trade name); employees.
Processes	Management and operational processes.
Outputs	The intended outputs include food, drinks and service.

2.6.30.110   We believe that the acquired set of restaurants is a business. This is notwithstanding the fact that it does not contain all of the inputs and processes necessary for it to be capable of creating outputs to provide a return to P because S's procurement system was not acquired.

2.6.30.120   The acquired activities and assets do not need to be self-sustaining to be a business. The fact that some elements of a business are not taken over does not mean that what is acquired is not a business. A market participant could integrate the procurement needs of the acquired restaurants into its own procurement process. In fact, not taking over the procurement system of the acquiree may be a part of the synergies that a market participant would intend to obtain by entering into the business combination.

2.6.30.130   Because the acquired group of assets is a business, the acquisition is accounted for as a business combination.

EXAMPLE 1C – IDENTIFYING A BUSINESS – NO PROCESS ACQUIRED

2.6.30.140   Assume the same facts as in Example 1A except that P acquires only the land, buildings, leased assets and leasehold improvements, and equipment. S had closed the restaurants comprising the acquired set for a significant period of time before the acquisition by P. P does not acquire employees, the rights to the trade name or the processes from S. The elements in the acquired set include the following.

Inputs	Non-current assets (land, buildings, leased assets, leasehold improvements, equipment).
Processes	None.
Outputs	The intended outputs include food, drinks and service.

2.6.30.150   We believe that the acquired set of restaurants is *not* a business. A business consists of inputs and processes applied to those inputs that have the ability to create outputs. In this example, no processes are acquired. Therefore, we believe that there is no business and consequently no business combination; instead, the acquisition is accounted for as an asset acquisition (see 2.6.10.30–35). Even if a market participant would be capable of acquiring the land, buildings and equipment and integrating these into its own business to create outputs, the acquired set is not a business.

2.6.30.160   The seller may retain an option to repurchase key components of the business sold. In such cases, it is necessary to consider the nature of those components to determine whether the assets and activities acquired would meet the definition of a business in their absence. The terms and substance of the option are also considered.

EXAMPLE 1D – IDENTIFYING A BUSINESS – CALL OPTION OVER KEY PERSONNEL

2.6.30.170   Company P acquires Company S's R&D business. However, at the same time the parties agree on an option for S to reacquire the service contracts of the key research personnel in the business, exercisable at any time over the next two years. The R&D activities acquired are extremely specialised and the research personnel have unique knowledge that is not readily available in the marketplace.

2.6.30.180   Without the research personnel, one of the key elements necessary for the group of assets to comprise a business is missing. Therefore, in this example we believe that there is no business and consequently no business combination; instead, the acquisition is accounted for as an asset acquisition (see 2.6.10.30–35).

2.6.30.190   IFRS 3 contains a rebuttable presumption that a set of assets and activities in which goodwill is present is a business. However, a business does not need to have goodwill. Therefore, the presence of goodwill implies that the acquired set is a business. However, the acquirer should consider whether all of the tangible and intangible assets acquired have been correctly identified, recognised and valued before concluding that goodwill is present. [*IFRS 3.B12*]

2.6.30.200   IFRS 3 provides some example factors to consider in determining whether an integrated set of activities and assets in the development stage is a business, including:
- planned principal activities have commenced;
- there are employees, intellectual property and other inputs and there are processes that could be applied to those inputs;
- a plan to produce outputs is being pursued; and
- there will be an ability to obtain access to customers who will purchase the outputs. [*IFRS 3.B10*]

2.6.30.210   Not all of these factors need to be present for the acquired set to be considered a business. [*IFRS 3.B10*]

2.6.40   Investment property

2.6.40.10   If investment property is acquired, then a careful analysis of what is acquired is often needed to determine whether it constitutes a business. In our experience, it can be difficult to decide whether the acquired set meets the definition of a business, and judgement is required. However, IFRS 3 (and not IAS 40) is the primary standard in applying judgement to determine whether an acquired investment property qualifies as a business. Factors that may be relevant in making the determination include whether property management services are acquired and the nature of those services, and the level and nature of ancillary services – e.g. security, cleaning and maintenance (see 3.4.100). [*IAS 40.14A*]

EXAMPLE 1E – IDENTIFYING A BUSINESS – INVESTMENT PROPERTY

2.6.40.20   Company P purchases four investment properties (shopping malls) that are fully rented to tenants. P also takes over the contract with the property management company, which has unique knowledge related to investment properties in the

area and makes all decisions, both of a strategic nature and related to the daily operations of the malls. Ancillary activities necessary to fulfil the obligations arising from these lease contracts are also in place, specifically activities related to maintaining the building and administering the tenants.

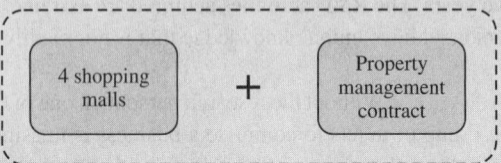

2.6.40.30   The elements in the acquired set include the following.

Inputs	Non-current assets (land and buildings) and contracts.
Processes	Management with unique knowledge related to investment properties in the area.
Outputs	The intended outputs include rental income.

2.6.40.40   We believe that the acquired set is a business because it contains all of the inputs and processes necessary for it to be capable of creating outputs to provide a return to P.

2.6.40.50   In contrast, if the property management is not taken over, then the group of assets might not be a business. The acquired set might not represent an integrated set of activities and assets because the key element of the infrastructure of the business, property management, is not taken over. If so, then P would account for the transaction as the purchase of individual investment properties, and not as the purchase of a business. It is necessary to consider all of the relevant facts and circumstances and significant judgement may be required.

2.6.50   OVERVIEW OF ACQUISITION METHOD

2.6.50.10   IFRS 3 requires acquisition accounting to be applied to all business combinations in its scope. Below are the steps to follow in applying acquisition accounting for a business combination, which are discussed in more detail throughout this chapter. [*IFRS 3.4–5*]

REQUIREMENT	REFERENCE
Identify the acquirer	2.6.60
Determine the date of acquisition	2.6.180

REQUIREMENT	REFERENCE
Identify the consideration transferred in the business combination, and elements of the transaction that should be accounted for separately from the business combination	2.6.260, 340
Measure the consideration transferred	2.6.260
Identify the identifiable assets acquired and liabilities assumed in the business combination	2.6.560
Measure the identifiable assets acquired and liabilities assumed in the business combination	2.6.600
Measure NCI	2.6.930
Determine the amount of goodwill or the gain on a bargain purchase	2.6.1010
Recognise any measurement period adjustments	2.6.1020

2.6.60   IDENTIFYING THE ACQUIRER

2.6.60.10   An acquirer is identified for each business combination. The acquirer is the combining entity that obtains control of the other combining business or businesses. The concept of control is discussed in chapter 2.5. [*IFRS 3.6, A*]

2.6.60.20   In most business combinations, identifying the acquirer is straightforward because it will be clear which one of the combining entities has obtained control. The acquirer is identified in the following steps.
1. Apply the guidance in IFRS 10 to determine who has control.
2. If an acquirer cannot be identified clearly from the guidance in IFRS 10, then the additional factors identified in IFRS 3 are considered. These consist mainly of examining the form of the consideration transferred, the relative size of the combining entities, relative voting rights and the composition of the board of directors and senior management. [*IFRS 3.7, B13–B18, 10.5–18*]

2.6.60.30   In our view, the IFRS 10 guidance discussed in chapter 2.5 should not be the sole focus of identifying an acquirer even if it appears that an acquirer can be identified; the additional guidance in IFRS 3 should also be taken into account. Otherwise there is a risk that the analysis of which party is the acquirer may lead to an answer that conflicts with what we believe is the intention of IFRS 3. For example, only applying the IFRS 10 guidance on control would mean that a reverse acquisition (see 2.6.170) could not arise, because the investor that controls all of the voting rights of an investee will always be assessed to have power if the investee is controlled by means of voting rights (see 2.5.130).

2.6.70   Combinations effected primarily by transferring cash/other assets or by incurring liabilities

2.6.70.10   In business combinations effected primarily by the transfer of cash or other assets or by incurring liabilities, the acquirer is usually the entity that transfers the cash or other assets or incurs the liabilities. For example, if Company P acquires Company S by transferring cash to the owners of S, then P would usually be identified as the acquirer in the business combination, assuming that S meets the definition of a business (see 2.6.20). [*IFRS 3.B14*]

2.6.80   Combinations effected primarily by exchanging equity interests

2.6.80.10   In most business combinations effected primarily through the exchange of equity interests, the acquirer is the entity that issues the new equity interests. One exception to this general principle is a reverse acquisition, in which the issuing entity is the acquiree (see 2.6.170). Another exception arises when a new entity is created to issue equity instruments to effect a business combination (see 2.6.150). [*IFRS 3.B15, B18*]

2.6.80.20   Although it is not an exhaustive list, other factors to consider in identifying the acquirer are discussed in 2.6.90–140. The factors have no hierarchy, and some factors may be more relevant to identifying the acquirer in one combination and less relevant in others. Judgement is required when the various factors individually point to different entities being the acquirer.

2.6.90   *Relative voting rights*

2.6.90.10   The acquirer is usually the combining entity whose owners, as a group, hold the largest portion of the voting rights in the combined entity. Typically, the weight attached to this factor increases as the portion of the voting rights held by the largest interest holder increases – e.g. a split of 80 percent to 20 percent is likely to be determinative in the absence of other factors. In making this determination, consideration is given to the existence of any unusual or special voting arrangements, and potential voting rights such as options, warrants or convertible securities that are 'substantive' (see 2.5.140). [*IFRS 3.B15(a)*]

2.6.90.20   In some cases, the exercise of potential voting rights may be subject to regulatory approval. In our view, the rights are considered substantive only when regulatory approval is deemed a mere formality. The nature of regulatory approval, together with all relevant facts and circumstances, should be considered when making this assessment.

2.6.90.30   In some transactions, the voting rights of one or more classes of shares automatically change at a future date or on the occurrence of specified events. For example, a class of shares may be designated as non-voting for a limited time period following the business combination. All of the facts and circumstances of the transaction are evaluated to determine how this affects the identification of the acquirer. The discussion in 2.6.110 may also be helpful in evaluating whether the period of time for which the shares are non-voting is substantive.

2.6.100   *Large minority voting interest*

2.6.100.10   If there is a large minority voting interest and no other owner or organised group of owners has a significant voting interest, then the acquirer is usually the combining entity whose single owner or organised group of owners holds the largest minority voting interest in the combined entity. For example, if one investor owns 40 percent of the newly combined entity and the remaining 60 percent is shared equally by six other investors who are not organised as a group, then the combining entity previously owned by the investor holding 40 percent of the combined entity is likely to be the acquirer. For an illustration of this principle, see Example 2C. [*IFRS 3.B15(b)*]

2.6.110 *Composition of governing body*

2.6.110.10   The acquirer is usually the combining entity whose shareholders (owners) have the ability to appoint or remove a majority of the members of the governing body – e.g. board of directors – of the combined entity. [*IFRS 3.B15(c)*]

2.6.110.20   IFRS 3 is silent on whether these rights need to exist only at the date of acquisition, or for a period of time thereafter. However, if control of the governing body by a shareholder group is temporary, then consideration is given to whether that control is substantive. In making this determination, the period of time for which each governing body member is entitled to hold their position is also considered, taking into account scheduled retirements and elections after the date of acquisition.

2.6.110.30   Although there is no minimum duration required for a shareholder group to be in control of the governing body for it to be deemed substantive, in our view control should generally extend for a sufficient duration to allow the governing body to consider and act on substantive matters following the acquisition. These may include matters related to corporate governance, the appointment and compensation of senior management, the issue of debt or equity securities, and substantive business integration, exit and disposal activities. If the period of control of the governing body is temporary, then judgement is required in determining whether that control is substantive.

2.6.120 *Composition of senior management*

2.6.120.10   The acquirer is usually the combining entity whose former management dominates the management of the combined entity. [*IFRS 3.B15(d)*]

2.6.120.20   IFRS 3 is silent on what is meant by 'management'. In our view, it is consistent with 'key management personnel' defined in IAS 24 as being those persons having authority and responsibility for planning, directing and controlling the activities of the entity. The definition of key management personnel includes directors (both executive and non-executive) of an entity or any of the entity's parents (see 5.5.40). [*IAS 24.9*]

2.6.130 *Terms of exchange*

2.6.130.10   The acquirer is usually the combining entity that pays a premium over the pre-combination fair value of the equity interests of the other combining entity or entities. This factor applies equally when the equity instruments exchanged are not publicly traded. [*IFRS 3.B15(e)*]

EXAMPLE 2A – IDENTIFYING THE ACQUIRER – LEVEL OF INFLUENCE

2.6.130.20   Company P acquires 100% of the shares of public Company S. P obtains 15% of these shares for a cash payment at a premium of 10% above the market price. It acquires the remaining shares in exchange for 58% of the shares in P.

2.6.130.30   The former shareholders of S also obtain warrants in P. If they were exercised, then this would increase their interest in P to 71%. However, the warrants cannot be exercised for three years from the date of the acquisition.

2.6.130.40   The board of directors of the combined entity consists of five nominees of P and four nominees of S for a two-year term. The removal of board members requires a vote of at least two-thirds of the shareholders. The chairman and the CEO of P retain their positions in the combined company. No other relevant circumstances exist with respect to voting, ownership of significant blocks of shares, or management.

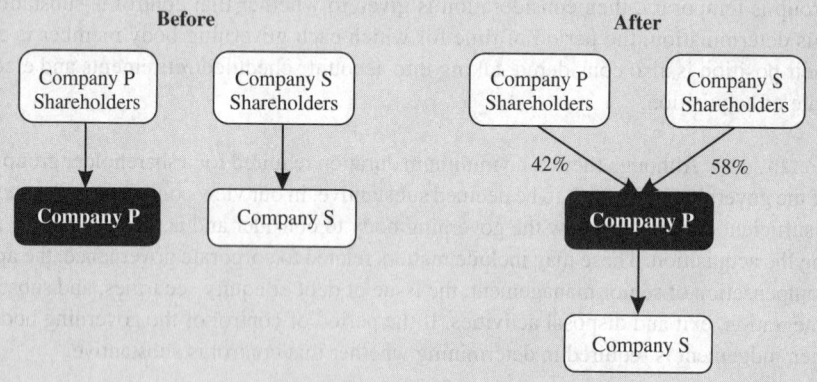

2.6.130.50   In our view, P is the acquirer, notwithstanding the voting majority of the former shareholders of S. Although S's former shareholders will own the majority of the shares in the combined company, they will not own two-thirds of the shares for at least three years following the business combination; accordingly, they will not be able to vote out the board of directors in place immediately after the business combination. P paid partly in cash, including a premium above market price, and dominates the board of directors and senior management of the combined entity. Therefore, we believe that P is the acquirer because its former shareholders have the most influence over the combined entity.

2.6.140   *Relative sizes*

2.6.140.10   The acquirer is usually the combining entity that is significantly larger than the other combining entity or entities. Size can be measured with reference to, for example, assets, revenue or profit. Other examples of relative size include operating cash flows and market capitalisation. If assets are being used to compare relative size, then in our view it is the fair value of the assets that should be used. [*IFRS 3.B16*]

2.6.140.20   Judgement is required in comparing the combining entities based on their relative size. If each combining entity is involved in similar businesses, then a comparison of relative size might be straightforward. However, if the combining entities are involved in different businesses, then a comparison of relative size might not be straightforward and certain adjustments to amounts reported in the financial statements may be required. Information other than the amounts reported in the financial statements is also considered.

EXAMPLE 2B – IDENTIFYING THE ACQUIRER – USING FAIR VALUES

2.6.140.30   Two companies' principal revenue-generating assets are intangible. In one case, the assets were internally developed and did not qualify for recognition in the statement of financial position; in the other case, the assets were acquired in a series of business combinations and therefore are recognised in the statement of financial position. Accordingly, comparing the reported assets of the two companies may not be appropriate. As noted in 2.6.140.10, we believe that the fair value of the assets should be used.

2.6.140.40   Similarly, comparing the amount of reported revenues without considering the nature and source of those revenues may not be appropriate. For example, comparing revenues generated by an entity with high volumes and low gross margins (e.g. a grocery store chain) with revenues generated by an entity with low volumes and high gross margins (e.g. a designer and manufacturer of specialised equipment) might not be meaningful.

2.6.150   New entity formed to effect business combination

2.6.150.10   A new entity (Newco) formed to effect a business combination is not necessarily the acquirer. If the new entity issues shares to effect the business combination, then one of the combining entities that existed before the combination is identified as the acquirer by considering the additional factors provided in IFRS 3 (see 2.6.70–140 and 160). [*IFRS 3.B18*]

2.6.150.20   A newly formed entity that pays cash rather than issuing shares in a business combination might be identified as the acquirer; however, it will not always be the acquirer. All facts and circumstances are considered in identifying the acquirer in a business combination and judgement is required. [*IFRS 3.B18*]

2.6.150.30   A business combination in which two or more entities transfer net assets that constitute businesses to a newly formed entity, or the owners of those entities transfer their equity interests to a newly formed entity, is a business combination in the scope of IFRS 3; in some countries, such a business combination is referred to as a 'roll-up' or 'put-together' transaction. For an example of such a business combination, see Example 2C. [*IFRS 3.B18*]

2.6.150.40   For a discussion of contributions that constitute a business on formation of a joint venture, see 3.6.350.

2.6.160   Combinations involving more than two entities

2.6.160.10   There is only one acquirer in a business combination. In business combinations involving more than two entities, determining the acquirer includes consideration of, among other things, which of the combining entities initiated the combination and the relative size of the combining entities. [*IFRS 3.B17*]

2.6.160.20   The guidance in respect of combinations involving the exchange of equity interests, which indicates that the acquirer is usually the combining entity whose single owner or organised group of owners holds the largest minority voting interest in the combined entity (see 2.6.100), may be particularly helpful in identifying the acquirer in some combinations involving more than two entities.

EXAMPLE 2C – IDENTIFYING THE ACQUIRER – DOMINANT SHAREHOLDER

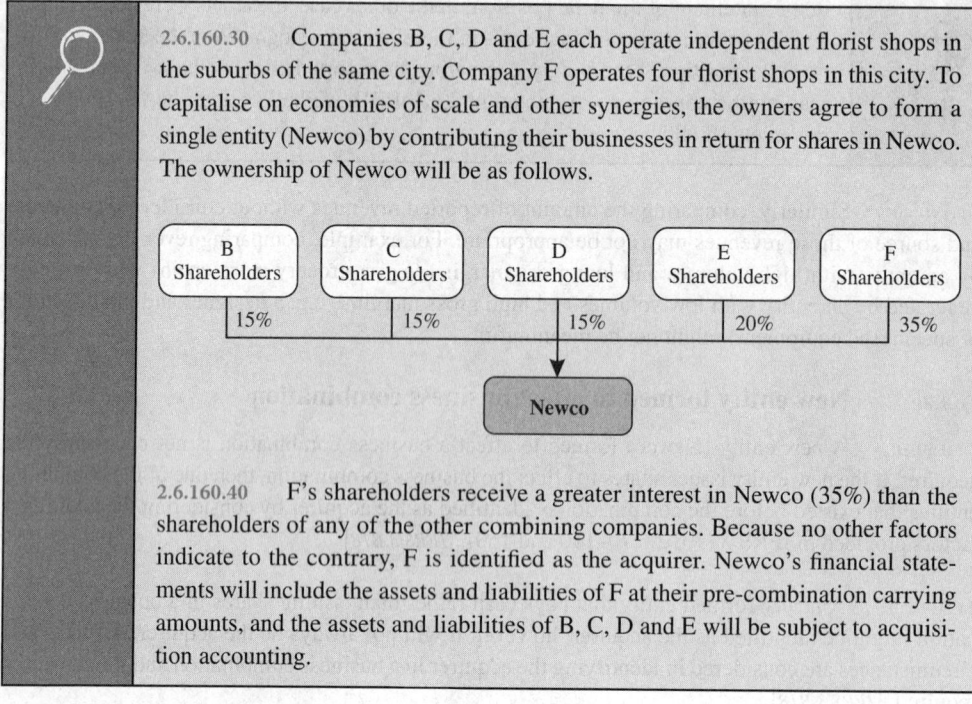

2.6.160.30   Companies B, C, D and E each operate independent florist shops in the suburbs of the same city. Company F operates four florist shops in this city. To capitalise on economies of scale and other synergies, the owners agree to form a single entity (Newco) by contributing their businesses in return for shares in Newco. The ownership of Newco will be as follows.

2.6.160.40   F's shareholders receive a greater interest in Newco (35%) than the shareholders of any of the other combining companies. Because no other factors indicate to the contrary, F is identified as the acquirer. Newco's financial statements will include the assets and liabilities of F at their pre-combination carrying amounts, and the assets and liabilities of B, C, D and E will be subject to acquisition accounting.

2.6.170   Reverse acquisitions

2.6.170.10   A 'reverse acquisition' is a business combination in which the legal acquirer – i.e. the entity that issues the securities – becomes the acquiree for accounting purposes and the legal acquiree becomes the acquirer for accounting purposes. It is the application of the guidance in IFRS 3 on identifying the acquirer that results in the identification of the legal acquiree as the accounting acquirer in a reverse acquisition (see 2.6.60). [*IFRS 3.B19*]

2.6.170.20   For example, an unlisted operating entity may wish to obtain a stock exchange listing but wants to avoid a public offering. The unlisted entity arranges for a listed entity to acquire its equity interests in exchange for the equity interests of the listed entity. In this example, the listed entity is the legal acquirer because it issued its equity interests, and the unlisted entity is the legal acquiree because its equity interests were acquired. However, application of the guidance in IFRS 3 on identifying the acquirer may result in identifying the listed entity as the accounting acquiree and the unlisted entity as the accounting acquirer. In this case, if the listed entity is:
- a business (see 2.6.20), then IFRS 3 applies; or
- not a business, then the IFRS Interpretations Committee noted that IFRS 2 applies to the transaction once the acquirer has been identified following the principles in IFRS 3 (see 4.5.2360). [*IFRS 3.B19, IU 03-13*]

2.6.170.30   The Committee has also confirmed that the acquirer in a reverse acquisition is not required to be a legal entity if it is a reporting entity. [*IU 09-11*]

2.6.170.35   Consolidated financial statements prepared following a reverse acquisition are legally those of the legal acquirer but are described in the notes as a continuation of the amounts from the (consolidated) financial statements of the legal acquiree. Consequently, the reverse acquisition is reflected in the consolidated financial statements of the legal acquirer, but not in any consolidated financial statements of the legal acquiree. [*IFRS 3.B21, IU 03-13*]

2.6.170.40   A reverse acquisition may also arise in a subgroup. Example 2D illustrates this.

EXAMPLE 2D – IDENTIFYING THE ACQUIRER – SUBGROUP PERSPECTIVE

2.6.170.50   Company X has a 100% shareholding and control over Company Y. X contributes its share in Y to Company Z in exchange for newly issued equity interests in Z. As a result, X obtains control over Z and retains control over Y. X, Y and Z are operating entities – i.e. businesses in accordance with IFRS 3 – that are controlled by means of voting rights.

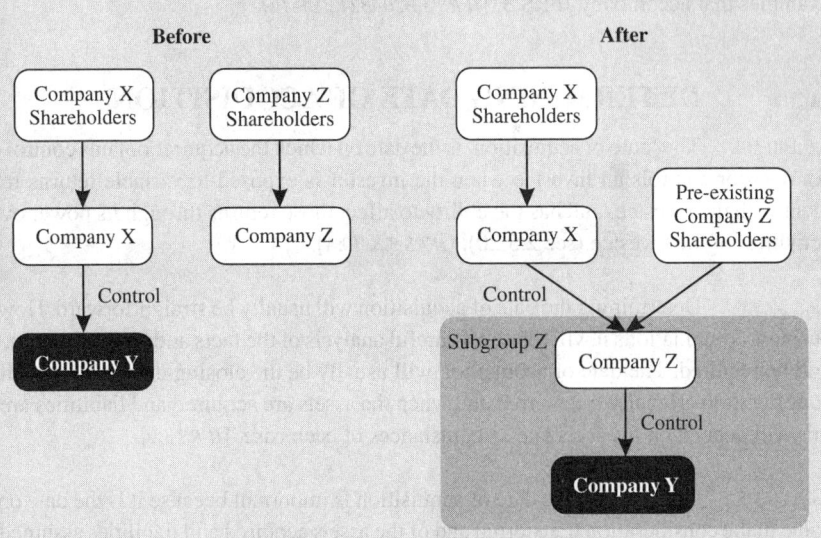

2.6.170.60   From X's perspective, this is an acquisition of Z in exchange for transferring to Z's shareholders shares in Y – i.e. X is the acquirer and Z is the acquiree in the business combination.

2.6.170.70   If Z prepares financial statements for its subgroup, then it is necessary to identify an acquirer within that subgroup. If the guidance in IFRS 10 alone were to be applied, then Z would be identified as the acquirer because Y is an entity controlled by means of voting rights and Z controls all of the voting rights in Y. However, as discussed in 2.6.60.30 the IFRS 10 guidance is not the sole basis for identifying an acquirer even if it seems that an acquirer can be identified and the guidance in IFRS 3, which takes into account control by the former shareholders of one of the combining entities, should also be considered. Consequently, from the perspective of Z's subgroup, this is a reverse acquisition – i.e. Y is the accounting acquirer and Z the accounting acquiree. This is because Y's previous shareholder X obtains control over Z through the majority of the voting rights.

2.6.170.80   In this example, the accounting acquiree from the perspective of X's financial statements and the perspective of Z's financial statements is the same – i.e. Z.

2.6.170.90   In applying acquisition accounting to a reverse acquisition, it is the identifiable assets and liabilities of the legal acquirer (accounting acquiree) that are measured at fair value. For further guidance on recognising and measuring the identifiable assets acquired and liabilities assumed in a business combination, see 2.6.560. [*IFRS 3.B22*]

2.6.170.100   Paragraphs B20 to B24 of IFRS 3 provide guidance on applying the acquisition method to reverse acquisitions, and the accounting for reverse acquisitions is illustrated in the illustrative examples that accompany IFRS 3. [*IFRS 3.B20–B24, IE1–IE15*]

2.6.180   DETERMINING DATE OF ACQUISITION

2.6.180.10   The 'date of acquisition' is the date on which the acquirer obtains control of the acquiree. An investor controls an investee when the investor is exposed to variable returns from its involvement with the investee, and has the ability to affect those returns through its power over the 'relevant activities' of the investee (see 2.5.20). [*IFRS 3.8, 10.A*]

2.6.180.20   Determining the date of acquisition will usually be straightforward. However, in certain business combinations it will require a careful analysis of the facts and circumstances, and judgement will be required. The date of acquisition will usually be the closing date – i.e. the date on which the consideration is legally transferred and when the assets are acquired and liabilities are assumed – but this will depend on the facts and circumstances of each case. [*IFRS 3.9*]

2.6.180.30   Determining the date of acquisition is important because it is the date on which the fair value of the consideration transferred and of the assets acquired and liabilities assumed is determined, and the date on which NCI and goodwill are measured and recognised. It is also only from this date that the results of the acquiree are included in the consolidated financial statements of the acquirer.

2.6.190   Designating an effective date of acquisition

2.6.190.10   It is not possible to designate an effective date of acquisition other than the actual date on which control is obtained. However, in some cases it may be acceptable for an acquirer to consolidate a subsidiary from the start/end of a reporting period close to the date of acquisition for convenience, if the effect thereof is immaterial. For example, a subsidiary acquired on 13 October might be consolidated with effect from 1 October, provided that the effect of the 13 days is immaterial to the consolidated financial statements. For disclosure purposes, the date of acquisition would still be 13 October.

2.6.200 Agreements with retroactive effect

2.6.200.10   In some cases, an agreement will provide that the acquisition is effective on a specified date. Irrespective of any date specified in an agreement, the date of acquisition is the date on which the control is actually obtained. This may or may not correspond to a specified date in an agreement.

EXAMPLE 3A – DATE OF ACQUISITION – STATED EFFECTIVE DATE

2.6.200.20   Company P and Company S commence negotiations on 1 January 2018 for P to acquire all of the shares in S. On 1 March 2018, the agreement is finalised and P obtains the power to control S's operations on that date. However, the agreement states that the acquisition is effective as of 1 January 2018 and that P is entitled to all profits after that date. In addition, the purchase price is determined with reference to S's net asset position as at 1 January 2018.

2.6.200.30   Notwithstanding that the price is based on the net assets at 1 January 2018 and S's shareholders do not receive any dividends after that date, in this example the date of acquisition for accounting purposes is 1 March 2018. This is because it is only on 1 March 2018 that P has the power to direct the relevant activities of S so as to affect its returns from its involvement with S.

2.6.210 Shareholder approval

2.6.210.10   In some cases, management may agree on an acquisition subject to receiving shareholder approval, sometimes referred to as a 'revocable' agreement. In our view, the date of acquisition cannot be before shareholder approval if the passing of control is conditional on such approval – e.g. the voting rights do not transfer or the board of directors remains unchanged until the acquisition is approved by the shareholders. However, it is necessary to consider the substance of the requirement of the shareholder approval to assess the impact that it has on obtaining control.

EXAMPLE 3B – DATE OF ACQUISITION – SHAREHOLDER APPROVAL

2.6.210.20   Company P enters into an agreement with the shareholders of Company S on 1 March 2018 to acquire a controlling interest in S. The agreement states that the effective date of transfer is 1 April 2018 and is subject to approval by the shareholders of P at a meeting scheduled for 1 May 2018. The voting rights are not transferred and the board of directors remains unchanged until the approval of P's shareholders.

1 March 2018	1 April 2018	1 May 2018
P enters into agreement to acquire S	Effective date of transfer in the agreement	Expected approval by the shareholders of P

2.6.210.30   We believe that the date of acquisition cannot be before P's shareholders approve the transaction, because the passing of control is conditional on their approval – i.e. the voting rights are not transferred and the board of directors remains unchanged until the approval of P's shareholders. For a discussion of agreements with retroactive effect, see 2.6.200.

2.6.220   **Regulatory approval**

2.6.220.10   In some cases, a business combination cannot be finalised before regulatory approval is obtained. Although at the date of acquisition the acquirer is required to have the ability to direct the relevant activities of the acquiree (see 2.5.90), this does not necessarily require the transaction to be finalised legally. It is necessary to consider the nature of the regulatory approval in each case and the impact that it has on the passing of control.

EXAMPLE 3C – DATE OF ACQUISITION – REGULATORY APPROVAL SUBSTANTIVE

2.6.220.20   Company P and Company S are manufacturers of electronic components for a particular type of equipment. P makes a bid for S's business and the competition authority announces that the proposed transaction is to be scrutinised to ensure that competition laws will not be breached. P and S agree the terms of the acquisition and the purchase price before competition authority clearance is obtained, but the contracts are made subject to competition authority clearance.

2.6.220.30   In this example, the date of acquisition cannot be earlier than the date on which approval is obtained from the competition authority because this is a substantive hurdle to be overcome before P is able to control S's operations.

EXAMPLE 3D – DATE OF ACQUISITION – REGULATORY APPROVAL NOT SUBSTANTIVE

2.6.220.40   Company P acquires the shares in Company S on 1 April 2018. However, before the sale of shares becomes legally binding, the transaction needs to be registered, a process that takes up to six weeks. The registration of the shares is a formality in this jurisdiction and there is no risk that the sale could be rejected. In this example, the date of acquisition could be 1 April 2018 because the registration of the sale does not prevent the passing of control.

2.6.220.50   However, if the facts of this case were different and the registration was not a formality because the authorities were required to consider and accept or reject each transaction, then it is likely that the date of acquisition could not be earlier than the date of registration.

2.6.230   **Public offers**

2.6.230.10   If a public offer is made for the acquisition of shares, then it is necessary to consider the impact of the nature and terms of the offer and any other relevant laws or regulations in determining the date of acquisition.

2.6.230.20   In some jurisdictions an offer, at a certain minimum price, to buy the shares of all other shareholders is made once a shareholder owns a certain percentage of the voting rights in an entity (a 'mandatory offer'). Typically, the acquirer obtains the voting rights associated with each share as each individual shareholder accepts the offer.

EXAMPLE 3E – DATE OF ACQUISITION – SHARES TRANSFER WHEN PUBLIC OFFER CLOSES

2.6.230.30   Company P makes an offer to acquire all of the shares in Company S and each shareholder can decide individually whether to accept or reject the offer; the offer is conditional on at least 75% acceptance. The offer is made on 15 September 2018 and closes on 15 November 2018, at which time ownership of the shares, and the rights associated with ownership, will be transferred. At 20 October 2018 enough offers have been accepted to give P its minimum 75% of the shares of S.

2.6.230.40   P has the power to control S at 20 October 2018 if its rights are substantive such that, as of that date onwards, P is able to make decisions when they need to be made and therefore impose its will on S's operations. Local laws and regulations in respect of public offers need to be considered in this assessment. If P does not have the power to control S's operations until the public offer has closed, then the date of acquisition could not be earlier than 15 November 2018.

EXAMPLE 3F – DATE OF ACQUISITION – SHARES IN PUBLIC OFFER TRANSFER PROGRESSIVELY

2.6.230.50   Company P increases its shareholding in Company S to above 30% and in accordance with local law makes a mandatory offer on 15 March 2018 to acquire all of the shares in S. Each shareholder can decide individually whether to accept or reject the offer, and P obtains the voting rights and all other rights associated with each share as each individual shareholder accepts. The offer is not conditional on a minimum level of acceptance. The offer closes on 15 June 2018 but on 1 May 2018 enough shareholders have accepted the offer for P's interest in S to exceed 50%.

2.6.230.60   In this example, the date of acquisition is 1 May 2018 because P obtains control of S on this date. After 1 May 2018, any additional acquisition of shares would be treated as an acquisition of NCI (see 2.5.620).

2.6.240   Acquirer consulted on major decisions

2.6.240.10   In most cases, the seller in a business combination agrees to consult the acquirer on major business decisions during the period between signing the agreement and completing the transaction. In our view, if such rights are aimed at ensuring that no fundamental changes occur – i.e. on completion, the acquirer receives the acquiree in a condition that is similar to its condition on signing the agreement – then the acquirer's rights during that period are protective rights. As such, they cannot give the acquirer power over the relevant activities or remove such power from the seller during that period (see 2.5.110.10). In our experience, most of such rights are found to be protective, but it is necessary to consider all relevant facts and circumstances to determine the substance of the rights agreed between the parties. [*IFRS 10.14, B26–B27*]

EXAMPLE 3G – DATE OF ACQUISITION – CONSULTATION ON MAJOR DECISIONS

2.6.240.20   Company P enters into an unconditional sale-and-purchase agreement (SPA) to buy all of the shares in Company S, which is wholly owned by Company Q. The SPA is signed on 1 April 2018 and the transaction is completed on 1 July 2018.

2.6.240.25   Before the sale, Q controls S through voting rights. Q holds these voting rights and has the ability to appoint the board of directors of S until 1 July 2018. The SPA prevents Q from changing S's articles of association and business strategy without P's consent in the period between 1 April and 1 July 2018.

2.6.240.30   In this example, the rights granted to P by the SPA are protective (see 2.5.110.20). In the period between signing the SPA and completing the transaction, P cannot direct the relevant activities of S because the rights it has obtained on signing the SPA relate to fundamental changes to S's activities only. Therefore, we believe that Q retains power over S's relevant activities until 1 July 2018 (see 2.5.110.10) and the completion date is the date of acquisition in this example.

2.6.250   Date of acquisition in business combination achieved in stages

2.6.250.10   Sometimes control is obtained in successive share purchases – i.e. the acquirer obtains control of an acquiree in which it held an equity interest immediately before the date of acquisition. Such a business combination is commonly referred to as a 'business combination achieved in stages' or a 'step acquisition'. Consistent with all other business combinations in the scope of IFRS 3, for a step acquisition the date of acquisition is the date on which the acquirer obtains control of the acquiree. [*IFRS 3.8, 41*]

2.6.250.20   For a discussion of the accounting for a business combination achieved in stages, see 2.6.1140.

2.6.260   CONSIDERATION TRANSFERRED

2.6.260.10   The consideration transferred to obtain control of an acquiree in a business combination consists of the assets transferred by the acquirer, the liabilities incurred by the acquirer to former owners of the acquiree and the equity interests issued by the acquirer. It includes contingent consideration (see 2.6.280) and certain elements of share-based payment awards exchanged for awards held by the acquiree's employees (see 2.6.420). However, a number of items are excluded from consideration transferred (see 2.6.340). Consideration is often transferred directly to the former owners of the acquired business; however, consideration given in exchange for an acquired business may be transferred indirectly – e.g. if the acquirer contributes a business to an acquired subsidiary (see 2.6.550). [*IFRS 3.37*]

2.6.260.20   In some cases, the consideration transferred in a business combination will relate not just to the acquirer obtaining control over the acquiree, but also to other elements of the overall transaction. Amounts that are not part of the exchange for control over the acquiree are excluded from the accounting for the business combination; instead, they are accounted for as separate transactions in accordance with other relevant standards. [*IFRS 3.51*]

2.6.260.30   The consideration transferred in a business combination is measured at fair value except for any portion of the acquirer's share-based payment awards issued to replace awards held by the acquiree's employees, which are measured in accordance with IFRS 2 (see 2.6.420). [*IFRS 3.37*]

2.6.260.40   Fair value is measured in accordance with IFRS 13, which is the subject of chapter 2.4. That chapter includes general guidance on applying the principles of IFRS 13 in measuring fair value, as well as application guidance on specific items that might be relevant to a business combination.

2.6.270   Deferred consideration

2.6.270.10   Deferred consideration comprises obligations to pay specified amounts at future dates – i.e. there is no uncertainty about the amount to be paid. Deferred consideration is recognised and measured at fair value at the date of acquisition and is included in the consideration transferred. The unwinding of any interest element of deferred consideration is recognised in profit or loss.

2.6.270.20   For a discussion of the classification of cash flows arising from the settlement of deferred consideration, see 2.3.20.16–17.

2.6.280   Contingent consideration

2.6.280.10   Contingent consideration is an obligation by the acquirer to transfer additional assets or equity interests to the former owners of an acquiree as part of the exchange for control of the acquiree if specified future events occur or conditions are met. Contingent consideration may also include an acquirer's right to the return of previously transferred consideration if certain conditions are met – e.g. a repayment to the acquirer of consideration transferred to the former owners of an acquired business is required if that business does not meet financial or operating targets that were specified in the acquisition agreements. [*IFRS 3.A*]

2.6.280.20   Contingent consideration may include the transfer of additional cash, the issue of additional debt or equity securities, or the distribution of other consideration on resolution of contingencies based on post-combination earnings, post-combination security prices or other factors. All contingent consideration is measured at fair value on the date of acquisition and included in the consideration transferred in the acquisition. [*IFRS 3.39*]

2.6.280.30   Obligations of an acquirer under contingent consideration that meet the definition of a financial instrument are classified as equity or a financial liability in accordance with IAS 32 (see 7.3.270). For a discussion of the subsequent measurement of contingent consideration, see 2.6.1120. [*IFRS 3.40*]

2.6.280.40   For a discussion of the classification of cash flows arising from the settlement of contingent consideration, see 2.3.20.18.

2.6.290   Assets transferred or liabilities assumed by acquirer

2.6.290.10   Assets transferred or liabilities assumed by the acquirer as part of the consideration transferred in a business combination are generally measured at their acquisition date fair values; any gain or loss is recognised in profit or loss in accordance with the relevant IFRS. However, this guidance applies only if the acquirer does not retain control of the assets or liabilities transferred after the acquisition (see 2.6.550). [*IFRS 3.38*]

2.6.300   Business combination with no consideration transferred

2.6.300.10   A business combination can occur without the acquirer transferring consideration. Examples include:
- an acquiree repurchases a sufficient number of its own shares so that an existing shareholder obtains control of the acquiree;
- veto rights held by another equity holder expire; and
- business combinations achieved by contract alone – e.g. stapling arrangements (see 2.6.305) – or the formation of a dual-listed entity. In these business combinations, the acquirer transfers no consideration in exchange for control of an acquiree and obtains no equity interests in the acquiree on obtaining control. [*IFRS 3.43*]

2.6.300.20   In business combinations in which no consideration is transferred, an acquirer uses the acquisition date fair value of its interest in the acquiree, instead of the acquisition date fair value of the consideration transferred, to determine the amount of goodwill. [*IFRS 3.33, B46*]

EXAMPLE 4 – NO CONSIDERATION TRANSFERRED

2.6.300.30   Company P owns 45% of Company S. On 31 October 2018, S repurchases a number of its shares such that P's ownership interest increases to 65%. The repurchase transaction results in P obtaining control of S. Therefore, the transaction is a business combination and P is the acquirer.

2.6.300.40   The following additional information is relevant for this example.

Carrying amount of P's 45% interest in S in P's financial statements immediately before the share repurchase	40
Immediately after the share repurchase:	
• Fair value of 65% of S	65
• Fair value of 35% of S	35
• Fair value of identifiable net assets of S	80

2.6.300.50   P elects to measure NCI at fair value at the date of acquisition (see 2.6.940), and records the following entry.

	DEBIT	**CREDIT**
Identifiable net assets of S	80	
Goodwill[1]	20	
Investment in S		40
NCI (equity)		35
Gain on previously held interest in S (profit or loss)[2]		25
To recognise acquisition of S		

Notes

1. Goodwill is calculated as follows.

Fair value of interest in S after the share repurchase	65
Plus NCI	35
Less fair value of identifiable net assets acquired	(80)
Goodwill	20

Because P elects to measure NCI at fair value at the date of acquisition, goodwill includes 7 attributable to NCI – i.e. 35 - (80 x 35%). If P had elected to measure NCI at its proportionate interest in the fair value of the identifiable net assets of S, then NCI would be recognised at 28 (80 x 35%) and goodwill would be reduced to 13.

2. The gain on previously held interest in S is calculated as follows.

Fair value of interest in S after the share repurchase	65
Carrying amount of interest in S before the share repurchase	(40)
Gain on previously held interest in S	25

2.6.300.60   In a business combination achieved by contract alone, the acquirer receives no additional equity interests in the acquiree. Therefore, if the acquirer held no equity interest in the acquiree before the business combination, then 100 percent of the acquiree's equity would be attributed to NCI. If in such circumstances the acquirer elects to measure NCI at fair value at the date of acquisition, then in our view this does not include any control premium (see 2.4.840) because it is a non-controlling interest. [*IFRS 3.44*]

EXAMPLE 5 – BUSINESS COMBINATION ACHIEVED BY CONTRACT ALONE

2.6.300.70   Company P obtains control of Company S in a business combination achieved by contract alone on 1 January 2018. P had no equity interest in S before the business combination.

2.6.300.80   The following facts at the date of acquisition are relevant for this example.

Fair value of identifiable net assets of S	150
Fair value of 100% of the equity interests in S	200

2.6.300.90   P elects to measure NCI at fair value at the date of acquisition (see 2.6.940), and records the following entry. The credit to NCI reflects the fact that P has no equity interest in S.

	DEBIT	CREDIT
Identifiable net assets of S	150	
Goodwill (200 - 150)	50	
NCI (equity)		200
To recognise acquisition of S		

2.6.305   *Stapling arrangements*

2.6.305.10   A stapling arrangement is an example of a business combination in which no consideration is transferred (see 2.6.300.10). It is a contractual arrangement between two or more entities or their shareholders in which the equity securities of the entities or other similar instruments are 'stapled' together and each of these entities has the same owners. The stapled securities are quoted as a single security – i.e. the equity securities of each entity are not traded independently.

2.6.305.20   The IFRS Interpretations Committee discussed the application of IFRS 3 in a stapling arrangement that combines separate entities and businesses by unifying ownership and voting interests in the combining entities. The Committee noted the following about the accounting for these arrangements.
- The arrangement meets the definition of a business combination (see 2.6.20).
- As a result, one of the combining entities needs to be identified as the acquirer. In this regard, several factors addressed in IFRS 3 are also taken into account to identify the acquirer (see 2.6.60). In a stapling arrangement, relative voting rights may be particularly relevant among these factors (see 2.6.90).
- The combining entity in a stapling arrangement that is the acquirer in accordance with IFRS 3 is also identified as the parent for the purpose of applying IFRS 10 and therefore prepares consolidated financial statements of the combined entity. [*IU 05-14*]

2.6.310   Business combination involving mutual entities

2.6.310.10   If a business combination takes place between mutual entities, then acquisition accounting is applied. In a combination involving mutual entities, the acquirer and acquiree exchange only equity interests. If the fair value of the equity or member interests in the acquiree is more reliably measurable than the fair value of the member interests transferred by the acquirer, then the acquirer determines the amount of goodwill by using the acquisition date fair value of the acquiree's equity interests instead of the acquirer's equity interests transferred as consideration. [*IFRS 3.33, B47*]

2.6.320   Business combination effected through derivatives

2.6.320.10   IFRS 9 does not apply to certain forward contracts between the acquirer and the seller that will result in a business combination to buy an acquiree at a future date. Therefore, if an entity effects a business combination by entering into a *forward contract*, then an issue arises about whether the contract to acquire the target should be accounted for as a derivative in accordance with IFRS 9 or as an unrecognised executory contract before the date of acquisition, or if it leads to consolidation when the derivative forward contract grants present access to ownership benefits. These issues are discussed in 2.5.730 and 7.1.160–170. [*IFRS 9.2.1(f)*]

2.6.320.20   Before the date of acquisition, an *option* to acquire a business is a derivative that falls in the scope of IFRS 9 (see 7.1.170.20); the scope exemption discussed in 2.6.320.10 does not extend to options because in that case an acquisition is conditional on the option being exercised. Therefore, the option will be measured at fair value through profit or loss, and the consideration transferred includes the fair value of the derivative at the date of acquisition. For a discussion of the accounting for an unexercised call option from the date of acquisition onwards, see 2.5.750. [*IFRS 9.BCZ2.41*]

2.6.330   Hedging future business combination

2.6.330.10   A firm commitment to acquire a business in a business combination can be a hedged item only for foreign exchange risk because other risks cannot be specifically identified and measured. In our view, an entity may also hedge the foreign exchange risk of a highly probable forecast business combination. In our view, in the consolidated financial statements, a cash flow hedge of the foreign exchange risk of a firm commitment to acquire a business or a forecast business combination relates to the foreign currency equivalent of the consideration paid. In a cash flow hedge designation, the effective portion of the gain or loss arising from the hedging instrument is recognised in OCI. [*IFRS 9.B6.3.1*]

2.6.330.20   For a discussion of when and how the amount recognised in OCI is recognised as an adjustment to goodwill or reclassified to profit or loss, see 7.9.470.

2.6.340   DETERMINING WHAT IS PART OF BUSINESS COMBINATION

2.6.340.10   Determining what is part of the business combination transaction involves an analysis of the elements of the overall arrangement. Generally, a transaction entered into by or on behalf of the acquirer or primarily for its benefit or that of the combined entity, rather than being entered into before the combination primarily for the benefit of the acquiree or its former owners, is likely to be a separate transaction. [*IFRS 3.52*]

2.6.340.20   IFRS 3 provides three examples, which are not intended to be exhaustive, of transactions that are not part of a business combination and which are therefore accounted for separately in accordance with other relevant standards. The three examples are transactions that:
- in effect settle a pre-existing relationship between the acquirer and the acquiree (see 2.6.350);
- remunerate employees or former owners of the acquiree for future services (see 2.6.400); and
- reimburse the acquiree or its former owners for paying the acquirer's acquisition-related costs (see 2.6.530). [*IFRS 3.52*]

2.6.340.30   The implementation guidance to IFRS 3 provides the following factors that entities should consider in assessing whether a transaction is part of a business combination or is a separate transaction that should be accounted for separately:
- the reasons for the transaction;
- who initiated the transaction; and
- the timing of the transaction. [*IFRS 3.B50*]

2.6.340.40   These factors are not mutually exclusive or individually conclusive. An acquirer determines whether any portion of the amounts transferred by the acquirer relate to transactions other than the acquisition of a business that should be accounted for separately from the consideration exchanged for the acquiree and the assets acquired and liabilities assumed in the business combination. [*IFRS 3.B50*]

2.6.340.50   For example, the acquirer in a business combination may have outstanding debt with terms that could result in an increase in the interest rate in the event of an acquisition. If the interest rate on debt of the acquirer is increased as a result of a business combination, then in our view the additional interest costs are not part of the business combination and therefore should not be included in the consideration transferred. This is because changes in the acquirer's interest rate are not part of the exchange for control of the acquiree. The acquirer should account for the variable interest feature and any related additional interest expense in accordance with IFRS 9.

2.6.350   Pre-existing relationships

2.6.350.10   A 'pre-existing relationship' is any relationship that existed between the acquirer and the acquiree before the business combination was contemplated. Such relationships may be contractual or non-contractual, and include defendant and plaintiff, customer and vendor, licensor and licensee, lender and borrower, and lessee and lessor relationships. In our view, the guidance in respect of pre-existing relationships should also be applied to relationships entered into while the business combination is being contemplated but before the date of acquisition. [*IFRS 3.B51*]

2.6.350.20   Because the acquirer consolidates the acquiree following a business combination, pre-existing relationships are effectively settled as a result of the combination. Therefore, such pre-existing relationships are accounted for separately from the business combination. [*IFRS 3.BC122*]

2.6.350.30   The settlement of a pre-existing relationship gives rise to a gain or loss that is recognised by the acquirer in profit or loss at the date of acquisition. How the resulting gain or loss is calculated depends on whether the pre-existing relationship was contractual or non-contractual in nature. In general:
- settlement of a relationship that is favourable to the acquirer results in a gain being recognised by the acquirer, subject to adjustment in respect of any existing carrying amount in the financial statements of the acquirer; and
- settlement of a relationship that is unfavourable to the acquirer results in a loss being recognised by the acquirer, subject to adjustment in respect of any existing carrying amount in the financial statements of the acquirer. [*IFRS 3.B52*]

2.6.350.40   For a discussion of the income tax effects of the effective settlement of a pre-existing relationship, see 3.13.890.

2.6.360   *Non-contractual relationships*

2.6.360.10   An example of a pre-existing non-contractual relationship between the acquirer and acquiree is a lawsuit related to a non-contractual matter in which the two parties had a relationship as plaintiff and defendant. [*IFRS 3.B51*]

2.6.360.20   The gain or loss on effective settlement of a non-contractual relationship is measured at fair value. The difference between the fair value of the lawsuit and any amounts previously recognised by the acquirer in accordance with applicable standards is recognised as a gain or loss at the date of acquisition. [*IFRS 3.B52(a)*]

EXAMPLE 6A – PRE-EXISTING RELATIONSHIP – NON-CONTRACTUAL

2.6.360.30   Company P is the defendant in a lawsuit in which Company S is the plaintiff. P has recognised a liability related to this lawsuit in accordance with IAS 37. On 1 January 2018, P acquires S in a business combination, and pays cash consideration of 100,000 to S's shareholders. The acquisition effectively settles the lawsuit.

2.6.360.40   The following additional information is relevant for this example.

Carrying amount of P's liability related to the lawsuit immediately before the acquisition	8,000
Fair value of the lawsuit obligation as at 1 January 2018	5,000

2.6.360.50   P recognises a 3,000 gain on the effective settlement of the lawsuit at the date of acquisition in profit or loss, being the difference between the 8,000 liability previously recognised under IAS 37 less the 5,000 fair value of the lawsuit at the date of acquisition.

	DEBIT	CREDIT
Liability for litigation	8,000	
Gain on settlement (profit or loss)		3,000
Consideration transferred		5,000
To recognise settlement of pre-existing relationship		

2.6.360.60   In accounting for the acquisition, the consideration transferred to acquire S is 95,000, being the total amount paid to the shareholders of 100,000 less the 5,000 recognised in connection with the effective settlement of the lawsuit. KPMG's *Guides to financial statements* series illustrates disclosure regarding pre-existing relationships that are accounted for separately from the business combination.

2.6.370   *Contractual relationships*

2.6.370.10   Examples of pre-existing contractual relationships between the acquirer and acquiree include a customer-vendor relationship, a licensor-licensee relationship and a lender-borrower relationship. [*IFRS 3.B51*]

2.6.370.20   The gain or loss on effective settlement of a contractual relationship is measured at the lower of:
- the amount by which the contract is favourable or unfavourable compared with market (i.e. off-market) from the perspective of the acquirer; and

- the amount of any stated settlement provisions in the contract available to the counterparty to whom the contract is unfavourable. [*IFRS 3.B52(b)*]

2.6.370.30   This valuation of the off-market component of a contract is the same as would be done for the valuation of a contract with a third party. However, instead of being included in the valuation of the contract recognised in the statement of financial position, the resulting value is included in the accounting for the settlement of the pre-existing relationship.

2.6.370.40   The difference between the amount calculated in 2.6.370.20 and any amounts previously recognised by the acquirer is recognised as a gain or loss at the date of acquisition. [*IFRS 3.B52*]

EXAMPLE 6B – PRE-EXISTING RELATIONSHIP – SUPPLY CONTRACT

2.6.370.50   Company P sells goods to Company S under a long-term, fixed-price supply agreement. The supply agreement commenced on 1 June 2016 and expires on 1 June 2021. A clause in the agreement states that either party has the right to cancel the agreement on payment of a penalty of 5,000. P acquires S on 1 June 2018, when the supply agreement has three years left to run.

2.6.370.60   At the time of the acquisition, P determines that, although the contract currently remains profitable, the pricing under the contract is less than the current market price for the goods – i.e. the agreement is unfavourable to P. P values the off-market component of the contract at 3,000.

2.6.370.70   Because the cancellation penalty is higher than the off-market value of the contract, the loss on settlement of the pre-existing relationship is measured based on the value of the off-market component of the contract from P's perspective – i.e. at the lower amount.

	DEBIT	CREDIT
Loss on settlement (profit or loss)	3,000	
Consideration transferred		3,000
To recognise settlement of pre-existing relationship		

2.6.370.75   If in this example the penalty had been 2,000 instead of 5,000, then the above entry would have been the same except that the loss and corresponding credit to consideration transferred would have been 2,000 – i.e. based on the cancellation penalty in the contract (see 2.6.370.20).

2.6.370.80   In respect of a lender-borrower relationship, there will frequently not be a stated settlement provision in the contract available to the counterparty to whom the contract is unfavourable. In that case, the amount by which the contract is favourable or unfavourable compared with market – i.e. fair value as compared with the carrying amount – results in the recognition of a gain or loss on settlement.

EXAMPLE 6C – PRE-EXISTING RELATIONSHIP – FINANCIAL INSTRUMENTS

2.6.370.90   Company P issued five-year bonds on 31 December 2016, which are held entirely by Company S. P acquires S on 1 June 2018. The following additional information at the date of acquisition is relevant for this example.

Carrying amount of the bonds in P's financial statements	1,000
Fair value of the bonds	850

2.6.370.100   P recognises the settlement of the pre-existing relationship as follows.

	DEBIT	CREDIT
Liability for bonds	1,000	
Gain on settlement (profit or loss)		150
Consideration transferred		850
To recognise settlement of pre-existing relationship		

2.6.380   *Prepaid contracts*

2.6.380.10   If the pre-existing relationship between the acquirer and acquiree is a prepaid contract – e.g. a prepaid licence or prepaid lease agreement – then an issue arises about how to determine the favourable or unfavourable aspect of the pre-existing relationship from the acquirer's perspective. Any amount paid or received by the acquiree or the acquirer before the business combination is not itself recognised in the acquisition accounting (see also 2.6.910). Instead, the favourable/unfavourable element at the date of acquisition is determined by comparing the actual future payment stream under the contract with the market rate that would need to be paid to the counterparty based on the future periods in the contract if the contract were entered into anew for those remaining periods.

2.6.380.20   In the case of downstream prepaid transactions, applying the mechanical calculation (see 2.6.370.20) will indicate that the pre-existing relationship is unfavourable compared with market from the perspective of the acquirer because the acquirer will not receive any future payments from the acquiree. However, in such transactions the acquirer may also have recognised a liability in its financial statements before the business combination; the carrying amount of this liability is derecognised at the date of acquisition. [*IFRS 3.B52*]

EXAMPLE 6D – PRE-EXISTING RELATIONSHIP – DOWNSTREAM PREPAID LEASE

2.6.380.30   Company P (lessor) entered into a five-year operating lease with Company S (lessee). The contractual rental payments of 10,000 were fully prepaid by S on entering into the contract and P recognised deferred income of 10,000 in its statement of financial position. The contract was concluded at market terms and there are no stated settlement provisions. P acquires S in a business combination two years later. At the date of acquisition, P's balance of deferred income is 6,000 ((10,000 / 5) x 3 remaining years).

2.6.380.40   At the date of acquisition, a market participant granting a lease for a similar asset over a three-year period would expect to receive a present value of lease payments of 6,600 (whether as an up-front payment or over three years with interest). As a result of the business combination, P will receive rental payments of zero. Therefore, the pre-existing relationship is unfavourable by 600 compared with market from P's perspective. This amount is recognised as a settlement loss after the derecognition of P's deferred income of 6,000.

	DEBIT	CREDIT
Deferred income	6,000	
Loss on settlement (profit or loss)	600	
Consideration transferred		6,600
To recognise settlement of pre-existing relationship		

2.6.380.50   In the case of upstream prepaid transactions, applying the mechanical calculation (see 2.6.370.20) will indicate that the pre-existing relationship is favourable compared with market from the perspective of the acquirer because the acquirer will not make any future payments to the acquiree. However, in such transactions the acquirer may also have recognised an intangible asset (see 3.3.100) or prepaid rent (see 5.1.310.20) in its financial statements before the business combination; the carrying amount of any such asset will be derecognised at the date of acquisition. [*IFRS 3.B52*]

EXAMPLE 6E – PRE-EXISTING RELATIONSHIP – UPSTREAM PREPAID LEASE

2.6.380.60   Company P (lessee) enters into a five-year operating lease with Company S (lessor). The contractual rental payments of 10,000 were fully prepaid by P on entering into the contract, and P recognised prepaid rent of 10,000 in its statement of financial position. The contract was concluded at market terms and there are no stated settlement provisions. P acquires S in a business combination two years later. At the date of acquisition, P's balance of prepaid rent is 6,000 ((10,000 / 5) x 3 remaining years).

2.6.380.70   At the date of acquisition, a market participant entering into a lease contract for a similar asset over a three-year period would expect to pay a present value of lease payments of 6,600 (whether as an up-front payment or over three years with interest). As a result of the business combination, P will pay zero for the right to use the asset. Therefore, the pre-existing relationship is favourable by 600 compared with market from P's perspective. This amount is recognised as a settlement gain after the derecognition of P's asset for prepaid rent of 6,000.

	DEBIT	CREDIT
Consideration transferred	6,600	
Prepaid rent		6,000
Gain on settlement (profit or loss)		600
To recognise settlement of pre-existing relationship		

2.6.380.80   In our experience, further complexity is likely to arise because contracts between the acquirer and the acquiree may include prepayments as well as ongoing payments. Additionally, in downstream transactions the contractual relationship can also give rise to a reacquired right (see 2.6.390).

2.6.390   *Reacquired rights*

2.6.390.10   The pre-existing relationship may take the form of a right granted by the acquirer to the acquiree before the business combination. For example, an acquirer may have previously granted the acquiree the right to use the acquirer's trade name under a franchise agreement. As a result of the business combination, the acquirer effectively reacquires that previously granted right. Rights of this kind reacquired by an acquirer in a business combination are identifiable intangible assets that the acquirer recognises separately from goodwill (see 2.6.690). [*IFRS 3.29, B35–B36*]

2.6.390.20   The following table summarises the accounting for the settlement of pre-existing 'upstream' relationships and 'downstream' relationships under which a licence is granted by one party to another involved in a business combination.

FAVOURABLE FOR	UPSTREAM RELATIONSHIP[1]	DOWNSTREAM RELATIONSHIP[2]
Licensee	• Licensee is the acquirer • Settlement gain arises	• Licensee is the acquiree • Settlement loss arises (see Example 7)
Licensor	• Licensor is the acquiree • Settlement loss arises	• Licensor is the acquirer • Settlement gain arises

Notes
1.   The acquiree previously granted a licence to the acquirer.
2.   The acquirer previously granted a licence to the acquiree.

EXAMPLE 7 – FRANCHISE RIGHTS REACQUIRED

2.6.390.30   Franchiser P acquires the business of operating Franchisee S for 30,000. In connection with the acquisition, P reacquires previously granted franchise rights.

2.6.390.40   The following facts at the date of acquisition are relevant for this example.

Fair value of the identifiable net assets of S, excluding the franchise right		17,000
Reacquired franchise right:		
• Value of the right measured in accordance with IFRS 3 (see 2.6.690)		3,000
• Cancellation penalty in the franchise contract		5,000
• Amount by which contract is unfavourable for P relative to the terms of current market transactions for similar items		4,000

2.6.390.50   The cancellation penalty is higher than the off-market value of the contract; therefore, the loss on settlement of the pre-existing relationship is measured based on the value of the off-market component of the contract from P's perspective – i.e. at the lower amount (see 2.6.370.20). P records the settlement of the pre-existing relationship and the reacquisition of the franchise right as follows.

	DEBIT	CREDIT
Loss on settlement (profit or loss)	4,000	
Consideration transferred		4,000
To recognise settlement of pre-existing relationship		
Reacquired rights (intangible asset)	3,000	
Other identifiable net assets of S	17,000	
Goodwill	6,000	
Consideration transferred		26,000
To recognise reacquired right as part of acquisition accounting		

2.6.400   Payments to employees or former owners of acquiree

2.6.400.10   An acquirer may enter into an arrangement for payments to employees or selling shareholders of the acquiree that are contingent on a post-acquisition event. The accounting for such arrangements depends on whether the payments represent contingent consideration issued in the business combination (which are included in the acquisition accounting), or are separate transactions (which are accounted for in accordance with other relevant standards). [*IFRS 3.B54*]

2.6.400.20   Contingent consideration issued in a business combination is an obligation of the acquirer to transfer additional consideration to the former owners of an acquiree as part of the exchange for control of the acquiree if specified future events occur or conditions are met. Such additional consideration may be in the form of cash, other assets or equity interests. Contingent consideration may also give the acquirer the right to the return of previously transferred consideration if specified conditions are met or fail to be met. [*IFRS 3.A*]

2.6.400.30   Arrangements for contingent payments to employees or selling shareholders that do not meet the definition of contingent consideration – i.e. payments that are not part of the exchange for control of the acquiree and are not part of the accounting for the business combination – are accounted for separately in accordance with other relevant standards. [*IFRS 3.51*]

2.6.400.40   The application guidance of IFRS 3 provides indicators to be evaluated when determining whether contingent payments to employees or selling shareholders comprise contingent consideration or are a transaction to be accounted for separately from the business combination. Judgement will frequently be required in this respect. [*IFRS 3.B55*]

2.6.400.50   An arrangement under which contingent payments are automatically forfeited if employment terminates is compensation for post-combination services. Although this requirement is included within a group of indicators to assist in identifying amounts that are part of consideration transferred, the language in the standard is plain and rules out an alternative interpretation; this has been confirmed by the IFRS Interpretations Committee. Therefore, this is the case even if an evaluation of some, or even all, of the other indicators suggests that the payments would otherwise be considered to be additional consideration transferred in exchange for the acquiree; and even if the relevant employee is entitled to remuneration at rates comparable with those earned by people in similar roles. [*IFRS 3.B55(a), IU 01-13*]

2.6.400.60   In a discussion of this interpretation, the Committee noted that the service condition should be substantive. A non-substantive service condition related to contingent payments linked to continuing employment would be extremely rare and occur only in the most obvious of circumstances. For example, an arrangement in which there is an employment requirement by the selling shareholders for one day, and there are no duties that have to be performed. This may be a case in which the service condition is not substantive. [*IU 01-13*]

EXAMPLE 8 – CONTINGENT PAYMENTS LINKED TO CONTINUING EMPLOYMENT

2.6.400.70   Company P acquires all of the outstanding shares of Company S in a business combination. S had four shareholders with equal shareholdings, two of whom were also senior-level employees of S.
- The non-employee shareholders each receive 100.
- The employee shareholders each receive 60, plus an additional payment of 150 to 200 based on a multiple of earnings over the next two years. Each of these shareholders forfeits their additional payment if they leave S's employment at any time during the two years following its acquisition by P; and each of them also receives a salary that is considered reasonable remuneration for their services.

2.6.400.80   Some might propose that of the total amount of 210 to 260 payable to each employee shareholder (60 + 150 to 200), 100 can be attributed to consideration in exchange for their share of the acquired business and not compensation. This is because 100 is the fair value of a shareholding only, evidenced by the amount paid to the non-employee shareholders. However, this would not be an appropriate conclusion under paragraph B55(a) of IFRS 3.

> 2.6.400.90   The additional consideration of 150 to 200 represents compensation for post-combination services, because this part of the payment is forfeited if the former shareholder does not remain in the employment of S for two years following the acquisition – i.e. only 60 is attributed to consideration in exchange for the acquired business. Any evaluation of other factors related to the arrangement would not change this conclusion.

2.6.400.100   In our view, contingent payments that are forfeited at the discretion of the acquirer if employment terminates are also compensation for post-combination services. In such arrangements, it is generally the fact that continuing employment is required to be provided by the recipient of the contingent payment that is relevant. However, in our view careful consideration should be given to arrangements in which a related party of the beneficiary of such an award is required to provide continuing services. For example, a contingent payment arrangement may be structured so that the spouse of an employee will benefit from payments that are contingent on the employee's continued employment. Such arrangements may, in substance, be compensation for post-combination services.

2.6.400.110   If all or part of a contingent consideration arrangement is not affected by employment termination, then other indicators are considered in determining whether the arrangement is part of the business combination or a separate transaction. [*IFRS 3.B55(b)–(h)*]

2.6.410   Forgiveness of full-recourse loans

2.6.410.10   Full-recourse loans granted to employees of an acquiree may be forgiven in connection with a business combination. This could include loans granted to employees in connection with the exercise of share options, as well as loans granted for other purposes. If it is not clear whether the forgiveness of the loans is part of the exchange for the acquiree or is a transaction separate from the business combination, then all relevant facts and circumstances are considered in making the determination, paying particular attention to the factors in 2.6.340.30.

2.6.410.20   For example, if the loans were entered into before the commencement of negotiations for the business combination, and the original terms of the loans require forgiveness in the event of a change in control, then in our view such forgiveness should generally be accounted for as part of the acquisition accounting. However, if such forgiveness includes any post-combination service requirements, or is tied to another agreement that includes post-combination service requirements, then in our view the forgiveness should be accounted for separately.

2.6.410.30   In another example, if the acquisition agreement includes a clause requiring forgiveness of the loans, then determining why the clause was included, as well as reviewing other arrangements entered into with the participating employees, will be helpful in making a determination. For example, if the clause was included at the request of the acquirer, and a termination agreement was also entered into with the employee before the combination, then the forgiveness might in substance constitute a severance payment to the employee that should be accounted for as a transaction separate from the business combination. In our view, an acquirer cannot avoid the recognition of a severance cost that it would otherwise expect to incur immediately following a business combination by arranging for the acquiree to make the payment before the business combination, or by putting clauses in an acquisition agreement that effectively provide for the payments.

2.6.410.40   In reviewing arrangements such as those discussed in 2.6.410.10–30, all arrangements with the participating employees are considered. For example, if two arrangements are entered into at about the same time, such as an arrangement providing for the forgiveness of a loan with no service requirement and a second arrangement that includes a service requirement, then in our view it should be considered whether the service requirement included in the second arrangement should impact the determination of whether the first arrangement is part of the exchange for the acquiree or is a transaction separate from the business combination.

2.6.420   Acquirer share-based payment awards exchanged for acquiree awards

2.6.420.10   The consideration transferred might include certain elements of share-based payment awards exchanged for awards held by the acquiree's employees. Typically, the grant of a share-based payment replacement award is an example of a transaction with an element that is part of the consideration transferred and an element that is accounted for outside the acquisition accounting. IFRS 3 contains detailed attribution requirements that determine the amount of a share-based payment included in consideration transferred – i.e. increasing goodwill or decreasing a gain on bargain purchase – and the amount recognised outside the acquisition accounting as post-combination remuneration cost of the acquirer in accordance with IFRS 2 (see 2.6.1130). [*IFRS 3.B56*]

2.6.420.20   For an in-depth discussion of acquirer share-based payment awards exchanged for acquiree awards in a business combination, see our *IFRS Handbook: Share-based payments*.

2.6.430   *Voluntary replacement of expired acquiree awards*

2.6.430.10   An award may expire when a business combination occurs – i.e. the employee is no longer entitled to the share-based payment and the award lapses. If such an award is replaced voluntarily, then all of the market-based measure of the replacement award is recognised as post-combination remuneration cost. None of the market-based measure of the replacement awards is attributed as consideration transferred in the business combination. [*IFRS 3.B56*]

2.6.430.20   A replacement is considered voluntary unless the acquirer is obliged to issue replacement awards. An acquirer is obliged to issue replacement awards if the acquiree or its employees are able to enforce replacement. Such obligations may arise from various sources, including:
- the terms of the acquisition agreement;
- the terms of the acquiree's awards; or
- applicable laws or regulations. [*IFRS 3.B56*]

2.6.440   *Mandatory replacement of acquiree awards*

2.6.440.10   When the acquirer mandatorily issues replacement awards to employees of an acquiree in exchange for unexpired share-based payment awards issued previously by the acquiree, such exchanges are accounted for as modifications of share-based payment awards under IFRS 2. As a result, all or a portion of the market-based measure of the acquirer's replacement awards is included in measuring the consideration transferred in the business combination. [*IFRS 3.B56*]

2.6.440.20   In some instances, a portion of the value of the replacement awards is allocated to post-combination service and accounted for separately from the business combination. This occurs when post-combination service is required to be rendered by the employees of the acquiree in connection with the acquirer issuing replacement awards or if the market-based measure of the replacement awards exceeds the market-based measure of the acquiree awards. [*IFRS 3.B59*]

2.6.440.30   The amount of the market-based measure of the replacement awards treated as consideration transferred is determined in the following manner.

---

1.   Determine at the date of acquisition, in accordance with IFRS 2:
  •   the market-based measure of the acquiree's awards (FVa); and
  •   the market-based measure of the replacement awards (FVr). [*IFRS 3.B57*]

2.   Determine:
  •   the period for which services have been provided by the employees before the date of acquisition (A in the diagram below);
  •   the original vesting period of the acquiree's awards (B in the diagram);
  •   the post-combination vesting period, if any, for the replacement awards (C in the diagram); and
  •   the greater of the total vesting period (the sum of A plus C) and the original vesting period of the acquiree's awards (B).

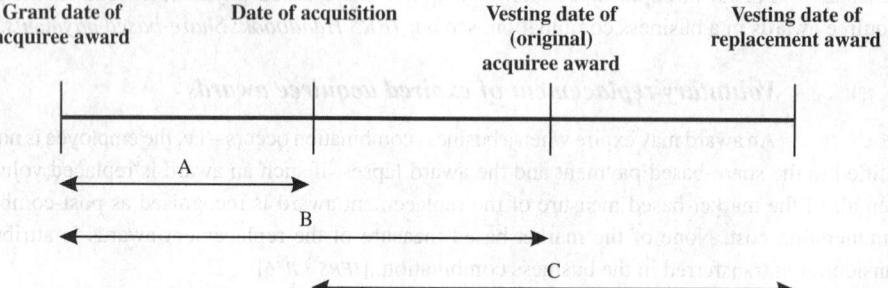

| Grant date of acquiree award | Date of acquisition | Vesting date of (original) acquiree award | Vesting date of replacement award |

In our experience, the total vesting period of the original awards may be longer than the sum of the pre-combination period for which service has been provided plus the post-combination vesting period of the replacement awards. However, in other cases a change-in-control clause is included in the original terms of an acquiree award and the clause is triggered by an acquisition of the acquiree such that unvested awards immediately vest at the date of acquisition (see 2.6.480).

3.   Calculate the portion of the replacement awards attributable to consideration transferred in the business combination as the product of:
  •   the market-based measure of the acquiree's awards at the date of acquisition; and
  •   the ratio of the pre-combination vesting period to the greater of the total vesting period and the original vesting period of the acquiree's awards. [*IFRS 3.B58*]

$$\text{Amount included in consideration transferred} = \text{FVa} \times \frac{A}{\text{Greater of }(A + C)\text{ and } B}$$

Any remaining amount of the market-based measure of the replacement awards after deducting the amount attributed to consideration transferred is treated as post-combination remuneration cost. [*IFRS 3.B59*]

2.6.440.40   These requirements for determining the portions of a replacement award attributable to pre- and post-combination service apply regardless of whether the replacement award is classified as cash-settled or as equity-settled in accordance with IFRS 2. [*IFRS 3.B61*]

2.6.440.50   The process in 2.6.440.30 demonstrates several points.
- The acquirer measures both the replacement awards given to employees by the acquirer and the acquiree awards at the date of acquisition. The measurement and attribution of replacement awards issued in a business combination are independent of the original grant-date value of the acquiree awards.
- IFRS 3 sets two limits on the amount of the replacement awards' value that is included in the consideration transferred:
  - the amount cannot exceed the market-based measure at the date of acquisition of the *acquiree* awards; and
  - the amount includes only the portion of the value attributed to *pre-combination* service.
- Any incremental value of the replacement awards over the value of the acquiree awards at the date of acquisition is attributed to post-combination service and is not part of the consideration transferred, even if all service has been rendered as at the date of acquisition. In this case, the excess value is recognised immediately as remuneration cost in the post-combination financial statements of the combined entity. If additional service is required, then the remuneration cost is recognised in the post-combination financial statements by applying the requirements of IFRS 2 (see 2.6.1130).
- Even if the acquiree awards are fully vested at the time of a business combination, a portion of the replacement awards is allocated to post-combination service if the acquiree's employees are required to render service in the post-combination period for the replacement awards to vest. [*IFRS 3.B57–B59*]

EXAMPLE 9 – SHARE-BASED PAYMENT AWARDS

2.6.440.60   On 1 January 2016, Company S granted equity-settled share-based payment awards with a grant-date fair value of 100 to its employees, subject to a three-year service condition.

2.6.440.70   Company P buys 100% of S's shares on 1 January 2018 and as part of the acquisition agreement is required to issue equity-settled replacement awards to S's employees. At the date of acquisition, the market-based measure of the original awards is 120; the market-based measure of the replacement awards is 140. The replacement awards have a one-year vesting condition.

2.6.440.80   Assuming that all employees are expected to meet the service condition, the following points are relevant to determining the amount attributed to the pre-combination service.
- The period for which service has been provided by S's employees before the date of acquisition is two years.
- The vesting period of the original (acquiree) awards is three years.
- The vesting period of the replacement awards is one year.
- The total vesting period and the original vesting period are both three years. The greater of those two periods is therefore also three years.

2.6.440.90   In its consolidated financial statements, P records the following entries.

	DEBIT	CREDIT
Consideration transferred	80	
Equity		80
To recognise replacement awards attributed to pre-combination service as part of consideration transferred		
Remuneration cost	60	
Equity		60
To recognise replacement awards attributed to post-combination service in accordance with IFRS 2 (60 x (1 year / 1 year))		

Notes

Amount attributed to pre-combination service

$120^{(1)}$ x 67% (2 years / 3 years)$^{(2)}$ = 80

1. Market-based measure of acquiree awards at the date of acquisition.
2. Ratio of service rendered as at 1 January 2018 compared with the greater of the original vesting period (3 years) and the sum of the pre-combination period for which service has been provided (2 years) plus the post-combination vesting period (1 year); both periods are three years.

Amount attributed to post-combination service

$140^{(3)}$ - $80^{(4)}$ = 60

3. Market-based measure of replacement awards at the date of acquisition.
4. Amount attributed to pre-combination service (see above).

2.6.450   *Replacement awards with expected forfeitures*

2.6.450.10   The recognition of remuneration cost in respect of share-based payment awards is based on the best available estimate at the date of acquisition of the total number of replacement awards expected to vest. Accordingly, the determination of the amount of replacement awards to be attributed to pre- and post-combination service takes into account the expected rate of forfeitures of the replacement awards arising from expected failure to meet vesting conditions other than market conditions (see 4.5.540.60). [*IFRS 2.19–20, 30, 3.B60*]

2.6.450.20   Consistent with the guidance in IFRS 2, changes in estimated forfeitures are reflected as an adjustment to post-combination remuneration cost in the period in which the change in estimate occurs. Therefore, the acquirer does not adjust consideration transferred in periods subsequent to the date of acquisition if actual forfeitures differ from the forfeitures estimated at the date of acquisition. [*IFRS 3.B60*]

2.6.450.30   Likewise, an acquirer does not adjust the amount of consideration transferred when other changes result in a change in the estimate of the number of awards expected to vest – e.g. those related to non-market performance conditions or modifications occurring after the date of acquisition. Accordingly, all relevant information is taken into account when determining the probability of meeting a non-market performance condition at the date of acquisition. For example, if at the date of acquisition it is not probable that a non-market performance condition for the replacement awards will be met, then no amount is attributed to pre-combination service and recognised as part of the consideration transferred. If the non-market condition of the replacement award is ultimately met, then the whole amount of the acquisition date market-based measure of that award is recognised as post-combination remuneration cost.

2.6.460   *Replacement awards with market conditions*

2.6.460.10   A share-based payment may contain a market condition – e.g. a performance condition that determines whether a share-based payment vests that is related to the market price of the entity's equity instruments. [*IFRS 2.A*]

2.6.460.20   The attribution of the acquisition date market-based measure of the replacement awards to pre- and post-combination service follows the general requirements set out in IFRS 3. This applies regardless of the classification of the share-based payment as equity-settled or cash-settled. [*IFRS 3.B56–B61*]

2.6.460.30   However, the accounting for the replacement awards during the post-combination periods differs depending on the classification of the share-based payment – i.e. depending on whether the replacement awards with a market condition are classified as equity-settled or cash-settled.
- If the market condition of an equity-settled share-based payment is not met, then the accounting for the post-combination remuneration cost is not affected.
- If the market condition of a cash-settled share-based payment is not met, then the liability is reversed through profit or loss, even though the amount of the liability recognised for service attributed to pre-combination service remains in the consideration transferred.

2.6.460.40   For a discussion of vesting conditions, including market conditions, see 4.5.370 (classification), 4.5.540.50–70 (equity-settled share-based payments) and 4.5.930.30–50 (cash-settled share-based payments).

2.6.470   *Replacement awards with non-vesting conditions*

2.6.470.10   For equity-settled share-based payments, non-vesting conditions, similar to market conditions, are reflected in the market-based measure of the share-based payment at the date of acquisition. [*IFRS 2.21A*]

2.6.470.20   For cash-settled share-based payments, non-vesting conditions are also taken into account in the market-based measure of a cash-settled liability at the date of acquisition, similar to market conditions (see 4.5.960).

2.6.470.30   The accounting for replacement awards with a non-vesting condition during the post-combination periods depends on the classification of the share-based payment – i.e. whether it is equity-settled or cash-settled.

2.6.470.40   If an equity-settled replacement award contains a non-vesting condition, then the accounting consequences of not meeting such a condition depend on whether it was the employer, the employee or neither who could choose to meet that non-vesting condition.

2.6.470.50   For a discussion of non-vesting conditions, see 4.5.440 (classification), 4.5.550 (equity-settled share-based payments) and 4.5.960 (cash-settled share-based payments).

2.6.480   *Share-based payment award includes change-in-control clause*

2.6.480.10   Share options or other share-based payment plans often include a clause that provides for the acceleration of vesting in the event of a change in control of the issuer (a change-in-control clause). In other instances, existing awards are sometimes modified to add a change-in-control clause in contemplation of a change in control of an acquiree. The effect of the change-in-control clause that accelerates vesting on the attribution of an acquirer's replacement awards between pre- and post-combination service depends on how the change-in-control clause arose. For a discussion of share-based payments that expire on a change in control and are voluntarily replaced, see 2.6.430.

2.6.480.20   In some circumstances, a change-in-control clause is included in the original terms of an acquiree award and the clause is triggered by an acquisition of the acquiree such that unvested awards vest immediately at the date of acquisition. In such cases, the shortened vesting period resulting from the change in control was provided for by the terms of the acquiree award and, in our view, should be regarded as the original vesting period for the purpose of determining the amount of a replacement award to be attributed to pre- and post-combination service.

2.6.480.30   For example, an acquiree award that includes a change-in-control clause providing for the acceleration of vesting is exchanged for a replacement award that does not require post-combination service to vest. In this case, we believe that the original vesting period and the sum of the pre-combination vesting period plus the post-combination vesting period is the same for the purpose of attributing the replacement award to pre- and post-combination service. Accordingly, if in such situations the market-based measure of the replacement award is not in excess of that of the acquiree award, then we believe that the total market-based measure of the replacement award at the date of acquisition should be attributed to the consideration transferred in the business combination; no amount should be attributed to post-combination remuneration cost. Any market-based measure of the replacement award in excess of that of the acquiree award is recognised as post-combination cost, following IFRS 2.

2.6.490   *Acquirer requests modification of acquiree award in contemplation of change in control*

2.6.490.10   If a change-in-control clause that provides for the acceleration of vesting is added to the terms of the acquiree's share-based payment award at the request of the acquirer, and is replaced by a fully vested acquirer award, then in our view the accounting should be the same as if the acquirer issued a fully vested replacement award in exchange for an unvested acquiree award. This is consistent with the guidance in IFRS 3 that a transaction entered into by the acquirer and the acquiree during negotiations of the terms of the business combination for the benefit of the combined entity is more likely to be separate from the business combination. [*IFRS 3.52, B50*]

2.6.500   *Awards with graded vesting*

2.6.500.10   In some cases, share-based payment awards vest in instalments over the vesting period (graded-vesting awards). IFRS 2 requires each such instalment to be treated as a separate grant of share-based payment awards (see 4.5.680). Accordingly, an entity determines the portion of replacement awards to be attributed to the pre- and post-combination service separately for each tranche of a graded-vesting award. [*IFRS 2.IG11*]

2.6.510   **Unreplaced awards**

2.6.510.10   IFRS 3 also contains guidance about equity-settled acquiree awards that are not replaced (unreplaced awards). This guidance does not apply to cash-settled acquiree awards. [*IFRS 3.B62A–B62B*]

2.6.510.20   The accounting requirements for unreplaced acquiree awards distinguish between:
- acquiree awards that were vested at the date of acquisition; and
- acquiree awards that were not vested at the date of acquisition. [*IFRS 3.B62A*]

2.6.510.30   If equity-settled unreplaced acquiree options are vested but unexercised at the date of acquisition, then those acquiree awards form part of the NCI in the acquiree and are measured at their market-based measure at the date of acquisition in accordance with IFRS 2 (see 2.6.950). This assumes that the awards do not represent present ownership interests or entitle their holders to a proportionate share of the acquiree's net assets in the event of liquidation. The NCI are taken into account in the IFRS 3 acquisition accounting and affect the calculation of goodwill or a gain on bargain purchase. [*IFRS 3.19, B62A*]

2.6.510.40   If an equity-settled unreplaced acquiree award is not vested at the date of acquisition, then it is measured at its market-based measure as if the date of acquisition were the grant date under IFRS 2. In determining the portion of the market-based measure that is allocated to pre-combination service, all of the relevant data regarding the probability of meeting vesting conditions other than market conditions are taken into account. If the acquiree's awards have non-market performance conditions that are not probable of being met as at the date of acquisition, then no amount is allocated to pre-combination service and therefore no amount is allocated to NCI. [*IFRS 3.B62A*]

2.6.510.50   If the non-market performance condition is probable of being met such that a portion of the market-based measure is allocated to pre-combination service, then the market-based measure of the unvested share-based payment transaction is allocated to pre-combination service, and therefore to NCI, based on the ratio of the portion of the vesting period completed to the greater of the total vesting period or the original vesting period of the unreplaced awards. The balance is allocated to post-combination service. The attribution formula for unreplaced awards is the same as the formula for replaced awards (see 2.6.440.30). [*IFRS 3.B62B*]

2.6.510.60   The attribution requirements for replaced awards also apply to unreplaced awards in which the vesting period is modified. The portion of the market-based measure allocated to NCI is taken into account in the IFRS 3 acquisition accounting and affects the calculation of goodwill or a gain on bargain purchase.

(S) 2.6.520   ***Separate financial statements***

2.6.520.10   The requirements in IFRS 3 for the attribution of the market-based measure of re-placement awards were developed as part of the requirements for acquisition accounting in the consolidated financial statements of the acquirer (assuming that shares in the acquiree are acquired). It is not clear how replacement awards should be accounted for in the separate financial statements of the acquirer when shares in the acquiree are acquired.

2.6.520.20   If an entity accounts for its investments in subsidiaries at cost or using the equity method, then in our view one acceptable approach is to follow the attribution guidance in IFRS 3 by analogy. This is on the basis that, from the point of view of the separate financial statements, the issue of a replacement award may be considered to have been exchanged for two different items:
- as part of the cost of obtaining a controlling interest in the acquiree; and
- for post-acquisition services to be rendered by the acquiree's employees. [*IAS 27.10*]

2.6.520.30   If an entity is measuring its investments in subsidiaries in accordance with IFRS 9, then it follows the measurement requirements of IFRS 9 and IFRS 13 in determining the value of the investment at the date of acquisition. [*IAS 27.10*]

2.6.530   **Acquisition-related costs**

2.6.530.10   Acquisition-related costs incurred by an acquirer to effect a business combination are not part of the consideration transferred. Examples include professional and consulting fees, administrative costs and the costs of registering and issuing securities, such as stamp duty payable. [*IFRS 3.53*]

2.6.530.20   Such costs are accounted for as an expense in the period incurred, unless such costs are incurred to issue debt or equity securities, in which case they are recognised in accordance with IAS 32 (for equity, see 7.3.570) and IFRS 9 (for debt, see 7.7.50). [*IFRS 3.53*]

2.6.530.30   In some cases, judgement is required in determining whether a cost incurred is an acquisition-related cost or a cost that qualifies for capitalisation in accordance with, for example, IAS 38.

EXAMPLE 10 – THIRD PARTY PAYMENT FOR RIGHTS TO BE TRANSFERRED

2.6.530.40   Company P acquires Company S on 30 June 2018. Included in the assets acquired from S is an intangible asset that comprises rights to operate in a certain area of activity. However, P is required to make an additional payment to the regulator in S's jurisdiction in order for the rights to be transferred for use by P group.

2.6.530.50   In our view, in this example the payment to the regulator is an acquisi-tion-related cost. If the right was acquired separately – i.e. not as part of a business combination – then it would be capitalised as an intangible asset (see 3.3.30)

and the payment would be a transaction cost, like a transfer tax. Although the right is acquired as part of a business combination, the nature of the payment has not changed; accordingly, it is an acquisition-related cost incurred to effect the business combination and is expensed as it is incurred. We believe that the transfer of rights could not be construed as separate from the business combination because the transfer of the rights to P group is an integral part of the business combination itself.

2.6.530.60   If acquisition-related costs incurred by, or in substance on behalf of, an acquirer are paid by the acquiree or selling shareholders, then those costs are also accounted for as a separate transaction and are not part of the accounting for the business combination. [*IFRS 3.52(c)*]

2.6.530.70   An acquirer may incur costs related to equity securities issued to effect a business combination. Such costs may include, for example, fees charged by underwriters, attorneys, accountants and printers. These costs effectively reduce the proceeds from the issue, and therefore the amount is recognised in equity. An entity recognises as an expense in profit or loss all costs that are not *incremental* to the issue of the securities, because such costs would have been incurred even without the issue of the equity securities. [*IFRS 3.53, IAS 32.37*]

2.6.530.80   An acquirer may incur costs in connection with the issue of debt associated with a business combination. For example, such costs may include fees paid to creditors, attorneys and rating agencies. Debt issue costs reduce the proceeds from the debt issued and are an element of the effective interest cost of the debt; neither the source of the debt financing nor the use of the proceeds changes the nature of such costs. Only costs incurred in connection with a debt issue that are *directly attributable* to that debt issue are deducted from the amount initially recognised and amortised over the term of the debt as a component of interest cost. In our view, directly attributable costs comprise only those that are *incremental*. Costs that are not directly attributable to the issue of debt are recognised as an expense in profit or loss because such costs would have occurred even without the issue of debt. [*IFRS 3.53, 9.5.1.1*]

2.6.530.90   An entity may incur fees in connection with the issue of debt and also pay fees to the same service provider/creditor in a related business combination. The fees allocated to the debt issue and the cost of the acquisition (which are expensed), in our view should be representative of the actual services provided. For example, if an entity pays fees to an investment bank in connection with a business combination plus additional financing, then we believe that those fees should be allocated between the costs of the acquisition and debt issue costs, considering factors such as the fees charged by investment banks in connection with other similar recent transactions – e.g. fees charged by an investment bank solely for advisory services for an acquisition or fees charged by an investment bank solely for arranging financing.

2.6.530.100   In our view, costs incurred by the acquirer in respect of due diligence procedures, which may be internal or external costs, are generally acquisition-related costs rather than being related to financing. However, a final determination will depend on the facts and circumstances of each case.

2.6.530.110 In some circumstances, a vendor may commission due diligence procedures. Some vendor due diligence engagements are commissioned by selling shareholders, before potential buyers for a business are identified, to facilitate a rapid sale or to obtain a better transaction price. In other circumstances, an acquirer may be involved at some stage in setting the scope or procedures to be performed in such due diligence procedures. Factors to be taken into account in assessing whether the costs of such transactions borne by the vendor are in substance reimbursed by the acquirer include, but are not limited to:

- the extent to which the acquirer uses the vendor due diligence report;
- the extent to which the acquirer avoids paying for a due diligence process itself;
- the extent of the acquirer's involvement in the vendor due diligence process;
- the extent to which the vendor due diligence assists the former owners of the acquiree – e.g. by facilitating a quicker sale and/or a higher price; and
- who bears the cost of the due diligence if the business combination does not take place.

2.6.540 Written put option or forward

2.6.540.10 An entity may write a put option or enter into a forward with the non-controlling shareholders in an acquiree as part of acquisition of the subsidiary. In that case, in our view there is a rebuttable presumption that the transactions are linked and should be accounted for as a single transaction in the acquisition accounting. For a more in-depth discussion, see 2.5.680 and 730.

2.6.550 CONTROL MAINTAINED OVER ASSETS AND LIABILITIES TRANSFERRED

2.6.550.10 An acquirer may transfer a business or a subsidiary to the acquiree as consideration in a business combination. Other forms of consideration transferred may include assets and liabilities of a subsidiary or other assets of the acquirer. Regardless of the structure of the transaction, if the acquirer retains control of the transferred assets or liabilities after the acquisition, then it recognises no gain or loss in profit or loss and measures those assets and liabilities at their carrying amounts immediately before the acquisition. [*IFRS 3.38*]

2.6.550.20 Additionally, if an acquirer transfers an equity interest in a subsidiary, but continues to have a controlling interest in the subsidiary after the transfer, then the change in the parent's ownership interest in the subsidiary is accounted for as an equity transaction, and no gain or loss is recognised in profit or loss (see 2.5.580).

EXAMPLE 11A – EXISTING SUBSIDIARY TRANSFERRED TO ACQUIREE – NCI AT FAIR VALUE

2.6.550.30 Company P transfers its wholly owned Subsidiary S1 to Company S2 in exchange for a 60% interest in S2. The fair value of the consideration transferred (the proportionate fair value of S1) is equal to the fair value of the consideration received (the proportionate investment in S2) – i.e. there is no bargain purchase. It is also determined that there is no minority discount or control premium in this transaction. P elects to measure NCI at fair value.

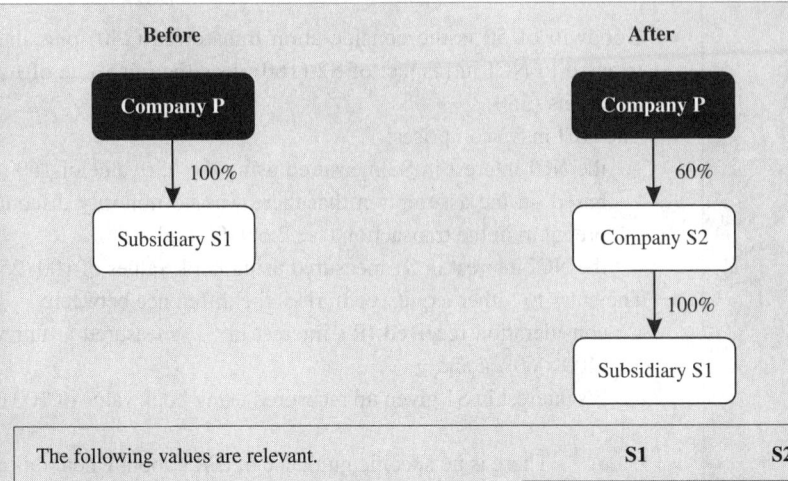

The following values are relevant.	**S1**	**S2**
Book value	250	200
Fair value of identifiable assets and liabilities	500	350
Fair value	600	400

2.6.550.40 P controls the transferred business (S1) directly before the transaction, and indirectly after the transaction through its control of S2. Therefore, P continues to measure the assets and liabilities of S1 following the acquisition at their carrying amounts immediately before the acquisition. However, as a result of the acquisition P has given up a 40% interest in S1. This decrease in interest is accounted for as an equity transaction.

Proof that the fair value of the consideration transferred is equal to the fair value of the consideration received.

Consideration transferred (40% of S1)	600 x 40% = 240
Consideration received (60% of S2)	400 x 60% = 240

2.6.550.50 P records the following entry.

	DEBIT	**CREDIT**
Identifiable net assets of S2	350	
Goodwill	50	
NCI (equity)		260
Other equity		140
To recognise acquisition of S2		

2.6.550.60 The above amounts are calculated as follows.
- The fair value of the identifiable net assets of S2 was given in the fact pattern. S1 is already consolidated and therefore its net assets are excluded from the above entry.

- Goodwill of 50 is the consideration transferred (240) plus the amount attributed to NCI in respect of S2 (160), less the fair value of its identifiable net assets (350).
- The NCI in S2 comprises:
  - the NCI interest in S2 measured using the fair value of 160 (400 x 40%), based on the assumption that there was no minority discount or control premium in the transaction (see 2.6.940); and
  - the NCI interest in S1 measured using book values of 100 (250 x 40%).
- The entry to 'other' equity comprises the difference between:
  - consideration received (P's interest in S2) measured at fair value of 240 (400 x 60%); and
  - P's interest in S1 given up measured using book value of 100 (250 x 40%).

2.6.550.70   There is no specific guidance in IFRS about where this credit should be recognised within equity; alternatives might include additional paid-in capital (share premium) and retained earnings.

EXAMPLE 11B – EXISTING SUBSIDIARY TRANSFERRED TO ACQUIREE – NCI AT PROPORTIONATE INTEREST IN IDENTIFIABLE NET ASSETS

2.6.550.80   Assume the same facts as in Example 11A except that P elects to measure NCI at their proportionate interest in the identifiable net assets of S2 at the date of acquisition.

2.6.550.90   P records the following entry.

	DEBIT	CREDIT
Identifiable net assets of S2	350	
Goodwill	30	
NCI (equity) (see 2.6.940)		240
Other equity		140
To recognise acquisition of S2		

2.6.550.100   The above entry differs from Example 11A as follows.
- Goodwill of 30 is the consideration transferred (240) plus the amount attributed to NCI in respect of S2 (140), less the fair value of its identifiable net assets (350).
- The NCI in S2 comprises:
  - the NCI interest in S2 measured using the fair value of the identifiable net assets of 140 (350 x 40%); and
  - the NCI interest in S1 measured using book values of 100 (250 x 40%).

2.6.550.110   An economically similar result would occur if S1 had issued new shares representing a 40% interest to the shareholders of S2 in exchange for all the ordinary shares of S2. The same accounting treatments as those described above would apply in such a transaction.

2.6.560   IDENTIFIABLE ASSETS ACQUIRED AND LIABILITIES ASSUMED

2.6.560.10   IFRS 3 contains general principles on the recognition and measurement of the identifiable assets acquired and the liabilities assumed as part of a business combination. There are limited exceptions to these recognition and measurement principles. For example, certain contingent liabilities assumed in a business combination are recognised separately as part of the acquisition accounting, and non-current assets (or disposal groups) classified as held-for-sale are measured at fair value less costs to sell. [*IFRS 3.10, 18, 23, 31*]

2.6.560.20   Subsequent to the business combination, assets and liabilities are generally measured in accordance with applicable standards; this subsequent measurement is outside the scope of this chapter other than for certain items in respect of which IFRS 3 contains guidance (see 2.6.1080).

2.6.570   Recognition principle

2.6.570.10   The recognition principle in IFRS 3 is that the identifiable assets acquired and the liabilities assumed as part of a business combination are recognised separately from goodwill at the date of acquisition, if they:

- meet the definition of assets and liabilities in the Conceptual Framework, which was in effect when IFRS 3 was developed but has been superseded since then; and
- are exchanged as part of the business combination, instead of as a separate transaction (see 2.6.340). [*IFRS 3.11–12*]

2.6.570.20   As a result of the recognition principle, the usual recognition criteria for assets and liabilities acquired in a business combination are always considered to be satisfied – i.e. probable inflow or outflow of economic benefits and that their values can be measured reliably. [*IFRS 3.BC126–BC130*]

2.6.570.30   Costs in respect of planned or future actions of the acquirer are not recognised as liabilities by the acquirer because they are not liabilities of the acquiree at the date of acquisition. For example, the cost of restructuring the acquiree is recognised as a liability as part of the acquisition accounting only if it is a liability of the acquiree at the date of acquisition. [*IFRS 3.11*]

2.6.570.40   There are limited exceptions to the recognition principle (see 2.6.640).

2.6.580   Classification and designation principles#

2.6.580.10   IFRS 3 provides a general principle that at the date of acquisition the acquirer classifies and designates identifiable assets acquired and liabilities assumed as necessary to apply other standards subsequently. Those classifications or designations are made based on the contractual terms, economic conditions, the acquirer's operating or accounting policies and other pertinent conditions at the date of acquisition. For a discussion of acquired financial instruments, see 2.6.590 and 7.4.20.30). [*IFRS 3.15*]

2.6.580.20   There are two exceptions to this general classification and designation principle: the classification by the acquiree of a lease as operating or finance in accordance with IAS 17 and the classification of a contract as an insurance contract in accordance with IFRS 4 are retained, unless the acquiree's classification was made in error. The classification and designation of these contracts are based on the contractual terms at inception of the contract, or at the date of the latest modification that resulted in a change of classification. [*IFRS 3.17*]

2.6.583   **FORTHCOMING REQUIREMENTS**

2.6.585   **LEASES**

2.6.585.10   IFRS 16 carries forward the IAS 17 distinction between operating and finance leases for lessors only. Under IFRS 16, a lessee applies a single, on-balance sheet lease accounting model and does not classify the lease as an operating or finance lease. Therefore, in a business combination the exception to the general classification and designation principle applies only to leases in which the acquiree is the lessor (see 5.1A.20.50). [*IFRS 3.17, 16.22, 61*]

2.6.587   **INSURANCE CONTRACTS**

2.6.587.10   IFRS 17 removes the exception to the general classification and designation principle for an insurance contract in its scope. [*IFRS 3.15, 17*]

2.6.590   *Financial instruments*

2.6.590.10   The acquirer goes through the process of designating financial instruments as hedging instruments and designating any hedging relationships of the acquiree, and reassessing whether separation of an embedded derivative from its host is required at the date of acquisition based on conditions as they exist at the date of acquisition. [*IFRS 3.16*]

2.6.590.20   This means that in its consolidated financial statements the acquirer cannot automatically continue to apply the hedge accounting model to the hedging relationship previously designated by the acquiree. Rather, if it wishes to apply hedge accounting, then the acquirer has to designate a new hedging relationship. This might involve the same financial instruments and hedged items, but the inception of the hedging relationship can be no earlier than the date of acquisition.

2.6.590.30   Designation can be made only if the hedging relationship meets all hedging requirements in IFRS 9 at the date of acquisition and can be made prospectively only from that date. This requires the acquirer to assess whether the hedge will be effective over the designated period. Hedge accounting is the subject of chapter 7.9; and for a discussion of assessing hedge effectiveness requirements, see 7.9.830.

2.6.600   **Measurement principle**

2.6.600.10   The measurement principle in IFRS 3 is that the identifiable assets acquired and the liabilities assumed as part of a business combination are measured at the date of acquisition at their fair values. There are limited exceptions to this measurement principle (see 2.6.640). [*IFRS 3.18*]

2.6.600.20   Fair value is measured in accordance with IFRS 13, which is the subject of chapter 2.4. That chapter includes general guidance on applying the principles of IFRS 13 in measuring fair value, as well as application guidance on specific items that might be relevant to a business combination.

2.6.600.30   IFRS 3 provides specific guidance on applying the fair value measurement principle to the following assets, which takes precedence over the general guidance in IFRS 13:
- assets with uncertain cash flows (valuation allowances) (see 2.6.610);
- assets subject to operating leases in which the acquiree is the lessor (see 2.6.620); and
- assets that the acquirer intends not to use or to use differently from the way in which other market participants would use them (see 2.6.630 and 2.4.330).

2.6.610   *Assets with uncertain cash flows (valuation allowances)*

2.6.610.10   IFRS 3 prohibits recognition at the date of acquisition of a separate valuation allowance on assets acquired that are measured at fair value. The rationale is that fair value incorporates uncertainties about cash flows. For example, because accounts receivable are recognised at fair value in accounting for a business combination, no separate valuation allowance for the contractual cash flows that are deemed uncollectable, or a loss allowance, are recognised. [*IFRS 3.B41*]

2.6.610.20   It appears that the guidance in 2.6.610.10 is provided specifically for the purpose of calculating goodwill, because any reduction in fair value by the loss allowance would have resulted in an increase in goodwill. Accordingly, it appears that under IFRS 9 an asset acquired in a business combination that is subject to IFRS 9's impairment requirements would attract a loss allowance at the first reporting date after it is recognised, even if that date is the date on which the business combination has taken place. This effectively means that, for the recognition of impairment, such assets are treated in the same way as other financial assets. For a further discussion, see 7.7.380, 7.8.20.50 and 7.10.270.40.

2.6.610.30   The acquirer discloses separately the fair value of the receivables acquired, as well as their gross contractual amounts and the best estimate of the amounts of the contractual cash flows that the acquirer does not expect to collect. [*IFRS 3.B64(h)*]

EXAMPLE 12 – FAIR VALUE OF TRADE RECEIVABLES LESS THAN FACE VALUE

2.6.610.40   Company P acquires Company S in a business combination on 31 December 2018. At the date of acquisition, the gross contractual amount of S's trade receivables is 100. The fair value of the trade receivables as at 31 December 2018 is 97 and the amount P expects to receive from the receivables is 95.

2.6.610.50   P recognises trade receivables at their acquisition date fair value of 97 in applying the acquisition accounting. Additionally, P recognises an impairment loss and loss allowances of 2 for expected credit losses for the receivables at the date of acquisition (see 2.6.610.20 and 7.8.20) separately from the acquisition accounting.

2.6.610.60   P discloses the fair value of the receivables acquired of 97, as well as their gross contractual amounts of 100 and the best estimate of the amounts of the contractual cash flows that it does not expect to receive of 5.

2.6.620   *Assets subject to operating leases with acquiree as lessor*

2.6.620.10   If the acquiree is the lessor in an operating lease, then the asset subject to the operating lease (e.g. a building) is recognised at fair value taking into account the terms of the related lease – i.e. the acquirer does not recognise a separate intangible asset or liability related to the favourable or unfavourable aspect of an operating lease relative to market terms or prices. For further guidance on leases acquired in a business combination, see 2.6.830. [*IFRS 3.B42*]

2.6.630   *Usage different from that of other market participants*

2.6.630.10   Many assets have different uses and often the value of an asset to an entity may be highly dependent on its specific use. Sometimes the acquirer intends to use an asset in a manner different from the way in which market participants would use it. In an extreme scenario, the acquirer in a business combination may intend not to use one of the assets acquired, whereas market participants would use and generate economic benefits from the asset. There can be a variety of reasons for this. An example is defensive intangible assets that the acquirer does not intend to use, but intends to hold and prevent others from gaining access to them, thereby increasing the value of the acquirer's existing (competing) assets. The question arises about how such assets should be valued in the acquisition accounting. [*IFRS 3.B43*]

2.6.630.20   The standards do not exempt an entity from recognising an asset acquired at fair value based on market participants' use of the asset because the entity does not intend to use that asset, or intends to use it in a way that is not similar to how market participants would be expected to use it. Therefore, such assets are recognised at fair value rather than based on the way in which the acquirer intends to use them (see 2.4.340.80). [*IFRS 3.B43*]

EXAMPLE 13 – ACQUIRED BRAND TO BE UNUSED

2.6.630.30   Company P, a confectionery company, acquires one of its main competitors, Company S, in a business combination on 31 October 2018. Although P intends to use S's production plant, distribution network and research facilities, it does not intend to use S's brand name for its confectionary. However, it is envisaged that other market participants would use that brand name.

2.6.630.40   Even though P does not intend to use S's brand name, it is still required to recognise and measure S's brand name at its fair value at the date of acquisition

 based on its use by other market participants. Therefore, P estimates the likely plans of market participants for the brand.

2.6.630.50   For a discussion of the amortisation of an intangible asset that the acquirer intends not to use or to use in a way that is different from how market participants would use them, see 3.3.235.

2.6.640   Exceptions to recognition and measurement principles#

2.6.640.10   IFRS 3 provides the following exceptions to the recognition and/or measurement principles. [*IFRS 3.21–31*]

EXCEPTION TO THE RECOGNITION PRINCIPLE	EXCEPTIONS TO BOTH THE RECOGNITION AND MEASUREMENT PRINCIPLES	EXCEPTIONS TO THE MEASUREMENT PRINCIPLE
• Contingent liabilities (see 2.6.650)	• Deferred taxes (see 2.6.660) • Indemnification assets (see 2.6.670) • Employee benefits (see 2.6.680)	• Reacquired rights (see 2.6.690) • Share-based payment awards (see 2.6.700) • Assets held for sale (see 2.6.710)

2.6.645   FORTHCOMING REQUIREMENTS

2.6.646   LEASES

2.6.646.10   IFRS 16 provides an additional exception to both the recognition and measurement principles for leases in which the acquiree is the lessee, see 2.6.915.

2.6.647   INSURANCE CONTRACTS

2.6.647.10   IFRS 17 provides an additional exception to the measurement principle such that an acquirer measures a group of contracts in the scope of IFRS 17 acquired in a business combination at the date of acquisition in accordance with IFRS 17 (see chapter 8.1A). [*IFRS 3.31A, 17.39, B93–B95*]

2.6.650   *Contingent liabilities*

2.6.650.10   A 'contingent liability' is:
- a possible obligation that arises from past events whose existence will be confirmed only by the occurrence or non-occurrence of one or more uncertain future events not wholly within the control of the entity; or
- a present obligation that arises from past events but is not recognised because it is not probable that economic outflow will be required to settle the obligation or it cannot be measured with sufficient reliability. [*IFRS 3.22, IAS 37.10*]

2.6.650.20   The following flowchart outlines the application of IFRS 3 in respect of contingent liabilities.

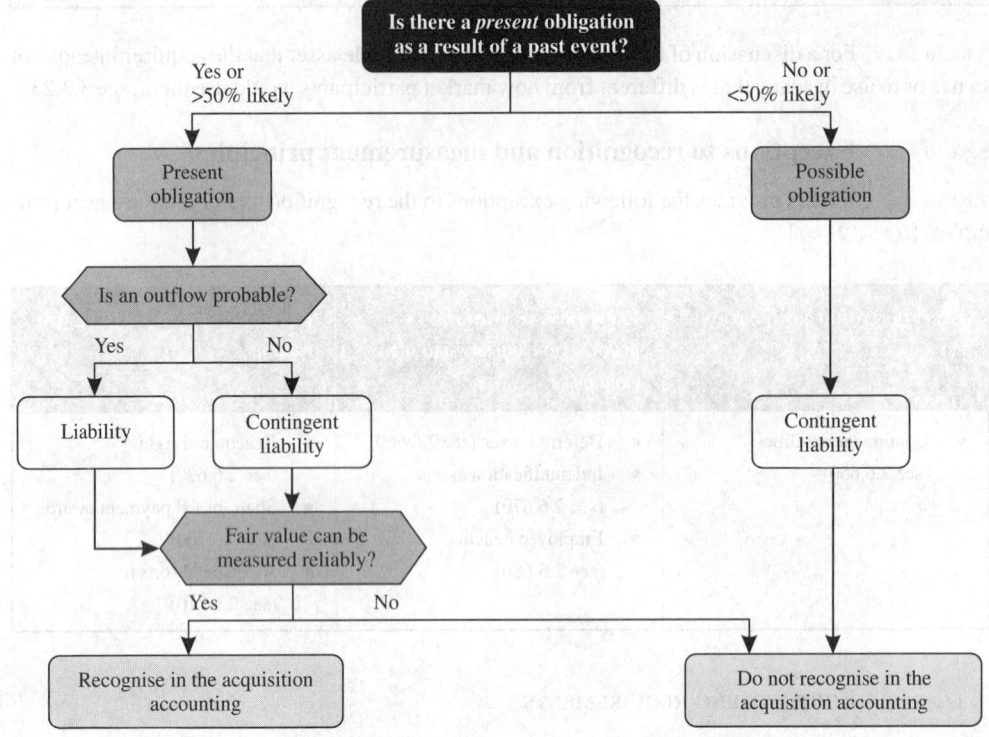

2.6.650.30   A contingent liability acquired in a business combination is recognised in the acquisition accounting if it is a present obligation and its fair value can be measured reliably; this is because it meets the definition of a liability in that case. A contingent liability that is a possible obligation is not recognised because it does not meet the definition of a liability. [*IFRS 3.23, BC274–BC275*]

2.6.650.40   In some cases, it will not be clear whether a present obligation exists – e.g. if the parties dispute the facts and circumstances giving rise to the contingent liability. In that case, IAS 37 clarifies that a past event is deemed to give rise to a present obligation if it is 'more likely than not' that a present obligation exists. Although this is not stated explicitly in IFRS 3, in our view it is appropriate to extend this requirement of IAS 37 in applying the acquisition method because IFRS 3 does not deal with the issue itself. [*IAS 37.15*]

2.6.650.50   The probability of payment being required is not relevant in determining whether a contingent liability that is a present obligation is recognised in a business combination, but this probability will impact its fair value. [*IFRS 3.23*]

2.6.650.60   Contingent liabilities may arise from actual or intended post-acquisition actions of the acquirer. Such contingent liabilities are not recognised as part of the acquisition accounting because the acquirer's intentions are not reflected in the acquisition accounting and the definition of a liability is not met at the date of acquisition. For example, risks arising from transactions after the date of acquisition to achieve tax optimisation for the acquirer would not be reflected as at the date of acquisition.

2.6.650.70   For a discussion of the subsequent measurement of contingent liabilities recognised in the acquisition accounting, see 2.6.1100.

2.6.650.80   Contingent assets are not recognised because a contingent asset is a 'possible' asset that does not meet the definition of an asset. [*IFRS 3.BC276, IAS 37.10*]

EXAMPLE 14 – CONTINGENT ASSET ACQUIRED

> 2.6.650.90   Company P acquires Company S in a business combination on 31 October 2018. S leases a property to Company Q under an operating lease. The terms of the lease state that if Q cancels the contract, then Q would be required to pay 100 to S. P would not recognise this contingent asset in accounting for the business combination.

2.6.660   *Deferred taxes*

2.6.660.10   Deferred tax assets and liabilities that arise from the assets acquired and liabilities assumed in a business combination are recognised and measured in accordance with IAS 12 rather than at fair value. Deductible temporary differences and unused tax losses of the acquiree are also accounted for in accordance with IAS 12. [*IFRS 3.24–25*]

2.6.660.20   For a discussion of the accounting for the income tax effects of business combinations, see 3.13.870.

2.6.670   *Indemnification assets*

2.6.670.10   Purchase agreements sometimes provide that the seller indemnifies the acquirer against a particular contingent liability outstanding at the date of acquisition. For example, a contingent liability could relate to a legal case of the acquiree for environmental pollution or to specific tax uncertainties. The seller may agree to reimburse the acquirer if the outcome of the legal case or resolution of the tax uncertainty requires payment by the acquiree. As a result, the acquirer obtains an indemnification asset. [*IFRS 3.27*]

2.6.670.20   If the seller is contractually obliged to indemnify the acquirer for a specific liability, then an asset is recognised at the same time and measured using the same measurement basis as the liability. This ensures that both the asset and the liability are measured on a consistent basis using similar assumptions, subject to management's assessment of collectability of the asset. [*IFRS 3.27–28*]

2.6.670.30   This accounting applies to indemnities related to a specific liability or contingent liability of the acquiree. It does not apply in accounting for general representations and warranties provided by the seller to the acquirer that do not create a specific right of reimbursement.

2.6.670.40   After initial recognition, an indemnification asset continues to be measured based on the assumptions used to measure the related liability, subject to management's assessment of collectability of the asset, limited to the amount of the liability to which it relates (see 2.6.1110). [*IFRS 3.57*]

EXAMPLE 15 – INDEMNIFICATION PROVIDED BY SELLER

2.6.670.50   Company P acquires Company S in a business combination on 31 October 2018. S is being sued by one of its customers for breach of contract. The sellers of S provide an indemnification to P for the reimbursement of any losses greater than 500. There are no collectability issues around this indemnification.

2.6.670.60   At the date of acquisition, it is determined that there is a present obligation and therefore the fair value of the contingent liability of 530 is recognised by P in the acquisition accounting. In the acquisition accounting, P also recognises an indemnification asset of 30 (530 - 500).

2.6.680   *Employee benefits*

2.6.680.10   Employee benefit liabilities (and assets, if there are any) are recognised and measured in accordance with IAS 19 and are the subject of chapter 4.4 except those to which IFRS 2 applies (see 2.6.700). [*IFRS 3.26*]

2.6.680.20   The measurement of the liability (or asset) does not take into account plan amendments, terminations or curtailments that the acquirer has no obligation to make at the date of acquisition; therefore, it does not take into account the acquirer's intentions or future actions, such as an intention to change the terms of the plan to conform to the acquirer's existing plan.

2.6.690   *Reacquired rights*

2.6.690.10   The acquisition of a right that had been previously granted to the acquiree to use one of the acquirer's assets (recognised or unrecognised) is a reacquired right, which is recognised as part of the acquisition accounting. The reacquired right represents an identifiable intangible asset that is recognised separately from goodwill. [*IFRS 3.B35*]

2.6.690.20   Reacquired rights are measured by taking into account only the remaining contractual term of the related contract. Any potential renewals are ignored even if a market participant would take these into account in its determination of fair value. This is consistent with the requirement that the amortisation period of reacquired rights cannot take into account expected renewals (see 2.6.1090). [*IFRS 3.29, 55*]

2.6.700   *Share-based payment awards*

2.6.700.10   In certain instances, an acquirer's share-based payment awards (replacement awards) may be exchanged for awards held by the acquiree's employees (acquiree awards). Such payments are accounted for as modifications in accordance with IFRS 2. Any liability or equity instrument related to a share-based payment award is measured in accordance with IFRS 2, which is a market-based measurement principle rather than a fair value measurement principle. For a discussion of the accounting for share-based payment awards, see 2.6.420. [*IFRS 3.30*]

2.6.710   *Assets held for sale*

2.6.710.10   Non-current assets (or disposal groups) acquired solely with the intention of disposal in the short term are consolidated. However, they are classified separately as non-current assets (or disposal groups) held-for-sale if they meet the criteria for classification as held-for-sale in IFRS 5 within a short period of time after the date of acquisition – generally three months or less. Such non-current assets (or disposal groups) classified as held-for-sale are measured at fair value less costs to sell in accordance with IFRS 5 (see 5.4.260). [*IFRS 3.31, 5.11*]

2.6.720   **Intangible assets**

2.6.720.10   All *identifiable* intangible assets acquired in a business combination are recognised separately from goodwill and are initially measured at their acquisition date fair values. This often involves identifying and recognising intangible assets not previously recognised by the acquiree in its financial statements. Therefore, the identification, recognition and measurement of intangible assets is an important part of the acquisition accounting that often requires considerable time and attention. For a discussion of measuring the fair value of intangible assets, see chapter 2.4 in general, supplemented by the specific guidance in 2.4.1010.

2.6.720.20   In general, an intangible asset is recognised only if it meets the asset recognition criteria – i.e. it is *probable* that the expected future economic benefits attributable to the asset will flow to the entity, and its cost can be measured reliably. For identifiable intangible assets acquired in a business combination, these recognition criteria are always considered to be satisfied. Therefore, all identifiable intangible assets acquired in a business combination are recognised separately from goodwill. [*IAS 38.21, 33*]

2.6.720.30   IAS 38 provides guidance on the subsequent accounting for intangible assets acquired in a business combination (see 3.3.190–320).

2.6.720.40   An asset is identifiable if either it is separable or it arises from contractual or other legal rights, regardless of whether those rights are transferable or separable from the entity or from other rights and obligations (see 3.3.40). [*IAS 38.12*]

2.6.720.50   The implementation guidance to IFRS 3 provides examples of intangible assets that meet the identifiability criteria for recognition as intangible assets separately from goodwill – i.e. either arise from contractual-legal rights or are separable. The intangible assets are grouped into the following categories:
- marketing-related;
- customer-related;
- artistic-related;
- contract-based; and
- technology-based. [*IFRS 3.IE16–IE44*]

2.6.720.60   Sometimes an intangible asset acquired is separable only together with a related contract, identifiable asset or liability. In this case, it is recognised separately from goodwill, but generally together with the related item. [*IFRS 3.B34, IAS 38.36*]

2.6.720.70 Examples of intangible assets that may be separable only together with a related item include:

- a trademark for a product because this may be separable only together with the recipe or documented but unpatented technical expertise used to manufacture that product;
- a trademark for natural spring water because this may relate to a particular spring and be separable only together with that spring;
- a group of depositor relationships because this may be separable only together with the related deposit liabilities; and
- a licence to operate an item because this may be separable only together with the related item – e.g. a licence to operate a nuclear power plant or an airport. [*IFRS 3.B32(b), B34*]

EXAMPLE 16A – INTANGIBLE ASSETS ACQUIRED – CORE DEPOSITS

2.6.720.75 Commercial Bank B acquires Savings Bank S in a business combination on 31 October 2018. B expects that part of the short-term deposits of S (current accounts and savings deposits) will remain deposited in S for a significant period of time and that the useful life of the related customer relationships is longer than the contractual duration.

2.6.720.76 The interest rates on the acquired deposits are lower than the cost of alternative sources of funding – e.g. deposits at interbank market rates. B estimates that this will result in substantially reduced annual funding costs for the bank.

2.6.720.77 In this example, B recognises an intangible asset ('core deposits'), which to a large extent represents the value of the reduced funding cost provided by the deposits.

2.6.720.80 Sometimes a group of complementary identifiable intangible assets may be acquired – e.g. a trademark for a drug and its related trade name, formula, recipe and technological expertise. In this case, the group of complementary assets may be recognised together as a single asset separate from goodwill provided that the individual assets have similar useful lives. [*IAS 38.37*]

2.6.720.90 Many intangible assets arise from rights conveyed legally by contract, statute or similar means. An intangible asset that meets the contractual-legal criterion is identifiable, regardless of whether it meets the separability criterion. Examples of intangible assets that may meet the contractual-legal criterion include:

- franchises granted – e.g. in respect of fast-food outlets, restaurant chains or car dealers;
- trademarks;
- patents;
- contracts negotiated with customers or suppliers and related relationships;
- licence agreements;
- the favourable terms of an acquired operating lease compared with current market terms, regardless of whether the lease terms prohibit the acquirer from selling or otherwise transferring the lease; and
- licences to operate, regardless of whether the licence can be sold or otherwise transferred separately from the related item – e.g. licences to operate a nuclear power plant or an airport. [*IFRS 3.B32(a)–(c)*]

2.6.720.100   Contractual or other legal rights are not defined in IFRS 3, but it is clear from the examples in the standard that the definition is intended to be broad. For example, customer relationships may meet the contractual-legal criterion at the date of acquisition even if there is no contract in place with the customer at the date of acquisition, if the acquiree has a practice of establishing contracts with customers. [*IFRS 3.IE30(c)*]

2.6.720.110   Sometimes a contract may be cancellable by the customer, but this does not affect it meeting the contractual-legal criterion. [*IFRS 3.IE25, IE30*]

2.6.720.120   Sometimes the terms of a contract may prohibit its sale or transfer separately from the acquiree. This does not affect it meeting the contractual-legal criterion, but it may in some cases affect its fair value (see 2.4.70). [*IFRS 3.IE26*]

2.6.720.130   'Goodwill' is an asset representing the future economic benefits arising from other assets acquired in a business combination that are not individually identified and separately recognised. An intangible asset acquired in a business combination that meets neither the separability criterion nor the contractual-legal criterion at the date of acquisition is subsumed into goodwill. Similarly, any value attributable to items that do not qualify as assets at the date of acquisition is subsumed into goodwill. For a discussion of the recognition and measurement of goodwill, see 2.6.1010. [*IFRS 3.A, B37–B38*]

2.6.720.140   Examples of items that are not identifiable include:
- the assembled workforce of the acquiree – i.e. an existing collection of employees that permits the acquirer to continue to operate an acquired business from the date of acquisition;
- potential future contracts at the date of acquisition, although there may be a related customer relationship intangible asset (see 2.6.760);
- synergies from combining the acquiree's net assets with those of the acquirer; and
- market share. [*IFRS 3.B37–B38, BC163, BC179*]

2.6.720.150   Although individual employees may have employment contracts that are intangible assets, the assembled workforce as a whole does not have such a contract and it is not separable. [*IFRS 3.BC178*]

2.6.720.160   A collective bargaining agreement typically dictates the terms of the employment – e.g. wage rates – but normally does not oblige the covered employees to remain with the employer for a specified period. The assembled workforce of the acquiree is not recognised as an intangible asset because it is not identifiable. In our view, the existence of a collective bargaining agreement does not change this for the employees covered by that agreement. However, in our view the underlying collective bargaining contract could meet the criteria for recognition as a separate intangible asset (favourable contract terms) or a liability (unfavourable contract terms). In our experience, the separate recognition of a collective bargaining agreement intangible asset is rare.

2.6.720.170   In our view, a group of individual employment contracts entered into by an acquiree with a broad group of employees should not be viewed, collectively, as an assembled workforce. However, the facts and circumstances in each situation should be evaluated. For example, non-compete clauses included in such contracts are evaluated separately for possible recognition as identifiable intangible assets.

2.6.720.180   If an item acquired in a business combination is included in goodwill – e.g. because it is not identifiable at the date of acquisition – then the acquirer does not subsequently reclassify that value from goodwill for events that occur after the date of acquisition. For a discussion of subsequent adjustments to the acquisition accounting, see 2.6.1020. [*IFRS 3.45–50, B38*]

2.6.730   *Customer-related intangible assets*

2.6.730.10   Customer-related intangible assets may meet the contractual-legal and/or the separability criterion (see 2.6.720.40). Identifying, recognising and measuring customer-related intangible assets is an area that often requires careful analysis and attention. The relationship that an acquiree has with its customers may encompass a number of distinct intangible assets that need to be recognised separately from each other – e.g. a specific contract with a customer may need to be recognised separately from the relationship with that customer. This can pose challenges in the acquisition accounting. Examples of customer-related intangible assets include:

- customer lists (non-contractual);
- order or production backlog (contractual);
- customer contracts and related customer relationships (contractual); and
- non-contractual customer relationships. [*IFRS 3.IE23*]

2.6.740   *Customer lists*

2.6.740.10   A customer list consists of information about customers, such as names and contact information. It may also be a database that includes other information about customers, such as order histories and demographic information. Customer lists do not generally arise from contractual or other legal rights, but are frequently sold, leased or exchanged. A customer list that is separable might meet the definition of an intangible asset even if the acquiree does not control the customer relationship. However, not all customer lists are separable. In some countries, regulations prevent an entity from selling, leasing or exchanging the information in such a list. Sometimes there are terms of confidentiality or other agreements that prohibit an entity from selling, leasing or otherwise exchanging information about its customers. The existence of such regulation or similar agreements prevents recognition because the list would not be separable in such cases. [*IFRS 3.B33, IE24*]

2.6.740.20   It is important to distinguish between a customer list and a customer base. A customer list includes specific information about the customer, such as name, contact information, order history and demographic information. A customer base represents a group of customers that are neither known nor identifiable to the entity – e.g. the customers that visit a particular fast-food restaurant. A customer base does not meet the criteria for recognition separately from goodwill because a customer base meets neither the contractual-legal nor the separability criterion.

EXAMPLE 16B – INTANGIBLE ASSETS ACQUIRED – CUSTOMER LIST

2.6.740.30   Company P acquires Company S, a medical testing company, in a business combination on 31 October 2018. S provides testing services to patients, such as blood screening, based on referrals from their general practitioners (medical practitioners who provide primary care to patients). S maintains a database with each patient's information, such as name, address, telephone number, doctor's name, insurer's name and policy number. However, this patient information is protected by privacy laws and S cannot sell, license, transfer or otherwise exchange it.

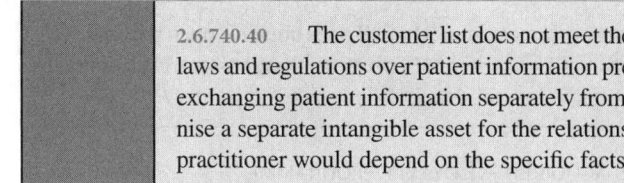

2.6.740.40   The customer list does not meet the separability criterion because privacy laws and regulations over patient information prevent selling, transferring, licensing or exchanging patient information separately from the acquiree. Whether P could recognise a separate intangible asset for the relationship with the patients and the general practitioner would depend on the specific facts and circumstances of each case.

2.6.750   *Order or production backlog*

2.6.750.10   Order or production backlog arises from contracts such as purchase or sales orders. An order or production backlog acquired in a business combination meets the contractual-legal criterion even if the purchase or sales orders are cancellable by the customer (see 2.6.720.110). [*IFRS 3.IE25*]

2.6.760   *Customer contracts and related customer relationships*

2.6.760.10   Customer relationships are identifiable intangible assets if they arise from contractual or legal rights, or are separable. The following criteria need to be met to conclude that a customer relationship exists:

- the acquiree has information about, and regular contact with, the customer; and
- the customer has the ability to make direct contact with the acquiree. [*IFRS 3.IE28*]

2.6.760.20   Care is taken to distinguish between a customer contract and the related customer relationship because they may represent two distinct intangible assets, which may need to be recognised separately from each other because they may have different useful lives. [*IFRS 3.IE27*]

2.6.760.30   If an entity establishes relationships with its customers through contracts, then those customer relationships arise from contractual rights and therefore meet the contractual-legal criterion. This is unaffected by confidentiality or other contractual terms that prohibit the sale or transfer of a contract separately from the acquiree. The interpretation of what is a contractual customer relationship is broad. [*IFRS 3.IE26, IE30*]

EXAMPLE 16C – INTANGIBLE ASSETS ACQUIRED – CUSTOMER CONTRACTS AND RELATIONSHIPS

2.6.760.40   Company P acquires Company S in a business combination on 31 October 2018. S has a practice of using purchase orders when entering into transactions with its customers. At the date of acquisition, S:
- has a backlog of open purchase orders with 75% of its recurring customers; and
- does not have open purchase orders, or other contracts, with the other 25% of its recurring customers.

2.6.760.50   Regardless of whether they are cancellable, the purchase orders from the 75% of S's recurring customers meet the contractual-legal criterion. The related relationships with those customers also meet the contractual-legal criterion. Therefore, both the contracts and the relationships are recognised as intangible assets separately from goodwill, and separately from each other because they represent two distinct intangible assets. Because S has a practice of establishing customer relationships with customers through purchase orders, the customer relationships

> with the 25% of recurring customers with whom S does not have open purchase orders also meet the contractual-legal criterion. Therefore, these customer relationship assets are recognised at fair value, separately from goodwill. [*IFRS 3.IE29, IE30(c)*]

EXAMPLE 16D – INTANGIBLE ASSETS ACQUIRED – LOYALTY PROGRAMME

2.6.760.60   Company P acquires Company S, a department store, in a business combination on 31 October 2018. S runs a loyalty programme and has access to relevant customer information and the ability to contact customers participating in the loyalty programme. In addition, the customers have the ability to make direct contact with S. On the basis of the information presented in this example, the customer relationship is recognised as an intangible asset separately from goodwill at its acquisition date fair value.

2.6.770   *Overlapping customer relationships*

2.6.770.10   Sometimes both the acquirer and the acquiree can have relationships with the same customer. In our view, the acquirer should still recognise the acquiree's relationship with that customer at its fair value at the date of acquisition if that relationship is identifiable.

EXAMPLE 16E – INTANGIBLE ASSETS ACQUIRED – OVERLAPPING CUSTOMER RELATIONSHIPS

2.6.770.20   Company P acquires Company S in a business combination on 31 October 2018. P and S operate in the same industry and both sell their products to Customer C. Assuming that the relationship meets the separability or contractual-legal criterion, an issue arises about whether P should recognise an intangible asset for S's relationship with C separately from goodwill because P already has a relationship with C.

2.6.770.30   We believe that P should recognise a customer relationship intangible asset for S's relationship with C, because it meets the definition of an identifiable intangible asset. The relationship is measured at its fair value at the date of acquisition from a market participant's perspective.

2.6.780   *Acquiree has pre-existing customer relationship with acquirer*

2.6.780.10   Sometimes the acquiree may have a pre-existing customer relationship with the acquirer, and the question arises about whether the acquirer recognises this relationship in the acquisition accounting. In our view, the acquirer should not recognise an intangible asset separately from goodwill for a customer relationship that the acquiree has with the acquirer because, from the perspective of the consolidated group, the definition of an asset is not met because no future economic benefits will be derived from outside the group; the asset cannot be disposed of and the contract is between members of the consolidated group.

2.6.780.20   In contrast, a reacquired right previously granted by the acquirer to the acquiree to use an asset of the acquirer is recognised in the acquisition accounting (see 2.6.390). The reason for the difference is that in the case of a reacquired right, the acquirer regains the right to use one of its assets; however, in the case of a customer relationship that the acquiree has with the acquirer, the acquirer is not obtaining an identifiable asset because from the group's perspective the acquirer and acquiree are part of the same reporting entity. [*IFRS 3.B35*]

2.6.790 *Purchased legal relationships with customers*

2.6.790.10   Sometimes an acquiree may have a purchased legal relationship with customers, but does not have direct contact with those customers. In our view, purchased legal relationships with customers may meet the criteria to be recognised as contract-based intangible assets even if the entity does not have a direct contact with its customers and only limited or no information about their identity, if the relationship is established through contractual or other legal rights.

EXAMPLE 16F – INTANGIBLE ASSETS ACQUIRED – FUNDS MANAGEMENT

2.6.790.20   Company P acquires Company S, a fund management company, in a business combination on 31 October 2018. S has a portfolio of customers (investors) who invest their money in the funds run by S and pay a management fee to S as the fund manager.

2.6.790.30   There is no contact between S and its investors, and S does not have any information about its investors. Rather, intermediaries advertise S's funds to their customers and enable them to invest in the funds. By doing so, the investors agree to the terms and conditions included in a prospectus that is issued by the fund, which includes all relevant provisions, including those applying to the management fee.

2.6.790.40   In this example, we believe that P should recognise a contract-based intangible asset as part of the acquisition accounting, based on the terms and conditions contained in the prospectus. The intangible asset is effectively the right of S to receive management fees.

2.6.800 *Non-contractual customer relationships*

2.6.800.10   A customer relationship that does not meet the contractual-legal criterion can be identifiable if it meets the separability criterion. Separability is demonstrated if the entity has the ability to dispose of the asset, or for the asset to be disposed of as a package with a related asset, liability or related contract, but not as part of a business combination. Therefore, in our view if an asset is capable of being divided from the entity, then separability is demonstrated by the following:

- there is a market for the same or similar assets to be exchanged in transactions that are not business combinations; and
- the entity has access to this market – i.e. the entity would be able to sell its customer relationship in that market. [*IFRS 3.B33–B34, IE31*]

2.6.810 *IPR&D assets*

2.6.810.10   In-process research and development (IPR&D) may be acquired in a business combination.

- 'Research' is original and planned investigation undertaken with the prospect of gaining new knowledge and understanding. Outside a business combination, research costs are expensed as incurred (see 3.3.120).
- 'Development' is the application of research findings or other knowledge to a plan or design for the production of new or substantially improved materials, products, processes etc before the start of commercial production or use. It does not include the maintenance or enhancement of ongoing operations (see 3.3.120). [*IAS 38.8, 54*]

2.6.810.20   IFRS 3 does not contain an exception to the recognition or measurement principles for IPR&D. Therefore, IPR&D is recognised separately from goodwill and measured at its fair value at the date of acquisition, if it is identifiable (see 2.6.720.40) and otherwise meets the definition of an intangible asset (see 3.3.30). This is irrespective of whether the acquiree had recognised the asset in its financial statements before the business combination. Similar to other intangible assets acquired in a business combination, the asset recognition criteria of probable future economic benefits and being able to measure its cost reliably are considered to be satisfied in all cases (see 2.6.720.20). If there is uncertainty about the outcome of a project, then this is reflected in the measurement of its fair value. [*IAS 38.34*]

2.6.810.30   At the date of acquisition, IPR&D is capitalised as an intangible asset not yet ready for use. The subsequent measurement of an acquired IPR&D project and the treatment of subsequent expenditure on it are in accordance with IAS 38 (see 3.3.120 and 210).

EXAMPLE 16G – INTANGIBLE ASSETS ACQUIRED – IPR&D

2.6.810.40   Company P acquires Company S, a pharmaceutical company, in a business combination on 31 October 2018. The identifiable net assets acquired by P include an IPR&D project for a new drug. S has capitalised 1,000 in accordance with IAS 38 in respect of this project. The fair value of the project at the date of acquisition is 3,000.

2.6.810.50   As part of its acquisition accounting, P recognises separately from goodwill an intangible asset of 3,000 for the IPR&D project.

2.6.820   *Usage different from that of other market participants*

2.6.820.10   Sometimes the acquirer may intend not to use an acquired intangible asset, or it may intend to use it in a way that is not its highest and best use. There are a variety of reasons why an acquirer may intend not to use an acquired asset – e.g. for competitive reasons or because the asset was incidental to the acquisition. Nevertheless, it is measured at its fair value at the date of acquisition based on its use by other market participants (see 2.4.1010 and 2.6.630). [*IFRS 3.B43*]

2.6.830   **Leases#**

2.6.830.10   If the acquiree in a business combination is a party to lease agreements at the date of acquisition, then the acquirer needs to account for these leases assumed as part of the acquisition accounting. This may result in the recognition of assets and liabilities. The type of lease – i.e. operating or finance – and whether the acquiree is the lessee or the lessor will impact how the assets and liabilities are recognised. The terms of the lease compared with market terms at the date of acquisition will impact the determination of the fair value of the asset or liability.

2.6.830.20 The following is a summary of the treatment of leases in the acquisition accounting, which is explained in more detail in 2.6.840–910.

LEASE TYPE	ACQUIREE AS		ASSETS AND LIABILITIES TYPICALLY RECOGNISED BY ACQUIRER	
	LESSOR	LESSEE	ASSETS	LIABILITIES
Operating lease		✗	• Leasehold improvements • Favourable lease contract terms	• Unfavourable lease contract terms
	✗		• Leased asset • Favourable lease contract terms (incorporated into fair value of leased asset) • Customer relationships and other identifiable intangible assets • Leasehold improvements	• Unfavourable lease contract terms (incorporated into fair value of leased asset)
Finance lease		✗	• Leased asset (fair value of leasehold interest in property) • Leasehold improvements	• Finance lease obligations
	✗		• Net investment in the lease (lease receivable and unguaranteed residual value of leased asset) • Customer relationships and other identifiable intangible assets	

2.6.840   *Operating leases*

2.6.850   *Acquiree is the lessee in an operating lease*

2.6.850.10 If the acquiree is the lessee in an operating lease, then the underlying asset that is the subject of the lease is not recognised by the acquiree or the acquirer. However, the acquirer recognises a separate intangible asset or liability in respect of operating leases of the acquiree that are acquired in a business combination; in respect of an asset, these lease agreements meet the contractual-legal criterion (see 2.6.720.40). The lease contract asset or liability is recognised at its fair value at the date of acquisition. Factors that affect the fair value include, for example, the lease not being priced at market rates at the date of acquisition, the existence of renewal options and the difficulty in securing such a lease. Leasehold improvements of the acquiree are recognised as tangible assets at their fair values at the date of acquisition. [*IFRS 3.B28–B29*]

EXAMPLE 17A – OPERATING LEASE ACQUIRED – ACQUIREE IS LESSEE

2.6.850.20   Company P acquires Company S in a business combination on 31 December 2018. S entered into an operating lease for a building as the lessee during 2016. The rent under the agreement is fixed for five years and is substantially lower than market rates at the date of acquisition. The contract has a fair value estimated at 500, which includes consideration of renewal options.

2.6.850.30   P recognises an intangible asset of 500 separately from goodwill and does not recognise the underlying building.

2.6.860   *Acquiree is the lessor in an operating lease*

2.6.860.10   If the acquiree is the lessor in an operating lease, then the asset subject to the operating lease (e.g. a building) is recognised at fair value taking into account the terms of the related lease – i.e. the acquirer does not recognise a separate intangible asset or liability related to the favourable or unfavourable aspect of an operating lease relative to market terms or prices. For a discussion of measuring the fair value of investment property, see chapter 2.4 in general, supplemented by the specific guidance in 2.4.610. [*IFRS 3.B42*]

2.6.860.20   If the asset that is the subject of the operating lease is measured subsequent to the acquisition using the cost model in accordance with IAS 16, then the off-market value of the lease, favourable or unfavourable, becomes a separate component of the asset for the purpose of calculating depreciation. [*IAS 16.44*]

2.6.860.30   In addition to recognising the lease contract, an intangible asset may be recognised for the relationship that the lessor has with the lessee at its fair value at the date of acquisition, because the contractual-legal criterion is satisfied (see 2.6.720.40).

EXAMPLE 17B – OPERATING LEASE ACQUIRED – ACQUIREE IS LESSOR

2.6.860.40   Company P acquires Company S in a business combination on 31 December 2018. One of the assets acquired by P is a building with an operating lease to a third party, which qualifies as investment property in accordance with IAS 40.

2.6.860.45   The following information is relevant for this example.
- The lease contract with the third party has 12 years remaining, and the estimated remaining useful life of the building is 30 years.
- The estimated fair value of the building is 30,000, which excludes any favourable or unfavourable aspect of the operating lease relative to its market terms.
- Because the lease is at a fixed rate that is above current market rates, the lease has an estimated fair value of 600, which represents the favourable aspect of the operating lease relative to its market terms.

2.6.860.50   As part of its acquisition accounting, P recognises the building initially at a fair value of 30,600 (30,000 + 600).

2.6.860.60   If P subsequently measures investment property using the cost model under IAS 16, then the building will be depreciated over its remaining useful life of 30 years, and the lease component will be amortised over its remaining useful life of 12 years. Assuming that P uses the straight-line depreciation method and there is no residual value, depreciation expense in the first year after the acquisition will be 1,050 ((30,000 / 30) + (600 / 12)).

2.6.860.70   If P subsequently measures investment property using the revaluation model under IAS 40, then the building is not depreciated. Each time the fair value of the building is determined, the fair value of the lease contract asset or liability is incorporated into the fair value of the building.

2.6.870   **Finance leases**

2.6.880   *Acquiree is the lessee in a finance lease*

2.6.880.10   If the acquiree is the lessee in a finance lease, then the acquirer recognises the fair value of both the asset held under the finance lease and the related liability. Depending on the terms of the lease, the fair value of the leased asset may be less than the fair value of the asset itself. This is because the acquirer acquires as part of the business combination the right to use an asset over the remaining term of the lease, which could be shorter than the economic life of the asset. In other words, although the asset is accounted for according to its type – e.g. property, plant and equipment – the acquirer measures the fair value of the asset based on the fair value of the leasehold interest acquired rather than on the underlying asset itself.

2.6.890   *Acquiree is the lessor in a finance lease*

2.6.890.10   If the acquiree is the lessor in a finance lease, then the acquirer recognises a receivable for the net investment in the finance lease. This is measured at its acquisition date fair value, determined based on the assumptions about discount rates and other factors that market participants would use. In our view, an acquirer would not recognise separately an additional asset or liability related to favourable or unfavourable contracts, because measurement of the fair value of the lease receivables and the unguaranteed residual values at fair value would consider all of the terms of the lease contracts.

2.6.890.20   In addition, an intangible asset may be recognised for the relationship that the lessor has with the lessee (see 2.6.730).

2.6.900   **Contingent rent**

2.6.900.10   Outside a business combination, contingent rent is not generally recognised until it becomes payable. However, in our view the existence of contingent rent in a lease contract, acquired in a business combination, should be incorporated into the fair value measurement of the asset or liability arising from the lease that is recognised as part of the acquisition accounting. [*IAS 17.25*]

EXAMPLE 17C – OPERATING LEASE ACQUIRED – CONTINGENT RENT

2.6.900.20   Company P acquires Company S in a business combination on 31 October 2018. S is a retailer and leases its retail outlets under operating lease contracts. One of S's operating lease agreements, with a remaining lease period of eight years, requires a fixed annual lease payment of 500 plus an additional contingent rental payment equal to 2.5% of annual sales in excess of 10,000.

2.6.900.30   At the date of acquisition, the market rate of an eight-year lease for a similar property is a fixed annual lease payment of 500 plus an additional contingent rental payment equal to 2% of annual sales in excess of 10,000. P has determined that all other terms of the lease contracts are consistent with market terms.

2.6.900.40   In applying acquisition accounting, P recognises a liability for an unfavourable lease contract, because of the unfavourable contingent rental payments relative to market terms for the remaining eight years of the lease term – i.e. the contingent rental payments of 2.5% on annual sales in excess of 10,000 is unfavourable to the market rate of 2% on a comparable lease.

2.6.910   *Prepaid or accrued rent recognised by acquiree on operating leases*

2.6.910.10   In accordance with IAS 17, lease payments under an operating lease are usually recognised on a straight-line basis over the lease term; if the timing of lease payments does not represent the time pattern of the lessee's benefits under the lease agreement, then prepaid rent or accrued liabilities for rental payments is recognised (see 5.1.310.20). Such prepaid rent or accrued liability does not meet the definition of an asset acquired or a liability assumed (see 2.6.380 and 560).

2.6.910.20   Therefore, prepaid or accrued rent previously recognised by an acquiree to recognise lease payments under an operating lease on a straight-line basis in accordance with the requirements of IAS 17 is not recognised by the acquirer in the acquisition accounting; this is regardless of whether an acquiree is the lessee or lessor. Instead, the favourable/unfavourable element of the lease contract, which is recognised in the acquisition accounting, is determined by comparing the actual future payment stream under the operating lease with the market rate that would need to be paid based on the future periods in the contract as if a new contract were granted in respect of those periods. This either forms the basis of an acquiree asset or liability, or is included in the accounting for the settlement of a pre-existing relationship (see 2.6.350). [*IAS 17.33*]

EXAMPLE 17D – OPERATING LEASE ACQUIRED – ACCRUED RENT PAYABLE

2.6.910.30   Company P acquires Company S in a business combination on 31 December 2018. S leases its headquarters under an operating lease. The lease terms included an incentive of the first year of the lease being rent-free. At the date of acquisition, S had recognised a liability of 1,000 for accrued rent as a result of recognising the lease expense on a straight-line basis in accordance with IAS 17.

2.6.910.40   As a part of its acquisition accounting, P does not recognise the accrued rent recognised by S, because it does not meet the definition of a liability. However, P recognises an intangible asset or liability for the fair value of the operating lease, depending on whether the required future rental payments are favourable or unfavourable. An intangible asset or a liability would be amortised to lease expense during the post-combination period on a straight-line basis over the remaining term of the operating lease.

2.6.915 FORTHCOMING REQUIREMENTS

2.6.915.10 IFRS 16 introduces a new exception to both the recognition and the measurement principles for leases in which the acquiree is the lessee. Under IFRS 16, for leases in which the acquiree is the lessee, an acquirer generally recognises and measures:

- a lease liability at the present value of the remaining lease payments as if the acquired lease were a new lease at the date of acquisition; and
- a right-of-use asset at the same amount as the lease liability, adjusted to reflect favourable or unfavourable terms of the lease when compared with market terms – i.e. such terms are reflected in the measurement of the right-of-use asset, rather than recognised as a separate intangible asset (liability). [*IFRS 3.28A–28B*]

2.6.920 Customer contract liabilities

2.6.920.10   The acquirer in a business combination recognises a liability in respect of a contract liability of the acquiree only if the acquiree has an obligation to perform subsequent to the acquisition. The obligation to perform is measured at fair value at the date of acquisition in accordance with the general measurement principle.

EXAMPLE 18 – CONTRACT LIABILITIES – OBLIGATION TO PERFORM

2.6.920.20   Company X has built a fibre-optic network. A five-year right to specified amounts of capacity and routes is sold to large corporations for an up-front payment. X accounts for the up-front payments as a contract liability and recognises the revenue over the five-year term of the contracts.

2.6.920.30   X has an obligation to perform under the contracts, which relates to the provision of services – i.e. X should provide the capacity and routes to customers.

2.6.920.40   Company Y acquires X in a business combination. As part of the acquisition accounting, Y recognises a liability measured at fair value for the obligation of X to perform under the contracts.

2.6.930 MEASUREMENT OF NCI

2.6.930.10   NCI can be categorised by:
- present ownership interests that entitle their holders to a proportionate share of the entity's net assets in liquidation (ordinary NCI – see 2.6.940); and
- all other NCI (other NCI – see 2.6.950). [*IFRS 3.19*]

Measuring ordinary NCI

2.6.940.10   If less than 100 percent of a subsidiary is acquired, then the acquirer can elect on a transaction-by-transaction basis to measure ordinary NCI either at:

- fair value at the date of acquisition, which means that goodwill, or the gain on a bargain purchase, includes a portion attributable to ordinary NCI; or
- the holders' proportionate interest in the recognised amount of the identifiable net assets of the acquiree, which means that goodwill recognised, or the gain on a bargain purchase, relates only to the controlling interest acquired. [*IFRS 3.19*]

2.6.940.20   This accounting policy choice relates only to the initial measurement of ordinary NCI. After initial recognition, the option of measuring ordinary NCI at fair value is not available.

2.6.940.30   Fair value is measured in accordance with IFRS 13, which is the subject of chapter 2.4.

2.6.940.40   The implication of recognising ordinary NCI at their proportionate interest in the recognised amount of the identifiable assets and liabilities of the acquiree is that both the NCI and goodwill are lower because no goodwill is ascribed to the NCI. However, an issue arises in recognising ordinary NCI at their proportionate interest when both ordinary and other NCI are present (see 2.6.960).

EXAMPLE 19A – ORDINARY NCI MEASURED AT FAIR VALUE

2.6.940.50   On 31 October 2018, Company P acquires 60% of Company S for cash of 1,000. The following additional facts at the date of acquisition are relevant for this example.

Fair value of the identifiable net assets of S	1,500
Fair value of 40% of S	650

2.6.940.60   If P elects to measure ordinary NCI in S at fair value, then in its consolidated financial statements P recognises the identifiable net assets of S at 1,500 (full fair value), NCI at 650 (full fair value) and the resulting goodwill at 150 (1,000 + 650 - 1,500); for the calculation of goodwill, see 2.6.1010. P records the following entry in its consolidated financial statements.

	DEBIT	CREDIT
Identifiable net assets of S	1,500	
Goodwill	150	
NCI (equity)		650
Cash		1,000
To recognise acquisition of S		

EXAMPLE 19B – ORDINARY NCI MEASURED AT PROPORTIONATE INTEREST IN IDENTIFIABLE NET ASSETS

2.6.940.70   Assuming the same facts as in Example 19A, if P elects to recognise ordinary NCI in S at their proportionate interest in the recognised amount of the identifiable assets and liabilities, then in its consolidated financial statements P recognises the identifiable net assets of S at 1,500 (full fair value), NCI at 600 (1,500 x 40%) and the resulting goodwill at 100 (1,000 + 600 - 1,500); for the calculation of goodwill, see 2.6.1010. P records the following entry in its consolidated financial statements.

	DEBIT	CREDIT
Identifiable net assets of S	1,500	
Goodwill	100	
NCI (equity)		600
Cash		1,000
To recognise acquisition of S		

2.6.950   Measuring other NCI

2.6.950.10   The accounting policy choice in 2.6.940.10 does not apply to other NCI, such as equity components of convertible bonds or options under share-based payment arrangements. Such instruments are measured at fair value or in accordance with other relevant standards – e.g. share-based payments that give rise to NCI are measured using the market-based measure in accordance with IFRS 2. [*IFRS 3.19*]

2.6.960   Measurement if both components of NCI present

2.6.960.10   If both components of NCI are present in an acquisition and the acquirer intends to measure ordinary NCI at their proportionate interest in the identifiable net assets of the acquiree, then an issue arises about how that proportionate interest should be calculated.

2.6.960.20   The following fact pattern is used in the discussion in 2.6.970–1000 to illustrate the different accounting approaches.
- Company P acquires 80 percent of the ordinary shares of Company S for 1,600.
- P elects to measure ordinary NCI at their proportionate interest in the identifiable net assets of S. The identifiable net assets are determined under IFRS 3 as 1,800.
- S also has outstanding 200 equity-classified preference shares that have a preference in liquidation and participate with a fixed amount of 1 per share in liquidation; none of these shares were acquired by P. Because the preference shares do not entitle the holders to a proportionate share of net assets in the event of liquidation, they are not eligible for the measurement choice and are measured in the acquisition accounting at fair value, which is determined to be 240.

2.6.960.30   In our view, there are two possible approaches for determining the proportionate interest in identifiable net assets in measuring ordinary NCI (see 2.6.970 and 980); a third approach has been identified that we do not believe is appropriate (see 2.6.990). In our view, an entity should choose an accounting policy, to be applied consistently, between Approach 1 and Approach 2 for all business combinations in which ordinary NCI are measured at their proportionate interest in the identifiable net assets.

2.6.970   *Approach 1: Fair value of other NCI*

2.6.970.10   Under Approach 1, the proportionate interest in the identifiable net assets of ordinary NCI is determined using the following steps.
1. Start with the recognised amount of the identifiable net assets of the acquiree, measured in accordance with IFRS 3.
2. Deduct the values assigned to other NCI – e.g. the market-based measure of a share-based payment – from the identifiable net assets of the acquiree. This step is the key difference between the approaches.
3. Multiply the determined subtotal by the percentage interest attributable to ordinary NCI.

2.6.970.20   Applying Approach 1 to the fact pattern in 2.6.960.20, ordinary NCI are measured as follows at the date of acquisition.

Step 1: Identifiable net assets of S	1,800
Step 2: Minus share of preference shareholders (fair value)	(240)
Residual identifiable net assets	1,560
Step 3: Measure ordinary NCI (1,560 x 20%)	312

2.6.970.30   Under Approach 1, it is argued that other NCI also have a share in the identifiable net assets of the acquiree. Accordingly, ordinary NCI are measured after taking account of the value of the interests in the identifiable net assets attributable to other NCI. The value taken into account (deducted) for such other NCI is represented by the amount recognised under IFRS 3 (fair value in this example).

2.6.970.40   By way of contrast with Approach 2 in 2.6.980, Approach 1 assumes that a proportionate share in liquidation is the trigger for allowing the measurement option in IFRS 3. However, this trigger does not direct how ordinary NCI should be measured.

2.6.980   *Approach 2: Participation in liquidation*

2.6.980.10   Approach 2 is based on the idea that a proportionate share in liquidation should not only be the trigger for allowing the measurement option in IFRS 3, but also directs the measurement of ordinary NCI. Under Approach 2, Step 2 in 2.6.970.10 comprises the amount that other NCI would receive in liquidation; this deduction is determined based on an assumed liquidation on the date of acquisition.

2.6.980.20   Applying this approach to the fact pattern in 2.6.960.20, ordinary NCI are measured as follows at the date of acquisition.

Step 1: Identifiable net assets of S	1,800
Step 2: Minus share of preference shareholders (in liquidation)	(200)
Residual identifiable net assets	1,600
Step 3: Measure ordinary NCI (1,600 x 20%)	320

2.6.990 *Approach 3: No adjustment*

2.6.990.10   Another possible approach is to determine the proportionate share of identifiable net assets of ordinary NCI without any adjustment for other NCI – i.e. without Step 2 illustrated in 2.6.970.20 and 980.20. We do not believe that Approach 3 is acceptable because it fails to take into account any value attributable to other stakeholders' interests in the acquiree and therefore overvalues ordinary NCI.

2.6.990.20   If this approach were applied to the fact pattern in 2.6.960.20, then ordinary NCI would be measured as follows at the date of acquisition.

Step 1: Identifiable net assets of S	1,800
Step 2: Minus share of preference shareholders	-
Residual identifiable net assets	1,800
Step 3: Measure ordinary NCI (1,800 x 20%)	360

2.6.1000 *Goodwill calculation*

2.6.1000.10   Depending on the approach taken, there is a consequential effect on the calculation of goodwill. Applying the acceptable approaches in 2.6.970 and 980 to the fact pattern in 2.6.960.20, goodwill is determined as follows.

	APPROACH 1 (2.6.970)	APPROACH 2 (2.6.980)
Consideration transferred	1,600	1,600
NCI – preference shares	240	240
Ordinary NCI	312	320
Total NCI	552	560
Minus identifiable net assets	(1,800)	(1,800)
Goodwill	352	360

2.6.1000.20   In these calculations, the amount attributed to preference shareholder NCI is 240 in both cases – i.e. fair value. This is because the different approaches to measuring other NCI are solely for the purpose of measuring ordinary NCI. These calculations have no effect on the amount at which other NCI are stated in the statement of financial position at the date of acquisition. Instead, it is the calculation of goodwill that is affected.

2.6.1010   GOODWILL OR GAIN ON BARGAIN PURCHASE*

2.6.1010.10   Goodwill is recognised at the date of acquisition, measured as a residual. Goodwill previously recorded by the acquiree is not recorded as a separate asset by the acquirer. [*IFRS 3.32*]

GOODWILL IS MEASURED AS THE EXCESS OF **A** OVER **B**	
A. The aggregate of: • consideration transferred, which is generally measured at fair value (see 2.6.260); • the amount of any NCI in the acquiree, which for 'ordinary' NCI may be measured either at fair value or at their proportionate share in the recognised amount of the identifiable assets and liabilities of the acquiree (see 2.6.940); and • in a business combination achieved in stages, the acquisition date fair value of the acquirer's previously held equity interest in the acquiree (see 2.6.1140.30).	B. The net of the acquisition date amounts of the identifiable assets acquired and the liabilities assumed, measured in accordance with IFRS 3 (see 2.6.560).
A gain on a bargain purchase arises when B is greater than A. [*IFRS 3.34*]	

2.6.1010.20   A bargain purchase may arise for a number of reasons; these include a forced liquidation or distressed sale or because of applying the measurement requirements of IFRS 3, which require in certain instances measurement of the identifiable assets acquired and liabilities assumed at amounts other than fair value (see 2.6.640). A business combination does not, however, need to exhibit any particular characteristics such as evidence of a forced or distressed sale in order for a bargain purchase to be recognised. Such a gain is the result of applying the formula, regardless of other factors, such as the economic rationale for the transaction. [*IFRS 3.35*]

2.6.1010.30   Before recognising a gain on a bargain purchase, the acquirer reassesses whether it has correctly *identified* all of the assets acquired and the liabilities assumed. In our view, the acquirer should also reassess whether it has correctly identified any NCI in the acquiree, any previously held equity interest in the acquiree, and the consideration transferred. Following that reassessment, the acquirer reviews the procedures used to *measure* the following amounts required to be recognised at the date of acquisition to ensure that the measurements reflect consideration of all available information as at the date of acquisition:
• the identifiable assets acquired and liabilities assumed;
• any NCI in the acquiree;
• for a business combination achieved in stages, the acquirer's previously held equity interest in the acquiree; and
• the consideration transferred. [*IFRS 3.36*]

2.6.1010.40   In our view, an acquirer should also review the procedures used to identify amounts that are not part of what the acquirer and acquiree exchanged in the business combination. For example, a business combination may:

- result in the effective settlement of a pre-existing relationship between the acquirer and the acquiree – e.g. a supply agreement or an operating lease arrangement (see 2.6.350);
- include transactions that compensate employees or former owners of an acquiree for future services (see 2.6.400); or
- include transactions that reimburse the acquiree or its former owners for paying the acquirer's acquisition-related costs (see 2.6.530).

2.6.1010.50   Such transactions are not part of the business combination transaction and are therefore accounted for as separate transactions. Accounting for such arrangements as separate transactions, rather than as part of the acquisition, affects the determination of goodwill or the gain from a bargain purchase that arises from the business combination.

2.6.1010.60   Any remaining gain from a bargain purchase after completing the reassessment is recognised in profit or loss at the date of acquisition. Disclosure is required of the amount of any recognised gain from a bargain purchase, the line item in profit or loss in which the gain is recognised, and a description of the reasons why the transaction resulted in a gain. [*IFRS 3.34, B64(n)*]

2.6.1020   MEASUREMENT AFTER ACQUISITION ACCOUNTING

2.6.1030   Measurement period

2.6.1030.10   The initial accounting for a business combination comprises a number of steps, including identifying and/or measuring:
- consideration transferred (see 2.6.260);
- the identifiable assets acquired and liabilities assumed (see 2.6.560);
- any NCI (see 2.6.930);
- goodwill or the gain on a bargain purchase (see 2.6.1010); and
- any pre-existing equity interest in the acquiree (see 2.6.1140).

2.6.1030.20   The measurement period cannot be longer than one year from the date of acquisition. However, the standard does not allow an 'open' one-year period following the date of acquisition. Instead, the measurement period ends when the acquirer receives the information that it was seeking about facts and circumstances existing at the date of acquisition, or learns that more information is not available. Although the final outcome of some items may not be known within a year – e.g. a liability for which the outcome was uncertain at the date of acquisition – the purpose of the measurement period is to provide time to obtain the information necessary to measure items at the date of acquisition; determining the ultimate outcome of, for example, provisions, is not part of the acquisition accounting. [*IFRS 3.45, BC392*]

2.6.1030.30   An entity reflects measurement period adjustments by revising its comparative financial statements as if the new information had been known when the business combination was accounted for initially (see 2.6.1060.30). [*IFRS 3.45*]

2.6.1040   **Reporting if acquisition accounting incomplete**

2.6.1040.10   If the acquisition accounting is not complete in any financial statements issued during the measurement period, then the acquirer reports provisional amounts for the assets, liabilities, equity interests or items of consideration for which the accounting is incomplete. [*IFRS 3.45*]

2.6.1040.20   IFRS 3 does not provide specific guidance on determining provisional amounts. Those amounts are determined based on the available information at the date of acquisition, consistent with the recognition and measurement requirements of the standard. In our view, entities should make a reasonable effort to determine provisional amounts. Accordingly, we believe that it would not be appropriate to assign only nominal amounts, or no amounts, solely because the acquirer anticipates receiving additional information about facts and circumstances that existed at the date of acquisition.

2.6.1040.30   Until the accounting for a business combination is complete, the acquirer is required to disclose the following in its annual financial statements and in any interim financial statements:
- the reasons why the initial accounting for the business combination is incomplete;
- the assets, liabilities, equity interests or items of consideration for which the initial accounting is incomplete; and
- the nature and amount of any measurement period adjustments recognised during the period. [*IFRS 3.B67(a), IAS 34.16A(i)*]

2.6.1050   **Adjustments to provisional amounts**

2.6.1050.10   Measurement period adjustments are analogous to adjusting events after the reporting date under IAS 10 (see chapter 2.9). 'Adjusting events' are events that occur after the reporting date but before the financial statements are authorised for issue and that provide evidence of a condition that existed at the reporting date; such events are reflected in the financial statements. Similarly, the effects of information that first becomes available during the measurement period and that provides evidence of conditions or circumstances that existed at the date of acquisition are reflected in the accounting at the date of acquisition. All other changes to amounts included in the acquisition accounting that occur after the date of acquisition, including those occurring within the measurement period, do not generally affect the acquisition accounting (see 2.6.1070). [*IFRS 3.BC399*]

EXAMPLE 20A – PROVISIONAL ACCOUNTING – ACQUISITION ACCOUNTING VS PROFIT OR LOSS

2.6.1050.20   Company P acquires Company S in a business combination on 30 April 2018. Provisional amounts are recognised for certain of the assets acquired and liabilities assumed, including a liability related to a contractual dispute between S and one of its customers. Shortly before the date of acquisition, S's customer claimed that certain amounts were due by S under penalty clauses for completion delays included in the contract.

2.6.1050.30   P evaluates the dispute based on the information available at the date of acquisition and concludes that S was responsible for at least some of the delays in completing the contract. P recognises a provisional amount for this liability of 1,000 in its acquisition accounting, which is its best estimate of the fair value of the liability to the customer based on the information available at the date of acquisition.

	DEBIT	**CREDIT**
Goodwill	1,000	
Liability		1,000
To recognise liability at date of acquisition based on provisional estimates		

2.6.1050.40   The interim consolidated financial statements of P for the six months ending 30 June 2018 include appropriate disclosure in respect of the provisional accounting.

2.6.1050.50   P obtains no new information about the possible outcome of the dispute until September 2018, when the customer presents additional information in support of its claim. Based on this information, P concludes that the fair value of the liability for the customer's claim at the date of acquisition was 2,000. Accordingly, P records the following entry in its consolidated financial statements.

	DEBIT	**CREDIT**
Goodwill	1,000	
Liability		1,000
To increase liability within measurement period		

2.6.1050.60   P continues to receive and evaluate information related to the claim after September 2018. Its evaluation does not change until May 2019, when it concludes, based on additional information and responses received from the customer to enquiries made by P, that the liability for the claim at the date of acquisition was 1,900. P determines that the amount that would be recognised with respect to the claim under IAS 37 at May 2019 would be 2,200. Accordingly, P records the following entry in its consolidated financial statements.

	DEBIT	**CREDIT**
Profit or loss	200	
Liability		200
To increase liability after end of measurement period		

2.6.1050.70   The information resulting in the decrease in the estimated fair value of the liability for the claim in May 2019 was obtained after the measurement period, and therefore the decrease is not recognised as an adjustment to the acquisition accounting.

> **2.6.1050.80** If the amount determined in accordance with IAS 37 subsequently exceeds the previous estimate of the fair value of the liability, then P recognises an increase in the liability. Because this change relates to the subsequent measurement of the liability, it is recognised in profit or loss (see 2.6.1100).

2.6.1050.90 It is important to distinguish new information about conditions that existed at the date of acquisition from information about changes in the value of acquired assets or liabilities that result from events that occur subsequent to the date of acquisition. Only the former results in adjustments to the acquisition accounting.

2.6.1050.100 A degree of tension exists between the general requirement in IFRS 3 to measure amounts recognised in the acquisition accounting at fair value and the requirement to amend acquisition accounting retrospectively for measurement period adjustments. In our view, additional information that becomes available during the measurement period that, had it been known, might have affected observable market data on which the measurement of an item included in the acquisition accounting is based should not give rise to a measurement period adjustment. This is because such information does not affect the basis of estimation of the fair value of an asset or liability at the date of acquisition – i.e. the price that would be received to sell an asset or paid to transfer a liability in an orderly transaction between market participants. In contrast, if fair values are estimated based on other than observable market data, then the measurement of such values in the acquisition accounting is adjusted if new information obtained during the measurement period represents a basis for a better estimate of fair value at the date of acquisition. For a discussion of the discovery of a fraud after the reporting date, see 2.9.70.

2.6.1060 Changes in recognition of assets and liabilities

2.6.1060.10 Measurement period adjustments may affect not only the measurement of assets and liabilities but also their recognition. Therefore, during the measurement period the acquirer recognises additional assets or liabilities if new information is obtained about facts and circumstances that existed at the date of acquisition that, had it been known, would have resulted in the recognition of those assets and liabilities at that date. [*IFRS 3.45*]

2.6.1060.20 Generally, it is expected that the possibility of subsequent adjustments to the acquisition accounting during the measurement period would have been identified in the disclosures in any financial statements of the acquirer issued subsequent to the business combination but before the adjustments are identified. Accordingly, unless an acquirer has a high level of confidence that it has identified all contingent liabilities assumed, it is advisable for the acquirer to disclose the status of its identification of such liabilities in financial statements that include the measurement period.

2.6.1060.30 Adjustments made during the measurement period are recognised retrospectively and comparative information is revised – i.e. as if the accounting for the business combination had been completed at the date of acquisition. These adjustments include adjustments to the assets acquired, liabilities assumed and goodwill or gain on a bargain purchase recognised at the date of acquisition, and any change in depreciation, amortisation or other effects on comprehensive income that arise as a result of the adjustments. [*IFRS 3.45, 49*]

EXAMPLE 20B – PROVISIONAL ACCOUNTING – ADJUSTMENT OF COMPARATIVES

2.6.1060.40   Company P acquired Company S on 30 November 2018. As part of the acquisition accounting, P recognised a provisional amount of 10,000 in respect of a patent developed by S, based on the historical earnings attributable to products developed using that patent. However, the technology covered by the patent was new and P expected the cash flows to be generated by the patent to increase beyond those being generated at the time. Accordingly, P commissioned an independent valuation report from a third party consultant, which was not expected to be finalised for several months. P assessed the useful life of the patent to be 10 years. Goodwill of 20,000 was recognised in the provisional accounting.

2.6.1060.50   The consolidated financial statements of P at 31 December 2018 included appropriate disclosure about the provisional accounting (see 2.6.1040).

2.6.1060.60   The valuation report is finalised subsequent to the issue of the 2018 financial statements but before the end of the measurement period. Based on the valuation, P concludes that the fair value of the patent was 15,000 as at 30 November 2018. Management does not revise the estimated useful life of the patent, which remains at 10 years. As a result of this measurement period adjustment, the comparative information presented in the 2019 financial statements is revised as follows.

	31 DECEMBER 2018	
	AS STATED ORIGINALLY	REVISED
Profit or loss (patent amortisation)	(83)[1]	(125)[2]
Goodwill	20,000	15,000[3]
Patent	9,917[4]	14,875[5]

Notes
1.   10,000 x 1 / 10 x 1 / 12.
2.   15,000 x 1 / 10 x 1 / 12.
3.   20,000 - 5,000.
4.   10,000 - 83.
5.   15,000 - 125.

2.6.1070   Adjustments after measurement period

2.6.1070.10   After the measurement period ends, the acquisition accounting is adjusted only to correct an error or, in our view, to reflect a change in accounting policy in certain circumstances. Other adjustments are accounted for in accordance with the relevant standards. [*IFRS 3.50*]

2.6.1070.20   If an error in the acquisition accounting is discovered after the measurement period, then the acquisition accounting is adjusted in accordance with IAS 8 (see 2.8.80) and comparative amounts are restated. In addition, it is also likely that the entity will be required to present a statement of financial position as at the beginning of the earliest comparative period (see 2.8.140). [*IFRS 3.50, IAS 1.10, 40A, 8.41*]

2.6.1070.30   The measurement of certain identifiable assets acquired and liabilities assumed is an exception to the general fair value measurement principle (see 2.6.640). For example, deferred taxes and employee benefits are not measured at fair value in the acquisition accounting; instead, they are measured in accordance with IAS 12 and IAS 19, respectively (see 2.6.660 and 680). An issue therefore arises about whether the acquisition accounting is adjusted when the accounting for those items changes.

2.6.1070.40   This issue arose in applying the amendments to IAS 19 (issued in June 2011) that changed the accounting for defined benefit plans, which were effective for annual periods beginning on or after 1 January 2013. Under the revised standard, plan administration costs – other than the costs of managing plan assets – are recognised in the periods in which the related administration services are provided (see 4.4.980.50). Previously, these costs might have been included in the assumptions used to measure the defined benefit obligation. The amendments were applied retrospectively.

2.6.1070.50   In our view, if changes in accounting policy affect items that were initially measured in accordance with a specific standard at an amount other than fair value and those changes are effective retrospectively, then the acquisition accounting should be adjusted to reflect the change in accounting policy.

2.6.1070.60   In some instances, particularly if a new standard is applicable fully retrospectively, retrospective adjustment of the acquisition accounting may present practical difficulties. In such cases, entities consider the requirements of IAS 8 to determine whether full retrospective adoption is impracticable (see 2.8.90).

2.6.1080   SUBSEQUENT MEASUREMENT AND ACCOUNTING

2.6.1080.10   IFRS 3 provides specific guidance on the subsequent measurement of the following items, which are discussed in this chapter:
- reacquired rights (see 2.6.1090);
- contingent liabilities (see 2.6.1100);
- indemnification assets (see 2.6.1110); and
- contingent consideration (see 2.6.1120).

2.6.1080.20   Additionally, some issues arise in respect of the subsequent accounting for share-based payment awards issued in a business combination (see 2.6.1130).

2.6.1090   Reacquired rights

2.6.1090.10   For a discussion of the concept of reacquired rights and their measurement at the date of acquisition, see 2.6.690.

2.6.1090.20   The acquirer amortises a reacquired right over the remaining contractual period of the related contract in which the right was granted, regardless of the likelihood of renewals. This is consistent with the exception to the fair value measurement principle for the initial measurement of a reacquired right, which does not take into account potential contract renewals. [*IFRS 3.29, 55*]

2.6.1100   Contingent liabilities that are present obligations

2.6.1100.10   A contingent liability assumed in a business combination is recognised and measured at fair value at the date of acquisition, if it represents a present obligation that arises from past events and can be measured reliably (see 2.6.650). Subsequently, such contingent liabilities are recognised at the higher of:

- the amount recognised initially less, if appropriate, the cumulative amount of income recognised in accordance with the principles of IFRS 15; and
- the amount that would be recognised in accordance with IAS 37. [*IFRS 3.56*]

2.6.1100.20   These requirements do not apply to contracts accounted for under IFRS 9. [*IFRS 3.56*]

2.6.1100.30   Subsequent adjustments to the carrying amount of a contingent liability recognised in the acquisition accounting might be recognised as a change to the acquisition accounting or be recognised in profit or loss subsequent to the acquisition. In determining the appropriate accounting, an entity considers whether the events or conditions that result in such an adjustment existed at the date of acquisition. If new information is discovered within the measurement period that relates to conditions that existed at the date of acquisition, then the acquisition accounting is adjusted (see 2.6.1050). If such new information relates to events subsequent to the business combination or is discovered subsequent to the expiry of the measurement period, then the remeasurement of the contingent liability is recognised in profit or loss (see 2.6.1050 and 1070).

2.6.1100.40   A contingent liability initially recognised in a business combination is not derecognised until it is settled, cancelled or expires. In our view, if a contingency for which a liability is recognised in the acquisition accounting is reassessed subsequently as 'probable to occur', then the guidance in 2.6.1100.10 in respect of subsequent measurement still applies even if the amount recognised exceeds the amount that the entity expects to pay notwithstanding that a similar liability recognised initially, other than in a business combination, would be measured under IAS 37. This effectively establishes a 'floor' on the amount recognised in respect of a contingent liability initially recognised in a business combination. [*IFRS 3.56*]

EXAMPLE 21A – SUBSEQUENT ACCOUNTING – CONTINGENT LIABILITY

2.6.1100.50   Company P acquires Company S in November 2017. Before the date of acquisition, Company X filed a lawsuit against S. Based on the legal foundations of the lawsuit, P's management determines that a present obligation exists; however, based on previous experience, the likelihood of the case being decided against S is less than probable. Taking these factors into account, P recognises a liability of 5,000 in respect of the contingent liability as part of the acquisition accounting.

2.6.1100.60   In December 2018, P reassesses the likelihood of the lawsuit being settled or determined in court and determines that settlement is now probable,

although the amount at which the liability is now estimated to be settled is less than management previously considered possible. Management's best estimate of the amount of settlement is 4,000.

2.6.1100.70   We believe that the liability should continue to be measured at 5,000 until it is settled – i.e. the fair value of the contingent liability at the date of acquisition.

2.6.1110   Indemnification assets

2.6.1110.10   Indemnification assets are an exception to the recognition and measurement principles of IFRS 3. An acquirer recognises indemnification assets at the same time and measures them on the same basis as the indemnified item, subject to contractual limitations and adjustments for collectability, if applicable (see 2.6.670). [*IFRS 3.27*]

2.6.1110.20   Subsequent to initial recognition, the acquirer continues to measure an indemnification asset on the same basis as the related indemnified asset or liability. For example, an indemnification asset related to an asset or liability measured at fair value, such as an indemnification related to a forward contract accounted for at fair value under IFRS 9, is itself measured at fair value. [*IFRS 3.57*]

2.6.1110.30   The initial and subsequent accounting for indemnification assets recognised at the date of acquisition applies equally to indemnified assets and liabilities that are recognised and measured under the principles of IFRS 3 and those that are subject to exceptions to the recognition or measurement principles of IFRS 3 (see 2.6.670). For example, an acquirer would initially recognise and measure an indemnification asset related to a defined benefit pension obligation using assumptions consistent with those used to measure the indemnified item – i.e. assumptions consistent with IAS 19; this basis of measurement would continue subsequent to the business combination. [*IFRS 3.28, 57*]

2.6.1110.40   An acquirer may hold an indemnification related to an item that is not recognised at the date of acquisition. For example, an indemnification may relate to a contingent liability that is not recognised because it cannot be measured with sufficient reliability (see 2.6.670.30). In our view, notwithstanding that no amount was recognised in the acquisition accounting, in these circumstances the indemnification asset should be recognised and measured at the same time and on the same basis as the indemnified item subsequent to the business combination, subject to any contractual limitations on the amount of the indemnification and adjustments for collectability. [*IFRS 3.28*]

EXAMPLE 21B – SUBSEQUENT ACCOUNTING – INDEMNIFICATION ASSET

2.6.1110.50   Company P is fully indemnified for any obligation arising from a contingent liability assumed in the acquisition of Company S. The fair value of the contingent liability recognised at the date of acquisition was 10,000. P also recognised an indemnification asset of 10,000 at the date of acquisition – i.e. there were no concerns about the collectability of the indemnification asset.

	DEBIT	CREDIT
Indemnification asset	10,000	
Contingent liability		10,000
To reflect contingent liability and associated indemnification asset as part of acquisition accounting		

2.6.1110.60 Following the acquisition, P obtains new information about events subsequent to the date of acquisition and, based on this new information, concludes that the liability would be measured at an amount of 5,000 under IAS 37; this does not impact the measurement of the contingent liability at the date of acquisition (see 2.6.1050.10). P still has no concerns about the collectability of the indemnification asset.

2.6.1110.70 Because the acquisition date fair value of the contingent liability of 10,000 is higher than the IAS 37 amount of 5,000, the carrying amount of the liability remains at 10,000, notwithstanding that payment is now probable (see 2.6.1100.40). Under IFRS 3, the measurement of the indemnification asset follows the measurement of the liability, subject to management's assessment of collectability and contractual limitations. Because there are no concerns over the collectability of the indemnification asset or contractual limitations on the amount of the indemnification, P continues to recognise the indemnification asset at 10,000.

2.6.1110.80 Collectability of the indemnification asset may affect its measurement. For indemnification assets measured at fair value, management's assessment of collectability is considered in determining fair value. For items measured at other than fair value, the carrying amount of the indemnification asset is reduced to reflect management's assessment of any uncollectable amounts under the indemnity. [*IFRS 3.27, 57*]

2.6.1110.90 The measurement of an indemnification asset is subject to any contractual limitations on its amount. [*IFRS 3.28, 57*]

2.6.1110.100 The acquirer derecognises an indemnification asset only when it collects the asset, sells it or otherwise loses the right to it. [*IFRS 3.57*]

2.6.1110.110 If the amounts recognised by an acquirer for an indemnified liability and a related indemnification asset recognised at the date of acquisition do not change subsequent to the acquisition and ultimately are settled at the amounts recognised in the acquisition accounting, then there will be no net effect on profit or loss providing that those amounts are the same.

2.6.1120 Contingent consideration

2.6.1120.10 The fair value of contingent consideration is initially recognised by an acquirer at the date of acquisition as part of the consideration transferred, measured at its acquisition date fair value (see 2.6.280). [*IFRS 3.39*]

2.6.1120.20 Subsequent changes in the fair value of contingent consideration that result from additional information about facts and circumstances that existed at the date of acquisition that the acquirer obtains during the measurement period are measurement-period adjustments; therefore, the acquisition accounting is adjusted (see 2.6.1050). [*IFRS 3.58*]

2.6.1120.30 The accounting for changes in the fair value of contingent consideration after the date of acquisition, other than measurement-period adjustments, depends on whether the contingent consideration is classified as equity, an asset or a liability. For a discussion of the classification of contingent consideration, see 7.3.270.

2.6.1120.40 Contingent consideration classified as equity is not remeasured and its subsequent settlement is accounted for within equity. [*IFRS 3.58(a)*]

2.6.1120.50 Contingent consideration classified as an asset or a liability is subsequently remeasured to fair value at each reporting date until the contingency is settled, with changes in fair value recognised in profit or loss. [*IFRS 3.58(b)*]

EXAMPLE 21C – SUBSEQUENT ACCOUNTING – CONTINGENT CONSIDERATION

2.6.1120.60 Company P acquires Company S in September 2018 for cash. Additionally, P agrees to pay 5% of profits in excess of 5,000 generated over the next two years in cash in a lump sum at the end of the two years. P determines the fair value of the contingent consideration liability to be 45 at the date of acquisition. In its consolidated financial statements, P records the following entry.

	DEBIT	CREDIT
Goodwill	45	
Liability for contingent consideration		45
To recognise contingent consideration at fair value as part of acquisition accounting		

2.6.1120.70 A year after the acquisition, S has performed better than projected initially by P and a significant payment is now expected to be made at the end of year two. The fair value of this financial liability is 185 at the end of the first year. Accordingly, P recognises the remeasurement of the liability in profit or loss. P records the following entry in its consolidated financial statements.

	DEBIT	CREDIT
Profit or loss	140	
Liability for contingent consideration (185 - 45)		140
To remeasure contingent consideration		

> **2.6.1120.80**   The adjustment to the financial liability to reflect the final settlement amount (final fair value) will also be recognised in profit or loss if the amount differs from the fair value estimate at the end of the first year.

2.6.1130   Acquirer share-based payment awards exchanged for acquiree awards

2.6.1130.10   Neither IFRS 2 nor IFRS 3 provides explicit guidance on how to account for the amount allocated to post-combination service. In our view, an entity should choose an accounting policy, to be applied consistently, to account for the recognition of the remuneration cost in post-combination periods under either the new grant approach or the modification approach.

2.6.1130.20   Because IFRS 3 provides guidance on how to allocate the market-based measure of the replacement awards between pre- and post-combination service, the cumulative amount recognised will be the same under either the new grant approach or the modification approach. This is because the allocation between pre- and post-combination service will always be undertaken in accordance with the method set out in 2.6.440.30. [*IFRS 3.B59*]

2.6.1130.30   Under the new grant approach, in line with the basic attribution principle in IFRS 2, the amount attributed to post-combination service is recognised over the vesting period of the replacement award.

2.6.1130.40   If, instead, the modification approach is followed, then the attribution period may be different because the IFRS 2 requirements for recognising awards differ for new grants and modifications (see 4.5.1190). For example, to apply modification accounting the acquirer has to determine whether the terms of the replacement award, as compared with the terms of the acquiree award, are beneficial to the employee. If the replacement is considered to be non-beneficial – e.g. replacement award with no incremental value and an extension of the vesting period – then the amount allocated to post-combination service is recognised over a shorter period under the modification approach than under the new grant approach.

2.6.1140   BUSINESS COMBINATION ACHIEVED IN STAGES#

2.6.1140.10   Sometimes control is obtained in successive share purchases – i.e. the acquirer obtains control of an acquiree in which it held a non-controlling equity interest immediately before the date of acquisition. Such a business combination is commonly referred to as a 'business combination achieved in stages' or a 'step acquisition'. For example, Company P acquires a 10 percent interest in Company S, and an additional 60 percent interest some years later to gain control. [*IFRS 3.41*]

2.6.1140.20   The acquisition method is applied in the normal manner to a business combination achieved in stages, including:
- determining the date of acquisition (see 2.6.180);
- recognising and measuring the consideration transferred (see 2.6.260); and
- recognising and measuring the assets acquired and liabilities assumed (see 2.6.560).

2.6.1140.30   In a step acquisition, the fair value of any non-controlling equity interest in the acquiree that is held immediately before obtaining control is used in the determination of goodwill – i.e. it is remeasured to fair value at the date of acquisition with any resulting gain or loss recognised in profit or loss or OCI, as appropriate. For a discussion of the fair value of a non-controlling interest, see chapter 2.4 in general and 2.4.830 in relation to valuing investments in associates and joint ventures. [*IFRS 3.32(a)(iii), 42*]

2.6.1140.40   This treatment effectively considers that any investment in the acquiree that was held before obtaining control is sold and subsequently repurchased at the date of acquisition. Accordingly, in our view the disclosure of that gain or loss should be on the same basis as if the investment had been disposed of to a third party.

2.6.1140.50   On obtaining control, any amounts recognised in OCI related to the previously held equity interest are recognised on the same basis as would be required if the acquirer had disposed of the previously held equity interest directly. [*IFRS 3.42, BC389*]

2.6.1140.60   Equity investments in the scope of IFRS 9 are measured at fair value with changes in fair value recognised in either profit or loss or OCI (see 7.4.60 and 410). Any fair value gains or losses recognised in OCI may remain in accumulated OCI or may be transferred to retained earnings, but reclassification to profit or loss on disposal of the investment (or in other circumstances) is prohibited (see 7.7.160.10). [*IFRS 9.4.1.4, 5.7.5, B5.7.1*]

2.6.1140.70   Also, for investments not accounted for under IFRS 9 before obtaining control, unrealised gains or losses may have been recognised in OCI – e.g. foreign exchange gains or losses, and revaluation surpluses on property, plant and equipment. The treatment of these amounts on obtaining control is consistent with how they would be treated if the previously held equity interest was disposed of to a third party. For example, foreign exchange gains or losses previously recognised in OCI are reclassified from equity to profit or loss on the date on which control is obtained, while revaluation surpluses on property, plant and equipment may be reclassified within equity to retained earnings. [*IFRS 3.42, IAS 16.41, 21.48–48A*]

EXAMPLE 22 – STEP ACQUISITION – FOREIGN CURRENCY TRANSLATION RESERVE

2.6.1140.80   On 1 January 2017, Company P acquired 30% of the voting ordinary shares of Company S for 80,000. P equity accounts its investment in S under IAS 28. At 31 December 2017, P recognised its share of the net asset changes of S using equity accounting as follows.

Share of profit or loss	7,000
Share of exchange differences in OCI	1,000
Share of revaluation reserve of property, plant and equipment in OCI	500

2.6.1140.90   The carrying amount of the investment in the associate on 31 December 2017 was therefore 88,500 (80,000 + 7,000 + 1,000 + 500).

2.6.1140.100   On 1 January 2018, P acquired the remaining 70% of S for cash of 250,000. The following additional information is relevant at that date.

Fair value of the 30% interest already owned[1]	90,000
Fair value of S's identifiable net assets	300,000

2.6.1140.110   P records the following entry in its consolidated financial statements.

	DEBIT	CREDIT
Identifiable net assets of S	300,000	
Goodwill[2]	40,000	
Foreign currency translation reserve	1,000	
Property, plant and equipment revaluation reserve	500	
Cash		250,000
Investment in associate S		88,500
Retained earnings[3]		500
Gain on previously held interest in S recognised in profit or loss[4]		2,500
To recognise acquisition of S		

Notes

1. For a discussion of the fair value measurement of investments in associates, see 2.4.830.

2. Goodwill is calculated as follows.

Cash consideration	250,000
Fair value of previously held equity interest in S	90,000
Total consideration	340,000
Fair value of identifiable net assets acquired	(300,000)
Goodwill	40,000

3. The credit to retained earnings represents the reversal of the unrealised gain of 500 in OCI related to the revaluation of property, plant and equipment. In accordance with IAS 16, this amount is not reclassified to profit or loss.

4. The gain on the previously held equity interest in S is calculated as follows.

Fair value of 30% interest in S at 1 January 2018	90,000
Carrying amount of interest in S at 1 January 2018	(88,500)
	1,500
Unrealised gain previously recognised in OCI	1,000
Gain on previously held interest in S recognised in profit or loss	2,500

2.6.1140.120   Notwithstanding that on obtaining control amounts recognised in OCI are recognised on the same basis as would be required if the acquirer had disposed of the previously held equity interest directly, in our view classification of the previously held equity interest as held-for-sale or as a discontinued operation is not appropriate because there is no actual sale of the investment. [*IFRS 3.BC384, 5.6–8, IASBU 05-09*]

2.6.1140.130   For a discussion of the accounting when the investor obtains control over an existing associate or joint venture that does not meet the definition of a business, see 3.5.580.30.

2.6.1145   **FORTHCOMING REQUIREMENTS**

2.6.1145.10 *Annual Improvements to IFRSs 2015–2017 Cycle – Amendments to IFRS 3* clarify that when a party to a joint arrangement, which had rights to the assets and obligations to liabilities, obtains control over a joint operation that is a business, the transaction is accounted for as a business combination achieved in stages. The acquirer applies the requirements for a business combination achieved in stages and remeasures its previously held interest in the joint operation (see 2.6.1140). [*IFRS 3.42A*]

2.6.1150   PUSH-DOWN ACCOUNTING

2.6.1150.10   'Push-down accounting' – whereby fair value adjustments recognised in the consolidated financial statements are 'pushed down' into the financial statements of the subsidiary – is not addressed by, and is not applicable under, IFRS. However, some fair value adjustments could be reflected in the acquiree as revaluations if this is permitted by the relevant standards, as long as the revaluations are kept up to date subsequently.

EXAMPLE 23 – PUSH-DOWN ACCOUNTING PROHIBITED

2.6.1150.20   On 31 March 2018, Company P acquired all of the shares of Company S and as part of the acquisition accounting recognised land and buildings at 500 (the previous cost-based carrying amount was 300) and a trademark at 150 (which was not previously recognised).

2.6.1150.30   S could recognise the fair value adjustment of 200 in respect of land and buildings in its own financial statements for the period ended 31 December 2018 if it changed its accounting policy to one of revaluation and complied with all of the revaluation requirements, including the need to keep revaluations up to date (see 3.2.300).

2.6.1160   DISCLOSURES

2.6.1160.10   The overall objective of the disclosure requirements of IFRS 3 is for the acquirer to provide information that enables the users of its financial statements to evaluate:

- the nature and financial effects of a business combination that occurs either during the current reporting period, or after the reporting date but before the financial statements are authorised for issue; and
- the financial effects of adjustments recognised in the current reporting period that relate to business combinations that occurred in the current or previous reporting periods. [*IFRS 3.59, 61*]

2.6.1160.20   If the specific disclosures do not meet the overall disclosure objective, then the acquirer discloses whatever additional information is required to meet that objective. [*IFRS 3.63*]

2.6.1160.30   The disclosure requirements cover:

- general information on the business combination;
- consideration transferred;
- assets acquired and liabilities assumed;
- goodwill (or a gain on a bargain purchase);
- transactions that are not part of the business combination;
- business combinations in which the acquirer holds less than 100 percent of the acquiree;
- business combinations achieved in stages – i.e. step acquisitions;
- pro forma information about revenue and profit or loss; and
- adjustments, including measurement-period adjustments and contingent consideration adjustments. [*IFRS 3.B64–B67*]

2.6.1160.40   The disclosures are required for each material business combination, or in aggregate for individually immaterial business combinations that are collectively material. [*IFRS 3.B65, B67*]

2.6.1160.50   The disclosures are required as at the date of acquisition even if the acquirer consolidates the subsidiary from a different date for convenience (see 2.6.190.10).

2.6.1160.60   Disclosures are generally required in respect of a business combination that occurs after the reporting date but before the financial statements are authorised for issue. The only exception is if the initial accounting is incomplete when the financial statements are authorised, in which case the entity discloses why the disclosures cannot be given. [*IFRS 3.B66*]

2.6.1160.70   The disclosure requirements also apply for interim financial statements prepared in accordance with IAS 34. [*IAS 34.16A(i)*]

2.6.1160.80   The disclosure requirements of IFRS 3 are illustrated in KPMG's *Guides to financial statements* series.

2.6.1170   FUTURE DEVELOPMENTS

2.6.1170.10   In June 2015, the IASB published *Post-implementation Review of IFRS 3 Business Combinations – Report and Feedback Statement*, which followed its public consultation in 2014. The statement identifies the following areas as highly significant that have been added to the IASB's agenda:
- challenges in applying the definition of a business (see 2.6.20);
- the identification and measurement of intangible assets in a business combination (see 2.6.720); and
- the accounting for goodwill (see 2.6.1010 and chapter 3.10).

2.6.1170.20   In June 2016, the IASB published Exposure Draft *Definition of a Business – Proposed Amendments to IFRS 3*. The exposure draft proposed to clarify the definition of a business and introduce tests to assess whether a set of acquired assets and activities constitutes a business (see 2.6.20). The final amendments are expected in the second half of 2018.

2.6.1170.30   The IASB is also working on a research project to improve goodwill impairment accounting in response to the difficulties in applying these requirements in practice. It expects to publish a consultation document, and has tentatively decided:

- to consider ways to ensure timely recognition of goodwill impairment;
- not to consider amortisation of goodwill; and
- to explore whether some identifiable intangible assets could be subsumed within goodwill.

2.7 Foreign currency translation

2.7 Foreign currency translation

CURRENTLY EFFECTIVE REQUIREMENTS

This publication reflects IFRS in issue at 1 August 2018, and the currently effective requirements cover annual periods beginning on 1 January 2018.

The requirements related to this topic are mainly derived from the following.

STANDARD	TITLE
IAS 21	The Effects of Changes in Foreign Exchange Rates
IAS 29	Financial Reporting in Hyperinflationary Economies
IFRIC 22	Foreign Currency Transactions and Advance Consideration

The currently effective requirements include newly effective requirements arising from the following.

- IFRS 9 *Financial Instruments*, which is effective for annual periods beginning on or after 1 January 2018. Transition requirements for IFRS 9 are the subject of chapter 7.11. The impact of the new requirements on foreign currency translation is reflected in 2.7.95.
- IFRIC 22 *Foreign Currency Transactions and Advance Consideration*, which is effective for annual periods beginning on or after 1 January 2018. The new requirements may be applied retrospectively or prospectively to items initially recognised on or after:
  - the beginning of the reporting period in which the entity first applies the interpretation; or
  - the beginning of a prior reporting period presented as comparative information in the financial statements of the reporting period in which the entity first applies the interpretation. See 2.7.90.20–80.

FORTHCOMING REQUIREMENTS

The currently effective requirements are affected by the following forthcoming requirements. They are highlighted with a # and the impact is explained in the accompanying boxed text at the reference indicated.

In May 2017, the IASB issued IFRS 17 *Insurance Contracts*, which is effective for annual periods beginning on or after 1 January 2021. See 2.7.125. IFRS 17 is the subject of chapter 8.1A.

FUTURE DEVELOPMENTS

For this topic there are no future developments.

2.7.10   **DEFINITIONS**

2.7.20   **Reporting entity**

2.7.20.10   A 'reporting entity', as used in this chapter, refers to an entity that may have a foreign operation. Although that entity may not be a parent as defined in IFRS 10, for simplicity it is referred to as a 'parent' throughout this chapter. [*IAS 21.11*]

2.7.25   **Foreign operation**

2.7.25.10   A 'foreign operation' is an entity that is a subsidiary, associate, joint arrangement or branch of a reporting entity, the activities of which are based or conducted in a country or currency other than those of the reporting entity. [*IAS 21.8*]

2.7.30   **Functional currency**

2.7.30.10   An entity's 'functional currency' is the currency of the primary economic environment in which it operates (see 2.7.70). [*IAS 21.8*]

2.7.35   **Foreign currency**

2.7.35.10   'Foreign currency' is a currency other than the functional currency of the entity. [*IAS 21.8*]

2.7.40   **Presentation currency**

2.7.40.10   An entity's 'presentation currency' is the currency in which the financial statements are presented. [*IAS 21.8*]

2.7.40.20   Although an entity measures items in its financial statements in its functional currency, it may decide to present its financial statements in a currency or currencies other than its functional currency. For example, an entity with a euro functional currency may choose to present its financial statements in US dollars because its primary listing is in the US. [*IAS 21.38*]

2.7.40.30   If an entity presents its financial statements in a presentation currency that is not its functional currency, then there is no requirement for it to present additional financial information in its functional currency.

2.7.50   **Monetary items**

2.7.50.10   'Monetary items' are units of currency held, and assets and liabilities to be received or paid, in a fixed or determinable number of units of currency (see 2.7.120). [*IAS 21.8*]

2.7.55   **Exchange rate**

2.7.55.10   The 'exchange rate' is the ratio of exchange for two currencies. The 'spot exchange rate' is the exchange rate for immediate delivery. [*IAS 21.8*]

2.7.60 SUMMARY OF APPROACH TO FOREIGN CURRENCY TRANSLATION

2.7.60.10   The following is a summary of the approach under IFRS to foreign currency translation, which is explained in more detail in 2.7.80–310.20.

- An entity determines its functional currency. All transactions that are not denominated in its functional currency are foreign currency transactions. These transactions are translated into the entity's functional currency at the spot exchange rate at the transaction date.
- At the reporting date, assets and liabilities denominated in a currency other than the entity's functional currency are translated as follows:
  - monetary items are translated at the spot exchange rate at the reporting date;
  - non-monetary items measured at historical cost are not retranslated – they remain at the exchange rate at the date of the transaction; and
  - non-monetary items measured at fair value are translated at the spot exchange rate when the fair value was determined.
- Next an entity determines the functional currency of each of its branches, subsidiaries, associates and joint arrangements, including consideration of whether this is the same as the entity's own functional currency.
- The financial statements of the parent, branches, subsidiaries, associates and joint arrangements are translated into the group presentation currency if their functional currencies are different from the group presentation currency. Two methods for such translation exist.
  - *The step-by-step method:* The financial statements of the foreign operation are translated into the functional currency of any intermediate parent, and the financial statements of the intermediate parent that include the foreign operation are then translated into the functional currency of the ultimate parent (or the presentation currency, if it is different).
  - *The direct method:* The financial statements of the foreign operation are translated directly into the functional currency of the ultimate parent (or the presentation currency, if it is different).
- The result of all of the above is that the entity will present its financial statements or consolidated financial statements in either the functional currency of the parent entity or another chosen presentation currency. [*IAS 21.BC18, IFRIC 16.17*]

2.7.70 DETERMINING THE FUNCTIONAL CURRENCY

2.7.70.10   An entity measures its assets, liabilities, equity, income and expenses in its functional currency. All transactions in currencies other than the functional currency are foreign currency transactions (see 2.7.80). [*IAS 21.IN7, 20*]

2.7.70.20   Each entity in a group has its own functional currency. There is no concept of a group-wide functional currency under IFRS. For further discussion of this issue, see 2.7.180.

2.7.70.30   In determining its functional currency, an entity emphasises the currency that determines the pricing of the transactions that it undertakes, rather than focusing on the currency in which those transactions are denominated. The following factors are considered in determining an appropriate functional currency:

- the currency that mainly influences sales prices for goods and services – this will often be the currency in which sales prices are denominated;
- the currency of the country whose competitive forces and regulations mainly determine the sales prices of its goods and services; and
- the currency that mainly influences labour, material and other costs of providing goods and services – this will often be the currency in which these costs are denominated and settled. [*IAS 21.9*]

2.7.70.40   The factors in 2.7.70.30 are the 'primary' indicators of an entity's functional currency. These factors are provided as an inclusive list; however, this should not be interpreted as meaning that *all* of these factors should indicate a certain currency in order for that currency to be the entity's functional currency. Additional, or 'secondary', factors may exist that provide supporting evidence to determine an entity's functional currency, namely:

- the currency in which funds from financing activities are generated; this would be the currency in which the entity's debt and equity instruments are issued; and
- the currency in which receipts from operating activities are usually retained. [*IAS 21.10*]

2.7.70.50   Furthermore, when determining the functional currency of a foreign operation, it is necessary to consider whether it is the same as the functional currency of its parent (see 2.7.180). [*IAS 21.11*]

2.7.70.60   In our experience, entities often operate in a mixture of currencies and consideration of the factors in 2.7.70.30 and 40 may not result in an obvious conclusion on the entity's functional currency. In such cases, management has to exercise judgement to determine the functional currency that most faithfully represents the economic effects of the underlying transactions, events and conditions based on the specific facts and circumstances. In doing so, priority is given to the primary indicators before considering the secondary indicators (see 2.7.70.30). [*IAS 21.12*]

2.7.70.70   In many cases, an entity's functional currency is its local currency.

EXAMPLE 1A – FUNCTIONAL CURRENCY IS LOCAL CURRENCY (1)

2.7.70.75   Company R in Russia produces goods that are exported throughout Europe. Selling prices are denominated in euro for the convenience of trade and consistency in pricing, and some of R's cash reserves are held in euro. However, all of the other factors, including the currency that mainly influences the costs of providing goods, indicate that the rouble is R's functional currency.

2.7.70.77   In our view, the functional currency is the rouble because there is not enough evidence to indicate that the euro overcomes the presumption that the rouble *best* reflects the economic substance of the underlying events and circumstances relevant to R.

EXAMPLE 1B – FUNCTIONAL CURRENCY IS LOCAL CURRENCY (2)

2.7.70.80   Company C is a manufacturer of steel products in Chile. C has analysed its operations as follows.

- The majority of raw material purchases are from local suppliers and are denominated in Chilean pesos, based on the price of steel, quoted in US dollars, on the London Metal Exchange.
- The majority of products are sold in the local Chilean market. The local sales price is set based on a US dollar-denominated international steel price, as the starting point, and then adjusted based on the requirements of local laws and regulations, and local supply and demand.
- These sales and raw material purchases are invoiced and settled in Chilean pesos like most other expenses, including payroll and processing costs.
- A significant amount of financing is in US dollars to match the currency used as the starting point for setting the selling price.
- Cash reserves are held in Chilean pesos.

2.7.70.90   In this example, C concludes that its functional currency is the Chilean peso for the following reasons.
- C primarily generates and spends cash in Chilean pesos in the Chilean economy.
- Although C uses the US dollar-denominated international spot price for steel as the starting point for pricing its domestic sales, such domestic sales prices are ultimately determined by competitive forces in the Chilean economy and denominated and settled in Chilean pesos.
- The fact that the US dollar-denominated international steel price influences the cost of its raw materials is not a determining factor in the analysis. The international market price of steel is driven by international forces of supply and demand, but quoted in US dollars because it is a stable and widely traded currency. Other costs of providing goods and services are generally sourced locally and mainly determined by competitive forces and regulations in Chile. Purchases of steel and most other expenses are invoiced and settled in Chilean pesos.
- The fact that financing is obtained in US dollars is a secondary factor (see 2.7.70.40) that does not override the conclusion reached by C in considering the primary factors above.

2.7.70.100   However, it cannot be assumed that the local currency is always the functional currency.

EXAMPLE 2A – FUNCTIONAL CURRENCY IS NOT LOCAL CURRENCY (1)

2.7.70.110   Company P in the Philippines manufactures sports clothing that is exported to the US. Selling prices are established having regard to prices in the US, and are denominated in US dollars. Sales are settled in US dollars and the receipts are converted to Philippine pesos only when necessary to settle local expenses. The majority of P's borrowings are denominated in US dollars and the cost of the manufacturing equipment, which is P's major item of property, plant and equipment, is denominated in US dollars. Management's salaries – which represent the significant portion of labour costs – are denominated and paid in US dollars. Other labour costs, as well as all material costs, are denominated and settled in Philippine pesos. In this example, P concludes that its functional currency is the US dollar.

EXAMPLE 2B – FUNCTIONAL CURRENCY IS NOT LOCAL CURRENCY (2)

2.7.70.112   Company B operates a mine in Vietnam and generates its revenue from the sale of tungsten and bismuth. B has analysed its operations as follows.

- 80% of B's sales are exports to various countries. The selling prices are denominated in US dollars based on or indexed to international commodity exchanges. Export contracts are influenced by global supply and demand and are invoiced and settled in US dollars. The remaining sales are invoiced in Vietnamese dong.
- B's cost structure is as follows:
    - 45%: import of mining reagents, which are denominated and settled in US dollars;
    - 20%: payroll, mainly relating to expatriate workers whose pay is denominated and settled in US dollars;
    - 20%: depreciation of mining plant and equipment that is imported and is priced in US dollars; and
    - 15%: other expenses that are mainly denominated in Vietnamese dong.
- Approximately half of B's financing is in US dollars and half in Vietnamese dong.
- Receipts from sales are retained in US dollars in order to pay expenses and repay financing denominated in US dollars.

2.7.70.113   B's management concludes that the above indicators are mixed and therefore exercises its judgement to determine the currency that most faithfully represents B's economic environment. In doing so, it gives priority to the primary indicators (see 2.7.70.30) before considering secondary indicators (see 2.7.70.40).

2.7.70.114   Management considers that 80% of B's revenues are denominated and settled in US dollars; these selling prices are not determined by local competitive forces and regulations, but rather by worldwide competition and global forces of supply and demand in the international metals market. The expenses are predominately salaries of expatriate workers and the pricing of imported reagents, mining plant and equipment, which are denominated in US dollars and are also primarily driven by factors affecting the international markets for these items, rather than conditions in the Vietnamese economy.

2.7.70.115   These factors indicate that B generates cash predominantly in US dollars and spends most of it in US dollars; and that there is no other currency, and no single country, that mainly influences selling prices and costs. This conclusion is further supported by the fact that receipts from sales are retained in US dollars and is not contradicted by B having financing in both US dollars and Vietnamese dong.

2.7.70.117   Based on this analysis, B concludes that the US dollar is its functional currency because it is the currency that most faithfully represents the economic effects of its activities and transactions.

2.7.70.120   In some cases, an analysis of the underlying events and circumstances relevant to an entity may indicate that two (or more) currencies are equally relevant.

EXAMPLE 3 – FUNCTIONAL CURRENCY IS NOT OBVIOUS

2.7.70.130   T is a Turkish company that has analysed its operations as follows.

- The majority of short- and long-term debt is financed in US dollars and the balance is financed in Turkish lira.
- The activities of T are financed mainly by its own capital that is denominated in Turkish lira and currencies other than the US dollar.
- The majority of cash reserves are held in US dollars.
- Export sales that are priced and denominated largely in US dollars make up approximately 95% of total sales.
- The majority of operating expenses are priced and denominated in Turkish lira and the balance is denominated in US dollars.

2.7.70.140   In this example, T concludes that both the Turkish lira and the US dollar are key to its operations. However, because an entity can have only one functional currency, management applies judgement to determine whether the Turkish lira or the US dollar is T's functional currency. In doing so, greater weighting will be given to the primary indicators.

2.7.70.150   In this example, further consideration would need to be given to the specific facts and circumstances and the environment in which T operates. For example, it would have to be considered whether the US dollar is used to achieve stability in T's financial results and position rather than because the US economy is a determining factor for those results and position. However, in the absence of further evidence, it seems that in this example the US dollar might be considered T's functional currency.

2.7.70.160   An entity may not choose to adopt a functional currency other than that determined under IAS 21. An entity whose functional currency is that of a hyperinflationary economy may not avoid applying hyperinflationary accounting by choosing a different stable currency as its functional currency. [*IAS 21.14*]

2.7.70.170   Once an entity has determined its functional currency, it is not changed unless there is a change in the relevant underlying transactions, events and circumstances (see 2.7.320).

2.7.80   TRANSLATION OF FOREIGN CURRENCY TRANSACTIONS

2.7.80.10   A 'foreign currency transaction' is a transaction that is denominated or requires settlement in a currency other than an entity's functional currency (i.e. in a foreign currency). Before applying this definition and the guidance on foreign currency transactions, an entity first considers whether there is a foreign currency or other embedded derivative that requires separation. For a discussion of embedded derivatives, see 7.2.110; and for a discussion of embedded foreign currency derivatives, see 7.2.260–265.

2.7.80.20 If an embedded derivative is separated from a hybrid contract, then the guidance on foreign currency transactions is applied to the host contract if the host contract is denominated in a foreign currency. For a discussion of the accounting for separated embedded derivatives, see 7.2.370; and for a discussion of the accounting for separable foreign currency derivatives, see 7.2.370.50–80 and 7.2.370.100–140. [*IAS 21.20, IFRIC 22.BC26–BC27*]

2.7.90   At the transaction date

2.7.90.10 Each foreign currency transaction is initially recorded in the entity's functional currency at the spot rate of exchange at the date of the transaction, or at spot rates that approximate the actual exchange rates. An average of spot exchange rates for a specific period may be a suitable approximate rate for transactions during that period, particularly if spot exchange rates do not fluctuate significantly. [*IAS 21.21–22*]

2.7.90.20 The date of a transaction is the date on which the transaction first qualifies for recognition under IFRS. [*IAS 21.22*]

2.7.90.30 If an entity recognises a non-monetary asset or liability arising from the payment or receipt of consideration for a foreign currency transaction in advance of recognising the related asset, expense or income (the 'related item'), then the date of the transaction is the date on which the entity initially recognises the non-monetary asset or liability arising from the payment or receipt of the advance consideration. The date of the transaction is used to determine the spot exchange rate for translating the related item on its initial recognition. If there are multiple payments or receipts in advance, then an entity determines the date of the transaction for each advance payment or receipt separately. [*IFRIC 22.8–9*]

2.7.90.40 The guidance in 2.7.90.30 does not apply in the following cases:
- if the asset or liability arising from the payment or receipt of advance consideration is monetary rather than non-monetary and therefore is retranslated for changes in the spot exchange rate between its initial recognition and settlement with the resulting exchange differences included in profit or loss (see 2.7.110); and
- if the related item is measured on initial recognition either at its fair value or at the fair value of the consideration paid or received using a measurement date different from the date of initial recognition of the non-monetary asset or liability relating to the advance consideration – e.g. if the related item is measured at the fair value of the consideration determined at the date of initial recognition of the related item, then the spot exchange rate at that date is used. [*IFRIC 22.4–5, BC12, BC14*]

2.7.90.50 In addition, an entity is not required to apply the guidance in 2.7.90.30 to income taxes, insurance contracts that it issues or reinsurance contracts that it holds. [*IFRIC 22.6*]

EXAMPLE 4– FOREIGN CURRENCY CONSIDERATION RECEIVED PARTLY BEFORE AND PARTLY AFTER SALE OF GOODS

2.7.90.60 On 1 March 2018, Entity Z, whose functional currency is FC, enters into a contract to deliver goods on 1 December 2018 to its customer for a price in foreign currency (AC) of AC 500. An amount of AC 100 is due and received on 1 June 2018, with the remaining balance due on 31 December 2018.

Spot exchange rate at	AC	FC
1 June 2018	1.0	2.0
1 December 2018	1.0	3.0

2.7.90.70 Z recognises a non-monetary contract liability of FC 200 on 1 June 2018 by translating AC 100 into its functional currency at the spot exchange rate on 1 June 2018. Z does not revise the translated amount of the non-monetary liability.

2.7.90.80 Z recognises revenue on 1 December 2018, the date on which it transfers control over the goods to the customer. The date of the transaction for the revenue relating to the advance consideration of AC 100 is 1 June 2018 and the date of the transaction for the remainder of the revenue is 1 December 2018.

2.7.90.90 On 1 December 2018, Z:
- derecognises the contract liability of FC 200 and recognises revenue of FC 200 using the spot exchange rate on 1 June 2018; and
- recognises additional revenue of FC 1,200 and a corresponding receivable in respect of the remaining balance of AC 400 using the 1 December 2018 spot exchange rate. The receivable is a monetary item and is retranslated until the receivable is settled.

2.7.93 *Multiple exchange rates and lack of exchangeability*

2.7.93.10 When several exchange rates are available, an entity uses the one at which the future cash flows represented by the transaction or balance could have been settled if those cash flows had occurred at the measurement date. [*IAS 21.26*]

2.7.93.20 Some countries have dual exchange rates: the official exchange rate and an unofficial parallel exchange rate. In our view, individual transactions should be translated using the exchange rate that will be used to determine the rate at which the transaction is settled. This will normally be the official rate. However, the use of an unofficial exchange rate may be more appropriate in very limited circumstances – e.g. if it is a legal rate (i.e. domestic and foreign entities can and do purchase and sell foreign currency on a local market at this rate legally) and represents the rate at which the transaction can be settled because long-term lack of liquidity in the exchange market means that sufficient amounts of cash are not available at the official rate. See 2.7.250.20 for discussion about disclosures of significant judgements made in determining the exchange rate to use. [*IAS 21.26*]

2.7.93.30 When exchangeability between two currencies is temporarily lacking, an entity uses the first subsequent rate at which exchanges could be made. IFRS does not provide specific guidance for situations in which there is a longer-term lack of exchangeability. [*IAS 21.26, IU 11-14*]

2.7.95 *Hedged foreign currency transactions*

2.7.95.10 The initial measurement of an asset or liability may be adjusted if its acquisition or incurrence has been hedged with respect to foreign exchange risk. This depends on the nature of the hedging relationship and, for a cash flow hedge, whether the entity applies the hedge accounting requirements in IFRS 9 or continues to apply those in IAS 39 (see 7.11.220.10).

- If an entity hedges in a fair value hedge a firm commitment, then the initial carrying amount of the asset or liability that results from the entity meeting the firm commitment is adjusted to include the cumulative change in the fair value of the firm commitment attributable to the hedged risk that was recognised in the statement of financial position (see 7.9.170.30–40 and 7I.7.50.20).
- If an entity hedges in a cash flow hedge a forecast transaction or a firm commitment that results in the recognition of a non-financial asset or non-financial liability, then:
  - under IFRS 9, it includes the gain or loss on the hedging instrument accumulated in equity in the initial carrying amount of that asset or liability – this is commonly referred to as a 'basis adjustment' (see 7.9.200.70 and 470.60); or
  - under IAS 39, it may either include the gain or loss on the hedging instrument accumulated in equity in the initial carrying amount of that asset or liability (basis adjustment) or retain the amount in equity and reclassify it to profit or loss when the asset or liability affects profit or loss (see 7I.7.80.70–80 and 265.70). [*IFRS 9.6.5.8(b), 6.5.9, 6.5.11(d)(i), IAS 39.93–94*]

2.7.95.20   For example, inventory bought in a foreign currency is measured on initial recognition at the spot exchange rate. This measurement may be impacted if the entity hedges its future inventory purchases to minimise its exposure to movements in exchange rates and has a policy of applying a basis adjustment. [*IFRS 9.6.5.11(d)(i), IAS 39.94, 98*]

EXAMPLE 5 – INVENTORY PURCHASED IN FOREIGN CURRENCY – INITIAL MEASUREMENT WHEN HEDGE ACCOUNTING APPLIED

2.7.95.30   Company B plans to purchase inventory at a price denominated in a foreign currency. In anticipation of the transaction, B enters into a forward exchange contract to purchase the foreign currency for an amount of functional currency. B does not pay any advance consideration to the seller. The inventory is measured on initial recognition at the spot exchange rate.

2.7.95.40   The forward contract was designated and determined effective as a cash flow hedge of the foreign currency exposure on the anticipated inventory purchase.

2.7.95.50   If B applies the hedge accounting requirements in IFRS 9, then it includes the gain or loss on the hedging instrument accumulated in equity in the initial carrying amount of inventory (commonly referred to as a 'basis adjustment').

2.7.95.60   If B continues to apply the hedge accounting requirements in IAS 39, then it may choose an accounting policy, to be applied consistently, to account for the effective portion of the gain or loss on the hedging instrument using one of the following approaches:
- add to or deduct from the inventory amount initially recognised (basis adjustment); or
- retain in equity and reclassify to profit or loss, usually when the inventory affects profit or loss (see 7I.7.80.70).

2.7.95.70   For a discussion of the accounting for cash flow hedges, see 7.9.180 and 7I.7.60. For a discussion of the accounting for the tax impact of a basis adjustment, see 3.13.160.50–100.

2.7.100   At the reporting date

2.7.110   *General requirements*

2.7.110.10   At the reporting date, assets and liabilities denominated in a currency other than the entity's functional currency are translated as follows:

- monetary items are translated at the exchange rate at the reporting date;
- non-monetary items measured at historical cost are not retranslated; they remain at the exchange rate at the date of the transaction; and
- non-monetary items measured at fair value are translated at the exchange rate when the fair value was determined. [*IAS 21.23*]

2.7.120   *Monetary vs non-monetary items#*

2.7.120.10   'Monetary items' are units of currency held, and assets and liabilities to be received or paid, in a fixed or determinable number of units of currency. Conversely, non-monetary items lack such a feature. An entity may need to apply judgement in determining whether an item is monetary or non-monetary. Examples of non-monetary items include:

- prepaid expenses and income received in advance, on the basis that no money will be paid or received in the future; and
- equity securities held and share capital, on the basis that any future payments are not fixed or determinable. [*IAS 21.8, 16, IFRIC 22.BC17*]

2.7.120.20   Most debt securities are considered monetary items because their contractual cash flows are fixed or determinable. There is no exemption from this classification when the security is classified as fair value through OCI if the future cash flows are fixed or determinable (see 7.7.470.10). [*IFRS 9.B5.7.2A*]

2.7.120.30   The appropriate treatment of deferred taxes is not clear in IFRS. Deferred taxes comprise both monetary and non-monetary components. Treatment as a monetary item is based on the view that deferred tax represents future amounts of cash that will be paid to/received from the tax authorities. In our experience, deferred tax is normally treated as a monetary item. An entity that normally considers deferred tax as a monetary item may nonetheless consider individual deferred tax items as non-monetary if an event that would result in realisation of the asset or liability is not expected to occur and not result in a cash flow – e.g. temporary differences arising on revaluation of a non-depreciable asset that an entity does not plan to sell. If this approach is taken, then in our view a review to determine the appropriate treatment should be performed for all deferred tax items, and consistent criteria should be applied. If a portion of a deferred tax item is likely to result in realisation of the asset or liability, then in our view the item should be treated as a monetary item in its entirety. [*IFRIC 7.BC21–BC22*]

2.7.120.40   When a non-monetary asset (see 2.7.110.10) is measured at fair value, an issue may arise about how to distinguish the change in fair value from the related foreign exchange gain or loss.

EXAMPLE 6 – FOREIGN EXCHANGE GAIN OR LOSS ON NON-MONETARY ASSET MEASURED AT FAIR VALUE

2.7.120.50   Company Y, whose functional currency is FC, owns an investment property. The fair value of the investment property as at 31 December 2017 was AC 1,000 with the exchange rate being AC 1: FC 1.5. Therefore, in Y's 31 December 2017 financial statements, the property was recorded at FC 1,500. Y measures all investment property at fair value (see 3.4.140). As at 31 December 2018, the fair value of the property has increased to AC 1,200 and the exchange rate at the same date is AC 1: FC 1.7.

2.7.120.60   In our view, the foreign exchange gain or loss may be calculated as the difference between the fair value recorded at the spot rate at 31 December 2017 and the same fair value measured at the exchange rate at 31 December 2018 – i.e. a foreign exchange gain of 200 (1,000 x (1.7 - 1.5)). Under this approach, the fair value gain excluding the impact of changes in foreign currency rates is FC 340 ((1,200 - 1,000) x 1.7). This reflects recognition of the foreign currency amount of the fair value gain at the spot rate at the reporting date. The total gain in this example is 540 ((1,000 x 1.5) - (1,200 x 1.7)), which comprises the foreign exchange gain of 200 and the fair value gain of 340.

2.7.120.70   However, Y is not precluded from performing revaluations on a more frequent basis than at each reporting date. In this case, Y could calculate the foreign exchange gain or loss on the revaluation date as the difference between:
● the fair value recorded at the previous revaluation date using the exchange rate at that date; and
● the same fair value using the exchange rate at the current revaluation date.

2.7.120.75   Alternatively, if the fair value gain or loss determined in the foreign currency is considered to have accrued through the period, then Y may use the average exchange rate for the period to translate the fair value gain or loss into a functional currency amount in accordance with 2.7.90.10. The foreign exchange gain or loss would represent the difference between:
● the fair value recorded at the previous revaluation date using the spot exchange rate at that date plus the fair value gain or loss for the period translated at the average of spot exchange rates; and
● the fair value recorded at the current revaluation date using the spot exchange rate at the current revaluation date. [*IAS 21.22, IFRS 9.IG.E.3.3*]

2.7.120.80   Although both the exchange gain or loss and the change in the fair value of the investment property measured at fair value are recognised in profit or loss, they are disclosed separately if they are material. [*IAS 1.35, 21.52*]

2.7.120.90   For a discussion of how to distinguish between foreign exchange gains or losses included in profit or loss and other fair value gains and losses included in OCI on monetary financial assets measured at fair value through OCI, see 7.7.470.

2.7.125 **FORTHCOMING REQUIREMENTS**

2.7.125.10   IFRS 17 requires an entity to treat a group of insurance contracts that generate cash flows in a foreign currency as a monetary item, including the contractual service margin. [*IFRS 17.30*]

2.7.130 *Intra-group transactions*

2.7.130.10   Although intra-group balances are eliminated on consolidation (see 2.5.550), any related foreign exchange gains or losses will not be eliminated. This is because the group has a real exposure to a foreign currency because one of the entities will need to obtain or sell foreign currency to settle the obligation or realise the proceeds received. [*IAS 21.45*]

EXAMPLE 7 – FOREIGN EXCHANGE LOSS ON INTRA-GROUP LOAN

2.7.130.20   Parent P has a functional currency of AC, and Subsidiary S has a functional currency of FC. P, whose year end is 31 December, lends AC 100 to S on 1 June 2018. S converted the cash received into FC on receipt.

	AC	FC
Exchange rate at 1 June 2018	1.0	1.5
Exchange rate at 31 December 2018	1.0	2.0

Entries in S	**DEBIT (FC)**	**CREDIT (FC)**
1 June 2018		
Cash	150	
Intra-group payable		150
To recognise intra-group loan on issue		
31 December 2018		
Exchange loss	50	
Intra-group payable		50
To recognise exchange loss on intra-group loan		

2.7.130.30   In S's second entry in 2.7.130.20, the liability is remeasured as at 31 December 2018 and a translation loss is recorded. P records the following entry.

Entry in P	**DEBIT (AC)**	**CREDIT (AC)**
Intra-group receivable	100	
Cash		100
To recognise intra-group loan on issue		

2.7.130.40   On consolidation at 31 December 2018, the FC 200 converts to AC 100 (see 2.7.220) and the receivable and payable are eliminated.

2.7.130.50   However, the exchange loss equivalent to FC 50 for the year ending 31 December 2018 remains on consolidation. This is appropriate because S will need to obtain AC to repay the liability; therefore, the group as a whole has a foreign currency exposure. It is not appropriate to transfer the exchange loss to OCI on consolidation unless the loan forms part of P's net investment in S (see 2.7.150).

2.7.140   Recognition of foreign exchange gains and losses

2.7.140.10   Foreign exchange gains and losses are generally recognised in profit or loss. Exceptions relate to monetary items that in substance form part of the reporting entity's net investment in a foreign operation (see 2.7.150) and hedging instruments in a qualifying cash flow hedge or hedge of a net investment in a foreign operation (see chapters 7.9 and 7I.7). Also, when a gain or loss on a non-monetary item is recognised in OCI, the foreign exchange component is recognised in OCI. For example, because IAS 16 requires gains and losses arising on a revaluation of property, plant and equipment to be recognised in OCI (see 3.2.300), the related exchange difference is also recognised in OCI. [*IAS 21.28, 30, 32*]

2.7.150   *Net investment in foreign operation*

2.7.150.10   A monetary item receivable from or payable to a foreign operation may form part of the net investment in a foreign operation. To qualify, settlement of the monetary item should be neither planned nor likely to occur in the foreseeable future. To form part of the net investment in a foreign operation, the entity that has the monetary item receivable or payable may be the reporting entity or any subsidiary in the group. However, an investment in a foreign operation made by an associate of the reporting entity is not part of the reporting entity's net investment in that operation because an associate is not a group entity. [*IAS 21.15–15A, 32–33, BC25F*]

2.7.150.12   A monetary item, settlement of which is neither planned nor likely to occur in the foreseeable future, may be in the form of a loan with no stated maturity on which interest is payable periodically until the loan is settled. For example, an entity may have a loan to its subsidiary, the settlement of which is neither planned nor likely to occur in the foreseeable future. Assume that the loan's principal is 100, which is equal to its carrying amount, and the loan is not impaired. It is unclear whether in such a case the net investment in a foreign operation should include:
- 100, on the basis that interest payments should not be regarded as the settlement of a loan; or
- only the present value of 100, on the basis that only the settlement of the principal amount is neither planned nor likely to occur in the foreseeable future.

2.7.150.13   In our view, both approaches discussed in 2.7.150.12 are acceptable. However, in our experience the predominant practice is to apply the first approach. Because the settlement of the principal is neither planned nor likely to occur in the foreseeable future, under the second approach the present value of the principal amount of the loan might be close to zero.

2.7.150.15   In the financial statements that include the reporting entity and its foreign operation (e.g. the consolidated financial statements), foreign exchange gains and losses arising from monetary items that in substance form part of the net investment in the foreign operation are recognised in OCI and are presented within equity in the foreign currency translation reserve (see 2.7.260).

2.7.150.20   The exception in 2.7.150.15 applies only in the financial statements that include both the reporting entity and the foreign operation. In the separate financial statements of the reporting entity or the foreign operation, the foreign exchange gains and losses are recognised in profit or loss. [*IAS 21.32–33*]

EXAMPLE 8A – GAINS AND LOSSES ON MONETARY ITEMS THAT ARE PART OF NET INVESTMENT IN FOREIGN OPERATION – RECOGNITION (1)

2.7.150.30   Parent P has a functional currency of AC, and Subsidiary S has a functional currency of FC. P sells inventory to S for FC 300. At the reporting date, S has not yet paid the amount it owes to P, but payment is expected to be made in the foreseeable future. Accordingly, the exchange gain or loss incurred by P is recognised in profit or loss in both its consolidated and separate financial statements. Even if repayment was not due for three years (for example) or even longer, in our view if repayment is still planned, then the gain or loss should be recognised in profit or loss.

2.7.150.40   In addition to the trading balances between P and S, P lends an amount of FC 500 to S that is not expected to be repaid in the foreseeable future. P regards the amount as part of its permanent funding to S. In this case, the exchange gain or loss incurred by P on the FC 500 loan is recognised in profit or loss in P's separate financial statements, but recognised in OCI and presented within equity in its consolidated financial statements.

2.7.150.50   If the loan was denominated in AC rather than in FC (i.e. in P's functional currency rather than S's functional currency), then S would incur an exchange gain or loss. In its separate financial statements, S would recognise the gain or loss in profit or loss. On consolidation, the gain or loss would be recognised in OCI.

2.7.150.60   When the exchange gain or loss incurred by either P or S is recognised in OCI on consolidation, any related deferred or current tax is also recognised in OCI (see 3.13.280.40 and 530).

2.7.150.70   P and/or S could avoid recognising an exchange gain or loss only if the funding did not meet the definition of a financial liability (see 7.3.20.20), which is unlikely to be the case in our experience. If that were the case, then P's 'contribution' of FC 500 that is not required to be repaid would be classified as a capital contribution in S's financial statements and would not be retranslated subsequent to initial recognition (see 2.7.100). Similarly, in P's separate financial statements, the funding would be classified as part of P's investment in the equity instruments of S, which also would not be retranslated if P has a policy of measuring investments in subsidiaries at cost in its separate financial statements.

EXAMPLE 8B – GAINS AND LOSSES ON MONETARY ITEMS THAT ARE PART OF NET INVESTMENT IN FOREIGN OPERATION – RECOGNITION (2)

2.7.150.80   Modifying the fact pattern in 2.7.150.30–40 of Example 8A, suppose that the 'permanent' funding extended to Subsidiary S is made via another entity in the group, Subsidiary T, rather than from Parent P directly; this is done for tax reasons.

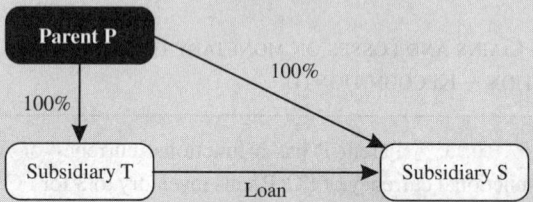

2.7.150.90   Any exchange difference in respect of the loan is recognised in OCI in the consolidated financial statements because from the group's point of view the funding relates to an investment in a foreign operation. This is the case irrespective of the currency in which the loan is denominated. So if the loan is denominated in T's functional currency, and this is different from that of S, then exchange differences are still recognised in OCI in the consolidated financial statements. [*IAS 21.15A, 32–33*]

2.7.160   *Presentation of items in profit or loss*

2.7.160.10   Disclosure is required of the amount of exchange differences recognised in profit or loss for the period, except for those arising on financial instruments measured at fair value through profit or loss. However, the standard does not specify the line item in which such differences should be presented. [*IAS 21.52*]

2.7.160.20   In our experience, the most common practice is for all such exchange differences related to monetary items to be included as part of finance costs. However, it is also acceptable to allocate the exchange differences to the various line items affected. For example, an entity might classify exchange differences on trade payables arising from the purchase of inventory as part of cost of sales, and exchange differences arising from loans as part of finance costs. If exchange differences are allocated in this way, then this should be done consistently from period to period having regard to the guidance in IAS 1 on offsetting (see 4.1.200), and in our view it would be necessary to disclose the entity's allocation policy, if it is significant, in the financial statements. For further discussion, see 4.1.120.10–30, 7.10.45 and 70.20.

2.7.170   **FOREIGN OPERATIONS**

2.7.170.10   A 'foreign operation' of an entity is a subsidiary, associate, joint arrangement or branch whose activities are conducted in a country or currency other than those of the reporting entity. IFRS defines the terms subsidiary (see chapter 2.5), associate (see chapter 3.5) and joint arrangement (see chapter 3.6). However, a branch is not defined in IFRS and therefore issues arise regarding the level and nature of activities that can comprise a foreign operation (see 2.7.190). [*IAS 21.8*]

2.7.180 **Functional currency of foreign operation**

2.7.180.10 The guidance provided on determining an entity's functional currency also applies to determining the functional currency of a (potential) foreign operation of the entity. This guidance places greater emphasis on the currency that determines the pricing of transactions than on the currency in which transactions are denominated. Especially relevant in the case of a foreign operation is whether it has the same functional currency as the reporting entity. To determine this, the relationship between the foreign operation and the reporting entity needs to be considered. In considering the relationship between the foreign operation and the reporting entity, in addition to the primary and secondary indicators discussed in 2.7.70, the following factors are relevant:

- whether the activities of the foreign operation are conducted as an extension of the reporting entity rather than with a significant degree of autonomy;
- whether a high or low proportion of the foreign operation's activities comprise transactions with the reporting entity;
- whether cash flows from the foreign operation's activities directly affect the cash flows of the reporting entity and are readily available for remittance to it; and
- whether the foreign operation generates sufficient cash flows from its own activities to service existing and normally expected debt obligations without additional funds from the reporting entity. [*IAS 21.11*]

2.7.180.20 The factors in 2.7.180.10 are relied on only to provide additional supporting evidence to determine a foreign operation's functional currency. When the indicators are mixed and the functional currency is not obvious, priority is still given to the primary indicators (see 2.7.70.30). [*IAS 21.9, 12*]

2.7.180.30 In our view, the conclusion about a foreign operation's functional currency should be the same irrespective of whether the analysis is performed on a stand-alone basis or with reference to the foreign operation's relationship with the reporting entity. In other words, if an entity determines that its functional currency is the same as that of the reporting entity with reference to the factors noted in 2.7.180.10 in the consolidated financial statements of the reporting entity, then it should use the same functional currency to measure items in its separate financial statements.

2.7.190 *Issues in determining whether foreign operation has same functional currency as reporting entity*

2.7.190.10 A significantly different accounting result may be achieved depending on whether the foreign operation is considered to have the same functional currency as the reporting entity. When the foreign operation has the same functional currency as the reporting entity, but undertakes a large number of transactions in a foreign currency, the effect of these transactions will be reflected in profit or loss. To reduce or eliminate volatility, the reporting entity may choose to hedge its exposure and therefore may be able to apply hedge accounting. Conversely, if it is concluded that the foreign operation has a functional currency different from that of the reporting entity, then foreign exchange gains or losses on translation of the foreign operation into the group presentation currency will be recognised in OCI because it is part of a net investment in a foreign operation. This avoids profit or loss volatility. These issues are particularly significant when the activities are conducted through an entity that is constituted to accomplish a specific narrow objective ('limited-purpose vehicle') (see 2.7.210.10).

2.7.190.20 For a discussion of some of the issues that require particular attention when determining the functional currency of a foreign operation, see 2.7.200–210.

2.7.200   *Separate legal entity*

2.7.200.10   In our view, the analysis of whether a foreign subsidiary consists of more than one operation should be based on the substance of the activities of the foreign operation, rather than its legal structure. Accordingly, we believe that a single legal entity may comprise multiple foreign operations with different functional currencies in certain circumstances.

EXAMPLE 9 – MULTIPLE FOREIGN OPERATIONS IN SINGLE LEGAL ENTITY

2.7.200.20   Parent P is based in the US and its functional currency is the US dollar. Subsidiary S is based in the UK. S has three distinct operations (X, Y and Z), which are conducted from the UK but under different economic environments as a result of differences in the nature of their products and markets. Separate accounting records are kept for each of the operations. In our view, the functional currency of each of X, Y and Z should be determined separately.

2.7.200.30   Care should be taken in assessing whether X, Y and Z could indeed have different functional currencies. The fact that they are part of the same legal entity will normally make it more difficult to demonstrate that any of them is independent and not an integral part of the reporting entity. In particular, if separate accounting records for each operation are not kept or if their operations and cash flows are managed on a unified basis, then in our view it would not be appropriate to conclude that each is a foreign operation. [*IAS 21.BC6*]

2.7.210   *An operation*

2.7.210.10   In our view, a foreign operation should carry out its own activities. We do not believe that an ad hoc collection of assets comprises an operation. Furthermore, when the foreign operation under consideration is a limited-purpose vehicle, in our view in order for the foreign operation to have a functional currency that differs from the reporting entity, it is necessary that:
- there is a substantive business reason for establishing a separate entity to conduct these activities;
- there is a substantive business reason for choosing the currency in which that entity transacts; and
- both substantial cash inflows and substantial third party funding are denominated in that currency.
  [*IAS 21.BC6–BC7*]

2.7.210.20   In our view, an example of a substantive business reason would be providing security for an external borrowing. However, we believe that obtaining a natural hedge or avoiding the need for hedge accounting would not, on its own, be a sufficient business reason for the purpose of determining whether a limited-purpose vehicle has its own functional currency.

EXAMPLE 10A – FUNCTIONAL CURRENCY OF LIMITED-PURPOSE VEHICLE (1)

2.7.210.30   Company B in New Zealand sets up a limited-purpose vehicle, V, to finance the acquisition of a cargo ship. V obtains a loan from an external bank, buys the ship and then leases the ship to B on normal commercial terms for a period of seven years (compared with the 25- to 30-year life of the ship). The ship serves as security for the loan. The interest and capital repayments on the loan will be financed partly through the lease payments, with the outstanding balance to be settled with the proceeds from the sale of the ship after seven years. All of these transactions are denominated in US dollars. B's functional currency is the New Zealand dollar.

2.7.210.40   In our view, V can have a functional currency that differs from the functional currency of B. By acquiring the ship, B is able to isolate the ship as security in favour of the external bank and therefore it has a substantive business reason. Because most ship purchase and sale transactions are denominated in US dollars, it follows that V's transacting currency would be the US dollar. Also, the loan from an external party is provided and settled in US dollars. Although the lease payments are mostly internal, these would not be sufficient to settle the entire loan and the settlement is effected by using the proceeds from the sale of the ship to an external party.

2.7.210.45   In such circumstances, in our view the functional currency of V would be the US dollar, in part because of the substantial residual US dollar value risk.

EXAMPLE 10B – FUNCTIONAL CURRENCY OF LIMITED-PURPOSE VEHICLE (2)

2.7.210.50   Company K establishes a limited-purpose vehicle, D, to lease a production plant to a third party. D obtains a loan from K, buys the plant and then leases the plant to a third party. The lease payments are sufficient to finance the interest and capital repayments on the loan. All of these transactions are denominated in US dollars. K's functional currency is the euro.

2.7.210.60   In our view, in this case D cannot have a functional currency that differs from that of K because there is no substantive business purpose for establishing a separate entity through which to purchase the production plant and effect the lease agreement. K could have acquired the production plant and entered into the lease agreement itself. D does not operate with a significant degree of autonomy from K. K determines the asset profile and future cash flows of D because K has written the lease agreement and provided the funding for the purchase of the production plant.

2.7.210.65   Also, there is no clear reason for choosing US dollars as the transacting currency. Any currency could have been chosen as the transacting currency, which means that it is not relevant that substantially all of D's assets, liabilities, income and expenses are denominated in a currency different from that of K. The US dollar cash flows of D directly affect the cash flows of the reporting entity because they are remitted immediately to the K in the form of interest and principal payments.

2.7.210.70   We believe that K and D will have the same functional currency, which in this case will be determined by analysing the combined operations.

2.7.220 TRANSLATION OF FOREIGN CURRENCY FINANCIAL STATEMENTS

2.7.230 Foreign operations

2.7.230.10   The financial statements of foreign operations are translated into the group presentation currency as follows:

- assets and liabilities are translated at the spot exchange rate at the reporting date;
- items of income and expense are translated at exchange rates at the dates of the relevant transactions, although appropriate average rates may be used;
- the resulting exchange differences are recognised in OCI and are presented within equity – generally referred to as the 'foreign currency translation reserve' or 'currency translation adjustment'; and
- cash flows are translated at exchange rates at the dates of the relevant transactions, although appropriate average rates may be used (see 2.3.80). [*IAS 7.26, 21.39–40, 44, 52*]

2.7.230.20   The objective of the translation approach is not to change the way in which underlying items are measured but to express the underlying amounts – as measured in the functional currency – in the different presentation currency. Accordingly, in our experience items of income and expense are determined by taking the amount recognised in functional currency and translating it at the actual or approximate spot exchange rate for the date on which the income or expense was recognised. This would be the case even when the income or expense arises from a foreign currency transaction (i.e. a transaction denominated in a currency other than the functional currency) that was measured in the functional currency using the exchange rate for an earlier date – e.g. when an entity receives advance consideration as specified in 2.7.90. [*IAS 21.21–22, 39(b), BC16, IFRIC 22.8–9*]

EXAMPLE 11 – TRANSLATION OF FOREIGN CURRENCY INCOME AND EXPENSE FROM FUNCTIONAL CURRENCY TO PRESENTATION CURRENCY

2.7.230.30   Company C's functional currency is FC and its presentation currency is PC. On 1 January 2018, C agrees to sell specified goods to Customer D at a price of PC 100. The following facts are also relevant for this example.

- Goods are to be delivered on 31 December 2018.
- D pays the price of PC 100 on 1 January 2018. This deposit is not refundable.
- C delivers the goods to D on 31 December 2018.
- The cost of the goods sold is FC 120.
- C applies the practical expedient in IFRS 15 (see 4.2.130) and does not adjust the consideration for a significant financing component.
- Relevant exchange rates are as follows.

	PC	FC
1 January 2018	1	1.5
Exchange rate at 31 December 2018	1	1.2

2.7.230.40   Although PC is C's presentation currency, the sale transaction is a foreign currency transaction because PC is not C's functional currency. C concludes that the advance consideration received gives rise to a non-monetary liability, which it measures in its functional currency at the exchange rate on 1 January 2018 – i.e. PC 100 x 1.5 = FC 150. Applying the guidance in 2.7.90, the date of the transaction for the purpose of measuring the revenue in C's functional currency is also 1 January 2018.

2.7.230.50   On 31 December 2018, C recognises the following income and expense in its functional currency. To present these amounts in its presentation currency, C translates them from its functional currency using the exchange rate at 31 December 2018.

	FC	RATE	PC
Revenue	150	1.2	125
Cost of sales	(120)	1.2	(100)
Gross profit	30		25

2.7.230.60   The resulting amounts in C's presentation currency reflect the functional-currency gross profit of FC 30 translated at the rate on the date it was recognised and maintain the relationship between revenue and cost of sales measured in the functional currency. If C had instead translated the revenue using the exchange rate on 1 January 2018 (i.e. as PC 100), then the functional-currency gross profit of FC 30 would effectively have been remeasured as a gross profit of nil in the presentation currency.

2.7.230.70   Although IFRS is not explicit on these points, in our view:
● capital transactions (e.g. dividends) should be translated at exchange rates at the dates of the relevant transactions; and
● components of equity should not be retranslated – i.e. each component of equity is translated once, at the exchange rates at the dates of the relevant transactions (see 2.7.260.10).

2.7.230.80   IFRS does not specifically discuss the exchange rate to be applied when reclassifying gains and losses from OCI to profit or loss – e.g. gains and losses reclassified from the cash flow hedge reserve. In our view, an entity should choose an accounting policy, to be applied consistently, to use one of the following approaches to translate reclassification adjustments into the presentation currency.
● *Historical rate approach:* Use the historical exchange rate used to measure the gain or loss when it was originally included in OCI. This approach views the transaction date as the date on which the gain or loss was first recognised and is consistent with the accumulated balance of OCI not being retranslated following initial recognition of the gain or loss (see 2.7.230.70).
● *Current rate approach:* Use the exchange rate at the date on which the gain or loss is reclassified from OCI to profit or loss, with the effect of any difference between this rate and the historical rate being included in retained earnings. This approach views the reclassification adjustment as a separate transaction giving rise to a new transaction date and the use of an updated exchange rate as better meeting the objective of reflecting the reclassification adjustment as measured in the functional currency.

EXAMPLE 12 – TRANSLATION OF RECLASSIFICATION ADJUSTMENT

2.7.230.90   Company E's functional currency (FC) is different from its presentation currency (PC). At 1 January 2017, E has an outstanding debt instrument denominated in PC in the amount of PC 100. Additionally, E generates some of its sales revenue in PC. Because PC is not the entity's functional currency, these are foreign currency transactions.

2.7.230.100   On 1 January 2017, E designated the PC 100 debt instrument as the hedging instrument in a cash flow hedge of foreign currency risk on highly probable forecast PC 100 sales that are expected to – and do – occur on 31 March 2018.

2.7.230.110   E translates the debt instrument into its functional currency as follows.

	PC	FC
1 January 2017	1	1.4
31 December 2017	1	2.0
Average exchange rate for 2017	1	2.0
31 March 2018	1	2.4
Average exchange rate for Q1 2018	1	2.4

	LIABILITY (PC)	RATE	LIABILITY (FC)	AOCI (FC)	AOCI (PC)
1 January 2017	100	1.4	140	0	0
31 December 2017	100	2.0	200	(60)	(30)
31 March 2018	100	2.4	240	(100)	(47)

2.7.230.120   On 31 December 2017, E retranslates the debt instrument into its functional currency equivalent of FC 200 (100 x 2.0) and recognises a translation loss of FC 60 (100 x (2.0 - 1.4)) in OCI. On 31 March 2018, E retranslates the debt instrument into the functional currency equivalent of FC 240 (100 x 2.4) and recognises a translation loss of FC 40 (100 x (2.4 - 2.0)) in OCI. At 31 March 2018, E has an accumulated balance of OCI in the cash flow hedge reserve of FC 100.

2.7.230.130   We believe that E should choose one of the approaches in 2.7.230.80 to determine the rate at which to translate the reclassification of the loss of FC 100 from OCI to profit or loss on 31 March 2018 when the hedged item affects profit or loss. The approach chosen impacts the amount of revenue that E presents in its presentation currency even though the cash flow hedge has mitigated foreign currency risk (see 4.1.15).

Historical rate approach

	RECLASSIFICATION ADJUSTMENT (FC)	RATE	RECLASSIFICATION ADJUSTMENT (PC)
31 December 2017	(60)	2.0	(30)
31 March 2018	(40)	2.4	(17)
Total	(100)		(47)

Revenue (presented in profit or loss)

	FC	RATE	PC
Revenue before hedge accounting	240	2.4	100
Reclassification from OCI	(100)	Historical	(47)
Revenue after hedge accounting	140	Mixed	53

2.7.230.140   Under the historical rate approach, E recognises revenue before hedging of PC 100 and translates the reclassification from OCI to profit or loss at PC 47, computed using the historical exchange rates at the date of the relevant transaction that were used to translate the losses and the balance in the cash flow hedge reserve (see 2.7.230.10 and 70). Therefore, E's revenue, net of hedging adjustments, is PC 53 under the historical rate approach.

Historical rate approach

	RECLASSIFICATION ADJUSTMENT (FC)	RATE	RECLASSIFICATION ADJUSTMENT (PC)
31 December 2017	(60)	2.0	(30)
31 March 2018	(40)	2.4	(17)
Total	(100)		(47)

Revenue (presented in profit or loss)

	FC	RATE	PC
Revenue before hedge accounting	240	2.4	100
Reclassification from OCI	(100)	Historical	(47)
Revenue after hedge accounting	140	Mixed	53

2.7.230.150 Under the current rate approach, E translates the reclassification of the hedging loss from OCI at the spot exchange rate on the date of reclassification. Accordingly, E presents a reclassification of PC 42 from OCI to profit or loss and makes an adjustment to retained earnings of PC 5 to reflect the elimination of the remaining balance in the cash flow hedge reserve. Under the current rate approach, E recognises revenue, net of hedging adjustments, of PC 58.

2.7.230.160 E's hedging strategy was to eliminate foreign exchange risk associated with the PC 100 revenues to be recognised on 31 March 2018 relative to the exchange rate of 1.40 when the hedging relationship was designated on 1 January 2017. Accordingly, net revenue in functional currency terms is measured at FC 140. The historical rate approach effectively translates the FC 140 into the presentation currency at different rates from different dates. However, the current rate approach results in translating the FC 140 into the presentation currency at the exchange rate on the date on which the revenue is recognised.

2.7.230.170 As stated in 2.7.230.20, translating capital transactions should be done using exchange rates at the dates of the relevant transactions. For practical reasons, in our view this may be approximated by use of an average of spot exchange rates, as used for the translation of income and expenses, if appropriate – e.g. for the translation of gains and losses on financial assets measured at fair value through OCI (see 2.7.240).

2.7.230.180 Goodwill and fair value acquisition accounting adjustments related to a foreign operation are treated as assets and liabilities of the foreign operation. In other words, they are considered to be expressed in the functional currency of the foreign operation and are translated at the exchange rate at the reporting date like other assets and liabilities. [*IAS 21.47*]

2.7.230.190 For the purpose of impairment testing, goodwill may be allocated to a CGU that is an operation with a functional currency different from that of the acquired foreign operation. In that case, in our view the entity should choose an accounting policy, to be applied consistently, to use either of the following approaches to denominating the goodwill for the purposes of translation into the presentation currency.
- *Denominate the goodwill in the functional currency of the acquired foreign operation:* The rationale for this approach is that the goodwill arose on the acquisition of the foreign operation.
- *Denominate the goodwill in the functional currency of the CGU to which it is allocated:* The rationale for this approach is that it is the cash flows generated by the CGU that support the continued recognition of the goodwill, and the allocation of goodwill to the CGU indicates that the goodwill is an asset of that CGU. [*IAS 21.47, BC29–BC31*]

2.7.230.200 The reporting date of a foreign operation that is a subsidiary, associate or joint venture may be before that of the parent (see 2.5.440 and 3.5.200). In that case, adjustments are made for significant movements in exchange rates – up to the reporting date of the parent – for group reporting purposes. [*IAS 21.46, 28.34, IFRS 10.B92–B93*]

2.7.240   **Using average exchange rates**

2.7.240.10   In determining whether average exchange rates may be used to translate income and expenses (and cash flows), in our view fluctuations in the exchange rate and the volume and size of transactions should be considered. For example, if the flow of transactions (by size and volume) is fairly stable over the period and exchange rates have not altered significantly, then it may be acceptable to update exchange rates only quarterly. In this case, the translated amounts for each quarter would be combined to obtain the annual total. However, at the other extreme, daily exchange rates might be used for an entity with complex operations in which there is an uneven flow of transactions, or if exchange rates are not stable. [*IAS 21.22*]

2.7.250   **Multiple exchange rates and lack of exchangeability**

2.7.250.10   As noted in 2.7.93, in some countries there are dual exchange rates: the official exchange rate and an unofficial parallel exchange rate. In our view, when a foreign operation operates in a dual exchange rate environment, subject to the considerations highlighted above, its financial statements should be translated using the rate applicable to dividends and capital repatriation because this is how the investment in the foreign operation will be recovered.

2.7.250.15   In our view, the determination of which rate to use in these circumstances may be a matter of judgement and the conclusion may change over time. For example, although an entity may legally apply to a government agency for foreign currency at the official rate for the purpose of paying dividends, it may also be able to effect dividends or capital repayments through parallel market transactions. We believe an entity should consider all relevant facts and circumstances in determining what is the more appropriate rate to use for the purposes of translation, including:

- practical difficulties, uncertainties or delays associated with applying for foreign currency at the official rate;
- whether an entity would plan to remit a dividend or repayment of the net investment through an application for funds at the official rate or through parallel market transactions;
- past and current practice in relation to the remittance of dividends or capital; and
- the ability to source funds for dividend or capital repayments through parallel market transactions.

2.7.250.20   An entity discloses judgements that management makes in applying the entity's accounting policies that have the most significant effects on the amounts recognised in the financial statements. This may include the judgements made and the reasons for selecting one specific foreign exchange rate rather than another when more than one foreign exchange rate exists. In our view, the financial statements should disclose the reasons for not applying an official exchange rate as well as information about the rate used, if a rate other than the official rate has been used. [*IAS 1.122*]

2.7.260   **Foreign currency translation reserve**

2.7.260.10   The net exchange difference that is recognised in the foreign currency translation reserve in each period represents the following.

- In respect of income, expenses and capital transactions, the difference between translating these items at actual or average spot exchange rates, and using the spot exchange rate at the reporting date.

- In respect of the opening balance of equity, the difference between translating the balance at the spot exchange rate used at the previous reporting date, and using the rate at the current reporting date. [*IAS 21.41*]

2.7.260.20   The proof of the foreign currency translation reserve is illustrated in Example 15.

2.7.260.30   In addition, the foreign currency translation reserve may include exchange differences arising from loans that form part of an entity's net investment in a foreign operation (see 2.7.150) and gains and losses related to hedges of a net investment in a foreign operation (see 7.9.210 and 7I.7.90).

2.7.260.40   In some cases, the foreign currency translation reserve may have a debit balance. A debit balance on the reserve is not reclassified to profit or loss simply because it represents a 'loss'. It is reclassified to profit or loss only on disposal of the foreign operation (see 2.7.340).

2.7.260.50   When there is an NCI in a foreign operation subsidiary, the amount of accumulated exchange differences attributable to the NCI is allocated to and recognised as part of the NCI. [*IAS 21.41, IFRS 10.B94*]

2.7.270   Hyperinflation

2.7.270.10   The functional currency of a foreign operation may be the currency of a hyperinflationary economy. In that case, the foreign operation's financial statements are first restated into the measuring unit current at the reporting date. This does not apply for the comparative amounts if the group's presentation currency is not the currency of a hyperinflationary economy. All amounts in the financial statements (excluding the comparatives noted above) are then translated using the exchange rate at the current reporting date. [*IAS 21.42–43, 29.8*]

2.7.270.20   If the financial statements of a hyperinflationary foreign operation are translated into the currency of a non-hyperinflationary economy, then the comparative amounts are not adjusted for changes in the price level or exchange rate since the relevant comparative reporting date. In other words, the comparatives are those previously presented. [*IAS 21.42*]

EXAMPLE 13 – TRANSLATION OF FINANCIAL STATEMENTS OF HYPERINFLATIONARY FOREIGN OPERATION

2.7.270.30   Company X prepares financial statements as at and for the year ending 31 December 2018 with comparative information as at and for the year ended 31 December 2017.

2.7.270.40   If the functional currency and presentation currency are the currencies of hyperinflationary economies, then the 2017 and 2018 financial statements are restated to be presented in the measuring unit current at 31 December 2018. Accordingly, the relevant exchange rate at 31 December 2018 is applied in translating the financial information for both years.

> 2.7.270.50   However, if the presentation currency is not the currency of a hyperinflationary economy but the functional currency is the currency of a hyperinflationary economy, then the 2018 financial statements are restated in terms of the measuring unit current at 31 December 2018, and translated using the exchange rate at 31 December 2018. The 2017 comparative amounts, however, remain unchanged and are presented as they were in 2017 – i.e. they reflect the measuring unit and exchange rates at 31 December 2017.

2.7.270.60   If the presentation currency is a non-hyperinflationary currency, then the approach described in 2.7.270.10–50 leads to changes in the equity of the foreign operation during the current period as a result of adjusting non-monetary assets and liabilities and equity balances for hyperinflation under IAS 29. In addition, there are changes in equity in respect of the translation of all IAS 29 restated amounts in the financial statements to the closing exchange rate. The standards are not clear on how these changes should be presented in these circumstances. In the absence of any specific guidance and considering the economic inter-relationship between inflation and exchange rates, in our view an entity may use one of following approaches, which should be applied consistently.

APPROACH	DESCRIPTION	RATIONALE
Approach 1	Present the entire amount of these changes as an adjustment to equity in the statement of changes in equity.	The changes in equity result from changes in the measuring unit applied to the net investment in the foreign operation. IAS 29 does not view these changes as giving rise to gains or losses, but instead treats them as adjustments to the corresponding equity balances. [*IAS 29.25*]
Approach 2	Present the entire amount of these changes in OCI and accumulate them in a separate component of equity.	The changes in equity arise on retranslation of the financial statements of a foreign operation and should be presented in the same way as for a foreign operation whose functional currency is not hyperinflationary. Accordingly, on disposal of the foreign operation, the accumulated amount of the adjustments should be reclassified to profit or loss. [*IAS 21.39, 48*]
Approach 3	Present the component arising from reflecting changes in the price level under IAS 29 as an adjustment to equity (as under Approach 1) and the component arising from changes in the foreign exchange rate used for translation in OCI (as under Approach 2).	The changes in equity are the result of two economically linked events, the remeasurement under IAS 29 and the retranslation under IAS 21, which are presented separately.

2.7.270.70   The gain or loss on the net monetary position of the foreign operation is recognised in profit or loss in accordance with IAS 29 regardless of the approach followed (see 2.7.270.60). [*IAS 29.28*]

EXAMPLE 14 – CHANGES IN EQUITY ARISING FROM HYPERINFLATIONARY FOREIGN OPERATION PRESENTED IN NON-HYPERINFLATIONARY CURRENCY

2.7.270.80   Company X, whose presentation currency of PC is not hyperinflationary, has a wholly owned Foreign Subsidiary Y, whose functional currency of FC is hyperinflationary. In December 2017, Y issued shares and bought land for 200. During 2018, Y undertakes no transactions. Over the same period, the general price index of the economy in which Y operates increases by 50%. The following facts are also relevant for this example.

Exchange rate at:	FC	PC
31 December 2017	1.0	0.5
31 December 2018	1.0	0.25

General price index of the economy in which Y operates at:	
31 December 2017	100
31 December 2018	150

Extract from Y's statement of financial position

	HISTORICAL PURCHASING POWER (FC)	IAS 29 INFLATION ADJUST- MENT	RESTATED IN ACCORDANCE WITH IAS 29 (FC)	EXCHANGE RATE	RESTATED IN ACCORDANCE WITH IAS 29 (PC)
December 2017					
Land	200	100 / 100	200	0.5	100
Share capital	200	100 / 100	200	0.5	100
December 2018					
Land	200	150 / 100	300	0.25	75
Share capital	200	150 / 100	300	0.25	75

2.7.270.90   In Y's 2017 financial statements, presented in FC, the land and share capital are reported at FC 200. In Y's 2018 financial statements, presented in FC, the carrying amounts of the land and of share capital are each restated to FC 300 in the statement of financial position at both 31 December 2017 and 31 December 2018 and no gain or loss or other movement in equity is reported in 2018.

2.7.270.100   However, from the perspective of X's consolidated financial statements presented in PC, comparative information is not changed and hence the net investment in Y has decreased by PC 25 during 2018 from PC 100 at 31 December 2017 to PC 75 at 31 December 2018. X determines that this net decrease results from:

- the change in the FC price level during 2018 – an increase of PC 25 (i.e. increase of FC 100 in the carrying amount of the land and share capital translated at the closing exchange rate of 0.25); and
- the change in the PC:FC exchange rate – a decrease of PC 50 (i.e. effect of translating the opening balance of FC 200 at a closing rate of 0.25 compared with the opening rate of 0.5).

2.7.270.110   X applies Approach 3 in 2.7.270.60 for presenting changes in the equity of Y, and presents the following amounts in its 2018 financial statements.

OTHER COMPREHENSIVE INCOME	
Exchange difference (loss)	50
STATEMENT OF CHANGES IN EQUITY	
IAS 29 hyperinflation adjustment (credit)	(25)

2.7.270.120   For a discussion of the accounting treatment of hyperinflation, see chapter 2.10.

2.7.280   **Worked example**

EXAMPLE 15 – TRANSLATION OF FINANCIAL STATEMENTS OF FOREIGN OPERATION – COMPREHENSIVE EXAMPLE

2.7.280.10   As a result of the process of translating the financial statements of a foreign operation, the exchange difference recognised in the foreign currency translation reserve is a balancing figure; however, the amount can be proved, which is illustrated in this example. In addition, an exchange difference will arise in reconciling the opening and closing balances of the various assets and liabilities. The proof of these exchange differences is illustrated in 2.7.280.60 using property, plant and equipment as an example.

2.7.280.20   Subsidiary S was acquired on 1 January 2017. To simplify the example, assume that no goodwill or fair value adjustments arose in the business combination. Income and expenses since acquisition have been translated using annual average exchange rates (see 2.7.240). No dividends have been paid since acquisition. S's functional currency is FC; the group's presentation currency is PC.

	FC	PC
Exchange rate at 1 January 2017	1.0	1.0
Average exchange rate during 2017	1.0	1.25
Exchange rate at 31 December 2017	1.0	1.5
Average exchange rate during 2018	1.0	2.0
Exchange rate at 31 December 2018	1.0	2.5

The above rates are illustrative only and are not intended to indicate hyperinflation.

S's statement of financial position – 31 December 2018

	FC	RATE	PC	
Share capital	400	1.0	400	
Retained earnings – at acquisition	2,200	1.0	2,200	
Earnings of 2017 that were retained	900	1.25	1,125	
Net profit for the year – 2018	1,300		2,600	
Foreign currency translation reserve	-		5,675	(see 2.7.280.30)
Equity	4,800		12,000	
Property, plant and equipment	2,800	2.5	7,000	
Other assets and liabilities	2,000	2.5	5,000	
Net assets	4,800		12,000	

S's statement of profit or loss and OCI – 2018

	FC	RATE	PC	
Revenue	2,000	2.0	4,000	
Depreciation	(200)	2.0	(400)	
Other expenses	(500)	2.0	(1,000)	
Net profit for the year – 2018	1,300		2,600	
OCI				
Exchange difference on translating foreign operations – 2018	-		4,150	(see 2.7.280.45)
Total comprehensive income for the year	1,300		6,750	

2.7.280.30   The proof of the foreign currency translation reserve is demonstrated by taking the difference between the actual exchange rate used to translate each component of equity (i.e. the amount in FC recognised in the statement of financial position) and the closing exchange rate, and multiplying this by the balance of the item in FC. The proof of the translation reserve is a theoretical proof because each equity component is not actually retranslated to the closing exchange rate when presented in the consolidated financial statements.

Proof of foreign currency translation reserve

	ACTUAL RATE	CLOSING RATE	RATE DIFFERENCE	AMOUNT IN FC	DIFFERENCE IN PC
Share capital	1.0	2.5	1.5	400	600
Retained earnings – at acquisition	1.0	2.5	1.5	2,200	3,300
Earnings of 2017 that were retained	1.25	2.5	1.25	900	1,125
Net profit for the year – 2018	2.0	2.5	0.5	1,300	650
Translation reserve (accumulated)					5,675

2.7.280.40   Although the proof in this example is on a cumulative basis, in our experience the proof would be done on an annual basis.

2.7.280.45   The following proof of the change in the foreign currency translation reserve during 2018 is provided. This change is calculated based on the opening and closing exchange rates for balances that are brought forward from previous reporting periods and on the actual and the closing exchange rates for transactions that took place during 2018.

Proof of exchange difference – 2018

	OPENING OR ACTUAL RATE	CLOSING RATE	RATE DIFFERENCE	AMOUNT IN FC	DIFFERENCE IN PC
Share capital	1.5	2.5	1.0	400	400
Retained earnings – at acquisition	1.5	2.5	1.0	2,200	2,200
Earnings of 2017 that were retained	1.5	2.5	1.0	900	900
Net profit for the year – 2018	2.0	2.5	0.5	1,300	650
Translation reserve					4,150

2.7.280.50   The reconciliation of property, plant and equipment for 2018 will be disclosed as follows in the consolidated financial statements (assuming no additions or disposals). [*IAS 16.73*]

Property, plant and equipment – 2018	PC
Opening balance	4,500[1]
Depreciation	(400)[2]
Foreign exchange difference	2,900[3]
Closing balance	7,000

Notes
1.   Calculated as ((FC 2,800 + FC 200) x 1.5).
2.   Calculated as (FC 200 x 2).
3.   Proof of exchange difference calculation is shown below.

2.7.280.60   The proof of the exchange difference in the reconciliation of property, plant and equipment is demonstrated by taking the difference between the actual exchange rates used to translate each item and the closing exchange rate, and multiplying this by the amount of each item in FC.

Proof of exchange difference	ACTUAL RATE	CLOSING RATE	RATE DIFFERENCE	AMOUNT IN FC	DIFFERENCE IN PC
Opening balance	1.5	2.5	1.0	3,000	3,000
Current-year depreciation	2.0	2.5	0.5	(200)	(100)
Exchange difference					2,900

2.7.290   TRANSLATION FROM FUNCTIONAL TO PRESENTATION CURRENCY

2.7.300   General requirements

2.7.300.10   If an entity presents its financial statements in a presentation currency that is different from its functional currency, then the translation procedures are the same as those for translating foreign operations (see 2.7.230). [*IAS 21.39*]

2.7.300.20   The standard does not provide specific guidance on the translation of components of equity, other than in respect of the current year's income and expense.

2.7.300.30   In our view, the method of translation to any presentation currency should be consistent with the translation of a foreign operation for consolidation purposes. Therefore, after the initial translation into the presentation currency, components of equity at the reporting date should not be retranslated.

EXAMPLE 16 – TRANSLATION FROM FUNCTIONAL CURRENCY TO PRESENTATION CURRENCY

2.7.300.40   This example is similar to Example 15, which illustrates the translation of foreign operations. The functional currency of Company D is FC; however, the financial statements will be presented in presentation currency (PC). Income and expenses have been translated using an annual average exchange rate (see 2.7.240).

	FC	PC
Exchange rate at 31 December 2017	1.0	1.5
Average exchange rate during 2018	1.0	2.0
Exchange rate at 31 December 2018	1.0	2.5
Historical exchange rate used for opening retained earnings and share capital	1.0	1.0

Statement of financial position – 31 December 2018

	FC	RATE	PC
Share capital	400	1.0	400
Opening retained earnings	3,100	1.0	3,100
Net profit for the year – 2018	1,300		2,600
Foreign currency translation reserve	-		5,900[(1)]
Equity	4,800		12,000
Property, plant and equipment	2,800	2.5	7,000
Other assets and liabilities	2,000	2.5	5,000
Net assets	4,800		12,000

Statement of profit or loss and OCI – 2018

	FC		PC
Revenue	2,000	2.0	4,000
Depreciation	(200)	2.0	(400)
Other expenses	(500)	2.0	(1,000)
Net profit for the year	1,300		2,600
OCI			
Exchange differences on translation	-		4,150[(2)]
Total comprehensive income for the year	1,300		6,750

2.7.300.50   The proof of the foreign currency translation reserve is demonstrated by taking the difference between the actual exchange rate used to translate an item and the closing exchange rate, and multiplying this by the balance of the item in FC.

Proof of foreign currency translation reserve – 2018

	ACTUAL RATE	CLOSING RATE	RATE DIFFERENCE	AMOUNT IN FC	DIFFERENCE IN PC
Share capital	1.0	2.5	1.5	400	600
Opening retained earnings	1.0	2.5	1.5	3,100	4,650
Net profit for the year – 2018	2.0	2.5	0.5	1,300	650
Cumulative translation reserve					5,900

2.7.300.60   The following proof of exchange differences recognised in OCI and of the change in the foreign currency translation reserve during 2018 is provided. This change is calculated based on the opening and closing exchange rates for balances that are brought forward from previous reporting periods and on the actual and the closing exchange rates for transactions that took place during 2018.

Proof of exchange difference – 2018

	OPENING OR ACTUAL RATE	CLOSING RATE	RATE DIFFERENCE	AMOUNT IN FC	DIFFERENCE IN PC
Share capital	1.5	2.5	1.0	400	400
Opening retained earnings	1.5	2.5	1.0	3,100	3,100
Net profit for the year – 2018	2.0	2.5	0.5	1,300	650
Translation reserve					4,150

2.7.310   Hyperinflation

2.7.310.10   If both the entity's functional and presentation currencies are currencies of hyperinflationary economies, then all items in the financial statements (current period and comparatives) are translated into the presentation currency at the closing rate at the end of the most recent period presented after being restated for the effects of inflation. [*IAS 21.42–43*]

2.7.310.20   However, when the entity's functional currency is the currency of a hyperinflationary economy and its financial statements are to be translated into a presentation currency that is not the currency of a hyperinflationary economy, only the current period's amounts are remeasured for the effects of inflation in the current period, and then translated at the exchange rate at the reporting date. In this case, comparative amounts are not adjusted for changes in the price level or exchange rate during the current period – i.e. the comparatives reported as current in prior year financial statements are presented as they were previously (see illustration and discussion in 2.7.270.30–110). [*IAS 21.42*]

2.7.320   CHANGES IN FUNCTIONAL CURRENCY

2.7.320.10   Once an entity has determined its functional currency, it is not changed unless there is a change in the relevant underlying transactions, events and circumstances. If circumstances change and a change in functional currency is appropriate, then the change is accounted for prospectively from the date of the change. However, a prospective change triggers an issue with respect to the comparative financial information. [*IAS 21.13, 35–37*]

EXAMPLE 17 – CHANGE IN FUNCTIONAL CURRENCY

2.7.320.20   Company K incorporated in the UK with a 31 December year end had the euro as its functional and presentation currency until the end of 2017. From the beginning of 2018, the focus of K's operations changed and the appropriate functional currency is determined to be sterling going forward. Additionally, K changes its presentation currency to sterling.

2.7.320.30   At 1 January 2018, the financial position is translated from euro into sterling using the exchange rate at that date. From 2018, the financial statements will be prepared with any non-sterling transactions translated following the requirements for foreign currency transactions (see 2.7.80).

2.7.320.40   In our view, K should choose an accounting policy, to be applied consistently, to present the 2017 comparative information under either of the following approaches.
● The 2017 comparatives should be translated from euro – which is the functional currency for that period – into sterling using the amounts determined under the new functional currency as at 1 January 2018. Therefore, all comparative information will be translated at the exchange rate as at 1 January 2018. This is consistent with reflecting the change in functional currency prospectively from that date.

- The 2017 comparatives should be translated from the euro into sterling using the methodology specified in 2.7.290 in respect of the translation of financial statements from an entity's functional currency to its presentation currency – i.e. using appropriate 2017 exchange rates. This is consistent with the methodology applied on a change in presentation currency (see 2.7.330).

2.7.320.50   If, in this example, there is no change to the presentation currency (i.e. K's presentation currency is euro for both 2017 and 2018), then translation of comparative amounts into the new functional currency using the procedures that apply for translation into a different presentation currency (see 2.7.290) would allow K to avoid restatement of its comparatives – i.e. there would be no change in the 2017 comparatives presented in euro.

2.7.320.60   In our view, these procedures would apply equally when the legal currency of a country is changed. For example, on 1 January 2011 the legal currency in Estonia changed from the Estonian kroon to the euro.

2.7.330   CHANGES IN PRESENTATION CURRENCY

2.7.330.10   The same presentation currency is used for all periods presented. Generally, if an entity changes its presentation currency, then it presents its financial statements, including comparative amounts, as if the new presentation currency had always been the entity's presentation currency. The presentation of comparative information when there is a change in presentation currency connected with a change in functional currency is discussed in 2.7.320. In our view, the translation of comparative information into a new presentation currency is a change that would require, in accordance with IAS 1, presentation of a third statement of financial position as at the beginning of the preceding period presented when such information is considered material (see 2.1.20). [*IAS 1.40A–42, 46*]

2.7.330.20   The new presentation currency may differ from the reporting entity's functional currency or a foreign operation's functional currency. In such cases, adjusting comparative amounts retrospectively is achieved by translating comparatives in the functional currency to the presentation currency, based on the method described in 2.7.230 and 300.30 (unless the functional currency is hyperinflationary). Following this method, translating assets and liabilities, items of income and expense, and cash flows is relatively straightforward.
- Assets and liabilities are translated based on the exchange rate at the comparative reporting date.
- Items of income and expense, capital transactions and cash flows relating to transactions in a previous period are translated using the exchange rate prevailing at the transaction date or at an appropriate average rate (see 2.7.230.10). [*IAS 21.39*]

2.7.330.30   However, complexities may arise when translating components of equity because, in our view, such components are only translated once at the exchange rates at the dates of the relevant transactions (see 2.7.230.70). Therefore, retrospective application may require identification of the transactions that gave rise to the equity component and the historical rates applicable to these transactions. This may be especially relevant for equity components that have been accumulated over time, such as retained earnings.

DISPOSAL OF FOREIGN OPERATION

2.7.340.05   The following decision tree outlines the principles that apply to reclassification of the foreign currency translation reserve on disposal or partial disposal of a foreign operation.

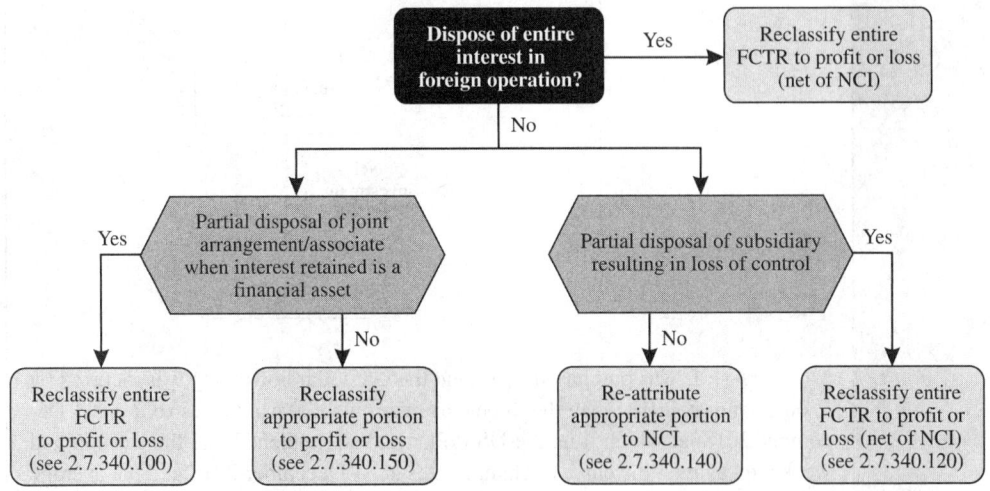

2.7.340.10   The cumulative exchange differences related to a foreign operation that have been included in the foreign currency translation reserve are reclassified to profit or loss when the foreign operation is disposed of. A disposal may arise, for example, through sale, liquidation or repayment of share capital. The standard does not specify in which line item this amount is included. In our experience, it is typically included as part of the gain or loss on the disposal. [*IAS 21.48–49*]

2.7.340.20   The cumulative exchange differences recorded and therefore subject to reclassification in respect of an individual foreign operation are affected by whether the entity uses the direct or step-by-step method of consolidation (see 2.7.60.10). However, if an entity uses the step-by-step method of consolidation, then it may adopt an accounting policy of determining the amount to be reclassified as if it had applied the direct method of consolidation to translate the financial statements of the foreign operation into the functional currency of the ultimate parent. [*IFRIC 16.17*]

EXAMPLE 18 – FOREIGN CURRENCY TRANSLATION RESERVE – EFFECT OF CONSOLIDATION METHOD ON RECLASSIFICATION

2.7.340.30   A group consists of Parent P with a euro functional currency, Intermediate Subsidiary B with a sterling functional currency, and Subsidiary C with a US dollar functional currency. B has a net investment in C of USD 300. The amount of the net investment remains the same in US dollar terms throughout its life. P has borrowed USD 300, which is designated as a hedge of the group's US dollar net investment in C against euro. The hedge is based on spot rates and has been fully effective throughout.

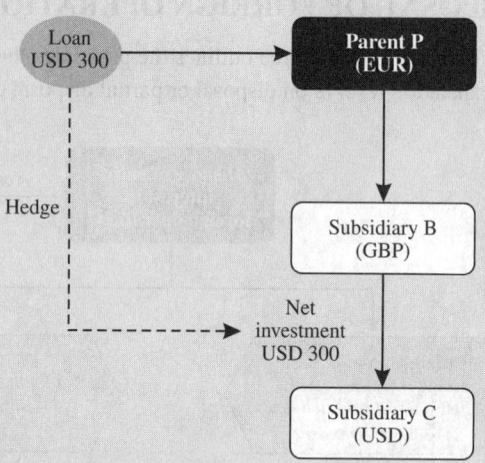

2.7.340.40 C was purchased by B, and the US dollar borrowing was incurred by P, on 1 January 2018 when the three currencies were at par. C was sold on 31 December 2018, at which time the US dollar had strengthened and the sterling had weakened against the euro. Exchange rates at 31 December 2018 and the average rates for the year then ended were as follows.

> USD 1 = EUR 1.25 = GBP 1.5 or
> GBP 1 = USD 0.67 = EUR 0.83

2.7.340.50 In its separate financial statements, P recognises a foreign exchange loss of EUR 75 ((300 x 1.25) - 300) on its US dollar liability. In P's consolidated financial statements, this is reclassified from profit or loss to the foreign currency translation reserve.

2.7.340.60 If P had used the direct consolidation method, then a corresponding foreign exchange gain of EUR 75 would have been recognised in the foreign currency translation reserve as a result of retranslating the USD 300 net investment into euro.

2.7.340.70 However, P has used the step-by-step consolidation method. B has first consolidated C, and recognises a foreign exchange gain in its foreign currency translation reserve of GBP 150 ((300 x 1.5) - 300). This is translated at the rate of 0.83 into euro, so that P Group's foreign currency translation reserve with respect to its net investment in C consists of:
- EUR 75 loss on the hedging instrument; and
- EUR 125 (150 x 0.83) gain recognised by B on B's net investment in C.

2.7.340.80 When P consolidates B, B's net assets, including B's net investment in C, are translated at the closing exchange rate from sterling into euro. This gives rise to a foreign exchange loss of EUR 50 ((300 x 0.83) - 300), which because of the consolidation method, is treated as part of the foreign currency translation reserve related to B Group.

2.7.340.90   On disposal of C, P may simply reclassify the net EUR 50 (125 - 75) gain to profit or loss that is presented in its foreign currency translation reserve related to C. Alternatively, it may additionally reclassify the loss of EUR 50 that relates indirectly to the net assets of C but was treated as part of the foreign currency translation reserve related to P's investment in B, as if it had applied the direct consolidation method. The second method better reflects the economic effect of the hedge transaction, which was designed to eliminate the effect of the exchange differences on the group's US dollar net investment in C.

2.7.340.100   In addition to the disposal of an entity's entire interest in a foreign operation, the following partial disposals are accounted for as disposals even if the entity retains an interest in the former subsidiary, associate or joint arrangement:

- if an entity loses control of a subsidiary that includes a foreign operation, regardless of whether the entity retains a non-controlling interest in its former subsidiary after the partial disposal; and
- if the retained interest after the partial disposal of an interest in a joint arrangement or an associate that includes a foreign operation is a financial asset – i.e. if the entity retains neither joint control nor significant influence. [*IAS 21.48A, BC36–BC40*]

2.7.340.110   For example, Parent P owns 100% of Subsidiary S, a foreign operation. P sells 60% of its investment and loses control of S. Therefore, the entire balance in the foreign currency translation reserve in respect of S is reclassified to profit or loss.

2.7.340.120   On disposal of a subsidiary that includes a foreign operation, the cumulative amount of the exchange differences related to that foreign operation that have been attributed to the NCI forms part of the NCI that is derecognised and is included in the calculation of the gain or loss on disposal, but it is not reclassified to profit or loss. [*IAS 21.48B*]

EXAMPLE 19 – FOREIGN CURRENCY TRANSLATION RESERVE – DISPOSAL OF SUBSIDIARY

2.7.340.125   Parent P acquired 90% of Subsidiary S that includes a foreign operation some years ago. P now sells its entire investment in S for 1,500. The following facts are also relevant for this example.

	S's TOTAL	P's SHARE: 90%	NCI: 10%
Net assets	1,000	900	100
Foreign currency translation reserve	200	180	20

> **2.7.340.127** P's gain on disposal would be calculated in the following manner.
>
> | | |
> |---|---:|
> | Sale proceeds | 1,500 |
> | Net assets of S | (1,000) |
> | NCI derecognised | 100 |
> | Foreign currency translation reserve | 180 |
> | Gain on disposal | 780 |

2.7.340.130 When a parent loses control of a subsidiary by contributing it to an associate or a joint venture, there is some ambiguity in IFRS on how the gain or loss on the loss of control should be calculated (see 2.5.810). If the entity applies the IFRS 10 approach and recognises the gain or loss in full in profit or loss, then the components of OCI of the former subsidiary are also reclassified in full as described in 2.7.340.120. If the entity applies the IAS 28 approach and eliminates a part of the gain or loss in respect of the continuing interest in the assets and liabilities contributed, then in our view the components of OCI of the former subsidiary should not be reclassified in full, but instead should be reclassified on a proportionate basis (see also 3.5.470.80).

2.7.340.140 Reductions in an entity's ownership interest in a foreign operation, except for those reductions described in 2.7.340.100, are regarded as partial disposals. In the case of the partial disposal of a subsidiary that includes a foreign operation, the entity re-attributes the proportionate share of the cumulative amount of the exchange differences recognised in OCI to the NCI in that foreign operation. For example, Parent P owns 100 percent of Subsidiary S that includes a foreign operation. P sells 20 percent of its investment and retains control over S. Therefore, 20 percent of the balance in the foreign currency translation reserve is reclassified to NCI. [*IAS 21.48C–48D*]

2.7.340.150 In any other partial disposal of a foreign operation, the entity reclassifies to profit or loss only the proportionate share of the cumulative amount of the exchange differences recognised in OCI. For example, Parent P owns 30 percent of Associate B that includes a foreign operation. P sells a 5 percent stake and retains significant influence over B. Therefore, one-sixth of the balance in the foreign currency translation reserve is reclassified to profit or loss. [*IAS 21.48C*]

2.7.350 Repayment of intra-group loans

2.7.350.10 A reporting entity may make a loan to a foreign operation that is classified as part of its net investment such that exchange differences on the loan are recognised in the foreign currency translation reserve (see 2.7.260). IFRS is silent on whether repayment of an inter-company loan forming part of the net investment is a partial disposal. In our view, an entity should choose an accounting policy, to be applied consistently, on whether repayment of an inter-company loan forming part of the net investment in a foreign operation is considered a partial disposal. We prefer that such a repayment not be considered a partial disposal because it does not change the percentage share interest held by the reporting entity. However, given historical practice, the definition of 'net investment' and its similarity to 'ownership interest', and the IASB's view that such loans are treated similarly to equity investments, an accounting policy that treats such repayments as partial disposals is also acceptable. [*IAS 21.8, 48D, BC25D*]

2.7.350.20   If an entity elects to treat repayment of a long-term inter-company loan forming part of the net investment as a partial disposal, then in our view the principles noted in 2.7.340.140 and 150 should be applied.

- *Loan to a subsidiary:* There would be no reclassification to profit or loss, only a re-attribution between the foreign currency translation reserve of the entity and NCI. However, if the subsidiary is wholly owned and there is no NCI, then no amount is re-attributed.
- *Loan to an associate or joint arrangement:* The proportionate share of the foreign currency translation reserve of the entity is reclassified to profit or loss. [*IAS 21.48C, 49*]

2.7.350.30   In our view, an entity should also consider whether the repayment of a loan results in substance in a liquidation of a subsidiary and a full disposal (see 2.7.360.30). [*IAS 21.49*]

EXAMPLE 20 – REPAYMENT OF LOAN FORMING PART OF NET INVESTMENT

2.7.350.40   Company P subscribed 100 in return for a 25% interest in Associate B, and extended 'permanent' funding of a further 50 at the same time. If B repays the loan of 50 and P's accounting policy is to treat repayment of a loan forming part of the net investment as a partial disposal, then we believe that one-third of the balance in the foreign currency translation reserve should be reclassified to profit or loss.

2.7.350.50   If P had extended the permanent funding sometime after the original investment, then we believe that the amount to be reclassified to profit or loss should be one-third of the change in the balance of the foreign currency translation reserve that arose while the funding was outstanding.

2.7.350.60   Alternatively, if P had tracked the actual foreign exchange differences arising on the permanent funding, then we believe that it would be acceptable for P to reclassify to profit or loss these actual foreign exchange differences that had been previously recognised in OCI.

2.7.360   Impairment, restructuring and liquidation

2.7.360.10   In the event of a write-down of the carrying amount of a foreign operation, either because of its own losses or because of an impairment recognised by the investor, the standard is clear that this does not constitute a partial disposal. Consequently, no amount of the foreign currency translation reserve is reclassified to profit or loss. [*IAS 21.49*]

2.7.360.20   In our view, a major restructuring that results in reducing the scale of operations of a foreign operation does not in itself trigger reclassification to profit or loss of any amount of the foreign currency translation reserve because the operations have not substantively ceased and the parent has not realised its investment in the foreign operation.

2.7.360.30   However, an entity may dispose of its interest in a foreign operation through liquidation or abandonment, including through sale of the business and assets of a foreign operation that was contained within a subsidiary. In our view, the substantive liquidation of a foreign operation should be treated as a disposal. For example, if an entity sells or abandons the business and assets of a foreign operation such that the operation is no longer active and the entity has no immediate plan to recommence activities, then the foreign operation has been in substance liquidated. The entity should treat such cases as a disposal of the foreign operation, even if the formal process of liquidating the legal body in which the foreign operation was carried on has not occurred and the entity continues to own all the equity interests in that legal body. In our view, determining whether a foreign operation has been in substance liquidated may involve judgement based on the specific facts and circumstances. [*IAS 21.49*]

2.7.370   DISPOSAL OF NON-FOREIGN OPERATIONS

2.7.370.10   IFRS is silent on the accounting for exchange differences on a disposal of a non-foreign operation if the group presentation currency is not the same as the parent's functional currency. For example, a German parent that presents its consolidated financial statements in US dollars but whose functional currency is the euro disposes of its entire interest in a directly owned German subsidiary whose functional currency is also the euro.

2.7.370.20   If the method used to prepare consolidated financial statements in US dollars was first to consolidate the financial statements of the subsidiary in euro and then second to translate these consolidated euro amounts into US dollars, then no exchange differences in respect of the subsidiary would be separately accumulated in the parent's consolidated financial statements. However, if the financial statements of the subsidiary had been directly translated into the presentation currency, then exchange differences would have been separately accumulated in respect of the subsidiary. In our view, no reclassification of these differences in respect of the subsidiary is required or permitted in the parent's consolidated financial statements because the subsidiary was not a foreign operation. [*IAS 21.8, BC18–BC20*]

2.7.380   CONVENIENCE TRANSLATIONS

2.7.380.10   A convenience translation occurs when an entity decides to present financial statements in addition to the financial statements required to be presented in accordance with IFRS. For example, an entity has a functional currency of Danish krone and a presentation currency of euro; in addition, it wishes to show US dollar figures for the most recent year's primary financial statements, but it will not publish a full set of US dollar financial statements. [*IAS 21.BC14*]

2.7.380.20   There is a difference between a convenience translation and a translation to the presentation currency. An entity that presents its financial statements in a currency or currencies that are different from its functional currency describes the financial statements as complying with IFRS only if they comply with the translation method as set out in IAS 21. If an entity displays its financial statements or other financial information in a currency that is different from either its functional currency or its presentation currency and does not comply with the translation method set out under IAS 21, then it needs to provide disclosures – e.g. that the information in the convenience translation is supplementary, what the convenience currency is, and the functional currency and the method of translation used. A convenience translation may be used only for selected information and is provided only as supplemental information (see chapter 5.8). [*IAS 21.39, 42, 55, 57*]

2.8 Accounting policies, errors and estimates

2.8   Accounting policies, errors and estimates

CURRENTLY EFFECTIVE REQUIREMENTS

This publication reflects IFRS in issue at 1 August 2018, and the currently effective requirements cover annual periods beginning on 1 January 2018.

The requirements related to this topic are mainly derived from the following.

STANDARD	TITLE
IAS 1	Presentation of Financial Statements
IAS 8	Accounting Policies, Changes in Accounting Estimates and Errors

FORTHCOMING REQUIREMENTS

The currently effective requirements are affected by the following forthcoming requirements. They are highlighted with a # and the impact is explained in the accompanying boxed text at the references indicated.

- In May 2017, the IASB issued IFRS 17 *Insurance Contracts*, which is effective for annual periods beginning on or after 1 January 2021. See 2.8.35. IFRS 17 is the subject of chapter 8.1A.
- In March 2018, the IASB issued *Amendments to References to the Conceptual Framework in IFRS Standards*, which is effective for annual period beginning on or after 1 January 2020. See 2.8.25. The Conceptual Framework is the subject of chapter 1.2.

FUTURE DEVELOPMENTS

The currently effective requirements that may be affected by future developments are highlighted with a * and are briefly discussed in 2.8.150.

2.8.10   # SELECTION AND APPLICATION OF ACCOUNTING POLICIES*

2.8.10.10   Accounting policies are the specific principles, bases, conventions, rules and practices that an entity applies in preparing and presenting financial statements. [*IAS 8.5*]

2.8.10.20   For a discussion of the selection of accounting policies by an entity applying IFRS for the first time, see 6.1.170.

2.8.20   ## Hierarchy of accounting policy sources#

2.8.20.10   If an issue is specifically addressed by an IFRS, then an entity applies the accounting policy or policies required by that IFRS to that issue. [*IAS 8.7*]

2.8.20.20   If IFRS does not cover a particular issue, then management uses its judgement in developing and applying an accounting policy that results in information that is reliable and relevant to the economic decisions of users. There is a hierarchy of accounting literature to be used in arriving at the policy selected, which provides entities with a basic structure for resolving issues in the absence of specific guidance. [*IAS 8.10–12*]

2.8.20.30   If IFRS does not cover a particular issue, then an entity considers:
- in the first instance, the guidance and requirements in standards and interpretations dealing with similar and related issues; and then
- the Conceptual Framework (see chapter 1.2). [*IAS 8.11*]

2.8.20.40   The entity may also consider the most recent pronouncements of other standard-setting bodies (e.g. the FASB) and accepted industry practice, to the extent that they do not conflict with standards, interpretations and the Conceptual Framework (see chapter 1.2). [*IAS 8.12*]

2.8.20.50   The IFRS Interpretations Committee discussed whether, in following the hierarchy in IAS 8, it could be appropriate to consider only certain aspects of a standard that is applied by analogy or whether all aspects of that standard should be applied. The Committee noted that in developing an accounting policy through analogy to a standard dealing with similar and related issues, an entity uses its judgement in applying all relevant aspects of the IFRS to its particular issue. [*IU 03-11*]

2.8.25   **FORTHCOMING REQUIREMENTS**

2.8.25.10   In March 2018, the IASB issued the revised *Conceptual Framework for Financial Reporting* and *Amendments to References to the Conceptual Framework in IFRS Standards*. An entity that uses the Conceptual Framework to develop an accounting policy in the absence of specific IFRS guidance under the hierarchy in IAS 8 (see 2.8.20.30) applies the transitional provisions in the amendments to reflect the impact of the revisions on its accounting policies.

2.8.25.20   However, an entity cannot use the revised Conceptual Framework to develop accounting policies for regulatory account balances that do not fall in the scope of IFRS 14 (see chapter 6.2) and would continue using its existing accounting policies based on the previous version of the Conceptual Framework.

2.8.30   **Consistency#**

2.8.30.10   Unless an IFRS specifically permits otherwise, the accounting policies adopted by an entity are applied consistently to all similar items. For example, if an entity chooses to account for common control transactions in the consolidated financial statements of the acquirer at book value (see 5.13.50.30), then it uses that method consistently for all similar common control transactions in its consolidated financial statements; it cannot use IFRS 3 accounting for some common control transactions and book value accounting for other similar transactions. [*IAS 8.13*]

2.8.30.20   Certain standards permit the application of different methods of accounting to different categories of items. For example, IAS 2 requires the same cost formula to be used for all inventories having a similar nature and use to the entity, but also recognises that different cost formulas may be justified for inventories with a different nature or use. However, IAS 2 recognises that a difference in the geographical location of inventories, by itself, is not sufficient to justify the use of different cost formulas. For example, an oil refiner could not use a weighted-average costing formula for crude oil supplies in the US and use a FIFO costing formula at non-US locations. [*IAS 2.25–26, 8.13*]

2.8.30.30   However, a manufacturer may have computer chips that are used in industrial machinery, and computer chips that are used in domestic appliances; in our view, the cost of the computer chips for each end product could be measured differently because the two types of chips have different uses. However, in our view a difference in customer demographic – e.g. end user vs retailer – does not meet the IAS 2 criterion of inventories with a different nature or use to justify a difference in the costing formula.

2.8.30.40   Accounting policies within a group are applied consistently, including those that are established for the purposes of consolidation (see 2.5.440.60). An exception is that insurance contracts accounted for under IFRS 4 need not be accounted for consistently on a group-wide basis (see 8.1.60). [*IFRS 10.19, B87*]

2.8.30.50   For a discussion of the accounting policies followed in an interim reporting period, see 5.9.220.

2.8.35   **FORTHCOMING REQUIREMENTS**

2.8.35.10   There is no exception for insurance contracts under IFRS 17 – i.e. a group applies uniform accounting policies to all insurance contracts.

2.8.40   **Disclosures of judgements made in applying accounting policies**

2.8.40.10   In applying an entity's accounting policies, management makes a number of judgements that can significantly affect the amounts recognised in the financial statements. An entity discloses the judgements (other than estimates (see 2.8.120)) that have the most significant effect on the amounts that it recognises in its financial statements – e.g. whether an arrangement contains a lease. [*IAS 1.122–123*]

2.8.50   CHANGES IN ACCOUNTING POLICY*

2.8.50.10   A change in accounting policy is made when it is required by a new or revised IFRS. A voluntary change may be made if it will result in a reliable and more relevant presentation (see 2.8.70). In applying an IFRS that contains more than one acceptable accounting policy, in our view an entity may generally change its accounting policy from one acceptable accounting policy to another, because both methods are considered acceptable in providing a fair presentation. [*IAS 8.14–15*]

2.8.50.20   Notwithstanding our view in 2.8.50.10, in our view it is inappropriate for an entity to change an accounting policy multiple times without carefully considering the criteria to qualify for a voluntary change in accounting policy.

EXAMPLE 1 – CHANGING ACCOUNTING POLICY MULTIPLE TIMES

2.8.50.30   In 2016, Company B changed its accounting policy for property, plant and equipment from the cost model to the revaluation model. During 2018, B reassesses its accounting policy and decides to change its accounting policy back to the cost model. We believe that because B had previously demonstrated that the revaluation model was more appropriate, B would need to demonstrate that the need for a reversal of its previous change in accounting policy is due to a change in circumstances. Such a circumstance could occur as a result of the acquisition of B by a new parent if the new parent instructs B to change its accounting policy for property, plant and equipment to the cost model in order to align B's policy with the rest of the group.

2.8.50.40   IFRS specifically provides that in respect of investment property (see 3.4.130.20) it is 'highly unlikely' that a change in accounting policy from a fair value to a cost basis will result in a more relevant presentation in the financial statements. [*IAS 8.14(b), 40.31*]

2.8.50.50   The following changes in accounting policy are subject to special requirements.
- *First-time adoption of IFRS:* Changes in accounting policy that arise on the first-time adoption of IFRS are the subject of a separate standard, IFRS 1 (see 6.1.170). This includes changes in policies between interim and annual financial statements in the year of the first-time adoption of IFRS (see 6.1.1560).
- *Property, plant and equipment and intangible assets:* A change in accounting policy to revalue items of property, plant and equipment (see 3.2.360) or intangible assets (see 3.3.280) is accounted for as a revaluation in accordance with the relevant standard.
- *Insurance contracts:* An entity is permitted to change its existing IFRS accounting policy for insurance contracts only if the change improves either the relevance or the reliability of its financial statements without reducing either (see 8.1.90).
- *Exploration and evaluation activities:* An entity is permitted to change its existing IFRS accounting policy for exploration and evaluation activities only if the change makes the financial

statements more relevant and no less reliable, or more reliable and no less relevant, to the needs of users (see 5.11.340). [*IFRS 1.27–27A, 4.22, 6.13, IAS 8.17*]

2.8.50.60   In addition, individual standards may contain specific requirements for accounting policy changes that result from their adoption (see 2.8.60).

2.8.50.70   Neither the adoption of an accounting policy for new transactions or events, nor the application of an accounting policy to previously immaterial items, is a change in accounting policy. When a functional currency becomes hyperinflationary and the restatement requirements of IFRS are applied (see 2.10.140), in our view this is not a change in accounting policy because the restatement could not have been applied before the functional currency was judged hyperinflationary, which is similar to accounting for a new transaction or event. This view is notwithstanding the fact that purchasing-power adjustments are computed from the date on which non-monetary assets (liabilities) are acquired (incurred). [*IAS 8.16, IFRIC 7.3*]

2.8.50.80   For a discussion of the consistency of accounting policies in the consolidated financial statements, see 2.8.30.

2.8.50.90   The disclosures required in respect of changes in accounting policy include the reasons for the change and the amount of the adjustment for the current period and for each prior period presented. In our view, these disclosures should be made separately for each such change. A new, revised or amended standard may include transitional requirements that override the general requirements of IAS 8 (see 2.8.60). [*IAS 8.28–29*]

2.8.50.100   In addition, any accompanying financial information presented in respect of prior periods – e.g. historical summaries – is also restated as far back as is practicable to reflect the change in accounting policy (see 2.8.90.60). [*IAS 8.26*]

2.8.50.110   Although it is not specifically mentioned in IAS 8, the standard's implementation guidance shows the restated comparative financial statements with the heading 'restated'. In our view, this is necessary to highlight for users the fact that the comparative financial statements are not the same as the financial statements previously published (see 2.8.80.100).

2.8.50.115   Disclosures are also required about new standards that have been issued but are not yet effective, regardless of whether the entity adopts them early. These disclosures include known or reasonably estimable information relevant to assessing the possible impact that application of the new standard will have on the entity's financial statements in the period of initial application. [*IAS 8.30–31*]

2.8.50.120   For a discussion of the accounting for income taxes as a result of a change in accounting policy, see 3.13.540.

2.8.60   Accounting policy change on adoption of a new IFRS

2.8.60.10   If a change in accounting policy arises from the adoption of a new, revised or amended standard, then an entity follows the specific transitional requirements in that standard, which take precedence over the general requirements for changes in accounting policies. [*IAS 8.19*]

EXAMPLE 2 – SPECIFIC TRANSITIONAL REQUIREMENTS

2.8.60.20   Under the transitional requirements in IFRS 15, which is effective from 1 January 2018, an entity can apply this standard using the following methods.
- *Retrospective method:* By restating comparatives and adjusting retained earnings at the beginning of the comparative period (with or without optional practical expedients).
- *Cumulative effect method:* By adjusting retained earnings at the beginning of the year of initial application with no restatement of the comparative period.

2.8.60.30   These specific transitional requirements take precedence over the general requirements in IAS 8. For a discussion of the transitional requirements of IFRS 15, see 4.2.510. [*IFRS 15.C2–C8A*]

2.8.60.40   When an entity follows the specific transitional requirements of a standard, in our view it should nonetheless comply with the disclosure requirements of IAS 8 in respect of a change in accounting policy to the extent that the transitional requirements do not include disclosure requirements. Even though it could be argued that the disclosures are not required because they are set out in the requirements for *voluntary* changes in accounting policy, we believe that they are necessary in order to give a fair presentation. [*IAS 8.28–29*]

2.8.70   Voluntary change

2.8.70.10   An entity may change an accounting policy voluntarily if the new policy provides reliable and more relevant information. The early adoption of a new standard is not a voluntary change in accounting policy. [*IAS 8.14, 20*]

2.8.70.20   If, in the absence of a standard specifically addressing an accounting issue, an entity adopted an accounting policy based on the pronouncements of other standard-setting bodies (see 2.8.20.40) and chooses to change that accounting policy as a result of an amendment to the underlying pronouncement, then the change is accounted for and disclosed as a voluntary change in accounting policy. [*IAS 8.21*]

2.8.70.30   Generally, an entity applies a change in accounting policy retrospectively – i.e. as if the new accounting policy had always been applied – including any income tax effect. This is done by adjusting the opening balance of each affected component of equity for the earliest prior period presented and the other comparative amounts disclosed for each prior period presented, unless it is impracticable to determine either the period-specific or the cumulative effect of the change. [*IAS 8.22–23*]

2.8.70.40   If it is impracticable to determine the period-specific effects for one or more prior periods presented (see 2.8.90), then the entity restates the opening balances of assets, liabilities and equity for the earliest period for which retrospective application is practicable. [*IAS 8.24*]

2.8.70.50   If it is impracticable to determine the cumulative effect at the beginning of the current period of applying a new accounting policy to all prior periods (see 2.8.90), then the entity restates the comparative information prospectively from the earliest date that is practicable. Nevertheless, a change in accounting policy is permitted even if it is impracticable to apply the policy prospectively for any prior period. [*IAS 8.25, 27*]

2.8.70.60   The financial statements include disclosure regarding the change in accounting policy, including the reasons why applying a voluntary change in accounting policy provides reliable and more relevant information. [*IAS 8.29*]

2.8.80   ERRORS

2.8.80.10   Errors result from the misapplication of policies, oversight or the misinterpretation of facts and circumstances that exist at the reporting date and were made in a prior period. Examples include mathematical mistakes and fraud (see 2.9.70). [*IAS 8.5*]

2.8.80.20   Financial statements containing material errors, or immaterial errors made intentionally to achieve a particular result in the financial statements, do not comply with IFRS. Potential current-period errors are corrected before the financial statements are authorised for issue. Material prior-period errors are corrected by restating the comparative information presented in the current period's financial statements. [*IAS 8.41*]

2.8.80.30   The correction of a material prior-period error is made by either:
- restating the comparative amounts for the prior period(s) presented in which the error occurred; or
- restating the opening balances of assets, liabilities and equity for the earliest prior period presented if the error occurred before the earliest prior period presented. [*IAS 8.42*]

2.8.80.40   IAS 8 requires material prior-period errors to be corrected by restating the opening balance of equity and comparatives, unless it is impracticable to determine either the period-specific effects or the cumulative effect of the error. [*IAS 8.43*]

2.8.80.50   If it is impracticable to determine the period-specific effects of an error for one or more prior periods presented (see 2.8.90), then the entity restates the opening balances of assets, liabilities and equity for the earliest period for which retrospective restatement is practicable. [*IAS 8.44*]

2.8.80.60   If it is impracticable to determine the cumulative effect at the beginning of the current period of an error on all prior periods (see 2.8.90), then the entity restates the comparative information to correct the error prospectively from the earliest date practicable. [*IAS 8.45*]

EXAMPLE 3 – CORRECTING AN ERROR

2.8.80.70   During 2018, Company X discovered that prepayments of 400 made during 2016 had not been recognised in profit or loss as the related expenses were incurred. The prepayments should have been recognised as an expense of 100 in 2016; 250 in 2017; and 50 in 2018. The misstatement is material.

Extract from draft 2018 financial statements before correction of the error

	DRAFT 2018	2017
Extract from statement of profit or loss and OCI		
Revenue	6,000	4,000
Expenses	(5,500)	(3,600)
Net profit	500	400
Extract from statement of changes in equity		
Opening retained earnings	14,400	14,000
Current-year net profit	500	400
Closing retained earnings	14,900	14,400

2.8.80.80   The opening balance of retained earnings is adjusted and comparatives are restated when practicable to reflect the correction of the error. The restatement reflects any tax effects, which are ignored for the purposes of this example.

Extract from final 2018 financial statements after correction of the error

	2018	2017 RESTATED
Extract from statement of profit or loss and OCI		
Revenue	6,000	4,000
Expenses	(5,550)	(3,850)
Net profit	450	150
Extract from statement of changes in equity		
Opening retained earnings as reported previously	-	14,000
Correction of an error related to previous years (note reference)	-	(100)
Opening retained earnings (restated)	14,050	13,900
Current-year net profit	450	150
Closing retained earnings	14,500	14,050

2.8.80.90   In restating the comparatives, the adjustment will be included in the appropriate line item of the statement of profit or loss and OCI in the usual way (see chapter 4.1). For example, if the expense in Example 3 were insurance of Company X's head office and X classified its expenses by function, then the expense would normally be included in administrative expenses. In addition, the financial statements will include full disclosure regarding the error and the adjustments made to correct it. [*IAS 8.49*]

2.8.80.100   Although it is not mentioned specifically in IAS 8, the standard's implementation guidance shows the restated comparative financial statements with the heading 'restated'. In our view, this is necessary to highlight for users the fact that the comparative financial statements are not the same as the financial statements previously published. [*IAS 8.IG.Ex1*]

2.8.80.110   In Example 3, the component of equity affected by the error was retained earnings. If the error affects more components of equity, then the effect on each component of equity is disclosed separately. [*IAS 1.106(b)*]

2.8.90   IMPRACTICABILITY OF RETROSPECTIVE APPLICATION OR RESTATEMENT

2.8.90.10   The retrospective application of changes in accounting policies (see 2.8.50) and the restatement of material prior-period errors (see 2.8.80) are required, unless they are impracticable. Guidance is given on when retrospective application or restatement will be impracticable. [*IAS 8.5, 50*]

2.8.90.20   Retrospective application or restatement is done using only information that:
- would have been available in preparing the financial statements for that earlier period; and
- provides evidence of circumstances that existed on the date(s) when the transaction or event occurred. [*IAS 8.52*]

2.8.90.30   Other information – e.g. information that uses the benefit of hindsight – may not be used. [*IAS 8.53*]

2.8.90.40   Retrospective application or restatement is impracticable when it requires:
- significant estimates to be made that cannot, after making every reasonable effort, distinguish information that may be used from information that may not; or
- information regarding transactions or events that is not available to the entity after making every reasonable effort to retrieve the necessary information. [*IAS 8.5, 50, 52*]

2.8.90.50   In these cases, the financial statements are adjusted as at the beginning of the earliest period from which retrospective adjustment is practicable. [*IAS 8.24–25, 27, 44–45*]

2.8.90.60   If an entity presents any accompanying financial information in respect of prior periods – e.g. historical summaries – then in our view an inability to restate all of the periods presented in the historical summaries or other prior-period information is not a reason to conclude that none of the comparative information required by IFRS would be restated.

EXAMPLE 4 – INABILITY TO RESTATE ALL PERIODS IN HISTORICAL SUMMARIES

2.8.90.70   Company X prepares a 10-year historical summary as accompanying financial information to its annual report. As a result of a change in accounting policy, X attempts to adjust the historical summary for the entire 10-year period, but

concludes that it is impracticable to restate it beyond the last four years. Therefore, X restates the affected financial information as far back as practicable, being the last four years of the financial summary. [*IAS 8.23, 26*]

2.8.100   ACCOUNTING ESTIMATES

2.8.110   Changes in accounting estimates*

2.8.110.10   Estimates are an essential part of financial reporting and changes therein are accounted for in the period in which the change occurs. For example, a change in the estimate of expected credit loss is accounted for in the period in which the change in estimate is made. Disclosure of the nature and amount of such changes is required. [*IAS 8.32–33, 36–37, 39–40*]

2.8.110.20   In some cases, it can be difficult to determine whether a change represents a change in accounting policy or a change in estimate. In these cases, the change is treated as a change in estimate and appropriate disclosure is given. In our view, when an entity changes its method of measuring the cost of inventory (see 3.8.280) – e.g. from FIFO to weighted-average – this is a change in accounting policy notwithstanding the fact that both methods measure cost. [*IAS 8.35*]

2.8.110.30   A change in the estimate of the useful life or method of recognising the depreciation of property, plant and equipment (see 3.2.140) or the amortisation of an intangible asset (see 3.3.230) is accounted for prospectively as a change in estimate by adjusting depreciation or amortisation in the current and future periods. [*IAS 8.32, 36, 16.51, 61, 38.104*]

EXAMPLE 5 – ACCOUNTING FOR CHANGES IN ESTIMATES

2.8.110.40   Company C acquired a printing machine at the beginning of 2015 and its useful life was estimated to be 10 years. At the end of 2017, the carrying amount of the machine was 240. At the beginning of 2018, C revised the estimated useful life and reduced the remaining life of the machine to a further two years from that date. The residual value of the machine is zero.

2.8.110.45   Therefore, the carrying amount of 240 is depreciated over the next two years (2018 and 2019). In addition, the decrease in useful life may indicate that the carrying amount of the machine is impaired (see 3.10.110).

2.8.110.50   A change in estimate is different from the correction of an error because an error results from the misapplication of policy or misinterpretation of existing facts and circumstances. Changes in accounting estimates result from new information or new developments. An estimate takes into account all existing facts and circumstances, but changes over time as those facts and circumstances change or as the entity obtains more experience and/or knowledge. If an objective determination cannot be made of whether a change is a change in estimate or the correction of an error, then in our view it should be accounted for as a change in estimate; this is consistent with the approach taken to distinguishing between changes in estimates and changes in accounting policy. [*IAS 8.5, 34, 48*]

2.8.110.60   Any significant change in estimate made during the last interim period in a financial year is disclosed in a note to the annual financial statements, unless separate interim financial statements are published for this period. [*IAS 34.26*]

2.8.120   Disclosures of estimation uncertainties

2.8.120.10   In determining the carrying amounts of some assets and liabilities, management estimates the effects of uncertain future events on those assets and liabilities at the reporting date. An entity discloses the key assumptions it makes about the future, and other major sources of estimation uncertainty at the reporting date that have a significant risk of resulting in a material adjustment to the carrying amounts of assets and liabilities in the next financial year. [*IAS 1.125*]

2.8.120.20   The assumptions and other major sources of estimation uncertainty to be disclosed relate to the estimates that require management's most difficult, subjective or complex judgements that have a significant risk of resulting in material adjustments in the next financial year. These disclosures are intended to help users understand these judgements and the extent of estimation uncertainty. Examples of areas for which an entity considers the disclosure of assumptions and estimation uncertainties, if material, might include the following:

● discounted cash flow projections;
● recoverability of development costs;
● utilisation of tax losses;
● measurement of embedded derivatives;
● measurement of defined benefit obligations; and
● provisions and contingencies. [*IAS 1.126–127*]

2.8.130   CHANGE IN CLASSIFICATION OR PRESENTATION

2.8.130.10   In some cases, it may be appropriate to change the classification or presentation of items in the financial statements even though there has been no change in accounting policy, to achieve a more appropriate presentation. In these cases, comparative information is restated unless it is impracticable to do so, and appropriate explanatory disclosures are included in the financial statements. [*IAS 1.41, 45–46*]

EXAMPLE 6 – RESTATING COMPARATIVES FOR CHANGES IN PRESENTATION

2.8.130.20   In 2017, Company D aggregated its research and development (R&D) expenses together with other operating expenses in its statement of profit or loss and OCI. In 2018, D's management makes a strategic decision to increase investment in R&D. As a result, D recognises material amounts of R&D expenses in profit or loss during 2018 and these are expected to increase further in the future. D decides to separately present R&D expenses on the face of the statement of profit or loss and OCI in 2018. The 2017 comparatives are restated to present the equivalent amount of R&D expenses in the comparative period on the face of the statement of profit or loss and OCI. [*IAS 1.40A–40D, 31*]

2.8.140 **THIRD STATEMENT OF FINANCIAL POSITION**

2.8.140.10   A third statement of financial position is presented as at the beginning of the preceding period following a retrospective change in accounting policy, the correction of an error or a reclassification that has a material effect on the information in that statement of financial position. For further discussion of the third statement of financial position, see 2.1.20. [*IAS 1.10(f), 40A*]

2.8.150 **FUTURE DEVELOPMENTS**

2.8.150.10   The IASB is working on two maintenance projects on various issues related to accounting policies and accounting estimates.

- *Accounting Policies and Accounting Estimates – Proposed amendments to IAS 8:* In September 2017, the IASB published an exposure draft, which aimed at clarifying the distinction between a change in accounting policy and a change in accounting estimate in IAS 8. The comment period closed in January 2018 and the Board is considering the feedback received.
- *Accounting Policy Changes – Proposed amendments to IAS 8:* In May 2018, the IASB published an exposure draft, which proposed a relief from retrospectively applying changes in accounting policies resulting from agenda decisions published by the IFRS Interpretations Committee. Under the proposal, an entity would consider the expected benefits to users of financial statements from applying the new accounting policy retrospectively and the cost to the entity of determining the effects of retrospective application. The comment period closes in July 2018.

2.9   Events after the reporting date

2.9 Events after the reporting date

CURRENTLY EFFECTIVE REQUIREMENTS

This publication reflects IFRS in issue at 1 August 2018, and the currently effective requirements cover annual periods beginning on 1 January 2018.

The requirements related to this topic are mainly derived from the following.

STANDARD	TITLE
IAS 1	Presentation of Financial Statements
IAS 10	Events after the Reporting Period

FORTHCOMING REQUIREMENTS AND FUTURE DEVELOPMENTS

For this topic, there are no forthcoming requirements or future developments.

2.9.10   OVERALL APPROACH

2.9.10.10   The following diagram illustrates the scope of IAS 10, which deals with events that occur after the reporting date but before the financial statements are authorised for issue. [*IAS 10.3*]

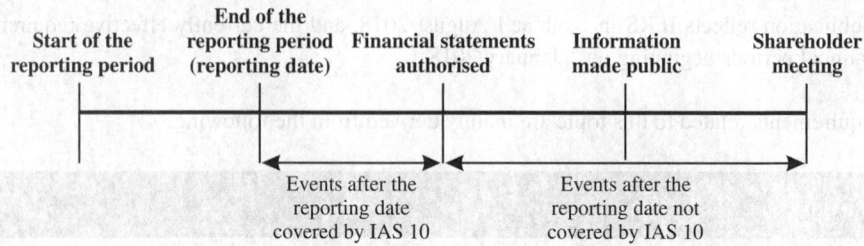

2.9.10.20   A number of terms are used, either in the literature or in practice, to describe the end of an entity's financial year, including 'reporting date', 'end of the reporting period', 'statement of financial position date', 'year end' and 'financial year end'. Generally, these terms are used interchangeably and have the same meaning. This publication consistently uses the term 'reporting date' throughout, which refers to the end of the reporting period and does not refer to the date on which the financial statements are prepared, authorised for issue, made public or filed.

2.9.15   Date on which the financial statements were authorised for issue

2.9.15.10   Disclosure is required in the financial statements of the date on which the financial statements were authorised for issue and who gave such authorisation, to inform users of the date to which events have been considered. If the shareholders have the power to amend the financial statements after issue, then the entity discloses that fact. [*IAS 10.17*]

2.9.15.20   The date on which the financial statements are authorised for issue is generally the date on which the financial statements are authorised for issue by management, either to the supervisory board or to the shareholders. Even if the shareholders are required to approve the financial statements, the date on which the financial statements are authorised for issue is the date of issue, not the date on which shareholders approve the financial statements. [*IAS 10.5–6*]

2.9.15.22   Identification of the date on which the financial statements are authorised for issue is a key area in the application of IAS 10. This is because any event that occurs after this date is not disclosed or reflected in the financial statements of the current period. However, the date on which the financial statements are authorised for issue is not always easily identifiable. In our view, the determination of this date should be based on all facts and circumstances, including the rights and responsibilities of the governing body and local governance rules on authorisation protocols. [*IAS 10.4–7*]

2.9.15.25   In our view, two different dates of authorisation for issue of the financial statements (dual dating of financial statements) should not be disclosed, because we believe that only a single date of authorisation for issue of the financial statements complies with IAS 10. [*IU 05-13*]

2.9.15.30   The financial statements of each entity have their own date of authorisation. For example, if financial statements of a subsidiary are authorised for issue after the publication of the consolidated financial statements of the group that includes this subsidiary, then the financial statements of the subsidiary have a later date of authorisation.

2.9.15.40   In our view, the authorisation for issue of the financial statements of the current period does not itself require the reconsideration of adjusting and non-adjusting events in respect of comparative information that is derived from financial statements (annual or interim) of a previous period that were themselves previously authorised for issue. [*IAS 1.38, 10.3, 8–11*]

2.9.20   ADJUSTING EVENTS

2.9.20.10   The financial statements are adjusted to reflect events that occur after the reporting date, but before the financial statements are authorised for issue, if either they provide evidence of conditions that existed at the reporting date (adjusting events) or they indicate that the going concern basis of preparation is inappropriate (see 2.9.55). [*IAS 10.3, 8, 14*]

EXAMPLE 1A – LEGAL CLAIM – DEFENDANT

2.9.20.20   Company T is being sued for breach of contract. At the reporting date, T asserted that it had not breached the contract and had legal opinions supporting this as the most likely outcome. Therefore, T had not recognised any provision in its draft financial statements (see chapter 3.12). Before the financial statements are authorised by the directors, the judge in the case delivers a preliminary ruling that T is guilty and liable for damages of 1,000. A final judgment is made after the financial statements have been authorised for issue.

| | Reporting date | | Financial statements authorised | |
| T sued for breach of contract | T's assessment not guilty | Preliminary ruling T is guilty | | Final judgment |

2.9.20.25   In our view, the financial statements should be adjusted and a provision of 1,000 recognised because the preliminary ruling provides enough evidence that an obligation existed at the reporting date, in the absence of any evidence to the contrary, notwithstanding the fact that a final judgment had not yet been reached.

2.9.20.30   For other examples of adjusting events, see paragraph 9 of IAS 10.

2.9.30   NON-ADJUSTING EVENTS

2.9.30.10   Financial statement amounts are not adjusted for non-adjusting events. Non-adjusting events are events that are a result of conditions that arose after the reporting date. An exception is when events after the reporting date indicate that the financial statements should not be prepared on a going concern basis (see 2.9.55). [*IAS 10.3, 10, 14*]

EXAMPLE 1B – LEGAL CLAIM – CLAIMANT

2.9.30.15   Continuing Example 1A from the point of view of Company V, which is suing Company T for breach of the contract, V is uncertain about the outcome of the legal proceeding at the reporting date. V's financial statements are authorised for issue after the final court judgment. V considers whether the favourable court ruling is an adjusting or non-adjusting event in respect of its claim, which has been treated as a contingent asset (see 3.12.107) because its realisation was probable but not virtually certain.

2.9.30.17   In our view, the change in probability of the realisation of income and the recovery of the related asset as a result of the court ruling is an event that should be reflected in the financial statements of the period in which the change occurs and should not be treated as an adjusting event in the prior-period financial statements. This is because the recognition of an asset for an item that is a contingent asset is specified as 'recognised in the period in which the change occurs'. [*IAS 37.33, 35*]

2.9.30.18   We believe that the phrase 'in which the change occurs' refers to the change in probability of the related inflows of economic benefits, which provides enough evidence that from that point in time the item meets the definition of and the recognition requirements for an asset. We believe that this specific guidance should be applied rather than considering the change in probability to be an event that provides additional information about circumstances at the reporting date, even though this is not symmetrical with the accounting by the counterparty (T). [*IAS 37.33, 35*]

2.9.30.20   Dividends declared (i.e. the dividends are authorised and no longer at the discretion of the entity) after the reporting date are non-adjusting events that are not recognised as a liability in the financial statements, but are disclosed in the notes to the financial statements. This is because no obligation exists at the reporting date. For further discussion of the timing of the recognition of dividends, see 7.3.680. [*IAS 10.12–13*]

2.9.30.25   A change in income tax rate or income tax law enacted or substantively enacted after the reporting date is a non-adjusting event that would generally result in disclosure (see 3.13.480.50). [*IAS 10.22(h), 12.46–47*]

2.9.30.28   An entity considers changes in market conditions after the reporting date to determine whether they indicate an adjusting or non-adjusting event. For example, if the assumptions made in determining recoverable amounts at the reporting date are consistent with market data at that date, then no further adjustment is necessary (see 3.10.180.70–110). However, the entity considers whether disclosure would be appropriate (see 2.9.30.30). [*IAS 10.11, 21*]

2.9.30.30   For material non-adjusting events, an entity discloses the nature of the event and an estimate of its financial effect or a statement that an estimate cannot be made. A non-adjusting event is considered to be material if it is of such importance that non-disclosure would affect the ability of users of the financial statements to make proper evaluations and decisions. In all cases, if a business combination happens after the annual reporting date but before the financial statements are authorised for issue, then an entity discloses information as prescribed by IFRS 3 (see 2.6.1160). [*IFRS 3.59–60, B66, IAS 10.21*]

2.9.30.40   For other examples of non-adjusting events, see paragraph 22 of IAS 10.

2.9.40   CURRENT VS NON-CURRENT CLASSIFICATION

2.9.40.10   Generally, the classification of long-term debt as current or non-current reflects circumstances at the reporting date. Refinancings, amendments, waivers etc that are agreed after the reporting date are not considered in determining the classification of debt, but are disclosed as non-adjusting events (see 2.9.30.30). However, if an entity expects, and has the discretion, at the reporting date to refinance or to reschedule payments on a long-term basis, then the debt is classified as non-current (see 3.1.40). [*IAS 1.72–76*]

2.9.50   EARNINGS PER SHARE

2.9.50.10   EPS is restated to include the effect on the number of shares of certain share transactions that happen after the reporting date even though the transactions themselves are non-adjusting events (see 5.3.530). [*IAS 33.64*]

2.9.55   GOING CONCERN

2.9.55.10   An entity does not prepare its financial statements on a going concern basis if management determines, after the reporting date but before the financial statements are authorised for issue, that it intends or has no alternative other than to liquidate the entity or to stop trading (see 1.2.70). [*IAS 10.14*]

2.9.60   IDENTIFYING THE KEY EVENT

2.9.60.10   In some cases, an event after the reporting date may actually have been triggered by an event that occurred before the reporting date. In such cases, it is necessary to determine the underlying causes of the event and its timing to determine the appropriate accounting. [*IAS 10.3*]

EXAMPLE 2A – THE KEY EVENT – CUSTOMER BANKRUPTCY

2.9.60.20   Company B receives notice after the reporting date that one of its major customers has gone into liquidation. In this case, the standard states that the bankruptcy of a customer after the reporting date usually confirms that the customer was credit-impaired at the reporting date. [*IAS 10.9*]

2.9.60.25   Therefore, B concludes that the bankruptcy is an adjusting event in determining whether the receivable is credit-impaired unless evidence to the contrary exists – e.g. the customer became bankrupt because its main operating plant was destroyed in a fire that happened after the reporting date (see also 7.8.237).

2.9.60.30   An entity considers whether adjusting events impact not only recognised items but also previously unrecognised items. [*IAS 10.9*]

EXAMPLE 2B – THE KEY EVENT – PREVIOUSLY RECOGNISED AND UNRECOGNISED ITEMS

2.9.60.35   Company M manufactures and sells luxury vehicles. All vehicles are guaranteed for 12 months and M determines that this is an assurance-type warranty (see 4.2.320). M introduces a new model, the R100, two months before the reporting date. At the reporting date, M recognises a warranty provision based on its previous experience with similar models. Historically, none of M's vehicles had manufacturing defects that would require a recall.

2.9.60.37   After the reporting date, M receives information on a technical malfunction that will require it to recall some of the R100 vehicles sold. M determines that the new information received is an adjusting event. Therefore, it recognises an additional provision in respect of the defective vehicles (see 3.12.360). [*IAS 10.9, 37.C1, IFRS 15.B28–B33*]

2.9.60.40   In other cases, multiple events may happen, some before and some after the reporting date, and it is necessary to determine which of the events triggers the recognition of the event in the financial statements.

2.9.70   DISCOVERY OF FRAUD AFTER REPORTING DATE

2.9.70.10   A fraud may be discovered after the financial statements have been authorised for issue. In our view, if information about the fraud could reasonably be expected to have been obtained and taken into account by an entity preparing financial statements when those financial statements were authorised for issue – e.g. in the case of a fraud within the entity itself – then subsequent discovery of such information is evidence of a prior-period error in those financial statements. In contrast, a fraud that occurred outside the entity and that had no direct effect on the entity's transactions might not reasonably be expected to have been known to the entity's management. Such a fraud could still have had an effect on the reported amounts of the entity if it had an effect on market prices; however, we believe that this is not a prior-period error because the definition of a prior-period error focuses on whether information was available or reasonably could have been obtained and taken into account (see 2.8.80). [*IAS 8.5, 10.9*]

2.9.70.20   In other circumstances, such an external fraud may be discovered after the reporting date but before the financial statements are authorised for issue. In our view, in concluding whether the discovery of the fraud should be treated as an adjusting or non-adjusting event related to reporting the fair value of financial assets under IFRS 9 in financial statements that have not yet been authorised for issue, management first identifies whether there is a question of existence, valuation or both.

2.9.70.30   In our view, if the discovery of a fraud raises issues related to the existence of the financial assets involved, then it should be treated as an adjusting event for financial statements that have not yet been authorised for issue. This is because the discovery of the fraud provides additional information about the existence of financial assets at the reporting date.

2.9.70.35   If, however, the fraud raises issues related only to the valuation of financial assets at the reporting date that do exist, then in our view it should be treated as a non-adjusting event for reporting the fair values of financial assets in the scope of IFRS 9. This is because of the following fair value measurement requirements.

- *Level 1 fair value measurement* – i.e. based on unadjusted quoted prices in active markets for identical assets or liabilities that the entity can access at the reporting date (see 2.4.280). In our view, although the market may have been mispricing the underlying value of the securities because of inaccurate or incomplete information, a quoted price for a financial instrument in an active market should not be overridden.

- *Level 2 or Level 3 fair value measurement* – i.e. based on inputs other than quoted prices included within Level 1 that are observable for the financial asset (Level 2) or unobservable inputs (Level 3) (see 2.4.290). The measurement objective for such fair value measurements is the same as that for a Level 1 fair value measurement: what the price was or would have been at the reporting date. Therefore, in our view any valuation that has as its objective fair value at the reporting date should not reflect information that neither was nor would have been reasonably available to market participants at that date. [*IFRS 13.9, 76, 81, 86*]

2.9.70.40   In some cases, it may be difficult to separate the existence and the valuation issues. In our view, if it is impracticable to separate the existence and the valuation issues, then the entire effect should be treated as an issue related to the existence of assets. For example, Fund Q reports an investment in government bonds and has its investment adviser, K, act as a custodian; Q discovers after the reporting date and before its financial statements have been authorised for issue that K has been charged with fraud. In this case, K is alleged to have reported these government bonds as assets of multiple investors and their owner of record is an affiliate of K. Although these government bonds were in existence at the reporting date, the existence of Q's claim to those assets is uncertain.

2.9.70.50   If an entity concludes that the subsequent discovery of a fraud is a valuation issue, and therefore it is treated as a non-adjusting event, then the non-adjusting event is disclosed if it is material. [*IAS 10.21*]

2.10 Hyperinflation

2.10   Hyperinflation

CURRENTLY EFFECTIVE REQUIREMENTS

This publication reflects IFRS in issue at 1 August 2018, and the currently effective requirements cover annual periods beginning on 1 January 2018.

The requirements related to this topic are mainly derived from the following.

STANDARD	TITLE
IAS 21	The Effects of Changes in Foreign Exchange Rates
IAS 29	Financial Reporting in Hyperinflationary Economies
IFRIC 7	Applying the Restatement Approach under IAS 29 Financial Reporting in Hyperinflationary Economies

FORTHCOMING REQUIREMENTS AND FUTURE DEVELOPMENTS

For this topic, there are no forthcoming requirements or future developments.

2.10.10   SCOPE

2.10.10.10   When an entity's functional currency (see 2.7.30) is hyperinflationary (i.e. it is the currency of a hyperinflationary economy), its financial statements are 'restated' so that all items are presented in the measuring unit current at the reporting date – i.e. it adopts the current purchasing power concept. Moreover, when an entity has foreign operations (e.g. a subsidiary, associate or joint arrangement) whose functional currency is the currency of a hyperinflationary economy, the investee's financial statements are restated before being translated and included in the investor's financial statements. Comparative amounts are excluded from the restatement requirement when the presentation currency of the ultimate financial statements into which they will be included is non-hyperinflationary (see 2.7.270). [*IAS 21.42–43, 29.8*]

2.10.10.20   Restatement for hyperinflation (see 2.10.20) is not elective. The IFRS Interpretations Committee discussed whether an entity, whose functional currency is not hyperinflationary, is permitted to use the concept of financial capital maintenance defined in terms of constant purchasing power units and, if so, whether it should follow the requirements in IAS 29 to present its financial statements. Under the concept of financial capital maintenance, a profit is earned only if the amount of net assets at the end of the period exceeds the amount of net assets at the beginning of the period, after excluding any distributions to and contributions from owners during the period. [*CF 8.3(a), 8.7, IU 01-14*]

2.10.10.30   The Committee noted that an entity is not permitted to apply a concept of financial capital maintenance that is in conflict with the requirements of a particular IFRS or to override the requirements of a particular standard. For example, IAS 29 cannot be applied simply because an entity whose functional currency is not hyperinflationary believes that the cumulative effects of inflation are significant and therefore that restatement would be helpful. In such cases, the entity may instead consider presenting supplementary current cost information (see chapter 5.8). [*IU 01-14*]

2.10.20   Indicators of hyperinflation

2.10.20.10   Under IFRS, it is a matter of judgement to determine when restatement for hyperinflation becomes necessary. Hyperinflation is indicated by the characteristics of an economy, which include but are not limited to the following.

- The general population prefers to keep its wealth in non-monetary assets or in a relatively stable foreign currency – amounts of local currency held are invested immediately to maintain purchasing power.
- The general population regards monetary amounts not in terms of the local currency but in terms of a relatively stable foreign currency – prices may be quoted in the stable currency.
- Sales and purchases on credit take place at prices that compensate for the expected loss of purchasing power during the credit period, even if the period is short.
- Interest rates, wages and prices are linked to a price index.
- The cumulative inflation rate over three years is approaching, or exceeds, 100 percent. [*IAS 29.3*]

2.10.20.20   Although the 100 percent numerical indicator is a key factor in identifying hyperinflation, it is not the only factor and should not be considered in isolation. Applying all of these factors could result in a country being considered hyperinflationary when its three-year cumulative inflation rate is, for example, only 80 percent.

2.10.20.30   Although judgement is involved in determining the onset of hyperinflation in a particular case, a preference is stated in the standard for all affected entities to apply the standard from the same date. [*IAS 29.4*]

2.10.30   MEASURING INFLATION RATE

2.10.40   Appropriate price index

2.10.40.10   For most countries there are two main indices that are generally used in measuring the general inflation rate: a consumer price index (CPI) and a producer or wholesale price index (PPI or WPI). The CPI measures the change in the cost of a fixed basket of products and services consumed by a 'typical household', generally including housing, electricity, food and transportation. The PPI or WPI measures wholesale price levels.

2.10.40.20   IFRS requires the use of a general price index that reflects changes in *general* purchasing power. In addition, two of the indicators of hyperinflation refer to the *general* population rather than a specific sector. For these reasons, in our view the CPI is the most appropriate index to use in measuring the inflation rate, because it is a broad-based measurement across all consumers in an economy. Some jurisdictions have multiple price indices published and further analysis and judgement may be required to determine an appropriate index that reliably reflects changes in general purchasing power. As noted in IAS 29, it is preferable that all entities that report in the currency of the same economy to use the same index. [*IAS 29.37*]

2.10.50   Cumulative inflation rate

2.10.50.10   IAS 29 refers to a cumulative inflation rate, but is silent on whether the calculation should be done on a simple or compounded basis. In our view, a compounded inflation rate should be calculated because the simple rate aggregates three discrete results without viewing the three-year period itself on a cumulative basis. [*IAS 29.3*]

EXAMPLE 1 – DETERMINING CUMULATIVE INFLATION RATE

2.10.50.20   The inflation rate in three consecutive years is 20%, 30% and 40%, respectively. The cumulative rate calculated on a simple basis is 90% (20 + 30 + 40). However, on a compounded basis the rate is 118%, which is calculated as follows.

- At the start of year 1, assume the index to be 100.
- At the end of year 1, the index is 120 (100 x 1.2).
- At the end of year 2, the index is 156 (120 x 1.3).
- At the end of year 3, the index is 218 (156 x 1.4), which gives a cumulative inflation rate of 118%, calculated as (218 - 100) / 100 or (((1 + 20%) x (1 + 30%) x (1 + 40%)) - 1).

2.10.60   **No index available**

2.10.60.10   When there is no index available, the standard requires an index to be estimated. The example it provides is using an estimate based on exchange rate movements between the functional currency and a relatively stable foreign currency. However, this approach might not be appropriate if the exchange rate is not freely floating. An estimate based on exchange rate movements might be adjusted for the effect of inflation, if there is any, in the foreign currency used as a benchmark. Although the standard uses this example in the context of the restatement of property, plant and equipment, in our view this method could be used for the restatement of the entire financial statements when no index is available. The same issue will arise when the official indices are considered unreliable, but this problem should be rare. [*IAS 29.17*]

2.10.60.20   If an entity estimates the index, then it discloses the following information:
- how the index was estimated;
- the level of the index at the reporting date; and
- movement in the index during the current and the previous reporting period. [*IAS 29.39(c)*]

2.10.70   **RESTATING FINANCIAL STATEMENTS FOR HYPERINFLATION**

2.10.70.10   To prepare a statement of financial position and a statement of profit or loss and OCI in a hyperinflationary economy, an entity needs to determine the impact of changes in purchasing power and restate its comparatives. To prepare these statements, there are four separate steps to be considered.
- *Step 1:* Restate the statement of financial position at the beginning of the reporting period.
- *Step 2:* Restate the statement of financial position at the end of the reporting period.
- *Step 3:* Restate the statement of profit or loss and OCI for the reporting period.
- *Step 4:* Calculate and separately disclose the gain or loss on the net monetary position. [*IAS 29.8–10*]

2.10.70.20   There will also be impacts on the statement of changes in equity and statement of cash flows from this process. [*IAS 29.33*]

2.10.80   **Step 1: Restate opening statement of financial position**

2.10.80.10   In the statement of financial position *at the beginning of the reporting period* both monetary and non-monetary items are 'indexed up' such that they are stated in the measuring unit current at the reporting date, and therefore reflect the purchasing power on that later date.

2.10.80.20   Non-monetary items, such as property, plant and equipment and inventory, may have been acquired many periods ago when the purchasing power of the currency was greater. Non-monetary items at the beginning of the reporting period are indexed up from the date of acquisition or contribution to reflect the purchasing power at the reporting date. However, if an asset or liability has been revalued, then it is indexed up only from the date of the most recent valuation. [*IAS 29.15, 18*]

2.10.80.30   Monetary items – i.e. money held and items to be received or paid in money – are, on any given date, always stated at their current purchasing power at that date. Therefore, the monetary items at the beginning of the reporting period also need to be indexed up to reflect their purchasing power at the reporting date – i.e. their opening balance is increased by the change in the price index during the reporting period to reflect the fact that the asset had higher purchasing power. The change in the price index is calculated by dividing the index at the reporting date by the index at the beginning of the reporting period. [*IAS 29.8, 12*]

2.10.80.40   Deferred income tax balances are calculated after the restatement of non-monetary items and require particular consideration. An entity calculates deferred tax balances in the opening statement of financial position applying the following methodology:

- remeasure the carrying amounts of non-monetary items by applying the measuring unit current at the date of the opening statement of financial position – i.e. by indexing up for the change in the price index from the date of acquisition or subsequent revaluation to the date of the opening statement of financial position;
- measure deferred tax at the date of the opening statement of financial position in accordance with IAS 12 based on those revised carrying amounts; and
- remeasure those deferred tax balances for the change in the measuring unit from the date of the opening statement of financial position to the reporting date – i.e. by indexing up for the change in the price index during the reporting period (see 2.10.140.20). [*IFRIC 7.4*]

2.10.80.50   If an entity applied IAS 29 in its previous period's financial statements, then the most efficient method of obtaining a restated opening statement of financial position is to restate all line items – i.e. monetary and non-monetary items – in the closing statement of financial position reported in the previous period's financial statements by applying the change in the price index during the current reporting period. This alternative approach achieves the same result because all items reported in the previous period's financial statements would have been previously restated to reflect changes in the price index to the previous reporting date. This is also consistent with how the previous period's financial statements are restated when included as comparative information in the current period's financial statements (see 2.10.130).

2.10.90   **Step 2: Restate closing statement of financial position**

2.10.90.10   The statement of financial position *at the reporting date* is also indexed up to current purchasing power terms.

2.10.90.20   Because monetary items are, on any given date, always stated at their current purchasing power at that date, this means that monetary amounts held at the reporting date do not require restatement.

2.10.90.30   Non-monetary items at the beginning of the reporting period are already restated to reflect the purchasing power at the reporting date in accordance with Step 1 (see 2.10.80.20). Therefore, assuming no changes to the non-monetary items in the reporting period – i.e. no additions or disposals and ignoring depreciation, amortisation and impairment – non-monetary items are carried at the same amount as in the adjusted statement of financial position at the beginning of the reporting period (i.e. the same for both years presented in the statement of financial position). If a non-monetary item is subject to depreciation or amortisation, then its carrying amount is adjusted to reflect depreciation or amortisation measured in terms of purchasing power at the reporting date.

2.10.90.40   For example, an item of land measured at cost at the beginning and at the end of the reporting period will be stated at the same amount in both statements of financial position, absent any impairment. Otherwise, a non-monetary asset purchased during the reporting period is indexed up to reflect the change in the price index from that at the date of acquisition to that at the reporting date. However, if an asset or liability has been revalued, then it is adjusted only from the date of the valuation. If the item is stated at the fair value at the reporting date (e.g. investment property), then it is not restated. [IAS 29.12–16, 18]

2.10.90.50   Deferred taxes are calculated in accordance with IAS 12 after the restatement of non-monetary items (see chapter 3.13).

2.10.100   Step 3: Restate statement of profit or loss and OCI

2.10.100.10   A hyperinflationary statement of profit or loss and OCI includes the gain or loss from holding monetary assets or liabilities and income and expenses during the period. The gain or loss from holding monetary assets or liabilities is included in profit or loss. Any income earned or expense incurred during the period will need to be indexed up from the date initially recorded to reflect the purchasing power at the reporting date. For practical reasons, average indexation rates may be acceptable if the overall result is not materially different from the result that would be obtained by indexing individual items of income and expense based on the date at which the transaction took place. In our experience, a single annual average often may not be appropriate because of the speed and exponential way in which the index rises in a hyperinflationary economy. [IAS 29.26]

2.10.100.20   The gain or loss from holding monetary assets or liabilities is an economic concept. Suppose that an entity held 1,000 of cash (and 1,000 of share capital), and had no other assets, liabilities or transactions throughout a year when the CPI index has moved from 100 to 150. The entity has made an economic loss in purchasing power terms, and current purchasing power accounting forces this to appear in the financial statements. The economic loss exists as follows: the entity would need 1,500 of cash at the reporting date to be in the same purchasing power position as having 1,000 of cash at the beginning of the reporting period, and a loss of 500 has actually occurred.

2.10.110   Worked example of IAS 29 restatements

Example 2 – Restatements to reflect purchasing power at reporting date

2.10.110.10   Company H was incorporated in December 2016 with a cash capital contribution of 100, and started its operations in 2017.

2.10.110.20   The following facts are also relevant for this example.
- In December 2017, H bought a piece of land for 600, and entered into a five-year loan. The land is measured at cost.
- In October 2018, H bought inventories, which remained unsold on 31 December 2018.
- H's functional currency has been considered hyperinflationary since 2016.

2.10.110.30 The following table shows a general price index of the economy in which H operates, on specified dates.

Price index at:	
31 December 2016	100
31 December 2017	150
31 October 2018	180
31 December 2018	200
Average price index during 2018	175

Statements of financial position before IAS 29 restatement

	HISTORICAL PURCHASING POWER	
	31 DEC 2018	**31 DEC 2017**
Share capital (contributed on 31 December 2016)	100	100
Retained earnings	1,050	800
Total equity	1,150	900
Land (acquired on 31 December 2017)	600	600
Investment securities held for trading	250	150
Inventories (acquired on 31 October 2018)	100	-
Trade receivables	500	200
Cash	100	350
Loan payable	(400)	(400)
Net assets	1,150	900

Statement of profit or loss and OCI before IAS 29 restatement

	2018
Revenue	1,150
Gain on change in fair value of investment securities	100
Interest on loan payable	(100)
Other expenses	(900)
	250

Step 1: Restate opening statement of financial position

2.10.110.40 The statement of financial position as at 31 December 2017 (1 January 2018) is restated so that it is expressed in the measuring unit current as at 31 December 2018. H can apply one of the following approaches.

- *Approach 1:* Restate the historical statement of financial position at the beginning of the reporting period:
  - non-monetary items in the statement of financial position as at 31 December 2017 are multiplied by the change in the index from the date the non-monetary items were acquired or contributed to 31 December 2018; and
  - monetary items as at 31 December 2017 are multiplied by the change in the index from 31 December 2017 to 31 December 2018 (1.33 = 200 / 150).
- *Approach 2:* Multiply all assets and liabilities reported in the hyperinflationary statement of financial position as at 31 December 2017 (i.e. as restated for changes in the price index to 31 December 2017) by the change in the index from 31 December 2017 to 31 December 2018 (1.33 = 200 / 150). [*IAS 29.34*]

2.10.110.50   This example does not include any income taxes. If H applied Approach 1, then to determine the opening balance of the deferred tax it would need to follow the methodology described in 2.10.80.40. Therefore, it will be more practical to apply Approach 2 because H can simply restate all the assets and liabilities including deferred tax items in its opening statement of financial position by applying the change in the price index during the current reporting period (see 2.10.80.50).

This example illustrates Approach 2.

Statement of financial position as at 1 January 2018

	31 DEC 2017 HISTORICAL PURCHASING POWER	31 DEC 2017 REPORTED IN PRIOR PERIOD[1]	1 JAN 2018 EXPRESSED IN 31 DEC 2018 PURCHASING POWER[2]
Share capital (contributed on 31 December 2016)	100	150[3]	200
Retained earnings	800	750[4]	1,000
Total equity	900	900	1,200
Land (acquired on 31 December 2017)	600	600	800
Investment securities held for trading	150	150	200
Inventories (acquired on 31 October 2018)	-	-	-
Trade receivables	200	200	267
Cash	350	350	467
Loan payable	(400)	(400)	(534)
Net assets	900	900	1,200

Notes
1. As included in the 2017 hyperinflationary financial statements.
2. As restated for inclusion as comparatives/opening position in the 2018 financial statements. All assets and liabilities are adjusted to be expressed in 31 December 2018 purchasing power. All amounts are calculated by multiplying the corresponding figures in the statement of financial position at 31 December 2017 as reported in the prior period by the change in the price index during 2018 – i.e. (200 / 150).
3. Calculated as historical purchasing power amount multiplied by change in price index from date of contribution to 31 December 2017 – i.e. (150 / 100).
4. Restated retained earnings are a balancing figure derived from the other amounts in the restated statement of financial position.

Step 2: Restate closing statement of financial position

2.10.110.60   The statement of financial position as at 31 December 2018 is restated so that it is expressed in the measuring unit current at that time. Non-monetary items – i.e. share capital, land and inventories – are restated from their acquisition or contribution date. The investment securities held for trading are not restated, because they are stated at fair value at the reporting date. Monetary items – i.e. trade receivables, cash and the loan payable – as at 31 December 2018 are not restated, because they are already expressed in purchasing power at that date. [*IAS 29.12, 14–15, 18*]

Statement of financial position as at 31 December 2018

	31 DEC 2018 HISTORICAL PURCHASING POWER	31 DEC 2018 EXPRESSED IN 31 DEC 2018 PURCHASING POWER
Share capital	100	200[1]
Retained earnings	1,050	1,161[2]
Total equity	1,150	1,361
Land	600	800[3]
Investment securities held for trading	250	250
Inventories	100	111[4]
Trade receivables	500	500
Cash	100	100
Loan payable	(400)	(400)
Net assets	1,150	1,361

Notes
1. Share capital contributed in 2016, calculated using the change in the index from 31 December 2016 to 31 December 2018 as ((200 / 100) x 100).
2. Restated retained earnings are a balancing figure derived from the other amounts in the restated statement of financial position. The increase reflects the net result for the period, which includes the monetary loss of 125 (see 2.10.110.70).

3. Land bought at end of 2017, calculated using the change in the index from 31 December 2017 to 31 December 2018 as ((200 / 150) x 600).

4. Inventory bought in October 2018, calculated using the change in the index from 31 October 2018 to 31 December 2018 as ((200 / 180) x 100).

Step 3: Restate statement of profit or loss and OCI

2.10.110.70   Income and expenses recorded in the statement of profit or loss and OCI are restated to reflect changes in the price index from the date on which they are recorded initially in the financial statements. In this example, an average index is applied. [*IAS 29.26*]

Statement of profit or loss and OCI

	31 DEC 2018 HISTORICAL PURCHASING POWER	RESTATEMENT	31 DEC 2018 EXPRESSED IN 31 DEC 2018 PURCHASING POWER
Revenue	1,150	165	1,315[1]
Gain on change in fair value of investments	100	14	114[2]
Interest on loan payable	(100)	(14)	(114)[3]
Other expenses	(900)	(129)	(1,029)[4]
Profit before gain or loss on net monetary position	250	36[6]	286
Loss on net monetary position	-		(125)[5]
Net profit	250		161

Notes
1. Revenue calculated using average index for 2018 – i.e. ((200 / 175) x 1,150).
2. Gain on change in fair value of investments calculated using average index for 2018 – i.e. ((200 / 175) x 100).
3. Interest on loan payable calculated using average index for 2018 – i.e. ((200 / 175) x 100).
4. Other expenses calculated using average index for 2018 – i.e. ((200 / 175) x 900).
5. See calculation in 2.10.110.80.
6. Restatement of items in the statement of profit or loss and OCI.

Step 4: Calculate gain or loss on net monetary position

2.10.110.80   The gain or loss on the net monetary position can be:
- derived as the difference resulting from the restatement of non-monetary assets, owners' equity and items in the statement of profit or loss and OCI and the adjustment of index linked assets and liabilities (Approach 1); or
- estimated by applying the change in the general price index to the weighted average for the period of the net amounts of monetary assets and liabilities (Approach 2). [*IAS 29.27*]

Approach 1: Difference from restatement of non-monetary items

	NON-MONETARY ITEMS			
	EXPRESSED IN PURCHASING POWER AT	AMOUNT	EXPRESSED IN PURCHASING POWER AT 31 DEC 2018	DIFFERENCE RESULTING FROM THE RESTATEMENT
Restatement of non-monetary assets				
Land	Dec 2017	600	800	200
Inventories	Oct 2018	100	111	11
Restatement of owner's equity				
Share capital	Dec 2017	(150)	(200)	(50)
Retained earnings	Dec 2017	(750)	(1,000)	(250)
Restatement of items in the statement of profit or loss and OCI (see 2.10.110.70)				(36)
Loss on net monetary position				125

Approach 2: Effect on the net monetary amounts

- Calculate the gain/loss on holding monetary items in the statement of financial position at the beginning of the reporting period based on the purchasing power as at 31 December 2018.
- Adjust the above amount for the effect of net monetary transactions that occurred during 2018 by comparing the restated carrying amounts to the historical transaction amounts.

Loss on net monetary position

	1 JAN 2018	NET CHANGE IN MONETARY ITEMS		31 DEC 2018
		RELATED TO TRANSACTIONS DURING 2018	RELATED TO TRANSACTIONS IN OCTOBER 2018	
Investment securities held for trading	150	100	-	250
Trade receivables	200	300	-	500
Cash	350	(150)	(100)	100
Loan payable	(400)	-	-	(400)

	1 JAN 2018	NET CHANGE IN MONETARY ITEMS		31 DEC 2018
		RELATED TO TRANSACTIONS DURING 2018	RELATED TO TRANSACTIONS IN OCTOBER 2018	
Net monetary position at historical purchasing power	300	250	(100)	450
Net monetary position at December 2018 purchasing power	400[(1)]	286[(2)]	(111)[(3)]	575[(4)]
Loss on net monetary position	(100)	(36)	11	(125)

Notes

1. Calculated by applying the change in the price index from that of December 2017 to that of December 2018 – i.e. ((200 / 150) x 300).
2. Calculated by applying the difference between the average price index of 2017 and that of December 2018 – i.e. ((200 / 175) x 250).
3. Calculated by applying the change in the price index from that of October 2018 to that of December 2018 – i.e. ((200 / 180) x 100).
4. Theoretical amount that net monetary assets and liabilities would have been if the historical amounts had maintained their purchasing power in line with changes in the price index– i.e. (400 + 286 - 111).

2.10.115 Presentation of gain or loss on net monetary position

2.10.115.10 The gain or loss on the net monetary position is recognised in profit or loss and disclosed separately. Adjustments to monetary assets and liabilities that are contractually linked or indexed to changes in prices are offset against the gain or loss on the net monetary position. Other income and expense items that are associated with the net monetary position include interest income and expenses and foreign exchange differences related to invested or borrowed funds. Although such items are disclosed separately, it may be helpful if they are presented together with the gain or loss on the net monetary position in the statement of profit or loss and OCI. [*IAS 29.9, 13, 28*]

2.10.120 Impairment of non-monetary assets

2.10.120.10 The restated amount of a non-monetary asset is reduced in accordance with the applicable standards if it exceeds the item's recoverable amount. For example, IAS 36 requires that if the recoverable amount of property, plant and equipment or goodwill is less than the asset's carrying amount, then the carrying amount of the asset is reduced to its recoverable amount and the reduction is an impairment loss that is recognised immediately in profit or loss. Similarly, IAS 2 requires inventories to be measured at the lower of cost and net realisable value with any write-down to net realisable value recognised as an expense in the period the write-down occurs. [*IAS 2.9, 34, 29.19, 36.59–60*]

2.10.120.20 Consistent with the requirements of those other standards, and with the objective of IAS 29 to reflect amounts in the financial statements based on their current purchasing power, in our view such reductions to recoverable amount should be included in profit or loss and determined based on amounts measured in purchasing power terms at the reporting date. [*IAS 29.8*]

EXAMPLE 3 – IMPAIRMENT OF INVENTORY

> 2.10.120.30   Company M's functional currency is considered to be hyperinflationary. M bought inventory some months before the reporting date for 100. The net realisable value of the inventory at the reporting date is 175, and the increase in the inflation index from the date of purchase to the reporting date is 100%. In current purchasing power terms, the inventory has a cost of 200. In this case, M writes down the inventory to 175 and recognises the loss of 25 in profit or loss for the period.

2.10.130   Comparative information

2.10.130.10   Comparative information in the functional currency is restated by taking the corresponding figures for the end of the previous period and applying a change in the general price index so that it is presented in terms of the measuring unit current at the reporting date. The same process that is used to calculate the statement of financial position at the beginning of the reporting period is used to calculate the comparative information (see 2.10.80). For a discussion of presenting comparative amounts in a different presentation currency, see 2.10.160. [*IAS 29.8, 34*]

2.10.130.20   If the comparative period's financial statements were themselves presented under IAS 29, then the previously published figures were in prior-period-end purchasing power. In that case, the restatement to purchasing power at the reporting date becomes a mathematical computation of multiplying up all those figures by the increase in the price index over the current reporting period. This multiplication is also applied to the gain or loss on net monetary position shown in the prior period's current purchasing power statement of profit or loss and OCI.

2.10.140   FIRST APPLICATION OF HYPERINFLATIONARY ACCOUNTING

2.10.140.10   At the reporting date in which an entity identifies its functional currency as hyperinflationary, it applies IAS 29 retrospectively, as if the currency had always been hyperinflationary. Non-monetary assets and liabilities at the beginning of both the current and the comparative periods are all restated for changes in prices from their dates of acquisition or incurrence (or revaluation, if applicable) into the purchasing power at the reporting date. Monetary items at the beginning of current and comparative periods are restated from those dates through to the purchasing power at the reporting date. [*IFRIC 7.3*]

2.10.140.20   IFRIC 7 provides guidance on the calculation of deferred tax in the period when an entity's functional currency is considered hyperinflationary, but has not been hyperinflationary in the previous period. At the reporting date, deferred taxes are recognised and measured in accordance with IAS 12 (see chapter 3.13). However, because deferred tax items are a function of carrying amounts of assets or liabilities and their tax bases, an entity cannot restate its comparative deferred tax items when it first applies IAS 29 by simply applying a general price index. Instead, the balance of deferred tax at the beginning of the current reporting period is calculated in accordance with IAS 12 after the nominal carrying amounts of non-monetary items at that date have been restated by applying the effects of inflation to that date. This remeasured deferred tax at the beginning of the reporting period is then restated by applying the effects of inflation to the reporting date. [*IFRIC 7.4*]

EXAMPLE 4 – RESTATING DEFERRED TAX

2.10.140.30   Continuing with the facts in Example 2, except that H identified the existence of hyperinflation during 2017. In addition, H's income tax rate is 40%. The tax base of the land was 590 at 31 December 2017 and it remained unchanged at 31 December 2018.

Restating deferred tax

	1 JANUARY 2018[1]	31 DECEMBER 2018
Accounting carrying amount	600	800
Tax base	590	590
Temporary difference	10	210
Deferred income tax liability expressed in 1 January 2018 purchasing power (as previously reported)	(4)[2]	
Deferred income tax liability expressed in 31 December 2018 purchasing power	(5)[4]	(84)[3]

The movement of deferred tax liability during 2018 is calculated as ((84) - (5) = (79)).

Notes
1.   Expressed in purchasing power at 1 January 2018, except for the restated opening deferred tax liability.
2.   Calculated as temporary difference multiplied by tax rate – i.e. (10 x 40%).
3.   Calculated as temporary difference multiplied by tax rate – i.e. (210 x 40%).
4.   Deferred tax liability at 1 January 2018, calculated by applying the change in the price index from 31 December 2017 to 31 December 2018 – i.e. ((200 / 150) x 4).

	DEBIT	CREDIT
Profit or loss	79	
Deferred tax liability		79
To recognise movement in deferred tax liability in 2018		

2.10.140.40   IAS 29 requires comparatives to be restated in the measuring unit current at the reporting date. However, if an entity's presentation currency is not hyperinflationary (see 2.10.160.10 and 2.7.270.20), then IAS 21 requires the comparative amounts to be those that were presented as current-year amounts in the prior-year financial statements. It is unclear whether on first application of hyperinflationary accounting the entity should restate its comparatives for price changes in prior periods if its presentation currency is not hyperinflationary. In our view, an entity should choose an accounting policy, to be applied consistently, on whether it restates its comparatives in these circumstances. If an entity chooses not to restate its comparatives in these circumstances, then in our view the entity should recognise directly in equity the gain or loss on the net monetary position related to price changes in prior periods. This will ensure that the gain or loss on the net monetary position recognised in profit or loss in the current period is consistent with the amount that would have been recognised had the entity always applied restatement under IAS 29. [*IAS 21.42, 29.8, 28*]

2.10.150 CESSATION OF HYPERINFLATIONARY ACCOUNTING

2.10.150.10   When an entity's functional currency ceases to be hyperinflationary, it discontinues preparing and presenting its financial statements in accordance with IAS 29 for reporting periods ending on or after the date on which the economy is identified as being non-hyperinflationary. The amounts expressed in the measuring unit current at the end of the last reporting period in which IAS 29 was applied are used as the basis for the carrying amounts in subsequent financial statements. Judgement is required in determining when the economy ceases to be hyperinflationary. [*IAS 29.38*]

2.10.160 TRANSLATION TO PRESENTATION CURRENCY DIFFERENT FROM FUNCTIONAL CURRENCY

2.10.160.10   When the financial information of an entity or foreign operation whose functional currency is hyperinflationary is translated into a different presentation currency, this is done in accordance with IAS 21 as follows.

- If the presentation currency is not hyperinflationary, then comparative amounts are not restated for changes in either the general price level in the functional currency (i.e. as otherwise required by IAS 29) or the exchange rate between the functional and presentation currencies. As such, the comparative amounts remain those amounts reported as current for the previous reporting period.
- If the presentation currency is hyperinflationary, then the comparative amounts are restated in accordance with both IAS 29 and IAS 21 for changes during the current reporting period in both the general price level in the functional currency and the applicable exchange rate. [*IAS 21.42–43, 29.8, 34*]

2.10.160.20   For further discussion of the issues addressed in 2.10.160.10, including the presentation of changes in equity arising during the current period when comparative amounts presented in a non-hyperinflationary currency are not restated, see 2.7.270 and 310.

2.10.170 SUPPLEMENTARY HISTORICAL COST INFORMATION

2.10.170.10   When restated financial statements are presented, in our view it is not appropriate to present additional supplementary financial information prepared on a historical cost basis. [*IAS 29.7*]

2.10.170.20   Because money rapidly loses its purchasing power in a hyperinflationary economy, reporting an entity's financial position and operating results in the currency of a hyperinflationary economy without restatement would be meaningless to users; comparative figures would also have little or no value. Therefore, the presentation of historical cost information in these cases may be misleading to users of the financial statements. [*IAS 29.2*]

2.10.180   **CHANGING PRICES**

2.10.180.10   Entities whose functional currency is not hyperinflationary may choose to disclose certain information about the effects of changing prices on a current cost basis as supplementary information to its financial statements (see chapter 5.8).

3. STATEMENT OF FINANCIAL POSITION

3.1 General

3. STATEMENT OF FINANCIAL POSITION

3.1 General

CURRENTLY EFFECTIVE REQUIREMENTS

This publication reflects IFRS in issue at 1 August 2018, and the currently effective requirements cover annual periods beginning on 1 January 2018.

The requirements related to this topic are mainly derived from the following.

STANDARD	TITLE
IAS 1	Presentation of Financial Statements

FORTHCOMING REQUIREMENTS

For this topic, there are no forthcoming requirements.

FUTURE DEVELOPMENTS

The currently effective requirements that may be affected by future developments are highlighted with a * and are briefly discussed in 3.1.60.

3.1.10 FORMAT OF STATEMENT OF FINANCIAL POSITION

3.1.10.10   IFRS generally requires an entity to present a classified statement of financial position, which distinguishes current from non-current assets and liabilities. However, entities may present assets and liabilities in order of liquidity if this presentation provides information that is reliable and more relevant. In our experience, presentation based on the order of liquidity is most commonly used by financial institutions and insurance entities. [*IAS 1.60*]

3.1.10.20   An entity may present some of its assets and liabilities using a current/non-current classification, and others in order of liquidity, if such a mixed presentation provides information that is reliable and more relevant. [*IAS 1.64*]

3.1.10.30   When relevant to an understanding of the entity's financial position, the statement of financial position includes line items, headings and subtotals in addition to the line items specified in IAS 1. Additional items may be presented because of their size or nature or to distinguish them from other items with different timing, liquidity or function. For example, an entity with significant trademarks may decide to present these separately in the statement of financial position, rather than combine them with other intangible assets. In another example, an entity that is the customer in a reverse factoring arrangement may decide to present amounts due in respect of a supplier factoring facility separately if their size or nature is sufficiently different from trade or other payables. For a discussion of the presentation and disclosure of liabilities related to reverse factoring arrangements in the statement of financial position, see 7.10.35.70–100. [*IAS 1.29–31, 54–55A, BC38A–BC38B*]

3.1.10.40   If an entity presents additional subtotals in the statement of financial position, then the subtotals:
- comprise line items made up of amounts recognised and measured in accordance with IFRS;
- are presented and labelled in a manner that makes the line items that constitute the subtotal clear and understandable;
- are consistent from period to period; and
- are displayed with no more prominence than other subtotals and totals presented in the statement of financial position. [*IAS 1.55A, BC38G*]

3.1.10.50   An entity can aggregate line items in the statement of financial position if the line items specified by IAS 1 are immaterial (see 1.2.40). [*IAS 1.54, BC38C*]

3.1.20 CURRENT VS NON-CURRENT CLASSIFICATION*

3.1.30 Assets

3.1.30.10   An asset is classified as current if it meets any of the following conditions:
- it is expected to be realised in, or is held for sale or consumption in, the entity's normal operating cycle;
- it is held primarily for trading purposes;
- it is expected to be realised within 12 months of the reporting date; or
- it is cash or a cash equivalent (see 2.3.10) that is not restricted from being exchanged or used to settle a liability for at least 12 months after the reporting date. [*IAS 1.66*]

EXAMPLE 1 – WORK IN PROGRESS

> 3.1.30.20   Company B constructs office buildings for third parties, control over which transfers to customers on completion of construction. Often, construction takes two to three years to complete. B's construction work in progress represents inventory and is classified as a current asset because construction over two to three years is B's normal operating cycle.

3.1.30.30   If an entity has different operating cycles for different parts of the business – e.g. retail and construction – then the classification of an asset as current is based on the normal operating cycle that is relevant to that particular asset. In our view, the entity need not identify a single operating cycle. [*IU 06-05*]

3.1.30.40   If a line item in the statement of financial position includes a combination of assets that are expected to be realised both before and after 12 months from the reporting date, then an entity discloses the amount expected to be realised after more than 12 months. For example, all trade receivables are classified as current assets (assuming that they are expected to be realised in their respective operating cycles), but an entity discloses in the notes the amount expected to be realised more than 12 months after the reporting date. [*IAS 1.61*]

3.1.30.45   Derivatives that meet the definition of held-for-trading in IFRS 9 but are not held primarily for trading purposes are classified as current or non-current assets based on their outstanding maturities; this is despite the fact that they meet the definition of held-for-trading in IFRS 9 (see 7.10.50.50). For other assets in the fair value through profit or loss category, see 7.10.50.60–70. [*IAS 1.68, BC38H–BC38K*]

3.1.30.50   A non-current asset is not classified as current unless it is classified as held-for-sale (see 5.4.110). [*IFRS 5.3, BC9–BC10, IAS 1.66*]

3.1.30.60   The current portion of a non-current financial asset is classified as a current asset. [*IAS 1.68*]

3.1.30.70   All assets that do not meet the definition of current assets are classified as non-current. [*IAS 1.66*]

3.1.40   Liabilities

3.1.40.10   A liability is classified as current if it meets any of the following conditions:
- it is expected to be settled in the entity's normal operating cycle;
- it is held primarily for trading purposes;
- it is due to be settled within 12 months of the reporting date; or
- it is not subject to an unconditional right of the entity at the reporting date to defer settlement of the liability for at least 12 months after the reporting date. [*IAS 1.69*]

3.1.40.20   Terms of a liability that could, at the option of the counterparty, result in its settlement by the issue of equity instruments do not affect its classification (see 7.10.50.40). [*IAS 1.69(d)*]

3.1.40.30   The IFRS Interpretations Committee discussed the classification of a loan with terms that enable the lender to call the loan at any time. The Committee noted that despite the fact that such a loan may not be due to be settled within 12 months of the reporting date, the presence of such a term means that the entity does not have an unconditional right to defer settlement for at least 12 months after the reporting date. Therefore, such a loan is classified as current. [*IAS 1.69(d), IU 11-10*]

3.1.40.40   Debt is usually classified as current or non-current based on whether it is due to be settled within 12 months of the reporting date. However, if a liability is part of the working capital used in the entity's normal operating cycle, then it is classified as current even if it is due to be settled more than 12 months after the reporting date. For example, an entity develops software for third parties that takes two years to complete and receives payment for this service up front. The contract liability recognised as a result of the up-front payment is classified as current even if the related service is not expected to be performed within 12 months of the reporting date. [*IAS 1.69(a), 70–71*]

3.1.40.50   As in the case of assets, if a line item in the statement of financial position includes a combination of liabilities that are expected to be settled both before and after 12 months of the reporting date, then an entity discloses the amount expected to be settled after more than 12 months. [*IAS 1.61*]

3.1.40.60   Derivatives that meet the definition of held-for-trading in IFRS 9 but are not held primarily for trading purposes are classified as current or non-current liabilities based on their outstanding maturities. This is despite the fact that they meet the definition of held-for-trading in IFRS 9 (see 7.10.50.50) and is consistent with the treatment of derivative financial assets that meet the definition of held-for-trading (see 3.1.30.45). For other liabilities in the fair value through profit or loss category, see 7.10.50.60–70. [*IAS 1.71, BC38H–BC38K*]

3.1.40.70   In our view, liabilities of a disposal group classified as held-for-sale should be classified as current in the statement of financial position as they are expected to be realised within 12 months of the date of classification as held-for-sale (see 5.4.110).

3.1.40.80   If an entity presents a classified statement of financial position and has a long-term financial liability that includes a portion due within 12 months of the reporting date and a portion due in later periods, then the liability is split into its current and non-current components. [*IAS 1.71*]

3.1.40.90   A lending agreement may include covenants that if breached render the related debt repayable before its contractual maturity date. Such an acceleration of required payments may be automatic or may be at the discretion of the lender. A liability that is repayable on demand because loan conditions have been breached is classified as current, even if the lender has agreed, after the reporting date but before the financial statements are authorised for issue, not to demand payment as a consequence of the breach. However, the debt is classified as non-current if the lender agrees by the reporting date to provide a period of grace ending at least 12 months after the reporting date. [*IAS 1.74–76, BC47*]

3.1.40.100   Loan agreements may include objective and/or subjective covenant clauses. Although subjective clauses may require greater judgement, in our view objective and subjective covenant tests should be dealt with consistently because both need to be assessed to determine whether an entity has an unconditional right to defer settlement of the liability. It is necessary to determine whether a covenant breach exists at the reporting date. This may require judgement, and more judgement may be needed to determine whether a subjective clause is breached at the reporting date.

3.1.40.110   In some circumstances, compliance with a loan covenant is assessed after the reporting date but the related tests for covenant compliance are based on financial information as at or before the reporting date. In our view, any breach of such a covenant that renders the related debt payable within 12 months after the reporting date should be treated as an adjusting subsequent event (see 2.9.20) and the related liability should be classified as current at the reporting date.

3.1.40.120   In our view, covenant tests that are based on information as at a date after the reporting date should be disregarded when assessing the classification of the liability at the reporting date, even when the entity assesses the likelihood of a breach at such future date as probable.

3.1.40.130   In some circumstances, an entity may – before the reporting date – obtain from a lender an agreement to amend a lending arrangement. Such amendments may defer the date as at which information is assessed for testing covenant compliance from a date at or before the reporting date to a later date. We believe that in such situations whether the entity would have breached the related covenant had the agreement not been amended does not affect the classification of the liability at the reporting date (see 3.1.40.120).

3.1.45   *Refinance and rollover*

3.1.45.10   The current portion of long-term debt is classified as current even if an agreement to refinance or reschedule payments on a long-term basis is completed after the reporting date but before the financial statements are authorised for issue. However, if at the reporting date an entity expects and is able – solely at its own discretion – to refinance or roll over an obligation for at least 12 months after the reporting date under an existing loan facility, then it classifies the obligation as non-current even if the loan otherwise would be current. [*IAS 1.72–73*]

EXAMPLE 2A – REFINANCING – SOLELY AT DISCRETION OF ENTITY

3.1.45.20   During the reporting period, Company D borrowed from a bank under a five-year revolving facility. Under the terms of the facility, D can borrow 1,000 in fixed tranches that have to be repaid 12 months after withdrawal. D expects and has the discretion to immediately re-draw that same 1,000 for a further 12 months.

3.1.45.25   In this example, D presents the borrowings under the facility as non-current liabilities because it has the intention and the discretion to refinance – i.e. to immediately re-draw an equivalent amount.

3.1.45.30   However, when the refinancing or rollover of an obligation is not solely at the discretion of the entity, the obligation is classified as current. [*IAS 1.73*]

EXAMPLE 2B – REFINANCING – NOT SOLELY AT DISCRETION OF ENTITY

3.1.45.35   Modifying Example 2A, the re-drawing is conditional on financial circumstances of D that are not within its control at the date on which the existing borrowing is due to be repaid. In this case, although D may expect to re-draw that same 1,000 (i.e. it has the intention), it does not have the discretion to re-draw an equivalent amount. D presents the borrowings under the facility as current liabilities because it does not have the discretion to refinance the borrowings.

3.1.45.40   The classification of debt based on the entity's intention and discretion to roll over may require careful consideration of the facts and circumstances. As explained in the preceding paragraphs, the existence of intention and discretion is based on the circumstances at the reporting date.

EXAMPLE 3 – CHANGES IN CIRCUMSTANCES AFTER REPORTING DATE

3.1.45.50   Company B is preparing its 31 December 2018 financial statements. B has a five-year loan that is due to be settled on 30 June 2019. In December 2018, B establishes a facility with the same lender that will replace the existing facility on 30 June 2019. Management of B intends to roll over the loan. The old and new facilities contain a proviso that B does not raise more than 5,000 in share capital. However, on 1 March 2019 management of B decides to and subsequently raises 6,000 in share capital.

3.1.45.60   In this example, at the reporting date B had the intention and discretion to roll over the original loan at its planned settlement date (six months after the reporting date). Therefore, the changes in circumstances after the reporting date are disregarded when assessing the classification of the loan at the reporting date. Accordingly, B classifies the loan as non-current as at 31 December 2018.

3.1.50   OFFSETTING

3.1.50.10   A financial asset and a financial liability are offset and reported net only when the entity currently has a legally enforceable right to set off and it intends to settle the asset and the liability either simultaneously or on a net basis (see 7.10.110.10). [*IAS 32.42*]

3.1.50.20   Non-financial assets and non-financial liabilities cannot be offset under IFRS. [*IAS 1.32–33*]

3.1.50.30   Specific offsetting rules exist for current and deferred tax assets and liabilities (see 3.13.630) and defined benefit plan assets and obligations (see 4.4.1080).

3.1.60   FUTURE DEVELOPMENTS

3.1.60.10   The IASB is working on a maintenance project to address the classification of liabilities. In February 2015, the IASB published Exposure Draft *Classification of Liabilities – Proposed*

amendments to IAS 1. The proposals were aimed at clarifying the criteria for classifying a liability as current or non-current by making it explicit that only rights in existence at the reporting date should affect the classification of a liability. Under the proposals, an entity would need to have a right – rather than an *unconditional right* – at the reporting date to defer settlement for at least 12 months in order to classify a liability as non-current, assuming that the other criteria are met (see 3.1.40). The Board will decide on the direction of the project in Q3 2018.

3.2 Property, plant and equipment

3.2　Property, plant and equipment

CURRENTLY EFFECTIVE REQUIREMENTS

This publication reflects IFRS in issue at 1 August 2018, and the currently effective requirements cover annual periods beginning on 1 January 2018.

The requirements related to this topic are mainly derived from the following.

STANDARD	TITLE
IFRS 13	Fair Value Measurement
IAS 16	Property, Plant and Equipment
IFRIC 1	Changes in Existing Decommissioning, Restoration and Similar Liabilities

The currently effective requirements include newly effective requirements arising from IFRS 15 *Revenue from Contracts with Customers,* which is effective for annual periods beginning on or after 1 January 2018. The new requirements may be applied using the retrospective method or the cumulative effect method (see 4.2.510). The impact of the new requirements on the accounting for property, plant and equipment is reflected in 3.2.20.40 and 380.10.

FORTHCOMING REQUIREMENTS

The currently effective requirements are affected by the following forthcoming requirements. They are highlighted with a # and the impact is explained in the accompanying boxed text at the references indicated.
- In January 2016, the IASB issued IFRS 16 *Leases*, which is effective for annual periods beginning on or after 1 January 2019. See 3.2.23 and 385. IFRS 16 is the subject of chapter 5.1A.
- In May 2017, the IASB issued IFRS 17 *Insurance Contracts*, which is effective for annual periods beginning on or after 1 January 2021. See 3.2.15. IFRS 17 is the subject of chapter 8.1A.

FUTURE DEVELOPMENTS

The currently effective requirements that may be affected by future developments are highlighted with a * and are briefly discussed in 3.2.410.

3.2.10   **SCOPE AND DEFINITION#**

3.2.10.05   IAS 16 is applied in accounting for property, plant and equipment. [*IAS 16.2*]

3.2.10.10   Property, plant and equipment comprises tangible assets held by an entity for use in the production or supply of goods or services, for rental to others or for administrative purposes, that are expected to be used for more than one period. Property, plant and equipment includes bearer plants – i.e. plants that:
- are used in the supply of agricultural produce;
- are expected to bear produce for more than one period; and
- have a remote likelihood of being sold as agricultural produce, except for scrap sales. [*IAS 16.6*]

3.2.10.15   The definition of property, plant and equipment is not restricted to assets that have an explicit link to an entity's revenue-generating operations (e.g. plant used in manufacturing goods for sale) or that form part of an entity's administrative infrastructure (e.g. corporate headquarters). For example, assets acquired as part of an entity's research activities meet the definition of property, plant and equipment if they are expected to be used in more than one period – even though research costs are expensed as they are incurred (see 3.3.120.10). Such assets are acquired to support the entity's ongoing supply of goods or services in the longer term.

3.2.10.20   Spare parts, stand-by equipment and servicing equipment – e.g. tools and consumable lubricants – are classified as property, plant and equipment if they meet the definition, including the requirement to be used over more than one period (see 3.2.10.10). Therefore, there is no requirement for such items to be used only in connection with an item of property, plant and equipment. [*IAS 16.8, BC12A*]

3.2.10.25   IAS 16 does not prescribe what constitutes an item of property, plant and equipment. Therefore, judgement is required in determining the unit of account to which the recognition and measurement requirements of IAS 16 are applied. For example, individually insignificant items, such as tools and dies, may be combined into a single unit of account in some circumstances. However, in our view an item that is separately identifiable and individually significant will generally constitute a unit of account under IAS 16. The assessment of whether an item is significant requires an entity to consider all facts and circumstances. For example, an entity might compare the total cost of the aggregated items to the cost of the item under review. Items of a dissimilar nature and used in an entity's operations constitute separate classes of property, plant and equipment (see 3.2.320) and may not be aggregated. [*IAS 16.9, 37*]

3.2.10.30   A long-term leasehold interest in a property classified as an operating lease may be classified as an investment property (see 5.1.250). In our view, any payment made to acquire such a leasehold interest should be classified as a lease prepayment rather than as property, plant and equipment.

3.2.15   **FORTHCOMING REQUIREMENTS**

3.2.15.10   Some entities operate an investment fund that provides investors with benefits determined by units in the fund or issue groups of insurance contracts with direct participation feature and hold the underlying items. Such funds or underlying items may include owner-occupied property.

3.2.15.20   Under consequential amendments to IAS 16 introduced by IFRS 17, an entity applies IAS 16 to owner-occupied property that is included within a fund or is an underlying item and it may elect to measure it using the fair value model under IAS 40. If the fair value model is applied, then the entity treats the property as a separate class of property, plant and equipment. [*IAS 16.29A–29B*]

3.2.20   INITIAL RECOGNITION AND MEASUREMENT#

3.2.20.10   Property, plant and equipment is recognised if, and only if, it is probable that future economic benefits associated with the item will flow to the entity and its cost can be measured reliably. [*IAS 16.7*]

3.2.20.20   Property, plant and equipment is recognised initially at cost. [*IAS 16.15*]

3.2.20.30   The cost of an item of property, plant and equipment comprises:
- its purchase price, including import duties and non-refundable purchase taxes, after deducting trade discounts and rebates;
- directly attributable expenditure (see 3.2.30); and
- decommissioning costs (see 3.2.70). [*IAS 16.16*]

3.2.20.40   If an entity receives an item of property, plant and equipment as a contribution from a customer to facilitate the entity's fulfilment of the contract, then the entity assesses whether it obtains control of that asset under the requirements in IFRS 15. If it obtains control of the contributed asset, then the entity recognises it as property, plant and equipment and measures it on initial recognition at fair value, if that can be reasonably estimated. If fair value cannot be reasonably estimated, then the asset is measured at the stand-alone selling price of the good or service that was promised in the contract in exchange for it. [*IFRS 15.66–69*]

3.2.23   FORTHCOMING REQUIREMENTS

3.2.23.10   IFRS 16 introduces consequential amendments to IAS 16, which specify that the cost of an item of property, plant and equipment may include costs incurred relating to leases of assets that are used to construct, add to, replace part of or service an item of property, plant and equipment – such as depreciation of right-of-use assets.

3.2.30   Directly attributable expenditure

3.2.30.10   Cost includes all expenditure directly attributable to bringing the asset to the location and condition necessary for its intended use. 'Intended use' means being capable of operating in the manner intended by management. [*IAS 16.16(b)*]

3.2.30.20   Borrowing costs that are directly attributable to the acquisition, construction or production of a qualifying asset form part of the cost of that asset (see 4.6.10).

3.2.30.30   The cost of an item of property, plant and equipment includes the estimated cost of its dismantlement, removal or restoration. This includes not only the initial estimate of such costs made at the time of installing the item, but also changes in that initial estimate and costs incurred through operations (use) for purposes other than producing inventory. For example, changes in the original estimate of dismantlement, removal or restoration costs are recognised as changes in the cost of the item (see 3.2.90). [*IAS 16.16(c), IFRIC 1.5(a)*]

3.2.30.40   The cost of employee benefits, including share-based payment transactions, that are incurred for employees working directly on the construction or acquisition of the asset are directly attributable costs of that item. [*IAS 16.17(a)*]

3.2.30.50   The costs incurred need not be external or incremental to be directly attributable.

EXAMPLE 1A – DIRECTLY ATTRIBUTABLE EXPENDITURE – LABOUR COSTS

3.2.30.55   Company G is installing a major piece of equipment at one of its factories. One of G's existing engineers is assigned to manage the installation on a full-time basis and installation is expected to take six weeks.

3.2.30.57   We believe that the cost of the engineer – including all employee benefits – during the period of installation should be included in the cost of the equipment even though those costs would have been incurred in any event. This is because the costs incurred need not be external or incremental to be directly attributable.

3.2.30.60   In some cases, an entity will incur expenditure in carrying out a feasibility study before deciding whether to invest in an asset or in deciding which asset to acquire. In our view, expenses incurred for feasibility assessment should be expensed as they are incurred because they are not linked to a specific item of property, plant and equipment. This is consistent with the approach taken under SIC-32 for the development of a website (see 3.3.130). However, in our view the cost of property, plant and equipment does include expenditure that is incurred only if an asset is acquired. For example, a fee may be payable to a broker or agent only if a suitable property is identified and bought. We believe that such a fee is directly attributable to the acquisition of the property acquired and therefore should be included in the cost of the property.

3.2.30.70   Often staff need to be trained in the use of a new item of property, plant and equipment. Training costs are not recognised as part of the cost of an item of property, plant and equipment. If the asset is installed by a third party and training is part of the total contract price, then in our view some part of the total price should be allocated to training and expensed as they are incurred. [*IAS 16.19(c)*]

3.2.30.80   The determination of whether operating lease costs are directly attributable costs requires judgement in light of all relevant facts and circumstances. The costs associated with opening a new facility, as well as general and administrative costs, are not part of the cost of an item of property, plant and equipment. Such costs are expensed as they are incurred. For example, Retailer B plans to open a new store and rents a retail space under an operating lease. In this example, the store could be opened immediately, but B first refurbishes the store so that it conforms with the design and branding of its other stores. B expects that the refurbishment will take three months. In our view, lease payments incurred during the refurbishment are costs associated with opening a new facility because they are not directly attributable to bringing the asset to the location and condition necessary for it to be capable of operating in the manner intended by management; therefore, these costs should be expensed as they are incurred. [*IAS 16.19(a), (d)*]

3.2.30.83   However, if a building is constructed on land that is leased under an operating lease, then in our view the operating lease costs for the land incurred during the construction period should be capitalised as part of the cost of the building if these costs are directly attributable to bringing the asset to the location and condition necessary for it to be capable of operating in the manner intended by management. [*IAS 16.16(b)*]

EXAMPLE 1B – DIRECTLY ATTRIBUTABLE EXPENDITURE – OPERATING LEASE COSTS

3.2.30.85   Company B enters into an operating lease of land on which there are several buildings in shell form – i.e. the interior and infrastructure is yet to be completed. The lease term is for a period of 20 years and management's intention is to use the premises as its corporate headquarters.

3.2.30.86   Because the buildings are in shell form, significant leasehold improvements are required before the premises will be ready for their intended use. Over a 10-month period, B constructs the interior of the buildings including ceilings and frames, electricity, lighting, air conditioning and work stations.

3.2.30.87   In this example, we believe that the construction of the leasehold improvements is similar to the construction of a building; therefore, the operating lease costs incurred during the construction period should be capitalised because they are directly attributable to bringing the premises to the condition necessary to be capable of operating in the manner intended by management – i.e. as its corporate headquarters.

3.2.30.90   Initial operating losses such as those incurred while demand for the item's output builds up are not part of the cost of an item of property, plant and equipment. [*IAS 16.20(b)*]

3.2.30.100   An entity may buy land with the intention of constructing a new building on the site within a reasonable timeframe. In our view, the costs of demolishing any existing building on the site should be capitalised as part of the cost of the property if they are directly attributable to bringing the asset to the location and condition necessary for its intended use. However, it may not be clear whether the demolition costs should be capitalised to the cost of the land or to the cost of the new building. This distinction is important because land and buildings are generally depreciated differently (see 3.2.140.10).

EXAMPLE 1C – DIRECTLY ATTRIBUTABLE DEMOLITION COSTS – CAPITALISED TO THE LAND

3.2.30.103   Company M buys land with a dilapidated building on it for the purpose of constructing an outside car park. The rationale behind the purchase is to acquire the land, rather than the land and the building. Management's intent at the

3.2 Property, plant and equipment

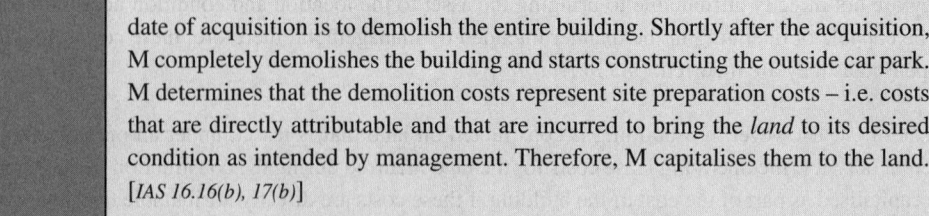

date of acquisition is to demolish the entire building. Shortly after the acquisition, M completely demolishes the building and starts constructing the outside car park. M determines that the demolition costs represent site preparation costs – i.e. costs that are directly attributable and that are incurred to bring the *land* to its desired condition as intended by management. Therefore, M capitalises them to the land. [*IAS 16.16(b), 17(b)*]

EXAMPLE 1D – DIRECTLY ATTRIBUTABLE DEMOLITION COSTS – CAPITALISED TO THE NEW BUILDING

3.2.30.105   Company T buys land with an old hotel for the purpose of constructing its headquarters. Management's intent at the date of acquisition is to demolish the entire hotel and construct a new building in its place. Shortly after the acquisition, T completely demolishes the hotel and starts constructing the new building. T determines that the demolition costs are directly attributable to the construction of the new building as intended by management. Therefore, T capitalises them to the new building. [*IAS 16.16(b)*]

3.2.30.110   A similar but less common example is when an entity agrees to relocate a community (or part thereof) in order to construct an asset – e.g. a golf course. In our view, the relocation costs should be capitalised because they are directly attributable to the construction of the asset.

3.2.30.120   Although it is common for the design of a complex asset to be modified and improved during construction, care should be taken to avoid double counting costs.

EXAMPLE 1E – DIRECTLY ATTRIBUTABLE EXPENDITURE – DESIGN MODIFICATION COSTS

3.2.30.125   Company E is constructing a hotel. The cost of designing the hotel has been capitalised as part of the cost of the asset. During construction, the directors of E reassess their plans and decide that a hotel is no longer viable in the current economic environment. Instead, the directors decide to develop the site into a retirement village, which requires a complete redesign of the site.

3.2.30.127   Although it is appropriate to capitalise the cost of designing the retirement village, we believe that the original hotel design costs should be written off because they are not part of the eventual asset and will result in double counting. A similar approach should be adopted for any other costs – e.g. construction costs – that do not form part of the eventual asset because of changes made in the course of construction.

3.2.30.130   In our view, cancellation costs incurred to acquire an item of property, plant and equipment are not directly attributable costs because they are not directly related to the acquisition of that item and are not required to bring the item to the location and condition necessary for it to be capable of operating in the manner intended by management. [*IAS 16.16(b)*]

EXAMPLE 1F – DIRECTLY ATTRIBUTABLE EXPENDITURE – CANCELLATION COSTS

3.2.30.135   Company T has signed a contract with Company S to buy several machines over the next five years. T can cancel the contract in relation to undelivered machines, but only if it pays a cancellation fee. One year after signing the contract, T receives an offer from Company Q to supply the remaining machines at a significantly lower cost. T cancels the contract with S and incurs the cancellation fee.

3.2.30.137   In this example, we believe that the cancellation fee should not be capitalised as part of the cost of the machines bought from Q. Instead, it should be expensed when it is incurred.

3.2.40   Abnormal waste

3.2.40.10   Similar to determining the cost of inventory (see 3.8.120), when an item of property, plant and equipment is constructed by an entity, the standard requires abnormal amounts of wasted material, labour and other resources to be expensed as they are incurred instead of being capitalised. A determination of what should be considered *abnormal* is subjective, but in our view the factors to consider include the level of technical difficulty involved with the construction, the scale of the project, the estimates and timelines included in the project planning, and the usual construction process for that type of asset. [*IAS 16.22*]

EXAMPLE 2A – COMMISSIONING COSTS

3.2.40.20   Company F is constructing a plant that produces plastic building blocks for children. During the commissioning phase – which is due to take two weeks – sample building blocks are produced to ensure that the plant is operating correctly. The engineers use the test results to finalise the calibration of the machines. Most of the building blocks produced during testing are unfit for sale and are disposed of. The commissioning phase lasts two weeks as scheduled.

3.2.40.25   In this example, the costs incurred as part of the testing are a normal part of the construction process and the related costs are capitalised.

EXAMPLE 2B – COMMISSIONING COSTS – ABNORMAL

3.2.40.30   Continuing Example 2A, if commissioning was due to take two weeks but actually took four weeks – e.g. because a trainee engineer had installed a machine incorrectly or because site management forgot to schedule machine operators for the testing phase – then we believe that any additional costs incurred as a result of such events should be considered abnormal and expensed as they are incurred. The additional costs could be measured with reference to the amount of testing that was planned.

3.2.40.40   However, if testing took four weeks instead of two because F was introducing a new and previously untested technology into its production process

> and unforeseen technical difficulties were experienced, then we believe that the
> additional costs incurred should be capitalised because the costs are not abnormal.

3.2.40.50   Abnormal waste is discussed in the context of assets that are constructed by the entity. In our view, these principles apply equally when the asset is not constructed by the entity, but the installation process nonetheless is necessary to bring the asset to its working condition. [*IAS 16.22*]

3.2.50   Pre-operating costs and losses

3.2.50.10   Start-up and pre-operating costs are not capitalised as part of the cost of property, plant and equipment unless those costs are necessary to bring the asset to its working condition. [*IAS 16.19, 20(b)*]

EXAMPLE 3A – PRE-OPERATING – GENERAL BUSINESS COSTS

3.2.50.15   Company G is opening a new plant in a town where it has not previously operated. In addition to obtaining a certificate to confirm that the plant meets environmental specifications, G is required to obtain general permits that allow it to conduct business in the town.

3.2.50.17   In this example, we believe that the cost of the permits should not be capitalised because they are a general business cost that does not relate specifically to the asset.

3.2.50.20   An entity may incur losses before the asset reaches its planned performance level. Such losses are not capitalised. [*IAS 16.20(a)*]

EXAMPLE 3B – PRE-OPERATING – OPERATING LOSSES

3.2.50.25   Continuing Example 2B, if after installation Company F runs the new plant at half capacity for a month while staff are trained in how to use it correctly, then any loss incurred during that period is recognised in profit or loss.

3.2.60   Interruptions

3.2.60.10   In some cases, construction will not be continuous and interruptions will occur during which time costs may still be incurred. For example, the entity may have to continue paying site insurance costs. IFRS is silent about whether such costs may be capitalised, but in our view the guidance in IAS 23 regarding the capitalisation of borrowing costs is relevant (see 4.6.10). [*IAS 23.21*]

3.2.60.20   Accordingly, we believe that costs incurred during an interruption should be capitalised only if:
* the interruption is temporary and is a necessary part of getting the asset into its working condition – e.g. the construction of a bridge is suspended while water levels are high – provided that such costs are not abnormal waste (see 3.2.40); or

- the costs are an integral part of getting the asset into its working condition even though physical construction has been suspended – e.g. the cost of delays for obtaining permits for the eventual operation of the asset.

3.2.70 Decommissioning costs

3.2.70.10   The cost of property, plant and equipment includes the estimated cost of dismantling and removing the asset and restoring the site to the extent that such cost is recognised as a provision (see 3.12.440). [*IAS 16.16(c)*]

EXAMPLE 4 – DECOMMISSIONING COSTS

3.2.70.20   Company H constructs a chemical plant that has a useful life of 30 years. Environmental laws require H to dismantle the plant at the end of its useful life. H recognises a provision for the dismantling and removal costs, which are capitalised as part of the cost of the asset. [*IAS 37.IE.C.Ex3*]

3.2.70.25   No provision is made, and no amount is capitalised, in respect of any environmental damage that has yet to occur – i.e. damage caused by future operations – rather than by the construction of the asset. This is because there is no present obligation for any environmental damage that has yet to occur. [*IAS 37.IE.C.Ex3*]

3.2.70.30   The cost of an item of property, plant and equipment includes not only the initial estimate of the costs related to the dismantlement, removal or restoration of property, plant and equipment at the time of installing the item, but also the costs incurred during the period of use for purposes other than producing inventory. Decommissioning and restoration costs incurred through the production of inventory are included as part of inventory costs (see 3.8.180).

EXAMPLE 5 – CLEAN-UP COSTS

3.2.70.40   Continuing Example 4, the installation and testing of Company H's new chemical plant results in contamination of the ground at the plant. H will be required to clean up the contamination caused by the installation when the plant is dismantled. H recognises a provision for restoration, which is capitalised as part of the cost of the asset.

3.2.70.50   Example 5 assumes that the contamination occurs when the asset is installed. If the contamination occurs as a consequence of the production of inventory, then the related cost is included in the cost of inventory or expensed in the period (e.g. if the costs are abnormal), as appropriate. [*IAS 16.18*]

3.2.80 *Changes to existing provisions*

3.2.80.10   Subsequent to initial recognition, the amount of a decommissioning provision will generally change because of the following:

- changes in the estimate of the amount or timing of expenditure required to settle the obligation;

- changes in the current market-based discount rate as defined in paragraph 47 of IAS 37; and
- the unwinding of the discount. [*IFRIC 1.3*]

3.2.80.20   The accounting for changes to an existing obligation because of changes in the estimated timing or amount of expenditure or changes in the discount rate is consistent with the accounting treatment for changes in estimates (see 2.8.100). This treatment is discussed further in 3.2.90–100. [*IFRIC 1.4–6*]

3.2.80.25   IFRS is not clear about how an entity should account for foreign exchange gains and losses arising on the retranslation of a decommissioning provision (see 3.12.470.40). Foreign currency denominated obligations are translated at current exchange rates when the obligation is a monetary liability. Non-monetary liabilities denominated in a foreign currency are not retranslated (see 2.7.110.10). [*IAS 21.23, 28*]

3.2.80.30   In our view, a decommissioning liability is:
- monetary to the extent that it is expected to be settled by payment in a fixed or determinable number of units of currency – e.g. future payments to employees or third parties for goods and/ or services; and
- non-monetary to the extent that it will be settled by the delivery, consumption or use of a previously recognised non-monetary asset – e.g. using materials on hand. [*IAS 21.16, 23*]

3.2.80.40   Generally, foreign exchange gains and losses arising on the retranslation of monetary items are recognised immediately in profit or loss (see 2.7.140.10). However, IFRIC 1 requires changes in a decommissioning provision resulting from changes in estimated cash flows to be added to or deducted from the cost of the related asset. In our view, an entity should choose an accounting policy, to be applied consistently, either to recognise foreign exchange gains and losses arising on the retranslation of decommissioning provisions in profit or loss, or to recognise them as adjustments to the cost of the related asset (see 3.12.470.40). [*IFRIC 1.5–6*]

3.2.90   *Cost model*

3.2.90.10   Under the cost model, all changes in the decommissioning provision (see 3.2.80.10), other than changes resulting from the unwinding of the discount, which are recorded in profit or loss, are added to or deducted from the cost of the related asset in the current period (see 3.12.150). However, the amount deducted from the cost of the asset cannot exceed its carrying amount – i.e. after considering the depreciation charged to date. Any excess is recognised immediately in profit or loss because an asset cannot have a negative carrying amount. [*IFRIC 1.5(a)–(b)*]

3.2.90.20   An increase in the cost of an asset may require consideration of whether there is an indication of impairment (see 3.10.120). [*IFRIC 1.5(c)*]

EXAMPLE 6A – REMEASUREMENT OF DECOMMISSIONING PROVISION – COST MODEL

3.2.90.30   Company X built a new plant that was brought into use on 1 January 2018. The cost to construct the plant was 1,500. The estimated useful life of the plant is 20 years and X accounts for the plant using the cost model.

3.2.90.40   The initial carrying amount of the plant included an amount of 100 for decommissioning, which was determined using a discount rate of 10%. At the end of 2018, X remeasures the provision for decommissioning to 130. Accordingly, X records the following entries in the year ending 31 December 2018.

	DEBIT	CREDIT
Depreciation (profit or loss)	75	
Accumulated depreciation (plant)		75
To recognise depreciation of plant calculated under straight-line method (1,500 x 5%)		
Interest expense (profit or loss)	10	
Provision for decommissioning		10
To recognise unwinding of discount on provision (100 x 10%) (see 3.12.840)		
Plant	20	
Provision for decommissioning		20
To recognise increase in provision (130 - (100 + 10))		

3.2.100   *Revaluation model*

3.2.100.10   Under the revaluation model, valuations are kept sufficiently up to date such that the carrying amount of the asset does not differ materially from its fair value at the reporting date (see 3.2.300). A change in the provision does not, of itself, affect the valuation of the asset, because the value of the provision is excluded from the asset valuation. [*IAS 16.34*]

3.2.100.20   The change in the provision affects the difference between the valuation and what would have been recognised under the cost model. Therefore, changes in the provision other than changes resulting from the unwinding of the discount (see 3.2.80.10), which are recorded in profit or loss, affect the revaluation surplus or deficit previously recognised in respect of that asset.
- A decrease in the provision is recognised in OCI, except to the extent that it reverses a revaluation deficit previously recognised in profit or loss, or when it would result in the depreciated cost of the asset being negative (see 3.2.100.30).
- An increase in the provision is recognised in profit or loss, except to the extent that any credit balance remains in the revaluation surplus in equity. [*IFRIC 1.6(a)–(b)*]

3.2.100.30   The depreciated cost of the asset cannot be negative.

EXAMPLE 6B – REMEASUREMENT OF DECOMMISSIONING PROVISION – REVALUATION MODEL (1)

3.2.100.35   The depreciated cost of an unimpaired asset is 25 and its revalued amount is 100, giving a revaluation surplus of 75.

> 3.2.100.37   If the decommissioning provision is reduced by 30, then 25 is recognised in OCI, which notionally reduces the depreciated cost to zero. The remaining 5 is recognised in profit or loss.

3.2.100.40   A change in the provision is an indicator that the fair value of the asset may also have changed and an entity should consider whether a revaluation is required. If a revaluation of the affected asset is required, then all other assets in the same asset class are revalued (see 3.2.300). [*IAS 16.36, IFRIC 1.6(c)*]

EXAMPLE 6C – REMEASUREMENT OF DECOMMISSIONING PROVISION – REVALUATION MODEL (2)

3.2.100.50   Company X built a new plant that was brought into use on 1 January 2018. The cost to construct the plant was 1,500. The estimated useful life of the plant is 20 years and, unlike in Example 6A, X accounts for the plant using the revaluation model.

3.2.100.60   The initial carrying amount of the plant included an amount of 100 for decommissioning, which was determined using a discount rate of 10%. At the end of 2018, X remeasures the provision for decommissioning to 130. X also revalues the plant at the end of 2018 to an amount of 1,800. Accordingly, X records the following entries in the year ending 31 December 2018.

	DEBIT	CREDIT
Depreciation (profit or loss)	75	
Accumulated depreciation (plant)		75
To recognise depreciation of plant calculated under straight-line method (1,500 x 5%)		
Interest expense (profit or loss)	10	
Provision for decommissioning		10
To recognise unwinding of discount on provision (100 x 10%) (see 3.12.840)		
Plant	375	
Revaluation surplus (OCI)		375
To recognise revaluation of plant (1,800 - (1,500 - 75))		
Revaluation surplus (OCI)	20	
Provision for decommissioning		20
To recognise increase in provision (130 - (100 + 10))		

EXAMPLE 6D – REMEASUREMENT OF DECOMMISSIONING PROVISION – REVALUATION MODEL (3)

3.2.100.70   Assume the same facts as in Example 6C except that Company X revalues the plant at the end of 2018 to an amount of 1,440. Accordingly, X records the following entries in the year ending 31 December 2018.

	DEBIT	CREDIT
Depreciation (profit or loss)	75	
Accumulated depreciation (plant)		75
To recognise depreciation of plant calculated under straight-line method (1,500 x 5%)		
Interest expense (profit or loss)	10	
Provision for decommissioning		10
To recognise unwinding of discount on provision (100 x 10%) (see 3.12.840)		
Plant	15	
Revaluation surplus (OCI)		15
To recognise revaluation of plant (1,440 - (1,500 - 75))		
Revaluation surplus (OCI)	15	
Profit or loss	5	
Provision for decommissioning		20
To recognise increase in provision (130 - (100 + 10))		

3.2.105   *Fully depreciated property, plant and equipment*

3.2.105.10   Once an item of property, plant and equipment has been fully depreciated and the asset has a net carrying amount (gross carrying amount less accumulated depreciation) of zero in the statement of financial position, further changes in any related provision for decommissioning are recognised in profit or loss. This applies under both the cost model and the revaluation model – i.e. regardless of whether any revaluation surplus remains recognised in equity. [*IFRIC 1.7*]

3.2.110   *New obligations*

3.2.110.10   IFRS contains no explicit guidance for a new obligation that arises subsequent to the initial recognition of the asset. In our view, the principles that apply to changes in estimates of existing obligations (see 3.2.80) should be applied in such circumstances even if the obligation arises only at the end of the useful life of the asset (see 3.12.440). However, the capitalisation of these costs should not result in the carrying amount of the asset exceeding its recoverable amount (see 3.10.180).

EXAMPLE 7 – DECOMMISSIONING COSTS – NEW OBLIGATION

3.2.110.20   Company H constructs a chemical plant and at the time that construction was completed there were no applicable environmental laws requiring decommissioning of the plant in the future. However, two years later the government introduces a new law requiring the plant to be dismantled at the end of its useful life. We believe that the principles that apply to changes in estimates of existing obligations should be applied and the amount of the provision should be recognised as part of the cost of the asset.

3.2.120   Incidental operations*

3.2.120.10   Generally, there are two types of incidental income.

- Incidental income from operating (including testing) a new asset is part of the directly attributable cost of the asset. The cost of testing the asset (less the income) is recognised as part of the cost of the item of property, plant and equipment. If the income from the testing activity is higher than the cost of testing the asset, then the net effect is a deduction from the cost of the asset.
- Other incidental operations are not considered necessary to bring the item to the location and condition necessary for it to be capable of operating in the manner intended by management. Therefore, income and expenses from incidental operations are recognised in profit or loss and included in their respective classifications of income and expense. [*IAS 16.17(e), 21*]

EXAMPLE 8A – INCOME INCIDENTAL TO OPERATIONS

3.2.120.20   Continuing Example 2A, Company F earns income from the sale of imperfect samples of building blocks produced during testing.

3.2.120.30   The income earned is deducted from the cost of testing the asset because the income is incidental to F's operations. The cost of testing the asset (less the income) is recognised as part of the cost of the item of property, plant and equipment. If the income from the testing activity is higher than the cost of testing the asset, then the net effect will be a deduction from the cost of the asset.

EXAMPLE 8B – INCOME INCIDENTAL TO CONSTRUCTION

3.2.120.40   Company K acquires a sports hall with the intention of constructing a supermarket on the site. While K waits to receive permits for the construction, it rents out the sports facilities to a local school.

3.2.120.50   The income earned, and any related expenses, are recognised in profit or loss (included in their respective classifications of income and expense) because the activity of renting out the sports facilities is not considered necessary to bring the item to the location and condition necessary for it to be capable of operating in the manner intended by management.

3.2.130   **Deferred payment**

3.2.130.10   When payment is deferred beyond normal credit terms, the cost of the asset is the cash price equivalent (i.e. current cash price) at the recognition date. This calculation is different from the calculation of the financial liability (the amount due in respect of the acquisition) that otherwise would be made under IFRS 9, which would require the cash flows to be discounted using a market rate of interest (see 7.7.90). However, in our view the requirements of IAS 16 should be applied because the standard specifically addresses deferred payment for property, plant and equipment. [*IAS 16.23*]

3.2.130.20   The difference between the cash price equivalent and the amount payable is recognised as interest expense over the period until payment, unless it is capitalised in accordance with IAS 23. In our view, the effective interest method should be applied as it would for other financial instrument liabilities (see 7.7.270) because there is nothing to the contrary in IAS 16.

3.2.140   **DEPRECIATION**

3.2.140.10   Subsequent to initial recognition, property, plant and equipment is depreciated on a systematic basis over its useful life. Each part of an item of property, plant and equipment with a cost that is significant in relation to the total cost of the item is depreciated separately. [*IAS 16.43*]

3.2.140.20   The useful life of an asset and the depreciation method applied is reviewed as a minimum at each annual reporting date. A change in the useful life or depreciation method is accounted for prospectively as a change in accounting estimate (see 2.8.100). [*IAS 16.51, 61*]

EXAMPLE 9 – CHANGE IN USEFUL LIFE

> 3.2.140.30   Company L acquired a printing machine at the beginning of 2015 and its useful life was estimated to be 10 years. At the end of 2017, the carrying amount of the machine was 240. At the beginning of 2018, L revised the estimated useful life and reduced the remaining life of the machine to a further two years from that date.
>
> 3.2.140.35   Therefore, the carrying amount of 240 is depreciated over the next two years (2018 and 2019). In addition, the decrease in useful life may indicate that the carrying amount of the machine is impaired (see 3.10.110).

3.2.140.40   The purpose of depreciation is not the recognition of decreases in the value of property, plant and equipment; rather, the purpose is to allocate the cost or revalued amount of an asset over its useful life on a systematic basis. Therefore, depreciation is recognised even if the value of the asset (e.g. a hotel) is being maintained by regular repairs and maintenance. [*IAS 16.6, 50, 60*]

3.2.140.50   The depreciation charge for each period is recognised as an expense in profit or loss, unless it is included in the carrying amount of another asset. For example, the depreciation of manufacturing plant and equipment is included in the cost of inventories. [*IAS 16.48*]

3.2.150 **Residual value**

3.2.150.10 An asset's depreciable amount is its cost, or revalued amount if it is carried under the revaluation model, less its residual value. Even though there might be uncertainty associated with the estimate of residual value, it is an estimate of the amount that an entity could receive from disposal of the asset at the reporting date if the asset were already of the age and in the condition that it will be in when the entity expects to dispose of it. Residual value does not include expected future inflation or expected increases or decreases in the ultimate disposal value. [*IAS 16.6*]

3.2.150.20 In many cases, the residual value will be insignificant or zero because the asset will be scrapped at the end of its useful life. However, if the residual value is significant, then changes in the estimated residual value could cause volatility in the depreciation charge. For example, ships and aircraft may have significant residual values that may be subject to significant volatility from period to period. The residual value of a ship that is intended to be used until the end of its economic life and sold as scrap may fluctuate significantly from period to period as a result of volatility in prices of steel. The residual value of a new aircraft intended to be sold on the second-hand market 10 years after its acquisition may fluctuate significantly as a result of volatility in the second-hand market price. [*IAS 16.6, 53*]

3.2.150.25 The residual value of an asset is reviewed as a minimum at each annual reporting date and changes are accounted for as a change in accounting estimate (see 2.8.100). [*IAS 16.51*]

EXAMPLE 10A – RESIDUAL VALUE – SALE IN THE SECOND-HAND MARKET

3.2.150.30 Company M buys a machine costing 400. M plans to use the machine for three years and then to sell it on the second-hand market. At the date of acquisition, a machine that is three years old is traded for 150 on the second-hand market.

3.2.150.33 Therefore, the residual value of the machine at the date of acquisition is 150. In this example, the depreciable amount of the machine to be recognised over the three-year holding period is 250.

EXAMPLE 10B – RESIDUAL VALUE – DISPOSAL AS SCRAP

3.2.150.35 Continuing Example 10A, Company N buys a similar machine costing 400. N plans to hold it until the end of its economic life of five years and then sell it as scrap. The machine is made primarily of steel. At the date of acquisition, N obtains a quote of 50 from a scrap steel broker.

3.2.150.37 Therefore, the residual value of the machine at the date of acquisition is 50. In this example, the depreciable amount of the machine to be recognised over the five-year economic (and useful) life is 350.

EXAMPLE 11 – CHANGE IN RESIDUAL VALUE ESTIMATE

3.2.150.40 On 1 January 2018, Company S buys a ship costing 4,000. S plans to hold it until the end of its economic life of 25 years and then sell it as scrap. The ship is made primarily of steel. Therefore, S uses a quote of 500 obtained from a

scrap steel broker at the date of acquisition for estimating the residual value of the ship. The depreciable amount for the ship on 1 January 2018 is therefore 3,500 (4,000 - 500) and the depreciation charge for 2018 is 140 (3,500 / 25).

3.2.150.45   Following a significant decrease in the price of steel in December 2018, S obtains a new quote from the scrap steel broker and reviews the residual value of the ship. Based on the new quote, the residual value of the ship at 31 December 2018 is 260. The new depreciable amount for 2019 is therefore 3,600 (4,000 - 140 - 260) and the annual depreciation charge going forward is 150 (3,600 / 24).

3.2.150.50   If the residual value of an asset increases to an amount equal to or more than the asset's carrying amount, then the depreciation charge will be zero. The entity would resume charging depreciation when the residual value falls below the asset's carrying amount. [*IAS 16.54*]

3.2.160   Methods of depreciation

3.2.160.10   The method of depreciation reflects the pattern in which the benefits associated with the asset are consumed, and is reviewed as a minimum at each annual reporting date. [*IAS 16.60–61*]

3.2.160.20   A change in the depreciation method is accounted for prospectively as a change in accounting estimate (see 2.8.100). [*IAS 16.61*]

3.2.160.30   IFRS does not require a specific method of depreciation to be used, and mentions the straight-line method, the diminishing-balance (or reducing-balance) method and the sum-of-the-units (or units-of-production) method. Other methods of depreciation that are not mentioned in the standard include the annuity method and renewals accounting. [*IAS 16.62*]

3.2.160.40   In our experience, the straight-line method (see 3.2.170) is used most commonly and is the easiest to administer. However, ultimately the method of depreciation is chosen to reflect most closely the pattern in which the future economic benefits associated with the asset are expected to be consumed. In making this determination, an entity considers not only the factors specific to its expected use of the asset – e.g. expected output – but other factors such as technical and commercial obsolescence, and any legal or similar restrictions on the use of the asset. [*IAS 16.56, 60, 62*]

3.2.170   *Straight-line method*

3.2.170.10   Under the straight-line method, depreciation is measured so that the amount each year is the same. It is calculated using the current gross carrying amount of the asset – i.e. cost or revalued amount – the expected residual value and its useful life.

EXAMPLE 12A – DEPRECIATION – STRAIGHT-LINE

3.2.170.20   A machine cost 150, has a residual value of 30 and a useful life of eight years. Therefore, the annual depreciation charge under the straight-line method is as follows.

YR 1	YR 2	YR 3	YR 4	YR 5	YR 6	YR 7	YR 8
15[1]	15	15	15	15	15	15	15

Note
1. Calculated as (150 - 30) / 8.

3.2.180 *Diminishing-balance method*

3.2.180.10   Under the diminishing-balance method, depreciation is measured as a percentage of the current carrying amount of the asset – i.e. cost or revalued amount less accumulated depreciation to date.

EXAMPLE 12B – DEPRECIATION – DIMINISHING BALANCE

3.2.180.15   Assuming the same facts as in Example 12A, the machine would be depreciated at 18.25[1]% per annum to reduce the carrying amount to the residual value of 30 at the end of eight years. Therefore, the annual depreciation charge under the diminishing-balance method is as follows.

YR 1	YR 2	YR 3	YR 4	YR 5	YR 6	YR 7	YR 8
28	22	18	15	12	10	8	7

Note
1. Calculated using the following formula: $R = 1 - n\sqrt{\dfrac{RV}{C}}$, with
    R – depreciation rate
    n – useful life in years
    RV – residual value of the asset
    C – cost of the asset

3.2.180.20   Under this method, the depreciation charge declines over the years, which is appropriate when the machine provides greater benefits to the entity in its earlier years – e.g. because it will be less capable of producing a high-quality product in later years, or because the machine will be less technologically advanced in later years.

3.2.190 *Units-of-production method*

3.2.190.10   Under the units-of-production method, depreciation is based on the level of output or usage expected to be achieved. Although this method may provide a more accurate picture of the consumption of an asset, it may be difficult to estimate the expected output over the life of the asset.

EXAMPLE 12C – DEPRECIATION – UNITS-OF-PRODUCTION

3.2.190.20   Continuing Example 12A, assume that the expected output over the life of the asset is 8,600 units and that the estimated annual output is as follows.

Yr 1	Yr 2	Yr 3	Yr 4	Yr 5	Yr 6	Yr 7	Yr 8
1,500	1,200	1,200	1,100	1,100	1,000	1,000	500

3.2.190.30   Therefore, the annual depreciation charge under the units-of-production method is as follows.

	ESTIMATED OUTPUT (A)	%[1] (B)	DEPRECIATION[2]
Yr 1	1,500	17%	21
Yr 2	1,200	14%	17
Yr 3	1,200	14%	17
Yr 4	1,100	13%	15
Yr 5	1,100	13%	15
Yr 6	1,000	12%	14
Yr 7	1,000	12%	14
Yr 8	500	5%	7
Total output	8,600	100%	120

Notes
1.   Calculated as (A / 8,600).
2.   Calculated as (150 - 30) x B, with 150 being the machine cost and 30 its residual value.

3.2.190.40   If this method of depreciation is used, then the estimates of future production are reviewed and revised if necessary at each reporting date in accordance with the requirement to review the expected useful life. The impact on depreciation expense of a revision to estimates of future production are treated as a change in estimate (see 2.8.100) and previous depreciation is not restated. [*IAS 16.51*]

3.2.200   *Annuity depreciation*

3.2.200.10   'Annuity depreciation' refers to depreciation methods under which the depreciation charge is adjusted to reflect the time value of money. Such depreciation methods result in lower depreciation charges in initial periods and larger depreciation charges in later periods. These methods are used under some national accounting practices – e.g. by operating lessors in order to recognise a level profit after considering financing costs related to the leased asset over the lease term. In our view, the financing costs of an asset should not impact the selection of a depreciation policy. IFRS requires depreciation to reflect the consumption of the economic benefits of an asset. We believe that this does not extend to consideration of financing costs or inflation adjustments.

3.2.210   *Renewals accounting*

3.2.210.10   Under some GAAPs, it has been common in certain industries (e.g. utilities) not to recognise depreciation on the basis that the assets are maintained at a certain performance or service level and that all maintenance costs, including costs incurred to replace components of the asset, are expensed immediately; this is often referred to as 'renewals accounting'. It has been argued that the amount recognised in profit or loss in respect of the upkeep of the assets is similar to the depreciation charge that would have been recognised.

3.2.210.20   A variation on renewals accounting is condition-based depreciation whereby the condition of the asset is assessed and depreciation is measured as the increased cost required to restore the asset to a predetermined performance or service level.

3.2.210.30   In our view, these methods of depreciation are not acceptable under IFRS unless the impact on the financial statements is immaterial.

3.2.215   *Revenue-based depreciation*

3.2.215.10   IAS 16 prohibits the use of a depreciation method that reflects the pattern of generation of economic benefits from the use of the asset in the business, instead of a pattern of consumption of expected future economic benefits of the asset. This means that an entity cannot use a revenue-based method of depreciation. [*IAS 16.62A*]

3.2.220   Commencement of depreciation

3.2.220.10   Depreciation of an asset begins when it is available or ready for use – i.e. when it is in the location and condition necessary for it to be capable of operating in the manner intended by management. In some cases, depreciation may commence before the asset is actually brought into use. [*IAS 16.55*]

EXAMPLE 13 – COMMENCEMENT OF DEPRECIATION

3.2.220.20   Company N buys computer equipment that it knows will be technologically obsolete after two years. The equipment is ready for use when acquired, but N does not bring it into use until six months after the acquisition.

3.2.220.25   In this example, depreciation commences when the asset is acquired because the asset is ready for use at this time.

3.2.220.30   If an item of property, plant and equipment is substantially complete, but is not yet in use, then an entity reviews the asset for potential indicators of impairment (see 3.10.20.30 and 120).

3.2.230   COMPONENT ACCOUNTING

3.2.230.10   If an item of property, plant and equipment comprises individual components for which different depreciation methods or rates are appropriate, then each component is depreciated separately. A separate component may be either a physical component or a non-physical component that represents a major inspection or overhaul. An item of property, plant and equipment is separated into parts (components) when those parts are significant in relation to the total cost of the item. [*IAS 16.43–47*]

3.2.230.20   Component accounting is mandatory if it would be applicable. However, this does not mean that an entity should split its assets into an infinite number of components if the effect on the financial statements would be immaterial. [*IAS 16.44, 46*]

3.2.230.30   If an entity depreciates some parts of an item of property, plant and equipment separately, then it depreciates the remainder of the item separately. The remainder consists of the parts of the item that are not significant individually. If an entity has varying expectations for these parts, then it uses approximation techniques to estimate an appropriate depreciation pattern for the remainder to reflect the consumption pattern and/or usefulness of its parts. [*IAS 16.46*]

EXAMPLE 14A – COMPONENT ACCOUNTING – INSIGNIFICANT COMPONENTS

3.2.230.40   Company Q buys a machine for 100. The machine consists of four components, of which two components comprise 80 of the total cost of 100. The remaining two components have a cost of 10 each, which is considered insignificant, and they have useful lives of four and six years respectively.

3.2.230.45   In this example, we believe that the two insignificant components could be combined to give a cost of 20 and a useful life of five years.

3.2.230.50   Although individual components are accounted for separately, the financial statements continue to disclose a single asset. For example, an airline would generally disclose aircraft as a class of assets, rather than disclosing separate information in respect of the aircraft body, hydraulics, engines, seating etc.

3.2.240   Physical components

3.2.240.10   If the component is a physical component – e.g. the motor in an engine – then the carrying amount of the component is determined with reference to its cost.

EXAMPLE 14B – COMPONENT ACCOUNTING – PHYSICAL COMPONENTS

3.2.240.15   Company O constructs a sports stadium that has an overall useful life of 50 years. One of the components of the stadium is the seating, which has an expected useful life of 10 years. The cost of the stadium in total is 500, which includes 50 in respect of the seating.

3.2.240.17   Therefore, the seating component is measured at 50 and has a useful life of 10 years.

3.2.240.20   In many cases, an entity acquires an asset for a fixed sum without knowing the cost of the individual components. In our view, the cost of individual components should be estimated either with reference to current market prices (if possible), in consultation with the seller or contractor, or using some other reasonable method of approximation – e.g. relative values.

3.2.250   **Major inspection or overhaul costs**

3.2.250.10   Major inspections and overhauls are identified and accounted for as a separate component if that component is used over more than one period. [*IAS 16.14*]

3.2.250.20   If a major inspection or overhaul cost is embedded in the cost of an item of property, plant and equipment, then it is necessary to estimate the carrying amount of the component. The carrying amount of the component is determined with reference to the *current* market price of such overhauls and not the expected future price. [*IAS 16.13–14*]

EXAMPLE 15A – OVERHAUL COSTS – CARRYING AMOUNT OF COMPONENT

3.2.250.30   Company P runs a merchant shipping business and has just acquired a new ship for 400. The useful life of the ship is 15 years, but it will be dry-docked every three years and a major overhaul carried out. At the date of acquisition, the dry-docking costs for similar ships that are three years old are approximately 80.

3.2.250.35   Therefore, the cost of the dry-docking component for accounting purposes is 80 and this amount would be depreciated over the three years to the next dry-docking. The remaining carrying amount, which may need to be split into further components, is 320. Any additional components will be depreciated over their own estimated useful lives.

3.2.250.40   Component accounting for inspection or overhaul costs is intended to be used only for major expenditure that occurs at regular intervals over the life of an asset. Costs associated with routine repairs and maintenance are expensed as they are incurred. [*IAS 16.12*]

3.2.260   *Costs to be included*

3.2.260.10   IFRS is silent about the specific costs that should be included in measuring the component attributable to major inspection or overhaul costs – i.e. whether they should be incremental and/ or external costs. In our view, the cost of a major inspection or overhaul includes internal as well as external costs, and there is no requirement for the costs to be incremental (see 3.2.30.50).

EXAMPLE 15B – OVERHAUL COSTS – INTERNAL VS EXTERNAL COSTS

3.2.260.20   Continuing Example 15A, the current market price of a dry-docking service is 80. However, Company P's currently employed technicians will carry out most of the work of future dry-dockings and the external costs incurred are likely to be only 30.

3.2.260.30   In this example, P concludes that it should attribute the entire cost of 80 to the component. This is on the basis that the cost of an item of property, plant and equipment includes internal as well as external costs, and there is no require-ment for the costs to be incremental.

3.2.270 *Relationship with physical components*

3.2.270.10   IFRS does not address the allocation of costs to a major inspection or overhaul when the underlying asset comprises a number of physical components. In our view, one acceptable method of allocating these costs is on the basis of the relative carrying amounts of the components of the underlying asset.

EXAMPLE 15C – OVERHAUL COSTS – MULTIPLE COMPONENTS

3.2.270.15   Continuing Examples 15A and 15B, Company P's ship comprises two physical components: the ship's body of 250 and the engines of 150. The dry-docking will involve servicing both of these components. In practice, the ship would comprise a number of other components; however, the example has been simplified for illustrative purposes.

3.2.270.20   In this example, P concludes that it will allocate the cost of the dry-docking component between the ship's body and the engines on the basis of their relative carrying amounts. On this basis, the components of the ship would be as follows.

Dry-docking costs		80
Body	(250 - (250 / 400) x 80)	200
Engines	(150 - (150 / 400) x 80)	120

3.2.270.30   This issue arises only before the first major inspection or overhaul being carried out because the component cost is assumed rather than actual.

3.2.280 **Replacing a component**

3.2.280.10   The remaining portion of a component that is replaced by a new component is derecognised. However, in our view any amount written off should be included in depreciation instead of being classified as a loss on disposal. We believe that the extra depreciation is in effect a revision of the estimated useful life of the component. [*IAS 16.13*]

EXAMPLE 15D – OVERHAUL COSTS – DERECOGNISED COMPONENTS

3.2.280.15   Continuing Example 15A, Company P carries out the dry-docking of its ship after two years instead of three as originally envisaged. The carrying amount of the overhaul at that date is 27 (80 / 3). The actual dry-docking costs are 100.

3.2.280.20   The remaining carrying amount of the component that has been replaced is written off immediately because the component effectively has been disposed of. The amount written off of 27 is included in depreciation because in effect it represents a revision of the estimated useful life of the dry-docking.

> 3.2.280.30   The actual dry-docking costs of 100 is capitalised to the cost of the ship and depreciated over the expected period until the next dry-docking.

3.2.290   SUBSEQUENT EXPENDITURE

3.2.290.10   Subsequent expenditure on an item of property, plant and equipment is recognised as part of its cost only if it meets the general recognition criteria – i.e. it is probable that future economic benefits associated with the item will flow to the entity and the cost of the item can be measured reliably. [*IAS 16.7, 12*]

3.2.290.20   Costs of the day-to-day servicing of property, plant and equipment are recognised in profit or loss as they are incurred. [*IAS 16.12*]

3.2.290.30   In some cases, an entity may incur costs in relocating assets. The standard requires that the recognition of costs as part of the carrying amount of an item of property, plant and equipment ceases when the item is in the location and condition necessary for it to be capable of operating in the manner intended by management. Therefore, costs of relocating or reorganising part or all of an entity's operations are not included in the carrying amount of an item of property, plant and equipment. [*IAS 16.20*]

3.2.290.40   Expenditure incurred to acquire safety or environmental equipment may be recognised as a separate item of property, plant and equipment if it enables the future economic benefits of other assets to be realised, even though the expenditure itself does not give rise directly to future economic benefits. [*IAS 16.11*]

EXAMPLE 16 – SUBSEQUENT EXPENDITURE REQUIRED BY LAW

> 3.2.290.50   The government introduces a new emissions law that requires aluminium smelters to be fitted with a new grade of filter; unless the new filters are fitted, smelters are no longer permitted to operate.
>
> 3.2.290.60   The cost of the new filters is capitalised as property, plant and equipment as long as the total carrying amount of the smelter plus the new filters does not exceed its recoverable amount (see 3.10.180).

3.2.300   REVALUATIONS

3.2.300.10   An entity may elect to measure a class of property, plant and equipment at fair value, if fair value can be measured reliably. If this accounting policy is chosen, then revaluations should be kept up to date, such that the carrying amount of an asset at the reporting date does not differ materially from its fair value. Any surplus arising on the revaluation is recognised in OCI except to the extent that the surplus reverses a previous revaluation deficit on the same asset recognised in profit or loss, in which case the credit to that extent is recognised in profit or loss. Any deficit on revaluation is recognised in profit or loss except to the extent that it reverses a previous revaluation surplus on the same asset, in which case the debit to that extent is recognised in OCI. Revaluation increases and decreases cannot be offset, even within a class of assets. [*IAS 16.31, 39–40*]

3.2.300.20   Land and any asset situated on the land – e.g. a building or specialised plant – are separate assets. Accordingly, increases and decreases in the fair value attributed to the land and to the building are recognised separately (see 2.4.580.20). [*IAS 16.58*]

3.2.310   Fair value

3.2.310.10   Fair value is measured in accordance with IFRS 13, which is the subject of chapter 2.4. That chapter includes general guidance on applying the principles of IFRS 13 in measuring fair value; specific points of interest in relation to property, plant and equipment, in particular the use of depreciated replacement cost to measure fair value, are discussed in 2.4.600.

3.2.320   All assets in class

3.2.320.10   If an asset is revalued, then all property, plant and equipment of the same class is revalued at the same time and these revaluations should be kept up to date. A class of assets is a grouping of items that have a similar nature and use in an entity's operations. The following are examples of classes of property, plant and equipment contained in IAS 16:

- land;
- land and buildings;
- machinery;
- ships;
- aircraft;
- motor vehicles;
- furniture and fittings; and
- office equipment. [*IAS 16.31, 36–38*]

3.2.320.20   In our view, different geographic locations do not justify concluding that the assets are in different classes.

EXAMPLE 17 – CLASS OF ASSETS

3.2.320.30   Company T has office buildings in Europe and Asia. The buildings in both regions are used for administrative purposes.

3.2.320.40   We believe that the buildings belong to the same class of property, plant and equipment, notwithstanding their different locations. Accordingly, the buildings in Europe should not be revalued without the buildings in Asia also being revalued.

3.2.330   Assets in course of construction

3.2.330.10   It is not clear from IAS 16 whether assets in the course of construction can be measured at fair value under a policy of revaluation. IAS 40 permits investment property in the course of construction to be measured at fair value (see 3.4.50), and it could be argued that the same logic applies to property, plant and equipment in the course of construction. IAS 16 itself does not preclude the revaluation model for assets in the course of construction. The ability to revalue such assets reliably is a matter of judgement because it may not be possible in all cases. For a discussion of the fair value measurement of investment property under construction, see 2.4.700. [*IAS 16.31*]

3.2.330.20   In considering a policy of revaluation for items of property, plant and equipment under construction, in our view such assets may be viewed as a separate class of property, plant and equipment (see 3.2.320) because an asset under construction is not yet used in the entity's operations.

EXAMPLE 18 – REVALUATIONS – ASSETS UNDER CONSTRUCTION

3.2.330.30   In 2018, Company X commissioned construction of a new office building that will become its corporate headquarters; X has a policy of revaluing land and buildings.

3.2.330.40   We believe that X should choose an accounting policy, to be applied consistently, to either:
- revalue the building under construction, consistent with its overall policy for the revaluation of property, plant and equipment; or
- account for the building under construction at cost until construction is complete, because assets under construction are a separate class of property, plant and equipment for which the cost basis of accounting is used.

3.2.340   Accumulated depreciation

3.2.340.10   When property, plant and equipment is revalued, an entity accounts for the revaluation using one of the following approaches.
- *Restatement approach:*
  - the gross carrying amount is adjusted in a manner that is consistent with the revaluation of the carrying amount of the asset – e.g. it is restated in proportion to the change in the carrying amount or with reference to observable market data; and
  - the accumulated depreciation is adjusted to equal the difference between the gross carrying amount and the carrying amount of the asset after taking into account accumulated impairment losses.
- *Elimination approach:* the accumulated depreciation is eliminated against the gross carrying amount of the asset. In our experience, this is the more common approach. [*IAS 16.35*]

3.2.340.20   An entity follows the same approach when fully depreciated assets are revalued.

EXAMPLE 19A – REVALUATIONS – RESTATEMENT APPROACH

3.2.340.30   Company V revalues all of its buildings at the beginning of 2018. The following information relates to one of the buildings.

Gross carrying amount		200
Accumulated depreciation		(80)
Carrying amount		120

Scenario 1: Proportionate restatement

3.2.340.40   V determines that the fair value of the building (i.e. the net carrying amount) is 150. Under the restatement approach, V uses this information to calculate the gross carrying amount on a proportionate basis; the accumulated depreciation is then the balancing number.

Gross carrying amount	(200 / 120) x 150	250
Accumulated depreciation	250 - 150	(100)
Carrying amount		150

Scenario 2: Disproportionate restatement

3.2.340.50   V determines that the fair value of the building (i.e. the net carrying amount) is 150, and the fair value of the building as new (i.e. the gross carrying amount) is 275. Under the restatement approach, V calculates the accumulated depreciation as the difference between the gross and net carrying amounts for which market data was obtained.

Gross carrying amount		275
Accumulated depreciation	275 - 150	(125)
Carrying amount		150

EXAMPLE 19B – REVALUATIONS – ELIMINATION APPROACH

3.2.340.60   Changing the approach in Example 19A, Company V accounts for the revaluation using the elimination approach, whereby the accumulated depreciation is eliminated against the gross carrying amount of the asset.

3.2.340.70   Under this approach, the gross carrying amount and the accumulated depreciation of the building are as follows.

Gross carrying amount		150
Accumulated depreciation		-
Carrying amount		150

3.2.350   Transferring revaluation surplus to retained earnings

3.2.350.10   The depreciable amount of a revalued asset is based on its revalued amount and not its cost. The depreciation charge for each period is recognised as an expense in profit or loss unless it is included in the carrying amount of another asset (see 3.2.140.50). [*IAS 16.6, 48*]

3.2.350.20   However, the revaluation surplus may be transferred directly to retained earnings as the surplus is realised. Realisation of the surplus may occur through the use (and depreciation) of the asset or on its disposal. The wording of the standard is not entirely clear, but in our view an entity should choose an accounting policy, to be applied consistently, to:

- not transfer any part of revaluation reserve to retained earnings;
- transfer all of the revaluation reserve to retained earnings on ultimate disposal; or
- transfer a relevant portion of the revaluation reserve to retained earnings as the asset is depreciated, with the balance being transferred on ultimate disposal. [*IAS 16.41*]

EXAMPLE 20 – REVALUATIONS – TRANSFERRING REVALUATION SURPLUS

3.2.350.30   Company P revalues its building at the beginning of 2018 from 120 to 150; the revaluation reserve is 30. At the date of the revaluation, the building has a remaining useful life of 15 years and is depreciated under the straight-line method.

3.2.350.40   P chooses the third option in 3.2.350.20 and each year transfers an amount of 2 from the revaluation reserve to retained earnings to match the additional depreciation of 2 that relates to the revalued portion of the asset (30 / 15).

3.2.360   Change in accounting policy

3.2.360.10   If an entity changes its accounting policy from the cost to the fair value model of accounting for property, plant and equipment, then the effect of the change is recognised as a revaluation (see 3.2.300.10). The opening balance of equity is not adjusted and comparatives are not restated. [*IAS 8.17*]

3.2.360.20   When an entity changes its accounting policy from the fair value to the cost model of accounting for property, plant and equipment, all previous revaluations, including subsequent depreciation charges, are reversed. In this case, the usual procedures for a change in accounting policy apply – i.e. the effect of the change is calculated retrospectively and the adjustment is generally recognised by adjusting the opening balance of retained earnings for the earliest prior period presented and restating comparative amounts presented (see 2.8.50). [*IAS 8.19*]

3.2.360.30   In our view, because IAS 16 allows two accounting treatments for the subsequent measurement of property, plant and equipment, an entity may change its accounting policy from one to the other accounting treatment because both treatments are considered acceptable in providing a fair presentation. However, care should be taken if an accounting policy is changed more than once to ensure that the requirement to qualify for a voluntary change in accounting policy is met (see 2.8.70).

3.2.370 COMPENSATION RECEIVED

3.2.370.10   Compensation for insurance recoveries, including the loss or impairment of property, plant and equipment, is recognised in profit or loss when receivable (see 3.2.370.40). The loss or impairment of the property, plant and equipment is recognised in profit or loss as an expense when it occurs. [*IAS 16.65–66*]

EXAMPLE 21 – INSURANCE RECOVERY

3.2.370.20   Company W's main operating plant is destroyed in a fire. The carrying amount of the plant was 600. W's insurers pay out an amount of 1,000, which comprises 800 for the rebuilding of the plant and 200 for loss of profits. The actual cost of rebuilding the plant is 900.

3.2.370.30   W records the following entries.

	DEBIT	CREDIT
At the time of the fire		
Loss (profit or loss)	600	
Property, plant and equipment		600
To recognise write-off of carrying amount of plant		
When the insurance proceeds are receivable		
Insurance claim receivable	1,000	
Income (profit or loss)		1,000
To recognise insurance claim receivable		
When the plant is reconstructed		
Property, plant and equipment	900	
Cash		900
To recognise cost of rebuilding plant		

3.2.370.40   Recognition of the loss or impairment may occur at a different point, and even in a different period, from the recognition of the compensation. In our view, income related to the compensation for damaged assets should be recognised when the damage giving rise to any loss or impairment has occurred and the entity has an unconditional contractual right to receive the compensation (see 3.12.198).

3.2.380 RETIREMENTS, DISPOSALS AND CHANGES IN USE#

3.2.380.10   When an item of property, plant and equipment is disposed of or permanently withdrawn from use, a gain or loss is recognised for the difference between any net proceeds received and the carrying amount of the asset. The amount of consideration included in the gain or loss on derecognition – and subsequent changes in that amount – is estimated under the requirements for determining the transaction price in IFRS 15 (see 4.2.90 and 200). [*IAS 16.71–72*]

3.2.380.15   The standard gives no guidance on the meaning of 'net proceeds'. In our view, in determining the *net* proceeds received, all directly attributable incremental costs of disposal – e.g. advertising, legal fees, stamp duty, agency fees and removal costs – should generally be deducted. We believe that it is also appropriate to deduct any amounts recognised as liabilities (see chapter 3.12) in relation to the disposal of the asset – e.g. provisions made for probable claims under warranties in the sales agreement, or for an agreed schedule of repairs to be done at the current owner's expense.

3.2.380.20   When part of an asset is disposed of or permanently withdrawn from use, the carrying amount of that part is derecognised. For example, when subsequent expenditure is recognised in the carrying amount of an item in respect of a replacement part, the carrying amount of the replaced part is derecognised, even if it had not been depreciated separately. [*IAS 16.70*]

3.2.380.30   The gain or loss on derecognition is generally included in profit or loss unless the transaction is a sale-and-leaseback and deferral is required (see 5.1.470), and is not classified as revenue. [*IAS 16.67–68, 71*]

3.2.380.35   Any attributable revaluation surplus may be transferred to retained earnings (see 3.2.350), but is not recognised in profit or loss. [*IAS 16.41*]

3.2.380.40   If an entity in the normal course of its business routinely sells items of property, plant and equipment that it previously held for rental to others, then it transfers such items to inventory when they cease to be rented and become held-for-sale. Such assets are outside the scope of IFRS 5. The items are transferred at their carrying amounts at the date of transfer, and the entity recognises the proceeds from the sale of such assets as revenue in accordance with IFRS 15. [*IAS 16.68A*]

EXAMPLE 22 – SALE OF ITEMS PREVIOUSLY HELD FOR RENTAL

3.2.380.50   Company Z operates a car rental business and also sells second-hand cars as part of its business model. Z acquires new cars with the intention of renting the cars for three years and then selling them. Z recognises the cars as property, plant and equipment during the rental period and transfers the cars to inventory at their carrying amount when they cease to be rented and become held-for-sale. Z recognises the proceeds from the sale of cars as revenue.

3.2.380.60   The date of disposal of an item of property, plant and equipment is the date on which the recipient obtains control of the asset under the guidance on the satisfaction of performance obligations in IFRS 15 (see 4.2.210), unless the disposal is by sale-and-leaseback. In our view, sale-and-leaseback accounting should be applied even if some of the general revenue recognition criteria have not been met (see 5.1.470). [*IAS 16.68–69*]

3.2.380.70   If an asset's carrying amount is to be recovered principally through a sale transaction or distribution rather than through continuing use, then the asset is classified as an asset (or disposal group) held-for-sale or held-for-distribution if certain criteria are met (see 5.4.30 and 37). Depreciation of that asset ceases at the earlier of the date on which the asset (or disposal group) is classified as held-for-sale and the date on which the asset (or disposal group) is derecognised. An entity measures such an asset (or disposal group) at the lower of its carrying amount and fair value less costs to sell (see 5.4.40). [*IFRS 5.6, 15–15A, IAS 16.55*]

3.2.380.80   Depreciation is recognised even if an asset is idle and retired from active use unless the asset is held for sale. However, under usage methods of depreciation (see 3.2.190), the depreciation charge can be zero while there is no production. [*IAS 16.55*]

3.2.380.90   For a discussion of exchanges of non-monetary assets, see chapter 5.7.

3.2.385   **FORTHCOMING REQUIREMENTS**

3.2.385.10   Under IFRS 16, a seller-lessee derecognises the underlying asset only if the transfer leg satisfies the requirements of IFRS 15 to be accounted for as a sale of the asset. [*IFRS 16.100*]

3.2.390   # GOVERNMENT GRANTS

3.2.390.10   A government grant may be related to an item of property, plant and equipment whether it is received in cash or is an asset received by way of non-monetary grant. For a discussion of the treatment of a government grant that relates to property, plant and equipment, see chapter 4.3. [*IAS 20.23–28*]

3.2.400   # DISCLOSURES

3.2.400.10   The disclosure requirements for property, plant and equipment, examples of which are included in KPMG's *Guides to financial statements* series, include a reconciliation between the carrying amount of property, plant and equipment at the beginning and end of the current reporting period and also the beginning and end of the comparative reporting period. [*IAS 16.73*]

3.2.400.20   The reconciliation includes separate line items for additions and acquisitions through business combinations. Therefore, acquisitions are split between property, plant and equipment acquired in a business combination and other acquisitions. However, all disposals are presented in a single line item in the reconciliation. [*IAS 16.73*]

3.2.400.30   In addition, the disclosure requirements of IFRS 13 apply to property, plant and equipment that is accounted for under the revaluation model (see 2.4.490). The disclosures under IFRS 13 are made for each class of asset; these classes may be determined under IAS 16 (see 3.2.320) only if this is consistent with the criteria for determining classes under IFRS 13 (see 2.4.510). [*IFRS 13.94*]

3.2.400.40   Under the revaluation model, an entity also discloses the amount at which the assets would have been stated had they been carried under the cost model. The amount to be disclosed includes borrowing costs capitalised in accordance with IAS 23 (see chapter 4.6). [*IU 05-14*]

<h1>3.2.410   FUTURE DEVELOPMENTS</h1>

3.2.410.10   In June 2017, the IASB published Exposure Draft *Property, Plant and Equipment – Proceeds before Intended Use – Proposed amendments to IAS 16*. The exposure draft proposed to clarify the accounting for the net proceeds from sales of items produced while bringing an item of property, plant and equipment to the location and condition necessary for it to be capable of operating in the manner intended by management (see 3.2.120.10–50). Under the proposal, an entity would not be allowed to deduct such proceeds from the cost of the asset. The comment period closed in October 2017. The Board is yet to determine the direction of the project.

3.3 Intangible assets and goodwill

3.3   Intangible assets and goodwill

CURRENTLY EFFECTIVE REQUIREMENTS

This publication reflects IFRS in issue at 1 August 2018, and the currently effective requirements cover annual periods beginning on 1 January 2018.

The requirements related to this topic are mainly derived from the following.

STANDARD	TITLE
IFRS 3	Business Combinations
IFRS 13	Fair Value Measurement
IAS 38	Intangible Assets
IFRIC 12	Service Concession Arrangements
SIC-32	Intangible Assets – Web Site Costs

The currently effective requirements include newly effective requirements arising from IFRS 15 *Revenue from Contracts with Customers,* which is effective for annual periods beginning on or after 1 January 2018. The new requirements may be applied using the retrospective method or the cumulative effect method (see 4.2.510). The impact of the new requirements on the accounting for intangible assets and goodwill is reflected in 3.3.30.50 and 310.10–20.

FORTHCOMING REQUIREMENTS

The currently effective requirements are affected by the following forthcoming requirements. They are highlighted with a # and the impact is explained in the accompanying boxed text at the references indicated.

In January 2016, the IASB issued IFRS 16 *Leases*, which is effective for annual periods beginning on or after 1 January 2019. See 3.3.33. IFRS 16 is the subject of chapter 5.1A.

FUTURE DEVELOPMENTS

The currently effective requirements that may be affected by future developments are highlighted with a * and are briefly discussed in 3.3.330.

3.3.10   **DEFINITION**

3.3.20   **Goodwill**

3.3.20.10   Goodwill arising in a business combination is measured as a residual at the date of acquisition in the following calculation, and is recognised in the statement of financial position. [*IFRS 3.32*]

GOODWILL IS MEASURED AS THE EXCESS OF A OVER B	
A. The aggregate of: • consideration transferred, which is generally measured at fair value (see 2.6.260); • the amount of any NCI in the acquiree, which for 'ordinary' NCI may be measured either at fair value or at their proportionate share in the recognised amounts of the net identifiable assets of the acquiree (see 2.6.930); and • in a business combination achieved in stages, the acquisition date fair value of the acquirer's previously held equity interest in the acquiree (see 2.6.1140.30).	B. The net of the acquisition date amounts of the identifiable assets acquired and the liabilities assumed measured in accordance with IFRS 3 (see 2.6.560).

3.3.30   **Intangible assets#**

3.3.30.10   An intangible asset is an identifiable non-monetary asset without physical substance. Unlike property, plant and equipment, an intangible asset can be held for any purpose, and need not be held for use in the production or supply of goods or services, for rental to others, or for administrative purposes. [*IAS 38.8, BC4–BC5*]

3.3.30.15   Licences are one example of an intangible resource that might meet the definition of an intangible asset. If a licence grants a right to use intellectual property, then it can be difficult to determine whether it is in the scope of IAS 17 or IAS 38 because IAS 17 does not clearly state that all licence arrangements are excluded from its scope. In our experience, licences are generally accounted for in accordance with IAS 38. [*IAS 17.2(b), 38.6*]

3.3.30.20   There may be instances in which an intangible asset is incorporated within a physical asset – e.g. knowledge contained in a book. In such circumstances, an entity assesses which aspect of the asset, tangible or intangible, is more significant and the asset is accounted for accordingly. In the example of the book, in our view it should be accounted for as an intangible asset because the knowledge in the book dominates the nature of the asset (and its value) as opposed to the tangible nature of the medium (the paper). [*IAS 38.4*]

3.3.30.25   In another example, the operating system on a computer is typically treated as part of the computer itself and the entire asset is accounted for in accordance with IAS 16. However, additional software acquired or developed for the computer will typically be treated as an intangible asset separate from the tangible asset (computer) on which it is installed. [*IAS 38.4*]

3.3.30.30 To meet the definition of an intangible asset, an item lacks physical substance and is:
- identifiable;
- non-monetary; and
- controlled by the entity and expected to provide future economic benefits to the entity – i.e. it meets the definition of an asset. [*IAS 38.8–17*]

3.3.30.40 These criteria apply to all intangible assets, whether acquired separately, acquired in a business combination or generated internally.

3.3.30.50 Incremental costs arising from obtaining a contract with a customer are not in the scope of IAS 38 but are in the scope of IFRS 15. Under IFRS 15, an entity recognises as an asset the costs of obtaining a contract with a customer if it expects to recover those costs (see 4.2.260). [*IAS 38.3(i), IFRS 15.91*]

3.3.33 **FORTHCOMING REQUIREMENTS**

3.3.33.10 The scope of IFRS 16 is largely based on the scope of IAS 17 – i.e. leases of intangible assets that are currently accounted for under IAS 38 are most likely to continue to be accounted for under this standard. However, IFRS 16 scopes out licences of intellectual property granted by a lessor in the scope of IFRS 15 (see 5.1A.20.20). [*IFRS 16.3(d)*]

3.3.33.20 Under IFRS 16, if an entity is a lessee, then it:
- applies IAS 38 to account for the rights held under licensing agreements for items such as motion picture films, video recordings, plays, manuscripts, patents and copyrights; and
- may apply IFRS 16 to account for any other leases of intangible assets (see 5.1A.20.30). [*IAS 38.6, IFRS 16.3(e), 4*]

3.3.40 *Identifiability*

3.3.40.10 In order for an intangible asset to be recognised it needs to be 'identifiable'. An item is identifiable if it:
- is separable – i.e. is capable of being separated or divided from the entity and sold, transferred, licensed, rented or exchanged either individually or together with a related contract, asset or liability; or
- arises from contractual or other legal rights, regardless of whether those rights are transferable or separable from the entity or from other rights and obligations. [*IAS 38.12*]

3.3.40.20 Therefore, separability is not a necessary condition for an item to be identifiable. For example, a business licence of a radio station that the station requires in order to operate is identifiable because it arises from legal rights, even though the licence is usually not separable from the station operator. [*IAS 38.12*]

3.3.40.30 In our experience, the decision of whether the identifiability criterion is met is often the critical factor in determining whether the definition of an intangible asset is met, and therefore whether an intangible asset qualifies for recognition.

EXAMPLE 1 – MARKET SHARE NOT IDENTIFIABLE

3.3.40.40   Company P is a successful engineering business. In past years, P has achieved a 25% market share for its products and it is contemplating recognising an intangible asset for this market share. In our view, market share does not meet the definition of an intangible asset because it is not separable and it does not arise from legal rights.

3.3.50   *Non-monetary*

3.3.50.10   Intangible assets are non-monetary. Monetary assets are subject to the requirements of other standards – e.g. financial instruments (see 7.1.30) and income tax receivables (see 3.13.70).

3.3.60   *Control*

3.3.60.10   To demonstrate control, an entity needs to have the power to obtain the future economic benefits arising from the item *and* be able to restrict the access of others to those benefits. [*IAS 38.13–16*]

EXAMPLE 2A – CONTROL NOT DEMONSTRATED

3.3.60.20   Company C has two key resources: customised software that it developed internally and for which a patent is registered; and the know-how of the staff that operate the software. Staff members are required to give one month's notice of their resignation.

3.3.60.30   It is clear that C controls the software. However, although it obtains economic benefits from the work performed by the staff, C does not have control over their know-how because staff could choose to resign at any time. Therefore, the know-how does not meet the definition of an intangible asset. [*IAS 38.15*]

EXAMPLE 2B – CONTROL DEMONSTRATED

3.3.60.40   Company D is a football club. D has acquired contracts with individual players that entitle it to receive that player's services and prevent that player from leaving the club or providing services to another club for a specified period of time.

3.3.60.50   Unlike in Example 2A, these contracts each meet the definition of an intangible asset because they give D control over any future economic benefits that may arise from the player's services, and restrict the access of others to those benefits. [*IAS 38.15*]

3.3.70   *Exchange transactions*

3.3.70.10   Control normally stems from legal rights that are enforceable in a court of law, which is equivalent to 'contractual or other legal rights' – a criterion for identifiability (see 3.3.40.10).

Control may be demonstrated by means other than legally enforceable rights, and therefore legal enforceability is not a necessary condition for control. In our view, the demonstration of separability through exchange transactions for the same or similar intangible assets generally provides evidence of control. [*IAS 38.13, 16, BC11–BC14*]

3.3.80 *Business combinations*

3.3.80.10   The identification of intangible assets acquired as part of a business combination can be a challenging exercise and IFRS 3 includes specific guidance to assist in understanding the types of assets acquired in a business combination that are likely to meet the definition of intangible assets; for further discussion, see 2.6.720–820.

3.3.90   INITIAL RECOGNITION AND MEASUREMENT

3.3.100   General requirements

3.3.100.10   An intangible asset is initially recognised at cost if:
- it is probable that future economic benefits that are attributable to the asset will flow to the entity; and
- the cost of the asset can be measured reliably. [*IAS 38.21, 24*]

3.3.100.20   These criteria are most important in assessing the recognition of internally generated intangible assets (see 3.3.120.40). When an intangible asset is acquired in a business combination, these criteria are assumed to be met (see 2.6.720.20). When an intangible asset is acquired in a separate acquisition – i.e. outside a business combination – the 'probability' criterion is assumed to be met; additionally, IAS 38 notes that the 'reliable measurement' criterion is usually met. [*IAS 38.25–26, 33*]

3.3.100.30   The cost of an intangible asset acquired in a business combination is generally its fair value. For a discussion of the general principles of determining fair value in a business combination, see 2.6.720. [*IAS 38.33–37*]

3.3.100.40   The cost of an intangible asset acquired in a separate acquisition is the cash paid or the fair value of any other consideration given. If the intangible asset acquired is exchanged for non-cash consideration or the intangible asset is one of a group of items acquired, then the cost is estimated based on the fair value of the consideration exchanged (see 5.7.20). The determination of the cost of an intangible asset acquired through the settlement of a derivative – e.g. a forward or call option – is discussed in 7.1.200.50. [*IAS 38.8, 26, 45–47*]

3.3.100.50   The cost of an internally generated intangible asset includes the directly attributable expenditure of preparing the asset for its intended use, and the principles discussed in respect of property, plant and equipment (see 3.2.30) apply equally to the recognition of intangible assets. Expenditure on training activities, identified inefficiencies and initial operating losses is expensed as it is incurred. [*IAS 38.27–30, 66–67*]

3.3.100.60   If payment is deferred beyond normal credit terms, then the cost of the asset is the cash price equivalent (i.e. current cash price) at the date of recognition. The issues that arise in accounting for deferred payment are similar to those in respect of property, plant and equipment (see 3.2.130). [*IAS 38.32*]

3.3.100.70 The determination of cost is more complicated if the consideration paid in exchange for receiving an intangible asset is wholly or partly variable. In our view, if variable payments are based on future revenues, then the cost of the intangible asset should be determined on the basis of the agreed minimum payments. The revenue-based payments are not a present obligation and therefore do not form part of the cost of the intangible asset. Instead, in general we believe that any additional payments should be expensed as the related sales occur. [*IU 03-16*]

EXAMPLE 3 – VARIABLE CONSIDERATION

3.3.100.80 Company Y buys a five-year licence to use technology owned by Company Z.

- Y agrees to pay a minimum amount of 200, 25% of which is due at the outset of the licence arrangement, with the remaining 75% due one year later.
- In addition to this minimum payment, Y also agrees to pay to Z 10% of the future revenues that will be generated with the licensed technology.
- Y's current best estimate of the revenues expected to be generated with the technology is 1,000 for each of the following five years.

3.3.100.90 The cost of Y's intangible asset (the licence) is determined on the basis of the agreed minimum payments – i.e. 50 plus the present value of 150. Any additional payments will be expensed as the related sales occur.

3.3.100.100 The minimum unconditional payments originally agreed for the acquisition of an intangible asset might change as a result of a contract renegotiation. Judgement is required to determine the appropriate accounting for any changes – other than in respect of finance cost (see 7.7.260.20) – in the carrying amount of the financial liability representing the total minimum unconditional amounts payable under the contract. The judgement is made based on a careful analysis of all relevant facts and circumstances. In the basic case of a renegotiation, which leads only to additional future payments relating solely to newly granted rights without modification of the originally agreed payments – e.g. an extension of the term of a licence – the whole change is likely to be recognised as a new financial liability given as consideration for an intangible asset. [*IAS 38.8*]

3.3.100.110 More complex contract renegotiations, which might lead to a change in the minimum unconditional payments originally agreed (i.e. a modification of the original financial liability), generally fall into two main categories, depending on whether new rights that cause an increase in the service potential of the intangible asset are granted. For guidance on derecognition and modification of terms of a financial liability applicable to both scenarios under IFRS 9, see 7.6.360–440. In our view, the following principles should be applied in accounting for such contract renegotiations.

- *Scenario 1 – No new rights granted*: If the renegotiation leads only to a change in the minimum unconditional payments originally agreed, without any grant of new rights, then we believe that it should be accounted for in accordance with the guidance on derecognition and modification of terms of a financial liability.
- *Scenario 2 – New rights granted:* If the renegotiation leads to both a change in the minimum unconditional payments originally agreed and a grant of new rights, then we believe that it comprises two transactions that should be accounted for separately:

–   the recognition of an intangible asset corresponding to the new rights granted (provided that the criteria for its recognition are met) and the related new financial liability representing its cost; and

–   a modification of the original financial liability, which should be accounted for in accordance with the guidance on derecognition and modification of terms of a financial liability.

3.3.100.120   In Scenario 2, we believe that the determination of the amounts attributed to each of the transactions will depend on the specific facts and circumstances. In some cases, attributing these amounts will be straightforward. However, in other cases a more in-depth analysis will be required.

3.3.110   Specific application

3.3.120   *Research and development*

3.3.120.10   'Research' is original and planned investigation undertaken with the prospect of gaining new scientific or technical knowledge and understanding. Research costs are expensed as they are incurred. For a discussion of property, plant and equipment used in research activities, see 3.2.10.15. [*IAS 38.8, 54*]

3.3.120.20   'Development' is the application of research findings or other knowledge to a plan or design for the production of new or substantially improved materials, devices, products, processes, systems or services before the start of commercial production or use. Development does not include the maintenance or enhancement of ongoing operations. [*IAS 38.8*]

3.3.120.30   Development does not need to be in relation to an entirely new innovation; rather it needs to be new to the specific entity. For example, an entity is developing a new IT system for processing its customer orders. The project meets the definition of development notwithstanding the fact that most of the entity's competitors use similar systems already.

3.3.120.40   If an internally generated intangible asset arises from the development phase of a project, then directly attributable expenditure is capitalised from the date on which the entity is able to demonstrate:
●   the technical feasibility of completing the intangible asset so that it will be available for use or sale;
●   its intention to complete the intangible asset and use or sell it;
●   its ability to use or sell the intangible asset;
●   how the intangible asset will generate probable future economic benefits;
●   the availability of adequate technical, financial and other resources to complete the development and to use or sell the intangible asset; and
●   its ability to reliably measure the expenditure attributable to the intangible asset during its development. [*IAS 38.57*]

3.3.120.50   In assessing how the intangible asset will generate probable future economic benefits, the entity needs to demonstrate the existence of a market for the output of the intangible asset or the intangible asset itself; or, if it is to be used internally, then the usefulness of the intangible asset. In carrying out this assessment, an entity uses the principles of IAS 36 (see chapter 3.10). If the asset will generate economic benefits only in combination with other assets, then the entity applies the concept of CGUs (see 3.10.60). [*IAS 38.57(d), 60*]

3.3.120.60   Although 'probable' is not defined in relation to intangible assets, it does not mean that a project needs to be certain to succeed before capitalising any development costs. For example, in our view a company should not expense all development costs as they are incurred simply because there is a possibility that a new product will not be approved for sale by the relevant authorities. Rather, an assessment should be made of the likelihood of success in each individual case. If a positive outcome is determined to be probable, then the company should capitalise the related development costs incurred from that point on.

3.3.120.70   Financial and other resources needed to complete the development are not required to be secured at the start of the project. An entity may be able to demonstrate its ability to secure these resources through business plans and external financing plans in which potential customers, investors or lenders have expressed interest. [*IAS 38.61*]

3.3.120.80   IFRS specifically prohibits the capitalisation of expenditure on internally generated intangible assets such as brands, mastheads, publishing titles, customer lists and similar items. An example of a 'similar item' is a database of information about the needs of potential customers that is used by the entity to help it secure contracts with customers. This is because the expenditure cannot be distinguished from developing the business as a whole. As a result, expenditure on these assets is viewed as not being reliably measurable. [*IAS 38.63–64*]

EXAMPLE 4 – DEVELOPMENT THAT IS PART OF THE BUSINESS

3.3.120.90   Company B has developed a successful business based on products that have a distinct house style and design. B uses its unique house style to develop a standard format for product development. In this example, the standard format does not meet the definition of an intangible asset because the asset is an integral part of the development of the business and cannot be separately identified.

3.3.120.100   If an entity acquires in-process research and development (IPR&D) in a business combination, then it is recognised as an intangible asset in the acquisition accounting (see 2.6.810). Typically, IPR&D acquired separately but outside a business combination will also meet the criteria to be recognised (see 3.3.100.10–20). However, any subsequent expenditure on the IPR&D projects is added to the carrying amount of the intangible asset only if it meets the recognition criteria for capitalising development costs (see 3.3.120.40). [*IAS 38.34, 42*]

3.3.130   *Website development costs*

3.3.130.10   Costs associated with websites developed for advertising or promotional purposes are expensed as they are incurred. [*SIC-32.8*]

3.3.130.20   In respect of other websites, costs incurred during the planning stage (pre-development) are expensed when they are incurred. Expenditure incurred during the application and infrastructure development stage, the graphical design stage and the content development stage is capitalised if the criteria for capitalising development costs (see 3.3.120.40) are met. This applies equally to internal and external costs. The costs of developing content for advertising or promotional purposes are expensed as they are incurred. [*SIC-32.9*]

3.3.140   *Goodwill*

3.3.140.10   Goodwill arising in a business combination is capitalised (see 3.3.20). [*IFRS 3.32*]

3.3.140.20   Internally generated goodwill is never recognised as an asset. [*IAS 38.48*]

3.3.150   *Items expensed as incurred*

3.3.150.10   Costs are expensed as they are incurred regardless of whether the general criteria for recognition appear to be met, if they are associated with:
- internally generated goodwill;
- start-up activities, unless they qualify for recognition as part of the cost of property, plant and equipment (see 3.2.20);
- training activities;
- advertising and promotional activities; or
- relocating or reorganising part, or all, of an entity. [*IAS 38.48, 69*]

3.3.150.20   Except for start-up costs, the costs in 3.3.150.10 cannot be capitalised either as stand-alone intangible assets or as a part of the cost of another intangible asset. In respect of advertising and other promotional costs, in our view it does not matter whether the activities relate to a specific product or to the business as a whole; the related expenditure should be expensed as it is incurred in either case.

3.3.150.30   Expenditure in respect of advertising and promotional activities is expensed when the benefit of those goods or services is available to the entity. In respect of the acquisition of goods, an expense is recognised when the entity has the right to access those goods. In respect of the acquisition of services, an expense is recognised when the services are received. This requirement does not prevent the recognition of an asset for prepaid expenses, but a prepayment is recognised only for payments made in advance of the receipt of the corresponding goods or services. [*IAS 38.69–70, IU 09-17*]

3.3.150.40   Catalogues are considered to be a form of advertising and promotional material, and not inventory, as the primary objective of catalogues is to advertise to customers. [*IAS 38.69, BC46G*]

3.3.160   *Emissions allowances*

3.3.160.10   IFRS does not have any specific guidance on accounting for emissions allowances. In our view, emissions allowances received by a participant in a 'cap and trade' scheme, whether bought or issued by the government, are intangible assets. For emissions allowances that are government grants, non-monetary government grants may be recognised either at fair value or at a nominal amount (see 4.3.50). Recognition of a non-monetary government grant at the amount paid (often zero) would result in no liability being recognised if the liability is measured at the carrying amount (zero) of the related assets. IAS 20 notes that fair value is the usual approach for non-monetary grants. [*IAS 20.23*]

3.3.160.20   Cap and trade schemes typically grant a number of certificates in relation to a specified period over which emissions will be measured (compliance period). Under some schemes, the relevant government might have identified a date by which it will determine and announce the allocation of the allowances for the next compliance period. This date might be before the date from which entities are entitled to their allowances and the date on which they are actually issued. For example, a national government announces that it will determine by 14 December 2018 the allocation of allowances to be issued on 28 February 2019. The grant is conditional on the entity being in business on 1 January 2019 to receive its allowances. In our view, provided that there are no other conditions attached to the grant, the entity should recognise the government grant and the intangible asset on 1 January 2019 because this is the date on which there is reasonable assurance that the entity will comply with the condition attached to the grant and that the grants will be received.

3.3.160.30   Subsequently, the general requirements for intangible assets apply (see 3.3.190–310). If the allowances are accounted for using the revaluation model for intangible assets (see 3.3.280), then any balance on the revaluation reserve in respect of the allowances that is derecognised when the entity settles its obligation under the scheme may be transferred directly to retained earnings within equity (see 3.3.310.40). This accounting treatment precludes any reclassification of fair value increments related to the allowances to profit or loss when the entity settles its obligations under the scheme. Conversely, if the entity accounts for its allowances under the cost method, then any difference between the carrying amount of the asset and the liability is recognised in profit or loss on settlement of the obligation.

3.3.160.40   For most allowances traded in an active market (see 3.3.280.10), no amortisation will be required as the condition of the asset does not change over time, and therefore the residual value will be the same as cost. As a result, the depreciable amount will be zero (see 3.3.220).

3.3.160.50   If the market value of the allowances falls below its cost, or other indicators of impairment exist, then the general impairment guidance is followed to determine whether the assets are impaired (see 3.10.120).

3.3.160.60   IFRS is silent on how an entity determines the carrying amount of an allowance for the purpose of calculating a gain or loss on disposal. Therefore, the hierarchy for selecting accounting policies is applied (see 2.8.20). In our view, the guidance for determining the cost of inventories should be applied by analogy (see 3.8.280). In some cases, the certificates will have unique identification numbers, and therefore it will be possible to apply the specific identification method if the holder tracks cost on an individual certificate basis. Otherwise, any reasonable cost allocation method may be used – e.g. average cost or first-in, first-out. The method used should be applied consistently.

3.3.160.70   For further discussion of the accounting for obligations arising from schemes for emissions allowances, see 3.12.510.

3.3.160.80   An entity might receive emissions allowances in a cap and trade scheme that are surplus to its expected usage requirements. In our view, the income from the sale of such allowances should not be recognised as revenue unless it arises in the ordinary course of the activities of the entity (see 4.2.10.10). [*IFRS 15.A*]

3.3.170   *REACH costs*

3.3.170.10   REACH is a regulation for the *Registration, Evaluation and Authorisation of CHemicals in the European Union* (EU). The REACH regulation requires manufacturers and importers to register all chemical substances not covered by other specific regulations – e.g. regulations regarding medicinal products – that they produce or import in quantities over a specified amount. The registration consists of submitting a technical report about the substance and paying a registration fee.

3.3.170.20   Once a chemical substance has been registered, another manufacturer has the right, and in certain cases the obligation, to use the registration documentation of the original registrant, who is obliged to grant the potential additional registrant access to all information, documentation and analyses. The potential additional registrant is required to reimburse the original registrant for a portion of the costs incurred in its original registration, and the regulation specifies a protocol for the sharing of data and costs. Claims are enforceable in the national courts.

3.3.170.30   An entity might incur significant costs in obtaining a REACH registration. In addition to the registration fee itself, costs incurred might relate to preparing the technical report, performing the chemical safety assessment – e.g. internal and external laboratory tests – and preparing the chemical safety report. Additional registrants incur costs for reimbursing previous registrants.

3.3.170.40   In our view, the registration costs under the REACH regulation are in the scope of IAS 38. We believe that the definition of an intangible asset and the general recognition criteria of IAS 38 will generally be met (see 3.3.30.30 and 100.10). However, an analysis specific to each registration should be performed to demonstrate the recovery of the actual costs by the specific entity.

3.3.170.50   In our view, REACH costs are a separately acquired intangible asset, similar to a product-specific licence. IAS 38 requires separately acquired intangible assets to be measured initially at cost, which comprises the purchase price and any directly attributable cost of preparing the asset for its intended use (see 3.3.100.40). For example, we believe that the labour costs for an employee while preparing the registration should be included if such costs are directly attributable. In contrast, administrative and other general overhead costs should not be included in the cost – e.g. the labour costs for an employee or external contractor administering the registration of substances to be registered. [*IAS 38.27–29*]

3.3.170.60   Normally, the probability test is considered to be met automatically for separately acquired intangible assets (see 3.3.100.20). However, in our view entities should explicitly consider the probability test for registration costs for REACH. We believe that this is appropriate because the acquisition of this intangible asset is mandated rather than being an unconstrained choice.

3.3.170.70   In our view, the costs that are directly attributable to a REACH registration are likely to include the preparation of a technical report, costs incurred for performing the chemical safety assessment, if any, and for documenting those results in the chemical safety report. Both internal and external costs may qualify for recognition, including internal and external laboratory costs.

3.3.170.80   However, in our view costs incurred in the following activities would not usually be directly attributable to a REACH registration and therefore should be expensed as they are incurred: evaluating the REACH requirements, assessing business impacts, database maintenance, and ongoing analyses after registration. We believe that these costs are feasibility and operating costs that are not directly attributable to a specific registration.

3.3.170.90   For registration based on a third party's previous registration, in our view the cost of the intangible asset should include the registration fee and the reimbursement to the original registrant.

3.3.170.100   Subsequent to initial measurement, in our view the intangible asset should be measured using the cost model. Because there is no active market for REACH registrations, the intangible asset would not qualify to be measured at fair value (see 3.3.280.10). [*IAS 38.78*]

3.3.170.110   An entity assesses whether the useful life of the intangible asset is finite or indefinite in the usual way (see 3.3.190). Although a registration itself generally has no time limit, an entity should consider the technological and commercial life cycles of the chemical substance and the related products – i.e. preparations and/or articles – in which it is to be used. Therefore, an intangible asset in respect of REACH registration will generally have a finite useful life. The most appropriate method of amortisation is determined by applying the general guidance in IAS 38 – i.e. it reflects the pattern of consumption of the economic benefits (see 3.3.230).

3.3.170.120   In our view, the reimbursement of costs by a potential additional registrant is an 'incidental operation' of the original registrant – i.e. an operation that is not necessary to bring the asset (registration) to the location and condition necessary for it to be capable of operating in the manner intended by management. The fact that a potential additional registrant can buy (at cost) work carried out by the original registrant does not affect whether the original registrant can obtain registration or how that registration is utilised in the pursuit of economic benefits.

3.3.170.130   Therefore, we believe that it is not appropriate to credit any reimbursement to the cost of the registration. In our view, the reimbursement should be recognised as income. It should not be recognised as revenue because it does not arise in the ordinary course of the activities of an entity (see 4.2.10.10). [*IFRS 15.A, IAS 38.31*]

3.3.170.140   In our view, the REACH regulation does not give rise to a present obligation because an entity makes its own decision about whether it will apply for registration. Because the cost of registration can be avoided by ceasing to use the chemical substance, we believe that a provision should not be recognised for estimated future registration costs in accordance with IAS 37 (see 3.12.90). We believe that the REACH registration requirement is similar to Example 6 of Appendix C to IAS 37 in respect of a legal requirement to fit smoke filters. [*IAS 37.19, IE.C.Ex6*]

3.3.180   *Regulatory assets*

3.3.180.10   In many countries, utility companies (or other entities operating in regulated industries) have contractual arrangements with the local regulator to charge a price based on a cost-plus model. Some arrangements will allow the entity to recover excess costs incurred through future price increases charged on future deliveries. Typically under such arrangements, the regulator approves the costs to be recovered based on conditions set out in the contractual arrangement. In our view, any excess cost that is incurred – and that may be recovered through future price increases charged on future deliveries – does not qualify for recognition as an asset because it does not meet the definition of an intangible asset and there is no contractual right to receive cash or other financial assets at the reporting date. The legal right to increase prices in the future is not sufficient to satisfy the definition of an intangible asset because the entity does not control the customers. The customers might decide not to buy or to buy less and thereby leave the entity with uncovered costs. For a discussion of regulatory liabilities, see 3.12.720.

3.3.185   *Service concession arrangements*

3.3.185.10   IFRIC 12 provides guidance to private sector entities on certain recognition and measurement issues that arise in accounting for public-to-private service concession arrangements.

3.3.185.20   IFRIC 12 addresses how service concession operators apply existing standards in accounting for the obligations that they undertake and the rights that they receive in service concession arrangements. IFRIC 12 focuses on arrangements in which the private sector entity (the operator) incurs expenditure in the early years of the arrangement as it constructs or upgrades public service infrastructure.

3.3.185.30   Under IFRIC 12, the operator recognises consideration receivable for construction (including upgrades of existing infrastructure) as a financial asset when it will be collected from the grantor and/or an intangible asset when the operator has the right to charge users of the public service. If an intangible asset is recognised, then the guidance provided in this chapter is relevant for recognition and measurement. Service concession arrangements are the subject of chapter 5.12.

3.3.190   CLASSIFICATION

3.3.190.10   The classification of an intangible asset depends on whether its useful life is finite or indefinite. An intangible asset has an indefinite useful life when, based on an analysis of all relevant factors, there is no foreseeable limit to the period over which the asset is expected to generate net cash inflows for the entity. [*IAS 38.88*]

3.3.190.20   Various external and internal factors need to be considered when assessing the useful life of an intangible asset.

3.3.190.30   External factors include:
- the term of any agreements and other legal or contractual restrictions on the use of the asset;
- the stability of the industry, changes in market demand and expected actions by competitors; and
- technological, commercial and other types of obsolescence. [*IAS 38.90*]

3.3.190.40   Internal factors include:
- the expected use of the asset and required maintenance;
- dependency on other assets; and
- typical product life cycles. [*IAS 38.90*]

3.3.190.50   If control of an intangible asset is based on legal rights that have been granted for a finite period, then the useful life cannot exceed that period unless:
- the legal rights are renewable; and
- there is evidence to support a conclusion that they will be renewed. [*IAS 38.94*]

3.3.190.60   In addition, the cost of renewal should not be significant. If the cost of renewing such rights is significant when compared with the future economic benefits expected to flow to the entity from renewal, then the renewal costs represent the cost to acquire a new intangible asset at the renewal date. [*IAS 38.94–96*]

3.3.190.70   Determining that an intangible asset has an indefinite useful life does not mean that its life is infinite. Conversely, an intangible asset that has no legal or contractual restrictions on its use does not necessarily mean that it has an indefinite useful life. For example, Company B is a fishery operating in various jurisdictions. One of the local governments wants to restrict fishing activities in its waters to preserve and ultimately rebuild its fish stocks. Accordingly, the local government intro-duces a temporary programme whereby each fishery should buy a permanent licence – i.e. it has no expiry date. This licence restricts the number of fish that B can catch for a particular species of fish (catch quota). The catch quota changes each year. In our view, B cannot automatically conclude that the licence has an indefinite useful life simply because the licence is permanent. All facts and cir-cumstances should be considered, including in this case an estimate of the duration of the programme and its effectiveness at maintaining fish stocks. [*IAS 38.91*]

3.3.190.80   Difficulties in determining useful life do not mean that an intangible asset has an indefinite useful life; nor does it mean that its useful life is unrealistically short. For example, Company T buys a wireless spectrum licence that covers various regions and frequencies. Although the licence has an unlimited life, it is expected that a new technology will eventually be developed that will require different frequencies and therefore render the licence obsolete. Although the timing of such obsolescence may be difficult to determine, T expects that at some point in the future the licence will cease to generate net cash inflows. Accordingly, T concludes that the licence has a finite useful life. However, T should not assign an unrealistically short useful life to the licence – e.g. one year – to avoid ongoing amortisation charges. In our view, the estimate of useful life should be consistent with management's estimate of the period over which the entity will receive cash flows from the licence. [*IAS 38.93*]

3.3.190.90   In our view, in assessing whether the useful life of a brand is finite or indefinite, an entity should consider the following factors in addition to the general factors outlined in 3.3.190.20–40, which are not exhaustive or necessarily in order of importance, in its assessment.

- *How well and for how long has the brand been established in the market? And what has been the brand's resilience to economic and social changes since its creation?* If the brand is mature and contributes significant value to the business and its abandonment would represent an unrealistic decision, then this might indicate an indefinite useful life.
- *How stable is the industry in which the brand is used?* In rapidly changing industries, it is less likely that a brand will have an indefinite useful life.
- *Is the brand expected to become obsolete at some point in the future – e.g. through a decline in market demand for the products sold under the brand, or because of the technological obsolescence of these products? Can the brand be deployed in more than one industry or with more than one technology?* If a brand is dependent on factors applying to a particular industry or technology, then it is less likely that it will have an indefinite useful life.
- *Is the brand used in a market that is subject to significant, enduring entry barriers?* If yes, then it is more likely that it will have an indefinite useful life.
- *Is sufficient ongoing marketing effort to support the brand included in the entity's financial fore-casts, such that benefits arising from the use of the brand are expected to be maintained beyond the foreseeable future? Is this level of marketing effort economically reasonable?* If the projected investment in marketing cannot assure the maintenance of the brand in the foreseeable future, then this does not indicate that the brand has an indefinite useful life.
- *Is the useful life of the brand dependent on the useful lives of other assets of the entity? If so, what are the useful lives of those assets?* If a brand is highly dependent on other assets with defined useful lives, then it is unlikely that the brand will be identified as having an indefinite useful life.

3.3.190.100   Further examples of determining whether an intangible asset has a finite or indefinite useful life are provided in the illustrative examples to IAS 38. [*IAS 38.IE*]

3.3.190.110   The events and circumstances relevant to the classification of an intangible asset as having either a finite or indefinite useful life may change over time. Therefore, an entity reviews the classification in each annual reporting period to decide whether the classification made in the past is still appropriate. A change in the assessment of the useful life from indefinite to finite is accounted for as a change in estimate under IAS 8 (see 2.8.110). [*IAS 38.109*]

3.3.200   INDEFINITE USEFUL LIVES*

3.3.200.10   Subsequent to initial recognition, goodwill and intangible assets with indefinite useful lives are measured at cost, or in some cases at a revalued amount (see 3.3.280), less accumulated impairment charges. Goodwill and intangible assets with indefinite useful lives are not amortised, but instead are subject to impairment testing at least annually (see 3.10.130). [*IAS 36.10, 38.107–108*]

3.3.200.20   The useful life of an intangible asset that is not being amortised is reviewed in each annual reporting period to determine whether events and circumstances continue to support an indefinite useful life for that asset (see 3.3.190.110). Reassessing the useful life of an intangible asset from indefinite to finite is an indicator that the asset might be impaired and the entity considers the need for an impairment test when such a change is identified (see 3.10.120). [*IAS 38.109–110*]

3.3.210   FINITE USEFUL LIVES

3.3.210.10   Subsequent to initial recognition, an intangible asset with a finite useful life is amortised on a systematic basis over its useful life, which is reviewed at least each annual reporting date. [*IAS 38.97, 104*]

3.3.210.20   A change in the useful life is accounted for prospectively as a change in estimate (see 2.8.110). [*IAS 38.104*]

EXAMPLE 5 – USEFUL LIFE REVISED

3.3.210.30   Company M acquired software – an intangible asset with a finite useful life – on 1 January 2011 and its useful life was estimated to be 10 years. At the end of 2017, the carrying amount of the software was 240. At the beginning of 2018, M revised the estimated remaining useful life and reduced it to two years as of that date.

3.3.210.40   Therefore, the carrying amount of 240 is amortised over the next two years (2018 and 2019). In addition, the decrease in useful life might indicate that the carrying amount of the software is impaired (see 3.10.120).

3.3.220   Residual value

3.3.220.10   The depreciable amount of an intangible asset with a finite useful life is determined after deducting its residual value. The residual value of an intangible asset is the estimated amount that an entity would obtain currently from disposal of the asset, after deducting the estimated costs of disposal, if the asset were in the condition expected at the end of its useful life. [*IAS 38.8, 102*]

3.3.220.20   However, unlike property, plant and equipment, the residual value of an intangible asset with a finite useful life is assumed to be zero unless:

- a third party has committed to buy the asset at the end of its useful life; or
- there is an active market (see 3.3.280.10) from which a residual value can be obtained, and it is probable that such a market will exist at the end of the asset's useful life. [*IAS 38.100*]

3.3.220.30   The effect of these criteria is that the residual value of an intangible asset with a finite useful life is generally assumed to be zero. A residual value other than zero implies that an entity expects to dispose of the intangible asset before the end of its economic life. [*IAS 38.101*]

3.3.220.40   The residual value of an intangible asset with a finite useful life is reviewed at least at each annual reporting date. A change in the asset's residual value is accounted for prospectively as a change in estimate (see 2.8.110). If the residual value of an intangible asset increases to an amount equal to or greater than the asset's carrying amount, then amortisation stops until its residual value subsequently decreases to an amount below the asset's carrying amount. [*IAS 38.102–103*]

3.3.230   **Methods of amortisation**

3.3.230.10   The method of amortisation of an intangible asset with a finite useful life reflects the pattern of consumption of the economic benefits embodied in the asset. The method used is reviewed at least at each annual reporting date and a change in the method applied is accounted for prospectively as a change in estimate (see 2.8.110). [*IAS 38.97, 104*]

3.3.230.20   No specific method of amortisation is required, and the straight-line method, the diminishing (or reducing-balance) method and the units-of-production method are cited as possible approaches; these methods are illustrated in 3.2.160. In determining the pattern of consumption of the economic benefits, and so the appropriate method of amortisation, an entity could consider the predominant limiting factor – e.g. the contract may specify the entity's use of the intangible asset as a predetermined number of years or number of units produced. If an entity cannot determine the pattern of consumption of the economic benefits reliably, then it uses the straight-line method. [*IAS 38.97–98, 98B*]

3.3.230.30   An entity is permitted to use revenue-based amortisation only when:

- it can demonstrate that revenue and the consumption of the economic benefits of the intangible asset are highly correlated; or
- the intangible asset is expressed as a measure of revenue – e.g. an entity may be granted a right to operate a toll road to generate a specific amount of revenue – such that revenue is the predominant limiting factor. [*IAS 38.98A, 98C*]

3.3.230.35   A high correlation between the revenue and the consumption of the economic benefits is a high threshold. This is because revenue is normally affected by other inputs and processes, selling activities and changes in sales volumes and prices that are not directly linked to the consumption of the economic benefits embodied in the intangible asset. In our view, an entity cannot simply assume that the consumption of economic benefits is based on revenue. This approach would not meet the requirement to demonstrate that the two variables – revenue and the consumption of economic benefits – are highly correlated. [*IAS 38.98A*]

3.3.230.40   In our view, if an intangible asset is expressed as a measure of revenue, then the fixed amount specified in the contract should represent an achievable threshold and not an unrealistically high amount. Otherwise, it will not represent the predominant limiting factor, because it would have no practical limiting effect on the consumption of the economic benefits embodied in the asset.

EXAMPLE 6 – REVENUE-BASED METHOD OF AMORTISATION

3.3.230.50   Company X acquires a concession to explore and extract gold that limits total cumulative revenue from the sale of gold to 2 billion. There are no limits for the time or the amount of gold to be extracted. The proved reserves of the gold mine multiplied by the gold market price at the date of the concession significantly exceed the revenue threshold of 2 billion. Therefore, X determines that the revenue threshold is achievable.

3.3.230.60   In this example, X concludes that revenue-based amortisation is an appropriate method. This is because the concession limits X's rights to a specified amount of revenue and that threshold is achievable. Therefore, revenue is the predominant limiting factor that represents the pattern in which the economic benefits of the concession are consumed.

3.3.230.70   For a discussion of the amortisation in a service concession arrangement, see 5.12.170.

3.3.235   *Usage different from other market participants*

3.3.235.10   An acquirer may intend not to use an acquired intangible asset, or it may intend to use it in a way that is not its highest and best use; determining the fair value of such an intangible asset is discussed in 2.4.340.80–120. However, an issue arises over the appropriate amortisation method to be applied to such an intangible asset. In our view, the guidance in 3.3.230 applies in the usual way, and it might not be appropriate to recognise an immediate impairment loss for the carrying amount of the asset simply because it will not be actively used.

EXAMPLE 7A – USEFUL LIFE – BRAND

3.3.235.20   Company P acquires Company S in a business combination. Both companies are involved in the manufacture of chocolate and other confectionery; while P's brands are dominant in the global marketplace, S's chocolate brand is a major competitor in certain markets. P does not plan to use S's brand after the acquisition, which will benefit P's brands by removing competition.

3.3.235.30   P concludes that it is likely to benefit from S's brand being removed from the marketplace for a period of five years. P further decides to use the straight-line method of amortisation. Accordingly, P amortises the carrying amount of S's brand on a straight-line basis over five years.

EXAMPLE 7B – USEFUL LIFE – DISTRIBUTION NETWORK

3.3.235.35   Changing the facts of Example 7A, one of Company S's assets is its distribution network. Company P will not use S's distribution network after the acquisition because it has its own network in the same areas. P estimates that it will take less than a year to move all of S's distribution to its own network. Additionally, removing S's distribution network from operation does not contribute to the value of P's own distribution network or its business in general.

3.3.235.37   Therefore, P concludes that the acquired distribution network, which is measured at fair value in the business combination, should be amortised over the period that it takes P to move all distribution to its own network, which will be less than a year.

3.3.235.40   In some cases, it may be possible to use the decline in fair value of the unused intangible asset (S's chocolate brand in Example 7A) over consecutive reporting periods as a proxy for measuring the consumption of economic benefits. However, whether such a method is indeed an appropriate proxy will depend on the specific facts and circumstances of a case.

3.3.235.50   For a discussion of the level at which impairment testing is carried out, see 3.10.125. In particular, because an intangible asset acquired for 'defensive' purposes does not generate independent cash inflows, it will be tested as part of the larger CGU that it benefits.

3.3.240   Commencement and cessation of amortisation

3.3.240.10   The amortisation of an intangible asset with a finite useful life begins when the asset is available for use – i.e. when it is in the location and condition necessary for it to be capable of operating in the manner intended by management. [*IAS 38.97*]

3.3.240.20   Except as discussed in 3.3.220.40, amortisation ceases at the earlier of the date on which the asset is:
- classified as held-for-sale (see 5.4.20); or
- derecognised. [*IAS 38.97*]

EXAMPLE 8A – AMORTISATION COMMENCES IMMEDIATELY

3.3.240.30   Company P develops new software for its human resources department. The software is completed in October 2018 and could be implemented at that date. However, management decides not to implement the software until early in 2019.

3.3.240.35   In this example, P determines that the software should be amortised from October 2018, because it is available for use from this date.

3.3.240.40   In contrast to Example 8A, in some cases an intangible asset is to be used only in conjunction with other assets that are not yet available for use. In such cases, judgement is required in determining when the consumption of the future economic benefits embodied in that asset commences to determine the commencement of amortisation.

3.3.240.50   In our view, there are two acceptable approaches to determining when amortisation should commence.

- The first approach is to commence amortisation of the asset once the asset group as a whole is ready to commence operations, because in effect it is from this point that the entity will realise the future economic benefits embodied in the asset. Applying this approach will require annual impairment testing because the asset is not yet available for use (see 3.10.130).
- The second approach considers the intangible asset's availability for use on a stand-alone basis – i.e. not as an integral part of a group of assets. Applying this approach, amortisation commences from the date of acquisition of the intangible asset because, on a stand-alone basis, it is available for use.

3.3.240.55   An entity's accounting policy choice in this regard should be applied consistently.

EXAMPLE 8B – AMORTISATION DELAYED

3.3.240.60   Company T, a telecom, acquires a wireless spectrum licence in 2018; T will complete the related infrastructure by 2020. The network is required in order for T to realise the future economic benefits embodied in the licence.

3.3.240.70   T elects to commence amortisation only when the network as a whole is ready, and in the meantime will perform annual impairment tests on the carrying amount of the licence.

3.3.250   Classification of amortisation expense

3.3.250.10   If an intangible asset with a finite useful life is used in the production of another asset – e.g. inventory – then the amortisation charge is included in the cost of that asset. Otherwise, amortisation is recognised in profit or loss. When an entity classifies its expenses by function (see 4.1.30), care should be taken in allocating the amortisation of intangible assets. [*IAS 38.99*]

EXAMPLE 9 – AMORTISATION EXPENSE PART OF ADMINISTRATION

3.3.250.20   Continuing Example 8A, Company P's human resources department is part of the administrative function of the business. Therefore, amortisation of the department's software will be included in administrative expenses.

3.3.260   Impairment*

3.3.260.10   Intangible assets with finite useful lives are tested for impairment when there is an indicator of impairment (see 3.10.120). Goodwill, intangible assets with indefinite useful lives and intangible assets not yet available for use are tested for impairment annually *and* when there is an indicator of impairment (see 3.10.130). [*IAS 38.111*]

3.3.270   # SUBSEQUENT EXPENDITURE

3.3.270.10   Subsequent expenditure to add to, replace part of, or service an intangible asset is recognised as part of the cost of an intangible asset if an entity can demonstrate that the item meets:
- the definition of an intangible asset (see 3.3.10); and
- the general recognition criteria for intangible assets (see 3.3.100). [*IAS 38.18*]

3.3.270.20   It will be rare for subsequent expenditure to be recognised in the carrying amount of an intangible asset except in the case of acquired IPR&D projects. Often it is difficult to attribute subsequent expenditure directly to a particular intangible asset rather than to the business as a whole. In addition, most subsequent expenditure is likely to be the cost to maintain the expected future economic benefits embodied in an existing intangible asset rather than an expenditure that meets the definition of an intangible asset (see 3.3.10) and the initial recognition criteria (see 3.3.100). [*IAS 38.20, 43*]

3.3.270.30   The general recognition criteria for internally generated intangible assets are applied to subsequent expenditure on IPR&D projects acquired separately or in a business combination. Therefore, capitalisation after initial recognition is limited to development costs that meet the recognition criteria (see 3.3.120). [*IAS 38.42, 54–62*]

3.3.270.40   Consistent with the requirements in respect of initial recognition (see 3.3.120.80), subsequent expenditure on items such as brands, mastheads, publishing titles and customer lists, and items similar in substance, is not capitalised. This is on the basis that the expenditure cannot be distinguished from developing the business as a whole, and therefore it cannot be identified separately from goodwill. [*IAS 38.20, 63*]

3.3.280   # REVALUATIONS

3.3.280.10   Intangible assets cannot be revalued unless there is an 'active' market, which requires a market in which transactions for the asset or liability take place with sufficient frequency and volume to provide pricing information on an ongoing basis. [*IAS 38.75, IFRS 13.A*]

3.3.280.20   Many intangible assets do not qualify for the revaluation model because they are considered unique, and therefore there is no active market for them; examples include customised software, brands, mastheads, publishing rights, patents and trademarks. An example of an intangible asset for which an active market may exist, thereby allowing such assets to be revalued, is an emissions allowance (see 3.3.160). [*IAS 38.78*]

3.3.280.30   If an intangible asset is revalued, then fair value is measured in accordance with IFRS 13, which is the subject of chapter 2.4. In that case, all intangible assets in that class are revalued to the extent that there is an active market for these assets. Revaluations are made with sufficient regularity such that at the reporting date the carrying amount of an asset does not differ materially from its fair value. [*IAS 38.72, 75*]

3.3.280.40   When an intangible asset is revalued, the revaluation is accounted for using one of the following approaches.

- *Restatement approach:*
  - the gross carrying amount is adjusted in a manner that is consistent with the revaluation of the carrying amount of the asset – e.g. it may be restated with reference to observable market data or in proportion to the change in the carrying amount; and
  - the accumulated amortisation is adjusted to equal the difference between the gross carrying amount and the carrying amount of the asset after taking into account accumulated impairment losses.
- *Elimination approach:* the accumulated amortisation is eliminated against the gross carrying amount of the asset. [*IAS 38.80*]

3.3.280.50   Any surplus arising on the revaluation is recognised in OCI (and presented in the revaluation reserve within equity) except to the extent that the surplus reverses a previous revaluation deficit on the same asset recognised in profit or loss, in which case a credit up to the amount of the deficit previously charged to profit or loss is recognised in profit or loss. Any deficit on revaluation is recognised in profit or loss except to the extent of any balance in the revaluation reserve on the same asset, in which case it is recognised in OCI (and deducted from the revaluation reserve in equity). Therefore, under IFRS, revaluation increases and decreases within a class of assets cannot be offset. [*IAS 38.85–86*]

3.3.290   RETIREMENTS AND DISPOSALS

3.3.300   Goodwill

3.3.300.10   When an operation to which goodwill relates is disposed of, the part of the carrying amount of goodwill that has been allocated to the respective CGU(s) is included in calculating the gain or loss on disposal (see 3.10.490). [*IAS 36.86*]

3.3.300.20   Goodwill previously recognised as a deduction from equity – e.g. before the adoption of IFRS and not restated on adoption (see 6.1.1060.30) – is not recognised in profit or loss when the entity disposes of all or part of the business to which that goodwill relates. [*IFRS 1.C4(i)*]

3.3.310   Intangible assets

3.3.310.10   An intangible asset is derecognised when:
- it is disposed of – in this case, the date of disposal is the date on which the recipient obtains control of the asset under the guidance on the satisfaction of performance obligations in IFRS 15 (see 4.2.240); or
- no further economic benefits are expected from it – i.e. neither from its future use nor from its future disposal. [*IAS 38.112, 114*]

3.3.310.20   The gain or loss arising from the derecognition of an intangible asset is the difference between the net proceeds received, if there are any, and the carrying amount of the intangible asset (see 3.2.380.70). The amount of consideration included in the gain or loss on derecognition – and subsequent changes in that amount – is estimated under the requirements for determining the transaction price in IFRS 15 (see 4.2.90 and 200). [*IAS 38.116*]

3.3.310.30   The gain or loss on derecognition is generally included in profit or loss unless the transaction is a sale-and-leaseback and deferral is required, and is not classified as revenue (see 5.1.470). [*IAS 38.113*]

3.3.310.40   Any attributable revaluation surplus may be transferred to retained earnings, but is not recognised in profit or loss (see 3.3.280). [*IAS 38.87*]

3.3.310.50   If an entity recognises the cost of replacing a part of an intangible asset in the carrying amount of an intangible asset, then it derecognises the carrying amount of the replaced part. If it is impracticable for the entity to determine the carrying amount of the replaced part, then it may use the cost of the replacement as an indication of the cost of the replaced part at the time when it was acquired or generated internally. [*IAS 38.115*]

3.3.310.60   The amortisation of an intangible asset with a finite useful life does not cease when the intangible asset is no longer used, unless the asset has been fully amortised, has been derecognised or is classified as held-for-sale. Non-current assets held for sale or distribution are presented separately from other assets in the statement of financial position and are not amortised or depreciated (see 5.4.40 and 110). [*IAS 38.112, 117*]

3.3.310.70   For a discussion of exchanges of non-monetary assets, see chapter 5.7.

3.3.320   DISCLOSURES

3.3.320.10   The disclosure requirements for intangible assets, which are illustrated in KPMG's *Guides to financial statements* series, include a reconciliation between the carrying amount of intangible assets at the beginning and end of the period. The reconciliation is required for both the current and the comparative period. [*IAS 38.118*]

3.3.320.20   The reconciliation for intangible assets other than goodwill includes separate line items for additions, indicating those internally developed, those purchased and those acquired through business combinations. However, all disposals may be presented in a single line item in the reconciliation. [*IAS 38.118*]

3.3.320.30   The calculation of the net exchange difference in respect of foreign operations, which is part of the reconciliation, is illustrated in 2.7.280. [*IAS 38.118*]

3.3.320.40   In addition, the disclosure requirements of IFRS 13 apply to intangible assets that are accounted for under the revaluation model (see 2.4.490).

3.3.330   FUTURE DEVELOPMENTS

3.3.330.10   The IASB is working on a goodwill and impairment research project. For further discussion of this project, see 3.10.880.

3.4   Investment property

3.4　Investment property

CURRENTLY EFFECTIVE REQUIREMENTS

This publication reflects IFRS in issue at 1 August 2018, and the currently effective requirements cover annual periods beginning on 1 January 2018.

The requirements related to this topic are mainly derived from the following.

STANDARD	TITLE
IFRS 13	Fair Value Measurement
IAS 16	Property, Plant and Equipment
IAS 17	Leases
IAS 40	Investment Property

The currently effective requirements include newly effective requirements arising from the following.

- IFRS 15 *Revenue from Contracts with Customers*, which is effective for annual periods beginning on or after 1 January 2018. The new requirements may be applied using the retrospective method or the cumulative effect method (see 4.2.510). The impact of the new requirements on the accounting for investment property is reflected in 3.4.250.10.
- *Transfers of Investment Property – Amendments to IAS 40*, which are effective for annual periods beginning on or after 1 January 2018. The amendments apply prospectively and require an entity, at the date of initial application, to reassess the classification of property held at that date and, if applicable, to reclassify property to reflect the conditions that exist at that date. Retrospective application is permitted, but only if it does not involve the use of hindsight. See 3.4.200.

FORTHCOMING REQUIREMENTS

The currently effective requirements are affected by the following forthcoming requirements. They are highlighted with a # and the impact is explained in the accompanying boxed text at the reference indicated.

- In January 2016, the IASB issued IFRS 16 *Leases*, which is effective for annual periods beginning on or after 1 January 2019. See 3.4.47, 115, 125, 135, 155, 175, 255 and 265. IFRS 16 is the subject of chapter 5.1A.
- In May 2017, the IASB issued IFRS 17 *Insurance Contracts*, which is effective for annual periods beginning on or after 1 January 2021. See 3.4.137. IFRS 17 is the subject of chapter 8.1A.

FUTURE DEVELOPMENTS

For this topic, there are no future developments.

3.4.10   **DEFINITION AND CLASSIFICATION**

3.4.10.10   IAS 40 is not a specialised industry standard. Therefore, determining whether a property is investment property depends on the use of the property rather than the type of entity that holds the property. Classification as investment property is mandatory if the criteria of IAS 40 are met, although there is a choice regarding how investment properties are measured subsequent to initial recognition (see 3.4.130). [*IAS 16.2, 40.2*]

3.4.10.20   Investment property is property held to earn rental income or for capital appreciation, or both, rather than for:
- use in the production or supply of goods or services or for administrative purposes; or
- sale in the ordinary course of business. [*IAS 40.5*]

3.4.10.30   For example, a retail site owned by Company G, but leased out to third parties in return for rental income, is an investment property. However, a factory owned and used by Company H is not an investment property because it is used in the production of goods.

3.4.10.40   Although the definition in 3.4.10.20 appears relatively straightforward, determining what is or is not investment property raises some difficult practical issues. Some of these issues are discussed in 3.4.20–100. [*IAS 40.14–14A*]

3.4.10.50   The following items are specifically excluded from the scope of IAS 40 because they are subject to requirements contained in other standards:
- biological assets on land related to agricultural activities (see chapter 3.9); and
- mineral rights and reserves such as oil, natural gas and similar non-regenerative resources (see chapter 5.11). [*IAS 40.4*]

3.4.20   **Property**

3.4.20.10   An investment property may comprise:
- land;
- a building or part of a building; or
- both. [*IAS 40.5*]

3.4.20.20   Land and assets situated on that land are generally separate assets. However, in some cases a structure that is not a building in its own right may be regarded as an integral part of the related land and therefore might still meet the definition of investment property – e.g. golf courses and car parks that are not separate structures. If the investment property is being accounted for under the cost model (see 3.4.170), then it is necessary to assess whether these structures are separately depreciable as components. [*IAS 16.58*]

3.4.30   **Equipment and furnishings**

3.4.30.10   Equipment and furnishings physically attached and integral to a building are considered to be part of the investment property. For example, lifts, escalators, air conditioning units, decorations and installed furniture, such as built-in cabinetry, would be included as part of the cost and fair value of the investment property and would not be classified separately as property, plant and equipment. [*IAS 40.50*]

3.4.30.20   If investment property contains furniture, then its fair value may also include the value of the existing furniture if it is impractical to determine the fair value without inclusion of such items (see 3.4.45.60). In such cases, the furniture would not be accounted for as a separate asset if the investment property is accounted for at fair value (see 3.4.140). If the investment property is accounted for using the cost model (see 3.4.170), then the related furniture is accounted for under IAS 16 as separate components. This is consistent with the components approach required by IFRS (see 3.2.230). However, in our view care should be taken to ensure that the disclosure of the fair value of the investment property is not misleading when the fair value of the property includes the fair value of the furniture. [*IAS 40.50*]

3.4.40   Leased property#

3.4.40.05   The following table explains which standard applies to each category of lease.

LESSEE		LESSOR	
OPERATING LEASE	FINANCE LEASE	OPERATING LEASE	FINANCE LEASE
Can elect to apply IAS 40 if the definition of investment property is met.	Apply IAS 40 if the definition of investment property is met.	Apply IAS 40 if the definition of investment property is met.	IAS 40 does not apply; apply IAS 17.

3.4.40.10   IAS 17, rather than IAS 40, applies to property leased out under a finance lease in the financial statements of a lessor (see chapter 5.1).

3.4.40.20   A lessee under an operating lease may elect to classify its leasehold interest as investment property, provided that the leasehold interest meets the rest of the definition of an investment property. In such cases, the lessee accounts for the lease as if it were a finance lease, by recognising the asset at the lower of fair value and the present value of the minimum lease payments, and an equivalent liability (see 5.1.250). This election is available on a property-by-property basis. If a lessee follows this election for one such property, then it is required to apply the fair value model to all its investment property. In a lease of land and buildings, when the building is held under a finance lease, the land may qualify as investment property even if it is held under an operating lease by the lessee. [*IAS 40.6*]

EXAMPLE 1 – CLASSIFICATION OF LEASEHOLD INTEREST

3.4.40.30   Company D acquires a 30-year leasehold interest in a piece of empty land. D constructs and owns a retail building on the land and assesses that the lease of the land is an operating lease. D can choose to classify the operating lease of the land as investment property if the fair value model is applied.

3.4.45   *Multiple components*

3.4.45.10   If a lease includes both land and building elements, then an entity determines the classification of each element based on the classification criteria of IAS 17 (see 5.1.240). [*IAS 17.15A*]

3.4.45.20   In certain circumstances, a building may be treated as being owned outright by the lessee of the land, even if the underlying land is held under an operating lease (see 5.1.417). This might be the case if, for example, during the lease term the lessee is entitled to build or remove any structures on the leased land and the lessee would have both the right to remove the building and the obligation to do so if the lessor so required, should the lease terminate. In this case, the building may be an investment property, even if the land, separately classified as held under an operating lease, is not treated as an investment property.

3.4.45.30   IAS 17 applies to property held by a lessee under an operating lease that is not classified as investment property (see 3.4.40.30). For a discussion of the accounting for leases, see chapter 5.1; and for specific discussion of the classification of leases that cover both land and buildings, see 5.1.240.

3.4.45.40   In certain circumstances, land and/or buildings may be leased together with other assets under a single contract and the group of assets may generate a single cash flow stream. This might be the case if, for example, a lessee enters into a single lease contract for a shipping port – e.g. land, buildings, cranes, vehicles, shipping containers etc. In this case, judgement is required to determine whether any of the other assets – i.e. not the land or building – included in the leasing arrangement should be classified as investment property.

3.4.45.50   The lease classification principles are generally applied on an asset-by-asset basis (see 5.1.260). Therefore, to determine whether the leased assets are eligible for investment property classification, it is necessary to consider whether some or all of the other assets included under a single contract are held under a finance lease, particularly from the lessor's perspective. Lease classification is generally determined before evaluating whether the underlying leased asset may be classified as investment property (see 3.4.40.10).

3.4.45.60   In our view, factors that should be taken into consideration by lessees and lessors in assessing whether a group of assets held under a single lease agreement meets the definition of investment property include, but are not limited to, the following.

FACTOR	HOW THE FACTOR IS APPLIED	EXAMPLES OF OTHER ASSETS THAT MAY BE ELIGIBLE FOR INVESTMENT PROPERTY CLASSIFICATION	EXAMPLES OF OTHER ASSETS THAT OFTEN CANNOT BE CLASSIFIED AS INVESTMENT PROPERTY
The nature of the other assets under the single lease agreement	Other assets under the single lease agreement that are deemed to be an integral part of the land and/or building components should generally be included as part of investment property classification.	A lease of farmland includes the use of an underground pipeline system for irrigation. The underground pipeline cannot easily be relocated and is integral to the generation of the cash flows of the group of assets. Therefore, the pipeline may be classified as part of an investment property rather than as a separate item.	A lease of farmland includes the use of a tractor. The tractor can easily be moved to another location or sold to another farm. Therefore, the tractor should be excluded from investment property classification.

Factor	How the factor is applied	Examples of other assets that may be eligible for investment property classification	Examples of other assets that often cannot be classified as investment property
The nature of the other assets under the single lease agreement (continued)	Assets that cannot easily be relocated to another location are generally integral to the generation of the cash flows of the group of assets and may be included as part of investment property classification. [*IAS 40.50(a)*]		
The practicability of determining the fair value of the land and building components without the inclusion of the other assets in the single lease agreement	Other assets that do not directly impact the ability to measure the land and/or building under the fair value model should generally be excluded from investment property classification.	When performing a valuation of a building, it may be impracticable to exclude items such as office furniture. Therefore, such items are generally included as part of investment property (see 3.4.30.20). [*IAS 40.50(b)*]	When performing a valuation of a building used as a brewery, it is not generally necessary or common practice to include fermentation tanks and other equipment housed in the brewery in order to determine the fair value of the land and/or building. Therefore, if the entire brewery is leased out under a single lease agreement, then generally only the land and building components are eligible for investment property classification.
The entity's business model	Investment property is held either to earn rental income or for capital appreciation rather than for use in the production or supply of goods or services in order to be eligible for classification as investment property. [*IAS 40.5*]	A manufacturer enters into a finance lease for an existing plant. The facility includes a large warehouse that the manufacturer will rent to a third party under a finance lease. The warehouse may be eligible for investment property classification (see 3.4.90).	A manufacturer enters into an operating lease of land, on which it intends to construct a factory to be used for its own use. Because the property will be held for the manufacturer's own use and not to earn rental income or for capital appreciation, it is not eligible for investment property classification. [*IAS 40.7*]

3.4.45.70   If a piece of equipment is deemed to be an integral component of the investment property, then it is important to ensure that the measurement of the investment property does not double count any assets or liabilities that are recognised as separate assets or liabilities (see 2.4.720). [*IAS 40.50(a)*]

3.4.47   FORTHCOMING REQUIREMENTS

3.4.47.10   Under IFRS 16, a lessee applies a single, on-balance sheet lease accounting model to all of its leases unless it elects the recognition exemptions for short-term leases and/or leases of low value assets (see 5.1A.140). A lessee recognises a right-of-use asset representing its right to use the underlying asset and a lease liability representing its obligation to make lease payments. [*IFRS 16.5, 22*]

3.4.47.20   A lessee applies IAS 40 to account for a right-of-use asset if the underlying asset would otherwise meet the definition of investment property. Therefore, in contrast to the current option for property held under operating leases (see 3.4.40.20), all leasehold property will be treated as investment property if the definition is met. An entity applies its chosen valuation model (cost or fair value) to all its investment property, whether leased or owned. [*IAS 40.2, 5, IFRS 16.48, 56*]

3.4.47.30   IFRS 16 substantially carries forward the lessor accounting requirements in IAS 17. Therefore, if a lessor enters into an operating lease of investment property, then it continues to recognise the investment property. In contrast, if a lessor enters into a finance lease of investment property, then it derecognises the investment property and instead recognises a net investment in the lease. However, an intermediate lessor classifies a sub-lease as being a finance lease or an operating lease with reference to its right-of-use asset under the head lease rather than the underlying asset (see 5.1A.510, 530 and 600). [*IFRS 16.B58*]

3.4.50   Investment property under construction or development

3.4.50.10   Property under construction or development for future use as an investment property (investment property under construction) is accounted for under the requirements of IAS 40, using the measurement model elected for investment property (see 3.4.130). [*IAS 40.8(e), 65*]

3.4.60   Investment property vs inventory or property, plant and equipment

3.4.60.10   Property that is held by an entity for sale in the ordinary course of business, or that is in the process of construction or development for such sale, is classified as inventory (see chapter 3.8) rather than as investment property. [*IAS 40.9(a)*]

3.4.60.20   Property that is held by an entity for use in the production or supply of goods or services, or for administrative purposes, is classified as property, plant and equipment (see chapter 3.2) rather than as investment property. [*IAS 40.7*]

3.4.60.30   Similar types of property can be used differently. Therefore, judgement is required to determine whether a property should be classified as investment property, based on the specific facts and circumstances. In our view, the entity's business model – i.e. the entity's intentions regarding that property – should be the primary criterion to consider in determining whether classification as investment property is appropriate.

3.4.60.40   Examples 2A to 2D illustrate how to consider the entity's business model in determining the classification of property using a car park scenario. For a discussion of property operated by a third party under a management contract, see 3.4.100.40.

EXAMPLE 2A – BUSINESS MODEL – CAR PARK IS PART OF LARGER INVESTMENT PROPERTY

3.4.60.50   Company G owns an apartment building, which is held solely to earn rental income and is classified as investment property. G also owns a car park, which is attached to the apartment building. Only residents of the apartment building are allowed to enter the car park, and the parking fee is included in the monthly rental associated with the apartment building. G is also the operator of the car park. In this example, G classifies the car park as investment property because it forms part of a larger building that is held by the same owner for the same business purpose.

EXAMPLE 2B – BUSINESS MODEL – CAR PARK IS INVENTORY

3.4.60.60   Company H develops a car park and sells individually designated parking spaces to owners of an adjacent apartment building. H provides security and maintenance services for the car park, which are considered to be insignificant (see 3.4.100.10). H is also the operator of the car park. In this example, H classifies the car park as inventory rather than investment property, because the parking spaces are held for sale in the ordinary course of business (see 3.4.60.10).

EXAMPLE 2C – BUSINESS MODEL – CAR PARK IS PROPERTY, PLANT AND EQUIPMENT

3.4.60.70   Modifying the fact pattern in Example 2B, Company H rents out parking spaces on an hourly basis. The parking spaces are not assigned to any specific customers and customers are free to park in any unoccupied space. Because an individual parking space has not been designated and it is relatively easy for H to provide an alternative parking space, the arrangement does not involve a specified asset; rather H provides a service to customers. Therefore, in this example, classification as investment property is not appropriate because the car park is not being held to earn rentals or for capital appreciation. Instead, H classifies the car park as property, plant and equipment, because it is held for use in the supply of goods or services (see 3.4.60.20).

EXAMPLE 2D – BUSINESS MODEL – CAR PARK IS INVESTMENT PROPERTY

3.4.60.80   Modifying the fact pattern in Example 2C, Company H enters into formal agreements with customers to rent out specified spaces in the car park. Every space in the car park is rented out under a standard agreement. Under the

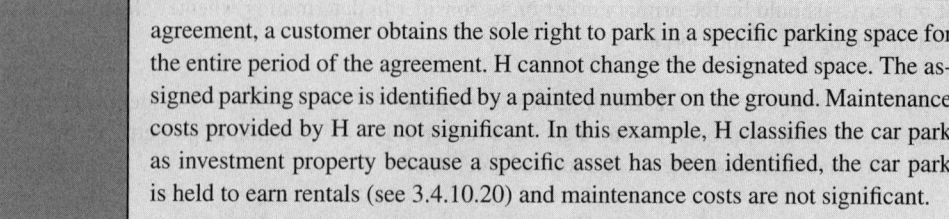

agreement, a customer obtains the sole right to park in a specific parking space for the entire period of the agreement. H cannot change the designated space. The assigned parking space is identified by a painted number on the ground. Maintenance costs provided by H are not significant. In this example, H classifies the car park as investment property because a specific asset has been identified, the car park is held to earn rentals (see 3.4.10.20) and maintenance costs are not significant.

3.4.60.90   In some cases, it may be difficult to distinguish between property held for sale in the ordinary course of business (inventory) and property held for capital appreciation (investment property). The standard gives examples of land held for long-term capital appreciation (investment property), land held for short-term sale (inventory), and property acquired exclusively with a view to subsequent disposal in the near future (inventory). 'Short-term', 'long-term' and 'near future' are not defined in IFRS and various interpretations are possible. [*IAS 40.8–9*]

3.4.60.100   As noted in 3.4.60.30, the business model of an entity – i.e. the entity's intentions regarding that property – should be the primary criterion for classification of a property. The holding period (short- or long-term) is considered in the context of the business model rather than as a 'bright line'. Therefore, an entity that trades in properties would classify its property as inventory if it intended to dispose of the property in the course of its normal operating cycle. [*IAS 1.68*]

EXAMPLE 3 – PROPERTY TO BE SOLD IN NORMAL COURSE OF BUSINESS

3.4.60.110   Company F, a property developer, acquires empty land with the intention of building residential homes that will be sold on completion. Because empty land is an asset held in the process of production for a future sale, F classifies the land and subsequently the buildings it constructs as inventory.

3.4.60.120   However, if land is held for an undetermined future use, then it is classified as investment property because the land is considered to be held for capital appreciation. [*IAS 40.8(b)*]

EXAMPLE 4A – UNDETERMINED FUTURE USE OF PROPERTY

3.4.60.130   Company E pays 400 to acquire an interest in a piece of empty land. E has not yet decided what it will do with the land, but it acquired the interest because it considered the asking price to be a bargain. E classifies the land as investment property, because the land is held for an undetermined future use; it is transferred to inventory if and when development for sale commences (see 3.4.200).

3.4.60.140   In some cases, the determination of whether land has an undetermined future use requires judgement and is dependent on the specific facts and circumstances. In our view, if there is significant uncertainty about whether an entity is able to develop land for its own use or for sale in the ordinary course of business as intended by management, then the land is deemed to be held for an undetermined future use and is classified as investment property. We believe that factors to take into account to determine if property is held for an undetermined future use include, but are not limited to, the following.

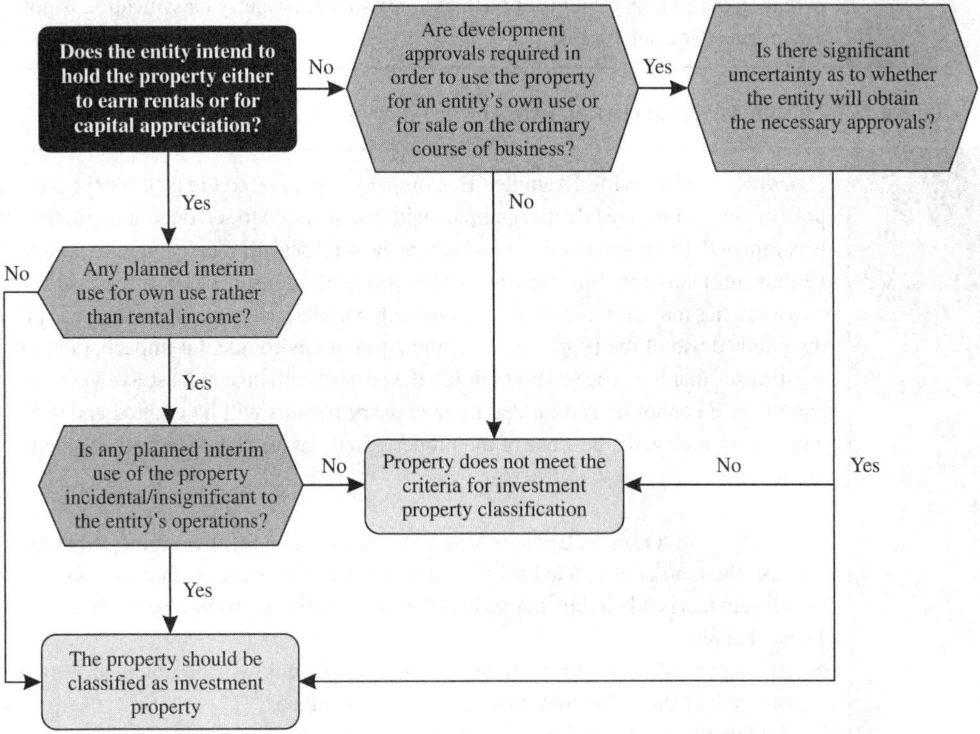

```
┌─────────────────┐        ┌──────────────┐         ┌──────────────┐
│ Does the entity │   No   │ Are          │   Yes   │ Is there     │
│ intend to hold  │ ─────▶ │ development  │ ──────▶ │ significant  │
│ the property    │        │ approvals    │         │ uncertainty  │
│ either to earn  │        │ required in  │         │ as to whether│
│ rentals or for  │        │ order to use │         │ the entity   │
│ capital         │        │ the property │         │ will obtain  │
│ appreciation?   │        │ for an       │         │ the necessary│
└─────────────────┘        │ entity's own │         │ approvals?   │
        │                  │ use or for   │         └──────────────┘
        │ Yes              │ sale on the  │
        ▼                  │ ordinary     │
┌─────────────────┐        │ course of    │
│ Any planned     │        │ business?    │
│ interim use for │        └──────────────┘
│ own use rather  │              │ No
│ than rental     │              ▼
│ income?         │        ┌──────────────┐
└─────────────────┘        │ Property     │
        │                  │ does not meet│
        │ Yes              │ the criteria │
        ▼                  │ for          │
┌─────────────────┐   No   │ investment   │
│ Is any planned  │ ─────▶ │ property     │
│ interim use of  │        │ classification│
│ the property    │        └──────────────┘
│ incidental/     │
│ insignificant to│
│ the entity's    │
│ operations?     │
└─────────────────┘
        │
        │ Yes
        ▼
┌─────────────────┐
│ The property    │
│ should be       │
│ classified as   │
│ investment      │
│ property        │
└─────────────────┘
```

3.4.60.150   The determination of the degree of uncertainty surrounding the ability to use the property as intended and the significance of any planned interim use will require judgement based on the specific facts and circumstances.

EXAMPLE 4B – UNDETERMINED FUTURE USE – INVENTORY OR OWNER OCCUPIED

3.4.60.160   Modifying Example 4A, Company E evaluates two development options: construction of a hotel that it will own and operate, and construction of a residential complex with a view to selling individual units in the complex in the ordinary course of business. E's ultimate decision will depend on the outcome of detailed project development proposals and market analysis. This process is expected to take two years to complete and management has already begun the process of developing the alternative proposals and has obtained the necessary permits to construct either development option.

3.4.60.170   We believe that the criteria for investment property classification are not met because management intends to hold the developed property either for its own use or for sale in the ordinary course of business. Because the developed property will not be held to earn rental income or for capital appreciation, and there is no uncertainty about whether the property can be developed for own use or sale in the ordinary course of business, investment property classification is not appropriate (see 3.4.10.20).

EXAMPLE 4C – UNDETERMINED FUTURE USE – OBTAINING PERMITS

3.4.60.180   Modifying Example 4B, Company E purchased the land for the purpose of developing a residential complex with the intention to sell once construction is completed. In the jurisdiction in which the land is located, E is required to obtain various substantive permits from the local government authority before any construction activities may commence. Receipt of such permits is dependent on approval of the planned use of the property and completion of environmental impact studies. E estimates that the process of obtaining the permits will take at least five years to complete. E cannot be certain that the necessary permits will be granted and will continue to review the best use of the property in order to maximise its investment in the land.

3.4.60.190   In this case, E cannot begin physical development work immediately because the land is not zoned for the intended use. Therefore, E should consider all relevant facts and circumstances in order to assess the appropriate classification. These include:

- the degree of uncertainty about whether the permits will be obtained – e.g. probability that all required permits will be obtained;
- the length of time to obtain the permits;
- existence of regulatory restrictions on the use of the property; and
- the other options that E may pursue to realise the value of the land – e.g. using the land as owner-occupied property.

3.4.60.195   In this example, considering all facts and circumstances, if there is significant uncertainty about whether E will be able to use the land as planned for sale, then we believe that E should classify the land as investment property.

3.4.60.200   Generally, property investors classify their properties as investment property. However, in our view a property investor should classify properties as inventory when, at the date of acquisition, the properties are 'marked' as trading properties – i.e. the investor has the intention of selling them in the ordinary course of business.

EXAMPLE 5 – PROPERTY INVESTOR

3.4.60.210   Company H, an investor in commercial buildings, buys portfolios of properties (including commercial and residential buildings) on a regular basis. Historically, residential buildings have generally been sold shortly after acquisition.

> If, at the date of acquisition, H has the intention of selling the residential buildings in its ordinary course of business, then we believe that they should be classified as inventory, irrespective of whether they are occupied by tenants.

3.4.60.220   Classification requires more judgement when, for example, an entity decides to hold a residential property until a tenant moves out and plans to sell the property only when it is unoccupied. Depending on particular circumstances and the entity's intentions, the waiting period may be viewed as part of preparing the property for sale at its best price or it may be more appropriate to classify the residential property as investment property.

3.4.60.230   Completed developments held for sale in the ordinary course of business are classified as inventory. However, if the intention of the developer entity is to hold a completed development for a certain period and the developer rents the property out during that holding period, then in our view the developer should consider whether continuing to classify the property as inventory is appropriate or whether the property should be classified to investment property. [*IAS 40.9*]

3.4.60.240   Similarly, if an entity decides to redevelop an existing investment property with the intention of selling the property on completion, then it considers whether continuing to classify the property as investment property is appropriate or whether the property should be transferred to inventory (see 3.4.200). However, a decision to dispose of an investment property without redevelopment does not result in a reclassification to inventory. In this case, the property continues to be classified as investment property until the time of disposal unless it is classified as held-for-sale (see 5.4.20). [*IAS 40.57(b), 58*]

3.4.60.250   Property previously classified as investment property that is being redeveloped for continued use as investment property is treated as investment property during its redevelopment (see 3.4.240.10). [*IAS 40.58*]

3.4.60.260   For further discussion of transfers to and from investment property, see 3.4.190.

3.4.70   Property as collateral

3.4.70.10   Financial institutions sometimes take possession of property that was originally pledged as security in full and final settlement of a mortgage for loans (see 7.8.240). If a financial institution acquires a property in this way, then the property is classified based on the buyer's intended use of the property – e.g. as investment property or property, plant and equipment (see chapter 3.2) – or is classified as held-for-sale if appropriate (see 5.4.20). [*IFRS 5.IG.E3*]

3.4.70.20   If a financial institution is uncertain of its intentions with respect to land and buildings that it has repossessed, then in our view those properties should be classified as investment property. This is consistent with the treatment of land held for an undetermined future use (see 3.4.60.120). [*IAS 40.8(b)*]

3.4.80   Consolidated and separate financial statements

3.4.80.10   In determining the classification of a property in consolidated financial statements, the assessment is made from the point of view of the group as a single reporting entity. Although this is consistent with the requirement for the consolidated financial statements to be presented as those of a single reporting entity (see 2.1.100), it means that a property might be classified differently in consolidated financial statements from any separate financial statements (see 2.1.120). [*IAS 27.4, 40.15*]

EXAMPLE 6A – SEPARATE VS CONSOLIDATED FINANCIAL STATEMENTS – DIFFERENT CLASSIFICATION

3.4.80.20   Company G leases an office block to its Subsidiary H, which uses the offices as its administrative head office. In G's separate financial statements the property is classified as investment property (assuming that the lease is an operating lease). However, in the consolidated financial statements the property is classified as property, plant and equipment because the property is owner-occupied (see 3.4.60.20).

3.4.80.30   In our view, the principles in 3.4.80.10 do not apply to property leased to an associate or joint venture, because they are not part of the group. [*IAS 27.4*]

EXAMPLE 6B – SEPARATE VS CONSOLIDATED FINANCIAL STATEMENTS – SIMILAR CLASSIFICATION

3.4.80.35   Changing Example 6A, if G leased the office block to Associate J, then the property would be classified as investment property in both G's individual or separate financial statements and the consolidated financial statements.

3.4.80.40   When assessing the classification of a property leased to, or occupied by, another group entity in the entity's separate financial statements, an issue arises over whether transactions that are not conducted on an arm's length basis should impact the classification. For example, a subsidiary may be instructed to lease a property to another group entity at a price other than market rent. [*IAS 40.15*]

3.4.80.50   In our view, property leased to related parties, other than own employees, should be regarded as investment property, provided that the asset meets the definition of an investment property. This is irrespective of whether the rents charged are on an arm's length basis. The existence of related party relationships and the disclosure of transactions with related parties would also have to be addressed (see chapter 5.5). Property leased to own employees is considered owner-occupied and may also trigger related party disclosures if the employees are key management personnel. [*IAS 40.9(c), 15*]

3.4.90   Dual-use property

3.4.90.10   Property often has dual purposes whereby part of the property is used for own-use activities that would result in the property being considered to be property, plant and equipment and part of the property is used as an investment property. A portion of a dual-use property is classified as an investment property only if the portion could be sold or leased out separately under a finance lease; in some countries, the ability to sell a portion of a property is referred to as 'strata title' or 'condominiumisation'. [*IAS 40.10*]

EXAMPLE 7A – DUAL-USE PROPERTY – PORTION SOLD OR LEASED OUT SEPARATELY

> 3.4.90.20   Company M owns an office block and uses two floors as its own office; the remaining 10 floors are leased out to tenants under operating leases. Under the laws in M's country, M could sell legal title to the 10 floors while retaining legal title to the other two floors. In this example, the 10 floors would be classified as investment property.

3.4.90.30   In some countries, the right to sell legal title to a portion of a property is not an automatic right and it is necessary first to apply to the relevant local authority for permission. In our view, the entity should be regarded as having the ability to sell legal title to a portion of a property if the process for obtaining that right is relatively straightforward and procedural, rather than being subject to a review process in which the chance of rejection is more than remote (see also 3.4.120.40–45).

3.4.90.40   If a portion of the property cannot be sold or leased out separately under a finance lease, then the entire property is classified as investment property only if the portion of the property held for own use is insignificant. 'Insignificant' is not defined, but in our view should be assessed on a property-by-property basis with reference to value and/or usable floor space. In our view, an own-use portion below five percent of the measure used will generally be insignificant. [*IAS 40.10*]

EXAMPLE 7B – DUAL-USE PROPERTY – AMOUNT HELD FOR OWN USE INSIGNIFICANT

> 3.4.90.50   Company N uses 10% of the office floor space of a building as its head office. N leases the remaining 90% to tenants, but is unable to sell the tenants' space or to enter into finance leases related solely to it. We believe that N should not classify the property as an investment property because the 10% of floor space used by N is more than an insignificant portion.

3.4.90.60   The following are examples of dual-use properties owned by an investor that also operates the properties. The examples illustrate:
- portions of the property that would generally be classified as investment property, assuming that they could be sold or leased out under finance leases separately, subject to ancillary services being relatively insignificant (see 3.4.100); and
- portions of the property that often cannot be classified as investment property because they cannot be sold or leased out separately under finance leases.

EXAMPLES OF DUAL-USE PROPERTIES	EXAMPLES OF PORTIONS THAT MIGHT BE CLASSIFIED AS INVESTMENT PROPERTY	EXAMPLES OF PORTIONS THAT OFTEN CANNOT BE CLASSIFIED AS INVESTMENT PROPERTY
Hotel complex	• Separate retail premises • Office block	• Hotel bedrooms • Restaurant facilities within the hotel complex • Kiosks in the reception hall

EXAMPLES OF DUAL-USE PROPERTIES	EXAMPLES OF PORTIONS THAT MIGHT BE CLASSIFIED AS INVESTMENT PROPERTY	EXAMPLES OF PORTIONS THAT OFTEN CANNOT BE CLASSIFIED AS INVESTMENT PROPERTY
Retail area	• Separate retail premises with their own separate entrances or a retail area within another building – e.g. a shopping mall or a hotel	• Retail concessions or franchises within a department store
Airports	• Separate buildings within the airport perimeter, such as hotels, warehousing, airline office blocks, courier facilities	• Retail concessions in the airport terminal

3.4.100   **Ancillary services and exposure to operating risks**

3.4.100.10   In many cases, the owner of a property provides ancillary services to tenants. In such cases, the key to identifying investment property is to decide whether the services provided are a 'relatively insignificant component of the arrangement as a whole'. The standard gives two examples of properties for which ancillary services are provided:

• an owner-managed hotel is not an investment property because the ancillary services provided are a significant component of the arrangement; and

• an office building for which security and maintenance services are provided by the owner is an investment property because the ancillary services are generally an insignificant component of the arrangement. [*IAS 40.11–12*]

3.4.100.20   Classification difficulties arise in respect of properties that fall between these two extreme examples – e.g. serviced apartments and business centres. The standard acknowledges that judgement is required in assessing whether the definition of investment property is met and requires an entity to develop criteria that are applied consistently in making that assessment. In our view, an entity should decide in each situation whether the substance of the arrangement is more like the example of the owner-managed hotel (not investment property) or the example of the office building with security and maintenance services provided by the owner (investment property). [*IAS 40.13*]

EXAMPLE 8A – SERVICED APARTMENTS – OWNER-MANAGED HOTEL

3.4.100.23   Company P owns serviced apartments that are located within one of its hotel complexes. Tenants have full access to the hotel facilities and P provides a full daily cleaning service and room service menu. The only significant difference between this accommodation and a hotel suite is a lower price per night, based on a weekly rather than a daily rate. We believe that these serviced apartments are not investment property because they are similar to an owner-managed hotel.

EXAMPLE 8B – SERVICED APARTMENTS – SIMILAR TO SERVICED OFFICES

> **3.4.100.26** Company Q owns serviced apartments that are located within an apartment block. Q provides security and maintenance services and offers an optional weekly cleaning and laundry service. The leases have a minimum term of three months and references are generally required. The arrangement may be similar to an office building with security and maintenance services. We believe that these serviced apartments qualify as investment property.

3.4.100.30 A similar approach applies when classifying business centres. Some business centres provide a high level of services (such as secretarial support, teleconferencing and other computer facilities) and tenants sign relatively short-term leases or service agreements; we believe that these facilities are more like an owner-managed hotel (and not an investment property). Other business centres require the user to sign up to a minimum period and may provide only basic furnishings in addition to services such as security and maintenance; we believe that these additional services are relatively insignificant and the property would be investment property.

3.4.100.40 If a property is operated by a third party under a management contract, then it is necessary to apply judgement in assessing whether the definition of investment property is met. The standard acknowledges that the terms of management contracts vary widely and requires an entity to develop criteria that are applied consistently in making an assessment. [*IAS 40.13–14*]

3.4.100.50 The standard gives two examples of hotels managed by others:
- at the one extreme, the entity's position is that of a passive property investor and therefore the property is an investment property; and
- at the other extreme, the entity has simply outsourced certain day-to-day functions to a property manager and retains significant exposure to the variation in cash flows from operating the property, and so the property is not an investment property. [*IAS 40.13*]

3.4.100.60 In our view, to classify properties that fall between these two extremes, the relevant factors to be considered include the following.

CONSIDERATION	EXAMPLE
Under the management contract, the party that has the power to make the significant operating and financing decisions regarding the operations of the property	• If the lessor has the power to decide: – hiring, firing and remuneration of staff and to set staffing levels; – opening hours (if applicable); – terms and conditions offered to customers; and – products on offer. • The more power the lessor has to decide and/or influence the items noted above, the more indicative it is that the property is not investment property for the lessor.

CONSIDERATION	EXAMPLE
Calculation of the lessor's return	• A fixed or variable return based on property values is more indicative of investment property for the lessor. • An insignificant proportion of revenue/turnover is more indicative that the property is investment property for the lessor. • A direct percentage of operating profit/result accruing to the owner as earned from the operations of the property is more indicative that the property is not investment property for the lessor. • A significant exposure to variations in net cash flows of the lessee (considering both operating profits and revenues) is more indicative that the property is not investment property for the lessor. For further discussion, see 3.4.100.80.
Lessor's power of intervention under the management contract	• If the lessor's power of intervention is greater than might be expected from a normal landlord-tenant relationship, then this is more indicative that the property is not investment property.
Duration of the contract	• If the contract is on an annual renewal basis with early cancellation clauses, then it is more indicative that the property is not investment property. • If the contract is for a long fixed period of time relative to the life of the asset, then this is more indicative of investment property.

3.4.100.70   In our view, if a property owner shares substantial operating risks with the property manager, then the owner is in effect participating in the delivery of goods and services. This may still be the case even if the day-to-day running of a hotel has been entrusted to a third party hotel management entity, because such arrangements may still leave the owner of the hotel significantly exposed to the variations in the cash flows of the hotel's operations. In such cases, the property is not investment property.

3.4.100.80   The determination of whether the owner is exposed to significant variations in cash flows of operations requires judgement and will depend on the facts and circumstances of the situation. A variable cash flow component will not automatically preclude investment property classification as long as it does not result in the realisation of substantially all of the cash flows from operations. However, if the owner has the right to substantially all of the net cash flows or operating profit of an underlying property, then the property would not qualify as investment property.

EXAMPLE 9 – VARIABLE CASH FLOW COMPONENT OF OWNER'S RETURN ON PROPERTY

3.4.100.90   If the owner is not responsible for the day-to-day activities of the property and receives a fee of 2% of revenues, then the property is investment property. However, if the owner receives a fee of 98% of net operating profit, then the property is not investment property. For examples lying between these two extremes, judgement will be required, and consideration of the other factors outlined in the table in 3.4.100.60.

3.4.110 RECOGNITION#

3.4.110.10 Investment property is recognised as an asset when and only when:

- it is probable that the future economic benefits that are associated with the investment property will flow to the entity; and
- the cost of the investment property can be measured reliably. [*IAS 40.16*]

3.4.110.20 These recognition criteria are applied to all investment property costs – initial costs to acquire an investment property and subsequent costs to add to or replace a part of an investment property (see 3.4.180) – when the costs are incurred. [*IAS 40.17*]

3.4.115 FORTHCOMING REQUIREMENTS

3.4.115.10 An investment property held by a lessee as a right-of-use asset is recognised in accordance with IFRS 16 (see 5.1A.270). [*IAS 40.19A, IFRS 16.22*]

3.4.120 INITIAL MEASUREMENT#

3.4.120.05 Judgement is required to determine whether the acquisition of investment property is a business combination. Such judgement is outside the scope of IAS 40 and is applied based on the guidance outlined in IFRS 3. If investment property acquired constitutes a business – e.g. a property management contract that is taken over together with the acquisition of investment property – then it is accounted for as a business combination (see 2.6.40). [*IAS 40.14A*]

3.4.120.10 Investment property is initially measured at cost except when the asset is:

- transferred from another category in the statement of financial position (see 3.4.210);
- received as a government grant (see 4.3.50);
- acquired in a share-based payment arrangement granted by the acquiring entity (see 4.5.1800); or
- acquired in a business combination (see 2.6.560). [*IAS 40.20*]

3.4.120.15 The cost of investment property is the amount of cash or cash equivalents paid or the fair value of other consideration given to acquire the investment property at the time of its acquisition or construction. [*IAS 40.5*]

3.4.120.20 The cost of investment property includes transaction costs and directly attributable expenditure on preparing the asset for its intended use. The principles discussed in respect of attributing cost to property, plant and equipment (see 3.2.20) apply equally to the recognition of investment property. In addition, clearly identified inefficiencies and initial operating losses are expensed as they are incurred, which is similar to the accounting for property, plant and equipment (see 3.2.40–50). [*IAS 40.20–23*]

3.4.120.25 Under IAS 23, an entity capitalises borrowing costs directly attributable to the acquisition, construction or development of an investment property that is a qualifying asset. However, an entity is not required to capitalise borrowing costs in this way if it measures the investment property at fair value. [*IAS 23.4(a), 8–9*]

3.4.120.30 If payment is deferred, then the cost of the investment property is the cash price equivalent. The issues that arise in accounting for the deferred payment are similar to those in respect of property, plant and equipment (see 3.2.130). [*IAS 40.24*]

3.4.120.35 In some cases, determining the date of acquisition, and therefore determining cost, is not straightforward.

EXAMPLE 10 – DETERMINING DATE OF ACQUISITION

3.4.120.40 On 15 February 2018, Company D enters into a contract to buy a shopping centre for 500 in cash, subject to competition authority approval (see also 2.6.220). If such approval is obtained, then the contract stipulates that the sale is effective from 1 January 2018 and D is entitled to the returns made from that date – i.e. the purchase price is adjusted for those returns. On 10 June 2018, the approval is obtained.

3.4.120.45 If the approval from the competition authority is considered to be a substantive hurdle to be overcome (see also 2.6.220.20–30), then in our view control of the shopping centre passes only when such approval is obtained – i.e. on 10 June 2018. Assuming that the returns made between 1 January 2018 and 10 June 2018 are 30, we believe that the cost of investment property recognised at 30 June 2018 is 470 (500 - 30).

3.4.125 FORTHCOMING REQUIREMENTS

3.4.125.10 An investment property held by a lessee as a right-of-use asset is measured initially at its cost in accordance with IFRS 16 (see 5.1A.290). [*IAS 40.29A, IFRS 16.23–25*]

3.4.130 SUBSEQUENT MEASUREMENT#

3.4.130.10 Subsequent to initial recognition, an entity chooses an accounting policy, to be applied consistently, either to:
- measure all investment property using the fair value model, subject to limited exceptions that are discussed in 3.4.160; or
- measure all investment property using the cost model (see 3.4.170). [*IAS 40.30, 32A*]

3.4.130.20 The standard implies a preference for measuring investment property at fair value, noting that it will be very difficult to justify a voluntary change in accounting policy from the fair value model to the cost basis of measurement. In our view, a change in accounting policy from the fair value to the cost model attributed solely to changes in market conditions is not justifiable. Entities adopting the cost model on initial recognition are required to disclose the fair value on the same basis as those adopting the fair value model. [*IAS 40.31, 79(e)*]

3.4.130.30 If a lessee elects to classify one of its properties that is held under an operating lease as investment property, then the entity is required to use the fair value model for all of its investment property (see 3.4.40.20). However, the lessee's election to classify its operating leases as investment property is made on a property-by-property basis – i.e. not all operating leases qualifying for investment property classification need be classified as investment property. [*IAS 40.6, 34*]

3.4.130.40   If the entity has issued liabilities that pay a return linked to a group of assets that includes investment property, then the entity may make a separate election for the investment properties that back the linked liabilities. [*IAS 40.32A*]

3.4.133   FORTHCOMING REQUIREMENTS

3.4.135   LEASES

3.4.135.10   Under IFRS 16, an entity applies its chosen accounting policy for subsequent measurement of investment property – i.e. cost or fair value – to owned investment property and right-of-use assets that meet the definition of investment property (see 5.1A.360). [*IAS 40.30, 32A, IFRS 16.29, 34*]

3.4.137   INSURANCE CONTRACTS

3.4.137.10   Under IFRS 17, if an entity issues direct participating contracts and the underlying items include investment property, then the property held by the fund (or property that is an underlying item) cannot be measured partly at cost and partly at fair value. This is similar to the currently effective requirements. [*IAS 40.32B*]

3.4.140   Fair value model

3.4.150   *General requirements#*

3.4.150.10   If an entity chooses to measure investment property using the fair value model, then it measures the property at fair value at each reporting date, with changes in fair value recognised in profit or loss. [*IAS 40.33–35*]

3.4.150.20   Fair value is measured in accordance with IFRS 13, which is the subject of chapter 2.4. That chapter includes general guidance on applying the principles of IFRS 13 in measuring fair value; specific points of interest in relation to investment property, including the valuation of investment property under construction, are discussed in 2.4.610.

3.4.150.30   Once the fair value of investment property has been measured, an entity ensures that it does not double count assets or liabilities that are recognised as separate assets or liabilities (see 2.4.720). The entity is also exempt from applying IAS 36. [*IAS 40.50, 36.2(f)*]

3.4.155   FORTHCOMING REQUIREMENTS

3.4.155.10   IFRS 16 introduces consequential amendments to IAS 40, which specify that if a lessee uses the fair value model to measure an investment property that is held as a right-of-use asset, then it measures the right-of-use asset and not the underlying property at fair value. [*IAS 40.40A*]

3.4.160   *Exemption from fair value*

3.4.160.10   In exceptional cases, there will be clear evidence on initial recognition of a particular investment property that its fair value cannot be measured reliably on a continuing basis. In such cases, the property in question is measured using the cost model as if it were property, plant and equipment (see 3.4.170), except that the residual value is deemed to be zero in all cases. The exemption applies only when comparable market transactions are infrequent and alternative estimates of fair value – e.g. based on discounted cash flow projections – are not available. [*IAS 40.53*]

3.4.160.20   An assessment of whether the exemption applies is made only once, when the investment property is initially recognised – following either acquisition or transfer from another category in the statement of financial position. The exemption cannot be used after initial recognition if it was not invoked at the time of initial recognition, even if comparable market transactions become less frequent and alternative estimates of fair value become less readily available. [*IAS 40.55*]

3.4.160.30   Once the exemption is applied, the property continues to be measured in accordance with IAS 16 until its disposal. [*IAS 40.53*]

3.4.160.40   However, if the fair value of an investment property under construction cannot be measured reliably, but the entity expects the fair value of the completed property to be reliably measurable, then such investment property under construction is accounted for using the cost model until the earlier of the date on which the fair value of the property can be measured reliably or the date on which the construction is completed. [*IAS 40.53–53B*]

3.4.170   Cost model#

3.4.170.10   If an entity chooses to measure investment property using the cost model, then the property is accounted for in accordance with the cost model for property, plant and equipment – i.e. at cost less accumulated depreciation (see 3.2.140) and less any accumulated impairment losses (see 3.10.380). However, the property continues to be classified as investment property in the statement of financial position. [*IAS 40.56*]

3.4.170.20   If an entity adopts the cost model for measuring investment property, then it is also required to disclose the fair value of the investment property measured on the same basis as under the fair value model. In this regard, the guidance in IFRS 13 in respect of measuring fair value applies (see 3.4.150.20), as well as the exemptions from fair value measurement (see 3.4.160). [*IAS 40.79(e)*]

3.4.170.30   If a property accounted for using the cost model is classified as held-for-sale (see 5.4.20), then the measurement requirements of IFRS 5 apply from the date on which the criteria are met. In particular, such property is not depreciated when it is classified as held-for-sale. [*IFRS 5.2, 15, 25, IAS 40.56*]

3.4.175   **FORTHCOMING REQUIREMENTS**

3.4.175.10   After initial recognition, an entity that chooses the cost model for subsequent measurement accounts for an investment property that is held as a right-of-use asset in accordance with IFRS 16 if it is not held for sale in accordance with IFRS 5. [*IAS 40.56(b), IFRS 16.30–33*]

3.4.180   SUBSEQUENT EXPENDITURE

3.4.180.10   Expenditure incurred subsequent to the completion or acquisition of an investment property is capitalised only if it meets the general asset recognition criteria – i.e. it is probable that future economic benefits associated with the item will flow to the entity and the cost of the item can be measured reliably. The standard is explicit that under this recognition principle an entity does not recognise in the carrying amount of investment property the cost of the day-to-day servicing of such a property. Instead, such costs are expensed as they are incurred. An example of such maintenance activity is the repair of a leaking roof. [*IAS 40.16–18*]

3.4.180.20   Parts of investment property acquired through replacement are capitalised and included in the carrying amount of the investment property if the general asset recognition criteria are met. The carrying amount of the part replaced is derecognised. These requirements are consistent with the requirements in respect of property, plant and equipment (see 3.2.280). [*IAS 40.19*]

3.4.180.30   The issues that arise in accounting for subsequent expenditure are similar to those in respect of property, plant and equipment (see 3.2.290).

3.4.190   TRANSFERS TO OR FROM INVESTMENT PROPERTY

3.4.200   Timing of transfers

3.4.200.10   Although an entity's business model plays a key role in the initial classification of property (see 3.4.60.30), the subsequent reclassification of property is based on an actual change in use rather than on changes in an entity's intentions. [*IAS 40.57–58*]

3.4.200.15   However, a decision to dispose of an investment property without redevelopment does not result in it being reclassified as inventory. The property continues to be classified as investment property until the time of disposal unless it is classified as held-for-sale (see 5.4.20). [*IFRS 5.2, 5(d), IAS 40.56, 58*]

EXAMPLE 11A – CHANGE IN USE – REDEVELOPMENT FOR SALE

3.4.200.20   Company S owns a retail site that is an investment property. S decides to modernise the site and then to sell it. The investment property is transferred to inventory at the date on which the redevelopment of the site commences; this evidences the change in use.

3.4.200.30   To reclassify inventories to investment property, a change in use is required. This will generally be evidenced by the inception of an operating lease to another party. In some cases, a property (or a part of a property) classified as inventory (see chapter 3.8) is leased out temporarily while the entity searches for a buyer. In our view, the inception of such an operating lease, solely by itself, does not require the entity to transfer the property to investment property provided that the property continues to be held for sale in the ordinary course of business. Any rental income is incidental to such sale (see 3.2.120.10). [*IAS 40.57*]

3.4.200.40   An entity may no longer have the intention or the ability to develop property classified as inventory for sale in the ordinary course of business as originally planned because of fluctuations in property and capital markets. Depending on the facts and circumstances of the situation, it may be appropriate to reclassify a property originally classified as inventory to investment property if there is a change in the business model of the entity that evidences a change in the use of the property. Examples of such situations include the following.

- Property development of land has completely ceased and it is being rented in its current condition (not on a temporary basis).
- Property development has completely ceased and all of the development plans for resale have been deferred indefinitely, and the entity continues to hold the property awaiting improvement in the property market; in effect, the property or land is now being held for rental and/or capital appreciation.

3.4.200.45   A change in management's intention alone would not be sufficient evidence for reclassification and would need to be supported, for example, by an actual change in the use of the property that in certain circumstances could be evidenced by a cessation of further development as originally planned. [*IAS 40.57, BC27*]

3.4.200.50   A reclassification of an investment property to inventory or property, plant and equipment is performed only when an entity's use of the property has changed. For example, the commencement of construction for sale or own use would usually mean that the property is no longer available for rent to third parties. Therefore, a change in use occurs on commencement of redevelopment and reclassification is appropriate at that point. [*IAS 40.57, BC26, BC29*]

EXAMPLE 11B – CHANGE IN USE – REDEVELOPMENT FOR OWN USE

> 3.4.200.60   Company G has previously classified a property as an investment property. G has decided to use the property as its administrative headquarters because of an expansion of its business and commences redevelopment for own use in February 2018 – e.g. builders are on site carrying out the construction work on G's behalf. The redevelopment of the property for future use for administrative purposes effectively constitutes owner occupation. Therefore, G should reclassify the property on commencement of the redevelopment in February 2018.

3.4.210   **Measurement of transfers**

3.4.220   *Cost model*

3.4.220.10   If an entity chooses to measure investment property using the cost model, then transfers to and from investment property do not alter the carrying amount of the property. Therefore, revaluations recognised for property, plant and equipment carried at fair value (see 3.2.300) are not reversed when the property is transferred to investment property. [*IAS 40.59*]

3.4.220.20   IAS 40 does not state specifically whether the property's carrying amount should be brought up to date under its current policy immediately before the transfer. In our view, an adjustment to bring the property's carrying amount up to date is required if the effect would be material to the way in which the results for the period are presented in the statement of profit or loss and OCI.

EXAMPLE 12 – CARRYING AMOUNT OF PROPERTY BEFORE TRANSFER

> 3.4.220.30   Company T has a property classified as inventory. Some time after acquisition, management decides to hold the property indefinitely because the market is currently depressed, and leases out the property to another party under an operating lease.

> 3.4.220.35   When the lease is entered into, the net realisable value of the property is 450, which is lower than its cost of 480. We believe that T should write down the property to 450 before transferring it to investment property and the loss of 30 (450 - 480) should be presented in profit or loss in the same line as other inventory write-downs.

3.4.220.40   IAS 40 is silent on the treatment of an existing revaluation reserve when revalued property is transferred from property, plant and equipment to investment property, where it will be measured under the cost model. In our view, any revaluation reserve accumulated while the property was accounted for as property, plant and equipment should be accounted for in accordance with IAS 16 – i.e. the reserve may be transferred to retained earnings when the amount is realised either through higher depreciation charges while the asset is being used or on disposal. Alternatively, none of the reserve is transferred to retained earnings. For further discussion of issues that arise in respect of this treatment, see 3.2.350. [*IAS 16.41, 40.62*]

3.4.230   *Fair value model*

3.4.230.10   If an entity chooses to measure investment property using the fair value model, then investment property transferred from another category in the statement of financial position is recognised at fair value on transfer. The treatment of the gain or loss on revaluation at the date of transfer depends on whether the property was previously held for own use. [*IAS 40.61–65*]

3.4.230.20   If the property was previously held for own use, then it is accounted for as property, plant and equipment up to the date of the change in use. Any difference at the date of the change in use between the carrying amount of the property and its fair value is recognised as a revaluation of property, plant and equipment in accordance with IAS 16, even if the property was previously measured using the cost model under IAS 16. Any existing or arising revaluation surplus previously recognised in OCI is not transferred to profit or loss at the date of transfer or on subsequent disposal of the investment property. However, on subsequent disposal, any existing revaluation surplus that was recognised when the entity applied the IAS 16 revaluation model to the property may be transferred to retained earnings. [*IAS 40.61, 62(b)(ii)*]

3.4.230.30   If the property is inventory that is being transferred to investment property, then the gain or loss on revaluation, based on the asset's carrying amount at the date of transfer, is recognised in profit or loss. [*IAS 40.63–64*]

3.4.230.40   IFRS is silent on where any gain or loss arising at the point of transfer should be recognised. In our view, any gain or loss on property previously classified as inventory should be included in the same line as other gains or losses on inventory.

3.4.230.50   The gain or loss is identified separately if it is material (see 4.1.80).

3.4.230.55   An entity may measure investment property at fair value but cannot reliably measure the fair value of investment property under construction, as a result of which it measures such investment property at cost until construction is completed (see 3.4.160.40). In this case, there will typically be a difference between the carrying amount and the fair value of investment property on completion of construction. Any difference between the fair value of the property at that date and its previous carrying amount is recognised in profit or loss. [*IAS 40.65*]

3.4.230.60   When a property is transferred from investment property measured at fair value (whether to own-use properties or to inventories), the transfer is accounted for at fair value. The fair value at the date of transfer is then deemed to be the property's cost for subsequent accounting under IAS 2 or IAS 16 (see chapters 3.8 and 3.2, respectively). Any difference between the carrying amount of the property before transfer and its fair value on the date of transfer is recognised in profit or loss in the same way as any other change in the fair value of investment property. [*IAS 40.60*]

3.4.230.70   If an investment property measured using the fair value model is classified as held-for-sale in accordance with IFRS 5 (see 5.4.20), then the measurement requirements of IAS 40 still apply (see 5.4.20.20). [*IFRS 5.2, 5, IAS 40.33–52*]

3.4.240   REDEVELOPMENT

3.4.240.10   When an entity redevelops an existing investment property, the property is not transferred out of investment property during redevelopment. This means that an investment property undergoing redevelopment continues to be measured under the cost model or at fair value (depending on the entity's accounting policy). [*IAS 40.58*]

3.4.240.20   However, consideration is given to whether any of the property has been disposed of during the course of redevelopment. For example, significant items of equipment installed in the building, or even the building itself, may have been scrapped. In our view, any such disposals should be accounted for as follows.

- If investment property is measured under the cost model, then components of the property should be accounted for as separate items of property, plant and equipment (see 3.2.230). Accordingly, such components should be written off as disposals.
- If an investment property is measured at fair value, then information may not exist to enable the entity to account for the disposals separately. We believe that it is acceptable to include the disposals as part of the change in fair value (see 3.4.250.20).

3.4.240.30   If an entity obtains a loan for the redevelopment of existing investment property that is a qualifying asset under IAS 23 (see 4.6.20), then the interest expenditure on the loan used for the incremental cost of redevelopment incurred during the period of construction is capitalised in accordance with IAS 23. If the redevelopment involves a complete redevelopment of a site, then in our view an entity could also capitalise interest expenditure on the historical cost of the land if a loan that was obtained to fund its initial acquisition is still outstanding. However, an entity is not required to capitalise borrowing costs in this way if it measures the investment property at fair value. [*IAS 23.4(a)*]

3.4.250   DISPOSALS#

3.4.250.10   The gain or loss on disposal of investment property is measured as the difference between the net disposal proceeds and the carrying amount of the property, unless the transaction is a sale-and-leaseback (see 5.1.470). The standard gives no guidance on the meaning of 'net' in this context. In our view, it should be determined in the same manner as for property, plant and equipment (see 3.2.380.15). The amount of consideration included in the gain or loss on derecognition, and subsequent changes in that amount, are estimated under the requirements for determining the transaction price under IFRS 15 (see 4.2.90 and 200). [*IAS 40.69–70*]

3.4.250.20   IAS 40 does not state explicitly how to determine the carrying amount on disposal of investment property that is measured at fair value. One approach is to consider the carrying amount at the date of the last published statement of financial position (whether annual or interim), because paragraph 5 of IAS 40 defines 'carrying amount' as the amount at which an asset is recognised in the statement of financial position. For further discussion of how to measure fair value, see chapter 2.4. [*IFRS 13.9, IAS 40.5, 40*]

EXAMPLE 13A – GAIN/LOSS ON DISPOSAL – BASED ON FAIR VALUE AT LAST REPORTING DATE

3.4.250.30   Company V measures investment property at fair value. V's last published statement of financial position was as at the end of its half-year interim period, 30 September 2017. The carrying amount of one particular retail site was 500 on that date. On 28 February 2018, V obtained an independent valuer's report that stated that the fair value of the retail site had dropped to 470, and this was recognised in V's management accounts. On 31 March 2018, the property was sold for 490. A loss on disposal of 10 (490 - 500) would be recognised in profit or loss.

3.4.250.33   An alternative approach is to update the fair value measurement immediately before the sale and then to compare that updated fair value with the sale proceeds when calculating the gain or loss on disposal.

EXAMPLE 13B – GAIN/LOSS ON DISPOSAL – BASED ON MOST RECENT EVIDENCE OF FAIR VALUE

3.4.250.35   Using the figures in Example 13A to illustrate the alternative approach, the statement of profit or loss includes a loss of 30 (470 - 500) as part of the line including all investment property fair value changes, and a profit of 20 (490 - 470) on disposal, which is presented separately. However, if V assesses at 31 March that the selling price of 490 provides the best evidence of the fair value of the retail site at that date, then the gain or loss on disposal would be zero and an amount of 10 would be presented as fair value changes.

3.4.250.37   In our view, an entity should choose an accounting policy, to be applied consistently, to apply one of the approaches outlined in 3.4.250.20 and 33. A consequence of the accounting policy choice may be the presentation of the gain or loss from disposal in the statement of profit or loss, as indicated by the preceding examples. If the policy noted in 3.4.250.20 is adopted, then the entire gain or loss arising from the disposal calculated based on the fair value per the entity's last year end will be recorded as a gain/loss on disposal, which may be presented as a separate line item caption in the statement of profit or loss from revaluation gains of investment property. However, under the policy choice noted in 3.4.250.33, the change in the fair value immediately before the sale will be included as a revaluation gain in profit or loss, and any remaining portion, if there is any, will be recorded as a gain/loss on disposal, which may or may not be included in the same line item caption in the statement of profit or loss.

3.4.250.40   The date of disposal of an investment property is the date on which the recipient obtains control of the asset, under the guidance on the satisfaction of performance obligations in IFRS 15 (see 4.2.210). If the disposal is achieved by entering into a finance lease or a sale-and-leaseback, then IAS 17 applies. In our view, sale-and-leaseback accounting should be applied even if the general revenue recognition criteria have not been met (see 5.1.470). [*IAS 40.67*]

3.4.255   FORTHCOMING REQUIREMENTS

3.4.255.10   IFRS 16 applies to a disposal effected by entering into a finance lease and to a sale-and-leaseback (see 5.1A.600, 680). Under IFRS 16, a seller-lessee derecognises the underlying asset only if the transfer leg satisfies the requirements of IFRS 15 to be accounted for as a sale of the asset. [*IAS 40.67, IFRS 16.100*]

3.4.260   PRESENTATION AND DISCLOSURES#

3.4.260.10   Investment property is presented separately in the statement of financial position. [*IAS 1.54(b)*]

3.4.260.20   Applicable disclosures under IAS 17 continue to apply to investment property. [*IAS 40.74*]

3.4.260.30   The disclosure requirements of IFRS 13 apply to the fair value of investment property, either under the fair value model or for disclosure purposes (see 2.4.490). The disclosures under IFRS 13 are made for each class of asset, which may require an entity's investment property portfolio to be disaggregated instead of being disclosed as a single class of asset (see 2.4.510).

3.4.260.40   In addition, IAS 40 itself includes a number of disclosures in respect of investment property. Because IAS 40 makes no reference to making disclosures on a class-by-class basis, it could be assumed that the minimum requirement is to make the disclosures on an aggregate basis for the whole investment property portfolio. If investment property represents a significant portion of the assets, then it may be appropriate to disclose additional analysis – for example:

- analysing the portfolio into different types of investment property – such as retail, offices, manufacturing and residential; and
- identifying separately any properties currently under redevelopment, vacant, whose use is undetermined and/or that are intended for sale. [*IAS 1.77, 40.74–79*]

3.4.265   FORTHCOMING REQUIREMENTS

3.4.265.10   Under IFRS 16, a lessee applies the disclosure requirements in IAS 40 to right-of-use assets that are investment property, and is not required to provide certain of the disclosures normally required under IFRS 16. [*IAS 40.74, IFRS 16.56*]

3.5 Associates and the equity method

3.5 Associates and the equity method

CURRENTLY EFFECTIVE REQUIREMENTS

This publication reflects IFRS in issue at 1 August 2018, and the currently effective requirements cover annual periods beginning on 1 January 2018.

This chapter deals with the classification of investees as associates, and the accounting for associates and joint ventures (equity-accounted investees). The classification of joint arrangements as joint ventures or joint operations is the subject of chapter 3.6. The disclosures related to interests in equity-accounted investees are discussed in chapter 5.10.

The requirements related to this topic are mainly derived from the following.

STANDARD	TITLE
IAS 28	Investments in Associates and Joint Ventures

The currently effective requirements include newly effective requirements arising from the following.
- IFRS 9 *Financial Instruments*, which is effective for annual periods beginning on or after 1 January 2018. Transition requirements for IFRS 9 are the subject of chapter 7.11. The impact of the new requirements on accounting for associates and the equity method is reflected in 3.5.500 and 530.
- *Annual Improvements to IFRSs 2014–2016 Cycle – Amendment to IAS 28,* which is effective for annual periods beginning on or after 1 January 2018. The new requirements apply retrospectively. See 3.5.100.10 and 200.60.

FORTHCOMING REQUIREMENTS

The currently effective requirements are affected by the following forthcoming requirements. They are highlighted with a # and the impact is explained in the accompanying boxed text at the references indicated.
- In September 2014, the IASB issued *Sale or Contribution of Assets between an Investor and its Associate or Joint Venture – Amendments to IFRS 10 and IAS 28*. However, the effective date was deferred indefinitely.
- In May 2017, the IASB issued IFRS 17 *Insurance Contracts*, which is effective for annual periods beginning on or after 1 January 2021. See 3.5.207. IFRS 17 is the subject of chapter 8.1A.
- In October 2017, the IASB issued *Long-term Interests in Associates and Joint Ventures – Amendments to IAS 28*, which is effective for annual periods beginning on or after 1 January 2019. See 3.5.425 and 505.

FUTURE DEVELOPMENTS

For this topic, there are no future developments.

| 3.5.10 | **ASSESSING WHETHER INVESTEE IS AN ASSOCIATE** |
| 3.5.20 | **Definitions of associate and significant influence** |

3.5.20.10   An 'associate' is an entity over which an investor has significant influence. [*IAS 28.3*]

3.5.20.20   'Significant influence' is the *power* to participate in an entity's financial and operating policy decisions, but it is not control or joint control of those policies. Significant influence may exist over an entity that is controlled by another party. More than one party may have significant influence over a single entity. [*IAS 28.3, 5*]

| 3.5.30 | **Assessing whether significant influence exists** |
| 3.5.40 | *Voting rights* |

3.5.40.10   Significant influence is presumed to exist when an investor holds 20 percent or more of the voting power of another entity. Conversely, it is presumed that significant influence does not exist with a holding of less than 20 percent. These presumptions may be overcome if an ability, or lack of ability, to exercise significant influence is clearly demonstrated. [*IAS 28.5*]

| 3.5.50 | *Ability to exercise vs actual exercise* |

3.5.50.10   In determining whether an entity has significant influence over another entity, the focus is on the *ability* to exercise significant influence. It does not matter whether significant influence is actually exercised. [*IAS 28.7–8*]

| 3.5.60 | *Potential voting rights* |

3.5.60.10   In assessing significant influence, an entity takes into account the effects of potential voting rights that are currently exercisable, both those held by the investor and those held by other parties. Potential voting rights include warrants, call options, debt or equity instruments that are convertible into ordinary shares, and other similar instruments that have the potential, if they are exercised or converted, to give the holder voting power. IFRS 10 requires consideration of whether potential voting rights are 'substantive' in the determination of control (see 2.5.100), but IAS 28 was not amended as a result of IFRS 10. As a result, the evaluation of whether significant influence exists is based on whether potential voting rights are currently exercisable and not whether they are substantive. Accordingly, the assessment of whether significant influence exists considers, for example, call options that are out of the money but currently exercisable. [*IAS 28.7–8*]

| 3.5.70 | *Indirect holdings* |

3.5.70.10   In assessing whether voting rights give rise to significant influence, it is necessary to consider both direct holdings of the investor and holdings of the investor's subsidiaries. In our view, holdings of the investor's joint ventures and other associates should not be included in this evaluation. [*IAS 28.5*]

| 3.5.80 | *Qualitative factors* |

3.5.80.10   IAS 28 states that significant influence is usually evidenced by one or more of the following:
- representation on the board of directors or equivalent governing body of the investee;
- participation in the investee's policy-making processes;
- material transactions between the investor and the investee;
- an interchange of managerial personnel; or
- provision of essential technical information. [*IAS 28.6*]

3.5.80.20   In our view, additional factors that may indicate significant influence include:
- a right of veto over significant decisions;
- influence over dividend or reinvestment policies;
- guarantees of indebtedness, extensions of credit, ownership of warrants, debt obligations or other securities; or
- the relative size and dispersion of the holdings of other shareholders; however, significant influence may exist over an entity that is controlled by another party (see 3.5.20.20).

3.5.80.30   In our view, 'one or more' in paragraph 6 of IAS 28 does not mean that a single factor in isolation necessarily indicates significant influence. For example, providing management services to an entity does not in itself result in the entity being an associate. Similarly, entering into material transactions with an entity does not necessarily give rise to significant influence over that entity. However, meaningful representation on the governing body of an entity generally indicates significant influence. Therefore, the analysis requires judgement considering all facts and circumstances.

3.5.80.35   Severe long-term restrictions that impair an investee's ability to transfer funds to the investor do not in themselves preclude significant influence over the investee. However, an entity considers these restrictions when assessing its ability to exercise significant influence. [*IAS 28.BCZ18*]

3.5.80.40   The IFRS Interpretations Committee discussed how a fund manager assesses significant influence over a fund that it manages and in which it has an investment when the IFRS 10 analysis led to the conclusion that the fund manager is an agent and therefore does not control the fund (see 2.5.350–390). The Committee noted that when IFRS 10 was issued, neither the definition of significant influence nor any requirements on how to assess significant influence in IAS 28, as described above, were modified. Therefore, unlike IFRS 10, IAS 28 does not address decision-making authority held in the capacity of an agent in the assessment of significant influence. [*IFRS 10.17–18, IU 03-17*]

3.5.80.45   However, in our view, if the financial and operating policies of an investee are largely predetermined, then most of the factors described in 3.5.80.10 for assessing significant influence are not relevant. Therefore, in this case, we believe that the entity should generally account for its interest in the investee as a financial asset in accordance with IFRS 9 (see chapters 7.4, 7.6 and 7.7).

3.5.85   *Nature and extent of investor's rights*

3.5.85.10   In many cases, investors have certain rights that need to be considered when determining significant influence. These rights can be derived from law, the entity's constitution or shareholders' agreement.

3.5.85.20   In our view, it is necessary to consider the nature and extent of the rights of investors in determining significant influence, including the distinction between rights that allow investors to participate in significant decisions that would be expected to be made in the ordinary course of business, and rights that protect the investors.

3.5.85.30   For example, investors' approval may be necessary for:
- amendments to an entity's constitution;
- the pricing of related party transactions;

- the liquidation of the entity or launching of bankruptcy proceedings; or
- share issues or repurchases.

3.5.85.40   In our view, these rights are granted to investors to protect their interests, and do not overcome the presumption that an investor holding less than 20 percent voting rights does not have significant influence.

3.5.85.50   However, in other cases investors may participate in:
- appointing and removing governing body members, including setting their remuneration; or
- making operating and capital decisions, including approving budgets, in the ordinary course of business.

3.5.85.60   In our view, such rights give investors the right to participate in financial and operating policy decisions (see 3.5.80.10). Therefore, these rights may overcome the presumption that an investor holding less than 20 percent voting rights does not have significant influence.

3.5.90   **EXEMPTIONS FROM EQUITY METHOD**

3.5.90.10   An entity (the investor) is required to account for investments in associates and joint ventures using the equity method except:
- when the entity is exempt from preparing consolidated financial statements, unless it chooses to do so on a voluntary basis (see 2.1.100.30, 35 and 60);
- when all of the following apply:
  - the entity is a wholly owned subsidiary, or is a partially owned subsidiary and its other owners (including those not otherwise entitled to vote) have been informed about, and do not object to, the entity not applying the equity method;
  - the entity's debt or equity instruments are not traded in a public market (see 5.2.10.12), including stock exchanges and over-the-counter markets;
  - the entity did not file, and is not in the process of filing, its financial statements with a regulatory organisation for the purpose of issuing any class of instruments in a public market; and
  - the ultimate or any intermediate parent of the entity produces financial statements that comply with IFRS – i.e. in those financial statements, subsidiaries are consolidated or are measured at fair value through profit or loss in accordance with IFRS 10 – and are available for public use;
- when the entity is a venture capital or similar organisation, including an investment entity (see 3.5.100);
- when the entity classifies the investment (or a portion thereof) as held-for-sale (see 3.5.160); or
- in any separate financial statements prepared by the investor (see 3.5.640). [*IAS 28.17–20, IFRS 10.B85L(b)*]

3.5.90.20   Difficulty in obtaining the financial information from an associate needed to apply the equity method is not grounds for not applying equity accounting. It is presumed that the investor, by virtue of its ability to exercise significant influence, is able to obtain the necessary information from associates.

3.5.100   **Venture capital or similar organisations, including investment entities**

3.5.100.10   IFRS contains an exemption from the requirement to apply equity accounting to investments in associates and joint ventures held by, or indirectly held through, an entity that is a venture capital organisation, mutual fund, unit trust or similar entity, including an investment-linked insurance fund. Such entities may elect to measure investments in those associates and joint ventures at fair value through profit or loss in accordance with IFRS 9 (see chapters 7.4 and 7.7). This election is available on an investment-by-investment basis. [*IAS 28.18*]

3.5.100.20   A venture capital or similar organisation that qualifies as an investment entity for the purpose of applying the exemption from consolidation (see chapter 5.6) measures its investments in associates and joint ventures at fair value through profit or loss in accordance with IFRS 9. This is one of the requirements for qualifying as an investment entity. [*IFRS 10.B85L(b)*]

3.5.110   *Qualifying as venture capital or similar organisation*

3.5.110.10   IAS 28 does not provide criteria for determining whether an investor qualifies as a venture capital or similar organisation. In our view, it is necessary to consider the nature and extent of an entity's investment activities as well as the entity's organisation and its relationship with its investees when determining whether it meets the definition of a venture capital or similar organisation. We believe that entities that apply the exception for venture capital or similar organisations should generally meet the following criteria:
- the investor's *primary business activity* is investing for current income, capital appreciation or both (see 3.5.120);
- the investor's investment activities are *clearly and objectively distinct* from any of its other activities (see 3.5.130); and
- the investees are separate *autonomous businesses* from the investor (see 3.5.140).

3.5.120   *Primary business activity*

3.5.120.10   In our view, evidence that the investor's primary business activity is investing for current income, capital appreciation or both includes, but is not limited to:
- the investor's expressed business purpose is to be a venture capital or similar organisation;
- the investor holds multiple investments or has an investment plan to acquire multiple investments;
- the investor has no activities other than investment activities and has no significant assets or liabilities other than those related to its investment activities; and
- the investor has an exit strategy for each investment.

3.5.130   *Clearly and objectively distinct*

3.5.130.10   In order for the investor's investment activities to be *clearly and objectively distinct* from any of its other activities, in our view the activities should be:
- in a separate legal entity; or
- part of a legal entity conducting investment activities that are clearly and objectively distinct from the entity's other activities.

3.5.130.15   In addition, the legal structure of an entity or a group should not determine whether an investor – or a clearly and objectively distinguished part of an entity – whose primary activity is investing in separate autonomous businesses meets the definition of a venture capital or similar organisation.

3.5.130.20   For the purpose of assessing whether an entity's investment activities are clearly and objectively distinct from its other activities, we believe that the investor should consider organisational and financial factors such as, but not limited to:

- whether the investment activity is carried out as an extension of the other activities, rather than being carried out with a significant degree of autonomy or separation from other activities;
- whether there is management that has been identified separately that has specific responsibility for the investment activities;
- whether the investment activity has its own control and reporting systems, including separate reporting to management and/or the board; and
- whether the investment activity is identified as a separate operating segment (see 5.2.50), although materiality considerations may mean that it is not reported separately.

3.5.130.30   Some of these factors may be demonstrated more readily when the investor's activities are performed in a separate legal entity.

3.5.140   *Autonomous businesses*

3.5.140.10   In our view, investees are not separate autonomous businesses from the investor if, for example:

- the investor obtains benefits, or has the objective of obtaining benefits, that extend beyond those generally afforded to the residual interest holders. Relationships or activities that would fall into this category include, for example:
  - the acquisition, use, exchange or exploitation of the processes, intangible assets or technology of investees by the investor;
  - significant purchases or sales of assets between the investee and the investor; or
  - other transactions that are on terms that are not considered to be at arm's length;
- the investor provides significant administrative or support services to investees;
- investees provide financing guarantees or collateral for borrowing arrangements of the investor;
- compensation of the investee's employees or management depends on the financial results of the investor; or
- the investor directs the integration of operations of investees or the establishment of business relationships between investees.

3.5.150   *Partial use of venture capital exemption*

3.5.150.10   If an investor has significant influence over an entity and a portion of the investor's interest in this entity is held by a subsidiary that qualifies as a venture capital or similar organisation (see 3.5.110), then the investor can, in its consolidated financial statements, apply the exemption in IAS 28 to the venture capital subsidiary's interest in the associate. If the investor makes that election, then it applies the equity method to the remaining portion of the associate. However, a similar exemption is not provided for a portion of an investment in a joint venture. [*IAS 28.19, BC21–BC22*]

EXAMPLE 1A – INDIRECT HOLDINGS – SIGNIFICANT INFLUENCE

3.5.150.20   Parent P has two wholly owned subsidiaries, S and V.
- V is a venture capital organisation.
- S owns 10% of Company C and V owns 20% of C.
- V assesses that it has significant influence over C and applies the venture capital exemption in its consolidated financial statements.

- P assesses that it has significant influence over C as a result of its indirect combined 30% shareholding in C.

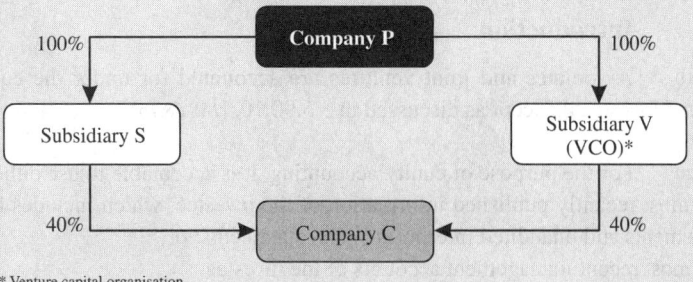

* Venture capital organisation

3.5.150.30   In its consolidated financial statements, P may account for the 10% of C held by S under the equity method and for the 20% held by V as a financial asset measured at fair value through profit or loss.

3.5.150.40   However, if the parent has control over an entity and a portion of the parent's interest in this entity is held by a subsidiary that qualifies as a venture capital or similar organisation, then IFRS 10 does not provide any exemption that would allow the NCI held via a subholding to be exempt from consolidation.

EXAMPLE 1B – INDIRECT HOLDINGS – CONTROL

3.5.150.50   Parent P has two wholly owned subsidiaries, S and V.
- V is a venture capital organisation.
- S and V each own 40% of Company C.
- S and V both conclude that they have significant influence over C.
- S applies equity accounting in its consolidated financial statements and V applies the venture capital exemption in its consolidated financial statements.
- P assesses that it has control over C as a result of its indirect combined 80% shareholding in C.

* Venture capital organisation

3.5.150.60   The exemption in V's consolidated financial statements to measure its investment in C at fair value through profit or loss is not available at the group level. Therefore, in its consolidated financial statements, P consolidates C with 20% NCI.

3.5.160   Associates and joint ventures classified as held-for-sale

3.5.160.10   An investment, or a portion of an investment, in an associate or joint venture that meets the criteria to be classified as held-for-sale (see 5.4.20 and 280) is measured at the lower of its existing carrying amount and fair value less costs to sell. Equity accounting ceases at the time of reclassification of the whole interest. [*IAS 28.20*]

3.5.160.15   In the case of a partial disposal, an entity applies the equity method to any portion of the investment that has not been classified as held-for-sale until disposal of the portion classified as held-for-sale. After disposal, any retained interest in the investment is accounted for in accordance with IFRS 9 (see chapters 7.4, 7.6 and 7.7) or by using the equity method if the retained interest continues to be an associate or joint venture. [*IAS 28.20*]

3.5.160.20   In our view, when an entity plans to obtain control over an existing associate or joint venture in a business combination achieved in stages (see 2.6.1140), classification of the previously held interest as held-for-sale or as a discontinued operation is not appropriate, because there is no actual sale of the investment. [*IFRS 3.BC384, 5.6–8, IASBU 05-09*]

3.5.160.30   For a discussion of intended distributions of investments in associates and joint ventures by the investor, see 7.3.690. [*IFRIC 17.11–13*]

3.5.160.40   If an investment, or a portion of an investment, in an associate or joint venture ceases to be classified as held-for-sale, then the investor reverts to applying the equity method. The comparative amounts disclosed for periods since the classification as held-for-sale are restated (see 5.4.100.10). [*IAS 28.21*]

3.5.170   APPLYING THE EQUITY METHOD

3.5.170.10   The discussion in 3.5.180–500 refers to equity-accounted investees, which encompasses associates and joint ventures (see 3.6.240).

3.5.180   Introduction

3.5.180.10   Associates and joint ventures are accounted for under the equity method (equity-accounted investees) except as discussed in 3.5.90.10. [*IAS 28.16*]

3.5.180.20   For the purpose of equity accounting, it is acceptable to use either:
- the most recently published information of the investee, which includes both audited financial statements and unaudited interim financial statements; or
- the most recent management accounts of the investee.

3.5.180.30   The equity method is described as a method of accounting whereby the investment is initially recognised at cost and adjusted thereafter for the post-acquisition change in the investor's share of net assets of the investee. [*IAS 28.3*]

3.5.180.40   The investment in the equity-accounted investee is further described as being initially recognised at cost and subsequently increased or decreased to recognise:
- the investor's share of the profit or loss of the investee;
- the investor's proportionate interest in the investee arising from changes in the investee's OCI; and
- the dividends received from the investee. [*IAS 28.10*]

3.5.180.50   These descriptions of the equity method in paragraphs 3 and 10 of IAS 28 are not entirely consistent. In particular, it is unclear how the investor should account for changes in the net assets of an equity-accounted investee that are recognised directly in the investee's equity. This is because paragraph 3 of IAS 28 seems to imply that the investor would adjust the investment by its share in these changes in equity whereas paragraph 10 of IAS 28 could be read as precluding the recognition of an increase or decrease in the investment for such changes. [*IAS 28.3, 10*]

3.5.180.60   In our view, the description in paragraph 3 of IAS 28 is more authoritative. We believe that the list of adjustments in paragraph 10 was not meant to be exhaustive and therefore that the definition in paragraph 3 takes precedence. For further discussion of this issue, see 3.5.370.

3.5.190   *Link between equity accounting and consolidation*

3.5.190.10   It is not clear whether equity accounting should be understood as a one-line consolidation or as a measurement approach.
- On the one hand, paragraph 26 of IAS 28 states that many of the procedures applicable to consolidation and the concepts underlying the accounting procedures for the acquisition of a subsidiary apply to equity accounting and the acquisition of an equity-accounted investee.
- On the other hand, the basis for conclusions to IFRS 9 notes that the linkage between acquisition accounting and equity accounting is only in respect of accounting 'methodology' and not in respect of 'principles'. [*IAS 28.26, IFRS 9.BCZ2.42*]

3.5.190.20   In our view, the following are examples of accounting methodology in IFRS 10 and IFRS 3 that should be extended to the application of equity accounting (see chapters 2.5 and 2.6, respectively):
- determining the date of acquisition and the fair value of identifiable net assets in the acquisition of an equity-accounted investee;
- retrospectively adjusting provisional amounts recognised at the date of acquisition during the measurement period; and
- accounting for initial and subsequent measurement of contingent consideration (see 3.5.250).

3.5.190.30   In contrast, we believe that the following are examples of accounting 'principles' in IFRS 10 and IFRS 3 that should *not* be extended to the application of equity accounting:
- accounting for an equity-settled share-based payment issued by an equity-accounted investee (see 3.5.400); and
- accounting for a change in ownership interest in an equity-accounted investee while maintaining significant influence or joint control (see 3.5.540–550).

3.5.190.40   In some situations, it is not clear whether the treatments in IFRS 10 or IFRS 3 should be extended to equity accounting. These include:

- accounting by the investor for purchases or sales of NCI by an equity-accounted investee (see 3.5.370);
- eliminating interest income or expense (see 3.5.460); and
- transactions between equity-accounted investees (see 3.5.490).

3.5.200   *Accounting periods and policies#*

3.5.200.10   Unless it is impracticable, an investee's financial statements used to apply the equity method are prepared for the same accounting period as that of the investor. If different periods are used, then the length of reporting periods and the gap between reporting dates are consistent from period to period. [*IAS 28.33–34*]

3.5.200.20   The difference between the reporting date and the date of the financial statements of an investee used when applying the equity method may not exceed three months. [*IAS 28.34*]

3.5.200.30   When different reporting periods are used to apply the equity method, adjustments are made for the effects of any significant events or transactions that happen between the two reporting dates. In our view, the same accounting applies when an equity-accounted investee changes its reporting date to align with that of the investor as when a subsidiary aligns its reporting date with that of the parent. For a discussion of the position in respect of subsidiaries, see 2.5.440. [*IAS 28.34*]

3.5.200.40   When applying the equity method, the financial information of all investees is prepared on the basis of IFRS. Uniform accounting policies are used in preparing the investor's financial statements, with exceptions in relation to investment entities (see 3.5.200.50) and insurance contracts (see 8.1.60). Accordingly, when an equity-accounted investee applies different policies in its own financial statements, adjustments are required to conform to the investor's accounting policies. [*IAS 28.35–36*]

3.5.200.50   A non-investment entity investor may have an interest in an equity-accounted investee that is an investment entity and has subsidiaries. When applying the equity method to its interest in such an equity-accounted investee, the non-investment entity investor can elect to retain the fair value accounting applied by its investment entity equity-accounted investees to their subsidiaries. This approach is different from the unwinding of the fair value accounting by an investment entity subsidiary because a non-investment entity parent is required to consolidate such a subsidiary (see 5.6.210 and 3.5.200.60). [*IAS 28.36A, BC46A–BC46G*]

3.5.200.60   A non-investment entity investor makes the election to retain the fair value accounting applied by its investment entity equity investees to their subsidiaries (see 3.5.200.50) separately for each investment. This election is made at the later of the date on which the investee:
- is initially recognised by the non-investment entity investor;
- becomes an investment entity; and
- first becomes a parent. [*IAS 28.36A*]

3.5.207   FORTHCOMING REQUIREMENTS

3.5.207.10   There is no exception for insurance contracts under IFRS 17 – i.e. uniform accounting policies are applied in preparing the investor's financial statements.

3.5.210   **Acquisition of equity-accounted investee**

3.5.220   *Applicability of common control exemption*

3.5.220.10   In our view, the common control exemption in respect of business combinations under IFRS 3 applies equally to acquisitions of investments in equity-accounted investees among entities under common control (see 5.13.20.30). For a discussion of the accounting for common control transactions, see chapter 5.13.

3.5.230   *Starting to apply equity method*

3.5.230.10   An investment in an equity-accounted investee is accounted for under the equity method from the date on which the investor obtains significant influence or joint control over the investee. [*IAS 28.32*]

3.5.240   *Determining initial carrying amount*

3.5.240.10   An issue arises about how the initial carrying amount of an investment accounted for under the equity method should be determined. The IFRS Interpretations Committee discussed this issue and noted that the cost of an investment in an equity-accounted investee determined in accordance with IAS 28 comprises the purchase price and other costs directly attributable to the acquisition of the investment, such as professional fees for legal services, transfer taxes and other transaction costs. [*IU 07-09*]

3.5.240.20   In our view, costs directly attributable to the acquisition of an investment in an equity-accounted investee normally do not include costs incurred after the acquisition is completed. Examples of post-acquisition costs that should be expensed are integration costs and costs to determine the fair value of the investor's share in the investee's net assets. An exception to expensing post-acquisition costs applies to the acquisition of additional interests. For a discussion of contingent consideration as part of the initial carrying amount of the investment, see 3.5.250.

3.5.240.30   In our view, costs that are directly attributable to a probable future acquisition of an investment accounted for under the equity method should be recognised as a prepayment (asset) in the statement of financial position. The costs should be included in the initial carrying amount at the date of acquisition, or recognised in profit or loss if the acquisition is no longer expected to be completed.

3.5.240.40   Investments in equity-accounted investees are not qualifying assets for the capitalisation of borrowing costs (see 4.6.20.20). Therefore, interest incurred on a loan obtained for the purpose of acquiring an investment in an equity-accounted investee cannot be capitalised. [*IAS 23.7, BC22*]

3.5.250   *Contingent consideration*

3.5.250.10   In our view, the IFRS 3 treatment in respect of contingent consideration arising on the acquisition of subsidiaries should be applied to contingent consideration arising from the acquisition of an equity-accounted investee (see 3.5.190.20). Accordingly, we believe that the contingent consideration should be initially recognised at fair value as part of the cost of acquisition (see 2.6.280.20) and subsequently accounted for as follows.
- *Contingent consideration classified as equity:* An entity should not remeasure it and should account for its settlement in equity.

- *Contingent consideration classified as an asset or a liability:* An entity should remeasure it to fair value at each reporting date until the contingency is settled, with changes in fair value recognised in profit or loss (see 2.6.1120.50). [*IFRS 3.58, IAS 28.26*]

EXAMPLE 2 – CONTINGENT CONSIDERATION

3.5.250.20　　On 1 January 2018, Investor D acquires Associate A and agrees to pay 100 up front, plus 5% of profits over 5,000 generated in the two years following the acquisition, in cash as a lump sum at the end of the two years – i.e. at 31 December 2019. The fair value of the obligation is estimated at 45 at the date of acquisition. D records the following entry.

	DEBIT	CREDIT
Investment in associate	145	
Cash		100
Financial liability (contingent consideration)		45
To recognise acquisition of associate		

3.5.250.25　　At the end of 2018, A has performed better than was initially projected by D, such that a significant payment is now expected to be made at the end of 2019. The fair value of this financial liability is 185 at 31 December 2018. D recognises the difference between the initial fair value at acquisition and the fair value at 31 December 2018 (the reporting date) as an additional liability with a charge to profit or loss as follows.

	DEBIT	CREDIT
Profit or loss (finance expense)	140	
Financial liability (contingent consideration)		140
To recognise change in fair value of contingent consideration		

3.5.250.27　　The adjustment to the liability to reflect the final settlement amount (final fair value) will be recognised in profit or loss in the same way if the amount differs from the fair value estimate at the end of 2018.

3.5.260　　*Forward contract to acquire equity-accounted investee*

3.5.260.10　　A forward contract to acquire an investment that will then become an equity-accounted investee is a derivative that is in the scope of IFRS 9. The scope exemption in paragraph 2.1(f) of IFRS 9 for business combinations (see 2.6.320) cannot be applied by analogy to the acquisition of an interest in an equity-accounted investee because the latter represents the acquisition of a financial instrument. Therefore, the derivative is measured at fair value through profit or loss, and the cost of investment includes the fair value of the derivative at the date of acquisition. [*IFRS 9.BCZ2.42*]

3.5.270   *Goodwill*

3.5.270.10   On the date of acquisition of an equity-accounted investee, fair values are attributed to the investee's identifiable assets and liabilities as explained in 2.6.560. Any positive difference between the cost of the investment and the investor's share of the fair values of the identifiable net assets acquired is goodwill. [*IAS 28.32*]

3.5.270.20   Goodwill is included in the carrying amount of the investment in the equity-accounted investee and is not shown separately. Goodwill is not amortised and therefore amortisation is not included in the determination of the investor's share of the investee's profit or loss. Goodwill attributable to the investment is not tested annually for impairment (see 3.10.580). [*IAS 28.32, 42*]

3.5.270.30   Any excess in the investor's share in the fair value of identifiable net assets over cost is included in the investor's share of the investee's profit or loss in the period in which the investment is acquired. [*IAS 28.32*]

3.5.270.40   The investor's share of depreciation charges to be included with the share of the investee's profit or loss in the investor's financial statements reflects any fair value adjustments for depreciable assets at the date of acquisition. The fair value adjustments are made only for the proportion of net assets acquired. [*IAS 28.32*]

3.5.280   *Obligation or potential obligation to buy equity instruments*

3.5.280.10   An entity may write a put option or enter into a forward purchase agreement with the non-controlling shareholders in an existing *subsidiary* on their shares in that subsidiary. If the put option or forward purchase agreement granted to the non-controlling shareholders provides for settlement in cash or in another financial asset by the entity, then the entity recognises a liability for the present value of the exercise price of the option or of the forward price, and in our view accounts for such agreement under the anticipated-acquisition method or the present-access method (see 2.5.680). [*IAS 32.23*]

3.5.280.20   It could be questioned whether, by analogy, the exercise of a put option to buy an equity-accounted investee's equity instruments – in other words, the purchase of the underlying interests – should be anticipated. However, in our view an obligation or potential obligation to buy an equity-accounted investee's equity instruments should not generally be anticipated. We believe that the recognition of a liability in relation to subsidiaries arises because of the specific requirement in paragraph 23 of IAS 32 to recognise a financial liability for an obligation or potential obligation to buy group equity instruments, whereas equity-accounted investees are not part of the group. Therefore, the obligation or potential obligation to buy the equity instruments in an equity-accounted investee does not give rise to a financial liability for the present value of the redemption amount. We believe that such an obligation or potential obligation is therefore in the scope of IFRS 9 and should be measured as a derivative at fair value with changes recognised in profit or loss (see 7.3.240).

3.5.290   Determining investor's share in equity-accounted investee

3.5.300   *Percentage attributable to investor*

3.5.300.10   In some cases, the economic interests of investors will not equal their shareholding (voting interest). For example, an entity may control 30 percent of the voting power of an equity-accounted investee but have only a 20 percent interest in the profits and net assets of the investee. In our view, in these cases the investor should account for the 20 percent interest, because equity accounting is described with reference to the investor's share in net assets and profit or loss (see 3.5.180.30). [*IAS 28.3, 10*]

3.5.310   ***Interest in investee held via subsidiary***

3.5.310.10   An interest in an equity-accounted investee may be held via a subsidiary. If the subsidiary is not wholly owned by the investor, then a share of the income or expense recognised under the equity method is allocated to NCI. [*IFRS 10.B94*]

EXAMPLE 3A – INDIRECT HOLDINGS – VIA SUBSIDIARY

3.5.310.20   Company P owns 70% of Subsidiary S, which in turn has an investment of 40% in Associate A. S applies equity accounting to its 40% investment in A. Subsequently, P consolidates S.

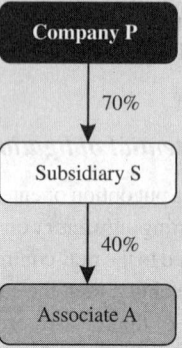

3.5.310.30   Assume that A's profit for the year is 100. Therefore, in the consolidated financial statements of P, the equity-accounted profit of A is 40.

3.5.310.40   Of this amount, 70% is allocated to the equity holders of P (i.e. effectively 28% of A's profit) and 30% to the NCI (i.e. effectively 12% of A's profit).

3.5.320   ***Other indirect holdings***

3.5.320.10   Shareholdings of the parent and all of its subsidiaries are taken into account in applying the equity method. However, shareholdings of other equity-accounted investees are not considered. [*IAS 28.27*]

EXAMPLE 3B – INDIRECT HOLDINGS – VIA EQUITY-ACCOUNTED INVESTEE

3.5.320.20   In addition to several subsidiaries, Company H has a 50% shareholding in a joint venture, J, and a 25% holding in Associate A. J also holds 10% of the share capital of A.

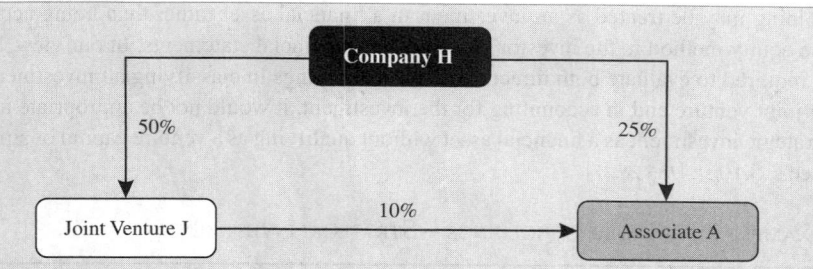

3.5.320.30 A reports a profit of 200 and pays a dividend of 100. In its consolidated financial statements, H will apply the equity method for its 25% interest in A and will not apply the equity method to the additional interest, effectively 5%, held through J.

3.5.320.35 Therefore, H will recognise its share of A's profit of 50 (200 x 25%). H will also reduce the carrying amount of its investment in A by the dividends received of 25 (100 x 25%). J has classified its investment in A as a financial asset measured at fair value through OCI under IFRS 9 and therefore recognises dividends received of 10 in profit or loss (see 7.7.510). Accordingly, in accounting for its interest in J, H will include J's share of the dividend received from A of 5 (100 x 50% x 10%).

3.5.320.40 This is different from the treatment that would result if H had taken into account J's 10% holding and therefore treated A as a 30% associate (25% + (50% x 10%)). Under that method, the share of profits would have been 60 (200 x 30%) and the amount applied against the carrying amount of A for the dividends received, assuming that J passed the dividend onto H, would have been 30 (100 x 30%). This approach is not appropriate because H does not control J, and shareholdings of other equity-accounted investees are not considered in applying the equity method.

In H's consolidated financial statements	IAS 28 METHOD[1]	IF ALL EQUITY ACCOUNTED
Share of profit of A	50	60
Dividends received from A	(25)	(30)
Increase in carrying amount of investment in A	25	30
Share of dividend received by J from A recognised in profit or loss	5	-

Note
1. Ignoring any fair value gain or loss recognised by J on its investment in A.

3.5.320.50 An issue may arise when an entity acquires an indirect interest in shares in an associate or joint venture for strategic and potentially for trading purposes. The issue is whether such a holding may be treated as an investment in a financial asset rather than being accounted for under the equity method in the investor's consolidated financial statements. In our view, because an entity is required to evaluate both direct and indirect holdings in classifying an investment as an associate or joint venture and in accounting for the investment, it would not be appropriate to account for any strategic investment as a financial asset without qualifying as a venture capital or similar organisation (see 3.5.100). [*IAS 28.27*]

EXAMPLE 3C – INDIRECT HOLDINGS – STRATEGIC INVESTMENT

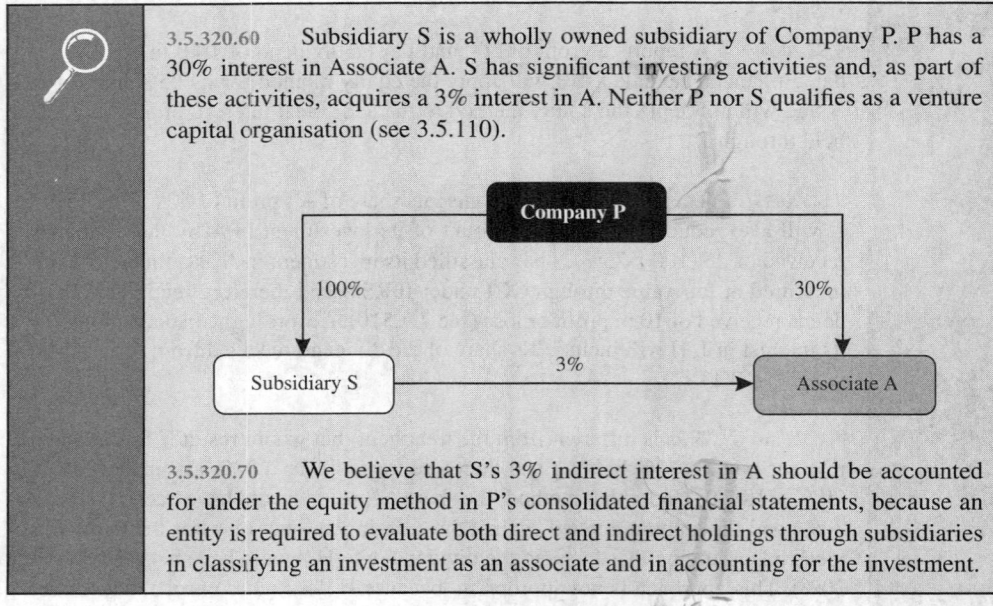

3.5.320.60   Subsidiary S is a wholly owned subsidiary of Company P. P has a 30% interest in Associate A. S has significant investing activities and, as part of these activities, acquires a 3% interest in A. Neither P nor S qualifies as a venture capital organisation (see 3.5.110).

Company P

100%

30%

Subsidiary S

3%

Associate A

3.5.320.70   We believe that S's 3% indirect interest in A should be accounted for under the equity method in P's consolidated financial statements, because an entity is required to evaluate both direct and indirect holdings through subsidiaries in classifying an investment as an associate and in accounting for the investment.

3.5.330   **Potential voting rights**

3.5.330.10   Although an investor may have taken into account potential voting rights when assessing whether it has significant influence (see 3.5.60), the share of comprehensive income recognised under the equity method is based on current ownership interests, unless the potential voting rights in substance give the investor access to the returns associated with an ownership interest. [*IAS 28.12–13*]

EXAMPLE 4 – POTENTIAL VOTING RIGHTS

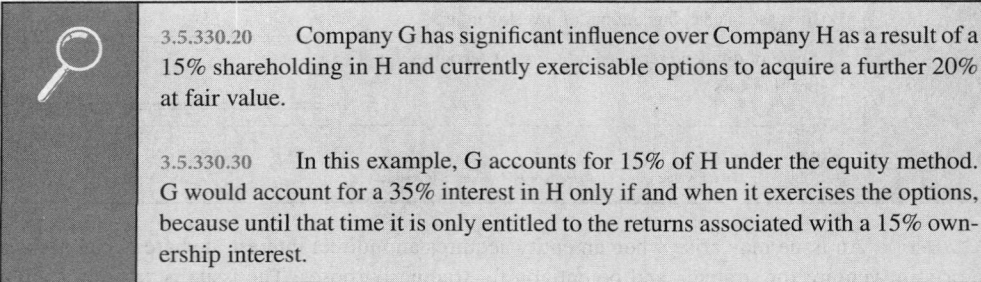

3.5.330.20   Company G has significant influence over Company H as a result of a 15% shareholding in H and currently exercisable options to acquire a further 20% at fair value.

3.5.330.30   In this example, G accounts for 15% of H under the equity method. G would account for a 35% interest in H only if and when it exercises the options, because until that time it is only entitled to the returns associated with a 15% ownership interest.

3.5.340   **Treasury shares held by investee**

3.5.340.10   An equity-accounted investee may have an investment in its investor. This means that the carrying amount of the investee under the equity method includes the investor's share of the investee's investment in the investor's own shares. In our view, the investor should not make any adjustment in respect of treasury shares held by an equity-accounted investee. For further discussion of this issue, see 7.3.550.

3.5.350   **Crossholdings**

3.5.350.10   Two entities may have an ownership interest in each other that results in mutual significant influence or joint control. For example, an entity could be an investor in an associate and that investee could be an investor in the entity and have significant influence over it. However, the accounting for such a crossholding when applying the equity method is unclear because of the reciprocal relationship. In the absence of specific guidance, in our view, an acceptable approach is to interpret the term 'the investor's share' in IAS 28 as the investor's *effective* share.

3.5.350.15   Under this effective ownership interest approach, an investor determines its share of comprehensive income of an investee on the basis of the investor's effective interest in the investee. The effect of the reciprocal interests is incorporated into the investee's financial statements through the investee's own equity accounting – i.e. the investee's comprehensive income would already include the equity pick-up for its own equity interest in the investor.

EXAMPLE 5 – CROSSHOLDINGS

3.5.350.20   Company C owns 30% of Company B, and B owns 25% of C. Each company has significant influence over the other and therefore applies the equity method.

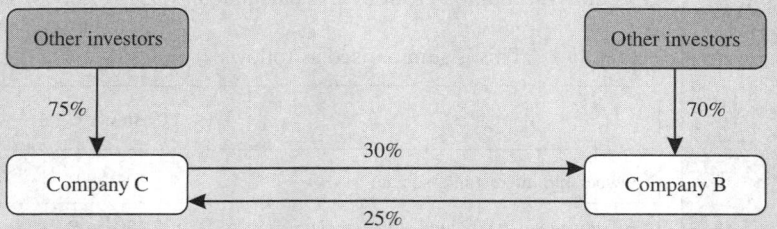

3.5.350.30   C has effectively acquired 7.5% of its own shares (30% x 25%), and B has acquired 7.5% of its own shares (25% x 30%). Accordingly, an investor in either C or B would effectively have increased its share in each of these entities by a factor of 1.081 (1 / (100% - 7.5%)). From an investor's perspective, an investee's holding of its own shares through a crossholding structure has the same effect on the investor's effective share of the interest of the investee as other share buy-backs. However, an investor does not make any adjustment in respect of treasury shares held by an equity-accounted investee (see 3.5.340 and 7.3.550.20).

3.5.350.40   Under the equity method, the investment is initially recognised at cost and is adjusted thereafter for the post-acquisition change in the investor's share of the net assets of the investee. The comprehensive income of C includes C's share of post-acquisition comprehensive income of B, and the comprehensive income of B includes B's share of post-acquisition comprehensive income of C.

3.5.350.50   Under the effective ownership interest approach, C determines its share of comprehensive income of B on the basis of its effective interest in B. The effect of the reciprocal interests is incorporated into B's financial statements through its own equity accounting – i.e. B's comprehensive income would already include the equity pick-up for its own equity interest in C.

3.5.350.60   Assume that C and B both have a profit of 1,000 before taking into account their reciprocal investments. C's effective share of B's profit is 32.43% (30% / (1 - 25% x 30%)). Therefore, C's effective interest takes into consideration the fact that B holds 7.5% of its own equity. Therefore, the shares that are outstanding represent 92.5% of all shares (100% of shares minus 7.5% of shares held by B via its investment in C).

3.5.350.65   As a result, C's interest in B is in effect higher than 30%; it equals 30% of 92.5% of shares 'outstanding'. Therefore, the effective interest is calculated by dividing 30% by 92.5%. The resulting effective ownership interest of 32.43% is used to recognise C's share of profit of B. The profit or loss of B already includes B's share of profit or loss of C of 250 (1,000 x 25%). Therefore, C's equity-accounted profit of B is 405 ((1,000 + 250) x 32.43%).

3.5.350.70   Similarly, B's effective share of C's profit is 27.03% (25% / (1 - 25% x 30%) or 25% divided by 92.5%). B's effective ownership interest is applied to the profit of C, which includes the share of C in B of 300 (1,000 x 30%). Therefore, B's equity-accounted profit of C is calculated as 351 ((1,000 + 300) x 27.03%).

3.5.350.80   This is summarised as follows.

	COMPANY C	**COMPANY B**
Ownership interest in associate	30% in B	25% in C
Effective ownership interest in associate	32.43% in B *(30% / 92.5%)*	27.03% in C *(25% / 92.5%)*
Profit or loss for the period *before* equity pick-up	1,000	1,000
Calculation of profit or loss of C and B including the equity pick-up for their respective interests in each other based on ownership interest (without taking into consideration the crossholding)	300 *(1,000 x 30%)*	250 *(1,000 x 25%)*

	COMPANY C	COMPANY B
Profit or loss for the period *after* equity pick-up (without taking into consideration the crossholding)	1,300	1,250
Equity pick-up based on the effective ownership interest (taking into consideration the crossholding)	405 *(1,250 x 32.43%)*	351 *(1,300 x 27.03%)*
Total including equity pick-up based on effective interest	1,405	1,351

3.5.350.90   As a result, C's total profit would be 1,405, of which 1,054 (1,405 x 75% or 1,405 - 351) is attributable to shareholders other than B. B's total profit would be 1,351, of which 946 (1,351 x 70% or 1,351 - 405) is attributable to shareholders other than C. The total allocation to 'external' shareholders is 2,000 (1,054 + 946), which equals the total profit of C and B (1,000 + 1,000).

3.5.350.100   A proof of this allocation to C's external shareholders (75% = 100% - 25%) can be determined on the basis of their effective share of B's profit.

(75% / (1 - (25% x 30%))) x (1,000 + 300) = 1,054

3.5.350.110   For a shorter, simpler calculation of the figures in 3.5.350.60–100, the total profit of C and total profit of B can be determined by solving the following simultaneous equations, whereby C is profit of C and B is profit of B.

If   B = 1,000 + (25% x C) and C = 1,000 + (30% x B)

Then   B = 1,000 + 25% x (1,000 + (30% x B))
            B = 1,351

Therefore   C = 1,000 + (30% x 1,351)
            C = 1, 405

These figures are then multiplied by the nominal share that B and C own in each other (i.e. 25% and 30%, respectively) to determine the profit that should be considered in applying the equity method in respect of both investments. Consequently, C recognises income of 405 (1,351 x 30%) in respect of its investment in B, and B recognises income of 351 (1,405 x 25%) in respect of its investment in C.

3.5.350.120   It might be claimed that there is an element of double counting under the effective ownership interest approach. However, in our view this effect is similar to not adjusting for treasury shares held by equity-accounted investees (see 3.5.340). It reflects the total profit flows into the entity from a non-group entity – e.g. as if the entities made full distribution – and has the result that the investor determines its share of the investee in the same way as other investors in the investee would determine their share of their investment in the investee; therefore, for example, B's financial statements reflect B's shareholders' economic interest.

3.5.360   **Equity-accounted investee is a group**

3.5.370   *Interest in entity held via investee*

3.5.370.10   An investor's equity-accounted investee may have non-wholly owned subsidiaries. In the investor's consolidated financial statements, the NCI in the equity-accounted investee's subsidiary are not reflected. This is because the investor takes into account only its share in the comprehensive income and net assets of the equity-accounted investee's subsidiaries, associates and joint ventures. The investor's interest or entitlement is determined after the investee non-controlling shareholders have been attributed their interest in the investee. [*IAS 28.27*]

3.5.370.20   The equity-accounted investee may buy or sell NCI in its subsidiaries and account for these transactions as equity transactions in its consolidated financial statements. In our view, the investor should account for these transactions because they change the net assets of the equity-accounted investee, and changes in the investee's net assets are required to be reflected in the investor's accounting. However, it is unclear how these transactions should be reflected in the investor's consolidated financial statements.

3.5.370.30   In our view, there are two possible approaches to accounting for these transactions.
- *Approach 1:* The transaction is accounted for as a third party transaction, with decreases in interests recognised in profit or loss (see 3.5.370.40–45), and increases in interests recognised using the 'partial step-up' approach (see 3.5.540).
- *Approach 2:* The transaction is accounted for as a post-acquisition change in the net assets of the investee, with the adjustment recognised directly in equity (see 3.5.370.48).

3.5.370.35   An investor should choose an accounting policy, to be applied consistently to all transactions with NCI at the equity-accounted investee level.

3.5.370.40   Under Approach 1, such transactions are not considered as equity transactions from the investor's perspective because the NCI of the equity-accounted investee do not meet the definition of NCI at the investor's level. Therefore, this is a transaction with third parties from the perspective of the investor and is accounted for accordingly.

3.5.370.45   If an equity-accounted investee sells equity interests in its subsidiaries to its non-controlling shareholders in an equity transaction, then it transfers its group equity instruments (equity interests in a member of the investee's own group) to third parties (the investee's non-controlling shareholders); this represents a dilution of the investor's indirect interest in the subsidiary of the investee and gives rise to the recognition of a gain or loss in the investor's consolidated financial statements. Similarly, if an equity-accounted investee buys equity interests from its non-controlling shareholders, then the investor recognises an increase in its interest in the investee and follows the guidance in 3.5.540.

3.5.370.48   Under Approach 2, such a transaction is reflected directly in equity at the investor level, based on the fact that it reflects the post-acquisition change in the net assets of the investee (see 3.5.180.30). Maintaining the entry in equity at the investor's level is consistent with the guidance in IAS 28, which states that many of the procedures appropriate for the application of the equity method are similar to consolidation procedures described in IFRS 10. In this case, the investor would replicate the equity-accounted investee's accounting by reflecting the investor's share of the investee's adjustment to its equity. [*IAS 28.3, 26*]

EXAMPLE 6 – DECREASE IN ASSOCIATE'S HOLDING IN SUBSIDIARY

3.5.370.50   Company P owns 40% of Associate A, which has several subsidiaries. On 1 January 2018, A sells 30% of Subsidiary S, one of its wholly owned subsidiaries, for 80 but retains control over S.

3.5.370.60   The carrying amount of S in A's consolidated financial statements is 200. As a result, A records the following entry.

In A's financial statements	DEBIT	CREDIT
Cash	80	
NCI (200 x 30%)		60
Shareholders' equity (parent)		20
To recognise increase in NCI		

3.5.370.70   Under Approach 1 (see 3.5.370.40), at P's level the increase in equity becomes a dilution gain and P records a gain of 8 (20 x 40%) in profit or loss. This amount would be adjusted at P's level if necessary due, for example, to any acquisition fair value adjustments allocated to S at P's level.

In P's financial statements (Approach 1)	DEBIT	CREDIT
Investment in associate (20 x 40%)	8	
Dilution gain (profit or loss)		8
To recognise dilution of P's interest in S		

3.5.370.80   Applying Approach 2 (see 3.5.370.48) would result in 8 (20 x 40%) being recorded directly in equity at P's level. Again, this amount would be adjusted at P's level if necessary due, for example, to any acquisition fair value adjustments allocated to S at P's level.

In P's financial statements (Approach 2)	DEBIT	CREDIT
Investment in associate (20 x 40%)	8	
Shareholders' equity (parent)		8
To recognise P's share in associate's increase in equity		

3.5.380   **Equity-accounted investee issues instruments to parties other than investor**

3.5.390   *Preference shares*

3.5.390.10   If an equity-accounted investee has issued cumulative preference shares that are classified as equity, then before applying the equity method the investor adjusts the profit or loss of the investee by the amount of any dividends payable on the preference shares, whether or not these dividends have been declared. [*IAS 28.37*]

3.5.400   *Equity-settled share-based payments*

3.5.400.10   When an equity-settled share-based payment is issued by an equity-accounted investee to its own employees, in our view the investor should record its share of the investee's share-based remuneration expense as part of its share of the investee's profit or loss. However, in our view the investor does not account for a share in the credit to shareholders' equity recognised by the investee. Instead, the offsetting credit entry should reduce the investment in the investee, because we believe that the equity instruments of the investee that have been granted to third parties represent a dilution of the investor's interest in the equity-accounted investee.

EXAMPLE 7A – SHARE OPTIONS ISSUED TO ASSOCIATE EMPLOYEES – ENTRIES DURING VESTING

3.5.400.20   Company C has 2,000 shares outstanding and issues 1,000 share options to its employees, which can be converted into 1,000 shares in C. The grant-date fair value of each option issued is 1; the total grant-date fair value of the options issued is 1,000 (1,000 x 1). The options will vest over five years and all 1,000 options are expected to vest.

3.5.400.25   C recognises share-based remuneration expense of 200 (1,000 / 5) in profit or loss and an offsetting credit to equity in the current year. Company B holds 600 shares of C, which represents a 30% interest (600 / 2,000), and has significant influence over C. B recognises its share of the remuneration expense (i.e. 60) in profit or loss as part of income from equity-accounted investees but records the offsetting credit as a reduction of its investment in C.

3.5.400.30   C and B record the following entries each year over the five-year vesting period.

In C's financial statements	DEBIT	CREDIT
Share-based payment remuneration (profit or loss)	200	
Shareholders' equity (parent)		200
To recognise share-based payment at associate level		
In B's financial statements		
Income from equity-accounted investees (profit or loss)	60	
Investment in associate		60
To recognise share-based payment at investor level		

3.5.400.40   On exercise, it will be necessary to true up the charge because at that point the nature of the third party interest changes. The true-up will bring the cumulative credit against the investment to an amount equal to the share of the equity-accounted investee's net assets lost as a result of the dilution of the investor's original interest, less the investor's share of the exercise proceeds.

3.5.400.45   In our view, this true-up should not be anticipated because doing so would amount to reclassifying the arrangement as a cash-settled share-based payment or not classifying the arrangement as a share-based payment at all, neither of which would be appropriate.

EXAMPLE 7B – SHARE OPTIONS ISSUED TO ASSOCIATE EMPLOYEES – ENTRIES ON EXERCISE

3.5.400.50   Continuing Example 7A, assume that at the end of the vesting period all options vest and are exercised. Each option has an exercise price of 3. Company C records the following entry.

In C's financial statements	DEBIT	CREDIT
Cash	3,000	
Shareholders' equity (parent)		3,000
To recognise exercise of options at associate level *(1,000 x 3)*		

3.5.400.60   The issue of new share options results in a dilution of Company B's interest in C by 10% (30% - (600 / (2,000 + 1,000))); B maintains significant influence over C (see 3.5.550.60). Immediately before the shares are issued, C has net assets totalling 11,000. B records the following entry.

In B's financial statements	DEBIT	CREDIT
Loss on dilution (profit or loss)	200	
Investment in associate		200
To recognise dilution of investment in associate at investor level		
Calculation of loss on dilution		
B's share of net assets before exercise (11,000 x 30%)		3,300
B's share of net assets after exercise ((11,000 + 3,000) x 20%)		(2,800)
Cumulative adjustment required		500[1]
Less: adjustment previously recognised for share-based payment expense (60 x 5 years)		(300)
Loss on dilution		200
Note		
1. Net assets lost (11,000 x 10%)		(1,100)
Share of proceeds on exercise of options (3,000 x 20%)		600
Cumulative adjustment required		500

3.5.410 *Warrants*

3.5.410.10   In our view, when an equity-accounted investee issues a warrant (option) to a third party for cash, no entry should be recognised by the investor because both the debit entry to recognise the investor's share of the proceeds and the offsetting credit entry are made to the investor's interest in the investee (see 3.5.400.10). If the warrant is unexercised, then we believe that an investor should choose an accounting policy, to be applied consistently, of either recognising an entry in profit or loss or recognising it in equity. Example 8 illustrates both approaches.

3.5.410.15   Under the first approach, the investor recognises a gain in profit or loss when the warrant expires, on the basis that there has been an increase in the investor's net assets in the investee. This approach views the event as an increase in the net assets in the investee, as though the investee bought back the warrant for no consideration. This also results in similar accounting to that applied if an additional interest in the investee were received for no consideration, with the resulting excess being recognised in profit or loss.

3.5.410.17   Under the second approach, the investor recognises an adjustment in equity when the warrant expires. This is on the basis that the investor's share of the expired warrant should also be recognised because it represents additional net assets of the investee that are to the benefit of its shareholders that have been realised with no additional ownership interests being issued. Under this approach, recognising a gain in profit or loss would not be appropriate because no equivalent gain is recognised by the investee.

EXAMPLE 8 – WARRANTS ISSUED BY ASSOCIATE

3.5.410.20   Investor Q holds 40% of Associate A. A issues a warrant to a third party for a cash premium of 100, exercisable in two years. After two years, the third party does not exercise the warrant and it expires. A's net assets are 1,000 – unchanged during the period except for the cash received on issuing the warrant. On issue, A records the receipt of cash and the warrant issued. Q does not record an entry.

In A's financial statements	DEBIT	CREDIT
Cash	100	
Equity		100
To record receipt of cash on issue of warrant		

3.5.410.30   Under the first approach (see 3.5.410.15), the investor recognises a gain in profit or loss when the warrant expires. Accordingly, Q records the following entry.

In Q's financial statements	DEBIT	CREDIT
Investment in associate (100 x 40%)	40	
Gain on lapse of warrants (profit or loss)		40
To record expiration of warrant		

3.5.410.40   Under the second approach (see 3.5.410.17), the investor recognises an adjustment in equity when the warrant expires. Accordingly, Q records the following entry.

In Q's financial statements	DEBIT	CREDIT
Investment in associate (100 x 40%)	40	
Equity		40
To record expiration of warrant		

3.5.420   ### Equity-accounted investees that are loss-making#

3.5.420.10   The investor's share of losses of an equity-accounted investee is recognised only until the carrying amount of the investor's equity interest in the investee is reduced to zero. For a discussion of dividends received by the investor from a loss-making investee, see 3.5.440.10. [*IAS 28.38*]

3.5.420.20   After the investor's interest is reduced to zero, a liability is recognised only to the extent that the investor has an obligation to fund the investee's operations or has made payments on behalf of the investee. [*IAS 28.39*]

3.5.420.30   The equity interest in an equity-accounted investee includes, for this purpose, the carrying amount of the investment under the equity method and other long-term interests that in substance form part of the entity's net investment in the associate or joint venture – e.g. a loan for which settlement is neither planned nor likely to happen in the foreseeable future. Other long-term interests do not include trade receivables, trade payables or any long-term receivables for which adequate collateral exists – e.g. secured loans. [*IAS 28.38*]

3.5.420.35   When losses recognised under the equity method exceed the investor's investment in ordinary shares, the excess is applied to other components of the investor's interest in an equity-accounted investee in the reverse order of their seniority. [*IAS 28.38*]

3.5.420.40   In our view, the share of losses of an equity-accounted investee corresponds to the investor's share of total comprehensive income – i.e. it includes both the profit or loss component and the OCI component. When total comprehensive income is a loss and comprises a loss component and a profit component, in our view the profit component should be fully recognised and the loss component recognised only until the carrying amount of the investor's equity interest is reduced to zero. This is because the loss component is the one that is the subject of the limitation. [*IAS 28.38*]

EXAMPLE 9A – LOSS-MAKING ASSOCIATE

3.5.420.50   Company P owns 40% of the shares in Associate A. A has negative equity of 200 in applying the equity method in P's consolidated financial statements – i.e. the equity of A after making the adjustments necessary in applying the equity method, such as fair value adjustments on initial recognition. Therefore, P's share of the equity of A is -80 (-200 x 40%).

3.5.420.55   However, P is not committed to financing the losses of A and has not provided any guarantees of A's obligations. Therefore, once P reduces its interest in A to zero, it does not absorb any further losses of A.

3.5.420.57   If A earns a profit in subsequent periods, then P recognises profits only after all unrecognised losses have been eliminated.

EXAMPLE 9B – LOSS-MAKING ASSOCIATE – PROFIT BUT OCI NEGATIVE

3.5.420.60   Modifying Example 9A, assume that the carrying amount of P's interest in A was 5 at the beginning of the period. During the year, A has a profit of 50, but total comprehensive income of -25 resulting from a net change of -75 in its cash flow hedging reserve. Therefore, P's share of the equity of A at the end of the period is -5 (5 + (-25 x 40%)).

3.5.420.65   Assuming that P is not committed to financing the losses of A and has not provided any guarantees of A's obligations, P once again reduces its interest in A to zero but does not absorb any further losses of A.

3.5.420.67   In its statement of profit or loss and OCI, we believe that P should recognise its share of the profit of A of 20 (50 x 40%) and limit its share of A's OCI to -25 (-75 x 40%, capped at the carrying amount of 5 + 20).

3.5.425   **FORTHCOMING REQUIREMENTS**

3.5.425.10   *Long-term Interests in Associates and Joint Ventures – Amendments to IAS 28* clarify that for those long-term interests that are not accounted for under the equity method, an entity applies IFRS 9. It applies IFRS 9 to these instruments before applying the loss absorption requirements in 3.5.420. [*IAS 28.14A*]

3.5.430   Transactions with equity-accounted investees

3.5.430.10   Unrealised profits on transactions with equity-accounted investees are eliminated to the extent of the investor's interest in the investee, regardless of whether that unrealised profit is in the investor, a subsidiary in the same group as the investor, or the investee – i.e. in both 'upstream' and 'downstream' transactions. [*IAS 28.26, 28*]

3.5.430.20   If a downstream transaction results in a loss, then no portion of the loss is eliminated to the extent that it provides evidence of a reduction in the net realisable value or of impairment of the asset to be sold or contributed. If an upstream transaction provides evidence of a reduction in the net realisable value of the assets to be purchased, then the investor recognises its share in those losses. [*IAS 28.29*]

3.5.430.30   In an upstream sale of assets – i.e. the equity-accounted investee sells to the investor – IFRS does not specify whether the elimination should be presented as a reduction in the investment in the investee or as a reduction in the underlying asset (e.g. inventory). In our view, either approach is acceptable.

EXAMPLE 10A – DOWNSTREAM SALE OF INVENTORY

3.5.430.40   This example illustrates the elimination in a downstream sale of inventory by the investor during 2018 to a 20% associate. The inventory has not been sold by the associate at the 2018 annual reporting date.

	INVESTOR	ASSOCIATE
Cost of inventory	50	150
Selling price of inventory	150	Not yet sold
Profit related to the transaction	100	

3.5.430.50   The investor records the following entry in 2018 to eliminate its 20% interest in the profit from this transaction.

	DEBIT	CREDIT
Revenue (150 x 20%)	30	
Cost of sales (50 x 20%)		10
Investment in associate (100 x 20%)		20
To eliminate unrealised profit on downstream transaction		

3.5.430.60   The credit is recognised against the carrying amount of the investment in the associate and not against inventory because the inventory is an asset of the associate, and is included in the 'investment in associate' line item in the statement of financial position.

3.5.430.70   If the associate sells the inventory during 2019, then the investor records the following entry to recognise the profit from the transaction in its consolidated financial statements in 2019.

	DEBIT	CREDIT
Cost of sales (50 x 20%)	10	
Investment in associate (100 x 20%)	20	
Revenue (150 x 20%)		30
To recognise realised profit on downstream transaction		

3.5.430.80   In this example, a portion of the whole transaction is eliminated against both revenue and cost of sales. Alternative approaches are possible – e.g. eliminating only the unrealised profit (i.e. the net 20) against revenue, with the 20 flowing through later as part of the share of associate income in the year of sale by the associate.

EXAMPLE 10B – UPSTREAM SALE OF INVENTORY

3.5.430.90   Modifying Example 10A, the 20% associate makes an upstream sale of inventory to the investor.

	INVESTOR	ASSOCIATE
Cost of inventory	150	50
Selling price of inventory	Not yet sold	150
Profit related to the transaction (100 x 20%)	20	100

3.5.430.100   The investor's share of earnings from the associate will include 20 that represents the investor's share of the associate's profit on the transaction with the investor. This share of profit is eliminated. The investor records the following entry.

	DEBIT	CREDIT
Share of profit or loss of associate	20	
Investment in associate *or* inventory (see 3.5.430.30)		20
To eliminate unrealised profit on upstream transaction		

3.5.430.110　This entry will be reversed when the inventory is sold by the investor to a third party.

3.5.440　*Downstream transactions in excess of investee's carrying amount*

3.5.440.10　An investor may enter into a downstream transaction with an equity-accounted investee for which its share of the gain arising from the transaction exceeds its interest in the investee. In our view, there are two possible approaches for such an excess and an entity should choose an accounting policy, to be applied consistently to all downstream transactions with equity-accounted investees. The same issue arises when dividends are paid by the investee in excess of the carrying amount of the investment and the chosen accounting policy for downstream transactions should also be applied for such dividend distributions.

3.5.440.20　In our view, the accounting policy should also be consistent with any policy chosen for the sale of a subsidiary to an existing or newly created equity-accounted investee when the investor applies the 'IAS 28 approach' (see 3.5.470).

3.5.440.30　Under the first approach, once the investor's interest in the equity-accounted investee has been reduced to zero (see 3.5.420), any remaining portion of the investor's share of the gain should not be eliminated because the resulting credit in the statement of financial position does not meet the definition of a liability. Therefore, it is possible that the investor's share of the gain will not be fully eliminated in the investor's financial statements. If the investee earns a profit in subsequent periods, then the investor should recognise its share of the profit only after adjusting for the excess gain that was not previously eliminated. [*IAS 28.38*]

3.5.440.40　The discussion in 3.5.440.30 assumes that the equity-accounted investee has the related goods in its statement of financial position. If the goods purchased were sold by the investee or used in production and therefore recognised as an expense, then no elimination entry would be necessary.

3.5.440.45　Under the second approach, the investor eliminates its share of the gain in full. The amount of the elimination in excess of the carrying amount of the investor's interest in the equity-accounted investee is presented as deferred income. If the investee earns a profit in subsequent periods and the carrying amount of the investment in the investee becomes positive, then the investor should change its presentation of the deferred income so that it is offset against the investment in the investee in the usual way. This approach is based on the view that the requirement to eliminate the investor's share of gains on downstream transactions with equity-accounted investees is not subject to a 'floor' of a zero net investment. [*IAS 28.28*]

EXAMPLE 10C – DOWNSTREAM SALE OF INVENTORY – ELIMINATION EXCEEDS INVESTEE CARRYING AMOUNT

3.5.440.50　This example illustrates the elimination in a downstream sale of inventory by the investor to a 50% associate.

	INVESTOR	ASSOCIATE
2018		
Cost of inventory	600	900
Selling price of inventory	900	Not yet sold
Profit related to the transaction	300	
Carrying amount of associate	100	
2019		
Net profit	-	1,000

3.5.440.60 Under the first approach (see 3.5.440.30), the investor's entry required to eliminate its 50% interest in the profit from this transaction is limited to the carrying amount of the investment in the associate. The investor records the following entry in 2018. For an alternative presentation of the elimination entry, see 3.5.430.70.

	DEBIT	CREDIT
Revenue ((900 x 50%) x (100 / 150))	300	
Cost of sales ((600 x 50%) x (100 / 150))		200
Investment in associate ((300 x 50%) limited to 100)		100
To eliminate unrealised profit on downstream		
transaction subject to zero net investment limitation		

3.5.440.70 The investor records the following entry in 2019 to adjust the share of profit for the previously unrecognised elimination, which assumes that the inventory was not sold by the associate in 2019.

	DEBIT	CREDIT
Investment in associate	450	
Share of profit or loss of associate ((1,000 x 50%) - 50)		450
To adjust equity-accounted earnings in 2019 for		
limitation of elimination applied in 2018		

3.5.440.80 Under the second approach (see 3.5.440.45), the following entries fully eliminate the investor's share of the profit from the transaction and the corresponding presentation of deferred income in a downstream sale of inventory. The investor records the following entry in 2018.

	DEBIT	CREDIT
Revenue (900 x 50%)	450	
Costs of sales (600 x 50%)		300
Investment in associate ((300 x 50%) limited to 100)		100
Deferred income ((300 x 50%) - 100)		50
To eliminate fully unrealised profit on downstream transaction		

3.5.440.90   The investor records the following entries in 2019.

	DEBIT	CREDIT
Investment in associate	500	
Share of profit or loss of associate (1,000 x 50%)		500
To recognise equity-accounted earnings of associate		
Deferred income	50	
Investment in associate		50
To offset deferred income as associate earns profits		

3.5.450 *Elimination of balances*

3.5.450.10   IFRS requires the elimination of the investor's share of profits or losses on transactions with equity-accounted investees when applying the equity method. Balances such as receivables or payables and deposits or loans to or from equity-accounted investees are not eliminated. [*IAS 28.28*]

3.5.460 *Elimination of interest income or expense*

3.5.460.10   The elimination of interest income or expense arising on balances with equity-accounted investees is not specifically addressed in IFRS. The fact that many of the procedures appropriate for equity accounting are similar to consolidation procedures suggests that elimination should be performed (see 3.5.190). However, the examples of upstream and downstream transactions in the standard are sales of assets, which suggest that transactions that do not involve assets should not be eliminated. This is consistent with the fact that balances with equity-accounted investees are not eliminated (see 3.5.450). [*IAS 28.26, 28*]

3.5.460.15   In our view, in general an entity should choose an accounting policy, to be applied consistently, on whether to eliminate such transactions. The accounting policy selected by the entity affects only the presentation of comprehensive income, because it affects the split between finance costs and equity-accounted earnings.

3.5.460.20   As an exception, if one of the parties has capitalised the interest (see 4.6.10), then in our view the transaction should be eliminated. In this case, the transaction is viewed as an upstream or downstream transaction because it gives rise to an asset in the entity that has been charged the interest expense (see 3.5.430). [*IAS 28.28*]

3.5.470   ***Contribution of subsidiary to existing or newly created investee***

3.5.470.10   Sometimes a parent may sell or contribute a controlling interest in a subsidiary to an existing equity-accounted investee. Significant influence or joint control in a former subsidiary may also be retained via an interest in the acquirer. In such cases, it is unclear how the gain or loss should be calculated, because there appears to be some ambiguity in IFRS in this regard. IFRS 10 requires any resulting gain or loss to be recognised in full in profit or loss when control of a subsidiary is lost (see 2.5.760) – i.e. no elimination is made for a continuing interest in the assets and liabilities contributed. However, IAS 28 requires an elimination to be made for a continuing interest in the assets and liabilities contributed. [*IFRS 10.25, IAS 28.28, 30*]

3.5.470.20   In our view, this conflict means that the entity should choose an accounting policy, to be applied consistently, to follow either the IFRS 10 approach or the IAS 28 approach.
- *The IFRS 10 approach:* Under this approach, no elimination of the gain or loss is performed and the fair value of the retained investment is its deemed cost for the purposes of subsequent accounting.
- *The IAS 28 approach:* Under this approach, the gain or loss is eliminated to the extent of the retained interest in the former subsidiary.

EXAMPLE 11A – SUBSIDIARY SOLD TO ASSOCIATE

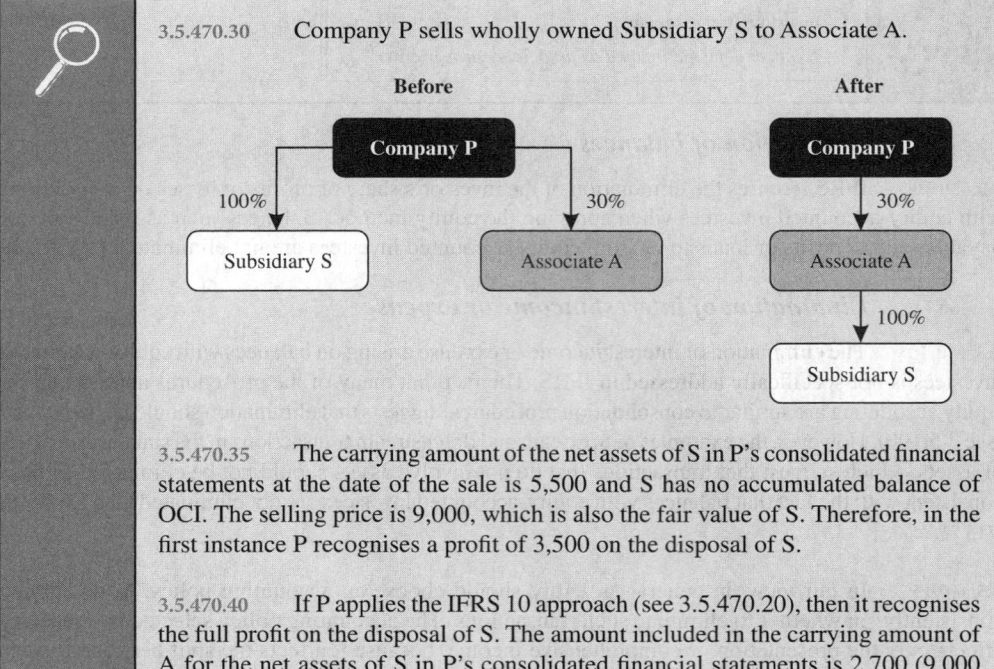

3.5.470.30   Company P sells wholly owned Subsidiary S to Associate A.

3.5.470.35   The carrying amount of the net assets of S in P's consolidated financial statements at the date of the sale is 5,500 and S has no accumulated balance of OCI. The selling price is 9,000, which is also the fair value of S. Therefore, in the first instance P recognises a profit of 3,500 on the disposal of S.

3.5.470.40   If P applies the IFRS 10 approach (see 3.5.470.20), then it recognises the full profit on the disposal of S. The amount included in the carrying amount of A for the net assets of S in P's consolidated financial statements is 2,700 (9,000 x 30%).

3.5.470.50   If P applies the IAS 28 approach (see 3.5.470.20), then it eliminates 30% of the profit recognised on the disposal of S against the carrying amount of the investment in A.

3.5.470.60   In applying the IAS 28 approach, P records the following entries for the transaction and the subsequent elimination.

	DEBIT	CREDIT
Cash	9,000	
Net assets of S		5,500
Gain on disposal (profit or loss)		3,500
To recognise disposal of S		
Gain on disposal (profit or loss) (3,500 x 30%)	1,050	
Investment in associate		1,050
To recognise elimination of 30% of profit on disposal of S		

3.5.470.70   The amount included in the carrying amount of A for the net assets of S in P's consolidated financial statements, following the elimination, is 1,650 (9,000 x 30% - 1,050). This corresponds to the carrying amount of the net assets of S in P's financial statements before the disposal, which was 1,650 (5,500 x 30%).

3.5.470.80   The investor's accounting policy choice has consequences for the treatment of reserves of the former subsidiary. In effect, if the entity applies the IAS 28 approach (see 3.5.470.20), then in our view the components of OCI of the former subsidiary are not reclassified in full, but instead should be reclassified on a proportionate basis (see 2.7.340). This is because we believe that the requirement in IAS 21 to reclassify in profit or loss a proportionate share of the cumulative amount of the exchange differences recognised in OCI applies in such circumstances. We also believe that a similar approach should be applied to other components of OCI. [*IAS 21.48C*]

EXAMPLE 11B – SUBSIDIARY SOLD TO ASSOCIATE – OTHER RESERVES

3.5.470.90   Modifying Example 11A, assume that Subsidiary S has a foreign currency translation reserve of 300 (accumulated gains) and an available-for-sale revaluation reserve of 200 (accumulated gains) on the date that it is sold to Associate A.

3.5.470.100   If Company P applies the IAS 28 approach (see 3.5.470.20), then the profit on disposal of 2,450 (3,500 - 1,050) calculated in Example 11A is adjusted for the reclassification of amounts previously recognised in OCI by 350 ((300 + 200) x 70%). The profit recognised is therefore 2,800.

3.5.470.110   An issue arises when an entity applies the IAS 28 approach (see 3.5.470.20) and the carrying amount of the entity's interest in the equity-accounted investee is insufficient to support the elimination of part or all of the gain attributable to the retained interest.

3.5.470.115   In our view, there are two possible approaches to eliminate the excess profit and an entity should choose an accounting policy, to be applied consistently, consistent with the approach taken to the elimination of gains on downstream transactions in excess of the investee's carrying amount (see 3.5.440).

- Under the first approach, once the investor's interest in the investee has been reduced to zero, any remaining portion of the investor's share of the gain should not be eliminated. If the investee earns a profit in subsequent periods, then the investor should recognise its share of the profit only after adjusting for the excess gain that was not previously eliminated.
- Under the second approach, the investor eliminates in full its share of the gain. The amount of the elimination in excess of the carrying amount of the investor's interest in the investee is presented in the statement of financial position as deferred income.

EXAMPLE 11C – SUBSIDIARY SOLD TO ASSOCIATE – ELIMINATION EXCEEDS CARRYING AMOUNT

3.5.470.120   Company X owns 100% of Company X1, and Company Y owns 100% of Company Y1. X, Y and Company Z incorporate a new entity (Newco) and invest cash of 875, 875 and 750, respectively, giving an interest of 35%, 35% and 30%, respectively. X, Y and Z each have significant influence over Newco. Newco obtains a loan of 7,500 and uses its cash of 10,000 (7,500 plus the 2,500 contributed on formation) to acquire X1 and Y1. In effect, X and Y have each disposed of a subsidiary with significant influence retained.

3.5.470.130   The carrying amounts and fair values of X1 and Y1 are as follows.

	X1	Y1
Carrying amount	1,000	2,500
Fair value	7,000	3,000

3.5.470.140   The shareholdings in Newco, X1 and Y1 after the transaction are as follows.

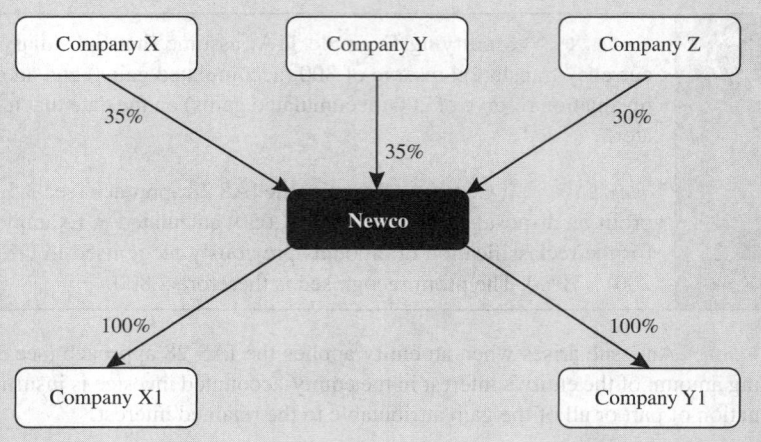

3.5.470.150   The statement of financial position of Newco after the transaction is as follows.

560

Investment in X1	7,000
Investment in Y1	3,000
	10,000
Non-current liability	7,500
Equity	2,500
	10,000

3.5.470.160 Under the first approach (see 3.5.470.115), once X's interest in the associate has been reduced to zero, any remaining portion of X's share of the gain should not be eliminated. If Newco earns a profit in subsequent periods, then X should recognise its share of the profit only after adjusting for the excess gain that was not previously eliminated.

3.5.470.170 X records the following entry to recognise its disposal of X1.

	DEBIT	CREDIT
Cash	7,000	
Net assets of X1 (carrying amount)		1,000
Gain on disposal (profit or loss)		6,000
To recognise disposal of X1		

3.5.470.180 X records the following entry to recognise its investment in Newco.

	DEBIT	CREDIT
Investment in Newco	875	
Cash		875
To recognise investment in Newco		

3.5.470.190 X then records the following entry to eliminate the effect of its continued 35% interest in X1 via Newco, limited to the carrying amount of the investment in Newco.

	DEBIT	CREDIT
Gain on disposal (profit or loss) (6,000 x 35% limited to 875)	875	
Investment in Newco		875
To eliminate gain on contribution to Newco subject to zero net investment limitation		

3.5.470.200   Under the second approach (see 3.5.470.115), X should eliminate in full its share of the gain. The amount of the elimination in excess of the carrying amount of X's interest in the associate is presented in the statement of financial position as deferred income.

3.5.470.210   After recording the entries to recognise its disposal of X1 (see 3.5.470.170) and the investment in Newco (see 3.5.470.180), X records the following entry to eliminate the effect of its continued 35% interest in X1 via Newco.

	DEBIT	CREDIT
Gain on disposal (profit or loss) (6,000 x 35%)	2,100	
Investment in Newco (limited to investment)		875
Deferred income		1,225
To fully eliminate gain on contribution to Newco		

3.5.470.220   If Newco earns a profit in subsequent periods and the carrying amount of the investment becomes positive, then X will change its presentation of the deferred income so that it is offset against its investment in Newco in the usual way.

3.5.480   *Contribution of associate or joint venture to existing or newly created associate or joint venture that gains control*

3.5.480.10   An entity may contribute an associate or joint venture to another associate or joint venture that in turn gains control over the contributed associate or joint venture. In such scenarios, it may be unclear whether significant influence or joint control still exists over the contributed investee. In our view, the accounting relationship is established with the direct investee whose entire group/investees will be equity accounted (see also 3.5.320). Therefore, the contributed investee will be equity accounted as a matter of course and the relationship of significant influence or joint control is retained.

EXAMPLE 12 – ASSOCIATE GAINS CONTROL OVER ANOTHER OF INVESTOR'S ASSOCIATES

3.5.480.15   Company B has a 40% associate, Company X. Company C holds 15% of X. The other 45% of X is held by other investors. Both B and C contribute their stakes in X to a newly created company, Newco, and C makes an additional cash payment to B. Newco now controls X.

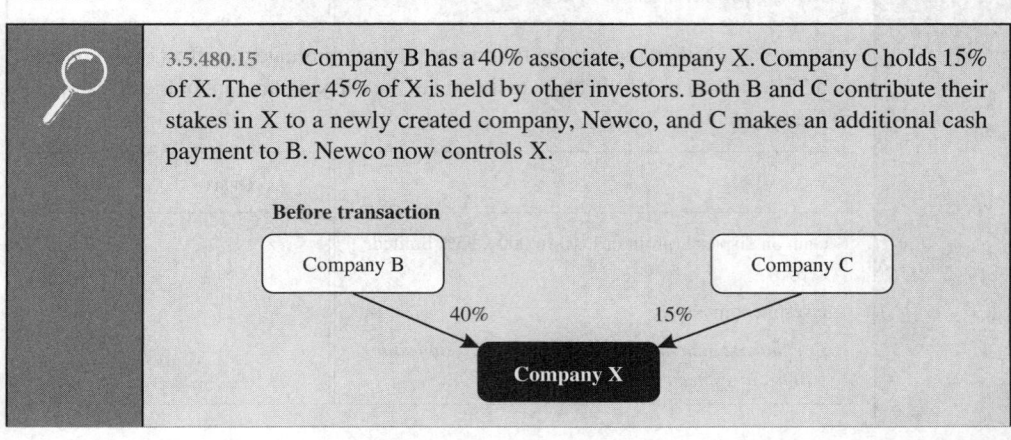

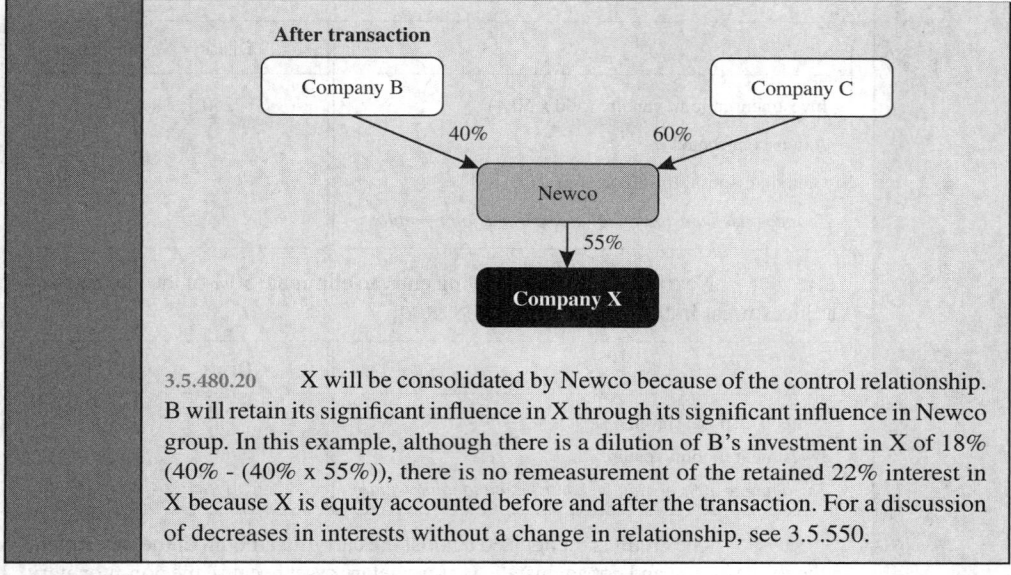

After transaction

Company B — 40% → Newco ← 60% — Company C

Newco — 55% → Company X

3.5.480.20   X will be consolidated by Newco because of the control relationship. B will retain its significant influence in X through its significant influence in Newco group. In this example, although there is a dilution of B's investment in X of 18% (40% - (40% x 55%)), there is no remeasurement of the retained 22% interest in X because X is equity accounted before and after the transaction. For a discussion of decreases in interests without a change in relationship, see 3.5.550.

3.5.485   *Contribution of non-monetary asset to investee*

3.5.485.10   If an entity contributes a non-monetary asset to an equity-accounted investee in exchange for an equity interest in the investee, then it recognises a gain or loss following the guidance on upstream and downstream transactions (see 3.5.430). The gain on disposal of the non-monetary asset is recognised to the extent of the interest of other investors in the equity-accounted investee – i.e. in proportion to the interest in the asset given up. The gain is determined as the difference between the fair value of the asset disposed of and its carrying amount, multiplied by the other investor's percentage interest; this means that the value of the retained interest in the asset is not stepped up, as illustrated in Example 13A. [*IAS 28.30*]

3.5.485.15   However, if the transaction lacks commercial substance (see 5.7.20.20), then no gain or loss is recognised. [*IAS 28.30*]

EXAMPLE 13A – DOWNSTREAM CONTRIBUTION OF NON-MONETARY ASSET

3.5.485.20   Company P and Company Q contribute non-monetary assets to their joint venture as follows in a transaction that has commercial substance.

	P	Q
Carrying amount of non-monetary assets contributed	100	130
Fair value of non-monetary assets contributed	250	250
Share in the joint venture	50%	50%

3.5.485.30   P records the following entry to recognise its contribution.

	DEBIT	CREDIT
Investment in joint venture (500 x 50%)	250	
Assets contributed		100
Gain on disposal (profit or loss)		150
To recognise contribution of assets to the joint venture		

3.5.485.40   Next P records the following entry to eliminate 50% of the gain against the investment in the joint venture. [*IAS 28.30*]

	DEBIT	CREDIT
Gain on disposal (profit or loss)	75	
Investment in joint venture		75
To eliminate 50% of gain on contribution to joint venture		

3.5.485.50   The credit is recognised against the carrying amount of the investment in the joint venture and not against the non-monetary asset because the non-monetary asset is an asset of the joint venture, and is included in the 'investment in the joint venture' line item in the statement of financial position.

3.5.485.55   The effect of this elimination is that P will recognise its share of the assets that it contributed at their carrying amounts at the date of the transfer and its share of the assets contributed by Q at fair value. As a result, P's share in the joint venture is 175.

Non-monetary assets contributed by P (100 x 50%)	50
Non-monetary assets contributed by Q (250 x 50%)	125
Total	175

EXAMPLE 13B – DOWNSTREAM CONTRIBUTION OF NON-MONETARY ASSET AND CASH

3.5.485.60   Modifying Example 13A, P contributes cash to the joint venture in addition to contributing non-monetary assets. The respective contributions of P and Q are as follows.

	P	Q
Carrying amount of non-monetary assets contributed	100	130
Fair value of non-monetary assets contributed	250	300
Cash contributed	50	-
Share in the joint venture	50%	50%

3.5.485.70   P records the following entry to recognise the contribution.

	DEBIT	CREDIT
Investment in joint venture (600 x 50%)	300	
Non-monetary assets contributed		100
Cash contributed		50
Gain on disposal (profit or loss)		150
To recognise contribution to joint venture		

3.5.485.80   Next P records the following entry to eliminate 50% of the gain against the investment in the joint venture.

	DEBIT	CREDIT
Gain on disposal (profit or loss)	75	
Investment in joint venture		75
To eliminate 50% of gain on contribution to joint venture		

3.5.485.90   As a result, P's share in the joint venture amounts to 225.

Non-monetary assets contributed by P (100 x 50%)	50
Cash contributed by P (50 x 50%)	25
Non-monetary assets contributed by Q (300 x 50%)	150
Total	225

3.5.490   Transactions between equity-accounted investees

3.5.490.10   IFRS is silent on whether unrealised profits or losses on a transaction between two equity-accounted investees should be eliminated. There is a conceptual argument to suggest that some of the profit should be eliminated, but it is not clear whether a transaction between two equity-accounted investees is analogous to an intra-group transaction between subsidiaries.

3.5.490.20   In our view, an entity should choose an accounting policy, to be applied consistently, of either:

- not eliminating the unrealised profit or losses from transactions between two equity-accounted investees; or
- eliminating some of the profit or losses from these transactions, by multiplying the investor's interest in the first investee by its interest in the second investee; this follows the requirements for downstream and upstream transactions (see 3.5.430) by analogy. [*IAS 28.26, 28*]

3.5.500 **Impairment#**

3.5.500.10 An investment in an equity-accounted investee may be impaired, even if the investee has already accounted for any impairment of the underlying assets. Therefore, investments in equity-accounted investees are subject to impairment testing requirements. [*IAS 28.40*]

3.5.500.20 Fair value adjustments and goodwill recognised on acquisitions of equity-accounted investees are not recognised separately. Goodwill recognised on the acquisition of an equity-accounted investee is not subject to an annual impairment test. Instead, after applying equity accounting, the investment is tested for impairment when there is an indication of a possible impairment. The guidance in IAS 28 is used to determine whether it is necessary to perform an impairment test for investments in equity-accounted investees (see 3.10.570). If there is an indication of impairment, then the impairment test applied follows the principles in IAS 36 (see 3.10.575). [*IAS 28.40–42*]

3.5.500.30 The requirements of IAS 36 are applied to the entire carrying amount of an investment in an equity-accounted investee without 'looking through' the investment to the investor's carrying amount of individual assets within the investee. Therefore, after applying the equity method, any impairment loss on an investment in an equity-accounted investee is not allocated to the underlying assets that make up the carrying amount of the investment, including goodwill. Accordingly, any such impairment loss is reversed if the recoverable amount increases subsequently (see 3.10.585). [*IAS 28.42*]

3.5.505 **FORTHCOMING REQUIREMENTS**

3.5.505.10 *Long-term Interests in Associates and Joint Ventures – Amendments to IAS 28* clarify that for those long-term interests that are not accounted for under the equity method, an entity applies IFRS 9. It applies IFRS 9 to these instruments before applying the impairment requirements in 3.5.500 to determine whether the net investment in the associate or joint venture is impaired. [*IAS 28.14A*]

3.5.510 **CHANGES IN STATUS OF EQUITY-ACCOUNTED INVESTEES**

3.5.520 **Overview**

FROM: TO:	FINANCIAL ASSETS	EQUITY-ACCOUNTED INVESTEES
Financial assets	N/A	Gain or loss for the difference between (a) the sum of the fair value of any retained investment, any proceeds on disposal and the amount reclassified from OCI; and (b) the carrying amount of the investment (see 3.5.570.10). Retained investment initially measured at fair value for the purpose of applying IFRS 9 (see 3.5.570.30). All reserves reclassified or transferred (see 3.5.570.20–30).

FROM: To:	FINANCIAL ASSETS	EQUITY-ACCOUNTED INVESTEES
Equity-accounted investees	Accounting policy choice: • Transfer fair value gains or losses recognised in OCI to retained earnings. • Keep fair value gains or losses recognised in OCI in accumulated OCI (see 3.5.530).	Additional interest purchased: • No remeasurement of previously held interest. No re-classification or transfer of reserve (see 3.5.540.10). • Allocation approach for additional interest (see 3.5.540.20). A portion of interest sold: • No remeasurement and no reclassification or transfer of the reserve for the retained interest (see 3.5.550.10). • Gain or loss on sale and reclassification or transfer of the reserve for the portion of interest sold (see 3.5.550.20–30).

3.5.530 Investment becomes equity-accounted investee

3.5.530.10 An investment may become an equity-accounted investee when:
• the investor acquires an additional holding; or
• there is a change in circumstances that results in significant influence or joint control being obtained.

3.5.530.20 Previously held investments in equity instruments have been measured at fair value under IFRS 9 with changes in fair value recognised in either profit or loss or OCI (see 7.4.60 and 410). Under IFRS 9, reclassification of fair value gains or losses recognised in OCI to profit or loss on disposal of the investment, or in other circumstances, is prohibited (see 7.7.160.10). This requirement applies when an equity investment becomes an equity-accounted investee. Any fair value gains or losses recognised in OCI may be transferred to retained earnings or remain in accumulated OCI. [*IFRS 9.4.1.4, 5.7.5, B5.7.1*]

EXAMPLE 14 – STEP ACQUISITION TO ACHIEVE SIGNIFICANT INFLUENCE

3.5.530.30 Company P acquired 10% of Company M for 200 on 30 January 2018. M is a listed entity and on 31 December 2018 the quoted price of the investment is 300. On 1 January 2019, P acquires an additional 20% of M for 600. The fair value of the identifiable net assets of M is 2,500 on 1 January 2019.

3.5.530.40 P's original investment was accounted for as a financial asset under IFRS 9. Assuming that on initial recognition P elected to measure the investment at fair value through OCI, in 2018 P recognised a fair value gain of 100 (300 - 200) in OCI (fair value reserve – equity instruments). P's accounting policy is to transfer fair value gains or losses recognised in OCI to retained earnings on changes in holding.

3.5.530.50 On 1 January 2019, P obtains significant influence and records the following entry.

	Debit	**Credit**
Investment in associate	900	
Fair value reserve (equity instruments)	100	
Cash		600
Investment in financial asset		300
Retained earnings		100
To recognise acquisition of additional 20% interest in M to achieve significant influence		

3.5.530.60 In determining the value of any goodwill included in the investment of an associate, P adds the consideration paid for the new acquisition to the fair value of the previously held investment as follows.

Fair value of investment in financial asset at 1 January 2019	300
Additional consideration	600
Total investment in associate at 1 January 2019	900
30% share of fair value of net assets (2,500 x 30%)	(750)
Goodwill	150

3.5.540 ## Acquisition of additional interests while continuing to apply equity accounting

3.5.540.10 If an entity acquires additional interests while continuing to apply equity accounting, then it does not remeasure the existing interest if an acquisition results in a change in status from an associate to a joint venture, or vice versa. Therefore, in our view an existing interest should also not be remeasured if the increase does not change the classification as an associate or as a joint venture. We believe that reserves, such as the cumulative foreign currency translation reserve, should not be reclassified to profit or loss or transferred to retained earnings, because doing so would be inconsistent with the continuation of equity accounting and the existing carrying amount. [*IAS 28.24*]

3.5.540.20 IFRS is silent on how to account for the additional interest. In our view, an entity should apply an 'allocation' approach similar to that applied when an interest is acquired in a new equity-accounted investee, whereby goodwill is calculated on the incremental interest acquired as a residual after valuing the incremental share of identifiable net assets at fair value. This results in identifiable net assets being valued on a mixed measurement basis.

EXAMPLE 15 – ADDITIONAL INTERESTS ACQUIRED – ALLOCATION APPROACH

3.5.540.30 Company P owns 25% of Associate A (Tranche 1). On 1 October 2018, P acquires an additional 10% of A for 250 (Tranche 2), and A remains an associate. The investment in A immediately before the acquisition of Tranche 2 is 583, which includes goodwill of 50. The fair value of identifiable net assets as at 1 October 2018 is 2,300.

3.5.540.40   The investment in A as at 1 October 2018 can be analysed as follows.

	GOODWILL	IDENTIFIABLE NET ASSETS	TOTAL INVESTMENT IN A
Tranche 1 (25%)	50	533	583
Tranche 2 (10%)	20[1]	230[2]	250
Total	70	763	833

Notes
1.   Calculated as 250 - (2,300 x 10%).
2.   Calculated as 2,300 x 10%.

3.5.550   Decrease in interest while continuing to apply equity accounting

3.5.550.10   If an entity disposes of an interest while continuing to apply equity accounting, then it does not remeasure the retained interest if the decrease results in a change in status from associate to joint venture, or vice versa. Therefore, in our view a retained interest should also not be remeasured if the decrease does not change the classification as an associate or as a joint venture. We believe that reserves, such as the cumulative foreign currency translation reserve, relating to the retained interest should not be reclassified to profit or loss or transferred to retained earnings, because doing so would be inconsistent with the continuation of equity accounting and the existing carrying amount. For a discussion of a contrasting case regarding the treatment of reserves relating to the portion of the interest disposed of, see 3.5.550.20. [*IAS 28.24*]

3.5.550.20   If an entity's ownership interest is reduced, but the entity continues to apply equity accounting, then it reclassifies to profit or loss any equity-accounted gain or loss previously recognised in OCI in proportion to the reduction in the ownership interest. This reclassification applies only if that gain or loss would be reclassified to profit or loss on disposal of the related asset or liability – e.g. a foreign currency translation reserve. Otherwise, the portion of reserves remains within equity – e.g. revaluation reserve or fair value reserve (equity instruments). In our view, the difference between the proceeds from the sale and the cost of the investment sold should be recognised in profit or loss. [*IAS 28.25*]

3.5.550.30   IFRS is silent on how to determine the cost of the investment sold and the portion of reserves that is reclassified or transferred. In our view, the guidance on cost formulas for inventories should be applied to determine the cost of financial assets sold when the financial assets are part of a homogeneous portfolio (see 3.8.280 and 7.6.230.50). Therefore, an entity should choose an accounting policy, to be applied consistently, to use any reasonable cost allocation method – e.g. weighted-average cost or first-in, first-out – in determining the cost of the investment sold. We believe that the portion of reserves reclassified or transferred should be calculated consistently with the gain or loss of the partial disposal.

EXAMPLE 16A – DECREASE IN INTEREST – WEIGHTED-AVERAGE COST METHOD

3.5.550.40   Company P owns 30% of Associate A. The contribution of A to P's consolidated statement of financial position immediately before the decrease in ownership interest is as follows.

Investment in associate (A)	120
Net assets	120
Foreign currency translation reserve	24
Fair value reserve (equity instruments)	18
Revaluation reserve	15
Retained earnings	63
Total shareholder's equity	120

3.5.550.50   On 1 January 2018, P sells 10% of A for cash of 50 while maintaining significant influence. P's accounting policy is to transfer fair value gains or losses recognised in OCI to retained earnings on changes in holding. P records the following entry, electing to use the weighted-average cost method in calculating the gain or loss on disposal.

	DEBIT	CREDIT
Cash	50	
Foreign currency translation reserve (24 x 10% / 30%)	8	
Fair value reserve (equity instruments) (18 x 10% / 30%)	6	
Revaluation reserve (15 x 10% / 30%)	5	
Retained earnings (5 + 6)		11
Gain (50 - 40 + 8)		18
Investment in associate (120 x 10% / 30%)		40
To recognise decrease in interest in A while maintaining significant influence		

3.5.550.60   A decrease in interest while an investment continues to be classified as an associate or joint venture can also result from a dilution. A dilution of an interest in an equity-accounted investee may happen, for example, when the investee issues shares to other parties. The dilution gain or loss is the difference between the carrying amounts of the investment in the equity-accounted investee, immediately before and after the transaction that resulted in the dilution. The gain or loss on the dilution of an interest in an equity-accounted investee is recognised in profit or loss; the amount of profit or loss arises from the new (reduced) ownership interest in the assets subscribed for the new shares – e.g. the cash paid by the other party – compared with the reduction in ownership interest in the previous carrying amount of the investment in the equity-accounted investee. Such a transaction is not a transaction with equity holders in their capacity as equity holders, and therefore any resulting gain or loss is recognised in profit or loss. For a discussion of dilutions resulting in equity accounting ceasing, see 3.5.560. [*IAS 28.25*]

EXAMPLE 16B – DECREASE IN INTEREST – LOSS ON DILUTION

3.5.550.70   Company P owns 30% of Associate A. The carrying amount of the investment in A in P's consolidated statement of financial position is 120, which includes goodwill and fair value adjustments in respect of A's identifiable net assets (see 3.5.270).

3.5.550.80   On 1 January 2018, A issues shares to other parties for cash of 50. P's interest in A is decreased to 25% as a result of the shares issued. P's gain or loss on dilution is calculated as follows.

Dilution of previous interest (120 x 5% / 30%)	(20.0)
Interest in the cash subscribed (50 x 25%)	12.5
Loss	(7.5)
Carrying amount of the investment before the transaction	120.0
Loss on dilution	(7.5)
Carrying amount of the investment after the transaction	112.5

3.5.560   Loss of significant influence or joint control

3.5.560.10   The equity method continues to apply until joint control or significant influence ceases, or until the investment is classified as held-for-sale (see 3.5.160). This may happen when:
- the investment or a portion of the investment is sold;
- there is a dilution in shareholding;
- there is a change in facts and circumstances; or
- the investor obtains control of an associate or joint venture. [*IAS 28.9, 22*]

3.5.560.15   However, if an investment in an associate becomes an investment in a joint venture or vice versa, then the equity method continues to be applied. For a discussion of the change resulting from the acquisition of additional interests, see 3.5.540. For a discussion of the change resulting from a decrease in interest, see 3.5.550. [*IAS 28.24*]

3.5.560.20   In our view, once an investment has been classified as an associate or joint venture, the investor will be regarded as continuing to have significant influence or joint control until a specific, identifiable event or transaction changes the circumstances. Insignificant or temporary changes in the relationship between the investor and the investee would not normally result in the cessation of joint control or significant influence.

3.5.570   *Discontinuing equity accounting without obtaining control of an existing associate or joint venture*

3.5.570.10   If an entity discontinues equity accounting without obtaining control of an existing associate or joint venture, then it recognises a gain or loss in profit or loss calculated as the difference between:

- the sum of:
    - the fair value of any proceeds from the interests disposed of;
    - the fair value of any retained investment; and
    - the amount reclassified from OCI (see 3.5.570.20); and
- the carrying amount of the investment at the date on which significant influence or joint control is lost. [*IAS 28.22*]

3.5.570.20   Amounts recognised in OCI in relation to the associate or joint venture are accounted for on the same basis as would be required if the investee had disposed of the related assets and liabilities directly. Some amounts are reclassified to profit or loss and some are not.
- The investor's share of the following amounts is reclassified to profit or loss:
    - exchange differences that were recognised in OCI in accordance with IAS 21;
    - changes in the fair value of debt instruments previously recognised in OCI in accordance with IFRS 9; and
    - the effective portion of gains and losses on hedging instruments in a cash flow hedge previously recognised in OCI in accordance with IFRS 9.
- The investor's share of the following amounts is not reclassified to profit or loss:
    - revaluation reserve (see 3.2.350.20); and
    - changes in the fair value of equity instruments previously recognised in OCI in accordance with IFRS 9 (see 7.10.90.10). [*IAS 28.22–23*]

3.5.570.30   When an investment ceases to be an associate or joint venture and is accounted for in accordance with IFRS 9, the fair value of the investment at the date on which it ceases to be an associate or a joint venture is regarded as its fair value on initial recognition as a financial asset in accordance with IFRS 9 (see 7.4.420.60). [*IAS 28.22*]

3.5.580   *Accounting for gain of control of existing associate or joint venture*

3.5.580.10   Obtaining control of an existing associate or joint venture that meets the definition of a business is an economic event that changes the nature of the investment. It is as if any investment in the acquiree that was held before obtaining control was sold and subsequently repurchased at the date of acquisition. [*IFRS 3.41–42, BC384*]

3.5.580.20   For a discussion of the accounting when the investor obtains control over an existing associate or joint venture that meets the definition of a business (a business combination achieved in stages), see 2.6.1140.

3.5.580.30   IFRS does not provide specific guidance for cases in which an investor obtains control over an existing associate or joint venture that does not meet the definition of a business. In our view, one acceptable approach is to account for an existing associate or joint venture at cost – i.e. without remeasurement. [*IFRS 3.2(b)*]

3.5.590   *Investor's elimination of profits on previous downstream transactions*

3.5.590.10   The investor's elimination of profits on previous downstream sales to associates or joint ventures is effectively reversed on a loss of significant influence or joint control.

EXAMPLE 17 – LOSS OF SIGNIFICANT INFLUENCE – PREVIOUS PROFIT ELIMINATION

3.5.590.20   Company F was previously a 20% associate of Company P. On 1 April 2018, P sells half of its investment in F and no longer has significant influence over F. Therefore, P discontinues the use of the equity method.

3.5.590.30   In a previous period, P sold land to F at a profit of 100. P eliminated the portion of the profit attributable to its interest in F of 20 against the equity-accounted carrying amount of its investment in F (see 3.5.430.50).

3.5.590.40   As the former carrying amount, which was reduced by the elimination, is replaced by the sale proceeds and the fair value of the retained interest, the elimination is automatically reversed, resulting in a correspondingly larger profit.

3.5.600   *Dividends received after loss of significant influence or joint control*

3.5.600.10   There is no specific guidance on how an investee that was previously an associate or joint venture should account for dividends declared from earnings that accrued in a period when it was accounted for as an associate or joint venture. Because the loss of significant influence or joint control is an economic event that changes the nature of an investment, in our view the dividends received should be accounted for in accordance with IFRS 9 with no specific adjustment needed. [*IFRS 9.5.7.1A*]

3.5.610   Retained investment in associate or joint venture following loss of control of subsidiary

3.5.610.10   Any retained investment in a former subsidiary that represents an associate or joint venture is remeasured to its fair value at the date on which control is lost (see 2.5.760). The remaining investment is accounted for in accordance with IAS 28 from the date on which control is lost, and the fair value at the date on which control is lost is the deemed cost of the investee in applying the equity method (see 3.5.240). An exception arises when the subsidiary is contributed to an associate or joint venture and the entity elects to apply IAS 28 approach in 3.5.470.20 – i.e. it eliminates the gain or loss to the extent of the retained interest in the former subsidiary. [*IAS 28.28*]

3.5.620   PRESENTATION

3.5.620.10   An entity presents each of the following for equity-accounted investees in the statement of profit or loss and OCI:
- the investor's share of the post-tax profit or loss in a single amount, which may result in a reconciling item in the tax rate reconciliation (see 3.13.640.20); and
- the investor's share of OCI, distinguishing the part that will be reclassified to profit or loss in the future when certain conditions are met and the part that will never be reclassified to profit or loss (see 3.5.570.20–30, 4.1.240). [*IAS 1.82(c), 82A, BC54K, IG6*]

3.5.620.20   For the statement of changes in equity, in our view an entity should choose an accounting policy, to be applied consistently, of either:
- allocating the investor's share of the comprehensive income of equity-accounted investees to the appropriate components of equity. In that case, for example, profit or loss will be allocated to

retained earnings, and exchange differences recognised in OCI will be allocated to the foreign currency translation reserve (see 2.7.230.10); or

- presenting the investor's share of the comprehensive income of equity-accounted investees separately.

3.5.630 **Disposals and impairment losses**

3.5.630.10   In our view, gains or losses arising on disposal of an equity-accounted investee, or the impairment of a loan to an equity-accounted investee, are not part of the investor's share of the equity-accounted earnings. We believe that it would be most appropriate for these items to be recognised in the same line item as other gains and losses on financial assets or sales of subsidiaries.

Ⓢ 3.5.640   # SEPARATE FINANCIAL STATEMENTS

3.5.640.10   In separate financial statements, investments in subsidiaries, associates and joint ventures are accounted for either:

- at cost;
- in accordance with IFRS 9 (see 7.4.20.10); or
- using the equity method as described in IAS 28. [*IAS 27.10*]

3.5.640.20   When an investment measured at cost or using the equity method is classified as held-for-sale or held-for-distribution (or included in a disposal group classified as held-for-sale or held-for-distribution), it is accounted for in accordance with IFRS 5, which is the subject of chapter 5.4. The measurement of investments accounted for in accordance with IFRS 9 is not changed when they are classified as held-for-sale. [*IAS 27.10*]

3.5.640.30   If an investor qualifies as a venture capital or similar organisation and elects to measure investments in associates or joint ventures at fair value through profit or loss in its consolidated financial statements (see 3.5.100), then these investments are accounted for in the same way in the separate financial statements. [*IAS 27.11*]

3.5.640.40   The same accounting policies are applied for each category of investments – i.e. each of subsidiaries, associates and joint ventures. In our view, those categories can be further divided into sub-categories only if a sub-category can be defined clearly and objectively and results in information that is relevant and reliable. This is because IAS 8 requires consistent accounting policies to be applied to similar transactions, other events and conditions unless another IFRS specifically permits categorisation of items for which different policies may be appropriate. We believe that whether these latter tests are met should be judged similarly to choosing an accounting policy under the hierarchy for the selection of accounting policies (see 2.8.20). [*IAS 27.10, 8.13*]

3.5.640.50   For example, an investment entity parent is required to measure the investment in an investment entity subsidiary at fair value through profit or loss in its separate financial statements. However, it is not clear how an investment entity parent should account for a non-investment entity subsidiary whose main purpose is to provide services that relate to the investment entity's investment activities in its separate financial statements (see 5.6.100). In our view, non-investment entity subsidiaries can be considered a sub-category and therefore be measured other than at fair value through profit or loss in the parent's separate financial statements. [*IFRS 10.31, IAS 27.11A*]

3.5.640.60   All dividends from an associate or joint venture are recognised in the separate financial statements of the investor when the right to receive the dividend is established. Dividends are recognised in profit or loss unless the investor elects to use the equity method. If the investor uses the equity method, then it recognises the dividend as a reduction of the carrying amount of the investments. In our view, recognition in profit or loss in the separate financial statements of the investor may also be applied when the distribution is in excess of the retained profits of the investee. In addition, the receipt of dividend income may be an indicator of impairment (see 3.10.600.30). [*IAS 27.12, 36.12(h)*]

3.5.650   Changes in interests in investee under the cost method

3.5.650.10   If an entity loses control but retains significant influence over a subsidiary that was held at cost in its separate financial statements, then in our view the entity should continue to account for the remaining investment using the cost approach without remeasurement. We believe that the nature of the investment in the separate financial statements does not change after the sale of the interest – i.e. it remains an investment (see 7.6.230.50).

3.5.660   Changes in interests in investee under the equity method

3.5.660.10   An entity that obtains control over a former associate or a joint venture that was accounted for using the equity method in its separate financial statements may choose to continue applying the equity method for its accounting for the subsidiary (if it is applied consistently for each category of investments). In our view, an entity should choose one of the following accounting policies, to be applied consistently, to account for such a transaction:

● *apply the guidance on step acquisitions in IFRS 3:* This is on the basis that obtaining control over a subsidiary is a significant economic event, which is accounted for by analogy to the guidance in IFRS 3 (see 2.6.1140); or

● *apply the guidance on acquisitions of additional interests in an equity-accounted investee:* This is on the basis that equity accounting continues to be applied and therefore there is no change in the accounting model (see 3.5.540).

3.5.660.20   In our view, a similar accounting policy choice, to be applied consistently, is available in the opposite scenario in which an entity loses control and continues to apply the equity method in its separate financial statements for its retained interest in the associate or joint venture:

● *apply the guidance on the loss of control in IFRS 10:* This is on the basis that losing control over a subsidiary is a significant economic event, which is accounted for by analogy to the guidance in IFRS 10 (see 2.5.760); or

● *apply the guidance on a decrease in interests in an equity-accounted investee:* This is on the basis that equity accounting continues to be applied and therefore there is no change in the accounting model (see 3.5.550).

3.5.660.30   In our view, an entity should choose an accounting policy, to be applied consistently, for both of these scenarios (gaining and losing control).

● Applying the guidance in IFRS 3 and IFRS 10 means that interests will be remeasured to fair value when control is obtained or lost.

● Applying the guidance in IAS 28 means that interests will *not* be remeasured to fair value when control is obtained or lost.

3.6   Joint arrangements

3.6 Joint arrangements

CURRENTLY EFFECTIVE REQUIREMENTS

This publication reflects IFRS in issue at 1 August 2018, and the currently effective requirements cover annual periods beginning on 1 January 2018.

The disclosures related to joint arrangements are discussed in chapter 5.10.

The requirements related to this topic are mainly derived from the following.

STANDARD	TITLE
IFRS 11	Joint Arrangements

FORTHCOMING REQUIREMENTS

The currently effective requirements are affected by the following forthcoming requirements. They are highlighted with a # and the impact is explained in the accompanying boxed text at the references indicated.

In December 2017, the IASB issued *Annual Improvements to IFRSs 2015–2017 Cycle – Amendments to IFRS 11*, which are effective for annual periods beginning on or after 1 January 2019. See 3.6.318.

FUTURE DEVELOPMENTS

The currently effective requirements that may be affected by future developments are highlighted with a * and are briefly discussed in 3.6.370.

3.6.10   IDENTIFYING JOINT ARRANGEMENTS

3.6.10.10   A 'joint arrangement' is an arrangement over which two or more parties have 'joint control', being the contractually agreed sharing of control – i.e. unanimous consent is required for decisions about the relevant activities. [*IFRS 11.4, 7*]

3.6.10.20   To identify a joint arrangement, an entity:
- first assesses whether collective control exists (see 3.6.20); and
- then assesses whether the arrangement gives two or more parties *joint* control over the arrangement (see 3.6.30). [*IFRS 11.8, B5–B6*]

3.6.10.30   IFRS 11's two-step process is described in 3.6.20–30. However, in many scenarios it will be simpler to identify a joint arrangement by determining:
- whether a contract exists whereby two (or more) parties are required to exercise together, on a unanimous consent basis, their powers in relation to an arrangement; and
- whether those powers amount to control.

3.6.10.40   For example, three parties each have one third of the voting power in an entity and decisions are made by a simple majority. In the absence of a shareholders' contract that requires unanimous consent or two predefined parties to agree, it is clear that joint control does not exist because there is more than one combination of parties that can agree to reach the simple majority. Therefore, the two-step approach in 3.6.10.20 is not relevant. [*IFRS 11.B8*]

3.6.10.50   Conversely, if a shareholders' contract exists, then each of the parties can immediately analyse whether unanimous consent is required for decisions about the relevant activities. Then the next question is whether any unanimous consent requirement extends to sufficient matters such that joint control, rather than sole control, exists.

3.6.10.60   In our experience, it is uncommon for an entity whose shares are publicly traded to be subject to contractually established joint control.

3.6.20   Determining whether there is collective control

3.6.20.10   In the first step of the assessment, an entity assesses whether control exists and is collective. An investor *controls* an investee when it:
- is exposed to (has rights to) variable returns from its involvement with the investee; and
- has the ability to affect those returns through its power over the investee. For further discussion of control, see chapter 2.5. [*IFRS 10.6, 11.B5*]

3.6.20.20   All of the parties, or a group of parties, control the arrangement collectively if they have to act together to direct the activities that significantly affect the returns of the arrangement – i.e. the relevant activities as defined in IFRS 10 (see 2.5.60). [*IFRS 11.8, B5*]

EXAMPLE 1 – COLLECTIVE CONTROL

3.6.20.30   An arrangement is set up in which Company X holds 50%, Company Y holds 30% and Company Z holds 20%. The contractual terms between the companies specify that a minimum of 75% of the votes are required to make decisions about the relevant activities of the arrangement.

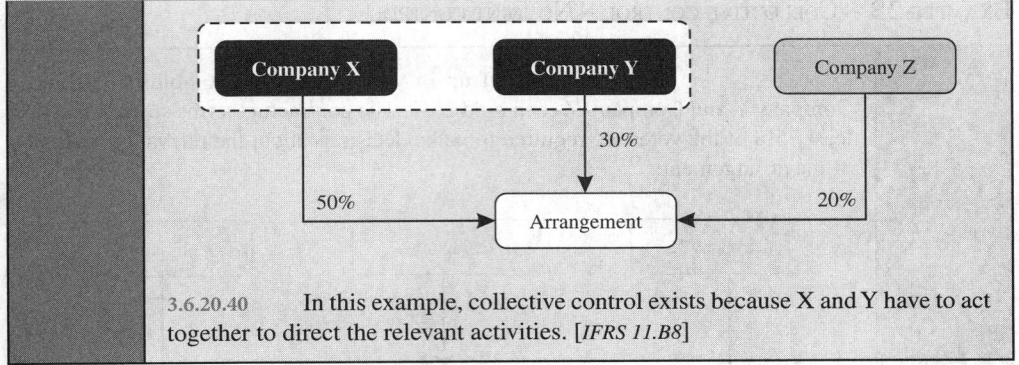

3.6.20.40   In this example, collective control exists because X and Y have to act together to direct the relevant activities. [*IFRS 11.B8*]

3.6.20.50   If collective control exists, then the second step of the analysis is performed. If such control does not exist, then that arrangement is not a joint arrangement. [*IFRS 11.B6*]

3.6.30   Determining whether control is joint control

3.6.30.10   'Joint control' is the contractually agreed sharing of control of an arrangement. Joint control exists only when decisions about the relevant activities – i.e. those that significantly affect the returns of the arrangement – require the unanimous consent of the parties sharing control of the arrangement. Therefore, decisions relating to fundamental changes in the activities of the arrangement, or that apply only in exceptional circumstances (i.e. protective rights), are not considered in this assessment. For further discussion of substantive and protective rights, see 2.5.100. [*IFRS 10.B26, 11.A, 7, 9, B6, B9*]

3.6.30.20   An enforceable contractual arrangement can be evidenced in several ways; however, it is often in writing and usually in the form of a contract or documented discussions between the parties. Statutory mechanisms can also create enforceable contractual arrangements on their own or in conjunction with contracts between parties. [*IFRS 11.B2*]

EXAMPLE 2A – COLLECTIVE CONTROL – JOINT CONTROL

3.6.30.30   Continuing Example 1, joint control exists implicitly, because no decisions can be made about the relevant activities of the arrangement without both X and Y agreeing. Therefore, the arrangement is a joint arrangement. [*IFRS 11.B8*]

3.6.30.40   Example 2A illustrates that unanimous consent over the relevant activities can be implicit rather than explicit. That is, the shareholdings of the individual parties mean that unanimous consent of specific parties is always required – even though there is no explicit shareholders' agreement provision in this regard. This often happens when:
- two parties each have 50 percent of the voting rights; and
- the contractual arrangement requires that the decisions about the relevant activities are made by simple majority – i.e. 51 percent. [*IFRS 11.B7*]

3.6.30.50   The existence of collective control does not automatically result in the conclusion that joint control also exists.

EXAMPLE 2B – COLLECTIVE CONTROL – NO JOINT CONTROL

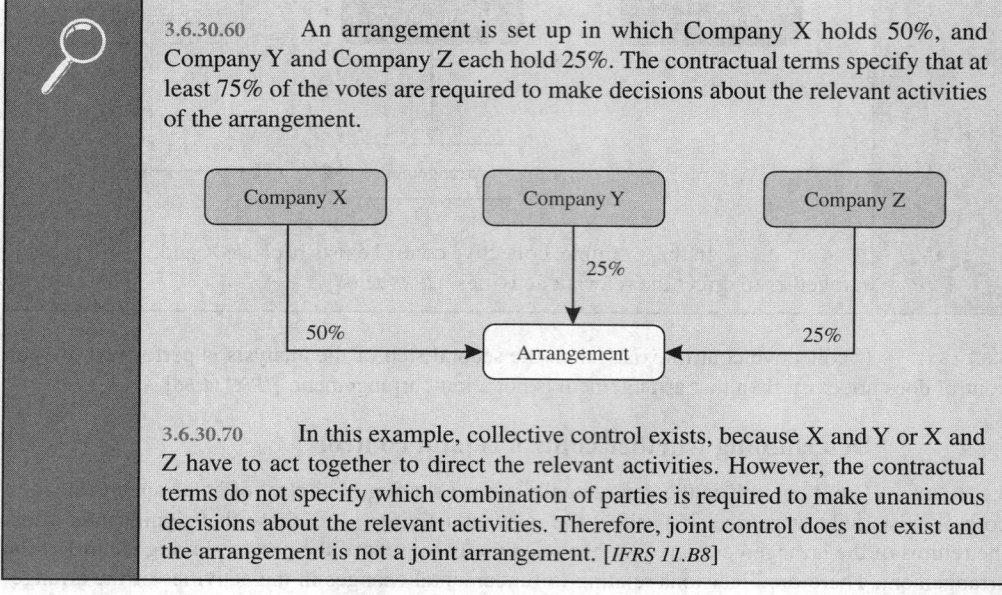

3.6.30.60   An arrangement is set up in which Company X holds 50%, and Company Y and Company Z each hold 25%. The contractual terms specify that at least 75% of the votes are required to make decisions about the relevant activities of the arrangement.

3.6.30.70   In this example, collective control exists, because X and Y or X and Z have to act together to direct the relevant activities. However, the contractual terms do not specify which combination of parties is required to make unanimous decisions about the relevant activities. Therefore, joint control does not exist and the arrangement is not a joint arrangement. [*IFRS 11.B8*]

3.6.30.80   An arrangement can be a joint arrangement even when not all parties to the arrangement share in the joint control of the arrangement – e.g. minority shareholders in a joint arrangement structured as a company; see also 3.6.200.180. [*IFRS 11.11*]

3.6.30.90   Agreeing to act in the best interests of another party does not in itself establish joint control.

EXAMPLE 2C – COLLECTIVE CONTROL – CONTROL VS ACTING IN BEST INTERESTS

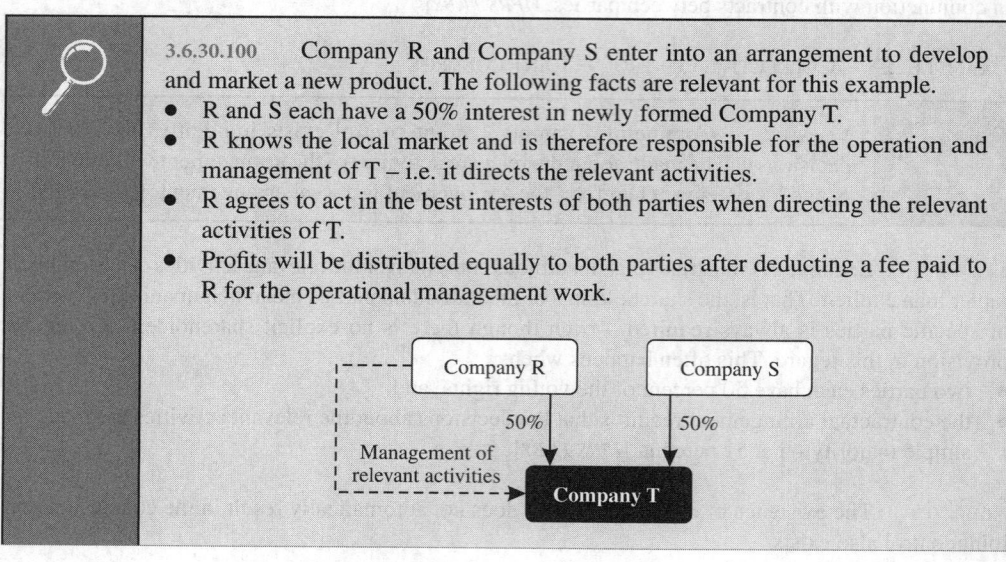

3.6.30.100   Company R and Company S enter into an arrangement to develop and market a new product. The following facts are relevant for this example.
- R and S each have a 50% interest in newly formed Company T.
- R knows the local market and is therefore responsible for the operation and management of T – i.e. it directs the relevant activities.
- R agrees to act in the best interests of both parties when directing the relevant activities of T.
- Profits will be distributed equally to both parties after deducting a fee paid to R for the operational management work.

> 3.6.30.110   Unless S has other rights that enable it to block policy decisions made by R – i.e. substantive rights (see 2.5.100) – R has sole power over the relevant activities of T. Therefore, T is a subsidiary of R and not a joint arrangement. T would be a joint arrangement only if decisions about its relevant activities required the unanimous consent of R and S.

3.6.30.120   The assessment of joint control requires judgement and consideration of all facts and circumstances. A change in the facts and circumstances requires reassessment of whether joint control still exists. [*IFRS 11.12–13*]

3.6.40   *Joint de facto control*

3.6.40.10   Joint control exists only when it is *contractually agreed* that decisions about the relevant activities require the unanimous consent of the parties that control the arrangement collectively. Therefore, even when the parties can demonstrate past experience of voting together in the absence of a contractual agreement to do so, that requirement will not be satisfied. In other words, de facto joint control is not possible in this scenario.

3.6.40.20   However, it is possible for parties to establish joint de facto control – i.e. power is based on de facto circumstances (see 2.5.160) – and the parties sharing that control have contractually agreed to share that control.

EXAMPLE 3 – JOINT DE FACTO CONTROL

3.6.40.30   Company X holds 23% of the voting rights of Company Z and Company Y holds 25% of the voting rights. The remaining voting rights are held by thousands of shareholders, none individually holding more than 1% of the voting rights.

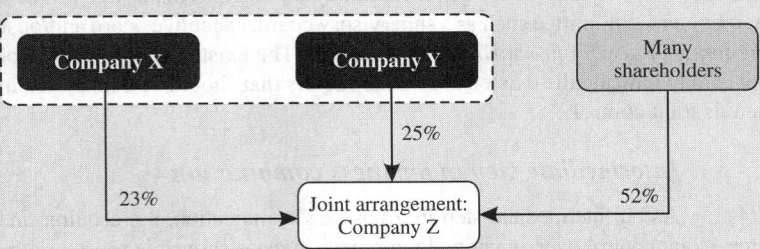

3.6.40.40   X and Y have contractually agreed that, on decisions about the relevant activities of Z, casting their combined 48% voting power requires their unanimous consent. None of the other shareholders has any arrangements to consult each other or make collective decisions.

3.6.40.50   In this example, X and Y's combined shareholding results in de facto control over the arrangement. Accordingly, X and Y conclude that they have joint de facto control over Z.

3.6.50   ***Factors that may be relevant in assessing joint control***

3.6.50.10   Although the contractual terms may require the unanimous consent of the parties that control the arrangement collectively, a significant disparity in holdings may require some caution in assessing whether joint control exists. For example, consider an arrangement in which one party holds 75 percent and another party holds 25 percent. The significant disparity in holdings may indicate that joint control does not exist, because a party holding 75 percent of the arrangement may be unlikely to accept the sharing of control of the arrangement.

3.6.50.20   The contractual terms may include clauses on resolving disputes, such as arbitration, so that decisions can be made in the absence of unanimous consent of the parties that have joint control. However, the existence of such clauses does not automatically preclude the arrangement from being assessed as a joint arrangement. In our view, for joint control to exist, dispute resolution procedures should be neutral and not favour one of the parties – e.g. a mutually agreed-on independent arbitrator should be used. [*IFRS 11.B10*]

3.6.50.25   Consideration should also be given to rights over relevant activities that are exercisable only in the event of deadlock (see 2.5.140.70–100).

3.6.50.30   In our view, other factors that may be relevant in assessing joint control include the following.
- *The terms of shareholder agreements:* If there are clauses in the shareholder agreements or financial arrangements that give additional rights to one of the parties, then this may indicate that joint control does not exist.
- *The termination provisions:* If termination clauses give an advantage to one of the parties, then this may indicate that joint control does not exist.
- *Subsequent transactions:* Transactions that are contemplated when the joint arrangement is set up – e.g. a sell-off by one of the parties – might indicate that joint control does not exist.
- *Governance structure:* It is unlikely that joint control exists when one party has the power to appoint or remove the majority of the governing body members. This power can be exercised through a shareholders' committee such as a supervisory board, executive board and/or steering committees.
- *The terms of any profit-sharing arrangements:* The existence of uneven profit-sharing arrangements may indicate the existence of other factors that should be considered in assessing whether there is joint control.

3.6.60   ***Intermediate step in business combination***

3.6.60.10   As an intermediate step in a business combination, the acquirer and seller may appear to exercise joint control over an entity. In our view, in these cases it is necessary to consider the overall economic effect of all the transactions related to the business combination as a whole. If the facts and circumstances indicate that the joint control is not substantive – e.g. because the joint control is for too short a period to have any real economic effect – then the entity should not be treated as a joint arrangement. For a discussion of the general accounting requirements for business combinations, see chapter 2.6.

3.6.70   # CLASSIFYING JOINT ARRANGEMENTS

3.6.80   ## Overview

3.6.80.10   Joint arrangements are classified either as:

- a *joint operation*, whereby the jointly controlling parties, known as the 'joint operators', have rights to the assets and obligations for the liabilities relating to the arrangement; or
- a *joint venture*, whereby the jointly controlling parties, known as the 'joint venturers', have rights to the net assets of the arrangement. [*IFRS 11.14–16*]

3.6.80.20   The rights and the obligations of the parties arising from the arrangement in the normal course of business are key to determining the type of the arrangement, and therefore the subsequent accounting. [*IFRS 11.14, B14*]

3.6.80.30   The following flowchart provides an overview to classifying joint arrangements using a four-test approach. [*IFRS 11.B33*]

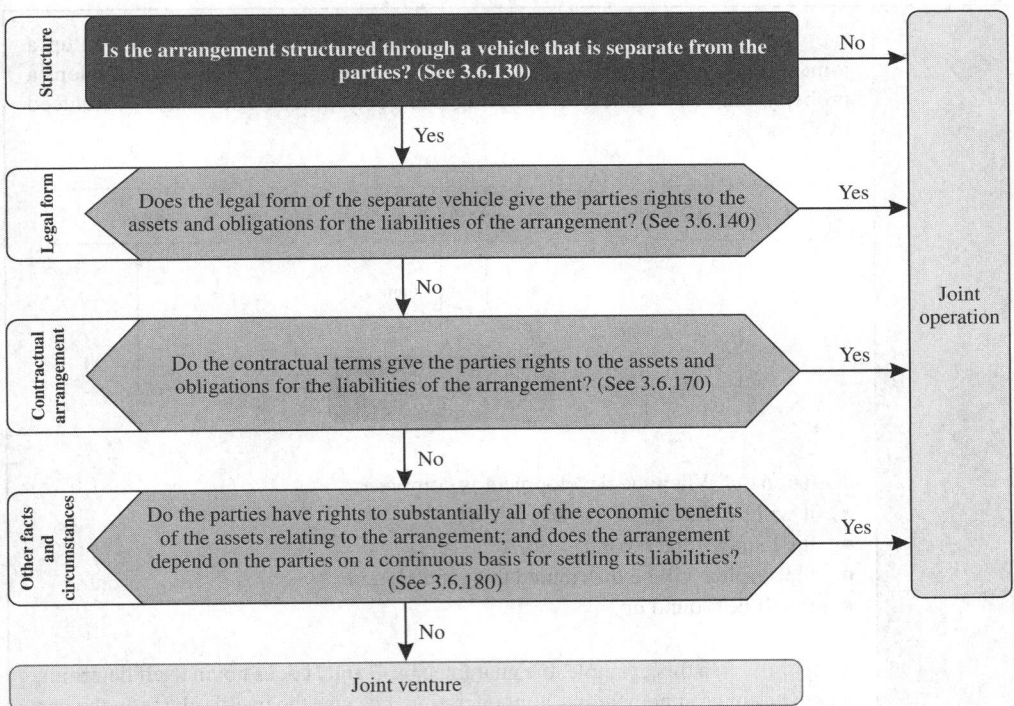

3.6.80.40   An entity reassesses the type of joint arrangement if facts and circumstances change. [*IFRS 11.19*]

3.6.90   *Rights to assets and obligations for liabilities*

3.6.90.10   A party needs to have rights to the assets *and* obligations for the liabilities relating to the arrangement in order to be classified as a joint operation. A party has rights to the assets when, for example, it has rights, title or ownership in the individual assets of the arrangement. A party has obligations for liabilities when, for example, it is liable to third parties for individual liabilities.

3.6.90.20   Therefore, the parties are required to have *both* rights to the assets *and* obligations for the liabilities, rather than either, in order for an arrangement within a separate vehicle to be classified as a joint operation. When the parties have only rights to assets without obligations for liabilities, or vice versa, the joint arrangement is a joint venture. [*IFRS 11.B30*]

3.6.100   *Primary, not secondary, obligation for liabilities*

3.6.100.10   A guarantee to third parties provided by the parties to the arrangement – e.g. for services provided by or financing provided to the arrangement – does not in itself determine that a joint arrangement is a joint operation. This is because it represents a secondary rather than a primary obligation. [*IFRS 11.B27*]

EXAMPLE 4 – PRIMARY OBLIGATION FOR LIABILITIES

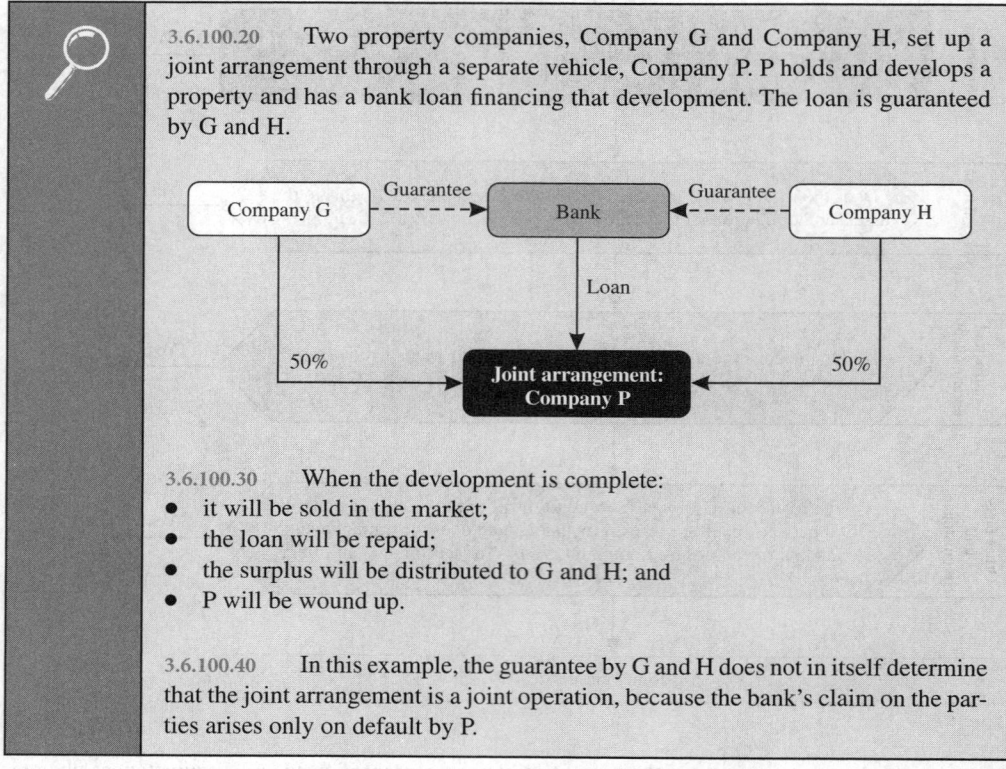

3.6.100.20   Two property companies, Company G and Company H, set up a joint arrangement through a separate vehicle, Company P. P holds and develops a property and has a bank loan financing that development. The loan is guaranteed by G and H.

3.6.100.30   When the development is complete:
- it will be sold in the market;
- the loan will be repaid;
- the surplus will be distributed to G and H; and
- P will be wound up.

3.6.100.40   In this example, the guarantee by G and H does not in itself determine that the joint arrangement is a joint operation, because the bank's claim on the parties arises only on default by P.

3.6.100.50   Similarly, an obligation for unpaid or additional capital does not result in joint operation classification, because this also does not represent a primary obligation. [*IFRS 11.B27*]

3.6.100.60   Therefore, in our view in order to have obligations for the liabilities, the obligation should:
- be a primary, rather than a secondary, obligation; and
- represent a non-contingent, ongoing obligation, rather than an obligation that will be settled if and when a certain event occurs.

3.6.110   *Unit of account*

3.6.110.10   The unit of account of a joint arrangement is the *activity* that two or more parties have agreed to control jointly. A party assesses its rights to the assets and obligations for the liabilities relating to that activity. The whole of an activity is classified, in its entirety, as either a joint operation or a joint venture. [*IFRS 11.BC35*]

3.6.110.20   The parties could undertake different activities within a single vehicle and have different rights to the assets and obligations for the liabilities relating to these different activities. However, even though this situation is conceptually possible, it is expected to be rare in practice. [*IFRS 11.BC36*]

3.6.110.30   Although the unit of account is the activity, it is not clear how this concept should be applied in practice. For example, IFRS 11 includes an illustrative example of a joint arrangement that undertakes both manufacturing and distribution activities to third party customers. Although the joint arrangement appears to have two activities, the type of joint arrangement in this illustrative example is determined at the vehicle level, rather than the activity level. This implies that when the arrangement is structured through a single vehicle, the unit of account could not generally be at a lower level than the vehicle itself. [*IFRS 11.IE23–IE28*]

3.6.120   *Framework agreements*

3.6.120.10   Parties may be bound by a framework agreement that sets up the general contractual terms for:
- undertaking one or more activities; and
- establishing different joint arrangements for specific activities that form part of the agreement. [*IFRS 11.18*]

3.6.120.20   Even though those joint arrangements are governed under the same framework agreement, the classification of each arrangement may differ if the parties' rights and obligations differ. Therefore, joint operations and joint ventures can co-exist when the parties undertake different activities that form part of the same framework agreement. [*IFRS 11.18*]

EXAMPLE 5 – FRAMEWORK AGREEMENT COVERING MULTIPLE JOINT ARRANGEMENTS

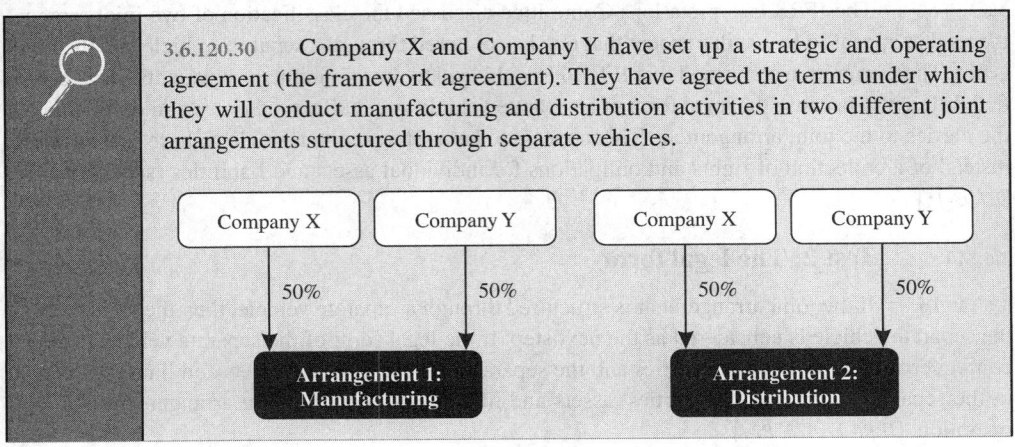

3.6.120.30   Company X and Company Y have set up a strategic and operating agreement (the framework agreement). They have agreed the terms under which they will conduct manufacturing and distribution activities in two different joint arrangements structured through separate vehicles.

> **3.6.120.40**   Each joint arrangement is analysed individually and separately to determine its classification, even though both joint arrangements are governed by a single framework agreement. This could result in one arrangement being classified as a joint venture and the other being classified as a joint operation. [*IFRS 11.IE14–IE28*]

3.6.130   Test 1: The structure

3.6.130.10   A joint arrangement not structured through a separate vehicle is classified as a joint operation. A joint arrangement structured through a separate vehicle can be either a joint venture or a joint operation. [*IFRS 11.B16, B19*]

3.6.130.20   A 'separate vehicle' is a separately identifiable financial structure – including separate legal entities or entities recognised by statute, regardless of whether those entities have legal personality. [*IFRS 11.A*]

3.6.130.30   In our view, in order to have a 'separately identifiable financial structure' and therefore a separate vehicle, the structure should have some sort of legal form – i.e. entities recognised by law or statute. This means that the following examples, in isolation, would not be separate vehicles: a set of accounting records, a bank account, or an operating segment in the context of IFRS 8.

3.6.130.40   This interpretation gives meaning to the test of whether there is a separate vehicle, which would be unnecessary if the threshold were as low as a bank account, for example. It is also consistent with the subsequent tests relating to legal form (see 3.6.140) and contractual arrangements (see 3.6.170).

3.6.130.50   The structure of a joint arrangement may therefore be decisive in determining the parties' rights and obligations arising from the arrangement, because the absence of a separate vehicle means that the joint arrangement is a joint operation. In such situations, entities need not consider the additional steps of the classification analysis.

3.6.130.60   The IFRS Interpretations Committee discussed the classification of two joint arrangements that appear to be similar except that one is structured through a separate vehicle and the other is not. The Committee confirmed that IFRS 11 could lead to the two joint arrangements being classified differently because the legal form of a separate vehicle could affect the rights and obligations of the parties to the joint arrangement. This appears to be a reference to a single right to the net assets instead of a collection of rights and obligations for individual assets and liabilities (see 3.6.80.10). [*IU 03-15*]

3.6.140   Test 2: The legal form

3.6.140.10   If the joint arrangement is structured through a separate vehicle, then the legal form of the separate vehicle is considered as the next step. If the legal form of the separate vehicle does not confer separation between the parties and the separate vehicle – i.e. the assets and liabilities placed in the separate vehicle are the parties' assets and liabilities – then the joint arrangement is a joint operation. [*IFRS 11.B22, B24*]

EXAMPLE 6 – LEGAL FORM DOES NOT CONFER SEPARATION

3.6.140.20   Company X and Company Y set up a joint arrangement through a separate vehicle, Company D, to perform construction services. The main feature of the legal form of the separate vehicle is that X and Y themselves, and not D, have rights to the assets and obligations for the liabilities.

3.6.140.30   In this example, the legal form of the separate vehicle does not confer separation between the parties and the vehicle. Therefore, the joint arrangement is classified as a joint operation, and no consideration of the additional steps of the classification analysis is required. [*IFRS 11.IE2–IE8*]

3.6.150 *Separate vehicles with no legal personality*

3.6.150.10   In most cases, we expect that a separate vehicle will confer legal separation between the parties and the vehicle. Therefore, for joint arrangements structured through separate vehicles, the parties will need to consider further steps in the classification analysis to determine how to classify the joint arrangement.

3.6.150.20   As an exception, in some jurisdictions partnerships confer no separation between the parties and the vehicle itself – i.e. the assets and liabilities placed in the separate vehicle are those of the partners. Those partnerships are therefore classified as joint operations.

3.6.160 *Unlimited liability vehicles*

3.6.160.10   It is possible for a separate vehicle to have a separate legal personality and for the parties to have unlimited liability. In such cases, the unlimited nature of the parties' liability will not, in itself, cause the joint arrangement to be classified as a joint operation.

3.6.160.20   This is because such an unlimited liability vehicle usually provides the parties with a secondary obligation for all of the vehicle's liabilities, rather than a primary obligation for each of the vehicle's liabilities (see 3.6.100). If the liabilities are those of the vehicle, then the unlimited nature of the parties' liability is essentially:
- a guarantee of all of the vehicle's liabilities; or
- an open-ended obligation for uncalled capital, which is not a direct and primary obligation for the vehicle's liabilities.

3.6.160.30   In addition, in such vehicles the parties are unlikely to have rights to the assets, which is also required for joint operation classification (see 3.6.90).

3.6.170 **Test 3: The contractual arrangement**

3.6.170.10   The test at Step 3 of the analysis is to identify whether, in spite of the structure and legal form indicating that the arrangement is a joint venture, the contractual terms specify that the parties have rights to the assets and obligations for the liabilities of the arrangement. If so, then the arrangement is a joint operation. [*IFRS 11.B26–B27*]

EXAMPLE 7 – OPERATING AGREEMENT CONFERS DIRECT RIGHTS AND OBLIGATIONS

3.6.170.20   Company X and Company Y set up a joint arrangement through a separate vehicle, Company H, to undertake oil and gas exploration, development and production. H's legal form confers separation between the parties and the separate vehicle – i.e. the assets and liabilities of the separate vehicle are considered to be its own.

3.6.170.30   In addition, X and Y set up a joint operating agreement (contractual arrangement). This specifies that the rights and obligations arising from H's activities are shared between X and Y in proportion to each party's holdings. In particular, X and Y share the rights and obligations arising from:
- the exploration and development permits granted to H;
- the production obtained; and
- all related costs.

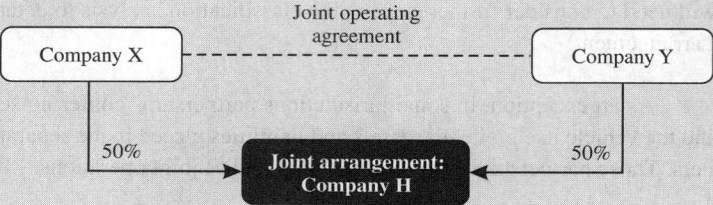

3.6.170.40   Because the arrangement is structured through a separate vehicle, X and Y consider the legal form. The legal form confers separation between the parties and the separate vehicle, which is an initial indication that the joint arrangement is a joint venture. However, because the contractual terms provide the parties with rights to the assets and obligations for the liabilities, that initial indication is reversed and the joint arrangement is concluded to be a joint operation.
[*IFRS 11.IE34–IE43*]

3.6.170.50   In our view, in order for the contractual terms to result in classification as a joint operation, the contractual terms need to give primary obligations for the liabilities and direct rights to the assets, in spite of there being a vehicle with separate legal personality. This may be difficult to achieve in many jurisdictions. We expect that relatively few arrangements structured through separate vehicles will be joint operations as a result of this step of the classification analysis. For further discussion, see 3.6.230.

3.6.180   **Test 4: Other facts and circumstances**

3.6.180.10   The last step of the analysis is to identify whether, in spite of the legal form and contractual arrangement indicating that the arrangement is a joint venture, other facts and circumstances:
- give the parties rights to *substantially all* of the economic benefits relating to the arrangement (asset test); and

- cause the arrangement to depend on the parties on a *continuous* basis for settling its liabilities (liability test). [*IFRS 11.B29–B32*]

3.6.180.20   If so, then the arrangement is a joint operation. [*IFRS 11.B30*]

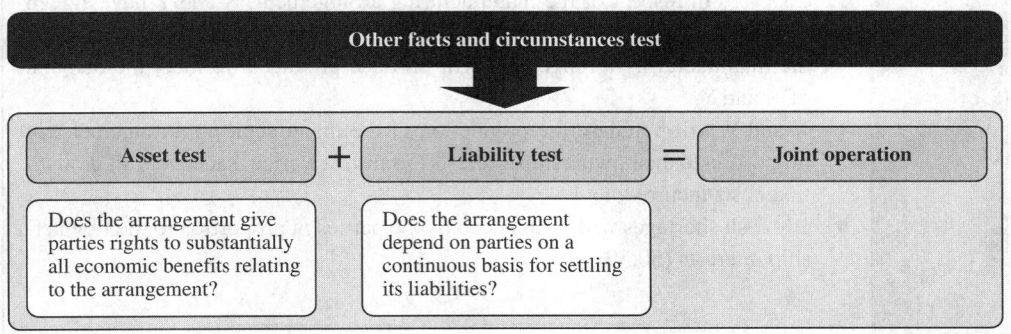

3.6.180.25   The IFRS Interpretations Committee noted that the test of other facts and circumstances is *not* a test of whether the parties are closely or fully involved with the operation of the separate vehicle. [*IU 03-15*]

3.6.180.30   The Committee also clarified that the other facts and circumstances test focuses on whether those facts and circumstances create enforceable rights to the assets and obligations for the liabilities. [*IU 03-15, 05-14*]

3.6.180.40   Only when both the asset test *and* the liability test are met, is the arrangement classified as a joint operation. [*IFRS 11.B30*]

3.6.180.50   The discussion that follows in 3.6.190–230 starts with a base case that is derived from IFRS 11; the base case establishes the principle in the standard in analysing other facts and circumstances. The base case is followed by variations that deal first with the asset test (see 3.6.200) and then the liability test (see 3.6.210).

3.6.190   *The base case*

3.6.190.10   When the activities of an arrangement are designed to provide output to the parties and the arrangement is limited in its ability to sell to third parties, this indicates that the parties may have rights to substantially all the economic benefits of the arrangement's assets. Such an arrangement also results in the liabilities incurred by the arrangement being, in substance, satisfied by the cash flows received from the parties through their purchase of the output. When the parties are substantially the only source of cash flows contributing to the arrangement's operations, this indicates that the parties have an obligation for the liabilities relating to the arrangement. [*IFRS 11.B31–B32*]

EXAMPLE 8A – OTHER FACTS AND CIRCUMSTANCES – BASE CASE

3.6.190.20   Company X and Company Y set up a strategic and operating agreement (the framework agreement). The agreement sets out the terms under which they will conduct the manufacturing and distribution of product P. The joint manufacturing arrangement is structured through a separate vehicle whose legal form confers separation between the parties and the separate vehicle.

3.6.190.30   In respect of the manufacturing arrangement, X and Y have agreed the following:

- the manufacturing arrangement will produce product P to meet the demand of X and Y;
- X and Y will purchase the production of the manufacturing arrangement, in proportion to their ownership interests (50:50), at a price that covers all production costs incurred; and
- any cash shortages will be financed by the parties in proportion to their ownership interests (50:50).

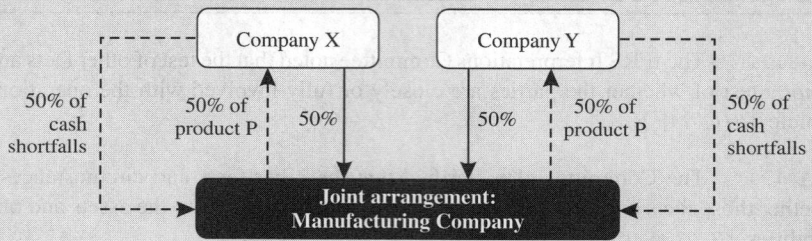

3.6.190.40   In this example, the manufacturing arrangement is structured through a separate vehicle whose legal form confers separation from the parties. There is therefore an initial indication that the arrangement is a joint venture. The contractual terms do not amend or change the rights and obligations of the parties, and therefore do not reverse that initial indication.

3.6.190.50   However, considering other facts and circumstances leads to the conclusion that the arrangement is a joint operation because X and Y:

- have committed to purchase all of the production manufactured and therefore have rights to substantially all the economic benefits of the arrangement's assets; and
- have an obligation for the arrangement's liabilities, because they are required to provide sufficient cash flows through purchases and additional cash calls to enable the arrangement to settle its liabilities on a continuous basis.
[*IFRS 11.IE14–IE18*]

3.6.200   *The asset test*

3.6.200.10   The discussion that follows considers variations from the base case in 3.6.190 that deal with the asset test – i.e. whether the parties have rights to substantially all of the economic benefits relating to the arrangement. Examples 8B to 8H are modifications of Example 8A.

EXAMPLE 8B – OTHER FACTS AND CIRCUMSTANCES – JOINT ARRANGEMENT SELLS SUBSTANTIALLY
ALL OUTPUT TO THIRD PARTIES

3.6.200.20   Modifying Example 8A, if the manufacturing arrangement distributes the products to third party customers instead of to X and Y, then it becomes a self-financed arrangement that has a trade of its own. The arrangement assumes demand, inventory and credit risks, and does not depend on the parties to be able to carry out its activities on a continuous basis. In addition, because X and Y do not have the right to purchase the products, they do not have rights to substantially all of the economic benefits of the arrangement's assets.

3.6.200.30   Therefore, in this example, the arrangement fails the asset test and is classified as a joint venture. [*IFRS 11.IE23–IE28*]

3.6.200.40   For further discussion about the level of output that could be sold to a third party without failing the requirement for the parties to have rights to 'substantially all' economic benefits of the arrangement, see 3.6.200.210–290.

3.6.200.50   Following the IFRIC clarification in 3.6.180.30, for the parties to have rights to the economic benefits relating to the arrangement, those rights have to be legal or contractual. Accordingly, an intention by the parties to take substantially all of the output of the arrangement is not in itself sufficient to conclude that the parties have rights to economic benefits of the arrangement. This is because having an intention to purchase output does not amount to an enforceable right. [*IU 03-15, 05-14*]

EXAMPLE 8C – OTHER FACTS AND CIRCUMSTANCES – INTENTION TO PURCHASE OUTPUT

3.6.200.60   Modifying Example 8A, Company X and Company Y intend to purchase all of product P; however, they have no contractual right or obligation to do so. Therefore, X and/or Y could legally refuse to take the output or the joint arrangement could legally refuse to sell to X and Y, and instead sell to third parties.

3.6.200.70   Without a contract to purchase the output, the parties do not have an enforceable right to take the output produced by the joint arrangement. Therefore, the requirement for the parties to have rights to substantially all of the economic benefits relating to the arrangement is not met. Accordingly, in this example, the asset test is failed and the arrangement is a joint venture. [*IU 03-15, 05-14*]

3.6.200.80   Although Example 8C focuses on the asset test, the example is also relevant to the liability test (see 3.6.210). This is because the parties cannot have an in-substance obligation for the liabilities of the arrangement unless they have an obligation to purchase substantially all of the output.

EXAMPLE 8D – OTHER FACTS AND CIRCUMSTANCES – PURCHASE OF OUTPUT DISPROPORTIONATE TO INTERESTS

3.6.200.90   Modifying Example 8A, Company X and Company Y are contracted to purchase product P in the ratio of 70:30, even though they have a 50:50 interest in the joint arrangement.

3.6.200.100   IFRS 11 refers to 'the parties' as having rights to substantially all economic benefits of the assets of the arrangement. The standard refers to the parties collectively, and does not address the relative rights of the parties and how those rights are split among the parties. For further discussion of the definition of 'parties' in IFRS 11, see 3.6.200.180. [*IFRS 11.B31*]

3.6.200.110   Therefore, in our view the disproportionate purchase of output in relation to the parties' interests in the joint arrangement would meet the asset test. Accordingly, in the absence of other indicators to the contrary, the joint arrangement is a joint operation.

3.6.200.120   In Example 8D, the difference between the parties' obligation to purchase output and their interests is plus or minus 40 percent. However, in some cases the difference may be more extreme – e.g. one of the parties might take 100 percent of the output – and it may be unclear whether the asset test is met. In these cases, careful analysis would be needed to identify the reason why the parties take the output in such extreme proportions and to identify who has the rights and obligations to the arrangement.

EXAMPLE 8E – OTHER FACTS AND CIRCUMSTANCES – ONE PARTY PURCHASES 100% OF OUTPUT

3.6.200.130   Modifying Example 8A, assume that the joint arrangement is an oil refinery to which Company X and Company Y supply oil to be refined. However, in the beginning of the operation only X is supplying oil to the refinery and receiving 100% of the output produced. Y's field will only start its production in two years' time because it is still under development. Once the production starts, each party will have a right to supply oil to the refinery and receive output in proportion to their ownership interests.

3.6.200.140   In our view, even with an extreme disproportionate purchase of the output in relation to the parties' interests, the asset test would still be met. In this example, the current output taken by X is temporary and as soon as both parties start production, the output will be shared on a proportionate basis. Accordingly, in the absence of other indicators to the contrary, the joint arrangement is a joint operation.

3.6.200.150   Another example in which extreme disproportion arises on a temporary basis, which is common in the energy and natural resources sector, is carried interest arrangements. In such arrangements, the parties may agree that one party funds the other party's share of development costs in return for receiving the other party's share of the output until the full amount is repaid; in many cases, this agreement is between the parties to the arrangement and does not affect the joint arrangement itself.

This agreement results in one party taking 100 percent of the output until the carried interest is repaid. In our view, in the absence of other indicators to the contrary, such joint arrangements should be classified as joint operations.

3.6.200.160   In Example 8E, the output of the joint arrangement is a service – refining oil. IFRS 11 does not state that the output needs to be physical; the standard only requires that by taking the output the parties to the arrangement receive substantially all of the economic benefit of the joint arrangement's assets. In our view, it is reasonable to assume that if the economic benefit provided by the arrangement is a service, then that is the output. [*IFRS 11.B31*]

3.6.200.170   Examples 8D and 8E assume that the parties that have joint control take all of the output of the joint arrangement. They do not deal with the situation in which a third party investor in the joint arrangement – i.e. a party who does not share the joint control – commits to take part of the output.

3.6.200.180   Throughout IFRS 11, the term 'parties' is used to denote any party to the arrangement, whereas the term 'parties that have joint control' (or similar) is used to refer to those with joint control. On this basis, when assessing whether 'the parties' have rights to the economic benefits of the arrangement, in our view the joint controllers *and* other investors in the arrangement should be considered. In this context, 'other investors' do not necessarily have to be equity investors. [*IFRS 11.11*]

EXAMPLE 8F – OTHER FACTS AND CIRCUMSTANCES – INVESTOR WITHOUT JOINT CONTROL PURCHASES SOME OUTPUT

3.6.200.190   Modifying Example 8A, assume that Company X and Company Y each have a 40% interest in the joint arrangement, with investor Z having a 20% interest. Z does not share in joint control. X, Y and Z are contracted to purchase the output in proportion to their interests in the joint arrangement.

3.6.200.200   In our view, because IFRS 11 does not restrict which parties have rights to the economic benefits of the arrangement, in this example the asset test is met and, in the absence of other indicators to the contrary, the joint arrangement is a joint operation.

3.6.200.210   Examples 8A and 8D to 8F assume that the arrangement is designed to provide 100 percent of its output to the parties. IFRS 11 requires the parties to have rights to *substantially* all economic benefits; therefore, a low percentage of output could be sold to a third party without failing the asset test. [*IFRS 11.B31*]

3.6.200.220   IFRS 11 does not provide a bright-line for 'substantially all' and judgement is required in determining whether substantially all of the economic benefits of the arrangement are taken by the parties. It is necessary to determine whether the level of output sold to third parties means that it cannot be concluded that the parties take substantially all of the output and economic benefits from the arrangement.

3.6.200.225   The IFRS Interpretations Committee discussed whether volumes or monetary values of output should be the basis for determining whether the parties to the joint arrangement are taking substantially all of the output. The Committee noted that the economic benefits of the assets of the joint arrangement relate to the cash flows arising from the parties' rights to, and obligations for, the assets. Consequently, the Committee noted that the assessment is based on the monetary value of the output, instead of physical quantities. [*IU 03-15*]

3.6.200.230   IFRS 11 states that if the activities of an arrangement are designed to provide output to the parties and the arrangement is limited in its ability to sell to third parties, then this indicates that the parties have rights to substantially all of the economic benefits of the arrangement's assets. Examples 8A to 8D and 8F assume that the output of the arrangement can be stored. However, in some cases the output cannot be stored and it is unclear whether, in these cases, the output could be sold directly to third parties without failing the asset test. [*IFRS 11.B31*]

3.6.200.235   In some cases, the output of a joint arrangement will be fungible (i.e. exchangeable or interchangeable) and in other cases it will be bespoke (i.e. customised or tailored). The IFRS Interpretations Committee discussed whether this distinction determines the classification of a joint arrangement when performing the asset test. The Committee noted that whether the output is fungible or bespoke is not a determinative factor for the classification of the joint arrangement. [*IU 03-15*]

EXAMPLE 8G – OTHER FACTS AND CIRCUMSTANCES – OUTPUT SOLD DIRECTLY TO THIRD PARTIES WITH PARTIES HAVING RIGHTS TO GROSS PROCEEDS

3.6.200.240   Modifying Example 8A, assume that the joint arrangement produces electricity. Even though Company X and Company Y are contracted to purchase the output, the electricity cannot be stored and has to be sold directly into the grid. Accordingly, X and Y have rights to receive the gross proceeds from the sale of the electricity (directly and without any offset for costs) rather than the electricity itself. The parties are therefore exposed to the credit and price risks relating to the gross proceeds.

3.6.200.250   In our view, the requirement for the parties to have rights to substantially all of the economic benefits of the arrangement is met in this example. In effect, the joint arrangement is delivering the output as a sales agent for the parties because the output cannot be stored. Accordingly, the asset test is met and, in the absence of other indicators to the contrary, the joint arrangement is a joint operation.

3.6.200.260   In Example 8G, the only output of the joint arrangement is electricity. However, in other cases there may be additional outputs – e.g. emissions allowances or by-products of production processes that are sold. In such cases, the parties need to meet the asset test with respect to *all* of the outputs of the joint arrangement – including, for example, the emissions allowances – and the asset test is based on the monetary value of all types of outputs (see 3.6.200.225). [*IU 03-15*]

3.6.200.270   In Example 8G, the output of the joint arrangement cannot be stored. This raises the question of whether the asset test would be met if the output could be stored but is nonetheless sold directly by the joint arrangement with the parties having rights to the *gross proceeds*. In our view, the asset test could still be met in these cases, but before reaching a conclusion it would be necessary to consider who has rights to the output – i.e. is the joint arrangement selling the output on its own behalf (which would fail the asset test, as in Example 8B) or as an agent for the parties (who also assume inventory risk and risks relating to the gross proceeds)?

3.6.200.280   In Example 8A, the manufacturing vehicle sells the output directly to the parties of the arrangement. However, the manufacturing vehicle may sell the output to a distribution vehicle of the same parties. If the distribution vehicle is classified as a joint operation – e.g. because its legal form does not confer separation between the parties and the vehicle itself (see 3.6.140) – then, in our view the asset test could still be met by the manufacturing vehicle. This is because the nature of the joint operation is that the assets and liabilities of the distribution vehicle are effectively those of each party, which is effectively the same as the parties purchasing the output directly. However, in order to achieve this outcome, we believe that the distribution vehicle should have substance – i.e. it is not structured only to achieve a joint operation classification for the manufacturing vehicle.

3.6.200.290   Conversely, if the distribution vehicle is classified as a joint venture, then in our view the manufacturing vehicle would fail the other facts and circumstances test. This is because the parties have no direct rights to the assets or obligations for the liabilities of the distribution vehicle, which means that in effect the output of the manufacturing vehicle is *not* being sold directly to the parties of the arrangement.

3.6.200.300   In our view, the assessment of whether the parties have rights to substantially all of the economic benefits relating to the arrangement should be made at the beginning of the arrangement by looking forward for the entire life of the arrangement (or for the life of the underlying assets, if longer). This is because this assessment considers whether the parties are receiving substantially all of the benefits of the joint arrangement's assets.

EXAMPLE 8H – OTHER FACTS AND CIRCUMSTANCES – PARTIES PURCHASE ALL OUTPUT FOR ONLY PART OF ARRANGEMENT'S LIFE

3.6.200.310   Modifying Example 8A, assume that the joint arrangement is a renewable energy generation plant with a limited life of 25 years. However, Company X and Company Y are contracted to purchase all of the output of the arrangement (energy and green credits) for only five years. Any extension of the parties' purchase agreement after five years requires the agreement of both parties.

3.6.200.320   In this example, X and Y have a contractual right and obligation to purchase the output of the arrangement only for a period that is substantially shorter than the whole life of the arrangement and the output may be sold to third parties after expiry of that period. The extension clause is not considered, because the parties do not have an unconditional right *and* obligation to extend the purchase agreement. [*IU 03-15*]

3.6.200.330   Therefore, we believe that because it is predetermined that the parties do not have rights to substantially all of the future economic benefits relating to the arrangement for the whole life, the asset test is failed and the arrangement is a joint venture.

3.6.210   **The liability test**

3.6.210.10   The discussion that follows considers variations from the base case in 3.6.190 that deal with the liability test – i.e. whether the arrangement depends on the parties on a continuous basis for settling its liabilities. Examples 8I to 8J are mainly modifications of Example 8A.

3.6.210.20   If the liability test is met, then the joint arrangement will be a joint operation if the asset test is also met (see 3.6.200).

EXAMPLE 8I – OTHER FACTS AND CIRCUMSTANCES – TRANSFER PRICING

3.6.210.30   Modifying Example 8A, assume that Company X and Company Y pay a transfer price rather than cost price to purchase product P. The transfer price ensures that the joint arrangement will always make a profit. Additionally, the joint arrangement has no access to funding facilities, not even from the parties.

3.6.210.40   X and Y will provide the cash flow to settle the joint arrangement's liabilities through the transfer price paid for product P; and because the joint arrangement cannot access finance from other sources, this is the only currently available source of cash flow.

3.6.210.50   Therefore, in our view the requirement for the parties to have an in-substance obligation for the liabilities relating to the arrangement is met. This is because the parties are the only source of cash to settle the liabilities of the joint arrangement, and the pricing arrangement ensures that the joint arrangement has sufficient cash to settle its obligations on a continuous basis (see 3.6.210.100). Accordingly, the arrangement meets the liability test and, in the absence of other indicators to the contrary, the joint arrangement is a joint operation.

3.6.210.60   Example 8I illustrates a transfer pricing arrangement that ensures that the joint arrangement receives sufficient cash to settle its obligations on a continuous basis.

EXAMPLE 8J – OTHER FACTS AND CIRCUMSTANCES – MARKET PRICES

3.6.210.70   Modifying Example 8A, assume that Company X and Company Y pay market price rather than cost price to purchase product P. This pricing arrangement means that the joint arrangement could make a profit or a loss (if prices decline). As in Example 8A, the joint arrangement has a liquidity facility provided by the parties.

3.6.210.80   Despite the pricing arrangement, in our view X and Y are still the only source of cash flow to settle the liabilities of the arrangement through purchasing product P. Further, in the event that the price paid for product P does not cover the expenditure incurred by the arrangement, X and Y are the only source of funding available through the liquidity facility that they have provided. Accordingly, X and Y provide sufficient cash to the joint arrangement in order to meet its obligations on

> a continuous basis. Therefore, the liability test is met and, in the absence of other indicators to the contrary, the joint arrangement is a joint operation.

3.6.210.90   In Example 8J, the risk of the pricing arrangement not covering all of the joint arrangement's liabilities is mitigated by the liquidity arrangement provided by the parties. However, in our view the liability test might still be met even without the liquidity arrangement, depending on the relevant facts and circumstances.

3.6.210.100   The IFRS Interpretations Committee discussed whether the fact that the output from the joint arrangement is sold to the parties at *market price* prevents the joint arrangement from being classified as a joint operation. The Committee noted that, on its own, this is not a determinative factor for the classification of the joint arrangement. Instead, the parties consider whether the cash flows provided to the joint arrangement through their purchase of output, along with any other funding that the parties are obliged to provide, will be sufficient to enable the joint arrangement to settle its liabilities on a continuous basis. Therefore, if the parties are contracted to purchase output at market price, then they need to exercise judgement and consider all relevant facts and circumstances when evaluating whether their obligations to provide cash to the joint arrangement are sufficient for the joint arrangement to settle its liabilities on a continuous basis, as well as being substantially the only source of such cash. [*IU 03-15*]

3.6.215   *Financing from a third party*

3.6.215.10   The IFRS Interpretations Committee observed that if the cash flows to the joint arrangement from the sale of output to the parties, along with any other funding that the parties are obliged to provide, satisfy the joint arrangement's liabilities, then third party financing alone would not preclude the classification of the joint arrangement as a joint operation irrespective of whether the financing occurs at inception or during the course of the joint arrangement's operations. The Committee also noted that in this situation, the joint arrangement will, or may, settle some of its liabilities using cash flows from third party financing, but the resulting obligation to the third party finance provider will, in due course, be settled using cash flows that the parties are obliged to provide. [*IU 03-15*]

3.6.220   **Summary of observations**

3.6.220.10   The following table summarises the observations made in 3.6.200–215, indicating whether, in our view each factor considered would preclude classification as a joint operation. The starting point for the summary is the base case discussed in 3.6.190.

	VARIATION FROM THE BASE CASE	PRECLUDE JOINT OPERATION?	REFERENCE
Asset test	Joint arrangement sells substantially all output to third parties	Yes	Example 8B
	Intention to purchase output	Yes	Example 8C
	Purchase of output disproportionate to interests	No	Example 8D

	VARIATION FROM THE BASE CASE	PRECLUDE JOINT OPERATION?	REFERENCE
Asset test (continued)	One party purchases 100% of the output	No, but careful analysis required	3.6.200.120–150 Example 8E
	Output is a service	No	3.6.200.160
	Investor without joint control purchases some output	No	Example 8F
	Small percentage of output sold to a third party	No	3.6.200.210–225
	Output sold directly to third parties with parties having rights to gross proceeds	No	Example 8G, 3.6.200.260–270
	Joint arrangement sells substantially all output to distribution vehicle (joint operation) of the same parties	No	3.6.200.280
	Joint arrangement sells substantially all output to distribution vehicle (joint venture) of the same parties	Yes	3.6.200.290
	Parties purchase all output for only part of arrangement's life	Yes	Example 8H
Liability test	Transfer pricing that ensures a profit	No	Example 8I
	Market prices	No, but careful analysis required	Example 8J, 3.6.210.90–100
	Financing from a third party	No, but careful analysis required	3.6.215

3.6.230 *Comparison with contractual arrangement test*

3.6.230.10   In the contractual arrangement test (see 3.6.170), the contract needs to give the parties rights to the assets and obligations for the liabilities. The facts and circumstances test differs from that.

- In respect of assets, it requires rights to substantially all of the economic benefits of the assets, rather than to ownership of or legal rights to the assets themselves.
- In respect of liabilities, it considers whether the arrangement depends on the parties on a continuous basis for settling its liabilities – i.e. what might be termed an enforceable indirect obligation to provide cash to the arrangement, rather than a direct legal obligation for the arrangement's liabilities.

3.6.230.20   The contractual terms may, however, be facts and circumstances to be considered in this step. Even though contractual terms do not specify that the parties have legal rights to the assets, they may give rights to their economic benefits; and even though they do not explicitly impose legal obligations, they may give enforceable indirect obligations.

3.6.230.30   For example, in certain jurisdictions, a contractual arrangement may override the legal form of a separate vehicle and give the joint operators direct legal rights to the assets and direct obligations for the liabilities of the joint arrangement. This type of contractual arrangement is considered in Test 3 (see 3.6.170). Conversely, a contractual arrangement for the output of the joint arrangement does not provide direct legal rights to the assets or direct obligations for the liabilities. Therefore, this contractual arrangement is only relevant in Step 4 of the analysis (see 3.6.180).

3.6.240 ACCOUNTING FOR JOINT ARRANGEMENTS

3.6.240.10 All parties to a joint arrangement are in the scope of IFRS 11, even if all of those par- ties do not have joint control. The following table is a simplified overview of the general accounting requirements for all parties to a joint arrangement. [*IFRS 11.3*]

	CONSOLIDATED FINANCIAL STATEMENTS	SEPARATE FINANCIAL STATEMENTS
Joint operator	Recognises its assets, liabilities and transactions, including its share of those incurred jointly (see 3.6.260).	
Other party to a joint operation	Recognises its assets, liabilities and transactions, including its share of those incurred jointly, if it has rights to the assets and obligations for the liabilities. Otherwise, it accounts for the joint operation in accordance with the IFRS applicable to that interest – e.g. IAS 28 or IFRS 9. For further discussion, see 3.6.310.	
Joint venturer	Applies the equity method in accordance with IAS 28 (unless certain exemptions in that standard apply). For a discussion of the application of the equity method, and the exemptions therefrom, see chapter 3.5.	Choice between equity method, cost method and in accordance with IFRS 9 (see 3.5.640).
Other party to a joint venture	Applies the equity method in accordance with IAS 28 (unless certain exemptions in that standard apply) if significant influence exists; otherwise, in accordance with IFRS 9 (see 3.6.300).	Choice between equity method, cost method or in accordance with IFRS 9 if significant influence exists; otherwise, in accordance with IFRS 9 (see 3.6.300).

3.6.250 Applicability of common control exemption

3.6.250.10 In our view, the common control exemption in accounting for business combinations also applies to the transfer of investments in joint ventures between investors under common control (see 5.13.20.30). Although IAS 28 does not include an explicit exemption for common control transactions, equity accounting follows the methodology of acquisition accounting. Therefore, we believe that it is appropriate to extend the application of the business combinations common control exemption. For a discussion of the accounting for common control transactions, see chapter 5.13.

3.6.260 Joint operators

3.6.260.10 A joint operator recognises its assets, liabilities and transactions, including its share of those incurred jointly, in both its consolidated and its separate financial statements. These assets, liabilities and transactions are accounted for in accordance with the relevant standards. The joint operator does not additionally account in its consolidated or separate financial statements for its shareholding in the separate vehicle. [*IFRS 11.20–21, 26(a), IU 03-15*]

3.6.260.20 If a joint operation is classified as such because of its structure (see 3.6.130), legal form (see 3.6.140) or contractual arrangement (see 3.6.170), then determining the joint operator's rights and obligations to individual assets and liabilities is generally straightforward. This is because in these cases the contractual terms will usually be clear about the joint operator's rights and obligations to individual assets, liabilities and transactions relating to the joint arrangement.

EXAMPLE 9A – JOINT OPERATION – NO SEPARATE VEHICLE – CONTRACT ESTABLISHES JOINT LEGAL TITLE

3.6.260.30   Company X and Company Y set up a joint arrangement to construct and operate an oil pipeline. The contractual terms between X and Y do not establish a separate vehicle through which these activities are conducted. Therefore, the arrangement is a joint operation (see 3.6.130).

3.6.260.40   Under the contractual terms, X and Y hold joint legal title to all of the assets and are jointly liable for all of the liabilities relating to the arrangement. A joint bank account is set up to handle the cash flows of the arrangement.

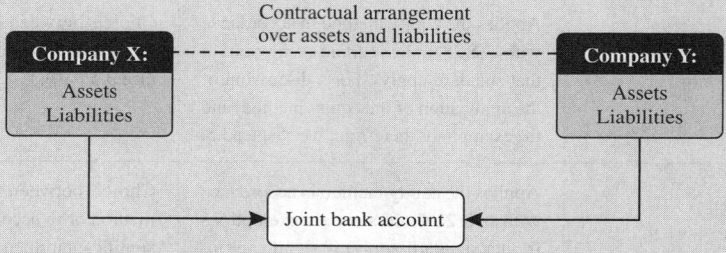

3.6.260.50   At inception of the arrangement, X and Y each contribute 500 to the joint bank account. During the first year of operation, the bank account is used to purchase property, plant and equipment of 100 and to settle expenses of 100.

3.6.260.60   In this example, the contractual terms between X and Y establish their respective rights to the assets and obligations for the liabilities relating to the arrangement, and their respective rights to the corresponding revenues and obligations for the corresponding expenses.

3.6.260.70   Accordingly, X and Y each recognise cash of 400, property, plant and equipment of 50 and expenses of 50 for their respective interest in the arrangement.

EXAMPLE 9B – JOINT OPERATION – SEPARATE VEHICLE DOES NOT CONFER SEPARATION

3.6.260.80   Company X and Company Y set up a joint arrangement in the form of a partnership in which each company has a 50% interest. In accordance with applicable laws, the partnership structure has no legal personality and does not confer separation between the partners and the partnership (see 3.6.150.20) – i.e. the assets and liabilities of the partnership are those of X and Y. Accordingly, the arrangement is a joint operation (see 3.6.140).

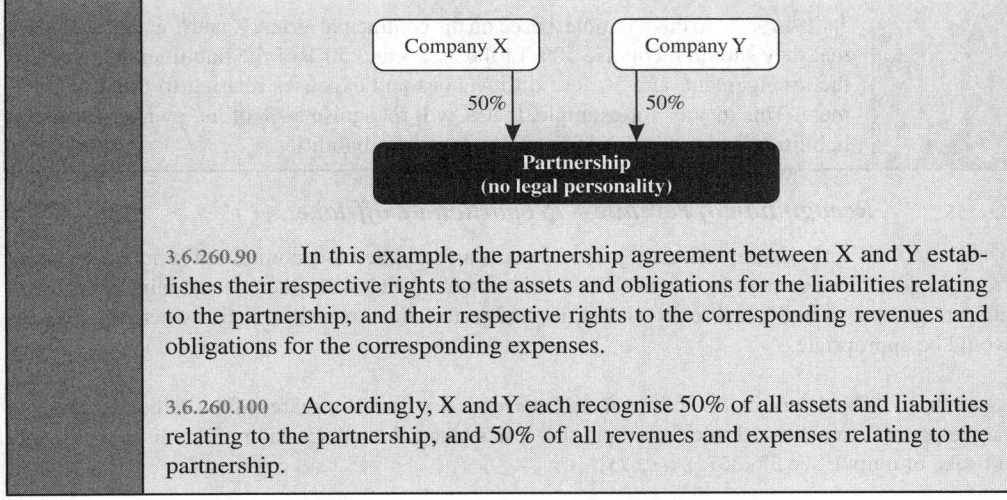

3.6.260.90   In this example, the partnership agreement between X and Y establishes their respective rights to the assets and obligations for the liabilities relating to the partnership, and their respective rights to the corresponding revenues and obligations for the corresponding expenses.

3.6.260.100   Accordingly, X and Y each recognise 50% of all assets and liabilities relating to the partnership, and 50% of all revenues and expenses relating to the partnership.

3.6.260.110   In some cases, the accounting is more complex because the joint operators retain legal title to their respective assets and an obligation for their respective liabilities. However, the contractual terms govern the transactions under the joint arrangement, including the acquisition and disposal of capital assets.

3.6.260.120   In our view, the joint operators may base their accounting in these cases on the contractual terms governing the arrangement's assets and liabilities. Although other approaches might be appropriate depending on the facts and circumstances, we believe that it would not be acceptable for a joint operator to recognise its share of the assets and liabilities on an inconsistent basis – e.g. its share of assets (based on the contractual terms) but 100 percent of its liabilities (not in accordance with the contractual terms).

EXAMPLE 9C – JOINT OPERATION – NO SEPARATE VEHICLE – NO JOINT LEGAL TITLE

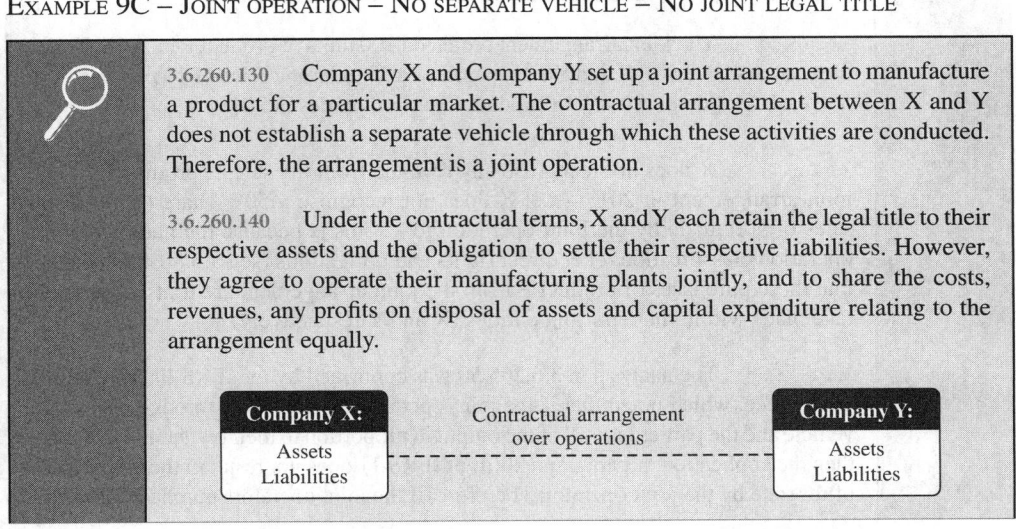

3.6.260.130   Company X and Company Y set up a joint arrangement to manufacture a product for a particular market. The contractual arrangement between X and Y does not establish a separate vehicle through which these activities are conducted. Therefore, the arrangement is a joint operation.

3.6.260.140   Under the contractual terms, X and Y each retain the legal title to their respective assets and the obligation to settle their respective liabilities. However, they agree to operate their manufacturing plants jointly, and to share the costs, revenues, any profits on disposal of assets and capital expenditure relating to the arrangement equally.

> **3.6.260.150** In this example, based on the contractual terms, X and Y each conclude that they should recognise 50% of the assets and 50% of the liabilities relating to the arrangement, and 50% of all revenues and expenses relating to the arrangement. This means, for example, that X will recognise 50% of its 'own' assets and liabilities, and recognise 50% of Y's assets and liabilities.

3.6.265   ***Recognition of revenue – Proportionate off-take***

3.6.265.10   If, as in Example 8A, the joint operators are contractually committed to purchase output from the joint arrangement in proportion to their ownership interests, then determining their rights and obligations to individual assets, liabilities and transactions based on their ownership interests would be appropriate.

3.6.265.20   The determination of revenue, however, is not based on shares of the vehicle's sales, but on the parties' own onward sales of output that it has taken; for a discussion of the disproportionate off-take of output, see 3.6.267. [*IU 03-15*]

EXAMPLE 9D – JOINT OPERATION – PURCHASE OF OUTPUT PROPORTIONATE TO INTERESTS

3.6.265.30   Continuing Example 8A, the following diagram is a brief recap of the structure (joint operation).

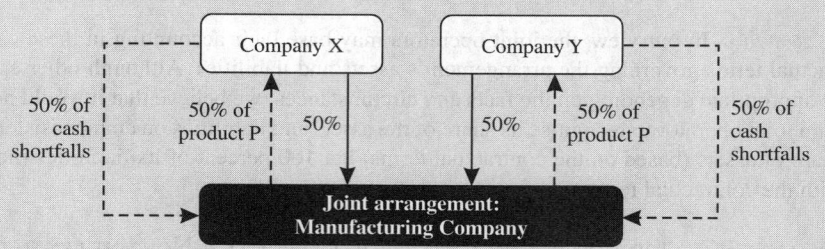

3.6.265.40   The joint arrangement produced 100 units of product P in 2018. Under the contractual terms, X and Y each purchased 50 units at a price of 10 per unit – i.e. 500 each. X did not sell any of product P to third parties in 2018.

3.6.265.50   X does not recognise any revenue from the sale of product P by the joint arrangement in 2018 – i.e. X does not recognise a 50% share (250) of the sales of 500 made by the joint operation to Y. This is because the nature of joint operation classification – i.e. direct rights and obligations (see 3.6.80.10) – means that these purchases of product P from the joint arrangement are transactions that take place within the reporting entities (X and Y respectively).

3.6.265.55   The analysis in 3.6.265.50 was confirmed by the IFRS Interpretations Committee, which noted that if the joint operation is structured through a separate vehicle and the parties take all of the output in proportion to their ownership interests, then the application of paragraph 20(d) of IFRS 11 does not result in the recognition of revenue by the joint operator. Therefore, if the joint operators purchase all of the output from the joint operation in proportion to their rights, then they recognise 'their' revenue only when they sell the output to third parties. For this purpose, third parties do not include other parties that have rights to the assets and obligations for the liabilities relating to the joint operation. [*IFRS 11.20(d), IU 03-15*]

3.6.265.60   In 2019, X sells all of product P to third parties at a price of 11 per unit, and recognises revenue of 550 (50 x 11). Therefore, the total revenue recognised by X (zero in 2018 plus 550 in 2019) does not exceed the revenue from the sale of the output to third parties.

3.6.267   *Recognition of revenue – Disproportionate off-take*

3.6.267.10   As Example 8D illustrates, the joint operators' rights and obligations in respect of the joint arrangement's output may not align with their ownership interests in the arrangement. The IFRS Interpretations Committee noted that the identification of the reasons for the difference between the percentage of ownership interest and the percentage share of the output may provide relevant information and that judgement will be needed to determine the appropriate accounting. [*IU 03-15*]

3.6.267.20   In our view, for transactions between the joint operation and the joint operators that are based on a market price, one acceptable approach is for each joint operator to recognise assets, liabilities and expenses in proportion to its ownership interest and to treat the disproportion in output taken as a sale between it and the other joint operator(s). This approach represents the arrangement as if each joint operator received its share of the output for its ownership interest at cost and then one joint operator sold some of its output to the other joint operator at market price.

3.6.267.30   In our experience, in arrangements in which parties purchase output in disproportion to their ownership interests, transactions are likely to be based on market prices. This is because using market prices ensures a fair sharing of the economic benefits amongst the parties.

EXAMPLE 9E – JOINT OPERATION – PURCHASE OF OUTPUT DISPROPORTIONATE TO INTERESTS

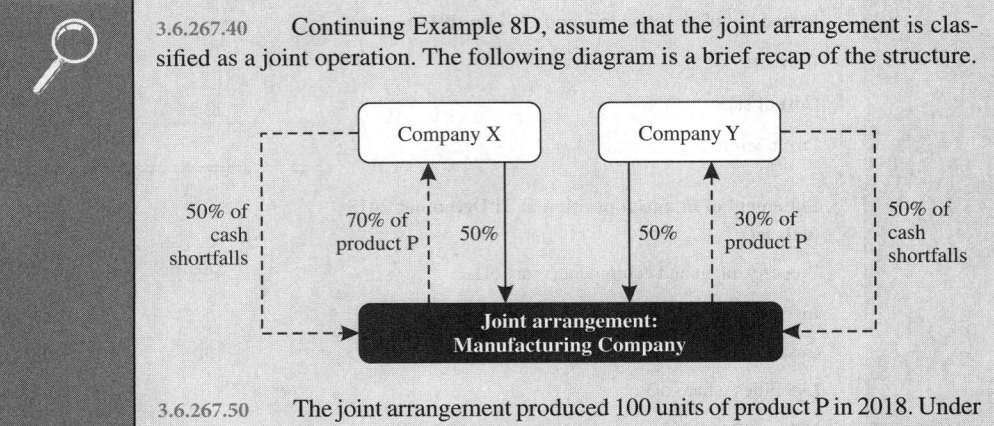

3.6.267.40   Continuing Example 8D, assume that the joint arrangement is classified as a joint operation. The following diagram is a brief recap of the structure.

3.6.267.50   The joint arrangement produced 100 units of product P in 2018. Under the contractual terms, X purchased 70 units and Y purchased 30 units at market price.

3.6.267.60   The following facts are also relevant for this example.

DURING 2018	
Market price of P in 2018 (per unit)	1
Revenue in 2018 (100 units x 1 per unit)	100
P's production costs in 2018 (100 units x 0.7 per unit)	70
Depreciation in 2018 (included in production costs)	10

BALANCES AT 31 DECEMBER 2018	
Property, plant and equipment	990
Liabilities (unpaid expenses)	20
Cash (sale proceeds of 100 minus expenses paid of 40)	60

3.6.267.70   Applying the approach in 3.6.267.20, both X and Y recognise 50% of the arrangement's assets, liabilities and costs. Therefore, each of X and Y recognise 50 units at cost. X recognises the additional 20 units as if they were purchased at market price, and Y recognises revenue from the sale of those 20 units. No other revenue or costs are illustrated in 2018, to isolate the effect of the disproportionate purchase of output.

3.6.267.80   X and Y present the following amounts in the statement of financial position and in the statement of profit or loss and OCI in respect of their interests in the arrangement. [*IFRS 11.20*]

	X	Y
Statement of profit or loss and OCI for 2018 (extract)		
Revenue	-	20[1]
Cost of sales	-	(14)[2]
Profit before tax	-	6
Statement of financial position at 31 December 2018 (extract)		
Property, plant and equipment (share of)	495[3]	495[3]
Inventory (own)	55[4]	21[5]
Cash (share of)	30	30
Liabilities (share of)	(10)	(10)
Net assets	570	536

Notes
1.   Calculated as 20 units x 1 (market price).
2.   Calculated as 20 units x 0.7 (cost).
3.   Calculated as 990 x 50%; the same approach applies to cash and liabilities.
4.   Calculated as (50 units x 0.7) + (20 units x 1).
5.   Calculated as 30 units x 0.7.

3.6.267.90   If the arrangement were to distribute its 2018 profit of 30 (100 - 70), then X and Y would recognise their share of the cash received of 15; at the same time, their respective share of the joint arrangement's cash balance would decrease by 15. Consequently, the distribution would have no effect on the financial statements of X and Y.

3.6.267.100   In circumstances other than those described in Example 9E – e.g. if the joint operators are contracted to purchase output at cost or at a price designed to achieve a break-even result – it may be appropriate to apply an approach based on the joint operators' contractual rights for the output of the arrangement.

3.6.270   Sale, contribution or purchase of assets between joint operator and its joint operation

3.6.270.10   When a joint operator sells or contributes assets to a joint operation – i.e. a downstream transaction – such transactions are in effect transactions with other parties to the joint operation. The joint operator recognises gains and losses from such transactions only to the extent of the other parties' interests in the joint operation. The full amount of any loss is recognised immediately by the joint operator, to the extent that these transactions provide evidence of impairment of any assets to be sold or contributed. [*IFRS 11.22, B34–B35*]

3.6.270.20   When a joint operator purchases assets from a joint operation – i.e. an upstream transaction – it does not recognise its share of the gains or losses until those assets have been sold to a third party. The joint operator's share of any losses is recognised immediately, to the extent that these transactions provide evidence of impairment of those assets. [*IFRS 11.22, B36–B37*]

3.6.280   Joint venturers

3.6.280.10   Joint venturers account for their interest in the joint venture in accordance with IAS 28 (see chapter 3.5). [*IFRS 11.24*]

3.6.280.20   Joint venturers may also enter into transactions with the joint venture itself. For a discussion of transactions between a joint venturer and its joint venture, see 3.5.430–485.

3.6.290   Other parties to joint arrangement

3.6.290.10   Other parties to a joint arrangement are also required to determine the type of joint arrangement for those parties with joint control, because this subsequently determines their accounting (see 3.6.300–310). This may be difficult when that party has limited information on the contractual terms and other facts and circumstances relating to those parties with joint control. [*IFRS 11.23, 25*]

3.6.290.20   In practice, one scenario in which an issue may arise is if the other party has rights to, and obligations for, the underlying assets and liabilities in a joint venture. In this scenario, the parties with joint control have rights to only the net assets of the arrangement. We expect such scenarios to be unlikely in practice, because this would result in the other party having more direct rights to, and obligations for, the underlying assets and liabilities than the parties with joint control themselves.

3.6.300   *Other party to joint venture*

3.6.300.10   In their consolidated financial statements, other parties to a joint venture account for their interests in the joint venture in accordance with IFRS 9, or IAS 28 if significant influence exists. [*IFRS 11.25*]

(S) **3.6.300.20**   In their separate financial statements, other parties to a joint venture account for their interest in the joint venture in accordance with IFRS 9. If significant influence exists, then the interest may also be accounted for at cost or using the equity method (see 3.5.640). [*IFRS 11.27(b), IAS 27.10*]

(S) **3.6.300.30**   However, if the interest in the joint venture, when significant influence exists, is accounted for in accordance with IFRS 9 in the consolidated financial statements (see 3.5.100), then the same accounting is adopted for the separate financial statements. [*IAS 27.11*]

(S) 3.6.310   *Other party to joint operation*

3.6.310.10   If other parties to a joint operation have rights to the assets and obligations for the liabilities of that joint operation, then in both their consolidated and their separate financial statements they account for their interests in the same way as a joint operator (see 3.6.260–270 and 317). If such a party does not have those rights and obligations, then it accounts for its interest in accordance with the standard applicable to that interest. That is, if the joint operation is a separate legal entity, then the other party accounts for its interest in accordance with IAS 28 – if it has significant influence (see 3.5.30) – or IFRS 9. If the joint operation is not a separate legal entity, then the other party accounts for the assets and liabilities relating to its interest in accordance with the standards applicable to them – e.g. IAS 16 for property, plant and equipment. [*IFRS 11.23, 27(a)*]

3.6.310.20   However, IFRS 11 does not specify whether the assessment of other parties' rights to the assets and obligations for the liabilities is to be performed in the same way as the assessment for a joint operator – e.g. in response of a joint arrangement, in which the classification of the joint operation is the result of the other facts and circumstances test (see 3.6.180). In this case, in our view, one approach is to perform the same assessment as for a joint operator. Under this approach, if the other party to a facts-and-circumstances joint operation has the equivalent rights to the assets and obligations for the liabilities as the joint operators, then it accounts for its interest in the joint operation in accordance with the guidance in IFRS 11 (see 3.6.260–270 and 317).

3.6.310.30   We believe that this approach is acceptable even if the other party has significant influence, because the accounting for the rights and obligations that the other party has in the joint operation follows the guidance in IFRS 11. In such a case, no conflict with IAS 28 arises because, through the lens of the other party's IFRS 11 analysis and accounting, there are no remaining net assets or results in the separate legal entity to which equity accounting could be applied.

3.6.313	**CHANGES OF INTERESTS AND CHANGES IN STATUS OF JOINT ARRANGEMENTS**

3.6.315   Joint ventures

3.6.315.10   For a discussion of changes in the status of joint ventures, see 3.5.510–610.

3.6.316   Joint operations*

3.6.317   *Acquisition of interest in joint operation#*

3.6.317.10   If a joint operator acquires an interest in a joint operation that constitutes a business, then the joint operator applies the relevant principles for business combination accounting (see chapter 2.6). This includes the recognition of goodwill, the recognition of deferred taxes arising from initial recognition of the identifiable assets acquired and liabilities assumed, and recognising acquisition-related costs in profit or loss. However, the principles for business combination accounting do not apply if the formation of the joint operation coincides with the formation of the business. [*IFRS 11.21A, B33A–B33B*]

3.6.317.15   These principles apply to the acquisition of both the initial interest and additional interests of the joint operation in respect of the acquired interest. However, when an additional interest is acquired (without obtaining control), previously held interests in the joint operation are not remeasured. [*IFRS 11.21A, B33C*]

EXAMPLE 10A – ACQUISITION OF INTEREST IN JOINT OPERATION

3.6.317.20   Company P acquires 50% of the shares of existing Joint Operation J for cash of 1,100, and incurs transaction costs of 20. J operates a producing oil field and is considered by P to be a business.

3.6.317.30   The fair value of J's identifiable net assets is 2,000, which includes a fair value uplift of 500 on the assets. The tax base of the net assets in J's financial statements is equal to their carrying amount at the date of acquisition – i.e. 1,500. The tax rate is 20%.

3.6.317.40   P records the following entries.

	DEBIT	CREDIT
Identifiable assets acquired (2,000 x 50%)	1,000	
Goodwill (1,100 - (1,000 - 50[(1)]))	150	
Deferred tax ((500 x 20%) x 50%) (see 3.13.850)		50
Cash		1,100
To record acquisition of joint control in J		
Profit or loss	20	
Cash		20
To record acquisition costs		

Note
1.   Deferred tax on the fair value uplift.

609

EXAMPLE 10B – ACQUISITION OF ADDITIONAL INTEREST IN JOINT OPERATION

3.6.317.50   Continuing Example 10A, five years later Company P acquires an additional interest of 10% in Joint Operation J for cash of 300, and incurs transaction costs of 10. J remains a joint operation.

3.6.317.60   The fair value of J's identifiable net assets is 2,500, which includes a fair value uplift of 1,000 on the assets. The tax base of the net assets in J's financial statements is equal to their carrying amount at the date of acquisition – i.e. 1,500. The tax rate is 20%.

3.6.317.70   P records the following entries.

	DEBIT	CREDIT
Identifiable assets acquired (2,500 x 10%)	250	
Goodwill (300 - (250 - 20⁽¹⁾))	70	
Deferred tax ((1,000 x 20%) x 10%) (see 3.13.850)		20
Cash		300
To record acquisition of additional interest in J		
Profit or loss	10	
Cash		10
To record acquisition costs		

Note
1.   Deferred tax on the fair value uplift.

3.6.317.80   Previously held interests in J (50%) are not remeasured as a result of the additional interest acquired.

3.6.317.90   The requirements above do not apply if the joint operation does not represent a business. The IFRS Interpretations Committee discussed whether previously held interests in the assets and liabilities of a joint operation that does not constitute a business should be remeasured if the investor obtains joint control or control over the joint operation. The Committee noted that a cost-based approach is used for an asset acquisition in which the asset or group of assets does not meet the definition of a business, and that any existing assets are generally not remeasured. [*IFRS 3.2(b), 3.A, IU 01-16*]

3.6.318   FORTHCOMING REQUIREMENTS

3.6.318.10   *Annual Improvements to IFRSs 2015–2017 Cycle – Amendments to IFRS 11* clarify how an entity accounts for an increase in its interest in a joint operation that meets the definition of a business. Under the amendments, when an entity that participates in a joint operation subsequently obtains joint control, it does not remeasure its previously held interests. [*IFRS 11.B33CA*]

3.6.319   *Change in status of joint operation*

3.6.319.10   A change in circumstances in a joint operation can lead to a change in status in such a way that joint control no longer exists and the arrangement is no longer a joint operation. In our view, such a change can also affect the accounting of other parties, who had rights to the assets and obligations for the liabilities of the former joint operation. Because the arrangement is no longer a joint operation, the requirements in IFRS 11 for those other parties (see 3.6.310.10) no longer apply. We believe that another party to a facts-and-circumstances joint operation that had selected the approach described in 3.6.310.20–30 should stop accounting for its interest under IFRS 11 once the arrangement is no longer a joint operation. In these cases, the other party subsequently recognises its interest as follows.

- If it has significant influence and accounts for its interest in accordance with IAS 28, then it uses the net carrying amount of the assets and liabilities previously recognised under IFRS 11 as the deemed cost for the equity-accounted investment.
- If it accounts for its interest in accordance with IFRS 9, then it initially recognises it at fair value. Any difference between fair value and the net carrying amount of the assets and liabilities previously recognised under IFRS 11 is recognised immediately in profit or loss. [*IAS 28.10, IFRS 9.5.1.1*]

3.6.320   FINANCIAL STATEMENTS OF JOINT VENTURES

3.6.330   Accounting by joint ventures for contributions received

3.6.330.10   IFRS addresses the accounting for joint ventures from the point of view of the joint venturers. However, IFRS is silent on what treatment should be applied by the joint venture itself. If a joint venture prepares its own financial statements, then issues arise about how the joint venture should account for contributions received.

3.6.330.20   The accounting treatment applied by the venturers is independent of the treatment applied by the joint venture itself – i.e. the joint venturers will reverse the accounting applied by the joint venture when they account for their interest in the joint venture. This issue is therefore relevant only to the financial statements of the joint venture.

3.6.340   *Contributed assets do not comprise a business*

3.6.340.10   If assets not comprising a business are contributed to a joint venture in exchange for equity instruments, then the joint venture applies IFRS 2 and measures the contributed assets at fair value (see 4.5.90). The contribution of assets is in the scope of IFRS 2 because the joint venture has received goods and paid for these goods in shares (see 4.5.20.10). [*IFRS 2.5*]

3.6.350   *Contributed assets comprise a business*

3.6.350.10   An issue arises about how to account for contributed assets that constitute a business when that business is contributed on formation of the joint venture. This is because IFRS 2 scopes out any contribution that constitutes a business (see 4.5.260) and IFRS 3 contains a scope exception for a business that is contributed on the formation of a joint venture in the financial statements of the joint venture itself. [*IFRS 2.5, 3.2(a)*]

3.6.350.20   In the absence of specific guidance, some entities use fair values and others use book values to record the contributions received from venturers. In our view, the joint venture should choose an accounting policy to recognise such contributions at either fair values or book values. This accounting policy should be applied consistently to similar contributions on formation of a joint venture.

3.6.350.30   If the contribution is measured using fair values, then we believe that the joint venture should apply IFRS 3 (see 2.6.600) by analogy in accounting for the contributed assets at fair value. Acquisition accounting under IFRS 3 is the subject of chapter 2.6.

3.6.350.35   If the contribution is measured using book values, then we believe that the joint venture should apply the guidance described in 5.13.60.10 by analogy.

3.6.350.40   However, in our view this applies only to a contribution received by a newly created joint venture. We believe that the step-up to fair value should not be applied when the joint venture is itself a former subsidiary, in relation to its own assets. This is because there is no contribution received and the change of control of an entity is not a reason for this entity to step up its own assets.

3.6.350.50   The contribution of a business that occurs subsequent to the formation of the joint venture is accounted for in accordance with IFRS 3. This is because the IFRS 3 scope exception applies only on formation. [*IFRS 3.2(a)*]

3.6.360   FINANCIAL STATEMENTS OF JOINT OPERATION STRUCTURED AS SEPARATE ENTITY

3.6.360.10   IFRS addresses the accounting for joint operations from the point of view of the joint operators. However, IFRS is silent on what treatment should be applied by the joint operation itself.

3.6.360.20   The IFRS Interpretations Committee noted that the financial statements of the joint operation itself should comply with all relevant standards – i.e. they include the assets, liabilities, revenue and expenses of the separate vehicle. However, the Committee noted that, in identifying those assets and liabilities, it is necessary to understand the joint operators' rights and obligations relating to the assets and liabilities and how those rights and obligations affect those assets and liabilities. [*IU 03-15*]

3.6.360.30   If a joint operation is a separate legal entity that prepares its own financial statements, then an issue arises about how the joint operation should account for contributions received.

3.6.360.40   The accounting treatment applied by the joint operators is independent of the treatment applied by the joint operation itself – i.e. the joint operators will reverse the accounting applied by the joint operation when they account for their interest in the joint operation. This issue is therefore relevant only to the financial statements of the joint operation.

3.6.360.50   The scope exclusion for joint ventures in respect of contributed assets that constitute a business when that business is contributed on formation (see 3.6.350.10) also applies to joint operations. In our view, the guidance in 3.6.340–350 in respect of contributions received should also apply in the financial statements of a joint operation housed in a separate vehicle. This is because we believe that the general principles discussed in that guidance have general applicability. [*IFRS 3.2(a)*]

3.6.370   FUTURE DEVELOPMENTS

3.6.370.10   In June 2016, the IASB published Exposure Draft *Definition of a Business – Proposed Amendments to IFRS 3*. The exposure draft proposed to clarify the definition of a business and introduce tests to assess whether a set of acquired assets and activities constitutes a business (see 3.6.317). The final amendments are expected in the second half of 2018.

3.8 Inventories

3.8   Inventories

CURRENTLY EFFECTIVE REQUIREMENTS

This publication reflects IFRS in issue at 1 August 2018, and the currently effective requirements cover annual periods beginning on 1 January 2018.

The requirements related to this topic are mainly derived from the following.

STANDARD	TITLE
IAS 2	Inventories

The currently effective requirements include newly effective requirements arising from IFRS 15 *Revenue from Contracts with Customers,* which is effective for annual periods beginning on or after 1 January 2018. The new requirements may be applied using the retrospective method or the cumulative effect method (see 4.2.510). The impact of the new requirements on the accounting for inventories is reflected in 3.8.10.20, 90, 100.10–20, 230.10–15, 30, 260.10 and 400.30.

FORTHCOMING REQUIREMENTS

The currently effective requirements are affected by the following forthcoming requirements. They are highlighted with a # and the impact is explained in the accompanying boxed text at the references indicated.

In January 2016, the IASB issued IFRS 16 *Leases*, which is effective for annual periods beginning on or after 1 January 2019. See 3.8.209. IFRS 16 is the subject of chapter 5.1A.

FUTURE DEVELOPMENTS

For this topic, there are no future developments.

3.8.10   SCOPE AND DEFINITION

3.8.10.10   Inventories are assets:
- held for sale in the ordinary course of business (finished goods);
- in the process of production for sale (work in progress); or
- in the form of materials or supplies to be consumed in the production process or in the rendering of services (raw materials and consumables). [*IAS 2.6*]

3.8.10.20   Inventory may include intangible assets that are being produced for resale – e.g. software. Inventory also includes properties that have been bought or are being developed for resale in the ordinary course of business (see 3.4.60). If an entity incurs costs under a contract with a customer and those costs do not give rise to inventories or assets in the scope of another standard, then the entity considers whether those costs represent 'costs to fulfil a contract' under IFRS 15 (see 4.2.270). [*IAS 2.8, 38.2–3, 40.5, 9*]

3.8.10.30   Financial assets, such as investments held for trading for short-term profit making, are not inventory (see 7.1.30). [*IAS 2.2(b)*]

3.8.20   Property, plant and equipment held for sale

3.8.20.10   Inventories encompass assets bought or constructed with the intention of resale in the ordinary course of business. This includes items that would meet the definition of property, plant and equipment – e.g. buildings – had they been bought or constructed with the intention of use in the production or supply of goods or services, for rental to others or for administrative purposes. [*IAS 2.6, 8*]

3.8.20.20   However, it is not appropriate to reclassify an existing item of property, plant and equipment – e.g. a building – as inventory when the entity decides to sell it. In our view, this is also the case when management, during construction of a building, changes its intention in such a way that the building will be sold once construction is finished, unless the entity sells buildings in the ordinary course of business. For further discussion of the accounting for non-current assets held for sale, see chapter 5.4. [*IFRS 5.3, IAS 1.66*]

3.8.20.30   Items of property, plant and equipment that are rented and then subsequently sold on a routine basis – e.g. rental cars – are transferred to inventories at their carrying amount when they cease to be rented and become held-for-sale (see 3.2.380.40). [*IAS 16.68A*]

3.8.25   Investment property

3.8.25.10   The classification of property as held-for-sale in the ordinary course of business (inventory) or as held-for-capital-appreciation (investment property) can be complex and may require judgement. An entity's business model plays a key role in the classification of property on initial recognition (see 3.4.60.30). A property is subsequently reclassified if there is an actual change in use (see 3.4.200). [*IAS 40.57–58*]

3.8.30   Spare parts

3.8.30.10   Spare parts, stand-by and servicing equipment – e.g. tools and consumable lubricants – are classified as property, plant and equipment if they meet the definition, including the requirement to be used over more than one period (see 3.2.10.10–20); otherwise, they are classified as inventory.

This applies to assets held for use within the entity and to those held to provide maintenance services to others. [*IAS 16.8, BC12A*]

EXAMPLE 1 – SPARE PARTS USED IN CONNECTION WITH PROPERTY, PLANT AND EQUIPMENT

3.8.30.20   Company F, an aircraft charter company that offers aircraft maintenance services, has spare parts. Some of the spare parts will be used in less than one period in the day-to-day repair and maintenance of aircraft on behalf of customers. Others will be used only in connection with F's own aircraft.

3.8.30.30   The spare parts to be used in the servicing business do not meet the definition of property, plant and equipment, because they are consumed in less than one period in rendering maintenance services. Therefore, they are accounted for as inventory. Conversely, the spare parts that F will use in its own aircraft meet the definition of property, plant and equipment because they are consumed over more than one period.

3.8.40   Re-usable and returnable packaging or parts

3.8.40.10   Packaging or parts that are sold to a customer, but will be returned to the seller to be re-used, are not inventory if the items will be used over more than one period.

EXAMPLE 2 – RE-USABLE BOTTLES

3.8.40.20   Company C produces and distributes bottled drinks. C receives a deposit for the bottles when drinks are sold. C is required to buy back empty bottles, which are used again in future periods. Bottles are used over more than one period and are not bought for the purposes of resale. Therefore, the bottles are not inventory; they are an item of property, plant and equipment (see 3.2.10.20).

3.8.40.30   For a discussion of the accounting for refundable deposits from customers, see 3.12.370.

3.8.50   Samples

3.8.50.10   For advertising and promotional purposes, some entities may manufacture samples that they intend to hand out free of charge – e.g. beauty products. The costs of manufacturing such samples are expensed as they are incurred; they are not recognised as inventory. [*IAS 38.69–70*]

3.8.50.20   Other entities may buy such samples that they intend to hand out free of charge. The costs of purchasing those samples are expensed when the entity receives, or otherwise has the right to access, the samples; they are not recognised as inventory. A prepayment (asset) for such samples can be recognised in the statement of financial position only for payments made in advance of the receipt of the samples (see 3.3.150.30). However, if a producer sells products to a retailer and the retailer gives samples to customers free of charge, then the samples would be treated as inventory of the producer. [*IAS 38.69–70*]

3.8.60   Catalogues

3.8.60.10   Catalogues that are distributed free of charge to prospective customers and describe the entity's products and services are not inventory or property, plant and equipment. Instead, catalogues are considered to be a form of advertising and promotional material because their primary objective is to advertise. Therefore, the cost of catalogues is recognised as an expense when the entity receives, or otherwise has the right to access, the catalogues. A prepayment (asset) can be recognised in the statement of financial position only for payments made in advance of the receipt of the catalogues (see also 3.3.150.30–40). [*IAS 38.69–70, BC46G*]

3.8.70   Commodities

3.8.70.10   The measurement requirements of IAS 2 do not apply to minerals and mineral products held by producers that are measured at net realisable value (NRV) in accordance with well-established practices in certain industries. If such inventories are measured at NRV, then changes in value are recognised in profit or loss. This exemption applies only to producers of these inventories. There is no exemption for entities that process or convert these products. [*IAS 2.3(a)*]

3.8.70.20   The measurement requirements of IAS 2 also do not apply to inventories held by commodity broker-traders who measure their inventories at fair value less costs to sell. All changes in the fair value less costs to sell of such inventories are recognised in profit or loss. Such inventories are normally acquired with the purpose of selling them in the near future and generating a profit from fluctuations in price or broker-traders' margin. [*IAS 2.3(b), 5*]

3.8.70.25   In assessing whether an entity acts as a commodity broker-trader, the term 'near future' needs to be interpreted. In our view, such an assessment may vary from entity to entity and the factors considered in this assessment include the business model of the entity. The entity should consider the extent to which it provides additional services related to the underlying commodities, such as distribution, storage or repackaging services, as well as the fact that entities that sell goods in the near future after receipt generally do not have significant storage capacity. If an entity acts as a commodity broker-trader, then the own-use exemption under IFRS 9 will not generally be available (see 7.1.200). [*IAS 2.3, 5*]

EXAMPLE 3A – COMMODITIES – RESOLD IN SAME CONDITION

3.8.70.30   Wholesaler C buys gold and resells it in the same condition a short period after physical delivery. The commodity received under such a contract is accounted for under IAS 2, except for the measurement requirements for inventories. The commodity is measured at fair value less costs to sell.

EXAMPLE 3B – COMMODITIES – SERVICES PERFORMED BEFORE RESALE

3.8.70.35   In another example, Company L performs significant services for Company M by cutting and shaping gold into small retail units and then selling it. In this case, L accounts for the transaction in accordance with IAS 2, including measurement. However, if L is acting as an agent, then it will not recognise any inventories under IAS 2 (see 4.2.340).

3.8.70.37   IFRS does not contain specific guidance on accounting for emissions allowances. In general, emissions allowances (or carbon credits) are accounted for as intangible assets (see 3.3.160). However, if such allowances are held for sale in the ordinary course of business, then in our view they may be inventories (see 3.8.10.20). Notwithstanding the fact that they do not have physical substance, in our view they may be classified as commodities. 'Commodities' is not defined in IFRS and an emissions allowance is not a financial asset (see 7.1.30), which means that there is no definitional restriction on classifying emissions allowances as commodities. [*IAS 38.3(a)*]

3.8.70.38   In our view, if such allowances are held as a commodity for resale and they are measured at fair value less costs to sell, then the measurement requirements of IAS 2 do not apply to those emissions allowances. For a discussion of the accounting for emissions allowances received by a participant in a 'cap and trade' scheme, see 3.3.160; and for a discussion of the accounting for obligations arising from such schemes, see 3.12.510. [*IAS 38.3(a)*]

3.8.70.40   The presentation and disclosure requirements of IAS 2 apply to items of inventory held by producers or commodity broker-traders. [*IAS 2.4, 5*]

3.8.80   Agricultural produce

3.8.80.10   IAS 2 applies to agricultural produce from the point of harvest. For a discussion of the accounting for biological assets before harvest, see chapter 3.9. [*IAS 2.3(a), 41.3*]

3.8.80.20   However, if the following are measured at NRV in accordance with well-established industry practices, then the measurement requirements of IAS 2 do not apply:
- producers' inventories of agricultural and forest products; and
- producers' inventories of agricultural produce after harvest. [*IAS 2.3*]

3.8.80.30   The presentation and disclosure requirements of IAS 2 apply to such items. [*IAS 2.4*]

3.8.90   RECOGNITION AND DERECOGNITION

3.8.90.10   IAS 2 does not include specific guidance on the timing of recognition of purchased inventories. In the absence of specific guidance in IAS 2, in our experience entities generally refer to the revenue recognition requirements. Applying that guidance, inventory is recognised on the date on which the entity obtains control of it (see 4.2.240). [*IFRS 15.31*]

3.8.90.15   An entity has control of inventory when it is able to direct its use and obtain substantially all of its remaining benefits. This may occur at a point in time or over time. Indicators that control has passed include the entity having:
- a present obligation to pay;
- physical possession;
- legal title;
- the risks and rewards of ownership; and
- accepted the asset. [*IFRS 15.38*]

3.8.90.17   The indicators of transfer of control are factors that are often present if an entity has control of inventory. However, they are not individually determinative, nor are they a list of conditions that have to be met. An entity needs to evaluate all available evidence when determining if it has obtained control of inventory.

3.8.90.20   A relevant consideration in evaluating at which point in time an entity obtains control of inventory is the shipping terms of the arrangement. Shipping terms alone do not determine when control transfers – i.e. an entity considers them along with the other indicators of control in 3.8.90.15. However, shipping terms often indicate the point in time when the entity has legal title, the risks and rewards of ownership and a present obligation to pay, which are all indicators that control has transferred. For example, when goods are shipped 'free on board' (FOB), an entity usually receives the bill of lading and takes over the risk of loss or damage to the goods when they are loaded onto the ship. This may indicate that the entity obtains control over the goods when they are loaded onto the ship at the port of the seller. If this is the case, then inventory includes items bought FOB that are in transit at the reporting date.

3.8.90.25   If an entity is an intermediary in an arrangement, then it needs to determine if it acts as a principal or an agent – i.e. whether it controls inventory before it is transferred to the customer. To do so, the entity first applies the general guidance on the transfer of control. If this assessment is not conclusive, then the entity considers the specific principal vs agent indicators (see 4.2.340.30–35). If the entity determines that it acts as a principal in the arrangement, then it recognises inventory in its statement of financial position. Conversely, if the entity determines that it acts as an agent, then it does not recognise inventory.

3.8.90.30   The carrying amount of inventories is recognised as an expense when the inventories are sold unless they form part of the cost of another asset – e.g. property, plant and equipment under construction. Therefore, derecognition depends on the timing of revenue recognition (see chapter 4.2). As such, inventory does not include:

● items sold, even if a normal level of returns is expected (see 4.2.310); or
● items shipped to customers on or before the reporting date unless control over those items has not transferred to the buyer – e.g. before goods are loaded onto the ship in an FOB arrangement they would be included in inventory of the seller. [*IAS 2.34*]

3.8.90.40   For a discussion of sales with a right of return and accounting for an asset for the right to recover returned goods, see 4.2.310.

3.8.100   Consignment stock

3.8.100.10   In some cases, a seller may deliver goods to another party but retain control of those goods – e.g. the goods may be delivered to a dealer or distributor for sale to an end customer. These types of arrangements are called 'consignment arrangements'. Indicators of a consignment arrangement include, but are not limited to, the following:

● the goods are controlled by the seller until a specified event occurs – e.g. the sale of the good to a customer of the intermediary – or until a specified period expires;
● the seller is able to require the return of the goods, or transfer the goods to another intermediary; and
● the intermediary does not have an unconditional obligation to pay for the goods, although it might be required to pay a deposit. [*IFRS 15.B77–B78*]

3.8.100.20   The principles in 3.8.90 also apply in respect of consignment inventory. Therefore, items controlled by an entity that are held on consignment at another entity's premises are included as inventory of the consignor. Items held on consignment on behalf of another entity are not included as inventory of the consignee. For a discussion of the recognition of revenue, see 4.2.350.

3.8.110 MEASUREMENT

3.8.110.10   Inventory is measured at the lower of cost and NRV (see 3.8.120 and 330, respectively). [*IAS 2.9*]

3.8.110.20   As an exception to this general rule, producers' inventories of agricultural and forest products and mineral ores may be stated at NRV if this is accepted industry practice (see 3.8.70.10). Also, inventory held by commodity broker-traders may be measured at fair value less cost to sell (see 3.8.70.20). In these cases, changes in value are recognised in profit or loss. [*IAS 2.3*]

3.8.110.30   A group with diverse operating activities could measure the inventories held by commodity broker-traders within the group at fair value less costs to sell (see 3.8.70.20) and other inventories at the lower of cost and NRV.

3.8.120 COST

3.8.120.10   The cost of inventories comprises:
- purchase costs (see 3.8.130);
- production or conversion costs (see 3.8.170); and
- other costs incurred in bringing inventory to its present location and condition, including attributable non-production overheads (see 3.8.220). [*IAS 2.10, 15*]

3.8.130 Purchase costs

3.8.130.10   Purchase costs include the purchase price, transport and handling costs, taxes that are not recoverable and other costs directly attributable to the purchase. [*IAS 2.11*]

3.8.130.20   A purchase price may be attributable to several assets – e.g. if an entity buys all of its inventories from a particular supplier. In our view, one possible method is to allocate the purchase price to the individual assets based on their relative fair values.

3.8.140 *Sales tax*

3.8.140.10   Sales tax paid – e.g. value added tax – is not included in the cost of inventory if the tax is recoverable. For items on which the sales tax is not recoverable, or for entities that are not entitled to a full refund, the non-refundable portion of sales tax paid is included as part of the cost of the inventory. [*IAS 2.11*]

3.8.150 *Deferred payment*

3.8.150.10   If payment for inventory is deferred beyond normal credit terms, then the arrangement contains a financing element and interest is imputed if the impact is material. [*IAS 2.18*]

3.8.150.20   If interest is imputed, then the cost of the inventory is based on a cash price equivalent. Generally, the cash price equivalent is the price for normal credit terms. In our view, if a cash price equivalent is not available, then cost should be determined by discounting the future cash flows at an interest rate determined with reference to market rates. The difference between the total cost and the deemed cost should be recognised as interest expense over the period of financing under the effective interest method (see 7.7.270). [*IAS 2.18*]

3.8.150.30   In our view, the length of normal credit terms will depend on the entity, the industry and the economic environment. Periods of high interest rates or high inflation levels may also affect the length of normal credit terms.

3.8.155   *Long-term prepayment*

3.8.155.10   The IFRS Interpretations Committee discussed whether an entity that makes a long-term prepayment for inventory should accrete interest on the prepayment and recognise interest income resulting in an increase in the cost of inventories. The Committee did not take the issue onto its agenda and noted that judgement is required to identify when an individual long-term contract contains a financing element that should be accounted for separately. [*IU 11-15*]

3.8.160   *Discounts and rebates on purchases*

3.8.160.10   Cash, trade or volume discounts and rebates received are deducted from the cost of purchase. [*IAS 2.11*]

3.8.160.20   There is no specific guidance on the timing of recognition of rebates or volume discounts. In our view, if it is probable that the rebate or volume discount will be earned and the amount can be estimated reliably, then the discount or rebate should be recognised as a reduction in the purchase price when the inventory is bought. This assessment should be reviewed on an ongoing basis.

EXAMPLE 4A – VOLUME DISCOUNT – PROBABLE TO BE EARNED

> 3.8.160.30   Company Z is a furniture retailer. Z buys beds from Company Y at a cost of 100 each. Y has agreed to grant Z a 10% refund on all purchases if Z buys at least 10,000 beds in a 12-month period. Based on past experience, it is probable that Z will buy 10,000 beds from Y. Therefore, we believe that Z should record the beds at the expected cost of 90 per unit and recognise a receivable for the anticipated rebate.

3.8.160.40   If it is not probable that the required criteria to earn the rebate will be met, or the amount of the rebate cannot be estimated reliably, then the purchase cost is measured at the gross amount payable, until such time as it becomes probable that a rebate will be received and the amount of that rebate can be estimated reliably.

3.8.160.50   If the discount or rebate is recognised subsequent to when the item is sold, then in our view the proportion of the discount attributable to the sold items should be recognised as an adjustment to cost of sales at the same time as the discount or rebate is recognised.

EXAMPLE 4B – VOLUME DISCOUNT – NOT PROBABLE TO BE EARNED

3.8.160.60   If, in the fact pattern described in Example 4A, it had not initially been probable that Z would buy the required 10,000 beds, then Z would have recorded each of the beds bought at a gross unit cost of 100 each.

3.8.160.65   Assume that after nine months, Z has bought 9,000 beds and concludes that it is now probable that it will meet the minimum purchase of 10,000 beds and will receive the 10% rebate. At that date, 3,000 beds are still on hand. The other 6,000 beds have been sold.

3.8.160.67   We believe that Z should reduce the cost of each of the remaining beds by 10 – i.e. 30,000 (3,000 x 10) of the rebate should be allocated to reduce the cost of inventory. The remaining 60,000 should be recognised in profit or loss immediately as a reduction of cost of sales.

3.8.160.70   In our view, incentives for early payment (settlement discounts) should be treated as a reduction in the purchase price. Generally, when such discounts are not taken, the cost of inventory is the higher amount payable before discount, provided that payment is not deferred beyond normal credit terms (see 3.8.150). This approach is consistent with the assumption that there is no financing element when payment is within normal credit terms.

3.8.170   Production or conversion costs

3.8.170.10   The production or conversion costs include all direct costs such as labour, material and direct overheads and an allocation of fixed and variable production overheads. These include the depreciation and maintenance of factory buildings and equipment; amortisation of intangible assets such as software used in the production process; and the cost of factory management and administration. Labour costs include taxes and employee benefit costs associated with labour that is involved directly in the production process. The costs do not need to be external or incremental. [*IAS 2.12*]

3.8.170.20   The following are recognised as an expense and are not allocated to the cost of inventory in the statement of financial position:
- impairment losses, including goodwill impairment losses;
- abnormal amounts of wasted material, labour or other production costs (see 3.8.190); and
- general administration costs unrelated to the production of inventory – e.g. the costs of operating a finance department.

3.8.180   *Decommissioning and restoration costs*

3.8.180.10   Decommissioning and restoration costs incurred as a consequence of the production of inventory in a particular period are part of the cost of that inventory (see 3.2.70.30). Accordingly, the effect of any changes to an existing obligation for decommissioning and restoration costs related to items that have been sold are recognised in profit or loss. [*IAS 16.16(c), 18, IFRIC 1.4*]

3.8.190   ***Allocation of fixed production overheads***

3.8.190.10   The allocation of fixed production overheads is based on the normal capacity of production facilities. Any inefficiency is recognised in profit or loss. If an entity classifies expenses based on function, then the inefficiency is allocated to the appropriate function. Conversely, if an entity classifies expenses based on nature, then the inefficiency is included in 'other expenses'. [*IAS 2.13, 38*]

3.8.190.20   In determining what constitutes normal capacity, an entity considers the following factors:
- the nature of the business, economic factors, the status of product life cycles and the reliability of forecasts;
- the maximum capacity and expected utilisation of production facilities, including planned maintenance and shut-downs; and
- the expected levels of activity to be achieved on average over a number of periods, adjusted for unusual fluctuations or circumstances.

EXAMPLE 5 – ALLOCATING FIXED PRODUCTION OVERHEADS

3.8.190.30   Assume that under normal operating conditions Company J expects to produce 100 coffee machines a year. Budgeted and actual fixed production overheads for 2018 are 800. Therefore, the fixed overhead cost per machine based on normal production levels is 8.

3.8.190.40   During 2018, because of problems with the production machinery and decreased demand, J produces only 80 coffee machines. The production overheads are allocated based on the normal production levels of 100 (i.e. 8 per unit). Therefore, of the total production overheads of 800, only 640 (80 x 8) is allocated to inventory. The other 160 is recognised as an expense as it is incurred.

3.8.190.50   However, if during 2018 in response to increased demand for coffee machines J increased production shifts and produced 130 machines, then the amount allocated to the inventory would be limited to the actual expenditure. Therefore, if the total production overheads remain constant at 800, then a cost of 6.15 (800 / 130) is allocated to each machine.

3.8.190.60   If actual production differs substantially from the normal capacity over a period of time, then an entity considers whether it needs to revise the normal capacity used in the allocation of fixed production overheads.

3.8.190.70   Issues may arise when an entity has a planned plant shut-down. For example, Company F is involved in freezing and canning fresh fruit. Production takes place during the first six months of the reporting period when the fresh fruit is picked. During the second six months of the reporting period, the production plant is closed and maintenance is performed. No inventory is on hand during the shut-down period. The maintenance costs do not comprise a separate component of the plant (see 3.2.250). In determining the normal capacity over which production costs will be allocated, F takes into account the annual scheduled plant shut-down.

3.8.190.80   However, in our view the maintenance cost in the second half of the reporting period cannot be accrued over the production in the first six months of the reporting period. This is because a provision cannot be recognised during the first half for the maintenance costs to be incurred in the second half of the reporting period (see 3.12.540).

3.8.190.90   In our view, the maintenance costs also cannot be capitalised and allocated to the following period's production. If F were to attribute the maintenance cost incurred in the second half of the reporting period as a cost of producing the inventory in the following reporting period, then this would result in the maintenance costs being recognised as an asset in the statement of financial position. We believe that the maintenance costs do not give rise to an asset as defined in the Conceptual Framework (see 1.2.30) and therefore they should be expensed as they are incurred.

3.8.200   *Common costs as part of inventory*

3.8.200.10   Properties for sale in the ordinary course of business or in the process of construction or development for such sale are accounted for under IAS 2 rather than IAS 40 (see 3.4.60.10 and 3.8.10.20). If an entity is constructing individual units as part of a single complex with the objective of selling them, then the entity needs to identify and distinguish between costs specifically attributable to each unit (e.g. flooring) and common costs attributable to the complex as a whole (e.g. land). In our view, the common costs should be allocated to each unit on a systematic and rational basis that provides a reasonable approximation of the cost attributable to the individual items of inventory. We believe that the allocation method applied should reflect the construction efforts as well as the cost of a unit. [*IAS 40.9(a)*]

3.8.200.15   Common costs are allocated to individual items of inventory with reference to the relative fair values of individual items of inventory only if fair value is a reasonable approximation of cost. If there is a considerable difference between individual inventory items' cost and fair value, then using an allocation of relative fair values could result in a misallocation of common costs. [*IAS 2.14*]

3.8.208   *Capitalisation of operating lease costs as part of inventory#*

3.8.208.10   There is no specific guidance on capitalisation of operating lease costs incurred in the production of inventory – i.e. whether they should be capitalised as part of the inventory cost of each unit or kept as a prepayment until sale. For example, Company P leases land under an operating lease that is not classified as investment property because it does not meet the conditions under IAS 40 (see 3.4.40). The lease payments are required to be paid in advance. P develops a multi-unit condominium complex on the land and the condominiums will be sold in the ordinary course of business (see also 3.8.200). In our view, P should include the cost of the operating lease in the cost of inventory. P can do so by including the lease payment in inventory directly. Alternatively, the cost of inventory may be determined by initially recording the lease premium as a prepayment, amortising it in accordance with IAS 17 (see 5.1.310), and capitalising the operating lease expense as inventory. [*IAS 40.6*]

3.8.209   FORTHCOMING REQUIREMENTS

3.8.209.10   Under IFRS 16, a lessee applies a single, on-balance sheet lease accounting model to all of its leases unless it elects the recognition exemptions for short-term leases and/or leases of low value assets (see 5.1A.140). A lessee recognises a right-of-use asset representing its right to use the underlying asset and depreciates it. [*IFRS 16.5, 22, 31*]

3.8.209.20   The depreciation of the right-of-use assets used in the production process is capitalised as a cost of conversion of inventories. [*IAS 2.12*]

3.8.210   *Interruptions*

3.8.210.10   Interruptions in production may happen while costs are still being incurred. For example, an entity may continue to pay rent on a factory during an unplanned plant shut-down or labour strike. IAS 2 does not deal specifically with such circumstances, but in our view guidance from IAS 23 should be used by analogy (see 4.6.160), because this standard deals specifically with a similar issue. [*IAS 23.20*]

3.8.210.20   Accordingly, we believe that costs incurred during an interruption should be capitalised to inventory only if:
- the interruption is planned, is temporary and is a necessary part of getting the inventory ready for sale – e.g. the inventory requires time to mature; or
- the costs are costs of purchase – e.g. purchases of additional raw materials during the shut-down period.

3.8.210.30   Therefore, in our view rent costs during a strike would not be recognised as part of inventory, but rent costs during scheduled maintenance shut-downs might be.

3.8.215   *Learning curve costs*

3.8.215.10   In certain industries, 'learning curve costs' are incurred on the early units produced – e.g. in producing multiple units of complex goods for sale. Learning curve costs are costs that are expected to be incurred on early units as production issues are resolved and are expected to decrease each time a unit is produced. This is based on the observation that repetition of the same operation results in less time or effort expended on that operation.

3.8.215.20   As a result of these learning curve costs, actual production costs on the earlier units produced may exceed the NRV of these units and therefore result in losses on initial production. However, profits may be made on later individual units. Losses on the earlier units may be incurred even if all these units are sold subject to one contract and that overall contract is profitable.

3.8.215.30   Abnormal additional costs are expensed as they are incurred (see 3.8.170.20). However, in our view learning curve costs incurred in the production process should be included in the cost of inventory (subject to recoverability – see 3.8.335.10) when there is clear objective evidence that these costs are not abnormal costs. We believe that such costs are not abnormal if they are planned and anticipated as part of the production process, and if they can be measured reliably.

3.8.220   **Other costs**

3.8.220.10   Any other costs that are directly related to bringing inventories to the point of sale and getting them ready for sale are also allocated to inventories. These may include non-production overheads or the costs of designing products for specific customers including, for example, the amortisation of development costs related to a specific product or process. [*IAS 2.15, 38.97*]

3.8.220.20   Selling and advertising costs cannot be included in the cost of inventory. [*IAS 2.16*]

3.8.230   *Distribution, packaging and transport costs*

3.8.230.10   In some arrangements, an entity delivers goods to a location specified by its customer. In these cases, the entity first needs to determine if transporting goods is a separate performance obligation. If so, then it applies the guidance in IFRS 15 (see 4.2.347.20).

3.8.230.15   If transport and distribution costs form part of a single performance obligation for the sale of goods, then the entity considers if they represent costs that are necessary to get the inventory to its present location or condition for sale. If so, then they are included in the cost of inventory. Examples of such costs include, but are not limited to, the following:
- the cost of transporting goods from the supplier if the entity is an intermediary and acts as a principal in the arrangement;
- transport or distribution costs that are incurred at an intermediate stage in the production process; and
- transport or distribution costs to get the inventory from a central warehouse to the point of sale.

3.8.230.20   Similarly, packaging costs incurred to prepare inventory for sale are part of the cost of inventory.

3.8.230.30   Other distribution costs and the costs of transporting goods to customers – i.e. those that do not relate to a separate performance obligation and are not necessary to get the inventory to its present location or condition for sale – are recognised as an expense as they are incurred; they are not allocated to inventory.

3.8.240   *Storage or holding costs*

3.8.240.10   Storage or holding costs are generally expensed as they are incurred unless:
- storage is necessary before a further stage in the production process;
- the inventory is produced as a discrete project – e.g. custom-built furnishings when the storage cost will be charged to the customer; or
- the inventory requires a maturation process to bring it into a saleable condition – e.g. whisky, wine or cheese. [*IAS 2.16(b)*]

3.8.250   **Joint products and by-products**

3.8.250.10   A production process may result in more than one output being produced. For example, in the wine-making process, grappa is produced from the liquid distilled from the fermented residue of grapes after they have been pressed. [*IAS 2.14*]

3.8.250.20   If the cost related to the individual products cannot be identified, then the total production costs are allocated between the products on a rational and consistent basis. One possible method is to allocate the total production costs based on the relative selling prices of each product. If this method is used, then it is reasonable to assume the same profit margin for each product unless there is a more accurate method of making the allocation. [*IAS 2.14*]

3.8.250.30   If a production process results in products that are incidental to the primary product, then the cost allocated to these by-products may be based on their NRV, which is then deducted from the cost of the main product. [*IAS 2.14*]

3.8.260   Borrowing costs

3.8.260.10   Borrowing costs are capitalised as part of the cost of inventories if the inventories are qualifying assets. Inventories that are routinely manufactured in large quantities or that are produced on a repetitive basis in a short time are not qualifying assets (see 4.6.20). [*IAS 2.17, 23.4, 5, 7, BC6*]

3.8.270   Agricultural produce

3.8.270.10   The fair value less costs to sell of agricultural produce at the date of harvest is the deemed cost of the produce for the purpose of applying IAS 2 (see 3.9.90.10). [*IAS 2.20*]

3.8.280   Cost formulas

3.8.280.10   If items of inventory are not interchangeable or comprise goods or services produced for specific projects, then cost is determined on an individual item basis. This is appropriate for unique items, such as custom-built furnishings, property developments, antiques and works of art. [*IAS 2.23*]

3.8.280.20   A cost formula may be used when there are many interchangeable items. The cost formula used is first-in, first-out (FIFO) or weighted-average. [*IAS 2.25*]

3.8.280.30   The last-in, first-out (LIFO) method is prohibited. [*IAS 2.BC9*]

3.8.280.40   Under the weighted-average cost formula, the cost of each item is determined from the weighted average of the cost of similar items at the beginning of a period and the cost of similar items bought or produced during the period. The average may be calculated on a periodic basis or as each additional shipment is received. [*IAS 2.27*]

EXAMPLE 6A – APPLYING COST FORMULAS – FIFO AND WEIGHTED-AVERAGE COST METHODS

3.8.280.50   This example illustrates the application of each of the methods in an entity that uses a periodic inventory system. The following information pertains to December 2018.

	UNITS	UNIT COST	TOTAL COST
Opening inventory	200	10	2,000
Purchases	50	11	550
Purchases	400	12	4,800
Purchases	350	14	4,900
	1,000		12,250

At the end of the period, there are 400 units in inventory.

FIFO method		
Closing inventory	350 units @ 14	4,900
	50 units @ 12	600
		5,500
Cost of sales for the period	12,250 - 5,500	6,750
Weighted-average cost method		
Weighted-average unit cost	12,250 / 1,000	12.25
Closing inventory	400 x 12.25	4,900
Cost of sales for the period	12,250 - 4,900	7,350

3.8.290 *Standard cost method*

3.8.290.10   The standard cost method may be used for convenience if the results approximate actual cost. Under a standard costing system, the cost of a product is determined using predetermined rates for the material, labour and overhead expenses based on manufacturing specifications. [*IAS 2.21*]

3.8.290.20   To be acceptable as a basis for measuring cost, standard costs take into account normal levels of materials and supplies, labour efficiency and capacity utilisation, or are adjusted for variances. Standard costs should be reviewed regularly, in our view at least at each reporting date, and adjusted to take into account changes in circumstances.

3.8.290.30   If standard costs are not updated to approximate the actual costs, then it is necessary to analyse the variance accounts and to apportion part of the variances to inventory.

EXAMPLE 6B – APPLYING COST FORMULAS – ADJUSTING STANDARD COSTS FOR VARIANCES

3.8.290.40   If the standard unit cost in Example 6A was 10, then the closing standard cost of inventory would be 4,000 (400 x 10) before adjusting for variances.

3.8.290.50   Applying FIFO, the adjustment to closing inventory would be an increase of 1,500. The adjustment is computed by allocating the purchase-price variance applicable to the 400 units of inventory as follows: 350 x (14 - 10) + 50 x (12 - 10).

3.8.290.60   Applying the weighted-average cost method, the adjustment to closing inventory would be an increase of 900. The adjustment is computed by allocating the purchase-price variance applicable to the 400 units of inventory as follows: 400 x (12.25 - 10).

3.8.300   *Retail method*

3.8.300.10   The retail method may be used if the result approximates the actual cost. This assessment should be reviewed regularly, in our view at least at each reporting date. Under the retail method, inventory is recorded based on its selling price. The cost of the inventory is derived by deducting the profit margin from the selling price. Adjustments are made when inventory has been marked down to below its original selling price. An average percentage for each retail department may be used if the margins on all the products within that department are similar. [*IAS 2.21–22*]

EXAMPLE 6C – APPLYING COST FORMULAS – RETAIL METHOD

3.8.300.20   This example illustrates the retail method.

	COST	RETAIL PRICE
Opening inventory	6,250	8,000
Purchases	19,500	34,000
Inventory on hand		(23,000)
Sales for the period		19,000
Retail method		
Cost	6,250 + 19,500	25,750
Retail price	8,000 + 34,000	42,000
Cost percentage of retail price	25,750 / 42,000	61%
Closing inventory	23,000 x 61%	14,030
Cost of sales for the period	6,250 + 19,500 - 14,030	11,720

3.8.300.30   The example does not consider the impact of mark-ups or mark-downs on the selling price, which would add to the complexity of the calculation under the retail method.

3.8.310   *Base stock method*

3.8.310.10   The base stock method is often used in the hospitality industry – e.g. by hotels and restaurants in accounting for linen or silver and glassware. Under the base stock method, the cost of initial purchases of equipment to be used in operations is recognised as inventory and carried unamortised as base stock. The cost of replacement items is expensed when they are acquired.

3.8.310.20   IFRS does not specifically allow for the base stock method. In our view, the base stock method may be used for practical reasons if the result obtained approximates the result that would be obtained by applying IFRS. This assessment should be reviewed regularly, in our view at least at each reporting date.

3.8.310.30   The treatment that is applied under IFRS depends on whether the equipment will be used for more than one period. If it will be used for more than one period, then it meets the definition of property, plant and equipment and is recognised at cost and depreciated over its estimated useful life (see 3.2.10). Otherwise, it is treated as inventory. If it is inventory, then it is measured at the lower of cost and NRV and items are expensed as they are consumed (replaced).

3.8.315   *Minimum inventory levels*

3.8.315.10   Sometimes entities maintain minimum inventory levels. In our view, this does not by itself justify a different cost formula for the minimum level of inventory compared with inventory above the minimum level. In our view, a different cost formula for the minimum inventory level may be acceptable if, and only if, it reflects the inventory flows in the entity. [*IAS 2.24–25, BC15–BC19*]

3.8.320   *Consistency*

3.8.320.10   The same type of cost formula need not be used for all inventory. However, the same cost formula is applied to all inventories having a similar nature and use to the entity. [*IAS 2.25*]

3.8.320.20   A difference in geographic locations does not, by itself, justify different cost formulas. However, raw materials used by one segment may have a different use from the same raw materials used in another segment and this may justify a different treatment. [*IAS 2.26*]

EXAMPLE 7 – COST FORMULAS IN DIFFERENT SEGMENTS

3.8.320.30   Company J buys gold and refines it. Some of the refined gold is sold by the wholesale segment. The remainder is used by a segment that manufactures jewellery. The wholesale and jewellery segments may use different cost formulas to account for the refined gold.

3.8.320.40   A change in cost formulas is justified only if it results in reliable and more relevant information (see 2.8.70).

3.8.320.50   However, if an entity buys inventory items that it did not have in a previous period, then a new method may be used for the new inventories if they have a different nature and use from other items of inventory.

3.8.330   NET REALISABLE VALUE

3.8.330.10   NRV is the estimated selling price in the ordinary course of business less the estimated costs of completion and sale. The costs of sale include directly attributable marketing and distribution costs. NRV is an entity-specific value. [*IAS 2.6*]

3.8.335   Write-downs of inventories and reversals of write-downs

3.8.335.10   Any write-down of inventories to NRV is recognised as an expense in the period in which the write-down occurs. [*IAS 2.34*]

3.8.335.20   A previous write-down of inventories to their NRV is reversed if it subsequently increases. The amount of the reversal is limited to the amount of the original write-down, such that the new carrying amount is the lower of cost and the revised NRV. Reversals of previous write-downs are recognised in profit or loss in the period in which the reversal occurs as a reduction in the amount of inventories recognised as an expense in the period. [*IAS 2.33–34*]

EXAMPLE 8 – WRITE-DOWNS AND REVERSALS

3.8.335.30   On 31 December 2017, Company P writes down its inventory from a carrying amount of 100 to its NRV of 95. During 2018, the inventory is still on hand and its NRV increases to 103.

3.8.335.40   In this example, P recognises a reversal of 5, such that the new carrying amount of the inventory is the lower of its cost of 100 and its revised NRV of 103.

3.8.340   Groups of items

3.8.340.10   NRV write-downs are normally determined on an individual item basis. However, in some cases it may be appropriate to evaluate similar products in groups. That may be the case for items of inventory related to the same product line that have similar purposes or end uses, are produced and marketed in the same geographic area and cannot be practicably evaluated separately from other items in that product line. [*IAS 2.29*]

3.8.340.20   In the clothing textile industry it may not be possible to determine selling prices for each textile individually and therefore it may be necessary to perform the NRV assessment on all textiles that will be used to produce clothing for a particular season.

3.8.340.30   However, retailers do not generally determine NRV write-downs on the basis of the whole department store because different departments usually have different margins.

3.8.350   Intended use

3.8.350.10   The estimated selling price takes into account the intended use of the items. [*IAS 2.31*]

EXAMPLE 9 – EXCESS MATERIALS IN DETERMINING NRV

3.8.350.20   Company B has excess inventories of materials that it will not be able to use in production. B has made the decision to sell the excess materials. The NRV of the excess materials is based on their anticipated sale.

3.8.350.25   If materials and other supplies are held for use in the production of inventories, then NRV is based on the estimated selling price of the finished products in which they will be incorporated (less the estimated costs of completion and sale). Therefore, such materials and supplies are not written down below cost if the finished products in which they will be incorporated are expected to be sold at or above cost. If, however, an entity intends to sell materials in their current form rather than incorporate them into finished products, then NRV is based on the estimated selling price of the materials in their current form. [*IAS 2.32*]

EXAMPLE 10A – CALCULATING NRV – INTENDED USE IS MANUFACTURE

3.8.350.26   Company P, a cabinet manufacturer, has raw material timber inventory on hand at 31 December 2018 with a carrying amount of 100. The current market value of that timber is 95. P intends to use the timber to manufacture cabinets. Therefore, the NRV is based on the finished cabinets and not on the timber in its raw material form. P estimates costs to completion and sale of 50 and a selling price for the cabinets of 160.

3.8.350.27   P does not write down inventory at 31 December 2018 because the NRV of the timber of 110 (160 - 50) is higher than its carrying amount of 100. If, however, P intended to sell the timber in its current raw material form, then it would write down the timber by 5 plus the estimated costs of sale.

EXAMPLE 10B – CALCULATING NRV – INTENDED USE IS DEVELOPMENT

3.8.350.28   Company Q, a property developer, has undeveloped land inventory at 31 December 2018 with a carrying amount of 1,000. The current market value of that undeveloped land is 950. Q intends to develop houses on the land. In this example, the NRV of the land is based on the estimated selling prices of the finished houses less the estimated costs of completion and sale.

3.8.350.29   Therefore, the land will not be written down at 31 December 2018 if Q estimates that the finished houses will be sold above cost. If, however, Q intended to sell the land in its current form, then it would write down the land by 50 plus the estimated costs of sale.

3.8.350.30   Operating losses do not result in an automatic write-down of inventory.

EXAMPLE 11 – OPERATING LOSSES

3.8.350.40   Company T is a tractor producer and also has a servicing division that is operating at a loss. T has some parts that will be used in the servicing business and others that will be used in the production of tractors.

3.8.350.50   In this example, T evaluates the NRV of the parts to be used in tractors separately from the NRV of the parts to be used in the servicing division. The losses in the servicing division may result in a write-down of the parts that will be used by that division, but not of those that will be used in production.

3.8.360   Events after reporting date

3.8.360.10   Estimates of NRV take into consideration fluctuations in price or cost to the extent that they provide evidence of conditions existing at the reporting date (see 2.9.20). Events after the reporting date may provide evidence that the cost of inventory exceeds its NRV at the reporting date. In these cases, the inventory is written down to its NRV at the reporting date. [*IAS 2.30*]

EXAMPLE 12 – EVENT AFTER REPORTING DATE

> 3.8.360.20   On 31 December 2018, the carrying amount of Company P's inventory is 100. On that date, P estimates that the NRV of the inventory is 110.
>
> 3.8.360.30   Events in January 2019 provide evidence that the NRV of the inventory on 31 December 2018 was 95. Therefore, P writes down its inventory to 95 in its 31 December 2018 financial statements.

3.8.370   Replacement cost

3.8.370.10   Lower replacement costs do not lead automatically to a NRV write-down. However, a write-down would be recognised if the fall in prices means that the finished products will be sold for less than production cost.

3.8.380   Changes in exchange rates

3.8.380.10   Changes in exchange rates may require a NRV write-down (see chapter 2.7).

EXAMPLE 13 – EFFECT OF EXCHANGE RATES ON NRV

> 3.8.380.20   Company Z is a book dealer. On 1 December, Z orders 20 books at a cost of foreign currency AC 110 each. The expected selling price of the books is functional currency FC 120. The spot exchange rate is AC 1:FC 0.9 on 1 December. On 20 December when the books are received, the exchange rate is AC 1:FC 1.5.
>
> 3.8.380.30   Assuming that Z had not hedged the foreign exchange risk on its order, the recorded unit cost of the books would be FC 165, because the inventory is measured based on the spot exchange rate at the purchase date. The anticipated selling price of FC 120 has not changed. Therefore, Z recognises a NRV write-down of FC 45 on each book, assuming no further costs of sale.

3.8.390   Sales contracts

3.8.390.10   The determination of NRV takes into account firm sales contracts that have been entered into. The NRV of inventory held to satisfy firm sales contracts is based on the selling price under those contracts. The NRV of inventory held in excess of firm sales contracts is based on general selling prices without regard to the firm sales contracts. [*IAS 2.31*]

EXAMPLE 14 – FIRM SALES CONTRACTS

> 3.8.390.20   Company P has 100 units of inventory on hand at its annual reporting date recorded at a carrying amount of 10 per unit. The current market price is 8 per unit. P has a firm sales contract with Company Q to sell 60 units to Q at 11 per unit, which cannot be settled net (see 7.1.200).

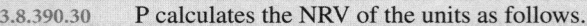

> 3.8.390.30   P calculates the NRV of the units as follows.
> - For the 60 units that will be sold to Q, NRV is 11 per unit less estimated selling costs.
> - For the remaining 40 units, NRV is 8 per unit less estimated selling costs.
>
> 3.8.390.40   Therefore, P writes down the 40 units by 80 (40 x (10 - 8)) plus estimated selling costs.

EXAMPLE 15 – FIRM SALES CONTRACTS – SALES COMMITMENT DERIVATIVES

> 3.8.390.50   Company E manufactures semi-finished copper and copper alloy products. E enters into forward contracts to manage its copper inventory level and those forward contracts fall in the scope of IFRS 9 and are accounted for under its guidance (see 7.1.200.50).
>
> 3.8.390.60   In our view, the NRV of the inventory held to satisfy firm sales contracts should be based on the contract price including the fair value of the related sales commitment derivatives (see 7.1.200.50). However, the NRV of inventory held in excess of firm sales contracts should be based on the general selling prices without regard to the specific sales contracts.

3.8.390.70   If an entity has a contract to sell inventory for less than the cost of fulfilling the obligations under the contract, then the inventory held to satisfy that contract is written down by the amount that the cost of fulfilling the obligations exceeds the selling price. If that excess is greater than the carrying amount of the inventory, then an onerous contract provision may be recognised (see 3.12.630). [*IAS 2.31*]

3.8.400   PRESENTATION AND DISCLOSURES

3.8.400.10   Inventories are current assets. However, an entity discloses the amount of inventories that are expected to be recovered after more than 12 months from the reporting date. [*IAS 1.61, 66–68*]

3.8.400.20   Advance payments made in respect of purchases of inventories are not classified as inventory. Generally, such payments are either a right to receive inventory or a refund of cash.

3.8.400.30   Advance payments received from customers in respect of goods to be sold are not netted against inventories. Instead, an entity recognises a contract liability for its obligation to transfer goods or services to a customer (see 4.2.470). [*IFRS 15.105–106*]

3.8.400.40   The carrying amount of each class of inventory is disclosed separately. Classes of inventories include raw materials, work in progress and finished goods. The inventories of a service provider are normally described as work in progress. [*IAS 2.36–37*]

3.8.400.50   The amount of inventories recognised as an expense during the period and the amount of any write-down of inventories recognised as an expense is disclosed. [*IAS 2.36(d)–(e)*]

3.8.400.60   If an entity chooses to allocate expenses by function, then the cost of inventories sold during the period is disclosed. If an entity chooses an allocation of expenses by nature, then the costs recognised as an expense for raw materials and consumables, labour costs and other costs together with the amount of the net change in inventories for the period are disclosed. For further discussion of presentation in the statement of profit or loss and OCI, see chapter 4.1. [*IAS 2.36, 39*]

3.8.400.70   In our view, write-downs of inventory to NRV as well as any reversals of such write-downs should be presented in cost of sales.

3.8.400.80   The amount of a reversal of a write-down to NRV is disclosed separately. A gain on the sale of inventory previously written down is viewed as evidence of an increase in NRV, triggering this disclosure requirement in the period of sale. [*IAS 2.36(f)*]

EXAMPLE 16 – DISCLOSURE OF REVERSALS

3.8.400.90   Company X owns inventory with an original cost of 100, which was written down to its NRV of 80. In the following period, the item is sold for 120. This gain is viewed as evidence of an increase in NRV at the subsequent reporting date. Therefore, a reversal of the write-down of 20 is disclosed in the period in which the inventory is sold.

3.9   Biological assets

3.9 Biological assets

CURRENTLY EFFECTIVE REQUIREMENTS

This publication reflects IFRS in issue at 1 August 2018, and the currently effective requirements cover annual periods beginning on 1 January 2018.

The requirements related to this topic are mainly derived from the following.

STANDARD	TITLE
IFRS 13	Fair Value Measurement
IAS 41	Agriculture

FORTHCOMING REQUIREMENTS

For this topic, there are no forthcoming requirements.

FUTURE DEVELOPMENTS

The currently effective requirements that may be affected by future developments are briefly discussed in 3.9.110.

3.9.10   **DEFINITION AND SCOPE**

3.9.10.10   'Biological assets' are living animals or plants. Biological assets, except for bearer plants (see 3.9.10.13), are in the scope of IAS 41 if they are:
- transformed by a process of management (i.e. agricultural activity); and
- capable of biological transformation into either agricultural produce (thereafter accounted for as inventory (see chapter 3.8) or under other applicable standards) or even into additional biological assets.

3.9.10.13   A 'bearer plant' is a plant that:
- is used in the supply of agricultural produce;
- is expected to bear produce for more than one period; and
- has a remote likelihood of being sold as agricultural produce, except for scrap sales. [*IAS 41.5*]

3.9.10.15   'Biological transformation' comprises the processes of growth, degeneration, production and procreation that cause qualitative or quantitative change in a biological asset. IAS 41 applies, for example, to the following activities: raising livestock, forestry, growing annual or perennial crops, cultivating orchards and plantations, floriculture and aquaculture (including fish farming). [*IAS 41.5–6*]

3.9.10.20   Determining whether an asset is a biological asset or inventory sometimes depends on the purpose for which the asset is held. For example, fertilised eggs held for hatching chicks are biological assets, whereas eggs held for sale are inventory.

3.9.10.30   Animals or plants that are not subject to a process of management of biological transformation are not in the scope of IAS 41. Such management of biological transformation distinguishes agricultural activity from other activities. For example, an entity that is a pet shop buys baby animals from breeders and then sells them. The pets are accounted for as inventory and not as biological assets because the entity does not manage the biological transformation of the animals.

3.9.10.40   Harvesting from unmanaged sources, such as ocean fishing and deforestation, is another activity that does not involve a process of management of biological transformation and is therefore outside the scope of IAS 41.

3.9.10.50   Similarly, animals or plants that are used primarily in activities in which there is no management of biological transformation, such as recreational parks or game parks, are outside the scope of IAS 41.

EXAMPLE 1 – BIOLOGICAL TRANSFORMATION

3.9.10.55   Company G owns horses that it trains and uses for racing. The racehorses are owned primarily for activities that do not involve biological transformation (i.e. racing) and therefore are not accounted for as biological assets. Instead, the horses are recognised as assets and depreciated over their estimated useful lives applying the principles for property, plant and equipment (see 3.2.140). However, if G used the racehorses primarily for breeding purposes, then those horses would be in the scope of IAS 41.

3.9.10.60   Although IAS 41 requires bearer plants to be accounted for in accordance with IAS 16, the produce growing on bearer plants is a biological asset in the scope of IAS 41. IAS 41 applies to agricultural produce only at the point of harvest. IAS 2 or other applicable standards apply after the agricultural produce is harvested (see 3.9.90). The following table provides examples of biological assets, agricultural produce and products that are the result of processing after harvesting. [*IAS 41.2(b), 3–4*]

BIOLOGICAL ASSETS		AGRICULTURAL PRODUCE	PRODUCTS THAT ARE THE RESULT OF PROCESSING AFTER HARVEST
IAS 41	IAS 16	IAS 41	IAS 2
Sheep		Wool	Yarn, carpet
Dairy cattle		Milk	Cheese
Pigs		Carcass	Sausages, cured hams
	Trees in a plantation forest	Felled trees	Logs, lumber
	Cotton plants	Cotton	Thread, clothing
	Sugarcane	Harvested cane	Sugar
	Tea bushes	Leaf	Tea
	Vines	Grapes	Wine
	Fruit trees	Picked fruit	Processed fruit

3.9.10.70   IAS 41 does not deal with the measurement of contracts for the future sale of biological assets or agricultural products. Such contracts may be in the scope of IAS 39 if the contract can be settled net in cash or by another financial instrument, as if the contract were a financial instrument (see 7.1.200). A contract that is not in the scope of IFRS 9 may be an onerous contract, in which case a provision would be recognised in accordance with IAS 37 (see 3.12.630). [*IAS 41.B54*]

3.9.20   RECOGNITION

3.9.20.10   Biological assets are recognised when the asset is controlled by the entity, its cost or fair value can be measured reliably and it is probable that future economic benefits associated with the asset will flow to the entity. [*IAS 41.10*]

3.9.30   MEASUREMENT

3.9.30.10   Biological assets are measured at fair value less costs to sell. The presumption that a biological asset can be measured at fair value less costs to sell can be rebutted only on initial recognition when quoted market prices are not available and alternative fair value measurements are determined to be clearly unreliable. If the fair value of a biological asset cannot be measured reliably at the date of initial recognition, then the asset is stated at cost less any accumulated depreciation and impairment losses (see 3.9.60). If fair value subsequently becomes reliably measurable, then the asset is measured at fair value less costs to sell. [*IAS 41.12, 30*]

3.9.30.20   Once a biological asset has been measured at fair value less costs to sell, it continues to be measured on that basis until disposal. [*IAS 41.31*]

3.9.30.25   A gain may arise on initial recognition of a biological asset, such as when a calf is born or on initial recognition of agricultural produce as a result of harvesting. Losses may also arise in such circumstances due to the deduction of costs to sell in measuring fair value. Gains or losses arising on initial recognition are recognised in profit or loss in the period in which they arise. [*IAS 41.26–29*]

3.9.30.30   Changes in fair value less costs to sell are recognised in profit or loss. [*IAS 41.26*]

3.9.30.40   Biological assets measured at fair value less costs to sell are excluded from the measurement scope of IFRS 5 (see 5.4.20). However, once a biological asset meets the criteria to be classified as held-for-sale, or is included in a disposal group that is classified as held-for-sale, in accordance with IFRS 5, it is presumed that fair value can be measured reliably. [*IFRS 5.5, IAS 41.30*]

3.9.40   **Fair value model**

3.9.40.10   Fair value is measured in accordance with IFRS 13, which is the subject of chapter 2.4. That chapter includes general guidance on applying the principles of IFRS 13 in measuring fair value; specific points of interest in relation to biological assets are discussed in 2.4.730.

3.9.40.20   The costs involved in developing biological assets are expensed as they are incurred. Essentially, the entity's profit for the period is the difference between the increase in fair value of the biological asset and the costs incurred in that period.

3.9.50   *Costs to sell*

3.9.50.10   Costs to sell are incremental costs directly attributable to the disposal of an asset, excluding finance costs and income taxes. Transport costs are included in the measurement of fair value (see 2.4.110). [*IAS 41.5*]

3.9.60   **Cost model**

3.9.60.10   If fair value cannot be measured reliably, then the cost model is used instead. The presumption that fair value can be measured reliably can be rebutted only on initial recognition when quoted market prices are not available and alternative fair value measurements are determined to be clearly unreliable. For biological assets that have short transformation cycles, in most cases it will be possible to estimate a fair value reliably. [*IAS 41.30, BC4C*]

3.9.60.20   The IFRS Interpretations Committee discussed fair value measurement of produce growing on bearer plants; in particular, whether fruits growing on palm oil trees can be an example of a biological asset for which an entity might rebut the fair value presumption as discussed in 3.9.60.10. The Committee noted that to rebut the presumption, an entity needs to demonstrate that any fair value measurement is clearly unreliable and that this may occur when an entity encounters significant practical difficulties on initial measurement. However, the converse is not necessarily true – i.e. if an entity encounters significant practical difficulties, then this does not always mean that any fair value measurement of produce is clearly unreliable. The Committee also noted that possible differences in supportable assumptions used for fair value measurement are not evidence of significant practical difficulties even if they could result in significantly different valuations. Such differences, in and of themselves, do not automatically mean that any fair value measurement of produce is clearly unreliable. [*IU 06-17*]

3.9.60.25   In our view, the level of uncertainty required to conclude that a fair value measurement is clearly unreliable is a high threshold. The following are examples of factors that we believe are not determinative on their own and therefore would not support such a conclusion:

- the absence of market prices;
- regulations that limit the effect of global market prices on prices in the local market;
- large fluctuations in the prices of the biological asset or its agricultural produce (may be reflected in the valuation model); and
- a history of large variations in the outcomes of the biological transformation process (may be reflected in the valuation model).

3.9.60.30   There is no specific guidance on determining cost for biological assets. The general guidance on determining cost, as described in 3.2.20 and 3.8.120, applies. The general depreciation and impairment considerations described in 3.2.140 and chapter 3.10 are also relevant. [*IAS 41.33*]

3.9.60.40   IAS 23 requires the capitalisation of certain borrowing costs as part of the cost of qualifying assets (see 4.6.10–20).

3.9.70   # GOVERNMENT GRANTS

3.9.70.10   IAS 20 applies to government grants related to biological assets to which the cost model applies (see 3.9.60 and 4.3.60). [*IAS 41.37*]

3.9.70.20   An unconditional government grant related to biological assets that are measured at fair value less costs to sell is recognised in profit or loss when it becomes receivable. However, if the government grant is conditional, then it is recognised in profit or loss only when the conditions are met. [*IAS 41.34–35*]

EXAMPLE 2 – TERMS AND CONDITIONS OF GOVERNMENT GRANT

3.9.70.30   Company X receives 100 as a government grant under the condition that it grow and harvest fruit trees in a certain location for at least the next 10 years. If X stops these activities at any time during the 10 years, then the full amount of the grant is repayable to the government. Accordingly, the 100 is deferred in the statement of financial position and will be recognised in profit or loss once the 10-year period has expired.

> **3.9.70.35**   If the facts were different and X became entitled to retain the grant on a pro rata basis as time passed, on a straight-line basis over the 10 years, then X would recognise 10 in profit or loss as each year of activity is completed. [*IAS 41.36*]

3.9.70.40   IAS 41 differs from IAS 20 to avoid government grants related to biological assets measured at fair value less costs to sell being recognised in profit or loss immediately when conditions are attached. In such circumstances, if an entity were to deduct the government grant from the carrying amount of the asset, and subsequently measure the related biological asset at fair value, then in effect the government grant would be recognised in profit or loss immediately. [*IAS 41.B66*]

3.9.80   LEASED ASSETS

3.9.80.10   A lease of a biological asset is classified as a finance lease or an operating lease under IAS 17 (see 5.1.100). IAS 41 applies to the presentation and measurement of lease contracts of biological assets in the statement of financial position of the lessee (finance lease) or lessor (operating lease). [*IAS 41.B82(n)*]

3.9.90   AGRICULTURAL PRODUCE

3.9.90.10   Agricultural produce, which is the harvested product of an entity's biological assets, is measured at fair value less costs to sell at the point of harvest. Fair value is measured in accordance with IFRS 13; see chapter 2.4 in general and 2.4.730 for specific points of interest in relation to biological assets (and agricultural produce). In our experience, market prices are normally available for agricultural produce. After harvest, agricultural produce is treated as inventory (see chapter 3.8). [*IAS 41.3, 13, 32*]

3.9.90.20   Some harvested produce may be subject to processing that may be a logical and natural extension of biological activity. For example, the processing of grapes into wine or making cheese from milk may include an element of biological transformation. However, these assets are subject to the principles of accounting for inventory, rather than the requirements for biological assets, because IAS 41 does not deal with processing of agricultural produce after harvest. [*IAS 41.IN2*]

3.9.100   PRESENTATION AND DISCLOSURES

3.9.100.10   Detailed disclosures about biological assets are required by IAS 41. Examples of such disclosures are included in KPMG's *Guides to financial statements* series, and include a reconciliation of changes in the carrying amount of the biological asset. [*IAS 41.40–57*]

3.9.100.20   When biological assets are measured at cost because fair value cannot be estimated reliably, detailed additional disclosures are required. [*IAS 41.54–55*]

3.9.100.30   In addition, the disclosure requirements of IFRS 13 apply to biological assets measured at fair value less costs to sell (see 2.4.490). The disclosures under IFRS 13 are made for each class of assets (see 2.4.510).

3.9.110   **FUTURE DEVELOPMENTS**

3.9.110.10   The IFRS Interpretations Committee discussed a request to remove the current requirement in IAS 41 to exclude taxation cash flows (i.e. use pre-tax cash flows) when measuring the fair value of biological assets using a present value technique. The Committee recommended and the IASB agreed to amend IAS 41 as part of the next *Annual Improvements to IFRSs Cycle*. The proposals would enable fair value measurement of biological assets on a post-tax basis.

FUTURE DEVELOPMENTS

3.10 Impairment of non-financial assets

3.10 Impairment of non-financial assets

CURRENTLY EFFECTIVE REQUIREMENTS

This publication reflects IFRS in issue at 1 August 2018, and the currently effective requirements cover annual periods beginning on 1 January 2018.

The requirements related to this topic are mainly derived from the following.

STANDARD	TITLE
IFRS 13	Fair Value Measurement
IAS 36	Impairment of Assets
IFRIC 10	Interim Financial Reporting and Impairment

The currently effective requirements include newly effective requirements arising from IFRS 9 *Financial Instruments*, which is effective for annual periods beginning on or after 1 January 2018. Transition requirements for IFRS 9 are the subject of chapter 7.11. The impact of the new requirements on impairment of non-financial assets is reflected in 3.10.565, 570, 585 and 660.

FORTHCOMING REQUIREMENTS

The currently effective requirements are affected by the following forthcoming requirements. They are highlighted with a # and the impact is explained in the accompanying boxed text at the references indicated.
- In January 2016, the IASB issued IFRS 16 *Leases*, which is effective for annual periods beginning on or after 1 January 2019. See 3.10.675. IFRS 16 is the subject of chapter 5.1A.
- In May 2017, the IASB issued IFRS 17 *Insurance Contracts*, which is effective for annual periods beginning on or after 1 January 2021. See 3.10.25. IFRS 17 is the subject of chapter 8.1A.

FUTURE DEVELOPMENTS

This topic is subject to future developments that may affect several aspects of the accounting for impairment of goodwill. See 3.10.880.

3.10.10 STEPS IN IMPAIRMENT TESTING

3.10.10.10   There are a number of steps in performing impairment testing, which are discussed in more detail throughout this chapter.

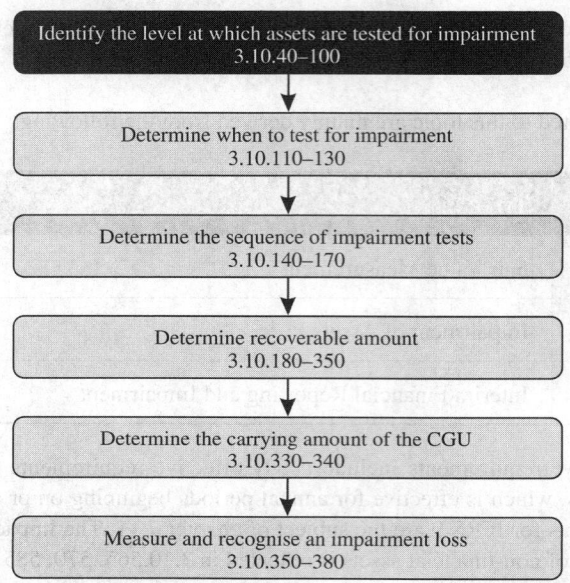

3.10.20 SCOPE#

3.10.20.10   IAS 36 covers the impairment of all non-financial assets except for:
- investment property that is measured at fair value (see chapter 3.4);
- inventories (see chapter 3.8);
- biological assets that are measured at fair value less costs to sell (see chapter 3.9);
- deferred tax assets (see chapter 3.13);
- contract assets and contract costs to obtain or fulfil a contract with customers (see 4.2.285 and 7.8.390);
- assets arising from employee benefits (see chapter 4.4);
- non-current assets (or disposal groups) classified as held-for-sale (see 5.4.20); and
- deferred acquisition costs and intangible assets arising from an insurer's contractual rights under insurance contracts (see chapter 8.1). [*IAS 36.2–5*]

3.10.20.15   The standard does not cover financial assets (see chapters 7.7 and 7.8) other than investments in subsidiaries, associates and joint ventures. [*IAS 36.2(e), 4*]

3.10.20.20   The above assets are excluded from the scope of IAS 36 because other standards deal with their measurement. However, that does not mean that the assets are ignored entirely in the impairment testing process (see 3.10.330–340). [*IAS 36.3*]

3.10.20.30   There is no scope exemption for assets that are not ready for use or sale – e.g. a building under construction (see 3.10.250.120).

3.10.30 KEY DEFINITIONS AND OBJECTIVE

3.10.30.10 There are certain key definitions in IAS 36 that are used in this chapter. Here we give a general description as an aid to understanding the concepts in IAS 36 as the chapter progresses.

3.10.30.20 A CGU is the smallest group of assets that generates cash inflows from continuing use that are largely independent of the cash inflows of other assets or groups thereof. In our experience, in most cases impairment testing is performed at the CGU level – i.e. assets are tested in groups, rather than on a stand-alone basis. CGUs are discussed in 3.10.60. [*IAS 36.6*]

3.10.30.30 In testing for impairment, the carrying amount of an asset or CGU is compared with its 'recoverable amount', which is the higher of:
- the asset's or CGU's fair value less costs of disposal; and
- value in use. [*IAS 36.6*]

3.10.30.40 'Fair value less costs of disposal' is the price that would be received to sell an asset or CGU in an orderly transaction between market participants at the measurement date, less the costs of disposal. IAS 36 refers to IFRS 13 for determining fair value, and there is no special guidance in IAS 36 (see 3.10.190). [*IAS 36.6*]

3.10.30.50 'Value in use' is the present value of the future cash flows expected to be derived from an asset or CGU. Value in use is a valuation concept that is specific to IAS 36 and not used in other standards. It combines entity-specific estimates of future cash flows – from continuing use and eventual disposal of the asset or CGU – with a market participant-based discount rate. IAS 36 includes detailed rule-based requirements on determining value in use (see 3.10.220–350). [*IAS 36.6*]

3.10.30.60 'Corporate assets' are assets other than goodwill that contribute to the future cash flows of both the CGU under review and other CGUs. IAS 36 includes specific requirements on how to test corporate assets for impairment because they benefit multiple CGUs. For a discussion of the general requirements related to corporate assets, see 3.10.150 and 170; and for application issues, see 3.10.480. [*IAS 36.6*]

3.10.40 IDENTIFY LEVEL AT WHICH ASSETS ARE TESTED FOR IMPAIRMENT

3.10.50 Individual assets

3.10.50.10 Whenever possible, IAS 36 is applied to the individual asset. However, a single asset is not generally tested for impairment on a stand-alone basis when it generates cash inflows only in combination with other assets as part of a larger CGU. There are exceptions to this basic rule, which are explored in 3.10.125. [*IAS 36.22, 66–67*]

3.10.50.20   In our experience, most single assets do not qualify to be tested alone. This means that most assets are tested for impairment in CGUs (see 3.10.125). An example of a single asset that might be tested individually is an investment property measured under the cost model (see 3.4.170).

3.10.60   Cash-generating units

3.10.60.10   Assets are grouped together into the smallest group of assets that generates cash inflows from continuing use that are largely independent of the cash inflows of other assets or groups thereof – e.g. a plant or division of a larger entity. Such a group is known as a CGU. A CGU is identified consistently from period to period for the same asset or types of assets, unless a change is justified. [*IAS 36.6, 72*]

3.10.60.20   The identification of CGUs requires judgement, and can be one of the most difficult areas of impairment accounting. Although the key test is the identification of independent cash inflows, IAS 36 also refers to other factors – e.g. the manner in which management monitors operations and makes decisions about continuing or disposing of assets and/or operations. In our view, these additional factors are intended to assist in identifying parts of the business that have independent cash inflows, and are not alternative tests. [*IAS 36.68–69*]

3.10.70   *Independent cash inflows*

3.10.70.10   In determining whether a group of assets is a CGU, the IFRS Interpretations Committee has confirmed that emphasis is placed on independent cash inflows, rather than net cash flows; therefore, cash outflows in themselves are not relevant. For example, an individual store location with largely independent sales is a CGU. The fact that the store may share infrastructure, human resources, marketing and other operating expenses with other stores is not relevant in making this determination. [*IU 03-07*]

3.10.70.20   In our view, two considerations are particularly useful in identifying groups of assets that have independent cash inflows, although neither of them is likely to be determinative in isolation.
- *Revenue separation:* Are the streams of revenue derived from these groups of assets independent of one another?
- *Asset separation:* Are assets operated together to such an extent that they do not generate independent revenue streams? In making this assessment, the assets referred to are not corporate assets; rather, they are the core operating assets of the business (see 3.10.95).

3.10.70.30   IAS 36 clarifies that if an active market exists for the output from a group of assets, then that group of assets is a separate CGU – even if the output is sold only to other units of the same entity. This is because that group of assets *could* generate independent cash inflows. [*IAS 36.70–71*]

3.10.70.40   This clarification is particularly relevant for vertically integrated businesses, in which one unit produces a product and transfers it to another unit within the same reporting entity for further processing or sale. In this case, it is likely that each unit will be a separate CGU, regardless of how the business is run. [*IAS 36.IE5–IE10*]

3.10.70.50   CGUs are not constrained by country borders, and a single CGU might cover different countries and functional currencies (see 2.7.30).

3.10.75 *Revenue separation*

3.10.75.10   Revenue separation is likely to be the key consideration in businesses that operate a large number of smaller businesses – e.g. retail outlets – or that sell bundled products or have a large amount of referred business. Examples 1A to 1E illustrate revenue separation.

EXAMPLE 1A – REVENUE SEPARATION IN IDENTIFYING CGUs – SEPARATE CUSTOMER BASES

3.10.75.20   Company R operates retail outlets in a number of cities within a country; the retail outlets are supplied via regional distribution centres. The customer base of one outlet is separate from the customer bases of other outlets – i.e. their cash inflows are independent. Therefore, R concludes that each retail outlet is a separate CGU. The regional distribution centres may be corporate assets (see 3.10.90). [*IAS 36.IE1–IE4*]

EXAMPLE 1B – REVENUE SEPARATION IN IDENTIFYING CGUs – SIGNIFICANT CASH INFLOWS

3.10.75.25   Company C operates a network of retail outlets. Cash inflows come from sales to customers and volume rebates from suppliers. Volume rebates are based on purchases by all retail outlets and represent around 10% of revenue income.

3.10.75.26   C has daily sales information, and monthly statements of profit or loss are produced for each individual retail outlet. This information is used to make decisions about continuing to operate individual retail outlets.

3.10.75.27   Notwithstanding that the volume rebate income is based on the combined purchases by all retail outlets, C concludes that each retail outlet is a separate CGU. This is because the volume rebate income is insignificant compared with sales, and C monitors and makes decisions about its assets and operations at the individual retail outlet level.

EXAMPLE 1C – REVENUE SEPARATION IN IDENTIFYING CGUs – SINGLE CUSTOMER BASE AND CENTRAL PRICING

3.10.75.30   Company M is a multinational with manufacturing operations split between two countries, and sales offices in a number of countries around the world. Engines are manufactured in Country X and parts are manufactured in Country Y.

3.10.75.35   Almost all customers that buy an engine also buy original spare parts through the same sales office; customers do not buy parts unless they have also bought an engine. Products and pricing are controlled by head office, and the price of an engine takes into account the almost inevitable subsequent sale of parts and maintenance services – i.e. the engine is often sold at a discounted price.

3.10.75.37   In this example, M concludes that it has a single CGU, for the following reasons:
- it has a single customer base for engines and parts; and
- pricing is set centrally by head office across all products. [*IAS 36.IE5–IE10*]

> 3.10.75.40   The analysis in this example may be more complex if M has a series of product lines, each with its own engine series and related spare parts.

EXAMPLE 1D – REVENUE SEPARATION IN IDENTIFYING CGUs – BUNDLED PRODUCTS (1)

> 3.10.75.50   Company U is a utility company that caters to the residential customers in a particular region. It offers a 'value-pack' to its customers, which is a bundle of two products: gas and electricity. Although customers can elect to buy the elements of the package separately, 75% of customers choose the value-pack.
>
> 3.10.75.55   In this example, U concludes that its business as a whole comprises a single CGU, because the cash inflows of each operation are not generated largely independently.

EXAMPLE 1E – REVENUE SEPARATION IN IDENTIFYING CGUs – BUNDLED PRODUCTS (2)

> 3.10.75.60   Modifying Example 1D, only 45% of customers choose the value-pack. In this example, Company U concludes that it has two CGUs: a gas CGU and an electricity CGU.

3.10.80   *Asset separation*

3.10.80.10   Asset separation is likely to be the key consideration in businesses that use a single asset base to generate different revenue streams – e.g. telecoms that use a single network to deliver services. Examples 1F to 1H illustrate asset separation.

EXAMPLE 1F – ASSET SEPARATION IN IDENTIFYING CGUs – ALLOCATION NOT POSSIBLE

> 3.10.80.20   Company T is a telecommunications company that offers fibre-to-the-premise services with the 'last mile' – i.e. the connection from the exchange or the cabinet to the customer's residence – being either copper or fibre. Both services are provided from a single fibre network, the backbone, which is the core operating asset.
>
> 3.10.80.25   In this example, T concludes that its business is a single CGU because its core operating asset, the network, services all customers. Although the cash inflows can be separated to the customer level, the asset cannot be separated between the two types of customers (copper vs fibre) except on an arbitrary basis.

EXAMPLE 1G – ASSET SEPARATION IN IDENTIFYING CGUs – NO DISCRETION TO CLOSE OPERATIONS

> 3.10.80.30   Company X operates in the transportation industry, and was recently awarded a licence by the government to provide bus services throughout Country Y, based on minimum service levels. X charges a separate fare for each passenger on each bus route and is therefore able to measure revenues by route; however, X

does not have discretion to choose the areas in which it will operate, because the contract requires it to supply the entire country with bus services. [*IAS 36.68*]

3.10.80.35   In this example, X concludes that all of the assets dedicated to the contract form a single CGU. This is because X does not have the ability to make decisions about the allocation of assets at a lower level. Although the cash inflows can be separated by route, the terms of the licence agreement require the assets to be operated as part of a single network such that the routes do not generate *independent* revenue streams. [*IAS 36.68*]

3.10.80.37   This conclusion would be reached even if cash inflows could be determined at a lower level – e.g. for each region or route – because X is not able to close an unprofitable route under the terms of the contract. [*IAS 36.68*]

EXAMPLE 1H – ASSET SEPARATION IN IDENTIFYING CGUs – DISCRETION TO CLOSE OPERATIONS

3.10.80.40   Modifying Example 1G, the terms of the licence do not prescribe minimum service levels for the country overall – i.e. the licence allows Company X to withdraw bus services from routes that are unprofitable. X manages its fleet of buses by region; the buses are similar and are used interchangeably in a particular region.

3.10.80.45   Revenue separation is possible. Therefore, in this example, X concludes that each region is a separate CGU, because its core assets are managed at this level – even if each route has a separate customer base.

3.10.80.50   In our view, the conclusion in Example 1H would not change even if Company X could theoretically interchange the buses used in different regions. This is because IAS 36 emphasises the way in which a business actually is run and not how it could be run. [*IAS 36.69*]

3.10.85   **Review of CGU determination**

3.10.85.10   IAS 36 requires that a CGU be identified consistently from period to period unless a change is justified. In our view, this requirement indicates that the application of the standard is not intended to result in a different outcome each year if there has been no significant change in the business; instead, an entity should look for significant trends over time. [*IAS 36.72*]

EXAMPLE 2 – IDENTIFYING CGUs – CHANGE IN BUSINESS

3.10.85.20   Continuing Example 1D, between 2013 and 2017 around 75% of customers chose the value-pack; Company U concluded that its business as a whole comprised a single CGU. In 2018, that percentage drops to 55% even though U's product offering has remained the same.

3.10.85.30   In this example, we would not expect U to change the basis of identifying its CGUs in 2018 in the absence of a clear reason for the change – e.g. a sustained change in customer preferences because of new technology or products offered by competitors.

> **3.10.85.40**   However, a change in CGU determination may be appropriate if the trend continues in 2019 – even if the reason for the trend cannot be specifically identified.

3.10.90   Corporate assets

3.10.90.10   By definition (see 3.10.30.60), corporate assets contribute to the future cash inflows of two or more CGUs, without generating their own cash inflows that are largely independent. Therefore, a corporate asset is not tested for impairment as an individual asset on a stand-alone basis, unless management has decided to dispose of the asset (see 3.10.50). Instead, IAS 36 includes specific requirements about how a corporate asset is tested for impairment as part of the testing of CGUs. For a discussion of the general requirements related to corporate assets, see 3.10.150; and for application issues, see 3.10.480. [*IAS 36.100–101*]

3.10.90.20   IAS 36 notes that examples of corporate assets include headquarter buildings, computer equipment and research centres. Other examples of corporate assets might be a warehouse shared by several retail units, or plant and machinery shared by production lines. In our experience, such assets are sometimes referred to as 'shared' rather than 'corporate' assets; however, they fall under the definition of a corporate asset in IAS 36 if they contribute to the cash flows of more than one CGU. [*IAS 36.100*]

3.10.95   Asset separation vs corporate assets

3.10.95.10   In 3.10.80, we refer to the core operating assets of a business being used collectively to generate revenue. This could be seen as similar to a corporate asset that contributes to the future cash inflows of two or more CGUs (see 3.10.90.10). Therefore, a question arises about why corporate assets do not result in CGUs being identified at a higher level. Such a conclusion would result in a different analysis of CGUs, and may result in a different impairment outcome.

3.10.95.20   Making the distinction between core operating assets and corporate assets requires judgement and a careful analysis of the facts and circumstances. In our view, the core operating assets are the key to revenue generation within the business, whereas corporate assets are peripheral to the generation of revenue. Returning to telecommunications Company T in Example 1F, the backbone network is the core operating asset because it drives the amount of revenue earned; however, T's headquarters relate to the administration of the business as a whole, and are classified as a corporate asset.

3.10.100   Goodwill

3.10.100.10   Similar to corporate assets, goodwill does not generate cash inflows independently of other assets or groups of assets, and therefore is not tested for impairment separately. Instead, IAS 36 includes specific requirements about how goodwill is tested for impairment as part of the testing of CGUs. For a discussion of the general requirements related to goodwill, see 3.10.160–170; and for a discussion of application issues, see 3.10.430. [*IAS 36.80*]

3.10.110   DETERMINE WHEN TO TEST FOR IMPAIRMENT

3.10.110.10   Impairment testing is required:
- at each reporting date for an asset or CGU when there is an indication of possible impairment (a triggering event); and
- annually for the following assets, regardless of whether there is a triggering event:

- intangible assets with an indefinite useful life (see 3.3.200);
- intangible assets not yet available for use; and
- CGUs to which goodwill has been allocated (see 3.10.430). [*IAS 36.9–10*]

3.10.110.20   The annual impairment test is required *in addition* to any impairment tests performed by the entity as a result of a triggering event. [*IAS 36.10*]

3.10.120   Indicator-based impairment testing

3.10.120.10   An entity assesses at each reporting date whether there is an indication, based on either internal or external sources of information, that an asset or a CGU may be impaired. [*IAS 36.9*]

3.10.120.20   The following are examples of *internal* indications of impairment that are considered in assessing whether indicator-based impairment testing is necessary:
- the obsolescence or physical damage of an asset;
- significant changes in the extent or manner in which an asset is (or is expected to be) used that have (or will have) an adverse effect on the entity;
- a plan to dispose of an asset before the previously expected date of disposal;
- indications that the performance of an asset is, or will be, worse than expected;
- cash flows for acquiring the asset, operating or maintaining it that are significantly higher than originally budgeted;
- net cash flows or operating profits that are lower than originally budgeted; and
- net cash outflows or operating losses. [*IAS 36.12(e)–(g), 14*]

3.10.120.30   The following are examples of *external* indications of impairment that are considered in assessing whether indicator-based impairment testing is necessary:
- a significant and unexpected decline in market value;
- significant adverse effects in the technological, market, economic or legal environment;
- an increase in market interest rates that will increase the discount rate used to determine an asset's value in use (see 3.10.300); and
- the carrying amount of the net assets of an entity exceeding its market capitalisation. [*IAS 36.12(a)–(d)*]

3.10.120.40   In our view, if the price paid to acquire NCI by a parent entity is less than the carrying amount of those interests in the consolidated financial statements, then this might be an indication that certain assets of the subsidiary are impaired. In such cases, we believe that the parent should consider whether any of the underlying assets are impaired before accounting for the change in ownership interests (see 2.5.670).

3.10.120.50   The examples in 3.10.120.20–40 are indications of possible impairment that are considered in assessing whether impairment testing is required; they do not automatically lead to mandatory impairment testing. For example, an entity assesses whether the magnitude or effect of a change in interest rates, or the gap between its net assets and market capitalisation, requires the determination of recoverable amounts. [*IAS 36.12, 16*]

3.10.125   *Testing single asset vs CGU*

3.10.125.10   The nature of the indication of impairment, and in some cases the nature of the asset, determines the level at which impairment testing is carried out. In some cases, it is clear that a CGU rather than an individual asset should be tested for impairment.

EXAMPLE 3A – IMPAIRMENT INDICATORS – OPERATING LOSSES

3.10.125.20 Company C's business comprises three CGUs: X, Y and Z. CGUs X and Y are profitable. However, a downturn in the market for the product sold by CGU Z has resulted in operating losses for that CGU, which management concludes is an indication of possible impairment.

3.10.125.30 As a result, C tests CGU Z for impairment. However, C does not test CGUs X and Y, unless such testing is required because of the allocation of corporate assets and/or goodwill (see 3.10.150–170).

EXAMPLE 3B – IMPAIRMENT INDICATORS – FALL IN MARKET CAPITALISATION

3.10.125.40 Company B is a listed multinational with various manufacturing operations. All CGUs that make up the company continue to be profitable despite downward pressure on margins; however, B's market capitalisation has fallen significantly below the carrying amount of its recognised net assets.

3.10.125.50 B is not able to identify a specific area of operations that is the driver for the fall in market capitalisation, and therefore concludes that all CGUs should be tested for impairment.

3.10.125.60 In other cases, the indication of possible impairment is at the level of the single asset. In this case, to determine the level at which impairment testing is carried out, IAS 36 includes a series of steps to be considered based on the nature of the asset and how it generates cash inflows. Those steps are shown in the following flowchart.

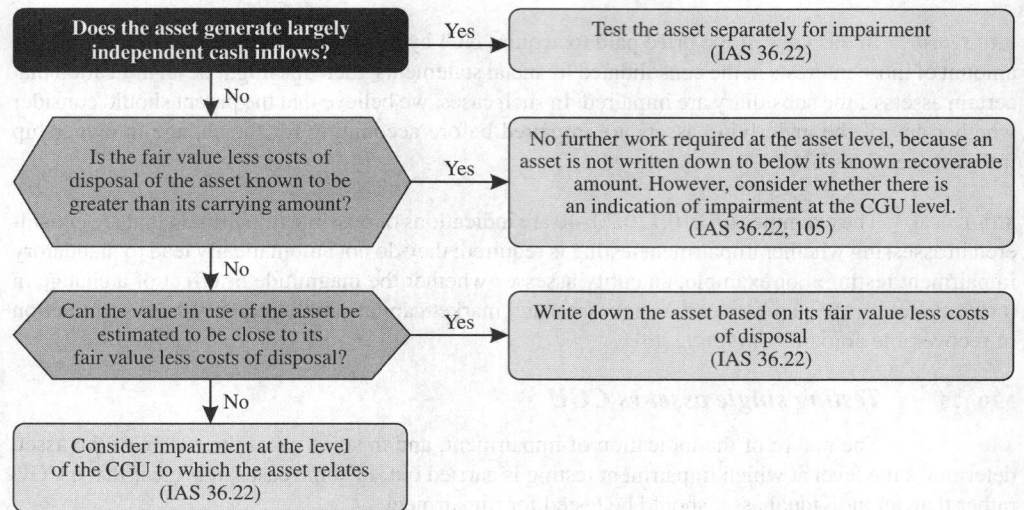

EXAMPLE 4A – TESTING SINGLE ASSET VS CGU (1)

3.10.125.70 Company C operates one factory that comprises a single CGU. There is no indication of impairment at the CGU level. However, a key piece of equipment is damaged and, although it is operational at a reduced capacity and able to be repaired, C has decided to replace the machine and has ordered a newer model.

3.10.125.80 C ascertains that there is a market for second-hand machines in an overseas market, and identifies a selling agent. C plans to continue using the damaged machine until the new one arrives, at which point it will be refurbished and sold. This process is expected to take about six weeks.

3.10.125.90 The selling agent has indicated an estimated selling price for the refurbished machine, from which C is able to estimate the fair value less costs of disposal of the machine in its current condition. In addition, C estimates that its value in use is close to its fair value less costs of disposal. This is because, based on the short period until the machine is sold, cash flows from its continuing use are estimated to be negligible.

3.10.125.100 Applying the steps in the flowchart in 3.10.125.60, C concludes that the damaged machine should be written down to its fair value less costs of disposal. Although the machine does not generate largely independent cash inflows, in this example the asset's value in use can be estimated to be close to its fair value less costs of disposal (which can be measured).

EXAMPLE 4B – TESTING SINGLE ASSET VS CGU (2)

3.10.125.110 Company Z comprises a single CGU engaged in the retail industry, which is profitable overall. Z acquired a new office building in 2013, from which it runs its operations. The building has a relatively generic design with no special features.

3.10.125.120 There is no indication of impairment at the CGU level even though an ongoing property slump causes Z to question whether the carrying amount of the building should be impaired. A report indicates that the fair value less costs of disposal of Z's building is greater than its carrying amount.

3.10.125.130 Applying the steps in the flowchart in 3.10.125.60, Z concludes that no further work is required. Although the building does not generate largely independent cash inflows, in this example the asset's fair value less costs of disposal is greater than its carrying amount, which means that no loss is recorded. In addition, Z concludes that there is no indication of impairment at the CGU level.

EXAMPLE 4C – TESTING SINGLE ASSET VS CGU (3)

> 3.10.125.140 Company X has two CGUs, A and B, each of which operates under its own brand name. CGU B has been incurring losses, and X concludes that it should be tested for impairment. Within CGU B, the brand is the most significant asset.
>
> 3.10.125.150 X is aware from a recent preliminary report prepared by a valuation specialist that the fair value of the brand is lower than its carrying amount. However, X has no intention of disposing of the brand, which is an integral part of its business.
>
> 3.10.125.160 Applying the steps in the flowchart in 3.10.125.60, X concludes that the CGU as a whole should be tested for impairment – i.e. the brand should not be tested as a stand-alone asset. This is because the brand does not generate largely independent cash inflows, and Z answers 'no' to the other two questions in the flowchart.

3.10.130 Mandatory annual impairment testing

3.10.130.10 Impairment testing is required:
- annually for intangible assets with indefinite useful lives and intangible assets not yet available for use, irrespective of whether there is an indication that the related assets may be impaired; and
- whenever there is an indication that they may be impaired. [*IAS 36.9–10*]

3.10.130.20 Similarly, CGUs to which goodwill has been allocated are tested for impairment annually and whenever there is any indication of impairment. [*IAS 36.10*]

3.10.130.30 The annual impairment test for the following items may be performed at any time within an annual reporting period, provided that the test is performed at the same time every year:
- a CGU (or group of CGUs) to which goodwill has been allocated;
- intangible assets not yet available for use; and
- intangible assets with indefinite useful lives. [*IAS 36.10, 96*]

3.10.130.40 Different assets (and CGUs) can be tested for impairment at different times. [*IAS 36.10, 96*]

3.10.130.50 There may be circumstances in which an entity wishes to change the timing of its annual impairment testing. In our view, a change in timing is acceptable provided that it is justified under the circumstances and not made to achieve a specific outcome – e.g. to avoid, delay or reduce an impairment charge. For example, an entity may wish to change the timing of its annual impairment testing to better align with its internal financial budgeting/forecasting cycle or in the context of a significant acquisition.

3.10.130.60 If the period between the revised annual impairment testing date and the previous date exceeds 12 months, then a question arises about whether two impairment tests need to be performed in the same annual period in which the change in testing date occurs; once at the previous testing date and again at the revised testing date. In our view, the approach taken should ensure that any impairment charge is reported in the appropriate reporting period. Determining whether an additional impairment test is required at the previous testing date will depend on the specific facts and circumstances, including but not limited to:

- the length of time between the previous and revised annual testing dates;
- the frequency of interim reporting;
- the outcome of the previous impairment test – i.e. the size of the difference between recoverable amount and the carrying amount (headroom);
- changes in market conditions; and
- the existence of any indications of impairment (see 3.10.120) between the previous and revised testing dates.

3.10.130.70   For example, a change in the annual testing date from February to September – a potential gap of 19 months from February 2018 to September 2019 – will generally require more comprehensive impairment testing considerations than a change in testing date from February to March.

3.10.130.80   Intangible assets with an indefinite useful life or not yet available for use are also tested for impairment in the period in which they were initially recognised. [*IAS 36.10*]

EXAMPLE 5 – ACQUISITION OF INDEFINITE-LIFE INTANGIBLE ASSET

3.10.130.90   In-process research and development (see 3.10.640) is acquired in April 2018 by a company with a year end of 31 December 2018. In this case, the first impairment test is performed not later than 31 December 2018. For a discussion of the testing of goodwill for the first time, see 3.10.460.

3.10.140   DETERMINE SEQUENCE OF IMPAIRMENT TESTS

3.10.140.10   The sequence of impairment tests becomes complicated when there are corporate assets or goodwill that relate to more than one CGU.

3.10.150   Corporate assets

3.10.150.10   A portion of a corporate asset is allocated to a CGU when the allocation can be done on a reasonable and consistent basis. [*IAS 36.102(a)*]

3.10.150.20   When a portion of a corporate asset cannot be allocated to a CGU on a reasonable and consistent basis, two levels of impairment tests are carried out.

- The first test is performed at the individual CGU level without the corporate asset (bottom-up test), and any impairment loss is recognised (see 3.10.350).
- The second test is applied to the minimum collection of CGUs to which the corporate asset can be allocated reasonably and consistently (top-down test). [*IAS 36.102(b)*]

EXAMPLE 6A – ALLOCATION OF CORPORATE ASSET (1)

3.10.150.30   Company S and Company T both have two CGUs, A and B, and there is no goodwill attributable to any of the CGUs. Both CGUs in each company benefit from the use of an IT system (corporate asset) that is administered by their respective head offices. In each company there is an indication that CGU B is impaired.

3.10.150.35   S concludes that a portion of the IT system can be allocated to CGU B's carrying amount on a reasonable and consistent basis. Accordingly, S carries out one impairment test: CGU B, including a portion of the IT system.

3.10.150.37   T concludes that a portion of the IT system cannot be allocated to CGU B on a reasonable and consistent basis. Accordingly, T carries out the following two impairment tests.
- CGU B, excluding any portion of the IT system from its carrying amount.
- CGU A plus CGU B plus the IT system.

3.10.150.40   There is no guidance in IAS 36 on what a 'reasonable and consistent' basis means, and therefore judgement is required in this regard. Depending on the nature of the asset, potential bases for allocation may include square metres occupied, headcount or transactions processed. However, in many cases it is likely that the basis of an intra-group charge will provide a reasonable and consistent basis for allocating a corporate asset to CGUs.

3.10.150.50   In some cases, the indication of impairment may be specific to a corporate asset rather than to the CGUs to which the corporate asset relates.

EXAMPLE 6B – ALLOCATION OF CORPORATE ASSET (2)

3.10.150.60   Continuing Example 6A, the IT system of S has become technically obsolete, but otherwise there is no indication of impairment in any of the CGUs in general. Because the corporate asset contributes exclusively to the cash flows of S as a whole, S is identified as the relevant group of CGUs to be tested. [*IAS 36.101*]

3.10.150.70   For specific guidance on determining value in use when there are corporate assets, see 3.10.480.

3.10.160   Goodwill

3.10.160.10   There are two scenarios in which goodwill is tested for impairment:
1. a CGU or a group of CGUs to which goodwill has been allocated is being tested for impairment when there is an indication of possible impairment (see 3.10.120); or
2. goodwill is being tested for impairment in the annual mandatory impairment testing, without there being an indication of impairment in the underlying CGUs.

3.10.160.20   In the first scenario in 3.10.160.10 (indicator-based impairment test), the way in which impairment testing is carried out depends on whether goodwill has been allocated to individual CGUs or to a group of CGUs. If goodwill has been allocated to a group of CGUs, then impairment testing is performed in the following steps.

- The first impairment test is performed at the individual CGU level without goodwill (bottom-up test), and any impairment loss is recognised (see 3.10.350).
- The second impairment test is applied to the collection of CGUs to which the goodwill relates (top-down test). [*IAS 36.97*]

3.10.160.30   However, if the goodwill has been allocated to an individual CGU, then there is no need for a two-step approach, and the entire CGU (including goodwill) is tested for impairment.

3.10.160.40   In the second scenario in 3.10.160.10 (annual impairment test), the collection of CGUs to which the goodwill relates is tested for impairment, and there is no requirement for two-stage (bottom-up and top-down) testing.

EXAMPLE 7 – GOODWILL IMPAIRMENT TEST

3.10.160.50   Company P has determined that there is an indication of impairment in CGU R (carrying amount of 100). Goodwill (carrying amount of 50) relates not only to CGU R, but also to two other CGUs, S and T (carrying amounts of 60 and 40, respectively).

3.10.160.55   Company P performs impairment testing as follows.
1. *Bottom-up test:* The carrying amount of CGU R is 100 and its recoverable amount is determined to be 80. An impairment loss of 20 is recognised.
2. *Top-down test:* The carrying amount of CGU (R + S + T), including goodwill, is 230 (80 + 60 + 40 + 50) – i.e. the carrying amount of CGU R is after recognising the impairment loss in the bottom-up testing. This carrying amount is used in determining the impairment loss, if there is any, in the top-down test.

3.10.160.60   For a discussion of the impairment testing of goodwill when there are NCI in a subsidiary, see 3.10.510.

3.10.170   Corporate assets and goodwill

3.10.170.10   IAS 36 contains guidance on testing each of corporate assets (see 3.10.150) and goodwill (see 3.10.160); however, there is no guidance on how the testing interacts when there are corporate assets *and* goodwill present. In our view, the testing requirements overlap rather than being done in consecutive steps.

EXAMPLE 8A – CORPORATE ASSETS AND GOODWILL (1)

3.10.170.20   Company Z allocates goodwill to the group of CGUs A, B and C. Z uses the same IT system (corporate asset) for all its CGUs, A, B, C and D. Management concludes that the corporate asset's carrying amount cannot be allocated to each CGU on a reasonable and consistent basis (see 3.10.150.20). There is an indication of impairment for CGU B.

3.10.170.30   Therefore, Z carries out impairment testing in the following sequence.
1. CGU B is tested for impairment without goodwill and without any allocation of the corporate asset to its carrying amount.
2. The group of CGUs A+B+C is tested for impairment with goodwill, but without any allocation of the corporate asset to its carrying amount.
3. The group of CGUs A+B+C and CGU D are tested together for impairment with goodwill and with the corporate asset included in the carrying amount of the combined group.

EXAMPLE 8B – CORPORATE ASSETS AND GOODWILL (2)

3.10.170.40   Assume that the facts in Example 8A were different and Z concluded that it could allocate the corporate asset's carrying amount to CGUs on a reasonable and consistent basis.

3.10.170.50   In this case, Z would carry out impairment testing in the following sequence.
1. CGU B would be tested for impairment without goodwill but with an allocation of the corporate asset included in its carrying amount.
2. CGU A+B+C would be tested for impairment with goodwill and with an allocation of the corporate asset (an allocation relevant to all three CGUs) to its carrying amount.

3.10.170.60   Examples 8A and 8B illustrate the additional burden in impairment testing if corporate assets are not allocated to CGUs. For further discussion of allocating goodwill to CGUs or groups of CGUs, see 3.10.430.

3.10.180   DETERMINE RECOVERABLE AMOUNT

3.10.180.10   The recoverable amount of an asset or CGU is the higher of its:
- fair value less costs of disposal; and
- value in use. [*IAS 36.6*]

3.10.180.20   The purpose of impairment testing is to determine whether the recoverable amount is greater than the carrying amount. If it is greater – based on *either* fair value less costs of disposal or value in use – then there is no requirement to refine the determination of the recoverable amount to a single number. However, if it is not greater, then more detailed work is required to determine the recoverable amount in order to calculate the impairment loss.

3.10.180.30   Therefore, it is not always necessary to determine both an asset's or CGU's fair value less costs of disposal *and* value in use. For example, assume that fair value less costs of disposal exceeds the carrying amount of an asset or a CGU, or if there is no reason to believe that the asset's or CGU's value in use materially exceeds its fair value less costs of disposal. In this case, it is not necessary to calculate value in use. However, assume that it is not possible to determine fair value less costs of disposal, because there is no basis for making a reliable estimate of fair value. In this case, value in use is used as the recoverable amount. [*IAS 36.19–22*]

3.10.180.40   Despite these general requirements, if the impairment testing of another asset – e.g. goodwill – causes the CGU to be tested for impairment, then all assets within that CGU are included in the impairment test. However, in allocating any impairment loss, an individual asset is not written down to below its known recoverable amount or zero (see 3.10.380). [*IAS 36.105*]

3.10.180.50   As acknowledged in IAS 36, in some cases forms of shortcut testing may be appropriate. Therefore, in estimating the recoverable amount, conservative assumptions – i.e. assumptions that would understate recoverable amount – can be used initially. Only if the resulting recoverable amount is less than the carrying amount of the asset or CGU will it be necessary to refine the assumptions, either:

- to show that the recoverable amount does exceed the carrying amount; or
- to calculate an actual recoverable amount in order to determine the impairment loss. [*IAS 36.23*]

3.10.180.60   Sometimes a CGU (with or without goodwill) that has been acquired recently is tested for impairment. In these situations, the consideration paid to acquire that CGU in an arm's length transaction, adjusted for disposal costs and any changes in value arising from factors since acquisition, may provide the best evidence of the CGU's fair value less costs of disposal – and therefore the recoverable amount if value in use is lower. Consequently, in our view impairment losses on recently acquired CGUs should occur infrequently in practice. [*IAS 36.BC69–BC70*]

3.10.180.70   Market conditions that arise after the reporting date are considered to determine whether they are an adjusting or non-adjusting event (see chapter 2.9). If the assumptions made in determining recoverable amount at the reporting date are consistent with the assumptions that a market participant would make at that date, then no further adjustment is necessary. This applies to assumptions used in determining either fair value less costs of disposal or value in use. However, the entity should consider whether disclosure would be appropriate in accordance with IAS 10 if the assumptions that a market participant would make change subsequent to the reporting date. [*IAS 10.3, 8, 10*]

EXAMPLE 9 – CHANGE IN MARKET CONDITIONS AFTER REPORTING DATE

3.10.180.80   Company R, with a year end of 31 December 2018, comprises a single CGU that provides domestic logistics services. R performs annual impairment testing at the reporting date because the CGU includes goodwill.

3.10.180.90   At 31 December 2018, the government of R's jurisdiction was considering deregulating the logistics services sector to allow foreign companies to operate in R's domestic logistics market. Such deregulation would have a negative impact on R's future sales and overall profitability. However, at 31 December 2018, most market and economic commentators believed that deregulation would not be implemented because of the potential negative impact on employment in the sector. On this basis, R prepared alternative cash flow forecasts, including one that assumed a low likelihood of the deregulation being implemented; as a result, no impairment loss was recognised.

3.10.180.100   On 25 February 2019, before R's financial statements are authorised for issue, the government deregulates the logistics services sector with immediate effect. R expects a decline in sales in 2019 and concludes that it might be required to recognise an impairment loss in the following reporting period.

3.10.180.110   In this example, R does not adjust its impairment calculations at 31 December 2018, because the assumptions used were consistent with the assumptions that a market participant would have made at that time. However, in the notes to its financial statements R discloses that the sector has been deregulated and that this might result in an impairment loss in the following period.

3.10.180.120   For the impairment testing of goodwill and intangible assets with indefinite useful lives, an entity may use the most recent determination of recoverable amounts – made in a preceding reporting period – provided that the following criteria are met:

- the assets and liabilities making up the CGU (when the asset is tested as part of a CGU) have not changed significantly since the last determination of recoverable amount;
- the last determination of recoverable amount resulted in the asset's or CGU's carrying amount being exceeded by a substantial margin; and
- management assesses, based on an analysis of the facts and circumstances, that the likelihood of an impairment loss is remote. [*IAS 36.24, 99*]

3.10.185   DIFFERENCES BETWEEN FAIR VALUE AND VALUE IN USE

3.10.185.10   The following table summarises the differences between fair value and value in use.

CHARACTERISTICS	FAIR VALUE LESS COSTS OF DISPOSAL (FVLCD)	VALUE IN USE (VIU)
RELEVANT STANDARD	IFRS 13	IAS 36
GENERAL		
Unit of account	Single asset, CGU or group of CGUs (see 2.4.820).	Single asset, CGU or group of CGUs (see 3.10.40).
Definition	The price that would be received to sell an asset or paid to transfer a liability in an orderly transaction between market participants at the measurement date under current market conditions, less incremental costs directly attributable to the disposal of an asset or CGU, excluding finance costs and income tax expense (see 2.4.20.10). [*IAS 36.6, IFRS 13.9, B2*]	The present value of the future cash flows expected to be derived from an asset or CGU from both its continuing use and ultimate disposal (see 3.10.220.10). [*IAS 36.6*]

CHARACTERISTICS	FAIR VALUE LESS COSTS OF DISPOSAL (FVLCD)	VALUE IN USE (VIU)
RELEVANT STANDARD	IFRS 13	IAS 36
GENERAL (CONTINUED)		
Valuation viewpoint	Market participant Fair value **excludes** the following if they are not available to market participants: • additional value derived from the grouping of assets; • entity-specific synergies; • legal rights or legal restrictions specific to the current owner; and • tax benefits or tax burdens specific to the current owner. [*IFRS 13.2, IAS 36.53A*]	Entity-specific Value in use **includes** the following factors specific to the entity: • additional value derived from the grouping of assets; • entity-specific synergies; • legal rights or legal restrictions specific to the current owner; and • tax benefits or tax burdens specific to the current owner. [*IAS 36.53A*]
Valuation technique	• Market approach • Income approach • Present value technique. [*IFRS 13.B5–B30*]	Present value technique.
Cash flow premises	• Exit price (see 2.4.60.20). • Principal or most advantageous market, in the absence of a principal market (see 2.4.100). • For non-financial assets, highest and best use (see 2.4.330). [*IFRS 13.2, 16, 27*]	Current use based on management's best estimate. [*IAS 36.30(a), 33(a)*]
Starting point for cash flows	Entity-specific budgets and forecasts, when applying a present value technique, adjusted for market conditions.	Entity-specific budgets and forecasts. Significant differences between a market participant's perspective and the entity's perspective need to be justified.
FORECAST PERIOD		
Forecast period	Reflect assumptions that market participants would use (see 2.4.160.40). [*IFRS 13.B14(a)*]	Maximum of five years, unless a longer period can be justified. Cash flow projections after the forecast period are extrapolated over the useful life of the CGU using a steady or declining growth rate that is consistent with that of the product, industry or country (see 3.10.230.10). [*IAS 36.33(b)–(c)*]

CHARACTERISTICS	FAIR VALUE LESS COSTS OF DISPOSAL (FVLCD)	VALUE IN USE (VIU)
RELEVANT STANDARD	IFRS 13	IAS 36
CASH FLOW ASSUMPTIONS		
Capital expenditure	Include, if consistent with a market participant perspective.	Exclude expansionary capital expenditure, unless already committed to by the entity (see 3.10.250.10). [*IAS 36.33b, 44b*]
Restructuring	Include, if consistent with a market participant perspective.	Exclude, unless already committed to by the entity (see 3.10.260.20). [*IAS 36.33b, 44a*]
Corporate overhead	Include if consistent with a market participant perspective. Excluding a portion of corporate overhead costs may be supportable to the extent to which the costs would be viewed as a market participant synergy in a fair value transaction.	Allocate to CGUs, with limited exceptions (see 3.10.240.70).
DISCOUNT RATE		
Discount rate premise	Rate reflects assumptions that a market participant would use (see 2.4.160.40). [*IFRS 13.B14(a)*]	Rate reflects current market assessment of time value of money and risks (see 3.10.300.10). [*IAS 36.55*]

3.10.190 FAIR VALUE LESS COSTS OF DISPOSAL

3.10.190.10   The fair value element of fair value less costs of disposal is measured in accordance with IFRS 13, which is the subject of chapter 2.4. That chapter includes general guidance on applying the principles of IFRS 13 in measuring fair value; specific points of interest in relation to impairment are discussed in 2.4.820.

3.10.200   Costs of disposal

3.10.200.10   Costs of disposal are *incremental* costs directly attributable to the disposal of an asset or CGU. These costs include, for example, legal costs necessary to effect the sale, transaction taxes and other costs to prepare the asset or CGU for its sale. Finance costs and income tax expense are excluded, as are costs already recognised as a liability. [*IAS 36.6, 28*]

3.10.210   Reasonableness tests of fair value less costs of disposal

3.10.210.10   When the recoverable amount of a CGU is determined on the basis of fair value less costs of disposal, and substantial parts of an entity are tested for impairment, the entity generally performs a high-level comparison between market capitalisation and the recoverable amount. In our view, in that case it may be appropriate to add a control premium to market capitalisation in performing the comparison (see 2.4.840). This approach differs from that when the recoverable amount is based on value in use (see 3.10.320.20).

3.10.210.20   Earnings multiples resulting from the fair value less costs of disposal calculation can also be checked for reasonableness by comparison with:
● market multiples for the entity; and
● comparable quoted entities.

3.10.210.25   Comparable transactions may also provide some support. Multiples to consider include price/earnings (P/E) ratios, as well as EBIT and EBITDA multiples (see 3.10.320.30).

EXAMPLE 10 – REASONABLENESS TEST – EARNINGS MULTIPLES

3.10.210.30   The fair value less costs of disposal of CGU X is estimated to be 100. In arriving at this estimate, some of the assumptions include current EBITDA of 8, terminal year EBITDA of 15 and a terminal value of 170. These figures can be used to calculate implied earnings multiples that can be compared with market multiples for reasonableness.

Implied current Enterprise Value / EBITDA multiple (100 / 8)	12.5
Implied terminal Enterprise Value / EBITDA multiple (170 / 15)	11.3
Market multiples of Enterprise Value / EBITDA	5–7

3.10.210.40   The difference between the implied and market multiples suggests that the fair value less costs of disposal estimate is inconsistent with market pricing. This is because the implied multiples are significantly higher than those of comparable businesses. Such differences may be justified in terms of lower risk, higher growth rates etc between the CGU and comparable entities. However, this might also indicate that the fair value less costs of disposal estimate is too high. For example, there may be increased uncertainty about achieving forecast growth; this may need to be reflected, for example, by adding a forecasting risk premium in the discount rate (see 3.10.300.170).

3.10.220   VALUE IN USE

3.10.220.10   Value in use is the present value of the future cash flows expected to be derived from an asset or CGU, both from its continuing use and ultimate disposal.

3.10.220.20   The determination of an asset's value in use reflects considerations such as:
1. the estimated future cash flows that the entity expects the asset to earn;
2. possible variations in the amount or timing of those future cash flows;
3. the time value of money, which is reflected by using a discount rate based on the current market risk-free rate of interest;

4. the price for the uncertainty inherent in the asset; and
5. other factors, such as illiquidity, that would be reflected in valuing the expected future cash flows from the asset. [*IAS 36.30*]

3.10.220.30   The second, fourth and fifth of these elements can be reflected either as adjustments to the future cash flows or as adjustments to the discount rate. [*IAS 36.32*]

3.10.220.40   Appendix A of IAS 36 discusses two approaches to projecting cash flows in order to calculate present value:
● the traditional approach, which uses a single cash flow projection, or most likely cash flow; and
● the expected cash flow approach, which uses multiple, probability-weighted cash flow projections. [*IAS 36.A4–A14*]

3.10.220.50   Whichever approach an entity adopts for measuring the value in use of an asset, the rate used to discount cash flows should not reflect adjustments for factors that have been incorporated into the estimated cash flows and vice versa. Otherwise, the effect of some assumptions will be double counted. [*IAS 36.55–56*]

3.10.220.60   The traditional approach uses a single estimate of future cash flows – i.e. generally the most likely outcome – and does not involve adjustments to the cash flows for their risk. Under this approach, the discount rate used should comprise three components:
● *Component 1*: risk-free rate – i.e. time value of money;
● *Component 2*: the appropriate risk premium; and
● *Component 3*: uncertainty about the future cash flows. [*IAS 36.A4*]

3.10.220.70   In contrast, the expected cash flow approach uses a range of cash flow outcomes, weighted by the estimated probability of each. Because uncertainty about the future cash flows – i.e. Component 3 in 3.10.220.60 – is considered directly in arriving at the expected cash flows, it is not reflected in the discount rate under this approach. Therefore, the discount rate used with expected cash flows only includes the risk-free rate and the appropriate risk premium – i.e. Components 1 and 2 in 3.10.220.60. In our view, it would not be appropriate to use a risk-free discount rate with expected cash flows because a risk premium has not been incorporated into the cash flows. [*IFRS 13.B26, IAS 36.A7*]

3.10.220.80   In theory, an alternative to using either a single estimate of future cash flows or expected cash flows would be to use certainty-equivalent cash flows. Under this method, Components 2 and 3 in 3.10.220.60 are reflected directly in the cash flows such that an investor would be indifferent between investing in the risky cash flows of the asset or CGU and alternative cash flows from a risk-free investment. In this case, a risk-free discount rate is used. However, cash risk premiums are difficult to estimate, especially where assets or liabilities with comparable cash flow profiles are not readily identifiable. Therefore, in our experience certainty-equivalent cash flows are not often used and we expect a risk premium to be incorporated into the discount rate in the value in use calculation. [*IFRS 13.B25*]

3.10.220.90   The following flowchart illustrates the approaches described in paragraphs 3.10.220.60–80.

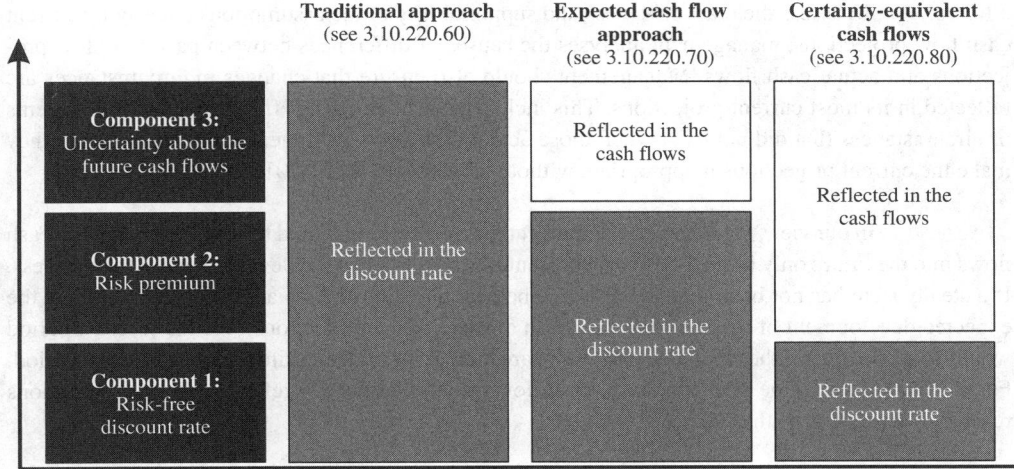

	Traditional approach (see 3.10.220.60)	Expected cash flow approach (see 3.10.220.70)	Certainty-equivalent cash flows (see 3.10.220.80)
Component 3: Uncertainty about the future cash flows		Reflected in the cash flows	Reflected in the cash flows
Component 2: Risk premium	Reflected in the discount rate	Reflected in the discount rate	
Component 1: Risk-free discount rate			Reflected in the discount rate

3.10.230   Forecast period

3.10.230.10   The value in use calculation is based on reasonable and supportable assumptions concerning projections of cash flows approved by management (as part of the budget) and adjusted to the requirements of IFRS. These cash flow forecasts should cover a maximum of five years, unless a longer period can be justified. The cash flows after the forecast period are extrapolated into the future over the useful life of the asset or CGU. For such cash flows, an entity uses a steady or declining growth rate that is consistent with that of the product, industry or country, unless there is clear evidence to suggest another basis. These cash flows form the basis of what is referred to as the terminal value. [*IAS 36.33, 35*]

3.10.230.20   When economies enter a difficult period, in our view it may be necessary to determine the terminal value in two stages to reflect the impact of economic contraction and a subsequent return to maintainable earnings.

- In the first stage, growth rates (potentially on a year-by-year basis) are applied to take the cash flows:
    - to a level at which they can be regarded as reflecting maintainable earnings; and
    - to the period in a mid-point of the cycle – i.e. not at the peak or trough of the cycle.
- The second stage is an extrapolation of those maintainable earnings until the end of the asset's life. In accordance with IAS 36, this growth rate should not exceed the long-term average growth rate appropriate to the asset or CGU, unless a higher rate can be justified. [*IAS 36.33(c)*]

EXAMPLE 11 – EXTRAPOLATION OF CASH FLOWS

3.10.230.30   An entity has detailed forecasts for the next two years. It envisages recessionary conditions continuing for the year after that (the third year), with a slow recovery in the fourth and fifth years. The projection for the third to fifth years reflects that assumption (first stage). The entity believes that the position expected at the end of the fifth year represents the stable long-term position. Therefore, it extrapolates those cash flows into the future using a steady growth rate (second stage).

3.10.230.40   To assess the reasonableness and supportability of the assumptions underlying current cash flow projections, management analyses the causes of differences between past cash flow projections and actual cash flows. Management should also ensure that changes in circumstances are reflected in its most current projections. This includes considering the effects of subsequent events or circumstances that did not exist when those actual cash flows were generated, and whether they make the current projections inappropriate without adjustment. [*IAS 36.34*]

3.10.230.50   In our view, the final year of management projections should be used to extrapolate cash flows into the future only if the final year represents a steady state in the development of the business. If a steady state has not been reached, then we believe that adjustments are necessary to reflect the expected development of the business. Using an average of the projections over the forecast period would be misleading if the estimated cash flows are increasing or decreasing over the forecast period. For a CGU that is in the start-up phase, cash flow projections should reflect realistic assumptions regarding revenue growth.

3.10.230.60   If a CGU consists of several assets that are essential to the ongoing business, then the impairment test is determined based on the essential asset with the longest useful life, and the replacement of assets with shorter lives is considered to be part of the day-to-day servicing of that CGU. For example, if a CGU includes a specialised factory that has a 50-year useful life and machinery with a 10-year useful life, then the cash flow projections are based on the 50-year useful life of the factory. [*IAS 36.49*]

3.10.230.70   In some cases, a CGU may contain an intangible asset with an indefinite useful life or goodwill. In our view, an entity cannot conclude automatically that the intangible asset with an indefinite useful life or goodwill is the essential asset. All facts and circumstances are considered to determine which asset is essential to the operations of the CGU. In our view, in the case of a service business, it is likely that intangible assets with indefinite useful lives or acquired goodwill will be the assets with the longest useful life that are essential to the ongoing operations of the CGU. However, in the case of a nuclear power plant, we believe that it is likely that the plant itself, which has a finite life, will be the asset essential to its ongoing operations.

3.10.230.80   After analysing all relevant facts and circumstances, an entity may determine that an intangible asset with an indefinite useful life or allocated goodwill is essential to the ongoing operations of the CGU. In this case, cash flow projections are prepared for an indefinite period. In our view, entities could, as an approximation, project cash flows for a limited period and then estimate a terminal value at the end of the projection period; the limited period is subject to the rebuttable five-year maximum forecast period (see 3.10.230.10). [*IAS 36.33(c)*]

3.10.230.90   In our view, an essential asset need not be an asset recognised in the statement of financial position. For example, depending on the facts and circumstances of the CGU, it might be appropriate to conclude that the essential asset is a right to use land and other properties under a long-term operating lease, or an unrecognised brand.

3.10.240   Composition of cash flows

3.10.240.10   The cash flows used in determining value in use are those specific to the entity.

3.10.240.20   Cash flows include:
- cash inflows from continuing use;
- cash outflows necessary to generate the cash inflows (including overhead costs); and
- net cash flows from the ultimate disposal of the asset or CGU. [*IAS 36.39, 41*]

3.10.240.30   Overhead costs generally consist of costs to provide identifiable services to CGUs and other corporate costs, including stewardship costs. Stewardship costs may include remuneration to directors and senior officers and the costs of external financial reporting.

3.10.240.40   An entity considers the following two criteria when determining whether overhead costs, including stewardship costs, should be included in the value in use calculation of a CGU:
- the costs can be attributed directly or allocated on a reasonable and consistent basis to the CGU; and
- the costs are necessarily incurred to generate cash inflows from the CGU. [*IAS 36.39(b), 41*]

3.10.240.50   In some cases, it may be challenging to determine whether stewardship costs meet the criteria in 3.10.240.40. The first criterion is usually met because an entity generally has in place a reasonable and consistent basis to allocate stewardship costs. For example, a 'reasonable and consistent basis' could be based on the relative estimated future revenue of the CGUs.

3.10.240.60   In our experience, stewardship costs are generally considered necessary to generate cash inflows at the CGU level. In limited circumstances, this conclusion could be challenged when there is little or no apparent link between the stewardship costs incurred at a higher level and the CGU's cash inflows. An example of such circumstances could be a multinational conglomerate with multiple CGUs and a decentralised corporate structure, in which the stewardship costs are incurred at a significantly higher level than the level at which the impairment test is being performed. In addition, in this example facts may indicate that the stewardship costs to be incurred at the higher level will have no contribution to the generation of cash inflows at the CGU's level. A careful assessment of the underlying facts and circumstances is required to rebut the presumption that stewardship costs are necessarily incurred to generate cash inflows at the CGU level.

3.10.240.70   Stewardship costs are allocated to and included in a CGU's value in use calculation in the same manner as corporate assets are allocated to a CGU's carrying amount. In our view, in the limited circumstances in which stewardship costs are not allocated (see 3.10.240.60), two impairment tests at two levels should be carried out by applying the guidance for corporate assets that are not allocated to CGUs (see 3.10.500). We believe that stewardship costs should not be allocated to the level at which there are no sufficient non-financial assets in the scope of IAS 36 that are tested for impairment.

3.10.240.80   Particular care is required when considering the cash flows related to corporate assets (see 3.10.480).

3.10.240.90   The net cash flows from the disposal of an asset at the end of its useful life is the amount that an entity expects to obtain from the disposal in an arm's length transaction, after deducting the estimated costs of disposal. An entity uses current prices at the date of the estimate for similar assets that:
- have reached the end of their useful life; and
- have been used in conditions similar to those in which the asset will be used. [*IAS 36.52–53*]

3.10.240.100   These prices are adjusted for the effect of future price increases or decreases specific to the asset. If the effect of inflation is not taken into consideration in estimating those prices, then the discount rate also does not take into consideration the effect of inflation. [*IAS 36.53(b)*]

3.10.240.110   In our view, in the case of an asset or CGU that is in the start-up phase, the cash flow projections should reflect outflows to be incurred in making the asset or CGU fully operational. [*IAS 36.42*]

3.10.240.120   The carrying amount of a CGU does not include the carrying amount of any recognised liability, unless an entity needs to consider a recognised liability to determine the recoverable amount of a CGU. This may occur when the disposal of a CGU would require the buyer to assume the liability – e.g. a decommissioning liability. The IFRS Interpretation Committee discussed this scenario and noted that in such cases the carrying amount of the liability is deducted both from the CGU's carrying amount and from its value in use. This approach makes the comparison between the CGU's carrying amount and its recoverable amount meaningful because both amounts are determined consistently. However, if the recoverable amount of a CGU is determined using fair value less costs of disposal, then the liability is deducted only from the carrying amount because it is already reflected in the fair value of the CGU. [*IAS 36.29, 78, IU 05-16*]

3.10.240.130   When for practical reasons the recoverable amount of a CGU is determined after consideration of assets (e.g. receivables or other financial assets) or liabilities (e.g. payables, pensions or other provisions) that are not part of a CGU, the carrying amount of the CGU is increased by the carrying amount of those assets or decreased by the carrying amount of those liabilities. Additionally, inflows from assets that generate inflows that are largely independent of the cash inflows from the asset or CGU under review – e.g. surplus property – are not included; the carrying amount of such assets is also excluded from the carrying amount of the CGU. [*IAS 36.43, 79*]

3.10.240.140   Cash flows exclude those arising from financing activities and tax (but see 3.10.710). [*IAS 36.50–51*]

3.10.240.150   In some cases, an entity may wish to determine cash flows based on historical or projected net profits for the asset or CGU. However, net profits do not generally equate to net cash flows. Therefore, in our view this approach may be acceptable only if the net profit is adjusted to exclude the effects of non-cash items – including depreciation, amortisation and accounting revaluations – and to include gross cash flows from the ultimate disposal of the asset or CGU and other cash flows that are not recognised as income or expenses in the respective future periods of the cash flow forecast – e.g. the replacement of assets with shorter useful lives in a CGU, or the replacement of the components of an asset with shorter useful lives.

3.10.250   *Capital expenditure*

3.10.250.10   Cash flow estimates reflect the asset in its current condition. Therefore, they exclude future capital expenditure that will improve or enhance the asset's performance, or restructurings to which the entity is not yet committed and the related benefits (see 3.12.230); and they include future capital expenditure that will maintain the asset's performance. For specific guidance on capitalised development expenditure, see 3.10.630–650. [*IAS 36.44, 47*]

3.10.250.20   The benefits from capital expenditure to improve or enhance an asset's performance are taken into account in the future net cash flow estimation only once the expenditure is incurred. In our view, capital expenditure should be considered incurred once the project has substantively commenced, rather than it being necessary for the project to have been completed. [*IAS 36.48*]

EXAMPLE 12A – CAPITAL EXPENDITURE – SUBSTANTIALLY COMPLETE PROJECT

3.10.250.30   Company S commences a capital expenditure project related to CGU V in 2018. The project is forecast to take three years to complete at a cost of 80. Once the project is completed, CGU V expects its annual cash inflows to increase by 35. At the end of 2018, costs of 20 have been incurred and capitalised – i.e. the project is 25% complete based on a cost measure.

3.10.250.40   In determining the cash flow forecasts for the value in use calculation, management includes the benefit of the additional annual cash inflows of 35 resulting from completion of the project, because the project has substantively commenced. The cash flow forecast also includes the remaining cash outflows of 60 to complete the project.

3.10.250.50   However, capital expenditure necessary to maintain the performance of an asset, and maintenance expenditure, are taken into account when estimating the future net cash flows. Therefore, these are treated like day-to-day servicing costs. Assume that a CGU consists of assets with different useful lives, all of which are essential to the ongoing operation of the unit. In this case, the replacement of assets and components with shorter lives is considered to be part of the day-to-day servicing of the unit when estimating the cash flows of the CGU. [*IAS 36.49*]

EXAMPLE 12B – CAPITAL EXPENDITURE – DAY-TO-DAY SERVICING

3.10.250.60   A company has a CGU that includes a factory with a useful life of 30 years and some equipment with a useful life of 10 years. The roof of the factory requires replacement after 15 years.

3.10.250.70   If the factory is the essential asset of the CGU that determines the forecast period (see 3.10.230.60–90), then other assets – e.g. the maintenance of an asset, components of assets with shorter useful lives including the equipment and the roof – are considered to be part of the day-to-day servicing of the CGU.

3.10.250.80   In many cases, maintenance expenditure will also include an element of improvement simply because of the natural process of technological advancement that is unrelated to a conscious effort to increase the value of the business. An entity uses its judgement to assess whether capital expenditure is more akin to maintenance expenditure or capital improvements. In making this determination, an entity considers factors such as whether the old equipment is still available and the overall level of enhancement to the business.

3.10.250.90   If the entity concludes that part of its maintenance expenditure is more akin to capital improvements, then it should be excluded from the estimation of value in use unless the entity is committed (see 3.10.250.10–40).

EXAMPLE 12C – CAPITAL EXPENDITURE – IMPROVEMENT VS REPLACEMENT EXPENDITURE

3.10.250.100   Company P provides broadband internet services in Country C. Technology is regularly upgraded, allowing competitors to propose ever faster broadband connections.

3.10.250.110   P's budgets include expenditure to replace its equipment with new upgraded equipment in order to keep pace with technological developments. P concludes that its programme of switching to new upgraded equipment is more akin to maintenance expenditure. This is because the upgrade is required for P to maintain its position in the market. As a result, P includes its budgeted expenditure in estimating value in use.

3.10.250.120   When an asset that is not in use requires future expenditure to prepare it for use – e.g. a building under construction – these expected cash outflows are incorporated into the estimated cash flows in impairment testing. [*IAS 36.42*]

3.10.260   *Restructuring*

3.10.260.10   For accounting purposes, an entity is committed to a restructuring only when it meets the criteria to recognise a restructuring provision (see 3.12.230).

3.10.260.20   Typically, management includes planned cash flows related to a restructuring in its internal budgets and forecasts. For the purposes of impairment testing, budgets are adjusted to exclude these amounts until the entity is committed to the restructuring. [*IAS 36.46–47*]

3.10.270   *Relocation costs*

3.10.270.10   Relocation costs are not included in any restructuring provision recognised, because they relate to the ongoing activities of the entity (see 3.12.330). However, in our view if assets that will be relocated are tested for impairment, then the relocation costs should be included in the estimation of future cash outflows.

3.10.280   *Transfer pricing*

3.10.280.10   The cash inflows generated by an asset or CGU may be affected by internal transfer pricing. In this case, an entity uses:

- management's best estimate of future prices that could be achieved in arm's length transactions, rather than internal transfer prices (if they are different), in estimating the future cash inflows used to determine the asset's or CGU's value in use; and
- the future cash outflows used to determine the value in use of other assets or CGUs affected by the internal transfer pricing. [*IAS 36.70*]

3.10.280.20   If the two CGUs are in separate legal entities, then in our view the actual transaction 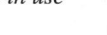 price should be used when determining the value in use and calculating any impairment loss for the purposes of the separate or individual financial statements (see 2.1.110–120) of the individual entities. If such transactions take place, then IFRS requires related party disclosures in the separate or individual financial statements, including their nature and amounts (see chapter 5.5). [*IAS 24.18*]

3.10.290   Foreign currency cash flows

3.10.290.10   When an asset or a CGU generates cash flows in a foreign currency, those cash flows are estimated in the foreign currency. They are discounted using a discount rate appropriate for the currency in which the cash flows are generated. [*IAS 36.54*]

3.10.290.20   When an asset being tested for impairment is non-monetary and is measured in a foreign currency, the following are compared:
- the carrying amount in the functional currency (see 2.7.30), determined in accordance with IAS 21 (see 2.7.110); and
- the recoverable amount determined in the foreign currency and translated into the functional currency at the spot exchange rate when the recoverable amount is determined. [*IAS 21.25*]

3.10.290.25   A non-monetary asset being tested for impairment may have a related decommissioning obligation that is a monetary liability denominated in a foreign currency. In our view, the entity should choose an accounting policy, to be applied consistently, either to:
- capitalise exchange differences related to the decommissioning obligation as part of the asset's carrying amount; or
- recognise exchange differences related to the decommissioning obligation immediately in profit or loss (see 3.12.470.40).

3.10.290.27   Accordingly, the accounting policy chosen in 3.10.290.25 may affect the carrying amount of the asset tested for impairment, and as a result whether an impairment loss is recognised and the amount thereof.

3.10.290.30   The recoverable amount of a foreign operation, and any resulting impairment loss, is calculated in the functional currency of the foreign operation. This is consistent with the principle that the functional currency is the currency in which an entity's transactions are *measured*. An impairment loss arises only if the recoverable amount in the functional currency of the foreign operation is less than its carrying amount in the functional currency. Any impairment loss determined in the functional currency is then translated into the presentation currency, which is the currency in which transactions are presented to users of the financial statements. A decline in the recoverable amount of a CGU that is a foreign operation may be due only to changes in the exchange rate from the functional currency of the foreign operation to the presentation currency of the group. Such a decline is recognised in the translation reserve in equity in accordance with IAS 21 (see 2.7.230).

EXAMPLE 13 – FOREIGN CURRENCY CASH FLOWS

 3.10.290.40   Group D's presentation currency is US dollars. D has an investment in Associate C, whose functional currency is the euro. At the reporting date, D's management determines that the carrying amount of its investment in C may be

impaired (see 3.10.560). The fair value less costs of disposal of C is lower than its carrying amount; therefore, D calculates C's value in use. C's value in use is calculated entirely in euro, and any resulting impairment loss is then translated into US dollars at the reporting date.

3.10.300   Discount rate

3.10.300.10   In determining value in use, projected future cash flows are discounted using a pre-tax discount rate that reflects:
- current market assessments of the time value of money; and
- the risks specific to the asset or CGU. [*IAS 36.55*]

3.10.300.15   The discount rate is based on the return that investors would require if they were to choose an investment that would generate cash flows of amounts, timing and risk profile equivalent to those of the asset or CGU. In other words, the discount rate is based on a market participant's view of the asset or CGU as at the current date. Therefore, although the cash flows in the value in use calculation are entity-specific, the discount rate is not. [*IAS 36.56, A16, BCZ53*]

3.10.300.20   In our experience, it is rare that a discount rate can be observed directly from the market. Therefore, an entity will generally need to build up a market participant discount rate that appropriately reflects the risks associated with the cash flows of the CGU being valued. In the absence of a discount rate that can be observed directly from the market, IAS 36 refers to other starting points in determining an appropriate discount rate:
- the entity's weighted-average cost of capital (WACC);
- the entity's incremental borrowing rate; and
- other market borrowing rates. [*IAS 36.A17–A18*]

3.10.300.30   In our experience, the most common approach is to estimate an appropriate rate using the WACC formula. Because a CGU-related rate is required, it is unlikely that the WACC of the entity as a whole can be used without adjustment. However, it may provide a useful reference point when determining the components of the appropriate WACC for the CGU. Adjustments to the entity's WACC should be made with the objective of developing a market participant discount rate.

3.10.300.40   WACC is a post-tax discount rate (see 3.10.710). It incorporates the market's view of how an entity would structure its financing using both debt and equity, with each having a different rate of return. The formula for WACC is as follows.

$$WACC = \left(\frac{E}{K} \times r_e\right) + \left(\frac{D}{K} \times b\,(1-t)\right)$$

E	= fair value of equity as a component of total capital
D	= fair value of debt as a component of total capital
K	= D + E = total capital
r_e	= cost of equity

b	=	cost of debt: the rate at which the entity could obtain financing for its operations, before any effects of interest reducing taxable income
t	=	corporate tax rate: used to reduce the debt rate to a post-tax rate, because debt typically results in a reduction in taxable income

3.10.300.50   The relative weights of debt and equity in a WACC calculation are based on the fair value, rather than on the carrying amount, of debt and equity. In addition, the weights are generally based on the estimated optimal long-term capital structure: therefore, the entity's actual debt/equity ratio is not determinative in the calculation.

3.10.300.60   In determining the cost of equity as an input to the determination of WACC, it is common to use the capital asset pricing model (CAPM). This estimates the cost of equity by adding risk premiums to the risk-free rate. The formula for the CAPM is as follows.

$$r_e = r_f + \beta \times (r_m - r_f) + \alpha$$

r_e	=	cost of equity
r_f	=	risk-free rate
β	=	beta, which is a measure of the correlation between a share's return in relation to the market return (or the return of a fully diversified portfolio of investments)
$(r_m - r_f)$	=	market return less the risk-free rate or the equity risk premium. This risk premium reflects systematic or market risk – i.e. the overall risk premium of a fully diversified portfolio of investments above the risk-free rate
α	=	alpha, or unsystematic (entity-specific) risk premium

3.10.300.70   The gearing – i.e. the proportion of asset or CGU financing that is funded by debt – and the cost of debt used in the WACC for the purpose of determining value in use are not entity-specific. IAS 36 notes that the discount rate is independent of the entity's capital structure and the way in which the entity financed the acquisition of the asset or CGU. Therefore, the gearing and cost of debt are those that the market participant would expect in relation to the asset or CGU being tested for impairment. In other words, the actual funding of the asset or CGU, which will often include intra-group debt, is not relevant in determining gearing for the purposes of the market participant's WACC. Instead, the WACC for the value in use calculation is based on the cost and amount of debt of a market participant investing in the cash flows of the asset or CGU. [*IAS 36.A19*]

3.10.300.80   The cost of debt is based on long-term rates being incurred at the date of valuation for new borrowings, rather than the rates negotiated historically in the debt market for existing borrowings. Determining appropriate rates includes considering the entity's incremental borrowing rate.

3.10.300.90   A key assumption underpinning WACC is a constant level of gearing throughout the cash flow period, including in the terminal value. If this assumption does not apply, then an entity will need to calculate WACC separately each year using different gearing levels as applicable, or else use alternative methods.

3.10.300.100   In considering gearing and the cost of debt, the following are possible sources of information, none of which is likely to be determinative in isolation:

- the cost of debt incurred by the entity at present, taking into account any need to refinance, as a proxy for the cost of debt of a market participant;
- the current market borrowings of comparable entities, considering both levels of debt and interest rates;
- recent industry acquisitions and refinancing; and
- information available from the entity's bank or other financial advisors.

3.10.300.110   The components of the cost of equity are defined in the CAPM formula – see 3.10.300.60, which also shows how they are used in the determination of WACC. The discussion in 3.10.300.120–170 describes each component.

3.10.300.120   The risk-free rate is generally obtained from the yield on government bonds that:
- are in the same currency; and
- have the same or a similar duration as the cash flows of the asset or CGU, often leading to 10- or 20-year government bonds being considered.

3.10.300.125   Typically, this information is readily available within a country – e.g. in newspapers – but the best sources for this data should be considered on a country-by-country basis.

3.10.300.130   An entity should consider whether the government bond yield selected represents a risk-free rate. For example, in a currency area that uses a common currency, zero-coupon bonds from the government in the currency area with the lowest yield should be used. This is because they are a better measure of the risk-free rate than bonds issued by other governments in the same currency with a higher yield, reflecting greater default risk. Similarly, when questions arise about the creditworthiness of government bonds, an entity may obtain an indication of default risk from credit default swap pricing on reference instruments in the same currency issued by the same government as the bonds from which the rate is derived. This may suggest that the government bonds do not reflect a risk-free rate. An entity should also consider the liquidity of the bonds used to estimate the risk-free rate.

3.10.300.140   'Beta factors' reflect the risk of a particular sector or industry relative to the market as a whole, and are a long-term rather than a short-term measure. Beta is typically calculated for individual listed companies using a regression analysis against an appropriate share index. When developing the cost of equity from a market participant's perspective, the selected beta is generally based on comparable entities' betas – even if the subject entity is a listed entity.

3.10.300.150   Careful consideration is given to the period over which the beta is measured, because any significant market volatility may have distorted the beta. In our experience, betas measured with reference to two-year or five-year historical data are typically used, with the five-year beta typically being favoured in volatile markets.

3.10.300.160   'Equity risk premium' is a measure of the long-term required rate of return on equities above the risk-free rate, and therefore should not be impacted significantly by short-term volatility. Various studies of equity risk premium based on historical data are available: these give a range of results depending on the exact period of the data included in the study and the method of calculation.

3.10.300.170 The 'alpha factor' represents an asset- or CGU-specific risk premium, and may need to be added to the cost of equity when a CGU is determined to carry additional risk that may not be reflected in the beta – i.e. risk that cannot be attributed to market risk. An alpha factor may include some or all of the following elements.

- *Size risk:* An additional premium that takes into account that smaller businesses are more risky than larger organisations. Size premiums are generally based on long-term information that is not impacted significantly by short-term volatility.
- *Financing risk:* An additional premium that takes into account the difficulty of funding working capital or maintainable capital expenditure in the short to medium term, based on the market's view of the asset or CGU rather than the entity's specific financing.
- *Country risk:* An additional premium that takes into account the additional risk associated with generating and incurring cash flows in a particular country. In some cases, country risk is incorporated into the equity risk premium; an entity should take care to avoid double counting.
- *Forecasting risk:* An additional premium that takes into account the additional risk associated with achieving forecasts. In our experience, the need for such an additional risk factor is often identified when the value in use calculation is cross-checked to other indications of value (see 3.10.320).
- *Illiquidity risk:* An additional premium that takes into account the difficulty of being able to sell an investment.

3.10.310 Inflation

3.10.310.10 The cash flows and the discount rate applied to them should be determined on a consistent basis. If the cash flows include the effect of general inflation – i.e. they are expressed in nominal terms – then the discount rate also includes the effects of inflation. Conversely, if the cash flows exclude the effects of inflation, then the discount rate also excludes the effects of inflation. [*IAS 36.40*]

3.10.320 Reasonableness tests of value in use

3.10.320.10 Having calculated value in use, in our experience it is important to perform a sensitivity analysis on:
- key cash flow assumptions;
- terminal value growth rates; and
- the discount rate generally.

3.10.320.15 In addition to sensitivity analysis, cross-checking to possible external evidence also provides support for the reasonableness of the discount rate and the cash flows used in determining value in use. [*IAS 36.33*]

3.10.320.20 When the recoverable amount of a CGU is determined on the basis of value in use and substantial parts of an entity are tested for impairment, a high-level comparison between market capitalisation and the total value in use for all CGUs provides some support that the assumptions and discount rate used are appropriate for the cash flows. In doing this comparison, market capitalisation is adjusted for the market value of debt and any surplus assets. However, in our view a control premium should not be added to the market price, because a value in use calculation incorporates all existing entity-specific synergies that are realisable for the use of the CGUs together. The addition of a control premium would assume a hypothetical acquisition, which is inconsistent with the concept of value in use. This approach differs from that when recoverable amount is based on fair value less costs of disposal (see 3.10.210). There may be circumstances in which it is supportable that an entity's value in use estimates exceed its debt-adjusted market capitalisation. However, because an entity's market capitalisation can be viewed as the equity market's estimate of the value of the entity's operations, differences should be carefully considered. If such differences exist, then an entity should carefully assess the reasonableness of the assumptions in its value in use calculations.

3.10.320.30   Earnings multiples implicit in the value in use calculation can also be compared with market multiples for the entity and comparable quoted entities, to check for reasonableness. Comparable transactions may also provide some support that the assumptions and discount rate used are appropriate for the cash flows. Multiples to consider include P/E ratios, as well as EBIT and EBITDA multiples (see Example 10).

3.10.330   DETERMINE CARRYING AMOUNT OF CGU

3.10.330.10   The carrying amount of a CGU is determined in a way that is consistent with the way that the recoverable amount of the CGU is determined. For example, the cash flow projections may include outflows in respect of recognised liabilities, or inflows in respect of assets that generate cash flows independently. In these cases, the carrying amount of the CGU that is used to determine the recoverable amount includes the related assets and liabilities. [*IAS 36.6, 43, 75*]

3.10.330.15   For example, an entity may purchase a machine with a government grant. In this case, in our view the carrying amount of the machine used to determine the impairment loss should be determined net of the government grant. This is irrespective of whether the grant is presented in the statement of financial position as deferred income or was deducted from the carrying amount of the asset (see 4.3.130). [*IAS 36.75*]

3.10.330.20   In another example, an entity may need to consider a recognised liability to determine the recoverable amount of a CGU if the disposal of a CGU would require the buyer to assume the liability – e.g. a decommissioning liability. As discussed in 3.10.240.120, in such cases the carrying amount of the liability is deducted both from the CGU's carrying amount and from its value in use. [*IAS 36.78, IU 05-16*]

3.10.340   Working capital

3.10.340.10   In our view, it is acceptable to include cash flows resulting from the realisation of working capital balances in cash flow projections and in the carrying amount of the CGU, even when such assets are excluded from the scope of IAS 36 (see 3.10.20). If the working capital is realised in the short term, and the effects of discounting are not material, then we believe that the working capital need not be discounted.

3.10.340.20   Alternatively, the cash flow projections may be adjusted to exclude the realisation of working capital balances. In this case, the carrying amount of the CGU also excludes working capital. However, even if working capital balances are not included in the carrying amount of a CGU, working capital cash flows related to amounts arising after the valuation date need to be reflected in the valuation analysis. Therefore, the cash flows related to the changes in working capital would be the assumed gross build-up in working capital. [*IAS 36.75*]

EXAMPLE 14 – WORKING CAPITAL

3.10.340.30   Working capital balances (net current assets of 100) are included in the carrying amount of the CGU.

3.10.340.35   In this case, the cash flow movement in working capital in year 1 would be the net change in working capital levels over the assumed working capital of 100. Accordingly, if the working capital at the end of year 1 is 120, then the cash flows for year 1 include a cash outflow of 20.

3.10.340.37   If the working capital balances of 100 are not included in the carrying amount of the CGU, then the cash flows shown in the impairment analysis for year 1 are an assumed gross build-up in working capital. This means a cash outflow of 120.

3.10.340.40   Example 14 illustrates that the inclusion or exclusion of opening working capital balances will have limited or no effect on whether an asset's value in use exceeds its carrying amount if the working capital is realised in the short term and the effect of discounting is not material. This is because the benefit of a lower carrying amount from excluding working capital is offset by increased cash outflows or, if the alternative approach is followed, the effect of including working capital is offset by lower cash outflows. The cash flows for future periods in both cases will include subsequent working capital movements.

3.10.350   MEASURE AND RECOGNISE IMPAIRMENT LOSS

3.10.350.10   An impairment loss is recognised to the extent that the carrying amount of an asset or CGU exceeds its recoverable amount. [*IAS 36.6, 59*]

3.10.350.20   Impairment losses are generally recognised in profit or loss unless the asset is carried at a revalued amount (see 3.10.360). [*IAS 36.60*]

3.10.350.30   In our view, after an entity has tested an asset for impairment, it should consider whether changes are required to the useful life, depreciation method and residual value of the asset. Any such changes are accounted for prospectively as a change in accounting estimate (see 3.2.140.20 and 150.25).

3.10.360   Revalued assets

3.10.360.10   Property, plant and equipment, along with intangible assets, that are measured at a revalued amount (see 3.2.300 and 3.3.280) are first revalued applying the principles in the relevant standard. Any impairment loss is calculated on the basis of the resulting carrying amount. The recoverable amount used in impairment testing is the higher of the asset's fair value less costs of disposal and its value in use; therefore, when fair value is determined on the basis of market values, any impairment loss to be recognised will generally be limited to the costs of disposal. [*IAS 36.5*]

3.10.360.20   Any impairment loss is recognised in OCI and presented in the revaluation reserve within equity, to the extent that it reverses a previous revaluation surplus related to the same asset. [*IAS 36.60*]

3.10.370   **Foreign operations**

3.10.370.10   In the consolidated financial statements, impairment losses related to foreign operations are calculated in the functional currency of the foreign operation and then translated into the group's presentation currency. Any translation gain or loss is recognised in the foreign currency translation reserve in equity and remains there until disposal of the foreign operation (see 2.7.340). For further discussion of this issue, see 3.10.290. [*IAS 21.49*]

(S) 3.10.370.20   In the separate financial statements, the recoverable amount of an asset or CGU is calculated in the relevant foreign currency and then translated into the functional currency of the reporting entity at the measurement date. This amount is compared with the carrying amount of the asset or CGU in the functional currency of the reporting entity, and any impairment loss is recognised in profit or loss (see also 3.10.290.20). [*IAS 21.25*]

3.10.380   **Allocating impairment losses**

3.10.380.10   The following table outlines the steps involved in allocating an impairment loss to assets in the scope of IAS 36. [*IAS 36.104–108*]

STEP 1	• Reduce the carrying amount of any goodwill allocated to the CGU.
STEP 2	• Allocate the remaining amount of the impairment loss pro rata to other assets in the CGU, on the basis of the carrying amount of each asset in the CGU (including intangible assets). • However, do not reduce the carrying amount of any asset below the highest of its recoverable amount (if it is determinable) and zero. Therefore, determine the recoverable amount of any of the individual assets or lower-level CGUs in the CGU being tested, if possible.
STEP 3	• If there is a remaining amount of the impairment loss after Step 2, then allocate it to the other assets in the CGU.
STEP 4	• Recognise a liability for any remaining amount of the impairment loss only if it is required by another standard.

3.10.380.20   For a discussion of the allocation of impairment losses related to goodwill when there are NCI in a subsidiary, see 3.10.510.

3.10.390   **REVERSAL OF IMPAIRMENT**

3.10.390.10   At each reporting date, an entity assesses whether there is an indication that a previously recognised impairment loss has reversed because of a change in the estimates used to determine the impairment loss. If there is such an indication, and the recoverable amount of the impaired asset or CGU subsequently increases, then the impairment loss is generally reversed. [*IAS 36.110, 114*]

3.10.390.20   The following are examples of *internal* indications that are considered in assessing whether an impairment may no longer exist or may have decreased:

- significant changes in the extent or manner in which an asset is (or is expected to be) used that have (or will have) a favourable effect on the entity; and
- indications that the performance of an asset is, or will be, better than expected. [*IAS 36.111(d)–(e)*]

3.10.390.30   The following are examples of *external* indications that are considered in assessing whether an impairment may no longer exist or may have decreased:
- a significant increase in an asset's value;
- significant favourable effects in the technological, market, economic or legal environment; and
- a decrease in market interest rates or other market rates of return on investments that will decrease the discount rate used to determine an asset's value in use (see 3.10.300). [*IAS 36.111(a)–(c)*]

3.10.390.40   If there are indications that an impairment of a CGU may no longer exist or has decreased – e.g. the overall profitability of the CGU has increased – then the CGU is assessed for a reversal of impairment. In our view, this is regardless of whether the composition of the assets in the CGU has changed since the impairment loss was recognised; this is because the unit of account for assessing impairment and for impairment reversal is the CGU in its entirety, and not the individual assets in the CGU. [*IAS 36.72–73, 117*]

EXAMPLE 15 – REVERSAL OF IMPAIRMENT – CHANGE IN COMPOSITION OF CGU

3.10.390.50   Company Z has a CGU (CGU X) that comprises various operating assets. As at 31 December 2017, Z recognised an impairment loss of 20 that resulted from a decline in profitability caused by the technical obsolescence of some of its assets. This resulted in the carrying amount of CGU X being written down to 80 from 100. No goodwill had been allocated to the CGU, and therefore the impairment loss was allocated pro rata to the non-financial assets in the CGU on the basis of their carrying amounts (see 3.10.380).

3.10.390.60   During 2018, in order to improve its technical capabilities, Z acquired new assets with a value of 30. They were added to CGU X because they were an integral part of that CGU and did not have their own independent cash inflows. At 31 December 2018, the addition of these assets had resulted in an increase in future cash inflows and in the recoverable amount of CGU X to 140.

3.10.390.70   In this example, Z concludes that it should recognise a reversal of impairment even though it resulted from the new assets that were added to CGU X. The reversal cannot exceed 20 (previous impairment) and is capped as described in 3.10.390.100. The amount of the reversal is allocated to the assets that were written down in 2017 and not to the newly acquired assets.

3.10.390.75   In our view, a reversal should be allocated only to previously impaired assets that are still used and are part of the CGU at the date of reversal, irrespective of the CGU in which the assets were originally impaired. For example, assets that were impaired in CGU X are transferred to CGU Y, which has also been impaired. A year after the transfer, indicators of reversal exist in CGU Y. We believe that any reversal of impairment in CGU Y should be allocated to both the original assets of CGU Y that were impaired and to the impaired assets received from CGU X. [*IAS 36.72–73, 117*]

3.10.390.80   An impairment loss is not reversed when the increase in recoverable amount is caused only by the unwinding of the discount used in determining the value in use. [*IAS 36.116*]

3.10.390.90   An impairment loss recognised for goodwill is not reversed in subsequent periods, even if it was recognised in an interim period of the same financial year. This is because any subsequent increase in the recoverable amount of goodwill is likely to be an increase in internally generated goodwill, rather than a reversal of the impairment loss recognised for the acquired goodwill. The recognition of internally generated goodwill is prohibited by IAS 38. Apart from this requirement, when testing a CGU for a reversal of an impairment loss, the allocation of the amount to be reversed follows the same principles as for the allocation of an impairment loss (see 3.10.380). [*IAS 36.122, 124–125, 38.48, IFRIC 10.8*]

3.10.390.100   In all cases, the maximum amount of the reversal is the lower of:
- the amount necessary to bring the carrying amount of the asset to its recoverable amount (if it is determinable); and
- the amount necessary to restore the assets of the CGU to their pre-impairment carrying amounts less subsequent depreciation or amortisation that would have been recognised. [*IAS 36.117, 123*]

3.10.390.110   A reversal of an impairment loss for an asset is generally recognised in profit or loss. A reversal of an impairment loss on a revalued asset is recognised in profit or loss to the extent that it reverses an impairment loss on the same asset that was previously recognised in profit or loss. Any additional increase in the carrying amount of the asset is treated as a revaluation increase. [*IAS 36.119*]

3.10.400   Impairment and reversal of impairment in same CGU

3.10.400.10   IAS 36 does not specifically address the following scenario:
- the fair value less costs of disposal of an asset within a previously impaired CGU increases, which would normally be expected to result in a reversal of impairment; and
- the recoverable amount of the CGU as a whole is further impaired.

3.10.400.15   This scenario may occur, for example, when:
- the fair value of real estate recovers; but
- the recoverable amount of the CGU as a whole, which includes the real estate, does not demonstrate a similar recovery.

3.10.400.20   In our view, in this scenario, an entity should choose an accounting policy, to be applied consistently, to either:
- assess the net impact from the perspective of the CGU as a whole – i.e. compare the carrying amount of the CGU to the recoverable amount of the CGU and recognise any impairment or reversal in one step; or
- apply a two-step approach whereby the entity:
   1. assesses and recognises a reversal of impairment at the individual asset level; and
   2. compares the revised carrying amount of the CGU, including the increase as a result of the reversal of impairment in Step 1, to its recoverable amount.

EXAMPLE 16 – REVERSAL OF IMPAIRMENT

3.10.400.30   Company X has one CGU that consists of the following assets: goodwill, land, a building and machinery. As at 31 December 2015, the carrying amount of the CGU was 800 and the CGU's recoverable amount was 250 (the higher of value in use of 250 and fair value less costs of disposal of 160). The fair value less costs of disposal of the land, building and machinery was 100, 35 and 25, respectively. In practice, we would not generally expect such a large difference between value in use and fair value less costs of disposal; however, this example has been simplified for illustrative purposes.

3.10.400.35   Based on this information, X determined that the CGU was impaired by 550 (800 - 250) and allocated the impairment loss as follows.

ASSET	CARRYING AMOUNT PRE-IMPAIRMENT	PRO RATA IMPAIRMENT ALLOCATION[(1)]	CARRYING AMOUNT AFTER PRO RATA IMPAIRMENT ALLOCATION[(2)]	RECOVERABLE AMOUNT BASED ON FAIR VALUE LESS COSTS OF DISPOSAL[(3)]	IMPAIRMENT LOSS ALLOCATED[(4)]	ALLOCATE REMAINING IMPAIRMENT LOSS[(5)]	CARRYING AMOUNT POST-IMPAIRMENT[(6)]
Goodwill	50	(50)	-		(50)	-	-
Land	200	(133)	67	100	(100)	-	100
Building	150	(100)	50	35	(100)	(9)	41
Machinery	400	(267)	133	25	(267)	(24)	109
Total	800	(550)	250	160	(517)	(33)	250

CGU recoverable amount	250
Impairment loss	(550)

Notes
1.   The impairment loss is allocated first by writing down the goodwill. Then, the remaining amount (500) is allocated pro rata based on the carrying amount of each asset in the CGU. For example, land is impaired by 133 - (200 / 750) x 500.
2.   Calculated as the carrying amount less the pro rata impairment allocation in column (1).
3.   Fair value less costs of disposal, which is relevant in determining the maximum impairment loss to be allocated to a single asset.
4.   Allocation of the impairment loss determined in column (1), capped such that no asset is written down to below its recoverable amount in column (3).
5.   Allocation of excess impairment loss of 33 in respect of land is allocated pro rata to the other assets in the CGU. For example, the building is impaired by a further 9 - (150 / (150 + 400)) x 33.
6.   Calculated as the pre-impairment carrying amount less the sum of columns (4) and (5).

3.10.400.40 The impact of depreciation is ignored for the remainder of this example. As at 31 December 2018, because of an impairment indicator of falling sales, X recalculates the CGU's recoverable amount at 210 (the higher of value in use of 210 and fair value less costs of disposal of 190). Accordingly, a further impairment loss of 40 (250 - 210) is recognised. For the allocation of the further impairment, X has calculated the fair value less costs of disposal of land, building and machinery as 130, 35 and 25, respectively.

3.10.400.50 Suppose that X chooses an accounting policy of assessing the net impact of the impairment and potential reversal from the perspective of the CGU as a whole (see 3.10.400.20). In this case, it follows the same one-step process as in the table in 3.10.400.35. Under this approach, the increase in the value of the land is not taken into account, other than to cap the allocation of the impairment loss.

ASSET	CARRYING AMOUNT POST-IM-PAIRMENT	PRO RATA IMPAIR-MENT ALLO-CATION	CARRYING AMOUNT AFTER PRO RATA IMPAIR-MENT ALLO-CATION	RECOV-ERABLE AMOUNT BASED ON FAIR VALUE LESS COSTS OF DISPOSAL	IMPAIR-MENT LOSS ALLO-CATED	ALLOCATE REMAINING IMPAIRMENT LOSS[1]	CARRYING AMOUNT POST-IMPAIR-MENT
Goodwill	-	-	-	-	-	-	-
Land	100	(16)	84	130	-	-	100
Building	41	(7)	34	35	(6)	-	35
Machinery	109	(17)	92	25	(17)	(17)	75
Total	250	(40)	210	190	(23)	(17)	210
CGU recoverable amount	210						
Impairment loss	(40)						

Note
1. Excess impairment loss of 16 related to the land (16 less cap of 0) and 1 related to the building (7 less cap of 6).

3.10.400.60 If X chooses an accounting policy of assessing the impairment and potential reversal separately (see 3.10.400.20), then it determines the impairment loss/reversal in two steps. Under this approach, the increase in the value of the land is taken into account.

3.10.400.70 In Step 1, X assesses and recognises a reversal of impairment at the individual asset level.

ASSET	CARRYING AMOUNT POST-IMPAIRMENT	RECOVERABLE AMOUNT BASED ON FAIR VALUE LESS COSTS OF DISPOSAL	REVERSAL OF IMPAIRMENT AT INDIVIDUAL ASSET LEVEL	REVISED CARRYING AMOUNT
Goodwill	-	-	-	-
Land	100	130	30	130
Building	41	35	-	41
Machinery	109	25	-	109
Total	250	190	30	280
		CGU recoverable amount		210
		Impairment loss		(70)

3.10.400.80 In applying Step 1, X reverses 30 (130 - 100) of the impairment loss previously recognised against land. The carrying amount of the CGU after Step 1 is 70 greater than its recoverable amount of 210. This impairment loss of 70 is allocated to the assets within the CGU in Step 2.

3.10.400.90 In Step 2, X compares the revised carrying amount of the CGU, including any increase as a result of impairment reversals in Step 1, to its recoverable amount. In Step 2, X follows the same process as in 3.10.400.35 and 50.

ASSET	POST-STEP 1 CARRYING AMOUNT	PRO RATA IMPAIRMENT ALLOCATION[1]	CARRYING AMOUNT AFTER PRO RATA IMPAIRMENT ALLOCATION	RECOVERABLE AMOUNT BASED ON FAIR VALUE LESS COSTS OF DISPOSAL	IMPAIRMENT LOSS ALLOCATED	ALLOCATE REMAINING IMPAIRMENT LOSS[2]	CARRYING AMOUNT POST-IMPAIRMENT
Goodwill	-	-	-	-	-	-	-
Land	130	-	130	130	-	-	130
Building	41	(19)	22	35	(6)	-	35
Machinery	109	(51)	58	25	(51)	(13)	45
Total	280	(70)	210	190	(57)	(13)	210
CGU recoverable amount	210						
Impairment loss	(70)						
Impairment reversal	30						
Net impairment loss	(40)						

691

> **Notes**
> 1. Pro rata allocation of the 70 (280 - 210) impairment loss to the building and machinery only. For example, the building is impaired by 19 - (41 / 150) x 70.
> 2. Excess impairment loss of 13 related to the building – i.e. 19 less cap of 6.

3.10.410 PRESENTATION

3.10.410.10   IAS 36 does not specify the line item in profit or loss in which an impairment loss should be recognised; however, it does require disclosure of the line items in which impairment losses are included. [*IAS 36.126*]

3.10.410.20   If an entity classifies expenses based on their function (see 4.1.30), then any loss is allocated to the appropriate function. In our view, in the rare case that an impairment loss cannot be allocated to a function, then it should be included in other expenses as a separate line item if it is significant – e.g. impairment of goodwill (see 4.1.30.10) – with additional information given in a note.

3.10.410.30   In our view, an impairment loss that is recognised in published interim financial statements should be presented in the same line item in the annual financial statements. We believe that this applies even if the asset is subsequently sold and the gain or loss on disposal is included in a line item different from impairment losses in the annual financial statements.

3.10.420 SPECIFIC APPLICATION ISSUES
3.10.430 Allocating goodwill to CGUs

3.10.430.10   The guidance in 3.10.160 discusses the impairment testing of goodwill. However, before the actual impairment testing, it is necessary to understand how goodwill is allocated to CGUs or groups of CGUs, and how that allocation may change over time.

3.10.440 *Level at which to allocate goodwill*

3.10.440.10   Each unit or group of units to which goodwill is allocated:
- should represent the lowest level within the entity for which information about goodwill is available and monitored for internal management purposes; and
- should not be larger than an operating segment, determined in accordance with IFRS 8 before applying the aggregation criteria of IFRS 8 (see 5.2.50). [*IAS 36.80–81*]

3.10.440.20   The allocation test related to operating segments in IFRS 8 applies regardless of whether the entity is required to present segment information (see 5.2.10).

3.10.440.30   Goodwill is allocated to the lowest level at which it is monitored for internal management purposes. This is to avoid the need to develop additional reporting systems to support goodwill impairment testing. However, this does not mean that entities can avoid testing goodwill at a level lower than an operating segment by simply not monitoring goodwill explicitly. [*IAS 36.82, BC140, BC144*]

EXAMPLE 17 – MONITORING GOODWILL

3.10.440.40   Company Z has three operating segments under IFRS 8, each with two product-oriented sub-units. Z believes that the goodwill acquired reflects the synergies created in four of its six sub-units.

3.10.440.50   However, these sub-units do not include goodwill in their internal performance reports to senior management. Instead, the target internal rate of return on the net assets of the sub-units (which do not include goodwill) was increased by senior management after the acquisition. These targets have been set to generate a desirable return on investment to shareholders.

3.10.440.60   Goodwill is not included explicitly in the management information delivered by the sub-units' management; however, to generate the expected return on investment, senior management indirectly takes into account goodwill by allocating it to the four sub-units. Consequently, Z allocates goodwill to the four sub-units.

3.10.450   *Method of allocating goodwill to CGUs*

3.10.450.10   Goodwill arising in a business combination is allocated to the acquirer's CGUs that are expected to benefit from the synergies of the business combination in which goodwill arose. This is irrespective of whether other assets or liabilities of the acquiree are assigned to those units. [*IAS 36.80*]

EXAMPLE 18A – ALLOCATION OF GOODWILL (1)

3.10.450.20   Company M is a producer of specialised electronic equipment. It acquires one of its main competitors, Company N, which operates in another geographic area. As part of its acquisition strategy, M will gradually shift N's customers onto M's products. M does not plan to support N's brand or product lines. M is planning to use the assets acquired from N, including its brand and products, defensively, and the fair value of the assets will be based on their highest and best use to market participants (see 2.4.1010.30–40).

3.10.450.25   In the absence of any factors to the contrary, one approach that M may follow is to allocate the majority of goodwill acquired to its existing CGUs that are expected to benefit from the acquisition of N's customers and the related synergies. Because N's brand and operations will have a short life, M attributes little, if any, goodwill arising from the business acquisition to N's CGUs at the date of acquisition.

3.10.450.30   In our view, the allocation of goodwill should generally take into account not only the expected synergies, but also the goodwill of the acquiree on a stand-alone basis ('stand-alone' goodwill).

3.10.450.40   The pre-acquisition analysis of the acquirer may be useful in allocating the goodwill to CGUs. This analysis may indicate the drivers behind the synergies that are expected to arise from the acquisition – e.g. incremental profits arising from:

- intellectual property synergies – e.g. the acquirer using the patented technology of the acquiree to enhance its own product development;
- revenue synergies – e.g. cross-selling opportunities, access to new markets or access to new distribution channels;
- cost saving synergies – e.g. enhanced capacity utilisation or reduced purchasing (or administration) costs as a result of the combined entity's larger scale; and
- other synergies – e.g. use of a joint sales force or co-marketing or the deployment of a skilled workforce.

3.10.450.50   IAS 36 does not prescribe any specific method of allocating goodwill to CGUs. Depending on the facts and circumstances, different methods of allocating goodwill to each benefiting CGU may be appropriate, including the following:

- based on the difference between the fair value of a CGU before and after the acquisition – i.e. 'with or without' method;
- based on the relative fair value of the identifiable net assets in each CGU;
- based on the relative fair value of the CGUs; and
- based on the proportions of other relevant indicators. For example, if goodwill arises from the highly skilled workforce of the acquiree, the goodwill allocation may be based on the deployment of that workforce in the group after the acquisition.

EXAMPLE 18B – ALLOCATION OF GOODWILL (2)

3.10.450.60   Company P acquires Company S for 100, having estimated the stand-alone value of S to be 70. P expects to realise potential synergies from the transaction with two of its existing CGUs, C and D. S comprises a single CGU and has identifiable net assets of 60, giving rise to goodwill of 40 on the acquisition (100 - 60).

3.10.450.70   In this example, P concludes that it is appropriate to allocate goodwill first to CGUs on the basis of the stand-alone goodwill attributable to S, with the residual goodwill being attributed to synergies between S and CGUs C and D.

3.10.450.80   Therefore, P allocates goodwill as follows.
- CGU S: 10 (70 - 60).
- CGUs C and D: 30 (100 - 70).

3.10.450.90   In this example, to allocate goodwill of 30 to CGUs C and D, which are expected to benefit from the synergies, P uses the 'with or without' method as follows.

	Pre-acquisition fair value	Post-acquisition fair value	Difference	Percentage of total	Goodwill
CGU C	80	100	20	40%	12
CGU D	120	150	30	60%	18
Total	200	250	50	100%	30

3.10.450.100   The difference between the pre- and post-acquisition fair values reflects the impact of the synergies arising from the acquisition. Therefore, P allocates the remaining goodwill of 30 between CGUs C and D based on the relative increase in their fair value resulting from the acquisition.

3.10.460   *Impact of measurement period on allocation of goodwill*

3.10.460.10   In accordance with IFRS 3, an entity is allowed up to a maximum of one year from the date of acquisition to finalise the acquisition accounting, and thereby determine the amount of goodwill (see 2.6.1020); until that time, the acquisition accounting is regarded as 'provisional'. [*IFRS 3.45*]

3.10.460.20   If goodwill allocated to a CGU has arisen in a business combination in the reporting period, then that goodwill is tested for impairment before that reporting date. However, if the acquisition accounting can be determined only provisionally, then it may also not be possible to finish allocating goodwill to CGUs before the end of the annual period in which the business combination occurred. In such cases, an entity discloses the amount of unallocated goodwill, together with the reason for not allocating the goodwill to CGUs. However, the allocation of goodwill to CGUs should be completed before the end of the first annual reporting period beginning after the date of acquisition. [*IAS 36.84–85, 96, 133*]

3.10.460.30   Judgement is required when the allocation process is not yet complete, but there is an indication of impairment in a CGU to which goodwill is expected to be allocated. In that case, in our view it is appropriate to test the goodwill for impairment based on a provisional allocation.

EXAMPLE 19 – GOODWILL ALLOCATION NOT COMPLETE

3.10.460.40   Company P acquires Company S in September 2018. The acquisition accounting is not yet complete; therefore, P is not able to complete the allocation of goodwill to CGUs before the end of the annual period in which the business combination occurred – i.e. 31 December 2018.

3.10.460.50   In this example, the allocation of goodwill to CGUs should be completed before 31 December 2019.

Impact of disposals and reorganisations on allocation of goodwill

3.10.470.10   An entity may dispose of an operation within a CGU or group of CGUs to which good-will has been allocated. In this case, a portion of the goodwill is included in the carrying amount of the operation disposed of when determining the gain or loss on disposal. In other words, part of the goodwill is derecognised when disposing of an operation. The portion of the goodwill allocated is measured based on the relative values of the operation disposed of and the portion of the CGU retained at the date of partial disposal – unless the entity can demonstrate that another method better reflects the goodwill associated with the operation disposed of. [*IAS 36.86, BC156*]

3.10.470.20   When the entity changes the composition of its CGUs, it reallocates goodwill using a relative value approach at the date of the reorganisation similar to that used when an entity disposes of an operation within a CGU – unless the entity can demonstrate that some other method provides a better allocation of goodwill to the reorganised units. [*IAS 36.87*]

EXAMPLE 20A – REALLOCATION OF GOODWILL – RELATIVE VALUE APPROACH

3.10.470.30   Company X produces and sells two types of machines and provides related services. X has two CGUs:
- *CGU A:* Production of Machine A and the related services in Country A; and
- *CGU B:* Production of Machine B and the related services in Country B.

3.10.470.40   X acquired a business in Country A engaged in the testing and monitoring of machines in that country, to enhance its service operations and streamline the production process of Machine A. On acquisition, the resulting goodwill of 12 was allocated solely to CGU A because there are no synergies with the operations in CGU B. There is no other goodwill from previous acquisitions.

3.10.470.50   Several years after the acquisition, technological developments increase the variety of services offered by X and enable it to provide most services from a distance. Consequently, X changes its business model to centralise all service operations in one place and starts selling service-only bundles. As a result, the composition of X's CGUs changes to:
- *CGU P$_A$:* Production and sale of Machine A in Country A;
- *CGU P$_B$:* Production and sale of Machine B in Country B; and
- *CGU S:* Service operations in both countries.

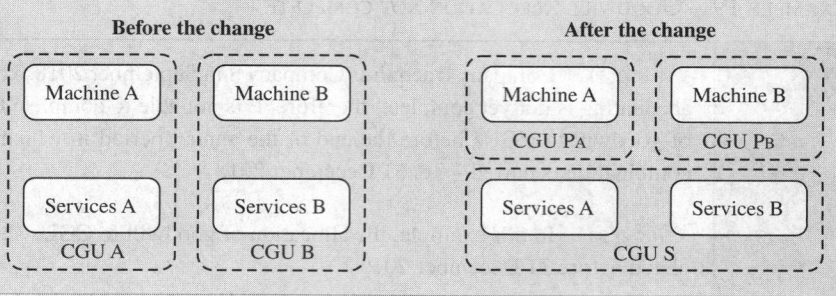

3.10.470.60   Following the changes in the composition of CGUs, the goodwill is reallocated to the units affected. Therefore, goodwill in CGU A is reallocated to CGU Pᴀ and CGU S. This is because the goodwill in CGU A can be identified or associated strictly with the asset groups of CGUs Pᴀ and S and not with the asset group of CGU Pʙ. [*IAS 36.87*]

3.10.470.70   Because there were indications of possible impairment, the goodwill in CGU A was assessed for impairment immediately before the reorganisation; no impairment was identified. For CGUs Pᴀ and S, the FVLCD is higher than the VIU and therefore the FVLCD is used to assess impairment. The fair values and carrying amounts for each CGU at the date of the reorganisation are as follows.

	CGU Pᴀ	CGU S	Tᴏᴛᴀʟ
Fair value/FVLCD[(1)]	45	15	60
Goodwill allocation	9[(2)]	3[(3)]	12
Carrying amount of identifiable net assets	38	4	42
Total net assets	47	7	54
Immediate impairment	2	-	2

Notes
1.   There are no material disposal costs and therefore the fair value of each CGU equals FVLCD.
2.   Calculated as 45 / 60 x 12 = 9.
3.   Calculated as 15 / 60 x 12 = 3.

3.10.470.80   Using the relative value approach, allocation of goodwill of 9 to CGU Pᴀ results in an impairment of 2 (45 - 47).

3.10.470.90   In Example 20A, because CGU Pᴀ is asset-intensive whereas CGU S is not, the allocation of goodwill based on the relative value approach may not appropriately reflect the goodwill associated with the operations of these CGUs.

3.10.470.100   In our view, an alternative approach of reallocating goodwill based on the relative current values of notional goodwill may be acceptable in the situation addressed in Example 20A. Under this alternative approach, a notional goodwill is determined by performing a purchase price allocation for each CGU based on the fair value of the CGU and its identifiable net assets as at the date of the reorganisation.

Eхᴀᴍᴘʟᴇ 20B – Rᴇᴀʟʟᴏᴄᴀᴛɪᴏɴ ᴏꜰ ɢᴏᴏᴅᴡɪʟʟ – Rᴇʟᴀᴛɪᴠᴇ ᴄᴜʀʀᴇɴᴛ ᴠᴀʟᴜᴇs ᴏꜰ ɴᴏᴛɪᴏɴᴀʟ ɢᴏᴏᴅᴡɪʟʟ

3.10.470.110   Using the same facts as in Example 20A, the table below illustrates the allocation of goodwill applying the relative current values of notional goodwill approach.

	CGU P$_A$	CGU S	TOTAL
Fair value/FVLCD[1]	45	15	60
Fair value of identifiable net assets	39	7	46
Current value of notional goodwill	6	8	14
Goodwill allocation	5[2]	7	12
Carrying amount of identifiable net assets	38	4	42
Total net assets	43	11	54

Notes
1. There are no material disposal costs and therefore the fair value of each CGU equals FVLCD.
2. Calculated as 12 x 6 / 14.

3.10.470.120   In this case, unlike in Example 20A, no impairment arises as a result of the goodwill reallocation using the relative current values of notional goodwill approach.

3.10.480   Corporate assets

3.10.480.10   The guidance in 3.10.150 discusses the impairment testing of corporate assets. However, complications may arise in respect of intra-group charges related to corporate assets in a value in use calculation.

3.10.490   *Corporate assets allocated to CGUs*

3.10.490.10   When an entity allocates a corporate asset to the underlying CGUs or to the group of CGUs that requires testing (see 3.10.150), it should ensure that the cash outflows attributable to the corporate asset are not double counted.

3.10.490.20   To avoid double counting, in our view the treatment of the recharge when a corporate asset(s) is allocated to a CGU should follow these steps.
1. Allocate the corporate asset(s) to the CGU.
2. Eliminate intra-group charges in respect of the corporate asset(s) from the CGU's cash flows.
3. Push down the corporate asset cash outflows incurred at the higher level to the CGU level.

EXAMPLE 21 – CORPORATE ASSETS – ALLOCATED TO CGUs

3.10.490.30   Company U owns and operates an IT system with a carrying amount of 100 that is used exclusively by CGU V and CGU W. Both CGU V's and CGU W's cash flows are dependent on the corporate asset. U charges each CGU an annual amount of 30 for use of the IT system. The actual running costs incurred by U in respect of the IT system are cash outflows of 20 a year.

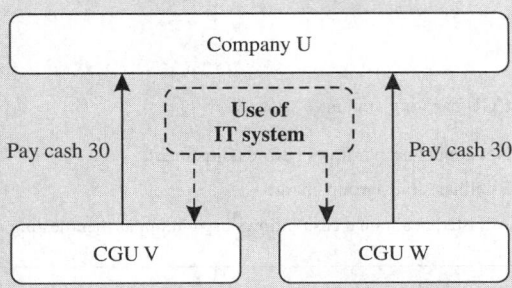

3.10.490.40 U performs the following three-step process outlined in 3.10.490.20.
1. U allocates the carrying amount of the IT system (100) to each CGU on the same basis used to allocate the intra-group charges (see 3.10.150.40). Both CGUs are charged the same amount of 30; therefore, the allocation to each CGU is 50.
2. U reverses the intra-group charges allocated to each CGU, thereby decreasing their cash outflows by 30.
3. The cash outflows for the corporate asset are pushed down to the CGU level, adding an amount of 10 to the outflows of each CGU.

	CGU V	CGU W
CGU carrying amount before adjustment	500	300
1. Allocate portion of corporate asset	50	50
Adjusted carrying amount used in impairment testing	550	350
Net annual cash inflows before adjustment	60	80
2. Eliminate intra-group charge	30	30
3. Push down actual cash outflows	(10)	(10)
Adjusted net annual cash inflows used in impairment testing	80	100

3.10.500   *Corporate assets not allocated to CGUs*

3.10.500.10   If a corporate asset is not allocated to the underlying CGUs, then no cash outflows associated with the corporate assets are included in the testing of the CGU. As outlined in 3.10.150.20, the CGUs are first tested without the corporate asset, and then grouped together to test the corporate assets and the related cash flows.

EXAMPLE 22 – CORPORATE ASSETS – NOT ALLOCATED TO CGUs

3.10.500.20   Continuing Example 21, assume that the IT system was only tested at the CGU V+W level. In this case, in the first stage of testing (bottom-up) the carrying amount of each CGU would not be adjusted, but the intra-group charges incurred would be reversed.

	CGU V	CGU W
CGU carrying amount	500	300
Net annual cash inflows before adjustment	60	80
Eliminate intra-group charge	30	30
Adjusted net annual cash inflows used in impairment testing	90	110

3.10.500.30   In the second stage of testing (top-down), CGUs V and W are tested together with the IT system (see 3.10.150). In that case, the total carrying amount of the combined assets is 900 (500 + 300 + 100) and the net annual cash inflow used in impairment testing is 180 (90 + 110 - 20).

3.10.510   Non-controlling interests

3.10.510.10   NCI may be measured either at fair value or based on their proportionate interest in the acquiree's identifiable net assets at the date of acquisition. The choice is available on a transaction-by-transaction basis. See 2.6.940.

3.10.510.20   NCI may have been measured at the date of acquisition at their proportionate interest in the identifiable net assets of the subsidiary (that is a CGU or group of CGUs). In this case, goodwill attributable to NCI is included in the recoverable amount of the related CGU or group of CGUs; however, it is not recognised in the parent's consolidated financial statements. [*IAS 36.C4*]

3.10.520   *Determining amount of goodwill in carrying amount of CGUs*

3.10.520.10   NCI may initially be measured based on their proportionate interest in the identifiable net assets of the subsidiary. In this case, the carrying amount of goodwill allocated to such a CGU or group of CGUs is grossed up to include the unrecognised goodwill attributable to the NCI. For impairment testing purposes, it is this adjusted carrying amount that is compared with the recoverable amount (see 3.10.330). This gross-up is not required if NCI were initially measured at fair value. [*IAS 36.C4*]

3.10.520.20   IAS 36 illustrates the gross-up of the carrying amount of goodwill allocated to a CGU or group of CGUs on the same basis as profit or loss is allocated to the parent and the NCI. However, in our view the standard does not preclude using another rational basis of gross-up – e.g. one that takes into account any control premium paid in the acquisition. [*IAS 36.C4, IE62–IE65*]

EXAMPLE 23A – GROSS-UP OF GOODWILL FOR NCI – CALCULATION OF IMPAIRMENT LOSS

3.10.520.30   Company P acquired 80% of Company S in a business combination several years ago, and paid a control premium of 15. NCI were measured at their proportionate interest in the identifiable net assets at the date of acquisition. The contribution of S to P's consolidated financial statements at the date of acquisition was as follows.

Goodwill	80
Identifiable net assets	1,000
Total net assets	1,080
Equity (parent)	880
Equity (NCI)	200
Goodwill share	-
Share of identifiable net assets	200
Total shareholders' equity	1,080

3.10.520.40 S is a CGU and goodwill arising on the acquisition is tested at this level. The recoverable amount of the CGU is determined to be 1,050.

3.10.520.50 A gross-up of goodwill on the same basis as the allocation of profit or loss (a 'mechanical' gross-up) would be calculated as 100 (80 / 80%). In that case, the impairment loss is 50 (1,050 - 1,100).

3.10.520.60 A rational way to gross up the goodwill would be to adjust the goodwill by the control premium before the gross-up. This would result in a grossed-up goodwill of 96 ((80 - 15) / 80% + 15). In that case, the impairment loss would be 46 (1,050 - 1,096).

3.10.530 *Allocating impairment loss to parent and NCI*

3.10.530.10 If a non-wholly owned CGU is impaired, then any impairment losses are allocated between the amount attributable to the parent and to the NCI. IAS 36 refers to allocating the impairment loss on the same basis as profit or loss is allocated to the parent and the NCI – i.e. a mechanical allocation. However, in our view the standard does not preclude using another rational basis of allocation – e.g. one that takes account of any control premium paid in the acquisition. [*IAS 36.C6*]

3.10.530.20 If a non-wholly owned CGU is impaired, then to the extent that the impairment loss is allocated to NCI that were measured initially at their proportionate interest in the identifiable net assets of the subsidiary, that impairment is not recognised in the financial statements. [*IAS 36.C6, C8, IE66–IE68*]

EXAMPLE 23B – GROSS-UP OF GOODWILL FOR NCI – ALLOCATION OF IMPAIRMENT LOSS

3.10.530.30 Continuing Example 23A, the impairment loss allocated to the parent is calculated as follows.

- *Mechanical gross-up of goodwill and mechanical allocation:* The impairment loss allocated to the parent would be 40 (50 x 80%).
- *Rational gross-up of goodwill and rational allocation:* The impairment loss allocated to the parent would be 38 (46 - ((46 / 96) x 20%) x (96 - 15)).
- *Rational gross-up of goodwill and mechanical allocation:* In our view, it would also be permitted to apply a rational gross-up of goodwill followed by a mechanical allocation of the impairment loss, in which case the part of the impairment loss allocated to the parent would be 37 (46 x 80%). We believe that this mixed method of rational gross-up and mechanical allocation is acceptable. This is because the rational gross-up results in total goodwill that is broadly similar to the position if NCI were measured initially at fair value; therefore, there is consistency. However, we believe that it would not be appropriate to apply a mechanical gross-up followed by a rational allocation.

3.10.530.40   No share of goodwill has been allocated to NCI and only the parent's share of the impairment loss is recognised in the consolidated financial statements. Therefore, the outcome under each of the approaches is as follows.

	MECHANICAL GROSS-UP AND ALLOCATION	RATIONAL GROSS-UP AND ALLOCATION	RATIONAL GROSS-UP AND MECHANICAL ALLOCATION
Calculated impairment loss	50	46	46
Recognised impairment loss	40	38	37
Parent's share	40	38	37
NCI share	-	-	-

3.10.540   *Choosing rational basis of gross-up and allocation*

3.10.540.10   If a non-wholly owned CGU is impaired, then as noted in 3.10.520.10–20, IAS 36 refers to a simple basis of gross-up and allocation on the basis of how profits are shared between the parent and NCI. This approach has the benefit of simplicity even though it may not reflect the true goodwill allocation between the parent and NCI.

3.10.540.20   Applying a different method of gross-up and allocation on a rational basis has the benefit of better reflecting the true goodwill allocation between the parent and NCI. However, the gross-up and allocation process could be more complex, and sophisticated records may need to be maintained to track the allocation of goodwill. This would depend on:

- the way in which the subsidiary's identifiable net assets were allocated to different CGUs;
- the allocation of the goodwill to the other CGUs of the acquirer on acquisition of the subsidiary; and
- other transactions between the parent and NCI.

3.10.550 **Associates and joint arrangements**

3.10.560 *Associates and joint ventures*

3.10.565 *Two-step impairment assessment*

3.10.565.10 From an investor's perspective, the impairment assessment in respect of an investment in a joint venture or associate (equity-accounted investees) comprises two successive steps.
1. Apply the equity method to recognise the investor's share of any impairment losses for the investee's identifiable assets.
2. When there is an indication of a possible impairment, test the investment as a whole and recognise any additional impairment loss. [*IAS 28.40–42*]

3.10.565.20 When applying the equity method (Step 1), appropriate adjustments are made to the investor's share of the investee's profit or loss after acquisition. For example, adjustments are made for the depreciation of assets based on their fair values at the date of acquisition. [*IAS 28.32*]

3.10.565.30 The equity method also requires appropriate adjustments to be made to the investor's share of the investee's profit or loss after acquisition for impairment losses recognised by the investee, such as in respect of goodwill or property, plant and equipment. Examples 24A to 24C illustrate different approaches that in our view are acceptable methods in performing Step 1 of the impairment testing. [*IAS 28.32*]

3.10.565.40 Goodwill resulting from the acquisition of an equity-accounted investee is not allocated to the investee's CGUs but instead is included in the carrying amount of the investment as a whole. Such goodwill is not subject to an annual impairment test. Instead, after applying equity accounting, the investment is tested for impairment when there is an indication of a possible impairment (Step 2). [*IAS 28.40–42*]

3.10.565.50 IAS 28 provides guidance for determining whether it is necessary to perform an impairment test for investments in equity-accounted investees (see 3.10.570). If there is an indication of impairment, then the impairment test applied follows the principles in IAS 36 described in this chapter. [*IAS 28.40, 42*]

3.10.570 *Objective evidence of impairment*

3.10.570.10 The net investment in an associate or joint venture is impaired if, and only if, objective evidence indicates that one or more events, which occurred after the initial recognition, have had an impact on the future cash flows from the net investment and that impact can be reliably estimated. It may not be possible to identify one specific event that caused the impairment because it may have been triggered by the combined effects of a number of events. [*IAS 28.41A*]

3.10.570.20 Observable data about the following loss events provides objective evidence that the net investment is impaired:
• significant financial difficulty of the associate or joint venture;
• a breach of contract – e.g. a default or delinquency in payments by the associate or joint venture;

- granting a concession because of the associate's or joint venture's financial difficulty that the entity would not otherwise consider;
- becoming probable that the associate or joint venture will enter bankruptcy or other financial reorganisation;
- the disappearance of an active market for the net investment because of financial difficulties of the associate or joint venture;
- information about significant changes with an adverse effect in the technological market, economic or legal environment in which the associate or joint venture operates, which indicate that the cost of the investment in the equity instrument may not be recovered; or
- a significant or prolonged decline in the fair value of an investment in an equity instrument below its cost. [*IAS 28.41A, 41C*]

3.10.570.30   The disappearance of an active market because the associate's or joint venture's equity or financial instruments are no longer publicly traded is not evidence of impairment. A downgrade of an associate's or joint venture's credit rating or a decline in the fair value of the associate or joint venture, is not of itself, evidence of impairment, although these events may be evidence of impairment when considered with other available information. [*IAS 28.41B*]

3.10.575   *Determining impairment loss*

3.10.575.10   In applying IAS 36, the investor compares the carrying amount of the investment after applying the equity method with its recoverable amount to determine any additional impairment loss (see 3.5.500). Any impairment loss recognised in Step 2 is applied to the investment as a whole. As a result, it has no effect on the application of the equity method (Step 1) in future periods. [*IAS 28.42*]

3.10.575.20   In our experience, different approaches to the two-step impairment assessment in respect of an investment in an associate are applied. These approaches are illustrated in Examples 24A to 24C.

EXAMPLE 24A – IMPAIRMENT OF ASSOCIATE – REPERFORMED FOR EACH CGU

3.10.575.30   Investor P acquired a 30% interest in Associate E for consideration of 300 on 1 January 2018. Both P and E prepare their consolidated financial statements in accordance with IFRS, and P applies the equity method to E.

3.10.575.40   The carrying amount and the fair value of E's identifiable assets at the date of acquisition were 700 and 800, respectively. E does not have liabilities at the date of acquisition. As a result, goodwill of 60 (300 - (800 x 30%)) was recognised on the acquisition of E, which forms part of P's investment in E.

3.10.575.50   Assume that E's financial statements at the date of acquisition also included goodwill of 50 that was recognised when E acquired another company in 2014. This pre-acquisition goodwill is reversed when P accounts for the acquisition of E in its consolidated financial statements (see 2.6.1010.10).

3.10.575.60   The following table provides details of the acquisition.

	CARRYING AMOUNT OF E'S ASSETS	LESS: CARRYING AMOUNT OF PRE-ACQUISITION GOODWILL	CARRYING AMOUNT OF E'S IDENTIFIABLE ASSETS	FAIR VALUE ADJUSTMENTS	CARRYING AMOUNT OF E'S IDENTIFIABLE ASSETS RECOGNISED BY P
CGU 1	250	-	250	50	300
CGU 2	180	(30)	150	-	150
CGU 3	320	(20)	300	50	350
Total	750	(50)	700	100	800
30% interest					240
Goodwill that forms part of P's investment in E					60
Carrying amount of P's investment in E (consideration paid)					300

3.10.575.70   Assume that there is no change in the carrying amount of E's assets, including the pre-acquisition goodwill, in 2018. At 31 December 2018, E performs an impairment test in preparing of its consolidated financial statements as follows.

	CARRYING AMOUNT OF E'S IDENTIFIABLE ASSETS RECOGNISED BY E	CARRYING AMOUNT OF PRE-ACQUISITION GOODWILL RECOGNISED BY E	CARRYING AMOUNT OF TOTAL ASSETS RECOGNISED BY E	RECOVERABLE AMOUNT	IMPAIRMENT LOSS RECOGNISED BY E
CGU 1	250	-	250	250	-
CGU 2	150	30	180	450	-
CGU 3	300	20	320	150	170
Total	700	50	750	850	170

3.10.575.80   As a result, E recognises an impairment loss of 170 for CGU 3. Of that amount, 20 is allocated to the pre-acquisition goodwill and 150 to the identifiable assets that belong to CGU 3 (see 3.10.380).

3.10.575.90   P does not recognise a loss of 51 – i.e. 30% of the impairment loss of 170 recognised in E's financial statements. Instead, when P applies the equity method to E, it recalculates the impairment loss recognised by E as follows.

	CARRYING AMOUNT OF E's IDENTIFIABLE ASSETS RECOGNISED BY P	RECOVERABLE AMOUNT	IMPAIRMENT LOSS	CARRYING AMOUNT OF E's IDENTIFIABLE ASSETS RECOGNISED BY P AFTER IMPAIRMENT
CGU 1	300	250	50	250
CGU 2	150	450	-	150
CGU 3	350	150	200	150
Total	800	850	250	550
30% interest	240		75	165

3.10.575.100 In the recalculation, the pre-acquisition goodwill of 50 in E's financial statements is not allocated to E's CGUs because, from P's perspective, it was eliminated when acquisition accounting was applied to E on 1 January 2018. Furthermore, the goodwill of 60 that P recognised on the acquisition of E is not allocated to E's CGUs; this is because the carrying amount of the investment in E as a whole, which includes that goodwill, is subject to impairment testing as a single asset after applying the equity method (see 3.10.565.40). The carrying amount of the investment in E after applying the equity method is calculated at 225 as follows.

	EQUITY METHOD	
	BEFORE IMPAIRMENT	AFTER IMPAIRMENT
30% interest of P in carrying amount of E's identifiable assets	240	165
Goodwill that forms part of P's investment in E	60	60
Carrying amount of P's investment in E	300	225

3.10.575.110 After applying the equity method, P identifies an indication that the investment in E might be impaired in accordance with IAS 28 (see 3.10.570). P compares the carrying amount of the investment in E after applying the equity method with its recoverable amount to determine any additional impairment loss to recognise on the investment in E.

3.10.575.120 Assume that the recoverable amount of P's investment in E is 280 from P's perspective. Because the recoverable amount is higher than the carrying amount of 225, P does not recognise an additional impairment loss on the investment in E as a whole. As a result, the total impairment loss recognised in relation to P's investment in E is 75, which results from applying the equity method.

> 3.10.575.130 In this example, P recognises impairment losses for CGUs 1 and 3 in applying the equity method whereas E recognises an impairment loss only for CGU 3. This is because the carrying amount of CGU 1 included in P's financial statements was higher than that in E's financial statements as a result of the fair value adjustments on the acquisition of E.

3.10.575.140 In Example 24A, the impairment loss recognised by E was recalculated using the recoverable amounts for each of E's separate CGUs. However, in our experience other methods that do not involve a full recalculation are also acceptable, as illustrated in Examples 24B and 24C; often, the approach taken depends on the level of information readily available.

EXAMPLE 24B – IMPAIRMENT OF ASSOCIATE – CGUs COMBINED

> 3.10.575.150 Changing the facts of Example 24A, the recoverable amounts of E's separate CGUs are not available to P although the total recoverable amount of 850 is available.
>
> 3.10.575.160 In this case, P compares the total carrying amount of CGUs 1, 2 and 3 in its financial statements of 800 with the total recoverable amount of 850. This results in no impairment loss in applying the equity method.
>
> 3.10.575.170 P would then need to compare the carrying amount of its investment in E of 300 with its recoverable amount of 280 (see 3.10.575.120) to determine the impairment loss on the investment in E as a whole, which would result in recognising an impairment loss of 20. The total impairment loss of 20 under this approach is different from the loss of 75 recognised in Example 24A. The following table summarises the details of the impairment testing under this approach.

	CARRYING AMOUNT OF E'S IDENTIFIABLE ASSETS RECOGNISED BY P	RECOVERABLE AMOUNT	IMPAIRMENT LOSS	CARRYING AMOUNT OF E'S IDENTIFIABLE ASSETS RECOGNISED BY P AFTER IMPAIRMENT
CGUs 1, 2 and 3	800	850	-	800
30% interest	240		_(a)	240
Goodwill that forms part of P's investment in E				60
Carrying amount of P's investment in E (after equity accounting)				300
Recoverable amount of P's investment in E				280
Impairment loss on P's investment in E as a whole				20(b)
Total impairment loss (a) + (b)				20

EXAMPLE 24C – IMPAIRMENT OF ASSOCIATE – FOCUS ON IMPAIRED CGUs

3.10.575.180 Again changing the facts of Example 24A, the recoverable amounts of CGUs 1 and 2 are not available to P, because E did not identify an impairment indication for those CGUs and therefore did not measure their recoverable amounts.

3.10.575.190 In this case, P recalculates the impairment loss for CGU 3 only; this would result in recognising an impairment loss of 60 (200 x 30%) in applying the equity method. P would then need to compare the carrying amount of the investment in E, after applying the equity method, of 240 (300 - 60) with its recoverable amount of 280 (see 3.10.575.120) to determine the impairment loss on the investment in E as a whole; this would result in no impairment loss. The total impairment loss of 60 under this approach is different from the loss of 75 recognised in Example 24A and the loss of 20 recognised in Example 24B.

3.10.575.200 The following table summarises the details of the impairment testing under this approach.

	CARRYING AMOUNT OF E'S IDENTIFIABLE ASSETS RECOGNISED BY P	RECOVERABLE AMOUNT	IMPAIRMENT LOSS	CARRYING AMOUNT OF E'S IDENTIFIABLE ASSETS RECOGNISED BY P AFTER IMPAIRMENT
CGU 1	300	Not available	-	300
CGU 2	150	Not available	-	150
CGU 3	350	150	200	150
Total	800	Not available	200	600
30% interest	240		60[a]	180
Goodwill that forms part of P's investment in E				60
Carrying amount of P's investment in E (after equity accounting)				240
Recoverable amount of P's investment in E				280
Impairment loss on P's investment in E as a whole				-[b]
Total impairment loss (a) + (b)				60

3.10.580   *Recoverable amount*

3.10.580.10   The value in use of an equity-accounted investee as a whole may be calculated by estimating the cash flows from the investment – i.e. future dividends and estimated cash flows from disposal of the shares – or by measuring the cash flows of the underlying operations of the entity as a whole. [*IAS 28.42*]

3.10.580.20   The forecast period should be over the useful life of the investee. In our view, because these assets relate to a portion of the net assets of an underlying business, the forecast period should be to perpetuity unless there is a planned disposal in the future or an expected termination of the business. If there is a planned disposal in the future but the asset is not classified as held-for-sale or held-for-distribution (see 5.4.20 and 35), then in our view cash flows should be forecast over the holding period and a disposal value should be estimated when determining value in use.

3.10.580.30   The recoverable amount of an equity-accounted investee should be based on cash flows that the investment will generate at its current ownership interest. In our view, an entity's plans to increase its interest in an investee to obtain control should not impact the cash flows associated with the value in use calculation in the current period if there is no binding commitment to do so before the reporting date.

3.10.580.40   When the shares of an equity-accounted investee are publicly traded, in our view the investor should carefully consider impairment analyses that suggest that value in use exceeds fair value less costs of disposal (see 3.10.320). [*IAS 36.22*]

3.10.580.50   For a discussion of any premium that might be included in the fair value less costs of disposal of an equity-accounted investee, see 2.4.830.

3.10.585   *Reversal of impairment*

3.10.585.10   As discussed in 3.10.565, any impairment loss recognised by the investor with respect to an equity-accounted investee is allocated to the carrying amount of the investment as a whole – i.e. it is not allocated to any assets, including goodwill, that constitute the carrying amount of the investment. Therefore, there is no restriction on the reversal of an impairment loss. [*IAS 28.42*]

3.10.585.20   Although an entity applies IAS 28 to determine if there is an indication of impairment (see 3.10.570), the standard is silent in respect of reversals of impairment. In our view, an entity applies IAS 36 to determine if there is an indication that an impairment should be reversed (see 3.10.390), because there is no exception that provides for a different treatment.

3.10.585.30   Any impairment loss is subsequently reversed only to the extent that the recoverable amount of the investment increases (see 3.10.390). This is confirmed by the wording in paragraph 42 of IAS 28 and supported by paragraph 114 of IAS 36, which refers to a reversal of an impairment loss only if there has been a change in the estimates used to determine the asset's recoverable amount, and only to the extent that the recoverable amount increases. Therefore, for example, an impairment loss is not reversed simply because the carrying amount of the investment has decreased because losses have been recorded. [*IAS 28.42, 36.114*]

EXAMPLE 25 – IMPAIRMENT OF ASSOCIATE – REVERSAL

3.10.585.40   In Example 24B, Company P recognised an impairment loss of 20 on its investment in Company E as a whole, thereby reducing the carrying amount of the investment from 300 (pre-impairment carrying amount) to 280 (recoverable amount).

3.10.585.50   The following year, E makes losses and the carrying amount of P's investment is further reduced to 220; however, the recoverable amount of E has increased 290.

3.10.585.60   P determines that there is an indication that the impairment loss has reduced under IAS 36, and records a reversal of the impairment loss of 10 (290 - 280). The reversal is limited to 10 because, in applying IAS 28, the impairment loss can be reversed only to the extent that the recoverable amount has increased. It would not be appropriate for P to reverse the entire impairment loss on the basis that recoverable amount (290) exceeds the latest carrying amount (220) by an amount that exceeds the previous impairment loss recorded.

3.10.590   *Joint operations*

3.10.590.10   An interest in a joint operation is accounted for on the basis of the joint operator's share of assets and liabilities (see 3.6.260). In that case, goodwill is tested for impairment annually in the same way as goodwill arising in a business combination. This is because under joint operation accounting, the investor accounts for its share of the individual assets (including goodwill) and liabilities of the joint operation – rather than an investment in equity instruments.

Ⓢ 3.10.600   **Separate financial statements**

3.10.600.10   Investments in subsidiaries, associates and joint ventures that an entity elects to account for in accordance with IFRS 9 are outside the scope of IAS 36. Instead, all of the requirements of IFRS 9 apply (see 7.8.10.20). [*IAS 27.10(b), 36.2(e)*]

3.10.600.20   If an entity elects to account for investments in subsidiaries, associates and joint ventures at cost in its separate financial statements, then the IFRS Interpretations Committee has noted that the requirements of IAS 36 apply – in terms of both indications of impairment (reversals) and in calculating the amount of any impairment loss (reversal). [*IAS 27.10(a), IU 01-13*]

3.10.600.30   In addition to the indicators of impairment in 3.10.120, the receipt of dividend income from a subsidiary, associate or joint venture is considered as a possible indication of impairment in separate financial statements when:
- the carrying amount of the investment in the separate financial statements exceeds the carrying amount in the consolidated financial statements of the investee's net assets (including any goodwill); or
- the dividend exceeds the total comprehensive income of the investee. [*IAS 36.12(h)*]

3.10.600.40   For investments in associates and joint ventures that are equity accounted, the same impairment requirements apply in both the investor's separate and consolidated financial statements. However, for investments in subsidiaries that are equity-accounted in the parent's separate financial statements, the impairment testing may result in a different outcome from that in the consolidated financial statements. This difference may arise because under the equity method goodwill is not tested for impairment separately, but instead the entire carrying amount of the investee (in this case, the subsidiary) is tested for impairment as a single asset (see 3.10.560). [*IAS 27.BC10G*]

3.10.603 *Functional currency of investee different from parent/investor* Ⓢ

3.10.603.10   A subsidiary, associate or joint venture may have a functional currency different from that of the parent/investor. In that case, in preparing separate financial statements, the recoverable amount of the investee is calculated in the relevant functional currency of the investee and translated into the parent/investor's functional currency at the reporting date (see 3.10.290.10–20). Therefore, movements in exchange rates may give rise to an impairment loss in the separate financial statements even if there is no such loss in the consolidated financial statements. For an overview of the difference in methodology between separate and consolidated financial statements, see 3.10.290. [*IAS 21.25(b)*]

EXAMPLE 26 – SEPARATE FINANCIAL STATEMENTS – IMPAIRMENT LOSS CAUSED BY CHANGE IN EXCHANGE RATE

3.10.603.20   Parent P's functional currency is FC, and the functional currency of Subsidiary S is AC. In 2016, P acquired its investment in S for AC 100, which was equivalent to FC 100 at that time. P accounts for S at cost in its separate financial statements.

3.10.603.30   At 31 December 2018 (P's year end) the recoverable amount of P's investment in S is AC 110, but the exchange rate has weakened and this translates to FC 80 – i.e. FC 20 less than the carrying amount in P's separate financial statements. As a result, P records an impairment loss of FC 20 in its separate financial statements.

3.10.605 *Investments in subsidiaries* Ⓢ

3.10.605.10   Because an investment in a subsidiary is an individual financial asset in the separate financial statements, it may be intuitive to conclude that it generates cash inflows largely independently of the cash inflows of other assets. Accordingly, the investment in the subsidiary would form a single CGU from the perspective of the separate financial statements, regardless of how CGUs are determined from the group's perspective.

3.10.605.20   Under this approach, once an indication of impairment has been identified, the impairment testing follows the same guidance as explained for Step 2 of the testing for equity-accounted investees (see 3.10.560).

EXAMPLE 27A – INVESTMENT IN SUBSIDIARY – SEPARATE CGU

3.10.605.30   Company P has a wholly owned subsidiary, S. In P's consolidated financial statements, S is identified as a separate CGU and goodwill recognised on the acquisition of S is fully allocated to S.

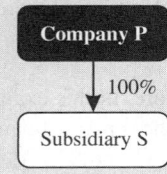

Company P

100%

Subsidiary S

> **3.10.605.40** If P identifies S as a separate CGU in its separate financial statements and consolidated financial statements, then in our experience the impairment testing in the separate financial statements would be performed on a basis similar to that in the consolidated financial statements.

3.10.605.50 However, a different approach might be appropriate if the assets of a subsidiary form part of a larger CGU from the group's perspective. In such situations, it may be necessary to conclude, from the perspective of the separate financial statements, that the investment in the subsidiary generates cash inflows largely independently only in combination with other assets within the group. Otherwise, an artificial impairment loss may be recognised.

3.10.605.60 Accordingly, the investment in the subsidiary would form part of a CGU that includes those other assets. In our view, it is appropriate in such situations for the entity to perform an impairment test for the separate financial statements at the level of such larger CGU, rather than based only on the investment in that subsidiary.

EXAMPLE 27B – INVESTMENT IN SUBSIDIARY – LARGER CGU

3.10.605.70 Company P has two wholly owned subsidiaries, S1 and S2. In P's consolidated financial statements, S1 and S2 are identified as a single CGU on a combined basis. In addition, goodwill recognised on the acquisition of S1 in P's consolidated financial statements was allocated to that larger CGU because of the synergies between the two subsidiaries.

3.10.605.80 In this example, if P identifies S1 as a separate CGU in the impairment test for the separate financial statements, then this may result in a day one impairment loss in the separate financial statements that would not be recognised in the consolidated financial statements. This is because the total amount of consideration for the acquisition of S1 is included in the carrying amount of the investment in S1 in the separate financial statements; however, the synergy effect of the acquisition of S1 is also expected in S2, and therefore may not be fully reflected in the recoverable amount of S1.

3.10.605.90 Therefore, in this example it may be necessary for P to perform an impairment test for the separate financial statements at the level of the larger CGU, which includes both S1 and S2.

3.10.605.100 When an entity is an intermediate parent within a larger group, from the perspective of the ultimate parent's consolidated financial statements, assets of the entity's subsidiary may form part of a CGU that includes assets of other entities within the group but outside the entity's subgroup. Similarly, goodwill arising on the acquisition of the entity's subsidiary may be allocated to a CGU or a group of CGUs that includes assets of other entities within the group but outside the intermediate parent's subgroup.

3.10.605.110 In such situations, impairment testing by the entity at the level of the investment in the subsidiary may result in a day one impairment loss in its separate and consolidated financial statements that would not be recognised in the ultimate parent's consolidated financial statements. This may occur, for example, because the synergy effect is expected within the ultimate parent's group but not within the entity's subgroup.

3.10.605.120 The intermediate parent cannot identify CGUs for impairment testing beyond the boundaries of the reporting entity (the subgroup). This means that an impairment loss may arise solely because of the group structure, which is driven by the ultimate parent. In that case, in our view it is acceptable for the entity to account for such impairment loss in its separate financial statements as an equity distribution.

EXAMPLE 27C – INVESTMENT IN SUBSIDIARY – BOUNDARIES OF REPORTING ENTITY

3.10.605.130 Parent P has two wholly owned subsidiaries, S1 and S2. S1 has a wholly owned subsidiary, X. In impairment testing in P's consolidated financial statements, each of X and S2 is identified as a separate CGU; however, goodwill recognised on the acquisition of X is allocated to the group of CGUs (X+S2) because of the effect of synergies.

3.10.605.140 In this example, if S1 identifies X as a separate CGU in the impairment testing in its separate financial statements, then a day one impairment loss will arise that would not be recognised in the consolidated financial statements. This is because the total amount of consideration for the acquisition of X is included in the carrying amount of the investment in X in the separate financial statements, although the synergies of the acquisition of X are also expected in S2.

3.10.605.150 However, unlike in Example 27B, S1 may not perform an impairment test for the separate financial statements at the level of the group of CGUs (X+S2) because S2 is outside the boundaries of the reporting entity that is the S1 subgroup.

> Therefore, S1 recognises an equity distribution for the amount of the impairment loss that arises solely because of the group structure.

3.10.610 Research and development

3.10.610.10   The treatment of R&D expenditure is not discussed explicitly in IAS 36, but such expenditure is key to the business models of many entities. In determining the appropriate treatment of R&D expenditure, it is necessary to consider each of the following:
- research expenditure, which is expensed as it is incurred;
- development expenditure, to the extent that it is capitalised (see 3.3.120); and
- acquired in-process research and development (IPR&D) expenditure before the capitalisation criteria are met, which is capitalised as part of the acquisition accounting (see 2.6.810).

3.10.620   *Research expenditure*

3.10.620.10   A research centre is a potential example of a corporate asset in IAS 36. This is because an entity's research activities may contribute to the future cash inflows of two or more CGUs. In that case, the asset (the research centre) and the related expenditure are tested for impairment following the guidance for corporate assets (see 3.10.90). [*IAS 36.100*]

3.10.630   *Capitalised development expenditure*

3.10.630.10   Capitalised development expenditure is recognised as an asset in the statement of financial position, and therefore the general guidance in IAS 36 applies.
- The asset is tested as an individual asset or as part of a larger CGU, as appropriate (see 3.10.40).
- The asset is tested at least at each annual reporting date before the product under development being available for use (see 3.10.130).

3.10.630.20   In determining recoverable amount on a discounted cash flow basis, future cash outflows will include all expenditure required to get the asset ready for sale or use.
- For fair value less costs of disposal, this will be based on the cash flow assumptions that a market participant would make, including in relation to capital expenditure (see 2.4.90).
- For value in use, this will include the expected cash outflow necessary to prepare the asset for use (see 3.10.250). [*IAS 36.42*]

3.10.630.30   Additionally, future cash flows over the entire expected product life cycle may need to be considered – forecast and then extrapolated as part of the terminal value – in establishing the recoverable amount. An arbitrary shorter period may artificially create or increase an impairment loss. This is because of the front loading of development costs and the level of capital investment required to launch the related product, and the back-ending of the receipt of benefits. This may be a circumstance in which a forecast period longer than five years is justified in determining value in use (see 3.10.230.10).

3.10.640   *Acquired in-process research and development*

3.10.640.10   The discussion in 3.10.630 in respect of capitalised development expenditure applies equally to acquired IPR&D. However, there is likely to be much more judgement involved because of the earlier stage of the project(s).

3.10.650   *Development expenditure incurred before capitalisation criteria met*

3.10.650.10   For many entities, one of the critical cash outflows in determining recoverable amount will be development expenditure incurred before the capitalisation criteria (see 3.3.120) are met. However, an issue arises about the assumptions that are appropriate in respect of the cash inflows that will potentially arise in the future.

- For fair value less costs of disposal, the recoverable amount will be determined based on the cash flow assumptions that a market participant would make (see 2.4.90).
- For value in use, IAS 36 is unclear. On the one hand, the potential cash inflows need to be included to show the benefit of the cash outflows, and in some cases to avoid artificially creating or increasing an impairment loss. But on the other hand, IAS 36 emphasises the need to test assets for impairment in their current condition (see 3.10.250.10).

3.10.650.20   In our view, development projects that do not yet meet the criteria for capitalisation should be included in the determination of value in use. This is to fairly reflect the current and ongoing activities of the CGU. Therefore, development expenditure incurred before the capitalisation criteria are met would be treated in the same way as capitalised development expenditure. However, there is likely to be much more judgement involved, because of the earlier stage of the project(s).

3.10.655   **Hedging**

3.10.655.10   Entities often enter into hedging instruments – e.g. commodity or foreign currency forwards – to manage risks that affect the future cash flows of a CGU. The treatment of such hedging instruments in impairment testing is not explicitly discussed in IAS 36.

3.10.655.20   IAS 36 requires the cash flow projections used in value in use calculations to be based on reasonable and supportable assumptions that represent management's best estimate of the range of economic conditions that will exist over the remaining life of the asset. It might therefore appear that hedging instruments should be factored into the calculation of value in use. [*IAS 36.33*]

3.10.655.30   However, financial assets in the scope of IFRS 9 are outside the scope of IAS 36. In addition, IAS 36 does not allow estimates of future cash flows to include cash inflows or outflows from financing activities. Therefore, it is unclear whether such hedging instruments should be included in determining a CGU's carrying amount and whether their cash flows should be included in estimating value in use. This issue arises regardless of whether the entity applies hedge accounting in accordance with IFRS 9 (see chapter 7.9). [*IAS 36.2(e), 50(a)*]

3.10.655.40   As set out in 3.10.330.10, the carrying amount of a CGU should be determined in a way that is consistent with how the recoverable amount of the CGU is determined. We believe that this principle takes precedence in determining the treatment of hedging instruments in estimating value in use. Therefore, in our view an entity should consider the impact of hedging instruments using either of the following approaches, which should be applied consistently.

- *Approach 1:* The hedging instrument is excluded from the carrying amount of the CGU and the cash flows expected from that instrument are excluded from the calculation of value in use.
- *Approach 2:* The hedging instrument is included in the carrying amount of the CGU and the cash flows expected from that instrument are included in the calculation of value in use.

3.10.655.50   The approach selected should be applied consistently.

3.10.655.60   These approaches should generally result in the same impairment conclusion, because they both determine the carrying amount of the CGU in a manner that is consistent with how value in use is determined. For example, in a simplified scenario, if the discount rate for the CGU applied under Approach 2 was close to the rate used to value a forward contract used as the hedging instrument, then the value of the hedging instrument included in the carrying amount of the CGU might be close to the net present value of the cash flows expected from the hedging instrument included in the value in use calculation, assuming no other factors affect the price of the forward contract.

3.10.655.70   However, the discount rate used in a value in use approach is a market-based rate that reflects the current market assessment of risks specific to the CGU as a whole. Therefore, judgement may be required in assessing whether the market-based discount rate adequately reflects the CGU's net risk exposures that are the subject of hedges.

- If an entity applies Approach 1 (exclude hedging instruments) and derives a discount rate used to calculate the recoverable amount under the value in use model from similar businesses with similar net risk exposures and hedging, then the entity may need to consider adjusting the discount rate used to calculate the value in use to take account of the effect of the hedging instruments.
- Conversely, if an entity applies Approach 2 (include hedging instruments) and the market-based discount rate does not reflect similar net risk exposures and hedging, then the entity may need to consider adjusting the discount rate to take account of the effect of the hedging instruments on the risks of the CGU's cash flows.

3.10.660   *Hedging reserve arising from business combination*

3.10.660.10   The foreign currency equivalent of the consideration paid in a business combination may have been subject to cash flow hedge accounting. This becomes relevant in testing the resulting goodwill for impairment; the hedge would have been a cash flow hedge of a firm commitment to acquire a business, or of a highly probable forecast business combination (see 7.9.470).

3.10.660.20   If a business was acquired through the purchase of an equity interest in an entity, rather than the acquisition of assets and liabilities that comprise the business, then we believe that an entity should choose an accounting policy, to be applied consistently, to designate the related cash flow hedge using one of the following approaches.

- *Hedge of a non-financial item:* If the hedge is designated as a hedge of a non-financial item, then the entity should recognise the gains or losses from the hedging instrument recognised in OCI as an adjustment to the initial carrying amount of the goodwill when the business combination occurs.
- *Hedge of a financial item:* If the hedge is designated as a hedge of a financial item, then the gains or losses on the hedging instrument recognised in OCI would continue to be recognised in the hedging reserve in equity until the related goodwill affects profit or loss, in part or in full (see 7.9.470.30–60).

3.10.660.30   Also, an entity may expect that all or a portion of a loss recognised in OCI will not be recovered in the future. In this case, it immediately reclassifies to profit or loss the amount that is not expected to be recovered. [*IFRS 9.6.5.11(d)(iii)*]

3.10.660.40   In our view, whether an entity designates the hedged item as a hedge of a non-financial item or a financial item should not impact the net amount of loss recognised in profit or loss as a result of future impairment assessments of the related goodwill. If the recognised amount of goodwill has been impacted by an adjustment (i.e. under the hedge of a non-financial item), then it is this adjusted carrying amount that is considered in impairment testing. If gains or losses on the hedging instrument continue to be recognised in the hedging reserve (i.e. under the hedge of a financial item), then the net loss recognised in profit or loss as a result of impairment or other lack of recoverability should equal:

- any excess of the carrying amount of the goodwill; plus (for debits) or minus (for credits)
- the amount included in the hedging reserve over the recoverable amount of the goodwill.

EXAMPLE 28 – HEDGING RESERVE ARISING IN BUSINESS COMBINATION

3.10.660.50   In 2017, Company P undertook a cash flow hedge, whereby it hedged the foreign currency risk of the consideration paid in a highly probable business combination that was effected through the purchase of an equity interest in the entity. The effective portion of changes in the fair value of the hedging instrument was recognised in OCI and presented in equity in a hedging reserve. On completion of the business combination, the amount in the hedging reserve was a debit of 10. Goodwill (exclusive of the hedging reserve) was 20. For simplicity, assume that the acquired business represents a separate CGU and that the only asset in the CGU is goodwill.

3.10.660.60   In 2018, P performs its annual goodwill impairment test and concludes that the recoverable amount of the CGU is 26.

Scenario 1 – P designates the hedge as a hedge of a non-financial item

3.10.660.70   Under this approach, on completing the business combination P adjusts the carrying amount of goodwill by the hedging reserve of 10, resulting in goodwill of 30 (20 + 10). In this case, P recognises an impairment loss of 4 (30 - 26).

Scenario 2 – P designates the hedge as a hedge of a financial item

3.10.660.80   Under this approach, on completing the business combination P does not make an adjustment to the carrying amount of goodwill. Therefore, a hedging reserve of 10 continues to be presented in equity, and the carrying amount of goodwill is 20. In this case, on the face of it goodwill is not impaired; this is because the carrying amount of the CGU (20) is lower than its recoverable amount (26). However, because the recoverable amount of the CGU is only 6 in excess of its carrying amount, the entity no longer expects to recover 4 (10 - 6) of the loss included in the hedging reserve. Therefore, 4 of the loss is reclassified from the hedging reserve to profit or loss.

3.10.670   **Leases**

3.10.670.10   IAS 36 does not explicitly discuss the treatment of leases in determining value in use. However, to identify an appropriate approach in determining the carrying amount and recoverable amount of a CGU, the principles of the standard can be followed – e.g. that financing items are excluded from impairment testing (see 3.10.240.140) and the carrying amount of a CGU does not include the carrying amount of any recognised liability, unless an entity needs to consider a recognised liability to determine the recoverable amount of a CGU (see 3.10.240.120).

3.10.670.20   The following table summarises the appropriate treatment of operating and finance leases from the perspective of both the lessee and lessor in determining value in use.

	LESSEE		LESSOR	
	OPERATING LEASE	FINANCE LEASE	OPERATING LEASE	FINANCE LEASE
CARRYING AMOUNT				
Lease asset	N/A. No asset recognised in statement of financial position[(1)].	Include leased asset in carrying amount[(2)].	Include underlying leased asset in carrying amount.	Lease asset is a financial asset. Therefore, follow impairment guidance in IFRS 9 (see 7.8.410).
Lease liability	N/A. No liability recognised in statement of financial position.	Exclude lease liability from carrying amount because it arises from financing. However, if on disposal of the CGU a buyer would assume the lease liability, then include liability in carrying amount (see 3.10.670.30).	N/A	N/A
RECOVERABLE AMOUNT				
Lease payments/ liability/receipts	Include future lease cash payments in cash flow forecasts.	Exclude future lease cash payments from cash flow forecasts. However, if on disposal of the CGU a buyer would assume the lease liability, then deduct the *carrying amount* of the lease liability (see 3.10.670.30).	Include future lease cash receipts in cash flow forecasts.	Lease asset is in the scope of impairment guidance in IFRS 9 (see 7.8.410).

Notes
1. An exception is when a lease prepayment gives rise to an asset. In this case, an entity would include the asset in the carrying amount of the CGU and there would be no (or fewer) future lease cash payments to consider when determining the recoverable amount.
2. An exception is when the lease asset is investment property measured at fair value, in which case the asset is outside the scope of IAS 36 (see 3.4.150).

3.10.670.30   A lessee's CGU may contain assets held under a finance lease and a finance lease liability. Under IAS 36, an entity considers a recognised liability in determining the recoverable amount of a CGU if the disposal of a CGU would require the buyer to assume the liability. In our view, this guidance applies to finance lease liabilities of a lessee. Therefore, in determining the recoverable amount of a CGU, a lessee should assess whether a buyer would assume the lease liability on disposal of the CGU. If the buyer would assume the lease liability then:

- if the recoverable amount of the CGU is determined using value in use, then the carrying amount of the liability is deducted both from the CGU's carrying amount and from its value in use (see 3.10.240.120); and
- if the recoverable amount of the CGU is determined using fair value less costs of disposal, then the liability is deducted only from the CGU's carrying amount because it is inherently reflected in the fair value of the CGU (see 3.10.240.120). [*IAS 36.29, 78, IU 05-16*]

3.10.675   **FORTHCOMING REQUIREMENTS**

3.10.675.10 IFRS 16 carries forward the IAS 17 distinction between operating and finance leases for lessors only.

3.10.675.20 Under IFRS 16, a lessee applies a single, on-balance sheet lease accounting model to all of its leases unless it elects the recognition exemption (see 5.1A.140). A lessee recognises a right-of-use asset representing its right to use the underlying asset and a lease liability representing its obligation to make lease payments. [*IFRS 16.5, 22*]

3.10.675.30 Under IFRS 16, a lessee applies IAS 36 to determine whether a right-of-use asset is impaired and to account for any impairment. For further discussion on impairment of the right-of-use asset, see 5.1A.350. [*IFRS 16.33*]

3.10.680   **Tax considerations in an impairment test – recoverable amount based on discounted cash flows**

3.10.680.10 The notion of 'tax' in this section refers only to income taxes in the scope of IAS 12 resulting from net cash inflows generated by an entity's asset or CGU.

3.10.680.20 This section applies when the recoverable amount of the asset or CGU that is tested for impairment is determined using a discounted cash flow technique – i.e. value in use or fair value less costs of disposal when the fair value is measured based on the present value of the future cash flows expected to be derived from the asset or CGU. Therefore, except for specific areas discussed in 3.10.700–710, 760.10–770.20 and 840.10–50, if an entity uses a discounted cash flow technique to determine the recoverable amount, then it follows the guidance in this section regardless of whether value in use or fair value less costs of disposal is used.

3.10.690   *Pre- or post-tax*

3.10.690.10 An issue often arises over whether the recoverable amount of an asset or CGU that is tested for impairment is to be determined using post-tax inputs (i.e. post-tax cash flows and a post-tax discount rate) or pre-tax inputs (i.e. pre-tax cash flows and a pre-tax discount rate).

3.10.700   *Application to fair value less costs of disposal*

3.10.700.10   For fair value less costs of disposal, IAS 36 refers to IFRS 13 for determining the fair value element. Both IAS 36 and IFRS 13 are silent on whether fair value is a pre-tax or a post-tax measure. When fair value is determined using a discounted cash flow technique, the assumptions used for the cash flows and discount rates reflect market participants' views (see 2.4.160.40). In our experience, it is common for market participants to determine the fair value less costs of disposal using post-tax assumptions – i.e. post-tax cash flows and post-tax discount rate. [*IFRS 13.B14, IAS 36.6*]

3.10.710   *Application to value in use*

3.10.710.10   When determining value in use, IAS 36 *prima facie* requires an entity to use pre-tax cash flows and a pre-tax discount rate. However, IAS 36 also requires the discount rate in a value in use calculation to be based on the market participant's view of the asset or CGU that is tested for impairment. An entity generally needs to build up a market participant discount rate that appropriately reflects the risks associated with the cash flows of the asset or CGU being valued. In our experience, the predominant approach is to use the WACC formula as a starting point to estimate an appropriate discount rate. WACC is a post-tax discount rate, which is why – despite the requirement in IAS 36 to use pre-tax inputs – in our experience, value in use calculations are predominantly performed on a post-tax basis (see 3.10.300.15–40). [*IAS 36.50(b), 55, A15–A21*]

3.10.720   *Consistency between pre- and post-tax*

3.10.720.10   Conceptually, the outcome of an impairment test should not be impacted by whether the impairment test uses post-tax inputs or pre-tax inputs. In other words, using post-tax inputs in an impairment test – e.g. because the only appropriate discount rate that is available is a post-tax discount rate such as WACC – should not result in a different outcome from when the pre-tax inputs are used. Therefore, when the recoverable amount is calculated using post-tax inputs, challenges may arise in applying a post-tax calculation appropriately so that the resulting outcome is equivalent to that of a pre-tax calculation. [*IAS 36.BCZ85*]

3.10.730   **Overview of the issues when performing an impairment test using post-tax inputs**

3.10.730.10   Paragraphs 3.10.740–840 discuss application issues that arise when performing an impairment test using post-tax inputs. These issues arise at different steps in performing an impairment test (e.g. when determining the cash flows or the carrying amount) and have interactions between them (e.g. whether the CGU's carrying amount should include the deferred tax liability depends on the approach taken to determine the post-tax cash flows). Overall, appropriately addressing these issues involves determining:

- a post-tax recoverable amount calculation so that the resulting outcome of the impairment test is equivalent to that of a pre-tax calculation (see 3.10.720); and
- the CGU's recoverable and carrying amounts on a consistent basis. [*IAS 36.75, BCZ85*]

3.10.730.20   The following diagram gives an overview of the application issues that arise when performing an impairment test using post-tax inputs and the interactions between them to achieve a consistent impairment outcome. As noted in 3.10.680.20, this section applies when the recoverable amount of the asset or CGU that is tested for impairment is determined using a discounted cash flow technique.

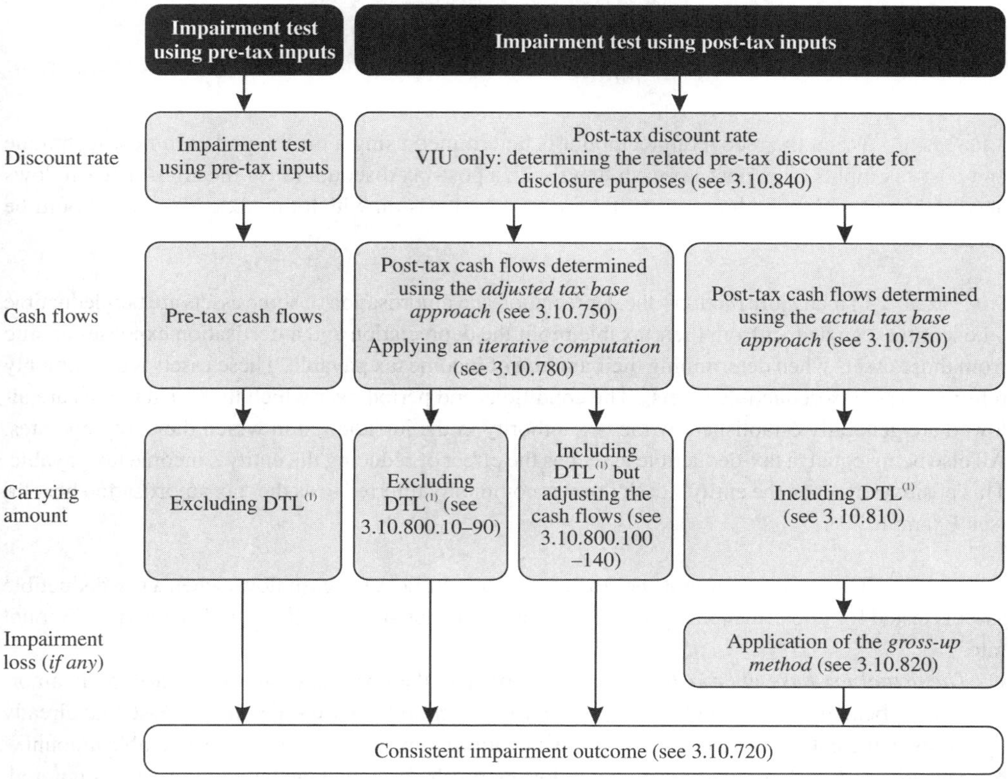
Impairment test using pre-tax inputs
Impairment test using post-tax inputs
Discount rate
Impairment test using pre-tax inputs
Post-tax discount rate
VIU only: determining the related pre-tax discount rate for disclosure purposes (see 3.10.840)
Cash flows
Pre-tax cash flows
Post-tax cash flows determined using the *adjusted tax base approach* (see 3.10.750)
Applying an *iterative computation* (see 3.10.780)
Post-tax cash flows determined using the *actual tax base approach* (see 3.10.750)
Carrying amount
Excluding DTL[1]
Excluding DTL[1] (see 3.10.800.10–90)
Including DTL[1] but adjusting the cash flows (see 3.10.800.100–140)
Including DTL[1] (see 3.10.810)
Impairment loss (*if any*)
Application of the *gross-up method* (see 3.10.820)
Consistent impairment outcome (see 3.10.720)

Note
1. Deferred tax liability.

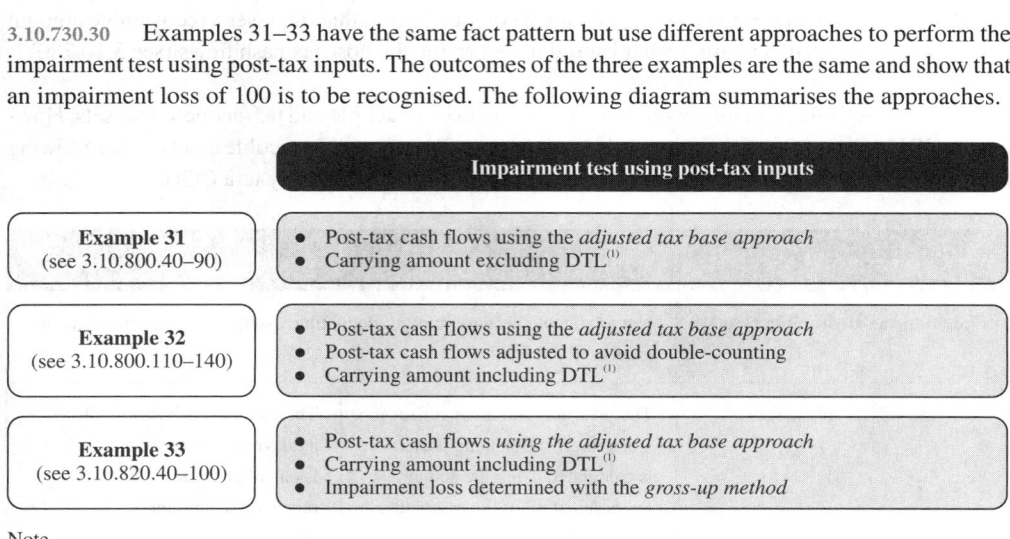

3.10.730.30 Examples 31–33 have the same fact pattern but use different approaches to perform the impairment test using post-tax inputs. The outcomes of the three examples are the same and show that an impairment loss of 100 is to be recognised. The following diagram summarises the approaches.

Impairment test using post-tax inputs
Example 31 (see 3.10.800.40–90)
Post-tax cash flows using the *adjusted tax base approach*
Carrying amount excluding DTL[1]
Example 32 (see 3.10.800.110–140)
Post-tax cash flows using the *adjusted tax base approach*
Post-tax cash flows adjusted to avoid double-counting
Carrying amount including DTL[1]
Example 33 (see 3.10.820.40–100)
Post-tax cash flows *using the adjusted tax base approach*
Carrying amount including DTL[1]
Impairment loss determined with the *gross-up method*

Note
1. Deferred tax liability.

3.10.740	***Determining the post-tax cash flows***
3.10.750	*Actual tax base vs adjusted tax base when determining the post-tax cash flows*

3.10.750.10   When the recoverable amount is determined using a discounted cash flow technique and post-tax inputs – i.e. post-tax cash flows with a post-tax discount rate – the after-tax cash flows need to be determined, which raises the issue of the basis on which the tax cash flows should be calculated.

3.10.750.20   In many jurisdictions, the depreciation and amortisation of some assets are tax-deductible – i.e. entities can deduct from their taxable profit the depreciation and amortisation expenses arising from those assets when determining their amount of income tax payable. These assets are commonly referred to as 'tax deductible assets'. The conditions and period over which these deductions are allowed are generally established by the tax authority in the jurisdiction in which the entity operates. All else being equal, a tax-deductible asset has the effect of reducing the entity's income tax payable. This positive effect on the entity's cash flows is commonly referred to as the 'tax amortisation benefit' (see Example 29).

3.10.750.30   There are two approaches to determining the post-tax cash flows when a tax-deductible asset is tested for impairment using post-tax inputs – i.e. post-tax cash flows with a post-tax discount rate.
- *The actual tax base approach:* Under this approach, the post-tax cash flows reflect a tax amortisation benefit that is calculated using the asset's *actual* tax base – i.e. the tax base that already exists in the entity. The asset's tax base is not adjusted/reset to the asset's recoverable amount.
- *The adjusted tax base approach:* Under this approach, the actual tax base of the asset is ignored. The post-tax cash flows reflect a tax amortisation benefit that is calculated using the asset's *adjusted* tax base – i.e. the asset's tax base is adjusted/reset to the asset's recoverable amount. This approach requires the use of an iterative computation so that the asset's recoverable amount equals its adjusted tax base, which is used to determine the post-tax cash flows (see 3.10.780).

3.10.750.40   A CGU generally contains a mix of non-tax-deductible and tax-deductible assets. However, a CGU may contain only non-tax-deductible assets or only tax-deductible assets. The following table summarises how the two approaches described in 3.10.750.30 apply to a CGU.

WHEN A CGU CONTAINS...	ACTUAL TAX BASE APPROACH	ADJUSTED TAX BASE APPROACH
Only non-tax-deductible assets	Not applicable because non-tax-deductible assets do not generate any tax amortisation benefit.	
Only tax-deductible assets	The post-tax cash flows reflect a tax amortisation benefit that is calculated using the actual tax bases of all of the assets that comprise the CGU.	The post-tax cash flows reflect a tax amortisation benefit that is calculated using the CGU's recoverable amount.

WHEN A CGU CONTAINS...	ACTUAL TAX BASE APPROACH	ADJUSTED TAX BASE APPROACH
Both tax-deductible and non-tax-deductible assets	The post-tax cash flows reflect a tax amortisation benefit that is calculated using the actual tax bases of only the tax-deductible assets.	The post-tax cash flows reflect a tax amortisation benefit that is calculated using the portion of the CGU's recoverable amount that corresponds to the tax-deductible assets.

3.10.760 *Application to fair value less costs of disposal*

3.10.760.10   In some jurisdictions, the impact of a sale transaction on an asset's tax base is dependent on how the transaction is structured. For example, in some jurisdictions, when assets are sold as part of a corporate structure and the buyer purchases shares of a legal entity, the assets' tax bases do not change. Alternatively, in some jurisdictions, when assets are sold outside a corporate structure or individually, the assets tax bases are adjusted to the transaction price.

3.10.760.20   When measuring fair value less costs of disposal using post-tax inputs, in determining how to consider the tax impacts on the post-tax cash flows (i.e. using the actual tax base approach or the adjusted tax base approach), an entity needs to consider how a hypothetical sale of the asset or CGU would be structured (see 2.4.100.110). This is because the fair value component of fair value less costs of disposal is a market-based measurement, rather than an entity-specific measurement, and is measured using assumptions that market participants would use in pricing the asset or CGU. [*IFRS 13.11*]

3.10.770 *Application to value in use*

3.10.770.10   When measuring value in use using post-tax inputs, it is not clear whether the tax cash flows should be determined using the actual tax base approach or the adjusted tax base approach (see 3.10.750.30). This is because:

- on the one hand, IAS 36 describes value in use as being an entity-specific measurement, as opposed to a market-based measurement. This supports the use of the actual tax base approach; and
- on the other hand, the basis for conclusions to IAS 36 provides a reason why value in use should be a pre-tax measure explaining that otherwise a post-tax calculation would require a complex iterative computation so that value in use itself reflects a tax base that equals the value in use. This supports the use of the adjusted tax base approach. [*IAS 36.BCZ81–BCZ84*]

3.10.770.20   In our view, when measuring value in use using post-tax inputs, it is acceptable to use either the actual tax base approach or the adjusted tax base approach.

EXAMPLE 29 – DETERMINING POST-TAX CASH FLOWS

3.10.770.30   In the context of an impairment test using post-tax inputs, Company Z determines the post-tax cash flows of one of its CGUs. The CGU contains only one asset that is fully tax-deductible in the year. This simplified example ignores the effect of discounting.

Tax base of asset	300
Statutory income tax rate	30%
Estimated future pre-tax net cash flows from use of the CGU	400

3.10.770.40   Based on the actual tax base approach (see 3.10.750.30), Z determines the CGU's post-tax cash flows as follows.

Estimated future pre-tax net cash flows from use of the CGU	400
Less income tax on those cash flows at tax rate (400 x 30%)	(120)
Plus tax amortisation benefit (TAB) (300 x 30%)	90
Recoverable amount – i.e. post-tax cash flows from use of the CGU	370

3.10.770.50   Based on the adjusted tax base approach (see 3.10.750.30), Z determines the CGU's post-tax cash flows as follows.

Estimated future pre-tax net cash flows from use of the CGU	400
Less income tax on those cash flows at tax rate (400 x 30%)	(120)
Plus TAB (see 3.10.770.60-70)	120
Recoverable amount – i.e. post-tax cash flows from use of the CGU	400

3.10.770.60   To understand how the TAB and recoverable amount are calculated under the adjusted tax base approach, Z solves the following two equations simultaneously.

1.	TAB = 30% x recoverable amount
2.	Recoverable amount = 400 - 120 + TAB

3.10.770.70   Inserting Equation 2 into Equation 1, the resulting TAB amounts to 120 and therefore the recoverable amount is 400.

TAB = 30% x (400 - 120 + TAB)

TAB = 84 + 30% TAB

70% TAB = 84

TAB = 120

3.10.770.80   Example 29 ignores discounting and the recoverable amount is determined based on a single year forecast period. In practice, determining post-tax cash flows using the adjusted tax base approach requires the use of an iterative computation (see 3.10.780).

3.10.780   *Applying an iterative computation when using the adjusted tax base approach*

3.10.780.10   In practice, determining post-tax cash flows using the adjusted tax base approach requires an iterative computation so that the asset's recoverable amount equals its adjusted tax base, which is used to determine the tax amortisation benefit.

EXAMPLE 30 – DETERMINING RECOVERABLE AMOUNT – ITERATIVE METHOD

3.10.780.20   Company Z determines the recoverable amount of one of its CGUs that is tested for impairment using post-tax inputs. The CGU contains only one asset, T, which is fully tax-deductible.

Statutory income tax rate	30%
Estimated future pre-tax net cash flows from use of T in year 1	200
Forecast period	3 years
Cash flows' expected growth rate during the forecast period	4%
Discount rate (based on WACC)	6%

3.10.780.30   Based on the adjusted tax base approach (see 3.10.750.30), Z determines the CGU's recoverable amount as follows. Z determines that asset T is tax-deductible on a straight-line basis over the next three years.

		YEAR 1	YEAR 2	YEAR 3	RECOVERABLE AMOUNT
Pre-tax cash flows	A	200	208	216	
Income tax on those cash flows at tax rate *(A x 30%)*	B	(60)	(62)	(65)	
Amortisation/ depreciation based on T's adjusted tax base *(recoverable amount / 3 years)*	C	177[1]	177[1]	177[1]	
TAB *(C x 30%)*	D	53	53	53	
Post-tax cash flows *(A + B + D)*	E	193	199	204	
Discounted post-tax cash flows *(E discounted at 6%)*	F	182	177	171	530

3.10.780.40   The iterative computation sets T's adjusted tax base (176.67 + 176.67 + 176.67) to equal the CGU's recoverable amount (530). T's adjusted tax base is used to calculate the TAB of 53 each year (176.67 x 30%).

> Note
> 1.   176.67 rounded to 177.

3.10.790   *Determining whether the deferred tax liability should be included in the CGU's carrying amount*

3.10.790.10   When a CGU is tested for impairment using post-tax inputs – i.e. post-tax cash flows and a post-tax discount rate – a question arises about whether the recognised deferred tax liability arising from the CGU's taxable temporary differences should be included in the CGU's carrying amount. This is because it could be argued that the disposal of a CGU would require the buyer to assume the CGU's taxable temporary differences. An entity needs to apply a consistent approach in determining the carrying amount and the recoverable amount (see 3.10.240.120). Therefore, whether the deferred tax liability is included in the CGU's carrying amount should be consistent with the way the post-tax cash flows are determined (see 3.10.800–810).

3.10.800   *Post-tax cash flows determined using the adjusted tax base approach*

3.10.800.10   In an impairment test using post-tax inputs, when the adjusted tax base approach is used, the post-tax cash flows are determined with a tax amortisation benefit calculated based on the CGU's recoverable amount (see 3.10.750.30–40). In this case, the tax amortisation benefit can be broken down into three components:
- *Component 1*: the future tax impacts arising from the CGU's actual tax base;
- *Component 2*: the future tax impacts arising from the difference between the CGU's carrying amount and its actual tax base; and
- *Component 3*: the future tax impacts arising from the difference between the CGU's recoverable amount and its carrying amount.

3.10.800.20   Under the adjusted tax base approach, the tax amortisation benefit – i.e. calculated based on the CGU's recoverable amount – is the sum of the three components in 3.10.800.10. Component 2, which is included in the tax amortisation benefit, is already captured by the deferred tax liability that is recognised on the balance sheet. Therefore, including the deferred tax liability under this approach leads to double-counting that results in deferring or underestimating the recognition of any impairment loss. This is because:
- on the one hand, the recoverable amount is increased by the lower tax cash outflows that include the tax amortisation benefit arising from the difference between the CGU's carrying amount and its actual tax base; and
- on the other hand, the carrying amount is decreased by the amount of the deferred tax liability that is calculated on the difference between the CGU's carrying amount and its actual tax base.

3.10.800.30   To avoid double-counting, the deferred tax liability arising from the CGU's taxable temporary differences is excluded from the CGU's carrying amount when the post-tax cash flows are determined using the adjusted tax base approach.

EXAMPLE 31 – ADJUSTED TAX BASE APPROACH – DEFERRED TAX LIABILITY EXCLUDED FROM CGU's CARRYING AMOUNT

3.10.800.40 Company Z tests for impairment one of its CGUs, which contains a single asset that is tax deductible in the year. The impairment test is performed using post-tax inputs. To determine the post-tax cash flows, Z applies the adjusted tax base approach. This simplified example ignores the effect of discounting.

Carrying amount of asset before impairment	500
Tax base of asset	300
Statutory income tax rate	30%
Temporary differences before impairment (500 - 300)	200
Deferred tax liability before impairment (200 x 30%)	60
Estimated future pre-tax net cash flows from use of the CGU	400

3.10.800.50 Using the adjusted tax base approach, Z determines the CGU's post-tax cash flows as follows (see 3.10.750.30).

Estimated future pre-tax net cash flows from use of the CGU	400
Less income tax on those cash flows at tax rate (400 x 30%)	(120)
Plus TAB (recoverable amount x 30%)	120
Recoverable amount – i.e. post-tax cash flows from use of the CGU	400

3.10.800.60 The TAB of 120 is calculated as shown in Example 29 in 3.10.770.60–70 and can be broken down into three components.

Component 1	The future tax impacts of the asset's actual tax base (300 x 30%)	90
Component 2	The future tax impacts of the difference between the asset's carrying amount and its actual tax base ((500 - 300) x 30%)	60
Component 3	The future tax impacts of the difference between the asset's recoverable amount and its carrying amount ((400 - 500) x 30%)	(30)

3.10.800.70 Component 2 in 3.10.800.60 – i.e. the future tax impacts of 60 arising from the difference between the CGU's carrying amount and its actual tax base – is also reflected in the recognised deferred tax liability.

3.10.800.80 Consequently, there is an impairment loss of 100 to be recognised – which is the difference between the recoverable amount of 400 and the CGU's carrying amount of 500, which excludes the deferred tax liability.

> **3.10.800.90** Including the deferred tax liability in the CGU's carrying amount would result in an impairment loss of 40 (400 - (500 - 60)). The impairment loss would be underestimated by an amount of 60 due to double counting. This is because the future tax impact of Component 2 – which amounts to 60 – would increase the recoverable amount and decrease the CGU's carrying amount due to the inclusion of the deferred tax liability.

3.10.800.100 As an alternative to excluding the deferred tax liability from the CGU's carrying amount, the double counting can be avoided by eliminating from the post-tax cash flows (determined using the adjusted tax base approach) the future tax impacts arising from the difference between the CGU's carrying amount and its actual tax base. However, this approach may create a discounting issue. [*IAS 36.BCZ86*]

EXAMPLE 32 – ADJUSTED TAX BASE APPROACH – INCLUDING THE DEFERRED TAX LIABILITY IN CGU's CARRYING AMOUNT AND ADJUSTING THE CASH FLOWS

> **3.10.800.110** Modifying Example 31, Company Z seeks to avoid double counting by adjusting the post-tax cash flows instead of excluding the deferred tax liability from the CGU's carrying amount. Z determines the asset's post-tax cash flows as follows.
>
> | | |
> |---|---:|
> | Estimated future pre-tax net cash flows from use of the CGU | 400 |
> | Less income tax on those cash flows at tax rate (400 x 30%) | (120) |
> | Plus TAB (see 3.10.800.50) | 120 |
> | Less adjustment for Component 2 of the TAB ((500 - 300) x 30%) | (60) |
> | Recoverable amount – i.e. post-tax cash flows from use of the CGU | 340 |
>
> **3.10.800.120** The carrying amount of the CGU includes the deferred tax liability arising from the CGU's temporary differences. Therefore, the CGU's net carrying amount is 440 (500 - 60).
>
> **3.10.800.130** Consequently, there is an impairment loss of 100 to be recognised, being the difference between the recoverable amount of 340 and the CGU's net carrying amount of 440.
>
> **3.10.800.140** This simplified example ignores the effect of discounting. In practice, including the deferred tax liability may create a discounting issue.

3.10.810 *Post-tax cash flows determined using the actual tax base approach*

3.10.810.10 In our view, the deferred tax liability arising from the CGU's taxable temporary differences should be included in the CGU's carrying amount when the post-tax cash flows are determined using the actual tax base approach. This is because, under the actual tax base approach, only Component 1 described in 3.10.800.10 – i.e. the future tax impacts arising from the CGU's actual tax base – is included in the tax amortisation benefit (see 3.10.750.30). Under that approach, Component 2 described in 3.10.800.10 – i.e. the future tax impacts arising from the difference between the CGU's carrying amount and its actual tax base – is not included in the tax amortisation benefit. Therefore, including the deferred tax liability arising from the CGU's taxable temporary differences in the CGU's carrying amount does not lead to double-counting. However, this may create a discounting issue. In addition, in the event of an impairment loss, this impacts the way the impairment loss is calculated (see 3.10.820).

3.10.820 *Impairment loss when deferred tax liability is included in the CGU's carrying amount*

3.10.820.10   When the impairment test is performed as described in 3.10.810.10 – i.e. the post-tax cash flows are determined using the actual tax base approach and the deferred tax liability is included in the CGU's carrying amount – in our view, in the event that an impairment exists, the impairment loss should be computed using the *gross-up method*. We believe that, the use of this method becomes necessary because of the interdependence between the impairment loss and the deferred tax liability:
- the impairment loss affects the deferred tax liability – i.e. the temporary differences change as a result of the write-down of the carrying amounts of the CGU's assets; and
- the deferred tax liability affects the impairment loss – i.e. the impairment loss changes as a result of the adjustment to the CGU's net carrying amount because the deferred tax liability changes. [*IAS 36.64*]

3.10.820.20   The gross-up method involves calculating the impairment loss in two steps.
- *Step 1*: Calculating the initial impairment loss, ignoring the impact of changes in the deferred taxes resulting from that loss.
- *Step 2*: Grossing-up (or recalculating) the initial impairment loss for the effect of the income tax.

3.10.820.30   If the gross-up method is not applied in the circumstances described in 3.10.820.10, then the CGU's net carrying amount after impairment – i.e. including the adjusted deferred tax liability – would still be higher than its recoverable amount.

EXAMPLE 33 – GROSS-UP METHOD – CGU CONTAINS A SINGLE TAX-DEDUCTIBLE ASSET

3.10.820.40   Company Z tests for impairment one of its CGUs, which contains a single asset that is tax-deductible in the year. To determine the post-tax cash flows, Z applies the actual tax base approach. This simplified example ignores the effect of discounting.

Carrying amount of asset before impairment	500
Tax base of asset	300
Statutory income tax rate	30%
Temporary differences before impairment (500 - 300)	200
Deferred tax liability before impairment (200 x 30%)	60
Estimated future pre-tax net cash flows from use of the CGU	400

3.10.820.50   Using the actual tax base approach, Z determines the CGU's post-tax cash flows as follows (see 3.10.750.30).

Estimated future pre-tax net cash flows from use of the CGU	400
Less income tax on those cash flows at tax rate (400 x 30%)	(120)
Plus TAB (actual tax base of 300 x 30%)	90
Recoverable amount – i.e. post-tax cash flows from use of the CGU	370

3.10.820.60 Because Z uses the actual tax base approach, the CGU's carrying amount includes the deferred tax liability arising from the CGU's temporary differences (see 3.10.810). Therefore, the CGU's net carrying amount is 440 (500 - 60).

3.10.820.70 Applying Step 1 in 3.10.820.20, there is an initial impairment loss of 70 being the difference between the CGU's recoverable amount of 370 and its net carrying amount of 440.

3.10.820.80 Assuming that the asset's tax base of 300 remains unchanged, if the initial impairment loss of 70 determined in Step 1 was not further adjusted, then the deferred tax liability would be 39 (((500 - 70) - 300) x 30%) and the CGU's net carrying amount would be 391 (500 - 70 - 39), which is still higher than the recoverable amount of 370.

3.10.820.90 Applying Step 2 in 3.10.820.20, Z calculates the impairment loss using the gross-up method as follows.

Impairment loss initially determined / (1 – tax rate)

70 / (1 - 30%) = 100

3.10.820.100 Assuming that the asset's tax base of 300 remains unchanged, Z adjusts the deferred tax liability to 30 (((500 - 100) - 300) x 30%). Therefore, the CGU's adjusted net carrying amount is 370 (500 - 100 - 30), which corresponds to its recoverable amount.

3.10.820.110 Complexity may arise for a CGU that contains both assets for which any allocation of impairment would trigger a change in the deferred taxes (e.g. identifiable assets initially acquired in a business combination) and assets for which any allocation of impairment would not trigger a change in the deferred taxes (e.g. non-tax-deductible goodwill or non-tax-deductible assets that are carried at cost and have been subject to the initial recognition exemption as discussed in 3.13.200). In our view, in this circumstance the gross-up method should be applied only to the initial impairment loss allocated to the assets for which any allocation of impairment would trigger a change in the deferred taxes.

EXAMPLE 34 – GROSS-UP METHOD – CGU CONTAINS TAX-DEDUCTIBLE ASSETS AND NON-TAX-DEDUCTIBLE GOODWILL

3.10.820.120 Company Z tests for impairment one of its CGUs that contains both tax-deductible assets and a non-tax-deductible goodwill. To determine the post-tax cash flows, Z applies the actual tax base approach. This simplified example ignores the effect of discounting.

Total carrying amount before impairment, of which:	500
– *Carrying amount of tax-deductible assets before impairment*	*300*
– *Carrying amount of non-tax-deductible goodwill before impairment*	*200*
Tax base of tax-deductible assets	100
Statutory income tax rate	30%
Temporary difference before impairment (300 - 100)	200
Deferred tax liability before impairment (200 x 30%)	60
Estimated future pre-tax net cash flows from use of the CGU	150

3.10.820.130   Using the actual tax base approach, Company Z determines the post-tax cash flows as follows (see 3.10.750.30).

Estimated future pre-tax net cash flows from use of the CGU	150
Less income tax on those cash flows at tax rate (150 x 30%)	(45)
Plus TAB (actual tax base x 30%)	30
Recoverable amount – i.e. post-tax cash flows from use of the CGU	135

3.10.820.140   Because Z uses the actual tax base approach, the CGU's carrying amount includes the deferred tax liability arising from the CGU's temporary differences (see 3.10.810). Therefore, the CGU's net carrying amount is 440 (500 - 60).

3.10.820.150   Applying Step 1 in 3.10.820.20, there is an initial impairment loss of 305, being the difference between the CGU's recoverable amount of 135 and its net carrying amount of 440.

3.10.820.160   Z allocates this initial impairment loss first to the goodwill (200), and the remaining amount of 105 (305 - 200) to the other assets. Because the impairment loss that is allocated to goodwill does not affect the deferred tax liability, Z does not apply the gross-up method to it.

3.10.820.170   Applying Step 2 in 3.10.820.20, Z uses the gross-up method to determine the impairment loss to be recognised in respect of the tax-deductible assets.

Impairment loss initially determined on the tax deductible assets / (1 - tax rate)
105 / (1 - 30%) = 150

3.10.820.180   Assuming that the tax base of the tax-deductible assets of 100 remains unchanged, Z adjusts the deferred tax liability to 15 (((300 - 150) - 100) x 30%). Therefore, the CGU's adjusted net carrying amount is 135 (500 - 200 - 150 - 15), which corresponds to its recoverable amount.

EXAMPLE 35 – GROSS-UP METHOD – CGU CONTAINS TAX-DEDUCTIBLE ASSETS AND A NON-TAX-DEDUCTIBLE ASSET OTHER THAN GOODWILL

3.10.820.190   Modifying Example 34, the CGU's carrying amount of 500 contains:
- tax-deductible assets for an amount of 300 before impairment; and
- a non-tax-deductible building for an amount of 200 before impairment – the building was acquired in a corporate shell that did not meet the definition of a business and is carried at cost.

3.10.820.200   As in Example 34:
- the CGU's net carrying amount is 440 (500 - 60); and
- there is an initial impairment loss of 305, being the difference between the CGU's recoverable amount of 135 and its net carrying amount of 440.

3.10.820.210   Company Z allocates this initial impairment loss to all of the assets of the CGU on the basis of their relative carrying amount (see 3.10.380.10). Therefore, Z allocates:
- 183 of the impairment loss to the tax-deductible assets (305 x 300 / 500); and
- 122 of the impairment loss to the building (305 x 200 / 500).

3.10.820.220   Because the impairment loss that is allocated to the building does not affect the deferred tax liability, Z does not apply the gross-up method to it.

3.10.820.230   Applying Step 2 in 3.10.820.20, Z uses the gross-up method to determine the impairment loss to be recognised in respect of the tax-deductible assets.

> Impairment loss initially determined on the tax deductible assets / (1 - tax rate)
>
> 183 / (1 - 30%) = 261

3.10.820.240   Assuming that the tax base of the tax-deductible assets of 100 remains unchanged, Z recognises a deferred tax asset of 18 (((300 - 261) - 100) x 30%). Therefore, the CGU's adjusted net carrying amount is 135 (500 - 122 - 261 + 18), which corresponds to its recoverable amount.

3.10.830   *Tax losses*

3.10.830.10   In our view, tax losses carried forward should not impact the outcome of an impairment test regardless of whether the corresponding deferred tax asset is recognised. Therefore, we believe that an appropriate approach to ensuring that tax losses carried forward at the date of the impairment test do not distort the outcome of the impairment test is to exclude them from both the carrying amount of the CGU and the cash flow forecasts. Instead, tax losses are accounted for in accordance with IAS 12 (see 3.13.350). This approach prevents the potential double counting the tax: once in the deferred tax asset and again in the recoverable amount. This approach also prevents the potential measurement mismatch because the cash flows comprising the recoverable amount are discounted, whereas any deferred tax asset related to tax losses is not.

3.10.840   *Determining a pre-tax discount rate from a post-tax value in use*

3.10.840.10   IAS 36 *prima facie* requires value in use to be determined using pre-tax cash flows and a pre-tax discount rate. However, in our experience, it is more common to use post-tax cash flows and a post-tax discount rate such as WACC (see 3.10.710).

3.10.840.20   Whichever rate is used (pre- or post-tax), the pre-tax discount rate needs to be disclosed. When value in use is determined using post-tax cash flows and a post-tax discount rate, the pre-tax discount rate needs to be calculated to comply with the disclosure requirements. [*IAS 36.134(d)(v)*]

3.10.840.30   In theory, discounting post-tax cash flows at a post-tax discount rate and discounting pre-tax cash flows at a pre-tax discount rate should give the same result (see 3.10.720.10). The pre-tax discount rate is usually not the-post tax discount rate grossed up by the standard tax rate. Differences arise because of the timing of future tax cash flows and discrepancies between the carrying amount of an asset and its tax base. [*IAS 36.BCZ85*]

3.10.840.40   An iterative method can be used to derive a pre-tax discount rate from the value in use calculated using the post-tax inputs. Under this method, the pre-tax discount rate is determined so that the value in use calculated using pre-tax inputs equals the value in use calculated using post-tax inputs. In practice, the pre-tax discount rate is changed until the discounted pre-tax cash flows equate to the value in use – i.e. already known from the post-tax calculation. [*IAS 36.BCZ85*]

3.10.840.50   Determining a pre-tax discount rate from a post-tax value in use requires an entity to adjust the post-tax cash flows to obtain the pre-tax cash flows. This requires the entity to determine:
- the allocation of tax cash flows to CGUs, because the actual tax return is normally calculated on the basis of legal entities;
- the timing of tax cash flows – because tax cash flows are subject to the discounting effect; and
- the assets' tax base.

3.10.850   *Tonnage tax*

3.10.850.10   Some entities – e.g. shipping companies – may elect to be taxed based on tonnage capacity. In this case, they are not subject to income tax. Tonnage tax is outside the scope of IAS 12, because it is not based on taxable profits (see 3.13.40). Therefore, in our view the cash flows in a recoverable amount calculation should be determined net of the tonnage tax cash out flows.

3.10.860   *Day one impairment loss arising from deferred taxes in a business combination*

3.10.860.10   In a business combination, there is no initial recognition exemption for deferred taxes except to the extent of taxable temporary differences arising from the initial recognition of goodwill (see 3.13.210.10). When temporary differences arise from the business acquired, deferred taxes are recognised with a corresponding entry in goodwill. If the fair value of an asset acquired in the business is higher than its tax base, then the deferred tax liability recognised increases the goodwill. When shortly after the business combination the goodwill is tested for impairment and the deferred tax liability is not included in the CGU's carrying amount, a day one impairment loss might arise simply as a result of the deferred tax liability recognised in the business combination. This is because:

- the recognition of a deferred tax liability in a business combination has the effect of grossing up the goodwill; and
- when the goodwill is tested for impairment, excluding the deferred tax liability from the CGU's carrying amount does not offset the gross-up of the goodwill.

3.10.860.20   In our view, a day one impairment loss cannot arise simply as a result of recognising a deferred tax liability in a business combination. We believe that this is not the intention of IAS 36. Therefore, we believe that, for the purposes of the impairment test only, the following are possible approaches to avoid this anomaly:
- reduce the carrying amount of goodwill by the amount of deferred tax liability recognised in the business combination; or
- reduce the carrying amount of the CGU by the amount of deferred tax liability recognised in the business combination.

3.10.860.30   Adjusting the carrying amount of goodwill or the CGU by the deferred tax liability recognised in the business combination to avoid the day-one impairment loss may create some complexity in subsequent periods. This is because, in our view, goodwill should be adjusted for the amount of the deferred tax liability based on temporary differences initially recognised in the business combination but not reversed at the date of the impairment test.

EXAMPLE 36 – DAY ONE IMPAIRMENT LOSS ARISING FROM DEFERRED TAXES IN A BUSINESS COMBINATION

3.10.860.40   On 6 October 2018, Company Z acquires 100% of Company S, which meets the definition of a business.

Consideration transferred	100
Fair value of the identifiable net assets of S	80
Tax base of the net assets of S	15
Statutory income tax rate	30%
Temporary differences (80 - 15)	65
Deferred tax liability recognised in the business combination (65 x 30%)	20

3.10.860.50   At the date of the business combination, Z recognises the following entry.

	DEBIT	CREDIT
Goodwill	40	
Identifiable net assets of S	80	
Deferred tax liability		20
Consideration transferred		100

3.10.860.60   Assume that between the date of the business combination and 31 December 2018:
- no significant event likely to impair the goodwill or the business acquired occurred; and
- the carrying amount of S did not change.

3.10.860.70   At 31 December 2018, Z performs an impairment test of the goodwill arising from the purchase of S. S comprises one CGU. Its recoverable amount is 100, which is consistent with the price paid for the acquisition of S, and its carrying amount is 120 (80 + 40). Therefore, an impairment loss should theoretically be recognised for the excess of 20 between the CGU's recoverable amount and its carrying amount.

3.10.860.80   However, in this case it is clear that this impairment loss arises solely because of the recognition of the deferred tax liability in the business combination. Therefore, for the purposes of the impairment test only, one appropriate approach for Z to avoid the impairment loss is to reduce the carrying amount of the goodwill by 20 – i.e. the amount of deferred tax liability recognised in the business combination – when comparing the CGU's carrying amount with its recoverable amount.

3.10.860.90   A similar situation can arise when unrecognised deferred tax assets related to tax losses are subsumed within goodwill in a business combination (see 3.13.870). In this case, in our view, for the purposes of the impairment test only, the future tax benefit that was subsumed in goodwill should be excluded from the carrying amount of the CGU when testing for impairment.

3.10.870   DISCLOSURES

3.10.870.10   IAS 36 includes a number of detailed disclosures, which can be grouped into two categories.
- Information related to an impairment loss recognised or reversed.
- Information related to goodwill and indefinite-lived intangible assets. [*IAS 36.126–137*]

3.10.870.20   When an impairment loss has been recognised or reversed during the period, the entity discloses the recoverable amount of the asset or CGU that was impaired. Although IAS 36 identifies goodwill as one of the assets whose recoverable amount might require disclosure, there is no discussion of how this requirement applies, because goodwill is never tested for impairment in its own right and any impairment loss is calculated following the specific allocation requirements of the standard (see 3.10.380). As a result, to the extent that an impairment loss is allocated to goodwill, the entity should disclose the recoverable amount of the related CGU or group of CGUs. [*IAS 36.130(e)*]

3.10.870.30   In our experience, the disclosures related to goodwill are the most challenging, requiring information about key assumptions made in estimating recoverable amount and a sensitivity analysis dealing with key assumptions that might reasonably change and thereby trigger an impairment loss. These disclosures are illustrated in KPMG's *Guides to financial statements* series. [*IAS 36.134(d)–(f)*]

3.10.870.40   Although IAS 36 specifically requires disclosures in respect of discount rates and growth rates, disclosures about key assumptions are not limited to these two items. Management needs to apply its judgement in determining the level of disclosures, to ensure that the level of aggregation in providing the disclosures – e.g. averages or ranges – does not obscure information that would be useful to users of the financial statements. In particular, the standard requires disclosure in respect of each individual CGU for which the carrying amount of goodwill or intangible asset with indefinite useful lives allocated to the CGU is significant in comparison to its carrying amount. [*IAS 36.134*]

3.10.870.50   Even if an entity uses a post-tax discount rate in its value in use calculation (see 3.10.840), then it nonetheless discloses the pre-tax discount rate. [*IAS 36.55, 134(d)(v)*]

3.10.880   FUTURE DEVELOPMENTS

3.10.880.10   The IASB is working on a goodwill and impairment research project to address various issues, including:
- using an unrecognised headroom as an additional input for testing goodwill. Headroom is the excess of the recoverable amount of a CGU over its carrying amount;
- simplifying the value in use calculation; and
- improving disclosures about goodwill and impairment.

3.10.880.20   The IASB is considering the form and the content of a consultation document and yet to determine the timing.

3.12 Provisions, contingent assets and liabilities

3.12 Provisions, contingent assets and liabilities

CURRENTLY EFFECTIVE REQUIREMENTS

This publication reflects IFRS in issue at 1 August 2018, and the currently effective requirements cover annual periods beginning on 1 January 2018.

The requirements related to this topic are mainly derived from the following.

STANDARD	TITLE
IAS 37	Provisions, Contingent Liabilities and Contingent Assets
IFRIC 1	Changes in Existing Decommissioning, Restoration and Similar Liabilities
IFRIC 5	Rights to Interests arising from Decommissioning, Restoration and Environmental Rehabilitation Funds
IFRIC 6	Liabilities arising from Participating in a Specific Market – Waste Electrical and Electronic Equipment
IFRIC 21	Levies

The currently effective requirements include newly effective requirements arising from IFRS 15 *Revenue from Contracts with Customers,* which is effective for annual periods beginning on or after 1 January 2018. The new requirements may be applied using the retrospective method or the cumulative effect method (see 4.2.510). The impact of the new requirements on the accounting for provisions is reflected in 3.12.20.10, 360–380, 590.40, 630 and 720.

FORTHCOMING REQUIREMENTS

The currently effective requirements are affected by the following forthcoming requirements. They are highlighted with a # and the impact is explained in the accompanying boxed text at the references indicated.

- In January 2016, the IASB issued IFRS 16 *Leases*, which is effective for annual periods beginning on or after 1 January 2019. See 3.12.625. IFRS 16 is the subject of chapter 5.1A.
- In June 2017, the IASB issued IFRIC 23 *Uncertainty over Income Tax Treatments*, which is effective for annual periods beginning on or after 1 January 2019. See 3.12.763.
- In May 2017, the IASB issued IFRS 17 *Insurance Contracts*, which is effective for annual periods beginning on or after 1 January 2021. See 3.12.106, 647 and 751. IFRS 17 is the subject of chapter 8.1A.

FUTURE DEVELOPMENTS

The currently effective requirements that may be affected by future developments are highlighted with a * and are briefly discussed in 3.12.880.

3.12.10   DEFINITIONS

3.12.10.10   A 'provision' is a liability of uncertain timing or amount. [*IAS 37.10*]

3.12.10.20   A 'liability' is a present obligation that arises from past events, which is expected to result in the outflow of the entity's resources on settlement. [*IAS 37.10*]

3.12.10.30   'Accruals' are liabilities to pay for goods or services that have been received or supplied but not yet paid for or invoiced. The uncertainty of timing and amount is generally less for an accrual than for a provision. Examples of accruals are fees for services rendered, such as audit or consulting fees, and certain employee benefits in the scope of IAS 19, such as holiday pay. [*IAS 37.11*]

3.12.10.40   A 'contingent liability' is an obligation of sufficient uncertainty that it does not qualify for recognition as a provision, unless it is assumed in a business combination. The uncertainty may arise from any of the following reasons.
- It is a *possible* obligation – i.e. one whose existence will be confirmed by the occurrence or non-occurrence of uncertain future events not wholly within the control of the entity. For example, if an entity is jointly and severally liable for an obligation, then the portion of the obligation that is expected to be met by other parties is an example of a possible obligation of the entity.
- It is a *present* obligation, but it is *not* more likely than not that there will be an outflow of resources embodying economic benefits, so that the probability of an outflow is 50 percent or less. An example is a claim against an entity, when the entity concludes that it is liable, but that it is likely to defend the case successfully.
- It is a *present* obligation, but its amount cannot be estimated reliably. These cases are expected to be extremely rare. [*IAS 37.10, 29*]

3.12.10.50   In our view, when a provision is measured at its best estimate, which is less than the amount that could be payable, the difference between the two amounts is *not* a contingent liability (see 3.12.110.40).

3.12.10.60   A 'contingent asset' is a possible asset that arises from past events and whose existence will be confirmed by the occurrence or non-occurrence of uncertain future events not wholly within the control of the entity. [*IAS 37.10*]

3.12.20   SCOPE

3.12.20.10   This chapter deals with all provisions other than income taxes including income tax exposures (see chapter 3.13), obligations for employee benefits (see chapter 4.4), liabilities for share-based payments (see chapter 4.5), liabilities for insurance contract obligations (see chapter 8.1), non-onerous leases (see chapter 5.1) and non-onerous executory contracts (see 1.2.130). Financial instruments, including guarantees that are in the scope of IFRS 9, are also not dealt with in this chapter (see chapter 7.1). [*IAS 37.1–2, 5*]

3.12.20.20   The term 'provision' may be used to refer to expected credit loss allowances of financial assets or impairment estimates. However, these are not provisions for liabilities but rather adjustments to the measurement of the relevant asset. For a discussion of the impairment of financial assets and other instruments in the scope of the impairment requirements of IFRS 9, see chapter 7.8; and for a discussion of the impairment of tangible and intangible assets, see chapter 3.10. [*IAS 37.7*]

3.12.20.30 IAS 37 applies only if another standard does not deal with that specific type of provision. For example, IFRS 4 applies to contractual rights and obligations under insurance contracts. Therefore, if an insurer is sued over an insurance policy or a claim, then it is necessary to consider whether the claim arising in respect of the lawsuit should be accounted for under IFRS 4 rather than under IAS 37. In our view, for an insurer, the determination of the applicable standard for a lawsuit related to an insurance policy depends on the basis for the respective claim. Assumptions and estimates that are part of the measurement of the insurance policy liabilities include litigation awards. Therefore, if the lawsuit relates to, for example, a dispute over whether an event is covered by the insurance or the adequacy of a settlement, then we believe that the lawsuit should be part of the measurement of the insurance policy liability under IFRS 4 (see 8.1.70). If, however, the lawsuit relates to sales practice – e.g. refusal to provide a certain type of coverage – then this claim would not arise from an insurer's contractual rights and obligations, and we believe that it should be in the scope of IAS 37. [*IFRS 4.IG32(e), IAS 37.1(c), 5(e)*]

3.12.30 RECOGNITION

3.12.30.10 A provision is recognised when:
- there is a legal or constructive obligation arising from past events or, in cases of doubt over the existence of an obligation (e.g. a court case), when it is more likely than not that a legal or constructive obligation has arisen from a past event;
- it is more likely than not that there will be an outflow of benefits; and
- the amount can be estimated reliably. [*IAS 37.14, 23*]

3.12.30.20 The following flowchart illustrates the application of these criteria in determining whether to recognise a provision.

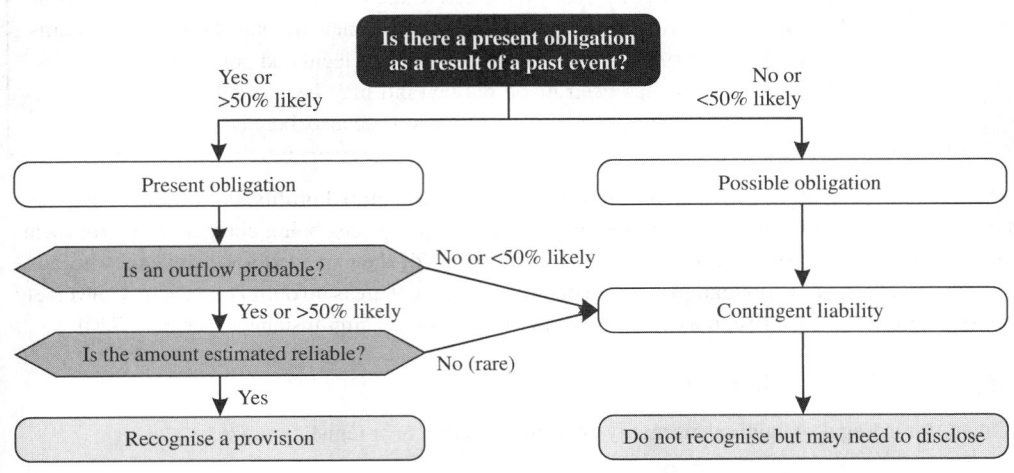

3.12.30.30 For a discussion of non-financial liabilities assumed as part of a group of assets that does not constitute a business, see 2.6.10 35.

3.12.40 Obligating event

3.12.40.10 An integral part of an obligation is that it arises from a past event. [*IAS 37.17*]

EXAMPLE 1A – OBLIGATING EVENT – NEW REGULATION – PROSPECTIVE OBLIGATION

> 3.12.40.20   A new regulation is passed that imposes a requirement on Company V, a motor vehicle manufacturer, to accept back and scrap all vehicles that it sells after 1 January 2018. A legal obligation to scrap the vehicles arises when enactment of the new legislation is virtually certain (see 3.12.50.20). The obligating events are sales of vehicles.
>
> 3.12.40.25   Therefore, V recognises a provision for the present value of the expected costs of scrapping each vehicle sold after 1 January 2018. This provision is recognised as the vehicles are sold (see 3.8.180). No provision is recognised for vehicles in inventory as at 1 January 2018, although the cost of scrapping would be considered in any net realisable value tests.

3.12.40.30   Expected future operating losses, even if they are probable, are not provided for unless they relate to an onerous contract (see 3.12.630). [*IAS 37.18, 63, 66*]

3.12.40.40   A provision is not recognised for general business risks. Although losses may be probable, and the amount of the expected losses can be estimated, until there is an event of loss there is no obligating event.

EXAMPLE 1B – OBLIGATING EVENT – GENERAL BUSINESS RISKS

> 3.12.40.50   Company P has announced to the public a business plan. As part of the plan, P is entering new overseas markets. The new markets expose P to significant increases in risk, including currency risk and legal and political uncertainties. Although the plan has been made public, and may be virtually certain of being implemented, P does not recognise a provision because there is no obligating event.

3.12.40.60   Similarly, a provision is not recognised for sub-optimal profits. For example, in a regulated industry, good results in one period may result in lower prices being charged in the following period. However, a provision is not recognised in respect of the expected lower revenues because, assuming that the future obligation is not an onerous contract, there is no obligating event. Conversely, the regulation may give rise to a contract liability under certain circumstances (see 3.12.720).

3.12.50   Legal obligation

3.12.50.10   Legal obligations normally arise from contracts or legislation. [*IAS 37.10*]

3.12.50.20   Possible new legislation is reflected only when it is virtually certain to be enacted as drafted. New legislation does not normally give rise to an obligation until it is enacted, because of uncertainties with respect to both whether it will be enacted and its final terms. [*IAS 37.22*]

3.12.50.30   IFRIC 21 provides specific guidance on determining the obligating event that gives rise to a liability under IAS 37 in connection with a levy imposed by a government (see 3.12.752). [*IFRIC 21.1*]

3.12.60 Constructive obligation

3.12.60.10 A 'constructive obligation' arises when an entity, by past practice or sufficiently specific communication to affected parties, has created a valid expectation in other parties that it will carry out an action. [*IAS 37.10*]

EXAMPLE 1C – OBLIGATING EVENT – CONSTRUCTIVE OBLIGATION

3.12.60.20 Company Y operates in the oil industry in a country that has no environmental clean-up requirements. However, Y has published an environmental policy indicating that it will clean up all contaminated sites and, in the past, has cleaned up such sites regardless of whether it was legally required to do so. Therefore, Y has a constructive obligation for the costs of cleaning up sites that are contaminated at the reporting date because its policy and past practice create a valid expectation that it will clean up the contamination.

3.12.60.30 A management decision alone does not give rise to a constructive obligation, because it does not create a valid expectation in other parties until that decision is communicated to them. Therefore, a board decision about a possible restructuring that has not been communicated does not trigger recognition of a provision. [*IAS 37.76*]

3.12.60.40 Business reasons or legal requirements may mean that an entity intends or is required to incur expenditure in the future. However, an intention or future requirement does not result in an unavoidable obligation. For example, an entity may need to fit a purifier in an oil plant or retrain staff to comply with new laws. The expenditure could be avoided by future actions, such as relocating its operations or hiring new staff, even if the entity does not plan to do so. Therefore, there is no obligating event. [*IAS 37.19, C6*]

3.12.60.50 In our view, in some cases an unconditional but not legally binding pledge may create a constructive obligation if the donor takes actions that mean that it has little or no alternative to fulfilling its pledge. We believe that this would involve considering not only past practice regarding fulfilling pledges, but also whether the donor's pledge has been communicated sufficiently widely and with sufficient detail to create valid expectations of performance. For a discussion of the accounting by a recipient of donations, see 5.7.60.

3.12.70 Uncertainty about whether obligation exists

3.12.70.10 In some cases, it may be disputed whether certain events have occurred or, particularly in the case of a legal claim, an entity may dispute whether there is an obligation even if it is clear that there is a past event. [*IAS 37.15–16*]

3.12.70.20 In such cases of uncertainty, a past event is deemed to give rise to a present obligation if, after taking account of all available evidence, it is more likely than not that a present obligation exists at the reporting date. [*IAS 37.15–16*]

Example 1D – Obligating event – Uncertainty about existence

> 3.12.70.30   Company F is a fish-canning company. A group is claiming that certain people suffered food poisoning from tuna canned by F. F disputes the claim. If it is more likely than not that F's tuna caused the food poisoning, then F is deemed to have a present obligation, even if F is planning to defend its position (see 3.12.740). [*IAS 37.16*]

3.12.75 *Examination by authorities*

3.12.75.10   An entity may be subject to penalties only if obligating events are detected. In our view, if an entity is obliged to self-report obligating events, then the detection risk (i.e. the possibility that the event will not be detected) should not be considered when measuring the obligation. Examples of events that generally require self-reporting include, but are not limited to, taxes and, in some countries, environmental contamination. When self-reporting is not required and there is uncertainty about the amount of an obligation in respect of a past event, then we believe that it may be appropriate to consider detection risk in measuring the provision (i.e. the possibility that the event will not be detected). For the accounting for income tax exposures, see 3.13.660. [*IFRIC 23.8*]

3.12.80 *Subsequent events that give rise to obligation*

3.12.80.10   An event that does not initially give rise to an obligation may give rise to one at a future date because of changes in the law or because of an entity's actions create a constructive obligation. [*IAS 37.21*]

Example 1E – Obligating event – New regulation – Retrospective and prospective obligation

> 3.12.80.20   Extending Example 1A, the new legislation requires Company V to accept back and scrap from 1 January 2018 all vehicles sold by it, *including* those sold before 1 January 2018. An issue arises about when V has an obligation in respect of vehicles sold before 1 January 2018 and not scrapped by 31 December 2017.
>
> 3.12.80.30   In our view, V should recognise a provision once it is virtually certain that the legislation will be enacted; the specific terms of the legislation are known, and it is possible to estimate the number of vehicles that will be in use and the scrapping costs. The obligation arises when the legislation is enacted or becomes virtually certain of being enacted and the obligating events are the past sales.

3.12.90 *Obligation dependent on future events*

3.12.90.10   If the existence of an obligation depends on the future actions of the entity, then a provision is not recognised until the obligation is unavoidable. [*IAS 37.19*]

EXAMPLE 1F – OBLIGATING EVENT – NEW REGULATION – FUTURE ACTION

3.12.90.20 As in Example 1A, a new regulation is passed that imposes an obligation on motor vehicle manufacturers in respect of scrapping costs. However, instead of being responsible for scrapping the vehicles, Company V will be required to pay a scrapping levy to the government. The scrapping levy in respect of vehicles sold before 2018 will be based on vehicle manufacturers' market share in 2018 regardless of their actual sales in previous periods. V could avoid the obligation – e.g. by selling vehicles in a different market.

3.12.90.25 Therefore, in our view the obligating event in this case occurs only in 2018 as V makes sales that establish its market share, and therefore its share of the costs of scrapping historical production by all manufacturers.

EXAMPLE 1G – OBLIGATING EVENT – NEW REGULATION – PARTICIPATION IN MARKET

3.12.90.30 Company M is a manufacturer of household equipment. M will become liable for waste management costs on historical household equipment based on its share of the market in a measurement period, defined as calendar year 2018. M is not required to recognise a provision until 2018. As of 2018, M recognises a provision only if it participates in the market, because the obligating event is M's participation in the market during the measurement period. For further discussion of costs of disposing of electrical and electronic equipment, see 3.12.520. [*IFRIC 6.9*]

3.12.100 *Identifying counterparty not required*

3.12.100.10 An obligation involves another party. However, an entity is not required to be able to identify the counterparty to the obligation before a provision is recognised. [*IAS 37.20*]

3.12.105 **Contingent liabilities#**

3.12.105.10 Contingent liabilities are not recognised in the statement of financial position except for certain contingent liabilities that were assumed in a business combination. [*IFRS 3.23, IAS 37.27*]

3.12.105.15 Contingent liabilities are reviewed continuously to assess whether an outflow of resources has become probable. If the recognition criteria are met, then a liability is recognised in the statement of financial position in the period in which the change in probability occurs. [*IAS 37.30*]

3.12.105.20 Contingent liabilities assumed in a business combination are recognised in accordance with the requirements of IFRS 3. An acquirer recognises a contingent liability assumed in a business combination if it is a *present* obligation and its fair value can be measured reliably (see 2.6.650). Such acquired contingent liabilities are subsequently measured at the higher of the amount that would be recognised as a provision (see 3.12.110) and the amount recognised on acquisition, less any subsequent amortisation when appropriate. For an example of accounting for a contingent liability assumed in a business combination related to a legal case, see 2.6.1100. A contingent liability that is a *possible* obligation is not recognised even if its fair value can be measured reliably. [*IFRS 3.23, 56*]

3.12.105.30   If a present obligation relates to a past event, the possibility of an outflow is probable and a reliable estimate can be made, then the obligation is not a contingent liability, but instead is a liability for which a provision is required (see 3.12.30). [*IAS 37.14*]

3.12.105.40   The expectation that an outflow related to an obligation will be reimbursed – e.g. that an environmental obligation will be covered by an insurance policy – does not affect the assessment of the probability of an outflow for the obligation. However, this may give rise to a reimbursement asset (see 3.12.190). [*IAS 37.53*]

3.12.105.50   An acquisition agreement in a business combination may require the seller to provide an indemnity of a specific contingent liability assumed by the acquirer in the acquisition. The existence of such an indemnity does not affect the amount recognised by the acquirer as a contingent liability in the accounting for the acquisition. However, it may give rise to an indemnification asset (see 2.6.1110).

3.12.105.60   If events after the reporting date confirm the existence of a liability, including the case in which the liability affects the entity's ability to continue as a going concern, then adjustments may be required (see 2.9.20).

3.12.105.70   Financial guarantee contracts issued are in the scope of IFRS 9 (see 7.1.60) unless the issuer of the contract has previously explicitly asserted that it regards such contracts as insurance contracts, and has used accounting applicable to insurance contracts, in which case the issuer may choose to apply either IFRS 9 or IFRS 4 (see 8.1.10) to the contracts. Generally, when a financial guarantee contract recognised under IFRS 4 becomes probable of being exercised, the provision is measured in accordance with IAS 37. However, the remaining requirements of IAS 37 – e.g. disclosures – do not apply. Non-financial guarantees related to products or services are addressed in 3.12.360, which deals with warranties. [*IFRS 9.2.1(e)*]

3.12.106   FORTHCOMING REQUIREMENTS

3.12.106.10   If an issuer of a financial guarantee contract accounts for it under IFRS 17, then it recognises and measures the contract in accordance with IFRS 17. [*IFRS 17.7(e)*]

3.12.107   Contingent assets

3.12.107.10   Contingent assets are not recognised in the statement of financial position because doing so may result in the recognition of income that may never be realised. [*IAS 37.31, 33*]

3.12.107.20   When realisation of a contingent asset is virtually certain, it is no longer considered contingent and is recognised as an asset. The asset is recognised in the period in which this change from contingent asset to asset occurs (see also 2.9.30.17). [*IAS 37.33, 35*]

746

EXAMPLE 2A – CONTINGENT ASSET – ARISES BEFORE REPORTING DATE

3.12.107.30   Company L leases a property to Company B under an operating lease. The contract is for 10 years and can only be cancelled on payment of a penalty. On 30 November 2018, before the end of the contract, B withdraws from the contract and is required to pay a cancellation penalty of 450.

3.12.107.40   In our view, L would generally recognise a receivable of 450 and corresponding income once B cancels the contract. However, L should not recognise the asset until the contract is cancelled.

EXAMPLE 2B – CONTINGENT ASSET – ARISES AFTER REPORTING DATE

3.12.107.50   Modifying the fact pattern in Example 2A, Company B cancels the contract on 28 February 2019. In this case, L would not recognise a receivable for the cancellation penalty as at 31 December 2018. The event that gives rise to the asset is the cancellation of the contract. Therefore, if the cancellation happens only after the reporting date, then an asset is not recognised at the reporting date (see 2.9.30).

3.12.110   MEASUREMENT

3.12.110.10   The amount recognised for a provision is the best estimate of the expenditure to be incurred. There is no option to have an accounting policy of measuring the provision based on the lowest or the highest anticipated outcome. [*IAS 37.36*]

3.12.110.15   In the extremely rare case in which no reliable estimate can be made, a liability exists that cannot be recognised. This liability is disclosed as a contingent liability (see 3.12.875). [*IAS 37.26*]

3.12.110.20   If the provision is being made for a large population of items, then the provision is measured at its expected value. This is the case, for example, for some forms of product warranties. Expected value considers all possible outcomes weighted based on their probabilities. If there is a continuous range of possible outcomes, and each point in the range is equally likely, then a provision is recognised for the mid-point in the range. For this distribution (probability) calculation to be meaningful, the items considered together using an expected value approach need to be similar in nature. [*IAS 37.39*]

3.12.110.30   If the provision is for a single item, then usually the most likely outcome is the best estimate.

EXAMPLE 3A – MEASURING PROVISION – SINGLE ITEM

3.12.110.35   If there is a 60% probability that Company D will have to pay damages of 600 in a legal case and a 40% probability that the claim against D will be dismissed, then the provision is measured at 600 because it is probable that D will

lose and if D loses, D will pay 600. The provision is not measured at 360 ((600 x 60%) + (0 x 40%)). [*IAS 37.40*]

3.12.110.40   In our view, when a provision is measured at its best estimate, which is less than the amount that could be payable, the difference between the two amounts is *not* a contingent liability.

EXAMPLE 3B – MEASURING PROVISION – BEST ESTIMATE LESS THAN AMOUNT THAT COULD BE PAYABLE

3.12.110.45   Company G has an obligation to rectify a fault in a plant constructed for a customer. G measures the provision based on the expected repair cost, which may be anywhere between 70 and 130. If the provision is measured at 90, then we believe that the remaining possible amount of 40 is not a contingent liability. This is because the unit of account is the obligation.

3.12.110.50   The uncertainty regarding the amount of the costs to be incurred is reflected in the measurement, although disclosure of the uncertainty regarding measurement needs to be considered. We believe that there is no separate obligation or past event for the unrecognised portion of the range of possible costs. [*IAS 1.125, 37.85(b)*]

3.12.120   Risk and discounting

3.12.120.10   If the effect is material, then the estimate is discounted at a pre-tax rate that reflects the time value of money and the risks specific to the liability, unless the future cash flows are adjusted for these risks. [*IAS 37.45, 47*]

3.12.120.20   Risk is reflected by adjusting either the cash flows or the discount rate. In our experience, when estimating the expenditure required to settle an obligation, it is generally easier to adjust the cash flows for risk and to discount the expected cash flows at a risk-free interest rate. Adjusting the discount rate for risk is often complex and involves a high degree of judgement. IAS 37 notes that the discount rate reflects the risks specific to the liability. Therefore, use of the entity's average or incremental borrowing rate would not be an automatic proxy for the risk of a specific liability. IAS 37 does not address whether an entity's own credit risk should be considered specific to an individual liability. In a discussion of this question, the IFRS Interpretations Committee noted its understanding that predominant practice is to exclude own credit risk and observed that own credit risk is generally viewed as a risk of the entity rather than a risk specific to the liability. [*IAS 37.47, IU 03-11*]

3.12.120.30   The risk-free rate may be determined by considering the interest rate on a government bond in the same currency as the obligation and with a similar maturity to the obligation. In our view, a government bond rate for a country that has a poor credit rating reflecting a risk of default should not be used. This is because, in this circumstance, a government bond rate is not a risk-free rate. In these cases, if there are other countries that use the same currency – e.g. the country is part of the euro zone – then we believe that the rate of the country with the lowest yield in that zone should be used as evidence of the risk-free rate. Alternatively, if there are no other countries that use the same currency, then the development of the price for respective credit default swaps may be an indicator for increasing risk in the bond yield, which should be eliminated for purposes of calculating the risk-free rate.

3.12.120.40   If an entity has set aside assets to fund an obligation, and the assets are intended to generate a sufficient return to meet the ultimate obligation, then an issue arises about whether the rate of return on the assets in the fund may be used as a risk-adjusted discount rate for the obligation. The variability of the cash flows on the liability is not normally correlated to the variability of the cash flows on the assets. Therefore, the return on the assets does not reflect the risks specific to the liability and in our view should not be used to discount the provision.

3.12.130   *Inflation adjustments*

3.12.130.10   IAS 37 provides no guidance on whether the discount rate should include the effects of inflation. In our view, if the cash flows are expressed in current prices, then the effects of inflation should not be included in the discount rate – i.e. a real discount rate should be used. If the cash flows include inflation, then the discount rate should include the effects of inflation – i.e. a nominal discount rate should be used. This approach is consistent with the requirement in IAS 36 for the estimates of future cash flows and the discount rate to reflect consistent assumptions about price increases attributable to general inflation (see 3.10.310).

EXAMPLE 3C – MEASURING PROVISION – ADJUSTMENT FOR INFLATION

3.12.130.20   Company M entered into a 10-year operating lease agreement in 2016 that requires it to make good any damage done during the lease. The make-good requirements include the requirement to remove leasehold improvements. M has recognised the costs of the leasehold improvements as property, plant and equipment, including the estimated costs of removing the leasehold improvements. At each reporting date, M estimates expected costs to make good the damage done, including costs to remove the leasehold improvements. This estimate reflects the damage done at the reporting date and is based on the expected costs at the end of the lease term (see 3.12.440.10–20). [*IAS 37.59*]

3.12.130.30   If M obtains a quote for making good damage incurred as at the reporting date, then in our view this quote should be adjusted to reflect the expected timing of the expenditure – i.e. at the end of the lease. We believe that this adjustment can be made by applying an inflation rate to the quote obtained and discounting that amount back to the reporting date using a nominal (i.e. including inflation) risk-free rate.

3.12.130.40   In this example, M prepares its financial statements for the year ending 31 December 2018 and obtains a quote for the costs to make good damage done as at that date. The estimated costs as at the reporting date are 100, the nominal risk-free rate is 6% and the projected inflation rate is around 4%. To estimate the expected costs at the end of the lease term, M should apply the inflation rate to the amount of 100 and discount it back at the nominal risk-free rate for the period of seven years. In this example, the estimated costs at the end of the lease term equal 87 $((100 \times 1.04^7) / 1.06^7)$ after discounting.

3.12.140 **Tax impact**

3.12.140.10   A pre-tax discount rate is used, because provisions are measured on a pre-tax basis. Any tax impact is accounted for separately (see chapter 3.13). [*IAS 37.47*]

3.12.150 **Remeasurement**

3.12.150.10   Provisions are remeasured at each reporting date based on the best estimate of the settlement amount. Changes to the best estimate of the settlement amount may result from changes in the amount or timing of the outflows or changes in discount rates. [*IAS 37.36, 59, IFRIC 1.4*]

3.12.150.20   For those provisions included in the cost of a related asset, the effects of any changes to an existing obligation, including those resulting from changes in the discount rate used, are generally added to or deducted from the cost of the related asset and depreciated prospectively over the asset's useful life (see 3.2.90). An exception is the periodic unwinding of the discount, which is recognised in profit or loss as a finance cost when it occurs because it is not a borrowing cost eligible for capitalisation. [*IFRIC 1.5, 8*]

EXAMPLE 3D – MEASURING PROVISION – REMEASUREMENT WHEN INCLUDED IN COST OF RELATED ASSET

3.12.150.30   Company W enters into an arrangement and obtains the right to operate an airport. In exchange for the right to operate, W is required by law to make one-off payments to local residents and businesses as compensation for the loss in the value of their property arising from the noise. In our view, the costs to be incurred for this compensation are a cost of obtaining the airport operating licence. We believe that these costs should be capitalised as an intangible asset (a licence) and amortised over the licence period (see 3.3.90 and 210).

3.12.150.40   We believe that the intangible asset should generally be recognised from the start of the arrangement if the right granted is usable from that date. However, in the unusual case that the estimated costs are not reliably measurable at the start of the licence and therefore the provision for payments is not recognised, then we believe that W should disclose a contingent liability. When the costs can be estimated, a provision will be recognised. In our view, these costs should be capitalised when they become reliably measurable as part of the cost of the licence. [*IAS 38.21*]

3.12.150.50   At the date on which the obligation can be measured reliably, W would recognise both the intangible asset and the corresponding liability at the same amount, being the present value of the expected future payments to the local residents and businesses as compensation for the loss in the value of their property.

3.12.150.60   The estimate of the costs of compensation may change over time. In our view, changes in the carrying amount of the liability, except for the unwinding of the discount recognised in profit or loss, should be accounted for as an adjustment to the carrying amount of the intangible asset. For a discussion of changes resulting from contract renegotiations, see 3.3.100.100–120.

3.12.160 **Future events**

3.12.160.10 Future events are reflected when measuring a provision if there is sufficient objective evidence that they will occur. For example, a technological development that would make decommissioning less expensive would be considered if there is evidence that the new technology will be available. In our view, an intention to reduce an obligation via negotiation or to avoid it by declaring bankruptcy is a future event that should not be anticipated. [*IAS 37.48*]

EXAMPLE 3E – MEASURING PROVISION – FUTURE INTENTION TO REDUCE OBLIGATION

3.12.160.20 Parent M owns 100% of Subsidiary G. As at 31 December 2018, G has net assets of 10. At its 2018 year end, M determines that its present estimate of G's environmental remediation obligation needs to be increased by 50. M is not required by the legislation to fund G's exposures. M determines that it will not fund G's deficit in the future, such that the net assets of G will not be sufficient to fund the full obligation. G intends to enter into negotiations with the relevant authorities to reduce, or be exempted from, the remediation obligation. If those negotiations fail, then G intends to start bankruptcy proceedings.

3.12.160.30 We believe that the measurement of G's obligation, both in G's own financial statements and in M's consolidated financial statements, should not be limited to G's net assets. Instead, we believe that G should recognise the full amount of the revised estimate of its environmental obligation. M should continue to consolidate G, including its full obligation, until it no longer controls G – e.g. after any bankruptcy proceedings have removed M's control (see 2.5.430).

3.12.170 **Gains**

3.12.170.10 Gains from the expected disposal of assets are not considered when measuring a provision. [*IAS 37.51*]

3.12.170.20 Therefore, if a provision is recognised for a restructuring (see 3.12.230), then gains on the related sale of any assets are not considered in measuring the provision. As a result, restructuring costs are likely to be recognised earlier than the gain on the related sale of assets.

EXAMPLE 3F – MEASURING PROVISION – EXPECTED GAIN ON SALE OF RELATED ASSET

3.12.170.30 Company K commits to a restructuring to outsource its distribution activities. This will involve closing one of its warehouses and cancelling leases of equipment used in the warehouse. K expects to sell the closed warehouse for a gain that exceeds the cancellation penalties on the equipment leases. The provision for the lease cancellation costs is not reduced by the expected gain from the sale of the warehouse.

3.12.180 **Associated costs**

3.12.180.10 Provisions are measured based on what an entity would rationally pay to settle or transfer the obligation. IFRS does not provide much guidance on the types of costs to be included in the measurement of a provision. However, the accrual of costs that need to be incurred to operate in the future is prohibited. [*IAS 37.18, 36–37*]

3.12.180.20   In our view, anticipated incremental costs that are directly related to the settlement of a provision should be included in the measurement of the provision to the extent that a third party who assumes the liability would require compensation. This is likely to be the case when the incremental costs are probable and can be estimated reliably.

3.12.180.30   Incremental costs are those in addition to normal operating expenses. Therefore, we believe that costs that are not incremental should not be included in the measurement of a provision, even if there is a reasonable basis for allocating a portion of these costs to the settlement of the provision. For example, costs to be incurred irrespective of a specific claim, such as salaries of employees in the claims department, are future operating costs; therefore, we believe that they should be excluded from the measurement of a provision. For further discussion of legal costs associated with claims, see 3.12.745.

3.12.180.40   In our view, the above principle applies to both external and internal costs. However, internal costs are less likely to be incremental and therefore would not normally be included in the measurement of a provision.

EXAMPLE 3G – MEASURING PROVISION – IDENTIFYING DIRECTLY RELATED INCREMENTAL COSTS

3.12.180.50   Company G maintains a risk management department that handles damage claims. The costs of the department are unlikely to be incremental for any specific claim and therefore G would not include these costs in the measurement of the provision for expected claims. However, if G engages an external adviser to negotiate the settlement of a specific matter, then this cost is incremental and would normally be included in the measurement of the related provision.

3.12.190   REIMBURSEMENTS

3.12.190.10   Reimbursements – such as insurance recoveries, indemnities and warranties – are recognised as a separate asset when recovery is virtually certain. The amount recognised is limited to the amount of the related provision. [*IAS 37.53*]

EXAMPLE 4A – REIMBURSEMENT – SETTLEMENT AMOUNT EXCEEDS PROVISION

3.12.190.20   One of Company M's customers has established a claim against M for 300 in respect of a defective product that the customer bought from M. M can recover the cost of the defect and a penalty of 12% from the supplier. The supplier has confirmed that it will pay 336 (300 + (300 x 12%)) to M as soon as M has paid the customer. M recognises a provision for the claim of 300.

3.12.190.25   Because the reimbursement is virtually certain, it is recognised as a separate asset. However, the amount recognised cannot exceed the amount of the provision recognised for the claim – i.e. 300. The expense and the reimbursement may be netted in profit or loss; however, the asset and the provision are not netted in the statement of financial position and are presented gross. M discloses the unrecognised reimbursement of 36 in the notes to the financial statements. [*IAS 1.34, 37.53–54, 56*]

3.12.190.30   An obligation and the related recovery are often recognised at the same time. However, if the party that will make the reimbursement cannot be identified, then the reimbursement is generally not virtually certain and cannot be recognised.

3.12.190.40   If the only uncertainty regarding the recovery of an insured loss is the amount of the recovery, then in our view the reimbursement amount will often qualify to be recognised as an asset.

EXAMPLE 4B – REIMBURSEMENT – SETTLEMENT AMOUNT UNCERTAIN

3.12.190.45   Company Y has recognised a provision for environmental contamination that it is obliged to clean up. Y's insurance company has confirmed that the accident that caused the contamination is an insured event, but has not yet finalised the settlement amount. We believe that Y should recognise its best estimate of the reimbursement, not exceeding the amount of the provision, as a separate asset.

3.12.190.50   In some cases, compensation for lost revenue may be received in non-cash form – e.g. as a non-financial asset. In our view, the difference in nature of the compensation does not result in different accounting outcomes and non-cash compensation should be treated in the same manner as cash compensation – i.e. it should be recognised when the event occurs that gives rise to the claim for compensation and the compensation becomes receivable.

EXAMPLE 4C – REIMBURSEMENT – COMPENSATION RECEIVED IN NON-CASH FORM

3.12.190.55   Company B is a railway operator and it has a delivery contract with Company G, which builds trains. The contract includes a clause for compensation for delivery delays of any committed purchases of railway cars on a fixed date. B agrees to accept spare parts free of charge in lieu of cash compensation if delays in delivery occur. In this example, we believe that B should recognise compensation for delays as delays occur and the compensation becomes receivable. The amount of compensation recognised would then become B's cost basis for the spare parts.

3.12.190.60   In certain cases, obligations can be settled by a parent company on behalf of its subsidiary.

EXAMPLE 4D – REIMBURSEMENT – OBLIGATION SETTLED BY PARENT

3.12.190.65   Company G manufactures and sells complex customised equipment and guarantees to reimburse its customers in the case of product malfunction. At the end of 2018, G receives a claim for 100 from one of its customers, but it does not have sufficient funds to settle this claim. G's parent, M, agrees to settle the claim on behalf of G without requiring further reimbursement by G.

3.12.190.70   In our view, the fact that M assumes the obligation without requiring further reimbursement does not exempt G from the requirement to recognise a liability arising from a contractual obligation. Therefore, G should recognise a provision in respect of the customer's claim of 100. When M agrees to settle the claim on behalf of G without requiring further reimbursement and acts in its capacity as shareholder, G should treat this reimbursement as an increase in equity for the shareholder contribution (see 1.2.190).

3.12.190.80   If a seller is contractually obliged to indemnify the acquirer for a specific liability assumed in a business combination, then IFRS 3 requires the acquirer to recognise an asset at the same time, measured using the same measurement basis as the related liability. For further discussion of indemnification assets under IFRS 3, see 2.6.670. [*IFRS 3.27*]

3.12.195   Compensation for impairment of non-financial assets or lost income

3.12.195.10   Under insurance contracts, the policyholder is compensated if a specified uncertain future event (an insured event) adversely affects the policyholder (see 8.1.20). An entity may hold an insurance contract under which it is compensated in some circumstances for the impairment of a non-financial asset or for lost income. The question arises about how to account for that compensation right. The first step is to determine which standard to apply or analogise to. IFRS 9 specifically excludes insurance contracts held from its scope and IFRS 4 does not address the accounting for insurance contracts by policyholders, other than the holders of reinsurance contracts (see 7.1.40–50 and 8.1.10). In our view, determining which standard to apply or analogise to depends on whether the compensation right is:
- a right under a financial guarantee contract, and if so whether that financial guarantee contract is an integral part of another financial instrument (see 7.1.60); or
- a right under another type of insurance contract – e.g. compensation for impairment of property, plant and equipment or compensation for lost profits. [*IFRS 4.2–4, A, 9.2.1(e)*]

3.12.195.15   We believe that compensation that is not related to a provision – e.g. for impairment of a non-financial asset or for lost revenue – is not a reimbursement right in the scope of IAS 37.

3.12.195.20   If the compensation right under an insurance contract is either a financial guarantee contract that the holder determines is not an integral element of the related debt instrument or is a right under another type of insurance contract, then in our view the accounting for this compensation right would depend on whether the loss event that creates a right for the entity to assert a claim has occurred at the reporting date.

3.12.198   *Compensation rights when loss event has occurred*

3.12.198.10   IAS 16 provides specific guidance on compensation for the impairment of property, plant and equipment (see 3.2.370). In our view, a consistent approach should be applied to other insurance contracts that compensate the holder for a loss event related to asset impairment or lost revenue/ profit. Therefore, if the loss event that creates a right for the entity to assert a claim has occurred, then we believe that the entity should recognise a receivable for the compensation when it has an unconditional contractual right to receive the compensation. The compensation receivable should be measured based on the amount and timing of the expected cash flows discounted at a rate that reflects the credit risk of the insurer. We believe that an entity would have an unconditional contractual right to receive compensation if:

- the entity has an insurance contract under which it can make a claim for compensation; and
- the loss event that creates a right for the entity to assert a claim at the reporting date has occurred and the claim is not disputed by the insurer. [*IAS 16.65–66*]

EXAMPLE 5A – COMPENSATION – CLAIM FOR LOST PROFITS

3.12.198.20   Company P has an insurance policy that allows it to claim for lost profits in the event of one of its key machines breaking down. Under the terms of the insurance contract, the amount of compensation is 10 for each full day that the machine is out of order. The machine breaks down on 1 October 2018 and P estimates that the machine will be out of order for the next six months. The amount of 10, being compensation receivable, is accrued for each working day that the machine has been out of order, because the loss event that creates a right for P to assert a claim occurs at the end of each working day. For further discussion of compensation for insurance recoveries for assets, see 3.2.370.

EXAMPLE 5B – COMPENSATION – CLAIM FOR DAMAGE TO ASSET

3.12.198.30   Company Q's building burns down and Q claims compensation for the impaired building under its fire insurance policy that covers this loss. The impairment of the building is recognised when the fire occurs. A receivable for the compensation is recognised when Q has an unconditional contractual right to receive compensation (i.e. when the damage has occurred) assuming that the loss event is not disputed by the insurer – e.g. by asserting arson, which is not covered by the insurance. For further discussion of compensation for insurance recoveries for assets, see 3.2.370.

3.12.199   *Compensation rights when loss event has not occurred*

3.12.199.05   In our view, a recognised impairment loss for which there is not yet a contractual right to assert a claim is similar in nature to a provision. A provision is a liability that is a present obligation arising from a past event, of uncertain timing or amount; an impairment recognised in advance of the event that allows an entity to assert a claim is an insured loss related to a past event, but there may be uncertainty about the timing or amount of the actual final loss. In some cases (e.g. a fire), there will be no timing gap between recognition of the impairment and the related loss event. In other cases (e.g. financial guarantee contracts), there may be a timing gap between recognition of the impairment and the related loss event.

3.12.199.10   For a further discussion of the accounting for compensation rights under financial guarantee contracts, see 7.1.138.

3.12.200   Environmental and similar funds

3.12.200.10   Funds may be set up to assist contributors to the fund to meet their decommissioning or rehabilitation obligations. If a contributor does not have control, joint control or significant influence over the fund, then the contributor recognises the right to receive compensation from the fund as a reimbursement right (see 3.12.190). [*IFRIC 5.9*]

3.12.210   USE OF PROVISIONS

3.12.210.10   Only expenditure related to the original nature of the provision is offset against the provision. [*IAS 37.62*]

3.12.220   SPECIFIC APPLICATION GUIDANCE

3.12.230   Restructuring

3.12.230.10   Specific guidance is provided regarding the recognition and measurement of restructuring provisions.

3.12.240   *Definition*

3.12.240.10   A 'restructuring' is a programme planned and controlled by management that materially changes the scope of the business or the manner in which it is conducted. [*IAS 37.10*]

3.12.250   *Obligating event*

3.12.250.10   A constructive obligation for a restructuring arises only when:
- there is a formal plan for the restructuring specifying:
  - the business or part of a business concerned;
  - the principal locations affected;
  - the location, function and approximate number of employees whose services will be terminated;
  - the expenditure to be incurred; and
  - when the plan will be implemented (see 3.12.290 for additional comments on timing); and
- the entity has raised a valid expectation in those affected that it will carry out the plan by either:
  - starting to implement the plan; or
  - announcing its main features to those affected by it. [*IAS 37.72*]

3.12.250.20   These requirements apply to all restructuring costs other than pension plan changes and redundancy payments (see 4.4.870–890 and 1440), and the impairment of assets as a result of a restructuring (see chapter 3.10). [*IAS 37.1(c), 5(d)*]

3.12.250.30   For a discussion of restructuring costs of an acquiree in a business combination, see 2.6.570.30. [*IFRS 3.51–52*]

3.12.260   *Sale transactions*

3.12.260.10   An obligation related to the sale of an operation arises only when there is a binding sale agreement. Therefore, even though the decision to sell an operation has been announced, no provision is recognised for obligations arising as a result of the sale until there is a binding sale agreement. [*IAS 37.78*]

3.12.260.20   Certain sale transactions may be subject to regulatory or shareholder approval. In these cases, the sale agreement is normally binding unless the approval is substantive and is considered to be a significant hurdle (see 5.4.30.85–87). In our view, a provision triggered by a sale agreement should be recognised once the agreement is finalised if it is more likely than not that the necessary approval will be obtained.

3.12.260.30   To the extent that the planned sale of an operation includes non-current assets (or disposal groups), the requirements for assets held for sale are relevant (see 5.4.20). Non-current assets (or disposal groups) that are classified as held-for-sale are subject to specific measurement requirements.

3.12.270   *Announcement*

3.12.270.10   There are no specific requirements for the contents of the announcement. However, it needs to be sufficiently explicit to create a valid expectation in those affected that the plan will be implemented. [*IAS 37.17(b), 72(b)*]

3.12.270.20   In our view, the announcement should include information about:
- the business or part of the business that is affected;
- the estimated timing; and
- the functions and approximate number of employees affected.

3.12.270.30   If the business is carried out in several locations, then the affected locations also need to be specified. However, we believe that it is not necessary for the estimated cost of the restructuring to be included in the announcement, because this is unlikely to be a key factor in raising an expectation that the restructuring will go ahead. [*IAS 37.72(a)(iii)*]

3.12.280   *Counterparty*

3.12.280.10   As noted in 3.12.100, IFRS does not require an entity to know the identity of the counterparty to the obligation before a provision is recognised. Therefore, it is not necessary to notify individual counterparties – e.g. each employee or vendor – before a provision is recognised. However, both the plan and the announcement of the plan need to have sufficient detail for those affected to identify the potential impact and to understand what their claim may be. [*IAS 37.20, 73*]

3.12.290   *Timing*

3.12.290.10   For a plan to create a constructive obligation, implementation needs to begin as soon as possible and be completed in a timeframe that would not allow for significant changes to the plan. [*IAS 37.74*]

3.12.290.20   There is no specified limit on the timing. The timeframe needs to be short enough that the plan is fixed and the possibility of it being changed is small. The longer the timeframe, the more difficult it will be to demonstrate that it is highly unlikely that the plan will be changed. [*IAS 37.74*]

3.12.300   *Contractual requirement to restructure*

3.12.300.10   An entity may enter into a contractual agreement to undertake a restructuring – e.g. as a result of an outsourcing arrangement.

EXAMPLE 6A – RESTRUCTURING – EXECUTORY OUTSOURCING CONTRACTS

3.12.300.20   Company K enters into a contract with Company L, under which L will take over and restructure K's existing IT department. Under the terms of the contract, all K's employees will be transferred to L. After that, L will perform the restructuring and K will reimburse L for all costs based on L's reports of work performed and costs incurred.

3.12.300.25   In our view, the agreement between K and L is an executory contract. Therefore, we believe that the restructuring costs should be recognised by K as L performs under the contract and reports to K, and not on signing the contract.

3.12.310   *Group-wide restructuring*

3.12.310.10   An entity that has a group-wide restructuring might not meet the criteria for recognising a provision for all locations at the same time.

3.12.310.20   In our view, the criteria should be applied to each part of the restructuring programme – e.g. each location – separately. Provisions should be recognised only for those locations that meet the criteria.

3.12.320   *Board decision*

3.12.320.10   Generally, a board decision in itself does not establish a constructive obligation – e.g. with respect to the termination of employees. [*IAS 37.75*]

3.12.320.20   However, a board decision may require communication with a decision-making body that includes employee representatives – e.g. a supervisory board. In such cases, approval of the plan by the supervisory board probably results in a constructive obligation even if there is no direct communication to the affected employees at that time. [*IAS 37.77*]

3.12.330   *Measurement*

3.12.330.10   Restructuring provisions include only incremental costs associated directly with the restructuring. Examples of costs that are considered in measuring the provision include:
- employee termination benefits that relate directly to the restructuring (see 4.4.1440);
- contract termination costs, such as lease termination penalties;
- onerous contract provisions (see 3.12.630);

- consulting fees that relate directly to the restructuring; and
- expected costs from when operations cease until final disposal. [*IAS 37.80*]

3.12.330.20   IFRS prohibits recognition of a provision for costs associated with ongoing activities. Therefore, provisions are not recognised for:

- expected future operating costs or expected operating losses unless they relate to an onerous contract (see 3.12.630);
- gains or losses on expected disposals or impairments of assets (see 3.12.350);
- investment in new systems;
- lower utilisation of a facility;
- the costs of training or relocating staff;
- staff costs for staff who continue to be employed in ongoing operations;
- loyalty bonuses or amounts paid to staff as an incentive to stay;
- the costs of moving assets or operations;
- administration or marketing costs;
- allocations of corporate overheads; or
- the costs of changing the name of an entity. [*IAS 37.80(b)–81*]

EXAMPLE 6B – RESTRUCTURING PROVISION – COSTS INCLUDED

3.12.330.30   Company C is a dairy but also produces cheese. The cheese-making operations are being restructured. The equipment that is used in the cheese-making operations will be redesigned and staff will be trained to use the new equipment. To the extent that the restructuring relates to C's ongoing operations, a provision is not recognised for these costs. Therefore, the costs of redesigning the operation and retraining staff are not included in the restructuring provision. The costs of new equipment and improvements to existing equipment are capitalised when they are incurred (see chapter 3.2).

3.12.340   *Employee termination payments*

3.12.340.10   For a discussion of the accounting for employee termination payments, see 4.4.1440.

3.12.350   *Asset disposals or impairment*

3.12.350.10   A restructuring may also entail asset disposals or trigger the impairment of assets. For a discussion of issues related to the impairment of assets, see chapter 3.10; and for a discussion of the classification of non-current assets (or disposal groups) as held-for-sale and their measurement, see chapter 5.4.

3.12.360   **Warranties**

3.12.360.10   An entity that has an established practice of repairing or replacing faulty or defective goods that are returned, even if it is not legally obliged to do so, generally has a constructive obligation to repair or replace products. The obligating event is the sale of goods that turn out to be defective or faulty, unless the warranty is a service-type warranty and is therefore accounted for as a separate performance obligation (see also 4.2.320). [*IAS 37.C1*]

3.12.360.20   A warranty provision is measured based on the probability of the goods requiring repair or replacement and the best estimate of the costs to be incurred in respect of defective products sold on or before the reporting date (see 3.12.110.20). [*IAS 37.C1*]

EXAMPLE 7 – ASSURANCE-TYPE WARRANTY – WARRANTY PROVISION

3.12.360.30   Company M manufactures and sells luxury vehicles. All vehicles are guaranteed for 12 months and M determines that this is an assurance-type warranty – i.e. it is not a separate performance obligation (see 4.2.320). M introduces a new model, the R100, two months before the reporting date. When the financial statements are prepared, no warranty claims have been made in respect of the R100. However, based on previous experience with similar models, it is probable that there will be claims for manufacturing defects.

3.12.360.35   M recognises a provision in respect of expected claims on the new model. The lack of claims history in respect of the R100 does not change this, because the sale of the defective vehicles is the obligating event. M considers claims patterns in respect of comparable models to determine the expected number of claims and the anticipated cost.

3.12.360.40   In our view, incremental staff costs that are directly attributable to handling individual warranty claims – e.g. amounts paid to contractors for call-outs or overtime pay – should be included in the measurement of provisions. However, costs that are not related to a specific warranty claim – e.g. the cost of maintaining a claims department – are not incremental and therefore should not be included in the measurement of the provision.

3.12.370   **Refundable deposits**

3.12.370.10   In some industries, customer refunds may relate to deposits collected for returnable containers.

EXAMPLE 8A – REFUNDABLE CONTAINER DEPOSITS – RETURNS EXPECTED

3.12.370.20   Company K sells gas in returnable cylinders. On delivery of gas to customers, K collects a deposit for each cylinder delivered and it has an obligation to refund this deposit when the customers return the cylinders. Based on its historical experience, K expects that all the cylinders will be returned. K accounts for the returnable cylinders as its property, plant and equipment and does not derecognise them as part of a sales transaction (see 3.8.40).

3.12.370.30   The IFRS Interpretations Committee discussed a similar scenario and noted that a deposit collected from a customer for a returnable container, which is not derecognised as part of a sales transaction, meets the definition of a financial liability because it is a contractual obligation to pay cash to the customer (see 7.1.30.50). Therefore, customer refunds related to deposits collected for returnable containers that are not derecognised as part of a sales transaction are outside the scope of IAS 37. [*IU 05-08*]

EXAMPLE 8B – REFUNDABLE CONTAINER DEPOSITS – RETURNS NOT EXPECTED

3.12.370.40   Modifying Example 8A, K derecognises cylinders as part of a sale transaction because it expects many of the cylinders to be retained by customers. However, K still collects a deposit from customers and has an obligation to return the deposit to a customer if the customer returns cylinders. The customer has a right but not an obligation to return the cylinders. K has no basis on which to estimate the number of customers that will return cylinders. In discussing a similar scenario, the IFRS Interpretations Committee noted that a deposit received for containers that are derecognised as part of a sales transaction would not meet the definition of a financial instrument. In our view, it would instead represent a consideration received for cylinders sold, and therefore is outside the scope of IAS 37 as well.

3.12.370.50   Because the customer has a right to return the cylinders bought and K is uncertain about the probability of return, we believe that it should apply the guidance in IFRS 15 on sales with a right of return (see 4.2.310). [*IFRS 15.B20–B25, IU 05-08*]

3.12.380   ## Self-insurance

3.12.380.10   Entities may elect not to insure against some risks or to obtain insurance that covers only a certain portion of incurred losses – e.g. because of high deductibles; this is sometimes referred to as 'self-insurance'.

3.12.380.20   A provision is not recognised for future losses or costs associated with self-insurance. However, a provision is recognised for qualifying costs related to events (insured or not) that occur before the reporting date. [*IAS 37.14, 18*]

EXAMPLE 9 – SELF-INSURANCE – OBLIGATING EVENT

3.12.380.30   Company D operates a chain of fast food outlets and decides not to insure against the risk of third party liability claims. Instead, D will self-insure this risk. Based on past experience, D expects losses of 100 each year in respect of third party liability claims for events that occurred within the year. In the first year of self-insurance, actual claims are 80. Assuming that all incurred losses have been reported, a provision cannot be recognised for the additional average claims of 20. Although it may be possible to estimate average annual expected claims reliably, there is no obligating event in the current year in respect of average claims in excess of actual claims.

> **3.12.380.40** However, D recognises a provision for losses that have been incurred, but not yet reported, at the reporting date (commonly referred to as 'IBNRs'), if there is a probable outflow of economic benefits and a reliable estimate of the losses can be made. If D believes that an extra 25 could be validly claimed by customers for loss events that occurred during the reporting period, then it would accrue that 25. This is because, although D has not yet received these claims, an obligating event has occurred. In our view, the calculation should take into account statistical experience of such events and the related amounts. Principles similar to those applied in the insurance industry may be helpful in measuring IBNR provisions.

3.12.390   *Risks assumed on behalf of third parties*

3.12.390.10   Specific requirements apply to obligations arising under an insurance contract (see chapter 8.1). Those requirements are not limited to entities regulated as insurance companies. [*IFRS 4.2(a)*]

EXAMPLE 10 – INSURANCE RISK ASSUMED ON BEHALF OF THIRD PARTY

> **3.12.390.20**   Company L owns and rents out properties. Under the rental agreement, L is responsible for repairing the properties in the case of fire. The rental payment includes a risk premium in respect of the possible loss because of fire. In our view, the properties are L's assets and therefore L should not recognise a provision for expected future damage – e.g. future fires. However, any further obligations – e.g. for damage to tenants' belongings – are an insurance contract and should be accounted for separately (see chapter 8.1).

3.12.390.30   Insurance contract liabilities arise only when risks are assumed on behalf of third parties. Risks assumed on behalf of group entities are self-insurance (as described in 3.12.380) in the consolidated financial statements. [*IFRS 4.A, B19(c)*]

3.12.400   *Captive insurance entities*

3.12.400.10   In some cases, separate entities are established for self-insurance arrangements. The administration of the entity is often handled by a third party insurance entity.

3.12.400.20   The guidance on consolidation (see chapter 2.5) applies in determining whether such entities should be consolidated.

3.12.400.30   If the insured entity consolidates the captive insurance entity, then the principles described above for self-insurance would apply (see 3.12.380). The insured entity would recognise a provision only when an event of loss occurs, and only for obligations incurred. For example, a self-insured entity would recognise impairment losses for property damaged in a fire rather than a provision to repair the property.

3.12.400.40   If the insured entity does not consolidate the captive insurance entity, then the arrangement has the same economic substance as an insurance contract and is accounted for in the same way as an insurance policy. An insurance policyholder recognises premiums as an expense over the period of the insurance. Losses are recognised only once the loss occurs, and reimbursement rights are recognised as separate assets (see 3.12.190).

3.12.400.50   For a discussion of the presentation and disclosure of self-insurance arrangements, see 8.1.130.

3.12.410   Environmental provisions

3.12.410.10   The recognition and measurement of a provision for environmental obligations follows the general requirements described in 3.12.30 and 110. Therefore, a provision is recognised when:

- there is either a legal or a constructive obligation to restore a site;
- the damage has already occurred;
- it is probable that a restoration expense will be incurred; and
- the costs can be estimated reliably. [*IAS 37.14*]

3.12.420   *Obligating event*

3.12.420.10   A constructive obligation may arise from published policies, past practices of environmental clean-ups or statements about clean-up policies made in the press or to the public. [*IAS 37.10*]

3.12.420.20   In-house standards and practices result in a constructive obligation only if they are communicated to third parties. [*IAS 37.10*]

EXAMPLE 11 – ENVIRONMENTAL PROVISION – OBLIGATING EVENT

3.12.420.30   Although no legal obligation exists, the board of Company G has instructed local management to clean up a site where land and ground water have been contaminated. The estimated cost of the clean-up is 250. If G does not have an established practice or published policies that would demonstrably commit it to cleaning up the site, then G would not recognise a provision based on the board decision alone. The board decision and instruction to clean up the site do not result in a constructive obligation if that decision is not communicated externally. The decision could still be reversed and the costs avoided.

3.12.420.40   Future changes in environmental legislation give rise to a legal obligation only once they are virtually certain of being enacted. [*IAS 37.22*]

3.12.430   *Measurement*

3.12.430.10   A provision is measured at the best estimate of the future clean-up costs. It reflects the amount that the entity would be required to pay to settle the obligation at the reporting date. [*IAS 37.36–37*]

3.12.430.20   In our experience, making the estimate may require specialised knowledge of environmental issues – e.g. the quantity and type of contaminants involved, the local geography and remediation costs. The estimates typically need to be made with input from environmental experts.

3.12.430.30   Future events that may affect the amount required to settle an obligation are reflected in the amount of the provision when there is sufficient objective evidence that they will occur. For example, anticipated cost savings arising from future improvements in technology are considered in measuring the provision if the existence of that technology is reasonably certain. [IAS 37.48–49]

3.12.430.40   The provision normally includes estimated incremental direct costs such as amounts paid to consultants, the costs of equipment dedicated to the clean-up, and the costs of employees performing the clean-up effort. In our view, the costs of the following activities should be included when measuring the provision:
- remedial investigation;
- risk assessment;
- feasibility studies;
- remedial action planning;
- remediation work;
- government oversight; and
- post-remediation monitoring.

3.12.430.50   Outflows in respect of environmental provisions may occur far in the future. Therefore, the effects of discounting are likely to be significant and, if so, the provision is measured at the present value of expected cash flows and remeasured when changes in interest rates impact the current estimate of the discount rate (see 3.12.120). [IAS 37.45, IFRIC 1.4]

3.12.440   *Decommissioning*

3.12.440.10   The obligation to make good environmental or other damage incurred in installing an asset is provided for in full immediately because the damage arises from a past event: the installation of the asset. For example, a provision is recognised for the expected cost of dismantling an oil rig when the rig is installed. [IAS 37.14, IE.C.Ex3]

3.12.440.20   When an obligation to restore the environment or dismantle an asset arises on the initial recognition of the asset, the corresponding debit is treated as part of the cost of the related asset and is not recognised immediately in profit or loss (see 3.2.70). The cost of an item of property, plant and equipment includes not only the initial estimate of the costs related to dismantlement, removal or restoration of property, plant and equipment at the time of installing the item, but also amounts recognised during the period of use for purposes other than producing inventory (see 3.2.110) – e.g. certain additional obligations for restoration costs. The provision recognised for dismantlement, removal or restoration of an item of property, plant and equipment is not reduced by the item's expected salvage value – instead, any salvage or other residual value would be taken into account when measuring the depreciable amount under IAS 16 (see 3.2.150). [IAS 16.6, 16(c), 53]

3.12.440.30   IFRS does not address how to account for new obligations – e.g. those triggered by a law enacted after an asset was acquired.

3.12.440.40   If an obligation to dismantle or decommission an asset or restore the environment arises after the initial recognition of the asset – e.g. because of changes in law or intent – then a provision is recognised at the time that the obligation arises. In our view, the estimated cost should be recognised as an adjustment to the cost of the asset and depreciated prospectively over the remaining useful life of the asset, assuming that the liability was not created through use of the item – e.g. to produce inventory (see 3.2.110 and 3.12.150.20). We believe that the principles that apply to changes in estimates of an existing obligation (see 3.2.80) should be applied in these circumstances. However, the capitalisation of these costs should not result in the asset's carrying amount exceeding its recoverable amount (see 3.10.180). [*IAS 37.14*]

3.12.440.50   In our view, the same approach should be taken even if the obligation arises only at the end of the useful life of the asset.

EXAMPLE 12A – DECOMMISSIONING PROVISION – OBLIGATING EVENT

3.12.440.55   Company Q operates a brewery close to the city centre. In 2018, because of new town planning restrictions, Q is required to stop operations immediately, move the brewery out of the town centre and clean up the site. Previously, Q had not recognised a provision for the clean-up, because there was no obligation. We believe that Q should recognise a provision for the site clean-up when the government informs Q of the need to move and clean up the site.

3.12.440.60   Because of the requirement to treat decommissioning as an element of the asset's cost, we believe that the provision should not be expensed immediately. Instead, the adjusted cost of the brewery will have to be tested for impairment (see 3.10.120). Further, if the brewery qualifies as an asset held for sale (see 5.4.20), then the requirement to measure the asset at the lower of its carrying amount and fair value less costs to sell may result in an impairment loss being recognised.

3.12.450   *Discounting*

3.12.450.10   Decommissioning, like the remediation of environmental damage, will often take place only far in the future. Therefore, the effects of discounting are normally material for decommissioning liabilities. In some industries – e.g. oil refining – the useful lives of assets requiring decommissioning might be very long. In our view, if there is uncertainty about the useful life of the asset, and therefore about the period over which the expected cash outflows related to the end-of-service decommissioning have to be discounted, then this uncertainty should be reflected in the measurement of the provision rather than used as a reason for not recognising the decommissioning liability (see 3.12.120). This is because we believe that uncertainty about the useful life of the assets should not lead to an inability to measure the provision reliably. However, if the useful life of the assets is very long, then the present value of the related decommissioning provision might not be material in early years. [*IAS 37.45*]

3.12.460   *Timing of outflow*

3.12.460.10   In determining the expected timing of the outflow, the expected useful life of the related asset should be considered. In our view, assumptions about future events should be supported by sufficient objective evidence because of the uncertainty of predicting events far into the future.

EXAMPLE 12B – DECOMMISSIONING PROVISION – MEASUREMENT (1)

3.12.460.15   Company Y has a chemical production plant with an anticipated useful life of 25 years. Clean-up is required only when the site is decommissioned. At the end of the useful life, it is possible that Y will construct a new production plant with a 25-year useful life on the site, in which case decommissioning will take place only in 50 years. Unless there is sufficient objective evidence that a new plant will be constructed, we believe that Y should assume that the decommissioning will take place in 25 years.

3.12.460.20   The assumptions also need to be consistent with the other assumptions about the use of the asset.

EXAMPLE 12C – DECOMMISSIONING PROVISION – MEASUREMENT (2)

3.12.460.25   Company T is required to remove an oil rig as soon as it stops pumping oil. If the estimated remaining useful life of the oil rig is 10 years, then we believe that T should assume that the decommissioning will take place in 10 years, even if there is a possibility that the oil rig may be used for longer.

3.12.460.30   An entity may not be required to, and may not be able to, decommission an asset immediately after it stops using the asset. In this case, the best estimate of the timing of the cash flows is used to measure the present value of the obligation. [*IAS 37.36*]

3.12.470   *Decommissioning liability in foreign currency*

3.12.470.10   IFRS does not provide clear guidance on the accounting treatment of exchange differences related to an obligation denominated in a foreign currency to settle a decommissioning obligation (see 3.2.80.25). For example, an entity constructs a plant. As the plant is constructed, the entity incurs a legal obligation to decommission the plant and the costs are denominated in a currency other than the entity's functional currency.

3.12.470.20   A foreign currency-denominated obligation is translated at the spot exchange rate at the reporting date if the obligation is a monetary liability, with translation gains and losses recognised in profit or loss. Non-monetary liabilities denominated in a foreign currency are translated at their historical exchange rate (see 2.7.110.10). In our view, a decommissioning liability is:

- monetary to the extent that it is expected to be settled by payment in a fixed or determinable number of units of currency – e.g. future payments to employees or third parties for goods and/or services; and
- non-monetary to the extent that it will be settled by the delivery, consumption or use of a previously recognised non-monetary asset – e.g. using materials on hand. [*IAS 21.16, 23*]

3.12.470.25   If a foreign currency-denominated obligation is a monetary liability, then in our view foreign currency-denominated cash flows should first be discounted to their present value in the foreign currency using a discount rate appropriate for the currency in which the cash flows will be incurred. Thereafter, the present value amount should be translated into the functional currency at the exchange rate at the reporting date. This approach is consistent with that required for impairment calculations (see 3.10.290). [*IAS 36.54*]

3.12.470.30   The analysis is complicated further because decommissioning costs are capitalised as part of the costs of the plant (see 3.12.440.20). Generally, changes in estimates for decommissioning are adjustments to the cost basis of the asset other than changes resulting from finance costs (unwinding of the discount). In some cases, foreign exchange gains or losses are regarded as borrowing costs (see 4.6.70), but generally under IFRS they are regarded as revisions of estimates of cash flows. [*IAS 23.6(e), IFRIC 1.4–7*]

3.12.470.40   In our view, the entity should choose an accounting policy, to be applied consistently, of either:

- capitalising exchange differences related to a decommissioning obligation in a foreign currency as part of property, plant and equipment and depreciating the amount prospectively over the remaining useful life of the asset; or
- recognising exchange differences related to a decommissioning obligation in a foreign currency immediately in profit or loss.

3.12.470.50   We believe that either treatment can be justified, because the gains or losses on remeasurement can be viewed either as finance costs that are not eligible for capitalisation or as revisions of estimated cash flows.

3.12.480   *Past vs future events*

3.12.480.10   A provision is recognised only if there are past events. Therefore, a provision reflects only damage incurred at the reporting date; a provision is not recognised for expected future damage.

EXAMPLE 12D – DECOMMISSIONING PROVISION – DAMAGE INCURRED VS FUTURE DAMAGE

3.12.480.20   Company U operates a nuclear power plant. Construction of the nuclear power plant was completed at the end of 2018 at a cost of 10,000. The estimated present value of the costs of dismantling the power plant and restoring the site for the damage caused by its construction at the end of its 25-year useful life is 980, which is not included in the construction cost of 10,000.

3.12.480.30   In addition, there will be ongoing damage to the environment by the emissions of various pollutants throughout the operating life of the power plant, which is expected to require remediation in 25 years, costing approximately 175 for each year of operation. The remediation resulting from ongoing damage will be carried out at the end of the plant's useful life. The obligation to dismantle the power plant and restore the site (980) is created as the power plant is constructed. The obligation in respect of the ongoing emissions arises as the emissions occur – i.e. over the useful life of the power plant.

3.12.480.40   U records the following entries in respect of the environmental damage.

	DEBIT	CREDIT
Nuclear power plant	980	
Obligation for remediation		980
To recognise liability for anticipated cost of site restoration and dismantling as part of cost of asset		
At 31 December 2018, assuming a 10% discount rate		
Interest cost (profit or loss)	98	
Obligation for remediation		98
To recognise unwinding of discount for year 1 on liability for site restoration and dismantling (980 x 10%)		
Depreciation of power plant (profit or loss)	439	
Accumulated depreciation – power plant		439
To recognise depreciation of power plant (10,980 / 25)		
Operating costs (profit or loss)	18	
Obligation for remediation		18
To recognise liability in respect of emissions during period (present value of 175 in 24 years)		

3.12.480.50   If U's estimates of the decommissioning costs remain unchanged, then in each of the following years during the useful life of the power plant, U will recognise:

- depreciation on the power plant of 439 (10,980 / 25);
- a provision for the present value of the additional obligation for remediation caused by emissions damage during the year; and
- assuming that there is no change in interest rates, the unwinding of the discount based on 10% of the accumulated obligation (for decommissioning and emissions damage) at the beginning of the year. Therefore, in 2019 U will recognise an interest cost of 110 ((980 + 98 + 18) x 10%). The unwinding of the discount is presented as a component of interest expense (see 3.12.840).

3.12.490   *Changes in estimate*

3.12.490.10   The effect of any changes to an existing obligation for dismantling costs is generally added to or deducted from the cost of the related asset and depreciated prospectively over the remaining useful life (see 3.2.140.20) of the asset – i.e. treated as a change in estimate (see 2.8.100). [*IFRIC 1.5*]

3.12.500   *Environmental and similar funds*

3.12.500.10   Sometimes funds are established to finance environmental or other remediation costs. Typically, funds reimburse entities for qualifying costs incurred but do not assume the primary responsibility for the decommissioning obligation. For example, to ensure that nuclear power plant operators have funding available to finance decommissioning costs, the government may require operators to make contributions to a fund. A fund may be set up to meet the decommissioning costs of a single contributor or of several contributors. The operator may have no control over the investment decisions of the fund and if the amount in the fund is insufficient to cover the decommissioning costs, then the operator will not be reimbursed for the additional costs.

3.12.500.20   The operator normally continues to bear the primary obligation for the decommissioning and therefore continues to recognise a provision for its obligation.

3.12.500.30   The operator's investment in the fund is accounted for as an asset. If the fund is a subsidiary, joint arrangement or associate of the operator, then it is consolidated (see chapter 2.5), accounted for based on the operator's rights and obligations to individual assets and liabilities or accounted for under the equity method, as appropriate (see chapters 3.5 and 3.6). Otherwise, if the operator does not have control, joint control or significant influence, then it recognises the right to receive compensation from the fund as a reimbursement right. The reimbursement right is measured at the lower of:

● the amount of the decommissioning obligation recognised; and
● the operator's share of the fair value of the net assets of the fund attributable to the operators. [*IFRIC 5.8–9*]

3.12.500.40   The change in the carrying amount of the reimbursement right other than from contributions to and payments from the fund is recognised in profit or loss in the period in which these changes occur. [*IFRIC 5.9*]

3.12.500.50   An obligation to make potential additional contributions – e.g. in the event of bankruptcy of another contributor – is treated as a contingent liability that is not recognised but is disclosed. A liability is recognised only if it is probable that additional contributions will be made. [*IFRIC 5.10*]

3.12.500.60   A residual interest in a fund that extends beyond a right to reimbursement, such as a contractual right to distributions once all the decommissioning has been completed, may be an equity instrument (see 7.1.30.60).

3.12.510   Emissions allowances

3.12.510.10   Certain jurisdictions operate a 'cap and trade' scheme, whereby an entity is required to deliver emissions certificates to a third party – e.g. a regulator – to be able to emit pollutants legally. The government grants a certain number of emissions certificates to an entity for use during a compliance period. The entity can then trade certificates with other parties to ensure that it has sufficient emissions certificates to match its emissions. IFRS does not contain specific guidance on accounting for cap and trade schemes involving emissions allowances.

3.12.510.20   In our view, emissions certificates received by a participant in a cap and trade scheme are intangible assets. Because these intangible assets are received from the government or government-related entity, the intangible may be measured initially at fair value or at a nominal amount (see 4.3.50.10 and 110.10). Subsequently, the allowances should be accounted for using the revaluation or cost model in IAS 38, and tested for impairment. For a more detailed discussion of the accounting for emissions certificates held by entities under such cap and trade schemes, see 3.3.160.

3.12.510.30   Provisions are measured at the best estimate of the expenditure required to settle the present obligation at the reporting date (see 3.12.110). Under cap and trade schemes, entities can generally settle their obligation created by the emission of pollutants only by surrendering emissions certificates to the local regulator. Generally, an entity cannot settle its obligation by making a cash payment or by transferring other assets. In our view, when other means of settlement are not possible, the provision could be measured based on the current carrying amount of the certificates on hand if sufficient certificates are owned to settle the current obligation, because that could be viewed as being the best estimate of the expenditure required to settle the obligation. Otherwise, the provision should be based on the current market value of the emissions certificates at the reporting date.

3.12.510.40   If at the reporting date the number of emissions certificates required to settle an entity's obligation exceeds the actual number of certificates on hand, then the best estimate of the expenditure required to settle the actual shortfall will generally be measured at the current market value of the emissions certificates needed to cover the shortfall. Consequently, if an entity chooses to sell emissions certificates during the year and in so doing creates a shortfall in the actual number of certificates held as compared with the total pollutants emitted at that date, then the portion of the obligation related to the actual shortfall at the reporting date at the current market value of the certificates will need to be remeasured if it is not already measured at the current market value of the emissions certificates at the reporting date.

3.12.520   Waste Electrical and Electronic Equipment

3.12.520.10   The EU's *Directive on Waste Electrical and Electronic Equipment* (WE&EE) requires the costs of disposing of such equipment in an environmentally acceptable manner to be borne by the producers, or by commercial users in some cases. Each member state is required to transform the EU directive on WE&EE into national law.

3.12.520.20   An entity has an obligation to contribute to waste management costs for historical household equipment (equipment sold to private households before 13 August 2005) based on its share of the market in a measurement period. The measurement period is specified in national law, which may vary from country to country. It is an entity's participation in the market during the measurement period that is the past event that triggers the recognition of an obligation to meet waste management costs. [*IFRIC 6.9*]

3.12.520.30   The disposal costs of new WE&EE (sold after 13 August 2005) and historical WE&EE from sources other than private households are allocated in different ways and are considered by the IFRS Interpretations Committee to be addressed adequately by the recognition criteria in IFRS. In our view, the facts and circumstances of each country's national law on the disposal of WE&EE should be analysed to determine the appropriate accounting under IFRS. [*IFRIC 6.7*]

EXAMPLE 13 – PROVISION FOR WASTE ELECTRICAL AND ELECTRONIC EQUIPMENT

3.12.520.40   Company C is a commercial user that owns historical WE&EE and is responsible for its disposal. Under recently enacted national legislation in the jurisdiction where C operates, C no longer has responsibility for the disposal of WE&EE if it replaces the equipment. Instead, on replacement of the equipment, the producer of the new equipment assumes responsibility for disposing of the old equipment.

3.12.520.50   In our view, the following accounting is appropriate.

- C should recognise a provision and capitalise the cost of disposal as part of the cost of the old equipment when the law is enacted.
- When the WE&EE is replaced, the waste disposal obligation for the equipment that is replaced is transferred to the producer of the replacement equipment. Therefore, the producer would recognise a provision for the disposal costs.
- C would derecognise the obligation and recognise any resulting gain or loss, depending on the amount paid to the producer for taking on the costs of disposal. We believe that C should separate the amount paid to the producer for taking on the costs of disposal from the amount paid for the new (replacement) equipment, even if this payment is embedded in the contracted purchase price of the new (replacement) equipment.

3.12.530   Obligation to acquire or replace assets

3.12.530.10   Generally, a legal or constructive obligation is recognised as a liability (provision) if the recognition criteria are met. However, a legal or contractual obligation to acquire or replace assets is recognised as a liability only to the extent of the performance of the obligation – i.e. the extent to which the costs of acquiring and replacing the asset have been incurred. For example, an entity is required to build infrastructure to satisfy the conditions of a licence. In our view, this should be treated the same way as an executory contract so that the obligation to incur costs for an item that will qualify for recognition as an asset in the future is not an obligation that requires recognition when the contract is agreed. Instead, an asset and liability will be recognised incrementally in accordance with the performance of the obligation, unless the contract is onerous (see 3.12.630). [*IAS 37.IE.C.Ex6*]

3.12.540   Repairs and maintenance

3.12.540.10   Repairs and maintenance of own assets cannot be provided for because these are costs associated with the future use of the assets. These costs are generally expensed as they are incurred (see 3.2.250). [*IAS 37.IE.C.Ex11*]

3.12.550   *Shut-downs*

3.12.550.10   Some entities periodically shut down facilities for repairs and maintenance.

EXAMPLE 14 – PERIODIC SHUT-DOWNS – OBLIGATING EVENT

3.12.550.20   Company Z operates a chain of hotels. Z closes each hotel every three years, for three months to perform repairs and maintenance. A provision cannot be recognised in respect of future repairs and maintenance, even though the costs can be estimated reliably and the repairs and maintenance are probable because they are necessary for Z to continue in operation. Until the expenditure is incurred, there is no obligating event because the expenditure is avoidable. The cost of repairs and

 maintenance is expensed as it is incurred unless the activity creates a separately recognisable component of the hotel asset (see 3.2.250).

3.12.560 *Legal requirement*

3.12.560.10   The prohibition on recognising a provision for future repairs and maintenance also applies when there is a legal requirement to undertake the specified repairs and maintenance activities.

3.12.560.20   For example, aviation laws require aircraft overhauls after a fixed number of flight hours. However, the overhaul can be avoided if the aircraft is withdrawn from use when or before it has flown the specified number of hours. Therefore, the cost of the overhaul is recognised only when the work is done. [*IAS 37.IE.C.Ex11B*]

3.12.560.30   As another example, in the UK, entities operating in the water industry agree a programme of maintenance with the regulator. If an entity does not spend the agreed amount within the specified period, then the regulator can require the water company to reduce the amount it charges to customers in future periods. In our view, both the future maintenance cost and any enforced reduction in revenues are amounts that relate to the future costs and therefore a provision should not be recognised for them. Instead, the costs and revenue reduction are recognised as they are incurred, unless the revenue reduction results in an onerous contract.

3.12.570 *Major inspection or overhaul costs*

3.12.570.10   When assets are subject to a major inspection or overhaul, a component approach to depreciation is applied. This results in the capitalisation of major inspection and overhaul costs and their depreciation over the period until the next major overhaul. For an explanation and an example of when the component approach is applied, see 3.2.250. [*IAS 16.14*]

3.12.580 *Replacement costs*

3.12.580.10   A provision is not recognised for the cost of replacing items of equipment that will be consumed in operations – e.g. the cost of replacing linen or crockery in the hospitality business.

3.12.580.20   Instead, the cost of the replacement items is recognised as equipment and depreciated if the items will be used for more than one period (see chapter 3.2), or as inventory when they are bought or produced. For a discussion of the base stock method of accounting for such items, see 3.8.310.

3.12.590 *Third party maintenance contracts*

3.12.590.10   Sometimes an entity will enter into a contract with an unrelated party to provide maintenance services – e.g. a lessor may agree to maintain a leased asset. In our view, the contract is executory and the service provider should not accrue for the expected cost of meeting its obligations under the contract unless the contract is onerous (see 3.12.630). The relevant costs should be recognised only when the services are performed. For a discussion of the accounting for the service element of lease payments, see 5.1.30.20.

3.12.590.20   Similarly, we believe that the customer (the lessee) should not recognise a provision in advance for the maintenance costs that will be payable under the contract. The maintenance contract is a service contract (an executory contract), and obligations under such contracts are not normally recognised until the service is provided unless the contract is onerous. Instead, the customer should accrue the costs only when they are due.

EXAMPLE 15 – POST-SALE MANUFACTURER SERVICES – OBLIGATING EVENT

3.12.590.30 Company D is a manufacturer and retailer of motor vehicles. D offers customers the option of post-sale services. Customers who elect to have these services pay a higher price for the vehicle. Under the terms of this arrangement, D maintains and services the vehicle for three years from the purchase date. We believe that D should not recognise a provision for the future service costs, unless the contract is onerous.

3.12.590.40 However, D assesses whether the post-sale services represent a separate performance obligation and accounts for them under IFRS 15 (see 4.2.60). [*IFRS 15.22, IAS 37.18*]

3.12.600 *Maintenance of leased assets#*

3.12.600.10 Lease contracts sometimes require the lessee to maintain the leased asset. In our view, the appropriate accounting treatment of the maintenance costs depends on:
- the nature of the costs;
- whether the lease is classified as a finance or an operating lease (see chapter 5.1); and
- the terms of the lease agreement. [*IAS 17.4*]

3.12.600.20 In our view, when the lessee is required to restore a leased asset to its original condition at the end of the lease term, the obligation to incur the hand-back cost arises when the damage occurs, which may be as the lessee uses the asset. The accounting for the obligation to restore and maintain the leased asset may vary depending on the nature of the lease agreement (see 3.12.610 and 620).

3.12.610 *Assets leased under finance lease#*

3.12.610.10 The substance of a finance lease is the purchase of an asset and a financing transaction (see 5.1.100). The accounting for a finance lease reflects this substance. Therefore, in our view the lessee should account for any overhauls or repairs and maintenance costs associated with an asset leased under a finance lease in the same way as it would for such costs related to its own assets.

3.12.610.20 As such, the lessee should apply the component approach to accounting for a leased asset that is subject to major repair or overhaul costs – i.e. the costs should be capitalised and depreciated over the useful life of the component (see 3.2.230). Other repair and maintenance costs should be expensed as they are incurred.

3.12.620 *Assets leased under operating lease#*

3.12.620.10 The issues are more complex for an asset leased under an operating lease because the asset and the future obligations under the lease are not reflected in the lessee's statement of financial position. There is no guidance in IFRS on whether component accounting is appropriate when the principal asset is not recognised in the financial statements.

3.12.620.20   In the case of an asset leased under an operating lease with no obligation to return the asset (or parts of the asset) in its original condition, the operating lease payments reflect the original condition of the asset and its anticipated condition at the end of the lease term. In other circumstances, if there is an obligation to return the asset (or parts of the asset) in its original condition, then the operating lease payments do not fully reflect the consumption of the asset during the lease term. In our view, the nature of the transaction determines the accounting treatment.

3.12.620.30   We believe that if repair or overhaul costs are included in the lease payments, then an entity should apply the 'component approach' (see 3.2.250) and recognise major repair or overhaul costs as a leasehold improvement. This approach may be applied on initial recognition to the extent that repair or overhaul costs are included in the lease payments, effectively treating a part of the lease contract as a finance lease (or owned asset) and the other part as an operating lease contract. Other maintenance costs would be recognised as an expense when they are incurred (see 3.2.290.20).

3.12.620.40   Conversely, if an entity has a contractual obligation to hand back the asset in its original condition, then it should apply the 'liability approach' and recognise a provision for the maintenance cost over the period of the lease as the original component is consumed. It recognises the corresponding charge in profit or loss. In our view, for this approach to be applied, the lease agreement should establish a clear obligation for the lessee to incur expenditure when 'damage' occurs; this may be proportionate to the use of the asset. The provision would be based on the extent of the damage at the reporting date.

EXAMPLE 16 – REFURBISHMENT PROVISION FOR LEASED PREMISES

3.12.620.50   To illustrate the two approaches in 3.12.620.30–40, assume that Company T leases a property under an operating lease. The property was refurbished two years before the lease commenced. T is required to fully refurbish the building every five years and the lease term is 13 years.

3.12.620.60   If the building may be handed back with a five-year-old refurbishment, then consumption of three years of refurbishment is included in the lease payments and the component approach in 3.12.620.30 should be applied. Under this approach, an asset (and a liability) would be recognised on initial recognition of the lease. Subsequently, when the refurbishment costs are incurred, T would capitalise those costs as leasehold improvements and depreciate the component over the period to the next refurbishment or to the end of the lease, if this is shorter. We believe that the component should not include the costs of day-to-day servicing of the building – e.g. cleaning (see 3.12.180.20–40).

3.12.620.70   In our view, if the building is required to be handed back newly refurbished, then the liability approach in 3.12.620.40 should be applied. Under this approach, T would recognise a provision for the refurbishment costs. The provision would be measured at the expected cost of the refurbishment based on the condition of the building at the reporting date. This results in a provision being recognised for the full cost of the refurbishment every five years.

3.12.625 **FORTHCOMING REQUIREMENTS**

3.12.625.10 IFRS 16 carries forward the IAS 17 distinction between operating and finance leases for lessors only. Under IFRS 16, a lessee applies a single, on-balance sheet lease accounting model and does not classify the lease as an operating or finance lease. In addition, the new standard may have an impact on accounting for lease maintenance costs. For further discussion of IFRS 16, see chapter 5.1A.

3.12.630 **Onerous contracts**

3.12.640 *Definition#*

3.12.640.10 An 'onerous contract' is one in which the unavoidable costs of meeting the obligations under the contract exceed the economic benefits expected to be received under the contract. [*IAS 37.10*]

3.12.640.20 A contract on unfavourable terms is not necessarily onerous.

EXAMPLE 17A – CONTRACT NOT ONEROUS – LEASE ON UNFAVOURABLE TERMS

> 3.12.640.25 Company B is the lessee of properties under operating leases. The lease payments on a number of the properties exceed normal market rentals for properties in the area. B does not have an onerous contract if the lease payments do not exceed the benefits that B will derive from using the properties (see 3.12.670).

3.12.640.30 Similarly, a contract that is not performing as well as anticipated, or as well as possible, is not onerous unless the costs of fulfilling the obligations under the contract exceed the benefits to be derived.

3.12.640.40 If an entity is assessing whether a contract for the sale of goods or services is an onerous contract, then in our view this assessment should be made based on the contract as a whole rather than on an item-by-item basis. This may be relevant when there are 'learning curve' costs that mean that inefficiencies are expected in the production of early units (see 3.8.215). However, entities should also consider the requirement for inventory to be tested for impairment generally on an item-by-item basis (see 3.8.340). If the contractual selling price is less than the unit cost, then a write-down to net realisable value may be required (see 3.8.330). Because this net-realisable-value test is applied to items of inventory, we believe that a write-down to net realisable value may be required for items produced under a contract that, taken as a whole, is not onerous. [*IFRS 15.BC294–BC296, BC315*]

EXAMPLE 17B – CONTRACT NOT ONEROUS – LEARNING CURVE COSTS

> 3.12.640.50 Company G builds three trains for a rail system. G concludes that it transfers control over trains to the customer at a point in time (see 4.2.240). The contract with the rail system is expected to be profitable overall. However, because of the customisation that requires use of a new technology, learning curve costs on the first of the three trains are expected to create a loss as detailed below, when considering only incremental costs (see 3.12.660).

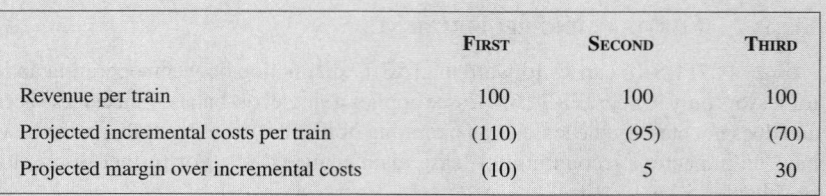

	FIRST	SECOND	THIRD
Revenue per train	100	100	100
Projected incremental costs per train	(110)	(95)	(70)
Projected margin over incremental costs	(10)	5	30

3.12.640.60   Because the contract as a whole is profitable – i.e. the expected margin in excess of incremental costs is 25 – in our view it is not onerous. However, because costs are being incurred to build the earlier units, G should consider whether any of the learning curve costs can effectively be deferred in the cost of inventory (see 3.8.215). G should also consider whether assets used to fulfil the contract are impaired (see chapter 3.10).

3.12.647   FORTHCOMING REQUIREMENTS

3.12.647.10 Under IFRS 17, an entity may choose to apply IFRS 15 or IFRS 17 to fixed-fee insurance service contracts if certain conditions are met. If an entity applies IFRS 15 to these contracts, then it continues to follow the onerous contract requirements in IAS 37. [*IFRS 17.8*]

3.12.650   *Determining whether contract is onerous*

3.12.650.10   In assessing whether a contract is onerous, it is necessary to consider:
- the unavoidable costs of meeting the contractual obligations, which is the lower of the net costs of fulfilling the contract and the cost of terminating it; and
- the economic benefits expected to be received. [*IAS 37.10*]

3.12.650.20   If a contract can be terminated without incurring a penalty, then it is not onerous. [*IAS 37.67*]

3.12.660   *Costs**

3.12.660.10   In determining the costs of fulfilling a contract, an entity considers the payments due in the period in which the contract cannot be cancelled. If there is an option to cancel the contract and pay a penalty, then the entity also considers the present value of the amount to be paid on cancellation of the contract, and measures the contract at the lowest net cost to exit. [*IAS 37.68*]

EXAMPLE 18A – DETERMINING WHETHER CONTRACT IS ONEROUS – CANCELLATION OPTION

3.12.660.20   Company F leases office space and pays an annual rental of 20. The remaining lease term is five years, although after two years F has an option to cancel the lease and pay the lessor a penalty of 25. The cost of fulfilling the contract is 85 (the present value of 20 x 5). The cost of terminating the contract is 60 (the present value of (20 x 2 + 25)). F uses the alternative that results in the lowest cost in determining whether the contract is onerous – i.e. 60. [*IAS 37.68*]

3.12.660.30   In our view, only unavoidable costs directly associated with meeting the entity's obligations to deliver the goods or services under the contract should be considered in determining whether the contract is onerous and in measuring any resulting provision. We believe that the unavoidable costs of meeting the obligations under the contract are only costs that:

- are directly variable with the contract and therefore incremental to the performance of the contract;
- do not include allocated or shared costs that will be incurred regardless of whether the entity fulfils the contract; and
- cannot be avoided by the entity's future actions.

EXAMPLE 18B – DETERMINING WHETHER CONTRACT IS ONEROUS – UNAVOIDABLE COSTS (1)

3.12.660.40   Company G services computers and charges clients a fixed monthly fee. On one of the service contracts, the servicing needs of the customer are significantly higher than anticipated. In determining whether the contract with that customer is onerous, we believe that G should consider the direct variable costs that it would need to incur to meet its obligations under the contract, but not costs that relate to the servicing business as a whole.

3.12.660.50   In our view, costs that would be incurred regardless of whether the contract is fulfilled are not incremental and therefore should not be considered in the onerous analysis of a contract to supply goods or services to others. Costs that are not incremental include fixed and non-cancellable costs, such as depreciation of property, plant and equipment, non-cancellable operating lease costs and personnel costs for employees who would be retained. We believe that costs that are not incremental should not be considered in the onerous contract analysis because they are costs to operate the business.

EXAMPLE 18C – DETERMINING WHETHER CONTRACT IS ONEROUS – UNAVOIDABLE COSTS (2)

3.12.660.60   Company Y provides data transmission services using a network infrastructure, which it leases partly from external carriers. The network infrastructure lease contracts are non-cancellable and are on fixed payment terms regardless of the volume or number of customers serviced by Y using the network.

3.12.660.70   For management purposes, Y uses a cost allocation methodology whereby the full cost of operating the network – including depreciation of owned equipment, rental of network infrastructure and personnel costs – is allocated to individual customer contracts.

3.12.660.80   We believe that depreciation of entity-owned equipment, rental of network infrastructure and personnel costs are fixed costs associated with operating the infrastructure and should not be included in the analysis of whether an individual customer contract is onerous. [*IAS 37.18*]

3.12.660.90   In some cases, to fulfil a customer contract an entity may need to lease an item under a non-cancellable operating lease. For example, in Example 18C Company Y needs to use the network equipment that it leases under a non-cancellable operating lease. We believe that the non-cancellable lease cost should not be considered an incremental cost of meeting the obligation under the individual customer contract, because this cost will be incurred whether or not the customer contract exists. However, we believe that Y should consider whether its lease of the network equipment is itself an onerous contract. Y would do this by comparing the economic benefits expected to be received from using the leased network equipment (see 3.12.670) with the unavoidable minimum payments to be made under the lease contract (see 3.12.680).

3.12.670 *Benefits*

3.12.670.10   The expected benefit under a contract is the net present value of the future inflows related to the contract. Estimating the future benefits to be derived may require judgement, possibly based on past experience or expert advice.

3.12.670.20   In considering the expected benefits under a contract, it may be necessary to evaluate the entity's expected use of a product.

EXAMPLE 18D – DETERMINING WHETHER CONTRACT IS ONEROUS – ASSESSING EXPECTED BENEFITS

3.12.670.30   Company B, a commercial bakery, has a forward contract to buy 100 tonnes of wheat at a price of 13,000 per tonne. The forward contract will be settled by physical delivery of the wheat and meets the own-use exemption (see 7.1.200). At the reporting date, the market price of wheat has dropped to 10,000 per tonne. However, B still expects to make a profit on the sale of the bread that will be made from the wheat delivered on settlement of the forward contract.

3.12.670.40   Therefore, the forward contract is not onerous and B does not recognise a provision for the above-market price. Instead, B measures the cost of the wheat at 13,000 per tonne when control of the wheat transfer to B.

3.12.670.50   An entity may enter into a derivative transaction to hedge its risk exposures arising from a sales contract. In our view, if an entity designates a derivative as a hedging instrument to hedge cash flows related to fulfilment of a sales contract, then in estimating the future benefits expected under the contract, it should consider benefits arising from the derivative (see 7.9.180). However, if hedge accounting is not applied, then we believe that benefits from a derivative used should not be included in the assessment in determining whether a contract is onerous.

EXAMPLE 18E – DETERMINING WHETHER CONTRACT IS ONEROUS – HEDGING EXPECTED CASH FLOWS

3.12.670.60   Company J is in the business of sourcing and supplying cocoa beans and providing related services to its customers – e.g. shipping, distribution and repackaging. J is not a broker-trader. The sales contracts with customers can be settled only by a physical delivery and meet the 'own-use' exemption – i.e. these contracts are not accounted for at fair value through profit or loss (see 7.1.200).

On 1 August 2018, J enters into a non-cancellable contract with Company Z to sell cocoa beans at 1,000 per tonne for delivery in 12 months.

3.12.670.70   To fulfil the sale contract with Z, J will need to purchase cocoa beans. To hedge the price risk of the expected purchase of inventory that will later be sold to Z, on 2 August 2018 J enters into a forward contract with Company B to purchase cocoa beans for 900 per tonne that will be settled net. The contract is designated as a hedging instrument in a cash flow hedge of a highly probable forecast purchase of inventory.

3.12.670.80   On 31 December 2018, the market price for cocoa beans is 1,200 per tonne and J determines that the hedging relationship continues to meet the hedge accounting criteria.

3.12.670.90   We believe that in determining whether the sales contract with Z is onerous, J should take the hedging instrument into account when estimating the costs to fulfil its obligation – i.e. as if the costs to purchase cocoa were fixed at the derivative's strike price of 900 per tonne. [*IAS 37.68, IFRS 9.2.4*]

3.12.680   *Leases*

3.12.680.10   In our view, when a lessee is assessing whether a lease is onerous, consideration should be given to any sub-lease income that could be earned from the leased asset. We believe that this applies even if the entity chooses not to sub-lease the asset – e.g. to avoid competitors gaining access to the area – or if a sub-lease requires the lessor's approval, provided that the approval cannot be withheld unreasonably. However, if a lease prohibits sub-leases, then potential sub-lease income should not be considered.

3.12.680.20   For further discussion of accounting for leases under IAS 17, see chapter 5.1. For further discussion of forthcoming requirements under IFRS 16, see chapter 5.1A.

3.12.690   *Timing of recognition*

3.12.690.10   Usually, a decision to terminate a contract at some date in the future does not result in a legal or constructive obligation at the date of the decision. Therefore, in our view the costs of cancelling or terminating a contract should not be recognised until the contract is actually terminated, unless the contract becomes onerous.

3.12.690.20   Before a separate provision for an onerous contract is recognised, an entity recognises any impairment loss that has occurred on assets dedicated to the contract (see chapter 3.10). [*IAS 37.69*]

3.12.700   *Overall loss-making operations*

3.12.700.10   Some contracts may be part of an overall loss-making operation. In our view, a provision should not be recognised for these contracts unless the cash flows related to the contract are clearly distinguishable from the operations as a whole. Otherwise, a provision would effectively be recognised for future operating losses, which is prohibited by IFRS.

EXAMPLE 18F – DETERMINING WHETHER CONTRACT IS ONEROUS – SEPARATELY IDENTIFIABLE VS OVERALL LOSS-MAKING

3.12.700.20   Company T is a tour operator. Among other services, T offers cruises on a lake. For this purpose, T leases a cruise ship under an operating lease. Because of increased competition for cruises, the costs of leasing the cruise ship exceed the income that T generates from its cruise operations. Given that the operating lease contract relates only to T's cruise operations, and the cash flows related to these operations are separately identifiable, in our view T should assess whether the lease contract is onerous. In performing this analysis, T should consider the costs of terminating the lease contract and alternative uses for the ship.

3.12.700.30   However, if T sold package tours, which included a cruise on the lake, and T's overall operations were loss-making, then the losses would relate to the business as a whole rather than specifically to the lease contract. In addition, it is likely that the cash inflows related to the cruise operations would not be clearly distinguishable from those related to the other operations. Therefore, in this case we believe that a provision for an onerous contract should not be recognised. However, T should consider whether the related recognised assets are impaired.

3.12.710   *Measuring the provision*

3.12.710.10   The present value of the obligation under an onerous contract is recognised as a provision. The amount of the provision is the lower of the cost of terminating the contract and the net cost of continuing with the contract after taking into account revenues directly related to a contract – i.e. the lowest net cost to exit. In our view, the lower of the cost of fulfilling the contract and of terminating the contract should be considered in measuring the provision, regardless of the entity's intention. [*IAS 37.66*]

EXAMPLE 19A – PROVISION FOR ONEROUS CONTRACT – MEASUREMENT – REVENUE DIRECTLY RELATED TO CONTRACT

3.12.710.20   Airline S owns a number of aircraft and has entered into a non-cancellable agreement under which it charters out one of its aircraft for 20 days for a fee of 10 per day. S incurs unavoidable costs of 15 a day to service the aircraft on any day that the aircraft is flown. The unavoidable costs of servicing the aircraft exceed the revenues. The anticipated loss on the contract is 5 per day for the 20 days – i.e. 100 (5 x 20). Before the onerous contract provision is calculated, S needs to test the aircraft for impairment (see chapter 3.10). [*IAS 37.69*]

3.12.710.30   If S is able to cancel the charter arrangement by paying a penalty of 40, then we believe that a provision of 40 rather than 100 should be recognised, regardless of whether S intends to cancel the contract.

3.12.710.40   In our view, an onerous contract should be measured using the same approach as was used for determining whether that contract is onerous (see 3.12.650). For example, an entity may have a choice either to produce goods itself or to buy them on the market in order to fulfil a contract with a customer. In our view, if the entity-specific marginal costs of producing the goods are lower than the cost of buying them on the market, then the entity-specific marginal costs should be used rather than the fair value of the goods on the market. This is consistent with the requirement to measure an onerous contract at the lowest net cost to exit. [*IAS 37.68*]

EXAMPLE 19B – PROVISION FOR ONEROUS CONTRACT – MEASUREMENT – MARKET PRICE VS MARGINAL COST TO PRODUCE

3.12.710.50   Company T has a non-cancellable fixed-price contract with a customer to deliver electricity. T has a variety of electricity-generating facilities, including nuclear, thermal hydro and wind power plants. If there is insufficient capacity to meet the customer demands, then T can buy electricity on the market. The market price for buying electricity is higher than T's incremental costs of producing electricity – i.e. fuel and labour – and both of these measures are higher than the revenue under the contract. We believe that T should measure the onerous contract provision based on the incremental costs of producing electricity, less the revenue to be earned from the customer. This is consistent with the requirement to measure an onerous contract at the lowest net cost to exit.

3.12.710.60   If a contract for the sale of goods is onerous, then the provision for the contract is used as the contract is fulfilled – e.g. to write down inventory that is acquired or produced at a cost that is greater than the revenue under the onerous contract (see 3.12.640.40).

EXAMPLE 20 – USING PROVISION FOR ONEROUS CONTRACT – WRITE-DOWN OF INVENTORY

3.12.710.70   Modifying Example 17B, assume that the revenue per train is 80, not 100. G enters into the agreement in the first quarter of 2018 and will produce and deliver one train in each of the next three quarters. G has the following projected revenues and costs measured on a net present value basis for the purpose of calculating the onerous contract provision.

	Q2	Q3	Q4	TOTAL
Revenue per train	80	80	80	240
Projected incremental costs per train	(110)	(95)	(70)	(275)
Projected margin over incremental costs	(30)	(15)	10	(35)

3.12.710.80   An onerous contract provision of 35 is recognised in the first quarter of 2018 when G enters into the contract because the contract is onerous overall. In our view, this provision is available for use as and when it becomes necessary in the second and third quarters to write down to net realisable value the individual trains whose unit cost exceeds the contractual selling price. The provision is used as follows.

	Q2	Q3	Q4
Movement in the onerous contract provision			
Opening balance	(35)	(5)	-
Use of provision to write down inventory	30	5	-
Closing balance	(5)	-	-

3.12.710.90   Therefore, in respect of this contract, G would recognise a loss of 35 in the first quarter of 2018, no gain or loss in the second quarter, a loss of 10 in the third quarter and a profit of 10 in the fourth quarter.

3.12.710.100   In our view, the direct variable operating costs necessary to fulfil an entity's obligations under a contract that cannot be avoided should be included when measuring the provision for an onerous contract. Costs that could be avoided by the entity's future actions or that are not related directly to the contract should not be included.

3.12.710.110   If a finance lease contract is onerous, then the leased asset is evaluated for impairment (see 3.10.110). An onerous contract provision is not recognised. Although the future lease payments under the contract may exceed the carrying amount of the asset because of future finance costs, an onerous contract provision cannot be recognised for future finance costs. Any component of the future lease payments that relates to services provided under the lease are evaluated separately to assess whether they give rise to an onerous contract (see 5.1.30.20).

3.12.710.120   Similarly, in our view if a contract (including an operating lease contract) is onerous, then assets dedicated to the contract, including any capitalised leasehold improvements, should be tested for impairment (see chapter 3.10) before the onerous contract provision is calculated. Therefore, in the case of the airline charter contract discussed in Example 19A, the fact that the operating costs exceed the revenues to be derived from the aircraft is an impairment indicator. Because the aircraft is S's recognised asset, S should test the aircraft for impairment before recognising a provision for an onerous contract. [*IAS 37.69*]

3.12.720   Regulatory liabilities

3.12.720.10   In many countries, utility companies and other entities operating in regulated industries have contractual arrangements with the local regulator to charge a price based on a cost-plus model. When costs incurred are below budget, some arrangements may require the regulated entity to return any 'excess margin' to customers through future price decreases. Under such arrangements, the regulator specifies the reduction in future prices, generally based on conditions set out in the agreement.

EXAMPLE 21 – ACCOUNTING FOR EXCESS MARGINS BY REGULATED ENTITY

3.12.720.20   In 2018, an electricity generator, U, was subject to rate regulation that limits the return on capital to 6%. Actual sales and costs resulted in U earning 8% and U knows that under the terms of its licence agreement it will have to reduce

2019 prices to achieve a target return of 4%. This expected future rate reduction is equal to 750 of 'excess' 2018 revenue.

3.12.720.30   The question is whether a liability for the expected future rate reduction of 750 should be recognised in the 2018 financial statements and, if yes, what type of obligation is being recognised and measured. In our view, when the claw-back of the excess margin is contingent on future activity and sales, U has no contractual obligation to deliver cash to a third party. Therefore, it does not have a financial liability in the scope of IAS 32 and IFRS 9 (see 7.3.30). However, if under the agreement U were required to pay the 750 to the local regulator if it stopped operating, or to another entity if that entity took over U's licence, then the 750 would be considered a financial liability. Further, because the mechanism for 'returning' current-year excess revenue is a reduction in prices on future sales, U does not have a present obligation in the scope of IAS 37 and a provision would be recognised only if U had an onerous contract – i.e. if it were obligated to provide future services at a loss.

3.12.720.40   In our view, in the circumstances described in 3.12.720.20–30, U would also have to consider, in preparing its 2018 financial statements, whether it had satisfied the revenue recognition requirements of IFRS 15 in respect of the 750 of excess revenue. This would include considering whether all of this amount relates to goods and services transferred to customers in 2018, and also whether some or all of the amount represents variable consideration that should be constrained. U would recognise any amounts received that do not satisfy the revenue recognition requirements of IFRS 15 as a contract liability at 31 December 2018.

3.12.720.50   For a discussion of regulatory assets, see 3.3.180.

3.12.720.60   If an entity is a first-time adopter of IFRS after 30 January 2014, then it is permitted to continue accounting for regulatory deferral account balances in accordance with its previous accounting policies. Subsequent to the adoption of IFRS, such balances are in the scope of IFRS 14, and not IAS 37. See chapter 6.2.

3.12.730   Software modification costs

3.12.730.10   When an external event, such as the introduction of a new currency, requires an entity to make a modification of its software in order to continue to operate once the new currency is introduced, the entity does not have a present obligation to modify software. In our view, a provision should not be recognised, because the entity would be able to avoid this expenditure by its future actions. However, an entity should consider whether costs incurred qualify for capitalisation as either property, plant and equipment or an intangible asset. [*IAS 37.19, IE.C.Ex11*]

3.12.730.20   The costs of modifying existing software are recognised as an expense when they are incurred unless they increase the expected utility of the asset and therefore qualify for capitalisation (see 3.3.270). [*IAS 16.12, 38.18*]

3.12.740 **Legal claims**

3.12.740.10   In our view, the relevant past event for a legal claim is the event that gives rise to the claim, rather than receipt of the claim itself. For example, in many jurisdictions a shop owner can be found liable for compensation when customers injure themselves on the shop premises. In such cases, we believe that the relevant past event is the incident, rather than the date on which the customer asserts a claim.

3.12.740.20   However, the mere existence of a present obligation as a result of a past event is not a sufficient basis on which to recognise a provision. In addition, the entity needs to consider whether it is probable that the obligating event will result in an outflow of resources. Such an assessment involves judgement by management on a case-by-case basis, taking into account past experience relating to the pattern of claims arising from any similar events and the circumstances surrounding the particular obligating event. For example, a retail chain may have noted that any claims arising from shop-floor accidents in their stores would typically be lodged within a relatively short period after the accident, indicating that the longer the delay in making such a claim, the less likely it is that the claim will ever be lodged. If a claim has not been lodged and is unlikely to be lodged, then the present obligation is treated as a contingent liability on the basis that it fails to meet the recognition criteria set out in paragraph 14(b) of IAS 37 (see 3.12.30.10). [*IAS 37.23*]

3.12.740.30   The assertion of a claim is not, in our view, determinative evidence that a present obligation exists. Instead, before determining whether a present obligation exists, any claim received will need to be assessed, taking account of all available evidence including, for example, the opinion of experts. [*IAS 37.16*]

3.12.740.40   When it is not clear whether a present obligation exists, management deems a present obligation to exist if, taking account of all available evidence, it is more likely than not that a present obligation exists. For example, if an entity disputes a legal claim but legal opinion advises that the defence will more likely than not be unsuccessful, then the entity would deem a present obligation to exist. Conversely, in our view if legal opinion supports the view that the defence will more likely than not be successful, then the entity should not deem a present obligation to exist. Instead, we believe that in such cases the legal claim gives rise to a contingent liability on the basis that the claim is indicative of a possible obligation. [*IAS 37.15*]

3.12.740.50   In our view, if an entity has been unsuccessful in defending a claim, but intends to appeal against the decision in a higher court, then any original assessment that a present obligation did not exist, and/or that an outflow of resources was not probable in respect of the claim, should be assessed to see whether there is sufficient evidence to support continuing with such a position. In many cases, evidence indicating that the appeal will more likely than not be successful will be lacking, in which case in our view a provision should be recognised based on and at the time of the lower court's ruling, rather than waiting until the outcome of the appeal.

3.12.745 *Legal costs associated with defending legal claims*

3.12.745.10   In our view, if the entity believes that there is no past obligating event, then expected legal costs to be incurred in defending the claim should not be accrued as a provision, even if these expected legal costs are incremental. We believe that the claim is not an obligating event with respect to the future legal costs if there is no past obligating event for the underlying claim. Instead, we believe that in such cases the probable future legal costs are future operating expenses and should be expensed when they are incurred.

3.12.745.15   In contrast, if the entity concludes that there is a past obligating event with respect to the underlying claim, then we believe that any incremental legal costs expected to be incurred in settling the claim should be included in measuring the provision.

3.12.750   Liabilities arising from financial guarantees#

3.12.750.10   Financial guarantee contracts are in the scope of IFRS 9 unless the issuer of the contract has previously explicitly asserted that it regards such contracts as insurance contracts, and has used accounting applicable to insurance contracts; in that case, the issuer may choose to apply either IFRS 9 or IFRS 4 to such contracts (see 7.1.50, 60). Generally, when a financial guarantee contract recognised under IFRS 4 becomes probable of being exercised, then the provision is measured in accordance with IAS 37. However, the remaining elements of this standard – e.g. the disclosure requirements – do not apply. For a discussion of non-financial guarantees for products or services, see 3.12.360. [*IFRS 9.2.1(e)*]

> 3.12.751   FORTHCOMING REQUIREMENTS
>
> 3.12.751.10 If an issuer of a financial guarantee contract accounts for it under IFRS 17, then it recognises and measures the contract in accordance with IFRS 17. [*IFRS 17.7(e)*]

3.12.752   Levies

3.12.752.10   IFRIC 21 provides guidance on determining the obligating event under IAS 37 in connection with a levy imposed by a government. The interpretation also applies to a liability to pay a levy whose timing and amount is certain. However, the guidance in IFRIC 21 is restricted to clarifying when to recognise a liability arising from a levy and other standards are applied to determine whether an asset or expense is recognised as a result. [*IFRIC 21.1–3, IU 01-15*]

3.12.753   *Scope*

3.12.753.10   A 'levy' in the scope of IFRIC 21 is defined as an outflow of resources embodying economic benefits from an entity imposed by a government in accordance with legislation. The following are not included in the scope of IFRIC 21:
- fines or penalties imposed for breaches of legislation;
- outflows in the scope of other standards – e.g. income taxes in the scope of IAS 12;
- payments to a government for purchases of assets or services; and
- amounts collected on behalf of a government and remitted to it– e.g. value added tax. [*IFRIC 21.4–5, BC6–BC8*]

3.12.753.15   In addition, an entity is not required to apply IFRIC 21 to liabilities arising from emission trading schemes (see 3.12.510). For a discussion of taxes levied on employers with respect to employee benefits in the scope of IAS 19, see 4.4.10.50. [*IFRIC 21.6, BC8*]

3.12.753.20   The definition of 'government' in IFRIC 21 is consistent with the one in IAS 20 (see chapter 4.3) and IAS 24 (see 5.5.70.10) and refers to government, government agencies and similar bodies whether local, national or international. [*IFRIC 21.4, BC6*]

3.12.754   *Recognition*

3.12.754.10   Under IFRIC 21, the obligating event that gives rise to a liability is the activity that triggers the payment of the levy in accordance with the legislation. An entity does not recognise a liability at an earlier date even if it has no realistic opportunity to avoid performing the activity that triggers the levy. The fact that an entity will continue operating in the future, and prepares its financial statements on a going concern basis, does not imply that the entity has a present or a constructive obligation to pay a levy that will be triggered by operating in a future period. [*IFRIC 21.8–10*]

3.12.754.20   The timing of liability recognition depends on the specific wording of the relevant legislation. A levy is recognised progressively over a period of time if the activity that triggers the payment of the levy occurs over a period of time. For example, if a levy is triggered by generating revenue over a period of time, then an entity recognises a liability for the levy at the same time as it generates that revenue. Conversely, if a levy is only payable if an entity operates in a specific market on a specified date (e.g. 1 January 2019) or if the entity reaches a specified minimum threshold (e.g. a specified level of revenue) then no liability is recognised until 1 January 2019 or until the minimum threshold is reached. [*IFRIC 21.11–12, IE1.Ex1, IE1.Ex3–IE1.Ex4*]

EXAMPLE 22A – LEVY – REVENUE ABOVE MINIMUM THRESHOLD

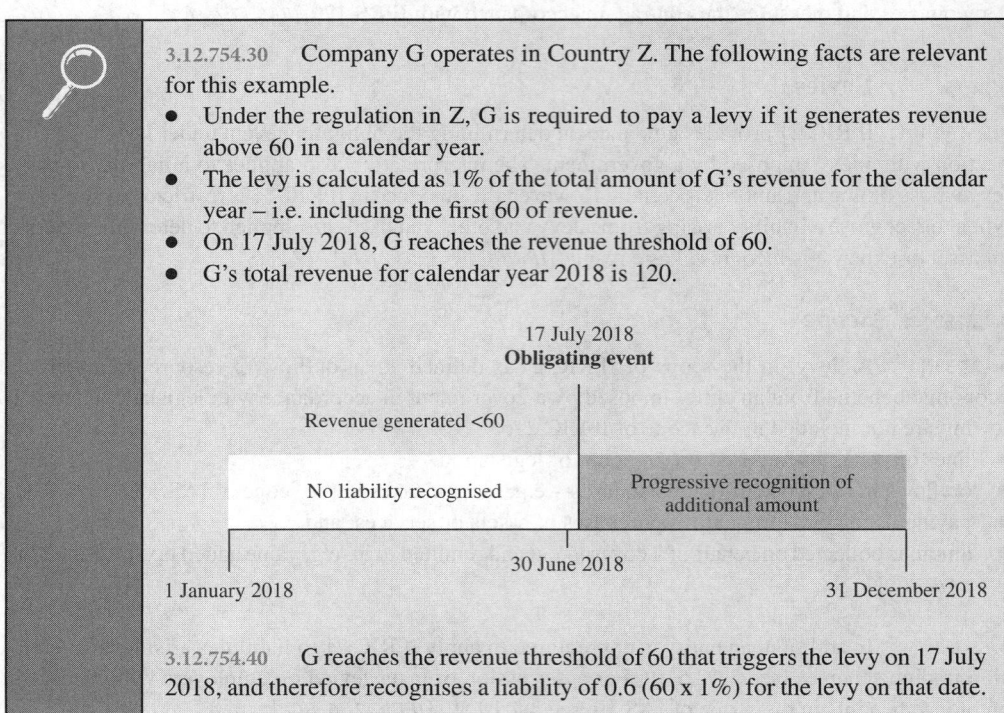

3.12.754.30   Company G operates in Country Z. The following facts are relevant for this example.
- Under the regulation in Z, G is required to pay a levy if it generates revenue above 60 in a calendar year.
- The levy is calculated as 1% of the total amount of G's revenue for the calendar year – i.e. including the first 60 of revenue.
- On 17 July 2018, G reaches the revenue threshold of 60.
- G's total revenue for calendar year 2018 is 120.

17 July 2018
Obligating event

Revenue generated <60

No liability recognised

Progressive recognition of additional amount

30 June 2018

1 January 2018

31 December 2018

3.12.754.40   G reaches the revenue threshold of 60 that triggers the levy on 17 July 2018, and therefore recognises a liability of 0.6 (60 x 1%) for the levy on that date.

Subsequently, G progressively recognises a liability for the levy related to revenue generated above the threshold between 17 July and 31 December 2018. The total liability for the calendar year is 1.2 (120 x 1%). [*IFRIC 21.IE1.Ex4*]

3.12.754.50   The IFRS Interpretations Committee discussed a scenario in which a levy was payable on reaching an annual threshold, which could be reduced pro rata to the respective number of days if the entity started or stopped the relevant activity during the year. The Committee noted that in this scenario an entity would be subject to a threshold that is lower than the threshold that applies at the end of the annual assessment period if, and only if, the entity stops the relevant activity before the end of the annual assessment period. In this case, the obligating event is the reaching of the threshold that applies at the end of the annual assessment period because until then the entity could avoid the payment of the levy by its future actions. The Committee also noted that there is a distinction between a levy with an annual threshold that is reduced pro rata on meeting a specified condition and a levy that is triggered progressively over time. Until the specified condition is met, the pro rata possibility of reduction in the annual threshold does not apply. [*IU 03-14*]

EXAMPLE 22B – LEVY – ANNUAL THRESHOLD THAT MAY BE REDUCED

3.12.754.60   Company G operates in Country Z. Under the regulation in Country Z, G is required to pay a levy if its revenue from activity B exceeds a threshold of 60 in a calendar year. If G stops activity B at any point in time, then the threshold is reduced pro rata to the actual number of days that G performed activity B during that calendar year. The levy is calculated as 1% of the total amount of G's revenue from activity B for the calendar year.

3.12.754.70   In the first quarter of 2018, G generates revenue of 20 from activity B. On 31 March 2018, G stops performing activity B in a manner that triggers the pro rata threshold assessment under the regulation. The pro rata threshold for the levy in 2018 is 15 (60 x 90 / 365). Because G's revenue from activity B exceeds the pro rata threshold of 15, G recognises a liability for the levy of 0.2 (20 x 1%) on 31 March 2018. However, if G had not ceased performing activity B, then no provision would be recorded until the annual revenue exceeded 60.

3.12.754.80   In some cases, a levy is payable only if multiple conditions or thresholds are met – e.g. some conditions may be determined at the entity level and some involve all entities operating in the same industry in a country meeting a specified threshold in aggregate. In our view, in these cases the obligating event occurs when the *last* condition (threshold) of all conditions (thresholds) in accordance with the legislation is met.

3.12.754.90   The same recognition principles apply in the annual and in the interim financial statements. An entity recognises a liability in the interim financial statements if a present obligation exists at the interim reporting date and does not recognise a liability if the obligating event has not yet occurred. This may result in uneven charges over the course of the year. [*IFRIC 21.13, BC29*]

3.12.755 **Tax exposures**

3.12.760 *Income tax#*

3.12.760.10   In our view, obligations for possible income tax exposures should be treated as current tax liabilities, and not provisions (see 3.13.660).

3.12.760.20   Interest and penalties related to income tax exposures are not explicitly included in the scope of IAS 12. The IFRS Interpretations Committee discussed the accounting for interest and penalties related to income taxes and noted that an entity first considers whether the interest or penalty is itself an income tax. If so, then it applies IAS 12. If the entity does not apply IAS 12, then it applies IAS 37 to that amount. The Committee also noted that this is not an accounting policy choice – i.e. an entity needs to apply judgement based on the specific facts and circumstances (see 3.13.45).

3.12.760.25   If an entity applies IAS 37, then it recognises a provision for the best estimate of interest and penalties payable related to previous tax years, if there is a probable outflow of resources and the amount can be estimated reliably. The provision is discounted if the effect of discounting is material. The interest and penalties will then be presented as other provisions (liabilities) in the statement of financial position and as interest and operating expenses respectively in the statement of profit or loss and OCI. For further discussion of income tax exposures, see 3.13.660. [*IAS 12.2, IU 09-17*]

3.12.760.30   In some countries, entities are subject to taxes that are calculated as a percentage of net revenues less certain specified costs. The list of deductible costs varies depending on the country. Although IAS 12 defines the taxable profit as a profit or loss for a period, determined in accordance with the rules established by taxation authorities, on which income taxes are payable, in some cases it may be difficult to determine whether a taxable amount is a 'taxable profit', and therefore whether a tax is an income tax in the scope of IAS 12. In our view, this determination should be based on the facts and circumstances of the particular case, including among other factors the relative significance of the deductions (see 3.13.40).

3.12.763   **FORTHCOMING REQUIREMENTS**

3.12.763.10   IFRIC 23 applies to current and deferred taxes if there is uncertainty about an income tax treatment, but does not address the accounting for the related interest or penalties. The guidance in IFRIC 23 is consistent with the guidance in 3.12.760.10. For further discussion of IFRIC 23, see 3.13.665. [*IFRIC 23.4*]

3.12.765   *Taxes related to share-based payment transactions*

3.12.765.10   For a discussion of the taxes related to share-based payment transactions, see 3.13.790 and 4.5.2070.

3.12.770   **PRESENTATION AND DISCLOSURES**

3.12.770.10   Provisions are disclosed as a separate line item in the statement of financial position. Provisions that will be used within one year or within an entity's normal operating cycle are classified as current liabilities, unless an entity presents its assets and liabilities in the statement of financial position in the order of liquidity when such a presentation provides information that is reliable and more relevant (see 3.1.10). [*IAS 1.54, 60, 70, 30A–31*]

3.12.780 Classes of provisions

3.12.780.10   Each class of provision is disclosed separately. The extent of disaggregation that is required will depend on the significance and nature of the individual provisions. Categories of provisions that are generally disclosed separately include provisions for:

- litigation;
- warranties;
- environmental obligations;
- onerous contracts; and
- restructuring costs. [*IAS 37.87*]

3.12.790 Movements schedule

3.12.790.10   Movements in each class of provision during the reporting period are disclosed. Comparative period information is not required. [*IAS 37.84*]

3.12.790.20   All movements are disclosed separately on a gross basis. Amounts that are reversed or used during the period may not be netted off against additional provisions recognised during the period. For example, if the provision for litigation for some matters has increased, but for others has decreased, then the gross amounts of the increases and decreases are shown.

3.12.800 Description of provisions

3.12.800.10   An entity discloses the following for each class of provision:

- a brief description of the nature of provisions and the expected timing of the outflows;
- an indication of the uncertainties and assumptions made in measuring the provisions; and
- the amount of any expected reimbursement, stating the amount of any asset that has been recognised for that expected reimbursement. [*IAS 37.85*]

3.12.800.15   An entity discloses the major assumptions concerning future events in accordance with paragraph 48 of IAS 37 if it is necessary to provide adequate information. The disclosure of uncertainties may be general in nature. In our view, for a legal claim it would normally be sufficient to say that the outcome depends on court proceedings. [*IAS 37.48, 85*]

3.12.800.20   However, an entity also considers the requirement to disclose key assumptions about the future, and other sources of estimation uncertainty that have a significant risk of causing a material adjustment to the carrying amounts of assets and liabilities within the next annual reporting period. [*IAS 1.125*]

3.12.800.30   Comparative information is included in the narrative information if it is relevant to an understanding of the current period's financial statements. For example, if a provision for a matter was made in a previous reporting period, then it may be useful for users of the financial statements to be given comparative narrative information to put the provision in its proper context. [*IAS 1.38*]

3.12.810   Disclosure exemption

3.12.810.10   There is an exemption from the disclosure requirements for provisions in extremely rare cases if providing the disclosure would seriously prejudice a dispute. For example, this exemption may apply to pending litigation, disputes with tax authorities (see 3.12.752 and 755) and claims subject to arbitration. [*IAS 37.92, 12.88*]

3.12.810.20   The exemption applies only to the disclosures required by IAS 37 and not to disclosures that may be required by other standards – e.g. disclosures about income tax liabilities or related party transactions.

3.12.810.30   The exemption would not often apply in consolidated financial statements because, for example, disclosure of litigation provisions is generally made in aggregate and as such it is unlikely that the disclosure would harm the entity's position in any one case.

3.12.820   Presentation of onerous contract provisions

3.12.820.10   In our view, when an entity has an onerous contract, any provision recognised should be presented as a liability. It should not be netted against the carrying amount of any related assets. [*IAS 1.32*]

3.12.830   Environmental and similar funds

3.12.830.10   A fund that is established to finance the costs associated with a provision is not offset against the related provision. Therefore, the operator recognises an obligation for decommissioning as a provision and recognises its interest in the fund as a separate asset, unless the fund relieves the contributor of its obligation to pay decommissioning costs (see 3.12.500). [*IFRIC 5.7*]

3.12.840   Effects of discounting

3.12.840.10   The unwinding of the discount on decommissioning or restoration provisions is not a qualifying borrowing cost that can be capitalised. In our view, the same applies to all imputed interest on non-financial liabilities, unless they represent a borrowing of funds (see 4.6.90). [*IAS 37.60, IFRIC 1.8*]

3.12.850   Reversals and other changes in estimate

3.12.850.10   A reversal of a provision is a change in estimate (see 2.8.100). Therefore, in our view the reversal should be presented in the same line item of the statement of profit or loss as the original estimate. For example, changes in provisions, whether they are additional amounts (debits) or reductions in amounts previously charged (credits), should be presented in distribution expenses if the original estimate was recorded in that classification. However, in some instances – e.g. on the basis of the size and incidence of the change in estimate – we believe that the effect of a reversal may be presented in other income (see 4.1.180 and 80).

3.12.850.20   Reversals of provisions are disclosed separately. Significant reversals of provisions may raise questions about the reliability of management estimates and need to be explained in the notes to the financial statements; this disclosure may also be required because of the size or incidence of the reversal. [*IAS 37.84(d), 1.98(g)*]

3.12.860   Reserves for general business risks

3.12.860.10   A provision cannot be recognised for costs associated with the risk of future losses. If an entity wishes to reflect risks not covered by provisions in the financial statements, then in our view it may establish a separate component of shareholders' equity – e.g. a non-distributable reserve – depending on the shareholders' approval, as may be required by the articles of incorporation or law. Amounts may be transferred to this reserve directly from retained earnings or from another category of equity. Any such transfers would be disclosed as part of the movements in equity (see 7.3.660).

3.12.870   Restructuring provisions

3.12.870.10   An issue often arises over whether restructuring costs may be presented as a separate line item in the statement of profit or loss and OCI, particularly when expenditure is classified according to its function. For a detailed discussion of this issue, see 4.1.70.

3.12.875   Contingent liabilities

3.12.875.10   Contingent liabilities are disclosed unless the likelihood of an outflow of resources embodying economic benefits is remote. Disclosures include a brief description of the nature of the contingency and, when this is practicable, the estimated financial effect, an indication of the uncertainties and the possibility of any reimbursement. When disclosure is impracticable, that fact is stated. [*IAS 37.86, 91*]

3.12.875.20   The type of information that is disclosed in respect of a contingent liability related to a legal claim includes:

- an explanation of the claim;
- the fact that no liability has been recognised;
- an explanation of why the entity does not accept liability under the claim;
- information about the estimated amount of the liability or an explanation of why this cannot be estimated reasonably; and
- information about any reimbursements that may be claimed if the defence is not successful – e.g. amounts that are reimbursable under an insurance policy.

3.12.875.30   In the extremely rare case that disclosure could seriously prejudice the entity's position in a dispute with another party, the entity need only disclose the general nature of the dispute and the reasons for not disclosing the information. The discussion in 3.12.810 applies equally to contingent liabilities. [*IAS 37.92*]

3.12.875.40   If crystallisation of a contingent liability would affect an entity's ability to continue as a going concern, then additional disclosures are required. [*IAS 1.25*]

3.12.876   Contingent assets

3.12.876.10   Contingent assets are disclosed when an inflow of economic benefits is considered more likely than not to occur. The disclosure includes the nature and, when it is practicable, the estimated financial effects of the contingent asset. When disclosure is impracticable, that fact is stated. The disclosures about contingent assets need to avoid giving misleading indications of the likelihood of income arising. [*IAS 37.89–91*]

3.12.876.20   Consistent with contingent liabilities, in the extremely rare case that disclosure of a contingent asset could seriously prejudice the entity's position in a dispute with another party, the entity need only disclose the general nature of the dispute and the reasons for not disclosing the information. [*IAS 37.92*]

3.12.880   **FUTURE DEVELOPMENTS**

3.12.880.10   The IFRS Interpretations Committee discussed how to account for loss-making contracts that were previously accounted for under IAS 11, after IFRS 15 becomes effective. In particular, which costs should be considered in assessing whether a contract is onerous under IAS 37. The Committee noted that an entity applies IAS 37 to assess whether a contract with a customer is onerous and cannot apply the previous requirements in IAS 11 on contract costs or the requirements in IFRS 15 on costs that relate directly to a contract. The Committee also discussed how the term 'unavoidable costs' should be interpreted – i.e. which costs should be taken into account when assessing whether a contract is onerous. It decided to develop a narrow-scope amendment to IAS 37 to clarify the meaning of 'unavoidable costs'. The forthcoming amendments may affect the guidance in 3.12.660.

3.12.880.20   The IFRS Interpretations Committee discussed whether a payment made on a disputed amount (e.g. a levy in the scope of IAS 37) meets the definition of an asset in the Conceptual Framework – i.e. it is a present economic resource controlled by the entity as a result of a past event. In these cases, the existence of the liability may not be probable and will be confirmed only on resolution of the dispute. The Committee noted that the payment meets the definition of an asset because it has the potential to produce economic benefits: if the entity wins the case it will recover the payment from the tax authority; if it loses the case, then the payment will be used to settle the liability. The Committee also noted that the payment is not a contingent asset, as defined in IAS 37, because it is an existing and not a possible asset. [*CF 4.3*]

3.13   Income taxes

CURRENTLY EFFECTIVE REQUIREMENTS

This publication reflects IFRS in issue at 1 August 2018, and the currently effective requirements cover annual periods beginning on 1 January 2018.

The requirements related to this topic are mainly derived from the following.

STANDARD	TITLE
IAS 12	Income Taxes
SIC-25	Income Taxes – Changes in the Tax Status of an Entity or its Shareholders

FORTHCOMING REQUIREMENTS

The currently effective requirements are affected by the following forthcoming requirements. They are highlighted with a # and the impact is explained in the accompanying boxed text at the references indicated.

- In June 2017, the IASB issued IFRIC 23 *Uncertainty over Income Tax Treatments*, which is effective for annual periods beginning on or after 1 January 2019. See 3.13.665.
- In December 2017, the IASB issued *Annual Improvements to IFRSs 2015–2017 Cycle – Amendments to IAS 12,* which is effective for annual periods beginning on or after 1 January 2019. See 3.13.775.

FUTURE DEVELOPMENTS

The currently effective requirements that may be affected by future developments are highlighted with a * and are briefly discussed in 3.13.1270.

3.13.10 OVERVIEW

3.13.10.10   The diagram below is a general step-by-step illustration of the considerations required in determining the accounting for income taxes. These steps are discussed in more detail in the rest of this chapter.

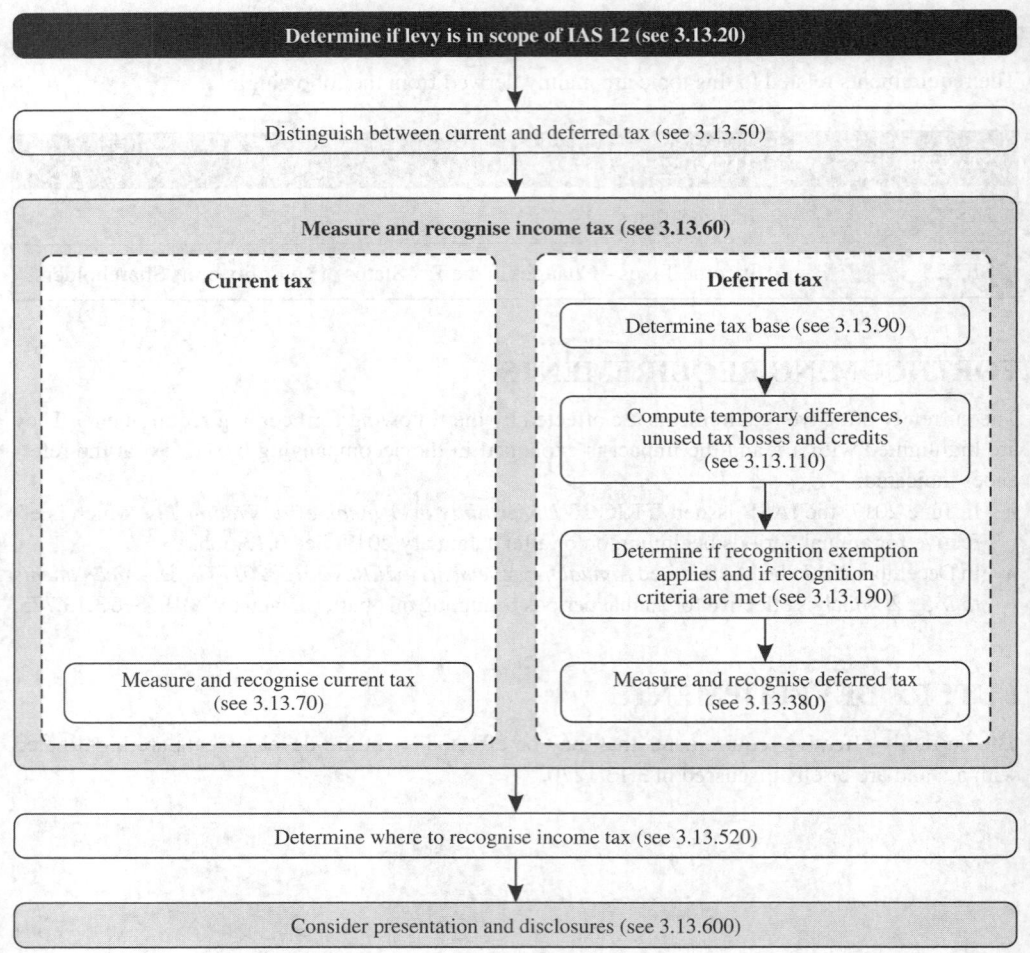

3.13.20 DETERMINE IF A LEVY IS IN SCOPE OF IAS 12

3.13.30 General principles

3.13.30.10   The scope of IAS 12 is limited to:

- income taxes, which are taxes based on taxable profits; and
- taxes (e.g. withholding taxes) that are payable by a subsidiary, associate or joint arrangement on distribution to the reporting entity. [*IAS 12.2*]

3.13.30.20   Taxable profit (tax loss) for a period is determined in accordance with the rules established by the taxation authorities, on which income taxes are payable (recoverable). [*IAS 12.5*]

3.13.30.30   Taxes that are not based on taxable profits are not in the scope of IAS 12. Examples include:
- social security taxes payable by an employer based on a percentage of employees' wages, which may be employee benefits (see chapter 4.4);
- taxes payable on capital and reserves; and
- levies imposed by a government that are in the scope of IFRIC 21 (see 3.12.752).

3.13.30.40   In our view, taxes that are not income taxes should generally be accounted for as provisions (see chapter 3.12) or as financial liabilities (see chapter 7.3), as appropriate. [*IAS 12.1–2, IU 03–06*]

3.13.30.50   The following are also excluded from the scope of IAS 12:
- government grants (see chapter 4.3); and
- investment tax credits (ITCs); however, for a discussion of the accounting for ITCs, including the application of IAS 12 by analogy, see 3.13.670. [*IAS 12.4*]

3.13.40   Taxable profit

3.13.40.10   Because taxable profit is determined in accordance with rules established by tax authorities, it is not necessarily the same as accounting profit. Taxes do not need to be based on a figure that is exactly accounting profit to be in the scope of the standard. However, the term 'taxable profit' implies that taxes in the scope of IAS 12 are levied on a net rather than on a gross amount. The IFRS Interpretations Committee discussed this issue and noted that taxes are not in the scope of IAS 12 if they are based on, for example:
- revenue (a gross figure);
- a fixed amount per unit of production; or
- notional income derived from tonnage capacity (see 3.10.850). [*IU 03-06, 05-09*]

3.13.40.20   In some cases, it is not clear whether a tax is based on taxable profit.

EXAMPLE 1A – SCOPE – SECONDARY TAX ON DIVIDENDS PAID TO SHAREHOLDERS

3.13.40.30   Companies in Country X pay a secondary tax on dividends paid to shareholders; the tax is levied on the company paying dividends and is not a shareholder withholding tax. The introduction of the secondary tax was accompanied by a reduction in the corporate income tax rate.

3.13.40.40   In our view, the secondary tax is in substance an income tax in the scope of IAS 12, because it taxes profits, even though the timing of the payment is linked to the payment of dividends (see 3.13.770). [*IAS 12.52B*]

EXAMPLE 1B – SCOPE – INCOME TAX ONLY PAYABLE IF PROFITS DISTRIBUTED

3.13.40.50   Companies in Country F pay a tax levied on (1) dividends paid out of profits to natural persons and non-residents, and on (2) certain other payments,

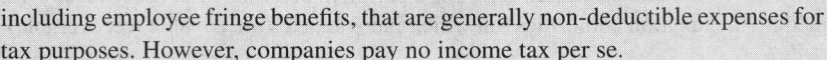

including employee fringe benefits, that are generally non-deductible expenses for tax purposes. However, companies pay no income tax per se.

3.13.40.60   Country F's tax system is an extreme example of a dual income tax rate system in the scope of IAS 12: it has a zero tax rate on undistributed taxable income, and a higher rate on distributed income. For further discussion of the tax consequences of dividends, see 3.13.70.30 and 770.

EXAMPLE 1C – SCOPE – TAX BASED ON EXCESS OF SELLING PRICE OVER SPECIFIED COSTS

3.13.40.70   Country Z levies value appreciation taxes on transfers of real estate. The tax is calculated based on a net amount, which is the excess of the selling price over specified costs – e.g. acquisition and development costs, financial and administrative expenses. In our view, such taxes are in the scope of IAS 12, because they are levied on a net amount.

EXAMPLE 1D – SCOPE – TAX BASED ON ASSESSED VALUE

3.13.40.80   Disposals of real estate in Country X are exempt from income tax. Instead, tax is levied on an amount calculated as the excess of:
- the assessed value at the time of disposal; over
- the assessed value at the time of acquisition plus improvement costs.

3.13.40.90   The assessed value for tax purposes is not the selling price but a value determined by tax authorities based on an index that does not entirely represent its fair value.

3.13.40.100   In our view, such a tax is still in the scope of IAS 12, because:
- the assessed value is close to, or has a relationship with, the proceeds from the disposal; and
- the tax is levied on a net amount.

EXAMPLE 1E – SCOPE – STATUTORY EMPLOYEE PROFIT-SHARING PLAN

3.13.40.110   Country Y has a statutory employee profit-sharing tax law under which a company has to share 10% of its taxable profit with its employees. Amounts to be paid to employees are calculated in accordance with the tax law.

3.13.40.120   The IFRS Interpretations Committee discussed this scenario and noted that this arrangement meets the definition of an employee benefit and is in the scope of IAS 19 (see 4.4.1270.40–50). Therefore, such an employee profit-sharing arrangement cannot be accounted for by analogy to IAS 12. [*IU 11-10*]

EXAMPLE 1F – SCOPE – TAXES PAYABLE BY AN ENTITY IN RESPECT OF REIMBURSEMENTS FROM A PLAN

3.13.40.123   Company F in Country Z sets up Fund X to fund its post-employment benefit plan. Under the arrangement, F makes payments for benefits to employees on behalf of the plan (advance payments) and subsequently receives reimbursements for these payments from X. For accounting purposes, the reimbursements are recorded as a settlement of advance payments in the statement of financial position – i.e. no income is recognised in the statement of profit or loss and OCI. For tax purposes, under Country Z's tax law:
- the reimbursements represent taxable income and are treated similarly to any other of F's investment income; and
- the advance payments do not impact taxable income because the tax deductions are received when the provision for the defined benefit obligations is recognised.

3.13.40.124   Unlike taxes payable by a plan (see 4.4.990), the accounting for taxes payable by the entity in respect of taxable income from the plan is not specifically addressed in IFRS. Therefore, F applies judgement to determine whether the amount of tax arising in relation to reimbursements is an income tax in the scope of IAS 12, a liability in the scope of IAS 37, or a cost of employee benefits in the scope of IAS 19 (see 4.4.1000.10).

3.13.40.125   F considers that under Country Z's tax law there is no separate tax regime for reimbursements. The reimbursement forms part of F's regular tax return and is treated as F's taxable income in its income tax calculation – i.e. the taxable income from the reimbursement can be reduced by any tax-deductible expenses. For example, if F's net result before income from reimbursements is a loss, then the income from reimbursement is offset against the loss. Based on this analysis, F concludes that the tax on the reimbursement is an income tax in the scope of IAS 12.

3.13.40.130   A variety of complex tax regulations are created by different tax authorities. Under these regulations, levies are not calculated based on taxable profit. Instead, the levies may take the form of royalties, extraction taxes and corporate taxes, or a combination thereof.

3.13.40.140   These types of levies are particularly prevalent in the extractive industries. For example, levies may be based on a percentage of 'operating profit' as determined on a mine-by-mine, field-by-field, ship-by-ship or other basis, after allowing for the deduction of certain expenses. To determine whether a levy or a tax is based on taxable profit, an entity considers the factors outlined in 3.13.40.10.

EXAMPLE 1G – SCOPE – MINING RIGHT ROYALTY

3.13.40.145   In Country M, companies that hold mining concessions are subject to a special mining right royalty calculated as 8% of profit from extractive activities after adding back depreciation of mining assets. The mining right royalty is based on monetary income from extractive activities, rather than on physical quantities,

and it is calculated based on the actual rather than a notional figure. The mining concession holders are also subject to a regular income tax of 30%, similar to other companies in M.

3.13.40.147   The special mining right royalty in this example is in the scope of IAS 12 because it is levied on a net amount (see 3.13.40.10). For a discussion of whether the initial recognition exemption applies on the introduction of such a mining right royalty to existing assets, see 3.13.215.

3.13.40.150   An entity assesses whether a levy is in the scope of IAS 12 based on its terms and conditions, which has consequences for recognition, measurement, presentation and disclosure. This assessment considers all facts and circumstances of each particular levy and may require judgement. For example, the definition of an obligating event under IAS 37 and further guidance in IFRIC 21 may lead to a levy being recognised earlier under IAS 12 than if it is accounted for under IAS 37 (see 3.12.754). In any event, the classification of items such as a levy is not an accounting policy choice. Therefore, an entity operating in multiple jurisdictions, or even in a single jurisdiction under multiple regulations with different terms, may have to recognise, measure and classify each tax differently. For further discussion of taxes that are not in the scope of IAS 12, see 3.12.760.30.

3.13.40.160   In some jurisdictions, entities are subject to a levy that is made up of two components (a 'hybrid tax'). One component may be calculated based on a gross amount such as revenues, while the other component may be calculated based on a net amount such as taxable profits. One of the components may be specified in the tax legislation as the 'minimum tax'. The objective is often to provide the tax authority with a minimum amount of revenue.

3.13.40.170   IFRS does not specifically address the accounting for a hybrid tax. In our view, irrespective of how a component is described or characterised in the tax legislation, an entity should choose an accounting policy, to be applied consistently, to do either of the following.
- Designate the component that is based on a gross amount as the minimum tax and recognise this minimum tax as an operating expense. Any excess over the minimum amount then is recognised as a current income tax expense in the scope of IAS 12.
- Designate the component that is based on a net amount as the minimum tax and recognise the amount resulting from the component that is calculated based on a net amount as a current income tax expense in the scope of IAS 12. Any excess over the minimum amount is then recognised as an operating expense.

EXAMPLE 2 – HYBRID TAX

3.13.40.180   Company X is subject to a statutory income tax rate of 30%; however, a minimum amount calculated at 2% of revenue is payable each year.

3.13.40.190   This example highlights the accounting policy choice in 3.13.40.170 based on two scenarios.
- In Scenario 1, the tax payable is based on revenue because this is the higher amount.

- In Scenario 2, the tax payable is based on taxable profit because this is the higher amount.

	SCENARIO 1	SCENARIO 2
Revenue	10,000	10,000
Expenses	(9,800)	(8,000)
Taxable profit	200	2,000
30% tax based on taxable profit	60	600
Minimum tax (2% of revenue)	200	200
Amount payable	200	600
Accounting policy choice 1: Designate the gross component as the minimum tax (operating expense)		
Operating expense	200	200
Income tax	-	400
Total	200	600
Accounting policy choice 2: Designate the net component as the minimum tax (income tax)		
Operating expense	140	-
Income tax	60	600
Total	200	600

3.13.40.200 Under the first accounting policy choice, the minimum tax of 200 is included in operating expense in both scenarios. In Scenario 1, income tax expense is zero because the minimum tax (200) exceeds the amount based on taxable income (60). In Scenario 2, income tax expense is 400 – i.e. the amount exceeding the minimum tax.

3.13.40.210 Under the second accounting policy choice, the income tax expense is 60 in Scenario 1 and 600 in Scenario 2.
- In Scenario 1, an amount of 140 is included in operating expense (200 minimum tax minus 60 recognised as income tax expense).
- In Scenario 2, no amount is presented as an operating expense, because the amount based on taxable profit exceeds the minimum tax.

3.13.40.220 The alternative accounting policies in 3.13.40.170 have different implications for determining deferred taxes.

3.13.40.230 Hybrid taxes do not include income taxes whereby a prepayment based on a gross amount is initially levied but the final liability is always adjusted to one based on a net amount. Such taxes are generally wholly in the scope of IAS 12.

3.13.45 Interest and penalties

3.13.45.10   Interest and penalties related to income taxes are not explicitly included in the scope of IAS 12. The IFRS Interpretations Committee discussed the accounting for interest and penalties related to income taxes and noted that an entity first considers whether interest or a penalty is itself an income tax (see 3.13.40). If so, then it applies IAS 12. If the entity does not apply IAS 12, then it applies IAS 37 to that amount (see 3.12.760.20). The Committee also noted that this is not an accounting policy choice. For a discussion of presentation of interest and penalties related to income taxes, see 3.13.610.15. [*IU 09-17*]

3.13.45.20   In our view, an entity should apply judgement, based on the specific facts and circumstances, including the substance of the tax legislation and the process of negotiation with the tax authorities in a specific jurisdiction, to determine whether interest or a penalty related to a particular income tax treatment, in its nature:

- is a separately identifiable financing charge or an operating expense, and therefore is *not an income tax* – e.g. when the interest and/or penalties arise because an entity underpays or overpays its income tax bill, whether deliberately to manage its cash flows, similar to its financing decisions in relation to any other settlement, or through oversight; or
- forms part of the tax treatment and therefore is itself *an income tax* – e.g. when an entity negotiates with tax authorities a single amount payable in relation to an uncertain tax treatment, including the interest and penalties charge.

3.13.50 DISTINGUISH BETWEEN CURRENT AND DEFERRED TAXES

3.13.50.10   Current tax is the amount of income taxes payable (recoverable) in respect of the taxable profit (loss) for a period. A current tax liability (asset) is recognised for income tax payable (paid but recoverable) in respect of all periods to date. [*IAS 12.5, 12*]

3.13.50.20   Deferred tax is the amount of income tax payable (recoverable) in future periods as a result of past transactions or events. The *Objective* of IAS 12 notes that it is inherent in the recognition of an asset or a liability that the entity expects to recover or settle the carrying amount of that asset or liability. If it is probable that recovery or settlement of that carrying amount will make future tax payments larger (smaller) than they would be if such recovery or settlement were to have no tax consequences, then the entity recognises a deferred tax liability (deferred tax asset), with certain limited exceptions. [*IAS 12.5*]

EXAMPLE 3 – CURRENT VS DEFERRED TAXES

3.13.50.30   Company X is subject to the tax rules in Country Y. Taxable profit in Country Y is determined in the same manner as accounting profit except for the treatment of property, plant and equipment. The following facts are also relevant for this example.
- For tax purposes, the cost of property, plant and equipment is fully deductible in the year of acquisition.
- For accounting purposes, such property, plant and equipment is depreciated on a straight-line basis over the estimated useful life of three years.

- X acquired an item of property, plant and equipment for 300 at the beginning of year 1 and did not acquire further property, plant and equipment in years 2 and 3.
- The income tax rate is 20%.

3.13.50.40   Extracts from X's statements of financial position and statements of profit or loss and OCI for years 1 to 3, prepared in accordance with IFRS and the applicable tax laws respectively, are set out below; for simplicity, tax balances are not shown in the statements of financial position.

	ACCOUNTING BASIS			TAX BASIS		
	YR 1	YR 2	YR 3	YR 1	YR 2	YR 3
Statement of financial position as at 31 December (extracts)						
Other net assets	1,000	1,330	1,710	1,000	1,330	1,710
Property, plant and equipment	200	100	-	-	-	-
Total net assets	1,200	1,430	1,710	1,000	1,330	1,710
Statement of profit or loss and OCI for the year ended 31 December (extracts)						
Profit before depreciation and tax	350	330	380	350	330	380
Depreciation	(100)	(100)	(100)	(300)	-	-
Profit before tax	250	230	280			
Taxable profit				50	330	380
Income tax expense on taxable profit for the year (20%)				10	66	76

3.13.50.50   As shown above, X is liable to pay income tax of 10 in respect of taxable profit in year 1, 66 in respect of taxable profit in year 2, and 76 in respect of taxable profit in year 3. These amounts are current tax for the respective years.

3.13.50.60   Although the statutory income tax rate remains unchanged throughout the period, the relationship between X's current tax expense and the accounting profit before tax is inconsistent, as illustrated below.

	Yr 1	Yr 2	Yr 3
Current tax expense for the year	10	66	76
Profit before tax	250	230	280
Effective tax rate	4%	29%	27%

3.13.50.70   The above table illustrates the tax impact of the mismatch in the recognition of income and expenses for accounting and tax purposes. As a result, although X's financial statements reflect the income tax payable as assessed for the current period, they do not fully reflect the future tax consequences of the property, plant and equipment recognised in the financial statements. Because the carrying amount of property, plant and equipment for accounting purposes exceeds the corresponding carrying amount for tax purposes, it is likely that the amount of future economic benefits that will be taxable when the asset is recovered will exceed the amount that will be deductible for tax purposes, making X's future tax payments larger than they would be if the recovery were to have no tax consequences.

3.13.50.80   To resolve this mismatch and to fully reflect the future tax consequences, deferred tax is recognised for the tax effect of the difference between the carrying amounts of the property, plant and equipment for accounting and for tax purposes, as illustrated below.

	Carrying amounts		Difference between carrying amounts[1]	Tax effect of difference	Change in tax effect of difference
	Accounting basis	Tax basis			
	(A)	(B)	(C) = (A)-(B)	(D) = (C) x 20%	(E)
Year 1	200	-	200	40	40
Year 2	100	-	100	20	(20)
Year 3	-	-	-	-	(20)

Note
1.   Only differences that will lead to a higher (lower) tax payment in future periods are considered.

3.13.50.90   The difference between the carrying amounts of the asset for accounting and for tax purposes of 200 (200 - 0) will result in a higher tax payable in future periods when the carrying amount of the asset is recovered, because the future economic benefits that will be taxable as the asset is recovered in the future will no longer come with any corresponding tax deduction. Accordingly, the tax effect of this difference of 40 (200 x 20%) is recognised in year 1 as a deferred tax liability to reflect the fact that the asset has been fully deducted for tax purposes during that year.

3.13.50.100   Because the difference between the carrying amount of the asset for accounting and for tax purposes is reduced during the useful life of the asset, the amount of the deferred tax liability also reduces. As illustrated in the following table, the accounting for deferred tax seeks to resolve the mismatch in the recognition of income and expenses for accounting and for tax purposes and to restore the relationship between X's tax expense and its accounting profit before tax.

	YR 1	YR 2	YR 3
Current tax expense for the year	10	66	76
Deferred tax expense (income)	40	(20)	(20)
Total income tax charge	50	46	56
Profit before tax	250	230	280
Effective tax rate	20%	20%	20%

3.13.60   MEASURE AND RECOGNISE INCOME TAX

3.13.60.10   Although the recognition and measurement requirements for current and deferred tax share some similarities, there are some important differences. These differences generally arise because of the different nature of the taxes.

3.13.70   CURRENT TAX

3.13.70.10   A current tax liability (asset) is recognised for income tax payable (paid but recoverable) in respect of all periods to date. [*IAS 12.12*]

3.13.70.20   The measurement of current tax liabilities and assets is based on tax law that is enacted or substantively enacted by the reporting date. Although in certain circumstances, this may include announcements of future changes; in general, the effects of future changes in tax laws or rates are not anticipated (see 3.13.480). [*IAS 12.46*]

3.13.70.30   Current tax liabilities (assets) are generally measured at the amount expected to be paid (recovered). However, any income tax consequences of dividends on the tax rates are recognised when a liability to pay the dividend is recognised (see 3.13.770). [*IAS 12.46, 52A–52B*]

3.13.70.40   In some tax jurisdictions, entities are able to negotiate the payment of large tax balances. This means that the payment of amounts that would ordinarily be settled within 12 months under the tax legislation is deferred. Typically, an entity negotiates a series of payments with the tax authorities. If the restructured tax liability does not bear interest at a market rate, then an issue arises about whether the liability should be discounted to net present value at the date on which the terms of payment are agreed. In our view, an entity should discount restructured tax liabilities by analogy to the treatment in IFRS 9 (see 7.7.80). The same rationale applies to current tax receivables of an entity with deferred payment terms. Conversely, deferred tax amounts are not discounted (see 3.13.510.10). [*IFRS 9.B5.1.1–B5.1.2, 12.53, IU 06-04*]

3.13.70.50   Actual taxes payable (receivable) might differ from the amounts recognised as current tax liabilities (assets). Such adjustments reflect changes in the estimated amounts to be paid to (recovered from) the tax authorities. These changes could arise in the course of an entity finalising its tax position for prior years. Unless there is an indication that the adjustment is the result of an error, such changes to current tax are treated as a change in estimate. They are recognised in the tax expense (income) of the period in which the adjustment occurs (see chapter 2.8); this results in a separately disclosed component of tax expense (income) and a reconciling item in the explanation of the relationship between tax expense (income) and accounting profit in the notes. [*IAS 12.80(b), 81(c)*]

3.13.80   DEFERRED TAX

3.13.80.10   Deferred tax is recognised for the estimated future tax effects of temporary differences (see 3.13.110.10), unused tax losses carried forward and unused tax credits carried forward. Adjustments to deferred taxes are accounted for retrospectively only if there is an indication that they are a result of an error, similar to current taxes (see 3.13.70.50). [*IAS 12.5*]

3.13.90   DETERMINE TAX BASE

3.13.90.10   The tax base of an asset or a liability is the amount attributed to that asset or liability for tax purposes. The tax base of an asset is the amount that will be deductible for tax purposes against any taxable economic benefits that will flow to the entity when it recovers the carrying amount of the asset. The tax base of a liability is its carrying amount, less any amount that will be deductible for tax purposes in future periods. Some items have a tax base even though they are not recognised as assets or liabilities (see 3.13.120). [*IAS 12.5, 7–9*]

3.13.90.20   In our view, in determining the tax base of an asset or a liability, an entity should not carry out an assessment of how probable it is that the respective amounts will ultimately be deducted or taxed (see 3.13.320.30). Instead, the probability assessment is part of the analysis required for the recognition of deferred tax assets (see 3.13.330.10). [*IAS 12.5, 7–8, 24*]

EXAMPLE 4A – DETERMINE TAX BASE – LOSSES EXPECTED FOR FORESEEABLE FUTURE

3.13.90.30   Tax law allows Company T to deduct the acquisition cost of an asset of 150 from taxable profit, by depreciating the cost over the asset's useful life. T expects to suffer ongoing losses for the foreseeable future.

3.13.90.40   We believe that the tax base of the asset is 150 even though T may not be able to obtain a tax benefit in the future from the depreciation of the asset – i.e. from the tax base. However, because T expects to make ongoing losses, it is unlikely that T will be able to obtain a benefit. T makes further analysis to determine

> whether it can recognise a deferred tax asset in respect of any deductible temporary difference arising from the tax base of 150 (see 3.13.330).

3.13.90.50   In some cases, an entity is entitled to a tax deduction on the sale of an asset only if it utilises its tax losses carried forward. In such cases, in our view the entity should choose an accounting policy, to be applied consistently, to do either of the following:

- include the conditional deduction in the tax base of the asset; or
- treat the conditional deduction as a separate tax credit.

3.13.90.60   We believe that under either policy, the entity should factor any uncertainty about whether it will benefit from the conditional deduction into the assessment of the recoverability of any deferred tax asset related to the tax losses carried forward or the tax credit (see 3.13.350).

EXAMPLE 4B – DETERMINE TAX BASE – CONDITIONAL TAX DEDUCTION

3.13.90.70   Tax law provides that a tax deduction will be available on the sale of an asset, subject to prior utilisation of tax losses carried forward. Company M acquires an asset for 150 and later revalues it to 200. On disposal of the asset, M receives a tax deduction of 150 in all cases. In addition, if M has utilised its tax losses carried forward, then M receives a further tax deduction of 50 on disposal of the asset (conditional deduction).

3.13.90.80   We believe that M should choose an accounting policy (see 3.13.90.50), to be applied consistently, to do either of the following.

- *Include the conditional deduction in the tax base of the asset:* Under this approach, the tax base of the asset is 200. Any uncertainty about whether M will benefit from the conditional deduction should be factored into the assessment of any deferred tax asset related to the tax losses carried forward.
- *Treat the conditional deduction as a separate tax credit:* Under this approach, the tax base of the asset is 150 giving rise to a taxable temporary difference of 50; the additional potential tax credit of 50 should be treated as a separate deductible temporary difference. Any uncertainty about whether M will benefit from the conditional deduction should be factored into the assessment of any deferred tax asset related to that deductible temporary difference.

3.13.100   Management's intention

3.13.100.10   In some jurisdictions, different tax deductions are available for an asset depending on how its carrying amount is recovered. In such cases, the tax base of an asset is generally determined based on management's intent. However, there is specific guidance for non-depreciable assets measured using the revaluation model and there is a rebuttable presumption that the carrying amount of investment property measured at fair value will be recovered through sale (see 3.13.410.10 and 430). [*IAS 12.51, 51B–51C*]

3.13.100.20   In some jurisdictions, no deduction is allowed when an asset is depreciated, but a deduction is allowed when the asset is disposed of, abandoned or scrapped. Sometimes an asset may be recovered through use and then scrapped at the end of its useful life. In this case, in our view the tax base should be determined assuming that the carrying amount is recovered through use and scrapping together. Therefore, we believe that the tax base should include the tax deduction that will be received when the asset is scrapped.

EXAMPLE 4C – DETERMINE TAX BASE – TANGIBLE ASSET THAT BECOMES TAX-DEDUCTIBLE WHEN SOLD OR SCRAPPED

3.13.100.30   An item of property, plant and equipment is bought for 100. The asset will be depreciated for accounting purposes over its 10-year useful life to a residual value of zero. No tax deductions will be received while the asset is being used. However, when the asset is sold or scrapped, a tax deduction is received for the initial cost of the asset of 100. We believe that the tax base of the asset is 100.

EXAMPLE 4D – DETERMINE TAX BASE – INTANGIBLE ASSET THAT BECOMES TAX-DEDUCTIBLE ON EXPIRY

3.13.100.40   Company X paid 100 to acquire the right to mine a specific area for 40 years, which is recognised as an intangible asset. The asset is not depreciable for tax purposes, but is amortised for accounting purposes (see 3.3.210).

3.13.100.50   If the right is used until expiry, then on expiry X will receive a tax deduction for the initial cost of 100. However, no deduction is available if the right is disposed of or the mine is abandoned in the future.

3.13.100.60   We believe that if management's intention is to use the right until it expires, then the tax base is 100. However, if management's intention is to sell the right after 10 years, then the tax base of the intangible asset is zero.

3.13.100.70   Management normally needs to demonstrate its intent clearly in order for it to be reflected in the determination of the tax base. However, in our view it is not always required that the entity perform a formal act demonstrating this intention. Instead, depending on the facts and circumstances, we believe that it may be sufficient to assume that management will act in the most economically advantageous way.

EXAMPLE 4E – DETERMINE TAX BASE – DEMONSTRATING MANAGEMENT INTENT

3.13.100.80   Company P acquires an item of property, plant and equipment for 100, the cost of which is only deductible for tax purposes on disposal.

3.13.100.90   If P's management estimates a positive residual value of the asset under IAS 16, then we believe that this demonstrates its intention to sell the asset at the end of its useful life. Accordingly, we believe that the tax base of the asset is 100.

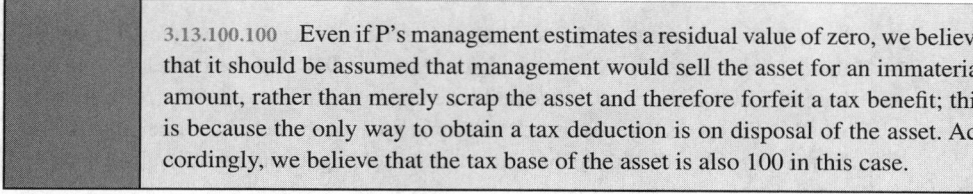

3.13.100.100   Even if P's management estimates a residual value of zero, we believe that it should be assumed that management would sell the asset for an immaterial amount, rather than merely scrap the asset and therefore forfeit a tax benefit; this is because the only way to obtain a tax deduction is on disposal of the asset. Accordingly, we believe that the tax base of the asset is also 100 in this case.

3.13.100.110   Management's intention may also be relevant in determining which tax rates to apply in calculating deferred tax (see 3.13.390).

3.13.110   COMPUTE TEMPORARY DIFFERENCES, UNUSED TAX LOSSES AND CREDITS

3.13.110.05   An entity computes any temporary differences, unused tax losses and credits for which the recognition of deferred tax needs to be considered.

3.13.110.10   A temporary difference is the difference between the tax base of an asset or liability (see 3.13.90) and its carrying amount in the financial statements. Such a temporary difference will result in taxable or deductible amounts in future periods when the carrying amount is recovered or settled. Therefore, in determining the amount of deferred tax to recognise, the analysis focuses on the carrying amounts in the statement of financial position rather than on the differences between profit or loss and taxable profits – i.e. it is a 'balance sheet' approach, rather than a 'timing differences' or an 'income statement' approach. Temporary differences may be either:

- taxable – i.e. they will result in taxable amounts in future periods; or
- deductible – i.e. they will result in tax deductions in future periods. [*IAS 12.5*]

3.13.110.20   The existence of a deductible temporary difference depends solely on a comparison of the carrying amount of an asset and its tax base at the reporting date, and is not affected by possible future changes in the carrying amount or expected manner of recovery of the asset. [*IAS 12.26(d)*]

EXAMPLE 5A – TEMPORARY DIFFERENCE – DEBT INSTRUMENT MEASURED AT FAIR VALUE

3.13.110.30   Company E purchases a debt instrument for 1,000 at the beginning of year 1. The following facts are also relevant for this example.
- The debt instrument's nominal value is 1,000.
- The maturity date is at the end of year 5.
- Interest is payable annually at 2%.
- For accounting purposes, the debt instrument is measured at fair value.
- The instrument's tax base is its cost of 1,000.

3.13.110.40   At the end of year 2, the debt instrument's fair value decreases to 918 as a result of an increase in market interest rates. However, E estimates that it will be able to collect all of the contractual cash flows, including the full nominal amount of 1,000, if it continues to hold the debt instrument until its maturity.

> **3.13.110.50**   At the end of year 2, the difference between the carrying amount of the debt instrument in E's financial statements of 918 and the corresponding tax base of 1,000 gives rise to a deductible temporary difference of 82, irrespective of whether E expects to recover the carrying amount of the debt instrument by sale or by use – i.e. by selling the debt instrument or holding it until maturity. [*IAS 12.26(d), BC39–BC44*]

3.13.110.60   In consolidated financial statements, temporary differences are determined by comparing the carrying amounts of assets and liabilities in the consolidated financial statements with the appropriate tax base. The IFRS Interpretations Committee discussed this issue and noted that when entities in the same consolidated group file separate tax returns, separate temporary differences arise in those entities. Consequently, when an entity prepares its consolidated financial statements, deferred tax balances are determined separately for those temporary differences, using the applicable tax rates for each entity's tax jurisdiction. [*IAS 12.11, IU 05-14*]

EXAMPLE 5B – TEMPORARY DIFFERENCE – ACCRUED INTEREST RECEIVABLE

> **3.13.110.70**   Company R accrues interest of 100, which will be taxed only when R receives the cash payment. The statement of financial position includes an asset (receivable) of 100. However, tax base of the asset equals zero, because the interest will be taxed in the future. This difference is a taxable temporary difference, because the amount will be taxed in a future period – i.e. when the cash is received. [*IAS 12.IE.A.1*]

EXAMPLE 5C – TEMPORARY DIFFERENCE – REVALUATION FOR ACCOUNTING PURPOSES

> **3.13.110.80**   Company B's accounting policy is to measure property, plant and equipment at fair value, and B revalues its production plant above its original cost (see 3.2.300). The tax base does not include such revaluation and the revaluation itself will not be directly taxed – i.e. the tax base of the production plant is unchanged.
>
> **3.13.110.90**   The revaluation results in a taxable temporary difference, because B will use the plant to generate future economic benefits that are expected to result in taxable profits, but the corresponding tax deduction (i.e. depreciation charge) will be limited to the original cost of the plant. As a consequence, the revaluation will be taxed indirectly. [*IAS 12.20, IE.A.11*]

3.13.110.100   In our view, when assets are revalued for tax purposes, to the extent that the tax base is increased to the same level as the carrying amount, this increase represents the reversal of the previously determined taxable temporary difference, rather than the origination of a deductible temporary difference – i.e. these are not separate temporary differences for the property, plant and equipment and its subsequent revaluation (see 3.13.570.120).

EXAMPLE 5D – TEMPORARY DIFFERENCE – REVALUATION FOR TAX PURPOSES

3.13.110.110   Company C's property, plant and equipment is revalued for tax purposes. The revaluation surplus is tax-deductible in future years. No revaluation is recognised under IFRS, in accordance with C's accounting policy for property, plant and equipment.

3.13.110.120   The three scenarios illustrate the effect of different tax bases before and after the tax revaluation.

		SCENARIO 1	SCENARIO 2	SCENARIO 3
Carrying amount	(a)	100	100	100
Tax base before revaluation	(b)	120	60	60
Tax base after revaluation	(c)	180	90	180
Temporary difference before revaluation of tax base – deductible (taxable)	(d) = (b) - (a)	20	(40)	(40)
Temporary difference after revaluation of tax base – deductible (taxable)	(e) = (c) - (a)	80	(10)	80

3.13.110.130   In Scenario 1, the revaluation results in an increased deductible temporary difference. In Scenario 2, the revaluation results in a reduced taxable temporary difference. In Scenario 3, we believe that the revaluation results in both. The taxable temporary difference is reduced to zero and a deductible temporary difference arises. This is because C will receive future tax deductions for the additional value recognised for tax purposes.

3.13.120   No recognised asset or liability

3.13.120.10   In our experience, it is common for entities to be entitled to future tax deductions relating to transactions that do not result in any asset or liability being recognised in the statement of financial position. For example, a transaction might be accounted for directly in equity or give rise to a gain or loss in the statement of profit or loss and OCI.

3.13.120.20   In our view, the future tax allowance available should generally be compared with the related carrying amount of zero in the statement of financial position – a temporary difference would therefore exist. This is in line with IAS 12, which states that some items have a tax base, even though they are not recognised as assets or liabilities – e.g. research costs that are expensed immediately for accounting purposes but are tax-deductible over a future period of time. [*IAS 12.9*]

EXAMPLE 6A – NO RECOGNISED ASSET OR LIABILITY – INTRA-GROUP RESTRUCTURING

3.13.120.30   Company P undertook a restructuring in which P's investment in Subsidiary S was sold from one wholly owned subsidiary, IP1, to another, IP2. The sale was executed at fair value, which resulted in a profit for IP1 because the fair

value of the investment in S exceeded its carrying amount. Under the tax rules, the transaction led to the creation of a tax-deductible 'premium' (effectively the profit on the sale) in IP2 which is amortised systematically over 10 years.

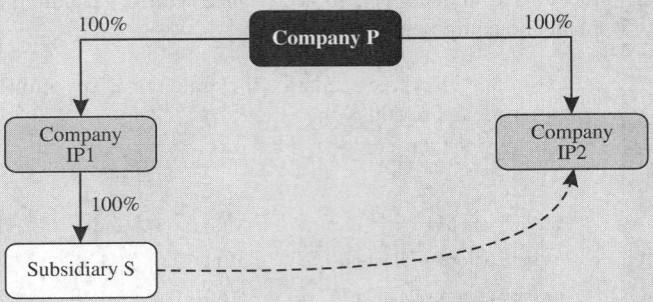

3.13.120.40   In P's consolidated financial statements, the impact of the intra-group transaction is eliminated and, consequently, the profit on sale and corresponding premium do not exist in the consolidated financial statements. However, for tax purposes:

- IP1 has a current tax liability for the tax on the capital gain from the sale; and
- IP2 will be entitled to annual tax deductions associated with the premium for the next 10 years.

3.13.120.50   Even though the intra-group transaction (and consequently the capital gain and premium) is fully eliminated on consolidation, we believe that IAS 12 applies in this situation because it is applicable to accounting for income taxes overall. We believe that a deductible temporary difference for the premium exists despite there being no recognised asset or liability for accounting purposes. Therefore, subject to recoverability (see 3.13.330), P should recognise a deferred tax asset for the deductible temporary difference related to the premium. The premium is not subject to the initial recognition exemption (see 3.13.200) because the transaction that gives rise to the temporary difference affects taxable profit.

3.13.120.60   In some tax jurisdictions, a tax deduction is available in relation to treasury shares – e.g. on disposal. For these treasury shares, it can be difficult to determine whether a temporary difference exists because no asset is recognised in the statement of financial position.

3.13.120.70   Generally, any amounts paid by an entity to acquire treasury shares are debited directly to equity, and no asset or liability arises (see 7.3.500).

3.13.120.80   In our view, there are two approaches to identifying any temporary difference in relation to treasury shares. An entity should choose an accounting policy based on one of these approaches, to be applied consistently, to determine whether a temporary difference exists.

- Under the first approach, an entity determines whether a temporary difference exists by comparing the tax base of the treasury shares to the amount deducted from equity.

- Under the second approach, although there is a tax base for the shares, there is no corresponding asset or liability recognised in the statement of financial position. Therefore, a deductible temporary difference arises. However, because of the initial recognition exemption (see 3.13.200), no deferred tax asset is recognised in respect of this temporary difference. [*IAS 12.9, 24, 32.33*]

3.13.120.90   For a discussion of the presentation of tax effects of transactions involving an entity's own shares, see 3.13.590; and for a discussion of other presentation items, see 3.13.520.

EXAMPLE 6B – NO RECOGNISED ASSET OR LIABILITY – TREASURY SHARES

3.13.120.100   Company Y purchases treasury shares on the market for 1,000. Y intends to hold the shares from a legal perspective – i.e. not cancel them – for a number of reasons. Y might consider selling them on the market, or exchanging the shares as consideration for the acquisition of a business. In Y's tax jurisdiction, proceeds from the sale of treasury shares (if ever disposed of) are taxed and the original cost is deducted from this taxable income.

3.13.120.110   Under the first approach in 3.13.120.80, Y compares the tax base of 1,000 with the acquisition cost of 1,000 deducted from equity; therefore, at inception there is no temporary difference between the tax base and the carrying amount of the equity component recognised in the statement of financial position.

3.13.120.120   Under the second approach in 3.13.120.80, a deductible temporary difference of 1,000 (tax base 1,000 with no corresponding accounting asset) arises, but because of the initial recognition exemption (see 3.13.200), no deferred tax asset is recognised.

EXAMPLE 6C – NO RECOGNISED ASSET OR LIABILITY – SHARE-BASED PAYMENTS

3.13.120.130   Modifying Example 6B, Company Y holds the treasury shares to settle a share-based payment transaction. Y expects to receive a tax deduction based on the cost of the treasury shares. In this case, the cost of the treasury shares will be factored into the measurement of the tax base of the share-based payment transaction (see 3.13.820).

3.13.130   Financial instruments

3.13.140   *Compound financial instruments*

3.13.140.10   Under IFRS 9, on initial recognition a financial asset or financial liability is measured at fair value plus or minus directly attributable transaction costs, unless the instrument is classified as at fair value through profit or loss or is a trade receivable that does not have a significant financing component. Normally, the fair value on initial recognition is the transaction price (see 7.7.10.10). However, on initial recognition of a compound financial instrument, IAS 32 requires an issuer to split compound financial instruments into a financial liability and an equity component. For further discussion of compound instruments, see 7.3.310. Because of these requirements, the carrying amount of the financial liability component may not equal its par or nominal value. In most tax jurisdictions, the tax base of the financial liability would be its par or nominal value – i.e. the sum of the liability and equity components – and this will result in a taxable temporary difference. [*IFRS 9.5.1.1, 5.13, IAS 12.23, 32.15, 28*]

3.13.150 *Obligation to purchase own equity instruments*

3.13.150.10 IAS 32 requires an entity to recognise a financial liability for the present value of the redemption amount if:

- the entity has committed to acquire its own shares for cash or other financial assets (see 7.3.240); or
- in the consolidated financial statements, it has committed to acquire the shares held by NCI in a subsidiary (see 2.5.680). [*IAS 32.23*]

3.13.150.20 This also applies to contracts under which the NCI in the consolidated financial statements can put the shares of a subsidiary back to the entity (see 2.5.680). Example 7A illustrates how to determine the temporary difference associated with such contracts.

EXAMPLE 7A – TEMPORARY DIFFERENCE – WRITTEN PUT LIABILITY

3.13.150.30 Company Z enters into a transaction on 1 May 2018 to acquire 60% of Company S's shares from Company M and obtains control of S. Before the transaction, M wholly owns S. At the same date, Z writes a put option ('written put') to M. Through this, M is entitled to put all of its remaining shares in S (40%) on 1 May 2018, at a formulaic price based on EBITDA.

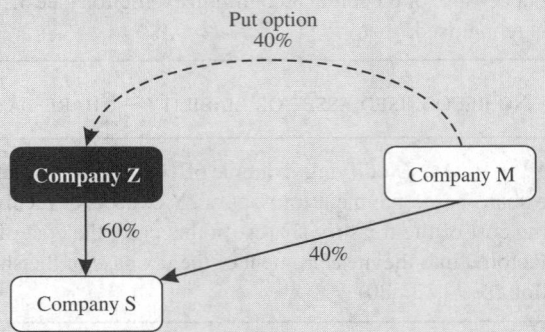

3.13.150.40 On 1 May 2018, the present value of the redemption amount (variable based on EBITDA) is 500. Therefore, a financial liability for 500 is recognised in Z's financial statements. In Z's tax jurisdiction, no tax deduction is available on the written put liability.

3.13.150.50 In our view, the tax base of the written put liability is equal to its carrying amount of 500 minus the deductible amount of zero; therefore, no temporary difference exists and no deferred tax should be recognised. This is consistent with the definition of the tax base of a liability (see 3.13.90.10).

3.13.160   *Derivatives*

3.13.160.10   Under IFRS 9, derivative financial instruments are measured on initial recognition and subsequently at fair value (see 7.7.10 and 150.10). Consequently, if the carrying amount of a derivative financial instrument becomes different from its tax base, then a temporary difference arises. [*IFRS 9.5.1.1, 5.2.1, 12.7–8*]

EXAMPLE 7B – TEMPORARY DIFFERENCE – INTEREST RATE SWAP

3.13.160.20   Company D enters into a pay-fixed receive-floating interest rate swap with an initial fair value of zero. D does not designate the swap as a hedging instrument.

3.13.160.30   The swap is taxed on a cash basis. That is, if D makes a net cash payment under the swap, then D receives a tax deduction; conversely, if D obtains a net cash receipt under the swap, then the receipt is taxable.

3.13.160.40   Remeasurement of the interest rate swap results in the following temporary differences.

- If the swap has a positive fair value of 100 at the reporting date – i.e. the swap is an asset – then this indicates that D expects to obtain net cash receipts in the future. The tax base of the asset is zero. A taxable temporary difference of 100 arises, resulting in a deferred tax liability.
- If the swap has a negative fair value of 100 at the reporting date – i.e. the swap is a liability – then this indicates that D expects to make net cash payments in the future. The tax base of the liability is zero. A deductible temporary difference of 100 arises, resulting in a potential deferred tax asset.

3.13.160.50   For further discussion of temporary differences arising from cash flow hedging of forecast transactions, see 3.13.730.

3.13.170   **Foreign currencies and hyperinflation**

3.13.170.10   Sometimes, temporary differences are created when changes in exchange rates lead to changes in the tax basis rather than the book basis. This situation usually arises when an entity has a functional currency that is different from the currency of the country in which it is domiciled. For example, an entity based in the UK may have some operations in Germany for which sterling is the functional currency (see 2.7.30). As a result, non-monetary property, plant and equipment in Germany is translated from euro into sterling once, using the historical rate at the transaction date. [*IAS 12.41, 21.23(b)*]

3.13.170.20   If the asset is part of a unit paying tax in Germany, then the tax base in euro is retranslated from euro to sterling at the exchange rate at the reporting date. Therefore, book value remains at the historical value, whereas the tax base is translated to the current rate at each reporting date. This translation difference may create temporary differences. Deferred tax is recognised for this temporary difference in line with the general principles for recognising income tax assets and liabilities (see 3.13.320 and 330). [*IU 01-16*]

3.13.170.30   This applies even when the non-monetary assets are part of a foreign branch that has the same functional currency as its parent. In that case, the special recognition criteria regarding investments in subsidiaries, branches and associates, and interests in joint arrangements (see 3.13.260) do not apply. This is because the non-monetary assets are those of the entity itself, not the overall investment. [*IAS 12.41, IE.A.17, IE.B.13*]

3.13.170.40   The foreign currency translation reserve arising from the translation of foreign operations in the consolidated financial statements does not in itself result in deferred tax assets or liabilities. The foreign currency translation reserve is neither an asset nor a liability, and does not give rise to temporary differences. However, exchange differences arising on the translation of the financial statements of foreign operations might have associated tax effects that affect the financial statements. For example, an entity intends to sell an investment in a subsidiary in the foreseeable future. In this case, it recognises deferred taxes on temporary differences arising from that investment (see 3.13.260.40–50). Suppose that part of these differences arises from translating the financial statements of foreign operations; in this case, the deferred tax effect in respect of these differences will be recognised in OCI (see 3.13.530.10).

3.13.170.50   In some jurisdictions, foreign currency gains and losses are netted for tax purposes, and the net gain (loss) is taxable (deductible) in instalments over several years. In our view, if a single tax base exists under applicable tax law, then it is appropriate to present a net deferred tax liability (asset). [*IAS 12.5*]

3.13.170.60   An entity operating in a hyperinflationary economy will make current purchasing power adjustments to its assets (see chapter 2.10). Although the carrying amount in the financial statements is increased, the tax base remains stated in the historical measuring unit. In such cases, temporary differences arise and are recognised in full. [*IAS 12.IE.A.18*]

3.13.180   Other differences

3.13.180.10   Some differences that arise between IFRS and the corresponding tax treatment may not give rise to a deferred tax liability (asset), because an item that affects the accounting will not be taxable or deductible in the future. Although there is no definition of such items in IFRS, they are often referred to as 'permanent' differences.

EXAMPLE 8 – 'PERMANENT' DIFFERENCES

3.13.180.20   One of Company D's investees has declared a dividend of 100. D has recognised a receivable in its financial statements. In D's jurisdiction, dividends are tax-exempt. In this case, no deferred tax liability is recognised, following either of the following analyses.
- The tax base of the receivable is zero and therefore there is a temporary difference of 100; however, a tax rate of zero will apply when the cash is received. Therefore, no deferred tax liability is recognised.

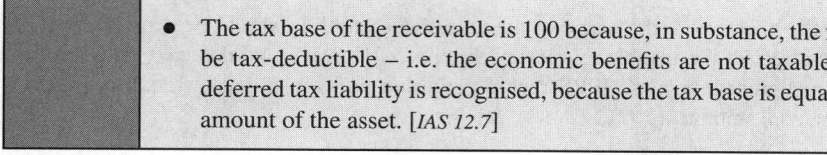

- The tax base of the receivable is 100 because, in substance, the full amount will be tax-deductible – i.e. the economic benefits are not taxable. Therefore, no deferred tax liability is recognised, because the tax base is equal to the carrying amount of the asset. [*IAS 12.7*]

3.13.190   DETERMINE IF RECOGNITION EXEMPTION APPLIES AND IF RECOGNITION CRITERIA ARE MET

3.13.200   Initial recognition exemption

3.13.210   *General principles*

3.13.210.10   Deferred tax is not recognised for certain temporary differences that arise on the initial recognition of assets and liabilities. The exemption is not conceptual in nature and is one of the more difficult aspects of the standard to apply. The exemption applies to:
- a deferred tax liability (but not a deferred tax asset) that arises from the initial recognition of goodwill (see 3.13.1020); and
- a deferred tax asset or liability that:
  - arises from the initial recognition of an asset or liability in a transaction that is not a business combination; and
  - affects neither accounting profit nor taxable profit at the time of the transaction (see 3.13.200).
  [*IAS 12.15, 22(c), 24, 32A, 33, IU 03-17*]

3.13.210.15   In consolidated financial statements, an entity assesses whether an asset or a liability is being recognised for the first time for the purpose of applying the initial recognition exception from the perspective of the consolidated financial statements. For example, the initial recognition exemption may not apply to goodwill transferred within a group (see Example 60C), whereas the exemption is likely to apply to temporary differences arising from originated inter-company loans. [*IU 05-14*]

3.13.210.20   The issues that arise in respect of the initial recognition exemption for deferred tax assets are similar to those in respect of deferred tax liabilities.

EXAMPLE 9A – INITIAL RECOGNITION EXEMPTION – NON-TAXABLE GOVERNMENT GRANT

3.13.210.25   Company G receives a non-taxable government grant. A temporary difference arises on the initial recognition of the grant, irrespective of whether G deducts it from the cost of the asset or presents it as deferred income (see 4.3.120). G does not recognise any deferred tax asset because the temporary difference arises at the time of the transaction and affects neither accounting nor taxable profit. [*IAS 12.33, IE.B.7*]

EXAMPLE 9B – INITIAL RECOGNITION EXEMPTION – NON-DEDUCTIBLE COSTS

3.13.210.30   Company F acquires a building for 100. The cost of the building will never be deductible for tax purposes, even on its eventual disposal. Therefore, the tax base is zero and a taxable temporary difference of 100 arises. In the absence

of the exemption, the carrying amount of the building would be grossed up for the effect of the taxable temporary difference. However, no deferred tax liability is recognised, because IFRS regards grossing up as resulting in less transparent financial statements. [*IAS 12.15(b), 22*]

3.13.210.40   F applies the exemption, and no deferred tax is initially recognised; no deferred tax will be recognised subsequently as the carrying amount of the asset is depreciated or impaired. At the end of year 1, the carrying amount of the building is 95 after recognising depreciation. No deferred tax is recognised for the difference of 5 created in year 1. [*IAS 12.22*]

3.13.210.50   If the temporary difference that arises from the initial recognition of an asset qualifies for the initial recognition exemption, and the asset is subsequently revalued, then in our view the initial recognition exemption is irrelevant for the consequences of the revaluation, and the related deferred tax liability should be recognised. We believe that the revaluation is a subsequent event in the life of the recognised asset, and therefore the revaluation creates a new temporary difference. In our view, an entity should choose an accounting policy, to be applied consistently, to measure that deferred tax liability based on either:

- the excess of the revalued amount over the original cost; or
- the impact of the revaluation – i.e. the difference between the revalued amount and the carrying amount before revaluation.

EXAMPLE 9C – INITIAL RECOGNITION EXEMPTION – ASSET SUBSEQUENTLY REVALUED

3.13.210.60   Continuing Example 9B, Company F revalues the building at the end of year 3. At this point, the original cost less accumulated depreciation is 85, and the new carrying amount after revaluation is 120.

3.13.210.70   We believe that the initial recognition exemption is irrelevant for the consequences of the revaluation, and a deferred tax liability should be recognised as a result of the revaluation. We believe that F should choose the accounting policy to measure the deferred tax liability based on either:
- the excess of the revalued amount over the original cost of 20 (120 - 100); or
- the difference between the revalued amount and the original cost less accumulated depreciation of 35 (120 - 85).

3.13.210.80   In our view, if assets or liabilities with temporary differences that did not give rise to the recognition of any deferred taxes because of the initial recognition exemption are subsequently acquired in a business combination, then a deferred tax liability or asset should be recognised as part of the acquisition accounting.

EXAMPLE 9D – INITIAL RECOGNITION EXEMPTION – ASSET ACQUIRED IN A BUSINESS COMBINATION

3.13.210.90   Continuing Example 9B, at the end of year 1 – i.e. before the revaluation – Company M acquires Company F in a business combination. The fair value of the building on acquisition is 95, which is equal to the carrying amount in F's

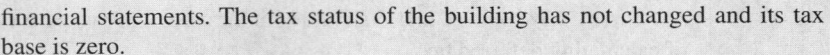

financial statements. The tax status of the building has not changed and its tax base is zero.

3.13.210.100   The building is recognised by M in its consolidated statement of financial position for the first time at the time of the business combination. Because the building is acquired in a business combination, the initial recognition exemption does not apply. Therefore, M recognises a deferred tax liability in its consolidated statement of financial position.

3.13.215   *Other taxes in the scope of IAS 12*

3.13.215.10   In some cases, a new levy in the scope of IAS 12 may be introduced in addition to the existing income tax. If some assets or liabilities are treated differently for the purposes of the new levy – e.g. the new tax levy does not allow deduction of depreciation of property, plant and equipment – then this would affect the tax bases of an entity's existing assets or liabilities (see 3.13.90) and new temporary differences would arise. In our view, the initial recognition exemption does not apply to such temporary differences, because they arise *after* the assets and liabilities have been recognised. However, the initial recognition exemption does apply to assets and liabilities recognised on or after the date on which the tax law is enacted or substantively enacted. [*IAS 12.15, 24*]

EXAMPLE 9E – INITIAL RECOGNITION EXEMPTION DOES NOT APPLY

3.13.215.20   Company F operates in the mining industry in Country M. On 15 November 2018, the government in M introduces a new special mining right royalty calculated as 8% of profit from extractive activities after adding back depreciation of mining assets. This is in addition to its regular income tax of 30%. The tax law becomes effective immediately. The mining right royalty is in the scope of IAS 12 (see Example 1G).

3.13.215.30   The book value of F's mining assets on 15 November 2018 is 2,000. Depreciation of mining assets is not deductible for the purpose of calculating the mining right royalty. Therefore, the tax base of the mining assets for the purpose of the mining right royalty is zero and a taxable temporary difference of 2,000 arises. We believe that the initial recognition exemption does not apply to F's mining assets that have been acquired before 15 November 2018 – i.e. before the new tax law is enacted; however, it does apply to mining assets acquired on or after 15 November 2018.

3.13.220   *Partial deductions*

3.13.220.10   In some cases, the cost of an asset is partially deductible for tax purposes. In our view, the asset should be split into two parts for the purpose of calculating deferred tax.

EXAMPLE 10A – PARTIAL DEDUCTION

3.13.220.20   Company G acquires machinery for 200. For tax purposes, 80% of the cost can be deducted; the remaining 20% can never be deducted, even on disposal.

> 3.13.220.30   We believe that G should split the asset into two parts for the purpose of calculating deferred tax.
> - The initial recognition exemption should apply to a cost of 40 (200 x 20%). Therefore, no deferred tax will be recorded on initial recognition, or as this portion of the asset is depreciated subsequently.
> - The general requirements should apply to a cost of 160 (200 x 80%). This means that no deferred tax will be recognised initially, because the carrying amount and tax base of the asset are both 160. However, if a temporary difference arises as the asset is depreciated, then deferred tax should be recognised.

3.13.220.40   The original cost of an asset may be partially deductible for tax purposes, and that asset may be depreciated, impaired or revalued after initial recognition. If this is the case, then in our view the entity may calculate deferred tax by:
- splitting the carrying amount of the asset in proportion to the deductible and non-deductible portions of the asset; and
- considering the two parts of the asset separately, consistent with our views expressed in 3.13.210.50 and 220.30 – i.e. applying the initial recognition exemption to the non-deductible portion and the general requirements to the deductible portion.

EXAMPLE 10B – PARTIAL DEDUCTION – ASSET SUBSEQUENTLY IMPAIRED

> 3.13.220.50   Continuing Example 10A, for accounting purposes, Company G recognises an impairment loss that reduces the carrying amount of the machinery to 180. The impairment has no effect on the tax base of the machinery, which remains at 160. For simplicity, both tax and accounting depreciation are zero at the date of impairment.
>
> 3.13.220.60   In this example, G calculates deferred tax as follows.
> - G splits the impaired amount of 180 in proportion to the non-deductible and the deductible portions of the asset – i.e. 36 (180 x 20%) and 144 (180 x 80%), respectively.
> - G applies the initial recognition exemption to the impaired amount of 36, because this is a subsequent change in the initially unrecognised temporary difference.
> - G compares the impaired amount of 144 with the tax base of 160 (200 x 80%). Subject to recoverability (see 3.13.330), G recognises a deferred tax asset on a deductible temporary difference of 16.

EXAMPLE 10C – PARTIAL DEDUCTION – ASSET SUBSEQUENTLY REVALUED

> 3.13.220.70   Continuing Example 10A, for accounting purposes, Company G subsequently revalues the machinery bought upwards to 220. There is no effect on the tax base of 160. For simplicity, both tax and accounting depreciation are zero at the date of the revaluation.

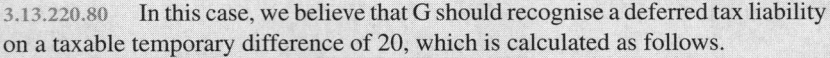

3.13.220.80   In this case, we believe that G should recognise a deferred tax liability on a taxable temporary difference of 20, which is calculated as follows.

- The revalued amount of 44 (220 x 20%) is compared with the original cost of 40 (200 x 20%), giving a taxable temporary difference of 4. This is a new temporary difference and the initial recognition exemption is not relevant (see 3.13.210.50).
- The revalued amount of 176 (220 x 80%) is compared with the tax base of 160 (200 x 80%), giving a taxable temporary difference of 16.

3.13.230   *Finance leases**

3.13.230.10   Applying the initial recognition exemption to finance leases can be particularly difficult, depending on the treatment allowed by the tax authorities. Examples 11A and 11B illustrate this issue.

3.13.230.20   When an entity enters into a finance lease as a lessee, it records the purchase of the leased asset and a corresponding liability in its statement of financial position. In some tax jurisdictions, the lease payments are deductible on a cash basis. Although there is an asset under IFRS, there is no corresponding asset for tax purposes, and therefore a temporary difference arises on the initial recognition of the asset. Similarly, a liability is recognised under IFRS that has a tax base of zero; therefore, a temporary difference arises on the initial recognition of the liability. Furthermore, the transaction affects neither accounting nor taxable profit on initial recognition. Therefore, a question arises about whether the initial recognition exemption applies. [*IAS 12.7–9*]

3.13.230.30   In our view, in the circumstances described in 3.13.230.20, the application of the initial recognition exemption is not appropriate. We believe that the asset and liability that arise for accounting purposes under a finance lease are integrally linked. Accordingly, they should be regarded as a net package (the finance lease) for the purpose of recognising deferred tax. This is consistent with the way in which the lease transaction is viewed for tax purposes.

EXAMPLE 11A – LEASES – LESSEE RECEIVES TAX DEDUCTION FOR LEASE PAYMENTS

3.13.230.40   Company H acquires a piece of property, plant and equipment through a finance lease and records the acquired asset and the corresponding liability. For tax purposes, the whole amount of the lease payment is deductible on a cash basis. At the date of acquisition and at the end of year 1, H records the following entries before considering any deferred income tax.

	DEBIT	CREDIT
Property, plant and equipment	100	
Lease liability		100
To recognise finance lease liability and related asset		
Depreciation (profit or loss)	10	
Property, plant and equipment		10
To recognise depreciation in respect of year 1		

	DEBIT	CREDIT
Interest expense (profit or loss)	8	
Lease liability	12	
Cash		20
To recognise lease repayment and unwinding of discount on lease liability for year 1 at 8%		

3.13.230.50   On initial recognition of the transaction, we believe that a taxable temporary difference of 100 arises on the asset, and a deductible temporary difference of 100 arises on the liability. This gives a net temporary difference of zero. Therefore, no deferred tax is recognised. The initial recognition exemption does not apply because there is no temporary difference.

	CARRYING AMOUNT	TAX BASE	(TAXABLE) DEDUCTIBLE DIFFERENCE
Property, plant and equipment	100	-	(100)
Lease liability	(100)	-	100
Net	-	-	-

3.13.230.60   At the end of year 1, a taxable temporary difference of 90 exists on the asset, and a deductible temporary difference of 88 exists on the liability. This gives a net taxable temporary difference of 2. We believe that H should recognise a deferred tax liability for this net difference.

	CARRYING AMOUNT	TAX BASE	(TAXABLE) DEDUCTIBLE DIFFERENCE
Property, plant and equipment	90	-	(90)
Lease liability	(88)	-	88
Net	2	-	(2)

3.13.230.70   H records the following additional entry at the end of year 1, based on a tax rate of 50%.

	DEBIT	CREDIT
Income tax expense	1	
Deferred tax liability		1
To recognise deferred tax at end of year 1		

3.13.230.80   If an entity is the lessor in a finance lease, then it derecognises the leased asset and recognises a receivable at an amount equal to the net investment in the lease, although it retains title to the leased asset during the lease term. In some tax jurisdictions, the lease receipts are taxed on a cash basis. Similar to a lessee, a question arises for lessors about whether the initial recognition exemption applies.

3.13.230.90   Similar to the position of the lessee discussed in 3.13.230.20–30, in our view in the circumstances described in 3.13.230.80, the finance lease asset and the tax deductions that arise on the leased asset are integrally linked; therefore, they should be considered together for the purpose of recognising deferred tax.

EXAMPLE 11B – LEASES – LESSOR DEDUCTS TAX DEPRECIATION ON LEASED ASSET

3.13.230.100   Company J is the lessor in the agreement discussed in Example 11A. At inception of the finance lease, J derecognises the item of property, plant and equipment and recognises a receivable at an amount equal to the net investment in the lease. For tax purposes, the lease receipts are taxed on a cash basis. For tax purposes, J deducts the cost of the asset on a straight-line basis over 10 years.

3.13.230.110   J measures the leased asset at 100 immediately before commencement of the lease. J also recognises a receivable with a carrying amount of 100 on commencement of the lease. As a result, no temporary difference arises on commencement of the lease.

	CARRYING AMOUNT	TAX BASE	(TAXABLE) DEDUCTIBLE DIFFERENCE
Finance lease receivable	100	-	(100)
Leased asset	-	(100)	100
Net	100	(100)	-

3.13.230.120   In later years, a temporary difference will arise to the extent that the carrying amount of the finance lease receivable differs from the tax base of the leased asset. In effect, the tax base of the leased asset is attributed to the finance lease receivable.

3.13.240   *Decommissioning provisions**

3.13.240.10   When considering the initial recognition exemption, it can also be difficult to apply the requirements to decommissioning provisions that are capitalised as part of the cost of property, plant and equipment (see 3.2.70).

3.13.240.20   In some tax jurisdictions, the decommissioning expenditure is deducted on a cash basis. As a consequence, the tax base of the liability is zero (as is the related portion of the asset). This deductible temporary difference arises on initial recognition of the provision, but does not affect either accounting or taxable profit.

3.13.240.30   Under one interpretation of the initial recognition exemption, deferred tax would not be recognised in respect of the provision, either initially or as the asset is depreciated. In our view, the non-recognition of the tax effect of this deductible temporary difference is not an appropriate application of the exemption. Consistent with our analysis for finance leases (see Example 11A), in our view the asset and liability that arise in accounting for a decommissioning provision are integrally linked. They should therefore be regarded as a net package for the purpose of recognising deferred tax.

EXAMPLE 12 – DECOMMISSIONING PROVISION

3.13.240.40   Company K recognises a provision for site restoration of 100, which is capitalised. For tax purposes, the expenditure will be deducted only when incurred. K records the following entries before the impact of any deferred income tax.

	DEBIT	CREDIT
Property, plant and equipment	100	
Provision		100
To recognise provision against related asset		
Depreciation (profit or loss)	10	
Property, plant and equipment		10
To recognise depreciation in respect of year 1		
Interest expense (profit or loss)	8	
Provision		8
To recognise unwinding of discount for year 1 on provision at a discount rate of 8%		

3.13.240.50   On initial recognition of the transaction, we believe that a taxable temporary difference of 100 arises on the capitalisation of the decommissioning provision, and a deductible temporary difference of 100 arises on the provision. This gives a net temporary difference of zero. Therefore, no deferred tax is recognised. The initial recognition exemption does not apply because there is no temporary difference.

	CARRYING AMOUNT	TAX BASE	(TAXABLE) DEDUCTIBLE DIFFERENCE
Property, plant and equipment	100	-	(100)
Provision	(100)	-	100
Net	-	-	-

3.13.240.60   At the end of year 1, a taxable temporary difference of 90 exists on the asset, and a deductible temporary difference of 108 exists on the provision. This gives a net deductible temporary difference of 18.

	CARRYING AMOUNT	TAX BASE	(TAXABLE) DEDUCTIBLE DIFFERENCE
Property, plant and equipment	90	-	(90)
Provision	(108)	-	108
Net	(18)	-	18

3.13.240.70   K records the following entry at the end of year 1 to recognise deferred tax on the net deductible temporary difference of 18 based on a tax rate of 50%, subject to recoverability (see 3.13.330).

	DEBIT	CREDIT
Deferred tax asset	9	
Income tax expense		9
To recognise deferred tax at end of year 1		

3.13.250   *Compound financial instruments*

3.13.250.10   When an entity issues a compound financial instrument, it records both a financial liability component and an equity component for that instrument (see 7.3.310). The initial recognition exemption is not triggered by a difference in liability or equity classification between the financial statements and the tax base that creates a temporary difference. If there is a temporary difference between the carrying amount of a financial liability component and its tax base on initial recognition, then an entity recognises the corresponding deferred tax. [*IAS 12.23*]

3.13.250.20   The standard refers to compound financial instruments in general. However, the standard illustrates only the example of a convertible bond.

EXAMPLE 13A – CONVERTIBLE DEBT

3.13.250.30   Company L issues convertible debt for proceeds of 100; a liability of 80 is recognised and the remaining 20 is recognised as equity (see 7.3.410). The tax base of the liability is 100.

3.13.250.40   The temporary difference arises from a difference in the classification of the instrument, rather than from a difference in initial recognition – the total carrying amount in both cases is 100. Therefore, the initial recognition exemption does not apply; deferred tax in respect of the taxable temporary difference of 20 is recognised in equity. [*IAS 12.23, 62A(b), IE.A.9, IE.Ex4*]

3.13.250.50   Compound financial instruments include many types of financial instruments. The common characteristic of compound financial instruments is the existence of a liability and an equity component. In our view, the specific requirements mentioned in 3.13.250.10, which apply to taxable temporary differences for which the initial recognition exemption is overridden, should not be restricted to taxable temporary differences arising from a convertible bond, as illustrated in the standard. Instead, they should extend to all temporary differences arising from the initial recognition of any compound financial instrument. This includes, for example, any deductible temporary difference arising from a mandatorily convertible bond in a jurisdiction where the tax deduction is based on the interest calculated on the par value of the bond and low-interest loans from shareholders.

EXAMPLE 13B – LOW-INTEREST LOAN FROM SHAREHOLDER

3.13.250.60   Company M receives a loan of 100 from its parent; the loan is repayable after six years, and no interest is payable on it. M recognises a liability at fair value of 70 and a capital contribution of 30, to reflect the fact that the difference between the fair value of a loan with a market rate of interest and the amount of cash received by M is a contribution from the parent (see 7.7.80, 110.40). The tax base of the loan is 100. [*IFRS 9.B5.1.1*]

3.13.250.70   The temporary difference arises from a difference in initial classification of the liability component of 70 separately from the equity component of 30, rather than from a difference in initial recognition of the instrument as a whole. We therefore believe that a taxable temporary difference of 30 arises to which the initial recognition exemption does not apply (see 3.13.250.10). As a result, M should recognise the deferred tax liability with a corresponding entry in equity. [*IAS 12.23*]

EXAMPLE 13C – CONVERTIBLE DEBT – MANDATORY CONVERSION AND TAX DEDUCTION BASED ON INTEREST

3.13.250.80   Company Z issues a mandatorily convertible bond to a third party investor paying non-discretionary interest in cash. This compound financial instrument is separated at inception between a financial liability (the interest strip) and an equity component (as a residual). The following are characteristics/values of the mandatorily convertible bond at inception.

Liability component	18
Equity component	82
Interest cash outflows over the life of the convertible bond, which will be tax-deductible when paid	20

3.13.250.90   No amount will be repaid on maturity, because the bond is mandatorily convertible. The only cash flow exchanged is the interest of 20 paid to the bond holders. The cash flow accounts both for the repayment of the principal and for the interest on the liability recognised by Z. All of these cash flows are deductible for tax purposes in Z's tax jurisdiction, where the tax rate is 30%.

3.13.250.100   We believe that based on the definition in paragraph 8 of IAS 12, the tax base of the liability component of the bond is zero. This is the difference between the carrying amount of the liability component (i.e. 18), and all repayments deductible for tax purposes (i.e. 20, which actually exceeds the carrying amount of 18). Therefore, a deductible temporary difference of 18 arises from the initial recognition of the mandatorily convertible bond. According to the specific requirements on compound financial instruments that override the initial recognition exemption (see 3.13.250.10), this difference should result in a deferred tax asset of 5.4 (18 x 30%) which Z recognises in equity, subject to recoverability (see 3.13.330). [*IAS 12.8, 23, 61A*]

3.13.250.110   If a subsidiary issues a convertible bond, as described in Examples 13A and 13C, to a party external to the group, then in the consolidated financial statements of the parent the equity component of the convertible bond is presented as NCI (see 2.5.450). However, it is unclear how the related deferred tax that was recognised by the subsidiary in equity should be treated in the consolidated financial statements – i.e. whether it should be attributed entirely to NCI or to owners of the parent and any 'ordinary' NCI (see 2.5.460.10) in proportion to their ownership interests in the subsidiary. [*IAS 1.81B*]

3.13.250.120   In our view, an entity should choose an accounting policy, to be applied consistently in the consolidated financial statements, to attribute the deferred tax effect resulting from the issuance of the convertible bond by a subsidiary using one of the following approaches.
- *Approach 1:* Attribute the deferred tax effect related to the convertible bond entirely to NCI, on the basis that paragraph 23 of IAS 12 indicates that the tax effect is attributed specifically to the equity component of the convertible bond.
- *Approach 2:* Attribute the deferred tax effect related to the convertible bond to the owners of the parent and to any ordinary NCI in proportion to their ownership interests, on the basis that the tax effect relates to the temporary difference associated with the liability component, and therefore only the existing shareholders of the subsidiary are exposed to the tax consequences. Although paragraph 23 of IAS 12 requires the tax effects to be recognised in equity, it does not specify which component of equity. [*IAS 12.8, 23, 61A, IFRS 10.B94*]

3.13.250.130   Any tax effect that is recognised in NCI remains in NCI even after the subsequent reversal of the related temporary difference. Subsequent changes in the related deferred tax liability (asset) are recognised in profit or loss. [*IAS 12.23*]

3.13.250.140   The accounting policy choice in 3.13.250.120 does not affect the subsequent attribution of profit or loss of the subsidiary, which is generally attributed to the owners of the parent and any ordinary NCI in proportion to their ownership interests in the subsidiary (see 2.5.500).

EXAMPLE 13D – CONVERTIBLE DEBT ISSUED BY SUBSIDIARY – ALLOCATION OF TAX EFFECT TO
NCI AND OWNERS OF PARENT

3.13.250.150   Continuing Example 13C, Company P is the parent of Company Z
with an 80% shareholding. The applicable tax rate in both Z's and P's tax jurisdictions is 30%.

3.13.250.160   Z records the following entries in respect of the issuance of the convertible bond and the related deferred tax.

In Z's financial statements	DEBIT	CREDIT
Cash	100	
Liability		18
Equity		82
To record issuance of convertible bond		
Deferred tax asset (18 x 30%)	5.4	
Equity		5.4
To record deferred tax on initial recognition of convertible bond		

3.13.250.170   In P's consolidated financial statements, the equity component of 82 is
reclassified as NCI (see 2.5.460.40). From the consolidated perspective, P records
the following entry for the issuance of the convertible bond.

In P's consolidated financial statements	DEBIT	CREDIT
Cash	100	
Liability		18
NCI		82
To record issuance of convertible bond		

3.13.250.180   The entry for the deferred tax related to the issuance of the convertible bond by Z in P's consolidated financial statements depends on its
accounting policy. The following entries illustrate both approaches discussed
in 3.13.250.120.

Approach 1: Attribute deferred tax effects entirely to NCI	DEBIT	CREDIT
Deferred tax asset	5.4	
NCI		5.4
To record deferred tax on initial recognition of convertible bond		

Approach 2: Attribute deferred tax effects to owners of the parent and to ordinary NCI in proportion to their ownership interests	DEBIT	CREDIT
Deferred tax asset	5.4	
NCI (5.4 x 20%)		1.1
Other equity (5.4 x 80%) (see 2.5.570.80)		4.3
To record deferred tax on initial recognition of convertible bond		

3.13.250.190 Subsequent changes in the deferred tax asset are recognised in profit or loss, which is subject to normal parent/NCI attribution, regardless of the accounting policy chosen by P for the initial attribution of the deferred tax (see 3.13.250.140).

3.13.250.200 If the interest to the holders of the bond is paid in a lump sum, then P records the following entries in its consolidated financial statements.

In P's consolidated financial statements	DEBIT	CREDIT
Liability	18	
Interest expense	2	
Cash		20
To record interest payment on convertible bond		
Current tax (statement of financial position)	6	
Current tax expense (profit or loss)		6[1]

Attributable to:
    Owners of the parent: 4.8 (6 x 80%)
    NCI: 1.2 (6 x 20%)		

To record current income tax effect of interest payment (20 x 30%)		
Tax expense (profit or loss)	5.4[1]	

Attributable to:
    Owners of the parent: 4.3 (5.4 x 80%)
    NCI: 1.1 (5.4 x 20%)		

Deferred tax asset		5.4
To reverse deferred tax asset when liability repaid		

Note
1. Current income tax credit of 6 on the tax deductible interest expense of 20 exceeds deferred tax asset of 5.4 on the 18 deductible temporary difference by 0.6 (6 - 5.4) and therefore reflects the tax benefit of the interest expense recognised in profit or loss (2 x 30%).

3.13.250.210 The following table illustrates the allocation of the income tax effect of (6) related to the convertible bond to P's owners and to NCI based on the two approaches discussed in 3.13.250.120.

	APPROACH 1 ATTRIBUTE TO NCI ONLY		APPROACH 2 ATTRIBUTE TO P'S OWNERS AND NCI	
	OTHER EQUITY/ RETAINED EARNINGS	NCI	OTHER EQUITY/ RETAINED EARNINGS	NCI
Deferred tax on initial recognition of convertible bond	-	5.4	4.3	1.1
Income tax effect of interest payment on convertible bond	4.8	1.2	4.8	1.2
Reversal of deferred tax asset on repayment of liability	(4.3)	(1.1)	(4.3)	(1.1)
Net income tax effect	0.5	5.5	4.8	1.2

3.13.260 Exceptions for investments in subsidiaries, branches and associates, and interests in joint arrangements

3.13.260.10 Temporary differences may arise in relation to the carrying amounts of the individual assets and liabilities of a subsidiary, branch or an interest in a joint operation and the tax bases of such assets and liabilities. In our experience, such temporary differences are commonly referred to as 'inside basis differences'; the tax effects of these temporary differences are subject to the general recognition and measurement principles of IAS 12.

3.13.260.20 Additionally, the difference between the tax base of a parent or investor's investment in a subsidiary, branch or associate, or the interest in a joint arrangement and the carrying amount of the related net assets in the parent or investor's consolidated financial statements is a temporary difference. This is despite the fact that the investment may be eliminated in the consolidated financial statements. In practice, such temporary differences are commonly referred to as 'outside basis differences'. They can arise, for example, because of undistributed profits of a subsidiary, branch or associate, or joint arrangement that affect the carrying amount of the investment but not its tax base. [*IAS 12.38*]

(S) 3.13.260.30 Temporary differences may also arise in respect of other investments in the parent or investor's separate financial statements – e.g. when the investment is measured at fair value in accordance with IFRS 9 but the tax base of the investment is its original cost. [*IAS 27.10*]

3.13.260.40   Tax effects on *taxable* temporary differences in respect of investments in subsidiaries, branches and associates, and interests in joint arrangements are not recognised if:

● the investor is able to control the timing of the reversal of the temporary difference; and
● it is probable that the temporary difference will not reverse in the foreseeable future (see 3.13.280).
  [*IAS 12.39*]

3.13.260.50   Tax effects on *deductible* temporary differences in respect of investments in subsidiaries, branches and associates, and interests in joint arrangements are recognised only to the extent that it is probable that:

● the temporary difference will reverse in the foreseeable future; and
● taxable profit will be available, against which the temporary difference can be utilised. [*IAS 12.44*]

3.13.270   *Timing and nature of reversal*

3.13.270.10   The temporary differences associated with investments in subsidiaries, branches and associates, and interests in joint arrangements will fluctuate from period to period. This may be due, for example, to movements in exchange rates and the profitability of the investee. In our view, the reversal of a temporary difference means its crystallisation rather than its fluctuation. For example, we believe that changes in exchange rates do not cause the reversal of a temporary difference, but instead change the amount of the temporary difference. Conversely, if an entity disposes of an investment, or if that investee pays a dividend, then the temporary difference reverses, either in full or partially.

3.13.270.20   The reversal of temporary differences associated with investments in subsidiaries, branches and associates, interests in joint arrangements can occur through:

● sale;
● dividend;
● other means, such as liquidation; or
● a combination of those means of reversal.

3.13.270.30   The IFRS Interpretations Committee discussed the measurement of deferred taxes relating to an investment in an associate when local tax legislation prescribes different tax rates depending on a manner of reversal – e.g. dividends, sale and liquidation. The Committee noted that an entity measures deferred tax liabilities and deferred tax assets using the tax rate and the tax base that are consistent with the expected manner of recovery or settlement (see 3.13.100). Therefore, in such cases, if one part of the temporary difference is expected to reverse through dividends and another part is expected to reverse on sale or liquidation, then different tax rates apply to the parts of the temporary difference to be consistent with the expected manner of reversal. [*IU 03-15*]

EXAMPLE 14A – 'OUTSIDE BASIS DIFFERENCES' – MANNER OF REVERSAL FOR INVESTMENT IN ASSOCIATE

3.13.270.40   Company C has an investment in Associate K. As a result of undistributed profits and dilution gains (see 3.5.550), the tax base of the investment becomes different from its carrying amount. Therefore, a temporary difference arises. The following facts are also relevant for this example.

● Management believes that the portion of the temporary difference that relates to undistributed profits will be reversed through dividends.

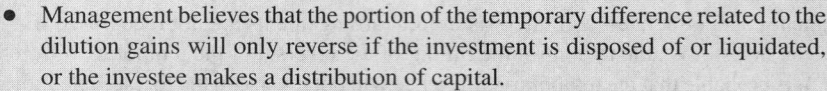

- Management believes that the portion of the temporary difference related to the dilution gains will only reverse if the investment is disposed of or liquidated, or the investee makes a distribution of capital.
- Management has no plans to dispose of its investment in K.
- In C's tax jurisdiction, distributions of capital for tax purposes are treated differently from dividend distributions of undistributed profits.

3.13.270.50   C measures the resulting deferred tax liability taking into account the different rates that are applicable to the different manners of recovery or settlement. For example, to the extent that the temporary difference relates to undistributed profits and is expected to reverse through dividends, C applies the rate applicable to dividends from undistributed profits. To the extent that the temporary difference will reverse only through sale, liquidation or a distribution of capital, C uses the relevant rate(s).

3.13.270.60   When a taxable temporary difference associated with an investment in a subsidiary, branch or associate, or an interest in a joint arrangement crystallises, an entity will sometimes receive a related tax deduction. For example, paying a dividend may reverse a temporary difference associated with an investment in a subsidiary. It may also generate a dividend credit or other tax benefit for the parent. In our view, the tax effect of the reversal of the temporary difference should be considered net of the tax benefit related to the dividend (see 3.13.810 and 1220).

3.13.280   *Foreseeable future*

3.13.280.10   The recognition criteria for both deferred tax assets and liabilities refer to 'foreseeable future'; however, the term 'foreseeable future' is not defined. In our view, it is necessary to consider in detail a period of 12 months from the reporting date, and also to take into account any transactions that are planned for a reasonable period after that date. [*IAS 12.39, 44*]

3.13.280.20   In practice, an entity assesses 'foreseeable future' on a case-by-case basis, taking into account the entity's history and the certainty of its plans.

EXAMPLE 14B – 'OUTSIDE BASIS DIFFERENCES' – ASSESSING LENGTH OF FORESEEABLE FUTURE

3.13.280.30   Parent P plans to draw dividends of 200 from Subsidiary S in 18 months' time; P estimates that 150 of that amount will relate to post-acquisition earnings already recognised in the financial statements. We believe that 18 months is within the foreseeable future, and that the deferred tax related to the planned 150 distribution should therefore be recognised.

3.13.280.40   If a loan to an investee is accounted for as an integral part of the investor's investment, then in our view it should be assumed that any temporary difference associated with the loan will not reverse in the foreseeable future through repayment. This is because the requirement for net investment accounting requires that repayment should not be planned or likely to occur in the 'foreseeable future'; this is to allow classification as part of the investment (see 2.7.150). [*IAS 21.15*]

3.13.290   *Investments in subsidiaries or branches*

3.13.290.10   An entity controls an investment in a subsidiary or branch; therefore, there is generally no need to consider whether the entity can control the timing of the reversal of a taxable temporary difference. The key issue is whether the temporary difference will reverse in the foreseeable future, and if so, how it will reverse; and in relation to a deductible temporary difference, whether the asset recognition criteria are met. [*IAS 12.39, 44*]

EXAMPLE 14C – 'OUTSIDE BASIS DIFFERENCES' – INVESTMENT IN SUBSIDIARY

3.13.290.20   If Subsidiary S pays dividends to Parent P, then a dividend tax of 10% will be incurred. However, if P disposes of its investment, then tax of 30% will be incurred on the reversal of the temporary difference. P plans to dispose of its investment in S within the next two years.

3.13.290.30   We believe that P should measure deferred tax in line with the manner in which it expects to recover the carrying amount of the investment. Because P plans to dispose of its investment in S in the foreseeable future, the deferred tax liability is calculated using the tax rate of 30%. [*IAS 12.51*]

3.13.300   *Investments in associates*

3.13.300.10   An investor does not control an associate (see chapter 3.5); it is therefore not generally in a position to control the timing of the reversal of a taxable temporary difference related to the investment in the associate. Therefore, it recognises a deferred tax liability unless the investor can otherwise control the timing of the reversal of the temporary differences – e.g. if the associate has agreed that profits will not be distributed in the foreseeable future. [*IAS 12.42*]

3.13.300.20   In our view, if the investor does not control the reversal of a temporary difference, and recognises a deferred tax liability, then the measurement of the deferred tax liability should be analysed as follows.

- If the entity has a plan to dispose of its investment in the associate in the foreseeable future, then the deferred tax liability should be based on the tax consequences of disposal; the entity should take into account any recovery of the carrying amount through dividends until the date of disposal.
- In other cases, the entity should determine the most likely manner of recovery of the temporary difference – e.g. dividend, payment out of capital or liquidation. It may be that different tax rates apply to different manners of reversal of different elements of the temporary difference. In this case, the entity should consider such differences in measuring the deferred tax liability (see 3.13.270.30). [*IAS 12.42*]

EXAMPLE 14D – 'OUTSIDE BASIS DIFFERENCES' – DIVIDENDS RECEIVED FROM ASSOCIATE TAX-EXEMPT

3.13.300.30   Company C acquired a 25% equity interest in Associate D for 1,000. Since acquisition, D has followed a dividend policy of distributing a third of its profit for the year; however, there is no shareholders' agreement in this respect.

3.13.300.40   The following additional facts are relevant for this example.
- At the end of 2018, the carrying amount of D in C's consolidated financial statements is 1,500. The tax base of the investment is 1,000.
- The tax laws under which C operates stipulate that dividends received from associates are tax-exempt.
- On disposal of the investment, any realised capital gains are subject to tax at a rate of 40%.
- C has no intention of selling its investment in D.

3.13.300.50   In this example, we believe that C should measure deferred tax in line with the manner in which it expects to recover the carrying amount of the investment. Because C has no intention to dispose of the investment in the foreseeable future, the deferred tax liability should be calculated using the tax rate applicable to dividends, which is zero in this case.

EXAMPLE 14E – 'OUTSIDE BASIS DIFFERENCES' – DIVIDENDS RECEIVED FROM ASSOCIATE TAXABLE

3.13.300.60   Modifying Example 14D, dividends received by C are taxed at a rate of 20%. In this example, we believe that C should recognise a deferred tax liability of 100 ((1,500 - 1,000) x 20%).

3.13.310   *Interests in joint arrangements*

3.13.310.10   Whether a joint venturer or a joint operator is in a position to control a joint arrangement's dividend policy will depend on the terms of the joint arrangement. In our view, the ability of a joint venturer or a joint operator to veto the payment of dividends is sufficient to demonstrate control for the purpose of recognising deferred tax. [*IAS 12.43*]

3.13.320   **Liability recognition criteria**

3.13.320.10   A deferred tax liability is recognised for all taxable temporary differences, unless the deferred tax liability arises from:
- the initial recognition of goodwill; or
- the initial recognition of an asset or liability in a transaction that:
  - is not a business combination; and
  - at the time of the transaction, affects neither accounting profit nor taxable profit (see 3.13.200).
  [*IAS 12.15*]

3.13.320.20   An additional exemption applies to taxable temporary differences related to investments in subsidiaries, branches and associates, and interests in joint arrangements, if certain criteria are met (see 3.13.260). [*IAS 12.39*]

3.13.320.30   The standard requires the tax effects of all taxable temporary differences to be fully recognised as a deferred tax liability except when a specific exemption applies (see 3.13.200). It does not allow the partial recognition method. Therefore, the fact that some or all of the differences may not be expected to crystallise in the future is not relevant under IFRS. [*IAS 12.15*]

EXAMPLE 15 – TAXABLE TEMPORARY DIFFERENCES NOT EXPECTED TO CRYSTALLISE

3.13.320.40   Company E owns machinery with a revalued carrying amount of 150 and a tax base of 80 (original cost was 100). When the machinery is sold, any capital gain is deductible against the cost of similar replacement assets.

3.13.320.50   E expects its business to grow, and that the machinery will be replaced. Therefore, E does not expect the difference of 70 between the carrying amount and the tax base to crystallise and generate a tax liability. Nevertheless, IFRS requires the deferred tax liability to be recognised. [*IAS 12.20*]

3.13.330   Asset recognition criteria

3.13.330.10   Unlike deferred tax liabilities, a deferred tax asset is recognised in respect of deductible temporary differences only to the extent that it is *probable* that taxable profit will be available, against which the deductible temporary differences can be utilised. Similar to deferred tax liabilities, no deferred tax asset is recognised if it arises from the initial recognition of an asset or liability in a transaction that:
- is not a business combination; and
- at the time of the transaction, affects neither accounting profit nor taxable profit (see 3.13.200). [*IAS 12.24*]

3.13.330.20   An additional exemption exists in respect of deductible temporary differences related to investments in subsidiaries, branches and associates, and interests in joint arrangements (see 3.13.260). This is similar to the treatment for taxable temporary differences. [*IAS 12.44*]

3.13.330.30   Although an entity is required to consider the probability of realising the benefit of deductible temporary differences, 'probable' is not defined in IAS 12. In our experience, entities often use a working definition of 'more likely than not', which is consistent with the definition of 'probable' in other standards – e.g. in respect of provisions (see 3.12.30). [*IAS 12.24, IFRIC 23.9, BC14–BC15*]

3.13.330.40   In determining whether taxable profit will be available in the future, an entity considers:
- taxable temporary differences that will reverse – i.e. will become taxable – in the same period that deductible temporary differences reverse – i.e. will become deductible (see 3.13.340); and
- the periods into which a tax loss or tax credit arising from a deductible temporary difference can be carried back or forward.

3.13.330.50   If the amount of taxable temporary differences is insufficient to recognise a deferred tax asset in full, then an entity also considers:
- the probability of generating future taxable profits in the periods that the deductible temporary differences reverse (see 3.13.360); and
- tax planning opportunities (see 3.13.370). [*IAS 12.28–29*]

3.13.330.60   All deductible temporary differences are assessed together unless, under tax law, their use is restricted to deductions against income of a specific type. [*IAS 12.27A*]

3.13.340   *Taxable temporary differences*

3.13.340.10   When considering whether taxable temporary differences are available in order to recognise a deferred tax asset, an entity needs to estimate the periods in which the reversals are expected to occur.

EXAMPLE 16A – ASSET RECOGNITION – REVERSAL OF EXISTING TAXABLE TEMPORARY DIFFERENCES

3.13.340.20   Company N has the following temporary differences at the end of year 1:
- a deductible temporary difference of 100 in respect of a liability for employee benefits because for tax purposes the expenditure is deducted when paid, which is expected to be in year 2; and
- a taxable temporary difference of 300 in respect of property, plant and equipment. Of this amount, 150 is expected to reverse in year 2, and the remaining 150 in year 3.

	TEMPORARY DIFFERENCE	TIMING OF EXPECTED REVERSAL		
		YR 1	YR 2	YR 3
Deductible temporary difference	100	-	100	-
Taxable temporary difference	(300)	-	(150)	(150)

3.13.340.30   N recognises the deferred tax asset associated with the employee benefit liability, because the reversing deferred tax liability associated with property, plant and equipment will generate sufficient taxable profit to enable that deferred tax asset to be utilised.

3.13.340.35   This is the case even if N is loss-making and expects to continue to incur tax losses in the future. [*IU 05-14*]

EXAMPLE 16B – ASSET RECOGNITION – REVERSAL OF FUTURE TAXABLE TEMPORARY DIFFERENCES (1)

3.13.340.40   Modifying Example 16A, the employee benefit expenditure is expected to be paid in year 10. There are no existing taxable temporary differences that are expected to reverse in the same or a later period. However, N expects to continue investing in property, plant and equipment. It fully expects that future taxable temporary differences will be available 10 years from now, and that they will be sufficient to absorb the deductible temporary difference.

> 3.13.340.50   In this case, IAS 12 is specific that taxable temporary differences expected to arise in the future cannot be taken into account. Therefore, subject to an analysis of other sources of taxable profit, N is not able to recognise a deferred tax asset. [*IAS 12.28–29, IU 05-14*]

3.13.340.60   In some cases, it is not clear when a deductible temporary difference reverses – e.g. an expected credit loss (ECL) provision for a receivables portfolio measured on a collective basis. In our view, for short-term receivables the provision reverses each year and is replaced by a new provision against new trade receivables.

EXAMPLE 16C – ASSET RECOGNITION – REVERSAL OF FUTURE TAXABLE TEMPORARY DIFFERENCES (2)

> 3.13.340.70   Company O recognises an ECL provision for a receivables portfolio (see chapter 7.8). For tax purposes, the allowance cannot be deducted; instead, bad receivables are deducted in accordance with criteria established by the tax authorities. Because the ECL provision remains constant or grows slightly year on year, O believes that the deductible temporary difference will never reverse as long as it remains in business.

> 3.13.340.80   We believe that the ECL provision reverses each year and is replaced by a new provision for new trade receivables. Therefore, in assessing whether a deferred tax asset should be recognised, O considers its recoverability assuming a full reversal in the following year.

3.13.350   *Unused tax losses and tax credits*

3.13.350.10   The requirement to consider the sources of taxable profit in respect of deductible temporary differences also applies when assessing whether a deferred tax asset arising from unused tax losses and unused tax credits should be recognised. For a discussion of tax credits in respect of specific investments, see 3.13.670.

3.13.350.20   A deferred tax asset is recognised for unused tax losses and unused tax credits carried forward, to the extent that it is probable that future taxable profits will be available. [*IAS 12.34*]

3.13.350.30   In our view, in determining whether probable future taxable profits are available, the probability threshold is applied to portions of the total amount of unused tax losses or tax credits, rather than to the entire amount.

EXAMPLE 17 – ASSET RECOGNITION – APPLYING PROBABILITY THRESHOLD TO PORTIONS OF UNUSED TAX LOSSES

> 3.13.350.40   Company R has cumulative tax losses of 1,000 carried forward at the end of year 1. R expects to recover a portion of that amount in year 2, because it has just signed a major contract that will be performed during year 2. However, it is uncertain whether the contract will be extended for subsequent years.

> 3.13.350.50   At the end of year 1, R assesses that it is highly probable that a taxable profit of 400 will be available in year 2, but that it is not yet probable that any further taxable profit will be available from year 3 onwards. Therefore, R does not believe that the total 1,000 of tax losses is more likely than not to be fully recovered.
>
> 3.13.350.60   In determining whether it should recognise a deferred tax asset, we believe that R should assess whether any portion of the tax losses carried forward is recoverable through probable future taxable profits. Therefore, as at the end of year 1, R should recognise a deferred tax asset related to the deductible temporary difference of 400.

3.13.350.70   The standard provides the following additional guidance.
- If an entity has a history of recent losses, then a deferred tax asset is recognised only to the extent that:
    - the entity has sufficient taxable temporary differences; or
    - there is convincing evidence that sufficient taxable profit will be available against which the tax losses or tax credits can be utilised.
- An entity considers whether any unused tax losses arise from identifiable causes that are unlikely to recur; if so, this makes it easier to justify recognition of the resulting deferred tax asset. [IAS 12.35–36]

3.13.350.75   The IFRS Interpretations Committee discussed the recognition and measurement of deferred tax assets by loss-making entities and noted that an entity recognises a deferred tax asset for the carry forward of unused tax losses to the extent of the taxable temporary differences of an appropriate type that reverse in an appropriate period. The reversal of those taxable temporary differences enables the utilisation of the unused tax losses and justifies the recognition of deferred tax assets. Consequently, future tax losses are not considered. The Committee also noted that if tax law limits the extent to which unused tax losses can be recovered against future taxable profits in each year, then the amount of a deferred tax asset from unused tax losses is restricted as specified by the tax law. This is because when the suitable taxable temporary differences reverse, the amount of tax losses that can be utilised by that reversal is reduced as specified by the tax law. [IU 05-14]

3.13.350.80   In our view, an entity in the start-up phase should not recognise a deferred tax asset in respect of tax losses if it does not have sufficient taxable temporary differences. This is because we believe that it is not appropriate to forecast profits when a business is in a start-up phase, unless there is convincing evidence that future taxable profits will be available – e.g. signed contracts are in place and it is clear that the business can operate at a cost level that will result in taxable profits.

EXAMPLE 18 – ASSET RECOGNITION – START-UP OPERATIONS

> 3.13.350.90   Company T was established one year ago and is in its start-up phase. In its first year of operations, T has a loss of 500 for tax purposes. T does not have any taxable temporary differences. T expects to be profitable by its third year of operations, and expects all tax losses to be utilised by the end of its fifth year of operations. In the absence of convincing evidence that future taxable profits will be available, we believe that T should not recognise a deferred tax asset in respect of tax losses.

3.13.360   ***Future taxable profits***

3.13.360.10   In our view, an entity should take into account all factors concerning its expected future profitability, both favourable and unfavourable, when assessing whether a deferred tax asset should be recognised on the basis of the availability of future taxable profits. In our view, a deferred tax asset should be recognised if:

- an entity has a stable earnings history;
- there is no evidence to suggest that current earnings levels will not continue into the future; and
- there is no evidence to suggest that the tax benefits will not be realised for some other reason.

EXAMPLE 19A – ASSET RECOGNITION – FORECASTS OF FUTURE PROFITS

3.13.360.20   Company M has a deductible temporary difference in respect of a liability for employee benefits. The majority of this difference is expected to reverse in 20 years' time. M prepares budgets and forecasts for a period of only two years into the future.

3.13.360.30   However, M has a history of being profitable; and based on an assessment of M's business prospects, there is no reason to believe that it will not be profitable in the future. Therefore, in this example, we believe that a deferred tax asset should be recognised, regardless of the limited period for which budgets and forecasts are available.

3.13.360.35   An estimate of probable future profits may include the recovery of some of the assets for more than their carrying amounts if there is sufficient evidence that it is probable that a higher amount will be realised. For example, this may apply to fixed-rate debt instruments that are measured at fair value and whose fair value is lower than the nominal amount if an entity expects to hold them to maturity and collect all contractual cash flows. [*IAS 12.29A*]

3.13.360.40   If the estimated fair value of an asset accounted for under the cost model is higher than its revalued tax base, then this is a factor taken into account in assessing the probability of whether taxable profits will be available to offset the deductible temporary difference in the future. In our view, the assessment should also take into account the appropriate scheduling of the reversal of such temporary differences. If the assessment is favourable, then a deferred tax asset should be recognised for the deductible temporary difference. [*IAS 12.24, 29(a)*]

EXAMPLE 19B – ASSET RECOGNITION – TIMING OF FUTURE PROFITS UNCERTAIN

3.13.360.50   Company Q is a wine maker and the land from which it operates is vital to its operations. The following facts are relevant for this example.
- The land is revalued for tax purposes (but not under IFRS) and the revaluation surplus is deductible from the sales proceeds when the land is sold. Therefore, the tax revaluation creates a deductible temporary difference that will reverse when the land is sold (see 3.13.110.110).

- At the reporting date:
  - carrying amount of the land: 60;
  - estimated fair value of the land: 100;
  - revalued tax base of the land: 70; and
  - a taxable profit of 30 would be generated on sale of the land.
- Q needs to maintain possession of the land on which the grapes are grown in order to continue its business of producing wine; therefore, it is not possible to forecast when or if the land will be disposed of.

3.13.360.60   We believe that the difficulty of estimating the timing of the reversal of the temporary difference is not in itself a reason for not recognising a deferred tax asset. However, it is a relevant factor in assessing the probability of the availability of future tax profits.

3.13.360.70   In this case, we believe that the taxable profit of 30 could be taken into account when assessing the factors concerning the entity's expected future profitability, both favourable and unfavourable (see 3.13.360.10). If the recoverability assessment is favourable, then a deferred tax asset should be recognised for the deductible temporary difference of 10 (70 - 60).

3.13.360.80   Taxable profit used for the asset recognition test is different from taxable profit on which income taxes are payable (see 3.13.30.20). To avoid double counting, an entity excludes reversals of existing taxable and deductible temporary differences in determining whether sufficient future taxable profits are available to recognise deferred tax assets in excess of taxable temporary differences. In addition, an entity does not include in that assessment new deductible temporary differences that originate in future periods. [*IAS 12.29(a), BC56, IE.Ex7*]

EXAMPLE 19C – ASSET RECOGNITION – REVERSAL OF EXISTING TEMPORARY DIFFERENCES

3.13.360.90   Company C has deductible temporary differences of 5,750, which are expected to reverse over the next four years. In addition, C has taxable temporary differences of 2,000 reversing over the same period. C does not expect to generate taxable profits in the near future.

3.13.360.100   As a first step, C considers taxable temporary differences that reverse in the same period as the deductible temporary differences and concludes that it should recognise a deferred tax asset for deductible temporary differences of at least 2,000 (see 3.13.340).

3.13.360.110   Because there are insufficient taxable temporary differences to recognise the deferred tax asset in full, as a next step C prepares a projection of future taxable profits (see 3.13.330.50). To avoid double counting, C adjusts its projection of taxable profits to exclude the reversals of the existing taxable temporary differences as follows.

	Yr 1	Yr 2	Yr 3	Yr 4	Total
Future tax losses	(250)	-	-	(500)	(750)
Reversal of existing taxable temporary differences	(500)	(500)	(500)	(500)	(2,000)
Reversal of existing deductible temporary differences	750	1,000	1,500	2,500	5,750
Taxable profit adjusted for reversals of existing temporary differences	-	500	1,000	1,500	3,000

3.13.360.120   To determine the total amount of the deferred tax asset to recognise, C adds up reversing taxable temporary differences and the adjusted taxable profit for each period. As a result, C recognises a deferred tax asset for deductible temporary differences of 5,000 (500 + 1,000 + 1,500 + 2,000).

EXAMPLE 19D – ASSET RECOGNITION – FUTURE PROFITS FROM ORIGINATING DEDUCTIBLE TEMPORARY DIFFERENCE

3.13.360.130   Company R has a calendar year end. R has a deductible temporary difference of 400, which is expected to reverse over the next three years. R assesses its expected future profits, to determine whether to recognise the deferred tax asset.

	Yr 1	Yr 2	Yr 3
Future taxable profits	250	150	150
Of which new deductible differences	(200)	(120)	(100)
Future taxable profits available for recovery of deferred tax assets	50	30	50

3.13.360.140   Although R expects to generate sufficient future taxable profits in the next three years, a large part of those profits arises from new deductible temporary differences. To assess recoverability of the deferred tax asset, R determines future taxable profits arising in the relevant period exclusive of the effects of originating temporary differences.

3.13.360.150   These future profits of 130 (50 + 30 + 50) support the recognition of a deferred tax asset associated with a deductible temporary difference of 130. The recognition of the remaining deferred tax asset associated with the temporary difference of 270 (400 - 130) would depend on the availability of other sources of taxable profits, such as tax planning opportunities (see 3.13.370).

3.13.370   *Tax planning opportunities*

3.13.370.10   'Tax planning opportunities' are actions that an entity would take to create or increase taxable income for a specific period to utilise tax losses or tax credits carried forward or deductible temporary differences. An example includes deferring the claim for certain deductions from taxable

843

profits to a later period. However, these opportunities do not include creating taxable profit in the future from future originating temporary differences (see 3.13.360.80). [*IAS 12.30*]

3.13.370.20   In our view, it should be management's intention to take advantage of tax planning opportunities, or at least it should be more likely than not that they will take advantage of these opportunities, before they can be used to justify the recognition of deferred tax assets. In most cases, it can be presumed that the entity will take advantage of any opportunity to reduce its overall tax burden. However, taking advantage of the opportunities may involve, for example, making an irrevocable election that may have other, disadvantageous, implications for the future. In this event, management should determine whether it is probable that it will make the election (see also 3.13.100 and 960.10).

3.13.370.30   Including or excluding entities from a tax group – i.e. a group of entities that are treated as a single entity for tax purposes – may qualify as a tax planning opportunity. In some situations, entities – e.g. a parent and its subsidiaries – are automatically included in the same tax group. If this is the case, then in our view income taxes should be determined on a combined basis. If, however, participation within a tax group is discretionary, then we believe that management should consider its intention as described in 3.13.370.20 when evaluating whether discretionary elections related to tax groups would qualify as a tax planning opportunity.

3.13.380   MEASURE AND RECOGNISE DEFERRED TAX

3.13.380.10   Deferred tax assets and liabilities are measured based on:
- the expected manner of recovery (asset) or settlement (liability) (see 3.13.390); and
- the tax rate expected to apply when the underlying asset (liability) is recovered (settled), based on rates that are enacted or substantively enacted at the reporting date (see 3.13.480). [*IAS 12.47, 51*]

3.13.390   Expected manner of recovery or settlement

3.13.390.10   The measurement of deferred tax assets or liabilities reflects management's intention regarding the manner of recovery of an asset or settlement of a liability. [*IAS 12.51*]

3.13.390.20   In some tax jurisdictions, the applicable tax rate or tax base depends on how the carrying amount of an asset or liability is recovered or settled. In such cases, management's intention is key in determining the amount of deferred tax to recognise. [*IAS 12.51A*]

EXAMPLE 20A – DETERMINING MANNER OF RECOVERY – MANAGEMENT'S INTENTION

3.13.390.30   Company V owns an operating plant that it intends to continue to use in its operations. If the plant was sold, then any gain would attract capital gains tax of 20%. The income tax rate is 30%.

3.13.390.40   In this example, deferred tax is measured using a rate of 30%, because management intends that the carrying amount will be recovered through use. Even if the plant is revalued, deferred tax would be measured at a rate of 30%. This is because the plant will be recovered through operations and taxable operating income is generated, which would therefore be taxed at a rate of 30%.

3.13.390.50   Special provisions apply for non-depreciable assets and investment property (see 3.13.410–430). [*IAS 12.51B–51C*]

3.13.400   *Dual intention*

3.13.400.10   In many cases, management has a dual intention with respect to assets. That is, it intends to operate the asset and then to sell it. In this case, the carrying amount will be recovered in two ways, and the calculation of deferred tax should reflect that dual intention. If different tax rates apply to usage and sale of the asset, then in our view deferred tax should be calculated using what is sometimes called a 'blended rate' approach.

EXAMPLE 20B – MEASURING DEFERRED TAX – DUAL INTENTION

3.13.400.20   Company C acquires an asset in a business combination. The following facts are relevant for this example.
- C determines that the fair value of the asset on the date of acquisition is 150.
- For accounting purposes, C depreciates the asset over five years to its expected residual value of 50.
- The asset is not depreciated for tax purposes; instead, a tax deduction is received on sale. C expects to sell the asset for its residual value, at which time it will receive a tax deduction of 100.
- The income tax rate is 30% and the capital gains tax rate is 10%.

3.13.400.25   There may be different approaches to arriving at a blended rate.

Approach 1

3.13.400.30   One approach in these circumstances is to treat the asset as having a single tax base of 100. This results in a single temporary difference of 50 (carrying amount of 150 less tax base of 100). Considering the expected manner of recovery of the carrying amount of 150, a deferred tax liability of 25 is recognised in the acquisition accounting as follows.

	CARRYING AMOUNT	TAX BASE	TEMPORARY DIFFERENCE	DEFERRED TAX
Use (tax rate = 30%)	100	-	100	30
Sale (tax rate = 10%)	50	100	(50)	(5)
Net amount recognised	150	100	50	25

Approach 2

3.13.400.40   Alternatively, it could be argued that the use and sale consequences should be considered separately, subject to the manner in which C expects to recover the carrying amount of the asset. By considering the two components of the above calculation separately, C would recognise a deferred tax liability of 30 and a deferred tax asset of 5, subject to recoverability (see 3.13.330).

	Carrying Amount	Tax base	Temporary Difference	Deferred tax
Use (tax rate = 30%)	100	-	100	30
Sale (tax rate = 10%)	50	100	(50)	(5)

Approach 3

3.13.400.50 A third, less common, approach is to treat the asset as having a single tax base of 100, but first to apply the income tax rate to the 'top slice' of the temporary difference. C would then apply the capital gain tax rate to any 'bottom slice' of the temporary difference. The top slice is the lower of the portion of the carrying amount that will be recovered through usage and the temporary difference; the bottom slice is the temporary difference less the top slice.

	Carrying Amount	Tax base	Temporary Difference	Deferred tax
Total	150	100	50	
Top slice			50[1]	15[3]
Bottom slice			-[2]	-

Notes
1. The lower of the portion of the carrying amount that will be recovered through usage (100) and the temporary difference (50).
2. Temporary difference (50) less the top slice (50).
3. 50 x 30% (income tax rate).

3.13.400.60 Subsequently, as the carrying amount of the asset reduces, the temporary difference falls to zero and the deferred tax liability is released. When the carrying amount falls below the tax base, a deductible temporary difference arises for the first time. This is recognised at the capital gain rate of 10%.

3.13.400.70 The third approach can be seen more clearly if the figures in this example are changed. For example, if the deduction available on sale had been only 40, such that the taxable temporary difference was 110, then the income tax rate would have been applied to the first 100 of the temporary difference and the capital gain tax rate would have been applied to the remaining 10 of the temporary difference.

	Carrying Amount	Tax base	Temporary Difference	Deferred tax
Total	150	40	110	
Top slice			100[1]	30[3]
Bottom slice			10[2]	1[4]

Notes
1. The lower of the portion of the carrying amount that will be recovered through usage (100) and the temporary difference (110).
2. Temporary difference (110) less the top slice (100).
3. 100 x 30% (use rate).
4. 10 x 10% (sale rate).

3.13.410 *Non-depreciable property, plant and equipment*

3.13.410.10   The question of which tax rate and tax base to use can arise in the context of non-depreciable property, plant and equipment. When a non-depreciable item of property, plant and equipment is revalued, the deferred tax on the revaluation is measured using the tax rate that applies on disposal. [*IAS 12.51B*]

EXAMPLE 21 – REVALUATION OF NON-DEPRECIABLE TANGIBLE ASSET

3.13.410.20   Company X owns a piece of land that is not depreciated. For tax purposes, the cost of the land is 300 and it is depreciated over 15 years. At the reporting date, the carrying amount of the land under IFRS is 300, and the tax base is 160.

3.13.410.30   X revalues the land to 400 in accordance with the revaluation model for property, plant and equipment (see 3.2.300); the revaluation is not recognised for tax purposes. If the land is ever sold, then any recovery of the depreciated original cost will be taxed at the income tax rate of 30%; the proceeds in excess of the original cost will not be taxed.

3.13.410.40   In this case, the deferred tax calculations are as follows.
* Before the revaluation, X recognises a deferred tax liability of 42 ((300 - 160) x 30%).
* As a result of the revaluation, X does not recognise any further deferred tax liability. This is because there will never be any taxation consequences arising from the revaluation above original cost.

3.13.420 *Non-amortisable intangible assets*

3.13.420.10   The question of which tax rate and tax base to use (see 3.13.100.10 and 390.20) also arises in the context of non-amortisable intangible assets.

3.13.420.20   The IFRS Interpretations Committee discussed how to measure deferred taxes relating to non-amortisable intangible assets and noted that an entity applies the general measurement requirements in IAS 12 – i.e. it considers whether the asset is expected to be recovered through use and/or through sale. The Committee also noted that the guidance in paragraph 51B of IAS 12 is limited to non-depreciable property, plant and equipment (see 3.13.410) and cannot be applied by analogy to non-amortisable intangible assets. [*IAS 12.51–51B, IU 11-16*]

EXAMPLE 22 – NON-AMORTISABLE INTANGIBLE ASSET

3.13.420.30   Company Y acquires, in a business combination, a licence that is renewable without limitation, and therefore has an indefinite useful life (see 3.3.190.50–60). The carrying amount of the licence will therefore be its fair value determined as part of the acquisition accounting, until an impairment loss is recognised, or the licence is sold.

3.13.420.40   If the fair value of the licence determined in the acquisition accounting is higher than its tax base, then a temporary difference arises and Y recognises a deferred tax liability. The income tax rate in Y's jurisdiction is 30% and the capital gains tax rate is 10%.

3.13.420.50   If the management of Y determines that it expects to recover the entire carrying amount of the licence through use, then the deferred tax liability is measured at 30%. Conversely, if management determines that it expects to recover the entire carrying amount of the licence through sale, then the deferred tax liability is measured at 10% (see 3.13.100 and 390). If management has dual intention with respect to the licence, then it measures the deferred tax liability at a blended rate and applies one of the approaches in Example 20B to calculate it.

3.13.430   *Investment property*

3.13.430.10   IAS 40 allows investment property to be measured either at fair value or under the cost model (see 3.4.130). A specific measurement requirement applies to a deferred tax asset or liability that arises from investment property measured at fair value. This requirement establishes a rebuttable presumption that the carrying amount of investment property measured at fair value will be recovered through sale. Therefore, unless the presumption is rebutted, the measurement of a deferred tax asset or liability pertaining to the investment property reflects the tax consequences of recovering the carrying amount of the investment property entirely through sale. [*IAS 12.51C*]

3.13.430.20   The presumption is rebutted if the investment property is depreciable and is held within a business model whose objective is to consume substantially all the economic benefits embodied in the investment property over time, rather than through sale. If the presumption is rebutted, then the normal requirements of measuring deferred tax assets or liabilities are applicable (see 3.13.380). [*IAS 12.51C*]

3.13.430.30   If an investment property comprises land only, then because the land would not be depreciated, the presumption cannot be rebutted. Similarly, if a single investment property comprises land and buildings, then the presumption may be rebutted for the building component only. If this is the case, then the fair value of the investment property is split into component parts to determine the amount of deferred tax. In some cases, this may result in additional valuation work being required to determine the split.

EXAMPLE 23 – INVESTMENT PROPERTY – LAND AND BUILDING COMPONENTS

3.13.430.40   Company Y acquired an investment property in year 1. The cost of the investment property was 600, which Y split into 540 for the land and 60 for the building. Y elects to account for its investment property at fair value, but rebuts the presumption that the carrying amount of the building will be recovered though sale. For tax purposes, the building component is depreciated over 20 years; the land component is not depreciated but is deductible against any capital gain, which is imposed on sale of the land.

3.13.430.50   At the end of year 1, the fair value of the property is 700, of which 650 relates to the land and 50 to the building. The income tax rate in Y's jurisdiction is 35% and the capital gains tax rate is 40%.

	LAND		BUILDING	
	CARRYING AMOUNT	TAX BASE	CARRYING AMOUNT	TAX BASE
Cost	540	540	60	60
Depreciation	-	-	-	(3)
Change in fair value	110	-	(10)	-
Amount at the end of year 1	650	540	50	57

3.13.430.60   On revaluing the property at the end of year 1, Y recognises deferred tax as follows.

- The building has a carrying amount of 50 under IFRS and a tax base of 57. Therefore, a deferred tax asset of 2 (7 x 35%) arises, subject to recoverability (see 3.13.330). The income tax rate of 35% is used to measure the deferred tax relating to the building component, because Y has determined that the building component will be recovered through use, rather than sale.
- The land has a carrying amount of 650 under IFRS and a tax base of 540. Therefore, at the end of the year 1 a deferred tax liability of 44 (110 x 40%) arises. The capital gains tax rate of 40% is used to measure the deferred tax relating to the land component, because the land component is non-depreciable and therefore the sale presumption cannot be rebutted.
- This results in an overall net deferred tax liability of 42 (44 - 2).

3.13.440   *Special tax regimes for investment property companies*

3.13.440.10   In some jurisdictions, entities may elect to take advantage of special tax regimes for investment property companies. Typically, the entity will pay a one-off amount to the tax authorities in order to enter the special tax regime – i.e. an 'entry tax'. The entry tax may be based on a percentage of the value of the entity's investment property portfolio. Alternatively, it may be equivalent to the current tax that would be payable if the entity were to dispose of its portfolio on the date of entry to the special tax regime. Once it has entered the special tax regime, the entity may pay income taxes at a rate that is lower than the prevailing rate; alternatively, it may be exempt from income taxes. For a discussion of presentation of a change in tax status, see 3.13.550.

3.13.440.20   There may be a delay between the date of the management decision to enter the special tax regime and the date on which the entity actually enters the regime. In our view, the entity should measure deferred taxes at the entry tax rate from the date of the management decision – provided that there are no substantive conditions for entry to the regime that are outside the control of the entity.

3.13.440.30   Conversely, if entry to the special tax regime is subject to conditions that are not within the control of management – e.g. shareholder approval, regulatory approvals etc – then in our view the entity should consider whether those conditions are substantive. Depending on the outcome of that assessment, the entity may need to continue to calculate deferred tax at the prevailing tax rate until such time as the substantive conditions are met.

EXAMPLE 24 – ENTRY TO SPECIAL TAX REGIME

3.13.440.40 Company Z is an unlisted investment property company in a juris-diction whose normal corporate tax rate on income and asset disposals is 30%. However, a special tax regime exists under which listed investment property companies pay no income taxes.

3.13.440.50 To enter the regime, Z needs to pay a one-off entry tax. This is cal-culated as the tax that would arise on disposal of Z's entire property portfolio, at the special entry tax rate of 20%. Z's management decides in July 2018 that Z will enter the special tax regime with effect from 1 April 2019.

3.13.440.60 Management considers that the listing condition is the only substan-tive condition for entry to the special tax regime that Z does not meet at the date of its decision. As at 31 December 2018, we believe that Z should measure deferred tax at the normal tax rate of 30% if it remains unlisted, or recognise the entry tax measured at 20% as a liability if it has completed its listing at that date.

3.13.440.70 For a discussion of the timing of a change in tax status, see 3.13.485.

3.13.450 *Corporate structure*

3.13.450.10 The tax treatment of an asset may be different depending on whether the asset is treated as an individual asset or as part of a corporate structure. For example, in some jurisdictions it is more tax-efficient to dispose of the shares of the entity that holds the asset, rather than to dispose of the underlying asset itself. In our view, the tax base in the consolidated financial statements should be determined based on the tax treatment of individual assets and liabilities on an item-by-item basis. [*IAS 12.11, 51–51A*]

3.13.450.15 In an extreme case, an asset (e.g. a building) might be held by a group as the sole asset within a corporate shell for tax planning reasons. The IFRS Interpretations Committee discussed the recognition of deferred tax for a single asset in a corporate shell and noted that if a tax law attributes separate tax bases to the asset and the shares, then in the consolidated financial statements an entity recognises two deferred taxes: the deferred tax related to the asset and the deferred tax related to the shares. For example, an asset held within a corporate shell, when sold individually, would not be tax-deductible and therefore has a tax base of zero. However, the original cost of the investment in the shares of the corporate shell is tax-deductible when disposed of by the holding company. In this case, the entity determines two deferred taxes in the consolidated financial statements – i.e. the deferred tax related to the asset, which is determined by comparing the carrying amount of the underlying asset with its tax base of zero, and the deferred tax related to the investment in the corporate structure. [*IU 07-14*]

3.13.450.20 In our view, this principle applies even on classification of the corporate structure as a disposal group as held-for-sale or held-for-distribution (see 5.4.20 and 35). We believe that any deferred taxes on the individual assets (liabilities) should not be affected by the corporate structure of the corresponding disposal group. However, classification as a disposal group is a factor that should be considered when analysing whether deferred tax on the corporate structure itself should be recognised (see 3.13.260). [*IAS 12.39, 44*]

EXAMPLE 25 – ASSETS HELD IN CORPORATE STRUCTURE

3.13.450.30   Subsidiary S has two individual assets, B and C, and no liabilities. S meets the criteria in IFRS 5 to be classified as a disposal group. After applying the measurement requirements in IFRS 5, the carrying amounts of asset B and asset C in Parent P's consolidated financial statements are 300 and 400, respectively. The tax bases of the assets in accordance with the tax accounts of S are 200 for each asset. When P disposes of the shares in S, an amount of 800 will be deductible for tax purposes. P's income tax rate is 10%.

	CARRYING AMOUNT	TAX BASE	TAXABLE TEMPORARY DIFFERENCE
Asset B	300	200	100
Asset C	400	200	200
Total	700	400	300

	NET ASSETS OF S IN P'S CONSOLIDATED FINANCIAL STATEMENTS	TAX BASE FOR SHARES	DEDUCTIBLE TEMPORARY DIFFERENCE
Investment in S	670[1]	800	(130)

Note
1.   Calculated as carrying amounts of asset B and asset C minus deferred tax liability (700 - (300 x 10%)).

3.13.450.40   We believe that P should consider the tax base of 400 (rather than 800) in its consolidated financial statements for assets B and C. Consequently, despite the planned disposal of S, P continues to recognise a deferred tax liability based on the taxable temporary difference of 300.

3.13.450.50   However, the difference between the consolidated net assets of S of 670 and the tax base of P's investment in S of 800 represents an additional temporary difference of 130. Because S meets the criteria to be recognised as a disposal group, it is probable that this deductible temporary difference will reverse in the foreseeable future. Therefore, the recognition exemption for the deductible temporary difference no longer applies and P recognises a separate deferred tax asset (see 3.13.260), subject to recoverability (see 3.13.330). [*IAS 12.15, 44, IFRS 5.6–8*]

3.13.460   ***Financial assets***

3.13.460.10   In our view, the tax treatment of financial assets should be consistent with the entity's business model in which the asset is held (see 7.4.70). For example, for financial assets held to trade to realise fair value changes, we believe that the entity should assume that the carrying amount of the asset will be recovered through sale. For financial assets held for both to collect and for sale (see 7.4.130), in our view management should determine whether it intends to recover the carrying amount of the asset through:

- sale; or
- the receipt of interest, and the repayment of principal.

3.13.460.20   When there is a dual intention with respect to the recovery of the carrying amount of a financial asset, a more detailed analysis will be required. This will follow the same methodology as illustrated in 3.13.400.

3.13.460.30   When the financial asset is an investment in a subsidiary, branch or associate, or an interest in a joint arrangement, special recognition criteria apply to determine whether any deferred tax should be recognised (see 3.13.260).

3.13.470   Applicable tax rate

3.13.470.10   In our view, the tax rate expected to apply is based on the statutory tax rate and not an entity's effective tax rate. For example, Company U is subject to a statutory tax rate of 30 percent. However, after tax deductions it usually pays tax of around 20 percent. We believe that deferred tax should be recognised using the statutory tax rate of 30 percent and that U should not anticipate future deductions.

3.13.480   *Enacted or substantively enacted*

3.13.480.10   In most cases, the calculation of deferred tax will be based on tax rates that have been enacted. However, in some jurisdictions it may be clear that a change in tax rate is going to be enacted – even though the legal process necessary to effect the change has not yet been completed. In these circumstances, the determination of whether a tax rate is 'substantively enacted' may require judgement. [*IAS 12.47–48*]

EXAMPLE 26A – SUBSTANTIVELY ENACTED TAX RATE

3.13.480.20   The president of Country Z indicated to the public in July 2018 that he would like to reduce the corporate tax rate from 40% to 30%. The issue was debated by the government in August and September, and on 30 November the government formally announced that the reduction in tax rate would take effect in January 2019. However, the change in tax rate was not written into law until a presidential decree confirming the change in law was signed in February 2019. In Country Z, the signing of a presidential decree is a mere formality and the president cannot override decisions formally announced by the government.

3.13.480.30   In our view, the tax rate of 30% is substantively enacted on 30 November 2018 and should be used in the calculation of deferred tax from that date.

EXAMPLE 26B – NOT SUBSTANTIVELY ENACTED TAX RATE

3.13.480.40   Modifying Example 26A, the president of Country Z has the power to override or veto decisions made by the government, although the current president has never done so.

3.13.480.50   In our view, the new tax rate of 30% should not be used until enacted in February 2019. The fact that there have been no precedents of the president overriding decisions of the government is not indicative that he would not do so. However, if the new tax rate is enacted before authorisation of the financial statements, then the notes should include disclosure of this non-adjusting event (see 2.9.30.25). [*IAS 10.22(h)*]

3.13.480.60   In some countries, entities are able to negotiate a rate of tax with the government that is different from the general statutory rate. In our view, the negotiated rate should not be used in determining deferred tax until a formal agreement is in place confirming the rate. This is because the negotiated rate is not 'enacted' or 'substantively enacted' for that particular entity until agreement has been reached with the government.

3.13.485   *Timing of a change in tax status*

3.13.485.10   In some jurisdictions, the tax status of an entity or its shareholders may change following the entity's own decision or events outside the entity's control. The tax status may affect both the tax rates that an entity is subject to and the tax base of its assets and liabilities. In some circumstances, although the decision to change the tax status has been made, the timing or the impact of the change may be uncertain. IFRS does not address the timing of a change in tax status. Although SIC-25 provides guidance on where to recognise tax consequences of a change in the tax status of an entity or its shareholders (see 3.13.550), it does not elaborate on how to determine when this change occurs.

3.13.485.20   In our view, an entity should consider the following factors when determining the timing of a change in tax status.
- *Whether the change is subject only to the entity's decision:* We believe that changes in tax status that are solely subject to the entity's decision should generally be reflected when its management decides to change the tax status. If a change in tax status is subject to other factors, then the entity should consider the nature of the contingency – i.e. whether the condition is within or outside the entity's control.
- *Nature of the contingency.*
  - *Events or requirements that are within an entity's control:* We believe that if the event or requirements triggering the change are within an entity's control, then it should reflect the change when it demonstrates the ability and intent to meet all the requirements.
  - *Events or requirements that are outside an entity's control:* We believe that if a change is subject to *substantive* contingencies that are outside an entity's control (e.g. shareholders' decision, regulatory approval, further tax legislation or decisions to be made by the external party), then an entity should reflect the change only when all of the following conditions are met:
    - the contingency is resolved;
    - the relevant tax law is enacted or substantively enacted, if applicable (see 3.13.480); and
    - the entity can reliably determine how the tax status has changed. [*IAS 12.46–49*]

3.13.485.30   The diagram below summarises the factors in 3.13.485.20.

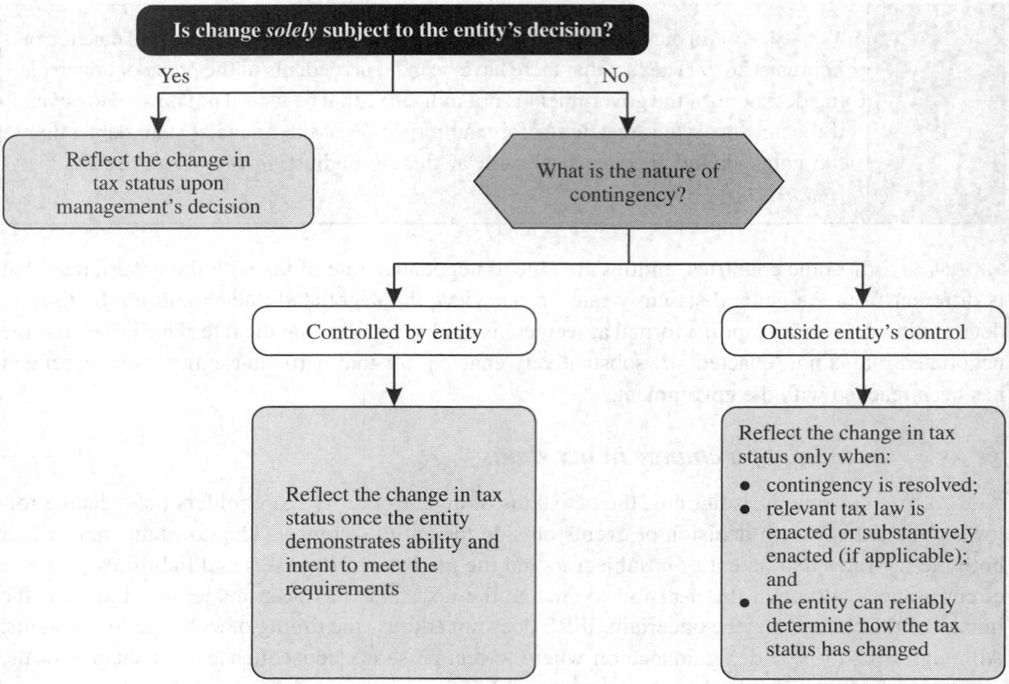

Is change *solely* subject to the entity's decision?

Yes — Reflect the change in tax status upon management's decision

No — What is the nature of contingency?

Controlled by entity — Reflect the change in tax status once the entity demonstrates ability and intent to meet the requirements

Outside entity's control — Reflect the change in tax status only when:
- contingency is resolved;
- relevant tax law is enacted or substantively enacted (if applicable); and
- the entity can reliably determine how the tax status has changed

EXAMPLE 27 – TIMING OF A CHANGE IN TAX STATUS – GOVERNMENT DECISION

3.13.485.40   Company P, incorporated in Country L, holds an investment in Associate S, incorporated in Country F. Under a tax treaty between Countries L and F, distributions of profits from affiliates incorporated in F to holding companies in L are not subject to withholding tax in F. This is different from distributions to companies in non-treaty countries, which are subject to a withholding tax of 5%. Therefore, P uses a zero tax rate when calculating deferred tax arising from the investment in S (see 3.13.300).

3.13.485.50   In December 2018, L commenced a process, under which the tax treaty between L and F will be replaced by 1 January 2020. Therefore, any distribution of profits from companies in F occurring after this date may be subject to a withholding tax, as determined in the future tax treaty. If no agreement between the countries is reached, then distributions will be subject to a 5% withholding tax, similar to non-treaty countries.

3.13.485.60   We believe that in December 2018 P should continue using a zero tax rate when calculating deferred tax arising from the investment in S. This is because even though the tax status of F is expected to change, possibly to a company resident in a non-treaty country, the other conditions in 3.13.485.20 are not met.

> - *Events are outside P's control:* The change is a result of a government decision, rather than P's decision.
> - *The contingency is not resolved:* The change is contingent on either the conclusion of negotiations between Countries L and F, or the default to a non-treaty countries status.
> - *Inability to reliably determine how the tax status has changed:* The impact of the change can be reliably determined only once the terms of the new treaty are agreed on or it is decided that F will become a non-treaty country.

3.13.485.70   For a discussion of:
- timing of changes in tax regimes for investment property companies, see 3.13.440;
- timing of reflecting a commencement of a tax holiday, see 3.13.500;
- timing of changes in tax regimes for effectively tax-exempt entities, see 3.13.1240; and
- presentation of changes in current and deferred tax that are caused by a change in a tax status of an entity or its shareholders, see 3.13.550.

3.13.490   *Split tax rates*

3.13.490.10   When different statutory tax rates apply to different levels of taxable income, the entity determines the average statutory rates that are expected to apply when the temporary difference reverses. In our view, an entity should prepare forecasts in order to estimate the tax rate that will apply when temporary differences reverse; in each period, the forecast should be updated and the balance of deferred tax should be revised as a change in estimate (see 2.8.110), if necessary. [*IAS 12.49*]

EXAMPLE 28A – SPLIT RATES – DIFFERENT RATES FOR DIFFERENT LEVELS OF TAXABLE INCOME

> 3.13.490.20   Company F is domiciled in Country C, where entities pay a different income tax rate depending on their level of taxable profit.
> - An income tax rate of 20% applies to the first 2 million of taxable profit.
> - An income tax rate of 30% applies to any taxable profit in excess of 2 million.
>
> 3.13.490.30   We believe that F needs to prepare forecasts in order to estimate the tax rate that will apply when temporary differences reverse; in each period, the forecast should be updated and the balance of deferred tax should be revised as a change in estimate.

3.13.490.40   We believe that Example 28A is different from using an effective tax rate to recognise deferred tax (see 3.13.470.10). This is because in this example the statutory rate varies depending on the level of taxable income, not depending on what tax deductions are available.

EXAMPLE 28B – SPLIT RATES – CAPITAL ASSETS SUPPORT MULTIPLE MARKETS WITH DIFFERENT RATES

> 3.13.490.50   Company Z is domiciled in Country B, where entities pay a different income tax rate depending on the source of taxable profit.
> - An income tax rate of 20% applies to taxable profit from local market.

- An income tax rate of 10% applies to taxable profit from exports.
- Deductions in respect of capital assets used to support the business in both markets (e.g. property, plant and equipment) are taxed at a weighted-average rate based on the proportion of profits earned in each market.

3.13.490.60   Similar to Example 28A, we believe that Z needs to prepare forecasts in order to estimate the tax rate that will apply when temporary differences associated with both markets reverse. These forecasts should be updated at each reporting date and the balance of deferred tax should be revised as a change in estimate.

3.13.500   *Tax holidays*

3.13.500.10   Some countries provide tax holidays – i.e. periods in which no tax is payable – for entities in a start-up phase or that meet certain investment criteria. In our view, it is not appropriate to base the recognition of deferred tax on the tax rate that applies when a temporary difference originates; instead, we believe that the entity should consider the rate of tax expected to apply when the underlying asset (liability) is recovered (settled).

EXAMPLE 29 – TAX HOLIDAY

3.13.500.20   Company C has a two-year tax holiday; from the third year, a tax rate of 33% applies. At the start of the tax holiday, C bought a machine for 100 that will be depreciated over its estimated useful life of five years; for tax purposes, the machine will be depreciated over four years. In this example, the temporary difference partly originates during the tax holiday in years 1 and 2, and reverses only in year 5.

3.13.500.30   Therefore, we believe that deferred tax should be provided during the tax holiday – i.e. in years 1 and 2 – applying a 33% tax rate, as shown in the following table.

END OF YEAR	ASSET BALANCE		TEMPORARY DIFFERENCE	DEFERRED TAX BALANCE	DEFERRED TAX MOVEMENT
	CARRYING AMOUNT	TAX BASE			
1	80	75	(5)	(2)	(2)
2	60	50	(10)	(3)	(1)
3	40	25	(15)	(5)	(2)
4	20	-	(20)	(7)	(2)
5	-	-	-	-	7

3.13.500.40   Sometimes a tax holiday is available for a limited period of time but commences only when cumulative taxable profit exceeds zero. In this case, if an entity is currently in a tax loss position, then in our view deferred tax assets and liabilities should be measured at the tax rate expected to apply when the temporary differences reverse. The measurement should not take account of the tax holiday.

3.13.500.50   Therefore, until the date on which all tax losses carried forward are utilised, the entity would not apply a zero tax rate, because:
- the entity only benefits from the advantageous rate if it generates a cumulative taxable profit; and
- the benefit would be received only if the temporary differences reversed during the limited period of the tax holiday.

3.13.500.60   For a discussion of the timing of a change in tax status, see 3.13.485.

3.13.510   Discounting

3.13.510.10   Deferred taxes are not discounted. Instead, the nominal amount is presented in the statement of financial position, even if the effect of discounting would be material. Conversely, current tax liabilities (assets) are in some cases discounted (see 3.13.70.40). [*IAS 12.53*]

3.13.520   DETERMINE WHERE TO RECOGNISE INCOME TAX

3.13.530   General principles

3.13.530.10   Accounting for the current and deferred tax effects of a transaction or other event is consistent with the accounting for the transaction or event itself. Therefore, current and deferred tax is generally recognised in profit or loss, except to the extent that it arises from:
- a business combination; or
- items recognised in the current or previous period, outside profit or loss – i.e. in OCI or directly in equity. [*IAS 12.57–58, 61A*]

3.13.530.20   The total tax expense (income) related to profit or loss from ordinary activities is presented as part of profit or loss as a separate line item in:
- a single statement of profit or loss and OCI; or
- in the separate statement of profit or loss, if two statements are presented. [*IAS 1.82(d), 12.77*]

3.13.530.30   Where exchange differences on deferred foreign tax liabilities or assets are recognised in profit or loss, such differences may be classified as deferred tax expense (income) if that presentation is considered to be the most useful to financial statement users (see 2.7.160). There is no guidance in IAS 12 on where exchange differences arising from current foreign currency tax liabilities or assets should be presented in profit or loss. In our view, the guidance on deferred taxes in foreign currency should apply equally to current taxes in foreign currency (see 3.13.170). [*IAS 12.78*]

3.13.530.40   When an enacted or substantively enacted tax rate changes, an entity undertakes a detailed review of the components of the net deferred tax position. This is to determine whether any items comprising the balance were previously charged or credited to OCI – e.g. in respect of available-for-sale securities or the revaluation of property, plant and equipment – or equity.

3.13.530.50   A change in the net deferred tax position may result from a change in tax rates related to items recognised outside profit or loss. If this is the case, then the effect of the change is also recorded outside profit or loss – i.e. in OCI or directly in equity. In exceptional circumstances, it may be difficult to determine the amount that should be recorded outside profit or loss – e.g. when a change in tax rate affects an item that was only partly recognised outside profit or loss. In such circumstances, an entity may use a reasonable pro rata allocation method to determine the amount of tax consequence to be recognised outside profit or loss (see 3.13.590). [*IAS 12.63*]

3.13.530.60   An entity may present each component of OCI either net of the related tax effects, or gross of tax with the tax effects shown separately; this is discussed in more detail in 4.1.250.20. IFRS gives no explicit guidance about the reserve in equity in which deferred tax should be recognised. In our experience, deferred tax is generally recognised in the same reserve as the underlying item to which it relates. For example, deferred tax related to a revaluation of property, plant and equipment is usually recognised in the revaluation reserve. [*IAS 1.90–91, IG6*]

3.13.540   Change in accounting policy

3.13.540.10   Changes in the carrying amount of deferred tax balances that relate to changes in the underlying temporary differences are generally recognised in profit or loss. Other changes – e.g. those resulting from changes in tax rates – are recognised in profit or loss, unless they relate to items previously recognised outside profit or loss. [*IAS 12.61A, 62A*]

3.13.540.20   When an entity applies a new accounting policy retrospectively (see 2.8.50), the impact on assets and liabilities, including related changes to deferred tax assets and liabilities, is credited or charged directly to equity. However, it is unclear where the entity should recognise subsequent adjustments to the deferred tax that are recognised as part of a change in accounting policy. [*IAS 12.62A*]

3.13.540.30   In our view, an entity should choose an accounting policy, to be applied consistently, to do either of the following.
- Recognise any subsequent changes in deferred taxes that were originally recognised directly in equity as a result of a change in accounting policy as though the new accounting policy had always been applied. Depending on the policy in question, and therefore on how the underlying transaction is accounted for, the change in deferred tax will be recognised either:
  - in profit or loss;
  - in OCI; or
  - directly in equity.
- Recognise any subsequent changes in deferred taxes that were recognised originally directly in equity as a result of a change in accounting policy directly in equity.

EXAMPLE 30 – CHANGE IN DEFERRED TAX RESULTING FROM CHANGE IN ACCOUNTING POLICY

3.13.540.40   Company B has an investment property. The following facts are relevant for this example.
- Unrealised changes in the fair value of the investment property do not affect taxable profit. However, if B's investment property is sold, then any reversal

of the cumulative tax depreciation and any excess of the sales proceeds over cost will be taxed at 40%.

- For tax purposes, the investment property is depreciated on a straight-line basis with an annual charge of 40.
- At the beginning of 2017, B voluntarily changed its accounting policy for investment property from the cost model to the fair value model. Because B presents one year of comparative information in its annual financial statements, in its 2017 financial statements, B restated the opening statement of financial position at 1 January 2016 as follows:
  - increasing investment property by 800 (remeasurement to fair value);
  - recognising deferred tax liability of 320 (temporary difference of 800 x 40%); and
  - increasing opening retained earnings by 480 (800 - 320).
- Before the change in accounting policy, there were no temporary differences related to the investment property.
- During 2016 and 2017, the temporary difference related to the investment property changed as follows.

	2016	2017
Temporary difference at the beginning of the year	800	740
• Decrease in carrying amount as a result of fair value remeasurement	(100)	(80)
• Decrease in tax base as a result of tax depreciation	40	40
Decrease in temporary difference relating to investment property	(60)	(40)
Temporary difference at the end of the year	740	700

- At the beginning of 2018, the applicable tax rate decreased unexpectedly from 40% to 30%. Accordingly, B calculated the impact of the reduction in the tax rate on the recognised deferred tax liability as follows.

Impact of tax rate reduction on recognised deferred tax liability	
• Adjustment to retained earnings at 1 January 2016 upon the change in accounting policy (800 x 10%)	80
• Change in temporary difference recognised in profit or loss during 2016 (60 x 10%)	(6)
• Change in temporary difference recognised in profit or loss during 2017 (40 x 10%)	(4)
Total decrease in deferred tax liability (700 x 10%)	70

3.13.540.50   Of the total decrease in deferred tax liability, 10 (6 + 4) is recognised as deferred tax income in profit or loss in 2018. This is because it relates to fair value remeasurement recognised in profit or loss during 2016 and 2017, and the depreciation that is recognised for tax purposes.

3.13.540.60   The change in deferred tax liability of 80 relates to the cumulative effect on opening retained earnings of a change in accounting policy that was recognised directly in equity (retained earnings). In the 2018 financial statements, we believe that B should choose an accounting policy, to be applied consistently, to recognise the decrease of 80 either:

- in profit or loss as deferred tax income because had the accounting policy always been applied, then fair value changes would have been recognised in profit or loss; or
- directly in retained earnings because the change relates to a previous change in accounting policy that was recognised directly in equity (retained earnings).

3.13.540.70   We believe that IFRS is not clear about subsequent changes in deferred tax balances resulting from changes in accounting policies or other retrospective adjustments to retained earnings. However, in other circumstances involving items recognised outside profit or loss (e.g. the revaluation of property, plant and equipment), the standard is quite explicit that any subsequent changes are recorded outside profit or loss (see 3.13.530.10). [*IAS 12.57–58, 61A*]

3.13.550   Presentation of a change in tax status

3.13.550.10   An entity follows the general principles outlined in 3.13.530.10 when recognising changes in current and deferred tax that are caused by a change in its own, or its shareholders', tax status. The change in current and deferred tax is recognised in profit or loss – except to the extent that it relates to an item (e.g. a revaluation of property, plant and equipment) recognised outside profit or loss in the current or in a previous period. For a discussion of timing of a change in tax status, see 3.13.485. [*SIC-25.4*]

3.13.560   Reassessment of recoverability of deferred tax assets

3.13.560.10   At every reporting date, an entity assesses whether it has any previously unrecognised deferred tax assets that now fulfil the recognition criteria of probable future taxable profits (see 3.13.330). The entity recognises any previously unrecognised deferred tax assets to the extent that it has become probable that future taxable profit will allow the deferred tax assets to be recovered. [*IAS 12.37*]

3.13.560.20   In our view, if a deferred tax asset previously considered not recoverable is recognised, then the presentation of the deferred tax income should follow the presentation of the item that originally gave rise to the potential deferred tax asset.

EXAMPLE 31 – REASSESSMENT OF RECOVERABILITY OF DEFERRED TAX ASSET – ALLOCATION OF IMPACT

3.13.560.30   Company K's management reassesses the recoverability of a deferred tax asset associated with tax losses carried forward and previously not recognised. Management concludes that the deferred tax asset is recoverable following the revaluation of a financial asset measured at fair value through OCI. The revaluation is recognised in OCI in accordance with IFRS 9.

3.13.560.40   We believe that the deferred tax income associated with the tax losses carried forward should be recognised in profit or loss. This is despite the fact that the revaluation of the fair value through OCI financial asset and its related deferred tax are recognised in OCI. This is because the item that gave rise to the deferred tax asset was the tax loss of a prior period.

3.13.560.50   For a discussion of the allocation of income taxes between continuing and discontinued operations, see 3.13.620.

3.13.560.60   Deferred tax recognised as part of the acquisition accounting for an entity acquired in a business combination is adjusted against goodwill on initial recognition. However, this is not the case if the deferred tax asset is a previously unrecognised asset of the acquirer. In this case, the acquirer recognises the deferred tax asset as tax income in profit or loss (see 3.13.900). [*IAS 12.58, 67*]

3.13.570   Revaluations and changes in fair value

3.13.570.10   Whether an entity recognises the deferred tax related to a revaluation in or outside profit or loss depends on how it treats the revaluation under IFRS. When an entity revalues property, plant and equipment, it recognises the revaluation in OCI in accordance with the revaluation model (see 3.2.300); in this case, the related deferred tax is also recognised in OCI. [*IAS 12.61A, 62, 64*]

3.13.570.20   Subsequent changes in the deferred taxes that arise as the asset is depreciated are recognised in profit or loss. The entity does not adjust the balance in the revaluation reserve.

EXAMPLE 32A – REVALUATION OF PROPERTY, PLANT AND EQUIPMENT – RECOGNITION OF TAX IMPACTS

3.13.570.30   Company C acquires machinery for 100 at the beginning of year 1, which is depreciable over a five-year period for both accounting and tax purposes.

3.13.570.40   For accounting purposes, machinery is revalued to fair value. C performs revaluations of machinery at the end of years 2 and 4, and the related changes in the carrying amount are recognised in OCI. Depreciation is determined based on revalued amounts. For tax purposes, the carrying amount of machinery is determined based on the cost.

3.13.570.50 The following table shows the changes in the carrying amount, tax base and temporary differences in relation to the machinery between years 1 to 5.

	YR 1	YR 2	YR 3	YR 4	YR 5
Carrying amount at the beginning of the year	100	80	90	60	42
Depreciation	(20)	(20)	(30)	(30)	(42)
Revaluation	-	30	-	12	-
Carrying amount at the end of the year	80	90	60	42	-
Tax base	(80)[1]	(60)	(40)	(20)	-
Taxable temporary difference	-	30	20	22	-
Change in taxable temporary difference	-	30	(10)	2	(22)
Causes of changes in taxable temporary difference:					
Revaluation	-	30	-	12	-
Difference in depreciation	-	-	(10)[2]	(10)	(22)[2]

Notes
1. Calculated as cost minus tax depreciation (100 - (100 / 5)).
2. Calculated as accounting depreciation minus tax depreciation (30 - (100 / 5) and (42 - (100 / 5))).

3.13.570.60 The applicable tax rate is 50%. C recognises the tax effect of the change in the temporary differences caused by revaluations in OCI as follows:
- year 2: 15 (30 x 50%); and
- year 4: 6 (12 x 50%).

3.13.570.70 C recognises the effect of the differences in depreciation in profit or loss as follows:
- years 3 and 4: 5 (10 x 50%); and
- year 5: 11 (22 x 50%).

3.13.570.80 In the case of property, plant and equipment, an entity is permitted but not required to make transfers from the revaluation reserve to retained earnings as the revaluation is realised – e.g. through depreciation. In such cases, any transfer would be made net of the related deferred tax (see 3.2.350.20). [*IAS 12.64*]

EXAMPLE 32B – REVALUATION OF PROPERTY, PLANT AND EQUIPMENT – TRANSFER TO RETAINED EARNINGS

3.13.570.83 Continuing Example 32A, Company C's accounting policy is to transfer a relevant portion of the revaluation surplus from the revaluation reserve to retained earnings as it is realised (third option in 3.2.350.20).

3.13.570.85   The following table shows the carrying amounts and the related deferred taxes of the revaluation reserve and net transfers to retained earnings at the end of each year from year 3 to year 5.

	REVALUATION RESERVE	DEFERRED TAX RELATED TO REVALUATION RESERVE	RETAINED EARNINGS
Year 2	30	(15)	-
Transfer	(10)	5	5
Year 3	20	(10)	5
Transfer	(10)	5	5
Additional revaluation	12	(6)	-
Year 4	22	(11)	10
Transfer	(22)	11	11
Year 5	-	-	21

3.13.570.90   In our view, when IFRS requires valuation gains that were initially recognised in OCI to be reclassified to profit or loss upon disposal, the deferred tax on the valuation gains that were previously recognised in OCI should also be reclassified to profit or loss accordingly. In addition, in our view such reclassification should not net off the reclassified gain against the tax charge.

EXAMPLE 33 – RECLASSIFICATION ADJUSTMENTS ON DISPOSAL OF FAIR VALUE THROUGH OCI FINANCIAL ASSETS

3.13.570.100   Company J acquires a debt instrument measured at fair value through OCI for 100 in 2018. The following facts are also relevant for this example.
- J records interest income of 5 during 2018. No temporary differences arise from the accretion of interest.
- J revalues the asset to 125 at 31 December 2018.
- As at 31 December 2018, J recognises a deferred tax liability of 5 in OCI ((125 - 105) x 25%).
- J sells the asset for 125 on 1 January 2019, reclassifying the gain of 20 to profit or loss.
- J pays tax on the gain of 20 at the applicable tax rate of 25%.
- The example does not illustrate the impact of expected credit losses.

3.13.570.110   We believe that in 2019 J should, in effect, reclassify the tax amount on disposal of the asset, by crediting the deferred tax liability of 5 to OCI and charging current tax of 5 to profit or loss. We believe that J should not net off the reclassified

> gain of 20 against the tax charge of 5 in profit or loss, but should present a pre-tax
> gain of 20 and a current tax expense of 5.

3.13.570.120 The situation is different when the revaluation is carried out for tax rather than for accounting purposes – e.g. when the tax authorities permit or require adjusting the tax base of property, plant and equipment. In such cases, the change in deferred tax is recognised in profit or loss (see 3.13.790.60–80). However, this is not the case if the tax revaluation is linked to an accounting revaluation, either in the past or in a future period, that was (or will be) recognised in OCI (see 3.13.110.100). [*IAS 12.65*]

3.13.570.130 In our view, the principle in 3.13.570.120 also applies to other situations in which the tax base of an asset changes but its carrying amount remains the same. For example, an asset may be transferred from a wholly owned group entity to another group entity that is not wholly owned. In some jurisdictions, the tax base of this asset may be changed, to the extent of the NCI in the receiving entity. For a discussion of intra-group transactions, see 3.13.1160.

EXAMPLE 34 – CHANGE IN TAX BASE RESULTING FROM INTRA-GROUP TRANSFER

> 3.13.570.140 Company P transfers an item of property that has a carrying amount
> and tax base of 1,000 to its 75% subsidiary, Company S. The carrying amount of
> the property in P's consolidated financial statements will be unchanged at 1,000.
> However, in line with applicable local tax legislation, the tax base of the asset is
> reduced to 750 – i.e. by the extent of the NCI in S. In our view, P should recognise
> a deferred tax liability and deferred tax expense in consolidated profit or loss at the
> time of the transfer to reflect the decrease in the tax base of the property.

3.13.580 Defined benefit post-employment plans

3.13.580.10 Under IAS 19, some components of the defined benefit cost are recognised in profit or loss – e.g. service costs or net interest on the defined benefit liability – and some components are recognised in OCI – e.g. remeasurements (see 4.4.830). Entities may make cash contributions to funded post-employment benefit plans – e.g. to maintain day-to-day funding of current service costs, to cover a deficit arising from past net actuarial losses or to contribute towards past service costs. These cash payments do not affect the statement of profit or loss and OCI but they do affect the statement of financial position because they reduce the net defined benefit liability or increase the net defined benefit asset, and therefore affect the related deferred tax asset or liability. In some jurisdictions, entities receive current tax deductions for such cash contributions rather than for the related IAS 19 pension expense that they recognise in profit or loss and OCI.

3.13.580.20 The general principle in IAS 12 is that the current and deferred taxes are recognised in profit or loss, OCI or equity consistent with the accounting for the related transaction or event (see 3.13.530). In cases of cash contributions to funded post-employment benefit plans, it may be difficult to determine how the related current income taxes should be allocated between profit or loss and OCI because the cash contribution itself does not affect the profit or loss or OCI and it may not be clear what the cash contribution is funding. This allocation does not affect the total amount of income tax recognised in profit or loss and OCI in relation to a post-employment benefit plan, the total amount of current tax or the total amount of deferred tax for the period in relation to a post-employment benefit plan. However, an issue arises because it is necessary to disclose the amount of deferred taxes recognised in profit or loss. [*IAS 12.81(g)(ii)*]

3.13.580.30   In our view, the allocation of the current income tax effect to profit or loss and OCI should reflect the nature of the cash contribution, unless it is impracticable to identify whether the cost, to which the funding relates, affects profit or loss or OCI. For example, it is clear that past service cost is recognised in profit or loss, but a deficit may arise from a combination of remeasurements recognised in OCI and current service contributions being less than the current service cost recognised in profit or loss. We believe that a number of allocation approaches are acceptable if the nature of the cash contribution is unclear, including the following.

- *Approach 1:* Allocate current income taxes first to profit or loss, to the extent of the tax effects of the total service cost and net interest recognised in profit or loss in the current period, and then allocate any residual amount to OCI. Under this approach, it is argued that the contribution relates primarily to service cost and net interest recognised in profit or loss in the current period only.
- *Approach 2:* Allocate the entire amount of current income tax related to contributions to profit or loss. Under this approach, it is argued that the contribution relates to service cost and net interest recognised in profit or loss in the current and prior periods.
- *Approach 3:* Allocate the entire amount of income tax related to contributions to OCI. Under this approach, it is argued that the contribution is made to fund a deficit arising from an identifiable cause – e.g. changes in actuarial assumptions – and relates to remeasurements recognised in OCI in the current and prior periods. [*IAS 12.58, 61A, 63*]

EXAMPLE 35 – DEFINED BENEFIT PLANS – ALLOCATION OF INCOME TAXES RELATED TO CONTRIBUTIONS

3.13.580.40   Company T has a post-employment defined benefit plan. The following facts are relevant for this example.

	AMOUNTS RELATED TO DEFINED BENEFIT PLAN	RELATED INCOME TAX CREDIT AT 40%
Contributions paid to the plan (tax deductible on payment)	(120)	48
Service cost and net interest recognised in profit or loss	(100)	40
Remeasurements recognised in OCI	(80)	32

3.13.580.50   T needs to determine how to allocate the income tax credit of 40 recognised in profit or loss between current and deferred tax elements and how to allocate the income tax credit of 32 recognised in OCI between current and deferred tax elements. The following table highlights the known amounts and the amounts that T needs to determine.

Income tax	Profit or Loss	OCI	Total
Current tax	?	?	48
Deferred tax	?	?	24[1]
Total income tax	40	32	72

Note
1. Calculated as 72 - 48.

Approach 1

3.13.580.60   Under Approach 1 discussed in 3.13.580.30, the current tax effect of 48 on the contributions is first allocated to profit or loss to the extent of the service cost and net interest recognised in profit or loss in the current period multiplied by the relevant statutory tax rate (100 x 40% = 40). The remaining amount of the current tax of 8 (48 - 40) is attributed to OCI.

3.13.580.65   As a next step, the deferred tax is allocated to profit or loss and then to OCI. The amount of deferred tax allocated to profit or loss is calculated as the total amount of income tax recognised in profit or loss of 40 minus the current tax allocated to profit or loss of 40. The amount of deferred tax allocated to OCI is calculated as the total amount of income tax recognised in OCI of 32 minus current tax allocated to OCI of 8.

Income tax – Approach 1	Profit or Loss	OCI	Total
Current tax	40[1]	8[2]	48
Deferred tax	-[3]	24[4]	24
Total income tax	40	32	72

Notes
1. Calculated as 100 x 40%.
2. Calculated as total current tax of 48 minus current tax allocated to profit or loss of 40.
3. Calculated as total amount of income tax recognised in profit or loss of 40 minus current tax allocated to profit or loss of 40.
4. Calculated as total deferred tax of 24 minus deferred tax allocated to profit or loss of 0. Alternatively, it can be calculated as total income tax recognised in OCI of 32 minus current tax allocated to OCI of 8.

Approach 2

3.13.580.70   Under Approach 2 discussed in 3.13.580.30, the entire amount of current tax of 48 is allocated to profit or loss. The deferred tax is then allocated to profit or loss and OCI in a manner similar to that discussed under Approach 1.

Income tax – Approach 2	PROFIT OR LOSS	OCI	TOTAL
Current tax	48	–[1]	48
Deferred tax	(8)[2]	32[3]	24
Total income tax	40	32	72

Notes
1. Calculated as total current tax of 48 minus current tax allocated to profit or loss of 48.
2. Calculated as total amount of income tax recognised in profit or loss of 40 minus current tax allocated to profit or loss of 48.
3. Calculated as total deferred tax of 24 minus deferred tax allocated to profit or loss of (8).

Approach 3

3.13.580.80   Under Approach 3 discussed in 3.13.580.30, the entire amount of current tax of 48 is allocated to OCI. The deferred tax is then allocated to profit or loss and OCI in a manner similar to that discussed under Approach 1.

Income tax – Approach 3	PROFIT OR LOSS	OCI	TOTAL
Current tax	–[1]	48	48
Deferred tax	40[2]	(16)[3]	24
Total income tax	40	32	72

Notes
1. Calculated as total current tax of 48 minus current tax allocated to OCI of 48.
2. Calculated as total amount of income tax recognised in profit or loss of 40 minus current tax allocated to profit or loss of 0.
3. Calculated as total deferred tax of 24 minus deferred tax allocated to profit or loss of 40.

3.13.590 Transactions involving an entity's own shares

3.13.590.10   Transactions involving an entity's own shares – e.g. the issue, purchase and reissue of treasury shares – are recognised in equity; therefore, the resulting deferred tax (if any) is also recognised in equity. [*IAS 12.61A*]

EXAMPLE 36A – TRANSACTION COSTS ON ISSUANCE OF SHARES – FULL RECOGNITION OF DEFERRED TAX ASSET

3.13.590.20   In 2018, Company J issues shares and incurs transaction costs of 100 (recognised in equity), which are deductible for tax purposes. The tax rate is 30%. However, J's taxable profit for 2018 before deducting the transaction costs is zero and the deduction cannot be utilised in 2018. J has determined that it is probable that the tax losses will be utilised before they expire (see 3.13.350). Accordingly, the deferred tax asset is recognised in full. Therefore, the credit for the amount of the deferred tax asset related to the transaction costs of 30 is recognised directly in equity.

3.13.590.25   In some circumstances, if it is difficult to determine the amount of income tax that relates to items recognised outside profit or loss, IAS 12 allows an entity to make a reasonable pro rata allocation or to use another method that achieves a more appropriate allocation in the circumstances. [*IAS 12.63*]

EXAMPLE 36B – TRANSACTION COSTS ON ISSUANCE OF SHARES – PARTIAL RECOGNITION OF DEFERRED TAX ASSET

3.13.590.30   Modifying Example 36A, J's tax loss for 2018 is 150; including the 100 in respect of the transaction costs. After considering the probability of utilising the tax losses before they expire, J concludes that a deferred tax asset for only 50% of the losses can be recognised.

3.13.590.40   In this case, it is difficult to attribute the part of the tax loss recognised to specific items; and IAS 12 allows J to make a reasonable allocation between profit or loss and equity. In our view, in this example it would be reasonable to conclude that 50% of the tax attributable to the transaction costs is recoverable and therefore that 15 (100 x 50% x 30%) should be recognised in equity. [*IAS 12.63*]

3.13.590.50   The tax effect of items recognised outside profit or loss is recognised outside profit or loss. This requirement extends beyond the initial recognition of a deferred tax liability (asset) to any subsequent revisions to the tax balance. [*IAS 12.61A*]

EXAMPLE 36C – TRANSACTION COSTS ON ISSUANCE OF SHARES – SUBSEQUENT RECOGNITION OF DEFERRED TAX

3.13.590.60   Continuing Example 36B, in the following year J revises its estimate and concludes that the full deferred tax asset can be recognised. In this case, the additional 15 of deferred tax related to the transaction costs is also recognised in equity.

3.13.590.70   When the transaction costs are actually deducted for tax purposes, a current tax asset will arise. This will be offset by the reversal of the deferred tax asset. In our view, both the current tax and the related deferred tax reversal should be recognised in equity, resulting in a net effect of zero on equity.

EXAMPLE 37 – DISPOSAL OF ENTITY'S OWN SHARES

3.13.590.80   Company K acquires its own shares for 100 for the purpose of using them as consideration in acquiring a subsidiary at a later date. At the reporting date, the fair value of the shares has increased to 120. At this date, K disposes of the shares by using them as consideration in acquiring a subsidiary and, as a consequence, K is taxed on the difference of 20 (taxable income of 120 minus original cost of 100). We believe that any tax effect on this difference should be recognised in equity because the underlying item – i.e. the share transaction – was recognised in equity. [*IAS 12.5, 9, 61A*]

3.13.590.90   An entity might pay remuneration for goods or services in shares, share options or other equity instruments that are considered to be equity-settled share-based payments (see chapter 4.5). In this case, a temporary difference may arise, for example, when the entity receives a tax deduction for share-based payments at the exercise date, whereas the expense is recognised in profit or loss over the vesting period. Any deferred tax on temporary differences arising from such transactions is generally recognised in profit or loss. However, this is not the case when the underlying transaction is a business combination or is recognised outside profit or loss. If the tax deduction (or estimated future tax deduction) for that share-based payment transaction exceeds the amount of the related cumulative remuneration expense, then this indicates that the tax deduction relates not only to remuneration expense but also to an equity item. Accordingly, the excess of the associated deferred tax is recognised directly in equity (see 3.13.820). [*IAS 12.68A–68C, IE.Ex5*]

3.13.600   PRESENTATION AND DISCLOSURES

3.13.610   General principles

3.13.610.10   Tax assets and tax liabilities are presented separately from other assets and liabilities in the statement of financial position. In addition, current tax assets and current tax liabilities are distinguished from deferred tax assets and deferred tax liabilities in the statement of financial position. This requirement applies whether or not an entity presents a classified statement of financial position. For a discussion on presenting a classified statement of financial position, see 3.1.10. [*IAS 1.54*]

3.13.610.15   Interest and penalties are presented in the statement of financial position and in the statement of profit or loss and OCI, consistent with the standard applicable to their nature (see 3.13.45), as follows.
- *If IAS 37 applies:* As other provisions (liabilities) in the statement of financial position and as operating (penalties) and interest expenses respectively in profit or loss.
- *If IAS 12 applies:* As current/deferred tax payables in the statement of financial position and as income tax expense in the statement of profit or loss and OCI.

3.13.610.20   Deferred tax liabilities and assets are always classified as non-current when a classified statement of financial position is presented (see 3.1.10). This applies even though some part of the deferred tax balance may be expected to reverse within 12 months of the reporting date. [*IAS 1.56*]

3.13.620   Discontinued operations

3.13.620.10   There is no explicit guidance in IAS 12 on allocating income tax income and expense between continuing and discontinued operations when an entity presents discontinued operations in accordance with IFRS 5 (see chapter 5.4). Complexities can arise in practice. [*IFRS 5.33*]

EXAMPLE 38 – ALLOCATION OF TAX BETWEEN CONTINUING AND DISCONTINUED OPERATIONS

3.13.620.20   Company G has two principal lines of business: B and C. For several years, B has been profitable and C has been loss-making. Tax losses in C have exceeded the taxable income in B. Overall, G has accumulated tax losses carried forward. However, G has not previously recognised a deferred tax asset – this is because management considered that there would be insufficient taxable profit to utilise the losses.

3.13.620.30   G then abandons C's line of business and presents C as a discontinued operation. Management concludes that the tax losses carried forward generated in the past by C will be utilised against future profits in B; therefore, G recognises a deferred tax asset. A question arises about whether the deferred tax income arising on recognition of this deferred tax asset should be presented as:
- part of discontinued operations, because the tax losses arose originally in C; or
- part of continuing operations, because the tax losses will be utilised against future profits in B.

3.13.620.40   In our view, either presentation is acceptable.

3.13.630   Offsetting

3.13.630.10   An entity offsets current tax assets and current tax liabilities only when:
- it has a legally enforceable right to set off current tax assets against current tax liabilities; this will normally be the case only when the tax payable or receivable relates to income taxes levied by the same taxation authority, and the taxation authority permits the entity to make or receive a single net payment; and
- it intends either to settle on a net basis, or to realise the asset and settle the liability simultaneously. [*IAS 12.71–72*]

3.13.630.20   Therefore, within a group, current tax assets and current tax liabilities of different group entities are offset only if the entities:
- have a legally enforceable right to make or receive a single net payment; and
- intend to make or receive such a net payment or to recover the asset and settle the liability simultaneously. [*IAS 12.73*]

3.13.630.30   Deferred tax liabilities and assets are offset if:
- the entity has a legally enforceable right to set off current tax liabilities and assets; and
- the deferred tax liabilities and assets relate to income taxes levied by the same tax authority on either:
  - the same taxable entity; or
  - different taxable entities, but these entities intend to settle current tax liabilities and assets on a net basis, or their tax assets and liabilities will be realised simultaneously for each future period in which these differences reverse. [*IAS 12.74*]

3.13.630.40   The standard further explains that the offsetting requirements allow an entity to avoid having to schedule the timing of reversal of temporary differences. In our view, this relates only to the presentation of deferred tax liabilities and assets, and not to the underlying recognition criteria (see 3.13.320–330). [*IAS 12.75*]

3.13.640   Disclosures

3.13.640.10   Extensive disclosures are required for deferred tax. These are illustrated in KPMG's *Guides to financial statements* series. This commentary focuses on areas of uncertainty in practice. [*IAS 12.79–88*]

3.13.640.20   A reconciliation between the applicable statutory tax rate and the entity's effective tax rate (expressed in percentages or in absolute numbers) is required. For a group that operates in multiple tax jurisdictions, the applicable tax rate can be determined in one of two ways:

- based on the statutory tax rate applicable to the parent entity; in this case, the reconciliation will include a separate line item representing the effect of tax rates in different jurisdictions; or
- using the average statutory tax rate applicable to the group, calculated on a weighted-average basis. [*IAS 12.81(c), 85*]

3.13.640.30   An entity discloses taxable temporary differences on investments in subsidiaries, branches and associates, and interests in joint arrangements (see 3.13.260) for which deferred tax liabilities have not been recognised. The disclosure is not the amount of unrecognised deferred tax; instead, it is the gross temporary difference. [*IAS 12.81(f)*]

EXAMPLE 39 – DISCLOSURE OF TAXABLE TEMPORARY DIFFERENCES ON INVESTMENT IN SUBSIDIARY

> 3.13.640.40   Company P acquired Subsidiary S and has recognised S's post-acquisition earnings of 500 in its consolidated financial statements. If these earnings were distributed, then tax of 50 would be payable by P. P did not recognise this deferred tax liability because it met the criteria for non-recognition (see 3.13.260).
>
> 3.13.640.50   The temporary difference of 500 is disclosed in the notes to the financial statements of P. In addition, entities are encouraged to disclose the tax consequences of a distribution, 50 in this example. [*IAS 12.81(f), 87, IE.Ex3*]

3.13.640.60   An entity is required to disclose, in respect of each *type* of temporary difference, the amount of deferred tax assets and liabilities recognised in the statement of financial position. In our view, this could be interpreted in one of two ways.

- Disclosure based on the statement of financial position captions – e.g. disclosure of deferred tax assets and deferred tax liabilities (separately) in respect of property, plant and equipment. This method of presentation is shown in KPMG's *Guides to financial statements* series.
- Disclosure based on the reason for the temporary difference – e.g. excess of wear and tear tax deductions over depreciation and amortisation. [*IAS 12.81(g)*]

3.13.640.70   In our view, it is not appropriate to disclose the tax effects of both recognised and unrecognised deferred tax assets as a single amount – e.g. similar to the 'gross' approach under US GAAP – because under IFRS, it is *recognised* deferred tax assets that are required to be disclosed.

EXAMPLE 40 – DISCLOSURE OF DEDUCTIBLE TEMPORARY DIFFERENCES

> 3.13.640.80   The following example illustrates gross and net methods of disclosure. As discussed in 3.13.640.70, we believe that it is not appropriate to disclose gross deductible temporary differences. [*IAS 12.81*]

Deductible temporary differences	INAPPROPRIATE	APPROPRIATE
Property, plant and equipment	1,000	800
Intangible assets	400	300
Valuation allowance	(300)	-
Total deductible temporary differences	1,100	1,100

3.13.640.90   An entity discloses both the amount of the deferred tax asset and the nature of the evidence supporting its recognition when:

- the recoverability of a deferred tax asset depends on future taxable profits in excess of the profits arising from the reversal of existing taxable differences; and
- the entity has suffered a tax loss in the current or preceding period in a tax jurisdiction, in respect of which a deferred tax asset has been recognised in the financial statements. [*IAS 12.82*]

3.13.650   OTHER APPLICATION ISSUES

3.13.650.10   Other application issues discussed in this chapter include the following.

- Income tax exposures (see 3.13.660).
- Investment tax credits (see 3.13.670).
- Cash flow hedge accounting (see 3.13.730).
- Dividends (see 3.13.760).
- Share-based payments (see 3.13.820).
- Business combinations (see 3.13.870).
- Other group issues (see 3.13.1130).
- Foreign investment (see 3.13.1220).
- Investments in pass-through entities (see 3.13.1230).
- Effectively tax-exempt entity (see 3.13.1240).
- Acquiring tax losses other than in a business combination (see 3.13.1250).
- Derecognition (see 3.13.1260).

3.13.660   INCOME TAX EXPOSURES#

3.13.660.10   The term 'income tax exposures' generally refers to positions taken by an entity that:
- may be challenged by the tax authorities; and
- may result in:
  - additional taxes;
  - penalties or interest;
  - changes in the applicable tax rate;
  - changes in the tax base of assets or liabilities; or
  - changes in the amount of available tax losses carried forward or tax credits that would reduce a deferred tax asset or increase a deferred tax liability.

3.13.660.20   Whether an income tax exposure is present depends both on the specific position taken by an entity and on the applicable tax law. Therefore, income tax exposures often occur:
- when the applicable tax law is not very clear or is not consistently understood; or
- in tax regimes where the amounts finally payable to the tax authorities are the outcome of lengthy negotiations involving a high degree of subjectivity and discretion, or are even random.

3.13.660.30   Examples of tax exposures include:
- deductions taken on tax returns that may be disallowed by the tax authorities;
- transactions structured to utilise existing tax losses carried forward that may otherwise expire unused;
- transactions that could affect an entity's non-taxable or tax-exempt status; and
- an unresolved dispute between the entity and the relevant tax authority about the amount of tax due.

3.13.660.40   Income tax exposures are not discussed directly in IFRS. However, the following definitions are relevant.
- Current tax is the amount of income tax payable (recoverable) in respect of the taxable profit (tax loss) for a period.
- Deferred tax liabilities are the amounts of income taxes payable in future periods in respect of taxable temporary differences. [*IAS 12.5*]

3.13.660.50   A tax exposure falls under the definition of current tax to the extent that it affects the calculation of income tax in respect of the current or prior periods (see 3.13.70.50). A tax exposure falls under the definition of deferred tax to the extent that it affects the carrying amount of an asset or liability for accounting or tax purposes. [*IAS 12.5*]

3.13.660.60   Potential income tax exposures are analysed individually and separately from the calculation of income tax, and in our view the amount of tax provided for should be determined in accordance with IAS 12; this is because we believe that income tax exposures are income taxes in the scope of that standard. In our view, consistent with the definition of current tax, the amount to be provided for is the best estimate of the tax amount expected to be paid. In our experience, the best estimate of the amount expected to be paid may be determined using different methods. For example, if there are only two possible outcomes, then it may be appropriate to use a most likely outcome method (see 3.12.110.30). If there are a number of possible outcomes, then it may be appropriate to use an expected value method (see 3.12.110.20). [*IAS 12.12, 46, IU 05-14*]

3.13.660.70   Exposures related to taxes that are not income taxes – e.g. taxes on sales such as value added tax – are recognised and measured in accordance with IAS 37, unless they are dealt with specifically in another standard – e.g. IAS 19 for social security taxes (see 3.12.760.30).

3.13.665   FORTHCOMING REQUIREMENTS

3.13.665.10   IFRIC 23 applies to current and deferred taxes if there is uncertainty about an income tax treatment, but does not address the accounting for the related interest or penalties. The guidance in IFRIC 23 is consistent with the guidance in 3.13.660.50–60. [*IFRIC 23.4*]

3.13.665.20 If there is uncertainty about an income tax treatment, then an entity considers whether it is probable that a tax authority will accept the entity's tax treatment included or planned to be included in its tax filing. The underlying assumption in the assessment is that a tax authority will examine all amounts reported and will have full knowledge of all relevant information. [*IFRIC 23.8–9*]

3.13.665.30 Based on the assessment, an entity reflects uncertainty about a tax treatment in measuring its current and deferred taxes as follows.

- *Tax authority is likely to accept the entity's tax treatment:* If an entity concludes that it is probable that the tax authority will accept its tax treatment, then it measures current and deferred taxes consistently with the tax treatment used or planned to be used in its income tax filing.
- *Tax authority is unlikely to accept the entity's tax treatment:* If an entity concludes that it is not probable that the tax authority will accept its tax treatment, then it reflects the effect of that tax uncertainty in determining the related taxable profit (tax loss), tax bases, unused tax losses, unused tax credits and tax rates. To do so, an entity uses either the most likely amount or the expected value method – whichever better predicts the resolution of the uncertainty. [*IFRIC 23.10–11*]

3.13.665.40 The definition of 'tax authority' in IFRIC 23 covers all bodies that decide whether a particular tax treatment is acceptable under the tax law, including a court. In some cases, a specific tax treatment may be challenged by a local tax authority, but ultimately be defendable if it is escalated to a higher tax authority – e.g. to court. However, some entities may have an intention of settling the claim instead of taking it to a higher level, considering the costs and efforts involved in defending the claim. In these cases, the entity needs to determine which tax authority is relevant for its assessment of whether it is probable that a tax treatment would be accepted. In our view, in determining the relevant tax authority for this assessment, the entity should consider management's intention to settle the claim. Therefore, the analysis should focus on acceptance by the local tax authority, rather than the court. This approach would better reflect the expected manner of resolving the tax uncertainty. [*IAS 12.46–47, 51, IFRIC 23.9*]

EXAMPLE 41 – UNCERTAIN INCOME TAX TREATMENT – EXPECTED SETTLEMENT

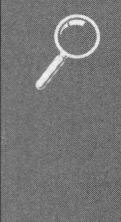

3.13.665.50 Company X donated 10,000 widgets to charity and claimed a deduction in its 2018 tax filing. Under the local tax law, deductions for donated assets are determined based on the market price of the assets. The deduction claimed was based on X's list price of 10 per widget and amounted to 100,000 (10,000 x 10). Similar widgets produced by other companies are sold on the market for a range of 9 to 11 per unit. In 2019, the local tax authority examined X's tax filing and argued that the deduction had to be based on the lowest observable market price of 9 per unit – i.e. it should have been 90,000 (10,000 x 9).

3.13.665.60 X believes that if it takes this case to court, then it is probable that it will be able to defend its position based on similar precedents. However, the costs of doing so would be higher than the amount of additional tax claimed by the local tax authority. Therefore, X intends to settle the claim.

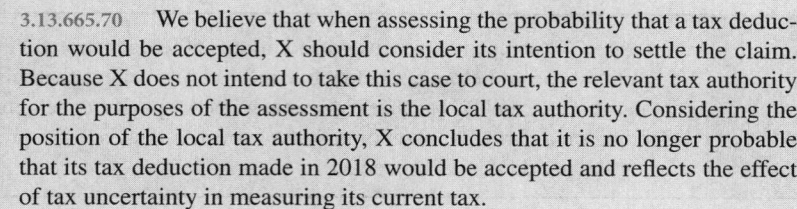

3.13.665.70   We believe that when assessing the probability that a tax deduction would be accepted, X should consider its intention to settle the claim. Because X does not intend to take this case to court, the relevant tax authority for the purposes of the assessment is the local tax authority. Considering the position of the local tax authority, X concludes that it is no longer probable that its tax deduction made in 2018 would be accepted and reflects the effect of tax uncertainty in measuring its current tax.

3.13.665.80 Companies with more than one uncertain tax treatment assess uncertainties separately or together, depending on which approach better predicts the resolution of the uncertainty – e.g. how the entity supports the tax treatment, or what approach it expects the taxation authority to take during an examination. [*IFRIC 23.6–7*]

3.13.665.90 An entity reassesses estimates and assumptions if facts and circumstances change or new information emerges. If changes in facts and circumstances occur, or new information emerges, between the reporting date and the date when the financial statements are authorised for issue, then the entity applies IAS 10 to identify whether its estimates and assumptions need to be adjusted to reflect those events (see chapter 2.9). [*IFRIC 23.13–14, A1–A3, IAS 8.36–37, 10.8, 10*]

3.13.670   INVESTMENT TAX CREDITS

3.13.680   Definition and scope

3.13.680.10   There is no formal definition of investment tax credits (ITCs) under IFRS, but such government incentives are typically delivered through the tax systems – e.g. in the form of reductions in income tax liabilities or increases in tax-deductible expenses. Accounting for ITCs is not addressed directly in IFRS because they are scoped out of IAS 12 and IAS 20. However, IAS 12 applies to all temporary differences arising from ITCs. In our view, in determining the accounting for ITCs it is necessary to consider all the relevant facts and circumstances, and in particular the indicators in 3.13.700.10. [*IAS 12.4, 20.2(b)*]

3.13.690   Identifying investment tax credits

3.13.690.10   The substance of a tax incentive may be more akin to a credit received for investment in a certain area – i.e. specific expenditure on a particular asset or activity – or simply a reduction in the applicable tax rate. The former is an ITC, whereas the latter falls in the scope of IAS 12.

EXAMPLE 42A – INVESTMENT TAX CREDIT – R&D EXPENSES

3.13.690.20   Under the applicable tax regulations, Company B receives an additional 50% tax deduction for incurring certain R&D expenses. We believe that this tax incentive is an ITC because it relates to specific expenditure on R&D activities.

3.13.690.30   Separately, B receives an additional 50% deduction for expenditure on a qualifying asset – e.g. highly specialised manufacturing equipment. We believe that this tax incentive is an ITC because it relates to expenditure on a specific asset.

EXAMPLE 42B – INVESTMENT TAX CREDIT – PROFITABILITY

> 3.13.690.40   Company C receives an additional 50% deduction for employee costs if it makes a profit before tax below five million. We believe that this tax benefit is not in substance an ITC because it does not relate to specific expenditure or required spending on a particular asset or activity; instead it relates to the profitability of C during the period that it is received.

3.13.700   Accounting for investment tax credits

3.13.700.10   In practice, because ITCs are typically government incentive schemes delivered through the tax systems, entities generally account for ITCs using IAS 12 or IAS 20 by analogy. Applying one or the other standard by analogy will have different recognition, measurement, presentation and disclosure consequences. In our view, management needs to choose an accounting approach that best reflects the economic substance of the ITC. This determination requires judgement in light of all relevant facts and circumstances.

3.13.710   *Applying IAS 20 by analogy*

3.13.710.10   If the substance of an ITC is more akin to a government grant, then we believe that the application of IAS 20 by analogy is more appropriate. In determining whether the economic substance of an ITC is more akin to a government grant, the definition of a government grant in IAS 20 (see 4.3.10) and the following indicators are considered.

- The amount of tax incentive is independent of the amount of taxable profit or tax liability. For example, a government provides an ITC to entities that invest in retirement homes for the elderly. An eligible entity is required to first carry forward and offset the ITC against its income tax liability for a specified period; if there is insufficient income tax liability to offset the ITC after the specified period, then any excess ITC is paid by the government in cash at the end of the period. In such a situation, the ITC incentivises an entity to invest in retirement homes. Therefore, the benefit may not be akin to a tax allowance.
- As well as the condition that expenditure is made on a particular asset or activity, there are other substantive conditions attached to an ITC that relate to the operating activity of an entity. This may be the case when, for example, as well as the condition that expenditure is incurred on a particular asset, an ITC stipulates another condition such as requiring that a certain number of local workers are employed to operate the asset. Therefore, if other substantive conditions are attached to an ITC, then these conditions may indicate that the benefit is more akin to a government grant.

3.13.710.20   Following IAS 20 by analogy, ITCs are recognised as income over the periods necessary to match them with related costs for which they are intended to compensate. ITCs are presented in the statement of financial position by setting up the grant as deferred income or, if the grant relates to an asset, then either as deferred income or as a deduction in arriving at the carrying amount of an asset. ITCs are subsequently presented in profit or loss either as other income or as a deduction from the related expense, as appropriate (see 4.3.40, 80 and 120).

3.13.720   *Applying IAS 12 by analogy*

3.13.720.10   We believe that the application of IAS 12 is more appropriate when the economic substance of an ITC is akin to a tax allowance. For example, under a general R&D tax incentive scheme, which is available to all taxable entities, a government allows entities to claim an additional 15% tax deduction for a broad range of generic R&D expenditure in the period in which the expenditure is incurred. If the additional deduction exceeds taxable income, then the resulting tax loss can be carried forward and utilised in a future period of up to three years. If any part of the ITC remains unclaimed after three years, then the ITC expires. In this case, in the absence of any other relevant indicators, we believe that the economic substance of the ITC is more akin to a tax allowance and should be accounted for by analogy to IAS 12.

3.13.720.20   Following IAS 12 by analogy, ITCs are presented in profit or loss as a deduction in current tax expense to the extent that an entity is entitled to claim the credit in the current reporting period. Any unused ITC is recognised as a deferred tax asset and income if it meets the recognition criteria (see 3.13.330).

3.13.730   CASH FLOW HEDGE ACCOUNTING

3.13.730.10   Under IFRS 9, if a cash flow hedge of a forecast transaction (see 7.9.180) subsequently results in the recognition of a non-financial asset (liability), then the entity removes the accumulated amount of changes in fair value of the hedging instrument from the cash flow hedge reserve and includes it directly in the initial cost or other carrying amount of the asset (liability) (see 7.9.200.70). This adjustment is commonly referred to as a 'basis adjustment'. If an entity continues to apply the hedging requirements in IAS 39, as permitted by IFRS 9, then it may apply a similar accounting policy (see 7I.7.80.70). Basis adjustments can give rise to temporary differences. This is because they affect the carrying amount of the asset (liability), but usually not its tax base. [*IFRS 9.6.5.11(d)(i)*]

3.13.740   Initial recognition exemption

3.13.740.10   On initial recognition of a hedged non-financial asset (liability), a question arises over whether the initial recognition exemption applies to a temporary difference resulting from a basis adjustment (see 3.13.730.10). Generally, any gain or loss arising from the hedging instrument has tax consequences. In our view, the initial recognition exemption does not apply in these circumstances. This is because the hedging instrument and the recognition of the hedged non-financial asset (liability) are integrally linked and the hedging instrument affects the taxable profit (tax loss) at the time of the basis adjustment. [*IAS 12.15, 24*]

3.13.750   Presentation of current and deferred tax

3.13.750.10   Applying the general principle for accounting for the current and deferred tax effects consistently with the accounting for the transaction itself (see 3.13.530.10) may be challenging in the case of cash flow hedging of a forecast transaction that results in the recognition of a non-financial asset (liability). The challenges relate to tax effects of both a hedging instrument and a hedged item and arise because of the mechanics of cash flow hedge accounting under IFRS 9 (see 7.9.200).

3.13.750.20   Under IFRS 9, the effective portion of changes in fair value of a hedging instrument is recognised in OCI and accumulated in the cash flow hedge reserve in equity. The related tax effects are accounted for in the same manner. On recognition of a hedged non-financial asset (liability), an entity removes the accumulated amount from the cash flow hedge reserve and includes it directly in the initial cost or other carrying amount of the asset (liability) – i.e. makes a basis adjustment (see 3.13.730.10). These amounts are not reclassified from OCI (see 7.9.200.70) and a question arises over whether deferred tax related to the hedging instrument should be removed from the cash flow hedge reserve as well and, if so, where it should be recognised. Another question related to the hedging instrument is where to recognise a current tax effect on its settlement because the settlement of a hedging instrument generally does not affect the accounting profit or loss, but generally affects the taxable profit (tax loss). Similar questions arise in relation to the hedged item – i.e. where to recognise the deferred tax on a temporary difference arising from a basis adjustment and its reversal.

3.13.750.30   In our view, one possible approach to accounting for the current and deferred tax effects of a cash flow hedge of a forecast transaction that results in the recognition of a non-financial asset (liability) is as follows:

- *current tax on the hedging instrument* – recognise on settlement in profit or loss;
- *deferred tax on the hedging instrument (reversal)* – recognise a reversal of the deferred tax previously recognised in OCI (i.e. deferred tax that relates to the effective portion of the changes in fair value; see 7.9.200.10) on settlement also in OCI; and
- *deferred tax on the hedged item* – recognise in profit or loss. [*IAS 12.58, 61A, 65*]

EXAMPLE 43 – BASIS ADJUSTMENT IN CASH FLOW HEDGE

3.13.750.40   Company S's risk management policy is to hedge its exposure to cash flow fluctuations from changes in foreign currencies arising from inventory purchases. On 1 January 2018, S enters into a foreign currency forward contract to hedge the currency exposure on a future purchase of inventory. The fair value of the forward at inception is zero.

3.13.750.50   S designates and documents the full fair value changes of the forward in a cash flow hedge of a highly probable forecast purchase transaction that is expected to occur on 31 December 2018. For the purposes of this example, the hedge is considered fully effective (see 7.9.840).

3.13.750.60   On 31 December 2018, S buys the inventory and its cost translated at the spot rate is 100,000. This is also the tax base of the inventory. On the same date, S receives a net amount of 10,000 on settlement of the forward – i.e. immediately before settlement, the forward is an asset with a fair value of 10,000, which is included in taxable profit on receipt. The income tax rate is 30%.

3.13.750.70   S determines that all criteria for hedge accounting have been met and records the following entries.

	DEBIT	CREDIT
31 December 2018		
Forward (asset)	10,000	
Hedging reserve (OCI)		10,000
To recognise change in fair value of the forward		

	DEBIT	CREDIT
Deferred tax expense (OCI)	3,000	
Deferred tax liability		3,000
To recognise deferred tax on the forward (see 3.13.160)		
Cash	10,000	
Forward (asset)		10,000
To recognise cash received on settlement of the forward		
Current tax expense (profit or loss)	3,000	
Current tax liability		3,000
To recognise current tax payable on gains from settlement of the forward (10,000 x 30%)		
Deferred tax liability	3,000	
Deferred tax income (OCI)		3,000
To reverse deferred tax when the forward is settled		
Inventory	100,000	
Cash		100,000
To recognise purchase of inventory		
Hedging reserve (equity)	10,000	
Inventory		10,000
To recognise basis adjustment (see 7.9.200.70)		
Deferred tax asset[1,2]	3,000	
Deferred tax income (profit or loss)		3,000
To recognise deferred taxes on the hedged inventory, arising from basis adjustment (see 3.13.740.10)		

Notes
1. The recognition of the deferred tax asset is subject to the criteria in 3.13.330.
2. Calculated as (100,000 - 90,000) x 30%.

3.13.750.60   On 31 March 2019, S sells the inventory for 120,000. S is liable to tax of 6,000 on taxable income of 20,000 ((120,000 - 100,000) x 30%). S records the following entries.

	DEBIT	CREDIT
31 March 2019		
Cash	120,000	
Revenue from contracts with customers		120,000
To recognise revenue for the sale of inventory		

	Debit	Credit
Costs of goods sold	90,000	
Inventory		90,000
To derecognise hedged inventory sold		
Current tax expense (profit or loss)	6,000	
Current tax liability		6,000
To recognise current tax payable on sale of the inventory ((120,000 - 100,000) x 30%)		
Deferred tax expense (profit or loss)	3,000	
Deferred tax asset		3,000
To reverse deferred tax when inventory is sold		

3.13.760 DIVIDENDS

3.13.770 Income taxes triggered by payment of dividends#

3.13.770.10   Under IAS 32, distributions to holders of an equity instrument are recognised directly in equity. However, income taxes that are linked to the payment of dividends are generally linked more directly with past transactions and events than with the actual distribution to shareholders. Therefore, an entity follows the same general principles as outlined in 3.13.530.10 in attributing the income tax between consequences of dividends in profit or loss, OCI and equity. [*IAS 32.35A, 12.52B*]

3.13.775 FORTHCOMING REQUIREMENTS

3.13.775.10 *Annual Improvements to IFRSs 2015–2017 Cycle – Amendments to IAS 12* clarify that an entity presents income tax consequences of all distributions of profit (i.e. dividends) in profit or loss, unless the transactions or events that generated those distributable profits were recognised outside profit or loss. That is, the amendments clarify that the requirements in paragraph 52B of IAS 12 are not limited to the circumstances described in paragraph 52A of IAS 12. Therefore, income tax consequences of payments on financial instruments that are classified as equity but treated as liabilities for tax purposes are recognised in profit or loss if those payments are distributions of profits previously recognised in profit or loss.

3.13.780 Tax rate dependent on profit distribution

3.13.780.10   In some jurisdictions, income taxes are payable at a higher or lower rate if part or all of the net profit or retained earnings is distributed. In these cases, deferred tax is based on the tax rate applicable to undistributed profits. When a liability for the payment of dividends is recognised in the financial statements, the tax consequences of the distribution are also recognised. In this case, the specific requirement in relation to the tax consequences of dividend payments takes precedence over the principle that deferred taxes are measured at the amount expected to be paid (recovered). For a discussion of how to present the tax effects of profit distribution, see 3.13.770, 810 and 1220. [*IAS 12.47, 52A–52B*]

EXAMPLE 44 – RECOGNITION OF INCOME TAX CONSEQUENCES OF DIVIDENDS

3.13.780.20   In jurisdiction X, the tax rate applicable to undistributed investment income is 50%. The tax rate applicable to distributed investment income is 30%. Company F earns investment income of 100 in year 1 and pays a dividend of 80 in year 2. F has a history of annual dividend payments and it intends to continue this policy in the future.

3.13.780.30   F did not recognise the dividend as a liability at the end of year 1 because the dividend was approved after the reporting date. In this case, the specific requirement regarding the tax consequences of dividend payments takes precedence over the general requirement regarding the amount expected to be paid (recovered). Therefore, in year 1 F recognises current tax expense of 50 (100 x 50%); in year 2, F recognises current tax income of 16 (80 x (30% - 50%)) as a result of the dividend.

3.13.790   Tax-exempt reserves

3.13.790.10   In some countries, the tax authorities allow gains on the disposal of property, plant and equipment to be added to a tax-exempt reserve. This reserve is taxed only when it is distributed in the form of dividends or on liquidation.

EXAMPLE 45A – TAX-EXEMPT RESERVES – CAPITAL GAIN

3.13.790.20   In Country E, any capital gain on the disposal of certain machines is not taxable, provided that the capital gain is not distributed and is recorded in a 'reserve not available for distribution'. If the capital gain is distributed, then it is taxed at the income tax rate of 40%.

3.13.790.30   Company M in Country E sells a machine with a carrying amount of 250 for 350. It therefore makes a gain on disposal of 100. For tax purposes, the 100 gain on disposal will be taxed in future periods only if distributed.

3.13.790.40   The income tax consequences of the disposal gain is calculated at the income tax rate for undistributed earnings. In this case, the tax rate is zero; therefore, no tax liability is recognised (100 x 0%). M recognises income tax payable of 40 (100 x 40%) only when a liability to distribute the reserve is recognised.

3.13.790.50   In some countries, the tax authorities allow revaluations for tax purposes. In some cases, part of the tax revaluation is recorded in a tax-exempt reserve, which will be taxed only on distribution of dividends out of this tax-exempt reserve. In such cases, no deferred tax liability is recognised for the additional tax to be paid on distribution until the related dividend is recognised. [*IAS 12.52A–52B*]

EXAMPLE 45B – TAX-EXEMPT RESERVES – REVALUATION

3.13.790.60   In Country F, companies may revalue property, plant and equipment for tax purposes. The revaluation is taxed immediately at 25% and subsequent depreciation based on the revalued amount is tax-deductible at the income tax rate of 40%.

3.13.790.70   The revaluation is credited to a revaluation reserve in equity (for tax purposes). On distribution of the revaluation reserve, further income tax is payable at a rate of 15% (the normal income tax rate of 40% minus the 25% tax already paid).

3.13.790.80   Company C revalues its property, plant and equipment for tax purposes, but no revaluation is recognised under IFRS. On 31 December 2018, the carrying amount under IFRS equals the tax base before a revaluation of 100. C records the following entries.

	DEBIT	CREDIT
Income tax (profit or loss)	25	
Income tax payable		25
To recognise current tax (100 x 25%)		
Deferred tax asset	40	
Income tax (profit or loss)		40
To recognise deferred tax asset (100 x 40%)		

3.13.790.90   No tax liability is recognised for the additional tax to be paid on distribution until the related dividend is recognised (see 3.13.780.10). The recognition of the deferred tax consequences of the tax revaluation, which in Example 45B is in profit or loss, is discussed in 3.13.570.120.

3.13.800   **Dividend withholding tax**

3.13.800.10   In some tax jurisdictions, a dividend withholding tax is payable on distributions to shareholders. Such taxes are not attributable to the entity paying the dividend; instead, the entity collects and pays them to the tax authorities on behalf of the shareholder. Therefore, such taxes are recognised directly in equity as part of the distribution to shareholders. [*IAS 12.65A*]

EXAMPLE 46 – DIVIDEND WITHHOLDING TAX

3.13.800.20   Company M declares a dividend of 200, 20% of which is payable to the tax authorities. M records the following entry.

	DEBIT	CREDIT
Distribution (equity)	200	
Liability (to shareholders)		160
Liability (to the tax authorities)		40
To recognise distribution of dividend and resulting withholding tax		

3.13.800.30 For a discussion of the accounting for the potential income tax effects of such distributions in the financial statements of a parent, see 3.13.260.

3.13.800.40 In our view, withholding taxes attributable to investment income (e.g. dividends received) should be recognised as part of income tax expense, with the investment income recognised on a gross basis. This is because neither IFRS 9 nor IAS 12 provides any mechanism for income tax paid to be offset against the underlying income. [*IAS 12.2*]

3.13.810   Dividend credits

3.13.810.10 In some tax jurisdictions, an entity may 'attach' credits to a dividend payment that are used by the shareholder to offset tax payable on the dividend. These credits provide relief from double taxation, because the profits from which the dividend is paid have already been taxed at the entity level.

EXAMPLE 47A – CREDIT ATTACHED TO DIVIDEND PAYMENT

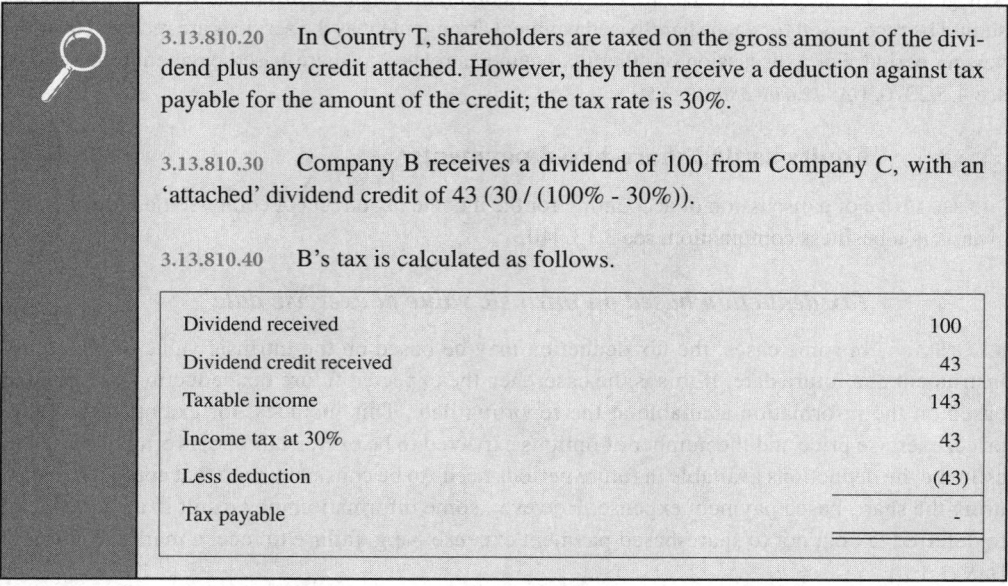

3.13.810.20 In Country T, shareholders are taxed on the gross amount of the dividend plus any credit attached. However, they then receive a deduction against tax payable for the amount of the credit; the tax rate is 30%.

3.13.810.30 Company B receives a dividend of 100 from Company C, with an 'attached' dividend credit of 43 (30 / (100% - 30%)).

3.13.810.40 B's tax is calculated as follows.

Dividend received	100
Dividend credit received	43
Taxable income	143
Income tax at 30%	43
Less deduction	(43)
Tax payable	-

3.13.810.50 For accounting purposes, an entity needs to determine how it should present the dividend received in profit or loss – either net or gross of the dividend credit.

3.13.810.60 In our view, net presentation is more appropriate. This is because the dividend credit is simply a mechanism to ensure that certain dividends (or parts thereof) are tax-exempt. We believe that the net presentation reflects that substance.

EXAMPLE 47B – CREDIT ATTACHED TO DIVIDEND PAYMENT – GROSS VS NET PRESENTATION

3.13.810.70 Continuing Example 47A, the table below illustrates the net and gross presentation of the dividend credit for Company B. As noted in 3.13.810.60, we believe that the net presentation reflects the substance of the transaction.

	NET	GROSS
Profit before tax	100	143
Income tax	-	(43)
Net profit	100	100

3.13.820 SHARE-BASED PAYMENTS

3.13.820.10 In some tax jurisdictions, an entity may receive a tax deduction that differs in amount and/or timing from the cumulative share-based payment expense recognised in profit or loss. This will generally result in deferred tax on the temporary differences. In our view, the deferred tax should be recognised for each share-based payment arrangement as the services are received over the vesting period. For a discussion of other tax payments related to share-based payment transactions, see 4.5.2070. [*IAS 12.68A–68B, IE.Ex5*]

3.13.830 Equity-settled share-based payments

3.13.830.10 For a discussion of accounting for the income tax effects of equity-settled replacement awards in a business combination, see 3.13.940.

3.13.840 *Tax deduction based on intrinsic value at exercise date*

3.13.840.10 In some cases, the tax deduction may be based on the intrinsic value of the equity instrument at a future date. If this is the case, then the expected future tax deduction is estimated based on the information available at the reporting date. This includes, for example, the share price, exercise price and the number of options expected to be exercised. The information used to estimate the deductions available in future periods needs to be consistent with that applied in measuring the share-based payment expense. However, some information may result in an adjustment to deferred tax but not to share-based payment expense – e.g. failure to meet a market condition. [*IAS 12.68B*]

3.13.840.20   An issue arises if the amount of the tax deduction (or estimated future tax deduction) exceeds the amount of the related cumulative share-based payment expense. This indicates that the tax deduction relates not only to remuneration expense, but also to an equity item. In this case, the excess of the associated income tax is recognised directly in equity. Any subsequent reduction in the excess is also recorded in equity. Such an excess benefit over the share-based payment expense may arise when the method of calculating the tax deduction differs from the method of calculating the IFRS 2 measure. An example is when the future tax deduction is measured based on the intrinsic value of share options rather than the grant-date fair value. [*IAS 12.68C*]

3.13.840.30   The excess is determined at each reporting date on a cumulative basis. The amount recognised in equity equals the excess multiplied by the tax rate. To achieve this, the movements in the excess also flow through equity. That is, if an excess recognised in equity is later reversed, partially or in full, then the reversal is also recognised directly in equity.

3.13.850   *Other tax deductions*

3.13.850.10   An entity may settle a share-based payment transaction by transferring treasury shares, and receive a tax deduction based on the cost of the treasury shares. In this case, the entity estimates its expected future tax deduction based on the cost of the treasury shares.

3.13.850.20   In other cases, current tax deductions are available based on the intrinsic value of a share-based payment award at grant date. In these circumstances, in our view an entity should choose an accounting policy, to be applied consistently, based on one of the following approaches.
- Recognise deferred tax between points in time at which the share-based payment cost is recognised and the associated tax deduction is given. This results in a similar approach of recognising deferred tax irrespective of whether the tax deduction is received before or after the share-based payment expense is recognised.
- Recognise the current tax deduction entirely in equity at grant date and then reclassify it to profit or loss over the vesting period, such that no deferred tax is recognised.
- Recognise a deferred tax liability when the tax deduction is received and build up a deferred tax asset as the share-based payment expense is recognised. The resulting asset and liability are then offset at the end of the vesting period.

3.13.860   Cash-settled share-based payments

3.13.860.10   For a cash-settled share-based payment arrangement, sometimes a tax deduction is received for an amount equal to the ultimate payment when it is made. In these cases, a question arises about whether the temporary difference should reflect:
- the carrying amount of the share-based payment liability, which is measured at fair value under IFRS 2; or
- the intrinsic value based on the price of the underlying share at the reporting date.

3.13.860.20   Determining the temporary difference with reference to fair value would be consistent with general practice for calculating deferred tax on revalued items (see 3.13.110). Conversely, the guidance on deferred tax inserted into IAS 12 as a result of the issuance of IFRS 2 refers explicitly to *intrinsic* value in the case of equity-settled share-based payments. In our view, an entity should choose an accounting policy, to be applied consistently, in these circumstances. [*IAS 12.IE.Ex5*]

BUSINESS COMBINATIONS

General principles

3.13.880.10   An entity generally recognises deferred tax assets and liabilities for temporary differences that arise in respect of recognised identifiable assets and liabilities in a business combination. However, it does not recognise deferred tax for:
- taxable temporary differences related to the initial recognition of goodwill (see 3.13.200); and
- temporary differences related to acquired investments in subsidiaries, branches and associates, and interests in joint arrangements, when the relevant criteria are met (see 3.13.260).

3.13.880.20   In addition, the entity recognises any deferred tax assets only to the extent that it is probable at the date of acquisition, that future taxable profits will be available against which the related deductible temporary differences can be used (see 3.13.330). For general guidance on the accounting for business combinations, see chapter 2.6. [*IAS 12.15, 19, 24, 66*]

3.13.880.30   Deferred taxes are recognised in accordance with the principles in IAS 12 in the acquisition accounting for unused tax losses and unused tax credits of the acquiree, and on temporary differences between the tax bases of identifiable assets acquired and liabilities assumed in a business combination and the related amounts recognised in the acquisition accounting. Assets acquired and liabilities assumed in a business combination are measured in the acquisition accounting in accordance with IFRS 3. [*IAS 12.19, 66, 68*]

3.13.880.40   In some jurisdictions, depending on how the transaction is structured, the tax bases of those assets and liabilities may not be affected by the business combination; alternatively, the tax bases may be measured in a different way, which can give rise to temporary differences. Such temporary differences arise for different reasons, including the following.
- *Recognition:* If the acquiree applied the initial recognition exemption to temporary differences, then they would not meet the criteria for that exemption from the perspective of an acquirer in a business combination (see 3.13.210.80). Additionally, temporary differences may arise on assets and liabilities that were not recognised in the acquiree's financial statements, such as certain intangible assets or contingent liabilities recognised in accordance with IFRS 3 (see 2.6.650).
- *Measurement:* Amounts recognised in respect of acquisition accounting for assets acquired and liabilities assumed in many cases will differ from those recognised in the acquiree's financial statements.
- *Assessment of recoverability:* The acquirer's assessment of whether deferred tax assets are recoverable may differ from that of the acquiree. This may be because of a change in circumstances of the combined entity compared with those of the acquiree on a stand-alone basis. [*IAS 12.15(b), 19, 24, 26(c)*]

3.13.880.50   The interaction of the acquirer's and acquiree's tax attributes may affect the deferred tax recognised in the acquisition accounting. It may also affect the acquirer's existing temporary differences. Such attributes might include, for example, current and deferred tax balances, tax rates, taxable income and tax jurisdiction.

3.13.880.60   Generally, the effects of the acquisition on the acquiree's deferred taxes are recognised as part of the acquisition accounting, whereas the effects of the acquisition on the acquirer's deferred taxes are recognised separately from the acquisition accounting. [*IAS 12.66–67*]

3.13.880.70   Future changes in tax rates are not anticipated for the purpose of measuring deferred taxes in a business combination. Deferred tax assets and liabilities are measured based on rates that are enacted or substantively enacted at the date of acquisition (see 3.13.480). This applies even if expected tax rate changes were considered in negotiating the consideration transferred or a change in tax rates was substantively enacted after the date of acquisition but during the measurement period (see 2.6.1030). The effect of changes in tax rates is recognised in profit or loss separately from the acquisition accounting in the period in which the change is enacted or substantively enacted. [*IAS 12.46*]

3.13.890   Contingent consideration

3.13.890.10   When determining the income tax effects of contingent consideration, an entity considers all relevant factors. These may include the nature, measurement and timing of any tax deduction in respect of the contingent consideration, and the classification of the related contingent consideration. For a discussion of contingent consideration, see 2.6.280.

3.13.890.20   The tax treatment of contingent consideration may vary depending on the jurisdiction in which a business combination takes place. It may also depend on the legal form of the transaction. For example, contingent consideration may affect the tax base of the identifiable assets and liabilities acquired or of goodwill deductible for tax purposes. Alternatively, it may affect only the tax base of an acquired investment in a subsidiary.

3.13.890.30   A liability (asset) in relation to contingent consideration recognised in the acquisition accounting may result in amounts that are taxable (deductible) in future periods. In this case, deferred taxes are generally recognised for the resulting temporary differences. In our view, the tax effects of such contingent consideration should be recognised in the acquisition accounting consistently with the recognition of the contingent consideration. [*IAS 12.66*]

3.13.890.40   When contingent consideration affects the tax base of an acquired investment in a subsidiary, the acquirer considers whether:
- it is appropriate to recognise deferred taxes in relation to a temporary difference related to that investment; or
- the exception to the recognition of deferred tax in relation to such investments applies (see 3.13.980). [*IAS 12.38–45*]

3.13.890.50   If contingent consideration is classified as an asset or a liability, then changes in the fair value after the date of acquisition of the investment are generally recognised in profit or loss (see 2.6.1120). The deferred tax effects of changes in temporary differences are recognised in the same manner as the related changes in the fair value of the contingent consideration – i.e. in profit or loss. [*IAS 12.61A*]

EXAMPLE 48A – CONTINGENT CONSIDERATION

3.13.890.60   Company P acquires Company S in a business combination. The following information is relevant for this example.
- In addition to consideration transferred at the date of acquisition, contingent consideration of 300 is potentially payable in cash. This depends on the future earnings of S.

- P classifies the contingent consideration as a liability, and recognises changes in fair value in profit or loss.
- The fair value of the contingent consideration is 140 at the date of acquisition.
- Before accounting for the tax effects of the contingent consideration, P calculates goodwill of 600 for financial reporting purposes. Of this amount, 400 is tax-deductible.
- P anticipates adequate future taxable income to support recognition in full of all deferred tax assets arising from its deductible temporary differences.

3.13.890.70   The payment of contingent consideration will affect the tax base of the goodwill recognised by P. Therefore, the recognition of deferred taxes in the acquisition accounting depends on whether the related temporary difference is a taxable or deductible temporary difference – i.e. on whether goodwill for accounting purposes exceeds that for tax purposes or vice versa (see 3.13.1020).

3.13.890.80   Assume that the related liability is settled at its carrying amount at the date of acquisition. The resulting tax goodwill at that date is 540 (400 + 140). Accordingly, P does not recognise deferred tax for the resulting taxable temporary difference, because of the exemption for the initial recognition of goodwill (see 3.13.1020). [*IAS 12.21A*]

EXAMPLE 48B – CONTINGENT CONSIDERATION – FAIR VALUE REMEASUREMENT

3.13.890.90   Modifying Example 48A, the payment of contingent consideration attracts a tax deduction when the related liability is settled. The applicable tax rate is 40%. In this example, P recognises a deferred tax asset of 56 (140 x 40%) on the contingent consideration as part of the acquisition accounting. This reduces the goodwill recognised in the business combination.

3.13.890.100   After the date of acquisition, the fair value of the contingent consideration is remeasured to 250. P recognises the change in the fair value of the contingent consideration and related tax effects in profit or loss.

3.13.900   **Items that are not part of business combination**

3.13.910   *Changes in acquirer's deferred tax assets*

3.13.910.10   The interaction of the tax positions of the acquirer and acquiree frequently results in a change in the assessment of the recoverability of the acquirer's deferred tax assets. For example, assume that the *acquirer* did not previously recognise a deferred tax asset for its tax losses. It might determine that, as a result of the business combination, it is able to use these tax losses against the future taxable profit of the combined entity. Such changes are recognised separately from the acquisition accounting. Also, changes to the acquirer's deferred taxes occurring subsequent to the date of acquisition are recognised outside the acquisition accounting. [*IAS 12.67*]

3.13.910.20   In our view, the deferred tax consequence of an acquisition for the acquirer should be determined as the difference between:

- the acquirer's net deferred tax asset or liability measured just before the acquisition; and
- its net deferred tax asset or liability measured on those same temporary differences just after the acquisition.

3.13.910.30   For a discussion of the general principles of asset recognition and tax groups, see 3.13.330 and 1170.

EXAMPLE 49 – CHANGE IN RECOGNITION OF ACQUIRER'S DEFERRED TAX ASSETS AT DATE OF ACQUISITION

3.13.910.40   Company P acquires 100% of Company S in a business combination. The following facts are relevant for this example.
- P has cumulative tax losses of 200 at the date of acquisition.
- Before the acquisition, P's management had determined that it was less than probable that P would realise its tax losses. In making that determination, P's management considered future taxable profits, the existence of taxable temporary differences and tax planning opportunities.
- P's tax losses have an indefinite carry-forward period.
- S has no unused tax losses or tax credits. All of the taxable temporary differences of S relate to finite-lived assets.
- In its consolidated financial statements, P records the acquisition of S and recognises identifiable net assets acquired of 460 and goodwill of 240.
- The tax rate applicable to both P and S is 40%.
- Goodwill arising in the business combination is not tax-deductible.

3.13.910.50   The following table presents amounts recognised in the acquisition accounting and their related tax bases.

	FINANCIAL STATEMENTS	TAX BASE
Identifiable net assets acquired (excluding deferred tax)	500	400
Deferred tax liability ((500 - 400) x 40%)	(40)	-
Goodwill	240	-
Consideration transferred	700	

3.13.910.60   Under the local tax law, P and S are included in the same tax group. There is no restriction on utilising the tax losses of P against the taxable profits of other entities in that tax group. The reversal of the taxable temporary differences of S plus the anticipated profits projected to be generated by S after the acquisition provide evidence that P's unused tax losses are recoverable. Therefore, P recognises the deferred tax asset of 80 (200 of tax losses at the applicable tax rate of 40%) as tax income in profit or loss separately from the business combination.

> 3.13.910.70   Modifying the facts in 3.13.910.60, P may not be able to include S in the same tax group, and may be unable otherwise to support a conclusion that it is probable that it will be able to recover its unused tax losses against the taxable profit of S. In this case, the deferred tax asset in respect of P's losses remains unrecognised as of the date of acquisition.

3.13.920   *Settlement of pre-existing relationships*

3.13.920.10   Pre-existing relationships between the acquirer and the acquiree are effectively settled as a result of the business combination. They are accounted for separately from the business combination as a gain or loss at the date of acquisition (see 2.6.780). Accordingly, an entity also recognises the tax effects of the settlement outside the business combination.

3.13.920.20   The tax treatment of the settlement of a pre-existing relationship will vary depending on the tax laws of the relevant jurisdiction. If the tax treatment is the same as that for accounting, then the current tax income or expense is recognised in the same manner as the related settlement loss or gain. If, however, the tax treatment of the settlement gain or loss differs from the accounting treatment, then a temporary difference may arise. The accounting for that temporary difference will depend on the tax treatment of the gain or loss. This might, for example, result in an adjustment to goodwill deductible for tax purposes or another intangible asset, or an adjustment to the tax base of the acquirer's investment in its subsidiary.

3.13.930   *Acquisition-related costs*

3.13.930.10   Acquisition-related costs in a business combination are expensed as they are incurred and the services are received, unless the costs are related to the issue of debt or equity securities. Acquisition-related costs may include finder's fees, advisory fees, legal fees, accounting fees, valuation fees and other professional or consulting fees (see 2.6.530). [*IFRS 3.53*]

3.13.930.20   For tax purposes, these costs may be:
- immediately deductible;
- capitalised;
- included as part of goodwill deductible for tax purposes; or
- included in the tax base of the investment acquired.

3.13.930.30   The ultimate tax treatment might depend on the treatment of the business combination for tax purposes and whether the business combination is ultimately consummated.

3.13.930.40   When determining the accounting before the date of acquisition for the tax effects of acquisition-related costs incurred, an entity considers the expected ultimate tax treatment of those costs. An entity may expect that the transaction costs will result in a tax deduction subsequent to incurring such costs. In such cases, the entity recognises a deferred tax asset with respect to those costs, subject to recoverability (see 3.13.330). Conversely, an entity may expect that the transaction costs will be treated as part of the cost of investment for tax purposes; furthermore, it may not expect to recognise deferred taxes on temporary differences related to that investment. In this situation, it will not recognise a deferred tax asset (see 3.13.260).

3.13.930.50   The deferred tax effects attributed to acquisition-related costs are recognised outside the business combination. This is because the costs themselves are accounted for separately from the acquisition accounting.

3.13.940   *Equity-settled replacement awards issued*

3.13.940.10   An acquirer may issue an equity-settled replacement award (see 2.6.420) that will result in a tax deduction at a later date. In this case, it recognises a deferred tax asset as part of the acquisition accounting for the deductible temporary difference that relates to the portion of the award attributed to pre-combination employee service. For portions of the award attributable to post-combination employee service, it recognises a deferred tax asset in the period in which the cost is recognised for financial reporting purposes. In this respect, it follows the same principles discussed in 3.13.590.90.

3.13.940.20   The deferred tax asset recognised as part of the acquisition accounting may subsequently be remeasured for changes in the amount expected to be received as a tax deduction – e.g. because of fluctuations in the market price of the related shares. IAS 12 does not stipulate how such changes in the deferred tax asset arising from the expected tax deduction should be recognised. In our view, an entity should choose an accounting policy, to be applied consistently, to:

- recognise all such changes in profit or loss;
- recognise all such changes directly in equity; or
- recognise the effect of estimated future tax deductions in excess of a certain amount directly in equity and other such changes in profit or loss ('asymmetric' accounting policy).

3.13.940.30   An entity that adopts the 'asymmetric' accounting policy in 3.13.940.20 recognises changes in the expected tax deduction differently depending on whether the total estimated tax deduction attributed to the pre-combination service element of an award exceeds the amount of the acquisition date market-based measure of that element of the award. To the extent that the expected tax deduction exceeds the market-based measure, the related tax effects are recognised in equity. All other such changes are recognised in profit or loss.

3.13.940.40   For a discussion of the classification and presentation of current and deferred taxes, see 3.13.520.

3.13.950   Identifiable assets acquired and liabilities assumed

3.13.960   *Acquiree's deferred tax assets*

3.13.960.10   In assessing whether to recognise deferred tax assets of the combined entity, the acquirer considers tax planning opportunities that the combined entity intends to take to realise a tax benefit that otherwise may not be realised – e.g. because of the expiration of an unused tax loss existing at the date of acquisition. An acquirer may be permitted under tax law to include the acquiree in its tax group. In this case, the acquirer may need to consider this possibility in evaluating qualifying tax planning opportunities (see 3.13.370). [*IAS 12.29(b)–30*]

3.13.960.20   In some situations, tax law restricts acquired tax benefits from being recovered through future taxable income of the combined entity after the acquisition. In such cases, only the acquiree's separate past and expected future results of operations are used in determining whether recognition of the acquiree's existing deferred tax assets is appropriate. A similar situation arises when the combined entity is not permitted to include the acquirer and acquiree in the same tax group. In those circumstances, taxes payable resulting from the reversal of existing taxable temporary differences of the acquirer would not be reduced by reversing deductible temporary differences of the acquiree.

3.13.960.30   The acquirer should take care to distinguish tax planning opportunities from post-acquisition events or its post-acquisition actions (see 3.13.1070). Tax planning opportunities affect the recoverability or measurement of deferred tax assets already existing at the date of acquisition. Post-acquisition events or the acquirer's post-acquisition actions create or change temporary differences. They are therefore not anticipated in determining the recognition or measurement of deferred taxes in the acquisition accounting. For a discussion of subsequent changes to deferred tax benefits of the acquiree, see 3.13.1060.

3.13.970   *Identifiable intangible assets*

3.13.970.10   Identifiable assets for tax purposes might not match exactly the identifiable assets or goodwill recognised for accounting purposes. For example, an entity may receive tax deductions for a single 'tax intangible'. For accounting purposes, this is recognised as several different identifiable intangible assets and goodwill as a residual. In our view, the deduction attached to the tax intangible should be treated as the combined tax base of the relevant intangible assets, including goodwill, for the purpose of determining any temporary difference arising from the business combination.

EXAMPLE 50 – SINGLE TAX DEDUCTION FOR MULTIPLE INTANGIBLE ASSETS

3.13.970.20   Company P acquires Company S's business, as opposed to the acquisition of the legal entity. The following facts are relevant for this example.
- In the acquisition accounting, P recognises various identifiable intangible assets (A, B and C), each with a carrying amount of 100.
- The residual (goodwill) amounts to 200.
- P is entitled to a total tax deduction of 500 in respect of the identifiable intangible assets and goodwill ('tax intangible').
- Economically, the tax intangible is a combination of the identifiable intangible assets recognised for accounting purposes and goodwill.

3.13.970.30   We believe that the deduction attached to the tax intangible should be treated as the combined tax base of the relevant intangible assets (A, B and C) and goodwill for the purpose of determining any temporary difference arising from the business combination. In this case, no temporary difference arises because the combined tax base of 500 equals the combined carrying amount of relevant assets (A, B, C and goodwill).

3.13.980   *Acquiree's investments in subsidiaries, branches and associates, and interests in joint arrangements*

3.13.980.10   The difference between the tax base of the acquirer's investment in the acquiree and the carrying amount of the acquiree's net assets in the acquirer's consolidated financial statements is a temporary difference. This is despite the fact that this investment is eliminated in the consolidated financial statements (see 3.13.260). In our experience, at the date of acquisition the tax base of the investment and the carrying amount of the related net assets in the consolidated financial statements are often equal, being the fair value at the date of acquisition – i.e. no temporary difference related to the investment exists at acquisition. However, a temporary difference may exist at acquisition if the tax base of the investment is adjusted, for example, to include acquisition-related costs or to reflect a pre-existing relationship, or if the acquisition results in a bargain purchase (see 3.13.1030). [*IAS 12.38*]

3.13.980.20   An acquiree may be a group itself – i.e. the acquiree may have its own investments in subsidiaries, branches and associates, and interests in joint arrangements. The acquirer determines whether a deferred tax liability (asset) is recognised for a taxable (deductible) temporary difference at the date of acquisition; it does so without regard to the acquiree's previous assertions about meeting the criteria in paragraph 39 and 44 of IAS 12 (see 3.13.260) in respect of the acquiree's investments.

- If the relevant criteria are met from the acquirer's perspective, then no deferred tax liability (asset) is recorded at acquisition.
- If the criteria are not met, then a deferred tax liability (asset) is recognised in the acquisition accounting.

3.13.980.30   If there are subsequent changes in the assessment of whether a deferred tax asset or liability is recognised for temporary differences, then the entity accounts for them separately from the acquisition accounting. For example, a deferred tax liability may not be recognised at the date of acquisition because the acquirer determines that it is probable that the temporary difference will not reverse in the foreseeable future. In this case, a deferred tax liability because of a change in circumstances is subsequently recognised outside the business combination.

3.13.980.40   A deferred tax asset is recognised for a deductible temporary difference related to investments in subsidiaries, branches and associates, and interests in joint arrangements only if it is probable that the temporary difference will reverse in the foreseeable future (see 3.13.260.50), subject to recoverability (see 3.13.330). Situations may also arise in which a deferred tax asset is not recognised at the date of acquisition because it does not meet the 'foreseeable future' requirement (see 3.13.280), but is subsequently recognised. In such circumstances, the related benefit is recorded as a reduction in income tax expense separately from the acquisition accounting, unless it is considered a measurement-period adjustment (see 3.13.1050). [*IAS 12.44*]

3.13.990   *Pre-existing tax-deductible goodwill of acquiree*

3.13.990.10   In a business combination, an acquiree may have tax-deductible goodwill from its prior acquisitions. For accounting purposes, in the acquirer's consolidated financial statements, the carrying amount of the pre-existing goodwill is subsumed into the goodwill arising from the current business combination (see 2.6.1010.10). In such cases, an entity faces a question about how to determine the amount of any temporary difference associated with the goodwill arising from the current business combination.

3.13.990.20   In our view, in determining the amount of any temporary difference associated with the goodwill arising from the current business combination, there is a rebuttable presumption that the financial statement carrying amount of the newly created goodwill should be compared with the tax base including that of the pre-existing goodwill of the acquiree. This is because goodwill is measured as a residual for accounting purposes, and therefore its sources – in particular, if they relate to the pre-existing goodwill of the acquiree – are generally indistinguishable. [*IFRS 3.BC328*]

3.13.990.30   We believe that the above presumption can be rebutted only when the tax deduction associated with the pre-existing goodwill is clearly unrelated to the financial statement carrying amount of the goodwill arising from the current business combination.

EXAMPLE 51A – PRE-EXISTING TAX-DEDUCTIBLE GOODWILL OF ACQUIREE IN BUSINESS COMBINATION – NO REBUTTAL OF PRESUMPTION

3.13.990.40   Company P acquires all of the shares in Company S. The following facts are relevant for this example.
- Before the acquisition, S had been entitled to a tax deduction on goodwill that arose from its previous acquisition of Company T, on a straight-line basis over the life determined by the tax authority.
- When P acquired S, the remaining tax deduction associated with S's pre-existing goodwill was 30. S will be entitled to continue to claim the tax deduction on the pre-existing goodwill.
- P's acquisition of S resulted in the recognition of goodwill of 100 in P's consolidated financial statements.
- Neither P nor S is entitled to any additional tax deduction in relation to goodwill apart from the 30 that relates to S's pre-existing goodwill.

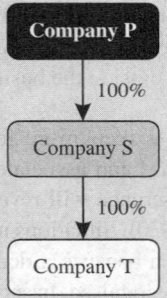

3.13.990.50   In determining the amount of the temporary difference associated with the goodwill arising from the business combination involving P and S, we believe that there is a rebuttable presumption that P should compare the consolidated financial statement carrying amount of the goodwill (100) with the tax base including that of S's pre-existing goodwill (30). In the absence of clear facts and circumstances to the contrary, the accounting goodwill is regarded as partially tax-deductible and the amount of related temporary difference is 70 (100 - 30).

3.13.990.60   Accordingly, we believe that the initial recognition exemption applies to the above taxable temporary difference and therefore P should not recognise deferred tax for this temporary difference either initially or subsequently. After the date of acquisition, as S claims the tax deduction on a straight-line basis in respect of its pre-existing goodwill, an additional taxable temporary difference arises. Following the guidance in 3.13.990.40, a deferred tax liability is recognised in P's consolidated financial statements for such temporary difference.

EXAMPLE 51B – PRE-EXISTING TAX-DEDUCTIBLE GOODWILL OF ACQUIREE IN BUSINESS COMBINATION – REBUTTAL OF PRESUMPTION

3.13.990.70   Continuing Example 51A, if P identifies facts and circumstances that indicate that the tax deduction associated with S's pre-existing goodwill is clearly unrelated to the financial statement carrying amount of the goodwill arising from the current business combination, then we believe that the goodwill arising from the current business combination has a tax base of zero.

3.13.990.80   As a result, at the date of acquisition there will be the following two separate temporary differences arising from the transaction.
- A taxable temporary difference of 100, being the difference between the carrying amount of the goodwill (100) and the corresponding tax base (zero). No deferred tax is recognised in respect of this taxable temporary difference because it arises from the initial recognition of goodwill (see 3.13.990.10–20).
- A deductible temporary difference of 30, being the difference between the tax base for the tax deduction associated with S's pre-existing goodwill (30) and the corresponding financial statement carrying amount (would generally be zero). The initial recognition exemption does not apply to this deductible temporary difference (see 3.13.990.50); accordingly, a deferred tax asset is recognised, subject to recoverability (see 3.13.330).

3.13.1000   *Indemnification assets*

3.13.1000.10   Entities may enter into indemnification arrangements whereby the seller of a business contractually agree to reimburse the acquirer for certain tax liabilities of the acquiree. In our view, the acquirer should account for such income tax exposures under IAS 12 (see 3.13.660.60). For a discussion of indemnification assets in a business combination, see 2.6.670. [*IFRS 3.27–28, 57*]

3.13.1010   Goodwill or gain on bargain purchase

3.13.1020   *Goodwill*

3.13.1020.10   Deferred tax liabilities are not recognised at the date of acquisition for taxable temporary differences that arise between the tax base of goodwill and its financial statement carrying amount. In other words, they are not recognised when the carrying amount of goodwill is greater than its tax base (see 3.13.1080). [*IAS 12.15(a)*]

3.13.1020.20   A temporary difference may also arise on the initial recognition of goodwill if the goodwill is not tax-deductible. No deferred tax liability is recognised on this temporary difference; this is because goodwill is measured as a residual, and recognising a deferred tax liability would gross up the amount of goodwill. If the temporary difference decreases in subsequent periods – e.g. because of the impairment of goodwill – then the exemption still applies and no deferred tax is recognised. In our view, this guidance also applies to a portion of goodwill that is only partially deductible (see 3.13.1020.40). [*IAS 12.21A*]

3.13.1020.30   The situation in 3.13.1020.20 differs from scenarios in which goodwill is tax-deductible, but no temporary difference arises because the carrying amount of goodwill in the financial statements equals its tax base. If the carrying amount and the tax base of such goodwill differ in subsequent periods – e.g. because of impairment for accounting purposes that is not deductible for tax purposes until later periods – then the entity recognises deferred tax (see 3.13.1080.20). [*IAS 12.15(a), 21B*]

3.13.1020.40 IFRS does not provide explicit guidance in respect of goodwill that is only partially tax-deductible when recognised initially. In our view, goodwill with a carrying amount higher than its tax base should be split into two parts.

1. To the extent that the carrying amount equals the tax base, no temporary difference arises. If temporary differences arise in subsequent periods, then the entity recognises deferred tax on this portion of the goodwill, subject to recoverability (see 3.13.1080 and 330).
2. The excess of the carrying amount of goodwill over the tax base is not tax-deductible. The exemption for not recognising deferred tax for goodwill applies both initially and subsequently to any temporary differences that arise in respect of the non-tax-deductible portion of the goodwill. [*IAS 12.15(a), 21A–21B*]

3.13.1020.50 An entity recognises deferred tax assets in respect of the initial recognition of goodwill for which the tax base of that goodwill is in excess of its carrying amount. This is subject to the existence of appropriate future taxable income (see 3.13.330). In our view, an appropriate method of determining the amount of the deferred tax asset to recognise in such a situation is by determining an adjustment both to deferred taxes recognised in the acquisition accounting and to goodwill, such that the deferred tax asset recognised for goodwill equates to the related temporary difference multiplied by the relevant tax rate. This may be done by resolving the following equation. [*IAS 12.32A*]

$$\begin{array}{ccc} \text{Deferred tax} & & \text{Initial net temporary} \\ \text{asset recognised} \end{array} = \begin{array}{c} \text{Initial net temporary} \\ \text{difference} \end{array} \times \left(\dfrac{\text{Tax rate}}{(1 - \text{tax rate})} \right)$$

EXAMPLE 52 – DEFERRED TAX ASSET ON INITIAL RECOGNITION OF GOODWILL

3.13.1020.60 Company P acquires Company S in a business combination. The following facts are relevant for this example.

- Goodwill for financial reporting purposes before any adjustment for deferred tax assets arising on goodwill is 600.
- Tax-deductible goodwill of 900 arises in the business combination.
- The relevant tax rate is 40%.

3.13.1020.70 Using the formula in 3.13.1020.50, the deferred tax asset to be recognised, and the associated adjustment to accounting goodwill, is 200 ((900 - 600) x (40% / (1 - 40%)). Accordingly:

- goodwill recognised in the acquisition accounting is 400 (initially determined goodwill of 600 minus the adjustment to goodwill of 200); and
- the deferred tax asset of 200 equates to the temporary difference of 500 (900 - 400) related to the goodwill, multiplied by the tax rate of 40%.

3.13.1020.80 Deferred taxes are determined separately for each tax-paying component in each tax jurisdiction. Accordingly, an entity determines the carrying amount and tax base of goodwill separately for each tax-paying component, rather than at the reporting entity level. [*IAS 12.11*]

3.13.1030   *Gain on bargain purchase*

3.13.1030.10   A gain on a bargain purchase is determined after deferred taxes have been recognised in the acquisition accounting. The gain may create or change a temporary difference. For example, in a bargain purchase the tax base of the acquirer's investment in the acquiree may be less than the related carrying amount of the identifiable net assets recognised in the consolidated financial statements. In this case, the acquirer assesses whether a deferred tax liability is recognised for such a temporary difference (see 3.13.290). In our view, because the gain is recognised immediately in profit or loss, the related tax effects of the resulting temporary difference, if there are any, should also be recognised in profit or loss. For a discussion of a gain on a bargain purchase, see 2.6.1010. [*IFRS 3.34, IAS 12.38–43*]

3.13.1040   **Measurement after acquisition accounting**

3.13.1050   *Measurement period*

3.13.1050.10   An acquirer may obtain new information about facts and circumstances that existed at the date of acquisition; if it had been known, then this information would have affected the measurement of the amounts recognised. In certain circumstances, the acquirer adjusts provisional amounts recognised in the acquisition accounting as a result of this (see 2.6.1030). [*IFRS 3.45–50*]

3.13.1050.20   Amounts included in the acquisition accounting may be subject to changes in estimates related to the tax attributes of the acquiree. The acquisition accounting may also be subject to changes in estimates related to amounts included for the carrying amounts of assets acquired and liabilities assumed. These changes may affect temporary differences on which deferred taxes were recognised as part of the acquisition accounting. Tax-related amounts included in determining deferred taxes in the acquisition accounting may be based on estimates as well. For example, an entity may need to estimate the tax base at the date of acquisition of significant capital assets, or the amount and availability of unused tax losses. These estimated amounts may be revised as more information is available. Changes in estimates of tax-related amounts are accounted for in the same manner as changes in estimates of other amounts recognised in the acquisition accounting (see 2.6.1050–1060).

3.13.1060   *Changes in acquiree's deductible temporary differences, unused tax losses or unused tax credits*

3.13.1060.10   The accounting for subsequent changes in the recognition of acquired deferred tax assets depends on:
- whether such changes occur during or after the end of the measurement period; and
- whether such changes result from new information about facts and circumstances that existed at the date of acquisition, or from events that occur after the business combination.

3.13.1060.20   Measurement-period changes in the recognition of acquired deferred tax assets may result from new information about facts and circumstances that existed at the date of acquisition. These changes are generally recognised by adjusting the acquisition accounting retrospectively (see 2.6.1030). However, recognition of such deferred tax assets during the measurement period may result in the carrying amount of goodwill recognised in the business combination being reduced to zero. In this case, any remaining deferred tax benefit is recognised in profit or loss (see 3.13.1030). [*IAS 12.68(a)*]

3.13.1060.30 Taxes recognised in the acquisition accounting may be adjusted because of events that occur after the date of acquisition. In this case, subsequent recognition or derecognition of the acquiree's tax benefits occurs separately from the acquisition accounting, even if the event occurs during the measurement period. Such events might include:
- changes in enacted or substantively enacted tax laws; and
- changes in expected levels of future taxable income caused by events occurring subsequent to the date of acquisition. [*IAS 12.68(b)*]

EXAMPLE 53 – MEASUREMENT AFTER ACQUISITION ACCOUNTING – ADJUSTMENT TO ACQUIRED DEFERRED TAX ASSET AFTER DATE OF ACQUISITION

3.13.1060.40 Company P acquires Company S in a business combination. The following facts are relevant for this example.
- At the date of acquisition, management of P concludes that full recognition is appropriate for an acquired deferred tax asset.
- During the measurement period, S loses a significant customer. This event will result in significantly less future taxable income than was estimated at the date of acquisition.
- As a result, management of P concludes that recoverability of the acquired deferred tax asset is not probable, and derecognises the deferred tax asset.

3.13.1060.50 Because the change is the result of an event that occurred subsequent to the date of acquisition, in its consolidated financial statements P accounts for the derecognition as an adjustment to income tax expense, instead of as an adjustment to the acquisition accounting.

3.13.1070 Subsequent measurement and accounting

3.13.1070.10 An entity recognises deferred taxes that result from a business combination as part of the acquisition accounting. However, in our view, except for limited circumstances (see 3.13.1070.30), the tax effect of post-acquisition events, or the acquirer's post-acquisition actions, should not be anticipated.

EXAMPLE 54A – SUBSEQUENT MEASUREMENT AND ACCOUNTING – TAX EFFECT OF POST-ACQUISITION RESTRUCTURING NOT PART OF ACQUISITION ACCOUNTING

3.13.1070.20 Company P acquires Company S in a business combination and plans to restructure the acquired business shortly after the acquisition. It does this to transfer non-tax-deductible goodwill or another intangible asset to a jurisdiction with more favourable tax treatment. We believe that P should not recognise the tax consequences of this post-acquisition restructuring as part of the acquisition accounting. [*IAS 12.66*]

3.13.1070.30 However, depending on the facts and circumstances of a transaction and the applicable tax laws, we believe that it may be appropriate in rare cases to regard some non-substantive post-acquisition actions as an integral part of the business combination, and therefore reflect the tax effect of these actions in the accounting for the business combination. This may be the case when the applicable tax laws allow the deductibility of the acquisition date goodwill, but only if certain defined non-substantive actions are taken after acquisition. In this regard, it is necessary to consider whether such actions are substantive hurdles to overcome in obtaining the tax benefits – e.g. whether these actions would involve substantive fees or approvals by shareholders or tax authorities that cannot be regarded as a formality.

EXAMPLE 54B – SUBSEQUENT MEASUREMENT AND ACCOUNTING – TAX EFFECT OF POST-ACQUISITION RESTRUCTURING IS PART OF ACQUISITION ACCOUNTING

3.13.1070.40   In Country Z, Company P acquires Company S in a business combination. The following facts are relevant for this example.

- For accounting purposes, goodwill before any deferred tax adjustment is 600.
- For tax purposes, the tax benefit associated with the goodwill is determined to be 900 at the date of acquisition. This amount can be deductible for tax purposes only if P affects an upstream merger of S after the acquisition.
- The amount of tax benefit associated with the goodwill is not adjusted for any subsequent transactions that occur between the date of acquisition and the merger.
- No approval is required to effect an upstream merger.
- There is no time limit for the completion of the merger process and the timing is within P's control.
- No fees, except for administrative duties, are payable to effect the upstream merger.
- Generally, acquisitions in Country Z are followed by the subsequent merger and the impact of the tax-deductibility of goodwill is factored into the pricing of the transaction.
- P effects the merger shortly after the acquisition.
- The relevant tax rate is 40%.

3.13.1070.50   In this example, P concludes that the post-acquisition upstream merger of S into P is an integral part of the business combination and takes into account the tax-deductibility of goodwill in the acquisition accounting.

3.13.1070.60   Applying the method described in 3.13.1020.50 and subject to recoverability (see 3.13.330), P recognises a deferred tax asset of 200 ((900 - 600) x (40% / (1 - 40%)) and an adjusted accounting goodwill of 400.

3.13.1080   *Recognition of deferred taxes related to goodwill subsequent to business combination*

3.13.1080.10   Even when deferred taxes are not recognised in respect of goodwill at the date of acquisition (see 3.13.1020), they may need to be recognised subsequently. Such recognition may be required as a result of changes in the difference between the tax base of goodwill and the related financial statement carrying amount that arise after the acquisition. Whether and how those subsequent changes are recognised depends on:

- whether goodwill has a tax base – i.e. whether goodwill is deductible for tax purposes; and
- whether the financial statement carrying amount of goodwill at the date of acquisition is less than, equal to or greater than the tax base of goodwill at the date of acquisition. [*IAS 12.21A–21B*]

3.13.1080.20 Goodwill deductible for tax purposes may have a tax base equal to or less than its carrying amount on initial recognition in a business combination. In this case, no deferred taxes are recognised in the acquisition accounting (see 3.13.1020.20–30). However, suppose that a temporary difference arises or changes in subsequent periods – e.g. because of amortisation of the goodwill for tax purposes or impairment of the carrying amount of goodwill for financial reporting purposes in later periods. In this case, deferred tax is recognised, subject to a recoverability assessment for deferred tax assets (see 3.13.330). [*IAS 12.21B*]

EXAMPLE 55 – SUBSEQUENT MEASUREMENT AND ACCOUNTING – DEFERRED TAX LIABILITY ARISING FROM AMORTISATION OF TAX-DEDUCTIBLE GOODWILL

3.13.1080.30 Company R recognises goodwill of 400 as part of its accounting for a business combination. The goodwill is deductible for tax purposes; the carrying amount of the goodwill for tax purposes is also 400. In this case, no deferred tax is recognised at the date of initial recognition.

3.13.1080.40 Goodwill is deductible for tax purposes over 10 years on a straight-line basis. In this case, temporary differences will arise after the date of initial recognition of the goodwill, because goodwill is not amortised under IFRS (see 3.3.200.10).

3.13.1080.50 At the end of year 1, the carrying amount of the goodwill under IFRS is still 400 and the carrying amount for tax purposes is 360 (400 - 40). If the tax rate is 25%, then R will recognise a deferred tax liability of 10 ((400 - 360) x 25%).

3.13.1080.60 There is no tax effect from the impairment of non-deductible goodwill. [*IAS 12.21A*]

3.13.1090 Business combination achieved in stages

3.13.1100 *Changes in deferred tax recognised on previously held investment in associate or interest in joint arrangement*

3.13.1100.10 An entity may obtain control over a previously held investment in an associate or interest in a joint arrangement in a business combination that has been achieved in stages; such an entity may change its assessment about the recognition of deferred taxes on that investment (see 3.13.260).

3.13.1100.20 For example, an entity may have been unable to control the timing of reversal of a temporary difference related to its investment in an associate; therefore, it recognised deferred taxes on a temporary difference related to that investment. If that entity acquires an additional interest in that associate such that it obtains control, then as a parent the entity controls the dividend policy and may be able to assert that:

- it can control the timing of reversal of the temporary difference; and
- it is not probable that such reversal will occur in the foreseeable future. [*IAS 12.39–40*]

3.13.1100.30   In our view, because such changes in deferred taxes are an indirect consequence of the business combination, they should be recognised separately from the acquisition accounting. [*IAS 12.58(b)*]

3.13.1110   *Tax consequences of remeasuring previously held associate or joint venture*

3.13.1110.10   A business combination that is achieved in stages requires the acquirer to remeasure to fair value its previously held equity interest at the date of acquisition (see 2.6.1140). [*IFRS 3.41–42*]

3.13.1110.20   Remeasuring an equity-accounted investee on obtaining control of the investee increases or decreases the financial statement carrying amount of the previously held investment. In some jurisdictions, such a transaction may not cause a change in the tax base of the investment; therefore, in such cases the temporary difference related to the investment changes. In our view, any deferred tax income or expense in respect of the change in temporary difference related to the entity's investment should be recognised separately from the acquisition accounting. This treatment is consistent with the gain or loss on remeasurement of the previously held investment, which is recognised in profit or loss (see 2.6.1140.30–40).

EXAMPLE 56 – SUBSIDIARY ACQUIRED IN BUSINESS COMBINATION ACHIEVED IN STAGES

3.13.1110.30   On 1 January 2017, Company P purchases 25% of Company S for 10,000, which is equal to the tax base of its investment. The investment is accounted for under the equity method.

3.13.1110.40   S is taxed at a rate of 20%. P is taxed on any dividend income received at 35%; however, P receives a 20% tax credit for taxes paid by S, which leads to the marginal rate at which P pays tax on dividends received from S of 15%. P records the following entry for its investment in S.

	DEBIT	CREDIT
Investment in S	10,000	
Cash		10,000
To recognise initial investment in S		

3.13.1110.50   On 31 December 2017, P calculates its share of S's after-tax profits to be 1,000. No other changes in P's investment in S occurred during the year. P is not able to control the timing of reversal of the temporary difference associated with its investment in S and therefore recognises a deferred tax liability of 150 (1,000 x 15%) associated with that investment attributable to undistributed earnings (see 3.13.270.60).

3.13.1110.60 P records the following entries for its share of the earnings of the investee.

	DEBIT	CREDIT
Investment in S	1,000	
Equity-accounted earnings of associate		1,000
To recognise P's share of earnings of S		
Deferred tax expense (income)	150	
Deferred tax liability		150
To recognise tax effect of P's share of earnings of S		

3.13.1110.70 On 1 January 2018, P acquires the remaining 75% of S for 60,000. The fair value of the equity investment at that date is 14,000. Accordingly, P remeasures its equity investment to fair value and records a gain of 3,000 (14,000 - 11,000). P also recognises an additional deferred tax liability of 450 (3,000 x 15%) associated with the temporary difference created by the gain on remeasurement. P records the following entries.

	DEBIT	CREDIT
Investment in S	3,000	
Gain on remeasurement (profit or loss)		3,000
To recognise gain on investment in S on obtaining control		
Deferred tax expense (income) (profit or loss)	450	
Deferred tax liability		450
To recognise tax effect of gain on investment in S on obtaining control		

3.13.1110.80 On 1 January 2018, immediately before the acquisition accounting, the carrying amount and tax base of the investment in S is as follows.

	CARRYING AMOUNT	TAX BASE
Initial investment in S	10,000	10,000
Equity earnings	1,000	-
Gain on remeasurement	3,000	-
Total	14,000	10,000

3.13.1110.90 P has recognised a deferred tax liability of 600 on the temporary difference associated with its investment in S of 4,000 (14,000 - 10,000) before the acquisition accounting. P determines that its investment in S now meets the criteria for the exception to recognition of a deferred tax liability related to its investment in S, because it is now able to control the timing of reversal of any temporary difference and does not expect such temporary differences to reverse in the foreseeable future. On 1 January 2018, P records the following entry to eliminate that deferred tax liability separately from the acquisition accounting. [*IAS 12.39*]

	DEBIT	**CREDIT**
Deferred tax liability	600	
Deferred tax expense (income)		600
To derecognise deferred tax liability associated with P's investment in S separately from acquisition accounting		

3.13.1110.100 However, if P had determined that it had not met the criteria for exemption from recognition of deferred taxes, then it would not derecognise this deferred tax liability. [*IAS 12.39*]

3.13.1120 *Reverse acquisition*

3.13.1120.10 In a reverse acquisition (see 2.6.170), deferred tax is recognised as part of the acquisition accounting on the difference between the tax bases and the fair values of the identifiable assets and liabilities of the accounting acquiree in the consolidated financial statements. This is despite the fact that the accounting acquiree is the legal acquirer. [*IAS 12.66*]

3.13.1120.20 In our view, changes to the accounting acquirer's deferred tax assets (liabilities) generated by a reverse acquisition should be recognised in profit or loss and not as part of the acquisition accounting. This is despite the fact that the accounting acquirer is the legal acquiree. [*IAS 12.67*]

EXAMPLE 57 – REVERSE ACQUISITION

3.13.1120.30 Company Z acquires 100% of the share capital of Company Y in a reverse acquisition – i.e. Y is considered to be the acquirer for accounting purposes. In Y and Z's jurisdiction, the tax bases of the legal acquiree's assets and liabilities are adjusted to reflect the cost of the legal acquirer's investment. The cost of Z's investment in Y is 'pushed down' to adjust the tax bases of Y's assets and liabilities, despite the fact that Y is the acquirer for accounting purposes.

3.13.1120.40 We believe that in the consolidated financial statements, the resulting adjustments to Y's deferred tax assets and liabilities should be recognised in profit or loss, and not against goodwill.

3.13.1130   **OTHER GROUP ISSUES**

3.13.1140   **Changes in ownership interests while retaining control**

3.13.1140.10   In a parent's consolidated financial statements, changes in its ownership interest in a subsidiary while retaining control are accounted for as equity transactions (see 2.5.560).

3.13.1140.20   Examples of the tax effects of transactions with NCI include current tax payable by a parent on the sale of shares to these parties and the effects of changes in the composition of a tax group. Membership of such tax groups is frequently restricted to subsidiaries in which the parent owns more than a specified minimum interest. Accordingly, transactions with NCI may affect the tax attributes of the tax group or its members because of a change in the parent's ownership interest, including:

- a change in the ability to recognise deferred tax assets – e.g. the anticipated future profits of a subsidiary that becomes a member of a tax group may provide evidence that supports the recognition of previously unrecognised deferred tax assets;
- a change in tax rates – e.g. adding an entity to a tax group may increase overall taxable profits to a level that results in a different tax rate applying to the profits of the entire tax group; and
- a change in tax bases of assets and liabilities – e.g. in some jurisdictions, an entity becoming part of a tax group may have its assets and liabilities rebased for tax purposes.

3.13.1140.30   Accounting for the current and deferred tax effects of a transaction or other event is consistent with the accounting for the transaction or event itself (see 3.13.530.10). Therefore, in our view the direct tax effects relating to a change in a parent's ownership interest in a subsidiary while retaining control, which is accounted for as an equity transaction, should be recognised directly in equity. In our view, the amounts regarded as direct tax effects will generally be limited and do not necessarily include the full current tax crystallised by such transaction. [*IAS 12.57*]

3.13.1140.40   Sometimes, a transaction with NCI crystallises certain tax effects, but not all of these tax effects are directly related to the equity transaction. In our view, tax effects that are not directly related to an equity transaction should be recognised separately from the accounting for that equity transaction. To determine whether a tax effect is a direct or an indirect effect of an equity transaction, an entity considers all relevant indicators. Factors that may indicate that a tax effect of a transaction is indirect include the following.

- The tax effect depends on a specific election or action of the entity, rather than being an automatic consequence of the transaction with the NCI.
- The tax effect depends on the entity-specific attributes of the parent or its subsidiaries, rather than being an effect of the transaction with the NCI that would apply to a market participant. For example, a change in an entity's assessment of recoverability of deferred tax assets is dependent on the financial condition of the members of that tax group.

3.13.1140.50   For example, a partial disposal of a subsidiary while retaining control may trigger the parent entity to reassess whether it expects to reverse part or all of the 'outside basis difference' – namely, the temporary difference between:

- the tax base of its investment in the subsidiary; and
- the carrying amount of the related consolidated net assets.

3.13.1140.60   This in turn would result in the recognition of some of this previously unrecognised deferred tax (see 3.13.260).

3.13.1140.70   In our view, such tax effects are not directly related to, and should be recognised separately from, any tax arising from the accounting 'gain or loss' recognised in equity on the sale of ownership interest. Even though the crystallisation of a portion of the outside basis difference, and therefore the recognition of the related tax liability, is triggered by the disposal, we believe that the tax effect arising from the recognition of previously unrecognised outside basis difference arises from a change in the parent's expectation about the realisation of its investment in a subsidiary. Accordingly, the crystallisation of the outside basis differences should be recognised separately from the equity transaction, in line with the original underlying transactions or other events that give rise to such differences.

EXAMPLE 58 – DIRECT AND INDIRECT TAX EFFECTS OF PARTIAL DISPOSAL OF SUBSIDIARY WHILE MAINTAINING CONTROL

3.13.1140.80   Parent P owns 100% of Subsidiary S. P sells 20% of its interest in S to a third party for 1,100 while retaining control. At the date of the partial disposal, the net assets in S are 5,200 and the tax base of the investment is the original cost of 5,000.

3.13.1140.90   The accounting 'gain' on disposal of S in P's consolidated financial statements, which is recognised directly in equity, is 60 (1,100 - (5,200 x 20%)). The taxable gain on disposal is 100 (1,100 - (5,000 x 20%)). P's tax rate is 25%.

3.13.1140.100   Before the disposal, S had undistributed profits of 200 (its net assets amount to 5,200), which represented the entire taxable outside basis difference in respect of P's investment in S. P did not recognise any deferred tax liability on the taxable outside basis difference, because P was able to control whether the retained earnings of S were distributed, and had determined that it would not distribute these earnings in the foreseeable future (see 3.13.260.40).

3.13.1140.110   It was not until the sale that the part of the outside basis difference relating to the disposed interest failed to satisfy the recognition exception for outside basis differences.

3.13.1140.120   At the date of the sale, P also reassesses its assertion regarding the reversal of the remaining outside basis difference associated with the retained interest in S, and determines that it is still probable that that part of the outside basis difference will not reverse in the foreseeable future.

3.13.1140.130   In this example, we believe that the current tax of 25 comprises both direct and indirect components, which should be accounted for separately.
- The part of the current tax relating to P's accounting 'gain' on the sale – i.e. 15 (60 x 25%) – is a direct tax effect of the equity transaction and should therefore be recognised directly in equity (see 3.13.1140.30).
- The balance of the current tax, which in accounting terms is the crystallisation of the outside basis difference on the change in P's interest in S – i.e. 10 (200 x 20% x 25%), or ((100 - 60) x 25%) – is not directly related to, and should therefore be recognised separately from, the equity transaction.

3.13.1140.140 We believe that the same analysis applies irrespective of whether the actual sale and change in expectation occur at the same time, or at different points in time.

3.13.1140.150 In Example 58, the recognition of the income tax liability arising from a change in P's expectation about the realisation of its investment in S relates to a portion of undistributed profits from past earnings results. Accordingly, this income tax effect is also recognised in profit or loss, consistent with the accounting for the original transaction that gave rise to the outside basis difference. In other cases, the taxable temporary difference may be related to an item originally recognised in OCI or directly in equity – e.g. a temporary difference resulting from changes in the fair value of an available-for-sale investment. In these other cases, the related tax effect would be 'traced' back to those items and recorded in OCI or directly in equity; in the exceptional circumstances when it is difficult to make this determination, an entity may make a reasonable pro rata allocation to recognise part of the tax effect outside profit or loss. [*IAS 12.58, 60–62, 63*]

3.13.1140.160 The type of transaction will determine whether the direct tax effects of these transactions are current or deferred. For example, if an entity's subsidiary sells its own shares to a third party, then the transaction might not result in a current tax effect for the parent, but instead increase the temporary difference related to the parent's investment in the subsidiary. As such, this transaction would result in the recognition of deferred tax in the parent's consolidated financial statements, which would be recognised in equity. However, if an entity sells a portion of its interest in a subsidiary to a third party at a taxable gain, then that tax gain would result in a current tax effect that is recognised as discussed in 3.13.1140.50–70.

3.13.1140.170 In our view, similar to the accounting for the tax effects of business combinations discussed in 3.13.1070.10, the tax effect of events that occur, or actions that are undertaken, subsequent to a transaction with an NCI should not be anticipated.

Ⓢ **3.13.1150** **Common control business combination in separate financial statements**

3.13.1150.10 A common control business combination may take the form of the individual assets being acquired and liabilities being assumed, rather than the shares in the business being acquired. In that case, the acquirer has a choice to account for the transaction using book value accounting or IFRS 3 accounting in its separate financial statements (see 5.13.50.40). If the acquirer elects book value accounting, then an issue arises about how the acquirer should account for any initial recognition exemption that applied when the individual assets or liabilities were originally recognised by the acquiree (see 3.13.200).

3.13.1150.20 In the above case, the acquirer recognises in its separate financial statements the assets and liabilities, including any deferred tax assets and liabilities, of the entity whose book values are carried over in accounting for the transaction. In our view, this should include the carry-over of any initial recognition exemption that applied when the individual assets or liabilities were recognised. This is because book value accounting assumes that the pre-existing accounting is continued.

EXAMPLE 59 – COMMON CONTROL BUSINESS COMBINATION – SEPARATE FINANCIAL STATEMENTS

3.13.1150.30 Company S1 and Company S2 are both wholly owned subsidiaries of Company P; both S1 and S2 are operating entities. S1 has, among its business assets, a building with a book value of 400. From S1's perspective, the building has always had a tax base of zero because there are no deductions available for tax purposes. No deferred taxes were recognised by S1 on the building because of the initial recognition exemption.

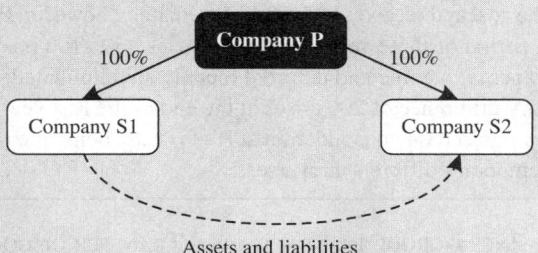

Assets and liabilities

3.13.1150.40 In 2018, S2 acquires all of the assets and liabilities of S1 in a business combination. There is no change in the tax status of the building – i.e. no amounts are tax-deductible; the tax base remains zero. In its separate financial statements, S2 elects to recognise the common control transaction using the book values of the transferred entity, S1. S2 therefore recognises the building at its book value of 400, but does not recognise related deferred taxes in its separate financial statement – i.e. the initial recognition exemption is carried over from S1 to S2.

3.13.1160   Intra-group transactions

3.13.1160.10 Intra-group transactions are eliminated on consolidation (see 2.5.550). It may be intuitive to reverse not only the transaction itself, but also the tax effects thereof in order to fully eliminate the transaction in the consolidated financial statements. The IFRS Interpretations Committee discussed intra-group transactions and noted that transferring assets or liabilities between entities in the consolidated group affects the consolidated financial statements in terms of the recognition, measurement and presentation of deferred tax if the intra-group transaction affects:

• the tax base of assets or liabilities;
• the tax rate applicable to the recovery or settlement of those assets or liabilities;
• the recoverability of any related deductible temporary differences and therefore the recognition of deferred tax assets; and
• the extent to which deferred tax assets and liabilities of different entities in the group are offset in the consolidated financial statements. [*IAS 12.IE.A.14, IE.B.11, IU 05-14*]

EXAMPLE 60A – INTRA-GROUP TRANSACTIONS – TRADING

3.13.1160.20 Company V sells inventory to fellow subsidiary Company W for 300. This results in a profit of 50 in V's separate financial statements. V pays current tax of 15 on the profit. On consolidation, the profit of 50 is reversed against the carrying amount of the inventory of 300. Therefore, the carrying amount of the inventory on consolidation is 250. However, the carrying amount of the inventory for tax purposes will depend on the legislation in W's jurisdiction. Assuming that the carrying amount of the inventory for tax purposes is 300, a deductible temporary difference of 50 arises. This is recognised on consolidation at W's tax rate, subject to the general asset recognition requirements (see 3.13.330).

EXAMPLE 60B – INTRA-GROUP TRANSACTIONS – ROYALTIES

3.13.1160.30 Parent P bills royalties of 300 to its foreign Subsidiary S. S expenses the cost and receives tax relief immediately; however, P recognises the income over a period of three years for tax purposes – i.e. 100 per year. On consolidation, the expense, income and deferred income are eliminated. However, a taxable temporary difference of 200 arises at the end of the first year of the arrangement. This is recognised on consolidation at P's tax rate, being the rate that will apply when the temporary difference reverses.

EXAMPLE 60C – INTRA-GROUP TRANSACTIONS – TRANSFER OF GOODWILL

3.13.1160.40 In January 2014, Company P acquired Business C and recognised goodwill of 100 on acquisition. The goodwill is depreciated for tax purposes over 10 years.

3.13.1160.50 On 31 December 2018, P carries out an internal reorganisation. The following facts are relevant for this example.
- P sets up a new wholly owned Subsidiary S.
- P transfers C, including the accounting goodwill of 100 to S. However, for tax purposes, the remaining goodwill of 50 (100 - 100 / 10 x 5) is retained by P.
- P is taxed at 20% and S is taxed at 30%.
- P and S file separate tax returns.

3.13.1160.60 Because P and S are subject to different tax rates, the internal reorganisation affects the consolidated financial statements in terms of the recognition, measurement and presentation of deferred tax (see 3.13.1160.10).

3.13.1160.65 In the consolidated financial statements, transferring the goodwill from P to S as a result of the internal reorganisation does not meet the initial recognition exemption because the goodwill is not recognised for the first time from the perspective of the consolidated financial statements (see 3.13.210.15). This is different from *origination* of inter-company balances – e.g. origination of an inter-company loan.

3.13.1160.70 P calculates the deferred tax amount related to the goodwill of C in its consolidated financial statements for 2018 as follows.

In P's tax jurisdiction	
Carrying amount of goodwill from Business C	-
Tax base	50
Deductible temporary difference	(50)
Deferred tax asset at the tax rate of 20%	10[1]

In S's tax jurisdiction	
Carrying amount of goodwill from Business C	100
Tax base	-
Taxable temporary difference	100
Deferred tax liability at the tax rate of 30%	(30)

Note
1.   The recognition of the deferred tax asset is subject to the criteria in 3.13.330.

3.13.1160.80   The deferred tax asset and liability are not offset in the consolidated financial statements, unless P and S have both an enforceable right and the intention to set off current tax liabilities and assets (see 3.13.630.30). [*IAS 12.74*]

3.13.1160.90   In some jurisdictions, a change in tax base may result from an intra-group transfer of an asset to an entity that is not wholly owned by the group (see 3.13.570.130).

3.13.1170   Tax groups

3.13.1180   *Tax-consolidated groups*

3.13.1180.10   In some countries, tax-consolidation systems permit groups comprising a parent entity and its wholly owned subsidiaries to elect to be treated as a single entity for income tax purposes. Subsidiaries that are not wholly owned or not directly owned might also be eligible for this treatment if certain criteria are met. The tax-consolidation systems are generally elective rather than compulsory. Under these systems, a tax-consolidated group generally prepares a single consolidated annual tax return. In most cases, the parent entity will become liable for the income tax liabilities of the entire group.

3.13.1180.20   The entities in a tax-consolidated group may enter into a tax-sharing agreement (including a tax-funding or contribution agreement) to allocate tax expenses to subsidiaries on a predetermined, ongoing basis.

3.13.1180.30   In our view, in the absence of specific guidance in IFRS, an entity should choose an Ⓢ accounting policy, to be applied consistently, to account for income taxes in the separate or individual financial statements of entities within a tax group. Various approaches are acceptable under IFRS, two of which are illustrated in 3.13.1190–1200.

3.13.1190   *Approach 1*

3.13.1190.10   Current and deferred income taxes are recognised by each entity within the group, regardless of who has the legal liability for settlement or the legal right for recovery of the tax.

3.13.1190.20   Under this approach, a view is taken that in substance each entity in the tax-consolidated group remains taxable. This is because income taxes are payable and recoverable on the subsidiary's profits or losses as determined in accordance with the applicable tax rules. This is true even if the taxes are payable or recoverable by the parent entity and not the subsidiary itself.

3.13.1190.30 Current and deferred tax amounts for each entity within the tax group are determined and recognised under a systematic, rational and consistent method. A difference may arise from current and deferred taxes recognised and the amounts paid to or received from the parent entity. This is disclosed in the tax reconciliation or recognised as a contribution from or a distribution to the parent entity (see 3.13.1210.20).

3.13.1190.40 We believe that an entity should choose an accounting policy, to be applied consistently, for measuring the current and deferred taxes to be recognised by each entity within a tax-consolidated group. In our view, there are several acceptable ways to measure the current and deferred taxes to be recognised by each entity within a tax-consolidated group, including the following.

- *'Stand-alone taxpayer' approach:* Under this approach, current and deferred taxes are recognised as if the entity were taxable in its own right.
- *'Separate taxpayer within the group' approach:* Under this approach, current and deferred taxes are measured on the basis that the entity is part of a tax group; this results in adjustments related to the entity's transactions that have tax consequences for the entity but do not have tax consequences (or have different tax consequences) at the group level – e.g. intra-group transfers of inventories or property, plant and equipment, and management fees.
- *'Group allocation' approach:* Under this approach, current and deferred taxes of the tax group are allocated in a systematic manner.

3.13.1190.50 Various allocation methods might be applied. However, in our view a method is not appropriate if it results in:
- only current taxes being allocated to an entity in the group that has temporary differences;
- no deferred taxes being allocated to an entity with temporary differences because the tax group has none;
- current taxes being allocated only to entities with accounting profit; or
- current taxes and deferred taxes being allocated on a basis inconsistent with IAS 12 – e.g. based on revenue, total assets, net assets or operating profit.

3.13.1200   *Approach 2*

3.13.1200.10 Under this approach, each entity (subsidiaries and parent entity) recognises current income taxes based on the amounts actually paid by the individual legal entities. These amounts are generally based on a contractual agreement between the entities within the group. Deferred income taxes are also recognised in each entity's financial statements based on the amounts expected to be settled by the entity in the future.

Ⓢ 3.13.1210   *Group relief*

3.13.1210.10 In some jurisdictions, each entity within a group prepares its own tax return and is liable for any tax payable. However, an entity that makes tax losses may transfer those losses to another entity within the same group. Practice varies regarding whether the receiving entity pays the surrendering entity. In our view, if entities within a group transfer tax losses between themselves for no payment, then in their separate financial statements the entities should choose an accounting policy, to be applied consistently, to disclose such transfers in their tax reconciliations or to recognise them as contributions/distributions as appropriate.

EXAMPLE 61 – TRANSFER OF TAX LOSSES WITHIN A GROUP

3.13.1210.20 Subsidiary S is subject to a tax rate of 25% and has tax losses of 100. Initially, S recognises a related deferred tax asset of 25. S agrees to transfer its tax losses of 100 to its parent, Company P, at the end of the year. Consider the following cases.

- *Case 1:* P pays 25 to S in consideration for the transfer and S records the cash receipt against its deferred tax balance.
- *Case 2:* P pays nothing in consideration for the transfer and S records the transfer of its tax asset as a distribution.
- *Case 3:* P pays nothing in consideration for the transfer and S writes off its deferred tax asset and discloses the transfer in its tax reconciliation.

3.13.1210.30 S records the following entries for the initial recognition and subsequent transfer of the tax losses in cases 1, 2 and 3.

	DEBIT	CREDIT
Deferred tax asset	25	
Income tax (profit or loss)		25
To initially recognise deferred tax on tax losses (100 x 25%)		
Case 1		
Cash	25	
Deferred tax asset		25
To recognise tax loss transfer		
Case 2		
Distribution (equity)	25	
Deferred tax asset		25
To recognise tax loss transfer		
Case 3		
Income tax (profit or loss)	25	
Deferred tax asset		25
To recognise tax loss transfer		

3.13.1220 **FOREIGN INVESTMENT**

3.13.1220.10 Many jurisdictions provide tax relief for entities with an element of foreign ownership. This relief may be structured in a variety of ways. In general, as in the case of dividend credits (see 3.13.270.60 and 810), when the result of a tax scheme is to reduce the effective tax rate attributable to certain income, in our view any benefit should be recognised as part of income taxes.

EXAMPLE 62 – REDUCTION OF EFFECTIVE TAX RATE FROM FOREIGN INVESTMENT

3.13.1220.20   In Country F, the tax rate is 35%. However, when a dividend is received by an overseas shareholder, that shareholder receives a cash rebate directly from F's tax authorities. The rebate is 20% of the underlying taxes paid; this reduces the effective tax rate on that dividend income to 28% (35% x 80%).

3.13.1220.30   Overseas shareholder G (who resides in Country F for tax purposes) receives a dividend of 100 from Company H, and thereby becomes entitled to receive a cash rebate of 7 (100 x 35% x 20%). We believe that G's statement of profit or loss and OCI should be presented as follows.

Profit before tax	100
Income tax	(28)
Net profit	72

3.13.1220.40   Suppose that G is the parent of H. In this case, we believe that on consolidation the effect of the rebate should continue to be disclosed as part of income taxes. This is because the overall effect is still to reduce the group's effective tax rate. Intra-group dividend income is eliminated on consolidation, so there will be a difference between taxable income and accounting income. As a result, the effect of any income tax expense relating to the eliminated dividend income is reflected in the tax rate reconciliation. [*IAS 12.81(c)*]

3.13.1230   INVESTMENTS IN 'PASS-THROUGH' ENTITIES

3.13.1230.10   In many tax jurisdictions, some entities are not subject to income taxes directly. Rather, their income is passed through to and is taxed in the hands of their investors, as if it were the income of the investors. As such, in our experience these entities are often called 'pass-through' or 'tax-transparent' entities. An example of a pass-through entity may be a partnership that is not subject to income tax directly but each of its partners is liable for tax on its share of the profits or capital gains of the partnership. The types of structures and detailed tax treatments vary across jurisdictions. These pass-through tax treatments are, however, distinct from tax schemes that tax entities on distributions. Generally, a pass-through entity does not recognise any current or deferred tax of its own, because income tax is levied on its investors rather than on the entity.

3.13.1230.20   An investor in a pass-through entity accounts for the current and deferred tax associated with its investment following the general principles in IAS 12. If the pass-through entity is the investor's subsidiary, branch, associate or joint arrangement, then the investor determines the extent to which the temporary differences between the investment's tax base and the carrying amount of the related net assets or investment in its financial statements (commonly referred to as 'outside basis differences') should be recognised (see 3.13.260).

3.13.1230.30   A parent of a pass-through entity does not generally recognise deferred tax on the temporary differences between the pass-through entity's individual assets and liabilities and their tax bases (commonly referred to as 'inside basis differences') in its consolidated financial statements, on the

912

basis that these differences are often passed through to, and are therefore embedded in, the outside basis differences associated with the investment. In addition, under this approach, when a parent considers whether a portion of the outside basis differences associated with an investment in a pass-through entity will reverse in the foreseeable future (see 3.13.280), it considers whether the reversal of inside basis differences within the pass-through entity would effectively be passed through to the parent. Example 62 illustrates how the outside basis difference of a parent associated with an investment in a pass-through subsidiary can reverse in a way that does not involve the sale, disposal or distribution of the investment.

EXAMPLE 63 – INVESTMENT IN PASS-THROUGH ENTITY

3.13.1230.40 At the beginning of year 1, Company P established a partnership such that the partnership was wholly owned by P at the consolidated level. The initial investment was 100, with which the partnership acquired certain property, plant and equipment. The property, plant and equipment is depreciated over four years for accounting purposes and is immediately fully deductible for tax purposes.

3.13.1230.50 During year 1 and year 2, the partnership had taxable income of 250 and 270 respectively, before tax depreciation. In addition, during year 1, the partnership had tax-exempt income of 30 that will only be taxed as part of the capital gain when the partnership interest is sold. The partnership is a pass-through entity for tax purposes; in accordance with the applicable tax rules, the tax base of P's investment in the partnership equals P's initial investment cost plus its share of the partnership's taxable income less its share of distributions received from the partnership.

3.13.1230.60 In P's consolidated financial statements, the inside basis differences associated with P's investment in the partnership, and the accounting and taxable profits of the partnership, are calculated as follows.

	YR 1			YR 2			CHANGE IN INSIDE BASIS DIFFERENCE
	CARRYING AMOUNT	TAX BASE	INSIDE BASIS DIFFERENCE	CARRYING AMOUNT	TAX BASE	INSIDE BASIS DIFFERENCE	
	(A)	(B)	(C)=(A)-(B)	(D)	(E)	(F)=(D)-(E)	(G)=(F)-(C)
Property, plant and equipment	75	-	75	50	-	50	(25)
Other assets	280	280	-	550	550	-	-
Net assets	355	280	75	600	550	50	(25)
Taxable income	250	250		270	270		
Tax-exempt income	30	-		-	-		
Depreciation	(25)	(100)		(25)	-		
Net profit	255	150		245	270		

3.13.1230.70   The deferred tax related to the change in inside basis difference of 25 during year 2 is not recognised by the partnership itself because the partnership is not taxed on its own. In addition, deferred tax related to the change is not recognised by P because this change is effectively embedded in the change in the outside basis difference associated with the investment, as shown below.

3.13.1230.80   The outside basis difference associated with P's investment in the partnership in P's consolidated financial statements is calculated as follows.

	YR 1			YR 2			
	NET ASSETS OF INVESTMENT	INVESTOR'S TAX BASE	OUTSIDE BASIS DIFFERENCE	NET ASSETS OF INVESTMENT	INVESTOR'S TAX BASE	OUTSIDE BASIS DIFFERENCE	CHANGE IN OUTSIDE BASIS DIFFERENCE
	(H)	(I)	(J)=(H)-(I)	(K)	(L)	(M)=(K)-(L)	(N)=(J)-(M)
Tax base at the beginning of the year		100			250		
Taxable profit for the year		150			270		
Tax base at the end of the year	355	250[1]	105	600	520[1]	80	(25)

Note
1.   The tax base excludes a reduction for the tax-exempt income of 30 that will only be taxed as part of the capital gain when the partnership interest is sold.

3.13.1230.90   The outside basis differences comprise the following.

	YR 1	YR 2
Temporary difference arising from income during year 1 that is tax-exempt until the partnership interest is sold or otherwise disposed of	30	30
Temporary difference arising from the accelerated tax depreciation of property, plant and equipment for tax purposes	75	50
Total	105	80

3.13.1230.100   Consequently, although the partnership is P's subsidiary, a portion of the outside basis difference associated with P's investment in the partnership may reverse as the inside basis differences of the partnership are recovered during the operations of the partnership. In this example, of the 105 total outside basis difference at the end of year 1, 75 would reverse during the operations of the partnership as the inside basis difference associated with the property, plant and equipment of the partnership reverses; the remaining 30 associated with tax-exempt income would reverse when the partnership interest is sold or otherwise disposed of.

3.13.1230.110 The change in the outside basis difference between year 1 and year 2 of 25 corresponds to the depreciation of the partnership's property, plant and equipment, because the whole of the cost of 100 was deducted for tax purposes in year 1. Effectively, the reversal of the inside basis difference associated with the partnership's property, plant and equipment is passed through to P because of its tax status. This is irrespective of the fact that P may not have any intention to sell or otherwise recover its investment in the foreseeable future.

3.13.1230.120 Accordingly, at the end of year 1, even though P does not have any intention to sell or otherwise dispose of the investment in the partnership, P determines that the tax effect of 75 out of the total outside basis difference of 105 needs to be recognised because it is probable that this portion of the outside basis difference will reverse in the future, as the partnership's property, plant and equipment is depreciated.

3.13.1230.130 P's tax rate is 20% and it records the following entries in year 1.

	DEBIT	CREDIT
Income tax expense (150 x 20%)	30	
Current tax payable		30
To recognise current tax payable on P's share of profits passed through from partnership		
Income tax expense (75 x 20%)	15	
Deferred tax liability		15
To recognise deferred tax liability related to part of outside basis difference associated with P's investment in partnership expected to reverse in foreseeable future		

3.13.1240 EFFECTIVELY TAX-EXEMPT ENTITY

3.13.1240.10 In some jurisdictions, certain types of entities – e.g. investment vehicles or real estate investment trusts – may be subject to a special tax regime. Under the special tax regime, qualifying entities can be fully taxed on a particular type of income – e.g. rental income or dividends from subsidiaries originating from such income – and then be entitled to a full tax deduction when they distribute all or virtually all of that income further to their investors every year. In essence, such entities are 'pass-through' (see 3.13.1230.10) and can be regarded as effectively tax-exempt in relation to the specified income.

3.13.1240.20   In our view, to qualify as effectively tax-exempt under such special tax regime, an entity should meet all of the following criteria:

- the entity should be economically compelled to distribute to its investors all or virtually all of the specified income that otherwise would be taxable;
- the entity should meet, and expect and intend to continue to meet, the requirements under the relevant tax laws, including conditions other than distribution requirements – e.g. requirements on debt/equity ratios;
- there should be no indication that the entity will fail to meet those requirements; and
- the entity should be eligible to claim a tax deduction for distributions paid to its investors in future periods.

3.13.1240.30   For a discussion of timing of a change in tax status, see 3.13.485.

3.13.1250   ACQUIRING TAX LOSSES OTHER THAN IN BUSINESS COMBINATION

3.13.1250.10   An entity recognises a deferred tax asset for unused tax losses/credits carried forward to the extent that it is probable that future taxable profits will be available against which the unused tax losses/credits can be utilised. In our view, this principle should be applied to both:

- internally generated tax losses; and
- tax losses acquired in a transaction that is not a business combination. For a discussion of the acquisition of tax losses in a business combination, see 3.13.960; and for a discussion of transfers of tax losses within a group, see 3.13.1210. [*IAS 12.34*]

3.13.1250.20   In our view, the initial recognition exemption is not applicable to acquired tax losses, because IAS 12 deals with tax losses and tax credits separately from temporary differences. Therefore, we believe that on initial recognition an entity should recognise a deferred tax asset for the acquired tax losses at the amount paid – provided that it is probable that future taxable profits will be available against which the acquired tax losses can be utilised (see 3.13.330). The deferred tax asset is then remeasured in accordance with the general measurement principles in IAS 12. [*IAS 12.24, 34–36*]

EXAMPLE 64 – ACQUIRED TAX LOSSES

3.13.1250.30   Company P acquires Company S, a shell company with accumulated tax losses of 450 for cash of 100. This transaction is not a business combination. P has a tax rate of 30%. P and S form a tax group and it is probable that future taxable profit will be available against which the acquired tax losses can be utilised. Therefore, P recognises a deferred tax asset for the acquired tax losses at the amount paid of 100. The deferred tax asset is then remeasured in accordance with IAS 12 to 135 (450 x 30%). The remeasurement of 35 (100 - 135) is credited to profit or loss.

3.13.1260   DERECOGNITION

3.13.1260.10   Current and deferred tax assets and liabilities are not financial instruments. This is because they arise from tax legislation, and not from a contract between the taxable entity and the tax authorities. Therefore, income tax assets and liabilities are not subject to the measurement requirements of IFRS 9 (see 7.1.30.100). [*IAS 32.11, 13, AG11–AG12, IFRS 9.3.1.1*]

3.13.1260.20   However, IAS 12 is silent on the derecognition of tax assets when, for example, an entity transfers to another party its right to receive cash from the tax authorities. In our view, an entity may apply the derecognition requirements of IFRS 9 by analogy in such situations to assess whether it is appropriate to derecognise tax assets (see 7.6.60).

3.13.1270   **FUTURE DEVELOPMENTS**

3.13.1270.10   In March 2018, the IFRS Interpretations Committee discussed fact patterns under which an entity recognises an asset and a liability at the commencement date of a lease, or recognises a liability and includes in the cost of an item of property, plant and equipment the costs of decommissioning that asset. Under the fact patterns discussed, the lease payments and decommissioning costs are deductible for tax purposes when paid. The Committee decided to research developing an interpretation aimed at addressing the recognition and measurement of deferred tax under these fact patterns.

3.13.1270.20   In June 2018, the Committee decided to recommend that the IASB propose a narrow-scope amendment to IAS 12 to clarify that the initial recognition exemption in paragraphs 15 and 24 of IAS 12 does not apply to transactions that give rise to both deductible and taxable temporary differences to the extent that an entity would otherwise recognise a deferred tax asset and a deferred tax liability of the same amount in respect of those temporary differences. The Board is yet to consider this issue.

4. STATEMENT OF PROFIT OR LOSS AND OCI

4.1 General

4. STATEMENT OF PROFIT OR LOSS AND OCI

4.1 General

CURRENTLY EFFECTIVE REQUIREMENTS

This publication reflects IFRS in issue at 1 August 2018, and the currently effective requirements cover annual periods beginning on 1 January 2018.

The requirements related to this topic are mainly derived from the following.

STANDARD	TITLE
IAS 1	Presentation of Financial Statements

The currently effective requirements include newly effective requirements arising from the following.

- IFRS 9 *Financial Instruments*, which is effective for annual periods beginning on or after 1 January 2018. Transition requirements for IFRS 9 are the subject of chapter 7.11. The impact of the new requirements on the statement of profit or loss and OCI is reflected in 4.1.15.10, 20.40, 130.10 and 180.10.
- IFRS 15 *Revenue from Contracts with Customers*, which is effective for annual periods beginning on or after 1 January 2018. The new requirements may be applied using the retrospective method or the cumulative effect method (see 4.2.510). The impact of the new requirements on the statement of profit or loss and OCI is reflected in 4.1.15.20–30.

FORTHCOMING REQUIREMENTS

For this topic, there are no forthcoming requirements.

FUTURE DEVELOPMENTS

This topic is subject to future developments that may affect several aspects of the structure and content of the statement of profit or loss and OCI. See 4.1.260.

4.1.10 FORMAT OF STATEMENT OF PROFIT OR LOSS AND OCI

4.1.10.05   Profit or loss and OCI may be presented in either:
- a single statement that includes all components of profit or loss and OCI in two separate sections; or
- two separate statements, a 'statement of profit or loss' displaying components of profit or loss followed immediately by a 'statement of comprehensive income' beginning with profit or loss and displaying components of OCI. [*IAS 1.10–10A*]

4.1.10.10   Although the formats of the statement of profit or loss and OCI are not prescribed, certain items are required to be presented in the statement to the extent they are material. In our experience, there is limited flexibility over the order of these items, which tends to follow the order of the items set out in IAS 1. [*IAS 1.81A–82A*]

4.1.10.20   The chosen format for the statement of profit or loss and OCI is applied consistently. In our view, if an entity has no items of OCI, then it may present a single performance statement ending at a line 'profit or loss and total comprehensive income for the year' (or similar) that is titled 'statement of profit or loss and OCI'; such a statement should not be titled 'statement of profit or loss'. [*IAS 1.45*]

4.1.10.30   Additional line items, headings and subtotals are presented when this is necessary for an understanding of the entity's financial performance (see 4.1.80). [*IAS 1.85*]

4.1.10.40   Both formats for presenting the statement of profit or loss and OCI are illustrated in KPMG's *Guides to financial statements* series.

4.1.15 PRESENTATION OF REVENUE

4.1.15.10   An entity is required to present revenue as a separate line item in the statement of profit or loss, presenting separately interest revenue calculated using the effective interest method (see 7.10.60.10–30). [*IAS 1.82(a)*]

4.1.15.20   Conversely, an entity is not required to disclose the 'revenue from contracts with customers' as a separate line item in the statement of profit or loss as long as it is disclosed separately in the notes (see 4.2.480.20–30). [*IFRS 15.113, IAS 1.82(a)*]

4.1.15.30   The term 'revenue' is defined as income arising in the course of an entity's ordinary activities. An entity's 'ordinary activities' may be broader than those generating revenue from contracts with customers in the scope of IFRS 15 or generating interest revenue calculated using the effective interest method. As such, the revenue line item in the statement of profit or loss may include other revenue amounts that are not in the scope of IFRS 15. [*IFRS 15.A*]

4.1.20 CLASSIFICATION OF EXPENSES

4.1.20.10   Expenses recognised in profit or loss are classified according to their function (e.g. cost of sales, distribution and administration) or nature (e.g. staff costs, depreciation and amortisation).

This analysis may be presented in the primary statement or in the notes. Presenting the analysis in the primary statement may constitute more prominent disclosure. However, if an entity chooses to present the analysis of expenses in the notes to the financial statements, then it ensures that its presentation in the primary statement is not misleading and is relevant to an understanding of the financial statements (see 4.1.90). [*IAS 1.99–100*]

4.1.20.20   IAS 1 requires management to select the most relevant and reliable presentation of expenses; an entity's choice often depends on the nature of the entity and the industry in which it operates. [*IAS 1.99, 105*]

4.1.20.30   The chosen classification is generally applied consistently from one period to the next. A change of classification is made only if a new or revised IFRS requires a change in presentation or if the change will result in more relevant information – e.g. following a significant change in the nature of operations (see 2.8.130). [*IAS 1.45*]

4.1.20.40   An entity that presents the analysis of expenses by function or by nature in the statement of profit or loss and OCI may face challenges in determining how this presentation interacts with the specific requirements to present the effect of some events or circumstances as a single amount in the statement of profit or loss and OCI – e.g. impairment losses determined in accordance with section 5.5 of IFRS 9 (see 4.1.80, 90). An entity applies judgement in determining an appropriate presentation. In doing so, it needs to ensure that the chosen presentation is not misleading and is relevant to the users' understanding of its financial statements. [*IAS 1.82, 85, 97, 99*]

4.1.30   Classification by function

4.1.30.10   If expenses are classified according to function, then they are allocated to, for example, cost of sales, distribution or administrative activities. As a minimum, under this method an entity discloses its cost of sales separately from other expenses. [*IAS 1.103*]

4.1.30.20   There is no guidance in IFRS on how specific expenses are allocated to functions. An entity establishes its own definitions of functions – such as cost of sales, distribution and administrative activities – and applies these definitions consistently. It may be appropriate to disclose the definitions used.

4.1.30.30   All expenses – including staff costs, depreciation and amortisation – are allocated to the appropriate functions (see 4.1.20.40). In our view, staff costs, depreciation and amortisation can be allocated to specific functions in almost every case. Only expenses that cannot be allocated to a specific function are classified as 'other expenses'.

4.1.30.40   In our view, cost of sales includes only expenses directly or indirectly attributable to the production process, such as direct materials, labour costs, the depreciation of assets used in manufacturing, and repair and maintenance costs related to production. Other costs not attributable to the production process, such as marketing and advertising expenses, are classified as selling and distribution costs.

4.1.30.50   Additional information based on the nature of expenses – e.g. depreciation, amortisation and staff costs – is disclosed in the notes to the financial statements. [*IAS 1.104*]

4.1.40 Classification by nature

4.1.40.10   If classification by nature is used, then expenses are aggregated according to their nature – e.g. purchases of materials, transport costs, depreciation and amortisation, staff costs and advertising costs. [*IAS 1.102*]

4.1.50   EMPLOYEE BENEFITS AND RESTRUCTURING EXPENSES

4.1.60   Employee benefits (staff costs)

4.1.60.10   Staff costs are presented separately if expenses are classified by nature. In addition, staff costs are required to be disclosed in the notes if expenses are classified by function. [*IAS 1.102, 104*]

4.1.60.20   IAS 1 does not contain specific guidance on what to include in staff costs. In our view, staff costs comprise all costs directly attributable to personnel, including salaries, social security expenses, pension costs, health benefits and share-based compensation received in the capacity as an employee.

4.1.60.30   In some countries, housing and other infrastructure assets (e.g. schools) are provided to staff and their families. In this case, in our view any rent paid by the entity should be included in staff costs. If the property is owned by the employer, then in our view depreciation and maintenance of the property should also be included in staff costs.

4.1.70   Restructuring expenses

4.1.70.10   If an entity chooses to disclose 'results of operating activities' (see 4.1.120), then restructuring costs are normally presented as part of operating results because they represent the costs of restructuring ongoing operations. If the restructuring charge is significant, then it may be appropriate to present or disclose the effect(s) of the restructuring charge either in the statement of profit or loss and OCI (following an appropriate presentation (see 4.1.90)) or in the notes to the financial statements. [*IAS 1.BC56*]

4.1.80   ADDITIONAL LINE ITEMS

4.1.80.10   An entity presents additional items of income or expense, headings or subtotals in the statement of profit or loss and OCI when they are relevant to an understanding of the entity's financial performance. [*IAS 1.85*]

4.1.80.13   If an entity presents additional subtotals in the statement of profit or loss and OCI, then the subtotals:
- comprise line items made up of amounts recognised and measured in accordance with IFRS;
- are presented and labelled in a manner that makes the line items that constitute the subtotal clear and understandable;
- are consistent from period to period (see 4.1.10.20 and 20.30);
- are displayed with no more prominence than other subtotals and totals presented in the statement of profit or loss and OCI; and
- are reconciled in the statement of profit or loss and OCI with the subtotals and totals required by IAS 1. [*IAS 1.85A–85B, BC38G, BC58B*]

4.1.80.15   Additional line items are described appropriately in accordance with their nature or function, consistent with the way that the entity presents its analysis of expenses (see 4.1.20). Factors to consider when determining whether to present additional items include materiality and the nature and function of the components of income and expenses. [*IAS 1.86*]

4.1.80.20   In our view, when assessing materiality, the effect of a transaction or an event as a whole should be considered even if, for presentation purposes, the effect will be allocated to different line items for classification by nature or function.

EXAMPLE 1 – PRESENTATION OF ADDITIONAL LINE ITEMS – ASSESSMENT OF MATERIALITY

4.1.80.30   Company P has incurred restructuring costs related to various parts of its business. If P analyses its expenses by function, then it allocates the total restructuring costs to the identified functions to ensure that the analysis of expenses is presented using a consistent classification method. However, we believe that in assessing materiality, P should assess the total restructuring costs instead of the allocated amounts independently of each other. [*IAS 1.86, 97–98*]

4.1.90   Presentation and disclosures

4.1.90.10   Disclosure in the notes to the financial statements is sufficient for many items that are material individually. Separate presentation in the statement of profit or loss and OCI may be appropriate only when it is necessary for an understanding of the entity's financial performance. In such cases, the entity discloses in the notes to the financial statements an additional explanation of the nature of the amount presented. [*IAS 1.29–30A, 97, 112*]

4.1.90.20   In our view, the nature of an item does not change merely because it is individually material. We believe that individually material items should generally be presented within, or adjacent to, the remaining aggregated amounts of the same nature or function, consistent with the classification of items that are not individually material (see 4.1.20). For example, a separately presented material write-down of inventory damaged in a fire is classified as cost of sales because other impairment losses on inventories are included in that line item (see 3.8.400.70). [*IAS 1.29, 45, 99*]

4.1.90.30   It may be appropriate for an entity to include a subtotal of all items classified as having the same nature or function. For example, when an individually material cost of sale (e.g. a write-down of inventory damaged in a fire) is presented separately from 'other cost of sales', a subtotal for the line item 'cost of sales' may also be presented. For guidance on factors that an entity needs to consider when presenting subtotals in the statement of profit or loss and OCI, see 4.1.80.

4.1.90.40   If the effect of a particular transaction, event or circumstance is pervasive and affecting a number of line items, then it may be appropriate to disclose in the notes to the financial statements the total impact of the event. In this case, in our view an analysis of related amounts and the line items affected should be disclosed in the notes, with a description of the circumstances. An entity may also wish to disclose in the statement of profit or loss and OCI the related element of each line item affected. This may be achieved in a number of ways – e.g. by sub-analysing (and subtotalling) the appropriate line items or by presenting the individually material items in a separate column, with a column in which the total for each line item is presented.

EXAMPLE 2 – ALTERNATIVE PRESENTATIONS OF INDIVIDUALLY MATERIAL ITEMS

4.1.90.50   Set out below are extracts from statements of profit or loss and OCI illustrating possible presentations of individually material items.

Approach 1: Use of parenthesis

Revenue	1,600
Cost of sales (including loss of inventory destroyed in fire of 175)	(1,000)
Gross profit	600

Approach 2: Use of subtotals

Revenue		1,600
Cost of sales		
Loss of inventory destroyed in fire	175	
Other cost of sales	825	
		(1,000)
Gross profit		600

Approach 3: Use of columns

	EXCLUDING RESTRUCTURING	RESTRUCTURING COSTS	TOTAL
Raw materials and consumables	2,500	50	2,550
Employee benefit expense	1,000	200	1,200
Depreciation and amortisation	750	100	850
Other expenses	400	50	450

4.1.90.60   If an item of income or expense is presented or disclosed separately in the current period, then comparable amounts recognised in the comparative period are presented or disclosed as comparative information. This may arise, for example, when expenses in respect of a single event or transaction are recognised in both the current and the comparative periods. The presentation of comparative amounts for an individually material item of income or expense may be appropriate even if the item was not presented or disclosed separately in the annual financial statements of the prior period. [*IAS 1.38, 38B, 41–44*]

4.1.100   USE OF DESCRIPTION 'UNUSUAL' OR 'EXCEPTIONAL'

4.1.100.10   IFRS does not describe events or items of income or expense as 'unusual' or 'exceptional'. However, if an entity labels an item of income or expense as 'unusual' or 'exceptional' in the statement of profit or loss and OCI, then such items cannot be characterised as 'extraordinary' (see 4.1.110).

4.1.100.20   In our view, an item is not exceptional or unusual merely because there is a requirement to present or disclose that item separately, either in the statement of profit or loss and OCI or in the notes to the financial statements. [*IAS 1.17(c), 97*]

4.1.100.30   In our view, if the description 'exceptional' or 'unusual' is used, then its use should be infrequent and reserved for items that justify a prominence greater than that achieved by separate presentation or disclosure. For example, it may be appropriate to characterise items such as costs associated with a natural disaster as exceptional or unusual.

4.1.100.40   If an item is characterised as 'exceptional' or 'unusual', then in our view the description used should include the nature of the item (e.g. exceptional impairment loss on property affected by earthquake) and the notes to the financial statements should include an additional explanation of the nature of the amount and its characterisation as exceptional or unusual. We believe that the description of an item simply as an exceptional or unusual item does not meet the requirement for amounts to be classified by their nature or function.

4.1.100.50   In our view, any amount described as unusual or exceptional should be classified by nature or function, in the same way as usual or non-exceptional amounts (see 4.1.20).

4.1.100.60   If an entity chooses to use a descriptor that is not defined in IFRS (e.g. 'exceptional'), then it uses the term consistently and describes the term in the notes to the financial statements to provide clarity for users of financial statements.

4.1.100.70   Describing items of a similar nature or function as exceptional or unusual in consecutive periods is inconsistent with a characterisation of these items as unusual or non-recurring, unless the amounts relate to a single transaction or event that is recognised over several financial periods.

4.1.100.80   A restructuring is one example of an event that may give rise to amounts that are individually material. In our view, such events are not exceptional or unusual and should not generally be described as such. However, it may be appropriate nonetheless to present or disclose the effect(s) of a significant restructuring separately as described in 4.1.70.10.

4.1.110   EXTRAORDINARY ITEMS

4.1.110.10   IFRS makes no distinction between ordinary and extraordinary activities. The presentation, disclosure or characterisation of items of income and expense as 'extraordinary items' in the statement of profit or loss and OCI or in the notes is prohibited. [*IAS 1.87*]

4.1.120   OPERATING RESULT

4.1.120.10   The disclosure of the results of *operating* activities is not required as a separate line item in profit or loss. However, entities may voluntarily provide a subtotal before profit or loss for the year. In our view, 'results from operating activities' may be an appropriate subtotal. [*IAS 1.82, 85–85A, BC55–BC56*]

4.1.120.20   The terms 'operating' and 'non-operating' are not defined in the context of profit or loss. However, the standard on the statement of cash flows defines operating activities as 'the principal revenue-producing activities of an entity'. If an entity wishes to present a subtotal for operating result, then this definition may be an appropriate starting point in determining the components of operating income. [*IAS 7.6*]

4.1.120.30   Only items that are clearly not related to operating activities are presented outside the operating result. [*IAS 1.BC56*]

4.1.120.40   In our view, gains and losses on the disposal of property, plant and equipment are generally part of the operating activities of an entity and should be shown below gross profit (when such a subtotal is presented) but within operating results, perhaps as part of other operating income or expense. This is an example of when the effect of a single transaction is classified differently in the statement of cash flows and the statement of profit or loss and OCI. The cash proceeds from the sale generally would be presented within investing activities in the statement of cash flows and not as an operating cash inflow (see 2.3.20 and 3.2.380.40).

4.1.130   SALES OF FINANCIAL INVESTMENTS

4.1.130.10   Gains (losses) on the disposal of financial investments are generally included in finance income (finance costs). However, presentation as a separate line item in the statement of profit or loss and OCI may be required (see 4.1.20.40, 80.10–90.10 and 7.10.60–70). [*IAS 1.82(aa)*]

4.1.130.20   In our view, entities that routinely trade in financial instruments, or for which investing activities are part of the ordinary operations, should present the net results of these activities within operating results. The gross proceeds on disposal of investments are not generally presented as revenue in the statement of profit or loss and OCI.

4.1.140   SHARE OF PROFIT OF EQUITY-ACCOUNTED INVESTEES

4.1.140.10   The share of profit or loss of equity-accounted investees (associates and joint ventures) attributable to an investor (i.e. after tax and NCI) is presented as a separate line item before tax in profit or loss. This presentation generally results in a reconciling item in the tax rate reconciliation (see 3.13.640.20). [*IAS 1.82(c), BC54L, IG6, 28.10*]

4.1.150   ALTERNATIVE EARNINGS MEASURES

4.1.150.10   An entity may wish to present alternative earnings measures such as EBITDA, EBIT or 'headline earnings' in the statement of profit or loss and OCI. IFRS does not prohibit the presentation of subtotals, including certain alternative earnings measures, if relevant criteria are met. In our view, if a measure – e.g. EBITDA or EBIT – is made up of amounts recognised and measured in accordance with IFRS, then it may be considered an additional subtotal under IAS 1. [*IAS 1.85–85A*]

4.1.150.15   When an entity presents additional subtotals – e.g. EBIT or EBITDA – in the statement of profit or loss and OCI, the requirements for presentation of those subtotals, including a reconciliation with the subtotals and totals required by IAS 1, apply (see 4.1.80.13). [*IAS 1.85A–B, BC38G*]

4.1.150.20   National regulators may have more restrictive requirements. In some jurisdictions, regulations may prohibit various presentation formats, or give guidance on when it is and is not appropriate to use alternative measures in financial reports or documents related to financial reports, and therefore these requirements are also considered. For example, according to the US Securities and Exchange Commission's *Final Rule: Conditions for Use of Non-GAAP Financial Measures* (e.g. EBITDA, 'special' EPS), such measures are shown outside the financial statements.

4.1.150.30   In the EU, the European Securities and Markets Authority issued *Guidelines on Alternative Performance Measures* (APMs), which seek to enhance transparency and comparability of APMs that are presented outside the financial statements and to ensure that their use is not misleading (see 5.8.10.40). The International Organization of Securities Commissions issued a *Statement on Non-GAAP Financial Measures* with a similar purpose.

4.1.160   EBITDA

4.1.160.10   The presentation of EBITDA in the statement of profit or loss and OCI depends on the classification of expenses adopted, and whether that classification is given in the statement of profit or loss and OCI or in the notes to the financial statements.

4.1.160.20   In our view, the presentation of EBITDA is usually possible by presenting a sub-analysis of earnings while classifying items of income and expense to the appropriate line items.

EXAMPLE 3 – POSSIBLE ALTERNATIVE PRESENTATIONS OF EBITDA IN STATEMENT OF PROFIT OR LOSS AND OCI

4.1.160.30   Set out below are extracts from statements of profit or loss and OCI illustrating possible presentations of EBITDA.

4.1.160.40   **Approach 1: Classification of expenses by function or nature**

Revenue	500
Expenses[1]	(400)
Analysis of profit from operations	
Profit before interest, tax, depreciation and amortisation (EBITDA)	**120**
Depreciation and amortisation	(20)
Results from operating activities	100

Note
1.   Classified by function or nature either in the statement of profit or loss and OCI or in the notes.

4.1.160.50	**Approach 2: Classification of expenses by nature**
Revenue	500
Other income	10
Raw material and consumables used	(210)
Staff costs	(100)
Other expenses, other than depreciation and amortisation	(80)
Profit before interest, tax, depreciation and amortisation (EBITDA)	**120**
Depreciation and amortisation	(20)
Results from operating activities	100

4.1.160.50   As an alternative, an entity could disclose EBITDA:

- as a footnote to the statement of profit or loss and OCI beneath EPS;
- in a note to the financial statements; or
- as supplemental information (see chapter 5.8).

4.1.170   **EBIT**

4.1.170.10   It is possible to show EBIT in the statement of profit or loss and OCI, regardless of the classification of expenses or the entity's definition of interest for the purposes of EBIT.

EXAMPLE 4 – POSSIBLE PRESENTATION OF EBIT IN STATEMENT OF PROFIT OR LOSS AND OCI

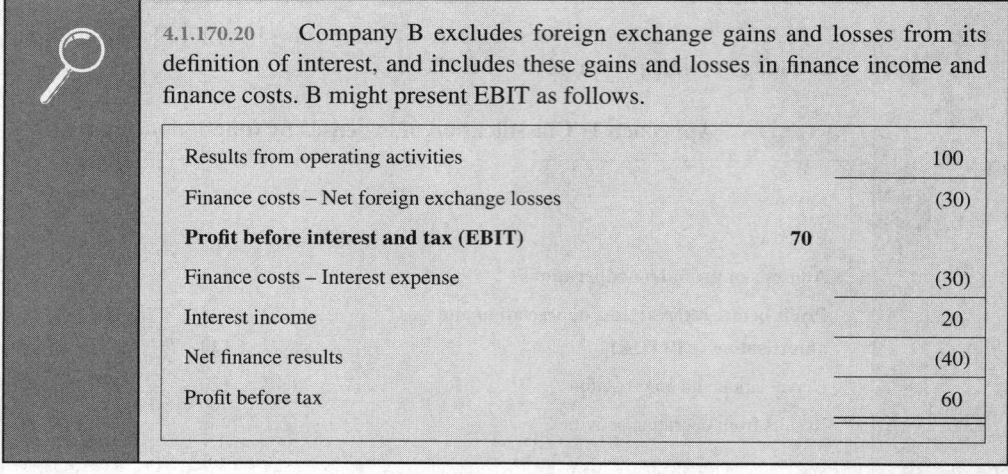

4.1.170.20   Company B excludes foreign exchange gains and losses from its definition of interest, and includes these gains and losses in finance income and finance costs. B might present EBIT as follows.

Results from operating activities		100
Finance costs – Net foreign exchange losses		(30)
Profit before interest and tax (EBIT)	**70**	
Finance costs – Interest expense		(30)
Interest income		20
Net finance results		(40)
Profit before tax		60

4.1.170.30   Although finance costs are required to be presented separately in the statement of profit or loss and OCI, in our view the above split between interest and other finance costs is acceptable.

Some entities that present EBIT include all finance costs in the interest line. In our view, this alternative presentation is also acceptable as long as the definition of EBIT is clear. [*IAS 1.82*]

4.1.180 CHANGES IN ESTIMATES

4.1.180.10   In our view, changes in estimates – e.g. reversals of provisions or impairment losses – should generally be presented in the same line item (classification) in the statement of profit or loss and OCI as the original estimate. However, impairment losses (including reversals of impairment losses or impairment gains) determined in accordance with section 5.5 of IFRS 9 are specifically required to be presented as a separate line item. [*IAS 1.82(aa)*]

4.1.180.20   Therefore, if the original estimate was classified as cost of sales, then we believe that changes in the estimate, whether they are additional charges (debits) or reductions in amounts previously charged (credits), should also be presented in cost of sales. An entity discloses the nature and amount of a change in accounting estimate that affects the current period or is expected to have an impact on future periods. [*IAS 8.39*]

4.1.180.30   Sometimes, however, it may be acceptable to present the effect of a reduction in an estimate of an expense in other income even if the original estimate was classified as other expenses. This might be appropriate when, for example, the reversal is significant and would otherwise result in the line item 'other expenses' being a net credit. In this situation, it would be logical to present 'other income' and 'other expenses' in consecutive line items to help users with comparability.

4.1.190 INCOME TAX

4.1.190.10   In our view, all items of profit or loss should be presented in the primary statement before the effect of income tax (i.e. gross) unless they are specifically required by another IFRS to be presented after the effect of income tax – e.g. share of profit of equity-accounted investees (see 4.1.140) and amounts related to discontinued operations (see 4.1.220). For a discussion of the presentation of income tax associated with items of OCI, see 4.1.250. [*IAS 1.82(d), 12.77, 28.10, IFRS 5.33–33A*]

4.1.200 OFFSETTING

4.1.200.10   Items of income and expense are offset when this is required or permitted by an IFRS; or when gains, losses and related expenses arise from the same transaction or event or from similar individually immaterial transactions and events. In our view, if an entity buys and then within a short timeframe sells foreign currency, then the transactions should be presented on a net basis in the statement of profit or loss and OCI. [*IAS 1.32–35*]

4.1.200.20   In our view, if a financial asset and financial liability qualify to be offset (see 7.10.110), then the related income and expense items should also be offset.

4.1.210 Finance costs

4.1.210.10   Finance costs are required to be presented as a separate line item in the statement of profit or loss and OCI. In our view, the presentation should not be of 'net finance results' unless finance costs and finance income are also presented as separate line items in the statement of profit or loss and OCI, with the net amount being a subtotal of finance costs and finance income (see 4.1.170.30). For further discussion, see 7.10.70. [*IAS 1.82(b)*]

4.1.220 Discontinued operations

4.1.220.10   If an entity has discontinued operations during the period, then it is required to disclose separately in the statement of profit or loss and OCI a single amount comprising the total of:

- the post-tax profit or loss on discontinued operations; and
- the post-tax gain or loss recognised on:
  - the measurement to fair value less costs to sell; or
  - the disposal of the assets/disposal group(s) constituting the discontinued operations. [*IAS 1.82(ea),* *IFRS 5.33(a)*]

4.1.220.20   For further discussion of the presentation of discontinued operations, see 5.4.220.

4.1.230 Pro forma income statement

4.1.230.10   If there have been significant changes in the structure of an entity – e.g. following a major business combination – then the entity may wish to present a pro forma income statement. IFRS does not prohibit such presentation, but in our view any pro forma information should be identified clearly as such and presented in a manner that is not misleading. Also, the basis of preparation of the pro forma information should be explained clearly.

4.1.230.20   Although a pro forma income statement may be appropriate as supplemental information, it is not a substitute for an income statement that complies with IFRS.

4.1.230.30   For further discussion of the presentation of pro forma information, see 2.1.130.

4.1.240 OTHER COMPREHENSIVE INCOME

4.1.240.10   OCI comprises items of income and expense, including reclassification adjustments, that are not recognised in profit or loss as required or permitted by IFRS. [*IAS 1.7*]

4.1.240.20   Certain items initially recognised in OCI are subsequently reclassified (formerly referred to as 'recycled') to profit or loss. Generally, IFRS specifies whether and when amounts previously recognised in OCI are reclassified to profit or loss. [*IAS 1.93*]

4.1.240.30   In the OCI section of the statement of profit or loss and OCI, items are classified by nature (including share of OCI of equity-accounted investees) and grouped into those that in accordance with other IFRSs:

- may be reclassified to profit or loss in the future when certain conditions are met; and
- will never be reclassified to profit or loss. [*IAS 1.82A, BC54H, BC54K, IG6*]

4.1.240.40   Examples of items of income and expense that are not subsequently reclassified to profit or loss include:

- revaluation of property, plant and equipment (see 3.2.300) and intangible assets (see 3.3.280);

- remeasurements of defined benefit plans (see 4.4.950);
- gains and losses on fair value through OCI equity instruments (see 7.4.10.10 and 7.7.160); and
- the income tax effect of the above items (see chapter 3.13).

4.1.240.50   Examples of items of income and expense that may subsequently be reclassified to profit or loss include:
- foreign exchange differences on the translation of foreign operations (see 2.7.230 and 300);
- the effects of cash flow hedging (see 7.9.180);
- cost of hedging reserve (see 7.9.690.10);
- gains and losses on fair value through OCI debt instruments (see 7.4.10.10 and 7.7.160); and
- the income tax effect of the above items (see chapter 3.13).

4.1.240.60   Changes in the valuation of property, plant and equipment and intangible assets may be transferred to retained earnings in subsequent periods as the asset is used or when it is derecognised (see 3.2.350). [*IAS 1.96*]

4.1.240.70   Reclassification adjustments to profit or loss of amounts previously recognised in OCI are disclosed separately for each component of OCI. An entity may present these reclassification adjustments either in the statement of profit or loss and OCI or in the notes to the financial statements. If the entity chooses the latter approach, then it presents the components of OCI after any related reclassification adjustments. [*IAS 1.92, 94, IG6*]

4.1.250   Effect of income tax

4.1.250.10   The amount of income tax related to each component of OCI, including reclassification adjustments, is disclosed either in the statement of profit or loss and OCI or in the notes to the financial statements. [*IAS 1.90*]

4.1.250.20   An entity may present components of OCI either net of the related tax effects or gross of tax with a separate line item for the tax effects related to those components. The latter presentation is illustrated in our series of illustrative financial statements. If an entity presents items of OCI before the related tax effects, then it allocates the tax amount between items that may be reclassified subsequently to profit or loss and those that will never be reclassified. [*IAS 1.90–91*]

4.1.260   FUTURE DEVELOPMENTS

4.1.260.10   The IASB is working on a research project on primary financial statements. This project considers potential targeted improvements to the structure and content of the primary financial statements focusing primarily on the statements of financial performance and cash flows (see 2.1.160). A consultation document is expected in the first half of 2019.

4.2   Revenue

4.2   Revenue

CURRENTLY EFFECTIVE REQUIREMENTS

This publication reflects IFRS in issue at 1 August 2018, and the currently effective requirements cover annual periods beginning on 1 January 2018.

The requirements related to this topic are mainly derived from the following.

STANDARD	TITLE
IFRS 15	Revenue from Contracts with Customers

KPMG's publication *Revenue – Issues In-Depth* provides a comprehensive analysis of IFRS 15. The publication is more in-depth than this chapter and includes additional clarification of the requirements of IFRS 15 and of our interpretative guidance. It provides extensive illustrative examples to elaborate or clarify the practical application of IFRS 15.

FORTHCOMING REQUIREMENTS

The currently effective requirements are affected by the following forthcoming requirements. They are highlighted with a # and the impact is explained in the accompanying boxed text at the references indicated.

- In January 2016, the IASB issued IFRS 16 *Leases*, which is effective for annual periods beginning on or after 1 January 2019. See 4.2.405. IFRS 16 is the subject of chapter 5.1A.
- In May 2017, the IASB issued IFRS 17 *Insurance Contracts*, which is effective for annual periods beginning on or after 1 January 2021. See 4.2.15. IFRS 17 is the subject of chapter 8.1A.

FUTURE DEVELOPMENTS

For this topic, there are no future developments.

4.2.10   SCOPE#

4.2.10.10   IFRS 15 applies to contracts to deliver goods or services to a customer. A 'customer' is a party that has contracted with an entity to obtain goods or services that are an output of the entity's ordinary activities. [*IFRS 15.6*]

4.2.10.20   A counterparty to a contract is not a customer if, for example, it has contracted with the entity to participate in an activity or process in which the parties to the contract share in the risks and benefits that result from the activity or process, rather than to obtain the output of the entity's ordinary activities – e.g. developing an asset in a collaboration arrangement. [*IFRS 15.6*]

4.2.10.30   IFRS 15 does not apply to:
- lease contracts in the scope of IAS 17 (see chapter 5.1);
- insurance contracts in the scope of IFRS 4 (see chapter 8.1);
- financial instruments and other contractual rights or obligations in the scope of IFRS 9 (see section 7), IFRS 10 (see chapter 2.5), IFRS 11 (see chapter 3.6), IAS 27 (see chapter 2.5) and IAS 28 (see chapter 3.5); and
- non-monetary exchanges between entities in the same line of business to facilitate sales to customers or potential customers. [*IFRS 15.5*]

4.2.10.40   A contract with a customer may be partially in the scope of IFRS 15 and partially in the scope of another accounting standard or interpretation. If the other accounting standard or interpretation specifies how to separate and/or initially measure one or more parts of a contract, then an entity first applies those requirements. Otherwise, the entity applies the guidance in IFRS 15 to separate and/or initially measure the separately identified parts of the contract. [*IFRS 15.7*]

4.2.10.50   The following flowchart highlights the key considerations when determining the accounting for a contract that is partially in the scope of IFRS 15.

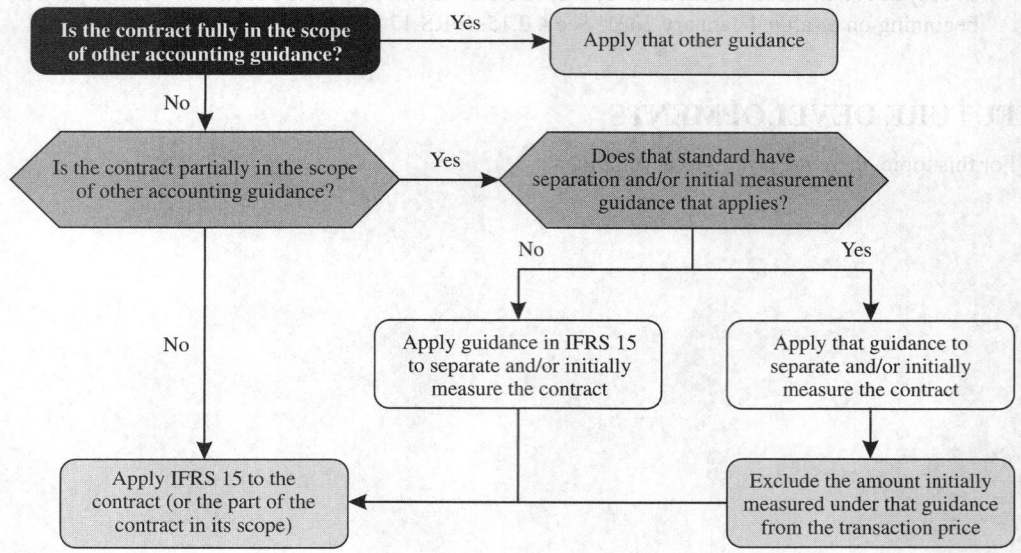

4.2.10.60   In some cases, an entity may receive a contribution of cash or other assets in a non-reciprocal transfer. Such a non-reciprocal transfer is not an exchange transaction – i.e. the contribution is not given in exchange for goods or services that are an output of the entity's ordinary activities. Accordingly, such contributions are not transactions with a customer and therefore are not in the scope of IFRS 15. For a discussion of non-reciprocal transfers, see 5.7.60. [*CF 6.80(b), 82, IFRS 15.BC28*]

4.2.15	**FORTHCOMING REQUIREMENTS**

4.2.15.10   IFRS 15 does not apply to contracts in the scope of IFRS 17, similar to the scope exception for IFRS 4 which is replaced by IFRS 17. However, if certain conditions are met, then an entity may choose to apply IFRS 15 rather than IFRS 17 to fixed-fee insurance service contracts. [*IFRS 17.8*]

4.2.20   OVERVIEW OF THE REVENUE MODEL

4.2.20.10   Entities apply a five-step model to determine when to recognise revenue, and at what amount. The model specifies that revenue should be recognised when (or as) an entity transfers goods or services to a customer, measured at the amount to which the entity expects to be entitled. Depending on whether certain criteria are met, revenue is recognised:
- over time, in a manner that depicts the entity's performance; or
- at a point in time, when control of the goods or services is transferred to the customer.

4.2.20.20   The following table summarises the steps in the revenue model, which are explained in the rest of this chapter.

STEP	REFERENCE
Step 1: Identify the contract	**4.2.25**
Step 2: Identify the performance obligations in the contract	**4.2.60**
Step 3: Determine the transaction price	**4.2.90**
Step 4: Allocate the transaction price to the performance obligations in the contract	**4.2.160**
Step 5: Recognise revenue	**4.2.210**

4.2.25   STEP 1: IDENTIFY THE CONTRACT

4.2.30   Criteria to determine whether a contract exists

4.2.30.10   A 'contract' is an agreement between two or more parties that creates enforceable rights and obligations. Contracts can be written, oral or implied by an entity's customary business practices. [*IFRS 15.10*]

4.2.30.20   A contract with a customer is in the scope of the standard when it is legally enforceable and all of the following criteria are met:

- the contract is approved and the parties are committed to their obligations;
- rights to goods or services and payment terms can be identified;
- the contract has commercial substance; and
- collection of consideration is probable. [*IFRS 15.9*]

4.2.30.25   In some cases, an entity may be entitled to consideration for services performed only if a specific outcome is achieved and the customer can withdraw from the contract at any time before that event without compensating the entity. These arrangements are often referred to as 'success-based fee arrangements'. They are common in the services industry – e.g. real estate agents and travel agents. It appears that these arrangements, in which the entire amount of the promised consideration is contingent on the achievement of a specific outcome, are not contracts with a customer in the scope of IFRS 15 before the specific outcome is achieved. This is because, in such arrangements, the entity does not have enforceable rights to payment for the services that it has performed to date and, similarly, the customer has no obligations. [*IFRS 15.9, 12*]

4.2.30.30   To determine whether the collectability criterion in 4.2.30.20 is met, an entity may use a portfolio of historical data. This type of analysis may be appropriate when an entity has a high volume of homogeneous transactions. These estimates are then used as an input into the overall assessment of collectability for a specific contract. [*IFRS 15.4*]

4.2.30.40   If a contract does not meet the criteria in 4.2.30.20, then the entity continually reassesses the criteria and applies the requirements of the standard to the contract from the date on which the criteria are met. [*IFRS 15.14*]

4.2.30.50   Generally, when an entity concludes that a contract does not exist because the collectability threshold is not met, the entity does not record a receivable for consideration that it has not yet received, for the goods or services transferred to the customer.

4.2.30.60   Any consideration received under a contract with a customer that does not meet the criteria in 4.2.30.20 is recognised as a liability until either:
- there are no remaining obligations to transfer goods or services and all, or substantially all, of the promised consideration has been received and is non-refundable; or
- the contract is terminated and the consideration that has been received is non-refundable. [*IFRS 15.15*]

4.2.30.70   When there is a significant change in facts and circumstances, an entity is required to reconsider if a contract still meets the criteria in 4.2.30.20. An entity does not reassess the collectability criterion in 4.2.30.20 unless the significant change in facts and circumstances results in a significant deterioration in the customer's creditworthiness. The determination of whether there is a significant deterioration in the customer's creditworthiness is based on specific facts and circumstances and requires judgement. Judgement is also required in evaluating whether the likelihood that an entity will not receive the full amount of stated consideration in a contract gives rise to a collectability issue or a price concession. If an entity determines that the criteria are no longer met, then it ceases to apply the standard to the contract. [*IFRS 15.13, 52, BC45*]

4.2.30.80   In some cases, an entity may continue to deliver services to a customer under the terms of a contract after it has expired – e.g. when the terms of the new contract to replace the existing contract are not finalised before the expiry date of the existing contract. If the entity has legally enforceable rights and obligations related to these services, then the services delivered are accounted for using the general guidance in IFRS 15. Conversely, if the entity does not have legally enforceable rights and obligations for the services delivered after the contract expires, then it applies the guidance on accounting for consideration received before a contract exists (see 4.2.30.60). Making the assessment of whether enforceable rights and obligations exist will often be complex and may require an entity to seek legal advice to determine whether it has enforceable rights and obligations after the expiry date of the contract.

4.2.33   Framework agreements

4.2.33.10   Generally, a framework agreement that includes no minimum purchase quantities only establishes the terms under which orders to purchase goods or services may be placed, rather than creating enforceable rights and obligations for the parties – i.e. it does not create a contract. However, enforceability is a matter of law in the relevant jurisdiction and each framework agreement will need to be evaluated based on its terms and conditions and local law.

4.2.33.20   When a framework agreement on its own does not create enforceable rights and obligations, it will normally be the purchase order in combination with the framework agreement that creates the enforceable rights and obligations between the entity and the customer. Therefore, the purchase order in combination with the framework agreement will be evaluated to determine whether the criteria in 4.2.30.20 are met and a contract exists.

4.2.33.30   An entity needs to consider whether the pricing of individual purchase orders is inter-related and:
- the purchase orders need to be combined (see 4.2.40); or
- there are implicit or explicit promises in the framework agreement – i.e. whether it includes a material right (see 4.2.330), or any variable consideration (see 4.2.100) – e.g. a rebate or discount.

4.2.35   Term of the contract

4.2.35.10   IFRS 15 is applied to the contractual period in which the parties to the contract have presently enforceable rights and obligations. [*IFRS 15.11*]

4.2.35.20   A contract does not exist if each party to the contract has a unilateral enforceable right to terminate a wholly unperformed contract without compensating the other party (or parties). A contract is 'wholly unperformed' if both of the following criteria are met:
- the entity has not yet transferred any promised goods or services to the customer; and
- the entity has not yet received, and is not yet entitled to receive, any consideration in exchange for promised goods or services. [*IFRS 15.12*]

4.2.35.30   If a contract can be renewed or cancelled by either party at discrete points in time without significant penalty, then an entity accounts for its rights and obligations as a separate contract for the period during which the contract cannot be cancelled by either party.

4.2.35.40   If only the customer has the right to terminate the contract without penalty and the entity is otherwise obliged to continue to perform until the end of a specified period, then the contract is evaluated to determine whether the option gives the customer a material right (see 4.2.330).

4.2.35.45   If an entity enters into a month-to-month contract that automatically renews and is cancellable by either party without penalty, then it cannot automatically assume that a contract period extends beyond the current period (e.g. the current month) because the contract is no different from a contract that requires the parties to actively elect to renew the contract each period (e.g. place a new order, sign a new contract).

4.2.35.50   If a contract can be terminated by compensating the other party and the right to compensation is considered substantive, then its duration is either the specified period or the period up to the point at which the contract can be terminated without compensating the other party. In making the assessment of whether the right to compensation is substantive, an entity considers all relevant factors, including legal enforceability of the right to compensation on termination. If an entity has a past practice of not enforcing a termination penalty and that practice changes the legally enforceable rights and obligations, then this could affect the contractual term. If a contract can be terminated by either party without substantive compensation, then its term does not extend beyond the goods and services already provided.

4.2.35.60   A payment to compensate the other party on termination is any amount (or other transfer of value – e.g. equity instruments) other than a payment due as a result of goods or services transferred up to the termination date. It is not restricted only to payments explicitly characterised as termination penalties.

4.2.35.70   It appears that an economic incentive to renew a contract is not relevant when evaluating the term of the contract because it does not give rise to enforceable rights or obligations.

EXAMPLE 1 – TERM OF THE CONTRACT – ECONOMIC INCENTIVE

4.2.35.80   Company X enters into a month-to-month wireless contract with Customer Y that includes a handset and voice and data services. Y makes no up-front payment for the handset, but will pay the stand-alone selling price of the handset through monthly instalments over a 12-month period. If Y fails to renew the monthly wireless contract, then the remaining balance for the handset becomes immediately due.

4.2.35.90   In addition, Y pays a monthly service fee for the voice and data services, which represents its stand-alone selling price. The contract does not include any payments other than for the handset and the services.

4.2.35.100   In assessing the enforceability of the contract, X considers the amounts due if Y decides not to renew at the end of Month 1. X observes that the requirement to repay the remaining balance for the handset when the service contract is not renewed is an economic incentive for Y to renew. We believe that this economic incentive is not a substantive termination penalty, but instead is a repayment of a loan for goods already transferred.

4.2.35.110   Because X cannot enforce the service contract for a period longer than one month, X concludes that the contract term is one month.

4.2.40 Combining contracts

4.2.40.10   Contracts entered into at or near the same time with the same customer (or related parties – see 5.5.30) are combined if one or more of the following criteria are met:
- the contracts are negotiated as a package with a single commercial objective;
- the consideration in one contract depends on the price or performance of the other contract; or
- the goods or services promised in the contracts (or some of the goods or services promised in each of the contracts) are a single performance obligation (see 4.2.60.10). [*IFRS 15.17*]

4.2.50 Portfolio approach

4.2.50.10   IFRS 15 specifies the accounting for an individual contract with a customer. However, as a practical expedient, an entity may apply IFRS 15 to a portfolio of contracts (or performance obligations) with similar characteristics if the entity reasonably expects that the financial statement effects of applying the standard to the portfolio or to individual contracts (or performance obligations) within that portfolio would not be materially different. [*IFRS 15.4*]

4.2.60 STEP 2: IDENTIFY THE PERFORMANCE OBLIGATIONS IN THE CONTRACT

4.2.60.10   A 'performance obligation' is the unit of account for revenue recognition. An entity assesses the goods or services promised in a contract with a customer and identifies as a performance obligation either:
- a good or service (or a bundle of goods or services) that is distinct (see 4.2.70); or
- a series of distinct goods or services that are substantially the same and that have the same pattern of transfer to the customer (see 4.2.80). [*IFRS 15.22*]

4.2.60.20   Promises to transfer a good or service can be explicitly stated in the contract, or be implicit based on established business practices or published policies that create a valid expectation that the entity will transfer the good or service to the customer. [*IFRS 15.24*]

4.2.70 Distinct goods or services

4.2.70.10   A single contract may contain promises to deliver to the customer more than one good or service. At contract inception, an entity assesses the goods or services explicitly or implicitly promised in a contract and identifies as a performance obligation each promise to transfer a distinct good or service. [*IFRS 15.22(a)*]

4.2.70.20   A good or service that is promised in a contract is 'distinct' if both of the following criteria are met.
- *Criterion 1:* The customer can benefit from the good or service either on its own or together with other resources that are 'readily available' to the customer.
- *Criterion 2:* The entity's promise to transfer the good or service to the customer is separately identifiable from other promises in the contract. [*IFRS 15.27*]

4.2.70.30   The customer can benefit from the good or service if it can be used, consumed, sold for an amount other than scrap value, or otherwise held in a way that generates economic benefits. If a good or service is regularly sold separately, then this is an indicator that the customer can benefit from a good or service on its own. [*IFRS 15.28*]

4.2.70.40   'Readily available' resources are goods or services that are sold separately by the entity or by another entity, or resources that the customer has already obtained from the entity – e.g. a good or service delivered up-front – or from other transactions or events. [*IFRS 15.28*]

4.2.70.50   The objective when assessing whether an entity's promises to transfer goods or services are distinct within the context of the contract is to determine whether the nature of the entity's overall promise in the contract is to transfer a combined item or items to which the promised goods or services are inputs. The following factors suggest that two or more promises to transfer goods or services are not 'separately identifiable'.
- The entity provides a significant service of integrating the good or service (or bundle of goods or services) into the bundle of goods or services for which the customer has contracted. This occurs when the entity is using the goods or services as inputs to produce or deliver the output or outputs specified by the customer. A combined output (or outputs) might include more than one phase, element or unit.
- One or more of the goods or services significantly modifies or customises, or is significantly modified or customised by, one or more of the other goods or services promised in the contract.
- The goods or services are highly interdependent or highly inter-related, such that each of the goods or services is significantly affected by one or more of the other goods or services. In making this assessment, an entity considers whether there is a transformative relationship between the two items in the process of fulfilling the contract, rather than merely whether one item, by its nature, depends on the other (i.e. whether there is a functional relationship). [*IFRS 15.29, BC116K*]

4.2.70.53   In evaluating whether goods or services are separately identifiable, an entity considers whether the risks that it assumes to fulfil its obligations to transfer goods or services are inseparable. The IFRS Interpretations Committee discussed a scenario in which an entity enters into a contract with a customer to transfer a plot of land and to construct a building on that plot of land. The Committee noted that in determining whether there is a significant service of integrating the land and the building into a combined output, an entity considers whether the risks that it assumes in transferring the land to the customer are inseparable from the risks that it assumes in constructing the building – i.e. whether its performance obligations would be any different if it did not also transfer the land and vice versa. [*IFRS 15.BC105, BC116J–BC116K, IU 18-03*]

4.2.70.54   The Committee also noted that in determining whether the land and the building are highly interdependent or highly inter-related, the entity considers whether it would be able to fulfil its promise to transfer the land if the customer used another party to construct the building and whether it would be able to fulfil its promise to construct the building if the customer purchased the land from another party. If this is the case, then the risks that the entity assumes to fulfil each promise are separable and the transfer of the land and construction of the building are distinct performance obligations. [*IFRS 15.BC105, BC116J–BC116K, IU 18-03*]

4.2.70.55   IFRS 15 does not include a hierarchy or weighting of the indicators of whether a good or service is separately identifiable from other promised goods or services within the context of the contract. An entity evaluates the specific facts and circumstances of the contract to determine how much emphasis to place on each indicator. Certain indicators may provide more compelling evidence than others in different scenarios or types of contracts. For example, factors such as the degree of customisation, complexity, customer's motivation for purchasing goods or services, contractual restrictions and the functionality of individual goods or services may have differing effects on the distinct analysis for different types of contracts. In addition, the relative strength of an indicator, in light of the specific facts and circumstances of a contract, may lead an entity to conclude that two or more promised goods or services are not separable from each other within the context of the contract. This may occur even if other indicators might suggest separation.

EXAMPLE 2A – SINGLE PERFORMANCE OBLIGATION

4.2.70.60   Company X enters into a contract to design and build a hospital. X is responsible for the overall management of the project and identifies various promised goods and services, including engineering, site clearance, foundation, procurement, construction of the structure, piping and wiring, installation of equipment, and finishing.

4.2.70.70   X identifies that many of the goods and services to be provided meet Criterion 1 in 4.2.70.20. This is because the customer could benefit from the goods or services on their own – each construction material is sold separately by numerous suppliers or could be resold for more than scrap value by the customer – or together with other readily available resources such as additional materials or the services of another contractor.

4.2.70.80   However, X determines that Criterion 2 in 4.2.70.20 is not met because it provides a significant service of integrating the goods and services to produce the output (the hospital) for which the customer has contracted.

4.2.70.90   As a result, because Criterion 2 is not met, X accounts for the contract as a single performance obligation.

EXAMPLE 2B – MULTIPLE PERFORMANCE OBLIGATIONS

4.2.70.100   Company Y enters into a contract to sell a machine to Customer C and provide a standard installation service. The installation service is also offered by third party providers.

4.2.70.110   Y determines that Criterion 1 in 4.2.70.20 is met for the machine because C can use it with a readily available resource (services from a third party installer). It is also met for the installation service because the service can be used with a resource owned by C (the machine).

4.2.70.120   Y further considers the principle and the factors in 4.2.70.50 and determines that Criterion 2 in 4.2.70.20 is met for the machine and installation service because:

> - Y does not provide a significant integration service that would combine the machine with the installation services to produce a combined output;
> - the installation service does not significantly customise or modify the machine; and
> - the installation service and the machine do not each significantly affect the other because they are not highly interdependent or highly inter-related.
>
> 4.2.70.130   As a result, because both criteria are met, Y accounts for the machine and installation as separate performance obligations.

4.2.70.140   If a promised good or service is not distinct, then it is combined with other promised goods or services in the contract until the entity identifies a bundle of goods or services that is distinct. [*IFRS 15.30*]

4.2.70.150   The performance of tasks to fulfil a contract that do not transfer goods or services to the customer are not performance obligations – e.g. administrative tasks to set up a contract. [*IFRS 15.25*]

4.2.80   Series of distinct goods or services

4.2.80.10   As an exception to the general requirement to treat distinct goods or services as a performance obligation, an entity treats a series of distinct goods or services as a single performance obligation if the goods and services are substantially the same and both of the following criteria are met:
- each distinct good or service is a performance obligation satisfied over time; and
- the same method is used to measure progress towards satisfaction of each distinct good or service in the series. [*IFRS 15.22(b), 23*]

4.2.80.20   If the series guidance requirements are met for a group of goods or services, then the series is treated as a single performance obligation – i.e. the series guidance is not optional. To apply the series guidance, it is not necessary for the goods to be delivered or services performed consecutively over the contract period. There may be a gap or an overlap in delivery or performance, and this does not affect the assessment of whether the series guidance applies.

4.2.80.30   To determine whether the series guidance applies, an entity first determines the nature of its promise. For example, if the nature of the promise is to deliver a specified quantity of a good or service, then the evaluation considers whether each good or service is distinct and substantially the same. Conversely, if the nature of the entity's promise is to stand ready or to provide a single service for a period of time (i.e. there is not a specified quantity to be delivered), then the evaluation would probably focus on whether each time increment, rather than the underlying activities, is distinct and substantially the same.

EXAMPLE 3 – SERIES OF DISTINCT SERVICES TREATED AS SINGLE PERFORMANCE OBLIGATION

> 4.2.80.40   Company X enters into a two-year service contract with a customer to provide a weekly cleaning service for a fixed fee of 100 per week.

4.2.80.50   X determines that its performance of the cleaning services is satisfied over time, because the customer consumes and receives the benefit from the services as they are provided – i.e. the customer benefits from cleaning services as X performs (see 4.2.220).

4.2.80.60   X determines that each increment of its services – e.g. month, day etc – is distinct, because the customer benefits from that period of service on its own and each increment of service is separable from those preceding and following it – i.e. one service period does not significantly affect, modify or customise another.

4.2.80.70   X determines that its contract with the customer is a single performance obligation to provide two years of cleaning services because:
- services are substantially the same;
- each of the distinct increments of services is satisfied over time; and
- a consistent measure of progress to recognise revenue is used.

4.2.90   STEP 3: DETERMINE THE TRANSACTION PRICE

4.2.90.10   The 'transaction price' is the amount of consideration to which an entity expects to be entitled in exchange for transferring goods or services to a customer. The transaction price may include amounts that are not paid by the customer. For example, a healthcare company may include amounts to be received from the patient, insurance companies and government organisations in determining the transaction price. In another example, a retailer may include in the transaction price the amounts received from the manufacturer as a result of coupons or rebates issued by the manufacturer directly to the end customer. [*IFRS 15.47, BC187*]

4.2.90.13   The transaction price excludes amounts collected on behalf of third parties – e.g. certain sales taxes (see 4.2.345). [*IFRS 15.47*]

4.2.90.15   An entity estimates the transaction price at contract inception, including any variable consideration, and updates the estimate each reporting period for any changes in circumstances. When determining the transaction price, an entity assumes that the goods or services will be transferred to the customer based on the terms of the existing contract, and does not take into consideration the possibility of a contract being cancelled, renewed or modified. [*IFRS 15.49*]

4.2.90.20   An exception to the principles of measurement of the transaction price exists for sales- and usage-based royalties arising from licences of intellectual property (see 4.2.460). [*IFRS 15.58*]

4.2.90.30   In determining the transaction price, an entity considers the effect of the following:
- variable consideration, including constraining estimates of variable consideration (see 4.2.100);
- the time value of money (see 4.2.130);
- consideration payable to the customer (see 4.2.140); and
- non-cash consideration (see 4.2.150). [*IFRS 15.48*]

4.2.100   **Variable consideration**

4.2.100.10   If the consideration promised in a contract includes a variable amount, then an entity estimates the amount of consideration to which it will be entitled in exchange for transferring the promised goods or services to a customer. Examples of variable consideration include discounts, rebates, refunds, credits, early settlement discounts, price concessions, incentives, performance bonuses, penalties, rights of return and consideration contingent on the occurrence or non-occurrence of a future event – e.g. minimum rental guarantees in a sale of an apartment building in which consideration may vary based on the actual level of rentals. [*IFRS 15.50–51*]

4.2.100.20   Variable consideration may be explicitly identified in the contract. In addition, consideration is variable if either of the following circumstances exists:
- the customer has a valid expectation arising from an entity's customary business practices, published policies or specific statements that the entity will accept an amount of consideration that is less than the price stated in the contract – i.e. the contract contains an implicit price concession, or the entity has a history of providing price concessions or price support to its customers; or
- other facts and circumstances indicate that the entity's intention, when entering into the contract with the customer, was to offer a price concession to the customer. [*IFRS 15.52, BC190–BC194*]

4.2.100.25   In some contracts, the actual quantity delivered may be confirmed after control transfers to the customer (see 4.2.210). For example, a mining entity transfers control of copper concentrate to a customer and then the customer determines the actual quantity of copper delivered after processing the concentrate. The final amount paid by the customer is based on this actual quantity. It appears that such arrangements, in which the transaction price may vary depending on the quantity subject to confirmation after delivery, represent variable consideration under IFRS 15.

4.2.100.27   Some contracts may contain provisional pricing features under which the transaction price is based on the spot rate of the commodity at the payment due date (see Example 14 in chapter 7.2). This may be later than the date at which the performance obligation is satisfied. In contrast with the scenarios discussed in 4.2.100.25, variability arising solely from changes in the market price after control transfers is not subject to the variable consideration guidance in IFRS 15. This is because at the delivery date a receivable already exists and it is in the scope of IFRS 9. [*IASBU 12-15*]

4.2.100.30   When an entity enters into a contract with a customer for an undefined quantity of output at a fixed contractual rate per unit of output, the consideration may be variable. In some cases there may be substantive contractual terms that indicate that a portion of the consideration is fixed – e.g. contractual minimums. For contracts with undefined quantities, it is important to appropriately evaluate the entity's underlying promise to determine how the variability created by the unknown quantity should be treated under IFRS 15. For example, the entity's underlying promise could be a series of distinct goods or services (see 4.2.80), a stand-ready obligation or an obligation to provide the specified goods or services. Unknown quantities could also represent customer options for which the entity will need to consider whether a material right exists (see 4.2.330).

4.2.100.40   Different structures of discounts and rebates may have a different effect on the transaction price. For example, some agreements provide a discount or rebate that applies to all purchases made under the agreement – i.e. the discount or rebate applies on a retrospective basis once a volume threshold is met. In other cases, the discounted purchase price may apply only to future purchases once a minimum volume threshold has been met.

4.2.100.50   If a discount applies retrospectively to all purchases under the contract once the threshold is achieved, then the discount represents variable consideration. In this case, the entity estimates the volumes to be purchased and the resulting discount in determining the transaction price and updates that estimate throughout the term of the contract. However, if a tiered pricing structure provides discounts for future purchases only after volume thresholds are met, then the entity evaluates the arrangement to determine whether the arrangement conveys a material right to the customer (see 4.2.330). If a material right exists, then this is a separate performance obligation, to which the entity allocates a portion of the transaction price. If a material right does not exist, then there are no accounting implications for the transactions completed before the volume threshold is met, and purchases after the threshold has been met are accounted for at the discounted price.

4.2.100.60   If a contract is denominated in a foreign currency, then changes in exchange rates may affect the amount of revenue recognised by an entity in its functional currency. This does not constitute variable consideration for the purpose of applying IFRS 15 because the variability relates to the form of the consideration (i.e. the currency) and not to other factors, and an entity applies the guidance on foreign currency transactions and translation (see chapter 2.7). [*IFRS 15.68*]

4.2.105   *Estimating the amount of variable consideration*

4.2.105.10   Variable consideration is estimated using whichever of the following methods the entity expects to better predict the amount of consideration to which it will be entitled.
- *Expected value:* The sum of the probability-weighted amounts in a range of possible amounts. An expected value may be an appropriate estimate of the amount of variable consideration if an entity has a large number of contracts with similar characteristics.
- *Most likely amount:* The single most likely amount in a range of possible consideration amounts. The most likely amount may be an appropriate estimate of the amount of variable consideration if the contract has only two possible outcomes. [*IFRS 15.53*]

4.2.105.20   An entity applies one estimation method consistently throughout the contract and to similar types of contracts when estimating the effect of an uncertainty on an amount of variable consideration to which it will be entitled. [*IFRS 15.54, BC195*]

4.2.105.30   An entity may use a group of similar transactions as a source of evidence when estimating variable consideration, particularly under the expected value method. The estimates using the expected value method are generally made at the contract level, not at the portfolio level. Therefore, using a portfolio of data as a source of evidence in this way is not itself an application of the portfolio approach (see 4.2.50). The entity needs to use judgement to determine whether the number of similar transactions is sufficient to develop an expected value that is the best estimate of the transaction price for the contract and whether 'the constraint' (see 4.2.110) should be applied. An entity also uses judgement to determine whether:
- its contracts with customers are sufficiently similar;

- the contracts with customers from which the expected value is derived are expected to remain consistent with subsequent contracts; and
- the volume of similar contracts is sufficient to develop an expected value.

4.2.105.40   If an entity uses a portfolio of data to estimate variable consideration, then the transaction price may be an amount that is not a possible outcome for an individual contract but that is still representative of the expected transaction price.

EXAMPLE 4 – ESTIMATING VARIABLE CONSIDERATION – USING PORTFOLIO OF DATA

4.2.105.50   Company M enters into a large number of similar contracts whose terms include a fixed fee and a performance bonus. Depending on the outcome of each contract, M either will receive a bonus of 100 or will not receive any bonus. Based on its historical experience, M expects to receive a bonus of 100 in 60% of the contracts. M determines that the number of similar transactions is sufficient to develop an expected value that is the best estimate of the transaction price.

4.2.105.60   To estimate the transaction price for future individual contracts of this nature, M considers its historical experience and estimates that the expected value of the bonus is 60.

4.2.105.70   In this example, M determines that the estimated expected value of the bonus of 60 does not need to be constrained (see 4.2.105.30).

4.2.110   *Constraining estimates of variable consideration*

4.2.110.10   An entity includes estimates of variable consideration in the transaction price only to the extent that it is 'highly probable' that a significant reversal in the amount of cumulative revenue recognised will not occur when the uncertainty associated with the variable consideration is resolved. [*IFRS 15.56*]

4.2.110.20   To assess whether – and to what extent – the 'constraint' should be applied, entities consider both:
- the likelihood of a revenue reversal arising from an uncertain future event; and
- the potential magnitude of the revenue reversal when the uncertainty related to the variable consideration has been resolved. [*IFRS 15.57*]

4.2.110.30   When constraining its estimate of variable consideration, an entity assesses the potential magnitude of a significant revenue reversal relative to the cumulative revenue recognised – i.e. for both variable and fixed consideration, rather than a reversal of only the variable consideration. The assessment of magnitude is relative to the transaction price for the contract, rather than the amount allocated to the specific performance obligation.

4.2.110.40   Factors indicating that including an estimate of variable consideration in the transaction price could result in a significant revenue reversal include, but are not limited to, the following:

- the amount of consideration is highly susceptible to factors outside the entity's influence, including volatility in a market, weather conditions and/or a high risk of obsolescence of the promised good or service;
- the uncertainty about the amount of consideration is not expected to be resolved for a long period of time;
- the entity's experience (or other evidence) with similar types of contracts is limited;
- the entity has a practice of either offering a broad range of price concessions or changing the payment terms and conditions of similar contracts in similar circumstances; and
- the contract has a large number and broad range of possible consideration amounts. [*IFRS 15.57*]

4.2.110.50   Depending on the circumstances, an entity may include none, some or all of the variable consideration in the transaction price. [*IFRS 15.56*]

EXAMPLE 5 – CONSTRAINING REVENUE AMOUNT

4.2.110.60   Investment Manager M enters into a two-year contract with a customer, a non-registered investment partnership (Fund), to provide investment management services. Fund's investment objective is to invest in equity instruments issued by large listed companies.

4.2.110.70   For providing the investment management services, M receives:
- a quarterly management fee of 2% per quarter for assets under management – the assets used to determine the management fee are the fair value of the net assets at the end of the most recent quarter; and
- a performance-based incentive fee of 20% of the fund's return in excess of an observable market index over the contract period.

4.2.110.80   M determines that the contract includes a single performance obligation that is satisfied over time.

4.2.110.90   M identifies that both the management fee and the performance fee are variable consideration.

4.2.110.100   Before including the estimates of consideration in the transaction price, M considers whether the constraint should be applied to either the management fee or the performance fee.

4.2.110.110   At the end of year 1, M makes the following assessment of whether any portion of the consideration is constrained.
- *Management fee:* M determines that the cumulative amount of consideration from the management fee to which it is entitled at the end of the year is not constrained, because it is calculated based on asset values at the end of each quarter; therefore, once the quarter finishes the consideration for the quarter is known. M determines that it can allocate the entire amount of the fees to the

completed quarters, because the fee relates specifically to the distinct services provided for those quarters (see 4.2.190.30).

- *Performance fee:* M determines that the full amount of the performance fee is constrained and therefore excluded from the transaction price because:
  - the performance fee has a high variability of possible consideration amounts and the magnitude of any downward adjustment could be significant;
  - although M has experience with similar contracts, that experience is not predictive of the outcome of the current contract because the amount of consideration is highly susceptible to volatility in the market based on the nature of the assets under management; and
  - there is a large number of possible outcomes.

4.2.110.120   As a result, M determines that the revenue recognised during the year is limited to the quarterly management fees.

4.2.120   *Reassessment of variable consideration*

4.2.120.10   At each reporting date, an entity updates the estimated transaction price – including its assessment of whether an estimate of variable consideration is constrained – for the circumstances present at the reporting date and the changes in circumstances that occurred during the reporting period. [*IFRS 15.59*]

4.2.130   **Time value of money**

4.2.130.10   To estimate the transaction price in a contract, an entity adjusts the promised amount of consideration for the time value of money if the contract contains a significant financing component. [*IFRS 15.60*]

4.2.130.20   The objective when adjusting the promised amount of consideration in a contract to reflect the time value of money is for an entity to recognise revenue at an amount that reflects what the cash selling price would have been if the customer had paid cash for the promised goods or services when they are transferred to the customer. [*IFRS 15.61*]

4.2.130.30   The time value of money is reflected in the entity's estimate of the transaction price if the contract has a significant financing component. An entity considers all relevant factors when determining if a significant financing component exists, including:
- the difference, if any, between the amount of promised consideration and the cash selling price of the goods or services; and
- the combined effect of the length of time between the transfer of the goods or services to the customer and payment, and the prevailing interest rates in the relevant market. [*IFRS 15.61*]

4.2.130.40   When the consideration to be received for a good or service with extended payment terms is the same as the cash selling price, the implied interest rate is zero. However, a significant financing component may still exist. For example, retailers sometimes offer a promotional incentive that allows customers to buy items such as furniture and pay the cash selling price two years after delivery. Judgement is required to evaluate whether in these circumstances an entity is offering a discount or other promotional incentive for customers who pay the cash selling price at the end of the promotional period equal to the financing charge that would otherwise have been charged in exchange for financing the purchase.

4.2.130.45   Under some long-term contracts for which revenue is recognised over time, the payment of the promised consideration may be scheduled for part-way through the performance period – e.g. under a 26-month construction contract the promised consideration is to be paid in full at the end of Month 13. It appears that in these cases, a significant financing component may exist. We believe that an entity should assess the contract as a whole and exercise judgement in determining whether the financing component is significant.

4.2.130.50   A contract with a customer does not include a significant financing component if:
- the timing of payment for, or transfer of, goods or services to a customer is at the discretion of the customer – e.g. a prepaid phone card or customer loyalty point;
- a substantial portion of the consideration is variable and the amount or timing of that consideration is not substantially within the customer's or entity's control – e.g. a transaction whose consideration is a sales-based royalty; or
- the difference between the amount of promised consideration and the cash selling price of the promised goods or services arises for reasons other than the provision of finance – e.g. protection from the counterparty not completing its obligations under the contract. [*IFRS 15.62*]

4.2.130.60   As a practical expedient, an entity is not required to reflect the time value of money in its estimate of the transaction price if it expects at contract inception that the period between customer payment and the transfer of goods or services will not exceed one year. [*IFRS 15.63*]

4.2.130.70   In a contract with two or more performance obligations, identifying the period between customer payment and the transfer of goods or services may present challenges, especially when the performance obligations are satisfied at different points in time and consideration is paid over time or all at once. In some contracts that include consideration paid over time, one performance obligation is completed in the early stages of a contract, whereas a second performance obligation continues for an extended period of time. In these cases, the entity generally allocates each payment received to both performance obligations in the contract on a pro rata basis to calculate the financing component and determine whether the practical expedient applies (rather than allocating payments to a single performance obligation until it has been fully paid, as would be the case with a FIFO allocation).

4.2.130.80   In other contracts with two or more performance obligations, consideration includes an up-front payment and performance obligations are completed consecutively over time. An entity evaluates all relevant evidence, including termination clauses, to determine whether it is appropriate for an up-front cash payment to be allocated to the first performance obligation when determining whether the practical expedient can be applied at the contract level.

4.2.130.90   If a contract includes a significant financing component, then an entity uses the discount rate that would be reflected in a separate financing transaction between it and the customer at inception of the contract. This discount rate is not generally updated for a change in circumstances. [*IFRS 15.64*]

4.2.130.100   The financing component is recognised as interest expense (when the customer pays in advance) or interest income (when the customer pays in arrears). [*IFRS 15.65*]

EXAMPLE 6A – SIGNIFICANT FINANCING COMPONENT – TWO-YEAR CONTRACT

4.2.130.110   Company K enters into a contract with a customer to construct and deliver a piece of equipment. K determines that the contract contains a single performance obligation that is satisfied at a point in time when the equipment is delivered to the customer. Construction is expected to take two years.

4.2.130.120   K and the customer agree consideration of 80, which is payable and paid on the date the contract is signed.

4.2.130.130   K considers the terms of the sale and determines that the contract includes a significant financing component because:
- there is a significant period between payment and delivery of the asset;
- the asset is regularly sold at a higher price; and
- there is no evidence to suggest the advance is for another reason.

4.2.130.140   K determines the discount rate, based on its credit characteristics, to be 12%.

4.2.130.150   Therefore, to reflect the financing that it is receiving from the advance payment, K recognises interest expense of 20 in the construction period and revenue of 100 (80 x 1.12^2) on the delivery date.

4.2.130.160   If after contract inception there is a change in the expected period between customer payment and the transfer of goods or services, then it appears that the transaction price – i.e. the promised amount of consideration adjusted for the significant financing component – should not be revised for the effect of the change in the expected period between payment and performance. Instead, an entity should revise the period over which it recognises the difference between the transaction price and the promised consideration as interest. This is because the cash selling price of the goods or services is agreed by the parties at contract inception and does not vary in response to changes in the estimated timing of the transfer of the goods or services. If the entity had used the revised timing at the inception of the contract, then this would have changed either the amount of promised consideration or the implied interest rate.

EXAMPLE 6B – SIGNIFICANT FINANCING COMPONENT – CHANGE IN EXPECTED COMPLETION DATE

4.2.130.170   Modifying Example 6A, after year 1 Company K determines that the construction will take three rather than two years.

4.2.130.180   We believe that K should revise the period over which it recognises the difference between the transaction price and the promised consideration as interest expense. K should not revise the transaction price of 100.

4.2.140   Consideration payable to a customer

4.2.140.10   Consideration payable to a customer includes cash amounts that an entity pays or expects to pay to the customer, or to other parties that purchase the entity's goods or services from the customer. Consideration payable also includes credit or other items – e.g. a coupon or voucher – that can be applied against amounts owed to the entity, or to other parties that purchase the entity's goods or services from the customer. [*IFRS 15.70*]

4.2.140.20   Payments made to a customer that are not specified in the contract may still represent consideration payable to a customer. The determination of how broadly payments within a distribution chain should be evaluated requires judgement. An entity need not always identify and assess all amounts ever paid to a customer to determine if they represent consideration payable to a customer. Consideration payable to a customer includes amounts paid to a customer's customer – i.e. amounts paid to end customers in a direct distribution chain. However, in some cases an entity may conclude that it is appropriate to apply the guidance more broadly – i.e. to amounts paid outside the direct distribution chain. Judgement is required to evaluate a specific fact pattern to determine whether a payment to a party outside a direct distribution chain is treated as consideration payable to a customer. [*IFRS 15.70, BC92, BC255*]

EXAMPLE 7 – CONSIDERATION PAYABLE TO A CUSTOMER

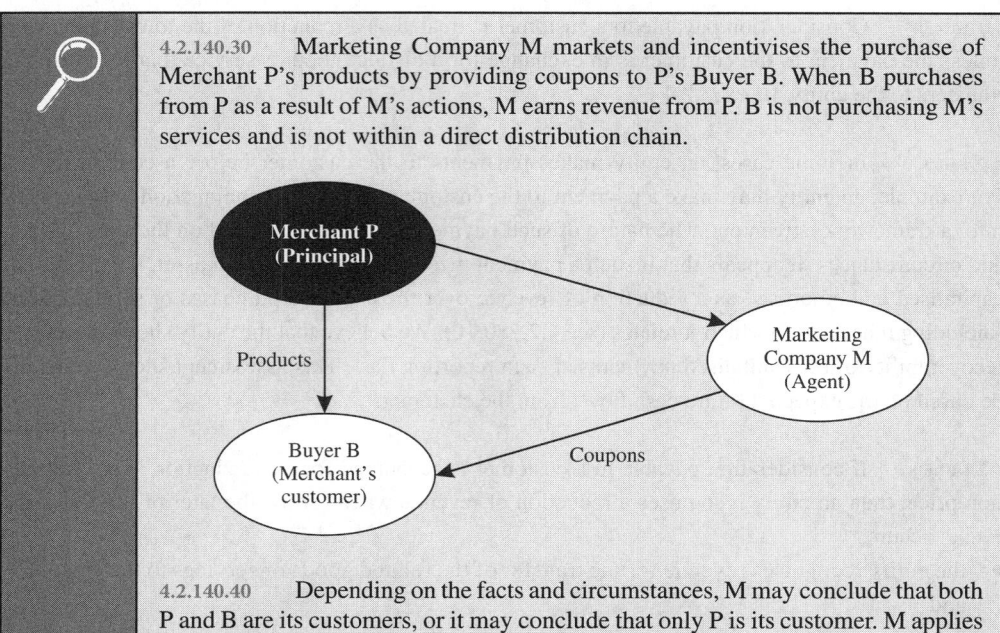

4.2.140.30   Marketing Company M markets and incentivises the purchase of Merchant P's products by providing coupons to P's Buyer B. When B purchases from P as a result of M's actions, M earns revenue from P. B is not purchasing M's services and is not within a direct distribution chain.

4.2.140.40   Depending on the facts and circumstances, M may conclude that both P and B are its customers, or it may conclude that only P is its customer. M applies judgement in making this assessment (see 4.2.10.10–20).

4.2.140.45   The following flowchart highlights the key considerations when determining the accounting for the consideration payable to a customer. [*IFRS 15.70–72*]

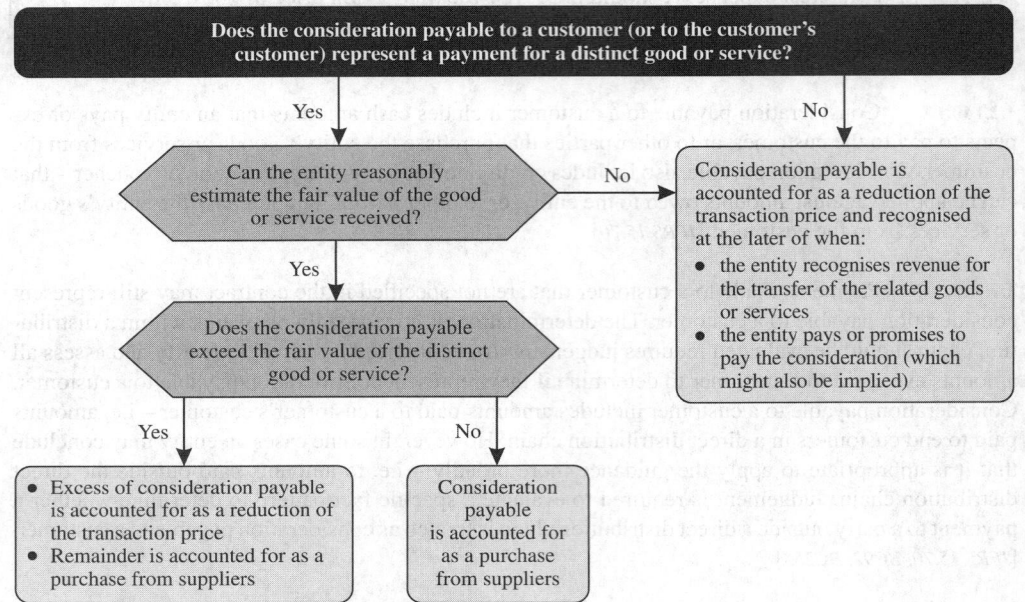

4.2.140.50   Consideration payable to a customer is treated as a reduction of the transaction price, unless the payment to the customer is in exchange for a distinct good or service that the customer transfers to the entity. [*IFRS 15.70*]

4.2.140.55   In some cases, an entity makes payments to the customer before a contract exists. For example, an entity may make a payment to the customer under, or in conjunction with entering into, a framework agreement. The nature of such payments is evaluated based on the specific facts and circumstances. It appears that if such a payment meets the definition of an asset, then it may be capitalised and amortised as a reduction of revenue over the expected purchases or service period (including renewals) to which it relates (see 4.2.280.10). We believe that the entity should assess the recoverability of the capitalised payments at each reporting date. This assessment should generally be based on the expected future cash flows from the customer.

4.2.140.60   If consideration payable to a customer is accounted for as a reduction in the transaction price, then an entity recognises a reduction of revenue when (or as) the later of the following events occurs:

- the entity recognises revenue for the transfer of the related goods or services to the customer; and
- the entity pays or promises to pay the consideration; this promise might be implied by the entity's customary business practices. [*IFRS 15.72*]

4.2.140.70   If the consideration payable to the customer is a payment for a distinct good or service from the customer, then the entity accounts for it in the same way as it accounts for other purchases from suppliers. However, if the consideration payable exceeds the fair value of the distinct goods or services that the entity receives from the customer, then the excess is accounted for as a reduction of the transaction price. If the fair value of the good or service received from the customer cannot be reasonably estimated, then all of the consideration payable to the customer is accounted for as a reduction of the transaction price. [*IFRS 15.71*]

4.2.145   *Slotting fees*

4.2.145.10   Slotting fees are payments made by an entity to a retailer for product placement in the retailer's store. Judgement is required to determine whether slotting fees are:
- *paid in exchange for a distinct good or service that it receives from the customer:* these are recognised as a purchase from the supplier – i.e. as a prepayment or an expense; or
- *sales incentives granted by the entity:* these are recognised as a reduction of the transaction price.

4.2.145.20   When making this judgement, an entity carefully considers its particular facts and circumstances.

4.2.150   Non-cash consideration

4.2.150.10   When a customer promises consideration in a form other than cash – i.e. non-cash consideration – it is measured at fair value (see chapter 2.4). If a reasonable estimate of fair value cannot be made, then the estimated selling price of the promised goods or services is used for reference. [*IFRS 15.66–67*]

4.2.150.15   Estimates of the fair value of non-cash consideration may vary. Although this may be due to the occurrence or non-occurrence of a future event, it can also vary due to the form of consideration – e.g. variations due to changes in the price per share if the non-cash consideration is an equity instrument. If the fair value of non-cash consideration varies for reasons other than the form of consideration, then those changes are reflected in the transaction price and are subject to the guidance on constraining variable consideration (see 4.2.110). [*IFRS 15.68*]

4.2.150.20   If a customer contributes goods or services – e.g. materials, equipment or labour – to facilitate an entity's fulfilment of the contract, then the entity assesses whether it obtains control of these contributed goods or services. If it does, then the entity accounts for the contributed goods or services as non-cash consideration received from the customer. [*IFRS 15.69*]

4.2.160   STEP 4: ALLOCATE THE TRANSACTION PRICE TO THE PERFORMANCE OBLIGATIONS IN THE CONTRACT

4.2.160.10   The objective when allocating the transaction price is for an entity to allocate the transaction price to each performance obligation in an amount of consideration to which the entity expects to be entitled in exchange for transferring the promised goods or services to the customer. [*IFRS 15.73*]

4.2.160.20   An entity generally allocates the transaction price to each performance obligation on a relative stand-alone selling price basis. Discounts and variable consideration are allocated on a different basis when specific criteria are met (see 4.2.190). [*IFRS 15.74*]

4.2.160.30   For a performance obligation that includes a series of distinct goods or services (see 4.2.80), the transaction price can be allocated to the individual distinct goods or services underlying the performance obligation. [*IFRS 15.75*]

4.2.170   Estimating the stand-alone selling price

4.2.170.10   The 'stand-alone selling price' is the price at which an entity would sell a promised good or service separately to a customer. The best evidence of this price is an observable price from stand-alone sales of that good or service to customers with similar characteristics. A contractually stated price or list price may be the stand-alone selling price of that good or service, although this is not presumed to be the case. In some cases, an entity may sell a good or service separately for a range of observable prices. When this is the case and the stated contract price is within a sufficiently narrow range of observable selling prices, it may be appropriate to use a stated contract price as the estimated stand-alone selling price of a good or service. [*IFRS 15.77*]

4.2.170.20   When an observable selling price is not available, an entity considers all information that is reasonably available when estimating a stand-alone selling price – e.g. market conditions, entity-specific factors and information about the customer or class of customer. It also maximises the use of observable inputs and applies consistent estimation methods to estimate the stand-alone selling price of other goods or services with similar characteristics. [*IFRS 15.78*]

4.2.170.30   The standard describes three estimation methods. [*IFRS 15.79*]

Adjusted market assessment approach	Evaluate the market in which goods or services are sold and estimate the price that customers in the market would be willing to pay
Expected cost plus a margin approach	Forecast the expected costs of satisfying a performance obligation and then add an appropriate margin for that good or service
Residual approach (limited cases)	Subtract the sum of the observable stand-alone selling prices of other goods or services promised in the contract from the total transaction price

4.2.170.40   An entity may estimate the stand-alone selling price with reference to the total transaction price less the sum of the observable stand-alone selling prices of other goods or services promised in the contract. This is often referred to as the 'residual approach'. The residual approach can be applied only if the stand-alone selling price of one or more goods or services is highly variable or uncertain. This is the case if one of the following criteria is met:

- the entity sells the same good or service to different customers for a broad range of amounts; or
- the entity has not yet established a price for that good or service and the good or service has not previously been sold on a stand-alone basis. [*IFRS 15.79(c)*]

4.2.170.42   If one of the criteria in 4.2.170.40 is met and an entity estimates the stand-alone-selling price using the residual approach, then it appears that the total transaction price should include the estimated amount of any variable consideration before applying the constraint (see 4.2.110). This approach is consistent with the allocation objective because the estimated variable consideration is the amount of consideration to which the entity expects to be entitled.

4.2.170.45   The residual approach is an estimation technique, not an allocation method. Therefore, the timing of the transfer of control of each performance obligation – i.e. delivered vs undelivered goods or services – is not relevant when applying the residual approach. Additionally, it may be arbitrary if the residual approach results in no, or very little, consideration being allocated to a performance obligation. This is because a distinct good or service has value to the customer on a stand-alone basis. [*IFRS 15.BC273*]

4.2.170.50   If two or more goods or services in a contract have highly variable or uncertain stand-alone selling prices, then an entity may need to use a combination of methods to estimate the stand-alone selling prices of the performance obligations in the contract. For example, an entity may use:

- the residual approach to estimate the aggregate stand-alone selling prices for all of the promised goods or services with highly variable or uncertain stand-alone selling prices; and then
- another technique to estimate the stand-alone selling prices of the individual goods or services relative to the estimated aggregated stand-alone selling price that was determined by the residual approach. [*IFRS 15.80*]

4.2.180   Allocating the transaction price

4.2.180.10   At contract inception, the transaction price is generally allocated to each performance obligation on the basis of relative stand-alone selling prices. However, when specified criteria are met a discount or variable consideration may be allocated to one or more, but not all, performance obligations in the contract (see 4.2.190). [*IFRS 15.76*]

EXAMPLE 8 – ALLOCATING TRANSACTION PRICE

4.2.180.20   Company T enters into a one-year mobile contract in which a customer is provided with a phone and a data/calls/texts plan (the wireless plan) for a price of 35 per month. T has identified the phone and the wireless plan as separate performance obligations.

4.2.180.30   The phone can be purchased from the manufacturer's website for a price of 200 and T offers a 12-month plan without a phone that includes the same level of data/calls/texts for a price of 25 per month, providing observable evidence of stand-alone selling prices for both performance obligations.

4.2.180.40   Therefore, the transaction price of 420 (35 x 12 months) is allocated to the performance obligations based on their relative stand-alone selling prices as follows.

PERFORMANCE OBLIGATION	STAND-ALONE SELLING PRICES	SELLING PRICE RATIO	PRICE ALLOCATION
Phone	200	40%	168[1]
Wireless plan	300[2]	60%	252[3]
Total	500	100%	420

Notes
1.   Calculated as 420 x 40%.
2.   Calculated as 12 x 25.
3.   Calculated as 420 x 60%.

4.2.190   *Allocating discounts and variable consideration*

4.2.190.10   An entity allocates any discount proportionately to all performance obligations in the contract, except when there is objective evidence that the discount relates to one or more specific performance obligations. [*IFRS 15.81*]

4.2.190.20   This evidence exists, and a discount is allocated entirely to one or more, but not all, of the performance obligations, if the following criteria are met:
- the entity regularly sells each distinct good or service, or each bundle of distinct goods or services, in the contract on a stand-alone basis;
- the entity also regularly sells, on a stand-alone basis, a bundle (or bundles) of some of those distinct goods or services at a discount to the stand-alone selling prices of the goods or services in each bundle; and
- the discount attributable to each bundle of goods or services is substantially the same as the discount in the contract, and an analysis of the goods or services in each bundle provides observable evidence of the performance obligation(s) to which the entire discount in the contract belongs. [*IFRS 15.82*]

4.2.190.30   Variable consideration is allocated to only part of the contract if the terms of a variable payment relate directly to that part of the contract and allocating the variable payment to only that part of the contract is consistent with the allocation objective (see 4.2.160.10). Judgement is required based on careful consideration of all facts and circumstances to determine whether a variable payment relates directly to a specific performance obligation, especially when variation in the price is not directly linked to a change in effort – e.g. if pricing in the contract is based on a market price or an index. [*IFRS 15.85*]

EXAMPLE 9 – ALLOCATING VARIABLE CONSIDERATION – EACH SHIPMENT IS A DISTINCT
PERFORMANCE OBLIGATION

4.2.190.40   Mining company M enters into a contract to deliver 12 monthly shipments of gold ore to Customer C. Each shipment is priced based on the spot rate
for gold at the date of the shipment. M determines that each shipment is a distinct
performance obligation. M considers that the amount paid by C for a specific shipment of gold ore is independent of past or future shipments – i.e. the amount paid
is resolved entirely as a result of delivering one specific shipment. Therefore, M
concludes that the variability resulting from changes in market price relates directly
to each distinct monthly shipment and that allocating this variable consideration to
each shipment is consistent with the allocation objective.

4.2.190.50   In some cases, a contract that contains a series of distinct goods or services (see 4.2.80)
may contain both fixed and variable consideration. In these cases, variable consideration may be attributed to one or more, but not all, distinct goods or services promised in the series. This allows an
entity, in some cases, to attribute the reassessment of variable consideration to only the satisfied
portion of a performance obligation if that performance obligation is a series of distinct goods or
services. [*IFRS 15.BC285*]

EXAMPLE 10A – ALLOCATING VARIABLE CONSIDERATION – SERIES OF DISTINCT SERVICES

4.2.190.60   Company X is an electricity provider. X enters into a contract with
Customer C to supply electricity for one year on the following terms.
● The amount and the timing of the electricity supply are at C's discretion – i.e.
  the quantity is variable.
● The fee includes a fixed and a usage-based component.
● Fixed fee is 1,200 and it is payable in monthly instalments.
● Usage-based fee is a standard price of 1 per kWh and it is payable at the end of
  each month. The price per kWh is fixed for the whole contract period.

4.2.190.70   X determines that it has a stand-ready obligation to supply electricity
because the amount and timing of the supply is at C's discretion. X also determines
that this stand-ready obligation is a series because:
● each increment of X's services – e.g. month, day etc – is distinct and has the
  same pattern of transfer to the customer;
● the customer simultaneously receives and consumes the benefits of the electricity
  as it is provided (see 4.2.220); and
● X would use the same time-based method to measure its progress to transfer
  each increment of its service to the customer (see 4.2.80).

4.2.190.80   X allocates the fixed fee on a straight-line basis throughout the year
and the variable fee based on the daily/monthly electricity consumption. This is
because, under the terms of the contract, the variable payment relates to the amount

of electricity used during a period and therefore variable consideration is attributed only to the satisfied portion of a performance obligation. This allocation is consistent with the allocation objective (see 4.2.160.10). The pricing is consistent throughout the contract and the rates charged are consistent with X′s standard pricing practices with similar customers. [*IFRS 15.BC285*]

EXAMPLE 10B – ALLOCATING VARIABLE CONSIDERATION – MULTIPLE PERFORMANCE OBLIGATIONS

4.2.190.90   Company X enters into a contract with Customer C for two intellectual property licences (Licences A and B). X determines that the promises to transfer the licences represent two distinct performance obligations, each of which is satisfied at a point in time. The prices stated in the contract are as follows:
- Licence A – a fixed fee of 2,000; and
- Licence B – 3% of C's future sales of products that use that licence.

4.2.190.100   X estimates that its sales-based royalties (i.e. the total variable consideration) will be 1,500. The stand-alone selling prices of Licence A and B are 1,800 and 1,700, respectively.

4.2.190.110   X determines that the royalty relates directly to Licence B and that allocating all of the variable consideration to Licence B is consistent with the allocation objective. Therefore, it allocates the total variable consideration of 1,500 entirely to Licence B.

4.2.190.120   X allocates the fixed consideration as follows:
- 1,800[1] to Licence A; and
- 200[1] to Licence B.

> **Note**
> 1.   In this example, the entire variable consideration is allocated to Licence B and the fixed consideration is allocated to Licence A in an amount equal its stand-alone selling price. The remaining amount of fixed consideration of 200 (2,000 - 1,800) is allocated to Licence B.

4.2.190.130   In some cases, a contract may contain both variable consideration and a discount. For example, an entity may sell products in a bundle at a discount to the aggregate stand-alone selling prices of the products in the bundle. In addition, the transaction price may include a variable element. In these cases, an entity applies the guidance on allocating variable consideration before it applies the guidance on allocating discounts. That is, the standard includes an allocation hierarchy. When a contract contains both variable consideration and a discount, applying the allocation guidance in the reverse order may result in an incorrect allocation of the transaction price. [*IFRS 15.86*]

4.2.190.140   Some contracts contain features that may be variable consideration and/or a discount – e.g. a rebate. In these cases, an entity evaluates the nature of the feature. If the rebate causes the transaction price to be variable – e.g. the amount of the rebate depends on the number of purchases that a customer makes – then the entity follows the hierarchy and applies the guidance on allocating variable consideration first. Conversely, if a rebate is fixed and not contingent – e.g. the rebate is simply a fixed discount against the aggregate stand-alone selling prices of the items in a bundle – then an entity applies the guidance on allocating discounts and does not consider the guidance on allocating variable consideration. [*IFRS 15.86*]

4.2.200   Changes in the transaction price

4.2.200.10   After initial allocation, changes in the transaction price are generally allocated to performance obligations on the same basis as the transaction price was allocated at contract inception. [*IFRS 15.88*]

4.2.200.20   A change in the transaction price is allocated to one or more distinct goods or services only if the specified criteria relating to allocating variable consideration are met (see 4.2.190.20). [*IFRS 15.89*]

4.2.200.30   Any portion of a change in transaction price that is allocated to a satisfied performance obligation is recognised as revenue – or as a reduction in revenue – when the transaction price changes. [*IFRS 15.88*]

4.2.200.40   Changes in the transaction price resulting from a contract modification are accounted for under the modifications guidance (see 4.2.290). If a change in the transaction price occurs after a contract modification, then it is allocated to the performance obligations in the modified contract – i.e. those that were unsatisfied or partially unsatisfied immediately after the modification – unless the:

- change is attributable to an amount of variable consideration that was promised before the modification; and
- modification was accounted for as a termination of the existing contract and creation of a new contract.

4.2.210   STEP 5: RECOGNISE REVENUE

4.2.210.10   An entity recognises revenue when (or as) it satisfies a performance obligation by transferring a good or service to a customer. An entity 'transfers' a good or service to a customer when the customer obtains control of that good or service. Control may be transferred either at a point in time or over time. The analysis of when control transfers is performed primarily from the perspective of the customer. [*IFRS 15.31–32, BC121*]

4.2.210.20   IFRS 15 contains specific guidance on when to recognise revenue from a distinct licence of intellectual property (see 4.2.420).

4.2.220   Performance obligations satisfied over time

4.2.220.10   An entity recognises revenue over time when one or more of the following criteria is met. [*IFRS 15.35*]

	CRITERION	EXAMPLE
1	The customer simultaneously receives and consumes the benefits provided by the entity's performance as the entity performs, and another entity would not need to substantially reperform the work that the entity has completed to date.	Routine or recurring services.
2	The entity's performance creates or enhances an asset that the customer controls as the asset is created or enhanced.	Building an asset on a customer's site.
3	The entity's performance does not create an asset with an alternative use to the entity (see 4.2.220.40–60) and the entity has an enforceable right to payment for performance completed to date (see 4.2.220.70–120).	Building a specialised asset that only the customer can use, or building an asset to a customer order.

4.2.220.20   In evaluating Criterion 1 and determining whether another party would not need to substantially reperform, the entity disregards potential contractual restrictions or practical limitations and presumes that another party would not have the benefit of any asset that the entity presently controls and would continue to control if that other party took over the performance obligation. This evaluation is hypothetical. [*IFRS 15.B3–B4*]

4.2.220.30   In evaluating Criterion 2 and assessing whether a customer controls an asset as it is created or enhanced, an entity considers the guidance on control in IFRS 15, including the indicators of the transfer of control (see 4.2.240.20). [*IFRS 15.B5*]

4.2.220.35   In evaluating Criterion 2 in sales of real estate, an entity focuses on the real estate unit itself rather than on the right to sell or pledge a right to obtain the real estate in the future. This is because the latter does not provide evidence of control of the real estate unit. [*IU 03-18*]

4.2.220.40   In evaluating Criterion 3, an asset does not have an alternative use to an entity if the entity is either restricted contractually from readily directing the asset for another use during the creation or enhancement of that asset, or limited practically from readily directing the asset in its completed state for another use. The assessment of whether an asset has an alternative use is made at contract inception and is not subsequently updated, unless a contract modification substantially changes the performance obligation (see 4.2.290). [*IFRS 15.36*]

4.2.220.50   For an asset to have no alternative use to an entity, a contractual restriction on the ability to direct its use has to be substantive – i.e. an enforceable right. If an asset is largely interchangeable with other assets and could be transferred to another customer without breaching the contract or incurring significant incremental costs, then the restriction is not substantive. [*IFRS 15.B7*]

4.2.220.60   A practical limitation on an entity's ability to direct an asset for another use – e.g. design specifications that are unique to a customer – exists if the entity would:
- incur significant costs to rework the asset; or

- be able to sell the asset only at a significant loss. [*IFRS 15.B8*]

4.2.220.70   An entity that is constructing an asset with no alternative use is effectively constructing the asset at the direction of the customer. The contract will often contain provisions providing some economic protection against the risk of the customer terminating the contract and leaving the entity with an asset of little or no value. Therefore, to demonstrate that a customer controls an asset that has no alternative use as it is being created, an entity evaluates whether it has an enforceable right to payment for the performance completed to date. An entity has an enforceable right to payment for performance completed to date if it has a right to receive an amount that approximates the selling price of the goods or services transferred if the contract is terminated by the customer or another party for reasons other than failure to perform as promised. The likelihood that the customer would terminate the contract or that the entity would exercise its right to payment are not relevant in making this assessment. [*IFRS 15.37, IU 03-18*]

4.2.220.80   To meet this part of Criterion 3, the entity's right to payment has to be for an amount that approximates the selling price of the goods or services transferred – e.g. a right to recover costs incurred plus a reasonable profit margin. The amount to which the entity is entitled does not need to equal the contract margin, but has to be based on either a reasonable proportion of the entity's expected profit margin or a reasonable return on the entity's cost of capital. However, if an entity would only recover its costs, then it would not have the right to payment for performance completed to date and this part of Criterion 3 would not be met. [*IFRS 15.B9–B13*]

4.2.220.85   In some cases, an entity may enter into a contract with a customer that is expected to be loss-making from the outset. This usually happens when an entity pursues a specific economic objective – e.g. to enter into a new market, an entity agrees to sell a product in that market for a price that is below cost. It appears that a contract with a negative margin may still meet the conditions in 4.2.220.80 if the amount to which the entity is entitled from the customer on termination is reasonable in proportion to the expected margin for the contract and the performance completed to date.

4.2.220.90   The following table includes other factors to consider.

Factor	Impact
Payment terms	- An unconditional right to payment is not required, but rather an enforceable right to demand or retain payment for the performance completed to date if the contract is terminated by the customer for convenience.
Payment schedule	- A payment schedule does not necessarily indicate whether an entity has an enforceable right to payment for performance to date.
Contractual terms	- If a customer acts to terminate a contract without having a contractual right at that time to do so, then the contract terms may entitle the entity to continue to transfer the promised goods or services and require the customer to pay the corresponding consideration promised.

Factor	Impact
Legislation or legal precedent	• Even if a right is not specified in the contract, jurisdictional matters such as legislation, administrative practice or legal precedent may confer a right to payment to the entity. • By contrast, legal precedent may indicate that rights to payment in similar contracts have no binding legal effect, or that an entity's customary business practice not to enforce a right to payment may result in that right being unenforceable in that jurisdiction.
Payment in scope of the analysis	• Only payments under the existing contract with the customer are relevant for the analysis. Amounts received or to be received from a third party if the asset is resold are not payments for performance under the existing contract. [*IU 03-18*]

4.2.220.100   When a right to payment on termination is not specified in the contract with the customer, an entity may still have a right to payment under relevant laws or regulations. The fact that the entity may sue a customer who defaults or cancels a contract for convenience does not in itself demonstrate that the entity has an enforceable right to payment. Generally, a right to payment exists only if taking legal action entitles the entity to a payment for the cost incurred plus a reasonable profit margin for the performance completed to date. Factors to consider when determining if an entity has a right to payment include:

• relevant laws and regulations;
• customary business practices;
• the legal environment;
• relevant legal precedents; and
• legal opinions on the enforceability of rights. [*IFRS 15.B11–B12, BC147*]

4.2.220.110   Each individual factor may not be determinative on its own. An entity needs to determine which factors are relevant for its specific set of circumstances. In cases of uncertainty – e.g. when the factors in 4.2.220.100 are inconclusive or provide contradictory evidence about the existence of a right to payment – an entity considers all relevant factors and applies judgement in reaching its conclusion.

4.2.220.120   In some cases, an entity may have an apparent right to payment described in its contract with the customer, or under a relevant law or regulation, but there may be uncertainty over whether the right is enforceable. This may be the case when there is no legal precedent for the enforceability of the entity's right. In these cases, an entity may need a legal opinion to help it assess whether it has an enforceable right to payment. However, all facts and circumstances need to be considered in assessing how much weight (if any) to place on the legal opinion. [*IFRS 15.B12*]

4.2.220.130   Potential contractual restrictions or practical restrictions may prevent the entity from transferring the remaining performance obligation to another entity (Criterion 1) or directing the asset for another use (Criterion 3). IFRS 15 provides guidance on whether these facts or possible termination affect the assessment of those criteria. It provides the following guidance on the assumptions that an entity should make when applying Criteria 1 and 3. [*IFRS 15.B4, B6–B8, BC127*]

DETERMINING WHETHER	CONSIDER CONTRACTUAL RESTRICTIONS?	CONSIDER PRACTICAL LIMITATIONS?	CONSIDER POSSIBLE TERMINATION?
• another entity would not need to substantially reperform (Criterion 1)	No	No	Yes
• the entity's performance does not create an asset with an alternative use (Criterion 3)	Yes	Yes	No

EXAMPLE 11A – APPLYING THE OVER-TIME CRITERIA – PROFESSIONAL CONSULTANT

4.2.220.140   Company B enters into a contract to provide a consulting service to a customer that results in B providing a professional opinion based on facts and circumstances specific to the customer. If the customer were to terminate the consulting contract for reasons other than B's failure to perform as promised, then the contract requires the customer to compensate B for its costs incurred plus a 15% margin. The 15% margin approximates the profit margin that B earns from similar contracts.

4.2.220.150   B applies the criteria in 4.2.220.10 and determines the following.
- If B does not issue the professional opinion and the customer hires another consulting firm, then that other firm would need to substantially reperform the work completed by B to date because it would not have the benefit of any work in progress performed by B. Accordingly, the customer does not simultaneously receive and consume the benefits of B's performance and Criterion 1 in 4.2.220.10 is not met.
- B is not creating or enhancing an asset that the customer obtains control of as B performs. This is because B delivers the professional opinion to the customer only on completion. B therefore determines that Criterion 2 in 4.2.220.10 is not met.
- The development of the professional opinion does not create an asset with alternative use to B because it relates to facts and circumstances that are specific to the customer. Therefore, there is a practical limitation on B's ability to readily direct the asset to another customer. The contract's terms provide B with an enforceable right to payment for its performance completed to date for costs incurred plus a reasonable margin. B therefore determines that Criterion 3 in 4.2.220.10 is met.

4.2.220.160   Because Criterion 3 is met, B recognises revenue over time as it provides the consulting services.

EXAMPLE 11B – APPLYING THE OVER-TIME CRITERIA – BOTTLE MANUFACTURER

4.2.220.170   Company C enters into a framework agreement to manufacture bottles for Customer B under the following terms.

- The design of the bottles is the intellectual property of B.
- The sales price is cost plus 10%.
- There is no stated minimum purchase quantity.
- C is required to maintain a specific level of inventory of raw materials and finished goods.
- If B terminates the framework agreement, then it is required to purchase inventory of raw materials at cost and work in progress and finished goods on hand at the agreed sales price at the date of termination.
- The manufacturing process does not result in material amounts of work in progress.

4.2.220.180   C determines that the nature of the promise to B under the framework agreement is to manufacture bottles for use in B's operation.

4.2.220.190   C applies the criteria in 4.2.220.10 and determines that it does not create an asset with an alternative use because C is legally prevented from selling the asset to another customer. The contract's termination clause provides C with an enforceable right to payment for its performance completed to date – i.e. for costs incurred plus a reasonable margin. C therefore determines that Criterion 3 in 4.2.220.10 is met.

4.2.220.200   Because Criterion 3 is met, C recognises revenue over time as it manufactures bottles.

EXAMPLE 11C – APPLYING THE OVER-TIME CRITERIA – REAL ESTATE (1)

4.2.220.210   Real Estate Developer D in Country Y enters into a contract with Customer C for sale of a real estate unit in a multi-unit residential complex. The contract contains the following terms.

- C pays a 10% deposit at contract inception and the remainder of the purchase price after construction is complete.
- D retains legal title until C has paid the full purchase price.
- C has the right to terminate the contract at any time before construction is complete.
- On termination, D is required to make reasonable efforts to resell the unit to a third party.
- If the resale price obtained from the third party is less than the original purchase price in the contract with C, then C must pay the difference to D.

4.2.220.220   D applies the criteria in 4.2.220.10 and determines that its performance does not create an asset with an alternative use under Criterion 3. However, the consideration to which D is entitled from C on termination is limited to reimburse-ment of any loss of profit on resale. This does not approximate to the selling price of the part-constructed real estate unit, and therefore does not compensate D for its performance completed to date. Based on its analysis, D concludes that Criterion 3 in 4.2.220.10 is not met. [*IU 03-18*]

4.2.220.230   Because Criterion 3 is not met, D recognises revenue at the point in time when control of the unit transfers to C.

EXAMPLE 11D – APPLYING THE OVER-TIME CRITERIA – REAL ESTATE (2)

4.2.220.240   Modifying the fact pattern in Example 11C, the contract between Real Estate Developer D and Customer C contains the following terms.
- C pays 20% of the purchase price in instalments as the unit is constructed and the remainder of the purchase price after construction is complete.
- D retains legal title to the unit during construction.
- C has the 'in rem' right to the unit during construction (i.e. the legal right to the unit), which it can resell or pledge to a new buyer.

4.2.220.250   The contract cannot be terminated under Country Y's local law. How-ever, the courts in Country Y have accepted requests to terminate similar contracts in some circumstances – e.g. when the customer becomes unemployed or ill. In these cases, the courts have allowed the developer to retain approximately 10% of the payments made as a termination penalty.

4.2.220.260   D concludes that the 'in rem' right to the unit does not give C the ability to direct the use of the unit itself during construction; therefore, Criterion 2 in 4.2.220.10 is not met. [*IU 03-18*]

4.2.220.270   Although the contract does not give C a termination right, D concludes that the legal precedent permits the termination of contracts for reasons other than its failure to perform as promised. Further, the termination penalty of approximately 10% of the payments which the courts have allowed the developer to retain does not compensate the developer for performance to date. Therefore, D concludes that Criterion 3 in 4.2.220.10 is not met. [*IU 03-18*]

4.2.220.280   Because none of the criteria for over-time revenue recognition are met, D recognises revenue at the point in time when control of the unit transfers to C.

4.2.220.290   An entity that agrees to deliver a commodity considers the nature of its promise to determine whether to recognise revenue over time or at a point in time. In many contracts to deliver commodities, an entity has promised to transfer a good and will consider the point-in-time guidance to determine when control transfers. However, there may be scenarios in which an entity has promised to provide a service of delivering a commodity that the customer immediately consumes and therefore immediately receives the benefits. For example, a contract to deliver natural gas to temporary storage may represent a promise to deliver a good, whereas a contract to provide natural gas to the customer for on-demand consumption may represent a service that meets Criterion 1 for over-time recognition.

4.2.220.300   To determine whether the customer immediately consumes the assets and receives the benefits as the performance obligation is satisfied, the entity evaluates:
- the inherent characteristics of the commodity;
- the contract terms;
- information about the infrastructure and other delivery mechanisms; and
- other relevant facts and circumstances.

4.2.230   *Measuring progress*

4.2.230.10   For each performance obligation satisfied over time, an entity selects a single method for measuring progress and applies it consistently. The objective is to depict the transfer of control of the goods or services to the customer. An entity uses either an output method or an input method to measure progress. However, it does not have a free choice. In selecting the method, the entity considers the nature of the good or service being delivered. [*IFRS 15.39–41, BC159*]

4.2.230.20   An entity recognises revenue over time only if it can reasonably measure its progress towards complete satisfaction of the performance obligation. In circumstances when it cannot reasonably measure the outcome, but expects to recover the costs incurred in satisfying the performance obligation, an entity recognises revenue only to the extent of the costs incurred. [*IFRS 15.44–45*]

4.2.230.30   Input methods measure performance based on the entity's efforts or inputs towards satisfying the performance obligation relative to the total expected inputs. Examples include resources consumed, costs incurred, time elapsed, labour hours expended and machine hours used. [*IFRS 15.B18*]

4.2.230.40   If an input method provides an appropriate basis to measure progress and an entity's inputs are incurred evenly over time, then it may be appropriate to recognise revenue on a straight-line basis. [*IFRS 15.B18*]

4.2.230.50   An entity applying an input method excludes the effects of any inputs that do not depict its performance in transferring control of goods or services to the customer. In particular, when using a cost-based input method – e.g. cost-to-cost – an adjustment to the measure of progress may be required when an incurred cost:
- does not contribute to an entity's progress in satisfying the performance obligation – e.g. unexpected amounts of wasted materials, labour or other resources (these costs are expensed as they are incurred); or
- is not proportionate to the entity's progress in satisfying the performance obligation – e.g. uninstalled materials (see 4.2.230.60). [*IFRS 15.B19*]

4.2.230.60   For uninstalled materials, a faithful depiction of performance may be for the entity to recognise revenue only to the extent of the cost incurred – i.e. at a zero percent profit margin – if, at contract inception, the entity expects all of the following conditions to be met:
- the good is not distinct;

- the customer is expected to obtain control of the good significantly earlier than it receives services related to the good;
- the cost of the transferred good is significant relative to the total expected costs to completely satisfy the performance obligation; and
- the entity is acting as the principal, but procures the good from a third party and is not significantly involved in designing and manufacturing the good. [*IFRS 15.B19(b)*]

4.2.230.70   If an entity determines that the cost of uninstalled materials should be excluded from the measure of progress, then revenue and the related costs are recognised on transfer of control of the uninstalled materials to the customer (see 4.2.230.50–60). In determining when control transfers to the customer, it appears that an entity should consider all relevant indicators, including both point-in-time and over-time indicators (see 4.2.220 and 240).

4.2.230.75   When an entity excludes the cost of uninstalled materials from the measure of progress, it appears that it may be appropriate not to attribute any profit margin to the uninstalled materials and recognise a higher profit margin as the other costs are incurred and reflected in the measure of progress. Other approaches to recognising the profit margin on uninstalled materials may also be acceptable.

4.2.230.80   Output methods measure performance based on the value of the goods delivered relative to those undelivered. Examples include surveys of performance to date, appraisals of results achieved, milestones reached, time elapsed, units delivered and units produced. [*IFRS 15.B15*]

4.2.230.90   Although IFRS 15 lists milestones as an example of a possible measure of progress when using an output method, it remains necessary to consider whether milestones faithfully depict performance, particularly if they are widely spaced. This is because control generally transfers continuously as the entity performs, rather than at discrete points in time. Normally, a milestone method would need to incorporate a measure of progress between milestone achievements to faithfully depict an entity's performance.

4.2.230.100   If an entity's performance has produced a material amount of work in progress or finished goods that are controlled by the customer, then output methods such as 'units of delivery' or 'units of production' may not faithfully depict progress. This is because not all of the entity's performance is included in measuring the output. [*IFRS 15.B15, BC165*]

4.2.230.110   Work in progress for an over-time performance obligation is generally expensed as a fulfilment cost when it is incurred because control of the work in progress transfers to the customer as it is produced and not at discrete intervals. However, inventory to support multiple contracts that has an alternative use is recognised as an asset until it is dedicated to a specific contract.

4.2.230.120   When measuring performance, as a practical expedient, if the entity has a right to invoice a customer in an amount that corresponds directly with its performance to date, then it can recognise revenue in that amount. For example, in a service contract an entity may have a right to bill a fixed amount for each unit of service provided. [*IFRS 15.B16*]

4.2.230.130   The determination of whether the invoice amount represents the value to the customer may be more difficult in scenarios with multiple performance obligations or where the fixed amount per unit changes over time. This might occur with contracts that have declining unit prices, rates with forward market curves, rates with contractual minimums, or contracts with volume rebates. In these cases, judgement is required to determine whether the changes in pricing are in response to a change in the underlying value to the customer. If a contract includes fixed fees in addition to per-unit invoicing, substantive contractual minimums or payments to the customer such as rebates, discounts or signing bonuses, then the use of the practical expedient may be precluded because the fixed fees cause the invoiced amounts not to correspond to the value that the customer receives. Further, to apply the practical expedient to a contract, all goods and services in the contract need to qualify. [*IFRS 15.B16*]

4.2.230.140   Judgement is required to determine an appropriate measure of progress for a stand-ready obligation. When making the judgement, an entity considers the substance of the stand-ready obligation to ensure that the measure of progress aligns with the nature of the underlying promise. In assessing the nature of the obligation, the entity considers all relevant facts and circumstances, including the timing of transfer of goods or services, and whether the entity's efforts (e.g. costs) are expended evenly throughout the period covered by the stand-ready obligation. [*IFRS 15.26(e)*]

4.2.230.150   In many cases, a straight-line measure of progress will be appropriate for recognising revenue on a stand-ready obligation. However, it is not always appropriate. For example, in a contract for unspecified software upgrades or a health club contract, revenue is generally recognised on a straight-line basis because the pattern of benefit to the customer as well as the entity's efforts to fulfil the contract are generally even throughout the period. In contrast, a straight-line basis of recognition would not generally be appropriate in an annual contract to provide snow removal services in an area where snowfall is highly seasonal. The pattern of benefit of these services, as well as the entity's effort to fulfil the contract, would not generally be even throughout the year, because snow is expected only in the winter. [*IFRS 15.26(e), IE92–IE94, BC160*]

4.2.240   Performance obligations satisfied at a point in time

4.2.240.10   If a performance obligation is not satisfied over time, then the entity recognises revenue at the point in time at which it transfers control of the good or service to the customer. An entity has control of a good or service when it has the ability to direct the use of, and obtain substantially all of the remaining benefits from, the good or service. [*IFRS 15.32–33*]

4.2.240.15   The benefits of an asset are the potential cash flows – inflows or savings in outflows – that can be obtained directly or indirectly, including by:
- using the asset to:
  - produce goods or provide services (including public services);
  - enhance the value of other assets; and
  - settle liabilities or reduce expenses;
- selling or exchanging the asset;
- pledging the asset to secure a loan; and
- holding the asset. [*IFRS 15.33*]

4.2.240.20   Indicators that control has passed to the customer include the customer having:
- a present obligation to pay;
- physical possession;
- legal title;

- the risks and rewards of ownership; and
- accepted the asset. [*IFRS 15.38*]

4.2.240.30   Relevant considerations include the following.
- In some cases, possession of legal title is a protective right and may not coincide with the transfer of control of the goods or services to a customer – e.g. when a seller retains title solely as protection against the customer's failure to pay.
- In consignment arrangements (see 4.2.350) and some repurchase arrangements (see 4.2.380), an entity may have transferred physical possession but still retain control. Conversely, in bill-and-hold arrangements (see 4.2.360) an entity may have physical possession of an asset that the customer controls.
- In some arrangements, a customer may obtain control of an asset before it has physical possession – e.g. a bank purchasing a fixed amount of gold from a mine may be able to sell the gold for immediate physical settlement before the refinement process is completed.
- When evaluating the risks and rewards of ownership, an entity excludes any risks that give rise to a separate performance obligation in addition to the performance obligation to transfer the asset – e.g. if an entity has transferred control of an asset but not yet satisfied an additional performance obligation to provide maintenance services related to the transferred asset. In some cases, the customer may have the rewards of ownership, but not the risks. This does not necessarily preclude the customer from having control. An entity considers whether the other indicators are more relevant and the customer's ability to direct the use of and obtain substantially all of the benefits from the asset.
- An entity needs to assess whether it can objectively determine that a good or service provided to a customer conforms to the specifications agreed in a contract.

4.2.240.35   Another relevant consideration in evaluating at which point in time control transfers to the customer is shipping terms of the arrangement. Shipping terms alone do not determine when control transfers – i.e. an entity considers shipping terms along with other indicators of control to assess when the customer has the ability to direct the use of, and obtain substantially all of the benefits from, the asset. However, shipping terms often indicate the point in time when the customer has legal title, the risks and rewards of ownership and a present obligation to pay which are all indicators that control has transferred. Incoterms of the International Chamber of Commerce are used frequently in international purchase-and-sales contracts. They include standard trade terms such as 'free on board' (FOB), 'cost, insurance and freight' (CIF) and 'ex works' (EXW) (see 3.8.90). In the case of FOB, when the goods are loaded onto the ship the customer usually receives the bill of lading and takes over the risk of loss or damage to the goods. This may indicate that the customer obtains control when the goods are loaded onto the ship and the bill of lading has been transferred to the customer. If control of the goods transfers to the customer before delivery to the final destination, then an entity considers whether the transportation service is a distinct performance obligation and if so, whether it acts as a principal or an agent for the shipping service (see 4.2.347).

4.2.240.37   When goods are shipped, the risk of loss may often be transferred to a third party while the goods are in transit. The fact that the seller transfers its risk of loss to another party (i.e. the third party shipping company or insurance company) does not mean that the customer has the ability to direct the use or obtain substantially all the benefits from the goods or services. An entity needs to consider this when assessing at which point in time control transfers to the customer.

4.2.240.40   Customer acceptance clauses included in some contracts are intended to ensure the customer's satisfaction with the goods or services promised in the contract. The table below illustrates examples of customer acceptance clauses. [*IFRS 15.B83–B86*]

IF THE ENTITY...	THEN...	FOR EXAMPLE...
Can objectively verify that the goods or services comply with the specifications underlying acceptance	Customer acceptance would be a formality, and revenue could be recognised before explicit acceptance	The customer acceptance clause is based on meeting objective size and weight specifications
Cannot objectively determine whether the specifications have been met	It is unlikely that the entity would be able to conclude that the customer has obtained control before formal customer acceptance	The customer acceptance clause is based on a modified product functioning in the customer's new production line
Delivers products for trial or evaluation purposes and the customer is not committed to pay any consideration until the trial period lapses	Control of the product is not transferred to the customer until either the customer accepts the product or the trial period lapses	The customer acceptance clause specifies that the customer may use prototype equipment for a specified period of time

4.2.240.50   The indicators of transfer of control are factors that are often present if a customer has control of an asset; however, they are not individually determinative, nor are they a list of conditions that have to be met. IFRS 15 does not suggest that certain indicators should be weighted more heavily than others, nor does it establish a hierarchy that applies if only some of the indicators are present. However, it remains possible that in some circumstances, certain indicators will be more relevant than others and so carry greater weight in the analysis. Judgement may be required to determine the point in time at which control transfers. This determination may be particularly challenging when there are indicators that control has transferred alongside 'negative' indicators suggesting that the entity has not satisfied its performance obligation. [*IFRS 15.BC155*]

4.2.240.60   Many entities sell through distributors and resellers. These transactions will require judgement to determine if the transfer of control occurs on delivery to the intermediary (sell-in model) or when the good is resold to the end customer (sell-through model). Entities need to consider the guidance on consignment sales (see 4.2.350) and variable consideration (see 4.2.100) to determine which model is appropriate.

4.2.250   CONTRACT COSTS

4.2.260   Costs to obtain a contract

4.2.260.10   An entity capitalises incremental costs incurred as a result of obtaining a contract – e.g. sales commissions – if the entity expects to recover these costs. [*IFRS 15.91–92*]

4.2.260.20   Costs that are incurred regardless of whether the contract is obtained – including costs that are incremental to trying to obtain a contract – are expensed as they are incurred unless they meet the criteria to be capitalised as fulfilment costs. [*IFRS 15.93*]

4.2.260.30   As a practical expedient, an entity is not required to capitalise the incremental costs to obtain a contract if the amortisation period of the resulting asset would not exceed one year. The assessment of whether the practical expedient applies is made at the contract level. If a contract includes multiple performance obligations, and one or more of them will be satisfied beyond one year, then the practical expedient will not usually apply. This will be the case when the asset relates to all of the goods and services in the contract and more than one performance obligation is present, which means that the amortisation period of the capitalised costs will be longer than a year. For a discussion of the amortisation period, see 4.2.280. [*IFRS 15.94*]

4.2.260.40   In some cases, an additional commission may be payable, or the original commission amount adjusted, at a future date. In these cases, an entity considers the enforceable rights and obligations created by the arrangement to determine when the liability is accrued and whether to capitalise a commission, and in what amount. Examples include commissions:
- paid for renewal of the contract;
- earned on contract modifications;
- contingent on future events;
- subject to claw-back; and
- that are tiered, subject to a threshold.

EXAMPLE 12A – COMMISSIONS FOR CONTRACT RENEWAL – CAPITALISING ON RENEWAL

4.2.260.50   Company N pays commission of 100 on commencement of a contract with a non-cancellable two-year term and agrees to pay further commission of 100 if the customer renews the contract at the end of two years.

4.2.260.60   In this example, N capitalises only the initial commission of 100 on contract commencement. N capitalises the second commission of 100 only when the customer renews the contract. This is because the contract creates enforceable rights and obligations for both parties only for the initial contract period of two years, and N does not accrue the second commission payment until it has a present obligation.

EXAMPLE 12B – COMMISSIONS FOR CONTRACT RENEWAL – CAPITALISING ON COMMENCEMENT

4.2.260.70   Modifying Example 12A, N pays commission of 100 on commencement of a contract with a non-cancellable two-year term and agrees to pay additional commission of 100 on the first anniversary of the contract.

4.2.260.80   In this example, N capitalises 200 on contract commencement. This is because the contract creates enforceable rights and obligations for both parties for the contract period of two years. Also, N accrues the second payment because it has a present obligation, and its payment depends only on the passage of time.

4.2.270   **Costs to fulfil a contract**

4.2.270.10   If costs incurred to fulfil a contract with a customer are not in the scope of another standard, then an entity recognises an asset for fulfilment costs that meet the following criteria:

- they relate directly to an existing contract or specific anticipated contract;
- they generate or enhance resources of the entity that will be used to satisfy the performance obligations in the future; and
- they are expected to be recovered. [*IFRS 15.95*]

4.2.270.15   If costs to fulfil a contract with a customer fall in the scope of another standard and that standard precludes their capitalisation, then the costs cannot be capitalised under IFRS 15. [*IFRS 15.BC307*]

4.2.270.20   The following table illustrates some examples of costs to fulfil a contract and indicates whether they relate directly to the contract. [*IFRS 15.97–98*]

DIRECT COSTS THAT ARE ELIGIBLE FOR CAPITALISATION IF OTHER CRITERIA IN **4.2.270.10** ARE MET	COSTS REQUIRED TO BE EXPENSED WHEN THEY ARE INCURRED
Direct labour – e.g. employee wages	General and administrative costs – unless they are explicitly chargeable under the contract
Direct materials – e.g. supplies	Costs that relate to satisfied performance obligations
Allocation of costs that relate directly to the contract – e.g. depreciation and amortisation	Costs of wasted materials, labour or other contract costs
Costs that are explicitly chargeable to the customer under the contract	Costs that do not clearly relate to unsatisfied performance obligations
Other costs that were incurred only because the entity entered into the contract – e.g. subcontractor costs	

4.2.280   **Amortisation**

4.2.280.10   Capitalised costs to obtain and/or fulfil a contract are amortised on a systematic basis, consistent with the pattern of transfer of the good or service to which the asset relates. This includes not only goods and services in an existing contract, but also those to be transferred under a specific anticipated contract – e.g. services to be provided under renewal of an existing contract. If the contract contains multiple performance obligations satisfied at different points in time, then the entity takes this into account when determining the appropriate amortisation period and pattern. [*IFRS 15.99*]

4.2.280.20   Some entities pay sales commissions on all contracts executed with customers, including new contracts – i.e. new services and/or new customers – and renewal or extension contracts. If the commission paid by an entity on a new contract will be followed by corresponding commissions for each renewal period – i.e. the salesperson will receive an incremental commission each time the customer renews the contract, or does not cancel it – then the entity applies judgement to determine whether the original commission on the new contract should be amortised over only the initial contract term, or over a longer period.

4.2.280.30   The capitalised asset is generally recognised over the period covered by the commission. If the renewal commission is commensurate with the initial commission, then the initial commission is amortised over the original contract term and the renewal commission is amortised over the renewal period. Commissions are generally considered commensurate with each other when they are reasonably proportional to the respective contract value.

4.2.285   Impairment

4.2.285.10   An impairment related to the capitalised costs is recognised in profit or loss to the extent that the carrying amount exceeds the recoverable amount. 'Recoverable amount' is defined as:

- the remaining expected amount of consideration to be received in exchange for the goods or services to which the asset relates; less
- the costs that relate directly to providing those goods or services and that have not been recognised as expenses. [*IFRS 15.101–102*]

4.2.285.20   When determining the consideration expected to be received in the contract costs impairment analysis, an entity includes cash flows from both existing contracts and specific anticipated contracts and does not constrain its estimate of variable consideration. However, the entity excludes from the amount of consideration the portion that it does not expect to collect, based on an assessment of the customer's credit risk. [*IFRS 15.102*]

4.2.285.30   An entity recognises a reversal of any impairment recorded when impairment conditions improve. However, following the reversal of an impairment, the carrying amount of the asset cannot exceed the carrying amount that would have been determined if no impairment had been recognised and the asset had continued to be amortised. [*IFRS 15.104*]

4.2.290   CONTRACT MODIFICATIONS

4.2.290.10   A 'contract modification' is a change in the scope or price (or both) of a contract that is approved by the parties to the contract. The modification is 'approved' when it creates legally enforceable rights and obligations on the parties to the contract. Consistent with the determination of whether a contract exists in Step 1 of the model, this approval may be written, oral or implied by customary business practices, and should be legally enforceable. If the parties have not approved a contract modification, then an entity continues to apply the requirements of IFRS 15 to the existing contract until approval is obtained. [*IFRS 15.18*]

4.2.290.20   If a change in scope has been approved but the corresponding change in price has not yet been determined, then an entity estimates the change to the transaction price by applying the guidance on estimating variable consideration and constraining the transaction price (see 4.2.100). [*IFRS 15.19*]

4.2.290.30   An entity accounts for modifications either as a separate contract (i.e. on a prospective basis) or as part of the original contract (i.e. on a cumulative catch-up basis). The key decision points to consider when determining whether a contract modification should be accounted for as part of the original contract or as a separate contract are illustrated in the following flowchart. [*IFRS 15.20–21*]

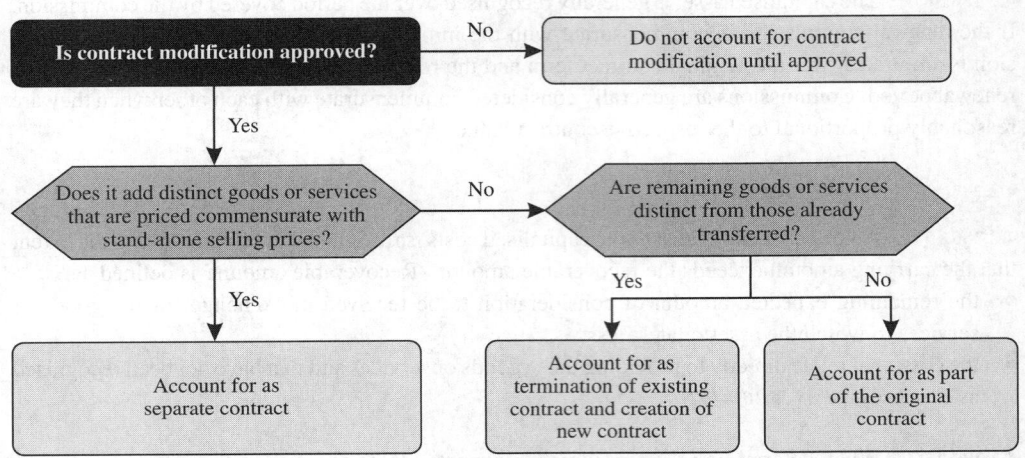

4.2.290.40   A contract modification is treated as a separate contract (i.e. prospective treatment) if the modification results in:

- a promise to deliver additional goods or services that are distinct (see 4.2.70); and
- an increase in the price of the contract by an amount of consideration that reflects the entity's stand-alone selling price of those goods or services adjusted to reflect the circumstances of the contract. [*IFRS 15.20*]

4.2.290.50   If these criteria are not met, then the entity's accounting for the modification is based on whether the remaining goods or services under the modified contract are distinct from those transferred to the customer before the modification. [*IFRS 15.21*]

4.2.290.60   If the goods or services are distinct, then the entity accounts for the modification as if it were a termination of the existing contract and the creation of a new contract. In this case, the entity does not reallocate the change in the transaction price to performance obligations that are completely or partially satisfied on or before the date of the contract modification. Instead, the modification is accounted for prospectively and the amount of consideration allocated to the remaining performance obligations (or to the remaining distinct goods or services in a series treated as a single performance obligation) is equal to the:

- consideration included in the estimate of the transaction price of the original contract that has not been recognised as revenue; plus or minus
- increase or decrease in the consideration promised by the contract modification. [*IFRS 15.21(a)*]

4.2.290.70   If the modification to the contract does not add distinct goods or services, then the entity accounts for it on a combined basis with the original contract, as if the additional goods or services were part of the initial contract – i.e. as a cumulative catch-up adjustment. The modification is recognised as either an increase in or reduction of revenue at the date of modification. [*IFRS 15.21(b)*]

EXAMPLE 13 – APPROVAL OF CONTRACT MODIFICATION

4.2.290.80   Company C agrees to construct a specialised cruise ship for a customer. Halfway through the project, the customer decides to modify the original plans to accommodate additional passengers. The change is communicated orally, but no written change order for the additional material, design services or labour has been executed.

4.2.290.90   C has built cruise ships for the customer before, and the customer has been willing to pay for the incremental services and materials, together with a margin, as long as C can show that the costs are reasonable given the changes requested.

4.2.290.100   The contract specifies that all changes need to be agreed in writing and there is no legal precedent for oral agreements being enforceable in the jurisdiction.

4.2.290.110   C has not yet commenced any work with respect to the agreed modifications and the construction work undertaken to date on the cruise ship is not affected by the modification.

4.2.290.120   In this example, C does not yet adjust the contract for the modification, because it is not approved. The fact that C has experience with the customer paying for such modifications is not relevant in making the assessment, because an oral agreement is not legally enforceable in the jurisdiction.

4.2.290.130   If the transaction price changes after a contract modification, then an entity applies the guidance on changes in the transaction price (see 4.2.200). [*IFRS 15.90*]

4.2.300   APPLICATION ISSUES

4.2.310   Sale with a right of return

4.2.310.10   A 'sale with a right of return' is a transaction in which an entity transfers control of a product to a customer and also grants the customer the right to return the product for various reasons.

4.2.310.20   An entity applies the guidance for a sale with a right of return when a customer has a right to:
- a full or partial refund of any consideration paid;
- a credit that can be applied against amounts owed, or that will be owed, to the entity; or

- another product in exchange, unless it is another product of the same type, quality, condition and price – e.g. exchanging a red sweater for a white sweater (see 4.2.310.40). [*IFRS 15.B20*]

4.2.310.30   In addition to product returns, the guidance also applies to services that are provided subject to a refund. An entity does not account for its stand-ready obligation to accept returns as a performance obligation. [*IFRS 15.B21*]

4.2.310.40   The guidance for a sale with a right of return does not apply to:
- exchanges by customers of one product for another of the same type, quality, condition and price; and
- returns of faulty goods or replacements, which are instead evaluated under the guidance on warranties (see 4.2.320). [*IFRS 15.B26–B27*]

4.2.310.50   An entity that transfers products with a right of return recognises the following items.
- *Revenue:* This is initially measured at the amount of consideration to which the entity expects to be entitled, based on the expected level of returns. The entity applies the general guidance on estimating the transaction price to measure revenue, including the guidance on estimating variable consideration and the constraint (see 4.2.100). The entity may consider historical experience with similar contracts to make estimates and judgements (see 4.2.105.30).
- *A refund liability:* This is initially measured at the amount of consideration received or receivable to which the entity does not expect to be entitled. Again, the entity applies the general guidance on estimating the transaction price to measure the refund liability. If a right of return allows the customer to return a product for a partial refund, then the refund liability is measured based on the portion of the transaction price expected to be refunded. The nature of such a refund liability is different from contract liabilities and it therefore is not presented as such (see 4.2.470).
- *An asset (and a corresponding adjustment to cost of sales) for the right to recover products from customers:* This is initially measured with reference to the previous carrying amount of the products transferred, less expected recovery costs (including potential decreases in the value to the entity of returned products). The nature of this asset is different from trade and other receivables and it therefore is not presented as such. [*IFRS 15.B21, B23, B25*]

4.2.310.60   An entity updates the measurement of the refund liability at each reporting date for changes in expectations about the amount of the refunds. It recognises:
- adjustments to the refund liability as revenue; and
- adjustments to the refund asset as an expense. [*IFRS 15.B24–B25*]

EXAMPLE 14 – SALE WITH RIGHT OF RETURN

4.2.310.70   Company B sells 100 products at a price of 100 each and receives a payment of 10,000. Under the sale contract, the customer is allowed to return any undamaged products within 30 days and to receive a full refund in cash. The cost of each product is 60.

4.2.310.80   B estimates that three products will be returned, and that a subsequent change in the estimate would not result in a significant revenue reversal. B also estimates that the costs of recovering the products will be insignificant and expects that the products can be resold at a profit.

4.2.310.90   B records the following entries on transfer of the products to the customer to reflect its expectation that three products will be returned.

	DEBIT	CREDIT
Cash	10,000	
Refund liability		300[1]
Revenue		9,700
To recognise sale excluding revenue relating to products expected to be returned		
Return asset	180[2]	
Costs of sales	5,820	
Inventory		6,000
To recognise cost of sales and right to recover products from customers		

Notes
1.   Calculated as 100 x 3 products expected to be returned.
2.   Calculated as 60 x 3 products expected to be returned, assuming that the cost to recover the products is insignificant.

4.2.310.100   An entity sometimes charges a customer a restocking fee when a product is returned. This fee is generally intended to compensate the entity for costs associated with the product return (e.g. shipping costs and repacking costs) or the reduction in the selling price that an entity may achieve when reselling the product to another customer. A right of return with a restocking fee is similar to a right of return for a partial refund. Therefore, a restocking fee is included as part of the estimated transaction price when control transfers – i.e. the refund liability is based on the transaction price less the restocking fee. Similarly, the entity's expected costs related to restocking are reflected in the measurement of the return asset when control of the product transfers. This is consistent with the guidance in IFRS 15 that any expected costs to recover returned products should be included by reducing the carrying amount of the asset recorded for the right to recover those products. [*IFRS 15.55, B23–B25*]

EXAMPLE 15 – RIGHT OF RETURN WITH RESTOCKING FEE

4.2.310.110   Company Z sells 20 widgets to a customer for 30 each and the cost of each widget is 15. The customer has the right to return a widget but is charged a 10% restocking fee. Z expects to incur restocking costs of 2 per widget returned. Z estimates returns to be 5%.

4.2.310.120   When control of the widgets transfers to the customer, Z recognises the following.

ITEM	WHAT TO INCLUDE	AMOUNT	CALCULATION
Revenue	Widgets not to be returned plus restocking fee	573	$(19^{(1)} \times 30) +$ $(1 \times 3^{(2)})$
Refund liability	Widget expected to be returned less restocking fee	27	$(1 \times 30) - 3^{(2)}$
Return asset	Cost of widget expected to be returned less restocking cost	13	$(1 \times 15) - 2$

Notes
1. Widgets not expected to be returned calculated as 20 widgets sold less one (20 x 5%) expected to be returned.
2. Restocking fee calculated as 30 x 10%.

4.2.310.130 IFRS 15 does not distinguish between conditional and unconditional rights of return, and both are accounted for similarly. However, for a conditional right of return the probability that the return condition would be met is considered in determining the expected level of returns. For example, a food production company only accepts returns of its products that are past a sell-by date. In this example, the food production company assesses the probability that the products will become past their sell-by date and estimates their return rate based on its historical experience. [*IFRS 15.55, B23*]

4.2.320 **Warranties**

4.2.320.10 If an entity provides a warranty with the sale of a product, then it assesses whether the warranty is a performance obligation. Only a warranty that provides a customer with a service in addition to assurance that the product complies with agreed specifications is a performance obligation. [*IFRS 15.B28*]

4.2.320.20 An entity distinguishes the types of product warranties as follows. [*IFRS 15.B29–B30*]

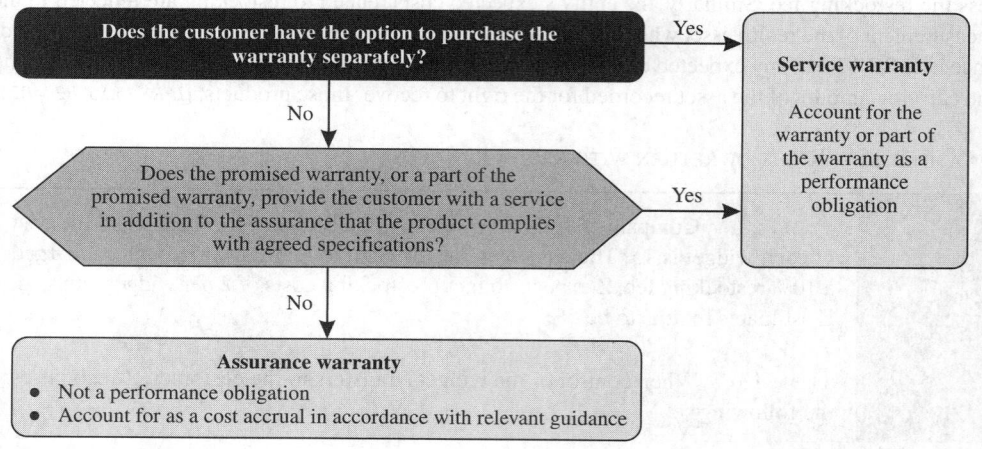

4.2.320.30   To assess whether a warranty or part of the promised warranty provides a customer with a service in addition to assurance that the product performs as specified, an entity considers factors such as:

- whether the warranty is required by law – such requirements typically exist to protect customers from the risk of purchasing defective product;
- the nature of the tasks that the entity agrees to perform; and
- the length of the warranty coverage period – the longer the coverage period, the more likely it is that the entity is providing a service rather than just protecting the customer against a defective product. [*IFRS 15.B31*]

4.2.320.40   IFRS 15 lists the length of the warranty period as a factor to consider when assessing whether the warranty provides a customer with a service. However, it is only one of several factors. An entity usually considers the length of the warranty in the context of the specific market, including geography and product line. In addition to the length of the warranty period, the nature of costs incurred in performing the warranty work may provide evidence of the nature of the warranty promise. [*IFRS 15.B31*]

4.2.320.50   A warranty that is marketed as an 'extended warranty' may be a service-type warranty, but the facts will need to be evaluated to determine whether it provides services beyond the assurance that the product meets the agreed specifications. The mere labelling of a warranty as 'extended' or 'enhanced' is not determinative. An entity considers all facts and circumstances and the factors included in IFRS 15 in making that determination.

EXAMPLE 16 – LIFETIME WARRANTY

4.2.320.60   Luggage Company L is a leading manufacturer in the specialty luggage industry. L provides a lifetime warranty on all bags. If a bag is broken or damaged, then L will repair or replace the bag free of charge. There are no regulations in the luggage industry on warranties.

4.2.320.70   L assesses whether the lifetime warranty is a service-type warranty as follows.

FACTOR	RATIONALE
No legal requirement	In this example, there is no law that requires L to make a promise for the lifetime of the product. Therefore, this factor suggests that the warranty is a separate performance obligation.
Longer coverage period	In this example, the length of the warranty is for the life of the baggage, as compared with other manufacturers that offer warranty for a specific period. Therefore, this factor suggests that the warranty is a separate performance obligation.
Promises beyond agreed specifications	In this example, the nature of the tasks not only includes repairing or replacing baggage that does not meet the promised specifications, but also includes repairing damage that occurs after the customer obtains control of the baggage. Therefore, the baggage warranty goes beyond

FACTOR	RATIONALE
	the promise that the baggage complies with agreed specifications, which suggests that it is a separate performance obligation.

4.2.320.80   Based on its analysis, L concludes that the lifetime warranty provides a service in addition to the assurance that the product complies with agreed specifications. It therefore accounts for the service as a separate performance obligation. [*IFRS 15.B31*]

4.2.320.90   If an entity provides a warranty that includes both an assurance element and a service element and the entity cannot reasonably account for them separately, then it accounts for the warranties together as a performance obligation. [*IFRS 15.B32*]

4.2.320.100   If the warranty or part of the warranty is considered to be a performance obligation, then an entity allocates a portion of the transaction price to that performance obligation by applying the requirements of Step 4 of the model (see 4.2.160). [*IFRS 15.B29, B32*]

4.2.320.110   An entity may offer compensation in the form of cash or credit to a customer, rather than repairing or replacing the defective product. Unlike returns of faulty goods or replacements, this refund is generally accounted for using the guidance on a sale with a right of return (see 4.2.310), and not the guidance on warranties. [*IFRS 15.B20–B27*]

4.2.320.120   In a contract for the delivery of services, an entity may offer to 'make good' or offer a refund. If an entity offers to 'make good' – e.g. to repaint an area that a customer was not pleased about – then it considers this in determining the timing of the transfer of control and revenue recognition. If an entity offers a refund to customers who are dissatisfied with the service provided, then it applies the guidance on a sale with a right of return (see 4.2.310), and follows the guidance on estimating variable consideration in determining the transaction price for the service being provided (see 4.2.105). [*IFRS 15.B20–B27*]

4.2.320.130   A legal requirement to pay compensation if products cause harm or damage is not a performance obligation, and is accounted for under IAS 37 (see chapter 3.12). [*IFRS 15.B33*]

4.2.330   Customer options for additional goods and services

4.2.330.10   In a contract with a customer, the entity may grant the customer an option to acquire additional goods or services. Such an option gives rise to a performance obligation in the contract if the option provides a material right that the customer would not receive without entering into that contract. [*IFRS 15.B40*]

4.2.330.20   An option does not provide a customer with a material right if the option for additional goods and services provides a right to purchase the goods or services at a price that reflects the stand-alone selling price for those goods or services. [*IFRS 15.B41*]

4.2.330.30   The following flowchart helps analyse whether a customer option is a performance obligation. [*IFRS 15.B40–B41*]

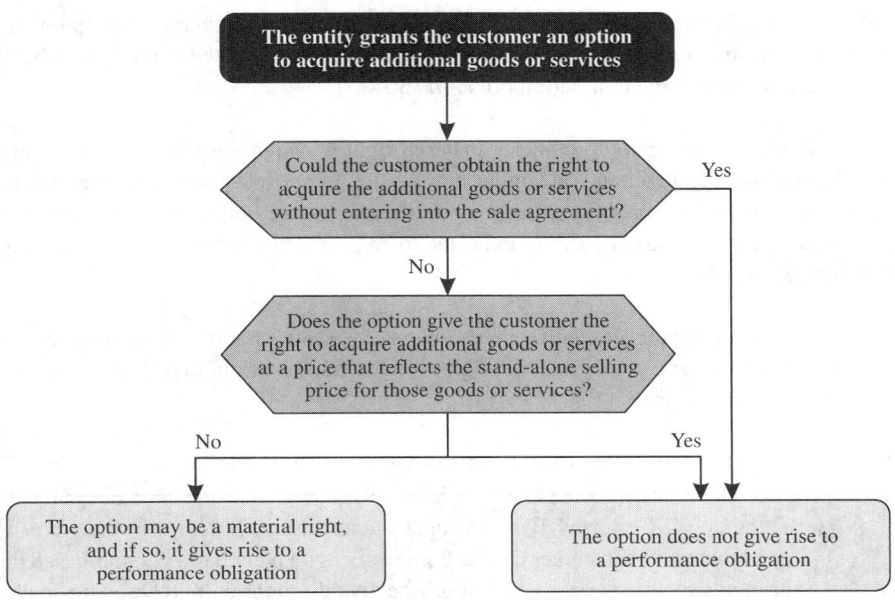

4.2.330.40 In many cases, the rights that an entity grants to its customers accumulate as the customer makes additional purchases. For example, in a customer loyalty programme, the points granted in an initial transaction are typically used in conjunction with points granted in subsequent transactions. Further, the value of the points granted in a single transaction may be low, but the combined value of points granted over an accumulation of transactions may be much higher. In such cases, the accumulating nature of the right is an essential part of the arrangement. When assessing whether these customer options represent a material right, an entity considers the cumulative value of the rights received in the transaction, the rights that have accumulated from past transactions and additional rights expected from future transactions. An entity considers all relevant quantitative and qualitative factors.

4.2.330.50 If the option is a material right that gives rise to a performance obligation, then a portion of the transaction price is allocated to the option on a relative stand-alone selling price basis (see 4.2.160). [*IFRS 15.B42*]

4.2.330.60 If the stand-alone selling price for a customer's option to acquire additional goods or services is not directly observable, then the entity estimates it. The estimate of the stand-alone selling price for a customer's option to acquire additional goods and services reflects the discount that the customer obtains when exercising the option, adjusted for the following:
- any discount that the customer receives without exercising the option; and
- the likelihood that the option will be exercised. [*IFRS 15.B42*]

4.2.330.70 The initial estimate of the likelihood that the customer will exercise the option is not subsequently revised because it is an input into the estimate of the stand-alone selling price of the option. Under IFRS 15, an entity does not reallocate the transaction price to reflect changes in stand-alone selling prices after contract inception. The customer's decision to exercise the option or allow the option to expire affects the timing of recognition of the amount allocated to the option, but it does not result in reallocation of the transaction price. [*IFRS 15.88*]

4.2.330.80   If a customer option provides a material right to acquire goods or services similar to the original ones in the contract and on similar terms – e.g. when the customer has an option to re-new the contract – then the transaction price may be allocated to the optional goods or services with reference to the optional goods or services expected to be provided and the corresponding expected consideration. [*IFRS 15.B43*]

4.2.330.83   It appears that the alternative approach in 4.2.330.80 is not limited to contract renewals and may be applied to other types of material rights – e.g. a material right to purchase similar goods or services at a discounted price.

EXAMPLE 17 – TIERED DISCOUNTS UNDER A FRAMEWORK AGREEMENT

4.2.330.85   Company B is a widget manufacturer. B enters into a framework agreement with Customer C. The framework agreement has a volume-based tiered pricing structure – i.e. there is a prospective discount on purchases made after a specified threshold is met. We believe that B may apply the alternative approach in 4.2.330.80 when determining the transaction price for purchases made under the agreement. Under the alternative approach, B would allocate the transaction price with reference to the total number of widgets that it expects C to purchase under the framework agreement and the corresponding expected consideration from those purchases – i.e. revenue would be recognised at the average price per unit based on total expected purchases. [*IFRS 15.B43*]

4.2.330.90   Revenue for material rights is recognised when the future goods or services are trans-ferred or when the option expires. If the option is a single right with a binary outcome – i.e. it will either be exercised in full or expire unexercised – then there is nothing to recognise before the option is exercised or expires. Conversely, if the option represents multiple rights or it does not expire, then it appears that an entity may apply the guidance on unexercised rights – i.e. breakage (see 4.2.410). We believe that an entity may apply the breakage guidance to customer loyalty programmes regard-less of whether the points expire because they represent multiple rights (see 4.2.335.75). [*IFRS 15.B40, B44–B46*]

4.2.330.100   When a customer exercises a material right for additional goods or services, an entity may account for it using one of the following approaches.
- *Continuation of the original contract:* Under this approach, an entity treats the consideration allocated to the material right as an addition to the consideration for the goods or services under the contract option – i.e. as a change in the transaction price.
- *Contract modification:* Under this approach, an entity applies the contract modification guidance to evaluate whether the goods or services transferred on exercise of the option are distinct from the other goods or services in the contract. The outcome of this evaluation will determine whether the modification is accounted for prospectively or with a cumulative catch-up adjustment.

EXAMPLE 18 – EXERCISE OF A MATERIAL RIGHT

Scenario 1

4.2.330.110   Service Provider S enters into a contract with Customer M to provide Service A for two years for 100. It also offers M an option to purchase two-year Service B, which is typically priced at 400, for 300. S determines that the option gives rise to a material right and therefore is a separate performance obligation. Assume that S allocates 75 to Service A and 25 to the option to purchase Service B, based on their stand-alone selling prices. Six months into the contract, M exercises the option to purchase Service B.

Scenario 2

4.2.330.120   Modifying Scenario 1, Services A and B are not distinct. It is assumed that the measure of progress on the date of the exercise of the option changes from 25% to 10%. The other assumptions are the same.

4.2.330.130   The table below explains how S accounts for the exercise of the option under each approach in Scenario 1 and Scenario 2.

CONTINUATION OF THE ORIGINAL CONTRACT	CONTRACT MODIFICATION	
PROSPECTIVE	DISTINCT – PROSPECTIVE	NOT DISTINCT – CUMULATIVE CATCH-UP
Scenarios 1 and 2	**Scenario 1**	**Scenario 2**
Recognise revenue of 325 (25 + 300) for Service B over two years.	Recognise revenue of 325 (25 + 300) for Service B over two years.	Update the transaction price to 400 (100 + 300).
No changes to the amount or timing of revenue recognition for Service A.	No changes to the amount or timing of revenue recognition for Service A.	Update the measure of progress from 25% to 10%.
		Recognise a catch-up adjustment of 21.25 (400 x 10% - (75 x 6 / 24)).
		Recognise revenue of 360 (400 - (400 x 10%)) over the remaining 18 months.

4.2.330.140   An entity can use a portfolio of similar transactions as a source of data to estimate expected breakage for an individual contract if it has a sufficiently large number of similar transactions or other history. Doing so is not using the portfolio approach (see 4.2.50).

4.2.335   *Customer loyalty programmes and other incentives*

4.2.335.10   A customer loyalty programme that provides a customer with a material right is accounted for as a separate performance obligation. [*IFRS 15.B40*]

EXAMPLE 19 – CUSTOMER LOYALTY PROGRAMME

4.2.335.20 Company C operates a customer loyalty programme at its store, rewarding customers 1 point per 10 spent. Each point is redeemable for a cash value of 1 on future purchases. No other discounts or rebates are offered by C to customers.

4.2.335.30 During year 1, customers purchase products from the store for 100,000 and earn 10,000 points redeemable for future purchases at the store. C expects customers to redeem 97% of the points. The redemption estimate is made on the basis of C's past experience, which it assesses as being predictive of the amount of consideration to which it will be entitled. The stand-alone selling price of the products sold to customers without points is 100,000.

4.2.335.40 Because the points provide a material right to the customers that they would not receive without having purchased products from the store, C concludes that the points are a separate performance obligation of the contracts for the sale of those products – i.e. the customers paid for the points when purchasing products from the store.

4.2.335.50 C allocates the transaction price between the product and the points on a relative stand-alone selling price basis as follows.

PERFORMANCE OBLIGATION	STAND-ALONE SELLING PRICES	SELLING PRICE RATIO	PRICE ALLOCATION
Products	100,000	91%	91,000[1]
Points	9,700[2]	9%	9,000[3]
Total	109,700	100%	100,000

Notes
1. Calculated as 100,000 x 91%.
2. Calculated as 10,000 x 1 x 97%.
3. Calculated as 100,000 x 9%.

4.2.335.60 During year 2, 4,500 of the points are redeemed, and C continues to expect that 9,700 points will be redeemed in total. C calculates the revenue to be recognised and the corresponding reduction in the contract liability as follows.

$$4,175 = 9,000 \times 4,500 / 9,700$$

– i.e. price allocated to points multiplied by points redeemed in year 2 divided by total points expected to be redeemed.

4.2.335.70 During year 3, a further 4,000 points are redeemed. C updates its estimate, because it now expects 9,900 rather than 9,700 points to be redeemed. C calculates the revenue to be recognised and the corresponding reduction in the contract liability as follows.

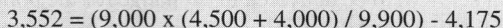

$$3{,}552 = (9{,}000 \times (4{,}500 + 4{,}000) / 9{,}900) - 4{,}175$$

– i.e. price allocated to points multiplied by points redeemed in year 2 and year 3 divided by total points expected to be redeemed minus revenue recognised in year 2.

4.2.335.75   Under some loyalty programmes, points expire, whereas under others they do not. It appears that an entity may apply the breakage guidance in 4.2.410 to both types of programmes to determine when to recognise revenue for points that are not expected to be exercised.

4.2.335.80   Customer loyalty programmes do not generally include a significant financing component even though the time period between when the customer loyalty points are earned and redeemed may be greater than one year. This is because the transfer of the related goods or services to the customer – i.e. use of the loyalty points – occurs at the discretion of the customer. [*IFRS 15.62, BC233*]

4.2.335.90   If an entity sells gift cards or coupons in stand-alone transactions with customers and grants gift cards or coupons in the same denomination in transactions in which customers purchase other goods and services, then the stand-alone selling price of the gift card or coupon identified as a material right may differ from the stand-alone selling price of a gift card or coupon sold separately. This is because customers who receive the gift card or coupon as a material right may be significantly less likely to redeem it than customers who purchase a gift card or coupon in a separate transaction. Therefore, an entity may conclude that there is no directly observable stand-alone selling price for a free gift card or coupon provided to a customer in connection with the purchase of another good or service. In this case, the entity estimates the stand-alone selling price using the guidance in Step 4 of the model (see 4.2.170). [*IFRS 15.B42*]

4.2.335.100   Retail stores often print coupons at the register after a purchase is completed. These coupons are often a form of marketing offer, and customers can often access similar discounts without making a purchase – e.g. if coupons are printed in a newspaper or freely available in-store or online. Typically, these coupons have little or no effect on the revenue accounting when they are granted. If there is no general marketing offer, then the entity assesses whether the coupon conveys a material right. This assessment includes consideration of the likelihood of redemption, which will often be low and therefore reduces the likelihood that the coupon will be identified as a material right. As a result, the coupons are often recognised as a reduction in revenue on redemption. [*IFRS 15.B42*]

4.2.337   *Awards supplied by a third party*

4.2.337.10   Some customer loyalty programmes may involve multiple parties. If another party is involved in the customer loyalty programme, then an entity needs to assess whether it acts as an agent or as a principal with respect to the loyalty points and, if relevant, the goods or services to be delivered in exchange for the points (see 4.2.340). Loyalty programmes may be structured in different ways which impacts this assessment. Typical arrangements include the following.

- *Points are issued by the entity and can be redeemed only for goods or services provided by the entity:* In such arrangements, an entity is usually a principal with respect to the loyalty points and the goods or services to be delivered in exchange for the points because it does not satisfy its performance obligation until the goods or services are transferred to the customer.

- *Points are issued by the entity and can be redeemed for goods or services provided by the entity or by a third party at the customer's discretion:* In such arrangements, an entity is usually a principal with respect to the loyalty points because it is obliged to 'stand ready' until the customer has made its choice. The entity satisfies its performance obligation and recognises revenue only when the customer redeems the points, either from the entity or from the third party. An entity assesses whether it acts as an agent or as a principal with respect to the goods or services to be delivered in exchange for the points.
- *Points can be redeemed for goods or services provided only by a third party:* In such arrangements, an entity assesses whether it acts as an agent or as a principal with respect to the points (i.e. does it control the points before they are transferred to the customer). In some cases, it may be challenging. For example, a bank may offer its credit card customers a loyalty programme under which the customer earns points to be redeemed with a specific airline. Judgement is required to determine whether the bank controls the points before they are transferred to the customer (see 4.2.340). Under this type of arrangement, an entity typically satisfies its obligation when the points are transferred to the customer. [*IFRS 15.BC383–BC385*]

4.2.337.20   If the entity acts as an agent, then the net amount retained is recognised as revenue – i.e. the difference between the revenue allocated to the points and the amount that the entity pays to the third party. [*IFRS 15.B36, BC383–BC385*]

EXAMPLE 20A – THIRD PARTY CUSTOMER LOYALTY PROGRAMME – PRINCIPAL VS AGENT (1)

4.2.337.30   Company L participates in a customer loyalty programme operated by a third party. Under the programme, members earn points for purchases made in L's stores. Programme members redeem the accumulated award points for goods supplied by the third party. At the end of 2018, L has granted points with an allocated transaction price of 1,000 and owes the third party 700. The amount of revenue to be recognised depends on whether L acts as an agent or a principal with respect to the points.

L is an agent

4.2.337.40   If L is acting as an agent with respect to the points, then it recognises revenue of 300 in relation to the award points when its products are sold to customers and L has satisfied its obligation to arrange for the points to be provided to the customer. L records the following entry.

	DEBIT	CREDIT
Cash	1,000	
Revenue (1,000 - 700)		300
Payable to third party		700
To recognise revenue when acting as agent for issuance of the points		

L is a principal

4.2.337.50   If L is acting as a principal with respect to the points, then it recognises revenue of 1,000 and an expense of 700 when its products are sold to customers and the points are transferred to the customer. L records the following entry.

	DEBIT	CREDIT
Cash	1,000	
Expense	700	
Revenue		1,000
Payable to third party		700
To recognise revenue when acting as principal for issuance of the points		

EXAMPLE 20B – THIRD PARTY CUSTOMER LOYALTY PROGRAMME – PRINCIPAL VS AGENT (2)

4.2.337.60   Company M participates in a customer loyalty programme operated by a third party. Programme members earn points for purchases made in 2018 in M's stores and can redeem the accumulated points for goods supplied by either M or the third party until 31 December 2019.

4.2.337.70   At the end of 2018, M has recognised contract liabilities of 2,000, representing 1,000 awards expected to be redeemed. In 2019, 500 awards are redeemed with the third party, 400 awards are redeemed directly with M and 100 awards expire without being redeemed. The third party invoices M 1.75 for each award redeemed by members and M determines that it acts as an agent when the third party supplies the awards. The cost of the inventory for the goods supplied for points redeemed directly with M is 600.

4.2.337.80   In 2019, M recognises a liability of 875 (500 x 1.75), derecognises the contract liabilities of 2,000 and recognises revenue of 1,125, which represents revenue of 800 (400 x 2) for awards redeemed directly, 125 (500 x 0.25) for awards redeemed through the third party, and 200 (100 x 2) for lapsed awards.

	DEBIT	CREDIT
Contract liabilities	2,000	
Cost of goods sold	300	
Revenue		1,125
Payable to third party		875
Inventory		600
To recognise revenue from the loyalty programme in 2019		

4.2.337.90   When an entity participates in a loyalty programme operated by a third party, it may be required to pay the third party for:
- carrying out administrative tasks with respect to the programme; and
- assuming the obligation to supply the awards.

4.2.337.100   It appears that it is appropriate for the entity to recognise amounts payable to the third party for carrying out administrative tasks in profit or loss as an expense over the period in which the loyalty programme is in effect.

4.2.337.110   It appears that it is appropriate for the entity to recognise amounts payable to the third party for assuming the obligation to supply the awards when the third party becomes obliged to supply the awards, by analogy to the principle for recognising revenue in IFRS 15. In Example 20B, this occurs when a customer chooses to redeem its awards from the third party in 2019.

4.2.340   Principal vs agent

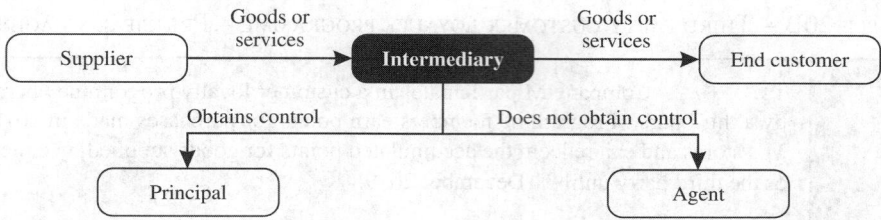

4.2.340.10   When an entity provides goods or services directly to its customers and no other parties are involved, the entity is the principal. However, when other parties are involved, the entity determines whether the nature of its promise is a performance obligation to provide the specified goods or services itself, or to arrange for them to be provided by another party – i.e. whether it is a principal or an agent. This determination is made by identifying each specified (i.e. distinct) good or service promised to the customer in the contract and evaluating whether the entity obtains control of the specified good or service before it is transferred to the customer. Because an entity evaluates whether it is a principal or an agent for each good or service to be transferred to the customer, it is possible for the entity to be a principal for one or more goods or services and an agent for others in the same contract. [*IFRS 15.B34–B34A*]

4.2.340.20   If an entity obtains control of the goods or the right to the services in advance of transferring those goods or services to the customer, then the entity is a principal. Otherwise, it is an agent. [*IFRS 15.B35–B36*]

4.2.340.25   When another party is involved, an entity that is a principal obtains control of:
- a good from another party that it then transfers to the customer;
- a right to a service that will be performed by another party, which gives the entity the ability to direct that party to provide the service on the entity's behalf; or
- a good or a service from another party that it combines with other goods or services to produce the specified good or service promised to the customer. [*IFRS 15.B35A*]

4.2.340.30   To determine if it controls a specified good or service before it is transferred to the customer, the entity acting as an intermediary applies the general guidance on transfer of control (see 4.2.240). The following indicators may be helpful in this analysis.

- *Intermediary does not obtain control – agent:* The supplier has a substantive unconditional right to recall the inventory before sale to an end customer, or the supplier and the intermediary enter into a consignment arrangement and control only passes on sale to the end customer.
- *Intermediary obtains control – principal:* The supplier and the intermediary enter into a bill-and-hold arrangement and all of the criteria for the transfer of control in 4.2.360.20 are met. [*IFRS 15.B77–B78, B81*]

4.2.340.35   If the assessment based on the general guidance on transfer of control is not conclusive, then an entity considers the specific indicators of whether it acts as a principal. These indicators include, but are not limited to, the following. [*IFRS 15.B34A, B37*]

INDICATOR	RELEVANT CONSIDERATIONS
The entity is primarily responsible for providing specified goods or services	The entity: • has discretion with respect to accepting and rejecting orders from customers; • can source the good or service ordered by the customer from more than one supplier; • is responsible for delivery and any loss or damage between pick up from the supplier and delivery to the end customer; • is responsible for the sales strategy; and • is the party the customer believes is responsible for fulfilling the promise.
The entity has inventory risk	The entity: • is liable for damage and product loss for inventory in its possession before sale to the end customer, including loss in inventory value; • is liable for customer returns; • commits to a minimum order quantity; and • has no right to return unsold inventory to the supplier.
The entity has discretion in establishing prices for specified goods or services	The amount paid to the supplier is: • a fixed price per unit; and • not a commission or fee basis, which is fixed in terms of either an amount of currency or a percentage of the value of the underlying goods or services.

4.2.340.40   The indicators in 4.2.340.30 and 35 are not exhaustive. To assess whether it obtains control, an entity needs to carefully assess its facts and circumstances, including the nature of the specified goods or services and the terms and conditions of the contract. There is no specific hierarchy for the indicators, and all of the indicators are considered in making the assessment. [*IFRS 15.B37A*]

4.2.340.50   The evaluation focuses on the promise to the customer, and the unit of account is the specified good or service. A 'specified good or service' is a distinct good or service (or a distinct bundle of goods or services) to be provided to the customer. That is, the analysis of whether an entity acts as a principal or an agent is performed at the performance obligation level. If individual goods and services are not distinct from one another, then they represent inputs into a combined promise that is the specified good or service that the entity assesses. [*IFRS 15.B34, BC385Q*]

4.2.340.60 When a customer contracts for a combined output of significantly integrated goods or services and the entity is the party that provides the significant integration service, the entity is the principal for the combined output. In these cases, the entity controls the specified good or service (the combined output) before it transfers control to the customer because it controls the inputs necessary to perform the significant integration service. [*IFRS 15.B35A(c), BC385R*]

4.2.340.70 The specified good or service to be transferred to the customer may in some cases be a right to an underlying good or service that will be provided by another party. For example, a travel website may sell an airline ticket that gives the customer the right to fly on a particular airline, or an entity may provide a voucher that gives the holder the right to a meal at a specified restaurant. In these cases, the principal vs agent assessment is analysed based on who controls the right to the underlying good or service. That is, an entity may be a principal in a transaction relating to a right (e.g. sale of a voucher that gives the customer the right to a meal) even if another party controls and transfers the underlying good or service (e.g. the flight or the meal) to the end customer. [*IFRS 15.B35A(b)*]

4.2.340.80 An entity may be a principal in a transaction relating to a right if it has the ability to direct the use of the right to the underlying service because it has committed itself to purchase the right and has inventory risk. The entity's ability to establish the price that the customer would pay for the right may also be a relevant indicator to consider. [*IFRS 15.IE239–IE248F*]

4.2.340.90 If the entity is a principal, then revenue and the related costs are recognised on a gross basis – corresponding to the consideration to which the entity expects to be entitled. For example, if an entity providing restructuring advice and engaging external lawyers determines that it acts as a principal, then it reports revenue and legal fees paid to lawyers on a gross basis. [*IFRS 15.B35B*]

4.2.340.100 In some arrangements in which the entity is a principal, it may not know the price paid by the end customer to the intermediary because it receives a fixed amount per unit regardless of the price paid. This may be the case when the intermediary has flexibility in setting prices or procures the good or service on behalf of the end customer. An entity that is a principal would generally be expected to be able to apply judgement and determine the consideration to which it is entitled using all relevant facts and circumstances. Such cases do not represent variable consideration. [*IFRS 15.BC385X–BC385Z*]

4.2.340.110 If the entity acts as an agent, then its performance obligation is to arrange for the provision of the specified good or service. Therefore, it recognises revenue on a net basis corresponding to any fee or commission to which it expects to be entitled. An entity's fee or commission might be the net amount of consideration that the entity retains after paying other parties. An entity recognises revenue when its obligation to arrange for the provision of the specified good or service is fulfilled, which may be before it is provided to the customer by the principal. [*IFRS 15.B36*]

EXAMPLE 21 – REVENUE RECOGNITION BY AN AGENT

4.2.340.120   Company V operates a website from which it sells Company T's products. Customers place orders directly on the website and provide credit card details for payment. V receives the order and authorisation from the credit card company, and passes the order on to T, which ships the product directly to the customer. V does not take title to the product and has no risk of loss or other responsibility for the function or delivery of the product. T is responsible for all product returns and defects. T sets the price of the product at 175, from which V receives a commission of 25.

4.2.340.130   V considers that it does not take title to the product, is not primarily responsible for providing the product, does not have inventory risk, and does not have discretion in establishing prices. Therefore, V determines that it does not control the product before it is transferred to the customer and acts as an agent. As a result, V recognises its fee of 25 as revenue when it passes the order to T.

4.2.340.140   Amounts collected by an agent on behalf of a third party are accounted for as a payable in the statement of financial position until they are settled and do not gross up revenue and expenses. Similarly, amounts prepaid by an agent to a third party on behalf of customers are recognised as a receivable until recovered and do not gross up revenues and expenses. [*IFRS 15.47, B35B–B36*]

4.2.345   *Sales taxes*

4.2.345.10   Revenue does not include amounts collected on behalf of tax authorities – e.g. some sales taxes, excise duties or value added taxes (VAT). The amount of taxes or duties may be computed as a percentage of either the selling price or the production cost. [*IFRS 15.47*]

4.2.345.20   To determine how to account for sales taxes or duties, an entity assesses whether it is primarily obligated for payment of the taxes or whether it collects the amount from the customer on behalf of the tax authorities. This determination is made based on the analysis of the local regulatory requirements. [*IFRS 15.BC188B*]

EXAMPLE 22A – SALES TAXES – GROSS ACCOUNTING FOR EXCISE DUTIES

4.2.345.30   Excise duties may be determined based on production levels and are payable to the authorities regardless of whether goods are sold – i.e. the tax payments are not refunded by the authorities if the goods are not sold. It appears that in these cases the seller is primarily responsible for the tax and it is another production cost to be recovered in the pricing of the goods. Accordingly, it does not collect the tax from the customer on behalf of the tax authorities and the transaction price would be determined on a gross basis, including the excise duties recouped from customers. As a result, any excise duties recouped from a customer should be included in the revenue line item, and any excise duties incurred should be included in the 'cost of goods sold' line item.

EXAMPLE 22B – SALES TAXES – NET ACCOUNTING FOR EXCISE DUTIES

> 4.2.345.40   Excise duties may be recouped from the authorities if the buyer defaults. It appears that in such cases, the seller is likely to be collecting the tax from the customer on behalf of the tax authorities because it is not primarily responsible for the tax and does not bear any risk. Under this approach, the amount of excise tax should be excluded from revenue and amounts collected should be reported as a liability.

EXAMPLE 22C – SALES TAXES – GROSS ACCOUNTING FOR EXPORT TAXES

> 4.2.345.50   The tax authorities in Country X impose an export tax on certain commodities sold to overseas customers; an entity cannot reclaim the tax if the customer defaults. It appears that this example is similar to Example 22A – i.e. the seller is primarily obligated for payment of the taxes rather than collecting the amounts on behalf of the tax authorities. Therefore, the transaction price is determined on a gross basis, including any export tax recouped from customers. As a result, the export tax is included in the revenue line item, and export tax incurred is included in expenses or 'cost of goods sold'.

4.2.345.60   The accounting for sales or excise duties may vary depending on the different tax regimes in various jurisdictions. This might lead to different accounting for different sales or excise duties by entities within a multinational group. Depending on how the legal or regulatory requirements are applied, the determination of whether an entity is primarily responsible for the tax may require significant judgement. It appears that if excise taxes are significant, then the entity should disclose the judgements made and the line item(s) in which amounts are included, if applicable.

4.2.347   *Transporting goods to customers*

4.2.347.10   In some arrangements, an entity delivers goods to a location specified by its customer and incurs transport costs. To determine how to account for these costs, an entity needs to consider whether the transportation service is a distinct performance obligation (see 4.2.60) and when control of the goods transfers to the customer.

4.2.347.20   If control of the goods transfers to the customer on delivery to the final destination – i.e. transport and distribution costs form part of a single performance obligation for the sale of goods – then the entity recognises revenue when the goods are delivered and applies the guidance on inventory in IAS 2 on accounting for transport costs (see 3.8.230).

4.2.347.30   If control of the goods transfers to the customer before the goods are transported, then this may indicate that the transportation service is a separate performance obligation and the entity needs to determine whether it is a principal or an agent in relation to it (see 4.2.340).
- If the entity acts as a principal for the transportation service, then it recognises the gross revenue as the service is provided and applies the guidance in IFRS 15 on fulfilment costs.
- If the entity acts as an agent for the transportation service, then it recognises the net revenue when the service is arranged. [*IFRS 15.B34, BC116S*]

4.2.347.40   The following flowchart summarises how an entity may analyse transport costs.

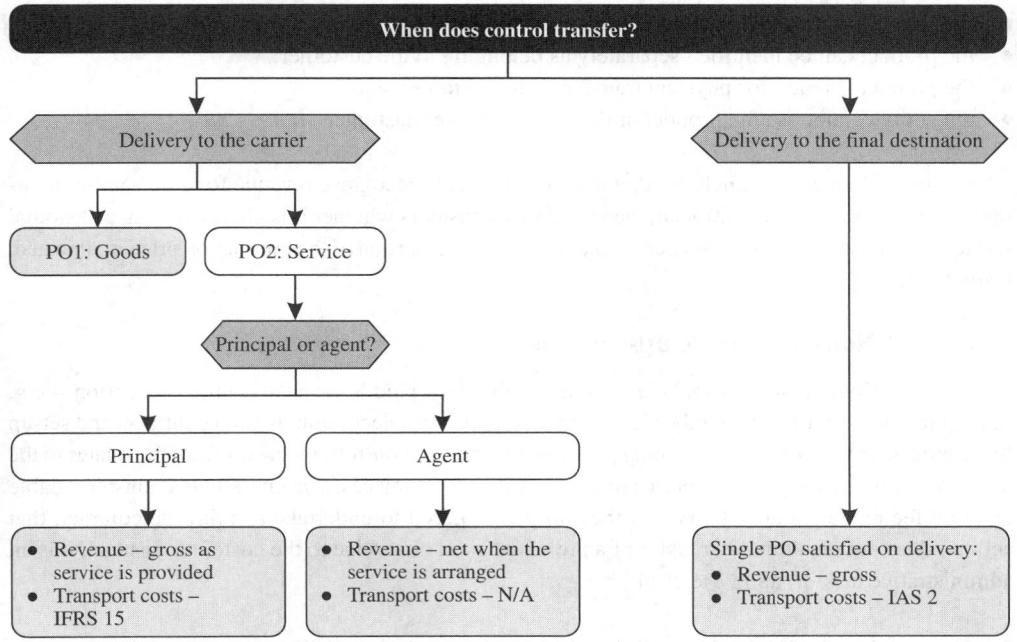

4.2.350   Consignment arrangements

4.2.350.10   In some cases, an entity may deliver goods to another party but retain control of those goods – e.g. an entity may deliver a product to a party, such as a dealer or distributor, for sale to an end customer. These types of arrangements are called consignment arrangements. [*IFRS 15.B77*]

4.2.350.20   Indicators that an arrangement is a consignment arrangement include, but are not limited to, the following:
● the product is controlled by the entity until a specified event occurs, such as the sale of the product to a customer of the intermediary, or until a specified period expires;
● the entity is able to require the return of the product, or transfer the product to another intermediary; and
● the intermediary does not have an unconditional obligation to pay for the product, although it might be required to pay a deposit. [*IFRS 15.B78*]

4.2.360   Bill-and-hold arrangements

4.2.360.10   Bill-and-hold arrangements occur when an entity bills a customer for a product but retains physical possession of the product until it is transferred to the customer at a future point in time – e.g. because of a customer's lack of available space for the product or delays in the customer's production schedules. An entity recognises revenue for a bill-and-hold arrangement when the customer obtains control of the product, which may in some cases be before delivery to the customer. [*IFRS 15.B79–B80*]

4.2.360.20   For an entity to have transferred control of a product in a bill-and-hold arrangement, all of the following criteria are required to be met:
- the reason for the bill-and-hold arrangement is substantive;
- the product can be identified separately as belonging to the customer;
- the product is ready for physical transfer to the customer; and
- the entity cannot use the product or direct it to another customer. [*IFRS 15.B81*]

4.2.360.30   If an entity concludes that it is appropriate to recognise revenue for a bill-and-hold arrangement before a good is shipped, then the entity considers whether it is also providing a custodial service that constitutes a performance obligation to which a portion of the transaction price is allocated. [*IFRS 15.B82*]

4.2.370   Non-refundable up-front fees

4.2.370.10   Some contracts include non-refundable fees paid at or near contract inception – e.g. joining fees for health club memberships, activation fees for telecommunication contracts and set-up fees for outsourcing contracts. An entity assesses whether the non-refundable up-front fee relates to the transfer of a promised good or service to the customer. In many cases, even though a non-refundable up-front fee relates to an activity that the entity is required to undertake to fulfil the contract, that activity does not result in the transfer of a promised good or service to the customer. Instead, it is an administrative task. [*IFRS 15.B48–B50*]

4.2.370.20   If the activity does not result in the transfer of a promised good or service to the customer, then the up-front fee is an advance payment for performance obligations to be satisfied in the future and is recognised as revenue when those future goods or services are provided. [*IFRS 15.B49*]

4.2.370.25   In the funds industry, there are usually two separate contracts: the first between the investor and the fund's manager (brokerage or sales contract, whereby the fund manager acts as an agent for the fund); and the second between the fund's manager and the fund itself (investment management contract). The fund manager assesses whether the up-front fee receivable for the sale of units of a (retail) fund relates to the transfer of a promised service (i.e. a brokerage service) or if it is an advance payment for an investment management service to be satisfied in the future. By contrast, in the insurance industry, it appears that there is generally no distinct brokerage service because insurers enter into a single contract with policyholders (investors) and the contract is sold as a net package.

4.2.370.30   If the up-front fee gives rise to a material right for future goods or services, then the entity attributes all of it to the goods and services to be transferred, including the material right associated with the up-front payment. [*IFRS 15.B49*]

4.2.370.40   When assessing whether a non-refundable up-front fee provides the customer with a material right, an entity considers both quantitative and qualitative factors from the customer's perspective – i.e. how likely the non-refundable up-front fee is to impact the customer's decision on whether to exercise the option to continue buying the entity's product or service. This is consistent with the notion that an entity considers valid expectations of the customer when identifying promised goods or services.

4.2.370.50   An entity recognises revenue from up-front fees when the goods or services to which they relate are provided to the customer. [*IFRS 15.B49*]

4.2.370.60   In some cases, an entity may charge a non-refundable fee in part as compensation for costs incurred in setting up the contract. If the set-up activities do not represent a performance obligation, then the up-front fees are not recognised as revenue until or as the entity satisfies its performance obligations. [*IFRS 15.B51*]

4.2.370.70   An entity needs to consider whether the receipt of an up-front payment gives rise to a significant financing component within the contract. All relevant facts and circumstances will need to be evaluated, and an entity needs to apply judgement in determining whether a significant financing component exists (see 4.2.130). [*IFRS 15.60*]

4.2.380   Repurchase arrangements#

4.2.380.10   An entity enters into a repurchase agreement if the entity sells an asset to a customer and promises or has the option to repurchase it, or if the customer has the option to put it back to the entity. The option to repurchase the asset may be in the same contract or in another contract. A contract creates enforceable rights and obligations and can be written, oral or implied by an entity's customary business practices (see 4.2.30). [*IFRS 15.10, B64*]

4.2.380.20   If an entity does not have a contractual right to repurchase a good, but decides to do so after transferring control of that good to a customer, then this does not constitute a repurchase arrangement. This is because the customer is not obliged to resell that good to the entity under the original contract. [*IFRS 15.BC423*]

4.2.380.30   Repurchase agreements may be in the form of:
- a forward or a purchase call option; or
- a written put option. [*IFRS 15.B65*]

4.2.390   *Repurchase arrangements in a form of forward or purchase call option*

4.2.390.10   If the repurchase arrangement is in the form of a forward or a call option, then the entity has not transferred control of the asset to the customer and accounts for the arrangement as:
- a lease, if the repurchase price is less than the original selling price; or
- a financing arrangement, if the repurchase price equals or exceeds the original selling price. [*IFRS 15.B66*]

4.2.390.20   When comparing the repurchase price with the selling price, the entity considers the time value of money. [*IFRS 15.B67*]

4.2.390.30   In a financing arrangement, the entity continues to recognise the asset and recognises a financial liability for any consideration received. The difference between the consideration received from the customer and the amount of consideration to be paid to the customer is recognised as interest, and processing or holding costs if applicable. If the option expires unexercised, then the entity derecognises the liability and the related asset, and recognises revenue. [*IFRS 15.B68–B69*]

4.2.400 *Repurchase arrangements in a form of written put option*

4.2.400.10   If the repurchase arrangement is in the form of a written put option, then the arrangement is accounted for as:

- a lease, if the customer has a significant economic incentive to exercise the option and the exercise
  price is less than the original selling price;
- a financing arrangement, if the exercise price equals or exceeds the original selling price and is
  more than the expected market value of the asset; or
- a sale with right of return, if the customer does not have a significant economic incentive to
  exercise the option at a price that is:
    - lower than the original selling price; or
    - equal to or higher than the original selling price and lower than or equal to the expected market
      value of the asset. [*IFRS 15.B70, B72–B74*]

4.2.400.20   The following flowchart illustrates the analysis of how to account for a repurchase
agreement in the form of a written put option.

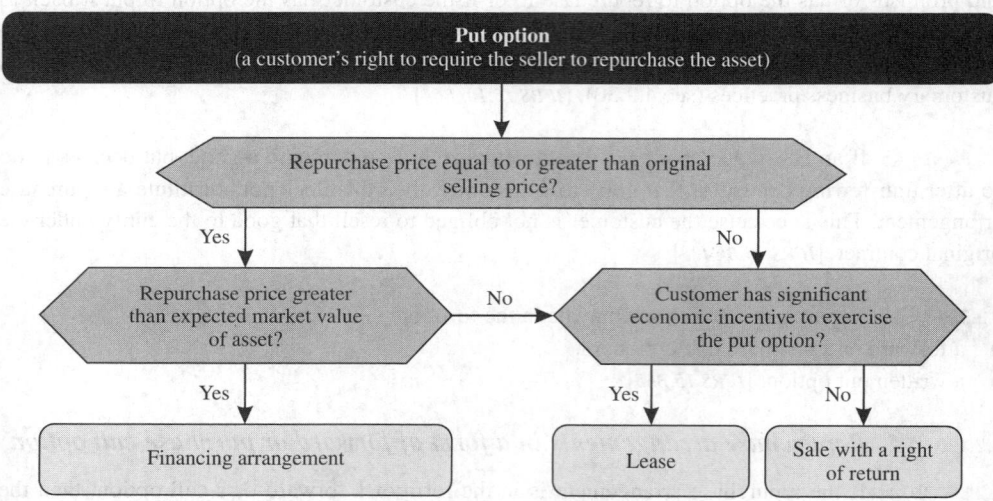

4.2.400.30   To assess whether the customer has a significant economic incentive, an entity considers
factors including:

- the relationship of the repurchase price to the expected market value of the asset at the date of
  repurchase; and
- the amount of time until the right expires. [*IFRS 15.B71*]

4.2.400.40   If an arrangement is accounted for as a financing arrangement (see 4.2.390.30) and
the option expires unexercised, then the entity derecognises the liability and the related asset and
recognises revenue at the date on which the option expires. [*IFRS 15.B76*]

4.2.400.50   When comparing the repurchase price with the selling price, the entity considers the
time value of money. [*IFRS 15.B75*]

4.2.405.10   IFRS 16 introduces consequential amendments to IFRS 15 in relation to sale and re-purchase agreements. Under the amended guidance, if the contract is part of a sale-and-leaseback transaction, then the entity treats the arrangement as a financing arrangement and accounts for the financial liability in accordance with IFRS 9. [*IFRS 15.B66(a), B70, 16.103*]

4.2.410   Customers' unexercised rights (breakage)

4.2.410.10   An entity may receive a non-refundable prepayment from a customer that gives the customer the right to receive goods or services in the future. Common examples include gift vouchers and non-refundable tickets. However, prepaid stored-value products (e.g. a gift card) that meet the definition of financial liabilities are excluded from the scope of IFRS 15 and accounted for in accordance with IFRS 9.

4.2.410.20   An entity recognises a prepayment received from a customer as a contract liability and recognises revenue when the promised goods or services are delivered in the future. However, a portion of the contract liability recognised may relate to contractual rights that the entity does not expect to be exercised – i.e. a breakage amount. [*IFRS 15.B44–B45*]

4.2.410.30   The timing of recognition of revenue related to breakage depends on whether the entity expects to be entitled to a breakage amount. [*IFRS 15.B46*]

4.2.410.40   To determine whether an entity expects to be entitled to a breakage amount, it applies the constraint requirements in Step 3 of the model (see 4.2.110). It determines the amount of break-age to which it is entitled as the amount for which it is considered highly probable that a significant reversal will not occur in the future. This amount is recognised as revenue in proportion to the pattern of rights exercised by the customer (proportional method) when the entity expects to be entitled to breakage. Otherwise, the entity recognises breakage when the likelihood of the customer exercising its remaining rights becomes remote (remote method). [*IFRS 15.B46*]

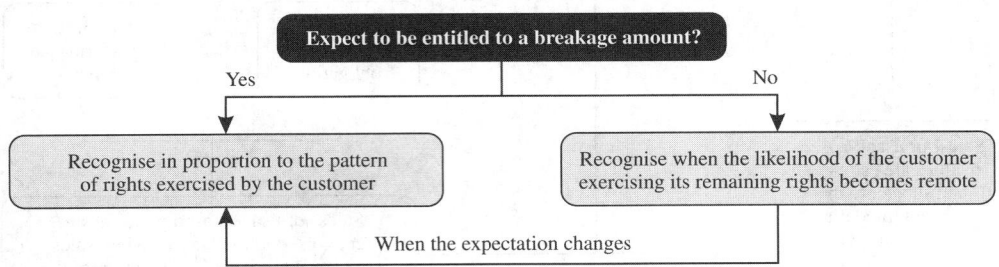

4.2.410.50   Although an entity considers the variable consideration guidance to determine the amount of breakage, breakage itself is not a form of variable consideration because it does not affect the transaction price. It is a recognition, rather than a measurement concept in IFRS 15. [*IFRS 15.B46*]

4.2.410.60   If an entity is required to remit unclaimed funds from a customer balance to a govern-ment entity – e.g. in accordance with unclaimed property laws – then it recognises a liability instead of revenue. [*IFRS 15.B47*]

4.2.420   **Licensing**

4.2.420.10   A licence establishes a customer's rights to the intellectual property of an entity – for example:

- software and technology;
- movies, music and video games;
- franchises;
- patents, trademarks and copyrights; and
- scientific compounds. [*IFRS 15.B52*]

4.2.420.20   The following flowchart summarises how IFRS 15 applies to licences of intellectual property.

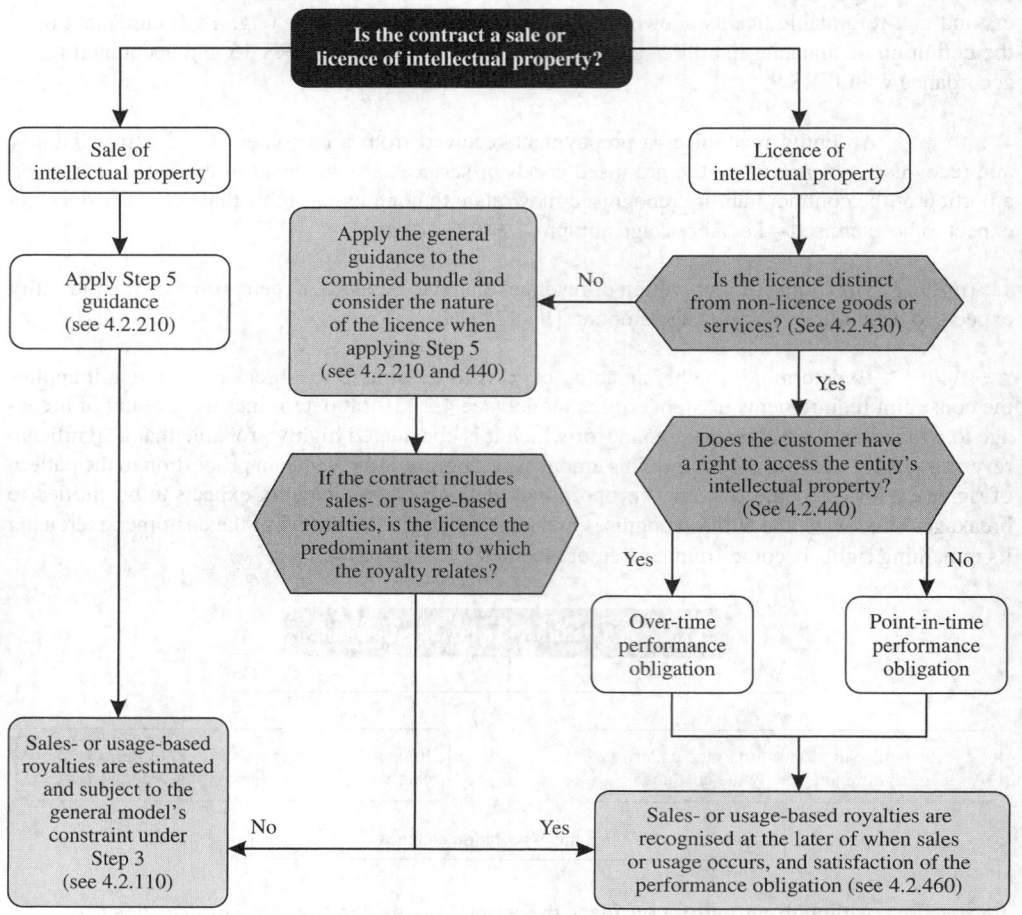

4.2.430   *Determining if a licence is distinct*

4.2.430.10   A contract to transfer a licence to a customer may include promises to deliver other goods or services in addition to the promised licence. These promises may be specified in the contract or implied by an entity's customary business practices. [*IFRS 15.B53*]

4.2.430.20   An entity applies Step 2 of the model (see 4.2.60) to identify each of the performance obligations in a contract that includes a promise to grant a licence in addition to other promised goods or services. This includes an assessment of whether:
- the customer can benefit from the licence on its own or together with other resources that are readily available; and
- the licence is separately identifiable from other goods or services in the contract. [*IFRS 15.B53*]

4.2.430.30   In some cases it may be necessary to consider the nature of the entity's promise in granting a licence that is not distinct. An entity considers the nature of its promise in granting a licence that is the primary or dominant component of a combined performance obligation. [*IFRS 15.BC414X*]

4.2.430.40   If the licence is not distinct, then an entity accounts for it in accordance with the general requirements of IFRS 15. Examples of licences that are not distinct are:
- a licence that forms part of a tangible good and that is integral to the functionality of that good; and
- a licence that the customer can benefit from only in conjunction with a related service. [*IFRS 15.B54*]

4.2.440   *Nature of a distinct licence*

4.2.440.10   If an entity grants a licence that is distinct from other promised goods or services in the contract, then it evaluates the nature of the licence to determine if it is:
- a right to access the entity's intellectual property as it exists throughout the licence period. If this is the case, then revenue from the licence is recognised over time; or
- a right to use the entity's intellectual property as it exists at the point in time at which the licence is granted. If this is the case, then revenue from the licence is recognised at a point in time. [*IFRS 15.B56*]

4.2.440.20   The nature of the licence is a right to access if all of the following criteria are met:
- the contract requires, or the customer reasonably expects, that the entity will undertake activities that significantly affect the intellectual property to which the customer has rights;
- the rights granted by the licence directly expose the customer to any positive or negative effects of the entity's activities that significantly affect the intellectual property; and
- those activities do not result in the transfer of a good or a service to the customer as those activities occur. [*IFRS 15.B58*]

4.2.440.30   To determine whether a customer could reasonably expect the entity to undertake activities that do not result in the transfer of a good or service to the customer that significantly affect the intellectual property, the entity considers its customary business practices, published policies and specific statements, and whether there is a shared economic interest between the entity and the customer. [*IFRS 15.B59*]

4.2.440.40   An entity significantly affects the intellectual property when either:
- activities are expected to change the form (e.g. the design or content) or functionality (e.g. the ability to perform a function or task) of the intellectual property; or
- the ability to obtain benefit from the intellectual property is substantially derived from, or dependent on, those activities (e.g. the ability to benefit from a brand is often dependent on the entity's ongoing activities to support or maintain the value of that brand). [*IFRS 15.B59A*]

4.2.440.50 An entity's ongoing activities do not significantly affect the intellectual property when that intellectual property has significant stand-alone functionality, unless they change that functionality. Intellectual property that often has significant stand-alone functionality includes software, biological compounds or drug formulas, and completed media content (e.g. films, television shows and music recordings). [*IFRS 15.B59A*]

4.2.440.60 If the criteria in 4.2.440.20 are not met, then the nature of the licence is a right to use the entity's intellectual property as that intellectual property exists at the date the licence is granted. This is because in this case the customer can direct the use of, and obtain substantially all of the remaining benefits from, the licence at the point in time it transfers. When the nature of the licence is a right to use the entity's intellectual property, it is accounted for as a performance obligation satisfied at a point in time. [*IFRS 15.B61*]

4.2.440.70 Contractual provisions relating to time, geographical region or use could represent:
- additional licences if they create a right to use or access intellectual property that the customer does not already control; or
- only attributes of a promised licence to intellectual property that the customer controls. [*IFRS 15.B62*]

4.2.440.80 If these provisions do not represent multiple licences, then they are not considered when determining the nature of the entity's promise in granting a licence – i.e. whether a right-to-use or right-to-access licence. [*IFRS 15.B62*]

4.2.440.90 A guarantee provided by the licensor that it has a valid patent to the underlying intellectual property and that it will maintain and defend that patent is also not considered when determining whether the licence provides a right to access or a right to use the entity's intellectual property. [*IFRS 15.B62*]

EXAMPLE 23A – LICENCE FOR RIGHT TO ACCESS INTELLECTUAL PROPERTY

4.2.440.100 Franchisor Y licenses the right to open a store in a specified location to a franchisee. The store bears Y's trade name and the franchisee will have a right to sell Y's products for 10 years. The franchisee pays an up-front fixed fee. The franchise contract also requires Y to maintain the brand through product improvements, marketing campaigns etc.

4.2.440.110 The licence provides the franchisee access to the intellectual property as it exists at any point in time in the licence period. This is because:
- Y is required to maintain the brand, which will significantly affect the intellectual property by affecting the franchisee's ability to obtain benefit from the brand;
- any action by Y may have a direct positive or negative effect on the franchisee; and
- these activities do not transfer a good or service to the franchisee.

4.2.440.120 Therefore, Y recognises the up-front fee over the 10-year franchise period.

EXAMPLE 23B – LICENCE FOR RIGHT TO USE INTELLECTUAL PROPERTY

4.2.440.130   Company X has contracted to license software, on a non-exclusive basis, to a customer for three years.

4.2.440.140   The licence gives the customer the right to use the software for the licence period and the customer will not receive any upgrades to the software during the licence period.

4.2.440.150   The licence is a right to use intellectual property because the customer can use the licence in its current form and it does not expect X to undertake any activities that will significantly affect the intellectual property – i.e. the transaction is similar to the sale of a tangible good.

4.2.440.160   Therefore, X recognises revenue for the licence at a point in time.

4.2.450   *Timing and pattern of revenue recognition*

4.2.450.10   The nature of an entity's promise in granting a licence to a customer is to provide the customer with either a right to:
- access the entity's intellectual property; or
- use the entity's intellectual property. [*IFRS 15.B56*]

4.2.450.20   A promise to provide the customer with a right to access the entity's intellectual property is satisfied over time because the customer simultaneously consumes and receives benefit from the entity's performance of providing access to its intellectual property as that performance occurs. The entity applies the general guidance for measuring progress towards the complete satisfaction of a performance obligation satisfied over time in selecting an appropriate measure of progress (see 4.2.230). [*IFRS 15.B60*]

4.2.450.30   A promise to provide the customer with a right to use the entity's intellectual property is satisfied at a point in time. The entity applies the general guidance on performance obligations satisfied at a point in time to determine the point in time at which the licence transfers to the customer (see 4.2.240). However, revenue cannot be recognised before the beginning of the period during which the customer can use and benefit from the licence (i.e. before the start of the licence period). [*IFRS 15.B61*]

4.2.450.40   Although the point at which the customer can begin to use and benefit from the licence is typically easily determinable, the transfer of control indicators may not be applied to licences as easily as they might be to physical goods. For example, there may not be 'legal title' to a licence and it may be difficult to assess whether the customer has the significant risks and rewards of a licence. However, the contract can be viewed as analogous to title to a licence, and availability of a copy of the intellectual property (when applicable) as the equivalent to 'physical possession'. Assessing the entity's right to payment in a licence contract should not be significantly different from that assessment in other scenarios. Consequently, control of a licence will generally transfer to the customer when:

- there is a valid contract between the parties;
- the customer has a copy or the ability to obtain a copy of the intellectual property; and
- the customer can begin to use and benefit from the licence. [*IFRS 15.38*]

4.2.450.50   An entity may enter into a contract with a customer to renew or extend an existing licence to use the entity's intellectual property. If the renewal is agreed before the start of the renewal period, then a question arises about when to recognise revenue for the renewal. It appears that an entity should choose an accounting policy, to be applied consistently, to recognise revenue for the renewal when:
- the renewal is agreed – on the basis that the renewal is regarded as a modification of an existing contract in which the licence has already been delivered; or
- the renewal period starts – on the basis that this is the date from which the customer can use and benefit from the renewal.

4.2.460 *Sales- or usage-based royalties*

4.2.460.10   Sales- or usage-based royalties that are attributable to a licence of intellectual property, are recognised at the later of:
- when the subsequent sale or usage occurs; and
- the satisfaction or partial satisfaction of the performance obligation to which some or all of the sales- or usage-based royalty has been allocated. [*IFRS 15.B63*]

4.2.460.20   This is an exception to the general requirements and it applies when the:
- royalty relates only to a licence of intellectual property; or
- licence is the predominant item to which the royalty relates (e.g. when the customer would ascribe significantly more value to the licence than to the other goods or services to which the royalty relates). [*IFRS 15.B63A*]

4.2.460.30   An entity does not split a royalty into a portion that is subject to the exception and a portion that is subject to the guidance on variable consideration, including the constraint (see 4.2.100). [*IFRS 15.B63B*]

4.2.460.40   An entity may be entitled to a sales-based or usage-based royalty in exchange for a licence and other goods or services in the contract, which may or may not be distinct from the licence. For example:
- software licences are commonly sold with post-contract customer support and other services – e.g. implementation services – or hardware where there is a single consideration in the form of a sales- or usage-based royalty;
- franchise licences are frequently sold with consulting or training services or equipment, with ongoing consideration in the form of a sales-based royalty;
- biotechnology and pharmaceutical licences are often sold with research and development services and/or a promise to manufacture the drug for the customer, with a single consideration in the form of a sales-based royalty; or
- licences to digital media and a promise for promotional activities may be sold with a single consideration in the form of a sales-based royalty. [*IFRS 15.B63A*]

4.2.460.50   The guidance specifies that the royalties exception applies when the licence is the predominant item to which the royalty relates. 'Predominant' is not defined in IFRS 15. Significant judgement may be required to determine whether a licence is the predominant item in an arrangement. For example, an entity may determine that a licence of intellectual property is the predominant item when it represents the major part or substantially all of the value or utility of the bundle. Another entity may conclude that the exception would apply when a licence of intellectual property is the largest single item in a bundle of goods or services. These different interpretations may give rise to differences in the transaction price and timing of revenue recognition, because they could affect the conclusion on whether the royalties exception applies to an arrangement. [*IFRS 15.B63A*]

4.2.460.60   The royalties exception generally applies to milestone payments based on the customer's subsequent sales. However, this does not extend to milestone payments that are determined with reference to other events or indicators – e.g. regulatory approval or enrolment in clinical trials. For example, arrangements in the life sciences industry often include a licence of intellectual property of a drug and an obligation to perform research and development services, with a substantial portion of the fee being contingent on achieving milestones such as regulatory approval of the drug.

4.2.465   Transfers of assets from customers

4.2.465.10   In certain industries, it is common for entities to receive transfers of property, plant and equipment (or cash to acquire it) from their customers in return for a network connection and/or an ongoing supply of goods or services.

4.2.465.20   The nature of such arrangements can vary widely. In some arrangements, the party that transfers the assets (the transferor) is the party that receives access to a supply of goods or services (the ultimate customer). In other arrangements, the transferor is not the ultimate customer or is the ultimate customer for only a short period of time. For example, a property developer builds a residential complex in an area that is not connected to the water mains. To connect to the water mains, the property developer is required to install a network of pipes and to transfer them to the water supply company, which will supply future services to the residents of the complex.

4.2.465.30   An entity that receives such contributed assets evaluates all relevant facts and circumstances to determine the appropriate accounting, including whether the contribution is part of a contract with a customer in the scope of IFRS 15 (see 4.2.10). If the contract is in the scope of IFRS 15, then the entity determines whether:
- the connection to the supply of future services transfers a distinct good or service to the customer (see 4.2.60); and
- the contributed assets are non-cash consideration to be included in the transaction price (see 4.2.150).

4.2.465.40   An entity considers all of its obligations under the contract to determine the appropriate timing of revenue recognition.

4.2.467   Tooling

4.2.467.10   Tooling arrangements are typically contracts or master service agreements in which an entity builds or receives a tool that is used for the production of customised parts ordered by the customer. Such arrangements are common, for example, in the automotive and aerospace and defence industries. The tools are usually unique and cannot be used for another customer. The entity is usually responsible for maintaining the tool, which remains physically with it for use in the production process. Such tooling arrangements vary widely with respect to which entity is responsible for development, payment terms and whether title of the tool or ownership of the intellectual property passes to the customer.

4.2.467.20   To determine the appropriate accounting for a tooling arrangement, an entity first assesses whether the arrangement is a sale, a lease or development of its own property, plant and equipment (or other asset) to be used in the production process. This assessment requires judgement. The following flowchart illustrates the key considerations once the nature of the arrangement is determined.

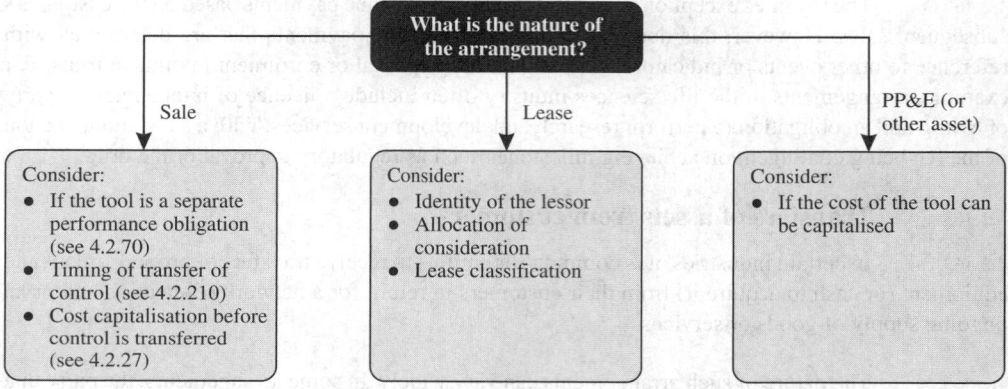

4.2.467.30   If an entity determines that a tooling arrangement is in the scope of IFRS 15, then it assesses whether the tool is transferred to the customer.
- If the tool is transferred to the customer, then the entity assesses whether the tool is a separate performance obligation (see 4.2.70) and determines the timing of transfer of control (see 4.2.210).
- If the tool is not transferred to the customer, then the entity assesses whether the cost of the tool may be capitalised under IAS 16 (see chapter 3.2), IFRS 15 (see 4.2.270) or other guidance.

4.2.470   PRESENTATION

4.2.470.10   When either the entity or the customer has performed, the entity presents a contract asset or contract liability in its statement of financial position. If the entity has an unconditional right to consideration, then this is presented separately as a receivable. [*IFRS 15.105*]

4.2.470.20   A 'contract asset' is a right to consideration that is conditional on something other than the passage of time. [*IFRS 15.A, 107*]

4.2.470.30   A 'contract liability' is an obligation to transfer goods or services for which consideration has been received or is due from the customer. [*IFRS 15.A, 106*]

4.2.470.40   When a contract contains multiple performance obligations, it is possible that at a given point in time some performance obligations could be in a contract asset position, and others in a contract liability position. In this case, an entity presents a single contract asset or liability representing the net position of the contract as a whole. The entity does not present both a contract asset and a contract liability for the same contract. It may be challenging to determine a single net position in some circumstances if, for example, different systems are used for different performance obligations. In addition, if under the contract combination guidance (see 4.2.40) an entity combines two or more contracts and accounts for them as a single contract, then it presents a single contract asset or contract liability for that combined contract. This is consistent with the guidance on the combination of contracts that specifies determining the unit of account based on the substance of the transaction, rather than its legal form. [*IFRS 15.BC317*]

4.2.470.50   A single contract is presented either as a net contract asset or as a net contract liability. However, if an entity has multiple contracts, then it cannot present on a net basis contract assets and contract liabilities of unrelated contracts (i.e. contracts that cannot be combined under Step 1). Therefore, it presents total net contract assets separately from total net contract liabilities, rather than a net position on all contracts with customers. An asset arising from the costs of obtaining a contract is presented separately from the contract asset or liability. [*IFRS 15.BC301, BC317–BC318*]

4.2.470.60   Receivables are accounted for in accordance with IFRS 9 (see 7.7.20), as appropriate. A right to consideration is unconditional if only the passage of time is required before payment of that consideration is due. [*IFRS 15.108*]

4.2.470.70   An entity is not prohibited from using alternate terms to describe contract assets and contract liabilities in its statement of financial position. In that case, the entity needs to provide sufficient information for the user to distinguish the amount from receivables. [*IFRS 15.109*]

4.2.480   DISCLOSURES

4.2.480.10   The objective of the disclosure requirements is for an entity to disclose sufficient information to enable users of financial statements to understand the nature, amount, timing and uncertainty of revenue and cash flows arising from contracts with customers. [*IFRS 15.110*]

4.2.480.20   Entities disclose, separately from other sources of revenue, revenue recognised from contracts with customers (i.e. from contracts in the scope of IFRS 15), and any impairment losses recognised on receivables or contract assets arising from contracts with customers. If an entity elects either the practical expedient not to adjust the transaction price for a significant financing component (see 4.2.130.60), or the practical expedient not to capitalise costs incurred to obtain a contract (see 4.2.260.30), then it discloses this fact. [*IFRS 15.113, 129*]

4.2.480.25   It appears that an entity is not required to present revenue from contracts with customers as a separate line item in the statement of profit or loss and may aggregate it with other types of revenue considering the requirements in IAS 1 (see 4.1.80). However, in providing a separate disclosure of revenue from contracts with customers – either in the notes or in the statement of profit or loss – we believe that an entity should not include amounts that do not fall in the scope of IFRS 15. [*IFRS 15.113, IAS 1.29–30, 85*]

4.2.480.30   The standard includes specific disclosure requirements regarding the disaggregation of revenue, contract balances, performance obligations, significant judgements and assets recognised to obtain or fulfil a contract to achieve the overall disclosure objective. These disclosures are illustrated in KPMG's *Guide to annual financial statements – IFRS 15 supplement.* [*IFRS 15.114–128, B87–B89*]

4.2.490 EFFECTIVE DATE AND TRANSITION

4.2.500 Effective date

4.2.500.10   The standard is effective for annual periods beginning on or after 1 January 2018. Early adoption is permitted. [*IFRS 15.C1*]

4.2.510 Transition

4.2.510.10   An entity can apply the standard to all of its contracts with customers using either:
- the retrospective method (see 4.2.520); or
- the cumulative effect method (see 4.2.530). [*IFRS 15.C3*]

4.2.510.20   For the purposes of transition:
- the date of initial application is the start of the reporting period in which an entity first applies the standard. For an entity with a calendar year end applying the standard for the first time as of the mandatory effective date, the date of initial application would be 1 January 2018; and
- a contract is a 'completed contract' if all of the goods or services identified in accordance with IAS 11, IAS 18 and related interpretations that the entity has an obligation to deliver and the customer has a right to receive have been transferred before the date of initial application. It appears that the assessment of whether a contract is complete should take into account the entity's current stated accounting policies. [*IFRS 15.C2*]

4.2.510.30   It appears that if on initial application an entity has a deferred balance related to a completed contract, then it should continue to account for it in accordance with its existing accounting policy after the date of initial application. [*IFRS 15.BC445E*]

EXAMPLE 24 – TRANSITION – DEFERRED BALANCE RELATING TO A COMPLETED CONTRACT

4.2.510.40   In 2017, Company C enters into a framework agreement with Customer B to supply widgets. The framework agreement specifies the following volume-based tiered pricing:
- 1 to 2,000 items: 5 per item; and
- over 2,000 items: 4 per item.

4.2.510.50   There is no stated minimum purchase quantity. Before 31 December 2017, B orders and C delivers 1,800 items.

4.2.510.60   Under IAS 18, C estimates that B's total expected purchases under this framework agreement will be 2,500 items – i.e. B will qualify for the discount. Therefore, C recognises revenue based on the total expected purchases at the average price per item of 4.8 ((5 x 2,000 + 4 x 500) / 2,500). As a result, C recognises 360 ((5 - 4.8) x 1,800) as deferred revenue in its statement of financial position at 31 December 2017.

> **4.2.510.70**   C applies IFRS 15 in the reporting period beginning on 1 January 2018 using the cumulative effect method. C determines that each purchase order under the framework agreement is a separate contract and the orders fulfilled constitute completed contracts at 1 January 2018 because all of the items ordered were delivered under IAS 18.
>
> **4.2.510.80**   We believe that C should continue to account for the deferred revenue of 360 in accordance with IAS 18 – i.e. to recognise it as revenue when it grants discounts to B on subsequent sales.

4.2.510.90   IFRS 15 introduces consequential amendments to several other standards. For example, it amends IAS 38 such that the amount of consideration to be used in calculating the gain or loss on disposal of an intangible asset is determined under the requirements for determining the transaction price in IFRS 15 (see 3.3.310). A question arises over how to apply consequential amendments to other standards on transition to IFRS 15. It appears that it would be appropriate to apply consequential amendments in a manner that is consistent with the transition method chosen for IFRS 15 – i.e. retrospective or cumulative effect method. However, it may also be acceptable to apply consequential amendments to other standards retrospectively under the general requirements of IAS 8 (see 2.8.60).

4.2.520   Retrospective method

4.2.520.10   When an entity applies the standard using the retrospective method, it recognises the cumulative effect of applying the standard at the start of the earliest comparative period. [*IFRS 15.C3(a)*]

4.2.520.20   An entity may choose to apply one or more of the following practical expedients:
- for completed contracts, an entity need not restate contracts that:
  - begin and end within the same annual reporting period; or
  - are completed contracts at the beginning of the earliest period presented;
- for completed contracts that have variable consideration, an entity may use the transaction price at the date on which the contract was completed, rather than estimating amounts for variable consideration in each comparative reporting period;
- for contracts that were modified before the beginning of the earliest period presented, an entity need not retrospectively restate the contract for those contract modifications in accordance with the requirements in 4.2.290.30. Instead, an entity may reflect the aggregate effect of all of the modifications that occur before the beginning of the earliest period presented in:
  - identifying the satisfied and unsatisfied performance obligations;
  - determining the transaction price; and
  - allocating the transaction price to the satisfied and unsatisfied performance obligations; and
- for all periods presented before the date of initial application, an entity need not disclose the amount of the transaction price allocated to the remaining performance obligations, nor an explanation of when it expects to recognise that amount as revenue. [*IFRS 15.C5*]

4.2.520.25   The practical expedient for contract modification essentially allows an entity to use hindsight when assessing the effect of a modification on a contract. However, it does not exempt an entity from applying other aspects of the requirements to a contract – e.g. identifying the performance obligations in the contract and measuring the progress towards complete satisfaction of those performance obligations.

4.2.520.30   If an entity elects to apply one or more practical expedients, then it discloses the expedient(s) elected and a qualitative assessment of the estimated effect of applying each expedient. [*IFRS 15.C6*]

EXAMPLE 25 – TRANSITION – RETROSPECTIVE METHOD

4.2.520.40   Company Y entered into a contract with a customer to provide a software licence and telephone support for two years for a fixed amount of 400,000. The software was delivered and operational on 1 July 2016.

4.2.520.50   Under IAS 18, Y treats the contract as a single performance obligation, and recognises revenue for the arrangement on a straight-line basis over the 24-month contract term at 16,667 per month.

4.2.520.60   Under IFRS 15, Y determines that the contract consists of two performance obligations: the software licence and the telephone support. Y allocates 300,000 of the transaction price to the software licence and 100,000 to the telephone support.

4.2.520.70   Y determines that the software licence is a performance obligation satisfied at a point in time. Therefore, Y would have recognised revenue of 300,000 on the delivery date of 1 July 2016.

4.2.520.80   Y determines that the telephone support is a performance obligation satisfied over time, and its progress is best depicted by direct labour hours as follows:
- 2016: 30,000;
- 2017: 50,000; and
- 2018: 20,000.

4.2.520.90   Y also considers the effect of the change in revenue recognition on related costs balances and adjusts them accordingly.

4.2.520.100   Y's year end is 31 December and it decides to apply the retrospective method, with the following consequences.
- Y records an adjustment to opening equity at 1 January 2017 for the additional revenue related to 2016 that would have been recognised if IFRS 15 had always applied.
- The first practical expedient in 4.2.520.20 is not available because the contract does not begin and end in an annual reporting period.
- The second practical expedient in 4.2.520.20 is not available because the consideration is not variable and the contract is not completed before the date of initial application.

- The third practical expedient in 4.2.520.20 for modified contracts is not available because the contract is not modified.
- The fourth practical expedient in 4.2.520.20 is available to be applied when preparing the disclosures for the annual financial statements.

4.2.520.110   The following table illustrates the revenue amounts presented in Y's financial statements for the year ended 31 December 2018.

	2017	2018
Revenue	50,000	20,000
Adjustment to opening equity	230,000[1]	-

Note
1. Calculated as 300,000 for the software plus 30,000 for the services (for 2016 that would have been recognised under IFRS 15 up to 1 January 2017) minus 100,000 recognised under IAS 18 (6 months x 16,667).

4.2.520.120   An entity is also required to comply with the disclosure requirements for a change in accounting policy, including the amount of the adjustment to the financial statement line items and earnings per share amounts affected. However, an entity that adopts the standard retrospectively is not required to disclose the impact of the change in accounting policy on the financial statement line items and earnings per share amounts for the year of initial application. [*IFRS 15.C4*]

4.2.530   Cumulative effect method

4.2.530.10   When an entity applies the cumulative effect method, it recognises the cumulative effect of applying the standard as of the date of initial application, with no restatement of comparative information. [*IFRS 15.C7*]

4.2.530.20   An entity can choose to apply the requirements of IFRS 15 to:
- only contracts that are not completed contracts at the date of initial application; or
- all contracts at the date of initial application. [*IFRS 15.C7*]

4.2.530.30   An entity that applies the cumulative effect method may also use the contract modifications practical expedient (see 4.2.520.20). An entity can choose to apply the practical expedient to all contract modifications that occur before the:
- beginning of the earliest period presented; or
- date of initial application. [*IFRS 15.C7A*]

4.2.530.40   If an entity elects the cumulative effect method, then it is also required to disclose:
- the amount by which each financial statement line item is affected in the current period as a result of applying the standard; and
- an explanation of the significant changes between the reported results under the standard and under the previous revenue requirements – i.e. IAS 11 and IAS 18. [*IFRS 15.C8*]

EXAMPLE 26 – TRANSITION – CUMULATIVE EFFECT METHOD

4.2.530.50   Modifying Example 25, Y decides to apply the cumulative effect method, with the following consequences.

- Y does not adjust the comparative period (2017).
- Y records an adjustment to opening equity at the date of initial application (1 January 2018) for the additional revenue related to 2016 and 2017 that would have been recognised if IFRS 15 had applied.
- Y also considers the effects of the revenue adjustments on related cost balances and adjusts them accordingly.
- Y discloses the amount by which each financial statement line item is affected in the current period as a result of applying the standard.

4.2.530.60   The following table illustrates the revenue amounts presented in Y's financial statements for the year ended 31 December 2018.

	2017	2018
Revenue	200,000[(1)]	20,000[(2)]
Adjustment to opening equity	-	80,000[(3)]

Notes
1. Calculated in accordance with IAS 18.
2. Calculated in accordance with IFRS 15.
3. Calculated as 300,000 for the software plus 80,000 for the services (for 2016 and 2017) minus 300,000 recognised under IAS 18 (18 months x 16,667).

4.2.540   Summary of the transition options

4.2.540.10   The following table illustrates the basis on which an entity's revenue numbers would be reported if the entity has a calendar year end, applies the standard for the first time from the effective date and presents one year of comparatives.

Approach	2017	2018	Date of equity adjustment
Full retrospective – no practical expedients	IFRS 15	IFRS 15	1 January 2017
Partial retrospective – practical expedients	Mixed requirements[(1)]	IFRS 15	1 January 2017
Cumulative effect	IAS 11, 18	IFRS 15 / IAS 11, 18[(2)]	1 January 2018

Notes
1. Includes a mix of IFRS 15 for the restated contracts and IAS 18/IAS 11 for those items that the practical expedient was applied to.
2. See disclosure requirement set out in 4.2.530.40.

4.3 Government grants

4.3 Government grants

CURRENTLY EFFECTIVE REQUIREMENTS

This publication reflects IFRS in issue at 1 August 2018, and the currently effective requirements cover annual periods beginning on 1 January 2018.

The requirements related to this topic are mainly derived from the following.

STANDARD	TITLE
IAS 20	Accounting for Government Grants and Disclosure of Government Assistance
IAS 41	Agriculture
SIC-10	Government Assistance – No Specific Relation to Operating Activities

FORTHCOMING REQUIREMENTS AND FUTURE DEVELOPMENTS

For this topic, there are no forthcoming requirements or future developments.

4.3.10 **DEFINITIONS**

4.3.10.10   Government grants are transfers of resources to an entity by a government entity in return for compliance with certain past or future conditions related to the entity's operating activities – e.g. a government subsidy. The definition of 'government' refers to governments, government agencies and similar bodies, whether local, national or international. [*IAS 20.3*]

4.3.10.15   Government assistance that is provided for an entity in the form of benefits that are available in determining taxable profit or tax loss, or are determined or limited on the basis of income tax liability, are not in the scope of IAS 20. [*IAS 20.2(b)*]

4.3.10.20   Government assistance meets the definition of a government grant even if the conditions are only a requirement to operate in certain regions or industry sectors. [*SIC-10*]

4.3.10.30   IAS 20 establishes accounting requirements only for government assistance in the form of grants. Therefore, the distinction between government grants and other forms of government assistance is important. Government assistance is not considered a government grant if the assistance cannot reasonably have a value placed on it or is a transaction with a government body that cannot be distinguished from the normal operating transactions of the entity. [*IAS 20.3, 34–38*]

4.3.10.35   If a government provides free technical or marketing advice or other services or guarantees, then the assistance is not normally recognised in the financial statements. Similarly, a government procurement contract, or similar arrangement, whereby a government body agrees to buy certain output produced by an entity is not normally distinguished from the normal operations of the entity and is not treated as a government grant. The extent of government assistance that does not take the form of a grant is, however, disclosed if it is significant and benefits the entity directly. [*IAS 20.3, 34–38*]

4.3.10.40   In addition, if the government provides support to an entity and is also a shareholder in that entity, then the entity needs to assess whether the government is acting in its capacity as shareholder or as government (see 7.7.375.40). If there are no terms attached to a government contribution requiring the entity to comply with certain conditions, then that contribution is most likely not a government grant. For example, a local bus company receives buses from the government; the government is also the sole shareholder of the bus company and a similar contribution is not available to other bus companies. There are no further conditions attached to the contribution of the buses, but there is a general expectation that the company will provide bus services to the local community. To determine the proper accounting for the contributed assets, the economic substance of the transaction needs to be analysed. In our view, providing public transportation in the local area is an objective of the company itself, and not a condition of the contributed assets. In addition, the contribution is not available to other companies. Therefore, we believe that in this example the contributed assets do not meet the definition of a government grant; the government is acting in its capacity as a shareholder and the asset contribution should be recognised as a capital contribution. For a discussion of the evaluation of shareholder transactions, see 1.2.190. [*IAS 20.3*]

4.3.20 **Forgivable loans**

4.3.20.10   A government may extend a loan that will be forgiven if certain prescribed conditions are met (a forgivable loan). A forgivable loan is treated as a government grant only when there is reasonable assurance that the entity will meet the terms for forgiveness of the loan. Otherwise, the loan is recognised as a liability (see 4.3.100). Careful analysis of all facts and circumstances is required to determine whether cash received from a government meets the definition of a forgivable loan under IAS 20. [*IAS 20.3, 10, IU 05-16*]

EXAMPLE 1A – GOVERNMENT FINANCING – LOAN FORGIVABLE IF CERTAIN CONDITIONS MET

4.3.20.20 Company C is launching an airline. Government Z provides C with financing to fund the launch. The financing is in the form of a loan that will be repayable by C if the business is successful, but the amount advanced will not be repaid if the airline is launched but the business is unsuccessful. In our view, C should recognise the amount received as a liability. We believe that the liability would become a government grant (forgivable loan) if, and only if, the venture does not succeed – i.e. when it is reasonably assured that the business is not successful.

EXAMPLE 1B – GOVERNMENT FINANCING – LOAN NOT FORGIVABLE

4.3.20.30 Company D receives cash from Government X to help finance a research and development project. The amount received is repayable in cash only if D chooses to commercialise the results of the research phase of the project. If D does not commercialise the results, then it is required to transfer the rights to the research to X to settle the loan. X does not undertake to waive repayment of the loan, but instead requires settlement either in cash or by transfer of the rights to the research. Therefore, D concludes that the cash received from X is not a forgivable loan under IAS 20, but a financial liability (see chapter 7.1). D also considers whether the difference between the fair value of the financial liability and the cash received represents a government grant (see 4.3.100). [*IU 05-16*]

4.3.30 **Waiver of expenses**

4.3.30.10 In some cases, instead of providing a cash grant, a government may waive amounts payable by the entity – e.g. a liability for taxes. In our view, these qualify as government grants because in substance there is a transfer of resources, although it is in the form of a waiver of expenses (see 4.3.80).

4.3.40 **RECOGNITION AND MEASUREMENT**

4.3.40.10 Government grants are recognised when there is reasonable assurance that the entity will comply with the relevant conditions and the grant will be received. [*IAS 20.7*]

4.3.40.20 Grants are recognised in profit or loss on a systematic basis as the entity recognises as expenses the costs that the grants are intended to compensate. [*IAS 20.12*]

4.3.40.30 Grants that relate to the acquisition of an asset are recognised in profit or loss as the asset is depreciated or amortised. For a discussion of the presentation of such grants in the statement of financial position and in the statement of profit or loss and OCI, see 4.3.130. [*IAS 20.17*]

4.3.40.40   If a grant relates to a non-depreciable asset, then an entity considers the conditions related to the grant. For example, an entity is granted land on the condition that it operates a building on that land. The entity recognises the land at its fair value. In this case, the grant is recognised in profit or loss as the building is depreciated because the operation of the building is the condition attached to the grant. [*IAS 20.18*]

4.3.40.50   In some cases, a grant may relate to an asset that will be used both to fulfil the conditions of the grant and for other activities of the entity. In our view, the grant should be recognised in profit or loss systematically based on the cost incurred in meeting the conditions of the grant – i.e. excluding consideration of the timing of recognition of the costs of activities that are not related to the conditions of the grant.

EXAMPLE 2 – GRANT OF LAND – CONDITIONAL ON CONSTRUCTION AND OPERATION

> 4.3.40.60   Company D receives a grant of land. D recognises the land at its fair value. The conditions of the grant require D to construct on the land and to operate, for a given period, a sports stadium. D assesses whether the arrangement is in the scope of IFRIC 12 (see 5.12.01) and concludes that it is not. The piece of land is larger than is required to construct the stadium and D disposes of the excess land to a third party. In our view, the whole of the grant (i.e. the value of all of the land granted) should be recognised systematically based on the costs incurred in fulfilling the conditions of the grant – i.e. the costs of operating the stadium.

4.3.40.70   A grant that is compensation for expenses or losses already incurred, or for which there are no future related costs, is recognised in profit or loss in the period in which it becomes receivable. Therefore, if a government provides an entity with annual grants that do not relate to future costs, then the grant in respect of each period is recognised as it becomes receivable. [*IAS 20.20*]

4.3.50   Non-monetary grants

4.3.50.10   If a government grant is in the form of a non-monetary asset, then an entity chooses an accounting policy, to be applied consistently, to recognise the asset and grant at either the fair value of the non-monetary asset or the nominal amount paid (nominal value). For example, Government X gives Company Y an item of property, plant and equipment with a fair value of 50 for no consideration. Y measures both the item of property, plant and equipment and the grant either at 50 or at nominal value, which in this case is zero. IAS 20 notes that fair value is the usual approach. [*IAS 20.23*]

4.3.50.20   Fair value is measured in accordance with IFRS 13, which is the subject of chapter 2.4.

4.3.60   Grants related to biological assets

4.3.60.10   As an exception to the general recognition principle, an unconditional government grant related to biological assets that are measured at fair value less costs to sell (see 3.9.70.20) is recognised in profit or loss when it becomes receivable. If the government grant is conditional, then it is recognised in profit or loss when the condition is met. IAS 20 applies to government grants related to biological assets to which the cost model applies (see 3.9.70.10). [*IAS 41.34–35, 37*]

4.3.70 **Grants related to other assets measured at fair value through profit or loss**

4.3.70.10 Although there is specific guidance on accounting for government grants related to biological assets that are measured at fair value less costs to sell (see 4.3.60), there is no similar guidance for government grants related to other assets that are measured at fair value with changes therein recognised in profit or loss – e.g. investment property for which the entity applies the fair value model (see 3.4.150). In our view, in such cases, the treatment required for government grants related to biological assets should be applied by analogy. Therefore, we believe that a grant related to an asset measured at fair value with changes therein recognised in profit or loss should be recognised in profit or loss when it becomes receivable, provided that any attached conditions are fulfilled.

EXAMPLE 3A – GRANT OF INVESTMENT PROPERTY – UNCONDITIONAL

4.3.70.20 On 25 January 2018, Local Government F grants Company G a property with a fair value of 450; ownership of the property is transferred to G at the same time. G classifies the property as investment property, which it measures at fair value. The fair value of the property on 31 December 2018 is 480. There are no conditions attached to the grant.

4.3.70.23 We believe that the government grant of 450 should be recognised in profit or loss on 25 January 2018. A gain on revaluation of the property of 30 is recognised on 31 December 2018 when the investment property is revalued in accordance with the requirements of IAS 40 (see chapter 3.4).

EXAMPLE 3B – GRANT OF INVESTMENT PROPERTY – CONDITIONAL

4.3.70.25 On 30 September 2018, Company H buys a residential building, which is partially funded by a grant from local government. H classifies the building as investment property and measures it at fair value. The nominal value of the grant is repayable if specified works intended to improve the energy efficiency of the building are not finished by 30 June 2019. The specified works are finalised in May 2019.

4.3.70.30 At the end of 2018, H revalues its investment property and recognises any changes in fair value in profit or loss. Notwithstanding the fact that H received the grant attached to the building before the end of 2018, H defers recognition of the grant in profit or loss until the date on which the conditions are met. Accordingly, H recognises income from the grant on completion of the specified works in May 2019; for a discussion of repayable grants, see 4.3.90.

4.3.80 **Grants in form of waiver of expenses**

4.3.80.10 In our view, the general recognition principles apply to grants in the form of a waiver of expenses. Therefore, we believe that such grants should be recognised in profit or loss on a systematic basis as the entity recognises as expenses the costs the grant is intended to compensate.

EXAMPLE 4 – WAIVER OF CURRENT TAX PAYABLE

4.3.80.20   Company N receives an investment tax credit (ITC) in the form of a waiver of current taxes payable and it concludes that accounting for the ITC by analogy to a government grant is appropriate (see 3.13.710).

4.3.80.25   If the expenditure to which the grant relates is incurred in the period in which the tax is waived, then the benefit of the tax relief is reflected in that period. If the expenditure will be incurred in a future period, then the benefit of the tax relief is deferred in the statement of financial position until the expenditure is incurred.

4.3.80.27   Similarly, if the grant relates to the acquisition of an asset, then the benefit of the tax relief is deferred in the statement of financial position and recognised in profit or loss as the related asset is depreciated.

4.3.80.30   For guidance on the presentation of grants in the form of a waiver of expenses, see 4.3.150.

4.3.90   **Repayment**

4.3.90.10   A government grant may be required to be repaid under certain conditions – e.g. if the actual costs to which the grant relates are lower than expected.

4.3.90.20   If the amount is recognised as a government grant and subsequently some or the entire amount becomes repayable unexpectedly, then the repayment is accounted for as a change in estimate (see 2.8.110). In our view, the effect of the change in estimate should be recognised in the period in which management concludes that it is no longer reasonably assured that the terms for forgiveness will be met. In our view, a financial liability should be recognised at the same time for the amount of the repayment, based on the general requirements of IFRS 9 – i.e. at fair value (see 7.7.10). The amount would differ from the face value of the grant if the interest rate is not a market rate of interest (see 4.3.100). In our view, the repayable portion of the credit previously recognised should be reversed as follows:

- the credit may have been shown as deferred income or a credit to an asset, in which case the reversal should be against the appropriate line item in the statement of financial position; and/or
- the credit may have been recognised as a reduction in depreciation or amortisation of an asset or as income, in which case the reversal should be against the appropriate line item in profit or loss. [*IAS 20.32*]

4.3.90.30   For grants related to an asset, the reversal of the credit previously recognised may result in an increase in the carrying amount of the asset. An entity also considers whether the change in circumstances that gave rise to the repayment of the loan is an indication of impairment of the new carrying amount of the asset (see 3.10.110). [*IAS 20.32–33*]

4.3.90.40   In some circumstances, a financial liability in respect of a grant that becomes repayable may be forgiven; for a discussion of forgivable loans, see 4.3.20. In our view, if there is reasonable assurance that the entity will meet the terms for forgiveness of such a loan, then it should be accounted for as a government grant and the amount received recognised over the compliance period. Otherwise, we believe that the loan should be treated as a financial liability.

4.3.100   Low-interest loans

4.3.100.10   The benefit of a government loan at a below-market interest rate is accounted for as a government grant, unless the definition of a government grant is not met (see 4.3.10.30). The loan is initially recognised and subsequently measured in accordance with IFRS 9. IFRS 9 requires loans at below-market rates to be initially measured at their fair value – e.g. the present value of the expected future cash flows discounted at a market-related interest rate (see 7.7.80). The benefit that is the government grant is measured as the difference between the fair value of the loan on initial recognition and the amount received, which is accounted for according to the nature of the grant. [*IAS 20.10A, IFRS 9.5.1.1, B5.1.1*]

4.3.100.20   In some situations, a government may provide a loan at market rate that will be modified to a lower rate when the entity spends the funds provided on qualifying research and development activities. In our view, the difference between the fair value of the loan at a market interest rate and the fair value of the low interest rate loan should be accounted for as a government grant. Payments on research activities are expensed as they are incurred, whereas payments on development activities are capitalised when the criteria set out in IAS 38 are met (see 3.3.120). Therefore, in this situation, we believe that the part of the government grant related to research activities and development costs that are not capitalised should be recognised in profit or loss when the related costs are incurred; we also believe that an entity should choose an accounting policy, to be applied consistently, either to deduct the grant related to capitalised development costs from the related intangible asset or to recognise such grants as deferred income and release them to profit or loss as the capitalised development costs are amortised; for a discussion of the presentation of grants related to assets, see 4.3.130. In this way, the benefit of the grant is recognised on a systematic basis because the entity recognises, as expenses, the costs the grant is intended to compensate.

4.3.110   Emissions allowances

4.3.110.10   IFRS does not have any specific guidance on accounting for emissions allowances received in a 'cap and trade' scheme. In our view, if an allowance is received from a government for less than its fair value, then the entity should choose an accounting policy, to be applied consistently, either to recognise the resulting government grant at fair value (as the difference between the fair value of the allowance and the consideration (if any) paid) or to recognise it at the nominal amount paid for the certificate. IAS 20 notes that fair value is the usual approach for non-monetary grants (see 3.3.160 and 4.3.50.10). The grant is recognised as deferred income and recognised in profit or loss on a systematic basis over the compliance period, regardless of whether the allowance received continues to be held by the entity. Disposals of certificates or changes in their carrying amount – e.g. because of impairment, which is the subject of chapter 3.10 – do not affect the manner in which grant income is recognised. As an alternative to the deferred income approach, we believe that an entity may present an allowance net of the deferred government grant. For further discussion of the accounting for emissions allowance schemes, see 3.12.510. [*IAS 20.23*]

4.3.110.20   Fair value is measured in accordance with IFRS 13, which is the subject of chapter 2.4.

4.3.120 **PRESENTATION AND DISCLOSURES**

4.3.130 **Presentation of grants related to assets**

4.3.130.10   Government grants related to assets other than biological assets measured at fair value less costs to sell and other assets measured at fair value with changes therein recognised in profit or loss (see 4.3.70), may be either deducted from the cost of the asset (net presentation) or presented separately as deferred income that is amortised over the useful life of the asset (gross presentation). In our view, this approach also applies to grants related to assets held by a lessee under a finance lease. An entity chooses a presentation format in the statement of financial position, to be applied consistently to all government grants related to assets. [*IAS 8.13, 20.24*]

4.3.130.15   If net presentation in the statement of financial position is used, then the grant reduces the cost and therefore reduces the depreciation expense recognised. However, if an entity presents government grants related to assets (other than biological assets measured at fair value less costs to sell and other assets measured at fair value with changes therein recognised in profit or loss) gross in the statement of financial position, then IAS 20 does not require a specific presentation in the statement of profit or loss and OCI. In our view, an entity should choose an accounting policy, to be applied consistently, to present such grants either as income or as a reduction in the related expense. [*IAS 20.27*]

EXAMPLE 5A – GRANT RELATED TO ASSET – PRESENTATION IN STATEMENT OF FINANCIAL POSITION AND DEPRECIATION

4.3.130.20   Company F received a government grant of 200 to acquire machinery. The machinery costs 700 and has an estimated useful life of five years. If F presents the grant as a deduction from the cost of the machinery, then the asset is shown in the statement of financial position at its net cost of 500 (700 - 200). The grant is recognised in profit or loss over the useful life of the depreciable asset and presented as a reduction in the annual depreciation expense of 100 (500 / 5).

4.3.130.30   If the grant is presented as deferred income, then the machinery is shown at its gross cost of 700 and annual depreciation on the machinery is 140 (700 / 5). In addition, F presents deferred income of 200. Each year, 40 (200 / 5) is recognised in profit or loss.

4.3.130.35   In our view, the choice of net or gross presentation (see 4.3.130.10) has no impact on the timing of recognition in profit or loss.

EXAMPLE 5B – GRANT RELATED TO ASSET – PRESENTATION OF DEPRECIATION AND AMORTISATION OF DEFERRED INCOME

4.3.130.40   Continuing Example 5A, assume that the machinery is used in F's production plant for producing inventories for sale in the ordinary course of business. The depreciation of the machinery is reflected in the cost of inventories. In accordance with F's accounting policies, the machinery is shown at its gross cost – i.e. the grant is presented as deferred income.

> 4.3.130.45   In our view, the amortisation of the deferred income should be included in the cost of inventory. This means that the amortisation of the deferred income will be recognised in profit or loss at the same time as the depreciation on the machinery – i.e. as inventory is sold. This approach is consistent with the principle in IAS 20 that the benefit of a government grant is recognised at the same time as the expenses to which it relates.

4.3.130.50   In our view, if an entity presents government grants as a deduction from the related asset, but the grant is received before the asset is recognised, then the grant should be shown as deferred income until the asset is built or acquired.

4.3.130.60   The deferred income is generally classified as a non-current liability when an entity presents a classified statement of financial position (see 3.1.10.10).

4.3.140   Presentation of grants related to income

4.3.140.10   An entity chooses a presentation format, to be applied consistently, either to offset a grant related to income against the related expenditure or to include it in other income. For example, Company P receives a government grant of 100 to fund research costs of 500. P has a choice of presenting net research costs of 400, or gross research costs of 500 and other income of 100. Regardless of P's choice, it is applied consistently. [*IAS 8.13, 20.29*]

4.3.150   Presentation of grants in form of waiver of expenses

4.3.150.10   In our view, either a net or a gross approach may be used to present a grant in the form of a waiver of expenses.

4.3.150.20   For a discussion of the accounting and presentation consequences of a waiver of taxes that is determined to be an ITC, see 3.13.670.

4.3.160   Related party disclosures

4.3.160.10   If the government is also a shareholder, then additional related party disclosures are required (see chapter 5.5).

4.4   Employee benefits

4.4 Employee benefits

CURRENTLY EFFECTIVE REQUIREMENTS

This publication reflects IFRS in issue at 1 August 2018, and the currently effective requirements cover annual periods beginning on 1 January 2018.

The requirements related to this topic are mainly derived from the following.

STANDARD	TITLE
IAS 19	Employee Benefits
IFRIC 14	IAS 19 – The Limit on a Defined Benefit Asset, Minimum Funding Requirements and their Interaction

FORTHCOMING REQUIREMENTS

The currently effective requirements are affected by the following forthcoming requirements. They are highlighted with a # and the impact is explained in the accompanying boxed text at the reference indicated.

In February 2018, the IASB issued *Plan Amendment, Curtailment or Settlement – Amendments to IAS 19*, which are effective for annual periods beginning on or after 1 January 2019. See 4.4.935 and 945.

FUTURE DEVELOPMENTS

For this topic, there are no future developments.

4.4.10   **SCOPE**

4.4.10.10   IAS 19 deals with all employee benefits except those to which IFRS 2 applies (see chapter 4.5). IFRIC 14 applies to all post-employment plans and other long-term employee defined benefit plans. The interpretation may also apply to entities that have plan deficits. [*IAS 19.2, IFRIC 14.4–5*]

4.4.10.20   Employee benefits are all forms of consideration given by an entity in exchange for services provided by employees or for the termination of employment, and include benefits provided directly to employees, to their dependants and to others. [*IAS 19.6, 8*]

4.4.10.30   IAS 19 does not define the term 'employee'. Under IAS 19, an employee may provide services on a full-time, part-time, permanent, casual or temporary basis, and employees include directors and other management personnel. [*IAS 19.7*]

4.4.10.40   In our view, IAS 19 does not apply to benefits provided to agents in a principal-agent relationship. For example, an entity engages agents to sell its goods or services. The agents are paid for sales made by receiving commission payments. In addition, agents engaged by the entity for a period specified in the contract – e.g. 10 years – are entitled to receive additional commission payments on a triggering event – e.g. contract termination. We believe that the benefits provided to the agents in this type of principal-agent relationship are outside the scope of IAS 19 because agents are not employees.

4.4.10.50   In some countries, a tax, other than an income tax that is in the scope of IAS 12, may be levied on employers with respect to employee benefits in the scope of IAS 19 – e.g. cash bonuses. IFRS is not clear about whether the tax liability levied on the employer is in the scope of IAS 19 or IAS 37. In our view, an entity should choose an accounting policy, to be applied consistently, for which standard should be applied to tax liabilities levied on the employer. It can be argued that the tax liability would be considered an employee benefit to be accounted for under IAS 19, the rationale being that the tax liability levied on the employer is part of the benefit to which it relates – i.e. a tax levied on an employer in respect of a cash bonus is part of the bonus – or that it is similar to an administrative cost. However, such arrangements may also be considered to be in the scope of IAS 37 based on the tax liability being treated separately from the bonus. When this is the case, the timing of the recognition of the cash bonus (see 4.4.1270 and 1350), administrative cost (see 4.4.1000.10) or tax levy (see 3.12.754) might be different.

4.4.20   **Share-based payment or IAS 19 employee benefit**

4.4.20.10   Employee benefits in the form of share-based payments are generally not in the scope of IAS 19 but in the scope of IFRS 2. However, as discussed in 4.4.30–70 some transactions may require detailed analysis to conclude whether they are in the scope of IAS 19 or IFRS 2. [*IAS 19.2*]

4.4.30   *Components with different features*

4.4.30.10   In our view, the components of a payment to an employee should be accounted for separately if the award contains both an employee benefit and a share-based payment. For example, a payment to an employee may have both a cash and a share component. The terms of the bonus plan may require settlement of 75 percent of the award in a fixed amount of cash and 25 percent in shares. We believe that the 75 percent cash bonus is an employee benefit in the scope of IAS 19, whereas the 25 percent bonus that is paid in shares represents a share-based payment in the scope of IFRS 2 (see 4.5.2000).

4.4.30.20   Certain arrangements (such as profit-sharing plans) may provide, at the discretion of the employee, a choice of two settlement alternatives that are mutually exclusive – e.g. one equity-settled share-based payment component that would be a share-based payment transaction in the scope of IFRS 2 and one profit-sharing component that, if it were granted separately, would be an employee benefit in the scope of IAS 19. In our view, the entire arrangement should be accounted for as a share-based payment, applying the IFRS 2 requirements for compound instruments by analogy (see 4.5.1120 and 2010).

4.4.40   *Equity instruments of entities outside group*

4.4.40.10   Equity-settled and cash-settled entity and group share-based payment transactions are in the scope of IFRS 2 (see 4.5.110). However, if employees of an entity are granted rights to equity instruments in an entity that is not a group entity (e.g. an associate or joint venture), then in our view the transaction is not a share-based payment transaction (see 4.5.1480.60–70). Because a benefit is provided to employees, we believe that such a transaction is an employee benefit in the scope of IAS 19.

4.4.50   *Tax payments related to share-based payments*

4.4.50.10   In some countries, a share-based payment arrangement may be subject to a tax payment and the employer may pay employees an amount of cash to cover social taxes and/or income taxes related to share-based payment transactions in addition to the share-based payment arrangement. In our view, if the cash payment is not based on the price or value of the entity's shares, then this portion of the plan should be treated as an employee benefit under IAS 19. In our view, if the cash payment is based on the value of the entity's shares, then it may be appropriate to treat this portion of the plan as a cash-settled share-based payment transaction in the scope of IFRS 2 (see 4.5.2080.20).

4.4.60   *Cash payments based on estimates of fair value*

4.4.60.10   Arrangements involving payments tied to the performance of an entity require evaluation of the substance of the transaction. For example, an arrangement in which employees of an entity receive a cash payment based on the increase in the entity's net assets may be a profit-sharing arrangement or a share-based payment arrangement depending on the facts and circumstances (see 4.5.1930.10). In our view, if the net asset value of the entity does not reflect the fair value of its own equity instruments (e.g. the change in net assets primarily represents the profit or loss from operations and does not include fair value changes of assets and liabilities), then the transaction is, in substance, a profit-sharing arrangement that should be accounted for as an employee benefit (see 4.4.1270 and 1350).

4.4.70   *Cash payments depending on share price vs based on share price*

4.4.70.10   A cash payment may depend, but not be based, on the share price. If it is based on the share price, then the payment is a share-based payment. Judgement is required to define the border between 'depending on' and 'being based on'. For example, an employee is entitled to a cash payment of 100 if the share price remains at least at the current price of 8 over the next year. If the share price falls, then the employee is not entitled to the payment. In our view, although the cash payment depends on the share price, it is not based on the share price. Therefore, we believe that the cash payment is not a share-based payment but an employee benefit in the scope of IAS 19 (see 4.5.1950.10).

4.4.70.20   A cash payment may be based on but not equal to the share price. If an employee is entitled to a payment equal to the share price at vesting date, then the employee participates one-to-one in share price increases. In our view, a payment determined as a linear function of the share price (or its movements) is based on the share price and therefore is a share-based payment. For example, if the employee is entitled to 60 percent of the share price or to 200 percent of the share price, then we believe that the payment is based on the value of the equity instruments and therefore is a share-based payment (see 4.5.1950.20–30).

4.4.80   Types of employee benefit

4.4.80.10   Employee benefits are all forms of consideration given by an entity in exchange for service rendered by employees or for the termination of employment. [*IAS 19.8*]

4.4.80.20   IAS 19 sets out the requirements for four types of employee benefit:
- provided in exchange for services rendered by employees:
  - post-employment benefits (see 4.4.90);
  - short-term employee benefits (see 4.4.1220); and
  - other long-term employee benefits (see 4.4.1310); and
- provided in exchange for termination of employment:
  - termination benefits (see 4.4.1440). [*IAS 19.5*]

4.4.90   POST-EMPLOYMENT BENEFITS

4.4.100   Definition and scope of post-employment benefits

4.4.100.10   Post-employment benefits are employee benefits (other than termination benefits and short-term employee benefits) that are payable after the completion of employment (before or during retirement) – e.g. pensions, lump sum payments on retirement or medical benefits after employment. [*IAS 19.5(b), 8, 26*]

4.4.100.20   Some plans are specifically established to provide benefits both during and after the completion of employment. For example, Company K has a fund for paid annual leave. Any surplus in the fund is used to make pension payments. In our view, a plan that is established specifically to pay benefits both during and after the completion of employment should be treated as a long-term employee benefit plan (see 4.4.1310), rather than as a post-employment benefit plan.

4.4.100.30   If a plan offers different benefits (i.e. under different benefit formulas) to different groups of beneficiaries (e.g. active employees vs retirees) and is funded by separate pools of assets or a single pool of assets but with appropriate controls in place, then the benefits offered during employment and post-employment are accounted for separately because separate promises are made to employees and retirees, and under different benefit formulas. As such, benefits offered to retirees are accounted for as a post-employment benefit (see 4.4.200.20–30 and 330.20).

4.4.100.40   Long-term disability benefits are an example of other long-term employee benefits (see 4.4.1410). However, if a long-term disability benefit is payable only after termination of employment, then in our view the benefit is a post-employment benefit. In addition, in our view a long-term disability benefit that is payable only if an employee remains employed but is no longer providing services should also be accounted for as a post-employment benefit. We believe that this is, in substance, the same as if employment ends for the employee. [*IAS 19.155, 157*]

4.4.110   *Severance payments*

4.4.110.10   Severance payments and other amounts that are always payable on cessation of employment, regardless of the reason for the employee leaving, are post-employment benefits, rather than termination benefits. For example, Company B makes payments to its employees on cessation of employment regardless of the reason that the employee leaves B's employment. The employee is entitled to one week's salary for each year of service provided, based on the employee's final salary. Because the amount is payable on cessation of employment regardless of the reason for leaving, the plan is a post-employment benefit plan. [*IAS 19.164*]

4.4.110.20   The normal principles apply in determining whether such post-employment plans give rise to defined benefit or defined contribution plans. The amount of the payments is often based on factors such as the number of years of service or final salary. Therefore, these plans often give rise to a defined benefit plan. The principles set out in 4.4.300–1200, including the requirements to discount the obligation and to use the projected unit credit method, apply to any defined benefit arrangements and therefore also to these plans. Example 31, illustrating the year one calculations for an other long-term employee benefit, also applies to severance payments.

4.4.120   Constructive obligations

4.4.120.10   Post-employment benefit plans include not only formal arrangements but also informal practices that give rise to 'constructive obligations'. Therefore, the accounting treatment is the same, regardless of whether an obligation is legal or constructive. [*IAS 19.61*]

4.4.120.20   Constructive obligations arise when an entity has no realistic alternative but to pay the employee benefits. They may arise from informal past practices or communication with employees. For further discussion of:
- classification, see 4.4.130.60;
- actuarial assumptions, see 4.4.430; and
- general guidance on constructive obligations, see 3.12.60.

4.4.130   Distinction between defined contribution and defined benefit plans

4.4.130.10   Post-employment plans are classified as either defined contribution or defined benefit plans. The classification determines the accounting treatment. [*IAS 19.27*]

4.4.130.20   A post-employment plan is classified as a defined contribution plan if the entity pays fixed contributions into a separate entity (a fund) and will have no further obligation (legal or constructive) to pay further amounts if the fund has insufficient assets to pay all employee benefits relating to current and prior service. All other post-employment plans are defined benefit plans. [*IAS 19.8, 28*]

4.4.130.30   The classification of post-employment plans is based on the entity's obligation to make further contributions, rather than on the benefit to which the employees are entitled. [*IAS 19.8, BC29*]

4.4.130.40   Employee benefit plans may promise employees a defined benefit – e.g. payment of a specified amount or an amount to be determined using a specified formula, such as a percentage of average or final salary. In many cases, the entity's current funding obligation – e.g. under local social legislation – is limited to a fixed amount or satisfaction of a funding level that is lower than the estimate of the present value of the future obligation calculated under IAS 19 – i.e. the defined benefit obligation (see 4.4.380). In our view, a requirement to satisfy only current funding obligations does not provide a sufficient basis for classifying the plan as a defined contribution plan.

4.4.130.50   In some cases, it may be difficult to determine whether a plan that has promised specified benefits to employees is a defined benefit or a defined contribution plan for the entity. If the plan bears all the risk of funding shortfalls and members would have to accept reduced benefit levels in the event of a shortfall, then the plan is likely to be a defined contribution plan.

4.4.130.60   However, if a defined benefit promise has been made to employees (either by the entity or by the pension plan), then in our view it is generally very difficult for the entity to demonstrate that it does not have a constructive obligation to fund any shortfalls; in this case, the plan will be a defined benefit plan.

4.4.130.70   For a discussion of group plans with pooled assets and with both a defined contribution component and a defined benefit component, see 4.4.200.20–30.

4.4.130.80   IAS 19 provides specific guidance on the classification of plans with insured benefits (see 4.4.1170).

4.4.140   *Minimum benefit guarantees*

4.4.140.10   In certain cases, a plan that would otherwise be a defined contribution plan contains certain minimum benefit guarantees. For example, the entity may guarantee a minimum return on the investment of contributions. In our view, a minimum benefit guarantee causes a plan to be a defined benefit plan.

4.4.150   *Impact of vesting conditions*

4.4.150.10   If a plan that has characteristics of a defined contribution plan contains vesting conditions – e.g. a service condition – then there is a potential for the entity to benefit (from refunds or reduced future contributions) if the vesting conditions are not met (see 4.4.260). In our view, such a plan should nevertheless be classified as a defined contribution plan, if the entity bears no downside risk and would not be required to make additional contributions to cover shortfalls.

4.4.160   *Change in classification*

4.4.160.10   A plan may be reclassified from a defined benefit plan to a defined contribution plan or vice versa. There is no specific guidance on how to account for any gain or loss that might arise in this situation. A plan may be reclassified as a result of:
- a change in circumstances leading to a change in the way that the plan is accounted for, when its nature remains unchanged; or
- a change in the nature of the plan itself that leads to a need to reclassify.

4.4.160.20   The facts and circumstances that cause the reclassification of a defined benefit plan to a defined contribution plan or vice versa affect the determination of the accounting treatment and classification of that change. This is because in some instances a reclassification results from a change that is akin to a change in accounting estimate (see 4.4.1030) and in others the change is akin to the plan being settled or amended (see 4.4.160.30–40). A change that is akin to a change in estimate can, for example, occur if there is a change in the accounting for a multi-employer defined benefit plan, as discussed in 4.4.190; and either can occur if there is a change in the basis of accounting for a group plan (see 4.4.230).

4.4.160.30   The nature of a defined benefit plan may change from defined benefit to defined contribution, resulting in a change in classification. This change in classification is accounted for as a settlement of the defined benefit plan because the entity's obligation has been eliminated (see 4.4.910). [*IAS 19.111*]

4.4.160.40   Conversely, a change to the terms of a defined contribution plan may cause it to become a defined benefit plan – e.g. new laws may change the obligation of the entity even if it does not change the benefit to be received by the employee. In our view, if a change to the terms of a plan results in its reclassification from a defined contribution to a defined benefit plan, then this should be treated as the introduction of a new defined benefit plan – i.e. a plan amendment. If, under the revised terms of the plan, the present value of the defined benefit obligation less the fair value of the related plan assets differs from the previous defined contribution obligation, then that change should be treated as a past service cost – i.e. the past service cost is equal to the increase in the obligation less the fair value of the related assets (see 4.4.880).

4.4.170   Multi-employer plans

4.4.170.10   Multi-employer plans are plans that pool the assets contributed by various entities that are not under common control to provide benefits to employees of more than one entity. For a discussion of group plans, see 4.4.200. In multi-employer plans, contribution and benefit levels are not determined based on the identity of the employer. [*IAS 19.8*]

4.4.170.20   Multi-employer plans are classified as either defined contribution or defined benefit plans and accounted for in the same way as single-employer plans, considering the characteristics of the scheme and the obligation of the employer. [*IAS 19.32*]

4.4.170.30   If sufficient information is available to apply defined benefit accounting to a multi-employer defined benefit plan, then an entity accounts for its proportionate share of the defined benefit obligation, plan assets and cost associated with the plan in the same way as for any other defined benefit plan. If insufficient information is available, then the plan is treated as a defined contribution plan and additional disclosures are required (see 4.4.1160). [*IAS 19.33–34*]

4.4.170.40   If an entity applies defined contribution plan accounting to a multi-employer defined benefit plan that has a contractual agreement with its participants determining how a surplus in the plan would be distributed or a deficit in the plan funded, then the asset or liability that arises from the contractual agreement is recognised. Any changes in the amount of the obligation (asset) are recognised in profit or loss because recognition outside profit or loss is available only under defined benefit accounting. [*IAS 19.36–37*]

4.4.170.50 Whether an entity applies defined benefit or defined contribution accounting, it applies IAS 37 in determining when to recognise and how to measure a liability that arises from the wind-up of a multi-employer defined benefit plan or the entity's withdrawal from a multi-employer defined benefit plan (see chapter 3.12). [*IAS 19.39*]

4.4.180 *Availability of sufficient information*

4.4.180.10 It is clear from their definition that multi-employer plans expose participating entities to the actuarial risk of other entities' employees, yet the standard envisages that it may be possible for an entity to apply defined benefit accounting to its proportionate share of the plan. Therefore, exposure to the actuarial risk of other entities' employees alone is not enough to justify the application of defined contribution accounting to a defined benefit multi-employer plan. In our view, sufficient information is available for defined benefit accounting to be applied for participation in a multi-employer defined benefit plan if:

- the participant in the multi-employer plan has access to information about all components of the plan (e.g. plan assets, defined benefit obligation, remeasurements, service cost, net interest) and not only knowledge of the net deficit or surplus (i.e. an actuarial valuation on an IAS 19-compliant basis for the plan as a whole is available to participating entities); and
- the stated basis for allocating the deficit or surplus is reasonably stable. For this to be the case, the methodology for allocating the deficit or surplus should remain consistent and the allocation should not result in significant variability of the entity's proportion of the deficit or surplus. [*IAS 19.36*]

4.4.180.20 In our view, the assessment of whether the stated basis for allocating the deficit or surplus is reasonably stable should be made in relation to the entity participating in the plan. As such, the size of the entity's share of the plan may affect this assessment.

EXAMPLE 1 – MULTI-EMPLOYER PLAN – ASSESSING STABILITY OF ALLOCATION BASIS

4.4.180.30 Companies B and D, together with other companies, participate in a multi-employer benefit plan. The plan allocates the deficit or surplus based on a plan-wide contribution rate that is calculated based on each company's relative percentage of pensionable earnings. B and D estimate that their relative percentage of pensionable earnings may increase or decrease by five percentage points from year to year. B's share of the plan is significant, and therefore it determines that a five percentage point change in its relative percentage of pensionable earnings would not result in significant variability in the proportion of the deficit or surplus that would be allocated. Conversely, D does not have a significant share of the plan and it determines that a five percentage point change in its relative percentage of pensionable earnings would result in significant variability, and therefore this may not be considered a reasonably stable basis for allocating the deficit or surplus.

4.4.190 *Change in accounting treatment*

4.4.190.10 If an entity has been accounting for a multi-employer defined benefit plan as a defined benefit plan and the information that was previously available becomes unavailable, then the plan is accounted for going forward as if it were a defined contribution plan. In our view, this should be treated as a change in estimate following the specific requirements for changes in estimates related to defined contribution plans – i.e. as a change in estimate recognised as part of the defined contribution cost in profit or loss in the period. [*IAS 19.36*]

4.4.190.20   If an entity has been accounting for a multi-employer defined benefit plan as a defined contribution plan but sufficient information then becomes available that enables it to account for that plan as a defined benefit plan (see 4.4.300), then in our view this should be treated as a change in estimate following the specific requirements for changes in estimates related to defined benefit plans – i.e. as remeasurements in the period (see 4.4.950). We believe that any deficit or surplus at the date of reclassification of the plan should be included in the calculation of remeasurements of the net defined benefit liability (asset) as if the gain or loss arose in the first year in which defined benefit accounting is applied as a result of new information becoming available. It is not a plan amendment (see 4.4.880) because the entity neither introduces a defined benefit plan nor changes the benefits payable under an existing defined benefit plan. [*IAS 19.104*]

4.4.200   Group plans

4.4.200.10   Defined benefit plans in which entities under common control share risks are group plans rather than multi-employer plans. Group plans are classified as either a defined contribution plan or a defined benefit plan in accordance with the terms of the plan (see 4.4.130). Under IAS 19, the accounting for defined benefit group plans in separate or individual financial statements (see 2.1.110–120) depends on whether there is a contractual agreement or stated policy for charging the net defined benefit cost to individual group entities (see 4.4.210–220). [*IAS 19.40–41*]

4.4.200.20   IAS 19 does not specifically address group plans that have both defined contribution and defined benefit components – e.g. defined benefit for all employees of some group entities and defined contribution for all employees of other group entities.

EXAMPLE 2 – GROUP PLAN WITH DEFINED CONTRIBUTION AND DEFINED BENEFIT COMPONENTS

4.4.200.30   Companies C and B are under the common control of Parent P. C and B participate in a single plan with P for the benefit of their employees, with a stated policy for charging the IAS 19 cost for the plan as a whole (see 4.4.210.10). C's employees are entitled to a defined contribution award on retirement and B's employees are entitled to a defined benefit award on retirement. The contributions made by C and B and their employees are held in a single asset pool in a trust. C and B might wish to account for the defined contribution and defined benefit components of the plan separately – i.e. C accounts for the plan as a defined contribution plan whereas B accounts for it as a defined benefit plan. In our view, for this to be appropriate, as a minimum there should be controls in place within the trust that prevent any use of assets related to defined contribution members to settle obligations related to defined benefit members and vice versa. If such restrictions on availability are not in place, then we believe that the plan as a whole should be accounted for as a single plan and defined benefit accounting should be applied at a group level (see 4.4.210.10).

4.4.210   *Contractual agreement or stated policy exists*

4.4.210.10   If a contractual agreement or stated policy exists for charging individual group entities the IAS 19 cost for the plan as a whole, then an entity recognises the net defined benefit cost allocated to it under the agreement or policy. The net defined benefit cost to be allocated to and recognised by group entities under a contractual agreement or a stated policy is measured in accordance with IAS 19 and is therefore, in aggregate, equal to the amount recognised at the group level in profit or loss and in OCI (see 4.4.830). [*IAS 19.41, 120*]

4.4.210.20   IFRS is silent on where the allocated net defined benefit cost should be recognised in the financial statements of group entities (see 2.1.110–120). In our view, participants in a group plan should not generally recognise any of the allocated amount outside profit or loss; instead, they should recognise it as a single expense within personnel expenses (see 4.4.1120). However, there may be circumstances in which recognition of a portion of the allocated amount outside profit or loss is appropriate – e.g. if there is a reasonable basis for allocating remeasurements to group entities.

EXAMPLE 3A – GROUP DEFINED BENEFIT PLAN – ALLOCATION OF COST UNDER STATED POLICY (1)

4.4.210.30   Company G participates in a group defined benefit plan for which the net defined benefit cost is allocated to group entities in accordance with a stated policy. Under the stated policy, the cost allocated to participating entities is based on the obligation attributable to plan participants. This assessment includes identifying which specific participating entities have incurred an obligation for particular plan members. The stated policy is intended to reflect as closely as possible each group entity's share of the underlying financial position and performance of the plan, including any remeasurements attributable to those entities. In our view, it may be appropriate for G to apply full defined benefit accounting to its share of each component of the net defined benefit cost, and therefore to recognise allocated remeasurements in OCI in its financial statements. For complex group plans, it may be necessary to involve an actuary to determine the group entities to which the defined benefit obligation relates.

EXAMPLE 3B – GROUP DEFINED BENEFIT PLAN – ALLOCATION OF COST UNDER STATED POLICY (2)

4.4.210.40   Company B participates in a group defined benefit plan for which 90% of the defined benefit obligation is attributable to its active employees and retirees. B is not the legal sponsor of the plan and the net defined benefit cost is allocated to group entities in accordance with a stated policy. Under that policy, the net defined benefit cost is allocated based on an assessment of either the defined benefit obligation or the current service cost attributable to other participants, with the balance allocated to B. In our view, it may be appropriate for B to apply full defined benefit accounting to its share of each component of the net defined benefit cost, and therefore to recognise allocated remeasurements in OCI. We believe that this would be appropriate on the basis that 90% of the defined benefit obligation is attributable to B's active employees and retirees, and not simply as a result of the stated policy of allocation.

Ⓢ 4.4.220   ***No contractual agreement or stated policy in place***

4.4.220.10   If there is no contractual agreement or stated policy in place, then the net defined benefit cost is recognised by the group entity that is legally the sponsoring employer for the plan. The other participants in the plan recognise in profit or loss an amount equal to their contributions payable for the period. In our view, the net defined benefit cost recognised by the legal sponsor should be equal to the net defined benefit cost for the plan as a whole less the contributions of other plan participants. [*IAS 19.41*]

4.4.220.20   IFRS does not address how this net cost should be recognised by the legal sponsor. In our view, the appropriate accounting treatment by the legal sponsor will depend on the facts and circumstances of the plan, and in particular the basis of the contributions made by other entities.

EXAMPLE 4A – GROUP DEFINED BENEFIT PLAN – ACCOUNTING BY LEGAL SPONSOR – OTHER ENTITIES CONTRIBUTE ONLY CURRENT SERVICE COST

> 4.4.220.30   Company C is the legal sponsor of a group plan for which the contributions of participants relate only to their current service cost for the period. Because the remeasurements for the plan are being borne wholly by C, in our view it may be appropriate for C's cost in profit or loss to be recognised net of the contributions of other entities.

4.4.220.40   A situation may arise in which the contributions of participants other than the legal sponsor exceed the defined benefit cost of the plan as a whole recognised in profit or loss. IFRS does not provide guidance on the treatment by the legal sponsor of the excess of contributions received. The appropriate accounting treatment by the legal sponsor will depend on the facts and circumstances of the plan.

4.4.220.50   One possible approach is to offset contributions of other entities first against the amount recognised in profit or loss in the current period, with the excess contributions offset against remeasurements recognised in OCI, because the contributions may include an element of funding a deficit related to remeasurement losses recognised in prior periods.

EXAMPLE 4B – GROUP DEFINED BENEFIT PLAN – ACCOUNTING BY LEGAL SPONSOR – OTHER ENTITIES CONTRIBUTE IN EXCESS OF CURRENT SERVICE COST

> 4.4.220.60   Company D is the legal sponsor of a group plan for which the net defined benefit cost is 100, including a remeasurement loss of 20. Contributions by other participants are 90. Under the approach in 4.4.220.50, in its financial statements, D would first offset the contributions against the 80 recognised in profit or loss, with the remaining contribution of 10 being recognised in OCI as an adjustment to the remeasurement.

4.4.230   *Introduction or removal of stated policy or contractual agreement*

4.4.230.10   If a legal sponsor introduces a stated policy or contractual agreement or removes a policy or agreement, but the plan remains a defined benefit plan, then in our view the general principles of changes in the classification of a multi-employer defined benefit pension plan should be applied to the respective recognition and derecognition of a share of an existing deficit or surplus (see 4.4.190) – i.e. the resulting change in estimate should be accounted for under whichever of defined contribution or defined benefit accounting principles is to be applied after the event causing the change in classification. Accordingly, if the plan has a deficit and:

- a policy or agreement is removed by a legal sponsor, then other participants should derecognise their portion of the deficit and recognise the gain resulting from that change in estimate in profit or loss (see 4.4.190.10), whereas the sponsor should account for a remeasurement loss on the net defined benefit liability (see 4.4.190.20); or
- a policy or agreement is introduced, then this would result in a remeasurement gain on the net defined benefit liability for the legal sponsor and a remeasurement loss equal to the newly recognised share of net defined benefit liability for other participants.

4.4.240   State plans

4.4.240.10   State plans are established by legislation to cover all, or specific groups of, entities and are not operated by the employer. [*IAS 19.44*]

4.4.240.20   State plans are accounted for in the same way as multi-employer plans. If the employer has an obligation only to pay contributions and has no legal or constructive obligation to pay future benefits, then state plans are defined contribution plans. Otherwise, they are defined benefit plans. [*IAS 19.43, 45*]

4.4.240.30   In our experience, there is generally insufficient information available about defined benefit state plans to apply defined benefit accounting. Therefore, defined contribution accounting is normally applied to such state plans.

4.4.250   DEFINED CONTRIBUTION PLANS

4.4.250.10   An entity accounts for its contributions to defined contribution plans on an accrual basis. An asset or liability may result from advance payments or payments due, respectively, to a defined contribution fund. [*IAS 19.51*]

4.4.260   Vesting conditions and advance contributions

4.4.260.10   If contributions are made to a defined contribution plan in advance of services being rendered, or if a defined contribution plan has vesting conditions, then some believe that under paragraph 51(a) of IAS 19 the contributions should be recognised as a prepayment and that the prepayment should be expensed as the employee provides services that entitle them to the benefits. However, under IAS 19 the entity's obligation for each period is determined by the amounts to be contributed for that period. The IFRS Interpretations Committee discussed the issue of vesting conditions and noted that each contribution to a defined contribution plan is recognised as an expense over the period of service that obliges the employer to pay this contribution to the defined contribution plan, rather than over the period of service that entitles the employee to receive the benefit. [*IAS 19.51, IU 07-11*]

4.4.270   Refund of contributions or contribution holiday

4.4.270.10   In unusual cases, an entity may be entitled to a refund of contributions, to a contribution holiday or to a reduction in future contributions in respect of past services under a defined contribution plan – e.g. if the plan has vesting conditions and an employee forfeits benefits as a result of failing to meet the required service conditions. The IFRS Interpretations Committee discussed a scenario in which an entity is entitled to a refund of contributions and noted that a refund is recognised as an asset and as income when the entity becomes entitled to it – e.g. by the employee failing to meet the vesting condition. In our view, a contribution holiday or a reduction in contributions for past services, the cost of which has already been recognised as personnel expenses, should be treated in the same way as a refund. Accordingly, we believe that a contribution holiday or a reduction in future contributions that will accrue in future periods for services to be provided after the reporting date should not be anticipated. Instead, the benefit should be recognised by way of a lower (or no) contribution expense in those future periods. [*IU 07-11*]

EXAMPLE 5 – DEFINED CONTRIBUTION PLAN WITH POTENTIAL REFUND OF CONTRIBUTIONS

4.4.270.20   Company Y makes contributions to a defined contribution plan on behalf of its employees. Each employee's vested interest is 100% if employment ends after age 60; 75% if employment ends after age 55; and 50% if employment ends before age 55. To the extent that the interest does not vest, Y is entitled to a contribution refund. Y expenses 100% of the defined contributions that fall due in respect of each period. If an employee does not complete the required service to become entitled to 100% of the contributions, then Y recognises an asset and income when it becomes entitled to the resultant refund – i.e. on a termination of employment.

4.4.280   *Refund or contribution holiday for multi-employer plan*

4.4.280.10   An employer that participates in a defined benefit multi-employer plan may become entitled to a refund of contributions (see 4.4.840) or to a contribution holiday if the plan is in surplus. In our view, an asset should not be recognised for an anticipated refund of contributions or a contribution holiday for a defined benefit multi-employer plan that is accounted for as a defined contribution plan because insufficient information is available to apply defined benefit accounting. This is because the factors that give rise to the exemption from defined benefit accounting – i.e. the inability to obtain sufficient information to calculate the entity's proportionate share – and therefore the exemption from recognising an asset or liability, apply until the refund is received or receivable. However, the surplus and the implications – i.e. the expected reduction in contributions – should be disclosed. [*IAS 19.148(d)(iv)*]

4.4.290   **Presentation and disclosures**

4.4.290.10   Assets and liabilities related to defined contribution plans are classified as current or non-current in accordance with the general classification requirements (see 3.1.20).

4.4.290.20   The amount recognised as an expense for defined contribution plans is disclosed. Information about contributions to defined contribution plans for key management personnel is also disclosed, if applicable. [*IAS 19.53–54, 24.17*]

4.4.300   **DEFINED BENEFIT PLANS**

4.4.310   **Basic principles**

4.4.310.10   IAS 19 establishes requirements for the basis of the valuation as well as principles for the actuarial assumptions to be used in valuing defined benefit plans.

4.4.310.20   Estimates, averages and computational shortcuts may be used only if they provide a reliable approximation of the detailed computations that are required. Computational shortcuts may be appropriate in practice when performing a roll-forward of a previous valuation – e.g. from valuation date to a subsequent reporting date (see 4.4.350). [*IAS 19.58, 60*]

4.4.320   *Interest in a fund*

4.4.320.10   An entity offsets qualifying plan assets against the related obligation to employees; it does not consolidate the fund that holds the plan assets. For further discussion, see 4.4.1490. [*IAS 19.57(a)(iii), 113*]

4.4.330   *Inter-related post-employment benefit plans*

4.4.330.10   An entity may have more than one post-employment benefit plan. In our view, if the post-employment benefits are financed through a single scheme, funded by one asset pool, and therefore share the same investment risk, then they should generally be considered and reported as a single plan, and the terms of each component of the plan should be disclosed separately.

4.4.330.20   Conversely, if different benefits are funded through different funds or are administered by one fund but have different arrangements, subject to different investment risk, then we believe that they should be considered as separate plans. They may be combined in preparing disclosures for the financial statements if they are all in a net surplus or a net liability position. Otherwise, offsetting is appropriate only if there is a legal right to set off between underfunding of one plan and overfunding of another plan (see 4.4.1080). [*IAS 19.131*]

4.4.330.30   In our view, the fact that there are the same beneficiaries in two different plans does not automatically result in a single plan even if one plan may have certain rights to the surplus in the other plan. For example, access of an unfunded post-employment medical benefit plan under specific circumstances to part of the surplus of another post-employment plan does not generally result in a plan asset in the medical benefit plan if the amount of the surplus is not transferred but only 'reserved' – i.e. the surplus 'reserved' for the medical benefit plan would decline if the investments decreased or the defined benefit obligation increased in the original post-employment benefit plan. Treating such an arrangement as one plan could result in disguising the true position of the arrangement, because the 'unreserved' surplus of the post-employment plan could be offsetting the deficit of the medical plan. However, if there is a right to set off, then the 'reserved' surplus may be a plan asset of the medical plan. In this case, an entity needs to consider its legally enforceable right to use a surplus in one plan to settle obligations under another plan and its intention to settle the plans on a net basis (see 4.4.1080).

EXAMPLE 6 – DEFINED BENEFIT PLANS – INTER-RELATED POST-EMPLOYMENT BENEFIT PLANS

4.4.330.40   Company H is required by law to make severance payments to employees when they retire or leave. Severance payments reduce pension entitlement. If H anticipates that the severance payments will be such that no pension payments will be required, then we believe that the net defined benefit liability (asset) should reflect only the severance payments. If pension payments will be required in addition to the severance payments, then the pension liability should reflect the amounts that will be payable as a top-up to the severance payment. In any case, we believe that the calculation of the severance liability and the pension liability should reflect consistent actuarial assumptions, such as estimated future salary increases, but may have different inputs – e.g. benefits may be based on the final salary for the pension scheme, but on the average salary for the severance liability.

4.4.340   **Recognition and measurement**

4.4.340.10   Accounting for defined benefit plans involves the following steps.

- Determining the deficit or surplus in the plan, by:
  - determining the present value of the defined benefit obligation (see 4.4.380); and
  - deducting the fair value of any plan assets (see 4.4.550).
- Adjusting the amount of the deficit or surplus for any effect of limiting a net defined benefit asset to the asset ceiling (see 4.4.690).
- Determining the amounts to be recognised in profit or loss (see 4.4.830).
- Determining the remeasurements of the net defined benefit liability (asset) to be recognised in OCI (see 4.4.950). [*IAS 19.57*]

4.4.350   *Timing and frequency of actuarial valuations*

4.4.350.10   To determine the present value of the defined benefit obligation, an entity needs to obtain an actuarial valuation. The timing or frequency of actuarial valuations is not mandated by IFRS. Actuarial valuations are required to be regular enough for the amounts recognised in the financial statements not to differ materially from the amounts that would be determined at the reporting date. Therefore, a valuation a few months before the reporting date is acceptable if it is adjusted for material subsequent events – e.g. discount rate changes – up to the reporting date. [*IAS 19.58*]

4.4.350.20   IFRS is silent on the treatment of a change in the timing of actuarial valuations. In our view, because the change in the timing does not change the measurement objective, it is not a change in accounting policy (see chapter 2.8). In our view, such a change can be made if the measurement of the obligation would still not be materially different from a measurement based on an actuarial valuation obtained at the reporting date.

EXAMPLE 7 – DEFINED BENEFIT PLANS – TIMING OF ACTUARIAL VALUATION

4.4.350.30   Company D previously measured its defined benefit obligation based on an actuarial valuation obtained at the reporting date; the most recent actuarial valuation was obtained at 31 December 2017. We believe that D may measure the obligation at 31 December 2018 based on an actuarial valuation obtained at 30 September 2018 if it adjusts the obligation for material subsequent events up to 31 December 2018.

4.4.350.40   In our view, asset values should generally be determined at the annual reporting date, even if the valuation of the obligation is done in advance and is adjusted forward, because these values are generally observable in the market. [*IAS 19.58*]

4.4.360   *Interim reporting*

4.4.360.10   The preparation of interim financial information does not necessarily involve obtaining an updated actuarial valuation. Although the basic requirement of IAS 19 is that remeasurements are recognised in the period in which they arise, for interim financial statements a greater degree of estimation may be appropriate. Determining whether an updated valuation of the net defined benefit liability (asset) is necessary at the interim reporting date requires judgement (see 5.9.150). [*IAS 34.B9, 19.BC59*]

4.4.360.20   Entities may nevertheless choose to update their actuarial valuation at the each interim reporting date.

4.4.360.30   An updated valuation of the net defined benefit liability (asset) at the interim reporting date does not affect the measurement of service cost and net interest for the remainder of the current annual reporting period. Their measurement continues to be based on the assumptions at the prior annual reporting date. [*IAS 19.BC63–BC64*]

4.4.370   Net defined benefit liability (asset)

4.4.370.10   The net defined benefit liability (asset) is recognised in the statement of financial position and is determined as follows.
- *Step 1:* Present value of the defined benefit obligation (see 4.4.380) minus the fair value of any plan assets (see 4.4.550) equals the deficit or surplus in the defined benefit plan.
- *Step 2:* Adjustment for any effect of limiting a net defined benefit asset to the asset ceiling (see 4.4.690). [*IAS 19.8, 63–64*]

4.4.380   DEFINED BENEFIT OBLIGATION

4.4.390   Actuarial valuation method

4.4.390.10   The projected unit credit method is used to determine the present value of the defined benefit obligation. This involves projecting future salaries and benefits to which an employee will be entitled at the expected date of leaving. [*IAS 19.67–68*]

EXAMPLE 8 – MEASURING DEFINED BENEFIT OBLIGATION AND CURRENT SERVICE COST

4.4.390.20   Company F operates a defined benefit plan that provides an annual pension of $\frac{1}{60}$ of final salary for each year of service. The total expected annual salary on retirement of employees covered by the plan is 600,000. All the employees are expected to retire in 10 years and have worked for five years to date. After retirement, the employees are expected to live for 15 years.

4.4.390.30   The defined benefit obligation is the present value of the expected payment of 750,000 ($\frac{5}{60}$ x 600,000 x 15). The employee cost for the period (current service cost) is equal to ($\frac{1}{60}$ x 600,000 x 15) discounted to its present value, adjusted for the actuarially determined probability of the outcome.

4.4.395   *Contribution-based promises*

4.4.395.10   Contribution-based promises are defined benefit plans with a promised return on actual or notional contributions that is based on either or both of the following features:
- a guaranteed return of a fixed amount or rate; and/or
- a benefit that depends on future asset returns.

4.4.395.20   IAS 19 is silent on the accounting for contribution-based promises. Because these plans are defined benefit plans, the projected unit credit method generally applies to the measurement of the related defined benefit obligation. However, in our experience, in some jurisdictions entities predominantly apply the methodology of IFRIC Draft Interpretation D9 *Employee Benefit Plans with a Promised Return on Contributions or Notional Contributions* and therefore measure benefits that depend on future asset returns at the fair value of the related assets.

4.4.395.30   The IFRS Interpretations Committee discussed this issue and acknowledged that divergence in practice exists; however, it decided not to proceed with a project on the issue. In our view, an entity applying IFRIC D9 should update its approach as necessary to comply with the currently effective IAS 19 – e.g. to reflect the amended calculation of net interest – because IFRIC D9 was based on an earlier version of the standard. [*IU 05-14*]

4.4.400   Attributing benefits to periods of service

4.4.400.10   Benefits are attributed to periods of service in accordance with the plan's benefit formula, unless that formula is back-end-loaded – i.e. service in later periods will lead to a materially higher level of benefit than service in earlier periods – in which case a straight-line attribution is used. [*IAS 19.70*]

4.4.400.20   In determining whether straight-line attribution is required, an entity considers whether an employee's service throughout the period will ultimately lead to benefits at that higher level. [*IAS 19.73*]

EXAMPLE 9A – DEFINED BENEFIT OBLIGATION – ATTRIBUTING BENEFITS TO PERIODS OF SERVICE

4.4.400.30   Company G sponsors a pension plan in which employees earn defined benefits for service provided between the ages of 25 and 65. As part of the pension plan, G offers an early retirement scheme under which employees earn early retirement benefits for service provided between the ages of 47 and 62. The early retirement benefits are earned regardless of the period of service before the age of 47 – i.e. an employee joining G at age 46 is entitled to the same early retirement benefit as an employee who has been employed since the age of 26. Because services provided from the age of 47 to 62 lead to the early retirement benefit, the obligation for the early retirement scheme is attributed to services provided from the age of 47 through to 62.

4.4.400.40   If a straight-line attribution is used, then benefits are attributed from the date on which service first leads to benefits under the plan until the date on which further service by the employee will lead to no material amount of further benefits under the plan, other than from salary increases. This method of attribution is required because the employee's service throughout the period will ultimately lead to benefits at a higher level. [*IAS 19.70, 73*]

4.4.400.50   An entity evaluates the terms of a plan to determine the date on which service first leads to benefits under the plan, because it may not necessarily be the date of hire.

EXAMPLE 9B – DEFINED BENEFIT OBLIGATION – DETERMINING START OF ATTRIBUTION PERIOD

4.4.400.60   Company H offers post-employment medical benefits to its retirees under the following conditions:
- they provided 20 years of service; and
- they were employed at the age of 60.

> 4.4.400.70   The start of the attribution period may differ depending on whether the benefit is earned after 20 years of cumulative service or 20 years of consecutive service. In the cumulative service (first) scenario, the employee may leave at the age of 35 after seven years of service and return at the age of 38 and still earn the benefit. If 20 years of cumulative service is required, then the benefit would be attributed from the date of original hire – i.e. when the employee was 28 – because the services provided from that date contribute to the benefits earned. However, if 20 years of consecutive service is required, then the attribution would start from the age of 40 because the first seven years of employment did not give rise to benefit entitlement. However, all facts and circumstances need to be considered – e.g. an entity does not rehire former employees in practice – to ensure that the appropriate attribution period is used.

4.4.400.80   IFRS is silent on whether the benefits previously attributed to earlier years of service should be revised if the structure of benefits offered by a plan is amended but benefits earned from the past service are unchanged. In our view, if an amendment offers improved benefits for future services and benefits accrued in respect of past service remain unaffected, then the benefits should not be attributed over the entire service period but rather split into two distinct periods, with the change accounted for prospectively.

EXAMPLE 9C – DEFINED BENEFIT OBLIGATION – ATTRIBUTION OF BENEFITS FOLLOWING PLAN AMENDMENT

> 4.4.400.90   A defined benefit plan offers different benefit accrual rates for different groups of participants – e.g. one category accrues a benefit of $^1/_{60}$ of the final salary per year whereas the other accrues a benefit of $^1/_{50}$. From 1 January 2018, the plan is amended to offer all members benefits at the more advantageous accrual rate of $^1/_{50}$ and this change applies prospectively – i.e. only to benefits earned after 1 January 2018. We believe that because the benefits earned in respect of service provided until 31 December 2017 are not affected by the amendment, the benefits should not be attributed over the entire working lives of members but instead should be attributed separately over two distinct periods of service – i.e. one before and one after the amendment.

4.4.410   Actuarial assumptions

4.4.410.10   Actuarial assumptions comprise the following.
- Demographic assumptions, such as:
  - mortality (see 4.4.420.10);
  - rates of employee turnover, disability and early retirement (see 4.4.420.20); and
  - the take-up of any benefit payment options available under the plan (see 4.4.440).
- Financial assumptions, such as:
  - future salary (see 4.4.430.30);

- benefit levels (excluding any cost of the benefits to be met by employees or third parties) (see 4.4.430–490);
- certain taxes payable by the plan (see 4.4.500); and
- the discount rate (see 4.4.510). [*IAS 19.76*]

4.4.410.20   Actuarial assumptions represent the entity's best estimates of the variables that will determine the ultimate cost of settling the defined benefit obligation. They are unbiased (neither imprudent nor excessively conservative) and mutually compatible – e.g. the economic relationship between increases in salaries and future inflation-linked pension increases reflects the same expectations. [*IAS 19.76–78*]

4.4.410.30   The financial assumptions are based on current market expectations of future events – e.g. medical cost inflation – and are determined in nominal (stated) terms unless real (inflation-adjusted) terms would be more appropriate. [*IAS 19.79–80*]

4.4.420   *Demographic assumptions*

4.4.420.10   Mortality assumptions are determined with reference to the entity's current best estimate of the mortality of plan members both during and after employment. Existing mortality tables might therefore need to be adjusted for expected changes in mortality. [*IAS 19.81–82, BC142*]

4.4.420.20   Although an entity makes estimates of voluntary early retirements, it does not take into account future redundancies or other plan curtailments in determining the defined benefit obligation until the termination or curtailment is recognised (see 4.4.890).

4.4.430   *Benefits*

4.4.430.10   The calculation takes into account not only the stated plan benefits, but also any constructive obligations. Constructive obligations include those established by informal practices, which the entity has no realistic alternative but to continue, such as 'discretionary' inflationary increases in pensions that would be very difficult for an employer to stop granting. [*IAS 19.87, 88(a)*]

4.4.430.20   The actuarial assumptions take into account future benefit changes that are set out in the formal terms of a plan. This includes estimated future changes in state benefits that affect benefits payable under the plan and for which there is reliable evidence that the change will happen. [*IAS 19.87–88*]

4.4.430.30   The measurement of the defined benefit obligation reflects expected future salaries. Therefore, for average salary plans, the *projected* average salary rather than the current average salary is used in measuring the liability. Similarly, even if the plan benefits are expressed in terms of current salaries, expected future salaries are taken into account. [*IAS 19.70, 87(b)*]

4.4.430.40   Other future changes that the employer currently has a constructive obligation to make – e.g. inflation increases – are also reflected in the measurement of the obligation. However, future changes to the terms of a plan, as long as the employer does not have a constructive obligation to make these changes, are not anticipated in the measurement of the obligation. Therefore, if, for example, the terms of a plan are changed from covering a select group of employees to covering all employees, then the change is treated as a plan amendment that may give rise to a past service cost (see 4.4.870), or as a new plan, rather than as an actuarial loss. [*IAS 19.89*]

4.4.440 *Optionality included in the plan*

4.4.440.10   A plan may give its members the option to receive a lump-sum payment at retirement instead of ongoing payments. An assumption is made about the proportion of plan members who will select each form of settlement option available under the plan terms. Therefore, when the employees are able to choose the form of the benefit – e.g. lump-sum payment vs annual pension – the entity makes an actuarial assumption about what proportion will make each choice. As a result, an actuarial gain or loss will arise if the choice of settlement taken by the employee is not the one that the entity has assumed will be taken. [*IAS 19.8*]

EXAMPLE 10 – DEFINED BENEFIT OBLIGATION – OPTION TO CHOOSE LUMP-SUM PAYMENT OR ANNUAL PAYMENTS

4.4.440.20   Under the terms of its defined benefit pension plan, Company Z gives its employees the option to receive a lump-sum payment at retirement instead of ongoing payments. Z expects that none of its employees will opt for the lump-sum payment and therefore applies an assumption of zero in measuring its defined benefit obligation. Eventually, however, some employees elect to take that option. These lump-sum payments are not considered to be a settlement (see 4.4.910) because a zero assumption is nevertheless an assumption made about an issue that Z was required to consider, based on the terms of the arrangement. Therefore, they will result in an actuarial gain or loss.

4.4.450 *Performance targets or other criteria*

4.4.450.10   Certain pension promises may be based on achieving specific performance targets or other criteria. The actuarial assumptions include the best estimate of the effect of these variables on the cost of meeting the benefit promise – i.e. on the measurement of the defined benefit obligation. For example, the terms of a plan may state that it will pay reduced benefits or require additional contributions from employees if the plan assets are insufficient. Such criteria are reflected in the measurement of the defined benefit obligation, regardless of whether the changes in benefits resulting from the criteria either being or not being met are automatic or are subject to a decision by the entity, by the employee or by a third party such as the trustee or administrators of the plan. [*IAS 19.88(c), BC150(c)*]

4.4.460 **Risk-sharing arrangements**

4.4.460.10   The measurement of the defined benefit obligation takes into consideration risk-sharing features and contributions from employees or third parties that are not reimbursement rights.

4.4.470 *Sharing a surplus*

4.4.470.10   The terms of a plan may include specific surplus-sharing provisions or the terms of allocation may be defined in a separate agreement between the employer and the employees. For example, the terms of a plan may provide that if the plan has a surplus, then 30 percent of the surplus is allocated to employees and the remainder to the employer (see 4.4.700). The portion of the surplus allocated to the participants in the defined benefit plan is reflected in the actuarial assumptions about future benefit changes, because it is reflected in the formal terms of the plan. [*IAS 19.88(b)*]

4.4.480   *Limit on employer contributions*

4.4.480.10   Any limits to the contributions that an entity is required to make are included in the calculation of the ultimate cost of the benefit. The effect is determined over the shorter of the expected life of the entity and the expected life of the plan. [*IAS 19.91*]

4.4.490   *Employee and third party contributions*

4.4.490.10   Some defined benefit plans require employees or third parties to contribute to the cost of the plan. Contributions by employees reduce the cost of the benefits to the entity. An entity considers whether third party contributions reduce the cost of the benefits to it or are a reimbursement right (see 4.4.640). [*IAS 19.92*]

4.4.490.20   Contributions from employees or third parties that reduce the cost to the entity of those benefits may be reflected in measuring the defined benefit obligation. IAS 19 distinguishes between discretionary contributions and contributions that are set out in the formal terms of the plan, and provides guidance on accounting for both.
- Discretionary contributions by employees or third parties reduce service cost on payment of the contributions to the plan – i.e. the increase in plan assets is recognised as a reduction of service costs.
- Contributions that are set out in the formal terms of the plan either:
  - reduce service cost, if they are linked to service (see 4.4.490.30); or
  - affect remeasurements of the net defined liability (asset), if they are not linked to service. An example of these are contributions that are required to reduce a deficit arising from losses on plan assets or actuarial losses (see 4.4.960). [*IAS 19.87(d), 92–93*]

4.4.490.30   Contributions that are set out in the formal terms of the plan and linked to service reduce the service cost as follows.
- If the amount of the contributions is dependent on the number of years of service, then those contributions are attributed to periods of service using the attribution method required by paragraph 70 of IAS 19 for the gross benefit – i.e. either using the plan's contribution formula or on a straight-line basis, as appropriate (see 4.4.400).
- If the amount of the contributions is independent of the number of years of service, then the entity is permitted as a practical expedient to recognise those contributions as a reduction of the service cost in the period in which the related service is rendered, instead of using the attribution method required by paragraph 70 of IAS 19. Examples of contributions that are independent of the number of years of service include those that are a fixed percentage of the employee's salary, a fixed amount throughout the service period or dependent on the employee's age. [*IAS 19.93*]

4.4.490.40   For a discussion of the accounting for state subsidies paid to employers, see 4.4.640.50–80.

4.4.500 **Taxes payable by plan**

4.4.500.10   IAS 19 distinguishes between taxes payable by the plan on contributions relating to service before the reporting date or on benefits resulting from that service, and all other taxes payable by the plan. An actuarial assumption is made about the first type of taxes, which are taken into account in measuring current service cost and the defined benefit obligation, because they are seen as part of the cost of providing the benefits. All other taxes payable by the plan are included in the return on plan assets and therefore form part of remeasurements (see 4.4.970). [*IAS 19.8, 76(b)(iv), 130*]

EXAMPLE 11 – DEFINED BENEFIT OBLIGATION – TAXES ON CONTRIBUTIONS RELATING TO SERVICE BEFORE REPORTING DATE

4.4.500.20   Company Z has a defined benefit pension plan. The plan is required to pay a 10% tax on all contributions it receives – a 'contributions tax'. Without considering the impact of investment earnings that might also fund the future benefits, the plan needs to receive contributions of 100 to retain sufficient post-tax plan assets to pay a benefit of 90, effectively increasing Z's cost of the benefit. This type of tax is included in determining the defined benefit obligation at the end of each reporting date. Changes in the expected timing or amount of contributions tax payable will lead to actuarial gains and losses, which are recognised in OCI.

4.4.500.30   Estimating the amount of contributions tax payable to be included in the calculation of the defined benefit obligation involves making various assumptions, including the following:
- the expected timing of contributions tax payments, which might occur periodically over the employment period; and
- the level of plan assets already held by the plan, because they limit the need for additional contributions and the related taxes.

4.4.510 **Discount rate**

4.4.510.10   The obligation for estimated future payments is measured on a discounted basis. The obligation is discounted using a high-quality corporate bond rate (see 4.4.520) or a government bond rate if there is an insufficiently deep high-quality corporate bond market (see 4.4.530). The currency and maturity of the bonds need to be consistent with the currency and maturity of the defined benefit obligation. [*IAS 19.83, IU 06-17*]

4.4.520 *High-quality corporate bonds*

4.4.520.10   In our view, 'high-quality' should be interpreted as a bond with one of the two highest ratings – i.e. AAA and AA (Standard & Poor's rating) or Aaa and Aa (Moody's rating) – or equivalent from other ratings agencies.

4.4.520.20   We believe that consideration should be given to adjustments for downgrades subsequent to the reporting date. In some cases, bonds that are included in data underlying a yield curve or bond-matching model (see 4.4.540.10) may be downgraded by a credit rating agency subsequent to the reporting date so that the bonds no longer meet the criteria to be considered high-quality. In other cases, the market index may include corporate bonds that are no longer high-quality. In either of these cases, the facts and circumstances should be evaluated to determine if there is an adjusting event or a non-adjusting event after the reporting date (see 2.9.20–30).

4.4.520.30   In our view, the incremental borrowing rate of an entity is not an appropriate rate to use, because it reflects the credit quality of the entity. [*IAS 19.84, BC134*]

4.4.530   *Deep market*

4.4.530.10   The depth of the market for high-quality corporate bonds is assessed at the currency level. [*IAS 19.83*]

4.4.530.20   An entity that operates in a country with a currency without a sufficiently deep high-quality corporate bond market uses government bonds issued in the same currency to determine the discount rate. In our view, such an entity cannot construct a synthetic equivalent using a bond market in another country's currency and notional or actual currency swaps. We believe that the hierarchy specified in the standard, which requires a default to the government bond rate, means that the government bond rate should be used. IAS 19, however, is not specific about what level of government should be used to determine the appropriate government bond rate. [*IAS 19.83*]

4.4.530.30   If bonds with a maturity that matches the maturity of the defined benefit obligation are not available, then an appropriate discount rate is estimated by extrapolating interest rates on shorter-term bonds using the yield curve and considering any available evidence about likely longer-term interest rates. [*IAS 19.86*]

4.4.540   *Discount rate methodologies*

4.4.540.10   Approaches to determining an IAS 19 discount rate may vary from entity to entity. In our experience, the prevalent methods are a yield curve approach, a bond-matching model or a market index approach under which an entity selects a representative discount rate from a published index representing high-quality corporate bonds (see 4.4.520).

4.4.540.20   In practice, an entity often uses a single weighted-average discount rate to measure the defined benefit obligation, reflecting the estimated timing and amount of benefit payments and the currency in which the benefits are to be paid. In such cases, the entity also uses the same rate to calculate current service cost and interest cost. However, in our view, in measuring the defined benefit obligation, current service cost and interest cost, an entity might instead use different weighted-average discount rates derived from the same yield curve for different categories of plan members in order to match more closely the expected timing of the benefit payments for each category. [*IAS 19.85*]

4.4.540.30   For example, different weighted-average rates might be used for pensioners and for members still in employment. In this case, rather than using a single weighted-average discount rate, an entity might calculate the defined benefit obligation, current service cost and interest cost separately for pensioners and active members, using the more specific weighted-average discount rate from the same yield curve attributable to each category. This calculation would result in different overall weighted-average discount rates for the defined benefit obligation and current service cost of the entire plan – i.e. when aggregating all categories – because current service is provided only by active members (see 4.4.860). [*IAS 19.85*]

EXAMPLE 12 – DEFINED BENEFIT OBLIGATION – USING SEPARATE DISCOUNT RATES FOR PENSIONERS AND ACTIVE MEMBERS

4.4.540.40   Company G calculates the defined benefit obligation, current service cost and interest cost separately for pensioners and active members of its defined benefit plan by using the weighted-average discount rate attributable to each category from the same yield curve. The weighted-average discount rates used for the calculations are as follows:

- pensioners – 4.6%; and
- active members – 4.8%.

4.4.540.50   When aggregating the two categories, the overall weighted-average discount rate that effectively has been used to measure the defined benefit obligation and the interest cost for the entire plan is 4.72% (reflecting that in this plan a higher proportion of the defined benefit obligation is attributable to active members than to pensioners).

4.4.540.60   However, in measuring the current service cost for the overall plan, G uses the discount rate of 4.8%. This is because current service is provided only by active members in the plan.

4.4.540.70   We believe that the approach described in 4.4.540.30–60 is not limited to broad categories of plan members and may be applied on a more granular basis to sub-categories of plan members (e.g. using separate discount rates for different sub-categories of pensioners) or even separately for each member in the plan (which is the most granular basis) as long as it is applied consistently in the calculation of the defined benefit obligation, current service cost and interest cost for each category of plan members. [*IAS 19.85*]

4.4.540.75   In our view, an entity may also calculate the defined benefit obligation, current service cost and interest cost using the following approach:

- estimate the timing and expected benefit payments for each year at a plan level; and
- apply to the expected benefit payments the corresponding spot rate from a single yield curve that aligns to the expected year of payment.

4.4.540.80   In our view, an entity cannot calculate the interest cost for the year by applying the one-year forward rate to the defined benefit obligation at the beginning of the year. This is because the net interest is calculated by applying the discount rate used for the measurement of the defined benefit obligation to the net defined benefit liability (asset) at the beginning of the year. [*IAS 19.83, 123, BC74*]

4.4.540.90   In line with our experience discussed in 4.4.540.110, whichever of the approaches discussed in 4.4.540.10–75 is used by the entity, it should generally be applied consistently from period to period.

4.4.540.100   In addition, if an entity applies an approach that results in different overall weighted-average discount rates effectively being used to measure the defined benefit obligation and current service cost for the entire plan, as discussed in 4.4.540.30–70, then it considers whether separate disclosure should be made of the different weighted-average rates effectively applied for the defined benefit obligation and current service cost – e.g. 4.72 percent and 4.8 percent respectively in Example 12. [*IAS 19.144*]

4.4.540.110   In our experience, entities generally determine discount rates for defined benefit plans using methodologies and data sources that are consistent from period to period. It may be appropriate, in certain circumstances, to consider the appropriateness of previously used methodologies, especially in response to any significant changes in market conditions. In our view, a change in the method used to select a discount rate may be appropriate when that change results in a more reliable estimate. We believe that this would be a change in an accounting estimate as opposed to a change in accounting policy in accordance with IAS 8. If an entity changes its approach to determining a discount rate, then it provides disclosures under IAS 8. In such cases, an entity discloses the nature and amount of a change in an accounting estimate that affects the current period or is expected to have an impact on future periods. [*IAS 8.39*]

4.4.540.120   In our view, any adjustments and changes to the previously used methodologies require assessment. We believe that it may be appropriate for an entity to exclude certain bonds from those to be included in a yield curve, a bond-matching model or a market index to more reliably reflect changing market conditions – e.g. by excluding 'outlier' bonds from an index. Such adjustments should be made on an objective and rational basis. For example, some entities express this in terms of the number of standard deviations of a bond's yield compared with the median or mean.

4.4.540.130   We believe, however, that certain approaches would not be appropriate – e.g. weighting the yields on outlier bonds differently from those on bonds deemed to be more representative of the overall market, because such weighting would be arbitrary and, accordingly, would not be consistent with the measurement requirements of IAS 19. Similarly, eliminating bonds issued by financial institutions solely on the basis that they are issued by financial institutions may be difficult to support because these bonds are an integral part of the market; however, if the elimination of bonds issued by such entities is a consequence of the use of a systematic and rational method of eliminating outliers, then this might be acceptable. Additionally, we believe that averaging observed bond yields for some period of time – e.g. a period before and after the reporting date – would be inconsistent with the requirement to determine an appropriate discount rate with reference to market yields at the reporting date. [*IAS 19.83*]

4.4.550   **PLAN ASSETS**

4.4.560   **Criteria for qualifying as plan assets**

4.4.560.10   'Plan assets' comprise:
- assets held by a legally separate fund that exists solely to pay or fund employee benefits, which:
  - can be used only to pay or fund employee benefits;
  - are not available to the entity's creditors (even in the case of bankruptcy) (see 4.4.570); and
  - cannot be returned to the entity except as reimbursement for employee benefits paid (see 4.4.580) or if the fund is in surplus (see 4.4.840); and
- qualifying insurance policies (see 4.4.660). [*IAS 19.8*]

4.4.560.20   In our view, if an entity controls the voting rights of shares contributed to and held by the fund, then this does not preclude the shares from qualifying as plan assets; however, the entity would take into account the lack of voting rights when determining the fair value of the shares (see 4.4.620).

4.4.560.30   Although there is no explicit requirement in IFRS about the nature of plan assets that can be held, there may be such requirements in local pension regulations, which may have to be considered.

4.4.570   *Restriction on availability*

4.4.570.10   In our view, the restriction on the availability of the assets to creditors of the entity applies both to claims arising from liquidation or similar court proceedings and from normal operations.

4.4.570.20   In our view, the protection from claims of other parties to the assets should not be capable of being overridden by other contracts (e.g. mortgages) or legislation and the assets should be prevented legally from being made available to the entity or its creditors under any circumstances, other than for permitted purposes.

4.4.580   *Reimbursement for benefits paid*

4.4.580.10   The definition of plan assets refers to the return of plan assets to the reporting entity for benefits that have already been paid. Therefore, in our view the definition of plan assets is not met if an entity has the ability to receive reimbursement in advance, *before* the reimbursable benefit payments are made. It is possible that a reimbursement right asset might arise in those circumstances (see 4.4.640). [*IAS 19.8, 116–119*]

4.4.590   *Ability to use plan assets*

4.4.590.10   When determining whether assets qualify as plan assets, in addition to meeting the general criteria for treatment as plan assets (see 4.4.560 and 600.10), in our view it is necessary for the plan to have the ability to use those assets to fund employee benefit payments both legally and in substance; the plan should not be prevented by the entity from accessing the economic benefits attaching to the assets. For example, it is possible for operating assets used by the entity to be plan assets. IAS 19 does not impose any additional conditions for such assets to be classified as plan assets but, if the assets in question are critical to the continued existence of the entity, or highly specialised and/or transferability restrictions are imposed on the plan in connection with those assets, then the plan may not have the ability to use those assets to fund employee benefits both legally and in substance. An analysis of the facts and circumstances may be required in performing this assessment. [*IAS 19.8, 114, BC177*]

4.4.600   *Financial instruments issued by entity*

4.4.600.10   Plan assets include *transferable* financial instruments issued by the reporting entity if the criteria for treatment as plan assets are met (see 4.4.560). Examples of such transferable financial instruments may include shares issued by the reporting entity (including by its subsidiaries) or loans granted by post-employment benefit plans to the reporting entity (or its subsidiaries) (see 4.4.1500). In our view, transfer would need to be possible both legally and in substance. IAS 19 precludes non-transferable financial instruments issued by the reporting entity from being plan assets in all cases. [*IAS 19.8, 114, BC177*]

4.4.600.20   For a discussion of insurance policies issued to the plan by the reporting entity or a related party of the reporting entity, see 4.4.660.

4.4.600.30   Plan assets exclude contributions receivable from the reporting entity and other financial instruments issued by the reporting entity and held by the fund that cannot be transferred to third parties – e.g. non-transferable loans by the fund to the reporting entity (see 4.4.1500). [*IAS 19.8, 114*]

4.4.600.40   In our view, the requirement for financial instruments to be transferable to qualify as plan Ⓢ assets applies to instruments issued by all entities that are part of the group – i.e. parent, intermediate and ultimate parent, and subsidiaries – in both separate and consolidated financial statements.

4.4.600.50   In our view, financial instruments of associates and joint ventures in which group enti- Ⓢ ties have invested qualify for treatment as plan assets if they are transferable and the other criteria for treatment as plan assets are met. If financial instruments issued by associates and joint ventures are not transferable, then we believe that an entity can still treat them as plan assets – in both separate and consolidated financial statements – because they are not part of the group. This is an accounting policy choice that should be applied consistently.

4.4.610   *Replacement assets*

4.4.610.10   In some cases, assets of the fund can be returned to the entity in situations other than when it is for reimbursement of employee benefits paid or when the fund is in surplus. In these cases, the entity is typically required to provide replacement assets to the fund. In our view, an entity's ability to replace existing plan assets does not preclude classification of the assets as plan assets, if the current fair value of the replacement assets is required to be equal to or higher than the fair value of the assets replaced and the substitution can be made only if the trustees of the fund agree. We believe that this is similar to the sale of the assets by the fund. However, it is critical in such cases that the entity delivers equivalent or greater current fair value to be considered similar to a sale. This is because any below-market exchange represents a transfer of value to the entity, which would preclude the assets from qualifying as plan assets (see 4.4.560).

4.4.620   Measurement

4.4.620.10   Plan assets are measured at fair value in accordance with IFRS 13, which is the subject of chapter 2.4. For assets measured at fair value that have a bid and ask price, IFRS 13 requires the use of the price within the bid-ask spread that is the most representative of fair value in the circumstances. Under IFRS 13, the use of bid prices for long positions and ask prices for short positions is permitted but not required. For further discussion of the use of inputs based on bid and ask prices in measuring fair value, see 2.4.250. [*IAS 19.57(a)(iii), 113, IFRS 13.70*]

4.4.620.20   The requirement to measure plan assets at fair value overrides the requirements of other standards. Therefore, in our view if the plan has a controlling interest in another entity, then the investment should be measured at fair value and the underlying entity should not be consolidated (see 4.4.1490). Similarly, shares of the plan sponsor (employer) that qualify as plan assets should be measured at fair value and not presented as a deduction from equity, which is normally the treatment of treasury shares (see 7.3.500).

4.4.620.30   Plan assets may include non-financial assets such as property; in our view, they should also be measured at fair value, even if they were transferred to the fund by the entity in settlement of contributions due to the fund and were previously measured at cost by the entity. The measurement of fair value under IFRS 13 reflects any special characteristic of the assets – e.g. their location or age (see 2.4.70). Differences between the carrying amount of the asset derecognised by the entity and the fair value of the contribution made may result in a gain or loss on contribution in profit or loss.

EXAMPLE 13 – PLAN ASSETS – TRANSFER OF NON-FINANCIAL ASSETS TO PLAN

> 4.4.620.40   Company B contributes property to its plan with a carrying amount of 100 and a fair value of 160 in settlement of contributions due to the fund of 160. Because B has transferred the control of that property to the fund and the plan assets are not consolidated by B, we believe that B should recognise a gain of 60 on the contribution in profit or loss in the period in which the asset is contributed.

4.4.620.50   In some cases, the entity may continue to use the asset after the asset has been contributed into the plan – e.g. a leaseback of a contributed office building. In such cases, the entity considers the requirements for the transfer of risks and rewards of ownership under IAS 17, which may affect the assessment of whether a gain should be recognised (see 5.1.470).

4.4.630   Assets that do not qualify as plan assets

4.4.630.10   In our view, investments held by employee benefit plans that do not qualify as plan assets should be accounted for by the entity in the same way as its other financial assets (see chapters 7.1–7.10) but also might be classified as a reimbursement right (see 4.4.640). If the investments include shares of the entity itself, then the requirements for treasury shares apply (see 7.3.500).

4.4.640   Reimbursement rights

4.4.640.10   If an entity will be reimbursed for expenditure that is required to settle a defined benefit obligation, but the reimbursement right does not give rise to a plan asset (see 4.4.560), then the reimbursement right is recognised as a separate asset when recovery is virtually certain. For example, an insurance policy that is not a plan asset generally gives rise to a reimbursement right. [*IAS 19.48, 116*]

(S) 4.4.640.20   In our view, the reimbursement right needs to be due from a party outside the group (which may include an associate or joint venture (see 4.5.120.60)). Therefore, a right to receive assets from another group entity – e.g. parent, subsidiary – to fund employee benefit obligations is not treated as a reimbursement right in the consolidated financial statements. However, it may be appropriate to recognise a reimbursement right in the separate financial statements of the entity providing that the criteria in paragraph 116 of IAS 19 are met. [*IFRS 4.IG2.Ex1.21*]

4.4.640.30   Reimbursement rights are accounted for in the same way as plan assets – i.e. they are measured at fair value and the changes in fair value of the reimbursement rights are accounted for in the same way as the changes in the fair value of plan assets. Remeasurements arising on reimbursement rights are recognised in OCI (see 4.4.830.10). However, reimbursement rights are presented differently from plan assets, being shown as a separate asset in the statement of financial position rather than being netted against the related defined benefit obligation. [*IAS 19.116*]

EXAMPLE 14A – REIMBURSEMENT RIGHT

4.4.640.40   Company O has a defined benefit pension plan for all of its employees. O outsources some of its employees to Company P, a third party. The outsourced employees continue to participate in O's pension plan but O is entitled to recover the costs of the outsourced employees, including costs associated with the defined benefit plan, from P. O accounts for the full net defined benefit liability under the defined benefit plan. If it is virtually certain that P will reimburse O for the pension costs, then O recognises an asset for the reimbursement, which is accounted for in the same way as a plan asset. However, O shows the reimbursement right as a separate asset and does not deduct it from the carrying amount of the defined benefit obligation.

4.4.640.50   In some countries, governments introduce a state subsidy to plan sponsors for costs incurred under plans that meet certain criteria making them equivalent to a specified state plan. Some people believe that such a state subsidy paid to the plan sponsors is a reimbursement right, whereas others believe that it is similar to a state benefit (see 4.4.430.20) that affects the net benefit payable by the entity, the estimated amount of which has now changed. In our view, an entity should choose an accounting policy, to be applied consistently, to treat the state subsidy paid to the sponsor either as a reimbursement right or as a state benefit. In our view, the initial recognition of the state subsidy, regardless of whether it is considered to be a reimbursement right or a state benefit, should be accounted for as a remeasurement gain and not as a plan amendment (see 4.4.950 and 880.30–40). For a discussion of state subsidies that are paid to the plan and treated as third party contributions, see 4.4.490). [*IAS 19.87(e), 92–93, 116*]

EXAMPLE 14B – REIMBURSEMENT RIGHT OR STATE BENEFIT – STATE SUBSIDY TO PLAN SPONSOR

4.4.640.60   Company M provides post-retirement medical benefits to its employees. The defined benefit obligation at 31 December 2018 is 150, excluding any effects of a state subsidy, and the plan assets are 50. As a result, without the effect of the state subsidy, M would recognise a net defined benefit liability of 100 (net of plan assets of 50) in the 2018 financial statements.

4.4.640.70   M determines that its plan is equivalent to the specified state plan and that, based on its actuarial assumptions about expected costs, M will receive a subsidy of 20. M chooses to treat the state subsidy as a reimbursement right and therefore recognises it as a separate asset. Because the creation of the reimbursement right is a remeasurement gain, M records the following entry. [*IAS 19.92, 116*]

	DEBIT	CREDIT
Reimbursement right (separate asset)	20	
Remeasurement (OCI)		20
To recognise reimbursement right asset		

> **4.4.640.80** If M chooses to treat the state subsidy as a state benefit, then the subsidy of 20 would be incorporated into the measurement of the benefit obligation. In this case, M would not recognise or present a separate asset. Instead, M would record the following entry. [*IAS 19.87(e)*]
>
> | | DEBIT | CREDIT |
> |---|---|---|
> | Net defined benefit liability | 20 | |
> | Remeasurement (OCI) | | 20 |
> | *To recognise state benefit as reduction of entity's obligation (net recognition)* | | |

4.4.650   Insurance policies

4.4.660   *Insurance policies that qualify as plan assets*

4.4.660.10 Insurance policies may be held by the plan or by the entity. If the policy is held by the entity (i.e. benefits the entity), then it is treated as a plan asset if it is a qualifying insurance policy – i.e. if:
- it is not issued by a related party of the entity (see 5.5.30); and
- the proceeds of the policy:
  - can be used only to pay or fund defined benefit obligations;
  - are not available to the entity's creditors (even in the case of bankruptcy); and
  - cannot be returned to the entity except as reimbursement for employee benefits paid or when the proceeds are surplus to requirements. [*IAS 19.8*]

4.4.660.20 IAS 19 requires financial instruments issued by the reporting entity to the plan to be transferable for them to be treated as plan assets. The IFRS Interpretations Committee discussed this issue and noted that this requirement also applies to insurance policies issued *to the plan* by the entity or a related party of the entity (see 5.5.30). [*IAS 19.8, 114, IU 01-08*]

4.4.660.30 In our view, the requirements that should be met for insurance policies held by the entity to qualify as plan assets do not apply to policies held by the plan. This is because we believe that the definition of qualifying insurance policies applies only to policies issued by related parties *to* the entity and not to policies issued *by* the entity or a related party of the entity to the plan. The following table illustrates the classification of insurance policies as plan assets.

HELD BY: / ISSUED BY:	SPONSOR	PENSION PLAN
Related party	Do not qualify as a plan asset (definition of qualifying insurance policy in IAS 19.8)	Qualify as plan assets if *transferable* (definition of assets held by a long-term employee benefit fund in IAS 19.8)
Unrelated party	Qualify as a plan asset (definition of qualifying insurance policy in IAS 19.8)	Qualify as a plan asset (definition of assets held by a long-term employee benefit fund in IAS 19.8)

4.4.670   *Measurement*

4.4.670.10   An insurance policy that qualifies as a plan asset is measured at fair value. A qualifying insurance policy is included with other plan assets held by the fund that are deducted from the related defined benefit obligation. [*IAS 19.57, 113*]

4.4.670.20   If the timing and amount of payments under a qualifying insurance policy exactly match some or all of the benefits payable under a plan, then the present value of the related obligation is determined and is deemed to be the fair value of the insurance policy. Generally, the fair value of such insurance policies held by the fund is determined in the same way – i.e. matching that of the related obligation. [*IAS 19.115*]

4.4.670.25   In our view, when the timing and amount of payments under a qualifying insurance policy exactly match only *some* of the benefits payable for some or all of the individuals under the plan, then the present value of the related part of the obligation should be determined and be deemed to be the fair value of the insurance policy, provided that those benefits can be separately identified and reliably measured on a consistent basis.

4.4.670.30   The entity's cost of acquiring such an 'exactly matching' policy is typically greater than the amount at which the policy is required to be measured – i.e. the present value of the related obligation – because of factors such as:
- different actuarial assumptions used by the insurer;
- profit margin required by the insurer; and
- future administration costs to be incurred by the insurer.

4.4.670.40   In our experience, it is often difficult or impracticable to determine the different components giving rise to the excess premium paid for an exactly matching insurance policy. In such instances, an issue arises about how the excess premium paid should be recognised. If it is clear that a portion of the excess relates solely to administration costs of the insurer, and that portion can be reliably measured, then in our view those costs should be expensed in profit or loss when the administration services are provided to the entity (see 4.4.980). If it is not clear what the portion relates to, or the portion relating solely to administration costs cannot be reliably measured, then we believe that it is acceptable to recognise the entire amount in OCI as part of the total return on plan assets, excluding amounts included in net interest. In our experience, the stated administration costs of an insurance policy may not be representative of the actual costs to be incurred under the plan. Therefore, the determination of whether administration costs of the insurer can be reliably measured should be made irrespective of stated contract costs per the insurance policy. [*IAS 19.130, BC125*]

4.4.670.50   A longevity swap transfers the risk of plan members living longer (or shorter) than expected from the plan to an external party – usually an insurance company or a bank. Under a longevity swap, the plan pays fixed amounts and receives variable amounts (a variable leg), being the amounts actually paid to plan members. These amounts are settled on a net basis. The IFRS Interpretations Committee discussed whether an entity should account for a longevity swap as a single instrument or split the swap into two components in which the variable leg is measured as a qualifying insurance policy in accordance with 4.4.670.20. The Committee noted that the predominant practice is to account for a longevity swap as a single instrument, and to measure it at fair value as part of the plan assets (see 4.4.620), with changes in the fair value recognised in OCI (see 4.4.830.10). [*IAS 19.8, 113–114, 120(c), IU 03-15*]

4.4.680   *Insurance policies that do not qualify as plan assets*

4.4.680.10   A right to reimbursement that arises from an insurance policy that is not a plan asset is recognised as a separate asset rather than as a deduction in determining the net defined benefit liability. However, in all other respects the insurance policy is treated in the same way as plan assets (see 4.4.640). [*IAS 19.118*]

4.4.690   **ASSET CEILING**

4.4.690.10   If a plan is in surplus, then the amount recognised as an asset in the statement of financial position is limited to the 'asset ceiling'. The asset ceiling is the present value of any economic benefits available to the entity in the form of:
- a refund (see 4.4.740); or
- a reduction in future contributions (see 4.4.770). [*IAS 19.8, 64, IFRIC 14.7*]

4.4.690.20   If the plan is in deficit and there is a minimum funding requirement, then the effect of the asset ceiling might result in recognition of an additional liability if payments under the minimum funding requirement would create a surplus in excess of the asset ceiling (see 4.4.780–800).

EXAMPLE 15 – ASSET CEILING – IMPACT OF CEILING

4.4.690.30   Company E's defined benefit plan has the following characteristics.

Present value of obligation	11,000
Fair value of plan assets	(14,200)
Computed net asset	(3,200)

4.4.690.40   The present value of available reductions in future contributions as a result of the plan surplus is 1,000. E does not have an unconditional right to a refund. As a result, the adjustment required to limit the net defined benefit asset to the asset ceiling is 2,200 (3,200 - 1,000). Therefore, E recognises an asset of 1,000 in its statement of financial position.

4.4.690.50   Both the initial recognition of a surplus restriction or an additional liability that is recognised when payments under a minimum funding requirement creates a surplus in excess of the asset ceiling (see 4.4.780) and any change in that effect, except for amounts included in net interest on the net defined benefit liability (asset), are recognised immediately in OCI as a part of remeasurements (see 4.4.950.10).

4.4.700   **Sharing benefits**

4.4.700.10   If any surplus is required to be shared between the entity and employees, or if past practice has established a valid expectation that the benefit will be shared, then the portion that will be made available to the employees increases the defined benefit obligation, and as a consequence decreases the amount that could be recognised as a net asset by the entity (see 4.4.470.10). [*IAS 19.88(b)*]

4.4.710   Economic benefits available

4.4.710.10   Issues often arise about whether a surplus is available to the entity. An economic benefit, in the form of a refund or a reduction in future contributions, is available to an entity if, in accordance with the terms of the plan and applicable statutory requirements, it is realisable during the life of the plan or on the settlement of the plan liabilities. [*IFRIC 14.7–8*]

4.4.710.20   Determining whether the economic benefit is available to an entity requires a detailed analysis of the facts and circumstances in each case, including the terms of the plan and applicable legislation (see 4.4.730–800).

4.4.720   *Intended use of surplus*

4.4.720.10   The economic benefit available to an entity does not depend on how it intends to use the surplus. An entity determines the maximum economic benefit that is available from refunds, reductions in future contributions or a combination of both, but not based on mutually exclusive assumptions. [*IFRIC 14.9*]

4.4.720.20   In our view, unless agreement is required, an entity does not need to have made a request, or intend to make a request, for a refund or reduction in future contributions to factor in these methods of realising benefits when applying the asset ceiling. This is because the asset ceiling test is not based on management intentions.

4.4.720.30   Sometimes, an entity may decide to use an available surplus to improve the benefits. In our view, unless there is a legal or constructive obligation to improve the benefits, the surplus should be considered as being available to the entity in determining the amount of the asset to recognise.

4.4.720.40   If the entity enters into a legal or constructive obligation to improve the benefits, then any resulting increase in the obligation (and decrease in the surplus) is treated as a past service cost (see 4.4.870) rather than a change in the effect of the asset ceiling (see 4.4.950.10). [*IAS 19.102*]

4.4.730   Economic benefit available as refund

4.4.740   *The right to a refund*

4.4.740.10   A refund is available to an entity only if the entity has an unconditional right to a refund:
- during the life of the plan, without assuming that the plan liabilities are settled;
- over time until all members have left the plan, assuming the gradual settlement of the plan liabilities; or
- on plan wind-up, assuming the full settlement of the plan liabilities in a wind-up. [*IFRIC 14.11*]

4.4.740.20   The economic benefit available as a refund under each of these scenarios might vary.

4.4.740.30   If the entity's right to a refund of a surplus depends on the occurrence or non-occurrence of one or more uncertain future events not wholly within its control, then the entity does not have an unconditional right and does not recognise an asset. [*IFRIC 14.12*]

4.4.740.40   In our view, if the trustees, or any other third party responsible for governing the plan, have an unconditional right to wind up the plan at any time, then the entity does not have an unconditional right to a refund assuming the gradual settlement of the plan liabilities over time. The entity may have an unconditional right to a refund assuming wind-up but, as explained in 4.4.750.20, this may not support recognition of an asset. In our view, an unconditional right of the entity to a refund should not be assessed based on probability or past practice.

4.4.740.50   In analysing whether an entity has an unconditional right to a refund, care should be taken to understand the terms of the plan, terms of the trust deed and applicable legislation that may influence the existence of such a right. In analysing trustees' rights to wind up the plan, we believe that consideration should be given to whether such rights can be exercised 'with cause' or 'without any cause'. In the latter case, the unconditional right of the entity to a refund after gradual settlement over time is presumed not to exist unless there is evidence to the contrary. However, if the trustees can exercise their right only 'with cause' and such cause is within the entity's control, then we believe that the entity may have an unconditional right to a refund under this scenario, because the entity can avoid by its own actions the trustees' wind-up of the plan. In our experience, determining whether an economic benefit is available as a refund can be complex and often depends on entity- and country-specific facts and circumstances. [*IFRIC 14.11(b)*]

EXAMPLE 16 – ASSET CEILING – UNCONDITIONAL RIGHT TO REFUND

> 4.4.740.60   Company P has a pension plan. The trustees governing the plan have an unconditional right to wind it up in the event of a change in control of P. In this case, in our view P does not have an unconditional right to a refund assuming the gradual settlement of the plan liabilities over time. This is because we believe that a change-in-control event is an uncertain future event that is not within the control of P (see 7.3.40.80).
>
> 4.4.740.70   However, if the trustees had an unconditional right to wind up the plan in the event of a change in control of P only if P reduced its contributions to the plan, then we believe that this does not preclude P from having an unconditional right to a refund. P can avoid the trustees' wind-up of the plan by not reducing contributions to the plan, because reducing its contributions to the plan is within P's control.

4.4.750   *Measurement of economic benefit*

4.4.750.10   The economic benefit available as a refund is measured as the amount of the surplus at the reporting date – i.e. the fair value of the plan assets less the present value of the defined benefit obligation – that the entity has a right to receive as a refund, less any associated costs. In measuring the amount available when the plan is wound up, the costs of settling the liabilities and making the refund are taken into account. The entity also needs to have an unconditional right to the refund (see 4.4.740). [*IFRIC 14.11, 13–14*]

4.4.750.20   In our experience, even if the entity has an unconditional right to a refund assuming the wind-up, the costs to settle plan liabilities may often be too high to result in the recognition of an asset.

4.4.760   *Taxes on a surplus*

4.4.760.10   If an entity will be required to pay income tax on the realisation of a surplus, then it may be required to recognise a related deferred tax liability (see chapter 3.13).

4.4.760.20   If a refund will be subject to a tax other than income tax, then the available surplus is determined net of tax. [*IFRIC 14.13*]

4.4.770   **Economic benefit available as reduction in contributions**

4.4.770.10   If there is no minimum funding requirement, then the economic benefit available as a reduction in future contributions is measured as the present value of the future service cost to the entity for each year over the shorter of the expected life of the plan and the expected life of the entity. If there is a minimum funding requirement, then the economic benefit is measured following the approach set out in 4.4.790. [*IFRIC 14.16–17*]

4.4.780   **Minimum funding requirements**

4.4.780.10   Some entities are subject to requirements that specify a minimum level of contributions to be made to a post-employment benefit plan over a period of time (a minimum funding requirement). Under a minimum funding requirement, an entity may have a present obligation to make minimum contributions to a plan. If the fair value of plan assets is in excess of the defined benefit obligation, or would be once the committed contributions were made (see 4.4.800), then the entity considers whether the asset ceiling may limit the amount that the entity may recognise as an asset. If the minimum funding requirement contribution could be recovered as a refund, either from the ongoing plan or on settlement or termination of the plan, then the net plan asset would normally qualify for recognition. However, if this amount could not be recovered as a refund but only through a reduction in future contributions, then the minimum funding requirement may limit the amount of the asset that can be recognised. As a result, some or all of the minimum funding requirement contribution may have to be recognised in OCI in the current period if it is not recoverable (see 4.4.690.50). [*IAS 19.64, IFRIC 14.20, 24*]

EXAMPLE 17 – ASSET CEILING – MINIMUM FUNDING REQUIREMENT

4.4.780.20   Under a minimum funding requirement, Company Q has a present obligation to make minimum contributions for services that it has received to date. The minimum funding requirement also limits the reduction in future contributions based on a ratio calculated as a percentage of plan assets divided by the obligations to employees as determined under statutory requirements. If the plan is over-funded by a specified percentage – e.g. 110% – then Q is entitled to a reduction in future contributions. Q currently has a funding ratio that is less than 110% and it is therefore required to make minimum funding requirement contributions – i.e. above the normal ongoing contributions for current service – to raise the asset-to-liability ratio to the minimum funding level. Q is allowed to make contributions over the next several years and is not currently entitled to a reduction in future contributions. However, Q has projected that, for the services that it has received to date, a reduction in future contributions will be available to it in the future based on its expected return on plan assets and future expected service costs assumed for the purposes of its funding valuation and on the resulting current minimum funding requirement contributions. Q therefore assesses whether sufficient economic benefit is available to it to support recognition of an asset.

> 4.4.780.30   The economic benefit, in the form of a refund from the plan or a reduction in future contributions, may be considered available even if it is not immediately realisable at the reporting date. Therefore, because a reduction in contributions will be available to Q in the future, an asset can be recognised. [*IFRIC 14.8*]

4.4.780.40   Minimum funding requirements are classified into two types:
- those relating to contributions in respect of future service (see 4.4.790); and
- those relating to contributions to cover an existing shortfall on the minimum funding basis in respect of services already received (see 4.4.800). [*IFRIC 14.18*]

4.4.790   *Minimum funding requirement for future service*

4.4.790.10   If there is a minimum funding requirement for contributions relating to future service, then the measurement of the economic benefit available as a reduction in future contributions set out in 4.4.770 does not apply. The economic benefit is instead the sum of:
a.   any prepaid amount that reduces future minimum funding requirement contributions; and
b.   the present value of the estimated future service cost to the entity in each year less the estimated minimum funding requirement contributions that would be required for future service in the given year if there were no prepayment of future minimum funding requirement contributions. This amount can never be less than zero. [*IAS 19.64, IFRIC 14.20, 22*]

4.4.790.20   Under IFRIC 14, a prepayment of an entity's future minimum funding requirement contributions for future service is recognised as an asset. The asset is recognised on the basis that the entity has a future economic benefit from the prepayment in the form of reduced cash outflows in future years in which minimum funding requirement payments would otherwise be required. Such a benefit is available even if the future minimum funding requirement contributions exceed the future IAS 19 service cost. The essence is that the prepayment reduces future contributions that cover not only future service costs but also future excess of minimum funding requirement contributions over service cost. [*IFRIC 14.20–22, IE22–IE27, BC30A*]

4.4.790.30   The IFRS Interpretations Committee discussed whether an entity should assume continuation beyond the fixed period of a future minimum funding requirement for contributions relating to future service in arrangements for which:
- the contribution rate is renegotiated with the pension fund trustees – e.g. on an annual or triennial basis; and
- a pension regulation or a contractual arrangement, or both, requires the entity and the trustees to renew the agreement to decide the schedule of contributions regularly under the existing funding principles, if the plan is continued – i.e. although the level of contributions is subject to future negotiations, the entity must continue to make contributions if the plan continues after the fixed period. [*IU 07-15*]

4.4.790.40   The Committee noted that for such arrangements – i.e. when neither a plan wind-up nor a plan closure to future accrual has been decided and agreed with the trustees – the entity needs to assume a continuation of those factors establishing the minimum funding basis in estimating the minimum funding requirement contributions for future service beyond the minimum fixed period – i.e. it cannot assume a zero contribution rate. This is because such an estimate does not include changes that require future negotiations with the trustees. Furthermore, the Committee noted that for any factors that are not determined by the trustees, the assumptions used to estimate the future minimum funding requirement contributions beyond the fixed period need to be consistent with those used for determining future service costs. [*IFRIC 14.17, 21, BC30, IU 07-15*]

4.4.800 *Minimum funding requirement to cover existing shortfall*

4.4.800.10   If a plan has a funding shortfall on the minimum funding basis for services already received, then the entity may have to pay additional contributions to cover the shortfall. Such minimum funding requirements have to be recognised as a liability if a surplus arising from the payment of the extra contributions is not fully available as a refund or reduction in future contributions. [*IFRIC 14.23–24*]

4.4.810 **Multi-employer plans**

4.4.810.10   The principles for assessing the asset ceiling set out in 4.4.690–800 also apply in determining whether a surplus is available to an entity that participates in a multi-employer plan (see 4.4.170) to which defined benefit accounting is applied.

4.4.820 **DEFINED BENEFIT COST**
4.4.830 **Components of defined benefit cost**

4.4.830.10   The defined benefit cost is the entire periodic change in the net defined benefit liability (asset), excluding changes caused by contributions to or refunds from the plan, benefit payments from the plan or the effects of business combinations and disposals. Except to the extent that another standard requires or permits their inclusion in the cost of an asset, the components of the defined benefit cost are recognised as follows:
*   service cost, in profit or loss (see 4.4.850);
*   net interest on the net defined benefit liability (asset), in profit or loss (see 4.4.940); and
*   remeasurements of the net defined benefit liability (asset), in OCI (see 4.4.950). [*IAS 19.120*]

4.4.830.20   Some standards require or permit the capitalisation of certain employee benefit costs as part of the cost of assets – e.g. inventories (see 3.8.170) or property, plant and equipment (see 3.2.30.40). Any post-employment costs capitalised in the cost of such assets include the appropriate proportion of the components listed in 4.4.830.10. The interaction of the requirements in those standards with the requirement in IAS 19 to capitalise only 'the appropriate proportion' of each component – i.e. service cost, net interest and remeasurements – may be complex, because that proportion might vary between the components of the overall cost. In our experience, it is a matter of judgement to assess the 'appropriate proportion' of each component of defined benefit cost to be included in the cost of the related assets. [*IAS 19.121*]

4.4.840 *Refunds of contributions*

4.4.840.10   If an entity receives a refund of contributions paid to a defined benefit plan, then the refund is recognised as a reduction in the net defined benefit asset or an increase in the net defined benefit liability. Receipt of the cash does not trigger the recognition of income, because the measurement of the net defined benefit liability (asset) would have reflected the expected refund.

4.4.840.20   However, if there was a surplus in the fund that was previously not regarded as recoverable, and therefore was not recognised, then the refund gives rise to a gain. IFRS is silent about how the gain should be recognised, but in our view it should be treated as a remeasurement gain and therefore be recognised in OCI because it is part of the effect of a change in the asset ceiling. [*IAS 19.127(c)*]

4.4.850   SERVICE COST#

4.4.850.10   Service cost comprises:
- current service cost (see 4.4.860);
- past service cost, consisting of plan amendments and curtailments (see 4.4.870); and
- any gain or loss on settlement (see 4.4.910). [*IAS 19.8*]

4.4.860   Current service cost

4.4.860.10   The current service cost is the increase in the present value of the defined benefit obligation resulting from employee service in the current period. [*IAS 19.8*]

4.4.860.20   It is therefore determined using the same actuarial methodology and assumptions as are used in determining the present value of the defined benefit obligation (see 4.4.380). [*IAS 19.67*]

4.4.860.30   Under IAS 19, interest accumulates on service cost; however, it is unclear where that interest should be recognised. In our view, the interest that arises on service cost should be recognised in profit or loss and it would be appropriate for that interest to be classified as part of service cost. We believe that it would not be appropriate to recognise this interest element in OCI, because it does not meet the definition of a remeasurement in IAS 19 (see 4.4.830.10 and 950.10). For a discussion of where service cost and net interest cost are presented, see 4.4.1100.10.

4.4.870   Past service cost

4.4.870.10   Past service cost, which can be positive or negative, is the change in the present value of a defined benefit obligation for employee service provided in prior periods resulting from:
- a plan amendment (see 4.4.880); or
- a curtailment (see 4.4.890). [*IAS 19.8, 102, 106*]

4.4.870.20   Before determining past service cost, an entity remeasures the net defined benefit liability (asset) – i.e. plan assets, the defined benefit obligation and the effect of the asset ceiling – based on the current fair value of the plan assets and current actuarial assumptions (including current market interest rates and other current market prices), reflecting the benefits offered under the plan before the plan amendment or curtailment, in the same way as for a settlement (see 4.4.920.90). [*IAS 19.99*]

4.4.880   *Plan amendment*

4.4.880.10   A plan amendment occurs when an entity introduces or withdraws a defined benefit plan or changes the benefits payable under an existing defined benefit plan. [*IAS 19.104*]

4.4.880.20   Examples of plan amendments that may give rise to past service cost include:
- changing the retirement age from 65 to 60;
- increasing the benefits that are payable on early retirement;

- changing the final salary on which the pension is based to include bonuses;
- changing the salary on which the pension is based from final salary to average salary; and
- expanding the employee groups covered by the plans, with retrospective effect.

4.4.880.30   In our view, for a change to be a plan amendment there should be a change in the agreement between the entity and the employee. This is because guidance in IAS 19 on plan amendments focuses on benefits payable and not on the entity's net cost. For example, if a government makes a state subsidy available to a sponsor of a qualifying benefit plan (see 4.4.640.50), then in our view the introduction of such a subsidy does not result in a plan amendment if it has no direct impact on the benefit received by the employees and does not lead to a change in the agreement between the entity and its employees. Therefore, we believe that the effect of the introduction of such a subsidy should be treated as a remeasurement (actuarial gain). [*IAS 19.104*]

4.4.880.40   The IFRS Interpretations Committee discussed whether the source of a change should affect the accounting. The Committee noted that it does not and, therefore, the accounting for changes caused by government is the same as for changes made by an entity. [*IU 11-07*]

4.4.880.50   Sometimes it is difficult to determine whether a change in the defined benefit obligation is the result of a benefit change or is an actuarial gain or loss.

EXAMPLE 18 – DEFINED BENEFIT COST – CHANGE IN BENEFIT OR IN ASSUMPTION

4.4.880.60   Company P operates a defined benefit plan in which benefits are based on final salary. During 2018, the salaries of P's employees are reduced by 10%. As a result, the present value of the defined benefit obligation reduces. A question arises about whether the reduction in the defined benefit obligation is a negative past service cost or an actuarial gain. In this example, we believe that it is an actuarial gain; there has been no change to the benefit entitlement because the employees still receive the same percentage of final salary. Instead, the defined benefit obligation reduction is the result of a difference between previous and revised actuarial assumptions about final salary.

4.4.880.70   In our view, past service cost also includes granting entitlements to employees joining a plan – e.g. in connection with a newly acquired business – when members of one defined benefit plan may transfer to another defined benefit plan and their past service entitlements are also transferred. In our view, the gain or loss arising on the introduction of new members to a plan, together with past service entitlement, meets the definition of a past service cost and not actuarial gains or losses. We believe that this past service cost should be calculated net of any related assets transferred – i.e. the past service cost is equal to the increase in the obligation in respect of the transferred employees less the fair value of the related assets transferred.

4.4.890   *Curtailment*

4.4.890.10   A curtailment occurs if there is a significant reduction by the entity in the number of employees covered by the plan. A curtailment may arise from an isolated event, such as the closing of a plant, from discontinuance of an operation or from termination or suspension of a plan. [*IAS 19.105*]

4.4.890.20 If the reduction in the number of employees covered by the plan is not significant, then the entity needs to determine whether the change is:
- a change in estimated employee turnover resulting in an actuarial gain or loss; or
- a change in the benefits offered resulting in a plan amendment. [*IAS 19.BC162*]

4.4.900 *Timing of recognition of past service cost*

4.4.900.10 Past service cost is recognised immediately, at the earlier of the following:
- when the plan amendment or curtailment occurs;
- when the related restructuring costs are recognised, if the plan amendment or curtailment arises as part of a restructuring (see 3.12.230); and
- when the related termination benefits are recognised, if the plan amendment or curtailment is linked to termination benefits (see 4.4.1440). [*IAS 19.8, 103*]

4.4.900.20 If a plan amendment or curtailment occurs in isolation – i.e. it is not connected with a termination benefit or restructuring – then determining when the plan amendment occurs requires judgement. The timing of recognition depends on the individual facts and circumstances and how they interact with the requirements of IAS 19 regarding constructive obligations (see 4.4.120). [*IAS 19.61–62, BC158*]

4.4.900.30 In our view, an amendment of the terms of a plan may occur before the formal signing of the amended terms provided that the entity has a right to enforce the amended terms of the plan and is not in the process of negotiations with an uncertain outcome that is outside its control.

EXAMPLE 19 – DEFINED BENEFIT COST – PLAN AMENDMENT – TIMING OF RECOGNITION

4.4.900.40 Company B negotiates with its employees amendments to the terms of the defined benefit pension plan to fix the benefits at the current salary level. A binding agreement with the employees was achieved in principle in May 2018. The employees are allowed a three-month period during which they can decide to accept the plan amendment by either:
- remaining in the plan, albeit with reduced future benefits; or
- remaining in the plan as deferred members but transferring their future benefits into a defined contribution plan.

4.4.900.50 We believe that the plan amendment occurred when the employees agreed in May 2018 to accept the terms of the arrangement in principle. At this point in time, B had no realistic alternative to proceeding with the plan amendment and has to accept the choices made by the employees at the end of the three-month period.

4.4.900.60 In certain circumstances, it may be necessary to defer recognition of a plan amendment to a later date as a result of matters that are outside the entity's control. For example, this may be necessary if the entity is in the process of negotiations to amend the terms of a defined benefit plan with an uncertain outcome that is outside the entity's control, or if the approval of another party, substantive in nature, is required.

4.4.900.70   If there are multiple amendments to the same plan, then the specific facts and circumstances of those plan amendments need to be considered. In our view, there is an initial presumption that the amendments should be considered and accounted for in aggregate rather than each in isolation. However, this presumption may be rebutted if it can be demonstrated that the amendments were negotiated separately with separate member groups – e.g. employees vs retirees – as opposed to being negotiated as a package. [*IAS 19.107*]

4.4.900.80   In many cases, plan amendments that result in a past service cost are economically linked to a restructuring transaction or other termination benefits. Therefore, those linked components are recognised at the same time. [*IAS 19.103*]

4.4.910   Settlements#

4.4.920   *Definition and scope*

4.4.920.10   A settlement is a transaction that eliminates all further legal or constructive obligations for part or all of the benefits provided under a defined benefit plan, other than a payment of benefits to, or on behalf of, employees that are set out in the terms of the plan and included in the actuarial assumptions. [*IAS 19.8, 111*]

4.4.920.20   Examples of transactions that may give rise to settlements include:
- a one-off transfer of significant obligations of the entity under the plan to an insurance company through the purchase of an insurance policy with no recourse to the entity (see 4.4.1180.20); and
- the termination of a plan that as a result ceases to exist. [*IAS 19.111*]

4.4.920.30   A lump-sum cash payment, under the terms of the plan, to plan participants in exchange for their rights to receive ongoing payments is not a settlement (see 4.4.440). [*IAS 19.111*]

4.4.920.40   There may be situations in which a large number of employees choose the lump-sum payment option at the same time in response to the entity's actions, such as offering enhanced lump-sum payments. In our view, in such cases an entity should consider whether the payments remain within the terms of the plan. If they do, then the payments are not considered as settlements; instead, they may give rise to an actuarial gain or loss. However, if the payments go beyond the terms of the plan, then we believe that settlement accounting might apply for at least part of the total cost. [*IAS 19.111*]

4.4.920.50   In our view, an increase or a decrease in contingent benefits that does not arise from a plan amendment is not a settlement or past service cost, but rather a potential outcome that was contemplated as part of the original pension plan. Therefore, the change should be accounted for as a remeasurement (actuarial gain or loss).

EXAMPLE 20A – DEFINED BENEFIT COST – CONTINGENT BENEFITS – SETTLEMENT OR REMEASUREMENT

4.4.920.60   Under Company D's pension plan, benefits granted to employees are contingent on the funding level of the plan. If the funding level is above 100%, then the contingent benefits payable under the plan increase from 4% to 6% of salary for each year of service. If the funding level falls below 100%, then the benefits payable

under the plan decrease from 4% to 2% of salary for each year of service. We believe that both increases and decreases in contingent benefits as a result of fluctuations in the underlying contingency should be accounted for as remeasurements (actuarial gains or losses), because those changes are contemplated in the terms of the plan.

4.4.920.70   A settlement occurs together with a plan amendment and curtailment if a plan is terminated with the result that the obligation is settled and the plan ceases to exist. However, the termination of a plan is not a settlement if the plan is replaced by a new plan that offers benefits that are, in substance, the same. For example, as part of a restructuring, benefits and assets for a group of participants in a multi-employer plan are transferred to a new plan without any amendments to the accrued benefits or future benefits. In substance, this is only restructuring the existing arrangement with no change in benefits for the employees or in the obligation of the entity. Consequently, the inherited deficit is also carried over to the new plan. [*IAS 19.101*]

4.4.920.80   The gain or loss on a settlement is the difference between:
- the present value of the defined benefit obligation being settled, as determined on the date of settlement; and
- the settlement price, including any plan assets transferred and any payments made directly by the entity in connection with the settlement. [*IAS 19.109*]

4.4.920.90   Before determining a gain or loss on settlement, an entity remeasures the net defined benefit liability (asset) – i.e. plan assets, the defined benefit obligation and the effect of the asset ceiling – based on the current fair value of plan assets and current actuarial assumptions (including current market interest rates and other current market prices), reflecting the benefits offered under the plan before the settlement, in the same way as for past service cost (see 4.4.870.20). [*IAS 19.99*]

4.4.920.100   It is unclear whether the amount of the 'plan assets transferred' used in determining the gain or loss on a settlement (see 4.4.920.80) includes not only the fair value of the 'plan assets transferred' but also the effect of limiting a net defined benefit asset to the asset ceiling (see 4.4.690) that arises from remeasuring the net defined benefit asset before determining the gain or loss on settlement (see 4.4.920.90). In the absence of specific guidance, in our view an entity should choose one of the following accounting policies, to be applied consistently, in determining the amount of the plan assets transferred as part of the settlement price.
- *Approach 1:* Adjust the amount of the plan assets transferred for the effect of the asset ceiling. This is on the basis that the 'plan assets transferred' that were part of the net defined benefit asset whose measurement was limited to the asset ceiling could be regarded as being reduced directly by the effect of the asset ceiling. Moreover, if the effect of the asset ceiling is not included in the settlement price by restricting the value of the 'plan assets transferred', but is instead reversed through OCI as part of the pre-settlement remeasurement of the net defined benefit asset (as under Approach 2), then the loss (gain) on settlement recognised in profit or loss will be larger (smaller) as a result. This might be seen as effectively reclassifying the asset ceiling restriction of the net defined benefit asset from OCI to profit or loss, which is prohibited by paragraph 122 of IAS 19.
- *Approach 2:* Determine the amount of the plan assets transferred based on the deficit or surplus in the plan – i.e. before any adjustment for the asset ceiling – and then separately reverse the effect of the asset ceiling through OCI. This is on the basis that the assessment of the asset

ceiling could be regarded as a distinct step from the calculation of the gain or loss on settlement and not part of it.

EXAMPLE 20B – DEFINED BENEFIT COST – RELATIONSHIP BETWEEN SETTLEMENT AND ASSET CEILING

4.4.920.110   Company C settled its defined benefit plan in full on 31 October 2018. C does not make any payment in connection with the settlement.

4.4.920.120   The defined benefit obligation, determined based on actuarial assumptions at the date of settlement, and the fair value of plan assets at the date of settlement are shown in the following table.

	BEFORE SETTLEMENT
Defined benefit obligation	(800)
Fair value of plan assets	900
Surplus	100
Effect of asset ceiling	100
Net defined benefit asset	-

4.4.920.130   Although the plan had a surplus of 100 before the settlement, the present value of the economic benefits available in the form of refunds from the plan or reductions in future contributions to the plan – i.e. the future service cost for periods of the expected life of the plan – was zero. Therefore, C did not recognise a net defined benefit asset before the settlement – i.e. there was still an asset ceiling effect of 100 at the date of settlement (see 4.4.690). [*IAS 19.8, 64, IFRIC 14.17*]

4.4.920.140   In this example, the amount of the plan assets transferred for the defined benefit obligation being settled of 800 is determined as follows.
●   Under Approach 1 in 4.4.920.100, as 800 – i.e. the fair value of the plan assets of 900 less the effect of the asset ceiling of 100. Under this approach, C reports neither a gain nor a loss on settlement, reflecting the fact that it has made no payment to settle its net defined benefit asset of zero.
●   Under Approach 2 in 4.4.920.100, as 900 – i.e. the fair value of the plan assets before adjustment for the effect of the asset ceiling. Under this approach, C reports a loss of 100 on settlement through profit or loss, reflecting the difference between the defined benefit obligation settled and the plan assets transferred. C then adjusts the asset ceiling by 100 through OCI.

4.4.930   *Timing of recognition*

4.4.930.10   An entity recognises a gain or loss on the settlement of a defined benefit plan when the settlement occurs. [*IAS 19.110*]

4.4.930.20   In our view, the occurrence of a settlement relates to the transfer of an obligation rather than the actual payment. We believe that the absence of a lump-sum payment, or the fact that an actual transfer of plan assets has not yet been made, does not preclude recognition of a settlement. Nevertheless, payment may be considered an indicator of whether a settlement has occurred. Evaluation of the facts and circumstances is required to determine whether the entity has entered into a transaction that eliminates all further legal or constructive obligations for part or all of the benefits under a plan.

4.4.930.30   An entity need not distinguish between past service cost resulting from a plan amendment, past service cost resulting from a curtailment and a gain or loss on settlement if these transactions occur together. [*IAS 19.100*]

4.4.930.40   However, in some cases a plan amendment occurs before a settlement – e.g. when an entity changes the benefits under the plan and settles the amended benefits later. In those cases, an entity recognises past service cost before any gain or loss on settlement – e.g. if a plan restructuring is executed in stages and the criteria for past service cost are met before the settlement occurs. In our experience, this is common when changes to a plan are caused by the government. However, evaluation of the facts and circumstances of the arrangement is required to assess when the criteria for past service cost (see 4.4.900) and settlement are met. [*IAS 19.100*]

4.4.935   FORTHCOMING REQUIREMENTS

4.4.935.10   *Plan Amendment, Curtailment or Settlement – Amendments to IAS 19* clarify that when a plan amendment, curtailment or settlement occurs:
- the updated actuarial assumptions used in remeasuring the plan are applied to determine the current service cost and net interest for the remainder of the annual reporting period; and
- the effect of the asset ceiling is disregarded when calculating the gain or loss on any settlement of the plan and is dealt with separately in OCI. [*IAS 19.101A, 120–126*]

4.4.935.20   This clarification is consistent with Approach 2 in 4.4.920.100.

4.4.940   NET INTEREST#

4.4.940.10   Net interest on the net defined benefit liability (asset) is the change during the period in the net defined benefit liability (asset) that arises from the passage of time. It is determined by applying the discount rate used to measure the defined benefit obligation at the start of the annual period to the net defined benefit liability (asset) at the start of the annual period, taking into account any changes in the net defined benefit liability (asset) during the period as a result of contributions and benefit payments. [*IAS 19.8, 123*]

4.4.940.20   The net interest on the net defined benefit liability (asset) can be seen as the total of:
- interest cost on the defined benefit obligation;
- interest income on plan assets; and
- interest on the effect of the asset ceiling. [*IAS 19.124*]

4.4.950   # REMEASUREMENTS

4.4.950.10   Remeasurements of the net defined benefit liability (asset) comprise:
- actuarial gains and losses (see 4.4.960);
- the return on plan assets, excluding amounts included in net interest on the net defined benefit liability (asset) (see 4.4.970); and
- any change in the effect of the asset ceiling, excluding amounts included in net interest on the net defined benefit liability (asset). For a discussion of the asset ceiling, see 4.4.690; and for a discussion of the effect of the asset ceiling arising from a minimum funding requirement, see 4.4.780. [*IAS 19.8, 127*]

4.4.960   ## Actuarial gains and losses

4.4.960.10   Actuarial gains and losses arise from changes in the present value of the defined benefit obligation as a result of:
- experience adjustments – i.e. the effects of differences between the previous actuarial assumptions and the actual outcome; and
- the effects of changes in actuarial assumptions. [*IAS 19.8, 128*]

4.4.960.20   Actuarial gains and losses do not include changes in the present value of the defined benefit obligation caused by the introduction, amendment, curtailment or settlement of the defined benefit plan, or changes to the benefits payable under the defined benefit plan. In some cases, judgement is required to distinguish actuarial gains and losses from past service cost (see 4.4.870). [*IAS 19.129*]

4.4.960.30   Contributions from employees or third parties set out in the formal terms of the plan affect remeasurements if they are not linked to service – e.g. if the contributions are required to reduce a deficit arising from losses on plan assets or actuarial losses (see 4.4.490.20). In addition, changes in employee or third party contributions that are linked to service and depend on the number of years of service (see 4.4.490.30) which are set out in the formal terms of the plan result in actuarial gains or losses. However, if changes in employee or third party contributions that are linked to service and depend on the number of years of service are not set out in the formal terms of a plan, then they result in current and past service cost (see 4.4.860–870). [*IAS 19.93–94*]

4.4.970   ## Return on plan assets

4.4.970.10   The return on plan assets comprises interest, dividends and other income derived from the plan assets, as well as realised and unrealised gains or losses on the plan assets, less:
- any costs of managing plan assets; and

- any tax payable by the plan itself, other than tax included in the actuarial assumptions used to measure the present value of the defined benefit obligation. [*IAS 19.8, 130*]

4.4.980 *Administration costs*

4.4.980.10   IAS 19 distinguishes between the costs of managing plan assets and all other types of administration cost. Costs of managing plan assets reduce the return on plan assets. IAS 19 specifies how to calculate the part of the total return on plan assets that is recognised in profit or loss, as part of net interest (see 4.4.940), and that amount does not include the costs of managing plan assets. Therefore, those costs are recognised as part of remeasurements in OCI. [*IAS 19.8, 130*]

4.4.980.20   IAS 19 does not specify what internal costs – e.g. costs of an internal treasury department – qualify as costs of managing plan assets. In our view, consideration should be given to whether internal costs are incurred exclusively for managing plan assets – i.e. directly attributable only to managing those plan assets. For example, personnel expense of a dedicated asset manager would clearly qualify, whereas the personnel expense of an asset manager who has a dual role may need to be allocated with care. [*IAS 19.8*]

4.4.980.30   IAS 19 does not provide specific requirements for the accounting for other administration costs, except for stating that they are not deducted from the return on plan assets. [*IAS 19.130*]

4.4.980.40   However, IAS 19 specifies that in the case of a defined benefit plan offering medical benefits, the actuarial assumptions about future medical costs include an assumption about claim handling costs, which are therefore included in the measurement of the defined benefit obligation. [*IAS 19.76(b)(iii)*]

4.4.980.50   Administration costs other than the costs of managing plan assets and the costs of handling medical claims are recognised when the related administration services are provided to the entity and in our view they should be treated as an expense within profit or loss. [*IAS 19.BC125, 1.88*]

4.4.990 *Taxes payable by plan*

4.4.990.10   The actuarial assumptions made in measuring current service cost and the defined benefit obligation include an assumption about taxes payable by the plan on contributions relating to service before the reporting date or on benefits resulting from that service (see 4.4.500). The costs of any other types of tax payable by the plan itself, such as taxes on investment income, are deducted in determining the return on plan assets. As a result, they are charged to OCI as part of the excess or shortfall of the overall return on plan assets over the amount included in net interest on the net defined benefit liability (asset) – i.e. as part of the remeasurement of plan assets. [*IAS 19.8, 76(b)(iv), 130, BC121–BC124*]

EXAMPLE 21 – REMEASUREMENTS – TAXES INCLUDED IN RETURN ON PLAN ASSETS

4.4.990.20   Company M has a defined benefit plan and it prepares a calculation of the return on plan assets as part of calculating remeasurements for the annual period ending 31 December 2018. The following facts are also relevant for this example:
- fair value of plan assets at 1 January 2018 – 2,000;

- interest income on plan assets – 10%;
- tax payable by the plan – 15%; and
- actuarial assumption at 1 January 2018 of the discount rate on the defined benefit obligation – 6%.

Opening fair value of plan assets		2,000
Interest income (actual)	200	
Other fair value changes (actual)	100	
Gross return on plan assets	300	
Tax payable on gross return (300 x 15%)	(45)	
Change in fair value of plan assets, net of taxes payable (net change)		255
Closing fair value of plan assets		2,255
Portion of net change in value recognised in profit or loss as part of net interest (2,000 x 6%)		120
Portion of net change recognised in OCI as part of remeasurements		135
		255

4.4.1000 *Taxes payable by entity*

4.4.1000.10 Although IAS 19 provides specific guidance on the treatment of taxes payable by the plan, the accounting for taxes payable by the entity in respect of the plan is not specifically addressed. A wide variety of taxes on pension costs exists around the world and it is a matter of judgement whether they are income taxes in the scope of IAS 12, liabilities in the scope of IAS 37, or costs of employee benefits in the scope of IAS 19. In our view, an entity should choose an accounting policy, to be applied consistently, to account for taxes on pension costs that are not income taxes in the scope of IAS 12 under IAS 37 or IAS 19. If an entity applies IAS 19, unless the tax is considered to be part of the benefit to which it relates (see 4.4.10.50), we believe that taxes payable by the entity are similar to the administrative costs of running a defined benefit plan and that consideration should be given to the nature of the taxes payable by the entity. In our view, an entity should therefore recognise the tax expense as follows:

- in OCI as part of the remeasurement of the return on plan assets, if the tax is a cost of managing plan assets (see 4.4.980.10); or
- in profit or loss, if it is any other tax payable by the entity. [*IAS 19.BC124*]

4.4.1010 *Net defined benefit liability (asset) denominated in foreign currency*

4.4.1010.10 A net obligation under a defined benefit plan may be denominated in a foreign currency – e.g. an entity may have an obligation to employees working abroad that is denominated in the local currency of the country in which they work. It is unclear whether the obligation should be translated into the entity's functional currency before or after measuring the obligation. In our view, the net defined benefit liability (asset) should first be calculated in the currency in which it is denominated and the resulting net amount should be translated into the entity's functional currency. As a result, foreign exchange gains and losses on the net defined benefit liability (asset) are recognised together with other exchange gains and losses rather than as part of the IAS 19 remeasurement. In our view, the same treatment would apply to all plans that have a functional currency different from that of the entity. [*IAS 19.141(e)*]

4.4.1020 Determining remeasurements

4.4.1020.10   To determine remeasurements, an entity prepares a schedule of movements in the obligation, the plan assets and the effect of the asset ceiling (if any). The difference between the opening balance, adjusted for expected movements during the period, contributions and refunds, benefit payments and the effect of any business combinations or disposals, and the closing balance represents the remeasurement for the period.

EXAMPLE 22 – DETERMINING REMEASUREMENTS

4.4.1020.20   Company W has a defined benefit plan and it prepares a calculation of the remeasurements for the annual period ending 31 December 2018. The following facts are also relevant for this example.
- For simplicity, net interest is based on the position at the beginning of the period and does not take into account contributions made into and benefits paid out of the plan during the year; these would generally be reflected (see 4.4.940).
- The discount rate is 6%.
- The asset ceiling is 700.

Plan assets	
Fair value at 1 January 2018	16,000
Interest income (16,000 x 6%)	960
Contributions for 2018 (actual amounts received by the fund)	1,050
Employee benefits paid in 2018 (actual benefits paid by the fund)	(1,500)
Projected amount of assets at 31 December 2018	16,510
Fair value at 31 December 2018	16,920
Remeasurement gain for 2018	410

Alternative calculation of remeasurement gain on plan assets	
Difference between closing and opening balance of plan assets (16,920 - 16,000)	920
Net contributions received and benefits paid in 2018 (1,500 - 1,050)	450
Less interest income	(960)
Remeasurement gain for 2018	410

Defined benefit obligation

Obligation at 1 January 2018 (based on actuarial calculation at 31 December 2017)	15,000
Interest cost (15,000 x 6%)	900
Current service cost (based on actuarial calculation at 31 December 2017)	800
Employee benefits paid in 2018 (actual benefits paid by the fund)	(1,500)
Expected obligation at 31 December 2018	15,200
Actual obligation at 31 December 2018 (based on actuarial calculation at 31 December 2018)	17,410
Remeasurement (actuarial) loss for 2018	2,210

Effect of the asset ceiling

Opening balance at 1 January 2018 (surplus 1,000 (16,000 - 15,000) - ceiling 700)	300
Interest cost (300 x 6%)	18
Expected effect of asset ceiling at 31 December 2018	318
Actual effect of asset ceiling at 31 December 2018 (deficit 490 (16,920 - 17,410))	-
Remeasurement gain for 2018	318

Alternative calculation of remeasurement gain on the effect of the asset ceiling

Difference between closing and opening balance of effect of asset ceiling (0 - 300)	300
Plus interest expense	18
Remeasurement gain for 2018	318

Total remeasurement gain (loss) for 2018

Remeasurement gain on plan assets	410
Remeasurement loss on defined benefit obligation	(2,210)
Remeasurement gain on asset ceiling	318
Total remeasurement loss for 2018	(1,482)

4.4.1030 Change in estimate

4.4.1030.10 Under IAS 19 changes in estimates are treated as remeasurements and are recognised in OCI. In our view, changes in the amount of a defined benefit obligation as a result of changes in the method of measuring the obligation – e.g. as a result of applying a different measurement method under the projected unit credit method – are actuarial gains or losses and therefore remeasurements that are recognised in OCI. For a discussion of changes in estimate resulting from changes in the accounting treatment of multi-employer defined benefit plans, see 4.4.190. [*IAS 19.8*]

4.4.1030.20   Benefits are attributed to periods of service in accordance with the plan's benefit formula unless that formula is back-end-loaded (see 4.4.400.10). In our view, any changes in the overall approach to measuring the obligation – e.g. changing from using the projected unit credit method to attribute the benefits to periods of service to using a straight-line attribution method – would not be a change in estimate and should be considered as a correction of an error (see 4.4.1050), unless the plan's benefit formula has changed. We believe that there is a distinction between changing the method for measuring the obligation (see 4.4.1030.10) and changing the overall approach to measuring the obligation, which would change the overall attribution method. [*IAS 19.70*]

4.4.1040   Recognition of remeasurements

4.4.1040.10   Remeasurements of the net defined benefit liability (asset) are recognised in OCI and are not reclassified to profit or loss in a subsequent period. However, the entity may transfer cumulative amounts recognised through OCI to another component of equity. [*IAS 19.122*]

4.4.1050   ERRORS

4.4.1050.10   An incorrect classification of an employee benefit plan – e.g. as a defined contribution plan instead of a defined benefit plan – is an error.

4.4.1050.20   Calculation errors may arise if the assumptions used in the calculation are incorrect – e.g. if certain eligible employees were not included in the calculation of the obligation.

4.4.1050.30   Material prior-period errors are prior-period adjustments (see 2.8.80).

4.4.1060   PRESENTATION AND DISCLOSURES OF DEFINED BENEFIT PLANS

4.4.1070   Presentation

4.4.1080   *Offsetting*

4.4.1080.10   Net liabilities and net assets arising on different plans are presented separately, except for the rare circumstances when there is a legal right to set off and an intention to settle the plans on a net basis. [*IAS 19.131*]

4.4.1090   *Current and non-current presentation*

4.4.1090.10   A distinction between current and non-current assets and liabilities arising from post-employment benefits is not required. [*IAS 19.133*]

4.4.1090.20   Generally, assets and liabilities related to defined benefit plans are presented as non-current, because a distinction between current and non-current portions may sometimes be arbitrary.

However, if the distinction between the current and non-current portions is clear, then split presentation is possible. For example, an entity may choose to present as the current portion of its employee benefit obligation an amount equal to its contributions payable to a plan within the next 12 months. However, in our experience the common approach is for the total liability to be presented as non-current unless it is part of a disposal group that is held for sale or distribution (see 5.4.20 and 35). [*IAS 19.BC200*]

4.4.1100   *Service cost and net interest*

4.4.1100.10   IAS 19 does not specify where service cost and net interest on the net defined benefit liability (asset) are presented. It also does not specify whether an entity presents service cost and net interest separately or as components of a single item of income or expense. An entity therefore chooses an approach, to be applied consistently, to the presentation of service cost and net interest on the net defined benefit liability (asset) in profit or loss. [*IAS 19.134, BC201, 1.45*]

4.4.1110   *Curtailments or settlements*

4.4.1110.10   In our view, if a curtailment or settlement arises as a result of the disposal of an operation, including a subsidiary, then the resulting gain or loss may be shown as an adjustment to the gain or loss on disposal of the operation or as a component of personnel expenses. In our view, an entity should choose a presentation format, to be applied consistently, for the presentation of curtailment or settlement gains or losses. For a discussion of disclosure requirements, see 4.4.1130.40.

4.4.1120   *Group plans*   Ⓢ

4.4.1120.10   If there is a contractual agreement or a stated policy for charging the costs of a group plan, then an entity that participates in that plan recognises the defined benefit cost allocated to it under the agreement or policy. In such a case, questions may arise about how to account for and present the allocated cost. In our view, the amount of the allocated cost recognised in profit or loss (see 4.4.210) should generally be presented as a single expense within personnel expenses. [*IAS 19.41*]

4.4.1120.20   If there is no such contractual agreement or stated policy, then the net defined benefit cost is recognised by the group entity that is legally the sponsoring employer for the plan. In our view, any amount of the net defined benefit cost recognised in profit or loss by the legal sponsor (see 4.4.220) should generally be presented as a single expense within personnel expenses. [*IAS 19.41*]

4.4.1130   Disclosures

4.4.1130.10   The disclosures required by IAS 19 are based on the following three objectives:
- to explain the characteristics of, and risks associated with, defined benefit plans;
- to identify and explain the amounts in the financial statements arising from defined benefit plans; and
- to describe how defined benefit plans may affect the amount, timing and uncertainty of future cash flows. [*IAS 19.135*]

4.4.1130.20   If those disclosures are insufficient to meet these objectives, then an entity is required to provide more detail to meet them. In considering the objectives, an entity takes into account whether the users of the financial statements need additional information to evaluate the quantitative information that is being disclosed. [*IAS 19.136–137*]

4.4.1130.30   An entity considers the level of detail necessary to satisfy its disclosure objectives and how much emphasis to place on each of the various requirements. It also assesses whether all or some disclosures need to be disaggregated to distinguish between plans or groups of plans with materially different risks. [*IAS 19.136, 138*]

4.4.1130.40   Past service cost and gains and losses arising from settlements need not be disclosed separately if they occur together. [*IAS 19.141(d)*]

4.4.1140   *Expected contributions and benefit payments*

4.4.1140.10   An entity discloses the contributions expected to be paid to the plan for the next annual reporting period. It also discloses information about the maturity profile of the defined benefit obligation, which may include information about the distribution of the timing of benefit payments such as a maturity analysis of the benefit payments. This disclosure is not restricted to funded plans, and therefore provides information about the entity's cash flows in the immediate future with respect to both funded and unfunded plans. [*IAS 19.147(b)–(c)*]

4.4.1150   *Related party disclosures*

4.4.1150.10   IAS 24 requires disclosure of key management compensation in total and for each of the following categories:
- short-term employee benefits;
- post-employment benefits;
- other long-term benefits;
- termination benefits; and
- share-based payments (see 5.5.110). [*IAS 24.17*]

4.4.1160   *Multi-employer plans and group plans*

4.4.1160.10   The extent of disclosure to be made by an entity participating in a multi-employer or group defined benefit plan depends on whether it accounts for its participation on a defined benefit basis, under a stated policy or contractual agreement or, alternatively, on a defined contribution basis. [*IAS 19.148–149*]

4.4.1160.20   Some of the information required to be disclosed by an entity participating in a group plan can be disclosed by cross-reference to disclosures about the plan in another group entity's financial statements. However, this approach may be taken only if those other financial statements are available to users of the entity's financial statements on the same terms as, and no later than, its own financial statements. This requirement may limit the practical use of the exemption. [*IAS 19.150*]

4.4.1170   INSURED BENEFITS

4.4.1180   General principles

4.4.1180.10   If employee benefits are insured, then the accounting treatment depends on the nature of the obligation retained by the entity. [*IAS 19.46*]

4.4.1180.20   If an entity buys an insurance policy from an unrelated third party and in so doing settles its legal and constructive obligations under a defined benefit plan – e.g. the insurance policy is in the name of a specified plan participant and the entity does not have any legal or constructive obligation to cover any loss on the policy – then the purchase of the insurance policy is treated as a settlement of some or all of the entity's obligations. The premiums paid under the policy are recognised as an expense (in effect, defined contribution accounting). For a discussion of purchases of insurance policies based on current salary and other policies that do not cover the entire obligation, see 4.4.1200. [*IAS 19.46, 49, 112*]

4.4.1180.30   If the entity retains an indirect obligation – e.g. if actuarial risk will be transferred back to the entity by way of increased premiums, or the entity retains an obligation to pay the benefits through a plan – then the plan continues to be treated as a defined benefit plan. The insurance policy is treated as a plan asset, or as a separate asset, depending on the circumstances as explained in 4.4.660. [*IAS 19.48*]

4.4.1180.40   If an unrelated third party – e.g. an independent insurance company – takes on the actuarial risk and the primary obligation to the employees, then the entity may nevertheless retain a contingent obligation to make additional payments if the third party defaults. If the risk of the entity having to make additional payments is remote, then in our view such a plan is normally treated as a defined contribution plan and the entity's potential obligation is a contingent liability that would not be recognised (see 3.12.105).

4.4.1190   Insurance policies qualifying as plan assets

4.4.1190.10   Not all insurance policies qualify as plan assets. The distinction between those that qualify and those that do not, and their measurement, is discussed in 4.4.660.

4.4.1200   Current salary policies and other limited cover

4.4.1200.10   An entity may buy insurance policies each period to settle all of its defined benefit obligations. In this case, recognising as an expense the cost of the policies bought (in effect, defined contribution accounting) will have the same effect as applying defined benefit accounting and recognising a settlement gain or loss. Although the accounting may be similar to defined contribution accounting, the disclosure requirements for defined benefit plans may still be relevant.

4.4.1200.20   An assessment of whether an entity settles all of its defined benefit obligations through the purchase of insurance policies is made on a plan-by-plan basis. For example, an entity has a pension plan with an annual benefit based on current salary levels. The entity pays an annual premium under an insurance policy based on the same current salary levels and the insurer guarantees all of the benefits earned to date by employees based on current salary levels. If the entity does not retain an indirect obligation in respect of the plan (see 4.4.1180.30), then it may be appropriate for the entity to treat the plan as a defined contribution plan. This is because the entity may have settled all of its obligations with regard to benefits earned to date through the purchase of insurance policies. [*IAS 19.46*]

4.4.1200.30   However, an insurance policy may not cover the entity's entire obligation. An insured benefit cannot be treated as a defined contribution plan if the entity has an obligation to make payments if the insurer does not pay *all* future employee benefits related to employee service in the current and prior periods. Therefore, in our view such a plan should be accounted for as a defined benefit plan even if some of its obligations have been settled and are no longer recognised.

EXAMPLE 23 – INSURED BENEFITS – LIMITED COVER INSURANCE POLICY

> 4.4.1200.40   Company Q has a pension plan with a payment based on final salary. Q pays premiums to Insurer R under an insurance policy based on current rather than projected salary levels. R guarantees all the benefits earned to date based on current salary levels. Because defined benefit obligations are based on projected rather than current salary levels (see 4.4.390.10), there is a difference between Q's defined benefit obligation and the obligations assumed by R under the insurance policy. We believe that Q therefore has a defined benefit plan. Although the insurance policy bought by Q is based on current rather than projected salary levels, in our view this should be treated as a partial settlement to the extent that the liability (based on current salary levels) is settled by the purchase of an insurance policy (see 4.4.910). [*IAS 19.46*]

4.4.1210   DEATH-IN-SERVICE BENEFITS

4.4.1210.10   Entities may offer death-in-service benefits to employees as part of their employment packages. These benefits may be offered:
- through a post-employment plan, within which the benefits may or may not be insured; or
- on a stand-alone basis, which may or may not be insured.

4.4.1210.20   Often, the actuarially determined measurement of the obligation for a post-employment plan reflects expected death in service. In our view, expected death-in-service benefits should be treated consistently in measuring the post-employment benefit obligation and the death-in-service obligation. Therefore, we believe that if death-in-service benefits are provided through a post-employment plan and are not insured, and the measurement of the post-employment benefit plan obligation reflects expected death in service – i.e. is reduced for retirement benefits that will not be paid because of death in service – then the entity should recognise the cost of death-in-service benefits. This is done by including their present value in the post-employment benefit obligation and recognising the service cost as the service that gives rise to the entitlement is provided.

4.4.1210.30   If death-in-service benefits are provided through a post-employment plan and are insured, then in our view an entity should choose an accounting policy, to be applied consistently, from the following options:
- recognise the cost of the benefits by including their present value in the post-employment benefit obligation and recognise the insurance policy as a plan asset or reimbursement right (see 4.4.640); or
- recognise the cost of the benefit as the insurance premiums are payable.

4.4.1210.40   In our view, if death-in-service benefits offered on a stand-alone basis are insured or reinsured with third parties, then the cost of the benefit should be recognised as the insurance premiums are payable. We believe that if death-in-service benefits offered on a stand-alone basis are not insured or reinsured with third parties, then the benefit should be recognised as an expense to the extent that deaths have occurred by the reporting date.

4.4.1220   **SHORT-TERM EMPLOYEE BENEFITS**

4.4.1230   **Definition and scope**

4.4.1230.10   'Short-term employee benefits' are defined as employee benefits (other than termination benefits) that are expected to be settled wholly before 12 months after the annual reporting date in which the employees render the related service. These benefits are accounted for using normal accrual accounting. [*IAS 19.8*]

4.4.1230.20   If employee benefits do not meet the definition of short-term, then they are classified as post-employment benefits (see 4.4.90) or other long-term employee benefits (see 4.4.1310) and a more complex accounting model is applied.

4.4.1230.30   IAS 19 does not directly specify the unit of account for assessing when a benefit is expected to be 'wholly settled'. Possibilities might include, for example, the overall benefit level for all employees, or each benefit for each individual employee or certain subgroups of the workforce. However, the basis for conclusions to IAS 19 explains that the classification needs to reflect the characteristics of the benefits, rather than the demographic or financial assumptions at a point in time. It also explains that classification on an employee-by-employee basis would not be practical and would not meet the objectives of the classification. Therefore, in our view the classification should be done for the benefits as a whole, for all employees. [*IAS 19.BC20–BC21*]

EXAMPLE 24 – SHORT-TERM EMPLOYEE BENEFITS – EXPECTED TO BE SETTLED WHOLLY WITHIN 12 MONTHS

4.4.1230.40   Company B has a sick leave programme that entitles an employee to five sick days per year; any unused sick days are accumulated. On retirement, the employee is entitled to a 50% payout of the accumulated unused sick leave based on final salary, provided that the employee is a qualifying pensioner – i.e. aged at least 50 with two years of service or aged at least 45 with 20 years of service. If employment is terminated before the retirement date, then all unused sick leave is forfeited.

4.4.1230.50   B classifies this plan as a short-term or a long-term benefit depending on its expectation about whether all of the benefit will be settled within 12 months after the end of the period in which the benefit was earned. If B expects that unused sick days will be settled – i.e. taken by employees – wholly within those 12 months, then the whole benefit is classified as a short-term benefit. However, if B expects that a significant portion of the benefit as a whole, for all employees, will not be settled within 12 months after the end of the period in which the benefit was earned, then we believe that the whole benefit should be classified as a long-term employee benefit.

4.4.1230.60   An employee's annual benefit entitlements – e.g. salary or annual leave entitlement to be taken during the related annual period of service – will often depend on seniority and/or length of service. In our experience, the predominant practice is to treat higher salaries and such annual leave entitlements based on seniority or length of service as short-term employee benefits. For a discussion of one-off jubilee or milestone anniversary benefits that are classified as other long-term employee benefits, see 4.4.1320.70.

EXAMPLE 25 – SHORT-TERM EMPLOYEE BENEFITS – INCREASING ANNUAL SALARY AND LEAVE ENTITLEMENTS

4.4.1230.70   Company P has a policy of promoting employees to manager level after five years and to senior manager after a further five years. Before promotion to manager, employees receive an annual salary of 20,000 and an annual leave entitlement of 25 days. Managers receive an annual salary of 25,000 and an annual leave entitlement of 30 days. Senior managers receive an annual salary of 30,000 and an annual leave entitlement of 35 days. All annual leave must be taken during the annual reporting period in which it is earned.

4.4.1230.80   In this example, future salary increases and annual leave entitlements are not anticipated in measuring current employee costs – e.g. the annual expense for a manager's salary is 25,000. The fact that annual salary and leave entitlement increase as employees' length of service and seniority increase does not make the additional benefit a long-term benefit.

4.4.1240   Change in classification

4.4.1240.10   An entity does not reclassify a short-term employee benefit as long-term if its expectations of the timing of settlement change only temporarily. However, if the entity's expectations of the timing of settlement change other than temporarily, or the characteristics of the benefit change – e.g. from a non-accumulating to an accumulating benefit (see 4.4.1250) – then the short-term benefit is reclassified. [*IAS 19.10*]

4.4.1250   Paid absences

4.4.1250.10   An entity accrues the obligation for paid absences if the obligation both relates to employees' past services and accumulates – i.e. can be carried forward to a future period. [*IAS 19.13*]

4.4.1250.20   A liability is recognised whether or not the benefits are vesting – i.e. whether or not employees are entitled to payment of their unused benefits if they leave. For example, if entitlement to annual leave pay accumulates, then it is accrued even if it does not vest – i.e. even if employees do not get paid for unused annual leave when their employment ends. [*IAS 19.15*]

4.4.1250.30   If the paid absence is expected to be settled wholly before 12 months after the end of the annual reporting period in which it is earned, then it is classified as a short-term benefit. If not, then it is classified as an other long-term benefit (see 4.4.1230.30 and 1320.20).

EXAMPLE 26A – PAID LEAVE – SHORT-TERM EMPLOYEE BENEFIT

4.4.1250.35   Company D has a compensated leave policy that provides employees with 12 days of paid leave per year. Legally, employees are able to accumulate their leave without limit. Accumulated unused balances are paid to employees on ceasing employment. D actively monitors leave balances and encourages employees to take their leave frequently.

> 4.4.1250.36   Assessing the appropriate classification of the compensated leave requires judgement. At each reporting date, D expects the outstanding balance of compensated leave to be settled wholly within 12 months. In this example, annual leave is therefore a short-term employee benefit.

EXAMPLE 26B – PAID LEAVE – LONG-TERM EMPLOYEE BENEFIT

> 4.4.1250.37   Modifying Example 26A, Company D allows employees to accumulate up to 24 days of unused leave before it starts to manage further accumulation. As a result, many employees accumulate balances greater than 12 days.
>
> 4.4.1250.38   At each reporting date, D expects that a significant portion of the annual leave earned during the reporting period will be settled more than 12 months after the reporting date. In this example, annual leave is therefore a long-term employee benefit. For a discussion of the presentation of long-term employee benefits, see 4.4.1430.

4.4.1250.40   In most cases, an entitlement to maternity or paternity leave is contingent on a future event and does not accumulate. Therefore, these costs are recognised only when the absence starts. In our view, this applies even if employees are required to complete a minimum service period before being entitled to the benefit, or if the length of the leave entitlement depends on the period of service. [*IAS 19.13, 18*]

4.4.1250.50   Similarly, no accrual is recognised for amounts to be paid to employees in future periods in respect of public holidays because the entitlement to pay does not accumulate.

4.4.1260   *Measurement*

4.4.1260.10   The liability for paid absences that are a short-term benefit is measured as the undiscounted amount that the entity expects to pay for the unused entitlement. [*IAS 19.11, 16*]

4.4.1260.20   Therefore, the accrual for paid annual leave classified as a short-term benefit is based on the expected amount of unused annual leave – i.e. the number of days of leave at each reporting date that employees are entitled to but have not used and that can be used (or paid) in future periods.

4.4.1260.30   If the benefits are vesting – i.e. employees will receive payments for unused benefits when they leave – then a liability is recognised for the total amount.

4.4.1260.40   In measuring an obligation for non-vesting benefits, an entity takes into account the possibility that employees may leave before they use their entitlement. For example, an entity would recognise a liability for an entitlement to sick leave that can be carried forward to the next annual reporting period, but that will not be paid for if the employee leaves, only to the extent that it expects employees to take sick leave in that future period. [*IAS 19.15*]

4.4.1270   **Profit-sharing and bonus plans**

4.4.1270.10   A provision is recognised for the expected cost of bonus or profit-sharing plans if an entity has a present legal or constructive obligation and a reliable estimate of the obligation can be made. For a discussion of whether a liability is recognised at the reporting date, see chapter 2.9. [*IAS 19.19*]

4.4.1270.20   Some bonus plans may have aspects that are similar to long-term benefits (see 4.4.1310). For example, under a bonus plan employees are entitled to higher bonuses the longer that they remain with the entity. However, the bonuses are calculated and settled quarterly. Such a bonus plan raises the following questions.
● Does one year of service earn the employee the right to one year of benefit?
● Does continuous employment earn the right to an accumulated benefit?

4.4.1270.30   In our view, such an arrangement is more like a salary benefit and the incremental bonus should be treated in the same way as expected future salary increases. Therefore, the benefit is a salary benefit based on the current year's service, which is settled in full within 12 months of the end of the period in which the service is provided.

4.4.1270.40   Some bonus or profit-sharing plans may be statutory arrangements. For example, in some jurisdictions certain entities are required to pay employees a fixed percentage share of an entity's taxable profit. The IFRS Interpretations Committee discussed such scenarios and noted that although such a statutory employee profit-sharing arrangement calculates amounts payable to employees in accordance with tax law, it meets the definition of an employee benefit and should be accounted for in accordance with IAS 19. Therefore, an entity measures its liability for the profit-sharing arrangement in accordance with IAS 19:
● at the undiscounted amount expected to be paid, if the arrangement is short-term in nature; or
● in accordance with the recognition and measurement criteria of IAS 19 for other long-term employee benefits, if the arrangement is long-term in nature. [*IAS 19.24, 155, IU 11-10*]

4.4.1270.50   The objective of IAS 19 is to record compensation expense only when the employee has provided the related services. Consequently, the Committee noted that an entity should not recognise an asset or liability related to future expected reversals of differences between taxable profit and accounting profit in connection with such an employee profit-sharing arrangement. [*IU 11-10*]

EXAMPLE 27A – SHORT-TERM EMPLOYEE BENEFITS – PROFIT-SHARING ARRANGEMENT BASED ON TAXABLE PROFIT

4.4.1270.60   Company M has accounting profit of 1,000, including accrued interest income of 100. In accordance with tax law, interest income is included in taxable profit on a cash basis. The law prescribes that the employee profit-sharing arrangement is determined at 10% of taxable profit. Under IAS 19, M recognises a liability of 90 ((1,000 - 100) x 10%), reflecting the amount expected to be paid as employee benefit for the current period. An additional liability of 10 (100 x 10%), reflecting the amount by which the employee benefit is expected to be measured on a basis higher than accounting profit in future years (the 'deferred component'), is not recognised. This is because the additional 10 is considered to relate to future

employee services and no amount is recognised in respect of the deferred component of the employee benefit.

4.4.1280 *Measurement*

4.4.1280.10 The amount provided is the best estimate of the undiscounted amount that the entity expects to pay. [*IAS 19.20, BC55*]

4.4.1280.20 If payment is conditional – e.g. on the employee remaining in service – then the conditions (and the possibility of forfeiture) are taken into account in measuring the obligation. [*IAS 19.20, BC55*]

EXAMPLE 27B – SHORT-TERM EMPLOYEE BENEFITS – MEASUREMENT OF ANNUAL PROFIT-SHARING PLAN

4.4.1280.30 Company P, with a year end of 31 December 2018, offers its employees a profit-sharing plan. On 31 March 2019, P will pay an amount to participants for services provided during 2018, provided that they remain in employment on that date. The total amount payable to employees is calculated as 5% of the profit for 2018. Each employee's entitlement is determined at 31 December 2018; there is no reallocation of the bonus entitlement for participants who are no longer employed at 31 March 2019. P estimates that 3% of the participants will stop employment between 31 December 2018 and 31 March 2019. P will offer its employees a similar plan in future periods.

4.4.1280.40 Because the amount payable is calculated in respect of achieving a performance condition at 31 December 2018 and there will be a similar plan each year, in our view the amount payable by P for services received in 2018 should be accrued over the 12-month service period in 2018 – i.e. excluding the three-month 'loyalty' period between 31 December 2018 and 31 March 2019. The measurement of the obligation at 31 December 2018 includes an estimate of expected forfeitures – i.e. the 3% of participants who are expected to cease employment between 31 December 2018 and 31 March 2019. [*IAS 19.20*]

4.4.1280.50 If the events or circumstances on which payment is conditional result in part of the payment being expected to be settled more than 12 months after the annual reporting date in which the services are rendered, then the profit-sharing or bonus plan is an other long-term employee benefit (see 4.4.1310). [*IAS 19.24*]

4.4.1290 **Low-interest loans**

4.4.1290.10 Loans given to employees at lower-than-market interest rates are generally short-term employee benefits. IFRS does not directly address how to account for such low-interest employee loans.

4.4.1290.20 Loans granted to employees are financial instruments in the scope of IFRS 9. Therefore, low-interest loans to employees are measured at fair value – i.e. the present value of the anticipated future cash flows discounted using a market interest rate (see 7.7.90.10). In our view, any difference between the fair value of the loan and the amount advanced is an employee benefit. [*IFRS 9.5.1.1*]

4.4.1290.30   We believe that loans to employees at below-market interest rates granted by an entity that is in the business of making loans, such as a bank, should also be measured initially at fair value.

4.4.1290.40   The fair value of the loans to employees is calculated in accordance with IFRS 13, which is the subject of chapter 2.4. This may require assumptions to be made about employee turnover and, if the loans do not have a fixed maturity, about estimated repayment dates. Because these loans are in the scope of IFRS 9, if expectations about the repayment date or employee turnover change, then the entity adjusts the carrying amount of the loan. These adjustments are recognised in profit or loss. [*IFRS 9.B5.4.6*]

4.4.1290.50   If the favourable loan terms are not dependent on continued employment, then in our view there should be a rebuttable presumption that the interest benefit relates to past services, and the cost should be recognised in profit or loss immediately. If the benefit relates to services to be rendered in future periods – e.g. if the interest benefit will be forfeited if the employee leaves or is a bonus for future services – then in our view the amount of the discount may be treated as a prepayment and expensed in the period in which the services are rendered. If the services will be rendered more than 12 months into the future, then the entire benefit is a long-term benefit (see 4.4.1310).

4.4.1290.60   Loans to key management personnel, whether or not they are at below-market interest rates, are related party transactions that require additional disclosure (see chapter 5.5). [*IAS 19.25, 24.9, 17*]

4.4.1290.70   We believe that the issue of shares to employees using the proceeds of a loan made by the issuer, when the loan has recourse only to the shares, is an option grant and not an employee benefit (see 4.5.2280).

4.4.1300   **Non-monetary benefits**

4.4.1300.10   If the short-term employee benefit is in the form of a benefit in kind (e.g. free or discounted goods or services), then in our view its measurement could be based on the entity's net marginal cost of providing the benefit, unless other standards specifically require fair value measurement of the asset or obligation (e.g. the benefit represents a share-based payment in the scope of IFRS 2 or the benefit is in the form of low-interest loans to employees (see 4.4.1290)). [*IAS 19.11*]

EXAMPLE 28 – SHORT-TERM EMPLOYEE BENEFITS – BENEFIT IN KIND

4.4.1300.20   Company C owns apartments that it leases to its employees at below-market rental rates. It is unclear whether the below-market element of the rental should be recognised as an employee benefit. Although the accounting requirements for low-interest loans require financial assets to be measured at fair value, there are no similar requirements in IFRS for non-monetary benefits. Therefore, in our view C is not required to impute a notional income – i.e. the difference between a market rental and the rental actually charged – in order to impute a corresponding expense, which would represent the employee benefit. Instead, C's credit to profit or loss could simply be the actual rental received from the employee. This is the case even if C's core business is investment property.

4.4.1310   OTHER LONG-TERM EMPLOYEE BENEFITS

4.4.1320   **Definition and scope**

4.4.1320.10   Other long-term employee benefits are defined as all employee benefits other than short-term employee benefits, post-employment benefits and termination benefits. [*IAS 19.8*]

4.4.1320.20   Other long-term employee benefits may include accumulating annual leave that can be carried forward and used more than 12 months after the end of the annual reporting period in which the employees render the related services; paid long-service leave; other long-service benefits – e.g. a bonus or extra salary after 20 years of service – and profit-sharing and other bonus schemes that are not expected to be settled wholly before 12 months after the end of the annual reporting period in which the employees render the related services. As discussed in 4.4.1230.30, IAS 19 does not directly specify the unit of account for assessing when a benefit is expected to be 'wholly settled' but in our view the classification should be done for the benefit as a whole, for all employees (see Examples 29A and 29B). [*IAS 19.8, 153, BC20–BC21*]

4.4.1320.30   Although the definition of long-term employee benefits relates to benefits expected to be settled *during* employment, or they would instead be post-employment benefits, in our view a long-term disability benefit that is payable only if an employee remains employed but is no longer providing services should be accounted for as a post-employment benefit (see 4.4.100.40).

4.4.1320.40   Long-term benefits are accounted for as such in their entirety; these benefits are not split between the short- and long-term portions for measurement purposes. For a discussion of the presentation of long-term employee benefits as current or non-current, see 4.4.1430 and Examples 29A and 29B. [*IAS 1.69*]

EXAMPLE 29A – LONG-TERM CLASSIFICATION OF PLAN AS A WHOLE – PROFIT-SHARING BENEFIT

4.4.1320.50   Company M has a three-year annual bonus plan under which employees receive a bonus based on the financial performance of M during the annual reporting period. However, bonuses are paid 30 days after the end of year 3 only to employees who are still in employment with M at the end of year 3. The plan is designed to provide an incentive for employees to remain committed to M and is commonly referred to as a 'profit-sharing benefit' (see 4.4.1350). For years 1 and 2, the employee cannot require settlement before 12 months after the end of the annual reporting period in which the employee rendered the related service. Considering the above, this arrangement is classified as a long-term employee benefit for measurement purposes. The liability is presented in the statement of financial position as non-current at the end of years 1 and 2, and as current at the end of year 3 (see 4.4.1430). We believe that the timing of the physical payment of the bonus is not relevant in determining whether the benefit is short-term or long-term – e.g. if part of the bonus is paid on account once the financial statements for years 1 and 2 are authorised for issue.

EXAMPLE 29B – LONG-TERM CLASSIFICATION OF PLAN AS A WHOLE – LONG-SERVICE LEAVE

4.4.1320.60   Company N has a retention plan providing employees with a one-off benefit of 15 additional days of annual leave after they have rendered five years of continuing service to N. The additional leave vests only at the end of year 5 – i.e. the employees are not entitled to a portion of the leave before the end of year 5. Such an arrangement is commonly referred to as 'long-service leave'. Because the employee can require settlement only after the end of year 5 – this arrangement is classified at the outset and throughout its life as a long-term employee benefit for measurement purposes. The liability is presented in the statement of financial position as non-current for those employees within the first four years of providing service, and as current for employees within year 5 of providing service.

4.4.1320.70   A similar treatment to that in Example 29B would apply to a plan providing employees with a one-off jubilee or milestone anniversary benefit of one month's salary after they have rendered five years of continuing service to the entity. [*IAS 19.8, 153*]

4.4.1320.80   In our view, benefits that are payable on the earlier of cessation of employment and a specified date more than 12 months after the end of the annual reporting period in which services are provided should be treated as other long-term benefits and not as post-employment benefits.

EXAMPLE 30 – LONG-TERM BENEFITS VS POST-EMPLOYMENT BENEFITS VS FINANCIAL INSTRU-MENTS

4.4.1320.90   Company Y makes lump-sum payments to expatriate employees of one month's salary for each year of service. The amounts are paid every five years, or at the date of cessation of employment if the employee leaves within the five-year period. Because the benefits are payable during employment, we believe that they should be treated as long-term benefits and not as post-employment benefits. In our view, even if there is an obligation to pay cash, the benefits payable during employment are an obligation to provide employee benefits under IAS 19 and are not a financial liability in the scope of IAS 32 and/or IFRS 9, because obligations to provide employee benefits are outside the scope of the financial instruments standards (see 7.1.40).

4.4.1330   Defined contribution long-term benefit plans

4.4.1330.10   Although IAS 19 implies that *all* long-term employee benefit plans are defined benefit plans, it does not specifically preclude defined contribution accounting for other long-term benefits. In some situations, other long-term employee benefit plans have the nature of defined contribution plans. In our view, defined contribution accounting should be used for these plans. [*IAS 19.154–156*]

4.4.1340   Accounting for defined benefit long-term benefit plans

4.4.1340.10   Other long-term employee benefit plans that are defined benefit plans are accounted for in a manner similar to post-employment defined benefit plans, except that the components of the defined benefit cost are not disaggregated. [*IAS 19.155*]

4.4.1340.20   Instead, the net total of the following amounts is recognised in profit or loss, except to the extent that another IFRS requires or permits their inclusion in the cost of an asset:
- service cost;
- net interest on the net defined benefit liability (asset); and
- remeasurements of the net defined benefit liability (asset). [*IAS 19.156*]

EXAMPLE 31 – LONG-TERM BENEFITS – EXTRA MONTH'S SALARY

4.4.1340.30   On 1 January 2018, Company P introduced a benefit of an extra month's salary after a further five years of service for those employees working for P at 1 January 2018. The aggregate amount of current monthly salaries of the employees eligible for the benefit is 480,000 and 60% of the employees are expected to work for five years until 31 December 2022 and receive the benefit. The expected annual salary increase over the next five years is 3%. The interest rate on high-quality corporate bonds is 10%.

4.4.1340.40   The statement of financial position obligation at 31 December 2018 for the eligible employees is calculated as follows.

Projected salary level after five years (future value of current salary with a 3% increase: present value = 480,000, i = 3%, n = 4)	540,244
Present value of projected salary level at 31 December 2018 (future value = 540,244, i = 10%, n = 4)	368,994
Adjusted benefit to take into account probability of employee working for the required five additional years (368,994 x 60%)	221,396
Benefit attributable to current year (221,396 / 5 years)	44,279
Fair value of plan assets at 31 December 2018	-
Amount to be recognised as a liability at 31 December 2018	44,279
Key i = interest rate; n = numbers of years of service	

4.4.1340.50   Therefore, an employee cost and a corresponding liability of 44,279 are recognised at 31 December 2018.

4.4.1340.60   In 2019, the calculation will be repeated. Assuming that the interest rate and the anticipated level of employees expected to work for the five years is constant, this will result in a net defined liability of 97,414 (present value of anticipated payment – i.e. 368,994 x 1.1 x 60% x 2 / 5). A net total of 53,135 will be recognised in profit or loss, made up of net interest of 4,428 (44,279 x 10%) and a service cost of 48,707 (97,414 - 44,279 - 4,428).

4.4.1350   Long-term profit-sharing and bonus plans

4.4.1350.10   As with post-employment benefits, the cost of long-term defined benefit employee benefits is attributed to the period in which the services that give rise to the obligation are rendered. [*IAS 19.155*]

4.4.1350.20   An entity considers the substance of a long-term profit-sharing or bonus plan in determining the attribution of benefits to periods of service (see 4.4.400).

EXAMPLE 32A – LONG-TERM BENEFITS – BONUS PLAN

4.4.1350.30   Company T has a bonus plan in which bonuses are based on the performance of T, as calculated on an annual basis. The bonus plan starts in 2018 and continues to 2022. The bonus is payable in cash to employees in two tranches, and the payments are conditional on the employee remaining in service for a specified time after the end of the performance period – i.e. the period that forms the basis for the bonus calculations annually under the bonus plan. Employees receive 50% of the bonus if they remain in service six months after the performance period, and the rest of the bonus is paid if the employee remains in service 18 months after the performance period (the 'stay periods'). In respect of the 2018 bonus, 50% of the bonus is payable on each of 30 June 2019 and 30 June 2020 if the employee remains in service on those dates.

4.4.1350.40   Because the employee becomes entitled to a portion of the bonus more than 12 months after the end of the annual reporting period in which the employee first renders the related service (which is the performance period in this example), the bonus plan is classified in its entirety as a long-term employee benefit for the purposes of recognition and measurement. For the definition of short-term employee benefits and a discussion of classification of other long-term employee benefits, see 4.4.1320. [*IAS 19.8*]

4.4.1350.50   In determining how to account for a long-term profit-sharing or bonus plan in which the entitlement to payment occurs at more than one date (staged vesting), as in Example 32A, in our view an entity should follow the approach set out below.

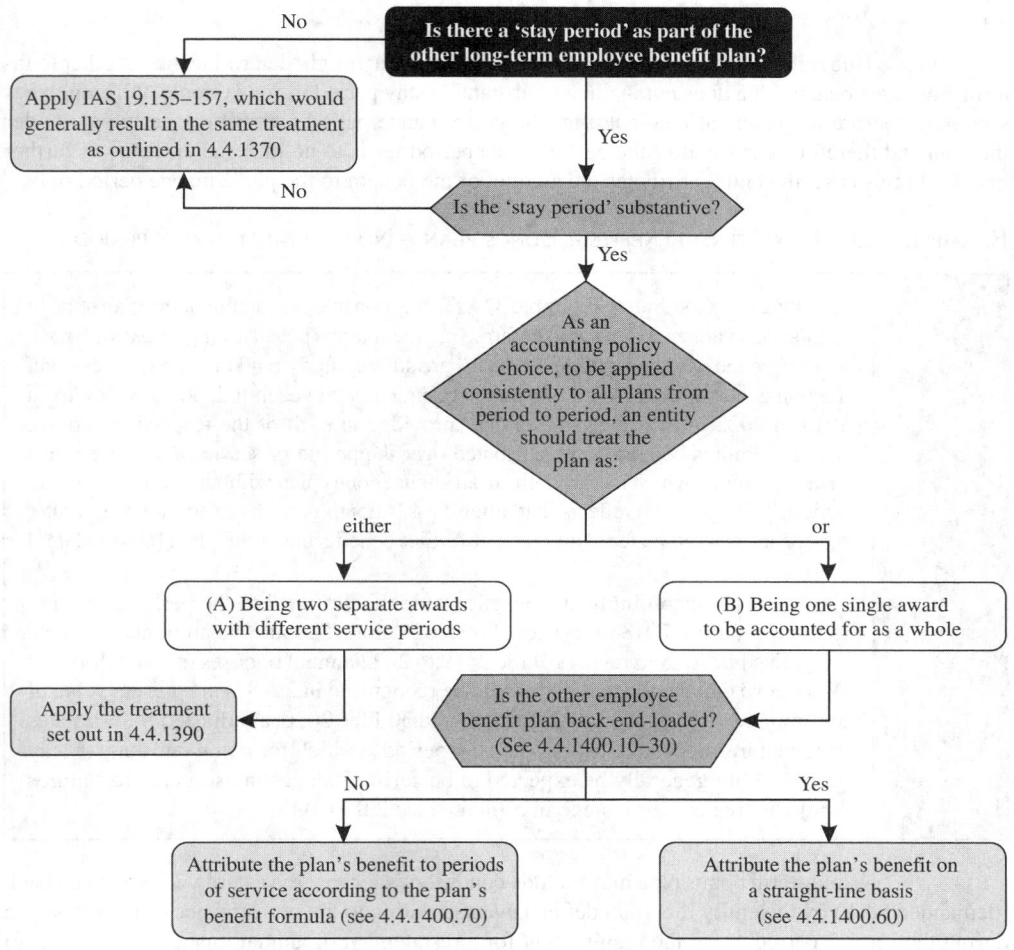

4.4.1360 *Stay period*

4.4.1360.10 The first step of the above approach is to determine if there is a stay period included in the other long-term employee benefit plan. If there is a stay period present, then the second step is to determine if the stay period is substantive. If there is no stay period or it is not substantive, then an entity applies the requirements of paragraphs 155–157 of IAS 19, which would generally result in the treatment outlined in 4.4.1370.10. Such situations may arise, for example, either if an employee earns a bonus for a period of service that is paid more than 12 months after the reporting date regardless of whether the employee remains in service (no stay period), or if employees who have left before the payment date of the bonus are regularly still paid the bonus (no substantive stay period). In such cases, we believe that the entire bonus should be attributed to the performance period.

4.4.1360.20 In our view, to support an assessment that the substance of an other long-term employee benefit plan with a stay period is that it is one with a 12-month service period, the plan should be an ongoing annual bonus arrangement, as opposed to a one-off bonus.

4.4.1370   *No substantive stay period*

4.4.1370.10   Under the approach set out in 4.4.1350.50, an entity might determine that its other long-term employee benefit plan does not include a substantive stay period if, for example, the employees who leave before the payment date but after the performance period are still regularly paid under the plan and therefore service after the performance period leads to no material amounts of further benefit. In this case, the entity attributes the amount of the benefit to the performance period only.

EXAMPLE 32B – LONG-TERM BENEFITS – BONUS PLAN – NO SUBSTANTIVE STAY PERIOD

4.4.1370.20   Continuing Example 32A, T may consider the nature of the plan to be in substance an annual bonus with deferred payment terms because employees who have left before the payment date of the bonus are still regularly paid the bonus. Therefore, the bonus plan is considered one that is being earned in each individual period from 2018 to 2022 in exchange for services provided in each of the respective periods. IAS 19 requires benefits to be attributed over the period of service under the plan's benefit formula, which is 12 months in an annual bonus plan without a substantive stay period. This approach reflects that, after the 12-month period, the employee's further service leads to no material amounts of further benefits under the plan. [*IAS 19.70, 155*]

4.4.1370.30   Accordingly, the benefit would be attributed to the performance period – e.g. during 2018 in respect of the 2018 annual bonus. No amounts would be recognised in 2018 in respect of the 2019 to 2022 annual bonuses (see 4.4.400.10). We believe that the amount that would be recognised in 2018 is the present value of the amounts to be paid on 30 June 2019 and 30 June 2020, as adjusted for estimates of forfeitures occurring during the stay periods (which for a non-substantive stay period would generally be expected to be zero). Changes in estimated forfeitures would be treated as a change in estimate (see 2.8.110).

4.4.1370.40   A long-term bonus plan may include conditions such that the award will be clawed back (demanded back) by the entity if certain defined events relating to the performance of the employee during the service period – e.g. the requirement for a restatement of annual financial statements to correct an overstatement of revenue resulting from the employee's activities – are detected during a predetermined period that follows the service period. In our view, for an award with such claw-back conditions, an entity should attribute the amount of the benefit to the performance (service) period only. This is because the employee can leave after the service period and keep the award with no risk of losing the award for events or actions *subsequent* to the service period – i.e. there is no substantive stay period. Therefore, in this situation service after the performance period leads to no material amounts of further benefit.

EXAMPLE 32C – LONG-TERM BENEFITS – BONUS PLAN – AWARD WITH A CLAW-BACK CONDITION

4.4.1370.50   Company R has a four-year bonus plan in which employees receive a lump-sum bonus after four years if certain performance conditions are met. However, R has the right to demand an employee to return the bonus if defined events relating to the performance of the employee during the four-year service period are detected within seven years of the original award date – i.e. in the three years after the bonus vests.

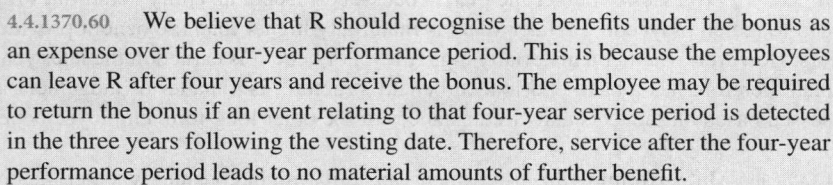

4.4.1370.60   We believe that R should recognise the benefits under the bonus as an expense over the four-year performance period. This is because the employees can leave R after four years and receive the bonus. The employee may be required to return the bonus if an event relating to that four-year service period is detected in the three years following the vesting date. Therefore, service after the four-year performance period leads to no material amounts of further benefit.

4.4.1380   *Substantive stay period*

4.4.1380.10   Under the approach set out in 4.4.1350.50, an entity might determine that its other long-term employee benefit plan includes a substantive stay period if, for example, the employees who leave before the payment date but after the performance period are not entitled to the award and therefore service after the performance period leads to material amounts of further benefit. In this case, we believe that the entity has an accounting policy choice, to be applied consistently to all plans from period to period, to treat each annual award under the plan as:
1. separate awards with different service periods; or
2. one single award to be accounted for as a whole.

4.4.1390   **Separate awards with different service periods**

4.4.1390.10   If an entity elects to apply accounting policy (1) outlined in 4.4.1380.10 and accounts for separate awards, then we believe that the entity should attribute the other long-term employee benefit plan's benefits over the different service periods as set out in 4.4.1390.20.

EXAMPLE 32D – LONG-TERM BENEFITS – BONUS PLAN – SEPARATE AWARDS WITH DIFFERENT SERVICE PERIODS

4.4.1390.20   Continuing Example 32A, T may select an accounting policy that considers each annual award under the other long-term employee benefit plan to be two separate awards with different service periods. Under this approach, the period of service is the period for which the employee is required to be employed by T before becoming unconditionally entitled to a part of the bonus payment. We believe that, under this accounting policy, the bonus expense for each award should be recognised over the respective service periods. As such, the two payments of the 2018 bonus would be considered separately: 50% of the 2018 bonus benefit would be attributed over 18 months (i.e. from 1 January 2018 to 30 June 2019) and the remaining 50% would be attributed over 30 months (i.e. from 1 January 2018 to 30 June 2020). Under this approach, the benefit would be attributed over the extended service period as opposed to the performance period only. [*IAS 19.70, 155*]

4.4.1400   *One single award*

4.4.1400.10   If an entity elects to apply accounting policy (2) outlined in 4.4.1380.10 and account for one single award as a whole, then in accordance with the usual attribution under IAS 19 the entity first determines if the other long-term employee benefit plan's benefit formula is back-end-loaded – i.e. the employee's service in later years will lead to a materially higher level of benefit than in earlier years. [*IAS 19.70*]

4.4.1400.20   To assess whether the plan is back-end-loaded, an entity determines if the benefit provided to the employee in the later years is materially higher than the benefit provided in the earlier years. However, whether a materially higher level of benefit is earned in the later years, and whether a plan therefore has a back-end-loaded benefit structure, is a matter of judgement and needs to be assessed based on the facts and circumstances of the other long-term employee benefit plan.

4.4.1400.30   In performing this assessment, an entity might consider whether the benefit earned by the employee per unit of time in the later years materially exceeds the benefit earned per unit of time in the earlier years.

EXAMPLE 32E – LONG-TERM BENEFITS – BONUS PLAN – ONE SINGLE AWARD

4.4.1400.40   Continuing Example 32A, T might carry out this assessment as follows.
- *Earlier years:* 1 January 2018 – 30 June 2019 equals 18 months' service for 50% of the bonus. Therefore, during the earlier years the employee earns a benefit of 2.8% per month (50% / 18).
- *Later years:* 1 July 2019 – 30 June 2020 equals 12 months' service for 50% of the bonus. Therefore, during the later years the employee earns a benefit of 4.2% per month (50% / 12). [*IAS 19.73.Ex1–Ex4, 155*]

4.4.1400.50   In this example, a materially higher level of benefit is earned in the later years (4.2% per month) when compared with earlier years (2.8% per month).

4.4.1400.60   If T determines that the other long-term employee benefit plan is back-end-loaded then, consistent with the guidance set out in Example 4 of the examples illustrating paragraph 73 of IAS 19, it attributes benefit on a straight-line basis under paragraph 70 of IAS 19. The period over which the benefits are attributed on a straight-line basis is from the date on which service by the employee first leads to benefits under the plan until the date on which further service by the employee will lead to no material amount of further benefit under the plan. As such, in this example T would recognise 100% of the benefit on a straight-line basis over 30 months (1 January 2018 – 30 June 2020).

4.4.1400.70   Conversely, if T determines that the other long-term employee benefit plan is *not* back-end-loaded, then it attributes the other long-term employee benefit plan benefits under the plan's benefit formula. In this example, and consistent with the guidance set out in Example 3 of the examples illustrating paragraph 73 of IAS 19, T would recognise 50% of the benefit over the first 18 months (1 January 2018 – 30 June 2019) and the remaining 50% over the last 12 months (1 July 2019 – 30 June 2020).

4.4.1400.80   Based on the fact pattern in this example and assuming that the actual amount of the bonus is 10,000, the following table illustrates the monthly accrual, in the relevant periods, that results from applying the guidance in 4.4.1350.50. Also, although the table illustrates the treatment under the guidance in 4.4.1400.70, it is provided only for illustrative purposes because in the example in 4.4.1350.30 the award is back-end-loaded and therefore the benefit formula would not be applied.

	To 31 DECEMBER 2018	To 30 JUNE 2019	To 30 JUNE 2020
MONTHLY ACCRUAL	FIRST 12 MONTHS	NEXT 6 MONTHS	LAST 12 MONTHS
4.4.1370.10 – annual bonus	833[1]	-	-
Tranche 1	277[2]	277	-
Tranche 2	167[3]	167	167
4.4.1390.20 – separate awards, different service periods	444[4]	444	167
4.4.1400.60 – single award, back-end-loaded, straight-line	333[5]	333	333
4.4.1400.70 – single award, *not* back-end-loaded, benefit formula	277[2]	277	416[6]

Notes
1. 10,000 / 12.
2. 5,000 / 18.
3. 5,000 / 30.
4. 277 + 167.
5. 10,000 / 30.
6. 5,000 / 12.

4.4.1400.90   In our view, under all accounting outcomes arising from applying the approach set out in 4.4.1350.50, the lower of the following two amounts should be presented as a current liability at 31 December 2018 (see 4.4.1430):
- the present value of the amount to be paid on 30 June 2019; and
- the amount of the liability in respect of the plan that has been recognised at 31 December 2018.

4.4.1410   Disability benefit

4.4.1410.10   Another form of other long-term employee benefit is long-term disability benefit. If the level of disability benefit depends on the length of service, then an obligation arises when the service is rendered. In our view, the accounting treatment of such disability benefits should be consistent with that for death-in-service benefits (see 4.4.1210) that are provided either through a post-employment plan or on a stand-alone basis and are insured or reinsured. [*IAS 19.157*]

4.4.1420   Long-term benefits not service-related

4.4.1420.10   If the amount of a long-term benefit is not dependent on the length of service, then the benefit is recognised only when the event that gives rise to an obligation to make the payment happens. A liability for long-term disability benefits (see 4.4.1410.10) is recognised only when an event that causes long-term disability happens, if the level of benefit is not dependent on years of service – e.g. disability benefit that is a flat percentage of salary at the time of disability. In our view, the lack of an explicit service period does not automatically lead to the conclusion that the benefit is not dependent on a service period – e.g. if a benefit is to be paid to an employee when a specific age is reached. [*IAS 19.157*]

4.4.1430 **Presentation and disclosures**

4.4.1430.10   Long-term employee benefits are accounted for as such in their entirety (see 4.4.1320.40). However, an entity distinguishes between current and non-current portions of obligations arising from long-term employee benefits if it does not have the ability to defer payment beyond 12 months from the reporting date. For example, an employee is eligible to receive an additional five weeks' leave after providing 10 years of continuous service to an entity; if the additional leave is not taken during employment, then it will be paid on termination of employment. The additional leave is a long-term employee benefit even after the benefit becomes unconditional – i.e. after the employee provides 10 years of continuous service. However, after the end of year 9 the entity no longer has the ability to defer settlement of the obligation beyond 12 months from the reporting date, and it therefore presents the obligation as current in the statement of financial position. [*IAS 1.69*]

4.4.1440 **TERMINATION BENEFITS**

4.4.1450 **Definition and scope**

4.4.1450.10   Termination benefits are those benefits provided in exchange for termination of an employee's employment as a result of either an entity's decision to terminate that employment before the employee's normal retirement date or an employee's decision to accept an offer of benefits in exchange for termination. [*IAS 19.8, 159*]

4.4.1450.20   Generally, post-employment benefits are accrued over the service period. However, an obligation for termination benefits arises from the termination and not from the employees' service. As a result of this difference in attribution, the obligation for termination benefits is not recognised over a service period but under the separate requirements for such benefits. Therefore, it is important to distinguish termination benefits from post-employment benefits. [*IAS 19.159, 165*]

4.4.1450.30   The terms of an early retirement arrangement require evaluation to determine whether the arrangement, or part of the arrangement, is a post-employment benefit rather than a termination benefit.

4.4.1450.40   IAS 19 notes two factors indicating that an employee benefit is provided in exchange for services rather than for termination of employment:
- the benefit is conditional on future service being provided, including if the benefit increases if further service is provided; and
- the benefit is provided in accordance with the terms of an employee benefit plan. [*IAS 19.162*]

4.4.1450.50   For example, if an entity makes an offer of benefits available for more than a short period, or there is more than a short period between the offer and the expected date of actual termination, then the entity considers whether it has established a new employee benefit plan and therefore whether the benefits offered under that plan are termination benefits or post-employment benefits. Employee benefits provided in accordance with the terms of an employee benefit plan are termination benefits if they both result from an entity's decision to terminate an employee's employment and are not conditional on future service being provided. [*IAS 19.163*]

4.4.1450.60   Some plans have features of both service-related and termination benefits.

EXAMPLE 33A – TERMINATION OR SERVICE BENEFITS – PLANS WITH ATTRIBUTES OF EACH

4.4.1450.65   Company N undergoes a restructuring and, for a limited period, offers an early retirement package to all employees aged 55 to 57. Employees aged 57 leave employment immediately. Employees younger than 57 who accept the offer have to continue to work until they reach age 57.

4.4.1450.67   The benefits provided to employees aged 57 are treated as termination benefits because those benefits are provided in exchange for termination of the employee's employment. Conversely, the early retirement benefits provided to employees younger than 57 are treated as post-employment benefits because those benefits are conditional on future services being provided, although the amount of early retirement package for employees younger than 57 is similar to the package offered to employees aged 57. [*IAS 19.8, 162*]

EXAMPLE 33B – TERMINATION OR SERVICE BENEFITS – FUTURE SERVICE REQUIREMENT

4.4.1450.70   *Altersteilzeit* plans in Germany are early retirement programmes offering bonus payments to employees in exchange for a 50% reduction in working hours. Their employment is terminated at the end of a required service period – typically one to six years. The bonus payments are wholly conditional on the completion of the required service period – i.e. if employment ends before the required service is provided, then the employees do not receive the bonus payments. Eligibility for the benefit would be on the basis of the employee's age but would also typically include a past service requirement. The IFRS Interpretations Committee discussed these plans and noted that the fact that the bonus payments under these plans are wholly conditional on completion of employee service over a period indicates that the benefits are in exchange for that service. Therefore, they do not meet the definition of termination benefits. Because the bonuses are payable after the completion of employment, the nature of the service benefits is that they are post-employment benefits. [*IAS 19.162(a), IU 01-12*]

4.4.1450.80   Termination benefits do not include employee benefits resulting from termination of employment at the request of the employee without an entity's offer, or as a result of mandatory retirement requirements, because those benefits are post-employment benefits. [*IAS 19.160*]

4.4.1450.90   Costs that are associated with ongoing activities are not recognised as a termination obligation.

EXAMPLE 33C – TERMINATION OR SERVICE BENEFITS – ONGOING ACTIVITIES

4.4.1450.100 Company M operates a chain of restaurants and decides to turn them into franchises. The restaurant managers, currently employees, will receive a redundancy payment if they agree to become franchisees. If they do not accept the offer, then they will remain as employees. Even if the plan has been communicated to the employees, M does not recognise a liability. The employees are being paid to become franchisees – i.e. the payments are not employee benefits – and therefore the cost is associated with M's ongoing activities (see 3.12.330.20).

4.4.1450.110 Some employee benefits are provided regardless of the reason for the employee's departure. The payment of such benefits is certain (subject to any vesting or minimum service requirements) but the timing of their payment is uncertain. Although such benefits are described in some jurisdictions as termination indemnities, termination gratuities or severance payments, they are post-employment benefits rather than termination benefits, and an entity accounts for them as post-employment benefits (see 4.4.90). [*IAS 19.159, 164*]

EXAMPLE 33D – TERMINATION OR SERVICE BENEFITS – LUMP-SUM PAYMENTS ON LEAVING SERVICE

4.4.1450.120 Company J, a restaurant, employs waiters and waitresses on short-term contracts and pays them a lump sum at the end of the contract period. In this case, J treats the lump-sum payments as post-employment benefits, rather than termination benefits, because the benefits are provided regardless of the reason for the employee's departure. The obligation does not accrue as a result of the decision to terminate employment. Therefore, the expense for the lump-sum payment is recognised over the service period.

EXAMPLE 33E – TERMINATION OR SERVICE BENEFITS – PAYMENT ON FAILURE TO RENEW CONTRACT

4.4.1450.130 Company P offers a manager a two-year contract with a right of renewal. P has the right to reject the renewal but in that case P will pay the employee a specified amount. In our view, the payment would be a termination benefit, because it is a one-off payment and the triggering event is the termination of the contract, rather than an amount related to the service obligation.

4.4.1450.140 Termination benefits are typically lump-sum payments, but may also include:
- enhancement of post-employment benefits (see Example 33F), either indirectly through an employee benefit plan or directly; and
- salary until the end of a specified notice period if the employee renders no further service that provides economic benefits to the entity. [*IAS 19.161*]

EXAMPLE 33F – TERMINATION OR SERVICE BENEFITS – ENHANCED PENSION

> 4.4.1450.150 Company M offers its CEO an enhanced pension package that increases the net present value of her pension entitlement to 300,000; her original pension entitlement per employment contract had a net present value of 200,000 (post-employment benefits). The enhanced pension entitlement of 100,000 has been offered as part of a termination agreement, because the CEO's employment will be terminated by M a year before the end of her five-year contract. In this case, the enhanced pension entitlement of 100,000 is a termination benefit.

4.4.1460 Recognition

4.4.1460.10   An entity recognises a liability and an expense for termination benefits at the earlier of:
- when it recognises costs for a restructuring in the scope of IAS 37 that includes the payment of termination benefits; and
- when it can no longer withdraw the offer of those benefits. [*IAS 19.165*]

4.4.1460.20   The factor determining both of these is the entity's inability to withdraw the offer of the termination benefits. Until the specified date is reached, the entity retains discretion to avoid paying the benefits.

4.4.1460.30   When the termination benefits are payable as a result of an employee's decision to accept an offer of benefits in exchange for the termination of employment – i.e. to take voluntary redundancy – the entity can no longer withdraw the offer of termination benefits at the earlier of:
- when the employee accepts the offer; and
- when a restriction (such as a legal, regulatory or contractual requirement) on the entity's ability to withdraw the offer takes effect. [*IAS 19.166*]

EXAMPLE 34A – TERMINATION BENEFITS – VOLUNTARY REDUNDANCY OFFER

> 4.4.1460.40   Company O is considering offering its employees voluntary redundancy. O has prepared and communicated to employees a formal detailed plan under which employees may request voluntary redundancy if it is offered by O – i.e. O retains a right of refusal to provide voluntary redundancies to employees who apply for it. O does not recognise an obligation because it has the ability to withdraw the offer of voluntary redundancies.

4.4.1460.50   If termination benefits are payable as a result of an entity's decision to terminate an employee's employment, then the entity can no longer withdraw the offer when it has communicated to the affected employees a plan of termination meeting all of the following criteria:
- actions required to complete the plan indicate that it is unlikely that significant changes to the plan will be made;
- the plan identifies:
  - the number of employees whose employment is to be terminated;
  - their job classifications or functions and their locations (although the plan need not identify these for individual employees); and

- the expected completion date; and
- the plan establishes the termination benefits that employees will receive in sufficient detail so that employees can determine the type and amount of benefits they will receive when their employment is terminated. [*IAS 19.167*]

4.4.1460.60   IAS 19 indicates that the specific employees who will be made redundant do not have to be informed about being made redundant – i.e. that the termination plan can instead be communicated to an employee group that includes the affected employees. For example, a board decision about a termination plan that has been approved by a decision-making body that includes employee representatives – e.g. a supervisory board – most likely results in a termination obligation even if there is no direct communication to the affected employees at that time (see 3.12.320.20).

EXAMPLE 34B – TERMINATION BENEFITS – VOLUNTARY REDUNDANCY UNDER RESTRUCTURING PLAN

4.4.1460.70   Modifying Example 34A, the formal detailed plan under which employees may request voluntary redundancy if it is offered by Company O is part of a wider restructuring plan that has been communicated to employees. O meets the criteria set out in IAS 37 to provide for the costs of that restructuring. Therefore, O recognises an obligation for the related termination benefits.

4.4.1470   Measurement

4.4.1470.10   Termination benefits are measured on initial recognition, and subsequent changes are measured and presented, in accordance with the nature of the employee benefit provided.
- If the termination benefits are provided as an enhancement to a post-employment benefit, then an entity applies the requirements for post-employment benefits (see 4.4.90), except that the requirements for the attribution of benefits are not relevant.
- If the termination benefits are expected to be settled wholly before 12 months after the end of the annual reporting period in which the termination benefit is recognised, then an entity applies the requirements for short-term employee benefits.
- If the termination benefits are not expected to be settled wholly before 12 months after the annual reporting date, then an entity applies the requirements for other long-term employee benefits. [*IAS 19.169–170*]

4.4.1480   Presentation and disclosures

4.4.1480.10   IAS 19 does not require specific disclosures about termination benefits. However, IAS 24 requires disclosures about employee benefits for key management personnel, and IAS 1 requires disclosure of employee benefits expense. [*IAS 19.171, 1.102, 104, 24.17*]

4.4.1490   CONSOLIDATION OF EMPLOYEE BENEFIT PLANS AND EMPLOYEE BENEFIT TRUSTS

4.4.1490.10   Post-employment benefit plans are classified as defined benefit or defined contribution plans (see 4.4.250). Defined benefit plans are accounted for as set out in 4.4.300 – i.e. the resulting obligation is presented on a net basis in the statement of financial position. The plans are not subject to normal consolidation principles.

4.4.1490.20   An employer may also set up a separate entity to provide other long-term employee benefits. Often, the entity holds assets that are transferred to it by the employer. The assets are then used by the entity to settle its obligations to employees. For example, an employee benefit trust may hold cash that will be used to pay bonuses. The employer often has control over the entity.

4.4.1490.30   An employer does not consolidate post-employment benefit plans or other long-term employee benefit plans in the scope of IAS 19. The employer accounts for its obligation under the employee benefit plan to provide the benefits in the same way as employee benefits that are settled directly by the employer – i.e. the employer recognises an obligation for the compensation that employees are entitled to receive based on services performed at each reporting date. However, other employee benefit vehicles are in the scope of IFRS 10 (see 2.5.10). [*IFRS 10.4A*]

4.4.1490.40   In our view, assets held by the fund that meet the definition of plan assets (see 4.4.560) should be measured at fair value and netted against the related liability. In our view, assets other than loans to the sponsor (see 4.4.1510) that do not meet the definition of plan assets (e.g. because of transferability restrictions) should be accounted for in accordance with the relevant IFRS (e.g. in accordance with IFRS 9 for financial instruments). These assets should be shown separately in the employer's statement of financial position. For a discussion of whether those financial instruments are treasury shares, see 7.3.500.

4.4.1500   Loans granted to and by post-employment or other long-term benefit plans

4.4.1500.10   Sometimes a post-employment or other long-term benefit plan may grant loans to, or receive loans from, the sponsoring entity. Examples 35A and 35B illustrate what in our view is the appropriate accounting treatment for such loans.

4.4.1510   *Pension plan loans to sponsor*

EXAMPLE 35A – PLAN LOAN TO SPONSOR – PLAN ASSET

4.4.1510.10   A pension plan grants a 10-year loan of 100 to Company P, the sponsoring entity, at a market rate of interest. The loan meets the criteria for classification as plan assets (see 4.4.600.10). We believe that P should record the following entries in its consolidated financial statements on initial recognition of the loan.

	DEBIT	CREDIT
Cash	100	
Loan payable		100
Plan assets (loan receivable)	100	
Plan assets (cash)		100
To recognise receipt of loan from pension plan		

4.4.1510.20 The net effect on plan assets is zero, because the cash transferred of 100 and the fair value of the loan receivable of 100 offset each other fully.

EXAMPLE 35B – PLAN LOAN TO SPONSOR – NOT PLAN ASSET

4.4.1510.30 A pension plan grants a 10-year loan of 100 to Company P, the sponsoring entity, at a market rate of interest; the loan is not transferable. The loan does not meet the criteria for classification as plan assets (see 4.4.560). We believe that P should record the following entry in its consolidated financial statements on initial recognition of the loan.

	DEBIT	CREDIT
Cash	100	
Plan assets (cash)		100
To recognise receipt of loan from pension plan		

4.4.1510.40 The net effect on plan assets is a decrease of 100, because the cash transferred to P of 100 decreases plan assets and the loan receivable by the plan from P does not meet the criteria for classification as plan assets. We believe that P in its statement of financial position should recognise neither the loan payable to the plan of 100 nor the loan receivable by the plan of 100. We believe that recognition of the loan receivable by the plan would result in P recognising a receivable from itself. Consequently, the plan assets decrease by the cash receipt of the sponsor and neither of the loans is recognised in the statement of financial position. However, P considers whether such loans should be disclosed. [*IAS 1.17(c)*]

4.5 Share-based payments

4.5   Share-based payments

CURRENTLY EFFECTIVE REQUIREMENTS

This publication reflects IFRS in issue at 1 August 2018, and the currently effective requirements cover annual periods beginning on 1 January 2018.

The requirements related to this topic are mainly derived from the following.

STANDARD	TITLE
IFRS 2	Share-based Payment

KPMG's publication *IFRS Handbook: Share-based payments* provides a comprehensive analysis of IFRS 2. The Handbook is more in-depth than this chapter and includes additional clarification of the requirements of IFRS 2 and of our interpretative guidance. It provides extensive illustrative examples to elaborate or clarify the practical application of IFRS 2.

The currently effective requirements include newly effective requirements arising from the following.
- IFRS 9 *Financial Instruments,* which is effective for annual periods beginning on or after 1 January 2018. Transition requirements for IFRS 9 are the subject of chapter 7.11. The impact of the new requirements on share-based payments is reflected in 4.5.310, 1740 and 2400.
- *Classification and Measurement of Share-based Payment Transactions – Amendments to IFRS 2,* which are effective for annual periods beginning on or after 1 January 2018. The amendments apply prospectively. Retrospective application is permitted, but only if it does not involve the use of hindsight. See 4.5.50, 920, 930, 1350, 1620 and 2160.

FORTHCOMING REQUIREMENTS AND FUTURE DEVELOPMENTS

For this topic, there are no forthcoming requirements or future developments.

4.5.10   OVERVIEW

4.5.10.10   The diagram below is a general step-by-step illustration of accounting for share-based payments. A brief overview of each step is provided in this section and the steps are discussed in more detail in the rest of this chapter.

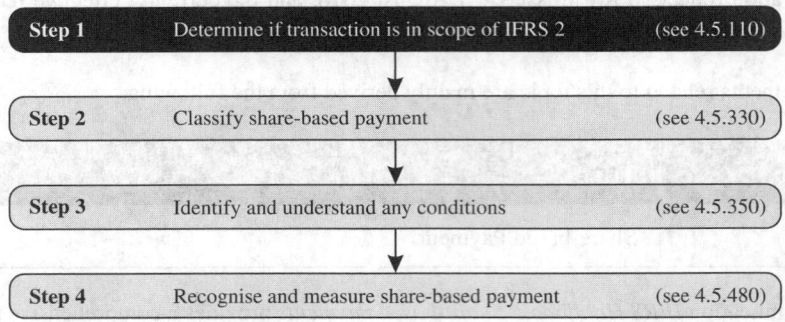

4.5.20   **Overview of Step 1: Determine if transaction is in scope of IFRS 2**

4.5.20.10   In a share-based payment transaction, an entity receives goods or services from a counterparty in exchange for consideration in the form of equity instruments, or cash or other assets for amounts that are based on the price (or value) of equity instruments of the entity or another group entity. A 'counterparty' can be an employee or any other party. This distinction is important because although the recognition requirements are similar for share-based payment transactions with employees and those with non-employees, the measurement requirements differ in many respects.

4.5.20.20   There are certain scope exclusions from IFRS 2, including the following:
- when the counterparty acts in its capacity as a shareholder (see 4.5.250);
- when the arrangement arises as part of a business combination (see 4.5.260); and
- when share-based payments are for the acquisition of certain financial instruments (see 4.5.310).

4.5.30   **Overview of Step 2: Classify share-based payment**

4.5.30.10   The following diagram illustrates the three different types of share-based payment transactions.

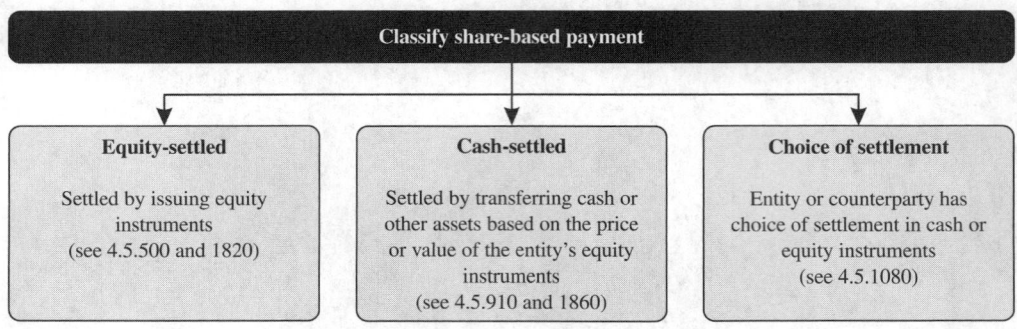

4.5.30.20　　For a further discussion of the classification of share-based payment transactions, including the impact of specific award features in determining classification, see 4.5.330. For a discussion of when the manner of settlement is not a choice within the control of the entity or the employee, but depends on an event outside both parties' control, see 4.5.2230.

4.5.40　Overview of Step 3: Identify and understand any conditions

4.5.40.10　　Share-based payment transactions, in particular those with employees, are often conditional on the achievement of conditions. The standard distinguishes between vesting conditions and non-vesting conditions as follows.

Vesting condition	A condition that determines whether an entity receives services that entitle the counterparty to receive cash, other assets or equity instruments of the entity. A vesting condition is either a service condition or a performance condition.
	<table><tr><td>**SERVICE CONDITION**</td><td>**PERFORMANCE CONDITION**</td></tr><tr><td>Vesting condition that requires the counterparty to complete a specified period of service during which services are provided to the entity. If the counterparty, regardless of the reason, ceases to provide services during the vesting period, then it has failed to satisfy the condition. The service requirement can be explicit or implicit.</td><td>Vesting condition that requires the counterparty to complete a specified period of service and specified performance target(s) to be met while services are rendered. A performance target can be one of the following conditions. • *Market condition:* If it is based on the price (or value) of the entity's equity instruments – e.g. achieving a certain share price target. • *Non-market performance condition:* If it is based on the entity's operations or activities – e.g. achieving a certain profit target.</td></tr></table>
Non-vesting condition	A condition other than a vesting condition that determines whether a counterparty receives the share-based payment – e.g. counterparty's choice of participation in a share purchase programme by paying monthly contributions.

4.5.40.20　　For a further discussion of the classification of conditions, see 4.5.350.

4.5.50　Overview of Step 4: Recognise and measure share-based payment

4.5.50.10　　The following table summarises the recognition and measurement principles for equity-settled and cash-settled share-based payments to employees, and highlights the accounting treatment for vesting and non-vesting conditions under each type of award. For a discussion of the measurement principles for equity-settled share-based payments to non-employees, see 4.5.90.

	EQUITY-SETTLED (SEE 4.5.500)	CASH-SETTLED (SEE 4.5.910)
Recognition	An entity recognises a cost (expense or asset) over the vesting period and a corresponding entry to equity.	An entity recognises a cost (expense or asset) over the vesting period and a corresponding liability.
Measurement	Measurement is based on the grant-date fair value of the equity instruments granted.	Measurement is based on the fair value of the liability at each reporting date, and it is remeasured until settlement date.
Impact of conditions	Market and non-vesting conditions are reflected in the initial measurement of fair value with no subsequent true-up if the conditions are not satisfied. An estimate is made for the number of equity instruments for which service and non-market performance conditions are expected to be satisfied, with a true-up to the number ultimately satisfied.	Market and non-vesting conditions are reflected in the measurement of fair value of the liability. An estimate is made for the number of awards for which service and non-market performance conditions are expected to be satisfied, with a true-up to the number ultimately satisfied.

4.5.50.20   Some share-based payment transactions provide one party with the choice of settlement in cash or in equity instruments. The following table summarises the difference in recognition and measurement depending on whether the employee or the entity has the choice of settlement.

	EMPLOYEE'S CHOICE OF SETTLEMENT (SEE 4.5.1100)	ENTITY'S CHOICE OF SETTLEMENT (SEE 4.5.1130)
Recognition and measurement	The share-based payment is accounted for as a compound instrument that includes a liability component (accounted for as cash-settled) and an equity component (accounted for as equity-settled).	The share-based payment is classified and accounted for as either equity-settled or cash-settled, depending on whether the entity has a present obligation to settle in cash.

4.5.60   Overview of other share-based payment considerations

4.5.60.10   The overview of Steps 1 to 4 in 4.5.20–50 addresses a simple basic scenario. However, some share-based payment arrangements may be more complex and involve other considerations, including modifications and cancellations, group transactions and arrangements with non-employees.

4.5.70 *Modifications and cancellations of employee share-based payment transactions*

4.5.70.10 Modifications of an equity-settled share-based payment arrangement are accounted for only if they are beneficial to the counterparty. If the fair value of the equity instruments granted has increased, then the incremental fair value at the date of modification is recognised in addition to the grant-date fair value. Modifications that are not beneficial to the counterparty do not affect the amount of the cost. However, reductions in the number of equity instruments granted are accounted for as cancellations.

4.5.70.20 In some cases, modifications may change the classification of a share-based payment arrangement. IFRS 2 does not contain explicit guidance on the accounting for such modifications.

4.5.70.30 Cancellations by the entity or by the counterparty are treated as an acceleration of vesting. If an entity grants new equity instruments to replace cancelled equity instruments, then this cancellation and replacement is accounted for by applying the principles of modification accounting.

4.5.70.40 For further discussion of modifications and cancellations of employee transactions, see 4.5.1190.

4.5.80 *Group share-based payments*

4.5.80.10 A share-based payment in which the receiving entity, the settling entity and the reference entity are in the same group from the perspective of the ultimate parent is a group share-based payment transaction from the perspective of both the receiving and the settling entities. In a group share-based payment transaction in which the parent grants a share-based payment to the employees of its subsidiary, the share-based payment is recognised in the consolidated financial statements of the parent, in the separate financial statements of the parent and in the financial statements of the subsidiary. For further discussion, see 4.5.1440.

4.5.90 *Share-based payments with non-employees*

4.5.90.10 Although the recognition requirements are similar for share-based payment transactions with employees and share-based payment transactions with non-employees, the measurement requirements differ in many respects.

4.5.90.20 Equity-settled share-based payment transactions with non-employees are generally measured at the fair value of the goods or services received (direct measurement), rather than at the fair value of the equity instruments granted at the time that the goods or services are received. If, in rare cases, the fair value of the goods or services received cannot be measured reliably, then the goods or services received are measured with reference to the fair value of the equity instruments granted (indirect measurement). For further discussion, see 4.5.1800.

Practical application issues

4.5.100.10   For a discussion of practical application issues relating to share-based payment transactions, as well as the interaction with other standards, see 4.5.1890.

4.5.110   **STEP 1: DETERMINE IF TRANSACTION IS IN SCOPE OF IFRS 2**

4.5.120   **Definition of share-based payment**

4.5.120.10   A share-based payment is accounted for under IFRS 2 if it meets the definition of a share-based payment transaction and the transaction is not specifically scoped out of the standard. For a discussion of transactions that are outside the scope of IFRS 2, see 4.5.240.

4.5.120.20   The standard does not contain a stand-alone definition of a share-based payment, but provides a complex two-step definition using the terms 'share-based payment arrangement' and 'share-based payment transaction'.

4.5.120.30   A 'share-based payment arrangement' is an agreement between the entity (or another group entity or any shareholder of any group entity) and another party (including an employee) that, provided the specified vesting conditions are met, entitles the other party to receive:
- cash or other assets of the entity for amounts that are based on the price (or value) of equity instruments (including shares or share options) of the entity or another group entity; or
- equity instruments (including shares or share options) of the entity or another group entity. [*IFRS 2.A*]

4.5.120.40   A 'share-based payment transaction' is a transaction in which the entity:
- receives goods or services from the supplier of those goods or services (including an employee) in a share-based payment arrangement; or
- incurs an obligation to settle the transaction with the supplier in a share-based payment arrangement when another group entity receives those goods or services. [*IFRS 2.A*]

4.5.120.50   Goods or services are provided either by employees (including others providing similar services) or non-employees. For a discussion on determining whether the transaction is with employees or non-employees, see 4.5.490. For a discussion of transactions with non-employees, see 4.5.1800.

4.5.120.60   In defining a share-based payment arrangement, a 'group' is defined as a parent and its subsidiaries as set out in IFRS 10 (see chapter 2.5). This determination is made from the perspective of the reporting entity's ultimate parent. The requirement to treat transactions involving instruments of another entity as share-based payments applies only to transactions involving equity instruments of a group entity (see 4.5.1440). [*IFRS 10.A*]

4.5.120.70   These definitions are complex because they include not only share-based payments that involve the reporting entity and the supplier, but also those that involve other group entities or shareholders. For a discussion of group share-based payments, see 4.5.1440.

4.5.130 Determining whether transaction is share-based payment transaction in scope of IFRS 2

4.5.130.10   The following flowchart illustrates the steps to analyse whether a transaction is a share-based payment transaction in the scope of IFRS 2. This analysis covers transactions that involve only the supplier of goods or services and the reporting entity – i.e. the reporting entity receives the goods or services and settles the transaction in its own equity instruments or a payment based on its own equity instruments. The reporting entity can be a group or a separate legal entity.

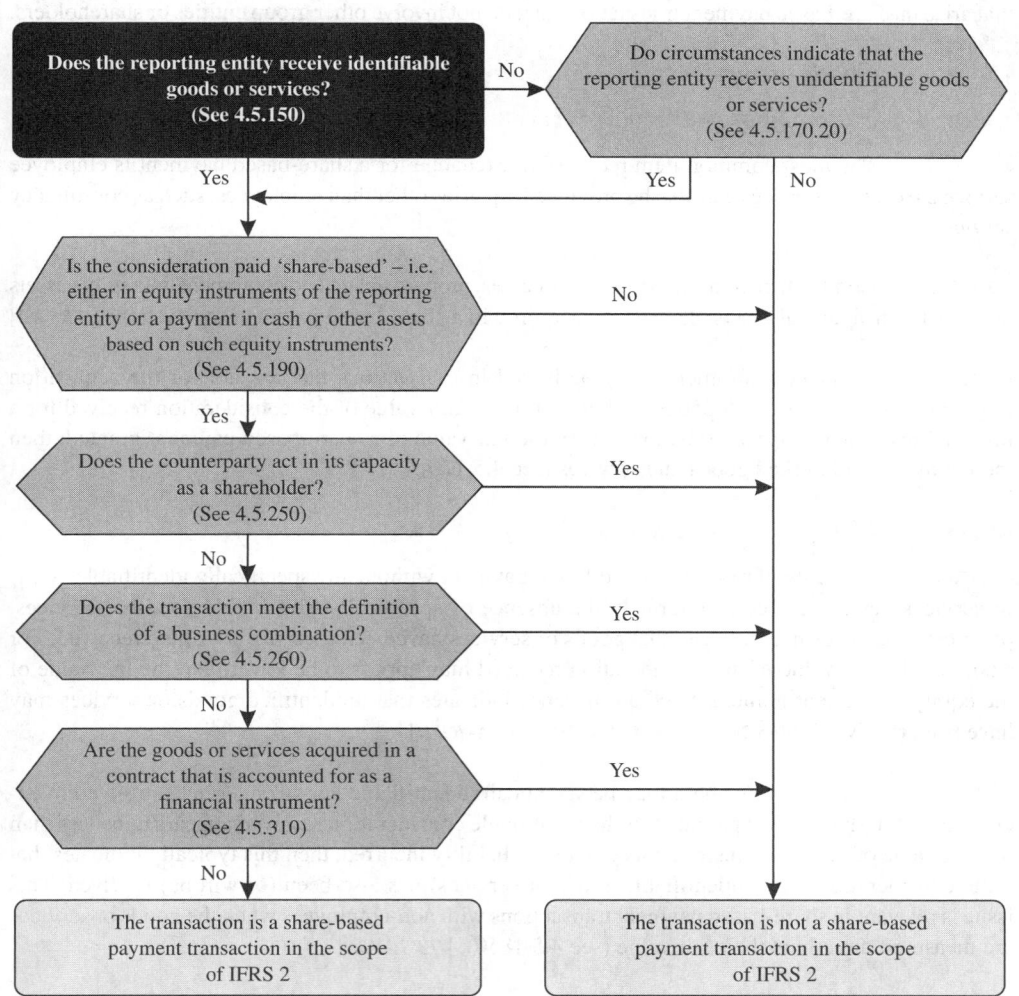

4.5.130.20   If a transaction is in the scope of IFRS 2, then the requirements of the standard specify both the initial and the subsequent accounting for the equity instruments issued or liability incurred, including requirements for planned and unplanned repurchases of vested shares. For a discussion of the impact of an intent to repurchase on the classification of the share-based payment, see 4.5.2180–2200; and for discussion of the accounting for the repurchase, see 4.5.1410.10–30.

4.5.140   **Basic features of share-based payment transactions**

4.5.140.10   There are two basic features of a share-based payment transaction:
- the reporting entity receives goods or services (see 4.5.150); and
- the reporting entity settles the transaction in its own equity instruments or a payment based on its own equity instruments – i.e. the consideration is 'share-based' (see 4.5.190).

4.5.140.20   The reporting entity can be a group or a separate legal entity. This section addresses issues that arise in share-based payment transactions that do not involve other group entities or shareholders.

4.5.150   *Goods or services*

4.5.160   *Definition of goods or services*

4.5.160.10   The most common item received in exchange for a share-based payment is employee services. However, services can also be provided by parties other than employees, such as consultancy services.

4.5.160.20   Goods, such as inventories, consumables, property, plant and equipment, intangible assets and other non-financial assets, can also be acquired in a share-based payment transaction. [*IFRS 2.5*]

4.5.160.30   Financial instruments may be issued in transactions that are not for the acquisition of goods or services (see 4.5.250.30). However, if the fair value of the consideration received for a financial instrument appears to be lower than the fair value of a share-based payment granted, then there may be unidentified goods and services (see 4.5.170).

4.5.170   *Identification of goods or services*

4.5.170.10   An entity may grant a share-based payment without any specifically identifiable goods or services being received in return. In the absence of specifically identifiable goods or services, other circumstances may indicate that goods or services have been received or will be received. For example, the fair value of the consideration received may appear to be lower than the fair value of the equity instrument granted. Such a difference indicates that unidentified goods or services may have been received. [*IFRS 2.2, 13A, BC18A–BC18D, IG5A–IG5D*]

4.5.170.20   In other cases, there may be specifically identifiable goods or services received in exchange for the share-based payment. If the identifiable consideration received appears to be less than the fair value of the equity instruments granted or liability incurred, then this typically indicates that other consideration (i.e. unidentifiable goods or services) has also been (or will be) received. This issue is relevant in share-based payment transactions with non-employees when the goods or services are measured directly at their fair value (see 4.5.1850). [*IFRS 2.13A*]

4.5.170.30   For example, a grant of shares at a discount may indicate that unidentifiable goods or services have been or will be received, and that IFRS 2 therefore applies. [*IFRS 2.IG.Ex1*]

4.5.180   *Goods or services from a supplier*

4.5.180.10   The goods or services received or to be received by the entity need to be provided by the counterparty in its capacity as a supplier of goods or services. If the goods or services are provided by a counterparty in its capacity as a shareholder (see 4.5.250), then the transaction is not a share-based payment transaction.

4.5.190   *Consideration in form of share-based payment*

4.5.190.10   In its basic form, a share-based payment transaction requires the entity to settle the transaction by either transferring its own equity instruments or making a payment in cash or other assets for amounts that are based on the price (or value) of its equity instruments. [*IFRS 2.A*]

4.5.190.20   Depending on the type of consideration to be paid, the payment is referred to as either an 'equity-settled' or a 'cash-settled' share-based payment (see 4.5.330). Before classification is considered, it is necessary to consider what constitutes an equity instrument under IFRS 2 to decide if a transaction is in the scope of the standard. [*IFRS 2.A*]

4.5.200   *Definition of an equity instrument*

4.5.200.10   An 'equity instrument' is a contract that evidences a residual interest in the assets of an entity after deducting all of its liabilities. The most common examples of equity instruments used for share-based payments are ordinary shares and written call options, or warrants, issued over ordinary shares (share options). An equity instrument for the purposes of IFRS 2 can include redeemable shares (see 4.5.1970.10–20). [*IFRS 2.A*]

4.5.200.20   A share-based payment might involve granting preference shares or shares of one class of ordinary shares in circumstances in which there is more than one class of ordinary shares. In both of these cases, the instrument granted may be a right to a residual interest in an entity and therefore equity (see 4.5.1970.10–20).

4.5.210   *Equity instruments of the entity*

4.5.210.10   The issue of what is an equity instrument of the entity is of particular interest in consolidated financial statements. In the consolidated financial statements, equity instruments of the entity comprise the equity instruments of any entity that is included in the group – i.e. the parent and its subsidiaries; for a discussion of the relevance of the classification of instruments under IAS 32, see 4.5.1970.10–20. [*IFRS 2.A, B48–B50*]

4.5.220   *Basis of cash payments*

4.5.220.10   If the entity does not settle in its own equity instruments but in a payment of cash or other assets, then the amount is a share-based payment if it is based on the price (or value) of its equity instruments (or the equity instruments of another entity in the same group). [*IFRS 2.A*]

4.5.220.20   A common example of a cash payment based on an equity instrument of the entity is when an entity grants share appreciation rights (SARs) to its employees. SARs entitle the holder to receive a cash payment that equals the increase in value of the shares from a specified level over a specified period of time – e.g. from grant date to settlement date. In this case, the counterparty directly participates in changes in the value of the underlying equity instrument and, accordingly, the cash payment is based on the price or value of the equity instrument. Another common example of a cash-settled share-based payment is a payment based on the value of an equity instrument at a specific date – e.g. at vesting date or settlement date – rather than on the increase in value. [*IFRS 2.IG18–IG19*]

4.5.220.30   Sometimes it is difficult to assess whether the cash payment is based on the price or value of the equity instrument. For a more detailed discussion of the distinction between a cash payment that 'depends on' vs 'is based on' the price or value of the equity instrument, see 4.5.1950.

4.5.230   Basic scope examples

4.5.230.10   The following are basic scope examples that illustrate the analysis of the basic features of share-based payments in determining if a transaction is in the scope of IFRS 2.

SCENARIO	IN OR OUT OF SCOPE OF IFRS 2?	RATIONALE
Entity B grants 10 shares to its employees provided that they remain in service for the next 12 months.	In	This is an equity-settled share-based payment. The employees will receive the shares of B if they provide the required period of service to the entity.
Entity C grants employees a cash bonus equal to C's share price growth provided that they remain in service over the next 12 months.	In	This is a cash-settled share-based payment. C has an obligation to pay cash based on the change in share price to the employees who provide the required service; this award is also known as an SAR.
Entity E's share price is 120. E awards a cash bonus of 120 to employees, payable in one year to those who remain in service during the next 12 months.	Out	This is not a share-based payment. Although the payment to the employees is linked to the delivery of service from the employees, the payment is not based on the share price of E. For example, if the share price increases or decreases over the period, the employees would still receive the 120. The award is considered an employee benefit in the scope of IAS 19 (see chapter 4.4).
Entity D awards a cash bonus of 500 to employees, payable in one year to those who remain in service if D's share price exceeds a price of 10 per share during the next 12 months.	Out	This is not a share-based payment. Although D has an obligation if the share price-related target is met and the employees provide the required services, the amount of the payment is not based on the share price of D. The award is considered an employee benefit in the scope of IAS 19 (see chapter 4.4).

4.5.235   *Employee share purchase plans*

4.5.235.10   Often, broad-based share-based payment arrangements are designed as employee share purchase plans (ESPPs).

4.5.235.20   Sometimes, the shares are granted to the employees subject to a payment at a value below fair value. In this case, the entity receives past or future services in return for granting a discount and accordingly the transaction is a share-based payment. [*IFRS 2.IG.Ex11*]

4.5.235.30   If the terms appear to include a requirement for the employee to pay full fair value on grant date, then an example in the implementation guidance to IFRS 2 shows that there may be features in the terms and conditions that are required to be considered in determining the accounting. [*IFRS 2.IG.Ex11*]

4.5.235.40   It is not uncommon for such arrangements to contain some form of protection against any decline in value of the share between grant date and the date on which the employee is unconditionally entitled to the share. If this protection exists, then the arrangement is not the purchase of a share but instead is the granting of a share option. The exercise price of the share option is the amount paid on grant date. Because a share option with a prepaid exercise price has a positive value, there will be a cost to recognise for the employee services in such an arrangement. For further discussion on employee share purchase plans, see 4.5.2270.

4.5.240   Transactions outside scope of IFRS 2

4.5.240.10   The following transactions are not share-based payment transactions in the scope of IFRS 2:
- the counterparty acts in its capacity as a shareholder (see 4.5.250);
- the entity issues a share-based payment as consideration for the acquisition of a business (see 4.5.260); or
- the entity issues a share-based payment as consideration for a contract to acquire a non-financial item that is required to be accounted for as a derivative or other financial instrument under the financial instruments standards (see 4.5.310).

4.5.250   *Counterparty acts in capacity as shareholder*

4.5.250.10   Transactions with employees or other parties in their capacity as shareholders are outside the scope of IFRS 2. [*IFRS 2.4*]

4.5.250.20   If employees or other parties who are also shareholders participate in a transaction with the entity, then it may be difficult to determine in which capacity they act: as suppliers of goods or services to the entity, or as shareholders of the entity. If all shareholders have been offered the right to participate in a transaction, then this is an indication that the employees or other parties do not act as suppliers of goods or services but as shareholders. [*IFRS 2.4*]

4.5.250.30   Transactions in which equity instruments of an entity are issued in return for financial instruments of equal fair value are outside the scope of IFRS 2. Such transactions may be in the scope of IFRS 9 or IAS 32 (see chapter 7.1); for a further discussion of scope issues in practice relating to share-based payment vs shareholder transaction, see 4.5.1910. [*IFRS 2.6*]

4.5.260   *Acquisition of a business*

4.5.260.10   IFRS 2 does not apply to transactions in which the entity acquires goods as part of the net assets acquired in a:
- business combination as defined by IFRS 3;
- combination of entities or businesses under common control as described in paragraphs B1–B4 of IFRS 3; or
- contribution of a business on the formation of a joint venture as defined by IFRS 11. [*IFRS 2.5, BC23–BC24D, 3.A*]

4.5.260.20   Each of the scope exceptions set out in 4.5.260.10 is illustrated below. For other scope exceptions, see 4.5.1900. For a discussion of reverse acquisitions, see 4.5.2360.

4.5.270   *Business combinations and share-based payments*

4.5.270.10   In a business combination, equity instruments are often issued to the previous owners of the acquiree in exchange for control. If equity instruments are issued to previous owners of the acquiree who are also employees of the combined entity, then a question arises about whether the transaction with the employees is in exchange for control or in exchange for continued employee services. If the shares issued are part of the consideration transferred in exchange for control, then they are accounted for under IFRS 3. To the extent that the shares issued are granted to the employees in their capacity as employees – i.e. for continuing services – they are accounted for under IFRS 2. For further discussion, see 2.6.400–420. [*IFRS 2.5, 3.52(b)*]

4.5.270.20   The acquisition in exchange for equity instruments of a non-financial asset that does not constitute a business is in the scope of IFRS 2. As discussed in 4.5.250.30, transactions in which equity instruments are issued in return for financial instruments at the same fair value are outside the scope of IFRS 2. [*IFRS 2.5*]

EXAMPLE 1 – SINGLE ASSET (NOT A BUSINESS) ACQUIRED IN EXCHANGE FOR SHARES

4.5.270.30   Company C acquires a piece of vacant land from an unrelated party. C settles the purchase by issuing 1,000 new shares. The acquired asset – i.e. the vacant land – does not meet the definition of a business in IFRS 3. The transaction is in the scope of IFRS 2, and C accounts for the transaction as a share-based payment with non-employees. [*IFRS 2.5*]

4.5.270.40   If the presumption for share-based payments with non-employees is not rebutted, and the fair value of the goods received – i.e. the vacant land – can be measured reliably, then the transaction is measured at the fair value of the land (see 4.5.1850.20). Otherwise, it is measured indirectly at the fair value of the equity instruments granted. If the fair value of the land appears to be less than the fair value of the equity instruments issued, then typically this situation indicates that other consideration – i.e. unidentifiable goods or services – has been (or will be) received in addition to the land (see 4.5.1850.30). [*IFRS 2.13–13A*]

4.5.280   *Business combinations under common control*

4.5.280.10   A transaction in which the entity transfers share-based consideration to pay for net assets acquired in a business combination is outside the scope of IFRS 2. This exclusion applies to both business combinations in the scope of IFRS 3, and other transactions that meet the definition of a business combination but are outside the scope of IFRS 3 – e.g. combinations of entities or businesses under common control (see 2.6.20.10 and chapter 5.13). [*IFRS 2.5, BC24A–BC24D, 3.2(c)*]

4.5.290   *Contribution of business on formation of joint venture*

4.5.290.10   A transaction in which an investor contributes a business as part of the formation of a joint venture in the scope of IFRS 11 in return for shares in an entity is not in the scope of

IFRS 2 (see 3.6.10). Like business combinations under common control, these transactions are excluded from the scope of IFRS 3, and they are also outside the scope of IFRS 2. [*IFRS 2.5, BC24A–BC24D, 3.2(a)*]

4.5.290.20   If, instead, the assets contributed by an investor do not constitute a business, then the scope exception in IFRS 2 does not apply. As a result, such transactions would be in the scope of IFRS 2.

4.5.300   *Other transactions outside scope of IFRS 2*

4.5.300.10   In our view, the exclusion from IFRS 2 for business combinations extends beyond business combination transactions as defined in IFRS 3, and we believe that the following transactions are also outside the scope of IFRS 2:

- acquisition of NCI after control is obtained, because IFRS 10 is generally the specific standard applicable to the transaction (see 2.5.560);
- acquisition of associates, because IAS 28 is the specific standard applicable to the transaction (see 3.5.180); and
- acquisition of a joint controlling interest in a joint venture, because IAS 28 is the specific standard applicable to the transaction (see 3.5.180).

4.5.310   *Commodity contracts*

4.5.310.10   IFRS 2 includes a scope exception for contracts to acquire non-financial items that are in the scope of the financial instruments standards. Such contracts include those that fall directly in the scope of IFRS 9 and those that meet the own-use exemption but are designated as at fair value through profit or loss (see 7.1.200). [*IFRS 2.6, BC25–BC28, 9.2.4*]

4.5.320   Scope issues in practice

4.5.320.10   Other scope issues in practice discussed in this chapter include the following.
- Share-based payment vs shareholder transaction (see 4.5.1910).
- Share-based payment vs employee benefit (see 4.5.1920).
- Share-based payment vs financial instrument (see 4.5.2030).
- Tax payments related to share-based payments (see 4.5.2070).

4.5.330   STEP 2: CLASSIFY SHARE-BASED PAYMENT

4.5.340   Principles of classification as either equity-settled or cash-settled

4.5.340.10   A share-based payment transaction that is in the scope of IFRS 2 is classified as either an equity-settled or a cash-settled share-based payment transaction. The accounting requirements for each type of transaction differ significantly; for accounting for equity-settled share-based payments, see 4.5.500, and for accounting for cash-settled share-based payments, see 4.5.910. The differences between equity-settled and cash-settled awards are illustrated in the worked example included in 4.5.1010. If the counterparty has a choice of settlement, then the transaction is accounted for in two components (see 4.5.1100).

4.5.340.20   An equity-settled share-based payment transaction is a share-based payment transaction in which the entity:

- receives goods or services in exchange for its own equity instruments; or
- receives goods or services but has no obligation to settle the transaction with the supplier. [*IFRS 2.A*]

4.5.340.30   A cash-settled share-based payment transaction is a share-based payment transaction in which the entity acquires goods or services in exchange for a liability to transfer cash or other assets to the supplier of those goods or services for amounts that are based on the price (or value) of equity instruments of the entity (or equity instruments of another entity in the same group). [*IFRS 2.A*]

4.5.340.40   Generally, the classification as cash- or equity-settled is based on the entity's obligation to the counterparty – i.e. whether the entity is or can be required to settle in equity instruments or settle in cash – and the entity's intended settlement method.

4.5.340.50   The classification of a share-based payment transaction is not affected by how an entity obtains the equity instruments that it will use to settle its obligations. For example, to settle an obligation to transfer shares to the counterparty, an entity may expect to buy its own shares in the market, either because it is prohibited from issuing new shares or because it wishes to avoid dilution. However, this expectation is not taken into consideration when assessing the classification of the share-based payment transaction. [*IFRS 2.B49*]

4.5.340.60   All terms and conditions of the arrangement are considered when determining whether a share-based payment transaction is equity-settled or cash-settled. For example, a share-based payment transaction in which the employees are granted the right to shares that are redeemable – e.g. shares that are redeemable on cessation of employment – at the employee's option is a cash-settled share-based payment arrangement because the arrangement may ultimately be settled in cash. For a discussion of redeemable shares, see 4.5.980. [*IFRS 2.31*]

4.5.340.70   Some share-based payment transactions contain a grant of equity instruments with a cash alternative. The cash alternative may be the result of a contingent event (see 4.5.2230) or be subject to a choice of one of the parties:
- if the entity has the choice of settlement, then classification generally depends on the entity's intention (see 4.5.1130); or
- if the counterparty has the choice of settlement, then classification as equity-settled is precluded (see 4.5.1100).

4.5.340.80   In other cases, the type of settlement depends on the occurrence of an event that neither party can control (see 4.5.2230).

4.5.340.90   Other classification issues in practice discussed in this chapter include the following.
- Grants of equity instruments 'to the value of' (see 4.5.2110).
- Arrangements to transfer value to the employees on settlement date (see 4.5.2130).
- Grants of equity instruments that include redemption features (see 4.5.2170).
- Arrangements denominated in a currency other than the issuing entity's functional currency (see 4.5.2250).

4.5.350   STEP 3: IDENTIFY AND UNDERSTAND ANY CONDITIONS

4.5.360   Determining type of condition

4.5.360.10   Conditions that determine whether the counterparty receives the share-based payment are separated into vesting conditions and non-vesting conditions. 'Vesting conditions' are all conditions that determine whether the entity receives the services that entitle the counterparty to the share-based payment, and may be differentiated further between service and performance conditions. 'Performance conditions' are either market conditions or non-market performance conditions. All other conditions are considered non-vesting conditions. [*IFRS 2.IG4A, IG24*]

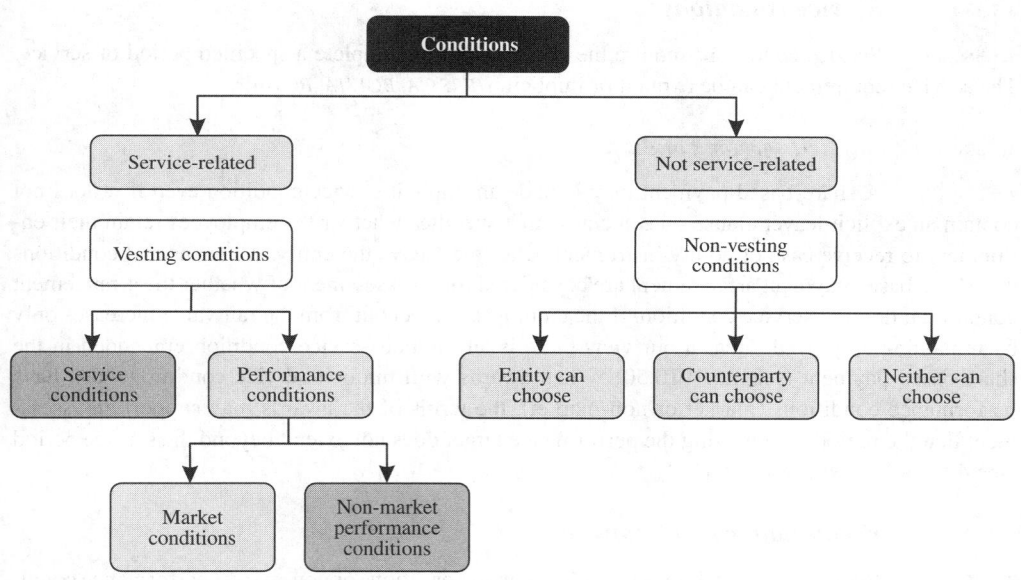

4.5.370   Vesting conditions

4.5.370.10   The definitions of 'vesting conditions' and 'market condition' in IFRS 2 were amended and the definitions of 'performance condition' and 'service condition' were added to IFRS 2 as part of the *Annual Improvements to IFRSs 2010–2012 Cycle*. These amendments are applied prospectively to share-based payment transactions for which grant date is on or after 1 July 2014 – i.e. they are currently effective requirements for entities with an annual reporting period ended on 31 December 2014. Earlier application is permitted.

4.5.370.20   For awards with a service condition (see 4.5.380), the amendments clarify that if the counterparty, regardless of the reason, ceases to provide service during the vesting period, then it has failed to satisfy the service condition. Therefore, if an employer terminates the services of an employee and prevents the required service from being provided, then such a termination is accounted for as a forfeiture. As a result of this amendment, the accounting policy choice discussed in 4.5.860.30–40 cannot be applied to share-based payment transactions for which grant date is on or after 1 July 2014.

4.5.370.30   The amendments also address circumstances in which an award is conditional on both a service condition and a specified performance target. They clarify that the specified performance target must be met while the counterparty is rendering services – i.e. the performance target is a performance (vesting) condition only if the performance assessment period coincides with the service period. Specifically, the period of achieving the performance target cannot extend beyond the end of the service period but may start before the service period, provided that the commencement date of the performance target is not substantially before the service commencement date. For further discussion of the period for achieving a performance target and the impact on whether the condition is a performance (vesting) or non-vesting condition, see 4.5.430.

4.5.380   *Service conditions*

4.5.380.10   Service conditions require the counterparty to complete a specified period of service. The service requirement can be explicit or implicit. [*IFRS 2.A, BC171A, BC346*]

4.5.390   *Implicit service conditions*

4.5.390.10   A share-based payment may include an implicit service condition even if it does not contain an explicit leaver clause – i.e. a clause that specifies whether the employees retain their entitlement to receive cash or equity instruments after they leave the entity. All terms and conditions of a share-based payment arrangement are considered for an assessment of whether the arrangement contains an implicit service condition. If the employee can benefit from the fair value increases only by remaining employed, then in our view there is an implicit service condition embedded in the share-based payment (see 4.5.1910.50). When awards with implicit service conditions also have performance conditions (market or non-market), the terms of the awards may support an assessment that the period of achieving the performance target does not extend beyond the service period (see 4.5.430). [*IFRS 2.A, BC346*]

4.5.400   *Performance conditions*

4.5.400.10   Performance conditions are either market conditions or non-market performance conditions that require the counterparty to:
- complete a specified period of service – i.e. a service condition, which can be either explicit or implicit (see 4.5.380); and
- meet specified performance targets while the counterparty is rendering the services. [*IFRS 2.A*]

4.5.400.20   The performance target in a market condition relates to the share price of the equity instruments of the entity or the equity instruments of another entity in the same group. [*IFRS 2.A*]

4.5.400.30   The performance target in a non-market performance condition relates to operations or activities of the entity itself or another entity in the same group – i.e. it is not related to the share price of the equity instruments of the entity (or the equity instruments of another entity in the same group). [*IFRS 2.A*]

4.5.410   *Market conditions*

4.5.410.10   'Market conditions' are conditions under which the vesting or exercisability of an equity instrument is related to the market price (or value) of the entity's equity instruments (or the equity instruments of another entity in the same group). Examples of market conditions include the following:

- attaining a specified share price;
- achieving a specified target that is based on the market price (or value) of the entity's equity instruments (or the equity instruments of another entity in the same group) relative to a stock-exchange index or an index of market prices of equity instruments of other entities; and
- achieving a specific share price or total shareholder return, measured based on the share price of an entity as adjusted for the reinvestment of dividends, or based on the share price of an entity relative to a stock-exchange index. [*IFRS 2.A*]

4.5.420   *Non-market performance conditions*

4.5.420.10   'Non-market performance conditions' are conditions under which vesting or exercisability of an equity instrument is related to specific performance targets associated with an entity's own operations or activities, or the operations or activities of another entity in the same group – e.g. a specified increase in profit or an EPS target. As such, non-market performance conditions are unrelated to the market price of the entity's equity instruments (or the equity instruments of another entity in the same group). [*IFRS 2.A*]

4.5.430   *Period of achieving performance target*

4.5.430.10   An award can require the counterparty to meet a performance target (market or non-market) in addition to a service condition, with a performance assessment period shorter or longer than the service period. Before the amendments introduced to IFRS 2 by the *Annual Improvements to IFRSs 2010–2012 Cycle,* it was not clear how the duration of a performance target should interact with the duration of the related service condition. The amendments confirmed that, in order for the target to be a vesting condition, the period of achieving the performance target:

- cannot extend beyond the end of the service period – inclusive of any implicit service period as discussed in 4.5.380; but
- may start before the service period on the condition that the commencement date of the performance target is not substantially before the commencement of the service period. [*IFRS 2.A*]

4.5.430.20   As such, the performance target is a performance (vesting) condition if the performance assessment period satisfies the requirements in 4.5.430.10. The performance target is a non-vesting condition if the performance assessment period extends beyond the end of the service period. This is because in the latter case the performance target does not determine whether the entity receives the services that entitle the counterparty to receive the share-based payment: the employee can leave the entity without losing entitlement to the award once the required service period has passed. For further discussion of this issue in the context of an initial public offering (IPO) or other exit event as either a vesting condition or for exercisability, see 4.5.460.

EXAMPLE 2A – PERIOD OF ACHIEVING PERFORMANCE TARGET – VESTING CONDITION (1)

4.5.430.30   Company S issued a share-based payment to its employees on 1 January 2018, subject to the conditions that the employees remain in service for two years and that S achieves a cumulative revenue target of 10,000 over those two years.

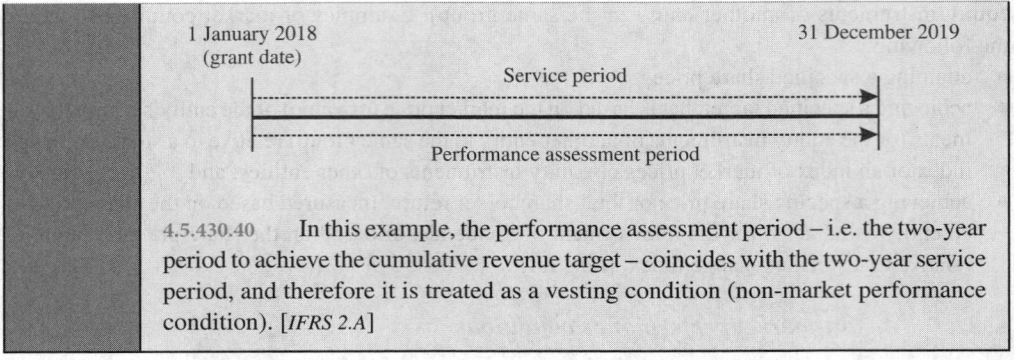

4.5.430.40 In this example, the performance assessment period – i.e. the two-year period to achieve the cumulative revenue target – coincides with the two-year service period, and therefore it is treated as a vesting condition (non-market performance condition). [*IFRS 2.A*]

EXAMPLE 2B – PERIOD OF ACHIEVING PERFORMANCE TARGET – VESTING CONDITION (2)

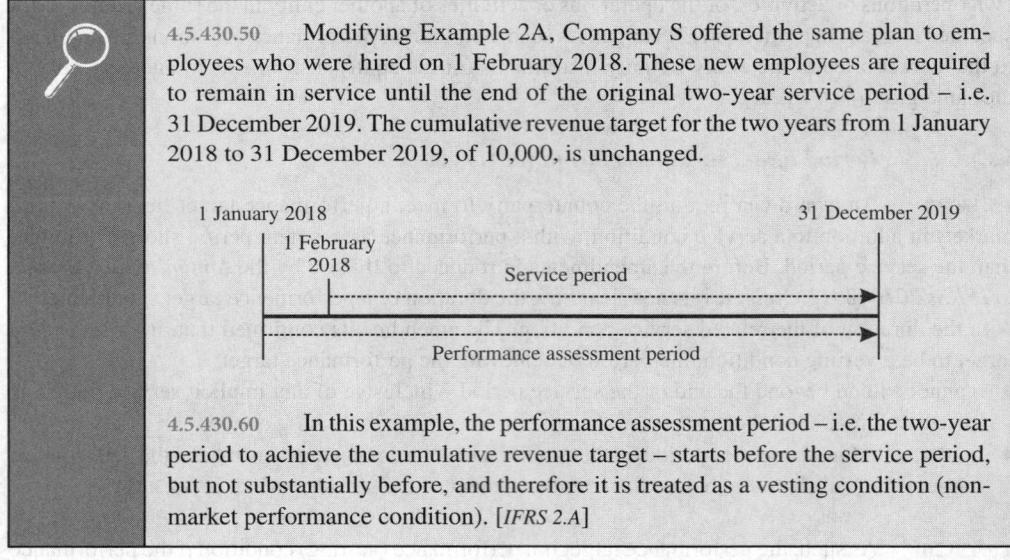

4.5.430.50 Modifying Example 2A, Company S offered the same plan to employees who were hired on 1 February 2018. These new employees are required to remain in service until the end of the original two-year service period – i.e. 31 December 2019. The cumulative revenue target for the two years from 1 January 2018 to 31 December 2019, of 10,000, is unchanged.

4.5.430.60 In this example, the performance assessment period – i.e. the two-year period to achieve the cumulative revenue target – starts before the service period, but not substantially before, and therefore it is treated as a vesting condition (non-market performance condition). [*IFRS 2.A*]

EXAMPLE 2C – PERIOD OF ACHIEVING PERFORMANCE TARGET – NON-VESTING CONDITION

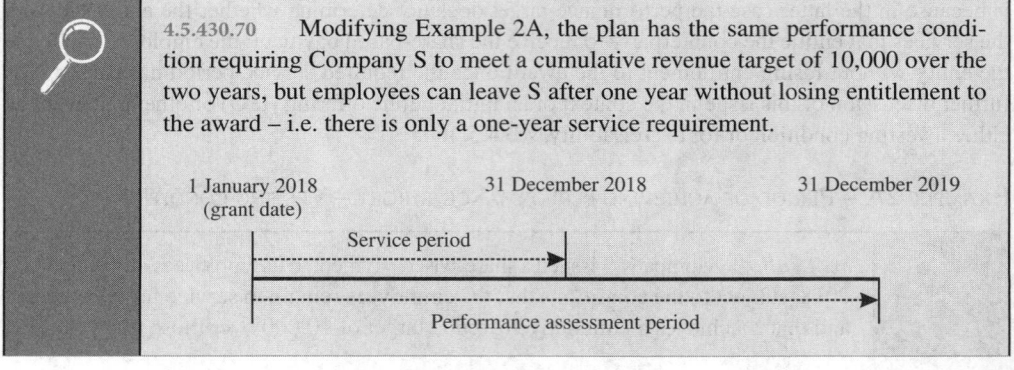

4.5.430.70 Modifying Example 2A, the plan has the same performance condition requiring Company S to meet a cumulative revenue target of 10,000 over the two years, but employees can leave S after one year without losing entitlement to the award – i.e. there is only a one-year service requirement.

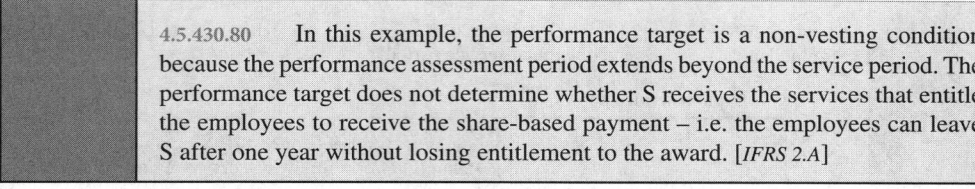

4.5.430.80   In this example, the performance target is a non-vesting condition because the performance assessment period extends beyond the service period. The performance target does not determine whether S receives the services that entitle the employees to receive the share-based payment – i.e. the employees can leave S after one year without losing entitlement to the award. [*IFRS 2.A*]

4.5.430.90   For a discussion of the impact of vesting conditions on the recognition and measurement of share-based payments, see 4.5.540.

4.5.440   Non-vesting conditions

4.5.440.10   The term 'non-vesting condition' is not explicitly defined in IFRS 2 but is inferred to be any condition that does not meet the definition of a vesting condition. [*IFRS 2.BC364*]

4.5.440.20   However, the standard does illustrate three types of non-vesting conditions that:
- the entity can choose to meet – e.g. continuation of the plan by the entity;
- the counterparty can choose to meet – e.g. participation in a share purchase programme by paying monthly contributions or transfer restrictions after vesting; or
- neither the entity nor the counterparty can choose to meet – e.g. an award can be exercised only when the price of gold does not exceed a specified price. [*IFRS 2.BC171B, IG24*]

4.5.440.30   Additionally, as discussed in Example 2C, a performance condition is a non-vesting condition if the performance assessment period extends beyond the service period. [*IFRS 2.A*]

4.5.440.40   For a discussion of the impact of non-vesting conditions on the recognition and measurement of share-based payments, see 4.5.550.

4.5.450   Classification of conditions in practice

4.5.460   *Requirement for IPO or other exit event*

4.5.460.10   Sometimes an award requires an IPO or other exit event – e.g. sale of the business – either as a vesting condition or for exercisability. For example, unlisted entities that are planning a listing in the future may issue a share-based payment that is conditional on a successful IPO.

4.5.460.20   The requirement for an exit event affects share-based payments in different ways depending on the timing of the condition. If the condition applies after the counterparty has become entitled to the share-based payment, then it is a non-vesting condition. If the condition is required to occur during the service period, then it is a non-market performance condition (see 4.5.430). [*IFRS 2.IG.Ex2*]

EXAMPLE 3A – IPO – NON-VESTING CONDITION

4.5.460.30   Company U granted a share option to an employee on 1 January 2018, subject to a three-year service condition. The option is exercisable only if an IPO occurs within the four years following the service period. If the employee leaves U after the service period but before the IPO, then the employee retains the option. There is no minimum IPO price required (see 4.5.460.80).

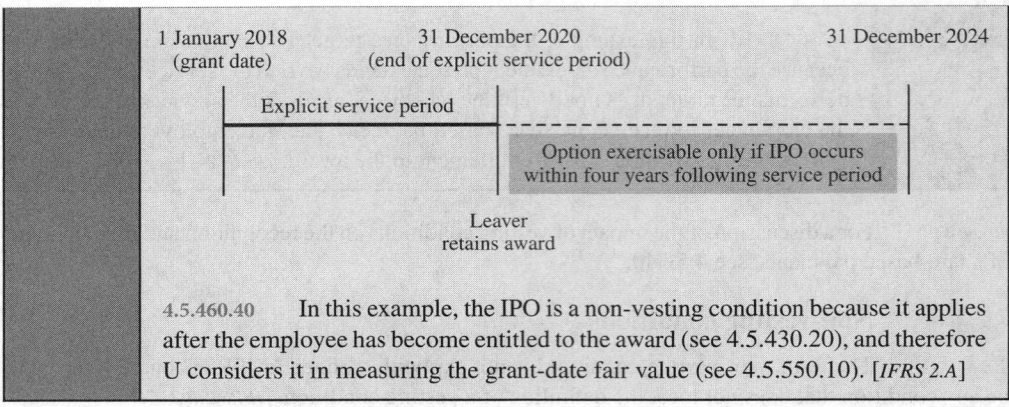

1 January 2018 (grant date) | 31 December 2020 (end of explicit service period) | 31 December 2024

Explicit service period

Option exercisable only if IPO occurs within four years following service period

Leaver
retains award

4.5.460.40   In this example, the IPO is a non-vesting condition because it applies after the employee has become entitled to the award (see 4.5.430.20), and therefore U considers it in measuring the grant-date fair value (see 4.5.550.10). [*IFRS 2.A*]

EXAMPLE 3B – IPO – NON-MARKET PERFORMANCE CONDITION

4.5.460.50   Modifying Example 3A, if the employee leaves Company U after the service period but before the IPO, then the employee is required to surrender the 'vested award' (or to sell it back at a nominal amount). In this case, the exit condition is in substance a vesting condition. Although the explicit service period is only three years, there is an implicit service period that runs until the exit event – i.e. the IPO – occurs. This is because if the IPO occurs after the explicit three-year period, the employee is entitled to the award only if the employee is still in service when the IPO occurs. [*IFRS 2.A*]

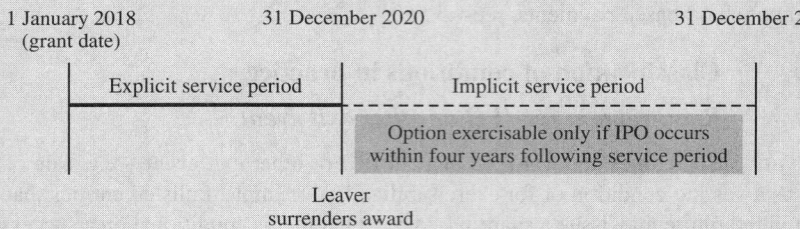

1 January 2018 (grant date) | 31 December 2020 | 31 December 2024

Explicit service period | Implicit service period

Option exercisable only if IPO occurs within four years following service period

Leaver
surrenders award

4.5.460.60   In this example, the IPO is a non-market performance condition because it is required to occur during the service period and there is no minimum IPO price (see 4.5.460.80). [*IFRS 2.A*]

4.5.460.70   U accounts for this arrangement as a grant with a variable vesting period (see 4.5.700) depending on a non-market performance condition. Because the IPO has no minimum price and therefore is not a market condition (see 4.5.460.80), U does not consider it in measuring the grant-date fair value; instead, it recognises the cost over the expected vesting period with true-up for the actual vesting period and the actual number of equity instruments granted. However, because the expected IPO condition influences the length of the estimated vesting period, it might affect inputs in measuring the grant-date fair value – e.g. the interest rate.

4.5.460.80   If there is a minimum price for the exit event, then it is unclear whether there is just one market condition – because the pricing is considered integral to the exit event – or one non-market performance condition (the occurrence of an IPO) and one market condition (reaching the minimum price). In our view, determining which approach is appropriate depends on the facts and circumstances of the transaction. We believe that it is appropriate to consider that an award has two separate conditions only if the non-market condition is substantive as a separate condition – e.g. it is possible that the entity would pursue an exit event even at a lower price. If this is not the case, then we believe that the award should be viewed as having only one integrated market condition.

4.5.470   *Cap in exercisability*

4.5.470.10   The exercisability of a share-based payment may be limited by a cap – e.g. the intrinsic value of the options exercised cannot exceed a certain percentage of an employee's annual salary. Such a condition may be structured as a limit on exercisability, but in substance it may be a vesting condition if it imposes further performance targets to receive the share-based payment.

4.5.470.20   In our view, if the cap reduces the number of exercisable options when the share price increases, then the cap meets the definition of a market condition rather than a non-vesting condition. This is because it is a condition on which the exercise price, vesting or exercisability of an equity instrument depends that is related to the market price of the equity instrument, even though market conditions are usually designed to reward, rather than penalise, increases in share price. [*IFRS 2.A*]

EXAMPLE 4 – SHARE-BASED PAYMENT WITH EXERCISE CAP

4.5.470.30   Company N grants an employee 1,000 share options with an exercise price of 10 per option. The employee may exercise the options at the end of the year subject to a service condition and a cap that depends on the employee's salary and the profit realised per option. The objective of the cap is to ensure that the intrinsic value on exercise does not exceed the employee's annual salary. Therefore, if the share price at exercise date is 60 and the employee's salary is 10,000, then the cap limits the number of exercisable options to 200 (10,000 salary divided by a profit of 50 per option) and the remaining options lapse.

4.5.470.40   In this example, we believe that the cap meets the definition of a market condition rather than a non-vesting condition, because the share price affects the number of options that can be exercised and potentially results in a number of options lapsing.

4.5.480   STEP 4: RECOGNISE AND MEASURE SHARE-BASED PAYMENT

4.5.490   Transaction with employee vs non-employee

4.5.490.10   Employees and others providing similar services are defined as individuals who render personal services to the entity and either:

- are regarded as employees for legal or tax purposes;

- work for the entity under its direction in the same way as individuals who are regarded as employees for legal or tax purposes; or
- render services similar to those rendered by employees. [*IFRS 2.A*]

4.5.490.20   The term 'employee' encompasses all management personnel – i.e. those persons having authority and responsibility for planning, directing and controlling the activities of the entity, including non-executive directors. [*IFRS 2.A*]

4.5.490.30   The requirements for transactions with employees are also applied to transactions with individuals who may not be employees, but who provide personal services similar to services provided by an employee. [*IFRS 2.11, A*]

4.5.490.40   Share-based payments with employees are classified as either:
- equity-settled transactions (see 4.5.500);
- cash-settled transactions (see 4.5.910); or
- employee transactions with a choice of settlement (see 4.5.1080).

4.5.490.50   For further discussion of the definition of non-employees and equity-settled and cash-settled share-based payments with non-employees, see 4.5.1800.

4.5.500   EQUITY-SETTLED TRANSACTIONS WITH EMPLOYEES

4.5.510   Basic principles of accounting for equity-settled share-based payment transactions with employees

	BASIC PRINCIPLES OF EQUITY-SETTLED TRANSACTIONS WITH EMPLOYEES	KEY STEPS
Recognition	Entity recognises a cost (expense or asset) over the vesting period and a corresponding entry to equity.	Determine the vesting period (see 4.5.520).
Measurement	Measurement is based on the grant-date fair value of the equity instruments granted.	Determine grant date (see 4.5.530) and the grant-date fair value (see 4.5.540).
Impact of conditions	Market and non-vesting conditions are reflected in the initial measurement of fair value, with no subsequent true-up if the conditions are not satisfied. An estimate is made for the number of equity instruments for which service and non-market performance conditions are expected to be satisfied, with a true-up to the number ultimately satisfied.	Apply the modified grant-date method (see 4.5.540).

4.5.510.10   For a worked example that illustrates the application of the key requirements on the recognition and measurement of equity-settled share-based payments, see 4.5.1010.

4.5.520   *Determine vesting period*

4.5.520.10   A 'vesting period' is the period over which all of the specified vesting conditions of a share-based payment arrangement are to be satisfied. [*IFRS 2.A*]

4.5.520.20   If the employee is not required to satisfy a specified vesting condition before becoming unconditionally entitled to the instruments granted, then the equity instruments vest immediately. Therefore, there is a presumption that the services rendered as consideration for these instruments have been received and the fair value of these instruments is recognised immediately with a corresponding increase in equity. [*IFRS 2.14*]

4.5.520.30   If the equity instruments do not vest until the employee completes a period of service, then the entity presumes that services are to be provided in the future. The entity accounts for the services as they are received during the vesting period. [*IFRS 2.15, IG.Ex1A–Ex2, IG.Ex5–Ex6*]

4.5.520.40   The costs are recognised over the vesting period, under the straight-line method for those equity instruments granted that are recognised following the modified grant-date method (see 4.5.540). [*IFRS 2.IG.Ex1A*]

4.5.520.50   For further discussion of how to determine the vesting period, see 4.5.660.

4.5.530   *Determine grant date*

4.5.530.10   Determining grant date is an important step because this is the date at which the fair value of the equity instruments is measured. For further discussion of how to determine grant date, see 4.5.570.

4.5.540   *Modified grant-date method*

4.5.540.10   The modified grant-date method is used to measure equity-settled share-based payment transactions. Under this method, the fair value of the equity instruments is measured at grant date, with some true-up for instruments that do not vest (commonly known as 'forfeiture'). [*IFRS 2.19–20, IG9*]

4.5.540.20   Equity-settled transactions are not remeasured subsequent to grant date for fair value changes, unlike cash-settled share-based payments (see 4.5.910).

4.5.540.30   The modified grant-date method requires entities to distinguish between the following types of conditions:
- vesting conditions:
  - service conditions; and
  - performance conditions:
    - market conditions; and
    - non-market performance conditions; and
- non-vesting conditions. [*IFRS 2.A, 19–21A, IG9*]

4.5.540.40   For further discussion of the definition and classification of conditions, see 4.5.350.

4.5.540.50 Market conditions are reflected as an adjustment (discount) to the initial estimate of fair value at grant date of the instrument to be received and there is no true-up for differences between estimated and actual vesting due to market conditions. The same applies to non-vesting conditions, which are discussed in more detail in 4.5.550. [*IFRS 2.21, IG24*]

4.5.540.60 The impact of service conditions and non-market performance conditions on vesting is estimated at grant date, but it is not reflected in the grant-date fair value itself. Instead, the accounting for the share-based payment is based on the number of equity instruments for which the service and non-market performance conditions are expected to be met. Subsequently, these estimates are trued up for differences between the number of instruments expected to vest and the actual number of instruments vested. There is no true-up for options that are forfeited because they vest but are not exercised. [*IFRS 2.20, IG24*]

4.5.540.70 The following flowchart provides a simplified overview of the treatment of different types of conditions in the modified grant-date method.

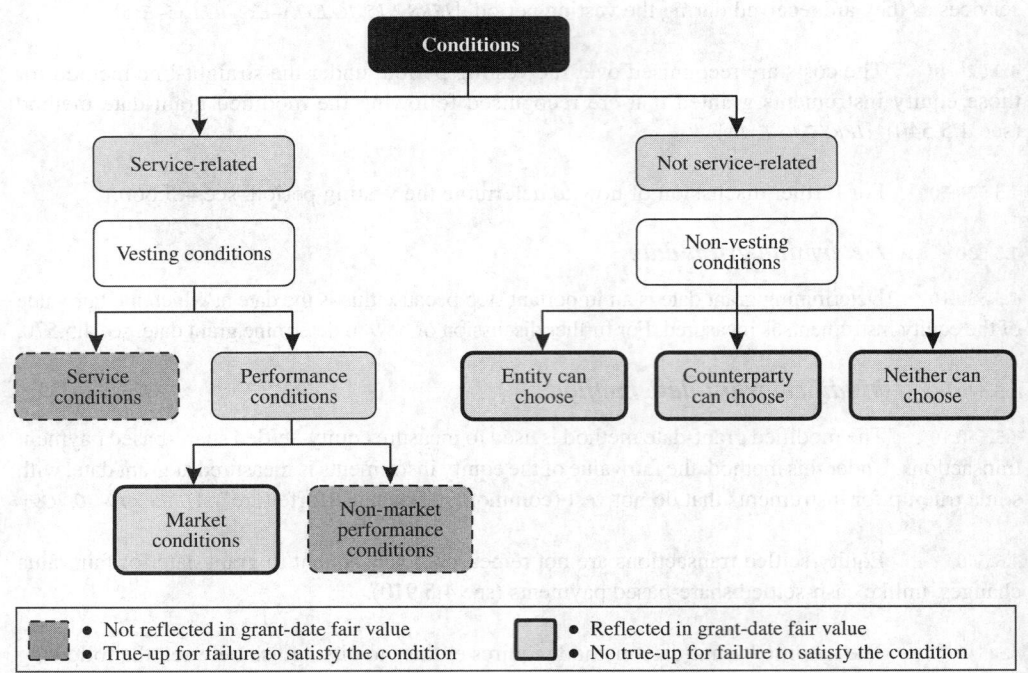

4.5.550 *Non-vesting conditions*

4.5.550.10 Like market conditions, non-vesting conditions (see 4.5.440) are reflected in measuring the grant-date fair value of the share-based payment and there is no true-up for differences between the expected and actual outcome of non-vesting conditions. Therefore, if all service and non-market performance conditions are met, then the entity will recognise the share-based payment cost even if the employee does not receive the share-based payment because of a failure to meet a non-vesting condition. [*IFRS 2.21A, IG24*]

4.5.550.20   If either the entity or the employee can choose whether to meet a non-vesting condition and one chooses not to do so during the vesting period, then such a failure to meet the condition is treated as a cancellation. Under cancellation accounting, the amount of the cost that would otherwise have been recognised over the remainder of the vesting period is recognised immediately, generally in profit or loss (see 4.5.1390.10). [*IFRS 2.28(a), 28A*]

EXAMPLE 5 – CHOOSING NOT TO MEET NON-VESTING CONDITION

4.5.550.30   When an employee stops contributing to an ESPP by monthly deductions from salary – i.e. the counterparty chooses not to meet a non-vesting condition – the unrecognised amount of the grant-date fair value of the equity instruments granted is recognised immediately. For a discussion of whether a plan is an ESPP or an option plan, see 4.5.2260.

4.5.550.40   If neither the entity nor the employee can choose whether to meet a non-vesting condition, then there is no change to the recognition if the non-vesting condition is not satisfied during the vesting period. The entity continues to recognise the cost over the vesting period. [*IFRS 2.21A, IG24*]

4.5.560   *Intrinsic value*

4.5.560.10   In rare circumstances, if the fair value of the equity instruments cannot be measured reliably, then an intrinsic value method is applied. The intrinsic value is remeasured at each reporting date and changes are recognised in profit or loss (to the extent that the cost is not eligible for capitalisation) until the instrument is settled – e.g. until the options are exercised. Example 10 in the implementation guidance to IFRS 2 provides an illustration of the intrinsic value method. [*IFRS 2.24–25, IG16*]

4.5.560.20   In our view, uncertainty about the future market price is not a reason for not being able to measure the fair value reliably. For example, in an ESPP in which employees pay a monthly contribution of 100 to buy shares at the end of the year at a discount of 20 percent of the then-current market price, there is uncertainty at grant date about what the future market price of those shares will be and accordingly how many shares the employees will be entitled to buy. However, this is not sufficient reason to conclude that the grant-date fair value cannot be measured reliably. For a discussion of the rare circumstances in which application of the intrinsic value method may be required, see 4.5.750.10.

4.5.570   **Determination of grant date**

4.5.570.10   The determination of grant date is important because this is the date on which the fair value of equity instruments granted is measured. Usually, grant date is also the date on which recognition of the employee services received begins. However, this is not always the case (see 4.5.670.20). [*IFRS 2.11*]

4.5.570.20   'Grant date' is the date at which the entity and the employee agree to a share-based payment arrangement, and requires that the entity and the employee have a shared understanding of the terms and conditions of the arrangement. [*IFRS 2.A*]

4.5.570.30   In order for the employer and the employee to 'agree' to a share-based payment transaction, there needs to be both an offer and an acceptance of that offer. [*IFRS 2.IG2*]

4.5.580   **Grant-date flowchart**

4.5.580.10   The determination of the grant date of a share-based payment that requires substantive approval can be illustrated as follows.

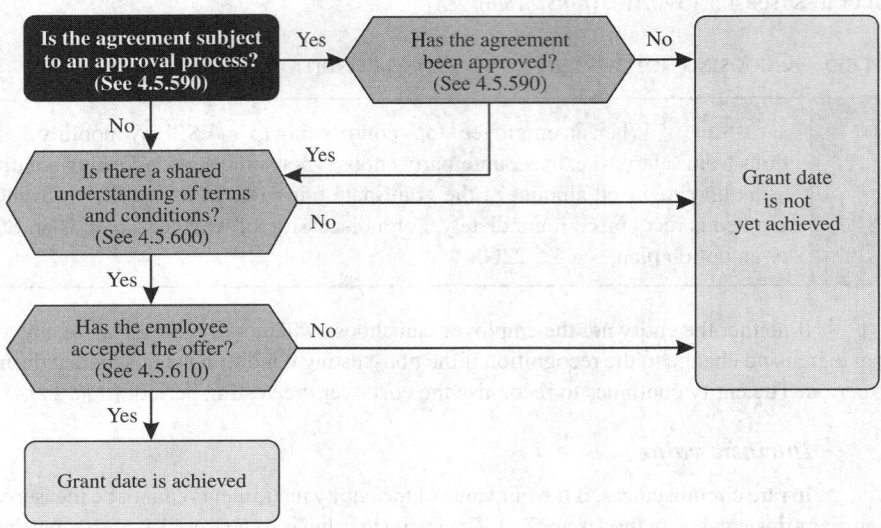

4.5.590   *Approval and communication by employer*

4.5.590.10   If the agreement is subject to an approval process, then grant date cannot be before the date on which that approval is obtained. If a grant is made subject to approval – e.g. by a board of directors – then grant date is normally when that approval is obtained. [*IFRS 2.A, IG1*]

4.5.590.20   In a broad-based unilateral grant of a share-based payment, there is often a period of time between board approval and communication of the terms of the award to individual employees. In some entities, the terms and conditions of the awards are communicated to each employee by their direct supervisor. Because of the varying schedules of employees and employers, it is possible that different employees may be informed of their awards on different dates. In some circumstances, the number and geographic dispersion of employees results in communication spanning several days or weeks. As a result, awards approved at a single board meeting may be subject to several different grant dates. However, using a single grant date for the purpose of valuing share-based payment transactions with the same terms that are granted at approximately the same date may not result in a material difference from the aggregate fair value that would otherwise be determined on grant date of each individual award.

EXAMPLE 6 – APPROVAL AND COMMUNICATION BY EMPLOYER

4.5.590.30   Each year on the first day of the year, multinational Company X issues share options to all employees who were employed by X for the three months before the end of the previous year. The number of options that each employee receives is based on their employee class and is a set amount each year. The exercise price of the share options is always 10% less than the market price on the day that the share plan is approved by the board, which is on the first day of the year. X's human resources policy requires that remuneration information be communicated to employees by their immediate superiors. Once the share plan has been approved by the board, the immediate superior of each employee is responsible for communicating the grant to the employee. On the day after the share plan was approved, X placed information regarding the share plan on the employee website.

4.5.590.40   We believe that grant date is the board approval date because the award is unilateral, communication to employees is purely administrative and soon after the board meeting X issues an entity-wide communication regarding the grant of the award, including the specific terms and conditions.

4.5.600   *Meaning of 'shared understanding'*

4.5.600.10   A shared understanding may not require the finalisation of all terms and conditions. For example, an offer may not specify the actual exercise price, but instead may state the formula that determines how the actual exercise price will be established. In our view, if the outcome is based on *objective* factors and different knowledgeable parties, independently of each other, would be able to make consistent calculations, then there is a shared understanding without having specified the actual grant terms. If, for example, the exercise price is based on the market price at a specified later date but the outcome of all other factors is already known, then there is a shared understanding at the date of the agreement of the way in which the exercise price will be determined. [*IFRS 2.A, IU 05-06*]

4.5.600.20   In our view, there will generally not be agreement on terms and conditions if the outcome is based primarily on *subjective* factors – e.g. if the number of shares to be awarded is a discretionary determination of a compensation committee at the end of the service period. Similarly, if the number of instruments issued to employees is determined based primarily on a *subjective* evaluation of the individual's performance over a period, then we believe that there is not a shared understanding until the number of instruments has been determined. The assessment of whether the evaluation of an individual's performance is primarily subjective may be difficult and requires judgement.

4.5.610   *Acceptance by employee*

4.5.610.10   Grant date is not reached until there is acceptance of the offer. The acceptance may be explicit (e.g. by signing a contract) or implicit (e.g. by commencing to render services). [*IFRS 2.IG2*]

EXAMPLE 7 – ACCEPTANCE BY EMPLOYEE

4.5.610.20   Company Q establishes a three-year share-based payment arrangement in which an employee is required to specify a monthly deduction percentage from their salary for buying shares at the then-current fair value (participation shares). For each participation share, the employee will receive an additional free share (matching share). Employees can state their monthly deduction in January 2018 for the entire three-year period – i.e. January 2018 to December 2020. An employee is required to make an explicit annual statement in January of each year in which they confirm the deduction percentage or amount. New joiners to the company can participate in the plan from the beginning of the next calendar year. The employee also has the right to reduce the monthly deductions at any time. If, for example, an employee stops the deductions from May 2018 onwards, then they will not lose entitlement to the matching shares previously received. Although the employee cannot increase the deduction amount subsequently during 2018, they can rejoin in January 2019 or January 2020 by stating a new monthly deduction percentage.

4.5.610.30   In this example, we believe that the statement of the deduction or investment amount is a required explicit acceptance. Therefore, grant date for the share-based payment of the matching shares could not be earlier than January each year because it is the date on which both parties agree to the arrangement.

4.5.610.40   In our view, 1 January each year is a new grant date because employees may increase or decrease their contributions and new employees are permitted to join at that date. In our view, in this example there is only one grant date per year because we believe that an ability to reduce, but not increase, contributions does not create new acceptance at each monthly purchase date of participation shares. This is because the absence of a reduction is not an implicit acceptance, and an explicit acceptance has already been made. We believe that the ability to reduce or stop deductions entirely is a cancellation right rather than an indication of a separate grant date because it is a one-directional change. If a reduction does take place, then that would be accounted for as a cancellation, which accelerates recognition of the related cost.

4.5.620   *Discretion clauses*

4.5.620.10   Some share-based payment arrangements may provide a remuneration committee (or an equivalent body) with differing degrees of discretion to amend the terms of awards. If a share-based payment arrangement contains a 'discretion clause', then it is necessary to consider the impact of the discretion clause:
- on the determination of grant date of the share-based payment (see 4.5.570); and
- whether modification accounting should be applied if discretion is exercised after grant date.

4.5.620.20   In our view, if the terms of a share-based payment arrangement provide the remuneration committee with discretion to amend the terms of an award, then a determination of whether there is a shared understanding with employees should be based on an analysis of the degree of subjectivity (i.e. discretion) afforded to the remuneration committee, as well as the factors over which the remuneration committee has discretion.

4.5.620.30   We believe that arrangements with discretion clauses should be categorised into the three categories in 4.5.630–650, depending on the degree of discretion available to the remuneration committee.

4.5.630   *Category 1: No delay to grant date, no modification*

4.5.630.10   Arrangements may contain clauses that are largely objective such that these may give little, if any, discretion to either the employee or the remuneration committee. In our view, such clauses that are largely objective do not result in a delay in grant date. We believe that subsequently invoking the clause does not result in modification accounting, if the changes are for predetermined adjustments (see 4.5.1290.20). We believe that adjustments made under a discretion clause are 'predetermined' if the following conditions are met:

- the arrangement clearly states the objective, method or outcome of the clause;
- both parties have a shared understanding of the clause at grant date; and
- the clause is invoked following a specified event.

4.5.630.20   Examples of predetermined adjustments are changes in the exercise price of options to reflect changes in capital structures, such as share splits or the recalculation of performance requirements. We believe that, in limited circumstances, a constructive obligation may exist if an entity, by its past practice or sufficiently specific communication to its employees, has created a valid expectation in the employees that it will exercise the discretion clause (see 3.12.60).

EXAMPLE 8 – CATEGORY 1 DISCRETION CLAUSE

4.5.630.30   Company B grants share options to its employees. The agreement contains an anti-dilution clause requiring B to restore the fair value of the employees' award following a change in the capital structure. B has discretion over the mechanism of restoring the fair value – e.g. by issuing additional share options or by lowering the exercise price. Both B and its employees have a shared understanding of the terms of the anti-dilution provision at grant date.

4.5.630.40   We believe that the anti-dilution provision in this example should be treated as a Category 1 discretion clause because the changes to the award are predetermined. In this case, both the event requiring the clause to be invoked and the objective of the clause are clearly defined in the agreement – i.e. B is required to invoke the clause to restore the fair value of the employees' award following a change in the capital structure.

4.5.630.50   However, if the fair value of the award increases rather than stays the same before and after changes in the capital structure, then B would treat this as a modification and recognise additional compensation cost (see 4.5.1230).

4.5.640   *Category 2: No delay to grant date, modification*

4.5.640.10   If the discretion clause does not result in a delay to grant date, then it is necessary to consider whether invoking the clause results in modification accounting (see 4.5.1190). In our view, modification accounting should be applied if a discretion clause is invoked and results in changes other than predetermined adjustments.

EXAMPLE 9 – CATEGORY 2 DISCRETION CLAUSE

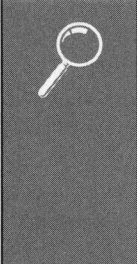

4.5.640.20   Company C grants share options to its employees. The agreement contains a discretionary anti-dilution clause that gives C discretion over whether to make an equitable adjustment to the employees' award following a change in capital structure.

4.5.640.30   We believe that the anti-dilution clause in this example should be treated as a Category 2 discretion clause, because the changes to the award are not predetermined. In this example, C has discretion over whether to invoke the clause.

4.5.640.40   When an entity exercises its discretion and modifies awards in conjunction with an equity restructuring, in our experience this often results in significant incremental compensation. This incremental compensation is measured as the difference between the fair value of the pre-modified award – considering how the equity restructuring would have affected the fair value of the award had it not been modified – and the fair value of the post-modified award. For further discussion of modification accounting, see 4.5.1190.

4.5.650   *Category 3: Delayed grant date*

4.5.650.10   If the discretion clause provides the remuneration committee with significant subjectivity such that there is no shared understanding of the terms and conditions before finalisation of the award, then grant date is not achieved until the period for exercising the discretion has passed. In our view, clauses that would be invoked only 'with cause' or in exceptional circumstances would not generally delay grant date. For example, a clause that is intended to be invoked with cause may be in relation to a specific employee action or an event that was not anticipated when the original performance condition was set, such as adjusting a revenue performance condition on the disposal of a significant business unit.

4.5.650.20   If an entity has the discretion to reduce or eliminate an award, then we believe that this would delay grant date. However, this does not result in delaying recognition of the share-based payment cost (see 4.5.670.20).

4.5.660   Determination of vesting period

4.5.670   *Service commencement date and grant date*

4.5.670.10   The 'vesting period' is the period during which all of the specified vesting conditions are to be satisfied in order for the employees to be entitled unconditionally to the equity instrument. Normally this is the period between grant date and vesting date. [*IFRS 2.A*]

4.5.670.20   However, services are recognised when they are received and grant date may occur after the employees have begun rendering services. Grant date is a measurement date only. If grant date occurs *after* the service commencement date, then the entity estimates the grant-date fair value of the equity instruments for the purpose of recognising the services from service commencement date until grant date. A possible method of estimating the fair value of the equity instruments is by assuming that grant date is at the reporting date. Once grant date has been established, the entity revises the earlier estimates so that the amounts recognised for services received are based on the grant-date fair value of the equity instruments. In our view, this revision should be treated as a change in estimate (see 2.8.110). [*IFRS 2.IG4*]

4.5.680 *Graded vesting*

4.5.680.10   In some situations, the equity instruments granted vest in instalments over the specified vesting period. Assuming that the only vesting condition is service from grant date to vesting date of each tranche, then each instalment is accounted for as a separate share-based payment. As a result, even though all grants are measured at the same grant date, there will be several fair values and the total cost recognised each period will be different, because both the grant-date fair values and the vesting periods are different. In our experience, instalments are not always on a yearly basis, but can also be on a monthly or even daily basis, which creates significantly more data complexities. [*IFRS 2.IG11*]

4.5.680.20   Application of the graded vesting method to grants that vest in instalments results in the recognition of a higher proportion of cost in the early years of the overall plan. This is because year 1 would bear the full cost for the instalment vesting in year 1 *and* a proportion of the cost of the instalment vesting over the next number of years – e.g. one-half of the year two instalment, one-third of the year three instalment etc. This effect is sometimes referred to as 'front-end loading'.

4.5.690 *Attribution to periods*

4.5.690.10   When allocating the cost of share-based payment awards that require the achievement of both service and performance conditions (see 4.5.380 and 400), in our view generally no greater significance should be placed on either the service or the performance condition; and the share-based payment cost should be recognised on a straight-line basis over the vesting period. Similar to the observation that it is not generally possible to identify the services received in respect of the individual components of an employee's remuneration package – e.g. services received in respect of healthcare benefits vs a company car vs share-based payment arrangements – it is very difficult to determine whether more services were received in respect of any given performance period as compared with the service period. [*IFRS 2.15, BC38*]

EXAMPLE 10 – IDENTIFYING ATTRIBUTION PERIOD

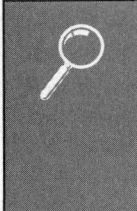

4.5.690.20   Company S issues to its employees share options that vest on the achievement of an EPS target after one year. In addition, the employee must remain employed with S for another two years after the EPS target is achieved. We believe that S should recognise the share-based payment cost on a straight-line basis over the three-year period in the absence of compelling evidence that a different recognition pattern is appropriate.

4.5.690.30   We believe that even if a grant is subject to a three-year service condition and a challenging one-year performance condition, both beginning at the same time – e.g. an increase in revenues of 20 percent while revenues have not increased by more than 10 percent over the last five years – this is not sufficiently compelling evidence to apply a method other than the straight-line method over three years.

4.5.700   *Variable vesting period*

4.5.700.10   In some share-based payments, the length of the vesting period varies depending on when a performance condition is satisfied. In this case, the length of the expected vesting period needs to be estimated. [*IFRS 2.15(b)*]

4.5.710   *Market condition with variable vesting period*

4.5.710.10   If the performance condition in such transactions is a market condition, then the length of the expected vesting period is estimated consistent with the assumptions used in estimating the grant-date fair value of the equity instruments granted. The length of the vesting period is not revised subsequently. [*IFRS 2.IG.Ex6*]

EXAMPLE 11A – SHARE-BASED PAYMENT WITH VARIABLE VESTING PERIOD

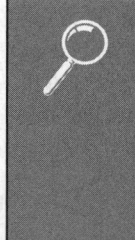

4.5.710.20   A share-based payment is subject to the condition that the employee remains in service until the share price achieves a certain target price at any time within the next five years. If the entity estimates that it will be met at the end of year 3, then the grant-date fair value is recognised over three years. The standard prohibits a subsequent revision of the expected length of the vesting period if the performance condition is a market condition. Therefore, in this example the entire grant-date fair value of the equity instruments granted is recognised in years 1 to 3, even if at the end of year 3 the market condition is not met. [*IFRS 2.15(b), IG.Ex6*]

4.5.710.30   IFRS 2 does not provide guidance on the accounting for the reverse scenario to that illustrated in Example 11A – i.e. if the market condition is met earlier than expected.

EXAMPLE 11B – SHARE-BASED PAYMENT WITH VARIABLE VESTING PERIOD – MARKET CONDITION MET EARLIER THAN EXPECTED

4.5.710.40   Continuing Example 11A, if the market condition is met in year 2, then in theory all of the expected services have been provided. Therefore, it could be argued that no cost should be recognised subsequent to that date, and instead that recognition should accelerate at that date.

4.5.710.50   In our view, the standard's explicit prohibition on revising the length of the vesting period should prevail – i.e. cost should continue to be recognised in accordance with the original three-year estimate – even though we believe that accelerated recognition would better reflect the economics of the scenario.

4.5.720   *Non-market performance condition with variable vesting period*

4.5.720.10   In contrast to a variable vesting period with a market condition, if the length of the vesting period is dependent on achieving a non-market performance condition, then the entity makes an estimate of the length of the expected vesting period at grant date based on the most likely outcome of the performance condition. Subsequently, the entity revises the estimate of the length of the vesting period until the actual outcome is known. [*IFRS 2.15(b), IG.Ex2*]

4.5.720.20   If the arrangement is accounted for as a grant with a variable vesting period, then the entity estimates at grant date whether (a) the employees will complete the requisite service period and (b) the non-market performance condition will be satisfied. A common example of a non-market performance condition with a variable vesting period is a requirement for an exit event – e.g. an IPO or sale – combined with a requirement that the employee is employed until the exit event occurs. The individual circumstances of each arrangement will have to be considered. The share-based payment cost is recognised if the exit event is more likely than not to be achieved; it is not necessary to be certain that the exit event will occur. [*IFRS 2.15, 20*]

4.5.720.30   In another example, an award of options is granted with a non-market performance condition and a service condition, but the vesting period automatically accelerates if the non-market performance condition is met during the period of required service. The award vests at the end of the service period regardless of whether the non-market performance condition is met. In addition, the options are exercisable at the same fixed date. Such an award contains two vesting alternatives.
- *Vesting alternative 1:* The period from grant date until the date on which the service condition is met. This would occur if the non-market performance condition is not met before the service condition is met.
- *Vesting alternative 2:* The period from grant date until the date on which the non-market performance condition is met before the date the service period is completed. This is because vesting is automatically accelerated if the non-market performance condition is satisfied before the service condition.

4.5.720.40   In our view, when accounting for such a share-based payment award, an entity should determine which vesting alternative to account for based on its assessment of which vesting alternative is the most likely outcome. This is because under IFRS 2 an entity generally accounts for the most likely outcome (see 4.5.720.10). In the example in 4.5.720.30, if an entity's initial assessment was that the most likely outcome was that the non-market performance condition would be met before the end of the service period, then it would estimate the expected vesting date for Vesting alternative 2. As long as the entity believes that the non-market performance condition will be met before the service condition, then it should base its accounting on its best estimate of the expected vesting period. If subsequent information indicates that the length of Vesting alternative 2 differs from the previous estimate, then the length of the vesting period should be revised and the entity should adjust the recognised share-based payment cost on a cumulative basis in the period in which the estimate is revised.

4.5.720.50   If an entity's assessment of the most likely outcome changes, then we believe that the accounting should switch to the alternative vesting period (see 4.5.830.20). The share-based payment cost recognised in the period of the change in estimate would adjust the cumulative cost recognised to the amount that would have been recognised if the new estimate had always been used.

4.5.730   Measurement principles

4.5.740   *Determining fair value of equity instruments granted*

4.5.740.10   Share-based payment transactions with employees are measured with reference to the fair value of the equity instruments granted. [*IFRS 2.11*]

4.5.740.20   The fair value of the equity instruments granted is determined as follows.

- If market prices are available for the equity instruments granted, then the estimate of fair value is based on these market prices.
- If market prices are not available for the equity instruments granted, then the fair value of equity instruments granted is estimated using a valuation technique. [*IFRS 2.16–17*]

4.5.750   *No track record of market price*

4.5.750.10   In many situations, a market price for equity instruments (e.g. share options) will not exist because equity instruments issued to employees often have terms and conditions (e.g. vesting conditions) different from those of instruments traded in the market; therefore, a valuation technique is used. A valuation technique requires the estimation of a number of variables, including the expected future volatility of the entity. In our view, if no equity instruments of the entity are traded, then an implied volatility should be calculated – e.g. based on actual experience of similar entities that have traded equity instruments. We believe that an entity, even one without a historical track record – e.g. a newly listed entity – should not estimate its expected volatility at zero. In rare cases, an entity may be unable to estimate, at grant date, expected volatility and therefore the fair value of the equity instruments cannot be measured. In such rare cases, use of the intrinsic value may be required (see 4.5.560). [*IFRS 2.B4, B26–B30*]

4.5.760   *Non-vesting conditions that employee can choose to meet*

4.5.760.10   Common examples of non-vesting conditions that the employee can choose to meet are certain non-compete agreements, transfer restrictions after vesting, savings conditions or a requirement to hold shares. Post-vesting restrictions are included in the grant-date measurement of fair value to the extent that the restriction affects the price that a knowledgeable, willing market participant would pay for that share. [*IFRS 2.B3, IG.Ex9A, IU 11-06*]

EXAMPLE 12 – SHARE-BASED PAYMENT WITH POST-VESTING RESTRICTION

> **4.5.760.20**   Company Z grants shares to employees conditional on one year of service. After the service period, the employees are entitled unconditionally to the shares. However, under the arrangement, they are not allowed to sell the shares for a further five-year period. The five-year restriction on the sale of the shares is a post-vesting restriction, which is a non-vesting condition (see 4.5.440), and is taken into account in the grant-date fair value measurement.

4.5.760.30   The IFRS Interpretations Committee discussed the fair value measurement of post-vesting transfer restrictions and noted that it is not appropriate to determine the fair value of equity instruments issued only to employees and subject to post-vesting restrictions, based on an approach that looks solely or primarily to an actual or synthetic market consisting only of transactions between an entity and its employees and in which prices, for example, reflect an employee's personal borrowing rate. This is because the objective of IFRS 2 is to estimate the fair value of an equity instrument and not the value from the employee's perspective. The Committee also noted that factors that affect only the employee's specific perspective of the value of the equity instruments are not relevant to estimating the price that would be set by a knowledgeable, willing market participant. Therefore, hypothetical transactions with actual or potential market participants willing to invest in restricted shares should be considered. [*IFRS 2.B3, B10, BC168, IU 11-06*]

4.5.770   *Dividends*

4.5.770.10   The treatment of expected dividends in measuring the fair value of the equity instruments depends on whether the employee is entitled to dividends. [*IFRS 2.B31*]

4.5.770.20   If the employees are not entitled to dividends declared during the vesting period, then the fair value of these equity instruments is reduced by the present value of dividends expected to be paid compared with the fair value of equity instruments that are entitled to dividends. [*IFRS 2.B34*]

4.5.770.30   If the employees are entitled to dividends declared during the vesting period, then in our view the accounting treatment depends on whether the dividends are forfeitable – i.e. whether dividends have to be paid back if vesting conditions are not met. [*IFRS 2.B32*]

4.5.770.40   For a discussion of the cost measurement and recognition for forfeitable and non-forfeitable dividend rights, see 4.5.2320.

4.5.780   **Variable number of equity instruments or variable exercise price**

4.5.790   *Shares 'to the value of'*

4.5.790.10   If a variable number of equity instruments to the value of a fixed amount is granted, commonly known as shares 'to the value of', then we believe that such an arrangement is an equity-settled share-based payment (see 4.5.2120).

4.5.790.20   A question arises about the measurement of such a grant if the date of delivery of the shares is in the future because there is a service requirement. In our view, there are two acceptable approaches in respect of measurement:
- as a fixed amount of cash that will be received in the future based on its discounted amount, similar to the net present value of a financial liability (Approach 1); or
- as a grant of free shares that are subject only to a service requirement – i.e. referenced to the share price, without discounting – because in contrast to a financial liability there is no outflow of resources (Approach 2).

4.5.790.30   Although IFRS 2 is silent on discounting in this fact pattern, other standards require discounting to reflect the time value of money. Therefore, measurement on a discounted basis is generally more appropriate if the payment is due to be settled more than 12 months after the reporting date.

EXAMPLE 13 – SHARES 'TO THE VALUE OF' – MEASUREMENT APPROACHES

4.5.790.40   Company C, which is listed on a stock exchange, grants shares to its CEO with a value equal to a fixed cash amount of 1,000, subject to a two-year service condition. The number of shares to be delivered depends on the share price on vesting date. C determines that the appropriate discount rate is 2%.

> 4.5.790.50   If C elects to apply Approach 1 in 4.5.790.20 to measure the grant, then the grant date fair value to recognise over the service period is 961 (1,000 / 1.02²) – i.e. a discounted amount. The difference between 961 and 1,000 is not subsequently recognised.
>
> 4.5.790.60   Conversely, if C elects to apply Approach 2 in 4.5.790.20 to measure the grant, then the grant date fair value to recognise over the service period is the total 1,000 – i.e. the undiscounted amount.

4.5.800   *Market condition and variable number of equity instruments*

4.5.800.10   Typically, a share-based payment is granted in which an employee receives a fixed number of equity instruments subject to vesting conditions. In such situations, the entity values the individual equity instruments granted to determine the grant-date fair value of the share-based payment.

4.5.800.20   Sometimes a share-based payment is granted to an employee in which the number of equity instruments that the employee receives varies based on the achievement of a market condition. In these situations, the employee has been granted a right to receive a variable number of equity instruments, and the value of this right depends on the outcome of the market condition.

4.5.800.30   If a share-based payment includes a market condition, then the grant-date fair value reflects the probability of satisfying the market condition. In the case in 4.5.800.20, the market condition creates variability in the number of equity instruments that will be received. Therefore, the entity determines the grant-date fair value of the right to receive a variable number of equity instruments reflecting the probability of different outcomes.

4.5.800.40   In our view, the grant-date fair value of the share-based payment for each right should be valued by applying a valuation technique that considers the different possible outcomes, such as binomial or Monte Carlo. We believe that the value of the share-based payment per right should not be adjusted subsequently for changes in the share price or related to the market condition, because it is a share-based payment with a market condition. Changes resulting from failure to meet a service condition are trued up as required.

4.5.810   Multiple vesting conditions

4.5.810.10   IFRS 2 provides examples in which share-based payments are subject to a single performance condition – i.e. a service requirement and one performance target. Examples in which a share-based payment is subject to two performance conditions are not included. In our experience, it is not unusual for a share-based payment arrangement to contain two performance conditions, often one market condition and one non-market performance condition. In some cases, both conditions need to be satisfied ('and' conditions); in other cases, only one condition needs to be satisfied ('or' conditions).

4.5.820 *Multiple cumulative performance conditions ('and' conditions)*

4.5.820.10   Vesting conditions may require two performance conditions to be satisfied – e.g. one market condition and one non-market performance condition.

4.5.820.20   In our view, in a share-based payment subject to both market and non-market performance conditions, the grant-date fair value used to measure the share-based payment should reflect the probability of not achieving the market condition.

4.5.820.30   In our view, if the non-market performance condition is not satisfied, then the entity should true up the cumulative share-based payment cost.

4.5.830 *Multiple alternative performance conditions ('or' conditions)*

4.5.830.10   Some share-based payment arrangements may require the satisfaction of both a service condition and at least one of two performance conditions – e.g. one market condition or one non-market performance condition – in order for the share-based payment arrangement to vest. Such arrangements with multiple vesting conditions are sometimes referred to as containing 'multiple interactive vesting conditions'. Share-based payment arrangements containing multiple interactive vesting conditions raise complicated accounting issues, because there is limited guidance in relation to grants of share-based payments that combine market and non-market performance conditions.

4.5.830.20   The implementation guidance to IFRS 2 contains an example of a share-based payment in which the exercise price varies with a non-market performance condition. This example illustrates that a 'switching' approach is taken when there are multiple mutually exclusive outcomes in a share-based payment arrangement. [*IFRS 2.IG.Ex4*]

4.5.830.30   In our view, this switching approach should be followed by analogy for a grant with multiple interactive vesting conditions. At grant date, the entity should estimate the fair value of the equity instruments for each possible outcome and account for the share-based payment based on the most likely outcome at each reporting date. The following table sets out all of the possible outcomes. [*IFRS 2.15, 21, IG.Ex4*]

POSSIBLE OUTCOMES (SEE 4.5.830.40–70)	MARKET CONDITION	NON-MARKET PERFORMANCE CONDITION
Scenario 1	Met	Not met
Scenario 2	Not met	Met
Scenario 3	Not met	Not met
Scenario 4	Met	Met

4.5.830.40   In estimating the fair value for each possible outcome, one fair value ignoring the probability of not achieving the market condition is calculated at grant date for the award assuming that all vesting conditions are met. In the discussion in 4.5.830.50, this is referred to as the 'non-adjusted fair value'. That fair value is used, with an adjustment to reflect the probability of not achieving the market condition, to measure the fair value of the award with the market condition; this is referred to as the 'adjusted fair value' in 4.5.830.70.

4.5.830.50   The non-adjusted fair value of the award is used to measure the fair value of the award with the non-market performance condition; with regard to the non-market performance condition, the estimate of the number of awards expected to vest is trued up to the actual number of instruments that vest because of the satisfaction of the non-market performance condition (see 4.5.540.60).

4.5.830.60   In our view, the entity should recognise the share-based payment cost based on the fair value of the equity instrument for the most likely outcome over the expected period of the most likely condition, with true-up if the required service condition is not met.

4.5.830.70   Effectively, this means the following.
- If vesting is achieved through the market condition only (Scenario 1 in 4.5.830.30), then the total cost recognised will be based on the fair value that reflects the grant-date estimate of the probability of achieving (or not achieving) the market condition – i.e. the adjusted fair value.
- If vesting is achieved through the non-market performance condition only (Scenario 2 in 4.5.830.30), then the eventual total cost recognised will be based on the fair value related to the non-market performance condition – i.e. the non-adjusted fair value.
- If neither the market nor the non-market performance condition is achieved (Scenario 3 in 4.5.830.30), then we believe that the entity should recognise the share-based payment cost based on the adjusted fair value – i.e. the fair value that was adjusted to reflect the probability of achieving the market condition. This is because there is no true-up for differences between estimated and actual vesting due to market conditions (see 4.5.540.50).
- If both conditions are met (Scenario 4 in 4.5.830.30), then we believe that the share-based payment cost should reflect the grant-date fair value without adjustment to reflect the probability of achieving the market condition. This is because we believe that, when both conditions are met, the share-based payment cost should not ignore the non-market fair value increment.

4.5.840   Good leaver clauses and retirees

4.5.840.10   Share-based payment arrangements may contain 'good leaver' clauses.

4.5.840.20   If a good leaver clause specifies that the share-based payment vests if an employee is eligible for retirement (retiree) before the end of the service period, then questions arise about how to recognise and measure the share-based payment. Usually, the service requirement for retirees differs from other employees because they only have to provide services until the earlier of the date on which they retire and the end of the service period. The grant-date fair value of an equity instrument granted to a retiree may also be different from the fair value of an identical equity instrument granted to other employees. This is because the fair value of an option partially depends on its expected exercise date, which in turn may be influenced by the vesting date, and the vesting date is earlier for the retirees. The terms of the share-based payment may also vary for the retirees and will need to be taken into account as usual – e.g. a shorter exercise period, pro rata vesting or adjustments to performance targets.

4.5.840.30   The following flowchart sets out the possible outcomes for a share-based payment arrangement that contains a good leaver clause under which employees who are good leavers retain their award, subject to the future outcomes of the original non-market performance condition(s).

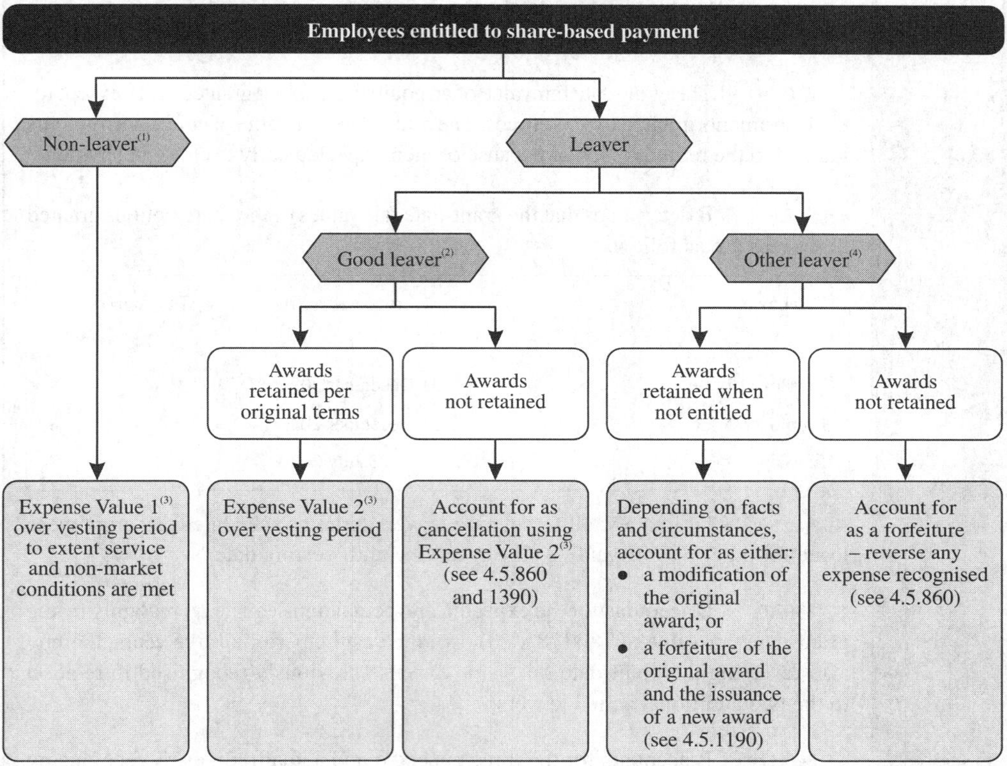

Employees entitled to share-based payment

Non-leaver[1]

Leaver

Good leaver[2]

Other leaver[4]

Awards retained per original terms

Awards not retained

Awards retained when not entitled

Awards not retained

Expense Value 1[3] over vesting period to extent service and non-market conditions are met

Expense Value 2[3] over vesting period

Account for as cancellation using Expense Value 2[3] (see 4.5.860 and 1390)

Depending on facts and circumstances, account for as either:
- a modification of the original award; or
- a forfeiture of the original award and the issuance of a new award (see 4.5.1190)

Account for as a forfeiture – reverse any expense recognised (see 4.5.860)

Notes
1.   An employee who stays in service until vesting date.
2.   An employee who leaves in circumstances that meet the good leaver clauses in the share-based payment arrangement.
3.   The entity calculates two grant date fair values for the arrangement (see 4.5.830).
- *Value 1:* Grant date fair value based on stated terms for a non-leaver.
- *Value 2:* Grant date fair value based on good leaver terms.
4.   An employee who leaves in circumstances other than as a good leaver.

EXAMPLE 14 – GOOD LEAVER CLAUSE FOR RETIREES

4.5.840.40   On 1 January 2018, Company B grants one share option each to 100 employees, subject to a five-year service condition. The share options can be exercised at any date from vesting to the end of 2024.

4.5.840.50   The arrangement contains a good leaver clause under which employees leaving before 31 December 2022 may keep the entitlement if their leaving is due to retirement. A retiree can exercise the option at any date from leaving B to the end of 2024.

4.5.840.60   On grant date, B estimates that:

- 80 employees will remain employed until 31 December 2022 (non-leavers);
- three employees will leave before 31 December 2022 as good leavers due to retirement before vesting date; and
- 17 employees will leave before 31 December 2022 for other reasons.

4.5.840.70   The grant-date fair value of an equity instrument granted is 10, except for the instruments granted to the retirees. The grant-date fair value of equity instruments granted to the retirees is lower because of their expected early exercise behaviour.

4.5.840.80   B determines that the grant-date fair values of the share options granted to retirees are as follows.

EMPLOYEE	RETIREMENT DATE	GRANT-DATE FAIR VALUE
Employee 1	31 December 2021	9
Employer 2	31 December 2020	8
Employer 3	23 July 2020	7

4.5.840.90   Ultimately, all three good leavers retire as scheduled, 19 employees leave for other reasons and 78 stay in service until vesting date.

4.5.840.100   B accounts for the expected and actual non-leavers by recognising the grant-date fair value of 780 (78 x 10) over the vesting period of five years, thereby also reversing the grant-date fair value expense previously recognised in relation to the two additional actual leavers.

4.5.840.110   B accounts for the three expected and actual retirees by recognising the grant-date fair values of 9, 8 and 7 for them over the respective service period from grant date to retirement date.

4.5.850   Separate grants

4.5.850.10   A share-based payment arrangement may include several awards. For example, a grant may contain one award that grants shares that vest subject to a one-year service condition and a market condition, and another award that grants shares that vest subject to a one-year service condition and a non-market performance condition. In our view, these two awards should be accounted for as separate share-based payments because their vesting is not interdependent.

4.5.850.20   For a discussion of the treatment of dividends when their vesting conditions differ from the conditions of the related share-based payment, see 4.5.2340.40.

4.5.860   Forfeiture or cancellation

4.5.860.10   Under the modified grant-date method, the estimated share-based payment cost is trued up for forfeitures that result from an employee failing to meet the service condition.

4.5.860.20   If an employee resigns before the end of the vesting period, then it is clear that the requested services have not been rendered and the termination is treated as a forfeiture.

4.5.860.30   Before the amendments introduced to IFRS 2 by the *Annual Improvements to IFRSs 2010–2012 Cycle*, it was not clear whether an award should be viewed as *forfeited* if an employer terminates the services of an employee and therefore prevents the required service from being provided. The amendments clarified that failure to complete the service period, regardless of the reason – i.e. whether an employee resigns voluntarily or is dismissed by the employer – results in the service condition not being met. Consequently, a failure to complete a service period is treated as a forfeiture. As noted in 4.5.370.20, the amendments are applied prospectively to share-based payment transactions for which grant date is on or after 1 July 2014, with earlier application permitted.

4.5.860.40   However, because IFRS 2 was not previously clear about this treatment, in our view there are two acceptable approaches to accounting for the termination of service by the employer in share-based payment transactions for which grant date is before 1 July 2014, provided that an entity does not elect to adopt the amendments early:
- treat it as a forfeiture because the employer has not received the agreed services; or
- treat it as a cancellation because it is the employer who is precluding the service from being provided – for a discussion of the accounting consequences of cancellations, see 4.5.1390. [*IFRS 2.19, IG24*]

4.5.860.50   Similarly, an employee may be precluded from providing services because of a sale of an operation that results in termination of employment. In our view, for share-based payment transactions for which grant date is before 1 July 2014, provided that an entity does not elect to adopt the amendments early, the approaches discussed in 4.5.860.40 are available in such circumstances – i.e. we believe that treatment as a forfeiture or as a cancellation is acceptable.

4.5.870   *Clauses setting out entitlement in case of failure to meet service condition because of action by employer*

4.5.870.10   In contrast to the situations addressed in 4.5.860.30 and 50, share-based payment arrangements may contain clauses setting out the employee's entitlement (e.g. acceleration of vesting) in relation to the share-based payment in the specific event of termination by the employer on sale of an operation. The accounting should reflect the terms of the arrangement in such cases. [*IFRS 2.15*]

4.5.880   **Presentation in financial statements**

4.5.890   *Presentation of share-based payment cost in profit or loss*

4.5.890.10   For a discussion of the presentation of share-based payments received in the capacity as an employee in profit or loss, see 4.1.60.20.

4.5.900   *Presentation of credit entry in equity*

4.5.900.10   IFRS 2 does not specifically address the presentation of the credit entry within equity. One method is to accrete the credit to equity as the employee cost is recognised.

4.5.900.20   Alternatively, at inception of the grant, the effect of an equity-settled share-based payment may be presented gross, in which case the total expected cost is recognised within equity – e.g. share options outstanding – with a corresponding and offsetting debit also recognised in equity for services to be received. As services are rendered and the related costs recognised, the offsetting debit for deferred cost is reduced. In our experience, predominant practice is to present only the cumulative cost within equity. However, this approach is not required by IFRS and in our view a gross presentation within equity is also permitted.

4.5.900.30   Except for those share-based payment transactions in which equity instruments of a subsidiary have been granted, IFRS does not address whether an increase in equity recognised in connection with a share-based payment transaction should be presented in a separate component within equity or within retained earnings. In our view, either approach is allowed under IFRS. If a separate component is presented, then the nature of the reserve should be disclosed. [*IAS 1.78(e), 79(b), 108*]

4.5.900.40   When equity instruments of a subsidiary have been granted to a counterparty who is not part of the consolidated reporting entity in a share-based payment transaction, the credit entry in equity in the consolidated financial statements of the parent is to NCI. This is because the definition of NCI refers to the equity in a subsidiary not attributable, directly or indirectly, to a parent (see 2.5.450.10). [*IFRS 10.A*]

4.5.910   CASH-SETTLED TRANSACTIONS WITH EMPLOYEES

4.5.920   Basic principles of accounting for cash-settled share-based payment transactions with employees

	BASIC PRINCIPLES OF CASH-SETTLED TRANSACTIONS WITH EMPLOYEES	KEY STEPS
Recognition	Entity recognises a cost (expense or asset) over the vesting period and a corresponding liability.	Determine the vesting period (consistent with equity-settled awards, see 4.5.660).
Measurement	Measurement is based on the fair value of the liability at each reporting date, and it is remeasured until settlement date.	Determine grant date (consistent with equity-settled awards, see 4.5.570).
Impact of conditions	Market and non-vesting conditions are reflected in the measurement of the fair value of the liability. An estimate is made for the number of awards for which service and non-market performance conditions are expected to be satisfied, with a true-up to the number ultimately satisfied.	Determine the initial fair value of the liability (see 4.5.930). Remeasure the fair value of the liability at each reporting date and ultimately at settlement (see 4.5.940).

4.5.920.10   For a worked example that illustrates the application of the key requirements relating to the recognition and measurement of cash-settled share-based payments, see 4.5.1010.

4.5.930   *Initial measurement*

4.5.930.10   Cash-settled share-based payment transactions result in a liability – generally an obligation to make a cash payment – based on the price of the equity instrument (e.g. share price). [*IFRS 2.30–31*]

4.5.930.20   Employee services received in a cash-settled share-based payment are measured indirectly at the fair value of the liability at grant date; the initial measurement of the liability is based on the fair value of the underlying instruments. Measurement of the liability takes into account the extent to which services have been rendered to date. [*IFRS 2.33*]

4.5.930.30   An entity measures the fair value of a cash-settled liability taking into account only market and non-vesting conditions. Service and non-market performance conditions affect the measurement of the liability by adjusting the number of rights to receive cash based on the best estimate of the service and non-market performance conditions that are expected to be satisfied. This means that the accounting for the effects of vesting and non-vesting conditions on cash-settled share-based payment transactions follows the approach used for equity-settled share-based payments (see 4.5.540). [*IFRS 2.33A–33D, IG.Ex12, BC371–BC382*]

4.5.930.40   The grant-date fair value of the liability is recognised over the vesting period. If no services are required, then the amount is recognised immediately. [*IFRS 2.32, BC243–BC245*]

4.5.930.50   The grant-date fair value of the liability is capitalised if the services received qualify for asset recognition. For further discussion relating to the capitalisation of the services received, see 4.5.950.10. [*IFRS 2.8*]

4.5.940   *Remeasurements*

4.5.940.10   At each reporting date, and ultimately at settlement date, the fair value of the recognised liability is remeasured. As described in 4.5.930.40, the grant-date fair value is recognised over the vesting period. Remeasurement applies to the recognised amount through vesting date. The full amount is remeasured from the vesting date to settlement date. The total net cost recognised in respect of the transaction will be the amount paid to settle the liability.

4.5.940.20   Remeasurements during the vesting period are recognised immediately to the extent that they relate to past services, and recognition is spread over the remaining vesting period to the extent that they relate to future services. That is, in the period of the remeasurement there is a catch-up adjustment for prior periods in order for the *recognised* liability at each reporting date to equal a defined proportion of the *total* fair value of the liability. The recognised proportion is generally calculated by dividing the period for which services have been provided as at the reporting date by the total vesting period. Remeasurements are recognised in profit or loss. [*IFRS 2.IG.Ex12*]

4.5.940.30   Remeasurements after the vesting period are recognised immediately in full in profit or loss. [*IFRS 2.32*]

4.5.940.40   A cash-settled share-based payment is remeasured to its actual settlement amount; therefore, the cumulative cost that will ultimately be recognised will be equal to the cash payment to the counterparty. This is different from equity-settled transactions for which there is no true-up of compensation cost for failure to satisfy a market condition (see 4.5.540.50). [*IFRS 2.BC249*]

4.5.950   *Capitalisation of services received*

4.5.950.10   Only the grant-date fair value of the arrangement may qualify for asset recognition under other standards. Accordingly, the remeasurement of the liability is recognised in profit or loss even if the grant-date fair value has been recognised as an asset. The carrying amount of that asset is not adjusted for the effects of the liability remeasurement. [*IFRS 2.IG19*]

4.5.960   Non-vesting conditions

4.5.960.10   Non-vesting conditions are also taken into account when estimating the fair value of a cash-settled liability, similar to market conditions. [*IFRS 2.33C*]

4.5.970   Presentation in profit or loss

4.5.970.10   The expense reflecting the recognition of the grant-date fair value of a cash-settled share-based payment to employees is presented as an employee cost, similar to expenses under equity-settled share-based payments (see 4.5.890).

4.5.970.20   There is no guidance on whether the remeasurement should be presented as an employee cost or as finance income or finance costs. In our view, an entity should choose an accounting policy, to be applied consistently, between these presentations. [*IFRS 2.BC252–BC255*]

4.5.970.30   If the remeasurement results in a credit to profit or loss in a period or cumulatively at the end of a period then, in determining how to present the credit in profit or loss, the entity considers the general requirements for offsetting income and expenses (see 4.1.200). [*IAS 1.32–35*]

4.5.980   Redeemable shares

4.5.980.10   Grants of equity instruments that are redeemable are classified as cash-settled share-based payments under certain conditions, depending on which party has the option to redeem (see 4.5.2180). For a discussion of what features may form part of the terms and conditions of the share-based payment arrangement, see 4.5.2170.10. [*IFRS 2.31*]

4.5.980.20   In our view, for a grant of options to acquire redeemable shares, the settlement of the share-based payment occurs only on redemption of the shares and not on exercise of the options. Therefore, we believe that an entity should recognise compensation cost and a corresponding cash-settled liability equal to the grant-date fair value of the options; this liability should be remeasured at each reporting date and ultimately at settlement date. [*IFRS 2.30–31*]

4.5.980.30   At the date on which the option is exercised, the redemption value of the share, and therefore of the liability recognised for the redeemable shares, will be equal to the sum of the exercise price and the intrinsic value of the option. Once the option is exercised, we believe that the entity should remeasure this cash-settled liability at fair value through profit or loss until the shares are redeemed. [*IFRS 2.30*]

4.5.990   **Disclosures**

4.5.1000   *Disclosures on measurement of fair value for cash-settled share-based payments*

4.5.1000.10   There are specific disclosure requirements on the measurement of fair value for share options. In our view, such disclosures should also be provided for cash-settled share-based payments – e.g. SARs. We believe that for cash-settled share-based payments, the following disclosures on measurement of fair value should be provided.

- *Awards granted during the period:* Disclosures on the measurement of fair value at grant date and at the reporting date.
- *Awards granted in previous periods but unexercised at the reporting date:* Disclosures on the measurement of fair value at the reporting date. [*IFRS 2.47(a), 50*]

4.5.1010   **WORKED EXAMPLE**

4.5.1010.10   This simple worked example illustrates the mechanics of applying key requirements in IFRS 2 to the recognition and measurement of equity-settled and cash-settled share-based payments.

EXAMPLE 15 – EQUITY-SETTLED AND CASH-SETTLED SHARE-BASED PAYMENTS – ACCOUNTING MECHANICS

4.5.1020   **Award with service condition only**

4.5.1020.10   On 1 January 2018, Company C granted two share-based payment awards to Employees E1 and E2. The following facts are relevant for this example.

- E1 will receive 100 share options provided that they remain in service for three years. If the service condition is met, then E1 can exercise their option at an exercise price of 50 per share. This is an equity-settled share-based payment.
- E2 will receive 100 SARs provided that they remain in service for three years. If the service condition is met, then E2 will receive the intrinsic value of the SARs at settlement date – i.e. any increase in the share price between grant date and settlement. This is a cash-settled share-based payment.

4.5.1020.20   Grant date for both awards is 1 January 2018 and on this date C, E1 and E2 have a shared understanding of the terms and conditions of the arrangement.

4.5.1020.30   The vesting period for both awards is from 1 January 2018 to 31 December 2020 – i.e. during this period the service condition should be satisfied for E1 and E2 to be unconditionally entitled to the awards. Settlement date for both awards is 15 February 2021.

4.5.1020.40   The grant-date fair value does not include the likelihood of E1 and E2 meeting the three-year service requirement, and C estimates this in determining how many awards are expected to vest (see 4.5.540.60). In this example, C expects E1 and E2 to complete the required service period; and both E1 and E2 meet the service requirement and the awards ultimately vest.

4.5.1020.50   C determines the following valuation information.

Share price at grant date – 1 January 2018	50
Grant-date fair value of award	9
Fair value of cash-settled award at 31 December 2018	10
Fair value of cash-settled award at 31 December 2019	12
Fair value of cash-settled award at 31 December 2020	14
Fair value of cash-settled award at 15 February 2021	15

4.5.1030   *Equity-settled award*

4.5.1030.10   Because C expects E1 to meet the service condition, it recognises an expense in 2018 based on the grant-date fair value of the award and the proportion of the total vesting period that has elapsed.

4.5.1030.20   C calculates the amount to be recognised as an expense in 2018 as follows.

$$300 = 100^{(1)} \times 9^{(2)} \times {}^1/_3{}^{(3)}$$

Notes
1.   Number of share options expected to vest.
2.   Grant-date fair value of the award.
3.   Elapsed portion of vesting period.

4.5.1030.30   C recognises the same expense in 2019 and 2020 because the expense is based on the grant-date fair value of the award and the expectation of achieving the service condition. Subsequent changes in the fair value of the award during the vesting period are ignored for equity-settled share-based payments (see 4.5.540.20).

4.5.1040   *Cash-settled award*

4.5.1040.10   In contrast to equity-settled share-based payments, the expense recognised for cash-settled share-based payments in each reporting period can differ because of changes in the fair value of the award. A cash-settled award is remeasured at each reporting date (see 4.5.940.10). Similar to equity-settled awards, the expected achievement of the service condition affects the expense recognised.

4.5.1040.20   In 2018, the expense recognised for the cash-settled award is based on the fair value at the reporting date – i.e. 31 December 2018. C calculates the amount to be recognised as an expense in 2018 as follows.

$$333 = 100^{(1)} \times 10^{(2)} \times {}^1/_3{}^{(3)}$$

Notes
1.   Number of instruments expected to vest.
2.   Reporting date fair value of the award.
3.   Elapsed portion of vesting period.

4.5.1040.30   In 2019 and 2020, the cumulative expense is based on the same criteria and C calculates the amount to be recognised as an expense in 2019 and 2020 as follows.

YEAR END	CUMULATIVE EXPENSE UNTIL END OF PERIOD	EXPENSE IN CURRENT PERIOD
31 December 2019	800	467
31 December 2020	1,400	600

CUMULATIVE EXPENSE AT **31 DECEMBER 2019**	EXPENSE FOR **2019**
$800 = 100^{(1)} \times 12^{(2)} \times {}^2/_3{}^{(3)}$	$467 = 800^{(4)} - 333^{(5)}$

CUMULATIVE EXPENSE AT **31 DECEMBER 2020**	EXPENSE FOR **2020**
$1,400 = 100^{(1)} \times 14^{(2)} \times {}^3/_3{}^{(3)}$	$600 = 1,400^{(6)} - 800^{(4)}$

Notes
1.   Number of instruments expected to vest.
2.   Reporting date fair value of the award.
3.   Elapsed portion of vesting period.
4.   Cumulative expense at 31 December 2019.
5.   Expense for 2018.
6.   Cumulative expense at 31 December 2020.

4.5.1040.40   An additional complication exists for cash-settled awards because the cash-settled liability is remeasured up to the date of settlement to ensure that the liability at settlement is equal to the cash payment (see 4.5.940.40). In this example, settlement occurs on 15 February 2021, and C recognises an additional expense of 100 in 2021 (100 x 15 - 1,400).

4.5.1040.50   The following table summarises the key differences between equity-settled and cash-settled share-based payments.

Amount of expense recognised in each period and cumulatively is likely to differ	• Equity-settled expense is based on the grant-date fair value. The grant-date fair value is not remeasured. • Cash-settled expense is based on the fair value as determined at each reporting date.
Periods over which expenses are recognised may differ	• Equity-settled expense is recognised over the vesting period. • Cash-settled expense is recognised until settlement.

4.5.1050 *Service condition not met*

4.5.1050.10 Assume that E1 resigns in 2019, and therefore does not satisfy the required service period. The cumulative equity-settled expense to be recognised at 31 December 2019 would be zero. If a service condition is not met, then the award does not vest and no cumulative expense is recognised (see 4.5.540.60).

4.5.1050.20 Therefore, C would recognise a credit of 300 in 2019 to reverse the expense recognised in 2018. This does not change the accounting in 2018, because that accounting was based on appropriate estimates at that time. This true-up approach for instruments that do not vest (because of service conditions not being met) applies to both equity-settled and cash-settled awards.

4.5.1060 **Award with service and non-market condition**

4.5.1060.10 Continuing with the example, on 1 January 2018, C also granted a share-based payment award to Employee E3. The following facts are relevant for this example.
- E3 will receive 100 share options provided that they remain in service for three years and if the profit for those three years is above 10,000.
- If the service condition and non-market performance condition are met, then the employee can exercise their option at an exercise price of 50 per share. This is an equity-settled share-based payment with both a service and a non-market condition.
- The grant-date fair value of the award is 9 – i.e. it is the same as the grant-date fair value of the award without the non-market condition.

4.5.1060.20 Similar to service conditions, the impact of non-market performance conditions on vesting is estimated at grant date, but not reflected in the grant-date fair value itself. Subsequently, these estimates are trued up for differences between the number of instruments expected to vest and the actual number of instruments vested. Changes in expectations can lead to the reversal of the cumulative share-based payment expense, similar to service conditions (see 4.5.540.60).

4.5.1070 **Award with service and market condition**

4.5.1070.10 Continuing with the example, on 1 January 2018 Company C also granted a share-based payment award to Employee E4. The following facts are relevant for this example.
- E4 will receive 100 share options provided that they remain in service for three years and if the share price of C increases by at least 20 points.
- If the service condition and market condition are met, then the employee can exercise their option at an exercise price of 50 per share.
- This is an equity-settled share-based payment with both a service and a market condition.

4.5.1070.20   C determines the following valuation information.

Share price at grant date – 1 January 2018	50
Grant-date fair value of award (includes the likelihood of achieving the market condition)	7.50
Share price at 31 December 2020	60

4.5.1070.30   C calculates the amount to be recognised as an expense in each of the years as follows.

$$250 = 100^{(1)} \times 7.50^{(2)} \times \frac{1}{3}^{(3)}$$

Notes
1.   Number of share options expected to vest.
2.   Grant-date fair value of the award.
3.   Elapsed portion of vesting period.

4.5.1070.40   Market conditions are reflected as an adjustment (discount) to the initial estimate of fair value at grant date and there is no true-up for differences between estimated and actual vesting – i.e. the equity-settled expense is recognised even if the market condition is not ultimately achieved (see 4.5.540.50). Therefore, even though the market condition of an increase by at least 20 points in share price by the end of the three-year period was not achieved – i.e. the share price only increased by 10 points – C recognises the same expense in all three periods, because the expense is based on the grant-date fair value and E4 met the service condition (see 4.5.540.70).

4.5.1070.50   This is different from a cash-settled award, which is remeasured to its actual settlement amount. Therefore, if a cash-settled award does not vest because of a failure to satisfy a market condition, then no cumulative expense is recognised – i.e. the cumulative cost that will ultimately be recognised will be equal to the cash payment to the counterparty (see 4.5.940.40).

4.5.1080   **EMPLOYEE TRANSACTIONS – CHOICE OF SETTLEMENT**

4.5.1090   **Basic principles of accounting for employee transactions with choice of settlement**

4.5.1090.10   If either the entity or the employee has a choice of settlement, then the transaction is accounted for at least in part as a cash-settled transaction if the entity granting the share-based payment will or can be required to settle in cash or other assets. [*IFRS 2.34*]

4.5.1090.20   The following flowchart illustrates the effect on accounting of a choice of settlement.

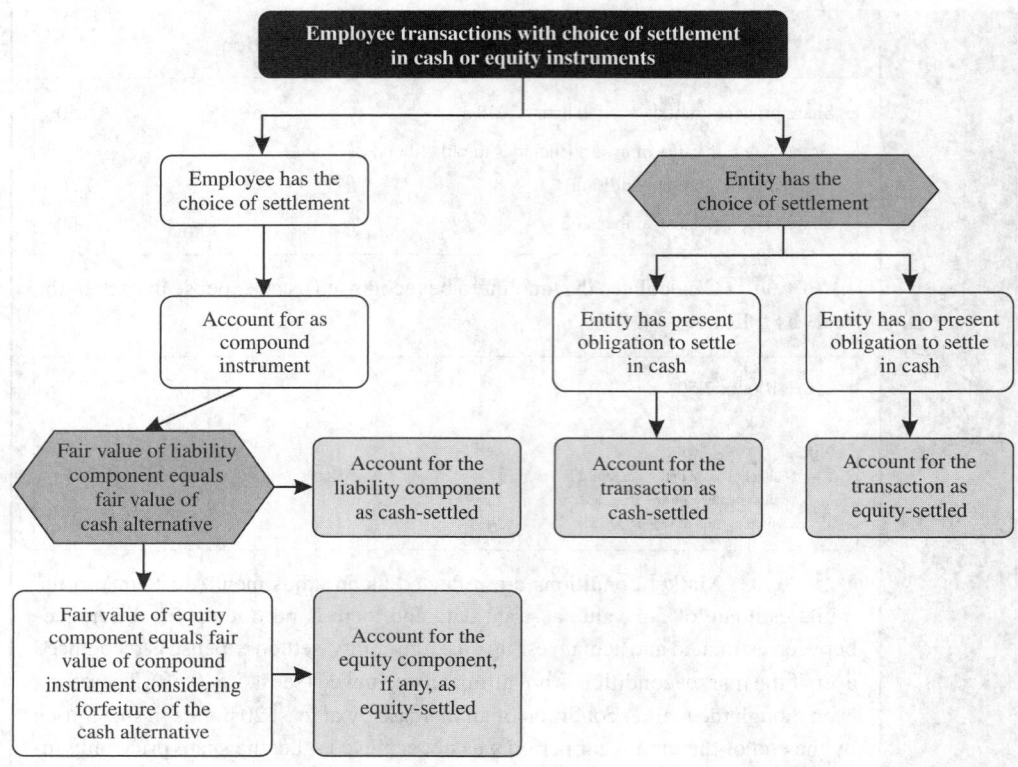

4.5.1090.30   If the manner of settlement is not a choice within the control of the entity or the employee, but depends on an event outside both parties' control, then we believe that instead an entity should determine whether to classify the share-based payment as equity-settled or cash-settled using an approach that is based on IAS 37 (see 4.5.2230).

4.5.1100   Share-based payment transactions in which employee has choice of settlement

4.5.1100.10   If the employee has the choice of settlement, then the entity has granted a compound financial instrument that includes a liability component and an equity component. [*IFRS 2.35–36, IG.Ex13*]

4.5.1100.20   At the measurement date, the fair value of the compound instrument (the value of services to be received) is the sum of the values of the liability component and the equity component. [*IFRS 2.37*]

4.5.1100.30   The liability component is measured first. It equals the fair value of the liability under the cash alternative. All of the fair value of the grant will be recognised as a liability if the employee would have to surrender the cash settlement right to receive the equity alternative with the same fair value. [*IFRS 2.37*]

4.5.1100.40   Next, the fair value of the equity component is measured. The fair value of the equity component takes into account that the employee forfeits their right to the cash alternative to receive the equity instruments. As a result, the incremental value of the equity component is zero, unless the employee receives a discount for choosing the equity alternative. [*IFRS 2.35–38*]

4.5.1110 *Different settlement dates*

4.5.1110.10 Determination of grant date and vesting date in respect of share-based payment arrangements that provide employees with a subsequent choice of cash settlement at one date or shares at a later date can be challenging because it may not be clear whether the date of cash settlement or the date of issuance of the shares should prevail.

4.5.1110.20 The IFRS Interpretations Committee discussed share-based payment transactions in which an employee has a choice of settlement and noted that as a consequence of the requirement to account for the cash settlement component and the share component separately, the vesting periods of the two components should be determined separately. [*IFRS 2.38, IU 05-06*]

4.5.1110.30 In our view, choosing one alternative – i.e. cash settlement or shares – before the end of the vesting period of the other alternative should be treated as a cancellation of the second alternative by one of the parties. We believe that the term 'forfeited' used in paragraph 40 of IFRS 2 should not be understood as forfeiture as used in applying the modified grant-date method. In the context of that method, forfeiture results in a reversal of previously recognised share-based payment cost. Reversal of the equity component when the cash alternative is selected is not appropriate, because services have been provided. Therefore, we believe that the equity component should be recognised as long as the required services have been provided to be eligible for cash settlement, notwithstanding the fact that the equity alternative is surrendered when cash settlement is chosen.

EXAMPLE 16 – SHARE-BASED PAYMENT WITH SETTLEMENT ALTERNATIVES ON DIFFERENT DATES

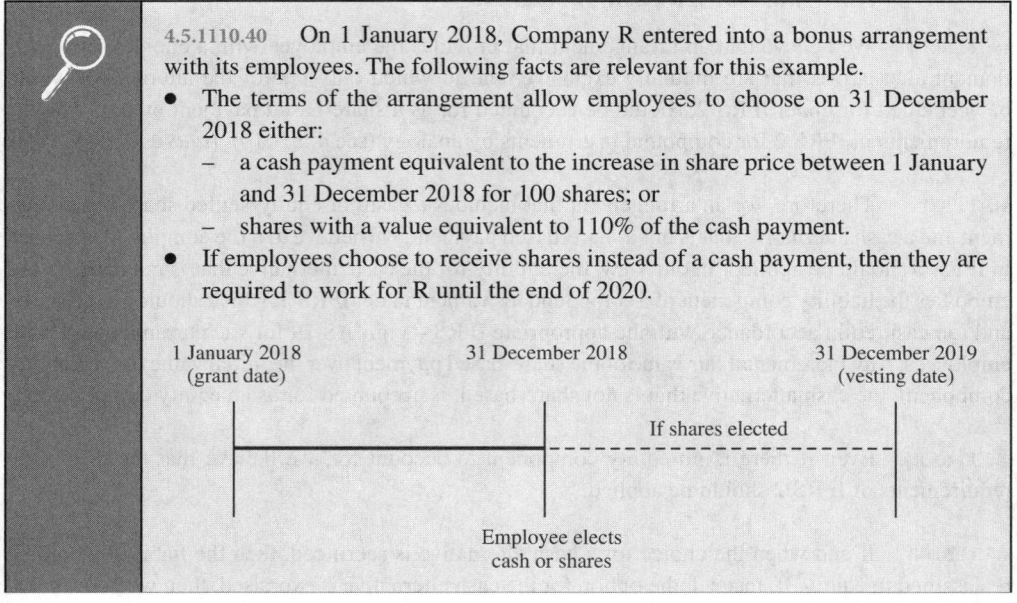

4.5.1110.40 On 1 January 2018, Company R entered into a bonus arrangement with its employees. The following facts are relevant for this example.
- The terms of the arrangement allow employees to choose on 31 December 2018 either:
  - a cash payment equivalent to the increase in share price between 1 January and 31 December 2018 for 100 shares; or
  - shares with a value equivalent to 110% of the cash payment.
- If employees choose to receive shares instead of a cash payment, then they are required to work for R until the end of 2020.

1 January 2018 (grant date) 31 December 2018 31 December 2019 (vesting date)

If shares elected

Employee elects cash or shares

4.5.1110.50   At the date on which the transaction was entered into, both the employer and employees understood the terms and conditions of the plan, including the formula that would be used to determine the amount of cash to be paid or the number of shares to be delivered to each employee; however, the exact amount of cash or number of shares would be known only at a future point in time. Nonetheless, if the outcome is based on objective factors and different knowledgeable parties, independently of each other, would be able to make consistent calculations, then we believe that there is a shared understanding without having specified the actual grant term (see 4.5.600.10). In this example, we believe that grant date is 1 January 2018. [*IU 05-06*]

4.5.1110.60   Continuing this example, a share-based payment transaction with cash alternatives at the choice of the employee is treated as a compound instrument with the liability and equity components of the compound instrument accounted for separately. Therefore, we believe that in this example the vesting periods for the liability and equity components are different: one year for the liability component and three years for the equity component. [*IU 05-06*]

4.5.1110.70   In this example, if the grant-date fair value of the liability component is 500 and the fair value of the equity component is 300, then at the end of 2018 R will have recognised the entire fair value of the cash component of 500 and 100 for the equity component (300 x $^1/_3$ = 100). If at the end of 2018 the employee elects to receive the cash payment, then we believe that this election should be treated as a cancellation of the equity component by the counterparty (see 4.5.1390). [*IFRS 2.39–40, IG.Ex13*]

4.5.1120   *Non-share-based cash alternative*

4.5.1120.10   We believe that an arrangement that provides the employee with a choice of two settlement alternatives that are mutually exclusive, and in which only one of the alternatives would be accounted for under IFRS 2, should be accounted for as a share-based payment by applying the requirements in IFRS 2 for compound instruments by analogy (see 4.5.2010). [*IFRS 2.35*]

4.5.1120.20   Therefore, for an arrangement that includes a cash- or equity-settled share-based payment and a cash alternative that is not a share-based payment, we believe that the compound approach in IFRS 2 should be applied. In our view, the liability for the cash alternative that is not share-based embodies the liability component of a compound instrument under IFRS 2, which should be measured and remeasured in accordance with the appropriate IFRS – e.g. IAS 19 for such arrangements with employees. Any incremental fair value of the share-based payment over the initial value of the liability component, the cash alternative that is not share-based, is accounted for as an equity component.

4.5.1120.30   Even if there is no equity component to account for, we believe that the disclosure requirements of IFRS 2 should be applied.

4.5.1120.40   If and when the choice for a cash alternative is sacrificed, then the liability would be reclassified to equity. If, instead, the option for the cash alternative is exercised, then we believe that the equity component would be treated as cancelled because the equity right had to be surrendered to receive the cash alternative. [*IFRS 2.39–40*]

4.5.1130   Share-based payment transactions in which entity has choice of settlement

4.5.1130.10   If the entity has the choice of settlement, then the entity accounts for the transaction either as a cash-settled share-based payment or as an equity-settled share-based payment in its entirety. The entity determines whether it has a present obligation to settle in cash. If it has a present obligation to settle in cash, then it accounts for the transaction as a cash-settled share-based payment; otherwise, it accounts for the transaction as an equity-settled share-based payment. [*IFRS 2.41–43*]

4.5.1130.20   Whether the entity has a present obligation to settle in cash depends on an assessment of the entity's:
- intent, if any, to settle in cash or in equity instruments;
- past practice, if any, of settling in cash or in equity instruments; and
- ability to settle in equity instruments.

4.5.1130.30   If the entity has the *stated* intent to settle in equity instruments, then the entity does not have a present obligation to settle in cash, unless it has a past practice of settling in cash or no ability to settle in equity instruments. The entity has a present obligation to settle in cash if the choice of settlement in equity instruments has no commercial substance – e.g. if the entity is legally prohibited from issuing or buying and reissuing shares. Therefore, to classify the share-based payment as equity-settled, the entity has to have the ability to settle in shares. Otherwise, the entity classifies the share-based payment as cash-settled. [*IFRS 2.41, BC265*]

4.5.1130.40   If the entity has the *stated intent to settle in cash*, then the entity has a present obligation to settle in cash, regardless of its past practice. [*IFRS 2.BC267*]

4.5.1130.50   If the entity does *not have a stated intent*, then it classifies the transaction as cash-settled if it has either a past practice of settling in cash or no ability to settle in equity instruments; otherwise, the transaction is classified as equity-settled. [*IFRS 2.41, BC265*]

4.5.1130.60   The basis of classification of share-based payments when the issuer has a choice of settlement differs from the classification criteria in the financial instruments standards, which focus more narrowly on whether the issuer has an obligation without considering its intent. [*IFRS 2.BC266*]

4.5.1130.70   IFRS 2 does not consider whether the basis of classification of a share-based payment in which the entity has a choice of settlement can or should be reconsidered after grant date if there is a change in circumstances (see 4.5.1160).

4.5.1140   *Settlement accounting when share-based payment is accounted for as cash-settled*

4.5.1140.10   When the entity accounts for the transaction as cash-settled, the entity applies the requirements for cash-settled share-based payments until settlement – i.e. the liability is remeasured to its fair value at each reporting date and ultimately at settlement date and the cash payment settles the liability. [*IFRS 2.42*]

4.5.1150   ***Settlement accounting when share-based payment is accounted for as equity-settled***

4.5.1150.10   When the entity accounts for the transaction as equity-settled, the accounting depends on whether the entity decides to settle in cash or in equity and whether it chooses the higher or lower fair value if there is a difference between the value of the equity or cash alternative. [*IFRS 2.43*]

4.5.1150.20   If the entity has classified the transaction as equity-settled and selects the type of settlement with the lower fair value at the date of settlement, then the accounting is as follows.

- If the entity settles in cash, then the cash payment is recognised as a deduction from equity, reflecting a repurchase of equity instruments.
- If the entity settles in equity as expected, then settlement does not require any more accounting entries, other than a possible transfer from one equity component to another. [*IFRS 2.43(a)–(b)*]

4.5.1150.30   If the entity chooses the type of settlement with the higher fair value at settlement date, then the entity recognises an additional expense for the excess value given. In our view, this expense represents the difference between the values of the equity alternative and the cash alternative at settlement date, rather than the difference from the grant-date fair value. [*IFRS 2.43(c), BC268*]

4.5.1160   ***Reassessment of classification***

4.5.1160.10   The classification as equity- or cash-settled of a transaction in which the entity has the choice of settlement is initially determined at grant date. In our view, an entity should reassess whether it has a present obligation to settle in cash if there is a change in circumstances before settlement date. Examples of changes in circumstances that would indicate that a reassessment of the classification is appropriate include a change in an entity's stated intent or a change in an entity's practice of settlement. In our view, whether the change in circumstances would lead to a change in classification of the share-based payment should be assessed based on the specific facts and circumstances of each arrangement.

4.5.1160.20   In our view, a change in circumstances that results in a change in classification of a transaction in which the entity has a choice of settlement should be accounted for prospectively. We believe that the change in intent of the entity should be treated as a change in the terms of the award. Therefore, the change in intent should be treated as a modification that changes the classification of the arrangement (see 4.5.1320).

4.5.1170   *Initial accounting as equity-settled*

4.5.1170.10   The communication of a change in the entity's intent from settling in equity to settling in cash is a change in circumstances that we believe should result in a reassessment of the classification of outstanding transactions, assuming that transactions were previously accounted for as equity-settled share-based payments. [*IFRS 2.BC267*]

4.5.1170.20   Consider the example of an entity that has the stated intent and ability to settle transactions in equity and has a past practice of doing so; at grant date, the arrangement is classified as equity-settled. However, if the entity changes its intent to settle in cash and communicates this to employees, then the entity would have a present obligation to settle in cash; therefore, we believe that the entity should reclassify the share-based payment arrangement to cash-settled.

4.5.1170.30   If the entity continues to have a stated policy of settlement in equity but subsequently settles a transaction in cash, then the question arises about whether the cash settlement results in the entity having a present obligation to settle other transactions in cash. In our view, if the entity's intention is to continue to settle in equity and the cash settlement was limited to an isolated circumstance – e.g. because of an illness in the employee's family – then equity-settled classification may continue to be appropriate. In this case, the isolated circumstance of cash settlement would not generally constitute a change in practice and would not generally result in the employees having an expectation that their awards will be settled in cash in the future. However, if the entity settles a number of transactions in cash, then we believe that it is more likely that the change in settlement should result in the share-based payment arrangement being reclassified to cash-settled because a past practice of settling in cash will have been established.

4.5.1180   *Initial accounting as cash-settled*

4.5.1180.10   In our view, if the share-based payment is classified at grant date as cash-settled, then it may be more difficult to support a conclusion that a change in circumstances results in the entity no longer having a present obligation to settle in cash. This is because the employees may have an expectation that the previous practice of settlement in cash will continue to be followed until a practice of settlement in equity is established. This is more difficult if the employee's ability to obtain cash by selling the equity instruments received in the share-based payment transaction would not be as easy as cash settlement by the entity – e.g. if there is not an active and liquid market available to the employees in which to sell the entity's equity instruments.

4.5.1180.20   For example, an entity has a past practice of settling in cash and, without communicating any change in policy to employees, the entity changes its intent such that it will settle future awards in equity. We believe that, before establishing a practice of settlement in equity, the entity should continue to classify the share-based payment arrangement as cash-settled. This is because, in the absence of communication of its change in intent and a change in practice, we believe that the employees will continue to have an expectation that the awards will be settled in cash and therefore the entity continues to have a present obligation to settle in cash.

4.5.1190   MODIFICATIONS AND CANCELLATIONS OF EMPLOYEE SHARE-BASED PAYMENT TRANSACTIONS

4.5.1200   Scope of this section

4.5.1200.05   This section contains guidance on modifications, cancellations and replacements of share-based payment transactions with employees. There are no specific requirements for cash-settled share-based payments that are modified or cancelled because cash-settled share-based payments are remeasured to the ultimate cash payment (see 4.5.940.40). Therefore, this section focuses on equity-settled share-based payments. For discussion on modifications that change the classification of an arrangement, see 4.5.1310.

4.5.1200.10   As a basic principle, IFRS 2 requires an entity to recognise, as a minimum, the original grant-date fair value of the equity instruments granted unless those equity instruments do not vest because of failure to meet any service and non-market performance conditions under the original terms and conditions.

4.5.1200.20 In addition to the original grant-date fair value, an entity recognises the effects of modifications that increase the fair value of the equity instruments granted or are otherwise beneficial to the employee. [*IFRS 2.27, B43(a)*]

4.5.1200.30 The entity cannot reduce the share-based payment cost that would be recognised under the original terms and conditions by modifying or cancelling a share-based payment. However, the timing of recognition of the cost of a share-based payment may change as a result of modifications. [*IFRS 2.BC237*]

4.5.1210   Modifications

4.5.1210.10 The accounting for a modification depends on whether the modification changes the classification of the arrangement and whether the changes are beneficial to the counterparty.

4.5.1220   *Modifications that do not change classification of arrangement*

4.5.1220.10 IFRS 2 distinguishes between different types of beneficial and non-beneficial modifications. The flowchart below provides an overview of the categories discussed and the respective accounting consequences, assuming that the modification does not affect the classification of the share-based payment. For a discussion on modifications that change the classification of an arrangement, see 4.5.1310. [*IFRS 2.B42–B44*]

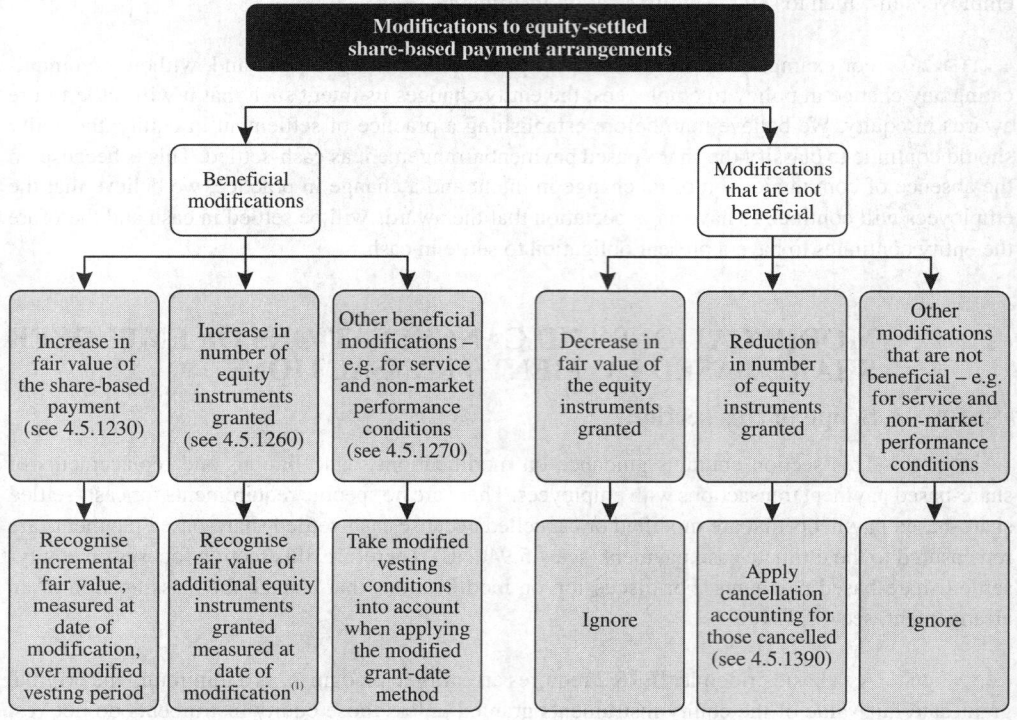

Note

1.   Over the period from date of modification to the end of the vesting period of the additional equity instruments.

4.5.1230 *Increases in fair value of share-based payment*

4.5.1240 Increases in fair value of equity instruments granted

4.5.1240.10 Sometimes a modification increases the fair value of the equity instruments granted – e.g. by reducing the exercise price of a share option granted. In such cases, the incremental fair value is recognised over the remaining modified vesting period, whereas the balance of the grant-date fair value is recognised over the remaining original vesting period. [*IFRS 2.B43(a), IG.Ex7*]

4.5.1240.20 The 'incremental fair value' is the difference between the fair value of the modified share-based payment and that of the original share-based payment, both measured at the date of the modification – i.e. the fair values as measured immediately before and after the modification. [*IFRS 2.B43*]

4.5.1250 Determining whether there is an increase in fair value of share-based payment

4.5.1250.10 In our view, when determining fair value at the date of modification, the same requirements as for determining the grant-date fair value apply – i.e. service conditions and non-market performance conditions are not taken into account in determining the fair value (see 4.5.540.60). If, for example, a share-based payment arrangement with a non-market performance condition is modified such that only the non-market performance target is modified, and all other terms and conditions remain the same, then the incremental fair value is zero (see 4.5.1270.10). This is because the fair value measured on an IFRS 2 basis – i.e. without adjustments for service and non-market performance conditions – is the same before and after the modification. [*IFRS 2.27, B43(a)*]

4.5.1250.20 If an award that contains a market condition is modified by an entity to make the market condition easier to meet, then this is a modification of a vesting condition that is beneficial to employees. The original market condition is taken into account in estimating the fair value of the original grant at the date of modification. If it is unlikely that the original market condition will be met at the date of modification, then the fair value of the original award at the date of modification may be significantly lower than the fair value of the original award as determined at grant date.

EXAMPLE 17 – MODIFICATION OF SHARE-BASED PAYMENT THAT IS BENEFICIAL

4.5.1250.30 On 1 January 2018, Company D granted 1,000 shares for no consideration to its CEO, subject to a two-year service condition and the share price achieving a target of 120. At grant date, the share price is 100 and the grant-date fair value of the equity instrument granted, including consideration of the possibility of not meeting the share price target, is 80.

4.5.1250.40 In July 2019, the share price decreases to 70 and D now estimates that it is highly unlikely that the share price target will be met. To motivate the CEO, the market condition is reduced to a share price target of 75. The fair value of the equity instrument granted, considering the market condition immediately before the modification, is 1 and immediately after the modification is 56; the incremental fair value is therefore 55 per share.

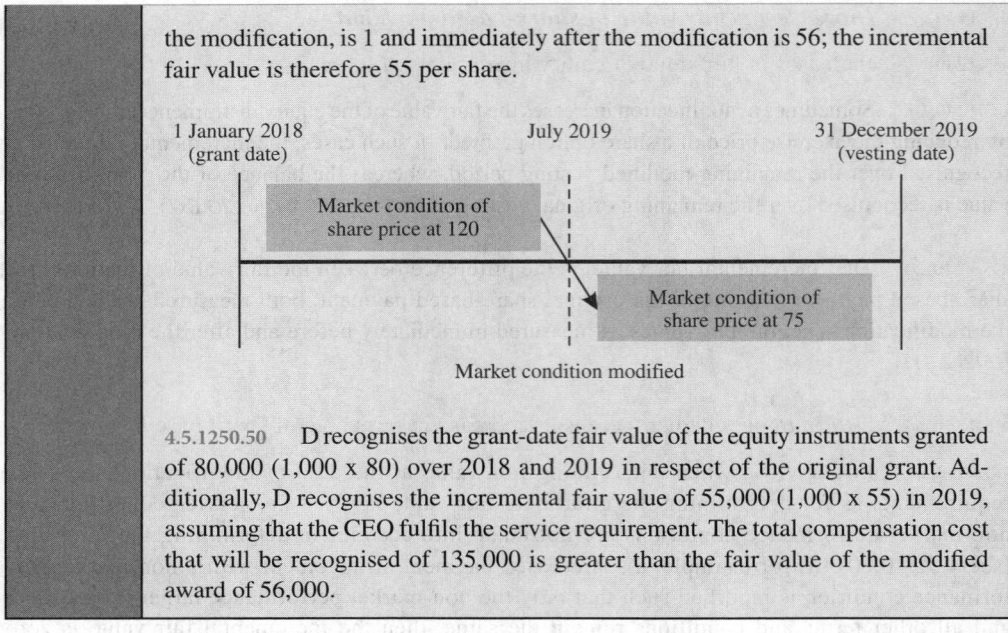

Market condition modified

4.5.1250.50 D recognises the grant-date fair value of the equity instruments granted of 80,000 (1,000 x 80) over 2018 and 2019 in respect of the original grant. Additionally, D recognises the incremental fair value of 55,000 (1,000 x 55) in 2019, assuming that the CEO fulfils the service requirement. The total compensation cost that will be recognised of 135,000 is greater than the fair value of the modified award of 56,000.

4.5.1260 *Increases in number of equity instruments granted*

4.5.1260.10 If a modification increases the number of equity instruments granted, then the entity recognises the fair value of the additional equity instruments measured at the date of modification. The additional share-based payment cost is attributed over the period from the date of modification to the end of the vesting period of the additional equity instruments. [*IFRS 2.B43(b)*]

4.5.1270 *Beneficial modifications of service and non-market performance conditions*

4.5.1270.10 If the modification changes a service condition or non-market performance condition in a manner that is beneficial to an employee – e.g. by reducing the vesting period or by modifying or eliminating a non-market performance condition – then the remaining grant-date fair value is recognised using the revised vesting expectations with true-up to actual outcomes (see 4.5.1280–1290). [*IFRS 2.B43(c)*]

4.5.1280 Modification of service condition

4.5.1280.10 If a service period is reduced, then the entity uses the modified vesting period when applying the requirements of the modified grant-date method. In the period of change, the entity calculates the cumulative amount to be recognised at the reporting date based on the new vesting conditions. [*IFRS 2.B43(c)*]

EXAMPLE 18 – SHARE-BASED PAYMENT WITH MODIFIED SERVICE CONDITION

4.5.1280.20 Company S grants an equity-settled share-based payment with a grant-date fair value of 1,000 subject to a five-year service period. At the beginning of year 3, the service period is reduced to four years. In this case, S calculates the cumulative amount

> to be recognised at the end of year 3 based on the new vesting period and recognises the difference to the amounts recognised in previous years ($(1,000 \times \frac{3}{4}) - 400 = 350$).

4.5.1280.30 If an employee leaves before vesting date, then an entity may respond by amending the terms of the share-based payment or granting a new award such that the award vests despite the employee not having completed the service period originally required. This fact pattern could be seen as a forfeiture of the original award and a grant of a new award. Forfeiture resulting from voluntary termination of employment by the employee would result in a true-up to zero of the original award. A grant of a new award would result in recognition of the new grant-date fair value immediately because no further services are provided. [*IFRS 2.27, B42, B43(c)*]

4.5.1280.40 In our view, if on termination of employment by either the employee or the employer, the employer accelerates the vesting period such that the employee receives the award despite not having completed the requisite service period, then this is a modification of the award and not a forfeiture of the original award (forfeiture would result in true-up to zero) and a grant of a new un-related award (which would result in recognising the new grant-date fair value immediately because no further services are provided). This is because IFRS 2 illustrates an acceleration of the vesting period as an example of a modification that is beneficial to an employee. The accounting would be the same if the acceleration of vesting were treated as the forfeiture of the original grant and a grant of a replacement award. This is because the grant of a replacement award is also treated as a modification (see 4.5.1430). [*IFRS 2.27*]

4.5.1280.50 Under modification accounting, there is only an incremental fair value to account for if the fair value has increased because of the modification, which is not the case when only a service condition is modified – e.g. waived on employee resignation. Therefore, under modification accounting the grant-date fair value of the original award is recognised immediately because at a minimum the original grant-date fair value is recognised over the revised vesting period of the share-based payment. [*IFRS 2.27–28*]

4.5.1290 Modification of non-market performance condition

4.5.1290.10 Like modifications of a service condition (see 4.5.1280), a modification of a non-market performance condition does not affect the modification date fair value of the share-based payment. The entity determines whether the modification is beneficial to the employee and, if it is, then the modified vesting conditions are taken into account when determining when to recognise the share-based payment cost (see 4.5.1250).

4.5.1290.20 Judgement may be necessary to decide if a change in the non-market performance conditions of a share-based payment arrangement should be considered as a modification. A change in the method of computation may not be a modification, but rather could be a predetermined adjustment that is not accounted for as a modification. As discussed in 4.5.630.10, we believe that a predetermined adjustment to a share-based payment would not result in modification accounting as described in 4.5.1290.10.

EXAMPLE 19 – SHARE-BASED PAYMENT WITH NON-MARKET PERFORMANCE CONDITION THAT IS
NOT MODIFIED

4.5.1290.30   Company P grants employees a share-based payment, the vesting of which depends on P's relative position within a comparator group of companies. P's relative position within this comparator group is based on market share determined with respect to revenue (a non-market performance condition). The agreement specifies that, should one of the comparator group companies need to be deleted from the list for reasons outside the control of P – e.g. de-listing of a competitor such that financial information is no longer available – then it will be replaced by the next company in a predetermined list. The agreement specifies that the objective of the clause is to ensure that the top five competitors by market share are included in the comparator group.

4.5.1290.40   We believe that any substitution in the comparator group in accordance with the original terms is not a modification because the composition of the group and the objective of the clause were clearly stated and defined in advance as part of the terms and condition of the original grant – i.e. the change was predetermined (see 4.5.630.10).

4.5.1290.50   However, if in Example 19 the agreement does not specify the objective of the clause or how a company in the comparator group will be replaced and the revision to the comparator group is a free choice or the change is made at the discretion of the entity, then we believe that this should be accounted for as a modification because of the subjectivity involved (see 4.5.640).

4.5.1300   *Give-and-take modifications*

4.5.1300.10   A package of modifications might include several changes to the terms of a grant, some of which are favourable to the employee and some not. For example, a share option grant can be modified by reducing the exercise price (give) and simultaneously reducing the number of granted options (take). In our view, it is appropriate to net the effects of both modifications, provided that they are agreed as part of a package. This is because the employee realises the net change rather than being able to earn the enhanced benefit of the reduction of the exercise price without suffering the loss in the total number of options. If the net effect is beneficial, then we believe that this net effect should be accounted for by applying the requirements for beneficial modifications to the net change.

4.5.1310   **Modifications that change classification of arrangement**

4.5.1320   *When change in classification should be treated as modification*

4.5.1320.10   Not all changes to the classification of a share-based payment arrangement are 'modifications'. In some cases, changes to the classification of an arrangement that contains multiple interactive vesting conditions may result from a change in the most likely outcome (see 4.5.2230.60).

In this case, in our view a switching approach (see 4.5.830.20–30) should be followed for the change in classification.

4.5.1320.20   There are also cases in which judgement is needed to determine whether modification accounting should be applied to the change in classification. In our view, the factors to consider in determining whether the change is a modification include the following:
• whether the different possible outcomes were contemplated when the award was granted; and
• whether the change is triggered by the entity or by an event that is outside the entity's control.

4.5.1320.30   The diagram below illustrates how we believe that these factors should be taken into account.

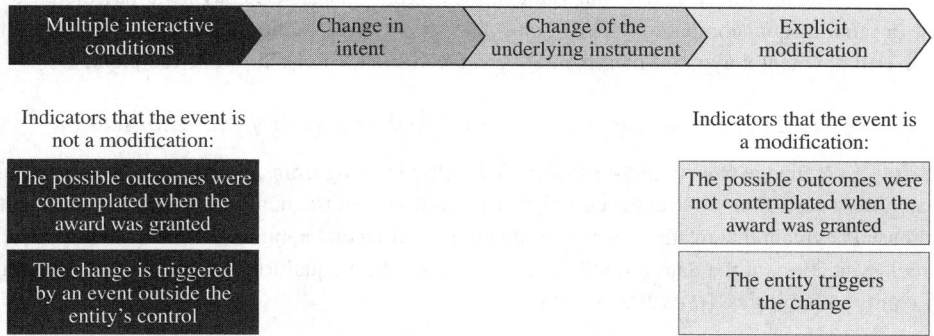

4.5.1320.40   For example, an entity has granted an award that gives it the choice of cash or equity set-tlement. The entity originally intended to settle in equity, and this has been its practice, but it changes its policy and begins to settle in cash; therefore, the entity reclassifies its outstanding share-based payments from equity-settled to cash-settled. We believe that this change in classification should be treated as a modification, because the entity triggered the change (see 4.5.1170.20).

EXAMPLE 20 – CHANGE TRIGGERED BY EVENT OUTSIDE ENTITY'S CONTROL

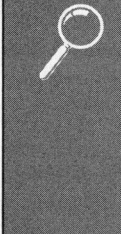

4.5.1320.50   Company N is an income trust under the relevant tax legislation in its jurisdiction. On 1 January 2018, N grants an award to its employees that is re-deemable at the option of the holder. N classifies the award as cash-settled because the units issued to its employees will ultimately result in a cash payment by N to its employees. On 1 January 2019, new tax legislation is enacted that requires all income trusts to be converted into traditional corporate structures. As a result, N's unit-based awards classified as cash-settled share-based payments will become equity-settled share-based payments.

4.5.1320.60   We believe that this change in classification should not be treated as a modification, because the change is triggered by an event outside the entity's

> control. In this case, we believe that a switching approach should be followed for the change in classification (see 4.5.830.20–30).

4.5.1330 *Modifications altering manner of settlement*

4.5.1330.10 A share-based payment may sometimes be modified to alter its manner of settlement. As a result, a share-based payment that was classified as equity-settled at grant date may be modified to become cash-settled or vice versa. IFRS 2 contains guidance on accounting for modifications that result in a change from cash-settled to equity-settled but no explicit guidance on the accounting for modifications that result in a change from equity-settled to cash-settled.

4.5.1330.20 The modification date fair value of the original share-based payment may increase, decrease or remain equal compared with its grant-date fair value. In addition, the terms of the modified share-based payment may grant incremental fair value (see 4.5.1240.20) to its recipient.

4.5.1340 *Change from equity-settled to cash-settled arising from modification*

4.5.1340.10 A change from equity-settled to cash-settled arising from a modification would occur if, for example, a cash alternative at the employee's discretion is subsequently added to an equity-settled share-based payment that results in a reclassification as a financial liability. Such a modification leads to a reclassification, at the date of modification, of an amount equal to the fair value of the liability from equity to liabilities. [*IFRS 2.27, IG.Ex9*]

4.5.1340.20 If the amount of the liability recognised on the date of modification is less than the amount previously recognised as an increase in equity, then no gain is recognised for the difference between the amount recognised to date in equity and the amount reclassified for the fair value of the liability; that difference remains in equity. Subsequent to the modification, the entity continues to recognise the grant-date fair value of equity instruments granted as the cost of the share-based payment. However, any subsequent remeasurement of the liability (from the date of modification until settlement date) is also recognised in profit or loss (see 4.5.970). In effect, this means that the cumulative amount recognised in profit or loss over the life of the award is the grant-date fair value plus or minus any subsequent changes in fair value after the change in classification. Therefore, the cumulative amount may be less than the original grant-date fair value. [*IFRS 2.IG.Ex9*]

4.5.1340.30 If the amount of the liability recognised on the date of modification is greater than the amount previously recognised as an increase in equity, then in our view two approaches are acceptable for recognising the excess liability. We believe that an entity should choose an accounting policy, to be applied consistently, to recognise either:

- the excess as an expense in profit or loss at the date of modification; or
- the entire liability as a reclassification from equity and not recognise any loss in profit or loss.

4.5.1340.40 The first approach of recognising the excess as an expense in profit or loss in effect transfers an amount recognised in equity in respect of the share-based payment to a liability and then remeasures that amount, through profit or loss, to its current fair value.

4.5.1340.50   The second approach of recognising the entire amount of the liability as a reduction in equity is consistent with the treatment applied when the liability is less than the amount recognised in equity, in that no gain is recognised in profit or loss for the difference between the amount recognised to date in equity and the initial fair value of the liability. In our view, it is appropriate for no gain or loss to be recognised in profit or loss when a change in the terms of the share-based payment leads to reclassification as a financial liability provided that the fair value of the liability at the date of modification is not greater than the fair value of the original share-based payment at the date of modification (see 4.5.1200.10–20). This is because under IFRS an entity does not recognise a gain or loss in profit or loss when it buys, sells, issues or cancels its own equity instruments – e.g. when treasury shares are repurchased for amounts greater than their issue cost (see 7.3.330.10, 480.10–20 and 510.10). [*IAS 32.33, AG32, IU 11-06*]

4.5.1350   *Change from cash-settled to equity-settled arising from modification*

4.5.1350.10   A change from cash-settled to equity-settled arising from a modification would occur if, for example, a new equity-settled share-based payment arrangement is identified as a replacement of a cash-settled share-based payment arrangement.

4.5.1350.20   At the modification date, an entity:
- derecognises the liability for the cash-settled share-based payment;
- measures the equity-settled share-based payment at its fair value as at the modification date and recognises in equity that fair value to the extent that the services have been rendered up to that date; and
- immediately recognises in profit or loss the difference between the carrying amount of the liability and the amount recognised in equity. [*IFRS 2.B44A–B44C, IG.Ex.12C*]

4.5.1360   *Modifications that change nature of arrangement*

4.5.1360.10   A modification may change the nature of an arrangement from a share-based payment transaction to an employee benefit in the scope of IAS 19.

4.5.1360.20   In our view, the accounting for modifications that change the classification of an equity-settled share-based payment arrangement to a cash-settled share-based payment arrangement should be applied by analogy to account for an IAS 19 employee benefit that is identified as a replacement of an equity-settled share-based payment arrangement. However, some adjustments should be made to reflect the fact that the new award is not a cash-settled share-based payment but an IAS 19 employee benefit – e.g. it may be necessary to change from a straight-line attribution method to a projected unit credit method. The employee benefit should be measured and recognised based on the general requirements of IAS 19 applicable to the type of employee benefit issued (see chapter 4.4).

4.5.1370   *Modified awards that are forfeited*

4.5.1370.10   As discussed in 4.5.860.10–40, equity-settled share-based payment cost is estimated and trued up for forfeiture because of an employee failing to provide service or failing to satisfy a non-market performance condition.

4.5.1370.20   There is no specific guidance regarding the amount to be reversed because of an employee failing to meet a non-market performance condition after a share-based payment has been modified. Therefore, a question arises about whether the amount to be reversed includes the amount that was recognised in respect of the original award (the grant-date fair value).

4.5.1370.30   In our view, if the employee meets the original condition but fails to meet a non-market performance condition that was added as part of the modification, then the amount to be reversed because of forfeiture is limited to any compensation cost recognised in respect of the modification. Therefore, if the original service condition (and non-market performance condition, if any) are met, then the entity should still recognise as the cost of the share-based payment, the original grant-date fair value of the equity instruments granted.

4.5.1370.40   We believe that this is the appropriate treatment because IFRS 2 states that "the entity shall recognise, as a minimum, the services received measured at the grant-date fair value of the equity instruments granted, unless those equity instruments do not vest because of failure to satisfy a vesting condition (other than a market condition) that was specified at grant date". IFRS 2 goes on to state that "this applies irrespective of any modifications to the terms and conditions on which the equity instruments were granted, or a cancellation or settlement of that grant of equity instruments". [*IFRS 2.27*]

4.5.1380   *Modifications after vesting date*

4.5.1380.10   In contrast to the general principle that no adjustment is made to the accounting for equity-settled share-based payments after vesting date, an adjustment is recognised for modifications occurring after vesting date. In this case, any incremental fair value is recognised immediately or over the new service period, if there is one. [*IFRS 2.B43*]

4.5.1390   **Cancellations or settlements**

4.5.1390.10   Cancellations or settlements of equity-settled share-based payments during the vesting period by the entity or by the counterparty are accounted for as accelerated vesting; therefore, the amount that would otherwise have been recognised for services received is recognised immediately. [*IFRS 2.28(a), IG.Ex.9A*]

4.5.1400   *Cancellation by employee*

4.5.1400.10   Cancellations by the employee can occur because the employee waives the share-based payment for their own reasons. In our experience, this does not occur often. Cancellations will occur more often as a consequence of the employee choosing not to meet a non-vesting condition that is part of the share-based payment arrangement. Failure to meet such a non-vesting condition is treated as a cancellation. [*IFRS 2.28A, BC237B*]

4.5.1400.20   A voluntary cancellation by the employee of an unvested share-based payment is accounted for as a cancellation. For example, a CEO may want to waive the entitlement to share options in difficult economic times. Even though this change is initiated by the employee and no compensation for waiving the entitlement is received, cancellation accounting is still applied.

4.5.1410   **Cancellation by entity**

4.5.1410.10   If the entity cancels a grant of equity instruments, then employees may expect compensation for the cancellation. [*IFRS 2.BC233*]

4.5.1410.20   Payments made for the cancellation are accounted for as repurchases of an equity interest to the extent that the payment does not exceed the fair value of the equity instruments granted, measured at the repurchase date. [*IFRS 2.28(b), 29*]

4.5.1410.30   If the payment made in exchange for the cancellation exceeds the fair value of the equity instruments granted, then the excess is recognised as an expense. The same principles apply to a repurchase of vested equity instruments. [*IFRS 2.28(b), 29*]

4.5.1410.40   For a discussion of a failure to provide service because of the termination of an employee's employment by the employer, see 4.5.860.10–40.

4.5.1420   **Accelerated amount**

4.5.1420.10   As indicated in 4.5.1390.10, the amount recognised when a share-based payment is cancelled is the amount that otherwise would have been recognised over the remainder of the vesting period if the cancellation had not occurred. The standard is not clear about what is meant by "the amount that otherwise would have been recognised for services received over the remainder of the vesting period" – i.e. whether it refers to the number of instruments that could have vested or that were expected to vest (see 4.5.1420.20). [*IFRS 2.28(a)*]

4.5.1420.20   In our view, an entity should choose an accounting policy, to be applied consistently, to follow either of these approaches.
- The share-based payment is recognised as if the service and the non-market performance conditions were met for the cancelled awards – i.e. those not forfeited already. This approach is supported by the wording in IFRS 2 that requires recognition for those equity instruments that were granted unless those equity instruments do not vest.
- The amount that would have been recognised is based on an estimate on the date of cancellation – i.e. estimating how many instruments are expected to vest at the original (future) vesting date. This approach is based on the view that on an ongoing basis the entity would have recognised only the grant-date fair value of those instruments that were expected to vest. [*IFRS 2.27*]

4.5.1430   **Replacements**

4.5.1430.10   Sometimes a share-based payment is granted as a replacement for another share-based payment that is cancelled. In this case, the principles of modification accounting are applied. The basis for conclusions to the standard explains that the reason for permitting a cancellation and a new grant to be accounted for as a modification is that the IASB could not see a difference between those two transactions and a repricing, being a change in the exercise price. [*IFRS 2.28(c), BC233*]

4.5.1430.20   To apply modification accounting, the entity identifies the new equity instruments granted as a replacement for cancelled equity instruments on the date on which the new equity instruments are granted. [*IFRS 2.28(c)*]

4.5.1430.30   If the entity does not identify a new equity-settled plan as a replacement for a cancelled equity-settled plan, then the two plans are accounted for separately. For example, if a new equity-settled share-based payment is offered and an old equity-settled share-based payment is cancelled – but the new plan is not identified as a replacement plan for the cancelled plan – then the new grant is recognised at its grant-date fair value and the original grant is accounted for as a cancellation. [*IFRS 2.28(c)*]

4.5.1430.40   The standard specifies that identification of a new grant as a replacement award is required on the date of the new grant. However, the standard is silent on the question of whether the cancellation should also be on the same date as the new grant. Judgement is required to determine if the facts and circumstances demonstrate that the arrangement is a modification when time has passed between the cancellation and the identification of a new grant.

4.5.1430.50   When modification accounting is applied, the entity accounts for any incremental fair value in addition to the grant-date fair value of the original award. In the case of a replacement, the incremental fair value is the difference between the fair value of the replacement award and the net fair value of the cancelled award, both measured at the date on which the replacement award is issued. The net fair value is the fair value of the cancelled award measured immediately before the cancellation, less any payment made to the employees on cancellation. [*IFRS 2.28(c)*]

4.5.1430.60   An entity may create a new, more beneficial share-based payment plan as a replacement for an old plan, but not formally cancel the old plan – e.g. because it would be disadvantageous for tax purposes to do so. Employees are expected to, and do, cancel their participation in the old plan and join the new one. Together, the entity and the employees are able to identify the new plan as a replacement, but the issue is whether it is eligible to be accounted for as a replacement when the old plan continues to exist. If there is sufficient evidence to establish a clear link between the employees' cancellation of participation in the old plan and acceptance of the share-based payment under the new plan and of the entity's expectation and intent for the new plan to replace the old plan, then in our view it is acceptable to apply replacement accounting. If the new plan is not identified as a replacement of the old plan, then cancellation accounting for the old plan would be applied (see 4.5.1420).

4.5.1440   # GROUP SHARE-BASED PAYMENTS

4.5.1450   ## Scope of this section

4.5.1460   ### *Background*

 4.5.1460.10   A share-based payment transaction in a group context may involve more than one entity in delivering the benefit to the group employees providing services. For example, a parent may grant its own equity instruments to employees of its subsidiary. From the perspective of the *parent's consolidated financial statements*, this transaction is a share-based payment in the scope of IFRS 2. As discussed in this section, the transaction is also a share-based payment in the scope of IFRS 2 from the perspective of the *parent's separate financial statements*, even though it is the subsidiary that receives the services from the employees. It is also a share-based payment in the scope of IFRS 2 from the perspective of the *subsidiary's financial statements*, even though it is the parent that has the obligation to settle the transaction and it is not the subsidiary's own shares that are granted to the employees. The requirements for group share-based payments apply to the separate, individual and consolidated financial statements of a group entity. This section focuses on the requirements in the separate financial statements of the parent and in the financial statements of the subsidiary for arrangements meeting the definition of a group share-based payment. [*IFRS 2.2, 3A*]

4.5.1470 *Definition and scope*

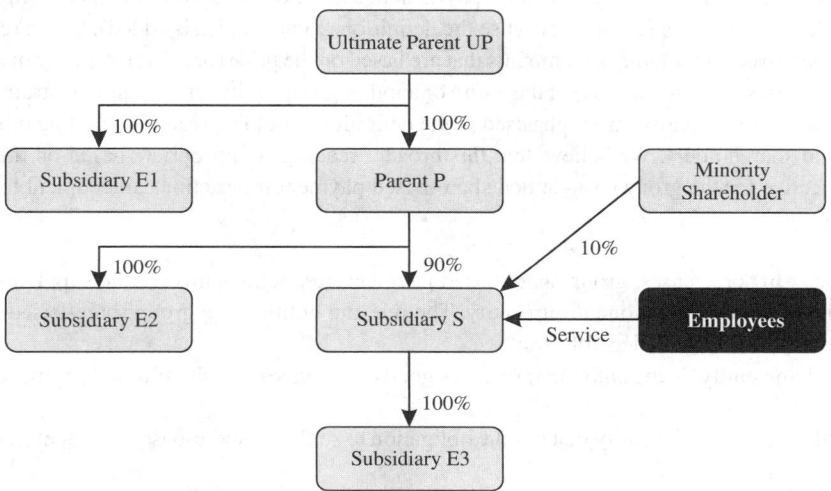

4.5.1470.10 Using this diagram, examples of a share-based payment arrangement that involves two entities include:

- Parent P grants its own equity instruments or a cash payment based on its own equity instruments to the employees of Subsidiary S; and
- S grants equity instruments of P or a cash payment based on the equity instruments of P to its own employees.

4.5.1470.20 P is not part of the reporting entity when S prepares its financial statements. Share-based payment arrangements that involve entities outside the reporting entity are referred to as 'group share-based payment arrangements', if the other entity is, from the perspective of Ultimate Parent UP, in the same group as the reporting entity.

4.5.1470.30 If, for example, a shareholder grants equity instruments of the reporting entity, or a cash payment based on those equity instruments, to parties that have supplied goods or services to the reporting entity, then such a transaction is a share-based payment transaction in the scope of IFRS 2 from the perspective of the reporting entity. Similarly, if the shareholder grants equity instruments, or a cash payment based on those equity instruments, of the reporting entity's parent or another entity in the same group as the reporting entity to parties that have supplied goods or services to the reporting entity, then that grant is a group share-based payment transaction. [*IFRS 2.3A*]

4.5.1470.40 If a reporting entity rather than, for example, the shareholder, grants equity instruments of its parent or equity instruments of another entity in the same group as the reporting entity – or a cash payment based on those equity instruments – to parties that have supplied goods or services to the reporting entity, then such a transaction is a share-based payment transaction in the scope of IFRS 2 from the perspective of the reporting entity. [*IFRS 2.B52(b)*]

4.5.1470.50   When considering the application of IFRS 2 to group share-based payments, the definition of a share-based payment arrangement may appear to be narrow. If in the definition the term 'entity' is read as the reporting entity, then a payment in cash or other assets of another group entity or a shareholder would not be covered because the definition reads (emphasis added): "… to receive (a) cash or other assets *of the entity* for amounts that are based on the price (or value) of equity instruments (including shares or share options) of the entity or another group entity, or (b) equity instruments … " In our view, the term 'entity' as emphasised in the definition should be read as including other group entities and shareholders. We believe that this broader reading is appropriate based on the IASB's stated objective for the group cash-settled share-based payment transactions amendment to IFRS 2. [*IFRS 2.A*]

4.5.1470.60   In some cases, group share-based payment transactions involve the supplier of goods and services and more than one group entity. The relevant entities in a group share-based payment transaction can be described as follows:
- a 'receiving entity' is the entity that receives goods or services in a share-based payment transaction; and
- a 'settling entity' is the entity that has the obligation to settle the share-based payment transaction.

4.5.1470.70   In some group share-based payments, intermediate entities are involved – e.g. when an entity's parent grants a share-based payment to a subsidiary of that entity. For further discussion, see 4.5.2380.

4.5.1470.80   Additionally, group share-based payments may involve equity instruments of another entity within the group or a cash payment based on the value of that other group entity's instruments. To help describe the scope and classification of group share-based payments, the term 'reference entity' is used in this section to describe the entity whose equity instruments are granted or on whose equity instruments a transfer of cash or other assets is based.

4.5.1470.90   The standard excludes from its scope only those transactions that are clearly for a purpose other than payment for goods or services supplied to the entity receiving them. In our view, the requirement for the transfer of, or a cash payment based on, equity instruments to be clearly for another purpose is a high threshold. We believe that any requirement for continued employment should be considered persuasive evidence that transfers of, or cash payments based on, equity instruments to employees are not clearly for another purpose and are share-based payment arrangements in the scope of IFRS 2. [*IFRS 2.3A, BC22*]

4.5.1470.100   If the share-based payment is consideration for services, then in some cases it might be difficult to determine whether it is the entity or the entity's shareholders that receive the service. For example, an entity's shareholder grants a share-based payment to members of the entity's management. The non-market performance condition is completion of a pending sale of the entity. In our view, management's services are received by the entity rather than received only by the shareholders, because it is one of management's normal duties to act in the best interest of the entity's shareholders. The entity might also benefit from the sale in other ways, such as additional sources of financing, enhanced liquidity, access to new markets etc. Therefore, this share-based payment should be reflected in the financial statements of the entity.

4.5.1470.110   The following flowchart summarises the requirements for determining whether a share-based payment that involves different entities is a group share-based payment.

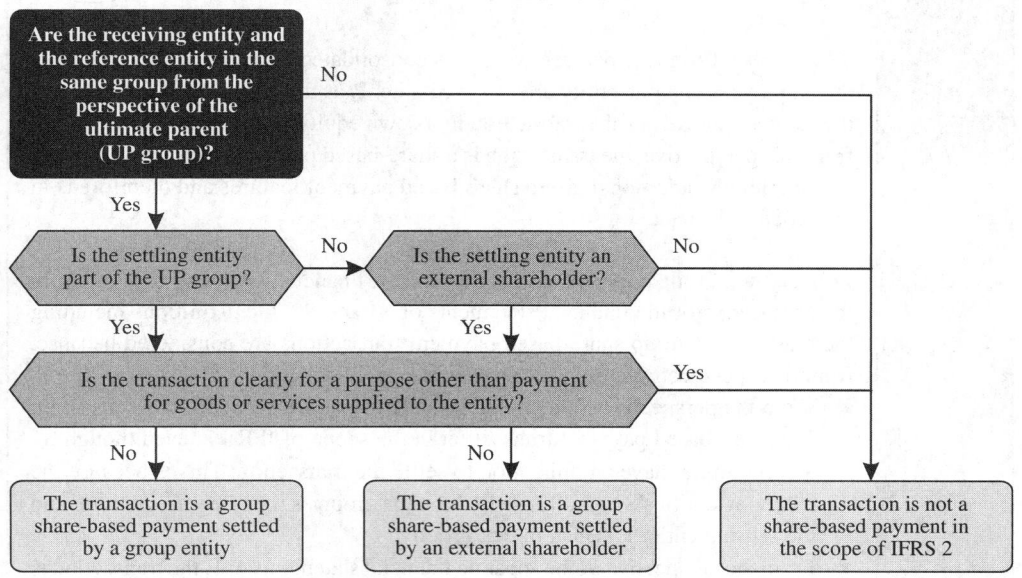

4.5.1480   ***Group share-based payment transactions settled by group entity***

4.5.1480.10   In all scenarios in which the receiving entity, the reference entity and the settling entity are in the same group from the perspective of the ultimate parent, the share-based payment transaction is in the scope of IFRS 2 in the financial statements of the receiving and the settling entity. A group entity that is only a reference entity does not account for the transaction because it is not a party to the arrangement. [*IFRS 2.43A–43C*]

4.5.1480.20   A common example of a group share-based payment transaction is one in which the parent grants its own shares to employees of its subsidiaries.

EXAMPLE 21 – PARENT GRANTS OWN SHARES TO EMPLOYEES OF SUBSIDIARIES   (S)

4.5.1480.30   Parent P grants its own shares to the employees of Subsidiaries S1 and S2. The grant is subject to the condition that the employees stay in service within P's group for a specified period.

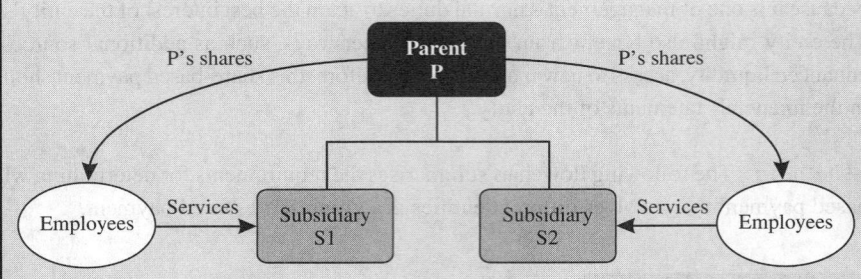

4.5.1480.40   From the perspective of P's consolidated financial statements, only the employees and one entity are involved – i.e. P, as the reporting entity, receives the services and settles the transaction in its own equity instruments. Accordingly, from this perspective, the transaction is a share-based payment transaction without considering the additional group share-based payment features and therefore is in the scope of IFRS 2.

4.5.1480.50   From the perspective of the separate financial statements of P, and from the perspective of the financial statements of S1 and S2, the definitions including the features for group share-based payment transactions are considered because, from their perspectives, multiple entities are involved.
- From the perspective of the financial statements of S1 and S2, the transaction is a share-based payment transaction in the scope of IFRS 2, even though S1 and S2 do not have an obligation to settle the transaction. This is because the receiving entities S1 and S2 are in the same group as the reference entity P and the settling entity P is also in that group.
- From the perspective of the separate financial statements of P, the transaction is a share-based payment in the scope of IFRS 2, even though P does not receive the services directly. This is because the settling entity P is also the reference entity and in the same group as the receiving entities.

4.5.1480.60   The requirement to treat transactions involving instruments of another entity as a share-based payment applies only to transactions involving the equity instruments of a group entity (see 4.5.120.60 and 1470.50–60). The determination of whether another entity is a group entity is based on the definition of a group – i.e. a parent and all of its subsidiaries – from the perspective of the ultimate parent. [*IFRS 2.2(a), 13A, A*]

4.5.1480.70   Therefore, a transaction in which the entity receives services from its employees and the employees receive equity instruments of a non-group shareholder is outside the scope of IFRS 2 from the perspective of the reporting entity.

4.5.1490   *Group share-based payment transactions settled by external shareholder*

4.5.1490.10   A group share-based payment transaction also includes transactions settled by a party that is an external shareholder, as long as the receiving entity and the reference entity are under common control by the same ultimate parent and are therefore in the same group. An 'external shareholder' is any shareholder that is outside that group but is a shareholder of any entity in the group. Examples of external shareholders include parties holding NCI in subsidiaries of the group or any shareholder of the ultimate parent. [*IFRS 2.3A*]

4.5.1490.20   Group share-based payment transactions that are settled by an external shareholder are in the scope of IFRS 2 from the perspective of the receiving entity if the reference entity is in the same group as the receiving entity. [*IFRS 2.3A, B50*]

4.5.1500   *Settlement by external shareholder when reference entity is in same group as receiving entity*

4.5.1500.10   If a shareholder that is not a group entity settles by granting equity instruments of the receiving entity (or a cash payment based on those equity instruments), then the transaction is in the scope of IFRS 2 from the perspective of the receiving entity. [*IFRS 2.3A*]

4.5.1500.20   However, in our view the transaction described in 4.5.1500.10 is not a share-based payment in the scope of IFRS 2 from the perspective of the shareholder. This is because the reference entity is not in the same group as the shareholder settling the transaction. [*IFRS 2.3A(b), B50*]

4.5.1500.30   If the reporting entity receives services from its employees and the employees receive equity instruments of a shareholder that is not a group entity, but the number of equity instruments received by the employees is based on the value of the reporting entity's equity instruments, then the transaction is in the scope of IFRS 2 from the perspective of the reporting entity. This is because in such a case the reporting entity is identified as the reference entity (see 4.5.1470.70–80) as the employees receive assets (the shareholder's equity instruments) based on the value of the reporting entity's equity instruments. The transaction is also in the scope of IFRS 2 from the perspective of the shareholder, for the reasons set out in 4.5.1510.10–20.

4.5.1510   *Settlement by external shareholder when reference entity is in shareholder's group*

4.5.1510.10   If an external shareholder settles in or based on its own equity instruments, rather than in the receiving entity's equity instruments, which is addressed in 4.5.1500, then the transaction is in the scope of IFRS 2 from the perspective of the shareholder. This is because the shareholder grants its own shares or a cash payment based thereon in return for receiving services. The fact that the shareholder receives the services only indirectly – i.e. via its investment, rather than directly – does not change this conclusion because the requirement to recognise unidentifiable goods or services applies. [*IFRS 2.2, 13A*]

4.5.1510.20   From the perspective of the receiving entity in which the shareholder invests, the transaction is generally not in the scope of IFRS 2 (see 4.5.1500.30). This is because the receiving entity and the reference entity are not in the same group, the reference entity being an external shareholder.

4.5.1510.30   IFRS 2 also applies to transactions in which the reporting entity grants equity instruments of the entity's parent or another entity in the same group as the reporting entity to parties that have supplied goods or services to another party in the group. [*IFRS 2.2*]

4.5.1520   **Classification of group share-based payment arrangements**

4.5.1530   *Classification principles*

4.5.1530.10   Classification of the share-based payment transaction depends on the nature of the award granted and whether the entity has an obligation to settle the transaction. If the entity has either an obligation to settle in its own equity instruments or no obligation to settle at all, then the transaction is accounted for as equity-settled. A settling entity that is not a receiving entity classifies a share-based payment transaction as equity-settled if it settles in its own equity instruments; otherwise, it classifies the transaction as cash-settled. [*IFRS 2.43A–43C*]

Ⓢ 4.5.1530.20   A share-based payment transaction is classified from the perspective of each reporting entity, rather than by making a single group-wide classification determination. In a typical group share-based payment transaction involving a parent and its subsidiary, separate classification assessments are made for a single transaction from the following three perspectives:
- the consolidated financial statements of the parent;
- the separate financial statements of the parent; and
- the consolidated and separate financial statements of the subsidiary. [*IFRS 2.43A, B45–B61*]

4.5.1530.30   Therefore, a single share-based payment transaction could be classified as equity-settled in the financial statements of a subsidiary that receives the services and cash-settled in the group's consolidated financial statements, or vice versa.

4.5.1540   *Equity instruments of another group entity: Own equity instruments vs cash or other assets*

4.5.1540.10   It is important to consider the perspective of the reporting entity and whether it is the separate entity or a consolidated group that is reporting when there is an obligation to settle the transaction in equity instruments of another group entity. This is because classification can differ between the separate and consolidated financial statements and can also differ between the various consolidated financial statements in a multiple-level group structure. [*IFRS 2.B50*]

Ⓢ 4.5.1540.20   From the perspective of the separate financial statements of the reporting entity, equity instruments of another entity in the group are classified as 'cash or other assets'. In contrast, from the group perspective equity instruments of an entity within the reporting entity's group are considered to be own equity instruments. This is because the shares in a subsidiary form part of the NCI in the ultimate parent's consolidated financial statements and are therefore considered to be equity for the purposes of the consolidated financial statements of the group (see 7.3.240.20).

4.5.1540.30   The scope assessment differs from the classification assessment. In the scope assessment, focus is placed on whether the reference entity is in or outside the group of the *ultimate parent* (see 4.5.1470.20). In the classification assessment, focus is placed on whether the equity instruments are those of the *reporting entity*.

4.5.1550   *Classification in financial statements of settling entity*

4.5.1560   Determining the settling entity

4.5.1560.10   Identifying the settling entity in a group share-based payment is not always straightforward. For example, Parent P issues its own shares to Subsidiary S and S uses those shares to settle a share-based payment granted by Subsidiary B to its employees. In our view, determining which of P and S is the settling entity depends on the facts and circumstances. We believe that if S is an operating entity managing its own cash flows, then it is likely that S is the settling entity. Conversely, we believe that if S fully depends on P for its financing and has no operating activity – e.g. it is an entity that is used only to settle this transaction – then it is likely that S is only an agent acting on P's behalf and that P is the settling entity. For a discussion of determining the fair value of equity instruments granted, see 4.5.740. For a discussion of an employee benefit trust used as the settling entity, see 4.5.2400.10.

4.5.1570   *Classification in financial statements of receiving entity without obligation to settle*

4.5.1570.10   A receiving entity that has no obligation to settle the transaction with the counterparty to the share-based payment transaction accounts for the transaction as equity-settled and recognises an expense, unless the goods or services received qualify for recognition as an asset, and an increase in its equity for the contribution received from the parent. [*IFRS 2.B53*]

4.5.1580   **Recognition and measurement**

4.5.1590   *Accounting for group share-based payment arrangement*

4.5.1590.10   After determining the classification of the share-based payment in the financial statements of the reporting entity, the recognition and measurement of the share-based payment transaction follows the accounting requirements for equity-settled share-based payments or for cash-settled share-based payments.

OBLIGATION TO SETTLE? \ NATURE OF THE AWARD:	OWN EQUITY INSTRUMENTS	CASH OR OTHER ASSETS
Yes	Equity-settled	Cash-settled
No	Equity-settled	Equity-settled

4.5.1600   *Accounting by direct parent that settles*

4.5.1600.10   A settling entity recognises an increase in equity or liabilities, depending on the classification of the share-based payment transaction. However, there is no explicit guidance on how a settling entity that is different from a receiving entity accounts for the debit entry.

4.5.1610   Equity-settled transactions

4.5.1610.10   When a parent grants rights to its equity instruments to employees of a subsidiary, the identifiable consideration received by the parent from the perspective of its separate financial statements for the equity instruments may be zero. If the identifiable consideration received is less than the fair value of the equity instruments granted (or liability incurred), then there is an indication that other consideration – i.e. unidentifiable goods or services – has been or will be received (see 4.5.170.20). [*IFRS 2.13A*]

4.5.1610.20   In our view, if a parent grants rights to its own equity instruments to employees of a subsidiary, then the parent receives goods or services indirectly through the subsidiary in the form of an increased investment in the subsidiary – i.e. the subsidiary receives services from employees that are paid for by the parent – thereby increasing the value of the subsidiary. Therefore, we believe that the parent should recognise in equity the equity-settled share-based payment, with a corresponding increase in its investment in the subsidiary in its separate financial statements. The amount recognised as an additional investment is based on the grant-date fair value of the share-based payment. In our view, the increase in investment and corresponding increase in equity for the equity-settled share-based payment should be recognised by the parent over the vesting period of the share-based payment. In recognising these amounts, the normal requirements for accounting for forfeitures should be applied (see 4.5.540).

Ⓢ 4.5.1620   Cash-settled transactions

4.5.1620.10   Accounting for a share-based payment transaction that has been classified as cash-settled in the parent's separate financial statements is more complex than for one classified as an equity-settled share-based payment.

4.5.1620.20   Assuming that an investment in a subsidiary is not different from any other asset measured on a cost basis, the same principles of recognition of the increase in the carrying amount of the asset for the services received in a cash-settled share-based payment apply – i.e. a parent would capitalise the grant-date fair value of the liability. The effects of changes in the estimated and actual outcome of service and non-market conditions would adjust the grant-date fair value cost of investment. Other remeasurements of the grant-date fair value would be recognised in profit or loss.

Ⓢ 4.5.1630   *Accounting by ultimate parent that settles*

4.5.1630.10   In some cases, the ultimate parent grants a share-based payment to a subsidiary in the group. As discussed in 4.5.1600.10, the settling entity – in this case, the ultimate parent – recognises an increase in equity or liabilities depending on the classification of the share-based payment transaction. However, there is no explicit guidance in IFRS 2 regarding the debit entry. In our view, the grant of a share-based payment by an ultimate parent to a group subsidiary increases the value of the ultimate parent's direct or indirect investment in the subsidiary. Therefore, we believe that the ultimate parent should recognise the cost of the share-based payment as a cost of investment in the subsidiary.

EXAMPLE 22 – SHARE-BASED PAYMENT SETTLED BY ULTIMATE PARENT

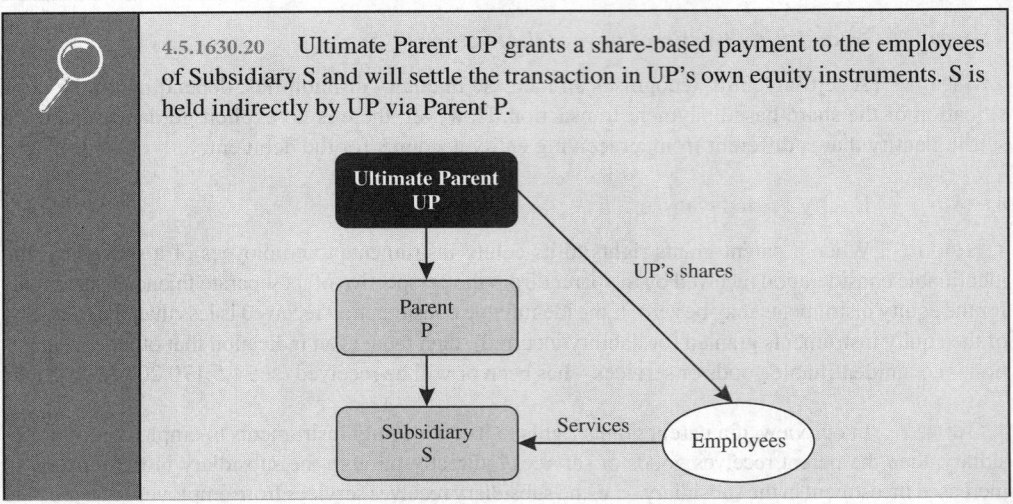

4.5.1630.20   Ultimate Parent UP grants a share-based payment to the employees of Subsidiary S and will settle the transaction in UP's own equity instruments. S is held indirectly by UP via Parent P.

> **4.5.1630.30** In our view, P, as an intermediate parent, should choose an accounting policy regarding whether to recognise a share-based payment in its separate financial statements (see 4.5.2380). We believe that, regardless of whether P recognises the transaction, the value of UP's investment in P increases by granting the share-based payment arrangement to S's employees, and therefore UP should recognise the cost of the share-based payment as a cost of investment in P.

4.5.1640   *Accounting by another group entity that settles*

4.5.1640.10   In our view, a settling entity with no direct or indirect investment in the entity receiving the services in a group share-based payment arrangement should recognise the cost of the share-based payment in equity as a distribution to its parent over the vesting period. This is because the entity could be seen to be settling the transaction on behalf of its parent.

EXAMPLE 23 – SHARE-BASED PAYMENT IN WHICH FELLOW SUBSIDIARY IS SETTLING ENTITY

> **4.5.1640.20**   Parent P has two subsidiaries, Q and R. Q grants a share-based payment to the employees of R and will settle the transaction in Q's own equity instruments.

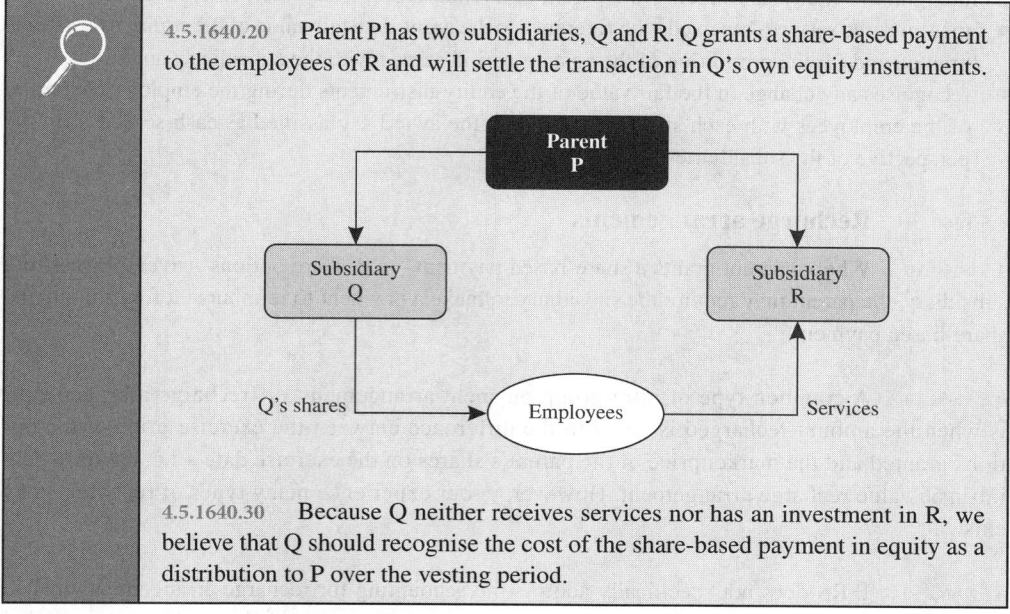

> **4.5.1640.30**   Because Q neither receives services nor has an investment in R, we believe that Q should recognise the cost of the share-based payment in equity as a distribution to P over the vesting period.

4.5.1650   *Accounting for transfers of employees*

4.5.1650.10   Employees may transfer within the group during the vesting period of a share-based payment arrangement. In some circumstances, the share-based payment may lapse or vest and the employee may be offered a new share-based payment. In such cases, the normal requirements for employees leaving and joining share-based payment arrangements usually apply from the perspective of each entity; for a discussion of the accounting for forfeitures, see 4.5.860.10–40.

4.5.1650.20   In other circumstances, a parent (or another group entity) may grant rights to its equity instruments to employees of a subsidiary that are conditional on the employees providing service within the group for a specified period of time. In such arrangements, the transfer of an employee will have no effect on the vesting of the share-based payment from the employee's point of view. [*IFRS 2.B59, B61*]

4.5.1650.30   If the subsidiaries have no obligation to settle the transaction with their employees, then the transaction is accounted for as equity-settled. Each subsidiary measures the services received from the employee with reference to the parent's grant-date fair value of the equity instruments. If an employee subsequently fails to satisfy a vesting condition other than a market condition, such that there is true-up of the share-based payment at the group level, then each subsidiary adjusts the amount previously recognised in its financial statements. If the employee transfers between two group entities during the vesting period, then this is not deemed to be a forfeiture from the perspective of the financial statements of the former employer or a new grant by the new employer. [*IFRS 2.B60–B61*]

4.5.1650.40   If the subsidiaries have an obligation to settle the transaction in cash or other assets, including in the equity instruments of a parent or another group entity, then each subsidiary:
- measures the services received with reference to the grant-date fair value of the equity instruments granted and for the proportion of the vesting period served with the subsidiary; and
- recognises any change in the fair value of the equity instruments during the employment period of the employees with each subsidiary, because the award is classified as cash-settled from the perspective of the subsidiaries. [*IFRS 2.B60*]

4.5.1660   Recharge arrangements

4.5.1660.10   When a parent grants a share-based payment – e.g. share options – to employees of a subsidiary, the parent may require the subsidiary to make a payment to reimburse it for granting the share-based payment.

4.5.1660.20   A common type of intra-group payment arrangement, or 'recharge arrangement', is when the amount recharged is equal to the difference between the exercise price of the options granted and the market price of the parent's shares on the exercise date – i.e. exercise date intrinsic value recharge arrangement. However, in our experience many types of recharges may exist.

4.5.1660.30   IFRS does not specifically address the accounting for recharge arrangements related to share-based payment transactions involving group entities or external shareholders. A receiving entity with no obligation to settle the transaction classifies the share-based payment in accordance with the normal classification requirements irrespective of the existence of any recharge arrangement. Therefore, the existence of a recharge arrangement between a parent and a subsidiary does not mean that in substance it is the subsidiary that has the obligation to the employees. [*IFRS 2.43D, B45*]

4.5.1660.40   Paragraphs 4.5.1670–1690 address the accounting in the financial statements of the subsidiary and the parent for recharge arrangements levied in respect of share-based payment arrangements that are classified as equity-settled in both the consolidated financial statements of the parent and the financial statements of the subsidiary (see 4.5.1530).

4.5.1660.50   The guidance may also be applied by analogy to other share-based payment arrangements – e.g. to those that are classified as cash-settled in the consolidated financial statements of the parent.

4.5.1660.60   In our experience, recharges from the parent settling the transaction to the subsidiary receiving the services are usually settled in cash. For a discussion of the recharge being settled by the subsidiary in shares of the parent rather than in cash, see 4.5.1740; and for a discussion of the recharge being settled by the subsidiary either in cash or in the subsidiary's own shares, see 4.5.1760.

4.5.1670   *Determining 'clearly linked' recharge arrangements*

4.5.1670.10   Determining the appropriate accounting treatment for a recharge arrangement will require judgement based on the terms and conditions of each arrangement. In our view, if the recharge is clearly linked to the share-based payment arrangement, then it should be accounted for separately from the share-based payment, but as an adjustment of the capital contribution recognised in respect of the share-based payment.

4.5.1670.20   In our view, in assessing whether a recharge is clearly linked to the share-based payment arrangement, the primary determinant should be whether the amount of the payment is based on the value of the share-based payment. The following are examples of situations in which we believe that a recharge would generally be considered to be clearly linked to the share-based payment:

- a payment based on the grant-date fair value of the equity-settled share-based payment (IFRS 2 charge);
- a payment based on the cost of the treasury share programme of the parent (parent's cost of acquiring the shares to settle its obligation to the employees of the subsidiary); or
- a payment based on the difference between the exercise price of the options and the market price of the parent's shares on exercise date (intrinsic value recharge).

4.5.1670.30   We believe that a recharge that is clearly linked to the share-based payment arrangement could also include, for example, some stated proportion of these bases.

4.5.1670.40   In addition, if a recharge that is based on the value of a share-based payment is also based on the number of awards that vest or are exercised, then we believe that this provides additional evidence that the recharge is clearly linked to the share-based payment arrangement.

4.5.1670.50   In our view, the timing of a recharge payment should not be a primary determinant of whether it is clearly linked to the share-based payment arrangement. However, if the parent articulates in advance of or at the same time as the grant that a recharge that is based on the value of the share-based payment is in respect of the share-based payment arrangement, then we believe that this provides evidence that the recharge is clearly linked. If a parent levies a recharge well after grant date – e.g. only when the options are exercised – with no prior communication of this intent and the parent having no history of having done so, then the timing of the recharge may weaken its link to the share-based payment arrangement.

4.5.1670.60   If a recharge arrangement that is clearly linked to a share-based payment is a contractual (oral or written) arrangement, then in our view the recharge transaction should be recognised and measured by analogy to the requirements for cash-settled share-based payment transactions (see 4.5.910). We believe that accounting for a contractual recharge by analogy to cash-settled share-based payments is appropriate because:

- IFRS 2 applies to expenses relating to share-based payments; and
- IFRS 9 does not apply to contractual expenses that are accounted for under IFRS 2. [*IFRS 9.2.1(h)*]

4.5.1670.70   Because the subsidiary recognises a capital contribution as part of the share-based payment arrangement, we believe that it is also appropriate for the subsidiary to recognise its reimbursement of the capital contribution to the parent as an adjustment of that capital contribution. The subsidiary should therefore recognise a recharge liability and a corresponding adjustment (debit) in equity for the capital contribution recognised in respect of the share-based payment.

4.5.1670.80   Similarly, because the parent recognises its capital contribution to the subsidiary as an increase in its investment in the subsidiary (see 4.5.1610.10–20), we believe that it is appropriate for the parent to account for the reimbursement by the subsidiary of this capital contribution by analogy to the requirements for cash-settled share-based payment transactions. The parent should therefore recognise a recharge asset and a corresponding adjustment (credit) to the carrying amount of the investment in the subsidiary.

4.5.1680   *Recognition and measurement of clearly linked recharge arrangements accounted for by analogy to IFRS 2*

4.5.1680.10   For recharges accounted for by analogy to the requirements for cash-settled share-based payments (see 4.5.1670.60), we believe that the recharge should be accounted for from the time when the parent and the subsidiary have a shared understanding of the terms and conditions of the contract; this will often be before the subsidiary makes a payment to the parent to settle its obligation under the recharge arrangement. We believe that the subsidiary and parent should measure the fair value of the recharge liability and asset initially at the date on which a shared understanding is established and, similar to the treatment of a share-based payment, the initial measurement of the recharge should be recognised as the services are provided in respect of the share-based payment.

4.5.1690   Varying recharges

4.5.1690.10   Additional complexities arise with regard to the accounting for a recharge in which the amount of the recharge varies – e.g. the amount recharged under an exercise date intrinsic value recharge arrangement varies with changes in share price (see 4.5.1660.10–20). Continuing to apply the guidance for cash-settled share-based payments by analogy, if such a recharge that is clearly linked to a share-based payment is recognised before the subsidiary makes a cash payment to the parent to settle its obligation, then we believe that the asset and liability arising from the recharge arrangement should be remeasured at the reporting date and ultimately at settlement date for changes in fair value (see 4.5.940.10).

4.5.1690.20   In our view, changes in the fair value of a linked recharge that is accounted for by analogy to the requirements for cash-settled share-based payments should not be recognised through profit or loss. This is because we believe that it is the nature of the payment that should determine the accounting treatment. We believe that the nature of a linked recharge is that of a reimbursement of a capital transaction and therefore that changes in the fair value of the recharge liability and asset from initial recognition to settlement should be treated as a true-up of the initial estimate of the net capital contribution.

4.5.1690.30   If a recharge liability is denominated in a currency that is not the functional currency of the subsidiary, then in our view IAS 21 should be applied. As a result, foreign exchange gains and losses that result from changes in the exchange rate should be recognised in profit or loss (see 2.7.130–140).

4.5.1700   *Recognition and measurement of clearly linked non-contractual recharge arrangements*

4.5.1700.10   In some cases, a well-established past practice or stated policy of applying recharges related to share-based payments may result in a recharge expense being considered a non-contractual constructive obligation. In our view, an entity should choose an accounting policy, to be applied consistently, to account for a constructive obligation for a non-contractual recharge either:
- by analogy to a cash-settled share-based payment in the scope of IFRS 2 (see 4.5.1670.60); or
- as a constructive obligation in the scope of IAS 37.

4.5.1700.20   Under IAS 37, a provision is recognised for a constructive obligation (see 3.12.30) when:
- a past event gives rise to a present obligation;
- it is probable there will be an outflow of resources required to settle the obligation; and
- a reliable estimate can be made of the amount of the obligation. [*IAS 37.14*]

4.5.1700.30   In our view, a present obligation for a non-contractual recharge arises when the related share-based payment has vested (vesting date). In determining whether an outflow of resources is probable, the following factors may be relevant:
- whether a share-based payment award is in the money;
- the volatility of the share price; and
- the tax consequences to the holder of exercising the share-based payment award. [*IAS 37.IE.C.Ex6–Ex7*]

4.5.1700.40   Once a provision has been recognised, it is remeasured at each reporting date and ultimately at settlement date. As discussed in 4.5.1670.10, if the recharge is determined to be clearly linked to the share-based payment, then the initial recognition and subsequent remeasurement of the provision should be recorded as an adjustment of the capital contribution recognised in respect of the share-based payment.

4.5.1710   **Excess recharges**   Ⓢ

4.5.1710.10   The amount recharged may be greater than the increase in the investment recognised by the parent in respect of the share-based payment. In our view, the excess should be treated by the subsidiary as a net capital distribution. In our view, in the absence of specific guidance in IFRS, more than one approach to the accounting by the parent for the excess may be acceptable. We believe that the parent should choose an accounting policy, to be applied consistently, with respect to the treatment of the excess of a recharge over the capital contribution recognised in respect of the share-based payment in its separate financial statements. The approaches in 4.5.1720–30 are examples of accounting policies that we believe are acceptable.

Ⓢ 4.5.1720   *Approach 1: Adjustment of capital contribution*

4.5.1720.10   Under this approach, the entire amount of the recharge, including the excess, is treated by the parent as an adjustment of the capital contribution to the subsidiary.

4.5.1720.20   If the recharge is greater than the recognised investment in the subsidiary, then we believe that the amount of the recharge in excess of the capital contribution recognised in respect of a share-based payment that is clearly linked to the recharge could be recognised as a return of capital. Under this approach, the initial recognition and subsequent remeasurement of that recharge would both be recognised as a reduction in the cost of the investment in the subsidiary and the excess of the recharge would cause a reduction in the net investment in the subsidiary.

Ⓢ 4.5.1730   *Approach 2: Dividend income*

4.5.1730.10   Under this approach, the excess is treated by the parent as dividend income.

4.5.1730.20   If the recharge is greater than the increase in the investment in the subsidiary, then we believe that the amount of the recharge in excess of the capital contribution recognised in respect of the clearly linked share-based payment could be recognised as dividend income. The determination of the excess that will ultimately be recognised as dividend income should be made on a grant-by-grant, employee-by-employee basis.

4.5.1740   **Alternative approaches for recharge arrangements that are settleable in shares of parent**

4.5.1740.10   A subsidiary may settle a recharge arrangement that is clearly linked to a share-based payment using the parent's shares rather than with cash. In our view, an entity should choose an accounting policy, to be applied consistently, to account for such a recharge arrangement either:
- by analogy to cash-settled share-based payment accounting (see 4.5.1680);
- by analogy to the requirements of the financial instruments standards; or
- if the arrangement is non-contractual, then in accordance with IAS 37 (see 4.5.1700).

4.5.1740.20   If financial instrument accounting is applied by analogy, then the subsidiary recognises a financial liability at fair value through profit or loss when the entity becomes a counterparty to the recharge agreement. Therefore, the entire fair value of the liability is recognised at once when the entity becomes a counterparty. Immediate recognition differs from the approach when a recharge arrangement is accounted for by analogy to a cash-settled share-based payment (see 4.5.1680). The debit is recognised in equity as an adjustment to the capital contribution that is recognised for the share-based payment transaction.

4.5.1740.30   Under the financial instrument accounting approach in 4.5.1740.20, subsequent changes in the fair value of the liability that arise from changes in estimates regarding employees not meeting the service or non-market performance conditions are recognised in equity. All other changes, such as unwinding the discount effect or changes in the value of the shares, are recognised in profit or loss.

4.5.1740.40   If, for example, the subsidiary has bought its parent's shares at grant date in order to have an economic hedge of its exposure to changes in the value of its parent's shares, then the investment in its parent's shares is accounted for as a financial asset, classified either at fair value through profit or loss or designated at fair value through OCI. For a financial asset classified at fair value through profit or loss, to account for changes in the liability for the recharge that arise from share price movements, any fair value changes with respect to the financial asset that are recognised in profit or loss are mirrored by a change in the value of the financial liability, which is also recognised in profit or loss. The net effect reflects the natural hedge of the transaction. If a financial asset is designated at fair value through OCI, then this natural hedge through profit or loss will not usually be achieved, because fair value changes on the asset are recognised in OCI instead of in profit or loss.

4.5.1760   *Recharge arrangements that are settleable in cash or in subsidiary's own shares*

4.5.1760.10   If the terms of a recharge arrangement that is clearly linked to a share-based payment offer the subsidiary a choice of settling in cash or in its own shares, then in our view the guidance for the classification of a share-based payment award as either equity-settled or cash-settled applies to determine the nature of the recharge obligation (see 4.5.330).

4.5.1770   *Recognition and measurement of recharge arrangements that are not clearly linked*

4.5.1770.10   Recharge arrangements that are not clearly linked are accounted for separately from the share-based payment arrangement. An entity considers whether such an arrangement is in the scope of another standard, in particular the financial instruments standards, and whether it is a transaction with a shareholder.

4.5.1780   *Modifications and replacements*

4.5.1780.10   A share-based payment between one group entity (e.g. a subsidiary) and its employees may be altered to change the settling entity to another group entity (e.g. the parent). Such alterations may also change the reference entity from the subsidiary to the parent.

4.5.1780.20   In our view, a share-based payment involving equity instruments of one group entity offered in exchange for a share-based payment arrangement of another group entity outside a business combination may be identified as a replacement plan in the consolidated financial statements of the group. For example, if Company P grants options over its shares to employees of Subsidiary Q in exchange for their options over shares of Q, then we believe that the grant of replacement options, if they are identified as such, should be accounted for in the consolidated financial statements of P as a modification of the original grant of options over shares of Q. This is because the shares in Q form part of NCI in P and are therefore considered to be equity for the purposes of the consolidated financial statements of the group.

(S) 4.5.1780.30   P accounts for the replacement as described in 4.5.1430.10 in its separate financial statements as an increase in the cost of investment and an increase in equity based on modification date fair value. From the date of modification, Q accounts for the transaction in its separate financial statements by recognising both the original cost at the grant-date fair value attributable to future services and any incremental value as a capital contribution from the parent.

4.5.1790   Presentation

4.5.1790.10   Generally, IFRS does not address presentation within equity for equity-settled share-based payment transactions (see 4.5.900).

4.5.1790.20   However, when equity instruments of a subsidiary have been granted to a counterparty that is not part of the consolidated reporting entity in a share-based payment transaction, the credit entry in equity in the consolidated financial statements of the parent is to NCI. This is because the definition of NCI in IFRS 10 refers to the equity in a subsidiary not attributable, directly or indirectly, to a parent (see 2.5.450).

4.5.1800   SHARE-BASED PAYMENTS WITH NON-EMPLOYEES
4.5.1810   Definition of non-employees

4.5.1810.10   Although the recognition requirements are similar for share-based payment transactions with employees and share-based payment transactions with non-employees, the measurement requirements differ in many respects. Therefore, it is important to determine the nature of the counterparty.

4.5.1810.20   The standard does not define a non-employee. However, it does indicate what the term 'employees or others providing similar services' encompasses (see 4.5.490) and notes that this includes non-executive directors. All other counterparties – i.e. those who are not considered 'employees or others providing similar services' – are considered non-employees. [*IFRS 2.A*]

4.5.1810.30   When assessing whether an individual is rendering services in a capacity as an employee or a non-employee, in our view the substance of the relationship between the entity and the individual should be considered, rather than simply the legal form of the arrangement. For example, an entity may consider one or more of the following factors in determining whether an individual is rendering services in a capacity as an employee. This list is not intended to be exhaustive and the assessment requires judgement.
- The entity is able to direct the individual's services in the same way as those of individuals regarded as employees for legal or tax purposes.
- The services rendered are similar to those rendered by employees.
- The service provider is able to determine when and how the services are provided. [*IFRS 2.A*]

EXAMPLE 24A – SHARE-BASED PAYMENT – COUNTERPARTY CLASSIFIED AS EMPLOYEE (1)

4.5.1810.40   Company B grants share options to Company Z, conditional on Z providing specified services to B. The services that Z is obliged to render are services of an individual, W, who is covering for an employee on long-term leave. Z is a 'one person' company set up by W for personal tax reasons. Although in this example Z is not an individual but a company, the services are similar to those rendered by employees, because the services comprise solely of the personal services of W. Therefore, we believe that the counterparty (Z) should be classified as an employee.

EXAMPLE 24B – SHARE-BASED PAYMENT – COUNTERPARTY CLASSIFIED AS NON-EMPLOYEE

4.5.1810.50   In contrast to Example 24A, Company C grants share options to Company Z, conditional on Z providing specified services to C. The services that Z is obliged to render are to design C's new logo. Z is a small company with multiple owners and several individuals are expected to work on the project.

4.5.1810.60   In this example, the services are not required from a specified individual, the services are not similar to those rendered by employees, Z can determine when and how the services are performed, and the share options are granted to Z – i.e. not to a specified individual. Therefore, we believe that the counterparty (Z) should be classified as a non-employee.

EXAMPLE 24C – SHARE-BASED PAYMENT – COUNTERPARTY CLASSIFIED AS EMPLOYEE (2)

4.5.1810.70   Company C receives specialised computer services from Mr K, an individual. Mr K is not a legal employee but works under a contract to provide services under the direction of C in the same way as individuals regarded as permanent employees under legislation in that jurisdiction. Mr K works one day a week for C and provides similar services to other companies for the rest of the week. As consideration for these services, C grants to Mr K a share-based payment.

4.5.1810.80   In this example, C has the ability to direct Mr K's services in the same way as those of its employees. Therefore, we believe that the counterparty (Mr K) should be classified as an employee.

4.5.1820   **Equity-settled share-based payments with non-employees**

4.5.1830   *Overview*

4.5.1830.10   The following flowchart summarises the requirements for equity-settled share-based payments with non-employees.

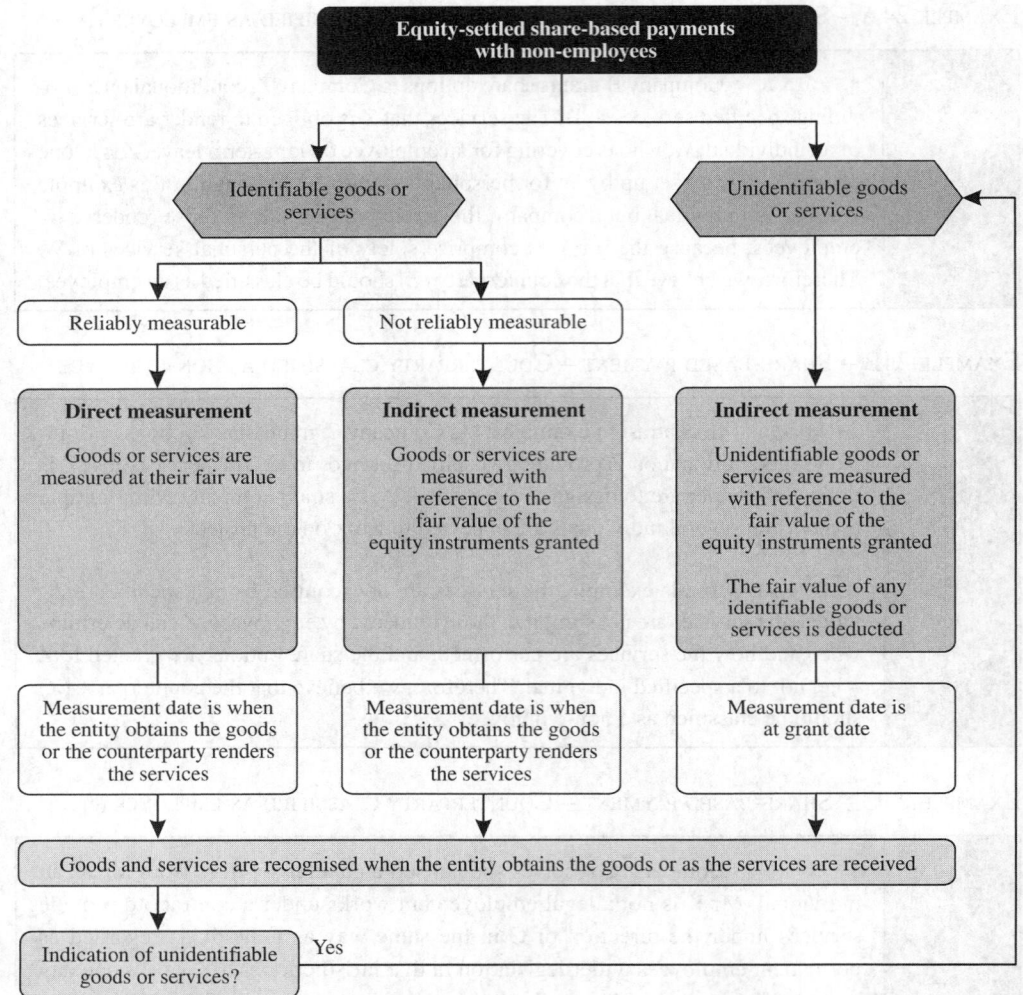

4.5.1840 *Recognition principles*

4.5.1840.10 In equity-settled share-based payments with non-employees, goods are recognised when they are obtained and services are recognised when they are received. If the goods or services do not qualify for recognition as assets, then they are expensed. This is similar to equity-settled share-based payments with employees. [*IFRS 2.7–8, 10, 14–15*]

4.5.1850 *Measurement principles*

4.5.1850.10 In contrast to equity-settled share-based payments with employees, which are measured at grant date, goods are measured when they are obtained and services are measured when they are rendered by the counterparty. Therefore, a single agreement with a non-employee can have multiple measurement dates, one for each delivery of goods or services. We refer to the 'measurement date' as the date on which the goods or services are received, which is consistent with the language used in IFRS 2. [*IFRS 2.7, 13, A*]

4.5.1850.20   What is being measured depends on whether the goods or services can be measured reliably. There is a rebuttable presumption that the goods or services from non-employees can be measured reliably, in which case the goods or services are measured at their fair value (direct measurement), with the share-based payment exchanged for the goods or services measured at an equal amount. If in rare cases the presumption is rebutted, then the goods or services are measured indirectly – i.e. with reference to the fair value of the equity instruments granted (indirect measurement) – as for equity-settled share-based payments with employees. [*IFRS 2.13*]

4.5.1850.30   If the consideration received in the form of those identifiable goods or services *appears* to be less than the fair value of the equity instruments granted, then the entity may be required to perform an 'indirect measurement test' to identify whether the entity has also received or will receive unidentifiable goods or services (see 4.5.170.20). An example of when the consideration appears to be less than the fair value of the equity instruments granted would be an obvious disparity in the values. If there are unidentifiable goods or services, then they are measured at grant date, which means that identifiable goods or services are measured twice on different dates: once for the purpose of valuing the unidentifiable goods or services, and again when the identifiable goods are obtained or services rendered. [*IFRS 2.13A, BC126, BC128B–BC128C*]

4.5.1860   Cash-settled share-based payments with non-employees

4.5.1870   *Recognition principles*

4.5.1870.10   In cash-settled share-based payments with non-employees, goods or services are recognised when they are received. If the goods or services do not qualify for recognition as assets, then they are expensed. This is the same as for equity-settled share-based payments with all counterparties and cash-settled share-based payments with employees. [*IFRS 2.7–8*]

4.5.1880   *Measurement principles*

4.5.1880.10   For cash-settled share-based payment transactions with non-employees, the liability is measured at its fair value. The liability is remeasured at each reporting date and ultimately at settlement date in the same way as cash-settled transactions with employees. [*IFRS 2.30*]

4.5.1880.20   In transactions in which the goods or services cannot be measured reliably, the goods or services and the liability incurred are measured at the fair value of the liability with reference to the value of the equity instrument on which the payment is based.

4.5.1880.30   In transactions in which the goods or services can be measured reliably, it is unclear whether the initial liability should be based on the fair value of the underlying instruments or if instead it should be based on the fair value of the goods or services received. In the latter case, it may be necessary to consider the requirements for unidentifiable goods or services (see 4.5.1850.30). From the first date of remeasurement, the liability would be equal under both approaches. In our experience, we expect this issue to be rare.

4.5.1890 **PRACTICAL APPLICATION ISSUES**

4.5.1890.10   Practical application issues discussed in this chapter include the following.
- Scope issues in practice (see 4.5.1900).
- Classification issues in practice (see 4.5.2100).
- Determination of the type of equity instruments granted (see 4.5.2260).
- Forfeitable and non-forfeitable dividend rights (see 4.5.2320).
- Reverse acquisitions (see 4.5.2360).
- Practice issues with group share-based payments (see 4.5.2370).
- Replacement awards in a business combination (see 4.5.2440).
- Share-based payments and income taxes (see 4.5.2450).
- Share-based payments and EPS calculations (see 4.5.2460).
- Hedging of share-based payment transactions (see 4.5.2470).
- Share-based payments issued by associate or joint venture (see 4.5.2480).

4.5.1900   **Scope issues in practice**

4.5.1910   ***Share-based payment vs shareholder transaction***

4.5.1910.10   In some transactions, it will be clear that the counterparties are acting in their capacity as shareholders. An example is when the entity grants all existing shareholders of a particular class of equity instruments the right to acquire additional equity instruments at a discount. Other cases will be less clear.

4.5.1910.20   IFRS 2 does not limit situations in which the counterparty acts in its capacity as a shareholder to transactions in which all existing shareholders are granted the same rights and restrictions. In particular, when the counterparty buys the equity instruments at fair value, it can appear as if the counterparty has paid the same amount as any other (new) shareholder would have paid. Distinguishing a share-based payment from a shareholder transaction can be difficult if the counterparty purchases the equity instruments at the same amount as other shareholders. [*IFRS 2.4*]

4.5.1910.30   The implementation guidance to the standard discusses ESPPs and illustrates the application of IFRS 2 to those transactions in which there is a discount on purchase or that contain option features. If an ESPP does not appear to fall within this guidance, then it may be difficult to determine whether the employee acts in the capacity of a shareholder or of a supplier of goods or services. For further discussion of ESPPs, see 4.5.2270.

4.5.1910.40   Factors that in our view may be relevant in determining whether a purchase of shares is in the scope of IFRS 2 include the following:
- the plan specifies that the realisation of a benefit is subject to future services; and
- the plan includes buy-back terms that do not apply to non-employee shareholders.

4.5.1910.50   For example, an employee may buy a share at a price that appears to be fair value, but may be required to sell the share back at the lower of fair value and the amount paid if they leave before a specified date.

4.5.1910.60   In another example, senior management of companies owned by private equity funds sometimes buy equity instruments with vesting being conditional on an exit event – e.g. an IPO or a sale of the company.

4.5.1910.70 The following analysis considers each of the indicators in 4.5.1910.40 in relation to the transactions described in 4.5.1910.50–60.

- Both arrangements contain a benefit that is subject to future services, because the employee can benefit from future increases in the value of the shares only by providing services for the specified period or by being employed when the exit event occurs.
- There is an apparent inconsistency in these arrangements between the proposition that the purchase of the shares is at fair value and the inclusion of the requirement to sell the shares back at the lower of fair value and the purchase price. This requirement is, in effect, a right that allows the entity to reacquire the shares, which has a positive value to the entity and has a negative value to the employee. If the amount paid was the fair value of a share without this condition, then the employee appears to have overpaid in purchasing the share from the entity by the value of the entity's right to reacquire the shares. If the requirement to sell back was not imposed on non-employee shareholders, then this may call into question the validity of the assertion that the purchase was at fair value in the first place.

4.5.1910.80 If applying these indicators results in the conclusion that a share purchase is a share-based payment, then a second issue is whether there is any cost to recognise if the transaction appears to be at fair value. Even if there is no cost to recognise – e.g. because the purchase price is equal to the grant-date fair value of the equity instruments granted – in our view the disclosure requirements of IFRS 2 still apply.

4.5.1910.90 However, in certain cases it may be difficult to determine that the purchase price is equal to the grant-date fair value of the equity instruments. This is particularly challenging when the shares bought by the employee are issued by an unlisted entity with a complex capital structure, such as in some private equity transactions.

4.5.1910.100 An entity may have multiple classes of shares. Sometimes the justification that the employee's share purchase is at fair value is with reference to purchases of other shares of that class held by non-employee shareholders. Particular difficulties can arise in allocating the fair value of an entity between classes of equity instruments if the non-employee shareholder transaction used as a reference involves more than one class (e.g. ordinary and preference shares) but the employee buys only one class (e.g. ordinary shares). This is because the buyers of more than one class of equity instrument benefit from their investment differently from buyers of a single class. When there are multiple classes of shares, complex capital structure valuation guidance may be relevant in deciding if the amount paid by the employee is below fair value.

4.5.1910.110 Sometimes a privately held entity, such as a wholly employee-owned entity, may require employees – e.g. by virtue of the entity's articles of association (see 4.5.2170.10) – to sell shares back to the entity if they cease to be employees; this might be required even if these shares were previously bought at fair value in a transaction that was a transaction with shareholders and not a share-based payment transaction. In our view, if the employee's obligation to sell the shares requires the entity to pay fair value at the time of repurchase and the original acquisition of the shares did not involve a share-based payment, then the obligation does not result in the transaction being a share-based payment. This is because there is no consideration received/paid beyond the shareholder transaction. However, the requirement to repurchase may affect the classification and measurement of these shares under the financial instruments standards (see 7.3.80). [*IFRS 2.4*]

4.5.1920 *Share-based payment vs employee benefit*

4.5.1920.10   Cash payments to employees for services rendered are generally accounted for under IAS 19 unless the cash payment is a share-based payment, in which case it is accounted for under IFRS 2. Although some of the accounting consequences are similar under both standards, there are some differences. A cash payment is a share-based payment if the payment is in cash or other assets for amounts that are based on the price (or value) of the equity instruments of the entity (or the equity instruments of another entity in the same group). In determining whether a payment to employees is a share-based payment, several issues may arise.

4.5.1930 *Cash payments based on approximations of price or value*

4.5.1930.10   Sometimes a payment is not based on the price or value of the entity's equity instruments but on an approximation of that measure. For example, employees of an entity receive a cash payment based on the increase in the *net asset value* of an unlisted entity – i.e. the change in shareholders' equity. The accounting for such an arrangement will depend on whether it is a profit-sharing arrangement or a share-based payment arrangement. In our view, if the net asset value of the entity does not reflect the fair value of its equity instruments – e.g. the change in net assets primarily represents the profit or loss from operations and does not include fair value changes of assets and liabilities – then the transaction is, in substance, a profit-sharing arrangement that should be accounted for as an employee benefit (see 4.4.1270). In our experience, this is the more typical situation.

4.5.1930.20   In some cases, the changes in net assets include substantially all changes in the fair value of the net assets of the entity. In these cases, the net asset value reflects the fair value of the equity instruments and this represents, in substance, the fair value of an equity instrument. Accordingly, in our view the transaction should be accounted for as a share-based payment. Judgement is needed on a case-by-case basis and we believe that only in limited circumstances will the change in net assets be substantially the same as the change in the value of an entity's shares.

4.5.1930.30   Sometimes newly listed or unlisted entities use an earnings basis for estimating the fair value of the entity's equity instruments. If such a measure uses a predetermined formula – e.g. a fixed multiple of EBITDA – to specify how the cash payment at settlement will be determined, then in our view such a payment is unlikely to be based on the price or value of an entity's equity instruments. This is because a market multiple will generally change over time. Accordingly, such payments should not be considered to be share-based payments, unless in limited cases the facts and circumstances provide evidence that the payment amount is based on the price or value of the entity's equity instruments. If the payment to an employee is not a share-based payment, then it would be considered an employee benefit in the scope of IAS 19. [*IFRS 2.B30*]

4.5.1940 *Date of determination of cash payments and link to service*

4.5.1940.10   To meet the definition of a share-based payment, a payment needs to be based on the price (or value) of the equity instrument of the entity or the equity instruments of another entity in the same group (see 4.5.190) and paid in return for goods or services provided to the entity (see 4.5.150).

4.5.1940.20   IFRS 2 does not specify the date that is relevant for the assessment of whether the payment is based on the price or value of the entity's equity instruments. In principle, a payment could be based on the price or value of the equity instrument at grant date, at vesting date, at settlement date or at another date.

4.5.1940.30   The implementation guidance to IFRS 2 illustrates that a payment based on the price (or value) of an equity instrument on the settlement date or on vesting date is regarded as share-based. It is less clear whether a payment based on the price (or value) of the equity instrument at grant date also meets the definition of share-based, because it is a fixed amount. [*IFRS 2.IG.Ex9, IG.Ex11*]

4.5.1940.40   Even if a payment is based on the price (or value) of an equity instrument, to establish that it is a share-based payment in the scope of IFRS 2 the payment is required to be in return for goods or services. As discussed in 4.5.2050–60, this issue can be difficult – e.g. if an employee buys a share at fair value and is required to sell back the share on termination of employment. [*IFRS 2.A*]

4.5.1940.50   If an equity instrument is bought at fair value on grant date and is redeemable only at the amount paid for it, then there is no net payment to the buyer. However, in our view if the payment on settlement date changes from being based on the value of an entity's equity instruments on the date the equity instruments are granted to be being based on the value of the entity's equity instruments on settlement date, then the payment meets the definition of a share-based payment.

EXAMPLE 25 – REDEMPTION AMOUNT THAT CHANGES FROM GRANT DATE TO SETTLEMENT DATE

4.5.1940.60   Company C grants a share to its employees in exchange for a cash payment at fair value. C is required to redeem the share at the end of employment. If the redemption occurs within the first three years after grant date, then the redemption amount equals the value of the share at grant date. If the redemption occurs after the three-year period, then the redemption amount becomes the current value of the share on redemption – i.e. on settlement date.

4.5.1940.70   We believe that the transaction is a share-based payment because the redemption amount is based on the value of the equity instrument and the net payment is in return for services, because the employees can participate in value increases only if they stay employed for a period of three years.

4.5.1950   *Cash payments depending on share price vs being based on share price*

4.5.1950.10   A cash payment may depend on, but not be based on, the share price. For example, an employee is entitled to a cash payment of 100 if the share price remains at least at the current share price of 8 over the next year. If the share price falls below 8, then the employee is not entitled to the payment. In our view, although this cash payment depends on the share price, it is not based on the share price. Therefore, we believe that the cash payment is not a share-based payment, but is likely to be an employee benefit in the scope of IAS 19 (see 4.4.70.10).

4.5.1950.20   If, in contrast, an employee is entitled to a payment equal to the share price at vesting date, then the employee participates one-to-one in the share price increases. In our view, a payment determined as a linear function of the share price or its movements is based on the share price, and therefore is a share-based payment.

4.5.1950.30   We believe that payments that entitle the employee to a percentage of the share price – e.g. to 60 percent of the share price or to 200 percent of the share price – also meet the definition of being based on the value of the equity instruments and are therefore share-based payments.

4.5.1950.40   If the mechanism to determine the amount of the cash payment is designed as something in between these extremes, then judgement is required to determine whether the mechanism is linked sufficiently to the price (or value) of the equity instruments. Therefore, judgement is required to define the border between 'depending on' and 'being based on'.

EXAMPLE 26 – CASH PAYMENTS DEPENDING ON SHARE PRICE

4.5.1950.50   Company B grants a cash bonus to its employees. The amount of the bonus depends on the share price achieved at the end of the year, as follows:
- if the share price is below 10, then the bonus amount is zero (level 1);
- if the share price is between 10 and 12, then the bonus amount is 1,000 (level 2); and
- if the share price is above 12, then the bonus amount is 1,500 (level 3).

4.5.1950.60   In this example, changes in the share price within a band – e.g. between 10 and 12 – will not result in a change in the bonus amount. We believe that the cash payment is not share-based because the size of the gaps between share price levels means that there is not sufficient linkage between the two. Therefore, we believe that the bonus is not a share-based payment in the scope of IFRS 2.

4.5.1960   *Capped payments*

4.5.1960.10   An arrangement may provide for a payment to be made that is based on the share price of an entity, but is subject to a cap. For example, Company E provides a bonus arrangement to its employees. The bonus is calculated as a fixed percentage of the share price of E (see 4.5.1950.30). However, if the share price exceeds a certain amount, then the payment is capped at a fixed amount. In our view, the arrangement should be accounted for as a cash-settled share-based payment if the payment is expected to be based largely on the share price of E; otherwise, it should be accounted for as an employee benefit.

4.5.1960.20   To determine whether the payment is expected to be based largely on E's share price, in our view the level of the cap and the expected volatility should be compared with the share price at grant date. If, at grant date, the cap is well in excess of the expected growth in E's share price in light of expected volatility, then we believe that the payment at grant date is based largely on E's share price. In our view, the assessment of whether the payment is expected to be based largely on an entity's share price – i.e. the significance of the cap relative to the expected volatility – should be made at each grant date of a new grant and should be reassessed subsequently only if the grant is modified (see 4.5.1190).

4.5.1970   *Relevance of classification under IAS 32 of instruments granted*

4.5.1970.10   One characteristic of a share-based payment transaction is that it is based on the price or value of the entity's *shares or other equity instruments.* An 'equity instrument' is a contract that evidences the residual interests in the assets of an entity after deducting all of its liabilities (see 1.2.120.30). Under the financial instruments standards, some instruments issued in the legal form of shares may be classified as liabilities. Some potential share-based payment arrangements require payments based on the change in the price of a share instrument that is a residual interest in an entity, but which would be classified as a liability under the financial instruments standards. [*IFRS 2.31, A, BC106–BC110, IAS 32.11, 96C*]

4.5.1970.20   The term 'equity instrument' is defined in IFRS 2 without reference to IAS 32, and it appears that classification under IAS 32 is not relevant. For example, IFRS 2 includes as an illustration of a cash-settled share-based payment a grant of puttable or redeemable shares or options over them. Such instruments would generally be classified as a financial liability under IAS 32. Under IFRS 2, payment based on the value of a puttable or redeemable share is a cash-settled share-based payment. [*IFRS 2.31, A*]

4.5.1980   *Deemed equity*

4.5.1980.10   An arrangement may require a cash payment to be made based on the price of a deemed share or a synthetic instrument. For example, a cash award may be based on the price (or value) of an amount that is a measure of equity of a business division that is not a separate legal entity. In our view, if the deemed equity or synthetic instrument is consistent with the definition of equity under IFRS (see 1.2.120.30), then the arrangement meets the definition of a cash-settled share-based payment. We believe that the reference to equity instruments in IFRS 2 does not require the instruments to be in the legal form of shares or other equity instruments. This view is based, in part, on the definition of a business in IFRS 3, which does not require there to be a separate legal entity (see 2.6.20.20). [*IFRS 3.A*]

4.5.1990   *Non-share-based elements*

4.5.2000   Separable non-share-based cash elements

4.5.2000.10   In our view, an award that contains both an employee benefit and a share-based payment should be separated and each component should be accounted for separately.

EXAMPLE 27 – PAYMENT WITH COMBINED SHARE-BASED PAYMENT AND EMPLOYEE BENEFIT FEATURE

4.5.2000.20   Company B grants a bonus payment to an employee that has both a cash and a share component. The terms of the bonus plan require settlement of 75% of the award in a fixed amount of cash and 25% in shares. The total value of the bonus payment is 1,000, to be settled by 750 in cash and the remaining amount of 250 in a variable number of shares at their current share price at settlement date.

4.5.2000.30   We believe that the 25% bonus that is paid in shares is a share-based payment in the scope of IFRS 2, whereas the cash bonus is an employee benefit in the scope of IAS 19 (see 4.4.30.10).

4.5.2010   Non-share-based cash alternative

4.5.2010.10   If a single arrangement provides a choice of two settlement alternatives that are mutually exclusive and at the discretion of the employee, in which only one of the alternatives would be accounted for under IFRS 2, then in our view the entire arrangement should be accounted for as a share-based payment applying the requirements for compound instruments in IFRS 2 by analogy. This is because such an arrangement is neither clearly in the scope of IAS 19 nor clearly in the scope of IFRS 2, but the requirements in IFRS 2 for compound instruments seem applicable by analogy.

EXAMPLE 28A – SHARE-BASED PAYMENT WITH NON-SHARE-BASED CASH ALTERNATIVE – AT EMPLOYEE'S DISCRETION

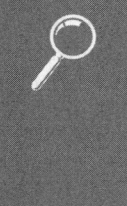

4.5.2010.20   Company B grants a payment to its employees conditional on a three-year service period. At the end of the service period, the employees will receive a bonus based on a predetermined percentage of the excess of the profit of B above 5,200. Each employee can choose to be paid in cash or to receive equity instruments of the entity to a value of 150% of the cash payment provided that they work for a further three years.

4.5.2010.30   We believe that the entire arrangement should be accounted for as a share-based payment and that the profit-sharing component should be separated using the guidance in IFRS 2 for compound instruments (see also 4.5.1120.10).

4.5.2010.40   For other examples of share-related payments that are accounted for under IAS 19, see 4.4.20.

4.5.2020   Non-share-based cash alternative at discretion of entity

4.5.2020.10   Some share-based payment arrangements provide the entity with a choice of settlement, but the amount of the cash settlement does not vary with changes in the share price of the entity.

EXAMPLE 28B – SHARE-BASED PAYMENT WITH NON-SHARE-BASED CASH ALTERNATIVE – AT ENTITY'S DISCRETION

4.5.2020.20   Company B grants its employees a fixed bonus that B may choose to settle in shares or cash. Because the cash settlement alternative does not vary with the value of B's shares or other equity instruments of B, the question arises about whether the arrangement is in the scope of IFRS 2.

4.5.2020.30   The IFRS Interpretations Committee discussed similar scenarios and noted that because consideration may be equity instruments of the entity and because plans that give the entity a choice of settlement are specifically addressed by IFRS 2, such plans are in the scope of the standard. [*IU 05-06*]

4.5.2020.40   In contrast to Example 28A, in this case B would not account for two components separately, but for the entire arrangement either as equity-settled or as a cash-settled liability, depending on B's past practice or stated policy to settle in equity or cash (see 4.5.1130). [*IU 05-06*]

4.5.2030 *Share-based payment vs financial instrument*

4.5.2030.10 Some share-based payment arrangements may be in the form of financial instruments that appear to be outside the scope of IFRS 2. Although the classification and subsequent measurement requirements of IFRS 2 are similar to those of the financial instruments standards, some differences exist and it is therefore important to determine the applicable standard.

4.5.2040 *Shares as legal mechanism*

4.5.2040.10 Sometimes, the share transaction in itself is not the share-based payment. In our view, if the issuance of shares represents only a legal mechanism to effect an arrangement, then it is not itself a share-based payment.

EXAMPLE 29 – ISSUANCE OF SHARES ONLY AS A LEGAL MECHANISM THAT IS NOT A SHARE-BASED PAYMENT

4.5.2040.15 Company S issues redeemable preference shares to its senior executives for a nominal amount. The preference shares are redeemable by the entity at the nominal amount if the executives leave the company or on liquidation. Redeemable preference shareholders are entitled to dividends, which are paid in the form of ordinary shares. The amount of the dividends payable is determined as 1% of S's profit for the year. The ordinary shares themselves do not contain vesting conditions.

4.5.2040.20 We believe that the redeemable preference shares in this example represent only a legal mechanism to effect a share-based payment, being the issue of equity instruments in the form of ordinary shares, and the preference shares are not themselves share-based payments. The identified share-based payment, being the issue of dividends in the form of ordinary shares, should be accounted for under IFRS 2 as an equity-settled share-based payment arrangement.

4.5.2040.30 For further discussion of share-based payment arrangements in the form of financial instruments in the scope of IFRS 2, see 4.5.2060.

4.5.2050 *Forfeiture payment based on lower of subscription price and fair value*

4.5.2050.10 A share purchase at fair value may contain a share-based payment.

EXAMPLE 30 – SHARE PURCHASE AT 'FAIR VALUE' THAT IS SHARE-BASED PAYMENT

4.5.2050.20 Company T sells ordinary shares to employees for cash consideration (subscription price) that appears to be equal to the fair value of the shares. The following facts are relevant for this example.
- The shares are subject to a condition that allows T to reacquire the shares when employment terminates.
- For the purpose of determining the reacquisition right exercise price, notionally the shares vest after five years of service.

- The reacquisition right exercise price of *vested* shares (i.e. after five years) is the fair value of the shares on the date of exercise. The exercise price of the reacquisition right for *unvested* shares (i.e. before five years) is the lower of the original subscription price plus 6% annual interest (not compounded) for each year from the purchase of the shares to exercise date of the reacquisition right, and the fair value at the exercise date.
- The subscription price of the ordinary share is 50.
- The share price at the end of three years is 67.
- The share price at the end of five years is 70.

4.5.2050.30   If an employee were to leave T at the end of three years, then T could acquire each of the employee's shares for 59 (50 x 118%) rather than for 67. However, if the employee were to leave T at the end of five years, then T could acquire each of the employee's shares for 70, not 65 (50 x 130%).

4.5.2050.40   In this example, the exercise price of the reacquisition right depends on whether the shares are considered vested or unvested. Shares vest – i.e. the reacquisition right exercise price varies – with employment. The exercise price for unvested shares limits the amount of fair value appreciation in which the employee can participate, but exposes the employee to all of the downside risk; and the ability to participate in fair value increases is dependent on future service. Therefore, in our view a share-based payment exists because, for the reacquisition right exercise price to equal fair value and the employee to benefit from increases in the share price, the employee is required to provide five years of services to T. Because the employees have written T a reacquisition right, this is an award in which T has a choice of settlement (see 4.5.2200.20 and 1130.10).

4.5.2060   *Requirement to buy and hold shares*

4.5.2060.10   An employee may be required to buy shares to participate in a share-based payment arrangement. If the employee pays fair value for the shares and the shares do not contain vesting conditions, then in our view the acquisition of shares by the employee does not form part of the share-based payment transaction; instead, it should be accounted for by the entity as an equity transaction in accordance with the financial instruments standards (see chapter 7.3). However, it is often difficult to determine whether shares are issued at fair value and entities should consider all facts and circumstances in determining whether the purchase of shares by employees is outside the scope of IFRS 2. The requirement to hold shares may be a non-vesting condition (see 4.5.1910.40).

EXAMPLE 31 – SHARE-BASED PAYMENT WITH REQUIREMENT TO BUY AND HOLD SHARES

4.5.2060.20   Company B grants a share-based payment in the form of share options to its employees. To receive the share options, an employee is required to buy a specified number of participation shares at fair value and hold the participation shares throughout the vesting period of the share-based payment. The employees

> are free to sell the participation shares during the vesting period; however, if the employees sell the shares, then the share options are forfeited (see 4.5.550.20). The requirement to hold the participation shares in order to exercise the share-based payment is treated as a non-vesting condition of the share-based payment arrangement (see 4.5.440.20).

4.5.2070 *Tax payments related to share-based payments*

4.5.2070.10   In some countries, a share-based payment arrangement may be subject to a tax payment related either to the employee's own tax obligations or to employee-based taxes levied on the employer. The tax is often based on the difference between the share price and the exercise price, measured at exercise date. Alternatively, the tax may be calculated based on the grant-date fair value of the grant.

4.5.2080 *Tax payments when employee has primary liability*

4.5.2080.10   In many cases, the tax obligation is a liability of the employee and not the employer, although the employer may have an obligation to collect it or withhold it. If the employer has an obligation to collect or withhold employee taxes, then the employer is either acting as an agent for the tax authorities by collecting the taxes, or acting as an agent for the employee by paying the tax authorities on the employee's behalf. In such situations, the guidance in 4.5.2160.10–20 applies.

4.5.2080.20   The employer may pay employees an amount of cash to cover social taxes and/or income taxes related to share-based payment transactions in addition to the share-based payment arrangement. In our view, if the cash payment is not based on the price or value of the entity's shares, then this portion of the plan should be treated as an employee benefit under IAS 19 (see 4.4.50.10). If the cash payment is based on the value of the entity's shares, then it may be appropriate to treat this portion of the plan as a cash-settled share-based payment transaction. [*IFRS 2.1*]

4.5.2090 *Tax payments when employer has primary liability*

4.5.2090.10   In some jurisdictions, the employer rather than the employee (see 4.5.2070.10 and 2080.10) may have the legal obligation to pay taxes on employee awards. If the employer is the obligor for the tax, then the employer recognises the cost and liability. In our view, an entity should choose an accounting policy, to be applied consistently, to treat the employer's obligation to pay the taxes either as a provision in accordance with IAS 37 or under IFRS 2.

4.5.2090.20   We believe that treatment as a provision would be appropriate if the obligation is of uncertain timing or amount, because this tax is not an income tax and therefore is not in the scope of IAS 12.

4.5.2090.30   The other alternative is to account for the tax obligation under IFRS 2. Under this alternative, if the amount of the tax is based on the price or value of the entity's equity instruments, then we believe that it should be accounted for as a cash-settled share-based payment. However, if the amount is not based on the value of an equity instrument, then it may be appropriate to consider the tax as an incidental expense associated with granting the share-based payment. The objective of IFRS 2 notes that the standard addresses share-based payments including associated expenses. [*IFRS 2.1*]

4.5.2090.40   The employer may be able to require the employee to reimburse the employer for tax paid by the employer. In our view, if the employer elects to collect the tax from the employee, then this agreement with the employee may be accounted for as a reimbursement right in accordance with IAS 37 (see 3.12.190). Alternatively, we believe that the recovery can be treated as an adjustment to the exercise price because from the entity's perspective it is a cash inflow from the employee that is conditional on exercise of the share-based payment. If the recovery is treated as an additional exercise price, then the estimation of the actual exercise price would affect the determination of the grant-date fair value. Differences between the estimated and the actual exercise price would not be trued up. If the reimbursement approach is taken, then the estimated recovery would be trued up to the actual amount recovered. [*IFRS 2.BC72*]

4.5.2090.50   In our view, the accounting policy choice regarding the treatment of the reimbursement right is independent of the accounting policy choice regarding accounting for the employer's obligation (see 4.5.2090.10–20).

4.5.2100   Classification issues in practice

4.5.2110   *Grants of equity instruments 'to the value of'*

4.5.2120   *Shares 'to the value of'*

4.5.2120.10   An equity-settled transaction is defined as a transaction in which the entity receives goods or services as consideration for equity instruments of the entity. Therefore, a transaction that is settled in a variable number of shares is generally classified as an equity-settled share-based payment transaction, even though this classification may differ from the debt vs equity classification under the financial instruments standards. [*IFRS 2.BC106–BC110*]

4.5.2120.20   In our view, classification as equity-settled applies even if the amount of money itself is variable.

EXAMPLE 32 – SHARE-BASED PAYMENT SETTLED IN VARIABLE NUMBER OF SHARES

4.5.2120.30   Company C, a listed entity, grants shares to its CEO, conditional on a one-year service period. The value of the grant depends on the share price level achieved at the end of the year and the share price on vesting date.
- If the share price is above 100 at the end of the year, then the CEO receives 1,000 settled in shares.
- If the share price is above 120 at the end of the year, then the CEO receives 2,000 settled in shares.

4.5.2120.40   We believe that C should classify the arrangement as equity-settled because equity instruments are issued in exchange for services. For a discussion of measurement aspects of grants with a variable number of equity instruments, see 4.5.800.

4.5.2120.50   For a discussion of how to account for a share-based payment in which the number of shares is variable – i.e. 'shares to the value of' – see 4.5.790.

4.5.2130   *Arrangements to transfer value to employees on settlement date*

4.5.2130.10   In some share-based payment arrangements, the entity's obligation is to deliver equity instruments, but the entity facilitates the sale of the shares on the market when employees want cash after settlement. In other arrangements, cash payments to be received from the counterparty – e.g. the exercise price of options or withholding taxes – are netted with the entity's obligation. In these circumstances, the question arises about whether such arrangements influence the classification of the share-based payment. Generally, if the counterparty has no ability to require a cash payment from the entity for its services, then the transaction is classified as equity-settled. This assessment does not change if the entity is required to make a cash payment as an agent on behalf of the counterparty. [*IFRS 2.A, 41, 43*]

4.5.2140   *Cashless exercise in variable number of shares*

4.5.2140.10   As illustrated in Example 33, a transaction that is settled in a variable number of shares is generally classified as an equity-settled share-based payment transaction, even though this classification may differ from the debt vs equity classification under the financial instruments standards (see chapter 7.3). In our view, an award that is net share settled, sometimes referred to in practice as 'cashless exercise', would be viewed as equity-settled if the recipient has no ability to require a cash payment for the equity instruments tendered. [*IFRS 2.BC106*]

EXAMPLE 33 – SHARE-BASED PAYMENT MAY REQUIRE OR PERMIT CASHLESS EXERCISE OF OPTIONS

4.5.2140.20   Company F grants an employee 10 options that entitle the employee to buy shares after three years at an exercise price of 100. At exercise date, the share price is 200. The exercise arrangement permits the employee to either:

- pay an exercise price of 1,000 and receive 10 shares worth 2,000 (i.e. net value of 1,000); or
- receive 5 shares worth 1,000 for no cash consideration (i.e. cashless exercise) by tendering all 10 options. The cash exercise price of 500 on these 5 shares is paid by tendering unexercised options with an intrinsic value of 500 ((200 - 100) x 5).

4.5.2140.30   We believe that F should classify the arrangement as equity-settled because F will not pay cash under either alternative.

4.5.2150   *Entity facilitates sale of equity instruments*

4.5.2150.10   An entity may facilitate the sale of shares or other equity instruments granted. For example, an entity might act as an agent for employees. In our view, if the employer bears no risk in respect of the sale of the shares – e.g. share price fluctuations, credit risks etc – then classification of the transaction as an equity-settled share-based payment arrangement is not precluded.

4.5.2150.20   Determining whether the entity is settling the arrangement in cash or acting as an agent requires an analysis of all terms and conditions. We believe that the following conditions are indicators of an agency relationship – i.e. that the equity instruments are sold on behalf of the recipient of the shares:

- the shares are sold to the market via an independent, third party brokerage firm;
- the entity has not agreed (explicitly or constructively) to buy the underlying shares from the brokerage firm;
- the entity does not guarantee, or underwrite in any way, the arrangement between the owner and the brokerage firm; and
- the entity is obliged to remit only the payments received from the broker and cannot be obliged to pay if the shares are not sold – e.g. in the event of unexpected market suspensions.

4.5.2160   *Settling net of withheld taxes*

4.5.2160.10   In some countries, an employee may be subject to taxes on receipt of a share-based payment arrangement. In some cases, the tax obligation is a liability of the employee and not the employer, although the employer may be obliged to collect or withhold the tax payable by the employee and transfer it to the tax authority. This type of arrangement is classified as equity-settled in its entirety if the share-based payment would otherwise be classified as equity-settled without the net settlement feature. This may be referred to as 'an exception' to the general requirements in IFRS 2. [*IFRS 2.33E–33H*]

4.5.2160.20   In our view, the amount that the entity is obliged to withhold under tax laws or regulations does not need to be a fixed amount but does need to reflect the employee's tax obligation related to the share-based payment. Any amounts withheld in excess of the employee's tax obligation associated with the share-based payment should be accounted for as cash-settled in accordance with 4.5.910.

4.5.2160.30   The exception discussed in paragraph 4.5.2160.10 does not apply to arrangements in which the entity is not required under tax law or regulation to withhold an employee's tax obligation associated with the share-based payment or any equity instruments that an entity withholds in excess of the employee's tax obligation associated with the share-based payment. [*IFRS 2.33H*]

EXAMPLE 34A – SHARE-BASED PAYMENT SETTLED NET OF TAX – STATUTORY RATE

4.5.2160.40   Company F grants its employees options that entitle them to buy shares after three years at an exercise price of 100. The arrangement includes a three-year service condition.

4.5.2160.50   Local tax law requires F to withhold an amount equal to 10% of the taxable gain on the share-based payment to settle the employee's tax obligation associated with share-based payment and transfer that amount in cash to the tax authority.

4.5.2160.60   F accounts for the arrangement in its entirety as an equity-settled share-based payment because it withholds the amount under local tax law and the

> arrangement would be classified as equity-settled in its entirety in the absence of the net settlement feature.

EXAMPLE 34B – SHARE-BASED PAYMENT SETTLED NET OF TAX – EMPLOYEE'S MARGINAL TAX RATE

4.5.2160.70   Modifying Example 34A, local tax law requires F to withhold tax at a minimum rate of 10% of the taxable gain to settle the employee's tax obligation associated with the share-based payment and transfer that amount in cash to the tax authority.

4.5.2160.80   The employee is required to pay tax on their income from the share-based payment arrangement at their marginal rate (i.e. the tax obligation is not limited to the minimum statutory withholding). Any difference between the amount withheld by F to meet the employee's tax obligation and the employee's final tax obligation is settled directly between the employee and the tax authority.

4.5.2160.90   F's current practice is to settle the share-based payment arrangement net at the employee's expected marginal tax rate of 35%.

4.5.2160.100   We believe that F should account for the arrangement in its entirety as an equity-settled share-based payment because it withholds an amount under local tax law and the arrangement would be classified as equity-settled in its entirety in the absence of the net settlement feature (see 4.5.2160.20).

4.5.2160.110   Conversely, if F chose to withhold at a fixed rate of 40% for administrative ease, rather than at the minimum statutory rate of 10% or the employee's expected marginal rate of 35%, then any excess over the employee's tax obligation withheld – i.e. in this case, over 35% – would generally be outside the scope of the exception discussed in 4.5.2160.20 because the excess withheld will not be used to settle the employee's tax obligation related to the share-based payment. The excess would instead be accounted for as a cash-settled share-based payment.

4.5.2170   *Grants of equity instruments that include redemption features*

4.5.2170.10   An entity may make a share-based payment using equity instruments that are redeemable, either mandatorily or at one party's option. The label under which these arrangements are seen in practice varies and includes 'buy-back arrangement', 'sell-back arrangement', 'put options' and 'call options'. Although the redemption features are sometimes included in the share-based payment agreement, they may also be part of the entity's articles of association or a separate agreement. In our view, redemption features that are associated with the instrument granted as part of a share-based payment form part of the terms and conditions of the share-based payment arrangement.

4.5.2170.20   Redemption features are generally observed in share-based payments of unlisted entities. Often, those grants are under the condition that the equity instruments are redeemable when the employee ceases employment with the entity. This is because the shareholders of unlisted entities often do not want to allow external parties to receive the benefit of subsequent increases in the value of the entity. Such a feature, however, does not always preclude the classification of the transaction as equity-settled, as discussed below in 4.5.2180–2200.

4.5.2180   *Mandatorily redeemable equity instruments*

4.5.2180.10   Sometimes share-based payments include both a grant of an equity instrument and an obligation to pay cash at a later date. Although such a share-based payment includes the grant of an equity instrument, classification as equity-settled is precluded if the instruments issued are redeemable mandatorily. This is because the entity is required to pay cash at some point in time – i.e. to settle the share-based payment in cash. [*IFRS 2.31*]

4.5.2190   *Equity instrument redeemable at employee's option*

4.5.2190.10   Classification as equity-settled is also precluded if the share-based payment results in the issuance of equity instruments that are redeemable at the option of the employee. The probability of the entity being required to pay cash is not considered. For further discussion of the accounting for redeemable shares, see 4.5.980. [*IFRS 2.31, 34*]

4.5.2190.20   The requirement to classify transactions involving puttable or redeemable shares as cash-settled share-based payment transactions is not limited to instruments with put or redemption terms that are exercisable immediately. Therefore, in our view instruments that require a minimum holding period before put rights are exercisable should be classified as cash-settled, regardless of the length of the minimum holding period. [*IFRS 2.31, 34*]

4.5.2200   *Equity instruments redeemable at entity's option*

4.5.2200.10   If the entity rather than the employee has the option to redeem the shares granted in a share-based payment, then the entity determines whether it has a present obligation to settle in cash and accounts for the share-based payment transaction accordingly. [*IFRS 2.41*]

4.5.2200.20   Even if the equity instruments are not puttable or redeemable, in our view the entity should consider whether the overall effect of the arrangements is that, in substance, the employer has a substantive choice of cash or equity settlement. A question may arise if, for example, the employee is required to offer shares back on ceasing employment and, although it is not required, the employer has a stated policy or past practice of accepting the offer and buying the shares back.

4.5.2200.30   However, a past practice of repurchasing shares issued in an equity-settled share-based payment transaction does not automatically require classifying future similar transactions as cash-settled because it can depend on the nature of the repurchase arrangements of each transaction. In our view, if there is no mandatory redemption feature and a repurchase arrangement is available to all shareholders, including non-employees, and is substantive, then in rare circumstances it may be appropriate to de-link the repurchase arrangement from the share-based payment, because it is considered more a shareholder-related term and condition. If the repurchase arrangement is de-linked in this manner, then it is not considered in the classification of the share-based payment, which is classified as equity-settled from grant date.

EXAMPLE 35A – REPURCHASE ARRANGEMENT DE-LINKED FROM SHARE-BASED PAYMENT

4.5.2200.40　Company B, an unlisted company, has established a discretionary share buy-back arrangement. The following facts are relevant for this example.

- Each year a share-dealing window operates around the annual general meeting date. A letter is distributed to all shareholders that advises them of the procedures for buying and selling B's shares and the fixed price at which the shares will be bought back as determined by an independent third party.
- These buy-back arrangements are available to all shareholders. Employees can leave B's employment and keep the shares that they have obtained through the share-based payment arrangements. Shareholders include employees, former employees, descendants of former employees and a pool of individual shareholders – i.e. not related to employees.
- Notwithstanding the existence of the buy-back arrangement, B is not obliged to repurchase the shares.

4.5.2200.50　In this example, we believe that B should classify the equity instruments issued to its employees under a share-based payment arrangement as equity-settled because the buy-back arrangement available to all other shareholders is substantive and B is not obliged to repurchase the shares from the employee – i.e. there is no mandatory redemption feature. B should also consider the terms of the buy-back arrangement to determine whether the offer to buy back shares is a written put in the scope of the financial instruments standards (see 7.3.240). [*IFRS 2.29*]

EXAMPLE 35B – REPURCHASE ARRANGEMENT LINKED TO SHARE-BASED PAYMENT

4.5.2200.60　Company C, an unlisted company, plans to issue shares to its employees. The following facts are relevant for this example.

- These equity instruments will be subject to discretionary share buy-back arrangements; C plans to make this buy-back available to all shareholders, but has not yet done so.
- Notwithstanding the proposal to establish a broad-based buy-back arrangement, C is not obliged to repurchase the shares. However, unlike in Example 35A, C is owned currently by a single shareholder. Following the share issue, a small percentage of C's shares will be held by other shareholders – i.e. employees. If they leave C's employment, then employees must offer their shares for sale to other employees or C, but C is still not obliged to repurchase the shares. Therefore, a body of ex-employee shareholders may in due course develop.

4.5.2200.70　In this example, we believe that there is not sufficient evidence to support a conclusion that it is appropriate to de-link the buy-back arrangement from the terms of the share-based payment arrangement. Therefore, we believe that considering the proposed buy-back arrangement as a shareholder arrangement

> (rather than a term of the employee share-based payment) is not appropriate because there is no body of existing shareholders outside the employee pool to demonstrate that the buy-back arrangement relates other than to employees who receive shares in their role as employees. In our view, the possible future development of a substantial external shareholding body should not be anticipated and the share-based payment should be classified following the requirements for share-based payment transactions in which the entity has the choice of settlement (see 4.5.1130).

4.5.2210 *Equity instruments redeemable at option of both parties*

4.5.2210.10   If the equity instruments are redeemable at the option of both parties, then a question arises about whether layering an entity's call option on top of an employee's put option changes the conclusion reached for the employee's put option. Because the entity can still be required to pay cash based on the employee's choice, such a transaction is classified as cash-settled. [*IFRS 2.31*]

4.5.2220 *Return of up-front payments on forfeiture of share-based payment*

4.5.2220.10   The scenarios in 4.5.2180–2210 cover equity instruments that are subject to redemption features once the equity instruments are vested. These redemption features affect the classification assessment and may result in classification as cash-settled. If the redemption feature applies to unvested equity instruments on forfeiture only, then in our view the assessment of classification may be different if the buy-back is only a mechanism for repaying an initial purchase price.

EXAMPLE 36 – RETURN OF UP-FRONT PAYMENT ON FORFEITURE OF SHARE-BASED PAYMENT

> 4.5.2220.20   The employees of Company G are eligible to buy shares from G at a discount from the market price and the employees become unconditionally entitled to the shares if they satisfy a service vesting condition. If an award is forfeited because employment terminates before the award is vested, then the employee is required to sell the shares back to G for an amount equal to the original purchase price. The discount from the grant-date fair value of the shares is a share-based payment with protection from a decline in value that is recognised over the service period. We believe that the requirement for the employee to sell the shares back to G at the original purchase price if the vesting condition is not satisfied does not result in the share-based payment being classified as cash-settled. In this case, we believe that the redemption feature is a mechanism to claw back unvested share-based payments.
>
> 4.5.2220.30   Because the employee is not unconditionally entitled to the shares during the vesting period, in our view the entity should recognise the purchase price received as a deposit liability until the share-based payment vests – i.e. the entity should initially recognise a liability to refund the purchase price rather than reflecting this in equity as an issuance of shares.

4.5.2230 *Contingently cash-settleable equity instruments*

4.5.2230.10   IFRS 2 provides guidance regarding the classification of share-based payments that contain a cash alternative that can be chosen by the entity or by the employee. However, it does not provide guidance regarding the classification of a share-based payment in which equity instruments are cash-settleable only on the occurrence or non-occurrence of a contingent event.

4.5.2230.20   In our view, if an entity issues a share-based payment that is contingently cash-settleable and the contingency is not within the control of the issuer or the counterparty, then it should determine whether to classify the share-based payment as cash or equity-settled based on the liability recognition criteria of IAS 37. This is because IFRS 2 does not base classification solely on the legal right to avoid cash payment – e.g. the standard also considers the intended manner of settlement. Therefore, in respect of contingently cash-settleable share-based payment arrangements, we believe that an entity is not required to analogise to the guidance in IAS 32 on the classification of instruments as a liability or equity (see 4.5.1970). [*IAS 37.14, IU 01-10*]

4.5.2230.30   Examples of contingent events outside the control of the issuer and of the counterparty include IPOs and changes in control of the entity. For a discussion of a change in control of the entity, see 4.5.2240.

4.5.2230.40   Based on the classification guidance in IAS 37, we believe that when determining whether a liability to the employee exists, the contingent feature would affect the classification only if the contingent event is probable – i.e. more likely than not (see 3.12.30.10). If the event's likelihood of occurrence is less than probable and the share-based payment would otherwise be classified as equity-settled, then we believe that it should be classified as equity-settled.

4.5.2230.50   In our view, after initial classification the entity should reassess at each reporting date the probability of cash outflow to determine whether the share-based payment is equity- or cash-settled. This is because IAS 37 requires reassessment of probabilities and estimates of expected cash flows at each reporting date (see 3.12.150.10). [*IAS 37.36*]

4.5.2230.60   If a change in the probability of cash outflows is such that the classification of the arrangement as either equity-settled or cash-settled changes, then in our view a switching approach should be followed to account for the change in classification, because there is one single grant with two possible outcomes from inception. This approach is the same as that for an award with multiple alternative performance conditions (see 4.5.830.20). We believe that it is not appropriate to account for the change in classification under the approach for changes in classification arising from modifications (see 4.5.1310).

EXAMPLE 37– CONTINGENTLY CASH-SETTLEABLE EQUITY INSTRUMENTS ON NON-OCCURRENCE OF IPO

4.5.2230.70   On 1 January 2018, Company H grants an award to employees with the following characteristics:
- if there is an IPO before 31 December 2022 and the employees are still in service, then H will settle the award in equity; and

- if there is no IPO before 31 December 2022 and the employees are still in service, then H will settle the award in cash.

4.5.2230.80　On 1 January 2018, it was not considered probable that an IPO would occur before 31 December 2022. Therefore, the award was initially classified as cash-settled. On 1 January 2019, it becomes probable that an IPO will occur before 31 December 2022.

4.5.2230.90　Therefore, on 1 January 2019 the award is reclassified as an equity-settled award; the cash-settled liability is reversed through profit or loss, and an expense for services provided to date for the equity-settled award is recognised using the grant-date fair value, with a credit to equity.

4.5.2240　*Change-in-control clause*

4.5.2240.10　A further issue arises when the contingent event is a change in the control of the entity. Often, a change in control requires approval of the entity's board and/or the shareholders. Generally, IFRS 2 regards shareholders as part of the entity, such as when it requires attribution to the entity of equity-settled grants made directly by the shareholders. Therefore, the shareholders of an entity are generally regarded as part of the entity for the purposes of the standard, unless it is clear that they are acting as an investor and not on behalf of the entity (see 7.3.40). In our view, in respect of a change in control, shareholders should be regarded as separate from the entity because they generally make decisions regarding whether to sell or retain their shares as investors based on the terms offered. Therefore, we believe that a change in control should not be regarded as an event within the control of the entity and should be considered a contingent event. This is consistent with our view on the impact of a change in the control clause of a financial instrument as debt or equity under the financial instruments standards (see 7.3.40).

EXAMPLE 38 – CONTINGENTLY CASH-SETTLEABLE EQUITY INSTRUMENTS ON CHANGE IN CONTROL

4.5.2240.20　On 1 January 2018, Company K issued share options to employees that vest after three years of service; the options are exercisable until 31 December 2022. If there is a change in control of K before 31 December 2022, then K must settle the share options in cash at their fair value at that date.

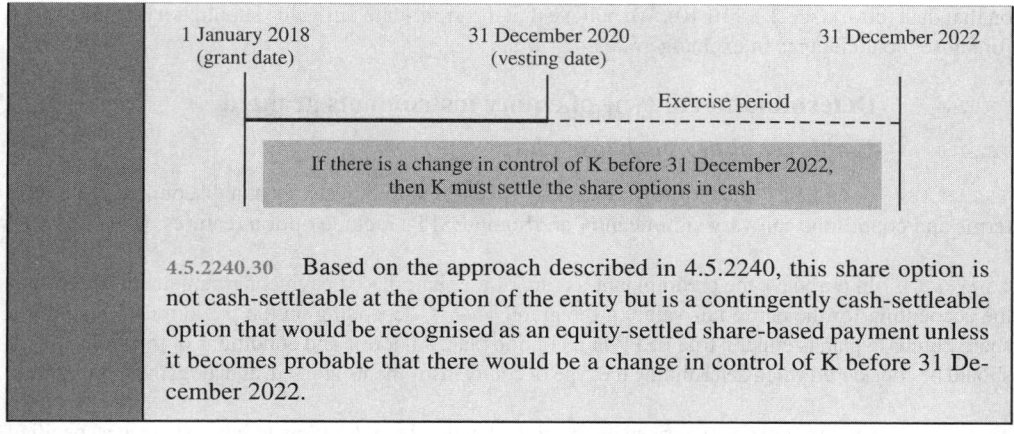

1 January 2018 (grant date)
31 December 2020 (vesting date)
31 December 2022

Exercise period

If there is a change in control of K before 31 December 2022, then K must settle the share options in cash

4.5.2240.30 Based on the approach described in 4.5.2240, this share option is not cash-settleable at the option of the entity but is a contingently cash-settleable option that would be recognised as an equity-settled share-based payment unless it becomes probable that there would be a change in control of K before 31 December 2022.

4.5.2250 **Arrangements denominated in currency other than issuing entity's functional currency**

4.5.2250.10 There is no specific guidance on the classification of share-based payment arrangements that are denominated in a currency other than the issuing entity's functional currency.

4.5.2250.20 Under IAS 32, derivative contracts that will be settled by an entity by delivering a fixed number of its own equity instruments for a variable amount of cash are classified as financial liabilities or financial assets (see 7.3.230.10). In the absence of specific guidance in IFRS 2, the question arises about whether the classification of the share-based payment should be consistent with that which would be required under the financial instruments standards. In our view, classification under IFRS 2 should be based on what form of consideration the entity is providing to its employees (see 4.5.2140.10 and 2120.10–20).

EXAMPLE 39 – SHARE-BASED PAYMENT NOT DENOMINATED IN ENTITY'S FUNCTIONAL CURRENCY

4.5.2250.30 Company C's shares are traded and quoted in euro, which is also C's functional and presentation currency. C issues options on its shares to employees of its US subsidiary with a fixed exercise price that is denominated in US dollars. Because the functional currency of C is the euro but the exercise price is denominated in US dollars, C will receive a variable amount of cash on exercise of the options for a fixed number of shares.

4.5.2250.40 We believe that the arrangement should be classified as equity-settled, because C is providing equity instruments to employees in exchange for services. Because there are a number of identified differences between IFRS 2 and the financial instruments standards, we do not believe that an analogy to the financial instruments standards is required in respect of these arrangements.

4.5.2250.50 In our view, in determining the grant-date fair value of the foreign currency-denominated option, the exercise price should be translated into the entity's functional currency at the exchange rate on that date (euro) (see 2.7.110.10). We believe that the grant-date fair value should not be remeasured for subsequent changes in exchange rates.

4.5.2260 Determination of type of equity instruments granted

4.5.2270 *Employee share purchase plans*

4.5.2270.10   In an ESPP, the employees are usually entitled to buy shares at a discounted price. The terms and conditions can vary significantly and some ESPPs include option features. [*IFRS 2.IG17*]

4.5.2270.20   In our view, the predominant feature of the share-based payment arrangement determines the accounting for the entire fair value of the grant. That is, depending on the predominant features, a share purchase plan is either a true ESPP or an option plan. All terms and conditions of the arrangement should be considered when determining the type of equity instruments granted, and judgement is required.

4.5.2270.30   Options are characterised by the *right*, but not the *obligation*, to buy a share at a specified price. An option has a value – i.e. the option premium – because the option holder has the benefit of any future gains and has none of the risks of loss beyond any option premium paid. The value of an option is determined in part by its duration and by the expected volatility of the share price during the term of the option. In our view, the principal characteristic of an ESPP is the right to buy shares at a discount to current market prices. ESPPs that grant short-term fixed purchase prices do not have significant option characteristics because they do not allow the grant holder to benefit from volatility. We believe that ESPPs that provide a longer-term option to buy shares at a specified price are, in substance, option plans, and should be accounted for as such. [*IFRS 2.B4–B41*]

EXAMPLE 40 – SHARE OPTION PLAN VS ESPP

4.5.2270.40   Employees are entitled to buy shares at a fixed price from the date of communication of the plan until two years later. Whether the predominant feature in this agreement is the option feature requires judgement based on all of the terms and conditions of the plan. In the absence of other indicators, we believe that this effectively is an option and should be accounted for as an option plan and not as an ESPP. This is because the employees have no obligation to buy the shares, but only the right. If the share price falls below the fixed exercise price, then the employees would not buy any shares. Therefore, the employees are protected from a decline in the value of the shares.

4.5.2270.50   Whether a plan is a true ESPP or an option plan affects:
- the determination of grant date;
- the number of instruments to account for; and
- the measurement of the grant-date fair value.

EXAMPLE 41 – IMPACT OF CLASSIFICATION AS TRUE ESPP OR AS OPTION PLAN

4.5.2270.60   On 1 January 2018, Company T granted a right to its employees to buy shares at a 20% discount to its share price. This grant is made to 1,000 of its employees and 700 employees buy shares.

4.5.2270.70   If the substance of the offer is an ESPP, then grant date is the date on which the employees accept the offer (e.g. February 2018) and recognition is based on the 700 employees accepting the offer.

4.5.2270.80   Conversely, if the substance of the offer is an option grant, then grant date is not dependent on the explicit acceptance by the employees and is therefore already achieved on 1 January 2018. Recognition is based on the option instruments granted to the 1,000 employees, assuming that the award vests, and not on the 700 employees who exercise their options – e.g. at the end of a two-year vesting period.

4.5.2280   *Share purchases funded through loans*

4.5.2280.10   All of the terms and conditions are analysed when determining the type of equity instruments granted. A share purchase funded through loans provided by or guaranteed by the granting entity may indicate that an ESPP is in substance an option plan. In our view, a plan that is, in substance, an option should be accounted for as such. In general, we believe that it is difficult to support recognition of shares and the loan as outstanding when the shares were paid for by a loan from the issuer to the buyer. If the substance of a share purchase arrangement is an option, then neither the shares nor the loan are outstanding until the options are exercised by paying the exercise price for the shares or the put option expires. Accordingly, until exercise of the options the shares issued to employees are treated as treasury shares and no financial asset for the loan receivable from the employees is recognised until this time.

EXAMPLE 42 – SHARE-BASED PAYMENT STRUCTURED AS SHARE PURCHASE ARRANGEMENT

4.5.2280.15   The employees of Company C received a right to and did buy shares immediately. At the same time, the employees received a loan for the amount of the purchase price. The loan accrues interest at a market rate. The employees receive a right to settle the loan in full by tendering the shares bought, either directly or via a right to put the shares back at the original purchase price plus market interest.

4.5.2280.20   In this example, the put option feature on the shares removes any risk for the employee of share price decreases while all rewards above the market rate of interest are retained, indicating that this share purchase agreement is in substance a share option.

4.5.2290   *Determining assets to which entity has recourse for loan repayment*

4.5.2290.10   In assessing whether shares paid for by a loan from the issuer are in substance a grant of options, an entity should consider whether it has full recourse to the employees in respect of the balance of the loan. For example, if the share price falls below the outstanding balance of the loan, then does the entity have recourse to the personal assets of the employee and will it pursue collection of the full loan balance?

4.5.2290.20   In our view, it is appropriate to account for the transaction as the issue of shares and a financial asset for the loan receivable only when it can be clearly demonstrated that the entity has and will pursue full recourse to the employees in respect of the loan. [*IU 11-05*]

4.5.2290.30   Whether the entity has full recourse to the employees in respect of the loan should be assessed based on all of the terms and conditions of the arrangement. We believe that for the loan to be considered full recourse, it should be documented as a full recourse loan and there should be no evidence that would indicate otherwise – e.g. a past history of the entity waiving all or a portion of similar loans. The following are examples of indicators that may support the conclusion that a loan is full recourse.

- The loan is reported by the entity to a credit agency in the same manner as commercial loans.
- The entity requests financial information from the employee to assess their ability to repay the loan.
- The entity has an ongoing process for monitoring the collectability of the loan.
- If applicable, the entity has a past history of collection in full of other employee loans – e.g. housing loans.

EXAMPLE 43 – ENTITY HAS RECOURSE TO ALL ASSETS OF EMPLOYEE

4.5.2290.40   Company C issues shares to its employees at the market price on the date of issue and the purchases are funded through a loan provided by C to its employees. C has recourse to all of the employees' assets and not just the shares bought with the loan. If C achieves a two-year cumulative EPS growth target of 15%, then 25% of the loan balance will be waived – i.e. the share purchase price will be reduced retrospectively by 25%. C has the intent and ability to pursue full collection of the outstanding loan balance and a past practice of collecting loans from employees.

4.5.2290.50   In Example 43, we believe that the arrangement is an issue of shares and a financial asset – this is because the loan is full recourse and therefore the arrangement is not in substance an option grant but rather should be treated as a share purchase. The employee may earn a discount to the share price subject to the achievement of a non-market performance condition. This is because the employee receives a waiver of 25 percent of the share price if a cumulative EPS target is met. In our view, the potential retrospective adjustment to the share purchase price is a share-based payment and not an employee benefit under IAS 19 because the payment is based on the share price. This is consistent with the example in IFRS 2 of a reduction in the exercise price of an option as a result of achieving a non-market performance condition – i.e. the shares ultimately can be bought by the employees at a discount from the purchase price specified originally. [*IFRS 2.IG.Ex4*]

4.5.2290.60   We believe that because the employee receives equity instruments – i.e. shares that may be bought at a discount – and does not receive a payment based on the price (or value) of the entity's shares or other equity instruments, the share-based payment in Example 43 should be classified as equity-settled (see 4.5.340.10).

4.5.2290.70   In our view, because the structure in Example 43 is viewed as a share purchase, the financial asset should be accounted for separately from the share-based payment and should be recognised and measured in accordance with the financial instruments standards. Under those standards, the initial and subsequent measurement of the financial asset reflect the likelihood of the employee receiving a discount as a result of the achievement of the non-market performance condition (see chapter 7.4 for classification and chapter 7.7 for measurement of financial instruments, and also 4.4.1290).

4.5.2290.80   If the loan issued to the employee does not bear interest at a market rate, then in our view the low-interest loan is a benefit conveyed to the employees that could be accounted for in accordance with IFRS 2. In some cases, such a loan is available only for financing share purchases, which suggests that the loan is an integral part of the share-based payment arrangement and therefore we believe that it should be accounted for under IFRS 2. However, it might also be appropriate to account for the discount as an employee benefit (see 4.4.1290) separately from the share-based payment, particularly if similar loans are available for other purposes.

4.5.2290.90   In other arrangements, a share purchase by employees may be funded only partially through a loan from the entity – e.g. the entity issues a loan to employees for 70 percent of the market price of its shares and the employee is required to pay in cash the remaining 30 percent of the purchase price. The entity has recourse only to the shares and the employees receive a right to settle the loan by tendering the shares bought, either directly or via a right to put the shares back to the entity. If the market price of the shares is less than the amount of the loan when the shares are to be tendered to the entity, then the entity receives the shares as settlement of the loan in full – i.e. the entity accepts the risk that its share price will decrease by greater than 30 percent. If the cash payment by the employee represents substantially all of the reasonably possible losses – based on the expected volatility of the shares – then in our view the fact that the loan has recourse only to the shares does not preclude accounting for the transaction as the issuance of shares and a financial asset. This is because, subsequent to the date of issuance, the employee is not only able to benefit from increases in the entity's share price, but is also at risk for substantially all of the reasonably possible decreases in the share price.

4.5.2300   *Accounting for interest and dividends in grant of share options*

4.5.2300.10   As a consequence of treating a share purchase funded through a non-full-recourse loan as an option, an issue arises about how to account for the share purchase, the loan issued, any interest on the loan and any dividends on the shares.

4.5.2300.20   In our view, the share purchase, loan issue, interest and dividends should be accounted for in accordance with the substance of the arrangement. If the share purchase funded through a non-full-recourse loan is in substance a share option, then we believe that neither the loan nor the shares should be recognised as outstanding and the repayment of the loan by the employee should be treated as the payment of the exercise price.

4.5.2300.30   Consequently, we believe that interest should not be accrued over the vesting period but should be recognised only as part of the exercise price when it is received. Interest therefore decreases the grant-date fair value of the option because of an increased exercise price. The right to receive dividends should also be taken into account in estimating the grant-date fair value of the option (see 4.5.2330.10) – i.e. the entitlement increases the grant-date fair value compared with an option without dividend entitlement. [*IFRS 2.B31*]

4.5.2300.40   However, we believe that forfeitable dividends declared but not paid out before exercise of the option should be recognised only when the loan amount, reduced for the dividends, becomes a recognised receivable on exercise. This is because the obligation to pay the dividends only reduces the unrecognised receivable due from the employee, rather than being a liability in its own right; this treatment is different from dividends declared on unvested shares (see 4.5.2350.20). In our view, the entity should choose an accounting policy, to be applied consistently, of either recognising the dividends by netting the amount with the proceeds from the exercise price or recognising a separate distribution in equity.

4.5.2310   *Free shares*

4.5.2310.10   In some share-based payment arrangements, employees are entitled to shares for no cash consideration; however, the grant is conditional on the fulfilment of specified vesting conditions. If the holders of such shares have the same rights as holders of shares not subject to a vesting condition, then the value of the shares granted is equal to the value of vested shares. However, if the holders of such shares are not entitled to dividends during the vesting period, then an adjustment is required for the expected future dividends that will not be received by employees.

4.5.2320   **Forfeitable and non-forfeitable dividend rights**

4.5.2330   *Cost measurement and recognition for forfeitable dividend rights*

4.5.2330.10   We believe that forfeitable dividends should be treated as dividend entitlements during the vesting period. If the vesting conditions are not met, then any true-up of the share-based payment would recognise the profit or loss effect of the forfeiture of the dividend automatically because the dividend entitlements are reflected in the grant-date fair value of the award; for a discussion of when a true-up applies, see 4.5.540.

4.5.2340   *Cost measurement and recognition for non-forfeitable dividend rights*

4.5.2340.10   In our view, two approaches are acceptable in accounting for non-forfeitable dividends. [*IFRS 2.B31–B36*]

4.5.2340.20   One approach is to treat non-forfeitable dividends as a dividend entitlement during the vesting period when determining the grant-date fair value of the share-based payment. The value of the dividend right is reflected in the grant-date fair value of the share-based payment, and therefore increases the cost of the share-based payment. If the share-based payment does not vest, then in our view the total amount previously recognised as a share-based payment cost should be split into:
- the value for the non-forfeitable dividends; and
- the balance of the share-based payment.

4.5.2340.30   We believe that only the balance of the share-based payment cost – i.e. the amount excluding the non-forfeitable dividends – would be subject to any true-up for failure to satisfy vesting conditions (see 4.5.540.60) to reflect the benefit retained by the employee.

4.5.2340.40   The other approach is to view non-forfeitable dividends as a payment for services with vesting conditions different from the vesting conditions of the underlying share-based payment. Under this approach, the dividend rights would be considered to be a benefit – e.g. under IAS 19 if the services are employee services – rather than a share-based payment because dividend amounts are unlikely to be based on the price or value of the entity's equity instruments. Accordingly, the grant-date fair value of the share-based payment would be lower than under the approach in 4.5.2340.20–30.

4.5.2340.50   Generally, dividends are considered to be part of the measurement of the grant-date fair value, which supports the approach in 4.5.2340.20 – i.e. to treat dividend entitlements as part of the share-based payment. However, in some circumstances there may be evidence that the share component of the transaction is merely a mechanism to deliver the dividend payments. In fact patterns in which the dividend payment is the primary consideration, the approach in 4.5.2340.40, which accounts separately for dividends, might be more relevant.

4.5.2350   *Dividend recognition*

4.5.2350.10   In our view, when the dividend rights are treated as dividend entitlements regardless of whether the dividends are forfeitable or non-forfeitable, dividends declared during the vesting period should be accounted for in accordance with the requirements of other standards (see 7.3.680) – i.e. as a distribution (see 4.5.770). Therefore, neither the declaration nor the payment of the dividends results in additional cost directly, because we believe that the recognition of cost for the grant of dividend rights should be considered separately as discussed in 4.5.2340.20–50. In particular, under the approach in 4.5.2340.20–30, if the dividend amounts are retained even if the vesting conditions are not met, then we believe that no adjustment of the dividend accounting is necessary because the portion of the share-based payment cost related to the non-forfeitable dividend would not be trued up.

4.5.2350.20   In relation to a grant of shares, in our view dividends that are declared during the vesting period but not paid until vesting should also be charged to equity and recognised as a liability when they are declared. For a discussion of the accounting for dividends declared in relation to a grant of share options, see 4.5.2300.

4.5.2350.30   In our view, if the share-based payment, and therefore forfeitable dividends thereon, are forfeited because of failure to satisfy a vesting condition, then the return of dividends or reduction in dividend payable should be accounted for as a transaction with a shareholder – i.e. the return should be recognised directly in equity as an adjustment of previously recognised dividends.

4.5.2360   **Reverse acquisitions**

4.5.2360.10   A reverse acquisition (see 2.6.170) may be in the scope of IFRS 2. For example, an unlisted operating entity that meets the definition of a business may want to obtain a stock exchange listing but want to avoid a public offering. The unlisted entity arranges for a non-operating listed entity (that does not meet the definition of a business) to acquire its equity interests in exchange for the equity interests of the listed entity. In this example, the listed entity is the legal acquirer because it issued its equity interests, and the unlisted entity is the legal acquiree because its equity interests were acquired.

4.5.2360.20   The IFRS Interpretations Committee discussed similar scenarios and noted that in such a case, the guidance in IFRS 3 on identifying the acquirer applies by analogy and would result in identifying the listed entity as the accounting acquiree and the unlisted entity as the accounting acquirer (see 2.6.170). However, because the listed entity is not a business, once the acquirer has been identified, IFRS 2 instead of IFRS 3 applies in accounting for the transaction. [*IU 03-13*]

4.5.2360.30   An issue arises about how to account for the difference between the fair value of the shares deemed to have been issued by the accounting acquirer (the unlisted entity) and the fair value of the accounting acquiree's (the non-operating listed entity's) identifiable net assets received. The Committee noted that the payment does not meet the definition of an intangible asset because it is not separable (see 3.3.40.10) and that the difference should be treated in its entirety as a payment for a stock exchange listing and expensed as it is incurred. [*IU 03-13*]

4.5.2360.35   Consolidated financial statements prepared following a reverse acquisition are legally those of the legal acquirer but are described in the notes as a continuation of the amounts from the (consolidated) financial statements of the legal acquiree. Consequently, the reverse acquisition is reflected in the consolidated financial statements of the legal acquirer, but not in any consolidated financial statements of the legal acquiree. [*IFRS 3.B21, IU 03-13*]

EXAMPLE 44 – REVERSE ACQUISITION INTO SHELL COMPANY

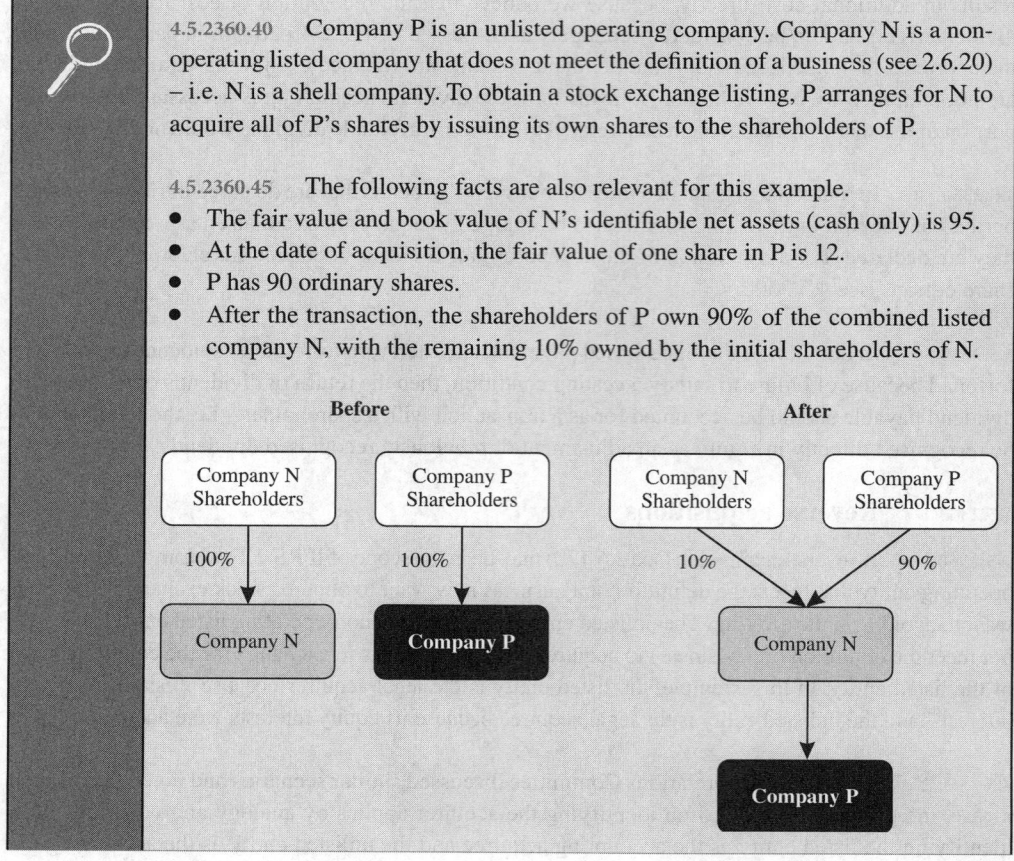

4.5.2360.40   Company P is an unlisted operating company. Company N is a non-operating listed company that does not meet the definition of a business (see 2.6.20) – i.e. N is a shell company. To obtain a stock exchange listing, P arranges for N to acquire all of P's shares by issuing its own shares to the shareholders of P.

4.5.2360.45   The following facts are also relevant for this example.
- The fair value and book value of N's identifiable net assets (cash only) is 95.
- At the date of acquisition, the fair value of one share in P is 12.
- P has 90 ordinary shares.
- After the transaction, the shareholders of P own 90% of the combined listed company N, with the remaining 10% owned by the initial shareholders of N.

Before

Company N Shareholders — 100% → Company N

Company P Shareholders — 100% → Company P

After

Company N Shareholders — 10%

Company P Shareholders — 90%

→ Company N → Company P

4.5.2360.50   In this example, the substance of the transaction is that P has acquired N for its listing status. As noted in 4.5.2360.20, because N is not a business the transaction is outside the scope of IFRS 3. The transaction is instead accounted for as a share-based payment transaction from the perspective of P.

4.5.2360.60   As such, P is deemed to have issued its own shares to acquire control of N. After the transaction, P's shareholders have a 90% interest in the combined entity – i.e. the shareholders have given up a 10% interest in P for a 90% interest in N. P would have to issue 10 shares to N for interests after the transaction to be held 90% (90 / 100) by P and 10% by N (10 / 100). Therefore, the fair value of the shares issued to N is 120 (10 shares x 12).

4.5.2360.70   In the consolidated financial statements of N, the following entry is recorded in respect of the transaction. As noted in 4.5.2360.30, the difference between the fair value of the shares deemed to have been issued and the fair value of the identifiable net assets acquired is recognised as an expense.

	DEBIT	CREDIT
Cash	95	
Listing expense (profit or loss)	25	
Equity (deemed issue of shares)		120
To recognise acquisition of N		

4.5.2370   Practice issues with group share-based payments

4.5.2380   *Intermediate parents*

4.5.2380.10   A shareholder may grant a share-based payment to employees of a subsidiary that is owned through an intermediate parent. For example, Ultimate Parent UP in a group may grant an equity-settled share-based payment to employees of Subsidiary S that is held through Intermediate Parent P. The share-based payment is recognised by the subsidiary in its financial statements (see 4.5.1460.10, and 1470.30 and 90). In our view, either of the following two approaches can be applied in the financial statements of P in respect of the group share-based payment transaction.

4.5.2380.20   We believe that P can conclude that it does not have a share-based payment to recognise in its separate financial statements because P, as the intermediate parent, is neither the receiving nor the settling entity in respect of the share-based payment. Under this approach, the share-based payment is effectively being accounted for as if UP holds the investment in S directly. P's consolidated financial statements, if it prepares any, would include the share-based payment recognised by S.

4.5.2380.30   Alternatively, we believe that P could recognise the share-based payment in its separate financial statements. Under this approach, attribution is appropriate because UP has only an indirect investment in S and can realise the benefits of the contribution only via P.

4.5.2380.40   If P chooses to account for the transaction, then P classifies the transaction as equity-settled in its separate financial statements. This is because P directly or indirectly receives the services without having an obligation to settle the transaction. By recognising a capital contribution from UP and an increase in investment in S, P mirrors the capital contribution recognised by the subsidiary and reflects the increase in investment by UP. [*IFRS 2.43B(b)*]

4.5.2390   *Employee benefit trusts*

(S) 4.5.2400   *Separate financial statements of sponsor*

4.5.2400.10   A plan sponsor may transfer or sell sufficient shares to enable a trust to meet obligations under share-based payment arrangements not only for current periods but also for future periods. In our view, the transfer of shares to an employee benefit trust does not represent a share-based payment transaction. Rather, the share-based payment arrangement is the arrangement between the employer and employees for which grant date needs to be identified. Therefore, we believe that grant date will generally be determined based on the date on which the sponsor enters into an agreement with the employees. We believe that the fact that the agreement will be satisfied by the trust, or even that, nominally, it is the trust that enters into the agreement with the employees, does not shift grant date to the date of transfer or sale of shares to the trust. We believe that a trust that would be required to be consolidated should usually be seen as an extension of the sponsor and therefore it may be appropriate to view actions that are nominally those of the trust as actions of the sponsor.

4.5.2400.20   IFRS does not provide specific guidance on the treatment in the entity's separate financial statements of transfers of cash to the trust to enable the trustee to buy shares of the entity on the market or from the entity. The share-based payment arrangement to the employee is accounted for by the entity under IFRS 2. In our view, from the perspective of the entity's separate financial statements, the entity should choose an accounting policy, to be applied consistently, as follows.

- *Treat the trust as a branch/agent of the entity:* The assets and liabilities of the trust are accounted for as assets and liabilities of the entity on the basis that the trust is merely acting as an agent of the entity. Under this treatment, the accounting in the entity's separate financial statements is the same as the accounting in the consolidated financial statements.
- *Account for the trust as a legal entity separate from the entity but as a subsidiary of the entity:* Any loan from the reporting entity to the trust is accounted for as a financial asset in accordance with its terms and the objective of the entity's business model (see chapter 7.4). If the trust is funded by the reporting entity making an investment in the trust, then the reporting entity recognises the investment in the subsidiary as an asset. The purchase of the reporting entity's shares in the market by the trust has no effect on the financial statements of the reporting entity. However, when the trust transfers those shares to employees, this is considered to be, in substance, two transactions: a distribution of the shares from the trust back to the reporting entity as treasury shares, followed by a distribution of those shares to the employees.

4.5.2400.30   Our view that an entity should choose an accounting policy to treat the trust as a branch/agent of the entity was developed for application to arrangements in which IFRS 2 requires the sponsor to recognise an expense in relation to shares held in trust for employees and should not be applied by analogy to other trust arrangements.

4.5.2410 *Consolidated financial statements of sponsor*

4.5.2410.10 Application of the criteria for consolidation often requires consolidation of a trust holding shares to meet obligations under a share-based payment arrangement by the grantor (see Example 14 in chapter 2.5). For a discussion of how to account for employee benefit trusts in separate financial statements, see 4.5.2390.

4.5.2420 *Accounting by sponsor's subsidiaries*

4.5.2420.10 The sponsor may require a subsidiary to transfer cash to an employee benefit trust to enable the trustee to settle the subsidiary's employees' share-based payment – e.g. by purchasing shares in the open market. If the subsidiary does not control the trust, then the share-based payment will be classified as equity-settled in the subsidiary's financial statements because the subsidiary has no obligation to settle the share-based payment (see 4.5.1570.10). In our view, the sponsor and the subsidiary should consider whether the cash transferred to the trust is in substance a recharge arrangement (see 4.5.1660).

4.5.2430 **Repurchase by the parent**

4.5.2430.10 A parent may be required to repurchase shares of a subsidiary that were acquired by employees of the subsidiary through a share-based payment arrangement.

4.5.2430.20 For example, a subsidiary issues options to its employees that it settles by issuing its own shares. On termination of employment, the parent entity is required to buy the shares of the subsidiary from the former employee.

4.5.2430.30 In our view, the classification of the share-based payment in the financial statements of the subsidiary should be based on the subsidiary's perspective. We believe that the repurchase arrangement is separate from the subsidiary's arrangement with its employees and therefore should not be considered in determining the classification of the share-based payment by the subsidiary. Because the subsidiary only has an obligation to deliver its own equity instruments, we believe that the arrangement should be classified as equity-settled in its financial statements.

4.5.2430.40 The arrangement should be classified as cash-settled in the consolidated financial statements of the parent because the parent has an obligation to settle in cash, based on the subsidiary's shares. This approach is consistent with the requirements for accounting for redeemable shares (see 4.5.2180).

4.5.2440 **Replacement awards in business combination**

4.5.2440.10 For a discussion of the initial recognition of replacement awards in a business combination, see 2.6.420–520; and for a discussion of their subsequent measurement, see 2.6.1130.

4.5.2450 **Share-based payments and income taxes**

4.5.2450.10 For a discussion of the classification and presentation of tax consequences related to share-based payment transactions, see 3.13.790.

4.5.2460   Share-based payments and EPS calculation

4.5.2460.10   For a discussion of the interaction of EPS with share-based payment arrangements, see 5.3.440.

4.5.2470   Hedging of share-based payment transactions

4.5.2470.10   An entity may buy treasury shares or derivative instruments as an economic hedge of the risk of share price fluctuations. Such arrangements raise the issue of whether hedge accounting can be applied.

4.5.2470.20   In our view, it is not possible to apply hedge accounting for the obligation to issue shares or other equity instruments to settle equity-settled share-based payment transactions. This is because market fluctuations in share price do not affect profit or loss (see 7.9.530).

4.5.2470.30   It may, in principle, be possible to apply cash flow hedge accounting for cash-settled share-based payment transactions. However, in our experience it may be difficult to meet the hedging requirements, and hedge accounting cannot be applied if the hedging instrument is itself equity (see 7.3.530.20). [*IFRS 9.B6.2.2*]

4.5.2480   Share-based payments issued by associate or joint venture

4.5.2480.10   For a discussion of accounting for an equity-settled share-based payment issued by an associate or joint venture, see 3.5.400.

4.6 Borrowing costs

4.6 Borrowing costs

CURRENTLY EFFECTIVE REQUIREMENTS

This publication reflects IFRS in issue at 1 August 2018, and the currently effective requirements cover annual periods beginning on 1 January 2018.

The requirements related to this topic are mainly derived from the following.

STANDARD	TITLE
IAS 23	Borrowing Costs

FORTHCOMING REQUIREMENTS

The currently effective requirements are affected by the following forthcoming requirements. They are highlighted with a # and the impact is explained in the accompanying boxed text at the reference indicated.

- In January 2016, the IASB issued IFRS 16 *Leases*, which is effective for annual periods beginning on or after 1 January 2019. See 4.6.45. IFRS 16 is the subject of chapter 5.1A.
- In December 2017, the IASB issued *Annual Improvements to IFRSs 2015–2017 Cycle – Amendments to IAS 23,* which are effective for annual periods beginning on or after 1 January 2019. See 4.6.115.

FUTURE DEVELOPMENTS

For this topic, there are no future developments.

4.6.10   # SCOPE AND RECOGNITION

4.6.10.10   Borrowing costs that are directly attributable to the acquisition, construction or production of a qualifying asset form part of the cost of that asset. Other borrowing costs are recognised as an expense in the period in which the entity incurs them. [*IAS 23.1, 8–9*]

4.6.10.20   This general requirement to capitalise directly attributable borrowing costs is not required to be applied to:
- qualifying assets measured at fair value – e.g. a biological asset or an investment property measured using the fair value model (see 3.4.140); or
- inventories that are manufactured or produced in large quantities on a repetitive basis. [*IAS 23.4*]

4.6.10.30   For a discussion of the capitalisation of borrowing costs related to exploration and evaluation assets, see 5.11.120.

4.6.20   # QUALIFYING ASSETS

4.6.20.10   A 'qualifying asset' is one that necessarily takes a substantial period of time to be made ready for its intended use or sale. Qualifying assets are generally those that are subject to major development or construction projects. [*IAS 23.5*]

4.6.20.20   Financial assets, and inventories that are manufactured or otherwise produced over a short period of time, are not qualifying assets. Investments, including, in our view, investments in subsidiaries, associates and joint ventures, are not qualifying assets. However, investment property may be a qualifying asset. [*IAS 23.7*]

4.6.20.30   An asset that is ready for its intended use or sale when acquired is not a qualifying asset, even if expenditure is subsequently incurred on the asset.

EXAMPLE 1A – QUALIFYING ASSET – CONSTRUCTION OF REAL ESTATE

4.6.20.40   In April 2018, Developer D undertakes a project to develop a multi-unit residential building. The construction is expected to take three years – i.e. a substantial period of time (see 4.6.20.90). D borrows funds to finance the development. Under applicable laws, the land on which the building is being constructed is and will continue to be owned by the government.

4.6.20.50   D starts marketing the units and commences the construction of the building. Successful marketing efforts result in entering into sales contracts with customers straight away.

4.6.20.60   D determines that revenue from the sale of individual units will be recognised over time in accordance with IFRS 15. This is because each unit has no alternative use to D and, under the standard terms of its contracts with customers, D will have an enforceable right to payment for the work in progress completed to date throughout the contract term (see 4.2.220.40–80). As a result, D does not expect to have material inventory or work in progress on its balance sheet for units sold because control over a specific unit under construction will, from the point of entering into a sales agreement, be continuously transferred to each individual customer.

4.6.20.70   At 31 December 2018, D has completed 10% of the construction work and sold 50% of the units in the building for a total consideration of 100,000. The actual costs incurred on the construction are 16,000. As a result, D recognises:
- revenue in profit or loss for the units sold of 10,000 (100,000 x 10%);
- construction costs in profit or loss for the units sold of 8,000 (16,000 x 50%); and
- inventory in the statement of financial position for the cost of the unsold units of 8,000 (16,000 x 50%).

4.6.20.80   D assesses whether the units under construction meet the definition of a qualifying asset.
- *Sold units:* D determines that the units sold do not meet the definition of qualifying assets, because any work in progress related to them is continuously sold in its existing condition to the customers and therefore recognised in profit or loss as costs are incurred.
- *Unsold units:* D determines that the unsold units also do not meet the definition of qualifying assets. This is because the inventory is currently being marketed, marketing efforts are intended to result in immediate sales contracts and each unit will be subject to immediate derecognition once there is a signed contract with a customer – i.e. the units are ready for their intended sale in their existing condition. [*IAS 23.5, 7*]

4.6.20.90   There is no specific guidance on how long a 'substantial period of time' is, but in our view it is a period well in excess of six months.

4.6.20.100   Inventories that take a long time to produce – e.g. whisky or property – can be qualifying assets. [*IAS 23.7*]

4.6.20.110   The term 'necessarily' is included in the definition of a qualifying asset to indicate that the nature of the asset has to be such that it takes a long time to get it ready for its intended use or sale. Therefore, in our view an asset that takes a long time to prepare for use or sale only because of inefficiencies in the development process is not a qualifying asset. [*IAS 23.5*]

4.6.20.120   IAS 23 does not specifically include contract assets in the list of possible qualifying assets. Contract assets represent conditional rights to future consideration in respect of goods and services already transferred to the customer. A contract asset that represents a conditional right to a financial asset (e.g. a receivable) is not measured at cost and its purpose is either to obtain cash or other financial assets or to generate finance income – i.e. it has no intended use for which it may take a substantial period of time to get ready. Therefore, in our view such contract assets are not qualifying assets. [*IAS 23.5, 7, IFRS 15.105–108*]

4.6.20.130   Conversely, a contract asset that represents a conditional right to a non-financial asset (e.g. an intangible asset; see 4.2.150 and 5.12.80.20) could be a qualifying asset if it does not accrue interest income (see 4.2.130). [*IFRC 12.19, 22, IE1, IE21*]

4.6.20.140   For a further discussion of the capitalisation of borrowing costs related to service concession arrangements, see 5.12.110.

4.6.30   Refurbishment

4.6.30.10   There is no guidance in IFRS regarding whether an asset that is being refurbished can be a qualifying asset. In our view, an asset being refurbished can be a qualifying asset if the refurbishment costs qualify for capitalisation (see 3.2.290) and the refurbishment will take a substantial period of time.

EXAMPLE 1B – QUALIFYING ASSET – REFURBISHMENT

4.6.30.20   Company X owns and manages a hotel, which is closed down for a major refurbishment. The refurbishment costs will be capitalised and the refurbishment will take 18 months. We believe that the borrowing costs related to the refurbishment should be capitalised, because the refurbishment costs are capitalised and the refurbishment takes a substantial period of time.

4.6.40   BORROWING COSTS ELIGIBLE FOR CAPITALISATION#

4.6.40.10   Borrowing costs eligible for capitalisation may include:
- interest expense calculated under the effective interest method (see 7.7.270);
- finance charges in respect of finance leases (see 5.1.300); and
- exchange differences to the extent that they are regarded as an adjustment to interest costs (see 4.6.70). [*IAS 23.6*]

4.6.40.20   The borrowing costs that are capitalised are those that would otherwise have been avoided if the expenditure on the qualifying asset had not been made. This includes interest on borrowings made specifically for the purpose of obtaining the qualifying asset (specific borrowings) and the cost of other borrowings that could have been repaid if expenditure on the asset had not been incurred (general borrowings). [*IAS 23.10*]

4.6.40.30   In our view, adjustments to the carrying amount of borrowings resulting from the re-estimation of expected cash flows under the contract (see 7.7.320.10) are an integral part of interest expense and therefore are eligible for capitalisation.

4.6.45   FORTHCOMING REQUIREMENTS

4.6.45.10   IFRS 16 introduces a single, on-balance sheet lease accounting model for lessees and eliminates the distinction between operating and finance leases. Therefore, interest in respect of any lease liability under IFRS 16 may be a borrowing cost eligible for capitalisation. [*IAS 23.6(d), 29C*]

4.6.50   Interest rate swaps

4.6.50.10   IFRS is silent on whether interest rate swaps that effectively alter borrowing costs should be considered in determining the amount of borrowing costs to capitalise.

4.6.50.20   In our view, payments and accruals of interest under interest rate swaps entered into as an economic hedge of eligible borrowing costs may be included in determining the amount of borrowing costs to capitalise even if they are not designated as hedging instruments in a qualifying hedging relationship. This is based on the principle that borrowing costs should include those costs that could have been avoided if expenditure on the qualifying asset had not been made. However, in our view it is not acceptable to consider the changes in fair value of interest rate swaps as a borrowing cost. The fair value of an interest rate swap is the present value of expected future cash flows, discounted at market rates, and does not represent borrowing costs incurred.

4.6.60   Tax

4.6.60.10   In our view, the amount of borrowing costs to be capitalised should be calculated on a pre-tax basis. Borrowing costs that are capitalised may give rise to deferred tax (see 3.13.80).

4.6.70   Foreign exchange differences

4.6.70.10   Borrowing costs may include foreign exchange differences to the extent that these differences are regarded as an adjustment to interest costs. There is no further guidance on the conditions under which foreign exchange differences may be capitalised and judgement is required to apply the requirements to the particular circumstances of the entity. [*IAS 23.6, 11, IU 01-08*]

4.6.70.20   In our view, exchange differences should not be capitalised if a borrowing in a foreign currency is entered into to offset another currency exposure unrelated to the qualifying asset. This is because such foreign exchange differences are part of the economic hedge of a separate currency exposure and not costs incurred in connection with the borrowing of funds that are directly attributable to the acquisition, construction or production of a qualifying asset. In other cases, we believe that the amount of foreign exchange differences to be capitalised should be restricted such that total capitalised borrowing costs are in the range between:
- interest incurred at the contractual rate (translated into the entity's functional currency); and
- interest that would have been incurred on a borrowing with identical terms in the entity's functional currency.

4.6.70.25   We believe that any foreign exchange differences arising on the amortised cost of a borrowing that would cause the total capitalised borrowing costs to exceed that range should be recognised in profit or loss. The extent to which any foreign exchange differences arising on the amortised cost of a borrowing – including any foreign exchange differences arising on accrued interest – are capitalised is an accounting policy choice that should be applied consistently.

4.6.70.30   If exchange differences qualify for capitalisation, then in our view both exchange gains and losses should be considered in determining the amount to capitalise.

EXAMPLE 2 – CAPITALISING FOREIGN EXCHANGE DIFFERENCES

4.6.70.40   Company R has a functional currency of FC and borrowed AC 1,000 on 1 January 2018 for two years at 3% per annum to finance the construction of a capital asset.

Scenario 1: Foreign exchange loss

4.6.70.50   The exchange rates for 2018 are as follows.

	AC	FC
1 January 2018	1.00	2.00
31 December 2018	1.00	2.16
Average for year	1.00	2.10

4.6.70.60   If R had borrowed the equivalent amount with identical terms in FC – i.e. FC 2,000 – on 1 January 2018, then the contractual interest rate would have been 5% per annum – i.e. FC 100. R has elected an accounting policy to capitalise all foreign exchange differences arising on the amortised cost of the borrowing – including foreign exchange differences arising on accrued interest – to the extent that total capitalised borrowing costs are in the range described in 4.6.70.20–25. R does not hedge the foreign exchange risk that arises from the borrowing.

4.6.70.70   R calculates the interest payable on the loan for the year ending 31 December 2018 in FC as follows.

	AC	RATE	FC
Interest	30[1]	2.1	63

Note
1.   Calculated as 1,000 x 3%.

4.6.70.80   R calculates the foreign exchange loss for the year ending 31 December 2018 on the translation of the amortised cost of the borrowing, including the accrued interest, as follows.

	AC	CHANGE IN RATE	FC
Principal	1,000	0.16[1]	160.0
Accrued interest	30	0.06[2]	1.8
Total foreign exchange loss			161.8

Notes
1.   Calculated as 2.16 - 2.00.
2.   Calculated as 2.16 - 2.10.

4.6.70.90   We believe that the foreign exchange difference that R capitalises for the year should be restricted such that total capitalised borrowing costs are in the range between interest incurred at the contractual rate – i.e. FC 63 – and interest that would have been incurred on a borrowing with identical terms in R's functional currency – i.e. FC 100. Therefore, out of the FC 161.8 foreign exchange loss on the amortised cost of the borrowing, only FC 37 – i.e. the FC 100 upper limit of the range less the FC 63 of interest incurred that is required to be capitalised – may be capitalised as borrowing costs, and the balance – i.e. FC 124.8 (161.8 - 37) – is recognised in profit or loss. The total capitalised borrowing costs would then be FC 100 – i.e. FC 63 of interest on foreign currency borrowings plus FC 37 foreign exchange difference on the amortised cost of the borrowing.

Scenario 2: Foreign exchange gain

4.6.70.100   Modifying the fact pattern in Scenario 1, the exchange rates for 2018 are as follows.

	AC	FC
1 January 2018	1.00	2.00
31 December 2018	1.00	1.82
Average for year	1.00	1.91

4.6.70.110   R calculates the interest payable on the loan for the year ending 31 December 2018 in FC as follows.

	AC	RATE	FC
Interest	30	1.91	57.3

4.6.70.120   R calculates the foreign exchange gain for the year ending 31 December 2018 on the translation of the amortised cost of the borrowing, including the accrued interest, as follows.

	AC	CHANGE IN RATE	FC
Principal	1,000	(0.18)[1]	(180.0)
Accrued interest	30	(0.09)[2]	(2.7)
Total foreign exchange loss			(182.7)

Notes
1. Calculated as 1.82 - 2.00.
2. Calculated as 1.82 - 1.91.

4.6.70.130   In this scenario, R recognises the entire FC 182.7 foreign exchange gain for the year to 31 December 2018 in profit or loss. This is because the foreign exchange difference that R can capitalise should be restricted such that total capitalised borrowing costs are in the range between interest incurred at the contractual rate – i.e. FC 57.3 – and interest that would have been incurred on a borrowing with identical terms in R's functional currency – i.e. FC 100. Capitalising any portion of the foreign exchange gain on the amortised cost of the borrowing would result in capitalised borrowing costs of less than FC 57.3, which would be outside the range.

4.6.80   Dividends

4.6.80.10   In our view, distributions and similar payments on instruments that are classified as liabilities – e.g. dividends on preference shares that are classified as a liability (see 7.3.390) – are eligible for capitalisation if those payments would otherwise be recognised in profit or loss (see 7.3.680.60). [*IAS 32.18, 20, 35*]

4.6.90   Imputed interest on non-financial liabilities

4.6.90.10   In our view, imputed interest on non-financial liabilities – e.g. the unwinding of the discount effect on provisions – does not meet the definition of borrowing costs under IAS 23, unless the non-financial liability represents a borrowing of funds. [*IFRS 15.60, BC229–BC230*]

4.6.90.20   Capitalising interest that is recognised from unwinding a discount on decommissioning or restoration provisions is not permitted because these liabilities do not represent a borrowing of funds. However, if an entity accrues interest on a contract liability that represents advance consideration received under a contract with a customer (see 4.2.130), then in our view this interest meets the definition of borrowing costs under IAS 23 because the interest represents the cost to the entity of borrowing funds from its customer. To the extent that the other criteria in IAS 23 are met, this interest should be capitalised. [*IFRIC 1.8, BC26, IFRS 15.60, BC229–BC230*]

4.6.100   Specific borrowings

4.6.100.10   The amount of specific borrowing costs capitalised is net of the investment income on any temporary investment of the funds pending expenditure on the asset. [*IAS 23.12*]

4.6.110   General borrowings#

4.6.110.10   If the interest costs to be capitalised relate to financing that is part of the entity's general borrowings, then the weighted-average interest cost (excluding the interest on any borrowings specific to any qualifying assets) is applied to the expenditure on the asset. The objective is to capitalise borrowing costs that would have been avoided if expenditure on the asset had not been incurred. In our view, an entity should determine general borrowings by excluding borrowings used to finance specific assets that are qualifying assets. However, we would not preclude the use of judgement in determining whether general borrowings include or exclude borrowings used to finance specific assets that are non-qualifying assets. [*IAS 23.14*]

4.6.110.20   In our view, the weighted-average accumulated expenditure on the asset during the period, reduced by any progress payments or grants received in respect of the asset, may be used in calculating the amount on which interest is capitalised. The amount capitalised may not exceed the actual interest incurred by the entity. [*IAS 23.14, 18*]

4.6.110.30   Unlike for specific borrowings (see 4.6.100.10), IAS 23 does not include guidance that allows an entity to reduce general borrowing costs that are eligible for capitalisation by the amount of any investment income.

4.6.115   FORTHCOMING REQUIREMENTS

4.6.115.10   *Annual Improvements to IFRSs 2015–2017 Cycle – Amendments to IAS 23* clarify that borrowings used specifically to finance the construction of a qualifying asset are transferred to the general borrowings pool after construction of the specific asset is completed. They also clarify that an entity includes funds borrowed specifically to obtain an asset other than a qualifying asset as part of general borrowings.

4.6.120   Calculation in consolidated financial statements

4.6.120.10   There is no specific guidance in IFRS relating to the calculation in consolidated financial statements, beyond the comment that in some cases the amount of borrowing costs to capitalise is based on a weighted-average borrowing rate applicable for a group rather than a weighted-average rate applicable to an individual entity's borrowings. [*IAS 23.15*]

4.6.120.20   In our view, the approach adopted for consolidated financial statements should be one that reflects the borrowing costs attributable to a particular qualifying asset. Entity-specific rates are likely to be the most appropriate for an individual entity within a group that is financed independently. For an entity that is largely financed by intra-group borrowings, a group borrowing rate is more appropriate. Only external borrowings should be considered in calculating a weighted-average group borrowing rate.

4.6.130   Calculation in separate financial statements   (S)

4.6.130.10   In our view, only borrowing costs incurred by the group entity that has incurred expenditure on a qualifying asset are eligible for capitalisation in the entity's separate financial statements.

EXAMPLE 3 – CAPITALISING BORROWING COSTS – SEPARATE FINANCIAL STATEMENTS

4.6.130.20   Parent P borrows funds on behalf of Subsidiary S. P makes an equity investment in S so that S can use the capital to construct a qualifying asset.

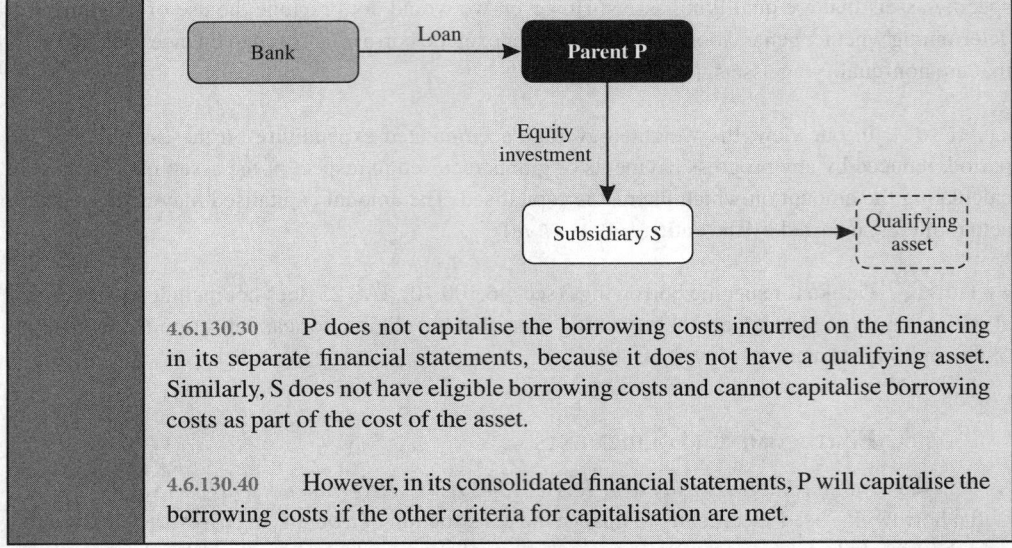

4.6.130.30   P does not capitalise the borrowing costs incurred on the financing in its separate financial statements, because it does not have a qualifying asset. Similarly, S does not have eligible borrowing costs and cannot capitalise borrowing costs as part of the cost of the asset.

4.6.130.40   However, in its consolidated financial statements, P will capitalise the borrowing costs if the other criteria for capitalisation are met.

4.6.140   PERIOD OF CAPITALISATION

4.6.150   Commencement

4.6.150.10   Capitalisation begins on the 'commencement' date. The commencement date for capitalisation is the date on which an entity first meets all of the following conditions:
- expenditure for the asset is being incurred;
- borrowing costs are being incurred; and
- activities that are necessary to prepare the asset for its intended use or sale are in progress. [*IAS 23.17*]

4.6.150.20   If funds are raised in advance to finance a major capital project, then capitalisation of borrowing costs cannot begin until the project starts. Capitalisation is limited to interest costs incurred after expenditure is incurred.

4.6.150.30   Expenditure on a qualifying asset includes only expenditure that has resulted in payments of cash, transfers of other assets or the assumption of interest-bearing liabilities. [*IAS 23.18*]

4.6.150.40   Activities that are necessary to get an asset ready may include technical and administrative work before construction begins, such as obtaining permits. Therefore, in the case of property constructed on purchased land, finance costs are capitalised in respect of the land once technical and administrative activities are in progress. [*IAS 23.19*]

4.6.160   Suspension

4.6.160.10   Capitalisation of interest is suspended during extended periods in which active development is interrupted. For example, capitalisation is suspended if development of a qualifying asset is suspended because an entity is waiting for parts to arrive. [*IAS 23.20*]

4.6.160.20   There is no guidance on what length of time is considered an extended delay.

4.6.160.30   Capitalisation may continue during a temporary delay that is caused by an external event, such as rain or flooding that is common in the region; or during an interruption caused by technical or legal obstacles that are a typical part of the process. Capitalisation may also continue during a period when active development is interrupted in order for *substantial* administrative or technical work to be carried out. In our view, if the administrative or technical work is not significant, then capitalisation should be suspended. [*IAS 23.21*]

4.6.170   **Cessation**

4.6.170.10   Capitalisation ceases when the activities necessary to prepare the asset for its intended use or sale are substantially complete.

EXAMPLE 4A – CESSATION – COMPLETE CONSTRUCTION

4.6.170.20   Company V has constructed a chemical plant. Construction is complete but minor modifications to the plant are required to meet the user's specifications before it is brought into use. V concludes that substantially all of the activities to prepare the plant for its use are complete when the construction is complete and stops capitalisation at that point.

EXAMPLE 4B – CESSATION – COMPLETE DEVELOPMENT

4.6.170.30   Company W has developed a residential property to lease out. The development process is complete, but the property requires minor decoration before it is leased out. W concludes that substantially all of the activities to prepare for the lease are complete when the development process is complete and stops capitalisation at that point.

5.   SPECIAL TOPICS

5.1   Leases

CURRENTLY EFFECTIVE REQUIREMENTS

This publication reflects IFRS in issue at 1 August 2018, and the currently effective requirements cover annual periods beginning on 1 January 2018.

The requirements related to this topic are mainly derived from the following.

Reference	Title
IAS 17	Leases
IFRIC 4	Determining whether an Arrangement contains a Lease
SIC-15	Operating Leases – Incentives
SIC-27	Evaluating the Substance of Transactions Involving the Legal Form of a Lease

The currently effective requirements include newly effective requirements arising from IFRS 15 *Revenue from Contracts with Customers,* which is effective for annual periods beginning on or after 1 January 2018. The new requirements may be applied using the retrospective method or the cumulative effect method (see 4.2.510). The impact of the new requirements on the accounting for leases is reflected in 5.1.30.40 and 515.

FORTHCOMING REQUIREMENTS

In January 2016, the IASB issued IFRS 16 *Leases*, which is effective for annual periods beginning on or after 1 January 2019. IFRS 16 is the subject of chapter 5.1A.

FUTURE DEVELOPMENTS

For this topic, there are no future developments.

5.1.10   **INTRODUCTION**

5.1.10.10   The accounting treatment of a lease does not depend on which party has legal ownership of the leased asset, but rather on which party bears the risks and rewards incidental to ownership of the leased asset. [*IAS 17.7*]

5.1.10.20   A lease is an agreement whereby the lessor conveys to the lessee the right to use an asset for an agreed period in return for a payment or series of payments. The definition of a lease includes contracts that are sometimes referred to as 'hire' or 'hire-purchase' contracts. Although legal definitions of a lease, hire or hire-purchase agreements may vary between different legal jurisdictions, IFRS focuses on the economic substance of the agreement. Therefore, lease accounting applies to contracts that meet the definition of a lease under IFRS and that are not exempt from IAS 17 or IFRIC 4, regardless of their legal name or definition. [*IAS 17.4, 6, IFRIC 4.4*]

5.1.10.30   Under IFRS, each lease is classified as either a finance lease or an operating lease; the classification determines the accounting treatment to be followed by the lessor and the lessee (see 5.1.100).

5.1.10.40   A lease is a finance lease if substantially all of the risks and rewards incidental to ownership of the leased asset are transferred from the lessor to the lessee by the agreement. Typical indicators assessed to determine whether substantially all of the risks and rewards are transferred include:
- the present value of the minimum lease payments that the lessee is required to make in relation to the fair value of the leased asset at inception of the lease;
- the duration of the lease in relation to the economic life of the leased asset; and
- whether the lessee will obtain ownership of the leased asset. [*IAS 17.8, 10*]

5.1.10.50   A lease that is not a finance lease is an operating lease. [*IAS 17.4*]

5.1.15   **SCOPE**

5.1.15.10   Leases to explore for or use minerals, oil, natural gas and similar non-regenerative resources (see 5.11.390) and licensing agreements for items such as motion picture films, video recordings, plays, manuscripts, patents and copyrights are excluded from the scope of IAS 17 (see 3.3.30.15). [*IAS 17.2*]

5.1.15.20   IAS 17 applies only to agreements or components of agreements that transfer the right to use assets. It does not apply to agreements that are contracts for services that do not transfer the right to use assets from one contracting party to the other. [*IAS 17.3*]

5.1.15.30   IAS 41 (see chapter 3.9) applies to the measurement of biological assets held by lessees under finance leases and for biological assets provided by lessors under operating leases. However, the requirements of IAS 17 apply for all other aspects of lease accounting for those assets. [*IAS 17.2*]

5.1.15.40   IAS 40 (see chapter 3.4) applies to the measurement of investment property provided by lessors under operating leases and for property held by lessees that is accounted for as investment property (see 5.1.250). However, the requirements of IAS 17 apply for all other aspects of lease accounting for those assets. For example, the accounting for lease incentives will be according to IAS 17 and SIC-15 requirements (see 5.1.310.110–140). However, if the investment property is measured at fair value, then an entity does not double count assets or liabilities that are recognised as separate assets or liabilities (see 3.4.150.30). [*IAS 17.2, 40.50*]

5.1.15.50   IFRS 3 applies to leases acquired in a business combination. The type of lease and whether the acquiree is the lessee or the lessor will impact how the assets and liabilities are recognised (see 2.6.830).

5.1.20   DEFINITIONS

5.1.20.10   The definitions in IAS 17 are important in determining classification as a finance lease or as an operating lease (see 5.1.100). This classification is the basis for the accounting for the lease by both the lessee and the lessor.

5.1.30   Minimum lease payments

5.1.30.10   Minimum lease payments are those payments that the lessee is, or can be, required to make to the lessor over the lease term. For further discussion of lease term, see 5.1.50; for a discussion of minimum lease payments in the context of lease classification, see 5.1.160; and for a discussion of minimum lease payments in the context of accounting for leases, see 5.1.280. [*IAS 17.4*]

5.1.30.11   From the lessee's point of view, minimum lease payments also include any amount guaranteed by the lessee or a party related to the lessee – e.g. residual value guarantee. From the lessor's point of view, minimum lease payments also include residual value guarantees by any third party unrelated to the lessor provided that party is financially capable of fulfilling the obligations under the guarantee. For further discussion of residual values, see 5.1.70. [*IAS 17.4*]

5.1.30.13   Both a lessee and a lessor include in minimum lease payments the exercise price of a purchase option over the leased asset held by the lessee only if it is reasonably certain at inception of the lease that the purchase option will be exercised. In addition, if the lease includes a put option under which the lessor can require the lessee to buy the asset at the end of the lease, then the lessee and the lessor include the exercise price of the put option in the minimum lease payments. This is because the put option functions economically as a residual value guarantee and the exercise price of the option is an amount that the lessee can be required to pay to the lessor. For further discussion of purchase options in the context of lease classification, see 5.1.140. [*IAS 17.4*]

5.1.30.17   Minimum lease payments do not include contingent rent amounts. For further discussion of contingent rent, see 5.1.80. [*IAS 17.4, IU 07-06*]

5.1.30.20   Minimum lease payments do not include costs for services and taxes to be paid by and reimbursed to the lessor. Amounts owed by a lessee to a lessor may include charges for repairs and maintenance or for other services. Similarly, payments due under a lease may include charges that are reimbursements for expenditure paid by the lessor on behalf of the lessee – e.g. taxes and insurance. If there are service elements or other reimbursements included in a single payment, then these elements are separated from the minimum lease payments that relate to the right of use of the leased asset. Accordingly, when calculating the present value of minimum lease payments to evaluate lease classification, such service charges and reimbursements are excluded. [*IAS 17.4*]

5.1.30.30   As described in 5.1.510.180, IFRIC 4 provides guidance on the allocation of payments between lease payments and payments related to other elements of the arrangement. In our view, because IFRIC 4 is an interpretation of IAS 17 and the most recent guidance on the allocation of lease payments, the allocation into the two components (right of use and other services/reimbursement) should be based on the guidance in IFRIC 4; therefore, it is based on the components' relative fair values. In some cases, the allocation will require the use of an estimation technique for the fair value of the components. For example:

- estimating the lease component with reference to a lease agreement for a comparable asset that contains no other components, and estimating the payments for the other components with reference to the cost of those components together with a reasonable profit; or
- estimating the payments for the other components with reference to comparable agreements and then deducting such payments from the total lease payments. [*IFRIC 4.12–15*]

5.1.30.35   The costs of services and taxes that the lessee is responsible for paying directly under other leases with similar types of property in similar locations may be used as a basis for estimating corresponding fair values under lease agreements in which these costs are included in the rental payments. Estimates of fair values for services and taxes may also be based on experience with similar property bought outright by the lessee or from other sources – for example:

- real estate taxes paid on similar property;
- property tax rate structures obtained from appropriate taxing authorities;
- estimates of insurance costs from insurance brokers; and
- experience in repairing or maintaining similar property.

5.1.30.37   Estimates of fair values for services and taxes include the anticipated fluctuations in these items over the lease term. For example, tax valuation methods vary by taxing authority, and these methods are taken into consideration in evaluating whether property taxes would be expected to increase or decrease. Experience with assets that the lessee owns may also provide a basis for estimating fluctuations in the fair values of services and taxes pertaining to leased assets.

5.1.30.40   A lessor in an arrangement that includes lease and non-lease components applies the separation guidance in IFRIC 4 before applying the separation guidance in IFRS 15 to the non-lease components – see 4.2.10.40. [*IFRS 15.7*]

5.1.30.50   For further discussion of lease arrangements that include service elements, see 5.1.375.

5.1.40   Inception date and commencement date of a lease

5.1.40.10   A distinction is made between the inception and commencement of the lease.

5.1.40.20   The inception of the lease is the earlier of the date of the lease agreement and the date of commitment by the parties to the principal terms of the lease. At this date:

- a lease is classified as either an operating or a finance lease; and
- in the case of a finance lease, the amounts to be recognised at the commencement of the lease are determined. [*IAS 17.4*]

5.1.40.30   The commencement of the lease term (also referred to as 'the commencement date') is the date from which the lessee is entitled to exercise its right to use the leased asset. This is the date of initial recognition of the lease. In other words, recognition of the lease takes place at the commencement date based on the amounts determined at the inception date. [*IAS 17.4*]

5.1.40.40 A significant amount of time may pass between the inception date and the commencement date – e.g. when parties commit to leasing an asset that has not yet been built. In such cases, a calculation of the present value of minimum lease payments prepared to help in determining the classification of the lease covers all lease payments made from the commencement of the lease term. In respect of the period between the inception date and the commencement date in such cases, an acceptable approach is to exclude the time-value effect of the period between the inception date and the commencement date from the calculation of minimum lease payments for both classification and measurement purposes – i.e. at the commencement date, the lease is recognised based on the present value of the minimum lease payments as at the commencement date, using the discount rate at the inception date. However, if the lease payments are adjusted for changes in the construction or acquisition cost of the leased asset, general price levels or the lessor's costs of financing the lease between the inception and commencement dates, then the effect of such changes is deemed to have taken place at inception. [*IAS 17.4–5*]

EXAMPLE 1 – CHANGES BETWEEN INCEPTION AND COMMENCEMENT DATES

5.1.40.45 Company B entered into a binding agreement on 1 January 2015 to lease a building from Company C. B will have the right to occupy the building from 1 January 2018, once C has finished construction of the building. The estimated fair value of the building on 1 January 2015, assuming that construction was completed at that date, was 11,000. The lease agreement states that the annual lease payments will be 10% of the construction costs incurred by C. The expected construction cost of the building was 9,000, such that the expected annual lease rental was 900 (9,000 x 10%). B starts occupying the building on 1 January 2018 as planned. The actual fair value of the building on this date is 13,000 and C's actual construction costs were 10,000, such that the annual lease payment is 1,000 (10,000 x 10%).

5.1.40.47 To assess the classification of the lease at inception, an acceptable approach is for B to consider the fair value of the building at inception of 11,000 and calculate the minimum lease payments using the actual construction costs of 10,000 discounted back to commencement date only – i.e. 1 January 2018 – using the discount rate at inception date. The minimum lease payments need not be discounted back to the inception date of 1 January 2015. If B assesses that the lease is a finance lease, then B will recognise the building as an asset on 1 January 2018, measured at the lower of 11,000 and the present value of the annual lease payments of 1,000 as at 1 January 2018 using the discount rate at inception date.

5.1.50 **Lease term**

5.1.50.10 The lease term commences when the lessee is entitled to start using the leased asset. This date may be earlier than the date on which actual use begins. For example, the lease term for a retail property may commence on 1 May 2018, but the lessee needs to customise the interior of the property before opening and operating its retail store on 1 July 2018. Even if the tenant could not start customisation until 1 June 2018, the commencement date of the lease is 1 May 2018 because this is the date on which the lessee is *entitled* to use the leased asset. [*IAS 17.4*]

5.1.50.20   The lease term includes the *non-cancellable* period of the contract and any further periods for which the lessee has an option to continue to lease the asset and for which, at the time of inception of the lease, it is judged reasonably certain that the lessee will exercise that option. A non-cancellable lease is a lease cancellable only on the occurrence of some remote contingency, with the permission of the lessor, if the lessee enters an equivalent lease, or on payment of a penalty such that continuation of the lease is reasonably certain. [*IAS 17.4*]

5.1.50.25   For example, if the lease term is nine years but the lessee can cancel the lease without penalty (and without the permission of the lessor) at the end of the third and sixth years, then the non-cancellable period of the contract would be three years. The substance of the arrangement is that at the end of the third and sixth years, the lessee has an option to extend the lease. If at the time of inception of the lease it is judged reasonably certain that the lessee will not cancel the lease and will effectively exercise its options to extend at the end of the third and sixth years, then the lease term will be nine years. [*IAS 17.4*]

5.1.50.30   IFRS does not provide specific guidance on how to assess when it should be considered 'reasonably certain' that a lessee would exercise an option to renew the lease. The assessment of the degree of certainty is based on facts and circumstances at inception of the lease rather than on the lessee's intentions. Factors relevant to the assessment may include, for example:
- the amount of the rentals payable in the secondary lease period compared with expected market rates for a similar asset during that period;
- the significance of continued use of the asset to the lessee's business model; and
- the ability of the lessee to recover costs that it incurs improving the leased asset.

5.1.50.40   In our view, if it is believed that a lessee will be economically compelled to renew a lease, then this indicates that renewal is reasonably certain. Conversely, if the lessee benefits from a modest discount on market rents in the secondary lease period, then this may increase the likelihood that the lessee will renew but, in the absence of other factors, will rarely demonstrate that renewal is reasonably certain.

5.1.60   Economic life and useful life

5.1.60.10   A leased asset's *economic* life is the period over which the asset is expected to be us-able – e.g. by the current lessee and any subsequent user. The economic life is used when comparing the lease term with the asset's life to evaluate whether the lease is an operating or a finance lease (see 5.1.100). A leased asset's *useful* life, which may be shorter than its remaining *economic* life, is the period over which the economic benefits of the asset are expected to be consumed by the lessee. A lessee depreciates an asset capitalised under a finance lease over the shorter of the *lease term* and the asset's *useful* life, unless it is reasonably certain that the lessee will obtain ownership by the end of the lease term, in which case the depreciation period is the useful life. [*IAS 17.4, 28*]

5.1.60.20   In our view, when an asset that was previously leased subsequently becomes the subject of a new lease, the economic life of the asset for the purpose of assessing the lease classification of the new lease is the *remaining* economic life of the asset measured from the *commencement date* of the new lease. If there is no modification to the original lease, then basing the classification on the leased asset's existing condition more accurately reflects the substance of the lease economics. [*IAS 17.4*]

EXAMPLE 2 – NEW LEASE CLASSIFICATION – ECONOMIC LIFE

> 5.1.60.30   Company L leases a new asset with an economic life of 10 years to Company M under a five-year lease with no option for renewal. At the end of the lease term, the remaining economic life of the asset is reassessed as seven years. Following expiry of the initial lease, L grants M a new five-year lease over the asset. The new lease does not contain a bargain purchase option and title does not transfer at the end of the lease term. For the purpose of determining the lease classification for the lessee, we believe that the economic life is seven years and that the contract life is five years.

5.1.70   Residual values

5.1.70.10   There are two types of residual value to be considered by the parties to a lease contract: *guaranteed* residual value and *unguaranteed* residual value. A 'guaranteed residual value' is the fixed or determinable amount that is required to be paid to the lessor at the end of the lease term or on disposal of the leased asset. An 'unguaranteed residual value' is the amount that the lessor expects to recover from the leased asset following the end of the term; however, realisation of that amount is not assured by a party external to the lessor. [*IAS 17.4*]

5.1.70.20   The amount of the minimum lease payments reflects whether the residual value is guaranteed or unguaranteed. The lessor includes in the determination of the minimum lease payments any residual value guaranteed by the lessee, a party related to the lessee or a third party unrelated to the lessor that is financially capable of discharging the obligations under the guarantee. The lessee includes a guaranteed residual value in the determination of the minimum lease payments only if the lessee or a party related to the lessee has guaranteed the residual value. For a lessee, the amount included in the minimum lease payments in respect of a residual value guarantee is the maximum amount that the lessee could, in any event, be required to pay. An unguaranteed residual value is always excluded from the determination of the minimum lease payments, but is nevertheless part of the lessor's gross investment in a finance lease (see 5.1.330.10). [*IAS 17.4*]

5.1.70.30   For further discussion of residual value guarantees and third party guarantees, see 5.1.378.

5.1.80   Contingent rent

5.1.80.10   The guidance in this section on the application of contingent rentals in determining minimum lease payments applies equally to both operating and finance leases and both lessees and lessors. 'Contingent rent' is the portion of lease payments that is not fixed in amount. This definition specifically refers to *future* amounts that are not fixed because they are potential incremental payments linked to future changes in indices, sales, use of equipment etc. The calculation of minimum lease payments includes the lease payments that are known at the lease inception date, based on the then-current variable market rate or current price level. [*IAS 17.4*]

5.1.80.20   This can be illustrated by considering an 'interest-only' lease, in which the periodic lease payments are calculated by multiplying an underlying monetary amount by a market interest rate and, in addition, there is a final lease payment of the underlying monetary amount. In such cases, the market interest rate is being used to set the periodic lease payments. The minimum lease payments therefore include the periodic lease payments based on the market interest rate at inception of the lease plus the final repayment of the underlying monetary amount. Differences between the actual lease payments and the minimum lease payments arising from *future* changes in the market interest rate after inception of the lease are contingent rents and are recognised as they are incurred.

EXAMPLE 3A – CONTINGENT RENTALS – INTEREST-BASED

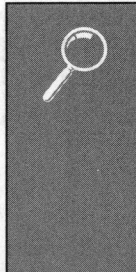

5.1.80.30   The annual rentals in a five-year lease are calculated as 1,000 x Euribor, with a 'bullet' repayment of 1,000 at the end of year 5. If Euribor is 5% on inception of the lease, then the minimum lease payments would be 50 each year (1,000 x 5%) plus the bullet repayment of 1,000 in year 5. If Euribor is actually 7% in year 1, then the contingent rent in year 1 would be 20 ((7% - 5%) x 1,000). If this lease were classified as an operating lease, then the lessee would recognise the total minimum lease payments on a straight-line basis over the term of the lease, giving an annual rental expense of (50 + 1,000 / 5) = 250, and would recognise the contingent rent as it is incurred.

5.1.80.40   Additional considerations may apply in more complex cases, such as indexed rental payments. One acceptable way of analysing such agreements is to consider whether the index at inception of the agreement is already included in the starting lease payments. For example, the lease agreement may identify a 'base' or 'starting' rent that is increased each year by the increase in a specified price index during that year. The agreement may state that the starting rent is 1,000 and that the annual lease payment will be 1,000 increased by the change in the consumer price index (CPI) since lease inception. Because CPI is the summary of past actual price levels, under this approach the price level on any given date will already include the CPI on that date – i.e. current prices are inclusive of the current level of CPI. Under this approach, any increases in lease payments after lease inception relate to future changes in CPI and therefore are contingent rents.

EXAMPLE 3B – CONTINGENT RENTALS – INDEXED RENTALS

5.1.80.50   Company Y entered into a five-year lease for a retail property. The inception and commencement date are 1 January 2014 and rentals are payable on 31 December each year. The lease agreement specifies a starting rent of 1,000 and requires the actual lease payment on 31 December of each year to be calculated as follows.

> Lease payment on 31 December in year X =
> 1,000 x (CPI at the end of year X / CPI at 1 January 2014)

5.1.80.60   Therefore, following the logic in 5.1.80.40, Y's minimum lease payments are 1,000 for every year of the lease. The starting rent of 1,000 already reflects the CPI at lease inception. Assuming that the CPI as at 1 January 2014 is 165 and it continues to rise in accordance with the indices below, then the actual rentals payable would be as follows.

Date	Base rent	CPI	Cumulative CPI increase	Annual rental with CPI variation	Contingent rentals
	(A)	(B)	(C)[1]	(D)[2]	(D - A)
31 December 2014	1,000	174	1.05	1,050	50
31 December 2015	1,000	186	1.13	1,130	130
31 December 2016	1,000	194	1.18	1,180	180
31 December 2017	1,000	198	1.20	1,200	200
31 December 2018	1,000	205	1.24	1,240	240

Notes
1. Calculated as (B / 165).
2. Calculated as (A x C).

5.1.80.70   Periodic fixed rental increases cannot be ignored when calculating the minimum lease payments for a lease agreement that also includes an indexation feature. The substance of the agreement helps in distinguishing between minimum lease payments and contingent rents. [*IU 11-05*]

5.1.80.73   If the base amount of rent is set using a fixed minimum rate of increase plus changes in CPI, then the fixed minimum rate of increase is used to determine the minimum lease payments at inception.

EXAMPLE 3C – CONTINGENT RENTALS – COMBINED WITH MINIMUM PAYMENTS

5.1.80.75   Company Y entered into a five-year lease of a retail property on similar terms to the lease illustrated in Example 3B, except that the lease agreement stated that the annual lease payments would be increased by the higher of (1) the increase in CPI as shown in the table in Example 3B and (2) 2% per annum. In this case, the minimum lease payments include the minimum fixed increase of 2% per annum, because Y is required to pay at least this amount irrespective of the future value of CPI.

5.1.80.80   If the base amount is expressed as the greater of a currency unit amount and the previous rent adjusted for CPI, then the minimum lease amounts at inception are determined using the currency unit amount, with any fluctuations considered contingent rental. For example, on each rent review date, if rent is set to be the greater of 5,000 or the base rent of 4,000 indexed to CPI, then the minimum lease payments are determined using the 5,000 minimum payment.

5.1.80.90   For further discussion of application issues involving contingent rent, see 5.1.390.

5.1.90   **Initial direct costs**

5.1.90.10   'Initial direct costs' are incremental costs, incurred by either the lessor or the lessee, that are directly attributable to negotiating and arranging a lease, except for such costs incurred by manufacturer or dealer lessors. For a discussion of the accounting for costs incurred by manufacturer or dealer lessors to negotiate and arrange a lease, see 5.1.340. [*IAS 17.4*]

5.1.90.20   Examples of initial direct costs include commissions, legal fees and internal costs that are incremental and directly attributable to negotiating and arranging a lease. Items that are not considered to be initial direct costs include allocations of internal overhead costs, such as those incurred by a sales and marketing team. [*IAS 17.4, 38*]

5.1.90.30   The initial recognition of and the subsequent accounting for initial direct costs depends on the classification of the lease (see 5.1.300.30, 310.170, 330.10, 340.10 and 350.40).

5.1.100   **CLASSIFICATION OF LEASE**

5.1.100.10   A 'finance lease' is a lease that transfers substantially all of the risks and rewards incidental to ownership of the leased asset from the lessor to the lessee; title to the asset may or may not transfer under such a lease. An 'operating lease' is a lease other than a finance lease. [*IAS 17.4, 7–8*]

5.1.100.20   For example, for a simple lease arrangement in which Company V leases an asset to Company W and no other parties are involved, the analysis will focus on the transfer of risks and rewards from V as lessor to W as lessee.

5.1.100.30   Additional factors may need to be considered in more complex, multi-party arrangements. For example, suppose that Company G leases an asset to Company K and G also enters into an agreement with Company Z whereby Z guarantees the residual value of the asset. Because Z is unrelated to K, the residual value is included in the minimum lease payments by G, but not by K. Depending on the facts and circumstances, this may result in G accounting for the arrangement as a finance lease and K accounting for the arrangement as an operating lease (see 5.1.160.50). [*IAS 17.9*]

5.1.100.40   Only risks and rewards incidental to ownership of the leased asset during the lease period are considered when determining lease classification. Relevant risks may include the possibility of losses from idle capacity or technological obsolescence and from decreases in the value of the asset; relevant rewards may include the gain from the increase in the value of the asset or realisation of the residual value at the end of the lease. Conversely, risks associated with construction of the asset before lease commencement, financing such construction and the costs of providing services using the leased asset are not incidental to ownership of the leased asset during the lease period and in our view should generally be disregarded in evaluating the classification of the lease. However, construction and financing risk may impact the assessment of who recognises the asset before the lease commences.

5.1.100.50   The classification of a lease is determined at inception of the lease and is not revised unless the lease agreement is modified (see 5.1.270). [*IAS 17.13*]

5.1.110   **Indicators of finance lease**

5.1.120   *Primary lease classification criteria*

5.1.120.10   The following are indicators that would normally individually or in combination lead to a lease being classified as a finance lease. Generally, the presence of any one indicator would point to classification as a finance lease. However, the lease classification is ultimately based on an overall assessment of whether substantially all of the risks and rewards incidental to ownership of the asset have been transferred from the lessor to the lessee or to the lessee and a third party residual value guarantor. [*IAS 17.8, 10*]

5.1.130   *Transfer of ownership*

5.1.130.10   If legal ownership of the asset ultimately transfers to the lessee, either during or at the end of the lease term, then the agreement will usually be classified as a finance lease. [*IAS 17.10(a)*]

5.1.140   *Purchase options*

5.1.140.10   The existence of a purchase option that is reasonably certain to be exercised, based on facts and circumstances at inception of the lease, means that title to the asset is expected to transfer. Therefore, a lease with such an option is normally classified as a finance lease. For example, if the lessee has the option to buy the leased asset at a price that is expected to be sufficiently lower than the expected fair value of the leased asset at the date the option becomes exercisable and therefore it is reasonably certain, at inception of the lease, that the option will be exercised, then the agreement is classified as a finance lease. [*IAS 17.10(b)*]

5.1.140.20   In our view, the following situations also normally lead to finance lease classification because in these situations it is reasonably certain, at lease inception, that the purchase option will be exercised.

* When the lessee is economically compelled for business reasons, not just because of a below-market price, to exercise a purchase option to buy the asset. For a further discussion of factors relevant to assessing economic compulsion, see 5.1.50.30–40.
* When the lessor has a put option with an exercise price that is expected to be sufficiently higher than the expected fair value of the leased asset at the date the option becomes exercisable. For a further discussion of lessor put options included in minimum lease payments, see 5.1.30.13. A put option is also a form of residual value guarantee; for a further discussion of how to assess residual value guarantees from a risk and rewards perspective, see 5.1.378.
* When the lessee has a call option to buy the asset at the end of the lease term at a fixed exercise price and the lessor has a matching put option for the same fixed exercise price. In such cases, depending on the fair value of the asset at the end of the lease, either the lessee or the lessor will generally be incentivised to exercise its option. We believe that a lease with such options should normally be classified as a finance lease because the combined effect of the options means that title to the asset is reasonably certain to transfer and the lessee bears residual value risk.

5.1.140.30   As discussed in 5.1.30.13, if the lease includes a put option under which the lessor can require the lessee to buy the asset at the end of the lease for a fixed price, then the lessee and the lessor include the exercise price of the put option in the minimum lease payments. [*IAS 17.4*]

5.1.150 *Major part of economic life*

5.1.150.10   If the lease term is for the major part of the economic life of the leased asset, then the agreement would normally be classified as a finance lease. [*IAS 17.10(c)*]

5.1.150.20   IFRS does not define what is meant by the 'major part' of an asset's economic life. Practice has been to look to the lease accounting guidance in US GAAP, which has quantitative criteria about what is considered to be the majority of an asset's economic life. US GAAP has a 'bright-line' threshold whereby a lease term equivalent to 75 percent or more of the economic life of an asset is considered to be the major part of the asset's economic life. Practice under US GAAP requires a lease that is very close to, but below, this bright-line cut-off – e.g. a lease term equivalent to 74 percent of the asset's economic life – to be classified as an operating lease if none of the other criteria for finance (capital) lease classification are met. In our view, although this 75 percent threshold may be a useful reference point, it does not represent a bright-line or automatic cut-off point under IFRS. We believe that it is necessary to consider all relevant factors when assessing the classification of a lease and it is clear that some leases may be for the major part of an asset's economic life even if the lease term is for less than 75 percent of the economic life of the asset.

5.1.160 *Present value of minimum lease payments is substantially all of fair value*

5.1.160.10   If at inception of the lease the present value of the minimum lease payments (see 5.1.30) amounts to substantially all of the fair value of the leased asset, then the agreement would normally be classified as a finance lease. [*IAS 17.10(d)*]

5.1.160.20   IFRS does not define what is meant by 'substantially all'. US GAAP has a bright-line threshold whereby if the present value of the minimum lease payments is 90 percent or more of the fair value of the leased asset at inception of the lease, then the lease is classified as a finance (capital) lease. Practice under US GAAP requires a lease that is very close to this bright-line cut-off – e.g. 89 percent – to be classified as an operating lease if none of the other criteria for finance (capital) lease classification are met. In our view, although the 90 percent threshold may provide a useful reference point, it does not represent a bright-line or automatic cut-off point under IFRS. We believe that it is necessary to consider all relevant factors when assessing the classification of a lease and it is clear that some leases may meet this criterion even if the present value of the minimum lease payments is less than 90 percent of the fair value of the leased asset at inception of the lease.

5.1.160.30   The discount rate to be used in assessing this criterion is determined using the guidance for calculating the present value of minimum lease payments when accounting for finance leases. Therefore, both the lessor and the lessee use the interest rate implicit in the lease as the discount rate for determining the present value of minimum lease payments for the lease classification test. However, in many cases, the lessee will not have enough information about the unguaranteed residual value of the leased asset to determine the lease's implicit interest rate, in which case the lessee instead uses its own incremental borrowing rate as the discount rate. Consistent with the definition of the lessee's incremental borrowing rate, the leased asset is considered as collateral. [*IAS 17.4, 20*]

5.1.160.40   Certain leases may, for example, have significant tax benefits that are reflected in the lease pricing such that the present value of the rentals, when discounted at the incremental borrowing rate, is less than 90 percent of the asset's fair value – not because the lessor has retained the risk of the leased asset to such extent, but because the tax benefits are greater than 10 percent. In these cases, judgement needs to be applied in determining whether the lease transfers substantially all of the risks and rewards incidental to ownership.

5.1.160.50   If a residual value guarantee is provided by someone other than the lessee or a party related to the lessee, then it is included in the calculation of minimum lease payments by the lessor but not by the lessee. This may result in the present value of the minimum lease payments at the inception date amounting to substantially all of the fair value of the leased asset for a lessor but not for a lessee. In some cases, this may indicate that substantially all of the risks and rewards were transferred from the lessor but were not passed on solely to the lessee (i.e. other parties also participated in some of the risks and rewards) and may result in a different classification of the lease by the lessor and the lessee (i.e. the lessor may classify the lease as a finance lease and the lessee may classify it as an operating lease).

5.1.160.60   In many long-term leases, it is not uncommon for the lessee to have a cancellation right with some penalty payments. In our view, the calculation of the minimum lease payments should include penalty payments if the lease term reflects the assessment that the lessee will exercise an option to terminate the lease. Such an approach determines the minimum lease payments based on whether the lessee is reasonably certain to exercise the termination option. For a discussion of the non-cancellable lease term, see 5.1.50.20–30.

5.1.170   *Specialised nature of asset*

5.1.170.10   If a leased asset is so specialised that only the lessee can use it without major modification, then the agreement would normally be classified as a finance lease. An asset built to the lessee's specifications may be a specialised asset. However, a machine that could be used by other entities in the same industry as the lessee – e.g. a printing press – would not be considered to be a specialised asset even if it had some degree of customisation. [*IAS 17.10(e)*]

5.1.180   **Supplemental indicators of finance lease**

5.1.180.10   The following are additional indicators that a contract may be a finance lease:
* the lessee can cancel the lease but the lessor's losses associated with the cancellation are borne by the lessee;
* gains or losses from the fluctuation in the fair value of the residual fall to the lessee – e.g. in the form of a rent rebate equalling most of the sales proceeds at the end of the lease; or
* the lessee can extend the lease at a rent that is substantially lower than the market rent. [*IAS 17.11*]

5.1.190   **Assessing the indicators**

5.1.190.10   IFRS does not provide a hierarchy to be applied when evaluating the indicators discussed in 5.1.130–180, and these indicators may not be conclusive. As a result, although the presence of any one indicator may point to classification as a finance lease, other facts or features may demonstrate that the lease does not transfer substantially all of the risks and rewards incidental to ownership. Therefore, judgement is required in determining lease classification based on an overall assessment of whether substantially all of the risks and rewards incidental to ownership of the leased asset have been transferred from the lessor to the lessee. [*IAS 17.12*]

EXAMPLE 4 – ASSESSING A PURCHASE OPTION

5.1.190.20   Company H leases an asset from Company J for 10 years. The lease includes a purchase option under which H may buy the asset from J at the end of the lease. The exercise price of the purchase option set at inception of the lease is the fair value of the asset at the date of exercise – i.e. the exercise price is variable. The continued use of the asset is significant to H's business model (see 5.1.50.30) and therefore H determines at lease inception that it is reasonably certain that the purchase option will be exercised.

5.1.190.30   In this example, legal ownership of the asset is expected to transfer to H. This is an indicator of a finance lease. However, because the exercise price is the fair value of the asset at the date of exercise, J continues to bear residual value risks and rewards – i.e. the fair value of the asset will be higher or lower than expected at the end of the lease. Because of the potential significance of the volatility of the future exercise price, judgement will be required to determine whether the lease has transferred substantially all of the risks and rewards incidental to ownership of the asset to H, and how the lease should be classified. [*IAS 17.12*]

5.1.190.40   Modifying the fact pattern, the exercise price of the purchase option is fixed. In this case, the residual value risks and rewards are instead borne by H. In this example, the expected transfer of title of the asset at a fixed price is an indicator that the lease has transferred substantially all the risks and rewards incidental to ownership of the asset to H and will generally result in the agreement being classified as a finance lease.

5.1.200   Other classification issues

5.1.210   *Evaluation of risks and rewards*

5.1.210.10   IFRS does not address how to consider probability when assessing whether a lease transfers substantially all of the risks and rewards incidental to ownership of an asset. In our view, an assessment of the risks and rewards should use a probability-weighted approach, taking into account who is more likely to be exposed to the expected risks and achieve the expected benefits, and not just the relative proportions of the risks and rewards. For a discussion of linked transactions in the legal form of a lease, see 5.1.500.

EXAMPLE 5A – PROBABILITY-WEIGHTED EVALUATION OF RISKS AND REWARDS (1)

5.1.210.20   Company R leases an asset to Company M for 14 years. The estimated economic life of the asset is 20 years. The fair value of the asset at inception of the lease is 1,000 and its estimated residual value at the end of the lease term is 250. All risks and rewards of ownership, other than the residual value risk, as discussed below, are transferred to M.

5.1.210.30   M agrees to reimburse R for the first 50 of losses on disposal of the asset at the end of the lease term (based on the estimated residual value of 250).

Therefore, if the asset is sold for 230, then M will pay 20 (250 - 230) to R. If the asset is sold for 200 or less, then M will pay 50 (250 - 200) to R. M has an option to buy the asset for 250, which is not a purchase option that is reasonably certain, at inception of the lease, to be exercised.

5.1.210.40   The present value of the minimum lease payments, *including* the guarantee of the first 50 of residual value, is 85% of the fair value of the asset.

5.1.210.50   Historical data suggests that the residual value of the asset at the end of the lease term is highly unlikely to fall below 200. Therefore, all of the most likely residual value risk is with M, although M does not bear the risk that the recoverable amount of the leased asset will be below 200 at the end of the lease term. Furthermore, M would receive any potential gains because M would be able to exercise the option to buy the asset for the fixed price of 250 if, at the end of the lease, the actual value was above 250.

5.1.210.60   We believe that the evaluation of the transfer of risks and rewards should reflect the probabilities of the realistically likely range of outcomes. In this example, substantially all of the reasonably possible risks and all rewards incidental to ownership of the asset are transferred to M. R has only an insignificant risk and no rewards in relation to the residual value. Therefore, in our view the lease should be classified as a finance lease.

EXAMPLE 5B – PROBABILITY-WEIGHTED EVALUATION OF RISKS AND REWARDS (2)

5.1.210.70   Company Q leases a building and is required to replace the building if it is destroyed by an earthquake during the lease term. In our view, the fact that Q bears these 'catastrophic' risks does not mean that the lease is necessarily a finance lease. Rather, the risks should be assessed after taking into account their likelihood. In an area in which earthquakes are very uncommon, Q's commitment to rebuild the building if it is destroyed by an earthquake may have little effect on the classification of the lease.

5.1.220   *Transactions structured to achieve a lease*

5.1.220.10   SIC-27 provides guidance for evaluating transactions that may involve specific structuring to achieve a lease transaction. When considering such structuring transactions, the substance of the arrangement is evaluated to assess whether it contains a lease and, if so, whether the lease has transferred to the lessee substantially all of the risks and rewards incidental to the ownership of the leased asset. In our experience, SIC-27 is applied in limited circumstances – e.g. when the only substantive effect of the agreement is to create and transfer tax benefits between parties (see 5.1.500). Arrangements that transfer the right to use an underlying asset, or otherwise change the allocation of the risks and rewards incidental to ownership of an underlying asset (other than tax benefits), are generally in the scope of IAS 17. [*SIC-27.3–5*]

Leases of land

5.1.230.10   The classification of a lease of land is assessed based on the general classification guidance. Consistent with the general leasing requirements, the assessment of the land classification is made at inception of the lease based on the expected conditions and outcomes at that time and is not revised merely because the value of the residual asset at the end of the lease increases over time. [*IAS 17.15A*]

5.1.230.20   In determining the lease classification, an important consideration is that land normally has an indefinite economic life. However, the fact that the lease term is normally shorter than the economic life of the land does not necessarily mean that a lease of land is always an operating lease; the other classification requirements are also considered. In our experience, it may be helpful to consider the indicators discussed further below when assessing the classification of a lease of land. However, ultimately, the lease classification is based on an overall assessment of whether substantially all of the risks and rewards incidental to ownership of the asset have been transferred from the lessor to the lessee. [*IAS 17.15A*]

5.1.231   *Lease term*

5.1.231.10   A lease of land will not typically cover the major part of the economic life of the land, because land normally has an indefinite economic life. However:
- in a 999-year lease of land and buildings, the significant risks and rewards associated with the land during the lease term are transferred to the lessee during the lease term, regardless of whether title will be transferred; and
- the present value of the residual value of the property with a lease term of 'several decades' would be negligible and therefore accounting for the land element as a finance lease is consistent with the economic position of the lessee. [*IAS 17.BC8B–BC8C*]

5.1.231.20   It follows that a long lease term may indicate that a lease of land is a finance lease. This is not because the lease term will thereby cover the major part of the economic life of the land, but because in a long lease of land the risks and rewards retained by the lessor through its residual interest in the land at the end of the lease are not significant when measured at inception. Conversely, a short lease of land is unlikely to be a finance lease because the risks and rewards retained by the lessor through its residual interest in the land at the end of the lease when measured at inception are likely to be significant.

5.1.231.30   It would not be appropriate to seek to determine a bright-line threshold lease term above which a lease of land would always be classified as a finance lease, because of the judgemental nature of the assessment. As an example, the basis for conclusions to IAS 17 notes that a 999-year lease of land, which is a common lease term in some jurisdictions, would normally be a finance lease. However, depending on the facts and circumstances, leases of land with terms as short as 50 years could be finance leases. In addition, a lease with a short minimum contractual period but a fixed-price renewal option that is reasonably certain to be exercised may also be a finance lease. [*IAS 17.BC8A–BC8C*]

EXAMPLE 6A – LEASES OF LAND – 50-YEAR TERM WITH INDEFINITE RENEWALS

5.1.231.40   In Country X, all land is owned by the government. Leases of land are granted to private sector entities under standard terms. The minimum contracted lease term is 50 years. The lease payments comprise a significant up-front amount

payable on lease commencement and an immaterial annual payment. At the end of the minimum contractual lease term of 50 years, the lessee may renew the lease on the same terms at its option; that is, annual lease payments continue to be immaterial and the lessee may renew the lease at the end of each subsequent renewal period. No additional premium is payable on renewal.

5.1.231.45   In this case, the lease term is very long, because at inception of the lease it is reasonably certain that the lessee will opt to renew the lease after 50 years, indeed indefinitely. Therefore, the lessee classifies the lease of land as a finance lease.

5.1.232   *Present value of minimum lease payments*

5.1.232.10   In our experience, many leases of land are granted for an up-front premium with immaterial annual lease payments. In such cases, the amount of the up-front premium generally approximates the present value of the lease payments. However, for leases of land that include material recurring lease payments it will often be difficult to assess whether the present value of the minimum lease payments amounts to substantially all of the fair value of the land, because of difficulties in estimating the rate implicit in the lease.

5.1.232.20   One approach is to discount the minimum lease payments first at a risk-free rate. In our view, if the present value of the minimum lease payments discounted at a risk-free rate amounts to less than substantially all of the fair value of the land, then this may indicate that the lease is an operating lease. The rationale for this view is that although the rate implicit in a lease of land is very difficult to estimate, it will always be higher than the risk-free rate – often very much higher. Therefore, if the present value of the minimum lease payments is less than substantially all of the fair value of the land when discounted at the risk-free rate, then there is little doubt that this would also be the case if the minimum lease payments were discounted at the (higher) interest rate implicit in the lease, if that rate were known.

EXAMPLE 6B – LEASES OF LAND – INABILITY TO RELIABLY DETERMINE INTEREST RATE IMPLICIT IN LEASE

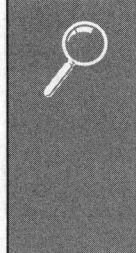

5.1.232.30   Company B rents a plot of land for 30 years from a third party on an arm's length basis and pays a fixed annual rent. B is unable to determine the rate implicit in the lease reliably. However, B notes that the yield on long-dated government bonds in its jurisdiction at the inception date of the lease is 6%. B calculates that the present value of the minimum lease payments payable over 30 years, discounted at the risk-free rate of 6%, equals 87% of the fair value of the land at inception, which B considers to be less than substantially all of the fair value of the land. We believe that B should classify the lease as an operating lease.

5.1.232.40   Applying this test using a risk-free rate will still require judgement – e.g. to determine the risk-free rate. Performing the calculation at other relevant discount rates may also help lease classification. For example, in markets in which property yields are readily ascertainable, discounting the minimum lease payments at a market property yield will help lease classification.

5.1.232.50   It may be helpful to perform a series of calculations to assist in the lease classification decision. For example, if calculations indicate that the present value of the minimum lease payments amounts to substantially all of the fair value of the leased land when discounted at a risk-free rate and when discounted at a market property yield, then this will indicate that the lease is a finance lease. However, if the present value of the minimum lease payments amounts to less than substantially all of the fair value of the leased land when discounted at a market property yield but more than substantially all of the fair value of the leased land when discounted at a risk-free rate, then additional indicators will need to be considered.

5.1.232.60   An alternative approach is to calculate the discount rate at which the present value of the minimum lease payments equals substantially all of the fair value of the leased land, and then compare that rate to other relevant information, such as the risk-free rate, market property yields, the lessee's incremental borrowing rate etc. Again, judgement will be required to interpret the results of these calculations.

5.1.232.70   Taking some lease terms seen commonly in practice, our calculations show that this indicator suggests that 150-year and 99-year leases in which the rentals are set at a market rate at inception of the lease could all be classified as finance leases under this approach. In some markets, leases as short as 50 years may be finance leases, in the absence of contra-indicators such as contingent rentals and other contingent payments as discussed below. However, in our experience it is rare for lease terms for less than 50 years to be considered finance leases.

5.1.233   *Contingent rentals*

5.1.233.10   Contingent rentals may indicate that a lease is an operating lease, if the nature of the contingency provides evidence that the lessor has not transferred substantially all of the risks and rewards of ownership of the land.

EXAMPLE 6C – LEASES OF LAND – RENTALS ADJUSTED TO MARKET RATES

5.1.233.20   Company B enters into a 99-year lease of land in Country Y. The starting rent under the lease is set at the prevailing market rate. Every five years, there is a market rent review under which rentals are reset to the market rate at the date of the rent review. Historical studies show a long-term trend of significant real-terms growth in land values in Country Y. In this case, the lessor's return depends on changes in the value of the land during the lease term through the rent review mechanism. In our view, B should classify the lease as an operating lease, because a key risk/reward of owning land is that its value may rise or fall and the lessor retains this risk/reward during the lease term.

5.1.233.30   The presence of contingent rentals does not automatically indicate that a lease of land is an operating lease. As part of the assessment of the lease, an entity would also consider:

- whether there are other indicators that the lease is a finance lease;
- the nature of the contingency and whether the contingency provides evidence about the extent to which the lease transfers risks and rewards of ownership of the land; and
- the materiality of the contingency in the context of the lease as a whole.

EXAMPLE 6D – LEASES OF LAND – ASSESSING SIGNIFICANCE OF CONTINGENT RENTALS

5.1.233.40   Company C enters into a 99-year lease of land in Country Z. The lessor is the local government authority. The lease payments comprise an up-front premium that equates to 50% of the fair value of the land, and annual rentals calculated initially at 3% of the market value of the land at inception. Subsequently, the annual rentals are set at the higher of the rent for the previous year and 3% of the current market value of the land. Historical data on land values in Country Z is limited but suggests that land values are fairly stable.

5.1.233.45   In this case, the lessor again retains exposure to changes in the value of the land during the lease term, this time through the calculation of annual rentals. However, the significance of this exposure is reduced because of the size of the up-front payment, the 'upwards-only' rent review mechanism and the relative stability of land values. In addition, the lease term is long and it appears likely that the present value of the minimum lease payments will exceed substantially all of the fair value of the land. To assess the most appropriate classification of the lease, C considers the significance of the contingent rentals.

5.1.233.47   In our view, on the basis of the facts in this example, C should classify the lease as a finance lease.

5.1.233.48   Contingent rentals adjusted for changes in CPI generally do not provide evidence about the extent to which the lease transfers the risks and rewards of ownership of the land.

EXAMPLE 6E – LEASES OF LAND – CPI-ADJUSTED RENTALS

5.1.233.50   Company D enters into a 50-year lease of land. The starting rent is set at the prevailing market rate. During the lease term, rentals are reset every five years by adjusting the previous rent by the cumulative change in CPI during the five-year period. In the five years before inception of the lease, annual changes in consumer prices have varied between 20% per annum and 10% per annum. In this case, the rentals are contingent and the effect of the contingency is expected to be significant. However, the contingency relates to changes in CPI, not changes in the market value of land.

5.1.233.60   In our view, the contingent rentals, based on the facts of this example, do not provide evidence about the extent to which the lease transfers the risks and rewards of ownership of the land; therefore, D should assess the classification of the lease with reference to other factors.

5.1.234   *Other contingent payments*

5.1.234.10   If there are other substantive mechanisms through which the lessor's return varies with changes in the fair value of the land during the lease term, then this may indicate that the lease is an operating lease. In practice, such mechanisms may include:

- renewal premiums based on the market value of the land at the date of renewal;
- purchase options for which the exercise price is the fair value of the land at the date on which the option is exercised;
- one-off payments due from the lessee to the lessor if there is a change in the planning status of the land; and
- the lessor's ability to terminate the lease and enter into a new lease on more favourable terms.

5.1.234.20   In each of these cases, similar principles to those in the contingent rentals discussed above apply. That is, it remains important to consider other potential indicators of lease classification.

EXAMPLE 6F – LEASES OF LAND – EARLY-TERMINATION RIGHT

5.1.234.30   Company E enters into a 50-year lease of land. The starting rent is set at the prevailing market rate. During the lease term, rentals are reset annually by adjusting the previous rent by CPI. E has no renewal or early-termination options. However, the lessor retains an option to terminate the lease without penalty by giving six months' notice.

5.1.234.40   In this case, the minimum lease payments include the rentals payable by the lessee over 50 years, because this is the period over which the lessee *can be required* to continue to make lease payments. However, although the lessee can be required to make lease payments for 50 years, the lessor has the right to terminate the lease early. This means that if the market value of land rises faster than CPI, then the lessor has an economic motive to terminate the lease and seek to secure a new tenant or buyer at the higher market price. Through this mechanism, the lessor retains a potential reward associated with ownership of the land, being the right to participate in future increases in the fair value of the land. In our view, this right indicates that the lease may be an operating lease.

5.1.235   *Economic indifference*

5.1.235.10   In our view, if it would make little economic difference to the entity whether it leased or bought an asset, then this indicates that the lease is a finance lease because the entity prima facie considers that any risks and rewards that are not transferred by the lease contract are not significant.

5.1.235.20   Examples 6G to 6I illustrate situations that suggest that it makes little economic difference to an entity whether it leases or buys an asset, such that the lease may be a finance lease.

EXAMPLE 6G – LEASES OF LAND – ECONOMICALLY EQUIVALENT TO OWNERSHIP (1)

5.1.235.30   Company F operates in Country Q, in which both freehold and lease-hold interests in land are common. F enters into a lease of land from Company G with the following terms and conditions.
- F makes a single lease payment of 1,000 at lease commencement.
- The lease term is for a period of 125 years.

- Title to the land does not transfer to F at the end of the lease.
- The market value of a freehold interest in the land is 1,000.

5.1.235.35   We believe that F should classify the lease as a finance lease, notwithstanding that it never obtains title to land, because it obtains risks and rewards typically associated with ownership of the land during the lease term and the pricing of the lease suggests that the risks and rewards associated with the residual interest in the land at the end of the lease are negligible. That is, in this example a 125-year lease is economically equivalent to an ownership interest in the land.

5.1.235.40   The finance lease asset will be amortised over the lease term, even though the underlying asset is land. In this example, because F prepays 100% of the rent, the amortisation charge is equivalent to the amount that would be recognised if the lease were classified as an operating lease. Conversely, if F were to pay for the lease over a period of time (e.g. 20 years), then F would recognise a finance lease obligation at lease commencement and subsequently amortise the obligation over the payment period using the effective interest method that would result in the recognition of a finance expense.

5.1.235.50   The conclusion in Example 6G would also follow from the guidance on the lease term in 5.1.231. However, an analysis of whether it makes little economic difference to a lessee between leasing and buying an asset may help in the analysis of more complex examples.

EXAMPLE 6H – LEASES OF LAND – ECONOMICALLY EQUIVALENT TO OWNERSHIP (2)

5.1.235.60   The following are modifications to Example 6G.
- A sales tax of 10% applies to sales of land but not to leases of land.
- Market participants commonly enter into 125-year leases of land to avoid the sales tax.
- The difference between the market value of a freehold interest in the land and the up-front rental payable on commencement of a 125-year lease is equivalent to the sales tax.

5.1.235.70   If it would make little economic difference to Company F whether it buys or leases the land, then we believe that F should classify any lease arising as a finance lease.

EXAMPLE 6I – LEASES OF LAND – ECONOMICALLY EQUIVALENT TO OWNERSHIP (3)

5.1.235.80   Foreign ownership of land is prohibited in Country R. Company H, a resident of Country R, is marketing a plot of land for sale to residents for 1,000 or lease to non-residents for annual rental payments of 50 that, when discounted at prevailing property yields, equate to 1,000. The lease payments are fixed in amount and the lease is non-cancellable.

5.1.235.90   If it would make little economic difference to H whether it transacts with residents or non-residents on this basis, then we believe that H should classify any lease arising as a finance lease.

5.1.240   *Land and building leases*

5.1.240.10   In the case of a combined lease of land and buildings, the land and buildings are considered separately to determine the classification, unless the value of the land at inception of the lease is deemed immaterial or it is clear that both elements are either finance leases or operating leases. In determining the classification, the minimum lease payments at inception of the lease are allocated to land and buildings in proportion to the relative fair values of the leasehold interests in the land element and the buildings element. If this allocation cannot be done reliably, then the entire lease is classified as a finance lease unless it is clear that both elements qualify as operating leases. [*IAS 17.15A–17, BC9–BC11*]

5.1.240.20   The fair value of the leasehold interest is different from the fair value of the leased asset. An allocation based on the relative fair values of the land and the building elements – rather than based on the relative fair values of the respective *leasehold interests* in the land and building element – is not generally appropriate because the land often has an indefinite economic life and therefore is likely to maintain its value beyond the lease term. Therefore, the lessor would not normally need compensation for using up the land. In contrast, the future economic benefits of a building are likely to be used up to some extent over the lease term (which is reflected via depreciation). Therefore, in allocating the minimum lease payments between the land and the building elements, it is reasonable to assume that the lease payments related to the building element (depreciable asset) are set at a level that enables the lessor not only to make a return on initial investment, but also to recover the part of the value of the building used up over the lease term. [*IAS 17.15A–17, BC9–BC11*]

5.1.240.30   If a lease contains no contingent rent, then lease payments are equal to minimum lease payments. In our view, one method of allocating the minimum lease payments between the land and building elements is to allocate to the land element the portion of the minimum lease payments that represents a financing cost for the land based on the land's fair value at the inception date of the lease and the lessee's incremental borrowing rate using the land as collateral. In that case, the residual should be allocated to the building element.

5.1.240.40   If a lease contains contingent rent, then in our view the contingent rent is allocated to both the land and the building elements of the lease. In our view, it is not appropriate to allocate the minimum lease payments, which do not include contingent rent, to the land element first and then to attribute the remaining minimum lease payments and the entire contingent rent to the building element. However, a significant amount of contingent lease payments might be an indication that the entire lease is an operating lease.

5.1.250   *Classifying operating lease property interests as investment property*

5.1.250.10   A lessee may elect to classify a property interest held under an operating lease as an investment property if the property would otherwise meet the definition of an investment property (see 3.4.40.20) and if the lessee applies the fair value model to all of its investment property. This election is available on a property-by-property basis. If the lessee makes this election for a given property interest, then the lessee accounts for that property interest as if it were a finance lease. For example, a lessee may acquire a 30-year ground lease that is classified as an operating lease and otherwise meets the definition of an investment property. To classify this leasehold interest as an investment property, the lessee is required to use the fair value model when accounting for all of its investment property. The lessee continues to account for the lease as a finance lease even if a subsequent event changes the nature of the lessee's interest so that it is no longer classified as investment property. [*IAS 17.19, 40.6*]

5.1.260   *Multiple leased assets*

5.1.260.05   The lease classification principles of IFRS are generally applied on an asset-by-asset basis. The underlying asset subject to the lease may be a stand-alone asset, a portion of a larger asset or a part of a single master lease arrangement. If an underlying identifiable asset represents a unit of account under either IAS 16 or IAS 38, then that asset is also a separate unit of account under IFRIC 4 and IAS 17. [*IFRIC 4.3*]

5.1.260.10   For example, a lessee may enter into an agreement to lease several buildings with varying economic lives and fair values. In our view, it would not be appropriate to determine a weighted-average economic life for the group of buildings to compare with the lease term. Further, we believe that it would not be appropriate to compare the net present value of the lease arrangement's minimum lease payments with the total fair value of all of the buildings.

5.1.260.20   The total lease payments are allocated to each leased asset and any other elements of the arrangement on the basis of their relative fair values (see 5.1.510.180). [*IFRIC 4.13*]

5.1.265   *Sub-leases and back-to-back leases*

5.1.265.10   An intermediate party may be involved in the lease arrangement. The intermediate party may lease an asset from the head lessor and subsequently enter into a sub-lease with a third party, the ultimate lessee. One of the key determinations is whether the intermediate party is acting as principal in its own right as both lessor and lessee or whether it is merely acting as agent for the head lessor or ultimate lessee. If the intermediate party is determined to be the principal, then offsetting the lessor lease receivable and lessee lease liability is unlikely to be appropriate. Lease receivables and payables may be derecognised only when the IFRS 9 criteria are met (see chapter 7.7). Lease receivables and payables may be offset only when the IAS 32 criteria are met (see 7.10.110); IAS 1 permits offsetting only if it is specifically permitted by an accounting standard (see 4.1.200.10).

5.1.265.15   Where the intermediate party is determined to be a principal, if the head lease is a finance lease and the sub-lease is also a finance lease, then the intermediate party recognises the liability for the head lease and derecognises the head lease asset; this is because the sub-lessee has the risks and rewards of ownership of the finance lease asset. Accordingly, the intermediate party recognises a sub-lease finance lease receivable. The head lease finance lease liability and the sub-lease finance lease receivable cannot be offset unless there is an intention and a legally enforceable right to set off (see 7.10.110).

5.1.265.20   Determining whether an entity is acting as an agent or principal requires judgement and all relevant facts and circumstances are considered. For a discussion of principal vs agent relationships, see 4.2.340; and for a discussion of linked transactions in the legal form of a lease, see 5.1.500.

5.1.270   **Subsequent changes to classification**

5.1.270.05   The following flowchart summarises the possible changes to lease classification resulting from lease modifications and other changes to lease terms.

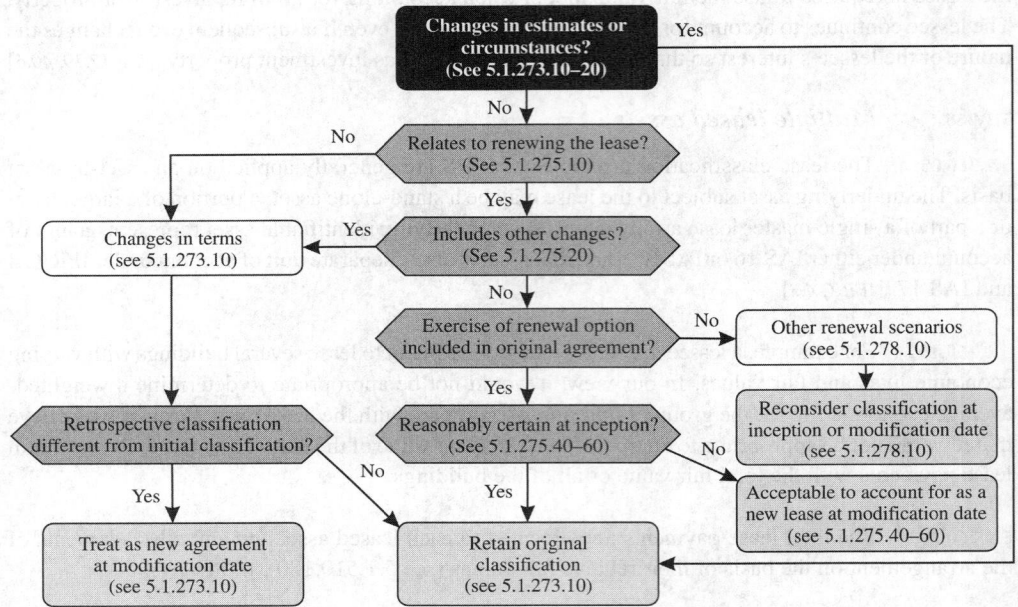

5.1.270.07   The rest of this section provides guidance on *when* a reclassification should be considered
or performed. For a discussion of the lessee's accounting for a finance lease modification that results
in a change in classification to operating lease and the accounting for a finance lease modification
that results in retaining a finance lease classification, see 5.1.410. For a discussion of the lessee's accounting for an operating lease modification that results in a change in classification to finance lease
and the accounting for an operating lease modification that results in retaining an operating lease
classification, see 5.1.415.

5.1.273   *Changes in terms vs changes in estimates or circumstances*

5.1.273.10   Leases are not reclassified for changes in estimates (e.g. of the economic life or the residual
value of the asset) or changes in circumstances (e.g. default by the lessee). If the terms of the lease are
modified other than by renewing the lease (see 5.1.275.10), then the modified agreement may have to
be treated as a new lease agreement, which may be classified differently from the original agreement.
IAS 17 requires a two-step test. First, to determine whether a modification results in a new lease agreement, the test is whether the lease would have been classified differently if the modified terms had been
in effect at inception of the lease. If the modified terms (e.g. changes to the lease payments) would have
resulted in a different classification based on the original estimates and circumstances, then the modified
agreement is regarded as a new lease agreement. In the second step, the 'new' agreement is classified
in accordance with its modified terms, based on estimates determined at the modification date – i.e. the
date of commitment by the parties to the modified terms of the lease. [*IAS 17.13*]

5.1.273.20   A lease is not reclassified because of a subsequent change in the likelihood that the lessee will renew a lease. For example, a lease may have a term of five years with a renewal option at the end of five years at a market rate. At inception of the lease, the lessee concludes that exercise of the renewal option is not reasonably certain and therefore bases its lease classification on the minimum lease payments and circumstances of the initial lease term only. If the lessee determines later that it is likely to renew the lease for an additional five years, then this would not, in itself, trigger a need to review the classification of the original lease because it is a change in estimate, not a change in the provisions of the lease. For a discussion of when the renewal option is exercised, see 5.1.275.40.

5.1.275   *Renewal of a lease*

5.1.275.10   The requirement to reconsider the classification of a lease at inception of the original lease when there is a change in the provisions of the lease (see 5.1.273.10) need not apply when there is a renewal of the lease. However, difficulties may arise in applying this exception, resulting from either:

- a lack of clarity with respect to the meaning of 'renewing the lease'; or
- a lack of guidance with respect to the required accounting when renewing the lease and meeting the exception to the modification accounting. [*IAS 17.13*]

5.1.275.20   Determining when the exception applies may be difficult, because the term 'renewing the lease' is not defined. In our view, this exception applies whenever a lessee exercises a renewal option in accordance with the provisions existing in the original lease agreement. Conversely, in our view if a lessee and lessor agree to renew a lease but also to change other provisions of the lease at the same time, then this exception does not apply.

EXAMPLE 7 – EXERCISE OF OPTION – CHANGE IN ORIGINAL LEASE

5.1.275.30   Company V leases a building from Company W under an operating lease with an initial term of 10 years, renewable for a further 10 years. During the ninth year of the lease, V and W agree to extend the lease for another 10 years at a new annual rental different from that in the original lease agreement. We believe that the exception from the need to reconsider the lease classification at inception of the original lease does not apply, because there has been a change to other provisions of the original lease.

5.1.275.40   The standard also does not specify the accounting required when the exception is applicable. Consider, for example, a lessee that exercises a renewal option included in the original lease agreement and thereby agrees to lease an asset for a secondary lease period that was not considered part of the lease term at inception. In some cases, the lessee may be required to give notice before the end of the initial lease term that it will exercise the renewal option. Although the standard is silent on the required accounting, in such a case an option has been replaced by a commitment and therefore the economic positions of the lessee and lessor have changed. Given the change in economic position, an acceptable treatment is to account for the secondary lease period as a new lease. Therefore, it is acceptable to account for the new lease, beginning on either the date on which the lessee commits to exercise the renewal option or the first day of the secondary lease period – i.e. when the new lease period commences. If this accounting is applied, then the classification of this new lease may be different from the original lease classification. Alternatively, it may be acceptable to consider the lessee's decision to exercise the option a change in estimate, because the renewal option was contained in the original lease agreement. In this case, the classification of the lease will remain the same as the original classification (see 5.1.273.10). In our view, the selection of accounting treatment – i.e. new lease or change in estimate – is an accounting policy decision that should be consistently applied.

EXAMPLE 8 – EXERCISE OF OPTION NOT REASONABLY CERTAIN AT INCEPTION – RENEWAL OPTION

5.1.275.50   Company G enters into a lease of an asset with an economic life of 10 years. The primary lease period is six years and G may extend the lease for a further three years at the original annual rent, provided that it exercises the renewal option by the end of year 5. At inception, it is not reasonably certain that G will exercise the renewal option. Based on the criteria in IAS 17, G concludes that the lease is an operating lease at inception.

5.1.275.60   Shortly before the end of year 5, G exercises the renewal option and agrees to continue to lease the asset in years 7 to 9. G determines that it will account for the secondary lease period as a new lease. G may account for the new lease starting either at the end of year 5 or at the beginning of year 7, and ending at the end of year 9. In our view, G should apply a consistent approach to similar transactions.

5.1.278   *Other renewal scenarios*

5.1.278.10   More complex situations may arise in practice – e.g. a secondary lease period may be added to a lease agreement that did not originally contain a renewal option, or the term of a secondary lease period may be lengthened or shortened. Because the phrase 'renewing the lease' is not discussed further, it is not clear whether in these situations the exception from the requirement to reconsider the classification of a lease at inception of the original lease applies. Therefore, in such cases, it is acceptable to reconsider the classification of the lease based on its new provisions, either at inception of the original lease or at the date on which the change is made to the lease agreement. Under the first alternative, to determine whether the modification results in a new lease agreement, an entity uses the two-step test described in 5.1.273.10.

5.1.278.20   A lease agreement that contains a purchase option may be classified at inception as an operating lease in some cases (see 5.1.140.10–30). The standard does not specify the accounting required when the lessee commits to exercise a purchase option in a lease classified as an operating lease. In our view, it is acceptable in this situation to:

- account for the agreement as a new lease beginning on the date on which the lessee commits to exercise the purchase option. This is because an option has been replaced by a commitment and therefore the economic positions of the lessee and lessor have changed. The classification of this new lease may be different from the original lease classification (see 5.1.110–190). In such a case, one key consideration in determining the classification of the new lease is the exercise price of the purchase option (see 5.1.190); or

- account for the lessee's commitment to exercise the purchase option as a change in estimate or circumstance and not a modification of the lease. This is because the option was contained in the original lease agreement and there has been no modification to the original terms. In this case, the lessee would continue to account for the existing lease as an operating lease when it commits to exercise the purchase option.

5.1.278.30   In our view, the selection of accounting treatment – i.e. new lease or change in estimate – is an accounting policy decision that should be consistently applied.

5.1.278.40   If a lease agreement contains a purchase option and is classified at its inception as a finance lease because it is reasonably certain that the purchase option will be exercised, then in our view the lease classification should not be reconsidered if subsequently the lessee determines that it is likely that the purchase option will no longer be exercised and there has been no change to the other provisions of the original lease. This is considered a change in estimate, not a modification to the lease, because the option was contained in the original lease agreement. Accordingly, the lease classification remains a finance lease. For a discussion of the accounting for this type of situation, see 5.1.410.50–120.

5.1.280   ACCOUNTING FOR LEASES

5.1.290   Lessee accounting

5.1.300   *Finance leases*

5.1.300.10   Unless the lease is acquired in a business combination, at commencement of a finance lease, the leased asset and the lease liability are recognised at the lower of:
- the fair value of the leased asset at the inception date; and
- the present value of the minimum lease payments at the inception date for the lease term (see 5.1.50). [*IAS 17.20*]

5.1.300.15   IFRS 3 applies to leases acquired in a business combination. The type of lease and whether the acquiree is the lessee or the lessor will impact how the assets and liabilities are recognised (see 2.6.830).

5.1.300.20   The discount rate used in determining the present value of the minimum lease payments is the interest rate implicit in the lease. The minimum lease payments include the exercise price of options to purchase the leased asset that are expected, at inception of the lease, to be exercised (see 5.1.30.13), as well as predetermined increases in the lease payments (see 5.1.80.70–90). Contingent rents are not included and are recognised as they are incurred (see 5.1.80). [*IAS 17.20, 25*]

5.1.300.30   The interest rate implicit in the lease is the discount rate that, at inception of the lease, causes the aggregate present value of the minimum lease payments and the unguaranteed residual value to be equal to the fair value of the leased asset plus any initial direct costs of the lessor. If the rate implicit in the lease cannot be determined, then the lessee's incremental borrowing rate is used. Initial direct costs incurred are capitalised as an addition to the cost of the asset. [*IAS 17.4*]

5.1.300.40   The periodic lease payments are split into two components: the interest charge for the period and the reduction (redemption) of the lease liability. The interest charge is determined so that a constant periodic rate of interest is recognised on the outstanding balance of the liability. Interest and redemption are determined on an effective interest rate basis, whereby the interest amount generally decreases over the lease term and the redemption amount generally increases each period. [*IAS 17.25*]

5.1.300.45   The lessee adjusts the carrying amount of the leased asset under a finance lease by adding the initial direct costs; this will affect the future depreciation of the asset. [*IAS 17.20*]

5.1.300.50   In our view, subsequent accounting for the asset under a finance lease should be similar to that for other owned assets, and assets under finance leases cannot be considered to be a separate class of asset solely on the basis that they were acquired under finance leases. For example, if a lessee has an accounting policy under which all property, plant and equipment is revalued (see 3.2.300), then this policy should also be applied to similar assets leased under finance leases.

5.1.300.60   The asset under a finance lease is depreciated in accordance with the depreciation policy used for comparable owned assets (see 3.2.140), over the shorter of the period of the asset's useful life and the lease term. An interest in land held under a finance lease is normally depreciated over the life of the lease. However, if at inception of the lease it is reasonably certain that the lessee will obtain ownership of the asset by the end of the lease term, then the asset is depreciated over its expected useful life (see 5.1.60.10). [*IAS 17.27*]

5.1.300.65   The asset under a finance lease is subject to impairment testing under IAS 36 (see 5.1.430). For a discussion of the treatment of leases when calculating value in use in impairment testing, see 3.10.670. [*IAS 17.30*]

5.1.300.70   The reduction of the lease liability is recognised under the effective interest method (see 7.7.280). However, depreciation of the asset is recognised on a different basis – e.g. straight-line (see 3.2.160). Consequently, the amounts included in the statement of financial position for the leased asset and the related liability are unlikely to be equal after commencement of the lease. In our view, the lessee cannot use a depreciation method such as annuity depreciation to reflect consumption of the asset on an after-interest basis (see 5.1.360). [*IAS 17.29*]

5.1.310   *Operating leases*

5.1.310.10   For an operating lease, other than one acquired in a business combination, a lessee does not recognise the leased asset in its statement of financial position, nor does it recognise a liability for rentals in respect of future periods, except for a property interest held under an operating lease that is accounted for as investment property (see 3.4.40.20 and 5.1.250.10). IFRS 3 applies to leases acquired in a business combination. The type of lease and whether the acquiree is the lessee or the lessor will impact how the assets and liabilities are recognised (see 2.6.830). [*IAS 17.19*]

5.1.310.20   For an operating lease, a lessee recognises rent expense on a straight-line basis over the lease term – i.e. between the commencement date and the end of the lease term – or on another systematic basis if it is more representative of the pattern of benefits to the lessee over time. If the timing of lease payments does not represent the time pattern of the lessee's benefits under the lease agreement, then prepaid rent or accrued liabilities for rental payments are recognised. [*IAS 17.33, IU 09-08*]

5.1.310.25   Although IAS 17 refers to 'lease payments' rather than the defined term 'minimum lease payments' when discussing how to recognise rent expense, in our experience minimum lease payments are generally recognised on a straight-line basis over the lease term. In our experience, the use of another systematic basis is rare. In addition, IAS 17 does not incorporate adjustments to reflect the time value of money; therefore, in our view recognising income or expense from annual fixed rate inflators – e.g. fixed rental step-ups intended to reflect inflation increases – as they arise to rental expense would not be consistent with the time pattern of the user's benefit. [*IAS 17.33–34, IU 09-08, 11-05*]

5.1.310.30   Contingent rentals are recognised as incurred (see 5.1.80). In our experience, contingent rentals are not generally included in the amounts recognised on a straight-line basis over the lease term. Some rentals may be entirely contingent – e.g. if they are based entirely on usage; in such cases, there will be no minimum lease payments to spread over the lease term and all payments will be recognised as they are incurred. [*IU 07-06*]

5.1.310.40   The definition of 'commencement date' refers to the date from which the lessee becomes entitled to exercise its right to use the leased asset and therefore receive the benefits of its use (see 5.1.40.30). This means that rent expense is recognised from this date even if the asset is not actually in use at that date. Even if an asset is not fully utilised for a period of time, lease expense is nevertheless recognised provided that the lessee has the right to use the asset and the asset is ready for use during that period for any purpose, which may be different from the purpose originally intended by the lessee. IAS 17 refers to 'the time pattern of benefits'; in this context, in our view the relevant benefit is the availability of the asset for use and its potential utility rather than the economic benefit expected to be realised by the lessee from its use. [*IAS 17.34, IU 09-08*]

EXAMPLE 9A – RENT EXPENSE – STRAIGHT-LINE BASIS

5.1.310.50   Company D leases 50,000 square metres of office space for five years under an operating lease agreement. D receives access to (but does not physically occupy) the entire 50,000 square metres at the commencement of the lease. D concludes that the lease agreement represents a single unit of account (see 5.1.260.05). Under the agreement, annual rentals are predetermined based on the actual space that D expects to occupy during each year.

5.1.310.60   The annual rentals that D will pay during the five-year period of the lease are as follows.

	SQUARE METRES	RENTALS
Year 1	20,000	320,000
Year 2	35,000	560,000
Year 3	45,000	720,000
Year 4	50,000	800,000
Year 5	50,000	800,000
Total	200,000	3,200,000

> 5.1.310.70   D recognises lease expense on a straight-line basis because another systematic basis is not more representative of the time pattern of D's benefit. Therefore, D recognises lease expense of 640,000 per year (3,200,000 / 5).

5.1.310.75   Conversely, if a lessee receives an additional right of use over the lease term – e.g. a lessee of two stories in an office building periodically receives access to additional rooms on a different floor during the lease term – then we believe that a pattern of lease expense based on the proportion of space available to the lessee during the lease term is generally appropriate. [*IAS 17.34, IU 09-08*]

EXAMPLE 9B – RENT EXPENSE – ANOTHER SYSTEMATIC BASIS

5.1.310.80   Modifying Example 9A, Company D's physical access to rental space increases periodically, while the rental payments remain fixed throughout the lease term and there is no difference in the market rent for any of the space that D receives. D concludes that the lease agreement represents a single unit of account (see 5.1.260.05). In addition, the lessor agrees to pay 175,000 towards the cost of leasehold improvements to be carried out by D.

5.1.310.90   D calculates expected annual rentals and the expected physical occupancy of the office space during the five-year period of the lease as follows.

	SQUARE METRES	RENTALS
Year 1	20,000	675,000
Year 2	35,000	675,000
Year 3	45,000	675,000
Year 4	50,000	675,000
Year 5	50,000	675,000
Total	200,000	3,375,000

5.1.310.100   In this example, D determines that the time pattern of its benefit depends on the actual physical occupancy of the office space and therefore a systematic basis other than the straight-line basis is more representative of the time pattern of D's benefit. D calculates lease expense to be recognised in profit or loss for year 1 as follows.

Total rent net of compensation for leasehold improvements	3,200,000[1]
Average price per square metre	16[2]
Rent for year 1	320,000[3]

Notes
1.   Calculated as 3,375,000 - 175,000.
2.   Calculated as 3,200,000 / 200,000.
3.   Calculated as 16 x 20,000.

5.1.310.110   Sometimes lessors provide incentives for the lessee to enter into a lease agreement; such incentives may include the reimbursement of relocation costs or costs associated with exiting lease agreements (see 5.1.417), or initial periods that are rent-free or at a reduced rate. These incentives are an integral part of the net consideration agreed for the use of the asset. Incentives granted to the lessee to enter into an operating lease are spread over the lease term using the same recognition basis as the rental payments – i.e. on a straight-line basis unless another systematic basis is representative of the time pattern over which the benefit of the leased asset is diminished. [*SIC-15.3, 5*]

EXAMPLE 10 – LEASE INCENTIVES

5.1.310.120   If a rent-free period of two years is agreed in a lease agreement covering 10 years at an annual amount of 1,000 for years 3 to 10, then the lessee (and the lessor) would recognise the net consideration of 8,000 systematically over the 10-year lease term.

5.1.310.130   Alternatively, if a lease agreement is for 10 years and the annual lease payment equals 800 in the first five years and 1,000 in years 6 to 10, then the lessee (and the lessor) would recognise the net consideration of 9,000 systematically over the 10-year lease term.

5.1.310.140   Assuming that the benefit is the same in each of the 10 years, the lessee would recognise rent expense of 900 in the first year and accrued rent of 100 at the end of the first year, whereas the lessor would recognise 900 of lease income and 100 of accounts receivable. For a discussion of the accounting for lease incentives, see 5.1.350.50 and Example 13.

5.1.310.150   In some jurisdictions where longer-term leases are common, there may be periodic rent reviews to adjust the lease payments up to the prevailing market rates. In our view, for leases that are subject to these periodic adjustments, the lease incentive, if any, should be spread over the *entire* lease term rather than the shorter period until the next market adjustment.

5.1.310.160   In our view, an up-front payment made to obtain the right to use the land that is classified as an operating lease should be capitalised as a lease prepayment and recognised over the lease term as an operating lease expense.

5.1.310.170   In our view, in the case of an operating lease, the lessee may either recognise the initial direct costs as an asset and expense them over the lease term, or expense them immediately.

5.1.310.180   Operating leases need to be assessed to determine whether they have become onerous, and whether a provision for an onerous contract is required – e.g. because of surplus lease space (see 3.12.680.10) or the payment of rates excessively above market that are not recoverable (see 3.12.640.25).

5.1.320   Lessor accounting

5.1.320.10   The definitions of finance and operating leases are the same for lessors as for lessees. However, the definition of minimum lease payments for a lessor also includes any residual value guaranteed by a financially capable independent third party, whereas the lessee includes only amounts guaranteed by the lessee and parties related to the lessee (see 5.1.30). [*IAS 17.4*]

5.1.330   *Finance leases*

5.1.330.10   Initially, the lessor recognises a finance lease receivable at the amount of its net investment, which comprises the present value of the minimum lease payments and any unguaranteed residual value accruing to the lessor. The present value is calculated by discounting the minimum lease payments due and any unguaranteed residual value, at the interest rate implicit in the lease (see 5.1.300.30). Initial direct costs are included in the calculation of the finance lease receivable, because the interest rate implicit in the lease, used for discounting the minimum lease payments, takes initial direct costs incurred into consideration (see 5.1.90). Contingent rentals are excluded from the minimum lease payments and are recognised as they are incurred (see 5.1.390). [*IAS 17.36–38*]

5.1.330.15   The lessor derecognises the leased asset and recognises the difference between the carrying amount of the leased asset and the finance lease receivable in profit or loss when recognising the finance lease receivable. This gain or loss is presented in profit or loss in the same line item as that in which the lessor presents gains or losses from sales of similar assets. For a discussion of manufacturer or dealer lessors, see 5.1.340.

5.1.330.20   Over the lease term, the lessor accrues interest income on the net investment. The receipts under the lease are allocated between reducing the net investment and recognising finance income, to produce a constant rate of return on the net investment. [*IAS 17.39–40*]

5.1.340   *Manufacturer or dealer lessors*

5.1.340.10   In some industries – e.g. office products, automotive – manufacturers or dealers often act as lessors of their products, either directly or through a finance entity subsidiary. A finance lease of an asset by a manufacturer or dealer results in two types of income: initial selling profit and finance income over the lease term. Manufacturer or dealer lessors recognise the selling profit or loss for the period in accordance with the entity's normal accounting policy for outright sales. Costs incurred in connection with negotiating and arranging a lease are recognised as an expense when the selling profit is recognised, which is generally at the commencement date of the lease term. [*IAS 17.38, 43–44, 46*]

5.1.340.20   If manufacturer or dealer lessors quote below-market interest rates – e.g. as a marketing tool – then selling profit is restricted to the amount that would have been earned if a market rate of interest had been charged. Using the lower rate would not be appropriate because it would overstate the selling profit and understate the financial income in subsequent periods. [*IAS 17.45*]

5.1.340.30   A manufacturer might lease its products to an end user under a finance lease through an intermediary party. In that case, the intermediary party applies the guidance on finance leases as both a lessee (lease with the manufacturer) and as a lessor (lease with the end user), in accordance with 5.1.265.10. The IFRS Interpretations Committee discussed such scenarios and noted that intermediary parties do not classify the finance lease asset received from a manufacturer as inventory. [*IU 06-05*]

5.1.350 *Operating leases*

5.1.350.10   If, before lease commencement, a lessor recognises an asset in its statement of financial position and leases that asset to a lessee under an operating lease, then the lessor does not derecognise the asset on lease commencement. Generally, future contractual rental payments from the lessee are recognised as receivables over the lease term as the payments become receivable. The asset subject to the operating lease is presented in the lessor's statement of financial position according to the nature of the asset – e.g. equipment. [*IAS 17.49*]

5.1.350.20   Generally, lease income from operating leases is recognised by the lessor in income on a straight-line basis over the lease term (see 5.1.310.25). It may be possible to recognise lease income using another systematic basis if that is more representative of the time pattern in which the benefit of the leased asset is diminished. [*IAS 17.50, SIC-15.3–4*]

5.1.350.30   Similarly, increases (or decreases) in rental payments over a period of time, other than contingent lease payments, are reflected in the determination of the lease income, which is recognised on a straight-line basis. For example, a contractual three percent per annum escalation of rents over the lease term is anticipated from commencement of the lease. Consequently, the lessor recognises lease income in excess of cash lease payments received in early periods of the lease and the opposite effect in later years.

5.1.350.35   The substance of an agreement is evaluated to determine whether indexed rentals should be included in the calculation of minimum lease payments or treated as contingent rentals and recognised as they are incurred (see 5.1.80).

5.1.350.40   Initial direct costs incurred by the lessor in arranging an operating lease are added to the carrying amount of the leased asset and cannot be recognised immediately as an expense. These initial direct costs are recognised as an expense on the same basis as the lease income. This will not necessarily be consistent with the basis on which the leased asset is depreciated. [*IAS 17.52*]

5.1.350.50   Incentives granted to the lessee in negotiating a new or renewed operating lease are recognised as an integral part of the net consideration agreed for the use of the asset. They are recognised as a reduction of rental income over the lease term using the same recognition basis as for the lease income – i.e. on a straight-line basis unless another systematic basis is representative of the time pattern over which the benefit of the leased asset is diminished. [*SIC-15.3–4, IU 08-05*]

5.1.350.60   The lessor depreciates the asset subject to the lease over the asset's useful life in a manner that is consistent with the depreciation policy that it applies to similar owned assets (see 3.2.140). [*IAS 17.53*]

5.1.360 *Annuity depreciation*

5.1.360.10   'Annuity depreciation' refers to depreciation methods under which the depreciation charge is adjusted to reflect the time value of money. Such depreciation methods result in lower depreciation charges in initial periods and larger depreciation amounts in later periods. These methods are used by lessors under some national accounting practices to recognise a level profit, after considering financing costs related to the leased asset, over the lease term. In our view, the way that an asset is financed should not impact the selection of a depreciation policy. IFRS requires depreciation to reflect the consumption of the economic benefits of an asset. We believe that this does not extend to consideration of the time value of money or inflation adjustments.

5.1.370 APPLICATION ISSUES

5.1.375 Complex lease arrangements with multiple elements

5.1.375.10   When assessing the components of complex lease transactions, it is often difficult to determine the appropriate accounting treatment. The following principle provides guidance on how to consider the multiple elements. Elements that are, in substance:

- costs or services are excluded from minimum lease payments (see 5.1.30.20);
- contingent rentals are excluded from minimum lease payments (see 5.1.80);
- residual value guarantees are included in full in minimum lease payments (see 5.1.70); or
- incentives are included in minimum lease payments (see 5.1.310.110 and 350.50).

5.1.378 Residual value guarantees and third party guarantees

5.1.378.10   A lessee that is required to provide the lessor with a guaranteed residual value may obtain a matching residual value guarantee from a third party. Unless the lessee is unconditionally released from the residual value guarantee by the lessor, minimum lease payments include the maximum amount that the lessee could, in any event, be required to pay under the residual value guarantee. The lessee's receivable from a third party cannot be offset against the residual value obligation under the lease, because there is no legal right and intention to set off (see 7.10.110).

5.1.378.20   If the terms of the lease require the lessee to pay for obtaining a third party residual value guarantee, then these are not costs for services, because they relate directly to the use of the asset. If the lessee is unconditionally released from the residual value guarantee by the lessor as a result of the lessee obtaining a residual value guarantee from a third party, then the lessee is in effect the agent for the lessor, and the payments made by the lessee to the third party are part of the minimum lease payments.

5.1.378.30   A lease agreement may include a short minimum term followed by several renewal periods. In such cases, the lease may require the lessee to give certain guarantees should the lessee not renew the lease. The lessee may guarantee that if the lessor sells the leased property at the end of the minimum term and reinvests the proceeds, then the lessee will make up any shortfall between the lessor's actual return on the reinvested funds and a specified rate of return on the reinvested funds for a period that typically extends to the end of the original renewal period(s) in the lease (known as 'make-whole premiums'). Make-whole premiums are a type of residual value guarantee and therefore are included in the minimum lease payments (see 5.1.70.20).

5.1.378.40   A lessee might indemnify a lessor for excess wear and tear of the leased asset. Judgement is necessary to determine whether lessee indemnifications are minimum lease payments, contingent rent or residual value guarantees.

5.1.378.50   If the lessee guarantees the lessor's debt, then judgement is necessary to determine whether the guarantee of the debt is an in-substance residual value guarantee or otherwise is part of the minimum lease payments. If the guaranteed debt is secured by the leased property with no recourse to other assets of the lessor, or the lessor has no significant asset other than the leased property, then the guarantee is, in substance, a residual value guarantee. An in-substance residual value guarantee represents the maximum amount the lessee could, in any event, be required to pay under the guarantee and is therefore included in minimum lease payments.

5.1.378.60   If the lessee's guarantee of the lessor's debt is not an in-substance residual value guarantee, and the guarantee is linked to the lease agreement, then it represents part of the consideration paid for the lease and is included in minimum lease payments based on its initial measurement under IFRS 9 (see 7.1.60).

5.1.378.70   Similarly, if the lessee provides a loan to the lessor, then judgement is required in determining whether the loan is an in-substance residual value guarantee or otherwise is part of the minimum lease payments. If the loan is secured by the leased property with no recourse to other assets of the lessor, or the lessor is a limited purpose vehicle with no significant asset other than the leased property, then the loan is, in substance, a residual value guarantee. If the loan is not an in-substance residual value guarantee, and is not at market terms, then the amount included in the minimum lease payments is the non-market value determined as the fair value of the loan according to IFRS 9 (see 7.7.10) less the actual cash amount of the loan.

5.1.380   Security deposits, key money payments and minimum lease payments

5.1.380.10   In some jurisdictions, the terms of property leases normally require the lessee to pay security deposits and advance rentals. The security deposit is held by the lessor throughout the term of the lease and is refunded in full to the lessee at the end of the lease term (if the lessee has performed fully and observed all of the conditions or provisions in the lease). However, the lessor may apply the security deposit to remedy the breach of any provisions in the lease contract and to indemnify any consequential costs and losses related to the leased property that are properly chargeable to the lessee under the contract. The security deposits do not normally carry any interest or the interest rate received is less than market interest rates.

5.1.380.20   In our view, the security deposit itself is not part of the lease payments and therefore is in the scope of IFRS 9 (see 7.1.20). Therefore, the security deposit should be measured at fair value on initial recognition. In our view, the difference between the initial fair value and the nominal value of the deposit is an additional lease payment made by the lessee.

5.1.380.30   In some jurisdictions, a new lessee pays the old lessee an amount to take over a lease on the existing lease terms. Such payments may be made to obtain rights to favourable lease terms or to gain access to a favourable trading location. These payments are commonly referred to as 'key money payments'. An acceptable approach is to apply IAS 17 and account for such payments as part of the lease arrangement. In such cases, the payment is treated in a similar manner to an up-front lease payment (see 5.1.310.160).

5.1.380.40   In some instances, the payment may also have characteristics that meet the definition of an intangible asset. For example, the right is separable from the lease agreement and is controlled by the lessee. In such cases, it is also acceptable to account for the payment separately from the lease arrangement in accordance with IAS 38 (see chapter 3.3).

EXAMPLE 11 – KEY MONEY PAYMENTS

5.1.380.50   Company Y makes a payment to Company X to take over a lease on its existing terms. Company Y has an option, not an obligation, to renew the lease on the same terms annually. In addition, Company Y may sell the rights to the lease agreement to a third party on the same terms and the lessor does not have the ability to cancel or change the terms of the lease.

5.1.380.60   In this example, the payment meets the definition of an intangible asset, and therefore Company Y could account for this payment either as a lease payment under IAS 17, or as an intangible asset under IAS 38. Under either approach, judgement is required to determine the amortisation period, which would depend on the facts and circumstances, particularly the lessee's right to sell and the lessee's intention to renew the lease.

5.1.390   Contingent rent

5.1.390.10   Contingent rent (as defined in 5.1.80) is included in profit or loss using the same presentation as for non-contingent rental income or expense. For example, a lease payment may be partially fixed, with additional rent based on total sales volume generated at the leased property. In our view, the fixed and contingent rent should be included in the lessee's financial statements as rental expense. Even though it might be appropriate to consider the contingent rent amount as a cost of sales if the function classification of expenses is used, it would not be appropriate to present the contingent rent as a reduction of sales revenue in the lessee's financial statements.

5.1.390.20   Leases to retailers often include contingent rental payments – e.g. one percent of sales in excess of 5,000 but less than 10,000, and two percent of sales of 10,000 or more. Limited guidance is provided in IAS 34 on a lessee's accounting for contingent lease obligations. IAS 34 requires recognition of an obligation before the minimum sales level is met if the required level of sales (5,000 and 10,000 in this example) is expected to be met over the measurement period for which rent payments are calculated. [*IAS 34.IE.B7*]

5.1.390.30   IFRS does not contain specific guidance on how to account for rent that was considered contingent at inception of the lease but is subsequently confirmed – e.g. after an upwards-only rent review on a property lease. One approach is to account for such a change prospectively by revising the minimum lease payments over the remaining term of the lease. This adjustment would impact both the disclosure of minimum lease payments and revenue and expense recognition. It would not trigger reconsideration of the lease classification. Alternatively, the confirmed rentals may be accounted for in the periods in which they are incurred. In our view, either of these approaches can be applied regardless of whether a confirmed contingent rent results in an increase or a decrease in future lease payments. In our view, an entity should choose an accounting policy for the treatment of contingent rent (either prospective adjustment or accrual basis), to be applied consistently to all similar leases with contingent rent provisions, including those with upwards-only adjustments and those under which future changes can be either upwards or downwards. The policy should also be applied to tax variation clauses when the additional rentals are considered to be contingent rent (see 5.1.460).

5.1.400   Derecognition of finance lease receivables

5.1.400.10   The derecognition of finance lease receivables is covered by the general derecognition guidance in IFRS 9 (see 7.6.60). For lease receivables to qualify for derecognition by the lessor, in full or in part, the transfer of the lease receivables needs to meet the derecognition criteria specified in IFRS 9. Depending on whether (part of) a financial asset has been transferred, the level of risks and rewards transferred and the extent to which control has been transferred, the transaction could result in full derecognition, partial derecognition under the continuing involvement approach or no derecognition of the transferred lease receivables. [*IFRS 9.2.1(b)(i), 3.2*]

5.1.410   Lessee accounting for finance lease modification

5.1.410.05   The following flowchart summarises the accounting for a finance lease modification in the financial statements of the lessee.

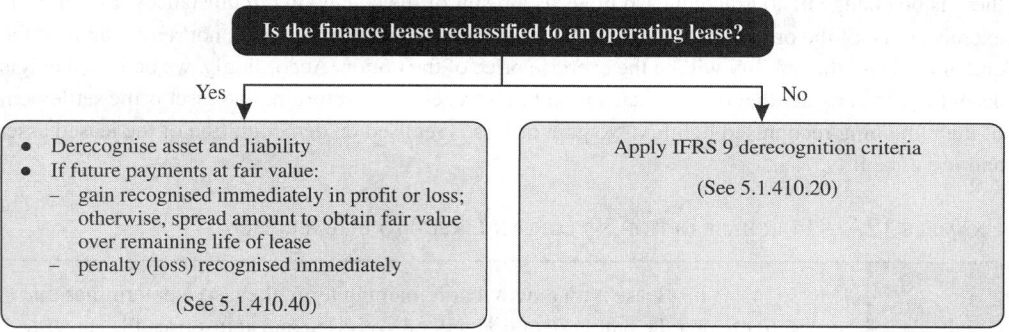

5.1.410.10   Finance lease liabilities recognised by a lessee are subject to the derecognition provisions of IFRS 9 (see 7.6.360). Finance lease liabilities are derecognised only when the lessee's obligation in terms of the lease contract is extinguished – i.e. the obligation is discharged or cancelled or expires. [*IFRS 9.2.1(b)(ii), 3.3.1*]

5.1.410.20   In our view, a finance lease modification that does not change the finance lease classification but results in a change to the contractual cash flows from those at inception triggers the application of the requirements of IFRS 9 (see 7.6.370) for derecognition of the financial liability. In that case, it is acceptable not to derecognise the leased asset, even if the IFRS 9 derecognition requirements will be met in respect of the lease liability, because the lease arrangement was not terminated or reclassified as an operating lease under the modification accounting. [*IFRS 9.2.1(b)*]

5.1.410.30   Similarly, if the lease arrangement was terminated by the exercise of a purchase option included in the lease term, then it is acceptable not to derecognise the leased asset, because, in substance, the asset is the same asset after the exercise of the purchase option as before; the only change is how it has been financed. This treatment is appropriate regardless of whether the option was considered reasonably certain to be exercised at inception of the lease.

5.1.410.40   If the modification changes the classification of the lease from a finance lease to an operating lease, then the leased asset and the finance lease liability will be derecognised. In our view, any resulting loss should be recognised immediately in profit or loss and any gain that results from the derecognition of the finance lease balances should be recognised immediately to the extent that the operating lease transaction is at fair value; otherwise, the gain should be recognised over the operating lease period.

5.1.410.50   If there is a change in circumstance that results in a purchase option that had been expected at lease inception to be exercised no longer being considered likely to be exercised before expiry of the lease, then in our view it is acceptable to:
- adjust the residual value of the asset to equal the purchase option exercise price;
- adjust the useful life of the asset to equal the remaining lease term; and
- not change the carrying amount or effective interest rate of the finance lease liability – i.e. the liability would continue to include the original expected purchase option exercise price.

5.1.410.60   The lease liability is not remeasured because there is no change in classification and there is no change in contractual cash flows as a result of the change in circumstances. Because the exercise price of the option is included in the lease liability and the liability is not remeasured, at the end of the lease the liability will be the exercise price of the option. Accordingly, we believe that it is acceptable to consider that the residual amount to be received on returning the asset is the settlement of the remaining recognised liability. No gain or loss is realised on derecognition of the leased asset and lease liability.

EXAMPLE 12A – PURCHASE OPTION NO LONGER LIKELY TO BE EXERCISED (1)

5.1.410.70   In a lease with a two-year remaining term, the lessee determines that it is unlikely that the purchase option will be exercised and at this time the carrying amount of the asset was 1,500 with an estimated residual value of 0 at the end of its useful life. The option exercise price is 1,000.

5.1.410.80   When the lessee determines that it is unlikely that it will exercise the purchase option, the residual value is reassessed to 1,000 (equal to the option exercise price) and depreciation is prospectively reassessed to 250 per annum ((1,500 - 1,000) / 2 years) over the remaining lease term. No initial loss is recorded.

5.1.410.90   At the end of the lease term, the lease liability of 1,000 and the asset of 1,000 are derecognised. Over the remaining two-year lease term, depreciation of 500 is recorded and no gain or loss is recognised on termination of the lease. The net profit or loss impact over the remaining two-year lease term is 500.

5.1.410.100   Alternatively, if the residual value of the asset is expected to be below the purchase option exercise price at the end of the lease term, then an entity may:
- adjust the residual value to the expected proceeds if the option were to be exercised and asset sold;

- adjust the useful life of the asset to equal the remaining lease term; and
- not change the carrying amount or effective interest rate of the finance lease liability – i.e. the liability would continue to include the original expected purchase option exercise price.

5.1.410.105   At the end of the lease term, on derecognition of the remaining liability (effectively the exercise price as noted in 5.1.410.60) and the leased asset (which has a carrying amount below the exercise price), the resulting gain is recognised in profit or loss. The impact of applying this approach rather than the approach discussed in 5.1.410.50, is the recognition of a higher depreciation charge over the remaining lease term offset by an equal gain recognised at the end of the lease term. If the asset's residual value is expected to be higher than the option exercise price, then the lessee is economically compelled to exercise the option, and therefore losses are not expected to occur.

EXAMPLE 12B – PURCHASE OPTION NO LONGER LIKELY TO BE EXERCISED (2)

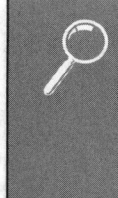

5.1.410.110   In a lease with a two-year remaining term, the lessee determined that it was unlikely that the purchase option would be exercised. The option exercise price is 1,000. When the lessee determined that it was unlikely to exercise the option, the carrying amount of the asset was 1,500 with an estimated residual value of 0 at the end of its useful life. The option is unlikely to be exercised as the anticipated resale value is 800 at the end of the lease term. Therefore, the residual value is reassessed to 800 and depreciation is reassessed to 350 per annum ((1,500 - 800) / 2 years).

5.1.410.120   At the end of the lease term, the lease liability of 1,000 and the asset of 800 are derecognised with a resulting gain of 200 (1,000 - 800). Over the remaining two-year lease term, depreciation of 700 is recognised. The net profit or loss impact over the remaining two-year lease term is 500, which is identical to the approach in Example 12A.

5.1.415   Lessee accounting for operating lease modification

5.1.415.10   The following flowchart summarises the accounting for an operating lease modification in the financial statements of the lessee.

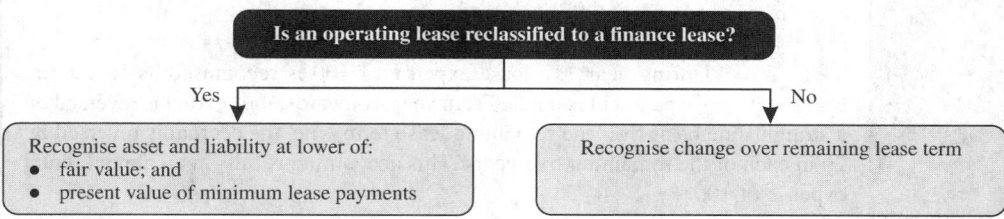

5.1.415.20   If a modification of an operating lease (see 5.1.270) results in the modification being treated as a new lease classified as a finance lease, then finance lease accounting applies (see 5.1.300).

5.1.415.30   If a modification of an operating lease does not result in a reclassification, then the new terms of the arrangement will be reflected in the rentals that are being recognised over the remaining lease term in a manner appropriate under the terms of the modified lease arrangement.

5.1.415.40   If a modification of an operating lease does not result in a reclassification, then the question of how to account for any remaining and new lease incentives arises.

EXAMPLE 13 – LEASE INCENTIVES IN OPERATING LEASE MODIFICATION

5.1.415.50   Company G enters into an operating lease of an asset on 1 January of year 1. The following facts are relevant for this example.
- The lease term is six years with an option to renew for four years.
- At inception, it was not reasonably certain that G would exercise the renewal option.
- G received a lease incentive of a one-year rent-free period.
- Annual rent is fixed at 120.

5.1.415.55   The lease incentive is spread over the six-year lease term as 20 per year (120 / 6) (see 5.1.310.110). The accounting for the lease incentive on a straight-line basis is performed by first determining the annual rental expense of 100 ((120 x 5) / 6), which takes into account the incentive. To record an annual rental expense of 100 over the lease term, an accrual is recognised and reversed as follows.

DATE	ANNUAL RENTAL PAYMENT (A)	ACCRUAL INCREASE/ (DECREASE) (B)	ANNUAL RENTAL EXPENSE (C)[1]	ACCRUAL PERIOD END BALANCE (D)[2]
Year 1	-	100	100	100
Year 2	120	(20)	100	80
Year 3	120	(20)	100	60
Year 4	120	(20)	100	40
Year 5	120	(20)	100	20
Year 6	120	(20)	100	-

Notes
1.   C = A + B.
2.   D = D prior year + B.

5.1.415.60   During year 1, a lease expense of 100 is recognised as an accrual because no lease payment is made. From year 2 onwards, the accrual is reversed on a straight-line basis over the remaining lease term – i.e. the accrual is reversed by 20 in each of the remaining five years. This accounting results in an annual rental expense of 100.

5.1.415.70   At the end of year 5, the remaining accrual balance is 20 and G exercises the renewal option for another 4 years – i.e. years 7 to 10 at 120 per year.

The renewal option also includes a new lease incentive that entitles G to a six-month rent-free period beginning at the start of year 7. As discussed in 5.1.275.40, in this case G may account for the change in the lease period as a new lease either at the commitment date (end of year 5) or at the first day of the renewal period (start of year 7).

5.1.415.80   If G elects to account for the secondary lease period as a new lease from the end of year 5 when the option is exercised, then an acceptable application of accounting for the change prospectively is to amortise the aggregate of the remaining lease incentive from the original lease (20) plus the renewal period incentive of 60 (6 / 12 months x 120) over the five-year remaining period to lease expiry – i.e. years 6 to 10. This accounting is achieved by reversing the remaining accrual of 20 over the new lease period of five years (4 per year) and in addition recognising the rental expense per year of 108 (120 x 4.5 / 5 years). The overall effect is that the annual rental expense is 104 in years 6 to 10 as follows.

Date	Annual Rental Payment (A)	Accrual Increase/ (Decrease) (B)	Annual Rental Expense (C)[1]	Accrual Period End Balance (D)[2]
Year 5	120	(20)	100	20
Year 6	120	(16)	104	4
Year 7	60	44	104	48
Year 8	120	(16)	104	32
Year 9	120	(16)	104	16
Year 10	120	(16)	104	-

Notes
1.   C = A + B.
2.   D = D prior year + B.

5.1.415.90   If G elects to account for the secondary lease period as a new lease from the beginning of the renewal period – i.e. in year 7 – then an acceptable application of accounting for the change prospectively is to continue amortising the residual balance of the original lease incentive over the remaining contractual period of the original lease – i.e. reverse the accrual of 20 in year 6 – and begin amortising the lease incentive for the renewal period over the four-year contractual term of the renewal period – i.e. years 7 to 10. The accounting for the renewal period lease incentive on a straight-line basis is performed by first determining the annual rental expense for the renewal period of 105 ((120 x 3.5) / 4), which takes into account the renewal period incentive. To record an annual rental expense of 105 over the renewal lease term, an accrual is recognised and reversed as follows.

Date	Annual Rental Payment (A)	Accrual Increase/ (Decrease) (B)	Annual Rental Expense (C)[1]	Accrual Period End Balance (D)[2]
Year 7	60	45	105	45
Year 8	120	(15)	105	30
Year 9	120	(15)	105	15
Year 10	120	(15)	105	-

Notes
1. C = A + B.
2. D = D prior year + B.

5.1.417 Lessor reimbursement of leasehold improvement

5.1.417.10   IFRS does not contain explicit guidance on the accounting for lessor reimbursements to the lessee for the cost of leasehold improvements. In our view, the appropriate accounting depends on whether the lessee or the lessor is the 'accounting owner' of the leasehold improvements – i.e. whether the lessee or the lessor accounts for the leasehold improvements as its property, plant and equipment.

5.1.417.20   In our experience, indicators that the lessee is the accounting owner of the leasehold improvements may include the following:
- the lessee is not contractually required to construct or install the leasehold improvements;
- the lessee is permitted to alter or remove the leasehold improvements without the consent of the lessor or without adequately compensating the lessor;
- the lessee is not required to provide evidence of costs incurred in order to receive reimbursement;
- the lessee bears the risk of cost overruns;
- the leasehold improvements are unique to the lessee's intended use of the leased asset; and
- the leasehold improvements are not available to the lessor in a lease to other parties.

5.1.417.30   This list of indicators is not exhaustive and judgement is required in determining the weighting of indicators based on the specific facts and circumstances.

5.1.417.40   We believe that some factors do not determine whether the lessee or lessor is the accounting owner of leasehold improvements – e.g. who has the legal title to the leasehold improvements, who has the insurable interests in the leasehold improvements and who receives the tax deduction for the lease improvements. This is because these factors may not capture the extent to which the parties benefit from, or are affected by, the future economic benefits associated with the leasehold improvements.

EXAMPLE 14 – LEASEHOLD IMPROVEMENTS – LESSEE IS THE ACCOUNTING OWNER

5.1.417.50   Company X leases office space from Company Y. The lease includes common facilities shared with another tenant on the same floor, such as hallways and bathrooms. X agrees to carry out the construction of the common facilities

before lease commencement, when X gets access to the office space. Y agrees to reimburse X for costs incurred up to the forecast of 10,000. Any overruns incurred by X will not be reimbursed by Y. In this example, it is assumed that X is the accounting owner of the leasehold improvements.

5.1.417.60   At the commencement date, the actual costs incurred by X are 11,000. The lease is classified as an operating lease by X and Y. X is not in the construction industry.

5.1.417.70   X recognises leasehold improvements of 11,000 as property, plant and equipment, which it will depreciate in accordance with IAS 16 over the shorter of the useful life of the leasehold improvements and the lease term (see 3.2.140). X recognises the 10,000 reimbursement from Y as a lease incentive (see Example 9B).

5.1.417.80   Y recognises the reimbursement payment as a lease incentive (see 5.1.350.50).

EXAMPLE 15 – LEASEHOLD IMPROVEMENTS – LESSOR IS THE ACCOUNTING OWNER

5.1.417.90   Modifying Example 14, Y is assumed to be the accounting owner of the leasehold improvements.

5.1.417.100   X recognises the 1,000 overrun as a lease expense over the lease term using the same recognition basis as other lease payments (see 5.1.310), because the overrun expenditure is essentially an adjustment to the lease payments.

5.1.417.110   Y recognises 11,000 as a transfer of property, plant and equipment from a customer (see 3.2.20.40 and 60), which will be depreciated in accordance with IAS 16 over its useful life (see 3.2.140). Y recognises the 1,000 overrun as an integral part of the net consideration agreed for the use of the asset, which will be recognised as part of lease income over the lease term using the same recognition basis as the lease income (see 5.1.350).

5.1.420   Embedded derivatives

5.1.420.10   If a lease contract contains terms or conditions with the characteristics of a derivative instrument, then the parties to the lease contract evaluate whether this embedded derivative component of the lease needs to be separated from the lease contract and accounted for separately (see 7.2.110 and 270.10). Examples of terms that may require separate recognition of an embedded derivative include leverage features built into the lease payments and lease payments that are based on an index that is unrelated to the lease contract (see 7.2.270.10). IFRS 9 does not provide a definition of leverage in the context of an index. However, factors to consider when assessing leverage are set out in 7.2.200.30. An index adjustment – e.g. twice CPI – may be an indication that the lease is leveraged. An embedded purchase option for a leased asset included in a lease contract is not separated because such an option is accounted for as part of the lease (see 7.2.120.100).

5.1.430   **Impairment**

5.1.430.10   The impairment of leased assets is dealt with in the same manner as the impairment of other non-financial assets (see chapter 3.10). [*IAS 17.30*]

5.1.430.20   In the case of an operating lease, impairment of the leased asset would be relevant to the lessor, unless the leased asset is an investment property that the lessor measures using the fair value model. Impairment of the asset under a finance lease would be relevant to the lessee. [*IAS 17.30, 54*]

5.1.430.30   Receivables due from the lessee under an operating lease are financial assets subject to the impairment requirements of IFRS 9 (see 7.8.410).

5.1.430.40   For a finance lease, the lessor recognises lease receivables rather than the leased asset itself. Because lease receivables are financial instruments, the lessor applies IFRS 9 to determine whether there is any impairment of the receivables that are recognised (see 7.8.410). The lessor's impairment assessment for a finance lease is based on the lessor's primary risk exposure, which is normally the creditworthiness of the lessee as opposed to potential decreases in value of the leased asset, which can be considered as collateral. [*IFRS 9.2.1(b)*]

5.1.430.50   In addition, operating leases need to be assessed to determine if they have become onerous and if a provision for onerous contract is required – e.g. because of surplus lease space or the payment of rates excessively above market that are not recoverable (see 3.12.640.25).

5.1.440   **Tax issues in finance leases**

5.1.450   *Post-tax methods of recognising finance income*

5.1.450.10   As noted in 5.1.330.20, a lessor recognises finance income from finance leases based on a pattern reflecting a constant periodic rate of return on its net investment in the lease. In our view, this calculation should be based on the carrying amount of the lease. The lessor may not adjust finance income to achieve a constant rate of return on the net cash investment, and thereby recognise a constant rate of return on a post-tax basis. IFRS does not specifically prohibit use of the net cash method. However, although recognition of finance income based on the net cash investment was previously permitted by IFRS, that option was removed in the 1997 revisions to IAS 17.

5.1.450.20   A finance lease may have significant tax benefits that are considered in the pricing of the lease transaction. This could result in the finance income from the lease being negative because of the present value of the minimum lease payments being less than the cost of the leased asset. On a pre-tax basis, the lease results in a loss. However, on a post-tax basis the lease would be profitable. In our view, the negative finance income should be spread over the lease term and recognised in line with the net investment in the lease. We believe that the pre-tax loss should not be recognised immediately.

5.1.460   *Tax variation clauses*

5.1.460.10   Some finance leases allow the lessor to obtain a tax benefit that is passed to the lessee in the form of reduced lease rentals. Virtually all such lease agreements contain a tax variation clause. Normally, these clauses are structured so that any tax disadvantage suffered by the lessor as a result of a change in tax rates or rules will be compensated by an increase in future lease payments.

5.1.460.20   IFRS does not have any guidance regarding the triggering of tax variation clauses. For example, the lessor may view the triggering of the tax variation clause as a contingency and recognise the contingent cash flows on a prospective basis over the remaining life of the lease. Alternatively, the lessor may determine that the trigger should be treated as a 'catch-up' in profit or loss. In our view, the method applied by the lessor should reflect the nature of the clause and whether the effect of the tax change is retrospective or prospective. The approach adopted for each type of variation clause should be applied consistently.

EXAMPLE 16 – TAX LEGISLATION CLAUSES

5.1.460.30   Lessor T borrows 1,000 at 6% to buy an asset. The asset is leased under a 20-year finance lease at an implicit interest rate of 5%. T is able to earn a small profit because tax cash flows allow T to repay the borrowing before the end of the lease term, generating interest cost savings.

5.1.460.40   After 10 years, the tax legislation changes and T is required to reimburse the tax authorities for the full amount of tax benefits previously obtained, including interest. Under the tax variation clause, the lease income over the remaining 10 years of the lease increases to 7%. Over the entire lease term, T achieves a return of 6%, the rate that would have applied to a loan with no particular tax advantages.

5.1.460.50   There are three possible ways to account for the triggering of the tax variation clause:

- prospectively, recognising future lease income at 7% (Option 1); or
- retrospectively, by restating the net investment in the lease, with a credit to income at the 'trigger' date, by discounting future lease rentals either at:
  - 5% – i.e. the original rate implicit in the lease (Option 2); or
  - 6% – i.e. the rate that would have applied had the tax benefit never been available to the lessee (Option 3).

5.1.460.60   If the additional rentals are considered as 'contingent rent', then the additional rental payments are recognised prospectively (Option 1), once the lessee is obliged to make them (see 5.1.80).

5.1.460.70   Retrospective adjustment as described in Option 2 is consistent with viewing the net investment in the lease as a financial asset and applying the guidance for changes in cash flow estimates under the effective yield method used to calculate returns on financial assets (see 7.7.330).

5.1.460.80   Retrospective adjustment as described in Option 3 results in the matching (to a degree) of the tax cost incurred by the lessor at the trigger date with the reimbursement of the related tax benefits recovered from the lessee.

> 5.1.460.90   In practice, tax variation clauses may take many forms. Changes in tax legislation can also take many forms. In some cases, rentals would be adjusted for any change in the tax rate applied to T; in others, T's tax benefit may be removed or adjusted prospectively. In our view, Option 1 and Option 2 may be appropriate depending on the circumstances. An entity should apply its chosen method consistently to similar circumstances. Option 3 has the effect of recognising future income at the date on which the change in future terms comes into effect, which in our view would not be appropriate.

5.1.470   SALE-AND-LEASEBACK TRANSACTIONS

5.1.470.10   A sale-and-leaseback transaction has two components: the sale of the asset from the seller to the lessor, and the leaseback of the asset from the buyer/lessor to the seller/lessee. Under IFRS, the two components are accounted for separately rather than the seller/lessee accounting for the net effect of the combined transaction. [*IAS 17.58*]

5.1.470.20   For example, a sale-and-leaseback transaction may result in a leaseback that is classified as a finance lease. IFRS requires sale-and-finance-leaseback transactions to be accounted for as a sale and a lease even though the transaction as a whole would not satisfy the revenue recognition criteria. [*IAS 17.4, 59*]

5.1.470.30   In our view, sale-and-leaseback transactions bypass the assessment of the *sale* transaction against the revenue recognition criteria. Therefore, we believe that the classification of the leaseback as an operating or finance lease should reflect not only the terms of the *lease* but also the risks and rewards retained by the seller/lessee under the sale agreement.

5.1.470.40   In a sale-and-leaseback transaction, the periodic lease payments are usually highly dependent on the selling price of the asset. The accounting for the gain or loss on the sale component of the transaction depends in part on the classification of the leaseback. [*IAS 17.58*]

5.1.480   Sale-and-finance-leaseback

5.1.480.10   If a sale-and-leaseback results in a finance lease, then any gain on the sale is deferred and recognised as income over the lease term. In our view, it is acceptable that the amortisation of the deferred gain be presented as a reduction of depreciation expense because the transaction is, in substance, a finance transaction. No loss is recognised unless the asset is impaired. [*IAS 17.59–60*]

5.1.490   Sale-and-operating-leaseback

5.1.490.10   If the leaseback is classified as an operating lease, then any gain is recognised immediately if the sale-and-leaseback terms are clearly at fair value. Otherwise, the sale and leaseback are accounted for as follows.
- If the selling price is at or below fair value, then the gain or loss is recognised immediately. However, if a loss is compensated for by future rentals at a below-market price, then the loss is deferred and amortised over the period in which the asset is expected to be used. In our view, the loss that

is deferred cannot exceed the present value of the difference – i.e. rental savings – between the below-market rents and the fair-market rents over the period in which such differences exist, as determined at inception of the lease.

- If the selling price exceeds fair value, then that excess is deferred and amortised over the period for which the asset is expected to be used.
- If the fair value of the asset is less than the carrying amount of the asset at the date of the transaction, then that difference is recognised immediately as a loss on the sale. [*IAS 17.61–63*]

5.1.500   LINKED TRANSACTIONS IN THE LEGAL FORM OF A LEASE

5.1.500.10   A series of linked transactions that take the legal form of a lease are accounted for in accordance with their economic substance. This situation may occur, for example, when a transaction is in the form of a lease but does not transfer the right of use of the asset from the lessor to the lessee. These transactions may be entered into in order to generate a tax saving (often cross-border) or to generate fees. Transactions in the legal form of a lease are considered to be 'linked' when the individual transactions cannot be understood without reference to the series as a whole. In this case, the series of transactions are accounted for as one transaction. Therefore, the net effect of the transaction is accounted for, instead of accounting separately for each component of the transaction. [*SIC-27*]

EXAMPLE 17 – LINKED TRANSACTIONS

5.1.500.20   Company P buys an aircraft from Company L and leases it back to L under a finance lease. Most of the payment to L for the aircraft is paid into a trust account securing lease payments to be made by L to P. P is entitled to significant tax deductions because of accelerated tax depreciation on the aircraft.

5.1.500.30   P has no residual or credit risks arising from the lease transaction because the lease payment is secured by the trust accounts. Therefore, in this example the risks and rewards of the leased assets have, in substance, not been transferred to P; the reason for the transaction is merely to achieve a tax benefit because, in substance, P pays a fee to the lessee to obtain tax benefits. Therefore, the transactions are included in the scope of SIC-27 and accounted for as linked transactions based on the economic substance.

5.1.510   LEASE TRANSACTIONS NOT IN THE FORM OF A LEASE

5.1.510.10   An arrangement may contain a lease even though the agreement is not in the legal form of a lease. For example, outsourcing arrangements may contain a lease of the underlying assets. The assessment of the substance of an agreement is carried out at its inception. The assessment depends on whether:

- fulfilment of the arrangement is dependent on the use of a specific asset or assets; and
- the arrangement conveys a right to use the asset(s). [*IFRIC 4.6*]

5.1.510.20   This assessment does not apply to arrangements that are excluded from the scope of IAS 17 or are in the scope of IFRIC 12 (see 5.12.01). [*IFRIC 4.4*]

5.1.510.30   The asset under the arrangement may be identified explicitly in the arrangement or it may be specified implicitly – e.g. if the supplier owns or leases only one asset with which to fulfil the obligation and it is not economically feasible or practicable for the supplier to use alternative assets to fulfil the arrangement. [*IFRIC 4.6–8*]

5.1.510.40   The arrangement conveys the right to use the asset if the buyer (lessee) obtains the ability or right to control the use of a specific asset. IFRIC 4 clarifies that the right to use an asset is transferred if any of the following conditions is met.

- The buyer has the ability or right to control the asset, including to direct how others should operate the asset, at the same time obtaining or controlling more than an insignificant amount of the asset's output.
- The buyer has the ability or right to control physical access to the asset, while obtaining or controlling more than an insignificant amount of the asset's output.
- The possibility that another party will take more than an insignificant amount of the asset's output during the term of the arrangement is remote and the price paid by the buyer for the output is neither a contractually fixed price per unit of output nor the market price per unit of output. [*IFRIC 4.9*]

EXAMPLE 18 – EMBEDDED LEASES – LIGHTING AS A SERVICE

5.1.510.45   Company L enters into an eight-year contract with Company M that requires M to install and maintain specific lighting equipment at L's stores. The terms of the contract are as follows.

- The equipment is designed and selected by M, subject to L's approval.
- M monitors the equipment remotely and performs maintenance on it as needed.
- L specifies the hours of operation and the level of brightness, and can direct M to change these specifications within a reasonable variance.
- The amount of consideration payable by L is based on usage – i.e. hours of operation and brightness impact the amount.
- The price paid to M is neither fixed per unit of output nor equal to the market price per unit of output at the time of its delivery.
- M has an option to upgrade the equipment following any future technological advancements, and an obligation to replace any damaged or defective equipment.
- The equipment is large and costly to transport and install. Therefore, it is not economically feasible or practicable for M to substitute alternative assets once the equipment is installed (the costs of substitution exceed the benefits).

5.1.510.47   The fulfilment of the arrangement is dependent on the use of specific assets. The cost of substitution for M exceeds the benefits and, as such, is not economically feasible. Therefore, the substitution rights are not substantive. Even if the substitution rights were substantive, IFRIC 4 would not preclude lease treatment before the date of substitution. M's obligation to replace broken equipment is a warranty-type obligation that also does not preclude lease treatment. Similarly, M's option to upgrade the equipment due to future technological advancements does not preclude lease treatment. [*IFRIC 4.7*]

> 5.1.510.48   The arrangement conveys to L the right to control the use of the assets because L:
>
> - specifies the hours of operation and the level of brightness and can direct M to change these specifications within a reasonable variance;
> - controls physical access to the lighting system because it is located in its facility; and
> - takes all of the assets' output (i.e. lighting), and the price paid to M is neither fixed per unit of output nor equal to the market price per unit of output at the time of its delivery. [*IFRIC 4.9*]
>
> 5.1.510.49   It is only necessary for one of the three circumstances in 5.1.510.48 to exist to conclude that L controls the use of the assets. In this example, the arrangement contains a lease because fulfilment of the arrangement is dependent on the use of the specific assets and the arrangement conveys to the purchaser (L) the right to control the use of the assets.

5.1.510.50   If a buyer agrees to buy 100 percent of the output of a specified asset and requires the asset to be operated at full capacity, then in our view there is a strong presumption that the buyer has effective control over the asset and therefore that the arrangement is or contains a lease. [*IFRIC 4.9(a)*]

5.1.510.60   In our view, this presumption can be rebutted only when the operator, although it is obliged to operate at maximum capacity, retains significant operational flexibility to influence the profitability of the arrangement – e.g. the mix of product quality/composition can be varied at the operator's discretion.

5.1.510.70   Generally, under IFRIC 4 a buyer controls an asset and a lease exists when the buyer is taking substantially all of the output, because others cannot obtain the output from the specified asset. However, an exemption was incorporated in paragraph 9(c) of IFRIC 4 so that arrangements in which the price is either contractually fixed per unit of output or equal to the market price per unit of output at the time of delivery of the output are not accounted for as leases. In our view, this exemption for fixed or market prices should be applied narrowly and only for arrangements in which the buyer clearly pays for the actual output. Therefore, except in the limited circumstances discussed in 5.1.510.130–170, if any variability is introduced to the price per unit (other than for unit pricing at a market rate at the time of delivery), then in our view such an arrangement does not meet the exemption for fixed or market prices. [*IFRIC 4.9(c), BC35–BC39*]

EXAMPLE 19A – APPLICATION OF PRICING EXEMPTION IN IFRIC 4 – PRICE CONTRACTUALLY FIXED

> 5.1.510.80   Company D enters into an arrangement to supply Company B with energy and builds a specific power plant to service this arrangement. Under the agreement:
>
> - it is remote that any other party will take more than an insignificant amount of D's plant output; and
> - B will pay D for each megawatt-hour (MWh) produced based on the current selling price per unit.

5.1.510.85   Because the price is contractually fixed and does not vary with output, the arrangement meets the exemption in paragraph 9(c) of IFRIC 4 and does not contain a lease. [*IFRIC 4.BC36(c)*]

EXAMPLE 19B – APPLICATION OF PRICING EXEMPTION IN IFRIC 4 – PRICE PER UNIT BASED ON ALLOCATION

5.1.510.90   Modifying Example 19A, assume the following.
- Company B makes pricing payments to Company D based on a set recovery of 90% of the monthly total operating costs of the plant plus a 25% profit mark-up for each MWh bought.
- This price is set in order to recover a portion of D's capital investment in the plant originally built to service the arrangement with B.

5.1.510.95   In substance, the payment reflects a variable allocation per MWh of the ongoing cost of the asset – i.e. the plant – rather than the cost of conversion for the MWh produced. The unit price of output is variable, and not reflective of current market price for the MWh, and accordingly does not meet the exemption in paragraph 9(c) of IFRIC 4. It may also be persuasive evidence that it is remote that parties other than B will take more than an insignificant amount of output of D's plant.

5.1.510.100   In our view, there is a strong presumption that any variability in the price per unit that depends on the volume of output of the asset means that the arrangement does not meet the exemption for fixed or market prices.

EXAMPLE 19C – APPLICATION OF PRICING EXEMPTION IN IFRIC 4 – PRICE PER UNIT DEPENDANT ON VOLUME

5.1.510.110   Modifying Example 19B, assume the following.
- Company B agrees to buy all of the electricity generated by a wind farm.
- B pays 10 per MWh generated based on a predetermined forecasted amount stated in the contract.
- If the actual electricity generated is 20% higher than the forecast, then the unit price is reduced by 10%.

5.1.510.115   We believe that this arrangement does not meet the exemption for fixed prices, because the price to be paid for each unit of output is not determined at the commencement of the arrangement.

5.1.510.120   Similarly, we believe that arrangements in which the unit price is subject to caps, floors or stepped adjustments that depend on the volume of output do not meet the exemption for fixed or market prices.

5.1.510.130   However, in our view the exemption for fixed prices may be met in certain limited circumstances. We believe that if the total volumes and total price for a contract are fixed (predetermined at inception of the contract), then regardless of how the pricing for the individual units occurs, the arrangement meets the exemption for fixed prices, because the price per unit is fixed on a total-contract basis.

5.1.510.140   We believe that if the buyer agrees to pay different prices at different times during the term of the arrangement and such a pricing structure is consistent with payments for output, then the arrangement meets the exemption for fixed prices, on the basis that the changes were predetermined at inception of the contract.

EXAMPLE 19D – APPLICATION OF PRICING EXEMPTION IN IFRIC 4 – PRICE PER UNIT CHANGES OVER CONTRACT TERM

5.1.510.150   Company C agrees to buy all of the electricity generated by a wind farm. C pays 8 per MWh generated in the summer months and 12 per MWh generated in the winter months. We believe that this arrangement meets the exemption for fixed prices because:
- the price to be paid for each unit of output is determined at the commencement of the arrangement; and
- the pricing structure is consistent with payments for output.

5.1.510.160   In our view, if an initial fixed price per unit is adjusted under the terms of the contract with reference to a general inflation index such that the price is fixed in real terms, then the arrangement meets the exemption for fixed prices. Reference to a specific inflation index – e.g. a specific commodity index related to the asset – would not satisfy the exemption because the price is not fixed in 'real terms'.

5.1.510.170   The entity reassesses the classification of the arrangement only when there is a change in the terms of the arrangement (see 5.1.270), a substantial change to the asset or a change in the determination of whether fulfilment of the arrangement is dependent on a specific asset. [*IFRIC 4.11*]

5.1.510.180   If an arrangement contains a lease, then the requirements of IAS 17 are applied only to the lease element of the arrangement. At the inception of such arrangement, payments required by the arrangement are split into lease payments and payments related to the other elements of the arrangement based on their relative fair values. In some cases, the separation of such payments will require the use of an estimation technique – e.g. with reference to a lease agreement for a comparable asset that contains no other elements or by estimating the payments for the other elements with reference to comparable agreements and then deducting these payments from total payments required. If it is impracticable to separate the lease payments, then:
- if the lease arrangement is a finance lease, then the lessee recognises an asset and a liability at an amount equal to the fair value of the asset that is identified as the subject of the lease; or
- if the lease arrangement is an operating lease, then the lessee classifies all payments as lease payments in order to meet the disclosure requirements of IAS 17. [*IFRIC 4.12–15*]

EXAMPLE 20 – SEPARATION OF LEASE PAYMENTS

5.1.510.190   Company L enters into an agreement with Company B, whereby:
- L will build and then own and operate for 25 years, a water and power plant;
- B will make a fixed monthly payment and a variable payment based on actual output from the water and power plant to L; and
- B will obtain 90% of the output from the water and power plant.

5.1.510.200   Both B and L conclude that the arrangement contains a lease agreement according to IFRIC 4 because:
- the agreement is based on a specific asset;
- the presence of the fixed monthly payment means that the amount B pays is not fixed per unit of output or equal to the market price; and
- B takes a high proportion of the output, making it remote that another party will take more than an insignificant part of the output.

5.1.510.210   Furthermore, the arrangement contains a service element and therefore the payments are allocated between the lease and the service elements.

5.1.515   OTHER ARRANGEMENTS THAT MAY CONTAIN A LEASE

5.1.515.10   Other arrangements may arise – e.g. a sale-and-repurchase arrangement – that are, in substance, leasing arrangements even though the agreement is not in the legal form of a lease.

5.1.515.15   IFRS 15 includes specific guidance for repurchase agreements (see 4.2.380). Under IFRS 15, an arrangement is accounted for as a lease in accordance with IAS 17 if the selling entity:
- has an obligation or a right to repurchase the asset at a price lower than the original selling price of the asset; or
- has an obligation to repurchase the asset at the customer's request at a price lower than the original selling price of the asset and the customer has a significant economic incentive to exercise its right (see 4.2.390.10, 400.10). [*IFRS 15.B66, B70*]

EXAMPLE 21 – SALE-AND-REPURCHASE ARRANGEMENT

5.1.515.20   Company B is a car manufacturer and enters into an arrangement with Company D, a rental car company, whereby:
- B sells vehicles that cost 85 to D for 100 on 1 January 2018;
- B is required to repurchase the vehicles one year after the sales date for 80;
- the present value of the future repurchase cost on 1 January 2018 is 78;
- on repurchase of the vehicles, B will resell them to other customers at market value, which is expected to be 70; and
- the economic life of each vehicle is five years.

5.1.515.30   Because B has an obligation to repurchase the vehicles (forward), B has not transferred control of the vehicles to D. Therefore, B is precluded from recognising revenue of 100 on the initial sale (see 4.2.390). Instead, because the repurchase price is lower than the original selling price, B accounts for the arrangement as a lease. [*IFRS 15.B66*]

5.1.515.40   B classifies the lease as an operating lease, because it does not transfer substantially all of the risks and rewards incidental to the ownership of the asset. On transfer of the vehicles to D, B recognises:

- cash of 100;
- a liability of 78 (present value of the future repurchase cost); and
- unearned rental income of 22 (100 - 78).

5.1.515.50   The unearned income is recognised on a straight-line basis over the rental period – i.e. one year. The vehicles are initially classified as property, plant and equipment with a value of 85 and the residual value of the vehicles is equal to their estimated resale price of 70. Accordingly, during the rental period the vehicles are depreciated by 15. The liability of 78 is accreted to 80 through an interest expense charge of 2. On repurchase, the liability of 80 is extinguished and the vehicles become held-for-sale and are transferred to inventory at their carrying amount of 70 (see 3.2.380.40).

5.1.515.60   B records the following entries.

	DEBIT	CREDIT
1 January 2018		
Cash	100	
Repurchase obligation		78
Unearned rental income (statement of financial position)		22
To recognise initial sale-and-repurchase obligation		
31 December 2018		
Unearned rental income (statement of financial position)	22	
Depreciation expense (profit or loss)	15[(1)]	
Interest expense (profit or loss)	2[(2)]	
Rental income (profit or loss)		22
Accumulated depreciation (statement of financial position)		15
Repurchase obligation		2
To recognise rental income, depreciation expense and interest expense		

	DEBIT	**CREDIT**
1 January 2019		
Repurchase obligation	80[3]	
Cash		80
Inventory (vehicles)	70[4]	
Property, plant and equipment (vehicles)		70
To recognise repurchase and transfer of vehicles to inventory		

Notes
1. Calculated as 85 - 70.
2. Calculated as 80 - 78.
3. Calculated as 78 + 2.
4. Calculated as 85 - 15.

5.1.515.70   Alternatively, if the fact pattern in this example was modified such that D was allowed but not required to sell the cars back to B (written put option) at a price lower than the original selling price and D had a significant economic incentive to exercise this option, then the arrangement would also be accounted for as a lease (see 4.2.400). [*IFRS 15.B66, B70*]

5.1.520   PRESENTATION AND DISCLOSURES

5.1.520.10   Lease receivables and lease payables are financial instruments and are treated as such for disclosure and presentation purposes (see chapter 7.10). [*IAS 32.4*]

5.1.520.20   For operating leases, a lessee presents its lease payments as expenses in profit or loss. A lessor presents the lease payments received as part of revenue in profit or loss. In our view, a lessee may not separate a finance component of its operating lease payment to present that component as part of interest expense.

5.1.520.30   In addition, lessors and lessees provide a general description of significant leasing arrangements. For lessees, this includes information about:
- the basis on which contingent rent payments are determined;
- the existence and terms of renewal or purchase options; and
- escalation clauses and restrictions imposed by lease arrangements, such as those concerning dividends, additional debt and further leasing. [*IAS 17.31, 35, 47, 56*]

5.1.520.40   For operating leases, both the lessor and the lessee disclose the non-cancellable minimum lease payments to be received or paid, respectively, over the remaining term of the lease. [*IAS 17.35, 56*]

5.1A   Leases: IFRS 16

5.1A   Leases: IFRS 16

FORTHCOMING REQUIREMENTS

In January 2016, the IASB published IFRS 16 *Leases*. IFRS 16 supersedes:

- IAS 17 *Leases;*
- IFRIC 4 *Determining whether an Arrangement contains a Lease*;
- SIC-15 *Operating Leases – Incentives*; and
- SIC-27 *Evaluating the Substance of Transactions Involving the Legal Form of a Lease*.

IFRS 16 applies for annual periods beginning on or after 1 January 2019. Early adoption is permitted for entities that apply IFRS 15 *Revenue from Contracts with Customers* on or before the date of initial application of IFRS 16.

The requirements related to this topic are mainly derived from the following.

STANDARD	TITLE
IFRS 16	Leases

FUTURE DEVELOPMENTS

For this topic, there are no future developments.

5.1A.10   OVERVIEW

5.1A.10.10   The following diagram illustrates how key elements of the standard are explained throughout this chapter. The corresponding section numbers are in brackets.

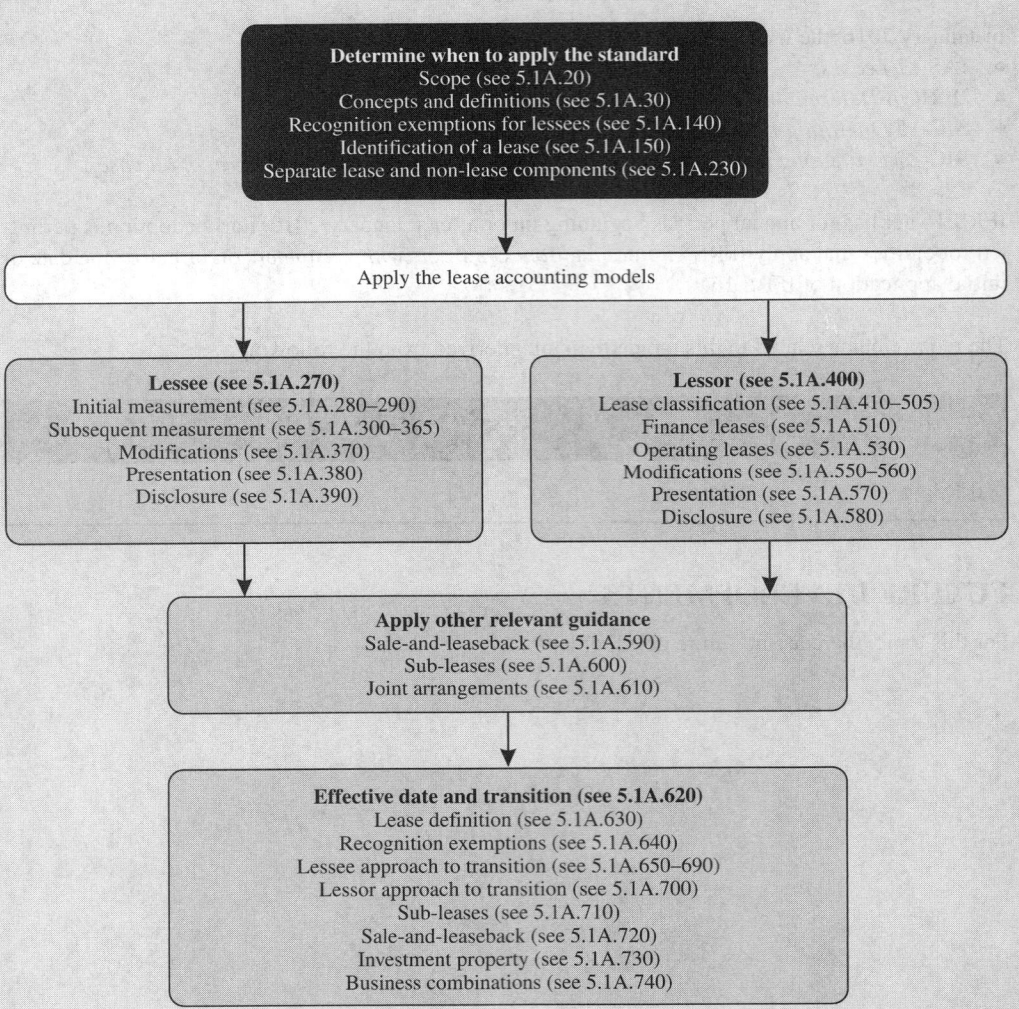

5.1A.10.20   A contract is, or contains, a lease if it conveys the right to control the use of an identified asset for a period of time in exchange for consideration. [*IFRS 16.9*]

5.1A.10.30   A lessee applies a single, on-balance sheet lease accounting model to all of its leases unless the lessee elects the recognition exemptions for short-term leases and/or leases of low-value assets (see 5.1A.140). A lessee recognises a right-of-use asset representing its right to use the underlying asset and a lease liability representing its obligation to make lease payments (see 5.1A.270–390). [*IFRS 16.IN10, 5, 22*]

5.1A.10.40 A lessor classifies leases as either operating or finance leases, depending on the substance of the transaction rather than the form of the contract. The classification determines the accounting treatment followed by the lessor. [*IFRS 16.61, 63*]

5.1A.10.50 A lease is classified as a finance lease by a lessor if substantially all of the risks and rewards incidental to ownership of an underlying asset are transferred from the lessor to the lessee by the agreement. The following are typical indicators that a lessor assesses to determine whether it has transferred substantially all of the risks and rewards:

- at the inception date, the present value of the lease payments in relation to the fair value of the underlying asset;
- the lease term in relation to the economic life of the underlying asset; and
- whether the lessee will obtain ownership of the underlying asset (see 5.1A.400–505). [*IFRS 16.61–63*]

5.1A.10.60 A lease that is not a finance lease is an operating lease for the lessor. [*IFRS 16.62*]

5.1A.20 SCOPE

5.1A.20.10 IFRS 16 applies to all leases, including leases of right-of-use assets in a sub-lease, except for those covered by the following paragraphs. [*IFRS 16.3*]

5.1A.20.20 IFRS 16 does not apply to:

- leases to explore for or use minerals, oil, natural gas and similar non-regenerative resources (see chapter 5.11);
- leases of biological assets in the scope of IAS 41 held by a lessee (see chapter 3.9);
- service concession arrangements in the scope of IFRIC 12 (see chapter 5.12);
- licences of intellectual property granted by a lessor in the scope of IFRS 15 (see chapter 4.2); and
- rights held by a lessee under licensing agreements in the scope of IAS 38 for items such as motion picture films, video recordings, plays, manuscripts, patents and copyrights (see chapter 3.3). [*IFRS 16.3*]

5.1A.20.30 A lessee may, but is not required to, apply IFRS 16 to leases of intangible assets other than rights held under licensing agreements in the scope of IAS 38 for items such as motion picture films, video recordings, plays, manuscripts, patents and copyrights (see 5.1A.20.20). [*IFRS 16.4*]

5.1A.20.40 IAS 40 (see chapter 3.4) applies to the recognition and measurement of investment property provided by lessors under operating leases and the subsequent measurement of right-of-use assets held by lessees that meet the definition of investment property (see 5.1A.360). The requirements of IFRS 16 apply to all other aspects of lease accounting for these assets. [*IFRS 16.29, 34*]

5.1A.20.50 IFRS 3 applies to leases acquired in a business combination. The accounting treatment depends on whether the acquiree is a lessee or a lessor and, if the acquiree is a lessor, on the type of lease (see 2.6.830, 5.1A.660.20 and 5.1A.675.140–160). [*IFRS 3.17(a), 28A–28B, B42*]

5.1A.25 Embedded derivatives

5.1A.25.10 Under IFRS, derivatives embedded in a lease that are considered not closely related to the lease host have to be separated and accounted for under IFRS 9 (see 7.2.110, 270.10). For example, if an entity has a lease agreement with variable lease payments adjusted for two times the change in

CPI, then the feature needs to be separated and accounted for under IFRS 9 because it is considered leveraged (see 7.2.270.10). Factors to consider when assessing leverage are set out in 7.2.200.30. Conversely, an inflation-indexed embedded derivative in a lease contract may be considered closely related to the lease and the whole payment accounted for under IFRS 16 if:

- the index relates to inflation in the country in which the leased asset is operated; and
- the feature is not leveraged.

5.1A.25.20   An embedded purchase option for a leased asset included in a lease contract is not separated because such an option is accounted for as part of the lease (see 7.2.120.100). [*IFRS 16.BC81*]

5.1A.30   CONCEPTS AND DEFINITIONS

5.1A.40   Period of use

5.1A.40.10   The 'period of use' is the total period of time over which an asset is used to fulfil a contract with a customer (including any non-consecutive periods of time). [*IFRS 16.A*]

EXAMPLE 1 – PERIOD OF USE – NON-CONSECUTIVE PERIODS

5.1A.40.20   Football Team V has an exclusive right to use a specific stadium for the months of September to May each year during its playing season. The contract runs for 10 years. From June to August, the owner of the stadium holds concerts and other events in the stadium.

5.1A.40.30   In this example, the period of use consists of 90 non-consecutive months. This is because V can use the stadium for nine months each year over the 10-year contract. The use of the same stadium by the owner in the remaining months of the year does not prevent the contract from being a lease (provided that the other aspects of the definition are met).

5.1A.50   Initial direct costs

5.1A.50.10   'Initial direct costs' are incremental costs of obtaining a lease that would otherwise not have been incurred, except for such costs incurred by manufacturer or dealer lessors in connection with finance leases. For a discussion of the accounting for costs incurred by manufacturer or dealer lessors to negotiate and arrange a lease, see 5.1A.515. [*IFRS 16.A*]

5.1A.50.20   Examples of initial direct costs include commissions and payments made by a potential lessee to an existing tenant to vacate the property so that the potential lessee can obtain the lease. Items that are not considered to be initial direct costs include allocations of internal overhead costs – e.g. those incurred by a sales and marketing team or a purchase team, costs of evaluating a prospective lessee's financial condition and costs to obtain offers for potential leases. Legal fees and internal costs that are incremental and directly attributable to negotiating and arranging a lease are considered initial direct costs only if they are contingent on the origination of a lease.

5.1A.50.30   A lessee includes any initial direct costs incurred in the cost of the right-of-use asset at the commencement date (see 5.1A.290.10). [*IFRS 16.24(c)*]

5.1A.50.40   For lessors, the initial recognition of and subsequent accounting for initial direct costs depend on the classification of the lease (see 5.1A.510–515, 530).

5.1A.60   Inception date and commencement date

5.1A.60.10   The 'inception date' of a lease is the earlier of the date of the lease agreement and the date of commitment by the parties to the principal terms and conditions of the lease. [*IFRS 16.A*]

5.1A.60.20   At the inception date:
- an entity assesses whether a contract is, or contains, a lease (see 5.1A.150); and
- a lessor determines whether a lease is classified as an operating or a finance lease (see 5.1A.410). [*IFRS 16.9, 66*]

5.1A.60.30   The 'commencement date' of a lease is the date on which a lessor makes an underlying asset available for use by a lessee. [*IFRS 16.A*]

5.1A.60.40   At the commencement date:
- a lessee recognises and measures the right-of-use asset and lease liability (see 5.1A.270); and
- a lessor recognises and measures finance leases (see 5.1A.510) and commences accounting for operating leases. [*IFRS 16.22–23, 26–27, 67, 70–71, 81*]

5.1A.60.50   The following table summarises the distinction between the inception and the commencement dates of a lease, and the respective accounting by a lessee and a lessor at those dates. [*IFRS 16.9, 22–23, 26–27, 66–67, 70–71, 81, A*]

	INCEPTION DATE	COMMENCEMENT DATE
Definition	Earlier of: • the date of a lease agreement; and • the date of commitment by the parties to the principal terms of a lease.	Date on which a lessor makes an underlying asset available for use by a lessee.
Lessee	• Assesses whether a contract is, or contains, a lease.	• Recognises and measures the right-of-use asset and lease liability.
Lessor	• Assesses whether a contract is, or contains, a lease. • Determines whether a lease is classified as operating or finance.	• Recognises and measures finance leases. • Commences accounting for operating leases.

5.1A.70   Lease payments

5.1A.70.10   'Lease payments' are payments made by a lessee to a lessor relating to the right to use an underlying asset during the lease term. Both the lessee and the lessor include the following in the lease payments:
- fixed payments, including in-substance fixed payments (see 5.1A.75), less any lease incentives;
- variable lease payments that depend on an index or a rate (see 5.1A.80);

- the exercise price of a purchase option if the lessee is reasonably certain to exercise that option (see 5.1A.95.10); and
- payments of penalties for terminating the lease, if the lease term reflects the assessment that the lessee will exercise an option to terminate the lease (see 5.1A.95.20). [*IFRS 16.A, 27, 70*]

5.1A.70.20   In some jurisdictions, the terms of property leases normally require the lessee to pay security deposits and advance rentals. The security deposit is held by the lessor throughout the term of the lease and is refunded in full to the lessee at the end of the lease term (if the lessee has performed fully and observed all of the conditions or provisions in the lease). However, the lessor may apply the security deposit to remedy the breach of any provisions in the lease contract and to indemnify any consequential costs and losses related to the leased property that are properly chargeable to the lessee under the contract. The security deposits do not normally carry any interest or the interest rate received is less than market interest rates.

5.1A.70.30   In our view, the security deposit itself is not part of the lease payments and therefore is in the scope of IFRS 9 (see 7.1.20). Therefore, the security deposit should be measured at fair value on initial recognition. In our view, the difference between the initial fair value and the nominal value of the deposit is an additional lease payment made by the lessee and it should therefore be included in the measurement of the right-of-use asset.

5.1A.70.40   KPMG's publication *Lease payments* provides a more in-depth discussion of determination of the lease liability than this chapter. This chapter summarises the key points.

5.1A.75   *Fixed and in-substance fixed payments*

5.1A.75.10   'In-substance fixed payments' are payments that are structured as variable lease payments, but which – in substance – are unavoidable. Examples include:
- payments that have to be made only if an event occurs that has no genuine possibility of not occurring;
- there is more than one set of payments that a lessee could make, but only one of those sets is realistic; and
- there are multiple sets of payments that a lessee could realistically make, but it has to make at least one set of payments. [*IFRS 16.B42*]

EXAMPLE 2A – IN-SUBSTANCE FIXED PAYMENTS – MINIMUM LEASE PAYMENT

5.1A.75.20   Company W leases a production line from Company L. The lease payments depend on the number of operating hours of the production line – i.e. W has to pay 1,000 per hour of use. The expected usage per year is 1,500 hours. If the usage is less than 1,000 hours, W must pay 1,000,000.

5.1A.75.30   This lease contains in-substance fixed payments of 1,000,000 per year, which are included in the initial measurement of the lease liability. The additional 500,000 that W expects to pay per year are variable payments that depend on usage and, therefore, are not included in the initial measurement of the lease liability but are expensed as the 'over-use' occurs. [*IFRS 16.27, 38(b), B42*]

5.1A.75.40   Variable lease payments that are highly probable to occur are not in-substance fixed payments if they are based on performance or use of the underlying asset and are therefore avoidable.

EXAMPLE 2B – IN-SUBSTANCE FIXED PAYMENTS – MINIMUM LEASE PAYMENT WITH NO COMMERCIAL SUBSTANCE

5.1A.75.50   Company R, an established retailer, leases space for a store within a mature retail development from Company Q. Under the terms of the lease, R is required to operate the store during normal working hours and is not permitted to leave the store vacant or to sub-let the store. The contract states that annual rentals payable by R will be:

- 100 if R makes no sales at the store; or
- 1 million if R makes any sales at the store during the term of the lease.

5.1A.75.60   In this example, the lease contains in-substance fixed lease payments of 1 million per year. The amount is not a variable payment that depends on sales. This is because there is no realistic possibility that R will make no sales at the store.

EXAMPLE 2C – IN-SUBSTANCE FIXED PAYMENTS – MULTIPLE OPTIONS AT END OF NON-CANCELLABLE PERIOD

5.1A.75.70   Lessee T leases a machine that has an expected useful life of five years. The non-cancellable period of the lease is three years. At the end of year 3, T has to either:

- purchase the machine for 200; or
- extend the lease for two years, by agreeing to pay 105 at the end of each year.

5.1A.75.75   T assesses at lease commencement that it is neither reasonably certain to purchase the machine at the end of year 3 nor reasonably certain to extend the lease for two years. That is, if T were to consider the purchase option and the renewal option separately, then it would include neither the exercise price of the purchase option nor the rentals payable in the renewal period in the lease liability at lease commencement.

5.1A.75.80   However, the arrangement contains an in-substance fixed payment at the end of year 3. This is because T is required to take one of the two options and, under all options, T is required to make a payment. The amount of the in-substance fixed payment is the lower of the present value of the exercise price of the purchase option (200) and the present value of the annual rentals in the renewal period (two payments of 105).

EXAMPLE 3 – LEASE PAYMENTS BASED ON OUTPUT OF SOLAR PLANT

5.1A.75.90   Utility Company C enters into a 20-year contract with Power Company D to purchase electricity produced by a new solar farm. C and D assess that the contract contains a lease. There are no minimum purchase requirements, and no fixed payments that C is required to make to D. However, C is required to purchase all of the electricity produced by the solar plant at a price of 10 per unit.

5.1A.75.100 C notes that it is highly probable that the solar plant will generate at least some electricity each year. However, the whole payment that C makes to D varies with the amount of electricity produced by the solar farm – i.e. the payments are fully variable. Therefore, C concludes that there are no in-substance fixed lease payments in this contract. C recognises the payments to D in profit or loss when they are incurred. [*IFRS 16.27, 38(b), B42*]

5.1A.75.110 Some lease contracts may specify that the lease payments are calculated periodically as the 'higher of' or 'lower of' two amounts. Often, these amounts are based on an index or a rate. Although both payment clauses are structured to be variable, leases with a 'higher of' clause may effectively include an in-substance fixed payment – because there may be a minimum payment that the lessee has no genuine possibility of avoiding, and the variability in the lease payment may exist only in how much the actual payment will exceed that minimum amount by.

EXAMPLE 4A – 'HIGHER OF' CLAUSE – IN-SUBSTANCE FIXED PAYMENTS

5.1A.75.120 Lessee X enters into a 10-year lease of retail space. Lease payments are made in advance. The first lease payment is 50,000 and subsequent lease payments are increased annually by the *higher of* the increase in CPI for the preceding 12 months and 5%. The CPI is 100 on lease commencement and 107 at the end of year 1 (i.e. inflation is 7% during the first year). X's discount rate is 4.5%.

5.1A.75.130 On commencement, X makes payment for year 1 and determines that the contract includes an in-substance fixed minimum (with a fixed escalation of 5% per year). X measures its lease liability at 460,905[1] and recognises a right-of-use asset at 510,905[2] (including the prepayment of 50,000).

5.1A.75.140 At the beginning of year 2, X adjusts the lease payment for year 2 to 53,500[3], based on the higher of the increase in CPI of 7% and 5%. To remeasure the lease liability at the beginning of year 2, X increases the lease payment of 53,500 by 5% for the remainder of the lease. Using an unchanged discount rate, the lease liability is increased from 481,646[4] to 490,819[5]. X records an adjustment to increase lease liability and the right-of-use asset by 9,173[6].

Notes
1.   Calculated as follows.

YEAR	LEASE PAYMENT	DISCOUNTED AT 4.5%
2	52,500	50,239
3	55,125	50,480
4	57,881	50,721
5	60,775	50,964
6	63,814	51,208
7	67,005	51,453
8	70,355	51,699
9	73,873	51,946
10	77,566	52,195
Lease liability at commencement		460,905

2. Calculated as 460,905 + 50,000 (prepayment).
3. Calculated as 50,000 × 1.07.
4. Calculated as 460,905 + 20,741 (interest for year 1).
5. Calculated as follows.

YEAR	LEASE PAYMENT	DISCOUNTED AT 4.5%
2	53,500	53,500
3	56,175	53,756
4	58,984	54,013
5	61,933	54,272
6	65,030	54,531
7	68,281	54,792
8	71,695	55,054
9	75,280	55,318
10	79,044	55,582
Lease liability at commencement		490,819

6. Calculated as 490,819 - 481,646.

5.1A.75.150 Unlike 'higher of' clauses, 'lower of' clauses generally do not have an in-substance fixed amount, and therefore result in variable lease payments.

EXAMPLE 4B – 'LOWER OF' CLAUSE – NOT IN-SUBSTANCE FIXED PAYMENT

5.1A.75.160 Modifying Example 4A, the lease payments are increased annually by the *lower of* the increase in CPI for the preceding 12 months and 5%. Because future CPI rates are unknown, Lessee X measures its lease liability at commencement as the present value of the nine remaining payments of 50,000.

5.1A.75.170   At the beginning of year 2, X adjusts the lease payment to 52,500[1]. Because future CPI rates are unknown, using an unchanged discount rate X re-measures the lease liability at the beginning of year 2 as the present value of the nine remaining payments of 52,500, and then makes payment for year 2.

Note
1.   Calculated as 50,000 × 1.05.

5.1A.80   *Variable payments depending on an index or rate*

5.1A.80.10   'Variable lease payments' are the portion of payments made by a lessee to a lessor for the right to use an underlying asset during the lease term that varies because of changes in facts or circumstances – other than the passage of time – occurring after the commencement date. [*IFRS 16.A*]

5.1A.80.20   Variable lease payments that depend on an index or a rate are included in the initial measurement of the lessee's lease liability and the initial measurement of the lessor's net investment in the lease, initially measured using the index or rate as at the commencement date – e.g. a lessee does not estimate future inflation, but measures the lease liability assuming no inflation for the remainder of the lease term. Such payments include payments linked to a consumer price index, payments linked to a benchmark interest rate (such as LIBOR) or payments that vary to reflect changes in market rental rates. [*IFRS 16.27–28, 70, BC166*]

5.1A.80.30   In practice, it is common for lease agreements to include periodic rent review clauses that depend on a published index. These clauses adjust contracted lease payments to reflect changes in inflation measures and other factors. Common indices include the following:
- consumer price index (CPI);
- producer price indices (PPIs);
- retail price indices (RPIs);
- house price indices; and
- average earnings indices.

EXAMPLE 5A – VARIABLE PAYMENTS – DEPENDING ON AN INDEX OR RATE

5.1A.80.40   Company Y rents an office building. The initial annual rental payment is 2,500,000. Payments are made at the end of each year. The rent will be increased each year by the change in CPI over the preceding 12 months.

5.1A.80.50   This is an example of a variable lease payment that depends on an index. The initial measurement of the lease liability is based on the value of the CPI on lease commencement – i.e. an annual rental of 2,500,000 for each year of the lease. If during the first year of the lease the CPI increases from 100 to 105 (i.e. the rate of inflation over the preceding 12 months is 5%), then at the end of the first year the lease liability is recalculated assuming future annual rentals of 2,625,000 (2,500,000 x ((105 - 100) / 100)). [*IFRS 16.28*]

Example 5B – Variable payments – Depending on libor

5.1A.80.60 Lessee C enters into a five-year lease of a car. On commencement, LIBOR is 2%, C's incremental borrowing rate is 5% and the initial fair value of the car is 10,000. The lease payments are paid at the beginning of each year and are determined as follows.

- Annual lease payments in years 1–4 are determined as LIBOR × 10,000, based on LIBOR at the date of payment.
- The payment in year 5 is determined as (LIBOR × 10,000) + 10,000.

5.1A.80.65 The lease contains a fixed lease payment and variable lease payments that depend on a rate. On commencement, C pays 200 for year 1 and records a right-of-use asset of 9,136[1] and a lease liability of 8,936[2].

5.1A.80.70 At the end of year 1, C records the following entries.

	Debit	Credit
Depreciation	1,827[3]	
Right-of-use asset		1,827
To recognise depreciation for year 1		
Interest expense	447[4]	
Lease liability		447
To recognise payment and expenses for year 1		

5.1A.80.80 At the beginning of year 2, LIBOR increases to 2.5%. Using a revised discount rate of 5.3%[5], C records the following entries to remeasure the lease liability and the right-of-use asset and the payment made for year 2.

	Debit	Credit
Right-of-use asset	109	
Lease liability		109
To recognise remeasurement of lease liability at beginning of year 2		
Depreciation expense	1,854[6]	
Right-of-use asset		1,854
To recognise depreciation for year 2		
Interest expense	490[7]	
Lease liability		240[8]
Cash		250[9]
To recognise payment for year 2		

Notes
1. Calculated as 200 + (200 x 0.95) + (200 x 0.95²) + (200 x 0.95³) + (10,200 x 0.95⁴).
2. Calculated as lease liability of 9,136 - 200 (prepayment for year 1).
3. Calculated as 9,136 / 5 years.
4. Calculated as 8,936 × 5%.
5. Revised discount rate assumed for the purposes of illustrating the example.
6. Calculated as 7,418 / 4 years.
7. Calculated as 9,492 × 5.3%.
8. Calculated as 490 - 250.
9. Because lease payments are determined using LIBOR at the date of payment, the lease payment for year 2 is calculated as 10,000 × 2.5%.

5.1A.85   *Variable payments depending on sales or usage*

5.1A.85.10   Variable lease payments that depend on sales or usage of the underlying asset are excluded from the lease liability. Instead, these payments are recognised in profit or loss in the period in which the performance or use occurs. [*IFRS 16.BC168–BC169*]

EXAMPLE 6 – VARIABLE PAYMENTS DEPENDING ON SALES – NOT DIRECTLY PROPORTIONAL TO SALES

5.1A.85.20   Company X leases a space for a new store. Historically, X's stores generate an average of 900,000 in revenue per month. Monthly lease payments for the new store are determined with reference to staggered sales targets as follows.

- Monthly revenue up to 600,000: 0.
- Monthly revenue 600,001–1 million: 20,000.
- Monthly revenue 1,000,001–2 million: 25,000.
- Monthly revenue above 2 million: 30,000.

5.1A.85.30   Even though the lease payments are not directly proportional to sales (i.e. not determined as a percentage of sales), the lease payments are still variable (i.e. there is no in-substance fixed minimum) and depend on sales. Genuine variability in the lease payments exist and the existence of a historical average or similar benchmark does not create a fixed minimum. Accordingly, X excludes the monthly lease payments from its measurement of the lease liability and measures the lease liability as zero.

5.1A.90   *Residual value guarantees*

5.1A.90.10   There are two types of residual value to be considered by the parties to a lease agreement.

- *Guaranteed residual value:* A guarantee made to a lessor by a party unrelated to the lessor that the value (or part of the value) of an underlying asset at the end of a lease will be at least a specified amount.
- *Unguaranteed residual value:* A portion of the residual value of the underlying asset, the realisation of which by the lessor is not assured or is guaranteed solely by a party related to the lessor. [*IFRS 16.A*]

5.1A.90.20   The amount of the lease payments reflects whether the residual value is guaranteed or unguaranteed. An unguaranteed residual value is always excluded from the determination of the lease payments, but is nevertheless part of the lessor's gross investment in a finance lease (see 5.1A.510.10). [*IFRS 16.A*]

5.1A.90.30   If a lessee provides a residual value guarantee, then it includes in the lease payments the amount that it expects to pay under that guarantee. Lease payments do not include payments allocated to non-lease components of a contract, unless the lessee elects to combine non-lease components with a lease component and to account for them as a single lease component (see 5.1A.255). [*IFRS 16.A, 15, 27*]

5.1A.90.40   For the lessor, lease payments include the full amount of any residual value guarantees provided to the lessor by the lessee, a party related to the lessee or a third party unrelated to the lessor that is financially capable of discharging the obligations under the guarantee. Lease payments do not include payments allocated to non-lease components. [*IFRS 16.A, 70*]

EXAMPLE 7 – RESIDUAL VALUE GUARANTEES – LESSEE

5.1A.90.50   Lessee Z has entered into a lease contract with Lessor L to lease a car. The lease term is five years. In addition, Z and L agree on a residual value guarantee – if the fair value of the car at the end of the lease term is below 400, then Z will pay to L an amount equal to the difference between 400 and the fair value of the car.

5.1A.90.60   At commencement of the lease, Z expects that the fair value of the car at the end of the term will be 400. Z therefore includes an amount of zero in the lease payments in respect of the residual value guarantee when calculating its lease liability.

5.1A.90.70   A lessee that is required to provide the lessor with a guaranteed residual value may obtain a matching residual value guarantee from a third party. Unless the lessee is unconditionally released from the residual value guarantee by the lessor, lease payments include the amount that the lessee expects to pay under the residual value guarantee. The lessee's receivable from a third party cannot be offset against the residual value obligation under the lease, because there is no legal right and intention to set off (see 7.10.110).

5.1A.90.80   A lease agreement may include a short minimum term followed by several renewal periods. In this case, the lease may require the lessee to give certain guarantees should it not renew the lease. For example, the lessee may guarantee that if the lessor sells the leased property at the end of the minimum term and reinvests the proceeds, then the lessee will make up any shortfall between the lessor's actual return on the reinvested funds and a specified rate of return on the reinvested funds for a period that typically extends to the end of the original renewal period(s) in the lease (known as 'make-whole premiums'). Make-whole premiums are a type of residual value guarantee.

5.1A.90.90   A lessee might indemnify a lessor for excess wear and tear of the leased asset. Judgement is necessary to determine whether lessee indemnifications are fixed lease payments, variable lease payments or residual value guarantees.

EXAMPLE 8A – INDEMNIFICATION FOR WEAR AND TEAR – RESIDUAL VALUE GUARANTEE

5.1A.90.100 Lessee Z enters into a contract with Lessor L to lease a new car. The lease term is five years. Z agrees to indemnify L for excess wear and tear on the vehicle. Under the clause, Z will pay for the difference between the actual sales price of the vehicle at the end of the lease term and the 'excellent condition' value for the five-year-old vehicle in accordance with a specific residual value benchmark.

5.1A.90.110 In this example, the indemnification is a residual value guarantee, because the amount that the lessee can be required to pay is the difference between the actual sales price and a value determined based on a benchmark.

5.1A.90.120 Z includes the expected amount payable in its lease liability. Subsequently, Z remeasures the lease liability if its expectation of the amount payable changes.

EXAMPLE 8B – INDEMNIFICATION FOR WEAR AND TEAR – VARIABLE LEASE PAYMENTS

5.1A.90.130 Modifying Example 8A, under the excess wear and tear clause Lessee Z will pay a fixed amount per mile above the normal mileage according to a specific residual value benchmark for a five-year-old car.

5.1A.90.140 In this example, the indemnification is a variable lease payment, because it is not a guarantee of value but a payment based on use.

5.1A.90.150 Z does not include the amount payable in the lease liability. Instead, Z recognises the amount payable as an expense in the periods in which the liability is incurred.

5.1A.95 *Purchase, renewal and termination options*

5.1A.95.10 A lessee determines whether it is reasonably certain that it will exercise a purchase option considering all relevant facts and circumstances that create an economic incentive to do so. This is similar to the approach for assessing whether a lessee expects to exercise a renewal option (see 5.1A.100). [*IFRS 16.27(d), B37*]

5.1A.95.20 At the commencement date, a lessee determines whether it is reasonably certain not to exercise an option to terminate the lease early. Unless the lessee is reasonably certain not to terminate the lease early, it reflects the early termination in the lease term and includes the termination penalty in the measurement of the lease liability. [*IFRS 16.27(e)*]

EXAMPLE 9 – LESSEE PURCHASE OPTION – ASSESSING IF REASONABLY CERTAIN TO BE EXERCISED

5.1A.95.30 Lessee E enters into a non-cancellable five-year lease with Lessor R to use a piece of equipment, with a plan to develop its own equipment to replace the leased asset, ready for use in five years' time. There is no renewal option, but

E has the option to purchase the equipment at the end of the lease for 500. Annual lease payments are fixed at 1,000 per year, paid at the end of each year. E's incremental borrowing rate is 5%.

5.1A.95.40 At the commencement date, E concludes that it is not reasonably certain to exercise the option. This is because E intends to develop its own equipment to replace the leased asset by the end of the lease. E excludes the exercise price of the option from its lease payments and measures its lease liability as 4,330[1].

5.1A.95.50 At the commencement date, the lease liability and right-of-use asset are expected to be amortised as follows.

Year	Lease Liability				Right-of-use Asset		
	Beginning	Lease Payment	Interest	Ending	Beginning	Deprecia-tion	Ending
1	4,330	(1,000)	217	3,547	4,330	(866)	3,464
2	3,547	(1,000)	177	2,724	3,464	(866)	2,598
3	2,724	(1,000)	136	1,860	2,598	(866)	1,732
4	1,860	(1,000)	93	953	1,732	(866)	866
5	953	(1,000)	47	-	866	(866)	-

Note
1. Calculated as $1{,}000 + (1{,}000 \times 0.95) + (1{,}000 \times 0.95^2) + (1{,}000 \times 0.95^3) + (1{,}000 \times 0.95^4)$.

5.1A.95.60 If a lease includes a put option under which the lessor can require the lessee to buy the asset at the end of the lease at a fixed price, then it appears that the lessee should include the exercise price in its lease liability. This is because the exercise of the option is outside the control of the lessee and therefore the exercise price under the put option is an amount that the lessee can be required to pay to the lessor (see 5.1A.70.10). For a discussion of lessor accounting for a fixed price put option, see 5.1A.545.

Example 10 – Lessor put option – Lessee accounting

5.1A.95.70 Lessee B enters into a five-year lease with Lessor D for a piece of machinery. The contract includes a put option under which D can require B to purchase the machinery at the end of the lease at a fixed price of 5,000. Due to the nature of the machinery, its residual value at the end of the lease term is expected to be no more than 6,000.

5.1A.95.80 Exercise of the put option is out of the control of B. B does not have an unconditional right to avoid payment, and we believe that it should include the exercise price – i.e. present value of 5,000 – in the measurement of the lease liability.

5.1A.100   Lease term

5.1A.100.10   Sometimes, the terms of a lease are enforceable only during a specified period. In this situation, the 'lease term' is the non-cancellable – i.e. enforceable – period of the lease, together with:
- optional renewable periods if the lessee is reasonably certain to extend; and
- periods after an optional termination date if the lessee is reasonably certain not to terminate early. [*IFRS 16.18*]

5.1A.100.20   A lease is no longer 'enforceable' when both the lessee and lessor have the right to terminate it without agreement from the other party with no more than an insignificant penalty. If only the lessee has the right to terminate a lease, then that right is considered to be an option available to the lessee to terminate the lease that an entity considers when determining the lease term. Termination options held by the lessor only are not considered when determining the lease term because, in this situation, the lessee has an unconditional obligation to pay for the right to use the asset for the period of the lease, unless the lessor decides to terminate the lease. [*IFRS 16.B34–B35, BC128*]

5.1A.100.30   For example, if the lease term is nine years but the lessee can cancel the lease without penalty (and without the permission of the lessor) at the end of the third and sixth years, then the non-cancellable period of the contract is three years. The substance of the arrangement is that at the end of the third and sixth years, the lessee has an option to extend the lease. If at the time of commencement of the lease it is judged reasonably certain that the lessee will not cancel the lease and will effectively exercise its options to extend at the end of the third and sixth years, then the lease term is nine years. [*IFRS 16.B37*]

5.1A.100.40   When determining the lease term, an entity considers all relevant facts and circumstances that create an economic incentive for the lessee to exercise an option to renew or not to exercise an option to terminate early. When assessing whether a lessee is reasonably certain to exercise an option to extend, or not to exercise an option to terminate early, the economic reasons underlying the lessee's past practice regarding the period over which it has typically used particular types of assets (whether leased or owned) may provide useful information. [*IFRS 16.B37, B40*]

5.1A.100.50   IFRS 16 provides examples of factors to consider when assessing whether it is 'reasonably certain' that a lessee would exercise an option to renew the lease. The assessment of the degree of certainty is based on the facts and circumstances at commencement of the lease, rather than on the lessee's intentions. The following table provides examples of factors that create an economic incentive to exercise or not to exercise options to renew or terminate early. [*IFRS 16.B37–B40*]

EXAMPLES OF RELEVANT FACTS AND CIRCUMSTANCES	
Contractual/market	**Asset**
• Level of rentals in any secondary period compared with market rates	• Nature of item (specialised)
• Contingent payments	• Location
• Renewal and purchase options	• Availability of suitable alternatives
• Costs relating to the termination of the lease and the signing of a new replacement lease	• Existence of significant leasehold improvements
• Costs to return the underlying asset	

5.1A.100.60   The shorter the non-cancellable period of a lease, the more likely a lessee is to exercise an option to extend the lease or not to exercise an option to terminate the lease. This is because the costs associated with obtaining a replacement asset are likely to be proportionately higher for a shorter non-cancellable period. [*IFRS 16.B39*]

5.1A.100.70   Different conclusions may be reached on whether a lessee is reasonably certain to exercise an option to renew, or not to exercise an option to terminate early, for options with similar terms (e.g. the same strike price and the same expected fair value of the underlying asset) depending on the particular facts and circumstances of a lease. For example, the following factors may affect the analysis.

- The longer the period until the option exercise date, the more compelling the evidence needs to be that the lessee will exercise the option. This is because estimates about economic conditions and incentives that may exist at the option date will be less precise. Such estimates include, but are not limited to, the fair value of the underlying asset, the availability of suitable alternative assets, and the tax environment.
- The nature of the underlying asset may significantly affect the assessment. Depending on the nature of the underlying asset, it may be more difficult for an entity to predict its future fair value – e.g. because the estimate may be subject to significant volatility – or the availability of suitable alternative assets.
- The location of the underlying asset could significantly affect relocation costs or the availability of alternative assets. For example, even for two identical underlying assets, considerations about relocation costs or available alternative assets could vary widely if one is deployed in a remote area and the other in an easily accessible area.
- The jurisdiction governing the lease could significantly affect the assumptions about laws and regulations (including tax consequences) affecting the assessment of the option – e.g. laws and regulations in some countries may be more stable and predictable than in other countries.

5.1A.100.80   The lease term for cancellable leases – i.e. those that automatically renew on a day-to-day, week-to-week or month-to-month basis (often referred to as 'evergreen leases') – is determined in the same manner as for all other leases. This involves considering whether the lessee is reasonably certain to exercise one or more of the renewal options. The assessment is based on all relevant facts and circumstances that create an economic incentive for the lessee to exercise the option to renew.

EXAMPLE 11 – NO STATED LEASE TERM

5.1A.100.90   Lessor R leases equipment to Lessee E. There is no stated duration for the lease in the contract. E can terminate the lease at any time by returning the underlying asset to R's location. For each day that the asset remains in E's possession, E will pay a fixed fee to R for the right to use that asset.

5.1A.100.100   The non-cancellable period of the lease is one day because E could elect to return the asset to R's location before the start of Day 2. If E has an ongoing need to use an asset similar to the underlying asset in its business, then the costs to E of terminating the lease (e.g. returning the underlying asset to R's location) and entering into a new lease (e.g. identifying another asset, entering

into a different contract and training employees to use a different asset) may provide a compelling economic reason for E to continue to use the same asset for a period that is longer than the non-cancellable period – i.e. the lease term may be more than one day.

5.1A.100.110 The lease term starts when the lessor makes the underlying asset available for use by the lessee – i.e. on the commencement date. It includes any rent-free periods provided to the lessee by the lessor. This date may be earlier than the date on which actual use begins. For example, the lease term for a retail property may commence on 1 May 2018, but the lessee may need to customise the interior of the property before opening and starting to operate its retail store on 1 July 2018. Even if the lessee could not start customisation until 1 June 2018, the commencement date of the lease is 1 May 2018 because this is the date on which the lessor made the underlying asset available for use by the lessee (see 5.1A.60). [*IFRS 16.A, B36*]

5.1A.110 Economic life and useful life

5.1A.110.10 'Economic life' is either the period over which an asset is expected to be economically usable by one or more users or the number of production or similar units expected to be obtained from an asset by one or more users. [*IFRS 16.A*]

5.1A.110.20 'Useful life' is the period over which an asset is expected to be available for use by an entity or the number of production or similar units expected to be obtained from an asset by an entity. [*IFRS 16.A, IAS 16.6*]

5.1A.110.30 When a lessor classifies a lease as an operating or a finance lease, the lessor compares the lease term to the economic life of the underlying asset (see 5.1A.440). [*IFRS 16.63(c)*]

5.1A.110.40 In our view, the economic life of the asset for the purpose of assessing lease classification is its *remaining* economic life measured from the *commencement date* of the lease.

EXAMPLE 12 – REMAINING ECONOMIC LIFE

5.1A.110.50 Company L leases a new asset with an estimated economic life of 10 years to Company M under a five-year lease with no option for renewal. At the end of the lease term, L now estimates that the remaining economic life of the asset is seven years. Following expiry of the initial lease, L leases the asset to Company N for five years. For the purpose of determining the lease classification in this second lease, we believe that the economic life is seven years.

5.1A.120 Discount rates

5.1A.120.10 At commencement date, a lessee (see 5.1A.270) uses the interest rate implicit in the lease if this can be readily determined. If this cannot be readily determined, then the lessee uses its incremental borrowing rate. At inception, a lessor determines the interest rate implicit in the lease and uses it for the purposes of lease classification (see 5.1A.445, 485) and to measure the net investment in a finance lease (see 5.1A.510.10). [*IFRS 16.26, 63(d), 68*]

5.1A.120.20   A lessee is required to identify a discount rate for all leases other than those for which it elects to apply the recognition exemptions for short-term leases and leases in which the underlying item is of low value. [*IFRS 16.5*]

5.1A.120.30   The accounting for leases applies to individual leases. However, lessees and lessors are permitted to use a portfolio approach to determine the discount rate for the lease. This is permitted for a portfolio of leases with similar characteristics, if the entity reasonably expects that the effects on the financial statements of applying the portfolio approach would not differ materially from applying the standard to individual leases within that portfolio. [*IFRS 16.B1*]

5.1A.120.40   KPMG's publication *Leases: Discount rates* provides a more in-depth discussion of determination of the discount rate than this chapter. This chapter summarises the key points.

5.1A.125   *Rate implicit in the lease*

5.1A.125.10   The 'interest rate implicit in the lease' is the discount rate at which the sum of the present value of the lease payments and the unguaranteed residual value equals the sum of the fair value of the underlying asset and any initial direct costs of the lessor. [*IFRS 16.A*]

EXAMPLE 13 – INTEREST RATE IMPLICIT IN THE LEASE

5.1A.125.20   Lessor B enters into a lease of a motor vehicle with a lease term of five years. The fair value of the motor vehicle is 10,000 and B expects that its fair value at the end of the lease (i.e. the unguaranteed residual value) will be 1,000. Lease rentals are 2,000 per year, payable in arrears. B incurs initial direct costs of 500.

5.1A.125.30   B calculates the interest rate implicit in the lease as follows.

Lease inception (outflows of 10,000 + 500)	(10,500)
Year 1 (inflow of 2,000)	2,000
Year 2 (inflow of 2,000)	2,000
Year 3 (inflow of 2,000)	2,000
Year 4 (inflow of 2,000)	2,000
Year 5 (inflows of 2,000 + 1,000)	3,000

5.1A.125.40   B therefore calculates the interest rate implicit in the lease as the rate that sets the discounted inflows in years 1–5 equal to the outflow at inception – i.e. the internal rate of return of the above flows. In this case, that rate is 1.48%.

5.1A.125.50   Lease payments are defined differently for lessors and lessees (see 5.1A.70). It appears that a lessee should use the lease payments as defined for the lessor when determining the interest rate implicit in the lease. This is because the interest rate implicit in the lease is specific to the lessor and it is an entity-specific measure.

5.1A.125.60   There is no separate definition of the interest rate implicit in the lease for the lessee and lessor. The lack of information available to the lessee (e.g. the lessor's initial direct costs, the initial fair value of the underlying asset and the lessor's expectations of the residual value of the asset at the end of the lease) will typically make it difficult for the lessee to determine the interest rate implicit in the lease. Therefore, it is likely to be difficult for lessees to readily determine the interest rate implicit for most leases.

5.1A.130   *Lessee's incremental borrowing rate*

5.1A.130.10   The lessee's 'incremental borrowing rate' is the rate of interest that a lessee would have to pay to borrow over a similar term, and with a similar security, the funds necessary to obtain an asset of a similar value to the right-of-use asset in a similar economic environment. [*IFRS 16.A*]

5.1A.130.20   In practice, lenders may only provide partial funding for the acquisition of big-ticket assets – e.g. aircraft, ships or buildings. It appears that the incremental borrowing rate should be calculated using a 'blended' or 'weighted' rate at which the lessee would raise finance for 100% of the cost of an underlying asset.

EXAMPLE 14A – LESSEE'S INCREMENTAL BORROWING RATE – BIG-TICKET LEASES WITH AN LTV RATIO

5.1A.130.30   Company B enters into a lease of a ship. If B were to buy the ship, a loan-to-value (LTV) ratio of 80% would apply (i.e. the lender would provide funding for only 80% of the value of the ship) and B would finance the remaining 20% of the value by equity.

5.1A.130.40   In this case, the 20% equity financing is excluded from the calculation of the incremental borrowing rate because it does not reflect a rate at which B would have to *borrow* the funds necessary to obtain the asset. Instead, B will consider other sources of debt finance for the remaining 20% (e.g. bank loans, overdrafts etc). We believe that B should then determine a 'blended' or 'weighted' rate as follows: (80% × rate for secured borrowing) + (20% × rate for general borrowings).

5.1A.130.50   This rate should be adjusted for other factors (as appropriate) – e.g. the lease term compared with the loan duration, the security's age and quality, and the lessee's credit rating.

EXAMPLE 14B – LESSEE'S INCREMENTAL BORROWING RATE – BIG-TICKET LEASES WITH 100% FINANCE AT A PREMIUM RATE

5.1A.130.60   Modifying Example 14A, if Company B were to buy the ship, then the lender would offer to finance 100% of the cost of a ship, but at a premium rate.

5.1A.130.70   B determines its incremental borrowing rate by considering how it would arrange its borrowings in practice. We believe that in this case the incremental borrowing rate would be the lower of:

- the 'blended' or 'weighted' rate described in Example 14A: i.e. (80% × rate for secured borrowing) + (20% × rate for general borrowings); or
- the premium rate that a lender would charge if it financed 100% of the purchase of a ship.

5.1A.130.80   This rate should be adjusted for other factors (as appropriate) – e.g. the lease term compared with the loan duration, the security's age and quality, and the lessee's credit rating.

5.1A.140   RECOGNITION EXEMPTIONS FOR LESSEES

5.1A.140.10   A lessee can elect not to apply the lessee accounting model to:
- leases with a lease term (see 5.1A.100) of 12 months or less that do not contain a purchase option (i.e. short-term leases); and
- leases for which the underlying asset is of low value when it is new (even if the effect is material in aggregate). [*IFRS 16.A, 5*]

5.1A.140.20   The election for short-term leases is made by class of underlying asset, whereas the election for leases of low-value assets can be made on a lease-by-lease basis. A 'class of underlying asset' is a grouping of underlying assets of a similar nature and use in the lessee's operations. When electing the short-term lease exemption for a particular class of underlying asset, an entity considers only underlying assets from leases that meet the definition of a short-term lease. [*IFRS 16.8*]

5.1A.140.30   If a lessee elects either of these recognition exemptions, then it recognises the related lease payments as an expense on either a straight-line basis over the lease term or another systematic basis if that basis is more representative of the pattern of the lessee's benefit. [*IFRS 16.6*]

EXAMPLE 15A – RECOGNITION EXEMPTION – SHORT-TERM LEASE

5.1A.140.40   Lessee L manufactures toys. L enters into a 10-year lease of a non-specialised machine to be used in manufacturing parts for Racing Car X1. It expects this model of toy to remain popular with customers until it completes development and testing of an improved model – Racing Car X2. The current machine can be easily replaced and the cost to install it in L's manufacturing facility is not significant. L and Lessor M each have the right to terminate the lease without a penalty on each anniversary of the lease commencement date.

5.1A.140.50   Although the contract is for 10 years, the non-cancellable period is one year because both L and M have a substantive termination right – both can terminate the lease without penalty and the cost to install the machine in L's manufacturing facility is not significant (5.1A.100.50). As a result, the lease term is one year and the lease qualifies for the short-term lease exemption. [*IFRS 16.B34*]

5.1A.140.60 If a lessee elects the short-term lease recognition exemption and there are any changes to the lease term – e.g. the lessee exercises an option that it had previously determined that it was not reasonably certain to exercise – or the lease is modified, then the lessee accounts for the lease as a new lease. [*IFRS 16.7*]

EXAMPLE 15B – RECOGNITION EXEMPTION – SHORT-TERM LEASE AND CHANGE IN LEASE TERM

Assessment on lease commencement

5.1A.140.70 Lessee S enters into a contract with Lessor T to lease a piece of non-specialised equipment for 12 months for construction work at one of its factories. The contract includes two 12-month renewal options with no change in payments. The lease does not contain a purchase option.

5.1A.140.80 At lease commencement, S determines that it is not reasonably certain to exercise the renewal options, considering all relevant economic factors. This is because S expects to complete its construction work within the first 12 months. S concludes that the lease term is 12 months.

5.1A.140.90 Therefore, the lease qualifies for the short-term exemption because the lease term is no longer than 12 months and there is no purchase option in the contract. On entering into this lease, S elects to apply the short-term lease exemption to all short-term leases of assets in the same class of underlying asset.

5.1A.140.100 In applying the short-term lease exemption, S recognises the lease payments as an expense on a straight-line basis over the lease term.

Short-term lease that no longer meets the definition after a change in the lease term

5.1A.140.110 Ten months after entering into the lease, S expands the scope and duration of construction work at its factory, so that it now expects to have an on-going need to use the equipment throughout the second year. Market prices have increased such that S has an economic incentive to extend the existing lease rather than enter into a new lease. S therefore gives binding notice that it will exercise its option to extend the lease for a further 12 months.

5.1A.140.120 Because there has been a change in the lease term, S accounts for a new lease. The new lease term is 14 months (two remaining months from the initial lease term plus 12 additional months), so it no longer meets the definition of a short-term lease. S therefore recognises a right-of-use asset and a lease liability.

5.1A.140.130 IFRS 16 does not specify a threshold for the low-value exemption, but the basis for conclusions states that the IASB 'had in mind' assets with a value of approximately USD 5,000 or less when they are new, such as small IT equipment (e.g. some laptops, desktops, tablets, mobile phones, individual printers) and some office furniture – i.e. 'inexpensive' assets. The exemption is not intended to capture underlying assets such as cars and most photocopiers. [*IFRS 16.B6, B8, BC98–BC104*]

EXAMPLE 15C – RECOGNITION EXEMPTION – LOW-VALUE ITEMS

5.1A.140.140 Lessee B is in the pharmaceutical manufacturing and distribution industry and leases the following:
- real estate, both office building and warehouse;
- inexpensive office furniture;
- company cars, both for sales personnel and for senior management and of varying quality, specification and value;
- trucks and vans used for delivery; and
- inexpensive IT equipment – e.g. laptops.

5.1A.140.150 B determines that the leases of inexpensive office furniture and laptops qualify for the recognition exemption on the basis that the underlying assets, when they are new, are individually of low value. Although the low-value exemption can be applied on a lease-by-lease basis, B elects to apply the exemption to all of these leases. In contrast, B applies the recognition and measurement requirements of IFRS 16 to its leases of real estate, company cars, trucks and vans. [*IFRS 16.IE3*]

5.1A.140.160 A lessee does not apply the low-value exemption to a lease of an individual asset in either of the following scenarios:
- if the underlying asset is highly dependent on, or highly inter-related with, other assets; or
- if the lessee cannot benefit from the underlying asset on its own or together with other readily available resources, irrespective of the value of that underlying asset. [*IFRS 16.B5*]

5.1A.140.170 The low-value exemption also does not apply to a head lease for an asset that is sub-leased or that is expected to be sub-leased. When a lessee neither enters into a sub-lease immediately nor expects to do so later, it may elect to apply the exemption. [*IFRS 16.B7*]

5.1A.140.180 However, if a lessee initially elects to use the low-value exemption – because it expects not to sub-lease the asset – but subsequently does enter into a sub-lease, then the lease would no longer qualify for the exemption. It appears that at the date of the change, the lessee should consider the lease to be a new lease. In these cases, the lessee also considers whether the reason for the change in intention provides evidence as to whether other leases of low-value items do or do not qualify for the exemption. [*IFRS 16.B7*]

5.1A.150 IDENTIFYING A LEASE

5.1A.160 Overview

5.1A.160.10 An entity assesses at inception of a contract whether that contract is, or contains, a lease. A contract is, or contains, a lease if it conveys the right to control the use of an identified asset for a period of time in exchange for consideration. [*IFRS 16.9*]

5.1A.160.20 The key elements of the definition are therefore as follows.

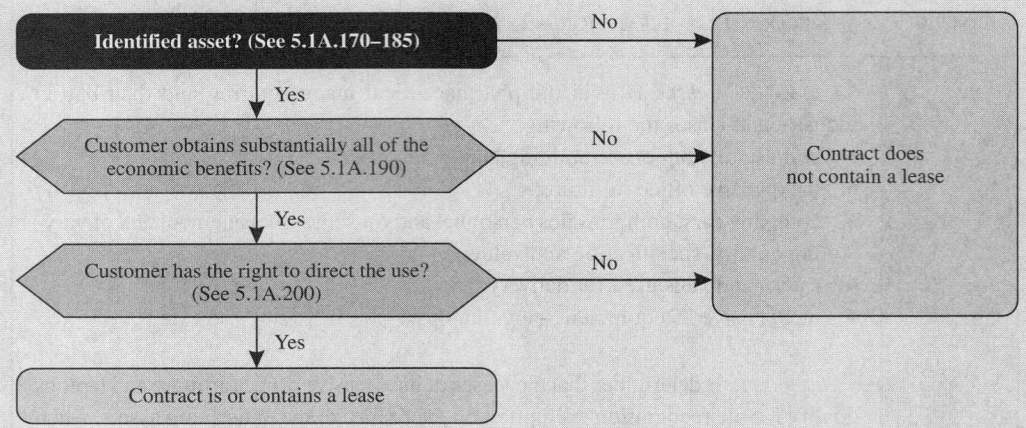

5.1A.160.30 KPMG's publication *Lease Definition* provides a more in-depth discussion of the identification of a lease than this chapter. This chapter summarises the key points. When discussing lease identification, we sometimes use the terms 'supplier' and 'customer' to refer to the parties to the contract that may be, or contain, a lease. That is, the supplier is the potential lessor and the customer is the potential lessee.

5.1A.170   Identified asset

5.1A.170.10   A contract contains a lease only if it relates to an identified asset.

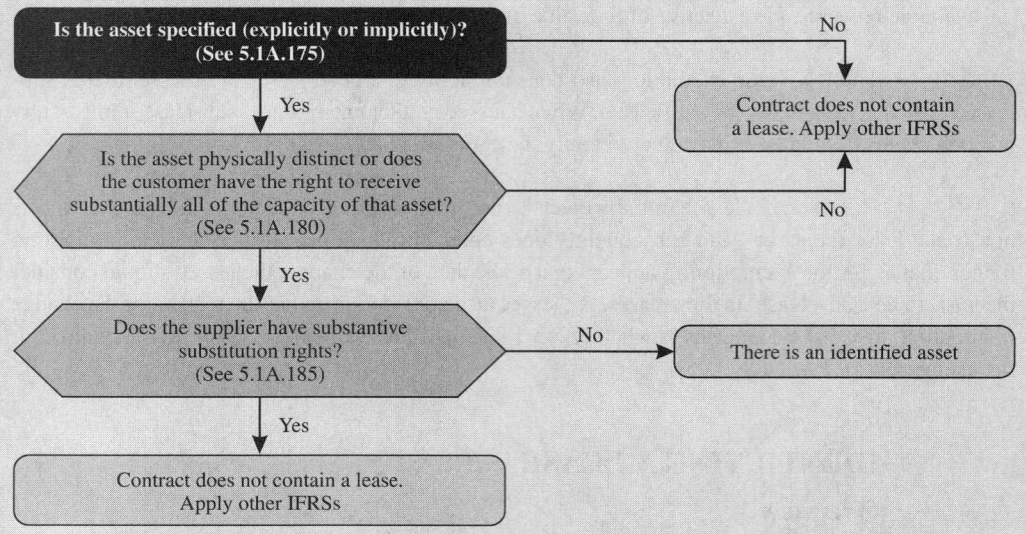

5.1A.175   *Specified asset*

5.1A.175.10   An asset can be either explicitly specified in a contract (e.g. by serial number or a specified floor of a building) or implicitly specified when it is made available for use by the customer. [*IFRS 16.B13*]

5.1A.175.20 An asset is implicitly specified if the facts and circumstances indicate that the supplier can fulfil its obligations only by using a specific asset. This may be the case if the supplier has only one asset that can fulfil the contract. For example, a power plant may be an implicitly specified asset in a power purchase contract if the customer's facility is in a remote location with no access to the grid, such that the supplier cannot buy the required energy in the market or generate it from an alternative power plant.

5.1A.175.30 In other cases, an asset may be implicitly specified if the supplier owns a number of assets with the required functionality, but only one of those assets can realistically be supplied to the customer within the contracted timeframe – i.e. the supplier does not have a substantive right to substitute an alternative asset to fulfil the contract. For example, a supplier may own a fleet of vessels but only one vessel that is in the required geographic area and not already being used by other customers.

5.1A.180 *Capacity portions*

5.1A.180.10 A capacity portion of an asset can be an identified asset if it is physically distinct – e.g. a floor of a building. In addition, a capacity portion that is not physically distinct is also an identified asset if it represents substantially all of the capacity of the asset. For example, a capacity portion of a fibre-optic cable is an identified asset if it represents substantially all of the capacity of the cable. [*IFRS 16.B20*]

5.1A.180.20 IFRS 16 does not define 'substantially all' in the context of the definition of a lease. For a discussion of the meaning of 'substantially all' in the context of the classification of a lease by a lessor, see 5.1A.445.20. In assessing rights over a capacity portion, an entity considers all relevant substantive rights, including rights of first refusal.

EXAMPLE 16A – IDENTIFIED ASSET – CAPACITY PORTION IS NOT AN IDENTIFIED ASSET

5.1A.180.30 Company D enters into an arrangement with Company E for the right to store its gas in E's specified storage tank. The storage tank has no separate compartments. At inception of the contract, D has the right to use up to 60% of the capacity of the storage tank throughout the term of the contract. E can use the other 40% of the storage tank as it sees fit.

5.1A.180.40 E has no substitution rights. However, the arrangement allows E to store gas from other customers in the same storage tank.

Storage tank

Storage rights of Company D 60%	Storage rights of other customers 40%

5.1A.180.50 In this example, there is no identified asset. This is because D only has rights to 60% of the storage tank's capacity and that capacity portion is not physically distinct – i.e. is not physically separated – from the remainder of the tank, and does not represent substantially all of the capacity of the storage tank.

EXAMPLE 16B – IDENTIFIED ASSET – CAPACITY PORTION IS AN IDENTIFIED ASSET

5.1A.180.60 Company C enters into an arrangement with Company S for the right to store C's products in a specified warehouse. Within this warehouse, Rooms V, W and X are contractually allocated to C for its exclusive use. S has no substitution rights. Rooms V, W and X represent 60% of the warehouse's total storage capacity.

Warehouse

Room V	Room W	Room X	Room Y	Room Z
Reserved for use by Company C				

5.1A.180.70 In this example, there is an identified asset. This is because:
- the rooms are explicitly specified in the contract;
- the rooms are physically distinct from the other storage locations within the warehouse; and
- S has no (substantive) substitution rights.

EXAMPLE 16C – IDENTIFIED ASSET – RIGHT OF FIRST REFUSAL

5.1A.180.80 Company O enters into a 10-year contract with Company B for 70% of the capacity of a specific gas pipeline. O also has a right of first refusal over the remaining 30% of the capacity of the pipeline.

5.1A.180.90 In this example, O is entitled to substantially all of the capacity of the pipeline, given that it uses 70% of the capacity and has the right of first refusal for the other 30%. Therefore, the pipeline is an identified asset.

5.1A.180.100 However, O's right of first refusal would not be considered if it is not substantive. For example, if the amount that Company O would be required to pay to use the additional 30% of capacity was so high that there was no realistic commercial possibility that O would ever purchase that additional capacity, then the pipeline would not be an identified asset.

5.1A.180.110 In some cases, there is a difference between an asset's nominal capacity and the capacity expected to be used by customers. Determining an asset's capacity for assessing whether the customer has the right to receive substantially all of the capacity of the asset may involve judgement and requires consideration of all facts and circumstances – e.g. considering the reason for the unused excess capacity.

EXAMPLE 16D – IDENTIFIED ASSET – EXPECTED CAPACITY

5.1A.180.120 Company O enters into a 30-year contract with Company B to transport gas through a pipeline. B builds and operates a new pipeline to transport O's gas. O determines the quantities of gas to be sent in the pipeline. B anticipates that O

will need additional capacity in the future and decides to build the pipeline with excess capacity – i.e. at commencement date, O uses only 70% of the pipeline's nominal capacity. The pipeline is located in an area where the probability that another customer would use the excess capacity is remote.

5.1A.180.130 B and O assess whether there is an identified asset based on the capacity expected to be used by O and other parties – i.e. 70%. This is consistent with assessing whether the customer has a right to obtain substantially all of the economic benefits from using the asset throughout the period of use (see 5.1A.190). Consequently, in this example O uses all of the expected capacity and, therefore, the pipeline qualifies as an identified asset.

5.1A.185 Substantive supplier substitution rights

5.1A.185.10 A customer (the potential lessee) does not control the use of an identified asset if the supplier (the potential lessor) has a substantive right to substitute an alternative asset. Such a right exists if the supplier:
- has the practical ability to substitute the asset throughout the period of use (see 5.1A.40 and 185.40–50); and
- would benefit economically from exercising its right to substitute the asset (see 5.1A.185.60–80). [*IFRS 16.B14*]

5.1A.185.20 An entity assesses whether substitution rights are substantive at inception of the contract. At that time, the entity considers all of the facts and circumstances – but not future events that are not likely to occur. [*IFRS 16.B16*]

5.1A.185.30 A right or obligation to substitute the asset for repairs and maintenance because the asset is not working properly – i.e. a 'warranty-type' obligation – or because a technical upgrade becomes available is not a substantive substitution right. [*IFRS 16.B18*]

5.1A.185.40 A supplier has the practical ability to substitute alternative assets when the customer cannot prevent it from substituting the asset and the supplier has alternative assets either readily available or available within a reasonable period of time. [*IFRS 16.B14(a)*]

5.1A.185.50 However, there is no practical ability to substitute the asset *throughout* the period of use (and therefore there is no substantive substitution right) if the substitution right applies, for example, only:
- to a part of the period of use or at or after a specific date; or
- on the occurrence of a particular event. [*IFRS 16.B15*]

5.1A.185.60 A supplier would benefit economically from the exercise of its right to substitute the asset when the economic benefits associated with substituting the asset are expected to exceed the related costs. [*IFRS 16.B14(b)*]

5.1A.185.70 Judgement is required to evaluate when the economic benefits associated with substituting the asset are expected to exceed the costs associated with doing so. Examples of factors to consider include:

- the availability of other assets to fulfil the contract;
- the alternative use of the asset and additional benefits for the supplier;
- the costs that would be incurred to substitute the asset (e.g. costs of relocation, disruption of activity during a period of time);
- the feasibility of substituting the asset (because of size, remote location etc); and
- whether the asset is located at the premises of the supplier or customer. [*IFRS 16.B17*]

5.1A.185.80 Because this analysis is performed from the supplier's perspective, it is more difficult for the customer to determine whether the substitution right is substantive. If this cannot be readily determined, then the customer presumes that any substitution right is not substantive. [*IFRS 16.B19, BC115*]

EXAMPLE 17A – IDENTIFIED ASSET – SUBSTANTIVE SUBSTITUTION RIGHT

5.1A.185.90 Company L enters into a five-year contract with Freight Carrier M for the use of rail cars from M to transport a specified quantity of goods. M uses rail cars of a particular specification, and has a large pool of similar rail cars that can be used to fulfil the requirements of the contract. The rail cars and engines are stored at M's premises when they are not being used to transport goods. The costs associated with substituting the rail cars are minimal for M.

5.1A.185.100 Relevant experience demonstrates that:
- M benefits economically from being able to deploy alternative assets as necessary to fulfil its contracts with customers; and
- the conditions that make substitution economically beneficial are likely to continue throughout the period of use.

5.1A.185.110 In this case, because the rail cars are stored at M's premises, it has a large pool of similar rail cars and substitution costs are minimal, M has the practical ability to substitute the assets – i.e. the rail cars are not implicitly specified. In addition, the substitution is economically beneficial to M throughout the period of use. Therefore, M's substitution rights are substantive and the arrangement does not contain a lease.

EXAMPLE 17B – IDENTIFIED ASSET – NO SUBSTANTIVE SUBSTITUTION RIGHT

5.1A.185.120 Company L enters into an eight-year contract with Company K that requires K to install and maintain specific lighting equipment at L's stores. The equipment is designed and selected by K, subject to L's approval. K has an option to upgrade the equipment for future technological advancements and an obligation to replace any damaged or defective equipment. However, the equipment is large and costly to transport and install. Therefore, it is not economically feasible or practicable for K to substitute alternative assets once the equipment is installed – i.e. the costs of substitution would exceed the benefits.

5.1A.185.130 Therefore, the substitution rights are not substantive and so fulfilment of the arrangement is dependent on the use of identified assets.

5.1A.190   **Economic benefits**

5.1A.190.10   To determine whether a contract conveys the right to control the use of an identified asset, an entity assesses whether the customer – the potential lessee – has the rights to:

- obtain substantially all of the economic benefits from using the identified asset throughout the period of use; and
- direct the use of the identified asset throughout the period of use (see 5.1A.200). [*IFRS 16.B9*]

5.1A.190.20   The economic benefits from using an asset include its primary output, by-products and other economic benefits from using the asset that could be realised from a commercial transaction with a third party (e.g. sub-leasing the asset). The benefits derived from *ownership* of the asset (e.g. income tax credits) are excluded from the analysis. [*IFRS 16.B21, BC118*]

5.1A.190.30   An entity considers the economic benefits that are in the defined scope of the right to use the asset – e.g. if a contract limits the use of a vehicle to only one particular territory during the period of use, then the entity considers only the economic benefits from use of the vehicle within that territory, and not beyond. [*IFRS 16.B22*]

EXAMPLE 18 – ECONOMIC BENEFITS – PRIMARY PRODUCTS AND BY-PRODUCTS

> 5.1A.190.40   Utility Company C enters into a 20-year contract with Power Company D to purchase all of the electricity produced by a new solar farm. D owns the solar farm and will receive tax credits relating to the construction and ownership of the solar farm, and C will receive renewable energy credits that accrue from use of the solar farm.
>
> 5.1A.190.50   C has the right to obtain substantially all of the economic benefits from use of the solar farm over the 20-year period because it obtains:
> - the electricity produced by the farm over the lease term – i.e. the primary product from use of the asset; and
> - the renewable energy credits – i.e. the by-product from use of the asset.
>
> 5.1A.190.60   Although D receives economic benefits from the solar farm in the form of tax credits, these economic benefits relate to the *ownership* of the solar farm. The tax credits do not relate to *use* of the solar farm and therefore are not considered in this assessment. [*IFRS 16.IE2.Ex9A*]

5.1A.190.70   The existence of variable lease payments derived from the use of an asset – e.g. a percentage of sales from use of a retail space – does not prevent an entity from having the right to obtain substantially all of the economic benefits from use of the asset. In these cases, although the entity passes on certain benefits to the supplier, the entity receives the cash flows arising from use of the asset. [*IFRS 16.B23*]

5.1A.190.80   Profit-sharing arrangements generally do not prevent an entity from obtaining all of the economic benefits from use of an identified asset throughout the period of its use. However, when the customer obtains a fixed rate of return and the supplier receives or absorbs all of the variability in net operating profits, it is not clear whether a contract contains a lease, particularly if the supplier also receives most of the economic benefits from use of the asset.

5.1A.190.90   For example, a supplier may receive most of the cash flows from the use of an asset in a business such as a casino, hotel or investment property, and the customer may receive a fixed return. In this situation, careful consideration needs to be given to the substance of the contract, including the nature of the arrangement between the parties, when determining which party receives the economic benefits from use of the identified asset. It is necessary to assess whether there is an agent-principal relationship between the parties, in which case there is no lease.

5.1A.190.100   For a discussion of the meaning of 'substantially all', see 5.1A.445.20.

5.1A.200   Right to direct the use

5.1A.205   *Overview*

5.1A.205.10   A customer – the potential lessee – has the right to direct the use of an identified asset in either of the following situations:
- the customer has the right to direct how and for what purpose the asset is used throughout the period of use (see 5.1A.210, 215); or
- all relevant decisions about how and for what purpose the asset is used are predetermined (see 5.1A.220) and:
    - the customer has the right to operate the asset (or to direct others to operate the asset in a manner that it determines) throughout the period of use, without the supplier having the right to change those operating instructions; or
    - the customer designed the asset (or specific aspects of the asset) in a way that predetermined how and for what purpose the asset will be used throughout the period of use. [*IFRS 16.B24*]

5.1A.205.20   The following diagram summarises the assessment of the right to direct the use.

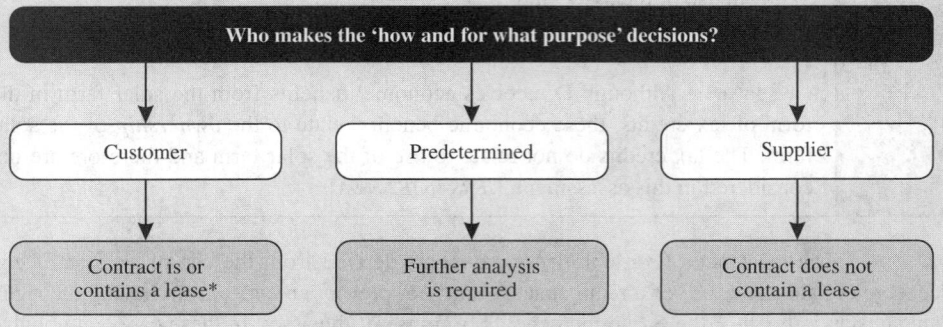

*   If other criteria are met (see 5.1A.160.20).

5.1A.205.30   IFRS 16 effectively requires a three-fold classification of decision-making rights into the following categories, which feature in the analysis in different ways.
- *'How and for what purpose' (or 'relevant') decisions:* Unless they are predetermined, these determine whether the arrangement contains a lease (see 5.1A.210–215).

- *Operating decisions:* These are ignored, unless the how and for what purpose decisions are pre-determined, in which case there is a lease if the customer makes the operating decisions and the other criteria for a lease are met (see 5.1A.220).
- *Protective rights:* These typically define the scope of the customer's right to use an asset but do not, in isolation, preclude a conclusion that there is a lease. However, when protective rights are too restrictive for the customer to have any substantive decision-making authority over the use of the asset, this could indicate that the how and for what purpose decisions are predetermined (see 5.1A.225).

5.1A.210 *How and for what purpose decisions*

5.1A.210.10   In assessing who has the right to direct how and for what purpose the asset is used, an entity considers the decision-making rights that are most relevant to changing how and for what purpose the asset is used during the period of use. Decision-making rights are 'relevant' when they affect the economic benefits derived from the use. [*IFRS 16.B25*]

5.1A.210.20   Examples of relevant decision-making rights that, depending on the circumstances, grant the right to change how and for what purpose the asset is used include the following.
- *What:* Rights to change the type of output that is produced by the asset – e.g. deciding whether to use a shipping container to transport goods or for storage.
- *When:* Rights to change when the output is produced – e.g. deciding when a power plant will generate power.
- *Where:* Rights to change where the output is produced – e.g. deciding on the destination of a truck or a ship.
- *Whether and how much:* Rights to change whether the output is produced, and the quantity of that output – e.g. deciding whether to produce energy from a power plant and how much energy. [*IFRS 16.B26*]

5.1A.210.30   Examples of decision-making rights that do not grant the right to change how and for what purpose the asset is used include: rights to operate an asset, rights to maintain an asset, or rights to take output that has already been produced. However, rights to operate an asset drive the analysis if the relevant decisions about how and for what purpose an asset is used are predetermined. [*IFRS 16.B27, B29*]

EXAMPLE 19A – RIGHT TO DIRECT THE USE – DECISION TO TAKE OUTPUT

5.1A.210.40   Company M enters into a 20-year contract with Company S, a solar developer, to install, operate and maintain a solar plant on M's facility. The solar plant has been designed by S to fulfil M's energy demand. M has the right to purchase any energy produced and S has the obligation to sell the energy to M whenever M wants to purchase it. Energy that is not purchased by M is sold into the grid – i.e. M has no obligation to purchase energy.

5.1A.210.50   In this example, M's decision as to whether to purchase the electricity from the solar plant affects only to whom the existing output is directed (to M or the grid). It does not affect when, where, whether or how much energy is produced (see 5.1A.210.30). Therefore, it is not a how and for what purpose decision.

5.1A.215 ***Determining who makes the how and for what purpose decisions***

5.1A.215.10 An entity has the right to direct how and for what purpose the asset is used if, in the scope of its rights of use defined in the contract, it can change how and for what purpose the asset is used throughout the period of use (see 5.1A.210). [*IFRS 16.B25*]

5.1A.215.20 In assessing whether an entity has the right to direct the use of an asset, only the rights to make decisions about the asset's use during the period of use are considered. Decisions that are predetermined before the period of use – i.e. commencement date – are not considered. [*IFRS 16.B29*]

EXAMPLE 19B – RIGHT TO DIRECT THE USE – HOW AND FOR WHAT PURPOSE DECISIONS – SHIP

5.1A.215.30 Company T enters into a five-year contract with Company U, a ship owner, for the use of an identified ship. T decides whether and what cargo will be transported, and when and to which ports the ship will sail throughout the period of use, subject to restrictions specified in the contract. These restrictions prevent T from sailing the ship into waters at a high risk of piracy or carrying explosive materials as cargo. U operates and maintains the ship, and is responsible for safe passage.

5.1A.215.40 T has the right to direct the use of the ship. The contractual restrictions are protective rights that protect U's investment in the ship and its personnel (see 5.1A.225). In the scope of its right of use, T determines how and for what purpose the ship is used throughout the five-year period because it decides whether, where and when the ship sails, as well as deciding the cargo that it will transport. T has the right to change these decisions throughout the period of use. Therefore, in this example the contract contains a lease. [*IFRS 16.IE2.Ex6B*]

EXAMPLE 19C – RIGHT TO DIRECT THE USE – HOW AND FOR WHAT PURPOSE DECISIONS – LIGHTING EQUIPMENT

5.1A.215.50 Continuing Example 17B, to optimise the lighting equipment's usage, Company K monitors the equipment remotely and performs maintenance on it as needed. However, Company L specifies the hours of operation and the level of brightness. These impact the amount of consideration that L pays, which is based on usage.

5.1A.215.60 In this example, L directs the use of the assets because it directs how and for what purpose the assets are used by specifying the following (including changes within a reasonable variance):
- the hours of operation (i.e. when, whether and how much output is produced); and
- the level of brightness (i.e. how much output is produced).

5.1A.215.70 An entity does not have to make all of the how and for what purpose decisions in order to have the right to direct the use of the asset – the decisions can be allocated between the parties. Judgement is required to assess the individual significance of the different how and for what purpose decisions – i.e. their impact on the economic benefits.

5.1A.215.80   If some decisions have greater significance than others, then the party that makes the more significant decisions generally directs the right to use the asset.

EXAMPLE 19D – RIGHT TO DIRECT THE USE – EACH PARTY TAKES SOME DECISIONS

5.1A.215.90   Retailer T enters into a contract with Landlord L to use a specific retail unit for a five-year period. The unit is part of a larger retail space with many retail units. The contract requires T to use the unit to operate its well-known store brand to sell its goods during the hours when the larger retail space is open. L can make reasonable changes to the opening hours of the larger retail space. T decides on the mix of goods sold from the unit, their pricing and the quantity of inventory held. [*IFRS 16.IE2.Ex4*]

5.1A.215.100   In this example, there are a number of how and for what purpose decisions that are not predetermined. L can make reasonable changes to the opening hours. However, by deciding on the mix of goods, their pricing and available quantities, T makes the decisions that will have a more significant impact on the economic benefits derived from the unit. Therefore, it is T who directs the right to use the unit.

5.1A.220   ***How and for what purpose decisions are predetermined***

5.1A.220.10   The decisions about how and for what purpose the asset is used can be predetermined in different ways. They could, for example, be agreed between the entity and the supplier in negotiating the contract, with neither party being able to change them after the commencement date, or they could, in effect, be predetermined by the design of the asset. However, situations in which *all* how and for what purpose decisions are predetermined are likely to be rare. [*IFRS 16.24, BC121*]

EXAMPLE 19E – RIGHT TO DIRECT THE USE – PREDETERMINED DECISIONS – SHIP

5.1A.220.20   Company R enters into a contract with Company S, a ship owner, for the transport of cargo from A Coruña to Hartlepool on an identified ship. The contract details the cargo to be transported on the ship and the dates of pick-up and delivery. The cargo will occupy substantially all of the capacity of the ship. S operates and maintains the ship and is responsible for the safe passage of the cargo on board the ship. R is prohibited from hiring another operator for the ship during the term of the contract or operating the ship itself.

5.1A.220.30   R does not have the right to control the use of the ship because it does not have the right to direct its use. R does not have the right to direct how and for what purpose the ship is used; these decisions are predetermined in the contract – i.e. the journey from A Coruña to Hartlepool transporting specified cargo within a specified timeframe. R does not have the right to operate the ship and did not design the ship in a way that predetermined how and for what purpose it would be used. R has the same rights over the use of the ship as if it were only one of many customers transporting cargo on the ship. Therefore, the contract does not contain a lease. [*IFRS 16.IE2.Ex6A*]

EXAMPLE 19F – RIGHT TO DIRECT THE USE – CUSTOMER DESIGNED THE ASSET

5.1A.220.40   Company C enters into a 20-year contract with Energy Supplier E to install, operate and maintain a solar plant for C's energy supply. C designed the solar plant before it was constructed; C hired experts in solar energy to help in determining the location of the plant and the engineering of the equipment to be used. C has the exclusive right to receive and the obligation to take all energy produced.

5.1A.220.50   In this example, the nature of the solar plant is such that all of the decisions about how and for what purpose the asset is used are predetermined because:
- the type of output (i.e. energy) and the production location are predetermined in the agreement; and
- when, whether and how much energy is produced are influenced by the sunlight and the design of the solar plant.

5.1A.220.60   Because C designed the solar plant and thereby programmed into it any decisions about how and for what purpose it is used, C is considered to have the right to direct the use. Although regular maintenance of the solar plant may increase the efficiency of the solar panels, it does not give E the right to direct how and for what purpose the solar plant is used. [*IFRS 16.IE2.Ex9A*]

5.1A.220.70   As illustrated in Example 19F, in some cases, an entity's (or its specialist's) decisions about the location of the asset and the engineering of the equipment could be sufficient to conclude that the entity designed specific aspects of the asset when the location is key for the performance of the asset (e.g. for solar or wind farms). However, judgement applies and the individual facts and circumstances need to be considered.

5.1A.225   *Protective rights*

5.1A.225.10   A contract may include certain terms and conditions designed to protect the supplier's interest in the identified asset or other assets, to protect its personnel or to ensure the supplier's compliance with laws or regulations. These protective rights typically define the scope of the right to use an asset but do not, in isolation, prevent an entity from having the right to direct the use of the asset within that scope. [*IFRS 16.B30*]

5.1A.225.20   For example, a contract may:
- specify the maximum amount of use of an asset or where or when the entity can use the asset;
- require an entity to follow particular operating practices; or
- require an entity to inform the supplier of changes in how an asset will be used. [*IFRS 16.B30*]

EXAMPLE 20 – DEFINITION OF A LEASE – PROTECTIVE RIGHTS

5.1A.225.30   Company L enters into a two-year contract with Company M, an aircraft owner, for the use of an identified aircraft. The contract details the interior and exterior specifications for the aircraft. It also contains contractual and legal restrictions on where the aircraft can fly. Subject to these restrictions, L determines where and when the aircraft will fly, and which passengers and cargo will be transported on it. M is responsible for operating the aircraft, using its own crew.

5.1A.225.40   The restrictions on where the aircraft can fly define the scope of L's right to use the aircraft. In the scope of its right of use, L determines how and for what purpose the aircraft is used throughout the two-year period of use because it decides whether, where and when the aircraft travels, as well as deciding the passengers and cargo that it will transport. L has the right to change these decisions throughout the period of use.

5.1A.225.50   The contractual and legal restrictions on where the aircraft can fly are protective rights and do not prevent L from having the right to direct the use of the asset. [*IFRS 16.IE2.Ex7*]

5.1A.230   SEPARATING LEASE AND NON-LEASE COMPONENTS

5.1A.230.10   If a contract is, or contains, a lease, then an entity accounts for each separate lease component separately from non-lease components following a two-step approach. [*IFRS 16.12*]

5.1A.240   Step 1: Identify the component(s)

5.1A.240.10   An entity considers the right to use an underlying asset as a separate lease component if it meets the following criteria:
- the lessee can benefit from using that underlying asset either on its own or together with other resources that are readily available; and
- the asset is neither highly dependent on, nor highly inter-related with, the other assets in the contract. [*IFRS 16.B32(a)–(b)*]

5.1A.240.20   Charges for administrative tasks or other costs incurred associated with the lease that do not transfer a good or service to the lessee do not give rise to a separate component. However, they are part of the total consideration that an entity allocates to the identified components. [*IFRS 16.B33*]

5.1A.250   Step 2: Account for the component(s)

5.1A.250.10   The following table summarises the process for accounting for lease and non-lease components from both the lessee and lessor perspectives. [*IFRS 16.13–17, B33*]

	LESSEE	LESSOR
When there is an observable stand-alone price for each component	Unless the practical expedient is elected (see below), separate and allocate based on the relative stand-alone price of components (see 5.1A.255.10–20).	Always separate and allocate following the IFRS 15 approach – i.e. on a relative stand-alone selling price basis (see 5.1A.260.10).
When there is no observable stand-alone price for some or all components	Maximise the use of observable information (see 5.1A.255.30).	

	LESSEE	LESSOR
Property taxes, insurance on the property and administrative costs	Activities (or costs of the lessor) that do not transfer a good or service to the lessee are not components in a contract. Include payments related to these costs as part of total consideration allocated to identified components (see 5.1A.240.20).	
Practical expedient: accounting policy election by class of underlying asset	Combine lease and any associated non-lease component(s) and account for them as a single lease component (see 5.1A.255.40).	N/A

5.1A.255 *Lessee perspective*

5.1A.255.10   If a contract contains a lease component and one or more additional lease or non-lease components, then the lessee allocates the consideration in the contract to each lease component on the basis of:

- the relative stand-alone price of each lease component; and
- the aggregate stand-alone price of the non-lease components. [*IFRS 16.13*]

5.1A.255.20   The lessee determines the relative stand-alone prices of lease and non-lease components based on the price that a lessor or a similar supplier would charge an entity for a similar component separately. [*IFRS 16.14*]

5.1A.255.30   If an observable stand-alone price is not readily available, then the lessee estimates the stand-alone price of the components by maximising the use of observable information. [*IFRS 16.14*]

5.1A.255.40   As a practical expedient a lessee can elect, by class of underlying asset, not to separate lease components from any associated non-lease components. A lessee that makes this election accounts for the lease component and the associated non-lease component(s) as a single lease component. [*IFRS 16.15*]

5.1A.255.50   If the lessee applies the practical expedient in 5.1A.255.40, then the nature of the individual components – e.g. whether they are fixed or variable depending on a rate or index – does not change.

EXAMPLE 21 – PRACTICAL EXPEDIENT TO COMBINE LEASE AND NON-LEASE COMPONENTS

5.1A.255.60   Lessee B enters into a five-year lease of a photocopier. The lease payments are 10,000 per year and the contract includes an additional maintenance charge calculated as 0.008 per page processed. Payments are due at the end of each year. B elects to apply the practical expedient to combine lease and non-lease components.

5.1A.255.70   At the commencement date, B measures the lease liability as the present value of the fixed lease payments (i.e. five annual payments of 10,000). Although B has elected to apply the practical expedient to combine non-lease components (i.e. maintenance costs) with the lease component, B excludes the non-lease costs from its lease liability because they are variable payments that depend on usage. That is, the nature of the costs does not become fixed just because B has elected not to separate them from the fixed lease payments. [*IFRS 16.15*]

5.1A.255.80   Unless a lessee applies the practical expedient, it accounts for non-lease components in accordance with other applicable standards. [*IFRS 16.16*]

EXAMPLE 22 – ACCOUNTING BY LESSEE FOR LEASE AND NON-LEASE COMPONENTS

5.1A.255.90   Lessee L enters into a five-year lease contract with Lessor M to use a ship, including crew. The contract includes maintenance services provided by M. M obtains its own insurance for the ship. Annual payments are 20,000, including 3,000 for maintenance services and 500 for insurance costs. L is able to determine that similar maintenance services and insurance costs are offered by third parties for 2,000 and 500 a year, respectively. L is also able to determine that similar leases for ships without crew, maintenance or insurance are offered by third parties for 15,000 a year and, using a cost-plus calculation, L estimates the annual cost of crew hire to be 5,000.

5.1A.255.100   In this case:
- the observable stand-alone price for maintenance services is 2,000;
- the estimated stand-alone price for the services rendered by the crew is 5,000;
- the observable stand-alone price for the lease is 15,000; and
- the insurance cost does not transfer a good or service to the lessee and therefore is not a separate component.

5.1A.255.110   Therefore, L allocates 13,636 ((15,000 / 22,000[1]) × 20,000) to the lease component.

> Note
> 1.   Total stand-alone prices of lease and non-lease components calculated as 2,000 + 5,000 + 15,000.

5.1A.260   *Lessor perspective*

5.1A.260.10   If a contract contains a lease component and one or more additional lease or non-lease components, then the lessor allocates the consideration in the contract in accordance with the requirements of IFRS 15 – i.e. according to the stand-alone selling prices of the goods and services included in each component. [*IFRS 16.17*]

5.1A.270   LESSEE ACCOUNTING

5.1A.270.10   A lessee applies a single lease accounting model under which it recognises all leases on-balance sheet at the commencement date, unless it elects to apply the recognition exemptions. A lessee recognises a right-of-use asset representing its right to use the underlying asset and a lease liability representing its obligation to make lease payments. [*IFRS 16.IN10, 5, 22*]

5.1A.280   Initial measurement of the lease liability

5.1A.280.10   At the commencement date, a lessee measures the lease liability at the present value of the future lease payments using the interest rate implicit in the lease if it is readily determinable. If the lessee cannot readily determine the interest rate implicit in the lease, then it uses its incremental borrowing rate at the commencement date (see 5.1A.70 and 125.60). [*IFRS 16.26*]

5.1A.280.20 Lease liabilities are financial liabilities measured in accordance with IFRS 16. However, they are subject to the derecognition requirements of IFRS 9. In addition, a derivative instrument embedded in a lease is accounted for in accordance with IFRS 9 (see 5.1A.25). [*IFRS 9.2.1(b), 9.4.3.3*]

5.1A.290 Initial measurement of the right-of-use asset

5.1A.290.10 At the commencement date, a lessee measures the right-of-use asset at cost, which includes the following:
- the amount of the initial measurement of the lease liability (see 5.1A.280);
- any lease payments made at or before the commencement date, less any lease incentives received;
- any initial direct costs incurred by the lessee (see 5.1A.50); and
- an estimate of costs to be incurred by the lessee in dismantling and removing the underlying asset, restoring the site on which it is located or restoring the underlying asset to the condition required by the terms and conditions of the lease, unless those costs are incurred to produce inventories. The lessee incurs the obligation for those costs either at the commencement date or as a consequence of having used the underlying asset during a particular period. [*IFRS 16.23–24*]

5.1A.300 Subsequent measurement of the lease liability

5.1A.305 *Measurement basis*

5.1A.305.10 After initial recognition, the lease liability is measured at amortised cost using the effective interest method. [*IFRS 16.36*]

EXAMPLE 23 – LEASE LIABILITY – MEASUREMENT AT AMORTISED COST

5.1A.305.20 Lessee X has entered into a contract with Lessor L to lease a building for seven years. The annual lease payments are 450, payable at the end of each year. X estimates that the incremental borrowing rate is 5.04% and uses it to measure the lease liability. The initial recognition of the obligation to make lease payments is 2,600.

5.1A.305.30 X performs the following calculations at the end of year 1.

		AMOUNT
Initial recognition of lease liability		2,600
Payment	(450)	
Repayment of interest	(131)[1]	
Repayment of principal	(319)[2]	(319)
Carrying amount of liability at end of year 1		2,281[3]

Notes
1. Calculated as 2,600 x 5.04%.
2. Calculated as 450 - 131.
3. Calculated as 2,600 - 319.

5.1A.305.40 A lessee cannot measure lease liabilities subsequently at fair value. [*IFRS 16.BC183*]

5.1A.310   *Remeasurement of the lease liability*

5.1A.310.10   A lessee remeasures the lease liability to reflect changes in the lease payments as follows. [*IFRS 16.36(c), 39–43, B42(a)(ii)*]

LESSEE REMEASURES LEASE LIABILITY USING REVISED LEASE PAYMENTS AND...

an *unchanged* discount rate when:	a *revised* discount rate when:
• the amount expected to be payable under the residual value guarantee changes; • future lease payments change to reflect market rates (e.g. based on a market rent review) or a change in an index or rate[(1)] used to determine the lease payments; or • the variability of payments is resolved so that they become in-substance fixed payments.	• future lease payments change as a result of a change in floating interest rates; • the lease term changes; or • the assessment of the exercise of a purchase option changes.

Note
1.   Other than changes in floating interest rates.

5.1A.315   *Variable lease payments that become fixed*

5.1A.315.10   If a lease payment is initially variable but subsequently becomes fixed, then it is treated as an in-substance fixed payment when the variability is resolved. The payment is therefore included in the lease liability from that point onwards. [*IFRS 16.B42(a)(ii)*]

EXAMPLE 24 – IN-SUBSTANCE FIXED PAYMENTS – PAYMENTS INITIALLY UNKNOWN BUT PARTIALLY FIXED AT END OF YEAR 1

5.1A.315.20   Lessee B enters into a 20-year lease of an item of machinery. The lease payments are paid at the end of each year and are determined as follows.
- Years 1–10: initially unknown but fixed at the end of year 1 based on capacity achieved in the second half of year 1.
- Year 11 onwards: variable, based on a fixed price per tonne processed.

5.1A.315.25   The capacity of the machine is unknown until it has been installed and it has been operating for a year.

Initial measurement of the lease liability

5.1A.315.30   At commencement, the future lease payments are unknown and B measures the lease liability as zero. B determines its discount rate.

Subsequent measurement of the lease liability as payments become fixed

5.1A.315.40   At the end of year 1, the lease payments for years 2–10 become fixed based on the capacity achieved in the second half of year 1. Using an unchanged discount rate (see 5.1A.310), B remeasures its lease liability and right-of-use asset as the present value of the fixed payments for years 2–10. The lease liability is

> reduced as the payments are made over years 2–10 (see 5.1A.305.10), and the right-of-use asset is depreciated over the remaining lease term of 19 years.

Variable lease payments depending on an index or rate

5.1A.320.10 After the commencement date, lessees remeasure the lease liability to reflect changes to the lease payments arising from changes in the index or rate. Any remeasurement is generally adjusted against the right-of-use asset. [*IFRS 16.36(c), 39*]

EXAMPLE 25A – LEASE LIABILITY – CHANGE IN VARIABLE PAYMENTS LINKED TO AN INDEX

5.1A.320.20 Lessee Y enters into a lease for a five-year term with Lessor L for a retail building, commencing on 1 January. Y pays 155 per year, in arrears. Y's incremental borrowing rate is 5.9%. Additionally, the lease contract states that lease payments for each year will increase on the basis of the increase in the CPI for the preceding year. At the commencement date, the CPI for the previous year is 120 and the lease liability is 655 based on annual payments of 155 discounted at 5.9% to commencement date.

5.1A.320.30 Assume that initial direct costs are zero and there are no lease incentives, prepayments or restoration costs. Y records the following entries for year 1.

	DEBIT	CREDIT
Right-of-use asset	655	
Lease liability		655
To recognise lease at commencement date		
Depreciation	131	
Right-of-use asset		131
Interest expense (655 x 5.9%)	39	
Lease liability (155 - 39)	116	
Cash (payment for year 1)		155
To recognise payment and expenses for year 1		

5.1A.320.40 At the end of year 1, the CPI increases to 125. Y calculates the revised payments for year 2 and beyond adjusted for the change in CPI as 161 (155 x 125 / 120). Because the lease payments are variable payments that depend on an index, Y adjusts the lease liability to reflect the change. The adjustment is calculated as the difference between the original lease payments (155) and the reassessed payment (161) over the remaining four-year lease term, discounted at the original discount rate of 5.9% (21).

5.1A.320.50 Remeasurements of variable lease payments that depend on an index and relate to future periods are reflected in the carrying amount of the right-of-use asset (see 5.1A.345.20). Y records the following entry.

	DEBIT	CREDIT
Right-of-use asset	21	
Lease liability		21
To recognise remeasurement		

EXAMPLE 25B – LEASE LIABILITY – PAYMENTS DESIGNED TO REFLECT EXPECTED CHANGES IN AN INDEX

5.1A.320.60   Lessee M enters into a contract with Lessor L to lease a piece of equipment for 10 years. The rent for year 1 is a fixed amount of 100, which increases by 5% in each subsequent year. The annual rent adjustment of 5% is designed to compensate L for the expected annual change in RPI, and is determined based on the average annual inflation over the past three years.

5.1A.320.70   The rents are fixed; they do not depend on the future value of RPI. On lease commencement, M includes in the lease liability the annual lease payments that increase by a fixed factor of 5% – i.e. 100, 105 (100×1.05), 110 (100×1.05^2), 116 (100×1.05^3) etc. There are no future changes in lease payments that require M to remeasure the lease liability.

5.1A.325   *Residual value guarantees*

5.1A.325.10   If a lessee provides a residual value guarantee, then it includes in the lease payments the amount that it expects to pay under the guarantee. If the amount expected to be payable under a residual value guarantee changes, then the lessee remeasures the liability. [*IFRS 16.27(c), 42–43*]

5.1A.330   *Purchase, renewal and termination options*

5.1A.330.10   A lessee remeasures the lease liability if it changes its assessment of whether it is reasonably certain to exercise a renewal or purchase option, or not to exercise an option to terminate the lease early. [*IFRS 16.36(c), 40*]

EXAMPLE 26 – LESSEE PURCHASE OPTION – REASSESSING IF REASONABLY CERTAIN TO BE EXERCISED

5.1A.330.20   Continuing Example 9, at the end of year 3 Lessee E makes a strategic decision to cut back on development projects, including the development of the replacement equipment. This decision is within E's control and represents a significant change in circumstances. E determines that the fair value of the equipment at the end of the lease will be 2,000.

5.1A.330.30   Accordingly, E concludes that it is now reasonably certain to exercise the option because it is unlikely to have a replacement asset available by the end of the lease, and the expected market value of the equipment at the end of the lease exceeds the exercise price by a substantial amount. E includes the exercise price in its lease payments. The appropriate discount rate at the end of year 3 is 5.5%. At this date, the remaining useful life of the underlying asset is reassessed to be four years (see 3.2.140.20).

5.1A.330.40   At the end of year 3, E remeasures the lease liability and the right-of-use asset to include the exercise price of 500 in its lease payments. Using the revised discount rate of 5.5%, at the end of year 3 E remeasures the lease liability from 1,860 to 2,296[1] and the right-of-use asset from 1,732 to 2,168[2], and records the following entries.

	DEBIT	CREDIT
Right-of-use asset	436	
Lease liability		436
To recognise remeasurement at end of year 3		

5.1A.330.50   The lease liability and right-of-use asset are expected to be amortised/depreciated as follows.

YEAR	LEASE LIABILITY				RIGHT-OF-USE ASSET		
	BEGINNING	LEASE PAYMENT	INTEREST	ENDING	BEGINNING	DEPRECIATION	ENDING
4	2,296	(1,000)	126	1,422	2,168	(542)	1,626
5	1,422	(1,500)	78	-	1,626	(542)	1,084
6					1,084	(542)	542
7					542	(542)	-

Notes
1.   Calculated as $(1,000 \times 0.945) + (1,000 \times 0.945^2)$.
2.   Calculated as 1,732 + 436.

5.1A.340   Subsequent measurement of the right-of-use asset

5.1A.345   *Measurement basis*

5.1A.345.10   Generally, a lessee measures right-of-use assets at cost less accumulated depreciation (see 5.1A.350) and accumulated impairment losses (see 5.1A.355). [*IFRS 16.29–30*]

5.1A.345.20   A lessee adjusts the carrying amount of the right-of-use asset for remeasurement of the lease liability (see 5.1A.310). If the carrying amount of the right-to-use asset has already been reduced to zero and there is a further reduction in the measurement of the lease liability, then a lessee recognises any remaining amount of the remeasurement in profit or loss. [*IFRS 16.30(b), 39*]

5.1A.345.30   The following diagram summarises the impact of changes in the carrying amount of the lease liability on the right-of-use asset. [*IFRS 16.38–39*]

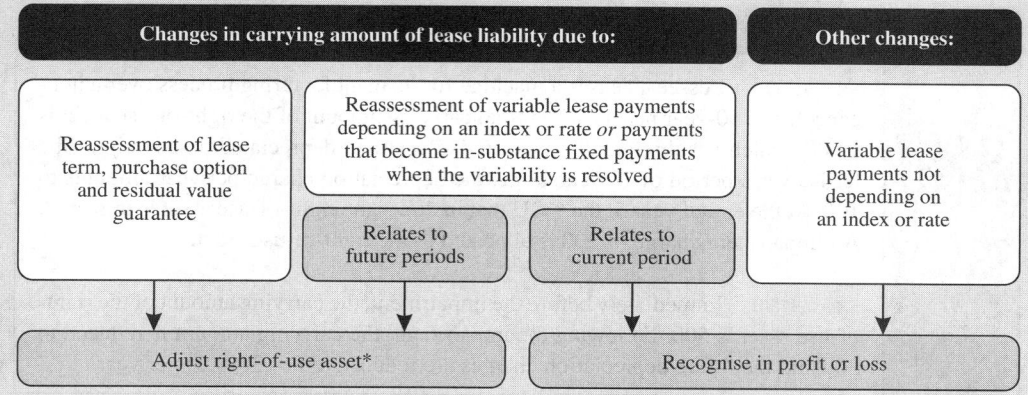

Changes in carrying amount of lease liability due to:		**Other changes:**

Reassessment of lease term, purchase option and residual value guarantee

Reassessment of variable lease payments depending on an index or rate *or* payments that become in-substance fixed payments when the variability is resolved

Variable lease payments not depending on an index or rate

Relates to future periods

Relates to current period

Adjust right-of-use asset*

Recognise in profit or loss

* If the carrying amount of the right-of-use asset is reduced to zero, then any further reductions are recognised in profit or loss.

5.1A.350 *Depreciation of the right-of-use asset*

5.1A.350.10 A lessee depreciates right-of-use assets in accordance with the requirements of IAS 16 – i.e. the depreciation method reflects the pattern in which the future economic benefits of the right-of-use asset are consumed. This will usually result in a straight-line depreciation charge. [*IFRS 16.31, IAS 16.60*]

5.1A.350.20 Depreciation starts at the commencement date of the lease. The period over which the asset is depreciated is determined as follows:
- if ownership of the underlying asset is transferred to the lessee, or the lessee is reasonably certain to exercise a purchase option, then the depreciation period runs to the end of the useful life of the underlying asset; otherwise
- the depreciation period runs to the earlier of:
  - the end of the useful life of the right-of-use asset; or
  - the end of the lease term. [*IFRS 16.32*]

EXAMPLE 27 – RIGHT-OF-USE ASSET – DEPRECIATION

5.1A.350.30 Lessee X enters into a non-cancellable, non-renewable five-year lease with Lessor L for a machine that will be used in X's manufacturing process. The useful life of the underlying machine is 10 years and ownership remains with L.

5.1A.350.40 Ownership does not transfer to X, therefore X depreciates the right-of-use asset from the commencement date over a period of five years (i.e. the end of the lease term).

5.1A.355 *Impairment of the right-of-use asset*

5.1A.355.10 A lessee applies IAS 36 to determine whether a right-of-use asset is impaired and to account for any impairment. After recognition of an impairment loss, the future depreciation charges for the right-of-use asset are adjusted to reflect the revised carrying amount. [*IFRS 16.33*]

EXAMPLE 28 – IMPAIRMENT OF THE RIGHT-OF-USE ASSET

> **5.1A.355.20** Lessee Y leases a machine for its manufacturing process over a non-cancellable 10-year period. The initial carrying amount of the right-of-use asset is 1,000, which is subsequently measured at cost and depreciated on a straight-line basis over a period of 10 years – i.e. the depreciation charge per year amounts to 100. At the end of year 5, the CGU that includes the right-of-use asset is impaired. An impairment charge of 200 is allocated to the right-of-use asset.
>
> **5.1A.355.30** Immediately before the impairment, the carrying amount of the right-of-use asset is 500. Following the impairment, the carrying amount is reduced to 300 and the future depreciation charges are reduced to 60 (300 / 5) per year.

5.1A.360 *Investment property model – IAS 40*

5.1A.360.10 An entity applies IAS 40 to account for a right-of-use asset if the underlying asset would otherwise meet the definition of investment property (see chapter 3.4). [*IFRS 16.34, 48, IAS 40.2*]

5.1A.360.20 Under IAS 40, an entity chooses as its accounting policy either the fair value model or the cost model for measuring its investment property. The entity applies the policy to all of its investment property – i.e. it applies the same policy to owned and leased investment property. However, in either case the entity complies with the disclosure requirement of IAS 40 – including disclosures of the fair value of the investment property (see chapter 3.4). [*IFRS 16.34, 56, IAS 40.30*]

5.1A.365 *Revaluation model – IAS 16*

5.1A.365.10 If right-of-use assets relate to a class of property, plant and equipment to which the lessee applies the revaluation model in IAS 16, then the lessee may elect to apply the revaluation model to all of the right-of-use assets that relate to that class of property, plant and equipment. [*IFRS 16.35*]

5.1A.370 **Lease modifications – Lessee**

5.1A.370.10 A 'lease modification' is a change in the scope of a lease, or the consideration for a lease, that was not part of the original terms and conditions of the lease – e.g. adding or terminating the right to use one or more underlying assets, or extending or shortening the contractual lease term. [*IFRS 16.A*]

5.1A.370.20 A lessee accounts for a lease modification as a *separate lease* if both of the following conditions exist:
- the modification increases the scope of the lease by adding the right to use one or more underlying assets; and
- the consideration for the lease increases by an amount commensurate with the stand-alone price for the increase in scope and any appropriate adjustments to that stand-alone price to reflect the circumstances of the particular contract. [*IFRS 16.44*]

5.1A.370.30 For a lease modification that is *not a separate lease*, at the effective date of the modification, the lessee accounts for the lease modification by remeasuring the lease liability by discounting the revised lease payments using a revised discount rate determined at that date and:

- for lease modifications that decrease the scope of the lease, the lessee decreases the carrying amount of the right-of-use asset to reflect the partial or full termination of the lease, and recognises a gain or loss that reflects the proportionate decrease in scope; and
- for all other lease modifications, the lessee makes a corresponding adjustment to the right-of-use asset. [*IFRS 16.45–46*]

5.1A.370.40   The following diagram summarises the accounting for lease modifications by a lessee.

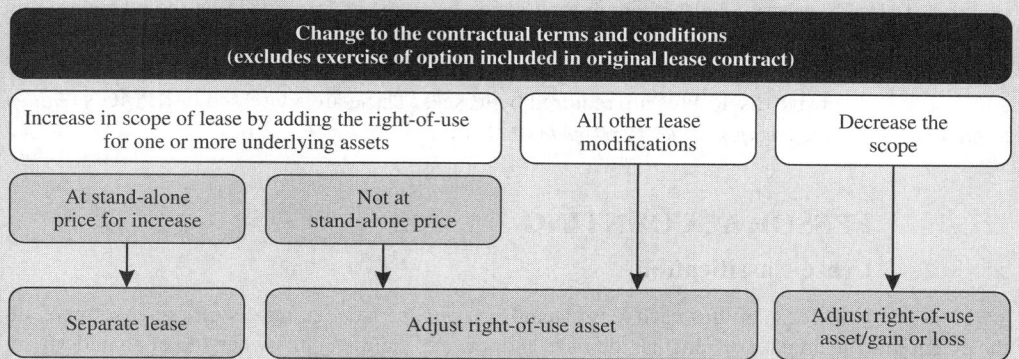

5.1A.380   **Lessee presentation**

5.1A.380.10   A lessee presents leases in its financial statements as follows. [*IFRS 16.47–50*]

STATEMENT OF FINANCIAL POSITION	STATEMENT OF PROFIT OR LOSS AND OCI	STATEMENT OF CASH FLOWS
Right-of-use asset Separate presentation in the statement of financial position[1] or disclosure in the notes to the financial statements. **Lease liability** Separate presentation in the statement of financial position or disclosure in the notes.	**Lease expenses** Separate presentation of interest expense on the lease liability from depreciation of the right-of-use asset. Presentation of interest expense as a component of finance costs.	**Operating activities** Variable lease payments not included in the lease liability. Payments for short-term and low-value leases (subject to use of recognition exemption). **Financing activities** Cash payments for principal portion of lease liability. **Depending on 'general' allocation** Cash payments for the interest portion are classified in accordance with other interest paid (see 2.3.50.20).

Note
1.   Right-of-use assets that meet the definition of investment property are presented within investment property (see 5.1A.360).

5.1A.390 Lessee disclosure

5.1A.390.10   A lessee discloses information that provides a basis for users of financial statements to assess the effect that leases have on financial position, financial performance and cash flows. [*IFRS 16.51*]

5.1A.390.20   A lessee discloses information about leases for which it is a lessee in a single note or separate section in the financial statements. However, a lessee does not need to duplicate information that is already presented elsewhere in the financial statements, provided that the information is incorporated by cross-reference in the single note or separate section about leases. [*IFRS 16.52*]

5.1A.390.30   Extensive disclosures are required by lessees. These are addressed in KPMG's *Guides to financial statements* series. [*IFRS 16.53–60, IAS 16.77*]

5.1A.400   LESSOR ACCOUNTING

5.1A.410   Lease classification

5.1A.410.10   A lessor classifies each lease as either a *finance lease* or an *operating lease* based on the extent to which the lease transfers the risks and rewards incidental to ownership of an underlying asset. [*IFRS 16.61, B53*]

5.1A.410.20   A 'finance lease' is a lease that transfers substantially all of the risks and rewards incidental to ownership of an underlying asset; title to the asset may or may not transfer under such a lease. An 'operating lease' is a lease other than a finance lease. [*IFRS 16.62–63*]

5.1A.410.30   Additional factors may need to be considered in more complex, multi-party arrangements. For example, suppose that Lessor G leases an asset to Lessee K, and G also enters into an agreement with Guarantor Z whereby Z guarantees the residual value of the asset. Because Z is a third party unrelated to G that is financially capable of discharging the obligations under the guarantee, the residual value is included in the lease payments of G (see 5.1A.90). Depending on the facts and circumstances, this may result in G accounting for the arrangement as a finance lease. [*IFRS 16.70(c)*]

5.1A.410.40   Only risks and rewards incidental to ownership of the underlying asset during the lease period are considered when determining lease classification. Relevant risks may include the possibility of losses from idle capacity or technological obsolescence and from decreases in the value of the asset. Relevant rewards may include a gain from the increase in the value of the asset or realisation of the residual value at the end of the lease. Conversely, risks associated with construction of the asset before lease commencement, financing the construction and the costs of providing services using the underlying asset are not incidental to ownership of the underlying asset during the lease period and in our view should generally be disregarded in evaluating the classification of the lease. However, construction and financing risk may impact the assessment of who recognises the asset before the lease commences. [*IFRS 16.B53*]

5.1A.410.50   The classification of a lease is determined at inception of the lease and is not revised unless the lease agreement is modified (see 5.1A.550). [*IFRS 16.66*]

5.1A.420 **Indicators of finance lease**

5.1A.425 *Primary lease classification criteria*

5.1A.425.10   The following are indicators that would normally individually or in combination lead to a lease being classified as a finance lease. Generally, the presence of any one indicator would point to classification as a finance lease. However, the lease classification is ultimately based on an overall assessment of whether substantially all of the risks and rewards incidental to ownership of the underlying asset have been transferred from the lessor to the lessee or to the lessee and a third party residual value guarantor. [*IFRS 16.63, 65*]

5.1A.430 *Transfer of ownership*

5.1A.430.10   If legal ownership of the underlying asset ultimately transfers to the lessee, either during or at the end of the lease term, then the agreement will usually be classified as a finance lease. [*IFRS 16.63(a)*]

5.1A.435 *Purchase options*

5.1A.435.10   The existence of a purchase option that is reasonably certain to be exercised, based on facts and circumstances at inception of the lease, means that title to the underlying asset is expected to transfer. Therefore, a lease with such an option is normally classified as a finance lease. For example, if the lessee has the option to buy the underlying asset at a price that is expected to be sufficiently lower than the expected fair value of the underlying asset on the date at which the option becomes exercisable and therefore it is reasonably certain, at inception of the lease, that the option will be exercised, then the agreement is classified as a finance lease. [*IFRS 16.63(b)*]

5.1A.440 *Major part of economic life*

5.1A.440.10   If the lease term is for the major part of the (remaining) economic life of the underlying asset – see 5.1A.110 – then the agreement would normally be classified as a finance lease by the lessor. For the classification of a sub-lease by an intermediate lessor, see 5.1A.600.30. [*IFRS 16.63(c)*]

5.1A.440.20   IFRS does not define what is meant by the 'major part' of an asset's economic life and an entity needs to exercise judgement in determining the reasonable threshold. In the absence of specific guidance, an entity may consider the most recent pronouncements under another accounting framework – e.g. US GAAP – using the hierarchy for selecting accounting policies in IAS 8. Under US GAAP, an entity is allowed but not required to use a 'bright-line' threshold whereby a lease term equivalent to 75 percent or more of the economic life of an asset is considered to be the major part of the asset's economic life. In our view, although this 75 percent threshold may be a useful reference point, it does not represent a bright-line or automatic cut-off point under IFRS. We believe that it is necessary to consider all relevant factors when assessing the classification of a lease and it is clear that some leases may be for the major part of an asset's economic life even if the lease term is for less than 75 percent of the economic life of the asset.

5.1A.445 *Present value of lease payments is substantially all of fair value*

5.1A.445.10   If at inception of the lease the present value of the lease payments (see 5.1A.70) amounts to substantially all of the fair value of the underlying asset, then the agreement would normally be classified as a finance lease. [*IFRS 16.63(d)*]

5.1A.445.20   IFRS does not define what is meant by 'substantially all' and an entity needs to exercise judgement in determining the reasonable threshold. Under US GAAP, an entity is allowed but not required to use a bright-line threshold whereby if the present value of the lease payments is 90 percent or more of the fair value of the underlying asset at inception of the lease, then the lease is classified as a finance (capital) lease. In our view, although the 90 percent threshold may provide a useful reference point, it does not represent a bright-line or automatic cut-off point under IFRS. We believe that it is necessary to consider all relevant factors when assessing the classification of a lease and it is clear that some leases may meet this criterion even if the present value of the lease payments is less than 90 percent of the fair value of the underlying asset at inception of the lease.

5.1A.445.30   The discount rate to be used in assessing this criterion is determined using the guidance for calculating the present value of lease payments when accounting for finance leases. Therefore, the lessor uses the interest rate implicit in the lease as the discount rate for determining the present value of lease payments for the lease classification test. [*IFRS 16.68*]

5.1A.445.40   If a residual value guarantee is provided by the lessee, a party related to the lessee or a third party unrelated to the lessor that is financially capable of discharging the obligations under the guarantee, then it is included in the calculation of the lease payments by the lessor (see 5.1A.90). This may result in the present value of the lease payments at the inception date amounting to substantially all of the fair value of the underlying asset for a lessor. In some cases, this may indicate that substantially all of the risks and rewards were transferred from the lessor but were not passed on solely to the lessee (i.e. other parties also participated in some of the risks and rewards). As a result, the lessor may classify the lease as a finance lease. [*IFRS 16.63(d), 70(c)*]

5.1A.445.50   A significant amount of time may pass between the inception date and the commencement date – e.g. when parties commit to leasing an underlying asset that has not yet been built. A lease contract may also include terms and conditions to adjust the lease payments for changes that occur between the inception date and the commencement date – e.g. a change in the lessor's cost of the underlying asset or a change in the lessor's cost of financing the lease.

5.1A.445.60   In such cases, the calculation of the present value of lease payments prepared to help a lessor determine the classification of the lease covers all lease payments made from the commencement of the lease term. However, if the lease payments are adjusted for changes in the construction or acquisition cost of the leased asset, general price levels or the lessor's costs of financing the lease between the inception and commencement dates, then the effect of these changes is deemed to have taken place at inception for the purpose of classifying the lease. [*IFRS 16.B54*]

5.1A.450   *Specialised nature of asset*

5.1A.450.10   If an underlying asset is so specialised that only the lessee can use it without major modification, then the agreement would normally be classified as a finance lease by the lessor. An asset built to the lessee's specifications may be a specialised asset. However, a machine that could be used by other entities in the same industry as the lessee – e.g. a printing press – would not be considered to be a specialised asset even if it had some degree of customisation. [*IFRS 16.63(e)*]

5.1A.455   *Supplemental indicators of finance lease*

5.1A.455.10   The following are additional indicators that a contract may be a finance lease:

- the lessee can cancel the lease but the lessor's losses associated with the cancellation are borne by the lessee;
- gains or losses from the fluctuation in the fair value of the residual fall to the lessee – e.g. in the form of a rent rebate equalling most of the sales proceeds at the end of the lease; or
- the lessee can extend the lease at a rent that is substantially lower than the market rent. [*IFRS 16.64*]

5.1A.460 *Assessing the indicators*

5.1A.460.10   IFRS does not provide a hierarchy to be applied when evaluating the indicators discussed in 5.1A.420–455, and these indicators may not be conclusive. As a result, although the presence of any one indicator may point to classification as a finance lease, other facts or features may demonstrate that the lease does not transfer substantially all of the risks and rewards incidental to ownership. Therefore, judgement is required in determining lease classification based on an overall assessment of whether substantially all of the risks and rewards incidental to ownership of the underlying asset have been transferred from the lessor to the lessee. [*IFRS 16.65*]

EXAMPLE 29 – ASSESSING THE INDICATORS – A PURCHASE OPTION AND OTHER INDICATORS

5.1A.460.20   Company J leases an asset to Company H for 10 years. The lease includes a purchase option under which H may buy the asset from J at the end of the lease. The exercise price of the purchase option set at inception of the lease is the fair value of the underlying asset at the date of exercise – i.e. the exercise price is variable. The continued use of the asset is significant to H's business model (see 5.1A.100.40–50) and therefore J determines at lease inception that it is reasonably certain that the purchase option will be exercised.

5.1A.460.30   In this example, legal ownership of the asset is expected to transfer to H. This is an indicator of a finance lease. However, because the exercise price is the fair value of the asset at the date of exercise, J continues to bear residual value risks and rewards – i.e. the fair value of the asset will be higher or lower than expected at the end of the lease. Because of the potential significance of the volatility of the future exercise price, judgement will be required to determine whether the lease has transferred substantially all of the risks and rewards incidental to ownership of the asset to H, and how the lease should be classified. [*IFRS 16.65*]

5.1A.460.40   Modifying the fact pattern, the exercise price of the purchase option is fixed. In this case, the residual value risks and rewards are instead borne by H. In this example, the expected transfer of title to the asset at a fixed price is an indicator that the lease has transferred substantially all of the risks and rewards incidental to ownership of the underlying asset to H and will generally result in the agreement being classified as a finance lease by J.

5.1A.465 **Other classification issues**

5.1A.470 *Evaluation of risks and rewards*

5.1A.470.10   IFRS does not address how to consider probability when assessing whether a lease transfers substantially all of the risks and rewards incidental to ownership of an asset. In our view, when assessing the risks and rewards, a lessor should consider the probabilities of outcomes – e.g. exercise of a purchase option – to determine who is more likely to be exposed to the expected risks and achieve the expected benefits, and not just the relative proportions of the risks and rewards.

EXAMPLE 30A – PROBABILITY EVALUATION OF RISKS AND REWARDS (1)

5.1A.470.20 Company R leases an asset to Company M for 14 years. The estimated economic life of the asset is 20 years. The fair value of the asset at inception of the lease is 1,000 and its estimated residual value at the end of the lease term is 250. All risks and rewards of ownership, other than the residual value risk, as discussed below, are transferred to M.

5.1A.470.30 M agrees to reimburse R for the first 50 of losses on disposal of the asset at the end of the lease term (based on the estimated residual value of 250). Therefore, if the asset is sold for 230, then M will pay 20 (250 - 230) to R. If the asset is sold for 200 or less, then M will pay 50 (250 - 200) to R. M has an option to buy the asset for 250, which is not a purchase option that is reasonably certain, at inception of the lease, to be exercised.

5.1A.470.40 For R, the present value of the lease payments, *including* the full amount of the residual value guarantee of 50, is 85% of the fair value of the asset (see 5.1A.90.40).

5.1A.470.50 Historical data suggests that the residual value of the asset at the end of the lease term is highly unlikely to fall below 200. Therefore, all of the most likely residual value risk is with M, although M does not bear the risk that the recoverable amount of the leased asset will be below 200 at the end of the lease term. Furthermore, M would receive any potential gains because M would be able to exercise the option to buy the asset for the fixed price of 250 if, at the end of the lease, the actual value was above 250.

5.1A.470.60 We believe that the evaluation of the transfer of risks and rewards should reflect the probabilities of the realistically likely range of outcomes. In this example, substantially all of the reasonably possible risks and all rewards incidental to ownership of the asset are transferred to M. R has only an insignificant risk and no rewards in relation to the residual value. Therefore, in our view the lease should be classified as a finance lease.

EXAMPLE 30B – PROBABILITY EVALUATION OF RISKS AND REWARDS (2)

5.1A.470.70 Company R leases a building to Company Q and Q is required to replace the building if it is destroyed by an earthquake during the lease term. In our view, the fact that Q bears these 'catastrophic' risks does not mean that the lease is necessarily a finance lease. Rather, the risks should be assessed after taking into

account their likelihood. In an area in which earthquakes are very uncommon, Q's commitment to rebuild the building if it is destroyed by an earthquake may have little effect on the classification of the lease by R.

5.1A.475 *Leases of land*

5.1A.475.10 The classification of a lease of land is assessed based on the general classification guidance. Consistent with the general leasing requirements, the assessment of the land classification is made at inception of the lease based on the expected conditions and outcomes at that time and is not revised merely because the value of the residual asset at the end of the lease increases over time. [*IFRS 16.B55*]

5.1A.475.20 In determining the lease classification, an important consideration is that land normally has an indefinite economic life. However, the fact that the lease term is normally shorter than the economic life of the land does not necessarily mean that a lease of land is always an operating lease; the other classification requirements are also considered. In our experience, it may be helpful to consider the indicators discussed further below (see 5.1A.480–505) when assessing the classification of a lease of land. However, ultimately, the lease classification is based on an overall assessment of whether substantially all of the risks and rewards incidental to ownership of the asset have been transferred from the lessor to the lessee. [*IFRS 16.B55*]

5.1A.480 Lease term

5.1A.480.10 A lease of land will not typically cover the major part of the economic life of the land, because land normally has an indefinite economic life. However:
- in a 999-year lease of land and buildings, the significant risks and rewards associated with the land during the lease term are transferred to the lessee during the lease term, regardless of whether title will be transferred; and
- the present value of the residual value of the property with a lease term of 'several decades' would be negligible and therefore accounting for the land element as a finance lease is consistent with the economic position of the lessee. [*IFRS 16.BCZ241–BCZ244*]

5.1A.480.20 It follows that a long lease term may indicate that a lease of land is a finance lease. This is not because the lease term will thereby cover the major part of the economic life of the land, but because in a long lease of land the risks and rewards retained by the lessor through its residual interest in the land at the end of the lease are not significant when they are measured at inception. Conversely, a short lease of land is unlikely to be a finance lease because the risks and rewards retained by the lessor through its residual interest in the land at the end of the lease when they are measured at inception are likely to be significant.

5.1A.480.30 It would not be appropriate to seek to determine a bright-line threshold lease term above which a lease of land would always be classified as a finance lease, because of the judgemental nature of the assessment. As an example, the basis for conclusions to IFRS 16 notes that a 999-year lease of land, which is a common lease term in some jurisdictions, would normally be a finance lease. However, depending on the facts and circumstances, leases of land with terms as short as 50 years could be finance leases. In addition, a lease with a short minimum contractual period but a fixed-price renewal option that is reasonably certain to be exercised may also be a finance lease. [*IFRS 16.BCZ241–BCZ244*]

EXAMPLE 31A – LEASES OF LAND – 50-YEAR TERM WITH INDEFINITE RENEWALS

5.1A.480.40   Company X leases land to other companies. The minimum contracted lease term is 50 years. The lease payments comprise a significant up-front amount payable on lease commencement and an immaterial annual payment. At the end of the minimum contractual lease term of 50 years, the lessee may renew the lease on the same terms at its option; that is, annual lease payments continue to be immaterial and the lessee may renew the lease at the end of each subsequent renewal period. No additional premium is payable on renewal.

5.1A.480.50   In this case, the lease term is very long, because at inception of the lease it is reasonably certain that the lessee will opt to renew the lease after 50 years – indeed, indefinitely. Therefore, X classifies the lease of land as a finance lease.

5.1A.485   Present value of lease payments

5.1A.485.10   In our experience, many leases of land are granted for an up-front premium with immaterial annual lease payments. In these cases, the amount of the up-front premium generally approximates the present value of the lease payments. However, for leases of land that include material recurring lease payments it will often be difficult to assess whether the present value of the lease payments amounts to substantially all of the fair value of the land, because of difficulties in estimating the rate implicit in the lease.

5.1A.485.20   One approach is to discount the lease payments first at a risk-free rate. In our view, if the present value of the lease payments discounted at a risk-free rate amounts to less than substantially all of the fair value of the land, then this may indicate that the lease is an operating lease. This is because although the rate implicit in a lease of land is very difficult to estimate, it will always be higher than the risk-free rate – often very much higher. Therefore, if the present value of the lease payments is less than substantially all of the fair value of the land when discounted at the risk-free rate, then there is little doubt that this would also be the case if the lease payments were discounted at the (higher) interest rate implicit in the lease, if that rate were known.

5.1A.485.30   Applying this test using a risk-free rate will still require judgement – e.g. to determine the risk-free rate. Performing the calculation at other relevant discount rates may also help to determine lease classification – e.g. in markets in which property yields are readily ascertainable, discounting the lease payments at a market property yield.

5.1A.485.40   It may be helpful to perform a series of calculations to assist in the lease classification decision. For example, if calculations indicate that the present value of the lease payments amounts to substantially all of the fair value of the leased land when it is discounted at a risk-free rate and when it is discounted at a market property yield, then this will indicate that the lease is a finance lease. However, if the present value of the lease payments amounts to less than substantially all of the fair value of the leased land when it is discounted at a market property yield but more than substantially all of the fair value of the leased land when it is discounted at a risk-free rate, then additional indicators will need to be considered.

5.1A.485.50 An alternative approach is to calculate the discount rate at which the present value of the lease payments equals substantially all of the fair value of the leased land, and then compare that rate with other relevant information, such as the risk-free rate, market property yields, etc. Again, judgement will be required to interpret the results of these calculations.

5.1A.485.60 Taking some lease terms seen commonly in practice, our calculations show that this indicator suggests that 99-year leases in which the rentals are set at a market rate at inception of the lease could be classified as finance leases under this approach. In some markets, leases as short as 50 years may be finance leases, in the absence of contra-indicators such as variable rentals and other variable payments as discussed below (see 5.1A.490–495). However, in our experience it is rare for lease terms of less than 50 years to be considered finance leases.

5.1A.490   Variable lease payments

5.1A.490.10 Variable lease payments (see 5.1A.80–85) may indicate that a lease is an operating lease, if the nature of the variable lease payment provides evidence that the lessor has not transferred substantially all of the risks and rewards of ownership of the land. [*IFRS 16.65*]

EXAMPLE 31B – LEASES OF LAND – RENTALS ADJUSTED TO MARKET RATES

5.1A.490.20 Company B leases land to Company C in Country Y under a 99-year lease. The starting rent under the lease is set at the prevailing market rate. Every five years, there is a market rent review under which rentals are reset to the market rate at the date of the rent review. Historical studies show a long-term trend of significant real-terms growth in land values in Country Y. In this case, B's return depends on changes in the value of the land during the lease term through the rent review mechanism. In our view, B should classify the lease as an operating lease, because a key risk/reward of owning land is that its value may rise or fall and B retains this risk/reward during the lease term.

5.1A.490.30 The presence of variable lease payments does not automatically indicate that a lease of land is an operating lease. As part of the assessment of the lease, an entity would also consider:
- whether there are other indicators that the lease is a finance lease;
- the nature of the variable lease payments and whether they provide evidence about the extent to which the lease transfers the risks and rewards of ownership of the land; and
- the materiality of the variable lease payments in the context of the lease as a whole.

EXAMPLE 31C – LEASES OF LAND – ASSESSING SIGNIFICANCE OF VARIABLE LEASE PAYMENTS

5.1A.490.40 Company Z leases land to other companies under 99-year leases. The lease payments comprise an up-front premium that equates to 50% of the fair value of the land, and annual rentals calculated initially at 3% of the market value of the land at inception. Subsequently, the annual rentals are set at the higher of the rent for the previous year and 3% of the current market value of the land. Historical data on the land values of Z is limited but suggests that land values are fairly stable.

> **5.1A.490.50** In this case, Z retains exposure to changes in the value of the land during the lease term through the calculation of annual rentals. However, the significance of this exposure is reduced because of the size of the up-front payment, the 'upwards-only' rent review mechanism and the relative stability of land values. In addition, the lease term is long and it appears likely that the present value of the lease payments will exceed substantially all of the fair value of the land. To assess the most appropriate classification of the lease, Z considers the significance of the variable lease payments.
>
> **5.1A.490.60** On the basis of the facts in this example, Z classifies the lease as a finance lease.

5.1A.490.70 In our view, variable lease payments adjusted for changes in CPI generally do not provide evidence about the extent to which the lease transfers the risks and rewards of ownership of the land. The other factors for lease classification should be considered.

EXAMPLE 31D – LEASES OF LAND – CPI-ADJUSTED RENTALS

> **5.1A.490.80** Company D leases land to Company E for 50 years. The starting rent is set at the prevailing market rate. During the lease term, rentals are reset every five years by adjusting the previous rent by the cumulative change in CPI during the five-year period. In the five years before inception of the lease, annual changes in consumer prices have varied between 20% per annum and 10% per annum. In this case, the rentals are variable and the effect of the variability is expected to be significant. However, the variability relates to changes in CPI, not changes in the market value of land.
>
> **5.1A.490.90** We believe that the variable rentals, based on the facts of this example, do not provide evidence about the extent to which the lease transfers the risks and rewards of ownership of the land; therefore, D should assess the classification of the lease with reference to other factors.

5.1A.495 Other variable lease payments

5.1A.495.10 If there are other substantive mechanisms through which the lessor's return varies with changes in the fair value of the land during the lease term, then this may indicate that the lease is an operating lease. In practice, such mechanisms may include:
- renewal premiums based on the market value of the land at the date of renewal;
- purchase options for which the exercise price is the fair value of the land at the date on which the option is exercised;
- one-off payments due from the lessee to the lessor if there is a change in the planning status of the land; and
- the lessor's ability to terminate the lease and enter into a new lease on more favourable terms.

5.1A.495.20 In each of these cases, an entity applies similar principles to those discussed in relation to the variable lease payments (see 5.1A.490). That is, it remains important to consider other potential indicators of lease classification.

EXAMPLE 31E – LEASES OF LAND – EARLY-TERMINATION RIGHT

5.1A.495.30   Company F leases land to Company E for 50 years. The starting rent is set at the prevailing market rate. During the lease term, rentals are reset annually by adjusting the previous rent by CPI. E has no renewal or early-termination options. However, F retains an option to terminate the lease without penalty by giving six months' notice.

5.1A.495.40   In this case, the lease payments include the rentals payable by E over 50 years, because this is the period over which E has an unconditional obligation to pay for the right to use the land. However, although E has an unconditional obligation to make lease payments for 50 years, F has the right to terminate the lease early. This means that if the market value of land rises faster than CPI, then F has an economic motive to terminate the lease and seek to secure a new tenant or buyer at the higher market price. Through this mechanism, F retains a potential reward associated with ownership of the land, being the right to participate in future increases in the fair value of the land. In our view, this right indicates that the lease may be an operating lease.

5.1A.500   Economic indifference

5.1A.500.10   In our view, if it would make little economic difference to the entity whether it leased or sold an asset, then this indicates that the lease is a finance lease because the entity prima facie considers that any risks and rewards that are not transferred by the lease contract are not significant.

5.1A.500.20   Examples 31F to 31H illustrate situations that suggest that it makes little economic difference to an entity whether it leases or sells an asset, such that the lease may be a finance lease.

EXAMPLE 31F – LEASES OF LAND – ECONOMICALLY EQUIVALENT TO OWNERSHIP (1)

5.1A.500.30   Company F operates in Country Q, in which both freehold and leasehold interests in land are common. F leases land to Company G with the following terms and conditions.
- G makes a single lease payment of 1,000 at lease commencement.
- The lease term is for a period of 125 years.
- Title to the land does not transfer to G at the end of the lease.
- The market value of a freehold interest in the land is 1,000.

5.1A.500.40   We believe that F should classify the lease as a finance lease, notwithstanding that it never transfers title to land, because it transfers risks and rewards typically associated with ownership of the land during the lease term and the pricing of the lease suggests that the risks and rewards associated with the residual interest in the land at the end of the lease are negligible. That is, in this example a 125-year lease is economically equivalent to an ownership interest in the land.

5.1A.500.50   The conclusion in Example 31F would also follow from the guidance on the lease term in 5.1A.480. However, an analysis of whether it makes little economic difference to a lessee between leasing and buying an asset may help in the analysis of more complex examples.

EXAMPLE 31G – LEASES OF LAND – ECONOMICALLY EQUIVALENT TO OWNERSHIP (2)

5.1A.500.60   The following are modifications to Example 31F.
- A sales tax of 10% applies to sales of land but not to leases of land.
- Market participants commonly enter into 125-year leases of land to avoid the sales tax.
- The difference between the market value of a freehold interest in the land and the up-front rental payable on commencement of a 125-year lease is equivalent to the sales tax.

5.1A.500.70   If it would make little economic difference to F whether it sells or leases out the land, then we believe that F should classify the lease as a finance lease.

EXAMPLE 31H – LEASES OF LAND – ECONOMICALLY EQUIVALENT TO OWNERSHIP (3)

5.1A.500.80   Foreign ownership of land is prohibited in Country R. Company H, a resident of R, is marketing a plot of land for sale to residents for 1,000 or lease to non-residents for annual rental payments of 50 that, when discounted at prevailing property yields, equate to 1,000. The lease payments are fixed in amount and the lease is non-cancellable.

5.1A.500.90   If it would make little economic difference to H whether it transacts with residents or non-residents on this basis, then we believe that H should classify any lease arising as a finance lease.

5.1A.505   *Land and building leases*

5.1A.505.10   In the case of a combined lease of land and buildings, the land and buildings are considered separately to determine the classification, unless the value of the land at inception of the lease is deemed immaterial or it is clear that both elements are either finance leases or operating leases. In determining the classification, the lease payments (including any lump-sum up-front lease payments) at inception of the lease are allocated to the land and buildings in proportion to the relative fair values of the leasehold interests in the land element and the buildings element. If this allocation cannot be done reliably, then the entire lease is classified as a finance lease unless it is clear that both elements qualify as operating leases. [*IFRS 16.B55–B57*]

5.1A.505.20   The fair value of the leasehold interest is different from the fair value of the underlying asset. An allocation based on the relative fair values of the land and the building elements – rather than based on the relative fair values of the respective leasehold interests in the land and building elements – is not generally appropriate because the land often has an indefinite economic life and therefore is likely to maintain its value beyond the lease term. Therefore, the lessor would not normally need compensation for using up the land. In contrast, the future economic benefits of a building are likely to be used up to some extent over the lease term (which is reflected via depreciation). [*IFRS 16.B56, BCZ245–BCZ247*]

5.1A.505.30   Therefore, in allocating the lease payments between the land and the building elements, it is reasonable to assume that the lease payments related to the:

- *building element (depreciable asset)* are set at a level that enables the lessor not only to make a return on initial investment, but also to recover the part of the value of the building used up over the lease term; and
- *land element (non-depreciable asset)* – assuming a residual value that equals its value at the inception of the lease – are set at a level that enables the lessor to make only a return on the initial investment. [*IFRS 16.BCZ245–BCZ247*]

5.1A.505.40   If a lease contains variable rentals, then in our view the variable rentals are allocated to both the land and the building elements of the lease. In our view, it is not appropriate to allocate the lease payments, which do not include variable rentals, to the land element first and then to attribute the remaining lease payments and the variable rent to the building element. However, a significant amount of variable rentals might be an indication that the entire lease is an operating lease.

5.1A.510   Finance leases

5.1A.510.10   Initially, the lessor recognises a finance lease receivable at an amount equal to its net investment in the lease, which comprises the present value of the lease payments and any unguaranteed residual value accruing to the lessor. The present value is calculated by discounting the lease payments and any unguaranteed residual value, at the interest rate implicit in the lease. Initial direct costs (see 5.1A.50) are included in the measurement of the finance lease receivable, because the interest rate implicit in the lease, used for discounting the lease payments, takes initial direct costs incurred into consideration (see 5.1A.125.10). [*IFRS 16.67–70*]

5.1A.510.20   The lessor derecognises the underlying asset and recognises the difference between the carrying amount of the underlying asset and the finance lease receivable in profit or loss when recognising the finance lease receivable. This gain or loss is presented in profit or loss in the same line item as that in which the lessor presents gains or losses from sales of similar assets. For a discussion of manufacturer or dealer lessors, see 5.1A.515.

5.1A.510.30   Over the lease term, the lessor accrues interest income on the net investment. The receipts under the lease are allocated between reducing the net investment and recognising finance income, to produce a constant rate of return on the net investment. [*IFRS 16.75–76*]

5.1A.515   *Manufacturer or dealer lessors*

5.1A.515.10   In some industries – e.g. office products, automotive – manufacturers or dealers often act as lessors of their products, either directly or through a finance entity subsidiary. A finance lease of an asset by a manufacturer or dealer results in two types of income: initial selling profit and finance income over the lease term. Manufacturer or dealer lessors recognise the selling profit or loss for the period in accordance with the entity's normal accounting policy for outright sales. Costs incurred in connection with negotiating and arranging a lease are recognised as an expense when the selling profit is recognised, which is generally at the commencement date of the lease term. [*IFRS 16.71–72, 74*]

5.1A.515.20   If manufacturer or dealer lessors quote below-market interest rates – e.g. as a marketing tool – then selling profit is restricted to the amount that would have been earned if a market rate of interest had been charged. Using the lower rate would not be appropriate because it would overstate the selling profit and understate the financial income in subsequent periods. [*IFRS 16.73*]

5.1A.520   ***Impairment and derecognition***

5.1A.520.10   A lessor applies the derecognition and impairment requirements of IFRS 9 to the net investment in the lease (see 7.6.60 and 7.8.410). A lessor regularly reviews estimated unguaranteed residual values used in computing the gross investment in the lease. If there is a reduction in the estimated unguaranteed residual value, then the lessor revises the income allocation over the lease term and immediately recognises any reduction in respect of amounts accrued. [*IFRS 16.77*]

5.1A.530   **Operating leases**

5.1A.530.10   If, before lease commencement, a lessor recognises an asset in its statement of financial position and leases that asset to a lessee under an operating lease, then the lessor does not derecognise the asset on lease commencement. Generally, future contractual rental payments from the lessee are recognised as receivables over the lease term as the payments become receivable. [*IFRS 16.81*]

5.1A.530.20   Generally, lease income from operating leases is recognised by the lessor in income on a straight-line basis from the commencement date over the lease term. It may be possible to recognise lease income using another systematic basis if that is more representative of the time pattern in which the benefit of the underlying asset is diminished. [*IFRS 16.81*]

5.1A.530.30   Similarly, increases (or decreases) in rental payments over a period of time, other than variable lease payments, are reflected in the determination of the lease income, which is recognised on a straight-line basis. For example, a contractual three percent per annum escalation of rents over the lease term is anticipated from commencement of the lease. Consequently, the lessor recognises lease income in excess of cash lease payments received in early periods of the lease and the opposite effect in later years.

5.1A.530.40   Initial direct costs incurred by the lessor in arranging an operating lease (see 5.1A.50) are added to the carrying amount of the underlying asset and cannot be recognised immediately as an expense. These initial direct costs are recognised as an expense on the same basis as the lease income. This will not necessarily be consistent with the basis on which the underlying asset is depreciated. [*IFRS 16.83*]

5.1A.530.50   Incentives granted to the lessee in negotiating a new or renewed operating lease are recognised as an integral part of the lease payments relating to the use of the underlying asset. They are recognised as a reduction of rental income over the lease term using the same recognition basis as for the lease income – i.e. on a straight-line basis unless another systematic basis is representative of the time pattern over which the benefit of the leased asset is diminished. [*IFRS 16.A, 81*]

5.1A.530.60   The lessor depreciates the underlying asset over the asset's useful life in a manner that is consistent with the depreciation policy that it applies to similar owned assets (see 3.2.140 and 3.3.210). [*IFRS 16.84*]

5.1A.540   **Annuity depreciation**

5.1A.540.10   'Annuity depreciation' refers to depreciation methods under which the depreciation charge is adjusted to reflect the time value of money. These depreciation methods result in lower depreciation charges in initial periods and larger depreciation amounts in later periods. They are used by lessors under some national accounting practices to recognise a level profit, after considering financing costs related to the underlying asset, over the lease term. In our view, the way that an asset is financed should not impact the selection of a depreciation policy. IFRS requires depreciation to reflect the consumption of the economic benefits of an asset. We believe that this does not extend to consideration of the time value of money or inflation adjustments.

5.1A.545   Fixed price lessor put options

5.1A.545.10   IFRS 16 does not address options held by a lessor that require the lessee to acquire the underlying asset at the end of the lease at a fixed price (i.e. fixed price lessor put options). The decision of whether the option will be exercised is within the lessor's control. Therefore, it appears that a lessor should choose one of the following accounting policies, to be applied consistently, to account for a lease that includes a fixed price lessor put option.

ACCOUNTING POLICY	DESCRIPTION	RATIONALE
Include full exercise price regardless of certainty to exercise	A lessor includes the full exercise price in its lease payments, regardless of whether it is reasonably certain to exercise the fixed price put option.	A lessor considers that the fixed price put option functions economically as a residual value guarantee. This is because the exercise price of the option is an amount that the lessee can be required to pay the lessor.
Assess whether it is reasonably certain to exercise	At the lease inception date, a lessor makes an assessment of whether it is reasonably certain to exercise the fixed price put option. If the lessor concludes that it is reasonably certain to do so, then it includes the exercise price in the lease payments. A lessor does not revise its initial assessment of whether it is reasonably certain to exercise the fixed price put option.	A lessor considers that the fixed price put option functions economically as a purchase option controlled by it. In doing so, the lessor assesses whether it is reasonably certain to exercise the fixed price put option based on all facts and circumstances.

5.1A.545.20   Generally, the presence of a fixed price lessor put option may indicate that the lease is a finance lease. This is because it may indicate that the lessor has transferred substantially all of the risks and rewards related to fluctuations in the fair value of the underlying asset to the lessee. Further, the lessor is likely to have an economic incentive to exercise the option and transfer the title of the underlying asset to the lessee at the end of the lease. However, there may be rare circumstances that would result in the lease being classified as an operating lease. This could occur, for example, if the lease payments before the exercise of the put option are fully variable depending on sales or usage.

5.1A.545.30   For the lessor, lease payments include any residual value guarantees provided to it by the lessee, a related party or a third party. A lessor does not double-count the exercise price in the measurement of its net investment in the lease. [*IFRS 16.70(c)*]

EXAMPLE 32A – FINANCE LEASE – FIXED PRICE PUT OPTION – LESSOR INCLUDES THE FULL EXERCISE PRICE

5.1A.545.40   Lessor T enters into a 10-year lease with Lessee M for a piece of machinery. The annual lease payments are 100 per year, paid at the end of each year. On lease inception, the asset's carrying amount is 1,000. The contract includes a put option under which T can require M to purchase the machinery at the end of the lease at a fixed price of 100. The fair value at the end of the lease (i.e. the unguaranteed residual value) is expected to be nil. The time value of money is disregarded for the purposes of this example.

5.1A.545.50   On commencement, T includes the put option exercise price in its lease receivables and records the following entry.

	DEBIT	CREDIT
Lease receivable[1]	1,100	
Property, plant and equipment		1,000
Gain[2]		100
To recognise lease at commencement date		

Notes
1.   T does not double count the exercise price (see 5.1A.545.30).
2.   Whether there is a gain or loss depends on the specific circumstances of each lease. In this example, the gain is a result of the fact that the time value of money is ignored. Because T uses the interest rate implicit in the lease – i.e. the rate that equates the present value of lease payments to the fair value of an underlying asset – to discount lease payments, there would generally be no gain or loss, except for any difference between the fair value and the carrying amount of the asset.

5.1A.545.60   At the end of the lease, T determines whether it will exercise the option. If T does exercise the option, then it records the following entry.

	DEBIT	CREDIT
Cash	100	
Lease receivable		100
To recognise exercise of put option		

5.1A.545.70   If T does not exercise the option, then the remaining lease receivable balance is transferred to the asset's carrying amount. Lessors usually exercise the option unless the asset's market value exceeds the exercise price of the put option. In this case, the asset will probably be re-leased or sold for a gain in a short time-frame. T records the following entry.

	DEBIT	CREDIT
Property, plant and equipment	100	
Lease receivable		100
Account for unexercised put option at end of lease		

EXAMPLE 32B – FINANCE LEASE – FIXED PRICE PUT OPTION – LESSOR ASSESSES WHETHER IT IS REASONABLY CERTAIN TO EXERCISE

5.1A.545.80   Modifying Example 32A, Lessor T chooses an accounting policy to assess whether it is reasonably certain to exercise the option. If at lease inception, T concludes that it is reasonably certain to exercise the put option, then the accounting outcome is the same as in Example 32A.

5.1A.545.90   However, if at lease inception T concludes that it is not reasonably certain to exercise the put option, and the option is:
- not subsequently exercised, then there is not accounting impact; or
- subsequently exercised, then T records the following entry.

	DEBIT	CREDIT
Lease receivable/Cash	100	
Gain on sale		100
To recognise exercise of put option		

5.1A.545.100   T does not revise its initial assessment of whether it is reasonably certain to exercise the option.

5.1A.550   Lease modifications – Lessor

5.1A.550.10   A 'lease modification' is a change in the scope of a lease, or the consideration for a lease, that was not part of the original terms and conditions – e.g. adding or terminating the right to use one or more underlying assets, or extending or shortening the contractual lease term. [*IFRS 16.A*]

5.1A.555   *Finance leases*

5.1A.555.10   A lessor accounts for a modification to a finance lease as a separate lease if both of the following conditions exist:
- the modification increases the scope of the lease by adding the right to use one or more underlying assets; and
- the consideration for the lease increases by an amount commensurate with the stand-alone price for the increase in scope and any appropriate adjustments to that stand-alone price to reflect the circumstances of the particular contract. [*IFRS 16.79*]

5.1A.555.20   If the modification is not a separate lease, then the lessor accounts for a modification to a finance lease as follows.
- If the lease would have been classified as an operating lease if the modification had been in effect at the inception date, then the lessor:
  - accounts for the lease modification as a new lease from the effective date of the modification; and
  - measures the carrying amount of the underlying asset as the net investment in the original lease immediately before the effective date of the lease modification.
- Otherwise, it applies the requirements of IFRS 9. [*IFRS 16.80*]

5.1A.560 *Operating leases*

5.1A.560.10   A lessor accounts for a modification to an operating lease as a new lease from the effective date of the modification, considering any prepaid or accrued lease payments relating to the original lease as part of the lease payments for the new lease. [*IFRS 16.87*]

5.1A.560.20   The following diagram summarises the accounting for lease modifications by a lessor.

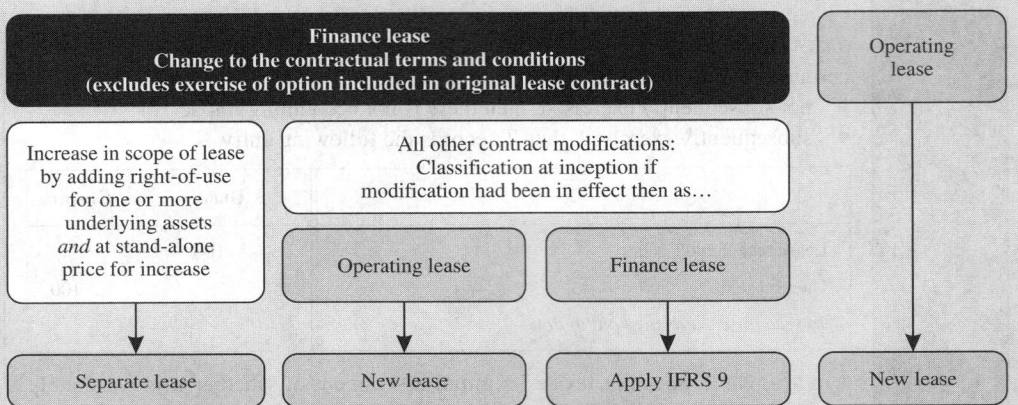

5.1A.570   Lessor presentation

5.1A.570.10   A lessor presents underlying assets subject to operating leases in its statement of financial position according to the nature of the underlying asset – e.g. equipment. [*IFRS 16.88*]

5.1A.570.20   A lessor recognises assets held under a finance lease in its statement of financial position and present them as a receivable at an amount equal to the net investment in the lease. [*IFRS 16.67*]

5.1A.580   Lessor disclosure

5.1A.580.10   A lessor discloses information that provides a basis for users of financial statements to assess the effect that leases have on financial position, financial performance and cash flows. Extensive disclosures are required by lessors for finance and operating leases. These are addressed in KPMG's *Guides to financial statements* series. [*IFRS 16.89*]

5.1A.590   SALE-AND-LEASEBACK TRANSACTIONS

5.1A.590.10   In a sale-and-leaseback transaction, an entity (the seller-lessee) transfers an underlying asset to another entity (the buyer-lessor) and leases that asset back from the buyer-lessor. [*IFRS 16.98*]

5.1A.590.20   To determine how to account for a sale-and-leaseback transaction, an entity first considers whether the initial transfer of the underlying asset from the seller-lessee to the buyer-lessor is a sale. The entity applies IFRS 15 to determine whether a sale has taken place (see chapter 4.2). This assessment determines the accounting by both the seller-lessee and the buyer-lessor, as follows. [*IFRS 16.99–103*]

	LESSEE (SELLER)	**LESSOR (BUYER)**
Transfer to buyer-lessor is a sale	• Derecognise the underlying asset and apply the lessee accounting model to the leaseback.[1] • Measure the right-of-use asset at the retained portion of the previous carrying amount (i.e. at cost).[1] • Recognise only the amount of any gain or loss related to the rights transferred to the lessor.[1]	Recognise the underlying asset and apply the lessor accounting model to the leaseback.[1]
Transfer to buyer-lessor is not a sale	• Continue to recognise the underlying asset. • Recognise a financial liability under IFRS 9 for any amount received from the buyer-lessor.	• Do not recognise the underlying asset. • Recognise a financial asset under IFRS 9 for the amount transferred to the seller-lessee.

Note
1. Adjustments are required if the sale is not at fair value or lease payments are off-market.

EXAMPLE 33 – SALE-AND-LEASEBACK TRANSACTION WHEN TRANSFER IS A SALE

5.1A.590.30   Company C sells an office building to Company D for cash of 1,000,000. Immediately before the transaction, the building is carried at a cost of 500,000. At the same time, C enters into a contract with D for the right to use the building for 15 years with annual payments of 80,000 payable at the end of each year. The transfer of the office building qualifies as a sale under IFRS 15.

5.1A.590.40   The fair value of the office building on the date of sale is 900,000. Because the consideration for the sale of the office building is not at fair value, C and D make adjustments to recognise the transaction at fair value. The amount of the excess sale price of 100,000 (1,000,000 - 900,000) is recognised as additional financing provided by D to C. The incremental borrowing rate of the lessee is 5.0% per annum. The present value of the annual payments is 830,400, of which 100,000 relates to the additional financing and 730,400 relates to the lease – corresponding to 15 annual payments of 9,634 and 70,366, respectively, when discounting at 5.0% per annum.

Seller-lessee perspective

5.1A.590.50   C recognises the transaction as follows.
• C measures the right-of-use asset retained through the leaseback of the office building as a proportion of its previous carrying amount, which is 405,778 (730,400 / 900,000 x 500,000).
• The total gain on the sale of the building amounts to 400,000 (900,000 - 500,000), of which:

- 324,622 (730,400 / 900,000 x 400,000) relates to the right to use the office building retained by C; and
- 75,378 ((900,000 - 730,400) / 900,000 x 400,000) relates to the rights transferred to D.
- C recognises only the portion of the gain on sale that relates to the rights transferred to D, which is 75,378. [*IFRS 16.IE11*]

5.1A.590.60   At the commencement date, C makes the following entries.

	DEBIT	CREDIT
Cash	1,000,000	
Right-of-use asset	405,778	
Building		500,000
Financial liability		830,400
Gain on sale-and-leaseback		75,378
To recognise sale-and-leaseback		

Buyer-Lessor perspective

5.1A.590.70   At the commencement date, D makes the following entries.

	DEBIT	CREDIT
Building	900,000	
Financial asset	100,000	
Cash		1,000,000
To recognise acquisition		

5.1A.590.80   After the commencement date, D accounts for the annual payments of 80,000 as follows:
- 70,366 are treated as lease payments; and
- 9,634 are accounted for as:
  - payments received to settle the financial asset of 100,000; and
  - interest revenue – applying the effective interest method. [*IFRS 16.IE11*]

5.1A.600   SUB-LEASES

5.1A.600.10   A sub-lease is a transaction in which a lessee (or 'intermediate lessor') grants a right to use the underlying asset to a third party, and the lease (or 'head lease') between the original lessor and lessee remains in effect. [*IFRS 16.A*]

5.1A.600.20   An entity applies IFRS 16 to all leases of right-of-use assets in a sub-lease. The intermediate lessor accounts for the head lease and the sub-lease as two different contracts. [*IFRS 16.3*]

5.1A.600.30   An intermediate lessor classifies the sub-lease as a finance lease or as an operating lease with reference to the right-of-use asset arising from the head lease. That is, the intermediate lessor treats the right-of-use asset as the underlying asset in the sub-lease, not the item of property, plant and equipment that it leases from the head lessor. However, if the head lease is a short-term lease for which the entity, as a lessee, has elected the short-term lease exemption (see 5.1A.140), then as an intermediate lessor it classifies the sub-lease as an operating lease. [*IFRS 16.B58*]

5.1A.600.40   At the commencement date of the sub-lease, if the intermediate lessor cannot readily determine the rate implicit in the sub-lease, then it uses the discount rate that it uses for the head lease, adjusted for any initial direct costs associated with the sub-lease to account for the sub-lease. [*IFRS 16.68*]

EXAMPLE 34 – SUB-LEASE CLASSIFIED AS A FINANCE LEASE

5.1A.600.50   Company L enters into a five-year lease for 5,000 square metres of office space (the head lease) with Company M (the head lessor). At the beginning of year 3, L sub-leases the 5,000 square metres of office space for the remaining three years of the head lease to Company N.

5.1A.600.60   L classifies the sub-lease with reference to the right-of-use asset arising from the head lease. Because the sub-lease is for the whole of the remaining term of the head lease – i.e. the sub-lease is for the major part of the useful life of the right-of-use asset – L classifies it as a finance lease.

5.1A.600.70   At the commencement date of the sub-lease, L:
- derecognises the right-of-use asset relating to the head lease that it transfers to N and recognises the net investment in the sub-lease;
- recognises any difference between the carrying amounts of the right-of-use asset and the net investment in the sub-lease in profit or loss; and
- continues to recognise the lease liability relating to the head lease, which represents the lease payments owed to the head lessor.

5.1A.600.80   During the term of the sub-lease, L recognises both interest income on the sub-lease and interest expense on the head lease. [*IFRS 16.IE8.Ex20*]

5.1A.610   JOINT ARRANGEMENTS

5.1A.610.10   When assessing whether a contract contains a lease, a joint arrangement (i.e. a joint venture or a joint operation) is considered to be the customer – and therefore a potential lessee – when the contract is either:
- entered into by the joint arrangement itself; or
- signed by one or more of the parties to the joint arrangement on behalf of the joint arrangement. [*IFRS 16.B11*]

5.1A.610.20   In this situation, it would not be appropriate to conclude that a contract does not contain a lease on the grounds that each of the parties to the joint arrangement either:
- obtains only a capacity portion that is not physically distinct;

- obtains only a portion of the economic benefits from use of the underlying asset; or
- does not unilaterally direct the use of the underlying asset. [*IFRS 16.B11, BC126*]

5.1A.610.30 When the joint arrangement is the customer, the contract contains a lease – and therefore the joint arrangement is a lessee – if the parties to the joint arrangement collectively have the right to control the use of an identified asset throughout the period of use through their joint control of the arrangement. [*IFRS 16.BC126*]

5.1A.610.35 In the following examples, assume that the parties have concluded that it is appropriate to account for the oil and gas activities as a joint arrangement.

EXAMPLE 35A – DRILLING RIG CONTRACT SIGNED BY THE JOINT OPERATION

5.1A.610.40 Joint Operation J is a separate vehicle with its own legal personality. J enters into a three-year contract with Supplier R, a service provider for the oil and gas industry, for the use of a drilling rig. The drilling rig is explicitly specified in the contract and R has no substitution rights. R is responsible for manning the rig, maintenance and safety. J makes all decisions about when and where to use the rig, as well as which geological targets to test.

5.1A.610.50 In this example, J is the customer because J entered into the contract on its own. Moreover, the contract contains a lease because the drilling rig is an identified asset, J obtains substantially all of the economic benefits from the use of the drilling rig and J directs the right to use it. Therefore, J is the lessee in the lease.

5.1A.610.60 Consequently, each of the parties to J recognises its share of the right-of-use asset and its share of the lease liability. [*IFRS 11.20*]

EXAMPLE 35B – DRILLING RIG CONTRACT SIGNED BY THE OPERATOR ON BEHALF OF THE JOINT OPERATION

5.1A.610.70 Parties X, Y and Z set up Joint Operation K as a separate vehicle with its own legal personality to explore a mineral interest. Each party to the joint operation contributes its undivided interest in that mineral interest to K as follows:
- X: 40%;
- Y: 30%; and
- Z: 30%.

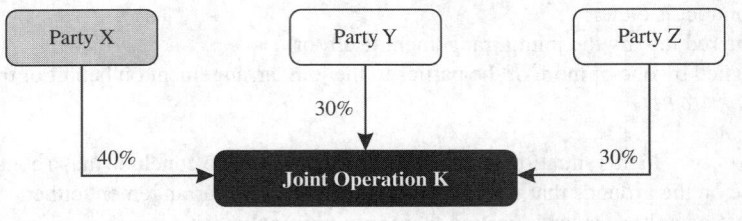

5.1A.610.80   X is appointed as the operator of K – i.e. X manages the day-to-day operations of K – and Y and Z are non-operators.

5.1A.610.90   X, on behalf of K, enters into a two-year contract with Supplier R, a service provider for the oil and gas industry, for the use of a drilling rig. The drilling rig is explicitly specified in the contract and R has no substitution rights. R is responsible for manning the rig, maintenance and safety. In accordance with the joint operation agreement, X, Y and Z jointly make all decisions about when and where to use the rig, as well as which geological targets to test.

5.1A.610.100   In this example, K is the customer because X enters into the contract on behalf of K. Moreover, the contract contains a lease because:
- the drilling rig is an identified asset;
- X, Y and Z collectively obtain substantially all of the economic benefits from using the drilling rig (by using it to explore K's mineral interest); and
- X, Y and Z jointly direct the use of the rig (i.e. they can collectively decide when, where and how to use the rig).

5.1A.610.110   Therefore, K is the lessee in a lease with R. Consequently, X, Y and Z account in their own financial statements for their share of the right-of-use asset and their share of the lease liability.

5.1A.610.120   In practice, questions may arise about whether a joint operator enters into a contract as a principal in its own name or on behalf of the joint operation. Judgement applies and the individual facts and circumstances – including the legal environment – need to be considered.

EXAMPLE 35C – DRILLING RIG CONTRACT SIGNED BY THE OPERATOR

5.1A.610.130   Modifying Example 35B, Party X – in its own name as a principal – enters into a four-year contract with Supplier R, a service provider for the oil and gas industry, for the use of a drilling rig. The drilling rig is explicitly specified in the contract and R has no substitution rights. R is responsible for manning the rig, maintenance and safety. In accordance with the contract, X makes all decisions about when and where to use the rig, as well as which geological targets to test.

5.1A.610.140   X is involved in a number of projects at various stages of development. X allocates the drilling rig to K for an initial two-year period. During this period, Y and Z reimburse X for their share of the costs. Afterwards the drilling rig is earmarked for another unrelated mineral interest project in the same geographic region for the remaining two years of the contract.

5.1A.610.150   In this example, X is the customer because X enters into the contract in its own name, as a principal, and not on behalf of K. Moreover, the contract contains a lease because:

- the drilling rig is an identified asset;
- X obtains substantially all of the economic benefits from using the drilling rig (by using it to explore its mineral interests and obtaining reimbursements from Y and Z for their share in the costs); and
- X directs the right to use the rig (i.e. X can decide when, where and how to use the rig).

5.1A.610.160 Therefore, X is the lessee in a lease with R. Consequently, X has the entire right-of-use asset and lease liability on its balance sheet.

5.1A.610.170 In addition, X will need to determine whether it has entered into a sub-lease of the drilling rig with K, in which X would be the lessor and K the lessee. When determining whether there is such a sub-lease, K needs to be analysed as the customer – i.e. X's share in the joint operation is included.
- If there is such a sub-lease, then X applies lessor accounting for the sub-lease. However, unlike when testing whether there is a sub-lease, lessor accounting for the sub-lease is restricted to Y's and Z's share in K because X cannot record a sub-lease to itself. Consistently, Y and Z account for their respective shares in the sub-lease between X and K.
- If there is no such sub-lease (e.g. because there is no collective control over the rig during the two-year period), then X (as receiver) and Y and Z (as payers) account for reimbursements related to the drilling rig as they would for other cost reimbursements.

5.1A.610.180 In some cases, all of the parties to a joint operation may sign *one* contract with a supplier, each in their own name and as a principal. If the joint operators enter into the contract collectively, then it appears that the accounting outcome should be the same as if the joint operation had entered into the contract itself. Consequently, we believe that in this case the joint operation is the customer in the contract. [*IFRS 16.BC126*]

5.1A.610.190 We believe that the same conclusion as in 5.1A.610.180 could be reached when the contract is instead signed by the joint operation on behalf of its joint operators or by one joint operator on behalf of all of the others.

5.1A.620 EFFECTIVE DATE AND TRANSITION

5.1A.620.10 IFRS 16 is effective for annual reporting periods beginning on or after 1 January 2019. Early adoption is permitted for entities that also adopt IFRS 15. [*IFRS 16.C1*]

5.1A.620.20 KPMG's publication *Leases – Transition Options* provides a more in-depth discussion of the transition provisions than this chapter. This chapter summarises the key points.

5.1A.630 Lease definition on transition

5.1A.630.10 On transition to IFRS 16, entities can choose whether to:
- apply the new definition of a lease to all of their contracts; or

- apply a practical expedient to 'grandfather' their previous assessment of which existing contracts are, or contain, leases. [*IFRS 16.C3–C4*]

5.1A.630.20   An entity that chooses to take advantage of the practical expedient:
- applies IFRS 16 to leases previously identified in accordance with IAS 17 and IFRIC 4;
- does not apply IFRS 16 to contracts previously identified as not containing leases in accordance with IAS 17 and IFRIC 4; and
- applies the IFRS 16 definition of a lease to assess whether contracts entered into (or modified) after the date of initial application of the standard are, or contain, leases. [*IFRS 16.C3*]

5.1A.630.30   The 'date of initial application' is the beginning of the annual reporting period in which an entity first applies the standard. For example, if an entity prepares financial statements for annual periods ending on 31 December and adopts IFRS 16 in 2019, then its date of initial application is 1 January 2019. [*IFRS 16.C2*]

5.1A.630.40   If it is chosen, then the practical expedient applies to all contracts entered into before the date of initial application, and the requirements of IFRS 16 apply to contracts entered into (or modified) on or after the date of initial application. An entity cannot elect to apply the new definition of a lease just to individual classes of underlying assets or when the entity acts only in the capacity of lessee or lessor. [*IFRS 16.C4*]

5.1A.640   Recognition exemptions on transition for lessees

5.1A.640.10   On transition, a lessee can elect not to apply the lessee accounting model to short-term leases and leases of low-value items. [*IFRS 16.5–6, 8*]

5.1A.640.20   For a discussion of the recognition exemptions, see 5.1A.140.

5.1A.650   Lessee approach to transition

5.1A.650.10   A lessee is permitted to:
- adopt the standard retrospectively; or
- follow a modified retrospective approach. [*IFRS 16.C5*]

5.1A.650.20   A lessee applies the election consistently to all of its leases. [*IFRS 16.C6*]

5.1A.650.30   The impact of the retrospective and modified retrospective approaches can be illustrated as follows. This diagram shows an entity with a calendar year end that presents one year of comparative financial information and adopts the new standard in its 2019 financial statements.

Approach	2018	2019	Date of equity adjustment
Retrospective	IFRS 16[(1)] / IAS 17[(1)]	IFRS 16	1 January 2018
Modified retrospective	IAS 17	IFRS 16	1 January 2019

Note
1.   The company will apply IAS 17 in preparing its financial statements for 2018. It will then apply IFRS 16 to prepare comparative financial information to be included in its 2019 financial statements.

Retrospective approach

5.1A.660.10 Under the retrospective approach, an entity applies the standard retrospectively in accordance with IAS 8. That is, the entity:

- applies the standard to all leases in which it is a lessee;
- restates its prior financial information;
- recognises an adjustment in equity at the beginning of the earliest period presented; and
- makes the disclosures required by paragraph 28 of IAS 8 on a change in accounting policy.
[*IFRS 16.C5(a)*]

Modified retrospective approach – Recognition and measurement

5.1A.670.10 Under a modified retrospective approach, an entity applies IFRS 16 from the beginning of the current period. To do this, it:

- calculates lease assets and lease liabilities as at the beginning of the current period using special rules included in IFRS 16;
- does not restate its prior-period financial information;
- recognises an adjustment in equity at the beginning of the current period; and
- makes additional disclosures specified in IFRS 16 and is exempt from certain of the disclosures usually required by paragraph 28 of IAS 8 on a change in accounting policy.

5.1A.670.20 A modified retrospective approach is applied as follows. [*IFRS 16.C8–C11*]

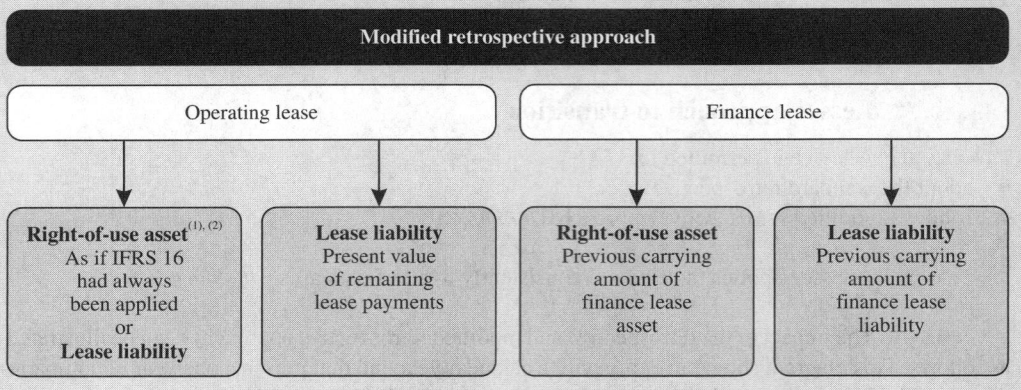

Notes

1. Under a modified retrospective approach, a lessee chooses on a lease-by-lease basis how to measure the right-of-use asset on transition to IFRS 16.

2. A lessee measures a right-of-use asset that will be accounted for as investment property using the fair value model in IAS 40 from the date of initial application. A lessee is not required to make any adjustments on transition for leases previously accounted for as investment property using the fair value model in IAS 40.

Operating leases

5.1A.675.10 For leases previously classified as operating leases, a lessee measures the lease liability at the date of initial application at the present value of the remaining lease payments. The discount rate is the lessee's incremental borrowing rate at that date. [*IFRS 16.C8*]

5.1A.675.20 For leases previously classified as operating leases, a lessee is permitted to choose, on a lease-by-lease basis, how to measure the right-of-use asset using one of two methods.

- *Option 1:* As if IFRS 16 had always been applied (but using the incremental borrowing rate at the date of initial application).
- *Option 2:* At an amount equal to the lease liability (subject to certain adjustments). [*IFRS 16.C8*]

EXAMPLE 36 – LEASE PREVIOUSLY CLASSIFIED AS OPERATING LEASE

Measuring the lease liability

5.1A.675.30 Retailer J leases a retail store for a fixed rental of 100 per annum, paid at the end of each year. The lease commenced on 1 January 2014, when J's incremental borrowing rate was 7%. The non-cancellable period of the lease was 10 years, renewable for a further five years. There were no initial direct costs.

5.1A.675.40 Under IAS 17, J classified the lease as an operating lease and recognised the lease payments as an expense on a straight-line basis – i.e. operating lease expense of 100 per annum.

5.1A.675.50 J adopts IFRS 16 using a modified retrospective approach with a date of initial application of 1 January 2019. At that date:

- J is not reasonably certain to exercise the renewal option. The remaining term of the lease is therefore five years; and
- J's incremental borrowing rate is 5%.

5.1A.675.60 J therefore calculates its lease liability as at 1 January 2019 based on the lease payments over the remaining lease term (five years at 100 per annum) discounted at its incremental borrowing rate at that date of 5% – giving a lease liability of 433.

Measuring the right-of-use asset

Option 1 – Retrospective but using the incremental borrowing rate at 1 January 2019

5.1A.675.70 J first calculates the carrying amount of the right-of-use asset on lease commencement – i.e. 1 January 2014. This is the present value of the lease payments over the 10-year term (10 years at 100 per annum) discounted at J's incremental borrowing rate at 1 January 2019 of 5% – giving an amount of 772.

5.1A.675.80 J's accounting policy is to depreciate right-of-use assets on a straight-line basis over the lease term. J therefore calculates the carrying amount of the right-of-use asset at 1 January 2019 as 5 / 10 x 772 = 386.

5.1A.675.90 Under Option 1, J records the following entry on initial recognition of this lease on 1 January 2019.

	DEBIT	CREDIT
Right-of-use asset	386	
Lease liability		433
Retained earnings	47	
To recognise the lease using Option 1		

Option 2 – Equal to the lease liability

5.1A.675.100   Under Option 2, J measures the right-of-use asset at 1 January 2019 to be equal to the lease liability of 433. J records the following entry on initial recognition of this lease on 1 January 2019.

	DEBIT	CREDIT
Right-of-use asset	433	
Lease liability		433
To recognise the lease using Option 2		

5.1A.675.110   If a lessee does not use the practical expedient to apply IAS 37 (see 5.1A.690.20) then it applies IAS 36 to right-of-use assets at the date of initial application. To do this, it appears that a lessee should follow the guidance in paragraphs 22 and 66–67 of IAS 36 (see 3.10.125) to determine whether impairment testing should be performed at the single asset or CGU level. [*IFRS 16.C8(c), C10(b)*]

5.1A.675.120   If a lessee determines that impairment testing should be performed at the CGU level, then it appears that an impairment test is required only when there is an indicator of possible impairment – i.e. a triggering event (see 3.10.110).

5.1A.675.130   If on transition a lessee elects to measure its right-of-use assets as if IFRS 16 had always been applied (see 5.1A.675.20), then for a lease previously classified as an operating lease this may result in a decrease in net assets because the carrying amount of right-of-use assets generally depreciates quicker than the lease liability amortises.

5.1A.680   *Finance leases*

5.1A.680.10   For a lease previously classified as a finance lease, a lessee measures the right-of-use asset and lease liability at the date of initial application at the carrying amount of the lease asset and lease liability under IAS 17. A lessee then applies IFRS 16 to account for the right-of-use asset and lease liability from that date. However, in some cases the lease payments included in the finance lease liability under IAS 17 may be different from those that would be included in a lease liability under IFRS 16 – e.g. if the lease includes a residual value guarantee or lease payments based on an index or a rate. If this is the case, then it appears that it is acceptable for a lessee to immediately remeasure its lease liability to reflect the lease payments that are included in the lease liability under IFRS 16. Although immediate remeasurement is not required, it eliminates the need for a catch-up adjustment for these changes if the lease is remeasured at a later date. Remeasurement of the lease liability is adjusted against the right-of-use asset. [*IFRS 16.C11, 39–43*]

5.1A.680.20   For leases previously classified as finance leases, it appears that a lessee adopting IFRS 16 using the modified retrospective approach can elect to apply the recognition exemptions for short-term leases and leases of low-value items. If it is elected, then on transition a lessee should 'derecognise' the finance lease assets and liabilities previously recognised under IAS 17 and record an adjustment in equity for the difference between the previous carrying amount of the finance lease assets and liabilities. [*IFRS 16.5*]

5.1A.690   *Modified retrospective approach – Practical expedients for operating leases*

5.1A.690.10   When applying a modified retrospective approach to previous operating leases, a lessee may use one or more of the following practical expedients on a lease-by-lease basis.

- Apply a single discount rate to a portfolio of leases with reasonably similar characteristics.
- Rely on a previous assessment of whether leases are onerous in accordance with IAS 37 immediately before the date of initial application as an alternative to performing an impairment review.
- Account for leases for which the lease term ends within 12 months of the date of initial application as short-term leases.
- Exclude initial direct costs from the measurement of the right-of-use asset at the date of initial application.
- Use hindsight, such as in determining the lease term if the contract contains options to extend or terminate the lease. [*IFRS 16.C10*]

5.1A.690.20   If an entity elects to apply the practical expedient to rely on its assessment of whether leases are onerous under IAS 37 rather than IAS 36 at the date of initial application, then it appears that an acceptable approach is to apply the expedient to any lease previously classified as an operating lease under IAS 17. For example, Retailer X leases 100 stores classified as operating leases under IAS 17. In 2018, X has vacated and intends to sublet 20 stores, 12 of which have been assessed as onerous leases. We believe that X can apply the practical expedient to all 100 leases, not only those for which it has previously recognised a provision. [*IFRS 16.C10(b)*]

EXAMPLE 37 – SHORT REMAINING TERM ON TRANSITION TO IFRS 16

5.1A.690.30   Company Q leases a vehicle for use in its business for an annual rental of 100. The lease commenced on 1 January 2017. The lease includes a three-year non-cancellable period, renewable at Q's option for a further two years at the same rental. The useful life of the vehicle is 10 years.

5.1A.690.40   In 2017, Q assesses that it is reasonably certain to exercise the renewal option and that the lease term is five years. Q notes that there are no indicators that the lease is a finance lease and so classifies the lease as an operating lease.

5.1A.690.50   Q adopts IFRS 16 using a modified retrospective approach with a date of initial application of 1 January 2019. At that date, Q assesses that it is no longer

> reasonably certain to exercise the renewal option – i.e. the remaining term of the lease is one year.
>
> **5.1A.690.60** Q can choose to account for the lease in one of two ways in 2019, as follows.
> - Q can apply the IFRS 16 lessee model to the lease and recognise a right-of-use asset and a lease liability. Under this approach, Q would measure the lease liability at 100, discounted at its incremental borrowing rate at 1 January 2019. It could then measure the right-of-use asset retrospectively, or at an amount equal to the lease liability. As a result, Q would recognise depreciation and interest expense in 2019.
> - Q can use the practical expedient to account for the lease as a short-term lease. Under this approach, Q would not recognise a right-of-use asset or lease liability for this lease. Instead, Q would recognise lease expense of 100 in 2019 and include this expense in its disclosure of total short-term lease expense.

5.1A.700 Lessor approach to transition

5.1A.700.10 Except for sub-leases (see 5.1A.710), a lessor does not make any adjustments on transition. Instead, a lessor accounts for its leases in accordance with IFRS 16 from the date of initial application. [*IFRS 16.C14*]

5.1A.710 Sub-leases on transition

5.1A.710.10 At the date of initial application, an intermediate lessor reassesses ongoing sub-leases that were classified as operating leases under IAS 17 to determine whether each sub-lease should be classified as an operating lease or a finance lease under IFRS 16. This assessment is made on the basis of the remaining contractual terms and conditions of the head lease and sub-lease. [*IFRS 16.C15*]

5.1A.710.20 For sub-leases classified as operating leases under IAS 17 but finance leases under IFRS 16, a lessor accounts for the sub-lease as a new finance lease entered into at the date of initial application. [*IFRS 16.C15*]

5.1A.720 Sale-and-leaseback on transition

5.1A.720.10 A seller-lessee does not reassess sale-and-leaseback transactions entered into before the date of initial application to determine whether a sale occurred in accordance with IFRS 15. [*IFRS 16.C16*]

5.1A.720.20 For a sale-and-leaseback transaction accounted for as a sale-and-finance lease in accordance with IAS 17, the seller-lessee:
- accounts for the leaseback in the same way as for any finance lease that exists at the date of initial application; and
- continues to amortise any gain on the sale over the lease term. [*IFRS 16.C17*]

5.1A.720.30 For a sale-and-leaseback transaction accounted for as a sale-and-operating lease in accordance with IAS 17, the seller-lessee:

- accounts for the leaseback in the same way as for any other operating lease that exists at the date of initial application; and
- adjusts the leaseback right-of-use asset for any deferred gains or losses that relate to off-market terms recognised in the statement of financial position immediately before the date of initial application. [*IFRS 16.C18*]

5.1A.730 Investment property

5.1A.730.10 A lessee measures a right-of-use asset that will be accounted for as investment property using the cost or fair value model in IAS 40 from the date of initial application. A lessee is not required to make any adjustments on transition for leases previously accounted for as investment property using the fair value model in IAS 40. [*IFRS 16.C9*]

5.1A.740 Business combinations

5.1A.740.10 An entity may have previously acquired an IAS 17 operating lease in a business combination for which the acquiree was the lessee. In this case, it appears that on transition the acquirer should account for the lease as a new lease at the date of the business combination. To do this, the acquirer should measure the lease liability at the present value of the remaining lease payments as if the acquired lease were a new lease at that date. The right-of-use asset should be measured at the same amount as the lease liability plus or minus any asset or liability previously recognised in the original business combination accounting for the favourable or unfavourable lease terms. There is no impact on goodwill. [*IFRS 16.C19*]

5.1A.740.20 An entity may have previously acquired an IAS 17 operating lease in a business combination for which the acquiree was the lessee. In this case, when measuring the right-of-use asset on transition as if IFRS 16 had always been applied (see 5.1A.675.20) it appears that the right-of-use asset should be measured as if it arose under a new lease on the date of the business combination, but using the discount rate at the date of initial application. The right-of-use asset should then be adjusted for any asset or liability previously recognised in the original business combination accounting for the favourable or unfavourable lease terms. The cumulative effect of these adjustments is recognised as an adjustment to the opening equity at the date of initial application. [*IFRS 16.C8(b)(i), C19*]

EXAMPLE 38 – OPERATING LEASE PREVIOUSLY ACQUIRED IN A BUSINESS COMBINATION – MODIFIED RETROSPECTIVE APPROACH

5.1A.740.30 Company Y is a lessee in an IAS 17 operating lease with a commencement date of 1 January 2010. Company X acquired Y on 1 January 2015. As a part of the business combination accounting, X recognised an asset of 1,000 for favourable lease terms. At the date of initial application:

- the lease has a remaining lease term of greater than 12 months;
- the asset for favourable lease terms has been amortised to 600; and
- X elects to transition to IFRS 16 using the modified retrospective approach and chooses to measure the right-of-use asset as if IFRS 16 had always been applied, but using its incremental borrowing rate at the date of initial application.

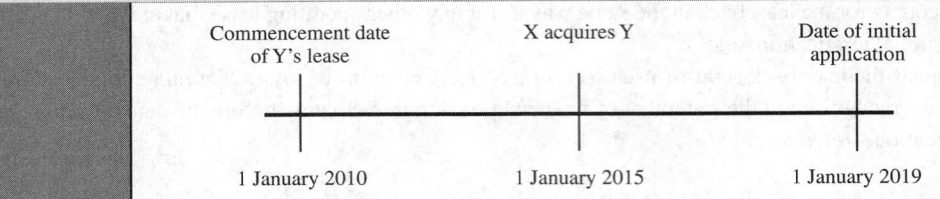

5.1A.740.40   In this example, X measures the lease liability at the present value of the remaining lease payments at 1 January 2019. We believe that when recognising the right-of-use asset at 1 January 2019, X should measure it as if it arose under a new lease on the date of the business combination (i.e. 1 January 2015), but using the discount rate at 1 January 2019. X derecognises the asset for favourable lease terms of 600 against the right-of-use asset. The cumulative effect of these adjustments is recorded against opening retained earnings at 1 January 2019.

5.2 Operating segments

5.2 Operating segments

CURRENTLY EFFECTIVE REQUIREMENTS

This publication reflects IFRS in issue at 1 August 2018, and the currently effective requirements cover annual periods beginning on 1 January 2018.

The requirements related to this topic are mainly derived from the following.

Reference	Title
IFRS 8	Operating Segments

FORTHCOMING REQUIREMENTS AND FUTURE DEVELOPMENTS

For this topic, there are no forthcoming requirements or future developments.

5.2.10   SCOPE

5.2.10.10   The disclosure of segment information is required only by those entities whose debt or equity instruments are traded in a public market (a domestic or foreign stock exchange or an over-the-counter market, including local and regional markets) or that file, or are in the process of filing, their financial statements with a securities commission or other regulatory organisation for the purpose of issuing any class of instruments in a public market. Segment disclosures are made within the financial statements. [*IFRS 8.2*]

5.2.10.12   IFRS 8 does not provide a definition for 'traded in a public market'. In our view, determining what is meant by traded in a public market depends on facts and circumstances, and can vary based on local requirements from securities commissions and/or regulators. We believe that if a buyer or a seller can contact a broker and obtain a quoted price, then this is an indicator that the debt or equity instruments are publicly traded, without regard to how often the instrument is traded.

5.2.10.13   The following factors may indicate that a fund is not traded in a public market.
- The fund is listed at a stock exchange for convenience listing or marketing purposes only, and cannot be traded on the stock market.
- The fund's shares are traded through a fund agent/administrator only – i.e. the subscriptions and redemptions of units are handled by a transfer agent/administrator directly associated with the fund.
- Buyer and seller set up prices based on the fund prospectus valuation principles and therefore prices would not be established by trading in a market.

5.2.10.14   The factors mentioned in 5.2.10.13 are not exhaustive and judgement is required when assessing if a fund falls in the scope of IFRS 8.

5.2.10.15   Segment information is required when an entity is in the process of issuing listed securities. In our view, segment information is required only when the entity has taken active steps to obtain a listing, rather than simply planning the listing. When an entity prepares financial statements for inclusion in a prospectus in preparation for a listing, segment information is included in those financial statements.

(S) 5.2.10.20   If an entity presents a financial report that includes both the consolidated financial statements of a parent that is required to present segment information and the parent's separate financial statements, then the segment disclosures are required only in the consolidated financial statements. [*IFRS 8.4*]

5.2.10.25   The consolidated financial statements of a group in which the parent is unlisted, but that has a listed non-controlling interest or a subsidiary with listed debt or equity instruments, are not in the scope of IFRS 8. [*IFRS 8.BC23*]

5.2.10.30   If an entity that is not required to provide segment information wishes to do so, but is unable to obtain all of the required information or wishes to disclose only limited information, then such information is not described as segment information. [*IFRS 8.3*]

5.2.10.40   Entities may also present segment information in the management commentary (or directors' report) accompanying the financial statements. Such information needs to be consistent, in all material respects, with the IFRS 8 disclosures in the financial statements (see 5.8.20.40).

5.2.20   CORE PRINCIPLE

5.2.20.10   The core principle of IFRS 8 is the disclosure of information that enables users of an entity's financial statements to evaluate the nature and financial effects of the business activities in which it engages and the economic environment in which it operates. The core principle is considered when forming judgements about how and what information is disclosed. [*IFRS 8.1*]

5.2.30   MANAGEMENT APPROACH

5.2.30.10   IFRS 8 requires segment disclosure based on the components of the entity that management monitors in making decisions about operating matters (the 'management approach'). Such components (operating segments) are identified on the basis of internal reports that the entity's CODM regularly reviews in allocating resources to segments and in assessing their performance. [*IFRS 8.BC4, BC9–BC10*]

5.2.30.20   The management approach is based on the way in which management organises the segments within the entity for making operating decisions and in assessing performance. Consequently, the segments are evident from the structure of the entity's internal organisation and the information reported internally to the CODM. The adoption of the management approach results in the disclosure of information for segments in substantially the same manner as they are reported internally and used by the entity's CODM for purposes of evaluating performance and making resource allocation decisions. In that way, financial statement users are able to see the entity 'through the eyes of management'. [*IFRS 8.BC4, BC9–BC10*]

5.2.35   FIVE-STEP APPROACH

5.2.35.10   The practical approach to segment reporting under IFRS 8 includes five steps, as presented in the chart below.

Step 1	Identify the CODM	(see 5.2.40)
Step 2	Identify operating segments	(see 5.2.50)
Step 3	Aggregate operating segments	(see 5.2.140)
Step 4	Determine reportable segments	(see 5.2.150)
Step 5	Disclose segment information	(see 5.2.180)

5.2.40   STEP 1: IDENTIFY THE CODM

5.2.40.10   The term CODM refers to a function, rather than to a specific title. The function of the CODM is to allocate resources to the operating segments of an entity and to assess the operating segments' performance. The CODM is usually the highest level of management (e.g. CEO or chief operating officer (COO)), but the function of the CODM may be performed by a group rather than by one person (e.g. a board of directors, an executive committee or a management committee). [*IFRS 8.7*]

5.2.40.15   Lower levels of management may make decisions about resource allocation that relate to less than the whole of the entity. These lower levels of management cannot be the CODM of the entity. However, they may be the segment manager for an operating segment (see 5.2.50.20). [*IFRS 8.9*]

5.2.40.20   An entity cannot have more than one CODM. [*IFRS 8.7*]

EXAMPLE 1A – IDENTIFYING THE CODM – A COMMITTEE

5.2.40.25   Company C has a CEO, a COO and a president. These individuals comprise the executive committee. The responsibility of the executive committee is to assess performance and to make resource allocation decisions across the whole entity. Each of these individuals has an equal vote. The executive committee is the CODM, because the committee is the highest level of management that performs these functions. The segment financial information provided to and used by the executive committee to make resource allocation decisions and to assess performance is the segment information that would be the basis for disclosure for external financial reporting purposes.

5.2.40.30   In our view, the mere existence of an executive committee, management committee or other high-level committee does not necessarily mean that one of those committees constitutes the CODM.

EXAMPLE 1B – IDENTIFYING THE CODM – AN INDIVIDUAL

5.2.40.35   Assume the same fact pattern as in Example 1A except that the CEO can override decisions made by the executive committee. Because the CEO essentially controls the committee and therefore has control over the operating decisions that the executive committee makes, in our view the CEO is the CODM for the purpose of applying IFRS 8.

STEP 2: IDENTIFY OPERATING SEGMENTS

5.2.50

5.2.50.10   The operating segments are identified based on the way in which financial information is organised and reported to the CODM. An operating segment is identified by IFRS 8 as a component of an entity:
- that engages in business activities from which it may earn revenues and incur expenses, including revenues and expenses related to transactions with other components of the same entity;

- whose operating results are regularly reviewed by the entity's CODM to allocate resources and assess its performance; and
- for which discrete financial information is available. [*IFRS 8.5*]

5.2.50.20   An operating segment generally has a segment manager. Essentially, the segment manager is directly accountable for the functioning of the operating segment and maintains regular contact with the CODM to discuss operating activities, forecasts and financial results. Like the CODM, a segment manager is a function, rather than a specific title. [*IFRS 8.9*]

5.2.50.30   There is no requirement to disaggregate information for segment reporting purposes if it is not provided to the CODM in a disaggregated form on a regular basis.

5.2.60   Types of operating segments

5.2.60.10   Under IFRS 8, operating segments are the individual operations that the CODM reviews for purposes of assessing performance and making resource allocation decisions. Operating segments could be identified on a number of different bases, including:

- products;
- services;
- customers;
- geography;
- legal entity;
- individual plant – e.g. an automotive supplier; and
- individual property – e.g. a real estate investment trust.

5.2.60.20   The operating segments and, ultimately, the reportable segments identified might not necessarily result in a single basis of segmentation – e.g. all geographic or all products.

EXAMPLE 2 – MORE THAN ONE BASIS FOR SEGMENTATION

5.2.60.25   Company M has six business components (A, B, C, D, E and F).

5.2.60.26   Three of these business components (A, B and C) are located in Germany and each manufactures and sells a different product to customers in Germany. The CEO (who has been identified as the CODM) assesses performance, makes operating decisions and allocates resources to these business components based on the financial information presented on a product-line basis.

5.2.60.27   The remaining three business components (D, E and F) are located in the US. These business components are organised to mirror the German operations – i.e. each manufactures and sells its products but to customers located in the US. However, the CODM assesses performance, makes operating decisions and allocates resources based on the financial information presented for the US operations as a whole. M's president of the US operations is responsible for assessing performance, making operating decisions and allocating resources to the business components in the US and is directly accountable to the CODM.

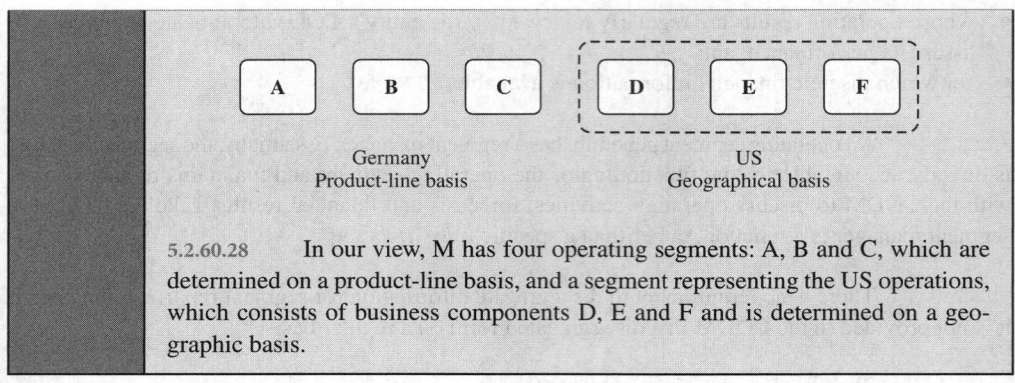

Germany
Product-line basis

US
Geographical basis

5.2.60.28   In our view, M has four operating segments: A, B and C, which are determined on a product-line basis, and a segment representing the US operations, which consists of business components D, E and F and is determined on a geographic basis.

5.2.60.30   Determining the industry in which a business component of an entity operates is generally not decisive for the purpose of identifying all of the operating segments under IFRS 8.

EXAMPLE 3 – IDENTIFYING OPERATING SEGMENTS AS BUSINESS COMPONENTS

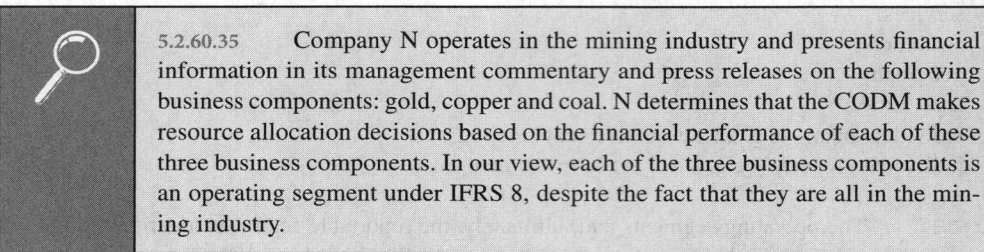

5.2.60.35   Company N operates in the mining industry and presents financial information in its management commentary and press releases on the following business components: gold, copper and coal. N determines that the CODM makes resource allocation decisions based on the financial performance of each of these three business components. In our view, each of the three business components is an operating segment under IFRS 8, despite the fact that they are all in the mining industry.

5.2.60.40   Operating segments can include, but are not limited to, start-up operations, vertically integrated operations, associates and joint arrangements. [*IFRS 8.5*]

5.2.70   *Start-up operations*

5.2.70.10   An operating segment may engage in business activities for which it has yet to earn revenue. Despite a lack of revenue, a start-up operation may qualify as an operating segment in accordance with IFRS 8. [*IFRS 8.5*]

EXAMPLE 4 – IDENTIFYING START-UP OPERATIONS AS OPERATING SEGMENT

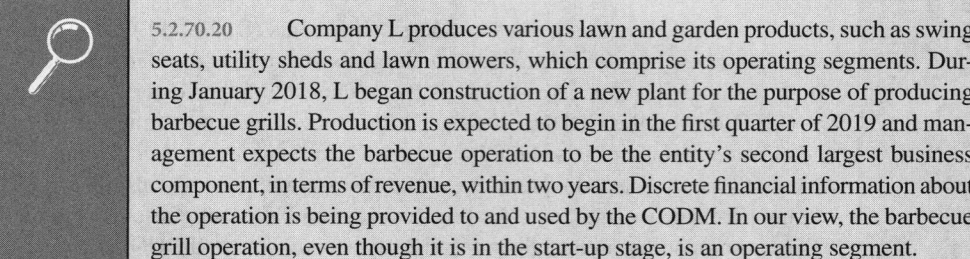

5.2.70.20   Company L produces various lawn and garden products, such as swing seats, utility sheds and lawn mowers, which comprise its operating segments. During January 2018, L began construction of a new plant for the purpose of producing barbecue grills. Production is expected to begin in the first quarter of 2019 and management expects the barbecue operation to be the entity's second largest business component, in terms of revenue, within two years. Discrete financial information about the operation is being provided to and used by the CODM. In our view, the barbecue grill operation, even though it is in the start-up stage, is an operating segment.

5.2.80   *Vertically integrated operations*

5.2.80.10   The definition of an operating segment includes components of an entity that sell primarily or exclusively to other operating segments of the entity if the entity is managed in that way. [*IFRS 8.A(a)*]

5.2.80.20   In certain vertically integrated businesses (e.g. oil and gas entities), information about the components engaged in each stage of production might be useful for the users of the financial statements because different activities within the entity might have significantly different prospects for future cash flows. However, the fact that an entity has vertically integrated operations does not necessarily mean that each of these individual operations will be considered separate operating segments for the purposes of IFRS 8. The identification of operating segments will depend on how the business is managed and how the financial information is organised and reported to the CODM.

EXAMPLE 5 – IDENTIFYING VERTICALLY INTEGRATED BUSINESSES AS OPERATING SEGMENTS

5.2.80.30   The CODM of an entity receives financial information organised by the following business components.

- Component A designs, manufactures, assembles and markets motorcycles.
- Component B provides consumer financial services, such as financing and leasing for new motorcycle purchases.
- Component C provides dealer financing.
- Component D designs advanced technology electronic systems for the telecommunications industry.

5.2.80.35   Component A contains four separate operations that:

- design the motorcycles;
- manufacture the necessary components;
- assemble the motorcycles; and
- market the motorcycles to consumers.

5.2.80.37   Component A is essentially a vertically integrated operation. No disaggregated information is provided to the CODM on the separate operations of Component A, and the CODM assesses operating performance and makes resource decisions about Component A based on the combined results of these operations.

5.2.80.40   In this example, the combined operations of Component A constitute an operating segment. However, if the fact pattern in this example is changed so that the disaggregated information on separate operations of Component A is regularly provided to and reviewed by the CODM to assess the separate operation's performance and to allocate resources, then in our view such operations would be separate operating segments.

5.2.80.50   Situations might exist in which an entity consists of vertically integrated operations, but no revenues are allocated to those different activities. To satisfy the definition of an operating segment under IFRS 8, a component of an entity has to engage in business activities from which it *may* earn revenues and incur expenses. It is the ability of a segment to earn revenues rather than the mere existence or an allocation of revenue that is determinative (see 5.2.90.40–50). [*IFRS 8.5(a)*]

5.2.85 *Joint arrangements and associates*

5.2.85.10   A joint operation, joint venture or an associate (the 'investee') could qualify as an operating segment under IFRS 8. Unilateral control over the investee's activities or control over the performance of the investee is not required in order to satisfy the definition of an operating segment under IFRS 8. Management might regularly review the operating results and performance of the investee for purposes of evaluating whether to retain the investor-investee relationship. IFRS 8 does not require that the CODM be responsible for making decisions about resources to be allocated *within* the segment, but rather for resources to be allocated *to* the segment. [*IFRS 8.5*]

5.2.85.20   To determine if an investee qualifies as an operating segment, an entity considers whether the CODM is responsible for making resource allocation decisions and for evaluating the financial performance of the investee. Resource allocation decisions may include whether to make additional investments in, or loans or advances to, the investee, or to sell any portion of its interest in the investee. In our view, if the primary responsibility for either of these functions resides at a lower level within the entity's organisation, then the investee might not be an operating segment.

5.2.90 *Functions and departments*

5.2.90.10   Under IFRS 8, not every part of an entity has to meet the definition of an operating segment or part of an operating segment. A corporate headquarters would probably carry out some, or all, of the functions in the treasury, legal, accounting, information systems and human resources areas. In certain situations, these corporate activities might even be reflected as a separate business unit for internal reporting purposes. However, corporate activities would not generally qualify as operating segments under IFRS 8, because typically they are not business activities from which the entity may earn revenues. [*IFRS 8.6*]

5.2.90.20   For the purposes of IFRS 8, an entity's pension and other post-employment benefit plans are not considered operating segments. [*IFRS 8.6*]

5.2.90.30   Assuming that amounts related to corporate activities are not allocated to operating segments – i.e. are not included in the measure of operating segment profit or loss reported to the CODM – the amounts for these activities would be reported in the reconciliation of the total reportable segment amounts to the financial statements (see 5.2.160.40). [*IFRS 8.16*]

5.2.90.40   Situations might exist in which a corporate activity may qualify as an operating segment. For example, the R&D activity or function may qualify as an operating segment if:
- sufficient and discrete financial information exists for an R&D activity and is reviewed by the CODM;
- the R&D activity has a segment manager;
- the R&D activity is not incidental to the entity; and
- the R&D activity is capable of earning revenues.

5.2.90.50   However, it is not essential for the R&D activity to earn revenue to qualify as an operating segment, as long as it is capable of doing so. [*IFRS 8.5*]

5.2.100   Information reviewed by CODM to make decisions

5.2.100.10   Under IFRS 8, entities are required to consider all types of information provided to the CODM when identifying operating segments. In addition, in our view if revenue and profitability information is released to analysts, the financial press or via an entity's website, then such information can be considered as well. Other forms of information to consider can include:

- management planning and budgeting materials;
- board of directors' reports; and
- media statements about how an entity operates its business, including information posted on its website. [*IFRS 8.5(b)*]

5.2.110   Discrete and sufficient financial information

5.2.110.10   To assess performance and to make resource allocation decisions, the CODM requires regular financial information about the business component. This information needs to be sufficiently detailed to allow the CODM to assess performance and to make resource allocation decisions. [*IFRS 8.5(c)*]

5.2.110.20   In rare cases, it is possible that the CODM receives only revenue information about the entity's business components and that measure is sufficient for the CODM to assess performance and to make resource allocation decisions about the business components. For example, if an entity provides different types of services and has fixed costs only – e.g. personnel costs, rent costs and the depreciation of office equipment – then the CODM may review only revenue information to assess the performance of, and to allocate the resources to, different operating segments.

5.2.120   Identification of operating segments when multiple types of segment information exist

5.2.120.10   Identifying the appropriate operating segments is not always obvious. Many entities – particularly multinational companies with diverse operations – organise and report financial information to the CODM in more than one way. As a result, operating segments might not be evident. [*IFRS 8.8*]

5.2.120.20   Judgement will be necessary in determining the single set of operating segments, and will depend on the individual facts and circumstances of the entity. In such situations, the entity determines which set of components constitutes the operating segments with reference to the core principle of IFRS 8 (see 5.2.20.10). The following additional factors can be considered in determining the appropriate operating segments:

- the nature of the business activities of each component;
- the existence of managers responsible for the components;
- information presented to the board of directors;
- information provided to external financial analysts and on the entity's website; and
- information presented in the front end of financial statements – e.g. a directors' report. [*IFRS 8.9–10*]

5.2.130   *Matrix organisations*

5.2.130.10   Some entities use a 'matrix' form of organisation, whereby business components are managed in more than one way. For example, some entities have segment managers who are responsible for geographic regions, and different segment managers who oversee products and services. If the entity generates financial information about its business components based on both geography and products or services (and the CODM reviews both types of information and both have segment managers), then the entity determines which set of components constitutes the operating segments with reference to the core principle of IFRS 8 (see 5.2.20.10). [*IFRS 8.10*]

5.2.140   STEP 3: AGGREGATE OPERATING SEGMENTS

5.2.140.10   Under IFRS 8, two or more operating segments may be aggregated into a single operating segment when the operating segments have characteristics so similar that they can be expected to have essentially the same future prospects. Aggregation is permitted only if:
- it is consistent with the core principle of IFRS 8 (see 5.2.20.10 and 142);
- the segments have similar economic characteristics (see 5.2.143); and
- the segments are similar in each of the following respects:
  - the nature of products and services (see 5.2.144);
  - the nature of the production processes (see 5.2.145);
  - the type or class of customer for their products and services (see 5.2.146);
  - the methods used to distribute their products or provide their services (see 5.2.147); and
  - if applicable, the nature of the regulatory environment – e.g. banking, insurance or public utilities (see 5.2.148). [*IFRS 8.12*]

5.2.140.15   The aggregation of operating segments is performed before determining which segments are reportable; therefore, operating segments may be aggregated even though individually they may exceed the quantitative thresholds for determining which ones are reportable (see 5.2.150.10). [*IFRS 8.IG7*]

5.2.140.20   The aggregation criteria are applied as tests and not as indicators. The ability to meet the criteria will depend on the individual facts and circumstances. A significant amount of judgement will be required when applying the aggregation tests (see 5.2.190).

5.2.141   Aggregation of investee operating segments

5.2.141.10   An investee can, by itself, qualify as an operating segment (see 5.2.85). In our experience, it may be difficult to satisfy the criteria under IFRS 8 to aggregate an investee operating segment with another operating segment because it is unusual for the CODM to review the performance of investees on an aggregated basis or together with other operating segments. Accordingly, in our view it will generally be inappropriate to aggregate an investee operating segment with another operating segment, including other investee operating segments. If the investee operating segment does not qualify as a reporting segment, then we believe that it should be included in the 'all other segments' category (see 5.2.160.40).

5.2.142   Consistency with core principle of IFRS 8

5.2.142.10   If an entity has very few operating segments, then it may be evident that the operating segments are also reportable segments. To be consistent with the objective and the core principle of IFRS 8, an entity cannot apply the aggregation provisions if the result would significantly impact the user's ability to understand the entity's performance, its prospects for future cash flows or the user's decisions about the entity as a whole. [*IFRS 8.1, BC32*]

EXAMPLE 6 – AGGREGATION – CORE PRINCIPLE OF IFRS 8

5.2.142.20   Company T is a tour operator providing services in three neighbouring European countries, each of which is determined to be an operating segment. The CODM reviews the operating results of each operation separately to assess the individual performance of and to allocate resources to each one.

5.2.142.30   In our view, although aggregation may be permitted in respect of economic characteristics and other similar factors, in T's case doing so would reduce users' ability to understand the entity's performance, its prospects for future cash flows and decisions about the entity as a whole. Therefore, we believe that T should disclose three reportable segments, which is consistent with the CODM's review of information by operating segment.

5.2.143   Similar economic characteristics

5.2.143.10   In determining similar economic characteristics, as an example IFRS 8 refers only to similar long-term average gross margins. However, in our view it may be appropriate to use other economic factors to determine if two or more operating segments have similar economic characteristics. We believe that those factors should be entity-specific and should be based on the primary factors that the CODM uses in reviewing the performance of, and allocating resources to, individual segments. Key performance indicators or other measures used in the industry or by the CODM might be more relevant than gross margins. [*IFRS 8.12*]

5.2.143.20   Useful measures to determine economic similarity may include:
- sales metrics – e.g. sales by square metres;
- trends in sales growth;
- rates of return on assets;
- levels of capital investments; and
- operating cash flows.

5.2.143.30   In addition to quantitative performance indicators, in our view the competitive and operating risks, currency risks and economic and political conditions associated with each operating segment may be considered. We believe that appropriate weight should be given to each of the various factors based on the individual facts and circumstances.

5.2.143.40   In our view, in assessing the similarity of economic characteristics, consideration should be given not only to the current measures, but also to future prospects. Operating segments that have historically been aggregated might not have similar economic characteristics in the current period. Management should analyse whether this change is due to temporary or abnormal circumstances. If the operating segments are expected to have similar economic characteristics in the foreseeable future, then the segments may be aggregated. In our view, if operating segments have similar economic characteristics in the current year (but historically do not) and it is *not* expected that they will continue to have similar economic characteristics in the future, then it may be appropriate *not* to aggregate the segments for the current year.

5.2.144 *Nature of products and services*

5.2.144.10   When determining whether the nature of the product or service is similar, it might be necessary to consider how broadly or narrowly the internal financial reporting and overall operations of an entity are defined. For example, an entity with a relatively narrow product range may consider two products not to be similar, whereas an entity with a broad product range may consider those same two products to be similar. Another factor to be considered is whether products and services have similar degrees of risk, opportunities for growth and end uses. [*IFRS 8.12(a)*]

5.2.145 *Nature of production processes*

5.2.145.10   In our view, the production processes of two or more operating segments may be considered similar if they share, or are able to share, common or interchangeable facilities and employees and use similar raw materials. The amount of capital vs labour intensiveness should also be considered. [*IFRS 8.12(b)*]

EXAMPLE 7 – AGGREGATION – NATURE OF PRODUCTION PROCESS

5.2.145.20   An automotive supplier produces two types of seats for a particular customer. Although the seats are manufactured through the same process, one is a bench seat for a van and the other is a bucket seat for a luxury coupe. Both products use similar raw materials, require the same amount of capital and labour intensiveness, can be produced interchangeably by existing employees and facilities, and use the same manufacturing machinery and equipment.

5.2.145.30   In this example, the production processes could be viewed as similar. However, all of the other aggregation criteria still need to be met in order to aggregate operating segments.

5.2.146 *Type or class of customer for products and services*

5.2.146.10   There are a number of factors to consider when assessing the similarity of the type or class of customers – e.g. the similarity of marketing or promotion methods, geographic areas and the nature and use of sales forces could be relevant factors. [*IFRS 8.12(c)*]

EXAMPLE 8 – AGGREGATION – TYPE OR CLASS OF CUSTOMER

5.2.146.20   An entity manufactures and sells a basic cleaning solution, but in two mixtures: one for home use and the other for commercial use. The commercial customer buys regularly in bulk orders, based on personal contact with the entity's sales representatives. The home customers buy products in small quantities and infrequently via a website order system.

5.2.146.30   In this example, even though the nature of the products and production processes may be viewed as similar, it may be difficult to conclude that the type or class of customer is similar to aggregate operating segments.

5.2.147   *Methods used to distribute products or provide services*

5.2.147.10   Whether methods used to distribute products or provide services are considered similar depends on how a particular entity is structured. [*IFRS 8.12(d)*]

EXAMPLE 9 – AGGREGATION – METHODS USED TO DISTRIBUTE PRODUCTS

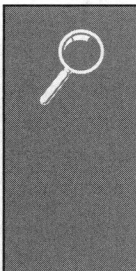

> **5.2.147.20**   A retailer sells its products through entity-owned stores located in shopping malls throughout Europe and also through the use of catalogues. The Director of Store Sales is responsible for all store operations and activities; the Director of Catalogue Sales is responsible for all catalogue sales. Separate financial information is reported by each director to the CODM on a regular basis. The CODM assesses performance and makes resource allocation decisions based on the separate financial information. The methods used to distribute products are not similar, and therefore such operating segments would not be aggregated.

5.2.148   *Nature of regulatory environment*

5.2.148.10   Even if all other criteria for two operating segments are determined to be similar, they may operate in different regulatory environments. If the effect of different regulatory environments is that operating segments are not similar, then they cannot be aggregated. [*IFRS 8.12(e)*]

5.2.148.20   Regulatory environment does not mean regulatory body. Regulatory bodies can be different but still relate to a similar regulatory environment.

5.2.150   **STEP 4: DETERMINE REPORTABLE SEGMENTS**

5.2.150.10   Under IFRS 8, an operating segment is required to be reported separately if any of the following quantitative thresholds is met.

- The segment's reported revenue (external sales and inter-segment transfers) is 10 percent or more of the combined revenue (internal and external) of all operating segments (see 5.2.156).
- The absolute amount of the segment's reported profit or loss is 10 percent or more of the greater, in absolute amount, of:
  - the combined reported profit of all operating segments that did not report a loss; and
  - the combined reported loss of all operating segments that reported a loss (see 5.2.157).
- The segment's assets are 10 percent or more of the combined assets of all operating segments (see 5.2.158). [*IFRS 8.13*]

5.2.150.20   'Combined' in each of the three tests in 5.2.150.10 means the total amounts for all operating segments before the elimination of intra-group transactions and balances – i.e. not the entity's financial statement amounts. It does not include reconciling items and activities that do not meet the definition of an operating segment under IFRS 8 – e.g. corporate activities (see 5.2.90.10).

5.2.150.25   Entities are required to ensure that the total external revenue of the identified reportable segments constitutes 75 percent or more of total consolidated revenue. If not, additional operating segments are required to be reported separately until at least 75 percent of total consolidated revenue is accounted for by the reportable segments. [*IFRS 8.15*]

5.2.150.30   The measures of the segment amounts used for these tests are based on the amounts reported to the CODM. As a result, these measures might not necessarily be in accordance with IFRS (e.g. information based on an adjusted operating profit, EBITDA or on a cash basis), and cannot be conformed to IFRS for purposes of applying the tests. [*IFRS 8.25*]

5.2.150.40   The CODM may use more than one measure of a segment's profit or loss, or more than one measure of a segment's assets or a segment's liabilities. In this case, the measure disclosed in reporting segment profit or loss, or segment assets or liabilities, is the measure that management believes is determined in accordance with the measurement principle most consistent with that used for the corresponding amounts in the entity's financial statements. [*IFRS 8.26*]

5.2.150.50   Operating segments that do not meet any of the quantitative thresholds may be considered reportable, and disclosed separately, if management believes that information about the segment would be useful to readers of the financial statements or more reportable segments need to be identified to meet the 75 percent test (see 5.2.160.20). [*IFRS 8.13*]

5.2.150.60   After applying the quantitative tests, an operating segment might be determined to be a reportable segment even though it was not considered to be a reportable segment in a previous period – e.g. a specific operating segment grew from 5 percent of total combined segment revenue in the previous period to 13 percent in the current period. In this situation, the entity discloses this operating segment as a reportable segment and restates all prior-period segment information to be consistent with the current period's segment presentation, unless the information is not available and the cost to develop it would be excessive; in this case, that fact is disclosed. [*IFRS 8.18*]

5.2.150.70   Conversely, an operating segment that has historically been a reportable segment might not exceed any of the quantitative thresholds in the current period. In this situation, if management expects it to be a reportable segment in the future, then the entity continues to treat that operating segment as a reportable segment to maintain the inter-period comparability of segment information. An operating segment that exceeds one of the quantitative tests – as a result of another operating segment dropping below the thresholds because of temporary or abnormal circumstances – would be a reportable segment. [*IFRS 8.17*]

5.2.155   Quantitative tests

5.2.156   *Revenue test*

5.2.156.10   The numerator in the revenue test is the revenue reported to the CODM attributable to the operating segment. The denominator is the combined revenue of all identified operating segments as reported to the CODM. The sum of all combined operating segment revenue might not necessarily equal consolidated revenue because of inter-segment sales and/or reconciling items. 'All identified operating segments' refers to the total of all operating segments reviewed by the CODM and should not be confused with reportable segments. [*IFRS 8.13(a)*]

EXAMPLE 10 – QUANTITATIVE TEST – REVENUE

5.2.156.15   After applying the aggregation criteria, Company X has four operating segments. The revenue test is applied as follows.

	REVENUES		
	EXTERNAL	INTERNAL	TOTAL
Segments A, B and C (aggregated)	4,000	1,000	5,000
Segment D	200	2,000	2,200
Segment E	500	100	600
Segment F	700	-	700
Combined	5,400	3,100	8,500
Reconciling items and eliminations	(300)	(3,100)	(3,400)
Consolidated	5,100	-	5,100

5.2.156.20   The reconciling items and eliminations include differences in revenue recognition policies between the measures of revenue reported to the CODM and the measures of revenue in the entity's financial statements, and the elimination of inter-segment sales. The threshold for the revenue test is 850 (8,500 x 10%). Therefore, Segments A, B and C (aggregated) and Segment D exceed the quantitative revenue threshold and are reportable segments. Segments E and F would be further evaluated to determine if they meet either the profit or loss or the asset quantitative threshold tests.

5.2.156.25   Situations might exist in which certain revenue relates to a business activity that is not an operating segment. It is not appropriate to include such revenue amounts in the denominator used to perform the segment revenue test. This could, in certain cases, result in additional operating segments being reported. [*IFRS 8.13(a)*]

5.2.157   *Profit or loss test*

5.2.157.10   To perform the profit or loss test, an entity uses the same measure of profit or loss as used by the CODM to allocate resources and to assess performance. The test is 10 percent or more of the greater, in the absolute amount, of:
• the combined reported profit of all operating segments that did not report a loss; and
• the combined reported loss of all operating segments that reported a loss. [*IFRS 8.13(b)*]

EXAMPLE 11 – QUANTITATIVE TEST – PROFIT OR LOSS

5.2.157.15   Company Y has five operating segments. The measure of segment profit or loss reported to and used by the CODM is profit before tax. The operating segment results are as follows.

	PROFIT OR (LOSS) BEFORE TAX
Segment G	10,800
Segment H	8,100
Segment I	(3,700)
Segment J	2,400
Segment K	(800)
Combined	16,800
Reconciling items and eliminations[1]	(1,800)
Consolidated	15,000

Note
1.   The reconciling items and eliminations include corporate expenses and the elimination of inter-segment profits.

5.2.157.20   Y calculates the following amounts for the profit or loss test.

	ABSOLUTE AMOUNT	10% OF ABSOLUTE AMOUNT
Combined segment profit for all operating segments that did not report a loss	21,300[1]	2,130
Combined segment loss for all operating segments that reported a loss	4,500[2]	450

Notes
1.   Calculated as 10,800 + 8,100 + 2,400.
2.   Calculated as 3,700 + 800.

5.2.157.25   Because 2,130 is the greater of the two amounts, this amount is the quantitative threshold used in the segment profit or loss test. Therefore, Segments G, H, I and J are reportable operating segments. Segment K would be further evaluated to see if it meets either the revenue or asset quantitative threshold tests.

5.2.157.30   Situations might exist in which certain profits or losses relate to a business activity that is not an operating segment – e.g. incidental revenue and expenses. It is not appropriate to include such profits or losses in the denominator used to perform the segment profit or loss test. This could, in certain cases, result in additional operating segments being reported. [*IFRS 8.13(b)*]

5.2.158   *Asset test*

5.2.158.10   All assets identifiable with an operating segment need not be included for purposes of performing the segment assets test. Only those assets included in the measure of segment assets reported to and used by the CODM for purposes of assessing performance and making resource allocation decisions are included in the asset test. [*IFRS 8.13(c)*]

EXAMPLE 12 – QUANTITATIVE TEST – ONLY PARTIAL ASSETS REPORTED TO CODM

5.2.158.15   Company S has 10 operating segments. The CODM receives and uses only receivables and inventory information in the measure of segment assets for purposes of assessing performance and making resource allocation decisions. Although it is evident which other assets (e.g. property, plant and equipment) could be identified with each of these specific operating segments, the measure of segment assets for purposes of the asset test is the total of segment receivables and inventory.

5.2.158.20   Changing the facts, assume that the segment receivables and inventory information is not reviewed or used by the CODM for purposes of assessing performance and making resource allocation decisions, although it is reported to the CODM. For purposes of applying the asset test, the entity includes the segment assets reported to the CODM, even if the information is not reviewed or used by the CODM. In this example, segment asset information is also required to be disclosed. The disclosure of segment assets would be the total of receivables and inventory, and is described as such.

5.2.160   REMAINING OPERATING SEGMENTS

5.2.160.10   An entity might be able to aggregate information about operating segments that fall below the quantitative thresholds based on the additional aggregation provisions stated in IFRS 8. Under IFRS 8, an entity is allowed to combine information about two or more such operating segments that do not meet the quantitative thresholds to produce a reportable segment only if the operating segments share a majority of the aggregation criteria listed in 5.2.140.10, provided that the aggregation is consistent with the core principle of IFRS 8 and the segments have similar economic characteristics. [*IFRS 8.14*]

5.2.160.20   IFRS 8 requires reportable segments to be identified until at least 75 percent of the total revenue reported in the financial statements is included in those segments (see 5.2.150.25). [*IFRS 8.15*]

5.2.160.30   When complying with the consolidated revenue test in 5.2.160.20, in our view entities have flexibility in determining which additional segments will be reported separately. We believe that the next largest operating segment is not required to be reported. Consideration should be given to reporting the additional segments that will be most useful to financial statement users, consistent with the core principle of IFRS 8.

5.2.160.40   IFRS 8 requires information about other business activities and operating segments that are not reportable to be combined and disclosed in an 'all other segments' category separate from other reconciling items in the reconciliations required by IFRS 8 (see 5.2.210). The sources of the revenue included in the 'all other segments' category are required to be described. [*IFRS 8.16*]

5.2.170   CHANGES IN COMPOSITION OF OPERATING SEGMENTS

5.2.170.10   Events might occur – e.g. a significant internal reorganisation or implementation of a new financial reporting system – that change the composition of the operating segments. In these cases, the financial results may be grouped and reported differently to the CODM.

5.2.170.20   Following a change in the composition of an entity's operating segments that results in a change in reportable segments, IFRS 8 requires previously reported segment information (including interim periods) to be restated, unless the information is not available and the cost to develop it would be excessive. The entity determines whether these limitations apply for each individual item of disclosure. The entity also discloses whether it has restated the comparative items of segment information for earlier periods. [*IFRS 8.29*]

5.2.170.30   If previously reported segment information is not restated, then IFRS 8 requires the entity to disclose current period segment information on both the old and new basis of segmentation in the year of change, and subsequently until all periods can be presented on the new basis, unless the information is not available and the cost to develop it would be excessive. [*IFRS 8.30*]

5.2.180   STEP 5: DISCLOSE SEGMENT INFORMATION

5.2.190   Annual disclosures

5.2.190.10   IFRS 8 requires an entity to disclose for each period for which a statement of profit or loss and OCI is presented:
- general information about the factors used to identify the entity's reportable segments, judgements made in applying the aggregation criteria, and the types of products and services from which each reportable segment generates its revenues;
- information about profit or loss, assets and liabilities; and
- reconciliations. [*IFRS 8.21*]

5.2.190.20   IFRS 8 does not provide any exemption from the required disclosures due to 'competitive harm'. [*IFRS 8.BC43–BC45*]

5.2.195   *General information*

5.2.195.10   The requirement to disclose general information about the identification of reportable segments, including the judgements made by management and the types of products and services, applies to all entities in the scope of IFRS 8. The disclosures include:
- how an entity has identified its reportable segments – e.g. products or services, geographic areas, regulatory environments or a combination of factors;
- a brief description of operating segments that have been aggregated; and
- economic indicators that have been assessed in determining that the operating segments have similar economic characteristics (see 5.2.143). [*IFRS 8.22*]

5.2.200   *Information about profit or loss, assets and liabilities*

5.2.200.10   IFRS 8 requires an entity to report a measure of profit or loss for each reportable segment, and a measure of total assets and liabilities for each reportable segment if such amounts are provided regularly to the CODM. It also requires an entity to disclose the following about each reportable segment if the specified amounts are included in the measure of segment profit or loss reviewed by the CODM or are otherwise provided regularly to the CODM, even if not included in that measure of segment profit or loss:

- revenues from external customers;
- revenues from transactions with other operating segments of the same entity;
- interest revenue;
- interest expense;
- depreciation and amortisation;
- material items of income and expense disclosed in accordance with IAS 1;
- equity-accounted earnings;
- income tax; and
- material non-cash items other than depreciation and amortisation. [*IFRS 8.23*]

5.2.200.20   If the amounts specified in 5.2.200.10 are inherent in the measure of segment profit or loss used by the CODM, then those amounts are required to be disclosed even if they are not explicitly provided to the CODM. [*IFRS 8.23*]

5.2.200.30   Adjustments and eliminations made in preparing the entity's financial statements – as well as allocations of revenue, expenses, gains or losses – are included in the reported segment profit or loss only if these items are included in the segment profit or loss measure used by the CODM. Additionally, allocations of amounts included in the measure of segment profit or loss are made on a reasonable basis. [*IFRS 8.25*]

5.2.200.35   To help users of financial statements understand an entity's segment disclosures, the entity provides sufficient explanation of the basis on which the information reported to the CODM was prepared. That disclosure includes differences in the basis of measurement between the consolidated amounts and the segment amounts and indicates whether allocations of items were made symmetrically. [*IFRS 8.20, 27, BCA90*]

5.2.200.40   IFRS 8 requires that a measure of total assets and total liabilities be disclosed for each reportable segment only if such information is regularly reported to the CODM. Total segment assets and total segment liabilities, or total identifiable assets by segment and total identifiable liabilities by segment, are not necessarily measures used by the CODM to assess performance and to make resource allocation decisions. Therefore, only those assets and liabilities that are included in the measure of the segment's assets and the segment's liabilities that is used by the CODM are reported for that segment. [*IFRS 8.23, 25*]

5.2.200.50   The following information is disclosed by each reportable segment if the specified amounts are included in the determination of segment assets reviewed by the CODM, or are otherwise regularly provided to the CODM even if they are not included in the determination of segment assets:

- interests in equity-accounted investees; and
- additions to non-current assets (including tangible and intangible assets) other than financial instruments, deferred tax assets, post-employment benefit assets and rights under insurance contracts. [*IFRS 8.24*]

5.2.200.60   IFRS 8 requires disclosure of the nature and effect of any asymmetrical allocation – e.g. if depreciation expense is included in the measure of segment profit or loss, but the related items of property, plant and equipment are not included in the measure of segment assets. [*IFRS 8.27(f)*]

5.2.203   *Joint arrangements and associates*

5.2.203.10   The segment information to be disclosed for an investee that is a reportable segment needs to be consistent with the concept of the management approach and the core principle of IFRS 8. Therefore, the segment information that is disclosed is determined on the same basis as it is reported to the CODM. [*IFRS 8.23–24*]

5.2.203.20   If the investee is identified as a reportable segment and the CODM receives financial statements of the investee, then the entity discloses the investee's revenue, a measure of profit or loss, assets and other amounts required by IFRS 8, as reported in the investee's financial statements. The difference between the amounts reported in the segment disclosure to the proportionate amounts reported in the entity's financial statements will be included in the reconciliation items (see 5.2.210).

5.2.203.30   In contrast, there might be situations in which the CODM only receives information about the investee that represents the entity's proportionate share in the investee's revenue, profits and loss, assets and other information. In those instances, in our view the entity should disclose the segment information of the investee using the proportionate amounts.

5.2.210   *Reconciliation disclosures*

5.2.210.10   An entity is required to provide reconciliations of the total of the reportable segments':
- revenues to the entity's revenues in the financial statements;
- measures of profit or loss to the entity's profit or loss before income tax and discontinued operations in the financial statements. However, if an entity allocates to reportable segments items such as income tax, then the entity may reconcile the total of the segments' measures of profit or loss to the entity's profit or loss after those items;
- assets to the entity's assets in the financial statements if segment assets are reported to the CODM;
- liabilities to the entity's liabilities in the financial statements if segment liabilities are reported to the CODM; and
- amounts for every other material item of information disclosed to the corresponding amount in the entity's financial statements. [*IFRS 8.28(a)–(e)*]

5.2.210.20   IFRS 8 requires all material reconciling items to be identified and described separately – e.g. the amount of each material adjustment made to reconcile the accounting policies used in determining segment profit or loss to the entity's amounts is identified and described separately. [*IFRS 8.28*]

5.2.210.30   Reconciliations of profit or loss amounts for reportable segments to the amounts reported in the entity's financial statements are required for each period for which a statement of profit or loss and OCI is presented.

5.2.210.40   Reconciliations of statement of financial position amounts for reportable segments to the amounts reported in the entity's financial statements are required for each date for which a statement of financial position is presented.

5.2.210.50   If a reconciling item results from an accounting policy used by an operating segment that is different from that used in the preparation of the entity's financial statements, then additional disclosures about the accounting policies used by the operating segment are required. Similarly, if a reconciling item results from an allocation method that is used by the entity, then additional disclosures about the nature and effect of any asymmetrical allocation to the operating segment are required. [*IFRS 8.27(b)–(d), (f)*]

5.2.220   Entity-wide disclosures

5.2.220.10   Entity-wide disclosures related to the following items are required, regardless of whether the information is used by the CODM in assessing segment performance.
- Revenue from external customers for products and services.
- Revenue from external customers by geographic areas.
- Geographic information about non-current assets other than financial instruments, deferred tax assets, post-employment benefit assets and rights arising from insurance contracts.
- Information on the extent of reliance on major customers. [*IFRS 8.31–34*]

5.2.220.20   The information in 5.2.220.10 is provided by both the entity's country of domicile and by an individual foreign country, if material. In our view, disclosing such information by region – e.g. Europe or Asia – does not meet the requirement to disclose information by an individual foreign country, if material. Such information is disclosed by an individual foreign country – e.g. France, the Netherlands or Singapore – when material. These disclosures apply to all entities subject to IFRS 8, including entities that have only one reportable segment. However, information required by the entity-wide disclosures need not be repeated if it is already included in the segment disclosures. [*IFRS 8.31, 33*]

5.2.220.30   An entity may allocate revenue from external customers to geographic areas as it deems most appropriate – e.g. by selling location, customer location or the location to which the product is transported, which might differ from the location of the customer. The selected method is applied consistently and disclosed in the financial statements. [*IFRS 8.33(a)*]

5.2.220.40   Some entities' segments may report revenues from a broad range of essentially different products and services, or more than one of the reportable segments might provide essentially the same products and services. Similarly, an entity's segments may hold assets in different geographic areas and report revenues from customers in different geographic areas, or more than one of its segments might operate in the same geographic area. These disclosures need to be provided only if they are not already disclosed as part of the reportable segment information required by IFRS 8.

5.2.220.50   The entity-wide disclosures are based on the same financial information that is used to produce the entity's financial statements – i.e. not based on the management approach. Accordingly, the revenue reported for these disclosures is equal the entity's total revenue. [*IFRS 8.32–33*]

5.2.220.60   IFRS 8 does not provide materiality thresholds for determining the entity-wide disclosures, other than for major customer information as described in 5.2.220.70. As a result, when otherwise not specified by the standard, judgement needs to be used to determine material items for entity-wide disclosure purposes. In our view, quantitative thresholds and qualitative reasons should be considered when determining material items for entity-wide disclosures.

5.2.220.70   Revenues from an individual external customer that represent 10 percent or more of an entity's total revenue are disclosed. Specifically, the total amount by significant customer and the identity of the segments that includes the revenue are disclosed. However, IFRS 8 does not require the identity of the customer or the amount of revenues that each segment reports from that customer to be disclosed. A group of entities known to be under common control are considered a single customer. Judgement of the extent of economic integration between the entities may be required in determining whether government-related entities are a single customer when government control is pervasive. [*IFRS 8.34, IAS 24.BC49(c)*]

5.2.230   Currency of segment disclosures

5.2.230.10   Segment information may be reported internally to the CODM in a currency that is different from the presentation currency used in the entity's financial statements. Some entities may decide that it is more useful for users to disclose such information in the presentation currency of the entity's financial statements; in such cases, an explanatory note may be appropriate. Conversely, other entities may decide that it is more useful to disclose segment information in the currency reported to the CODM; in such cases, the currency of such information may need to be carefully labelled and will result in additional reconciling items (see 5.2.210).

5.2.240   Interim disclosures

5.2.240.10   The following segment information is required to be disclosed in an entity's interim report only if the entity is in the scope of IFRS 8 for the purposes of its annual financial statements (see 5.9.60.20).
- Revenues from external customers, if included in the measure of segment profit or loss reviewed by the CODM or otherwise regularly provided to the CODM.
- Inter-segment revenues, if included in the measure of segment profit or loss reviewed by the CODM or otherwise regularly provided to the CODM.
- A measure of segment profit or loss.
- A measure of total assets and/or total liabilities for a particular reportable segment if:
    - the related amounts are regularly provided to the CODM; and
    - there has been a material change in the total assets or total liabilities for that segment from the related amounts disclosed in the last annual financial statements.
- A description of any differences from the last annual financial statements in the basis of segmentation or in the basis of measurement of segment profit or loss.
- A reconciliation of the total of the reportable segments' measures of profit or loss to the entity's profit or loss before income tax and discontinued operations. [*IAS 34.16A(g)*]

5.2.240.20   However, if an entity allocated to reportable segments items such as income tax, then the entity may reconcile the total of the segments' measures of profit or loss to profit or loss after those items. Material reconciling items are separately identified and described in the reconciliation. [*IAS 34.16A(g)(vi)*]

5.2.250   COMPARATIVE INFORMATION

5.2.250.10   IFRS 8 requires segment information for earlier periods presented to be restated in certain circumstances, such as changes in the composition of operating segments (see 5.2.170). Comparative segment information is required to be restated to conform to the requirements of IFRS 8, unless the information is not available and the cost to develop it would be excessive. In this case, that fact is disclosed. [*IFRS 8.29–30, 36*]

5.2.250.20   IFRS 8 does not provide guidance on whether prior-year amounts in entity-wide disclosures (see 5.2.220) need to be restated if there is a change in the current year – e.g. a previously immaterial country representing 3 percent of the external revenues included in the entity-wide geographic disclosures now represents 15 percent of external revenues. In our view, the prior-year information should be restated, if this is practicable, so that the disclosures from year to year are comparable.

5.2.260   ALLOCATION OF GOODWILL FOR IMPAIRMENT TESTING PURPOSES

5.2.260.10   IAS 36 requires that each unit or group of units to which goodwill is allocated cannot be larger than an operating segment before aggregation (see 3.10.460.10 and 5.2.140). [*IAS 36.80(b)*]

5.3 Earnings per share

5.3 Earnings per share

CURRENTLY EFFECTIVE REQUIREMENTS

This publication reflects IFRS in issue at 1 August 2018, and the currently effective requirements cover annual periods beginning on 1 January 2018.

The requirements related to this topic are mainly derived from the following.

Standard	Title
IAS 33	Earnings per Share

KPMG's publication *IFRS Handbook: Earnings per share* provides a comprehensive analysis of IAS 33. The Handbook is more in-depth than this chapter and includes additional clarification of the requirements of IAS 33 and of our interpretative guidance. It provides extensive illustrative examples of the calculation of both basic and diluted EPS.

FORTHCOMING REQUIREMENTS AND FUTURE DEVELOPMENTS

For this topic, there are no forthcoming requirements or future developments.

5.3.10   **OVERVIEW OF REQUIREMENTS**

5.3.10.10   Basic and diluted EPS are presented in the statement of profit or loss and OCI by entities whose ordinary shares or potential ordinary shares (see 5.3.100.10) are traded in a public market – i.e. a domestic or foreign stock exchange or an over-the-counter market, including local and regional markets – or that file, or are in the process of filing, their financial statements with a securities commission or other regulatory organisation for the purpose of issuing any class of ordinary shares in a public market. [*IAS 33.2*]

5.3.10.20   The consolidated financial statements of a group whose parent does not meet the scope requirement in 5.3.10.10 in its own capacity, but which has an NCI or a subsidiary that does meet the scope requirement, are not in the scope of IAS 33. [*IFRS 8.BC23*]

5.3.10.30   IAS 33 does not define the term 'traded in a public market'. In our view, determining what is meant by traded in a public market depends on facts and circumstances, and can vary based on local requirements from securities commissions and/or regulators. We believe that if a buyer or a seller can contact a broker and obtain a quoted price, then this is an indicator that ordinary shares or potential ordinary shares are publicly traded. This is without regard to how often the shares are traded.

5.3.10.40   If the relevant shares are shares or units in a fund, then the following factors may indicate that the fund is not traded in a public market.
- The fund is listed at a stock exchange for convenience listing or marketing purposes only, and cannot be traded on the stock market.
- The fund's shares are traded through a fund agent/administrator only – i.e. the subscriptions and redemptions of units are handled by a transfer agent/administrator directly associated with the fund.
- Buyer and seller set up prices based on the fund prospectus valuation principles and therefore prices would not be established by trading in a market.

5.3.10.50   The factors mentioned in 5.3.10.40 are not exhaustive and judgement will be required when assessing if a fund falls in the scope of IAS 33.

5.3.10.60   In our view, an entity is in the process of issuing ordinary shares only when the entity has taken active steps to obtain a listing, rather than simply planning the listing. We also believe that 'issuing' shares includes listing (registering) shares already in issue. Accordingly, when an entity prepares a prospectus in preparation for listing, EPS information should be included in the financial statements included in the prospectus.

5.3.10.70   If an entity's ordinary shares are untraded at the reporting date but are publicly traded by the time that the financial statements are authorised for issue, then the entity would generally have been in the process of filing its financial statements with a securities commission or other regulatory organisation for this purpose at the reporting date. Accordingly, we believe that the entity should disclose EPS information in its financial statements.

5.3.10.80   An entity's ordinary shares or potential ordinary shares may be publicly traded for only a portion of the current period – e.g. because the entity's ordinary shares or potential ordinary shares were listed for the first time during the period. In our view, in this situation the entity should present EPS information for all periods for which statements of profit or loss and OCI are presented, and not only for the periods during which the entity's ordinary or potential ordinary shares were publicly traded.

5.3.10.90   An entity that would not otherwise be required to present EPS information may wish or may be required by local regulations to present basic and/or diluted earnings per share or unit. If an entity voluntarily presents EPS information, then that information is calculated and presented in accordance with IAS 33. [*IAS 33.3*]

5.3.20   Presentation

5.3.20.10   Basic and diluted EPS for both continuing and total operations are presented in the statement of profit or loss and OCI for each class of ordinary shares, with equal prominence for all periods. An entity presenting profit or loss and OCI in two separate statements (see 4.1.10) discloses the information only in the statement displaying components of profit or loss. [*IAS 33.4A, 66–67A*]

5.3.20.20   If both separate financial statements and consolidated financial statements are prepared (S) by an entity (see 2.1.90), then EPS disclosures are required to be provided only on the basis of consolidated information. However, if an entity chooses to provide EPS amounts based on its separate financial statements, then it presents these additional amounts on the face of its own separate statement of profit or loss and OCI. IAS 33 does not permit these additional amounts to be presented on the face of the consolidated statement of profit or loss and OCI. [*IAS 33.4*]

5.3.20.30   EPS amounts are presented for all periods presented, including interim periods. However, for interim periods the presentation and disclosure requirements are limited (see 5.3.30, 560.70, 5.9.50). [*IAS 33.67*]

5.3.20.40   Presentation of EPS is required in the statement of profit or loss and OCI for the profit or loss from both continuing and total operations for the period. In addition, disclosure of separate EPS information is required for discontinued operations, either in the statement of profit or loss and OCI or in the notes to the financial statements (see 5.3.560.10). [*IAS 33.66, 68–68A*]

5.3.30   Interim financial statements

5.3.30.10   An entity is required to present basic and diluted EPS in its interim financial statements only when the entity is in the scope of IAS 33 (see 5.9.50). [*IAS 34.11*]

5.3.30.20   Neither IAS 33 nor IAS 34 is clear about the requirement to disclose EPS information when an entity's ordinary shares are untraded at the interim reporting date but are publicly traded by the time its interim financial statements for that period are authorised for issue. As noted in 5.3.10.70, in such circumstances the entity would generally have been in the process of filing its financial statements with a securities commission or other regulatory organisation for this purpose at the interim reporting date. Accordingly, in our view the entity should disclose EPS information in these interim financial statements.

5.3.30.30   In addition, neither IAS 33 nor IAS 34 is clear about the requirement to disclose EPS information when an entity's ordinary shares are publicly traded for only a portion of the current interim period – e.g. because the entity's ordinary shares or potential ordinary shares were only listed for the first time during the period. As noted in 5.3.10.80, in our view in this situation the entity should present EPS information in the interim financial statements for all periods for which statements of profit or loss and OCI are presented, and not only for the periods in which the entity's ordinary shares or potential ordinary shares are publicly traded.

5.3.40   Entities with more than one class of equity

5.3.40.10   An 'ordinary share' is an equity instrument that is subordinate to all other classes of equity instruments. Ordinary shares participate in profit for the period only after other types of shares such as preference shares have participated. If an entity has more than one class of ordinary shares, then EPS is disclosed for each class of ordinary shares. Ordinary shares of the same class are those shares that have the same right to receive dividends or otherwise share in the profit for the period. If an entity has shares with different rights, then it considers whether all the shares are in fact ordinary shares. [*IAS 33.5–6, 66*]

EXAMPLE 1 – TWO CLASSES OF ORDINARY SHARES

5.3.40.20   Company M has two classes of shares, A and B. The holders of class B shares are entitled to dividends equal to 50% of any dividends declared on the class A shares, but the shares are otherwise identical to class A shares. Both classes are subordinate to all other classes of equity instruments with respect to participation in profit. In this example, M concludes that both class A and B shares are ordinary shares despite the difference in entitlement to dividends. Therefore, disclosure of separate EPS amounts is required for both the class A and B ordinary shares.

5.3.40.30   In our view, an entity is not required to present separate EPS information for participating preference shares that are not considered to be a separate class of ordinary shares.

EXAMPLE 2 – PARTICIPATING PREFERENCE SHARES THAT ARE NOT ORDINARY SHARES

5.3.40.40   Company N has two classes of shares, X and Y. Shareholders of class X are entitled to a fixed dividend per share and have the right to participate in any additional dividends declared. The class Y shareholders participate equally with class X shareholders with respect to the additional dividends only.

5.3.40.50   In this example, N concludes that class X shares are not considered to be ordinary, because the fixed entitlement creates a preference over the class Y shares, and the class Y shareholders are subordinate to the class X shareholders. This is even if both classes participate equally in the residual assets on dissolution. The class Y shares are the only class of ordinary shares, and therefore the only class of shares for which disclosure of EPS is required. However, the participating rights of each class of these shares are considered in determining earnings attributable to ordinary equity holders (see 5.3.70). [*IAS 33.6*]

5.3.40.60   In our view, puttable instruments that qualify for equity classification instead of financial liability classification under IAS 32 (see 7.3.70) are not ordinary shares for the purposes of IAS 33. We believe that it is not appropriate to apply by analogy the limited scope exemption under IAS 32 for EPS calculation purposes. Accordingly, we believe that EPS presentation is not required for, or as a result of the existence of, such instruments. However, when determining the earnings that are attributable to the ordinary equity holders, the terms of these instruments are evaluated to determine if they are participating instruments (see 5.3.70). [*IAS 32.16A–16F*]

5.3.50   BASIC EPS

5.3.50.10   Basic EPS is the profit or loss attributable to ordinary equity holders of the parent entity for the period, divided by the weighted-average number of ordinary shares outstanding during the period. [*IAS 33.10*]

EXAMPLE 3 – BASIC EPS CALCULATION – SIMPLE EXAMPLE

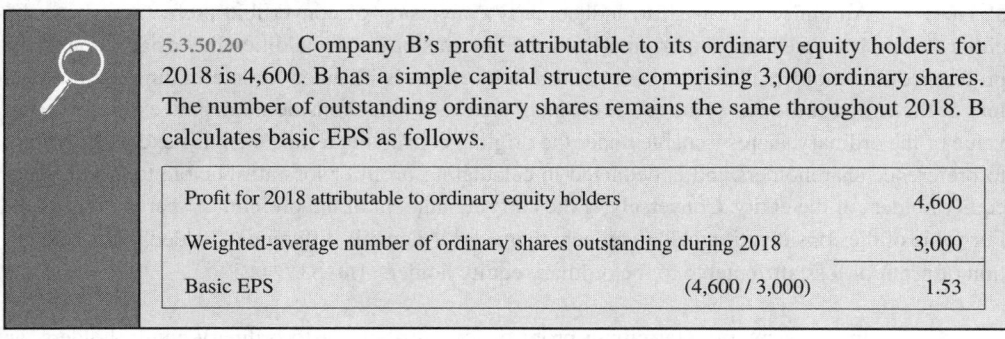

5.3.50.20   Company B's profit attributable to its ordinary equity holders for 2018 is 4,600. B has a simple capital structure comprising 3,000 ordinary shares. The number of outstanding ordinary shares remains the same throughout 2018. B calculates basic EPS as follows.

Profit for 2018 attributable to ordinary equity holders		4,600
Weighted-average number of ordinary shares outstanding during 2018		3,000
Basic EPS	(4,600 / 3,000)	1.53

5.3.50.30   In practice, the basic EPS calculation may be more complex than Example 3 and adjustments may be required to earnings (see 5.3.60–70) and/or the weighted-average number of shares outstanding during the period (see 5.3.80). The following are examples of instruments that may require adjustments to the basic EPS calculation:

- participating instruments and other classes of ordinary shares (see 5.3.70);
- partly paid ordinary shares (see 5.3.160);
- unvested shares and shares subject to recall (see 5.3.190 and 210);
- mandatorily convertible instruments (see 5.3.230); and
- share options exercisable for little or no consideration (see 5.3.260).

5.3.60   Earnings (the numerator)

5.3.60.10   The profit or loss attributable to ordinary equity holders of the parent entity – i.e. the numerator for basic EPS – is the profit or loss adjusted for:

- the post-tax amounts of dividends on preference shares classified as equity;
- gains or losses on the settlement of preference shares classified as equity; and
- other similar effects of preference shares classified as equity, including the amortisation of the premium or discount on the original issue of preference shares and the effects of payments to induce conversion (see 5.3.60.40). [*IAS 33.12–18*]

5.3.60.20   The post-tax amount of dividends on preference shares classified as equity is deducted to arrive at the profit or loss attributable to ordinary equity holders because those dividends represent income that is not attributable to ordinary equity holders. Cumulative preference dividends are deducted, whether they have been declared or not. Non-cumulative preference dividends are not deducted unless they have been declared by the reporting date. In our view, the profit or loss attributable to ordinary equity holders should not be adjusted for dividends on non-cumulative preference shares declared after the reporting date, even if these dividends relate to the reporting period. This is consistent with the requirement that dividends declared after the reporting date are non-adjusting events in accordance with IAS 10 because no obligation exists at the reporting date (see 2.9.30.20). [*IAS 33.14, A14(a)*]

5.3.60.30   Although non-cumulative preference dividends are generally ignored in the numerator for basic EPS until they are declared, separate consideration related to the allocation of earnings applies if the corresponding preference shares participate in dividends with ordinary shares as participating equity instruments (see 5.3.70).

5.3.60.40   An entity may wish to induce early conversion of convertible preference shares by either favourably amending the original conversion terms or paying additional consideration to the preference shareholders. The early conversion inducement is included in determining the profit or loss of the entity. If the fair value of the ordinary shares or other consideration paid exceeds the fair value of the ordinary shares issuable under the original conversion terms, then this excess is a return to preference shareholders and is deducted in calculating profit or loss attributable to the ordinary equity holders of the entity. Conversely, if the carrying amount of the preference shares exceeds the fair value of the consideration paid to redeem them early, then this difference is added in the calculation of profit or loss attributable to the ordinary equity holders. [*IAS 33.17–18*]

5.3.60.50   In our view, in determining profit or loss attributable to ordinary equity holders, an entity should also consider any obligations to cover losses attributable to any NCI regardless of the entity's accounting policy choice for how it accounts for these obligations (see 2.5.510).

EXAMPLE 4 – OBLIGATION TO COVER NCI LOSSES – EFFECT ON EPS

5.3.60.60   Company P owns 80% of Company S. P provides a guarantee to the NCI of S that it will cover any losses of S attributable to the NCI. P's consolidated profit for the year excluding S is 1,000 and S incurs a loss of 150. P has 100 ordinary shares outstanding throughout the year. If P was not obliged to cover the losses attributable to the NCI, then P would disclose EPS of 8.80 ((1,000 - 150 x 80%) / 100). However, because P has agreed to cover the losses attributable to the NCI, P discloses EPS of 8.50 ((1,000 - 150 x 100%) / 100).

5.3.70   Participating equity instruments and other classes of ordinary shares

5.3.70.10   The capital structure of some entities includes equity instruments that participate in dividends along with ordinary shares based on a predetermined formula ('participating equity instruments') and/or a separate class of ordinary shares with a dividend rate different from that of another class of ordinary shares but without prior or senior rights. These instruments may reduce the entitlement of an ordinary shareholder to the net profit or loss of an entity and therefore the numerator for basic EPS is adjusted for the effects of these instruments. To determine the profit or loss attributable to ordinary equity holders, profit or loss for the period is allocated to the different classes of ordinary shares and participating equity instruments. This allocation is made in accordance with the rights of the other class to participate in distributions if the entire profit or loss were distributed. [*IAS 33.A13–A14*]

EXAMPLE 5 – PARTICIPATING PREFERENCE SHARES THAT ARE NOT ORDINARY SHARES – EPS CALCULATION

5.3.70.20   Company P has two classes of shares, X and Y. The following facts are relevant for this example.
- Each X and Y class has 100 shares outstanding.
- Holders of class X are entitled to a fixed dividend per share and have the right to participate in any additional dividends declared. All dividends are discretionary.
- Holders of class Y participate equally with holders of class X with respect to the additional dividends only.
- Net profit for the period is 2,000.
- Preference dividends totalling 100 are paid to the holders of class X.

5.3.70.30   Even though P has no intention to pay additional dividends, to calculate the profit or loss attributable to the Y shares – being the only ordinary shares for P – the undistributed earnings are allocated to both the X and Y shares in accordance with their participation.

Net profit		2,000
Preference dividends paid to class X holders		(100)
Undistributed profits		1,900
Share of undistributed profits attributable to participating preference shareholders (class X)	(1,900 / 2)	(950)
Earnings attributable to ordinary shareholders of the parent (class Y)		950

EXAMPLE 6 – TWO CLASSES OF ORDINARY SHARES – EPS CALCULATION

5.3.70.40   Company R has two classes of ordinary shares, A and G. The following facts are relevant for this example.
- Class A has 30,000 shares outstanding.
- Class G has 10,000 shares outstanding.
- Class A shareholders participate in dividends at a rate of 1% higher than class G shareholders.

> - Net profit attributable to all shareholders for the period is 100,000.
> - R has not declared or paid any dividends for the period.
>
> 5.3.70.50   To calculate the profit or loss attributable to each class of shareholders, the net profit for the period is allocated to the class A and G shareholders in accordance with their rights to participate in these undistributed earnings, because there is a predetermined formula for dividend participation. R attributes the undistributed net profit for the period of 100,000 to class A and G shareholders as follows. [*IAS 33.A13–A14*]
>
> ---
>
> $(X^{(1)} \times 10{,}000) + (X \times 1.01 \times 30{,}000) = 100{,}000$
>
> $X = 2.48$ (rounded)
>
> | | | |
> |---|---|---|
> | Earnings attributable to class G shareholders | (2.48 x 10,000) | 24,800 |
> | Earnings attributable to class A shareholders | (2.48 x 1.01 x 30,000) | 75,144 |
>
> Note
> 1.   X represents the dividend per share to class G shareholders.

5.3.70.60   Some ordinary shares may be unvested (see 5.3.180) or contingently returnable to the entity – i.e. shares subject to recall (see 5.3.210). These shares may be entitled to non-forfeitable dividends during the vesting period or the period in which they are subject to recall. If this is the case, then to the extent that these dividends have not been recognised in profit or loss, in our view the profit or loss for the purpose of calculating basic EPS should be adjusted for these dividends and any undistributed earnings attributable to these shares, in accordance with their participating rights. This is because the numerator for basic EPS is intended to reflect amounts attributable to outstanding ordinary shares, and shares that are not yet vested or subject to recall are not considered to be outstanding. [*IAS 33.10, 24, A13–A14*]

5.3.70.70   The IFRS Interpretations Committee discussed whether a tax benefit arising from the hypothetical distribution of profit to participating equity holders should be reflected in the calculation of profit or loss attributable to ordinary shareholders. The Committee noted that, when calculating basic EPS, an entity adjusts profit or loss attributable to ordinary shareholders for the portion of any tax benefit attributable to those ordinary shareholders, regardless of whether the tax benefit is recognised in equity or in profit or loss. This is because the tax benefit is a direct consequence of the hypothetical distribution of profit to the participating equity holders underlying the determination of profit or loss attributable to ordinary equity holders (see 5.3.70.10). [*IAS 33.11, A14, IU 06-17*]

5.3.80   Weighted-average number of shares outstanding (the denominator)

5.3.80.10   When calculating basic EPS, the denominator is the weighted-average number of ordinary shares outstanding during the period. [*IAS 33.19*]

5.3.80.20   Example 7 illustrates the calculation of the weighted-average number of ordinary shares outstanding in a year. [*IAS 33.20, IE2*]

EXAMPLE 7 – CALCULATION OF WEIGHTED-AVERAGE NUMBER OF SHARES OUTSTANDING

5.3.80.25   In 2018, Company Z purchases treasury shares and issues new shares to settle a liability. The following facts are relevant for this example.

DATE	TRANSACTION	SHARES ISSUED	TREASURY SHARES (SEE **5.3.90**)	SHARES OUTSTANDING
1 January 2018	Balance at beginning of year	1,500	(250)	1,250
31 March 2018	Purchase of treasury shares for cash	-	(250)	1,000
30 June 2018	Issue of new shares to settle a liability	1,000	-	2,000
31 December 2018	Balance at end of year	2,500	(500)	2,000

5.3.80.30   Z calculates the weighted-average number of ordinary shares outstanding for 2018 as follows[1].

	NUMBER OF SHARES OUTSTANDING	TIME WEIGHTING	WEIGHTED-AVERAGE NUMBER OF SHARES
1 January to 31 March	1,250	3 / 12	312.5
1 April to 30 June	1,000	3 / 12	250
1 July to 31 December	2,000	6 / 12	1,000
		12 / 12	
Weighted-average number of ordinary shares outstanding			1,562.5

Note
1.   The weighted-average number of ordinary shares outstanding for 2018 can also be calculated as:
     (1,250 x 12 / 12) - (250 x 9 / 12) + (1,000 x 6 / 12).

5.3.80.40   Shares are usually considered outstanding for the purpose of determining the weighted-average number of ordinary shares outstanding from the date on which the corresponding consideration is receivable. The following table sets out some examples. [*IAS 33.21–23*]

ORDINARY SHARES ISSUED ...	TIME FROM WHICH SHARES ARE 'OUTSTANDING'
... for cash	When cash is receivable
... for another asset	When the asset is recognised

Ordinary shares issued ...	Time from which shares are 'outstanding'
... to settle a liability	Settlement date
... on conversion of a debt instrument	Date on which interest ceases to accrue
... in lieu of interest or principal on other financial instruments	Date on which interest ceases to accrue
... on voluntary reinvestment of dividends	Date on which dividends are reinvested
... as compensation for services received	When the services are rendered
... as consideration in a business combination	Date of acquisition
... on mandatory conversion of a convertible instrument	Date on which contract is entered into

5.3.80.50   The timing of the inclusion of ordinary shares is determined by the terms and conditions attaching to their issue after taking due consideration of the substance of any contract associated with their issue. [*IAS 33.21*]

EXAMPLE 8 – POTENTIAL ORDINARY SHARES – OPTIONS VESTED BUT UNEXERCISED

5.3.80.60   On 31 December 2016, Company D issued share options to its employees with an exercise price equal to the market price of D's shares at that date – i.e. the options represent potential ordinary shares. In 2018, all vesting conditions were satisfied; however, the employees have not exercised their options. Although all vesting conditions were met, the options are still potential ordinary shares outstanding (see 5.3.100.10) at 31 December 2018 and therefore the shares are not considered outstanding for the purposes of basic EPS.

5.3.80.70   The weighted-average number of ordinary shares outstanding in basic EPS may be affected if the number of ordinary shares outstanding is increased or decreased without a corresponding change in resources – e.g. as a result of a bonus or rights issue, share split, share consolidation (i.e. reverse share split) or stock dividend (see 5.3.530). [*IAS 33.26–29, 64, A2*]

5.3.90   *Treasury shares*

5.3.90.10   Treasury shares are not treated as outstanding ordinary shares and are therefore deducted from the number of shares outstanding. In consolidated financial statements, treasury shares include own shares that are held by a consolidated subsidiary (see 7.3.540). [*IAS 33.IE2*]

5.3.90.20   IFRS 10 excludes from its scope post-employment benefit plans or other long-term employment benefit plans to which IAS 19 applies (see 2.5.10.20 and 4.4.1490.30). Therefore, if an entity's ordinary shares are qualifying plan assets held by its employee benefit plan and are netted against the employee benefit obligation in accordance with IAS 19, then these shares are not the entity's treasury shares. Accordingly, in our view these shares should be considered outstanding when calculating EPS. However, if an entity's own shares held by its employee benefit plan do not meet the definition of plan assets, then they are presented as treasury shares, even though the plan is not consolidated by the employer (see 4.4.600.10 and 630.10); in this case, in our view these shares should not be considered outstanding when calculating EPS. [*IFRS 10.4A*]

5.3.90.30   Because the net presentation requirement for employee benefit plans under IAS 19 does not apply to equity-settled share-based payment plans, the consolidation requirements apply to a vehicle established in connection with equity-settled share-based payment plans (see 4.5.2410.10). If a reporting entity consolidates such a vehicle, then its ordinary shares held by that vehicle would be treasury shares; they are therefore not regarded as outstanding shares for basic EPS purposes. [*IAS 19.2*]

5.3.100   DILUTED EPS

5.3.100.10   To calculate diluted EPS, an entity adjusts the profit or loss attributable to ordinary equity holders of the parent entity (numerator) and the weighted-average number of shares outstanding (denominator) used in the basic EPS calculation for the effects of all dilutive potential ordinary shares. 'Potential ordinary shares' are financial instruments or other contracts that may entitle their holders to ordinary shares. Examples include:

- convertible debt or convertible preference shares, except for mandatorily convertible debt (see 5.3.240);
- share options, warrants and their equivalents (see 5.3.270); and
- shares that would be issued on satisfaction of certain conditions resulting from contractual arrangements, such as the purchase of a business that occurs before the reporting date (see 5.3.320). [*IAS 33.5, 30–31*]

5.3.100.20   Potential ordinary shares that were cancelled, have lapsed or have been converted to ordinary shares during the reporting period are reflected in the diluted EPS calculation, if they are dilutive, from the first day of the reporting period (if they were in existence at that date) to the day on which they lapse or are converted or cancelled. Potential ordinary shares issued during the reporting period are included in the diluted EPS calculation, if they are dilutive, from the day on which they are issued. [*IAS 33.36, 38*]

5.3.100.30   The effects of potential ordinary shares are reflected in diluted EPS only when they are dilutive – i.e. when their inclusion in the calculation would decrease EPS, or increase the loss per share, from continuing operations. [*IAS 33.41*]

5.3.100.40   When considering whether potential ordinary shares are dilutive or anti-dilutive and therefore whether to bring them into the diluted EPS calculation, each issue or series of potential ordinary shares is considered separately rather than in aggregate. For example, share options that have different exercise prices or dates need to be considered separately. The goal in computing diluted EPS is to calculate the maximum dilutive effect, and therefore each issue or series of potential ordinary shares is considered in sequence from the most dilutive to the least dilutive. To determine the sequence, it is necessary to calculate the effect that the conversion of the potential ordinary shares would have on both earnings from continuing operations and the number of shares. [*IAS 33.42, 44*]

5.3.100.50   Dilutive potential ordinary shares are determined independently for each period presented. The number of dilutive potential ordinary shares included in the annual (or year-to-date) period is not equal to a weighted average of the dilutive potential ordinary shares included in each interim computation. [*IAS 33.37*]

5.3.110   Adjustments to basic EPS

5.3.120   *Earnings*

5.3.120.10   To calculate diluted earnings, subject to the exception in relation to certain share-based payment costs (see 5.3.120.100), the numerator used for the calculation of basic EPS is adjusted for the post-tax effect of:

- any dividends, interest and other items related to the dilutive potential ordinary shares that are deducted in arriving at profit or loss attributable to ordinary equity holders – e.g. if a convertible debt is dilutive, then profit or loss attributable to ordinary equity holders is adjusted for the post-tax effect of the interest expense that would have been saved from the assumed conversion of the convertible debt (including any amortisation of initial transaction costs and discounts accounted for using the effective interest method, see 7.7.270); and
- any other changes in income or expense that would result from the assumed conversion of dilutive potential ordinary shares. Examples of such consequential effects on profit or loss may be:
  - an increase in the expense related to a non-discretionary employee profit-sharing plan; and
  - a decrease in depreciation expense if part of the interest on the debt is capitalised under IAS 23.
  [*IAS 33.33–35*]

EXAMPLE 9 – CONSEQUENTIAL EFFECTS ON PROFIT OR LOSS – CAPITALISED INTEREST

5.3.120.20   On 1 January 2018, Company B issued a convertible bond. The following facts are relevant for this example.

- In 2018, the interest on the debt recognised in accordance with IAS 32 and IFRS 9 is 9,000, of which:
  - 6,000 is recognised in profit or loss; and
  - 3,000 is capitalised into the cost of property, plant and equipment in accordance with IAS 23.
- Of the interest of 3,000 that is capitalised in 2018, 1,000 is recognised as part of the depreciation expense in 2018.
- Depreciation and interest expenses are tax-deductible.
- B's income tax rate is 30%.

5.3.120.30   B determines the consequential effect on profit or loss for the convertible debt as follows.

	BEFORE TAX	RELATED TAX AT 30%	AFTER TAX
Decrease in interest expense	6,000	(1,800)	4,200
Decrease in depreciation expense	1,000	(300)	700
Numerator adjustment	7,000	(2,100)	4,900

5.3.120.40   In our view, for an item to be treated as having a consequential effect on profit or loss as a result of the assumed conversion of dilutive potential ordinary shares, there should be a direct or automatic adjustment to profit or loss.

EXAMPLE 10 – NO CONSEQUENTIAL EFFECTS ON PROFIT OR LOSS – CALL OPTIONS AND SHARE SWAP ARRANGEMENTS

5.3.120.50   Company S issues share options to its employees. To fulfil its obligations in this regard, S writes a call option to Bank B to purchase its own shares at market price.

5.3.120.60   In this example, S concludes that this call option is not a derivative, because the value of the option does not depend on an underlying variable – i.e. it always has a fair value of zero (see 7.2.30.50). Therefore, as far as the call option between S and B is concerned, the assumed conversion of the employee share options would not lead to any consequential effect on profit or loss. Accordingly, no adjustment is made to the numerator in the diluted EPS calculation in this regard.

5.3.120.70   S also enters into a share swap arrangement with Bank C to reduce its exposure to an increase in the market price of its shares when the options become exercisable. The share swap has the following characteristics.
- S takes a notional loan from C with the principal amount equal to the purchase price of a notional number of shares at a notional share price.
- S pays interest on the notional loan and C pays dividends on the notional number of shares when S declares dividends.
- S may change the number of notional shares implicit in the notional loan by notifying C in advance, and S has the intention of reducing the number of notional shares in line with the reduction in share options outstanding. The difference between the notional price and the market price of shares is refunded by C if the number of shares decreases, and vice versa.

5.3.120.80   Although S may intend to adjust the notional amount under the swap arrangement to hedge its share-based payment obligations, the adjustment is not automatic and S has the discretion to adjust its exposure. Therefore, we believe that there is insufficient linkage between the swap arrangement with C and the exercise of options to consider changes in the swap arrangement with C to be a consequential change to profit or loss. Accordingly, no adjustment is made to the numerator in the diluted EPS calculation in this regard.

5.3.120.90   Therefore, neither of the arrangements in this example results in a consequential change to profit or loss and the numerator in the diluted EPS calculation is not adjusted.

5.3.120.100   In our view, the numerator should not be adjusted for equity-settled share-based payment costs when calculating diluted EPS (see 5.3.450.10). However, if there is a remeasurement expense from a liability of a cash-settled share-based payment that may also be settled in shares, then the numerator is adjusted for such an amount when calculating diluted earnings (see 5.3.520.40). [*IAS 33.58–59*]

5.3.130 *Weighted-average number of shares*

5.3.130.10   The denominator (the weighted-average number of ordinary shares) used for the calculation of basic EPS is adjusted for the weighted-average number of ordinary shares that would be issued on the conversion of all the dilutive potential ordinary shares into ordinary shares. [*IAS 33.36*]

EXAMPLE 11 – DILUTED EPS – ADJUSTMENTS TO WEIGHTED-AVERAGE NUMBER OF SHARES OUTSTANDING

5.3.130.20   Company B has the following transactions involving its non-cumulative preference shares during 2018. All of these preference shares are convertible into ordinary shares on the same conversion terms (1:1).
- On 1 January, 2,000 preference shares are outstanding.
- On 1 April, 500 shares are converted into ordinary shares.
- On 1 July, another 1,000 shares are issued.

5.3.130.30   B calculates the adjustments to the denominator in the diluted EPS for the preference shares as follows.

	NUMBER OF PREFERENCE SHARES OUTSTANDING	TIME WEIGHTING	WEIGHTED-AVERAGE NUMBER OF PREFERENCE SHARES
1 January to 31 March	2,000	3 / 12	500
1 April – preference shares converted	(500)		
1 April to 30 June	1,500	3 / 12	375
1 July – preference shares issued	1,000		
1 July to 31 December	2,500	6 / 12	1,250
		12 / 12	
Weighted-average for 2018			2,125

5.3.130.40   Similar to the denominator for basic EPS (see 5.3.80.70 and 530), the denominator for diluted EPS may be affected if the number of potential ordinary shares outstanding is increased or decreased without a corresponding change in resources – e.g. as a result of a bonus or rights issue, share split or share consolidation (i.e. reverse share split) or stock dividend. Each issue or series of potential ordinary shares in issue at the time of such a change in the number of ordinary shares may be required to be adjusted for the effect of the change. For further discussion of the impact on the denominator for diluted EPS, see 5.3.530.80. [*IAS 33.64*]

5.3.140 **APPLICATION TO SPECIFIC INSTRUMENTS**

5.3.150 **Partly paid shares**

5.3.160 ***Basic EPS***

5.3.160.10   If ordinary shares are not fully paid, then they are treated as a fraction of ordinary shares for the purposes of basic EPS. The fraction is calculated as the degree to which they are entitled to participate in dividends during the period relative to the dividend participation rights of a fully paid ordinary share. [*IAS 33.A15*]

5.3.170 ***Diluted EPS***

5.3.170.10   To the extent that partly paid shares are not entitled to participate in dividends during the period, they are treated as the equivalent of options or warrants (see 5.3.250). The treasury share method (see 5.3.270) is applied to the fraction of partly paid shares that is not entitled to participate in dividends. The unpaid balance of such shares is regarded as the proceeds from issuing shares. These proceeds are assumed to be used to purchase ordinary shares at the average market price for the period. The number of shares included in diluted EPS is the difference between the number of unpaid shares not included in basic EPS and the number of shares assumed to be purchased with the unpaid balance, if dilutive. Consistent with the view expressed in 5.3.270.50, the average market price should be determined based on the full reporting period, or the period for which the partly paid shares are outstanding, if this is shorter. [*IAS 33.A16*]

5.3.180 **Unvested ordinary shares**

5.3.180.10   This section covers unvested ordinary shares that are subject only to service- (time-) based vesting conditions. If unvested shares are subject to conditions other than time-based service – e.g. a market or a non-market performance condition – then they are treated as contingently issuable shares (see 5.3.320).

5.3.190 ***Basic EPS***

5.3.190.10   Unvested ordinary shares are not regarded as outstanding until they are vested. As a result, unvested ordinary shares are included only in calculating diluted EPS (see 5.3.200). Ordinary shares issued as compensation for services received are included in the denominator of basic EPS as the services are rendered and the vesting condition is met. As illustrated in Example 12, this averaging approach differs from the approach that is required when recognising share-based payment cost. [*IAS 33.21(g), 24, 48*]

EXAMPLE 12 – DENOMINATOR ADJUSTMENT FOR BASIC EPS VS GRADED-VESTING APPROACH FOR SHARE-BASED PAYMENT

5.3.190.20   Company Z has a share-based payment arrangement. The following facts are relevant for this example.
- Z grants 15,000 unvested shares to employees.
- The award vests rateably in three tranches of 5,000 after each year of service.

> **5.3.190.25**   In the basic EPS computation for year 2 of the three-year service period, the weighted-average number of shares outstanding includes 5,000 shares, being the first tranche that vested at the end of year 1. The second tranche of 5,000 only vested on the last day of year 2 and therefore carries a weighting of (0 / 365) in year 2. This averaging approach differs from the graded vesting approach that is required when recognising share-based payment cost (see 4.5.680).
>
> **5.3.190.30**   Conversely, if the entire award vests only on completion of three years' employment – i.e. no shares would be awarded if employment terminated before the end of the vesting period – then no shares are included in the basic EPS computation until the end of the three-year service period.

5.3.190.40   Some unvested shares that require service as a vesting condition are not entitled to dividends during the vesting period. However, if the unvested shares are entitled to non-forfeitable dividends during the vesting period, then to the extent that these dividends have not been recognised in profit or loss, in our view when calculating basic EPS, the numerator should be adjusted for these dividends and any undistributed earnings attributed to these unvested shares, in accordance with their participating rights (see 5.3.70.60).

5.3.200   *Diluted EPS*

5.3.200.10   Instruments with vesting conditions are considered in the denominator of the calculation of diluted EPS in a manner that depends on the nature of the vesting condition. If employee share options with fixed or determinable terms and unvested ordinary shares are subject only to service-(time-) based vesting conditions – i.e. no performance conditions – then they are treated as outstanding options (see 5.3.270) and are considered in the diluted EPS from grant date. [*IAS 33.48*]

5.3.210   *Ordinary shares subject to recall*

5.3.210.10   Similar to unvested shares, if ordinary shares are subject to recall, then they are not considered outstanding and are excluded from the calculation of basic EPS until the date on which they are no longer subject to recall. However, for the purpose of calculating basic EPS, an adjustment to the numerator may be required for any dividends and undistributed earnings attributable to these shares (see 5.3.70.60). Ordinary shares that are subject to recall are included in the calculation of diluted EPS (see 5.3.200). [*IAS 33.10, 24, A13–A14*]

5.3.210.20   In our view, shares that are subject to repurchase due to a written put option or a forward purchase contract should be excluded from the basic EPS calculation, similar to shares subject to recall (see 5.3.210.10). Similarly, an adjustment to the numerator may be required for any dividends and undistributed earnings attributable to these shares (see 5.3.70.60). However, the calculation of diluted EPS may require adjustment for the written put or forward (see 5.3.310).

5.3.220   **Convertible instruments**

5.3.230   *Basic EPS*

5.3.230.10   Generally, convertible instruments impact only the diluted EPS calculation (see 5.3.240). Ordinary shares issued on the conversion of convertible instruments are generally included in the denominator from the date on which interest ceases to accrue. However, ordinary shares to be issued under a mandatorily convertible instrument are included in the denominator for basic EPS from the date on which the contract is entered into (see 5.3.80.40). [*IAS 33.21(c)–(d), 23*]

5.3.240   *Diluted EPS*

5.3.240.10   Convertible instruments, other than those that are mandatorily convertible, are potential ordinary shares. The potential adjustments to the numerator include the post-tax amount of any dividends or interest, fair value gains or losses and other consequential changes in income or expense that would result from the assumed conversion (see 5.3.120). The potential adjustment to the denominator is based on the additional ordinary shares resulting from the assumed conversion. Conversion is assumed to have occurred at the beginning of the period or, if later, on the date of issuance of the convertible instrument. [*IAS 33.33–36, 49*]

5.3.240.20   In some cases, an entity may issue a financial instrument with more than one conversion feature. A question then arises over which conversion feature should be considered when determining the potential ordinary shares for inclusion in the diluted EPS calculation. The goal in computing diluted EPS is to calculate the maximum dilutive effect and therefore, the entity needs to calculate diluted EPS under the various conversion features to determine which feature is the most dilutive (see 5.3.100.40). [*IAS 33.44*]

5.3.240.30   Convertible bonds may be issued with two conversion features attached to the non-mandatory convertible instruments: an option for early conversion and an option for conversion at the end of a contingent period. In our view, the entity should compute separate diluted EPS calculations for the early conversion feature and the conversion at the end of the contingent period to evaluate which feature is most dilutive. The presentation of the diluted EPS should be based on the most dilutive scenario.

5.3.240.40   Options or warrants to purchase convertible instruments – e.g. an option to purchase convertible preference shares – are assumed to be exercised in diluted EPS only when:

- the average price of the convertible instrument exceeds the exercise price of the option;
- the average price of the ordinary shares obtainable on conversion exceeds the exercise price of the option; and
- the conversion of similar outstanding convertible instruments, if there are any, is also assumed. [*IAS 33.A6*]

5.3.240.50   However, IAS 33 is not clear on how to calculate the impact of options or warrants to purchase convertible instruments in diluted EPS. Because they are options, in our view one acceptable approach is to use the treasury share method in determining the impact on the denominator, assuming that the options would be exercised directly to obtain shares on conversion (see 5.3.270). The post-tax consequential changes in income or expense would be adjusted in the numerator.

5.3.250   **Options, warrants and their equivalents**

5.3.260   *Basic EPS*

5.3.260.10   Generally, options, warrants and their equivalents impact only the diluted EPS calculation (see 5.3.270). Options are included in the calculation of basic EPS once the option has been exercised. However, if options are exercisable for little or no further consideration after vesting, then in our view an entity should include the issuable shares in the denominator of basic EPS from the vesting date. This is because a vested share option with little or zero exercise price is in substance similar to a vested ordinary share, and the entity will receive no further substantive consideration when the option is exercised. [*IAS 33.21(g), 24, 48*]

5.3.270   *Diluted EPS*

5.3.270.10   To the extent that they are not included in the denominator for basic EPS, options, warrants and their equivalents are potential ordinary shares. To calculate diluted EPS, an entity assumes that dilutive share options, warrants and their equivalents are exercised so that ordinary shares are issued. Options, warrants and other potential ordinary shares issued subject to conditions – e.g. performance-based employee share options – may be contingently issuable potential ordinary shares (see 5.3.390). [*IAS 33.45*]

5.3.270.20   For options, warrants and similar instruments, rather than simply adding to the denominator the weighted-average number of ordinary shares that would be issued from the assumed conversion of options, IAS 33 prescribes a specific method, commonly referred to as the 'treasury share method'. The following diagram summarises the treasury share method. For a worked example illustrating the application of the treasury share method, see Example 19. [*IAS 33.45–46, IE5–IE5A*]

Step 1: Calculate the assumed proceeds Calculate the proceeds that would have been received from the assumed exercise of all options (see 5.3.270.40)	'Exercise price' x number of options
Step 2: Calculate the number of ordinary shares deemed to be repurchased at average market price Calculate the number of ordinary shares that would have been repurchased if the proceeds received in Step 1 were used to acquire these shares at their average market price during the period (see 5.3.270.50–80)	Assumed proceeds / average market price of shares
Step 3: Determine the bonus element Calculate the difference between the number of ordinary shares that would be issued at the exercise of the options and the number of ordinary shares deemed to be repurchased at the average market price	Number of shares that would be issued - number of shares deemed to be repurchased

5.3.270.30   Under the treasury share method, only the bonus element of the options – i.e. the number calculated under Step 3 in 5.3.270.20 – is reflected in diluted EPS. [*IAS 33.45*]

5.3.270.40   The 'exercise price' in Step 1 in 5.3.270.20 includes the fair value (measured in accordance with IFRS 2) of any goods or services to be supplied to the entity in the future under the share-based payment arrangement (see 5.3.450.30–70). [*IAS 33.47A*]

5.3.270.50   The average market price of an ordinary share is required in Step 2 in 5.3.270.20. The average market price should be determined based on the full reporting period, or, in our view, the period for which the potential ordinary shares are outstanding if this is shorter (see 5.3.270.60–80). For example, if options are outstanding for only four months of the reporting period, then in determining the bonus element the average market price should be based on the average market price during that four-month period.

5.3.270.60   In some cases, there may not be a quoted market price for the ordinary shares for the full period – e.g. because the entity does not have ordinary shares or potential ordinary shares that are publicly traded and the entity elects to disclose EPS, or the entity's ordinary shares or potential ordinary shares were not listed for the full period. In our view, if the average market price of the shares is necessary to calculate diluted EPS – e.g. because the entity has outstanding warrants or options – then the average market price used should be a meaningful average for the full reporting period, or the period for which the potential ordinary shares are outstanding if this is shorter.

EXAMPLE 13 – PERIOD TO CONSIDER WHEN APPLYING TREASURY SHARE METHOD – ENTITY ONLY QUOTED FOR PART OF PERIOD

5.3.270.65   Company C with a 31 December year end lists its ordinary shares on 7 November, so that it has a quoted market price for its shares only during the period from 7 November to 31 December. C has ordinary shares outstanding during the current and comparative periods.

5.3.270.70   In this example, we do not believe that an average market price for approximately two months would be meaningful for potential ordinary shares outstanding for the full year.

5.3.270.80   In our view, if there is no active market for ordinary shares, then an entity should determine fair value using valuation techniques. We believe that an entity should apply the guidance for measuring the fair value of financial instruments to determine the fair value of unquoted equity instruments (see 2.4.860) to estimate the average market price for the ordinary shares. Specialist expertise may be required in this assessment. In our view, the method used to determine the average market price should be disclosed in the notes to the financial statements.

5.3.270.90   A potential adjustment to the numerator when calculating diluted EPS may be required for the post-tax remeasurement income or expense for options and warrants when they are accounted for as liabilities under IFRS 2 or IAS 32. [*IAS 33.33–35*]

5.3.270.100   Options have a dilutive effect only if they are in the money – i.e. the exercise price, including the fair value of any goods or services to be supplied (see 5.3.270.40 and 450.30–70), is lower than the average market price of the ordinary shares. [*IAS 33.47*]

5.3.270.110   Options that require an entity to issue shares may also be present in agreements other than straight forward written options.

EXAMPLE 14 – OPTIONS TO ISSUE SHARES NOT IN FORM OF STRAIGHT FORWARD WRITTEN OPTIONS

5.3.270.120   Company G and Company B enter into an agreement whereby each contributes a certain portion of their business to Newco. G holds 45% of Newco and B holds 55%. The ordinary shares of B are quoted. B grants a put option to G, whereby G can put its 45% interest in Newco to B in exchange for 500-worth of B's ordinary shares.

5.3.270.130   B considers this put option in its calculation of diluted EPS. To determine if it would be dilutive, B needs to estimate the proceeds that it would receive from the issue of its ordinary shares to the value of 500 and compare those proceeds with the value of G's 45% of Newco. If the value of the 45% share of Newco is less than 500, then the put option is dilutive. If not, then it is anti-dilutive and is not reflected in the diluted EPS calculation, but B is required to disclose information about the existence and the effects of the anti-dilutive put option. [*IAS 33.70(c)*]

5.3.280   *Exercise price settled (or partially settled) by other instruments*

5.3.280.10   Some options may permit or require an entity to tender a debt or another instrument issued by the entity itself or its subsidiary in payment of all or a portion of the exercise price. The exercise of the options and the tendering of the instruments are assumed for diluted EPS if:

- the average market price of the ordinary share for the period exceeds the exercise price; or
- the selling price of the instrument to be tendered is below that at which the instrument may be tendered under the option and the resulting discount establishes an effective exercise price that is below the market price of the ordinary shares obtainable on exercise. [*IAS 33.A7*]

5.3.280.20   The post-tax interest on any debt assumed to be tendered for the dilutive instruments in 5.3.280.10 is added to the numerator for the purpose of calculating diluted EPS. IAS 33 is not clear on how to calculate the impact of such options on the denominator for diluted EPS. In our view, one acceptable approach is to use a similar approach to that for convertible instruments (see 5.3.240) – i.e. not the treasury share method. Therefore, for the portion for which the exercise price may be paid up by tendering debt or other instruments, the denominator should be adjusted for the total number of shares assumed to be issued. However, if the option may be settled in cash, then the cash alternative should be assumed if it is more advantageous to the option holder. In such cases, the treasury share method (see 5.3.270) should be used to determine the impact on the denominator for the diluted EPS. [*IAS 33.A7*]

5.3.290   *Proceeds used to redeem other instruments*

5.3.290.10   In some cases, the terms of options require the proceeds received from exercise to be used to redeem debt or other instruments of the entity (or its parent or a subsidiary). In determining diluted EPS, it is assumed that the proceeds are used first to purchase these instruments at their average market price, and the numerator is adjusted by the post-tax interest saving on the assumed redemption. If the proceeds to be received exceed the redemption amount, then the excess is assumed to be used to purchase ordinary shares under the treasury share method. [*IAS 33.A9*]

5.3.300   *Purchased put and call options*

5.3.300.10   If an entity has purchased options on its own shares, then these are excluded from diluted EPS because they are anti-dilutive; this is on the assumption that these options would be exercised only when they are in the money. [*IAS 33.62*]

5.3.310   *Written put options and forward purchase contracts*

5.3.310.10   If an entity has written a put option, or entered into a forward contract, on its own ordinary shares, then in our view the shares subject to the put or forward should be excluded from the denominator used to calculate basic EPS (see 5.3.210.20). However, we believe that even though the shares subject to written put options or forward purchase contracts should be excluded from basic EPS, their potentially dilutive effect should be considered in the calculation of diluted EPS. [*IAS 33.24, 63, A10*]

5.3.310.20   The dilutive effect of written put options and forward purchase contracts is calculated using a specific method prescribed in IAS 33, commonly referred to as 'the reverse treasury share method'. The method is similar to the treasury share method (see 5.3.270), but with an opposite assumption: instead of assuming that the assumed proceeds from the exercise of options are used to acquire ordinary shares at the average market price, as in the treasury share method, the reverse treasury share method assumes that additional ordinary shares are issued to raise enough proceeds to satisfy the exercise or settlement price. The dilutive effect – i.e. the bonus element – is therefore calculated as the difference between:
- the number of ordinary shares that would have to be issued at the average market price during the period to raise sufficient proceeds to fulfil the written puts or forwards; and
- the number of shares that would be repurchased under the terms of the written puts or forwards. [*IAS 33.63, A10*]

5.3.310.30   The following diagram summarises the reverse treasury share method. [*IAS 33.63, A10*]

Step 1: Calculate the proceeds assumed to be raised Calculate the proceeds that would need to be raised to satisfy the contract	Exercise or settlement price x number of shares subject to written put or forward purchase contracts
Step 2: Calculate the 'new' shares deemed to have been issued Calculate the number of ordinary shares that would be issued at the average market price during the period to raise proceeds to satisfy the contract	Assumed proceeds / average market price of shares
Step 3: Determine the bonus element Calculate the difference between the number of ordinary shares deemed to have been issued and the number of shares received from buying back the ordinary shares in the contract	Number of shares deemed to be issued - number of shares received from satisfying the contract

EXAMPLE 15 – THE REVERSE TREASURY SHARE METHOD – WRITTEN PUT OPTIONS

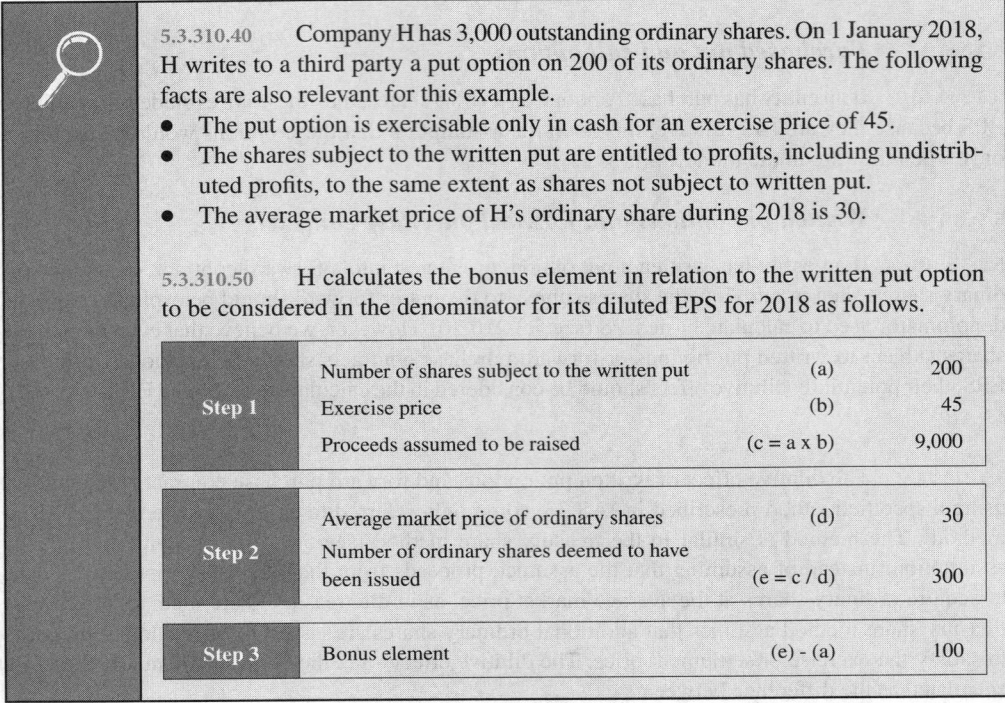

5.3.310.40   Company H has 3,000 outstanding ordinary shares. On 1 January 2018, H writes to a third party a put option on 200 of its ordinary shares. The following facts are also relevant for this example.
- The put option is exercisable only in cash for an exercise price of 45.
- The shares subject to the written put are entitled to profits, including undistributed profits, to the same extent as shares not subject to written put.
- The average market price of H's ordinary share during 2018 is 30.

5.3.310.50   H calculates the bonus element in relation to the written put option to be considered in the denominator for its diluted EPS for 2018 as follows.

Step 1	Number of shares subject to the written put	(a)	200
	Exercise price	(b)	45
	Proceeds assumed to be raised	(c = a x b)	9,000
Step 2	Average market price of ordinary shares	(d)	30
	Number of ordinary shares deemed to have been issued	(e = c / d)	300
Step 3	Bonus element	(e) - (a)	100

5.3.310.60   If a written put option or a forward purchase contract is accounted for as a liability in accordance with IAS 32 (see 7.3.240), then a potential adjustment to the numerator may be required for the post-tax remeasurement income or expense. [*IAS 33.33–35*]

5.3.310.70   In our view, any adjustments to the numerator for basic EPS for non-forfeitable dividends and undistributed earnings attributable to shares subject to written puts or forwards (see 5.3.210.20 and 70.60) should not be reversed in diluted EPS. This is consistent with the assumption in determining the denominator under the reverse treasury share method that shares will remain outstanding after the settlement of the written put or forward (see 5.3.310.20–30).

5.3.310.80   Consistent with the view expressed in 5.3.270.50, the average market price should be determined based on the full reporting period, or the period for which the written put options or forward purchase contracts are outstanding if this is shorter.

5.3.320   Contingently issuable ordinary shares

5.3.320.10   Contingently issuable ordinary shares are defined as ordinary shares issuable for little or no cash or other consideration on the satisfaction of specified conditions in a contingent share agreement. These do not include service conditions under IFRS 2 and the passage of time, which is a certainty. Therefore, shares that are issuable subject only to the passage of time (see 5.3.330.20), and unvested shares (see 5.3.180.10) and options that require only service for vesting, are not considered contingently issuable. Some potential ordinary shares that are subject to conditions other than service conditions and the passage of time are treated as contingently issuable potential ordinary shares (see 5.3.390). [*IAS 33.5, 21(g), 24, 48*]

5.3.330 *Basic EPS*

5.3.330.10   Contingently issuable ordinary shares are included in the calculation of the weighted-average number of shares outstanding for purpose of calculating basic EPS from the date on which the conditions are met, and not from any later date of actually being issued. [*IAS 33.5, 24*]

5.3.330.20   Shares that are issuable solely after the passage of time are not considered contingently issuable because the passage of time is a certainty. Instead, they are treated as outstanding for the purpose of calculating basic EPS only from the date on which the right to the shares comes into existence. Unvested shares and unvested employee share options that require only service for vesting cannot be contingently issuable shares. This is because their vesting is contingent only on the passage of time. [*IAS 33.24*]

5.3.340 *Diluted EPS*

5.3.340.10   To the extent that they are not yet taken into account in basic EPS, contingently issuable ordinary shares are potential ordinary shares. A potential adjustment to the numerator when calculating diluted EPS may be required when they are accounted for under IFRS 2 or IAS 32, similar to options (see 5.3.270.90). If the conditions are satisfied at the reporting date, then they are included in the denominator when calculating diluted EPS (if they are dilutive) from the later of the beginning of the reporting period or the date of the contingent share agreement. If the conditions are not satisfied, then the number of contingently issuable shares included in diluted EPS is based on the number of shares that would be issuable if the reporting date were the end of the contingency period. IAS 33 sets out specific requirements depending on the nature of the conditions (see 5.3.350–380). [*IAS 33.52*]

EXAMPLE 16A – CONTINGENTLY ISSUABLE ORDINARY SHARES – SERVICE AND PERFORMANCE CONDITION

5.3.340.20   Under the terms of a share-based payment arrangement, employees of Company Q need to complete three years of employment and Q needs to achieve a 20% increase in its net income over this same period in order for the shares to vest – i.e. a performance condition is included within the share-based payment arrangement. These shares are contingently issuable ordinary shares. The number of contingently issuable ordinary shares included in diluted EPS (if dilutive) is based on the number of shares that would be issuable if the reporting date were the end of the contingency period.

5.3.340.30   The test in 5.3.340.10 is at the reporting date and does not reflect expectations about the future. In other words, if the specified conditions would not be met if the reporting date were the end of the contingency period, then the contingently issuable ordinary shares are ignored in diluted EPS even though it is probable that the conditions will be met afterwards. This EPS treatment is different from the way in which similar conditions are accounted for under IFRS 2 (see 4.5.510 and 5.3.440).

5.3.340.40   Unvested shares and unvested employee share options that do not only require service as a vesting condition, but instead include market or non-market performance conditions, are treated as contingently issuable shares and options if they are issuable for little or no cash or other consideration.

Contingencies related to earnings target

5.3.350.10   If shares are contingently issuable based on achieving or maintaining a specified amount of earnings or a similar target – e.g. cost savings – and the entity attains the specified amount of earnings but is also required to maintain the level of earnings for an additional period after the reporting date, then the shares are considered only in the calculation of diluted EPS, if the effect is dilutive. The number of additional shares included in diluted EPS is based on the number of ordinary shares that would be issued if the amount of earnings at the reporting date were the amount of earnings at the end of the contingency period. These contingent shares are not considered outstanding for basic EPS, unless the earnings have been achieved or maintained for the required period. [*IAS 33.53*]

EXAMPLE 16B – CONTINGENTLY ISSUABLE ORDINARY SHARES – COST SAVINGS CONDITION

5.3.350.20   Company F hires a consultant to evaluate its operating costs and recommend ways to reduce them. The consultancy agreement includes the following performance targets.

- If the operating costs are reduced by at least 350 in year 1 or year 2, and this cost reduction is sustained for a further year, then the consultant will receive 1% of F's issued ordinary shares.
- If the operating costs are reduced by at least 700 in year 1 or year 2, and this cost reduction is sustained for a further year, then the consultant will receive 2% of F's issued ordinary shares.
- The consultant has three years to achieve these targets.

5.3.350.30   After year 1, the consultant achieves only 200 of cost savings. If this were the end of the contingency period, then no shares would be issued, and therefore there is no impact on either basic or diluted EPS.

5.3.350.40   At the end of year 2, cost savings of 400 have been achieved, but not yet sustained. There is no impact on basic EPS, because the cost savings have not been sustained. The potential ordinary shares (1% of F's issued ordinary shares) are included in the calculation of diluted EPS from the beginning of year 2, because the first target would be met if the end of year 2 were the end of the contingency period. When the cost savings have been sustained for one year, the effect of the shares to be issued will also be included in the calculation of basic EPS.

Contingencies related to price levels

5.3.360.10   The number of ordinary shares that are contingently issuable may depend on the future market price of the ordinary shares. In this case, if the effect is dilutive, then the calculation of diluted EPS is based on the number of ordinary shares that would be issued if the market price at the reporting date were the market price at the end of the contingency period. [*IAS 33.54*]

5.3.360.20   In our view, even if the share price had declined below the trigger level after the reporting date but before the financial statements were authorised for issue, the share price at the reporting date should still be used as the trigger in the calculation of the diluted EPS for the period.

5.3.370   *Contingencies related to earnings targets and price levels*

5.3.370.10   If the number of ordinary shares that are contingently issuable depends on future earnings and future prices of the ordinary shares, then such shares are included in the diluted EPS calculation only if both conditions are met at the reporting date. [*IAS 33.55*]

5.3.380   *Other contingencies*

5.3.380.10   Ordinary shares may be contingently issuable subject to a condition other than earnings or market price – e.g. opening of a specific number of retail stores. In such cases, the additional shares issuable are included in the denominator for diluted EPS according to the status at the reporting date. [*IAS 33.56*]

EXAMPLE 16C – CONTINGENTLY ISSUABLE ORDINARY SHARES – OTHER CONDITIONS

5.3.380.20   Company D enters into an agreement related to a business combination on 1 January 2018 in which it would be required to issue 5,000 additional shares for each new retail site opened during 2018. D opens a new retail site on 1 May 2018 and another one on 1 September 2018.

5.3.380.30   Because the condition is met during the year, additional shares are included in the denominator for basic EPS from the date on which the condition is met – i.e. 5,000 from 1 May and 5,000 from 1 September. [*IAS 33.IE7*]

5.3.380.40   The additional shares are included in the denominator for diluted EPS from the beginning of the period to the date on which they are included in the denominator for basic EPS – i.e. 5,000 from 1 January to 30 April and 5,000 from 1 January to 31 August. [*IAS 33.IE7*]

5.3.390   *Contingently issuable potential ordinary shares*

5.3.390.10   IAS 33 sets out how to treat instruments with conditions that cause them to be contingently issuable potential ordinary shares. First, an entity follows the guidance in paragraphs 52–56 of IAS 33 on contingently issuable shares (see 5.3.340–380) to determine whether the instrument is to be assumed to be issuable. If the instrument passes the tests, then the entity determines the impact on diluted EPS based on the relevant guidance for the instrument, as follows:
- for convertible instruments, see 5.3.240;
- for options or warrants, see 5.3.270; and
- for contracts that may be settled in ordinary shares or cash, see 5.3.410. [*IAS 33.57*]

EXAMPLE 16D – CONTINGENTLY ISSUABLE POTENTIAL ORDINARY SHARES – SHARE OPTION PLAN

5.3.390.20   Company N has an IFRS 2 share option plan with a three-year service and market condition. At the end of year 1, N determines based on paragraphs 52–56 of IAS 33 that all conditions would be met if the first reporting date were the end

of the contingency period. The number of contingently issuable potential ordinary shares to be included in diluted EPS is determined based on the guidance for options or warrants in IAS 33 (see 5.3.270).

5.3.390.30   Another case of contingently issuable potential ordinary shares is when a loan agreement allows the lender to convert the loan into ordinary shares of the borrowing entity under certain conditions.

EXAMPLE 16E – CONTINGENTLY ISSUABLE POTENTIAL ORDINARY SHARES – LOAN DEFAULT CONDITION

5.3.390.40   Company M (the borrower) has a loan from Bank B (the lender) that, on M's default or its credit rating downgrade (triggering events), allows B to convert the loan into ordinary shares of M.

5.3.390.50   The loan clause gives rise to contingently issuable potential ordinary shares. If M defaults during the period, then the conversion option would be exercisable. The number of shares to be included by M in the diluted EPS computation is based on the number of shares that would be issuable if the reporting date were the end of the contingency period. If a triggering event has occurred, then the ordinary shares are considered in the calculation of diluted EPS from the beginning of the reporting period (or from the date of the loan agreement, if this is later), and not from the triggering event. [*IAS 33.52*]

5.3.390.60   If B exercises the option, then the ordinary shares are outstanding and M includes them in the calculation of basic EPS from the exercise date, even if the shares have not yet been issued. This is because there are no further conditions or payments required and the issue of shares is contingent only on the passage of time. [*IAS 33.24*]

5.3.400   Other instruments impacting diluted EPS

5.3.410   *Contracts that may be settled in ordinary shares or cash*

5.3.410.10   If an entity issues a contract that may be settled in ordinary shares or cash at the entity's option, then the entity presumes that the contract will be settled in ordinary shares. This assumption is independent of the classification of the contract as a derivative, liability and/or equity under IAS 32 or, if it is a share-based payment, as a cash- or equity-settled arrangement (see 5.3.520 and 4.5.1080). This assumption is also independent of the entity's intended manner of settlement; this is different from the treatment of such instruments under IFRS 2 (see 4.5.1080). [*IAS 33.58, BC7–BC8*]

5.3.410.20   If the resulting potential ordinary shares are dilutive, then they are included in diluted EPS. Such a contract may have been classified either as a financial asset or financial liability or as a compound instrument. Therefore, instances may arise in which share-based payments are considered potential ordinary shares for EPS purposes even though they are classified as cash-settled share-based payment transactions. It is necessary to adjust the numerator in the diluted EPS calculation for any changes in profit or loss that would have resulted from classifying the contract as an equity instrument in its entirety (see 5.3.120 and 520.40). [*IAS 33.59*]

5.3.410.30   For contracts that may be settled in ordinary shares or cash at the holder's option, the entity uses the more dilutive of cash settlement and share settlement in calculating diluted EPS. Therefore, the EPS settlement assumption may not be consistent with the classification of the share-based payment (see 5.3.520.10). [*IAS 33.60*]

EXAMPLE 17 – OPTIONS SETTLEABLE EITHER IN CASH OR IN SHARES

5.3.410.40   Continuing Example 14, if on exercise of the put option by Company G, Company B has a choice to settle either in cash or by issuing shares, then B would presume that it will settle the contract by issuing shares and then determine whether the impact is dilutive. However, if the election to receive cash or shares were at G's option, then B would evaluate which is the more dilutive of cash or equity settlement and assume that option in the calculation of diluted EPS. [*IAS 33.58, 60*]

5.3.410.50   For a discussion of the interaction of EPS with IFRS 2, see 5.3.440.

5.3.420   *Potential ordinary shares of subsidiary, associate or joint venture*

5.3.420.10   Potential ordinary shares that are issued by a subsidiary, associate or joint venture (investee) to parties outside the group of the parent/investor and are convertible into either ordinary shares of the investee or ordinary shares of the parent/investor are included in the parent's or investor's calculation of diluted EPS if their effect is dilutive. The dilutive effect of potential ordinary shares that may entitle their holders to the investee's ordinary shares is determined based on a two-step approach.

- *Step 1:* They are included in diluted EPS of the investee. The impact on the investee's diluted EPS depends on the form of the instruments – e.g. if the instrument is an option, then the guidance in 5.3.270 is relevant.
- *Step 2:* The resulting diluted EPS of the investee is then included in the parent's or investor's diluted EPS based on the parent's or investor's holding of the instruments of the investee. [*IAS 33.40, A11(a), IE10*]

EXAMPLE 18 – POTENTIAL ORDINARY SHARES ISSUED BY NON-WHOLLY OWNED SUBSIDIARY – DILUTED EPS CALCULATION

5.3.420.20   Company S is a subsidiary of Company P. The following facts in respect of S are relevant for this example.
- S has 10,000 ordinary shares and 1,000 options outstanding, of which P owns 9,000 and 500, respectively.
- The options have an exercise price of 40.
- The average market price of S's ordinary share was 50 in 2018.
- In 2018, S's profit was 30,000.

5.3.420.25   The following facts in respect of P are also relevant for this example.
- P has 5,000 ordinary shares outstanding.

- In 2018, P's profit (excluding any distributed and undistributed earnings of subsidiaries) was 7,000.

5.3.420.30   To determine the diluted EPS of P, the diluted EPS of S is calculated first.

S's diluted EPS = $30,000^{(1)} / (10,000^{(2)} + 200^{(3)}) = 2.94$

Notes
1. S's earnings for the period.
2. Weighted-average ordinary shares.
3. Incremental shares related to weighted-average options outstanding. All options are dilutive because their exercise price is below the average market price of S's ordinary shares for the period. The incremental shares are calculated as follows.

Shares issued on assumed exercise of options	1,000
Less: shares that would be issued at average market price	(800)[i]
Incremental shares	200

    i.   Calculated as assumed proceeds from exercise of 40,000 (40 x 1,000), divided by average market price of 50.

5.3.420.40   Assuming that the options outstanding are dilutive at P's level (i.e. at the parent level), S's diluted EPS is then included in P's diluted EPS based on P's holding of S's equity instruments.

P's diluted EPS = $(7,000^{(1)} + 26,460^{(2)} + 294^{(3)}) / 5,000^{(4)} = 6.75$

Notes
1. P's earnings for the period.
2. P's share of S's earnings attributable to ordinary shares – i.e. ((9,000 / 10,000) x (2.94 x 10,000)).
3. P's share of S's earnings attributable to options – i.e. ((500 / 1,000) x (2.94 x 200)).
4. P's weighted-average ordinary shares outstanding.

5.3.420.50   In our view, the guidance in 5.3.420.10 also applies if options or warrants that entitle the holder to the ordinary shares of a subsidiary are issued by the parent rather than by the subsidiary itself.

5.3.420.60   Instruments of a subsidiary, associate or joint venture – e.g. convertible instruments or options – that may entitle their holders to the parent's or the investor's ordinary shares are considered among the potential ordinary shares of the parent or the investor. Their impact on the numerator or denominator depends on the form of the instruments – e.g. if they are convertible instruments, then the guidance in 5.3.240 is relevant. [*IAS 33.A11(b)*]

5.3.430   *Written put option over NCI*

5.3.430.10   In some circumstances, written put options may represent a (potential) obligation to purchase a subsidiary's equity instruments held by non-controlling shareholders (NCI puts) for cash or another financial asset. For these instruments, IAS 32 requires the parent to recognise a financial liability for the present value of the redemption price in its consolidated financial statements (see 7.3.240).

5.3.430.20   Although IAS 33 contains specific requirements on written puts on an entity's own ordinary shares (see 5.3.310), the EPS implications of NCI puts in the consolidated financial statements are less clear. This is because the guidance in paragraph A11 of IAS 33 that deals with instruments of subsidiaries, joint ventures or associates (see 5.3.420.10) does not address put options written on the shares of these entities. Therefore, in our view in determining its diluted EPS in the consolidated financial statements, an entity should choose an accounting policy, to be applied consistently, based on one of the following two approaches.

- *Approach 1:* Apply the guidance applicable to potential ordinary shares of a subsidiary (see 5.3.420.10) to NCI puts. This is on the basis that although paragraph A11(a) of IAS 33 does not address NCI puts, the approach that a subsidiary is required to apply to written put options on its own shares in accordance with paragraph 63 of IAS 33 should also be applied in the consolidated financial statements of the parent for NCI puts. Under this approach, it is assumed that the subsidiary would issue new shares to raise financing to buy the shares subject to the NCI put.
- *Approach 2:* Ignore the NCI puts. This is on the basis that paragraph A11(a) of IAS 33 does not address NCI puts. This approach does not assume that the subsidiary would issue new shares to raise financing to buy the shares subject to the put. Therefore, there would be no potential ordinary shares because once the NCI put is exercised the underlying shares would not be outstanding from the group's perspective. [*IAS 33.63, A10–A11*]

5.3.430.30   We believe that the accounting policy choice in 5.3.430.20 is available regardless of whether the NCI puts are written by the parent or the subsidiary – i.e. whether it is the parent or the subsidiary that has the obligation to settle. This is because economically, at a consolidated level, it makes no difference which group entity has written the instrument.

5.3.440   INTERACTION OF EPS WITH SHARE-BASED PAYMENTS

5.3.440.10   The nature of the vesting condition affects the determination of the impact on EPS of ordinary shares or potential ordinary shares issuable under a share-based payment arrangement. If the conditions are only service conditions, then the instruments under the arrangement are either unvested shares (see 5.3.180) or unvested potential ordinary shares. If the arrangement includes other conditions – e.g. market and/or non-market performance conditions – then the instruments under the arrangement are treated as either contingently issuable shares or contingently issuable potential ordinary shares (see 5.3.320). [*IAS 33.21(g), 24, 48*]

5.3.440.20   The classification of share-based payments (see 4.5.330) is considered in determining the impact of share-based payments on EPS (see 5.3.450–520). However, instances may arise in which the classification of share-based payments under IFRS 2 is different from the classification of share-based payments for the purposes of the calculation of EPS – e.g. when contracts may be settled in ordinary shares or cash (see 5.3.520).

5.3.450   Equity-settled share-based payments

5.3.450.10   For share-based payments that are classified as equity-settled under IFRS 2, in our view the numerator should not be adjusted when calculating diluted EPS. This covers both the share-based payment expenses incurred in the current period and the fair value of future goods or services included as a part of assumed proceeds when determining the adjustment to the denominator in a diluted EPS calculation (see 5.3.450.30). This is because:

- the share-based payment expenses incurred in the current period would not have been saved by the assumed conversion and are therefore not a consequential change in profit or loss (see 5.3.120); and
- the unrecognised share-based payment treated as assumed proceeds will be recognised in the numerator in basic EPS only over the remaining vesting period, as future services are provided. [*IFRS 2.BC57, IAS 33.47A, IE5A*]

5.3.450.20   If the instruments under a share-based payment arrangement are share options (see 5.3.270) or ordinary shares subject only to service conditions (see 5.3.180), then the impact in diluted EPS is determined using the treasury share method. [*IAS 33.48*]

5.3.450.30   In applying the treasury share method in 5.3.270 to share options and other share-based payment arrangements to which IFRS 2 applies, an entity adjusts the exercise price of potential ordinary shares to include the fair value of goods or services that will be recognised as a cost in future periods – i.e. the future share-based payment arrangements are included within assumed proceeds. [*IAS 33.47A, IE5A, IFRS 2.10–13A*]

5.3.450.40   IAS 33 is silent on how the future IFRS 2 charges to be added to the assumed proceeds (see 5.3.450.30) should be calculated. Outlined in 5.3.450.50–60 are two approaches to computing the assumed proceeds. In our view, there may be other approaches to computing the assumed proceeds – in particular, the value of the future services component of the calculation – that may be acceptable under IFRS.

5.3.450.50   Under the first approach, the value of the future services component of the assumed proceeds calculation is computed based on the outstanding options at the reporting date. This approach is illustrated in Example 19.

5.3.450.60   Alternatively, under the second approach, the value of the future services component of the assumed proceeds calculation is computed based on the average unearned compensation for the period. In our view, this approach is also acceptable because using the average unearned compensation for the period is consistent with including weighted-average options and warrants outstanding during the period in diluted EPS (if dilutive) and with the use of the average market price for the period to calculate the bonus element. This approach is also illustrated in Example 19.

5.3.450.70   In addition, the assumed proceeds from the exercise of a share option under a share-based payment will be affected by the number of employees who will exercise their options. To determine assumed proceeds, an entity factors actual forfeitures into the calculation because forfeitures will impact both the consideration received and the future services under the share-based payment. In our view, the consideration received on the exercise of the options component of the assumed proceeds should be based on the weighted-average number of options for the period. [*IAS 33.47A*]

EXAMPLE 19 – WORKED EXAMPLE OF BASIC AND DILUTED EPS CALCULATION – SHARE-BASED PAYMENT ARRANGEMENT

	5.3.460	**Background**

5.3.460.10   Company M is preparing its financial statements at and for the year ending 31 December 2018 and is calculating its basic and diluted EPS. M granted an option scheme to employees on 1 January 2018.

Profit attributable to ordinary equity holders of M (i.e. profit after recognition of share-based payment)	900,000
Ordinary shares outstanding at beginning and end of 2018	10,000
Average share price in 2018	44

5.3.460.20 The following details of the share-based payment arrangement are also relevant for this example.

- On 1 January 2018, M issued, for no consideration, 100 options to each of 10 employees – i.e. 1,000 options. The arrangement is conditional on the completion of three years of service – i.e. the options vest on 31 December 2020.
- M anticipates, at both grant date and the reporting date, that seven employees will provide the requisite service and vest in the shares – i.e. an overall vesting rate of 70%. Two employees leave on 30 June 2018 – i.e. actual forfeiture rate to date of 20%. At 31 December 2018, management continues to estimate that 70% of the options will vest – i.e. that overall 30% will be forfeited.
- The employees' options settle in shares at the completion of three years of service. The exercise price of the options is 31.50.
- At 1 January 2018, the market price of M's shares is 40 and the grant-date fair value of the employee option as measured in accordance with IFRS 2 is 6.75.
- For IFRS 2 purposes, the share options are classified as an equity-settled share-based payment arrangement.

5.3.465 *Share-based payment cost*

5.3.465.10 M calculates the share-based payment cost recognised in 2018 as follows.

$$1,575 = (1,000^{(1)} \times 6.75^{(2)} / 3^{(3)} \times 70\%^{(4)})$$

Notes
1. Number of options.
2. Grant-date fair value.
3. Number of years.
4. Expected vesting rate.

5.3.470 **Basic EPS**

Earnings		900,000
Weighted-average number of ordinary shares outstanding		10,000
Basic EPS	(900,000 / 10,000)	90

5.3.480 **Diluted EPS**

5.3.490 *Equity settlement*

5.3.490.10 To calculate diluted EPS, M assumes that any dilutive options are exercised. All of the options would be dilutive if they are in the money. Essentially, that means that the average market price of shares in 2018 exceeds the sum of the exercise price of the options and the fair value of any goods or services to be supplied to M in the future as measured in accordance with IFRS 2 under any respective IFRS 2 arrangements (see 4.5.730). The following table illustrates a simple way to determine if the options are dilutive.

Exercise price	31.50
Add	
Grant-date fair value of the option	6.75
	38.25
Compare with	
Average market price of shares in 2018	44

5.3.490.20   The average market price of shares in 2018 of 44 exceeds 38.25, and therefore the options are dilutive. [*IAS 33.47*]

5.3.500   *Denominator adjustment*

5.3.500.10   For the purpose of calculating the denominator for the diluted EPS, the denominator used in the basic EPS calculation is adjusted for the weighted-average number of ordinary shares that would be issued on the conversion of all dilutive potential ordinary shares into ordinary shares (see 5.3.130.10). For example, if the potential ordinary shares are cancelled or lapse during the period, then they are included only for the part of the period that they were outstanding (see 5.3.100.20). [*IAS 33.36*]

5.3.500.20   Furthermore, in the case of options or warrants, the treasury share method is used to calculate the weighted-average number of potential ordinary shares that is added to the denominator used in the basic EPS calculation. That is, the denominator is adjusted only for the bonus element contained in the option or warrant – i.e. the difference between the number of ordinary shares that would be issued at the exercise of the option and the number of ordinary shares that would have been issued at the average market price (see 5.3.270.20). In the case of options granted as part of a share-based payment arrangement, the 'exercise price' for the purposes of the treasury share method includes the fair value of any goods or services, measured in accordance with IFRS 2, to be supplied to the entity in the future under the share option or other share-based payment arrangement as well as the actual exercise price of the option (see 5.3.450.30). [*IAS 33.45–48*]

Approach 1 to computing assumed proceeds for IFRS 2 charges

5.3.500.30   Under the first approach in 5.3.450.50, M calculates the assumed proceeds and the bonus element as follows.

Step 1	Weighted-average number of options outstanding (and shares to be issued on exercise)	(a)	900[1]
	Exercise price	(b)	31.5
	Future services (IFRS 2)	(c)	3,600[2]
	Assumed proceeds	(d) = (a) x (b) + (c)	31,950

| Step 2 | Average market price of ordinary shares | (e) | 44 |
| | Number of ordinary shares deemed to have been issued | (f) = (d) / (e) | 726 |

| Step 3 | Bonus element | (a) - (f) | 174 |

Notes
1. The consideration to be received by M is based on the deemed exercise of the weighted-average number of options as described in paragraphs 36 and 48 of IAS 33, being the sum of 1,000 options outstanding at the beginning of the period (i.e. from grant date on 1 January 2018) and the 800 options outstanding at the end of the period (i.e. 31 December 2018), giving a weighted-average of 900. See 5.3.450.70.
2. The assumed proceeds from future services are based on outstanding options – i.e. on the unearned compensation for the remaining 8 employees.

| Unearned compensation at the end of the period (800 x 6.75 x $^2/_3$) | 3,600 |

Approach 2 to computing assumed proceeds for IFRS 2 charges

5.3.500.40   Under the second approach in 5.3.450.60, M calculates the assumed proceeds and the bonus element as follows.

Step 1	Weighted-average number of options outstanding (and shares to be issued on exercise)	(a)	900[1]
	Exercise price	(b)	31.5
	Future services (IFRS 2)	(c)	5,175[2]
	Assumed proceeds	(d) = (a) x (b) + (c)	33,525

| Step 2 | Average market price of ordinary shares | (e) | 44 |
| | Number of ordinary shares deemed to have been issued | (f) = (d) / (e) | 762 |

| Step 3 | Bonus element | (a) - (f) | 138 |

Notes
1. The consideration to be received by M is based on the deemed exercise of the weighted-average number of options outstanding during the period, as in the first approach.
2. The assumed proceeds from future services under this approach are based on average unearned compensation for the period.

Unearned compensation at the beginning of the period (1,000 x 6.75)	6,750
Unearned compensation at the end of the period (800 x 6.75 x $^2/_3$)	3,600
Average unearned compensation for the period ((6,750 + 3,600) / 2)	5,175

5.3.500.50   M calculates diluted EPS based on the two approaches as follows.

Diluted EPS based on Approach 1

Earnings		900,000
Weighted-average number of ordinary shares (for diluted EPS)	(10,000 + 174)	10,174
Diluted EPS	(900,000 / 10,174)	88.46

Diluted EPS based on Approach 2

Earnings		900,000
Weighted-average number of ordinary shares (for diluted EPS)	(10,000 + 138)	10,138
Diluted EPS	(900,000 / 10,138)	88.77

5.3.510   Cash-settled share-based payment

5.3.510.10   A cash-settled share-based payment that can be settled only in cash or other financial assets does not entitle the holder to an entity's equity instrument. Accordingly, it does not impact EPS. For a discussion of share-based payments that have settlement options but are classified as cash-settled share-based payments in accordance with IFRS 2, see 5.3.520.

5.3.520   Share-based payment arrangements with option to settle in ordinary shares or cash

5.3.520.10   If an entity issues a contract that may be settled in ordinary shares or cash at the entity's option, then the entity presumes that the contract will be settled in ordinary shares (see 5.3.410.10). However, if the counterparty – e.g. an employee – in a shared-based payment arrangement has the ability to require settlement of the options in either cash or equity, then for EPS purposes an entity uses the more dilutive of cash settlement and share settlement in calculating diluted EPS (see 5.3.410.30). This ignores the IFRS 2 classification of the share-based payment as a compound instrument for which part is a debt instrument for the right to be paid in cash and for which the remaining part is an equity instrument for the right to be settled in shares (see 4.5.1080). [*IAS 33.58, 60*]

5.3.520.20   If an entity is calculating diluted EPS under the cash settlement option, then there is no adjustment to the denominator because cash settlement does not result in any additional ordinary shares being issued. There is also no adjustment to the numerator in the diluted EPS, because the accounting for the liability under IFRS 2 is based on the fair value alternative – i.e. the cash settlement would not result in consequential changes to profit or loss.

5.3.520.30   Outlined in 5.3.520.40–50 are key factors to be considered in the calculation of diluted EPS for the equity settlement option.

5.3.520.40   *Adjustments to the numerator:* If an item is classified as cash-settled under IFRS 2 because of the settlement option, then a remeasurement expense will be incurred that would not have been recognised if the share-based payment were classified as equity-settled. The remeasurement expense on the liability recognised has a consequential effect on the numerator if the share-based payment were to be classified as equity-settled (for the purposes of the EPS calculation). Therefore, the post-tax remeasurement expense is reversed from the numerator so that the amount that remains within the numerator is based on what would have existed if the item had been classified as equity-settled under IFRS 2. [*IAS 33.59*]

5.3.520.50   *Adjustments to the denominator under the treasury share method:* An entity recognises a share-based payment cost for unvested cash-settled share-based payments over the remaining period until settlement date, which includes amounts arising from the remeasurement of the liability at each reporting date and finally at settlement date (see 4.5.940). In our view, the cost resulting from the remeasurement of cash-settled share-based payment arrangements should not be included in assumed proceeds in applying the treasury share method (see 5.3.450.20–70). This view is based on the fact that if the share-based payment is classified as equity-settled, then there is no remeasurement of the share-based payment. Instead, the future services are measured using the grant-date fair value of the cash-settled share-based payment in accordance with IFRS 2. [*IFRS 2.30, IG19, IAS 33.47A*]

5.3.530   RETROSPECTIVE ADJUSTMENT

5.3.530.10   The current- and prior-period amounts for basic and diluted EPS are adjusted for transactions that, other than the conversion of potential ordinary shares, adjust the number of ordinary shares outstanding without a corresponding change in resources. A change in the number of ordinary shares outstanding without a corresponding change in resources occurs, for example, with a bonus share issue, an issue of warrants with a bonus element (see 5.3.540.80–110), or a share consolidation or split, or if there is a bonus element in a rights issue (see 5.3.540). Basic and diluted EPS are also adjusted for a bonus issue, share split or reverse share split that occurs after the reporting date but before the financial statements are authorised for issue. The number of ordinary shares is adjusted as if the event had occurred at the beginning of the earliest period presented. [*IAS 33.26–27, 64*]

5.3.530.20   No such retrospective adjustment to the current- and prior-period amounts for basic and diluted EPS occurs when there is a share consolidation that is combined with a special dividend if together they have the overall effect of being the same as a share repurchase at fair value – i.e. the resulting decrease in the number of ordinary shares would come with a corresponding reduction of resources. In this case, the denominator is prospectively adjusted from the date on which the special dividend is recognised. [*IAS 33.29*]

5.3.530.30   If there is a change in the number of shares outstanding with a corresponding change in resources, then the weighted-average number of shares outstanding is adjusted from the date on which the change in resources is recognised.

EXAMPLE 20 – BONUS ISSUE AFTER REPORTING DATE

5.3.530.40   Company T has 700 shares outstanding during the year to 31 December 2018. On 1 January 2019, T issues:
- 300 shares for cash; and
- bonus shares to its equity holders, who receive one share for every share held immediately before the bonus issue.

5.3.530.50   Basic EPS and diluted EPS amounts are not restated for the impact of the issue of 300 shares for cash, but restatement of the 31 December 2018 basic and diluted EPS amounts is required for the subsequent bonus issue of shares because no additional resources were received by T in this regard. The number of shares to be used in the EPS calculation in respect of 2018 is 1,400 (700 x 2) (and the comparative EPS amounts for 2017 are restated to give retrospective effect to the bonus issue); and 2,000 (1,000 x 2) shares are used in respect of 2019.

5.3.530.60   The conversion of potential ordinary shares does not result in a retrospective adjustment to EPS. [*IAS 33.26, A2*]

5.3.530.70   Ordinary share or potential ordinary share transactions, other than those that adjust the number of shares outstanding without a corresponding change in resources, that occur after the reporting date are not accounted for retrospectively but are disclosed in the financial statements. [*IAS 33.64, 70(d)–71*]

5.3.530.80   When determining whether the weighted-average number of potential ordinary shares needs to be adjusted, an entity considers the terms and conditions underlying the potential ordinary shares. An entity makes an assessment of whether the terms and conditions of potential ordinary share arrangements allow for the exercise price and/or the conversion ratios to adjust automatically for any share issues without a change in resources. Unless the conversion ratio and/or the exercise price automatically adjusts, there will be no adjustment to the weighted-average number of potential ordinary shares in the diluted EPS calculation.

EXAMPLE 21 – WHEN TO ADJUST WEIGHTED-AVERAGE NUMBER OF POTENTIAL ORDINARY SHARES FOLLOWING BONUS ISSUE

5.3.530.90   Company J has a share option scheme in place when there is a bonus share issue to shareholders. None of the options have been exercised at the date of the bonus issue, the options are in the money just before the bonus issue and the market price of J's shares decreases following the bonus share issue.

5.3.530.100   If the terms and conditions of the share option scheme are that the exercise price of the options does not automatically adjust for the bonus share issue, then the options may become out of the money and may become anti-dilutive when considering the diluted EPS calculation for that period. However, if the terms of the scheme are such that the exercise price is adjusted for bonus issues – i.e. the exercise price and/or conversion rate will change in proportion to the bonus element – then the calculation of the diluted EPS in relation to these options is adjusted to reflect the effect of the bonus share issue.

5.3.530.110   Diluted EPS is not restated for any subsequent changes in assumptions made in calculating the effects of conversion of potential ordinary shares, such as the average market price or whether contingently issuable shares will be issued. [*IAS 33.65*]

5.3.540   Rights issue

5.3.540.10   In a rights issue, the exercise price is often less than the fair value of the ordinary shares. The inherent discount is economically similar to a bonus issue combined with an issue at fair value. Like a bonus issue, if there is a bonus element in a rights issue, then IAS 33 requires retrospective adjustments to the denominators for both basic and diluted EPS amounts for all periods before the rights issue. However, unlike a bonus issue, the bonus element inherent in a rights issue is measured by a prescribed formula that is specified in IAS 33 (see 5.3.540.20). [*IAS 33.27(b), A2*]

5.3.540.20   If the rights issue is offered to all existing shareholders, then the number of ordinary shares used in calculating basic and diluted EPS for all periods before the rights issue is the number of ordinary shares outstanding before the issue multiplied by a bonus factor. The bonus factor is calculated as follows. [*IAS 33.A2*]

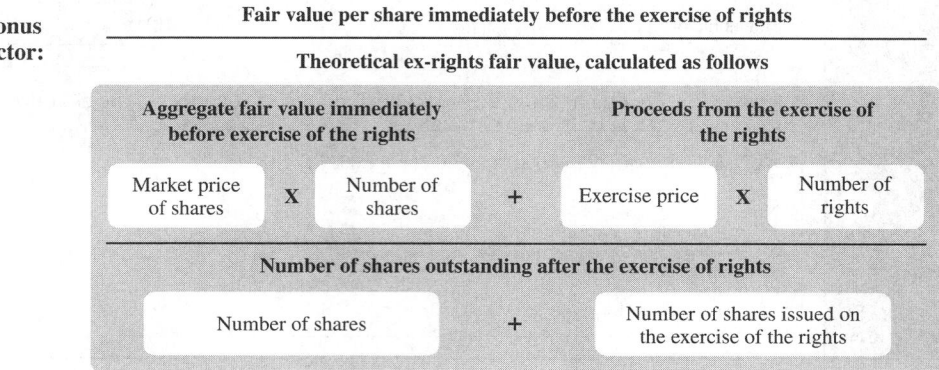

5.3.540.30   Generally, there is a time lapse between the announcement of a rights issue and the exercise of the rights. Accordingly, it may not be clear on which date the fair value of ordinary shares should be regarded as the 'fair value per share immediately before the exercise of rights' in the formula in 5.3.540.20. In our view, to the extent that the effect is material, the fair value per share immediately before (i.e. the last date) the exercise of rights to be used should be the market price of the ordinary shares immediately before the shares are traded without the rights attached. We believe that this price is the most consistent with the assumption underlying the calculation of the 'theoretical ex-rights fair value' and would therefore best reflect the bonus element when used to determine the adjustment factor for a rights issue. To use the price of ordinary shares on any later dates would incorporate price movements caused by factors other than the split of the rights in the determination of the bonus element.

EXAMPLE 22 – BONUS ELEMENT IN RIGHTS ISSUE

5.3.540.40   On 1 February 2018, Company E offers to its ordinary equity holders the right to subscribe to one new ordinary share for every three ordinary shares that they hold, at an exercise price that is below the fair value of the ordinary shares. The following facts are also relevant for this example.

- The number of outstanding ordinary shares before the rights issue is 3,000.
- The market price of ordinary shares on the last date the shares are traded with the rights attached (15 February) is 11.
- The exercise price for the rights is 7.
- All rights issues are exercised on 1 March.

5.3.540.50   The number of ordinary shares outstanding before the date on which the shares are exercised under the rights issue for the purpose of calculating both basic and diluted EPS in 2018 is increased by the bonus factor. E calculates the bonus factor as follows.

Fair value per share immediately before the exercise of the rights		11
Theoretical ex-rights fair value per share		10
Bonus factor	(11 / 10)	1.1

5.3.540.60   E calculates the theoretical ex-rights fair value per share as follows.

$$((11^{(1)} \times 3,000^{(2)}) + (7^{(3)} \times 1,000^{(4)})) / (3,000^{(2)} + 1,000^{(5)}) = 10$$

Notes
1.   Market closing price of the shares.
2.   Number of shares immediately before the exercise of the rights.
3.   Exercise price.
4.   Number of rights.
5.   Number of shares issued on the exercise of the rights.

5.3.540.70   In our view, the determination of whether a bonus element exists should be made once, at the time that the warrants are issued. At that time, if the exercise price is equal to the market price of the shares, then there is no bonus element. For example, the exercise price of a warrant is 10. This is equal to the market price of the shares on the date of issue of the warrants; therefore, there is no bonus element. Consequently, during periods when the market price exceeded the warrants' exercise price, the warrants would have been included in the determination of diluted EPS. In the basic EPS calculation, the issue of the ordinary shares on exercise of the warrants affects only the weighted-average number of ordinary shares outstanding during the period, without any further adjustment.

5.3.540.80   Bonus issues and rights issues of warrants that have a bonus element impact the computation of both basic and diluted EPS.

EXAMPLE 23 – BONUS ELEMENT IN ISSUE OF WARRANTS

5.3.540.90   Company G issues bonus warrants on the basis of one bonus warrant for every 10 ordinary shares outstanding for zero consideration. Each bonus warrant entitles the warrant holder to subscribe in cash for one new ordinary share at an exercise price of 2.50 during the exercise period. The market price of G's shares when the warrant was issued was 6 and therefore there is a bonus element.

5.3.540.100   The bonus element is applied retrospectively – i.e. this requires restatement of the prior period's basic and diluted EPS. The adjustment to the basic EPS amounts is calculated by adjusting the cumulative weighted-average number of shares outstanding at the time of the bonus issue.

5.3.540.110   Adjustments may also be made to diluted EPS amounts, but only if the potential ordinary shares are outstanding at the date on which the shares with a bonus element are issued. For example, a bonus share issue occurs on 31 March 2018 and options are issued on 30 April 2018; no adjustment to the diluted EPS calculation is made in relation to the options because they were issued after the date of the bonus share issue.

5.3.550   Stock dividends

5.3.550.10   In some circumstances, dividends are paid to the ordinary equity holders of an entity in the form of additional ordinary shares, rather than in cash. They are commonly referred to as 'stock dividends' (or 'scrip' or 'share dividends'). In our view, the treatment of stock dividends in the EPS calculation depends on whether the shareholders have an option to receive cash and whether there is an inherent bonus element.

- If shareholders have an option to receive either a cash dividend or a stock dividend of equal value, then the entity exchanges shares for an equal amount of cash savings and therefore we believe that the stock dividends increase the number of shares outstanding, with a corresponding change in resources – i.e. there is no bonus element. Accordingly, the shares issued as stock dividends should be factored into the calculation of EPS on a prospective basis, with no retrospective adjustment to EPS.
- If the stock dividends do not have any cash alternative, then we believe that their substance is that of a bonus issue that increases the number of shares outstanding without a corresponding change in resources. In this case, the additional shares issued as stock dividends should be treated as if they had been issued since the beginning of the earliest period presented, necessitating retrospective adjustment to EPS. [*IAS 33.21(b), 27(a)*]

EXAMPLE 24 – STOCK DIVIDEND WITH CASH ALTERNATIVE OF EQUAL VALUE

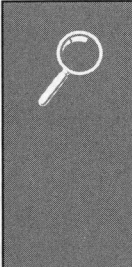

5.3.550.20   Company B grants a dividend whereby B's ordinary equity holders have the option to receive either cash of 2 or additional ordinary shares of B at a rate of 2 / x, whereby x is equal to the market price of B's ordinary shares. B has 100 ordinary shares outstanding with a market price of 5 per share. 30% of the ordinary equity holders opt to receive additional ordinary shares. These ordinary equity holders have opted to give up the cash value of 2, which is of equal value to the share dividend received. Therefore, B includes 12 (2 / 5 x 100 x 30%) additional shares in the calculation of basic EPS from the dividend payment date.

5.3.550.30   Under some dividend reinvestment programmes, the fair value of the stock alternative exceeds that of the cash alternative (often referred to as 'enhanced stock dividends'). In this case, we believe that there is a bonus element that requires retrospective adjustment to EPS amounts. In our view, the bonus element in stock dividends should be determined using the same formula as for determining a bonus element in a rights issue (see 5.3.540.20). [*IAS 33.A2*]

5.3.560   **DISCLOSURES**

5.3.560.10   Disclosure of separate EPS information is required for discontinued operations, if relevant, either in the statement of profit or loss and OCI or in the notes to the financial statements. [*IAS 33.68–68A*]

5.3.560.20   An entity provides a reconciliation of the earnings used in the basic and the diluted EPS calculations to profit or loss attributable to the parent entity. [*IAS 33.70*]

5.3.560.30   In some cases, there may be no difference between basic and diluted EPS. This will occur, for example, when the only potential ordinary shares are anti-dilutive and therefore excluded from the calculation of diluted EPS, or when there are dilutive potential ordinary shares but rounding creates the same amounts for basic and diluted EPS. In such cases, the entity is still required to disclose both basic and diluted EPS. This could be achieved by presenting only one line in the statement of profit or loss and OCI, labelled 'basic and diluted EPS'. In our view, if basic and diluted EPS are equal, then the entity does not need to disclose a reconciliation of the weighted-average number of ordinary shares used in the basic EPS calculation to the diluted EPS calculation, which would otherwise be required. However, if diluted EPS is reported for at least one period, then it should be reported for all periods presented, even if it equals basic EPS. In addition, an entity discloses potential ordinary shares that potentially could dilute EPS in the future, but are anti-dilutive for the current period presented. [*IAS 33.67, 70*]

5.3.560.40   Dividends and the related per-share amounts are disclosed either in the statement of changes in equity or in the notes to the financial statements, and not in the statement of profit or loss and OCI (see 2.2.10.30). [*IAS 1.107*]

5.3.560.50   Entities may wish to present additional EPS amounts based on alternative measures of earnings – e.g. an entity may disclose EBITDA per share (see 4.1.150 on the presentation of EBITDA).

These are presented in the notes to the financial statements only and not in the statement of profit or loss and OCI. [*IAS 33.73–73A*]

5.3.560.60   Both the basic and diluted additional amounts per share are disclosed in the notes to the financial statements for the alternative performance measure and each is disclosed with equal prominence. The entity describes the basis for determining the earnings amount, which should be consistent over time, and the earnings used are reconciled to a line item that is reported in the statement of profit or loss and OCI. The denominator used for the calculation of the additional basic and diluted per share amounts is the same as the weighted-average number of ordinary shares used in the basic and diluted EPS calculation as required under the standard. [*IAS 33.73–73A*]

5.3.560.70   The disclosure requirements in IAS 33 are not explicitly required in condensed interim financial statements prepared in accordance with IAS 34. Therefore, the general principle in IAS 34 is considered in determining the appropriate level of disclosure for an interim period (see 5.9.60.30). [*IAS 34.15, 15C, 25*]

5.4 Non-current assets held for sale and discontinued operations

5.4 Non-current assets held for sale and discontinued operations

CURRENTLY EFFECTIVE REQUIREMENTS

This publication reflects IFRS in issue at 1 August 2018, and the currently effective requirements cover annual periods beginning on 1 January 2018.

The requirements related to this topic are mainly derived from the following.

STANDARD	TITLE
IFRS 5	Non-current Assets Held for Sale and Discontinued Operations
IFRS 13	Fair Value Measurement
IFRIC 17	Distributions of Non-cash Assets to Owners

FORTHCOMING REQUIREMENTS

The currently effective requirements are affected by the following forthcoming requirements. They are highlighted with a # and the impact is explained in the accompanying boxed text at the references indicated.

In January 2016, the IASB issued IFRS 16 *Leases*, which is effective for annual periods beginning on or after 1 January 2019. See 5.4.33. IFRS 16 is the subject of chapter 5.1A.

FUTURE DEVELOPMENTS

For this topic, there are no future developments.

5.4.05   HELD FOR SALE OR DISTRIBUTION

5.4.10   General

5.4.10.05   The classification, presentation and measurement requirements for non-current assets or disposal groups held for sale also apply to those that are held for distribution to owners acting in their capacity as owners. Therefore, the requirements discussed in this chapter in respect of non-current assets and disposal groups that are classified as held-for-sale generally also apply to those classified as held-for-distribution. [*IFRS 5.5A, IFRIC 17.3*]

5.4.10.10   Classification as held-for-sale changes the measurement basis of most non-current assets and of disposal groups. Classification as held-for-sale also determines the presentation in the statement of financial position of such non-current assets and disposal groups.

5.4.10.20   A 'disposal group' is a group of assets to be disposed of together – by sale or otherwise – in a single transaction, and liabilities directly associated with those assets that will be transferred in the transaction. [*IFRS 5.A*]

5.4.10.30   Classification as a discontinued operation determines only the presentation of the operation in the statement of profit or loss and OCI, statement of cash flows and notes to the financial statements. There are no recognition or measurement impacts from classifying an operation as discontinued. However, a discontinued operation will generally include non-current assets or a disposal group or groups held for sale.

5.4.20   Held for sale

5.4.20.10   The *classification and presentation* requirements of the standard apply to all non-current assets and to disposal groups that are held for sale. [*IFRS 5.2*]

5.4.20.20   The *measurement* requirements for assets held for sale do not apply to certain assets. These assets are excluded either because measurement would be difficult (e.g. deferred tax assets) or because the assets are generally carried on the basis of fair value with changes in fair value recognised in profit or loss (e.g. investment property measured at fair value (see 3.4.140)). [*IFRS 5.2, 5*]

5.4.20.30   Excluded assets are *measured* using the standards that normally apply to these items, even if such assets are part of a disposal group. However, the disposal group as a whole is measured in a manner consistent with non-current assets that are held for sale. [*IFRS 5.4, 18–19, 23*]

5.4.20.40   As a result, non-current assets such as some financial assets may be classified and presented as held-for-sale but measured in accordance with other standards.

5.4.20.50   In the case of a disposal group, although the group as a whole is measured at the lower of carrying amount and fair value less costs to sell (see 5.4.40), some of the individual assets and liabilities within that disposal group may not be.

5.4.30   ***Classification#***

5.4.30.10   A non-current asset or disposal group is classified as held-for-sale when its carrying amount will be recovered principally through a sale transaction. [*IFRS 5.6*]

5.4.30.20   This is the case when the asset is *available for immediate sale* in its present condition subject only to terms that are usual and customary for sales of such assets or disposal groups, and its sale is *highly probable* – i.e. when it is significantly more likely than merely probable. [*IFRS 5.7, A*]

5.4.30.30   A need to obtain or construct a replacement asset (e.g. a new headquarters) or to cease operations that will not be transferred with the asset means that the asset is not available for immediate sale. Similarly, in our view if an asset is leased out and cannot be sold until the end of the lease term, then it is not available for immediate sale in its present condition. [*IFRS 5.IG.Ex1*]

5.4.30.40   A sale-and-operating-leaseback transaction results in the recognition of a completed sale of an asset (see 5.1.490). In our view, the general held-for-sale classification criteria should be applied to determine at what point the asset is held for sale. In particular, the likelihood of the planned arrangement being an operating lease and therefore a completed sale is relevant in determining whether and when the related asset could qualify as held-for-sale. [*IFRS 5.6–9, IAS 17.61*]

5.4.30.50   A sale-and-finance-leaseback transaction does not result in derecognition of the asset, and therefore the asset could not qualify as held-for-sale as a result of such a transaction. [*IFRS 5.8, IG.Ex4*]

5.4.30.60   An entity that is committed to a sale plan involving the loss of control of a subsidiary classifies all of the assets and liabilities of that subsidiary as held-for-sale in its consolidated financial statements when the criteria for classification as held-for-sale are met; this is regardless of whether the entity will retain a non-controlling interest in the subsidiary after the sale. A reduction in the level of ownership of a subsidiary that does not result in a loss of control is insufficient for the consolidated assets and liabilities to be classified as held-for-sale. [*IFRS 5.8A, BC24A–BC24E*]

5.4.30.65   An investment, or a portion of an investment, in an associate or joint venture is classified as held-for-sale when the relevant criteria are met; the entity continues to apply the equity method to any remaining portion of the investment that is not classified as held-for-sale. On disposal of the investment classified as held-for-sale, the accounting for any retained portion of the investment is reassessed:
- if the retained portion of the investment continues to qualify as an associate or joint venture, then the entity continues to apply the equity method and the disposal has no effect on this portion of the investment; or
- if the retained portion of the investment no longer qualifies as an associate or joint venture, then the investment is accounted for in accordance with IFRS 9 (see 3.5.630). [*IAS 28.20*]

5.4.30.70   To be highly probable, there needs to be commitment to a plan to sell by an appropriate level of management and that plan needs to have been initiated. This requires active marketing at a price that is reasonable in relation to the asset's fair value. There is an expectation that the sale will be completed within one year of the classification of assets or a disposal group as held-for-sale, subject to extension in certain circumstances. [*IFRS 5.8, IG.Ex5–7*]

EXAMPLE 1 – CLASSIFICATION AS HELD-FOR-SALE AND HELD-FOR-USE

5.4.30.75   Company X has commenced the process of selling an investment in a subsidiary and meets all of the criteria for classifying the assets and liabilities of the subsidiary as held-for-sale, including actively marketing the investment at a price that is reasonable in relation to the investment's fair value. A buyer is identified and the method of calculating the final agreed price for the investment is determined.

5.4.30.77   However, before finalising the sale, financial information regarding the subsidiary emerges that leads X to suspect that the final agreed price will be significantly below the price at which it is willing to sell its investment. Before receiving the results of the calculation, the management of X actively begins to consider alternatives to selling the investment.

5.4.30.78   In our view, in this situation the investment in the subsidiary no longer meets the held-for-sale criteria and should be reclassified as held-for-use (see 5.4.90), because management's consideration of other options is indicative of their unwillingness to sell at the current price.

5.4.30.80   In our view, when an active market exists, active marketing at a reasonable price will generally lead quickly to a sale. Accordingly, it is unlikely that a non-current asset with a quoted market price will be classified as held-for-sale for any significant period of time before disposal. [*IFRS 5.IG.Ex7*]

5.4.30.85   For some entities, the sale of significant non-current assets or disposal groups may be subject to shareholder approval. In our view, shareholder approval is considered as part of whether the sale is highly probable. Therefore, the requirement to obtain shareholder approval does not necessarily mean that the criteria for classification as held-for-sale are met only when shareholder approval is obtained. However, if substantive shareholder approval for a sale is required, then the sale might not be highly probable until shareholder approval is obtained. [*IFRS 5.8*]

5.4.30.87   The sale of significant non-current assets or disposal groups may also be subject to regulatory approval. Depending on particular circumstances, regulatory approval may be considered substantive or, on the contrary, viewed as a formality. In our view, if considering all available evidence management concludes that the pending regulatory approval does not prevent the sale from being highly probable, then it may not necessarily prevent the classification of the non-current assets or disposal groups as held-for-sale. [*IFRS 5.8–9, B1, IG.Ex5*]

5.4.30.90   Exchanges of non-current assets are a sale for the purposes of classification of a non-current asset or disposal group as held-for-sale, provided that the expected exchange has commercial substance (see 5.7.20). [*IFRS 5.10*]

5.4.30.100   Non-current assets that are to be abandoned or mothballed are not classified as held-for-sale because they will not be recovered principally through a sale transaction. [*IFRS 5.13*]

5.4.30.110   For a discussion of the classification of a non-current asset or a disposal group acquired exclusively with a view to its subsequent disposal, see 5.4.260. For other non-current assets or disposal groups, classification as held-for-sale is *prohibited* when the criteria are met only *after* the reporting date. Instead, disclosures are required in the notes to the financial statements. [*IFRS 5.12, IAS 10.22(c)*]

5.4.30.120   Statement of financial position comparatives are not re-presented to reflect the classification as held-for-sale at the current reporting date. [*IFRS 5.40, IG.Ex12*]

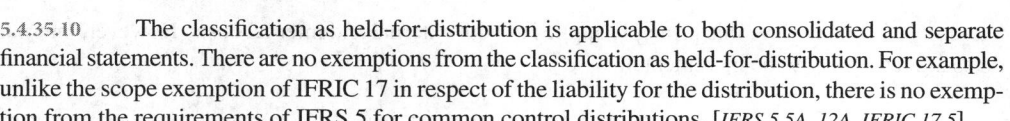

5.4.33   FORTHCOMING REQUIREMENTS

5.4.33.10   IFRS 16 carries forward the IAS 17 distinction between operating and finance leases for lessors only. Under IFRS 16, a lessee applies a single, on-balance sheet lease accounting model and does not classify the lease as an operating or finance lease. A seller-lessee derecognises the underlying asset only if the transfer leg satisfies the requirements of IFRS 15 to be accounted for as a sale of the asset. [*IFRS 16.100*]

5.4.35   Held for distribution (S)

5.4.35.10   The classification as held-for-distribution is applicable to both consolidated and separate financial statements. There are no exemptions from the classification as held-for-distribution. For example, unlike the scope exemption of IFRIC 17 in respect of the liability for the distribution, there is no exemption from the requirements of IFRS 5 for common control distributions. [*IFRS 5.5A, 12A, IFRIC 17.5*]

5.4.37   *Classification*

5.4.37.10   A non-current asset or disposal group is classified as held-for-distribution when the entity is committed to distributing the asset or disposal group to its owners. [*IFRS 5.12A*]

5.4.37.20   This is the case when the asset is *available for immediate distribution* in its present condition and its distribution is *highly probable* – i.e. when it is significantly more likely than merely probable. The criteria relevant to whether a distribution is highly probable are similar to those for classification as held-for-sale (see 5.4.30). [*IFRS 5.7, A*]

5.4.37.30   An entity may be committed to a distribution even if there is a requirement for shareholder approval of the distribution. The probability of shareholder approval is considered as part of the assessment of whether the distribution is highly probable. Accordingly, in some cases an entity may be committed to distributing a non-current asset or disposal group and therefore may be required to classify it as held-for-distribution before a liability is recognised for the distribution. [*IFRS 5.7, 12A*]

5.4.40   Measurement

5.4.40.10   The measurement requirements of IFRS 5 apply equally to non-current assets and to the assets and liabilities in a disposal group that are held for sale or held for distribution. [*IFRS 5.5A*]

5.4.40.20   The references to fair value in this section (as part of fair value less costs to sell) mean fair value measured in accordance with IFRS 13, which is the subject of chapter 2.4.

5.4.50   *Before classification as held-for-sale or held-for-distribution*

5.4.50.10   Before classification as held-for-sale or held-for-distribution, non-current assets and the assets and liabilities in a disposal group are measured in accordance with applicable IFRSs. For example, property, plant and equipment is tested for impairment. In our view, any resulting gains or losses should be recognised in accordance with the relevant standards. [*IFRS 5.18*]

5.4.60 *On initial classification as held-for-sale or held-for-distribution*

5.4.60.10   On initial classification as held-for-sale or held-for-distribution, disposal groups and non-current assets are measured at the lower of their:

* carrying amount; and
* fair value less costs to sell (or costs to distribute, as applicable). [*IFRS 5.15–15A*]

5.4.60.20   Costs to sell/distribute are incremental costs directly attributable to the disposal of an asset (or disposal group), excluding finance costs and income tax expense, that would not have been incurred by the entity had the decision to sell/distribute not been made. These costs include, for example, broker commission, legal and title transfer fees necessary to effect the sale/distribution and similar transaction taxes. For additional guidance on costs to distribute, see 7.3.570. [*IFRS 5.A, 15A*]

5.4.60.30   In our view, this principle applies to both external and internal costs. However, internal costs are less likely to be incremental.

5.4.60.35   In some cases, a disposal group may comprise the assets and liabilities of a subsidiary that is not wholly owned and the shares of that subsidiary may be quoted on an active market. Whether a control premium should be taken into account in measuring the fair value (less costs to sell) of the disposal group depends on the unit of account. Consistent with the discussion in 2.4.80.40, an entity should choose an accounting policy, to be applied consistently, to identify the unit of account either as the disposal group that corresponds to the subsidiary or the individual share in the subsidiary. For a discussion of this issue and the subsequent impact on measuring fair value, see 2.4.80 and 830.

5.4.60.40   Impairment losses on initial classification of a non-current asset or disposal group as held-for-sale are included in profit or loss even if the asset is, or the disposal group includes assets that are, measured at a revalued amount. The same applies to gains and losses on subsequent remeasurement (see 5.4.70). [*IFRS 5.20, IG.Ex10*]

5.4.60.50   Losses on a disposal group are allocated to the non-current assets in the disposal group that are in the scope of the *measurement* requirements of IFRS 5 in the order of allocation required by IAS 36 (see chapter 3.10). In the case of impairment losses, allocation would be first to goodwill and then to other assets on a pro rata basis. [*IFRS 5.23, IU 01-16*]

EXAMPLE 2 – ALLOCATION OF IMPAIRMENT LOSS TO ASSETS WITHIN DISPOSAL GROUP

5.4.60.60   A disposal group contains assets and liabilities that are not in the measurement scope of IFRS 5 (excluded assets) with a net carrying amount measured on the basis of the relevant standards of 270 (see 5.4.50). The carrying amount of assets in the measurement scope of IFRS 5 is 900. The fair value less costs to sell of the disposal group as a whole is 1,000.

> 5.4.60.70   A loss of 170 (1,000 compared with 1,170 (900 + 270)) is allocated to the assets in the measurement scope of IFRS 5 in the order of allocation required by IAS 36. The allocation is not restricted by the value in use or fair value less costs to sell of the individual assets as would be the case with an impairment loss recognised under IAS 36 (see 3.10.410).

5.4.60.80   The recognition and allocation of an impairment loss to the assets in a disposal group may have a consequential effect on the temporary differences and therefore the deferred taxes related to those assets. [*IFRS 5.15, 23*]

EXAMPLE 3 – INTERACTION BETWEEN IMPAIRMENT LOSS AND INCOME TAX

> 5.4.60.90   Company S has a disposal group that comprises assets A and B. Asset A has a carrying amount of 2,667 and a tax base of 0. Asset B has a carrying amount and a tax base of 400. The tax rate is 40%. Only asset A is in the measurement scope of IFRS 5. The disposal group includes a deferred tax liability of 1,067 (2,667 x 40%). The fair value less costs to sell of the disposal group is 1,400.
>
> 5.4.60.100   S calculates the impairment loss in two steps.
> - *Step 1:* Ignoring the impact of changes in the deferred tax resulting from recording the impairment loss, the impairment loss is 600 ((2,667 + 400 - 1,067) - 1,400).
> - *Step 2:* To arrive at an overall carrying amount for the disposal group of 1,400, S grosses up the impairment loss for the effect of tax. This results in an impairment loss of 1,000 (600 / 60%), and a revised deferred tax liability of 667 ((1,667 - 0) x 40%). The post-impairment carrying amount of the disposal group is 1,400 (1,667 + 400 - 667).

5.4.60.105   In some cases, the difference between the carrying amount and the fair value less cost to sell of a disposal group may exceed the carrying amount of non-current assets in the disposal group. The IFRS Interpretations Committee discussed whether the amount of the impairment loss recognised should be limited in such circumstances. [*IU 01-16*]

5.4.60.110   The Committee did not add this issue to its agenda and suggested that it could possibly be addressed by the IASB in the future. In our view, if the fair value less costs to sell of a disposal group is below its carrying amount, but the carrying amount of assets in the measurement scope of IFRS 5 is insufficient to absorb the impairment loss, then the amount of the impairment loss recognised is generally limited to the carrying amount of assets within the disposal group to which the measurement requirements of IFRS 5 apply. However, in some circumstances a different approach may be acceptable. [*IFRS 5.23, IU 01-16*]

5.4.60.120   A disposal group continues to be consolidated while it is held for sale or distribution. Accordingly, revenue (e.g. from the sale of inventory) and expenses (including interest) continue to be recognised. However, assets held for sale, including those within a disposal group, are not depreciated or amortised. [*IFRS 5.25*]

5.4.60.130   Foreign currency translation reserves in respect of a disposal group are transferred to profit or loss when the disposal group is disposed of (see 2.7.340) and not when the disposal group is classified as held-for-sale or held-for-distribution. [*IFRS 5.38, BC58, IAS 21.48–49*]

5.4.60.140   For a discussion of fair value measurement, see chapter 2.4.

5.4.70   *Subsequent remeasurement*

5.4.70.10   Subsequent to initial classification as held-for-sale, disposal groups and non-current assets that are measured at their fair value less costs to sell, are subject to a limit on the amount of any gain that can be recognised as a result of an increase in fair value less costs to sell before disposal. The maximum increase (and therefore gain) that can be recognised is the cumulative amount of impairment losses recognised in accordance with IFRS 5 and previously in accordance with IAS 36. Impairment losses allocated to goodwill are included in determining the maximum increase, and the disposal group as a whole continues to be measured at the lower of its carrying amount and fair value less costs to sell.

5.4.70.13   The reversal of the impairment loss is allocated to the assets in the disposal group that are subject to the measurement requirements of IFRS 5, except for goodwill, pro rata with the carrying amounts of those assets. In our view, reversals of impairment losses on subsequent remeasurement may result in individual assets in the disposal group being measured at amounts above their carrying amount if the non-current assets had not been classified as held-for-sale. However, the disposal group as a whole continues to be measured at the lower of its carrying amount and fair value less costs to sell. The allocation of gains and losses to individual assets will impact the amount of any temporary differences for deferred tax purposes (see chapter 3.13 and 5.4.60.80–100). [*IFRS 5.15, 20–23, IAS 36.122*]

5.4.70.15   Additional net assets that become part of a disposal group (e.g. because of profits being generated by the disposal group (see 5.4.60.120)) increase the carrying amount of the disposal group. For example, consider a disposal group that is held at 50, being its carrying amount at the date of classification as held-for-sale. There has not been an impairment previously for this disposal group. The disposal group recognises a profit of 10, together with an increase in debtors within the disposal group, between the date the disposal group was classified as held-for-sale and the following year end. In our view, at the reporting date the carrying amount would be 60 because there has been a change in the assets and liabilities in the disposal group. Also, in our view in such circumstances the recognition of the profit is not restricted by the absence of a cumulative impairment loss that can be reversed. The disposal group is then measured at the lower of the new carrying amount and its fair value less costs to sell. [*IFRS 5.19, 22(b)*]

5.4.70.20   On subsequent remeasurement of a disposal group, the carrying amount of any assets and liabilities excluded from the measurement requirements of IFRS 5 are remeasured in accordance with other applicable IFRSs. In our view, any gains and losses on this remeasurement should be recognised in accordance with the relevant standards. [*IFRS 5.19*]

5.4.70.30   Gains and losses on subsequent remeasurement to fair value less costs to sell are included in profit or loss regardless of whether the asset was, or the disposal group includes assets that were, previously measured based on revalued amounts. [*IFRS 5.37*]

5.4.70.40   Gains and losses from the remeasurement of a disposal group are allocated to the non-current assets in that group that are in the scope of the *measurement* requirements of IFRS 5 in the order of allocation required by IAS 36 (in the case of losses, first to goodwill and then to other assets on a pro rata basis). [*IFRS 5.23*]

5.4.70.50   A disposal group continues to be classified as held-for-sale even when part of the group (e.g. inventory) is sold separately, as long as the remaining items in the group continue to meet the criteria. [*IFRS 5.29*]

5.4.80   *On disposal*

5.4.80.10   Any gain or loss not recognised before the date of sale is recognised on the derecognition of the non-current asset or disposal group. [*IFRS 5.24*]

5.4.80.20   In respect of a distribution, any gain or loss will be recognised at the date of settlement of the dividend. The amount recognised in profit or loss will be the difference between the carrying amount of the liability for the dividend payable and the carrying amount of the non-current asset or disposal group. [*IFRIC 17.14*]

5.4.80.30   The derecognition of certain assets and liabilities may also result in the reclassification to profit or loss of amounts previously recognised in OCI – e.g. the cumulative amount of exchange differences related to a foreign operation (see 5.4.60.130).

5.4.80.40   In our view, costs to sell (see 5.4.60.20) should be expensed when they are incurred, rather than deferred until the sale is recognised, unless they meet the definition of an asset (e.g. they constitute a prepayment for services not yet received).

5.4.90   Reclassification as held-for-use and changes in method of disposal

5.4.90.10   Non-current assets and disposal groups are reclassified from held-for-sale or from held-for-distribution to held-for-use if they no longer meet the criteria to be classified as held-for-sale or held-for-distribution. [*IFRS 5.26, 29*]

5.4.90.20   On reclassification from held-for-sale or held-for-distribution to held-for-use, a non-current asset is remeasured at the lower of its recoverable amount and the carrying amount that would have been recognised had the asset never been classified as held-for-sale or held-for-distribution. The calculation of this carrying amount includes any depreciation that would have been recognised had the asset not been classified as held-for-sale or held-for-distribution. [*IFRS 5.27*]

5.4.90.30   Normally, reversals of impairments of goodwill are prohibited. In our view, reclassification as held-for-use and the requirement to remeasure on reclassification may create one of the rare circumstances when reversals of goodwill impairment are recognised. This may occur if the recoverable amount of goodwill exceeds its carrying amount as a result of impairment losses recognised in respect of the held-for-sale disposal group that were allocated to goodwill. [*IFRS 5.27, IAS 36.124*]

5.4.90.40   Any resulting adjustment is recognised in profit or loss unless the asset was measured at a revalued amount before its classification as held-for-sale or held-for-distribution. In these cases, the adjustment is recognised (in whole or in part) as a revaluation increase or decrease (see 3.2.300 and 3.3.280). [*IFRS 5.28*]

5.4.90.50   If an entity changes the method of disposal of non-current assets or disposal groups – e.g. reclassifies them from held-for-distribution to held-for-sale (or vice versa) without any time lag – then it continues to apply held-for-distribution or held-for-sale accounting. At the time of the change in method, an entity measures the non-current asset or a disposal group at the lower of its carrying amount and fair value less costs to sell/distribute and recognises any write-down or subsequent increase in their fair value less costs to sell/distribute. [*IFRS 5.26A*]

5.4.100   *Subsidiaries, joint arrangements and associates*

5.4.100.10   If a disposal group or a non-current asset that ceases to be classified as held-for-sale is a subsidiary, joint operation, joint venture, associate or portion of an interest in an associate or joint venture, then the financial statements for the periods since classification as held-for-sale are amended accordingly. In our view, this amendment should be made in the financial statements of the reporting period in which the change of classification occurs. To the extent that the amendment relates to earlier periods, it is recognised as a prior-period adjustment (i.e. the amendment is calculated retrospectively) and the opening balance of retained earnings and comparatives are restated (see chapter 2.8). [*IFRS 5.28, IAS 28.21*]

5.4.110   **Presentation**

5.4.110.10   Non-current assets and the assets of a disposal group classified as held-for-sale or held-for-distribution are presented separately from other assets in the statement of financial position. [*IFRS 5.38, 5A*]

5.4.110.20   The liabilities of a disposal group classified as held-for-sale or held-for-distribution are presented separately from other liabilities in the statement of financial position. [*IFRS 5.38, 5A*]

5.4.110.25   IFRS does not specifically address the presentation of NCI in a disposal group classified as held-for-sale or held-for-distribution. In our view, NCI in a disposal group classified as held-for-sale or held-for-distribution should continue to be presented within equity consistent with the requirement in IFRS 10 and should not be reclassified as a liability (see 2.5.530.30). [*IFRS 10.A*]

5.4.110.30   Non-current assets and assets of disposal groups classified as held-for-sale or held-for-distribution are classified as current in the statement of financial position. In our view, liabilities of such disposal groups should also be classified as current in the statement of financial position. Consequently, it would not generally be appropriate to present a three-column statement of financial position with the headings 'Assets/Liabilities not for sale', 'Assets/Liabilities held for sale' and 'Total' with the assets and liabilities held for sale or distribution included in non-current line items. [*IFRS 5.3, BC9–BC10, IAS 1.66*]

5.4.110.35   The disclosure requirements of IFRS 5 apply to non-current assets or disposal groups classified as held-for-sale. Disclosures required by other standards apply only when the requirements specifically refer to non-current assets (or disposal groups) classified as held-for-sale – e.g. the disclosure of EPS for a discontinued operation that is classified as held-for-sale. This includes the disclosure requirements of IFRS 13, which are applicable when a non-current asset or disposal group held for sale is measured at fair value less costs to sell (see 2.4.490). Disclosures required by other standards also apply when they relate to assets and liabilities in a disposal group that are not in the measurement scope of IFRS 5 (e.g. investment property measured at fair value) and such disclosures are not already provided in the other notes to the financial statements. Additional disclosures may be necessary to comply with the general requirements of IAS 1, in particular for a fair presentation and in respect of sources of estimation uncertainty. [*IFRS 5.5B, 41, 13.93, IAS 33.68*]

5.4.120   **DISCONTINUED OPERATIONS**

5.4.130   **Classification**

5.4.130.10   The presentation of an operation as a discontinued operation is limited to a component of an entity that either has been disposed of, or is classified as held-for-sale, and:
- represents a separate major line of business or geographic area of operations;
- is part of a co-ordinated single plan to dispose of a separate major line of business or geographic area of operations; or
- is a subsidiary acquired exclusively with a view to resale. [*IFRS 5.32*]

5.4.130.20   A component of an entity comprises operations and cash flows that can be distinguished clearly, both operationally and for financial reporting purposes, from the rest of the entity. In other words, a component will have been a CGU or a group of CGUs while being held for use (see 3.10.60). In our view, the disposal of a business that was previously part of an entity considered to be a single CGU does not qualify as a component of an entity, and therefore is not classified as a discontinued operation if it is disposed of. [*IFRS 5.31*]

5.4.130.25   It is possible for a component of an entity to be a separate major line of business or geographic area of operations with respect to a subsidiary's but not the parent's operations. In that case, the presentation in the subsidiary's financial statements may differ from the presentation in the parent's consolidated financial statements. For example, Subsidiary S cultivates pine trees and produces paper products in New Zealand. S disposes of all of its paper-producing facilities. Parent P has other subsidiaries producing paper in New Zealand. Because the disposed business is a component of S that represents a separate major line of business, the disposal is presented as a discontinued operation in S's financial statements, but not in P's consolidated financial statements.

5.4.130.30   It is not clear whether a business that will be disposed of by distribution to owners could be classified as a discontinued operation before its disposal. Although IFRS 5 was amended to extend the requirements in respect of non-current assets or disposal groups held for sale to such items held for distribution to owners, the cross-referencing in the amendments does not extend to discontinued operations. In our view, although the definition of a discontinued operation has not been extended explicitly, classification of non-current assets or disposal groups held for distribution to owners as a discontinued operation is appropriate if the remaining criteria of IFRS 5 are met. [*IFRS 5.5A*]

5.4.140   **Part of single plan**

5.4.140.10   An entity needs to have a single overall plan under which all or substantially all of a qualifying component of its operations is discontinued. Under the plan, the component may be disposed of in its entirety or by selling the assets and liabilities on a piecemeal basis. [*IFRS 5.32(b)*]

EXAMPLE 4 – ABSENCE OF SINGLE PLAN

5.4.140.20   During June 2017, Company D disposed of some of the manufacturing facilities within its kitchen segment. In the following year, other facilities within the segment were disposed of and the remaining operations combined with another business within D. None of the disposals met the criteria separately to be a discontinued operation. Although different parts of the kitchen segment were disposed of on a piecemeal basis, in this case there was no single plan to dispose of the segment. Therefore, D does not present its kitchen segment as a discontinued operation.

5.4.150   **Operating segment that is a separate major line of business or geographic area**

5.4.150.10   In our view, an operating segment (see 5.2.50) would normally represent a separate major line of business or geographic area of operation.

EXAMPLE 5 – DISPOSAL OF OPERATING SEGMENT THAT IS A SEPARATE MAJOR LINE OF BUSINESS

5.4.150.20   Company E has 5 different operating segments, one of which solely produces cigars. All of the cigar growing and production facilities are situated in Central America. E also has other operations in Central America for other operating segments. In April 2018, E disposed of its cigar segment. In our view, the cigar segment meets the definition of a component of a business and represents a separate major line of business, and would qualify for reporting as a discontinued operation.

5.4.160   *Discontinuance of products*

5.4.160.10   Abandoning or discontinuing products in a product line or replacing them with newer products is a part of the normal evolution of a business, and in our view does not constitute a discontinued operation. For example, Company Q has four segments: ice cream, chocolate, beverages and snack foods. Q has discontinued producing some of the chocolate bars containing nuts and instead has decided to add chocolate bars containing fruit to its product range.

5.4.160.20   In our view, ceasing to produce chocolate bars with nuts does not constitute a discontinued operation. Even though there may have been a single plan to cease the production of nut chocolate bars, the nut chocolate bars do not represent a separate major line of business.

5.4.160.30   In our view, the sale of a brand will also not meet the definition of a discontinued operation, unless it represents a separate major line of business of the entity.

5.4.170   *Closure of facility*

5.4.170.10   Closure of facilities resulting from productivity or other cost reasons is often a part of the general development within a business and does not necessarily meet the definition of a discontinued operation. For example, Company C has closed one of its seven facilities in North America because it is cheaper to manufacture its products in South East Asia. The facilities are included in the clothing segment together with other facilities in North America, South East Asia and Eastern Europe.

5.4.170.20   In our view, even if the closure of the facility is subject to a single plan, this transaction does not meet the definition of a discontinued operation because the same component of the business will continue to operate using different facilities. However, the closure may require the recognition of impairment charges and provisions triggered by the restructuring (see 3.10.110 and 3.12.230). Further recognition and measurement implications arise if the non-current assets used in this facility meet the definition to be classified as held-for-sale (see 5.4.20) or held-for-distribution (see 5.4.35).

5.4.180   *Disposal of subsidiary*

5.4.180.10   In our view, evaluation of whether an operation is a separate major line of business should be based on the nature and organisation of the entity's operations, and does not require alignment with legal entities within the organisation.

5.4.180.20   A subsidiary acquired exclusively for resale may be a discontinued operation (see 5.4.260).

5.4.180.30   In the case of an existing subsidiary, its sale or disposal is not automatically a discontinued operation if that subsidiary is not, on its own, a separate major line of business or geographic area of operation.

EXAMPLE 6 – DISPOSAL OF SUBSIDIARY THAT IS NOT A SEPARATE MAJOR LINE OF BUSINESS

5.4.180.40   Company B sells baby clothes, sports clothes, toys and gardening equipment and considers each product group as an operating segment. In July 2018, B disposed of D, a significant subsidiary included in the toy segment. B retains other operations in the toy segment.

5.4.180.50   In our view, even though the disposal of D may be significant for B, is subject to a single plan and can be distinguished operationally and for financial reporting purposes, the disposal of D should not be classified as a discontinued operation. This is because there are other operations within the same segment producing toys, and therefore D on its own does not represent a separate major line of business or geographic area of B.

5.4.180.60   However, because the disposal of D is significant, the impact of the disposal may require separate disclosure. [*IAS 1.97*]

5.4.190   *Venture capital investors*

5.4.190.10   Venture capital investors often acquire interests in a variety of businesses. Investments may be held for three to five years and then sold. Venture capital investors are required to consolidate entities that they control (see 2.5.10.40). Typically, when a new investment is proposed, a key feature of the proposal is the exit strategy. The disposal phase of an investment may be carried out in such a way that it may meet the definition of a discontinued operation.

5.4.190.20   In our view, if the investments to be sold in a particular year are a separate major line of business or geographic area of operations and the disposal is pursuant to a single plan, then the entity should present the disposal as a discontinued operation.

5.4.190.30   However, in our view the component is unlikely to be a discontinued operation from its date of acquisition because the disposal groups are unlikely to be held for sale at the date of acquisition (see 5.4.260).

5.4.200   Timing

5.4.200.10   Classification as a discontinued operation occurs at the date on which an operation meets the criteria to be classified as held-for-sale, when a group of assets ceases to be used or when an entity has disposed of an operation. [*IFRS 5.13, 32*]

5.4.200.20   In our view, an operation that will be disposed of by distribution to owners – e.g. a dividend in specie or a spin-off transaction – should not be classified as held-for-sale because no sale will occur; it should instead be classified as held-for-distribution when it meets the relevant criteria. An operation that meets the criteria to be classified as a discontinued operation that is to be distributed to owners is classified as discontinued at latest when the distribution occurs. [*IFRS 5.6–8, 12A, 32*]

5.4.210   Measurement

5.4.210.10   There are no recognition or measurement impacts from classifying an operation as discontinued. However, a discontinued operation will generally include non-current assets held for sale or a disposal group or groups. Therefore, the measurement requirements for discontinued operations are those of the individual assets and liabilities or disposal groups that comprise the operation (see 5.4.40).

5.4.210.20   An entity continues to recognise ongoing operating profits and losses from discontinued operations as they are incurred. The general prohibition on the accrual of future operating losses also continues to apply (see 3.12.40.30).

5.4.210.30   When a discontinued operation is disposed of, any profit or loss on the sale is recognised in the period in which the sale is recognised. [*IFRS 5.24*]

5.4.220   Presentation and disclosure

5.4.220.10   The results of discontinued operations are presented separately from continuing operations in the statement of profit or loss and OCI. Amounts included in profit or loss from discontinued operations are presented separately from OCI from discontinued operations. In our view, the results of the discontinued operations should not be presented net of NCI, because NCI are not an item of income or expense (see 2.5.530.10). An analysis of this single amount is presented either in the statement of profit or loss and OCI or in the notes to the financial statements. [*IFRS 5.33–33A, 10.B98*]

5.4.220.20   When presenting discontinued operations, it may be necessary to reconsider the allocation of revenue or expenses to a segment that is classified as a discontinued operation. In our view, revenue and expenses should not be presented as discontinued unless they will cease to be earned/incurred on disposal of the discontinued operation. For example, general corporate overhead expenses would not be allocated to a discontinued operation.

5.4.220.30   Although IFRS 5 is clear that the results of discontinued operations are presented separately from continuing operations in the statement of profit or loss and OCI as a single amount of profit or loss, it is unclear how the statement of profit or loss and OCI presentation requirements of IFRS 5 interact with those of IAS 1; specifically, whether amounts (e.g. of revenue and expenses) related to a discontinued operation are permitted or required to be excluded from the total of these line items presented in the statement of profit or loss and OCI.

5.4.220.40   In our view, this single amount of profit or loss for discontinued operations can be presented in different ways. An entity should choose a presentation format, to be applied consistently, to present the profit or loss for discontinued operations. One approach is to include amounts related to discontinued operations only in the single amount of profit or loss for discontinued operations, excluding amounts related to discontinued operations from all other amounts presented before that line. Alternatively, we believe that presenting the total of continuing plus discontinued for each line item is also acceptable in some instances – e.g. when a columnar approach is used to present the analysis of continuing and discontinued operations in the statement of profit or loss and OCI. However, when such a presentation is used, the 'continuing' amount should be presented separately for each line item. [*IFRS 5.IG.Ex11*]

5.4.220.50   Furthermore, it is not clear how the cash flow presentation requirements of IFRS 5 interact with those of IAS 7. IAS 7 requires a statement of cash flows to include all cash flows, therefore including both those from continuing and those from discontinued operations. Consequently, cash and cash equivalents include those of disposal groups classified as held-for-sale. IAS 7 also requires an analysis of cash flows classified into operating, investing and financing activities, and further analysis of the gross cash flows included in these activities (see 2.3.20). However, IFRS 5 requires presentation of the net cash flows attributable to operating, investing and financing activities of discontinued operations to be presented either in the statement of cash flows or in the notes. In our view, there are numerous ways in which these requirements may be met, including the following.

• Presenting the statement of cash flows split between continuing and discontinued cash flows with a total of the cash flows. The discontinued cash flows are analysed by operating, investing and financing activities and further analysis of these amounts is presented in the statement of cash flows or disclosed in the notes. This could be done through a columnar presentation showing continuing and discontinued operations with a total of the cash flows.
• Presenting a statement of cash flows that includes an analysis of all cash flows in total – i.e. including both continuing and discontinued operations. Amounts related to discontinued operations by operating, investing and financing activities are disclosed in the notes. This presentation is illustrated in KPMG's *Guides to financial statements* series. [*IAS 7.10, IFRS 5.33*]

5.4.220.60   The analysis of the result presented in the statement of profit or loss and OCI and cash flow information is not required for a disposal group that is a newly acquired subsidiary that is classified as held-for-sale on acquisition. [*IFRS 5.33(b)*]

5.4.220.70   The comparative statement of profit or loss and OCI and cash flow information is re-presented each period on the basis of the classification of operations as discontinued or continuing operations at the reporting date. [*IFRS 5.34*]

EXAMPLE 7 – COMPARATIVE INFORMATION FOR DISCONTINUED OPERATIONS

5.4.220.80   Company B has Segment D that is classified as discontinued in 2018. B re-presents the 2017 comparatives for the statement of profit or loss and OCI and cash flow information in respect of D as discontinued.

5.4.220.90   The investor's share of the discontinued operations of an associate or joint venture is presented as part of the share of profit or loss of equity-accounted investees and is also disclosed separately. In our view, such amounts should not be presented as part of the discontinued operations of the entity, unless they are discontinued operations of that entity itself. [*IAS 1.82*]

5.4.220.100   In our view, when a disposal or abandonment does not meet the definition of a discontinued operation, an entity may still present additional information about the disposal – i.e. similar information to that required by IFRS 5 – but the term 'discontinued operation' cannot be used. The amounts are presented in the appropriate line items within continuing operations. Such transactions will often meet the definition of a restructuring, and disclosure about provisions and contingent liabilities may also be required (see 3.12.770 and 875).

5.4.230   *Transactions between continuing and discontinued operations*

5.4 230.10   In some cases, there may be transactions between the continuing and discontinued operations – e.g. inter-segment sales and purchases. The IFRS Interpretations Committee discussed how to present intra-group transactions between continuing and discontinued operations and observed that IFRS 5 does not provide specific guidance on how an entity disaggregates consolidated results between continuing and discontinued operations in a way that reflects the elimination of intra-group transactions. The Committee suggested that this issue could possibly be addressed by the IASB in the future. [*IU 01-16*]

5.4.230.20   The Committee noted that under IFRS 10, notwithstanding the separate presentation and disclosure of the results of continuing and discontinued operations, intra-group transactions are required to be fully eliminated in the parent's consolidated financial statements (see 2.5.550). The Committee also noted that IFRS 5 requires the presentation and disclosure of information that enables users of the financial statements to evaluate the financial effects of discontinued operations. In the light of this objective, the Committee observed that, depending on the particular facts and circumstances, an entity may have to provide additional disclosures. [*IU 01-16*]

5.4.230.30   To illustrate the issue, in the case of the disposal of a downstream operation in a vertically integrated business, the revenue from continuing operations after the elimination of intra-group transactions against that amount would be zero, whereas the costs of sale of the continuing operations would continue to be as previously reported for the entity as a whole. Similarly, in the case of the disposal of an upstream operation in a vertically integrated business, the revenue from continuing operations after the elimination of intra-group transactions would continue to be as previously reported, whereas the costs of sale from continuing operations against that amount would be zero. Therefore, this may not provide sufficient information to enable users of the financial statements to evaluate the financial effects of discontinued operations.

5.4.230.40   In our view, considering that IFRS 5 does not specify how the elimination should be attributed to continuing and discontinued operations, an entity may present transactions between the continuing and discontinued operations in a way that reflects the continuance of those transactions, when that is useful to the users of the financial statements. It may be appropriate to present additional disclosure either on the face of the statement of profit or loss and OCI or in the notes. In our experience, if the additional disclosure is provided in the statement of profit or loss and OCI, then judgement may be required whether the disaggregated information should be presented as part of the statement itself or as an additional disclosure alongside the totals in that statement. Clear disclosure of the approach taken to the elimination of intra-group transactions will be relevant, including an explanation of any additional analysis of discontinued operations in the notes to the statement of profit or loss and OCI. [*IFRS 5.30, 33(b), IAS 1.85A–85B, IU 01-16*]

EXAMPLE 8 – TRANSACTIONS BETWEEN CONTINUING AND DISCONTINUED OPERATIONS

5.4.230.50   Company K has Segment G and Segment B. G sells a product to B for 10. B sells the product to external customers for 12. The sales, cost of sales and gross margins of G and B are as follows.

SEGMENT	G	B
Sales	10	12
Cost of sales	(6)	(10)
Gross margin	4	2

5.4.230.60   The transfer price between the two segments is on an arm's length basis. Assume that B does not hold any of this inventory at the beginning or end of the reporting period. B will be discontinued and meets the definition of a discontinued operation, but it is expected that the supply relationship between the segments will continue after the disposal.

5.4.230.70   We believe that if K presents the profit or loss from discontinued operations of B as a single line item in the statement of profit or loss and OCI (i.e. with the supporting disclosures in the notes to the financial statements (see 5.4.220.10)), then one acceptable approach for K is to present the statement of profit or loss and OCI by eliminating the sales and cost of sales in B. We believe that this presentation is also appropriate for the disclosures in the notes to the financial statements. Under this approach, K should include the gross margin obtained by B from the sales to external customers in discontinued operations because this gross margin will be discontinued after the disposal. The sales and cost of sales in G related to the discontinued B should be retained and shown as part of continuing operations, to reflect that the supply relationship will continue after the disposal.

5.4.230.80   In this example, K will show continuing revenues of 10, continuing cost of sales of 6 and discontinued operations as a single amount in the statement of profit or loss and OCI that includes the discontinued gross margin of 2. This allocation of revenue and expenses has the advantage of presenting the appropriate gross margin for the discontinued operations and also the appropriate revenue and expenses for the continuing operations.

5.4.240   *Disclosures*

5.4.240.10   The disclosure requirements of IFRS 5 apply to non-current assets or disposal groups classified as discontinued operations. Disclosures required by other standards apply when they refer specifically to non-current assets or disposal groups classified as discontinued operations – e.g. the disclosure of EPS for a discontinued operation. Disclosures required by other standards also apply when they relate to assets and liabilities in a disposal group that are not in the measurement scope of IFRS 5 (e.g. investment property measured at fair value) and such disclosures are not already provided in the other notes to the financial statements. Additional disclosures may be necessary to comply with the general requirements of IAS 1, in particular for a fair presentation and in respect of sources of estimation uncertainty. [*IFRS 5.5B, IAS 33.68*]

5.4.250   Reclassification as continuing

5.4.250.10   If the component ceases to be classified as held-for-sale (see 5.4.90), then the related operations are reclassified as continuing. The operations are presented as continuing in the current period and prior periods are re-presented consistently. [*IFRS 5.36*]

5.4.260   ACQUIRED EXCLUSIVELY WITH VIEW TO RESALE

5.4.260.10   A non-current asset or a disposal group acquired exclusively with a view to its subsequent disposal is classified as held-for-sale if it meets the held-for-sale criteria or if it is 'highly probable' that it will meet those criteria within a short period after acquisition (usually three months). In our view, any non-current asset or a disposal group that satisfies the criteria to be classified as held-for-sale at the date of its acquisition may be assumed to have been acquired exclusively with a view to its subsequent disposal. [*IFRS 5.11, BC72*]

5.4.260.20   A non-current asset or a disposal group acquired exclusively with a view to its subsequent disposal is measured on initial recognition at the lower of its:
* carrying amount had the asset or disposal group not been classified by the buyer as held-for-sale (e.g. cost); and
* fair value less costs to sell. [*IFRS 5.16*]

5.4.270   Subsidiaries

5.4.270.10   Subsidiaries are consolidated even if they are held exclusively with a view to subsequent disposal. They are classified as held-for-sale if they meet the relevant criteria. [*IFRS 10.A, 5.IG.Ex13*]

5.4.270.20   Consolidation requires the application of acquisition accounting, including an acquisition date fair value exercise (see chapter 2.6). Disclosure exemptions for disposal groups that are newly acquired subsidiaries and are classified as held-for-sale may simplify the application of these requirements (see 5.4.220.60). These exemptions allow certain analyses of statement of profit or loss and OCI and statement of financial position amounts to be omitted, reducing the need to determine the date-of-acquisition fair values of individual assets and liabilities. However, the date-of-acquisition fair value of certain non-current assets and liabilities outside the measurement scope of IFRS 5 may still have to be determined – e.g. a financial asset that is measured at fair value with changes recognised in OCI, and defined benefit post-employment benefits. [*IFRS 3.31, 5.33(b)*]

5.4.280   Associates and joint ventures

5.4.280.10   An investment in an associate or joint venture is classified as held-for-sale on acquisition if the classification criteria are met. It is not equity accounted. For further discussion of associates and joint ventures classified as held-for-sale, see 3.5.160. [*IFRS 5.11, IAS 28.15, 20*]

5.5   Related party disclosures

5.5 Related party disclosures

CURRENTLY EFFECTIVE REQUIREMENTS

This publication reflects IFRS in issue at 1 August 2018, and the currently effective requirements cover annual periods beginning on 1 January 2018.

The requirements related to this topic are mainly derived from the following.

REFERENCE	TITLE
IAS 24	Related Party Disclosures

FORTHCOMING REQUIREMENTS AND FUTURE DEVELOPMENTS

For this topic, there are no forthcoming requirements or future developments.

5.5.10   SCOPE

Ⓢ 5.5.10.10   Related party disclosure requirements apply to all entities, including parent entities and investors with joint control or significant influence over an investee, in their consolidated, separate and individual financial statements (see 2.1.90). There are no exemptions from the disclosure of intra-group transactions and outstanding balances in the separate financial statements of a parent or in the financial statements of subsidiaries. Such transactions and outstanding balances are eliminated in the consolidated financial statements of a group, except for those between an investment entity and its subsidiaries measured at fair value through profit or loss. [*IAS 24.3–4*]

5.5.10.20   A government-related entity (see 5.5.70.10) that applies IFRS is not exempt from providing related party disclosures; this is because the parties are under common control and therefore meet the definition of related parties. However, a government-related entity can elect to reduce the level of disclosure that would otherwise be required by IAS 24 (see 5.5.130). [*IAS 24.25–26*]

5.5.10.30   Local rules and regulations often require an entity to provide certain related party information – e.g. directors' individual remuneration or golden parachute agreements. Specific legal requirements may supplement but cannot override any requirement to provide related party disclosures under IFRS (see 5.5.80.20).

5.5.20   RECOGNITION AND MEASUREMENT

5.5.20.10   IAS 24 does not establish any recognition or measurement requirements for related party transactions. Related party transactions are accounted for in accordance with the requirements of relevant standards. For example, in an entity's separate financial statements, loans to other group entities are recognised and measured in accordance with IFRS 9 (see chapters 7.6, 7.7 and 7.8), and the disclosures required for financial instruments (see chapter 7.10) are provided in addition to those required for related party transactions.

5.5.20.20   Other standards may require the attribution of cost. For example, if a parent transfers its equity instruments directly to employees of a subsidiary as compensation for services provided to the subsidiary, then IFRS 2 requires recognition of the share-based payment compensation at the subsidiary level (see 4.5.1440). [*IFRS 2.3A, 43A–43D*]

5.5.20.30   Consistent with the identification of related party relationships, in our view the accounting for related party transactions should take into account their substance as well as their legal form. For example, when a shareholder forgives a loan to the entity, in most cases this would be accounted for as a capital contribution to the entity and not as a gain on extinguishment of a liability (see 7.3.450.50). [*IAS 24.10*]

5.5.30   IDENTIFYING RELATED PARTIES

5.5.30.10   The definition of a related party is not restricted to entities. It also includes persons, key management personnel and post-employment benefit plans. For example, entities that are under the common control of the same non-corporate shareholder – e.g. a person, a group of persons acting together or a trust – are related parties, even if the shareholder does not prepare consolidated financial statements. [*IAS 24.9*]

5.5.30.20   Examples of some related party relationships are illustrated below.

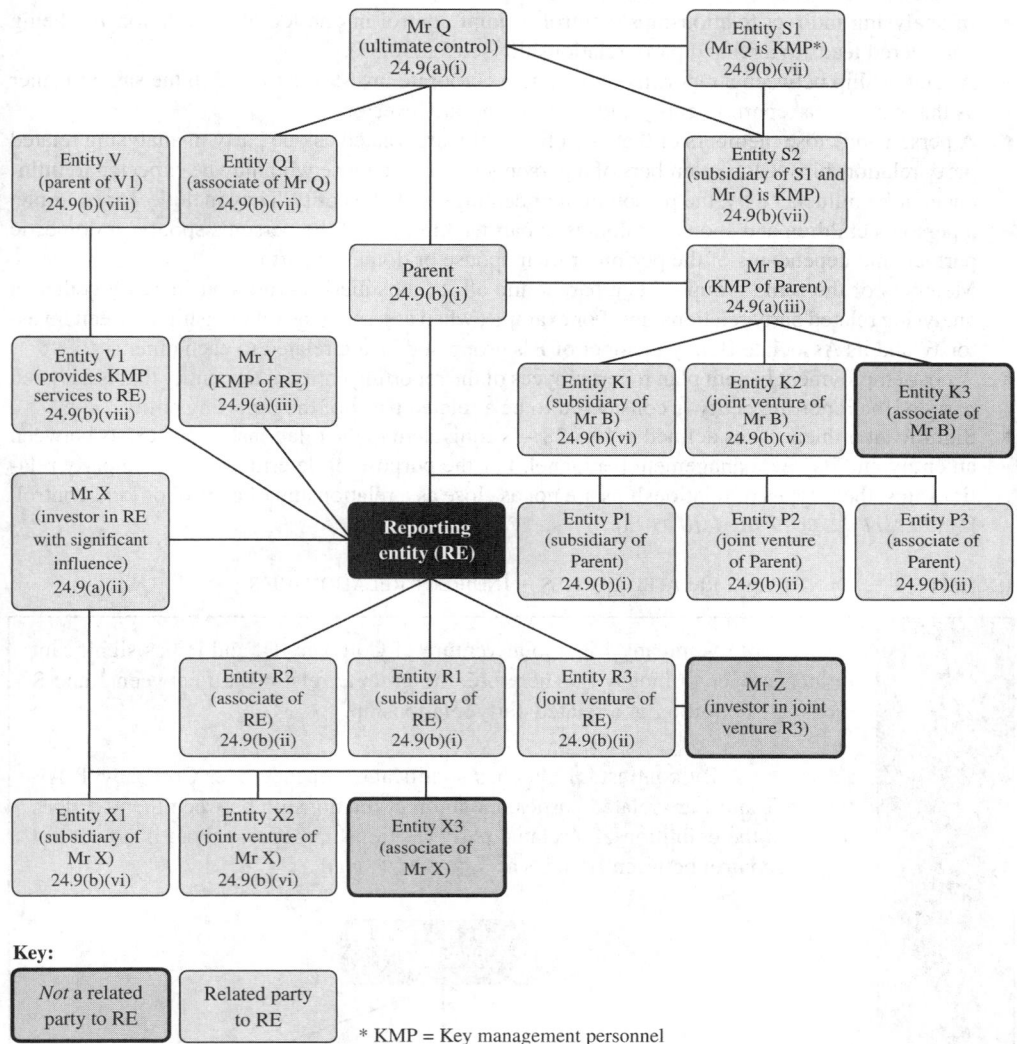

Key:

* KMP = Key management personnel

5.5.30.30   The following are some of the key principles applied in identifying related party relationships.

- Related party relationships are generally symmetrical – i.e. if B is related to C for the purposes of C's financial statements, then C is related to B for the purposes of B's financial statements.
- A management entity that provides key management personnel services to the reporting entity is a related party of the reporting entity. However, the relationship is not symmetrical – i.e. the reporting entity is not a related party of the management entity solely as a consequence of being a customer of the management entity, because the reporting entity cannot affect the management entity's activities.

- The definition includes relationships involving direct and indirect control, including common control, joint control and significant influence.
- In analysing indirect relationships, control or joint control in one leg of the relationship being considered leads to a related party relationship (see 5.5.30.35).
- A relationship between a reporting entity and a corporate investor is treated in the same manner as that between a reporting entity and a non-corporate investor.
- A person and close members of that person's family are treated as one party in analysing related party relationships. Close members of a person's family are those who may be expected to influence, or be influenced by, the person in their dealings with the entity. They include, for example, a person's children and spouse or domestic partner, children of the person's spouse or domestic partner, and dependants of the person or their spouse or domestic partner.
- Members of the same group – i.e. a parent and all its subsidiaries – are considered together in analysing related party relationships. For example, when assessing the relationship between Investor W and its Associate B, any member of B's group and W are related to each other.
- A post-employment benefit plan for employees of the reporting entity or any entity that is a related party of the reporting entity is considered to be a related party of the reporting entity.
- Significant influence – as defined in IAS 28 – is equivalent to the relationship that exists between an entity and its key management personnel. For the purpose of determining related party relationships, these types of relationships are not as close as a relationship of control or joint control.

[*IAS 24.9, 11–12, BC19, BC51, IU 05-15*]

EXAMPLE 1 – IDENTIFYING RELATED PARTIES – INDIRECT RELATIONSHIPS

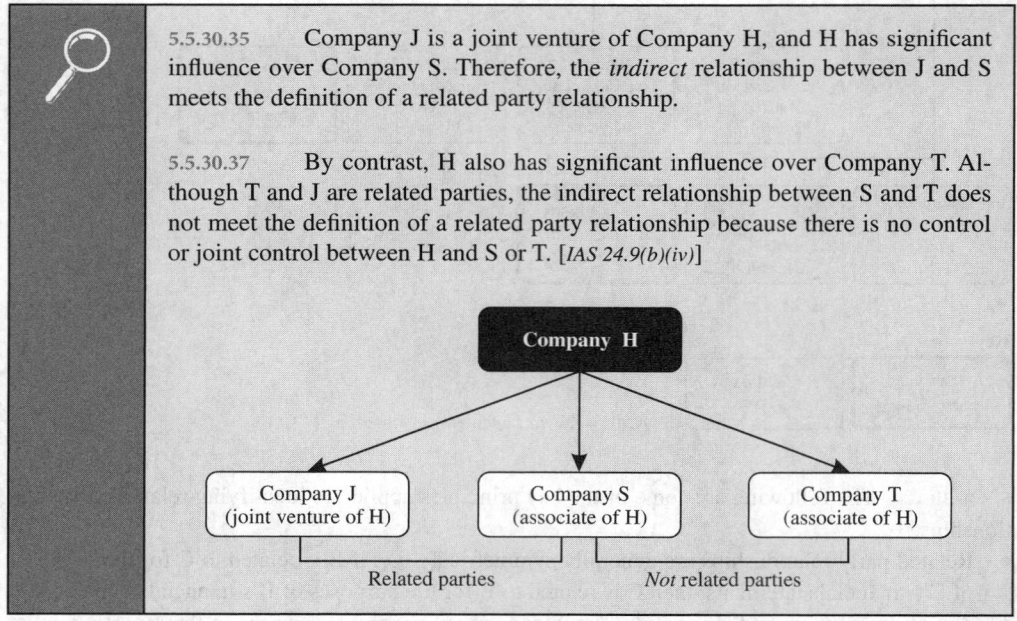

5.5.30.35   Company J is a joint venture of Company H, and H has significant influence over Company S. Therefore, the *indirect* relationship between J and S meets the definition of a related party relationship.

5.5.30.37   By contrast, H also has significant influence over Company T. Although T and J are related parties, the indirect relationship between S and T does not meet the definition of a related party relationship because there is no control or joint control between H and S or T. [*IAS 24.9(b)(iv)*]

Company H

Company J (joint venture of H) | Company S (associate of H) | Company T (associate of H)

Related parties   *Not* related parties

5.5.30.40   Although a branch is not formally defined in IFRS, in our experience it is generally understood to be an extension of an entity's activities. In our view, if a branch of an entity prepares its own financial statements, then it should disclose related party transactions and relationships, including those with its head office.

5.5.30.50   An entity or a person may become, or cease to be, a related party during the period covered by the financial statements. In our view, the determination of whether an entity or a person is a related party should be made considering their relationship during the reporting period, and not just the relationship at the reporting date. This is because the standard's objective is to provide users of the financial statements with the disclosures necessary to draw their attention to the possibility that the reporting entity's financial position and profit or loss may have been affected by the existence of related parties and by transactions and outstanding balances, including commitments, with such parties. For further discussion of the related party disclosures in such cases, see 5.5.100.30. [*IAS 24.1*]

5.5.40   **Key management personnel**

5.5.40.10   Key management personnel are those persons who have the authority and responsibility for planning, directing and controlling the activities of the entity – directly or indirectly. The definition of key management personnel includes directors (both executive and non-executive). In our view, the term also includes directors of any of the entity's parents to the extent that they have authority and responsibility for planning, directing and controlling the entity's activities. In our view, an entity's parent includes the immediate, intermediate and ultimate parent. [*IAS 24.9*]

5.5.40.20   In our view, a person is key management personnel of an entity even if that entity does not pay for the services received from the person. For example, a director of Parent B who also acts as a director of Subsidiary C is key management personnel of C, regardless of whether C reimburses B for the services received (see 5.5.110.50–70).

5.5.40.30   In our experience, an entity may have more than one level of management. For example, there may be a supervisory board whose members have responsibilities similar to those of non-executive directors, a board of directors that sets the overall strategy under which an entity operates and a management team that implements those strategies within the authority delegated to it by the board. The members of either board, including non-executive directors, will be considered to be key management personnel.

5.5.40.40   However, key management personnel are not limited to directors; in our view, other members of the management team may also be key management personnel. We believe that a person with significant authority and responsibility for planning, directing and controlling the entity's activities should be considered to be key management personnel. [*IAS 24.9*]

5.5.40.50   The role of key management personnel of a group of entities is performed by those who assume the authority and responsibility for planning, directing and controlling the activities of each separate entity in the group. Therefore, in our view in the consolidated financial statements of a group, key management personnel is not limited to the key management personnel of the parent entity, but may include key management personnel of other group entities, such as of subsidiaries.

EXAMPLE 2A – KEY MANAGEMENT PERSONNEL IN THE GROUP (1)

5.5.40.55   The management of Parent C directs the investment activities of the group, while the management of Subsidiary D – a significant operating subsidiary – directs the operations of D with minimal involvement from C's

> management. Because D contributes significantly to the group result, we believe that its key management personnel should be included as key management personnel of the group.

5.5.40.60   In our view, the definition of key management personnel in IAS 24 specifies a *role* and is not limited to a person. In our experience, the authority and responsibility for planning, directing and controlling the activities of an entity in some cases is assigned to an entity rather than to a person. For example, a bank may act as an investment manager for an investment fund and in doing so assume the roles and responsibilities of key management personnel. We believe that an entity that assumes the role of key management personnel should be considered a related party of the reporting entity. [*IAS 24.9(b)(viii)*]

5.5.40.70   Entities under the control or joint control of key management personnel (or their close family members) are also related parties of the reporting entity. [*IAS 24.9(b)(vi)*]

EXAMPLE 2B – KEY MANAGEMENT PERSONNEL IN THE GROUP (2)

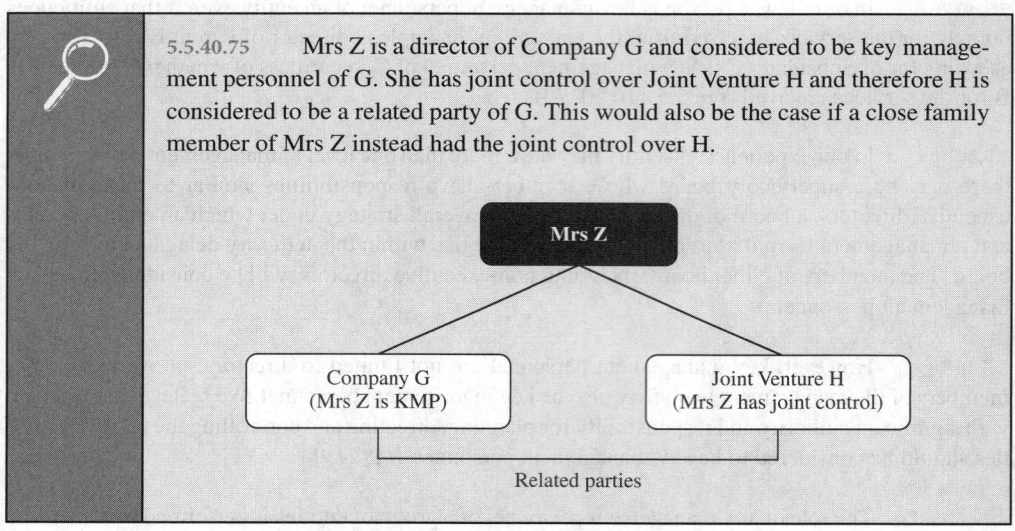

5.5.40.75   Mrs Z is a director of Company G and considered to be key management personnel of G. She has joint control over Joint Venture H and therefore H is considered to be a related party of G. This would also be the case if a close family member of Mrs Z instead had the joint control over H.

Mrs Z

Company G
(Mrs Z is KMP)

Joint Venture H
(Mrs Z has joint control)

Related parties

5.5.40.80   However, two entities are not related parties simply because they have a director or other member of key management personnel in common, or because a member of key management personnel of one entity has significant influence over the other entity. In Example 2B, if Mrs Z were a director of H, but as a person did not have control or joint control over H, then G and H would not be related parties solely because Mrs Z was a director of both. [*IAS 24.11(a)*]

5.5.50   **Post-employment benefit plans**

5.5.50.10   Related parties include post-employment benefit plans that benefit an entity's employees or the employees of any entity that is a related party of the reporting entity. [*IAS 24.9(b)(v)*]

EXAMPLE 3 – POST-EMPLOYMENT BENEFIT PLAN

> 5.5.50.13   Company B has significant influence over Company C. B and C each have a pension plan for the benefit of their respective employees. In addition, C transacts with B's pension plan in the ordinary course of business.
>
> 5.5.50.14   In this example, both pension plans are related parties of C and, accordingly, C discloses transactions with:
> - its own pension plan because it provides benefits to its employees; and
> - B's pension plan because it provides benefits to the employees of a related party (B).

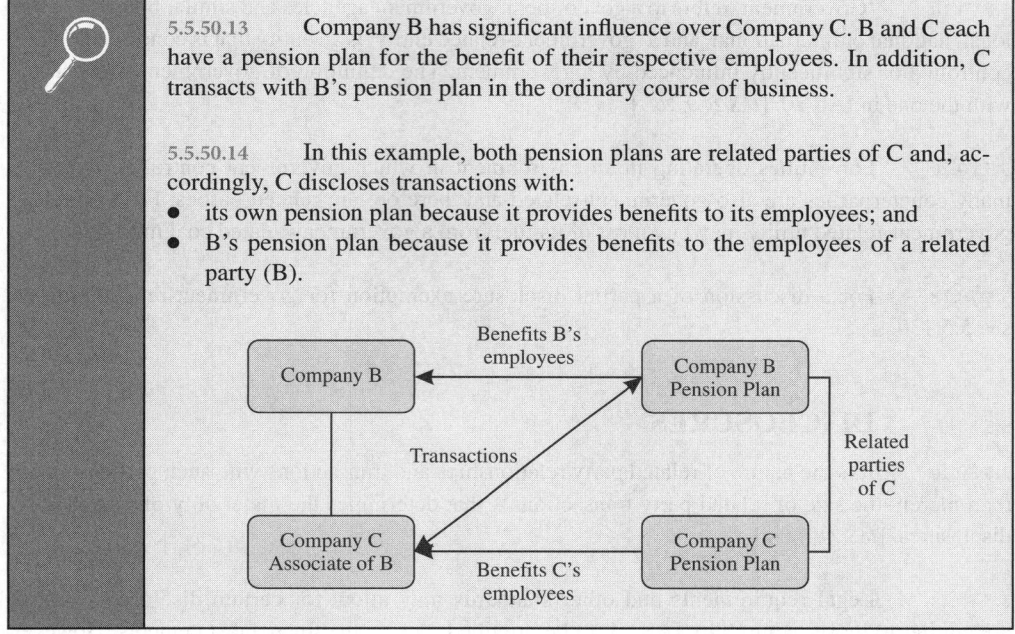

5.5.50.15   If the reporting entity is itself such a benefit plan, then the sponsoring employers are also related to the reporting entity. [*IAS 24.9(b)(v)*]

5.5.50.20   It is not clear whether a multi-employer plan that also benefits employees of unrelated parties should be included in the definition of a related party. The only condition in IAS 24 for the post-employment benefit plan to be regarded as a related party of the reporting entity is that it benefits the employees of the reporting entity, or of any entity that is a related party of the reporting entity. It does not require a specific level of influence or control. Therefore, in our view a multi-employer plan of which a reporting entity is one of the sponsoring entities is related to the reporting entity, even if the reporting entity does not have significant influence or control over the multi-employer plan. [*IAS 24.9(b)(v)*]

5.5.60   **Economic dependence**

5.5.60.10   An entity may be dependent, economically or operationally, on another party – e.g. a major customer or supplier. This dependency does not itself create a related party relationship. However, additional information about these relationships and the resulting transactions may be relevant to users of the financial statements. [*IAS 24.11(d), 1.17(c)*]

5.5.60.20   Providers of finance and similar entities are not related parties by virtue of their normal dealings with an entity, even though these parties may limit the actions of an entity or participate in its decision-making process. However, transactions in the ordinary course of business between related parties are disclosed. For example, a banking entity discloses transactions with its finance provider that is part of the same banking group even if these services are provided on the same terms as to unrelated customers. [*IAS 24.11(c)*]

5.5.70   Government-related entities

5.5.70.10   'Government' refers to a government, government agencies and similar bodies whether local, national or international, and a 'government-related entity' is an entity that is controlled, jointly controlled or significantly influenced by a government. The definition of government is consistent with the one in IAS 20. [*IAS 24.9, 20.3*]

5.5.70.20   For entities operating in an environment in which government control is pervasive, many counterparties are also government-related and therefore are related parties. For example, a government-related utility may buy most of its fuel from a government-related coal mine.

5.5.70.30   For a discussion of a partial disclosure exemption for government-related entities, see 5.5.130.

5.5.80   DISCLOSURES

5.5.80.10   It is the nature of related party relationships and transactions with such parties – rather than merely the size of related party transactions – that determines the materiality of related party disclosures. [*IAS 24.1, 5–8*]

5.5.80.20   Legal requirements and other standards may allow for certain disclosures, which are similar to those required by IAS 24, to be provided outside the financial statements. However, IAS 24 does not specifically allow the disclosures required by this standard to be provided outside the financial statements.

5.5.90   Control relationships

5.5.90.10   A reporting entity discloses the name of its parent and ultimate controlling party, if different. It also discloses the name of its ultimate parent if it is not disclosed elsewhere in information published with the financial statements. In our view, the *ultimate parent* and the *ultimate controlling party* are not necessarily synonymous. This is because the definition of 'parent' refers to an *entity*. Accordingly, an entity may have an ultimate parent and an ultimate controlling party. Therefore, if the ultimate controlling party of the reporting entity is a person or a group of persons, then the identity of that person or the group of persons and that relationship should be disclosed. [*IAS 1.138(c), 24.13*]

5.5.90.20   Parent and subsidiary relationships are disclosed regardless of whether there have been any transactions between the parties. Although it is not explicitly required by IAS 24, in our experience many entities include a list of significant subsidiaries in their consolidated financial statements similar to that required for separate financial statements by IAS 27. [*IAS 24.13–15, 27.16–17, IFRS 12.10(a), 12(a)–(b)*]

5.5.90.30   If neither the reporting entity's parent nor the ultimate controlling party produces consolidated financial statements available for public use, then the reporting entity discloses the name of the next most senior parent to the reporting entity's parent that produces financial statements available for public use. [*IAS 24.13, 16*]

5.5.90.40   Whereas parent and subsidiary relationships are disclosed regardless of whether transactions between the parties occurred, a reporting entity is not required to disclose related party relationships with other entities if control does not exist. [*IAS 24.13, 18–19*]

EXAMPLE 4 – CONTROL RELATIONSHIPS

5.5.90.50   Company M and Company B are owned and controlled by the same person, Mr X, and have the same directors. Both M and B have numerous subsidiaries. B holds shares in M, but not enough to give B control over M. M does not hold any shares in B.

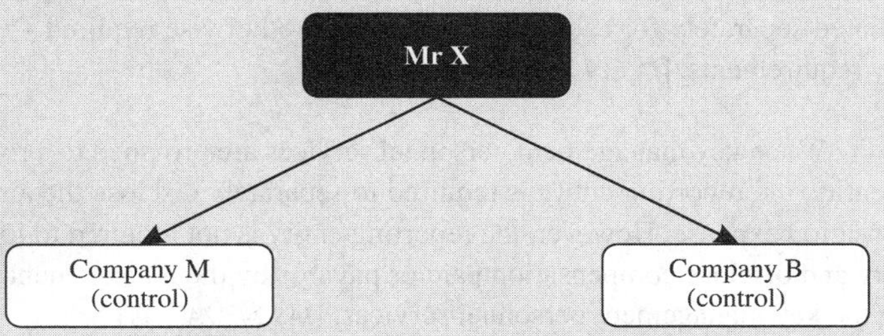

```
                        ┌──────────────┐
                        │     Mr X     │
                        └──────────────┘
                          ╱          ╲
                        ╱              ╲
                      ↙                  ↘
          ┌──────────────┐        ┌──────────────┐
          │  Company M   │        │  Company B   │
          │  (control)   │        │  (control)   │
          └──────────────┘        └──────────────┘
```

5.5.90.60   In its own financial statements, M discloses only its relationships with X and with M's own subsidiaries. M is not required to describe its *relationship* with B or any of B's subsidiaries if there have been no transactions with these entities. However, any *transactions* with B or its subsidiaries are disclosed as related party transactions.

5.5.90.70   Other standards may require a reporting entity to disclose the names of additional parties beyond those for which a control relationship exists – e.g. IFRS 12 (see chapter 5.10).

5.5.100   Transactions and balances, including commitments

5.5.100.10   Related party transactions that involve a transfer of resources, services or obligations are disclosed regardless of whether a price is charged. Therefore, disclosure is required in respect of guarantees, gifts or other non-reciprocal transfers of assets or services, asset swaps or other similar transactions between related parties. [*IAS 24.6, 18, 21*]

EXAMPLE 5 – RELATED PARTY TRANSACTION – NO PRICE CHARGED

5.5.100.20   Company E and Company F are related parties. F's business activities include providing fundraising and promotional activities and F makes use of E's employees to arrange these events. E does not charge F for these services. Accordingly, in both E's and F's financial statements, the nature and the extent of the use of E's employees by F are disclosed as a related party transaction.

5.5.100.30   In our view, related party disclosures should cover the period during which transactions could have been affected by the existence of the related party relationship. The disclosure of transactions occurring after parties cease to be related parties is not required (see 5.5.30.50). [*IAS 24.1*]

5.5.110   *Key management personnel compensation*

5.5.110.10   Key management personnel compensation, including that of non-executive directors, is disclosed in total and analysed into its components (short-term, post-employment, other long-term, termination and share-based benefits). Compensation amounts relate to services rendered to the reporting entity. For example, a reporting entity discloses the cost of goods or services recognised in relation to share-based payments and short-term employee benefits on an accruals basis. In our experience, disclosure of key management personnel compensation is generally aggregated rather than presented separately for each person unless it is otherwise required – e.g. by local statutory or regulatory requirements. [*IAS 19.7, 24.9, 17*]

5.5.110.15   When key management personnel services are provided to a reporting entity by a management entity, the reporting entity is required to separately disclose the amounts that it recognises as compensation expense. However, the reporting entity is not required to look through the management entity and disclose compensation paid or payable by the management entity to the individuals providing the key management personnel services. [*IAS 24.17A, 18A*]

5.5.110.20   In our view, materiality considerations cannot be used to override the explicit requirements for the disclosure of elements of key management personnel compensation. We believe that the nature of the key management personnel compensation always makes it qualitatively material. [*IAS 24.BC7–BC9*]

5.5.110.30   Compensation is not limited to amounts given by the reporting entity. Instead, it includes all amounts paid, payable or provided by the reporting entity, or on behalf of the reporting entity, in return for services received. Therefore, it includes employee benefits provided to the key management personnel but that are not recognised by the reporting entity in its financial statements – e.g. compensation paid by a parent entity to key management personnel of a subsidiary. [*IAS 24.9*]

5.5.110.40   Payments by an entity may relate to services provided to third parties, and not to the paying entity. If a reporting entity acts as an intermediary and makes payments to a party on behalf of another party, then in our view the reporting entity is required to disclose only compensation paid as consideration for services provided *to the reporting entity*.

EXAMPLE 6A – KEY MANAGEMENT PERSONNEL – PAYMENTS MADE ON BEHALF OF RELATED PARTY

5.5.110.50   Mr Y is a director of Parent Z. In addition to providing services to Z, Mr Y provides services to Subsidiary B. He is compensated by Z for the services provided to Z (in the amount of 800) as well as those provided to B (in the amount of 200). B reimburses Z for the amounts paid to Mr Y on its behalf. The relationships and payments can be illustrated as follows.

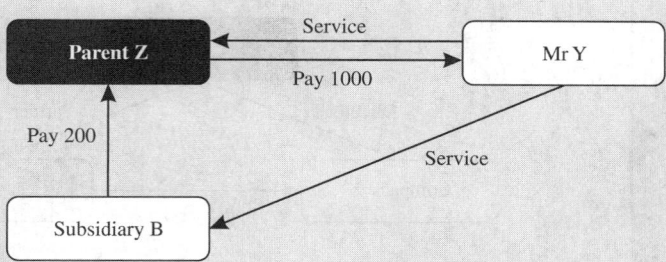

5.5.110.60   We believe that B discloses in its own financial statements the amount of 200 paid to Z in respect of the services provided by Mr Y to B as key management personnel compensation even though B pays this compensation to Z and not directly to Mr Y.

5.5.110.65   In Z's separate financial statements, we believe that disclosure of key management personnel compensation should include only the amount paid to Mr Y for services provided to Z – i.e. 800 (1,000 - 200). Z also discloses the reimbursement received from B (i.e. 200) for Mr Y's services as a related party transaction.

5.5.110.70   Now assume that B does not reimburse Z for the services provided by Mr Y to B. In our view, B should disclose in its own financial statements the apportioned amount of the compensation paid by Z for the service received by B from Mr Y (i.e. 200) and that the amount paid by B for these services was zero.

5.5.110.75   In Z's separate financial statements, we believe that disclosure of key management personnel compensation should include only the amount paid to Mr Y for services provided to Z (i.e. 800). Z also discloses the amount of the compensation paid for the services provided by Mr Y to B and that no consideration was received, as a related party transaction. [*IAS 24.17, 18*]

5.5.110.80   In Z's consolidated financial statements, Mr Y is considered to be key management personnel for both Z and the group as a whole. The compensation paid by Z therefore relates to services performed for the group, and therefore Mr Y's total compensation for services to both B and Z (i.e. 1,000) is disclosed. [*IAS 24.17*]

EXAMPLE 6B – KEY MANAGEMENT PERSONNEL – DUAL CAPACITY

5.5.110.90   Mrs B is a director of Company X and a partner of a legal firm Y that provides legal services to X. X and Y are not related parties. Mrs B is acting in two capacities in relation to X, as:
- a director; and
- a partner of a legal firm providing services to X.

5.5.110.100   This raises the issue of what is included as key management personnel compensation in the financial statements of X in relation to Mrs B. In our view, X should include within its disclosure of key management personnel compensation only the benefits provided to Mrs B in her capacity as director.

5.5.110.103   We believe that if Mrs B is closely involved in providing the legal services to X, by providing the services directly on behalf of Y or by supervising the service provided, then Mrs B is acting not only in the capacity as partner of Y; in substance the transaction is no different from a scenario in which Mrs B provides the legal services directly to X. In this example, X concludes that the fees paid to Y for legal services represent a related party transaction and are disclosed as 'other related party transactions' (see 5.5.120).

5.5.110.105   Conversely, if Mrs B does not provide legal services directly on behalf of Y, does not supervise the services and does not have the power to influence the services provided to X, then we believe that the service is not a related party transaction. [*IAS 24.11, 17, 18*]

5.5.110.110   In addition to key management personnel compensation, a reporting entity also discloses information about other transactions with key management personnel – e.g. personal finance transactions such as loans, current account balances and interest paid or received. For insurance entities, in our view disclosures should include the insurance cover provided to key management personnel by the reporting entity. [*IAS 24.18*]

5.5.120   *Other related party transactions*

5.5.120.10   As a minimum, the following disclosures are provided if there have been transactions between related parties:
- the nature of the related party relationship and information about transactions;
- the amount of the transactions;
- outstanding balances, including commitments, and their terms and conditions (including whether outstanding balances are secured);
- the nature of the consideration to be provided and details of guarantees given or received; and
- any allowance for doubtful debts and any amounts written off during the period. [*IAS 24.18*]

5.5.120.20   Commitments to do something if a particular event occurs or does not occur in the future, including executory contracts (recognised or unrecognised), are disclosed if they are with a related party. Commitments are not defined in IFRS, although IFRS 9 defines a 'firm commitment' as a binding agreement for the exchange of a specified quantity of resources at a specified price on a specified future date or dates, and describes a 'loan commitment' as a firm commitment to provide credit under pre-specified terms and conditions (see 7.9.990.30 and 7.1.260). Therefore, it may be useful for management to agree on a working definition for commitments, taking into account all types of commitments, and not only those that may result in a transfer of cash or other assets – e.g. a commitment to issue own equity instruments or to contribute services. [*IAS 24.21(i), IFRS 9.A, BCZ2.2*]

5.5.120.25   In our view, the disclosures about commitments with related parties should not be limited to those that are specifically required to be disclosed by standards other than IAS 24 – e.g. the disclosure of the amount of contractual commitments for the acquisition of property, plant and equipment, which is required by IAS 16. Therefore, to the extent material, we believe that an entity should provide disclosure of any commitments arising from its transactions with related parties, including:
- unconditional purchase or sales obligations;
- agreements that require the contribution of funds over a specified period; and
- commitments to contribute assets or services.

5.5.120.27   We believe that the information referred to in 5.5.120.25 is relevant to an understanding of the financial statements and consistent with the objective of IAS 24. [*IFRS 7.B10(d), 12.23(a), B18–B20, IAS 1.112(c), 114(c)(iv)(1), 16.74(c), 17.31(b), 35(a), 38.122(e)*]

5.5.120.30   In the consolidated financial statements, intra-group transactions and the profit on transactions with associates or joint ventures to the extent of the investor's interest (see 2.5.550, 3.5.430 and 3.6.280) are eliminated. In our view, a reporting entity should disclose the portions of transactions with associates and joint ventures that are not eliminated in applying equity accounting. [*IAS 24.4*]

5.5.120.40   Disclosure is provided separately for each category of related party. For example, sales to subsidiaries are not aggregated with sales to joint ventures. [*IAS 24.19*]

5.5.120.50   Items of a similar nature may be disclosed in aggregate as long as aggregation does not obscure the importance of individually significant transactions. For example, in a subsidiary's own financial statements, regular purchases or sales with other fellow subsidiaries may be aggregated. However, in our view details of a significant disposal of property, plant and equipment to a subsidiary should not be included in an aggregate disclosure of regular sales of goods to subsidiaries because they are not similar in nature. [*IAS 24.24*]

5.5.120.60   Related party transactions are required to be disclosed regardless of whether they are entered into on terms equivalent to those in an arm's length transaction. A reporting entity may include in its financial statements a statement that related party transactions were made on terms equivalent to those that prevail in an arm's length transaction only if that statement can be substantiated. [*IAS 24.23*]

5.5.120.70   In other situations, it is difficult to assess what information about transactions with related parties is required to be disclosed.
- For example, a mutual fund appoints an administrator to provide management services. In our view, the fund should disclose the following as a minimum: information about the services provided by the administrator – including the terms and conditions of the management agreement; the amount of the management fee paid to the administrator during the period; how the fee is calculated; and any fees outstanding at the reporting date.
- In another example, a parent entity may establish a captive insurance entity to provide self-insurance for the group. The captive insurance entity may then transfer the risk of losses to a third

party insurer. In our view, the relationship between the parent entity and the captive insurance entity should be disclosed in the captive insurance entity's own financial statements, including information about the nature of the insurance contracts, any outstanding balances, and revenues arising from those insurance contracts. We believe that the role of the third party insurer should also be disclosed. For a discussion of the accounting for captive insurance entities, see 3.12.400.

5.5.120.80   IAS 24 includes, as an example of a related party transaction, participation by a parent or subsidiary in a defined benefit plan that shares risks between group entities. In addition, IAS 19 requires certain disclosures for such defined benefit plans, including detail about the contractual agreement or stated policy for charging the net defined benefit cost or the fact that there is no such policy, and the policy for determining the contribution to be paid by the entity. [*IAS 24.22, 19.41–42, 149*]

5.5.130   *Government-related entities*

5.5.130.10   IAS 24 allows a reporting entity to reduce the level of disclosures about transactions and outstanding balances, including commitments, with:
- a government that has control, joint control or significant influence over the reporting entity; and
- another entity that is a related party because the same government has control, joint control or significant influence over both the reporting entity and the other entity. [*IAS 24.25, IE3*]

5.5.130.15   The following diagram highlights the government-related entities that may be in the scope of the exemption.

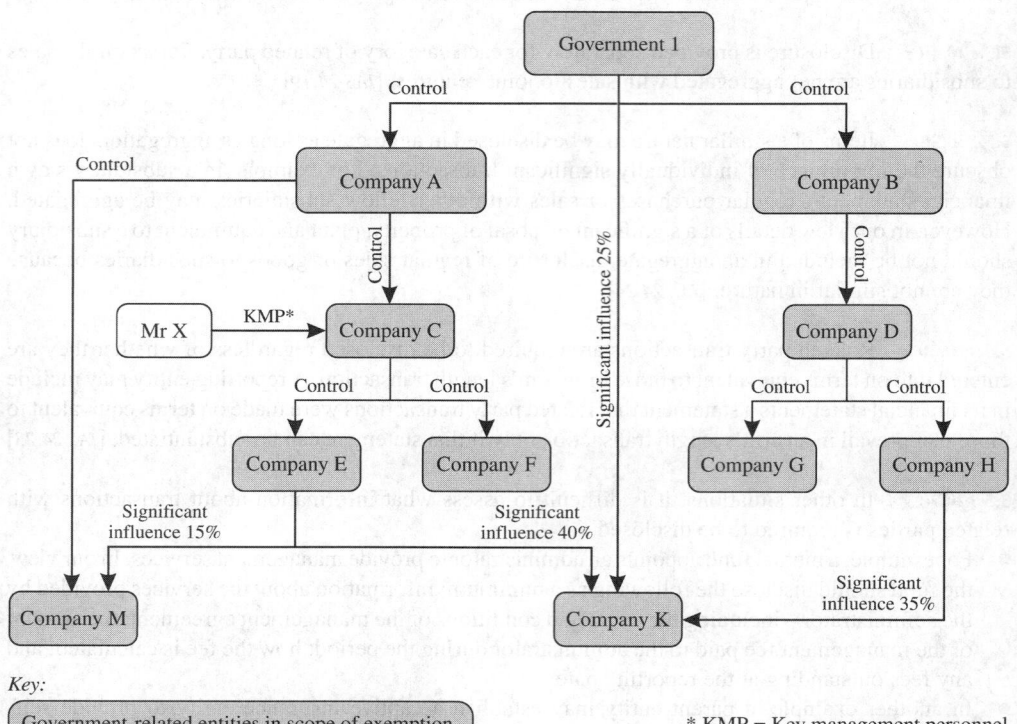

Key:

Government-related entities in scope of exemption

* KMP = Key management personnel

5.5.130.20   The exemption from the full related party disclosures could be a far-reaching exemption as a result of the broad definition of government-related entities (see 5.5.70.10) and the inter-relationship with the general definition of a related party because it applies to indirect relationships. For example, in the diagram in 5.5.130.15, it seems that Company E is in the scope of the exemption because Government 1 has indirect control over it. Therefore, direct or indirect government control, joint control or significant influence could bring entities into the scope of the exemption regardless of any other related party relationships between them.

5.5.130.30   However, the partial exemption does not apply to the relationships between an entity and a person in their capacity as an investor or as key management personnel. Again using the diagram in 5.5.130.15, this could mean that in E's financial statements the partial exemption applies to transactions with Government 1, Companies A, B, C, D, F, G, H, M and K. The partial exemption would not apply to transactions with Mr X. [*IAS 24.BC37, IE1–IE2*]

5.5.130.40   Almost all countries have multiple levels of governing public bodies – e.g. at city, provincial, state and perhaps federal levels. However, there may be significant differences from one country to the next in the relationships between these bodies and the extent to which one body is said to be under the control, joint control or significant influence of another body in the same country. Given this, identifying entities that are related to the 'same government' may not be straightforward. [*IAS 24.25*]

5.5.130.50   For example, in countries with a federal structure, if the federal government is independent of the state government, then in our view an entity controlled by the state government may not be a related party of an entity controlled at the federal level, even though both are controlled by government bodies in the same country. These bodies are not considered to be the same government for the purposes of the partial exemption. Therefore, if the two entities otherwise meet the definition of related parties in IAS 24, then transactions between the two entities would be subject to the full disclosure requirements of IAS 24.

5.5.130.60   Conversely, two entities controlled by different federal government bodies – e.g. one by the Department of Public Health and one by the Department of Education – in our view would seem to meet the criteria set out in the standard because these entities are under the control of the same federal government. In such cases, any transactions between the entities would fall in the scope of the partial exemption. [*IAS 24.25*]

5.5.130.70   As stated in 5.5.130.30, the partial exemption does not apply to individuals. For example, in E's financial statements (see diagram in 5.5.130.15), transactions between E and Mr X, who is a member of key management personnel of E's parent, C, are not eligible for the exemption. This also means that the partial exemption does not apply to a person who has control, joint control or significant influence over a reporting entity or who is a member of key management personnel of the reporting entity or its parent. For example, transactions with close family members of key management personnel of a government-related entity or with entities over which key management personnel have at least joint control would be subject to the full disclosure requirements by that government-related entity. [*IAS 24.9, 18, 25, IE2*]

5.5.130.80   The partial exemption is intended to meet the objective of IAS 24 by putting users of the entity's financial statements on notice that certain transactions or relationships could have an impact on the entity's operations or performance. They are not intended to require the reporting entity to either identify every government-related entity or quantify every transaction with such entities because this would defeat the purpose of the exemption. [*IAS 24.26, BC43*]

5.5.130.90   The following disclosures are required when a reporting entity applies the partial exemption:

- the name of the government and the nature of its relationship with the reporting entity – i.e. control, joint control or significant influence; and
- the following information in enough detail to enable users of the entity's financial statements to understand the effect of related party transactions on its financial statements:
    - nature and amount of each *individually significant* transaction; and
    - for other transactions that are *collectively, but not individually, significant,* a qualitative or quantitative indication of their extent. [*IAS 24.26, BC44–BC46*]

5.5.130.100   There are no quantitative indications or bright lines concerning the meaning of 'significant'. It may be useful for entities to establish criteria that they would apply consistently to determine whether transactions are individually or collectively significant. At a minimum, the reporting entity considers the closeness of the related party relationship and other factors relevant in establishing the level of significance of the transaction, such as whether it is:

- significant in terms of size;
- carried out on non-market terms;
- outside normal day-to-day business operations, such as the purchase and sale of businesses;
- disclosed to regulatory or supervisory authorities;
- reported to senior management; and/or
- subject to shareholder approval. [*IAS 24.27*]

5.5.130.110   Entities need to exercise judgement in deciding how much quantitative or qualitative information to disclose when transactions are collectively, but not individually, significant.

EXAMPLE 7 – DISCLOSURE OF COLLECTIVELY SIGNIFICANT TRANSACTIONS

5.5.130.115   Company B is considering the following disclosure alternatives for its sales of goods and purchases of raw materials to/from government-related entities, which are collectively significant:

- a large portion of Company B's sales of goods and purchases of raw materials are with entities controlled by Government G; or
- about 50% of Company B's sales of goods and about 35% of its purchases of raw materials are with entities controlled by Government G. [*IAS 24.26(b), IE3*]

5.5.130.120   Both disclosures give an indication of the extent of these collectively significant transactions, but arguably the version with percentages is more informative for the user. As a result, management needs to determine how much quantitative or qualitative information is sufficient for the user to understand the effect of related party transactions on the entity's financial statements.

5.5.130.130   In our view, the more clearly significant the transactions are to the entity, and/or the greater the likelihood that the transactions were affected by the existence of the related party relationship, generally the greater the need for more detailed information.

EXAMPLE 8 – DISCLOSURE OF INDIVIDUALLY SIGNIFICANT TRANSACTIONS

5.5.130.140   Company E makes the following disclosure in its financial statements about an individually significant transaction because of the size of the transaction.

The Company is controlled indirectly by Government X and in 2016 X entered into a procurement agreement with the Company, such that the Company would act as the sole supplier of electronic equipment to X's various agencies and departments for a term of three years from 2017 to 2019, with an agreed bulk discount of 10% compared with list prices that the Company would generally charge on individual orders. The aggregate sales value under the agreement for the year ended 31 December 2018 amounted to 350, and 280 for the year ended 31 December 2017. As at 31 December 2018, the aggregate amounts due from X amounted to 100, and 50 as at 31 December 2017. These balances are payable under normal credit terms of 30 days' credit.

5.5.130.150   An entity that qualifies for the partial exemption is required to disclose the name of the related government and the nature of its relationship to it. This disclosure relates to the basis on which the entity considers itself to be government-related, being the same basis on which it judges whether other entities are related to it by virtue of being related to that same government. In our view, the disclosure should therefore focus on identifying the highest level of government that has control, joint control or significant influence over the entity. In our experience, judgement may be required when identifying the relevant government when the entity operates in a country with multiple levels of government. [*IAS 24.25–26*]

5.6 Investment entities

5.6   Investment entities

CURRENTLY EFFECTIVE REQUIREMENTS

This publication reflects IFRS in issue at 1 August 2018, and the currently effective requirements cover annual periods beginning on 1 January 2018.

The disclosures related to interests in other entities by investment entities are discussed in chapter 5.10.

The requirements related to this topic are mainly derived from the following.

REFERENCE	TITLE
IFRS 9	Financial Instruments
IFRS 10	Consolidated Financial Statements
IFRS 13	Fair Value Measurement

The currently effective requirements include newly effective requirements arising from *Annual Improvements to IFRSs 2014–2016 Cycle – Amendment to IAS 28,* which is effective for annual periods beginning on or after 1 January 2018. The amendments apply retrospectively. See 5.6.210.50 and 60.

FORTHCOMING REQUIREMENTS AND FUTURE DEVELOPMENTS

For this topic, there are no forthcoming requirements or future developments.

5.6.10   **OVERVIEW OF INVESTMENT ENTITY MODEL**

5.6.10.10   The investment entities consolidation exception is mandatory for an entity that meets the criteria in 5.6.20. An investment entity is required to account for investments in controlled entities, as well as investments in associates and joint ventures, at fair value through profit or loss in accordance with IFRS 9 (see 7.4.440). However, this does not apply to subsidiaries that do not themselves qualify as investment entities and whose main purpose and activities are providing services that relate to the investment entity's investment activities. Such subsidiaries continue to be consolidated (see 5.6.100). [*IFRS 10.31–32, B85L(b)*]

5.6.10.20   The measurement of fair value is the subject of chapter 2.4. Specific points of interest in relation to investment entities are discussed in 2.4.830 (investments in subsidiaries, associates and joint ventures) and 2.4.930 (investment funds and similar investment vehicles).

5.6.10.30   An entity qualifies as an investment entity if it meets three 'essential' tests (see 5.6.20). The IFRS Interpretations Committee discussed this issue and noted that this is the case even if the entity does not have one or more of the 'typical' characteristics of an investment entity (see 5.6.130). Their absence only indicates that additional judgement may be required in determining whether the three essential tests are met. The flowchart below summarises this approach. [*IFRS 10.27–28, B85A, B85N, IU 03-17*]

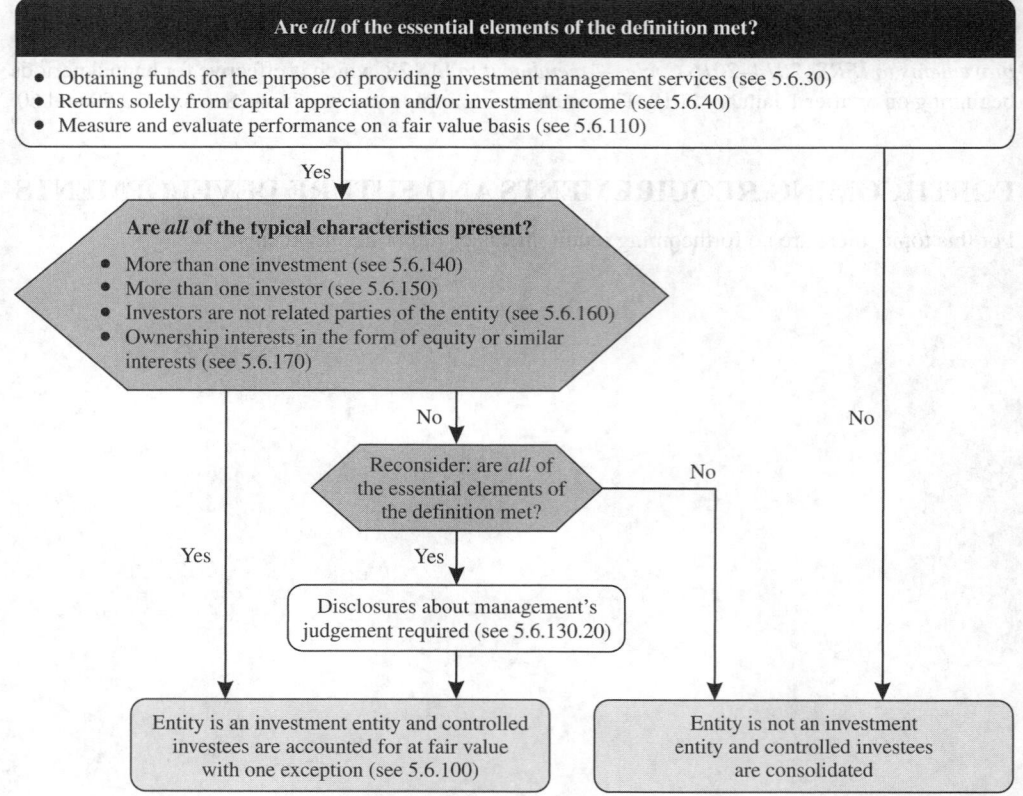

5.6.20 ESSENTIAL ELEMENTS

5.6.20.10 An entity needs to meet all of the essential elements of the definition of an investment entity to qualify for the consolidation exception. In making this determination, management is required to consider all facts and circumstances, including the purpose and design of the entity. [*IFRS 10.27, B85A–B85M*]

5.6.30 Investment management services

5.6.30.10 An investment entity obtains funds from investors to provide those investors with investment management services. Providing investment management services is necessary, though not on its own sufficient, to distinguish an investment entity from other types of entities. [*IFRS 10.27(a), BC237*]

5.6.30.20 IFRS 10 does not specify whether an investment entity responsible for providing investment management services has to perform them on its own. The performance of some or all of these services can therefore be outsourced to another party, as long as the services are provided by this party on behalf of the investment entity. [*IU 03-17*]

5.6.40 Returns solely from capital appreciation and/or investment income

5.6.40.10 An investment entity commits to its investors that its business purpose is to invest for returns solely from capital appreciation and/or investment income. This commitment could, for example, be included in the offering memorandum, investor communications and/or other corporate or partnership documents. [*IFRS 10.27(b), B85B*]

5.6.40.20 Certain types of transactions and relationships are prohibited, because they are inconsistent with the activities of an investment entity (see 5.6.70 and 90). However, investment-related services/activities are not prohibited (see 5.6.80–90).

5.6.50 *Exit strategies*

5.6.50.10 The investment plans of the entity need to provide evidence of its business purpose, demonstrating that an investment entity does not plan to hold its investments indefinitely (see 5.6.40). [*IFRS 10.B85F*]

5.6.50.20 A potential exit strategy documenting how the entity plans to realise capital appreciation is required for substantially all investments that could be held indefinitely. An entity is not required to have an exit strategy for its debt investments with a set maturity, because these investments have a limited life. However, a perpetual debt instrument or a debt instrument that has an equity conversion feature, exercisable at the option of either the issuer or the holder, could be held indefinitely (if they are converted) and therefore an exit strategy is required. [*IFRS 10.B85F, BC245, BC247*]

5.6.50.30 A potential exit strategy is not required for each investment, but rather for each type or portfolio of investments. Exit strategies that are put in place only for default events – e.g. a breach of contract or non-performance – are not considered exit strategies for the purposes of this assessment. [*IFRS 10.B85F*]

5.6.50.40   The following are examples of exit strategies for financial and non-financial instruments that could potentially be held indefinitely. [*IFRS 10.B85G*]

DEBT SECURITIES	EQUITY INVESTMENTS	INVESTMENT PROPERTY
• Private placement • Converting debt to equity with subsequent sale	• Initial public offering • Private placement • Distribution of ownership interests	• Sale on the open market • Private placement through an agent

5.6.50.50   An entity might not have a documented exit strategy for equity investments because *the entity* itself has a limited life. In other cases, *an investee* may have a limited life. In our view, the absence of a documented exit strategy in such cases does not necessarily preclude the entity from qualifying as an investment entity, because the limited life inherently implies no potential for investments to be held indefinitely. [*IFRS 10.B85F*]

EXAMPLE 1 – EXIT STRATEGY BY VIRTUE OF LIMITED LIFE

5.6.50.60   Fund F is a closed-ended fund with a 10-year life, without an option to extend. F has controlling equity interests in a number of companies, but it does not have a documented exit strategy for these investments.

5.6.50.70   In this example, we believe that F meets the exit strategy test. This is because its 10-year life means that it cannot hold the equity investments indefinitely or for an unreasonably long period.

5.6.50.80   In assessing the exit strategy of a limited-life entity or related to a limited-life investee, judgement may be required in terms of the length of life considered reasonable. For example, if Fund F in Example 1 had a 50-year life, then it is less likely that it could be concluded that F has an appropriate exit strategy for its investments.

5.6.50.90   In some circumstances, a fund may allow investors to redeem their units at short notice – e.g. by giving one month's notice. In our view, the existence of such a redemption feature is not in itself an exit strategy. We believe that an investor's economic compulsion to sell the underlying investment without an exit strategy is not sufficient for the fund to meet this condition. [*IFRS 10.B85F*]

5.6.50.100   An investment entity is not required to have a potential exit strategy for its investment in another investment entity that was formed in connection with the entity for legal, regulatory, tax or similar reasons, provided that the investment entity investee has a potential exit strategy for all of its investments that could be held indefinitely. For further discussion, see 5.6.180.50. [*IFRS 10.B85H, BC248*]

5.6.60   *Relationships, transactions and services*

5.6.60.10   There is specific guidance on certain relationships, transactions and services, which is summarised in the flowchart below.

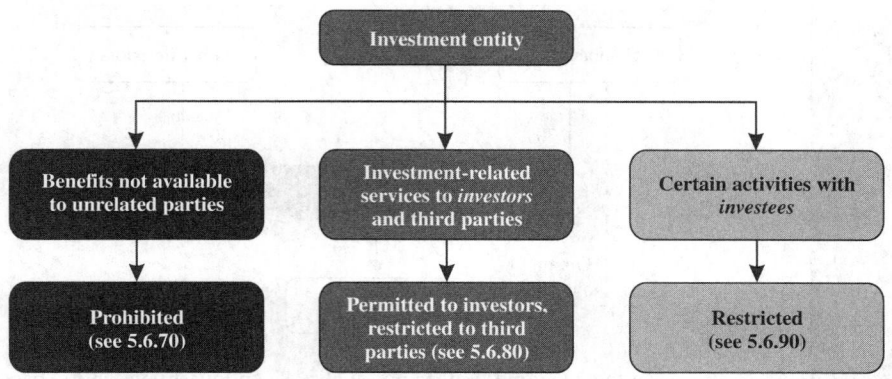

5.6.70 *Prohibited relationships and transactions*

5.6.70.10   Some relationships and transactions preclude an entity from qualifying as an investment entity; this is because they indicate that the entity is investing to earn benefits other than capital appreciation and/or investment income. These restrictions cover not only the entity, but also any member of the larger group of which it is a part – i.e. the group controlled by the investment entity's ultimate parent. [*IFRS 10.B85I*]

5.6.70.20   The following are examples of the relationships and transactions referred to in 5.6.70.10.
- Acquiring, using, exchanging or exploiting assets, technology or processes of an investee; this includes exclusive or disproportionate rights to acquire assets, technology, products or services – e.g. an option to buy an asset if its development is successful.
- Participation as a joint controller in a joint arrangement with the investee (see chapter 3.6), the purpose of which is to develop, produce, market or provide products or services.
- Obtaining a guarantee or collateral from an investee over the entity's borrowings; however, this does not preclude an investment entity from using its investment in an investee as collateral for borrowings.
- A related party of the entity holding an option to acquire ownership interests in the investee from the entity.
- Other transactions between the entity and an investee:
  - with terms that are not available to investors that are not related parties of either the investment entity or the investee;
  - that are not at fair value; or
  - that represent a substantial portion of the business activities of the investee or the entity. [*IFRS 10.B85I*]

EXAMPLE 2 – OPTION HELD BY RELATED PARTY

5.6.70.30   Fund F was formed by Company X to invest in technology start-up companies for capital appreciation. X has a 70% ownership interest in F, and the remaining 30% is owned by 10 unrelated investors. X holds an option to acquire the investments held by F at their fair value, if the underlying technology would benefit the operations of X.

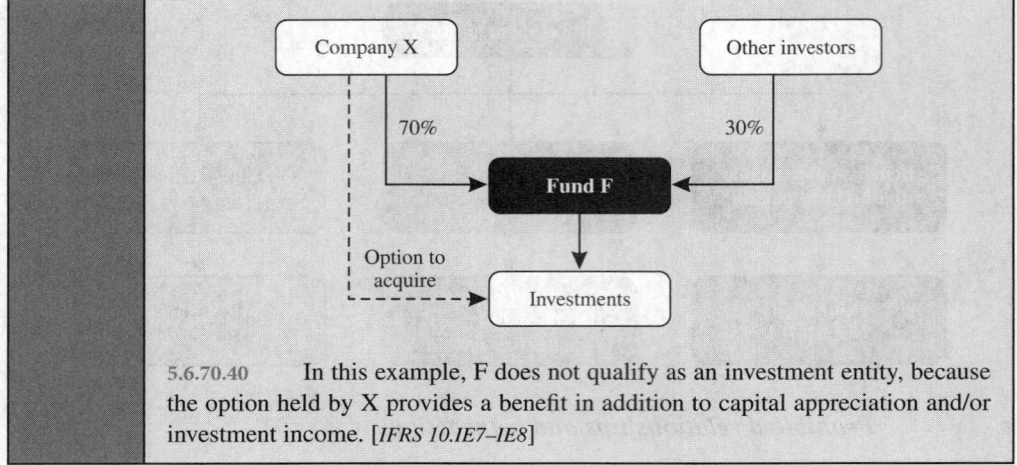

5.6.70.40   In this example, F does not qualify as an investment entity, because the option held by X provides a benefit in addition to capital appreciation and/or investment income. [*IFRS 10.IE7–IE8*]

5.6.80   **Permitted services to investors**

5.6.80.10   As part of its activities, an investment entity is permitted to provide investment-related services to its investors. Such services could include, for example, investment advisory services, investment management, investment support and administrative services. Even if the investment-related services are substantial and are also provided to third parties, this does not preclude an entity from qualifying as an investment entity. [*IFRS 10.B85C*]

5.6.80.20   If an entity provides investment-related services to third parties, then it needs to assess whether it still qualifies as an investment entity by assessing whether its provision of investment-related services to third parties is ancillary to its core investing activities and therefore does not change its business purpose. The definition of investment entity requires the purpose of the entity to be to invest solely for capital appreciation, investment income or both. Consequently, an entity whose main purpose is to provide investment-related services in exchange for consideration from third parties does not meet the definition of an investment entity. [*IFRS 10.B85C, BC240F, IU 03-17*]

5.6.80.30   The IFRS Interpretations Committee discussed this issue and noted that if investment management services are provided by a subsidiary, then the entity first assesses whether these services – including the ones provided to third parties – relate to the entity's investment activities. If they do, then the entity includes them when assessing whether the provision of investment-related services to third parties is ancillary to its core investing activities (see 5.6.80.20). For a discussion of further implications when these services are carried out through a subsidiary, see 5.6.100. [*IFRS 10.27(a), IU 03-17*]

5.6.90   **Restricted activities with investees**

5.6.90.10   Providing management services or strategic advice to an investee or providing financial support to an investee – e.g. through a loan, capital commitment or guarantee – is prohibited, unless these activities:
- do not represent a separate substantial business activity or a separate substantial source of income of the entity; and

- are undertaken to maximise the investment return from the investee. [*IFRS 10.B85D*]

5.6.90.20   For a discussion of the implications when these activities are carried out through a subsidiary, see 5.6.100.

5.6.100   *Investment-related services/activities carried out through subsidiary*

5.6.100.10   In determining whether an entity qualifies as an investment entity, the permitted services to investors in 5.6.80 and the allowed activities in 5.6.90 may be carried out through a subsidiary. [*IFRS 10.B85C–B85D, IU 03-17*]

5.6.100.15   An investment entity consolidates such a subsidiary rather than measuring it at fair value if:
- the main purpose and activities of the subsidiary are providing services that relate to the investment entity's investment activities; and
- the subsidiary does not itself qualify as an investment entity. [*IFRS 10.32, B85E, BC240*]

5.6.100.20   The treatment described in 5.6.100.15 is a mandatory exception from the general fair value requirement for investments of an investment entity.

EXAMPLE 3 – INVESTMENT ENTITY SUBSIDIARY PROVIDES INVESTMENT-RELATED SERVICES

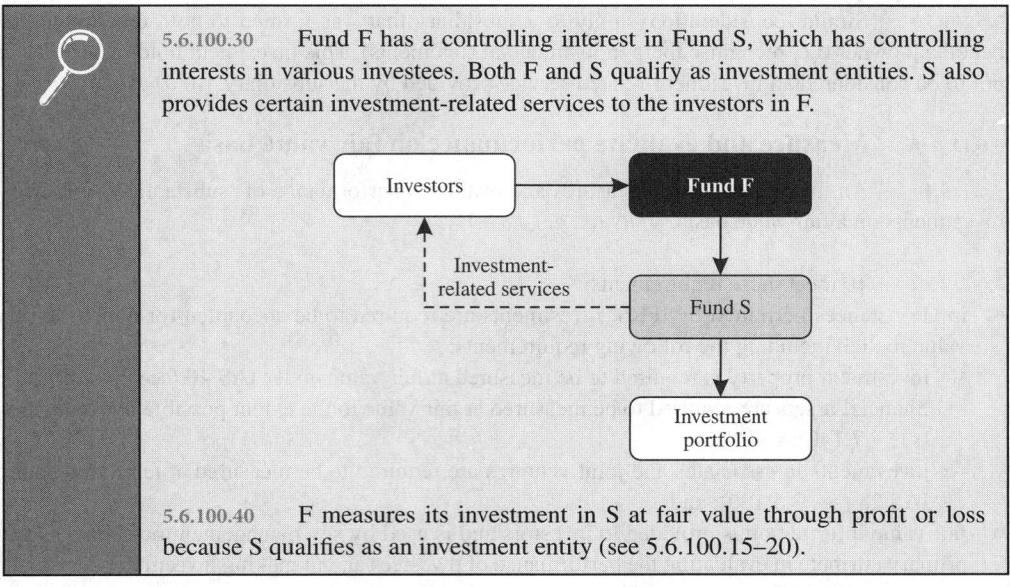

5.6.100.30   Fund F has a controlling interest in Fund S, which has controlling interests in various investees. Both F and S qualify as investment entities. S also provides certain investment-related services to the investors in F.

5.6.100.40   F measures its investment in S at fair value through profit or loss because S qualifies as an investment entity (see 5.6.100.15–20).

5.6.100.50   A subsidiary may be formed only for tax optimisation purposes. The IFRS Interpretations Committee has noted that when a subsidiary is established only for tax optimisation purposes, such that there is no activity within the subsidiary, then the subsidiary does not provide investment-related services. Therefore, an investment entity measures such a subsidiary at fair value through profit or loss. [*IU 03-14*]

EXAMPLE 4 – FUND FORMED FOR TAX OPTIMISATION PURPOSES ONLY

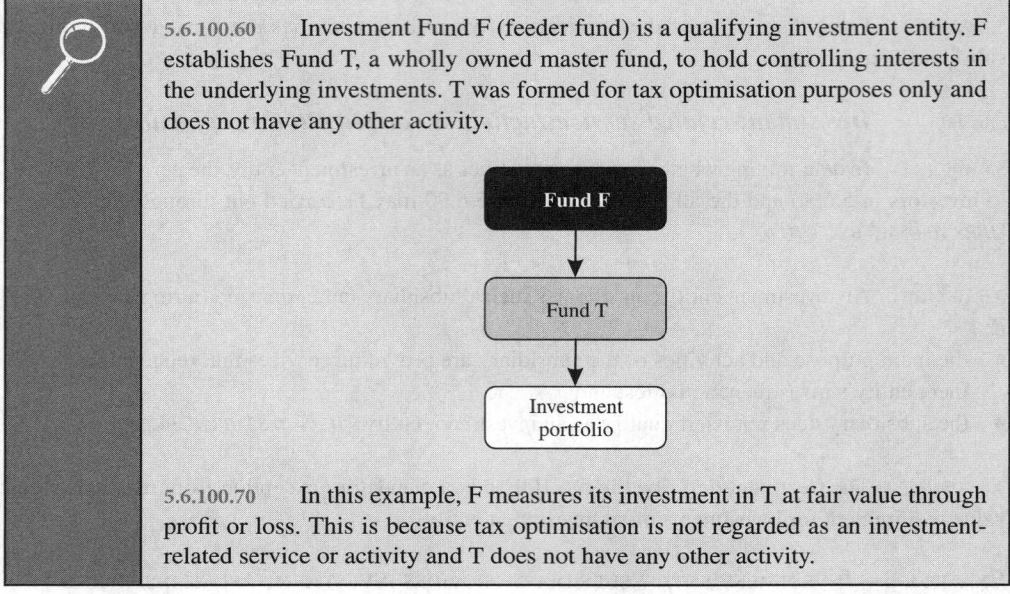

5.6.100.60   Investment Fund F (feeder fund) is a qualifying investment entity. F establishes Fund T, a wholly owned master fund, to hold controlling interests in the underlying investments. T was formed for tax optimisation purposes only and does not have any other activity.

5.6.100.70   In this example, F measures its investment in T at fair value through profit or loss. This is because tax optimisation is not regarded as an investment-related service or activity and T does not have any other activity.

5.6.100.80   Similar considerations apply to a subsidiary that was formed to hold investments as beneficial owner (i.e. recognise them in its financial statements). This investment holding activity is not to be considered an investment-related service provided by the subsidiary. [*IU 03-17*]

5.6.110   Measure and evaluate performance on fair value basis

5.6.110.10   An investment entity measures and evaluates performance of 'substantially all' of its investments on a fair value basis. [*IFRS 10.27(c), B85K*]

5.6.110.20   To meet these requirements:
- in all instances permitted by IFRS, investments are required to be accounted for under the fair value model, including the following requirements:
  - investment property is required to be measured at fair value under IAS 40 (see 3.4.140);
  - financial assets are required to be measured at fair value to the extent possible under IFRS 9 (see 7.7.140); and
  - investments in associates and joint ventures are required to be measured at fair value under IAS 28 (see 3.5.100); and
- fair value information is provided to investors and is used by key management personnel as the primary attribute in evaluating the performance of investees and in making investment decisions. [*IFRS 10.B85K–B85L*]

5.6.110.30   In our view, producing local GAAP financial statements in which an entity's investments are measured at cost does not result in the entity automatically failing the fair value measurement criterion and therefore not meeting the definition of an investment entity. This is because the local GAAP financial statements may not be the only way by which the entity evaluates or communicates the performance of its investments externally. For example, a wholly owned subsidiary may communicate and evaluate the performance of its investments to its parent primarily through a management information system that records investments at fair value. In such a case the entity would meet the fair value measurement criterion regardless of whether the local GAAP financial statements recognise and measure the investments at cost or at fair value.

5.6.110.40   The recognition of changes in fair value in OCI does not preclude an entity from qualifying as an investment entity – e.g. financial assets measured at fair value through OCI under IFRS 9 (see 7.7.160). [*IFRS 10.BC251*]

5.6.110.50   An entity that accounts for more than an insignificant portion of its investments at other than fair value does not qualify as an investment entity. However, non-investment assets – e.g. own-use property and equipment under IAS 16 (see chapter 3.2) – and financial liabilities (see 7.3.20.20) need not be measured at fair value. [*IFRS 10.B85M, BC250*]

5.6.110.60   There is no specific guidance on the threshold required for an entity to conclude that it measures and evaluates the performance of 'substantially all' investments on a fair value basis, and management needs to use its judgement. For example, an entity may account for investment property under the fair value model, but within that model some properties might be accounted for under the cost model because fair value cannot be determined reliably (see 3.4.160). In that case, the entity should assess the extent of its investment property accounted for under the cost model to determine if the 'substantially all' test is met.

5.6.110.70   In our experience, debt funds do not typically measure investments on a fair value basis and therefore would not qualify as investment entities. In many cases, this would not be relevant because the fund would not take a controlling stake in an investee. However, in certain situations following a financial restructuring, a debt fund may take a controlling equity stake, which may result in the requirement to consolidate the underlying investee; this is because the fund may still have debt investments that are measured on an amortised cost basis.

5.6.110.80   Fair value is measured in accordance with IFRS 13, which is the subject of chapter 2.4. That chapter includes general guidance on applying the principles of IFRS 13 in measuring fair value; specific points of interest in relation to investment entities are discussed in 2.4.830 (investments in subsidiaries, associates and joint ventures) and 2.4.930 (investment funds and similar investment vehicles).

5.6.120   Applying the definition

5.6.120.10   The following example is derived from the illustrative examples published with, but not forming an integral part of, IFRS 10.

EXAMPLE 5 – REAL ESTATE FUND

5.6.120.20   The following facts are relevant for this example.
- Real Estate Fund F develops, owns and operates retail, office and other commercial property through its wholly owned subsidiaries, each holding a separate property.

- Property investments held within the subsidiaries are accounted for by F and each of its subsidiaries at fair value under IAS 40.
- F does not have a set timeframe for disposing of its property investments, but uses fair value to identify the optimal time for disposal. F and its investors also consider other factors – e.g. expected cash flows – in making their decisions.
- Although fair value is a key performance indicator, key management personnel do not consider it a key attribute in assessing performance.
- F undertakes property and asset management activities, including property management, capital expenditure and tenant selection, which it outsources to third parties. These are a substantial part of F's business.

5.6.120.30   F does not qualify as an investment entity for any of the following reasons – i.e. any one of the following precludes F from qualifying as an investment entity.

- F's property and asset management activities are a substantial portion of its business activity – i.e. the benefits that F earns go beyond capital appreciation and/or investment income (see 5.6.70).
- F does not have exit strategies for its investments in real estate (see 5.6.50).
- Fair value is one of the performance indicators used by F. However, it is not the primary attribute used by key management personnel in evaluating performance and making investment decisions (see 5.6.110). [*IFRS 10.IE9–IE11*]

5.6.120.40   The wording of the illustrative example on real estate funds suggests that the IASB intends very few real estate funds to qualify as investment entities. In our experience, real estate funds may be involved in construction or development, and it is common for them to be involved in operations. Judgement is required to evaluate, based on the facts and circumstances for each case, whether these activities are a substantial portion of the business activities of the real estate fund or its investees.

5.6.130   TYPICAL CHARACTERISTICS

5.6.130.10   An entity considers the characteristics discussed in 5.6.140–170 in assessing whether it possesses all three essential elements of the definition of an investment entity (see 5.6.20). [*IFRS 10.B85N, IU 03-17*]

5.6.130.20   The absence of one or more of these typical characteristics does not necessarily disqualify an entity from being classified as an investment entity. Management may use its judgement to decide that the entity nonetheless meets the definition of an investment entity. The entity is required to disclose its reasons for concluding that it is nevertheless an investment entity if one or more of these characteristics are not met (see 5.10.300.10). [*IFRS 10.28, B85N, 12.9A*]

5.6.140   More than one investment

5.6.140.10   Generally, an investment entity is expected to hold multiple investments in order to diversify its risks and maximise returns. However, the standard acknowledges that this may not always be the case. [*IFRS 10.B85O*]

5.6.140.20   An investment entity might hold a single investment in the following situations, for example:

- in a start-up or wind-up period; or
- if its purpose and design is to provide investors with access to an investment to which they wouldn't otherwise have access – e.g. a feeder fund or because the entry price is too high. [*IFRS 10.B85P*]

5.6.150   More than one investor

5.6.150.10   An investment entity is generally expected to have multiple investors. This means that the entity (or entities in the same group) is less likely to earn returns other than capital appreciation and/or investment income (see 5.6.40). [*IFRS 10.B85Q*]

5.6.150.20   However, the standard acknowledges that in some cases a single investor is entirely credible. For example, a pension fund, government investment fund or family trust might be a single investor, representing a wider group of investors. Alternatively, there might be a single feeder fund in a master-feeder structure. [*IFRS 10.B85R*]

5.6.150.30   Sometimes a single investor will be temporary – e.g. in the investment entity's start-up or wind-up period. [*IFRS 10.B85S*]

5.6.160   Investors that are not related parties

5.6.160.10   Another typical characteristic of an investment entity is having investors that are not related parties (as defined in IAS 24 – see 5.5.30). This makes it less likely that the entity (or entities in the same group) is earning returns other than capital appreciation and/or investment income (see 5.6.40). [*IFRS 10.B85T*]

5.6.160.20   However, the standard provides the example of a fund set up for members of key management personnel that mirrors the investments of the entity's main investment fund. Such an arrangement does not preclude investment entity status. [*IFRS 10.B85U*]

5.6.170   Ownership interests that are equity

5.6.170.10   An investment entity is not required to be a legal entity, which means that the beneficial interests in the entity will not necessarily be in the form of equity or similar interests. [*IFRS 10.B85V*]

5.6.170.20   Each unit of ownership in an investment entity typically represents a specifically identifiable proportionate share in its net assets. However, it is also acceptable for an investment entity to have multiple classes of investors with separate investment pools per class or different proportionate shares of net assets or differential rights in the proportionate share of net assets – e.g. in a waterfall structure. [*IFRS 10.B85V*]

5.6.170.30   An investment entity may have significant ownership interests that are classified as liabilities under IAS 32 (see 7.3.10), as long as debt holders are exposed to variable returns from changes in the fair value of the entity's net assets. [*IFRS 10.B85W*]

MULTIPLE-FUND STRUCTURES FORMED FOR LEGAL, TAX AND SIMILAR REASONS

5.6.180.10   The discussion so far in this chapter has assumed that the entity being assessed against the investment entity criteria is a single entity. However, in practice two (or more) entities may be formed in connection with one another for legal, regulatory, tax or similar reasons. In this case, an issue arises in determining whether the entities meet the criteria for qualification as investment entities. Example 6 is derived from the illustrative examples published with, but not forming an integral part of, IFRS 10.

EXAMPLE 6 – MASTER-FEEDER STRUCTURE

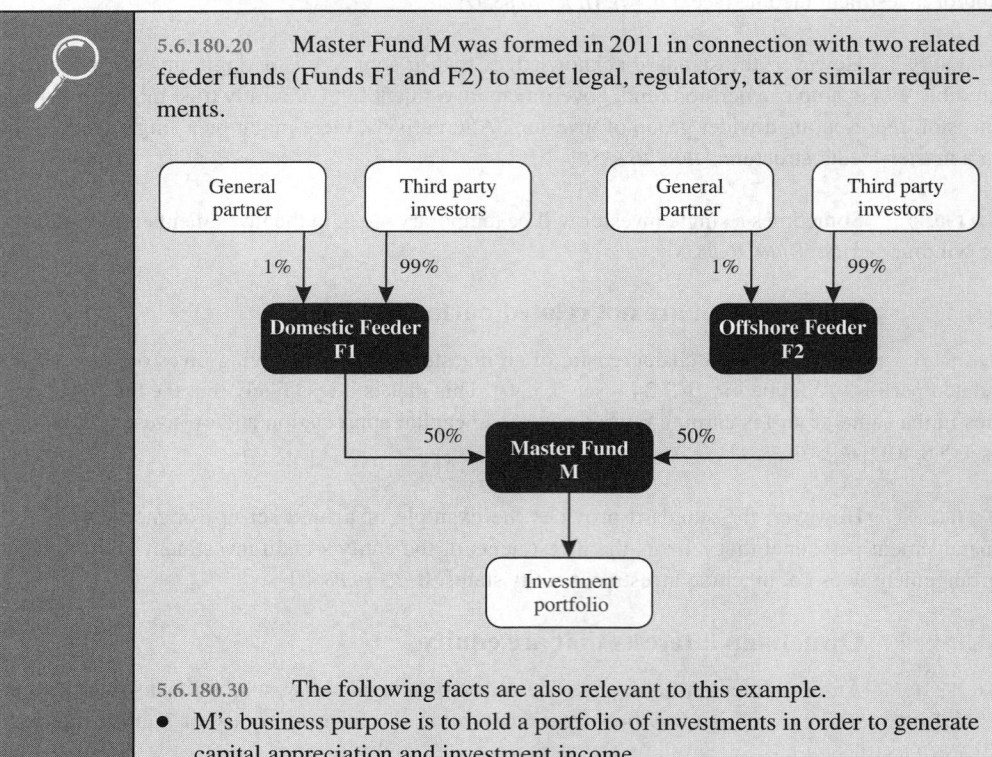

5.6.180.20   Master Fund M was formed in 2011 in connection with two related feeder funds (Funds F1 and F2) to meet legal, regulatory, tax or similar requirements.

5.6.180.30   The following facts are also relevant to this example.
- M's business purpose is to hold a portfolio of investments in order to generate capital appreciation and investment income.
- The investment objective communicated to investors is for the master-feeder structure to provide investment opportunities for investors in different markets to invest in large portfolios of assets.
- M has identified and documented exit strategies for the equity and non-financial investments that it holds.
- M measures and evaluates the performance of substantially all of its investments on a fair value basis, and investors in F1 and F2 receive financial information on a fair value basis.
- Ownership in M, F1 and F2 is represented through units of equity. [*IFRS 10.IE12–IE13*]

5.6.180.40   In this example, M, F1 and F2 were formed in connection with each other and when considered together they each meet the definition of an investment entity. [*IFRS 10.IE14*]

Essential elements of the definition of an investment entity

- M, F1 and F2 have obtained funds for the purpose of providing investors with investment management services (see 5.6.30).
- The master-feeder structure's business purpose, which was communicated to the investors of F1 and F2, is investing solely for capital appreciation and investment income (see 5.6.40).
- M has identified and documented potential exit strategies (see 5.6.50). Although F1 and F2 do not have an exit strategy for their investments in M, they can nevertheless be considered to have an exit strategy because M was formed in connection with F1 and F2 and holds investments on their behalf.
- M measures and evaluates the performance of its investments on a fair value basis, and investors in F1 and F2 receive financial information on a fair value basis (see 5.6.110). [*IFRS 10.IE14*]

Typical characteristics of an investment entity

- F1 and F2 indirectly hold more than one investment because M holds a portfolio of investments (see 5.6.140).
- Although M is wholly capitalised by F1 and F2, the feeder funds have multiple third party investors (see 5.6.150–160).
- Ownership in M, F1 and F2 is in the form of equity (see 5.6.170). [*IFRS 10.IE15*]

5.6.180.50   Example 6 illustrates that when two (or more) entities are formed in connection with each other for legal, regulatory, tax or similar reasons, the criteria for qualification as an investment entity are applied to the structure as a whole. In particular, the exit strategy and the fair value tests are considered with reference to the underlying investments. [*IFRS 10.B85H, IE12–IE15, BC248*]

5.6.180.60   A fund structure may be more complicated than that illustrated in Example 6, with multiple layers of funds. However, the principle remains the same and the issue is whether the entities have been formed in connection with each other for legal, regulatory, tax or similar reasons.

EXAMPLE 7 – EXIT STRATEGY DOCUMENTED BY INDIRECTLY CONTROLLED INVESTMENT

5.6.180.70   Funds F, S1 and S2 were formed in connection with each other for regulatory reasons. F has a controlling interest in S1, which has a controlling interest in S2. The underlying controlled equity investments are held by S2, which has a documented exit strategy for its investment portfolio. Neither F nor S1 has a documented exit strategy for S1 or S2.

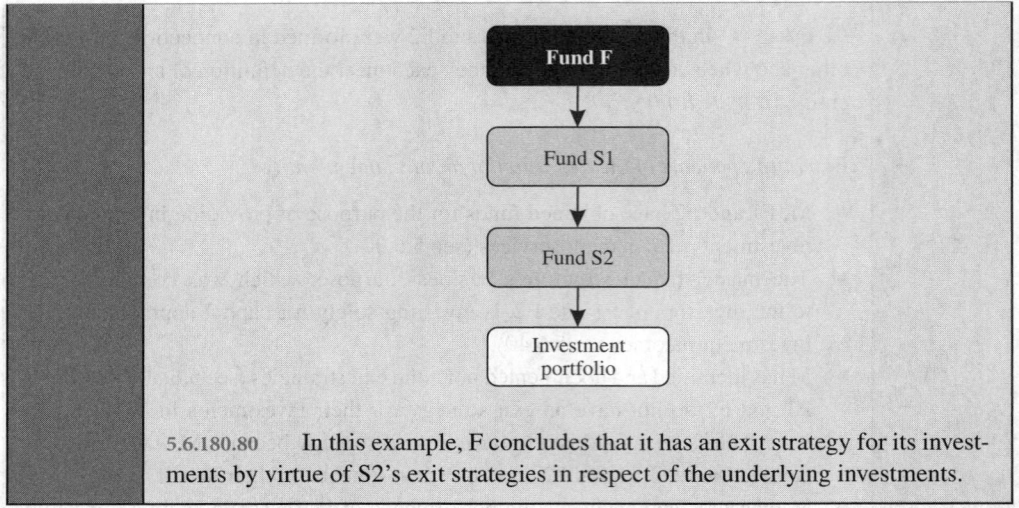

5.6.180.80   In this example, F concludes that it has an exit strategy for its investments by virtue of S2's exit strategies in respect of the underlying investments.

5.6.180.90   In many cases, funds that operate as a single unit will be established at the same time. However, in our view the phrase 'in connection with' used in IFRS 10 does not necessarily mean that funds must be formed or acquired at the same time; instead, the overriding factor should be whether the substance of the structure is that two (or more) entities operate as a single unit but are split into separate entities only for legal, regulatory, tax or similar reasons. [*IFRS 10.B85H, BC248, IE12, IE14–IE15*]

EXAMPLE 8 – INVESTMENT ENTITY SUBSIDIARY NOT FORMED AT SAME TIME AS PARENT

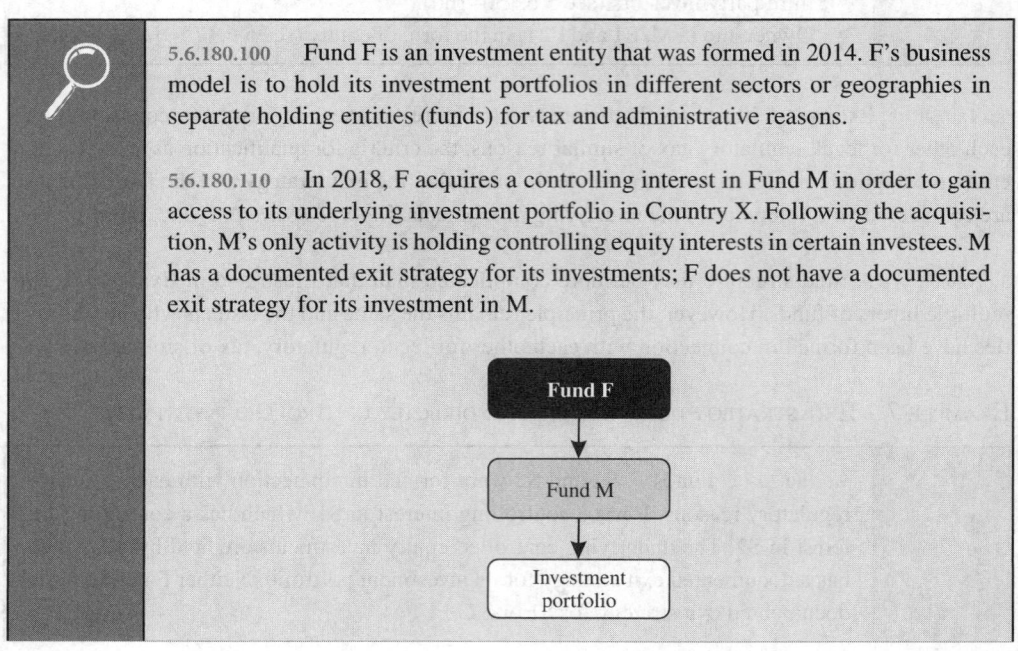

5.6.180.100   Fund F is an investment entity that was formed in 2014. F's business model is to hold its investment portfolios in different sectors or geographies in separate holding entities (funds) for tax and administrative reasons.

5.6.180.110   In 2018, F acquires a controlling interest in Fund M in order to gain access to its underlying investment portfolio in Country X. Following the acquisition, M's only activity is holding controlling equity interests in certain investees. M has a documented exit strategy for its investments; F does not have a documented exit strategy for its investment in M.

> 5.6.180.120   In this example, we believe that F continues to qualify as an investment entity following its acquisition of M, even though it does not itself have an exit strategy for the underlying investment portfolio (and assuming that the other criteria are met). Although F and M were not formed at the same time and in contemplation of one another, the substance of the structure is that F and M operate as a single unit.

5.6.190   PARENTS OF/INVESTORS IN INVESTMENT ENTITIES

5.6.200   Parent is investment entity

5.6.200.10   The investment entity consolidation exception is mandatory for the parent of an investment entity that itself meets the definition of an investment entity. In such cases, the parent entity is also required to account for its investments in controlled investees at fair value through profit or loss, even if the investment entity subsidiary was formed for specific legal, tax or regulatory purposes – e.g. in a master-feeder structure. [*IFRS 10.32–33*]

5.6.200.20   In addition, because the parent is an investment entity, any investments in associates and joint ventures are required to be accounted for at fair value through profit or loss (see 5.6.110.20). [*IFRS 10.B85L(b)*]

5.6.210   Parent/investor is not investment entity

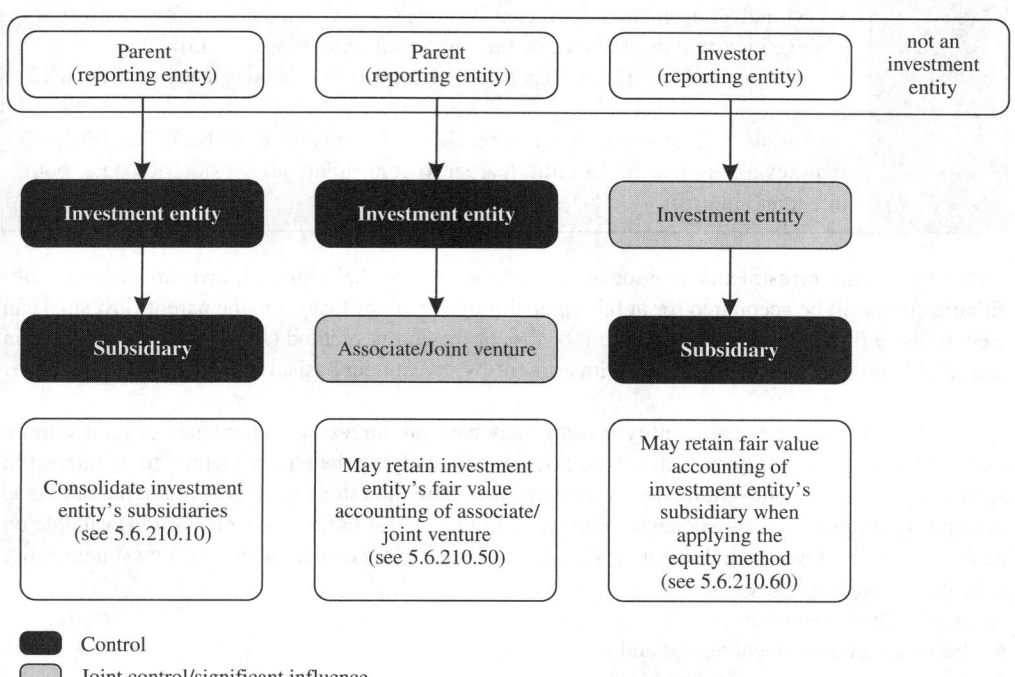

5.6.210.10 The consolidation exception is not carried through to the consolidated financial statements of a parent that is not itself an investment entity – i.e. the parent is nevertheless required to consolidate all subsidiaries. [*IFRS 10.33*]

EXAMPLE 9 – SPLIT HOLDING

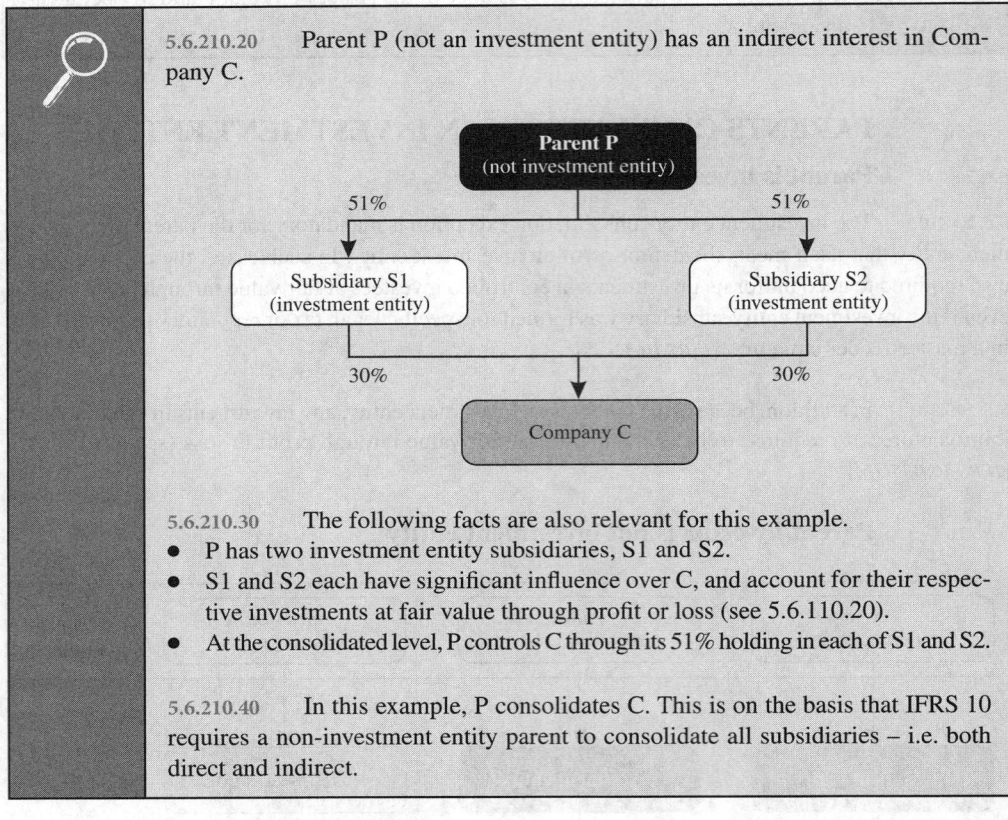

5.6.210.20 Parent P (not an investment entity) has an indirect interest in Company C.

5.6.210.30 The following facts are also relevant for this example.
- P has two investment entity subsidiaries, S1 and S2.
- S1 and S2 each have significant influence over C, and account for their respective investments at fair value through profit or loss (see 5.6.110.20).
- At the consolidated level, P controls C through its 51% holding in each of S1 and S2.

5.6.210.40 In this example, P consolidates C. This is on the basis that IFRS 10 requires a non-investment entity parent to consolidate all subsidiaries – i.e. both direct and indirect.

5.6.210.50 Any investments in associates and joint ventures held through investment-entity subsidiaries may still be accounted for at fair value through profit or loss – i.e. the parent (investor) can elect to use either fair value through profit or loss or the equity method (see 3.5.100). This election is available on initial recognition on an investment-by-investment basis. [*IAS 28.18–19*]

5.6.210.60 A non-investment entity investor may have an interest in an associate or joint venture that is an investment entity and has subsidiaries. When applying the equity method to its interest in such an associate or joint venture, the non-investment entity investor can elect to retain the fair value accounting applied by the associate or joint venture to its subsidiaries. This election is available on an investment-by-investment basis and is made at the later of the date on which the investment entity equity-accounted investee:
- is initially recognised;
- becomes an investment entity; and
- first becomes a parent. [*IAS 28.36A*]

EXAMPLE 10 – ASSOCIATE IS AN INVESTMENT ENTITY

5.6.210.70   Parent P (not an investment entity) has an interest in Associate X (an investment entity).

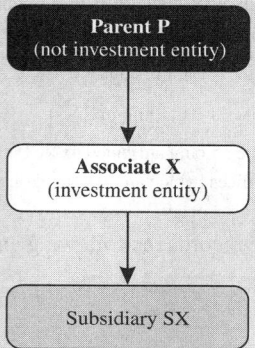

5.6.210.80   The following facts are also relevant for this example.
- X has a subsidiary, SX.
- In its consolidated financial statements, X measures SX at fair value through profit or loss.

5.6.210.90   When applying the equity method to its interest in X, P can elect to retain the fair value accounting applied by X to SX. [*IAS 28.36A*]

5.6.220   CHANGES IN STATUS

5.6.220.10   An entity reassesses its status if facts and circumstances indicate that there has been a change in any of the essential elements of the definition of an investment entity or in the typical characteristics. A change in status is accounted for prospectively. [*IFRS 10.29–30*]

5.6.230   Qualifying for first time

5.6.230.10   When an entity qualifies as an investment entity for the first time, it accounts for the change as a deemed loss of control of its subsidiaries. The difference between the previous carrying amount of the subsidiaries and their fair value at the date of the change in status is recognised as a gain or loss. Subsidiaries whose main purpose and activities are providing investment-related services and that are not themselves investment entities continue to be consolidated; see 5.6.100. [*IFRS 10.25–26, 32, B101*]

EXAMPLE 11 – QUALIFYING AS INVESTMENT ENTITY

5.6.230.20   Investment Fund F has consolidated Subsidiary S since its incorporation a number of years ago. F has a 60% holding in S. On 1 June 2018, F meets the criteria to qualify as an investment entity.

5.6.230.30 The following additional information is also relevant for this example.

At 1 June 2018

Carrying amount of S's net assets in F's consolidated financial statements, including any goodwill	1,000
Carrying amount of NCI in equity	400
Fair value of F's 60% holding in S	1,500
Credit (net of the amount attributed to NCI) recorded in a revaluation reserve related to S's offices, which are measured on a fair value basis (see 3.2.300)	150

5.6.230.40 F records the following entry at 1 June 2018. [*IFRS 10.B98–B99*]

	DEBIT	CREDIT
Investment in S	1,500	
NCI	400	
Revaluation reserve[(1)]	150	
Retained earnings[(1)]		150
Gain on deemed loss of control (profit or loss)		900
Various assets and liabilities		1,000
To deconsolidate S on qualifying as investment entity		

Note

1. The debit in the revaluation reserve is transferred directly to retained earnings, which is consistent with the treatment that would apply if the underlying property, plant and equipment had been disposed of directly. The transfer has no impact on the gain arising on the deemed loss of control. [*IFRS 10.B99, B101, IAS 16.41*]

5.6.240 Ceasing to qualify

5.6.240.10 When an entity ceases to qualify as an investment entity, it applies IFRS 3 at the date of change in status (the deemed date of acquisition) to any subsidiary that was previously measured at fair value in its consolidated financial statements. The fair value of the subsidiary at the date of the change becomes the deemed consideration transferred to obtain control of the investee. Acquisition accounting under IFRS 3 is the subject of chapter 2.6. [*IFRS 10.30, B100*]

EXAMPLE 12 – CEASING TO QUALIFY AS INVESTMENT ENTITY

5.6.240.20 Investment Fund F has been classified as an investment entity since it adopted the investment entity amendments to IFRS 10 on 1 January 2014; accordingly, its 60% holding in Subsidiary S has been accounted for at fair value through profit or loss. On 1 June 2018, F determines that it no longer meets the criteria to qualify as an investment entity.

5.6.240.30 The following additional information is also relevant for this example.

AT 1 JUNE 2018	
Carrying amount (fair value) of F's investment in S	1,500
Fair value of S's identifiable net assets	1,000
F elects to recognise NCI based on their interest in the identifiable net assets of S (see 2.6.940)	400 (1,000 x 40%)

5.6.240.40 F records the following entry at 1 June 2018. [*IFRS 10.B100*]

	DEBIT	CREDIT
Identifiable net assets	1,000	
Goodwill[1]	900	
NCI		400
Investment in S		1,500
To consolidate S on ceasing to qualify as investment entity		

Note

1. Goodwill is calculated as follows.

Consideration transferred	1,500
Plus NCI recognised	400
Less identifiable net assets	(1,000)
Goodwill [*IFRS 3.32*]	900

5.6.240.50 IFRS 3 is applied to all subsidiaries when an entity ceases to be an investment entity – i.e. the requirements do not distinguish between a business and a group of assets that is not a business – e.g. a single investment property in a corporate shell is often not a business. [*IFRS 10.B100, BC270*]

5.6.240.60 IFRS 3 provides specific guidance on the acquisition of an asset or group of assets (including any liabilities assumed), which would apply if the subsidiary is not a business. In such cases, the consideration transferred would be allocated to the individual identifiable assets and liabilities based on their relative fair values (see 2.6.10.30). [*IFRS 3.2(b)*]

5.7   Non-monetary transactions

5.7 Non-monetary transactions

CURRENTLY EFFECTIVE REQUIREMENTS

This publication reflects IFRS in issue at 1 August 2018, and the currently effective requirements cover annual periods beginning on 1 January 2018.

In the absence of a specific IFRS on non-monetary transactions, the requirements related to this topic are mainly derived from the following.

REFERENCE	TITLE
IFRS 15	Revenue from Contracts with Customers
IAS 16	Property, Plant and Equipment
IAS 38	Intangible Assets
IAS 40	Investment Property

The currently effective requirements include newly effective requirements arising from IFRS 15 *Revenue from Contracts with Customers,* which is effective for annual periods beginning on or after 1 January 2018. The new requirements may be applied using the retrospective method or the cumulative effect method (see 4.2.510). The impact of the new requirements on the accounting for non-monetary transactions is reflected in 5.7.10.30, 20.30, 30–50 and 90.

FORTHCOMING REQUIREMENTS AND FUTURE DEVELOPMENTS

For this topic, there are no forthcoming requirements or future developments.

5.7.10 INTRODUCTION

5.7.10.10   There is no definition of a 'non-monetary transaction' under IFRS. However, a non-monetary transaction can be considered to occur when there are exchanges of non-monetary assets, liabilities or services for other non-monetary assets, liabilities or services with little or no monetary consideration involved. An entity considers whether a group of monetary transactions that represents a non-monetary transaction in substance – i.e. the exchange of non-monetary assets or services accomplished through the exchange of monetary consideration – needs to be accounted for as described in this chapter. When addressing non-monetary transactions, the two most typical issues are:

- whether to measure the exchange based on historical cost or fair value; and
- whether to recognise revenue, gains or losses.

5.7.10.20   Guidance on certain specific non-monetary transactions is provided in chapters on other topics: business combinations (see chapter 2.6); contribution of non-monetary assets to an equity-accounted investee (see 3.5.485); share-based payments (see chapter 4.5); share splits and bonus issues (see 7.3.420); non-reciprocal capital contribution of non-monetary assets (see 7.3.450); and distributions of non-cash assets to owners and distributions in which the owners may elect to receive either the non-cash asset or a cash alternative (see 7.3.690).

5.7.10.30   Revenue for other non-monetary transactions is generally accounted for under IFRS 15 (see chapter 4.2). However, non-monetary exchanges between entities in the same line of business to facilitate sales to customers or potential customers other than the parties to the exchange are excluded from the scope of IFRS 15 (see 5.7.20.30 and 30). [*IFRS 15.5(d)*]

5.7.20 EXCHANGES OF ASSETS HELD FOR USE

5.7.20.10   All property, plant and equipment, intangible assets and investment property received in exchange for non-monetary assets are measured at fair value, unless:

- the exchange transaction lacks commercial substance; or
- the fair value of neither the asset received nor the asset given up is reliably measurable. Fair value is measured in accordance with IFRS 13, which is the subject of chapter 2.4. [*IAS 16.6, 24, 38.45, 40.27*]

5.7.20.20   Commercial substance is assessed by considering the extent to which future cash flows are expected to change as a result of the transaction. More specifically, an exchange transaction has commercial substance if the configuration of the cash flows – i.e. the amount, timing and uncertainty – of the assets received and transferred is different, or if the entity-specific value of the portion of the entity's operation affected by the transaction changes as a result of the exchange. The difference in both of these situations should be significant when compared with the fair value of the assets exchanged. [*IAS 16.25, 38.46, 40.28*]

5.7.20.30   Measurement of an exchange at fair value will result in the recognition of a gain or loss based on the carrying amount of the asset surrendered. To determine if a transaction results in the recognition of revenue, an entity considers whether the transaction is:

- incidental to its ordinary activities; and
- an exchange with another entity in the same line of business to facilitate sales to customers or potential customers (see 5.7.30). [*IFRS 15.5(d), A, IAS 1.34, 16.26, 38.45–47, 40.29*]

EXAMPLE 1 – COMMERCIAL SUBSTANCE

5.7.20.35   Company B signs an agreement with Company C to exchange its warehouse abroad for another in B's local city. This transaction is in line with B's strategy to focus on its domestic operations. Therefore, B estimates that the cash flows to be generated by the warehouse abroad will be lower than the cash flows to be generated by the domestic warehouse. The fair value of both warehouses is 200 and B's carrying amount of the surrendered warehouse is 140. B recognises the warehouse received at fair value (200), derecognises the surrendered warehouse (140) and recognises a gain of 60.

5.7.20.40   IAS 16, IAS 38 and IAS 40 contain guidance on when the fair value of an asset is reliably measurable in the context of asset exchanges. If a fair value can be measured reliably for either the asset received or the asset given up, then the fair value of the asset given up is used unless the fair value of the asset received is more clearly evident. For a discussion of fair value measurement, see chapter 2.4. [*IAS 16.26, 38.47, 40.29*]

5.7.20.50   In our view, the commercial substance test (see 5.7.20.20) applies only when assets held for use are exchanged. For a discussion of situations that involve non-current assets held for sale, see 5.4.30.90.

5.7.30   EXCHANGE OF GOODS AND SERVICES

5.7.40   Barter transactions

5.7.40.10   An entity recognises revenue for a non-monetary exchange, unless the transaction is incidental to its ordinary activities or is with a counterparty in the same line of business to facilitate sales to customers or potential customers. Revenue is measured at the fair value of the goods or services received. If an entity cannot reasonably estimate the fair value of the goods or services received, then it measures the non-cash consideration with reference to the stand-alone selling prices of the goods or services promised to the customer in exchange for the non-cash consideration (see 4.2.150). Fair value is measured in accordance with IFRS 13, which is the subject of chapter 2.4. [*IFRS 15.5(d), 66–67, A, IAS 1.34*]

5.7.40.20   Non-monetary transactions include barter transactions, typical examples of which include transactions involving commodities such as wheat or oil, or advertising barter transactions.

EXAMPLE 2 – EXCHANGE NOT IN THE SAME LINE OF BUSINESS

5.7.40.30   Natural Gas Company N sells gas to Steel Company S and receives in exchange a quantity of steel tubing. In this case, N is not in the same line of business of S. Therefore, N recognises revenue for gas sales equal to the fair value

of the steel tubing received, if it can be measured reliably. If the fair value of the tubing received cannot be determined reliably, then the revenue is measured with reference to the stand-alone selling price of the gas delivered.

5.7.50 DONATED ASSETS

5.7.60 General

5.7.60.10   An entity may receive assets from third parties for no consideration. Such non-reciprocal transfers include transfers such as government grants, gifts and donations. They may be received as cash, as other assets or as reductions in liabilities – e.g. forgiven loans – and may or may not have conditions or restrictions attached.

5.7.60.15   When assets are transferred to the entity by the government, these transfers normally meet the definition of a government grant (see 4.3.10). However, entities also consider the requirements of IFRIC 12 because certain assets transferred by the government would not necessarily be government grants. IFRIC 12 provides guidance to private sector entities on certain recognition and measurement issues that arise in accounting for public-to-private service concession arrangements (see chapter 5.12).

5.7.60.20   Assets or resources transferred to an entity by a shareholder for no consideration are normally equity contributions that would be accounted for directly in equity (see 7.3.450). [*CF 6.82*]

5.7.60.30   With the exception of assets or resources transferred to an entity by a shareholder or a government (via government grant), or arrangements in the scope of IFRS 15, there is no guidance on assets or resources received from other third parties. In our view, even though these transactions do not meet the definition of a government grant, government grant accounting should be applied by analogy to non-reciprocal non-monetary contributions by third parties other than shareholders or governments (see chapter 4.3), or those arrangements in the scope of IFRS 15 (see 5.7.80). Therefore, we believe that an entity should choose an accounting policy, to be applied consistently, to measure transferred or donated assets either at the fair value of the assets received or at the nominal amount paid. IAS 20 notes that fair value is the usual approach for measuring non-monetary grants. If the transactions are measured at fair value, then in our view the resulting income should be deferred and recognised in profit or loss on a systematic basis. [*IAS 20.12, 23*]

5.7.60.40   Gifts without conditions are likely to be rare in an arm's length relationship. In our view, if conditions are attached to a non-reciprocal transfer, then it is not generally appropriate to recognise the income immediately; instead, any income should be deferred until the conditions are satisfied. The income is recognised in profit or loss on a systematic basis as the entity recognises as expenses the costs that the grants are intended to compensate.

5.7.60.50   In our view, non-reciprocal transfers without conditions attached should be recognised by recipients as assets at the earlier of receipt of the asset or the existence of an enforceable right to receive future delivery of the asset, or as reduced liabilities when the transferor waives its right to receive a future payment.

5.7.60.60   In our view, if an entity elects an accounting policy for non-reciprocal transfers similar to the accounting for government grants related to biological assets measured at fair value less costs to sell (see 4.3.60), then transfers without conditions from non-shareholders should be recognised in profit or loss once such transfers become receivable. The amounts should be recognised as revenue if they arise in the course of ordinary activities, or as other income if they do not arise in the course of ordinary activities. Transfers with conditions should be recognised by recipients as a liability (contract liability or deferred income) until such time as the conditions are met, at which point they should be recognised as revenue or other income.

5.7.70   Not-for-profit entities

5.7.70.10   Donations are often received by charitable organisations and may be in the form of cash, goods, services or pledges (promises to pay at a future date). Donations may be 'earmarked' – e.g. if the donor requests that the donation be used for a particular purpose.

5.7.70.20   There is no specific guidance in IFRS on contributions received by not-for-profit entities. In our view, guidance may be obtained from the accounting for government grants related to biological assets measured at fair value less costs to sell (see 4.3.60) or from the general requirements for other assets as discussed above in 5.7.60.

5.7.80   TRANSFERS OF ASSETS FROM CUSTOMERS

5.7.80.10   IFRS 15 does not include specific guidance on accounting for the receipt of items of property, plant and equipment from customers in order to connect them to a network or to provide them with ongoing services.

5.7.80.20   Under the general requirements of IFRS 15, if a customer contributes goods to facilitate an entity's fulfilment of the contract, then the entity assesses whether it obtains control of the goods. If the entity obtains control of the goods, then it applies the guidance on non-cash consideration (see 4.2.150). Under this guidance, the entity measures the non-cash consideration received – i.e. the contributed asset – at fair value if that can be reasonably estimated; if not, then the entity uses the stand-alone selling price of the good or service that was promised in exchange for the non-cash consideration. [*IFRS 15.66–69*]

5.7.80.30   The timing of revenue recognition is based on the entity's obligations and depends on the facts and circumstances of each arrangement. A key consideration is whether a connection and ongoing access are distinct performance obligations (see 4.2.70).

5.8   Accompanying financial and non-financial information

5.8 Accompanying financial and non-financial information

CURRENTLY EFFECTIVE REQUIREMENTS

This publication reflects IFRS in issue at 1 August 2018, and the currently effective requirements cover annual periods beginning on 1 January 2018.

The requirements related to this topic are mainly derived from the following.

REFERENCE	TITLE
IAS 1	Presentation of Financial Statements

In addition, useful guidance related to this topic can be found in IFRS Practice Statement *Management Commentary*.

FORTHCOMING REQUIREMENTS

For this topic, there are no forthcoming requirements.

FUTURE DEVELOPMENTS

This topic is subject to future developments that may affect several aspects of the accompanying financial and non-financial information. See 5.8.40.

5.8.10 **GENERAL**

5.8.10.10 An entity considers its legal or regulatory requirements in assessing what is required to be, or prohibited from being, disclosed in its financial statements beyond the requirements of IFRS.

5.8.10.20 An entity ordinarily issues a document – e.g. an annual report – that includes its financial statements and accompanying information. The accompanying information may be presented in a narrative section of the annual report and may be provided either voluntarily or because of legal or regulatory requirements. The examples of such accompanying information include – but are not limited to – management commentary, management discussions and analysis operating and financial review, and a directors' report.

5.8.10.30 IFRS is not based on a particular legal or regulatory framework; it also does not contain any requirements for management commentary either as part of or outside the financial statements. However, the IASB has published guidance in the form of an IFRS Practice Statement *Management Commentary*. Its objective is to help management to provide useful management commentary for financial statements prepared in accordance with IFRS. The practice statement is not an IFRS and an entity need not comply with it in order to state compliance with IFRS.

5.8.10.40 An entity applying IFRS may be subject to national, regional or regulatory requirements or recommendations regarding the presentation of financial and/or non-financial information, regardless of whether the information is presented within or outside the financial statements. For example, in the EU, the European Securities and Markets Authority has issued guidelines on the disclosure of alternative performance measures outside the financial statements (see 4.1.150.30).

5.8.10.50 Information in addition to that required by IFRS is usually presented outside the financial statements as accompanying information – e.g. in a narrative section of the annual report. However, such information may be presented within the financial statements if this is appropriate. Factors that determine whether it is appropriate to present such information within the financial statements include:
- whether the information is required specifically by regulation;
- the nature and purpose of the information;
- its relationship to IFRS; and
- whether it is intended or required to be covered by the auditor's report.

5.8.10.60 For example, it may be appropriate to provide additional information within the financial statements when it is intended to provide further explanation of specific financial statement items presented in accordance with IFRS.

5.8.10.70 Alternatively, it may be inappropriate to provide additional information within the financial statements when it is provided voluntarily and is presented in a manner that could lead a user to conclude that it is in accordance with IFRS when in fact it is not. For example, if an unlisted entity wishes to provide segment information (see chapter 5.2), but is unable to obtain all of the required information, or wishes to disclose only limited segment information, then in our view that segment information should be presented outside the financial statements – e.g. as part of the directors' report. The discussion that accompanies the segment information should not imply that the information is prepared in accordance with IFRS when in fact it is not. [*IFRS 8.3*]

5.8.10.80   When accompanying information is presented outside the financial statements, it is important that it is presented in a manner that differentiates it clearly from the audited financial statements. [*IAS 1.49–50*]

5.8.10.90   Some standards allow certain specific disclosures to be presented outside the financial statements with a cross-reference to those disclosures from the financial statements, as long as the accompanying report or statement is available to users of the financial statements on the same terms as the financial statements and at the same time. Including all disclosures required by IFRS within the financial statements themselves helps users in differentiating between disclosures that are required by IFRS and other information. However, if such information is presented outside the financial statements, then in our view it should be marked clearly as being part of the disclosures required by IFRS and cross-referenced to the financial statements. An entity could identify such information as, for example, 'information that is an integral part of the audited financial statements' or 'disclosures that are required by IFRS'. [*IFRS 4.IG62, 7.B6, 14.31, IAS 34.16A*]

5.8.10.100   Accompanying information will normally be of interest to a wide range of users, but is often aimed at the needs of investors. In our view, an entity should apply the same guiding principles as those set out in the Conceptual Framework (see chapter 1.2) to ensure that the accompanying information is relevant, faithfully represented, understandable, timely, verifiable, and comparable. An entity may also consider the guiding principles set out in the IFRS Practice Statement *Management Commentary* in preparing such information.

5.8.10.110   An entity may consider the International Integrated Reporting Council's *International Integrated Reporting Framework* in developing its discussion of its operational performance in the context of its long-term strategy, and the resources and relationships on which this depends.

5.8.10.120   For a discussion of pro forma information, see 2.1.130.

5.8.20   TYPES OF FINANCIAL AND NON-FINANCIAL INFORMATION

5.8.20.10   Many entities present, outside the financial statements, a financial review by management that describes and explains the main features of the entity's financial performance and position, its progress and the principal uncertainties that it faces. IFRS does not include requirements for the presentation of this information. However, the IFRS Practice Statement *Management Commentary* provides guidance on the principles, qualitative characteristics and elements of management commentary. [*IAS 1.13, IPS 1.12–13*]

5.8.20.15   Among other things, the IFRS Practice Statement *Management Commentary* indicates that information in a management commentary supplements and complements the information presented in the financial statements and should include forward-looking information. [*IPS 1.12–13*]

5.8.20.20   Management commentary is often presented in the directors' report, chairman's report or other accompanying report or statement and may include a review of:
- the main factors and influences affecting the entity's performance, including:

- – changes in the environment in which the entity operates;
- – the entity's responses to those changes and their effects; and
- – its policy for investment to maintain and enhance performance, including its dividend policy;
- the entity's sources of funding, the policy on gearing (borrowing levels) and its risk management policies; and
- the entity's strengths and resources whose value is not reflected in the statement of financial position under IFRS – e.g. internally generated brands and trademarks.

5.8.20.30   In addition to the above, the directors' report or other accompanying report or statement may also include the following.
- General information:
  - – the nature of the business;
  - – mission statement and values;
  - – management's objectives and its strategies for meeting those objectives;
  - – list of directors and officers; and
  - – chairman's and CEO's statements.
- Business review:
  - – the entity's most significant resources, risks and relationships;
  - – performance during the period and future prospects;
  - – the critical performance measures and indicators that management uses to evaluate the entity's performance against stated objectives;
  - – market and product development, including research activities and competitor information; and
  - – acquisitions and disposals of businesses.
- Financial review:
  - – capital structure and financial position;
  - – stock exchange information, including share prices, dividends and shareholder information and profiles;
  - – tables of financial data and key figures for periods in addition to those covered in the financial statements and comparative periods – e.g. for the past five or ten years; and
  - – information about risk management and the sensitivity of key assumptions (in addition to the disclosures required by IFRS (see 7.10.480)).
- Other items:
  - – directors' interests and management philosophy;
  - – events subsequent to the reporting date;
  - – agenda for the annual general meeting;
  - – IT policies and significant investments; and
  - – specific disclosures required by laws and regulations. [*IPS 1.26–27, 29, 34–40*]

5.8.20.40   An entity may wish to discuss some of the above areas on a segment basis. IFRS 8 introduced the 'management approach', which requires disclosures about components of the entity that management monitors in making decisions about operational matters (see chapter 5.2). Accordingly, an entity needs to ensure that the information provided in the management commentary (or elsewhere in the narrative section of annual report) is, in all material respects, consistent with the IFRS 8 disclosures in the financial statements.

5.8.20.50   Some entities also present as accompanying information additional reports and statements, such as environmental reports and value-added statements, if management believes that this additional information will help in making investment decisions or that it will be of interest to other users. [*IAS 1.14*]

5.8.20.60   Disclosure of the domicile and legal form of the entity, the country of incorporation of the entity, the address of the registered office (or principal place of business), information about the length of the entity's life (if it is a limited-life entity) and a description of the nature of the entity's operations and its principal activities are often provided outside the financial statements. If they are not, then the entity provides these disclosures in the financial statements. [*IAS 1.138(a)–(b), (d)*]

5.8.20.70   IFRS does not prohibit an entity from providing a 'convenience translation' of its financial statements or other financial information. Such a translation presents financial statements or other financial information in a currency that is different from either its functional currency or its presentation currency as a convenience to users and does not comply with the translation method set out under IFRS. IAS 21 specifically requires that a convenience translation be clearly identified as supplementary information distinguished from the information that complies with IFRS (see 2.7.380.20). [*IAS 21.57*]

5.8.20.80   An entity may wish to present other supplementary information such as the following:
- information about the effects of changing prices on a current cost basis when an entity's functional currency is not hyperinflationary (see 2.10.180); and
- consolidated information when the entity disposed of its last subsidiary during the reporting period and, accordingly, is not required to issue consolidated financial statements at the reporting date (see 2.1.100.100 and 5.9.10.40).

5.8.20.90   For a discussion of whether the information in 5.8.20.80 should be presented within or outside the financial statements, see 5.8.10.50.

5.8.30   CORPORATE GOVERNANCE DISCLOSURES

5.8.30.10   IFRS does not provide guidance on the disclosure of corporate governance information. Often, a local legal or regulatory requirement specifies what corporate governance information should be disclosed and where such information should be presented (see 5.8.10.50).

5.8.30.20   Examples of corporate governance disclosures include:
- composition of the board of directors, including their responsibilities, criteria for election, term of office and the frequency of, and attendance at, board meetings;
- if there is a supervisory board, then the names of members of this board and a report of the supervisory board may be included in the annual report;
- names and responsibilities of the CEO and president;
- identification and responsibilities of executive and other management groups;
- identification, composition and responsibilities of various committees and sub-boards – e.g. advisory board, personnel committee, audit committee, nomination committee – and other entity-specific committees, such as a research and development committee or environmental committee;

- details of the remuneration of individual directors, including share or other incentive schemes;
- insider trading policies and practices;
- risk management disclosures, including board accountability and systems of control;
- sustainability disclosures, including social, ethical, safety, health and environmental policies and practices;
- a description of IT governance;
- management's assertion on effectiveness of internal controls; and
- a description or confirmation of compliance with rules, laws, codes and standards and reporting of any exceptions.

| 5.8.40 | **FUTURE DEVELOPMENTS** |

5.8.40.10   The IASB is working on a project to revise and update the IFRS Practice Statement 1 *Management Commentary* issued in 2010. This project considers how broader financial reporting could complement and support IFRS financial statements. The exposure draft is expected in the first half of 2020.

5.9 Interim financial reporting

5.9 Interim financial reporting

CURRENTLY EFFECTIVE REQUIREMENTS

This publication reflects IFRS in issue at 1 August 2018, and the currently effective requirements cover annual periods beginning on 1 January 2018.

The requirements related to this topic are mainly derived from the following.

STANDARD	TITLE
IAS 34	Interim Financial Reporting
IFRIC 10	Interim Financial Reporting and Impairment

The currently effective requirements include newly effective requirements arising from IFRS 15 *Revenue from Contracts with Customers*, which is effective for annual periods beginning on or after 1 January 2018. The new requirements may be applied using the retrospective method or the cumulative effect method (see 4.2.510). The impact of the new requirements on the interim financial reporting is reflected in 5.9.60.20 and 220.35.

FORTHCOMING REQUIREMENTS AND FUTURE DEVELOPMENTS

For this topic, there are no forthcoming requirements or future developments.

5.9.10   **SCOPE AND BASIS OF PREPARATION**

5.9.10.10   IFRS does not require the presentation of interim financial statements. Publicly traded entities are encouraged to provide interim financial statements at least for the first six months of their annual reporting period. Regulators may require interim financial statements to be prepared and may also specify the frequency of preparation – e.g. quarterly or half-yearly. An entity is not required to prepare interim financial statements in accordance with IAS 34 in order for its annual financial statements to comply with IFRS. [*IAS 34.1–2*]

5.9.10.20   An entity may prepare condensed interim financial statements in accordance with IAS 34, or a complete set of interim financial statements in accordance with IFRS. [*IAS 34.7*]

5.9.10.25   If an entity prepares condensed interim financial statements, then such financial statements state that they comply with IAS 34 if that is the case. [*IAS 34.19*]

5.9.10.28   Alternatively, if an entity prepares a complete set of financial statements in accordance with IFRS covering the interim period, then such financial statements comply with all requirements set out in IFRS, including those of IAS 1 and the measurement and any supplementary disclosure requirements of IAS 34. Such interim financial statements state that they comply either with IFRS or IFRS including the requirements of IAS 34. [*IAS 34.3, 7, 9, 19, 1.4*]

5.9.10.30   IAS 34 provides guidance on the structure and content of condensed interim financial statements. The overall considerations for preparing annual financial statements are also applicable to condensed interim financial statements. These include guidance on fair presentation and compliance with IFRS, the accrual basis of accounting, materiality and aggregation, offsetting and going concern. [*IAS 1.4, 15–35*]

5.9.10.31   Specific guidance in respect of materiality and its application to interim financial statements is included in IAS 34. Materiality is relevant to the recognition and measurement of items in interim financial statements (see 5.9.80.20) and the presentation and disclosure of items in those interim financial statements (see 5.9.60). Materiality is assessed based on information related to the interim period and not to the full annual reporting period. For example, an impairment charge may be material for the interim period even if it is not expected to be material for the annual period. If there is more than one interim period (e.g. in the case of quarterly reporting), then materiality is also assessed based on information related to the current financial year to date period. In assessing materiality, an entity considers the purpose of interim financial statements – i.e. to provide an update on the latest complete set of annual financial statements – which differs from the purpose of annual financial statements. For a discussion of materiality that is also applicable to interim financial statements, see 1.2.40. [*IAS 34.23–25, IPS 2.84–87*]

5.9.10.32   Information that is expected to be material to the annual financial statements need not necessarily be provided in interim financial statements if it is not material to the interim financial statements. However, such information may be regarded as material to the interim financial statements from a qualitative perspective, even if it does not meet any quantitative thresholds for the interim financial statements. [*IPS 2.85*]

EXAMPLE 1 – INFORMATION MATERIAL TO THE INTERIM FINANCIAL STATEMENTS – QUALITATIVE PERSPECTIVE

5.9.10.33   Company B sells mainly standardised products to private customers in its home market. B's annual reporting period ends on 31 December and its interim reporting period ends on 30 June. In the half-year interim reporting period, 98% of B's revenue was generated by sales of Product X. The remaining revenue was principally derived from a pilot sale of a new product line – Product Y – that B planned to launch in the third quarter of the year. B expects revenue from Product Y to increase significantly by the end of the annual reporting period, so that Product Y will provide approximately 20% of B's revenue for the full annual period.

5.9.10.34   B determines that the sales of Product Y are not quantitatively material to the interim financial statements. However, B considers that the information about revenue from Product Y is qualitatively material to the interim financial statements because it is a newly launched product with a growing revenue stream that is expected to be material to the annual financial statements. Therefore, when disaggregating revenue in accordance with paragraph 114 of IFRS 15 (see 5.9.60.20) in the half-year interim financial statements, B separately identifies revenue from Product Y. [*IPS 2.Ex Q*]

5.9.10.35   When making an assessment of uncertainties associated with an entity's going concern assumption, management takes into account all available information for a period of at least 12 months from the date of the interim financial statements. For example, an entity with a calendar year end that prepares half-yearly interim financial statements considers, for the purpose of preparing its 30 June 2018 condensed interim financial statements, information about a future period through, but not limited to, 30 June 2019 when assessing whether the going concern assumption is appropriate. [*IAS 1.4, 25–26*]

5.9.10.36   Some jurisdictions may impose local requirements that require a longer period of time to be considered in making a going concern assessment and as such will not conflict with the IAS 34 minimum requirement of at least 12 months. However, if a local jurisdiction permitted consideration of a period of less than 12 months from the interim reporting date, then reliance on that local permission would not be sufficient to allow an entity to state that its interim financial statements comply with IAS 34.

5.9.10.37   If management determines that a material uncertainty, relative to an entity's ability to continue as a going concern, exists at the date at which interim financial statements are authorised for issue, then such uncertainty is disclosed in those interim financial statements, whether or not it was disclosed in the most recent annual financial statements. [*IAS 1.4, 25–26, 10.16(b), 34.15*]

5.9.10.38   An entity may also disclose the absence of a material uncertainty and the significant judgement involved in reaching this conclusion. For example, management determined that a material uncertainty existed at the date of authorisation for issue of its most recent annual financial statements and provided disclosure of the material uncertainty in those financial statements. However, because no material uncertainty is identified at the date of authorisation for issue of subsequent interim financial statements, management provides disclosure about the change in circumstances and the significant judgement (see 1.2.80.10). [*IAS 1.122, 34.15, IU 07-14*]

5.9.10.40   Generally, the interim financial statements are prepared on a consolidated basis if the most recent annual financial statements were prepared on that basis. In our view, this approach is not required if an entity disposes of its last subsidiary during the interim period. In this case, because the entity no longer is a parent at the interim reporting date, consolidated financial statements are no longer required unless otherwise prescribed – e.g. by a local regulator (see 2.1.100.100). In such cases, we believe that interim financial statements – including the comparatives – should be presented as unconsolidated financial statements and identified as such. Disclosure of the previously reported consolidated information as supplementary information may be useful (see chapter 5.8). [*IAS 34.14*]

5.9.10.50   Interim financial statements – including the comparative information – may be included in one section in an interim report. However, there is no requirement in IFRS that prevents presentation or disclosure in another manner, as may be prescribed by local regulatory requirements or in response to other factors.

5.9.20   FORM AND CONTENT

5.9.30   Minimum components

5.9.30.10   Interim financial statements may be prepared in a condensed format, omitting most disclosures that are required to comply with IFRS when publishing a complete set of IFRS financial statements. Condensing and omitting disclosures is permitted assuming that financial statement users will have access to the most recent annual financial statements. Therefore, in our view the interim financial statements should focus on changes since the last annual financial statements. However, an entity should consider whether information disclosed in the last annual financial statements remains relevant. If changes in circumstances have made significant disclosures in the last annual financial statements less relevant, then in our view an entity should consider whether additional supplementary interim disclosures should be provided. [*IAS 34.10, 15A*]

5.9.30.20   Condensed financial statements include at least:
- a condensed statement of financial position at the end of the current interim period and at the end of the immediately preceding annual period;
- a condensed statement of profit or loss and OCI for the current interim period and cumulatively for the year to date, and for the comparable interim periods (current and cumulative) of the immediately preceding annual period;
- a condensed statement of changes in equity, cumulatively for the current year to date and for the comparable year-to-date period of the immediately preceding annual period;
- a condensed statement of cash flows, cumulatively for the current year to date and for the comparable year-to-date period of the immediately preceding annual period; and
- certain explanatory notes (see 5.9.60). [*IAS 34.8, 20*]

5.9.30.22   Unlike a complete set of interim financial statements, which in certain circumstances is required to include a statement of financial position as at the beginning of the preceding comparative period (see 2.1.10.10), there is no requirement to present an additional statement of financial position in condensed interim financial statements. However, disclosure is required for certain events and transactions, including a change of accounting policy or the correction of a material prior-period error (see 5.9.60.20, 40). [*IAS 34.5, 8, 15B(g), 16A(a), 1.BC33*]

5.9.30.23   Additionally, if an entity prepares a complete set of interim financial statements, then the (primary) financial statements are not condensed and full notes are required. [*IAS 34.5, 8–9*]

5.9.30.25   A condensed statement of profit or loss and OCI may be presented either:
- as a single statement; or
- as two separate statements:
  - a condensed statement of profit or loss displaying components of profit or loss; immediately followed by
  - a condensed statement of comprehensive income beginning with profit or loss and displaying components of OCI. [*IAS 34.8A, 1.10A*]

5.9.30.30   The approach adopted for the annual financial statements for the presentation of the statement of profit or loss and OCI as a single statement or as two statements is followed in the condensed interim financial statements. [*IAS 34.8A*]

5.9.30.40   IAS 34 defines an interim period as a "financial reporting period shorter than a full financial year". In our view, this means the period between the end of the last reporting period and the end of the current reporting period when an entity reports more than once during the financial year. An entity may not, for example, define an interim period as a year-to-date period to the current reporting date, and on that basis prepare a condensed statement of profit or loss and OCI for the year-to-date period only. For example, we believe that an entity reporting quarterly and claiming compliance with IAS 34 should present in its half-year interim report a statement of profit or loss and OCI for each of the three months and the six months ending on the current reporting date, as well as for the comparable periods of the immediately preceding financial year. [*IAS 34.4, 20, 22, IE.A2*]

5.9.40   Format of condensed financial statements

5.9.40.10   Condensed financial statements include, at a minimum, each of the headings and subtotals that were included in the most recent annual financial statements. Additional line items are included if their omission would make the financial statements misleading. [*IAS 34.10, IU 07-14*]

5.9.40.20   Although not required by IAS 34, in our view if an entity has operations that are discontinued at the interim reporting date or are disposed of during the interim period, then these operations should be presented separately in the condensed statement of profit or loss and OCI following IFRS 5 (see 5.4.220). In addition, in our view if an entity has non-current assets or a disposal group classified as held-for-sale or held-for-distribution at the interim reporting date, then we believe that these should be presented separately from other assets and liabilities in the condensed statement of financial position (see 5.4.110).

5.9.50   EPS in condensed financial statements

5.9.50.10   If an entity is in the scope of IAS 33, then it presents basic and diluted EPS (see 5.3.10.10 and 30) in the statement displaying the components of profit or loss. Although not required explicitly by IAS 34, EPS for continuing operations may be material to an understanding of the interim period, in which case it would be disclosed in addition to the EPS for total operations in the condensed financial statements. [*IAS 34.11–11A, 15*]

5.9.60 Explanatory notes in condensed financial statements

5.9.60.10   Entities are not required to repeat or provide insignificant updates to information already reported in the most recent annual financial statements. [*IAS 34.15A*]

5.9.60.20   Explanatory notes to the condensed financial statements include the following information if it is material, unless it is disclosed elsewhere in the interim report (see 5.9.10.50). [*IAS 34.16A, 21, 23, IFRS 3.59–63, 7.25–30, 10.27–30, 12.9A–B, 13.91–93(h), 94–96, 98–99, 15.114–115, B87–B89*]

AREA	DISCLOSURES[1]
Disaggregation of revenue from contracts with customers	An entity discloses (see 4.2.480.30): • a disaggregation of revenue recognised from contracts with customers into categories that depict how the nature, amount, timing and uncertainty of revenue and cash flows are affected by economic factors; and • sufficient information about the relationship between the disclosure of disaggregated revenue and revenue information that is disclosed for each reportable segment, if the entity applies IFRS 8 (see 'segment information' below).

Fair value of financial instruments	An entity discloses by class of financial instrument:
	• the fair value measurement at the interim reporting date;
	• for non-recurring fair value measurements, the reasons for the measurement;
	• the level of the hierarchy (see 2.4.260) in which the measurement is categorised;
	• for recurring fair value measurements, any transfers between Level 1 and Level 2, the reasons for those transfers, as well as the policy for the timing of recognising transfers between levels of the fair value hierarchy;
	• a description of the valuation technique and the inputs used in the fair value measurements for Level 2 and Level 3 measurements;
	• if a change in the valuation technique has been made, then the reasons for the change;
	• quantitative information about significant unobservable inputs for Level 3 measurements;
	• a reconciliation of Level 3 balances from opening to closing balances, including the amount of unrealised gains or losses related to assets or liabilities held at the reporting date;
	• for Levels 2 and 3:
	  – a description of valuation processes for Level 3 measurements;
	  – a quantitative sensitivity analysis for recurring Level 3 measurements; and
	  – if an accounting policy is made to measure offsetting positions on a net basis, then that fact;
	• the existence of an inseparable third party credit enhancement issued with a liability measured at fair value and whether it is reflected in the fair value measurement;
	• with limited exceptions, fair value of each class of instruments;
	• day one gain or loss information as required by IFRS 7 (see 7.10.470); and
	• information about contracts containing a discretionary participation feature (as described in IFRS 4) whose fair value cannot be measured reliably (see 7.10.460.30–40).

Debt and equity transactions	An entity discloses issues, repurchases and repayments of debt and equity securities, and dividends paid for ordinary and other shares.

AREA	DISCLOSURES[1]

Segment information	If an entity is required to disclose segment information in its annual financial statements in accordance with IFRS 8, then in its condensed interim financial statements it discloses (see 5.2.240):
	• a measure of segment profit or loss;
	• if included in the measure of segment profit or loss reviewed by, or otherwise provided regularly to, the chief operating decision maker:
	  – revenues from external customers; and
	  – inter-segment revenues;
	• a measure of total assets and/or total liabilities for a particular reportable segment if:
	  – the related amounts are regularly provided to the chief operating decision maker; and
	  – there has been a material change in the total assets or total liabilities for that segment from the related amounts disclosed in the last annual financial statements;
	• any change in the basis of segmentation or the basis of measuring segment profit or loss; and
	• a reconciliation between the total of the reportable segments' measures of profit or loss to the entity's profit or loss before income tax and discontinued operations.

Changes in accounting policies	An entity discloses the nature and effect of any change in accounting policy, or provides a statement that the interim financial statements reflect the same accounting policies as in the most recent annual financial statements (see 5.9.220).
Changes in estimates	An entity discloses the nature and amount of changes in estimates of amounts reported in prior interim periods of the current financial year or in prior annual reporting periods (see 5.9.210).
Effects of changes in the composition of an entity	The disclosure of changes in composition includes business combinations, acquisitions and disposals of subsidiaries and long-term investments, restructurings and discontinued operations. In respect of business combinations, an entity is required to disclose in its interim financial statements the information required by IFRS 3 (see 5.9.68).
Subsequent events	An entity discloses events that occurred after the interim reporting date that are not reflected in the interim financial statements.
Seasonality of activities	An entity explains the reasons for any seasonal fluctuations in its operations. Entities with highly seasonal activities are also encouraged to supplement the required disclosures with information for the 12-month period ending on the interim reporting date, as well as comparatives. There is no guidance on what additional information might be provided, and in our view such information may be limited to the information that is affected by seasonality – e.g. revenue and gross margin.
Unusual items	An entity discloses the nature and amount of items affecting assets, liabilities, equity, net income or cash flows that are unusual because of their nature, size or incidence.

Note

1. These disclosures may be either provided in the interim financial statements or disclosed 'elsewhere in the interim financial report' – i.e. incorporated by cross-reference from the interim financial statements to another part of the interim financial report that is available to users on the same terms and at the same time as the interim financial statements. [*IAS 34.16A*]

5.9.60.25   Unlike in a complete set of financial statements, for condensed interim financial statements there is no explicit requirement to disclose the date on which the condensed interim financial statements were authorised for issue and who gave such authorisation (see 2.9.15). However, it may be helpful to disclose the date of authorisation because any event that occurs after that date is not disclosed or adjusted in the condensed financial statements of the current interim period.

5.9.60.30   An entity provides an explanation of events and transactions that are significant to an understanding of the changes in its financial position and performance since the last annual reporting date. Information disclosed in relation to those events and transactions updates the relevant information presented in the most recent annual financial report. [IAS 34.15]

5.9.60.40   A non-exhaustive list of events and transactions for which disclosure would be required, if significant, is included in IAS 34. In our view, these disclosures are required only if they are material to an understanding of the current interim period:

- inventory write-downs and their reversal, and the recognition and reversal of impairment losses on any other assets (including financial assets and assets arising from contracts with customers) (see 5.9.80);
- acquisitions, disposals and commitments for the purchase of property, plant and equipment;
- litigation settlements and the reversal of restructuring provisions;
- any loan default or breach of a loan agreement that was not remedied on or before the interim reporting date;
- correction of prior-period errors;
- related party transactions;
- changes in the business or economic circumstances that affect the fair value of the entity's financial instruments, regardless of whether such items are accounted for at fair value;
- transfers of financial instruments between levels of the fair value hierarchy;
- changes in financial assets' classification – e.g. from amortised cost to fair value through profit or loss – as a result of changes in the entity's business model for managing the financial assets; and
- changes in contingent liabilities or contingent assets. [IAS 34.15B]

5.9.60.50   In respect of related party transactions, care should be taken in determining the level of disclosure that is necessary in condensed financial statements. If the nature and amounts of related party transactions are consistent with those previously reported, then no disclosure may be necessary in the condensed financial statements. However, if related party transactions are significant, then disclosure may be necessary even if the nature and amounts of those transactions are consistent with previous periods. [IAS 34.15B]

5.9.60.60   In our view, an entity does not generally have to update the disclosure of related party relationships unless there has been a significant change, such as a change in the controlling investor.

5.9.60.70   Other examples of items that may be material to an understanding of the interim period include:

- changes in significant judgements and assumptions made by management, as well as areas of estimation uncertainty as required by IAS 1;
- disclosures required by IFRS 7, if changes in an entity's financial risk management objectives and policies or in the nature and extent of risks arising from financial instruments occur during the interim period;

- disclosures required by IAS 36, if an entity's annual impairment testing of goodwill and intangible assets with indefinite useful lives occurs during an interim period;
- significant changes in the effective income tax rate;
- significant changes in the carrying amounts of assets and liabilities measured at fair value, in addition to IFRS 13 disclosures for financial instruments that are specifically required by IAS 34 (see 5.9.60.20);
- disclosures required by IFRS 2, if an entity grants a share-based payment award during the current interim period;
- disclosures required by IFRS 5, if an entity has operations that are discontinued at the interim reporting date or are disposed of during the interim period, or non-current assets or a disposal group classified as held-for-sale at the interim reporting date;
- acquisitions, disposals and commitments for the purchase of significant categories of non-current assets, in addition to property, plant and equipment, which is addressed in 5.9.60.40; and
- material movements in provisions during the interim period.

5.9.60.80   Any significant changes in estimates made during the final interim period are disclosed in the annual financial statements, unless separate interim financial statements are published for this period. [*IAS 34.26*]

5.9.60.90   Additional disclosures are required in the interim financial statements in the year that an entity adopts IFRS (see 6.1.1540).

5.9.68   *Business combinations*

5.9.68.10   IAS 34 requires disclosures about changes in composition of the entity during the interim period, including IFRS 3 disclosures in the case of business combinations. IAS 34 also requires disclosure of events after the interim period that have not been reflected in the financial statements for the interim period. A business combination that occurs after the end of the interim period may be an example of an event after the interim period that requires disclosure. [*IAS 34.16A(h)–(i), IFRS 3.59–63*]

5.9.70   Comparative information

5.9.70.05   An entity that prepares a complete set of interim financial statements (see 5.9.10.28) includes comparative information in accordance with the specific requirements of IAS 34 (see 5.9.30.20) and the general requirements of IAS 1. For further discussion of the requirements of IAS 1 in respect of quantitative and narrative comparative information, see 2.1.60. [*IAS 34.20, 1.4*]

5.9.70.10   An entity that prepares condensed financial statements is not required to apply the requirements of IAS 1 in respect of quantitative and narrative comparative information. [*IAS 1.4*]

5.9.70.20   IAS 34 itself contains specific requirements for the comparative primary statements (see 2.1.10.20) that are included in the condensed (and complete) interim financial statements (see 5.9.30.20). For example, in an initial public offering a set of half-yearly interim financial statements may be presented in addition to the most recent annual financial statements, which include comparative information. If the interim financial statements claim compliance with IFRS (for a complete set of financial statements) or IAS 34 (for condensed interim financial statements), then presentation of the comparative interim period is also required. [*IAS 34.20*]

5.9.70.30   However, IAS 34 is less specific in respect of the comparative information (both quantitative and narrative) that should be included in the selected explanatory notes. In our experience, entities generally include both quantitative and narrative comparative information in the explanatory notes because the disclosure is of continuing relevance to the current interim period. In our view, management should exercise judgement to decide what comparative information should be included in the explanatory notes. In some circumstances, it may be appropriate to omit certain disclosures related to the comparative period that were disclosed in the condensed financial statements of the comparative interim period and/or in the last annual financial statements. For example, a business combination occurred and was finalised during the previous annual period and was disclosed in accordance with IFRS 3 in the last annual financial statements. It may be appropriate to exclude from the condensed financial statements of the current interim period some of the disclosures in respect of the prior year business combination. However, certain information may need to be disclosed if necessary for the understanding of the current interim period. [*IAS 34.6, 15–15B, 16A*]

5.9.80   RECOGNITION AND MEASUREMENT

5.9.80.10   Generally, items are required to be recognised and measured as if the interim period were a discrete stand-alone period. However, the tax charge is based on the estimated weighted-average effective tax rate for the full year (see 5.9.160). [*IAS 34.29–30*]

5.9.80.20   The determination of materiality is made in relation to the interim period financial information, rather than in relation to the prior or current annual period (see 5.9.10.31–34). [*IAS 34.23–25*]

5.9.80.30   The conditions for recognising expenses and provisions are the same for interim financial statements as for annual financial statements. Therefore, losses, provisions, expenses and income are recognised as incurred or earned and may not be anticipated (see 3.12.30, 754.80). Similarly, costs and income that are incurred or earned unevenly during the financial year are anticipated or deferred at the interim reporting date if, and only if, it would also be appropriate to anticipate or defer that type of cost or income at the annual reporting date. [*IAS 34.37, 39*]

5.9.90   Inventory losses and manufacturing variances

5.9.90.10   Losses on inventories and interim period manufacturing cost variances are recognised using the same procedures as would be used at the annual reporting date. Therefore, they cannot be deferred on the basis that they are expected to be restored or absorbed by the annual reporting date. [*IAS 34.IE.B26–IE.B28*]

5.9.100   Volume rebates and discounts

5.9.100.10   Volume rebates and discounts are often granted by a supplier to a buyer on a 'stepped' basis, and calculated based on the volume or value of purchases during a certain period – e.g. a full year. A buyer anticipates volume rebates and other contractual price adjustments to the extent that it is probable that they will be earned. [*IAS 34.IE.B23*]

5.9.100.20   Discretionary rebates and discounts are not anticipated. [*IAS 34.IE.B23*]

5.9.110 **Seasonal results**

5.9.110.10   Revenue that is received seasonally, cyclically or occasionally within an annual period is not anticipated or deferred, but is recognised when it is earned. [*IAS 34.37–38*]

EXAMPLE 2 – REVENUE FROM SEASONAL RESULTS

> 5.9.110.20   Company K makes and sells printed directories. K derives income primarily from advertisements placed in the directories and recognises it as revenue when control over the advertisements transfers to K's customers, which occurs as the directories are delivered to the buyers of the directories.

5.9.110.30   Any related expenses – e.g. costs to produce the directories in Example 2 – are capitalised as inventory to the extent permitted (see chapter 3.8) until the revenue and the related cost of sales is recognised on sale of the directories to the buyers. Expenses that cannot be capitalised as part of inventory or costs to fulfil a contract under IFRS 15 (see 4.2.270) are expensed as they are incurred. [*IAS 34.39*]

5.9.120 **Amortisation and depreciation charges**

5.9.120.10   Intangible assets with finite useful lives are often amortised on a straight-line basis. In our view, the recognition of amortisation on a straight-line basis means evenly throughout the year. We believe that it is not acceptable to allocate amortisation to interim periods on the basis of seasonal revenues when an entity's accounting policy is to amortise intangible assets on a straight-line basis. [*IAS 34.39, IE.B24*]

5.9.120.20   In our view, this treatment should also be applied to other assets that are depreciated on a straight-line basis – e.g. property, plant and equipment.

5.9.130 **Major planned periodic maintenance or overhauls**

5.9.130.10   Costs of planned or periodic maintenance or overhauls are not anticipated for interim reporting purposes unless the requirements to recognise a provision are met at the end of the interim period (see 3.12.30). Similarly, other planned or budgeted (but not yet incurred) costs – e.g. employee training costs – are not anticipated. [*IAS 34.IE.B2*]

EXAMPLE 3 – MAINTENANCE AND REPAIR COSTS

> 5.9.130.20   Company B produces canned food using fresh vegetables. B's annual reporting period ends on 31 December. Production takes place from 1 January to 30 June and most workers are temporary. From 1 July to 31 December the plant is closed and maintenance work is performed.
>
> 5.9.130.30   Direct costs (labour) are largely incurred over the first six-month period, but other significant costs are incurred during the second six-month period – e.g. cleaning and maintenance of the factory. Depreciation of the plant and machinery are direct costs of production.

5.9.130.40   Maintenance and repair costs are recognised as they are incurred. B does not recognise a provision for the costs to be incurred during the second half of the year at the end of the first six-month period. However, B considers whether these costs should be either expensed as they are incurred or capitalised and depreciated as a separate component of the plant as they are incurred (see 3.2.230 and 250).

5.9.130.50   Depreciation of the plant and machinery is allocated on a systematic basis that reflects the pattern in which the asset is used in production. In our view, a unit-of-production method may be appropriate for these assets in circumstances as described above. If so, then the annual depreciation charges related to these assets would be spread over the first six months of the year. We believe that the planned maintenance shut-down for the second six months means that a straight-line time-based charge over the 12 months is unlikely to be appropriate for such assets.

5.9.140   Assets and liabilities measured at fair value

5.9.140.10   The carrying amount of assets that are measured at fair value – e.g. investment property – is determined at the interim reporting date. The fair value assessment may involve a higher degree of estimation than is used for the annual financial statements. In our experience, external valuers are often not used at the interim reporting date and entities may use extrapolations based on the balance at the previous annual reporting date, if appropriate. [*IAS 34.IE.C7*]

5.9.140.20   The fair value of liabilities for cash-settled share-based payment transactions is remeasured at each reporting date (see 4.5.940), often involving the use of valuation techniques (see 4.5.750.10). In our view, in assessing whether an updated valuation is required to be performed at the interim reporting date, an entity should consider the complexity of the valuation and the sensitivity of the fair value to changes in key inputs (e.g. the share price and interest rate risk) used in the valuation technique. Although we do not believe that a completely new valuation is required at the interim reporting date in all cases, the most recent valuation should be updated such that measurement of the obligation is not materially different from the measurement that would result if a new valuation were obtained at the interim reporting date.

5.9.140.30   IAS 34 is clear that the fair value measurement (IFRS 13) disclosure requirements in 5.9.60.20 relate only to financial instruments, even though the related disclosure requirements of IFRS 13 also apply to other assets and liabilities. In our view, this is also the case on first application of IFRS 13 in an interim period. However, fair value disclosures related to non-financial assets and non-financial liabilities may be necessary in some circumstances (see 5.9.60.30–40). [*IAS 34.16A(j)*]

5.9.150   Employee benefits

5.9.150.10   Determining whether there is a need to remeasure the net defined benefit liability (asset) for interim reporting purposes requires judgement. The basic requirement of IAS 19 is that remeasurements are recognised in the period in which they arise. Therefore, the potential materiality of the remeasurements is assessed in determining whether an updated valuation is necessary. Materiality is assessed in relation to the interim financial statements (see 5.9.80.20). [*IAS 19.58, BC60, 34.23–25*]

5.9.150.20   Reliable measurement of the net defined benefit liability (asset) in the statement of financial position at an interim reporting date may sometimes be achieved by adjusting the opening balance of the net defined benefit liability (asset) for items of income and expense, such as:

- current service cost;
- net interest on the net defined benefit liability (asset);
- other employee benefit income and expenses for the period; and
- contributions to the plan.

5.9.150.30   Obtaining an updated actuarial valuation is therefore not necessarily required at each interim reporting date, although entities may choose to update their actuarial valuation more frequently than required by IFRS. [*IAS 34.IE.B9, IE.C4, 19.58, BC59*]

5.9.150.40   Notwithstanding the general requirement in 5.9.150.10, an updated measurement of plan assets and obligations is required when a plan amendment, curtailment or settlement is recognised. In addition, significant market fluctuations may trigger the need for an updated actuarial valuation to remeasure the net defined benefit liability (asset). [*IAS 34.IE.B9, 19.99*]

EXAMPLE 4A – REMEASUREMENTS ARE MATERIAL

5.9.150.50   Company C applies a discount rate of 6% to its net defined benefit liability and therefore in calculating the interest income on plan assets for the period (see 4.4.940). The actual return on plan assets for the interim period is 8%. C has concluded that the financial assumptions at the interim reporting date would not differ materially from those made at the previous reporting date.

5.9.150.60   In this example, C concludes that the impact of the difference of 2% between the actual return on plan assets and the rate used to calculate the interest income on the plan assets for the period is material to the net defined benefit liability. Accordingly, C remeasures its net defined benefit liability at the interim reporting date.

EXAMPLE 4B – REMEASUREMENTS IN AGGREGATE ARE NOT MATERIAL

5.9.150.70   Changing the fact pattern of Example 4A, C now determines that the liability discount rate at the interim reporting date has decreased. C assesses that, in aggregate, the remeasurements to the net defined benefit liability – i.e. to plan assets, to the defined benefit obligation and to any effect of the asset ceiling – are not material. As a consequence, C decides not to obtain an updated actuarial valuation.

5.9.150.80   In our view, if it is necessary to update the actuarial valuation at the interim reporting date and internal expertise is not available to do so, then an actuary should perform the updated valuation.

5.9.150.90   An updated valuation of the net defined benefit liability (asset) at the interim reporting date does not affect the measurement of service cost and net interest for the remainder of the current annual reporting period. Their measurement continues to be based on the assumptions at the prior annual reporting date (see 5.9.210.30). [*IAS 34.28–29, IE.B9, 19.BC63–BC64*]

5.9.160   Income tax expense

5.9.160.10   The income tax expense recognised in each interim period is based on the best estimate of the weighted-average annual income tax rate expected for the full year applied to the pre-tax income of the interim period. [*IAS 34.30(c), IE.B12–IE.B16*]

5.9.160.20   This effective rate reflects enacted or substantively enacted changes in tax rates at the interim reporting date that are expected to take effect later in the year. Amounts accrued in one interim period may need to be adjusted in a subsequent interim period if the estimate of the annual effective tax rate changes (see 5.9.210). The income tax expense for an interim period comprises both current tax and deferred tax.

5.9.160.30   Anticipated tax benefits from tax credits are generally reflected in computing the estimated annual effective tax rate when the credits are granted and calculated on an annual basis. However, if the credits relate to a one-off event, then they are recognised in the interim period in which the event occurs. [*IAS 34.IE.B19*]

5.9.160.35   A change in tax rate that is substantively enacted in an interim period is analogous to a tax credit granted in relation to a one-off event. Consistent with the treatment of tax on a one-off event, an entity may recognise the effect of the change immediately in the interim period in which the change occurs. However, another acceptable approach would be to spread the effect of a change in the tax rate over the remainder of the annual reporting period via an adjustment to the estimated annual effective income tax rate. [*IAS 34.30(c), IE.B19*]

5.9.160.40   If different income tax rates apply to different categories of income – e.g. capital gains – or to different tax jurisdictions, then a separate rate is applied to each category in the interim period, to the extent practicable. However, a weighted-average rate across jurisdictions and income categories may be used if it is a reasonable approximation of the effect of using more specific rates. [*IAS 34.IE.B14*]

EXAMPLE 5 – APPLYING DIFFERENT INCOME TAX RATES FOR DIFFERENT SUBSIDIARIES

5.9.160.50   Companies B and C – two subsidiaries within a group – have different effective tax rates. Although C's activities are not seasonal, B has seasonal activities. The expected results for the full year are as follows.

	B	C	TOTAL
Pre-tax profit (loss) – first six months	(100)	60	(40)
Pre-tax profit – second six months	200	60	260
Total profit before tax	100	120	220
Expected tax expense	(33)	(12)	(45)
Effective tax rate	**33%**	**10%**	**20.5%**

5.9.160.60   In our view, it is not appropriate to use an annual consolidated effective tax rate of 20.5% to estimate the interim period tax expense. This is because it is unlikely that this weighted-average rate will be a reasonable approximation of the result of using separate rates for each component, because of the impact of the seasonality of B's operations and the difference in the effective rates of B and C.

5.9.160.70   We believe that the effective rate for each subsidiary should be applied to interim pre-tax profit (loss) to determine the interim income tax expense for the group, as follows.

First six months	B	C	TOTAL
Pre-tax profit (loss)	(100)	60	(40)
Income tax benefit (expense)	33	(6)	27
Effective tax rate	**(33%)**	**10%**	**(67.5%)**

Second six months	B	C	TOTAL
Pre-tax profit	200	60	260
Income tax expense	(66)	(6)	(72)
Effective tax rate	**33%**	**10%**	**27.7%**

5.9.160.80   There may be cases when a reliable estimate of the annual effective tax rate cannot be made. That situation may arise, for example, when relatively small changes in estimated pre-tax accounting income would produce a large change in the estimated annual effective tax rate. In our view, if a reliable estimate of the annual effective tax rate cannot be made, then the actual effective rate based on a year-to-date actual tax calculation may represent the best estimate of the annual effective tax rate.

5.9.170   *Non-tax-deductible items*

5.9.170.10   The average annual effective tax rate is based on the estimated pre-tax profit (loss) for the year. It is unclear whether the estimated pre-tax profit (loss) for the year should be adjusted to exclude non-tax-deductible items.

5.9.170.20   In our view, an entity should choose an accounting policy, to be applied consistently, to calculate the annual effective tax rate.
- One approach is to use the estimated pre-tax income (loss) for the year without adjustment to exclude non-tax-deductible items.
- However, another acceptable approach in some circumstances is to calculate the effective income tax rate based on the estimated *taxable* profit for the interim period. Under this approach, the accounting profit is adjusted for non-tax-deductible items (e.g. non-tax-deductible amortisation). This approach treats identifiable non-tax-deductible expenses (or non-taxable income) in a similar way to different categories of income (e.g. capital gains) to which a different tax rate is applied. In our view, this approach would be appropriate only if the amounts are significant

and separately identifiable, different tax rates are applied to *each* separate category of income, and an entity applies the same level of analysis to identify, in each tax jurisdiction, items taxed at both higher and lower rates.

EXAMPLE 6 – NON-TAX-DEDUCTIBLE AMORTISATION OF INTANGIBLE ASSETS

5.9.170.30   Group X is required to prepare quarterly interim financial statements in accordance with IAS 34. To estimate the amount of its income tax expense for the first quarter of 2018, X has prepared annual projections of income and tax.

5.9.170.40   X has made the following assumptions.
- The average enacted tax rate applicable to the group is 40%.
- No temporary difference will exist at the annual reporting date.
- The only non-tax-deductible item at the end of the year will be amortisation of an intangible asset.

Estimation of the average effective tax rate

	2018
Projected annual profit before tax and amortisation	1,200
Projected annual amortisation	(400)
Projected annual pre-tax profit	800
Projected annual income tax expense (1,200 x 40%)	480

There are two different approaches to estimating both the average annual effective tax rate and the income tax expense for the interim periods.

	TAX RATE
Method 1: (480 / 800)	60%
Method 2: (480 / 1,200)	40%

5.9.170.50   Under Method 1, X does not adjust the reported income for the non-tax-deductible amortisation, resulting in the estimated average annual effective tax rate of 60%. This expected annual effective tax rate differs from the average enacted tax rate because of the significance of the amortisation.

5.9.170.60   Under Method 2, X calculates the average annual effective tax rate by adjusting the reported income for the effect of the amortisation that is not tax-deductible.

5.9.170.70   The following illustrates the impact of applying either Method 1 or 2 in the interim financial statements when pre-amortisation profit is earned unevenly during the year.

Income tax expense estimation

	Q1	Q2	Q3	Q4	2018
Profit before tax and amortisation (a)	50	350	400	400	1,200
Amortisation	(100)	(100)	(100)	(100)	(400)
Pre-tax profit (loss) (b)	(50)	250	300	300	800
Income tax benefit (expense) – Method 1: (b) x 60%	30	(150)	(180)	(180)	(480)
Effective tax rate					60%
Income tax expense – Method 2: (a) x 40%	(20)	(140)	(160)	(160)	(480)
Effective tax rate					60%

5.9.170.80   We believe that X should choose an accounting policy, to be applied consistently, to calculate the annual effective tax rate either:

- using the estimated pre-tax income (loss) for the year without adjustment to exclude non-tax-deductible items; in this example, an effective tax rate of 60% is applied to the pre-tax accounting profit during each interim period (Method 1); or
- in some circumstances, based on the estimated *taxable* profit for the interim period; in this example, an effective tax rate of 40% is applied to the accounting profit *after* the adjustment for the effect of the amortisation (Method 2).

5.9.180   *Tax losses*

5.9.180.10   Tax losses may be carried forward from previous reporting periods or may be created during an interim period and reversed in subsequent interim periods.

5.9.180.20   The effect of any tax loss carried forward, originating in previous or current reporting periods, is considered in computing the average annual effective tax rate. The general criteria for recognition of a deferred tax asset are applied at each interim reporting date (see 3.13.330). The entity assesses whether it is probable that taxable profits will be available in future periods to utilise the tax benefit. [*IAS 34.IE.B21–IE.B22*]

EXAMPLE 7 – TAX LOSSES EXPECTED TO BE UTILISED IN LATER INTERIM PERIODS

5.9.180.30   Company B incurs a tax loss in the first quarter as a result of poor trading conditions, but anticipates making a profit for the year and paying tax for the full year. B estimates its tax expense for the year taking into account the losses

> in the first period and utilisation thereof in later interim periods. The effective tax rate is applied to the pre-tax loss and a deferred tax asset is recognised at the end of the first quarter.

5.9.180.40   If a tax loss arising in an interim period is available for a tax loss carry-back, then the related benefit is reflected in the interim period in which the loss is incurred. [*IAS 34.IE.B20*]

5.9.180.50   If management's estimate of the recoverability of unused tax losses changes during an interim period, then in our view it is acceptable for this change to be reflected in calculating the expected annual effective tax rate and apportioned between the interim periods.

EXAMPLE 8 – ALLOCATING UNRECOGNISED TAX LOSSES

> **5.9.180.60**   Company X has unrecognised tax losses of 2,000 at the beginning of the year. Profit for the first half year is 400 and estimated profit for the second half year is 600 – totalling 1,000 for the year. At the half-year interim reporting date, X reassesses the recoverability of the tax losses and believes that the entire tax loss will be utilised in current and future periods. Therefore, previously unrecognised tax losses of 800 would be allocated to the first half year (2,000 x (400 / 1,000)).

5.9.180.70   The change in the estimate of recoverability of the tax loss carried forward may result in a change in the expected annual tax rate as compared with previous interim periods of the same financial year – e.g. if the entity reports quarterly. In this case, previous interim periods are not restated, but the cumulative adjustment (calculation applied in 5.9.180.60 less the amount which has been recognised in previous interim periods) is recognised in the current interim period. This is consistent with the accounting for a change in estimate and the requirement in IAS 34 that amounts reported in interim financial statements be measured on a year-to-date basis (see 5.9.160.10, 210.10 and 30).

5.9.190   Current and deferred tax

5.9.190.10   Although IAS 34 provides guidance on how the income tax expense should be determined, it does not specify how the total amount should be split between current and deferred tax. An example of an appropriate method may be to split current and deferred tax based on the relative proportions expected at the annual reporting date. In our experience, most entities do not show this split.

5.9.190.20   Because the income tax expense is calculated by applying the estimated annual effective tax rate to the pre-tax profit or loss for the interim period, the resulting deferred tax asset or liability does not reflect the effect of temporary differences that do not impact profit or loss – e.g. temporary differences on the revaluation of property, plant and equipment. In our view, if material temporary differences arise in an interim period from items of income and expense recognised directly in equity or in OCI, then deferred tax should also be calculated and recognised for these items. In our view, it would be appropriate in such cases to measure deferred tax using the same principles as would apply at the end of the annual period – i.e. based on the temporary difference between the item's tax base and its carrying amount, and the tax rate expected to apply when the underlying asset/liability is recovered/settled (see 3.13.380).

5.9.200 **Impairment**

5.9.200.10 Reviews for indicators of impairment and any resulting impairment tests are performed at the interim reporting date in the same manner as at the annual reporting date. [*IAS 34.IE.B35–IE.B36*]

5.9.210 **Estimates**

5.9.210.10 Although measurements in both annual and interim financial statements are often based on reasonable estimates, the preparation of interim financial statements will generally require a greater use of estimation than annual financial statements. Changes to accounting estimates are applied to the current and future periods and do not involve the restatement of results for either the prior annual or interim periods in the current period (see 2.8.110). [*IAS 34.41, IE.C1–IE.C9*]

EXAMPLE 9 – CHANGE IN ESTIMATED USEFUL LIFE

5.9.210.20 Company D prepares quarterly interim financial statements. The carrying amount of one of its assets is 1,000, with the asset's useful life initially estimated to be 10 years. The resulting depreciation expense is 100 for the year and 25 for the first quarter. There is a change to the estimated useful life of the asset, which, at the beginning of the second quarter, is revised to be five years from that date. In our view, the depreciable amount at the end of the first quarter of 975 should be depreciated over the remaining useful life of five years because the change in estimate is applied prospectively. Therefore, depreciation of 48.75 will be recognised for each quarter (975 / 20 quarters) over the remaining useful life of the asset.

5.9.210.30 The measurement of annual results is not affected by the frequency of an entity's financial reporting – i.e. annual, half-yearly or quarterly – and amounts reported in interim financial statements are measured on a year-to-date basis. However, as an exception, an entity is prohibited from reversing an impairment loss recognised in a previous interim period in respect of goodwill. This specific prohibition is not applied by analogy to other transactions and events. [*IAS 34.28, IFRIC 10.8–9*]

5.9.210.40 Generally, in our view separate transactions and events should be accounted for as such during an interim period.

EXAMPLE 10 – GAIN ON DISPOSAL FOLLOWING IMPAIRMENT OF ASSET

5.9.210.50 Company P recognises an impairment loss in its interim financial statements for the first quarter. The asset is sold during a subsequent interim period and a gain is realised. In this example, we believe that the impairment loss should not be reclassified and offset against the gain on disposal merely because they occurred in two interim periods of a single year.

5.9.210.60 In addition, the gain does not automatically lead to the reversal of the earlier impairment loss. Instead, each of the impairment loss, any possible reversal of that loss and the gain on disposal are dealt with separately, in accordance with individual requirements of the standard applicable to the underlying item. However, recognition of a gain shortly after a loss may be an indicator that either the event giving rise to the impairment has reversed or that the estimates used should be reconsidered and, if necessary, revised.

5.9.210.70   Certain impairment losses may not be reversed if they have been recognised in interim financial statements that state compliance either with IFRS or with IAS 34 (see 5.9.10.20–25 and 210.30). It is not clear whether the requirements described in 5.9.210.30 apply when no such interim financial statements are prepared, but when an entity has prepared selected information in respect of an earlier interim period in which that impairment was recognised. In our view, judgement is needed and it may be relevant to consider whether the users of the selected interim financial information would have concluded that the impairment has been recognised in accordance with IFRS. For example, if the interim financial information is described as being prepared in accordance with the recognition and measurement principles of IFRS and includes a financial measure that reflects the impairment loss, then we believe that it may be appropriate not to reverse the impairment loss in the financial statements of subsequent interim (or annual) periods.

5.9.220   ACCOUNTING POLICIES

5.9.220.10   The accounting policies followed in the interim financial statements will generally be the same as those applied in the previous annual financial statements, except for changes in accounting policies made during the current period. [*IAS 34.28*]

5.9.220.20   Any change in accounting policy on adoption of a new or revised standard is accounted for in accordance with the transitional requirements specified in the relevant IFRS if such guidance is provided. Otherwise, the change in accounting policy is accounted for in accordance with the general guidance on changes in accounting policies in IAS 8 (see 2.8.50). [*IAS 34.43*]

5.9.220.30   The recognition and measurement requirements of any new or revised standards are applied to all interim periods within the annual period in which the new standards first are adopted – unless the transitional requirements of a standard permit or require different transition. For example, if an entity's annual reporting period ends on 31 December 2018, then it applies any new standards that are effective for periods commencing on or after 1 January 2018 in its interim financial statements at 31 March 2018, 30 June 2018 and 30 September 2018. The entity does not apply earlier versions of the standards in the interim financial statements and then change to the new standards for the annual financial statements. [*IAS 34.43(a), 44–45*]

5.9.220.35   The presentation and disclosure requirements of any new or revised standards are not directly applicable to the preparation of condensed financial statements unless those new requirements amend IAS 34 itself. However, an entity is required to describe the nature and effect of any change, which may result in further disclosure, even in condensed financial statements. For example, an entity presented condensed financial statements for an interim period within the annual period for which IFRS 15 was first applied. IAS 34 sets out the disclosure requirements in respect of the disaggregation of revenue from contracts with customers in condensed financial statements (see 5.9.60.20). However, to explain the nature and effect of the change in the first year of application of IFRS 15, the entity included additional disclosures – e.g. information about its performance obligations. [*IFRS 15.119, IAS 34.16A(a), (g)*]

5.9.220.40   Changes in accounting policy adopted after the first interim period are normally presented by restating the financial statements for prior interim periods of the current financial year and comparative interim periods presented. This may occur, for example, if a new or revised standard is published during the year and the entity early adopts the new standard. [*IAS 34.43–45*]

5.10 Disclosure of interests in other entities

5.10   Disclosure of interests in other entities

CURRENTLY EFFECTIVE REQUIREMENTS

This publication reflects IFRS in issue at 1 August 2018, and the currently effective requirements cover annual periods beginning on 1 January 2018.

The requirements related to this topic are mainly derived from the following.

STANDARD	TITLE
IFRS 12	Disclosure of Interests in Other Entities

FORTHCOMING REQUIREMENTS

The currently effective requirements are affected by the following forthcoming requirements. They are highlighted with a # and the impact is explained in the accompanying boxed text at the references indicated.

In May 2017, the IASB issued IFRS 17 *Insurance Contracts*, which is effective for annual periods beginning on or after 1 January 2021. See 5.10.145. IFRS 17 is the subject of chapter 8.1A.

FUTURE DEVELOPMENTS

For this topic, there are no future developments.

5.10.10   OBJECTIVE AND SCOPE

5.10.20   Objective

5.10.20.10   The objective of IFRS 12 is to provide disclosure that helps users of the financial statements to evaluate:

- the nature of, and risks associated with, an entity's interests in other entities; and
- the effects of those interests on the entity's financial position, financial performance and cash flows. [*IFRS 12.1*]

5.10.20.20   To meet this objective, IFRS 12 requires disclosure of the significant judgements and assumptions that an entity has made in determining the nature of its interest in another entity or arrangement. It also contains extensive disclosure requirements for interests in other entities. These disclosures are illustrated in KPMG's *Guides to financial statements* series, including our *IFRS 12 supplement*. [*IFRS 12.2*]

5.10.20.30   If the disclosures required by IFRS 12, together with disclosures required by other standards, do not meet this objective, then an entity discloses additional information that is necessary to meet the objective. [*IFRS 12.3*]

5.10.30   Scope

5.10.30.10   IFRS 12 applies to an entity that has an interest in any of the following:

- a subsidiary (see chapter 2.5);
- an associate (see chapter 3.5);
- a joint arrangement – i.e. a joint operation or joint venture (see chapter 3.6); or
- an unconsolidated structured entity (see 5.10.190). [*IFRS 12.5*]

5.10.30.20   The disclosure requirements in IFRS 12 also apply to an entity's interests that are classified (or included in a disposal group that is classified) as held-for-sale, held-for-distribution or as a discontinued operation in accordance with IFRS 5 (see chapter 5.4). However, if an entity's interest in a subsidiary, joint venture or associate is classified (or included in a disposal group that is classified) as held-for-sale, then the entity is not required to provide summarised financial information (see 5.10.90.10 and 140.20–150). [*IFRS 12.5A, B17, BC8C*]

5.10.30.30   The following are generally excluded from the scope of IFRS 12; however, IFRS 12 disclosures are required for certain areas. [*IFRS 12.6*]

SCOPE EXEMPTION	EXCLUSIONS FROM SCOPE EXEMPTION
Post-employment benefit plans or other long-term employee benefit plans to which IAS 19 applies (see chapter 4.4). [*IFRS 12.6(a)*]	None.
An entity's separate financial statements prepared in accordance with IAS 27. [*IFRS 12.6(b)*]	Certain disclosures apply in the following cases. • The entity has interests in unconsolidated structured entities and an entity's separate financial statements are its only financial statements (see 5.10.240.30–70).

SCOPE EXEMPTION	EXCLUSIONS FROM SCOPE EXEMPTION
	• The entity is an investment entity that measures all of its subsidiaries at fair value through profit or loss (see 5.10.280.10).
An interest held by an entity that participates in, but does not have joint control of, a joint arrangement. [*IFRS 12.6(c)*]	The disclosures do apply if that interest results in significant influence over the arrangement (see 5.10.130) or is an interest in an unconsolidated structured entity (see 5.10.240).
An interest in another entity that is accounted for in accordance with IFRS 9. [*IFRS 12.6(d)*]	The disclosures do apply if that interest is an interest in a joint venture or associate that is measured at fair value through profit or loss (see 3.5.100 and 5.10.130), or is an interest in an unconsolidated structured entity (see 5.10.240).

5.10.30.40   The following is a summary of whether the different disclosures discussed in this chapter Ⓢ apply to different types of financial statements (see 2.1.90).

INTERESTS IN:	CONSOLIDATED FINANCIAL STATEMENTS	SEPARATE FINANCIAL STATEMENTS	INDIVIDUAL FINANCIAL STATEMENTS	FINANCIAL STATEMENTS OF AN INVESTMENT ENTITY	REFERENCE
Consolidated subsidiaries	✓	N/A	N/A	✓ [1]	5.10.80
Unconsolidated subsidiaries	N/A	✗	N/A	✓	5.10.290
Joint arrangements and associates	✓	✗	✓	✓ [2]	5.10.130 and 300
Consolidated structured entities	✓	N/A	N/A	✓ [1]	5.10.230
Unconsolidated structured entities	✓	✓ [3]	✓	✓ [4]	5.10.240 and 300

Notes
1.   To the extent that subsidiaries are consolidated (see 5.6.100).
2.   The disclosures are less extensive for investment entities.
3.   The standard is unclear about the scope of the disclosures in separate financial statements (see 5.10.240.30–70).
4.   In general, only to the extent that the structured entity is not consolidated because the investment entity does not have control over it.

5.10.40   **DEFINITION**

5.10.50   **Interests in other entities**

5.10.50.10   For the purpose of applying IFRS 12, 'interests in other entities' are contractual and non-contractual involvement that exposes an entity to variability of returns from the performance of the other entity. These interests may, for example, take the form of equity or debt instruments, but the definition is broad and interests can also comprise other forms of involvement, such as the provision of funding, liquidity support, credit enhancement and/or guarantees. However, an interest in another entity does not exist solely as a result of a typical customer-supplier relationship. [*IFRS 12.A*]

5.10.50.20   Interests in another entity are the basis for many of the disclosures in IFRS 12. Understanding the purpose and design of the other entity may assist in identifying these interests. The reporting entity considers the risks that the other entity was designed to create and to pass on to the reporting entity and other parties. These concepts are discussed in chapter 2.5 in the context of consolidating subsidiaries (see 2.5.50 and 230). [*IFRS 12.B7*]

5.10.50.30   In addition, IFRS 12 requires an entity to provide disclosure about its relationship with unconsolidated structured entities that it sponsors even if it does not have an interest in them at the reporting date (see 5.10.270). [*IFRS 12.27–28*]

5.10.60   **Significant judgements and assumptions**

5.10.60.10   An entity discloses information about the significant judgements and assumptions that management has made in determining whether it has control, joint control or significant influence over another entity/arrangement, and in determining whether a joint arrangement structured through a separate vehicle is a joint venture or joint operation (see 3.6.70). These disclosures may also be relevant when facts and circumstances cause an entity to change its conclusion about the degree of control/influence over an investee during the reporting period. [*IFRS 12.7–8*]

5.10.60.20   Disclosures may be required in the following circumstances, which are not exhaustive:
- the entity does not control an investee even though it holds more than half of its voting rights;
- the entity controls an investee even though it holds less than half of its voting rights;
- the entity is an agent or principal;
- the entity does not have significant influence over an investee even though it holds 20 percent or more of its voting rights; and
- the entity has significant influence over an investee even though it holds less than 20 percent of its voting rights. [*IFRS 12.9*]

5.10.70   **Aggregation**

5.10.70.10   The disclosures required by IFRS 12 may be aggregated for interests in similar entities, with the method of aggregation being disclosed. A quantitative and qualitative analysis, taking into account the different risk and return characteristics of each entity, is made in order to determine the aggregation level. IFRS 12 gives the following examples of aggregation levels: by nature of activities, by industry or by geography for each of subsidiaries, joint ventures, joint operations, associates and unconsolidated structured entities. [*IFRS 12.B2–B6*]

5.10.70.20   However, in respect of the disclosure of summarised financial information for interests in *material* joint ventures and associates (see 5.10.140.20–130), the IFRS Interpretations Committee clarified that those disclosures need to be provided for each investee – i.e. they cannot be aggregated. [*IU 01-15*]

5.10.80   INTERESTS IN CONSOLIDATED SUBSIDIARIES

5.10.80.10   The disclosures in this section apply to an entity's consolidated financial statements, but do not apply to an investment entity's investments in unconsolidated subsidiaries in those financial statements (see 5.6.10.10).

5.10.80.20   An entity discloses information that helps users of its consolidated financial statements to understand the composition of the group and the interests of NCI in the group's activities and cash flows. This includes:
- the nature and extent of significant restrictions on its ability to access or use assets, or to settle liabilities of the group (see 5.10.100);
- the consequences of changes in its ownership interests in a subsidiary while retaining control (see 5.10.110);
- the consequences of losing control of a subsidiary (see 5.10.120); and
- the nature of, and exchanges in, the risks associated with the interests in consolidated structured entities (see 5.10.230). [*IFRS 12.10*]

5.10.80.30   If the financial statements of a subsidiary used in preparing the consolidated financial statements are as at a date or for a period that is different from that of the consolidated financial statements, then the entity discloses the reporting date of that subsidiary and the reason for using a different date or period. [*IFRS 12.11*]

5.10.90   Non-controlling interests

5.10.90.10   An entity discloses the following for each of its subsidiaries that has material NCI:
- the name of the subsidiary;
- its principal place of business, and country of incorporation (if this is different);
- the proportion of ownership interests held by NCI and, if it is different, the proportion of voting rights held;
- the profit or loss allocated to NCI during the reporting period;
- accumulated NCI at the reporting date; and
- summarised financial information about the subsidiary. [*IFRS 12.12*]

5.10.90.20   The summarised financial information may include, but is not limited to, current assets, non-current assets, current liabilities, non-current liabilities, revenue, profit or loss and total comprehensive income. The amounts disclosed are before intra-group eliminations. An entity also discloses dividends paid to NCI. [*IFRS 12.B10–B11*]

5.10.90.30   IFRS 12 does not provide a specific materiality threshold or approaches for determining the scope of subsidiaries with material NCI. The IFRS Interpretations Committee noted that the assessment of materiality is based on the consolidated financial information of the reporting entity. In making this assessment, both quantitative considerations (i.e. the size of the subsidiary) and qualitative considerations (i.e. the nature of the subsidiary) are considered. The Committee also noted that this judgement is made separately for each subsidiary or subgroup that has material NCI. [*IU 01-15*]

5.10.90.40   In a discussion about disclosing the profit or loss allocated to NCI and accumulated NCI (see 5.10.90.10), the Committee noted that an entity applies judgement in determining whether the disclosures are made on the basis of subgroups within the reporting entity (group) or for individual subsidiaries within those subgroups. [*IFRS 12.12(e)–(f), IU 01-15*]

5.10.90.50   In a discussion about disclosing summarised financial information (see 5.10.90.10), the Committee noted that the disclosures are prepared from the perspective of the reporting entity. For example, if the subsidiary was acquired in a business combination, then the amounts disclosed include the effects of acquisition accounting (see chapter 2.6). This means that the disclosures are consistent with the information included in the consolidated financial statements of the reporting entity. [*IFRS 12.12(g), B10(b)–B11, IU 01-15*]

5.10.90.60   The Committee did not note any specific approaches to disclosing summarised financial information about subsidiaries that have material NCI. It observed that an entity applies judgement in determining whether the disclosures are made on the basis of the subgroup or for individual subsidiaries within that subgroup. However, it noted that:
- transactions within the subgroup are eliminated when an entity prepares the information on a subgroup basis; and
- the information includes transactions between the subgroup or subsidiary (depending on the level at which the disclosures are made) and other members of the reporting entity's group – i.e. before eliminations. [*IFRS 12.12(g), B10(b)–B11, IU 01-15*]

EXAMPLE 1 – SUBSIDIARIES WITH MATERIAL NCI

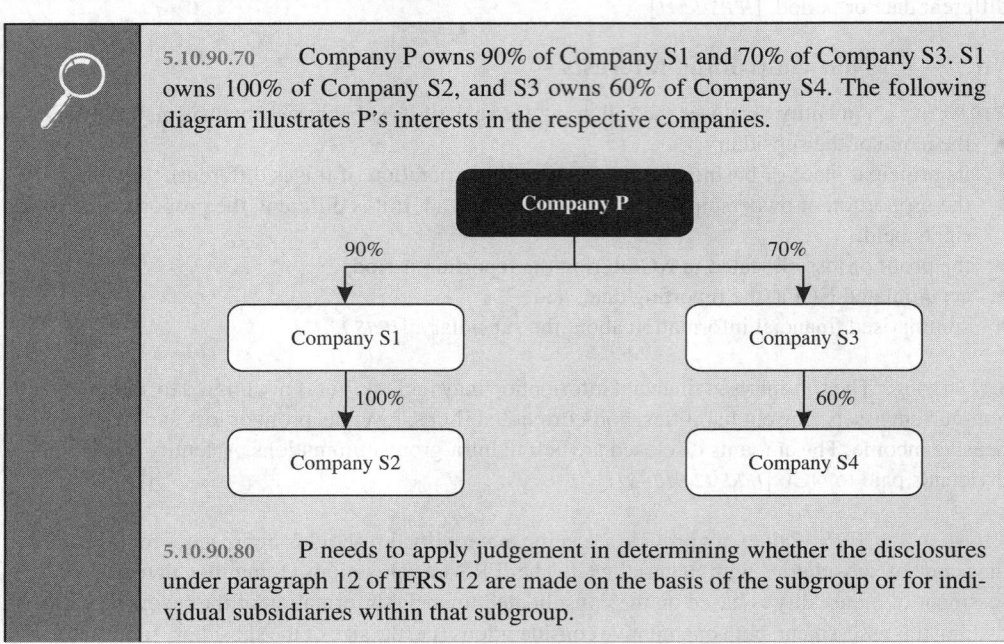

5.10.90.70   Company P owns 90% of Company S1 and 70% of Company S3. S1 owns 100% of Company S2, and S3 owns 60% of Company S4. The following diagram illustrates P's interests in the respective companies.

5.10.90.80   P needs to apply judgement in determining whether the disclosures under paragraph 12 of IFRS 12 are made on the basis of the subgroup or for individual subsidiaries within that subgroup.

5.10.90.90   Because there is a single, 10% NCI in the S1 subgroup, the subgroup approach for S1 (and therefore S2) results in a straightforward disclosure to provide and for the user to understand.

5.10.90.100   Conversely, there are two levels of NCI in the S3 subgroup: 30% in S3 itself and an additional 40% in S4, making a total of 58% in S4 (30% + 40% x 70%). Accordingly, P cannot provide the disclosure on the basis of a simple, single-NCI proportion in the subgroup. It needs to provide disclosures in one of the following ways, as it considers appropriate to meet users' information needs:
- in relation to a 30% NCI in the S3 subgroup and, separately, the further 28% NCI in S4; or
- on the individual subsidiary basis – i.e. in relation to a 30% NCI in S3 alone and separately for a 58% NCI in S4.

5.10.90.110   A question arises about whether the NCI disclosures apply to puttable instruments or instruments that impose on the issuing entity an obligation to deliver to another party a pro rata share of net assets of the entity only on liquidation, given that they are classified as equity in the financial statements of the issuer. In our view, the disclosures in respect of NCI do not apply to such instruments. Although they are classified as equity in the financial statements of the issuer if certain conditions are met (see 7.3.70), this presentation is an exception to the general principles for liability and equity classification. Such instruments are not equity instruments – and therefore are not NCI as defined (see 2.5.450.10) – and as a consequence are classified as financial liabilities in the consolidated financial statements.

5.10.100   Nature and extent of significant restrictions

5.10.100.10   An entity discloses significant restrictions on its ability to access or use assets or to settle liabilities of the group, and the carrying amount of the assets and liabilities to which those restrictions apply. The following are examples of such restrictions, which might be statutory, contractual or regulatory:
- restrictions on the ability of a parent or its subsidiaries to transfer cash or other assets to (from) other entities within the group; and
- guarantees that restrict dividends from being paid, or loans and advances being made (repaid) within the group. [*IFRS 12.10(b)(i), 13(a), (c)*]

5.10.100.20   A significant restriction requiring disclosure might arise from the protective rights of NCI – e.g. if the parent needs to settle the liabilities of a subsidiary before settling its own liabilities, or if NCI approval is required either to access the assets or to settle the liabilities of a subsidiary. [*IFRS 12.13(b)*]

5.10.110   Changes in ownership interests while retaining control

5.10.110.10   If an entity's ownership interests in a subsidiary change without it losing control – e.g. through a partial disposal of ownership interests (see 2.5.560) – then it discloses a schedule that shows the effects of such a change on the equity attributable to owners of the parent. [*IFRS 12.10(b)(iii), 18*]

5.10.120   Losing control

5.10.120.10   If an entity loses control of a subsidiary during the reporting period (see 2.5.760), then it discloses the following information:
- the gain or loss on the loss of control;
- the portion of that gain or loss attributable to measuring any retained investment at fair value; and
- if it is not presented separately, then the line item(s) in profit or loss in which the gain or loss is recognised. [*IFRS 12.10(b)(iv), 19*]

5.10.130   INTERESTS IN JOINT ARRANGEMENTS AND ASSOCIATES

5.10.130.10   An entity discloses information that helps users of its financial statements to evaluate the nature of its interests in joint arrangements and associates. This includes:
- the nature, extent and financial effects of its interests in such investees, including the nature and effects of contractual relationships with the other investors with joint control or significant influence; and
- the nature of, and changes in, the risks associated with its interests in such investees. [*IFRS 12.20*]

5.10.130.20   The following is a summary of how the key disclosures discussed in this section apply to different types of investees.

DISCLOSURES:	JOINT OPERATIONS	JOINT VENTURES	ASSOCIATES	REFERENCE
Significant restrictions	✗	✓	✓	5.10.130.30
Descriptive information	✓	✓	✓	5.10.140.10
Summarised financial information	✗	✓ (1)	✓ (1)	5.10.140.20–150
Immaterial investees	✗	✓	✓	5.10.160
Commitments	✗	✓	✗	5.10.170
Contingencies	✗	✓	✓	5.10.170

Note
1.   The disclosures are more extensive for joint ventures.

5.10.130.30   An entity discloses significant restrictions on the ability of a *joint venture or associate* to transfer cash dividends to the entity or to repay loans or advances made by the entity. These restrictions might arise from borrowing arrangements, regulatory requirements and/or contractual arrangements between investors. [*IFRS 12.22(a)*]

5.10.130.40   If the financial statements used in applying equity accounting are as at a date or for a period that is different from that of the consolidated or individual financial statements (see 3.5.200), then the entity discloses the reporting date of the financial statements of that investee, and the reason for using a different date or period. [*IFRS 12.22(b)*]

5.10.130.50   If an entity has ceased recognising its share of losses of an equity-accounted *joint venture or associate* (see 3.5.420), then it discloses its unrecognised share of losses of the investee, both for the reporting period and cumulatively. [*IFRS 12.22(c)*]

5.10.140   Nature, extent and financial effects of interests#

5.10.140.10   An entity discloses the following for each material *joint arrangement and associate*:
- the name of the investee;
- the nature of its relationship with the investee;
- its principal place of business, and country of incorporation (if this is different); and
- the proportion of ownership interests or participating shares held by the entity in the investee and, if it is different, the proportion of voting rights held. [*IFRS 12.21(a)*]

5.10.140.20   An entity discloses the following for each material *joint venture and associate*:
- whether the investee is accounted for using the equity method or at fair value (see 3.5.90);
- summarised financial information about the investee (see 5.10.140.30–130); and
- the fair value of the investee if it is equity accounted and has a quoted market price. [*IFRS 12.21(b)*]

5.10.140.30   The IFRS Interpretations Committee clarified that the disclosure of summarised financial information for interests in *material* joint ventures and associates needs to be provided for each investee – i.e. the disclosures cannot be aggregated (see 5.10.70). [*IU 01-15*]

5.10.140.40   An investment entity (see chapter 5.6) is not required to disclose summarised financial information. [*IFRS 12.21A*]

5.10.140.50   Summarised financial information for each material *joint venture and associate* includes, but is not limited to, current assets, non-current assets, current liabilities, non-current liabilities, revenue, profit or loss from continuing operations, post-tax profit or loss from discontinued operations, OCI and total comprehensive income. An entity also discloses dividends received from the investee. [*IFRS 12.B12*]

5.10.140.60   As part of the summarised financial information, an entity also discloses the following for each material *joint venture*:
- cash and cash equivalents;
- current financial liabilities, excluding trade and other payables and provisions;
- non-current financial liabilities, excluding trade and other payables and provisions;
- depreciation and amortisation;
- interest income;
- interest expense; and
- income tax expense or income. [*IFRS 12.B13*]

5.10.140.70   Except as noted in 5.10.140.120, the summarised financial information comprises amounts included in the IFRS financial statements of the joint venture or associate. The IFRS Interpretations Committee observed that these are the consolidated financial statements of the investee (if it has subsidiaries) or the individual financial statements of the investee (if it does not have subsidiaries). This means that the amounts relate to the whole investee and not the reporting entity's interest. [*IFRS 12.B14, IU 01-15*]

5.10.140.80 The amounts include adjustments made by the entity in applying the equity method – e.g. fair value adjustments made as part of the acquisition accounting. There is no guidance on whether these adjustments should be made on a net basis (reflecting only the reporting entity's interest) or grossed up to relate to the investee as a whole. The latter approach is illustrated in the *IFRS 12 supplement* forming part of KPMG's *Guides to financial statements* series. [*IFRS 12.B14*]

5.10.140.90 In addition, there is no guidance on how the following are dealt with in the summarised financial information:
- goodwill that forms part of the carrying amount of the equity-accounted investee (see 3.5.270); and
- inter-company eliminations – e.g. unrealised profit (see 3.5.430).

5.10.140.100 In the *IFRS 12 supplement* forming part of KPMG's *Guides to financial statements* series, these items are presented as follows.
- Goodwill is included in the reconciliation (see 5.10.140.110), because the determination of goodwill is very specific to the particular transaction between the parties.
- Inter-company eliminations are also included in the reconciliation. An alternative would be to present the summarised financial information after such eliminations because they are adjustments made in applying equity accounting (see 5.10.140.80).

5.10.140.110 An entity also presents a reconciliation of the summarised information presented to the carrying amount of its interest in the joint venture or associate in the statement of financial position. [*IFRS 12.B14(b)*]

5.10.140.120 The summarised financial information may be presented on the basis of the joint venture's or associate's financial statements, with appropriate disclosure of the basis of preparation, if:
- the investee is measured at fair value through profit or loss (see 3.5.100); or
- the investee does not prepare IFRS financial statements and the preparation of such statements would be impracticable or cause undue cost. [*IFRS 12.B15*]

5.10.140.130 The IFRS Interpretations Committee also noted that the summarised financial information needs to be disclosed even if the investee is listed and the local regulator prevents the investor from disclosing this information until the investee has released its own financial statements. This is because there is no exception in IFRS 12 that permits the non-disclosure of this information. [*IU 01-15*]

5.10.140.140 Summarised financial information is not required for interests in *joint operations*.

5.10.140.150 Uniform accounting policies for like transactions and events in similar circumstances are used in preparing the investor's financial statements, with an exception for insurance contracts (see 3.5.200.40 and 8.1.60). An equity-accounted investee may have accounting policies for items that do not apply to the investor. If disclosure of the accounting policies of the investee is considered necessary for an understanding of equity-accounted earnings, or the carrying amount of such investees in the statement of financial position, then in our view this information should be included in the accounting policy for equity-accounted investees.

5.10.150 Joint ventures and associates classified as held-for-sale

5.10.150.10   If an entity's interest (or a portion thereof) in a *joint venture or associate* is classified as held-for-sale in accordance with IFRS 5 (see chapter 5.4), then the entity is not required to disclose summarised financial information for that investee. [*IFRS 12.B17*]

5.10.160 Immaterial joint ventures and associates

5.10.160.10   An entity discloses the aggregate carrying amount of its interests in all individually immaterial *joint ventures* that are equity accounted and, separately, the aggregate carrying amount of its interests in all individually immaterial *associates* that are equity accounted. [*IFRS 12.B16*]

5.10.160.20   An entity also discloses – for all individually immaterial *joint ventures* together and, separately, for all individually immaterial *associates* together – its aggregated share of the following:
- profit or loss from continuing operations;
- post-tax profit or loss from discontinued operations;
- OCI; and
- total comprehensive income. [*IFRS 12.21(c), B16*]

5.10.160.30   An investment entity (see chapter 5.6) is not required to disclose this information. [*IFRS 12.21A*]

5.10.170 Commitments and contingencies

5.10.170.10   If an entity has unrecognised commitments relating to its interests in *joint ventures* that might give rise to a future outflow of cash or other resources, then it discloses the total commitments. Examples include commitments to provide financial support or to acquire ownership interests if a future event occurs/does not occur. [*IFRS 12.23(a), B18–B19*]

5.10.170.20   If an entity has contingent liabilities that require disclosure in accordance with IAS 37 (see 3.12.875), then the amounts related to the entity's interests in *joint ventures or associates* are disclosed separately from other contingent liabilities. This includes the entity's share of contingent liabilities incurred jointly with other investors with joint control or significant influence. [*IFRS 12.23(b)*]

5.10.180 Goodwill

5.10.180.10   On an ongoing basis, the carrying amount of goodwill allocated to an equity-accounted investee may require separate disclosure if that investee is considered to be a separate CGU in accordance with IAS 36 (see 3.10.870). The separate disclosure of goodwill may also be relevant for the reconciliation of the summarised financial information of associates and joint ventures to their carrying amount in the entity's consolidated or individual financial statements (see 5.10.140.90–110). [*IFRS 12.B14(b)(i)*]

5.10.190	**STRUCTURED ENTITIES**
5.10.200	**Overview of disclosure requirements**

5.10.200.10   The following disclosures are required under IFRS 12 in respect of structured entities.

DISCLOSURES	REFERENCE IN IFRS 12	REFERENCE IN INSIGHTS
The nature of and changes in the risks associated with its interests in *consolidated* structured entities	IFRS 12.10(b)(ii), 14–17	5.10.230
Information about its interests in *unconsolidated* structured entities	IFRS 12.26, 29–31, B25–B26	5.10.240–260
The sponsorship of an unconsolidated structured entity in which there is no interest at the reporting date	IFRS 12.25, 27–28	5.10.270

(S) 5.10.200.20   As noted in 5.10.30.30, IFRS 12 does not generally apply to separate financial statements. However, if an entity has interests in unconsolidated structured entities and prepares separate financial statements as its only financial statements, then the disclosure requirements in respect of *unconsolidated* structured entities apply (see 5.10.240), although the scope of those disclosures is unclear (see 5.10.240.30–70). [*IFRS 12.6(b)*]

5.10.200.30   The discussion in 5.10.210–220 is focused on determining the population of entities that are in the scope of the disclosure requirements discussed in 5.10.230–240.

5.10.210	**Definition and characteristics**

5.10.210.10   A 'structured entity' is an entity that has been designed so that voting or similar rights are not the dominant factor in deciding who controls the entity – e.g. when any voting rights relate only to administrative tasks and the relevant activities are directed by means of contractual arrangements. [*IFRS 12.A, B21*]

5.10.210.20   To supplement the definition in 5.10.210.10, IFRS 12 indicates that a structured entity often (i.e. not always) has some or all of the following characteristics:
- restricted activities;
- a narrow and well-defined objective;
- insufficient equity to permit the structured entity to finance its activities without subordinated financial support; and/or
- financing in the form of multiple contractually linked instruments issued to investors that create concentrations of credit or other risks (tranches). [*IFRS 12.B22*]

5.10.210.30   Although these characteristics are helpful in identifying structured entities, they may not be definitive in all cases.

5.10.210.40   Examples of entities with a narrow and well-defined objective that may be structured entities include those designed to effect a tax-efficient lease, carry out R&D activities, provide a source of capital or funding to an entity or provide investment opportunities for investors by passing on risks and rewards associated with the assets of the structured entity to investors. [*IFRS 12.B22(b)*]

5.10.210.50   Other examples of structured entities include securitisation vehicles, asset-backed financings and some investment funds. [*IFRS 12.B23*]

5.10.210.60   In assessing whether an investee is a structured entity, an investor considers how the power assessment was made under IFRS 10 (see 2.5.20–400), irrespective of the outcome of that analysis. This is because IFRS 10 requires entities to conduct the power analysis differently depending on whether voting rights are the dominant factor in assessing who controls the investee. Therefore, the analysis of the investee under IFRS 10 is directly relevant to a decision under IFRS 12 about whether the investee is a structured entity.

- If the decision was made on the basis of who held a majority of voting rights, or less than a majority but with de facto power over the investee (see 2.5.130), then the investee is *not* a structured entity.
- If the control analysis required a more in-depth consideration, such as of the purpose and design of the investee, and evidence of the practical ability to direct the relevant activities of the investee etc (see 2.5.170), then it is more likely that the investee is a structured entity.

EXAMPLE 2 – IDENTIFYING STRUCTURED ENTITIES – DEFINITION

5.10.210.70   Company C grants share options to its employees, subject to a service condition (see 4.5.380). C establishes Trust T for the purpose of acquiring and holding the shares that will be used to settle C's obligation under the share-based payment scheme (see 4.5.2390).

5.10.210.80   C concludes that it has power over the relevant activities of T because it has some rights, a special relationship and evidence of the practical ability to direct, as follows.[1]

- C can make and/or withdraw T's funding.
- In practice, T's relevant activities are carried out to suit C. This is indirect evidence of the practical ability to direct.
- T depends on the loan from C to acquire the shares and therefore to fund its operations; T's activities are conducted on behalf of C to settle its obligation under the share-based payment scheme; and C's exposure to returns from the loan and the residual – in fact, all of the variability of T – is greater than its voting or similar rights.

5.10.210.90   Because the power conclusion was *not* made on the basis of who holds the majority of voting rights, C concludes that T is a structured entity.

Note
1.   This example is based on Example 14 in chapter 2.5. That example details the facts supporting the consolidation conclusion, which are not repeated here.

5.10.210.100   Although in many cases structured entities are similar to the types of entities classified as special purpose entities (SPEs) under SIC-12, which was superseded by IFRS 10 and IFRS 12, the definition of a structured entity is broad. As a result, depending on the facts and circumstances, it is possible for an operating company to be classified as a structured entity.

5.10.210.110   Under IFRS 12, a structured entity is an *entity* that meets certain criteria (see 5.10.210.10). Accordingly, because a silo is considered 'a deemed separate entity', in our view a group of unincorporated assets and liabilities that is a silo and also meets the definition of a structured entity should be treated as a structured entity. However, if a group of unincorporated assets and liabilities is not a silo, then it will not be considered 'an entity' and therefore we believe that it should not be considered a structured entity even if the definition of a structured entity is otherwise met.

5.10.220   *'Similar' rights*

5.10.220.10   As noted in 5.10.210.10, a structured entity is an entity that has been designed so that voting or 'similar rights' are not the dominant factor in deciding who controls the entity. Therefore, it is important to understand the meaning of 'similar' rights.

5.10.220.20   In our view, an example of rights that are similar to voting rights is rights to appoint or remove members of an investee's key management personnel who have the ability to direct the relevant activities.

5.10.220.30   Conversely, in our view voting or similar rights would not generally include rights that derive from a contract that gives the holder the ability to direct the relevant activities of the investee (see 2.5.170). Such a contract might apply directly or indirectly as an override of the usual power that is derived from the voting rights of investors.

5.10.220.40   The approach in 5.10.220.10–30 focuses on how the investee is governed in order to consider what similar rights are; it does not focus on whether the activities of the investee are those of a conventional operating entity – e.g. a manufacturing company.

5.10.220.50   We believe that the following are examples of entities governed by voting or similar rights – i.e. they are *not* structured entities.
- A conventional operating company in which shareholders exercise voting rights, which determine the party that has power over the company.
- A joint arrangement in which the partners exercise voting rights, which determines that the parties have joint control. This is the case even if there are non-participating investors or if the voting rights held by the partners are disproportionate to their share of returns. Joint arrangements are the subject of chapter 3.6.

5.10.220.60   Conversely, the activities of the structured entities noted in 5.10.210.40–50 – e.g. securitisation vehicles, asset-backed financings and structures designed to effect a tax-efficient lease – are typically governed by a contract that specifies the rights and obligations of each party in the structure; they would not be governed by voting or similar rights.

5.10.230   Consolidated structured entities

5.10.230.10   In its consolidated financial statements, an entity discloses, if they are material, the terms of any contractual arrangements with consolidated structured entities that could require the parent or its subsidiaries to provide financial support. This explicitly includes events or circumstances that could expose the entity to loss. [*IFRS 12.14*]

5.10.230.20   If an entity in the group has provided financial or other support without having a con-tractual obligation – e.g. purchasing assets of or instruments issued by the structured entity without a contractual obligation to do so – then the type and amount of, and the reasons for, the support are disclosed in the consolidated financial statements. An entity also discloses any current intentions to provide financial or other support to a consolidated structured entity. These disclosures include providing assistance in obtaining financial support. [*IFRS 12.15, 17*]

5.10.230.30   If a parent or any of its subsidiaries has provided non-contractual financial or other support to a previously unconsolidated structured entity, which has resulted in the entity controlling the structured entity, then the entity discloses the factors that were relevant in reaching this conclusion. [*IFRS 12.16*]

5.10.230.40   The term 'support' is used broadly in IFRS 12. Therefore, entities need to analyse the kinds of support that they provide and may need to establish a monitoring system to obtain the information necessary to comply with the disclosure requirements.

5.10.240   Unconsolidated structured entities

5.10.240.10   If an entity has an interest (see 5.10.50) in an unconsolidated structured entity at the reporting date – e.g. a contract to provide management services – then it provides specific disclosures to help users of the financial statements to understand the nature and extent of its interests and to evaluate the nature of, and changes in, the risks in respect of its interests in unconsolidated structured entities. [*IFRS 12.24*]

5.10.240.20   The following is a summary of how the disclosures discussed in this section apply to different types of financial statements.

TYPES OF FINANCIAL STATEMENTS	APPLICABILITY OF DISCLOSURES
Consolidated financial statements	All disclosures apply.
Separate financial statements	IFRS 12 is unclear about the scope of the disclosures (see 5.10.240.30–70).
Individual financial statements	All disclosures apply.
Financial statements of an investment entity	Provided that the disclosures in 5.10.290 are made, the disclosures in this section apply only to the extent that the structured entity is not consolidated because the investment entity does not have control over it.

5.10.240.30   IFRS 12 is unclear about the population of structured entities that are considered 'uncon- solidated' in the separate financial statements: all structured entities, because none are consolidated in the separate financial statements; or only those structured entities that are not consolidated because they are not controlled by the reporting entity. [*IFRS 12.6(b), BC69*]

5.10.240.40   In our view, either of the following approaches is acceptable.
● *Approach 1:* An unconsolidated structured entity is a structured entity that the parent does not consoli-date regardless of the reason – i.e. *including* when the parent controls the structured entity but is not

preparing consolidated financial statements. This approach follows a plain reading of paragraph 6(b) of IFRS 12 – i.e. all subsidiaries are unconsolidated in a set of separate financial statements.

- *Approach 2:* An unconsolidated structured entity is a structured entity that the parent does not consolidate because it does not have control – i.e. *excluding* when the parent controls the structured entity but is not preparing consolidated financial statements. This approach is based on the IASB's intention of focusing on 'an entity's exposure to risk from interests in structured entities that the entity rightly does not consolidate because it does not control them'. To give effect to that intention, paragraph 6(b) is interpreted as a cumulative test, as follows.
  - Does the entity have interests in structured entities that would not be consolidated in any consolidated financial statements?
  - If yes, does the entity prepare only separate financial statements?
  - If yes, then disclosures are required. [*IFRS 12.6(b), BC69*]

Ⓢ EXAMPLE 3 – UNCONSOLIDATED STRUCTURED ENTITIES – INTERMEDIATE PARENT

5.10.240.50   Company IP, a wholly owned subsidiary of Ultimate Parent UP, is an intermediate parent that has two subsidiaries: S1, a manufacturing company that is not a structured entity; and S2, a structured entity. UP prepares consolidated financial statements for the group.

5.10.240.60   IP is exempt from preparing consolidated financial statements because UP prepares consolidated financial statements and all of the other exemption conditions are met (see 2.1.100). Therefore, IP presents only separate financial statements.

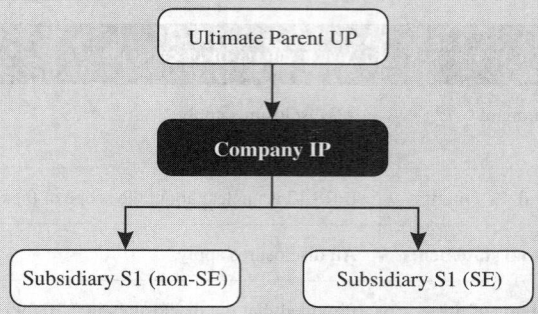

5.10.240.70   In this example, IP decides to adopt Approach 2 in 5.10.240.40 in respect of S2, and therefore does not disclose information about S2. This is on the basis that the non-consolidation of S2 is solely because IP is exempt from preparing consolidated financial statements, rather than because IP has concluded that S2 is not its subsidiary.

5.10.250   *Nature of interests*

5.10.250.10   IFRS 12 requires an entity to disclose general information about its interests in unconsolidated structured entities including, but not limited to, the nature, purpose, size and activities of the structured entity and how the structured entity is financed. [*IFRS 12.26*]

5.10.250.20   Judgement is required in assessing the appropriate level of detail so that the disclosure meets the objective of providing meaningful information to users of the entity's financial statements. [*IFRS 12.24*]

5.10.250.30   In our view, the key driver of the required disclosures is the entity's consideration of the purpose and design of the unconsolidated structured entity. The reporting entity considers the risks that the other entity was designed to create and to pass on to the reporting entity and other parties. These concepts are discussed in chapter 2.5 in the context of consolidating subsidiaries (see 2.5.50 and 230).

5.10.250.40   IFRS 12 does not specify how to measure the size of a structured entity. Therefore, management applies its judgement in determining an appropriate measure of size that provides sufficient and meaningful information about the assets held by unconsolidated structured entities. Example measurements that might be appropriate include the notional amounts of notes issued or of interest rate swaps for securitisation vehicles, or the net assets or funds under management for investment funds.

5.10.250.50   If an entity is exposed to variability of returns from its involvement with an unconsolidated structured entity through involvement that is unrelated to the purpose and design of the structured entity – e.g. in a typical customer-supplier relationship – then we believe that it is less likely that disclosure of the interest will be required (see 5.10.50).

EXAMPLE 4 – TYPES OF INTERESTS IN STRUCTURED ENTITIES

5.10.250.60   Structured Entity SE is set up by Real Estate Fund F and Property Manager M, a third party, for a specific project. The long-term purpose of SE is to acquire a tenanted commercial office building with a view to holding the building for rentals and capital appreciation.

5.10.250.70   Under IFRS 10, F concludes that it has control of SE (see 2.5.20). M's activities, acting as the agent of F, will include sourcing tenants and negotiating lease contracts, and providing ongoing building operations, maintenance and management services. M's management fees are based on the performance of SE.

5.10.250.80   SE contracts with Company Z to acquire the land on which the commercial office building will be constructed, and to design and construct the commercial office building. Z will receive payment over the following two years, but Z is not otherwise involved in SE.

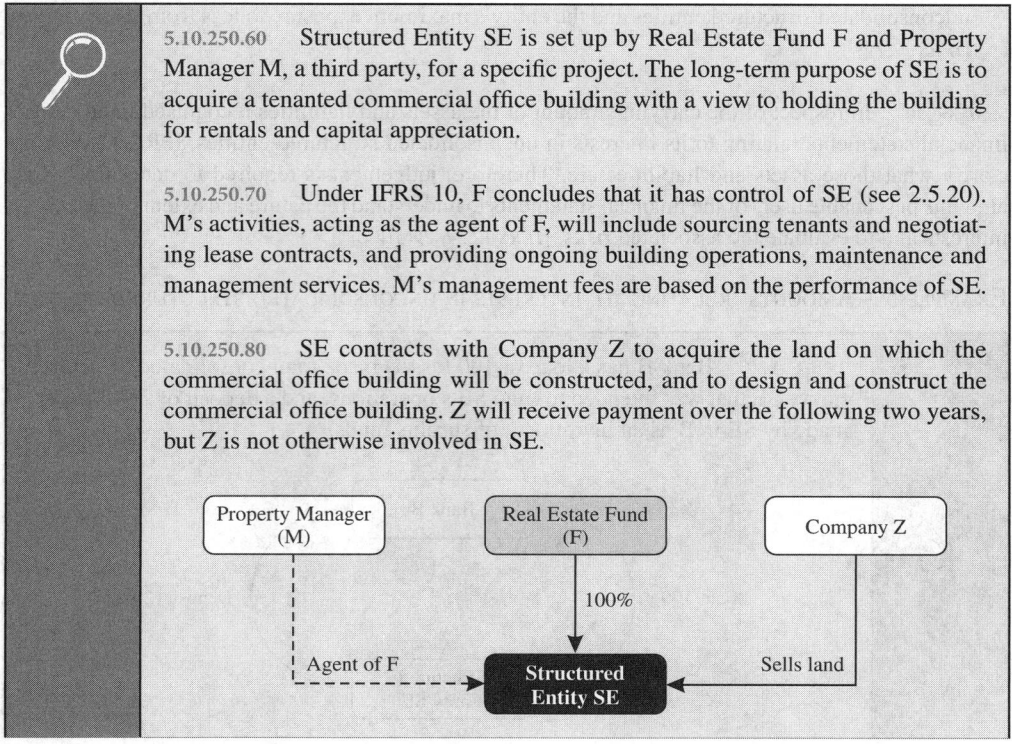

> 5.10.250.90   In this example, the parties conclude the following.
> - F, as the parent of SE, is subject to the IFRS 12 disclosures in respect of sub-sidiaries, which include disclosures related to consolidated structured entities (see 5.10.230).
> - M has an interest in SE through its contract to provide management services. M concludes that the IFRS 12 disclosures for interests in respect of unconsolidated structured entities apply (see 5.10.240–260).
> - Z has an interest in SE through its contract to sell land, which is yet to be settled. Z concludes that its involvement with SE does not require disclosure, because it is acting as a typical supplier in providing design and construction services.

5.10.260   *Nature of risks*

5.10.260.10   An entity provides disclosures that are sufficient to evaluate the nature of, and changes in, the risks in respect of its interests in unconsolidated structured entities, including:
- the carrying amount of the assets and liabilities recognised in its financial statements in relation to its interests in unconsolidated structured entities;
- the line items in the statement of financial position in which those assets and liabilities are recognised;
- the amount representing the entity's maximum exposure to loss from its interests in unconsolidated structured entities and how it is calculated; and
- a comparison of the carrying amount of the entity's assets and liabilities related to its interests in unconsolidated structured entities and the entity's maximum exposure to loss from those entities. [*IFRS 12.29*]

5.10.260.20   In respect of the carrying amount of the assets and liabilities recognised in an entity's financial statements relating to its interests in unconsolidated structured entities, IFRS 12 does not clarify what those assets and liabilities are. Therefore, judgement is required to determine which amounts best enable users of the financial statements to understand the nature and extent of the entity's interests and to evaluate the associated risks. [*IFRS 12.24, 29(a)*]

EXAMPLE 5 – AMOUNTS 'RELATING TO' INTERESTS IN UNCONSOLIDATED STRUCTURED ENTITIES

> 5.10.260.30   Bank B has a loan of 100 (asset) made to unconsolidated Structured Entity SE that was intended to fund SE's operations, and a deposit of 25 (liability) made by SE in B as an investment of surplus funds.

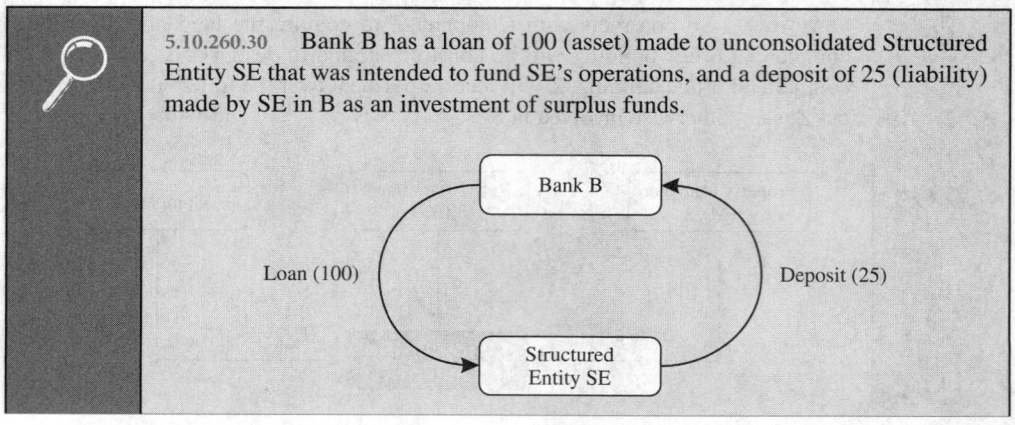

5.10.260.40   Although the parties have the right to set off the loan and the deposit, they are presented gross in B's statement of financial position because there is no intention to settle simultaneously or on a net basis (see 7.10.110).

5.10.260.50   In this example, B concludes that it should disclose both the asset and the liability because both are relevant to the measure of its risk exposure with SE.

5.10.260.60   However, if there was no right of offset, then B would disclose only the asset of 100 because the asset is the measure of its risk exposure with SE.

5.10.260.70   In disclosing an entity's maximum exposure to loss, there is no specific guidance in IFRS 12 regarding how it should be quantified. Management needs to apply its judgement to determine an appropriate measurement approach based on the specific facts and circumstances. This is acknowledged by the standard itself, which requires disclosure of how an entity measures its maximum exposure to loss. In respect of derivatives, this approach may lead some entities to adopt a single measurement – e.g. fair value by analogising to credit risk under IFRS 7 (see 7.10.520), notional amount by analogising to credit risk under the report of the Enhanced Disclosure Task Force (Enhancing Disclosures of Banks), or a varied approach depending on the type of derivative (e.g. fair value for a purchased option and notional amount for a credit default swap). [*IFRS 12.29(c), BC98*]

5.10.260.80   It may not always be possible to measure a maximum exposure to loss, such as when a financial instrument exposes an entity to theoretically unlimited losses – e.g. an interest rate swap. In this case, the entity discloses this fact and the reasons why it is not possible to calculate its maximum exposure to loss. [*IFRS 12.29(c), BC99*]

5.10.260.90   An entity also discloses the following in respect of unconsolidated structured entities in which it had or has an interest:
- the type and amount of any financial or other support provided during the reporting period when there was no contractual obligation to do so; this includes assisting the structured entity to obtain financial support; and
- the reasons for providing support. [*IFRS 12.30*]

5.10.260.100   If an entity has any intentions of providing future financial or other support to an unconsolidated structured entity, then it discloses those intentions, including intentions to help the structured entity in obtaining financial support. [*IFRS 12.31*]

5.10.260.110   An entity might need to provide disclosures in addition to the minimum specified in IFRS 12, if the minimum is not sufficient to meet the objective outlined in 5.10.250.10. The standard provides a list of potential additional disclosures, including information about any liquidity arrangements and financing difficulties encountered by an unconsolidated structured entity. [*IFRS 12.B25–B26*]

5.10.270   ***Sponsorship of an unconsolidated structured entity***

5.10.270.10   If an entity has no interest (see 5.10.50) in an unconsolidated structured entity at the reporting date, then the disclosures in 5.10.260 will not apply. However, if the entity has nonetheless 'sponsored' an unconsolidated structured entity, then it discloses the following instead:

- its method for determining which structured entities it has sponsored;
- income from those structured entities in the reporting period, including a description of the types of income; and
- the carrying amount at the time of transfer of all assets transferred to those structured entities during the reporting period. [*IFRS 12.27–28, BC90*]

5.10.270.20   The disclosures are based on the concept of an entity sponsoring an unconsolidated structured entity, which is not a term that is defined or explained in IFRS 12; the standard simply identifies sponsorship as a type of involvement in an unconsolidated structured entity. Whether a sponsorship relationship exists is therefore a matter of judgement. This is acknowledged by the standard itself, which requires disclosure of how an entity determined which structured entities it has sponsored. [*IFRS 12.27(a)*]

5.10.270.30   In addition, the sponsorship of an unconsolidated structured entity is not limited to periods in which the entity itself transacted or had a contractual involvement with the unconsolidated structured entity. Therefore, in our view the concept of sponsorship describes a relationship that, once it is established, can endure into future reporting periods. [*IFRS 12.25*]

5.10.270.40   As a result, entities face a practical issue over how to operationalise the requirements of IFRS 12, particularly because of the requirement to disclose all assets transferred to a structured entity in the reporting period. This disclosure:

- encompasses all assets transferred to a structured entity from any party – i.e. not just from the reporting entity; and
- applies regardless of whether the entity had any contractual involvement with the unconsolidated structured entity in that period. [*IFRS 12.25, 27(c), BC90*]

5.10.270.50   For this reason, there may be a temptation to provide every possible disclosure to ensure that there is no doubt that paragraph 27 of IFRS 12 has been complied with. However, this would not be consistent with the standard's overall objective (see 5.10.20.10), because information that is relevant to users of the financial statements may become hidden within the overall disclosures (see 1.2.40.20).

5.10.270.60   In identifying whether an entity needs to provide sponsorship-related disclosures about an unconsolidated structured entity in a particular reporting period, in our view the following factors may be useful to consider. The purpose of these factors, and the related questions, is to assess the extent or closeness of the relationship between the entity and the unconsolidated structured entity, as a measure of determining whether sponsorship exists and consequently whether disclosure under paragraph 27 of IFRS 12 is required.

PASSAGE OF TIME

- The closeness of entities may diminish with the passage of time. How long has it been since there have been any transactions with or related to the unconsolidated structured entity?

PURPOSE/DESIGN

- Was the reporting entity involved in set-up/design?
- Was the structured entity set up to provide some form of protection to the reporting entity?
- Does the reporting entity continue to rely on the unconsolidated structured entity in any way?
- Is there any warehousing taking place – i.e. placing assets in the unconsolidated structured entity to improve the reporting entity's capital position?
- Were assets acquired by the structured entity from the reporting entity or a third party?
- Does the reporting entity have representation on the governing body of the unconsolidated structured entity?

OTHER INVOLVEMENT

- To what extent has the reporting entity been involved with the unconsolidated structured entity?
- Is that involvement ongoing?
- Does the unconsolidated structured entity involve the development/introduction of a new product by the reporting entity?
- To what extent is the role of the structured entity an extension of the reporting entity?
- Is there any potential for future obligations/losses arising from past/present involvement?

BRAND/REPUTATIONAL ASSOCIATION

- To what extent is the reporting entity's brand associated with the unconsolidated structured entity?
- If the unconsolidated structured entity encounters difficulties (operational or financial), then how likely is it that they expose the sponsoring entity to brand or reputational harm such that the reporting entity would take action to mitigate such risks?

LEGAL ASSOCIATION/RISK

- Is the reporting entity exposed to current or future litigation arising from the activities of the unconsolidated structured entity?

TAX RISK

- Is the reporting entity exposed to current or future tax risk arising from the activities of the unconsolidated structured entity?

5.10.270.70   None of these factors is necessarily a conclusive indicator on its own. Instead, the relationship between the reporting entity and the unconsolidated structured entity should be considered from both a substance and an economic perspective.

EXAMPLE 6 – SPONSORSHIP

Scenario 1: Association by name

5.10.270.80   Entity X sets up a structured investment vehicle, called Entity X SIV. Apart from being involved in set-up, and in the absence of evidence to the contrary, the name of the SIV indicates the closeness of the relationship between Entity X and the SIV, because Entity X's brand is associated with the SIV.

5.10.270.90   In this example, Entity X concludes that Entity X SIV is in the scope of the sponsorship disclosures at every reporting date, not least as a result of brand/reputational risk and involvement.

Scenario 2: Involvement in set-up only

5.10.270.100   Entity X assists in setting up a structured investment vehicle, named ABC SIV, but has no involvement with ABC SIV after initial set-up and does not receive any ongoing income from ABC SIV.

5.10.270.110   In this example, Entity X concludes that the sponsorship disclosures apply:
- in the period of the initial set-up; and
- in the following reporting period, because of the potential legal risk arising from its involvement in the set-up.

5.10.270.120   Entity X concludes that no disclosure is required in subsequent reporting periods, because its relationship with ABC SIV is sufficiently remote based on the passage of time.

Scenario 3: Introducing parties

5.10.270.130   Entity X introduces two existing clients who have complementary interests, who together set up a structured investment vehicle. On the basis that Entity X has no other involvement in the dealings of the two clients, Entity X concludes that it has not sponsored the investment vehicle.

5.10.270.140   However, this conclusion might change if one or both of the clients were key customers such that Entity X would come to the aid of the resulting structure if there were problems – i.e. if Entity X had reputational risk arising from its role in the transaction between two key clients. This would be a matter of judgement in each case/reporting period.

5.10.275   **INVESTMENT ENTITIES**

5.10.280   **Overview of disclosure requirements**

5.10.280.10   The following table summarises which disclosure requirements of IFRS 12 apply to an investment entity. These requirements apply to all investment entities, including those that prepare only separate financial statements.

INTERESTS IN	DISCLOSURE REQUIREMENTS	REFERENCE
Consolidated subsidiaries, including those that are structured entities	General	5.10.80 5.10.230
Unconsolidated subsidiaries, including those that are structured entities	Specific	5.10.290
Structured entities that are not consolidated because they are not controlled	Both general and specific	5.10.240 5.10.300.20
Joint arrangements and associates	Both general and specific	5.10.130 5.10.300.20

5.10.290 Interests in unconsolidated subsidiaries

5.10.290.10   An investment entity discloses the following in respect of unconsolidated subsidiaries:
- the nature and extent of any significant restrictions on the ability of such investees to pay cash dividends to the investment entity or to repay loans or advances made by the investment entity;
- any commitment or intention to provide financial or other support to such investees; and
- the type and amount of financial or other support provided during the reporting period without a contractual obligation to do so, including the reasons for providing support. [*IFRS 12.19D–19E*]

5.10.290.20   For an unconsolidated subsidiary that is *a structured entity* (see 5.10.210), an investment entity discloses:
- contractual arrangements that could require the investment entity or its unconsolidated subsidiaries to provide financial support, including events or circumstances that could expose the investment entity to loss; and
- information about financial or other support provided during the reporting period without a contractual obligation to do so, including the relevant factors in deciding to provide support. [*IFRS 12.19F–19G*]

5.10.290.30   IFRS 12 also requires an investment entity to disclose the following basic information about all unconsolidated subsidiaries – i.e. both direct and indirect subsidiaries:
- the name of each subsidiary;
- its principal place of business, and country of incorporation (if this is different); and
- the proportion of ownership interests held and, if it is different, the proportion of voting rights held. [*IFRS 12.19B–19C*]

5.10.290.40   In addition, if an investment entity (parent) has an intermediate subsidiary that is also an investment entity, then the parent is permitted (but not required) to disclose the information in 5.10.290.30 by incorporating the financial statements of the investment entity subsidiary that include the relevant disclosures into its own financial statements. [*IFRS 12.19C*]

5.10.290.50   Investment entities apply the disclosure requirements set out in IFRS 7 and IFRS 13 to investees that are measured at fair value through profit or loss. For a discussion of these disclosures, see chapter 7.10 (IFRS 7) and 2.4.490 (IFRS 13).

5.10.290.60   Related party transactions and balances between an investment entity and its unconsolidated subsidiaries are disclosed in the investment entity's financial statements. Related party disclosures are the subject of chapter 5.5. [*IAS 24.4*]

5.10.300   Other disclosures

5.10.300.10   In addition to disclosing the fact that it is an investment entity, the entity discloses the significant judgements and assumptions made in determining that it qualifies as an investment entity. In particular, this includes how management concluded that the entity is an investment entity when it lacks one or more of the typical characteristics of such entities (see 5.6.130). [*IFRS 12.9A*]

5.10.300.20   In addition to disclosures about unconsolidated subsidiaries, an investment entity provides disclosure about the following.
- *Interests in joint arrangements and associates* (see 5.10.130). However, an investment entity is not required to disclose summarised financial information for interests in material joint ventures and associates (see 5.10.140.20–120), or interests in individually immaterial joint ventures and associates (see 5.10.160).
- *Interests in unconsolidated structured entities* (see 5.10.240). However, provided that the disclosures in 5.10.290 are made, the disclosures in 5.10.240 apply only to the extent that the structured entity is not consolidated because the investment entity does not have control over it. [*IFRS 12.21A, 25A*]

5.10.310   Change in status

5.10.310.10   An entity that qualifies as an investment entity for the first time (see 5.6.230), or ceases to qualify (see 5.6.240), discloses the change of status and the reasons for the change. [*IFRS 12.9B*]

5.10.310.20   An entity that qualifies as an investment entity for the first time (see 5.6.230) also discloses the effect of the change of status on the financial statements for the period presented, including:
- the total fair value of subsidiaries that ceased to be consolidated; and
- any gain or loss recognised as a result of the deemed loss of control, and the line item in which it is included in profit or loss. [*IFRS 12.9B*]

5.11 Extractive activities

5.11   Extractive activities

CURRENTLY EFFECTIVE REQUIREMENTS

This publication reflects IFRS in issue at 1 August 2018, and the currently effective requirements cover annual periods beginning on 1 January 2018.

The requirements related to this topic are mainly derived from the following.

REFERENCE	TITLE
IFRS 6	Exploration for and Evaluation of Mineral Resources
IFRIC 20	Stripping Costs in the Production Phase of a Surface Mine

FORTHCOMING REQUIREMENTS AND FUTURE DEVELOPMENTS

For this topic, there are no forthcoming requirements or future developments.

5.11.10 SCOPE

5.11.10.10   IFRS provides specific extractive industry guidance only for the recognition, measurement and disclosure of expenditure incurred on the exploration for and evaluation of (E&E) mineral resources. [*IFRS 6.3–4*]

5.11.10.20   E&E expenditure does not include amounts incurred in activities that precede the exploration for and evaluation of mineral resources (pre-exploration activities), such as expenditure incurred before obtaining the legal rights to explore a specific area. [*IFRS 6.5*]

5.11.10.30   Similarly, E&E expenditure does not include expenditure incurred after the technical feasibility and commercial viability of extracting a mineral resource are demonstrable (development activities). [*IFRS 6.5*]

5.11.10.40   IFRS 6 provides limited relief from the requirement to select accounting policies in accordance with the hierarchy for their selection (see 2.8.20), and from the general requirements for impairment testing (see 5.11.170). However, no such relief is provided for either pre-exploration activities or development activities; therefore, in our view these activities should fully comply with IFRS, including the hierarchy for selecting accounting policies. [*IFRS 6.7, 18*]

5.11.20 EXPLORATION AND EVALUATION EXPENDITURE

5.11.30 Accounting policy choice

5.11.30.10   An entity determines which of its expenditure meets the definition of E&E expenditure. As noted in 5.11.10, E&E expenditure does not include pre-exploration expenditure or development expenditure (see 5.11.230 and 260, respectively). [*IFRS 6.5*]

5.11.30.20   For each type of E&E expenditure, an entity chooses an accounting policy, to be applied consistently, of either immediately expensing the expenditure or capitalising it as an E&E asset. [*IFRS 6.9*]

5.11.30.30   In developing an accounting policy for E&E expenditure, an entity need not consider other IFRSs (by analogy) and need not refer to the definitions contained in the Conceptual Framework – i.e. an entity need not apply the hierarchy for selecting accounting policies. [*IFRS 6.7, IAS 8.11–12*]

5.11.30.40   However, the policy of expensing or capitalising reflects the extent to which the type of E&E expenditure can be associated with finding specific mineral resources. Typically, the more closely that expenditure relates to a specific mineral resource, the more likely that its capitalisation will result in relevant and reliable information. [*IFRS 6.9*]

5.11.30.50   The entity's accounting policy to capitalise or immediately expense each *type* of E&E expenditure is applied consistently to similar items and activities. In our view, the costs of activities that are similar are not different 'types' for the purpose of applying an E&E policy solely because they have different probabilities of leading to a project that is technically feasible and commercially viable. [*IAS 8.13*]

EXAMPLE 1 – EXPLORATORY DRILLING COSTS

5.11.30.60 Company X undertakes exploratory drilling activities across several regions of a country. X has identified that some regions have a high probability of success and others a low probability of success.

5.11.30.70 The exploratory drilling activities should be accounted for consistently based on X's accounting policy – i.e. either expensed or capitalised. The geographic location and the probability of whether the exploration will result in a project that is technically feasible and commercially viable are not considered in choosing the accounting policy.

5.11.40 Exploration and evaluation assets

5.11.40.10 Types of expenditure that might be included in the initial measurement of an E&E asset include:

- acquisition of rights to explore – e.g. exploration licences;
- topographical, geological, geochemical and geophysical studies;
- exploratory drilling;
- trenching;
- sampling; and
- activities in relation to evaluating the technical feasibility and commercial viability of extracting a mineral resource. [*IFRS 6.9*]

5.11.40.20 In some countries, an entity may make a contribution to the local community within which it wishes to commence E&E activities – e.g. a payment to relocate a village or to provide enhanced community services – to help gain permission to operate. In our view, such contributions may be capitalised as E&E assets and included in the cost of acquisition if an entity elects a policy of capitalising this type of E&E expenditure. [*IAS 8.13*]

5.11.50 Exploration and evaluation expenses

5.11.50.10 E&E expenditure for which an entity does not have a policy of capitalisation is expensed as it is incurred. In addition, E&E expenditure of a type that is not sufficiently closely related to a specific mineral resource to support capitalisation is expensed as it is incurred (see 5.11.30.40). For example, general seismic data costs might not be eligible for capitalisation as an E&E asset if they are not sufficiently closely related to finding a specific mineral resource. [*IFRS 6.9*]

5.11.60 Classification

5.11.60.10 An entity classifies each E&E asset as tangible or intangible based on the nature of the asset. Therefore, it is not possible to choose a single accounting policy with respect to the classification of all E&E expenditure. [*IFRS 6.15*]

5.11.60.20 E&E assets include the following.
- *Identifiable assets used for E&E:* Includes tangible items of property, plant and equipment such as exploration drilling rigs used only for E&E, and identifiable intangible assets such

as exploratory licences. These items are depreciated or amortised because they are used for E&E activities.

- *Costs incurred in connection with E&E activities that an entity elects to capitalise as E&E assets:* Might include, for example, labour costs, and the depreciation and amortisation of identifiable assets used for E&E.

5.11.60.30   Many identifiable E&E assets will clearly be tangible (e.g. vehicles, drilling rigs) and others clearly intangible (e.g. exploration licences). It is likely that there will also be a residual E&E asset that is less easily classified, and that a significant component of the residual E&E asset will consist of costs incurred in constructing exploratory wells or mines.

5.11.60.40   In our view, determining whether the nature of E&E assets is tangible or intangible should reflect whether the cost contributes to an item that is a physical (tangible) asset that will itself be used or, alternatively, to intangible knowledge about where, ultimately, to build a physical asset. For example, a well that will be used to extract reserves may be a tangible asset. However, an exploratory well may only provide knowledge. In our experience, costs relating to the building of exploratory wells or geological and geophysical activities tend to be classified as intangible E&E assets.

5.11.60.50   The classification of E&E assets as tangible or intangible is the basis for both the subsequent measurement of the assets and the related disclosures. [*IFRS 6.12, 15, 25*]

5.11.70   *Intangible assets*

5.11.70.10   Examples of E&E assets that might be classified as intangible include:
- drilling rights;
- acquired rights to explore;
- costs of conducting topographical, geological, geochemical and geophysical studies;
- exploratory drilling costs;
- trenching costs;
- sampling costs; and
- costs of evaluating the technical feasibility and commercial viability of extracting a mineral resource. [*IFRS 6.16*]

5.11.80   *Tangible assets*

5.11.80.10   IFRS does not define 'tangible'. However, most tangible assets will be identifiable items of property, plant and equipment (see 3.2.10).

5.11.80.20   Examples of E&E assets that might be classified as tangible assets include:
- equipment used in exploration, such as vehicles and drilling rigs;
- piping and pumps; and
- tanks. [*IFRS 6.16*]

5.11.80.30   To the extent that a tangible asset is consumed in developing an intangible asset, the amount reflecting that consumption is part of the cost of the intangible asset created. However, the asset being used remains a tangible asset. [*IFRS 6.16*]

EXAMPLE 2 – DEPRECIATION CAPITALISED

> 5.11.80.40   Company X has a drilling rig that is used only in the exploratory phase. The drilling rig is classified as a tangible asset (property, plant and equipment). The depreciation expense relating to the drilling rig is a cost of developing an intangible E&E asset and is therefore capitalised as part of the cost of the related E&E asset, which is the exploratory well.

5.11.90   Initial recognition and measurement

5.11.90.10   If an entity elects to capitalise E&E expenditure as an E&E asset, then that asset is measured initially at cost. [*IFRS 6.8*]

5.11.100   *Administrative and general overhead costs*

5.11.100.10   An entity chooses an accounting policy, to be applied consistently, of either expensing administrative and other general overhead costs, or capitalising those costs associated with finding specific mineral resources in the initial recognition and measurement of an E&E asset. In our view, the selected policy of expensing or capitalising administrative and other general overhead costs should comply, by analogy, with the guidance on capitalising similar costs incurred in relation either to inventories (see 3.8.120), intangible assets (see 3.3.90) or property, plant and equipment (see 3.2.30). [*IFRS 6.BC28*]

5.11.100.20   In our view, if an entity elects to capitalise administrative and other general overhead costs associated with finding specific mineral resources, then the following costs may qualify for inclusion as an E&E asset:
- payroll-related costs attributable to personnel working directly on a specific project, including the costs of employee benefits and share-based compensation for such personnel;
- certain management costs if the management roles are specific to a project;
- sign-up bonuses paid to contractors involved in a particular project;
- legal or other professional costs specific to the project – e.g. costs in respect of obtaining certain permits and certifications; and
- general office overheads for an office that is set up specifically to support E&E activities.

5.11.110   *Licence acquisition costs*

5.11.110.10   In accordance with its accounting policy, an entity may recognise an exploration licence as an E&E asset. In our view, the cost of that licence includes the directly attributable costs of its acquisition. We believe that entities should apply the guidance on costs that are directly attributable to intangible assets (see 3.3.90). Such costs may include non-refundable taxes and professional and legal costs incurred in obtaining the licence. [*IFRS 6.BC12*]

5.11.120   *Borrowing costs*

5.11.120.10   IAS 23 requires the capitalisation of borrowing costs as part of the cost of qualifying assets (see chapter 4.6). However, it is unclear how the requirements of IAS 23 interact with the requirements of IFRS 6. [*IAS 23.8–9*]

5.11.120.15   In our view, the requirements of IAS 23 do not override the exception in IFRS 6 that allows an entity a choice of either expensing or capitalising each type of E&E expenditure (see 5.11.30); this is because IFRS 6 defines E&E expenditure as expenditure incurred 'in connection with' E&E activities, which is broad enough to cover the related financing of such activities. Accordingly, we believe that an entity may choose to expense borrowing costs related to E&E assets. [*IFRS 6.A*]

5.11.130   *Decommissioning liabilities*

5.11.130.10   Many entities in the extractive industries incur an obligation in relation to site restoration and decommissioning as a result of undertaking E&E activities. A provision is recognised for the costs of any obligations for removal and restoration that are incurred as a consequence of having undertaken E&E activities (see 3.12.440). For example, a provision is recognised for the expected cost of dismantling a test drilling rig when it is installed. [*IFRS 6.11*]

5.11.130.20   Obligations that result from production – i.e. the extraction of reserves – are recognised only as extraction occurs. [*IAS 37.IE.C.Ex3*]

5.11.130.25   In general, if an obligation to dismantle an asset, or to restore the environment, arises on initial recognition of an asset, then the corresponding debit is treated as part of the cost of the asset and is not recognised immediately in profit or loss. For example, if a decommissioning liability arises in relation to drilling test bores and such expenditure is capitalised as an intangible E&E asset, then the initial estimate of the decommissioning liability is treated as part of the cost of the intangible asset. Similarly, the effect of any changes in the estimate of a decommissioning liability (except as related to the unwinding of the discount – see 5.11.130.40) is added to, or deducted from, the cost of the related asset. Additions to assets resulting from decommissioning liabilities are depreciated prospectively over the remaining useful life of the asset. [*IAS 16.16(c), IFRIC 1.5*]

5.11.130.30   However, in our view the cost of a decommissioning liability should be treated consistently with the treatment of the E&E expenditure that gave rise to the obligation. Entities may have differing treatments for different types of E&E expenditure. This may result in the cost of some decommissioning liabilities being recognised as part of the cost of the related E&E asset (whether it is classified as tangible or intangible), and the cost of other liabilities being recognised immediately in profit or loss.

5.11.130.40   A change in the estimate of a decommissioning liability that relates to the unwinding of the discount is always recognised in profit or loss. For a discussion of discounting in the measurement of decommissioning liabilities, see 3.12.450. [*IFRIC 1.8*]

5.11.140   **Subsequent measurement**

5.11.140.10   Subsequent to initial recognition, an entity applies either the cost model or the revaluation model, as appropriate, to each of its tangible and intangible E&E assets. [*IFRS 6.12*]

5.11.150   *Cost model*

5.11.150.10   Tangible assets used for E&E (and intangible assets with a finite life used for E&E) are depreciated (amortised) over their useful lives. The depreciable amount of a tangible asset (or an intangible asset with a finite useful life) is its cost less its residual value. The residual value of a tangible asset is the amount that an entity could receive for the asset at the reporting date if the asset were in the condition that it will be in when the entity expects to dispose of it. The residual value of an intangible asset with a finite useful life is assumed to be zero unless certain criteria are met (see 3.3.220). [*IAS 16.6, 53, 38.100*]

5.11.150.20   In our experience, it is very rare for an intangible asset used for E&E to be assessed as having an indefinite useful life. [*IAS 38.88*]

5.11.150.30   Depreciation or amortisation of a tangible or intangible asset commences only when the asset is available for use (see 3.2.220 and 3.3.240). Certain E&E assets (e.g. a vehicle or a drilling rig) may be available for use immediately; accordingly, such assets are depreciated or amortised during the E&E phase. Other E&E assets may not be available for use until a later date – e.g. when the mine or oil field is ready to commence operations. In that case, in our view there are two acceptable approaches for determining when depreciation/amortisation should commence.

- *Approach 1:* To commence depreciation or amortisation of the E&E assets once the mine or oil field is ready to commence operations, because in effect the entity will realise the future economic benefits embodied in those assets from this point.
- *Approach 2:* To commence depreciation or amortisation during the E&E phase because the assets are available for use when considered on a stand-alone basis. However, such depreciation or amortisation is capitalised to the extent that the E&E assets are used in the development of other assets; see, for example, 5.11.80.30 and Example 2. [*IFRS 6.16, IAS 16.49, 38.99*]

5.11.150.35   An entity's accounting policy choice in this regard should be applied consistently.

5.11.150.40   Regarding the method of depreciation or amortisation, the units-of-production method may reflect the pattern in which an E&E asset's future economic benefits are expected to be consumed by the entity better than the straight-line method. For a discussion of the application of the units-of-production method, see 5.11.320.20. [*IAS 16.62, 38.97–98*]

5.11.150.50   Both tangible and intangible E&E assets are tested for impairment in some circumstances (see 5.11.170).

5.11.160   *Revaluation model*

5.11.160.10   If an entity elects to apply the revaluation model, then the model applied is consistent with the classification of the assets as tangible or intangible. Tangible E&E assets are revalued using the property, plant and equipment model (see 3.2.300) and intangible E&E assets using the intangible asset model (see 3.3.280).

5.11.160.15   Both revaluation models apply the guidance in IFRS 13 in measuring fair value, which is the subject of chapter 2.4. In addition, intangible assets cannot be revalued unless there is an 'active' market, which requires a market in which transactions for the asset or liability take place with sufficient frequency and volume to provide pricing information on an ongoing basis. This requirement in effect rules out the revaluation of intangible E&E assets. [*IAS 38.75, IFRS 13.A*]

5.11.160.20   E&E assets are treated as a separate class of assets for disclosure purposes. IFRS generally defines a 'class of assets' as a grouping of items that have a similar nature and use in an entity's operations. A policy of revaluation is applied to all assets in a class (see 3.2.320). [*IFRS 6.25*]

5.11.160.30   In our view, tangible and intangible E&E assets are two separate classes of assets. We believe that generally all tangible assets used for E&E will form a separate class and that a policy of cost or revaluation should be applied consistently to all assets in that class. We believe that it is acceptable to apply the revaluation model to tangible E&E assets and the cost model to intangible E&E assets. [*IFRS 6.25*]

5.11.160.40   In our experience, the revaluation model is rarely used for tangible E&E assets.

5.11.165   Statement of cash flows

5.11.165.10   An entity presents cash flows during the period classified by operating, investing and financing activities in the manner most appropriate to its business (see 2.3.20). When an entity elects to expense E&E expenditure as it is incurred (see 5.11.30), the related cash flows are classified as operating activities. Cash flows from investing activities include only expenditure that results in the recognition of an asset. [*IAS 7.16*]

5.11.170   IMPAIRMENT

5.11.170.10   IAS 36 is applied to measure, present and disclose the impairment of E&E assets (see chapter 3.10). [*IFRS 6.18*]

5.11.170.20   However, relief is provided from the general requirements of IFRS in assessing whether there is any indication of impairment for E&E assets. Also, the level at which any impairment assessment is performed is specified and may be at a more aggregated level than is required for non-E&E assets. The assessment of impairment is then performed in accordance with general impairment requirements. [*IFRS 6.18–19*]

5.11.180   Indicators

5.11.180.10   E&E assets are assessed for impairment only when facts and circumstances suggest that the carrying amount of an E&E asset may exceed its recoverable amount, and on the transfer of E&E assets to development assets. Unlike for other assets, there is no requirement to assess whether an indication of impairment exists at each reporting date until an entity has sufficient information to reach a conclusion about the technical feasibility and commercial viability of extraction. [*IFRS 6.17–18, BC39*]

5.11.180.20   IFRS 6 includes industry-specific examples of facts and circumstances that, if one or more are present, indicate that an entity should test an E&E asset for impairment. One such indicator is that an entity's right to explore in the specific area has expired or will expire in the near future, and is not expected to be renewed. [*IFRS 6.20*]

5.11.180.30   'Near future' is not defined under IFRS. In our view, it should be a period sufficiently short such that no significant doubt exists about whether the area can be developed and any reserves extracted so as to recover the carrying amount of E&E assets before the right to explore lapses. In our view, the recoverable amount should be measured for any areas for which the rights to explore are due to expire within 12 months of the reporting date if the rights are not subject to a perfunctory renewal right. Other E&E assets are reviewed against the following list of indicators.

- Substantive expenditure on further exploration and evaluation activities in the specific area is neither budgeted nor planned.
- The entity has not discovered commercially viable quantities of mineral resources as a result of E&E activities in the area to date, and the entity has decided to discontinue such activities in the specific area.
- Even if development is likely to proceed, the entity has sufficient data indicating that the carrying amount of the asset is unlikely to be recovered in full from successful development or by sale.

5.11.180.40   These indicators are based on management information or intentions and decisions with respect to a given area of exploration.

5.11.180.50   In our view, the identification of the specific area being monitored is likely to be a significant factor in the frequency with which indicators exist, and therefore when it is necessary to review the recoverable amount of E&E assets. In our experience, it may be preferable for the level at which indicators are monitored and the level of E&E assets for which the recoverable amount is reviewed (see 5.11.190) to be consistent.

5.11.180.60   The list of impairment indicators is not exhaustive, and there may be additional facts and circumstances that suggest that an entity should review E&E assets for impairment. Such indicators may include, for example, significant adverse changes in commodity prices and markets or changes in the taxation or regulatory environment. In assessing whether an entity has sufficient cash to fund future planned or budgeted substantive exploration and evaluation, the entity's capacity to raise cash is considered if cash is not currently on hand. [*IFRS 6.20*]

5.11.190   **Level of testing**

5.11.190.10   An entity chooses an accounting policy, to be applied consistently, for allocating E&E assets to CGUs or groups of CGUs in assessing E&E assets for impairment. [*IFRS 6.21*]

5.11.190.20   An entity may be able to identify E&E assets for internal management purposes at a low level – e.g. at the level of a specific geological structure thought to contain hydrocarbons or a contiguous ore body. Although an entity may make an accounting policy choice to assess impairment at such a low level, there is no requirement to do so. Instead, entities are permitted to combine one or more CGUs in testing E&E assets for impairment (see chapter 3.10). [*IFRS 6.21–22*]

5.11.190.30   Entities should consider the level of impairment assessment to avoid assets being carried forward that would, if they were not aggregated with other assets, be impaired. For example, continuing to aggregate E&E costs for an area that will not be developed with other CGUs may result in knowingly carrying forward costs associated with assets even though a decision has been taken not to develop those mineral resources. In our view, a policy of recognising an impairment loss in respect of capitalised costs that relate to a specific area identified as not being capable of being developed into a producing asset is consistent with the encouragement to consider additional indicators of impairment, and may therefore be appropriate.

5.11.190.40   As seen in 5.11.190.20, an entity is permitted to aggregate CGUs to form a group of units in testing E&E assets for impairment. However, the grouping cannot be at a level of aggregation larger than that of the operating segment to which the CGU belongs (see 5.2.50). [*IFRS 6.21*]

5.11.190.50   In our view, the requirement that each CGU (or group of CGUs) may not be larger than an operating segment is not considered in absolute terms, such as segment profit or loss or total assets. Instead, we believe that impairment testing may not be performed at a level that results in the aggregation of E&E assets or CGUs belonging to different operating segments.

5.11.190.60   The identification of CGUs or groups of CGUs requires judgement and may be one of the most difficult areas of impairment testing for E&E assets. Its interaction with the indicators of impairment based on a specific area requires consideration.

5.11.190.70   On determining an accounting policy for allocating E&E assets to CGUs or groups of CGUs, the policy is applied consistently from period to period for the same types of assets. A change in accounting policy is permitted only if the criteria for a voluntary change in accounting policy are met (see 5.11.340). [*IAS 8.13*]

5.11.200   Recoverable amount

5.11.200.10   If facts and circumstances suggest that the carrying amount of a CGU or group of CGUs comprising E&E assets exceeds its recoverable amount, then the entity measures the recoverable amount of the CGU. Recoverable amount is the higher of fair value less costs of disposal and value in use. [*IFRS 6.18, IAS 36.9, 18*]

5.11.200.20   Many entities are likely to first determine the value in use of a potentially impaired asset, because the underlying information – i.e. cash flows based on management's estimates – will be more readily available than for fair value less costs of disposal. Only if this assessment highlights a potential impairment loss will the entity then be required to determine fair value less costs of disposal. For further discussion of measuring impairment, see 3.10.180–320.

5.11.210   *Value in use*

5.11.210.10   Cash flow projections to determine value in use are generally based on budgets approved by management that do not exceed five years (see 3.10.230). For most extractive activities, detailed budgets are prepared covering a period significantly in excess of five years – typically for the estimated field or mine life – which is generally based on resource and reserve reports; therefore, the period could be 20 years or more. In our view, if these budgets are considered reliable, then cash flow projections may be based on these longer budget periods. [*IAS 36.33, 35*]

5.11.210.20   When assessing impairment using a value-in-use model, future cash flows are estimated for the asset in its current condition (see 3.10.250). In the case of an asset that is not yet ready for use, which includes an E&E asset or related CGU, estimates include cash outflows expected to be incurred to bring the asset into use. [*IAS 36.42, 44*]

5.11.220   Reversals

5.11.220.10   Partial or full reversals of impairments of assets, other than impairments of goodwill, are recognised if there is an indication that a previously recognised impairment loss has reversed and the recoverable amount of the impaired asset has subsequently increased (see 3.10.420). [*IAS 36.110*]

5.11.230 PRE-EXPLORATION EXPENDITURE

5.11.230.10 Entities are required to identify and account for pre-exploration expenditure separately from E&E expenditure.

5.11.240 Identifying pre-exploration expenditure

5.11.240.10 Pre-licence costs are excluded from the scope of E&E costs. In our view, this exclusion implies that E&E activities commence on the acquisition of legal rights to undertake exploration activities in a certain area. [*IFRS 6.5(a)*]

5.11.240.20 Activities that take place before the acquisition of an exploration licence are pre-exploration, and will need to be identified separately. Pre-exploration expenditure typically includes the acquisition of speculative seismic data and expenditure on the subsequent geological and geophysical analysis of this data.

5.11.240.30 A formal process of bidding for licences may help the separate identification of activities that precede obtaining the licence. However, in some regions the licence process is less formal. For example, in certain areas in Africa a significant amount of E&E activity might commence while the formalities of obtaining a licence and government approval are being finalised, based on a valid expectation of a licence being granted. In our view, if the grant of the licence is subject only to administrative processes that are not substantive, then the licence may be deemed to have been granted. It is necessary to consider the nature of the regulatory approval in each case, because this determination is a matter of fact rather than accounting policy. Accordingly, it may be appropriate in some circumstances to capitalise E&E expenditure incurred before obtaining the licence, subject to an entity's accounting policy for such expenditure (see 5.11.30).

5.11.250 Accounting for pre-exploration expenditure

5.11.250.10 The recognition and measurement of pre-exploration expenditure is not addressed by IFRS. Therefore, an entity chooses an accounting policy, to be applied consistently, using the hierarchy for selecting accounting policies (see 2.8.20).

5.11.250.20 Pre-exploration expenditure cannot generally be associated with any specific mineral resources, because it is usually speculative in nature – e.g. costs incurred in reassessing previous seismic data. In our view, such expenditure should be expensed as it is incurred. [*IFRS 6.BC13*]

5.11.250.30 There may be some cases in which expenditure incurred in the pre-licence phase gives rise to an item that is an asset, even though it relates to E&E activities – e.g. the purchase of seismic data or analysis from a third party. [*IFRS 6.BC13*]

5.11.250.40 In addition, to the extent that pre-licence prospecting and exploration costs give rise to proprietary information that the entity has the ability to control, these costs may qualify for recognition as an intangible asset (see 3.3.30).

5.11.260
DEVELOPMENT EXPENDITURE

5.11.260.10   Entities identify and account for development expenditure separately from E&E expenditure.

5.11.270   Identifying development expenditure

5.11.270.10   IFRS does not contain a definition of development activities or expenditure in the context of extractive activities. From an accounting point of view, the term 'development' in the context of research and development is defined as "the application of research findings or other knowledge to a plan or design for the production of new or substantially improved materials, devices, products, processes, systems or services before the start of commercial production or use". One example of development expenditure for accounting purposes is costs related to the design, construction and operation of a pilot plant that is not of a scale economically feasible for commercial production. [*IAS 38.8, 59*]

5.11.270.20   In the extractive industries, 'development' often refers to the phase in which the technical feasibility and commercial viability of extracting a mineral resource have been demonstrated and an identified mineral reserve is being prepared for production – e.g. construction of access to the mineral reserves. In our view, these development activities are more akin to the construction of an asset to be used in commercial production than to expenditure incurred as part of development activities for accounting purposes. [*IFRS 6.5(b)*]

5.11.270.30   A significant factor in determining technical feasibility and commercial viability is likely to be the existence of proven and probable reserves. Entities make such assessments based on either their in-house, operators or third party reserve evaluations. In our view, in assessing commercial viability an entity should consider whether it has access to adequate resources to proceed with development activities.

5.11.280   Accounting for development expenditure

5.11.280.10   Once the technical feasibility and commercial viability of extracting a mineral resource are demonstrable, expenditure related to the development of that mineral resource is not recognised as part of E&E assets. IFRS does not prescribe when the technical feasibility and commercial viability of extracting a mineral resource are demonstrable. [*IFRS 6.5(b), 10*]

5.11.280.20   IFRS does not specify requirements for costs incurred on the development and extraction of mineral resources and an entity therefore chooses an accounting policy, to be applied consistently, using the hierarchy for selecting accounting policies (see 2.8.20).

5.11.280.30   If an entity identifies an (accounting) development phase once E&E activities have concluded, then it can generally identify an intangible asset and demonstrate that the asset will generate probable future economic benefits. In our view, to the extent that an entity incurs expenditure of an (accounting) development nature, the capitalisation of that expenditure as an intangible asset may be appropriate. [*IFRS 6.BC27*]

5.11.280.40   Alternatively, an entity may conclude that there is no (accounting) development phase between the determination of technical feasibility and commercial viability, and activities that are in preparation for production or extraction of a specific mineral reserve. In this case, it may be appropriate to capitalise development expenditure as part of the cost of an item of property, provided that those costs otherwise qualify for capitalisation.

5.11.290   Reclassifying exploration and evaluation assets

5.11.290.10   When the technical feasibility and commercial viability of extracting a mineral resource are demonstrable, an entity:
- stops capitalising E&E costs for that area;
- tests recognised E&E assets for impairment; and
- ceases classifying any unimpaired E&E assets (tangible and intangible) as E&E. [*IFRS 6.17*]

5.11.290.20   For E&E assets reclassified to development assets, an entity chooses an accounting policy, to be applied consistently, to classify such assets either as tangible or intangible development assets. Intangible E&E assets may be reclassified into tangible development assets or intangible development assets and vice versa.

5.11.300   *Identifiable exploration and evaluation assets*

5.11.300.10   Identifiable tangible assets that cease to be classified as E&E assets are generally classified as tangible development assets – e.g. a vehicle that will be used in production. Identifiable intangible E&E assets – e.g. an exploration licence – may continue to be classified as an intangible asset, or may be reclassified as a tangible asset if the intangible asset is considered to be integral to the tangible development asset and the tangible element of the asset is more significant.

5.11.310   *Non-identifiable exploration and evaluation assets*

5.11.310.10   Generally, when commercial and technical feasibility are demonstrable, a specific mineral reserve will have been identified for development. In our experience, mineral reserves are classified as either property assets (i.e. tangible) or intangible assets. In our view, an entity should choose an accounting policy, to be applied consistently, to classify mineral reserves either as tangible or as intangible assets. In our experience, mineral reserves, and by association the non-identifiable E&E assets, tend to be classified as tangible development assets.

5.11.310.20   Mineral reserves are excluded from the scope of both the intangible assets standard (IAS 38) and of the property, plant and equipment standard (IAS 16), and they are not in the scope of any other standard. Therefore, an entity chooses an accounting policy for mineral reserves by applying the hierarchy for selecting accounting policies (see 2.8.20). The limited relief from this hierarchy introduced by IFRS 6 (see 5.11.30) does not apply to mineral reserves that are not subject to E&E activities. The selected accounting policy is applied consistently. [*IFRS 6.3–4, IAS 16.3(c)– (d), 38.7*]

5.11.320   *Depreciation (amortisation)*

5.11.320.10   On reclassification of E&E assets, an entity depreciates (amortises) the resulting tangible development assets (and intangible developments assets with a finite life) over their useful lives. For both tangible and intangible development assets, the units-of-production method may be an appropriate method.

5.11.320.20   IFRS provides no specific guidance on how the units-of-production calculation should be performed. Specifically, there is no guidance on the reserves, or reserves and resources, measurement to be used in determining the ratio of current period production to total estimated production. For example, factors that would affect the measured reserves include the degree of probability used to assess the physical quantity of minerals in place and the economic assumptions used to assess the portion of this that can be commercially extracted. The relevant unit of measure may also be an area of judgement – e.g. using the amount of ore produced or the quantity of minerals contained in that ore. Accordingly, the basis of calculation is a matter of judgement such that the method used reflects the pattern in which the future economic benefits associated with the asset are consumed. The choice of measurement basis may also have implications for the cost base used in the units-of-production calculation.

5.11.320.30   For further discussion of the use of reserve and resource estimates in preparing financial statements, see 5.11.400.

5.11.330   *Impairment testing*

5.11.330.10   Before reclassification, E&E assets are assessed for impairment and any impairment loss is recognised in profit or loss. This impairment assessment is required regardless of whether facts and circumstances indicate that the carrying amount of the E&E asset is in excess of its recoverable amount. In our view, E&E assets can continue to be tested as part of the CGUs in which they have previously been included, as described in 5.11.170. This is because we believe that these assets are E&E assets to which the special aggregation relief applies. [*IFRS 6.17*]

5.11.330.20   Other than as described in 5.11.330.10, the impairment test on reclassification of E&E assets is performed in accordance with the general impairment testing requirements (see chapter 3.10). This will require an entity to develop additional accounting policies for allocating assets to CGUs and assessing recoverable amounts for these assets.

5.11.340   CHANGES IN ACCOUNTING POLICIES

5.11.340.10   IFRS 6 provides some relief from the requirements for a voluntary change in accounting policy (see 2.8.70). However, this modification relates only to E&E expenditure. Changes in accounting policies for pre-exploration activities and development expenditure are subject to the general requirements of IFRS for changes in accounting policy (see 2.8.50). [*IFRS 6.13*]

5.11.340.20   An entity may change its existing IFRS accounting policy for E&E expenditure if, and only if, the change makes the financial statements more relevant to the economic decision-making needs of users and no less reliable, or more reliable and no less relevant to those needs, judged by the criteria for voluntary changes in accounting policies (see 2.8.70). [*IFRS 6.13*]

5.11.340.30   In our view, the criteria in 5.11.340.20 prohibit entities from changing between certain policies used in current practice. For example, we believe that this requirement precludes entities in the oil and gas industry that account for exploration and development activities under IFRS using the successful-efforts method from changing to the full-cost method (see 5.11.370). Successful-efforts accounting refers to a practice of capitalising costs on a field-by-field basis with an assessment of commercial viability of the fields performed on a periodic basis. We believe that such a change in policy is not considered to result in more relevant and/or reliable information to the users of the financial statements because it may result in the capitalisation of unsuccessful costs – e.g. costs related to dry wells that do not represent future economic benefits.

5.11.340.40   Similarly, a mining company that currently expenses E&E costs is, in our view, precluded from changing to a policy of capitalisation of *all* such costs. This is because, without the temporary exemption from the accounting policy hierarchy, it is difficult to demonstrate the probability of future economic benefits from E&E expenditure. We therefore believe that such a change in policy is not considered to result in more relevant and/or reliable information to the users of the financial statements.

5.11.340.50   Conversely, we believe that a change in policy from the full-cost method to one based on the successful-efforts method or from capitalisation of all E&E expenditure to expensing (at least some) costs as incurred would be acceptable. In our view, expensing many such costs is more consistent with the Conceptual Framework because it is difficult to demonstrate that these costs meet the definition of an asset. Expensing these costs as they are incurred may therefore be viewed as more reliable.

5.11.350   STRIPPING COSTS

5.11.350.10   IFRS contains no specific guidance on the accounting for stripping costs incurred in the *pre-production* phase of surface mining. In our experience, pre-production stripping costs in surface mining are generally capitalised and amortised over the productive life of the mine under the units-of-production method.

5.11.350.20   Stripping costs incurred in the *production* phase of surface mining activities are in the scope of IFRIC 20. Such costs that give rise to benefits in the form of inventory produced are accounted for in accordance with IAS 2 (see chapter 3.8). However, production stripping costs that improve access to ore to be mined in the future are recognised as a non-current asset ('stripping activity asset') if, and only if, all of the following criteria are met.
- It is probable that the future economic benefit will flow to the entity.
- The entity can identify the component of the ore body to which access has been improved.
- The costs related to the stripping activity associated with that component can be measured reliably. [*IFRIC 20.6, 8–9*]

5.11.350.30   If the costs of the stripping activity asset vs inventory produced are not separately identifiable, then costs are allocated based on a relevant production method – e.g. based on the actual vs expected volume of waste extracted. [*IFRIC 20.13*]

5.11.350.40   The stripping activity asset is accounted for as a component of the existing asset of which it is a part – i.e. as a component of the mining assets. Therefore, the classification and measurement of the stripping activity asset is in line with that existing asset. [*IFRIC 20.14*]

5.11.350.50   The stripping activity asset is depreciated or amortised on a systematic basis over the expected useful life of the identified component of the ore body that becomes more accessible as a result of the stripping activity. The units-of-production method is applied unless another method is more appropriate. The expected useful life of the identified component of the ore body will differ from the life of the mine, except in limited circumstances when the stripping activity provides access to the whole of the ore body. [*IFRIC 20.15–16*]

5.11.360   **APPLICATION ISSUES**

5.11.370   **Compatibility of full-cost accounting with IFRS**

5.11.370.10   'Full-cost accounting' is a phrase used in the extractive industries to refer to the practice of capitalising a range of costs for a field or area under exploration. In our view, certain aspects of full-cost accounting are not fully compatible with IFRS, including:
- capitalising all pre-licence acquisition costs (see 5.11.230); and
- failing to disaggregate cost pools to a level that enables identification of when E&E for a particular resource ceases and allows impairment testing to be performed (see 5.11.170).

5.11.380   **Royalties and taxes**

5.11.380.10   In the extractive industries, levies not calculated based on taxable profit are often imposed on entities; they may take the form of royalties, extraction taxes, corporate taxes, or a combination thereof. The form and complexity of these arrangements will vary from country to country, or even within a country.

5.11.380.20   For example, in the oil and gas industry, royalties may be imposed based on a fixed percentage of gross production, either with reference to physical quantities or monetary values. Alternatively these levies, sometimes referred to as Petroleum Resource Taxes (PRTs), may be based on a percentage of operating profit as determined on a mine-by-mine or field-by-field basis, after allowing for the deduction of certain expenses. In other cases, PRTs are imposed in a way that may be viewed as creating a joint venture between the producing entity and the government.

5.11.380.30   In our view, the classification of arrangements such as PRT will depend on the relevant facts and circumstances, and is not an accounting policy choice. For a discussion of the classification of such arrangements, see 3.13.20.

5.11.390   *Extraction rights*

5.11.390.10   In some jurisdictions, entities may be required to pay royalties to land owners for the right to extract mineral resources located on the land. Such royalty payments do not fall in the scope of IFRS 6 because the technical feasibility and commercial viability of extracting the mineral resources would already have been demonstrated (see 5.11.10.30). They are also excluded from the scope of both IAS 17 and IAS 38. However, because extraction rights do not fall in the scope of other IFRSs, in our view an entity may account for the royalties by analogy to either IAS 17 or IAS 38 under the hierarchy for selecting accounting policies (see 2.8.20). [*IAS 17.2, 38.2*]

5.11.390.20   In our experience, the fee to be paid for the extraction rights (royalties) may be calculated under a variety of payment structures. Analysis may be required to determine whether the royalties are, in substance, a payment for the right to use the land – i.e. more like a lease agreement under IAS 17 – or are a payment for the right to extract mineral resources. Indicators that the royalties represent a right to extract mineral resources include calculations based on the quantity of resources extracted and cancellation clauses triggered by a reason related to the mineral resources, such as arrangements that are cancellable if the quality of the mineral deposit prevents exploration or if the mineral resource is exhausted.

5.11.390.30   If the royalties are not analogous to payments for the right to use the land, then a portion of these payments may qualify for capitalisation by analogy to IAS 38. In our view, if the extraction rights meet the definition of an intangible asset (see 3.3.30), then the present value of any non-refundable up-front payments, and non-refundable annual minimum payments, may be capitalised as an intangible asset. This is because the entity has a contractual obligation to make these payments and therefore these payments meet the definition of a financial liability when the contract is entered into (see 7.1.30.50).

5.11.390.40   In our view, variable payments should not be recognised until the obligating event occurs – e.g. as mineral reserves are extracted – because there is no contractual or present obligation before such time. Such payments are generally recognised in profit or loss as they are incurred unless they qualify for capitalisation – e.g. as part of the cost of inventory (see 3.8.120).

5.11.395   Going concern

5.11.395.10   The requirements of IFRS 6 are applied in the context of an entity preparing its financial statements on a going concern basis (see 1.2.70). However, if an entity has only E&E activities – e.g. a junior explorer – and there is no planned or budgeted substantive exploration and evaluation, then these factors may raise questions about the entity's ability to continue as a going concern (see 2.9.55). In such circumstances, it may also be relevant to consider access to capital and any reduction of planned capital expenditure.

5.11.400   Estimation uncertainties and judgements

5.11.400.10   Estimates of reserves and resources is generally an area of significant judgement and estimation for entities in the extractive industries.

5.11.400.20   Reserves and resources measurements affect the financial statements in a number of ways.
- Depreciation or amortisation charges based on the units-of-production method are directly affected by reserve estimates.
- Reserves estimates may be a key factor in determining the timing of decommissioning and site remediation costs, which affects the present value of any related liabilities.
- The estimated economic value of the remaining reserves is likely to be an important factor in impairment testing.
- Reserves may be a key input to fair value calculations in accounting for business combinations.
- Future profit expectations generated by reserves may be the basis for assessing whether deferred tax assets arising from unused tax losses should be recognised.

5.11.400.30   IFRS does not specifically require entities to disclose reserve information as part of their financial statements. However, an entity discloses the key assumptions about the future and other major sources of estimation uncertainty that have a significant risk of resulting in a material adjustment to the carrying amounts of assets and liabilities in the next annual period (see 2.8.120); and also discloses the judgements made in applying its accounting policies that have the most significant effect on the amounts recognised in the financial statements (see 2.8.40). [*IAS 1.122, 125*]

5.12 Service concession arrangements

5.12   Service concession arrangements

CURRENTLY EFFECTIVE REQUIREMENTS

This publication reflects IFRS in issue at 1 August 2018, and the currently effective requirements cover annual periods beginning on 1 January 2018.

The requirements related to this topic are mainly derived from the following.

REFERENCE	TITLE
IFRIC 12	Service Concession Arrangements
SIC-29	Service Concession Arrangements: Disclosures

The currently effective requirements include newly effective requirements arising from IFRS 15 *Revenue from Contracts with Customers,* which is effective for annual periods beginning on or after 1 January 2018. The new requirements may be applied using the retrospective method or the cumulative effect method (see 4.2.510). The impact of the new requirements on the accounting for service concession arrangements is reflected in 5.12.70–80, 120–130.

FORTHCOMING REQUIREMENTS

For this topic, there are no forthcoming requirements.

FUTURE DEVELOPMENTS

This topic is subject to future developments on the comprehensive project on rate-regulated activities. See 5.12.240.

5.12.01	**SCOPE**
5.12.05	**Introduction**

5.12.05.10   IFRIC 12 focuses on arrangements in which a private sector entity (the operator) operates and maintains a public service infrastructure. The infrastructure may already exist or may need to be constructed or upgraded by the operator during the concession period. The operator typically receives cash, either from the public sector body that awards the concession (the grantor) or from users, only once the infrastructure is available for use. [*IFRIC 12.1–3*]

5.12.05.20   IFRIC 12 applies to public-to-private service concession arrangements in which the public sector controls or regulates the services provided with the infrastructure and their prices, and controls any significant residual interest in the infrastructure. IFRIC 12 does not address all forms of infrastructure service arrangements (see 5.12.10.20) and does not address accounting by grantors. [*IFRIC 12.5–9*]

5.12.05.30   The determination of whether an arrangement is in the scope of IFRIC 12 affects the recognition and measurement of assets by the operator, notably whether the operator recognises service concession infrastructure as property, plant and equipment. IFRIC 12 includes the following guidance that may be relevant in determining whether an arrangement is in its scope:
- a description of the typical features of public-to-private service concession arrangements;
- specific scope criteria about control of the service concession infrastructure;
- application guidance on the scope criteria, which forms an integral part of the interpretation;
- an information note referring to the standards that apply to typical types of public-to-private service arrangements, which accompanies but is not part of IFRIC 12; and
- explanatory material in the basis for conclusions, which accompanies but is not part of IFRIC 12. [*IFRIC 12.1–9, AG1–AG8, IN2, BC2–BC19*]

5.12.05.40   The key requirements of the guidance in 5.12.05.30 are discussed below. In addition, IFRIC 4 states that service concession arrangements in the scope of IFRIC 12 are excluded from the scope of IFRIC 4 (see 5.1.510). [*IFRIC 12.BC29, 4.4(b)*]

5.12.10   **Public-to-private service concession arrangements**

5.12.10.10   Although IFRIC 12 does not define 'public-to-private service concession arrangements', it does describe the typical features of such arrangements. Typically, a public-to-private service concession arrangement in the scope of IFRIC 12 involves most of the following.
- *Infrastructure used to deliver public services:* This can take many forms and may be transport-related (e.g. roads, bridges, tunnels), a type of building (e.g. hospitals, prisons), utility-related (e.g. water distribution network, electricity supply plant) or specialist plant or equipment (e.g. medical equipment, vehicles). The infrastructure may include moveable and immoveable items – e.g. it may include a hospital building and related plant and equipment.
- *A contractual arrangement between the grantor and the operator:* This is referred to as a 'concession agreement'. The concession agreement specifies the services that the operator is to provide to the grantor and governs the basis on which the operator will be remunerated. Arrangements of this nature can vary greatly in duration, but terms of 30 years or more are not unusual.
- *Supply of services by the operator:* These may include the construction or upgrade of the infrastructure and the operation and maintenance of that infrastructure. Service concessions involving

a significant construction or upgrade element are sometimes called 'build-operate-transfer' or 'rehabilitate-operate-transfer' arrangements. The construction or upgrade services are often provided during the early years of the concession, but they may also be provided in stages during the concession period.

- *Payment of the operator over the term of the arrangement:* In many cases, the operator will receive no payment during the initial construction or upgrade phase. Instead, the operator will be paid by the grantor directly or will charge users during the period when the infrastructure is available for use.
- *Return of the infrastructure to the grantor at the end of the arrangement:* For example, if the operator has legal title to the infrastructure during the term of the arrangement, then legal title may be transferred to the grantor at the end of the arrangement, often for no additional consideration. [*IFRIC 12.3*]

5.12.10.20   The features in 5.12.10.10 give a broad indication of the types of arrangements to which the interpretation may relate. In our experience, a wide variety of service concession arrangements exist and not all of the arrangements that are in the scope of IFRIC 12 will have all of the features listed in 5.12.10.10.

5.12.10.25   IFRIC 12 states that a feature of public-to-private arrangements is "the public service nature of the obligation undertaken by the operator". In general, it is not necessary for the operator itself to provide services directly to the general public for an arrangement to be a public-to-private arrangement. However, an arrangement in which a public body outsources a routine service does not necessarily involve a public-to-private arrangement. [*IFRIC 12.3*]

EXAMPLE 1 – PUBLIC SERVICE OBLIGATION

5.12.10.30   An operator constructs and maintains a railway system, including tracks and stations, and procures the rolling stock under the terms of the concession agreement. The grantor employs the train drivers and station staff, and collects ticket revenues from passengers. In our view, this arrangement is a public-to-private arrangement because the services delivered using the infrastructure are provided to the public.

5.12.10.35   Conversely, if the government owned and operated all aspects of the railway system but contracted with a private sector company to perform routine maintenance of the trains, then this would not necessarily represent a public-to-private arrangement in the sense discussed in IFRIC 12. For a discussion of other types of arrangements between the public and private sector that may not be in the scope of IFRIC 12, see 5.12.45.

5.12.15   Scope criteria

5.12.15.10   The scope of IFRIC 12 is defined with reference to control of the infrastructure. An arrangement is in the scope of the interpretation if the grantor controls:
- what services the operator should provide with the infrastructure (control of services);
- to whom it should provide them (control of services);

- the price at which services are charged (control of pricing); and
- through ownership, beneficial entitlement or otherwise, any significant residual interest in the infrastructure at the end of the term of the arrangement (control of the residual interest). [*IFRIC 12.5*]

EXAMPLE 2 – ARRANGEMENTS IN SCOPE OF IFRIC 12

5.12.15.20   Grantor G awards a concession to Operator O to build and operate a new road to be used by the general public. Under the arrangement:
- G transfers to O the land on which the road is to be built, with adjacent land that O may redevelop or sell at its discretion;
- construction is expected to take five years, after which O will operate the road for 25 years;
- O has a contractual obligation to perform routine maintenance on the road and to resurface it as necessary, which is expected to be three times over the 25-year period;
- tolls for use of the road are set annually by G; and
- the road will revert to G at the end of the arrangement.

5.12.15.30   This arrangement is a public-to-private service concession arrangement as described in 5.12.10.10 because the road is built under general transport policy and is to be used by the public. The arrangement is in the scope of IFRIC 12 because the grantor controls:
- the services to be provided using the infrastructure and the price charged for those services – i.e. the grantor requires the infrastructure to be used as a road available to the public and sets the tolls; and
- the significant residual interest in the infrastructure, because the road reverts to the grantor at the end of the arrangement.

5.12.15.40   Conversely, a public-to-private service concession arrangement may contain some of the features indicated in 5.12.15.10 and not be in the scope of IFRIC 12.

EXAMPLE 3 – ARRANGEMENTS NOT IN SCOPE OF IFRIC 12

5.12.15.50   Company R, a private sector entity, enters into a contract with the Transport Ministry (the grantor) of Country S to acquire the right to operate the civil air navigation system in Country S. Under this contract:
- the grantor sells the air navigation system to R;
- R is required to upgrade and operate the system;
- R will charge users based on rates negotiated directly by R with individual users;
- there is no price-cap mechanism imposed by the grantor; and
- the contract is for an indefinite period and does not require R to transfer the air navigation system back to the grantor.

5.12.15.60   This arrangement has many characteristics of a public-to-private service concession arrangement – e.g. the grantor is a public sector body, the operator is a private sector body, the operator is responsible for the upgrade and operation

> of the service concession infrastructure and the infrastructure is used pursuant to public policy. However, under the terms of the contract the grantor does not control prices or any significant residual interest in the infrastructure. Therefore, the contract is not in the scope of IFRIC 12.

5.12.20   **Scope criteria: Control of services**

5.12.20.10   The grantor may control the services to be provided by the operator in a number of ways. For example, the services may be specified through the terms of the concession agreement and/or a licence agreement and/or some other form of regulation. All of these forms of control are consistent with the scope criteria of IFRIC 12. [*IFRIC 12.5, AG2*]

5.12.20.20   Furthermore, the degree of specification of the services may vary in practice. In some cases, the grantor will specify the services to be provided in detail and with reference to specific tasks to be undertaken by the operator – e.g. build a hospital according to the design and timetable in schedule B or complete the cleaning tasks in schedule C in each ward each evening. In other cases, the grantor will specify the services that the infrastructure should have the capacity to deliver – e.g. provide hospital accommodation suitable to support delivery of acute healthcare services to a local population of 10,000. In our view, the latter approach, using what is sometimes called an 'output specification', is also consistent with the scope criteria of IFRIC 12.

5.12.30   **Scope criteria: Control of pricing**

5.12.30.10   The grantor may control or regulate the pricing of the services to be provided using the infrastructure in a variety of ways. The IFRS Interpretations Committee discussed this issue and noted that the grantor does not need to have complete control over the pricing in order meet this criterion in IFRIC 12 – e.g. reviews or approvals by the grantor required by the agreement will generally be sufficient to consider pricing to be controlled by the grantor. For examples of price control, including price setting by an independent economic regulator, see 5.12.30.20–40. [*IFRIC 12.5, AG3, IU 07-09*]

5.12.30.20   In some cases, particularly when the grantor pays the operator directly, prices (or a price formula) may be set out in the concession agreement. In other cases, prices may be reset periodically by the grantor or the grantor may give the operator discretion to set unit prices but set a maximum level of revenue or profits that the operator may retain. All of these forms of arrangements are consistent with the scope criteria in IFRIC 12.

5.12.30.30   In some cases, prices may be indexed by, or reset periodically with reference to, a factor that is outside the control of the grantor. For example, prices may be indexed annually by a consumer price index (CPI) or a regulator may establish a price formula that depends on the value of an index – e.g. the regulator may specify that prices may rise by a maximum of CPI less X, with X being a value that is reset periodically by the regulator. Although the grantor cannot control the value of CPI, the grantor controls the framework in which the price is set. In our view, such price-setting mechanisms constitute price regulation that is consistent with the scope criteria in IFRIC 12.

5.12.30.40   An arrangement may be in the scope of IFRIC 12 when either the services to be provided or the pricing are controlled by an economic regulator acting in the public interest. For example, if the operator is a monopoly supplier of services in a geographic area, then an 'independent economic regulator' may be established to set prices and to monitor the operator's compliance with the conditions of its licence. The duties and powers of the regulator may be set out in legislation that requires the regulator to act in the public interest and constrains the government's ability to direct the operations of the regulator. [IFRIC 12.AG2]

5.12.30.50   If an entity operates in a regulated industry and has a legal right to charge a price based on a cost-plus model, then other considerations may apply. For a discussion of regulatory assets and liabilities, see 3.3.180 and 3.12.720.

5.12.30.60   For a discussion of other issues relating to pricing involving a competitive tender process or receipt of a government subsidy, see 5.12.42.

5.12.40   *Scope criteria: Control of residual interest*

5.12.40.10   The simplest ways in which the grantor may control the residual interest are for the concession agreement to require the operator to return all concession assets to the grantor, or to transfer the infrastructure to a new operator, at the end of the arrangement for no consideration. Such a requirement is a common feature of service concession arrangements involving concession assets with long useful lives, such as road and rail infrastructure. However, other forms of arrangements are also in the scope of IFRIC 12. [IFRIC 12.3, 5]

5.12.40.15   Some concession agreements may include certain provisions that if triggered would terminate the agreement and require the operator to return control of the infrastructure to the grantor. For example, there may be early termination provisions for non-compliance with quality, maintenance or environmental conditions. In our view, the existence of such terms would not in itself result in the grantor retaining control of any significant residual interest, provided that the condition triggering the termination is not under the control of the grantor. If the criteria triggering the termination are clearly stated in the agreement and the operator has the ability to control the use of the infrastructure to ensure that it is in compliance with the terms of the agreement, then the operator is able to control the residual interest of the infrastructure absent other aspects of the agreement that would convey control to the grantor. Similarly, we believe that a condition requiring the operator to remain solvent during the agreement would not in itself result in the grantor retaining control of any significant residual interest because this requirement does not have any bearing on the operator's use of the underlying infrastructure. Solvency is influenced by additional factors that are generally outside the service concession arrangement and are not considered when preparing the financial statements on a going concern basis.

5.12.40.20   The residual interest criterion may be met when the grantor holds an option to acquire the infrastructure assets at the end of the concession. Such an option gives the grantor the ability to control the use of the asset at the end of the concession period and restricts the operator's practical ability to sell or pledge any significant interest in the infrastructure. For example, an operator may acquire a site and develop a building that is to be used as a public healthcare facility. At the end of the arrangement, the grantor may have an option to acquire the site for its then fair value. This is an example of an arrangement in which the grantor controls the residual interest in the infrastructure but the operator bears residual value risk. [IFRIC 12.AG4]

5.12.40.30   Unlike IAS 17, which is based on a notion of risks and rewards, IFRIC 12 is based on a notion of control. Therefore, if the grantor bears the residual value risk but does not obtain control over the use of the infrastructure at the end of the concession, then the arrangement is not in the scope of IFRIC 12. [*IFRIC 12.5*]

EXAMPLE 4 – OPERATOR CALL OPTION

5.12.40.40   Operator O enters into an agreement to build and operate a pipeline for 20 years, O receives cash from Grantor G for this arrangement. O has an option to acquire the pipeline at the end of the arrangement for its then fair value. G does not have control over any conditions related to the purchase option. Once O exercises the option, G is no longer able to control the pipeline or the benefits to be generated from the pipeline in any way. The estimated useful life of the pipeline is 70 years; therefore, the residual asset of the pipeline at the end of the 20-year term is significant.

5.12.40.50   In this arrangement, G does not control the residual interest in the infrastructure, because O can acquire the pipeline at its fair value at its sole discretion. Therefore, the arrangement is not in the scope of IFRIC 12.

5.12.40.60   The residual interest criterion may also be met if the concession agreement establishes that the grantor holds the right to stipulate to whom the operator should transfer the assets at the end of the concession agreement. In our view, such a right effectively restricts the ability of the operator to sell or pledge the assets and gives the grantor control of the residual interest in the infrastructure. [*IFRIC 12.AG4*]

5.12.40.65   Conversely, an operator in a regulated industry may be permitted to retain control of the infrastructure – e.g. a power plant – at the end of an agreement. If the assets are expected to have a significant remaining economic life and residual value at the end of the agreement, then the arrangement is generally outside the scope of IFRIC 12 because the operator controls the significant residual interest in the infrastructure. In such a case, the operator accounts for the infrastructure assets in accordance with IAS 16. [*IFRIC 12.5(b), AG4*]

5.12.40.70   'Whole-of-life' arrangements – that is, arrangements for which the residual interest in the infrastructure is not significant – are in the scope of IFRIC 12 if the other scope criteria are met. The application guidance to IFRIC 12 states that the residual interest in the infrastructure is the estimated current value of the infrastructure as if it were already of the age and in the condition expected at the end of the term of the arrangement. For example, service concession arrangements for providing specialist medical equipment or IT infrastructure may have terms equivalent to the expected economic life of the equipment. Even if the operator retained ownership of the equipment at the end of the arrangement, the arrangement would be in the scope of IFRIC 12 because the equipment is not expected to have a significant economic value at the end of the arrangement. [*IFRIC 12.6, AG4*]

5.12.40.80   An operator may be required to replace part of an item of the infrastructure used under an existing service concession arrangement – e.g. the roof of a building. In determining if the grantor controls any significant residual interest in the replacement asset, IFRIC 12 requires the replaced asset to be considered as part of the whole infrastructure. In our experience, it is rare for a replacement asset to be deemed outside the scope of an existing service concession arrangement. In our view, only in limited circumstances when the operator is able to retain control of the residual interest of the replacement asset and is able to generate independent cash flows from its use, is the replacement asset out of the scope of IFRIC 12. In such instances, the operator accounts for the asset under IAS 16. [*IFRIC 12.6, AG6*]

EXAMPLE 5A – REPLACEMENT ASSETS – IN SCOPE OF IFRIC 12

5.12.40.90   Operator O enters into a service concession agreement with Grantor G to operate water supply infrastructure in jurisdiction X. O obtains the right to use land and existing infrastructure assets such as water mains and reservoirs for 50 years. During the 50-year period of the arrangement, O will need to replace certain assets that are essential to running the water plant including pumping systems and computer equipment. At the end of the arrangement, O will transfer all assets, including any replaced assets, back to G. O will not receive any compensation from G despite the fact that the replaced assets are expected to have significant residual value at the end of the arrangement.

5.12.40.100   We believe that the replaced assets are in the scope of IFRIC 12 because they:
- are essential to running the infrastructure as a whole;
- do not separately generate independent cash flow; and
- will revert back to G at the end of the concession period.

EXAMPLE 5B – REPLACEMENT ASSETS – OUT OF SCOPE OF IFRIC 12

5.12.40.110   Modifying the fact pattern in Example 5A, to facilitate the performance of its responsibilities under the service concession arrangement, Operator O also constructs an administrative building adjacent to a reservoir that will support administrative personnel and technical staff involved in the day-to-day operating activities of the water plant. At the end of the arrangement, O will retain title to the building and intends to lease out the office space. We believe that O should account for the building as its own asset under IAS 16.

5.12.42   *Other scope issues*

5.12.42.10   In our experience, many service concessions are granted following a process of competitive tender between prospective operators. In such cases, the bidders may be invited to propose the lowest price for which they would be prepared to perform the concession services, or may propose variants to the service levels requested by the grantor. In our view, the analysis of whether an arrangement is in the scope of IFRIC 12 should focus on the contractual, regulatory and other mechanisms that govern the concession period, not the process through which the concession is awarded. The fact that certain aspects of the services and prices are determined by a competitive process before the concession starts does not influence the assessment of whether the IFRIC 12 scope criteria about control of prices and services are met.

EXAMPLE 6 – CONTROL OF SERVICES AND PRICING – COMPETITIVE PROCESSES

> 5.12.42.20   Company X submits a bid to become the operator in a service concession arrangement in the telecommunications sector in response to a Request for Proposal (RFP) issued by the grantor. The RFP specifies the services that the operator is expected to provide and the maximum unit price that the operator will be permitted to charge users. X submits a variant bid in which it proposes to provide additional services not included in the RFP and to accept a lower maximum unit price. The grantor awards the concession to X under a concession agreement that features the services and price cap that X included in its variant bid. We believe that X should assess whether the arrangement is in the scope of IFRIC 12 by considering the terms of the final concession agreement; the fact that the services and prices are different from those set out in the RFP issued by the grantor is not relevant to this assessment.

5.12.42.30   Additional complexities may arise when assessing whether a business that receives a government subsidy is in the scope of IFRIC 12. For example, if the amount of the subsidy is specified in a contract or in regulation and the entity is required to perform specific services to receive the subsidy, then a question may arise over whether the arrangement meets the IFRIC 12 scope criteria about control of pricing and services.

5.12.42.40   In our view, when assessing whether a subsidised business meets the IFRIC 12 scope criterion for control of pricing, the primary focus of the analysis should be on whether the price that the operator charges users for the delivery of operating services is controlled or regulated. In general, if an operator charges a market price for the delivery of operating services, then the grantor does not control or regulate the price. Therefore, we believe that if an operator charges a market price for the delivery of operating services and receives a subsidy from the grantor, then there should not be a presumption that the existence of the subsidy constitutes price control.

5.12.42.50   However, depending on the facts and circumstances, a subsidy, or the combined effect of a subsidy and other elements of the arrangement, might in substance constitute price control. This might be the case, for example, in the following scenarios:
- the subsidy is received per unit of output sold and represents a significant proportion of the operating income of the operator; or
- the subsidy is a variable amount and is calculated to return excess revenues or profits to the grantor.

5.12.42.60   In such cases, an entity distinguishes the economic effects of caps and floors. If the effect was to cap the operator's return, then this would constitute price control under IFRIC 12. Conversely, if the effect was to guarantee the operator a minimum return with the operator also retaining exposure to variability in return above this minimum, then this would not constitute price control. [*IFRIC 12.AG3*]

5.12.42.70   If the subsidy constitutes price control, then it will be necessary to consider whether the remaining scope criteria of IFRIC 12 are met. If the arrangement is outside the scope of IFRIC 12, then the operator considers whether the subsidy is a form of government grant or other government assistance in the scope of IAS 20 (see chapter 4.3).

5.12.45 Other service arrangements

5.12.45.10   IFRIC 12 applies directly to public-to-private service concession arrangements. IFRIC 12 does not define 'public sector' or 'private sector'; these terms are also not defined elsewhere in IFRS. Application by analogy of IFRIC 12 to private-to-private service arrangements would be appropriate under the hierarchy for selecting accounting policies in IAS 8 (see 2.8.20). However, IFRIC 12 is silent on application to public-to-public service arrangements. [*IFRIC 12.BC14*]

5.12.45.20   Consider the following example. The government in Country X has established a limited liability entity, Company B, to act as the operator in a service concession arrangement. B's management has been recruited from the private sector and is encouraged to manage the day-to-day operations of B as if it were a commercial organisation. However, the government owns 100 percent of B's equity and controls 100 percent of the voting rights in B. For the purposes of this example, assume that all scope criteria in paragraph 5(a) and (b) of IFRIC 12 are met. The diagram below illustrates the relationship of the entities in the service concession arrangement.

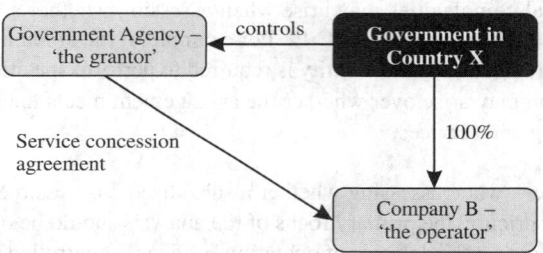

5.12.45.30   In our view, because the operator is 100 percent owned and controlled by the government, the arrangement is a public-to-public service concession arrangement and so is not directly in the scope of IFRIC 12.

5.12.45.40   Nevertheless, in accordance with IAS 8, B's management is required to use its judgement to develop and apply appropriate accounting policies. This will include considering the guidance and requirements in current accounting standards and interpretations dealing with similar and related issues, and the Conceptual Framework. Therefore, depending on the facts and circumstances, in our view application of IFRIC 12 by analogy may be appropriate. [*IAS 8.11, IFRIC 12.BC14*]

5.12.45.50   If in a subsequent accounting period the government sells a controlling interest in B to a private sector entity, then in our view B should reconsider its accounting treatment for the service concession arrangement, which may fall directly in the scope of IFRIC 12 at that time. Furthermore, if the operator is in the process of listing on a stock exchange or otherwise being privatised, then it should consider the application of IFRIC 12 under the hierarchy for selecting accounting policies. In both circumstances described above, using the accounting requirements set out in IFRIC 12 throughout will reduce the changes to B's accounting treatment of the service concession arrangement on change of control and/or listing.

5.12.45.60 In other cases, it may be appropriate to apply IFRIC 12 to some private-to-private arrangements. The basis for conclusions to IFRIC 12 states that application by analogy to private-to-private arrangements would be appropriate for arrangements that:

- meet the requirements set out in paragraph 5 – i.e. meet the scope criteria that establish that the grantor controls the use of the infrastructure; and
- have the characteristics described in paragraph 3 – i.e. have the general features of service concession arrangements described in that paragraph. [*IFRIC 12.BC14*]

5.12.45.70 IFRIC 12 identifies types of arrangements that may be very similar to leases. In some cases, the accounting by operators would be significantly different under IFRIC 4/IAS 17 and IFRIC 12. However, IFRIC 12 defines the border between leases and service concession arrangements that are in its scope: leases under IAS 17 convey a right to control the use of an asset, whereas under IFRIC 12 the grantor retains control of the right to use the infrastructure. [*IFRIC 12.AG7–AG8*]

5.12.45.80 In our view, the reference in IFRIC 12 to application by analogy is not intended to signify a free choice of whether to account for other arrangements either under IFRIC 4/IAS 17 or as service concession arrangements under IFRIC 12. Instead, IFRIC 12 may be relevant for identifying and accounting for those private-to-private arrangements in which the grantor retains control of the right to use the infrastructure.

5.12.45.90 In developing IFRIC 12, the IFRS Interpretations Committee considered the range of typical arrangements for private sector participation in the provision of public services; IFRIC 12 addresses only a subset of such arrangements. However, IFRIC 12 does include references to other standards that apply to typical types of public-to-private service arrangements. [*IFRIC 12.IN2, BC13*]

CATEGORY	LESSEE	SERVICE PROVIDER		OWNER	
Typical arrangement types	Lease (e.g. operator leases assets from grantor)	Service and/or maintenance contract (specific tasks – e.g. debt collection)	Rehabilitate-operate-transfer	Build-operate-transfer	Build-own-operate	100% divestment/ privatisation/ corporation
Asset ownership	Grantor				Operator	
Capital investment	Grantor		Operator			
Demand risk	Shared	Grantor	Operator and/or grantor		Operator	
Typical duration	8–20 years	1–5 years		25–30 years	Indefinite (or may be limited by licence)	
Residual interest	Grantor				Operator	
Relevant standards	IAS 17	IFRS 15	IFRIC 12		IAS 16	

5.12.45.100 These references to other standards represent a subset of the spectrum of such arrangements; no bright lines exist between the accounting requirements for different types of service concession arrangements. [*IFRIC 12.IN2*]

5.12.45.110   The analysis of whether an arrangement is in the scope of IFRIC 12 requires judgement and all relevant facts and circumstances need to be considered. Arrangements that appear to meet the scope criteria in paragraph 5 of IFRIC 12 but are purely service and/or maintenance contracts (e.g. debt collection on behalf of the grantor) are not in the scope of IFRIC 12. [*IFRIC 12.IN2*]

5.12.45.120   In some cases, the grantor gives the operator access to the existing infrastructure for the purpose of providing the public service and the arrangement does not require the operator to perform significant construction or upgrade services. In such cases, the operator assesses whether the arrangement is in the scope of IFRIC 12 by considering the specific facts and circumstances and the control criteria in paragraphs 5(a) and (b) of IFRIC 12. [*IFRIC 12.7, IU 09-16*]

5.12.45.130   In some service concession arrangements, the operator may enter into a lease agreement with a third party and may employ the underlying asset to fulfil its obligations under the concession agreement. The scope exemption in paragraph 4(b) of IFRIC 4 applies to the concession agreement between the operator and grantor but does not address other lease agreements. A question arises on how the operator should account for leases entered into in the context of a service concession arrangement but not dealt with by the scope exemption in paragraph 4(b) of IFRIC 4. The operator assesses whether the arrangement, including the leased infrastructure, is in the scope of IFRIC 12 by considering the specific facts and circumstances and the control criteria in paragraphs 5(a) and (b) of IFRIC 12. [*IU 09-16*]

EXAMPLE 7 – LEASES ENTERED INTO IN CONTEXT OF SERVICE CONCESSION ARRANGEMENTS

5.12.45.140   Operator O enters into a service concession arrangement, which is considered to be in the scope of IFRIC 12, with Grantor G to operate a rail service for 15 years. To deliver the service, O leases rolling stock with a useful life of 25 years from a third party. O has the obligation to pay the lessor. During the concession period, G controls the services that O delivers – e.g. by setting the timetable to which the rolling stock must be operated – and regulates the price that O charges passengers. At the end of the concession, G has an option to acquire the rolling stock or to otherwise direct its use.

5.12.45.150   In this example, O does not have the right to use the rolling stock. Instead, it has a contractual obligation under the concession to procure the right-of-use of the rolling stock. O transfers the right-of-use to G in exchange for an intangible asset, just as if it had delivered construction services in exchange for an intangible asset. Because O does not control the right to use the rolling stock, O does not apply IAS 17 to the lease agreement. Instead, O recognises a financial liability to make payments to the lessor and an addition to the carrying amount of its intangible asset on commencement of the lease agreement. [*IU 09-16*]

5.12.45.160   Modifying the fact pattern, G has the obligation to pay the lessor. However, O makes payments to the lessor and has an unconditional right to receive a reimbursement from G. In this case, O collects cash from G that it remits to the lessor on behalf of G. [*IU 09-16*]

5.12.45.170   The analysis about the accounting of lease agreements entered by the operator to purchase items necessary to fulfil its obligations under the concession requires judgement and all relevant facts and circumstances need to be considered.

5.12.50   KEY REQUIREMENTS

5.12.60   Operator's rights over infrastructure

5.12.60.10   The operator does not recognise public service infrastructure in the scope of IFRIC 12 as its property, plant and equipment, because the operator is considered to have a right of access rather than a right of use (see 5.1.510.40). This requirement applies to existing infrastructure of the grantor and to infrastructure that the operator builds or acquires for the purposes of the concession. [*IFRIC 12.11*]

EXAMPLE 8 – RIGHTS OVER INFRASTRUCTURE

5.12.60.15   Company C enters into a service concession arrangement with the government of Country Y to build and operate a hydroelectric power plant. C is responsible for acquiring the land on which the power plant will be built and other assets used in the construction. Because the land and the other assets used in the construction were not existing assets of C but rather were acquired to build the power plant under the terms of the service concession agreement, they are not recognised as assets of C.

5.12.60.20   IFRIC 12 does not apply to existing property, plant and equipment of the operator. The operator applies the derecognition criteria of IAS 16 to assess whether it should derecognise existing property, plant and equipment that it held and recognised before entering into the service concession arrangement and that it will use to fulfil its obligations under the arrangement. [*IFRIC 12.8*]

5.12.65   *Essential but uncontracted infrastructure enhancements*

5.12.65.10   In some cases, an operator in a service concession arrangement may need to construct additional public use assets that do not form part of the infrastructure but are essential for the arrangement to be operational. These assets might not be operated by the operator. In our view, even if these investments are not explicitly required by the arrangement, they should be accounted for as a part of the concession arrangement if the related assets are essential to providing the services.

EXAMPLE 9 – INFRASTRUCTURE ENHANCEMENTS – ESSENTIAL BUT UNCONTRACTED

5.12.65.20   Operator O enters into a service concession agreement with Grantor G to construct and operate a hydroelectric power plant in a remote area in Country K. To access the construction site, O constructs new access roads. The arrangement does

not specifically require O to construct the access roads, but they are necessary because there is no viable alternative to transport materials to the construction site. The government of Country K has given its permission to construct the access roads. O does not control or operate the new roads because they are the property of the government and accessible by the public.

5.12.65.30   In this example, we believe that the costs to build the access roads are in the scope of IFRIC 12. Although they do not directly contribute to the generation of cash flows by the hydroelectric power plant, they are essential to operating the plant, and G and O would have considered the costs in the pricing of the arrangement.

5.12.70   Recognition of construction or upgrade revenue

5.12.70.10   IFRIC 12 characterises operators as 'service providers' who construct or upgrade public infrastructure and operate and maintain that infrastructure. An operator recognises revenue and costs related to these services in accordance with IFRS 15 – i.e. when (or as) it satisfies its performance obligations by transferring control over goods or services to a customer (see chapter 4.2). [*IFRIC 12.12–14, 20, IFRS 15.31, 47*]

5.12.70.20   Depending on the type of concession contract, the consideration received/receivable by the operator may comprise a financial asset, an intangible asset or both (see 5.12.80). To the extent that the operator has an unconditional contractual right to receive cash or another financial asset from or at the direction of the grantor for the construction services, the operator recognises a financial asset. Conversely, to the extent that it receives a right to charge users of the public service, the operator recognises an intangible asset. [*IFRIC 12.15–17*]

5.12.70.30   If the operator receives an intangible asset, then the total revenue recognised by the operator over the concession term exceeds the total cash received by the operator over the concession term. This is because the revenue recognised by the operator includes construction revenue for which the consideration received is non-cash – i.e. an intangible asset. This is not the case if the operator receives a financial asset, because whereas interest accrual is recognised in the statement of profit or loss and OCI, the receipt of cash or other financial assets for the construction services is credited directly against the receivable. [*IFRIC 12.BC32, BC34*]

5.12.70.40   Usually, the operator provides more than one service – e.g. construction or upgrade services, operation services. To assess whether a service concession arrangement contains more than one service to the same customer, the operator applies the guidance in IFRS 15:
- to determine who the customer is – i.e. the grantor or the users of the infrastructure; and
- to identify performance obligations under the contract with that customer (see 4.2.60). [*IFRIC 12.13*]

5.12.70.50   Whether the customer in a service concession arrangement is the grantor and/or the user of the infrastructure depends on the type of concession and the services provided. The grantor is usually the customer for the construction or upgrade services. To the extent that the operator has an unconditional contractual right to receive cash or another financial asset from or at the direction of the grantor for services rendered, the grantor is also the customer for the operation services. However, if an operator receives an intangible asset, then the users of the infrastructure are typically the customers for the operation services. [*IFRIC 12.IE1, IE11, IE23, BC31–BC32*]

5.12.70.60   If a service concession arrangement includes more than one performance obligation to the same customer, then the operator allocates the total consideration to which it expects to be entitled over the concession period to each performance obligation based on its relative stand-alone selling price (see 4.2.160). [*IFRIC 12.13, IFRS 15.74, 84–85*]

5.12.70.70   This allocation is performed even if the concession agreement stipulates individual prices for certain services. This is because the amounts specified in the concession agreement may not necessarily be representative of the stand-alone selling prices of the services provided. The best evidence of this price is an observable price from stand-alone sales of that good or service to customers with similar characteristics. If this price is not available, then the operator estimates it considering all information that is reasonably available. For a discussion of how to estimate the stand-alone selling price, see 4.2.170. [*IFRIC 12.13, BC31, IFRS 15.79*]

5.12.70.80   Under the intangible asset model, the operator receives non-cash consideration in the form of a licence to operate the infrastructure. Under IFRS 15, the non-cash consideration is measured at its fair value. If a reasonable estimate of fair value cannot be made, then the estimated selling price of the promised service is used for reference. In practice, the estimated selling price of the construction services delivered may be the most appropriate method of establishing the amount of the consideration received or receivable for the construction services. [*IFRIC 12.13, 15, BC30, IFRS 15.66–67*]

EXAMPLE 10 – MEASUREMENT OF CONSTRUCTION REVENUE

5.12.70.90   Under the terms of a service concession arrangement, Company Q builds a toll road to a new development area. As consideration for building the toll road, Q receives a right to collect tolls from users of the road for 25 years. The value of this intangible asset will depend, among other things, on the expected number of users of the toll road. Traffic consultants have reported that the expected use of the road is uncertain and have prepared two projections: a high case and a low case. A valuation of the intangible asset using the high case suggests that the fair value of the intangible asset is 1,000; a valuation using the low case suggests that the fair value is 800. Based on its experience of other roads, Q considers that the stand-alone selling price of the construction services it performs in building this toll road is 950. In our view, Q should measure the intangible asset at 950 on initial recognition.

5.12.70.100   If the operator receives a right to operate the infrastructure plus a guarantee for a minimum return, then the transaction price for the construction services also includes the present value of the guaranteed amount.

5.12.70.110   When determining the total consideration to which it expects to be entitled, the operator adjusts the promised amount of consideration for the effect of the time value of money, if there is a significant financing component in the concession arrangement. Future cash receipts are discounted using the discount rate that would be reflected in a separate financing transaction between the operator and the grantor at inception of the contract. The operator may determine the rate as the rate of interest that discounts the nominal amount of the promised consideration to the price that would be paid in cash when control over the goods or services are transferred (see 4.2.130). [*IFRS 15.64*]

5.12.70.120   However, if the operator recognises consideration for construction services as an intangible asset (see 5.12.80), then in our view the arrangement does not include a significant financing component. This is because the intangible asset represents a right to charge users, and that right can only be exercised once the infrastructure being constructed is ready for use. As a result, the timing difference between the performance of construction services and receipt of the intangible asset arises for reasons other than financing. For a discussion of significant financing component, see 4.2.130.

5.12.70.130   Judgement may be required to determine stand-alone selling prices of different services. In particular, an operator may have to recognise different margins for different services under a single concession agreement. [*IFRIC 12.BC31*]

EXAMPLE 11 – DIFFERENT MARGINS FOR DIFFERENT SERVICES WITHIN SINGLE ARRANGEMENT

5.12.70.140   Company P enters into a service concession arrangement. Under the terms of the arrangement:
- P builds and operates a prison;
- P receives a fixed amount of cash for performing both construction and operation services; and
- total consideration received is 1,100.

5.12.70.150   P concludes that the service concession arrangement contains two performance obligations in the contract with the grantor in accordance with IFRS 15: construction services and operation services. P estimates that:
- the stand-alone selling price of the construction services it performs is 900 and the cost of construction services is 800; and
- the stand-alone selling price of the operation services is 300 and the cost of the operation services is 250.

5.12.70.160   P accounts for the arrangement by first allocating the total consideration between construction and operation services according to the relative stand-alone selling prices of the individual services. That is, P allocates revenue as follows:
- construction services – 825 ((900 / (900 + 300)) x 1,100); and
- operation services – 275 ((300 / (900 + 300)) x 1,100).

5.12.70.170   On this basis, P then expects to recognise a margin of 3% on performing construction services and a margin of 9% on performing operation services.

5.12.70.180   In some jurisdictions, it is common for a joint arrangement to be formed to undertake a specific service concession arrangement. The joint arrangement partners are typically a construction entity, a service provider and a financial institution. The joint arrangement partners may subcontract certain services required under the terms of the concession agreement to investors in the joint arrangement.

EXAMPLE 12 – MARGINS FOR SUBCONTRACTED SERVICES

5.12.70.190   Company B is a joint arrangement formed to act as the operator in a service concession arrangement to build and operate a hospital. B's investors include Company C, a construction entity. B subcontracts construction of the hospital to C. The key terms of the construction contract between B and C mirror the sections of the concession agreement dealing with construction of the hospital. B uses expected cost plus a margin approach to estimates stand-alone selling price.

5.12.70.200   In our view, B should estimate an appropriate construction margin applying the principles in IFRS 15 to the facts and circumstances of the specific arrangement. An appropriate construction margin is likely to reflect:
- the work performed by B to co-ordinate the various construction services required to be performed under the terms of the service concession arrangement; and
- the construction risks retained by B, which have not been passed on to C or other subcontractors.

5.12.80   Recognition of consideration receivable for construction or upgrade services

5.12.80.10   As mentioned in 5.12.70.20, the operator recognises consideration received or receivable for providing construction or upgrade services as:
- a financial asset to the extent that it has an unconditional right to receive cash irrespective of use of the infrastructure; and/or
- an intangible asset to the extent that its consideration is dependent on use of the infrastructure. [*IFRIC 12.15–17*]

5.12.80.20   Regardless of the nature of the consideration – i.e. financial asset, intangible asset or both – the operator recognises a contract asset during the construction or upgrade period in accordance with IFRS 15 (see 4.2.470). The financial and intangible assets are recognised after construction is completed. [*IFRIC 12.19*]

5.12.83   *Demand risk*

5.12.83.10   The operator recognises a financial asset only when its right to receive cash is not dependent on the use of the infrastructure. That is, the nature of the asset recognised by the operator depends on the allocation of the demand risk between the operator and the grantor. In simple cases, the operator recognises a financial asset to the extent that the grantor bears the demand risk, and an intangible asset to the extent that it bears the demand risk. The nature of the asset recognised by the operator depends on the allocation of the demand risk, not the significance of the demand risk in the context of the arrangement as a whole. [*IFRIC 12.16, BC42, BC47–BC48, BC52*]

EXAMPLE 13A – DEMAND RISK

5.12.83.20 Operator O enters into two separate concession agreements, each involving the construction and operation of a hospital.

5.12.83.30 In the first case (Hospital K), O receives fixed payments from the grantor during the concession period. In this case, the grantor bears the demand risk because the cash flows of O do not depend on the use of the hospital. Therefore, O recognises a financial asset as the consideration received for its construction services.

5.12.83.40 In the second case (Hospital L), the grantor pays O an amount calculated with reference to the average number of beds occupied by patients each month – i.e. the payment is calculated as the average occupancy multiplied by a rate per bed. In this case, O bears the demand risk because the cash flows of O depend on the use of the hospital. Therefore, O recognises an intangible asset as the consideration received for its construction services.

5.12.83.50 In some service concession arrangements, after examining all relevant facts and circumstances, it may remain unclear whether the grantor or the operator bears the demand risk. In such cases, if there is no clear indicator whether the consideration receivable by the operator is a financial asset or an intangible asset, then in our view the operator should choose to recognise a financial asset or an intangible asset and apply that choice consistently to similar types of arrangement.

EXAMPLE 13B – DEMAND RISK – GRANTOR AGREES TO PURCHASE ALL OUTPUT

5.12.83.60 Operator O enters into a service concession arrangement with Grantor G to build and operate a solar-generating power plant. G is contractually obliged to purchase all of the electricity produced by the plant at a fixed unit price. There is no guaranteed amount that G is obliged to pay O – i.e. O does not receive any consideration from G if the power plant does not generate electricity. O's income is solely dependent on the amount of electricity generated by the power plant.

5.12.83.70 In this case, it is unclear which party bears the demand risk. It could be argued that G bears the demand risk, because it is contractually required to purchase all of the electricity produced by the power plant, irrespective of the level of public demand for electricity. Following this approach, O would recognise a financial asset, because it does not bear the demand risk for the electricity produced.

5.12.83.80 Conversely, it could be argued that O bears the demand risk, because O's income and financial return depend entirely on the amount of electricity generated, with no minimum guaranteed income. Following this approach, O would recognise an intangible asset representing its right to charge G for any electricity produced.

5.12.83.90 Because it is unclear who bears the demand risk and whether O has a financial asset or an intangible asset, we believe that O should choose an accounting policy, to be applied consistently to all similar arrangements, to recognise either a financial asset or an intangible asset.

5.12.83.100   In more complex cases, the operator may recognise both a financial asset and an intangible asset.

EXAMPLE 13C – DEMAND RISK – MINIMUM AMOUNT GUARANTEED

5.12.83.110   Operator O builds and operates a hospital for the grantor, Hospital M. The grantor pays O based on occupancy as for Hospital L in Example 13A except that the monthly payment is subject to a minimum level –i.e. the monthly payment by the grantor is calculated as the higher of:
- average occupancy multiplied by a rate per bed; and
- a fixed monetary amount.

5.12.83.120   In this case, O recognises a financial asset representing the right to receive the fixed monetary amount and an intangible asset representing the right to charge for the use of the hospital above this fixed monetary amount.

5.12.83.130   The identity of the party that makes payments to the operator once the infrastructure is available for use does not affect how the operator classifies consideration receivable for construction or upgrade services.

EXAMPLE 13D – DEMAND RISK – PARTY MAKING PAYMENTS

5.12.83.140   Consider two separate concession agreements in which the operator builds and operates a road. In the first case, users of the road pay tolls to the operator based on use. In the second case, the grantor makes payments to the operator based on the number of users of the road; sometimes such an arrangement is described as a 'shadow toll'.

5.12.83.150   In both cases, the operator bears the demand risk and does not have an unconditional right to receive cash irrespective of use. Therefore, the operator recognises an intangible asset as consideration for construction services. [*IFRIC 12.BC39–BC40*]

5.12.90   *Unconditional right to receive cash*

5.12.90.10   The operator's right to receive cash is considered unconditional even when payment is contingent on the operator meeting future quality or efficiency performance requirements. For example, an operator may have a right to receive fixed amounts of cash from the grantor in return for the construction services, subject to deductions if the infrastructure is not available for use or is operating below a specified standard. In this case, the operator recognises a financial asset even though its right to receive cash is contingent on the satisfaction of other contractual conditions. When measuring the related revenue, the operator applies guidance in IFRS 15 on variable consideration (see 4.2.100). [*IFRIC 12.BC44*]

5.12.90.20   Some service concession agreements incorporate contractual clauses designed to elimi-nate substantially all variability in the operator's return. In such cases, it remains necessary to apply the criteria in 5.12.80.10 to determine whether the operator should recognise a financial asset and/ or an intangible asset. This is because the fact that the operator's asset is low-risk does not give the operator the unconditional contractual right to receive cash. [*IFRIC 12.BC52*]

EXAMPLE 14 – SUBSTANTIALLY FIXED RETURNS

5.12.90.30   Operator T enters in a service concession agreement with Country W to build and operate a toll bridge. The amounts receivable by T depend on the use of the bridge and will be paid directly by the users. The grantor regulates the toll prices that T may charge users based on a targeted rate of return – i.e. the rate is reset to reach an average return in the contract.

5.12.90.35   In this situation, although T has a substantially fixed return established in the service concession agreement, this does not give rise to a financial asset because T does not have an unconditional right to receive cash. Instead, T will recognise an intangible asset.

5.12.90.40   In some service concession arrangements, the operator receives an additional cash pay-ment at the end of the concession period. The amount of the payment may be based on, for example, the fair value of the service concession infrastructure at the end of the concession period. The treat-ment of this additional payment will depend on the facts and circumstances of the arrangement.

EXAMPLE 15A – END OF CONCESSION PERIOD – CASH PAYMENT

5.12.90.50   Company R builds and operates a toll road. In consideration for build-ing the toll road, R is entitled to charge users during the operating period and is entitled to receive a cash payment from the grantor based on the fair value of the toll road at the end of the concession.

5.12.90.55   In this case, the amount that R receives from users during the operating period depends on use of the infrastructure, but the amount that R receives from the grantor at the end of the concession does not. Therefore, R recognises an intangible asset for its right to charge users and a financial asset for its right to receive cash from the grantor.

EXAMPLE 15B – END OF CONCESSION PERIOD – CASH PAYMENT OR TITLE TRANSFER

5.12.90.60   Modifying the fact pattern in Example 15A, instead of being com-mitted to make an additional cash payment to Company R based on the fair value of the infrastructure at the end of the concession, the grantor has an option at the end of the concession to either:
- pay cash to R based on the fair value of the infrastructure at the end of the concession; or

> ● transfer to R the title to the infrastructure itself.
>
> 5.12.90.70   In this example, the key factor is that the grantor, and not R, controls the decision about which asset will be transferred at the end of the concession. Consequently, R does not have an unconditional right to receive cash. Instead, it has a right to receive either cash or the infrastructure at the end of the concession. Therefore, R does not recognise a financial asset but instead recognises its right to receive cash or a non-financial asset at the end of the concession as an intangible asset.

5.12.100   *Payments from operator to grantor*

5.12.100.10   IFRIC 12 addresses scenarios in which the operator receives consideration from the grantor for construction or upgrade services. In addition, in some cases the operator may make payments to the grantor at the inception of a service concession arrangement or over the concession period. In our view, the operator should recognise and measure any assets arising from such payments according to their substance, considering the terms of the arrangement as a whole.

5.12.100.15   The IFRS Interpretations Committee discussed how an operator accounts for payments that it makes to the grantor, other than those collected on behalf of and remitted to the grantor – e.g. sales taxes – and noted the following:

- if the service concession arrangement results in the operator having only a contractual right to receive cash from the grantor – i.e. the financial asset model applies (see 5.12.80) – then the operator accounts for those payments as a reduction of revenue. Under the financial asset model, the operator only has one customer (see 5.12.70.50), and therefore the amount paid to the grantor is part of the transaction price under the service concession contract. The operator applies the requirements of IFRS 15 to allocate this amount to the performance obligations that were identified under the contract;
- if the service concession arrangement results in the operator having only a right to charge users of the public service – i.e. the intangible asset model applies (see 5.12.80) – then it may be appropriate to consider that the operator has received an intangible asset (i.e. the licence to operate) in exchange for construction or upgrade services plus the payments to be made to the grantor. Consequently, the operator accounts for the payments applying IAS 38; and
- if payments are not for the right to a separate good or service or a separate right-of-use that is a lease, then the operator accounts for those payments as follows:
  - if the service concession arrangement results in the operator having only a contractual right to receive cash from the grantor – i.e. the financial asset model applies (see 5.12.80) – then the operator accounts for those payments as a reduction of revenue;
  - if the service concession arrangement results in the operator having only a right to charge users of the public service – i.e. the intangible asset model applies (see 5.12.80) – then the operator has received an intangible asset in exchange for construction or upgrade services and the payments to be made to the grantor. Consequently, the operator accounts for the payments applying IAS 38; and
  - if the operator has both a right to charge users of the public service and a contractual right to receive cash from the grantor – i.e. both the intangible asset and financial asset models apply – then the operator considers whether the payments represent payments made for the intangible asset or consideration payable to a customer, or both. [*IU 07-16*]

5.12 Service concession arrangements

5.12.100.17   This discussion is summarised in the following chart.

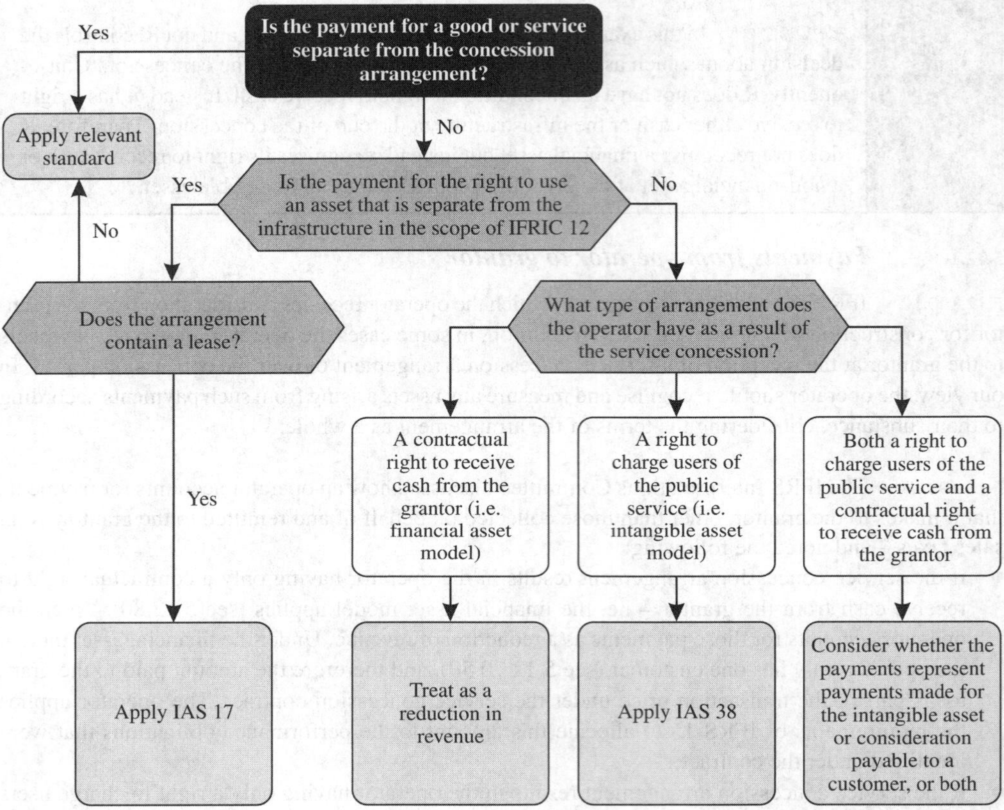

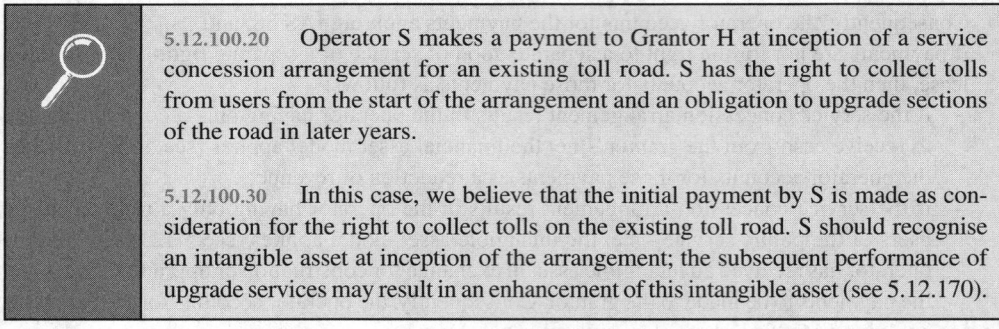

EXAMPLE 16A – PAYMENT FOR INTANGIBLE ASSET

> 5.12.100.20   Operator S makes a payment to Grantor H at inception of a service concession arrangement for an existing toll road. S has the right to collect tolls from users from the start of the arrangement and an obligation to upgrade sections of the road in later years.
>
> 5.12.100.30   In this case, we believe that the initial payment by S is made as consideration for the right to collect tolls on the existing toll road. S should recognise an intangible asset at inception of the arrangement; the subsequent performance of upgrade services may result in an enhancement of this intangible asset (see 5.12.170).

5.12.100.40   In some cases, an operator may be required to make a combination of fixed and variable payments over the concession period to acquire the right to collect tolls in this manner. In our view, the operator should include the fair value of the fixed element of the payments in the cost of the intangible asset and recognise a corresponding financial liability at inception of the agreement.

For a discussion of variable payments to acquire intangible assets, see 3.3.100.70. We believe that variable payments should generally be expensed as they are incurred.

EXAMPLE 16B – OTHER CONSIDERATION RECEIVED FOR INTANGIBLE ASSET

5.12.100.50   Operator R transfers to Grantor M, at inception of a service concession arrangement for a toll road, options to acquire equity instruments and other participation rights. The transfer is made as consideration for the right to charge the users for use of the road.

5.12.100.60   In this case, we believe that:
- the options to acquire equity instruments should be accounted for under IFRS 2 (see chapter 4.5);
- other participation rights, which are not share-based payments, should be accounted for under IFRS 9 (see chapter 7.3); and
- the fair value of the items transferred should be recognised as part of the cost of the intangible asset at inception of the arrangement.

EXAMPLE 16C – PAYMENTS NOT DEPENDENT ON FUTURE USE OF ASSET

5.12.100.70   Operator M makes a payment to Grantor L at inception of a service concession arrangement related to a new hospital. The terms of the arrangement are as follows.
- M is required to build a new hospital building.
- Once completed, M will receive monthly payments from L that do not depend on use of the hospital.
- The total cash receivable from L exceeds the fair value of the construction and operation services to be provided by M.

5.12.100.75   M identifies one customer – i.e. L – and two performance obligations – i.e. construction services and operation services.

5.12.100.80   In this example, the initial payment by M reduces the transaction price allocated to the performance obligations identified in the service concession contract in accordance with the allocation criteria of IFRS 15.

5.12.110   Borrowing costs

5.12.110.10   If the operator receives a right to charge for use of the public service infrastructure, then the operator is generally required to capitalise attributable borrowing costs for qualifying assets incurred during the construction or upgrade phase. Otherwise, the operator expenses borrowing costs as they are incurred. For a discussion of qualifying assets, see 4.6.20.120–130. [*IAS 23.1, 10, IFRIC 12.22, BC58*]

5.12.120   Items provided by the grantor

5.12.120.10   If the grantor provides items to the operator that the operator may retain or sell at its discretion – i.e. 'keep-or-deal' items – and those items form part of the consideration for the services provided, then the operator accounts for the items as part of the transaction price as defined in IFRS 15. [*IFRIC 12.27*]

5.12.120.20   Keep-or-deal items that the grantor transfers to the operator in consideration for services are not government grants. The distinction is important because the accounting for government grants and keep-or-deal items may be different. For example, the operator may account for a non-monetary government grant either at fair value or at nominal value (see chapter 4.3). In contrast, the operator measures non-cash consideration at fair value in accordance with IFRS 15. [*IFRIC 12.27, IFRS 15.66*]

5.12.120.30   The operator also distinguishes such keep-or-deal items from concession infrastructure controlled by the grantor and accounts for the two classes of items in different ways. The operator recognises keep-or-deal items such as inventory or property, plant and equipment, whereas the operator does not recognise concession infrastructure as property, plant and equipment. [*IFRIC 12.27*]

EXAMPLE 17 – KEEP-OR-DEAL ITEMS

5.12.120.40   Grantor G transfers to Operator O a property interest in a site containing a hospital building and a separate office building. Under the terms of the concession, O is required to rehabilitate and operate the hospital building for 20 years and then return the hospital building to G in a specified state. Conversely, O has discretion over the future use of the office building, which in practice it may occupy itself, redevelop and/or sell.

5.12.120.50   In this example, the hospital building is infrastructure in the scope of IFRIC 12 and so O does not recognise the hospital building as its property, plant and equipment. However, O has discretion to 'keep or deal' the office building. Therefore, O recognises the office building as its asset, measured at fair value on initial recognition.

5.12.130   Operation revenue

5.12.130.10   The operator recognises and measures revenue related to operation services in accordance with IFRS 15. The general principle in IFRS 15 is that an entity recognises revenue when it satisfies its performance obligation to transfer the operation services to the customer at the amount that reflects the consideration to which the entity expects to be entitled. [*IFRIC 12.20, IFRS 15.31, 46*]

5.12.130.20   If the operator recognises an intangible asset after the construction phase – i.e. it received a right to collect fees that are contingent on the extent of use of the public service – then it recognises operation revenue as it provides operation services to customers. For example, if an operator builds a toll road and receives the right to collect tolls from the users, then the operator recognises toll revenue as the road is used. [*IFRS 15.31*]

5.12.130.30   If the operator recognises a financial asset – i.e. it receives an unconditional right to receive cash that is not dependent on the extent of use of the public service – then a portion of payments received during the operation phase is allocated to the amortisation of this financial asset. The operator recognises revenue from the operation services and the financial asset resulting from them as it provides operation services to the customers and measures revenue at the amount that it expects to be entitled to for those services. For a discussion of how to allocate consideration, see 5.12.70.60 and 4.2.160. [*IFRS 15.31, 46*]

5.12.130.40   Further complexities may arise in service concession arrangements in which the operator recognises an intangible asset and a financial asset. In such cases, the consideration received or receivable under the arrangement will be allocated between the financial asset and the intangible asset. The consideration received or receivable for both components is recognised initially in accordance with IFRS 15. A portion of payments collected is allocated to the repayment of the financial asset. This is illustrated in Example 24, which is a comprehensive worked example. [*IFRIC 12.18, IE27*]

5.12.140   Maintenance obligations and upgrade services

5.12.140.10   Service concession agreements typically require the operator to maintain the infrastructure such that the infrastructure can deliver a specified standard of service at all times. In addition, service concession arrangements other than whole-of-life arrangements generally require the operator to hand back the infrastructure to the grantor or another party in a specified state at the end of the concession period. [*IFRIC 12.21*]

5.12.140.20   The operator recognises and measures contractual obligations to maintain or restore infrastructure in accordance with IAS 37 (see chapter 3.12), except for any upgrade element for which the operator recognises revenue and costs in accordance with IFRS 15. [*IFRIC 12.21*]

5.12.140.30   Judgement may be required to determine whether a particular activity to be undertaken by an operator under the contract is:
- an obligation arising under the terms of its licence to be recognised under IAS 37; or
- a service provided under the terms of the arrangement and therefore a separate performance obligation under IFRS 15 (see 4.2.320).

5.12.140.35   The illustrative examples in IFRIC 12 demonstrate situations in which major maintenance is accounted for as a revenue-generating activity and situations in which it is accounted for as a provision.
- *Revenue-generating activity:* Under a concession in which the operator receives a financial asset and is required to resurface a road at a specified time during the concession period, the resurfacing work is viewed as a separate performance obligation. Therefore, it is accounted for as a revenue component of the arrangement (see 5.12.70).
- *Provision:* Under a concession in which the operator receives an intangible asset and is required to resurface a road when it deteriorates below a specified condition, the resurfacing obligation is recognised and measured in accordance with IAS 37. The obligation arises as the road is being used – i.e. as the operating service is provided. Although it is not explicitly mentioned in the illustrative examples, under these arrangements the customer of the operating services may be determined as the user of the infrastructure. [*IFRIC 12.21, IE4, IE19, IE35*]

5.12.140.37   Notwithstanding the discussion in 5.12.140.35, in our view the most appropriate accounting treatment for maintenance activities will depend on the facts and circumstances of each arrangement, not only on whether the operator recognises a financial asset or an intangible asset as consideration for construction or upgrade services. [*IFRIC 12.21, IE4, IE19, IE35*]

EXAMPLE 18 – DISTINGUISHING OBLIGATIONS FROM SERVICES

5.12.140.40   Company H builds and operates a toll road and recognises an intangible asset. The service concession agreement requires H to maintain the toll road and, in practice, H expects to resurface the toll road every seven years. However, H has no contractual right to increase the toll price on the road after it finishes the resurfacing.

5.12.140.42   We believe that it would not be appropriate for H to treat the resurfacing activity as construction or enhancement revenue and record an increase in the carrying amount of the intangible asset. This is because the resurfacing activity does not provide a distinct service to the customers – i.e. the users of the infrastructure – and therefore is not a revenue-generating activity. H does not receive an additional right to charge users of the road when it resurfaces the road.

5.12.140.45   Judgement will be required in measuring an obligation to maintain or restore a concession asset and in determining the timing of its recognition. Generally, IAS 37 requires a provision to be measured at the best estimate of the expenditure to be incurred to transfer the present obligation at the reporting date. It will often be appropriate to recognise a provision for an obligation to restore a concession asset as the asset deteriorates. In such a case, the provision is likely to be measured at the costs expected to be incurred to perform the maintenance or restoration work, discounted by a rate that reflects the time value of money and the risks involved (see 3.12.110–120). [*IFRIC 12.21, IE20, IE36, IAS 37.37*]

5.12.140.50   Agreements in the scope of IFRIC 12 are generally executory when they are signed and rights and obligations under such contracts cannot be recognised to the extent that they are executory. However, if the facts and circumstances indicate that the operator accepts an obligation at inception of the service concession agreement as consideration for the rights that it acquires, then the operator will identify a (separate) performance obligation for the rehabilitation services and allocate part of the transaction price to it in accordance with the requirements of IFRS 15. The operator will recognise a contract liability for the rehabilitation services and the corresponding debit as part of the cost of the intangible asset at inception of the contract. [*IFRIC 12.BC68, BC55–BC56*]

EXAMPLE 19 – TIMING OF RECOGNITION AND MEASUREMENT

5.12.140.60   Company R enters into a concession arrangement to operate and maintain the existing water distribution network in Country S. There was no up-front fee paid by R; however, at inception of the contract R assumes an obligation to maintain and rehabilitate the existing water distribution network to reach certain standards of serviceability. Prices charged by R to customers are established by Country S at inception of the contract and are not subject to increases on the conclusion of the rehabilitation activity.

5.12.140.65   R identifies the rehabilitation services as a separate performance obligation under the contract with Country S in accordance with IFRS 15.

> 5.12.140.70   R recognises the intangible asset and the contract liability for the obligation assumed at inception of the agreement based on the stand-alone selling price of the expected future restoration services.

5.12.140.80   There may be situations in which the operator is reimbursed for some costs incurred in upgrading the service concession asset. In such cases, it is important to distinguish between revenue-generating services and obligations for maintenance under the terms of the concession arrangement. This determination is dependent on the specific facts and circumstances and requires judgement. If the operator concludes that the service to enhance the physical infrastructure is a revenue-generating service, then the operator will recognise the revenue and costs related to this service in accordance with IFRS 15 – i.e. as it delivers the service. Under this approach, the amount to be reimbursed by the grantor will form part of the consideration receivable for performing the construction services – i.e. a financial asset. [*IFRIC 12.14–15*]

EXAMPLE 20A – UPGRADE SERVICES – REVENUE-GENERATING

> 5.12.140.90   Company C operates a power plant under an arrangement that is in the scope of IFRIC 12. C has the right to charge users for electricity generated. C upgrades the plant to increase its production capacity and therefore increase the amount of revenue it is able to generate. The initial estimate of the fair value of the construction services required to complete the upgrade is 100. The cost of construction is 95. In addition, per the terms of the agreement the grantor agrees to reimburse 20% of the costs of the upgrade. C completes the upgrade within a single reporting period. C concludes that the requirement to enhance the physical infrastructure is a revenue-generating service and records the following entries.
>
> | | DEBIT | CREDIT |
> | --- | --- | --- |
> | Financial asset (95 x 20%) | 19 | |
> | Intangible asset | 81 | |
> | Construction revenue | | 100 |
> | Cost of sales (100 x (1 - 5%)) | 95 | |
> | Cash | | 95 |
> | *To recognise revenue for upgrade work* | | |

5.12.140.95   If the operator concludes that the requirement to perform construction services is an obligation arising under the terms of the agreement – e.g. a maintenance obligation – then the operator will recognise a provision for its obligation and a reimbursement right. The reimbursement right will be recognised when, and only when, it is virtually certain that the reimbursement will be received from the grantor in accordance with IAS 37. The provision to perform the upgrade services and the right to receive the reimbursement are presented separately (see 3.12.190). [*IFRIC 12.21, IAS 37.53*]

EXAMPLE 20B – UPGRADE SERVICES – OBLIGATION

5.12.140.100   Modifying the fact pattern in Example 20A, Company C is obligated under the terms of the agreement with the grantor to upgrade the plant but the upgrade is not expected to increase the plant's capacity. Under the agreement, the grantor reimburses C for the costs of the upgrade once C confirms that it will carry out the work. C concludes that the upgrade of the infrastructure is an obligation arising under the contract and is not a revenue-generating service.

5.12.140.110   C recognises a provision for the obligation to carry out the upgrade and a reimbursement asset assuming the reimbursement is in fact virtually certain to be received. The provision and the reimbursement are presented separately in the statement of financial position.

5.12.150   Subsequent accounting for financial and intangible assets

5.12.150.10   The operator accounts for any financial asset that it recognises in accordance with IFRS 9 (see chapter 7.6) and any intangible asset that it recognises in accordance with IAS 38 (see chapter 3.3). There are no exemptions from these standards for operators. [*IFRIC 12.23, 26*]

5.12.160   *Financial assets*

5.12.160.10   IFRIC 12 requires the operator to measure the financial asset at:
- amortised cost;
- fair value through OCI; or
- fair value through profit or loss. [*IFRIC 12.24*]

5.12.160.15   The operator classifies financial assets on an asset-by-asset basis; there is no requirement for an entity that recognises a number of financial assets arising from different service concession arrangements to apply the same classification in all cases. For further discussion of the classification of financial assets, see chapter 7.4.

5.12.170   *Intangible assets*

5.12.170.10   IAS 38 requires an intangible asset to be amortised over its expected useful life. The useful life of an intangible asset recognised in a service concession arrangement is the concession period. In our view, amortisation should begin when the asset is available for use – i.e. when the operator is able to charge the public for use of the infrastructure. [*IAS 38.97*]

EXAMPLE 21 – COMMENCEMENT OF AMORTISATION

5.12.170.20   Company D signs a service concession arrangement with the government of Country Z to build and operate a toll road. The concession agreement is for a 30-year period starting with the granting of the concession. The concession agreement requires D to construct the infrastructure in discrete sections, allowing D to build the individual sections of the road on completion of the construction services and start generating revenues by charging users for the use of these sections while other sections are still being built.

5.12.170.25 Because the concession agreement is represented by a series of intangible assets, we believe that D should start amortising the intangible asset(s) on a phased basis as each individual section begins operations.

5.12.170.30 No specific method of amortisation is required to be used, and the straight-line method, the diminishing (or reducing-balance) method, the units-of-production method and the revenue-based method are cited as possible approaches. However, the use of the revenue-based method is permitted only when revenue and the consumption of the economic benefits of the intangible asset are 'highly correlated' or the intangible right is expressed as a measure of revenue. All of these methods are illustrated in 3.3.230 and 3.2.160. If the pattern in which the asset's economic benefits are consumed cannot be determined reliably, then the straight-line method is used. IAS 38 and IFRIC 12 do not allow the use of 'interest' methods of amortisation, including the 'annuity method', which takes into account the time value of money. [*IAS 38.98–98A, IFRIC 12.BC64–BC65*]

5.12.170.40 Although the straight-line method may be appropriate for many service concession arrangements, other methods may also be acceptable, as is illustrated in the following examples. [*IAS 38.98*]

EXAMPLE 22 – UNITS-OF-PRODUCTION METHOD OF AMORTISATION

5.12.170.50 Company E builds and operates a toll road between two established population centres in a country with a stable economy. Tolls remain fixed for the duration of the concession. Traffic forecasts based on studies of similar projects in the country predict that use of the road will rise rapidly in the years following construction until the road reaches its capacity, and will remain stable for the rest of the concession term.

5.12.170.55 In our view, the use of a units-of-production method of amortisation (in which the unit of production would be the number of users of the toll road) is acceptable because E has developed a reliable estimate of expected traffic over the life of the concession arrangement.

EXAMPLE 23 – REVENUE-BASED METHOD OF AMORTISATION

5.12.170.60 Company F builds and operates a toll bridge. The concession has a variable term and ends when the total revenues collected by F from users of the bridge reach a predetermined level established in the concession contract – e.g. 10 million.

5.12.170.65 F uses the revenue-based method of amortisation because it represents the pattern in which the intangible asset's economic benefits are consumed. [*IAS 38.98A*]

5.12.170.70 Intangible assets with finite useful lives are tested for impairment using the general impairment requirements (see 3.10.110). [*IAS 38.111*]

5.12.180 WORKED EXAMPLE

5.12.180.10 This worked example illustrates the mechanics of applying IFRIC 12's key requirements on the recognition and measurement of revenue, and the recognition and measurement of the consideration for construction services. For simplicity, it does not illustrate the other requirements of IFRIC 12.

EXAMPLE 24 – SERVICE CONCESSION ARRANGEMENT TO PROVIDE PUBLIC HEALTH SERVICES

5.12.180.20 Municipality M (the grantor) contracts Company B (the operator) to build diagnostic medical equipment (a scanner) that will be used in providing public health services. The scanner will take one year to build. After its building, B will provide maintenance services and make the scanner available to the public health service facility for five years. B does not expect major repairs to be necessary during the concession period. At the end of the concession period, B must return the scanner to M for no additional consideration. Patients will pay B 100 each time the scanner is used, with M unconditionally guaranteeing a minimum annual payment of 60,000.

5.12.180.30 B also builds similar scanners in the normal course of business and estimates that the stand-alone selling price of the services provided in building the scanner is 350,000. The estimated interest rate of lending to M for a similar instrument is 5%.

5.12.180.40 B determines that M is the customer for the construction service. The consideration for this service comprises an intangible asset (i.e. the right to operate the scanner) and a fixed amount of 60,000 per year for five years. The patients of the scanner are the customer for the operating services.

5.12.180.45 B therefore identifies one performance obligation in the contract with M – i.e. construction of the scanner.

5.12.180.50 B also identifies one performance obligation in each of the contracts with users of the scanner for the operating services. Further, B recognises and measures the obligation to maintain the scanner in accordance with IAS 37, because it concludes that it is not a separate performance obligation.

5.12.190 Construction service

5.12.190.10 In exchange for the construction services, B receives a right to a fixed and determinable amount of cash of 60,000 per year for five years. B also receives a right to charge patients for use of the scanner and to retain the amount collected over and above the annual minimum. Therefore, B receives a financial asset and an intangible asset.

5.12.190.20   B recognises revenue from the construction service and a contract asset during the construction period – i.e. the first year. When the construction service is completed, B reclassifies the contract asset as a financial asset and an intangible asset.

5.12.190.30   The total consideration for the construction service is measured as the sum of present value of the guaranteed cash flows and the fair value of the intangible asset. However, because the fair value of an intangible asset is difficult to measure, B uses the stand-alone selling price of the scanner for measuring the total consideration received.

5.12.200   Measuring the financial asset

5.12.200.10   B reclassifies the portion of contract asset as a financial asset when it completes the construction service. B accounts for the financial asset received in the arrangement as a receivable under IFRS 9 and measures it at amortised cost, because the cash flows from the receivable are solely payments of principal and interest on the principal amount outstanding.

5.12.200.20   B measures the financial asset at the end of the first year (on completion of construction) by discounting the guaranteed future cash flows of 60,000 per year for five years at a discount rate of 5% per annum[1] – i.e. the rate of lending for a similar service concession agreement. The amount of consideration allocated to the financial asset is 259,769 (see 5.12.70.100–110). [*IFRIC 12.IE27, BC53*]

> Note
> 1.   In this example, the discount rate has not changed since inception of the concession.

5.12.210   Measuring the intangible asset

5.12.210.10   When both a financial and an intangible asset are recognised, the fair value of the intangible asset can be measured as the difference between the total consideration for the construction service – i.e. no element of the cash flows received from M relates to operating services – and the fair value of the financial asset received. [*IFRS 15.67, IFRIC 12.IE27, BC53*]

5.12.210.20   The total revenue from construction service will be equal to the stand-alone selling price of the construction service – i.e. 350,000. The 259,769 of consideration is received in the form of a financial asset (see 5.12.200.20). In this example, the remaining balance of 90,231 is allocated to the intangible asset, representing the right to charge patients.

5.12.210.30   In this example, B performs construction service only in the first year and therefore recognises the financial asset and intangible asset in full by the end of year 1. In more complex arrangements, it is likely that the operator will be required to perform construction services over the course of several years. In such cases, the operator will recognise revenue and a contract asset as it performs the construction services. When the construction services are completed, the operator will account for the financial asset and the intangible asset in accordance with IFRS 9 and IAS 38 (see illustrative example 3 of IFRIC 12). [*IFRIC 12.IE27–IE28, IE31*]

5.12.220   Accounting for revenue

5.12.220.10   Revenue for services provided is accounted for in accordance with IFRS 15 (see 5.12.70.10). In year 1, B recognises revenue from construction services of 350,000. In years 2 to 5, B recognises revenue from operating services.

5.12.220.20   Assume that actual demand for the scanner over the five years of operation is as follows.

	Yr 2	Yr 3	Yr 4	Yr 5	Yr 6
Number of times used	480	780	960	840	900

5.12.220.30   Based on the illustrative examples in IFRIC 12, in our view the cash receipts should be allocated between repayment of the receivable and revenue as follows.

	Yr 2	Yr 3	Yr 4	Yr 5	Yr 6
Use x 100	48,000	78,000	96,000	84,000	90,000
Amount received (subject to 60,000 minimum)	60,000	78,000	96,000	84,000	90,000
Allocated to receivable pay-down	60,000	60,000	60,000	60,000	60,000
Allocated to revenue from operation	-	18,000	36,000	24,000	30,000

5.12.220.40   Relevant amounts in the statement of profit or loss and OCI and statement of financial position over the concession period are as follows.

	Yr 1	Yr 2	Yr 3	Yr 4	Yr 5	Yr 6
Revenue	350,000	-	18,000	36,000	24,000	30,000
Finance income[1]	-	12,988	10,638	8,170	5,578	2,857
Amortisation expense[2]	-	(18,046)	(18,046)	(18,046)	(18,046)	(18,047)
Receivable[3]	259,769	212,757	163,395	111,565	57,143	-
Intangible asset	90,231	72,185	54,139	36,093	18,047	-
Cash	-	60,000	78,000	96,000	84,000	90,000

Notes
1. Receivable at the end of the previous period x 5%.
2. Intangible asset's initial carrying amount / 5 years.
3. Receivable at the end of the previous period + finance income for the period - payments for the period.

5.12.230   DISCLOSURES

5.12.230.10   The disclosure requirements applicable to service concession arrangements are contained in SIC-29. SIC-29 applies to both grantors and operators in service concession arrangements in which the operator receives a right and assumes an obligation to provide services to the public. [*IFRIC 12.10, SIC-29*]

5.12.240   FUTURE DEVELOPMENTS

5.12.240.10   On 30 January 2014, the IASB issued IFRS 14 *Regulatory Deferral Accounts*, which permits, but does not require, first-time adopters of IFRS to continue using previous GAAP to account for regulatory deferral account balances (see chapter 6.2) while the IASB completes its comprehensive project on rate-regulated activities.

5.12.240.20   The IASB has moved forward with a comprehensive project on rate-regulated activities. In September 2014, it published Discussion Paper *Reporting the Financial Effects of Rate Regulation*.

5.12.240.30   The discussion paper focused on a certain type of rate regulation – termed 'defined rate regulation' – which exhibits specific features of a formal regulatory pricing framework.

5.12.240.40   The discussion paper discussed four approaches to accounting for the financial effects of rate regulation:
- recognise the package of rights and obligations as an intangible asset;
- report using regulatory accounting requirements;
- develop specific IFRS requirements; and
- prohibit the recognition of regulatory deferral account balances.

5.12.240.50   The comment period on the discussion paper closed in January 2015 and the IASB discussed feedback in the first half of 2015. A new consultation document is expected in the first half of 2019.

5.13 Common control transactions and Newco formations

5.13 Common control transactions and Newco formations

CURRENTLY EFFECTIVE REQUIREMENTS

This publication reflects IFRS in issue at 1 August 2018, and the currently effective requirements cover annual periods beginning on 1 January 2018.

This chapter deals with business combinations among entities under common control. It does not deal with the wider issue of common control transactions – e.g. the transfer of a single item of property, plant and equipment between fellow subsidiaries.

The issues dealt with in this chapter are not covered explicitly in any of the standards. However, the following standards are relevant in understanding the accounting for common control transactions and Newco formations.

REFERENCE	TITLE
IFRS 3	Business Combinations
IFRS 10	Consolidated Financial Statements
IAS 27	Separate Financial Statements
IFRIC 17	Distributions of Non-cash Assets to Owners

FORTHCOMING REQUIREMENTS

For this topic, there are no forthcoming requirements.

FUTURE DEVELOPMENTS

This topic is subject to future developments that may affect several aspects of accounting for common control transactions in consolidated financial statements. See 5.13.250.

COMMON CONTROL TRANSACTIONS

5.13.10.10 A 'business combination involving entities or businesses under common control' is a business combination in which all of the combining entities or businesses are ultimately controlled by the same party or parties both before and after the combination, and that control is not transitory (see 5.13.30). The concept of control is discussed in chapter 2.5. [*IFRS 3.B1*]

5.13.10.20 A group of individuals is regarded as controlling an entity when, as a result of contractual arrangements, they exercise control. In our view, the requirement for there to be a contractual arrangement should be applied strictly and is not overcome by an established pattern of voting together. [*IFRS 3.B2*]

EXAMPLE 1A – COMMON CONTROL – SHAREHOLDERS' AGREEMENT

5.13.10.30 Company X and Company Y are owned by shareholders B, C, D and E, each of whom holds 25% of the shares in each company. B, C and D have entered into a shareholders' agreement in terms of which they exercise their voting power jointly. Therefore, both X and Y are under the control of the same group of individuals (B, C and D) and are under common control.

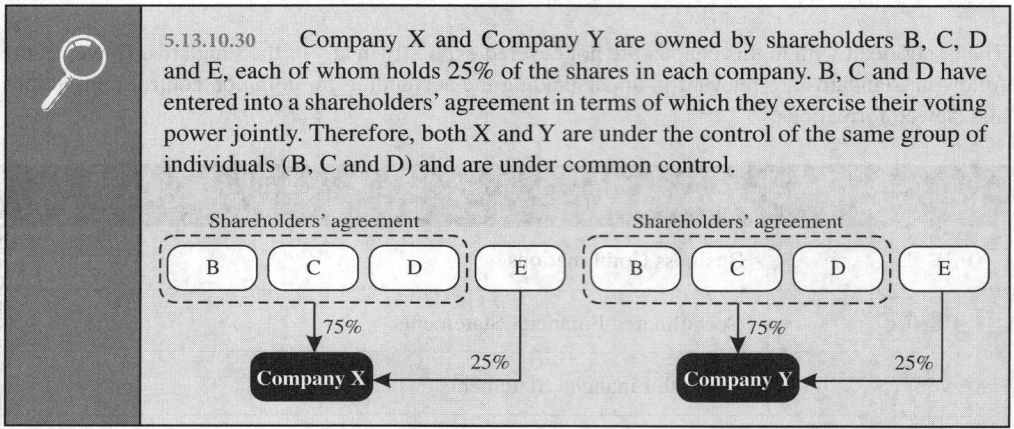

EXAMPLE 1B – COMMON CONTROL – FAMILY RELATIONSHIPS

5.13.10.40 Company Y and Company Z are owned by members and close relatives of a single family. The father owns 40% of the shares in each entity, each of his two brothers owns another 15% of the shares, and his son owns the remaining 30%. However, there are no agreements between the family members that they will exercise their voting power jointly.

5.13.10.45 Therefore, even though the shares are held within a single family who may have an established pattern of voting together, this group of individuals does not have a contractual arrangement to exercise control collectively over either company, and Y and Z are not under common control.

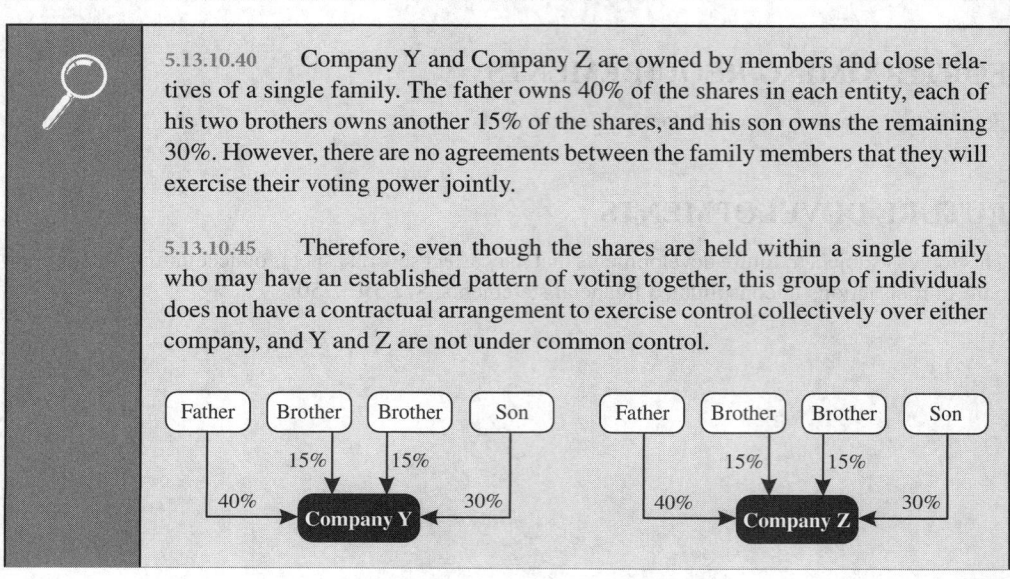

> **5.13.10.50** A different conclusion might be reached if, for example, the son were a child. However, judgement would be required to assess the facts and circumstances of each case.

5.13.10.60 In determining whether the combination involves entities under common control, it is not necessary that an individual, or a group of individuals acting together under a contractual arrangement to control an entity, be subject to the financial reporting requirements of IFRS. Also, the entities are not required to be part of the same consolidated financial statements. [*IFRS 3.B3*]

5.13.10.70 The extent of NCI in each of the combining entities before and after the business combination is not relevant in determining whether the combination involves entities under common control. However, transactions that affect the level of NCI are discussed in 5.13.65. [*IFRS 3.B4*]

5.13.20   Scope of common control exemption

5.13.20.10 In general, IFRS does not specify the accounting for common control transactions in (S) separate financial statements (see 2.1.120), if an entity elects to account for investments in subsidiaries at cost or using the equity method in accordance with IAS 27. The only exception is the establishment of a new parent in certain circumstances (see 5.13.150). In our view, an entity may apply the common control scope exclusion in IFRS 3 by analogy to the accounting for common control transactions in separate financial statements. The accounting for legal mergers and amalgamations in separate financial statements is further discussed in 5.13.230. [*IAS 27.10(a)*]

5.13.20.20 If an entity elects to account for investments in subsidiaries in accordance with IFRS 9 in its separate financial statements, then the common control exemption is not relevant and the requirements of IFRS 9 apply (see chapters 7.6–7.7). [*IAS 27.10(b)*]

5.13.20.30 In our view, the common control exemption in accounting for business combinations should also apply to the transfer of investments in associates and joint ventures between investors under common control. Although IAS 28 does not include an explicit exemption for common control transactions, equity accounting follows the methodology of acquisition accounting. Therefore, we believe that it is appropriate to extend the application of the common control exemption to those transfers. [*IAS 28.26*]

EXAMPLE 2 – INVESTMENTS IN ASSOCIATES

> **5.13.20.40** In the following group structure, the 30% investment in Associate A is transferred from Subsidiary S1 to Subsidiary S2, both of which are controlled by Company P. Accordingly, we believe that the transfer of A, in contrast to the acquisition of an associate from a third party, is outside the scope of the IFRS 3 methodology by virtue of the common control exemption in IFRS 3.

1633

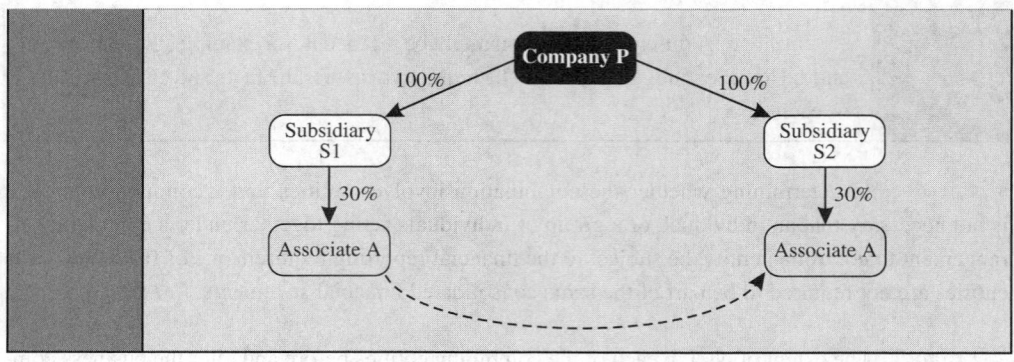

5.13.20.50   Questions have been raised about whether the view in 5.13.20.30 can continue to apply following comments made by the IASB in amending the scope of IAS 39 in respect of forward
contracts to enter into a business combination (see 7.1.170). The IASB noted that the exemption in
respect of forward contracts to enter into a business combination had not been extended to forward
contracts in relation to associates and joint ventures, and therefore that the scope exemption could not
be inferred to extend to IAS 28. This was on the basis that the linkage between acquisition accounting
and equity accounting is only in respect of accounting methodology and not the principles of the
accounting. However, we believe that the extension of the common control exemption is a matter
of accounting methodology and therefore that the common control exemption in IFRS 3 applies.
[*IFRS 9.BCZ2.42*]

5.13.20.60   An investor may have an investment in an associate that is controlled by a third party.
When the associate is involved in a transaction within the controlling group, it is a common control
transaction from the perspective of the associate. However, from the perspective of the investor, it is
not a common control transaction and is accounted for under the requirements of equity accounting
(see chapter 3.5).

EXAMPLE 3 – INVESTOR IN ASSOCIATE THAT ACQUIRES BUSINESS IN COMMON CONTROL TRANSACTION

5.13.20.70   In the following group structure, Company S3 acquires all of the shares
in Company S2 in a common control transaction. Investor X, which is unrelated to
P, has a 30% interest in S3 but no interest in S2 before the acquisition.

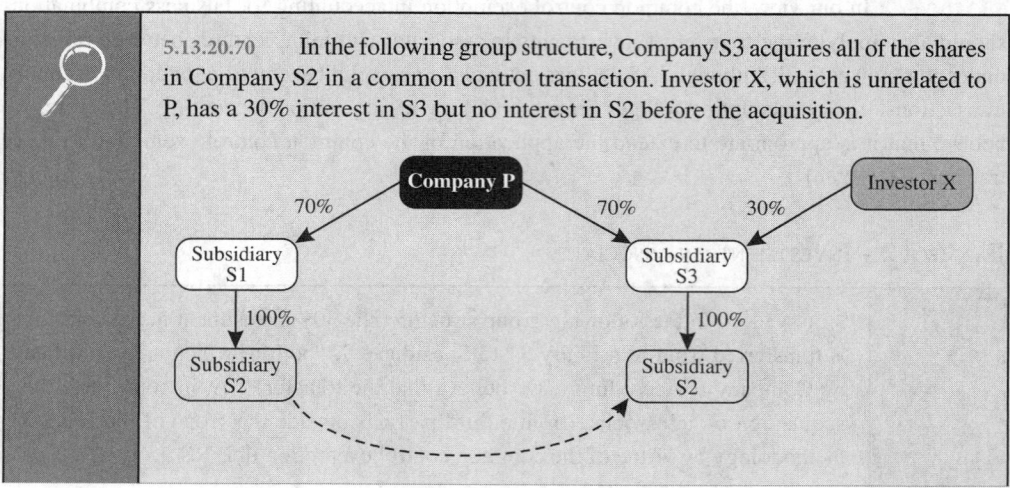

5.13.20.80   In this example, the transaction is not a common control transaction from the perspective of X. Therefore, the acquisition of S2 by S3 is accounted for as part of X's equity accounting of S3 in the usual way (see chapter 3.5).

5.13.30 Transitory common control

5.13.30.10   The term 'transitory' is not defined under IFRS. In our view, the notion of transitory is included in the common control definition as an anti-abuse measure to deal with so-called 'grooming' transactions – i.e. transactions structured to achieve a particular accounting treatment. Therefore, acquisition accounting applies to those transactions that look as though they are combinations involving entities under common control, but which in fact represent genuine substantive business combinations with unrelated parties.

5.13.30.20   In our view, the requirement that control not be transitory should be applied narrowly to give effect to its intention. We believe that transitory common control is relevant only if there is an intention to avoid applying acquisition accounting by structuring a series of transactions to place entities under common control before effecting the business combination.

EXAMPLE 4A – TRANSITORY COMMON CONTROL – INTERMEDIATE ACQUISITION

5.13.30.30   Company P has a subsidiary, Company B. P acquires all of the shares of Company C. Next, P combines the activities of B and C by transferring the shares in C to B. The question arises about how to account for the transfer of C into B in the consolidated financial statements of B.

5.13.30.40   If the intermediate step had been omitted and instead B had been the P group's vehicle for the acquisition of C – i.e. going straight to the 'after' position – then B would have been identified as the acquirer.

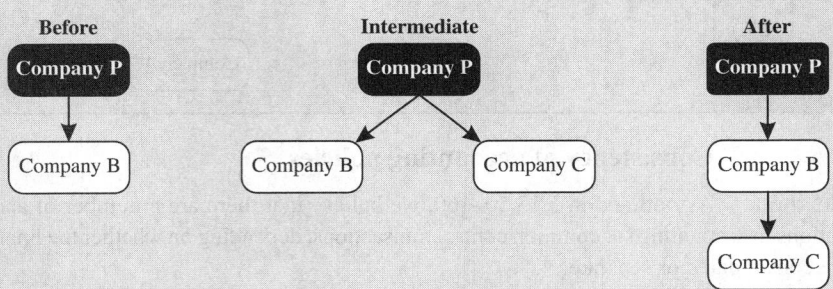

5.13.30.45   Because B and C are under common control, it might seem that acquisition accounting is not required because of the common control exemption. However, we believe that B should be identified as the acquirer and should account for its combination with C using acquisition accounting. This is because B would have applied acquisition accounting for C if B had acquired C directly rather than through P. Acquisition accounting cannot be avoided in the financial statements of B

> simply by placing B and C under the common control of P shortly before the transaction in what is a grooming transaction.

5.13.30.50 An assessment of whether control is transitory may require consideration of a wider series of transactions of which the business combination, which looks as though it involves entities under common control, is only one element.

5.13.30.60 Another issue with respect to common control transactions is whether an intention to dispose of a restructured or internally created group means that post-combination control is transitory and therefore that common control accounting does not apply to a restructuring within a group in preparation for disposal. In our view, an intention to dispose of restructured or internally created entities does not in itself result in control of the combined entities being transitory.

EXAMPLE 4B – TRANSITORY COMMON CONTROL – INTERMEDIATE RESTRUCTURING

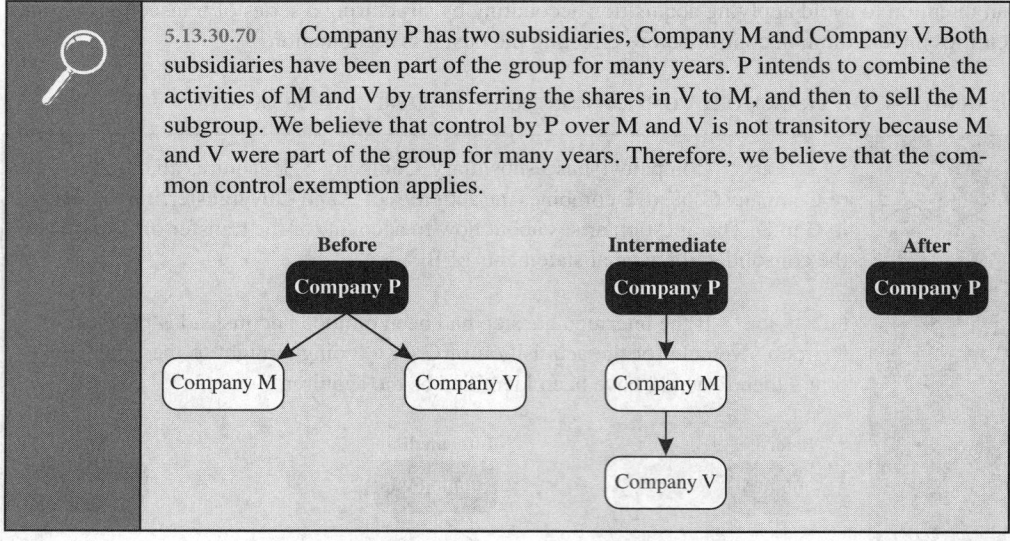

5.13.30.70 Company P has two subsidiaries, Company M and Company V. Both subsidiaries have been part of the group for many years. P intends to combine the activities of M and V by transferring the shares in V to M, and then to sell the M subgroup. We believe that control by P over M and V is not transitory because M and V were part of the group for many years. Therefore, we believe that the common control exemption applies.

5.13.40 Consistency of accounting policies

5.13.40.10 As outlined in 5.13.50–160, we believe that there are a number of accounting policy options in accounting for common control transactions, depending on whether the financial statements are consolidated or separate.

5.13.40.20 IFRS requires the application of consistent accounting policies for similar transactions. Accordingly, common control business combinations are accounted for using the same accounting policy in the consolidated financial statements to the extent that the substance of the transactions is similar. [*IAS 8.13*]

 5.13.40.30 Similarly, common control transactions are accounted for using the same accounting policy in the separate financial statements, independently of the choice for the entity's consolidated

financial statements, to the extent that the substance of the transactions is similar. This applies to both the accounting for acquisitions and disposals. [*IAS 8.13*]

5.13.40.40   Judgement is required in assessing the substance of a common control transaction to determine whether the specific facts and circumstances of a case warrant an accounting treatment that differs from that applied to previous common control transactions. [*IAS 8.13*]

5.13.40.50   However, in our view the nature of the investee does not affect the choice of accounting policy. For example, if the acquisition of a subsidiary in a common control transaction was previously accounted for using book value accounting (see 5.13.60), then we believe that the fact that a subsequent common control transaction involves the acquisition of an associate or joint venture is not sufficient in itself to support a different accounting policy being applied.

5.13.50   Common control transactions in consolidated financial statements of acquirer

5.13.50.10   This section provides general guidance for common control transactions and specific guidance for transactions involving a Newco, as well as legal mergers and amalgamations, as summarised in the diagram below.

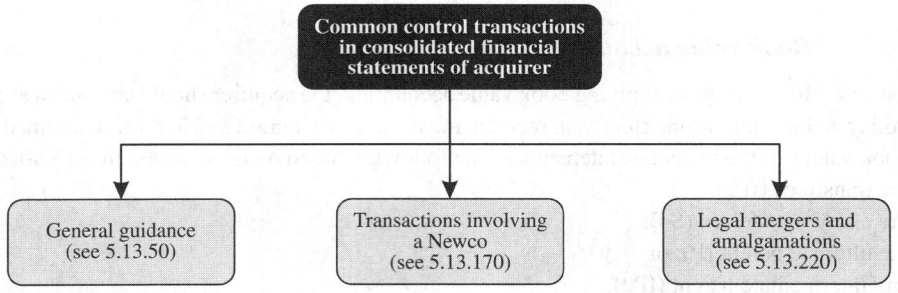

5.13.50.20   In the following group structure, all companies are a business as defined in IFRS 3 (see 2.6.20). If Company IP2 were to transfer its investment in Company S4 to Company S3, then S3 would be the acquirer for the purpose of applying the guidance that follows.

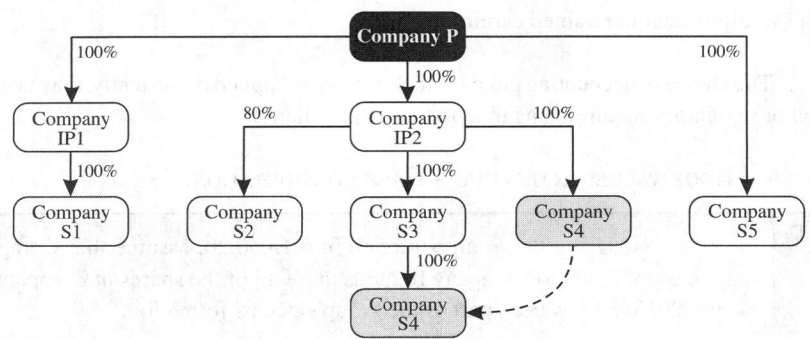

5.13.50.30   In our view, the acquirer in a common control transaction should use either of the following in its consolidated financial statements:
- book value (carry-over basis) accounting on the basis that the investment has simply been moved from one part of the group to another; or
- IFRS 3 accounting on the basis that the acquirer is a separate entity in its own right and should not be confused with the economic group as a whole.

5.13.50.40   The chosen accounting policy should be applied consistently to all similar common control transactions (see 2.8.30.10).

Ⓢ 5.13.50.50   In addition, the accounting policy choice in 5.13.50.30 also applies in the acquirer's separate financial statements if it acquires assets and liabilities constituting a business under IFRS 3 (from an entity under common control) rather than acquiring shares in that business.

5.13.50.60   Irrespective of the accounting policy choice selected in 5.13.50.30 by Company S3 in the group structure in 5.13.50.20, the consolidated financial statements of IP2 would not be affected. This is because at the IP2 subgroup level nothing has happened – the subgroup has a 100% interest in S4 both before and after the transaction. For a discussion of the accounting when changes in NCI occur, see 5.13.65; and for a general discussion of the accounting in the consolidated financial statements of the transferor, see 5.13.80.

5.13.60   *Book value accounting*

5.13.60.10   In our view, in applying book value accounting, the acquirer should choose an accounting policy, to be applied consistently, in recognising the assets acquired and liabilities assumed using the book values in the financial statements of the following based on the diagram in 5.13.50.20:
- the transferor (IP2);
- the entity transferred (S4);
- the ultimate parent (P); or
- any intermediate parent (IP2).

5.13.60.15   In applying book value accounting, an adjustment may be required in equity to reflect any difference between the consideration paid and the capital of the acquiree. The following are possible approaches to recognising the adjustment.
- Reflect the adjustment in a capital account, called a 'merger' reserve or similar.
- Reflect the adjustment in retained earnings.

5.13.60.17   The choice of accounting policy, which should be applied consistently, may be influenced by the legal or regulatory requirements in a particular jurisdiction.

EXAMPLE 5A – BOOK VALUE ACCOUNTING – CASH CONSIDERATION

5.13.60.20   Using the group structure in 5.13.50.20, assume that Company S3 pays cash of 2,000 to Company IP2 to acquire all of the shares in Company S4 on 1 July 2018. S4 has been part of the group since its formation.

5.13.60.21 The following illustrates the consolidated position of S3 at the transaction date, based on the book values in the financial statements of S4 (the entity transferred – see 5.13.60.10).

Financial position as at 1 July 2018, the date on which the transaction occurs

	S3 PRE-TRANSACTION	S4	EFFECT OF TRANSACTION AND ELIMINATIONS	S3 CONSOLIDATED
Assets	11,000	9,100	(2,000)[1]	18,100[2]
Liabilities	(5,000)	(6,000)	-	(11,000)
Net assets	6,000	3,100	(2,000)	7,100
Share capital	1,500	100	(100)[3]	1,500
Merger reserve	-	-	(1,900)[4]	(1,900)
Foreign currency translation reserve	200	100	-	300[5]
Retained earnings	4,300	2,900	-	7,200
Total equity	6,000	3,100	(2,000)	7,100

Notes
1. Cash paid.
2. Assets carried forward include any goodwill recognised by S4.
3. Share capital of S4 eliminated.
4. The surplus of the cash paid (2,000) over the share capital of S4 (100) is recognised in a merger reserve, which is a capital account (see 5.13.60.15). This accounting treatment may depend on legal or regulatory requirements (see 5.13.60.17).
5. Reserves in OCI carried forward include those recognised by S4 (see 5.13.61).

5.13.60.22 If S3 had instead elected to recognise the adjustment against retained earnings, then the components of equity would be as follows.

Equity as at 1 July 2018, the date on which the transaction occurs

	S3 PRE-TRANSACTION	S4	EFFECT OF TRANSACTION AND ELIMINATIONS	S3 CONSOLIDATED
Share capital	1,500	100	(100)	1,500
Foreign currency translation reserve	200	100	-	300
Retained earnings	4,300	2,900	(1,900)	5,300
Total equity	6,000	3,100	(2,000)	7,100

EXAMPLE 5B – BOOK VALUE ACCOUNTING – SHARES ISSUED

5.13.60.25   Changing the facts of Example 5A, assume that Company S3 issues shares for an amount of 400 (400 shares at a nominal value of 1 each) to acquire all of the shares in Company S4 from Company IP2 on 1 July 2018. The following illustrates the consolidated position of S3 at the transaction date, based on the book values in the financial statements of S4 (the entity transferred – see 5.13.60.10).

Financial position as at 1 July 2018, the date on which the transaction occurs

	S3 PRE-TRANSACTION	S4	EFFECT OF TRANSACTION AND ELIMINATIONS	S3 CONSOLIDATED
Assets	11,000	9,100	-	20,100
Liabilities	(5,000)	(6,000)	-	(11,000)
Net assets	6,000	3,100	-	9,100
Share capital	1,500	100	300[1]	1,900[2]
Merger reserve	-	-	(300)[3]	(300)
Foreign currency translation reserve	200	100	-	300
Retained earnings	4,300	2,900	-	7,200
Total equity	6,000	3,100	-	9,100

Notes
1.   Calculated as the issuance of shares less the elimination of S4's share capital – i.e. (400 - 100).
2.   S3's share capital beginning balance (1,500) plus the subsequent issuance (400).
3.   Balancing figure.

5.13.60.27   If Company S3 had instead elected to recognise the adjustment in retained earnings, then the components of equity would be as follows.

Equity as at 1 July 2018, the date on which the transaction occurs

	S3 PRE-TRANSACTION	S4	EFFECT OF TRANSACTION AND ELIMINATIONS	S3 CONSOLIDATED
Share capital	1,500	100	300	1,900
Foreign currency translation reserve	200	100	-	300
Retained earnings	4,300	2,900	(300)	6,900
Total equity	6,000	3,100	-	9,100

5.13.61   *Reserves*

5.13.61.10   As illustrated in Examples 5A and 5B, the application of book value accounting includes the transfer of OCI reserves – e.g. foreign currency translation reserve – previously recognised by the entity transferred (S4 in these examples). Using this approach ensures that the history of the combining entities is continued, which is consistent with book value accounting. In Example 5A, if the foreign currency translation reserve of S4 of 100 was not carried forward into post-combination S3, then a different profit or loss would be recognised when the underlying foreign operation is disposed of and the balance in the reserve is reclassified to profit or loss (see 2.7.340); that outcome would be inconsistent with the book value premise of a continuation of S4's accounting.

5.13.62   *Comparative information*

5.13.62.10   In our view, in its consolidated financial statements the acquirer is permitted, but not required, to re-present its comparatives and adjust its current reporting period before the date of the transaction as if the combination had occurred before the start of the earliest period presented. However, this restatement should not, in our view, extend to periods during which the entities were not under common control.

5.13.62.15   IFRS requires the application of consistent accounting policies for similar transactions. Accordingly, the chosen accounting policy regarding comparative information should be applied consistently to all similar common control transactions. [*IAS 8.13*]

EXAMPLE 6A – COMMON CONTROL PERIOD EXTENDS BEYOND START OF COMPARATIVE PERIOD

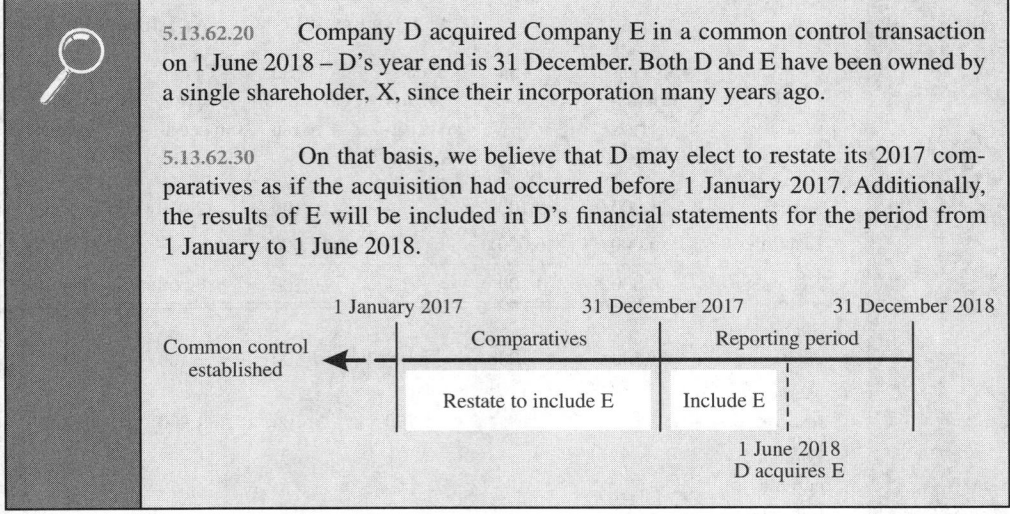

5.13.62.20   Company D acquired Company E in a common control transaction on 1 June 2018 – D's year end is 31 December. Both D and E have been owned by a single shareholder, X, since their incorporation many years ago.

5.13.62.30   On that basis, we believe that D may elect to restate its 2017 comparatives as if the acquisition had occurred before 1 January 2017. Additionally, the results of E will be included in D's financial statements for the period from 1 January to 1 June 2018.

EXAMPLE 6B – COMMON CONTROL PERIOD STARTED IN COMPARATIVE PERIOD

5.13.62.40   Company G acquired Company H in a common control transaction on 1 June 2018 – G's year end is 31 December. Both G and H are owned by a single shareholder, X. X acquired its investment in G in 2009, and its investment in H on 1 July 2017.

5.13.62.50 On that basis, we believe that G may elect to restate its 2017 comparatives as if the acquisition had occurred on 1 July 2017, but not earlier. Additionally, the results of H will be included in G's financial statements for the period from 1 January to 1 June 2018.

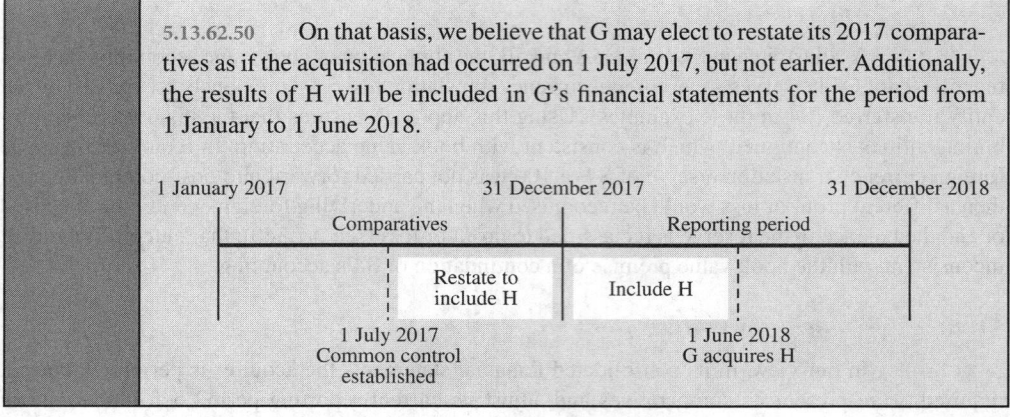

EXAMPLE 7A – COMPARATIVES RESTATED – CASH CONSIDERATION

5.13.62.60 Continuing Example 5A, Company S3 decides to restate the comparative information for 2017 in its 2018 financial statements. The example assumes no transactions during the year to highlight the effect of the restatement.

Financial position as at 1 January 2017 (start of comparative period) and 1 July 2018 (date on which the transaction occurs)

	S3 PRE-TRANS-ACTION	S4	AT 1 JANUARY 2017		AT 1 JULY 2018	
			TRANS-ACTION AND ELIMI-NATIONS	S3 CONSOLI-DATED	TRANS-ACTION AND ELIMI-NATIONS	S3 CONSOLI-DATED
Assets	11,000	9,100	-	20,100	(2,000)[(2)]	18,100
Liabilities	(5,000)	(6,000)	-	(11,000)	-	(11,000)
Net assets	6,000	3,100	-	9,100	(2,000)	7,100
Share capital	1,500	100	(100)[(1)]	1,500	(100)[(3)]	1,500
Merger reserve	-	-	100[(1)]	100	(1,900)[(4)]	(1,900)
Foreign currency translation reserve	200	100	-	300	-	300
Retained earnings	4,300	2,900	-	7,200	-	7,200
Total equity	6,000	3,100	-	9,100	(2,000)	7,100

Notes

1. This example illustrates the approach of not reflecting the cash paid of 2,000 in the comparative information, because the transaction takes place in 2018.
2. Cash paid.
3. Share capital of S4 eliminated.
4. The surplus of the cash paid (2,000) over the share capital of S4 (100) is recognised in a merger reserve, which is a capital account (see 5.13.60.15). This accounting treatment may depend on legal or regulatory requirements (see 5.13.60.17).

5.13.62.70   If S3 had instead elected to recognise the adjustment in retained earnings, then retained earnings would be increased by 100 as at 1 January 2017 and decreased by 1,900 as at 1 July 2018, and there would be no merger reserve.

EXAMPLE 7B – COMPARATIVES RESTATED – SHARES ISSUED

5.13.62.80   Continuing Example 5B, S3 decides to restate the comparative information for 2017 in its 2018 financial statements. The example again assumes no transactions during the year to highlight the effect of the restatement.

Financial position as at 1 January 2017 (start of comparative period) and 1 July 2018 (date on which the transaction occurs)

	S3 PRE-TRANSACTION	S4	AT 1 JANUARY 2017		AT 1 JULY 2018	
			TRANSACTION AND ELIMINATIONS	S3 CONSOLIDATED	TRANSACTION AND ELIMINATIONS	S3 CONSOLIDATED
Assets	11,000	9,100	-	20,100	-	20,100
Liabilities	(5,000)	(6,000)	-	(11,000)	-	(11,000)
Net assets	6,000	3,100	-	9,100	-	9,100
Share capital	1,500	100	300[(1)]	1,900[(2)]	300[(1)]	1,900[(2)]
Merger reserve	-	-	(300)[(3)]	(300)	(300)[(4)]	(300)
Foreign currency translation reserve	200	100	-	300	-	300
Retained earnings	4,300	2,900	-	7,200	-	7,200
Total equity	6,000	3,100	-	9,100	-	9,100

> **Notes**
> 1. Calculated as the issuance of shares less the elimination of S4's share capital – i.e. (400 - 100).
> 2. S3's share capital beginning balance (1,500) plus the subsequent issuance (400).
> 3. Balancing figure. In our experience, this approach to share capital is common in practice. However, an alternative would be to leave share capital unadjusted until the transaction occurs, similar to the approach in Example 7A.
> 4. Balancing figure.

> **5.13.62.90**   If S3 had instead elected to recognise the adjustment in retained earnings, then retained earnings would be decreased by 300 as at 1 January 2017 and 1 July 2018 and there would be no merger reserve.

5.13.65   *Non-controlling interests*

5.13.65.10   In our view, to the extent that the common control transaction involves transactions with NCI, the changes in NCI should be accounted for as acquisitions and/or disposals of NCI on the date on which the changes occur (see 2.5.560).

EXAMPLE 8 – CHANGE IN NCI

> **5.13.65.20**   Using the group structure below, 100% of the shares in Company S2 are transferred to Company S4 and the previous non-controlling shareholders in S2 obtain shares in S4. As a result, Company IP2's interest in S4 falls to 90%.

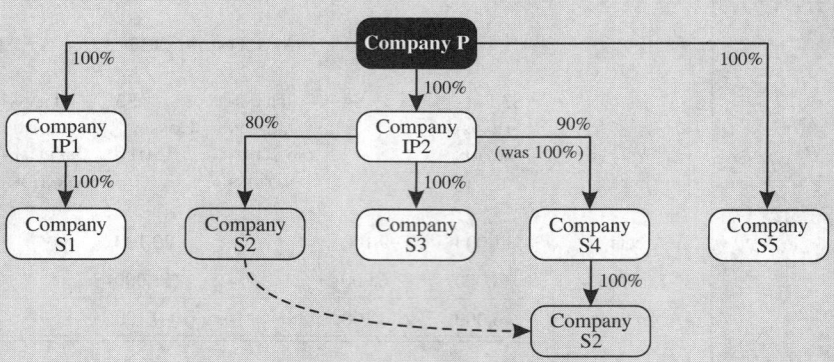

> **5.13.65.30**   Therefore, IP2 has sold a 10% interest in S4 (100% - 90%), which IP2 accounts for as a disposal without the loss of control (see 2.5.630); and has acquired a 10% interest in S2 (90% - 80%), which it accounts for as an acquisition of NCI (see 2.5.620).

> **5.13.65.40**   From S4's perspective, it has acquired a 100% interest in S2. However, if S4 chooses to restate comparatives, then it would not be appropriate for the restatement to be done as if S4 had always held a 100% interest in S2. This is because the group's holding in S2 was only 80% before the common control transaction. Instead, the restatement of comparatives is done on the basis of a historical 80% interest in S2, with the 20% NCI being acquired at the date of the transaction.

5.13.70   *Acquisition accounting*

5.13.70.05   In developing an accounting policy through analogy to an IFRS dealing with similar and related matters, an entity uses its judgement in applying all relevant aspects of the IFRS to its particular issue (see 2.8.20).

5.13.70.10   In our view, in applying acquisition accounting to a common control transaction, the methodology in IFRS 3 should be applied in its *entirety* by analogy because a common control transaction remains a business combination even though it is outside the scope of IFRS 3. This includes:

- identifying the business acquired;
- identifying the acquirer;
- identifying and measuring the consideration transferred;
- identifying and measuring the identifiable assets and liabilities; and
- recognising goodwill.

5.13.70.20   However, to the extent that the acquisition accounting gives rise to an apparent gain on a bargain purchase, in our view such amount should be recognised in equity as a capital contribution from the shareholders of the acquirer. This is on the basis that the profit relates to a transaction with shareholders acting in their capacity as shareholders.

5.13.70.30   Consistent with IFRS 3, the acquirer does not restate its comparatives when applying acquisition accounting to the transaction.

5.13.80   **Common control transactions in consolidated financial statements of transferor**

5.13.80.10   The requirements of IFRS 5 apply to the transferor in a common control transaction, regardless of whether the disposal occurs through non-reciprocal distribution of the shares in a subsidiary (a demerger or spin-off) or a sale (see 5.4.10 and 200).

5.13.80.20   In some cases, an agreement will purport that the transfer is effective on a specified date (perhaps even a date in the past). Irrespective of the date specified in an agreement, the date of derecognition of the transferred business is the date on which the control is actually lost. This may or may not correspond to the date specified in the agreement.

5.13.90   *Demergers*

5.13.90.10   Although IFRS 10 deals with the loss of control in general (see also 5.13.100), it does not deal with the loss of control through a demerger – i.e. non-reciprocal distributions of assets in the scope of IFRIC 17. However, the scope of IFRIC 17 excludes distributions in which the asset distributed is ultimately controlled by the same party or parties before and after the distribution. Therefore, common control transactions are excluded from the scope of IFRIC 17. [*IFRS 10.BCZ184, IFRIC 17.5*]

5.13.90.20   In our view, a demerger that is not in the scope of IFRIC 17 may be accounted for using either book values or fair values.

EXAMPLE 9 – DEMERGER OUTSIDE SCOPE OF IFRIC 17

5.13.90.30   In the following group structure, Company IP2 transfers its investment in Company S3 to Company S1 for no consideration. In effect, the shares in S3 have been distributed to the ultimate owner (Company P) who has then invested them in the IP1 subgroup. Alternatively, the direct transfer to S1 can be seen as benefiting P because its investment in IP1 is boosted by this undervalue transfer.

5.13.90.32   The carrying amount of S3 in IP2's consolidated financial statements is 100, and the fair value of S3 is 130.

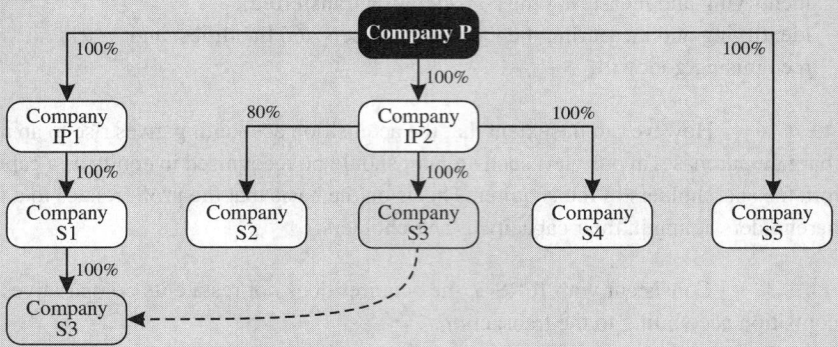

5.13.90.35   There is no change in the carrying amount or fair value of S3 between the date on which the distribution is authorised and the date on which it is effected. For a discussion of the implications of a distribution that is authorised and effected in different reporting periods, see 7.3.690.70.

5.13.90.40   If IP2 elects to account for the demerger using fair values, then it records the following entries, which are consistent with the accounting under IFRIC 17 (see 7.3.690).

	DEBIT	CREDIT
Equity	130	
Liability for distribution		130
To recognise liability at fair value of S3		
Liability for distribution	130	
Net assets of S3		100
Profit or loss		30
To derecognise liability and net assets of S3		

5.13.90.50   If IP2 elects to account for the demerger using book values, then it records the following entries with no impact on profit or loss.

	DEBIT	CREDIT
Equity	100	
Liability for distribution		100
To recognise liability at book value of S3		
Liability for distribution	100	
Net assets of S3		100
To derecognise liability and net assets of S3		

5.13.90.60   In our view, a disposal in which there is nominal consideration is an in-substance de-merger rather than a loss of control in the scope of IFRS 10, and should be accounted for using the entity's accounting policy choice in respect of demergers (see 5.13.90.20).

5.13.100   *Other disposals*

5.13.100.10   Other disposals that result in the loss of control fall in the scope of IFRS 10. In applying IFRS 10, on the face of it the gain or loss on disposal is calculated with reference to the fair value of the consideration received – i.e. the exchange amount is the basis for the accounting (see 2.5.760). However, in some cases it may be concluded that the use of the exchange amount would not reflect the substance of the transaction, and that in fact two transactions have occurred. [*IFRS 10.B98*]

EXAMPLE 10 – ACQUISITION AND SUBSEQUENT DISPOSAL

5.13.100.20   Using the group structure in Example 9, assume that Company IP2 ac-quired Company S3 in a common control transaction in 2017, which was accounted for using book values, and is disposing of S3 in a common control transaction in 2018. The following information is relevant.

	AT DATE OF ACQUISITION	AT DISPOSAL DATE
Book value of S3	80	100
Fair value of S3	100	130
Consideration paid (received)	100	(130)

5.13.100.30   Because IP2 accounted for the acquisition of S3 using book values (see 5.13.60), the gain recognised on disposal will be 30 (130 consideration re-ceived - 100 book value at date of disposal). However, if IFRS 3 had been applied to the acquisition (see 5.13.70), then the gain recognised on disposal would have been 10 (130 consideration received - (100 consideration paid + (100 - 80 increase in book values since date of acquisition))).

5.13.100.40   Therefore, depending on the facts and circumstances – such as the date of the acquisition of the entity being disposed of and how that acquisition was accounted for – an entity considers whether, in substance, a contribution or distribution has been made in addition to the disposal of the subsidiary.

5.13.100.50   In this example, IP2 concludes that in effect two transactions have occurred:
- a disposal of S3 for consideration equal to the carrying amount of S3 – i.e. 100 – which results in no gain or loss on disposal; and
- a capital contribution of 30 from P for the difference between the actual consideration received of 130 and the carrying amount of S3 of 100.

(S) 5.13.110   **Common control transactions in separate financial statements**

5.13.110.10   If a common control transaction is effected through the acquisition of assets and liabilities constituting a business under IFRS 3 (from an entity under common control) rather than by acquiring shares in that business, then the acquirer accounts for the transaction in its separate financial statements in accordance with the guidance in 5.13.50 in respect of consolidated financial statements.

5.13.110.20   The guidance that follows applies if an entity accounts for investments in subsidiaries at cost in its separate financial statements. [*IAS 27.10(a)*]

5.13.110.30   In our view, each of the acquirer and the transferor in a common control transaction should choose an accounting policy in respect of their separate financial statements, to be applied consistently to all similar common control transactions (see 5.13.40), to use one of the following approaches.
- *Book value accounting:* This is on the basis that the entities are part of a larger economic group, and that the figures from that larger group are the relevant ones. In applying book value accounting, the transaction is recognised as a distribution or contribution from a transaction with shareholders. In our view, the relevant book value is the carrying amount of the investee in the separate financial statements of the transferor.
- *Fair value accounting:* This is on the basis that the parties are separate entities in their own right and that the accounting for the transaction should be as if it had been carried out in an orderly manner between market participants.
- *Exchange amount accounting:* This is on the basis that the parties are separate entities in their own right and that the accounting should reflect the actual terms of the transaction.

5.13.110.35   However, we believe that it is not appropriate to use exchange amount accounting in common control transactions in which no consideration, or nominal consideration, has been transferred; this is because no exchange has occurred.

5.13.110.40   In the following paragraphs, we consider the application of these views to sideways transfers (see 5.13.120), downstream transfers (see 5.13.130) and upstream transfers (see 5.13.140).

(S) 5.13.120   *Sideways transfers*

5.13.120.10   In a 'sideways transfer', a subsidiary is transferred to a fellow subsidiary such that the transferor loses control of the subsidiary.

5.13.120.12   In applying fair value accounting, in our view the recognition of a gain or loss does not contradict the general principle that capital transactions with equity participants do not result in a gain or loss. The reason for recording a gain is the principle that the acquirer and acquiree are viewed as separate entities in their own right. Therefore, a gain should be recognised as if the transaction had been entered into with a third party.

EXAMPLE 11 – SEPARATE FINANCIAL STATEMENTS – SIDEWAYS TRANSFER

5.13.120.15   In the following transaction, Company S1 pays 80 to Company IP2 to acquire all of the shares in Company S3. The book value of IP2's investment in S3 is 100, and the fair value of S3 is 130.

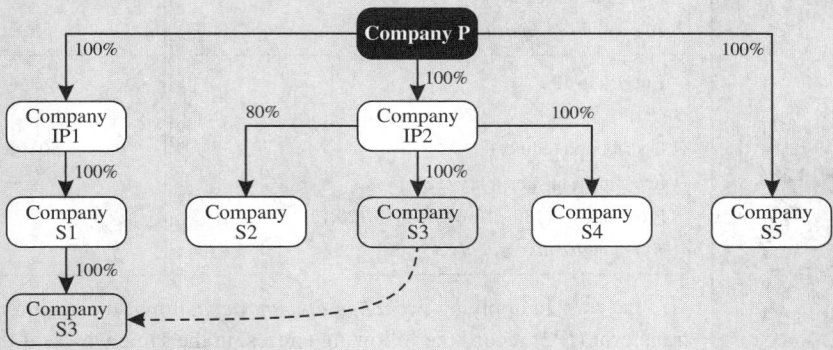

5.13.120.20   In applying *book value accounting*, the acquirer (S1) and the transferor (IP2) record the following entries, recognising the difference between the book value of the transferee (S3) and the consideration paid/received as an equity transaction with the shareholder (P) – i.e. as if S3 had been purchased for its book value of 100 and the difference of 20 paid back as a distribution made/contribution received.

	DEBIT	CREDIT
Entries in S1		
Investment in subsidiary (S3)	100	
Cash		80
Contribution (equity)		20
To recognise acquisition of S3		
Entries in IP2		
Cash	80	
Distribution (equity)	20	
Investment in subsidiary (S3)		100
To recognise disposal of S3		

5.13.120.30   In applying *fair value accounting*, the acquirer (S1) and the transferor (IP2) record the following entries, recognising the difference between the fair value of the transferee (S3) and the consideration paid/received as an equity transaction with the shareholder (P) – i.e. as if S3 had been purchased for its fair value of 130 and the difference of 50 paid back as a distribution made/contribution received.

	DEBIT	CREDIT
Entries in S1		
Investment in subsidiary (S3)	130	
Cash		80
Contribution (equity)		50
To recognise acquisition of S3		
Entries in IP2		
Cash	80	
Distribution (equity)	50	
Investment in subsidiary (S3)		100
Profit or loss (130 - 100) (see 5.13.120.12)		30
To recognise disposal of S3		

5.13.120.40   In applying *exchange amount accounting*, the acquirer (S1) and the transferor (IP2) record the following entries, in the same way as if the transaction had been with a third party for the actual price paid.

	DEBIT	CREDIT
Entries in S1		
Investment in subsidiary (S3)	80	
Cash		80
To recognise acquisition of S3		
Entries in IP2		
Cash	80	
Profit or loss	20	
Investment in subsidiary (S3)		100
To recognise disposal of S3		

(S) 5.13.130   ***Downstream transfers***

5.13.130.10   In a 'downstream transfer', a direct subsidiary of the transferor becomes an indirect subsidiary.

5.13.130.20   In a downstream transfer, the accounting in the acquirer's separate financial statements is unchanged from the accounting in a sideways transfer (see 5.13.120).

5.13.130.30 The accounting in the transferor's separate financial statements is affected because the transferee is now an indirect rather than a direct subsidiary of the transferor. In our view, there is no loss on such a transaction because the transferor does not lose any value. Accordingly, we believe that the transaction should be accounted for as follows.

- A surplus or deficit is computed in the same way as for a sideways transfer (see 5.13.120).
- The actual price received and the benchmark – i.e. book value, or fair value if fair value accounting is applied – are compared; any surplus in the price received is recognised as a dividend received and any deficit is recorded as an additional investment in the acquirer.

EXAMPLE 12 – SEPARATE FINANCIAL STATEMENTS – DOWNSTREAM TRANSFER

5.13.130.40 In the following transaction, Company S3 acquires all of the shares in Company S4 from Company IP2. The book value of IP2's investment in S4 is 100, and the fair value of S4 is 130.

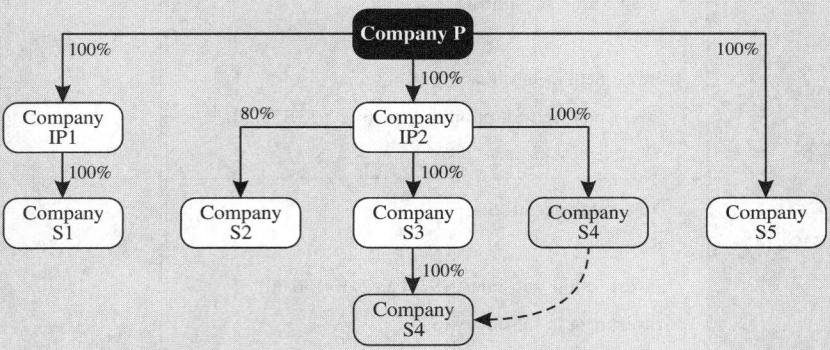

5.13.130.50 We believe that IP2 should record the following entries if the consideration paid by S3 is 80.

	DEBIT	CREDIT
Book value accounting		
Cash	80	
Investment in subsidiary (S3) (see 5.13.130.30)	20	
Investment in subsidiary (S4)		100
To recognise disposal of S4		
Fair value accounting		
Cash	80	
Investment in subsidiary (S3) (see 5.13.130.30)	50	
Investment in subsidiary (S4)		100
Profit or loss (130 - 100)		30
To recognise disposal of S4		

	DEBIT	CREDIT
Exchange amount accounting		
Cash	80	
Investment in subsidiary (S3) (see 5.13.130.30)	20	
Investment in subsidiary (S4)		100
To recognise disposal of S4		

5.13.130.60　If the consideration is 120 instead of 80, then we believe that IP2 should record the following entries.

	DEBIT	CREDIT
Book value accounting		
Cash	120	
Investment in subsidiary (S4)		100
Dividend received (profit or loss) (see 5.13.130.30)		20
To recognise disposal of S4		
Fair value accounting		
Cash	120	
Investment in subsidiary (S3) (see 5.13.130.30)	10	
Investment in subsidiary (S4)		100
Profit or loss (130 - 100)		30
To recognise disposal of S4		
Exchange amount accounting		
Cash	120	
Investment in subsidiary (S4)		100
Dividend received (profit or loss) (see 5.13.130.30)		20
To recognise disposal of S4		

Ⓢ 5.13.140　*Upstream transfers*

5.13.140.10　In an 'upstream transfer', an indirect subsidiary becomes a direct subsidiary.

5.13.140.20　The accounting in the acquirer's separate financial statements is affected because it already holds an investment in the transferee, although indirect. In our view, the transaction should be accounted for as if it had taken place at an amount set as the benchmark chosen – i.e. at book value, fair value or exchange amount – with any excess consideration being recognised as an additional investment and any deficit being recorded as a dividend received.

5.13.140.30   Following an upstream transfer, the acquirer should consider whether there are any indications that the carrying amount of its investment in the transferor may not be recoverable (see 3.10.120). However, in our view any resulting impairment 'loss' should generally first reduce to zero any entry for a dividend received, with the remainder being added to the carrying amount of the transferee, because it is in effect a contribution to that investment. Overall the transaction has moved investments and cash around the acquirer's group and there has been no loss of value. Therefore, in general we believe that it would be inappropriate to recognise a loss in profit or loss.

EXAMPLE 13 – SEPARATE FINANCIAL STATEMENTS – UPSTREAM TRANSFER

5.13.140.40   In the following transaction, Company P pays 80 to Company IP1 to acquire all of the shares in Company S1. The book value of IP1's investment in S1 is 100, and the fair value of S1 is 130.

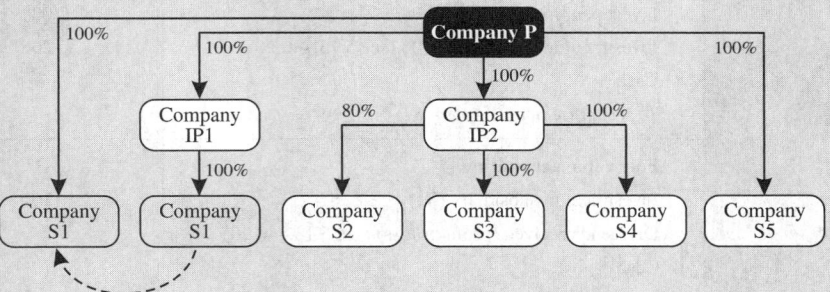

5.13.140.50   In an upstream transfer, the accounting in the transferor's (IP1's) separate financial statements is unchanged from the accounting in a sideways transfer (see 5.13.120.20–40).

5.13.140.60   We believe that P should record the following entries if it pays consideration of 80 to IP1.

	DEBIT	CREDIT
Book value accounting		
Investment in subsidiary (S1)	100	
Dividend received (profit or loss) (see 5.13.140.20)		20
Cash		80
To recognise acquisition of S1		
Fair value accounting		
Investment in subsidiary (S1)	130	
Dividend received (profit or loss) (see 5.13.140.20)		50
Cash		80
To recognise acquisition of S1		

	DEBIT	**CREDIT**
Exchange amount accounting		
Investment in subsidiary (S1)	80	
Cash		80
To recognise acquisition of S1		

5.13.140.70   If the consideration is 120 instead of 80, then we believe that P should record the following entries.

	DEBIT	**CREDIT**
Book value accounting		
Investment in subsidiary (S1)	100	
Investment in subsidiary (IP1) (see 5.13.140.20)	20	
Cash		120
To recognise acquisition of S1		
Fair value accounting		
Investment in subsidiary (S1)	130	
Dividend received (profit or loss) (see 5.13.140.20)		10
Cash		120
To recognise acquisition of S1		
Exchange amount accounting		
Investment in subsidiary (S1)	120	
Cash		120
To recognise acquisition of S1		

5.13.140.80   Following the transaction, P considers whether there are any indications that the carrying amount of its investment in IP1 may not be recoverable (see 5.13.140.30).

(S) 5.13.150   ***Establishment of new parent***

5.13.150.10   IAS 27 specifies the accounting in the *separate* financial statements of a newly formed entity that becomes the new parent entity of another entity in a group if:
- the new parent entity issues equity instruments as consideration in the reorganisation;
- there is no change in the group's assets or liabilities as a result of the reorganisation; and
- there is no change in the interest of the shareholder – either absolute or relative – as a result of the reorganisation. [*IAS 27.13–14*]

5.13.150.20   In such cases, if the new parent entity elects to measure the investment in the subsidiary at cost, then cost is determined as its share of total equity shown in the separate financial statements of the subsidiary at the date of the reorganisation. This represents a specific approach to determining cost and effectively rules out the application of fair value accounting in these circumstances. [*IAS 27.13*]

EXAMPLE 14A – NEW PARENT ESTABLISHED ABOVE ULTIMATE PARENT

5.13.150.30   Company P forms a Newco that becomes P's parent by issuing shares in exchange for P's shares. Because the only asset of Newco is its interest in P, there is no change in the assets and liabilities of the group headed by P and now by Newco. In addition, the shareholders remain the same. Therefore, the accounting in the separate financial statements of Newco is *in* the scope of paragraph 13 of IAS 27.

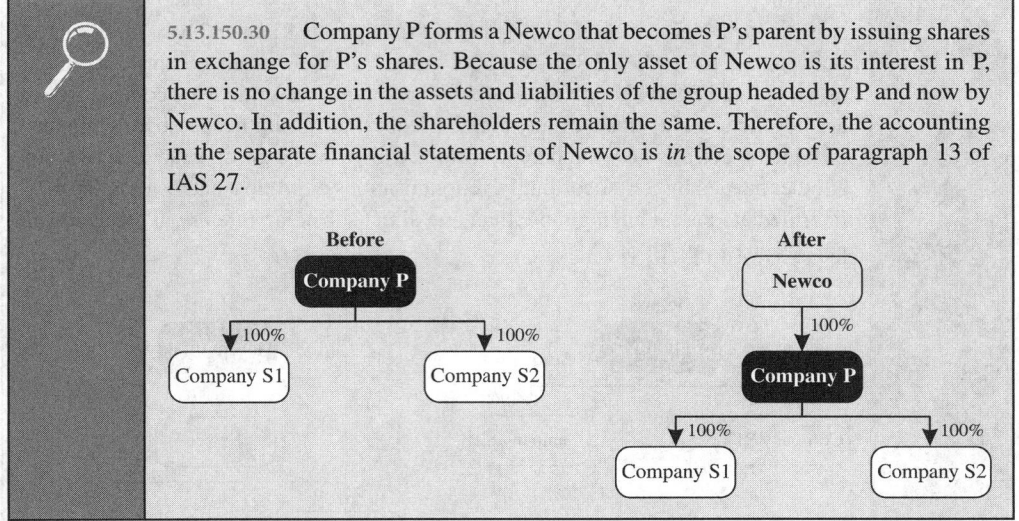

EXAMPLE 14B – NEW PARENT ESTABLISHED ABOVE SINGLE SUBSIDIARY

5.13.150.40   Newco becomes Company S1's parent by issuing shares to Company P in exchange for S1's shares. The only asset of Newco is its interest in S1. Both the net assets and shareholders of the group headed by S1 (being S1 itself, because it had no subsidiaries) and now by Newco, are the same before and after the reorganisation. Therefore, the accounting in the separate financial statements of Newco is *in* the scope of paragraph 14 of IAS 27.

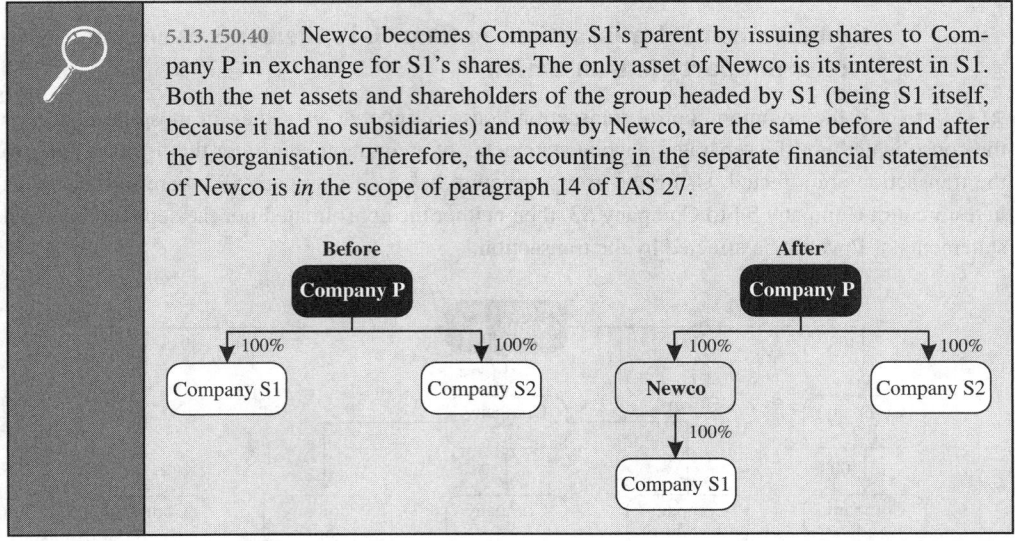

5.13.150.50   The IFRS Interpretations Committee discussed scenarios in which a reorganisation leads to a new parent entity having more than one subsidiary (see Example 14C). The Committee noted that the condition specified in 5.13.150.10 that requires no change to the group's assets and liabilities as a result of the reorganisation was not met in these cases and could not be applied by analogy. This was on the basis that the guidance in IAS 27 is an exception to the normal basis of determining the cost of an investment in a subsidiary. For such reorganisations the general principles in 5.13.110.30 apply. [*IAS 27.13–14, IU 07-11*]

EXAMPLE 14C – NEW PARENT ESTABLISHED ABOVE TWO SUBSIDIARIES

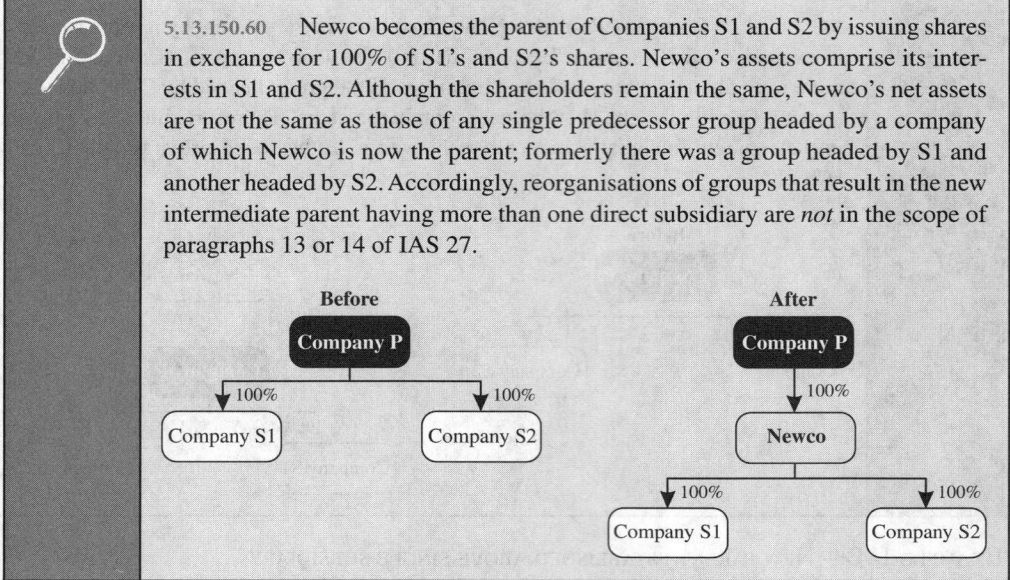

5.13.150.60   Newco becomes the parent of Companies S1 and S2 by issuing shares in exchange for 100% of S1's and S2's shares. Newco's assets comprise its interests in S1 and S2. Although the shareholders remain the same, Newco's net assets are not the same as those of any single predecessor group headed by a company of which Newco is now the parent; formerly there was a group headed by S1 and another headed by S2. Accordingly, reorganisations of groups that result in the new intermediate parent having more than one direct subsidiary are *not* in the scope of paragraphs 13 or 14 of IAS 27.

5.13.160   **Common control transactions in financial statements of common controller not party to transaction**

5.13.160.10   If the common control transaction does not involve NCI, then in most cases neither the consolidated nor the separate financial statements of a common controller that is not a party to the transaction are affected. Using the group structure below, if Company IP2 were to transfer its investment in Company S4 to Company S3, then neither the consolidated nor the separate financial statements of P would be affected by the transaction.

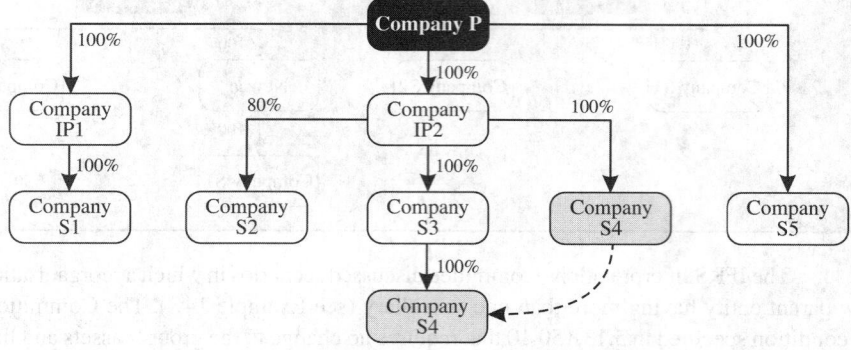

5.13.160.20   If the common control transaction involves NCI and the common controller's interest in the subsidiary is diluted, then the requirements of IFRS 10 in respect of transactions with NCI apply (see 2.5.580).

EXAMPLE 15 – DILUTION IN HOLDING

5.13.160.30   Using the group structure below, 100% of the shares in Company S2 are transferred to Company S4 and the previous non-controlling shareholders in S2 obtain shares in Company IP2; as a result, Company P's interest in IP2 falls to 98%. Therefore, P accounts for the dilution in IP2 as a transaction with NCI in its consolidated financial statements.

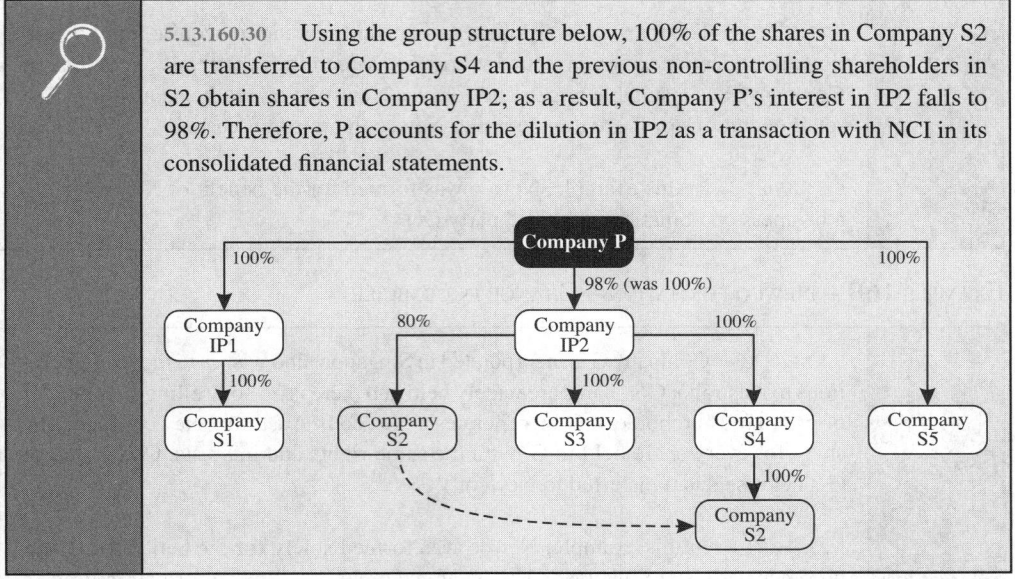

5.13.170   **TRANSACTIONS INVOLVING A NEWCO**

5.13.170.10   Although not a term that is defined in IFRS, in practice 'Newco' is a new entity and is referred to as such in the following discussions. However, a Newco can also be an existing entity that is not a business under IFRS 3.

5.13.170.20   A 'Newco formation' is a transaction that involves the formation of a new entity for the purpose of effecting a business combination or a transaction that purports to be a business combination. Generally, there is no guidance in IFRS on the accounting for such transactions in the financial statements of the newly formed entity (Newco). The discussion that follows relates to consolidated financial statements of Newco. For a discussion of the separate financial statements of a new parent established in a group structure, see 5.13.150.

5.13.170.30   In our view, the key step in analysing how a transaction involving a Newco should be accounted for is establishing whether a business combination has occurred (see chapter 2.6). This analysis involves understanding the economic drivers and rationale behind the transaction(s) – e.g. tax considerations or a restructuring of business activities before a listing transaction – which will vary from case to case. In effect, as the guidance in 5.13.180–205 illustrates, the key drivers of the accounting are identifying the party on whose behalf the Newco has been formed – i.e. the instigator of the transaction(s) – and identifying the business acquired.

5.13.170.40   Newco formations generally fall into two categories. They are either used to effect a business combination involving a third party, or in a restructuring among entities under common control.

EXAMPLE 16A – NEWCO FORMATION – PRIVATE EQUITY TRANSACTION

> 5.13.170.50   Company X is a private equity fund seeking to acquire retail operations that meet specified investment criteria. X identifies the retail operations of Company R as a suitable target, and forms a Newco to effect the acquisition. The retail operations of R are transferred to Newco in return for cash.
>
> 5.13.170.60   In this example, Newco was formed for the benefit of X in effecting a business combination by a third party (X).

EXAMPLE 16B – NEWCO FORMATION – CHANGE IN DOMICILE

> 5.13.170.70   Company G is incorporated in Singapore and wishes to move its operations to Australia. G's shares are widely held and there is no controlling shareholder or group of shareholders. G incorporates a Newco in Australia. Newco issues one share for every share held in G, with the same rights and interests. Ownership of G's net assets is transferred to Newco.
>
> 5.13.170.80   In this example, Newco was formed solely for the benefit of G and no other parties are involved. This is an example of a Newco formation used in a restructuring.

5.13.170.90   Not all situations are as clear as Examples 16A and 16B, and judgement may be required in determining the party for whom Newco acts and whether a business combination has occurred.

5.13.180   Newco used in business combination involving third party

5.13.180.10   The first issue in any Newco formation is establishing whether IFRS 3 applies.

EXAMPLE 17A – NEWCO FORMATION IN A BUSINESS COMBINATION – SINGLE ACQUISITION

> 5.13.180.20   Company P forms a Newco, which then acquires Company S from a third party in exchange for cash.
>
>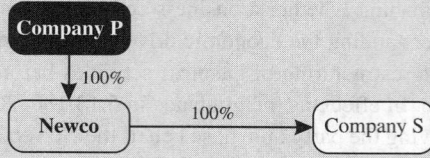
>
> 5.13.180.30   In this example, Newco is identified as the acquirer because Newco was used by P to acquire a business from a third party. Therefore, Newco will apply acquisition accounting as the acquirer.

EXAMPLE 17B – NEWCO FORMATION IN A BUSINESS COMBINATION – MULTIPLE ACQUISITIONS (1)

5.13.180.40   Newco is formed by a venture capital organisation (VCO), which transfers cash to Newco in exchange for a 52% equity interest in Newco. Company Q transfers Subsidiary S1 to Newco in exchange for a 25% interest in Newco, and Company R transfers Subsidiary S2 to Newco in exchange for a 23% interest in Newco. Through its 52% equity interest, VCO has the ability to appoint a voting majority of the board of directors of Newco. There are no other factors that indicate which of the combining entities is the acquirer.

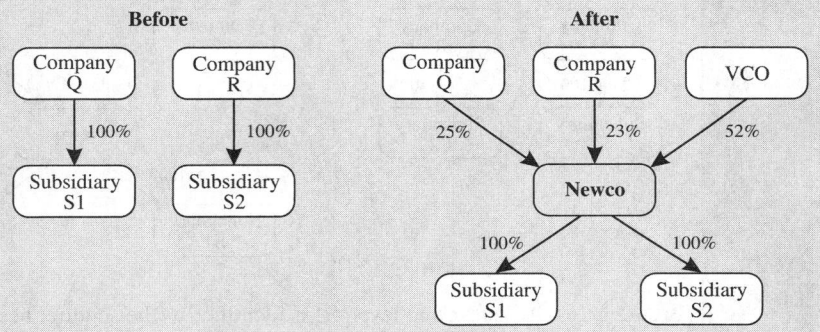

5.13.180.50   In this example, VCO is the acquirer in a business combination in which it has acquired control of S1 and S2 through Newco.

5.13.180.60   At the Newco level, Newco is identified as the acquirer, because it is the vehicle used by VCO to effect the acquisition. The number of shares in Newco issued to VCO exceeds the number of shares issued to the former owners of S1 and S2. Accordingly, the assets and liabilities of both S1 and S2 are subject to acquisition accounting.

5.13.180.70   In their consolidated financial statements, Q and R will account for the loss of control in S1 and S2, respectively, with a gain or loss being recognised in profit or loss (see 2.5.760 and 810); and will subsequently account for their interests in Newco as associates, assuming that significant influence exists (see 3.5.170).

5.13.180.80   If in this example Q, R and VCO had received equal shareholdings in Newco, then further analysis of the facts and circumstances would be required to identify the acquirer, or to determine whether Newco is in fact a joint arrangement (see 3.6.30).

5.13.180.90   Although in Examples 17A and 17B Newco is identified as the acquirer for the purposes of its own consolidated financial statements, this may not always be the case.

EXAMPLE 17C – NEWCO FORMATION IN A BUSINESS COMBINATION – MULTIPLE ACQUISITIONS (2)

5.13.180.100 Modifying Example 17B to remove VCO, Company Q contributes wholly owned Subsidiary S1, and Company R contributes wholly owned Subsidiary S2, to Newco. In exchange, Q receives a 52% equity interest in Newco and as a result has the ability to appoint a voting majority of the board of directors of Newco. R receives the remaining 48% equity interest in Newco. There are no other factors that indicate which of the combining entities is the acquirer.

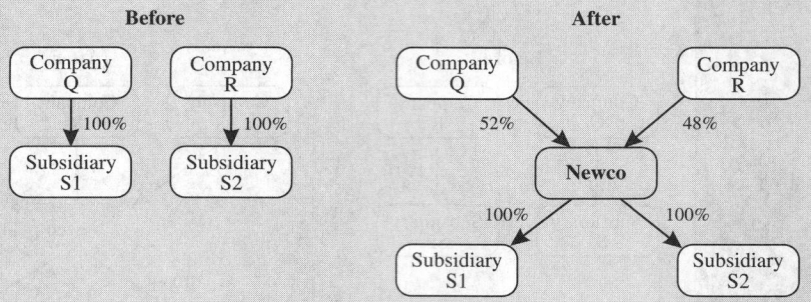

5.13.180.110 At the Newco level, S1 is identified as the acquirer because S1's parent (Q) received a 52% equity interest in Newco and there are no other factors that indicate which of the combining entities is the acquirer. Because S1 is the acquirer, its assets and liabilities will be recognised on a carry-over basis – i.e. at their pre-combination carrying amounts – and the assets and liabilities of S2 will be subject to acquisition accounting.

5.13.180.120 In this example, Q – through its vehicle Newco – is the acquirer from the perspective of Q's consolidated position, because it has effectively acquired control of S2 (by acquiring a 52% equity interest in Newco) in exchange for an NCI in S1 (through the 48% NCI in Newco acquired by R). In Q's consolidated financial statements, it continues to recognise the assets and liabilities of S1 at their pre-combination carrying amounts, and the assets and liabilities of S2 will be subject to acquisition accounting.

5.13.180.130 In R's consolidated financial statements, it has lost control of its former subsidiary, S2, and will recognise a gain or loss in profit or loss (see 2.5.760 and 810). R will also account for its investment in the Newco group as an associate, assuming that significant influence exists (see 3.5.170).

5.13.190 **Newco used in restructuring**

5.13.190.10 When a restructuring is facilitated through a Newco, as noted in 5.13.170.30, in our view it is necessary to determine whether there has been a business combination – i.e. whether it is possible to identify an acquirer and an acquiree. This is consistent with IFRS 3, which specifies that if a Newco issues equity securities, then one of the combining entities that existed before the business combination is identified as the acquirer. [*IFRS 3.B18*]

5.13.190.20   As a result, if two or more previously uncombined businesses are brought together under a Newco, then a business combination has taken place and one of the previously uncombined businesses will be the acquirer. When the business combination is amongst entities under common control, the guidance on accounting for common control transactions in the consolidated financial statements of the acquirer applies (see 5.13.50). However, if only one business is placed under Newco, then there is no business combination and book value accounting applies to the business transferred.

EXAMPLE 18A – NEWCO USED IN A RESTRUCTURING – SINGLE ACQUISITION

5.13.190.30   Company P forms a Newco, which then acquires Company X in exchange for shares of Newco. X is an existing subsidiary of P and comprises a group of three operating companies (A, B and C).

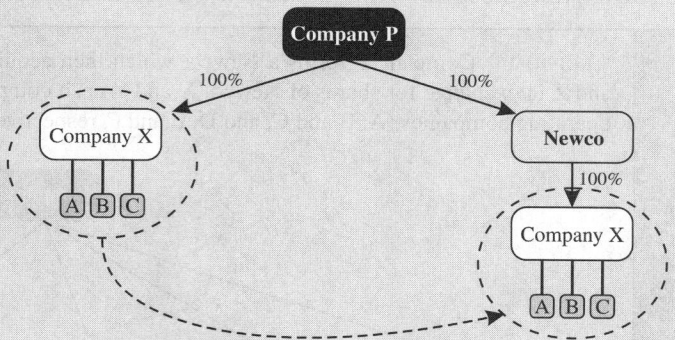

5.13.190.40   We believe that Newco should account for the restructuring using book value accounting in its consolidated financial statements; this is on the basis that there has been no business combination and in substance nothing has occurred. If IFRS 3 were applied, then X subgroup would be identified as the acquirer, but Newco is not a business and therefore cannot be the acquiree (see 2.6.20).

5.13.190.50   However, an issue arises about whether this is the only accounting that Newco could apply in its consolidated financial statements – i.e. is it possible to conclude that a business combination has occurred and therefore that acquisition accounting should be applied to part of the X group? In this example, we believe that the answer is 'no', because under IFRS 3 the entire X group would be identified as the acquirer. Newco cannot be the acquiree because it is not a business, and accordingly there is no business combination to which acquisition accounting can be applied. [*IFRS 3.B18*]

5.13.190.60   In Example 18A, we believe that the same conclusion would be reached even if Newco borrowed funds from a third party – e.g. from a bank – and subsequently paid cash to acquire Company X. We do not believe that financing from a third party changes the economics of the transaction, because no independent party has acquired X.

5.13.190.70   In addition, the conclusion in Example 18A would be the same if the transaction was structured differently such that the X group of companies was transferred under the control of Newco in consecutive stages rather than as a single transfer. In that case, we believe that the guidance on the linkage of transactions contained in IFRS 10 (see 2.5.770) is relevant.

5.13.190.80   In contrast with Example 18A, if two or more previously uncombined businesses are brought together under a Newco, it is then possible to identify an acquirer and acquiree(s) and to conclude that a business combination has occurred. In that case, the next step is to apply the principles of IFRS 3 to determine which of the entities (if any) transferred to Newco should be identified as the acquirer. Once the acquirer has been identified, the acquirer then determines its accounting policy in respect of common control transactions (see 5.13.50.30), having regard to the need for the consistency of accounting policies (see 5.13.40).

EXAMPLE 18B – NEWCO USED IN A RESTRUCTURING – MULTIPLE ACQUISITIONS

5.13.190.90   Company P forms a Newco, which then acquires Companies X, Y and Z in exchange for shares of Newco. X and Y each comprise a group of three operating companies (A, B and C, and D, E and F, respectively).

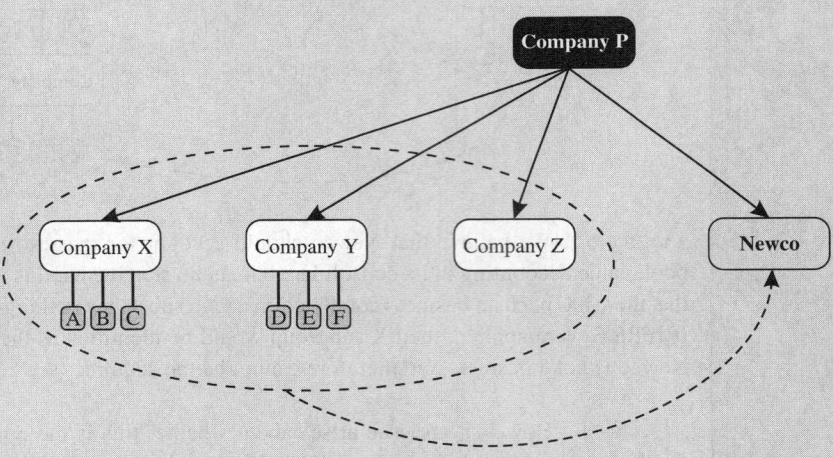

5.13.190.100   In this example, the transaction is analysed as follows.
- It is a business combination amongst entities under common control, because there are three previously uncombined businesses being brought together under a Newco.
- Applying the guidance in IFRS 3 (see 2.6.60), based on the facts and circumstances in this example, subgroup X is identified as the acquirer.
- Newco (as the vehicle of X) then chooses to apply IFRS 3 accounting in its consolidated financial statements (see 5.13.50.30) – i.e. Newco elects to apply acquisition accounting to subgroup Y and to Z.

> 5.13.190.110   The transaction has no impact on P's consolidated financial statements.

5.13.190.120   In Example 18B, Newco chose to apply IFRS 3 accounting. Instead, Newco could have chosen to apply book value accounting (see 5.13.50.30). In that case, Newco would have accounted for subgroups X and Y, and Z, on the basis of book values.

5.13.190.130   When Newco is used in a restructuring and book value accounting is applied, in our view the same considerations and choice of whether to restate comparatives apply as for common control transactions (see 5.13.62) – i.e. Newco may choose to present/re-present comparatives and the current period before the date of the transaction. The same approach should be followed for similar transactions. [*IAS 8.13*]

5.13.200   Newco used on emerging from bankruptcy

5.13.200.10   A Newco may also be used to restructure an entity following bankruptcy or as part of a restructuring to avoid bankruptcy. In this case, the general considerations in 5.13.170 apply and a determination is made of whether Newco is used in a business combination involving a third party – i.e. the creditors of the entity – or in a restructuring among entities under common control. This may depend on the involvement of different parties in forming the Newco, and judgement may be required in making a determination.

EXAMPLE 19 – NEWCO FORMATION ON EMERGING FROM BANKRUPTCY

5.13.200.20   Company P, which has two subsidiaries, Company X and Company Y, filed for creditor protection under local laws in 2018. To emerge from creditor protection, P has proposed the following restructuring plan, which is subject to approval by a majority of P's creditors:
- a Newco will be set up;
- P's current shares will be exchanged for shares of Newco;
- creditors will settle their outstanding claims against P in exchange for shares in Newco, which will strongly dilute the former shareholders of P; and
- Newco will be a holding company, owning 100% of the shares of the reorganised P. As a result, the creditors will represent almost all of the shareholders in P through their holdings in Newco.

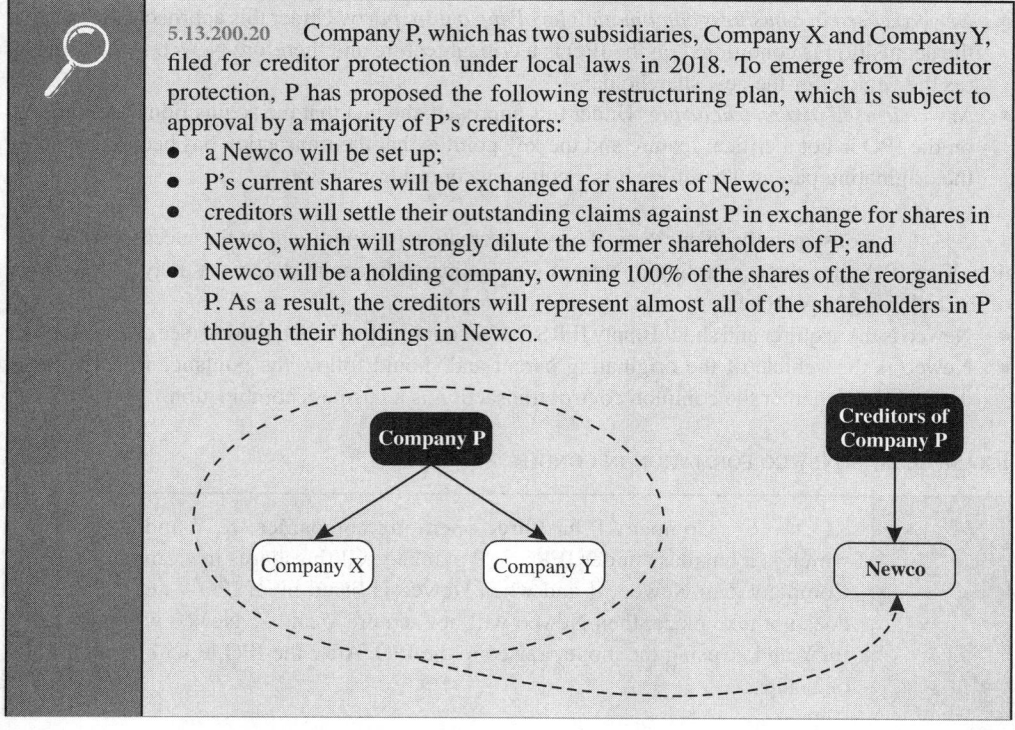

5.13.200.30   In this example, management concludes that a business combination involving a third party – i.e. the creditors of the entity – has occurred. Newco is identified as the acquirer, because it is the vehicle of the creditors to effect the transfer of ownership of P. Accordingly, Newco applies IFRS 3 in accounting for the acquisition of P and its subsidiaries.

5.13.205   Newco used in conditional IPO

5.13.205.10   In some cases, it may be difficult to identify on whose behalf a Newco is created and acting. This is the case if a Newco is created to acquire control of a number of businesses, but that acquisition is contingent on the completion of an initial public offering (IPO). In July 2011, the IFRS Interpretations Committee received a request for guidance on accounting for this type of scenario.

5.13.205.20   The Committee concluded its discussions by observing that the accounting for this scenario was too broad to be addressed through an interpretation or an annual improvement (see 1.1.130). Therefore, the Committee decided not to add the issue to its agenda and recommended that the IASB consider this scenario as part of its project on common control transactions (see 5.13.250). [IU 09-11]

5.13.205.30   However, the discussions of the Committee in effect identified two approaches in determining the appropriate accounting in such a Newco's consolidated financial statements.
- *Newco is used in a business combination involving a third party:* Under this approach, the fact that the acquisition is conditional on the IPO is a critical feature and therefore Newco is the acquirer (as the vehicle for the new shareholders).
- *Newco is used in a restructuring:* Under this approach, the fact that the acquisition is conditional on the IPO is not a critical feature and the key point is that the transaction has been initiated by the originating parent. Therefore, it is a common control transaction.

5.13.205.40   Consequently, in our view, if Newco's creation is conditional on the successful completion of an IPO, then the accounting in Newco's consolidated financial statements may follow either of the following approaches:
- Newco is the acquirer and should apply IFRS 3 in accounting for the acquisition (see chapter 2.6); or
- Newco is the vehicle of the originating parent and should follow the guidance in 5.13.190 in determining whether the common control transaction is a business combination.

EXAMPLE 20 – NEWCO FORMATION IN CONDITIONAL IPO

5.13.205.50   Company P has three operating companies, X, Y and Z, each of which is a business under IFRS 3. P plans to sell the shares in Company Y and Company Z to Newco, if and when Newco is listed in an IPO – i.e. if the IPO does not take place, then Newco will not acquire Y and Z. Newco will pay cash for Y and Z, using the money raised in the IPO. After the IPO, P will lose control of Y and Z.

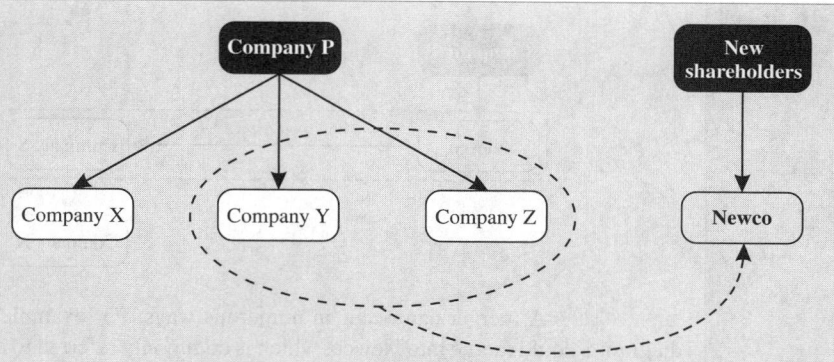

5.13.205.60   Under the first approach in 5.13.205.40, management of Newco concludes that a business combination has occurred in which Newco is the acquirer (as the vehicle for the new shareholders). Accordingly, Newco applies IFRS 3 to the acquisition of both Y and Z.

5.13.205.70   Under the second approach in 5.13.205.40, the transaction is analysed as follows.
- It is a business combination amongst entities under common control.
- Newco chooses to apply book value accounting (see 5.13.50.30) – i.e. Newco elects to account for both Y and Z on the basis of book values.

5.13.205.80   Under the second approach, Newco chose to apply book value accounting; as a result, it was not necessary for Y or Z to be identified as the acquirer. However, if Newco had chosen to apply IFRS 3 accounting (see 5.13.50.30), and assuming, based on the facts and circumstances in this example, that Y was determined to be the acquirer, then acquisition accounting would have been applied to Z.

5.13.210   LEGAL MERGERS AND AMALGAMATIONS

5.13.210.10   For the purposes of the discussion that follows, a 'merger' is a transaction that involves the combination of two or more entities in which one of the legal entities survives and the other ceases to exist, or in which both existing entities cease to exist and a new legal entity comes into existence. The latter is often referred to as an 'amalgamation'.

5.13.210.20   A merger can occur for a number of reasons, including achieving a tax benefit or to facilitate a listing.

EXAMPLE 21 – TYPES OF MERGERS OR AMALGAMATIONS

5.13.210.30   Company P forms a Newco and acquires Company S from a third party in exchange for cash. S is a holding company and the only asset that it holds is a 100% investment in operating Company X. Shortly after the acquisition, Newco and S merge.

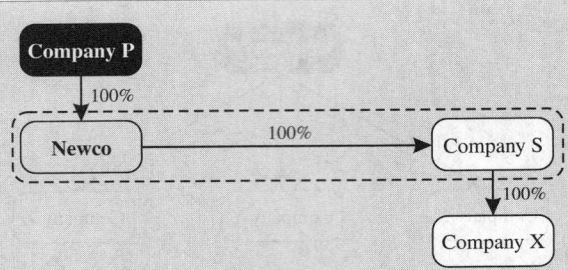

5.13.210.40 A merger can occur in numerous ways. For example, in the above diagram S could merge into Newco, which is commonly referred to as an upstream merger; in this case, S legally disappears and the legal entity that continues to exist is Newco. Alternatively, Newco could merge into S, which is commonly referred to as a downstream merger; in this case, Newco legally disappears and the legal entity that continues to exist is S.

5.13.210.50 In some jurisdictions, the merger between Newco and S may result in an amalgamation, in which a new entity, different from both Newco and S, legally survives after the merger. Judgement is required in assessing whether the form of the merger – which can vary from jurisdiction to jurisdiction – should result in a different accounting outcome.

5.13.210.60 Regardless of the nature of the merger, either upstream, downstream or as a new surviving entity, the result is economically the same as the merged entity will have identical net assets.

5.13.210.70 The guidance that follows in 5.13.220–230 applies equally to mergers and amalgamations of an existing holding company and an operating company. This is because the principles of such a merger/amalgamation are the same as a Newco and an operating company – i.e. one operating company and one non-operating company. However, this guidance would not apply when a Newco is created and then ceases to exist in an upstream merger designed simply to achieve a step-up in the carrying amounts of the net assets of an existing operating entity.

(S) **5.13.210.80** Further, this guidance does not apply if the transaction is between two operating entities that, before the merger or amalgamation, were substantive in their own right. In these cases, judgement is required to determine the appropriate values to reflect in the surviving entity for both its consolidated and separate financial statements.

(S) EXAMPLE 22 – MERGER OF OPERATING AND NON-OPERATING COMPANY

5.13.210.90 Company P has an investment in a wholly owned subsidiary, Company S, which is held via a holding company, Holdco. Other than its investment in S, Holdco has no other assets or liabilities and no activities. S in turn has a wholly owned subsidiary, Company X.

5.13.210.100 For tax reasons, P decides to effect a downstream merger of Holdco into S such that S is the surviving entity. Because this is a merger of one operating company and one non-operating company, we believe that S should apply the guidance in 5.13.220 in respect of its consolidated financial statements, and the guidance in 5.13.230 in respect of its separate financial statements.

Before	After
Company P	**Company P**
↓ 100%	
Holdco	↓ 100%
↓ 100%	
Company S	Company S
↓ 100%	↓ 100%
Company X	Company X

5.13.220   Consolidated financial statements

5.13.220.10 The issue that arises in a merger is determining which entity is the continuing entity for accounting purposes. For example, in Example 21, should the consolidated financial statements of the newly merged entity represent a continuation of the consolidated financial statements of S, or of the consolidated financial statements of Newco?

5.13.220.20 In our view, the legal form of the transaction is less important for the consolidated financial statements, because the focus in consolidated financial statements is the economic entity rather than the legal entity. Therefore, based on Example 21, in our view in respect of its consolidated financial statements the merged entity can do either of the following:

- use Newco consolidated as the consolidated financial statements of the newly merged entity on the basis that Newco was the acquirer in the business combination and therefore the newly merged entity should be a continuation of Newco consolidated; or
- use S consolidated as the consolidated financial statements of the newly merged entity on the basis that S continues to reflect the operations of the merged entity – from S's point of view, there has simply been a change in shareholding.

5.13.230   Separate financial statements

Ⓢ

5.13.230.10 Unlike in the consolidated financial statements, in our view the legal form of a merger may be more important in the context of separate financial statements because these have a different purpose, being the financial statements of a legal entity.

5.13.230.20   Legal form can have a range of consequences. For example, in certain jurisdictions the form of the merger (upstream, downstream or a new surviving entity) can result in different tax consequences, which represent different economic outcomes. In some jurisdictions, legal requirements mean that only one form of merger is available. Therefore, in our view the legal form of the transaction generally guides the accounting in the separate financial statements.

5.13.230.30   Continuing Example 21, if the merger of Newco and S takes the legal form of an upstream merger, then because the legal entity that continues to exist is Newco, we believe that it would be appropriate for the merged entity's statement of financial position to reflect the carrying amounts of the assets in Newco's consolidated statement of financial position – i.e. including goodwill and fair value adjustments.

5.13.230.40   Conversely, if the merger of Newco and S takes the legal form of a downstream merger, then because the legal entity that continues to exist is S, we believe that one approach for the merged entity's statement of financial position would be to reflect the carrying amounts of the assets on S's statement of financial position.

5.13.230.50   If the merger of Newco and S takes the legal form of a newly surviving entity (an amalgamation), then based on Example 21, we believe that in respect of its separate financial statements the merged entity can do either of the following.
- Use Newco as the separate financial statements of the newly merged entity on the basis that Newco was the acquirer in the business combination and therefore the newly merged entity should be a continuation of Newco.
- Use S as the separate financial statements of the newly merged entity on the basis that S continues to reflect the operations of the merged entity – from S's point of view, there has simply been a change in shareholding.

5.13.240   DISCLOSURES

5.13.240.10   In our view, an entity should disclose its accounting policy for common control transactions. [*IAS 1.10(e)*]

5.13.240.20   An entity provides additional disclosures in the financial statements if it is necessary for users to understand the effect of specific transactions. In our view, to meet this requirement, sufficient information about common control transactions should be disclosed in the financial statements in order that users can understand the effect thereof. [*IAS 1.15*]

5.13.240.30   If fair value accounting is applied, then in our view, for acquisitions of subsidiaries in consolidated financial statements, an entity should provide the disclosures required by IFRS 3 in respect of business combinations. If book value accounting is applied, then we believe that some of these disclosures will still be relevant to users of the financial statements – e.g. the amounts recognised for each class of assets and liabilities acquired, either at the date of the transaction (if comparative information is not re-presented) or at the beginning of the earliest period presented (if comparative information is re-presented). [*IFRS 3.59–63*]

5.13.250 **FUTURE DEVELOPMENTS**

5.13.250.10 The IASB is working on a research project *Business Combinations under Common Control*, aiming to develop requirements to be applied to accounting for business combinations under common control. It is expected to publish a discussion paper in the first half of 2019.

5.13.250.20 The IASB has discussed the types of transactions that are in the scope of the research project. The scope includes transactions under common control in which a reporting entity obtains control of one or more businesses, regardless of whether the reporting entity is the acquirer under IFRS 3. The project also includes transactions that are:

- preceded by an external acquisition and/or followed by an external sale of one or more of the combining parties; or
- conditional on a future sale – e.g. in an initial public offering.

6.   FIRST-TIME ADOPTION OF IFRS

6.1   First-time adoption of IFRS

6. FIRST-TIME ADOPTION OF IFRS

6.1 First-time adoption of IFRS

CURRENTLY EFFECTIVE REQUIREMENTS

This publication reflects IFRS in issue at 1 August 2018, and the currently effective requirements cover annual periods beginning on 1 January 2018.

The requirements related to this topic are mainly derived from the following.

STANDARD	TITLE
IFRS 1	First-time Adoption of International Financial Reporting Standards

The currently effective requirements include newly effective requirements arising from the following:
- IFRS 15 *Revenue from Contracts with Customers*, which is effective for annual periods beginning on or after 1 January 2018. See 6.1.1360.
- IFRS 9 *Financial Instruments*, which is effective for annual periods beginning on or after 1 January 2018. See 6.1.560.
- IFRIC 22 *Foreign Currency Transactions and Advance Consideration*, which is effective for annual periods beginning on or after 1 January 2018. See 6.1.1200.
- *Applying IFRS 9 Financial Instruments with IFRS 4 Insurance Contracts – Amendments to IFRS 4*, which are effective:
  - for the temporary exemption from IFRS 9 – for annual periods beginning on or after 1 January 2018; and
  - for the overlay approach – for annual periods beginning when an entity first applies IFRS 9. See 6.1.1460.20.
- *Annual Improvements to IFRSs 2014–2016 Cycle – Amendments to IFRS 1*, which are effective for annual periods beginning on or after 1 January 2018. The amendments remove a temporary mandatory exception for the investment entity assessment. See 6.1.1520.20.

FORTHCOMING REQUIREMENTS

The currently effective requirements are affected by the following forthcoming requirements. They are highlighted with a # and the impact is explained in the accompanying boxed text at the references indicated.
- In January 2016, the IASB issued IFRS 16 *Leases*, which is effective for annual periods beginning on or after 1 January 2019. See 6.1.245, 365 and 1425. IFRS 16 is the subject of chapter 5.1A.
- In May 2017, the IASB issued IFRS 17 *Insurance Contracts*, which is effective for annual periods beginning on or after 1 January 2021. See 6.1.1465. IFRS 17 is the subject of chapter 8.1A.

FUTURE DEVELOPMENTS

The currently effective requirements that may be affected by future developments are highlighted with a * and are briefly discussed in 6.1.1570.

6.1.10 GENERAL REQUIREMENTS

6.1.10.10   IFRS 1 contains all of the transitional recognition, measurement, presentation and disclosure requirements applicable for a first-time adopter preparing its first annual and interim financial statements in accordance with IFRS. A first-time adopter does not apply the transitional requirements of individual standards or interpretations unless specifically required to do so. [*IFRS 1.2*]

6.1.10.20   Entities already applying IFRS refer to the transitional requirements of individual standards and interpretations and to the general requirements applicable to changes of accounting policy (see 2.8.50). IFRS 1 does not apply to entities already reporting under IFRS that comply for the first time with a new standard. [*IAS 8.19, IFRS 1.5, 9*]

6.1.20   Key terms

6.1.20.10   A number of terms have been introduced in the context of the adoption of IFRS as an entity's reporting framework and are used throughout this chapter.

6.1.20.20   The following terms are applicable on first-time adoption of IFRS.
- The 'date of transition' is the beginning of the earliest period for which an entity presents full comparative information under IFRS in its first IFRS financial statements.
- An entity's 'first IFRS financial statements' are the first annual financial statements in which the entity adopts IFRS and in which it makes an explicit and unreserved statement of compliance with IFRS.
- The 'first IFRS reporting period' is the latest reporting period covered by an entity's first IFRS financial statements.
- A 'first-time adopter' is an entity that presents its first IFRS financial statements (see 6.1.30), except for an entity that re-adopts IFRS and chooses to apply IFRS retrospectively (see 6.1.50).
- The 'opening IFRS statement of financial position' is an entity's statement of financial position at the date of transition (see 6.1.130.10). [*IFRS 1.A*]

EXAMPLE 1 – KEY TERMS ON FIRST-TIME ADOPTION

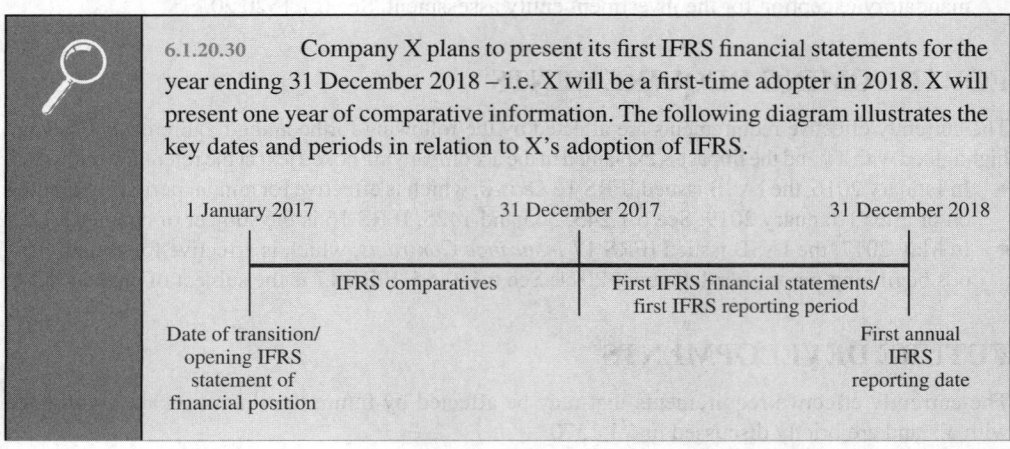

6.1.20.30   Company X plans to present its first IFRS financial statements for the year ending 31 December 2018 – i.e. X will be a first-time adopter in 2018. X will present one year of comparative information. The following diagram illustrates the key dates and periods in relation to X's adoption of IFRS.

1 January 2017	31 December 2017	31 December 2018
IFRS comparatives	First IFRS financial statements/ first IFRS reporting period	
Date of transition/ opening IFRS statement of financial position		First annual IFRS reporting date

6.1.20.40   In this diagram, the first-time adopter is presenting only one year of comparative information on the basis of IFRS and therefore has a date of transition of 1 January 2017. IFRS requires that comparative information be disclosed in respect of at least one previous reporting period (see 2.1.50). However, IFRS 1 does not prohibit the presentation of more than one year of comparative information. In such cases, the first-time adopter's date of transition would be at the start of the earliest comparative period presented on the basis of IFRS.

6.1.20.50   The following terms relate to other aspects of the adoption of IFRS.

- 'Deemed cost' is an amount used as a surrogate for cost or depreciated cost at a given date. Subsequent depreciation or amortisation assumes that the first-time adopter had initially recognised the asset or liability at the given date and that its cost was equal to the deemed cost.
- 'Fair value' is the price that would be received to sell an asset or paid to transfer a liability in an orderly transaction between market participants at the measurement date.
- 'Previous GAAP' is the basis of accounting that a first-time adopter used immediately before adopting IFRS (see 6.1.120). [*IFRS 1.A*]

6.1.30   Statement of compliance with IFRS

6.1.30.10   A first-time adopter is an entity that presents its first annual financial statements that include an explicit and unreserved statement of compliance with IFRS. The first-time adoption requirements also apply to interim financial statements prepared in accordance with IFRS (see chapter 5.9) for part of a period that will be covered by an entity's first IFRS financial statements. [*IFRS 1.2, A*]

6.1.30.12   IFRS 1 does not preclude an entity from applying the standard more than once if an entity has applied IFRS in a previous reporting period, but that entity's most recent previous annual financial statements did not contain an explicit and unreserved statement of compliance with IFRS by choice or necessity (see 6.1.50). [*IFRS 1.4A*]

6.1.30.15   Some jurisdictions use the term 'IFRS' as a starting point for describing their own reporting requirements. For example, some entities in the EU are required to prepare their consolidated financial statements in accordance with 'IFRSs as adopted by the EU' or 'EU IFRS'. The IFRS referred to in IFRS 1 is IFRS as issued by the IASB. [*IFRS 1.A*]

6.1.30.20   A first-time adopter does not describe financial statements as complying with IFRS unless it complies with all of the requirements of IFRS applicable to the first-time adopter. [*IAS 1.16*]

EXAMPLE 2 – ENTITIES THAT STOP USING PREVIOUS GAAP

6.1.30.30   Company X prepares its financial statements in accordance with previous GAAP. In 2018, X will stop preparing its financial statements in accordance with previous GAAP and instead will prepare them in accordance with IFRS. In 2018, X will be a first-time adopter if it makes an explicit and unreserved statement of compliance with IFRS in its 2018 financial statements. [*IFRS 1.3*]

EXAMPLE 3 – ENTITIES THAT DID NOT FULLY APPLY IFRS

> 6.1.30.35   Company S's financial statements for the year ended 31 December 2017 claimed compliance with IFRS except for IAS 39. In 2018, S will prepare financial statements that claim full compliance with IFRS. S will be a first-time adopter in its 2018 financial statements because the statement of compliance with IFRS in its 2017 financial statements was not unreserved. [*IFRS 1.3(a)(iii)*]

6.1.30.40   In general, the overriding criterion in assessing whether an entity is a first-time adopter is whether it includes an explicit and unreserved statement of compliance with IFRS in its first annual financial statements. However, there are also other common situations that arise in practice that are inter-related to this overriding criterion, some of which are discussed in 6.1.30.50–120. [*IFRS 1.3*]

6.1.30.50   Each entity that prepares financial statements – i.e. each reporting entity – can be a first-time adopter. In our view, financial statements that are prepared for a part of the reporting entity do not make the entity as a whole a first-time adopter.

EXAMPLE 4 – PART OF ENTITY PREVIOUSLY PRESENTED UNDER IFRS

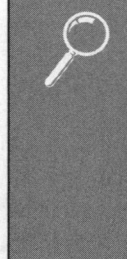

> 6.1.30.60   Company Y prepares its financial statements in accordance with previous GAAP. In 2018, Y will stop preparing its financial statements in accordance with previous GAAP and instead will prepare them in accordance with IFRS. However, for the year ended 31 December 2017 Y prepared a set of financial statements in accordance with IFRS for a single division of the company that it was planning to sell; these financial statements were presented to prospective buyers. In our view, the IFRS financial statements of the division as a separate reporting entity do not mean that Y as a whole has adopted IFRS for the first time. Instead, in 2018 the reporting entity, that is Y, will be a first-time adopter if it makes an explicit and unreserved statement of compliance with IFRS in its 2018 financial statements.

6.1.30.70   Even if previous GAAP is very similar to IFRS, or IFRS is referred to when national GAAP is silent, this is not sufficient to conclude that the entity is already applying IFRS (see 6.1.60). [*IFRS 1.3(a)(i), (iv)*]

EXAMPLE 5 – PREVIOUS GAAP NOT FULLY CONSISTENT WITH IFRS

> 6.1.30.80   Company Z prepares its financial statements in accordance with previous GAAP. In accordance with the requirements of previous GAAP, Z accounts for investment property following IAS 40 (see chapter 3.4) because previous GAAP has no specific guidance on that topic. However, previous GAAP is not necessarily consistent with IFRS in other respects. In 2018, Z will stop preparing its financial statements in accordance with previous GAAP and instead will prepare them in accordance with IFRS. In 2018, Z will be a first-time adopter if it makes an explicit and unreserved statement of compliance with IFRS in its 2018 financial statements.

6.1.30.90   In some cases, previous GAAP may require a reconciliation of key figures in the financial statements – e.g. profit or loss – to what they would have been if prepared in accordance with IFRS. However, because the entity does not fully comply with all of the requirements of IFRS, the reconciliation is not sufficient to conclude that the entity is already applying IFRS. [*IFRS 1.3(a)(v)*]

EXAMPLE 6 – RECONCILIATIONS TO IFRS IN PREVIOUS GAAP FINANCIAL STATEMENTS

6.1.30.100   Company P prepares its financial statements in accordance with previous GAAP. Although not required by previous GAAP, P reconciles its profit or loss under previous GAAP to IFRS in accordance with the requirements of the local stock exchange. In 2018, P will stop preparing its financial statements in accordance with previous GAAP and instead will prepare them in accordance with IFRS. In 2018, P will be a first-time adopter if it makes an explicit and unreserved statement of compliance with IFRS in its 2018 financial statements. Its previous reconciliation of profit or loss to IFRS did not constitute the adoption of IFRS.

6.1.30.110   An entity is a first-time adopter when it presents its first annual financial statements that include an explicit and unreserved statement of compliance with IFRS – it is not relevant whether the audit report (if any) is qualified. [*IFRS 1.4(c)*]

EXAMPLE 7 – QUALIFIED OPINION ON PREVIOUSLY PRESENTED IFRS FINANCIAL STATEMENTS

6.1.30.120   Company T's financial statements for the year ended 31 December 2017 contained an explicit and unreserved statement of compliance with IFRS; however, the audit report was qualified because T did not comply with certain requirements of IAS 39. In 2018, T will prepare financial statements that fully comply with IFRS and it expects to receive an unqualified audit report. T will not be a first-time adopter in its 2018 financial statements because the statement of compliance with IFRS in its 2017 financial statements was unreserved. The fact that T received a qualified audit report is not relevant to the determination of whether T is a first-time adopter.

6.1.40   *Dual compliance*

6.1.40.10   An entity may make an explicit and unreserved statement of compliance with both IFRS and another GAAP – e.g. EU IFRS. Such dual statements of compliance do not impact the assessment of whether an entity is a first-time adopter; the important fact is that the financial statements include an explicit and unreserved statement of compliance with IFRS. If in a subsequent year the entity drops the reference to its national GAAP while keeping its statement of compliance with IFRS, then the entity is not a first-time adopter in that year. This is because the most recent previous annual financial statements included an explicit and unreserved statement of compliance with IFRS. [*IFRS 1.4(a)*]

6.1.50   *Reinstating reference to IFRS*

6.1.50.10   An entity may have previously included an explicit and unreserved statement of compliance with IFRS and then subsequently dropped the reference to IFRS from its statement of compliance by choice or necessity. Because financial statements are generally prepared in accordance with at least one GAAP, this may arise if previous financial statements included a statement of compliance with both IFRS and another GAAP – e.g. EU IFRS – but the most recent annual financial statements stated compliance only with that other GAAP. If the entity subsequently reinstates the statement of compliance with IFRS, then the entity meets the criteria for applying IFRS 1. Notwithstanding this, the entity can choose either of the following approaches.

- Apply IFRS 1 in full, which includes disclosures about why the entity stopped and then resumed applying IFRS.
- Apply IAS 8 as if the entity had never stopped applying IFRS, and provide disclosures required by IFRS 1 regarding why the entity stopped and then resumed applying IFRS, as well as the reason for following this approach. [*IFRS 1.4A–4B, 23A–23B*]

EXAMPLE 8 – STATEMENT OF COMPLIANCE NO LONGER INCLUDED

6.1.50.20   Company B's financial statements for the year ended 31 December 2016 contained an explicit and unreserved statement of compliance with IFRS, although the audit report was qualified for non-compliance with IAS 39. B's financial statements for the year ended 31 December 2017 still did not comply with IAS 39 and therefore B decided not to include a statement of compliance with IFRS in the financial statements. B plans to comply fully with IFRS in its 2018 financial statements and will include an explicit and unreserved statement of compliance with IFRS in those statements. Accordingly, B will be a first-time adopter in 2018 if it chooses to apply IFRS 1 in full when it re-adopts IFRS, because its most recent previous financial statements did not include an explicit and unreserved statement of compliance with IFRS. Alternatively, B can apply IFRS retrospectively in accordance with IAS 8 as if it had never stopped applying IFRS.

6.1.60   *Previous omission of statement of compliance with IFRS*

6.1.60.10   A question also arises about whether an entity is a first-time adopter if it previously included only an explicit and unreserved statement of compliance with another GAAP which is equivalent to IFRS and it subsequently includes an explicit and unreserved statement of compliance with IFRS for the first time. In our view, although no statement of compliance with IFRS has ever been included in a previous set of financial statements in this case, the entity may apply either of the following approaches.

- *Approach 1:* The entity is a first-time adopter. This is because the definition of a first-time adopter is predicated on an entity stating explicit compliance with IFRS. The omission of a statement of compliance with IFRS would result in the entity being first-time adopter when it includes an explicit statement of compliance with IFRS (see 6.1.30).
- *Approach 2:* The entity is not a first-time adopter if it is determined that a statement of compliance with IFRS could have been made. The entity would need to assess, and make a determination of, whether it could have asserted dual compliance with both IFRS and the IFRS equivalent. If it is determined that dual compliance could have been possible, then the entity would not be a first-time adopter when it includes an explicit statement of compliance with IFRS.

6.1.70   *Subsidiary, associate or joint venture adopting IFRS before or after parent/investor*

6.1.70.10   IFRS includes specific requirements, some of which are mandatory, when a subsidiary (or associate or joint venture) becomes a first-time adopter later than its parent and when an entity becomes a first-time adopter later than its subsidiary (or associate or joint venture) (see 6.1.1240 and 1290). The question that arises is whether these requirements are also applicable when the relevant group entity has previously included an explicit and unreserved statement of compliance with an IFRS equivalent, but did not include a dual statement of compliance. As discussed in 6.1.60.10, we believe that the relevant group entity has a choice of two approaches, depending upon the facts and circumstances.

6.1.70.20   If the entity applies IFRS 1 and the approach taken results in the relevant group entities becoming first-time adopters at different dates, then the requirements in IFRS 1 that apply when a subsidiary, associate or joint venture adopts IFRS before or after its parent/investor are applicable. For further discussion, see 6.1.1240 and 1290.

EXAMPLE 9 – OMISSION OF COMPLIANCE STATEMENT WITH IFRS – GROUP ENTITIES

6.1.70.30   Company P becomes a first-time adopter in 2018. Subsidiary S included an explicit and unreserved statement of compliance with an IFRS equivalent in 2017 and includes an explicit and unreserved statement of compliance with IFRS as issued by the IASB in 2018. In this case, the way in which P measures the assets and liabilities of S in its consolidated financial statements in 2018 depends on whether S becomes a first-time adopter or is an existing IFRS reporter in 2018.

6.1.70.40   We believe that either of the following approaches, applied on a consistent basis, is acceptable.

- *Approach 1:* S becomes a first-time adopter in 2018. This is because the definition of a first-time adopter is predicated on an entity stating explicit compliance with IFRS and S did not include such statement in 2017. It would result in P becoming a first-time adopter in the same period as S.
- *Approach 2:* S is not a first-time adopter in 2018, if it is determined that a statement of compliance with IFRS could have been made in 2017. P would need to assess, and make a determination of, whether S could have asserted dual compliance with both IFRS and its IFRS equivalent in 2017. If it is determined that dual compliance could have been possible, then S is not a first-time adopter when it claims compliance with IFRS explicitly in 2018. In this instance, because P becomes a first-time adopter later than S, P would be required to follow the requirements in IFRS 1 for when a subsidiary, associate or joint venture adopts IFRS before its parent/investor.

6.1.80   *First-time adoption in different sets of financial statements*

6.1.80.10   An entity is a first-time adopter in relation to a set of financial statements – e.g. each of Ⓢ its separate and individual or consolidated financial statements – rather than in relation to the entity. Therefore, it is possible for an entity, through its different reporting entities, to be a first-time adopter more than once over a number of years, in respect of each set of financial statements that it prepares.

For example, an entity that prepares separate and consolidated financial statements can be a first-time adopter in its consolidated financial statements in one year and a few years later a first-time adopter in its separate financial statements. IFRS 1 includes specific requirements in respect of separate and consolidated financial statements when IFRS is adopted in each of the financial statements in different years (see 6.1.1230). [*IFRS 1.D17*]

6.1.80.20   However, in our view IFRS 1 cannot be applied more than once in respect of the same set of financial statements prepared for the same reporting period. In our experience, this issue is most likely to arise in connection with regulatory requirements dealing with the number of years of comparative information required to be included in the financial statements. Because IFRS requires only one year of comparatives plus a statement of financial position at the date of transition – i.e. any additional comparatives are presented on a voluntary basis – we believe that any such issue should be discussed with the relevant regulator.

EXAMPLE 10 – MULTIPLE SETS OF IFRS FINANCIAL STATEMENTS WITH DIFFERENT DATES OF TRANSITION

6.1.80.30   Company C will prepare its first financial statements in accordance with IFRS for the year ending 31 December 2018. The financial statements will include one year of comparative information, plus a statement of financial position at the date of transition of 1 January 2017. These financial statements will be filed with the securities regulator in Country M.

6.1.80.40   In early 2018, C plans to undertake an initial public offering in Country G. Under Country G's applicable regulatory requirements, C is required to file, in its offering document, its most recent financial statements prepared in accordance with IFRS, and those financial statements are required to include two years of comparative information. To satisfy Country G's regulatory requirements, C would have to prepare 2018 IFRS financial statements with two years of comparative information, which would mean that C would have a date of transition of 1 January 2016.

6.1.80.50   On the face of it, these two requirements mean that C requires two sets of first IFRS financial statements for the year ending 31 December 2018, which would show different results and financial positions because of the different starting points in preparing the financial statements – 1 January 2016 vs 1 January 2017. We believe that this would not be appropriate and that the date of transition in respect of C's first IFRS financial statements for the year ending 31 December 2018 should be either 1 January 2016 or 1 January 2017.

6.1.80.60   However, if the 2018 financial statements in 6.1.80.30 have already been filed with the securities regulator – i.e. made publicly available in Country M – then these are C's first IFRS financial statements. Because C has already made its *first* IFRS financial statements publicly available in Country M, C would not be able to have a second set of first IFRS financial statements under Country G's regulatory requirements; the date of transition will be 1 January 2017. However, the financial statements may include additional information to satisfy the requirements in Country G.

6.1.90 *Financial statements for internal use only*

6.1.90.10   Financial statements may be prepared for internal use only, without being distributed to external parties. In such cases the entity, even if the financial statements include an explicit and unreserved statement of compliance with IFRS, has not adopted IFRS. [*IFRS 1.3(b)*]

EXAMPLE 11 – IFRS FINANCIAL STATEMENTS FOR INTERNAL USE ONLY

6.1.90.20   Company D prepares financial statements in accordance with previous GAAP. For the year ended 31 December 2017, D prepared an additional set of financial statements in accordance with IFRS to assist management in assessing the potential impact of adopting IFRS in the future. The IFRS financial statements were not distributed to D's shareholders or to any other external parties. Although D may have complied with IFRS 1 on a voluntary basis in preparing the IFRS financial statements, it is not a first-time adopter for the purposes of those financial statements because they were not distributed externally. However, to avoid repeating the effort involved in preparing the opening statement of financial position when IFRS is adopted the following year – i.e. for the year ending 31 December 2018 – D can elect to present two years of comparative information in its first IFRS financial statements, to preserve the date of transition of 1 January 2016 (see 6.1.20.40).

EXAMPLE 12 – IFRS FINANCIAL STATEMENTS DISTRIBUTED TO AN EXTERNAL PARTY

6.1.90.30   Company E prepares financial statements in accordance with previous GAAP. For the year ended 31 December 2017, E prepared an additional set of financial statements in accordance with IFRS to assist management in assessing the potential impact of adopting IFRS in the future. The IFRS financial statements were not distributed to E's shareholders, but they were given to a bank that requested IFRS financial information in assessing a new loan facility for E. Because the IFRS financial statements were distributed to an external party (the bank), E is a first-time adopter for the purposes of those financial statements.

6.1.90.40   If in 2018 E is required to publish IFRS financial statements for statutory reporting purposes, then E would not be a first-time adopter and therefore would not be required to disclose, for example, an explanation of the impact of its transition from previous GAAP to IFRS (see 6.1.1520.60–80). Such disclosures would have been included in E's 2017 IFRS financial statements, which were not distributed to E's shareholders. E may therefore consider providing additional voluntary disclosures – e.g. similar disclosures to those provided in its 2017 IFRS financial statements – to assist the users of its 2018 IFRS statutory financial statements in understanding its transition from previous GAAP to IFRS.

6.1.100 *Group reporting packages*

6.1.100.10   A group reporting package that is prepared for the first time in accordance with IFRS for consolidation purposes, but which is not a complete set of financial statements in accordance with IAS 1 (see chapter 2.1), does not result in the entity being a first-time adopter. [*IFRS 1.3(c)*]

6.1.110 *No previous financial statements*

6.1.110.10 An entity is a first-time adopter if it did not present financial statements for previous periods. [*IFRS 1.3(d)*]

6.1.110.20 In practice, it is generally irrelevant to assess whether a Newco is a first-time adopter in its first ever financial statements because a Newco has no substantial assets and liabilities at the earliest date presented – i.e. the date of incorporation or creation. However, when a Newco is formed and pre-existing businesses are transferred to the Newco as part of a restructuring that is accounted for on a book value basis, in our view Newco might be a first-time adopter in respect of those businesses. This is because book value accounting in this type of transaction assumes that the pre-existing business (entity) is continued (see 5.13.190).

6.1.120 **Previous GAAP**

6.1.120.10 A first-time adopter could have prepared more than one set of financial statements of the same type for the same period – e.g. two sets of consolidated financial statements for the same annual period using different bases of accounting: e.g. one set under US GAAP and one set under Brazilian GAAP. The question that arises is which basis of accounting meets the definition of previous GAAP.

6.1.120.20 In our view, when assessing previous GAAP in these circumstances, it is necessary to consider the following:
- which financial statements are being replaced (see 6.1.120.30); and
- what will be more meaningful to the recipients of the IFRS financial statements (see 6.1.120.50).

EXAMPLE 13A – MORE THAN ONE SET OF PREVIOUS GAAP FINANCIAL STATEMENTS (1)

6.1.120.30 Company T previously prepared statutory financial statements in accordance with Brazilian GAAP and non-statutory US GAAP financial statements. T is adopting IFRS in its 2018 statutory financial statements. T's Brazilian and US GAAP financial statements are both publicly available, although the US GAAP financial statements are the more widely distributed set of financial statements. We believe that Brazilian GAAP is previous GAAP for the purposes of the first-time adoption of IFRS if the IFRS financial statements now being prepared are the statutory financial statements. We believe that previous GAAP is the GAAP applied in preparing the same financial statements published immediately preceding the period. We do not believe that IFRS 1 makes any distinction based on how widely distributed the previous GAAP financial statements were, provided that they were publicly available.

EXAMPLE 13B – MORE THAN ONE SET OF PREVIOUS GAAP FINANCIAL STATEMENTS (2)

6.1.120.40 Company G prepares statutory financial statements in accordance with Indian GAAP as well as non-statutory US GAAP financial statements. G is adopting IFRS in 2018 for non-statutory reporting purposes but will continue to prepare statutory financial statements in accordance with Indian GAAP. Previously G's non-domestic investors were provided only with G's US GAAP financial statements.

6.1.120.50   We believe that US GAAP is previous GAAP for the purposes of G's first-time adoption of IFRS for its non-statutory financial statements. We believe that if an entity's first IFRS financial statements are prepared for non-statutory purposes, then the accounting framework used immediately before the adoption of IFRS for its non-statutory filings is the previous GAAP. We believe that the users of G's first IFRS financial statements would be the users of G's US GAAP financial statements prepared for the preceding year and would therefore benefit most by assessing the effects of G's transition from US GAAP to IFRS rather than from Indian GAAP to IFRS. In our view, if G's non-domestic investors had access to both Indian and US GAAP financial statements, then it would be possible for G to select either Indian or US GAAP as previous GAAP for the purpose of adopting IFRS in the non-statutory financial statements. G would apply judgement in making a final determination.

6.1.130   OVERVIEW OF IFRS 1

6.1.130.10   The starting point for an entity's adoption of IFRS is the creation of a statement of financial position at the entity's date of transition, which involves the steps outlined below. [*IFRS 1.6*]

6.1.135   Recognise all assets and liabilities whose recognition is required by IFRS

6.1.135.10   Assets and liabilities that were not recognised under previous GAAP at the date of transition, but which meet the requirements for recognition under IFRS, are recognised in the opening IFRS statement of financial position. These may include, for example:
- defined benefit plan assets or liabilities;
- deferred tax assets or liabilities;
- provisions for restoration costs in respect of non-current assets; and
- amounts received that do not qualify for recognition as revenue – i.e. deferred income. [*IFRS 1.10(a)*]

6.1.140   Derecognise all assets and liabilities whose recognition is not allowed by IFRS

6.1.140.10   Assets and liabilities that were recognised under previous GAAP at the date of transition, but which do not meet the requirements for recognition under IFRS, are derecognised from the opening IFRS statement of financial position. For example:
- intangible assets that do not qualify for recognition – e.g. some internally generated intangible assets, all internally generated goodwill, capitalised start-up costs or research expenditure (see 3.3.110);
- liabilities for restructuring that do not meet the recognition requirements for a provision (see 3.12.30 and 230); and
- acquisition-related costs incurred and capitalised by an acquirer before the date of transition to effect a business combination in future that had not occurred by the date of transition (see 2.6.530).
[*IFRS 1.10(b)*]

6.1.150   **Reclassify assets, liabilities and components of equity as necessary**

6.1.150.10   Reclassification is required for items that were recognised under previous GAAP as one type of asset, liability or component of equity, but which are a different type of asset, liability or component of equity under IFRS. For example:

- some intangibles are reclassified as goodwill and vice versa;
- some equity items are reclassified as liabilities and vice versa; and
- reserves related to revaluations made under previous GAAP may be reclassified as retained earnings. [*IFRS 1.10(c)*]

6.1.160   **Apply IFRS in measuring all recognised assets and liabilities**

6.1.160.10   Assets and liabilities in the opening IFRS statement of financial position are remeasured in accordance with the relevant IFRS. For example:

- provisions are measured on a discounted basis (see 3.12.120);
- deferred tax liabilities and assets are measured on an undiscounted basis (see 3.13.510); and
- investment property is measured at fair value, when applicable (see 3.4.130). [*IFRS 1.10(d)*]

6.1.160.20   The measurement of assets and liabilities is in accordance with IFRS even if an item is measured under both previous GAAP and IFRS on a cost basis – i.e. the measurement requirements of IFRS are applied at a more detailed level. For example, IFRS does not permit inventories to be measured under the LIFO method and requires the same inventory cost formula to be applied by the entire reporting entity for inventories having a similar nature and use to the entity (see 3.8.280).

6.1.170   **Choose accounting policies**

6.1.170.10   In preparing its first IFRS financial statements, a first-time adopter selects accounting policies based on IFRS that are effective as at the first annual IFRS reporting date. This may include the early adoption of new standards or interpretations that are not effective for the first IFRS reporting period but for which early adoption is permitted. A first-time adopter does not apply earlier versions of standards that no longer are effective. [*IFRS 1.7–8*]

6.1.170.20   Generally, those policies are applied consistently at the date of transition to fully restate on a retrospective basis the opening statement of financial position on an IFRS basis, and in each of the periods presented in the first IFRS financial statements. This is the case even if a particular standard does not require retrospective application for existing users of IFRS. The retrospective application of IFRS effectively requires a first-time adopter to remeasure all transactions and events as at the date on which they originally arose using IFRS effective as at the entity's first annual IFRS reporting date. The mandatory exceptions and optional exemptions in IFRS 1 provide relief from these general principles (see 6.1.230–240). [*IFRS 1.7*]

6.1.170.30   A first-time adopter has a free choice over the accounting policies that it will use on an ongoing basis. The restrictions that apply to an existing user of IFRS in respect of voluntary changes in accounting policy, as set out in IAS 8, do not apply to a first-time adopter. A first-time adopter can adopt an accounting policy without the explicit need for the new policy to be reliable and more relevant than any alternative policies not adopted, provided that the policy complies with IFRS. Consequently, certain restrictions – e.g. on the change from the fair value model to the cost model for investment property under IAS 40 – do not apply to a first-time adopter. Therefore, the transition from previous GAAP to IFRS provides a first-time adopter with the opportunity to evaluate its accounting policies under IFRS and to take a 'clean sheet of paper' approach to selecting its IFRS accounting policies and practices. [*IFRS 1.5(a), 27, IAS 8.14(b)*]

6.1.170.40   Unless specifically allowed by IFRS 1, the transitional requirements of the standards and interpretations that apply to existing users of IFRS do not apply to first-time adopters. Instead, IFRS 1 includes specific guidance or refers to specific transitional guidance in certain standards and interpretations. [*IFRS 1.5, 9*]

6.1.180   Make judgements about estimates

6.1.180.10   The preparation of financial statements requires management to make judgements about estimates. IFRS 1 includes specific guidance on how to deal with changes in estimates that applies across all standards and interpretations. Essentially, the guidance is a modification of IAS 10. [*IFRS 1.14–16*]

6.1.180.20   The guidance in IFRS 1 applies from the date of transition to the first annual reporting date – i.e. it covers all periods presented in a first-time adopter's first IFRS financial statements. In developing the guidance on estimates, the IASB considered it more helpful for changes in estimates to be recognised when they were made, rather than pushing them back to the date of transition. This approach also reduces the ability of a first-time adopter to use hindsight when preparing its opening IFRS statement of financial position and IFRS comparatives. [*IFRS 1.17, BC84*]

6.1.190   *Estimates made under previous GAAP*

6.1.190.10   Estimates made by an entity in preparing its first IFRS financial statements at the date of transition and in the comparative reporting period(s) are consistent with estimates made under previous GAAP. Therefore, estimates are not updated for information received at a later date. If changes in estimates are appropriate, then they are accounted for prospectively. [*IFRS 1.14–17*]

6.1.190.20   The following are the only exceptions to this requirement.
- The estimate and related information under previous GAAP are no longer relevant because the entity elects a different accounting policy on the adoption of IFRS.
- There is objective evidence that the estimate under previous GAAP was in error. A prior-period error is an omission or misstatement arising from the failure to use, or the misuse of, reliable information that was available when financial statements for those periods were authorised for issue and could reasonably be expected to have been obtained and taken into account. [*IFRS 1.14, IAS 8.5*]

EXAMPLE 14 – ESTIMATE FOR PROVISION UNDER PREVIOUS GAAP

6.1.190.30   Company Y is a first-time adopter in 2018. On 31 December 2016, Y recognised a provision of 100 under previous GAAP in connection with a legal claim. The provision was calculated in the same way as under IFRS except that it was not discounted to its present value (see 3.12.120). The estimate of the provision under previous GAAP is not changed under IFRS except that the amount is discounted to its present value. In determining an appropriate discount rate, Y uses a discount rate that reflects market conditions at the date of transition (i.e. 1 January 2017) even if market conditions changed after that date. [*IFRS 1.16*]

6.1.200 *Estimates not made under previous GAAP*

6.1.200.10   If a first-time adopter needs to make an estimate under IFRS that was not required under previous GAAP, then the estimate reflects conditions that existed at the relevant year end – i.e. the date of transition, the end of the comparative period(s) and/or the latest year end. These estimates cannot reflect conditions that arose after the relevant year end, including changes in market prices, interest rates or foreign exchange rates. [*IFRS 1.16*]

6.1.210 Consider mandatory exceptions and optional exemptions

6.1.210.10   IFRS 1 includes numerous mandatory exceptions (see 6.1.230) and optional exemptions (see 6.1.240) from the requirements of the standards and interpretations that apply to existing users of IFRS. In general, their purpose is to ensure that the cost incurred by an entity in preparing its first IFRS financial statements does not exceed the benefits thereof. These exceptions and exemptions cannot be applied by analogy to any other items. [*IFRS 1.12, 18, B–E*]

6.1.220 Recognise adjustments from previous GAAP to IFRS

6.1.220.10   In preparing its opening IFRS statement of financial position, a first-time adopter will typically generate a series of adjustments. In certain cases, these adjustments are recognised in goodwill. Otherwise, they are generally recognised in the appropriate component of equity in the opening IFRS statement of financial position, which will often be opening retained earnings. [*IFRS 1.11, C4(g)*]

EXAMPLE 15 – ADJUSTMENTS FOR INVESTMENT PROPERTY CARRIED AT COST UNDER PREVIOUS GAAP

6.1.220.20   Company X measured an investment property at cost under previous GAAP and the carrying amount at the date of transition is 90. Under IFRS, X elects to measure it using the fair value model (see 6.1.460.50) rather than the cost model. As such, it is measured at fair value at the date of transition.

6.1.220.30   The fair value of the investment property, determined in accordance with IFRS 13, at the date of transition is 110. Therefore, investment property is recognised at 110 at the date of transition; the resulting adjustment of 20 on transition is recognised in opening retained earnings. [*IFRS 1.11, IG61*]

6.1.230 MANDATORY EXCEPTIONS

6.1.230.10   Retrospective application of some aspects of IFRS is prohibited. Unlike the optional exemptions (see 6.1.240), first-time adopters are required to use these exceptions from the general requirement for retrospective application. [*IFRS 1.13*]

6.1.230.20   The following table summarises the mandatory exceptions that are required to be applied by a first-time adopter. [*IFRS 1.14–17, B, D17, E6*]

MANDATORY EXCEPTION	EXCEPTION APPLIES TO	REFERENCE
Estimates	All estimates in the opening statement of financial position and IFRS comparative period.	6.1.180
Classification and measurement of financial instruments	Classification of financial assets and retrospective application of the effective interest method.	6.1.570–580
Derecognition of financial instruments	Financial assets and financial liabilities derecognised or not derecognised under previous GAAP before the date of transition.	6.1.640
Embedded derivatives	All hybrid contracts whose host is not a financial asset in the scope of IFRS 9.	6.1.650
Government loans	Existing below-market interest rate government loans at the date of transition.	6.1.680
Impairment of financial instruments	All financial instruments subject to impairment requirements of IFRS 9.	6.1.690
Hedge accounting	Hedging relationships accounted for as hedges under previous GAAP that still exist at the date of transition.	6.1.700
Non-controlling interests (NCI)	All subsidiaries.	6.1.1120
Assets and liabilities of subsidiaries, associates and joint ventures	Parent/investor that adopts IFRS *after* a subsidiary, associate or joint venture.	6.1.1240
Assets and liabilities of a parent	The separate and consolidated financial statements of all parent entities.	6.1.1230
Investment entities	The financial statements of a qualifying investment entity (see chapter 5.6).	6.1.1500

6.1.230.30   The last three mandatory exceptions noted in the table in 6.1.230.20 are discussed not in Appendix B, but rather in Appendix D or E of IFRS 1. However, these three exceptions are mandatory; if a first-time adopter meets the relevant criteria to which these exceptions apply, then it applies the exceptions.

6.1.240   OPTIONAL EXEMPTIONS#

6.1.240.10   Entities may elect to use one or more of the voluntary exemptions from the general requirement for retrospective application of IFRS. Some of these need to be applied to classes of items or transactions; others may be elected on an item-by-item basis.

6.1.240.20   These elections may not be applied to other items by analogy. [*IFRS 1.18*]

6.1.240.30   The following table summarises the optional exemptions available to a first-time adopter. [*IFRS 1.C–D*]

OPTIONAL EXEMPTION	EXEMPTION APPLIES TO	REFERENCE
Business combinations	All business combinations that occurred before the date of transition, or before an earlier date if so elected. Also applies to acquisitions of associates and interests in joint ventures.	6.1.950
Share-based payment transactions	Equity instruments granted on or before 7 November 2002, equity instruments granted after 7 November 2002 that vested before the date of transition, and liabilities for cash-settled awards that were settled before the date of transition.	6.1.850
Insurance contracts	Insurance contracts and financial instruments with a discretionary participation feature, and claims development information.	6.1.1460
Fair value or revaluation as deemed cost	Items of property, plant and equipment, certain intangible assets, and investment property measured under the cost model.	6.1.290, 390, 460
	Some or all assets and liabilities following a remeasurement event.	6.1.270
Deemed cost for oil and gas assets	Oil and gas properties accounted for in cost centres that include all properties in a large geographic area (often referred to as 'full cost accounting').	6.1.1470
Deemed cost for rate-regulated operations	Items of property, plant and equipment or intangible assets used in certain rate-regulated activities.	6.1.320, 400
Arrangements containing a lease	All arrangements outstanding at the date of transition.	6.1.1380, 1390
Cumulative translation differences	All cumulative translation differences existing at the date of transition.	6.1.1170
Investments in subsidiaries, associates and joint ventures	Separate financial statements of a parent/investor.	6.1.1490
Assets and liabilities of subsidiaries, associates and joint ventures	Subsidiary, associate or joint venture that adopts IFRS *after* the parent/investor.	6.1.1290
Restating comparatives for IFRS 9	Comparative information of an entity whose first IFRS reporting period begins before 1 January 2019.	6.1.565, 1530

OPTIONAL EXEMPTION	EXEMPTION APPLIES TO	REFERENCE
Compound financial instruments	All compound financial instruments in respect of which the liability component has been settled before the date of transition.	6.1.670
Designation of previously recognised financial instruments	All financial instruments that meet certain conditions.	6.1.570.20, 610
Designation of contracts to buy or sell a non-financial item	Contracts to buy or sell a non-financial item that meets the own-use exemption.	6.1.620
Fair value measurement of financial assets and financial liabilities on initial recognition	Certain financial assets or financial liabilities arising from transactions entered into on or after the date of transition.	6.1.630
Extinguishing financial liabilities with equity instruments	Renegotiation of the terms of a financial liability in which a debtor issues equity instruments to a creditor to extinguish all or part of the financial liability.	6.1.660
Decommissioning liabilities	All decommissioning liabilities that will be included in the carrying amount of property, plant and equipment.	6.1.800
Decommissioning liabilities related to oil and gas assets	Decommissioning liabilities related to oil and gas assets in the development or production phases for which the deemed cost exemption is used.	6.1.1470
Service concession arrangements	All service concession arrangements outstanding at the date of transition.	6.1.1430
Borrowing costs	Borrowing costs incurred on qualifying assets.	6.1.500
Moving from severe hyperinflation	All assets and liabilities held before the functional currency normalisation date, which is on or before the date of transition.	6.1.1190
Joint arrangements	All joint arrangements.	6.1.1210.60
Stripping costs in the production phase of a surface mine	Stripping costs in the scope of IFRIC 20.	6.1.1470.60
Revenue	Contracts with customers in the scope of IFRS 15.	6.1.1360
Foreign currency transactions and advance consideration	Assets, expenses and income in the scope of IFRIC 22.	6.1.1200

6.1.245   FORTHCOMING REQUIREMENTS

6.1.245.10   IFRS 16 introduces consequential amendments to IFRS 1, which include an option for a first-time adopter to apply the new lease definition to contracts existing at the date of transition based on facts and circumstances at that date (see 5.1A.630). [*IFRS 1.D9*]

6.1.245.20   If a first-time adopter is a lessee that recognises at the date of transition lease liabilities and right-of-use assets, then it is permitted to choose the following approaches to apply to all of its leases at the date of transition:
- measure the lease liability at the present value of the remaining lease payments, discounted using the lessee's incremental borrowing rate at the date of transition;
- measure a right-of-use asset, on a lease-by-lease basis, at either:
  - its carrying amount as if IFRS 16 had been applied since the commencement date of the lease, but discounted using the lessee's incremental borrowing rate at the date of transition to IFRS; or
  - an amount equal to the lease liability, adjusted by the amount of any prepaid or accrued lease payments relating to that lease recognised in the statement of financial position immediately before the date of transition to IFRS; or
- apply IAS 36 to the right-of-use asset at the date of transition to IFRS. [*IFRS 1.D9B*]

6.1.245.30   A first-time adopter that is a lessee measures the right-of-use asset at fair value at the date of transition to IFRS for leases that meet the definition of investment property in IAS 40 and are measured using the fair value model in IAS 40 from the date of transition (see 3.4.40, 150 and 5.1A.360). [*IFRS 1.D9C*]

6.1.245.40   A first-time adopter that is a lessee is permitted to apply the following optional exemptions at the date of transition on a lease-by-lease basis:
- apply a single discount rate to a portfolio of leases with reasonably similar characteristics;
- elect not to apply the measurement requirements in 6.1.245.20 to leases for which the lease term ends within 12 months of the date of transition or to leases for which the underlying asset is of low value. Instead, the first-time adopter recognises the lease payments associated with those leases as an expense on either a straight-line basis over the lease term or another systematic basis (see 5.1A.140);
- exclude initial direct costs from the measurement of the right-of-use asset; and
- use hindsight – e.g. in determining the lease term if the contract contains options to extend or terminate the lease.

6.1.250   Combining exceptions and exemptions

6.1.250.10   More than one exemption may be applied to a particular asset or liability. For example, a first-time adopter that elects not to restate a past business combination (see 6.1.950) may also choose to apply the fair value or revaluation as deemed cost exemption (see 6.1.290) to an item of property, plant and equipment acquired in an unrestated business combination (see 6.1.370.10). Under the business combination exemption, the previous initial measurement at acquisition of the assets and liabilities acquired in the business combination becomes their deemed cost under IFRS at the date of acquisition (see 6.1.1010.10). However, the additional application of the deemed cost exemption, at a date later than when the asset was acquired in the unrestated business combination, means that the valuation at that later date is adopted as the asset's deemed cost in the opening IFRS statement of financial position.

6.1.250.20   Certain exemptions may not be combined. For example, IFRS 1 requires assets and liabilities of subsidiaries that have adopted IFRS before a parent to be measured in the consolidated financial statements at the same carrying amounts as in the subsidiary's financial statements after adjusting for consolidation and the effects of the business combination (see 6.1.1270). In our view, this requirement generally prevents the use of another exemption that would alter these carrying amounts – e.g. the deemed cost exemption.

6.1.260   APPLICATION ISSUES

6.1.270   Event-driven fair value

6.1.270.10   The 'event-driven fair value' optional exemption in IFRS 1 is unlike other optional exemptions in that it may be applied selectively to some or all assets and liabilities of a first-time adopter if specific criteria are met – i.e. the exemption is not limited to a particular asset or liability. For example, unlike the fair value or revaluation as deemed cost optional exemption that applies only to property, plant and equipment (see 6.1.290), certain intangible assets (see 6.1.390) and investment property (see 6.1.460), in our view the event-driven fair value optional exemption may be applied to some or all of the assets and liabilities to which the event-driven fair values relate.

6.1.270.20   A first-time adopter may have established a deemed cost in accordance with previous GAAP for some or all of its assets and liabilities by measuring them at their fair value at one particular date because of an event such as a privatisation or initial public offering. If the measurement date is *at or before* the date of transition, then the first-time adopter may use such event-driven fair value measurements as deemed cost for IFRS at the date of that measurement. [*IFRS 1.D8(a)*]

6.1.270.30   If the measurement date is *after* the date of transition, but during the period covered by the first IFRS financial statements, then the event-driven fair value measurements may be used as deemed cost when the event occurs. The resulting adjustments are recognised directly in retained earnings (or, if appropriate, in another category of equity) at the measurement date. At the date of transition, the first-time adopter either establishes the deemed cost using paragraphs D5–D7 or measures assets and liabilities in accordance with the other requirements in IFRS 1 – i.e. a first-time adopter is not permitted to 'roll back' the fair value at the measurement date to the date of transition. [*IFRS 1.D8(b)*]

6.1.270.40   In our view, the reference in the exemption to fair value should be interpreted in accordance with the definition in IFRS 1 (see 6.1.20.50) – i.e. the price that would be received to sell an asset or paid to transfer a liability in an orderly transaction between market participants at the measurement date. Therefore, we believe that only remeasurements that could be referred to as fair value under IFRS qualify for the exemption. This is stricter than the 'previous GAAP revaluation as deemed cost' exemption that applies to property, plant and equipment (see 6.1.310.10), certain intangible assets (see 6.1.390.20) and investment property (see 6.1.460.30) because that exemption explicitly provides more flexibility in determining fair value. [*IFRS 1.D8*]

6.1.270.50   In our view, the reference in the exemption to "established a deemed cost in accordance with previous GAAP" and "by measuring them at their fair value" means that the fair values should have been recognised in the first-time adopter's previous GAAP financial statements. Therefore, for example, fair value information disclosed in the notes to the financial statements would not be sufficient to qualify for the exemption. [*IFRS 1.D8*]

6.1.270.60   Although the wording of the exemption implies that the remeasurement event is infrequent or non-routine, in our view privatisations and initial public offerings are just two examples of the events that qualify for the exemption.

(S) 6.1.270.70   We believe that other acceptable remeasurement events include, but are not limited to, fair values recognised by an entity emerging from bankruptcy and fair values recognised in applying acquisition accounting that were pushed down into the financial statements of the first-time adopter (acquiree). However, in the latter example we believe that the exemption would not apply if the acquisition accounting recognised by the parent had not been pushed down into the first-time adopter's (acquiree's) financial statements. This is because the fair values were not recorded in the first-time adopter's financial statements. Notwithstanding the fact that the fair values were pushed down into the financial statements of the first-time adopter (acquiree), the first-time adopter would not be permitted to recognise assets or liabilities that in themselves would not qualify for recognition in accordance with IFRS in the separate financial statements of the first-time adopter. Examples of such assets include goodwill, intangible assets and contingent liabilities recognised using business combination accounting principles.

EXAMPLE 16 – INTERNALLY GENERATED GOODWILL RECOGNISED UNDER PREVIOUS GAAP

6.1.270.80   Company P is a first-time adopter in 2018. P was privatised in 2015 and at the date of privatisation the carrying amounts of P's assets and liabilities were established with reference to their fair values. This exercise included the recognition of internally generated goodwill attributable to the business that was privatised as P.

6.1.270.90   At its date of transition of 1 January 2017, P wishes to continue to recognise the internally generated goodwill and to establish the carrying amount of property, plant and equipment using the fair value established in the privatisation, adjusted for depreciation between the date of privatisation and the date of transition. Therefore, the gross carrying amount of the property, plant and equipment in P's opening IFRS statement of financial position will be its fair value at the date of privatisation, with the subsequent depreciation representing the balance of accumulated depreciation at the date of transition. Depreciation recognised under previous GAAP was consistent with that required under IFRS.

6.1.270.100   However, we believe that P should not recognise the goodwill recognised in the privatisation in its opening IFRS statement of financial position because internally generated goodwill does not qualify for recognition under IFRS.

6.1.280   **Property, plant and equipment**

6.1.290   *Optional exemption to use fair value or revaluation as deemed cost*

6.1.290.10   The 'fair value or revaluation as deemed cost' optional exemption (also referred to as the 'deemed cost exemption') permits the carrying amount of an item of property, plant and equipment to be measured at the date of transition based on a deemed cost. If it is elected, then the deemed cost exemption may be based on any of the following. [*IFRS 1.D5–D6, D8, D24*]

Measurement basis	At what date?
Fair value (see 6.1.300)	Date of transition or any date before the date of transition
A previous GAAP revaluation that was broadly comparable to fair value under IFRS (see 6.1.310)	Date of revaluation, which is on or before the date of transition
A previous GAAP revaluation that was broadly comparable to cost or depreciated cost under IFRS, adjusted to reflect, for example, changes in a general or specific price index (see 6.1.310)	Date of revaluation, which is on or before the date of transition
An event-driven valuation – e.g. when an entity was privatised and at that point valued and recognised some or all of its assets and liabilities at fair value (see 6.1.270)	Date of valuation, which is on or before the date of transition

6.1.290.20   When the deemed cost exemption is used to establish the cost of an item of property, plant and equipment, it becomes the new IFRS cost basis at that date. Any accumulated depreciation recognised under previous GAAP before that date is set to zero. [*IFRS 1.IG9*]

6.1.290.30   If deemed cost is measured at a revalued or other fair value-based amount under previous GAAP before the date of transition, then the measurement of that asset between that date and the date of transition complies with IFRS. [*IFRS 1.IG9*]

6.1.290.40   A first-time adopter does not have to apply the deemed cost exemption to all classes of property, plant and equipment or to all items within a class of property, plant and equipment; instead, the exemption may be applied to individual items. [*IFRS 1.D5–D6, D8*]

6.1.290.50   The election of the deemed cost exemption is independent of the first-time adopter's accounting policy choice for the subsequent measurement of property, plant and equipment – i.e. a first-time adopter that elects to apply the deemed cost exemption is not required to apply the revaluation model subsequently.

6.1.300   *Fair value as deemed cost at date of transition*

6.1.300.10   Fair value is measured in accordance with IFRS 13, which is the subject of chapter 2.4. That chapter includes general guidance on applying the principles of IFRS 13 in measuring fair value; specific points of interest in relation to property, plant and equipment, in particular the use of depreciated replacement cost to measure fair value, are discussed in 2.4.560.

6.1.310   *Previous GAAP revaluation as deemed cost*

6.1.310.10   A first-time adopter may use a previous GAAP revaluation as the deemed cost of an item of property, plant and equipment if the revaluation under previous GAAP was broadly comparable to:
- fair value; or
- cost or depreciated cost under IFRS adjusted, for example, for changes in a general or specific price index. [*IFRS 1.D6*]

6.1.310.20   In our view, the reference in IFRS 1 to a previous GAAP revaluation means that the exemption is available only if the previous GAAP revaluation was reflected in the first-time adopter's previous GAAP financial statements. Further, in our view the deemed cost should be based on the most recent revaluation under previous GAAP on or before the date of transition.

6.1.310.30   By using the phrase 'broadly comparable', IFRS 1 allows some flexibility in allowing a deemed cost that is not identical to the amount that would have been determined if IFRS had been applied, or if an index had been applied to a fully IFRS-compliant cost. However, no further guidance is provided and the degree of acceptable flexibility is assessed based on a first-time adopter's specific facts and circumstances.

6.1.320   *Deemed cost for rate-regulated operations*

6.1.320.10   IFRS 1 includes an optional exemption that permits a first-time adopter to use the carrying amounts determined under previous GAAP as deemed cost for items of property, plant and equipment used in certain rate-regulated operations as defined in IFRS 1, even though these carrying amounts may include amounts that do not qualify for capitalisation under IFRS. This exemption may be applied on an item-by-item basis provided that each item to which it is applied is tested for impairment in accordance with IAS 36 at the date of transition. [*IFRS 1.31B, D8B*]

6.1.320.20   If a first-time adopter is eligible to apply IFRS 14 (see 6.2.10), then it is permitted to continue accounting for regulatory deferral account balances in accordance with its previous accounting policies. IFRS 14 is the subject of chapter 6.2, and 6.2.150 discusses application of the deemed cost exemption. [*IFRS 1.D8B*]

6.1.330   *Depreciation*

6.1.330.10   The requirements of IFRS in respect of depreciation are relevant to each item of property, plant and equipment as follows:
- from the date of acquisition if the first-time adopter does not elect the deemed cost exemption;
- from the date of transition if the first-time adopter elects the deemed cost exemption and deemed cost is determined at the date of transition; or
- from the date of the revaluation or other determination of fair value if the first-time adopter elects the deemed cost exemption and deemed cost is determined before the date of transition.

6.1.330.20   Estimates of depreciation made under previous GAAP may not be revised at the date of transition or in the first IFRS financial statements unless it is determined that they were made in error. On transition to IFRS, if errors are discovered with respect to depreciation recognised under previous GAAP, then those errors are corrected in the opening IFRS statement of financial position and disclosed separately in the reconciliations required from previous GAAP to IFRS (see 6.1.1520.70). [*IFRS 1.IG7*]

6.1.330.30   Depreciation is an accounting estimate and therefore changes in the depreciation method or changes in the estimate of useful lives are normally dealt with prospectively. However, if a first-time adopter previously depreciated an item of equipment based, for example, on tax allowances and without reference to the useful life of the asset or to its residual value as required by IFRS, then an adjustment to measure depreciation based on the useful life of the asset or its residual value is recognised as an adjustment to opening retained earnings. [*IFRS 1.IG7*]

6.1.330.40   In our view, when depreciation recognised in accordance with previous GAAP is not consistent with a method of depreciation permitted under IFRS, disclosure of the adjustment to cumulative depreciation does not result in disclosure of an error. This is because the depreciation recognised was in accordance with previous GAAP. [*IFRS 1.24(a)–(b), 26*]

6.1.340   *Component accounting*

6.1.340.10   There are no exemptions available from identifying components of property, plant and equipment that are required to be depreciated separately under IFRS. The identification and separate recognition of the depreciation of components are required in the opening IFRS statement of financial position. For example, IFRS requires major inspections and overhauls to be identified and depreciated as a separate component of the asset (see 3.2.250). Component depreciation affects the subsequent accounting for both cost and depreciation. Accordingly, both cost and accumulated depreciation are allocated to identified components separately. [*IFRS 1.IG12*]

6.1.340.20   When the original cost of a major inspection or overhaul is not available, the expected cost of the next overhaul may be used as the best estimate of the cost of the component. In our view, a similar approach is acceptable for measuring major inspection and overhaul costs in the opening IFRS statement of financial position. [*IAS 16.14*]

6.1.350   *Revaluation surplus under previous GAAP*

6.1.350.10   The treatment of any revaluation surplus under previous GAAP depends on whether the first-time adopter will apply the cost or revaluation model under IFRS after the date of transition. [*IAS 16.29*]

6.1.350.20   If a revaluation model was used under previous GAAP but the cost model will be used under IFRS, then any existing revaluation surplus at the date of transition is reclassified as a separate component of equity (not described as a revaluation reserve) or transferred to retained earnings. [*IFRS 1.11*]

6.1.350.30   If a first-time adopter elects to use the revaluation model under IFRS, then the revaluation surplus at the date of transition is measured as the difference between the carrying amount of the asset at that date and its cost or deemed cost. [*IFRS 1.IG10*]

EXAMPLE 17 – PROPERTY REVALUED UNDER PREVIOUS GAAP

6.1.350.40   Company B has an owner-occupied property with a cost of 60 under previous GAAP and of 55 under IFRS. Before the date of transition, the property was revalued to a fair value of 85 and a revaluation reserve of 25 was recognised under previous GAAP. Its fair value is 100 at the date of transition. Depreciation is ignored for the purposes of this example. B elects as its accounting policy under IFRS to measure the class of asset that includes this property on a fair value basis (see 3.2.300). Therefore, the carrying amount of the property at the date of transition will be 100.

6.1.350.50   Depending on the exemptions chosen by B, the IFRS revaluation reserve at the date of transition will be as follows.
- If the deemed cost exemption is not elected, then the IFRS revaluation reserve will be 45 (100 - 55), based on the IFRS cost of the asset.
- If the deemed cost exemption is applied on the basis of the fair value at the date of transition, then the IFRS revaluation reserve will be zero (100 - 100).
- If the deemed cost exemption is applied on the basis of the earlier revaluation, then the IFRS revaluation reserve at the date of transition will be 15 (100 - 85), based on that earlier revaluation as deemed cost.

6.1.360   *Deemed cost for property, plant and equipment held under finance lease#*

6.1.360.10   A first-time adopter applies the leasing requirements of IFRS to classify any leases in effect at its date of transition as operating or finance leases (see chapter 5.1 and 6.1.1400). Assets held under finance leases are accounted for as own assets – e.g. as property, plant and equipment – subject to the additional leasing requirements regarding initial recognition, measurement of cost and depreciation.

6.1.360.20   In our view, the deemed cost exemption for property, plant and equipment may also be applied to an asset acquired under a finance lease.

6.1.365   FORTHCOMING REQUIREMENTS

6.1.365.10   IFRS 16 introduces changes to the accounting by lessees and substantially carries forward the existing requirements for lessors in IAS 17. For lessees, IFRS 16 introduces a single, on-balance sheet lease accounting model and eliminates the distinction between operating and finance leases (see chapter 5.1A).

6.1.365.20   As a result, an optional exemption for first-time adopters that are lessees regarding the recognition and measurement of right-of-use assets has been added to IFRS 1 (see 6.1.245).

6.1.370   *Deemed cost for property, plant and equipment acquired in business combination*

6.1.370.10   In our view, the deemed cost exemption may be chosen by a first-time adopter that acquired an item of property, plant and equipment in a business combination that is not restated on transition to IFRS.

6.1.380   **Intangible assets and goodwill**

6.1.390   *Optional exemption to use fair value or revaluation as deemed cost*

6.1.390.10   The 'fair value or revaluation as deemed cost' optional exemption (also referred to as the 'deemed cost exemption') permits the carrying amount of an intangible asset to be measured at the date of transition based on a deemed cost. However, the exemption – which applies on an asset-by-asset basis – is available only when the following criteria are met:

● the asset qualifies for recognition under IAS 38; and
● the asset meets the criteria in IAS 38 for revaluation, including the existence of an active market (see 3.3.280). [*IFRS 1.D7(b)*]

6.1.390.20   To the extent that an active market exists and the deemed cost exemption is available for an intangible asset, the exemption applies in the same way as it does to property, plant and equipment. This means that deemed cost may be either fair value at the date of transition or a previous GAAP revaluation that meets certain criteria, with deemed cost determined at the date of the previous GAAP revaluation (see 6.1.290.10). [*IFRS 1.IG50*]

6.1.390.30   Fair value is measured in accordance with IFRS 13, which is the subject of chapter 2.4.

6.1.400   *Deemed cost for rate-regulated operations*

6.1.400.10   IFRS 1 includes an optional exemption that permits a first-time adopter to use the carrying amounts determined under previous GAAP as deemed cost for items of intangible assets used in certain rate-regulated operations, even though these carrying amounts may include amounts that do not qualify for capitalisation under IFRS. This exemption may be applied on an item-by-item basis provided that each item to which it is applied is tested for impairment in accordance with IAS 36 at the date of transition. [*IFRS 1.31B, D8B*]

6.1.400.20   If a first-time adopter is eligible to apply IFRS 14 (see 6.2.10), then it is permitted to continue accounting for regulatory deferral account balances in accordance with its previous accounting policies. IFRS 14 is the subject of chapter 6.2, and 6.2.150 discusses application of the deemed cost exemption. [*IFRS 1.D8B*]

6.1.410   *Internally generated intangible assets*

6.1.410.10   A first-time adopter recognises in its opening IFRS statement of financial position all internally generated intangible assets that qualify for recognition under IAS 38; similarly, it derecognises internally generated intangible assets that do not qualify for recognition. [*IFRS 1.IG44, IG47*]

6.1.410.20   In accordance with IAS 38, expenditure is capitalised only from the date on which the recognition criteria in the standard are met – i.e. prospectively. These criteria cannot be assessed using the benefit of hindsight. Therefore, to capitalise costs at the date of transition that were expensed under previous GAAP, it is required that the criteria for capitalisation were met at the time that the costs were incurred and that a system that measured such costs reliably was in place. [*IFRS 1.IG46–IG47, IAS 38.65, 71*]

6.1.410.30   In our view, the prohibition on the use of hindsight interacting with the requirements for the first-time adoption of IFRS should be interpreted as requiring either:

- contemporaneous evidence that all of the recognition requirements of IFRS were considered at the time that the expenditure was incurred. Expenditure should be capitalised only from the date on which it can be demonstrated that this information was available; or
- the existence of a process or control system to ensure that no expenditure of this nature is incurred without all recognition requirements having been considered. This might be the case, for example, if the first-time adopter had a well-managed product development programme that considered all of the recognition criteria and there is no reason to believe that the normal process or control system was not followed.

6.1.410.40   First-time adopters with extensive development programmes may have control procedures in place to assess the probability of future economic benefits periodically. In our view, if a first-time adopter has such a monitoring system, and if the costs incurred were measured reliably, then this information is likely to satisfy the requirements of IFRS for contemporaneous assessment of the probability of future economic benefits.

6.1.420   *Intangible assets acquired separately*

6.1.420.10   The considerations in 6.1.410 in respect of the recognition of an internally generated intangible asset apply equally to an intangible asset acquired separately – i.e. outside a business combination. However, in that case the criteria are generally easier to satisfy because a transaction involving a party separate from the first-time adopter occurred. [*IFRS 1.IG48*]

6.1.430   *Intangible assets acquired in business combination*

6.1.430.10   The requirements of IFRS 1 in respect of intangible assets acquired in a business combination are discussed in 6.1.1020.10.

6.1.440   *Amortisation*

6.1.440.10   The general requirements related to the amortisation of intangible assets are discussed in 3.3.200–210 and are relevant to a first-time adopter in relation to each intangible asset as follows:
- from the date of acquisition if the first-time adopter does not elect the deemed cost exemption;
- from the date of transition if the first-time adopter elects the deemed cost exemption and deemed cost is determined at that date; or
- from the date of the revaluation or other determination of fair value if the first-time adopter elects the deemed cost exemption and deemed cost is determined before the date of transition.

6.1.440.20   Estimates of amortisation made under previous GAAP may not be revised at the date of transition or in the first IFRS financial statements unless it is determined that they were made in error. On transition to IFRS, if errors are discovered with respect to amortisation recognised under previous GAAP, then those errors are corrected in the opening IFRS statement of financial position and disclosed separately in the reconciliations required from previous GAAP to IFRS (see 6.1.1520.70). [*IFRS 1.IG51*]

6.1.440.30   Amortisation is an accounting estimate and therefore changes in the amortisation method or changes in the estimate of useful lives are normally dealt with prospectively. However, if a first-time adopter previously amortised an intangible asset based, for example, on tax allowances, without reference to the useful life of the asset, then an adjustment to measure amortisation based on the useful life of the asset is recognised as an adjustment to opening retained earnings. [*IFRS 1.IG51*]

6.1.440.40   In our view, when amortisation recognised in accordance with previous GAAP is not consistent with a method of amortisation permitted under IFRS, disclosure of the adjustment to cumulative amortisation does not result in disclosure of an error; this is because the amortisation recognised was in accordance with previous GAAP. [*IFRS 1.24(a)–(b), 26*]

6.1.450   **Investment property**

6.1.460   *Optional exemption to use fair value or revaluation as deemed cost*

6.1.460.10   The 'fair value or revaluation as deemed cost' optional exemption (also referred to as the 'deemed cost exemption') permits the carrying amount of investment property to be measured at the date of transition based on a deemed cost. However, the fair value or revaluation as a deemed cost exemption for investment property is relevant only when a first-time adopter elects to use the cost model. [*IFRS 1.D7*]

6.1.460.20   The deemed cost exemption can be elected to be applied to individual investment properties on an item-by-item basis.

6.1.460.30   The deemed cost exemption applies in the same way as it does to property, plant and equipment. This means that deemed cost may be either fair value at the date of transition or a previous GAAP revaluation that meets certain criteria, with deemed cost determined at the date of the previous GAAP revaluation (see 6.1.290.10). [*IFRS 1.IG62*]

6.1.460.40   Fair value is measured in accordance with IFRS 13, which is the subject of chapter 2.4. That chapter includes general guidance on applying the principles of IFRS 13 in measuring fair value; specific points of interest in relation to investment property are discussed in 2.4.610.

6.1.460.50   If a first-time adopter elects to measure investment property using the fair value model, then all investment property at the date of transition is measured at fair value in accordance with IFRS 13 and the deemed cost exemption does not apply. This is because the first-time adopter's chosen accounting policy of fair value requires investment property to be measured at fair value, determined in accordance with IFRS 13, at the date of transition. [*IFRS 1.IG61*]

6.1.470   *Depreciation*

6.1.470.10   If the cost model is applied after initial recognition, then investment property is accounted for in accordance with the cost model for property, plant and equipment. In such cases, the relevant requirements of IFRS 1 on transition to IFRS in respect of depreciation of property, plant and equipment as discussed in 6.1.330 are also relevant to the depreciation of investment property.

6.1.470.20   If the fair value model is applied after initial recognition, then fair value changes at each reporting date are recognised in profit or loss and the investment property is not separately depreciated (see 3.4.150).

6.1.480   ***Deemed cost for investment property acquired in business combination***

6.1.480.10   In our view, the deemed cost exemption may be chosen by a first-time adopter that acquired an investment property in a business combination that is not restated on transition to IFRS.

6.1.490   **Borrowing costs**

6.1.500   ***Optional exemption for borrowing costs***

6.1.500.10   A first-time adopter is permitted to apply the requirements of IAS 23 from the date of transition or from an earlier date. If a first-time adopter applies the optional exemption for borrowing costs, then:

● it accounts for borrowing costs incurred on or after the chosen date of transition in accordance with IAS 23, including those incurred on qualifying assets already under construction; and

● it does not restate the borrowing costs capitalised under previous GAAP before the date of initial application of IAS 23. [*IFRS 1.D23, IAS 23.28*]

6.1.500.20   A first-time adopter that elects to apply the optional exemption in respect of borrowing costs is required to do so on a consistent basis across all relevant qualifying assets – the exemption cannot be applied on an asset-by-asset basis. If a first-time adopter does not elect to apply the optional exemption, then full retrospective application of IAS 23 is required. [*IFRS 1.7*]

6.1.510   ***Interaction with other requirements and exemptions***

6.1.510.10   The optional exemption in respect of borrowing costs is not relevant for a particular qualifying asset when the carrying amount of that asset is determined with reference to a deemed cost at the date of transition. This may be the case, for example, when the carrying amount of property, plant and equipment is determined with reference to fair value (see 6.1.300), or the carrying amount of an intangible asset is determined under the optional exemption for service concession arrangements (with reference to the carrying amount of property, plant and equipment under previous GAAP) (see 6.1.1430). In such circumstances, the carrying amount is reset for the purpose of accounting after the date of transition. [*IFRS 1.D23, IG23*]

EXAMPLE 18 – DEEMED COST EXEMPTION FOR CONSTRUCTION PROJECTS

6.1.510.20   Company B is a first-time adopter in 2018. B commenced a significant construction project in 2016 that represents a qualifying asset. B elects to apply IAS 23 as of 1 January 2016 (see 6.1.500.10) and capitalises 40 of IAS 23-compliant borrowing costs in the period from 1 January 2016 to 31 December 2016. At the date of transition (1 January 2017) B elects to use the fair value as the deemed cost optional exemption (see 6.1.300) and determines the fair value of the construction project to be 2,000.

6.1.510.30   Following the above election, B recognises the construction project at 2,000 at the date of transition and capitalises borrowing costs on the construction project thereafter in accordance with IAS 23. Therefore, B should not adjust the fair value of 2,000 at the date of transition to incorporate the borrowing costs of 40 capitalised during the period before the date of transition.

6.1.520 **Impairment of non-financial assets**

6.1.530 *Impairment testing at date of transition*

6.1.530.10   At the date of transition, a first-time adopter performs impairment tests in accordance with IAS 36 as follows.

- Goodwill that was acquired in an unrestated business combination (see 6.1.1020.10) is tested for impairment regardless of whether there is an indication of impairment. Although there is no specific requirement in IFRS 1, we prefer that goodwill acquired in a restated business combination also be tested for impairment at the date of transition (see 6.1.1070).
- In our view, goodwill that arose from the acquisition of an equity-accounted investee that is not restated – i.e. for which the business combinations exemption is applied (see 6.1.1210.40) – should be tested for impairment regardless of whether there is an indication of impairment. This is because the optional exemption for such investments requires application of all elements of the optional exemption for past business combinations – i.e. including the mandatory impairment test for goodwill that is not restated at the date of transition. However, for equity-accounted investees, the impairment testing is performed on the carrying amount of the investment as a whole (see 3.10.570).
- For other assets, detailed impairment testing is carried out at the date of transition if there is an indication of impairment. [*IFRS 1.C4(g)(ii), C5, IG39*]

6.1.530.20   Any impairment losses and reversals of impairment losses recognised at the date of transition are charged or credited to retained earnings unless another component of equity is appropriate. The latter would be the case, for example, when a revaluation surplus exists in respect of an item of property, plant and equipment, and the revaluation model will continue to be applied after transition (see 6.1.350).

6.1.540 *Reversal of impairment*

6.1.540.10   At the date of transition, a first-time adopter assesses whether there is an indication that a previously recognised impairment loss has reversed. If there is such an indication and the recoverable amount of the impaired asset or cash-generating unit subsequently increases, then the impairment loss is generally reversed (see 3.10.420). If there is no such indication, then the first-time adopter carries forward the previous GAAP carrying amount at the date of transition. It does not seek to recalculate the amount of the previous impairment loss. [*IFRS 1.IG43, IAS 36.110*]

6.1.540.20   However, in our view impairment losses should not be reversed if a first-time adopter elects to measure the related asset based on deemed cost (see 6.1.290, 390 and 460) at a date after the original impairment.

6.1.540.30   In practice, the accounting will often be more complex when previous GAAP differs from IFRS. Therefore, the reversal of any impairment loss requires careful consideration.

6.1.550 *Estimates made under previous GAAP*

6.1.550.10   Impairment testing typically requires the use of significant estimates. As discussed in 6.1.190, previous GAAP estimates made at the date of transition and at the end of the comparative period are not changed (except for the effect of differences between previous GAAP and IFRS), unless there is objective evidence that those estimates were in error. This prohibition on revising estimates applies to cash flow estimates that are the basis for impairment testing under IFRS, except when there is a difference between previous GAAP and IFRS regarding the composition and estimation of those cash flows. [*IFRS 1.IG40*]

6.1.550.20   Complying with IAS 36 may require a first-time adopter to make estimates that were not required under its previous GAAP – e.g. a first-time adopter might be determining value in use for the first time. In such cases, the additional estimates required by IFRS reflect conditions at the date of transition. They do not reflect conditions that arose after the date of transition. [*IFRS 1.IG41*]

6.1.560   Financial instruments

6.1.565   *Exemption from the requirement to restate comparatives for IFRS 9*

6.1.565.10   If a first-time adopter adopts IFRS for an annual period beginning before 1 January 2019 and applies IFRS 9 (2014), then the comparative information in its first IFRS financial statements does not have to comply with IFRS 9 (2014). If this option is taken, then in applying IFRS 9 (and the related IFRS 7 disclosures), the 'date of transition' is the beginning of the first IFRS reporting period (see 6.1.1530). [*IFRS 1.E1–E2*]

6.1.570   *Classification on transition*

6.1.570.10   For existing users of IFRS, financial assets are classified on initial recognition into one of four categories (see 7.4.10.10), and financial liabilities are generally classified on initial recognition into one of two categories (see 7.5.10.10). Subsequent reclassification is limited to specific circumstances (see 7.4.450).

6.1.570.20   The following table summarises the classification requirements that apply to a first-time adopter, which include some relief from the normal classification requirements of IFRS.

CATEGORY	DESCRIPTION
Financial assets at amortised cost	A financial asset is measured at amortised cost only if it meets both of the following conditions: • the asset is held within a business model whose objective is to hold assets to collect contractual cash flows (the held-to-collect business model); and • the contractual terms of the financial asset give rise on specified dates to cash flows that are solely payments of principal and interest on the principal amount outstanding – i.e. meet the SPPI criterion (see 7.4.100 and 150). [*IFRS 9.4.1.2*] A first-time adopter assesses whether these conditions are met based on the facts and circumstances that exist at the date of transition to IFRS. [*IFRS 1.B8*]
Debt financial assets at fair value through OCI	A debt instrument is measured at fair value through OCI only if it meets both of the following conditions: • the asset is held within a business model whose objective is achieved by both collecting contractual cash flows and selling financial assets; and • the contractual terms of the financial asset meet the SPPI criterion (see 7.4.130 and 150). [*IFRS 9.4.1.2A*] A first-time adopter assesses whether these conditions are met based on the facts and circumstances that exist at the date of transition to IFRS. [*IFRS 1.B8*]

CATEGORY	DESCRIPTION
Financial assets at fair value though profit or loss	Financial assets that do not meet the criteria for classification as subsequently measured at either amortised cost or fair value through OCI are classified as subsequently measured at fair value, with changes in fair value recognised in profit or loss (see 7.4.50.10). In addition, a first-time adopter may, on an instrument-by-instrument basis, designate a financial asset at fair value through profit or loss based on facts and circumstances at the date of transition. This designation is available only if it eliminates or significantly reduces a measurement or recognition inconsistency (see 6.1.610). [*IFRS 1.D19A*]
Financial assets – investments in equity instruments at fair value through OCI	On initial recognition, an entity may elect to present in OCI changes in the fair value of an investment in an equity instrument if it is not held for trading and is not contingent consideration for a business combination (see 7.4.410). A first-time adopter may, on an instrument-by-instrument basis, make this election based on the facts and circumstances at the date of transition (see 6.1.610). [*IFRS 9.D19B*]
Financial liabilities at fair value through profit or loss	Financial liabilities at fair value through profit or loss comprise financial liabilities held-for-trading and those designated under a fair value option (see 7.5.10.10). Under the fair value option an entity may, on an instrument-by-instrument basis, designate a financial liability as at fair value through profit or loss on initial recognition. Such classification is permitted only if, at the date of initial recognition: • the instrument is a hybrid instrument that contains an embedded derivative that can significantly modify the cash flows of the hybrid and it is clear with little or no analysis that separation of the embedded derivative is not prohibited; • when doing so results in more relevant information because: – a group of financial liabilities (or financial assets and financial liabilities) is managed on a fair value basis; or – the classification eliminates or significantly reduces a measurement or recognition inconsistency (an accounting mismatch) (see 7.5.40). A first-time adopter is permitted to designate a financial liability at FVTPL at the date of transition if the liability meets these criteria at that date (see 6.1.610). [*IFRS 1.D19, 9.4.2.2, 4.3.5*]
Financial liabilities at amortised cost	Financial liabilities that do not fall into the fair value through profit or loss category are generally measured at amortised cost (see 7.5.10.10).

6.1.580   *Financial assets – SPPI criterion*

6.1.580.10   In addition to the exceptions summarised in 6.1.570.20, IFRS 1 provides the following two exceptions to the general requirements for assessing whether the contractual cash flows of a financial asset meet the SPPI criterion.

- If it is impracticable to assess the modified time value of money element (see 7.4.180) based on the facts and circumstances that exist at the date of transition to IFRS, then the contractual cash flow assessment is made without taking into account the specific requirements for the modification of the time value of money element. In this case, the first-time adopter discloses the carrying amounts of the relevant assets until they are derecognised.
- If it is impracticable to assess whether the fair value of a prepayment feature is insignificant (see 7.4.220) based on the facts and circumstances that exist at the date of transition to IFRS, then the contractual cash flow assessment is made without taking into account the exception for certain prepayment features. In this case, the first-time adopter discloses the carrying amounts of the relevant assets until they are derecognised. [*IFRS 1.B8A–B8B, 7.42R–42S*]

6.1.590 *Financial instruments – Presentation*

6.1.590.10   Instruments issued by a first-time adopter are classified as equity or as liabilities in accordance with the specified criteria in 7.3.10. In determining the appropriate classification, a first-time adopter considers the facts and circumstances when an instrument was issued or at the date of any later change to its terms, and not the facts and circumstances at the date of transition. Other than in respect of compound financial instruments (see 6.1.670), there are no exemptions from this requirement. [*IFRS 1.IG35, IAS 32.15, 30*]

6.1.600 *Effective interest rate*

6.1.600.10   If it is impracticable to apply retrospectively the effective interest method in IFRS 9 to a financial asset or financial liability, then at the date of transition:
- the fair value of the financial asset is the new gross carrying amount of that asset; and
- the fair value of the financial liability is the new amortised cost of that liability. [*IFRS 1.B8C*]

6.1.610 *Designation at fair value*

6.1.610.10   The term 'designate' is used when referring to designating a financial asset, a financial liability or an 'own-use' contract as at fair value through profit or loss, or an investment in an equity instrument as at fair value through OCI. The term is not defined in IFRS, although the financial instruments standards do state that such designation for a financial asset or a financial liability as at fair value through profit or loss is similar to an accounting policy choice, it is not required to be applied consistently to all similar transactions (unlike an accounting policy choice). [*IFRS 9.B4.1.28*]

6.1.610.20   Because elective designations at fair value through profit or loss or fair value through OCI (see 6.1.570.20) are required to be made based on the facts and circumstances at the date of transition, it appears that there is no requirement for an act of designation to be performed at that date. We believe that the physical act of designation at fair value through profit or loss or fair value through OCI as at the date of transition may be made at any time during the course of preparing the financial statements in which IFRS is adopted for the first time (see also 7.11.120).

6.1.610.30   If an entity designates a financial liability as at fair value through profit or loss, then the amount of change in fair value that is attributable to changes in the credit risk of that liability is presented in OCI. However, if an entity determines that recognition in OCI would create or enlarge an accounting mismatch in profit or loss, then the entire fair value change of the liability is presented in profit or loss (see 7.7.180). A first-time adopter makes this determination on the basis of the facts and circumstances that exist at the date of transition to IFRS. [*IFRS 1.D19C, 9.5.7.7*]

6.1.610.40   Notwithstanding the guidance in 6.1.610.20, we believe that a first-time adopter should not use the benefit of hindsight to retrospectively designate only selected financial instruments at fair value through profit or loss or fair value through OCI in order to achieve a particular financial statement result because in that case the designation would not be made based solely on the facts and circumstances that exist at the date of transition and may instead reflect subsequent changes in facts and circumstances. For example, a first-time adopter could not retrospectively elect to designate investments in equity instruments as at fair value through OCI with the intention of any fair value losses arising after the date of transition being recognised in OCI.

6.1.620   *Own-use exemption*

6.1.620.10   In certain circumstances, it may be necessary to designate contracts into an 'own-use' category at their inception in order to qualify for the own-use exemption under IFRS 9. For further discussion, see 7.1.210.60. If a designation was made at inception of a contract for the application of a similar own-use exemption under previous GAAP, then this may be relevant evidence in determining whether application of the own-use exemption by the first-time adopter is appropriate.

6.1.620.20   In addition, under IFRS 9 a contract that meets the own-use exemption may be designated at inception as measured at fair value through profit or loss (see 7.1.200.40). This optional designation is permitted only if it eliminates or significantly reduces an accounting mismatch. A first-time adopter may designate as measured at fair value through profit or loss, at the date of transition to IFRS, contracts that already exist on that date, provided that the contracts meet the conditions for this designation at that date and the first-time adopter designates all similar contracts. [*IFRS 1.D33*]

6.1.630   *Optional exemption for fair value measurement on initial recognition*

6.1.630.10   IFRS 1 provides relief from the retrospective application of the requirements in respect of the recognition of 'day one' gains or losses (see 7.7.40). Under the optional exemption, the criteria for the recognition of gains and losses after the initial recognition of a financial asset or liability only need to be applied prospectively to transactions entered into on or after the date of transition to IFRS. [*IFRS 1.D20*]

6.1.640   *Mandatory exception for derecognition of financial instruments*

6.1.640.10   A first-time adopter needs to carefully assess the characteristics of its financial instruments recognised under previous GAAP, and consider:
- whether it should recognise financial assets at the date of transition that qualify for recognition in accordance with IFRS, but which were derecognised under previous GAAP; and
- whether it should derecognise financial assets at the date of transition that qualify for derecognition in accordance with IFRS but which continued to be recognised under previous GAAP.

6.1.640.20   An exception from applying the general requirements of IFRS in respect of the recognition/derecognition of financial instruments at the date of transition applies to transactions that took place before the date of transition. Under a mandatory exception in IFRS 1, a first-time adopter applies the derecognition requirements of IFRS prospectively to transactions occurring on or after the date of transition in respect of all non-derivative financial assets and financial liabilities. Under this exception, the previous GAAP accounting for transfers of financial assets and financial liabilities before the date of transition is not altered, which means that the opening IFRS statement of financial position is not adjusted in respect of such transactions. [*IFRS 1.B2*]

6.1.640.30   Despite this mandatory exception, a first-time adopter may elect to apply the derecognition requirements of IFRS retrospectively from any date before the date of transition, provided that the information required to do this was obtained at the time of initially accounting for those transactions. [*IFRS 1.B3*]

6.1.640.40   The exception from retrospective application of the derecognition requirements applies equally to financial instruments that would have qualified for derecognition under IFRS, but which were not derecognised under previous GAAP. [*IFRS 1.B2*]

6.1.640.50   The derecognition requirements of IFRS are particularly relevant when analysing the transfer of assets in a securitisation arrangement. Importantly, if assets are transferred to a structured entity (see 5.10.190) and IFRS is being adopted in the consolidated financial statements, then derecognition in the consolidated financial statements is not achieved if the structured entity is consolidated (see 7.6.210.20).

EXAMPLE 19 – DERECOGNITION OF FINANCIAL INSTRUMENTS

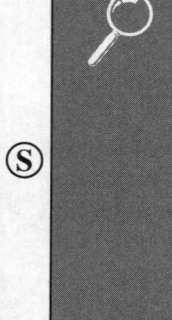

6.1.640.60   Company T is a first-time adopter in 2018. In December 2016, T transferred a portfolio of long-term receivables to Structured Entity SE. To finance the purchase of the receivables, SE issued notes to third party investors. Under its previous GAAP, T derecognised the receivables from its statement of financial position and SE was not consolidated. When applying the requirements of IFRS 1:

- T does not reinstate the receivables onto its separate – i.e. unconsolidated – opening IFRS statement of financial position; T also does not consider whether the derecognition requirements of IFRS are met because of the mandatory exception in respect of derecognition transactions occurring before the date of transition; and
- T determines that SE is consolidated under IFRS. As a result, T's consolidated financial statements include SE and also include the receivables that had been derecognised under previous GAAP.

6.1.650   *Derivatives and embedded derivatives*

6.1.650.10   Consistent with the general requirement of the financial instruments standards, all derivatives in the scope of IFRS 9, including embedded derivatives separated from host contracts, are measured at fair value in the opening IFRS statement of financial position. [*IFRS 1.B4(a), IG53, 9.B5.2.3*]

6.1.650.20   A first-time adopter assesses whether an embedded derivative is required to be separated from its host contract and accounted for as a derivative on the basis of the conditions that existed at the later of the date when the entity first became a party to the contract and the date of any change in the terms of the contract that significantly modified the cash flows required under the contract (see 7.2.220). [*IFRS 1.IG55, B9, 9.4.3.2, 4.3.3, B4.3.11*]

6.1.650.30   If the fair value of an embedded derivative that IFRS 9 requires to be separated cannot be determined reliably at the date of initial recognition on the basis of its terms and conditions, then the fair value of the embedded derivative can be calculated as the difference between the fair value of the hybrid instrument and the fair value of the host contract. If the fair value of such an embedded derivative cannot be determined using this technique, then the entire instrument is designated as at fair value through profit or loss and is measured at fair value. [*IFRS 1.IG55, 9.4.3.6–4.3.7*]

6.1.660   *Optional exemption for extinguishing financial liabilities with equity instruments*

6.1.660.10   IFRIC 19 addresses the accounting by a debtor when the terms of a financial liability are renegotiated and result in the debtor issuing equity instruments to a creditor to extinguish all or part of the financial liability (see 7.6.450). A first-time adopter is permitted to apply the transition provisions in IFRIC 19. [*IFRS 1.D25*]

6.1.660.20   These transition provisions require an entity to apply a change in accounting policy in accordance with IAS 8 from the beginning of the earliest comparative period presented (see 2.8.50). [*IFRIC 19.13*]

6.1.670   *Optional exemption for compound financial instruments*

6.1.670.10   A compound instrument is a financial instrument that, from the issuer's perspective, includes both a liability and an equity component. For a compound instrument in which the liability component is still outstanding at the date of transition, a first-time adopter separately identifies the liability and equity components. The equity component is split between the retained earnings component – i.e. cumulative interest on the liability portion – and the original (or 'true') equity component. The allocation between liabilities and equity is based on the circumstances at the date of issue of the instrument and the subsequent interest expense on the liability component is calculated under the effective interest method required by IFRS. [*IFRS 1.D18, IG35, IAS 32.28*]

EXAMPLE 20 – COMPOUND FINANCIAL INSTRUMENTS – SEPARATION OF EQUITY AND LIABILITY COMPONENTS

6.1.670.20   Company Q is a first-time adopter with a date of transition to IFRS of 1 January 2017. On 1 January 2013, Q issued an instrument for net proceeds of 1,000 with the following terms:
- a notional value of 1,000;
- a 5% coupon rate, payable at the end of each year;
- a maturity date of 31 December 2018; and
- the holder had an option to convert the instrument into a specified number of Q's shares at any time during 2018.

6.1.670.30   At the date of issue of 1 January 2013, the same instrument without the conversion feature would have had a fair value of 950. At the date of transition, the liability is still outstanding and therefore Q separately identifies and recognises a liability component and an equity component. At the date of issue, the liability component would be recognised at its fair value of 950, and the residual of 50 would be allocated to the equity component.

6.1.670.40   Under previous GAAP, interest is recognised on the notional amount of 1,000 at a constant rate of 5% over the term of the instrument and the carrying amount would remain at 1,000 at each reporting date. Under IFRS, interest is accrued on the liability component of 950 using the effective interest method over the term, and the interest and liability carrying amounts at each reporting date are calculated as follows.

	CARRYING AMOUNT AT 1 JANUARY	INTEREST ACCRUED AT 6.0175%	INTEREST PAID	CARRYING AMOUNT AT 31 DECEMBER
2013	950	57	(50)	957
2014	957	58	(50)	965
2015	965	58	(50)	973
2016	973	59	(50)	982

6.1.670.50   Therefore, the adjustment at the date of transition, 1 January 2017, is recorded as follows.

	DEBIT	CREDIT
Liability (1,000 - 982)	18	
Retained earnings	32	
Equity – conversion option		50
To recognise compound instrument on transition		

6.1.670.60   If the liability component in a compound instrument is no longer outstanding at the date of transition, then IFRS 1 contains an optional exemption that permits a first-time adopter to ignore the split illustrated in Example 20 between retained earnings and true equity. In our view, this optional exemption may be applied on an instrument-by-instrument basis. [*IFRS 1.D18, IG36*]

6.1.680   *Mandatory exception for government loans*

6.1.680.10   A first-time adopter of IFRS applies the requirements of the financial instruments standards and IAS 20 to a government loan with a below-market rate of interest prospectively from the date of transition. However, a first-time adopter may apply these requirements retrospectively if the information needed to do so was obtained at the time of initially recognising the government loan. [*IFRS 1.B10–B11*]

6.1.680.20   If under previous GAAP a first-time adopter did not recognise and measure the below-market interest rate government loan on a basis consistent with IFRS, then it uses the previous GAAP carrying amount of the loan as the carrying amount in its opening IFRS statement of financial position. Subsequently, the first-time adopter measures the loan at amortised cost, using an effective interest rate that is calculated at the date of transition. [*IFRS 1.B10–B11, 9.4.2.1*]

6.1.680.30   This mandatory exception does not preclude a first-time adopter from applying the optional exemption for designating previously recognised financial instruments at fair value through profit or loss to government loans (see 6.1.610). [*IFRS 1.B12*]

6.1.690   Impairment of financial instruments

6.1.690.10   A first-time adopter applies the impairment requirements of IFRS 9 retrospectively subject to the exemptions in 6.1.690.20–40. [*IFRS 1.B8D*]

6.1.690.20   At the date of transition, a first-time adopter uses reasonable and supportable information that is available without undue cost or effort to determine the credit risk at the date the financial instrument was initially recognised (or, for loan commitments and financial guarantee contracts, the date the first-time adopter became a party to the irrevocable commitment) and compares that with the credit risk at the date of transition to IFRS to assess whether there has been a significant increase in credit risk since initial recognition. [*IFRS 1.B8E, 9.5.5.6*]

6.1.690.30   In determining whether there has been a significant increase in credit risk since initial recognition, a first-time adopter is not required to undertake an exhaustive search for information, and may approximate the initial credit risk. However, if at the date of transition, such an assessment would require undue cost or effort, then the loss allowance is measured at an amount equal to lifetime expected credit losses (see 7.8.40) at each reporting date until that financial instrument is derecognised, unless the credit risk of the financial instrument at a reporting date is low. If this is the case, then the first-time adopter may apply the exemption in IFRS 9 relating to such instruments (see 7.8.150). [*IFRS 1.B8E, B8G, 9.B7.2.2–B7.2.3*]

6.1.690.40   In determining whether there has been a significant increase in credit risk since initial recognition, a first-time adopter may apply:
- the low credit risk exception (see 7.8.150); and
- the rebuttable presumption for contractual payments that are more than 30 days past due if a first-time adopter applies the impairment requirements by identifying significant increases in credit risk since initial recognition for financial instruments on the basis of past-due information (see 7.8.120). [*IFRS 1.B8F*]

6.1.700   Hedge accounting

6.1.710   *Mandatory exception on hedge accounting*

6.1.710.10   To prevent a first-time adopter from using hindsight to achieve a specific hedging result, a mandatory exception in IFRS 1 prohibits a first-time adopter from retrospectively designating transactions as hedges. Accordingly, the exception requires a first-time adopter to apply hedge accounting prospectively from the date of transition if the conditions for hedge accounting in IFRS are met. [*IFRS 1.B6*]

6.1.710.20   At the date of transition, a first-time adopter follows these steps:
- measure all derivatives at fair value;
- derecognise any deferred gains and losses related to derivatives that were reported as assets and liabilities under previous GAAP;
- identify whether a hedging relationship designated under previous GAAP is of a type that qualifies for hedge accounting under IFRS 9. For hedge accounting to be applied prospectively from the date of transition, a hedging relationship needs to meet, on or before the date of transition, the conditions for hedge accounting, including the designation, documentation and hedge effectiveness requirements specified in IFRS 9:
  - if a hedging relationship is of a type that does not qualify for hedge accounting under IFRS 9, then the first-time adopter does not reflect the hedging relationship in the opening IFRS statement of financial position (see 6.1.740.60); and
  - if a hedging relationship is of a type that qualifies for hedge accounting under IFRS 9, then the first-time adopter adjusts the previous GAAP carrying amounts of assets and liabilities and the components of equity in the statement of financial position at the date of transition as explained in 6.1.750. If hedge accounting for such a hedge is not to be applied prospectively from the date of transition, then the first-time adopter discontinues hedge accounting by applying paragraphs 6.5.6–6.5.7 of IFRS 9 (see 7.9.930). For a further discussion of hedging relationships under IFRS, see 6.1.740.50. [*IFRS 1.B4–B6, IG60, 9.6.5.6–6.5.7*]

6.1.720   *Measure all derivatives at fair value*

6.1.720.10   All derivatives are measured at fair value in the opening IFRS statement of financial position. Fair value is measured in accordance with IFRS 13, which is the subject of chapter 2.4. [*IFRS 1.B4(a)*]

6.1.730   *Derecognise deferred gains and losses previously reported as assets and liabilities*

6.1.730.10   Any assets and liabilities at the date of transition that represent deferred gains and losses on derivatives under previous GAAP are removed from the opening IFRS statement of financial position. [*IFRS 1.B4(b)*]

6.1.740   *Identify and designate IFRS hedging relationships*

6.1.740.10   A first-time adopter may apply hedge accounting from the date of transition only to hedging relationships that comply with the hedge accounting requirements of IFRS at that date. These requirements include the need for contemporaneous documentation. [*IFRS 1.IG60*]

6.1.740.20   For certain hedges designated under previous GAAP, although the hedging relationship is of a type that qualifies for hedge accounting under IFRS, the first-time adopter may have performed no effectiveness assessment or performed effectiveness assessments that do not comply with the IFRS 9 hedge effectiveness requirements (see 7.9.790). In these cases, provided that on or before the date of transition the first-time adopter specifies in the hedge documentation how it will assess whether the hedging relationship meets the hedge effectiveness requirements (including its analysis of the sources of hedge ineffectiveness and how it determines the hedge ratio), and assesses that the hedge meets the hedge effectiveness requirements, in our view the existing hedging relationship may continue on transition. [*IFRS 9.6.4.1(b), B6.4.12*]

EXAMPLE 21 – HEDGING RELATIONSHIPS DESIGNATED UNDER PREVIOUS GAAP – DESIGNATION UNDER IFRS 9

6.1.740.30   Company B is a first-time adopter in 2018 and its date of transition is 1 January 2017. On 1 October 2016, B designated a five-year interest rate swap as the hedging instrument in a cash flow hedge of the variability in interest payments attributable to changes in LIBOR on a floating rate bond. Under its previous GAAP, because the critical terms of the swap and the bond were matched, B was permitted to assume perfect effectiveness without performing any effectiveness assessment. On 31 December 2016, the deferred balance in equity, comprising the entire cumulative gain on the interest rate swap, was 1,000. On 1 January 2017, B adjusted its existing hedge documentation to specify how the hedge effectiveness requirements are assessed under IFRS 9 (see 7.9.790.30). B also performed a hedge effectiveness assessment under the documented method and the hedge was expected to be effective prospectively.

6.1.740.40   We believe that in this example there is no requirement for the first-time adopter to de-designate the existing hedging relationship and redesignate a new hedging relationship on account of the adjustment to the hedge documentation to specify how the hedge effectiveness requirements are assessed. Accordingly, because the existing hedging relationship continues after transition, for the purpose of assessing effectiveness and computing ineffectiveness to be recognised in profit or loss after transition, B takes into account the original hedge designation date. Therefore, if B decides to use a hypothetical derivative for assessing effectiveness and measuring ineffectiveness (see 7.9.855), then the terms of the hypothetical derivative could be determined as at 1 October 2016.

6.1.740.50   Conversely, if the hedge effectiveness requirements of IFRS 9 are not met on 1 January 2017 in Example 21, then hedge accounting has to be discontinued prospectively (see 7.9.960). It is possible to re-designate the hedging relationship later, if all of the conditions of IFRS 9 are met at that time. This qualifies as a new hedging relationship; however, the non-zero fair value of the interest rate swap at the subsequent designation date may create complexities in assessing hedge effectiveness and measuring ineffectiveness. For further discussion of methods for assessing hedge effectiveness, see 7.9.830. [*IFRS 1.B6*]

6.1.740.60   If the hedging relationship designated under previous GAAP is not of a type that qualifies for hedge accounting under IFRS 9 – e.g. the use of a stand-alone written option or a net written option as the hedging instrument, or the hedged item being a net position in a cash flow hedge for a risk other than foreign currency risk – then the hedging relationship is not reflected in the opening IFRS statement of financial position, except as explained in 6.1.740.70. [*IFRS 1.B5*]

6.1.740.70   If a first-time adopter has designated a net position as the hedged item under previous GAAP, then it may reflect the hedging relationship in its opening IFRS statement of financial position if the first-time adopter designates as a hedged item in accordance with IFRS either an individual item within that net position or a net position that meets the requirements for a group of items to be eligible as a hedged item (see 7.9.390), provided that it does so no later than the date of transition. Similarly, applying the same reasoning, it appears that a first-time adopter is also allowed in these circumstances to designate as a hedged item in accordance with IFRS a gross exposure that is a group of items (or a layer component thereof) within the net position designated under previous GAAP provided that the hedged item designated under IFRS meets the eligibility requirements (see 7.9.390) and the designation is done no later than the date of transition. [*IFRS 1.B5, 9.6.6.1*]

EXAMPLE 22 – REDESIGNATION OF HEDGING RELATIONSHIPS UNDER IFRS

6.1.740.80   Company Y is a first-time adopter with a date of transition to IFRS of 1 January 2017. Y's functional currency is FC. Y has certain cash inflows and outflows in a foreign currency (AC) related to the sale of its products and payments for goods, respectively. Y's risk management strategy is to manage its foreign currency risk exposure by analysing its AC inflows and outflows within cash flow time bands of three months – i.e. on a quarter-by-quarter basis. The cash flows within such time bands are considered highly probable forecast transactions.

6.1.740.90   Sales and purchases within the three months ended 31 March 2017 were expected to result in cash inflows of AC 1,000 and cash outflows of AC 700. As permitted under previous GAAP, Y designated as the hedged item its expected net inflows of AC 300 during the three months ended 31 March 2017.

6.1.740.100   Y may continue hedge accounting under IFRS 9 by meeting the following requirements for a cash flow hedge of foreign currency risk of a net position on or before the date of transition to IFRS (see 7.9.390).
● The forecast sales and purchases are individually eligible hedged items.
● The hedged items are managed together on a group basis for risk management purposes.
● The hedge designation specifies the reporting period in which the forecast transactions are expected to affect profit or loss as well as the nature and volume of these transactions (see 7.9.400.80–110). [*IFRS 9.6.6.1, B6.6.7*]

6.1.740.110   Alternatively, on transition to IFRS Y may be able to change the hedged item from a net position to a gross position that is a component of the net position. For example, Y could designate as the hedged item as at 1 January 2017 the first AC 300 of highly probable forecast sales in AC for the three months ending 31 March 2017 (i.e. a layer component of a group of items) if the relevant eligibility requirements are met (see 7.9.370 and 390) – i.e.:
● the forecast sales are individually eligible hedged items; and
● they are managed together on a group basis for risk management purposes.

6.1.740.120   IFRS 9 permits an entity to separate the foreign currency basis spread from a financial instrument that is designated as a hedging instrument. In this case, the foreign currency basis spread is excluded from the designation and accounted for as a 'cost of hedging' in a separate component of equity. It appears that it is possible for a first-time adopter, at the date of transition to IFRS, to separate the foreign currency basis spread from a financial instrument and recognise the accumulated amount of the 'cost of hedging' in a separate component of equity as if the first-time adopter had applied IFRS 9 from inception of the hedge. This is possible if the first-time adopter identifies existing hedging relationships that can qualify for hedge accounting under IFRS 9 and amends the hedge documentation to meet the relevant requirements in IFRS 9 before the date of transition to IFRS. [*IFRS 9.6.5.15–6.5.16, 7.2.26(b)*]

6.1.750 *Adjust previous GAAP carrying amounts*

6.1.760 *Fair value hedging relationships*

6.1.760.10   For a fair value hedging relationship that is of a type that qualifies for hedge accounting under IFRS, and for which, under previous GAAP, gains and losses either have been deferred or have not been recognised, the first-time adopter adjusts the carrying amount of the hedged item on the date of transition by the lower of:

- the portion of the cumulative change in the fair value of the hedged item since inception of the hedge that was not recognised under previous GAAP; and
- the portion of the cumulative change in fair value of the hedging instrument that, under previous GAAP, either was not recognised or was deferred in the statement of financial position as an asset or liability. [*IFRS 1.IG60A*]

EXAMPLE 23 – ADJUSTMENTS TO PREVIOUS GAAP CARRYING AMOUNTS

6.1.760.20   On 1 January 2015, Company G issued non-cancellable five-year bonds for 500. The interest rate on the bonds is fixed at the then market rate of 6% per annum and the bonds were issued at par. G's desired risk management strategy is to have variable rate funding and, therefore, on 1 January 2015 G also entered into a five-year interest rate swap with a notional amount of 500. The swap pays a floating interest rate based on LIBOR and receives a 6% fixed interest rate. Under previous GAAP, G had designated the swap as the hedging instrument in a fair value hedge of the exposure to changes in the fair value of the bonds attributable to changes in LIBOR. However, under previous GAAP fair value changes related to the swap were not recognised in G's financial statements and the carrying amount of the bond was measured at cost. Assume that, ignoring the effects of hedge accounting, on the date of transition the carrying amount of the bond under both previous GAAP and IFRS is 500.

6.1.760.30   At the date of transition, 1 January 2017, G documents the earlier hedge designation – i.e. of the interest rate swap – as a fair value hedge of interest rate risk for the issued bonds, and ensures that the hedging relationship meets the conditions for hedge accounting under IFRS 9, including effectiveness assessment. The hedging relationship is determined to meet the hedge effectiveness requirements because the critical terms of the hedged item and the hedging instrument are matched and the effect of credit risk is not expected to dominate the value changes that result from the economic relationship between the hedged item and the hedging instrument.

6.1.760.40   On 1 January 2017, the fair value of the bonds is 480. The change in fair value of 20 since inception comprises 15 related to changes in LIBOR and 5 related to changes in G's credit risk. The fair value of the swap as at 1 January 2017 is a liability of 18, all of which relates to changes in LIBOR.

6.1.760.50   When adjusting the carrying amount of the hedged liability at the date of transition, the carrying amount of the bond (liability) is reduced by 15, which is the lower of the cumulative change in the fair value of the hedged item since inception of the hedge resulting from the hedged risk (15) and the cumulative change in fair value of the hedging instrument (18) (see 6.1.760.10). When recognising the interest rate swap at the date of transition, the interest rate swap liability is reflected at 18.

6.1.760.60   In our view, the carrying amount of the hedged item to which the adjustment under 6.1.760.10 is applied is arrived at as follows.
1. Determine the carrying amount of the hedged item under IFRS on the date of transition as if hedge accounting was never applied. For example, a financial liability classified as subsequently measured at amortised cost is measured under the effective interest method.
2. The amount in (1) is then adjusted for the fair value hedge adjustments, if any, that were recognised under previous GAAP.

6.1.760.70   IFRS 1 does not appear to contemplate situations in which a first-time adopter applied fair value hedge accounting under previous GAAP in a manner similar to that required under IFRS 9 – i.e. by adjusting the carrying amount of the hedged item for fair value changes attributable to the hedged risk. In our view, if the fair value hedge accounting applied under previous GAAP results in substantially the same outcome as if IFRS 9 had been applied, then either of the following approaches, applied on a consistent basis, is acceptable at the date of transition to determine the carrying amount of the hedged asset or liability:
● the amount determined in accordance with guidance in 6.1.760.60; or
● the amount determined in (1) in 6.1.760.60, adjusted for the lower of the cumulative change in the fair value of the hedging derivative and the cumulative change in the fair value of the hedged item attributable to the hedged risk.

6.1.760.80   If the hedge accounting applied under previous GAAP does not qualify for hedge accounting under IFRS, then the hedged item is recognised in accordance with the IFRS that applies to that item, in which case it is likely that any adjustments to the hedged item under previous GAAP will be reversed (see 6.1.740.60).

6.1.770   *Cash flow hedging relationships*

6.1.770.10   If the hedged item is a forecast transaction that on the date of transition is no longer highly probable to occur but is still expected to occur, then any deferred gain or loss recognised under previous GAAP is transferred to a separate component of equity, typically referred to as a 'cash flow hedging reserve'. This amount remains in equity until:

- the forecast transaction subsequently results in the recognition of a non-financial asset or non-financial liability, at which time the entity removes the accumulated amount from the cash flow hedge reserve and includes it directly in the initial cost or other carrying amount of the non-financial asset or non-financial liability;
- the forecast transaction affects profit or loss, at which time the amount is transferred to profit or loss; or
- subsequent circumstances indicate that the forecast transaction is no longer expected to occur, in which case the amount is transferred to profit or loss. [*IFRS 1.IG60B, 9.6.5.11(d), 6.5.12*]

6.1.770.20   The requirements in 6.1.770.10 mean that any cumulative ineffectiveness before the date of transition that was recognised as deferred gains or losses may be recognised in the cash flow hedging reserve. However, hedge ineffectiveness arising after the date of transition will be recognised immediately in profit or loss (see 7.9.860.10). [*IFRS 1.IG60B, 9.6.5.11(c)*]

6.1.770.30   To the extent that the related forecast transaction is no longer expected to occur, any deferred gain or loss recognised under previous GAAP is transferred to retained earnings in the opening IFRS statement of financial position.

6.1.780   *Net investment hedging relationships*

6.1.780.10   Net investment hedging relationships are not dealt with specifically by IFRS 1. However, because IFRS accounts for net investment hedges in a manner similar to cash flow hedges, in our view the same basic process as set out in 6.1.770 should be followed.

6.1.780.20   However, if a first-time adopter takes advantage of the transitional relief included in IFRS 1 to set the cumulative translation reserve to zero at the date of transition (see 6.1.1170), then the related hedge reserve will also be set at zero with any adjustment arising from the recognition of the derivative or non-derivative hedging instrument being recognised in opening retained earnings.

6.1.790   **Provisions**

6.1.790.10   Generally, provisions for repairs and maintenance are derecognised in the opening IFRS statement of financial position (see 3.12.540). In our view, the derecognition of such a provision is an indication that a component of the relevant asset may need to be depreciated separately (see 3.2.230). For a discussion of the identification of components of property, plant and equipment on the first-time adoption of IFRS, see 6.1.340.

6.1.800   *Optional exemption for changes in decommissioning liabilities included in cost of property, plant and equipment*

6.1.800.10   If an obligation to restore the environment or dismantle an asset arises on the initial recognition of an item of property, plant and equipment, then the corresponding debit is treated as part of the cost of the related asset. This cost includes not only the initial estimate of the costs related to dismantlement, removal or restoration of the asset at the time of installing the item, but also amounts recognised during the period of use. Changes in the amount of the provision, other than those related to the production of inventories or the unwinding of the effect of discounting the provision, are ad-

1717

justed against the carrying amount of property, plant and equipment, and the adjusted depreciable amount is depreciated prospectively over the remaining useful life of the asset. [*IFRS 1.IG201–IG202, IAS 16.16(c)*]

6.1.800.20   IFRS 1 includes an optional exemption that allows a first-time adopter to calculate the amount of the provision capitalised in property, plant and equipment in its opening IFRS statement of financial position using the following steps:

- calculate the provision at the date of transition as if the obligation arose at that date, discounted using a current market-based discount rate;
- discount the provision back to the date on which the obligation first arose, using the first-time adopter's best estimate of the historical risk-adjusted discount rate(s) that would have applied between that date and the date of transition; and
- depreciate the resulting present value from the date on which the obligation first arose to the date of transition. [*IFRS 1.D21, IG203*]

EXAMPLE 24A – DECOMMISSIONING LIABILITY FOR ASSETS ACQUIRED BEFORE DATE OF TRANSITION (1)

6.1.800.30   On 1 January 2013, Company H acquired a manufacturing plant at a cost of 900. The plant has a useful life of 30 years and at the end of its useful life H will be required to decommission the plant in accordance with local regulations; the obligation arose as a result of the plant being built.

6.1.800.40   Under previous GAAP, there is no requirement to recognise a provision for decommissioning and the carrying amount of the plant is 750 at the date of transition, being 1 January 2018. H elects to use the optional exemption in IFRS 1 and as at 1 January 2018 H estimates that a decommissioning provision of 20 should be recognised – which is the present value using a current market-based discount rate at that date of the estimated amount that will be incurred when decommissioning occurs in 2042.

6.1.800.50   H discounts the 20 back five years to 1 January 2013, using a historical risk-adjusted discount rate, which results in an amount of 15. H then calculates depreciation based on the useful life of the plant of 30 years, arriving at an adjusted amount of 12.5 (15 - (15 / 30 x 5)) at the date of transition.

6.1.800.60   H records the following entry on transition.

	DEBIT	CREDIT
Manufacturing plant	15.0	
Retained earnings	7.5	
Accumulated depreciation		2.5
Decommissioning liability		20.0
To recognise decommissioning liability at date of transition		

6.1.810   *Interaction with deemed cost exemption*

6.1.810.10   A first-time adopter considers the interaction between the decommissioning provision and the fair value as deemed cost exemption (see 6.1.300), if elected, to establish the opening balance for property, plant and equipment at the date of transition. If fair value is used as deemed cost, then the valuation is grossed up for any provision for decommissioning, if the valuation reflects the price that a third party would pay for the asset and to assume the related obligation to decommission the asset – i.e. the amount of the asset less the provision is what the third party would pay. The decommissioning liability is measured in accordance with IFRS and the resulting adjustment is recognised in opening retained earnings.

6.1.810.20   If the valuation does not reflect the price that a third party would pay for the asset and to assume the related liability, then the difference between the fair value of the asset and the previous GAAP carrying amount is recognised as an adjustment to opening retained earnings. The decommissioning liability is measured in accordance with IFRS and the resulting adjustment is also recognised in opening retained earnings.

EXAMPLE 24B – DECOMMISSIONING LIABILITY FOR ASSETS ACQUIRED BEFORE DATE OF TRANSITION (2)

6.1.810.30   Modifying Example 24A, H chooses to apply the fair value as deemed cost exemption at the date of transition (see 6.1.300). The fair value of the plant at the date of transition is 850, which reflects the price a third party would pay for the asset and to assume the restoration obligation. At the date of transition, H records the following entries.

	DEBIT	CREDIT
Accumulated depreciation (900 / 30 x 5)	150	
Manufacturing plant		150
To reverse accumulated depreciation at date of transition		
Manufacturing plant (850 - 750)	100	
Retained earnings		100
To recognise plant at fair value at date of transition		
Manufacturing plant	20	
Decommissioning liability		20
To recognise decommissioning liability at date of transition		

6.1.810.40   If a first-time adopter uses the deemed cost exemption for oil and gas assets in the development or production phases (see 6.1.1470), then the amount of any adjustments required to measure decommissioning, restoration and similar liabilities in accordance with IAS 37 at the date of transition is recognised directly in retained earnings rather than adjusting the carrying amount of the underlying assets. [*IFRS 1.D21A*]

6.1.820   **Employee benefits**

6.1.830   *Estimates*

6.1.830.10   The measurement of employee benefit obligations under IFRS requires an entity to make demographic assumptions – e.g. to select mortality tables. A first-time adopter's estimates under IFRS at the date of transition are consistent with estimates made for the same date under previous GAAP (after adjustments to reflect any difference in accounting policies), unless there is objective evidence that those estimates were in error (see 6.1.190). In our view, if the assumptions made under previous GAAP are consistent with the methodologies and assumptions required under IFRS, then the same mortality tables should be used to determine the defined benefit obligation, unless there is objective evidence that those estimates were in error. [*IFRS 1.14, IAS 19.76(a), 81–82*]

6.1.830.20   However, IFRS may require a first-time adopter to make actuarial assumptions that were not required under previous GAAP, or were made using assumptions different from those under IFRS. For example, IAS 19 may require the use of a discount rate that is different from previous GAAP. In such cases, the first-time adopter uses estimates that reflect conditions at the date of transition; they do not reflect conditions that arose after that date (see 6.1.200). [*IFRS 1.IG20*]

6.1.840   **Share-based payment transactions**

6.1.850   *Transitional requirements and optional exemption*

6.1.850.10   The requirements of IFRS 1 in respect of share-based payment transactions match the transitional requirements that applied to existing users of IFRS when IFRS 2 came into effect in 2005. A first-time adopter is *required* to apply IFRS 2 to:
- equity instruments that were granted after 7 November 2002 that will vest *after* the date of transition;
- liabilities arising from cash-settled share-based payment transactions that will be settled *after* the date of transition; and
- awards that are modified *on or after* the date of transition, even if the original grant of the award is not accounted for in accordance with IFRS 2. [*IFRS 1.D2–D3, IG65*]

6.1.850.20   Additionally, a first-time adopter is *encouraged*, but not required, to apply IFRS 2 retrospectively to:
- equity instruments that were granted on or before 7 November 2002, or equity instruments that were granted after 7 November 2002 that vested before the date of transition. However, this application is allowed only if the first-time adopter had publicly disclosed the fair value of such awards determined at the measurement date in accordance with IFRS 2; and
- liabilities arising from cash-settled share-based payment transactions that were settled before the date of transition. [*IFRS 1.D2–D3, IG64*]

6.1.850.30   Awards for which retrospective application of IFRS 2 is encouraged but not required are referred to in this chapter as 'otherwise-exempt awards'. The optional exemption in IFRS 1 in respect of share-based payment transactions permits a first-time adopter to elect not to apply IFRS 2 to otherwise-exempt awards.

6.1.850.40   The following table demonstrates how application of the optional exemption impacts grants of equity-settled share-based payments made by entities with their first IFRS reporting date on 31 December 2018 or 31 March 2019.

REPORTING DATE	DATE OF TRANSITION	GRANT DATE	VESTING DATE	TREATMENT
31 December 2018	1 January 2017	On or before 7 November 2002	Before or after 1 January 2017	No share-based payment cost recognised[1]
		After 7 November 2002	Before 1 January 2017	No share-based payment cost recognised[1]
			On or after 1 January 2017	Recognise share-based payment cost for 31 December 2018 and 31 December 2017; and adjust 1 January 2017 retained earnings
31 March 2019	1 April 2017	On or before 7 November 2002	Before or after 1 April 2017	No share-based payment cost recognised[1]
		After 7 November 2002	Before 1 April 2017	No share-based payment cost recognised[1]
			On or after 1 April 2017	Recognise share-based payment cost for 31 March 2019 and 31 March 2018; and adjust 1 April 2017 retained earnings

Note
1. Only a modification to the terms of the award on or after the date of transition would result in the recognition of share-based payment cost (see 6.1.880), unless the first-time adopter applies IFRS 2 retrospectively to an otherwise-exempt award (see 6.1.860).

6.1.860   *Retrospective application to otherwise-exempt equity-settled awards*

6.1.860.10   A first-time adopter may apply the recognition and measurement requirements of the share-based payment standard retrospectively to equity instruments for which it is otherwise not required to do so *only* if:

- the first-time adopter had disclosed publicly the fair value of those equity instruments, measured in a manner consistent with IFRS 2; and
- the fair value was determined at the measurement date, as defined in IFRS 2. [*IFRS 1.D2*]

6.1.860.20   In our view, retrospective application of the recognition and measurement requirements of the share-based payment standard to otherwise-exempt awards may be applied on a grant-by-grant basis. We believe that a grant-by-grant election is possible because application of the standard to otherwise-exempt awards is encouraged when possible and the availability of the required fair value data may vary for grants made at different dates.

6.1.860.30   The publicly disclosed fair value is determined on the measurement date required by, and following the valuation methodology of, IFRS 2. [*IFRS 1.D2*]

6.1.860.40   In our view, the fair value should have been disclosed before publication of the first IFRS financial statements; however, it does not have to have been publicly disclosed when the award was granted.

6.1.860.50   If the first-time adopter has previously publicly disclosed fair value information at an aggregated level and that fair value is supported by sufficiently detailed calculations to permit estimates of the fair values of the separate share-based payment plans to be determined, then in our view the disclosure requirements for previous public disclosure have been met for the separate awards.

6.1.860.60   Certain of the disclosure requirements that apply to share-based payment transactions also apply to grants of equity instruments to which the recognition and measurement requirements of IFRS 2 have not been applied. [*IFRS 1.D2, 2.44–45*]

6.1.870   *Awards to which recognition and measurement requirements of IFRS 2 not applied*

6.1.870.10   IFRS does not specifically address the treatment in the opening IFRS statement of financial position of share-based payment cost recognised under previous GAAP for awards to which the recognition and measurement requirements of IFRS 2 are not applied (see 6.1.850.20). For example, under its previous GAAP a first-time adopter may have accounted for equity-settled share-based payment awards by debiting share-based payment cost in profit or loss and crediting a separate category of equity, such as contributed surplus or additional paid-in capital. As a result, for such equity-settled share-based payment awards, which are effectively 'grandfathered', it is unclear what, if any, adjustments should be made at the date of transition.

6.1.870.20   In our view, a first-time adopter should choose one of the following accounting approaches to be applied consistently at the date of transition.
- *Approach 1:* Share-based payment cost recognised in equity under previous GAAP is reversed in the opening IFRS statement of financial position. This is because IFRS 1 generally requires the opening IFRS statement of financial position to be prepared in accordance with IFRS, and the standard is usually explicit when an optional exemption permits the 'grandfathering' of previous GAAP. Because the optional exemption for share-based payment transactions does not explicitly permit the grandfathering of share-based payment cost recognised under previous GAAP, a first-time adopter may reverse the accounting under previous GAAP.
- *Approach 2:* Share-based payment cost recognised under previous GAAP is not reversed. This is because the circumstances in which IFRS 1 explicitly permits the grandfathering of previous GAAP generally relate to the accounting for assets and liabilities, and not to items of equity. This approach results in no adjustment at the date of transition, which may be seen as more in line with the objective of the share-based payment standard – i.e. that a first-time adopter recognises in profit or loss, and thereby equity, the effects of share-based payment transactions.

EXAMPLE 25 – SHARE-BASED PAYMENT COST RECOGNISED UNDER PREVIOUS GAAP

6.1.870.30   Company X is a first-time adopter in 2018. In 2012, X granted share options to its employees. Each option vests after a three-year service period. The aggregate fair value of the awards under previous GAAP was 200.

6.1.870.40   By 1 January 2017, all of the awards have vested and share-based payment cost of 200 was recognised in profit or loss under previous GAAP, with the corresponding credit being recognised as contributed surplus, which is a separate component of equity. Because the awards vested before X's date of transition, X is not required to apply IFRS to these awards.

6.1.870.50   Under Approach 1 in 6.1.870.20, X reverses the share-based payment cost recognised under previous GAAP at the date of transition by reallocating 200 from the contributed surplus to retained earnings.

6.1.870.60   Under Approach 2 in 6.1.870.20, X makes no accounting entry at the date of transition in respect of the share-based payment cost recognised under previous GAAP.

6.1.880   *Modification of awards*

6.1.880.10   An entity may modify the terms and conditions of a share-based payment arrangement – e.g. it may reduce the exercise price of the options granted, which would increase the fair value of those options.

6.1.880.20   Modifications to the terms or conditions of a grant of equity instruments will affect a first-time adopter as follows.
- *Modifications occurring before the date of transition:* The recognition and measurement requirements of IFRS 2 are not required to be applied if the original grant is not accounted for in accordance with IFRS 2.
- *Modifications occurring on or after the date of transition:* The recognition and measurement requirements of IFRS 2 are applied, even if the original grant was not accounted for in accordance with IFRS 2. However, in our view the modification accounting should be applied to the modification but not to the original grant – i.e. the original grant-date fair value should remain unrecognised and only the incremental fair value, if any, should be accounted for. This is because paragraph 57 of IFRS 2 specifically refers to the accounting for the modification. [*IFRS 1.D2*]

6.1.880.30   If an entity elects to apply IFRS 2 retrospectively to otherwise-exempt equity-settled or cash-settled awards (see 6.1.850.20–30), then in our view any modifications to those awards before the date of transition should also be accounted for in accordance with IFRS 2.

6.1.880.40   An equity-settled share-based award granted after 7 November 2002 with a vesting date after the date of transition is required to be accounted for in accordance with IFRS 2 (see 6.1.890.10). However, if such a grant is modified before the date of transition so that the instruments fully vest before this date, then in our view the transaction is not required to be accounted for under IFRS 2.

6.1.890   *Adjustments on transition for awards to which recognition and measurement requirements of IFRS 2 applied*

6.1.890.10   If the requirements of IFRS 2 are applied (see 6.1.850.10) or the first-time adopter applies IFRS to otherwise-exempt awards (see 6.1.850.20–30), then the recognition and measurement requirements of IFRS 2 are applied retrospectively. Any differences arising from this accounting at the date of transition are generally recognised in opening retained earnings.

6.1.900   *Share-based payment exemption and deferred taxes*

6.1.900.10   In some jurisdictions, entities receive a tax deduction based on the intrinsic value of equity-settled share-based payment transactions – e.g. share options – when the employees exercise their options and receive the equity instruments. IAS 12 provides specific guidance regarding the accounting for any tax deductions available on share-based payment transactions in the scope of IFRS 2 (see 3.13.820). In respect of options issued after 7 November 2002, a temporary difference arises between the tax base (based on the future tax deductions) of the share option and its carrying amount in the opening IFRS statement of financial position (zero, because the IFRS 2 share-based payment cost is offset by a corresponding credit entry in equity). A resulting deferred tax asset is recognised if the recognition criteria in IAS 12 are met. [*IFRS 1.IG5, IAS 12.9, 26(b), 68B*]

6.1.900.20   However, neither IFRS 1 nor IAS 12 provides specific guidance regarding the treatment of taxes on share-based payment transactions outside the scope of IFRS 2 – e.g. equity-settled share-based payment transactions granted before 7 November 2002. One approach is to identify the difference between the tax base of the share options and their carrying amount of zero as a temporary difference on which a deferred tax asset is recognised, subject to recoverability (see 3.13.330). In accordance with the principle in IAS 12 that the tax consequences of a transaction are recognised in a manner consistent with the accounting for the transaction itself, the deferred tax asset will be recognised in equity because the underlying transaction will affect equity on exercise of the options and issue of the shares. The initial recognition exemption in IAS 12 is not available because the difference only develops over time. Alternatively, the first-time adopter may elect not to identify a temporary difference and consequently not recognise any deferred tax on the basis that the share-based payments granted before 7 November 2002 have not been recognised in the IFRS financial statements and therefore there is no carrying amount, rather than a carrying amount of zero, recognised for accounting purposes. [*IAS 12.68C, IE.Ex5*]

6.1.910   **Deferred tax**

6.1.920   *Recognition of transition adjustments*

6.1.920.10   Deferred tax assets and liabilities are adjusted to reflect any adjustments to book value recognised as a result of adopting IFRS, and to measure deferred tax assets and deferred tax liabilities in accordance with the requirements of IFRS (see chapter 3.13). [*IFRS 1.C4(k)*]

6.1.920.20   If there is a taxable temporary difference in the opening IFRS statement of financial position, then a deferred tax liability is recognised in that opening IFRS statement of financial position. Adjustments to the balance of deferred tax at the date of transition are recognised in equity, generally in retained earnings, except in the following circumstances.
- If a business combination is restated, then the balance of deferred tax at the date of acquisition is determined as part of the reconstruction of the acquisition accounting (see 6.1.1070). The corresponding adjustment is against goodwill at the date of acquisition.
- If a business combination is not restated but an intangible asset is either subsumed into goodwill or recognised separately from goodwill at the date of transition (see 6.1.1020.10), then any related adjustment to deferred tax is recognised against goodwill. [*IFRS 1.IG5*]

6.1.920.30   A first-time adopter takes particular care to distinguish the adjustment for deferred tax made in the second bullet in 6.1.920.20 (related to a goodwill adjustment for an intangible asset) from any adjustment to deferred tax related to an unadjusted intangible asset. If deferred tax is recognised in relation to an intangible asset recognised under previous GAAP that was not adjusted in an unrestated business combination, then the adjustment is made to retained earnings and not to goodwill.

6.1.930   *Subsequent measurement*

6.1.930.10   Generally, changes in the carrying amount of deferred tax that relate to changes in the related temporary differences are recognised in profit or loss. Other changes – e.g. resulting from changes in tax rates – are recognised in profit or loss unless they relate to items previously recognised in OCI or directly in equity (see 3.13.530). [*IAS 12.61A*]

6.1.930.20   In our view, the first-time adopter should recognise any subsequent changes in deferred taxes in a manner consistent with how the deferred tax would originally have been recognised if the first-time adopter had been an existing user of IFRS.

6.1.930.30   In our view, the principle of recognising changes in deferred tax in accordance with IAS 12 after the date of transition applies equally to deferred tax arising in a business combination, regardless of whether the business combination was restated (see 6.1.940).

6.1.930.40   For a discussion of deferred taxes related to share-based payment transactions, see 6.1.900.

6.1.940   Business combinations

6.1.950   *Optional exemption for business combinations*

6.1.950.10   IFRS 1 provides an optional exemption whereby a first-time adopter may elect not to apply IFRS retrospectively to business combinations that occurred before the date of transition. However, all business combinations occurring on or after the date of transition are required to be accounted for in accordance with IFRS. [*IFRS 1.C1*]

6.1.950.20   For business combinations that occurred before the date of transition, entities have the following choices:
- restate all of these business combinations;
- restate all business combinations after a particular date; or
- do not restate any of these business combinations. [*IFRS 1.C1*]

6.1.950.30   If one business combination that is not required to be restated is voluntarily restated, then all subsequent business combinations and acquisitions (see 6.1.950.50) are restated. [*IFRS 1.C1*]

6.1.950.40   If business combinations are not restated, then the previous acquisition accounting remains unchanged. However, some adjustments – e.g. to reclassify intangibles and goodwill – may be required (see 6.1.970). [*IFRS 1.C1*]

6.1.950.50   The business combinations exemption applies equally to acquisitions of investments in associates, interests in joint ventures and interests in joint operations in which the activity of the joint operation constitutes a business that occurred before the date of transition. If a first-time adopter chooses to restate business combinations that occurred after a particular date before the date of transition, then that cut-off date applies equally to acquisitions of investments in associates, interests in joint ventures and interests in joint operations in which the activity of the joint operation constitutes a business (see 6.1.1210). [*IFRS 1.C5*]

6.1.960   *Definition of a business combination*

6.1.960.10   In our view, the business combination exemption is available to all transactions that would be considered to be a business combination under IFRS – i.e. to all business combinations as defined in IFRS 3 – regardless of how the transaction was accounted for under previous GAAP. We believe that the business combinations exemption is not available for transactions that are described as business combinations under previous GAAP, but which do not meet the definition of a business combination under IFRS. In our view, the exemption is available even if the business combination is outside the scope of IFRS 3 – e.g. a common control transaction.

EXAMPLE 26A – BUSINESS COMBINATION – COMMON CONTROL TRANSACTION

6.1.960.20   Company S's controlling shareholder, X, owns controlling interests in a number of other companies. In 2016, S acquired all of the shares in Company V, another operating company owned by X and in which S had no interest before the transaction. The transaction was a combination of businesses under common control. In assessing business combinations under previous GAAP, S applies the definition of a business combination in IFRS 3 – i.e. a transaction or other event in which an acquirer obtains control of one or more businesses. Because V is a business, the definition of a business combination is met and the exemption can be applied to the acquisition of V even though common control transactions are outside the scope of IFRS 3.

6.1.960.30   In our view, the business combination exemption also extends to any additional interest acquired between the date of the unrestated business combination and the date of transition.

EXAMPLE 26B – BUSINESS COMBINATION – ADDITIONAL INTEREST ACQUIRED

6.1.960.40   Company P is a first-time adopter in 2018. In 2012, P acquired 65% of Company S and in 2015 it acquired the remaining 35%. P elects not to restate business combinations that occurred before its date of transition – 1 January 2017. In our view, the business combination exemption should be applied to the 100% interest in the assets and liabilities of S. [*IFRS 1.B7*]

6.1.970   *Accounting for unrestated business combinations*

6.1.970.10   Once a first-time adopter has determined which business combinations under previous GAAP will not be restated on the adoption of IFRS, the following steps are relevant:
- maintain previous GAAP classification;
- determine whether any additional assets or liabilities are recognised;
- determine whether any recognised assets or liabilities are derecognised;

- remeasure the assets and liabilities after the business combination, if appropriate;
- adjust the measurement of goodwill, if appropriate; and
- eliminate any balance of negative goodwill.

6.1.970.20   Although it is not specifically mentioned in the section that follows, a first-time adopter considers the consequential effects on deferred tax and NCI whenever an adjustment is made. [*IFRS 1.C4(k)*]

6.1.980   *Maintain previous GAAP classification*

6.1.980.10   If a first-time adopter does not apply IFRS retrospectively to past business combinations, then it keeps the same classification of the business combination as under previous GAAP. For example, if under previous GAAP a business combination was treated as an acquisition by the legal acquirer, then this classification is maintained even if the transaction would have been classified as a reverse acquisition under IFRS. [*IFRS 1.C4(a), IG22.Ex2*]

6.1.990   *Determine whether additional assets or liabilities are recognised*

6.1.990.10   Even if the accounting for a business combination is carried forward from previous GAAP, the general requirements of IFRS 1 in respect of the recognition of assets and liabilities still apply (see 6.1.135). This requirement to assess recognition means, for example, that an asset cannot be omitted from the opening IFRS statement of financial position simply on the basis that it was not recognised in the accounting for the business combination under previous GAAP. [*IFRS 1.C4(b), C4(f)*]

6.1.990.20   However, an asset (including goodwill) or liability is not recognised in the first-time adopter's statement of financial position unless it would be recognised in the acquiree's own statement of financial position if it were prepared in accordance with IFRS. [*IFRS 1.C4(b)(ii), C4(f)*]

EXAMPLE 27A – UNRESTATED BUSINESS COMBINATIONS – CLASSIFICATION OF LEASES (1)

6.1.990.30   Company H will be a first-time adopter in 2018. H acquired subsidiary M in 2014 in a transaction that would be a business combination under IFRS. H elects not to restate the acquisition of M. As part of the accounting for the business combination under previous GAAP, a lease that had been entered into by M was classified as an operating lease and no asset or liability related to the lease was recognised in H's consolidated statement of financial position. However, under IFRS the lease would have been classified as a finance lease in M's statement of financial position based on an assessment of the facts and circumstances at inception of the lease. The lease remains in force as at 1 January 2017. Therefore, to comply with the recognition requirements of IFRS 1, the leased asset and the finance lease liability are recognised in H's opening IFRS statement of financial position (see 6.1.1410). [*IFRS 1.IG22.Ex7*]

6.1.990.40   An asset is not recognised in the parent's opening IFRS statement of financial position if it would be subject to the mandatory exception in IFRS 1 in respect of the derecognition of financial assets (see 6.1.640). In other words, the mandatory exception overrides the business combinations exemption. [*IFRS 1.C4(b)(i)*]

6.1.990.50   If an asset or liability acquired in an unrestated business combination is recognised for the first time as a result of applying this exemption, then it is measured at the amount that would have been recognised in the acquiree's own IFRS financial statements. Unless otherwise indicated, the resulting adjustment is recognised in opening retained earnings. [*IFRS 1.IG22.Ex2, Ex5, Ex7*]

EXAMPLE 27B – UNRESTATED BUSINESS COMBINATIONS – CLASSIFICATION OF LEASES (2)

6.1.990.60   Continuing Example 27A, Company H determines the adjustments required to its opening IFRS statement of financial position as follows.

- The leased asset is an item of property, plant and equipment. Therefore, H applies the guidance in respect of such assets (see 6.1.280) to determine the appropriate carrying amount at the date of transition. H elects to apply the fair value as deemed cost exemption at the date of transition. As a result, the asset has a deemed cost of 100.
- H applies the guidance in respect of finance leases (see 6.1.1410) to determine the appropriate carrying amount of the lease liability at the date of transition. H determines a carrying amount of 80, which is the amount of the lease liability that would have been recognised in M's own IFRS financial statements if the lease had been classified as a finance lease at its inception.

6.1.1000   *Determine whether any recognised assets or liabilities are derecognised*

6.1.1000.10   Assets and liabilities recognised in an unrestated business combination under previous GAAP are eliminated from the opening IFRS statement of financial position if they do not qualify for recognition under IFRS. [*IFRS 1.C4(c), IG22.Ex3–Ex4*]

EXAMPLE 27C – UNRESTATED BUSINESS COMBINATIONS – RECOGNISED LIABILITIES

6.1.1000.20   Company R is a first-time adopter in 2018. R acquired Subsidiary Y in 2016 in a transaction that would be a business combination under IFRS. R elects not to restate the acquisition of Y. As part of the accounting for the business combination under previous GAAP, R recognised a provision related to the future restructuring of Y's activities and the amount is still outstanding as at 1 January 2017. This restructuring liability does not qualify for recognition under IFRS at the date of acquisition in the financial statements of Y (see 3.12.230). Therefore, the liability is eliminated from R's opening IFRS statement of financial position.

6.1.1010   *Remeasure assets and liabilities after the business combination if appropriate*

6.1.1010.10   The carrying amount under previous GAAP of assets acquired and liabilities assumed in an unrestated business combination immediately after the business combination becomes their deemed cost at that date, even if a different amount would have been assigned under IFRS. [*IFRS 1.C4(e)*]

6.1.1010.20   The only exception to this principle is in the case of assets or liabilities that were assigned a deemed cost of zero and which are recognised because they would be recognised in the acquiree's statement of financial position if it were prepared in accordance with IFRS. [*IFRS 1.C4(f)*]

6.1.1010.30 In our view, the phrase 'immediately after the business combination' includes adjustments made to the carrying amounts of the assets and liabilities acquired during the measurement period under previous GAAP – i.e. for the period during which the business combination accounting is kept open for adjustments under previous GAAP. This would be the case even if the measurement period under previous GAAP ends after the date of transition.

EXAMPLE 27D – UNRESTATED BUSINESS COMBINATIONS – SUBSEQUENT REMEASUREMENT

6.1.1010.40 Company X is a first-time adopter in 2018. X acquired Subsidiary B in 2015 in a transaction that would be a business combination under IFRS. X elects not to restate the acquisition of B. Under previous GAAP, X was allowed, until the following reporting date – i.e. 31 December 2016 – to finalise the amounts assigned provisionally to the assets and liabilities acquired.

6.1.1010.50 During 2016, an appraisal report on the acquisition was completed and it indicated that certain of the equipment acquired had a fair value 20 higher than the amount assigned provisionally by X. Under previous GAAP, X adjusted the business combination accounting by increasing the carrying amount of equipment, with a corresponding adjustment to goodwill.

6.1.1010.60 We believe that the carrying amounts of equipment and goodwill immediately after the business combination are the adjusted amounts following receipt of the appraisal report.

6.1.1010.70 Having established deemed cost at the date of acquisition, the measurement requirements of IFRS are applied after that date. Therefore, property, plant and equipment is depreciated using a method and rate that is appropriate under IFRS and component accounting is applied (see 6.1.340). Similarly, investment property that the first-time adopter elects to measure using the fair value model is recognised at fair value in the opening IFRS statement of financial position (see 6.1.460). [*IFRS 1.C4(d)–(e), IG22.Ex2*]

6.1.1010.80 If the asset or liability qualifies for the fair value or revaluation as deemed cost exemption, then in our view this exemption is also available at the date of transition (see 6.1.290, 390 and 460).

6.1.1020 *Adjust measurement of goodwill if appropriate*

6.1.1020.10 The balance of goodwill at the date of transition, arising from an unrestated business combination, is adjusted only in respect of the following:

- to recognise separately certain intangible assets that were subsumed within goodwill under previous GAAP, including any consequential effect on deferred tax and NCI (see 6.1.920 and 1140);
- to subsume within goodwill certain intangible assets that were recognised separately under previous GAAP, including any consequential effect on deferred tax and NCI (see 6.1.920 and 1140);
- to correct any errors discovered on transition to IFRS; and
- to recognise any impairment loss on goodwill at the date of transition (see 6.1.530). [*IFRS 1.14, C4(b), C4(c)(i), C4(f), C4(g)*]

6.1.1020.20   No other adjustments to the balance of goodwill at the date of transition are made. This is the case even if goodwill was accounted for under previous GAAP, between the date of the business combination and the date of transition, using a method that did not comply with IFRS. For example, under previous GAAP goodwill may have been amortised, which is prohibited under IFRS. [*IFRS 1.C4(h), IG22.Ex2*]

6.1.1020.30   The above discussion assumes that goodwill was recognised as an asset under previous GAAP. If, for example, goodwill was written off against equity on the date of the business combination, then no adjustments are made that would create a goodwill balance at the date of transition. Instead, all adjustments are made against retained earnings. Additionally, in this example the goodwill cannot be reclassified to profit or loss as part of the gain or loss on disposal of the subsidiary. [*IFRS 1.C4(c)(i)–(ii), IG22.Ex5*]

6.1.1020.40   If a subsidiary was accounted for under the equity method under previous GAAP, then the balance of goodwill would have been embedded in the carrying amount of the investee. That amount becomes the carrying amount of goodwill for the purpose of applying IFRS 1 – i.e. the amount previously embedded in the carrying amount of the investee is presented separately when the subsidiary is consolidated under IFRS.

6.1.1020.50   Goodwill acquired in an unrestated business combination is tested for impairment at the date of transition in accordance with IFRS, with any resulting impairment loss recognised directly in retained earnings. This mandatory impairment testing is required regardless of whether there is any indication that the goodwill may be impaired. [*IFRS 1.C4(g)(ii)*]

6.1.1030   *Gain on bargain purchase*

6.1.1030.10   If a gain on a bargain purchase arises in a business combination under IFRS, then the acquirer reassesses the procedures on which its acquisition accounting is based and whether amounts included in the acquisition accounting have been appropriately determined. Any amount remaining after this reassessment is recognised immediately in profit or loss at the date of acquisition (see 2.6.1010). Consistent with IFRS, the balance of any gain on a bargain purchase that is still recognised in the first-time adopter's statement of financial position at the date of transition is eliminated against retained earnings. [*IFRS 3.34–36*]

6.1.1030.20   Under previous GAAP, a gain on a bargain purchase arising in a business combination may have been used to reduce the carrying amount of some or all of the assets acquired. In our view, the carrying amounts of any such assets should not be adjusted at the date of transition. This is because the carrying amount under previous GAAP of assets acquired and liabilities assumed in an unrestated business combination immediately after the business combination becomes their deemed cost at that date (see 6.1.1010.10). [*IFRS 1.C4(e)*]

6.1.1040   *Contingent consideration not recognised under previous GAAP*

6.1.1040.10   IFRS does not specifically address the treatment in the opening IFRS statement of financial position of contingent consideration that was not recognised under previous GAAP in an unrestated business combination and which remains outstanding at the date of transition. For a discussion of contingent consideration, see 2.6.1120.

6.1.1040.20   In our view, contingent consideration that was not recognised in an unrestated business combination and is determined to be non-equity-classified at the date of transition in accordance with IFRS should be recognised in the opening IFRS statement of financial position with a corresponding adjustment to retained earnings. The measurement of the non-equity-classified contingent consideration, both at the date of transition and subsequently, follows the guidance in IFRS 3. Any changes in the measurement of the non-equity-classified contingent consideration after the date of transition are recognised in profit or loss.

6.1.1040.30   If non-equity-classified contingent consideration was recognised under previous GAAP and meets the recognition criteria under IFRS at the date of transition, but was measured differently, then in our view the transition adjustment to reflect the measurement difference at the date of transition should be recorded against opening retained earnings.

6.1.1040.40   IFRS prohibits the remeasurement of equity-classified contingent consideration that arises in a business combination after the date of acquisition. Therefore if, in an unrestated business combination, equity-classified contingent consideration was not recognised, then it is unclear what, if any, adjustment is made at the date of transition.

6.1.1040.50   In our view, an entity should choose one of the following accounting approaches, to be applied consistently, in respect of equity-classified contingent consideration at the date of transition, if the recognition criteria under IFRS have been met at that date.
- *Approach 1:* The equity-classified contingent consideration is not recognised at the date of transition in the opening IFRS statement of financial position. This is because IFRS does not permit subsequent remeasurement of such equity instruments and IFRS 1 does not include a specific requirement to adjust for such instruments in an unrestated business combination at the date of transition.
- *Approach 2:* The equity-classified contingent consideration is measured in accordance with IFRS at the date of transition in the opening IFRS statement of financial position. This is because non-recognition of such instruments would go against the general principle of recognising assets and liabilities that qualify for recognition in the opening IFRS statement of financial position. Even though the general principle relates to assets and liabilities, we believe that it would also be appropriate to extend this principle to equity-classified contingent consideration in such situations. Under this approach, the corresponding adjustment on the date of transition would be recognised against opening retained earnings and the equity-classified contingent consideration would not be remeasured subsequently.

6.1.1050   *Subsidiary not consolidated under previous GAAP*

6.1.1050.10   Depending on the requirements of previous GAAP, a subsidiary might be consolidated for the first time at the date of transition. This might occur, for example, because previous GAAP did not require the preparation of consolidated financial statements, or because of a specific exclusion from the scope of consolidation.

6.1.1050.20   When a subsidiary is being consolidated for the first time, IFRS 1 includes a mandatory formula for the calculation of goodwill. For a discussion of the requirements related to previously unconsolidated subsidiaries, and the implications thereof, see 6.1.1100.

6.1.1060   *Accounting for restated business combinations*

6.1.1060.10   IFRS 1 permits a first-time adopter to restate past business combinations retrospectively in accordance with IFRS (see 6.1.950). However, retrospective restatement may be a very difficult and onerous exercise and may prove impracticable in certain circumstances. This is primarily because of the requirement that the information available to restate the past business combination be available at the time of the acquisition; the use of hindsight is prohibited. This may cause a practical difficulty for a first-time adopter, because it may not have been aware of all of the information to be collected at the date of acquisition in order to record the business combination on a basis consistent with IFRS.

6.1.1060.20   Some of the general issues that may be encountered are:
- calculating the consideration transferred in the business combination in accordance with IFRS and assessing whether any contingent consideration should be recognised without the use of hindsight;
- assessing whether to recognise contingent liabilities at the date of acquisition, again without the use of hindsight; and
- measuring the fair value of assets acquired and liabilities assumed at the date of acquisition on a basis consistent with IFRS.

6.1.1070   *Testing goodwill for impairment in a restated business combination*

6.1.1070.10   There is no specific requirement in IFRS that goodwill acquired in a restated business combination be tested for impairment at the date of transition. However, IFRS provides some guidance that suggests that IAS 36 is applied at the date of transition in determining whether any impairment loss exists at that date. Therefore, we prefer that a first-time adopter tests all goodwill for impairment at the date of transition even if there is no indication that an impairment exists at the date of transition. This is particularly important when the impairment requirements of previous GAAP differ significantly from the impairment requirements of IFRS. [*IFRS 1.BC39–BC40, IG39*]

6.1.1070.20   If goodwill acquired in a restated business combination is not tested for impairment at the date of transition, then it is required to be tested for impairment at some point during the first IFRS comparative period, unless there was an indication that a possible impairment existed at the date of transition (see 6.1.530).

6.1.1080   *Goodwill and fair value adjustments of foreign operations*

6.1.1080.10   IFRS requires any goodwill and fair value adjustments arising on the acquisition of a foreign operation to be treated as part of the assets and liabilities of the foreign operation and translated at the closing exchange rate at the reporting date. [*IAS 21.47*]

6.1.1080.20   A first-time adopter is not required to apply this requirement retrospectively to fair value adjustments and goodwill related to business combinations that occurred before the date of transition, regardless of whether the business combination is restated; however, it may choose to do so (see 6.1.1080.30). [*IFRS 1.C2–C3*]

6.1.1080.30   If the first-time adopter does not apply this requirement retrospectively, then it treats any goodwill and fair value adjustments as assets and liabilities of the parent. The amounts are therefore measured in the parent's functional currency as of the date of acquisition using the foreign currency translation requirements of the parent's previous GAAP. [*IFRS 1.C2, IG21A*]

6.1.1080.40   If a first-time adopter chooses to apply this requirement retrospectively, then it may apply it retrospectively to:
- all business combinations; or
- all business combinations that are being restated (see 6.1.1060). [*IFRS 1.C3*]

6.1.1090   Consolidation

6.1.1100   *Previously unconsolidated subsidiaries*

6.1.1100.10   IFRS requires the consolidation of all subsidiaries (except as noted in 2.5.10.20). However, a first-time adopter's previous GAAP may not have required consolidation of an entity that is considered a subsidiary under IFRS. This may occur because previous GAAP did not require the consolidation of:
- certain subsidiaries – e.g. because the subsidiary had dissimilar operations from the parent's, or the subsidiary was held for sale;
- subsidiaries held by venture capital or investment companies, or similar entities; or
- a subsidiary acquired and to be disposed of in the 'near future'. [*IFRS 1.IG26*]

EXAMPLE 28 – PREVIOUSLY UNCONSOLIDATED SUBSIDIARIES

> 6.1.1100.20   A subsidiary may have been classified as an investment in an associate or joint venture under previous GAAP because the definitions under previous GAAP of subsidiaries, associates and joint ventures are different from the definitions of those entities under IFRS (see chapters 2.5, 3.5 and 3.6). The exemption from the restatement of past business combinations also applies to past acquisitions of investments in associates and of interests in joint ventures. However, this exemption covers only the initial acquisition transaction. All subsidiaries are consolidated in the opening IFRS statement of financial position. [*IFRS 1.C4(j), C5*]

6.1.1110   *First-time consolidation of previously unconsolidated subsidiaries*

6.1.1110.10   When a subsidiary is being consolidated for the first time, the following steps are followed at the date of transition.
1. Measure the assets and liabilities of the subsidiary in the parent's opening IFRS consolidated statement of financial position based on the amounts that would be recognised in the subsidiary's financial statements if the subsidiary were applying IFRS.
2. Measure goodwill at the date of transition as the difference between:
   - the parent's interest in the amounts ascribed to the assets and liabilities of the subsidiary in (1) above; and
   - the cost of the investment in the subsidiary as it would be reflected in the parent's separate financial statements, if any are prepared. [*IFRS 1.C4(j), IG22.Ex6, IG27*]

6.1.1110.20   This calculation effectively increases goodwill by the amount of any post-acquisition losses and reduces goodwill by the amount of any post-acquisition profits.

6.1.1110.30   In our view, in determining the carrying amounts of the assets and liabilities of the subsidiary in (1) in 6.1.1110.10, the exceptions and exemptions in IFRS 1 apply as if the subsidiary were a first-time adopter.

EXAMPLE 29 – FIRST-TIME CONSOLIDATION OF PREVIOUSLY UNCONSOLIDATED SUBSIDIARIES

6.1.1110.40   Company L is a first-time adopter in 2018. L acquired all of the shares in Company J in 2012. J was not consolidated by L under previous GAAP because its business activities were dissimilar from those of the rest of the group. L acquired J for 100, which is the cost of the subsidiary in L's separate financial statements. The carrying amount of J's net assets is 60, which includes property, plant and equipment with a carrying amount of 35.

6.1.1110.50   In determining the carrying amount of J's assets and liabilities on an IFRS basis, L uses the fair value as deemed cost exemption (see 6.1.300) to measure property, plant and equipment at its fair value of 55. When recording its investment in J at the date of transition, L recognises various assets and liabilities at 80 (60 + 55 - 35), the cost of investment in J at 100 and goodwill as the difference of 20 (100 - 80).

6.1.1110.60   In many cases, applying the above formula for the calculation of goodwill will result in a gain on a bargain purchase at the date of transition. In that case, the difference is recognised in opening retained earnings because negative goodwill is recognised immediately in profit or loss under IFRS (see 6.1.1030). [*IFRS 3.34*]

6.1.1110.70   IFRS 1 is very specific in referring to the 'cost' of the investment in the subsidiary as the basis for the calculation of goodwill. Therefore, in our view any additional amounts included in the carrying amount of the investee in the parent's separate financial statements – e.g. fair value changes – should be eliminated against retained earnings at the date of transition. [*IFRS 1.C4(j)(ii)*]

6.1.1110.80   In our view, if a first-time adopter elected to measure its investment in subsidiary at a deemed cost at the date of transition, then this is the cost of the investment in subsidiary that should be used in the calculation referred to in (2) in 6.1.1110.10 (see 6.1.1490).

6.1.1110.90   The calculation of deemed goodwill applies to previously unconsolidated subsidiaries that were acquired in a business combination. If a subsidiary was not acquired in a business combination – i.e. it was created by the first-time adopter – then no goodwill is recognised. In such cases, if the adjusted net assets of the subsidiary are less than the cost of the investment in the parent's separate financial statements, then the resulting adjustment does not create goodwill, but is instead a debit to retained earnings. [*IFRS 1.IG27(c)*]

6.1.1120   Non-controlling interests

6.1.1130   *Business combinations restated*

6.1.1130.10   If a first-time adopter elects to restate any or all business combinations (see 6.1.950), then the balance of NCI at the date of transition related to all such restated business combinations is determined retrospectively, taking into account the impact of other elections made as part of the adoption of IFRS. In this case, IFRS 10 is applied (see 2.6.940), regardless of its application date for existing users of IFRS. [*IFRS 1.B7*]

6.1.1140   ***Business combinations unrestated***

6.1.1140.10   In respect of business combinations that are not restated on the adoption of IFRS (see 6.1.950), the balance of NCI under previous GAAP is not changed other than for adjustments made as part of the transition to IFRS. This means that the following specific requirements of IFRS in relation to NCI are applied prospectively from the date of transition:

- the attribution of total comprehensive income between NCI and the owners of the parent;
- the accounting for changes in ownership interests without the loss of control; and
- the accounting for the loss of control in a subsidiary. [*IFRS 1.B7, IG28, 10.23, B94, B96–B99*]

6.1.1140.20   If a subsidiary is being consolidated for the first time, then NCI are recognised as part of the initial consolidation adjustment.

EXAMPLE 30 – NCI OF PREVIOUSLY UNCONSOLIDATED SUBSIDIARIES

6.1.1140.30   Company X is a first-time adopter in 2018. X acquired 80% of the shares in Company Z in 2015. Z was not consolidated by X under previous GAAP because its business activities were dissimilar from those of the rest of the group. X acquired Z for 100, which is the cost of the subsidiary in X's separate financial statements. The carrying amount of Z's net assets on an IFRS basis would be 60. To consolidate Z at the date of transition, X records its investment in Z in its opening IFRS consolidated statement of financial position as follows.

	DEBIT	CREDIT
Various assets and liabilities	60	
Goodwill (100 - (60 x 80%))	52	
Non-controlling interests		12
Cost of investment in Z		100
To consolidate Z at date of transition		

6.1.1150   ***Agreements to acquire NCI***

6.1.1150.10   Agreements may be entered into as part of a business combination whereby a parent commits to acquire the shares held by NCI in a subsidiary, or whereby NCI in a subsidiary hold a put option that would require the parent to purchase its interests in the future. This is an area that requires careful analysis on transition to IFRS. For further discussion of the accounting treatment for such agreements, see 2.5.450 and 680.

6.1.1160   **Foreign currency translation**

6.1.1170   ***Optional exemption for cumulative foreign exchange differences***

6.1.1170.10   IFRS requires cumulative foreign exchange differences arising on the translation of a foreign operation to be recognised as a separate component of equity (see 2.7.230). A first-time adopter may either:

- apply IAS 21 retrospectively to determine the cumulative foreign exchange differences for each foreign operation that is recognised as a separate component of equity at the date of transition; or
- deem the cumulative foreign exchange differences to be zero at the date of transition, and reclassify any amounts recognised in accordance with previous GAAP at that date to retained earnings. [*IFRS 1.D13(a), BC53–BC55*]

6.1.1170.20   The optional exemption is not relevant for the translation of foreign currency transactions because such exchange differences are generally recognised in profit or loss.

6.1.1170.30   The optional exemption is applied consistently to all foreign operations, including interests in joint ventures and investments in associates that are foreign operations. The gain or loss on the subsequent disposal of any foreign operation *excludes* translation differences that arose before the date of transition if a first-time adopter elects to reset the cumulative foreign exchange differences to zero at the date of transition. [*IFRS 1.D13(b)*]

6.1.1170.40   Cumulative foreign exchange differences also arise when a first-time adopter presents its financial statements in a presentation currency that is different from its functional currency. This is because the translation procedures are the same as those for translating foreign operations. In our view, the optional exemption to deem cumulative foreign exchange differences to be zero also applies to cumulative foreign exchange differences that arise on translating financial statements from a first-time adopter's functional currency to a different presentation currency (see 2.7.290), even though such exchange differences do not relate to foreign operations and will not be reclassified to profit or loss. [*IAS 21.39*]

6.1.1180   *Determination of functional currency*

6.1.1180.10   IAS 21 includes specific requirements for the selection of an appropriate functional currency under IFRS (see 2.7.70). These requirements may differ from previous GAAP – e.g. when previous GAAP assumes a first-time adopter's functional currency to be that of the country in which the first-time adopter is domiciled.

6.1.1180.20   There is no optional exemption in IFRS 1 that allows a first-time adopter to determine its functional currency at the date of transition and to simply translate its opening IFRS statement of financial position into the functional currency using the spot rate at the date of transition. Therefore, a first-time adopter is required to consider the appropriate functional currency since inception because otherwise the carrying amount of non-monetary assets may be misstated in the opening IFRS statement of financial position. This may be another reason for a first-time adopter to consider using the deemed cost exemption for property, plant and equipment, intangible assets and investment property (see 6.1.290, 390 and 460, respectively). If the exemption is elected, then the deemed cost is translated into the first-time adopter's functional currency at the date of its determination. The following example illustrates the difficulty of determining the appropriate functional currency retrospectively.

EXAMPLE 31 – CHANGE IN FUNCTIONAL CURRENCY

6.1.1180.30   Under previous GAAP, Company X's functional currency was the euro. However, under IFRS it is determined that X's functional currency would always have been US dollars. Therefore, X reconstructs the carrying amount of property, plant and equipment on an IFRS basis at the date of transition, which is 1 January 2017, as follows.

Transaction	EUR	Rate	USD
Additions[(1)]	1,000	1.50	1,500
Depreciation[(2)]	(100)	1.45	(145)
Additions[(1)]	270	1.78	481
Depreciation[(2)]	(130)	1.30	(169)
Carrying amount	1,040		1,667

Notes
1. The historical exchange rate at the date of acquisition.
2. The average exchange rate for each year.

6.1.1180.40   If US dollars had been used as X's functional currency since the acquisition of property, plant and equipment, then its carrying amount at the date of transition would have been USD 1,667.

6.1.1180.50   Assuming that the spot rate as at 1 January 2017 is 1.35, a different result is obtained if X simply takes the carrying amount of the property, plant and equipment at the date of transition in euro and translates it to US dollars; in that case, the carrying amount would be USD 1,404, which would be inappropriate because, under IFRS, the carrying amount of non-monetary assets is not restated at the latest exchange rate at each reporting date.

6.1.1180.60   However, if X applies the 'fair value as deemed cost' exemption at the date of transition, then it would be appropriate to translate the fair value at that date using the 1.35 spot rate. If the deemed cost exemption is applied before the date of transition, then the roll-forward calculation is still required for the transactions occurring after the date on which the exemption is applied.

6.1.1190   *Hyperinflationary economies*

6.1.1190.10   IFRS 1 provides an optional exemption for a first-time adopter that was previously subject to severe hyperinflation and whose date of transition is on or after the functional currency normalisation date. This exemption allows a first-time adopter to measure assets and liabilities, held before the functional currency normalisation date, at fair value on the date of transition and use that fair value as the deemed cost of those assets and liabilities in the opening IFRS statement of financial position. For a discussion of the accounting for hyperinflation, see chapter 2.10. [*IFRS 1.D26, D29*]

6.1.1190.20   The functional currency is subject to severe hyperinflation if:
- a reliable general price index is not available to all entities with transactions and balances in the currency; and
- exchangeability between the currency and a relatively stable foreign currency does not exist. [*IFRS 1.D27*]

6.1.1190.30   The functional currency normalisation date is the date on which the entity's functional currency no longer has either, or both, of the characteristics in 6.1.1190.20, or on which there is a change in the entity's functional currency to a currency that is not subject to severe hyperinflation. [*IFRS 1.D28*]

6.1.1190.40   If the functional currency normalisation date falls within a 12-month comparative period, then the comparative period may be less than 12 months if the entity provides a complete set of financial statements for that shorter period. [*IFRS 1.D30, BC63J*]

6.1.1200   *Foreign currency transactions and advance consideration*

6.1.1200.10   Under IFRIC 22, the date of the transaction – which is used to determine the spot exchange rate for translating the related item on initial recognition – is the date of the initial recognition of the non-monetary asset or liability arising from the payment or receipt of the advance consideration. A first-time adopter need not to apply IFRIC 22 to items initially recognised before the date of transition. [*IFRS 1.D36*]

6.1.1210   **Associates and joint ventures**

6.1.1210.10   In the absence of any exemptions, a first-time adopter would be required to apply equity accounting, on an IFRS basis, to investments in associates and joint ventures from their date of acquisition. The difficulties associated with this approach are the same as those that apply to business combinations.

6.1.1210.20   To avoid such a process, the following requirements and optional exemptions in respect of investments in subsidiaries also apply to investments in associates and joint ventures.
- The optional exemption for business combinations also applies to acquisitions of investments in associates, interests in joint ventures and interests in joint operations in which the activity of the joint operation constitutes a business before the date of transition (see 6.1.950). If a first-time adopter chooses to restate business combinations that occurred after a particular date before the date of transition, then that cut-off date applies equally to associates, joint ventures and interests in joint operations in which the activity of the joint operation constitutes a business.
- Ⓢ The requirements that apply when a first-time adopter transitions to IFRS either before or after its parent (investor) also apply to associates and joint ventures (see 6.1.1220).
- The optional exemption for investments in subsidiaries in the separate financial statements of a parent also applies to associates and joint ventures (see 6.1.1490). [*IFRS 1.C5, D14–D17*]

6.1.1210.30   Additionally, the exemptions that apply to the assets and liabilities of a first-time adopter or its subsidiaries also apply to the assets and liabilities of an associate or joint venture for the purpose of applying the equity method of accounting. For example, the carrying amount of the property, plant and equipment of an associate at the date of transition can be based on its fair value (see 6.1.290).

6.1.1210.40   Goodwill recognised under previous GAAP in respect of an unrestated business combination is required to be tested for impairment at the date of transition (see 6.1.530). For acquisitions of associates or joint ventures that occurred before the date of transition and for which the business combination exemption is applied, goodwill recognised under previous GAAP is included in the carrying amount of the investment in the associate or joint venture and is not presented separately from the investment (see 3.5.270). [*IFRS 1.C4(g)(ii)*]

6.1.1210.50   For impairment testing of goodwill at the date of transition in respect of an unrestated acquisition of an associate or joint venture, see 6.1.530.

6.1.1210.60   A first-time adopter is permitted to use the transitional requirements in IFRS 11 when adopting IFRS. If the first-time adopter is changing from proportionate consolidation to the equity method, then it is always required to test the opening balance of the investment for impairment – i.e. regardless of whether there is an indication of impairment. Any impairment losses are recognised as an adjustment to retained earnings at the date of transition. [*IFRS 1.D31*]

6.1.1220   Assets and liabilities of subsidiaries, associates and joint ventures

6.1.1220.10   For a discussion of determining when an entity has adopted IFRS for the first time, see 6.1.30. It is possible that individual entities in a group – i.e. a parent and its subsidiaries – or their associates and joint ventures will adopt IFRS at different dates – i.e. each may have a different date of transition. There are special requirements and exemptions when this is the case. [*IFRS 1.D16–D17*]

6.1.1220.20   The exemptions and related requirements apply to subsidiaries, associates and joint ventures.

6.1.1230   *Adoption in parent's separate and consolidated financial statements*

6.1.1230.10   If a parent adopts IFRS in its separate financial statements earlier or later than in its Ⓢ consolidated financial statements, then it measures its assets and liabilities at the same amounts in both sets of financial statements, except for consolidation adjustments. [*IFRS 1.D17*]

6.1.1230.20   In our view, consolidation adjustments should include accounting policy alignments, as explained in 6.1.1250 and 1320 in relation to a parent adopting IFRS later or earlier than a subsidiary.

6.1.1240   *Parent/investor becomes first-time adopter later than subsidiary, associate or joint venture*

6.1.1240.10   The discussion that follows refers to a parent and its subsidiary. However, the requirements apply equally to an investor and its associate or joint venture, except as noted in 6.1.1240.50. [*IFRS 1.D17*]

6.1.1240.20   There are no optional exemptions available to a parent that adopts IFRS in its consolidated financial statements later than a subsidiary with respect to the measurement of assets and liabilities of the subsidiary that will be included in the parent's first IFRS consolidated financial statements. Except as noted in 6.1.1240.50, in the consolidated financial statements of the parent, the assets and liabilities of the subsidiary are measured at the same carrying amounts as in the financial statements of the subsidiary, after adjusting for the effects of consolidation procedures and business combination accounting. [*IFRS 1.D17*]

6.1.1240.30   In our view, the requirement for the parent to use amounts included in the financial statements of the subsidiary applies regardless of the subsidiary's basis of conversion to IFRS – e.g. the subsidiary might have applied SIC-8, which preceded IFRS 1.

6.1.1240.40   In general, the exceptions and exemptions in IFRS 1 are not applicable to the parent in respect of the measurement of the assets and liabilities of the subsidiary. However, there are circumstances in which the parent is not required to measure the assets and liabilities of the subsidiary in this manner:

- the parent elects accounting policies in its IFRS consolidated financial statements that are different from those used by the subsidiary in its IFRS financial statements (see 6.1.1250); and/or
- in the business combination accounting in which the subsidiary was acquired (see 6.1.1260).

6.1.1240.50   In addition, a parent that is not an investment entity does not apply the requirement for the parent to use amounts included in the financial statements of the subsidiary when the subsidiary is an investment entity (see 5.6.10). This is because the fair value accounting applied by an investment entity is not carried through to the consolidated financial statements of a parent that is not itself an investment entity – i.e. the parent is required to consolidate all subsidiaries (see 5.6.210). [IFRS 1.D17]

6.1.1250   *Consolidation adjustments*

6.1.1250.10   The consolidation adjustments required before incorporating the subsidiary's assets and liabilities into the parent's opening IFRS statement of financial position include the elimination of intra-group balances, transactions and accounting policy alignments.

6.1.1250.20   In our view, if consolidation adjustments include the alignment of accounting policies, then the optional exemptions in Appendix D are available to the parent in respect of the assets and liabilities of the subsidiary. This is because we believe that the availability of the optional exemptions overrides the requirement regarding subsidiaries when dealing with the alignment of accounting policies; otherwise, there would be no relief provided by IFRS 1.

6.1.1260   *Business combination accounting*

6.1.1260.10   When recognising the subsidiary's assets and liabilities in the parent's opening IFRS statement of financial position, the parent considers the effects of the business combination in which it acquired the assets, and assumed the liabilities, of the subsidiary. [IFRS 1.D17]

6.1.1260.20   The mandatory requirements when a parent adopts IFRS later than its subsidiary do not override the requirements in IFRS 1 with respect to past business combinations (see 6.1.950). Therefore, a parent applies Appendix C of IFRS 1 to account for the assets acquired and liabilities assumed in the business combination in which it acquired the subsidiary. [IFRS 1.D17, IG30(a)]

6.1.1260.30   However, for new assets acquired and liabilities assumed by the subsidiary after the business combination that are still held by the subsidiary at the parent's date of transition, the parent generally uses the carrying amounts in the IFRS financial statements of the subsidiary. [IFRS 1.IG30(a)]

6.1.1260.40   This means that it will be necessary for the parent to separate the assets and liabilities of the subsidiary at its date of transition into two categories – assets acquired and liabilities assumed:

- in the business combination in which the subsidiary was acquired; and
- by the subsidiary after the business combination.

6.1.1270   *Interaction with deemed cost exemption*

6.1.1270.10   A first-time adopter is able to elect to recognise certain assets at deemed cost at the date of transition (see 6.1.290, for example). However, in our view in general a parent may not apply the deemed cost exemption to establish the carrying amount of an asset of a subsidiary if the subsidiary adopted IFRS before the group. This is because the parent is required to measure the assets and liabilities of the subsidiary at the same carrying amounts as in the financial statements of the subsidiary.

6.1.1270.20   However, if a parent adopts a policy of revaluing property, plant and equipment, and the subsidiary has a policy of cost, then in our view this overrides the requirement regarding subsidiaries because it constitutes an accounting policy alignment (see 6.1.1250.10).

6.1.1270.30   Alternatively, if the subsidiary adopts a policy of revaluing property, plant and equipment, and the parent has a policy of cost, then in our view the deemed cost exemption is available to the parent with respect to the property, plant and equipment of the IFRS reporting subsidiary (see 6.1.1250.20).

6.1.1280   *Interaction with optional exemption for cumulative foreign exchange differences*

6.1.1280.10   A first-time adopter is able to deem cumulative translation differences to be zero at the date of transition and reclassify any such amounts determined in accordance with previous GAAP at that date to retained earnings. The optional exemption, when elected, is applied consistently to all foreign operations (see 6.1.1170).

6.1.1280.20   In our view, when a parent is a first-time adopter later than its subsidiary, the parent can elect to deem the cumulative foreign exchange differences to be zero and reclassify any amounts recognised in accordance with previous GAAP at that date as retained earnings, even if the subsidiary did not make this election in respect of its own IFRS financial statements. This is because the requirement to measure all assets and liabilities of the subsidiary at the same carrying amount as in the financial statements of the subsidiary is not affected by the cumulative translation adjustment exemption, which is a component of equity (see 6.1.1170).

EXAMPLE 32 – CUMULATIVE FOREIGN EXCHANGE DIFFERENCES OF SUBSIDIARIES

6.1.1280.30   Company P has three subsidiaries, Companies X, Y and Z, which are foreign operations from the perspective of P. The investment in Z is held by Y. Y was a first-time adopter in 2015 and elected to recognise the cumulative foreign exchange differences related to Z under previous GAAP in opening retained earnings.

6.1.1280.40   P elects to reset the cumulative foreign exchange differences related to X, Y and Z to zero at the date of transition. This includes the cumulative exchange differences for X and Y as determined under previous GAAP, as well as those for Z that have arisen between Y's date of transition of 1 January 2014 and P's date of transition of 1 January 2017, as determined under IFRS.

6.1.1290   *Subsidiary, associate or joint venture becomes first-time adopter later than parent/investor**

6.1.1290.10   The discussion that follows refers to a subsidiary and its parent. However, the requirements apply equally to an associate or joint venture and its investor. [*IFRS 1.D16*]

6.1.1290.20   A subsidiary may adopt IFRS later than its parent and may also have been reporting previously to the parent on an IFRS basis for group reporting purposes without presenting a full set of IFRS financial statements. Without any relief, the subsidiary is required to keep two sets of parallel accounting records: one set for group reporting purposes based on the parent's date of transition; and one set for the subsidiary's own financial statements based on its own date of transition.

6.1.1290.30   If a subsidiary adopts IFRS later than its parent, then the subsidiary may measure its assets and liabilities at either:
- the amounts included in the consolidated financial statements of the parent, based on the parent's date of transition, excluding the effects of consolidation procedures and the business combination in which the parent acquired the subsidiary; or
- the carrying amounts required by IFRS 1 based on the subsidiary's own date of transition. [*IFRS 1.D16, BC63*]

6.1.1290.40   The alternative of using the amounts included in the consolidated financial statements of the parent is not available to a subsidiary of an investment entity. This is because the parent will be accounting for the subsidiary at fair value through profit or loss. However, the subsidiary itself will either prepare consolidated financial statements (if it is not an investment entity) or measure its own investments at fair value through profit or loss at the date of transition (if it is an investment entity) following the mandatory exception discussed in 6.1.1500. [*IFRS 1.D16(a)*]

6.1.1290.50   The optional election to measure the assets and liabilities of the subsidiary based on the parent's date of transition provides relief in that it reduces, but does not eliminate, differences between the subsidiary's IFRS financial statements and the group reporting package. For example, because a reporting package does not constitute a full set of financial statements, the parent may have recorded certain material IFRS adjustments centrally – e.g. pension cost adjustments. Therefore, additional IFRS adjustments still may be required even if the subsidiary elects to measure its assets and liabilities based on the parent's date of transition. [*IFRS 1.BC61*]

6.1.1290.60   In addition, the group materiality threshold is likely to be higher for group reporting than for the subsidiary's own financial statements. If the materiality threshold for group reporting is well in excess of that in the financial statements of the subsidiary, then it may be particularly onerous for the subsidiary to determine all of the adjustments required when preparing its opening IFRS statement of financial position that were not recognised in its IFRS reporting package. The required adjustments would also need to be determined relative to the parent's date of transition, and then rolled forward from the parent's date of transition to the subsidiary's date of transition. In these cases, the subsidiary may effectively be precluded from electing the optional exemption altogether on practical grounds. [*IFRS 1.IG31*]

6.1.1290.70   The IFRS Interpretations Committee discussed whether a subsidiary that adopts IFRS later than its parent can recognise the cumulative translation differences at the amounts included in the consolidated financial statements of the parent, based on the parent's date of transition. The Committee noted that the relief in paragraph 16(a) of IFRS 1 cannot be applied to cumulative translation differences because cumulative foreign exchange differences arising on the translation of a foreign operation are recognised as a separate component of equity and are neither assets nor liabilities. The Committee observed that IFRS 1 does not allow applying an exemption by analogy. As such, the subsidiary that becomes a first-time adopter applies the existing exemption for cumulative foreign exchange differences in 6.1.1170.10. [*IU 09-17*]

6.1.1300 *Subsidiary elects to use IFRS 1 based on its own date of transition*

6.1.1300.10 If the subsidiary chooses to measure its assets and liabilities in accordance with IFRS 1 based on its own date of transition, then it applies the requirements of IFRS 1 without regard to the parent. In such cases, it is likely that the subsidiary will need to maintain two sets of parallel accounting records: one set for group reporting purposes based on the parent's date of transition and one set for the subsidiary's own financial statements based on its own date of transition. However, this option provides the subsidiary with additional flexibility to select optional exemptions that otherwise would not be available. [*IFRS 1.D16(b)*]

6.1.1310 *Subsidiary elects to use IFRS 1 based on parent's date of transition*

6.1.1310.10 In our view, the optional exemption for the subsidiary to use amounts included in the consolidated financial statements of the parent is available regardless of the parent's basis of conversion to IFRS – e.g. the parent might have applied SIC-8, which preceded IFRS 1.

6.1.1310.20 The requirement regarding subsidiaries means that a subsidiary, at its date of transition, is required to measure its assets and liabilities using the same carrying amounts as in the IFRS consolidated financial statements of the parent, after adjusting for the effects of consolidation procedures and the business combination in which the subsidiary was acquired. [*IFRS 1.D16(a)*]

6.1.1310.30 If the subsidiary elects the optional exemption, then the other exceptions and exemptions in IFRS 1 are generally not applicable to the subsidiary. However, there are circumstances in which the subsidiary is not required to measure its assets and liabilities in this manner:
- the subsidiary elects accounting policies in its IFRS financial statements that are different from those used by the parent in its IFRS consolidated financial statements (see 6.1.1320); and/or
- the assets and liabilities of the subsidiary were part of the net assets of the subsidiary at the time of the business combination in which the subsidiary was acquired by the parent (see 6.1.1340).

6.1.1320 *Consolidation procedures*

6.1.1320.10 The consolidation adjustments required before incorporating the carrying amount of the subsidiary's assets and liabilities in the parent's consolidated financial statements into the subsidiary's opening IFRS statement of financial position include the elimination of intra-group balances, transactions and accounting policy alignments (see 6.1.1230.20).

6.1.1320.20 In our view, if consolidation adjustments include the alignment of accounting policies, then the optional exemptions are available to the subsidiary in respect of its assets and liabilities. This is because we believe that the availability of the optional exemptions overrides the requirement regarding the parent when dealing with the alignment of accounting policies; otherwise there would be no relief provided by IFRS 1.

6.1.1330 *Business combination accounting*

6.1.1330.10 The requirements of IFRS 1 in respect of a subsidiary transitioning to IFRS later than its parent are complex, particularly for groups with numerous subsidiaries and in different jurisdictions.

6.1.1330.20   To apply the requirements of IFRS 1, it is necessary to understand the timing of the business combination in which the parent acquires the subsidiary and the subsidiary's acquisition of any subsidiaries in relation to the parent's date of transition and its own date of transition. [*IFRS 1.D16(a), IG30(a)*]

6.1.1340   *Business combination in which parent acquires subsidiary*

6.1.1340.10   When recognising the assets and liabilities in the subsidiary's opening IFRS statement of financial position, the subsidiary is required to eliminate the effects of the business combination in which it was acquired by the parent. [*IFRS 1.D16(a)*]

6.1.1340.20   Adjusting for the effect of the business combination in which the parent acquired the subsidiary effectively means that the requirements of paragraph D16(a) do not apply to assets acquired and liabilities assumed before the date on which the parent acquired the subsidiary. Accordingly, the mandatory exceptions and optional exemptions apply to such assets and liabilities (see 6.1.230–240). [*IFRS 1.IG30(a)*]

6.1.1350   *Business combinations after parent acquires subsidiary*

6.1.1350.10   After its acquisition by the parent but before its date of transition, a subsidiary that is transitioning to IFRS may have completed its own acquisitions of subsidiaries. In our view, when the subsidiary elects to use the carrying amounts in the financial statements of the parent, the requirements of Appendix C of IFRS 1 do not override the requirements for the subsidiary to measure its assets and liabilities at the carrying amounts in the parent's consolidated financial statements. [*IFRS 1.IG30(a)*]

6.1.1350.20   However, if the subsidiary's acquisition of its own subsidiaries during this period is before the parent's transition to IFRS, then the accounting for the acquisition in the subsidiary's IFRS consolidated financial statements will reflect the choices that the parent made in respect of accounting for the business combination in preparing its opening IFRS consolidated statement of financial position.

EXAMPLE 33 – BUSINESS COMBINATIONS AFTER PARENT ACQUIRES SUBSIDIARY

6.1.1350.30   Company S was acquired by Parent P on 1 January 2016 and Company T was acquired by S on 1 January 2017. Costs of 150 were incurred in respect of the restructuring of T in 2017 and goodwill of 650 was recognised. P elected not to restate the business combination in which S was acquired on its adoption of IFRS. Because the acquisition of T occurred before P's date of transition of 1 January 2018, it was accounted for in P's consolidated financial statements under previous GAAP in the same manner as it was accounted for in the financial statements of S. In addition, because P elected not to restate the acquisition in which S was acquired, the carrying amounts assigned to the assets and liabilities under previous GAAP became their deemed cost immediately after the date of acquisition.

6.1.1350.40   Therefore, P did not recognise an adjustment to goodwill in respect of the acquisition of T in its opening IFRS statement of financial position, even though goodwill under previous GAAP of 650 includes an amount of 150 that would not have been recognised in acquisition accounting under IFRS (see 6.1.1020). Because S is required to measure its assets and liabilities at the carrying amounts in the

> consolidated financial statements of P, the business combination exemption is not relevant to S, and S measures the goodwill of T in its opening IFRS statement of financial position at 650.

6.1.1350.50   If the subsidiary's acquisition of its own subsidiaries during this period is after the parent's transition to IFRS, then the accounting for the acquisition in the subsidiary's IFRS consolidated financial statements is in accordance with IFRS.

6.1.1360   Revenue

6.1.1360.10   A first-time adopter may use the optional exemption allowing it not to restate contracts with customers in the scope of IFRS 15 that were completed before the earliest period presented. For this purpose, a 'completed' contract is one for which the first-time adopter has transferred all of the goods or services identified in accordance with previous GAAP. [*IFRS 1.D35*]

6.1.1360.20   A first-time adopter is also permitted to use one or more of the following practical expedients in accordance with the transition provisions of IFRS 15:
- for contracts completed before the beginning of the first IFRS reporting period, a first-time adopter:
  - is not required to restate contracts that began and ended in the same annual reporting period; and
  - may use the transaction price at the date on which the contract was completed, rather than estimating variable consideration amounts in each comparative reporting period;
- for contracts that were modified before the beginning of the earliest period presented, a first-time adopter need not retrospectively restate the contract for those contract modifications in accordance with the requirements in 4.2.290.30. Instead, a first-time adopter may reflect the aggregate effect of all of the modifications that occur before the beginning of the earliest period presented in:
  - identifying the satisfied and unsatisfied performance obligations;
  - determining the transaction price; and
  - allocating the transaction price to the satisfied and unsatisfied performance obligations; and
- for all reporting periods presented before the beginning of the first IFRS annual reporting period, a first-time adopter is not required to disclose the amount of the transaction price allocated to any remaining performance obligations or an explanation of when it expects to recognise the amount as revenue. [*IFRS 1.D34, 15.C5*]

6.1.1360.30   If a first-time adopter elects to apply one or more of the practical expedients in 6.1.1360.20, then it needs to do so consistently for all contracts in all reporting periods presented. In addition, it discloses the expedients that have been used and a qualitative assessment of the estimated effect of applying each expedient, to the extent reasonably possible. [*IFRS 1.D34, 15.C6*]

EXAMPLE 34 – REVENUE FROM CONTRACTS WITH CUSTOMERS – APPLYING IFRS 15 ON ADOPTION OF IFRS

6.1.1360.40   Company M applies IFRS for the first time in its annual financial statements for the year ended 31 December 2018. M presents one year of comparative information in its financial statements, and therefore its date of transition to IFRS is 1 January 2017.

6.1.1360.50 M manufactures and sells cars to dealers with a promise to provide one free maintenance service to the end purchaser of a car. Under previous GAAP, M treated the free servicing component of the arrangement as a sales incentive, recognising a provision with a corresponding expense when the vehicle was sold to the dealer. In addition, it recognised revenue at the invoice price when the car was delivered to the dealer. Under IFRS 15, M determines that the arrangement consists of two performance obligations – the sale of the car and the right to one free maintenance service. This treatment results in a different pattern of revenue recognition from previous GAAP, because a portion of the transaction price is allocated to the free service and recognised as the performance obligation is satisfied.

6.1.1360.60 If M elects to apply IFRS 15 only to contracts that are not completed under previous GAAP at the date of transition to IFRS, then it applies the revenue standard to its contracts for the sales of cars as follows.
- M makes no opening adjustments at the date of transition – i.e. 1 January 2017 – for contracts relating to cars that have already been delivered to the dealer, because a first-time adopter is not required to analyse contracts that are completed under previous GAAP before the date of transition. This is because the cars have all been delivered and the free services are not considered to be part of the revenue transaction under previous GAAP.
- If M elects to apply the practical expedient under which contracts that begin and end in the same annual reporting period are not required to be restated, then it does not restate the comparative period – i.e. 2017 – because the car sales were recognised as point-in-time sales under previous GAAP.
- If M does not elect to apply this practical expedient, then it restates sales in the comparative period – i.e. 2017 – for the effect of allocating the transaction price between the car and the free maintenance service.

6.1.1360.70 Regardless of the approach selected for the comparative period, M applies IFRS 15 to all car sales made on or after 1 January 2018.

6.1.1370 **Leases#**

6.1.1380 *Optional exemption for arrangements containing a lease*

6.1.1380.10 IFRIC 4 requires an entity to assess whether an arrangement contains a lease at its inception on the basis of all facts and circumstances at that date. Arrangements are reassessed only if certain criteria are met. Any reassessment is based on the facts and circumstances at the date of reassessment (see chapter 5.1).

6.1.1380.20 First-time adopters might face practical difficulties in applying the requirements of IFRIC 4 retrospectively. Therefore, IFRS 1 includes an optional exemption that permits first-time adopters to apply the transitional requirements in IFRIC 4. If a first-time adopter elects the optional exemption, then it assesses arrangements existing at the date of transition based on the facts and circumstances existing at that date. [*IFRS 1.D9, BC63D, IG205, IFRIC 4.17*]

6.1.1390   *Optional exemption on reassessment of lease determination*

6.1.1390.10   In some jurisdictions, a first-time adopter's previous GAAP may have had the same accounting requirements as those of IFRS, the only difference being the effective date of the standard, differences in transitional requirements and/or slight differences in wording. The IASB recognised this to be the case with respect to IFRIC 4. Without any specific relief, a first-time adopter that had an IFRIC 4-equivalent standard in its previous GAAP, and elected the optional exemption for arrangements containing a lease, would be required to reassess its lease determination at the date of transition, even though it already would have performed such an assessment under previous GAAP. [*IFRS 1.BC63DA*]

6.1.1390.20   IFRS 1 includes an optional exemption under which a first-time adopter that made the same determination of whether an arrangement contains a lease under previous GAAP as that required by IFRIC 4, but at a date other than that required by IFRIC 4, need not reassess that determination for such arrangements when it adopts IFRS. For a first-time adopter to have made the same determination under previous GAAP as that under IFRS, the determination is required to give the same outcome as applying IAS 17 and IFRIC 4. [*IFRS 1.D9A, IG206*]

6.1.1390.30   In our view, the exemption is available even if the date on which an arrangement was assessed under previous GAAP was the same as the date that would have been required if IFRIC 4 had been applied, notwithstanding the phrase 'at a date other than that required by IFRIC 4'. We believe that interpreting the requirement literally as requiring the assessment to have been made at a date *other than that required by IFRIC 4* would be inconsistent with the intention of the IASB in providing relief. [*IFRS 1.BC63DA*]

6.1.1390.40   In our view, application of the exemption does not rely on the first-time adopter having applied the same accounting to the lease under previous GAAP as it would have done under IAS 17. We believe that the reference in the exemption to 'the same outcome as that resulting from applying IAS 17 and IFRIC 4' refers to the scope of IAS 17 rather than the accounting. This is consistent with the objective of IFRIC 4, which is to determine whether an arrangement falls in the scope of IAS 17. Interpreting IFRS 1 to require the same accounting as under IAS 17 would be inconsistent with the idea that, after applying this exemption, a first-time adopter goes on to apply the classification and accounting requirements of IAS 17 to leases at the date of transition. [*IFRS 1.D9A, IFRIC 4.BC13*]

6.1.1400   *Classification*

6.1.1400.10   A first-time adopter, at the date of transition, classifies leases as operating or finance leases based on circumstances existing at inception of the lease (unless the agreement is changed). The classification is based on IFRS effective at the reporting date for their first annual IFRS reporting date. [*IFRS 1.7, IG14*]

6.1.1400.20   If a lease agreement is changed between inception of the lease and the date of transition, then the classification of the lease under IFRS is tested using both the original and the revised terms based on the circumstances (and therefore the assumptions and estimates that were, or would have been, used) at the inception of the original lease. If the revisions would result in a different classification using the original assumptions, then the revisions are treated as a new lease from the modification date and the classification, recognition and measurement of the lease are determined using assumptions that were, or would have been, used as at the modification date. [*IFRS 1.IG14*]

6.1.1400.30   However, changes in estimates – e.g. changes in estimates of the economic life or of the residual value of the leased asset, or changes in circumstances such as default by the lessee – do not result in reclassification of leases. [*IFRS 1.IG14*]

6.1.1410   *Accounting for leases*

6.1.1410.10   With respect to finance leases, a lessee recognises, at the date of transition:

- the carrying amount of the leased asset determined as if IFRS had been applied from inception of the lease, subject to the requirements and/or optional exemptions of IFRS 1. For example, in our view the deemed cost exemption for property, plant and equipment may be applied to an asset acquired under a finance lease (see 6.1.290 and 360); and
- the carrying amount of the lease liability as a progression of the amount that would have been recognised at commencement of the lease, taking into account accrued interest and repayments. [*IFRS 1.IG14*]

6.1.1410.20   A lessor recognises a finance lease receivable in the statement of financial position at the amount of its net investment, which comprises the present value of the minimum lease payments and any unguaranteed residual value accruing to the lessor. If the lessor recognised the leased asset under previous GAAP, then it is derecognised at the date of transition. The carrying amount of the lease receivable at the date of transition is a progression of the amount that would have been recognised at commencement of the lease, taking into account accrued interest and repayments. [*IFRS 1.IG15, IAS 17.36*]

6.1.1410.30   With respect to operating leases, a lessee (lessor) recognises rent expense (income) on a straight-line basis over the lease term, or on another systematic basis if appropriate. Lease incentives are taken into account in determining the total lease expense (income) that is spread over the relevant period. [*IFRS 1.IG16, IAS 17.33, 50*]

6.1.1420   *Land and buildings*

6.1.1420.10   A lease of both land and a building is treated as two leases – one for the land, and one for the building – with each lease classified separately under IFRS (see 5.1.240). [*IAS 17.15A*]

6.1.1425   FORTHCOMING REQUIREMENTS

6.1.1425.10 IFRS 16 supersedes IAS 17 and IFRIC 4 and removes the optional exemption for arrangements containing a lease and the reassessment of lease determination from IFRS 1. An optional exemption for IFRS 16 has been added to IFRS 1 (see 6.1.245).

6.1.1430   **Service concession arrangements**

6.1.1430.10   Full retrospective application of the measurement requirements of IFRIC 12 (see chapter 5.12) may be impracticable for service concession arrangements that have been in existence for a long period of time. For example, obtaining information about construction costs incurred and estimating what would have been an appropriate service margin on construction services may be difficult for arrangements that started many years ago. IFRIC 12 provides transition relief to existing users of IFRS. IFRS 1 also makes this relief available, but not mandatory, to first-time adopters. [*IFRS 1.D22*]

6.1.1430.20 If retrospective application of IFRIC 12 at the date of transition is impracticable for any service concession arrangement, then the operator:

- reclassifies assets previously recognised under the service concession arrangement as a financial asset or an intangible asset at the date of transition, measured at the previous GAAP carrying amount; and
- tests those assets for impairment at the date of transition or, if that is impracticable, then at the start of the current reporting period. [*IFRIC 12.30*]

6.1.1430.30 The impairment test is undertaken in accordance with either IAS 36 (for an intangible asset) or IFRS 9 excluding assets classified and measured at fair value through profit or loss (for a financial asset).

6.1.1430.40 Neither IFRIC 12 nor IFRS 1 specifies how the operator should account for a financial asset recognised on transition at the carrying amount of the assets previously recognised.

6.1.1430.50 There is also no explicit guidance in IFRIC 12 on when an operator recognises both a financial asset and an intangible asset on transition to IFRS and how an allocation of the previous GAAP carrying amount should be made. In our view, an entity should choose a method, to be applied consistently to all such allocations.

- One acceptable method is to allocate the carrying amount to the financial asset and the intangible asset based on their relative fair values.
- Another acceptable method is to measure the financial asset by discounting the future guaranteed payments using a reasonable rate of lending to the grantor and assigning the remainder of the carrying amount to the intangible asset.

6.1.1440 *Interaction with other requirements and exemptions*

6.1.1440.10 In our view, the exemption in respect of service concessions takes precedence over other requirements and exemptions in IFRS 1. Therefore, a first-time adopter that follows the specific transitional requirements for service concession requirements does not further restate the previous GAAP carrying amount of the asset for elements that do not otherwise comply with IFRS – e.g. for borrowing costs included in the carrying amount.

6.1.1450 Insurance contracts#

6.1.1460 *Optional exemption for insurance contracts#*

6.1.1460.10 A first-time adopter is permitted to apply the transitional requirements of IFRS 4. Instead of applying the standard retrospectively, the transitional requirements allow a first-time adopter to apply the standard prospectively to reporting periods beginning on or after 1 January 2005. In addition, subsequent amendments to IFRS 4 in respect of financial guarantee contracts may be applied prospectively to reporting periods beginning on or after 1 January 2006 (see chapter 8.1). [*IFRS 1.D4, 4.40–41A*]

6.1.1460.20 A first-time adopter is permitted to apply the temporary exemption from IFRS 9 or overlay approach if it meets the specific eligibility criteria. In assessing its eligibility for the temporary exemption from IFRS 9, a first-time adopter uses carrying amounts determined under IFRS for its initial eligibility assessment – i.e. on its annual reporting date immediately before 1 April 2016. First-time adopters that apply the overlay approach restate comparative information to reflect the overlay approach only if they restate comparative information under IFRS 9 (see 6.1.1530). [*IFRS 4.20B(b), 20L, 35N*]

6.1.1465 **FORTHCOMING REQUIREMENTS**

6.1.1465.10 First-time adopters of IFRS are not permitted to apply IFRS 17 prospectively. Instead, they apply the transition provisions of Appendix C of IFRS 17 to contracts in the scope of IFRS 17. [*IFRS 1.B13, 17.C1–C24, C28*]

6.1.1470 Extractive activities

6.1.1470.10 There is no relief from the requirements of IFRS 6 for first-time adopters. The accounting for extractive activities under IFRS differs depending on the stage of activity in which the expenditure was incurred (see chapter 5.11).

6.1.1470.20 IFRS 1 includes an optional exemption that is applicable *only* to entities in the oil and gas industry that, under previous GAAP accounted for exploration and development costs for properties in the development or production phases in cost centres that included all properties in a large geographic area – this is often referred to as 'full cost accounting'. Generally, under full cost accounting, the historical information available under previous GAAP would have been aggregated at a much higher unit of account than the acceptable unit of account under IFRS. For many of these assets, the information available to recreate an IFRS-compliant carrying amount at the date of transition may not be available or, if it is available, then the recreation of an IFRS-compliant carrying amount at the date of transition would result in significant costs to preparers. [*IFRS 1.BC47A*]

6.1.1470.30 An optional exemption permits applicable first-time adopters to measure:
- exploration and evaluation assets at the carrying amount at the date of transition under previous GAAP; and
- assets in the development or production phases at amounts determined based on the related cost centre under previous GAAP, which are then allocated on a pro rata basis to the cost centre's underlying assets using reserve volumes or reserve values at the date of transition. [*IFRS 1.D8A*]

6.1.1470.40 If a first-time adopter elects to apply the optional exemption, then an impairment test of the assets to which the exemption is applied is required at the date of transition. For exploration and evaluation assets, a first-time adopter performs the impairment test in accordance with IFRS 6. For assets in the development or production phases, a first-time adopter performs the impairment test in accordance with IAS 36 (see chapter 3.10). [*IFRS 1.D8A*]

6.1.1470.50 For oil and gas assets in the development or production phases, there is an exception to the exemption in IFRS 1 in respect of decommissioning, restoration and similar liabilities (see 6.1.800). If a first-time adopter uses the deemed cost exemption for oil and gas assets in the development or production phases, then the amount of any adjustments required to measure decommissioning, restoration and similar liabilities in accordance with IAS 37 at the date of transition are recognised directly in retained earnings rather than adjusting the carrying amount of the underlying assets. [*IFRS 1.D21A*]

6.1.1470.60 If a first-time adopter is involved in surface mining and it incurs stripping costs in the production phase of a surface mine (see 5.11.350), then it applies IFRIC 20 which requires recognition of production stripping costs as an asset, subject to fulfilment of certain conditions. A first-time adopter may apply the transitional requirements in IFRIC 20 when adopting IFRS. [*IFRS 1.D32*]

6.1.1480   **Separate financial statements**

6.1.1490   *Optional exemption for investments in subsidiaries, associates and joint ventures*

6.1.1490.10   In separate financial statements, investments in subsidiaries, associates and joint ventures, unless they are classified as held-for-sale (see 5.4.20), are accounted for either:

- at cost;
- in accordance with IFRS 9 (see 7.4.20.10); or
- using the equity method in accordance with IAS 28 (see 3.5.640).

6.1.1490.20   The entity applies the same accounting for each category of investments (see 3.5.640.40). [*IAS 27.10*]

6.1.1490.30   If a first-time adopter chooses to measure any of these categories of investments at cost, then it may choose to measure the carrying amount of any such investments at the date of transition at an amount equal to:

- cost, determined in accordance with IAS 27; or
- deemed cost, which is either fair value at the entity's date of transition in its separate financial statements, or the previous GAAP carrying amount of the investment. [*IFRS 1.D15(a)–(b)*]

6.1.1490.40   If a first-time adopter chooses to account for any of these categories of investments using the equity method, then:

- it applies the optional exemption for business combinations to the acquisition of that investment (see 6.1.950); and
- if the entity adopts IFRS in its separate financial statements earlier than in its consolidated financial statements, and:
  - later than its subsidiary, then it applies the mandatory exception discussed in 6.1.1240; or
  - later than its parent, then it applies the optional exemption discussed in 6.1.1290. [*IFRS 1.D15A*]

6.1.1490.50   Fair value is measured in accordance with IFRS 13, which is the subject of chapter 2.4. In measuring the fair value of an investment in a subsidiary, associate or joint venture it is first necessary to decide on the unit of account, which determines whether a premium may be taken into account in measuring fair value (see 2.4.80 and 830).

6.1.1490.60   The deemed cost exemption is available on an investment-by-investment basis. [*IFRS 1.D15*]

EXAMPLE 35 – DEEMED COST EXEMPTION FOR INVESTMENT IN SUBSIDIARY

 6.1.1490.70   In accordance with local laws, Company J presents separate financial statements in addition to consolidated financial statements. J is a first-time adopter in 2018. J acquired 80% of the shares in Company H for 40 in 2016. J financed the

> acquisition through the issue of debt securities, and issue costs of 2 were incurred and capitalised as part of the carrying amount of the investment in H. Accordingly, at the date of transition – 1 January 2017 – the carrying amount of H is 42 in J's separate financial statements.
>
> 6.1.1490.80   If IFRS was applied retrospectively, then the issue costs would be adjusted against the carrying amount of the debt securities. However, J elects to apply the deemed cost exemption and to state its investment in H at its carrying amount under previous GAAP at the date of transition – i.e. 42.

6.1.1490.90   For a discussion of consolidation requirements, see 6.1.1090.

6.1.1500   Investment entities

6.1.1500.10   A qualifying investment entity is required to account for investments in controlled entities, as well as investments in associates and joint ventures, at fair value through profit or loss instead of preparing consolidated financial statements. The only exception is subsidiaries that do not themselves qualify as investment entities and whose main purpose and activities are providing services that relate to the investment entity's investment activities, which continue to be consolidated. Investment entities are the subject of chapter 5.6.

6.1.1500.20   A first-time adopter transitioning to IFRS on or after 1 January 2018 assesses whether it qualifies as an investment entity retrospectively. [*IFRS 1.39AD, BC99*]

6.1.1510   PRESENTATION AND DISCLOSURES

6.1.1520   First IFRS financial statements

6.1.1520.10   An entity's first IFRS financial statements include presentation of the opening statement of financial position. Therefore, an entity in its first IFRS financial statements presents three statements of financial position – i.e. as at the first annual IFRS reporting date; as at the previous annual reporting date; and as at the date of transition. The entity's first IFRS financial statements further include a statement of profit or loss and OCI (see 2.1.10.10), a statement of cash flows and a statement of changes in equity, including comparative information for the preceding period. Any additional comparatives presented on a voluntary basis need not comply with IFRS, provided that they are labelled clearly and explanatory disclosures are included. [*IFRS 1.6, 21–22*]

6.1.1520.20   In addition to presenting a third statement of financial position as at the date of transition, IFRS 1 also requires the presentation of 'related notes'. In our view, this requirement should be interpreted as requiring disclosure of those notes that are relevant to an understanding of how the transition from previous GAAP to IFRS affected the first-time adopter's financial position at the date of transition – i.e. not all notes related to the third statement of financial position are required in every circumstance. A first-time adopter might approach its decision about the relevant note disclosures by first assuming all notes are necessary and then considering which note disclosures are not relevant to an understanding of the effect of the transition to IFRS and may be omitted. In deciding which notes and other comparative information to omit, regard is given to materiality and the particular facts and circumstances of the first-time adopter, including legislative and other requirements of the jurisdiction in which the first-time adopter operates.

6.1.1520.30   For example, a first-time adopter may decide to include all of the notes disaggregating the line items in the statement of financial position at the date of transition, but to omit selected supporting (or descriptive) comparative information that it considers is not relevant to an understanding of the effect of transition at that date – e.g. the contractual maturity analysis for financial liabilities and the sensitivity analyses required by IFRS 7.

6.1.1520.40   The disclosure in the notes need not include information that relates to the period before the date of transition.

EXAMPLE 36 – INFORMATION RELATED TO PERIODS BEFORE DATE OF TRANSITION

6.1.1520.50   A first-time adopter presents a statement of financial position at its date of transition of 1 January 2017. The notes to the statement of financial position include the gross carrying amount and accumulated depreciation of each class of property, plant and equipment at that date and the amount of expenditure in the carrying amount of an item of property, plant and equipment in the course of its construction. However, a reconciliation of the carrying amount of property, plant and equipment in the period from 1 January 2016 to 31 December 2016 would not be required to be presented.

6.1.1520.60   Extensive disclosures are required in the first IFRS financial statements to explain how the transition from previous GAAP to IFRS affected the reported financial position, financial performance and cash flows of the first-time adopter. These disclosures include:
- reconciliations of equity reported under previous GAAP to equity reported under IFRS at the date of transition and at the end of the latest period presented in the entity's most recent annual financial statements under previous GAAP; and
- a reconciliation of total comprehensive income reported under previous GAAP for the latest period in the entity's most recent annual financial statements to its total comprehensive income reported under IFRS. [*IFRS 1.23–24*]

6.1.1520.70   The reconciliations show the material adjustments made to amounts reported under previous GAAP in order to determine corresponding amounts presented under IFRS, together with explanations of the reconciling items. The correction of errors made under previous GAAP is identified separately. [*IFRS 1.25–26*]

6.1.1520.80   A first-time adopter that presented a statement of cash flows under previous GAAP also explains the material adjustments to its statement of cash flows, if any. [*IFRS 1.25*]

6.1.1520.90   In our view, it is not sufficient to include a cross-reference to previously published disclosures of the impact of the transition to IFRS in the first IFRS financial statements. However, we believe that a reference to previously published additional voluntary information – e.g. a more detailed analysis – is permitted, if that information fully complies with all IFRS requirements and the reference does not imply that the previously published additional information has been audited if that is not the case.

(S) 6.1.1520.100 Some entities may have been required to prepare only separate – i.e. unconsolidated – financial statements under previous GAAP, but under IFRS are required to prepare consolidated financial statements. In our view, the non-preparation of consolidated financial statements is not a prior-period error. We believe that amounts reported under previous GAAP are those of the separate financial statements of the parent and IFRS 1 treats the transition to IFRS of an entity in its separate financial statements as a different transition from the same entity's transition in its consolidated financial statements. Because we have previously taken the view that reconciliations would generally be to the amounts reported in the same set of financial statements (see 6.1.80.10), in our view there are no relevant previous GAAP financial statements from which the first-time adopter is transitioning, and therefore no reconciliations between the first IFRS consolidated financial statements and the previous GAAP separate financial statements are required.

6.1.1520.110 The comparatives in a first-time adopter's first IFRS financial statements may be for a period shorter or longer than 12 months, but are for the same period as the previous GAAP financial statements. This also applies if the first-time adopter changes its annual reporting date during the period in which IFRS is adopted.

EXAMPLE 37 – FIRST IFRS FINANCIAL STATEMENTS SHORTER THAN 12 MONTHS

6.1.1520.120 Company B's previous GAAP comparative financial statements are for the 12-month period ended 30 June 2018; after 1 July 2018 B decides to change its annual reporting date from 30 June 2018 to 31 December 2018. Therefore, B's first IFRS financial statements are for the six-month period ended 31 December 2018 with comparatives for the 12-month period ended 30 June 2018, provided that this is in accordance with local laws and regulations.

6.1.1520.130 The disclosure requirements of IFRS 13 apply to classes of assets and liabilities measured at fair value as deemed cost on the date of transition (see 2.4.490).

6.1.1530   **Exemption from the requirement to restate comparatives for IFRS 9**

6.1.1530.10 If a first-time adopter adopts IFRS for an annual period beginning before 1 January 2019 and applies IFRS 9 (2014), then the comparative information in its first IFRS financial statements does not have to comply with IFRS 9 (2014). This exemption also includes IFRS 7 disclosures related to items in the scope of IFRS 9. If this option is taken, then:

- in applying IFRS 9 (and the related IFRS 7 disclosures), the 'date of transition' is the beginning of the first IFRS reporting period;
- previous GAAP is applied in comparative periods (rather than IFRS 9);
- the fact that the exemption has been applied as well as the basis of preparation of the comparative information are disclosed; and
- the adjustments arising on adoption of IFRS 9 are treated as a change in accounting policy and are recognised at the beginning of the first IFRS reporting period. Also, certain disclosures required by IAS 8 are made. [*IFRS 1.E1–E2*]

6.1.1530.20 The diagram below illustrates application by a first-time adopter in 2018 who has elected not to provide comparative information in accordance with IFRS 9.

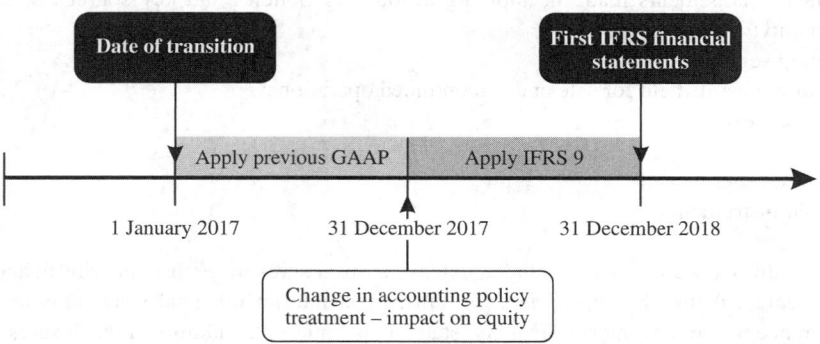

6.1.1540   Interim financial statements

6.1.1550   *Form, content and disclosures in interim IFRS financial statements*

6.1.1550.10   If an entity publishes a set of condensed interim financial statements in accordance with IFRS, then these financial statements contain, as a minimum, each of the headings and subtotals that were included in its most recent annual financial statements, together with selected notes required by IAS 34 (see chapter 5.9). In our view, a first-time adopter should apply this requirement by including at least all of the headings and subtotals that are expected to be included in its first annual IFRS financial statements. [*IAS 34.10*]

6.1.1550.20   The extensive disclosures required in the first IFRS financial statements (see 6.1.1520) are also provided in any interim financial statements prepared in accordance with IFRS (see chapter 5.9) for part of the period covered by the first IFRS financial statements. Alternatively, the interim financial statements include a cross-reference to another published document that contains those disclosures. [*IFRS 1.32(b)*]

6.1.1550.30   In addition, if the first-time adopter presented an interim financial report for the comparable interim period of the immediately preceding financial year, then additional reconciliations are included in its first interim IFRS financial statements. These are reconciliations of its equity at the end of that comparable interim period and total comprehensive income for that comparable interim period (current and year-to-date). [*IFRS 1.32(a)*]

6.1.1550.40   Unlike for the first IFRS financial statements, when a first-time adopter publishes its first condensed interim IFRS financial statements, IFRS is not explicit on whether to present the third statement of financial position as a primary financial statement or in the notes. Presentation of the third statement of financial position as a primary financial statement may be useful because this is consistent with how the first IFRS financial statements will be presented and it provides useful information to the readers of financial statements about the entity's starting point for its accounting in accordance with IFRS. [*IFRS 1.BC16*]

6.1.1550.50   In our view, when a first-time adopter prepares interim financial statements that claim compliance with IAS 34, these first interim IFRS financial statements should include a complete set of significant accounting policies. Significant judgement is then required in determining other areas that may require additional disclosure; these may include, but are not limited to:

- significant judgements made in applying accounting policies and key sources of estimation uncertainty;
- operating segments;
- non-current assets held for sale and discontinued operations;
- income tax expense;
- EPS;
- employee benefits; and
- financial instruments.

6.1.1550.60   In our view, having included extensive disclosures in the first interim financial statements presented, it may be appropriate for subsequent interim financial statements to include a cross-reference to the first interim financial statements, unless the additional disclosures would be material to an understanding of the subsequent interim financial statements. However, including extensive disclosures in interim financial statements is not a substitute for the required disclosures in the first annual IFRS financial statements and therefore a cross-reference in the first annual IFRS financial statements to an interim financial statement is not permitted (see 6.1.1520.90).

EXAMPLE 38 – DISCLOSURES IN FIRST IFRS INTERIM FINANCIAL STATEMENTS

6.1.1550.70   Company M's most recent annual financial statements under previous GAAP were prepared for the year ended 31 December 2017. M is required to prepare quarterly interim IFRS financial statements in the year of adoption and M also prepared quarterly interim financial statements under previous GAAP throughout 2017.

6.1.1550.80   In its *first* interim IFRS financial statements, for the three months ending 31 March 2018, M will disclose the following reconciliations.
- Reconciliations of equity under previous GAAP to equity under IFRS at:
  - the date of transition, being 1 January 2017;
  - the end of the comparative interim period, being 31 March 2017; and
  - the end of the comparative annual period, being 31 December 2017.
- Reconciliations of total comprehensive income under previous GAAP to total comprehensive income under IFRS for:
  - the comparative interim period, being the three months ended 31 March 2017; and
  - the comparative annual period ending 31 December 2017.

6.1.1550.90   In its interim IFRS financial statements for the six months ending 30 June 2018, M will disclose the following reconciliations.
- Reconciliation of equity under previous GAAP to equity under IFRS at the end of the comparative interim period, being 30 June 2017.
- Reconciliations of total comprehensive income under previous GAAP to total comprehensive income under IFRS for:
  - the comparative interim period, being the three months ended 30 June 2017; and

> – the comparative cumulative interim period, being the six months ended 30 June 2017. [*IFRS 1.32(a)–(b)*]

6.1.1560 *Changing accounting policies and/or use of optional exemptions in year of adoption*

6.1.1560.10 IFRS 1 governs the selection of accounting policies in the first annual IFRS financial statements and therefore the general requirements of IAS 8 do not apply to changes in accounting policies that occur during the period covered by the first financial statements. As such, it is acceptable for a first-time adopter to adopt an accounting policy or elect to use an optional exemption in its first annual IFRS financial statements that differs from that applied in any interim IFRS financial statements previously published during the year of adoption. It is also acceptable for a first-time adopter to adopt different accounting policies or use different optional exemptions between sets of interim IFRS financial statements before the issue of the first annual IFRS financial statements. [*IFRS 1.27*]

6.1.1560.20 If a first-time adopter changes its accounting policies or use of optional exemptions, then it:

- explains any such changes between the first interim and first annual financial statements or between sets of interim financial statements; and
- updates the reconciliation from previous GAAP to IFRS included in the previous interim financial information for those changes in the interim period in which the change is made. For further discussion of the required reconciliations in interim financial statements, see 6.1.1550.20–30 and 60–90. [*IFRS 1.27A, 32(c)*]

6.1.1560.30 Notwithstanding that changes in accounting policies between a first-time adopter's interim IFRS and first annual IFRS financial statements are not in the scope of IAS 8, some regulators may consider that the policies adopted in the first annual financial statements are more appropriate – e.g. on the basis of evolving best practice. When considering whether the policy is more appropriate, the criteria for voluntary changes in accounting policy in IAS 8 may be useful guidance (see 2.8.70).

6.1.1570 FUTURE DEVELOPMENTS

6.1.1570.10 The IFRS Interpretations Committee discussed whether a subsidiary that adopts IFRS later than its parent can recognise the cumulative translation differences at the amounts included in the consolidated financial statements of the parent, based on the parent's date of transition (see 6.1.1290). The Committee recommended and the IASB agreed to amend IFRS 1 as part of the next *Annual Improvements to IFRSs Cycle* to require a subsidiary that applies paragraph D16(a) of IFRS 1 to measure cumulative translation differences using the amounts reported by its parent, based on the parent's date of transition to IFRS (subject to any adjustments made for consolidation procedures and for the effects of the business combination in which the parent acquired the subsidiary).

6.2 Regulatory deferral accounts and first-time adoption of IFRS

6.2 Regulatory deferral accounts and first-time adoption of IFRS

CURRENTLY EFFECTIVE REQUIREMENTS

This publication reflects IFRS in issue at 1 August 2018, and the currently effective requirements cover annual periods beginning on 1 January 2018.

The requirements related to this topic are mainly derived from the following.

REFERENCE	TITLE
IFRS 14	Regulatory Deferral Accounts

An eligible entity can apply IFRS 14 only if it is a first-time adopter of IFRS. IFRS 14 permits, but does not require, first-time adopters of IFRS to continue using previous GAAP to account for regulatory deferral account balances while the IASB completes its comprehensive project on rate-regulated activities.

FORTHCOMING REQUIREMENTS

For this topic, there are no forthcoming requirements.

FUTURE DEVELOPMENTS

This topic is subject to future developments on the comprehensive project on rate-regulated activities. See 6.2.160.

SCOPE

6.2.10.10   An entity is eligible to apply IFRS 14 only if it:
- is subject to oversight and/or approval from an authorised body (the rate regulator);
- accounted for regulatory deferral account balances in its financial statements in accordance with the basis of accounting used immediately before adopting IFRS (previous GAAP); and
- elects to apply the requirements of IFRS 14 in its first IFRS financial statements. [*IFRS 14.5–6, BC15*]

6.2.10.20   The diagram below summarises the scope of IFRS 14.

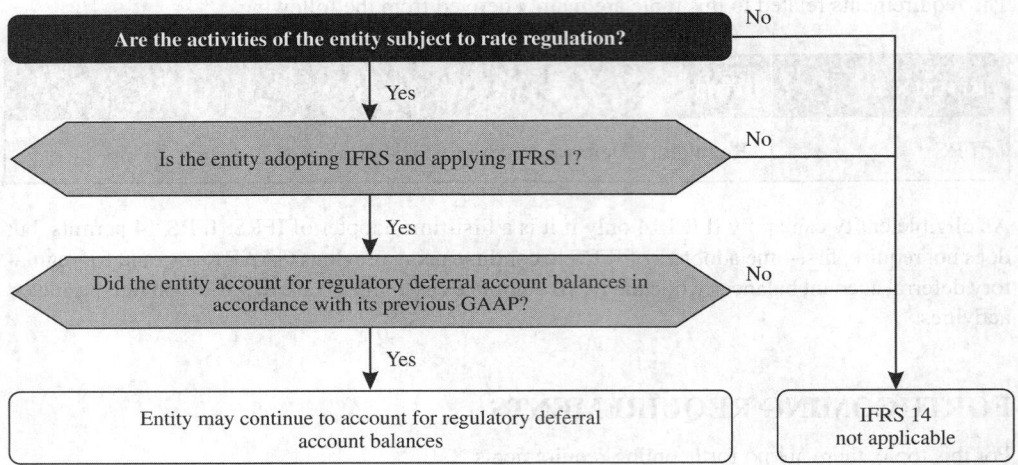

6.2.10.30   Price flexibility is a common feature of many rate-regulatory frameworks. For example, the rate regulator may: set different prices for different groups of customers; set a maximum price, but the entity can provide goods or services at a discount; or set a range of permitted prices. The definitions of 'rate regulation' and 'rate regulator' permit pricing based on the rate or range of rates established or approved by an authorised body. Therefore, if price flexibility is within clear restrictions established by the rate regulator, then activities subject to these types of rate-setting mechanisms are in the scope of IFRS 14. [*IFRS 14.BC57*]

6.2.10.40   Activities that are self-regulated are generally not in the scope of IFRS 14. For example, an entity with a dominant position in a market may decide to self-regulate to avoid external intervention. Because there is no formal rate regulator ensuring that a pricing framework is supported by statute or regulation, the oversight of these activities does not meet the definition of rate regulation. However, entities that are regulated by their own governing body or a related party can apply IFRS 14 if:
- the governing body establishes rates both in the interest of the customers and to ensure the overall financial viability of the entity within a specified pricing framework; and
- the framework is subject to oversight and/or approval by an authorised body that is empowered by statute or regulation. [*IFRS 14.B2, BC22–BC23*]

6.2.10.50   If an entity has been delegated regulatory power by the government and conducts previously state-run monopolistic activities, then such activities are in the scope of IFRS 14. In a similar way, a co-operative subject to some form of regulatory oversight – e.g. to obtain preferential loans, tax relief or other incentives to maintain the supply of essential or near-essential goods or services – falls in the scope of IFRS 14. [*IFRS 14.BC24, BC55*]

6.2.10.60   The application of IFRS 14 is optional but if an entity adopts the standard, then it has to apply *all* of its requirements to *all* regulatory deferral account balances that arise from *all* of its rate-regulated activities. An entity cannot, therefore, stop accounting for only certain regulatory deferral account balances on transition. However, it may elect not to apply IFRS 14 as a whole. [*IFRS 14.8, BC35*]

6.2.20   CORE REQUIREMENTS

6.2.20.10   A 'regulatory deferral account balance' is any expense (income) deferral or variance account that is included or is expected to be included by the rate regulator in establishing the rate(s) that can be charged to customers and that would not otherwise be recognised as an asset or liability under other standards. In other words, such balances reflect the differences that arise between regulatory accounting requirements and the accounting that would be required in the absence of IFRS 14. [*IFRS 14.A, B3, BC27*]

6.2.30   Grandfathering approach

6.2.30.10   If an entity meets the scope criteria of IFRS 14, then it can elect to apply its previous GAAP accounting policies to the recognition, measurement, impairment and derecognition of regulatory deferral account balances on transition to IFRS. The policies established are then applied consistently in subsequent reporting periods; any subsequent change in accounting policy – e.g. derecognition of balances – needs to meet the criteria to qualify as a voluntary change in accounting policy (see 2.8.70). [*IFRS 14.11–14, BC32–BC33*]

6.2.30.20   The following table summarises the position on subsequent changes in accounting policies.

	ENTITY ELECTING TO GRANDFATHER	ENTITY NOT ELECTING TO GRANDFATHER
Expand the range of regulatory deferral account balances recognised	✘	–
Reduce the range of regulatory deferral account balances recognised	✘	–
Derecognise all regulatory deferral account balances	✓	–
Start recognising regulatory deferral account balances	–	✘
✓ Allowed ✘ Prohibited		

6.2.30.30 An entity is not permitted to change an accounting policy to start recognising regulatory deferral account balances, or to recognise a wider range of such balances by modifying a previous GAAP policy. The rationale for these restrictions is that starting to recognise such balances would not make the financial statements more reliable under the requirements of IAS 8, given that the policy may need to change again following completion of the comprehensive project on accounting for rate-regulated activities under IFRS. [*IFRS 14.13, BC33–BC35*]

6.2.30.40 However, regulatory deferral account balances arising from timing differences that did not exist immediately before the date of transition to IFRS may be recognised, if they are consistent with the entity's established accounting policies. [*IFRS 14.B6*]

EXAMPLE 1 – TIMING DIFFERENCES THAT DID NOT EXIST IMMEDIATELY BEFORE TRANSITION

6.2.30.50 Company X has an accounting policy to recognise regulatory deferral account balances for storm damage costs that are expected to be recovered through the rate-setting framework. On 1 January 2018, X adopts IFRS 14 on its transition to IFRS. No storm damage costs have been incurred recently; therefore, no related regulatory deferral account balance is recognised in X's opening statement of financial position.

6.2.30.60 In March 2019, an ice storm causes significant damage to X's infrastructure. Based on historical experience and communication with the rate regulator, X expects the costs of repairing the damage to be recovered through an increase in future rates. Accordingly, X recognises a regulatory deferral account debit balance in the statement of financial position, consistent with its established accounting policies.

6.2.30.70 Similarly, accounting policy changes on first-time adoption or on the initial application of a new or revised standard may result in new timing differences between the recognition of items of income or expense for regulatory purposes and the recognition of those items for financial reporting purposes. An entity may recognise new or revised regulatory deferral account balances arising from such timing differences. [*IFRS 14.B6, BC59(a)(iii)*]

6.2.40 *Presentation requirements*

6.2.40.10 To isolate the impact of accounting for regulatory deferral account balances, these balances are presented separately from assets, liabilities, income and expenses recognised in accordance with other standards, as follows. [*IFRS 14.18–23, BC47*]

STATEMENT OF FINANCIAL POSITION	<ul><li>Regulatory deferral account balances are presented in separate line items.</li><li>Subtotals for assets and liabilities are calculated before the inclusion of regulatory deferral account balances.</li><li>Debit and credit balances are not offset.</li></ul>

OCI	• Net movements in all regulatory deferral account balances that relate to items recognised in OCI in the reporting period are presented separately. • Separate line items are presented depending on whether the net movement relates to items that will subsequently be reclassified to profit or loss.
PROFIT OR LOSS	• Remaining net movements are presented as a separate line item in profit or loss. • Net movements are distinguished from income and expenses that are presented in accordance with other standards by a subtotal calculated before their inclusion.

6.2.40.20   An entity does not classify regulatory deferral account balances as current or non-current line items in the statement of financial position. Instead, information is disclosed about the reporting period(s) over which regulatory deferral account balances are expected to be recovered or reversed. [*IFRS 14.21, BC47*]

6.2.40.30   A deferred tax asset (liability) and the related movement in that deferred tax asset (liability) resulting from the recognition of regulatory deferral account balances are presented with the regulatory deferral account balances and movements therein, rather than included within income tax line items; however, they are not netted against the related regulatory deferral account balances. An entity may present the deferred tax asset (liability) or movement in the deferred tax amount that arises as a result of recognising regulatory deferral account balances either:

• with the line items that are presented for the regulatory deferral account balances and movements therein (Approach 1); or
• as a separate line item alongside the regulatory deferral account balances or movements therein (Approach 2). [*IFRS 14.24, B11–B12*]

EXAMPLE 2A – REGULATORY DEFERRAL ACCOUNTS AND DEFERRED TAXES – PRESENTATION IN STATEMENT OF FINANCIAL POSITION

6.2.40.40   Company K has the following regulatory deferral accounts.

	OPENING	MOVEMENT	CLOSING
Regulatory deferral account debit balances[1]	30	20	50
Deferred taxes at 30%[2]	(9)	(6)	(15)
Regulatory deferral account credit balances[1]	(140)	(10)	(150)
Deferred taxes at 30%[2]	42	3	45

Notes
1. The net movement in regulatory deferral account balances is 10 (20 - 10).
2. Deferred tax assets and liabilities arising from the recognition of regulatory deferral account balances meet the offsetting criteria in paragraph 71 of IAS 12 (see 3.13.630.30). The closing net deferred tax asset is 30 (45 - 15) and the net movement in the deferred tax asset is (3) (3 - 6).

Approach 1: With debit and credit balances line items

Non-current assets	500
Current assets	300
Total assets	800
Regulatory deferral account debit balances and related deferred tax asset	**80**
Total assets and regulatory deferral account debit balances	880
Total equity	(200)
Non-current liabilities	(330)
Current liabilities	(200)
Total liabilities	(530)
Total equity and liabilities	(730)
Regulatory deferral account credit balances	**(150)**
Total equity, liabilities and regulatory deferral account credit balances	(880)

Approach 2: As a separate line item

Total assets	800
Regulatory deferral account debit balances	**50**
Deferred tax asset related to regulatory deferral account balances	**30**
Total assets and regulatory deferral account debit balances	880
Total equity and liabilities	(730)
Regulatory deferral account credit balances	**(150)**
Total equity, liabilities and regulatory deferral account credit balances	(880)

EXAMPLE 2B – REGULATORY DEFERRAL ACCOUNTS AND DEFERRED TAXES – PRESENTATION IN STATEMENT OF PROFIT OR LOSS AND OCI

6.2.40.50   Continuing Example 2A, Company K may present the regulatory deferral account balances and the related movement in deferred tax amounts in the statement of profit or loss and OCI using one of the following approaches.

Approach 1: With movements in regulatory deferral account balances

Revenue	300
Cost of sales	(200)
Gross profit	100
Other income	25
Expenses	(50)
Net finance cost	(20)
Profit before tax	55
Income tax expense	(15)
Profit for the year before net movements in regulatory deferral account balances	40
Net movement in regulatory deferral account balances related to profit or loss and the related deferred tax movement	**7**
Profit for the year and net movements in regulatory deferral account balances	47

Approach 2: As a separate line item

Profit for the year before net movements in regulatory deferral account balances	40
Net movement in regulatory deferral account balances related to profit or loss	**10**
Net movement in the deferred tax asset arising from regulatory deferral account balances related to profit or loss	**(3)**
Profit for the year and net movements in regulatory deferral account balances	47

6.2.40.60   Similarly, when an entity presents a discontinued operation or a disposal group (see 5.4.110 and 220), any related regulatory deferral account balances and the net movement in those balances are presented with the regulatory deferral account balances and movements therein, instead of within the disposal group or discontinued operations (see 6.2.90.30). [*IFRS 14.25, B20–B22*]

6.2.40.70   IFRS 14 does not provide specific guidance on how an entity should present cash flows relating to regulatory deferral account balances in the statement of cash flows and therefore the general requirements of IAS 7 apply (see chapter 2.3). The requirement to disclose information that enables users to assess the effects of rate regulation on an entity's cash flows suggests that the statement of cash flows should reflect the entity's rate-regulated activities. Taking into consideration the objective of IFRS 14 to isolate the impact of regulatory deferral account balances, activities relating to these balances are presented as a separate line item(s) in the statement of cash flows. [*IFRS 14.16, 27*]

6.2.40.80   Specific guidance is not provided on the application of IAS 34. Accordingly, the general requirements of IAS 34 apply (see chapter 5.9), including:
- at a minimum, inclusion of each of the headings and subtotals that were presented in the most recent annual financial statements and the selected explanatory notes required by IAS 34; and
- an explanation of any events and transactions that are significant to an understanding of the changes in financial position and performance of the entity. [*IFRS 14.BC60, IAS 34.10, 15–15A*]

6.2.50   APPLICATION OF OTHER STANDARDS

6.2.50.10   The normal requirements of other standards apply to regulatory deferral account balances, subject to some exceptions, exemptions and additional requirements that are specified in IFRS 14. Because only a limited population of entities is eligible to apply IFRS 14, and it is intended to be an interim solution, consequential amendments were not made to other IFRSs, with the exception of IFRS 1. [*IFRS 14.16–17, B7, BC37*]

6.2.50.20   The exceptions, exemptions and additional requirements have been developed to achieve two objectives:
- to resolve any conflicts between the grandfathered accounting policies and other IFRSs; and
- to better isolate regulatory deferral account balances from normal IFRS accounting.

6.2.50.30   In the absence of any specific exception, exemption or additional requirement in IFRS 14, if other IFRSs have different requirements from an entity's existing accounting policy under the previous GAAP, then those standards take precedence in recognising and measuring regulatory deferral account balances. [*IFRS 14.16*]

6.2.60   Income taxes

6.2.60.10   An entity applies IAS 12 to all of its activities, including rate-regulated activities, to identify the amount of income tax to be recognised. However, the amounts recognised related to regulatory deferral account balances are required to be presented separately rather than within tax line items (see 6.2.40.30). [*IFRS 14.B9–B12*]

6.2.60.20   An entity applying IFRS 14 might have recognised deferred tax with regard to temporary differences on regulatory deferral account balances in accordance with its previous GAAP. Because an existing policy on recognising deferred tax is not grandfathered, the entity accounts for deferred tax arising from temporary differences on regulatory deferral account balances in accordance with IAS 12. This may change the net amount of the regulatory deferral account balances compared with the pre-transition financial statements.

6.2.60.30   Under some rate-regulatory frameworks, future rates can be increased to recover some or all of an entity's income tax expense. In this case, the entity recognises a regulatory deferral account balance for income tax. On applying IAS 12, an additional temporary difference may arise on this regulatory deferral account balance, for which the entity might need to recognise more deferred tax. This interaction between deferred tax and regulatory deferral account balances grosses up the amount of both regulatory deferral account balances and deferred tax. [*IFRS 14.B10*]

6.2.70   Earnings per share

6.2.70.10   An entity that presents EPS (see 5.3.10.10) is required to present basic and diluted EPS amounts both including and excluding the movements in regulatory deferral account balances, with equal prominence. [*IFRS 14.26, B13–B14*]

6.2.80   Impairment of assets

6.2.80.10   Because an entity continues to apply its existing accounting policies under previous GAAP for the identification, recognition, measurement and reversal of impairment related to its regulatory deferral account balances, IAS 36 does not apply to such balances – i.e. such balances are outside the scope of IAS 36. [*IFRS 14.B15*]

6.2.80.20   Even though individual regulatory deferral account balances are not tested for impairment under IAS 36, they are relevant to impairment tests conducted under IAS 36. Specifically, items to which IAS 36 does not apply are nonetheless included in the carrying amount of a cash-generating unit (CGU) if this is consistent with the way in which the recoverable amount is measured (see 3.10.360.10). In a similar way, under IFRS 14 an entity applies the requirements of IAS 36 to a CGU that includes regulatory deferral account balances. Based on our experience, a regulatory deferral account balance forms part of a CGU and therefore is included in impairment testing at that level. [*IFRS 14.B15–B16*]

6.2.80.30   Regulatory deferral account balances relate to amounts that will be, or are expected to be, included in future rates charged to customers. These future rates are included in the measurement of the recoverable amount, regardless of whether it is calculated based on value in use or fair value less costs of disposal. Therefore, for consistency, regulatory deferral account balances are included in the carrying amount of the CGU that provides a rate-regulated activity. [*IFRS 14.B16*]

6.2.80.40   The recognition of regulatory deferral account balances impacts the carrying amount of a CGU but not its recoverable amount. Therefore, the inclusion of a regulatory deferral account debit balance in the carrying amount of a CGU might result in the recognition of an impairment loss (where otherwise none would have been recorded) or in a larger impairment loss. Alternatively, the inclusion of a regulatory deferral account credit balance in the carrying amount of a CGU might result in the recognition of no impairment loss (where otherwise one would have been recorded) or in a smaller impairment loss.

6.2.80.50   Because regulatory deferral account balances are excluded from the scope of IAS 36, a pro rata share of any impairment loss is not allocated to such balances included in an impaired CGU. Consequently, any impairment losses are allocated to the other assets in the CGU, as illustrated in Example 3. This means that application of IFRS 14 can affect not only the size of any impairment loss, but also the carrying amount of assets other than the regulatory deferral account balances recognised.

EXAMPLE 3 – ALLOCATION OF IMPAIRMENT LOSS

6.2.80.60   Company X has three CGUs: C, G and K. The following facts are relevant for this example.

- C carries out electricity distribution activities and X has elected to apply IFRS 14.

- C contains a regulatory deferral account debit balance of 80 and has been allocated goodwill of 40.
- At 31 December 2018, the carrying amount of C, including the regulatory deferral account balance, is 1,000.
- The recoverable amount of C, based on the higher of value in use and fair value less costs of disposal, is 850. Accordingly, X determines that C is impaired by 150 (1,000 - 850).
- The goodwill of 40 is written off and the remaining impairment of 110 is allocated on a pro rata basis to C's other assets in the scope of IAS 36.

6.2.80.70   X allocates the impairment loss of 150 as follows.

	CARRYING AMOUNT PRE-IMPAIRMENT	IMPAIRMENT LOSS ALLOCATION	CARRYING AMOUNT POST-IMPAIRMENT
Assets			
Property, plant and equipment	700	(87)[1]	613
Intangible assets	180	(23)[2]	157
Goodwill	40	(40)	-
Regulatory deferral account debit balance	80	-	80
Total	1,000	(150)	850

Notes
1. Calculated as (700 / 880[3]) x 110.
2. Calculated as (180 / 880[3]) x 110.
3. Calculated as 1,000 - 80 - 40.

6.2.90   Non-current assets held for sale and discontinued operations

6.2.90.10   The classification criteria of IFRS 5 for presenting non-current assets held for sale or discontinued operations apply to a disposal group or a discontinued operation that includes regulatory deferral account balances; however, those balances are outside the scope of IFRS 5 measurement requirements. [*IFRS 14.B19*]

6.2.90.20   Assets or liabilities that are not in the scope of the IFRS 5 measurement requirements are included in the carrying amount of a disposal group, but any impairment loss recognised for a disposal group is allocated only to the non-current assets that are in the scope of IFRS 5 measurement requirements (see 5.4.60.50). The recognition of regulatory deferral account balances impacts the carrying amount of a disposal group, but not the measurement of fair value less costs to sell and therefore may affect the size of any impairment loss. The carrying amount of the disposal group's non-current assets may also be affected because, similar to allocating an impairment loss within a CGU, an impairment loss is allocated to the disposal group's non-current assets in the scope of IFRS 5. [*IFRS 5.23*]

6.2.90.30   Notwithstanding the requirements of IFRS 5, an entity does not include the movement in regulatory deferral account balances that relates to a discontinued operation with the amounts presented as 'profit or loss from discontinued operations'. In the same way, an entity does not include regulatory deferral account debit or credit balances that relate to a disposal group with the amounts presented as 'non-current assets held for sale'. Rather, it presents these balances or movements either:

- within the line items that are presented for the regulatory deferral account balances and movements therein; or
- as a separate line item alongside the other regulatory deferral account balances or movements therein. [*IFRS 14.B20–B22*]

6.2.100   Group accounting policies

6.2.100.10   An entity's previous GAAP may not have required the accounting policies of subsidiaries to be harmonised on consolidation; however, IFRS 10 requires a parent to prepare consolidated financial statements using uniform accounting policies for similar transactions and for other events in similar circumstances (see 2.5.440.60). [*IFRS 10.19*]

6.2.100.20   A parent entity that has adopted IFRS 14 applies the same accounting policies to the regulatory deferral account balances of all of its subsidiaries in its consolidated financial statements, regardless of whether the subsidiaries account for those balances. Conversely, if the parent entity does not apply IFRS 14, then the consolidated financial statements do not include regulatory deferral account balances that may be recognised in the separate financial statements of a subsidiary. [*IFRS 14.B23*]

EXAMPLE 4 – UNIFORM ACCOUNTING POLICIES

6.2.100.30   Parent P controls Subsidiary B, which does not recognise regulatory deferral account balances in its own financial statements. On transition to IFRS, P elects to apply IFRS 14. Applying its grandfathered accounting policies, P recognises, in its consolidated financial statements, regulatory deferral account balances arising from B's rate-regulated operations.

6.2.100.40   IAS 28 also requires the use of uniform accounting policies when applying the equity method (see 3.5.200.40). Therefore, adjustments are made to an associate's or joint venture's accounting policies to conform them to those of the investor in applying the equity method. [*IFRS 14.B24*]

6.2.110   Business combinations

6.2.110.10   For the acquisition of a business that conducts rate-regulated activities, IFRS 14 provides a limited exception allowing the acquirer's previous GAAP accounting policies to be applied for the recognition and measurement of regulatory deferral account balances that have been acquired or assumed. Regulatory deferral account balances arising from the acquiree's rate-regulated activities are recognised by the acquirer, based on the acquirer's accounting policies – even if they were not recognised by the acquiree. [*IFRS 14.B17–B18*]

6.2.110.20   If an acquirer does not recognise regulatory deferral account balances in accordance with IFRS 14, then such balances cannot be recognised as a result of a business combination. [*IFRS 14.BC59(a)(ii)*]

6.2.120   **Disclosure of interests in other entities**

6.2.120.10   The disclosure requirements of IFRS 12 (see chapter 5.10) apply to an entity's interests in its subsidiaries, associates or joint ventures that contain regulatory deferral account balances. IFRS 14 specifies additional disclosures relating to the regulatory deferral account balances, or net movements therein, that are provided by an entity to which IFRS 12 disclosures apply. [*IFRS 14.B25–B28*]

6.2.120.20   An entity applying IFRS 14 discloses for each of its subsidiaries that have NCI that are material to the entity, or associates or joint ventures that are material to the entity:
- the regulatory deferral account balances;
- the net movement in those balances; and
- other summarised financial information required by IFRS 12 (see 5.10.90 and 140). [*IFRS 14.B26–B27*]

6.2.120.30   For each of its subsidiaries that have NCI that are material to the entity, an entity discloses the net movement in regulatory deferral account balances allocated to NCI. [*IFRS 14.B25*]

6.2.120.40   For all individually immaterial joint ventures or associates, the entity discloses the amounts listed in 6.2.120.20 in aggregate, separately for joint ventures and associates. [*IFRS 14.B26–B27*]

6.2.120.50   When an entity loses control over a subsidiary, it discloses the portion of gain or loss that is attributable to derecognising regulatory deferral account balances in the former subsidiary. [*IFRS 14.B28*]

6.2.130   **DISCLOSURES**

6.2.130.10   IFRS 14 requires disclosures that focus on providing users of the financial statements with information that enables them to evaluate the nature of, risks associated with and effects of rate regulation on an entity's financial position, financial performance and cash flows. [*IFRS 14.27–36*]

6.2.130.20   An entity considers the level of detail and extent of disclosures necessary to meet the specific needs of users in understanding the rate regulation to which the entity is subject. [*IFRS 14.29*]

6.2.130.30   If an entity elects not to apply IFRS 14, or is not eligible to apply it, then it is not required to apply any IFRS 14 disclosure requirements; however, it is not prohibited from voluntarily providing supplementary disclosures. [*IFRS 14.BC35*]

6.2.140   **TRANSITION**

6.2.140.10   Although IFRS 14 allows the grandfathering of existing accounting policies, it does not mean that an entity can necessarily carry forward the regulatory deferral account balances that it has recognised and measured in accordance with its previous GAAP to its first IFRS financial statements without adjustments. To determine the amount of regulatory deferral account balances for the statement of financial position at the entity's date of transition, other IFRSs need to be taken into account, and resulting adjustments need to be made to the amounts carried forward from the previous GAAP (see chapter 6.1). [*IFRS 14.7, 11, 16*]

6.2.150 Deemed cost exemption

6.2.150.10 The deemed cost exemption for rate-regulated operations (see 6.1.320) may be used by first-time adopters that elect to apply IFRS 14. If an entity elects to apply it, then regulatory deferral account balances already recorded in the cost of property, plant and equipment or intangible assets remain in these assets. Such balances are subject to IAS 16 or IAS 38 for subsequent accounting and IAS 36 for impairment testing. [*IFRS 1.D8B, 14.BC38*]

EXAMPLE 5 – APPLICATION OF DEEMED COST EXEMPTION

6.2.150.20 Company Y is a first-time adopter of IFRS in 2018. Y conducts rate-regulated activities. Y recognised amounts that qualify as regulatory deferral account balances under IFRS 14 as items of property, plant and equipment under its previous GAAP. Y elects to apply IFRS 14 in its first IFRS financial statements. At the date of transition – i.e. 1 January 2017 – these amounts do not qualify for capitalisation under IAS 16. The following facts are also relevant for this example.
- The amounts previously included in property, plant and equipment have a carrying amount of 100 at the date of transition and are depreciated over 10 years.
- A regulatory deferral account debit balance of 50 arises during the reporting period ended 31 December 2017.
- Y recovers 10% of the regulatory deferral account balance of 50 during the reporting period ended 31 December 2017.

6.2.150.30 The extracts below illustrate captions from Y's first IFRS financial statements for the following two scenarios.
- *Scenario 1:* Deemed cost exemption applied.
- *Scenario 2:* Deemed cost exemption is not applied.

6.2.150.40 The following extract from Y's financial statements demonstrates the accounting after adopting IFRS 14, depending on whether the deemed cost exemption is applied on the adoption of IFRS.

	SCENARIO 1 DEEMED COST EXEMPTION APPLIED		SCENARIO 2 DEEMED COST EXEMPTION NOT APPLIED	
	1 JANUARY 2017	31 DECEMBER 2017	1 JANUARY 2017	31 DECEMBER 2017
Property, plant and equipment	100	90[(1)]	-	-
Regulatory deferral account debit balances	-	45[(2)]	100	135[(3)]

Notes
1. Calculated as 100 - (1 x 100 / 10).
2. Calculated as 50 - (50 x 10%).
3. Calculated as (100 + 50) - (150 x 10%).

	SCENARIO 1 DEEMED COST EXEMPTION APPLIED		SCENARIO 2 DEEMED COST EXEMPTION NOT APPLIED	
	1 JANUARY 2017	**31 DECEMBER 2017**	**1 JANUARY 2017**	**31 DECEMBER 2017**
Net movement in regulatory deferral account balances[1]	N/A	45	N/A	35
Depreciation of property, plant and equipment	N/A	(10)	N/A	-

Note
1. The net movement in regulatory deferral account balances in 2017 is calculated as follows.

Balances arising in the period	50	50
Recovery of regulatory deferral account balances	(5)	(15)
Net movement in regulatory deferral account balances	45	35

FUTURE DEVELOPMENTS

6.2.160

6.2.160.10   The IASB has moved forward with a comprehensive project on rate-regulated activities. In September 2014, it published Discussion Paper *Reporting the Financial Effects of Rate Regulation*.

6.2.160.20   The discussion paper focused on a certain type of rate regulation – termed 'defined rate regulation' – which exhibits specific features of a formal regulatory pricing framework.

6.2.160.30   The discussion paper discussed four potential approaches to account for the financial effects of rate regulation:
- recognise the package of rights and obligations as an intangible asset;
- report using regulatory accounting requirements;
- develop specific IFRS requirements; and
- prohibit the recognition of regulatory deferral account balances.

6.2.160.40   The comment period on the discussion paper closed in January 2015 and the IASB discussed feedback in the first half of 2015. A new consultation document is expected in the first half of 2019.

APPENDICES AND INDEX

Appendix I

CURRENTLY EFFECTIVE REQUIREMENTS AND FORTHCOMING REQUIREMENTS

Below is a list of standards and interpretations, including the latest revisions or amendments to the standards and interpretations, in issue at 1 August 2018 that are effective for annual reporting periods beginning on 1 January 2018. This list notes the principal chapter(s) within which the requirements are discussed. It also notes forthcoming requirements in issue at 1 August 2018 that are effective for annual reporting periods beginning after 1 January 2018. This list does not include revisions or amendments to standards that became effective before 1 January 2018 or minor consequential amendments to standards or interpretations made as a result of a new or an amended IFRS.

STANDARD	RELATED CHAPTER(S)	LATEST EFFECTIVE AMENDMENTS OR REVISIONS	FORTHCOMING REQUIREMENTS
IFRS 1 *First-time Adoption of International Financial Reporting Standards*	6.1	IFRS 15 *Revenue from Contracts with Customers* *Issued:* May 2014 *Effective:* 1 January 2018	IFRS 16 *Leases* *Issued:* January 2016 *Effective:* 1 January 2019
		IFRS 9 *Financial Instruments* *Issued:* July 2014 *Effective:* 1 January 2018	IFRS 17 *Insurance Contracts* *Issued:* May 2017 *Effective:* 1 January 2021
		IFRIC 22 *Foreign Currency Transactions and Advance Consideration* *Issued:* December 2016 *Effective:* 1 January 2018	
		Applying IFRS 9 Financial Instruments with IFRS 4 Insurance Contracts – Amendments to IFRS 4 *Issued:* September 2016 *Effective:* 1 January 2018	

STANDARD	RELATED CHAPTER(S)	LATEST EFFECTIVE AMENDMENTS OR REVISIONS	FORTHCOMING REQUIREMENTS
IFRS 1 *First-time Adoption of International Financial Reporting Standards* (continued)		*Annual Improvements to IFRSs 2014–2016 Cycle – Amendments to IFRS 1* *Issued:* December 2016 *Effective:* 1 January 2018	
IFRS 2 *Share-based Payment*	4.5	IFRS 9 *Financial Instruments* *Issued:* July 2014 *Effective:* 1 January 2018 *Classification and Measurement of Share-based Payment Transactions – Amendments to IFRS 2* *Issued:* June 2016 *Effective:* 1 January 2018	-
IFRS 3 *Business Combinations*	2.4, 2.6, 3.3, 5.13	IFRS 15 *Revenue from Contracts with Customers* *Issued:* May 2014 *Effective:* 1 January 2018	IFRS 16 *Leases* *Issued:* January 2016 *Effective:* 1 January 2019 IFRS 17 *Insurance Contracts* *Issued:* May 2017 *Effective:* 1 January 2021 *Annual Improvements to IFRSs 2015–2017 Cycle – Amendments to IFRS 3* *Issued:* December 2017 *Effective:* 1 January 2019
IFRS 4 *Insurance Contracts*	8.1	IFRS 15 *Revenue from Contracts with Customers* *Issued:* May 2014 *Effective:* 1 January 2018 IFRS 9 *Financial Instruments* *Issued:* July 2014 *Effective:* 1 January 2018	IFRS 17 *Insurance Contracts* *Issued:* May 2017 *Effective:* 1 January 2021

Standard	Related chapter(s)	Latest effective amendments or revisions	Forthcoming requirements
IFRS 4 *Insurance Contracts* (continued)		*Applying IFRS 9 Financial Instruments with IFRS 4 Insurance Contracts – Amendments to IFRS 4* *Issued:* September 2016 *Effective:* 1 January 2018	
IFRS 5 *Non-current Assets Held for Sale and Discontinued Operations*	5.4	-	IFRS 16 *Leases* *Issued:* January 2016 *Effective:* 1 January 2019
IFRS 6 *Exploration for and Evaluation of Mineral Resources*	5.11	-	-
IFRS 7 *Financial Instruments: Disclosures*	7.1, 7.10, 7I.1, 7I.8	IFRS 9 *Financial Instruments* *Issued:* July 2014 *Effective:* 1 January 2018	IFRS 16 *Leases* *Issued:* January 2016 *Effective:* 1 January 2019 IFRS 17 *Insurance Contracts* *Issued:* May 2017 *Effective:* 1 January 2021
IFRS 8 *Operating Segments*	5.2	-	-
IFRS 9 *Financial Instruments*	7	*Issued:* July 2014 *Effective:* 1 January 2018 *Applying IFRS 9 Financial Instruments with IFRS 4 Insurance Contracts – Amendments to IFRS 4* *Issued:* September 2016 *Effective:* 1 January 2018	IFRS 16 *Leases* *Issued:* January 2016 *Effective:* 1 January 2019 IFRS 17 *Insurance Contracts* *Issued:* May 2017 *Effective:* 1 January 2021 *Long-term Interests in Associates and Joint Ventures – Amendments to IAS 28* *Issued:* October 2017 *Effective:* 1 January 2019

STANDARD	RELATED CHAPTER(S)	LATEST EFFECTIVE AMENDMENTS OR REVISIONS	FORTHCOMING REQUIREMENTS
IFRS 10 *Consolidated Financial Statements*	2.1, 2.5, 5.6, 5.13	*Annual Improvements to IFRSs 2014–2016 Cycle – Amendments to IAS 28* *Issued:* December 2016 *Effective:* 1 January 2018	IFRS 17 *Insurance Contracts* *Issued:* May 2017 *Effective:* 1 January 2021 *Sale or Contribution of Assets between an Investor and its Associate or Joint Venture – Amendments to IFRS 10 and IAS 28* *Issued:* September 2014 *Effective:* Deferred indefinitely
IFRS 11 *Joint Arrangements*	3.6	-	*Annual Improvements to IFRSs 2015–2017 Cycle – Amendments to IFRS 11* *Issued:* December 2017 *Effective:* 1 January 2019
IFRS 12 *Disclosure of Interests in Other Entities*	5.10	-	IFRS 17 *Insurance Contracts* *Issued:* May 2017 *Effective:* 1 January 2021
IFRS 13 *Fair Value Measurement*	2.4, 2.6, 3.2, 3.3, 3.4, 3.9, 3.10, 5.4, 5.6, 7.7, 7.10, 7I.6, 7I.8	IFRS 15 *Revenue from Contracts with Customers* Issued: May 2014 Effective: 1 January 2018 IFRS 9 *Financial Instruments* *Issued:* July 2014 *Effective:* 1 January 2018	IFRS 16 *Leases* *Issued:* January 2016 *Effective:* 1 January 2019 IFRS 17 *Insurance Contracts* *Issued:* May 2017 *Effective:* 1 January 2021
IFRS 14 *Regulatory Deferral Accounts*	6.2	-	-
IFRS 15 *Revenue from Contracts with Customers*	4.2, 5.7, 7I.6	*Issued:* May 2014 *Effective:* 1 January 2018	IFRS 16 *Leases* *Issued:* January 2016 *Effective:* 1 January 2019 IFRS 17 *Insurance Contracts* *Issued:* May 2017 *Effective:* 1 January 2021

STANDARD	RELATED CHAPTER(S)	LATEST EFFECTIVE AMENDMENTS OR REVISIONS	FORTHCOMING REQUIREMENTS
IFRS 16 *Leases*	5.1A	-	*Issued:* January 2016 *Effective:* 1 January 2019
IFRS 17 *Insurance Contracts*	8.1A	-	*Issued:* May 2017 *Effective:* 1 January 2021
IAS 1 *Presentation of Financial Statements*	1.1, 2.1, 2.2, 2.8, 2.9, 3.1, 4.1, 5.8, 7.10, 7I.8, 8.1A	IFRS 15 *Revenue from Contracts with Customers* *Issued:* May 2014 *Effective:* 1 January 2018 IFRS 9 *Financial Instruments* *Issued:* July 2014 *Effective:* 1 January 2018	IFRS 16 *Leases* *Issued:* January 2016 *Effective:* 1 January 2019 IFRS 17 *Insurance Contracts* *Issued:* May 2017 *Effective:* 1 January 2021 *Amendments to References to the Conceptual Framework in IFRS Standards* *Issued:* March 2018 *Effective:* 1 January 2020
IAS 2 *Inventories*	3.8	IFRS 15 *Revenue from Contracts with Customers* *Issued:* May 2014 *Effective:* 1 January 2018	IFRS 16 *Leases* *Issued:* January 2016 *Effective:* 1 January 2019
IAS 7 *Statement of Cash Flows*	2.3	-	-
IAS 8 *Accounting Policies, Changes in Accounting Estimates and Errors*	2.8	-	IFRS 17 *Insurance Contracts* *Issued:* May 2017 *Effective:* 1 January 2021 *Amendments to References to the Conceptual Framework in IFRS Standards* *Issued*: March 2018 *Effective*: 1 January 2020
IAS 10 *Events after the Reporting Period*	2.9	-	-

STANDARD	RELATED CHAPTER(S)	LATEST EFFECTIVE AMENDMENTS OR REVISIONS	FORTHCOMING REQUIREMENTS
IAS 12 *Income Taxes*	3.13	-	IFRIC 23 *Uncertainty over Income Tax Treatments* *Issued:* June 2017 *Effective:* 1 January 2019 *Annual Improvements to IFRSs 2015–2017 Cycle – Amendments to IAS 12* *Issued:* December 2017 *Effective:* 1 January 2019
IAS 16 *Property, Plant and Equipment*	2.4, 3.2, 3.4, 5.7	IFRS 15 *Revenue from Contracts with Customers* *Issued:* May 2014 *Effective:* 1 January 2018	IFRS 16 *Leases* *Issued:* January 2016 *Effective:* 1 January 2019 IFRS 17 *Insurance Contracts* *Issued:* May 2017 *Effective:* 1 January 2021
IAS 17 *Leases*	3.4, 5.1	IFRS 15 *Revenue from Contracts with Customers* *Issued:* May 2014 *Effective:* 1 January 2018	IFRS 16 *Leases* *Issued:* January 2016 *Effective:* 1 January 2019 IFRS 17 *Insurance Contracts* *Issued:* May 2017 *Effective:* 1 January 2021
IAS 19 *Employee Benefits*	4.4	-	*Plan Amendment, Curtailment or Settlement – Amendments to IAS 19* *Issued:* February 2018 *Effective:* 1 January 2019
IAS 20 *Accounting for Government Grants and Disclosure of Government Assistance*	4.3	-	-
IAS 21 *The Effects of Changes in Foreign Exchange Rates*	2.7, 2.10, 7.7, 7I.6	IFRS 9 *Financial Instruments* *Issued:* July 2014 *Effective:* 1 January 2018	-

STANDARD	RELATED CHAPTER(S)	LATEST EFFECTIVE AMENDMENTS OR REVISIONS	FORTHCOMING REQUIREMENTS
IAS 21 *The Effects of Changes in Foreign Exchange Rates* (continued)		IFRIC 22 *Foreign Currency Transactions and Advances Consideration* *Issued:* December 2016 *Effective:* 1 January 2018	
IAS 23 *Borrowing Costs*	4.6	-	IFRS 16 *Leases* *Issued:* January 2016 *Effective:* 1 January 2019 *Annual Improvements to IFRSs 2015–2017 Cycle – Amendments to IAS 23* *Issued:* December 2017 *Effective:* 1 January 2019
IAS 24 *Related Party Disclosures*	5.5	-	-
IAS 26 *Accounting and Reporting by Retirement Benefit Plans*	Not covered; see section *About this publication.*		
IAS 27 *Separate Financial Statements*	2.1, 5.13	-	-
IAS 28 *Investments in Associates and Joint Ventures*	2.1, 3.5	IFRS 9 *Financial Instruments* *Issued:* July 2014 *Effective:* 1 January 2018 *Annual Improvements to IFRSs 2014–2016 Cycle – Amendments to IAS 28* *Issued:* December 2016 *Effective:* 1 January 2018	*Sale or Contribution of Assets between an Investor and its Associate or Joint Venture – Amendments to IFRS 10 and IAS 28* *Issued:* September 2014 *Effective:* Deferred indefinitely IFRS 17 *Insurance Contracts* *Issued:* May 2017 *Effective: 1 January 2021*

STANDARD	RELATED CHAPTER(S)	LATEST EFFECTIVE AMENDMENTS OR REVISIONS	FORTHCOMING REQUIREMENTS
IAS 28 *Investments in Associates and Joint Ventures* (continued)			*Long-term Interests in Associates and Joint Ventures – Amendments to IAS 28* *Issued:* October 2017 *Effective: 1 January 2019*
IAS 29 *Financial Reporting in Hyperinflationary Economies*	2.7, 2.10	-	-
IAS 32 *Financial Instruments: Presentation*	7.10, 7I.1, 7I.3, 7I.8	-	IFRS 16 *Leases* *Issued:* January 2016 *Effective:* 1 January 2019 IFRS 17 *Insurance Contracts* *Issued:* May 2017 *Effective:* 1 January 2021
IAS 33 *Earnings per Share*	5.3	-	-
IAS 34 *Interim Financial Reporting*	5.9	IFRS 15 *Revenue from Contracts with Customers* *Issued:* May 2014 *Effective:* 1 January 2018	-
IAS 36 *Impairment of Assets*	2.4, 3.10	IFRS 9 *Financial Instruments* *Issued:* July 2014 *Effective:* 1 January 2018	IFRS 16 *Leases* *Issued:* January 2016 *Effective:* 1 January 2019 IFRS 17 *Insurance Contracts* *Issued:* May 2017 *Effective:* 1 January 2021
IAS 37 *Provisions, Contingent Liabilities and Contingent Assets*	3.12	IFRS 15 *Revenue from Contracts with Customers* *Issued:* May 2014 *Effective:* 1 January 2018	IFRS 16 *Leases* *Issued:* January 2016 *Effective:* 1 January 2019 IFRIC 23 *Uncertainty over Income Tax Treatments* *Issued:* June 2017 *Effective:* 1 January 2019

STANDARD	RELATED CHAPTER(S)	LATEST EFFECTIVE AMENDMENTS OR REVISIONS	FORTHCOMING REQUIREMENTS
IAS 37 *Provisions, Contingent Liabilities and Contingent Assets* (continued)			IFRS 17 *Insurance Contracts* *Issued:* May 2017 *Effective:* 1 January 2021
IAS 38 *Intangible Assets*	2.4, 3.3, 5.7	IFRS 15 *Revenue from Contracts with Customers* *Issued:* May 2014 *Effective:* 1 January 2018	IFRS 16 *Leases* *Issued:* January 2016 *Effective:* 1 January 2019
IAS 39 *Financial Instruments: Recognition and Measurement*	7I.1–7I.7	IFRS 9 *Financial Instruments* *Issued:* July 2014 *Effective:* 1 January 2018	-
IAS 40 *Investment Property*	2.4, 3.4, 5.7	IFRS 15 *Revenue from Contracts with Customers* *Issued:* May 2014 *Effective:* 1 January 2018 *Transfers of Investment Property – Amendments to IAS 40* *Issued:* December 2016 *Effective:* 1 January 2018	IFRS 16 *Leases* *Issued:* January 2016 *Effective:* 1 January 2019 IFRS 17 *Insurance Contracts* *Issued:* May 2017 *Effective:* 1 January 2021
IAS 41 *Agriculture*	2.4, 3.9, 4.3	-	-
IFRIC 1 *Changes in Existing Decommissioning, Restoration and Similar Liabilities*	3.2, 3.12	-	-
IFRIC 2 *Members' Shares in Co-operative Entities and Similar Instruments*	7.3, 7I.3	-	IFRS 17 *Insurance Contracts* *Issued: May 2017* *Effective:* 1 January 2021
IFRIC 4 *Determining whether an Arrangement contains a Lease*	5.1	IFRS 15 *Revenue from Contracts with Customers* *Issued:* May 2014 *Effective:* 1 January 2018	IFRS 16 *Leases* *Issued:* January 2016 *Effective:* 1 January 2019

Appendix I

STANDARD	RELATED CHAPTER(S)	LATEST EFFECTIVE AMENDMENTS OR REVISIONS	FORTHCOMING REQUIREMENTS
IFRIC 5 *Rights to Interests arising from Decommissioning, Restoration and Environmental Rehabilitation Funds*	3.12	-	-
IFRIC 6 *Liabilities arising from Participating in a Specific Market – Waste Electrical and Electronic Equipment*	3.12	-	-
IFRIC 7 *Applying the Restatement Approach under IAS 29 Financial Reporting in Hyperinflationary Economies*	2.10	-	-
IFRIC 9 *Reassessment of Embedded Derivatives*	7I.2	IFRS 9 *Financial Instruments* *Issued:* July 2014 *Effective:* 1 January 2018	IFRS 16 *Leases* *Issued:* January 2016 *Effective:* 1 January 2019
IFRIC 10 *Interim Financial Reporting and Impairment*	3.10, 5.9	IFRS 9 *Financial Instruments* *Issued:* July 2014 *Effective:* 1 January 2018	IFRS 16 *Leases* *Issued:* January 2016 *Effective:* 1 January 2019 IFRS 17 *Insurance Contracts* *Issued:* May 2017 *Effective:* 1 January 2021
IFRIC 12 *Service Concession Arrangements*	3.3, 5.12	IFRS 15 *Revenue from Contracts with Customers* *Issued:* May 2014 *Effective:* 1 January 2018	IFRS 16 *Leases* *Issued:* January 2016 *Effective:* 1 January 2019
IFRIC 14 *IAS 19 – Limit on a Defined Benefit Asset, Minimum Funding Requirements and their Interaction*	4.4	-	-
IFRIC 16 *Hedges of a Net Investment in a Foreign Operation*	7I.7	-	-
IFRIC 17 *Distributions of Non-cash Assets to Owners*	5.4, 5.13, 7.3, 7I.3	-	-

STANDARD	RELATED CHAPTER(S)	LATEST EFFECTIVE AMENDMENTS OR REVISIONS	FORTHCOMING REQUIREMENTS
IFRIC 19 *Extinguishing Financial Liabilities with Equity Instruments*	7.3, 7I.3	-	-
IFRIC 20 *Stripping Costs in the Production Phase of a Surface Mine*	5.11	-	-
IFRIC 21 *Levies*	3.12	-	-
IFRIC 22 *Foreign Currency Transactions and Advance Consideration*	2.7, 6.1	*Issued:* December 2016 *Effective:* 1 January 2018	-
IFRIC 23 *Uncertainty over Income Tax Treatments*	3.12, 3.13	-	*Issued:* June 2017 *Effective:* 1 January 2019
SIC-7 *Introduction of the Euro*	None	-	-
SIC-10 *Government Assistance – No Specific Relation to Operating Activities*	4.3	-	-
SIC-15 *Operating Leases – Incentives*	5.1	IFRS 15 *Revenue from Contracts with Customers* *Issued:* May 2014 *Effective:* 1 January 2018	IFRS 16 *Leases* *Issued:* January 2016 *Effective:* 1 January 2019
SIC-25 *Income Taxes – Changes in the Tax Status of an Entity or its Shareholders*	3.13	-	-
SIC-27 *Evaluating the Substance of Transactions Involving the Legal Form of a Lease*	5.1	-	IFRS 16 *Leases* *Issued:* January 2016 *Effective:* 1 January 2019
SIC-29 *Service Concession Arrangements: Disclosures*	5.12	-	-
SIC-32 *Intangible Assets – Web Site Costs*	3.3	-	-

TABLE OF CONCORDANCE

This table primarily shows how guidance that was included in the fourteenth edition has moved. The table of concordance does not include changes to paragraph numbers made as a result of forthcoming requirements, changes in the format of examples or editorial amendments.

2017/18 EDITION REFERENCE 14TH EDITION	CURRENT REFERENCE 15TH EDITION	2017/18 EDITION REFERENCE 14TH EDITION	CURRENT REFERENCE 15TH EDITION
2.4.300.100	2.4.300.100–120	3.12.199.05–30	7.1.139.20–40, 7I.1.85.10–40
2.4.920.15	2.4.920.30		
2.4.920.20	2.4.920.40	3.12.199.50–120	7.1.139.50–110, 7I.1.85.50–120
2.4.920.40	2.4.920.50		
2.4.970.30	2.4.970.05	3.12.199.40	7.1.140.20, 7I.1.87.20
2.7.90.20	2.7.93.20	3.12.375	3.12.370
2.7.90.25–60	2.7.95.10–75	3.12.390–475	3.12.380–470
2.7.230.20	2.7.230.70	3.12.640.50–70	3.12.640.40–60
3.2.380.60	3.2.380.35	3.12.754.80	3.12.754.90
3.2.380.70	3.2.380.15	3.12.760.20	3.12.760.25
3.2.380.80–110	3.2.380.60–90	3.13.160.50	3.13.730.10
3.4.250.40	Deleted	3.13.660.100	3.13.660.70
3.5.540.20–50	3.5.530.30–60	3.13.665.40–50	3.13.665.80–90
3.5.560–690	3.5.540–670	3.13.730–780	3.13.760–810
3.8.100.10	3.8.100.20	3.13.790–830	3.13.820–860
3.8.440.10–90	3.8.400.10–90		
3.10.310–330	3.10.680–860	3.13.840–1090	3.13.870–1020
3.10.340–586	3.10.310–585	3.13.1100–1180	3.13.1130–1210
3.10.680	3.10.870	3.13.1190	3.13.1220
3.12.196	7.1.130.20, 7I.1.83	3.13.1200	3.13.1230
3.12.197.10	3.12.195.20, 7I.1.83.10	3.13.1205–1210	3.13.1240–1250

2017/18 Edition REFERENCE 14TH Edition	CURRENT REFERENCE 15TH Edition
3.13.1210	3.13.1250
3.13.1220	3.13.1260
4.2A.190.32–38	4.2.190.50–80
4.2A.190.40	4.2.190.130
4.2A.190.50	4.2.190.140
4.2A.220.162–168	4.2.220.170–200
4.2A.220.170–180	4.2.220.290–300
4.2A.230.60–70	4.2.230.50–60
4.2A.290.80	4.2.290.30
4.2A.290.90–140	4.2.290.80–130
4.2A.380.20	4.2.380.30
4.5.930.30–50	Deleted
4.5.930.60–70	4.5.930.40–50
4.5.960.10	Deleted
4.5.1350.20–80	Deleted
4.5.2160.10–20	Deleted
4.6.10.40	4.6.20.140
5.1A.40	5.1A.110
5.1A.50	5.1A.60
5.1A.60	5.1A.50
5.1A.70.20	5.1A.90.30
5.1A.70.30	5.1A.95.10
5.1A.70.40–70	5.1A.95.30–50
5.1A.70.80	5.1A.90.40
5.1A.70.90–120	5.1A.75.10–40
5.1A.70.130–140	5.1A.75.90–100
5.1A.75.10–20	5.1A.80.10–20
5.1A.75.30–40	5.1A.80.40–50

2017/18 Edition REFERENCE 14TH Edition	CURRENT REFERENCE 15TH Edition
5.1A.80	5.1A.100
5.1A.90	5.1A.40
5.1A.100.10–20	5.1A.90.10–20
5.1A.100.50–130	5.1A.90.50–150
5.1A.110.10–240.40	5.1A.140.10–255.40
5.1A.240.50–270.20	5.1A.255.80–280.20
5.1A.270.30	5.1A.280.10
5.1A.270.40	5.1A.120.10, 130.10
5.1A.280.10–310.10	5.1A.290.10–315.10
5.1A.310.20–50	5.1A.320.20–50
5.1A.320–520	5.1A.340–465
5.1A.530–560.10	5.1A.475–490.10
5.1A.560.20–570.20	5.1A.490.30–495.20
5.1A.580–640.10	5.1A.500–540.10
5.1A.650–750.120	5.1A.550–675.100
5.1A.760.10	5.1A.690.10
5.1A.760.20–800.10	5.1A.690.30–730.10
5.7.40.30–40	5.7.40.20–30
5.7.60–90	5.7.50–80
5.12.70.20	5.12.70.90
5.12.70.25	5.12.70.20
5.12.70.28	5.12.70.30
5.12.70.65–80	5.12.70.140–170
5.12.70.90	5.12.70.180
5.12.70.100–110	5.12.70.190–200
5.12.85	5.12.90
6.1.600.20	Deleted
6.1.610	Deleted
6.1.620.10–20, 40–70	Deleted
6.1.620.30	6.1.610.40

2017/18 Edition REFERENCE 14TH Edition	CURRENT REFERENCE 15TH Edition
6.1.640	Deleted
7A.1.120.20	7.1.120.170
7A.1.120.30	7.1.120.180
7A.1.130.20	7.1.134.10, 136.10
7A.1.130.30–40	7.1.132.40–50
7A.1.130.50–60	7.1.132.130–140
7A.1.130.70	7.1.136.10, 139.20
7A.1.130.80–140	7.1.137.10–70
7.4.340.20	7.4.340.35
7A.6.95.10	7.6.95.25
7A.7.250.20–40	Deleted
7A.7.310.10–60	7.7.300.10–60
7A.7.310.70	7.7.300.70
7A.7.320	7.7.310
7A.7.330.10	7.7.320.10
7A.7.300.10	7.7.330.10
7A.7.300.20	7.7.330.40
7A.7.300.30	7.7.330.50
7A.7.300.40–50	7.7.330.70–80
7A.7.300.60–70	7.7.330.90–100
7A.7.350.22–25	7.7.350.260–270
7A.7.350.30	7.7.350.70–90
7A.7.350.40	7.7.350.100–120
7A.7.350.50–60	7.7.350.300–310
7A.7.350.70	7.7.350.320
7A.7.360.10	7.7.360.10–20
7A.7.375.10	7.7.370.30
7A.7.375.20	7.7.370.50–60
7A.7.370.10	7.7.375.10

2017/18 Edition REFERENCE 14TH Edition	CURRENT REFERENCE 15TH Edition
7A.7.370.15	7.7.375.20
7A.7.370.20–30	7.7.375.30
7A.7.370.40–50	7.7.375.40–50
7A.7.550	Deleted
7A.9.450.80	7.9.450.90
7A.9.850.70	7.9.853.10
7A.9.850.80–130	7.9.855.10–60
7A.9.960.40–50	7.9.960.90–100
7A.10.60.50	7.10.65.10
7A.10.60.60	7.10.65.30–40
7A.10.160.40–50	7.10.167.10–20
7.11.20.50–60	Deleted
7.11.20.80	7.11.50.30
7.11.30.30	7.11.50.30
7.11.50	Deleted
7.11.120.40–60	Deleted
3.12.196.10	7I.1.80.20
7.1.80.10	7I.1.80.50–60
7.1.190.40–60	Deleted
7.6.270.12–40	7I.6.270.30–100
7.6.740.10–20	7I.6.730.20–30
7.6.750.10	7I.6.730.40
7.6.760.20–50	7I.6.730.60–90
7.6.760.60	7I.6.730.130
7.7.80.40–50	7I.7.80.70–80
7.7.690.20–30	7I.7.690.70–80
7.8.225.25	Deleted
8.1.20.50	Deleted
8.1A.20.60–120	8.1A.20.130–190

2017/18 Edition REFERENCE 14TH Edition	CURRENT REFERENCE 15TH Edition
8.1A.20.130–150	8.1A.220–240
8.1A.20.160	8.1A.20.260
8.1A.20.170–180	8.1A.20.280–290
8.1A.30.30	8.1A.30.50
8.1A.60.10	8.1A.60.10, 20, 40
8.1A.70.10	8.1A.70.30
8.1A.80.10–20	8.1A.80.20–30
8.1A.80.30–50	8.1A.80.60–80
8.1A.80.60	8.1A.80.100
8.1A.80.70–110	8.1A.80.120–160
8.1A.110.20	Deleted
8.1A.110.30–90	8.1A.110.20–80
8.1A.110.110–150	8.1A.110.120–160
8.1A.140.40	8.1A.140.120
8.1A.160.20–80	8.1A.160.50–110
8.1A.160.90	8.1A.160.210, 240
8.1A.170.20–60	8.1A.170.50–90
8.1A.180.70	8.1A.180.90
8.1A.200.30–40	8.1A.20.40–50
8.1A.210.30	8.1A.210.40
8.1A.210.40	8.1A.210.60
8.1A.210.50	8.1A.210.100
8.1A.230.40	8.1A.230.50
8.1A.240.50–80	8.1A.240.60–90
8.1A.240.30–60	8.1A.240.40–70
8.1A.310.20	8.1A.310.20, 50
8.1A.310.30–50	8.1A.310.60–80
8.1A.310.60–80	8.1A.310.120–140
8.1A.370.30–40	8.1A.370.40–50

2017/18 Edition REFERENCE 14TH Edition	CURRENT REFERENCE 15TH Edition
8.1A.410.30	8.1A.410.40
8.1A.430.10–110	8.1A.430.20–120
8.1A.460.20	8.1A.460.30
8.1A.540.40	8.1A.540.50

Appendix III

LIST OF EXAMPLES

2.5 Consolidation

2.6   Business combinations

2.7   Foreign currency translation

2.8   Accounting policies, errors and estimates

2.9   Events after the reporting date

2.10   Hyperinflation

3.1 General

3.2 Property, plant and equipment

3.6   Joint arrangements

3.8 Inventories

3.9 Biological assets

3.10 Impairment of non-financial assets

3.12   Provisions, contingent assets and liabilities

3.13   Income taxes

4.1 General

4.2 Revenue

4.3   Government grants

4.4   Employee benefits

4.5   Share-based payments

5.1A Leases: IFRS 16

5.2 Operating segments

5.3   Earnings per share

5.4 Non-current assets held for sale and discontinued operations

5.5 Related party disclosures

5.6 Investment entities

5.7 Non-monetary transactions

5.9 Interim financial reporting

5.10 Disclosure of interests in other entities

5.11 Extractive activities

5.12 Service concession arrangements

5.13   Common control transactions and Newco formations

6.1 First-time adoption of IFRS

7.3 Equity and financial liabilities

7.4   Classification of financial assets

7.5 Classification of financial liabilities

7.6 Recognition and derecognition

7.7   Measurement

7.10   Presentation and disclosures

7.11   Transition to IFRS 9

7I.1   Scope and definitions

7I.2   Derivatives and embedded derivatives

7I.3 Equity and financial liabilities

7I.4   Classification of financial assets and financial liabilities

7I.5   Recognition and derecognition

7I.6   **Measurement and gains and losses**

7I.7   **Hedge accounting**

7I.8 Presentation and disclosures

8.1 Insurance contracts

8.1A Insurance contracts: IFRS 17

INDEX

A

Index

H

R

Notes

Notes

Notes

Notes

Notes

Notes

Notes

Notes

Notes

Notes

Notes

Notes

Notes

Notes

Notes

Insights into IFRS

**KPMG's practical guide to
IFRS Standards**

15th Edition 2018/19

Volume 2

The KPMG International Standards Group

SWEET & MAXWELL

THOMSON REUTERS

ISBN 978-0-414-06957-2

Printed and bound by L.E.G.O. S.p.A., Lavis (TN), Italy

EMBEDDING AND EXPLAINING THE CHANGES

After many years of deliberation and preparation, the new standards on revenue recognition and financial instruments are finally effective! Companies across the globe have worked hard to implement their requirements – now it's time to fully embed the changes and clearly explain their effects to investors and other stakeholders.

Under the new revenue standard, IFRS 15, companies will find that the analysis that needs to be performed and the disclosures required are very different – even if the numbers in their financial statements don't change significantly as a consequence of implementing the new requirements.

As for the new financial instruments standard, IFRS 9… The impairment requirements for banks may steal the limelight, but for corporates more broadly it brings opportunities for more effective hedge accounting, which could produce a more stable earnings environment – no small prize.

As you apply these new standards in your 2018 annual financial statements, I would encourage you to embrace the opportunity to think through how best to explain the changes. Remember that the quality and clarity of explanations of changes in accounting policies and their impacts are key. And that investors will be keenly interested in disclosures of key judgements and estimates.

At the same time, keep an eye on IFRS 16. The new leasing standard will be effective before we know it. And although many companies are well advanced with their preparations, no one can afford to become complacent.

And finally, let's not forget insurers, who face a major task in preparing for IFRS 17. For many, this will involve an overhaul of their business processes, with many taking advantage of the opportunity to streamline and achieve efficiencies.

With so many moving parts, *Insights into IFRS* provides in-depth guidance across the complete set of standards, including detailed information on existing standards as well as analysis of the new ones. Whether you read it in hard copy or e-book – or both – I hope it will prove a valuable companion as you embed and explain the changes.

Reinhard Dotzlaw, Global IFRS Leader
KPMG International Standards Group

OVERVIEW OF CONTENTS

ABOUT THIS PUBLICATION

Insights into IFRS, now in its 15th edition, emphasises the application of IFRS in practice and explains the conclusions that we have reached on many interpretative issues. Based on actual questions that have arisen in practice around the world, *Insights into IFRS* includes many illustrative examples to elaborate or clarify the practical application of IFRS.

Insights into IFRS is an interpretative guide to IFRS that builds on those standards and should be read alongside them.

ORGANISATION OF THE TEXT

This publication is organised into topics and is presented in two volumes.

Volume 1 includes separate sections dealing with:
- general issues such as business combinations and fair value measurement;
- specific items in the statement of financial position and statement of profit or loss and OCI;
- special topics such as leases; and
- issues relevant to those making the transition to IFRS.

Volume 2 includes separate sections dealing with:
- financial instruments;
- insurance contracts; and
- fair value measurement (the guidance included in Volume 1 is reproduced in Volume 2).

Both volumes include the following Appendices.
- Appendix I: List of standards and interpretations that comprise the currently effective requirements and the forthcoming requirements.
- Appendix II: Table of concordance showing how the guidance that was included in the 14th edition has moved.
- Appendix III: List of examples.

Paragraphs dealing with **separate financial statements** are indicated by an Ⓢ in the outer margin.

STANDARDS AND INTERPRETATIONS

This 15th edition of *Insights into IFRS* reflects IFRS in issue at 1 August 2018. The guidance differentiates between **currently effective requirements, forthcoming requirements** and **possible future developments**.

Currently effective requirements

The main text is based on those standards that are required to be aplied by an entity with an annual reporting period beginning on 1 January 2018 – i.e. an entity with an annual reporting date of 31 December 2018. These requirements are referred to as the **currently effective requirements**.

IFRS 15 *Revenue from Contracts with Customers* has come into force, so this edition of *Insights into IFRS* no longer contains the guidance on the superseded standards; chapter 4.2 now focuses on the newly effective requirements of IFRS 15.

This edition also contains detailed guidance on both the newly effective and predecessor financial instruments standards.
- *Section 7:* Provides guidance on IFRS 9 *Financial Instruments*, issued in 2014 and amended in 2017, and the related standards, including consequential amendments introduced by IFRS 9.
- *Section 7I:* Provides guidance on the predecessor standard – IAS 39 *Financial Instruments: Recognition and Measurement* – and the related standards, excluding any amendments introduced by IFRS 9.

An introduction to Sections 7 and 7I explains when an entity can continue to apply some or all of the requirements in the predecessor standard.

This publication does not consider the requirements of IAS 26 *Accounting and Reporting by Retirement Benefit Plans*. In addition, this publication does not address the requirements included in the *IFRS for Small and Medium-sized Entities* (IFRS for SMEs), which was published in July 2009, other than in a brief overview of the IFRS for SMEs in chapter 1.1.

Forthcoming requirements

A currently effective requirement may be subject to change by a new requirement that has been issued at 1 August 2018, but is not yet effective for an annual reporting period ending on 31 December 2018. These new requirements are referred to as **forthcoming requirements**.

In addition, the following chapters relate entirely to forthcoming requirements.

5.1A	IFRS 16 *Leases*
8.1A	IFRS 17 *Insurance Contracts*

Future developments

For some topics, we anticipate changes to IFRS in issue at 1 August 2018 – typically as a result of an IASB project. These changes are referred to as **future developments**.

REFERENCES

| Currently effective requirements | Our discussion of the current requirements of IFRS and our related interpretations are referenced to the 2018 *IFRS Standards required 1 January 2018* ('Blue Book').

References in square brackets after the text identify the relevant paragraphs of the standards or other literature – e.g. *IFRS 1.7* is paragraph 7 of IFRS 1; *IFRIC 12.IE27–IE28* is paragraphs 27 to 28 of the IFRIC 12 illustrative examples; and *IFRS 13.EM.02-13.13* is paragraph 13 of the educational material on fair value measurement (IFRS 13) issued in February 2013.

Currently effective requirements also refer to the IFRS Practice Statements – e.g. *IPS 2.70* is paragraph 70 of *IFRS Practice Statement 2: Making Materiality Judgements.* |
|---|---|
| Forthcoming requirements | The forthcoming requirements are referenced to the 2018 *IFRS Standards issued at 1 January 2018* ('Red Book'), except for *Plan Amendment, Curtailment or Settlement – Amendments to IAS 19* that were issued after the Red Book 2018 was published. |
| IFRS Interpretations Committee decisions and IASB tentative decisions | References to IFRS Interpretations Committee decisions and IASB tentative decisions, addressed in their publications *IFRIC Update* and *IASB Update*, respectively, are also referenced – e.g. *IU 03-11* is *IFRIC Update* March 2011; and *IASBU 05-09* is *IASB Update* May 2009. |

E-BOOK EDITION

Insights into IFRS is also now available as an e-book on ProView™. It makes your most complex searches efficient, lets you make notes, highlight text, bookmark text, share content (via email or PDF) and review your browsing history. But perhaps best of all is that your annotations will be automatically transferred to subsequent editions of *Insights*.

For more information on accessing your personal e-book, speak to your usual KPMG contact.

KEEPING IN TOUCH

For the latest on IFRS, visit kpmg.com/ifrs. To join the conversation, follow KPMG IFRS on LinkedIn.

Whether you are new to IFRS or a current user, you can find digestible summaries of recent developments, detailed guidance on complex requirements, and practical tools such as illustrative disclosures and checklists.

IFRS news	The latest need-to-know information on IFRS
IFRS toolkit	Insights into IFRS Guides to financial statements: • Illustrative IFRS disclosures • Disclosure checklist Newly effective standards Fair value measurement: Questions and Answers IFRS compared to US GAAP Combined and/or carve-out financial statements
Major new standards	Financial instruments Revenue from contracts with customers Leases Insurance contracts
Amendments to existing standards	Business combinations and consolidation Presentation and disclosure
Sectors	IFRS for banks IFRS 15: Are you good to go? • Aerospace and defence • Airlines • Automotive suppliers • Banks • Construction • Food, drink and consumer goods • Insurers • Investment management • Media • Pharma • Real estate • Retail • Technology IFRS 16 for: • Consumer markets and retail • Oil and gas • Telcos

For access to an extensive range of accounting, auditing and financial reporting guidance and literature, visit KPMG's Accounting Research Online. This web-based subscription service can be a valuable tool for anyone who wants to stay informed in today's dynamic environment. For a free 30-day trial, go to aro.kpmg.com and register today.

ABBREVIATIONS

The following abbreviations are used often within this publication.

CDO	Collateralised debt obligation
CDS	Credit default swap
CEO	Chief Executive Officer
CGU	Cash-generating unit
CODM	Chief operating decision maker
COO	Chief Operating Officer
CPI	Consumer price index
DPF	Discretionary participation feature
E&E	Exploration and evaluation
EBIT	Earnings before interest and taxes
EBITDA	Earnings before interest, taxes, depreciation and amortisation
ECL	Expected credit loss
EPS	Earnings per share
ESPP	Employee share purchase plan
EU	European Union
FASB	US Financial Accounting Standards Board
FIFO	First-in, first-out
FVOCI	Fair value through OCI
FVTPL	Fair value through profit or loss
GAAP	Generally accepted accounting principles/practices
IAS	International Accounting Standards
IASB	International Accounting Standards Board
IFRS	International Financial Reporting Standards
IPO	Initial public offering
IT	Information technology
LIBOR	London interbank offered rate
LIFO	Last-in, first-out
NCI	Non-controlling interests
Newco	New entity
NRV	Net realisable value
OCI	Other comprehensive income
POCI	Purchased or originated credit-impaired
R&D	Research and development
REACH	Regulation for the *Registration, Evaluation and Authorisation of CHemicals* in the European Union
SIC	Standing Interpretations Committee
SPPI	Solely payments of principal and interest
WACC	Weighted-average cost of capital

ACKNOWLEDGEMENTS

This publication was made possible by the invaluable input of many people working in KPMG member firms worldwide. The overview of the requirements of IFRS and the interpretative positions described reflect the work of both current and former members of the KPMG International Standards Group, for which the authors and editors are grateful.

Current members of the International Standards Group and a panel of reviewers from KPMG member firms around the world generously contributed their time for exhaustive and challenging reviews of this edition. A list of contributors to this edition who we would like to thank is included below.

KPMG MEMBER FIRMS' CONTRIBUTORS
Principal editors

Suzanne Arnold	United Kingdom
Stacy Brown	United Kingdom
Irina Ipatova	United Kingdom

Authors and principal contributors

Angie Ah Kun	South Africa
Kimber Bascom	United States
Ewa Bialkowska	United Kingdom
Jim Calvert	Ireland
Peter Carlson	Australia
Albert Chai	Hong Kong
Jessica Cheong	Hong Kong
Matthew Cook	United Kingdom
Gina Desai	United Kingdom
Bryce Ehrhardt	United States
Otilia Gheaus	Romania
Alan Goad	United States
Audrey Hamm	Switzerland
Hakob Harutyunyan	Canada
Kim Heng	Australia
Martijn Huiskers	The Netherlands
Irina Ipatova	United Kingdom
Ramon Jubels	Brazil
Prabhakar Kalavacherla	United States

Manish Kaushik	India
Gabriela Kegalj	Canada
Hagit Keren	United Kingdom
Sarah Kindzerske	United States
Joachim Kölschbach	Germany
Kirill Kulakov	Russia
Julia LaPointe	United States
Wolfgang Laubach	Germany
Jee Won Lee	Korea (Republic of)
Sylvie Leger	Canada
David Littleford	United Kingdom
Colin Martin	United Kingdom
Hirotaka Matsuo	Japan
Mike Metcalf	United Kingdom
Mark Northan	United States
Brian O'Donovan	United Kingdom
Andrea Schriber	United Kingdom
Anne Schurbohm	Germany
Agnieszka Sekita	United Kingdom
Marina Shu	Australia
Chris Spall	United Kingdom
Shunya Uchida	Japan
Anisa Vallee	South Africa
Fred Versteeg	The Netherlands
Ido Vexelbaum	United Kingdom
Avi Victor	Romania
Nicolas Vigneron	France
Anthony Voigt	United Kingdom
Guy Zmora	Israel

PANEL OF REVIEWERS

IFRS Panel

Archana Bhutani	India
Reinhard Dotzlaw (Global IFRS Leader)	Canada
Ramon Jubels	Brazil
Prabhakar Kalavacherla	United States
Dick Korf	The Netherlands
Michael Sten Larsen	Denmark
Wolfgang Laubach	Germany
Andrew Marshall	United Kingdom
Reyaz Mihular	Sri Lanka
Catherine Morley	Hong Kong
Brad Owen	Canada

Emmanuel Paret	France
Tara Smith	South Africa
Patricia Stebbens	Australia
Hirotaka Tanaka	Japan

Business Combinations and Consolidation Topic Team

Mahesh Balasubramanian	Bahrain
Nicholas Beggs	Czech Republic
Hanne Böckem	Germany
Peter Carlson (Deputy leader)	Australia
Heather de Jongh	South Africa
Ralph Menschel	Mexico
Mike Metcalf (Leader)	United Kingdom
Paul Munter	United States
Emmanuel Paret	France
Andrea Schriber	United Kingdom
Marilyn Stitt	Canada
Hirotaka Tanaka	Japan
Jim Tang	Hong Kong
Michael Voogt	Australia

Employee Benefits Topic Team

Kees Bergwerff	The Netherlands
Zola Beseti	South Africa
Rodrigo Corominas	Mexico
Regina Croucher	United States
Barbara Griessner	United Kingdom
Kim Heng (Leader)	Australia
Sarah Inglis	Australia
Gale Kelly	Canada
Ko Sin	China
Michael Sten Larsen	Denmark
Takanobu Miwa	Japan
Balasubramanian Sundaresan	India
Anthony Voigt	United Kingdom

Financial Instruments Topic Team

Aram Asatryan	Russia
Ewa Bialkowska	United Kingdom
Jean-François Dandé	France
Simon Fishley	Brazil
Erik Hoogcarspel	The Netherlands
Gale Kelly	Canada
Colin Martin (Deputy leader)	United Kingdom

Mark Northan (Deputy leader)	United States
Toshihiro Ozawa	Japan
Tara Smith	South Africa
Chris Spall (Leader)	United Kingdom
Patricia Stebbens	Australia
Venkataramanan Vishwanath	India
Danny Vitan	Israel
Andreas Wolsiffer	Germany
Ella Zhang	China

Income Taxes Topic Team

Syed Anjum	Pakistan
Yen San Chan	Singapore
Kayreen Handley	United States
Yuki Hayashi	Japan
Irina Ipatova	United Kingdom
Tomasz Książek	Poland
Benoit Lebrun	France
Jesus Luna	Mexico
Agnes Lutukai	Nigeria
Zuzana Paulech	Australia
Cheryl Robinson	Canada
Anne Schurbohm	Germany
Fred Versteeg (Leader)	The Netherlands

Insurance Contracts Topic Team

Jennifer Austin	United States
Erik Bleekrode	Hong Kong
Dana Chaput	Canada
Danny Clark	United Kingdom
Paolo Colciago	Italy
Frank Dubois	Singapore
Bhavesh Gandhi	Kuwait
Alan Goad (Deputy leader)	United States
Hagit Keren	United Kingdom
Joachim Kölschbach (Leader)	Germany
Viviane Leflaive	France
Csilla Leposa	Hungary
Ian Moyser	Australia
Esther Pieterse	South Africa
Chris Spall	United Kingdom
Danielle Torres	Brazil
Mary Trussell (Deputy leader)	Germany

Leases Topic Team

Kimber Bascom (Leader)	United States
Zola Beseti	South Africa
Archana Bhutani	India
Judit Boros	Hungary
Úna Curtis	Ireland
Karine Dupré	France
Ramon Jubels	Brazil
Wolfgang Laubach	Germany
Sylvie Leger	Canada
Andrew Marshall	United Kingdom
Brian O'Donovan (Deputy leader)	United Kingdom
Yen San Chan	Singapore
Julie Santoro	United States
Patricia Stebbens	Australia
Mag Stewart	Canada
Beth Zhang	China

Presentation Topic Team

Holger Erchinger	United States
Yoshiaki Hasegawa	Japan
Se Bong Hur	Korea (Republic of)
Gabriela Kegalj (Deputy leader)	Canada
Wietse Koster	The Netherlands
David Littleford (Leader)	United Kingdom
Esther Pieterse	South Africa
Luis Preciado	Mexico
Ruchi Rastogi	India
Edith Schwager	France
Agnieszka Sekita	United Kingdom
Sanel Tomlinson	Hong Kong

Revenue Recognition and Provisions Topic Team

Brian Allen	United States
Eric Damotte	Spain
Lise du Randt	South Africa
Yusuf Hassan	United Arab Emirates
Kim Heng	Australia
Ramon Jubels	Brazil
Prabhakar Kalavacherla (Leader)	United States
Reinhard Klemmer	Singapore
David Littleford	United Kingdom
Vijay Mathur	India

Allison McManus	Canada
Brian O'Donovan (Deputy leader)	United Kingdom
Emmanuel Paret	France
Esther Pieterse	South Africa
Anne Schurbohm (Deputy leader)	Germany
Mikhail Stepanov	Russia
Sachiko Tsujino	Japan

Valuations and Impairment Topic Team

Frederik Bort	United States
Jim Calvert (Deputy leader)	Ireland
Marc Castedello	Germany
Robert de Virion	Poland
Martin Friedhoff	Hong Kong
Gabriela Kegalj	Canada
Reinhard Klemmer	Singapore
Wolfgang Laubach (Leader)	Germany
Sylvie Leger (Deputy leader)	Canada
Mahesh Narayanasami	United States
Tomoo Nishigori	Japan
Thina Opperman	South Africa
Nirav Patel	India
Jean-Florent Rerolle	France
Didier Saintot	France
Kuldip Singh	Panama
Orazio Vagnozzi	Italy

Thanks to Camila Benedetti and Christopher Czarnecki from Babson College (United States) for their assistance.

APPLYING FINANCIAL INSTRUMENTS GUIDANCE – INTRODUCTION TO SECTIONS 7 AND 7I

The guidance on financial instruments is covered in two sections.
- *Section 7:* Provides guidance on IFRS 9 *Financial Instruments*, issued in 2014 and amended in 2017, and the related standards, including consequential amendments introduced by IFRS 9.
- *Section 7I:* Provides guidance on the predecessor standard – IAS 39 *Financial Instruments: Recognition and Measurement* – and the related standards, excluding any amendments introduced by IFRS 9.

APPLYING IFRS 9 OR IAS 39

IFRS 9 (2014) – i.e. the complete version of IFRS 9 – largely replaces IAS 39 and is effective for annual periods beginning on or after 1 January 2018. Unless they are specifically exempted, all entities are required to apply IFRS 9 (2014) instead of IAS 39 from that date. This includes entities that previously:
- applied an earlier version of IFRS 9 (i.e. one of the versions of IFRS 9 issued in 2009, 2010 or 2013); or
- elected to apply only the requirements of IFRS 9 on the presentation of gains and losses on financial liabilities designated as at FVTPL (i.e. the inclusion of gains and losses arising from changes in own credit risk in OCI).

Unless otherwise indicated, the term 'IFRS 9' refers to the complete version.

Hedge accounting

When an entity first applies IFRS 9, it may choose an accounting policy to continue to apply the hedge accounting requirements in IAS 39 in their entirety instead of those in chapter 6 of IFRS 9 until a new standard resulting from the IASB's ongoing project on accounting for dynamic risk management becomes effective (see 7.9.80). An entity making this election is required to comply with the disclosure requirements for hedge accounting introduced by IFRS 9 (see 7.10.380.10).

Even if an entity does not make this election, it may still apply the hedge accounting requirements in IAS 39 for a fair value hedge of the interest rate exposure of a portfolio of financial assets or financial liabilities (see 7.9.70).

Insurers applying IFRS 4

IFRS 4 *Insurance Contracts* provides options to insurers to defer application of IFRS 9 or to apply an overlay approach to presentation (see 8.1.160).

An insurer is permitted to continue to apply IAS 39 rather than IFRS 9 for annual periods beginning before 1 January 2021 – i.e. before IFRS 17 *Insurance Contracts* becomes effective – if it meets the following criteria.
- It has not previously applied any version of IFRS 9. This condition is met if the insurer has applied only the presentation requirements in IFRS 9 for gains and losses on financial liabilities designated as at FVTPL (see 7.5.40).

- Its activities are predominately connected with insurance.

If the insurer adopts IFRS 17 early, then it can no longer apply this temporary exemption. An insurer applying the temporary exemption is permitted to elect to apply only the IFRS 9 presentation requirements for financial liabilities referred to above while otherwise continuing to apply IAS 39.

When an insurer that does not apply IFRS 17 first applies IFRS 9, it is permitted to apply the overlay approach to designated financial assets. For those financial assets, the insurer adjusts its profit or loss for the difference between the amount reported in profit or loss under IFRS 9 and the amount that would have been reported in profit or loss for those assets if the insurer had applied IAS 39. The ability to use the overlay approach falls away when the insurer adopts IFRS 17.

For further discussion of these elections and the qualifying criteria, see 8.1.160.

Prepayment features with negative compensation

In October 2017, the IASB issued *Prepayment Features with Negative Compensation – Amendments to IFRS 9*, which allow an entity to measure financial assets containing prepayment features with negative compensation at amortised cost or at FVOCI if they meet the other relevant requirements of IFRS 9. The amendments are effective for annual periods beginning on or after 1 January 2019, with early adoption permitted. For further discussion of the amendments, see 7.4.225 and 7.11.95.

Possible permutations of IFRS 9 and IAS 39

From the effective date of IFRS 9 – i.e. 1 January 2018 – the following permutations of IFRS 9 and IAS 39 application are possible.

Entities applying IFRS 9

- Applying only IFRS 9, including its general hedging model.
- Applying IFRS 9, including its general hedging model and IAS 39's model for portfolio fair value hedges of interest rate risk.
- Applying IFRS 9, subject to electing to apply IAS 39's hedge accounting requirements in their entirety.
- Applying IFRS 9, including its general hedging model, together with the overlay approach.
- Applying IFRS 9, including its general hedging model and IAS 39's model for portfolio fair value hedges of interest rate risk, together with the overlay approach.
- Applying IFRS 9, subject to electing to apply IAS 39's hedge accounting requirements in their entirety, together with the overlay approach.

Insurers applying the temporary exemption from IFRS 9

- Applying only IAS 39.
- Applying IAS 39 and electing to apply the presentation requirements in IFRS 9 for gains and losses on financial liabilities designated as at FVTPL.

The table below provides more detailed information on where the relevant guidance is located for each topic and application scenario.

APPLICATION OF STANDARDS / TOPICS	INSURERS APPLYING THE TEMPORARY EXEMPTION FROM IFRS 9[1]	ENTITIES APPLYING IFRS 9 (INCLUDING GENERAL IFRS 9 HEDGE ACCOUNTING REQUIREMENTS)[2]	ENTITIES APPLYING IFRS 9 (EXCLUDING GENERAL IFRS 9 HEDGE ACCOUNTING REQUIREMENTS)[2]
Scope and definitions	7I.1	7.1	7.1
Derivatives and embedded derivatives	7I.2	7.2	7.2
Equity and financial liabilities	7I.3	7.3	7.3
Classification of financial assets	7I.4	7.4	7.4
Classification of financial liabilities	7I.4	7.5	7.5
Recognition and derecognition	7I.5	7.6	7.6
Measurement and gains and losses (other than impairment)	7I.6	7.7	7.7
Impairment	7I.6	7.8	7.8
Hedge accounting	7I.7	7.9[3]	7I.7
Presentation and disclosures	7I.8	7.10	7.10[4]
Transition to IFRS 9	N/A[1]	7.11	7.11[4]

Notes

1. For an insurer applying the temporary exemption from IFRS 9, see the guidance in 8.1.160. If the insurer elects to apply the presentation requirements in IFRS 9 for gains and losses on financial liabilities designated as at FVTPL, then see the guidance in 7.7.180, 7.10.210.40–80, 7.11.30.10–20, 110 and 150 for related presentation, disclosure and transition requirements. Insurers applying the temporary exemption are required to provide disclosures to enable users of financial statements to compare entities that apply the temporary exemption from IFRS 9 with those that do not (see 8.1.270). These insurers may find it useful to refer to relevant parts of section 7 when applying the disclosure requirements. Furthermore, the disclosures are prepared using the relevant transition requirements of IFRS 9 as if the date of initial application were the beginning of the first annual period after 1 January 2018.
2. For an insurer applying the overlay approach, see the additional guidance in 8.1.160.
3. For an entity applying IAS 39's model for portfolio fair value hedges of interest rate risk, see 7.9.70 and 500.
4. An entity applying IFRS 9 but electing to continue to apply IAS 39's hedge accounting requirements needs to provide the new disclosures on hedge accounting introduced by IFRS 9 (see 7.10.380.10). The transition requirements on hedge accounting in chapter 7.11 do not apply while IAS 39's requirements continue to be applied.

7.   FINANCIAL INSTRUMENTS

7.1   Scope and definitions

7.   FINANCIAL INSTRUMENTS

7.1   Scope and definitions

CURRENTLY EFFECTIVE REQUIREMENTS

This publication reflects IFRS in issue at 1 August 2018, and the currently effective requirements cover annual periods beginning on or after 1 January 2018.

The requirements related to this topic are mainly derived from the following.

STANDARD	TITLE
IFRS 7	Financial Instruments: Disclosures
IFRS 9	Financial Instruments
IFRS 15	Revenue from Contracts with Customers
IAS 32	Financial Instruments: Presentation

FORTHCOMING REQUIREMENTS

The currently effective requirements are affected by the following forthcoming requirements. They are highlighted with a # and the impact is explained in the accompanying boxed text at the references indicated.

- In January 2016, the IASB issued IFRS 16 *Leases*, which is effective for annual periods beginning on or after 1 January 2019. See 7.1.155. IFRS 16 is the subject of chapter 5.1A.
- In May 2017, the IASB issued IFRS 17 *Insurance Contracts*, which is effective for annual periods beginning on or after 1 January 2021. See 7.1.45 and 55. IFRS 17 is the subject of chapter 8.1A.
- In October 2017, the IASB issued *Long-term Interests in Associates and Joint Ventures – Amendments to IAS 28*, which are effective for annual periods beginning on or after 1 January 2019. See 7.1.165. IAS 28 is the subject of chapter 3.5.

FUTURE DEVELOPMENTS

For this topic, there are no future developments.

7.1.10 **OVERVIEW OF FINANCIAL INSTRUMENTS STANDARDS**

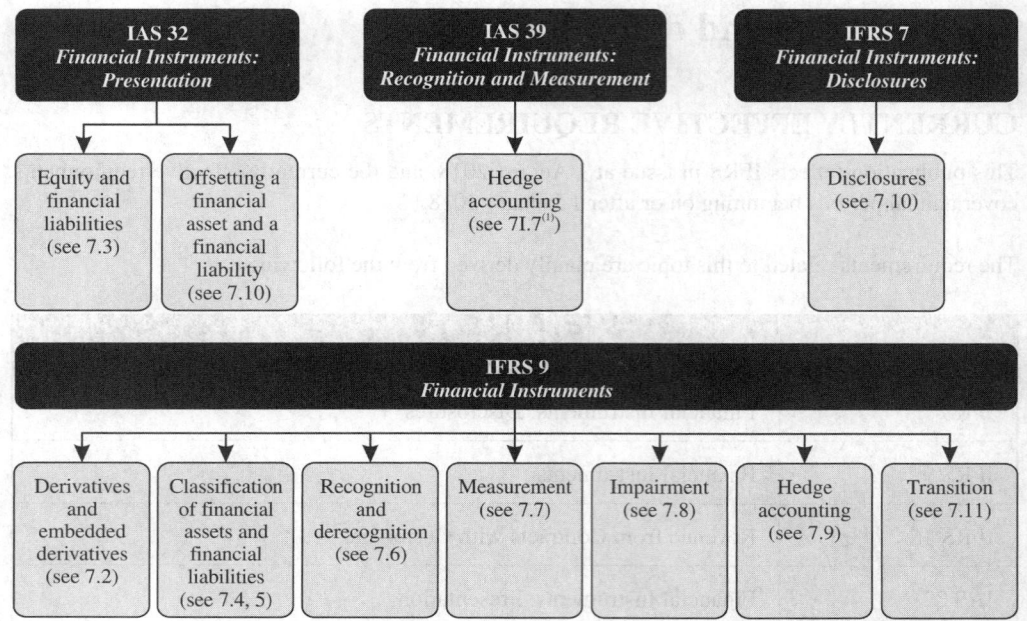

Note

1. IFRS 9 permits entities to choose, as an accounting policy, to continue to apply the hedge accounting requirements of IAS 39 instead of the requirements of IFRS 9. In addition, entities that choose to apply the hedge accounting requirements of IFRS 9 may apply the hedge accounting requirements of IAS 39 rather than IFRS 9 for a fair value hedge of the interest rate exposure of a portfolio of financial assets or financial liabilities.

7.1.20 SCOPE

7.1.20.10 The reporting of financial instruments is primarily addressed by three specific standards: IAS 32, IFRS 7 and IFRS 9. In addition, the measurement of fair value of financial instruments and disclosures about fair value are addressed by IFRS 13 (see chapter 2.4).

7.1.20.20 IAS 32 provides a definition of the term 'financial instrument'. It also defines the related concepts of financial assets, financial liabilities and equity instruments. IAS 32 provides guidance on whether a financial instrument is considered a financial asset, a financial liability or an equity instrument or whether it is a compound instrument that includes both liability and equity components. This guidance is focused largely on determining whether a financial instrument that an entity has issued is classified as a financial liability or as equity (see chapter 7.3). IAS 32 does not generally address recognition or measurement issues, but does contain accounting principles for derivatives on own equity instruments and for initial measurement, modification and conversion of compound instruments (see chapter 7.3). IAS 32 also addresses the presentation of interest and dividends (see chapter 7.3) and the offsetting of financial assets and financial liabilities (see chapter 7.10). [*IAS 32.4–10*]

7.1.20.30   IFRS 9 provides recognition and measurement requirements for financial assets and financial liabilities. This includes both primary financial instruments (e.g. cash, receivables, debt and shares in another entity) and derivative financial instruments (e.g. options, forwards, futures, interest rate swaps and currency swaps). [*IFRS 9.2.1–2.7*]

7.1.20.40   IFRS 7 requires entities to provide disclosures that enable users of their financial statements to evaluate the significance of financial instruments for the entity's financial position and performance, and the nature and extent of risks arising from financial instruments to which the entity is exposed and how the entity manages those risks. [*IFRS 7.3–5A*]

7.1.20.50   The scopes of the above three standards are not identical and are subject to different exclusions that are described in more detail in this chapter. Consequently, a scope exclusion in one standard cannot be assumed to apply equally in the other standards. In broad outline, IAS 32 generally applies to all financial instruments, including equity issued, whereas IFRS 9 applies only to financial assets and financial liabilities. IFRS 7 also generally applies to all financial instruments, although most of its disclosure requirements relate to financial assets and financial liabilities. However, certain financial assets and financial liabilities that are excluded from the scope of IFRS 9 are included in the scope of IFRS 7. In addition, IAS 32 and IFRS 9 require certain contracts to buy or sell non-financial items to be accounted for as if they were financial instruments (see 7.1.200). Derivatives embedded in non-financial contracts may also be accounted for in accordance with the financial instruments standards.

7.1.30   DEFINITIONS

7.1.30.10   A 'financial instrument' is any contract that gives rise to both a financial asset of one entity and a financial liability or equity instrument of another entity. [*IAS 32.11*]

7.1.30.20   Deferred revenue and prepaid expenses are not financial instruments because they are settled by the delivery or receipt of goods or services. [*IAS 32.AG11*]

7.1.30.30   A 'financial asset' is any asset that is:
- cash;
- a contractual right:
  - to receive cash or another financial asset; or
  - to exchange financial assets or financial liabilities under potentially favourable conditions;
- an equity instrument of another entity; or
- a contract that will or may be settled in the entity's own equity instruments and is:
  - a non-derivative for which the entity is or may be obliged to receive a variable number of the entity's own equity instruments; or
  - a derivative that will or may be settled other than by the exchange of a fixed amount of cash or another financial asset for a fixed number of the entity's own equity instruments. For this purpose, the entity's own equity instruments do not include: puttable financial instruments or instruments that impose on the entity an obligation to deliver to another party only on liquidation a pro rata share of the net assets of the entity that do not meet the definition of equity

instruments even if they are classified as equity instruments (see 7.3.70); or instruments that are contracts for the future receipt or delivery of the entity's own equity instruments. [*IAS 32.11*]

7.1.30.40   Gold bullion is a commodity and not a financial asset; therefore, it is not in the scope of IAS 32 or IFRS 9. Physical holdings of other commodities are also outside the scope of the financial instruments standards. However, contracts to buy or sell commodities or non-financial assets in the future are accounted for as derivatives if certain criteria are met (see 7.1.200). [*IFRS 9.IG.B.1, 2.4, IAS 32.8*]

7.1.30.50   A 'financial liability' is defined as:
- a contractual obligation:
  - to deliver cash or another financial asset to another entity; or
  - to exchange financial instruments under potentially unfavourable conditions; or
- a contract that will or may be settled in the entity's own equity instruments and is:
  - a non-derivative for which the entity is or may be obliged to deliver a variable number of its own equity instruments; or
  - a derivative that will or may be settled other than by the exchange of a fixed amount of cash or another financial asset for a fixed number of the entity's own equity instruments. For this purpose, rights, options or warrants to acquire a fixed number of the entity's own equity instruments for a fixed amount of any currency are equity instruments if the entity offers rights, options or warrants pro rata to all of its existing owners of the same class of its own non-derivative equity instruments. Also, for this purpose, the entity's own equity instruments are limited as described in 7.1.30.30. [*IAS 32.11*]

7.1.30.60   An 'equity instrument' is any contract that evidences a residual interest in the assets of an entity after deducting all of its liabilities (see chapter 7.3). [*IAS 32.11*]

7.1.30.70   The following two categories of financial instruments issued by an entity are exempt from liability classification even if they contain an obligation for the entity to deliver cash or another financial asset:
- puttable financial instruments that meet certain conditions; and
- an instrument, or a component of an instrument, that contains an obligation for the issuing entity to deliver to the holder a pro rata share of the net assets of the issuing entity only on its liquidation. [*IAS 32.16–16D*]

7.1.30.80   These instruments are classified as equity instruments provided that both the financial instrument and the issuing entity meet certain conditions (see 7.3.70).

7.1.30.90   IAS 32 provides a framework on the accounting for transactions in an entity's own equity instruments, including derivatives whose underlying is an entity's own equity instruments. IAS 32 also addresses the accounting treatment of treasury shares. For further discussion of these issues, see chapter 7.3. [*IAS 32.21–24, 33, AG27, AG36*]

7.1.30.100   The terms 'contract' and 'contractual' used in the definitions in 7.1.30.30 and 50 refer to an agreement between two or more parties that has clear economic consequences and that the parties have little, if any, discretion to avoid, usually because the agreement is enforceable by law. Contracts defining financial instruments may take a variety of forms and do not need to be in writing. An example of an item not meeting the definition of a financial instrument is a tax liability, because it is not based on a contract between two or more parties; instead, it arises as a result of tax law. [*IAS 32.13, AG12*]

7.1.40   **SPECIFIC EXEMPTIONS FROM FINANCIAL INSTRUMENTS STANDARDS#**

	IAS 32	IFRS 9	IFRS 7	APPLICABLE STANDARD
Interests in subsidiaries[1]	✘	✘	✘	IFRS 10 IAS 27
Interests in associates and joint ventures[1]	✘	✘	✘	IAS 28 IAS 27
Employers' rights and obligations under employee benefit plans	✘	✘	✘	IAS 19
Financial instruments, contracts and obligations under share-based payment transactions	✘	✘	✘	IFRS 2
Rights and obligations under insurance contracts (except embedded derivatives and certain financial guarantees)	✘	✘	✘	IFRS 4[2]
Financial instruments with a discretionary participation feature (except embedded derivatives)	✘[3]	✘	-	IFRS 4
Rights and obligations under leases	-	✘	-	IAS 17[4]
Equity instruments issued by the entity, including warrants and options that meet the definition of an equity instrument (for the issuer)	-	✘	-	IAS 32
Financial instruments issued by the entity that are classified as equity instruments in accordance with paragraphs 16A and 16B or paragraphs 16C and 16D of IAS 32 (for the issuer)	-	✘	✘	IAS 32
Forward contracts between an acquirer and a selling shareholder for the sale/acquisition of an acquiree that will result in a business combination at a future date of acquisition	-	✘	-	IFRS 3
Loan commitments that cannot be settled net in cash or another financial instrument that are not designated as at FVTPL and are not commitments to provide loans at below-market interest	-	✘[5]	-	-
Rights to reimbursement payments in relation to provisions	-	✘	-	IAS 37

	IAS 32	IFRS 9	IFRS 7	APPLICABLE STANDARD
Financial instruments that are rights and obligations in the scope of IFRS 15, except for those that IFRS 15 specifies are accounted for in accordance with IFRS 9 – e.g. receivables (see 4.2.470.60 and 7.8.10.10)	-	✗	-	IFRS 15

'✗' indicates a specific exclusion from the standard.

Notes
1. However, in some cases IFRS 10, IAS 27 or IAS 28 requires or permits an entity to account for an interest in a subsidiary, associate or joint venture in accordance with some or all of the requirements of IFRS 9 (see chapters 3.5 and 5.6), in which case the requirements of IAS 32, IFRS 9 and IFRS 7 apply. An entity applies IAS 32 to derivatives linked to interests in subsidiaries, associates or joint ventures. An entity also applies IFRS 9 and IFRS 7 to such derivatives, unless the derivative meets the definition of an equity instrument in IAS 32 (see 7.1.160 and 180).
2. IFRS 9 applies to an insurance contract that is an issued financial guarantee not accounted for under IFRS 4. IFRS 9 applies to a financial guarantee that arises when a transfer of a financial asset does not qualify for derecognition or when continuing involvement applies. Financial guarantee contracts held are not in the scope of IFRS 9. For a discussion of the accounting for financial guarantee contracts from the perspective of the holder, see 7.1.130. [*IFRS 9.4.2.1(b)*]
3. The issuer of such instruments is exempt from applying the financial liability/equity classification principles to the discretionary participation feature (see 8.1.110).
4. However, the following are subject to the specified provisions of IFRS 9 and to the requirements of IFRS 7: (1) lease receivables recognised by a lessor – derecognition and impairment provisions; (2) finance lease payables recognised by a lessee – derecognition provisions; and (3) derivatives embedded in leases – embedded derivative provisions (see 7.1.150).
5. However, the impairment requirements of IFRS 9 apply to such loan commitments issued and loan commitments are subject to the derecognition provisions of IFRS 9.

7.1.45   FORTHCOMING REQUIREMENTS

7.1.45.10   IFRS 4 applies to financial instruments that an entity issues with a discretionary participation feature (see 8.1.10.10). These instruments are scoped out of the measurement requirements of IFRS 9, but they are subject to the disclosure requirements of IFRS 7 and some of the presentation requirements of IAS 32.

7.1.45.20   By contrast, IFRS 17 applies to investments contracts with discretionary participation features only if the entity also issues insurance contracts (see 8.1A.40). Contracts in the scope of IFRS 17 are excluded from the scope of the disclosure requirements of IFRS 7 and all of the presentation requirements of IAS 32, as well as the measurement requirements of IFRS 9. Investment contracts with discretionary participation features issued by entities that do not issue insurance contracts are in the scope of IFRS 9, IFRS 7 and IAS 32. [*IFRS 7.3(d), 9.2.1(e), 17.3(c), IAS 32.4(d)*]

7.1.50   Insurance contracts#

7.1.50.10   There is a dividing line in IFRS between financial risk and insurance risk that is especially relevant for counterparty risk because it determines the nature of the contract as either an insurance contract to which IFRS 4 may apply or a financial instrument in respect of which IAS 32 and IFRS 9 apply.

7.1.50.20   An 'insurance contract' is a contract under which the insurer accepts significant insurance risk from the policyholder by agreeing to compensate the policyholder if a specified uncertain future event adversely affects the policyholder (see 8.1.20). [*IFRS 4.A*]

7.1.50.30   Although IAS 32 and IFRS 9 do not address the accounting for insurance contracts, they do not scope out insurance entities. Insurance entities apply IAS 32 and IFRS 9 to all financial instruments other than those that meet the definition of an insurance contract or a contract with a discretionary participation feature. Therefore, financial instruments that meet the definition of an insurance contract and that are in the scope of IFRS 4 are not subject to IFRS 9. However, IFRS 9 applies to a derivative that is embedded in a contract that is in the scope of IFRS 4, unless the derivative itself is in the scope of IFRS 4 (see 8.1.30). [*IFRS 9.2.1(e)*]

7.1.55   FORTHCOMING REQUIREMENTS

7.1.55.10   The definition of an insurance contract in IFRS 17 is almost the same as the definition in IFRS 4 (see chapter 8.1A). IFRS 17 does not change the scope requirements of IFRS 9 in respect of insurance contracts and derivatives embedded in those contracts. [*IFRS 9.2.1(e)*]

7.1.55.20   Consequential amendments introduced by IFRS 17 specify that investment components that are required to be separated from insurance contracts in the scope of IFRS 17 are subject to the requirements of IAS 32, IFRS 9 and IFRS 7. [*IFRS 7.3(d), 9.2.1(e), IAS 32.4(d)*]

7.1.60   **Financial guarantee contracts**

7.1.65   *Scope*

7.1.65.10   Financial guarantee contracts issued by an entity fall in the scope of IFRS 9 from the issuer's perspective except as discussed in 7.1.65.20. In our view, a financial guarantee contract held by an entity that is not an integral element of another financial instrument is not in the scope of IFRS 9 (see 7.1.136.10). [*IFRS 9.2.1(e)*]

7.1.65.20   Although financial guarantee contracts issued meet the definition of an insurance contract if the risk transferred is significant, they are generally outside the scope of IFRS 4 and are accounted for under IFRS 9. However, if an entity issuing financial guarantee contracts has previously asserted explicitly that it regards them as insurance contracts and has accounted for them as such, then the issuer may elect on a contract-by-contract basis to apply either IFRS 9 or IFRS 4. The election for each contract is irrevocable (see 8.1.10.30). [*IFRS 4.4(d), B18(g), 9.2.1(e), B2.5(a), BCZ2.12*]

7.1.65.30   For an entity whose business includes writing financial guarantee contracts, it will generally be clear from contract documentation, previously published financial statements and the entity's communications with customers and regulators etc whether it regards, and has previously accounted for, such contracts as insurance contracts. [*IFRS 9.B2.6*]

7.1.65.40   In other cases it may be less clear. For example, an entity might provide financial guarantees from time to time that are incidental to its main business, perhaps to support borrowings of its subsidiaries or major customers. In such cases, in our view judgement is required in determining whether previous assertions in financial statements or elsewhere are sufficiently explicit to continue to apply insurance accounting.

7.1.70   *Definition*

7.1.70.10   A 'financial guarantee contract' is a contract that requires the issuer to make specified payments to reimburse the holder for a loss that it incurs because a specified debtor fails to make payment when it is due in accordance with the original or modified terms of a debt instrument. [*IFRS 9.A*]

7.1.70.20   To be classified as a financial guarantee contract, a contract needs to comply with all of the following conditions.
- The reference obligation is a debt instrument (see 7.1.80).
- The holder is compensated only for a loss that it incurs (see 7.1.90).
- The contract does not compensate the holder for more than the actual loss that it incurs (see 7.1.100). [*IFRS 9.A*]

7.1.70.30   Financial guarantee contracts can have various legal forms, including certain letters of credit, credit default contracts and insurance contracts. However, the legal form of such contracts does not affect their accounting treatment. [*IFRS 9.B2.5*]

EXAMPLE 1 – FINANCIAL GUARANTEE CONTRACT – LETTER OF CREDIT

7.1.70.35   Bank B issues a letter of credit in the amount of up to 10,000 on behalf of its Customer C, identifying a foreign Supplier S as the beneficiary. Under the letter of credit, B promises to reimburse S for actual losses that S incurs if C fails to make the payments when due for its future specified purchases of 10,000 from S. The terms of the arrangement also require any subsequent recovery of reimbursed amounts from C to be returned to B.

7.1.70.37   The arrangement meets the definition of a financial guarantee contract. This is because under the terms of the letter of credit, B is required to reimburse S for a loss incurred if C – i.e. the specified debtor – fails to make a payment when it is due in accordance with the original debt instrument – i.e. the trade receivable. In other cases a letter of credit may meet the definition of a loan commitment as in Example 11E.

7.1.70.40   Credit-related contracts that require payment in circumstances other than those mentioned in 7.1.70.10 – e.g. if there is no failure by a specified debtor to make payment when it is due or if the holder would not incur a loss – are generally credit derivatives that are measured at fair value under IFRS 9. For the definition of derivatives, see 7.2.20. [*IFRS 4.IG2.1.12, 9.A, B2.5(b)*]

7.1.80   *Reference obligation is a debt instrument*

7.1.80.10   The first condition in the definition of a financial guarantee contract is that the contract should compensate the holder only for losses that it incurs on debt instruments – i.e. the 'reference obligation' in a financial guarantee contract should be a debt instrument. However, in our view this does not preclude a contract that contains a revolving portfolio as the reference obligation from being classified as a financial guarantee contract under IFRS 9. [*IFRS 9.A*]

7.1.80.20   IFRS 9 requires that a financial guarantee contract compensate the holder for losses that it incurs because of failure by 'specified debtors' to make payment when it is due. Consequently, in our view such a revolving portfolio structure does not violate the requirements of a financial guarantee contract if the following criteria are met.

- The portfolio of debt instruments is specified – i.e. the contract includes a list of debtors included in the reference portfolio at all times.
- All replacements to the portfolio are documented and contain restrictions, so that the replacement mechanism does not indirectly compensate the holder for any form of fair value loss on the reference portfolio. [*IFRS 9.A*]

7.1.80.30   The standard does not state what is meant by the term 'debt instrument' in the context of the definition of a financial guarantee contract. In our view, alternative approaches to the application of the definition are possible.

7.1.80.40   Based on a narrow reading, an entity may consider that the phrase is restricted to certain non-derivative debt instruments that are consistent with a basic lending arrangement – i.e. meet the SPPI criterion (see 7.4.150). Under this approach, the inclusion of a derivative instrument in the reference portfolio in 7.1.80.20 would violate the requirement that a financial guarantee contract compensate the holder only for losses that it incurs on debt instruments.

7.1.80.50   Alternatively, we believe that an entity may adopt a policy of applying the term to encompass derivatives and hybrid instruments that do or may give rise to an obligation of the debtor to make specified payments when they are due and that compensate the holder of the financial guarantee contract for failure to make timely payment of those specified amounts.

7.1.80.60   However, whatever the entity's policy, the definition of a financial guarantee contract is still met only if the contract compensates the holder solely for losses arising from the debtor's failure to make payment when it is due and not for losses arising from market risk.

EXAMPLE 2A – FINANCIAL GUARANTEE CONTRACT – HYBRID INSTRUMENTS

7.1.80.70   Investor Z buys structured notes that provide a return based on the movement in an equity index. Z also obtains a guarantee from a bank that, if the issuer of the notes fails to make payment of the full amount due on maturity of the notes, then the bank will pay the shortfall to Z. Such a contract may qualify as a financial guarantee contract depending on Z's accounting policy (see 7.1.80.50).

7.1.80.80   However, if the bank guaranteed to Z that it would pay any losses that Z incurred under the terms of the note because of a decrease in the equity index, then the contract would be a derivative and not a financial guarantee contract.

7.1.90   *Holder compensated only for a loss that it incurs*

7.1.90.10   The second condition that has to be met for a contract to be classified as a financial guarantee contract under IFRS 9 is that it should compensate the holder only for a loss that it incurs on the debt instrument. In our view, such a loss cannot be an opportunity loss or a fair value loss on a debt instrument but should be an actual loss that the entity incurs as a result of failure by a specified debtor to make payment when it is due. Consequently, contracts compensating the holder for losses arising from the restructuring of an entity do not lead automatically to a loss for the holder of the debt instrument other than a fair value loss, and it is possible that the holder will recover from the restructuring event. Therefore, we do not believe that a contract that compensates the holder for such losses meets the definition of a financial guarantee contract. [*IFRS 9.A*]

7.1.90.20   However, IFRS 9 is silent on when the cash flows should occur for compensation of a loss that an entity incurs. In our view, a contract may still meet the definition of a financial guarantee contract if the issuer makes payment to the holder for a past due amount provided that the contract requires any subsequent recovery of that amount from the specified debtor to be reimbursed to the issuer of the financial guarantee (see 7.1.100).

7.1.90.30   The definition of a financial guarantee contract does not require the holder of the guarantee also to hold the underlying debt instrument(s) as an asset, as long as the contract compensates the holder only for its losses arising from the debtor's failure to make payment when it is due on those debt instruments.

EXAMPLE 2B – FINANCIAL GUARANTEE CONTRACT – CREDIT-LINKED NOTES

7.1.90.40   Limited-purpose Vehicle L issues to investors 1,000 credit-linked notes with a stated 1,000 principal and 10% interest rate. Cash collected on an underlying pool of specified debt instruments held by L is used to fund distributions to investors. L has no other assets or operations and is prohibited from selling the debt instruments. Contractually, L is required to pay investors only to the extent that cash is collected from the underlying assets. A bank issues a guarantee to investors that they will receive the full 1,000 of principal and 10% interest from L. This is effected by the bank making payment of any shortfalls to an investor within 90 days, subject to the investor being required to reimburse any subsequent recoveries of such shortfalls to the bank.

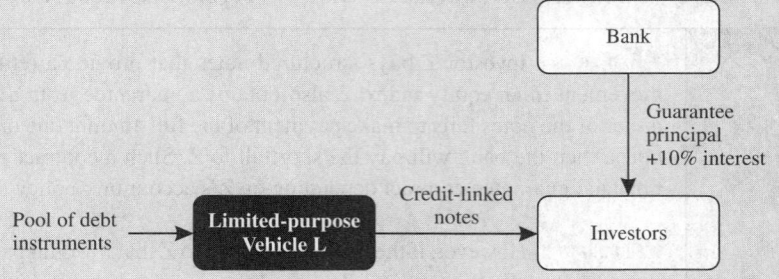

7.1.90.50   In this example, L's only exposure to risk that could lead to its failure to pay the stated return on the notes is the credit risk of the underlying pool of debt instruments. The investor would also suffer a loss if L were to fail to make payments when they were due in accordance with the terms of the notes even when L has obtained sufficient cash from its assets.

7.1.90.60   In our view, the guarantee agreement is a financial guarantee contract because the bank compensates the investor only for the loss that the investor would incur from a failure by specified debtors (either by the specified debtors in the underlying pool of debt instruments in L or by L itself) to make payment when it is due.

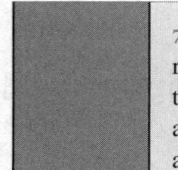

7.1.90.70   However, if the investor could fail to obtain the full 10% contractual return because of other risks – e.g. interest rate risk as a result of the portfolio containing floating rate loans – and the bank provided a guarantee covering shortfalls arising from those other risks, then the guarantee would not meet the definition of a financial guarantee contract.

7.1.90.80   Generally, a contract does not qualify as a financial guarantee contract if it provides for payments by the issuer in respect of amounts that are not past due. However, in many debt agreements non-payment of an amount that is due contractually would be an event of default that would trigger the entire remaining amount (principal and accrued interest) on the debt instrument to fall due.

7.1.90.90   For example, a contract between a guarantor and the holder of a loan with a maturity of five years allows for physical settlement – i.e. the guarantor is required to buy the entire outstanding debt amount at par plus accrued interest in the event of any non-payment by the debtor (e.g. a missed interest payment) that persists for 30 days beyond its due date. Under the terms of the loan, such a non-payment is an event of default. In our view, the contract would meet the definition of a financial guarantee contract if the non-payment condition that requires settlement of the guarantee also causes the entire outstanding debt amount to become immediately repayable. The issue of whether immediate repayment of the full amount of the debt instrument actually is requested by the creditor following the default does not affect the analysis.

7.1.90.100   Guarantee contracts that require payments to be made in response to changes in another specified variable – e.g. an interest rate, credit rating or credit index – are accounted for as derivatives in the scope of IFRS 9 provided that, in the case of a non-financial variable, the variable is not specific to a party to the contract (see 7.2.30.60). [*IFRS 9.B2.5*]

7.1.100   *Holder not compensated for more than actual loss that it incurs*

7.1.100.10   The third condition that needs to be satisfied is that the contract should not compensate the holder for an amount greater than the loss that it incurs on the debt instrument. Consequently, contracts that give rise to a leveraged payout that is greater than 100% of the loss do not meet the definition of a financial guarantee contract. For example, a contract such as a CDS that pays out to the protection buyer even if the holder does not have any exposure to the specified debt instrument does not meet the definition and is accounted for as a derivative. [*IFRS 4.IG2.1.12, 9.A*]

7.1.110   *Examples*

EXAMPLE 3A – FINANCIAL GUARANTEE CONTRACT – MEETING THE THREE CONDITIONS

7.1.110.10   A bank makes a loan to Company D. Company B issues a guarantee to the bank that if D fails to make a payment within 30 days after it falls due, then B will make the payment on behalf of D. The agreement states that if the bank subsequently recovers the payment from D, then the bank is required to immediately reimburse B for the amount received from D – i.e. the bank cannot retain an amount in excess of the loss that it ultimately incurs on the loan.

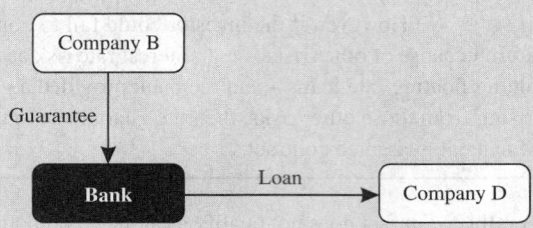

7.1.110.20   In this example, the contract meets the definition of a financial guarantee contract and is accounted for as such in B's financial statements. This is because the three conditions for classification as a financial guarantee contract have been met.

- The reference obligation is a debt instrument.
- The holder of the financial guarantee contract is compensated only for a loss that it incurs as a result of the debtor's failure to make a payment when it is due. In the example, the bank actually may or may not have incurred a loss when payment was not made within 30 days of the due date (because the debtor may make an appropriate payment later). However, as described in 7.1.90.10–20, if payment is made by the issuer before a loss is actually incurred by the holder, then the instrument can still qualify as a financial guarantee contract if the contract includes a provision that any subsequent recoveries of the overdue amount be repaid to the guarantor. This is because the inclusion of this provision ensures that the holder of the financial guarantee can be compensated only for its actual losses incurred.
- The financial guarantee contract does not compensate the holder for more than its actual losses incurred. In the example, this is achieved by the inclusion of the provision that any subsequent repayments of the overdue amount be repaid to the guarantor.

EXAMPLE 3B – FINANCIAL GUARANTEE CONTRACT – FAILING THE CONDITIONS

7.1.110.30   Modifying Example 3A, assume the same arrangement except that Company B will make payments to the bank based on changes in the credit rating of Company D.

7.1.110.40   In this example, the contract does not meet the definition of a financial guarantee contract, because B is required to make payments to the bank even if there is no failure by D to make payment when due and the bank does not incur a loss. Therefore, both B and the bank account for the contract as a derivative in their financial statements.

7.1.120   ***Accounting by the issuer***

7.1.120.10   If the issuer applies IFRS 9 to a financial guarantee contract, then it measures the contract:

- initially at fair value. If the financial guarantee contract was issued in a stand-alone arm's length transaction to an unrelated party, then its fair value at inception is likely to equal the premium received unless there is evidence to the contrary; and
- subsequently at the higher of:
  - the amount of the loss allowance determined in accordance with IFRS 9 (see chapter 7.8); and
  - the amount initially recognised less, when appropriate, the cumulative amount of income recognised in accordance with the principles of IFRS 15 (see chapter 4.2). [*IFRS 9.4.2.1(c), B2.5(a)*]

EXAMPLE 4A – FINANCIAL GUARANTEE ISSUED – MEASUREMENT

7.1.120.20   On 1 January 2019, Company C issues a financial guarantee to Company B and receives a premium of 300. Under the financial guarantee, C is required to reimburse B on 31 January 2022 for losses that B incurs from any non-payment between 2019 and 2021 on a bond held by B. C accounts for the financial guarantee under IFRS 9 and records the following entry on initial recognition.

	DEBIT	CREDIT
Cash	300	
Financial guarantee contract		300
To recognise the financial guarantee at fair value		

7.1.120.30   C determines the following amounts at each subsequent reporting date. The effect of discounting is disregarded for the purposes of this example.

31 DECEMBER	2019	2020	2021
Loss allowance	80	120	120
Amount initially recognised less cumulative amount of income recognised in accordance with the principles of IFRS 15	200	100	-

7.1.120.40   On 31 December 2019, the amount initially recognised less the cumulative amount of income recognised in accordance with the principles of IFRS 15 (200) is higher than the amount of the loss allowance (80). Accordingly, C measures the financial guarantee at 200 and does not recognise a loss allowance. C records the following entry.

	DEBIT	CREDIT
Financial guarantee contract	100	
Fee income		100
To recognise fee income from the financial guarantee for 2019		

7.1.120.50   On 31 December 2020, the amount of the loss allowance (120) is higher than the amount initially recognised less the cumulative amount of income recognised in accordance with the principles of IFRS 15 (100). Accordingly, C measures the financial guarantee at the amount of the ECL of 120. It first recognises income of 100 under IFRS 15, which reduces the carrying amount of the financial guarantee to 100. It then recognises an impairment loss of 20 in profit or loss, which increases the carrying amount of the financial guarantee to 120. C records the following entries.

	DEBIT	CREDIT
Financial guarantee contract	100	
Fee income		100
To recognise fee income from the financial guarantee for 2020		
Impairment loss	20	
Financial guarantee contract		20
To remeasure the financial guarantee to the amount of the loss allowance		

7.1.120.60   Applying the same principles, on 31 December 2021 C records the following entries.

	DEBIT	CREDIT
Financial guarantee contract	100	
Fee income		100
To recognise fee income from the financial guarantee for 2021		
Impairment loss	100	
Financial guarantee contract		100
To remeasure the financial guarantee to the amount of the loss allowance		

7.1.120.70   On 31 January 2022, C reimburses B for the actual losses that B incurs between 2019 and 2021 (represented by the loss allowance on the financial guarantee at 31 December 2021) and records the following entry.

	DEBIT	CREDIT
Financial guarantee contract	120	
Cash		120
To recognise cash paid under the financial guarantee		

7.1.120.80   IFRS 9 does not provide guidance on how the requirements in 7.1.120.10 should be applied if the issuer does not receive all of the premiums on initial recognition. Accordingly, it appears that the issuer should choose an accounting policy, to be applied consistently, to account for such contracts using one of the following approaches.

- *Gross approach:* Under this approach, the issuer recognises both:
  - a liability for its obligation to provide protection to the holder that is measured in accordance with 7.1.120.10 – i.e. the obligation to provide protection is measured at fair value on initial recognition. This fair value is likely to equal the sum of the premiums received and the fair value of the future premiums receivable; and
  - a financial asset in the scope of IFRS 9 for the future premiums receivable.
- *Net approach:* Under this approach, the issuer generally recognises a single net amount that is measured in accordance with 7.1.120.10.

7.1.120.90   If an issuer of a financial guarantee applies the net approach, then we believe that 'the amount initially recognised less, when appropriate, the cumulative amount of income recognised in accordance with the principles of IFRS 15' (see 7.1.120.10) should be increased by any premiums when they are received subsequent to initial recognition so that all premiums received are taken into account when measuring the financial guarantee.

7.1.120.100   In addition, under the net approach the ongoing recognition of income in accordance with the principles of IFRS 15 may cause, at particular points in time, the cumulative amount of income recognised to date to exceed the cumulative amount of premiums received to date. In such cases, the issuer of the financial guarantee accrues an amount in the statement of financial position representing the right to receive the excess from the holder. IFRS 9 does not specify how the 'higher of' measurement in 7.1.120.10 should be applied in such circumstances. It appears that an entity may choose an accounting policy, to be applied consistently, based on one of the following approaches.

- *Approach 1:* Exclude the accrued amount from the 'higher of' measurement and recognise it as a receivable separately from the financial guarantee contract liability. In this case, the issuer would measure the financial guarantee contract liability at the amount of the loss allowance. This is because 'the amount initially recognised less, when appropriate, the cumulative amount of income recognised in accordance with the principles of IFRS 15' would be considered to equal zero. Under this approach, the timing of income recognition is generally not affected by when the related premiums are received.
- *Approach 2:* Treat the accrued amount as representing a negative balance of 'the amount initially recognised less, when appropriate, the cumulative amount of income recognised in accordance with the principles of IFRS 15'. Under this approach, the financial guarantee contract would also be measured at the amount of the loss allowance. However, an accrued receivable would not be recognised separately from the financial guarantee contract liability. This approach reflects a strict application of the net approach but may result in swings in profit or loss depending on the timing of premium receipts – i.e. if premiums are received in arrears, then there may be losses reported during the early part of the coverage period that reverse out as cash premiums are received.

EXAMPLE 4B – PREMIUMS RECEIVED OVER THE LIFE OF A FINANCIAL GUARANTEE – NET APPROACH

7.1.120.110   Modifying Example 4A, Company C receives the total premiums of 300 in arrears in two instalments – 150 on 30 June 2020 and 150 on 31 December 2021.

C accounts for the financial guarantee under the net approach in 7.1.120.80 and Approach 1 in 7.1.120.100.

7.1.120.120   On 1 January 2019, C recognises the financial guarantee at its fair value of zero.

7.1.120.130   On 31 December 2019, C records the following entries to reflect:
- recognition of fee income of 100 for the year in accordance with the principles of IFRS 15 and a corresponding receivable; and
- remeasurement of the financial guarantee to the amount of the ECL of 80.

	DEBIT	CREDIT
Accrued fees receivable	100	
Fee income		100
To recognise fee income from the financial guarantee for 2019		
Impairment loss	80	
Financial guarantee contract		80
To remeasure the financial guarantee to the amount of the loss allowance		

7.1.120.140   On 31 December 2020, C records the following entries to reflect:
- receipt of premiums during the year of 150;
- recognition of fee income of 100 for the year in accordance with the principles of IFRS 15 and a corresponding receivable; and
- remeasurement of the financial guarantee to the amount of the ECL of 120.

	DEBIT	CREDIT
Cash	150	
Fee income		100
Accrued fees receivable		50
To recognise cash received and fee income from the financial guarantee for 2020		
Impairment loss	40	
Financial guarantee contract		40
To remeasure the financial guarantee to the amount of the loss allowance		

7.1.120.150   Applying the same principles, on 31 December 2021 C records the following entry.

	DEBIT	CREDIT
Cash	150	
Fee income		100
Accrued fees receivable		50
To recognise cash received and fee income from the *financial guarantee for 2021*		

7.1.120.160   On 31 January 2022, C reimburses B for the actual losses that B incurs between 2019 and 2021 (represented by the loss allowance on the financial guarantee at 31 December 2021) and records the following entry.

	DEBIT	CREDIT
Financial guarantee contract	120	
Cash		120
To recognise cash paid under the financial guarantee		

7.1.120.170   In the case of a guarantee provided by a parent over the liability of a subsidiary, even (S) if no consideration is or will be received by the parent, the parent is required to recognise a liability in its separate financial statements for the fair value of the guarantee. In our view, if no payments from the subsidiary to the parent are agreed for such a guarantee, then the parent has provided the guarantee in its capacity as a shareholder and accounts for the issuance of the guarantee as a capital contribution to the subsidiary.

7.1.120.180   An exception to the general measurement principles is provided for financial guarantee contracts that arise when a transfer of financial assets does not qualify for derecognition or results in continuing involvement. Such contracts are measured in accordance with specific provisions in IFRS 9 (see 7.6.240). [*IFRS 9.3.2.15–3.2.17, 4.2.1(b)*]

7.1.130   *Accounting by the holder*

7.1.130.10   In our view, the criteria for identifying a contract as a financial guarantee contract are the same for both the holder and the issuer.

7.1.130.20   An entity may buy a debt instrument whose terms include, or that is accompanied by, a guarantee of payments on the debt instrument, which is issued by a party other than the issuer of the debt instrument and which has the features of a financial guarantee contract. In our view, in determining its accounting for such a guarantee, the holder should determine whether the guarantee is an integral element of the debt instrument that is accounted for as a component of that instrument or is a contract that is accounted for separately.

7.1.132   *Determining whether a financial guarantee contract is integral to the debt instrument*

7.1.132.10   A financial guarantee is an integral element of a debt instrument and is accounted for as a component of that instrument if it is part of the contractual terms of the debt instrument and is

1797

not recognised separately. It appears that, to be integral, a financial guarantee does not have to be explicitly included in the contractual terms of the debt instrument. Judgement may be required in assessing whether a financial guarantee held is part of the contractual terms of an instrument. We believe that factors that may be relevant for this assessment include whether:

- the guarantee is implicitly part of the contractual terms of the debt instrument – e.g. because the loan agreement refers to it;
- the guarantee is required by laws and regulations that govern the contract of the debt instrument;
- the guarantee is entered into at the same time as and in contemplation of the debt instrument;
- the guarantee or the credit exposure that it covers can be assigned to a new holder independently from the other; and
- the guarantee is given by the parent of the borrower or another company within the borrower's group. [*IFRS 9.A, B5.5.55*]

7.1.132.20   If a guarantee or the credit exposure that it covers can be assigned independently from the other, then a question arises about whether the guarantee meets the definition of a financial guarantee – i.e. whether under the terms of the guarantee the holder is compensated only for a loss that it actually incurs on the guaranteed instrument (see 7.1.70).

7.1.132.30   If a financial guarantee is acquired at the time of initial recognition of a debt instrument and is considered to be an integral element of the debt instrument, then any premiums payable are a transaction cost of acquiring the financial asset and, where appropriate, are included in its initial carrying amount and the calculation of its effective interest rate (see 7.7.50). Conversely, if the premiums payable for a financial guarantee are required to be recognised separately, then the financial guarantee is not an integral element of the debt instrument. For example, if a financial guarantee is acquired after the initial recognition of the related debt instrument and not as part of a modification of the contractual terms of the debt instrument, then any premiums payable for the financial guarantee are recognised separately and accordingly the financial guarantee is not an integral element of the debt.

EXAMPLE 5A – FINANCIAL GUARANTEE – BOND QUOTED IN AN ACTIVE MARKET

7.1.132.40   Company B bought a bond issued by Company D that is quoted in an active market. The terms of the bond include an inseparable financial guarantee from D's parent.

7.1.132.50   In this example, we believe that the financial guarantee is an integral element of the bond because the bond was acquired with the benefit of the financial guarantee contract that is included in the terms of the bond and reflected in the quoted price of the bond.

EXAMPLE 5B – FINANCIAL GUARANTEE – REQUIRED BY LAWS AND REGULATIONS

7.1.132.60   Company E originates a loan. Local laws and regulations that govern the loan agreement require lenders to take out a financial guarantee contract for this type of debt. Accordingly, E purchases a financial guarantee from a third party and accounts for the premium paid as a transaction cost for the loan.

7.1.132.70   In this example, we believe that the financial guarantee is an integral element of the loan. This is because E has to buy the protection in order to grant the loan and the financial guarantee is not recognised separately.

EXAMPLE 5C – FINANCIAL GUARANTEE – CONCURRENT PURCHASE

7.1.132.80   Company F originates a loan. At the same time and in contemplation of the lending agreement, F purchases a financial guarantee from a third party in accordance with its credit risk management policy. The financial guarantee cannot be assigned independently from the loan.

7.1.132.90   In this example, we believe that F should develop an accounting policy on whether it considers the financial guarantee to be an integral element of the debt instrument. F may conclude that the financial guarantee:

- is an integral element of the loan, because it is entered into at the same time and in contemplation of the lending arrangement and it cannot be assigned independently from the loan; or
- is not an integral element of the loan, because it is entered into as a separate contract.

7.1.132.100   If F treats the financial guarantee as integral, then it accounts for the premiums payable as transaction costs of acquiring the related debt instrument. If F treats it as not integral, then it accounts for the premiums payable separately from the related debt instrument.

EXAMPLE 5D – FINANCIAL GUARANTEE – ACQUIRED FROM THE BORROWER'S PARENT

7.1.132.110   Company G originates a loan to Borrower H. Nine months later, following a decrease in the creditworthiness of H, G arranges for a parent of H to issue a financial guarantee in respect of the loan. G does not pay a premium for the guarantee.

7.1.132.120   We believe that the financial guarantee is an integral element of the loan, even if the guarantee is not an explicit part of the loan contract. This is because:

- H's parent could choose to support the subsidiary directly instead of becoming required to pay under the guarantee; and
- G does not pay any premium that would need to be recognised separately.

EXAMPLE 5E – FINANCIAL GUARANTEE – SUBSEQUENT ACQUISITION FROM A THIRD PARTY

7.1.132.130   Company J bought a bond issued by Company K that is quoted in an active market. Nine months later, J bought a financial guarantee contract on the bond from an unrelated third party bank.

7.1.132.140   In this example, we believe that the financial guarantee bought from the bank is not an integral element of the bond because the financial guarantee was

acquired from an unrelated third party (the bank) after J's initial recognition of the bond and the financial guarantee is neither included in the terms of the bond nor reflected in the quoted price of the bond. In addition, there is no modification of the contractual terms of the loan and J has to account for the premium paid separately.

7.1.134 *Accounting for integral financial guarantee contracts*

7.1.134.10   If the holder determines that the guarantee is an integral element of the debt instrument, then in our view the guarantee should not be accounted for separately. Instead, the holder should consider the effect of the protection when measuring the fair value of the debt instrument, when estimating the expected cash receipts from the debt instrument and when assessing impairment of the debt instrument.

7.1.136 *Accounting for non-integral financial guarantee contracts*

7.1.136.10   In our view, a financial guarantee contract held by an entity that is not an integral element of another financial instrument is not in the scope of IFRS 9. In our view, in general, the holder should account for such a financial guarantee contract as a prepayment of the guarantee premium (see 7.1.137) and a compensation right, by analogy to the guidance for reimbursements in IAS 37 (see 7.1.138–143). However, in our view an entity may also choose an accounting policy, to be applied consistently, to measure a non-integral financial guarantee contract that it holds at FVTPL if the contract:
- is held for trading, by analogy to the requirements for financial assets held for trading under IFRS 9; or
- guarantees a debt instrument that is measured at FVTPL, to reduce any accounting mismatch that would otherwise arise.

7.1.137 Premiums paid

7.1.137.10   If the holder accounts for a financial guarantee by analogy to the guidance for reimbursements in IAS 37 (see 7.1.136.10), then it also considers how to account for the premium paid for the financial guarantee. It appears that, for non-integral financial guarantees purchased for an existing financial asset that is not credit-impaired, the holder should choose an accounting policy, to be applied consistently, to measure the premium prepayment asset using one of the following approaches.
- *Approach 1:* Allocating all or part of the premium paid to acquisition of the recognised compensation right. Under this approach, all or part of the premium paid is viewed as consideration for acquisition of the recognised compensation right.
- *Approach 2:* Not allocating any part of the premium paid to acquisition of the compensation right. Under this approach, the premium and the compensation right are viewed as separate assets. The entire premium paid is considered as payment for coverage to be provided over the period of the guarantee.

EXAMPLE 5F – FINANCIAL GUARANTEE – PREMIUM PAID

7.1.137.20   On 31 December 2018, Company C paid 10 to purchase a financial guarantee contract not integral to the terms of the related loan. At that time, the loan was not credit-impaired and C had a loss allowance of 4 in respect of the loan.

7.1.137.30   C has adopted an accounting policy based on Approach 1 in 7.1.137.10. Accordingly, C records the following entries at its reporting date of 31 December 2018.

	DEBIT	CREDIT
Cash		10
Compensation right asset	4	
Deferred premium asset	6	

7.1.137.40   In subsequent periods, C expenses the deferred premium of 6 to profit or loss.

7.1.137.50   If C had adopted an accounting policy based on Approach 2 in 7.1.137.10, then it would recognise a compensation right of 4 in addition to the deferred premium of 10.

7.1.137.60   It appears that the accounting policy choice in 7.1.137.10 is not available if an entity purchases a financial guarantee contract over an existing financial asset that is credit-impaired. We believe that in such a case, the holder of a financial guarantee contract should treat part of the premium paid as relating to the purchase of the recognised compensation right – i.e. it should apply Approach 1 in 7.1.137.10.

7.1.137.70   In our view, the holder of a financial guarantee contract may apply by analogy the derecognition criteria for financial assets to any prepayment asset relating to a financial guarantee that is accounted for by analogy to IAS 37 (see 7.6.180.190). [*IAS 8.10–11*]

7.1.138   *Compensation rights*

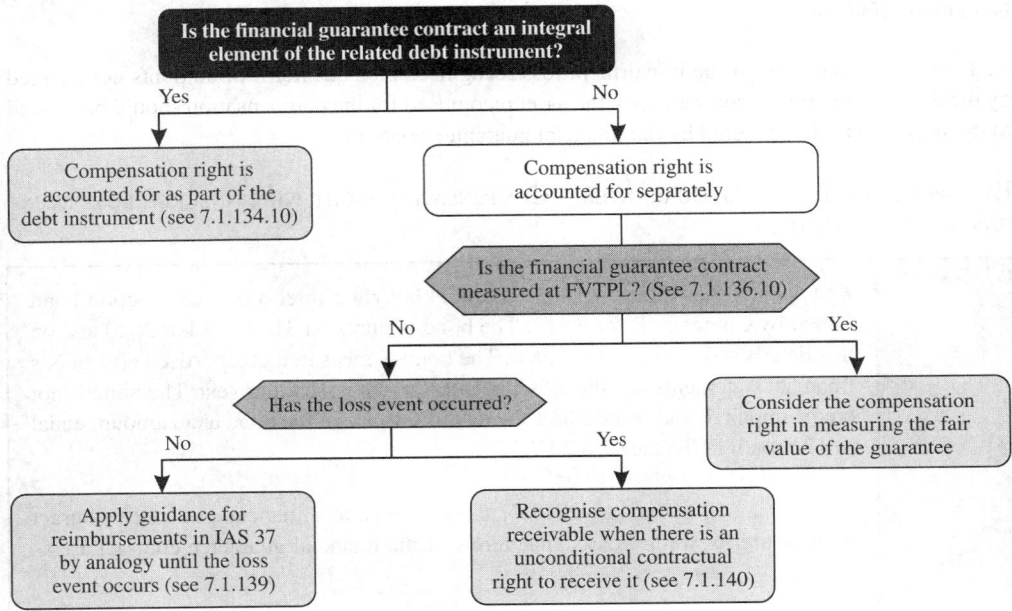

7.1.138.10   If the holder accounts for a non-integral financial guarantee contract by analogy to the guidance for reimbursements in IAS 37 (see 7.1.136.10), then in our view the accounting for any compensation right under the contract would depend on whether the loss event that creates a right for the holder to assert a claim has occurred at the reporting date.

7.1.139   *Compensation rights: Loss event has not occurred*

7.1.139.10   In our view, a recognised impairment loss for which there is not yet a contractual right to assert a claim is similar in nature to a provision as defined in IAS 37. A provision is a liability that is a present obligation arising from a past event, of uncertain timing or amount; ECLs are a loss that is recognised before the event that allows an entity to assert a claim, but there is uncertainty about the timing or amount of the ultimate actual loss that will be incurred. In the case of a financial guarantee contract, there is usually a timing difference between the recognition of the impairment loss and the related loss event.

7.1.139.20   If the loss event that creates a right for the entity to assert a claim at the reporting date has not occurred, but an impairment loss has been recognised under IFRS 9, then we believe that the compensation right should be accounted for by analogy to the guidance for reimbursements in IAS 37 because that is the guidance in IFRS dealing with the most similar issue (see 2.8.10). Therefore, we believe that the entity should recognise a compensation right when it recognises the related ECL, provided that it is virtually certain that the compensation will be received if the credit loss is actually suffered. [*IAS 8.10–11, 37.53*]

7.1.139.30   We believe that no net gain should be accrued when there is no current right to assert a claim under the financial guarantee contract. During the period between the initial recognition of the compensation right and the occurrence of the loss event that creates a right for the entity to assert a claim, the amount of the compensation right recognised should not exceed the amount of ECLs recognised. [*IAS 37.53*]

7.1.139.40   In our view, if the impairment loss recognised includes items or amounts not covered by the financial guarantee contract, then the asset recognised for the compensation should be limited to the impairment loss covered by the financial guarantee contract.

EXAMPLE 5G – FINANCIAL GUARANTEE – COMPENSATION RIGHT WHEN INSURED LOSS EVENT HAS NOT YET OCCURRED

7.1.139.50   On 1 January 2018, Bank N bought a three-year zero-coupon bond issued by Company B for 7,513. The bond matures on 31 December 2020 and on this date B is due to pay N 10,000. The bond is measured at amortised cost in N's financial statements and the effective interest rate is 10% per year. The bond is not credit-impaired and N measures the loss allowance of the bond at an amount equal to 12-month ECLs (see 7.8.20.70).

7.1.139.60   On 1 January 2018, N also entered into a financial guarantee contract with Insurer C, a third party. The terms of the financial guarantee contract are as follows.

- C will pay N up to 10,000 if B has not paid the full 10,000 to N by 31 January 2021.
- If B pays N less than the 10,000 owed, then C will pay N the difference between 10,000 and the amount received from B.
- If, after any payment from C to N, B subsequently repays any amount to N, then N is required to pay this amount to C – i.e. C will not compensate N for an amount greater than the loss incurred.

7.1.139.70   N considers that the financial guarantee contract is not integral to the bond (see 7.1.132.10 and 80–100) and accounts for it by analogy to the guidance for reimbursements in IAS 37 (see 7.1.136.10). The following facts at 31 December 2018 are also relevant to this example.

- The appropriate discount rate for C is 5%.
- N determines that credit risk has not increased significantly since initial recognition and measures the loss allowance at an amount equal to 12-month ECLs. N estimates that, as a result of default events that are possible in the following 12 months, the probability-weighted loss given default at maturity will be 3,000 with a 12-month probability of default of 1%.

7.1.139.80   N performs the following calculations at 31 December 2018.

	AMOUNT
Gross carrying amount of the bond	8,264[1]
Loss allowance on the bond	(25)[2]
Amortised cost of the bond	8,239
Present value of the compensation right	(27)[3]
Present value of the compensation right limited to the amount of ECLs	25

Notes
1. Calculated as the present value of the contractual cash flows at the original effective interest rate – i.e. 10,000 / (1 + 10%)².
2. Calculated as the 12-month ECLs on the bond, being the present value of the cash shortfalls – i.e. 3,000 x 1% / (1 + 10%)².
3. Calculated as the expected present value of the cash flows that could be claimed from C in respect of the shortfalls included in the recognised ECL discounted at a rate of 5%, reflecting the timing of the cash flows and the credit risk of C – i.e. 3,000 x 1% / (1 + 5%)². For simplicity, the compensation from C is discounted for two years rather than two years and one month.

7.1.139.90   N records the following entries[1] in the year ending 31 December 2018.

	DEBIT	CREDIT
Impairment loss (profit or loss)	25	
Loss allowance (statement of financial position)		25
To recognise the loss allowance on the bond		

	DEBIT	CREDIT
Compensation right (statement of financial position)	25	
Compensation right (profit or loss)[2]		25
To recognise compensation right		

Notes
1. This example does not illustrate N's accounting for the premiums paid to C. For a discussion of the accounting for premiums, see 7.1.137.
2. For a discussion of the presentation of compensation rights in profit or loss, see 7.1.143.

7.1.139.100 Continuing with the example, there are no changes to the amount and timing of the estimated shortfalls at 31 December 2019 and N performs the following calculations.

	AMOUNT
Gross carrying amount of the bond	9,090[1]
Loss allowance on the bond	(27)[2]
Amortised cost of the bond	9,063
Present value of the compensation right limited to the amount of ECLs	(27)[3]
Remeasurement of the compensation right	2[4]

Notes
1. Calculated as the opening gross carrying amount of 8,264 plus interest income accrued during the year of 826 (8,264 x 10%).
2. Calculated as the 12-month ECLs on the bond, being the present value of the cash shortfalls – i.e. 3,000 x 1% / (1 + 10%).
3. Being the ECL allowance of the bond under (2). In the absence of the imposed limit, the compensation right would have been 29 (3,000 x 1% / 1.05) – see note 3 to 7.1.139.80.
4. Calculated as 27 - 25.

7.1.139.110 N records the following entries in the year ending 31 December 2019.

	DEBIT	CREDIT
Gross carrying amount (statement of financial position)	826	
Interest income (profit or loss)		826
To accrete interest on the bond		
Impairment loss (profit or loss)	2	
Loss allowance (statement of financial position)		2
To remeasure the loss allowance on the bond		
Compensation right (statement of financial position)	2	
Compensation right (profit or loss)		2
To remeasure compensation right		

7.1.140   *Compensation rights: Loss event has occurred*

7.1.140.10   If the loss event that creates a right for the entity to assert a claim has occurred, then in our view the entity should recognise a receivable for the compensation when it has an unconditional contractual right to receive the compensation. The compensation receivable should be measured based on the amount and timing of the expected cash flows discounted at a rate that reflects the credit risk of the issuer of the financial guarantee contract. We believe that an entity would have an unconditional contractual right to receive compensation if:

- the entity has a contract under which it can make a claim for compensation; and
- the loss event that creates a right for the entity to assert a claim at the reporting date has occurred and the claim is not disputed by the issuer.

7.1.140.20   Any difference between the carrying amount of the previously recognised compensation right and the compensation receivable is recognised in profit or loss.

7.1.143   *Compensation rights: Presentation and disclosures*

7.1.143.10   It appears that an entity that accounts for a financial guarantee contract by analogy to the guidance for reimbursements in IAS 37 (see 7.1.136.10) should choose an accounting policy, to be applied consistently, to present gains or losses on a compensation right in profit or loss either:

- in the line item 'impairment losses (including reversals of impairment losses or impairment gains) determined in accordance with IFRS 9'; or
- in another appropriate line item.

7.1.143.20   Regardless of the accounting policy chosen in 7.1.143.10, the entity discloses the nature and amount of any gains or losses on compensation rights separately when they are material. [*IAS 1.97*]

7.1.145   **Share-based payments**

7.1.145.10   A separate standard provides guidance on the accounting for share-based payments. Accordingly, the initial classification and measurement, and subsequent measurement, of financial instruments arising from share-based payment transactions in the scope of IFRS 2 are subject to the requirements of that standard (see 4.5.2030). Without this scope exclusion, financial instruments arising from these transactions would generally fall in the scope of IAS 32 and IFRS 9. [*IAS 32.4(f), IFRS 9.2.1(h)*]

7.1.150   **Lease rights and obligations#**

7.1.150.10   Rights and obligations under leases are recognised and measured under IAS 17 (see chapter 5.1) and consequently are not subject to the general recognition and measurement requirements of IFRS 9. However, lease receivables recognised by a lessor are subject to the derecognition and impairment requirements of IFRS 9. Also, finance lease payables recognised by a lessee are subject to the derecognition principles of IFRS 9. [*IFRS 9.2.1(b)*]

7.1.150.20   Derivatives embedded in leases (both finance and operating leases) are subject to IFRS 9's embedded derivative requirements (see 7.2.120.100). [*IFRS 9.2.1(b)*]

7.1.150.30   A finance lease is a financial instrument. IFRS 7 applies to all financial instruments, and rights and obligations under leases are not specifically excluded from its scope. Consequently, recognised financial assets and financial liabilities arising from finance leases are subject to the financial instrument disclosure requirements (see chapter 7.10). [*IAS 32.AG9*]

7.1.155 FORTHCOMING REQUIREMENTS

7.1.155.10 IFRS 16 introduces changes to the accounting by lessees and substantially carries forward the existing requirements for lessors in IAS 17. For lessees, IFRS 16 introduces a single, on-balance sheet lease accounting model and eliminates the distinction between operating and finance leases (see chapter 5.1A).

7.1.155.20 As a result, the scope of IFRS 9 is amended to reflect the changes in the lease accounting. However, rights and obligations under leases continue to be scoped out of IFRS 9, except that the following are subject to the derecognition and impairment requirements of IFRS 9:
- finance and operating lease receivables recognised by a lessor; and
- lease liabilities recognised by a lessee. [*IFRS 9.2.1(b)*]

7.1.160 Investments in subsidiaries, associates and joint ventures#

7.1.160.10 Investments in subsidiaries, associates and joint ventures that are consolidated or equity accounted in the consolidated financial statements (see chapters 2.5, 3.5 and 3.6) are excluded from the scope of IAS 32 and IFRS 9. [*IAS 32.4(a), IFRS 9.2.1(a)*]

(S) 7.1.160.20 However, IFRS 9 applies to such investments in the separate financial statements of the parent or investor if it elects to account for those instruments in accordance with IFRS 9. In addition, IFRS 9 applies when an investment entity is required by IFRS 10 to measure its subsidiaries at FVTPL (see chapter 5.6). [*IAS 27.10(b), IFRS 10.31*]

7.1.160.30 IFRS 9 applies to derivatives on an interest in a subsidiary, associate or joint venture unless the derivative meets the definition of an equity instrument of the entity in IAS 32 (see 7.1.40 and 7.3.20.40). Such derivatives qualify for exemption from the scope of IFRS 9 when they may be settled only by the entity exchanging a fixed amount of cash or another financial asset for a fixed number of its own equity instruments (see 7.3.230.10). [*IAS 32.4(a), IFRS 9.2.1(a)*]

7.1.160.40 However, IFRS 9 does not apply to derivatives containing potential voting rights that in substance currently give access to the economic benefits associated with ownership interests in a subsidiary, associate or joint venture that are accounted for in accordance with 7.1.160.10. In this case, the derivatives are taken into account in determining the reporting entity's interest in the investee (see 2.5.140, 470 and 690). In our view, IFRS 9 also does not apply to derivatives to acquire NCI in a subsidiary that are accounted for under the anticipated-acquisition method (see 2.5.700). [*IFRS 10.B90–B91, 9.2.1(a)*]

7.1.160.50 Even if a derivative over shares in a subsidiary is not accounted for as a derivative under IFRS 9 (see 7.1.160.30–40), an entity is required to recognise a financial liability in its consolidated financial statements for an obligation to acquire equity instruments of the consolidated group (see 7.3.240) – e.g. a written put option or forward purchase contract over equity shares of a consolidated subsidiary.

7.1.160.60   A parent may invest in a convertible instrument issued by a subsidiary. In our view, if the Ⓢ convertible instrument is classified as equity by the subsidiary – e.g. because it is mandatorily convertible into a fixed number of ordinary shares (see 7.3.220) – then in the separate financial statements of the parent its investment in the convertible instrument should be considered to be an investment in a subsidiary and therefore would be excluded from the scope of IFRS 9 unless the parent has elected otherwise (see 7.1.160.20).

7.1.165   **FORTHCOMING REQUIREMENTS**

7.1.165.10   *Long-term Interests in Associates and Joint Ventures – Amendments to IAS 28* clarify that an entity applies IFRS 9 to long-term interests in an associate or joint venture that form part of the net investment in the associate or joint venture but to which the equity method is not applied (see 3.5.425). [*IAS 28.14A*]

7.1.170   Forward contracts between acquirer and selling shareholder in a business combination

7.1.170.10   IFRS 9 excludes from its scope forward contracts between an acquirer and a selling shareholder to buy or sell an acquiree that will result in a business combination at a future date of acquisition. The term of such a forward contract should not exceed a reasonable period normally necessary to obtain any required approvals and to complete the transaction. The scope exclusion applies from the perspectives of both the acquirer and a selling shareholder. [*IFRS 9.2.1(f)*]

7.1.170.20   To qualify for the scope exclusion, completion of the business combination should not be dependent on further actions of either party. Accordingly, the scope exclusion does not apply to option contracts, whether or not they are currently exercisable, that on exercise would result in a business combination; for a discussion of business combinations effected through derivatives, see 2.6.320. Option contracts allow one party to the contract discretion over whether a business combination occurs and therefore are not covered by the scope exemption. Similarly, in our view the scope exclusion does not apply to a combination of put and call options, often described as a 'synthetic forward'. [*IFRS 9.BCZ2.40–BCZ2.41*]

7.1.170.30   The completion of a business combination may be conditional on approval by the shareholders of either party or by a regulator or other governmental body. The purpose of the exclusion is to prevent particular contracts from being accounted for as derivatives while necessary regulatory and legal processes, including any required approvals, are completed. Therefore, in our view application of the scope exclusion is not usually precluded by the business combination being dependent on obtaining shareholder or regulatory approvals within a reasonable timeframe. We believe that this principle would extend to a contractual requirement for shareholder approval that has been included in the contract in the interests of good corporate governance, even though such an approval would not otherwise be required by law. [*IFRS 9.2.1(f), BCZ2.40–BCZ2.41*]

7.1.170.40   However, in some cases judgement may be required to determine whether contractual arrangements relating to approval have been designed so as to provide management of either party with an option over whether completion will happen or to allow deferral of completion beyond a reasonably necessary period such that application of the scope exclusion would not be appropriate. For example, this might be the case if completion of an agreement is permissible under law only if the seller obtains a specific regulatory approval but the agreement does not require the seller to make any effort to seek that approval but allows the seller instead to cancel the contract without penalty rather than applying for the approval.

7.1.170.50   The scope exemption does not apply by analogy to contracts to acquire investments in associates and similar transactions, such as investments in joint ventures (see 3.5.260). [*IFRS 9.BCZ2.42*]

7.1.180   Venture capital, mutual funds and similar entities

7.1.180.10   Venture capitalists, mutual funds, unit trusts and similar entities that do not qualify as investment entities under IFRS 10 (see chapter 5.6) may choose to account for investments in associates and joint ventures at fair value under IFRS 9, with all changes in fair value recognised in profit or loss, rather than applying the equity method. However, there is no exemption for these entities from the requirement to consolidate all entities that they control (see 3.5.100.10). [*IAS 28.18, IFRS 9.B2.3, 10.31–32*]

7.1.180.20   In our view, an entity that has substantive and separately managed venture capital operations may use the exemption from applying the equity method, even if the entity also has other operations. However, this exemption may be applied only to the investments held as part of the venture capital portion of the entity's operations.

7.1.180.30   For a discussion of whether an investor qualifies as a venture capital organisation and the accounting implications, see 3.5.100.

7.1.190   Reimbursements

7.1.190.10   Rights to reimbursement for expenditure that an entity is required to make to settle a liability recognised as a provision are outside the scope of IFRS 9. They are recognised and measured in accordance with IAS 37 (see 3.12.190). [*IFRS 9.2.1(i)*]

7.1.200   Purchases and sales of non-financial items

7.1.200.10   A contract to buy or sell a non-financial item may be required to be accounted for as a derivative, even though the non-financial item itself falls outside the scope of the financial instruments standards. Non-financial items include commodities such as gold, oil, wheat and soya beans, as well as motor vehicles, aircraft and real estate. If contracts to buy or sell non-financial items can be settled net in cash or another financial instrument, including if the non-financial item is readily convertible into cash, then they are included in the scope of the financial instruments standards. [*IAS 32.8, IFRS 9.2.4*]

7.1.200.20   There is an exception to this scope inclusion for contracts that are entered into and continue to be held for the receipt or delivery of a non-financial item in accordance with the entity's expected purchase, sale or usage requirements (the 'normal sales and purchases' or 'own-use' exemption). [*IAS 32.8, IFRS 9.2.4*]

7.1.200.30   The following flowchart illustrates when contracts to buy or sell a non-financial item are measured at FVTPL.

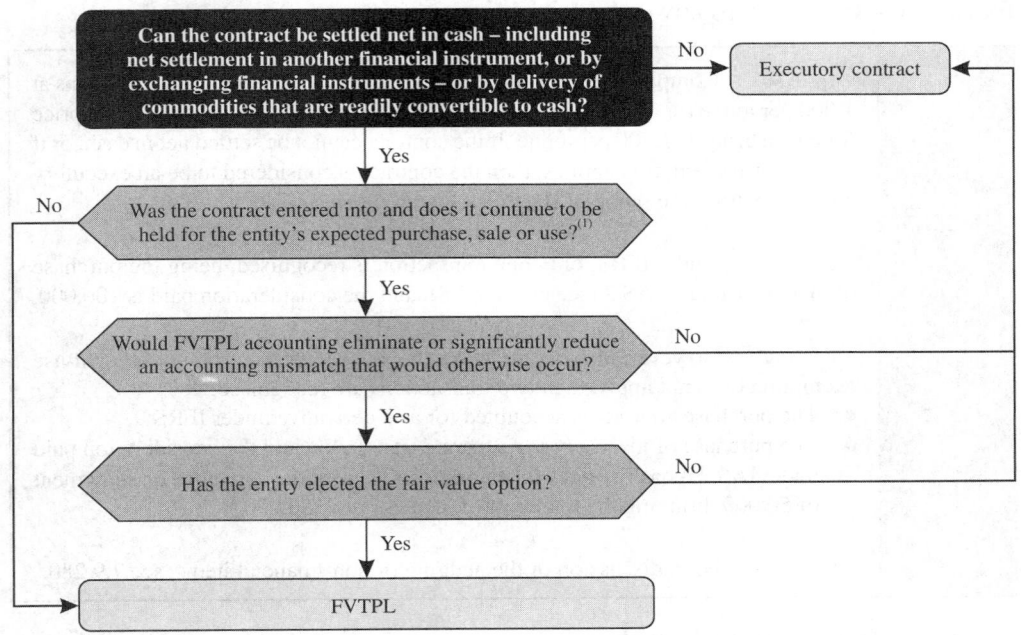

Note
1.   Assuming the contract meets the definition of a derivative.

7.1.200.40   In some cases, accounting mismatches can arise from own-use contracts being excluded from the scope of IFRS 9. For example, this could be the case if an entity entered into a derivative contract to economically hedge an own-use contract. To eliminate a resulting mismatch, an entity could apply hedge accounting. However, hedge accounting in these situations can be burdensome, because the commodity contracts are typically entered into in large volumes and managed on a net basis. As an alternative to hedge accounting, IFRS 9 provides an election whereby an entity can, at inception, irrevocably designate a contract to buy or sell a non-financial item that can be settled net in cash as measured at FVTPL even if the contract meets the own-use exemption. The designation can be made only if it eliminates or significantly reduces an accounting mismatch that would otherwise arise. [*IFRS 9.2.5, BCZ2.24*]

7.1.200.50   The accounting for a contract to buy non-financial items – e.g. commodities, property, plant and equipment, intangible assets and investment properties – differs depending on whether the purchase contract is regarded as a derivative. If the purchase contract is considered to be a derivative, then the purchase contract and the initial recognition of the non-financial item on settlement of the derivative are treated as separate transactions. The derivative is measured at FVTPL under IFRS 9 and the consideration paid for the non-financial item is the cash paid plus the fair value of the derivative on settlement. If the purchase contract is not regarded as a derivative, then it is treated as an executory contract (see 1.2.60). Under this approach there is only one transaction, being the purchase of a non-financial item under the contract, and the consideration paid for that non-financial item is the agreed price under the purchase contract.

EXAMPLE 6 – CONTRACT TO BUY NON-FINANCIAL ITEMS

7.1.200.60   Company J enters into a contract to buy 100 tonnes of cocoa beans at 1,000 per tonne for delivery in 12 months. On the settlement date, the market price for cocoa beans is 1,500 per tonne. If the contract cannot be settled net in cash, or if the own-use exemption applies, then the contract is considered to be an executory contract outside the scope of IFRS 9.

7.1.200.70   Under IFRS, only one transaction is recognised, being the purchase of inventory under IAS 2 (see chapter 3.8), and the consideration paid is 100,000.

7.1.200.80   However, if the contract can be settled net in cash and the own-use exemption does not apply, then two transactions are recognised.
- The purchase contract is accounted for as a derivative under IFRS 9.
- The purchase of inventory is a separate transaction and the consideration paid under IAS 2 is cash of 100,000 plus the fair value of the derivative on settlement of 50,000, bringing the total cost of inventory to 150,000.

7.1.200.90   For a discussion of the hedging of non-financial items, see 7.9.280.

7.1.210   *Settlement net in cash*

7.1.210.10   A commitment to buy or sell a non-financial item is considered settled net in cash if:
- the terms of the contract permit either party to settle net in cash or another financial instrument or by exchanging financial instruments – e.g. a written option that permits cash settlement;
- the entity has a past practice of settling similar contracts net in cash or other financial instruments or by exchanging financial instruments;
- the entity has a past practice of taking delivery of the underlying and selling it within a short period after delivery for trading purposes; or
- the non-financial item that is subject to the contract is readily convertible into cash. [*IAS 32.9, IFRS 9.2.6*]

7.1.210.20   A contract that can be settled net in cash or one with the underlying item readily convertible into cash may qualify as a contract entered into and held in accordance with the entity's expected purchase, sale or usage requirements as long as the entity has no past practice of settling similar contracts net or trading the underlying. [*IAS 32.8–9, IFRS 9.2.4*]

7.1.210.30   However, a contract cannot be considered entered into in accordance with the entity's expected purchase, sale or usage requirements if the entity has a past practice of settling similar contracts net in cash or other financial instruments or by exchanging financial instruments, or taking delivery of the underlying and selling it within a short period after delivery for trading purposes. Such contracts are in the scope of IFRS 9. [*IAS 32.9, IFRS 9.2.6*]

7.1.210.40   In our view, 'past practice' should be interpreted narrowly. Infrequent historical incidences of net settlement in response to events that could not have been foreseen at inception of a contract would not taint an entity's ability to apply the own-use exemption to other contracts. An example is an unplanned and unforeseeable breakdown (outage) in a power plant. However, any regular or foreseeable events leading to net settlements or closing out of contracts would taint the ability to apply the own-use exemption to similar contracts.

7.1.210.50   In our view, the concept of 'similar contracts' includes all contracts held for a similar purpose.

EXAMPLE 7A – CONTRACT HELD FOR SIMILAR PURPOSES

7.1.210.60   Power-generating Company P has sales contracts on electricity, each of which is held for one of the following purposes:
1. held for trading – i.e. P has entered or intends to enter into offsetting purchase contracts;
2. may result in delivery of the underlying power (commodity) but is available to be closed out from time to time as required – i.e. net cash settlement with the counterparty before or on the delivery date;
3. intended to be settled by delivery of the underlying power but may be closed out only in the case of *force majeure* or other similar unforeseen events; or
4. will always be settled by delivery of the underlying power.

7.1.210.70   Only contracts of types (3) and (4) qualify as own-use. However, in our view P should designate contract types (3) and (4) into an own-use category at inception in order to qualify for the exemption. Transfers out of these categories – e.g. closing out a contract other than because of an unforeseen one-off event – would taint P's ability to use the own-use exemption in the future.

7.1.210.80   Furthermore, P should be able to distinguish between contracts that qualify for the own-use exemption and other contracts. The designation need not refer specifically to the accounting treatment under IFRS, but it should be sufficient to ensure that the different purposes of each type of contract are clearly distinguished. For example, if an entity has two distinct business models for managing contracts to buy and sell commodities, each with different risk management policies, it may be sufficient if the entity clearly indicates at inception of each contract to which business model the contract relates.

EXAMPLE 7B – PHYSICAL AND DERIVATIVE CONTRACTS MANAGED TOGETHER

7.1.210.90   Company C is a chocolate manufacturer. C enters into a combination of physical contracts for the purchase of cocoa beans and cash-settled futures contracts. The physical contracts and the derivatives are managed together to hedge fixed-price sales contracts from an economic point of view.

7.1.210.100   In our view, the physical contracts and the derivatives would be regarded as similar in purpose and therefore the physical contracts would not qualify for the own-use exemption.

7.1.210.110   A contract for differences is a contract wherein two parties agree to pay or receive in cash the difference between the spot price and the fixed price on an underlying item, without actual delivery or receipt of that underlying item.

7.1.210.120   Sometimes the market structure in some countries or industries may preclude a supplier and customer from entering into a direct transaction for the purchase/sale of a non-financial item. In such situations, the supplier may enter into a contract with a market intermediary to sell the non-financial item at the spot price and the customer may enter separately into a contract with a market intermediary (possibly the same intermediary as that for the supplier) to buy the non-financial item at the spot price. Depending on the structure of the market, the market intermediary may act as a principal in its separate contracts with the customer and the supplier or, alternatively, it may act as an agent on behalf of the customer and the supplier. To fix the price for the non-financial item, the supplier and the customer may enter separately into a direct contract for differences between themselves and agree to pay/receive the difference between the spot price and a fixed price for that non-financial item.

7.1.210.130   If the market intermediary is acting as a principal in its separate contracts with the customer and the supplier, although the customer and supplier may be permitted to apply the own-use exemption to their respective contracts with the market intermediary to buy or sell the non-financial item, in our view the own-use exemption cannot be applied to the separate contract for differences between the customer and the supplier, because the contract for differences is not a contract to buy or sell a non-financial item that will be settled by the delivery or receipt of that non-financial item. [*IU 08-05*]

EXAMPLE 8A – CONTRACT FOR DIFFERENCES

7.1.210.140   Market regulations in the electricity market established by law may preclude an electricity generator and a customer (retailer) from contracting directly for the delivery and purchase of electricity – i.e. the generator has to deliver electricity to, and a customer can buy electricity only from, a central 'grid', whereby the grid acts as a principal in its separate contracts with the customer and the generator.

7.1.210.150   The generator and the customer manage their exposure to the risk of fluctuations in electricity spot prices by entering into a bilateral contractual arrangement (a contract for differences) that is settled outside the spot market, whereby the two parties – i.e. the generator and the customer – agree to exchange in cash the difference between the contractually agreed fixed price and the variable spot price that the customer pays in the market. The notional volume in such a contract for differences is generally determined either by the physical energy flow under the customer's contract with the grid to buy electricity or the generator's contract with the grid to deliver electricity.

7.1.210.160   In our view, the transactions comprising the customer's contract with the grid to buy electricity and the customer's contract for differences with the generator, or the generator's contract with the grid to deliver electricity and the generator's contract for differences with the customer, do not form a single arrangement because:
- these transactions have two distinct, separate purposes; and
- each contract is with different parties.

7.1.210.170 The structure is not considered to be a single accounting unit, and therefore the contract for differences and the customer's contract to buy electricity (or the generator's contract to deliver electricity) are analysed separately under IFRS 9. Because the contract for differences is settled in cash, it is precluded from qualifying for the own-use exemption, despite the linkage of the notional volume of the contract for differences to the physical energy flow under the customer's contract with the grid to buy electricity (or the generator's contract with the grid to deliver electricity). However, the customer's contract with the grid to buy electricity or the generator's contract with the grid to deliver electricity may qualify for the own-use exemption.

7.1.210.180 The customer/generator would, however, be able to designate a contract-for-differences derivative in a hedge of the variability in cash flows arising from the forecast purchases/sales of electricity at the spot rate if it satisfies the hedge designation and effectiveness criteria in IFRS 9 (see 7.9.240).

EXAMPLE 8B – INTERMEDIARY IN A WHOLESALE MARKET

7.1.210.190 Company B is an intermediary in a wholesale market. B enters into fixed-price contracts to buy aluminium in the market and sells it in the same condition to customers, who use it in their manufacturing processes. The market for aluminium is liquid. All contracts are intended to be settled physically. The specific purpose of these contracts is to generate stable profits from the margin between the purchase and sale prices. Open positions are kept to a minimum.

7.1.210.200 B aims to buy aluminium as cheaply as possible for its customers and it does not provide the customers with any additional services. The contracts are not and do not contain written options.

7.1.210.210 B concludes that the contracts are entered into and held for the purpose of generating profit from a dealer's margin, rather than for the purposes of the receipt or delivery of a non-financial item in accordance with its expected purchase, sale or use requirements. Accordingly, the contracts are in the scope of IFRS 9 and are measured at FVTPL.

7.1.210.220 Modifying the scenario, the conclusion may be different if B provided significant services to its customers – e.g. shipping, distribution or repackaging of the commodity into small retail units. Significant services are typically provided if the entity buys and sells in different markets (e.g. buys wholesale and sells retail). If additional services are provided, then determining whether a contract is entered into and held for the purposes of the receipt or delivery of a non-financial item in accordance with its expected purchase, sale or use requirements may involve significant judgement.

7.1.210.230	For a related discussion of the definition of a broker-dealer, see 3.8.70.25.

7.1.220 *Readily convertible into cash*

7.1.220.10   In our view, the following indicators are useful in determining whether a non-financial item is readily convertible into cash.

- There is an active market for the non-financial item. This refers to the spot market rather than the forward market. The relevant 'spot market' is the market where the entity sells its products based on its business model. An entity assesses whether this specific market is active, according to the guidance provided in IFRS 13 (see 2.4.280). It is important that buyers and sellers are present at any time. This is indicated, for example, by daily trading frequency (traded contracts) and daily trading volumes. Other indicators that might be considered are:
  - binding prices for the item are readily obtainable;
  - transfers of the item involve standardised documentation;
  - individual contract sales do not require significant negotiation or unique structuring;
  - the period required until the contract is finally closed is not extensive because of the need to permit legal consultation and document review; and
  - the difference between the transaction price and the entity's assessment of the value of the contract is insignificant (because a significant difference may indicate low liquidity).
- The non-financial item is fungible.
- Transaction costs, including commission, distribution and transport costs, are insignificant compared with gross sale proceeds. [*IFRS 13.A*]

7.1.230 *Written options*

7.1.230.10   A written option to buy or sell a non-financial asset that can be settled net in cash or another financial instrument – including when the non-financial item subject to the contract is readily convertible into cash – can never qualify for the own-use exemption because the entity cannot control whether the purchase or sale will take place. Therefore, such a contract cannot be entered into to meet an entity's expected purchase, sale or usage requirements. However, written options for commodities that cannot be settled net in cash (see 7.1.210) are not in the scope of IFRS 9. [*IAS 32.10, IFRS 9.2.7*]

7.1.230.20   Sometimes forward contracts, which may qualify for the own-use exemption, are combined with written options in one contract. For example, an agreement to sell a fixed amount of a product at a fixed price may be combined with a written option under which a customer may buy additional amounts. In our view, in such cases the contract may be split so that the forward element may qualify as own-use even though the written option component will not.

7.1.230.30   In the energy sector, it is common for a power company to provide 'whole of meter' contracts, under which the customer pays a fixed price per unit for the number of units of power it uses in a particular period. In our view, such contracts are not generally written options because the customer does not have the right to buy more or less of the product depending on the market price, nor does the customer have the ability to settle such contracts net in cash. In the case of electricity, the product cannot be stored or resold by customers and therefore from the perspective of the customer the power obtained under such contracts is not readily convertible into cash.

7.1.240   ***Embedded derivatives***

7.1.240.10   A contract to buy or sell a non-financial item may be required to be treated as a derivative and measured at FVTPL in the period between the trade date and the settlement date (see 7.6.20.50). [*IFRS 9.B3.1.4*]

7.1.240.20   If a contract to buy or sell a non-financial item is not a derivative but contains an embedded derivative, then an entity determines whether the embedded derivative should be separated from the host contract and accounted for separately (see 7.2.110). If the embedded derivative is accounted for separately, then in our view the host contract might still qualify for the own-use exemption.

7.1.240.30   For contracts to buy or sell non-financial items that are not treated as derivatives, the underlying purchase or sale transaction is accounted for in accordance with the relevant standard. Such contracts are generally executory contracts (see 1.2.60) to buy or sell the underlying non-financial item. However, if such contracts contain a 'price adjustment' clause, then an assessment is made about whether such a clause is an embedded derivative that requires separation under IFRS 9 (see 7.2.110). In our view, whether a contract to buy or sell a non-financial item has an embedded derivative that requires separation – e.g. in the form of a price adjustment clause – does not affect the conclusion about whether the host contract meets the own-use exemption under IFRS 9 (see 7.1.200.20). [*IFRS 9.2.4, 4.3.1, B3.1.2(b)*]

7.1.240.40   For a discussion of derivatives embedded in contracts in the scope of IFRS 15, see 7.1.270.10.

7.1.245   **Loan commitments**

7.1.250   *Scope*

7.1.250.10   A loan commitment may be an arrangement under which:
- both the lender and the borrower are committed to a future loan transaction – i.e. a forward contract to grant/receive a loan; or
- the lender is obliged contractually to grant a loan, but the borrower is not required to take the loan – i.e. lender's written option.

7.1.250.20   Generally, loan commitments, both issued and held, are excluded from the scope of IFRS 9 but are subject to the derecognition provisions of the standard and, for loan commitments issued, to the impairment requirements of the standard (see chapter 7.8). However, a loan commitment falls entirely in the scope of IFRS 9 when:
- the entity designates the loan commitment as a financial liability at FVTPL;
- the entity has a past practice of selling the assets resulting from its loan commitments shortly after their origination, in which case IFRS 9 applies to all loan commitments in the same class and they are treated as derivatives;
- the loan commitment can be settled net in cash or by delivering or issuing another financial instrument – i.e. such a loan commitment is a derivative; or
- the commitment is to provide a loan at a below-market interest rate. [*IFRS 9.2.1(g), 2.3*]

7.1.250.30   A loan commitment that is outside the scope of IFRS 9 (other than for the purposes of the impairment and derecognition requirements) may result in a loan mandatorily measured at

FVTPL. In our view, such a loan commitment may be designated as at FVTPL only if it meets the conditions for this designation in 7.5.40.10. [*IFRS 9.2.1(g)*]

EXAMPLE 9 – LOAN COMMITMENT RESULTING IN A LOAN MANDATORILY MEASURED AT FVTPL

7.1.250.40   Bank B has entered into a commitment to make a loan. If the loan is drawn down, then it will fail the SPPI criterion and as a result will be measured at FVTPL subsequent to initial recognition. The loan commitment does not meet any of the conditions in 7.1.250.20 for measurement at FVTPL in the absence of designation.

7.1.250.50   We believe that B cannot designate the loan commitment as at FVTPL because the commitment does not meet any of the conditions in 7.5.40.10. Therefore, the loan commitment is outside the scope of IFRS 9 other than for the purposes of its derecognition and impairment requirements. For guidance on measurement of a loan resulting from such a commitment, see 7.7.35.30.

7.1.250.60   A loan commitment that can be settled net in cash or by delivering or issuing another financial instrument is a derivative in the scope of IFRS 9 (see 7.1.250.20) – i.e. a loan commitment is excluded from the scope of IFRS 9 only if it cannot be settled net. Paying a loan out in instalments is not regarded as net settlement of a loan commitment. [*IFRS 9.2.3(b), BCZ2.5*]

EXAMPLE 10 – NET SETTLEMENT OF LOAN COMMITMENT

7.1.250.70   Bank B and Company L enter into an agreement that in two years' time, B will lend to L and L will borrow from B 100 for 10 years at a fixed interest rate.

7.1.250.80   B cannot terminate the loan commitment. However, the contract gives L an option to terminate the commitment on payment of a termination fee. The termination fee is calculated as the difference, if positive, between:
- the present value of the loan's contractual cash flows discounted at a risk-free market interest rate at the date of termination plus the original credit spread determined at the date the contract was signed; and
- the present value of the loan's contractual cash flows discounted at the fixed interest rate of the loan.

7.1.250.90   Because the loan commitment can be settled by L making a net cash payment based on the effect of changes in interest rates on the value of the loan commitment, B and L conclude that the loan commitment is a derivative in the scope of IFRS 9.

7.1.250.100   A loan commitment that is a hedged item in a fair value or cash flow hedge is accounted for as a hedged item under IFRS 9. In addition, if an entity manages the credit risk on a loan commitment using a derivative, then it may designate the loan commitment (or part of it) as measured at FVTPL, providing certain conditions are met (see 7.9.120). An entity may make this designation on initial recognition or subsequently or while the loan commitment is unrecognised. [*IFRS 9.2.3, 6.7.1*]

7.1.250.110   IFRS 9 includes specific requirements for the measurement of a loan commitment to provide a loan at a below-market interest rate when the loan commitment is not measured at FVTPL. Such a loan commitment is measured initially at fair value and subsequently at the higher of (1) the amount of the loss allowance in accordance with IFRS 9 (see chapter 7.8); and (2) the amount initially recognised less the cumulative amount of income recognised in accordance with the principles of IFRS 15 (see chapter 4.2). All loan commitments are subject to the derecognition requirement of IFRS 9. [*IFRS 9.2.1(g), 2.3(c), 4.2.1(d)*]

7.1.260   *Definition*

7.1.260.10   It appears that an arrangement is a loan commitment fully or partially in the scope of IFRS 9 (see 7.1.250.20) if it meets the following two conditions:

- it is a financial instrument as defined in IAS 32 (see 7.1.30); and
- it meets the description of a loan commitment in paragraph BCZ2.2 of IFRS 9 – i.e. it is a 'firm commitment to provide credit under pre-specified terms and conditions'. [*IFRS 9.2.1, BCZ2.2*]

7.1.260.20   For the purpose of applying the description of a loan commitment, it appears that the term 'pre-specified' does not mean that all the terms have to be fixed (e.g. the credit to be provided does not needs to have a fixed percentage interest rate) but rather that key terms have to be specified in advance – e.g. they could be specified by a formula. For example, we believe that a commitment to provide a loan with a variable rate of interest would meet the definition of a loan commitment. [*IFRS 9.BCZ2.2*]

EXAMPLE 11A – CREDIT CARD ISSUED BY A BANK

7.1.260.30   Bank B issues a credit card to a customer under pre-specified terms and conditions. The card can be used by the customer to buy goods or services from various third party retailers and service providers (merchants). B pays merchants for purchases made by the customer. B provides the customer with monthly statements of its purchases and the customer has an option to either repay B the outstanding amount in full by the due date or repay in instalments.

7.1.260.40   B's issuance of the card is a loan commitment that is either entirely in the scope of IFRS 9 or subject only to the impairment or derecognition requirements of IFRS 9 (see 7.1.250.20) because:
- the arrangement meets the definition of a financial instrument because B has a contractual obligation to deliver cash to third party merchants to pay for purchases made by the customer; and
- the arrangement meets the description of a loan commitment because B has a firm commitment to provide credit as it does not have the ability to prevent the customer from making purchases at the third party merchants and is required to honour such purchases until the card is cancelled.

EXAMPLE 11B – STORE CARD ISSUED BY A RETAILER THAT IS NOT PART OF A GROUP

7.1.260.50   Retailer R issues a store card to a customer. The card can be used by the customer to buy goods or services on credit from R. The store card cannot be used to withdraw cash or to buy goods or services from parties other than R. Also,

R is not obliged to provide any goods or services to the customer – i.e. R is not obliged to make any future sales to the customer – and R can cancel the card by giving notice to the customer.

7.1.260.60   R's issuance of the store card is not a loan commitment that could be either entirely in the scope of IFRS 9 or subject to its impairment or derecognition requirements because:

- R has no contractual obligation to deliver cash or another financial asset and, consequently, there is no financial instrument until R has supplied goods or services to the customer; and
- the agreement does not meet the description of a loan commitment in IFRS 9 because R has no obligation to sell goods or services and, consequently, does not have a firm commitment to provide credit.

EXAMPLE 11C – STORE CARD ISSUED BY A RETAILER THAT IS PART OF A GROUP

7.1.260.70   Modifying Example 11B, Retailer R is part of Group G and issues a store card to a customer that could be used by the customer to purchase goods from other Group G entities, but not from entities that are not part of Group G. In this example:

- in G's consolidated financial statements, the arrangement is not a loan commitment that could be either entirely in the scope of IFRS 9 or subject to its impairment or derecognition requirements for the reasons articulated in 7.1.260.60; and
- in R's individual and/or separate financial statements, the arrangement is a loan commitment that is either entirely in the scope of IFRS 9 or subject only to the impairment or derecognition requirements of IFRS 9 (see 7.1.250.20) because:
  - the arrangement meets the definition of a financial instrument because R would have a contractual commitment to deliver cash to other companies in the group to pay for purchases made by the customer; and
  - the agreement meets the description of a loan commitment because R has a firm commitment to provide credit as it does not have the ability to prevent the customer from making purchases at other Group G entities.

EXAMPLE 11D – LESSOR'S COMMITMENT TO A FINANCE LEASE

7.1.260.80   On 1 January 2018 (inception date of the lease), Company X enters into a binding agreement to lease an item of equipment to Company Y from 1 March 2018 (commencement date of the lease). The lease is determined to be a finance lease (see 5.1.40 and 110).

7.1.260.90   We believe that on 1 January 2018, X does not issue a loan commitment that could be either entirely in the scope of IFRS 9 or subject to its impairment or derecognition requirements because X has no contractual obligation to deliver cash or another financial asset. Instead, X has an obligation to make the equipment subject to the lease available to Y from 1 March 2018. Consequently, there is no

financial instrument until the commencement date; and IFRS 9 excludes from its scope rights and obligations under leases to which IAS 17 applies (subject to some exceptions that are not applicable to this question). [*IAS 17.4, IFRS 9.2.1(b)*]

EXAMPLE 11E – LETTER OF CREDIT

7.1.260.100   Bank B issues a letter of credit in the amount of 10,000 on behalf of its Customer C identifying a foreign Supplier S as the beneficiary. Under the terms of the letter of credit, B promises to pay 10,000 to S on presentation of documentary proof that it has shipped the goods to C. After B pays S, it collects the payment from C at a later date, in line with the agreed payment terms.

7.1.260.110   The arrangement is a loan commitment issued by B that is either entirely in the scope of IFRS 9 or subject only to the impairment or derecognition requirements of IFRS 9 (see 7.1.250.20) because B has a firm commitment to provide credit to C under the agreed credit terms by advancing cash to S.

7.1.260.120   It appears that a commitment to enter into a loan that is contractually convertible into a fixed number of equity instruments of the borrower does not meet the definition of a loan commitment. This is because such an instrument is partially a firm commitment to provide credit under pre-specified terms and conditions and partially a commitment to purchase an equity conversion option – i.e. it is not a loan commitment in its entirety. The basis for conclusions to IFRS 9 explains that the exemption for certain loan commitments from derivative accounting is aimed at simple lending transactions. Accordingly, we believe that a commitment to enter into a loan that is contractually convertible into a fixed number of equity instruments of the borrower is a derivative, which is measured at FVTPL by both the issuer and the holder. [*IFRS 9.BCZ2.2–BCZ2.3*]

7.1.270   Rights and obligations in the scope of IFRS 15

7.1.270.10   IFRS 9 excludes from its scope rights and obligations that are in the scope of IFRS 15, except for those that IFRS 15 specifies are accounted for in accordance with IFRS 9 – e.g. trade receivables. At the same time, IFRS 15 excludes from its scope financial instruments and other contractual rights and obligations that are in the scope of IFRS 9. IFRS 15 also states that a contract may be partially in its scope and partially in the scope of another standard, such as IFRS 9. In such cases, IFRS 15 states that if the other standard specifies how to separate and/or initially measure one or more parts of the contract, then an entity first applies the separation and/or measurement requirements of that other standard. For example, if a contract contains a financial instrument in the scope of IFRS 9, then the entity separates and measures that financial instrument using the guidance in IFRS 9 and excludes from the transaction price under IFRS 15 the amount initially measured in accordance with IFRS 9. Accordingly, the entity first considers whether the contract contains an embedded derivative that is in the scope of IFRS 9, and whether IFRS 9 requires it to be accounted for separately (see 7.2.110). [*IFRS 9.2.1(j), 15.5(c), 7, 108*]

7.1.270.20   The impairment requirements of IFRS 9 apply to contract assets in the scope of IFRS 15 (see 4.2.470 and 7.8.10.10). [*IFRS 9.2.2, 15.107*]

7.2 Derivatives and embedded derivatives

7.2   Derivatives and embedded derivatives

CURRENTLY EFFECTIVE REQUIREMENTS

This publication reflects IFRS in issue at 1 August 2018, and the currently effective requirements cover annual reporting periods beginning on 1 January 2018.

The requirements related to this topic are mainly derived from the following.

STANDARD	TITLE
IFRS 9	Financial Instruments

FORTHCOMING REQUIREMENTS

The currently effective requirements are affected by the following forthcoming requirements. They are highlighted with a # and the impact is explained in the accompanying boxed text at the references indicated.

- In January 2016, the IASB issued IFRS 16 *Leases*, which is effective for annual periods beginning on or after 1 January 2019. See 7.2.267. IFRS 16 is the subject of chapter 5.1A.
- In May 2017, the IASB issued IFRS 17 *Insurance Contracts*, which is effective for annual periods beginning on or after 1 January 2021. See 7.2.245. IFRS 17 is the subject of chapter 8.1A.

FUTURE DEVELOPMENTS

For this topic, there are no future developments.

7.2.10   DERIVATIVES

7.2.20   Definition

7.2.20.10   A 'derivative' is a financial instrument or other contract in the scope of IFRS 9 that has all of the following features:

- its value changes in response to one or more underlying variables – e.g. an interest rate (see 7.2.30);
- it has an initial net investment that is smaller than would be required for other instruments that have a similar response to the variable (see 7.2.40); and
- it will be settled at a future date (see 7.2.50). [*IFRS 9.A*]

7.2.20.20   The definition of a derivative does not require specific settlement features. As such, a contract that allows either net or gross settlement may be a derivative. [*IFRS 9.IG.B.3*]

7.2.20.30   The definition of a derivative is relevant in considering the treatment of both stand-alone contracts and features that are embedded in certain hybrid contracts (see 7.2.110). In our view, a stand-alone derivative should not be split into its component parts. For example, an interest rate collar should not be separated into an interest rate cap and an interest rate floor that are accounted for separately.

7.2.30   *Change in value based on an 'underlying'*

7.2.30.10   A derivative is a financial instrument that provides the holder or writer with the right (or obligation) to receive (or pay) cash or another financial instrument in amounts determined with reference to price changes in an underlying price or index, or changes in foreign exchange or interest rates, at a future date. A derivative may have more than one underlying variable. [*IFRS 9.IG.B.8*]

7.2.30.20   A derivative usually has a notional amount, which can be an amount of currency, a number of shares, a number of units of weight or volume or other units specified in the contract. However, in our view contracts without notional amounts or with variable notional amounts may also meet the definition of a derivative. The holder or writer is not required to invest in or receive the notional amount at inception of the contract. [*IFRS 9.BA.1*]

7.2.30.30   A contract to pay or receive a fixed amount on the occurrence or non-occurrence of a future event meets the definition of a derivative, provided that this future event depends on a financial variable or a non-financial variable not specific to a party to the contract. For example, an entity may enter into a contract under which it will receive a fixed payment of 100 if a specified index increases by a determined number of points in the next month. The settlement amount is not based on and does not need to change proportionately with an underlying. [*IFRS 9.BA.1*]

7.2.30.40   The underlying variable on which the fair value of a derivative instrument is based may be that of:

- the price of a financial instrument – e.g. a bond or equity security;
- the price of a commodity – e.g. gold, oil or wheat;
- a rate – e.g. an interest rate or a foreign exchange rate;
- an index of prices – e.g. a stock exchange index; or
- some other variable that has a measurable value – e.g. a climatic, geological or other physical variable. [*IFRS 9.IG.B.2*]

7.2.30.50   An option, forward or swap that is exercisable at the fair value of the underlying item always has a fair value of zero. Therefore, it does not meet the definition of a derivative because its value does not depend on an underlying variable. [*IFRS 9.A*]

7.2.30.60   The definition of a derivative excludes instruments with a non-financial underlying variable that is specific to a party to the contract. However, IFRS does not provide guidance on how to determine whether a non-financial variable is specific to a party to the contract. In our view, the analysis comprises two questions:
1. Is the variable non-financial or financial?
2. Is it specific to a party to the contract?

7.2.30.70   In our view, this exclusion is primarily intended to exclude insurance contracts. For example, a residual value guarantee on a motor vehicle, in which the holder is compensated not only for a decline in the market value of the vehicle but also for the condition of the vehicle, does not meet the definition of a derivative.

7.2.30.80   However, in our view items such as EBITDA, profit, sales volume, revenue or the cash flows of one counterparty may be considered to be non-financial variables that are specific to a party to the contract even though the contract, or the embedded feature being considered, does not meet the definition of an insurance contract (see 8.1.20). In addition, we believe that the gross domestic product of a counterparty that is a government or the non-viability of the issuer of a debt instrument – e.g. the issuer's regulatory capital ratio falling below a specified minimum threshold – may be considered to be a non-financial variable that is specific to a party to the contract. In our view, an entity should choose an accounting policy, to be applied consistently, on whether such items are considered to be non-financial variables that are specific to a party to the contract.

7.2.30.90   If an instrument has more than one underlying variable – i.e. it is dual-indexed – with one underlying being a non-financial variable specific to one of the parties, then judgement may be required in determining whether the instrument is a derivative.

7.2.30.100   The implementation guidance accompanying IFRS 9 identifies the following examples of a derivative.
*   A contract to exchange an amount of foreign currency determined by the sales volume of the entity at a fixed exchange rate at a future date.
*   An 'equity kicker' feature under which the lender of a subordinated loan is entitled to receive shares of the borrower free of charge, if the shares are listed. [*IFRS 9.IG.B.8, IG.C.4*]

7.2.30.110   Consistent with the equity kicker example described above, in our view a contractual feature in a debt instrument that converts the instrument into equity shares of the issuer on occurrence of a specified 'non-viability event' (e.g. the issuer's regulatory capital falling below a specified level) is a derivative component (see Examples 8A and 8B).

7.2.40   *No or 'smaller' initial net investment*

7.2.40.10   There is no quantified guidance on how much smaller the initial net investment should be, compared with the investment required for other contracts that would be expected to have a similar response to changes in market factors, for the contract to meet the definition of a derivative. The standard requires the initial net investment to be less than the investment needed to acquire the underlying non-derivative financial instrument. However, 'less than' does not necessarily mean 'insignificant' in relation to the overall investment and needs to be interpreted on a relative basis. [*IFRS 9.BA.3*]

7.2.40.20   Debt and equity securities are generally not derivatives, although their fair values respond to changes in the underlying – e.g. interest rates or a share price – in similar ways to derivatives on these instruments. This is because it is not possible to identify another instrument that would require a greater initial net investment and have a similar response to changes in the relevant market factors.

7.2.40.30   Many derivatives, such as at-market forward contracts, do not have any initial net investment.

7.2.40.40   Purchased options normally require the payment of an up-front premium, but the amount paid is normally small in relation to the amount that would be paid to acquire the underlying instrument. However, certain call options may have a very low exercise price, so that the amount paid to acquire the option is likely to be equivalent to the amount that would be paid to acquire the underlying asset outright at inception of the option. In our view, such options should be treated as a purchase of the underlying asset and not as derivatives. In other words, if an option is so deep in the money, at the date of issue or acquisition, that the cost of the option is almost equal to the value of the underlying asset at that date, then it should be accounted for as an investment in the underlying asset and not as a derivative. [*IFRS 9.IG.B.9*]

7.2.40.50   A cross-currency swap meets the definition of a derivative, even though there is an exchange of currencies at inception of the contract, because there is zero initial *net* investment. [*IFRS 9.BA.3*]

7.2.40.60   Any required deposits or minimum balance requirement held in margin accounts as security for derivatives are not considered part of the initial investment. For example, the initial margin required in respect of exchange-traded futures comprises cash collateral rather than being part of the initial investment in the underlying commodity. [*IFRS 9.IG.B.10*]

7.2.40.70   Sometimes one leg of a derivative is prepaid. Whether the remaining part still constitutes a derivative depends on whether all of the criteria in the definition are still met. [*IFRS 9.IG.B.4–IG.B.5*]

7.2.40.80   If a party to an interest rate swap prepays its pay-fixed obligation at inception but will continue to receive the floating rate leg over the life of the swap, then the floating-rate leg of the swap is still a derivative instrument. This is because all of the criteria for a derivative are met: the initial net investment – i.e. the amount prepaid by the entity – is less than investing in a similar primary financial instrument that responds equally to changes in the underlying interest rate; the instrument's fair value changes in response to changes in interest rates; and the instrument is settled at a future date. If the party prepays the pay-fixed obligation at a subsequent date, then this would be regarded as a termination of the old swap and an origination of a new instrument that is evaluated under IFRS 9. [*IFRS 9.IG.B.4*]

7.2.40.90   In the reverse situation, if a party to an interest rate swap prepays its pay-variable obligation at inception using current market rates, then the swap is no longer a derivative because the prepaid amount now provides a return that is the same as that of a fixed-payment annuity or an amortising fixed rate debt instrument in the amount of the prepayment. Therefore, the initial net investment equals that of other financial instruments with fixed annuities. [*IFRS 9.IG.B.5*]

7.2.50 *Settlement at a future date*

7.2.50.10   Derivatives require settlement at a future date. A forward contract is settled on a specified future date, an option has a future exercise date and interest rate swaps have multiple dates on which interest is settled. An option is considered settled on exercise or at its maturity. Therefore, even though the option may not be expected to be exercised when it is out of the money, it still meets the criterion of settlement at a future date. Any contract in which there is a delay between the trade date and settlement date is a derivative if the other criteria are also met. [*IFRS 9.IG.B.7*]

7.2.50.20   Settlement of a derivative, such as an interest rate swap, may be either a gross or a net exchange of cash or other financial instruments. [*IFRS 9.IG.B.3*]

7.2.50.30   A key element for a contract to buy or sell a non-financial item to be treated as a derivative in the scope of IFRS 9 is that the transaction should allow for net settlement in the form of cash or the right to another financial instrument (see 7.1.200). [*IFRS 9.IG.A.1–IG.A.2*]

7.2.60 **Exemptions from derivative treatment**

7.2.70 *Regular-way contracts*

7.2.70.10   'Regular-way contracts' are contracts to buy or sell financial assets that will be settled within the timeframe established by regulation or convention in the market concerned, not necessarily an organised market. Regular-way contracts are not treated as derivatives between the trade date and settlement date. [*IFRS 9.A, 3.1.2, B3.1.3–B3.1.6*]

EXAMPLE 1 – REGULAR-WAY CONTRACT

> 7.2.70.20   Company X purchases a security in a market in which three days is the normal settlement period for this type of transaction. X's commitment to settle the security in three days is not treated as a derivative because three days is the normal settlement period for this type of transaction in the environment in which the transaction takes place.
>
> 7.2.70.30   However, in a market with three-day settlement, if a contract entered into by X specifies that settlement will take place only in three months, then the exception would not apply and X would need to treat the contract as a derivative between the trade date and settlement date.

7.2.70.40   IFRS does not offer any specific guidance on how to treat a delay in the settlement of a regular-way contract. In our view, a delay would not preclude the use of the regular-way exemption if the contract requires delivery within the timeframe established by the convention in the market and the delay is caused by a factor that is outside the control of the entity.

7.2.80 *Derivatives on own equity*

7.2.80.10   Derivatives on own equity are excluded from the scope of IFRS 9 if they meet the definition of an equity instrument (see 7.3.20.40–50 and 130). [*IFRS 9.2.1(d)*]

7.2.90   *Gaming contracts*

7.2.90.10   A gaming institution may enter into different types of transactions with its customers. The following are examples.

- Transactions in which the gaming institution administers a scheme among its customers and receives a commission based on the amount wagered – e.g. parimutuel betting. In these transactions, the gaming institution will receive its commission regardless of the outcome of the wager.
- Transactions in which the gaming institution takes a position against its customers. In these transactions, the value of the individual contract is contingent on the outcome of a specified event and the gaming institution is not, therefore, normally guaranteed a specific commission or return – e.g. a bookmaker that lays fixed odds on the outcome of a sporting event.

7.2.90.20   In our view, the first type of transaction in 7.2.90.10 does not meet the definition of a derivative, because the value of such contracts does not fluctuate based on an underlying variable. We believe that these transactions should be accounted for under IFRS 15 (see chapter 4.2). Conversely, the second type of transactions in 7.2.90.10 will normally meet the definition of a derivative, because the value of such contracts varies depending on the likelihood of the occurrence of a specified event. In this case, such transactions will be accounted for under IFRS 9.

7.2.100   *Rights and obligations arising on transfer of financial asset*

7.2.100.10   Rights and obligations arising on a transfer of a financial asset that does not qualify for derecognition are not treated as derivatives under IFRS 9 if recognising the derivative would result in recognising the same rights or obligations twice (see 7.6.250.20). [*IFRS 9.B3.2.14*]

7.2.110   **EMBEDDED DERIVATIVES**

7.2.120   **Definition and outline**

7.2.120.10   A 'hybrid contract' is a contract that includes both a non-derivative host contract and one or more embedded derivatives. [*IFRS 9.4.3.1, B4.3.1*]

7.2.120.20   An 'embedded derivative' is a component of a hybrid contract that also includes a non-derivative host, such that some of the cash flows of the hybrid contract vary in a way similar to a stand-alone derivative. An embedded derivative causes modifications to some or all of the cash flows that would otherwise be required by the contract, according to a specified financial variable (e.g. interest rate, financial instrument price, commodity price, foreign exchange rate, index of prices or rates, credit rating or credit index) or non-financial variable that is not specific to a party to the contract (see 7.2.30.60). [*IFRS 9.4.3.1*]

7.2.120.30   When a hybrid contract contains a host that is a financial asset in the scope of IFRS 9, the entire hybrid contract, including all embedded features, is assessed for classification under IFRS 9 (see 7.4.150.50). [*IFRS 9.4.3.2*]

7.2.120.40   The IFRS 9 requirements on embedded derivatives do not apply when the host contract is a financial asset in the scope of IFRS 9. In other words, these requirements apply to embedded derivative features with host contracts that are either:

- financial liabilities; or
- not in the scope of IFRS 9 – e.g. rights under leases, insurance contracts or contracts to buy or sell a non-financial item that is not in the scope of IFRS 9 (see 7.2.120.100). [*IFRS 9.4.3.3*]

7.2.120.50   When a hybrid contract contains a host that is a financial liability or a contract that is not in the scope of IFRS 9, the hybrid contract is assessed to determine whether the embedded derivative(s) is (are) required to be separated from the host contract (bifurcated) in accordance with IFRS 9. Embedded derivatives in such a hybrid contract are separated if:

● the economic characteristics and risks of the embedded derivative are not closely related to those of the host (see 7.2.200);

● a separate instrument with the same terms as the embedded derivative would meet the definition of a derivative (see 7.2.20); and

● the hybrid contract is not measured at FVTPL (see 7.2.150). [*IFRS 9.4.3.3, B4.3.1*]

7.2.120.60   The following diagram illustrates how to apply the requirements for separating an embedded derivative from a hybrid contract.

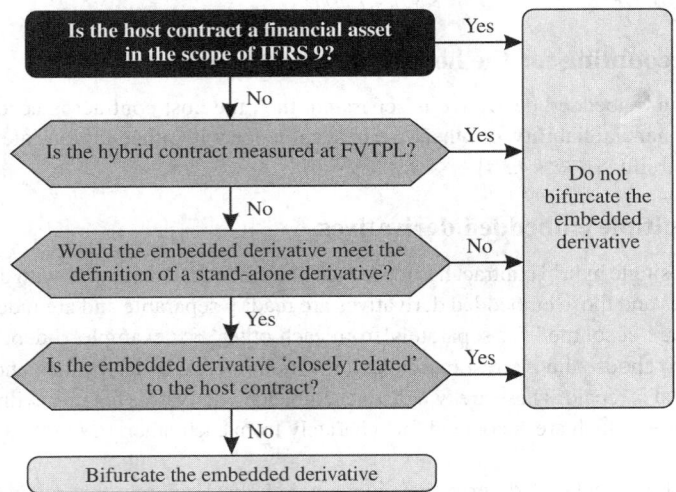

7.2.120.70   A derivative contract attached to a host contract that is transferable separately from the host contract, or that is added by a third party, is a stand-alone derivative and not an embedded derivative. For example, a finance lease or loan may have an associated interest rate swap. If the swap can be sold separately, then it is a stand-alone derivative and not an embedded derivative, even if both the derivative and the host contract have the same counterparty. [*IFRS 9.4.3.1*]

7.2.120.80   Each component of a 'synthetic instrument' is accounted for separately, unless there is a requirement to account for the separate instruments as a single hybrid instrument (see 7.6.40). A synthetic instrument is a combination of separate instruments that, viewed together, 'create' a different instrument.

EXAMPLE 2 – ACCOUNTING FOR COMPONENTS OF SYNTHETIC INSTRUMENT

7.2.120.90   Company D issues a five-year floating rate debt instrument and holds a five-year pay-fixed, receive-floating interest rate swap; together these two instruments create, for D, a synthetic five-year fixed rate financial liability. The individual

> components of the synthetic instrument are not embedded derivatives; instead, they are stand-alone instruments, which are accounted for separately. [*IFRS 9.IG.C.6*]

7.2.120.100   Although lease contracts and insurance contracts are generally excluded from the scope of IFRS 9, derivatives embedded in them are subject to the requirements for the separation of embedded derivatives. However, an embedded purchase option for a leased asset included in a lease contract is not separated because the option is accounted for as part of the lease (see chapter 5.1). All other derivatives embedded in lease contracts – e.g. foreign currency derivatives, leveraged escalation clauses etc – are considered for separation (see 7.2.267). If an embedded feature in an insurance contract itself transfers significant insurance risk, then the feature meets the definition of an insurance contract and therefore is not required to be separated under the embedded derivative guidance (see 8.1.30.50–70). [*IFRS 9.2.1(b), (e), B4.3.8(f), 4.7, B11*]

7.2.130   Accounting for the host contract

7.2.130.10   If an embedded derivative is separated, then the host contract is accounted for under IFRS 9 if it is a financial liability, or otherwise in accordance with other appropriate standards if it is not a financial liability. [*IFRS 9.4.3.4*]

7.2.140   Multiple embedded derivatives

7.2.140.10   If a single hybrid contract has more than one embedded derivative with different underlying risk exposures and those embedded derivatives are readily separable and are independent of each other, then they are accounted for separately from each other. For example, a debt instrument may contain options to choose the interest rate index on which interest is determined and the currency in which the principal is repaid. These are two distinct embedded derivative features with different underlying risk exposures, which are accounted for separately from each other. [*IFRS 9.B4.3.4*]

7.2.140.20   Multiple embedded derivatives in a single hybrid contract that relate to the same risk exposure, or that are not readily separable and independent of each other, are treated as a single compound embedded derivative (see 7.2.210). [*IFRS 9.B4.3.4*]

EXAMPLE 3 – ACCOUNTING FOR HOST CONTRACT

> 7.2.140.30   Company X issues a debt instrument that includes two embedded derivative features.
> - *Feature 1:* Varies the interest rate on the debt instrument.
> - *Feature 2:* Allows the holder of the debt instrument to put it back to the issuer.
>
> 7.2.140.40   X treats these two features as a single compound embedded derivative because they both relate to interest rate risk.

7.2.150   Hybrid contract measured at FVTPL

7.2.150.10   If the hybrid contract – i.e. the host contract plus the embedded derivative(s) – is measured at FVTPL, then separate accounting is not permitted. [*IFRS 9.4.3.3*]

7.2.150.20   If a contract contains one or more embedded derivatives and the host is not an asset in the scope of IFRS 9, then an entity may designate the entire hybrid contract as at FVTPL unless:
- the embedded derivative does not significantly modify the cash flows that would otherwise arise on the contract; or
- it is clear with little or no analysis when a similar hybrid instrument is first considered that separation would be prohibited. [*IFRS 9.4.3.5*]

7.2.150.30   The designation discussed in 7.2.150.20 is used only when:
- it reduces the complexities associated with separating embedded derivatives; or
- measuring the entire instrument at FVTPL is more reliable than measuring the fair value of the embedded derivative. [*IFRS 9.B4.3.9–B4.3.10*]

7.2.160   Inability to measure reliably

7.2.160.10   If the fair value of an embedded derivative cannot be measured reliably, although the characteristics are such that separation is required, then the entire hybrid contract – i.e. host contract and embedded derivative – is designated as at FVTPL. In our experience, this situation will be encountered only in rare circumstances (see 7.5.70.40). [*IFRS 9.4.3.6*]

7.2.170   Separation not voluntary

7.2.170.10   If an embedded derivative is not required to be separated, then IFRS 9 does not permit an entity to separate it – i.e. separation is not optional. [*IFRS 9.4.3.3*]

7.2.180   Existence of a contractual commitment

7.2.180.10   For an embedded derivative to exist, the contract needs to represent a contractual commitment. For example, forecast but uncommitted sales in a foreign currency, no matter how likely, cannot contain an embedded derivative. [*IFRS 9.4.3.1*]

7.2.190   When to separate

7.2.200   *Closely related criterion*

7.2.200.10   Determining whether an embedded derivative is closely related to the host contract requires consideration of the nature – i.e. the economic characteristics and risks – of the host contract and the nature of the underlying of the derivative. If the natures of both the underlying and the host contract are similar, then they are generally closely related. [*IFRS 9.4.3.3, B4.3.5–B4.3.8*]

7.2.200.20   In our view, a derivative with economic characteristics and risk types that are broadly similar to those of the host contract is not necessarily closely related to the host contract. This is the case in the following situations, for example.
- An equity host contract and an embedded equity index-linked derivative are not closely related unless they are both exposed to the equity characteristics of the same entity.
- The derivative embedded in an inflation-indexed lease contract is closely related to the lease only if the inflation index relates to the same economic environment as the lease contract. [*IFRS 9.B4.3.2, B4.3.8(f)*]

7.2.200.30   A leverage feature that is not insignificant usually causes an embedded derivative feature not to be closely related; an exception is discussed in 7.2.250. 'Leverage' in this context (for contracts other than options) means that the feature increases the variability of the contractual cash flows of the hybrid contract at a greater rate than would be inferred from the host contract's economic relationship with the relevant underlying. [*IFRS 9.B4.3.5, B4.3.8*]

7.2.200.40   Evaluating whether an embedded derivative is closely related to its host contract involves identifying the nature of the host contract. The nature of a host financial instrument – i.e. debt or equity – is not always obvious. A debt host contract is usually characterised by a fixed or determinable maturity and fixed or determinable payments, whereas an equity host contract has no stated or predetermined maturity and gives the holder a residual interest in the net assets of an entity. [*IFRS 9.B4.3.2*]

EXAMPLE 4 – HOST CONTRACT FOR STATED MATURITY INSTRUMENT LINKED TO SHARE PRICE

7.2.200.50   A five-year instrument has a principal of 100 that will be redeemed on a specified date at an amount equal to the principal plus the change in the fair value of 10 shares in a listed company over the term of the instrument.

7.2.200.60   Even though the redemption amount is linked to a listed company's share price, the instrument has a stated maturity and the host contract has the nature of a debt instrument.

7.2.210   *Multiple embedded derivatives*

7.2.210.10   As discussed in 7.2.140.20, in many cases multiple embedded derivatives are treated as a single compound embedded derivative. In our view, if there is specific guidance in IFRS 9 on whether one or more components of a compound embedded derivative are closely related to the host contract, then this guidance should be applied in assessing whether the compound embedded derivative should be separated. We believe that if the guidance requires a component of the compound derivative to be separated, then usually the compound derivative as a whole should be separated. [*IFRS 9.B4.3.5–B4.3.8*]

EXAMPLE 5 – SEPARATING MULTIPLE EMBEDDED DERIVATIVES

7.2.210.20   Company Y issues a 10-year debt instrument at 100 (par). The following are key terms of the debt instrument.
- *Interest rate:* The debt pays interest at a floating rate of three-month LIBOR plus a fixed margin.
- *Interest rate floor (embedded derivative 1):* The floating interest rate will not be lower than 5% for any period. The interest rate floor is in the money on issuing the debt – i.e. the floor is above the market rate of three-month LIBOR plus the margin on issuing the debt.
- *Prepayment option (embedded derivative 2):* Y may at any time voluntarily prepay the principal and related accrued interest outstanding in whole or in part plus a penalty of 1% of the outstanding amount.

7.2.210.30   Both embedded derivatives relate to the same risk – i.e. interest rate risk. They are also not readily separable and independent of each other, because the incentive to prepay increases as the floor becomes more in the money when interest rates fall, and prepaying extinguishes the floor.

7.2.210.40   In this example, a component of the compound embedded derivative, the interest rate floor, is not closely related to the host contract based on the specific guidance in IFRS 9, because it is in the money at inception. Therefore, Y concludes that the compound instrument as a whole is not closely related to the host contract and separates it. [*IFRS 9.B4.3.8(b)*]

7.2.220   *Reassessment of embedded derivatives*

7.2.220.10   The assessment of whether an embedded derivative is required to be separated from the host contract and accounted for as a derivative is made at inception of the contract – i.e. when the entity first becomes a party to the contract. Subsequent reassessment is prohibited unless there is a change in the terms of the contract that significantly modifies the cash flows that would otherwise be required under the contract, in which case reassessment is required. [*IFRS 9.B4.3.11*]

EXAMPLE 6 – REASSESSMENT OF EMBEDDED DERIVATIVES

7.2.220.20   Company X has not separated a foreign currency derivative embedded in a host one-year sales contract because the feature is not leveraged, it does not contain an option and the payments are denominated in the functional currency of the customer.

7.2.220.30   The functional currency of the customer changes three months after the inception of the contract. X does not reassess whether to separate the derivative embedded in the contract. This is because there have been no changes to the terms of the contract that significantly modify the cash flows that would otherwise be required under the contract.

7.2.220.40   However, if there are changes to the terms of the contract that significantly modify the cash flows that would otherwise be required under the contract, then X would be required to make a subsequent reassessment for embedded derivative separation.

7.2.230   *Extension features*

7.2.230.10   An option or automatic provision to extend the remaining term to maturity of a financial liability is not closely related to the host financial liability unless there is a concurrent adjustment to the approximate current market rate of interest at the time of the extension. However, depending on its terms, an entity may consider an extension feature in a host financial liability to be equivalent to a loan commitment that would not be in the scope of IFRS 9 and consequently would not be accounted for as a derivative if it were a separate instrument (see 7.1.245). In our view, when an entity adopts this approach it should not separate such an extension feature as the embedded derivative from the host financial liability. [*IFRS 9.4.3.3, B4.3.5(b)*]

7.2.240   *Calls, puts or prepayment options#*

7.2.240.10   A call, put or prepayment option embedded in a host financial liability or host insurance contract is closely related to the host contract in either of the following scenarios.

- The exercise price of the option is approximately equal on each exercise date to the amortised cost of the host financial liability or the carrying amount of the host insurance contract.
- The exercise price of the prepayment option reimburses the lender for an amount up to the approximate present value of lost interest for the remaining term of the host contract. 'Lost interest' is the product of the principal amount prepaid, multiplied by the interest rate differential. The 'interest rate differential' is the excess of the effective interest rate of the host contract over the effective interest rate that the entity would receive at the prepayment date if it reinvested the principal amount prepaid in a similar contract for the remaining term of the host contract. This exception is conditional on the exercise price compensating the lender for loss of interest by reducing the economic loss from reinvestment risk. [*IFRS 9.4.3.3, B4.3.5(e)*]

7.2.240.15   If a convertible debt instrument (see 7.3.310) contains a call or put option, then the assessment of whether the call or put option is closely related to the host debt contract is made before separating the equity element of the convertible debt instrument. [*IFRS 9.B4.3.5(e)*]

7.2.240.20   It is generally presumed that a call, put or prepayment option is closely related to the host contract if the exercise price is approximately equal to the amortised cost of the host financial liability at each exercise date. However, in our view, to evaluate whether a contingent call, put or prepayment option should be bifurcated, an entity should also consider the nature of the contingency. Accordingly, we believe that a contingent call, put or prepayment option with an exercise price approximately equal to the amortised cost of the host financial liability at each exercise date should not be bifurcated from the host contract if and only if the underlying contingent event that triggers exercisability of the option:

- is a non-financial variable that is specific to a party to the contract; or
- has economic characteristics and risks that are closely related to those of the host financial liability – e.g. based on the interest rate or credit risk of the host financial liability.

7.2.240.30   Examples of contingent events that would be a non-financial variable specific to a party to the contract or closely related might include a change in control of the issuer, a change in relevant taxation or law that specifically affects the instrument, the occurrence or non-occurrence of an IPO of the issuer or a change in the credit rating of the instrument.

EXAMPLE 7A – ISSUER REDEMPTION OPTION WITH SHARE PRICE BEING UNDERLYING RISK EXPOSURE

7.2.240.40   Company X issues a five-year bond containing an early-redemption option. The option allows X to redeem the bond at any time after the second anniversary of the issue date, subject to a 30-day notice period, if the volume-weighted-average price of X's shares, for at least 20 consecutive trading days, equals or exceeds 125% of X's share price at the issue date of the bond.

> 7.2.240.50   Because the redemption option's underlying risk exposure is X's share price, rather than the interest rate or credit risk of the host contract, X concludes that the call option should be separated from the host contract and measured at FVTPL (see 7.2.370.10).

EXAMPLE 7B – ISSUER REDEMPTION OPTION IN CONVERTIBLE BOND

> 7.2.240.60   Modifying Example 7A, the instrument is a convertible bond that the holder has the right to convert into a fixed number of shares any time after the second anniversary of the issue date. Company X determines that the conversion feature is an equity component (see 7.3.230). If X exercises its option to redeem the bonds, then the holder has the opportunity to convert within the 30-day notice period.
>
> 7.2.240.70   The economic effect of this call option is to incentivise the holder to convert, thereby limiting the value of the conversion feature from the holder's perspective.
>
> 7.2.240.80   X makes an assessment of whether the call option is closely related to the host contract before separating the equity element (see 7.2.240.15). X therefore considers the convertible bond, including the equity conversion option, in assessing whether the redemption feature has economic characteristics and risks that are closely related to those of the host contract.
>
> 7.2.240.90   Because both the host contract (including the conversion option) and the embedded call option include economic characteristics related to X's share price, it is possible that the call option would not be separated in the financial statements of X. This would depend on whether it can be demonstrated that the call option's exercise price is approximately equal on each exercise date to the amortised cost of the host contract (including the conversion option). [*IFRS 9.B4.3.5(e)*]

EXAMPLE 8A – DUAL-INDEXED EMBEDDED FEATURE – DERIVATIVE SEPARATED

> 7.2.240.100   Bank X issues a 20-year, fixed rate bond of 1,000 at par. The bond includes a contractual conversion feature that requires conversion of the bond into a variable number of equity shares of X if X's Common Equity Tier 1 ratio (as determined in accordance with applicable banking regulations) drops below 7.5% (the contingent event or the non-viability event). Under the conversion mechanism, the number of shares to be issued would be determined so as to have a fair value equal to the bond's par amount plus accrued interest but subject to a fixed cap on the number of shares to be issued. X does not classify the bond as measured at FVTPL.
>
> 7.2.240.110   X determines that the fair value of the conversion feature is mainly dependent on:

- *the probability of the contingent event occurring:* This is a non-financial variable specific to X, which is a party to the contract;
- *the fair value of the host bond:* The conversion feature would result in X issuing shares with a fair value equal to par plus accrued interest (subject to the cap), which may be different from the fair value of the bond received in exchange; and
- *the fair value of X's equity shares:* The cap on the number of shares to be issued means that if the share price is below a particular price level on the conversion date, then the number of shares to be issued would be capped and, consequently, the total fair value of the shares to be issued may be less than the bond's par amount plus accrued interest.

7.2.240.120   X has made an accounting policy choice to treat the contingent event as a non-financial variable that is specific to a party to the contract (see 7.2.30.80). However, X determines that the conversion feature meets the definition of a derivative (see 7.2.30.110). In this case, because the value of the conversion feature is dependent on changes in the fair value of X's equity shares, X concludes that the economic characteristics and risks of the conversion feature are not closely related to the host debt instrument. Therefore, X separates the conversion feature from the bond and accounts for the conversion feature at FVTPL (see 7.2.370).

EXAMPLE 8B – DUAL-INDEXED EMBEDDED FEATURE – DERIVATIVE NOT SEPARATED

7.2.240.130   Changing Example 8A, assume that the conversion feature does not include any cap on the number of shares to be issued. Therefore, changes in the fair value of X's equity shares no longer affect the value of the conversion feature. In this case, X determines that the fair value of the conversion feature is mainly dependent only on:
- the probability of the contingent event occurring; and
- the fair value of the host bond.

7.2.240.140   X does not separately account for the conversion feature as a derivative because the conversion feature is closely related to the host bond – i.e. the exercise price of the conversion feature at the time of conversion will be approximately equal at all times to the amortised cost of the host – and the exercise of the conversion feature is triggered only by the contingent event, which is a non-financial variable that is specific to a party to the contract (see 7.2.240.20).

7.2.240.150   Under IFRS 4, an insurer is not required to separate a policyholder's option to surrender an insurance contract for a fixed amount (or for an amount based on a fixed amount and an interest rate). [*IFRS 4.8*]

7.2.245   **FORTHCOMING REQUIREMENTS**

7.2.245.10   The exception for insurers discussed in 7.2.240.150 has not been carried forward to IFRS 17.

7.2.250   *Interest rate features in host financial liabilities and insurance contracts*

7.2.250.10   An exception to the requirement that all derivatives with leverage be separated is provided for embedded interest rate derivatives in which the underlying is an interest rate or index that can change the amount of interest that would otherwise be paid or received on an interest-bearing host debt contract or insurance contract. For a hybrid instrument with such an embedded derivative, leverage does not automatically result in separation unless:

- the embedded interest rate feature could prevent the holder of the hybrid instrument from recovering substantially all of its investment at settlement date; or
- the embedded interest rate feature could result in the holder receiving a rate of return on the hybrid instrument that is at least double its initial rate of return on the host instrument and could result in a rate of return that is at least twice the market return of an instrument with the same terms as the host instrument ('double-double test'). [*IFRS 9.B4.3.8(a)*]

7.2.250.20   In our view, this analysis should not be based on the likelihood of these limits being exceeded in practice, but rather on whether the contractual terms make it *possible* that the limits will be exceeded.

7.2.255   *Embedded interest rate caps and floors*

7.2.255.10   An embedded floor or cap on the interest rate on a debt contract or insurance contract is closely related to the host contract, provided that the cap is at or above the market rate of interest and the floor is at or below the market rate of interest when the contract is issued and the cap or floor is not leveraged in relation to the host contract. [*IFRS 9.B4.3.8(b)*]

7.2.255.20   The IFRS Interpretations Committee has discussed when an interest rate floor should be separated from a floating rate host contract and accounted for as a derivative. The Committee stated that:

- an entity should compare the overall interest rate floor (i.e. the benchmark interest rate referenced in the contract plus contractual spreads and if applicable any premiums, discounts or other elements that would be relevant to the calculation of the effective interest rate) for the contract to the market rate of interest for a similar contract without the interest rate floor (i.e. the host contract);
- in order to determine the appropriate market rate of interest for the host contract, an entity is required to consider the specific terms of the host contract and the relevant spreads (including credit spreads) appropriate for the transaction; and
- the term 'market rate of interest' is linked to the concept of fair value as defined in IFRS 13 and is described as the rate of interest 'for a similar instrument (similar as to currency, term, type of interest rate and other factors) with a similar credit rating' (see 7.7.10.30 and 80.20). [*IU 01-16, IFRS 9.B5.1.1*]

7.2.255.30   The Committee also noted that the requirements in paragraph B4.3.8(b) of IFRS 9 (see 7.2.255.10–20) should be applied to an interest rate floor in a negative interest rate environment in the same way as they would be applied in a positive interest rate environment because paragraph B4.3.8(b) of IFRS 9 does not distinguish between positive and negative interest rates. [*IU 01-16*]

7.2.255.40   In determining the unit of account for the purposes of the assessment in 7.2.255.10, in our view an entity should choose an accounting policy, to be applied consistently, to evaluate the cap or floor as one instrument or as a series of separate caplets or floorlets, one for each payment date.

7.2.255.50   If the cap or floor is assessed as one instrument, then we believe that the market rate of interest to which each cap or floor is compared could be the swap rate plus relevant spreads (including credit spreads). If the swap rate (i.e. the currently quoted rate for the fixed leg of an interest rate swap against a floating benchmark rate as determined by its particular market) is used, then it should be for the same period as the cap or floor. This is because the guidance in IFRS 9 in relation to 'market rate of interest' requires consideration of the rate of interest for a similar instrument with a similar term. Therefore, we believe that it would be inappropriate to use the spot rate for the first reset period as a proxy for the whole period of the cap or floor. If an entity determines, based on the assessment, that the embedded cap or floor is not closely related to the host contract, then in our view the entire cap or floor should be separated and not only those embedded caplets or floorlets that are in the money. This is consistent with the unit of account assessment. [*IFRS 9.B5.1.1*]

7.2.255.60   If the unit of account for the purposes of the assessment is a series of separate caplets or floorlets, then we believe that the market rate of interest with which each caplet or floorlet is compared should be the forward rate for the period of that particular caplet or floorlet plus relevant spreads (including credit spreads). If an entity determines, based on the assessment, that one or more – but not necessarily all – of the embedded caplets or floorlets are not closely related to the host contract, then in our view all caplets or floorlets should be separated and not only those embedded caplets or floorlets that are in the money. This is consistent with the guidance on multiple embedded derivatives (see 7.2.140 and 210).

7.2.260   Foreign currency derivatives embedded in non-financial or insurance contracts

7.2.260.10   A host contract that is an insurance contract or a non-financial instrument may be denominated in a foreign currency – e.g. the premiums on an insurance contract or the price of non-financial items in a purchase or sale transaction. In these circumstances, the foreign currency embedded derivative is not accounted for separately from the host contract, provided that it is not leveraged, does not contain an option feature and the payments required under the contract are denominated in one of the following currencies:

* the functional currency of one of the substantial parties to the contract;
* the currency in which the price of the related goods or services being delivered under the contract is routinely denominated in commercial transactions around the world; or
* the currency that is commonly used in contracts to buy or sell non-financial items in the economic environment in which the transaction takes place. [*IFRS 9.B4.3.8(d)*]

7.2.260.20   In our view, if the conditions in 7.2.260.10 are not met, then a foreign currency embedded derivative should be separated from the host contract. This is because those conditions are explicit requirements that should be satisfied in order for the host contract and the derivative to be considered 'closely related'.

EXAMPLE 9 – SEPARABLE FOREIGN CURRENCY DERIVATIVE EMBEDDED IN NON-FINANCIAL CONTRACT

7.2.260.30   Company E enters into a contract to provide goods and services to Company B. E and B have the same functional currency. The settlement of the host contract is to be made in that currency. However, certain of the goods and

> services that E will buy from unrelated third parties to fulfil its obligations will be denominated in a foreign currency. Accordingly, E and B agree that the final contract settlement price will be adjusted based on the movement in the foreign currency.
>
> 7.2.260.40   Because the embedded derivative is a foreign currency embedded derivative and does not meet the conditions in 7.2.260.10, both parties conclude that it should be separated from the host contract. This is notwithstanding that the foreign currency embedded derivative may have some economic relationship to the cost and value of the goods and services supplied.

7.2.260.50   IFRS 9 does not provide guidance on how to identify 'substantial parties to the contract'. In our view, the legal parties to a contract are not necessarily also the substantial parties to it. When determining who is a substantial party to a contract, an entity needs to consider all of the facts and circumstances related to the contract, including whether a legally contracting party possesses the requisite knowledge, resources and technology to fulfil the contract without relying on related parties. To make this assessment, an entity needs to look through the legal form of the contract to evaluate the substance of the underlying relationships. In our view, only one entity within a consolidated group can be deemed a substantial party with respect to a particular contract with an entity outside the group.

7.2.260.60   In our view, an entity that will provide the majority of the resources required under a contract is the substantial party to that contract. Identifying this entity is a subjective assessment and should be based on an analysis of both quantitative and qualitative factors. Certain resources – e.g. employees and material costs specifically used to fulfil the contract – can be quantified. Qualitative factors that may not be easily measured include developed technology, knowledge, experience and infrastructure.

7.2.260.70   'Routinely denominated', as noted in the second bullet in 7.2.260.10, should in our view be interpreted narrowly. Transactions qualifying for this exemption that may be considered to be routinely denominated in US dollars in commercial transactions around the world include:
- oil transactions;
- transactions related to large passenger aircraft; and
- transactions in certain precious metals – such as gold and silver – and diamonds. [*IFRS 9.IG.C.9*]

7.2.260.80   To qualify, the currency would have to be used in similar transactions around the world, and not just in one local area. For example, if cross-border transactions in natural gas are denominated in US dollars in North America and in euro in Europe, then neither the US dollar nor the euro is the currency in which natural gas is routinely denominated. [*IFRS 9.IG.C.9*]

7.2.260.90   In our view, 'routinely denominated in commercial transactions around the world' means that a large majority of transactions in international commerce around the world are traded in that currency. This implies that with respect to any particular commodity, transactions cannot be considered routinely denominated in more than one currency.

7.2.260.100   In our view, if transactions on a local or regional exchange are denominated in a local currency but are priced using the international price – e.g. US dollars per barrel of oil – at the spot exchange rate, then those transactions are, in effect, denominated in the international currency.

7.2.260.110   In addition, we believe that the existence of a relatively small proportion of transactions denominated in a local currency in one or two markets, or particular jurisdictions, does not preclude a commodity from meeting the definition of 'routinely denominated in commercial transactions around the world'.

7.2.260.120   The third exemption noted in 7.2.260.10 for a currency that is commonly used in the economic environment in which non-financial items are bought and sold may apply when a country's local currency is not stable, causing businesses in that environment to adopt a more stable and liquid currency for internal and cross-border trade. In our view, the application of this exemption is not limited to countries with a local currency that is not stable, and it may be applied in other countries as long as the 'commonly used currency' criterion is met. Accordingly, we believe that the exemption may also apply when the local currency is stable, but business practice has developed to commonly use a more liquid foreign currency such as the US dollar or the euro in either internal or cross-border trade. Before concluding that a currency, other than the local currency of a country, is commonly used in contracts to buy or sell non-financial items in that country, careful consideration needs to be given to business practices in that country.

7.2.260.130   In our view, the assessment of 'commonly used currency' in a specified environment requires judgement and should be evaluated in the context of the particular facts and circumstances in the jurisdiction, but not in the context of a specific industry. That judgement should be supported by an analysis of the specific economic environment in which the transaction takes place. We believe that the following parameters can provide evidence about whether a currency is commonly used in a particular jurisdiction:
- for a cross-border transaction, analysing the level of foreign trade transactions in that currency;
- for a domestic transaction, analysing the level of domestic commercial transactions in that currency; or
- as an alternative, for cross-border transactions and/or domestic transactions, analysing the level of all transactions – i.e. both foreign trade transactions and domestic commercial transactions – in that currency.

7.2.260.140   In our view, for the analysis in 7.2.260.130, an entity should establish criteria, to be applied consistently, to determine the extent to which transactions with entities whose functional currency is the currency being evaluated are considered. The following are possible approaches.
- *Exclude all of these transactions from the analysis:* Under this approach, to conclude that the euro is a currency that is commonly used in Country X (a non-eurozone country), for example, the transactions that require consideration are those entered into by entities in X with other entities that do not have the euro as their functional currency; this would exclude the majority of cross-border transactions with entities in the eurozone.
- *Include these transactions in the analysis:* Under this approach, to conclude that the euro is a currency commonly used in Country X, cross-border transactions with entities in the eurozone would be included in the analysis. However, we believe that it would be inappropriate to conclude that the exemption should apply based solely on the level of transactions with entities whose functional currency is the currency being evaluated. There should also be evidence that the currency is used in the relevant economic environment for other reasons, such as liquidity or convenience. For example, to conclude that the euro is a currency commonly used in X, there should be evidence that the euro is commonly used for other reasons linked to business practice in X and not only because of transactions with euro functional currency counterparties.

7.2.260.150   Furthermore, in our view the analysis of a commonly used currency should be performed on a country-by-country basis and not with reference to specific goods and services. For example, it is not appropriate to conclude that a particular currency is commonly used for cross-border leasing transactions and therefore that the foreign exchange embedded derivatives in all cross-border leases denominated in that currency do not require separation.

7.2.260.160   In our view, if a group entity has a separable foreign currency derivative, then the deriva- tive is separable both in its separate financial statements and in the consolidated financial statements even if the transaction is denominated in the functional currency of the parent, which may be chosen as the presentation currency of the consolidated financial statements (see 2.7.30–40). The consolidated entity does not have a functional currency and as such cannot be viewed as having a definable foreign currency exposure that would remove the need for separation on consolidation.

7.2.265   Foreign currency derivatives embedded in host debt instruments#

7.2.265.10   A host contract that is a debt instrument may contain a stream of principal or interest payments that are denominated in a foreign currency – e.g. a dual-currency bond. In these circumstances, the embedded foreign currency derivative is closely related to the host debt instrument. Such a derivative is not separated from the host contract because IAS 21 requires foreign currency gains and losses on monetary items to be recognised in profit or loss. [*IFRS 9.B4.3.8(c), IAS 21.28*]

7.2.267   FORTHCOMING REQUIREMENTS

7.2.267.10   IFRS 16 introduces a single, on-balance sheet lease accounting model for lessees and eliminates the distinction between operating and finance leases. Unless a lessee elects the recognition exemptions for short-term leases and/or leases of low value assets (see 5.1A.140), it recognises a lease liability for its obligation to make lease payments (see 5.1A.270.10). If the lease rentals are denominated in a foreign currency (without any leveraged or optional foreign currency features), then they will impact the lessee's embedded derivative assessment because the obligation to pay future rentals is a monetary liability in the foreign currency subject to retranslation under IAS 21 (see 7.2.265), rather than an embedded derivative in a non-financial contract. [*IAS 32.AG9, IFRS 16.22*]

7.2.267.20   If a lessee separated a foreign currency embedded derivative from a lease contract before the adoption of IFRS 16 and that derivative would no longer qualify for separation, then applying a modified retrospective approach under IFRS 16 (see 5.1A.670) would require it to account for the change in accounting policy on the date of initial application of IFRS 16 as follows.
- Eliminate the previously separated derivative through retained earnings.
- Recognise a lease liability and a right-of-use asset in accordance with IFRS 16 – i.e. the lease liability is recognised as a monetary item denominated in a foreign currency.
- Consider whether there is a different embedded derivative (e.g. foreign currency option-type derivative) that should be separated from the IFRS 16 lease liability.

7.2.267.30   If in a similar case, a lessee instead applies the full retrospective approach under IFRS 16, then the adjustments are required to be applied and measured retrospectively in accordance with IAS 8. In this case, the comparatives are restated and retained earnings are adjusted at the beginning of the comparative period.

7.2.270 Inflation-indexed embedded derivatives

7.2.270.10   Inflation-indexed lease payments are considered to be closely related to the host lease contract provided that there is no leverage feature (e.g. a multiple that would be applied to the inflation rate such that the lease payments would increase by x times inflation) and the index relates to inflation in the entity's economic environment (e.g. the consumer price index of the country in which the leased asset is operated). If the index is based on inflation rates in a different economic environment, then the embedded derivative is not closely related. [*IFRS 9.B4.3.8(f)*]

EXAMPLE 10 – SEPARABLE INFLATION-INDEXED DERIVATIVE EMBEDDED IN LEASE CONTRACT

7.2.270.15   Company L leases a building in Canada, with rental payments denominated in Canadian dollars. The rent is changed each year by multiplying the percentage change in the Canadian consumer price index by a factor of 1.5. Because the adjustments to the rents are higher than the actual inflation rate (i.e. there is a multiplier above 1 that has more than an insignificant effect), L concludes that the embedded derivative is leveraged and should be separated from the host lease contract.

7.2.270.20   In our view, inflation-indexed embedded derivatives in a financial liability are considered to be closely related to the host financial liability if the inflation index is one commonly used for this purpose in the economic environment of the currency in which the financial liability is denominated and it is not leveraged.

7.2.280 Specific hybrid financial instruments

7.2.280.10   Specific hybrid financial liabilities that may be encountered in practice, particularly in the financial services sector, are discussed in 7.2.290–350. The names of these instruments may vary from one country to another, but their accounting treatment is similar.

7.2.290 *Bonds with a constant-maturity yield*

7.2.290.10   Bonds with a constant-maturity yield have a floating rate interest rate that resets periodically on the basis of a market rate that has a duration extending beyond that of the reset period. For example, the interest rate on a 10-year bond resets semi-annually to the then-current weighted-average yield on identified treasury bonds with a 10-year maturity. The effect of this feature is that the interest rate is always equivalent to the market return on an instrument with 10 years' remaining maturity, even when the liability itself has a maturity of less than 10 years.

7.2.290.20   In our view, such a constant-maturity feature comprises an embedded derivative – i.e. a constant-maturity swap. The embedded derivative is not closely related to the host financial liability because it could potentially double the holder's initial rate of return and result in a rate of return that is at least twice what the market return would be for a contract with the same terms as the host contract, unless it has a cap at an appropriate level to prevent the doubling effect. [*IFRS 9.B4.3.8(a)–(b)*]

7.2.290.30   In the example in 7.2.290.10, after seven years the bond would still be yielding a return that is the same as that for an instrument with a 10-year maturity. It is possible that this would be twice the market rate on an instrument similar to the host contract without the constant-maturity feature and with three years left to maturity. However, if the bond also contained a cap that was not leveraged and was above the market rate of interest when the bond was issued, and which prevented the amount of interest increasing so as to double the holder's initial rate of return, then in our view the combined constant-maturity-and-cap feature would be considered closely related. [*IFRS 9.B4.3.8(a)–(b)*]

7.2.290.40   In our view, when assessing whether separation of the embedded derivative is required, the host financial liability can be assumed to be either a fixed rate or a variable rate instrument.

7.2.300 *Cash or share bond liabilities*

7.2.300.10   In a cash or share bond, the principal is determined with reference to movements in fair value of a single equity instrument or an equity index. If the fair value of the equity index or share price falls below a certain level, then it is the fair value of this equity index or share price that will be the basis for repayment – rather than the nominal value of the bond itself – or the bond will be settled by delivering the underlying shares. Therefore, the holder of the instrument might not recover substantially all of its initial investment. The bond will pay a higher coupon to compensate the holder for this increased level of risk.

7.2.300.20   The issuer of such a bond has in effect purchased a put option. In the example in 7.2.300.10, the underlying of the option is either the single equity instrument or the equity index. The option premium is embedded in the interest rate of the bond, which will therefore exceed the current market rate at the date of issuing the bond. This derivative embedded in the bond is not closely related to the host contract and is therefore separated. [*IFRS 9.B4.3.5(c)*]

7.2.310 *Bonds with interest payments linked to equity index*

7.2.310.10   If the interest payment on a bond is linked to movements in an equity index, then the fixed interest on the debt instrument is swapped against a variable return based on the movement in the equity index. The interest payments are not dependent on interest rate risk but on equity risk. Therefore, this swap is not closely related to the host liability and is separated. [*IFRS 9.B4.3.5(c)*]

7.2.310.20   An equity index typically comprises a number of equity instruments of different entities and therefore its movements arise from the changes in the fair value of numerous underlying equity instruments. To be considered closely related to the host contract, the embedded derivative needs to possess equity characteristics related to the issuer of the bond (host contract). Consequently, even if the host contract (bond) were to meet the definition of an equity instrument, it is unlikely that the embedded derivative could be considered closely related and therefore it is separated. [*IFRS 9.4.3.3(a), B4.3.2*]

7.2.320 *Step-down bonds*

7.2.320.10   Step-down bonds contain an interest feature such that the fixed interest rate declines over the life of the bond. For example, the first coupon is fixed at 10 percent whereas the last coupon is fixed at 5 percent.

7.2.320.20   The interest step-down feature alone would not be an embedded derivative that needs to be separated from the host contract. Instead, the step-down feature is taken into account in determining the amortised cost and the effective interest rate on the bond liability. Therefore, part of the interest paid early in the bond's life is deferred and released when the interest rate coupon falls below the effective interest rate of the bond (see 7.7.300). [*IFRS 9.IG.B.27*]

7.2.330 *Reverse (inverse) floating note liabilities*

7.2.330.10   Reverse (inverse) floating notes are bonds that have a coupon that varies inversely with changes in specified general interest rate levels or indexes – e.g. Euribor. For such bonds, coupon payments are typically made according to a pre-set formula such as the following.

X% - (Y x three-month Euribor on a specified date)
where X = a fixed interest rate and Y = a leverage factor

7.2.330.20   Such instruments can be viewed as a combination of a fixed rate debt instrument with a fixed-for-floating interest rate swap that is referenced to an interest rate index. Therefore, the liability contains an embedded derivative. The embedded derivative is not closely related to the host contract and needs to be separated if it could:

- prevent the investor from recovering substantially all of its initial recorded net investment in the bond (if the inverse floater contains no floor to prevent erosion of principal resulting from negative coupons); or
- increase the investor's rate of return on the bond to an amount that is at least twice the initial rate of return on the host contract and could result in a rate of return that is at least twice what the market rate would be for an instrument similar to the host contract. [*IFRS 9.B4.3.8(a)*]

7.2.330.30   If such a liability is capped at less than twice the market rate at the date of issue and floored at zero, then the embedded interest rate swap is considered closely related and is not separated. [*IFRS 9.B4.3.8(a)*]

EXAMPLE 11A – INVERSE RATE FEATURE – NOT CLOSELY RELATED

7.2.330.40   Company X issues a bond at par, which pays coupons linked to LIBOR. The bond includes a binary interest rate feature, whereby the bond pays:
- 9% coupon, if LIBOR is below 3%; and
- 1% coupon if LIBOR is 3% or above.

7.2.330.50   X needs to determine whether the binary interest rate feature is closely related to the host bond. To do so, X needs to identify the terms of the host contract. In this case, X identifies the host contract's terms as:
- excluding the binary interest rate feature; and
- issued at par and paying coupons of LIBOR plus a fixed spread of 0.5%. The spread is determined based on market data and results in an overall market rate of interest on the host contract that reflects its terms and its credit and liquidity risk. At the time of issuing the bond, LIBOR is 4% and therefore the initial rate of return on the host contract is 4.5%.

7.2.330.60   X now needs to compare possible rates of return on the hybrid bond containing the binary interest rate feature with those of the host instrument.

STEP	DETAIL	RESULT
Step 1	Calculate whether the binary interest rate feature could at least double the holder's initial rate of return on the host contract.	If LIBOR remains at or above 3%, the holder's rate of return on the hybrid contract would remain at 1% which is less than the initial rate of return on the host contract of 4.5%. However, if LIBOR declines below 3%, the return on the hybrid bond would increase to 9% which is double the initial rate of return on the host contract of 4.5%.
Step 2	For scenarios in which Step 1 is satisfied, calculate whether the binary interest rate feature could result in a rate of return that is at least twice the market return for a contract with the same terms as the host contract.	When LIBOR is below 3%, a contract with the same terms as the host contact would provide a market return of no more than 3.5% (i.e. LIBOR of 3% plus a fixed margin of 0.5%). Therefore, when LIBOR is below 3%, the hybrid bond would result in a rate of return of 9% that is more than twice what the market return would be on a contract with the same terms as the host contract.

7.2.330.70   Based on the analysis, X determines that the binary interest rate feature is not closely related to the host bond.

EXAMPLE 11B – INVERSE RATE FEATURE – CLOSELY RELATED

7.2.330.80   Modifying Example 11A, assume that the bond pays 7% coupons (instead of 9%) when LIBOR goes below 3% and all other information remains the same.

7.2.330.90   If LIBOR goes to below 3%, then the bond's coupon of 7%:
- would be at least double the market return on a contract with the same terms as the host contract (i.e. LIBOR of less than 3% plus a fixed margin of 0.5%); but
- could never double the initial rate of return on host contract of 4.5%.

7.2.330.100   Further, because the bond pays a minimum of 1% (when LIBOR goes above 3%), the binary interest rate feature would not prevent the holder of the bond from recovering substantially all of its recognised investment in the bond – i.e. the bond's par issuance amount. Accordingly, unlike in Example 11A, the binary interest rate feature in this example is considered closely related to the host bond.

7.2.340   ***Callable zero-coupon bonds***

7.2.340.10   Callable zero-coupon bonds typically have long maturities – e.g. 30 years. The issuer has the right to redeem the bond at predetermined dates before the contractual maturity at the accreted amount. In this case, the embedded derivative (call option) is closely related to the host financial liability if the bond is callable at an amount that is approximately equal to the amortised cost of the host financial liability at each predetermined date, and is not separated (see 7.2.240.10–20). [*IFRS 9.B4.3.5(e)*]

7.2.340.20   In our view, if the embedded call, put or prepayment option has other underlying financial risks (or non-financial risks that are not specific to a party to the contract) that are not closely related to those of the host contract – e.g. equity price risk – then the economic characteristics and risks of the embedded call, put or prepayment option are not closely related to the host contract and should be separated (see 7.2.240). [*IFRS 9.4.3.3, B4.3.5(e)*]

7.2.350   ***Perpetual reset bonds***

7.2.350.10   Perpetual reset bonds do not have a stated maturity, although the issuer may have the right to redeem the bonds at a specified date. If the issuer does not exercise this right, then the interest rate on the bonds will be reset to a new level (based on a predetermined formula) on this date.

7.2.350.20   In our view, it is a matter of judgement, based on all relevant facts and circumstances, whether the issuer should analyse such a perpetual reset bond as:
- a host perpetual debt instrument with an embedded call option and an embedded interest rate reset feature; or
- a host debt instrument with a fixed maturity (based on the reset date) and an embedded term-extension feature. [*IFRS 9.B4.3.3, IG.C.1*]

7.2.350.30   We believe that factors to consider when making this judgement, which is done on initial recognition, should include:
- the nature of the interest rate reset feature; and
- whether the probability of the entity calling the bond is determined to substantially exceed the probability of not exercising the call option, or vice versa.

7.2.350.40   If the host liability is considered to have a fixed maturity, then the embedded feature, which is an automatic provision to extend the term of the debt, is not closely related to the host contract unless there is a concurrent adjustment to the market rate of interest at the date of the extension. Because the resetting of the interest rate is based on a predetermined formula, this may or may not reflect current market rates, and consequently such a feature is not generally considered to be closely related and is separated as an embedded derivative unless it is considered to be equivalent to a loan commitment that would not be in the scope of IFRS 9 (see 7.2.230). [*IFRS 9.2.1(g), 2.3, B4.3.5(b)*]

7.2.360   **Specific hybrid non-financial contracts**

7.2.360.10   Embedded derivatives are often associated with financial instruments. However, they may arise in non-financial contracts – e.g. contracts for the delivery of goods and services. These embedded derivatives are also subjected to the analysis described in 7.2.120–270 and accounted for separately, when it is appropriate. In such cases, the host contract will not be a financial instrument, but will be accounted for under other appropriate standards. Examples 9 and 12 illustrate circumstances in which embedded derivatives exist in non-financial contracts. [*IFRS 9.4.3.1–4.3.3*]

EXAMPLE 12 – PRICE-INDEXATION OF A NON-FINANCIAL ITEM

7.2.360.20   Company X is a manufacturing company. It enters into a contract for the purchase of three specialised machines that will be delivered and installed at the end of 2018, 2019 and 2020 respectively. The price of each machine is determined with reference to a formula that uses the market price of such a machine at the end of 2017 as the base price. This base price is adjusted for twice the change in an employment cost index, as well as an index that reflects cost increases associated with the industry.

7.2.360.30   The indexation incorporates leverage into the pricing mechanism. Therefore, X considers this embedded derivative for separate accounting.

7.2.360.40   However, if X is able to demonstrate that the market prices of similar machines ordinarily move in tandem with the indexation – i.e. there is a high degree of correlation between the two – then separation would not be required.

EXAMPLE 13 – MAINTENANCE COST GUARANTEE

7.2.360.50   Company Y is a logistics company. Y buys its entire fleet of delivery vehicles from one vehicle manufacturer. The vehicle manufacturer provides a guarantee to Y under which it agrees to reimburse the logistics company for vehicle maintenance costs in excess of a specified level.

7.2.360.60   Whether this arrangement contains an embedded derivative within the purchase contract depends on the terms of the guarantee. If the fair value of an instrument changes in response to the change in a specified non-financial variable that is not specific to a party to the contract, then such an instrument meets the definition of a derivative under IFRS 9.

7.2.360.70   In our view, the variation in maintenance charges comprises a non-financial variable. Furthermore, this non-financial variable is specific to the fleet held by the logistics company because it is dependent on the condition of the company's own vehicles. Consequently, this feature of the contract does not meet the definition of a derivative and does not require separate accounting under IFRS 9.

7.2.360.80   When an obligation to deliver goods or services under a non-financial contract is settled, the purchaser usually will initially recognise a new financial liability in respect of the contractual obligation to pay the purchase price. It may therefore be necessary for purchaser to consider whether any embedded derivative is required to be separated from this new financial liability.

EXAMPLE 14 – PROVISIONAL PRICING OF COMMODITY CONTRACT

7.2.360.90   On 31 December 2017, Company R, a commodity producer, enters into an executory contract with Company B, a commodity processor, to deliver a specified amount of unrefined commodity X on 31 January 2018. The final purchase price is payable on 31 March 2018 and is determined with reference to the quoted spot market price for commodity X on that date (i.e. the purchase price is 'provisional' until that date). The parties have agreed that the purchase price is not determined until 31 March 2018 because it is expected that it will take B approximately two months to process the commodity for sale to its customers. The commodity contract is subject to the own-use exemption (see 7.1.200).

7.2.360.100   On 31 December 2017, R and B each consider whether the provisional pricing feature should be separated from the commodity contract and separately accounted for as an embedded derivative. They each conclude that the provisional pricing feature is closely related to the economic characteristics and risks of the host contact because:
- the final price is indexed to the spot market price of the commodity that is delivered under the host contract; and
- the timing lag between the delivery date and the price fixing date relates to the estimated time to process the commodity that is delivered under the host contract.

7.2.360.110   On 31 January 2018, R settles its contractual obligation to deliver the commodity and, as a result, R and B recognise a new financial asset and a new financial liability respectively in relation to the purchase price that is payable on 31 March 2018. The host contract is now a debt financial instrument.

7.2.360.120   R does not apply the embedded derivative requirements to its financial asset but instead assesses the classification of the hybrid financial instrument as a whole (see 7.4.150.50). R classifies the financial asset at fair value through profit or loss in its entirety because it has cash flows that are indexed to a commodity price and this means that the cash flows are not solely payments of principal and interest (see 7.4.150.60). On the other hand, B applies the embedded derivative requirements to its new financial liability and concludes that the provisional pricing feature needs to be separately accounted for as a derivative because payments indexed to a commodity price are not closely related to a host debt instrument because the risks inherent in the host and the embedded derivative are dissimilar. [*IFRS 9.4.3.2–4.3.3, B4.1.7A, B4.3.5(d)*]

7.2.370   **Accounting for separable embedded derivatives**

7.2.370.10   Separable embedded derivatives are required to be measured at fair value, with all changes in fair value recognised in profit or loss unless they form part of a qualifying cash flow or net investment hedging relationship (see chapter 7.9). [*IFRS 9.5.7.1, B4.3.1*]

7.2.370.20   The initial bifurcation of a separable embedded derivative does not result in any gain or loss being recognised. [*IFRS 9.B4.3.3, IG.C.1–IG.C.2*]

7.2.370.30   Because the embedded derivative component is measured at fair value on initial recognition, the carrying amount of the host contract on initial recognition is the difference between the carrying amount of the hybrid instrument and the fair value of the embedded derivative. If the fair values of the hybrid instrument and host contract are more reliably measurable than that of the derivative component – e.g. because of the availability of quoted market prices – then it may be acceptable to use those values to determine the fair value of the derivative on initial recognition indirectly – i.e. as a residual amount. [*IFRS 9.4.3.7, B4.3.3*]

7.2.370.40   When separating an embedded derivative that is a forward contract, the forward price is set such that the fair value of the embedded forward contract is zero at inception. The same applies if the embedded derivative is a swap. Consequently, the forward price needs to be at market on initial recognition. When separating an embedded derivative that is an option, the separation is based on the stated terms of the option feature documented in the hybrid instrument. As a result, the embedded derivative would have a fair value of other than zero on initial recognition of the hybrid instrument. However, the embedded derivative is valued based on terms that are clearly present in the hybrid instrument. [*IFRS 9.B4.3.3, IG.C.1–IG.C.2*]

EXAMPLE 15 – ACCOUNTING FOR SEPARABLE EMBEDDED FORWARD CONTRACT

7.2.370.50   Company G, whose functional currency is sterling, enters into a contract on 1 March 2018 to buy goods from Company B, whose functional currency is the euro. The purchase contract stipulates payment in US dollars and requires G to pay USD 380 on delivery of the goods in six months' time. The applicable exchange rates on 1 March 2018 are:
- spot rate: USD 1 = GBP 0.556; and
- six-month forward rate: USD 1 = GBP 0.526.

7.2.370.60   The contract between G and B contains a foreign currency derivative that requires separation under IFRS 9 because it does not fall under any of the exemptions for non-separation of embedded foreign currency derivatives (see 7.2.260).

7.2.370.70   The host contract is a purchase contract denominated in the functional currency of G – i.e. sterling. The embedded derivative is a foreign currency forward contract to sell USD 380 for sterling at 0.526 at 1 September 2018 – i.e. GBP 200. Because the forward exchange rate is the market rate on the date of the transaction, the embedded forward contract has a fair value of zero on initial recognition.

7.2.370.80   The embedded foreign currency forward contract is accounted for as if it were a freestanding derivative (see 7.2.370.10), and the host instrument as an executory contract (see 1.2.130).

7.2.370.90   If an executory contract to purchase goods or services with an embedded separable derivative related to variability in the price payable contains different delivery and payment dates, then a question arises about the maturity of the embedded derivative. In our view, an entity should choose an accounting policy, to be applied consistently, to determine the maturity of the embedded derivative as the delivery date or the payment date. We believe that regardless of the accounting policy chosen, the terms of the embedded derivative and its valuation should reflect the actual terms of the hybrid instrument and not presume cash flows on the delivery date if cash flows only occur after the delivery date. When the goods or services are delivered, a financial instrument should be recognised for the unconditional amount payable under the contract – i.e. the nature of the contract changes from an executory contract to a financial instrument contract. The separable embedded derivative may be a payment denominated in a third currency (see Example 15) or an embedded foreign currency option under which an entity can choose between different settlement currencies at the payment date based on an exchange rate fixed at inception of the executory contract. The accounting policy choice may have an impact on the holder's classification of its financial asset and on whether an embedded derivative continues to be separated subsequent to recognition of the financial instrument on the delivery date.

EXAMPLE 16 – EXECUTORY CONTRACT WITH SEPARABLE EMBEDDED DERIVATIVE

7.2.370.100   On 31 December 2017, Company M, whose functional currency is sterling, enters into a contract to sell goods to Company P, whose functional currency is euro. The contract is for delivery on 31 January 2018 and settlement in cash on 31 March 2018. After delivery of the goods, M's right to receive cash is not conditional on its future performance. The contract is subject to the own-use exemption (see 7.1.200). P can choose whether to settle the contract in sterling or euro at the time of payment. The exchange rate for each currency is fixed at inception of the executory contract and P can choose the most favourable currency depending on the foreign exchange rates at the payment date.

7.2.370.110   On 31 December 2017, M and P each consider that the embedded foreign exchange option should be separated from the executory contract and accounted for at FVTPL.

7.2.370.120   On 31 January 2018, M delivers the goods and, as a result, M and P recognise a new financial asset and a new financial liability, respectively, in relation to the purchase price that is payable on 31 March 2018. The contract is now a debt financial instrument. Both M and P consider the maturity of the embedded derivative to be at 31 January 2018 (i.e. delivery date).

7.2.370.130   M does not apply the embedded derivative requirements to its financial asset, but instead assesses the classification of the hybrid financial instrument as a whole (see 7.4.150.50). M classifies the financial asset at FVTPL in its entirety because it has cash flows that are dependent on two different foreign exchange rates – i.e. the cash flows are not solely payments of principal and interest (see 7.4.150.60). Conversely, P applies the embedded derivative requirements to its new financial liability. P concludes that an embedded foreign exchange option should continue to be separately accounted for as a derivative.

7.2.370.140   Modifying the fact pattern, if M and P consider the maturity of the embedded derivative to be at 31 March 2018 (i.e. payment date), then the embedded derivative that was separated at inception of the executory contract remains separated and is accounted for at FVTPL until 31 March 2018. M assesses the financial asset without considering the foreign exchange option. M concludes that because the cash flows are solely payments of principal and interest, the financial asset can be classified at amortised cost in line with its business model of holding assets to collect contractual cash flows. P has a financial liability, which is measured at amortised cost. [*IFRS 9.4.1.2, 4.3.2–4.3.3, B4.1.7A, B4.3.8(d)*]

7.2.370.150   Embedded derivatives accounted for separately may be designated as hedging instruments. The normal hedge accounting criteria outlined in 7.9.240 apply to embedded derivatives used as hedging instruments. [*IFRS 9.6.2.1, B6.2.1*]

7.2.380   Presentation and disclosures

7.2.380.10   IFRS 9 does not require separate presentation of separated embedded derivatives in the statement of financial position. In our view, under certain circumstances embedded derivatives that are separated from host financial liability should be presented together with the host contract (see 7.10.310). However, an entity is required to disclose separately financial instruments carried at amortised cost and those carried at fair value. Therefore, embedded derivatives that are separated from financial liabilities but not presented separately in the statement of financial position should be disclosed in the notes. [*IFRS 9.4.3.4, 7.8, B2(a)*]

7.3 Equity and financial liabilities

7.3 Equity and financial liabilities

CURRENTLY EFFECTIVE REQUIREMENTS

This publication reflects IFRS in issue at 1 August 2018, and the currently effective requirements cover annual periods beginning on or after 1 January 2018.

The requirements related to this topic are mainly derived from the following.

STANDARD	TITLE
IFRS 9	Financial Instruments
IAS 1	Presentation of Financial Statements
IAS 12	Income Taxes
IAS 32	Financial Instruments: Presentation
IFRIC 2	Members' Shares in Co-operative Entities and Similar Instruments
IFRIC 17	Distributions of Non-cash Assets to Owners
IFRIC 19	Extinguishing Financial Liabilities with Equity Instruments

FORTHCOMING REQUIREMENTS

The currently effective requirements are affected by the following forthcoming requirements. They are highlighted with a # and the impact is explained in the accompanying boxed text at the references indicated.

In May 2017, the IASB issued IFRS 17 *Insurance Contracts*, which is effective for annual periods beginning on or after 1 January 2021. See 7.3.515. IFRS 17 is the subject of chapter 8.1A.

FUTURE DEVELOPMENTS

This topic is subject to future developments that may affect how financial liabilities are distinguished from equity. See 7.3.700.

7.3.10	**CLASSIFICATION**

7.3.20	**Basic principles**

7.3.20.10   An instrument, or its components, is classified on initial recognition as a financial liability, a financial asset or an equity instrument in accordance with the substance of the contractual arrangement and the definitions of a financial liability, a financial asset and an equity instrument. [*IAS 32.15*]

7.3.20.20   An instrument is classified as a financial liability if it is:
- a contractual obligation:
  - to deliver cash or other financial assets; or
  - to exchange financial assets or financial liabilities with another entity under potentially unfavourable conditions (for the issuer of the instrument); or
- a contract that will or may be settled in the entity's own equity instruments and is:
  - a non-derivative that comprises an obligation for the entity to deliver a variable number of its own equity instruments; or
  - a derivative that will or may be settled other than by the entity exchanging a fixed amount of cash or other financial assets for a fixed number of its own equity instruments. [*IAS 32.11*]

7.3.20.30   An obligation to transfer cash may arise from a requirement to repay the principal or to pay interest or dividends.

7.3.20.40   In general, an 'equity instrument' is any contract that evidences a residual interest in the assets of an entity after deducting all of its liabilities. It meets both of the following conditions.
- There is no contractual obligation:
  - to deliver cash or another financial asset to another party; or
  - to exchange financial assets or financial liabilities with another party under potentially unfavourable conditions (for the issuer of the instrument).
- If the instrument will or may be settled in the issuer's own equity instruments, then it is either:
  - a non-derivative that comprises an obligation for the issuer to deliver a fixed number of its own equity instruments; or
  - a derivative that will be settled only by the issuer exchanging a fixed amount of cash or other financial assets for a fixed number of its own equity instruments. [*IAS 32.11, 16*]

7.3.20.50   As an exception to the general principles, the following are classified as equity instruments if certain conditions (discussed in more detail in 7.3.80–90) are met:
- puttable instruments; and
- instruments, or components of instruments, that impose on the entity an obligation to deliver to another party a pro rata share of the net assets of the entity only on liquidation. [*IAS 32.16A, 16C*]

7.3.20.60   Any financial instrument that an issuer could be obliged to settle in cash, or by delivering other financial assets, is a financial liability regardless of the financial ability of the issuer to settle the contractual obligation or the probability of settlement. The IFRS Interpretations Committee discussed this issue and noted that such a contractual obligation could be established explicitly or indirectly, but it needs to be established through the terms and conditions of the instrument. [*IAS 32.19–20, IU 11-06*]

EXAMPLE 1 – CLASSIFICATION AS LIABILITY OR EQUITY – LINKED INSTRUMENTS

7.3.20.70   Company K issues a non-redeemable financial instrument (the 'base' instrument) with dividends payable if interest is paid on another instrument (the 'linked' instrument). K is required to pay the interest on the linked instrument.

7.3.20.80   In this example, the linkage to the linked instrument, on which interest is contractually payable, creates a contractual obligation to pay dividends on the base instrument. Therefore, K concludes that this obligation should be classified as a liability.

7.3.20.90   When determining whether to classify a financial instrument as a financial liability or as equity, an entity assesses the substance of a contractual arrangement rather than its legal form. In assessing the substance of a contractual arrangement, the entity needs to consider all of the terms and conditions of the financial instrument, including relevant local laws, regulations and the entity's governing charter in effect at the date of classification (see 7.3.30.180). Therefore, it is possible for instruments that qualify as equity for legal or regulatory purposes to be classified as liabilities for the purposes of financial reporting. [*IAS 32.15, 18*]

7.3.20.100   The IFRS Interpretations Committee discussed the classification of a financial instrument as a liability or as equity and noted that in assessing the substance of a contractual arrangement, an entity needs to exclude a contractual term that lacks substance. The Committee also noted that IAS 32 does not require or permit factors not within the contractual arrangement to be taken into consideration in classifying a financial instrument as a liability or as equity. For example, economic compulsion should not be used as the basis for classification. This is because a contractual obligation could be established explicitly or indirectly, but it has to be established through the terms and conditions of the instrument (see 7.3.20.60). Therefore, by itself, economic compulsion does not result in a financial instrument being classified as a liability. [*IAS 32.20, IU 11-06, 01-14*]

7.3.20.110   Judgement is required to determine whether a contractual right – e.g. to avoid delivering cash, another financial asset or a variable number of the entity's own equity instruments – is substantive and therefore needs to be considered in determining the classification of an instrument as a financial liability or equity (see 7.3.30.80 and 220.100–140). [*IAS 32.15, 20, IU 01-14*]

7.3.20.120   Instruments commonly affected by these requirements include:
- preference shares;
- classes of shares that have special terms and conditions;
- subordinated instruments; and
- convertible and perpetual instruments.

7.3.20.130   Equity instruments include shares, options and warrants, and any other instrument that evidences a residual interest in an entity and meets the relevant conditions in 7.3.20.40–110.

7.3.20.140   The classification of an instrument as either liability or equity determines whether any interest, dividends, losses and gains related to that instrument are recognised as income or expense in profit or loss. [*IAS 32.36*]

7.3.20.150   If an instrument is classified as a liability, then coupon payments and any amortisation of discounts or premiums on the instrument are recognised as part of finance costs in profit or loss, under the effective interest method. Sometimes all of the fair value of the consideration received on issuing an instrument that includes a discretionary dividend feature is allocated to and recognised as a financial liability. For further discussion of the classification of discretionary dividends in such cases, see 7.3.290. [*IAS 32.35–36, AG37*]

7.3.20.160   If, however, some or all of an instrument is classified as equity, then discretionary distributions are accounted for directly in equity. See 7.3.290 and 680. [*IAS 32.35–36, AG37*]

7.3.20.170   The classification of an instrument, or its component parts, as either financial liability or equity is made on initial recognition. It is not generally revised as a result of subsequent changes in circumstances – with the exception of puttable instruments and instruments that impose on the entity an obligation only on liquidation (see 7.3.200). However, a reclassification between financial liability and equity or vice versa may be required in certain circumstances (see 7.3.470). [*IAS 32.15*]

(S) 7.3.20.180   The classification of financial instruments as equity or financial liabilities in the consolidated financial statements may differ from their classification in any separate or individual financial statements of entities within a group (see 7.3.240.20). [*IAS 32.AG29*]

(S) EXAMPLE 2 – CLASSIFICATION IN CONSOLIDATED AND SEPARATE FINANCIAL STATEMENTS

7.3.20.190   Company P has two subsidiaries, Companies B and G. G issues non-redeemable preference shares to a party outside the group. B writes a put option on the preference shares issued by G. The put option, if it is exercised, will require B to purchase the preference shares from the holder for cash.

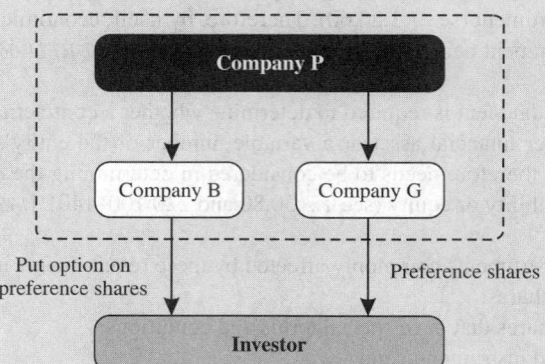

7.3.20.200   In its separate financial statements, G classifies the preference shares as equity because it does not have a contractual obligation to redeem the shares or to pay dividends. However, in the consolidated financial statements, the group as a whole has a contractual obligation to redeem the preference shares (through the put option written by B). P therefore classifies the preference shares as a financial liability in the consolidated financial statements.

7.3.30   Contractual obligation to deliver cash or another financial asset

7.3.30.10   The primary factor determining classification is whether the instrument establishes a contractual obligation for the issuer to make payments (principal, interest/dividends or both). A right on the part of the holder does not necessarily translate to a contractual obligation on the part of the issuer. [*IAS 32.17*]

7.3.30.20   The holder of an equity instrument might have the *right* to receive dividends if they are paid; however, the issuer does not have a *contractual obligation* to make payments until the dividend is appropriately authorised and is no longer at the discretion of the entity. The holder has a financial asset, whereas the issuer has an equity instrument rather than a financial liability. [*IAS 32.17*]

7.3.30.30   IAS 32 further clarifies that an instrument that creates an obligation is a financial liability if the entity does not have the unconditional right to avoid delivering cash or another financial asset in settlement of that obligation. A contractual obligation is not negated merely because of a lack of funds, statutory restrictions or insufficient profits or reserves. [*IAS 32.19, AG25*]

EXAMPLE 3A – LIABILITY FOR PREPAID CARD

7.3.30.32   Company C issues a prepaid card with the following features in exchange for cash:
- there are no expiry date or back-end fees;
- the balance on the card does not reduce unless it is spent by the cardholder;
- the balance on the card is non-refundable and cannot be exchanged for cash;
- the balance on the card is redeemable only for goods or services to a specified monetary amount at specified third party merchants; and
- when the cardholder purchases goods or services and redeems the balance at a merchant, C delivers cash to the merchant. [*IU 03-16*]

7.3.30.35   The liability for the prepaid card meets the definition of a financial liability because C:
- has a contractual obligation to deliver cash to the merchants on behalf of the cardholder when the cardholder uses the prepaid card to purchase goods or services; and
- does not have an unconditional right to avoid delivering cash to settle this contractual obligation. [*IU 03-16*]

EXAMPLE 3B – CONTRACTUAL OBLIGATION CONTINGENT ON COVENANTS IMPOSED BY LOCAL LAW

7.3.30.40   Company B has issued a loan, the terms of which stipulate that it is repayable only if its repayment does not violate certain covenants imposed by local law.

7.3.30.50   In this example, B does not have the unconditional right to avoid making payments; also, the breach of covenants that prevents repayment at a specific point in time defers, rather than negates, the obligation. Consequently, B classifies the loan as a financial liability.

7.3.30.60   An obligation that will be settled only if a holder exercises its right to redeem is a financial liability, irrespective of how likely or unlikely it is that the holder will actually exercise its right. [*IAS 32.19*]

7.3.30.70   When the terms of a financial instrument provide for cash settlement at the option of the holder, entities may obtain a letter of undertaking from the holder indicating that this option will not be called on. In our view, such an undertaking, unless it is legally enforceable and irrevocable, is not sufficient to warrant classification of the instrument as equity rather than as a financial liability. For example, assume that the holder of such an instrument has signed such a letter of undertaking but is able to sell the instrument. Furthermore, assume that the purchaser would not be restricted by the letter of undertaking that was signed by the seller. In this scenario, the instrument would be classified as a financial liability.

7.3.30.80   In most cases, the terms and conditions of an instrument establish a contractual obligation explicitly. However, such an obligation may also arise implicitly. For example, an instrument may include a non-financial obligation that is required to be settled if the entity fails to make distributions or redeem the instrument; this is a financial liability, because the entity can avoid payment only by settling the non-financial obligation. In another example, an instrument may provide that on settlement an entity delivers either cash or another financial asset, or its own shares whose value substantially exceeds the value of the cash or other financial asset; this is also a financial liability, because the value of the share settlement alternative is such that the entity will settle in cash. Therefore, the holder has in substance been guaranteed receipt of an amount that is at least equal to the cash settlement option. [*IAS 32.20, BC9*]

EXAMPLE 4 – NON-FINANCIAL OBLIGATION

7.3.30.90   Company G issues an instrument that includes a term under which G is required to deliver a property in settlement if the instrument is not redeemed after 10 years. The instrument is a financial liability because G can avoid settling the financial obligation only by settling the non-financial obligation.

EXAMPLE 5 – SHARE SETTLEMENT OPTION

7.3.30.100   Company B issues an instrument that is required to be settled either in cash or in a fixed number of B's own shares, the value of which will substantially exceed the amount of cash. The instrument is a financial liability because, although B does not have an explicit contractual obligation to settle in cash, the value of the share settlement option is so high that B will always settle in cash.

7.3.30.110   Instruments containing features that are classified as financial liabilities generally include the following:
- instruments that are redeemable at the option of the holder – e.g. redeemable preference shares;
- non-redeemable preference shares with dividends that are not discretionary (see 7.3.290);
- instruments that become redeemable on the occurrence of an uncertain future event that is beyond the control of both the holder and the issuer of the instrument (see 7.3.40); and
- subordinated liabilities.

7.3.30.120   As an exception to the general principles, some instruments that are redeemable, either at the option of the holder or on liquidation – which is either certain to occur and outside the control of the entity, or uncertain to occur but at the option of the instrument holder – are classified as equity instruments of the entity if certain conditions are met (see 7.3.80–90). [*IAS 32.16A, 16C*]

7.3.30.130   An entity also needs to distinguish between:
- a contractual obligation to deliver cash or another financial asset, which gives rise to a financial liability; and
- a statutory obligation, which does not necessarily result in a financial liability. [*IAS 32.AG12*]

7.3.30.140   For example, local law might require an entity to pay a minimum specified amount as dividends in each period for a particular instrument. In our view, such an obligation does not represent a contractual obligation and consequently the obligation is not classified as a financial liability under IAS 32. However, when an entity voluntarily incorporates a minimum specified amount of dividends into the terms of an instrument – e.g. to achieve a desired tax outcome or to achieve a certain regulatory status – in our view the payment of such dividends represents a contractual obligation of the entity and consequently the obligation is classified as a financial liability. [*IAS 32.AG12*]

EXAMPLE 6A – CONTRACTUAL OBLIGATIONS TO MAINTAIN TAX STATUS

7.3.30.150   Company S is a real estate investment trust (REIT). Under a contractual agreement with its shareholders, S is required to maintain its REIT tax status. To do so, under local tax law S needs to pay out a specified percentage of its taxable income as dividends each year. There is no legal obligation, outside the contractual terms in the shareholder agreement, for S to comply with those specific provisions of the local tax law. Instead, the decision to be taxed as a REIT is voluntary.

7.3.30.160   In this example, a contractual obligation to pay dividends is created indirectly (see 7.3.20.100) – i.e. it is a combination of the contractual requirement in the shareholder agreement to maintain the REIT tax status and the requirement in the local tax law to pay dividends in order to maintain that status. The tax law itself does not oblige S to make dividend payments because it is a voluntary election available to those that meet certain criteria. However, when viewed in combination with the contractual agreement with its shareholders, S has an obligation to make dividend payments. The clause under which S needs to comply with the REIT dividend requirements is a contractual obligation and not a statutory obligation. Therefore, this obligation is classified as a financial liability.

EXAMPLE 6B – NO CONTRACTUAL OBLIGATIONS TO MAINTAIN TAX STATUS

7.3.30.165   In contrast to Example 6A, the contractual terms of the shareholder agreement for Company T, another REIT, do not require the entity to maintain REIT tax status. Instead, the agreement provides the management of Company T with

> full discretion over the declaration of dividends even though a failure to declare and pay dividends may jeopardise its tax status. In this scenario, the legal requirement to pay dividends in order to maintain REIT tax status would not impact the classification of Company T's shares.

7.3.30.170   Some debt instruments issued by banks may be subject to a statutory provision requiring them to be converted into equity or written down when a supervisory authority determines that such an action is required. These instruments are commonly referred to as 'statutory bail-in instruments'. Bail-in occurs before a bank becomes insolvent – i.e. at the 'point of non-viability'. Statutory bail-in requirements do not impact the issuer's classification as financial liabilities or equity on initial recognition. However, bail-in features that are contractual terms of the instruments are considered in classification by the issuer.

7.3.30.180   Although only contractual obligations give rise to financial liability classification, in certain circumstances terms and conditions existing outside the contract can affect the classification of an instrument by giving the issuer an unconditional right to avoid payment. For example, the contractual right of the holder of a share issued by an entity to request redemption does not, in itself, require that financial instrument to be classified as a financial liability. Rather, the issuer is required to consider all of the terms and conditions of the instrument in determining its classification as a financial liability or equity. Those terms and conditions include relevant local laws, regulations and the entity's governing charter in effect at the date of classification. If a local law, regulation or the entity's governing charter gives the issuer of the instrument an unconditional right to avoid redemption, then the instrument is classified as equity. [*IFRIC 2.5–8*]

7.3.30.190   The overall context of IFRIC 2 is the classification of instruments, issued by co-operatives and similar entities, that are puttable instruments – defined in IAS 32 as financial liabilities but with equity classification required if certain criteria are met. Its focus is the interaction of contractual obligations to redeem an instrument and terms outside the contract that can affect the exercise of those contractual obligations. Accordingly, in our view IFRIC 2 should be interpreted such that restrictions on redemption outside the contract itself may negate the existence of a contractual obligation and lead to equity classification. However, we believe that it should not be interpreted to mean that a non-contractual obligation to make payments on an instrument that does not contain a contractual obligation will lead to financial liability classification of that instrument. For a discussion of members' shares in co-operative entities and similar instruments, see 7.3.60.

7.3.40   Contingent settlement provisions

7.3.40.10   An instrument may contain a contractual obligation to deliver cash or another financial asset depending on the outcome of an uncertain future event that is beyond the control of both the issuer and the holder of the instrument. Examples of such uncertain events are changes in:
- a stock market index;
- interest rate;
- taxation requirements; and
- the issuer's future revenues or debt-to-equity ratio. [*IAS 32.25*]

7.3.40.20   When an instrument contains such contingent settlement provisions, the issuer does not have the unconditional right to avoid making payments. Therefore, the instrument is a financial liability, unless one of the following applies:

- the part of the contingent settlement provision that could require settlement in cash or another financial asset is not genuine; or
- the issuer can be required to settle in cash or another financial asset only in the event of its own liquidation (as long as liquidation is neither predetermined nor at the option of the holder – see 7.3.40.170).

7.3.40.30   If the instrument containing such contingent settlement provisions is a puttable instrument, then it may qualify for classification as equity if it meets all of the relevant criteria (see 7.3.80). [*IAS 32.16A–16B*]

EXAMPLE 7A – CONTRACTUAL OBLIGATION IF IPO DOES NOT TAKE PLACE

7.3.40.40   Company Y issues a bond that is convertible automatically into a fixed number of ordinary shares when an IPO takes place. The offering is planned for two years' time, but is subject to the approval of a regulator. The bond is redeemable in cash only if the IPO does not take place.

7.3.40.50   In this example, Y cannot avoid the obligation, because it cannot ensure that regulatory approval will be received; nor can it ensure that the IPO will actually occur. In this scenario, the bond is potentially redeemable in cash and the contingency is beyond the control of both Y and the holder of the bond. The bond therefore contains a liability, regardless of the likelihood of cash settlement.

7.3.40.60   The contingent conversion feature qualifies as an equity instrument because the bond can convert only into a fixed number of equity shares (see 7.3.230 and 270.20). Therefore, the bond is accounted for as a compound instrument with liability and equity components (see 7.3.310). [*IAS 32.16(b)(ii), 28*]

EXAMPLE 7B – CONTRACTUAL OBLIGATION IF IPO TAKES PLACE

7.3.40.70   If the bond in Example 7A were redeemable in cash only if the IPO took place, then the instrument would be classified as equity. In this situation, the issuer would have the unconditional ability to avoid the obligation if it can decide whether to launch an IPO.

7.3.40.80   If an entity issues an instrument that becomes immediately redeemable in cash on the occurrence of a change in control of that entity, such as when a majority of the entity's shareholders choose to sell their shares to an acquiring party in a takeover, then in our view this feature should be classified as a financial liability. This is because we believe that such a change-in-control event is an uncertain future event that is not within the control of the entity; therefore, the entity does not have an unconditional right to avoid delivering cash. This would generally apply even if such a takeover required formal approval by a majority of shareholders at a general meeting, because it is reasonable to assume in this case that shareholders would be acting in their capacity as individual investors rather than as a body as part of the entity's internal corporate governance processes (see 7.3.40.90–130).

7.3.40.90   In our view, careful analysis of the specific facts and circumstances and judgement are required to assess whether the shareholders of an entity are acting as a body under the entity's governing charter – i.e. as issuer (part of the entity), or as individual investors (not as part of the entity).

7.3.40.100   When shareholders participate in the normal governance process, and in a routine manner related to the decision involved, they are generally acting as part of the entity. For example, assume that an entity has perpetual bonds with interest payments linked to dividends on ordinary shares, which need to be approved by the shareholders. These are classified as equity if the payment of dividends is at the discretion of the entity. The following may indicate that the entity's shareholders are acting as a body on behalf of the entity when approving or disapproving the payment of dividends on ordinary shares:
- dividend approvals are a recurring item on the agenda of the annual general meeting; and
- the dividend approval process is carried out consistently over the years as a matter of routine.

7.3.40.110   In such cases, we believe that the approval of dividends is within the control of the entity, that paragraph 25 of IAS 32 does not apply and that the term 'issuer' incorporates both the entity and its shareholders.

7.3.40.120   However, shareholders are not acting as a body under the entity's governing charter when they are acting as individual investors. For example, shareholders are generally considered to be acting outside the normal governance process when they are voting to dispose of their individual shareholding.

7.3.40.130   In such cases, we believe that a change in shareholding is not within the control of the entity, that paragraph 25 of IAS 32 applies and that the term 'issuer' does not incorporate both the entity and its shareholders.

7.3.40.140   As an exception, a contractual provision requiring settlement in cash or another financial asset that is considered non-genuine does not result in financial liability classification for that instrument. In our view, only in extremely rare, highly abnormal and very unlikely circumstances will a contingent settlement feature be considered 'non-genuine'. We believe that a contingent settlement feature should be considered non-genuine only if:
- it has no economic substance; and
- it could be removed by the parties to the contract without any compensation, either in the form of payment or by altering the other terms and conditions of the contract.

7.3.40.150   In our view, in all other cases such provisions should be considered genuine and therefore should affect classification. For example, an instrument may provide for cash settlement in the event of a change in tax law because the terms of the instrument were structured so that the holder and/or issuer could enjoy a specific tax benefit. However remote the chances of the tax law changing, such an instrument should be classified as a financial liability. A contingent settlement event – such as a tax change or a takeover of the issuer – would always be regarded as genuine unless it was inserted into the contract only to achieve financial liability classification. [*IAS 32.AG28*]

7.3.40.160   In our view, subsequent changes in circumstances that lead to a genuine contingent settlement feature becoming extremely rare, highly abnormal and very unlikely to occur – i.e. a change in probability – do not change the initial assessment that the contingent settlement feature is considered genuine and therefore do not result in reclassification of the instrument from financial liability to equity. Likewise, subsequent changes in circumstances that lead to a non-genuine contingent settlement feature becoming likely to occur do not result in a reclassification of an instrument from equity to financial liability. However, appropriate disclosure may be required (see 7.10.10.10).

7.3.40.170   As an exception, a contractual provision that requires settlement of a financial instrument only in the event of liquidation of the issuer does not result in financial liability classification for that instrument. However, the entity's liquidation date may be predetermined; alternatively, the holder of such an instrument may have the right to liquidate the issuer of the instrument. In those cases, the exception does not generally apply and financial liability classification may be required (see 7.3.90). [*IAS 32.16C, 25(b)*]

7.3.40.180   Unless the conditions for classification as equity under the exceptions to the general principles described in 7.3.90 are met, in our view the following liquidation rights should also result in financial liability classification:
- a liquidation right held by the instrument holder that becomes exercisable on the occurrence of an event that is not within the control of the entity – e.g. a change in control (see 7.3.40.80). This is because the entity cannot prevent the holder from obtaining the liquidation right if the uncertain event occurs. For example, if the liquidation right becomes exercisable on a change in control – e.g. when the majority of the issuer's shareholders choose to sell their shares in a takeover – then the contingent event is not the liquidation itself but the change in control, which is not within the discretion of the entity; and
- liquidation rights held by the instrument holders as a class rather than included in the individual instrument – e.g. the majority of preference shareholders have a contractual right to force the liquidation of the issuer. This is because the entity cannot avoid its potential obligation to deliver cash or another financial asset if the instrument holders make a decision to liquidate the entity.

7.3.40.190   However, we believe that financial liability classification is not generally appropriate when ordinary shareholders collectively have the right to force the liquidation of the entity. This is because the ordinary shareholders' right to liquidate the entity at a general meeting would generally be considered part of the normal or ordinary governance processes of the entity (see 7.3.40.100). Therefore, the ordinary shareholders acting through the general meeting would be considered to be acting as part of the entity.

7.3.40.200   A contract that would otherwise be settled by delivery of a fixed number of the entity's own equity instruments in exchange for a fixed amount of cash may provide for net cash settlement in the event of the counterparty's involuntary liquidation or bankruptcy. In our view, the existence of such a clause does not preclude the entity from classifying the contract as equity.

7.3.50   **Obligation to acquire own equity instruments**

7.3.50.10   Financial instruments that give the holder the right to 'put' them back to the issuer for cash or other financial assets ('puttable instruments') are financial liabilities of the issuer. However, if certain conditions are met, then they are classified as equity (see 7.3.80). The put option creates a contractual obligation that the issuer does not have the unconditional ability to avoid. In our view, the fact that the instrument may not be puttable immediately does not affect its classification as a financial liability, although that fact may affect its measurement (see 7.3.240) in addition to its classification as a current or non-current liability. [*IAS 32.16A, 18(b)*]

7.3.50.20   This principle applies even when:
- the amount of cash or other financial assets is determined on the basis of an index or other variable that has the potential to increase or decrease – e.g. a share index; or
- the legal form of the puttable instrument gives the holder a right to a residual interest in the assets of the issuer. [*IAS 32.18(b)*]

7.3.50.30   The amount payable to the holder of a puttable instrument might vary in response to an index or another variable whose economic characteristics are not closely related to those of the host contract. In this case, the instrument may contain an embedded derivative that requires separation (see 7.2.110). As a result, either:
- the entire puttable instrument (hybrid) is measured at FVTPL; or
- the embedded derivative is separated and accounted for at FVTPL (see 7.7.140).

7.3.50.40   Investors in many mutual funds, unit trusts and similar entities have the right to redeem their interests in exchange for cash that is equivalent to their share of the net asset value of the entity. This gives the issuer (the fund) a contractual obligation and therefore these instruments are classified as financial liabilities, unless they meet the conditions to be classified as equity (see 7.3.80–90). These instruments are financial liabilities independent of considerations such as when the right is exercisable, how the amount payable on exercise is determined and whether the instrument has a fixed maturity. However, these considerations may affect whether the instruments qualify for equity classification under the exceptions in 7.3.80–90. [*IAS 32.18(b)*]

7.3.50.50   The requirement addressed in 7.3.50.40 means that some entities do not present any equity. However, IAS 32 does not preclude such instruments from being included in the statement of financial position within a 'total members' interests' subtotal. [*IAS 32.IE32*]

7.3.60   *Members' shares in co-operative entities and similar instruments*

7.3.60.10   The principles in 7.3.50.40 apply equally to shares issued to members of a co-operative entity that give the holder the right to request redemption. Members' shares and similar instruments that would be classified as equity if they did not give the holder the right to request redemption are classified as equity only if:
- the entity has an unconditional right to refuse redemption; or
- redemption is unconditionally prohibited by local law, regulation or the entity's governing charter (see 7.3.30.150). [*IFRIC 2.2, 6–8*]

7.3.60.20   A distinction is made between unconditional and conditional prohibitions on redemption. Only an unconditional prohibition on redemption can lead to the classification of members' shares and similar instruments as equity.

7.3.60.30   An unconditional prohibition prevents an entity from incurring a liability for redemption, regardless of whether the entity will be able to satisfy the obligation. However, a conditional prohibition prevents *payments* from being made unless certain conditions are met – e.g. liquidity constraints. A conditional prohibition may only defer payment of a liability that has already been incurred. For example, members' shares can be redeemed as soon as the local liquidity or reserve requirements are met. [*IFRIC 2.BC14*]

7.3.60.40   An unconditional prohibition may be partial, in that it allows redemption but requires a stated minimum amount of members' shares or paid-in capital to be maintained at all times. In this case, the proportion of members' shares subject to the unconditional prohibition on redemption is classified as equity – even though each individual instrument may be redeemed. [*IFRIC 2.9*]

EXAMPLE 8 – PARTIAL UNCONDITIONAL PROHIBITION ON REDEEMING SHARES

7.3.60.50   Local law prohibits a co-operative from redeeming members' shares if that would cause the amount of paid-in capital from members' shares to fall below 75% of its highest ever reported amount. If the highest amount of paid-in capital from members' shares ever reported was 100, then 75 would always be classified as equity – even though each member could, individually, request redemption of their share.

7.3.60.60   An unconditional prohibition may be based on a factor that can change over a period of time. [*IFRIC 2.9*]

EXAMPLE 9 – PARTIAL UNCONDITIONAL PROHIBITION ON REDEEMING SHARES THAT CHANGES OVER TIME

7.3.60.70   The governing charter of Co-operative C states that 25% of the highest number of members' shares ever in issue should be maintained as equity. C decides to amend its governing charter by reducing this percentage to 20%. Assuming that all other factors remain the same, then the number of members' shares subject to the unconditional prohibition would reduce.

7.3.60.80   Consequently, C would increase its financial liability to redeem members' shares, while simultaneously decreasing the amount of members' shares classified as equity. This, and other such changes to the amount of members' shares or paid-in capital subject to an unconditional prohibition on redemption, are treated as transfers between financial liabilities and equity. [*IFRIC 2.9*]

7.3.60.90   For a discussion of changes in the effective terms of an instrument, see 7.3.490. [*IFRIC 2.9*]

7.3.60.100   In our view, an unconditional prohibition may also result in equity classification when it prohibits a contingent event from taking place. For a discussion of contingent events, see 7.3.40.

EXAMPLE 10 – CONTINGENT EVENT UNCONDITIONALLY PROHIBITED BY LAW

7.3.60.110   Company C has issued a put option on specified equity instruments that is exercisable if there is change in control of C. C is controlled by the government; for public interest reasons, the law unconditionally prohibits a change in control.

7.3.60.120   In this example, C concludes that no liability should be recognised for the potential obligation to redeem the equity instruments unless there is a change in the law to remove the prohibition.

7.3.60.130   On initial recognition, an entity measures its financial liability at fair value. In the case of members' shares with a redemption feature, the entity measures the fair value of the financial liability for redemption at no less than the discounted maximum amount payable under the redemption provisions of its governing charter or applicable law. The discount runs from the first date on which the amount could be required to be paid. [*IFRIC 2.10*]

7.3.70   Puttable instruments and obligations arising on liquidation classified as equity by exception

7.3.70.10   As exceptions to the general principles for liability and equity classification, a puttable instrument or an instrument (or a component of an instrument) that imposes on the entity an obligation only on liquidation is classified as equity if the conditions discussed in 7.3.80–90 are met.

7.3.70.20   Puttable instruments, and instruments that impose an obligation on the entity only on liquidation, are classified as equity in the separate or individual financial statements of the issuing entity (see 2.5.720.30). However, in the consolidated financial statements of the group, if the instrument is issued by a subsidiary and is not held by another member of the group, it is classified as a financial liability because the exception is not extended to classification as NCI in the consolidated financial statements. [*IAS 32.AG29A, BC68*]

7.3.80   *Puttable instruments*

7.3.80.10   A puttable instrument is a financial instrument that:
- gives the holder the right to put the instrument back to the issuer for cash or another financial asset; or
- is automatically put back to the issuer on the occurrence of an uncertain future event or the death or retirement of the instrument holder.

7.3.80.20   Even though a puttable instrument contains an obligation for the entity to deliver cash or another financial asset, it is classified as equity if all of the conditions in the following flowchart are met. [*IAS 32.16A–16B*]

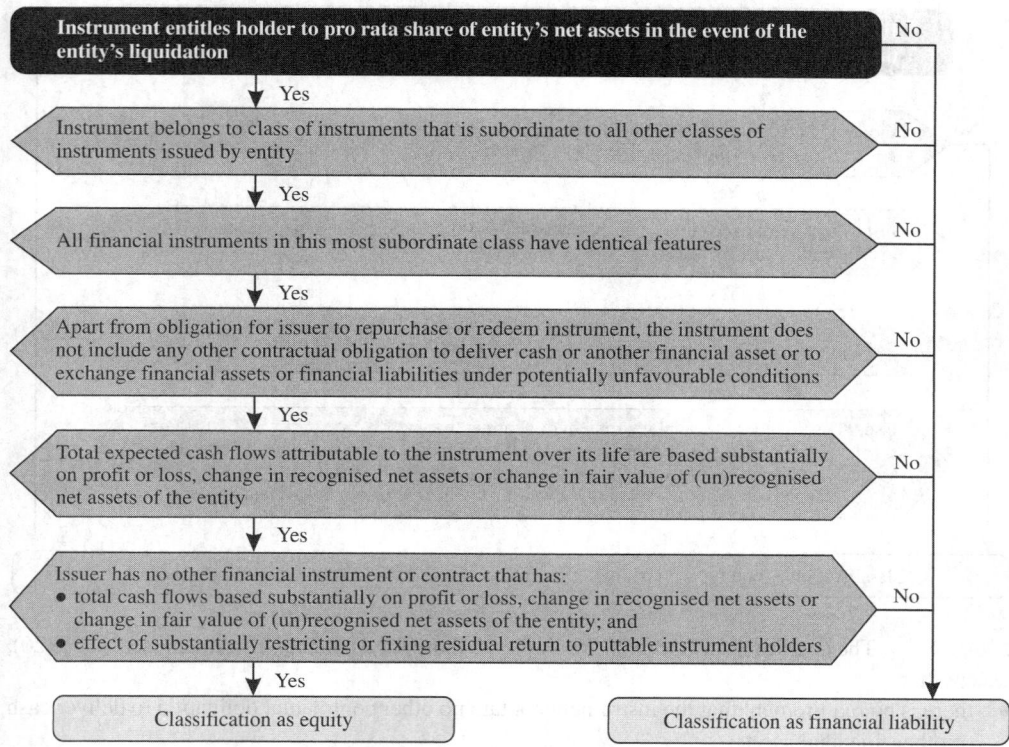

7.3.80.30   The issuer of a puttable instrument first evaluates the terms of the instrument to determine whether it is a financial liability or equity instrument in its entirety, or is a compound instrument that contains both a liability and an equity component, in accordance with the general definitions of liabilities and equity in IAS 32. If the puttable instrument is initially determined to be a financial liability, or to contain a financial liability component, then the whole instrument is tested for equity classification under the exception in 7.3.70.10. If the instrument meets all of the conditions for equity classification under the exception, then the whole instrument is classified as equity. If the whole instrument does not meet the conditions for equity classification under the exception, then it is classified wholly as a liability or is split into its liability and equity components in accordance with the general requirements on financial liability and equity classification in IAS 32. [*IAS 32.11, 16A, 28*]

7.3.90   *Instruments that oblige the entity on liquidation*

7.3.90.10   An entity may issue instruments that contain a contractual obligation for the entity to deliver to the holder a pro rata share of its net assets only on liquidation. In this case, the obligation arises if liquidation is either:

● certain to occur and is outside the control of the entity – e.g. a limited-life entity; or
● uncertain to occur but is at the option of the instrument holder – e.g. some partnership interests.

7.3.90.20   For such an instrument (or component) to qualify for equity classification by exception, all of the conditions in the following flowchart need to be met. [*IAS 32.16C*]

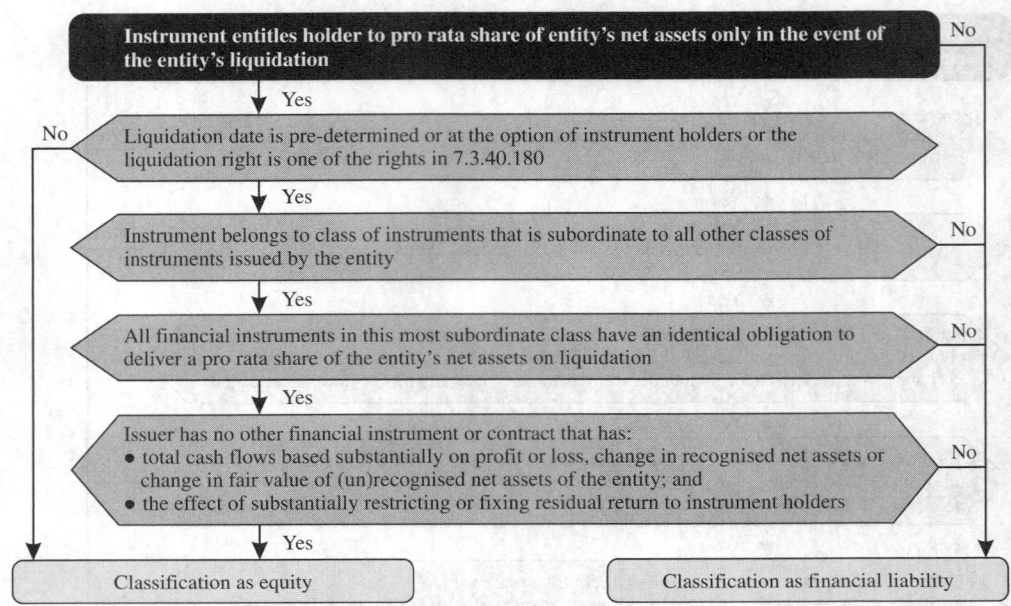

7.3.90.30   The conditions in 7.3.90.20 are similar to those for a puttable instrument (see 7.3.80.20), except that:

- there is no requirement that the instrument contain no other contractual obligation to deliver cash or other financial assets;
- there is no requirement to consider the total expected cash flows over the life of the instrument; and
- there is only one feature that needs to be identical among the instruments in the most subordinate class: this is the obligation for the issuing entity to deliver to the holder a pro rata share of its net assets on liquidation.

7.3.90.40   The reason for this distinction between a puttable instrument and an instrument that imposes on the entity an obligation only on liquidation is the difference in the timing of settlement of the obligations. A puttable instrument can be exercised before liquidation of the entity. Therefore, it is important to identify all contractual obligations that exist throughout its entire life to ensure that it always represents the most residual interest. However, for an instrument that imposes on the entity an obligation only on liquidation of the entity, it is appropriate to focus only on the obligations that exist at liquidation. [*IAS 32.BC67*]

7.3.100   *Components of instruments*

7.3.100.10   The exception in 7.3.90 applies to 'components of instruments that impose on the entity an obligation to deliver to another party a pro rata share of the net assets of the entity only on liquidation'. Therefore, if the instrument contains other contractual obligations, then those other obligations may need to be accounted for separately as financial liabilities in accordance with IAS 32.

7.3.100.20   An example of such an instrument is a unit holder's interest in a limited-life entity that:
- is not puttable; and

- includes only a right to:
  - fixed non-discretionary dividends each period; and
  - a pro rata share of the entity's net assets on its liquidation.

7.3.100.30   The obligation to pay fixed non-discretionary dividends represents a contractual obligation that is classified as a financial liability; the obligation to deliver a pro rata share of the entity's net assets on its liquidation is classified as equity, provided that all other criteria are met. However, if there is no mandatory dividend requirement, and dividends are entirely at the discretion of the entity, then the units are classified wholly as equity provided that all other criteria are met.

7.3.100.40   In our view, in applying the last condition set out in 7.3.90.20 when evaluating a component of an instrument for equity classification, an entity should choose an accounting policy, to be applied consistently, on whether the term 'other financial instrument' encompasses other components of that same financial instrument or only financial instruments other than the one that contains the component being evaluated.

7.3.110   Analysis not restricted to instruments other than the instrument under evaluation

7.3.110.10   An instrument may include an obligation to distribute mandatory dividends based on profits of the entity, and an obligation to distribute a pro rata share of the net assets on a fixed liquidation date. Assume that the entity applies the last condition in 7.3.90.20 to the component of the instrument that comprises the obligation arising only on liquidation; and that, to do this, its policy is to treat the mandatory dividend feature like another financial instrument. In this case, equity classification of the obligation arising only on liquidation would be precluded. This is because the mandatory dividends are based on profits and therefore the condition in paragraph 16D of IAS 32 is not met.

7.3.120   Analysis restricted to instruments other than the instrument under evaluation

7.3.120.10   However, assume that the entity's policy is to restrict the analysis under 7.3.90.20 to consider only financial instruments other than the one that contains the obligation arising on liquidation. In this case, the mandatory dividend feature in itself would not preclude equity classification of the obligation arising on liquidation. This is because the feature is part of the same instrument, and the condition for equity treatment in paragraph 16D of IAS 32 could be met. For further discussion of this condition for equity treatment, see 7.3.180.

EXAMPLE 11 – MANDATORY DIVIDEND FEATURE BASED ON PROFITS

7.3.120.20   Company C, which has a limited life, issues non-redeemable Instrument X that requires payment of a dividend equalling 90% of its profits. The holders of Instrument X will also participate in the liquidation of C on a pro rata basis.

7.3.120.30   The instrument is issued for its fair value of 1,000. The fair value of the mandatory dividend feature is 800 on issuance; this component of the instrument is classified as a financial liability.

Scenario 1: Analysis not restricted to instruments other than Instrument X

7.3.120.40   C's policy is to regard the mandatory dividend feature as another financial instrument for the purpose of applying the condition in 7.3.90.20 to the component that provides a pro rata participation in liquidation.

7.3.120.50   In this scenario, equity classification of the component that provides a pro rata participation in liquidation is precluded. This is because the mandatory dividends are substantially based on profits; therefore, the condition in paragraph 16D of IAS 32 is not met.

Scenario 2: Analysis restricted to instruments other than Instrument X

7.3.120.60   C's policy is to restrict the analysis under 7.3.90.20 to consider only financial instruments other than Instrument X.

7.3.120.70   In this scenario, the mandatory dividend feature of Instrument X in itself does not preclude equity classification of the component that provides a pro rata participation in liquidation. This is because the feature is part of the same financial instrument, and the condition for equity treatment in paragraph 16D of IAS 32 could be met.

7.3.130   *Pro rata share of entity's net assets on liquidation*

7.3.130.10   A pro rata share of the entity's net assets on liquidation is determined by:
- dividing the entity's net assets on liquidation into units of equal amount; and
- multiplying that amount by the number of units held by the financial instrument holder.
  [*IAS 32.16A(a), 16C(a)*]

7.3.130.20   In our view, the requirement in 7.3.130.10 means that each instrument holder has an entitlement to an identical monetary amount per unit on liquidation. For example, an instrument that entitles the holder to a fixed dividend on liquidation, in addition to a share of the entity's net assets, would not qualify under this requirement. Similarly, if payments to instrument holders on liquidation are subject to fees that are not computed on an identical per-unit basis – e.g. a fixed fee per holder rather than per unit – then the instrument would not satisfy this criterion. Furthermore, instruments that entitled the holder to a pro rata share of only a specific portion or component of the net assets of an entity would not satisfy this criterion.

7.3.140   *Class of instruments subordinate to all other classes*

7.3.140.10   In determining whether an instrument is in the most subordinate class, an entity evaluates the instrument's claim on liquidation as if it were to liquidate on the date on which it classifies the instrument. [*IAS 32.AG14B*]

7.3.140.20   IAS 32 does not preclude the existence of several types or classes of equity. The IFRS Interpretations Committee discussed the classification of puttable instruments that are subordinate to all other classes of instruments when an entity also has perpetual instruments that are classified as equity. The Committee noted that a financial instrument is first classified as a liability or equity instrument in accordance with the general requirements of IAS 32. As a second step, the entity considers the exceptions in paragraphs 16A and 16B, or 16C and 16D of IAS 32 (see 7.3.80–90), to determine whether a financial instrument should be classified as equity. It would do so if the financial instrument meets the definition of a financial liability because either:

- it is puttable to the issuer; or
- it imposes on the issuer an obligation on liquidation because liquidation is either:
  - certain to occur and outside the control of the entity; or
  - uncertain to occur but is at the option of the instrument holder. [*IU 03-09*]

EXAMPLE 12 – LEVEL OF SUBORDINATION

7.3.140.30   Company X issues two types of instruments. Instrument A is a perpetual instrument with no put rights; Instrument B is a puttable instrument. Both could qualify as equity, provided that all applicable criteria in IAS 32 are met. The existence of the puttable feature in Instrument B does not in itself imply that the instrument is less subordinate than Instrument A, because the level of an instrument's subordination is determined by its priority in liquidation.

7.3.140.40   If Instrument A and Instrument B are equally subordinate, then together they form the most subordinate class for the purposes of the 'identical features' test discussed in 7.3.150. However, in this case Instrument B would fail equity classification because of the existence of the put feature, which does not exist in Instrument A.

7.3.140.50   If Instrument B is more subordinate than Instrument A – e.g. if Instrument A is entitled to a fixed claim on liquidation and Instrument B is entitled to the residual net assets – then Instrument B may qualify for equity classification, provided that all other conditions in the exceptions are met.

7.3.140.60   Many investment funds have a nominal amount of founder shares that are issued to the fund manager. These shares are typically non-redeemable and have no entitlements to dividends. In our view, even a small amount of founder shares would disqualify investors' shares that are puttable from equity classification if the founder shares are subordinate to the puttable investors' shares. This is because the puttable investors' shares are not the most subordinate class of instruments.

7.3.140.70   If an investment fund issues redeemable participating shares and founder shares that rank pari passu in respect of their respective nominal amounts in liquidation and the founder shares have no further payment rights, then in our view the founder shares and participating shares together form the most subordinate class. However, because the redeemable participating shares have other rights, we believe that the participating shares would be classified as liabilities, because they do not have identical features to those of the founder shares (see 7.3.150).

7.3.150   *Identical features test*

7.3.150.10   In respect of puttable instruments, all financial instruments in the most subordinated class are required to have identical features to qualify for equity classification. No instrument holder in the most subordinate class of instruments can have preferential terms or conditions. In our view, this should be interpreted strictly to mean identical contractual terms and conditions. This includes non-financial features, such as governance rights, related to the holders of the instruments in their roles as owners of the entity. Differences in cash flows and contractual terms and conditions of an instrument attributable to an instrument holder in its role as non-owner are therefore not considered to violate the identical features test – provided that the transaction is on similar terms to an equivalent transaction that might occur between a non-instrument holder and the issuing entity. [*IAS 32.AG14C, AG14F–AG14G, AG14I*]

EXAMPLE 13 – GUARANTEE OF GENERAL PARTNERS IN LIMITED PARTNERSHIP

7.3.150.20   A general partner in Limited Partnership P provides a guarantee to P and is remunerated for providing that guarantee. If the guarantee and the associated cash flows relate to the general partner in its role as guarantor, and not in its role as owner of P, then P disregards the guarantee and the associated cash flows when assessing whether the contractual terms of the limited partnership instruments held by the general partner and limited partners are identical.

EXAMPLE 14 – ADDITIONAL INFORMATION RIGHTS

7.3.150.30   A fund manager that holds units in an investment fund may have access to certain information rights that are not granted to other unit holders. If these information rights are granted to the fund manager in its role as manager of the fund, then they are not considered to violate the identical features test.

Ⓢ 7.3.150.40   As discussed in 7.3.190, in our experience units issued by sub-funds within umbrella investment funds fail equity classification in the financial statements of the umbrella fund (when the umbrella fund and sub-funds form a single legal entity). In our view, contractual features that would violate the identical features test include:

- different rates of management fees;
- a choice *on issuance* by holders whether to receive income or additional units as distributions (such that the distributive or accumulative feature differs for each instrument after they are issued);
- different lock-up periods;
- different reference assets on which the pro rata share of net assets is calculated; or
- different currencies in which payments are denominated.

7.3.150.50   However, in our view the following features do not violate the identical features test, because there are no inherent differences in the features of each instrument within the most subordinate class:

- administrative charges based on the volume of units redeemed before liquidation, as long as all unit holders in the most subordinate class are subject to the same fee structure;
- different subscription fees payable on initial subscription, as long as all other features become identical once the subscription fees are paid;
- choice by holders *on each distribution date* to receive income or additional units as distributions, as long as the same ability to choose distributions or reinvestment is afforded to all of the unit holders in the most subordinate class – i.e. the choice is an identical feature for all of the instruments in this most subordinate class; and

- a term contained in identical instruments that carry equal voting rights that caps the maximum amount of voting rights that any individual holder may exercise.

7.3.160   *No other contractual obligation to deliver cash or another financial asset*

7.3.160.10   In respect of puttable instruments, one of the conditions for equity classification is that the instrument does not include any other contractual obligation to deliver cash other than the put feature. [*IAS 32.16A(d)*]

EXAMPLE 15 – ADDITIONAL CONTRACTUAL OBLIGATION TO DELIVER CASH

7.3.160.20   Unlisted unit trust T issues instruments that enable the holder to put the instrument back to T at any time. T is contractually required to distribute its net accounting profit on an annual basis.

7.3.160.30   In this example, T concludes that the requirement to distribute the net accounting profit annually is an additional obligation to deliver cash. Therefore, these instruments do not qualify for equity classification.

7.3.170   *Total expected cash flows attributable to instrument over its life*

7.3.170.10   In respect of puttable instruments, one of the conditions for equity classification is that the total expected cash flows attributable to the instrument over its life are based substantially on the profit or loss, the change in the recognised net assets, or the change in the fair value of the recognised and unrecognised net assets of the entity. In this context, profit or loss, and the change in recognised net assets, are measured in line with relevant standards. [*IAS 32.16A(e), AG14E*]

7.3.170.20   In some cases, an instrument may be puttable at a pro rata share of the entity's recog- nised net assets, as calculated in its *separate* financial statements. IFRS does not discuss whether such instruments could qualify for equity classification if the issuer is a parent entity required to present consolidated financial statements – i.e. in which it consolidates its investments in subsidiaries. IFRS includes no requirement for puttable instruments issued by a parent to be classified differently in the parent's separate financial statements and consolidated financial statements – provided that no additional arrangements exist between the holder of an instrument and subsidiaries of the issuer. Therefore, in our view when the entity is a parent, its profit or loss, change in recognised net assets or change in the fair value of the recognised and unrecognised net assets may be measured either on a separate or on a consolidated basis. For example, consider an instrument that is puttable at a pro rata share of a parent's recognised net assets as presented in its separate IFRS financial statements. This may qualify for classification as equity in both the separate and consolidated IFRS financial statements, provided that all other conditions in the exceptions are also met.

7.3.170.30   Instruments that are puttable at a pro rata share of recognised net assets determined in accordance with a different basis of accounting – e.g. local GAAP – may still satisfy the condition in 7.3.170.10, depending on the circumstances. For example, it may be possible to argue that the effect of differences between local GAAP and IFRS is immaterial when applied to the entity; or it might be argued that the effect is temporary and expected to converge over the life of the instrument, such that the total 'expected' cash flows are 'based substantially' on IFRS profit or loss or change in recognised net assets. In our view, the use of the terms 'expected' and 'based substantially' indicates that judgement should be exercised in determining whether the requirement is met in the individual circumstances of each specific situation, including consideration of how local GAAP and IFRS apply to the reporting entity's business and the terms of the instrument.

7.3.170.40   When the redemption amount of a puttable instrument is based on the change in fair value of the recognised and unrecognised net assets of the entity, judgement should still be applied to determine whether the total expected cash flows test is met but, in our experience, it will often be straightforward to determine.

7.3.180 *Other financial instruments or contracts*

7.3.180.10   An issuer may need to assess whether it has any other financial instrument or contract that precludes equity classification. In doing so, the entity does not consider a non-financial contract with the holder of the puttable instrument or the holder of the instrument that imposes an obligation only on liquidation. If there were such a contract, then the entity would have to determine that the non-financial contract has terms and conditions that are similar to those of an equivalent contract that might occur with a non-instrument holder. [IAS 32.16B, 16D, AG14J]

7.3.190 *Instruments issued by umbrella fund*

7.3.190.10   In certain jurisdictions, a collective investment scheme may be structured as an umbrella fund that operates one or more sub-funds, whereby investors purchase instruments that entitle the holder to a share of the net assets of a particular sub-fund. The umbrella fund and sub-funds together form a legal entity, although the assets and the obligations of individual funds are fully or partially segregated.

7.3.190.20   If the umbrella fund presents financial statements that include the assets and liabilities of the sub-funds, which together with the umbrella fund form a single legal entity, then the sub-fund instruments are assessed for equity classification in those financial statements from the perspective of the umbrella fund as a whole. Therefore, these instruments cannot qualify for equity classification under the conditions in 7.3.80–90. This is because they could not meet the 'pro rata share of the entity's net assets on liquidation' test (see 7.3.130) and, if they are puttable instruments, the identical features test (see 7.3.150).

7.3.190.30   In an alternative umbrella fund structure, the sub-funds may be subsidiaries of the umbrella fund. The umbrella fund may present consolidated financial statements in line with IFRS 10 that consolidate the sub-funds as subsidiaries. The exceptions to the general principles described in 7.3.80–90 are not extended to the classification of NCI in consolidated financial statements. Therefore, instruments issued by such sub-funds are classified as liabilities in the consolidated financial statements if they:
- qualified for equity classification under the conditions in 7.3.80–90 in the separate financial statements of each sub-fund; and
- represent NCI. [IAS 32.AG29A]

7.3.190.40   If the sub-funds are subsidiaries of the umbrella fund, but the umbrella fund qualifies as an investment entity, then the investments in the sub-funds are generally measured at FVTPL (see 5.6.10.10). The umbrella fund does not present consolidated financial statements and therefore no NCI arises in the umbrella fund's financial statements in respect of the investments in the sub-funds that are measured at FVTPL.

7.3.190.50   The umbrella fund may present combined financial statements. In this case, to the extent that they are expressed as being prepared in accordance with IFRS, in our view puttable sub-fund instruments would not qualify for equity classification in the combined financial statements for the reasons described in 7.3.190.20–30.

7.3.200   *Reclassification*

7.3.200.10   A puttable instrument or an instrument that imposes on the entity an obligation only on liquidation is reclassified as equity from the date on which it has all of the features and meets the conditions set out in 7.3.80.20 and 90.20. An instrument is reclassified from equity to financial liabilities from the date on which it ceases to have all of the features or meet all of the conditions for equity classification. [*IAS 32.16E*]

7.3.200.20   This indicates a continuous assessment model under which an entity reassesses its classification of instruments:
- whenever there are changes to the capital structure of the entity – e.g. when new classes of shares are issued or when existing shares are redeemed; or
- when there is a change in expectations over:
  - total expected cash flows; and
  - the evaluation of whether they are based substantially on IFRS profit or loss or change in recognised net assets.

7.3.200.30   When a puttable instrument, or an instrument that imposes on the entity an obligation only on liquidation, is reclassified from equity to financial liabilities, the liability is measured initially at the instrument's fair value at the date of reclassification. Any difference between the carrying amount of the equity instrument and the fair value of the financial liability at the date of reclassification is recognised in equity. [*IAS 32.16F(a)*]

7.3.200.40   When a puttable instrument, or an instrument that imposes on the entity an obligation only on liquidation, is reclassified from financial liabilities to equity, the equity instrument is measured at the carrying amount of the financial liability at the date of reclassification. [*IAS 32.16F(b)*]

7.3.200.50   In either case, there is no pre-tax profit or loss impact arising from the reclassification. Any potential income tax accounting implications under IAS 12 (see chapter 3.13.520) resulting from the reclassification need to be considered.

7.3.210   **Instruments to be settled in own equity**

7.3.210.10   A contract that will be settled by the entity issuing its own equity instruments does not create an obligation on the part of the entity to deliver cash or another financial asset. However, IAS 32 imposes additional requirements that have to be met in order to classify such instruments as equity. [*IAS 32.21*]

7.3.220   *Non-derivative contracts*

7.3.220.10   If a non-derivative contract will or may be settled in the issuer's own equity instruments, then it is a financial liability – provided that it includes a contractual obligation for the issuer to deliver a *variable number* of its own equity instruments. It is classified as a liability because the holder does not have a direct equity exposure, as would be the case if the issuer were obliged to deliver a fixed number of shares. [*IAS 32.11, 16(b)(i), 21, AG27(d)*]

7.3.220.20   Also, if a contract may be settled either in the issuer's own equity instruments (whether fixed or variable in number) or in cash or other financial assets, at the option of the *holder*, then the instrument is a financial liability or contains a liability component – e.g. a bond convertible into shares at the holder's option. [*IAS 32.11, 16(b)*]

7.3.220.30   The IFRS Interpretations Committee discussed the classification of a financial instrument as a liability or as equity and noted that if the *issuer* of a financial instrument has the contractual right to choose to settle the instrument either in cash or in a fixed number of its own shares, then the instrument meets the definition of an equity instrument provided that the instrument does not establish an obligation to deliver cash indirectly through its terms and conditions (see 7.3.20). This is because the issuer does not have a contractual obligation to deliver cash or to deliver a variable number of its own shares. [*IAS 32.16, AG25, IU 09-13*]

7.3.220.40   A contract is a financial liability if an entity has an obligation to deliver a number of its own equity instruments that varies so that the total fair value of the equity instruments delivered is equal to the amount of the contractual obligation. The amount of that contractual obligation could be fixed, or it could vary in response to changes in another market variable that is unrelated to the market value of the entity's equity instruments – e.g. the gold price. In these circumstances, the holder is not exposed to any gain or loss arising from movements in the fair value of the equity instruments. Consequently, in such instances the entity is using its equity instruments as currency. Such contracts are financial liabilities of the entity. [*IAS 32.21*]

7.3.220.50   The IFRS Interpretations Committee noted that a single obligation to deliver a variable number of an entity's own equity instruments is a non-derivative obligation that meets the definition of a financial liability and cannot be subdivided into components for the purpose of evaluating whether the instrument contains a component that meets the definition of equity. [*IAS 32.11, IU 05-14*]

EXAMPLE 16 – OBLIGATION TO DELIVER VARIABLE NUMBER OF SHARES SUBJECT TO CAP AND FLOOR

7.3.220.60   Company M has issued a financial instrument for 8,000. The instrument has a stated maturity date. At maturity, M must deliver a variable number of its own equity shares, as follows:

- if the share price is below 80, then M issues 100 shares (cap);
- if the share price is above 100, then M issues 80 shares (floor); and
- if the share price is between 80 and 100, then M issues a variable number of shares with a market value of 8,000.

7.3.220.70 The IFRS Interpretations Committee discussed a similar scenario and noted that the instrument in such an example is a financial liability because it comprises an obligation to deliver a variable number of shares. Although the variability is limited by a cap and a floor, the overall number of equity instruments that the issuer is obliged to deliver is not fixed and therefore the entire obligation meets the definition of a financial liability. It would not be appropriate to divide the instrument into components – e.g. the minimum number of shares to deliver under the floor – for the purpose of evaluating whether the instrument contains a component that meets the definition of equity. [*IU 05-14*]

7.3.220.80 The Committee also noted that such cap and floor features are embedded derivatives that need to be separated from the host liability – which in this example represents an obligation to deliver a variable number of shares with a fixed value of 8,000 – and to be measured at fair value, with all changes in fair value recognised in profit or loss, assuming that the instrument has not been designated in its entirety as at FVTPL (see 7.2.110 and 7.5.40). [*IU 05-14*]

7.3.220.90 This is because:

- the 'fixed-for-fixed' requirement is not met in respect of these features because the cap and floor are net settled derivatives which do not result in the exchange of a fixed amount of cash for a single fixed number of equity shares (see 7.3.230.10); and
- their values change in response to the price of the issuer's equity shares and therefore they are not closely related to the host debt contract. [*IU 05-14*]

7.3.220.100 An instrument may establish a contractual obligation to deliver a variable number of shares indirectly through its terms and conditions, even if the issuer has a contractual right to settle the instrument by delivering a fixed number of shares. This is illustrated in Example 17.

EXAMPLE 17 – CLASSIFICATION AS LIABILITY OR EQUITY – IS A CONTRACTUAL RIGHT SUBSTANTIVE?

7.3.220.110 Company Z issues a financial instrument that matures after five years.

- On maturity, the instrument is settled by delivering a variable number of Z's own equity instruments with a market value equal to a fixed cash amount, subject to a cap and a floor, similar to Example 16 – i.e. there are both a minimum and a maximum number of equity instruments that could be delivered if the price of a single equity instrument is higher or lower than certain amounts.
- Z also has a contractual right to settle the instrument at any time before maturity by delivering the maximum number of equity instruments specified in the contract – i.e. the cap amount.

7.3.220.120   In discussing a similar scenario, the IFRS Interpretations Committee noted that an entity cannot automatically assume that the financial instrument meets the definition of an equity instrument because it has a contractual right to settle early by delivering a fixed number of its own equity instruments. This is because this contractual right might not be substantive – because the issuer may have to deliver significantly more shares to settle early than it may otherwise be obliged to deliver at maturity – and therefore would not be considered in determining the classification of the instrument (see 7.3.20). [*IAS 32.15, 20, IU 01-14*]

7.3.220.130   Judgement is required to determine whether the early settlement option is substantive and therefore should be taken into account in classifying the instrument. In particular, Z needs to consider whether there are actual economic or other business reasons for it to exercise that option. [*IU 01-14*]

7.3.220.140   In making this assessment, Z considers the following factors:
- whether the instrument would have been priced differently if its early settlement option had not been included within the contractual terms;
- the width of the range between the cap and the floor; and
- Z's share price and its volatility. [*IU 01-14*]

7.3.230   *Derivative contracts*

7.3.230.10   A derivative contract is an equity instrument if it can be settled only by the entity receiving or delivering a fixed number of its own equity instruments for a fixed amount of cash or another financial asset (the so-called 'fixed-for-fixed' requirement). For example, an issued share option that gives the holder the right to buy a fixed number of the entity's shares for a fixed amount of cash or for a fixed stated principal amount of a bond is an equity instrument. IAS 32 also goes on to state that changes in the fair value of an instrument as a result of changes in market interest rates that do not affect the amount of cash or other financial assets to be received or paid, or the number of equity instruments to be received or delivered, do not impact classification as an equity instrument. A contract that is settled by an entity issuing a variable number of own shares for a fixed amount of cash, or a fixed number of own shares for a variable amount of cash, is a financial asset or financial liability of the entity. [*IAS 32.11, 16(b)(ii), 22*]

7.3.230.20   IAS 32 does not address an exchange of a fixed number of the entity's own equity instruments. In our view, a contract to exchange a fixed number of one class of non-derivative own equity instruments for a fixed number of a different class of non-derivative own equity instruments should be classified as an equity instrument. For example, an issued share option that gives the non-controlling shareholder of an entity's subsidiary the right to exchange a fixed number of shares in that subsidiary for a fixed number of shares in the parent entity is an equity instrument in the consolidated financial statements of the parent entity. [*IAS 32.16*]

7.3.230.30   For convertible bonds where the holder has the ability to convert into a fixed percentage of the issuer's outstanding shares, an issue arises over whether the conversion option meets the fixed-for-fixed requirement.

EXAMPLE 18 – BOND CONVERTIBLE INTO A FIXED PERCENTAGE OF AN ENTITY'S OUTSTANDING SHARES

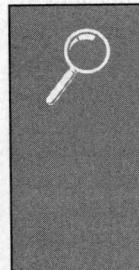

7.3.230.40   Company S issued a convertible bond for a principal amount of 5 million that matures in 10 years. The holder of the instrument has the option to convert the bond into ordinary shares of S. S may issue or redeem additional ordinary shares at any time. The number of ordinary shares to be received on conversion will represent a fixed percentage (i.e. 5%) of the issued and outstanding shares of S.

7.3.230.50   The conversion option does not meet the fixed-for-fixed requirement because the number of ordinary shares to be received upon conversion will vary when there are changes in the number of outstanding shares of S.

7.3.230.60   An obligation in a foreign currency represents a variable amount of cash. Consequently, contracts (both freestanding and embedded) are classified as financial assets or financial liabilities if they will be settled by an entity delivering a fixed number of its own equity instruments in exchange for a fixed amount of foreign currency. However, there is an exception for rights, options or warrants to acquire a fixed number of the entity's own equity instruments for a fixed amount of any currency. This exception requires that the entity offers the rights, options or warrants pro rata to all of its existing owners of the same class of its own non-derivative equity instruments. Under the exception, these rights, options or warrants are equity instruments. The exception does not extend to other instruments that grant the holder the right to purchase the entity's own equity instruments for a fixed amount denominated in a foreign currency (such as the conversion feature in bonds). For further discussion of foreign currency convertible bonds, see 7.3.350. [*IAS 32.11(b)(ii), 16(b)(ii), BC4F, BC4K*]

7.3.230.70   In our view, the requirement that a contract be settled by delivering a fixed number of its own shares for a fixed amount of cash, in order to be classified as equity, can also be met if the number of shares to be delivered or the amount of cash to be received changes over the life of the contract but the change is predetermined at inception of the contract.

EXAMPLE 19 – BERMUDAN OPTION

7.3.230.80   Company B issues an option, which the parties can exercise at predetermined dates (a Bermudan option). At each date, the option can be settled by B delivering a fixed number of its own shares for a fixed amount of cash. However, the number of shares and the amount of cash depend on the date of exercise of the option; the exact terms of the exchange at each exercise date were determined when B entered into the contract – i.e. the number of shares to be delivered is fixed for each date at inception.

7.3.230.90   Such a contract is in fact a series of European-style option contracts that would each be settled by B delivering a fixed amount of its own shares for a fixed amount of cash. Consequently, B concludes that the contract, assuming that it meets the other requirements, should be classified as an equity instrument.

7.3.230.100   Similarly, in our view adjustment clauses that alter the conversion ratio only to prevent dilution (anti-dilution) do not violate the fixed-for-fixed requirement and therefore do not result in the instrument being classified as a financial liability. 'Anti-dilution' refers to the adjustment of the conversion ratio to compensate holders of the instrument for changes in the number of equity instruments outstanding that relate to share issuances or redemptions not made at fair value – e.g. arising from rights issues or bonus issues. Anti-dilution can also include the adjustment of the conversion ratio to compensate holders of the instrument for dividend payments to existing shareholders that were not taken into account when the conversion ratio was initially set. Anti-dilution does not comprise any other form of compensation to the instrument holder for fair value losses – e.g. when compensation by adjusting the conversion ratio is given if the share price falls below a certain level or if new shares are issued at a then-current market price that is below the conversion price.

7.3.230.110   Many convertible bonds include takeover clauses that either allow or require the holder to exercise its conversion option at an enhanced conversion ratio if control of the issuer changes. A takeover may negatively affect bond holders relative to shareholders in a number of ways – e.g. if current shareholders are bought out by an acquirer, and the issuer's business is transferred to a new entity or the underlying shares are de-listed. The bond holder might suffer the loss of its conversion option (if conversion is required) or the loss of an option to convert into publicly traded shares (if the issuer's shares are no longer publicly traded). In the absence of compensation to the bond holder, the shareholders would benefit from the relative loss of value suffered by the bond holders. In our view, if a takeover clause provides an enhanced conversion ratio that is designed to compensate bond holders for this loss of optionality that arises on a takeover and is intended to preserve the relative economic interests of bond holders and shareholders, then it does not violate the fixed-for-fixed requirement.

7.3.230.120   Except as described in 7.3.230.100–110, in our view the requirement that a contract be settled by delivering a fixed number of the entity's own shares for a fixed amount of cash cannot be met when the right to the number of shares to be delivered is contingent on *both* the exercise date of the instrument *and* equity prices or any other index.

EXAMPLE 20 – PATH-DEPENDENT OPTION

7.3.230.130   Company G issues a convertible bond containing a right for the holder to convert the bond into shares of the issuer. The number of shares received at each exercise date is dependent on the average share prices prevailing three months before the exercise date – i.e. a path-dependent option.

7.3.230.140   G concludes that the instrument does not meet the fixed-for-fixed requirement, because there is not only variability in the date of exercise but also variability in the actual number of shares that will be issued at each exercise date. In Example 19, even though there was variability in the date of exercise, such a contract represents a series of European-style option contracts that will each be settled by delivering a fixed amount of own shares for a fixed amount of cash.

7.3.230.150   Any consideration received or paid for an instrument that is classified as an equity instrument – e.g. the option premium – is added to or deducted from equity. [*IAS 32.22*]

7.3.240   **Obligation to purchase own equity instruments**

7.3.240.10   An instrument that creates an obligation or potential obligation for an entity to purchase its own equity instruments for cash or another financial asset (see 7.3.50) gives rise to a financial liability. The amount of the liability is measured at the present value of the redemption amount. This is the case whether the exercise price is variable – e.g. based on a multiple of EBITDA – or fixed. A liability is recognised even if the contract itself is an equity instrument. Consequently, even if a contract entered into to purchase an entity's own equity instruments is classified as equity – i.e. a fixed amount of cash for a fixed number of equity instruments – an accounting entry is required to recognise a liability. The liability is accounted for at the present value of the redemption amount with a corresponding debit to equity. In effect, a reclassification is made from equity to reflect the obligation to repurchase the equity instruments in the future. If the contract expires without the obligation being settled – e.g. if a written put option expires unexercised – then the carrying amount of the liability at that time is reclassified to equity. For further discussion, see 7.3.490. [*IAS 32.23*]

7.3.240.20   This applies equally from a consolidated financial statements perspective to an (potential) obligation to purchase *a subsidiary's* equity instruments held by non-controlling shareholders because a subsidiary's equity constitutes the group's own equity in its consolidated financial statements. For a discussion of the subsequent accounting for changes in the carrying amount of liabilities resulting from forwards and put options over NCI, see 2.5.720. [*IAS 32.23, IFRS 10.22, IU 11-06*]

7.3.240.30   However, in our view an obligation or potential obligation – either in the form of forward or option contracts – to purchase an associate's or a joint venture's equity instruments should be classified as a derivative in the separate, individual and/or consolidated financial statements of the investor. This is because associates and joint ventures are not part of the group (see 3.5.280).

7.3.250   *Written put option to be settled in shares of parent*

7.3.250.10   The discussion in this section considers three different scenarios in which non-controlling shareholders have a right to put the subsidiary's equity shares to the parent in exchange for equity shares of the parent.

7.3.250.20   In Scenario 1, a subsidiary issues equity shares to non-controlling shareholders and a parent writes put options that give the non-controlling shareholders a right to put their equity shares in the subsidiary to the parent in exchange for a *fixed* number of the parent's equity shares. In this case, in the parent's consolidated financial statements, the option gives non-controlling shareholders a right to exchange a fixed number of one class of non-derivative own equity instruments for a fixed number of a different class of non-derivative own equity instruments. In our view, such a contract should be classified as equity (see 7.3.230.20).

7.3.250.30   In Scenario 2, a subsidiary issues equity shares to non-controlling shareholders and a parent writes put options that give the non-controlling shareholders the right to put their equity shares in the subsidiary to the parent in exchange for a *variable* number of the parent's equity shares. In this case, IAS 32 is not clear about how such instruments held by non-controlling shareholders should be classified in the parent's consolidated financial statements.

7.3.250.40   In our view, an entity should choose one of the following accounting policies, to be applied consistently, to account for such instruments.

- *Approach 1:* Classify the subsidiary's shares held by non-controlling shareholders together with the put options as financial liabilities. Under this approach, in accordance with paragraph AG29 of IAS 32, taking into account all of the terms and conditions agreed between members of the group and the holders of the instrument, the subsidiary's shares are effectively considered to be non-derivative contracts – i.e. a contractual obligation for the parent to deliver a variable number of its own equity shares – and there is no separate accounting for the put options (see 7.3.20.20 and 220.10).
- *Approach 2:* Account for the written put options separately as derivative liabilities. The basis of this approach is that the put option is a separate instrument and there is no obligation to deliver cash or another financial asset. Accordingly, the subsidiary's shares that are held by non-controlling interest holders are presented as equity reflecting existing ownership interests in the subsidiary and the put option is accounted for at FVTPL in accordance with IFRS 9 (see 7.3.230.10).

7.3.250.50   The put options in Scenario 2 in 7.3.250.30 may be written either together with the issuance of the shares to the non-controlling shareholders or subsequent to the issuance of these shares. When the put option is written subsequent to the issuance of the shares, under Approach 1 in 7.3.250.40, a reclassification would be required such that a financial liability is recognised and measured at fair value at that date. Under Approach 2 in 7.3.250.40, the put options are recognised as derivative liabilities regardless of the timing of their issuance.

7.3.250.60   Modifying Scenario 2, assume that the parent also has an option to settle by paying cash rather than delivering its own equity shares when the non-controlling shareholders exercise the options and deliver their shares in the subsidiary to the parent. If the parent's accounting policy is to consider the combination of the shares and the written put options as financial liabilities (Approach 1 in 7.3.250.40), then the existence of the parent's right to settle in cash does not affect its accounting treatment because the combination still represents a financial liability. However, if the parent's accounting policy is to account for the written put options separately (Approach 2 in 7.3.250.40), then in our view the parent should also choose one of the following accounting policies, to be applied consistently, in respect of the written put options.

- *Recognise a financial liability for the present value of the exercise price:* Under this approach, the written put option is a separate instrument that gives rise to a financial liability for the present value of the exercise price in accordance with paragraph 23 of IAS 32. The put option represents an obligation to purchase own shares in the group for cash. In this case, there is an issue of how to account for the debit side of the transaction because NCI are initially recognised separately from the written put option. For further discussion of the accounting for the shares in the subsidiary held by the non-controlling shareholders, see 2.5.690.
- *Account for the written put options as derivative liabilities at FVTPL:* Under this approach, the shares held by the non-controlling shareholders are classified as equity. The related put options are accounted for as derivative liabilities under IFRS 9 – i.e. at fair value with changes therein recognised in profit or loss. [*IAS 32.23, 26–27*]

7.3.250.70   We believe that the accounting policy choice in 7.3.250.60 arises because IAS 32 is not clear about the issuer's accounting for a written put option on its own equity instruments if it can avoid delivering cash or another financial asset (see 7.3.280.80). [*IU 11-16*]

7.3.250.80   To summarise the principles set out in 7.3.250.10–70, the following table contains the various scenarios and the respective classifications in the parent's consolidated financial statements.

SCENARIO	CLASSIFICATION
Subsidiary issues equity shares to non-controlling shareholders. Parent writes put options that give the non-controlling shareholders a right to put their equity shares in the subsidiary to the parent in exchange for a *fixed* number of the parent's equity shares.	Classify the subsidiary's shares held by non-controlling shareholders together with the put options as equity.
Subsidiary issues equity shares to non-controlling shareholders. Parent writes put options that give the non-controlling shareholders the right to put their equity shares in the subsidiary to the parent in exchange for a *variable* number of the parent's equity shares.	*Approach 1:* Classify the subsidiary's shares held by non-controlling shareholders together with the put options as financial liabilities. *Approach 2:* Classify the subsidiary's shares held by non-controlling shareholders as equity. Account for the written put options separately as derivative liabilities.
Subsidiary issues equity shares to non-controlling shareholders. Parent writes put options that give the non-controlling shareholders the right to put their equity shares in the subsidiary to the parent in exchange for a *variable* number of the parent's equity shares. Parent also has an option to settle by paying cash rather than delivering its own equity shares.	*Approach 1:* Classify the subsidiary's shares held by non-controlling shareholders together with the put options as financial liabilities. *Approach 2a:* Recognise a financial liability for the present value of the exercise price. For further discussion of the accounting for the shares in the subsidiary held by the non-controlling shareholders, see 2.5.690. *Approach 2b:* Classify the subsidiary's shares held by non-controlling shareholders as equity. Account for the written put options separately as derivative liabilities.

7.3.260 *Written put option to be settled in shares of another subsidiary*

7.3.260.10   A put option granted to the non-controlling shareholders might give them a right to put their equity shares in a subsidiary to the parent in exchange for a *variable* number of equity shares of another subsidiary of the same parent. Assuming that settlement of the option does not lead to deconsolidation of the other subsidiary, in our view in its consolidated financial statements, the parent should choose an accounting policy, to be applied consistently, from the alternatives set out in 7.3.250.40 – i.e. either to classify the subsidiary's shares together with the put options as financial liabilities or to account for the written put options as derivative liabilities.

7.3.260.20   However, if a put option granted to the non-controlling shareholders gives them a right to put their equity shares in the subsidiary to the parent in exchange for a *fixed* number of equity shares of another subsidiary of the same parent, then in the parent's consolidated financial statements the option gives the non-controlling shareholders a right to exchange a fixed number of one class of non-derivative own equity instruments for a fixed number of a different class of non-derivative own equity instruments. In our view, such a contract should be classified as equity (see 7.3.230.20).

7.3.270   Contingent consideration in business combination

7.3.270.10   Contingent consideration may be included in the consideration transferred in a business combination (see 2.6.280). IFRS 3 requires an obligation to pay contingent consideration to be classified as a liability or equity on the basis of the definitions of a financial liability and an equity instrument in paragraph 11 of IAS 32. That means that the obligation has to be to deliver a fixed number of shares in order for consideration that is settled in own equity instruments to be classified as equity. The subsequent accounting for the contingent consideration is dependent on this classification (see 2.6.1120). [*IFRS 3.40*]

7.3.270.20   In our view, the existence of any contingency regarding whether a fixed number of own shares will be delivered does not necessarily disqualify the contingent consideration from equity classification. We believe that if one of the possible outcomes in respect of the contingency is the delivery of neither shares nor other consideration, then this does not in itself preclude equity classification. This is because the delivery of no consideration does not constitute a 'settlement'. For example, if the arrangement involved issuing either zero or a single fixed amount of equity shares, then the fixed-for-fixed criterion would be met. This is because the only way that settlement could take place would be by delivering a single fixed amount of shares.

7.3.270.30   Also, in our view the classification analysis should be performed for an obligation to pay contingent consideration as referred to in IFRS 3 rather than for the entire contract. An entire-contract approach is not generally feasible, given that a contingent consideration arrangement is usually just one element of an overall sale-and-purchase agreement that governs all aspects of the business combination. We believe that a single business combination may involve more than one obligation to pay contingent consideration and that each obligation should be analysed separately for whether it is equity or liability. [*IFRS 3.40*]

7.3.270.40   In our view, an entity should choose an accounting policy, to be applied consistently, to analyse such relationships under one of two approaches.

- *Approach 1:* Obligations are separate when there is no necessary relationship between their outcomes or settlement (see 7.3.270.50).
- *Approach 2:* Obligations are separate only if there is no underlying causal relationship or significant correlation between their outcomes or settlement (see 7.3.270.60).

7.3.270.50   Under the first approach, one obligation is seen as separate from another obligation if there is no necessary relationship between the outcome or settlement of the obligations. For example, non-cumulative obligations to deliver shares based on different profit targets for different years may be seen as independent and therefore separate. This is because there is no necessary link between meeting the target for one year and meeting the target for another year. However, if there were an overlap between the periods, then the targets would not be independent.

7.3.270.60   Under the second approach, an obligation is seen as separate from another obligation only if there is no underlying causal relationship or significant correlation between the outcome or settlement of the obligations. Therefore, if this policy is chosen, non-cumulative requirements to deliver shares based on different profit targets for different years are seen as a single obligation. This is because the underlying operational and economic factors that influence performance in one year will tend to influence performance in another year. For example, an entity's performance across a number of years may be influenced by the successful development of, or failure to develop, a new product line.

EXAMPLE 21 – CONTINGENT CONSIDERATION IN BUSINESS COMBINATION

7.3.270.70   To illustrate the principles set out in 7.3.270.40–60, the following table contains several scenarios and the respective classification assessments.

SCENARIO	CLASSIFICATION
The vendor receives shares in the acquirer to the value of 50 if the acquiree's cumulative profits over a three-year period are at least 20.	Liability, because there is a single obligation to deliver a variable number of shares.
The vendor receives 50 shares in the acquirer if the acquiree's cumulative profits over a three-year period are at least 20.	Equity, because there is a single obligation to deliver a fixed number of shares.
The vendor receives 50 shares in the acquirer if the acquiree's cumulative profits over a three-year period are at least 20, and 100 shares if profits are at least 40.	Liability, because the arrangement involves settling with either 50 or 100 shares – i.e. a variable rather than a fixed number. The profit targets relate to the same period, and therefore they are not independent.
The vendor will receive one share in the acquirer for every 1 of profit in excess of 10.	Liability; the analysis is similar to the preceding scenario except that the number of shares is more obviously variable.
Share-settled contingent consideration is payable in three tranches: 1,000 shares if an earnings target is achieved for year 1; 1,000 shares if an earnings target is achieved for year 2; and 1,000 shares if an earnings target is achieved for year 3. Each target relates to annual earnings of the acquiree and is non-cumulative.	The classification depends on the policy adopted as described in 7.3.270.40–60. This may be considered three separate obligations to deliver a fixed 1,000 shares each (equity) or a single obligation to deliver 1,000, 2,000 or 3,000 shares (liability).

7.3.280   **Settlement options in derivative instruments**

7.3.280.10   A choice of the manner in which derivative financial instruments are settled – e.g. when the issuer or the holder could opt to settle net or gross – could determine their classification. IAS 32 states that a derivative financial instrument with settlement options is a financial asset or financial liability unless *all* of the settlement alternatives result in equity classification. Consequently, settlement options, even those that are at the discretion of the entity, could result in instruments being classified as financial assets or financial liabilities. [*IAS 32.26–27*]

EXAMPLE 22 – HOLDER SETTLEMENT OPTION

> **7.3.280.20**   Company K issues a warrant that gives the holder the right to acquire a fixed number of the issuer's own equity instruments for a fixed amount of cash. If the warrant expires unexercised, then the issuer will pay to the holder a fixed cancellation fee. K classifies the warrant as a financial liability because the holder may choose to receive cash or shares.

7.3.280.30   The provisions in IAS 32 regarding settlement options apply only to derivative financial instruments. Therefore, if an instrument does not meet the definition of a derivative, then its classification as a liability or as equity depends on whether the entity has a contractual obligation to deliver cash or other financial assets, or to deliver a variable number of its own equity instruments (see 7.3.20). [*IAS 32.11*]

EXAMPLE 23 – ISSUER SETTLEMENT OPTION

> **7.3.280.40**   Company H issues preference shares at par that are redeemable in five years and do not carry the right to receive dividends. At the end of five years, H has the option to redeem the shares, either in a fixed number of its own shares or in cash at an amount that is equal to the fair value of the shares.
>
> **7.3.280.50**   Under the terms of the instrument, H does not have an obligation to transfer cash or another financial asset, or to deliver a variable number of its own shares (see 7.3.220.30); nor does the entire instrument meet the definition of a derivative, because it fails the initial net investment criterion (see 7.2.40). Therefore, the provisions regarding settlement options do not apply, and H classifies the instrument as equity.
>
> **7.3.280.60**   For a discussion of whether the issuer's option to settle in cash should be separated as an embedded derivative, see 7.3.300.

7.3.280.70   Additionally, settlement options could determine the manner in which certain derivative instruments are accounted for. An entity is required to recognise a liability for the present value of the redemption amount if the contract contains an obligation to purchase its own equity instruments for cash or another financial asset. When the contract allows the counterparty discretion to require gross physical settlement, a gross liability for the present value of the redemption amount is recorded. The option is at the counterparty's discretion and therefore the entity cannot avoid gross physical settlement – i.e. the obligation to purchase its own equity instrument for cash or another financial asset (see 7.3.240). [*IAS 32.23, 26–27, IE6, IE31*]

7.3.280.80   However, IAS 32 is not clear on the effect of settlement options in a derivative instrument allowing the issuer discretion to choose gross or net settlement of a contract to purchase its own equity instruments for cash or another financial asset – e.g. a forward to purchase or a written put option. Therefore, in our view an entity should choose an accounting policy, to be applied consistently, from the following alternatives.

- *Recognise a liability for the present value of the redemption amount:* According to the illustrative examples that accompany the standard, an entity should recognise a liability for the present value of the redemption amount if one of the settlement alternatives is to exchange cash for shares (gross physical settlement).
- *Apply derivative liability accounting in accordance with IFRS 9:* Because the entity can choose net rather than gross settlement, it can avoid the obligation to purchase its own equity instruments for cash or another financial asset (see 7.3.240). [*IAS 32.23, 26–27, IE6, IE31*]

7.3.290   Discretionary payments – Dividends and other payments

7.3.290.10   A contractual requirement to pay dividends is an obligation to deliver cash; therefore, it gives rise to a financial liability. This does not change, even if the agreement to pay is conditional on the entity earning sufficient distributable profits; a restriction on the ability of an entity to satisfy a contractual obligation does not negate this obligation (see 7.3.30). [*IAS 32.19(a), 25, AG25*]

7.3.290.20   Dividends or other payments may be discretionary – i.e. there is no obligation to pay. For example, in many jurisdictions dividends on ordinary shares vary depending on the level of profitability; the entity can decide whether to pay dividends, and how much to pay. Although there may be an expectation that dividends will be paid if a certain level of profitability is achieved, this expectation is not a contractual obligation. Therefore, the entity is able to avoid the transfer of cash or another financial asset. [*IAS 32.19*]

7.3.290.30   Generally, when preference shares are non-redeemable, the appropriate classification is determined by the other rights that attach to them – in particular, distributions to holders. If the dividends are cumulative, then this suggests that the issuer may delay but cannot avoid the payment of dividends. However, if the issuer can choose to avoid the payment of dividends under all circumstances until liquidation of the entity, then the dividends are discretionary and do not give rise to an obligation. For example, if a non-redeemable preference share has a cumulative dividend, but payment is discretionary until liquidation and there are no other features that would lead to liability classification, then the instrument is classified as equity (see 7.3.390.10). [*IAS 32.AG26*]

7.3.290.40   If preference shares are redeemable and dividends are discretionary, then the issuer considers whether unpaid dividends are added to the redemption amount of the preference shares. If any unpaid dividends are added to the redemption amount and the entity does not have the unconditional ability to avoid redemption before liquidation, then the dividends are not in substance discretionary and the entire instrument including the discretionary dividend feature is a financial liability. Furthermore, if an entity is or may be obliged to redeem the instrument at fair value, then in our view unpaid dividends are implicitly added to the redemption amount if the payment of dividends decreases the fair value of the instrument being redeemed. Similarly, if an issuer of a puttable instrument is or may be obliged to repurchase the instrument at any time at an amount equal to a pro rata share of net assets, then we believe that unpaid dividends are implicitly added to the redemption amount if the payment of dividends decreases the amount of the entity's net assets and the amount that the entity is obliged to pay increases as a result of non-payment of dividends. [*IAS 32.AG37*]

7.3.290.50   There is an issue about whether to present discretionary dividends in profit or loss or equity if all of the fair value of the consideration received on issuing instruments with a discretionary dividend feature is allocated to and recognised as a financial liability. In principle, discretionary dividends may always be considered an equity feature, because an entity does not have a contractual obligation to deliver cash or another financial asset. However, when all of the fair value of the consideration received on issuing instruments is allocated to and recognised as a financial liability, IAS 32 is not clear about whether:

- discretionary dividends are presented in equity because, in principle, discretionary dividends are always an equity feature irrespective of whether any amount is allocated to equity; or
- discretionary dividends are presented in profit or loss because dividend payments on an instrument wholly recognised as a liability are recognised as an expense (see 7.3.20.150). [*IAS 32.36, AG37*]

7.3.290.60   Based on the reasoning in 7.3.290.50 and subject to the guidance in 7.3.290.40, in our view an entity should choose an accounting policy, to be applied consistently, to present the discretionary dividends in profit or loss or equity if none (or no more than a trivial amount) of the fair value of the consideration received on issuing instruments with a discretionary dividend feature is allocated to and recognised as equity.

7.3.290.70   The following flowchart shows the assessment required to determine whether discretionary dividends should be presented in profit or loss or equity.

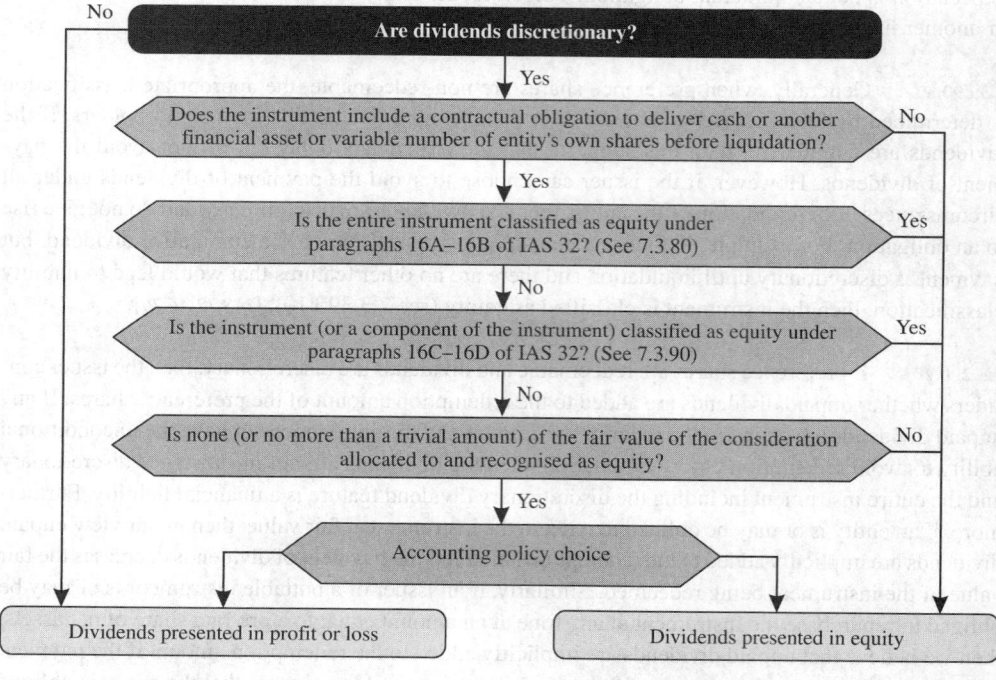

7.3.290.80   In our view, a similar assessment to that described in 7.3.290.50–70 applies to the assessment of the presentation of discretionary dividends on NCI shares subject to a put option written by the entity. If an entity chooses to apply the anticipated-acquisition method to account for NCI subject to a put option written by the entity, then the NCI are accounted for as if the put option had already been exercised. In this case, the NCI are derecognised and a financial liability is recognised for the present value of the redemption amount in the consolidated financial statements (see 2.5.700). Subject to the guidance in 7.3.290.40, we believe that an entity should choose an accounting policy from the alternatives described in 7.3.290.50–60, to be applied consistently to the presentation of discretionary dividends on NCI shares subject to a put option written by the entity. We believe that these accounting policy choices are available only if the subsequent changes in NCI put liabilities are recognised in profit or loss (see 2.5.700.40).

7.3.290.90   The following flowchart shows the assessment required to determine whether discretionary dividends on NCI shares subject to a put option written by the entity should be presented in profit or loss or equity.

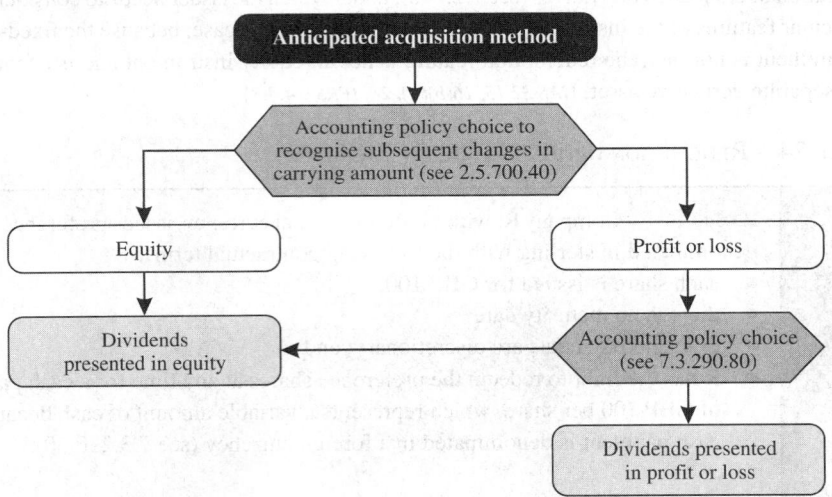

7.3.290.100   We believe that the accounting policy choice described in 7.3.290.80 is not available if the present-access method is applied to account for NCI, because the NCI continue to be recognised as equity when the put option is written. Discretionary dividends are paid on the NCI recognised as equity in the consolidated financial statements (see 2.5.710.10–20).

7.3.300   **Issuer's option to settle in cash**

7.3.300.10   An issuer's option to redeem a non-derivative equity instrument by delivering cash does not cause the instrument to be classified as a financial liability because the issuer does not have a contractual obligation to deliver cash or to deliver a variable number of its own shares under the instrument (see 7.3.220.30). [*IAS 32.16, AG25, IU 09-13*]

7.3.300.20   However, if the issuer of such an equity instrument has an option to redeem it by delivering a variable amount of cash, and therefore the fixed-for-fixed requirement is not met for this feature (see 7.3.230.10), then a question arises about whether the whole instrument should be considered as an equity instrument or whether the issuer's option to redeem the instrument is an embedded derivative that should be separated.

7.3.300.30   In our view, an entity should choose one of the following accounting policies, to be applied consistently, to account for such redemption options.

- *Account for the whole instrument as an equity instrument without separating the redemption option:* Under this approach, such a redemption option is not accounted for as an embedded derivative, but is considered part of the equity instrument. This is because the redemption option is already considered in determining that the entire instrument is a non-derivative equity instrument. In addition, discretionary payment features – such as discretionary dividends – are not usually separated from a non-derivative equity instrument but instead are considered an integral component of the instrument.
- *Separate the redemption option as an embedded derivative asset:* This approach is based on the guidance on compound financial instruments (see 7.3.310) and the guidance in IFRS 9 on the separation of embedded derivatives (see 7.2.110), under which the issuer needs to consider whether particular features of the instrument should be separated. In this case, because the fixed-for-fixed requirement is not met, the redemption feature is not an equity instrument and is accounted for as a separate derivative asset. [*IAS 32.15, 16(b)(ii), 28, IFRS 9.4.3.3*]

EXAMPLE 24 – REDEMPTION OPTION IN FOREIGN CURRENCY

7.3.300.40   Company R, with a euro functional currency, issues preference shares denominated in sterling with the following contractual terms:
- each share is issued for GBP 100;
- there is no maturity date;
- dividend payments are discretionary; and
- R has the right to redeem the preference shares at any time for a cash payment of GBP 100 per share, which represents a variable amount of cash because the cash payment is denominated in a foreign currency (see 7.3.230.30).

7.3.300.50   The preference shares meet the definition of an equity instrument because R does not have a contractual obligation to deliver cash or to deliver a variable number of its own shares. For the cash redemption option, we believe that R should choose an accounting policy, to be applied consistently, from the approaches discussed in 7.3.300.30 to either:
- account for the preference shares in their entirety as equity; or
- separate its option to redeem the shares in cash as an embedded derivative because the redemption amount is in a foreign currency and therefore the option does not meet the fixed-for-fixed requirement (see 7.3.230.30 and 350). Therefore, R recognises the amount of the consideration equal to the fair value of the redemption option on initial recognition as a derivative asset. Subsequently, R measures the derivative at fair value with changes therein included in profit or loss.

7.3.310   Compound instruments

7.3.310.10   An instrument may contain both a financial liability (e.g. an obligation to make interest and/or scheduled principal payments) and an equity component (e.g. a conversion feature in a convertible bond). Such an instrument is a compound instrument. [*IAS 32.29, AG31*]

7.3.310.20   The issuer of non-derivative compound instruments classifies the liability and equity components of the instrument separately as a financial liability and equity ('split accounting'). Components of compound instruments are analysed and classified in accordance with the basic classification principles in 7.3.20. [*IAS 32.28*]

7.3.310.30   A typical form of a compound instrument is a convertible bond, in which the holder is entitled to convert the instrument into equity instruments of the entity. Another form of compound instrument is one in which the equity characteristics lie in the dividend or interest stream rather than in the convertibility of the principal amount. For example, consider a non-cumulative mandatorily redeemable preference share, on which dividends are payable at the discretion of the issuer. In this case, the present value of the redemption amount represents the financial liability, with any remaining proceeds being attributed to equity. [*IAS 32.AG31*]

7.3.310.40   The same split accounting applies to share purchase warrants attached to debt instruments, irrespective of whether they are formally detachable from the debt instruments. The share purchase warrants are split and accounted for as an equity component by the issuer if the warrants meet the definition of an equity instrument. In this case, the amount allocable to the debt instrument is determined first, with any remaining proceeds being attributed to the warrants. [*IAS 32.31*]

7.3.310.50   Subject to 7.3.20.170, the initial classification of a convertible instrument into its liability and equity components is not revised subsequent to initial recognition – even if the likelihood of the conversion option being exercised changes over time. However, a reclassification may be required in certain circumstances (see 7.3.370 and 470). [*IAS 32.30*]

7.3.310.60   For a discussion of the measurement of the financial liability and equity components of a compound financial instrument, see 7.3.410.

7.3.320   *Accounting for early redemption*

7.3.320.10   On early redemption of a convertible instrument, the redemption payment is allocated to the liability and equity components. The method used is consistent with that used initially to allocate the instrument between its debt and equity components (see 7.3.410). The fair value of the liability component at the redemption date is compared with its carrying amount, giving rise to a gain or loss on redemption that is recognised in profit or loss. The remainder of the redemption payment is recognised in equity. [*IAS 32.AG33*]

7.3.330   *Accounting for conversion*

7.3.330.10   On conversion of a convertible instrument that is a compound instrument at maturity, the entity derecognises the liability component that is extinguished when the conversion feature is exercised and recognises the same amount as equity. The original equity component remains as equity, although it may be transferred within equity (see 7.3.630). No gain or loss is recognised in profit or loss. [*IAS 32.AG32*]

7.3.330.20   If the conversion feature is an American-style option that can be exercised before the redemption date, then a question arises about whether to derecognise the liability component based on its carrying amount (e.g. amortised cost based on the stated maturity ignoring the conversion option) at the time of early conversion, or to derecognise the liability component after remeasuring it to the redemption amount at conversion.

7.3.330.30   Under the first approach, the carrying amount of the liability on conversion (e.g. amortised cost based on the stated maturity ignoring the conversion option) is reclassified to equity and no gain or loss is recognised on conversion (see 7.3.330.10). Under the second approach, the liability is remeasured to the redemption amount at conversion, with additional interest expense being recognised in profit or loss under paragraph B5.4.6 of IFRS 9, because it is considered a prepayment of the liability component (see 7.7.320.10).

7.3.330.40   In our view, the first approach is appropriate because this conversion in effect represents a conversion at maturity, because of the way the American-style option operates. The financial liability component should be accounted for as a non-prepayable liability, and an American-style equity option recognised in equity. Consequently, we believe that there is no prepayment feature in the liability that leads to the recognition of a gain or loss arising from the revision of cash flow estimates (see 7.7.320.10).

7.3.330.50   However, a gain or loss may arise when convertible instruments contain embedded derivatives (see 7.3.360.50). If a convertible bond contains a prepayment feature that enables the issuer to call the bond and the prepayment feature has not been separately accounted for as a derivative, then in our view when the issuer announces its intention to exercise the call option it should recognise a catch-up adjustment to the amortised cost accounting for the financial liability under paragraph B5.4.6 of IFRS 9 (see 7.7.320.10).

7.3.330.60   We believe that the requirements for early redemption (see 7.3.320) do not apply because they address situations in which convertible debt is bought back not under the terms inherent in the instrument (call option) but instead through agreement between the issuer and holder to buy back at fair value without using any options embedded in the instrument – e.g. tender offers.

EXAMPLE 25A – CONVERTIBLE BOND WITH AMERICAN-STYLE OPTION

7.3.330.70   Company B issues a 10-year convertible bond that is convertible at any time after five years at the option of the holder (an American-style option). If the bond is not converted, then the par amount is repayable on maturity after 10 years. The conversion feature is classified at inception as equity, because it meets the fixed-for-fixed requirement (see 7.3.230.10). The host debt instrument is measured at amortised cost.

7.3.330.80   A question arises about whether to derecognise the liability component based on its amortised cost carrying amount at the time of early conversion, or to derecognise the liability component after remeasuring it to the par amount at conversion.

7.3.330.90   We believe that such conversion in effect represents a conversion at maturity. This is because the bond does not have a fixed maturity of 10 years, because of the way the American-style option operates. Consequently, we believe that there is no prepayment feature in the liability that leads to the recognition of a gain or loss arising from the revision of cash flow estimates.

7.3.330.100   The conversion arises from the exercise of the equity conversion option, which is an American-style option recognised in equity and not remeasured through profit or loss under IAS 32. Therefore, we believe that no gain or loss should be recognised in profit or loss on conversion of the bond.

EXAMPLE 25B – CONVERTIBLE BOND WITH AMERICAN-STYLE OPTION AND ISSUER PREPAYMENT OPTION

7.3.330.110   Modifying Example 25A, the convertible bond contains a prepayment feature that enables the issuer to call the bond at any time after five years at par. However, the holder still has the option to exercise its conversion right during a short period following the announcement of the issuer to call the bond. The prepayment option is not accounted for separately if it is closely related to the host liability contract (see 7.2.240).

7.3.330.120   We believe that when the issuer announces its intention to exercise the call option it should recognise a catch-up adjustment to the amortised cost accounting under paragraph B5.4.6 of IFRS 9 (see 7.7.320.10). This is because, in contrast to Example 25A, the issuer's call option is separate from the holder's conversion option. If the holder does not exercise the conversion option, then the conversion option is extinguished.

7.3.330.130   If the holder exercises the conversion option, then the liability component should be converted to equity. No gain or loss should be recognised in profit or loss on conversion or redemption because the carrying amount of the liability component has already been adjusted to the par amount before conversion or redemption.

7.3.330.140   In both Examples 25A and 25B, the carrying amount of the liability component at conversion is reclassified to equity on exercise of the conversion option. However, in Example 25A the carrying amount of the liability component is less than the par amount at the conversion date; in Example 25B, the carrying amount of the liability component is adjusted to par under paragraph B5.4.6 of IFRS 9 before conversion, with an impact on profit or loss.

7.3.340   *Amendment to induce early conversion*

7.3.340.10   An entity may amend the terms of a convertible instrument to induce early conversion – e.g. by offering a more favourable conversion ratio in the event of conversion before a specified date. When the terms are amended, the issuer recognises in profit or loss the difference between:

- the fair value of the consideration that the holder receives on conversion of the instrument under the revised terms; and

- the fair value of the consideration that the holder would have received under the original terms. [*IAS 32.AG35*]

7.3.350   **Foreign currency convertible bond**

7.3.350.10   If a convertible bond is denominated in a currency other than the functional currency of the entity, then an issue arises regarding the classification of the conversion option.

7.3.350.20   As discussed in 7.3.230.60, an obligation denominated in a foreign currency represents a variable amount of cash. Contracts, both freestanding and embedded, that will be settled by an entity delivering a fixed number of its own equity instruments in exchange for a fixed amount of foreign currency are classified as financial assets or financial liabilities. [*IAS 32.BC4K*]

EXAMPLE 26 – FOREIGN CURRENCY CONVERTIBLE BOND

7.3.350.30   Company G with a euro functional currency issues a convertible bond denominated in US dollars. The bond carries a fixed rate of interest and is convertible at the end of 10 years, at the holder's option, into a fixed number of euro-denominated shares of G. No settlement alternative is provided to the issuer.

7.3.350.40   The conversion option is an obligation for G to issue a fixed number of shares in exchange for a variable amount of cash. The cash is fixed in US dollar terms but variable in functional currency terms. Therefore, G classifies the conversion feature in the convertible bond as a derivative liability.

7.3.350.50   A related issue arises if a convertible bond denominated in a foreign currency is issued by a subsidiary that has a functional currency different from that of its parent, and that bond is convertible into the shares of the parent. The IFRS Interpretations Committee discussed a similar issue and noted that a group does not have a functional currency (see 2.7.70.20). In our view, two approaches are possible in the consolidated financial statements. We believe that an entity should choose an accounting policy, to be applied consistently, to base the classification in the consolidated financial statements on the functional currency of either the parent or the subsidiary. [*IU 11-06*]

7.3.350.60   In addition, in our view:
- if the bond is denominated in a currency other than the functional currency of either the parent or the subsidiary, then the conversion feature is a (derivative) liability;
- the currency in which the shares are denominated is not relevant to the analysis: the only requirement is that the number of shares is fixed; and
- the presentation currency or currencies of the group's consolidated financial statements (see 2.7.40) has no impact on the analysis.

7.3.350.70   Another issue arises in cases of inflation indexation. For example, an entity issues a convertible bond denominated in its functional currency. Both principal and interest payments of the instrument are indexed to changes in the CPI inflation of the economic environment of the entity. In our view, such indexation creates variability in the amount of cash being exchanged for a fixed number of shares and therefore the conversion feature should be classified as a financial liability. This principle applies even if the functional currency of the entity is the currency of a hyperinflationary economy (see chapter 2.10).

7.3.360 Cash settlement option in convertible bond

7.3.360.10   Many convertible bonds include a cash settlement option for the issuer if the holder exercises its right to convert the bonds into ordinary shares. For example, an entity with a euro functional currency issues euro-denominated fixed rate bonds with a 20-year maturity; the holder has the option to convert these into a fixed number of the issuer's ordinary shares at any time during the life of the bond. If the holder exercises its conversion option, then the issuer has the right to settle either:

- by delivering a fixed number of shares; or
- in cash at an amount equal to the market value of the shares to be issued.

7.3.360.20   Generally, a convertible bond is a compound instrument – i.e. having characteristics of both equity and a liability. In the example in 7.3.360.10 the convertible bond comprises the following features, which are clearly characteristics associated with a financial liability:

- an obligation to make fixed interest payments; and
- an obligation to deliver cash to the holder on redemption of the bond in the event of the holder not exercising its conversion option.

7.3.360.30   In addition, the instrument contains a conversion feature whereby there may be an exchange of a fixed number of shares for a fixed amount of cash. The issuer can settle the conversion option either by paying the holder the market value of the shares in cash, or by exchanging its own shares for cash – i.e. physical delivery. Consequently, the conversion option can be settled other than by the issuer exchanging a fixed number of shares for a fixed amount of cash. [*IAS 32.26*]

7.3.360.40   Because the conversion option is a derivative, the settlement option causes it to be classified as a financial liability instead of as an equity instrument. Therefore, in this case the convertible bond is not a compound instrument under IAS 32. Rather, it is a hybrid instrument comprising a host liability for the interest and principal amount plus an embedded derivative instrument for the conversion option (see 7.3.280). The host liability is measured at amortised cost and the derivative, not being closely related to the host, is measured at FVTPL; alternatively, the entire instrument is measured at FVTPL (see 7.5.70). For a discussion of the accounting for embedded derivatives, see 7.2.110.

7.3.360.50   In our view, in contrast to the accounting for conversion of a compound instrument (see 7.3.330.10), an entity should choose an accounting policy, to be applied consistently to all reclassifications from financial liability to equity because of a change in the effective terms when the contractual terms of the instrument have not changed, including for example the conversion of a hybrid instrument that is classified entirely as a financial liability. For a description of the acceptable accounting policies, see 7.3.490.110.

7.3.370 Restructuring a convertible bond

7.3.370.10   Continuing the example in 7.3.360.10–40, the issuer might restructure the convertible bond by removing the cash settlement alternative in the conversion option. As a result, the issuer would have a contract that requires it to physically deliver a fixed number of shares in exchange for a fixed amount of the bond on exercise by the holder. Such a contract meets the definition of an equity instrument, and so the conversion option is classified as such. However, the restructuring would not fall in the scope of IFRIC 19, because the entity does not issue equity instruments to extinguish the derivative component (see 7.3.460 and 7.6.450).

7.3.370.20   However, concluding that the restructured conversion option should be presented as equity is only the first step in accounting for the restructuring.

7.3.370.30   An entity also needs to consider whether the restructuring is deemed a significant modification of the terms of the bond, resulting in it being accounted for as a debt extinguishment (see 7.6.370).

7.3.370.40   IFRS 9 provides specific guidance when there is a modification in the cash flows of a debt instrument (see 7.6.370). However, when the terms of the conversion option are revised, there is no such cash flow effect. In such circumstances, in our view the impact of the modification from the holder's perspective should be considered.

7.3.370.50   Consider a convertible bond with a cash settlement option for the issuer if the holder exercises its right to convert the bonds into ordinary shares. If the holder exercises its conversion option, then the issuer has the right to settle either:
- by delivering a fixed number of shares; or
- in cash at an amount equal to the market value of the shares to be issued.

7.3.370.60   The holder might receive cash directly from the issuer at an amount equal to the market value of the shares, instead of receiving the shares and converting them into cash. The amount of cash accruing to the holder with or without the cash settlement option is almost the same. Consequently, removal of the cash settlement option does not in our view represent a substantial modification of the bond. As a result, the restructuring does not lead to the derecognition or extinguishment of the 'original' convertible bond and the recognition of a 'new' convertible bond. [*IFRS 9.B3.3.6*]

7.3.370.70   However, the restructuring does result in the extinguishment of the derivative component, because it is exchanged for an equity component (see 7.3.480.60). From the holder's perspective, this is an exchange of financial assets. However, because there is no cash transfer in the transaction, the consideration paid will usually be the fair value of the instrument received – i.e. the new conversion option without a cash settlement feature. Because the fair value of the 'old' conversion option is almost identical at the date of the restructuring to the fair value of the 'new' conversion option (see 7.3.370.80), no significant gain or loss arises.

7.3.370.80   From the issuer's perspective, the 'old' conversion option would have been measured at FVTPL until the restructuring of the convertible bond. At the date of restructuring, the derivative component is derecognised and a new instrument is recognised in equity at fair value – assuming that the fair value of both options is the same.

7.3.380   **Perpetual instruments**

7.3.380.10   Perpetual debt instruments normally provide the holder with a contractual right to receive an indefinite stream of interest payments at a market rate of interest, with no redemption of principal. Even though the holder will not receive repayment of the principal, such instruments are a liability of the issuer because there is a contractual obligation to make a stream of future interest payments to the holder. Assuming that the terms of the instrument are at the market rate, the face value or the carrying amount of the instrument reflects the present value of the holder's right to receive these interest payments in perpetuity. [*IAS 32.AG6*]

7.3.390 **Preference shares**

7.3.390.10   Preference shares that provide for redemption at the option of the holder give rise to a contractual obligation and are therefore classified as financial liabilities. If preference shares are not redeemable at the option of the holder, then the appropriate classification depends on the other terms and conditions associated with such shares – in particular, the attached dividend rights. If dividends are discretionary, then this fact supports the classification of the preference shares as equity instruments. If dividends are not discretionary, then they represent a contractual obligation, and the instrument is classified as a financial liability of the issuer (see 7.3.290.30). [*IAS 32.AG25–AG26*]

7.3.390.20   A typical example of a cumulative perpetual preference share is one with the following characteristics:
- the issuer has an obligation to pay dividends on preference shares only if it pays dividends on its ordinary shares; and
- the preference dividends are cumulative.

7.3.390.30   The fact that dividends are payable only if ordinary dividends, which are discretionary, are paid ('dividend stopper feature') does not create an obligation. However, because of the cumulative feature, the instrument is classified as equity only if:
- the accumulated dividends can be deferred indefinitely – i.e. until liquidation of the entity; and
- there is no other feature of the instrument that would lead to financial liability classification (see 7.3.40.170–180). [*IAS 32.25*]

7.3.390.40   The terms of certain preference shares provide for the accrual of interest on cumulative discretionary dividends even before such dividends are declared. In other words, interest accrues from the point in time at which the dividend *might* have been declared, such that if the dividend is declared, then an amount of interest becomes payable automatically. In our view, the accrual of interest alone does not cause such dividends to give rise to a contractual obligation to deliver cash or another financial asset as long as the dividends remain discretionary – i.e. the entity can avoid the payment of both dividends and interest on unpaid dividends until liquidation of the entity.

7.3.390.50   A preference dividend in which payment is contingent on the availability of future distributable profits differs from a discretionary dividend. With a discretionary dividend, the issuer is able to avoid the payment of dividends indefinitely. However, the payment of a contingent dividend cannot be avoided indefinitely (see 7.3.40). The fact that the issuer might currently be unable to pay the dividend has no bearing on its classification. Consequently, contingent dividends are classified as a liability. [*IAS 32.25*]

EXAMPLE 27A – PREFERENCE SHARES – SEPARATE FINANCIAL STATEMENTS

7.3.390.60   Company K issues preference shares with the following contractual terms:
- the shares are redeemable at the option of the issuer, at a fixed redemption price of 100 per share plus any accrued unpaid dividends;

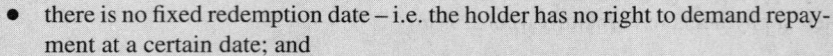

- there is no fixed redemption date – i.e. the holder has no right to demand repayment at a certain date; and
- the payment of dividends is at the discretion of the issuer. However, K is required to pay dividends if its parent pays dividends on its ordinary shares.

7.3.390.70   Therefore, in this example the payment of dividends is contingent on the occurrence of an uncertain future event that is beyond the control of both the issuer and the holder of the instrument.

7.3.390.80   Consequently, K recognises a financial liability. In substance, this instrument is a perpetual instrument with variable contingent dividend payments. Therefore, the amount of the initial investment represents the expected value of the variable contingent dividend payments, which are classified as a liability.

EXAMPLE 27B – PREFERENCE SHARES – CONSOLIDATED FINANCIAL STATEMENTS

7.3.390.90   The classification of the instrument in Example 27A would be different in the consolidated financial statements of the parent if the payment of dividends at the consolidated level were at the discretion of the parent (see 7.3.20.180).

7.3.400   RECOGNITION AND MEASUREMENT

7.3.400.10   IFRS does not have any specific measurement rules related to equity, other than in respect of:
- splitting compound instruments (see 7.3.410.10);
- the cost of equity transactions (see 7.3.570); and
- own equity instruments acquired and reissued or cancelled (see 7.3.510.10).

7.3.400.20   In part this is because the financial instruments standards do not generally apply to own equity. [*IFRS 9.2.1(d)*]

7.3.400.30   As a general principle, the definitions of income and expenses exclude transactions with holders of equity instruments. Therefore, no gains or losses are reported in profit or loss on transactions in equity instruments. All of the effects of transactions with owners are recognised directly in equity. However, certain derivatives on own equity, when they do not meet the definition of equity, will be treated as derivative assets or liabilities and will result in gains and losses recognised in profit or loss (see 7.7.140).

7.3.400.40   The recognition and measurement requirements for equity instruments that are issued in share-based payment transactions are specified by IFRS 2 (see chapter 4.5).

7.3.410   Compound instruments

7.3.410.10   When allocating the initial carrying amount of a compound instrument to the underlying financial liability and equity components, an entity first determines the fair value of the liability component. This includes any embedded derivatives – whether or not they have to be accounted for separately. The fair value of the liability component is determined with reference to the fair value of a similar stand-alone debt instrument (including any embedded non-equity derivatives). The amount allocated to the equity component is the residual amount after deducting the fair value of the financial liability component from the fair value of the entire compound instrument. For a discussion of the recognition of deferred tax liabilities on compound financial instruments, see 3.13.250. [*IAS 32.31–32*]

EXAMPLE 28 – ALLOCATING PROCEEDS OF ISSUED BOND TO COMPONENTS

7.3.410.20   Company Y issues 2,000 convertible bonds at the start of year 1. The bonds have a three-year term and are issued at par with a face value of 1,000 per bond, giving total proceeds of 2,000,000. The bonds have the following contractual terms:

- interest is payable annually in arrears at a nominal annual interest rate of 6%; and
- each bond is convertible at any time until maturity into 250 ordinary shares.

7.3.410.30   When the bonds are issued, the prevailing market interest rate for a similar liability without a conversion option is 9%.

7.3.410.40   The present value of the financial liability component is calculated using a discount rate of 9% (the market interest rate for similar bonds having no conversion rights).

Present value of the principal – 2,000,000 payable at the end of three years	1,544,367
Present value of the interest – 120,000 (2,000,000 x 6%) payable annually in arrears for three years	303,755
Total liability component	1,848,122
Equity component (balancing figure)	151,878
Proceeds of the bond issue	2,000,000

7.3.410.50   Coupon accruals and the unwinding of the discount are accounted for as interest expense. However, when dividends are declared post-conversion of the bonds, these relate to the equity component and are presented in equity as a distribution of profits.

7.3.420   Share splits and bonus issues

7.3.420.10   In the case of a simple split of shares or a bonus issue, IFRS does not require any adjustment to total equity or to individual components of equity presented in the financial statements, although they may affect basic and diluted EPS (see 5.3.530). However, the laws of the country of incorporation may require a reallocation of capital within equity.

7.3.420.20   There is no guidance in IFRS on whether a share dividend should be treated as a share split or bonus issue. For a discussion of the treatment of share dividends, see 7.3.680.90 and 7.7.520.

7.3.430   **Prepaid capital contributions**

7.3.430.10   Shareholders may pay for shares before they are issued. An issue then arises about whether the prepayment should be recognised directly in equity or shown as a liability.

7.3.430.20   If there is any possibility that the entity may be required to repay the amount received – e.g. if the share issue is conditional on uncertain future events – then in our view the amount received should be shown as a liability. However, if there is no possibility of the prepayment being refunded, so that the entity's obligation is to deliver only a fixed number of shares, then in our view the amount should be credited to a separate category of equity – e.g. a prepaid share reserve. The notes to the financial statements should disclose the prepayment and the terms of the shares to be issued.

7.3.440   **Receivables in respect of equity contributions**

7.3.440.10   An entity may be owed an amount:
- in respect of a contribution for new equity shares that have already been issued; or
- as an equity contribution for which no new shares will be issued (see 7.3.450).

7.3.440.20   In this case, an issue arises about when the equity should be recognised.

7.3.440.30   In our view, the equity and a corresponding receivable should be recognised if the receivable meets the definition of a financial asset. This requires the entity to have a contractual right to receive the amount at the reporting date. A 'contractual right' is more than an informal agreement or a non-contractual commitment.

7.3.440.40   If the shareholder is not committed contractually to making the contribution at the reporting date, then no receivable is recorded in respect of the transaction.

7.3.440.50   If a receivable is recognised but payment is not expected in the short term, then the amount is discounted and recorded, in both equity and receivables, at the present value of the amount to be received; unwinding of the discount on the receivable is accounted for as interest income (see 7.7.270).

7.3.440.60   An entity might decide to increase its share capital through a shareholders' resolution to issue new shares. However, in certain jurisdictions this does not establish a contractual right for the entity to receive cash or another financial asset; nor does it contractually bind the shareholders. In our view, unless and until there is a contractual right and the new shares are issued or outstanding, no receivable or outstanding shares should be recognised with respect to the transaction.

7.3.450   **Non-reciprocal capital contributions**

7.3.450.10   Sometimes an entity receives amounts from shareholders in the form of capital contributions, being either cash or other non-monetary assets, which are non-reciprocal – i.e. no financial or non-financial obligation exists. This may happen, for example, when an entity requires additional financing or is in financial difficulty. Amounts might be received from all shareholders or only certain shareholders. For a discussion in the context of NCI, see 2.5.520.

7.3.450.20   IFRS does not contain any specific guidance on transactions with shareholders. However, in applying the definitions of financial liabilities and equity, in our view the amount received should be accounted for in accordance with its substance.

- If there is any possibility of having to repay the amount received, then a liability should be recognised for the advance.
- If there is no requirement to repay the amount under any circumstances and any repayment would be entirely at the discretion of the entity that receives the contribution, then the economic substance will normally be an equity contribution and not income; this is because the shareholder is generally acting in its capacity as a shareholder in such cases. In our experience, it is highly unlikely that an entity would receive a non-reciprocal capital contribution from an unrelated third party.

7.3.450.30   If the amount is classified as equity, then the sub-classification within equity will be determined by the legal framework in which the entity operates. The legal framework may require or permit classification as additional paid-in capital, share premium and/or as a separate reserve – e.g. 'contributed assets'.

7.3.450.40   The recognition criteria for receivables in respect of equity transactions (see 7.3.440) should be applied in determining when a non-reciprocal capital contribution is recognised.

7.3.450.50   If a shareholder forgives debt, then it is likely that:
- the shareholder is acting in its capacity as a shareholder; and
- the forgiveness of debt should be treated as a capital transaction (see 7.7.375.40).

7.3.460   Extinguishing financial liabilities with equity instruments

7.3.460.10   A debtor and a creditor may renegotiate the terms of a financial liability with the result that the debtor extinguishes the liability fully or partially by issuing equity instruments to the creditor – i.e. a debt-for-equity swap. IFRIC 19 addresses the accounting by the debtor in a debt-for-equity swap transaction (see 7.6.450). [*IFRIC 19.1*]

7.3.470   RECLASSIFICATION OF INSTRUMENTS BETWEEN LIABILITY AND EQUITY

7.3.470.10   The following discussion of reclassification (see 7.3.470–490) applies to reclassifications of an instrument or its component parts between financial liability and equity and vice versa, with the exception of:
- puttable instruments (see 7.3.200);
- instruments that impose on the entity an obligation to deliver to another party a pro rata share of the net assets of the entity only on liquidation (see 7.3.200); and
- compound instruments on conversion at maturity (see 7.3.330).

7.3.470.20   As discussed in 7.3.20.170, the classification of an instrument, or its component parts, as either a financial liability or equity is made on initial recognition and is not generally revised as a result of subsequent changes in circumstances. However, a reclassification between financial liability and equity or vice versa may be required if:
- an entity amends the contractual terms of an instrument;
- the effective terms of an instrument change without any amendment of the contractual terms; or
- there is a relevant change in the composition of the reporting entity.

7.3.480   Reclassification due to amendment of contractual terms

7.3.480.10   An entity may amend the contractual terms of an instrument such that the classification of the instrument changes from a financial liability to equity or vice versa.

EXAMPLE 29 – RECLASSIFICATION FROM EQUITY TO FINANCIAL LIABILITY

> 7.3.480.20   Company J has perpetual preference shares, which it has classified as equity instruments. They were issued for 1,000 and carry the right to receive a discretionary dividend of 10%.
>
> 7.3.480.30   J later amends the terms of the instrument such that:
> - redemption is required in the event of a change in control of the entity; and
> - dividends are payable if interest is paid on another instrument on which the issuer is required to pay interest.
>
> 7.3.480.40   J no longer has the unconditional ability to avoid redemption, because a change in control is not within the control of the entity (see 7.3.40). Furthermore, a contractual obligation to pay dividends has been created (see 7.3.20.70–80). For these reasons, J reclassifies the instrument from equity to a financial liability.

7.3.480.50   In its discussions, the IFRS Interpretations Committee noted that a financial liability is initially recognised at the date of reclassification and it is initially measured at its fair value minus, in the case of a financial liability not at FVTPL, transaction costs that are directly attributable to the issue of the financial liability (see 7.7.10.10). Additionally, the original equity instrument is derecognised at the reclassification date and no gain or loss is recognised (see 7.3.510.10). If, in Example 29, the fair value of the financial liability on initial recognition amounts to 1,200, then an adjustment of 200 needs to be recognised in equity on derecognition of the equity instrument. [*IAS 32.33, IFRS 9.5.1.1, IU 11-06*]

7.3.480.60   However, when the classification of an instrument changes from a financial liability to equity due to an amendment of the contractual terms, in our view this represents the extinguishment of a financial liability and the issue of equity instruments. In this case, the resulting gain or loss on the extinguishment of the liability should be recognised in profit or loss (see 7.6.360.60 and 370) or, when appropriate, as an equity contribution (see 7.3.450.50). This view is in line with IFRIC 19 (see 7.3.460 and 7.6.450–460). For a discussion of the restructuring of convertible bonds, see 7.3.370.

7.3.490   Reclassification due to change of effective terms without amendment of contractual terms

7.3.490.10   In our view, the effective terms of an instrument are considered to have changed if relevant contractual provisions of an instrument become effective or cease to be effective as a result of:
- the passage of time;
- the action of a party; or
- other contingent events that are anticipated in the contractual terms of the instrument.

7.3.490.20   A change in the composition of the reporting entity may arise in consolidated financial statements from acquisitions or disposals of subsidiaries. In our view, such a change in group structure may trigger a reassessment of the terms and conditions agreed between members of the group and the holder of an instrument and reassessment of whether the group as a whole has an obligation to pay cash or other financial assets to the instrument holder.

7.3.490.30   The following are examples of changes in the effective terms of instruments.

EXAMPLE 30A – RECLASSIFICATION – FIXED EXERCISE PRICE AS RESULT OF PASSAGE OF TIME

7.3.490.40   Company X issues convertible debt with the conversion ratio based on the lower of a fixed amount and an amount indexed to the entity's share price one year after the date of issuance. At the end of that year, the conversion ratio would become fixed and therefore reclassification of the conversion option as equity would be appropriate. The exercise price of the derivative that is settled in the entity's own equity instruments therefore becomes fixed as a result of the passage of time.

EXAMPLE 30B – RECLASSIFICATION – EXPIRED PUT OPTION

7.3.490.50   Company Y issues a put option in an instrument that allows the holder to put the instrument back to Y for a fixed amount of cash during only the first three years of the instrument's life. If the put option expires unexercised at the end of the three years, then reclassification as equity would be appropriate.

EXAMPLE 30C – RECLASSIFICATION – REDEMPTION OF LINKED INSTRUMENT

7.3.490.60   Company Z issues a non-redeemable financial instrument (the 'base' instrument) with dividends payable if interest is paid on another instrument (the 'linked' instrument). Z is required to pay the interest on the linked instrument. When the linked instrument is redeemed, without any other changes in terms and conditions, the effective terms of the base instrument have changed. This is because it no longer contains a contractual obligation to make payments and therefore re-classification as equity is appropriate.

EXAMPLE 30D – RECLASSIFICATION – CHANGE IN COMPOSITION OF REPORTING ENTITY

7.3.490.70   Company Z writes a call option under which it has an obligation to deliver a fixed amount of equity shares in an unrelated party, Company X, in exchange for a fixed amount of cash.

7.3.490.80   Because equity shares in X are financial assets from the perspective of Z, Z classifies the option as a financial liability on initial recognition. However, if Z subsequently obtains control over and consolidates X, then Z would reclassify the option from financial liability to equity in its consolidated financial statements. This is because the option would now represent an obligation to deliver a fixed number of equity instruments in Z's group in exchange for a fixed amount of cash.

7.3.490.90   In our view, there is no difference between the accounting for reclassifications from equity to liability due to an amendment of the contractual terms (see 7.3.480.50) and such reclassifications due to a change in the effective terms. Therefore, we believe that a financial liability should be initially recognised at the date of reclassification. We believe that it should be initially measured at its fair value minus, in the case of a financial liability not at FVTPL, transaction costs that are directly attributable to the issue of the financial liability (see 7.7.10.10). Additionally, the original equity instrument should be derecognised at the reclassification date and no gain or loss should be recognised (see 7.3.510.10).

7.3.490.100   IAS 32 does not contain explicit general guidance on accounting for reclassifications from financial liability to equity because of a change in effective terms; and neither IAS 32 nor IFRS 9 provides comprehensive guidance on the measurement of an equity instrument on initial recognition. [*IAS 32.16F(b), 96B, AG33*]

7.3.490.110   Therefore, it is not clear whether it is appropriate to recognise a gain or loss in profit or loss on reclassification from financial liability to equity because of a change in the effective terms without any amendment of the contractual terms. In our view, an entity should choose an accounting policy, to be applied consistently, from the following alternatives.
- *By analogy to the conversion for compound instruments at maturity* (see 7.3.330): The equity instrument is measured at the carrying amount of the liability (component) and no gain or loss is recognised on reclassification.
- *By analogy to IFRIC 19* (see 7.3.460 and 7.6.450): The equity instrument is measured at its fair value and any difference between this fair value and the carrying amount of the liability is recognised in profit or loss.

7.3.500   TREASURY SHARES

7.3.510   Recognition and measurement#

7.3.510.10   Generally, any amounts paid by an entity to acquire its own equity instruments are debited directly to equity. This applies whether the equity instruments are cancelled immediately or held for resale – i.e. treasury shares. Amounts received on the sale of treasury shares are credited directly to equity. No gains or losses are recognised in profit or loss on any purchase, sale, issue or cancellation of own equity instruments, or in respect of any changes in the value of treasury shares. [*IAS 32.33*]

7.3.510.20   Own equity instruments held in connection with an equity compensation plan are presented as treasury shares (see 4.5.2280.10). [*IAS 32.4(f), 33–34*]

7.3.510.30   Assets held in respect of employee benefit plans other than equity compensation plans may include the employer's own shares. For a discussion of the treatment of these shares, see 4.4.620.20.

7.3.515   FORTHCOMING REQUIREMENTS

7.3.515.10   Some entities operate an investment fund that provides investors with benefits determined by units in the fund or issue groups of insurance contracts with direct participation features and hold the underlying items. Such funds or underlying items may include the entity's treasury shares.

7.3.515.20   Under consequential amendments to IAS 32 introduced by IFRS 17, an entity may elect to continue to account for such treasury shares as equity and to account for the reacquired instrument as if it were a financial asset measured at FVTPL. This election is irrevocable and is made on an instrument-by-instrument basis. [*IAS 32.33A*]

7.3.520   Treasury shares held for trading purposes

7.3.520.10   Some entities hold their own equity instruments for trading purposes; for example, they may be part of a portfolio of investments held for trading purposes.

7.3.520.20   There are no exemptions for treasury shares held for trading purposes. Such instruments are not recognised as assets or measured at fair value with gains and losses recognised in profit or loss, which is the treatment for other trading investments (see 7.7.140). [*IAS 32.33, AG36*]

7.3.530   Treasury shares held for hedging purposes

7.3.530.10   Treasury shares may be held for economic hedging purposes – e.g. to hedge an exposure to an issued index-linked structured note when the index includes the entity's own share price, or to hedge against the cost of a share-based payment arrangement. Holding treasury shares as an economic hedge is not sufficient to override the treasury share accounting requirements – even though this may give rise to a profit or loss mismatch. In this situation, the index derivative feature in the issued structured notes is measured at fair value with all changes therein recognised in profit or loss (see 7.7.140). Any own equity instruments held to hedge the index are accounted for as treasury shares, and changes in their value are not recognised.

7.3.530.20   In our view, the hedge accounting principles explained in chapter 7.9 do not apply to treasury shares. Treasury shares cannot be designated as a hedging instrument. The only non-derivatives that qualify as hedging instruments are financial assets or financial liabilities measured at FVTPL (except for financial liabilities designated as at FVTPL with changes in fair value attributable to changes in credit risk presented in OCI). Own equity is not considered to be a financial asset or financial liability. Also, treasury shares cannot be designated as the hedged item; the hedged risk should be one that could affect reported income whereas gains and losses on treasury shares are not recognised in profit or loss. [*IFRS 9.6.2.2, B6.2.2*]

7.3.540   Treasury shares held by subsidiaries

7.3.540.10   In consolidated financial statements, treasury share accounting applies to own equity instruments that are held by a consolidated subsidiary. [*IAS 32.33*]

EXAMPLE 31A – TREASURY SHARES HELD BY SUBSIDIARIES   Ⓢ

7.3.540.20   Company S is a subsidiary of Parent P. S has a 2% investment in P and S classifies its investment as at FVOCI in its separate financial statements. The following facts are also relevant for this example:
- the investment was acquired at a cost of 72; and
- the current fair value of the investment is 87.

7.3.540.30   P records the following entry in respect of the treasury shares on consolidation.

	DEBIT	CREDIT
Fair value revaluation reserve	15	
Treasury shares (equity)	72	
FVOCI investments		87
To eliminate FVOCI investment on consolidation and to recognise treasury shares		

EXAMPLE 31B – TREASURY SHARES HELD BY SUBSIDIARIES – SALE

7.3.540.40   Continuing Example 31A, in the next period S sells its investment in P for its fair value of 90. S will have recorded the investment in P at 90 (revalued to the date of sale) and accumulated 18 in its fair value revaluation reserve because there is no recycling of amounts presented in OCI. On consolidation, the amount recorded in equity should be reclassified within equity as a surplus on the sale of treasury shares (see 7.3.560.20).

7.3.540.50   For further discussion of the presentation of any surplus or deficit on the sale of treasury shares, see 7.3.560. Any current or deferred tax on the transactions is also recognised in equity (see 3.13.590).

7.3.550   **Treasury shares held by associates and joint ventures**

7.3.550.10   An associate or joint venture may have an investment in its investor. The carrying amount of the investee under the equity method will include the investor's share of the investee's investment in the investor's own shares. [*IAS 32.33*]

7.3.550.20   In our view, the investor should not make any adjustment in respect of treasury shares held by an associate or joint venture. We do not believe that the investor should reclassify this portion of the carrying amount of the investment in the associate or joint venture as a deduction from equity. Similarly, if dividends are declared on these equity instruments, then no adjustment should be made to the entity's share of the associate's or joint venture's profit during the year. We believe that the lack of control over an associate or joint venture, and the definition of a group – i.e. a parent and all of its subsidiaries (see 2.1.100.10) – distinguish these from cases in which treasury shares are held by a subsidiary. Information about own equity instruments held by associates or joint ventures should be disclosed in the notes to the financial statements. [*IAS 1.79, 32.33, IFRS 10.A*]

7.3.560   **Presentation**

7.3.560.10   IFRS does not mandate a specific method of presenting treasury shares within equity. However, local laws may prescribe the allocation method. Therefore, an entity needs to take into account its legal environment when choosing how to present its own shares within equity. An entity needs to choose a presentation format, to be applied consistently to all treasury shares. Possible presentation options are explained below, although other methods may also be used.

	PRESENTATION OF TREASURY SHARES	OUTCOMES
7.3.560.20	**Total cost of treasury shares as a separate category of equity**	• The cost of treasury shares purchased is debited to a separate category of equity. • When treasury shares are sold or reissued, the amount received for the instruments is credited to this category. • Any surplus or deficit on the sale of treasury shares is shown as an adjustment to share premium or reserves, including retained earnings, or a combination thereof. This method is illustrated in KPMG's *Guides to financial statements* series.
7.3.560.30	**Par value of treasury shares as a separate category of equity**	• The par value of treasury shares purchased is debited to a separate category of equity. • When treasury shares are sold or reissued, the par value of the instruments is credited to this category. • Any premium or discount to par value is shown as an adjustment to share premium or reserves, including retained earnings, or a combination thereof.
7.3.560.40	**Par value of treasury shares as a deduction from share capital**	• The par value of treasury shares purchased is debited to share capital. • When treasury shares are sold or reissued, the par value of the instruments is credited to share capital. • Any premium or discount to par value is shown as an adjustment to share premium or reserves, including retained earnings, or a combination thereof.

7.3.570 COSTS OF AN EQUITY TRANSACTION

7.3.570.10 Qualifying costs attributable to an equity transaction – e.g. issuing or buying back own shares – are debited directly to equity. In our view, this includes qualifying costs attributable to the distribution of a dividend because equity transactions include dividends to equity participants. Income tax relating to the transaction costs of an equity transaction are accounted for in accordance with IAS 12 (see 3.13.590). [*IAS 32.35–35A, 37*]

7.3.570.20 Issuing shares in a private placement for cash consideration is an equity transaction and, therefore, in our view the costs directly related to issuing equity instruments in a private placement should be recognised directly in equity.

7.3.570.30   Listing transactions often involve both listing existing shares and issuing new ones. In our view, the costs directly attributable to issuing new shares should be recognised directly in equity and any costs attributable to listing existing shares should be expensed as they are incurred.

7.3.570.40   In our view, similar to a listing of existing shares, secondary offerings – i.e. where existing shares are offered by the entity to new shareholders – and share splits do not result in new equity instruments being issued, so any costs associated with these transactions should be expensed as they are incurred. [*IAS 32.35–36*]

EXAMPLE 32 – LISTING OF SHARES ISSUED BY NEWCO – TRANSACTION IS NOT A BUSINESS COMBINATION

7.3.570.43   A Newco (see 5.13.180) is set up as the new parent of an existing Company C, whose shares are unlisted, to provide the existing shareholders in C with shares that are listed. Newco will issue shares to C's existing shareholders in exchange for their shares in C. Newco's share are listed and Newco incurs costs for issuing them. No additional cash is invested by the shareholders.

7.3.570.45   Because only one business is placed under Newco in this transaction, the transaction is not a business combination and so Newco applies book value (carry-over basis) accounting (see 5.13.60 and 190). Under this accounting, Newco's consolidated financial statements are considered as a continuation of those of C and therefore no equity transaction is reported in those financial statements. Therefore, we believe that the costs incurred by Newco in issuing the shares to the existing shareholders of C should be expensed in Newco's consolidated financial statements as they are incurred because those costs are in effect the costs of listing the existing shares of the continuing entity (via a restructuring) rather than costs of issuing new shares.

7.3.570.47   The requirement to record in equity all costs attributable to an equity transaction also applies to costs incurred on the issue of equity instruments in relation to a business combination (see 2.6.530). [*IFRS 3.53*]

7.3.570.50   Qualifying costs that relate to both existing shares and new shares are allocated on a rational and consistent basis – e.g. based on the number of shares. [*IAS 32.38*]

EXAMPLE 33 – ALLOCATION OF TRANSACTION COSTS BETWEEN EXISTING AND NEW SHARES

7.3.570.60   Company G issues 160 new shares and lists 80 existing shares in an IPO. The total costs related to both existing and new shares are 300. G allocates the cost between the listing of existing shares and the issue of new shares based on the number of shares. Therefore, the cost allocated to the new shares is 200 (300 x 160 / 240), which is recognised directly in equity. The cost allocated to listing the existing shares is 100 (300 x 80 / 240), which is recognised in profit or loss.

7.3.570.70   Only costs that relate to both listing existing shares and issuing new shares are allocated as explained in 7.3.570.50. We believe that costs that are directly attributable only to the listing itself should be recognised in profit or loss as they are incurred (see 7.3.570.30). The IFRS Interpretations Committee discussed this issue and noted that judgement may be required to determine which costs relate solely to activities other than equity transactions – e.g. listing existing shares – and which costs relate jointly to equity transactions and other activities. [*IU 09-08*]

7.3.580   Qualifying costs

7.3.580.10   Only incremental costs that are attributable directly to equity transactions such as issuing or buying back own equity instruments or distributing dividends are recognised in equity. These costs may be internal or external, but need to be incremental. Other costs are recognised in profit or loss even if they relate to newly issued shares. For further discussion of incremental internal transaction costs, see 7.7.50–60. [*IAS 32.37*]

7.3.580.20   Assume that an entity is issuing new shares and simultaneously listing them. The following are examples of costs related to the transaction that we believe should be recognised in equity, if they are incremental costs:

- fees for legal and tax advice related to the share issue;
- the cost of preparing and printing the prospectus;
- fees incurred in respect of valuing the shares;
- fees incurred in respect of valuing other assets – e.g. property – if the valuation is required to be disclosed in the prospectus;
- underwriting fees;
- fees and commissions paid to employees acting as selling agents that relate to the share issue;
- costs incurred in holding press conferences related to the share issue; and
- the cost of handling share applications.

7.3.580.30   In our view, few internal costs will meet the incremental test in practice because we believe that this will be difficult to demonstrate.

7.3.580.40   In our view, costs that relate to the listing itself and that are not directly attributable to the new share issue should be expensed. For example, stock exchange registration costs do not relate to the issue of shares but rather to the listing of the issued shares; accordingly, they should be expensed as they are incurred.

7.3.580.50   In our view, the costs of advertising a share issue should be recognised directly in equity if the advertising relates directly to the share issue and is not general advertising aimed at enhancing the entity's brand. An example may include incremental costs related to a road show in which the entity is specifically targeting potential investors. If only a part of the advertising relates to the share issue, then an apportionment of the costs may be appropriate.

7.3.590   Costs of anticipated equity transactions

7.3.590.10   Equity transaction costs may be incurred before the equity instrument is issued or bought back or before the dividend is distributed. IFRS is silent on how to treat costs incurred before the equity transaction has been recorded.

7.3.590.20   In our view, costs that are related directly to a probable future equity transaction should be recognised as a prepayment (asset) in the statement of financial position. The costs should be transferred to equity when the equity transaction is recognised, or recognised in profit or loss if the issue or buy-back is no longer expected to be completed or the dividend is no longer expected to be distributed.

7.3.600   Costs of issuing compound instruments

7.3.600.10   In the case of compound instruments, transaction costs are allocated to the individual components in proportion to the allocation of the proceeds. The costs related to the liability component are dealt with in accordance with the requirements for transaction costs associated with financial liabilities (see 7.7.50). However, the costs related to the equity component are reported as a deduction from equity. [*IAS 32.37–38*]

7.3.610   Related tax benefits

7.3.610.10   The tax effects of any transaction costs that are recognised in equity are generally also recognised directly in equity. [*IAS 32.35A, 12.61A(b)*]

7.3.610.20   If the tax benefits associated with the transaction costs are not probable, then the deferred tax asset is not recognised. In these cases, the gross transaction costs are deducted from equity. If in a subsequent period the tax benefits related to the transaction costs qualify for recognition, then the corresponding credit will generally be recognised directly in equity. For further discussion, see 3.13.590.

7.3.620   Presentation in equity

7.3.620.10   IFRS does not specify which component of equity the transaction costs recognised in equity should be charged against. In our view, an entity should choose an accounting policy, to be applied consistently, on the component of equity against which the transaction costs are recognised.

7.3.620.20   For a discussion about presenting income tax effects within equity, see 3.13.530.60.

7.3.620.30   If shares have a par value, then regulatory issues may prevent the amount from being deducted from share capital. In this case, the transaction costs may be presented as a deduction from share premium, other paid-in capital or retained earnings; or they might be shown as a separate reserve. If the transaction costs are presented as a deduction from share capital, then in our view the entity should disclose the impact.

EXAMPLE 34 – IMPACT OF TRANSACTION COSTS PRESENTED AS DEDUCTION FROM SHARE CAPITAL

7.3.620.40   Company C issues shares at their par value of 100. Transaction costs are 10. C provides the following disclosure:

Share capital (par value)	100
Transaction costs	(10)
Share capital in statement of financial position	90

7.3.620.50   Example 35 illustrates the combined application effect of the approaches explained in 7.3.610 and 620.30.

EXAMPLE 35 – RECOGNITION OF SHARE ISSUANCE, RELATED COSTS AND TAX

7.3.620.60   In year 1, Company Q issues additional shares for proceeds of 6,000. The total par value of these shares is 600. The costs of the transaction are 1,200. Under the local tax law, transaction costs are deducted only in year 2. Because it is probable that Q will earn sufficient taxable profit in year 2, Q recognises a deferred tax asset related to the transaction costs. The tax rate is 30%.

7.3.620.70   Q records the following entries in its financial statements.

	DEBIT	CREDIT
Cash	6,000	
Share capital		600
Share premium		5,400
To recognise share issuance		
Deferred tax asset (1,200 x 30%)	360	
Share premium	840	
Cash		1,200
To recognise transaction costs and related tax impact		

7.3.630   EQUITY PRESENTATION

7.3.630.10   There are no specific requirements in IFRS on how to present the individual components of equity. Therefore, in our view net accumulated losses may be deducted, on a decision by the shareholders or application of the articles of association, from another component of equity – e.g. additional paid-in capital – if this is permitted by applicable laws.

7.3.630.20   Laws in some countries require reserves to be established for specific purposes. For example, banks may be required to set aside amounts for general banking risks or losses on loans. Some entities also establish reserves if national tax laws grant exemptions from, or reductions in, tax liabilities when transfers to such reserves are made. IFRS neither requires nor prohibits the creation of such reserves, which are merely allocations and designations of components of equity. If such reserves are created, then in our view they should be classified as a separate component of equity and created by an appropriation from another category of equity – e.g. retained earnings. Transfers to these reserves and their related tax effects should be recognised directly within equity, and should not be recognised in profit or loss. Also, these reserves may not be recognised as liabilities in the statement of financial position. Disclosure of the nature and purpose of each reserve within equity is required. [*IAS 1.79(b)*]

7.3.640 **Income tax**

7.3.640.10   Income tax relating to distributions to holders of an equity instrument and to transaction costs of an equity transaction is accounted for in accordance with IAS 12. Current tax and deferred tax that relate to items that are recognised directly in equity are generally recognised directly in equity. For a further discussion of income taxes related to payment of dividends, see 3.13.740.

7.3.640.15   The amount of current and deferred tax recognised directly in equity is disclosed separately. There is no requirement to present the tax impact of items recognised in equity separately in the statement of changes in equity. In our experience, these tax effects are often disclosed in the notes to the financial statements (see 2.2.10). [*IAS 12.52B, 61A(b), 81(a), 32.35A*]

7.3.640.20   In our experience, the tax effects of equity transactions are generally presented in the same category of equity as the underlying transaction, as opposed to creating a separate category of equity for taxes (see 3.13.530.60).

7.3.650 **Non-controlling interests**

7.3.650.10   NCI are presented in the consolidated statement of financial position within equity, separately from the parent's shareholders' equity (see 2.5.530). Therefore, a statement of changes in equity includes an analysis of the amounts attributable to NCI. [*IAS 1.54(q), 106, IFRS 10.22*]

7.3.660 **CAPITAL DISCLOSURES**

7.3.660.10   An entity discloses information that enables users of its financial statements to evaluate the entity's objectives, policies and processes for managing capital. It discloses the following.
● Qualitative information, including a description of:
  – what it manages as capital;
  – when the entity is subject to externally imposed capital requirements:
    ● the nature of those requirements; and
    ● how those requirements are incorporated into the management of capital; and
  – how it is meeting its objectives for managing capital.
● Summary quantitative data about what it manages as capital. Some entities regard some financial liabilities – e.g. some forms of subordinated debt – as part of capital. Other entities regard capital as excluding some components of equity – e.g. components arising from cash flow hedges.
● Any changes in qualitative information and quantitative data from the previous period.
● Whether during the period it complied with any externally imposed capital requirements to which it is subject.
● When the entity has not complied with such externally imposed capital requirements, the consequences of such non-compliance. [*IAS 1.134–135*]

7.3.670 **CAPITAL MAINTENANCE**

7.3.670.10   IFRS does not establish requirements about what assets or net assets should be retained and what may be distributed. This is a legal issue that will depend on the regulatory environment in which an entity operates.

7.3.670.20   If there is a legal prohibition on the distribution of certain reserves, and an entity wishes to indicate these restrictions in the statement of changes in equity, then in our view the entity should transfer the restricted amounts to a separate component of equity – e.g. a non-distributable reserve or a capital reserve – if the applicable law permits. Any such transfer would be made through the statement of changes in equity (see chapter 2.2 and 7.3.630.20). In any case, the restrictions on distribution are disclosed in the notes to the financial statements. [*IAS 1.79(b)*]

7.3.680   **DIVIDENDS**

7.3.680.10   Dividends and other distributions to holders of equity instruments are recognised directly in equity (see 7.3.20.160).

7.3.680.20   A liability for a dividend payable is not recognised until an entity has an obligation to pay dividends. In the case of discretionary dividends, a liability for a dividend payable is not recognised until the dividend is both appropriately authorised *and* no longer at the entity's discretion – i.e. when the entity has an obligation to pay. In our view, it is not appropriate to recognise a liability based only on a constructive obligation. This is consistent with the basis for conclusions to IAS 10 and the definition of a financial liability in IAS 32 (see 7.3.20). Therefore, a constructive obligation cannot arise in connection with a dividend. [*IAS 10.12, BC4*]

7.3.680.30   In the case of discretionary dividends, the legal requirements of the particular jurisdiction are important in determining the point in time at which a liability is recognised. For example, suppose that the relevant law stated that a board decision or announcement required no further approval and was binding on the entity – e.g. the board has no discretion to withdraw its decision or announcement and no legal discretion to avoid making payment. In this case, the dividend liability is recognised on the board decision or announcement. However, suppose that the entity can choose to avoid payment until it is approved by the shareholders, or can withdraw its decision or announcement of the dividend (see 7.3.290). In this case, it would not be appropriate to recognise a liability at the time of the board decision or announcement.

7.3.680.40   In our view, an obligation to pay an interim dividend should be recognised when the entity has an obligation to make the payment and the amount to be paid can be determined reliably – i.e. the shareholders do not have an obligation to pay back the interim dividend.

7.3.680.50   Sometimes, in addition to the declaration or the approval process required as a condition for the payment of the dividends, additional conditions – e.g. the fulfilment/waiver of all conditions precedent for completion of a proposed business combination and the holder of the equity instruments continues to hold the securities until the record date on which the fulfilment/waiver of those conditions is announced – may determine the timing or amount of the dividend to be recognised. In this case, the liability is recognised when the obligation exists and for the amount that the entity has an obligation to pay.

7.3.680.60   Dividends on shares that are classified as liabilities are presented in profit or loss as a finance cost unless the dividends are discretionary. Even if the legal form of the payment is a dividend, it is not recognised directly in equity. For further discussion of the classification of discretionary dividends, see 7.3.290. Financing costs on shares classified as liabilities are determined under the effective interest method.

7.3.680.70   IFRS does not provide any guidance on accounting for share dividends – i.e. the issue of additional shares to shareholders characterised as a dividend.

7.3.680.80   Sometimes shares with a value equal to the cash dividend amount are offered as an alternative to the cash dividend. When the shares are issued, the liability is settled and a credit to equity is recognised as the proceeds of the issue. In our view, this practice is acceptable. Any reallocation of capital within equity needs to be in accordance with the applicable law.

7.3.680.90   In our view, a share dividend that is not an alternative to a cash dividend should be treated in the same way as a share split or a bonus issue – i.e. no entries are required (see 7.3.420).

7.3.690   Distributions of non-cash assets to owners

7.3.690.10   IFRIC 17 addresses specific forms of distributions. The interpretation deals with measurement and presentation issues in this respect.

7.3.690.20   A 'distribution' is a non-reciprocal transfer of assets from an entity to its owners, commonly referred to as a 'dividend'. There is no restriction placed on the term 'distribution' other than that it is non-reciprocal. Neither the reason for the transfer of assets nor its legal characterisation is a factor in determining whether it falls in the scope of the interpretation. Therefore, for example, a distribution that is in effect a return of capital is in the scope of the interpretation. [*IFRIC 17.2–3, BC4–BC5*]

7.3.690.30   IFRIC 17 addresses how an entity making distributions of non-cash assets to owners acting in their capacity as owners accounts for those distributions in its financial statements (separate, individual and/or consolidated). IFRIC 17 also applies to distributions in which each owner may elect to receive either their share of the non-cash asset or a cash alternative. Perhaps the most significant transactions included in the scope of the interpretation are demergers or spin-offs, in which an entity distributes its ownership interests in one or more subsidiaries to existing shareholders. [*IFRIC 17.3*]

7.3.690.40   IFRIC 17 does not apply to:
- common control transactions (see 5.13.90);
- distributions of part of the ownership interests in a subsidiary when control is retained; and
- distributions in which owners of the same class of equity instruments are not treated equally. [*IFRIC 17.4–7*]

7.3.690.50   IFRIC 17 also does not apply to the financial statements of the recipient of the distribution; recipients apply the requirements of IFRS 9 and IAS 27 to the receipt of dividends (see 7.7.500). [*IFRS 9.5.7.1A, IAS 27.12, IFRIC 17.8*]

7.3.690.60   A liability for the distribution is recognised when the distribution is authorised and is no longer at the entity's discretion. This timing will vary depending on the legal requirements of individual jurisdictions (see 7.3.680.20). [*IFRIC 17.10*]

7.3.690.70   The liability for the distribution is measured, initially and until the settlement date, at the fair value of the assets to be distributed. Any changes in the measurement of the liability are recognised in equity; this is consistent with the accounting for the liability at the time of initial recognition. For distributions in which the owners may elect to receive either non-cash assets or a cash alternative, the entity considers the fair value of each alternative and their associated probabilities when measuring the liability. [*IFRIC 17.11–13*]

7.3.690.80   Unless it is required by other standards – e.g. financial assets measured at FVTPL or FVOCI under IFRS 9 – the assets to be distributed are not remeasured to fair value when the liability is recognised. Instead, assets to be distributed that are in the measurement scope of IFRS 5 are measured in accordance with that standard (see 5.4.40). Assets to be distributed that are not in the measurement scope of IFRS 5 (e.g. deferred tax assets) continue to be measured in accordance with other standards (e.g. IAS 12).

7.3.690.90   At the date on which the distribution occurs – i.e. settlement date – the following takes place.
- The liability is remeasured based on the fair value of the assets to be distributed, with any change therein recognised in equity.
- The liability and the assets distributed are derecognised.
- Any difference between the fair value of the assets distributed and their carrying amount in the financial statements is recognised as a separate line item in profit or loss; this has a consequential effect on EPS.
- Any amounts recognised in OCI in relation to the assets distributed – e.g. fair value revaluation reserves – are reclassified to profit or loss or they may be transferred within equity depending on the derecognition requirements in other standards, on the same basis as would be required if the non-cash assets had been disposed of. [*IFRIC 17.13–15, BC38*]

7.3.690.100   In our experience, the amount recognised in profit or loss at the settlement date is not generally a loss. This is because, if the fair value of the assets had been lower than their carrying amount, an impairment loss would have been recognised before settlement. [*IFRIC 17.BC39*]

EXAMPLE 36 – DISTRIBUTION OF NON-CASH ASSETS TO OWNERS

7.3.690.110   Company P distributes items of property, plant and equipment as dividends to all of its owners acting in their capacity as owners. The carrying amount of the property, plant and equipment is 100 and the fair value is 130 at the date on which the distribution is authorised.

7.3.690.120   At the date of settlement of the distribution, the carrying amount of the property, plant and equipment is 95 and the fair value is 125.

7.3.690.130   Company P records the following entries in its financial statements.

	DEBIT	CREDIT
Equity	130	
Liability for distribution		130
To recognise liability at fair value of assets to be distributed		

	DEBIT	CREDIT
Liability for distribution	5	
Equity		5
To recognise change in carrying amount of liability up *to settlement date*		
Liability for distribution	125	
Property, plant and equipment		95
Profit or loss		30
To derecognise liability and assets distributed		

7.3.700   FUTURE DEVELOPMENTS

7.3.700.10   In February 2008, the IASB published Discussion Paper *Financial Instruments with Characteristics of Equity*. The objective of the IASB and FASB's joint project on the distinction between liabilities and equity was to have more relevant, understandable and comparable requirements for determining the classification of financial instruments that have the characteristics of liabilities, equity or both. In November 2010, the IASB amended its work plan and deferred work on a number of projects that were active at the time.

7.3.700.20   In July 2013, the IASB published Discussion Paper *A Review of the Conceptual Framework for Financial Reporting*, which included proposals on distinguishing liabilities from equity instruments. During the redeliberations, the IASB decided to further explore this subject in a separate research project *Financial Instruments with Characteristics of Equity*. In June 2018, the IASB published a second discussion paper, which is open for comment until January 2019.

7.3.700.30   KPMG's periodic *IFRS Newsletter: Financial Instruments* features the IASB's discussions and progress on this project. This publication, and other KPMG resources on financial instruments, are available at kpmg.com/ifrs.

7.4   Classification of financial assets

7.4   Classification of financial assets

CURRENTLY EFFECTIVE REQUIREMENTS

This publication reflects IFRS in issue at 1 August 2018, and the currently effective requirements cover annual periods beginning on 1 January 2018.

The requirements related to this topic are mainly derived from the following.

STANDARD	TITLE
IFRS 9	Financial Instruments

FORTHCOMING REQUIREMENTS

The currently effective requirements are affected by the following forthcoming requirements. They are highlighted with a # and the impact is explained in the accompanying boxed text at the references indicated.

- In October 2017, the IASB issued *Prepayment Features with Negative Compensation – Amendments to IFRS 9*, which are effective for annual periods beginning on or after 1 January 2019. See 7.4.225.
- In May 2017, the IASB issued IFRS 17 *Insurance Contracts*, which is effective for annual periods beginning on or after 1 January 2021. See 7.4.157. IFRS 17 is the subject of chapter 8.1A.

FUTURE DEVELOPMENTS

For this topic, there are no future developments.

7.4.10 **OVERVIEW**

7.4.10.10   The following flowchart provides an overview of the classification and measurement model for financial assets in IFRS 9. Each element of the model is explained further in this chapter.

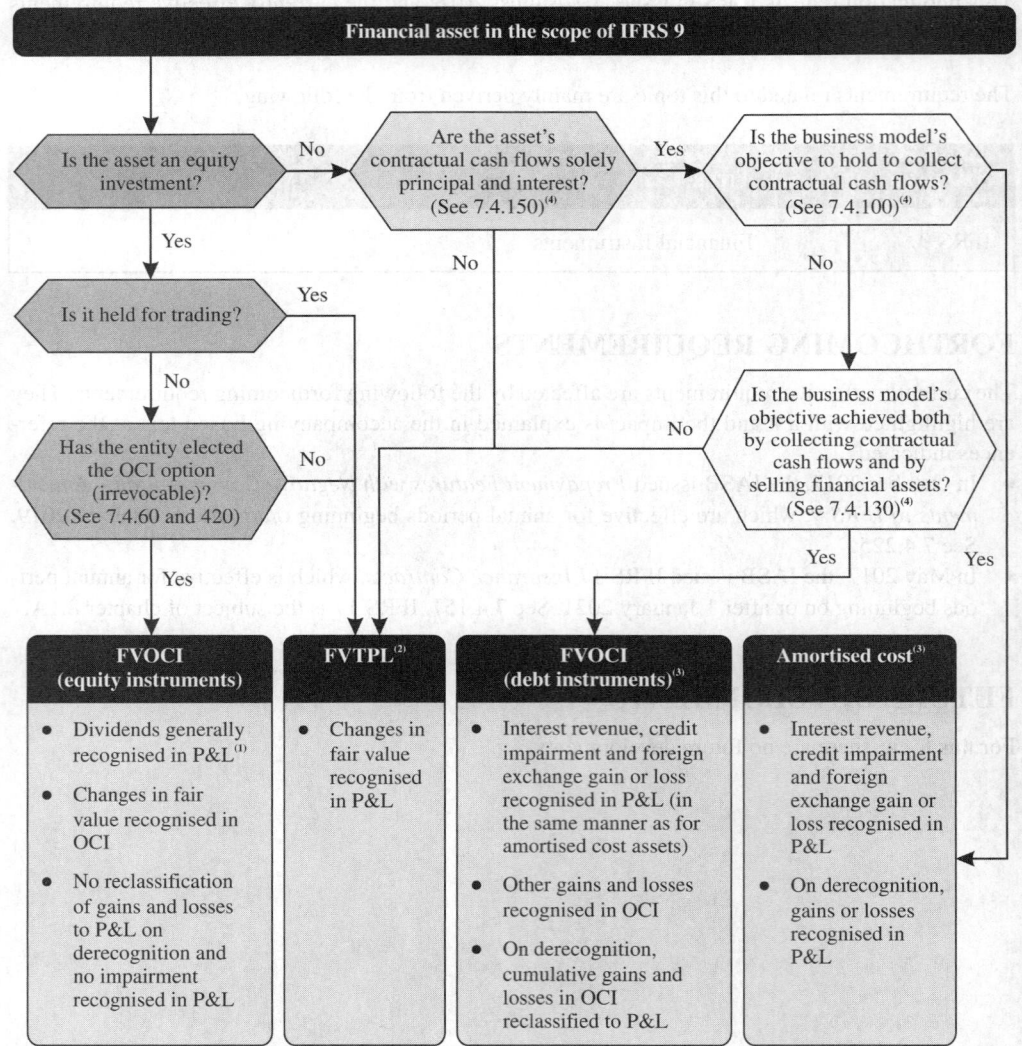

Notes

1.   P&L: profit or loss.
2.   Certain credit exposures can also be designated as at FVTPL if a credit derivative that is measured at FVTPL is used to manage the credit risk of all, or a part, of the exposure. [*IFRS 9.6.7.1*]
3.   Subject to an entity's irrevocable option to designate such a financial asset as at FVTPL on initial recognition if, and only if, such designation eliminates or significantly reduces a measurement or recognition inconsistency. [*IFRS 9.4.1.5*]
4.   The order in which the business model and assessments for the cash flow characteristics are performed does not impact the classification conclusion. [*IFRS 9.BC4.14*]

7.4.20   BASIC PRINCIPLES

7.4.20.10   On initial recognition, a financial asset is classified into one of three primary measurement categories:

- amortised cost;
- fair value through OCI (FVOCI); or
- fair value through profit or loss (FVTPL). [*IFRS 9.4.1.1*]

7.4.20.20   In addition, IFRS 9 provides presentation and designation options and other specific guidance for certain financial assets, as follows.

CLASSIFICATION OPTIONS	CLASSIFICATION IMPACT
Financial assets for which designation as at FVTPL eliminates or significantly reduces an accounting mismatch.	May be designated as at FVTPL (see 7.4.50.20 and 390).
Investments in equity instruments that are not held for trading (see 7.4.140.20–80).	Option to present changes in fair value in OCI (see 7.4.60 and 420).
Certain credit exposures if a credit derivative that is measured at FVTPL is used to manage the credit risk of all, or a part, of the exposure. This option is conditional on the entity having elected to apply the hedge accounting requirements in chapter 6 of IFRS 9 (see 7.9.120 and 7.11.20.50).	May be designated as at FVTPL (see 7.4.400).
Financial assets that: • continue to be recognised in their entirety when a transfer of the financial asset does not qualify for derecognition; or • continue to be recognised to the extent of their continuing involvement.	Specific guidance (see 7.6.60).

7.4.20.30   If an entity acquires financial instruments as part of a business combination (see 2.6.560), then it classifies the acquired financial instruments at the date of acquisition by applying the normal classification rules. If these classifications differ from the classifications made by the acquiree, then the reclassifications are not treated as transfers between portfolios in the consolidated financial statements of the acquirer. [*IFRS 3.16*]

7.4.20.40   If an entity grants an irrevocable loan commitment, then there may be a long period of time before the commitment is drawn down and there may be multiple draw-downs over the commitment period. A question therefore arises about whether loans drawn down under an irrevocable loan commitment should be assessed for classification based on conditions when the loan commitment was originated or when each loan was actually drawn down. It appears that an entity should choose an accounting policy, to be applied consistently, to make an assessment for classification based on the conditions at:

- *the loan commitment date:* under this approach, each loan is seen as a continuation of the loan commitment in line with the impairment requirements; or
- *each draw-down date:* under this approach, each loan is seen as a separate financial instrument, which is initially recognised at the point of each draw-down. [*IFRS 9.B5.5.47*]

7.4.20.50   The accounting policy choice in 7.4.20.40 is consistent with the accounting policy choice allowed for initial measurement of a loan measured at amortised cost resulting from a loan commitment outside the scope of IFRS 9 (see 7.7.33). We believe that the accounting policy selected for measurement should be consistent with the policy selected for classification.

7.4.30   Financial assets measured at amortised cost

7.4.30.10   A financial asset is measured at amortised cost only if it meets both of the following conditions:
- the asset is held within a business model whose objective is to hold assets to collect contractual cash flows (the held-to-collect business model); and
- the contractual terms of the financial asset give rise on specified dates to cash flows that are solely payments of principal and interest on the principal amount outstanding (the SPPI criterion). [*IFRS 9.4.1.2*]

7.4.40   Financial assets measured at FVOCI

7.4.40.10   A debt instrument is measured at FVOCI only if it meets both of the following conditions:
- the asset is held within a business model whose objective is achieved by both collecting contractual cash flows and selling financial assets; and
- the contractual terms of the financial asset meet the SPPI criterion. [*IFRS 9.4.1.2A*]

7.4.50   Financial assets measured at FVTPL

7.4.50.10   All other financial assets – i.e. financial assets that do not meet the criteria for classification as subsequently measured at either amortised cost or FVOCI – are classified as subsequently measured at fair value, with changes in fair value recognised in profit or loss.

7.4.50.20   In addition, an entity has the option on initial recognition to irrevocably designate a financial asset as at FVTPL if doing so eliminates or significantly reduces a measurement or recognition inconsistency – i.e. an 'accounting mismatch' – that would otherwise arise from measuring assets or liabilities, or recognising the gains and losses on them, on different bases.

7.4.60   Designation exception for investments in equity instruments

7.4.60.10   Investments in equity instruments fail the SPPI criterion and are therefore measured at FVTPL. However, on initial recognition an entity may make an irrevocable election to present in OCI the changes in the fair value of an investment in an equity instrument that is not held for trading (see 7.4.140.20–80). The election can be made on an instrument-by-instrument basis. [*IFRS 9.5.7.5, B5.7.1*]

7.4.60.20   The accounting under this election is as follows:

- the impairment requirements in IFRS 9 do not apply;
- all foreign exchange differences are recognised in OCI;
- amounts recognised in OCI are not reclassified to profit or loss; and
- only dividend income is recognised in profit or loss. [*IFRS 9.5.5.1, B5.7.1, B5.7.3*]

7.4.70   BUSINESS MODEL ASSESSMENT

7.4.70.10   An entity determines whether a financial asset that meets the SPPI criterion in 7.4.150 needs to be classified as measured at amortised cost, FVOCI or FVTPL. To do this, it needs to identify and assess the objective of the business model in which the asset is held. [*IFRS 9.4.1.1–4.1.2A*]

7.4.70.20   The following table summarises the key features of each type of business model and the resultant measurement category. [*IFRS 9.4.1.2–4.1.4*]

BUSINESS MODEL	KEY FEATURES	CATEGORY
Held-to-collect (see 7.4.100)	• The objective of the business model is to hold assets to collect contractual cash flows. • Sales are incidental to the objective of the model. • This model typically involves the lowest level of sales in comparison with other business models (in frequency and volume).	Amortised cost[1]
Both held to collect and for sale (see 7.4.130)	• Both collecting contractual cash flows and sales are integral to achieving the objective of the business model. • This model typically has more sales (in frequency and volume) than the held-to-collect business model.	FVOCI[1]
Other business models, including: • trading • managing assets on a fair value basis • maximising cash flows through sale (see 7.4.140)	• The business model is neither held-to-collect nor held to collect and for sale. • The collection of contractual cash flows is incidental to the objective of the model.	FVTPL[2]

Notes
1.   Subject to meeting the SPPI criterion.
2.   The SPPI criterion is irrelevant – i.e. assets in all business models are measured at FVTPL.

7.4.70.30   The objective of the entity's business model is not based on management's intentions with respect to an individual instrument, but rather is determined at a higher level of aggregation.

The assessment needs to reflect the way that an entity manages its business or businesses. A single reporting entity may have more than one business model for managing its financial instruments. It is possible for an entity to hold different portfolios being managed on different bases. In this case, the entity assesses the objective of the business model for each portfolio, rather than basing the classification on a single assessment at the reporting entity level. [*IFRS 9.B4.1.1–B4.1.2*]

7.4.70.40   Generally, an entity's business model is a matter of fact that can be observed from the way in which the entity is managed, and from the information provided to management. [*IFRS 9.BC4.20*]

EXAMPLE 1A – MORE THAN ONE BUSINESS MODEL – MULTIPLE PORTFOLIOS

7.4.70.50   Company X has one classification for a portfolio of investments that it manages in order to collect contractual cash flows. It has a different classification for financial assets in another portfolio of investments that it manages in order to trade to realise fair value changes. [*IFRS 9.B4.1.2*]

7.4.70.60   In some circumstances it may be appropriate to separate a portfolio of financial assets into sub-portfolios.

EXAMPLE 1B – MORE THAN ONE BUSINESS MODEL – SUB-PORTFOLIOS

7.4.70.70   Company Y acquires a portfolio of loans and manages some of the loans to collect their contractual cash flows and manages others with the objective of selling them. In this example, Y concludes that it is appropriate to separate its portfolio of financial assets into sub-portfolios. [*IFRS 9.B4.1.2*]

7.4.70.75   Similarly, in some circumstances it may be appropriate to separate a loan into portions.

EXAMPLE 2 – PORTIONS OF A LOAN

7.4.70.78   Company Z generally originates loans to collect contractual cash flows. However, it plans to sell portions of new loans that exceed the credit approval limits. In this example, Z concludes that it has two business models:
- held-to-collect model for loans (or portions of loans) that are intended to be held to collect contractual cash flows; and
- held-for-trading model for loans (or portions of loans) that are intended to be sold. [*IFRS 9.B4.1.2*]

7.4.70.80   The assessment is not performed on the basis of scenarios that the entity does not reasonably expect to occur – e.g. worst-case scenarios. For example, if an entity expects that it will sell a particular portfolio of financial assets only in a stress-case scenario, then that scenario will not affect the assessment of the business model for those assets if it is not reasonably expected that a stress scenario will occur. [*IFRS 9.B4.1.2A*]

7.4.80   Relevant and objective evidence

7.4.80.10   An entity assesses all relevant and objective evidence that is available at the date of the assessment to determine the business model for particular financial assets. The following are examples of relevant and objective evidence:

- how the performance of the business model (and the financial assets held within that business model) is evaluated and reported to the entity's key management personnel;
- the risks that affect the performance of the business model (and the financial assets held within that business model) and how those risks are managed; and
- how managers of the business are compensated – e.g. whether compensation is based on the fair value of the assets managed or the contractual cash flows collected. [*IFRS 9.B4.1.2B*]

7.4.80.20   In addition, an entity considers the frequency, volume and timing of sales in prior periods, the reasons for such sales and its expectations about future sales activity. However, information about sales activity is not considered in isolation, but as part of a holistic assessment of how the entity's stated objective for managing the financial assets is achieved and how cash flows are realised. Therefore, an entity considers information about past sales in the context of the reasons for those sales and the conditions that existed at that time compared with current conditions. [*IFRS 9.B4.1.2C*]

7.4.80.30   Although IFRS 9 states that an entity's business model for managing financial assets is a matter of fact, it also acknowledges that judgement is needed to assess the business model for managing particular financial assets. For example, the standard does not include 'bright lines' for assessing the impact of sales activity, but instead requires an entity to consider:

- the significance and frequency of sales activity; and
- whether both sales activity and the collection of contractual cash flows are integral or incidental to the business model. [*IFRS 9.B4.1.4B*]

7.4.80.40   In our view, in making the business model assessment, an entity should consider the stated objective of IFRS 9, which is to provide relevant and useful information to users of the financial statements for their assessment of the amounts, timing and uncertainty of the entity's future cash flows.

7.4.80.50   The more that a business model envisages holding financial assets for an extended period or until maturity to collect contractual cash flows, the more relevant and useful amortised cost information is. Conversely, the more that a business model envisages making sales of assets significantly before maturity, the more relevant and useful fair value information is. [*IFRS 9.BCE53–BCE56*]

7.4.90   Cash flows realised differently from expectations

7.4.90.10   Cash flows may be realised in a way that is different from expectations at the date on which the entity assessed the business model – e.g. if more or fewer financial assets are sold than was expected when the assets were classified. As long as the entity considered all relevant and objective information that was available when it made the business model assessment, this situation does not:

- give rise to a prior-period error in the entity's financial statements; or
- change the classification of the remaining financial assets held in that business model – i.e. those assets that the entity recognised in prior periods and still holds. [*IFRS 9.B4.1.2A*]

7.4.90.20 However, when an entity assesses the business model for newly acquired financial assets, it considers information about how cash flows were realised in the past, along with other relevant information. [*IFRS 9.B4.1.2A*]

EXAMPLE 3 – CASH FLOWS REALISED DIFFERENTLY FROM EXPECTATIONS

7.4.90.30 Company K has a portfolio of financial assets that it has previously determined to be subject to a held-to-collect business model. Previously, there were insignificant sales of assets to manage concentrations of credit risk. However, the portfolio has grown much larger than was previously expected, and considerable merger and acquisition activity among issuers in the portfolio is now anticipated.

7.4.90.40 As a result, K expects that there will be significant sales activity in the future to manage concentrations of credit risk, and concludes that its management of the portfolio is no longer consistent with a held-to-collect business model.

7.4.90.50 K concludes that the reclassification criteria for existing assets (see 7.4.450) have not been met. However, when new financial assets are acquired for the portfolio after the change, those new financial assets will not meet the held-to-collect criterion. This may lead to the portfolio being sub-divided, with existing financial assets in the portfolio being measured at amortised cost, and those acquired after the change being measured at fair value.

7.4.100   HELD-TO-COLLECT BUSINESS MODEL

7.4.100.10 Financial assets in a held-to-collect business model are managed to realise cash flows by collecting payments of principal and interest over the life of the instruments. That is, the assets held within the portfolio are managed to collect the contractual cash flows. [*IFRS 9.B4.1.2C*]

7.4.100.20 Although the objective of a business model may be to hold financial assets in order to collect contractual cash flows, the entity need not hold all of these assets until maturity. Therefore, a business model can be to hold financial assets to collect contractual cash flows even when some sales of financial assets have occurred or are expected to occur. [*IFRS 9.B4.1.3*]

7.4.100.30 An entity considers information about past sales and expectations about future sales, including the frequency, value and nature of such sales, when determining the objective of the business model. Sales or expected sales of financial assets may be consistent with a held-to-collect business model if those sales are incidental to the business model. The following are examples included in IFRS 9.

- The sales are due to an increase in the credit risk of a financial asset – e.g. a sale takes place because it no longer meets the credit criteria specified in the entity's documented investment policy; in the absence of such a policy, it may be demonstrated in other ways that the sale occurred because of an increase in credit risk. Irrespective of their frequency and value, sales due to an increase in the assets' credit risk are not inconsistent with a held-to-collect objective. This is because the credit quality of financial assets is relevant to the entity's ability to collect contractual cash flows. For a sale to be attributed to an increase in the credit risk of a financial asset, we expect the sale generally to occur within a reasonably short period after the increase in credit risk was identified.

- The sales are infrequent (even if they are significant), or are insignificant individually and in aggregate (even if they are frequent).
- The sales take place close to the maturity of the financial assets and the proceeds from the sales approximate the collection of the remaining contractual cash flows. [*IFRS 9.B4.1.3A–B4.1.3B, BC4.145*]

7.4.100.33   IFRS 9 does not contain any further guidance on how to assess whether sales are 'insignificant individually and in aggregate'. It appears that an entity should assess the significance of the amount of sales by comparing the portion sold with the overall size of the portfolio subject to the business model assessment, rather than other measures, such as the total assets in the entity's statement of financial position. We believe that the size of the portfolio is the relevant reference point because the objective is to assess the extent to which assets in the portfolio are sold as part of assessing the business model of the portfolio, not to compare the size of the transactions in the portfolio to other assets of the entity. We also believe that a comparison of gains and losses from sales with the total return of the portfolio could be used as an additional relevant reference point to indicate further cases in which the business model is not to hold assets in order to collect contractual cash flows.

7.4.100.35   In determining whether sales are insignificant in aggregate, it appears that an entity should consider expected sales over the expected lives of the instruments in the portfolio, rather than just over one reporting period. This is because the expected life is the period over which the contractual cash flows of an asset arise and during which the asset may potentially be sold. For example, if a portfolio comprised financial assets with expected maturities of between five and ten years, then we believe that it would not be appropriate to conclude that the entity held the assets to collect contractual cash flows only on the basis that it did not intend to make any sales during the next 12 months.

7.4.100.40   If there is more than an infrequent number of sales and those sales are more than insignificant, then an entity assesses whether and how those sales are consistent with the objective of a held-to-collect business model. An increase in the frequency or value of sales in a particular period is not necessarily inconsistent with an objective to hold financial assets in order to collect contractual cash flows, if an entity can explain the reasons for those sales and demonstrate why those sales do not reflect a change in the entity's business model. There is no quantitative bright-line measure on what frequency or value of anticipated sales would prevent a single business model from meeting the held-to-collect criterion. [*IFRS 9.B4.1.3B*]

7.4.100.50   Sales made in managing concentrations of credit risk (without an increase in the asset's credit risk) are assessed in the same way as any other sales made in the business model. [*IFRS 9.B4.1.3B*]

EXAMPLE 4 – HELD-TO-COLLECT BUSINESS MODEL – SALES

7.4.100.60   Company L has a portfolio of financial assets that it has determined to be part of a held-to-collect business model. A change in the regulatory treatment of these assets has caused L to undertake a significant rebalancing of its portfolio in a particular period. However, L does not change its assessment of the business model, because the selling activity is considered an isolated – i.e. one-time – event. [*IFRS 9.B4.1.4*]

> 7.4.100.70   By contrast, suppose that L were required by its regulator to routinely sell financial assets from a portfolio to demonstrate that the assets were liquid, and that the value of the assets sold was significant. In this case, L's business model for managing that portfolio would not be held-to-collect. [*IFRS 9.B4.1.4*]

EXAMPLE 5 – HELD-TO-COLLECT BUSINESS MODEL – FACTORS CONSIDERED IN ASSESSMENT

> 7.4.100.80   Company J holds investments to collect their contractual cash flows. The maturities of the investments are matched to J's estimated, and generally predictable, funding needs. In the past, sales of investments have typically occurred when the financial assets' credit risk has increased such that the assets no longer meet J's documented investment policy. In addition, infrequent sales have occurred as a result of unanticipated funding needs. Reports to management focus on the credit quality of the instruments and contractual returns. However, management also considers the financial assets' fair values from a liquidity perspective.
>
> 7.4.100.90   The following factors are relevant to the assessment of J's business model.
> * The stated objective of the business model is to hold assets to collect contractual cash flows. The fact that the investments' maturities match the generally predictable funding needs supports this objective.
> * Sales in response to an increase in the investments' credit risk because the investments no longer meet the entity's documented investment policy, and infrequent sales resulting from unanticipated needs, are not inconsistent with the held-to-collect business model.
> * Although management considers fair value information, it does so from a liquidity perspective, and the main focus of its review of financial information is on the credit quality and contractual returns, which is consistent with the held-to-collect business model. [*IFRS 9.B4.1.4.Ex1*]

7.4.110   Interaction with consolidation and derecognition requirements

7.4.110.10   A portfolio of financial assets acquired with the objective of selling to a securitisation vehicle may be consistent with a held-to-collect business model, depending on the circumstances. If selling the assets would result in derecognition, then the objective would be inconsistent with a held-to-collect objective. However, if selling the assets would not result in derecognition, then further analysis may be required.

(S) EXAMPLE 6 – FINANCIAL ASSETS ACQUIRED WITH OBJECTIVE OF SELLING TO SECURITISATION VEHICLE

> 7.4.110.20   Company D originates loans for the purpose of selling them to a securitisation vehicle, which D controls and consolidates (see chapter 2.5). The loans are derecognised from D's separate statement of financial position and recognised

by the securitisation vehicle. On consolidation, the loans remain within the consolidated group.

7.4.110.30   In the consolidated financial statements, the held-to-collect criterion is met, because the consolidated group originated the loans with the objective of collecting the contractual cash flows.

7.4.110.40   However, in D's separate financial statements, the held-to-collect criterion is not met. This is because the individual entity has originated the loans with the objective of selling them to the securitisation vehicle, rather than holding them to collect the contractual cash flows. [*IFRS 9.B4.1.4*]

7.4.110.50   An entity may hold a portfolio of financial assets for which its objectives include selling some of those financial assets to third parties in transactions that do not qualify for derecognition of the sold assets. In our view, whether such a portfolio is considered consistent with a held-to-collect business model depends on the circumstances.

EXAMPLE 7A – FINANCIAL ASSETS SOLD UNDER SALE-AND-REPURCHASE AGREEMENTS

7.4.110.60   Company M holds financial assets to collect the contractual cash flows through to maturity; however, its objectives include selling some of those financial assets as part of sale-and-repurchase agreements (repos). Under these agreements, M agrees to repurchase the financial assets at a later date before their maturity. During the term of the repos, the transferee is required to immediately remit to M an amount equal to any payments that the transferee receives from the transferred assets.

7.4.110.70   We believe that this scenario is consistent with a held-to-collect business model, based on:
- M's continuing recognition of the assets for accounting purposes; and
- the requirements to pass on interest received and to return the asset back to M before their maturity.

EXAMPLE 7B – FINANCIAL ASSETS SOLD UNDER FACTORING AGREEMENTS

7.4.110.80   Company R originates trade receivables and immediately sells them to a factor. The factor obtains outright legal ownership of the receivables and the debtors are required to remit funds directly to the factor. However, under the factoring agreement, R retains substantially all of the credit risk of the receivables through a guarantee given to the factor. Because of the guarantee, R continues to recognise the trade receivables in its statement of financial position.

7.4.110.90   In this case, in our view R should choose an accounting policy, to be applied consistently, on whether such receivables are held within a held-to-collect

business model. R may conclude that the assets are held within a held-to-collect business model consistent with its continuing recognition of the receivables. Alternatively, it may conclude that the held-to-collect criterion is not met, because:

- it immediately sells the assets; and
- it has no right to collect any of the contractual cash flows.

7.4.115 Financial assets held by a subsidiary or business unit that will be sold

7.4.115.10   A group may make a strategic decision to sell a subsidiary to a third party and meet the requirements to classify the subsidiary as held-for-sale in the group's consolidated financial statements. However, from the subsidiary's perspective the financial assets are considered to be held within a held-to-collect business model. It appears that an entity should choose an accounting policy, to be applied consistently, to make the business model assessment in the consolidated financial statements using one of the following approaches.

- *Approach 1:* Based on the group's intended disposal of the subsidiary.
- *Approach 2:* Based on the subsidiary's manner of managing the assets.

7.4.115.20   Under Approach 1 in 7.4.115.10, we believe that the strategic decision to sell the subsidiary should be considered in assessing how the group manages the financial assets held by the subsidiary. Similar to the considerations when a portfolio of assets is sold in a securitisation (see 7.4.110.10), if the sale transaction is expected to lead to derecognition of the financial assets in the consolidated financial statements, then the objective would be inconsistent with a held-to-collect business model. Under this approach, once the parent makes a decision to sell the subsidiary (including all of its assets and liabilities), the subsidiary's assets are considered as held in a business model whose objective is not to hold financial assets in order to collect contractual cash flows. Further, when an entity assesses whether there is a change in business model, the reclassification decision is generally based on the group's perspective (see 7.4.450.20).

7.4.115.30   Under Approach 2 in 7.4.115.10, the focus is on the level at which the group of assets is actually managed. The subsidiary may continue to manage the assets to realise cash flows by collecting contractual payments over the life of the instruments and the strategic decision at the group level may not change how:

- the assets are managed;
- performance is evaluated and reported to key management personnel;
- the risks that affect performance are managed; or
- managers of the business are compensated.

7.4.115.40   If the aspects discussed in 7.4.115.30 do not change, then we believe that the business model should remain held-to-collect in the consolidated financial statements. Further, if the subsidiary still originates new loans from the same business, then this would indicate that there has not been a change in the business model and the existing assets remain held-to-collect (see 7.4.450.30).

7.4.115.50   We believe that it does not make a difference whether the business that is held for sale is in a separate subsidiary or not. The accounting policy choice in 7.4.115.10 would apply similarly to a sale of a business unit as a going concern.

7.4.120 **Acquiring distressed assets**

7.4.120.10 Acquiring financial assets with incurred losses is not in itself inconsistent with a held-to-collect business model. For example, an entity may have a business model to acquire impaired loans for which it then collects the contractual cash flows by taking the necessary actions to maximise recoveries. [*IFRS 9.B4.1.4*]

7.4.130 **BOTH HELD TO COLLECT AND FOR SALE BUSINESS MODEL**

7.4.130.10 An entity may hold financial assets in a business model whose objective is achieved by both collecting contractual cash flows and selling financial assets. In order to make this business model assessment, it is necessary for the entity's key management personnel to conclude that both of these activities are integral to achieving the objective of the business model. [*IFRS 9.B4.1.4A*]

7.4.130.20 IFRS 9 clarifies that collecting contractual cash flows, or selling financial assets, or both, may not be the objective of the business model in itself. In particular, for the held to collect and for sale category, the business model is often to hold a portfolio of liquid assets in order to meet expected or unexpected commitments, or to fund anticipated acquisitions. Therefore, collecting contractual cash flows and/or selling financial assets may not be the objective of the business model in itself. In that case, the classification of the financial assets focuses not on the business model itself but rather on the way in which the assets are managed in order to meet the objectives of the business model. [*IFRS 9.B4.1.4A–B4.1.4C*]

7.4.130.30 Possible examples of such a business model include:
- a financial institution holding financial assets to meet its everyday liquidity needs; and
- an insurer holding financial assets to fund insurance contract liabilities. [*IFRS 9.B4.1.4A*]

7.4.130.40 A business model whose objective is achieved by both collecting contractual cash flows and selling financial assets will typically involve a greater frequency and value of sales than a held-to-collect business model. This is because selling financial assets is integral to achieving the business model's objective, rather than only incidental to it. However, there is no threshold for the frequency or amount of sales that may occur in this business model, because both activities are integral to achieving its objective. [*IFRS 9.B4.1.4B*]

EXAMPLE 8 – HOLDING INVESTMENTS IN ANTICIPATION OF CAPITAL EXPENDITURE

7.4.130.50 Company Z anticipates capital expenditure in five years. To be able to fund the expenditure, Z invests excess cash in short and long-term financial assets. Many of the financial assets have contractual lives that exceed Z's anticipated investment period.

7.4.130.60 Z intends to hold the financial assets but, when an opportunity arises, to sell them to invest in assets with a higher return. The portfolio's managers are remunerated based on the overall return from the portfolio of assets. Z's objective for managing the financial assets is therefore achieved by both collecting contractual cash flows and selling financial assets.

7.4.140   **OTHER BUSINESS MODELS**

7.4.140.10   Financial assets held in any other business model are measured at FVTPL. This category includes a portfolio that:
- is managed with the objective of realising cash flows through sale;
- is managed, and whose performance is evaluated, on a fair value basis (see 7.5.60); or
- meets the definition of held for trading. [*IFRS 9.B4.1.5–B4.1.6*]

7.4.140.20   A financial asset is held for trading if it is:
- acquired principally for the purpose of selling it in the near term;
- on initial recognition, part of a portfolio of identified financial instruments that are managed together and for which there is evidence of a recent actual pattern of short-term profit taking; or
- a derivative, except for a derivative that is a designated and effective hedging instrument. [*IFRS 9.A*]

7.4.140.30   'Trading' generally refers to the active and frequent buying and selling of an item. Financial assets and financial liabilities classified as held-for-trading are generally held with the objective of generating a profit from short-term fluctuations in price or dealer's margin. However, in our view these general characteristics are not a prerequisite for all financial instruments that the standard requires to be classified as held-for-trading. [*IFRS 9.BA6*]

7.4.140.40   The definition of 'held for trading' includes an asset or liability that is part of a portfolio of financial instruments that is managed together and for which there is evidence of trading activity. Although IFRS 9 does not define 'portfolio' explicitly, in this context it is possible to consider that a portfolio is a group of financial assets or financial liabilities that are managed as part of that group. [*IFRS 9.A, IG.B.11*]

7.4.140.50   The intention to profit from short-term fluctuations in price or dealer's margin need not be stated explicitly by the entity. Other evidence may indicate that a financial asset is being held for trading purposes. Evidence of trading may be inferred, based on the turnover and the average holding period of financial assets included in the portfolio. For example, an entity might buy and sell shares for a specific portfolio, based on movements in share prices. If this is done on a frequent basis, then the entity has established a pattern of trading for the purpose of generating profits from short-term fluctuations in price. Additional purchases of shares into this portfolio would also be considered as held-for-trading. [*IFRS 9.A, IG.B.11*]

7.4.140.60   In our view, if an entity makes an investment in a fund that is managed independently by a third party, then whether the entity should classify its investment in that fund as held-for-trading is not influenced by the fact that the underlying assets within the fund are actively traded. Therefore, the entity's investment in that fund would not meet the definition of an asset held for trading unless the entity actively trades in the investments that it holds in such funds. This situation may be contrasted with one in which an entity holds a portfolio of investments that are managed by a portfolio manager on the entity's behalf. In such cases, the entity determines the investment policies and procedures and, consequently, if the portfolio manager actively buys and sells instruments within the portfolio to generate short-term profits, then the instruments in the portfolio are considered held for trading and are classified as at FVTPL.

7.4.140.70   The standard does not define 'near term'. In our view, an entity should adopt a definition and apply a consistent approach to the definition used. If there is an intention to generate a profit from short-term fluctuations in price or dealer's margin, then the financial asset is classified appropriately as held-for-trading, even if the asset is not subsequently sold within a short period of time.

7.4.140.80   To generate short-term profits, traders may actively trade an asset's risks rather than the asset itself. For example, a bank may invest in a 30-day money market instrument for the purpose of generating profit from short-term fluctuations in the interest rate. When the favourable movement in the interest rate occurs, instead of selling the instrument the bank may issue an offsetting liability instrument. The 30-day money market instrument is classified as held-for-trading despite the fact that there is no intention to sell the instrument physically. The offsetting liability instrument is also classified as held-for-trading because it was issued for trading purposes and will be managed together with the related asset. [*IFRS 9.BA7*]

7.4.140.90   For a discussion of financial liabilities held for trading, see 7.5.30.

7.4.150   THE SPPI CRITERION

7.4.150.10   To determine whether a financial asset should be classified as measured at amortised cost or FVOCI, an entity assesses whether the cash flows from the financial asset represent, on specified dates, solely payments of principal and interest on the principal amount outstanding – i.e. the SPPI criterion. A financial asset that does not meet the SPPI criterion is always measured at FVTPL, unless it is an equity instrument for which an entity applies the OCI election (see 7.4.60 and 420). [*IFRS 9.4.1.2(b), 4.1.2A(b)*]

7.4.150.20   Contractual cash flows that meet the SPPI criterion are consistent with a basic lending arrangement. In such arrangements, consideration for the time value of money and credit risk are typically the most significant elements of interest. [*IFRS 9.B4.1.7A*]

7.4.150.30   The assessment of whether the SPPI criterion is met is made with reference to the currency in which the financial asset is denominated. In some cases, the par amount of a debt instrument is denominated in one currency and coupons are denominated in another currency – e.g. dual-currency bonds. It appears that a dual-currency bond would not meet the SPPI criterion because the coupons do not correspond to the currency in which the bond's par amount is denominated. [*IFRS 9.B4.1.8*]

7.4.150.40   An equity investment does not give rise to cash flows that are solely principal and interest. In addition, the dates of cash flows are not usually specified. Therefore, an equity investment is measured at fair value.

7.4.150.50   An entity does not separate embedded derivatives from host contracts that are financial assets in the scope of IFRS 9; instead, it assesses the hybrid financial instrument as a whole for classification under IFRS 9. [*IFRS 9.4.3.2*]

7.4.150.60   Many embedded derivative features may cause the entire hybrid financial asset to fail the SPPI criterion; this would result in the entire hybrid financial asset being classified as at FVTPL.

7.4.150.70   However, the existence of a derivative feature in a hybrid financial asset does not in itself preclude amortised cost classification of the financial asset if the feature is consistent with the SPPI criterion. For example, a prepayment or term extension option that is consistent with the SPPI criterion may allow the entire hybrid contract to be classified at amortised cost (see 7.4.190). [*IFRS 9.4.3.2, B4.1.10–4.1.11*]

EXAMPLE 9 – DERIVATIVE FEATURE IN HYBRID FINANCIAL ASSET

7.4.150.80   Company B has an investment in a convertible bond. Under the terms of the bond, the holder has the option to convert it into a fixed number of equity shares of the issuer. The convertible bond is analysed for classification in its entirety.

7.4.150.90   The presence of the conversion option causes the instrument to fail the SPPI criterion. This is because the embedded feature cannot be separated and the contractual terms of the convertible bond as a whole do not give rise solely to payments of principal and interest on the principal amount outstanding on the bond. Therefore, the convertible bond in its entirety is classified as at FVTPL. [*IFRS 9.B4.1.14*]

7.4.155   Deposit components separated from insurance contracts#

7.4.155.10   Some insurance contracts contain both an insurance component and a deposit component. In some cases, an insurer is required or permitted to unbundle those components (see 8.1.30). In assessing whether a deposit component that is unbundled meets the SPPI criterion, a question arises about which contractual terms are considered in the analysis. It appears that the SPPI assessment is based only on the contractual cash flows related to the unbundled deposit component. We believe that the contractual features that make up the unbundled insurance component should be ignored in the SPPI analysis. This is because each component is seen as a separate unit of account. Depending on how the contractual cash flows related to the deposit component are defined, the deposit component may or may not meet the SPPI criterion. [*IFRS 4.10–12*]

7.4.155.20   Lifetime mortgages (also sometimes referred to as 'equity release mortgages' or 'reverse mortgages') are loans secured against a property on which interest is accrued but not paid until the end of the mortgage along with the principal. This is usually when the borrower dies or moves into long-term care. The property is then sold and the proceeds are used to repay the mortgage balance, including the accrued interest. If the property is sold for more than the mortgage balance, then the excess is paid to the customer or their heirs. However, if there is a shortfall, then the loss is borne by the lender because these contracts include a 'no negative equity guarantee' clause – i.e. there is no recourse to the other assets of the borrower or their estate.

7.4.155.30   Lifetime mortgages generally qualify as insurance contracts if significant insurance risk is transferred (see 8.1.20.120). Under IFRS 4, the deposit component (the mortgage loan) may be unbundled from the insurance component (the 'no negative equity guarantee') if certain conditions are met. In our experience, there are various ways of determining how to unbundle the components under IFRS 4. These may include:
- a residual approach, under which the coupon payments on the mortgage are split in such a way that the fair value on initial recognition of the financial instrument component equals its par, with the remainder of the coupons being attributed to the insurance component as premiums; or

- attributing all of the coupon payments to the financial instrument component, which results in a fair value on initial recognition of the financial instrument component of greater than its par. This is because the coupons on lifetime mortgages are generally higher than the market rate of interest for vanilla mortgage loans. The financial instrument component is initially measured at this fair value and the excess of this amount above par is also regarded as a premium received for the insurance service. However, only the value of the expected pay-out under the 'no negative equity guarantee' is treated as the insurance component.

7.4.155.40   As such, the unbundled deposit component merely represents fixed and determinable payments through its life (even though the maturity of the deposit is linked to the death of the customer) and is assessed under IFRS 9.

7.4.157   FORTHCOMING REQUIREMENTS

7.4.157.10   IFRS 17 prohibits an entity to unbundle a component and account for it as a financial instrument unless it qualifies as a distinct investment component (as defined in IFRS 17) or is an embedded derivative that is required to be separated (see 8.1A.80). [*IFRS 17.11, 13, B31–B32*]

7.4.160   Principal

7.4.160.10   'Principal' is the fair value of the financial asset on initial recognition. However, the principal may change over time – e.g. if there are repayments of principal. [*IFRS 9.4.1.3(a), B4.1.7B*]

7.4.160.20   The definition of principal reflects the economics of the financial asset from the perspective of the current holder. This means that an entity assesses the asset's contractual cash flow characteristics by comparing the contractual cash flows to the amount that it actually invested. [*IFRS 9.BC4.182(a)*]

7.4.160.30   The principal may be different from the contractual par amount because principal is defined as the fair value on initial recognition. Prepayment features at par require careful analysis when instruments have been issued at a discount or premium to par (see 7.4.210–220). [*IFRS 9.BC4.187*]

7.4.170   Interest

7.4.170.10   'Interest' is consideration for the time value of money, for the credit risk associated with the principal amount outstanding during a particular period of time and for other basic lending risks (e.g. liquidity risk) and costs (e.g. administrative costs) as well as a profit margin that is consistent with a basic lending arrangement. [*IFRS 9.4.1.3, B4.1.7A, BC4.22*]

7.4.170.20   In extreme economic circumstances, interest can be negative if, for example:
- the holder of a financial asset either implicitly or explicitly pays a fee for the deposit of its money for a particular period of time; and
- that fee exceeds the consideration that the holder receives for the time value of money, credit risk and other basic lending risks and costs. [*IFRS 9.B4.1.7A*]

7.4.170.30   However, contractual features that introduce exposure to risks or volatility in the contractual cash flows that is unrelated to a basic lending arrangement, such as exposure to changes in equity prices or commodity prices, give rise to contractual cash flows that do not meet the SPPI criterion. [*IFRS 9.B4.1.7A*]

7.4.170.40   Leverage increases the variability of the contractual cash flows such that they do not have the economic characteristics of interest. Financial assets containing such features, for example, stand-alone options, forward contracts and swap contracts, do not meet the SPPI criterion. Another example of leverage is an interest rate that is set at two times LIBOR. [*IFRS 9.B4.1.9*]

7.4.170.45   It appears that if a financial asset's interest rate is determined by a floating rate multiplied by a positive factor less than one (e.g. LIBOR times 0.8), then it would not be leveraged. This is because it does not increase the variability of the contractual cash flows in a manner that is not consistent with a basic lending arrangement. An instrument with an indexation factor less than one can be explained as a combination of a floating rate asset and a fixed rate asset. If the interest rate is viewed as a benchmark component and a fixed component, then there is no need to perform a benchmark test (see 7.4.180.30) because the time value of money is not modified. Therefore, we believe that a financial asset with a positive indexation factor less than one would meet the SPPI criterion if there is no other element included in the contractual cash flows that is inconsistent with the SPPI criterion. [*IFRS 9.B4.1.13*]

7.4.170.50   Various types of loans, including inter-company loans, loans to employees, loans from governments and loans between suppliers and customers are interest-free or bear interest at below-market interest rates. It appears that these loans may meet the SPPI criterion. We believe that the fact that a loan has no contractual interest cash flows or bears interest at an off-market interest rate does not in itself cause failure of the SPPI criterion. This is because an entity measures the fair value of the financial instrument on initial recognition. This fair value on initial recognition is the principal amount of the financial instrument. As a result of the application of the effective interest method, even if there is no contractual interest, interest income is allocated over the expected life of the financial instrument. However, an interest-free or below-market rate loan often contains a prepayment feature that is exercisable at par and any prepayment features need to be analysed for compliance with the SPPI criterion (see 7.4.210–220). [*IFRS 9.4.1.3(a), B5.1.1, BC4.194*]

Ⓢ 7.4.170.60   It appears that intra-group loans granted on an interest-free basis with no fixed repayment terms and considered to be payable on demand by the lender (see 7.7.120.30–40) may meet the SPPI criterion. This is because the lender is not compensated for any other elements that are inconsistent with a basic lending arrangement. Also, the contract does not require the lender to keep the loan outstanding for any period so the contractual terms requiring no interest are not inconsistent with the SPPI criterion.

Ⓢ 7.4.170.70   Similarly, if an intra-group loan granted on an interest-free basis with no fixed repayment terms is repayable with one year's notice at the option of the lender and settlement is expected at the end of five years, then we believe that the loan could still meet the SPPI criterion. The fact that the lender does not charge or recognise additional interest if the loan is not called after one year does not change this assessment. Interest income is allocated over the expected life of the loan using the effective interest rate. The lender is not compensated for anything other than principal and interest. However, the impact of any prepayment features needs to be considered (see 7.4.210–220).

7.4.180   **Time value of money**

7.4.180.10   The 'time value of money' is the element of interest that provides consideration only for the passage of time and not for other risks and costs associated with holding the financial asset. To assess whether this element provides consideration only for the passage of time, an entity uses judgement and considers relevant factors including the currency in which the financial asset is denominated and the period for which the interest rate is set. Generally, there should be a link between the interest rate and the period for which the interest rate is set, because the appropriate rate for an instrument varies depending on the term for which the rate is set. In assessing the time value of money element, an entity also considers the currency in which the financial asset is denominated because interest rates vary by currency. [*IFRS 9.B4.1.9A, BC4.177(a)*]

7.4.180.20   IFRS 9 introduces the concept of 'modified time value of money', meaning that the relationship between the interest rate and the period for which the rate is set is imperfect. It gives the following examples:

- if the asset's interest rate is periodically reset but the frequency of that reset does not match the tenor of the interest rate – e.g. the interest rate resets every month to a one-year rate; or
- if the asset's interest rate is periodically reset to an average of particular short-term and long-term rates. [*IFRS 9.B4.1.9B*]

7.4.180.30   An entity assesses a modified time value of money feature to determine whether it meets the SPPI criterion. The objective of the assessment is to determine how different the undiscounted contractual cash flows could be from the undiscounted cash flows that would arise if the time value of money element was not modified (the benchmark cash flows). If the difference could be significant, then the SPPI criterion is not met. In some cases, an entity may be able to make this determination by performing only a qualitative assessment. In other cases, it may be necessary to perform a quantitative assessment (commonly referred to as the 'benchmark test'). In making the assessment, an entity has to consider all features that could affect future contractual cash flows. [*IFRS 9.B4.1.9C–B4.1.9D*]

7.4.180.35   A quantitative assessment could involve the projection of contractual cash flows and benchmark cash flows based on market implied forward rates and the determination of periodic and cumulative cash flow differences. The significance of these cash flow differences then needs to be assessed.

7.4.180.37   If an asset pays a variable market interest rate that is subject to a cap or floor, then it appears that the cap or floor is not a modified time value of money element and the existence of the cap or floor itself does not violate the SPPI criterion. IFRS 9 contains an example of a bond with a stated maturity date that pays a variable market interest rate that is capped. It explains that an instrument that is a combination of an instrument that has a fixed interest rate and an instrument that has a variable interest rate can have cash flows that meet the SPPI criterion because the contractual terms reduce cash flow variability by setting a limit on the variable interest rate. This suggests that a cap or floor is not regarded as a modification of the time value of money. [*IFRS 9.B4.1.13*]

7.4.180.38   If there is also a modified time value of money feature – e.g. a tenor mismatch – then we believe that the embedded cap or floor should be replicated in the benchmark cash flows for the purposes of any quantitative assessment. This is because the benchmark instrument should be designed with cash flows that would arise if the time value of money element was not modified. Therefore, all contractual features that are not a modification of the time value of money element, including the embedded cap or floor, should be replicated in the benchmark instrument. [*IFRS 9.B4.1.13*]

7.4.180.40   The relationship between the benchmark cash flows and the contractual cash flows could change over time. The entity considers the effect of the modified time value of money element in each reporting period and cumulatively over the life of the financial instrument. The term 'reporting period' is not defined in IFRS 9. It appears that an entity should choose an accounting policy, to be applied consistently, to interpret 'reporting period' for the purpose of performing the benchmark test as:

● financial reporting periods – Approach 1; or
● the reset period during which cash flow differences between the financial asset under assessment and the benchmark instrument may occur – Approach 2.

7.4.180.42   Under Approach 1, 'reporting period' is interpreted as not longer than the reporting period used to prepare financial statements.

7.4.180.43   Under Approach 2, 'reporting period' could be interpreted as a period that is shorter or longer than the entity's financial reporting period because cash flow differences between the financial asset under assessment and the benchmark instrument could occur in a period shorter or longer. For example, if the contractual interest rate is a one-month rate that is reset every six months, then a cash flow difference between the contractual one-month rate and the benchmark six-month rate can be observed twice a year. The maximum reporting period to be taken into consideration in this example would therefore be a six-month period. [*IFRS 9.B4.1.9C–B4.1.9D, IAS 1.36, 34.4*]

7.4.180.45   In assessing the significance of the modified time value of money element, an entity considers only reasonably possible scenarios, rather than every possible scenario. With the exception of regulated rates (see 7.4.180.100), the reason for the interest rate being set in a particular way is irrelevant to the analysis. [*IFRS 9.B4.1.9D*]

7.4.180.50   The assessment of the modified time value of money element requires judgement to:

● identify the characteristics of a benchmark instrument;
● identify reasonably possible scenarios; and
● determine whether the undiscounted contractual cash flows on the financial asset could (or could not) be significantly different from the undiscounted benchmark cash flows. [*IFRS 9.BC4.178*]

7.4.180.51   In some cases, the frequency with which coupons are paid on an instrument may differ from the frequency with which the coupons are reset. A question arises in this case about what the reset date of the benchmark instrument is for the purposes of the quantitative assessment. It appears that the reset date of the benchmark instrument should be the same as for the financial asset under assessment. This is because the benchmark instrument should have identical contractual terms and identical credit risk except that the interest rate is reset with a frequency that matches the tenor of the interest rate. For example, consider an instrument with a contractual interest rate that is indexed to a published one-month rate and reset every six months and on which coupons are paid every three months. The reset date of the benchmark instrument is therefore every six months – i.e. a six-month benchmark interest rate that is reset every six months but is paid every three months should be used in the benchmark test. [*IFRS 9.B4.1.9C, B4.1.13*]

7.4.180.53   It appears that several approaches may be followed to determine whether the differences between contractual and benchmark cash flows are 'significant' – e.g. a principal-based approach, a coupon-based approach or a mixture of the two. This is because the basis for assessing 'significant' is not defined in IFRS 9. We believe that an entity should select an approach and apply it consistently for all similar assets.

EXAMPLE 10A – MODIFIED TIME VALUE OF MONEY – DETERMINING THE DIFFERENCE BETWEEN CONTRACTUAL AND BENCHMARK CASH FLOWS ON A CUMULATIVE BASIS

7.4.180.55   Company S makes an assessment of the modified time value of money element for each reporting period and cumulatively over the life of the instrument. S determines that the following information represents a particular reasonably possible scenario when making the assessment on a cumulative basis:
● cumulative contractual cash flows – coupons – 35;
● cumulative benchmark cash flows – coupons – 30; and
● principal (invested on initial recognition, repayable on maturity) – 100.

7.4.180.57   S determines the following ratios for comparison with a threshold that it has predetermined for the cumulative analysis.

BASIS	RATIO
Absolute basis (principal-based)	(30 - 35) / 100 = 5.0%
Relative basis (coupon-based)	(30 - 35) / 30 = 16.6%
Mixed basis (principal- and coupon-based)	(30 - 35) / (100 + 30) = 3.8%

EXAMPLE 10B – MODIFIED TIME VALUE OF MONEY – INTEREST RATE RESETS MONTHLY

7.4.180.60   Company X holds an asset with a variable interest rate that resets every month to a one-year rate. To assess the modified time value of money feature, X compares the financial asset with a financial asset with identical contractual terms and identical credit risk – except that the variable interest rate is reset monthly to a one-month rate.

7.4.180.65   If the modified time value of money element could result in undiscounted contractual cash flows that are significantly different from the undiscounted benchmark cash flows, then the SPPI criterion is not met. [*IFRS 9.B4.1.9C*]

EXAMPLE 10C – MODIFIED TIME VALUE OF MONEY – CONSTANT MATURITY BOND

7.4.180.70   Company Y holds a constant-maturity bond with a five-year term and a variable interest rate that is reset semi-annually to a five-year rate. The interest rate curve at the time of initial recognition is such that the difference between a five-year rate and a semi-annual rate is insignificant. The benchmark instrument would be the one that resets semi-annually to a semi-annual interest rate.

7.4.180.75   The fact that the difference between a five-year rate and a semi-annual rate is insignificant at the time of initial recognition does not in itself enable Y to conclude that the modification of the time value of money results in contractual cash flows that are not significantly different from a benchmark instrument. Instead, Y considers whether the relationship between the five-year interest rate and the semi-annual interest rate could change over the life of the instrument such that the undiscounted contractual cash flows over the life of the instrument could be significantly different from the undiscounted benchmark cash flows. [*IFRS 9.B4.1.9D, B4.1.13*]

EXAMPLE 10D – MODIFIED TIME VALUE OF MONEY – PEGGED CURRENCIES

7.4.180.80   Bank D holds an instrument with principal and coupons denominated in Hong Kong dollars. However, the coupons are calculated based on US dollar LIBOR instead of HIBOR. The Hong Kong dollar is pegged to the US dollar (i.e. the exchange rate between the two is confined within a very narrow band).

7.4.180.85   If the principal and coupons are denominated in the same currency, but the currency of the reference interest rate differs from the currency of the instrument, then there is a modification of the time value of money element. D considers all reasonably possible scenarios individually to determine if there could be a significant difference between the contractual undiscounted cash flows and the undiscounted cash flows that would arise if there was no modification. D begins by assessing whether there is a sufficient link between the currency of denomination and the currency of the reference interest rate. [*IFRS 9.B4.1.9A, B4.1.9D*]

7.4.180.90   Because the currencies are pegged, D assesses whether it is reasonably possible that the peg could break during the life of the instrument. If it is reasonably possible that the peg could break, then there is no sufficient link between the currencies. Therefore, D determines based on a qualitative assessment that the SPPI criterion is not met. If D concludes that it is not reasonably possible that the peg could break during the life of the instrument, then D performs a quantitative benchmark test to determine whether the modified time value of money feature is significant. [*IFRS 9.B4.1.9B*]

7.4.180.95   Whether a scenario is considered 'reasonably possible' also depends on the maturity of the instrument – e.g. the shorter the maturity, the less likely it is that a break in the peg will occur over the life of the instrument.

7.4.180.100   In some jurisdictions, the government or a regulatory authority sets interest rates – e.g. as part of a broad macroeconomic policy, or to encourage entities to invest in a particular sector of the economy. In some of these cases, the objective of the time value of money element is not to provide consideration for only the passage of time. In spite of the general requirements for the modified time value of money, a regulated interest rate is considered to be a proxy for the time value of money if it:

- provides consideration that is broadly consistent with the passage of time; and
- does not introduce exposure to risks or volatility in cash flows that are inconsistent with a basic lending arrangement. [*IFRS 9.B4.1.9E*]

EXAMPLE 11 – REGULATED INTEREST RATES

> 7.4.180.110   Investor X places deposits on special savings accounts. The interest rate is determined by the central bank and the government according to a formula that reflects protection against inflation and remuneration that incentivises entities to use these accounts. This is because legislation requires some of the amounts collected to be lent to a government agency, which uses the proceeds for social programmes.
>
> 7.4.180.120   The time value element of interest on these accounts may not provide consideration only for the passage of time. However, X concludes that the contractual cash flows do not introduce risks or volatility that are inconsistent with a basic lending arrangement. Therefore, these savings accounts meet the SPPI criterion. [*IFRS 9.BC4.179–BC4.180*]

7.4.190   **Contractual provisions that change the contractual cash flows**

7.4.190.10   The contractual cash flows of some financial assets may change over their lives. For example, an asset may have a floating interest rate. Also, in many cases an asset can be prepaid or its term extended. For such assets, an entity determines whether the contractual cash flows that could arise over the life of the instrument meet the SPPI criterion. It does so by assessing the contractual cash flows that could arise both before and after the change in contractual cash flows. [*IFRS 9.B4.1.10, B4.1.12*]

7.4.190.20   IFRS 9 provides examples of contractual terms that change the timing or amount of contractual cash flows and meet the SPPI criterion. [*IFRS 9.B4.1.11*]

EXAMPLE	KEY FEATURES
Variable interest rate	A variable interest rate that consists of consideration for: • the time value of money; • the credit risk associated with the principal amount outstanding during a particular period of time – this may be a fixed credit margin determined on initial recognition; • other basic lending risks (e.g. liquidity risk) and costs (e.g. administrative costs); and • a profit margin.
Prepayment feature	A prepayment feature: • that permits the issuer (i.e. the debtor) to prepay a debt instrument or permits the holder (i.e. the creditor) to put the debt instrument back to the issuer before maturity; and • whose prepayment amount substantially represents unpaid amounts of principal and interest on the principal amount outstanding, which may include reasonable additional compensation for the early termination of the contract.

EXAMPLE	KEY FEATURES
Term extension feature	A term extension feature that: • permits the issuer or the holder to extend the contractual term of a debt instrument – i.e. an extension option; and • results in contractual cash flows during the extension period that are solely payments of principal and interest on the principal amount outstanding, which may include reasonable additional compensation for the extension of the contract.

7.4.200 *Variable interest rates*

7.4.200.10   An interest rate that is either fixed or variable may be consistent with the SPPI criterion. The component of a variable interest rate that represents compensation for credit risk may be fixed on initial recognition. However, in our experience compensation for credit risk is not always fixed at inception; it can vary in response to perceived changes in the creditworthiness of the borrower – e.g. if covenants are breached. If there are variations in the contractual cash flows of an instrument related to credit risk, then entities consider whether the variation can be regarded as compensation for credit risk and therefore whether the instrument may meet the SPPI criterion. In our view, it is not necessary for such a feature to reset to a current market credit spread to meet the SPPI criterion.

7.4.200.20   Some loans may include price ratcheting clauses. Under these clauses, the contractual interest rate is reset in accordance with a scale of predefined rates on the occurrence of one or more predefined trigger events that are linked to a deterioration in the borrower's credit risk, such as a specified gearing ratio of the borrower or interest cover of the borrower. These clauses are included to avoid the need to renegotiate the loan when the credit risk of the borrower changes. It appears that the SPPI criterion is met if the rates set at inception compensate the lender for increased credit risk and there are no other features that are inconsistent with a basic lending arrangement. In this case, the performance-based term – e.g. a gearing ratio or interest coverage ratio – is a reasonable proxy for the variation in credit risk of the financial asset.

7.4.200.30   An instrument whose interest rate is reset to a higher rate if the debtor misses a particular payment may meet the SPPI criterion because of the relationship between missed payments and an increase in credit risk. [*IFRS 9.B4.1.10*]

7.4.200.40   The cash flows in 7.4.200.20–30 can be contrasted with other circumstances in which the contractual cash flows are indexed to the debtor's performance but do not compensate the lender for changes in the credit risk of the instrument (e.g. interest payments equal to a percentage of the debtor's earnings or EBITDA). In these cases, the contractual feature would reflect a return that is inconsistent with a basic lending arrangement and would not meet the SPPI criterion. [*IFRS 9.B4.1.10, B4.1.13*]

7.4.200.50   A floating rate non-prepayable asset may be acquired at a deep discount to its stated par amount, either on original issue or in a secondary market. The discount usually represents a charge for credit risk and liquidity risk because investors typically demand a higher effective yield than the stated contractual interest rate due to credit and liquidity risk. A question arises whether the discount results in a leverage feature that would cause the instrument to fail the SPPI criterion. Leverage is a contractual cash flow characteristic of some financial assets which increases the variability of the contractual cash flows with the result that they do not have the economic characteristics of interest. The question arises in this case because the coupons are calculated by multiplying the stated floating interest rate by the stated par amount of the asset, which is greater than the principal amount as defined in IFRS 9. The way in which the coupons are calculated therefore results in increased variability in the contractual cash flows. [*IFRS 9.B4.1.9*]

7.4.200.60   It appears that if interest is payable based on an unleveraged floating rate applied to the par amount, the instrument contractually requires the borrower to repay the entire par amount and there are no other problematic features that would cause the instrument to fail the SPPI criterion, then the instrument would be consistent with a basic lending arrangement. This is because leverage has not been incorporated into the terms of the instrument and the discount reflects what market participants would demand for an increase in credit and/or liquidity risk. For a discussion of prepayment features at par, see 7.4.220. [*IFRS 9.B4.1.11(a)*]

EXAMPLE 12 – VARIABLE RATE INSTRUMENT ACQUIRED AT A DISCOUNT

7.4.200.70   Company X acquires a floating rate non-prepayable bond on the bond's issuance date at 80. The bond has a par amount of 100 and the borrower is contractually required to pay 100 on maturity. The bond pays interest on the par amount based on three-month LIBOR, reset every three months. The discount of 20 exists because investors demand a higher effective yield than the stated contractual interest rate due to credit risk and liquidity risk.

7.4.200.80   In this example, there is increased variability in contractual cash flows because interest is calculated by multiplying the three-month LIBOR rate by 100, which is greater than the principal of 80. However, the borrower is required to repay 100 on maturity. The bond therefore meets the SPPI criterion on the basis that leverage has not been incorporated into the instrument and the discount reflects what market participants would demand for an increase in credit and/or liquidity risk. [*IFRS 9.B4.1.11(a)*]

7.4.200.90   Modifying the fact pattern, if the borrower was contractually required to pay X only 80 on maturity, but with interest based on 100, then we believe that the bond would not meet the SPPI criterion because leverage would exist.

7.4.210   *Prepayment and extension features#*

7.4.210.10   The guidance for prepayment features (see 7.4.190.20) requires the prepayment amount to substantially represent 'unpaid amounts of principal and interest on the principal amount outstanding, which may include reasonable additional compensation for the early termination of the contract'. IFRS 9 does not discuss how the term 'unpaid amounts of principal and interest on the principal amount outstanding' should be interpreted or how these amounts should be calculated in this context. [*IFRS 9.B4.1.11(b)*]

7.4.210.20   It appears that to apply the guidance for prepayment features in 7.4.190.20, it is necessary to consider what the 'unpaid amounts of principal and interest' and the prepayment amount would be at each date on which the prepayment feature is exercisable to determine for all cases whether the prepayment amount substantially represents the former. We believe that determining 'unpaid amounts of principal and interest' requires consideration of the economic characteristics of the contract and may require judgement. In particular, it may be necessary to determine whether individual cash flows required by the contract (in the absence of the prepayment feature) represent payments of interest or repayments or advances of principal and how rights to interest are considered to arise over time. For example, for assets that are originated or purchased at a premium above the par amount repayable on maturity, contractual coupons (i.e. what the contract labels as interest) may represent in part repayments of principal for the purpose of evaluating the SPPI criterion.

7.4.210.30   One possible way to estimate 'unpaid amounts of principal and interest' would be to apply a methodology similar to the effective interest method (see 7.7.270). However, the starting point would be the fair value of the financial instrument on initial recognition, which excludes transaction costs, whereas the effective interest method includes transaction costs related to the acquisition of a financial asset in the calculation of an effective interest rate. Also, except for floating rate assets that reprice based on movements in market rates of interest, the effective interest method generally results in a single effective interest rate that applies across the expected life of a financial asset, whereas in some cases it may be appropriate for SPPI assessment purposes to represent the accrual of interest at different rates across time to best reflect the economic characteristics of the instrument (e.g. if a higher coupon rate is payable following exercise of an extension option).

7.4.210.40   It appears that it is possible that a loan acquired at a premium and prepayable only at a specific point in time following acquisition can meet the SPPI criterion. This is because if the premium is effectively repaid through coupon payments during the period before the prepayment date, then at the time when the prepayment option can and is expected to be exercised, a fixed prepayment amount may equal unpaid amounts of principal and interest. In this case, for SPPI assessment purposes, the implicit interest rate is different for the period before and the period after the prepayment date (assuming that the loan is not prepaid).

EXAMPLE 13 – ACQUISITION AT A PREMIUM TO PAR AMOUNT – LOAN ACQUIRED IN A BUSINESS COMBINATION

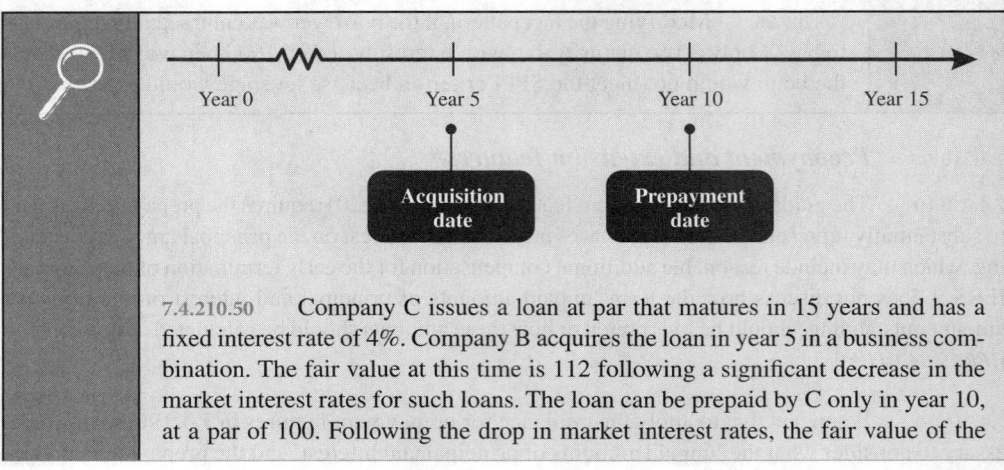

7.4.210.50   Company C issues a loan at par that matures in 15 years and has a fixed interest rate of 4%. Company B acquires the loan in year 5 in a business combination. The fair value at this time is 112 following a significant decrease in the market interest rates for such loans. The loan can be prepaid by C only in year 10, at a par of 100. Following the drop in market interest rates, the fair value of the prepayment feature at the date of the business combination was significant. Market participants valuing the loan at the date of acquisition would assume that it is highly likely that the prepayment option would be exercised at the prepayment date – i.e. 5 years after the acquisition.

7.4.210.60   The principal on initial recognition of the loan by B is 112, but this amount changes over time as a result of payments received. In this case, B determines that the premium of 12 relates to the first 5 years and that the coupon payments would represent in economic terms partly interest and partly repayments of principal. At the time when the prepayment option can and is expected to be exercised, the unpaid amount of principal will be 100 and the exercise price of the prepayment option will also be 100.

7.4.210.70   The loan therefore meets the SPPI criterion. [*IFRS 9.B4.1.11(b)*]

7.4.210.80   Modifying the fact pattern, if the prepayment option was exercisable at par at any time after acquisition of the loan but only in the event of a specified change in tax law that is considered very unlikely, then the prepayment amount would not substantially represent unpaid amounts of principal and interest. This is because the contingent event could occur at any time and the principal amount is currently 112 and the prepayment amount is 100. The SPPI criterion would therefore probably not be met. However, the loan may still be eligible for classification at amortised cost or FVOCI if the fair value of the prepayment feature is insignificant on initial recognition, because the loan was acquired at a premium and the prepayment amount substantially represents the contractual par amount and accrued contractual interest (see 7.4.220).

EXAMPLE 14 – TERM EXTENSION OPTIONS

7.4.210.90   Company D places an extendable deposit with Bank B by paying the principal amount to B. B is required to repay this principal amount at maturity. The terms of the extendable deposit include an initial five-year tenor and a fixed coupon rate agreed at inception. At the end of five years, B has the unconditional option to extend the deposit at the same fixed coupon rate for an additional five years. B is likely to choose to exercise the extension option only if the then-current market interest rate for five-year deposits is greater than the rate fixed in the contract.

7.4.210.100   In this example, B concludes that the contractual cash flows during the extension period are solely payments of principal and interest on the principal amount outstanding. This is because the coupon rate is fixed at inception of the deposit and is not leveraged. Furthermore, the contractual terms require payment at inception and repayment at maturity of the principal amount; they contain no other cash flow requirements or contingent features (see 7.4.210.150). [*IFRS 9.B4.1.10*]

EXAMPLE 15 – PREPAYMENT AT FAIR VALUE

7.4.210.110   Company M acquires a bond at par. The bond contains a call option that allows the issuer to prepay at the fair value of the bond on the date of exercise – i.e. the prepayment amount represents the present value of the future contractual principal and interest payments that would be due on the bond discounted at a current market rate.

7.4.210.120   In this example, the prepayment amount does not represent unpaid amounts of principal and interest. For example, the fair value of the bond may fall below the principal amount (in this case, the par amount) plus accrued interest – e.g. because of the deterioration in creditworthiness of the issuer. Interest includes consideration for the time value of money and for the credit risk associated with the principal amount outstanding during a particular period of time. If the prepayment amount is less than the principal amount plus accrued interest, then this is not consistent with the requirement that the holder be compensated for the time value of money and credit risk during the period the bond is in issue. The prepayment amount cannot be considered as providing additional compensation because it is less than the principal amount plus accrued interest – i.e. the holder suffers a loss on prepayment. [*IFRS 9.B4.1.11*]

7.4.210.125   Judgement is required in assessing whether a prepayment amount includes 'reasonable additional compensation for the early termination of the contract' because 'reasonable' is not defined in IFRS 9. The assessment may differ depending on whether:

- the prepayment penalty is fixed (e.g. 10 percent of the original contractual par amount) or variable and determined based on a formula (e.g. the present value of the remaining cash flows at the prepayment date discounted using a market rate, which may or may not include credit and other relevant spreads); and/or
- prepayment is at the option of the borrower or the lender.

7.4.210.127   The starting assumption is that the prepayment feature is genuine because non-genuine features would not usually be included in the contract. The fact that a termination penalty is regarded as common in the entity's jurisdiction is not on its own sufficient to determine that it is reasonable compensation for early termination. It appears that an entity should assess the nature and amount of the penalty based on the instrument's specific contractual cash flow characteristics. We believe that this assessment should include but not be limited to determining whether there is any exposure to non-SPPI risks – i.e. for the termination penalty to comply with the SPPI criterion, any variability should be based solely on the time value of money, credit risk, other basic lending risks and costs, as well as a profit margin. For example, if the penalty was indexed to equity prices or commodity prices, then it is not reasonable compensation. [*IFRS 9.B4.1.7A, BC4.178*]

7.4.210.130   There may be different considerations depending on whether the penalty is fixed or variable. In particular, for fixed penalties it appears that if the amount is insignificant relative to the outstanding principal and interest amounts, then it would generally be regarded as compliant with the SPPI criterion. This is because the prepayment amount would substantially represent the unpaid principal (or par amount) and accrued interest (see 7.4.210.10 and 220.10). In other cases, the entity needs to assess what the fixed penalty is designed to compensate for (e.g. administrative costs).

7.4.210.135   The evaluation of whether a penalty is reasonable is further affected by whether the lender or the borrower has the option to terminate the contract. For lender prepayment options, it appears that penalties may be seen as reasonable if they are designed to compensate the lender for:
- the impact of changes in market benchmark interest rates;
- an increase in fair value associated with changes in interest rates (which include credit and other relevant spreads); or
- other economic losses – e.g. break costs incurred in terminating a plain vanilla interest rate swap on prepayment of the loan that do not expose the lender to non-SPPI risks such as foreign exchange rate risk or equity price risk.

7.4.210.137   Conversely, penalties may not be reasonable for lender prepayment options if they could potentially result in large gains for the lender that cannot be justified as compensation. For example, this can be the case if the loan is long-term, early repayment is made shortly after advancing the loan and the prepayment amount is calculated by discounting the remaining contractual cash flows at the prepayment date using the market benchmark interest rate at the prepayment date. In this example, the penalty cannot be justified as compensation, and therefore would not be reasonable compensation for early termination because the lender would effectively receive the future credit spread even though it has chosen no longer to be exposed to the credit risk of the borrower.

7.4.210.140   For borrower prepayment options, it appears that there is more flexibility in determining what is 'reasonable' if the penalty would be voluntarily incurred by the borrower choosing to exercise the option. Penalties that could result in potentially large gains for the lender at or near origination may be reasonable in some circumstances. For example, the instrument described in 7.4.210.137 may be viewed as reasonable on the basis that the lender is receiving compensation (in this instance, for contractual interest payments that will not be received) as a result of the borrower's decision to terminate and the borrower can avoid the penalty.

7.4.210.145   However, for borrower prepayment options, despite the fact that there is more flexibility in determining what is 'reasonable', the terms of the penalty (including the magnitude of compensation) still need to be assessed. We believe that judgement should be applied to assess whether the penalty is designed to compensate the lender for the impact of the prepayment. Reasonable compensation for the lender could include, but is not limited to, interest payments that will not be received or other profits that will not be earned, costs incurred by the lender, reimbursement for economic losses or the cost of a replacement asset.

7.4.210.150   In some cases, contractual cash flows may change on the occurrence of a contingent event. In these cases, an entity assesses the nature of the contingent event. Although the nature of the contingent event is not in itself a determining factor in assessing whether the contractual cash flows meet the SPPI criterion, it may be an indicator. [*IFRS 9.B4.1.10*]

EXAMPLE 16 – CONTINGENT MANDATORY PREPAYMENT TERMS

7.4.210.160   Company X issues a bond to Company Y at par. It is mandatory for X to redeem the bond at par plus accrued unpaid interest if a specified default event occurs. The default events relate to a credit downgrade or loan covenant violations. If a default event occurs, then the prepayment amount substantially represents unpaid amounts of principal and interest on the principal amount outstanding.

7.4.210.170   In this example, the bond meets the SPPI criterion because the mandatory redemption feature protects the holder against credit deterioration of the issuer. [*IFRS 9.B4.1.10*]

EXAMPLE 17 – CONTINGENT PREPAYMENT FEATURE

7.4.210.180   Structured Entity SE issues a single tranche (Note N) to Investor M for 100. Note N is redeemable in five years at 100 and bears a fixed rate of interest. SE also holds a convertible bond and, in return for a premium, has written an equity call option to Bank B, which is the sponsor of SE. The written call option offsets the equity price risk embedded in the convertible bond.

7.4.210.190   Under the terms of Note N, SE is required to prepay Note N if and when B exercises its call option. The prepayment amount is 100 plus accrued interest.

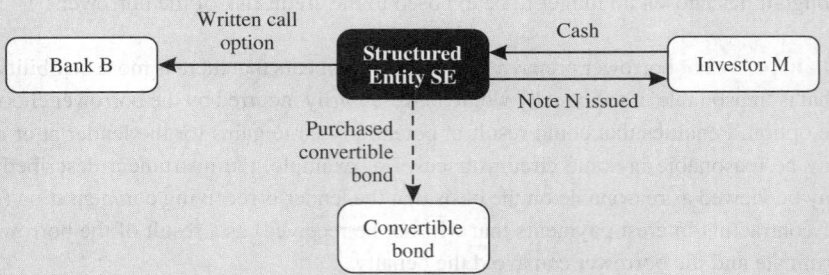

7.4.210.200   In this case, it appears that M's investment in Note N satisfies the SPPI criterion and that the nature of the contingent event is not relevant to that assessment. This is because:
- the interest receivable is set as a fixed rate of return for the period during which the instrument is outstanding, and the amount paid on termination (i.e. either on the date of prepayment or at the end of five years) substantially represents principal plus accrued interest;
- the premium received by SE from B is used by SE to add a margin to Note N. However, interest may include compensation for liquidity risk and a profit margin; and
- SE's other assets and liabilities (i.e. the convertible bond and the written call option) do not introduce exposure to risks or variability in the amount of

contractual cash flows that are inconsistent with a basic lending arrangement because the written call option offsets the risk of the equity call option embedded in the convertible bond.

7.4.220   *Exception for certain prepayment features at par*

7.4.220.10   If a financial asset would otherwise meet the SPPI criterion, but fails to do so only as a result of a contractual term that permits or requires prepayment before maturity, or permits or requires the holder to put the instrument back to the issuer, then the asset can be measured at amortised cost or FVOCI if:

- the relevant business model condition is satisfied (see 7.4.100 and 130);
- the entity acquired or originated the financial asset at a premium or discount to the contractual par amount;
- the prepayment amount substantially represents the contractual par amount and accrued (but unpaid) contractual interest, which may include reasonable compensation for early termination; and
- on initial recognition of the financial asset, the fair value of the prepayment feature is insignificant. [*IFRS 9.B4.1.12*]

7.4.220.20   IFRS 9 does not define the term 'contractual par amount'. If the contract does not define the term 'contractual par amount', then it appears that the 'contractual par amount' could be interpreted as either the nominal amount or the original issue price.

EXAMPLE 18 – CONTRACTUAL PAR AMOUNT FOR A ZERO-COUPON BOND

7.4.220.30   Company X issues for 80 a zero-coupon bond with a nominal amount of 100 and a maturity of four years. The contract includes a call option for X that is exercisable one year after issuance at an exercise price of 85. The contract does not refer to a 'contractual par amount' but describes 100 payable at maturity as the nominal amount.

7.4.220.40   Investor Y acquires the bond six months after its issuance for 60 due to a deterioration in credit risk of X. In analysing whether the bond meets the conditions to be measured at amortised cost or at FVOCI, we believe that Y can view the 'contractual par amount' as either the nominal amount of 100 or the original issue price of 80.

7.4.220.50   If the contractual par amount is considered to be 80, then Y may conclude that the prepayment amount of 85 substantially represents the contractual par amount plus accrued (but unpaid) contractual interest. [*IFRS 9.B4.1.12(b)*]

7.4.220.55   The fair value of the prepayment option may be determined by comparing the fair value of an otherwise identical loan without the prepayment option with the fair value of the same actual loan with the prepayment option (see 7.5.70.40). The fair value of the prepayment option cannot be determined by comparing the fair value on acquisition with the contractual par amount.

7.4.220.60   Some instruments may contain prepayment features that may qualify under this exception. Examples are:
- purchased credit-impaired assets acquired at a deep discount to par; and
- financial assets originated at below-market rates – e.g. a loan provided to a customer as a marketing incentive such that the loan's fair value on initial recognition is significantly below the contractual par amount advanced. [*IFRS 9.BC4.193–BC4.194*]

7.4.220.70   In these cases, the borrower may have the contractual ability to prepay at par, but the contractual prepayment feature would have an insignificant fair value because it is very unlikely that a prepayment will occur. [*IFRS 9.BC4.193–BC4.194*]

7.4.220.80   If an entity purchases credit-impaired assets acquired at a deep discount to par, then the prepayment is very unlikely because the financial asset is impaired and so the borrower is unlikely to have funds from which it could prepay the asset. [*IFRS 9.BC4.193*]

7.4.220.90   If an entity originates financial assets at below-market rates, then it is very unlikely that the customer will choose to prepay, because the interest rate is below-market and the financing is advantageous. Consequently, the amount at which the loan can be prepaid does not introduce variability that is inconsistent with a basic lending arrangement. [*IFRS 9.BC4.194*]

7.4.220.100   The above examples deal with circumstances in which a financial asset is originated or purchased at a discount to the par amount. However, the exception is equally relevant for assets that are originated or purchased at a premium. Possible examples might include:
- a fixed rate bond that is acquired at a substantial premium to par, but that is redeemable at par only at the option of the holder; or
- a bond that is acquired at a substantial premium to par but that is prepayable at par at the option of the issuer only in the event of a specified change in tax law that is considered very unlikely. [*IFRS 9.BC4.195*]

7.4.220.110   For some fixed rate retail mortgage or other loans, the borrower may have a prepayment option that is exercisable at the contractual par amount plus accrued unpaid interest at any time. If market interest rates fall, then this increases the likelihood that borrowers may exercise their prepayment options. However, not all borrowers act 'rationally' in an economic sense and they may not exercise their prepayment options even when it appears to be in their financial interest to do so. This reduces the fair value of the prepayment option, which is based on market participant views of the probability and possible timing of prepayment. If a loan is acquired or originated at a premium to the par amount and is prepayable at the par amount, and the fair value of the prepayment feature is significant on initial recognition, then the loan does not meet the exception in 7.4.220.10. [*IFRS 9.B4.1.12*]

EXAMPLE 19 – RETAIL MORTGAGE LOANS PREPAYABLE AT PAR

7.4.220.120   Bank B has a portfolio of fixed rate retail mortgage loans, each with a par value of 100. B acquired one of these loans in a business combination. Because the market interest rates have declined since origination of the loans, B acquired it at a premium – i.e. for 112. Borrower C can prepay the loan at the contractual par amount (i.e. 100) plus accrued unpaid interest at any time. Although the interest rate on the mortgage loan is above the current market interest rate that C would pay if C were to refinance with a new lender, historical experience and current expectations are that a significant proportion of customers, like C, do not seek a refinancing in these circumstances but will continue with the current product.

7.4.220.130   B determines the fair value of the prepayment option by comparing the fair value of an otherwise identical loan without the prepayment option with the fair value of the loan to C. The fair value of an otherwise identical loan without the prepayment option is 125. The fair value of the loan to C, which includes market-consistent assumptions about the likelihood of C exercising its prepayment option, is 112. Under this method, the fair value of the prepayment option is 13. B determines that the fair value of the prepayment feature of 13 is significant on initial recognition, and the loan therefore fails to qualify for measurement at amortised cost or FVOCI.

7.4.225   FORTHCOMING REQUIREMENTS

7.4.225.10   *Prepayment Features with Negative Compensation – Amendments to IFRS 9* allow particular financial assets with prepayment features that may result in negative compensation – e.g. the lender receives less than the par amount and accrued interest and effectively compensates the borrower for the borrower's early termination of the contract – to be measured at amortised cost or at FVOCI (subject to the business model assessment). Before the amendments, these instruments were measured at FVTPL because the SPPI criterion would not be met when the party that chooses to terminate the contract early may receive compensation for doing so.

7.4.225.20   The amendments clarify that irrespective of the event or circumstance that causes the early termination of the contract, either party may pay or receive reasonable compensation for that early termination. The amendments remove the requirement for the compensation to be 'additional'. Accordingly, a prepayment amount that is less than the unpaid amounts of principal and interest (or less than the contractual par amount plus accrued interest) may meet the SPPI criterion if it is determined to include reasonable compensation for early termination.

7.4.230   *Other contractual provisions that change the contractual cash flows*

7.4.240   *Lender's own funding costs*

7.4.240.10   In our experience, a lender's own funding costs often influence the interest rates charged to borrowers – e.g. home loan rates. A contract may specify that the lender is permitted to pass an increase in these costs on to the borrower or that these costs can only be passed on if they arise from the occurrence of a contingent event.

7.4.240.20   In our view, it may be appropriate to consider the lender's specific cost of funding (or changes therein) as a component of a return on a basic lending arrangement. This is because:

- IFRS 9 envisages the lender's own funding costs by referring to costs *associated* with holding the financial asset when describing the components of interest – i.e. this phrase is not limited to the direct costs of holding the financial asset; and
- interest can include a profit margin that is consistent with a basic lending arrangement and additional funding costs will affect the lender's profit margin. Therefore, the lender may seek to preserve its profit margin by passing on the increased costs to the borrower. [*IFRS 9.B4.1.7A, BC4.182(b)*]

7.4.240.30   For example, a clause that allows a bank to pass on its costs of wholesale funding or retail deposits may be consistent with a basic lending arrangement. However, a clause that allows the bank to pass on costs or losses related to derivative trading activities is not consistent with a basic lending arrangement. Similarly, the introduction of exposure to risks or variability that are unrelated to lending (e.g. exposure to equity or commodity price risk) is not consistent with a basic lending arrangement.

7.4.240.40   If a bank has discretion to adjust interest rates in response to a change in its funding costs, then the bank may be subject to various constraints – e.g. consumer regulation, borrower prepayment options and competition in the market. We believe that judgement is required in assessing whether constraints on the bank's ability to change the rate are sufficient to ensure that the contractual cash flows remain consistent with those of a basic lending arrangement. For a further discussion of the assessment of SPPI when a lending bank can adjust interest rates, see 7.4.280–285.

7.4.250   *Cross-selling clauses*

7.4.250.10   Some bank loans include 'cross-selling clauses' under which the interest rate is reduced prospectively if the borrower agrees to enter into other specified transactions or business arrangements with the bank. Under these clauses, the credit risk profile of the loan does not change but the bank expects to profit from the other business obtained from the borrower. This may include a reallocation of some overheads from the existing loan to the new business. It appears that such an embedded cross-selling clause may be consistent with the SPPI criterion if it in substance represents a reduction in the profit margin or compensation for administrative or similar costs associated with holding the financial asset (i.e. a reduction in components of interest as identified in 7.4.170.10) and the other cash flows of the financial asset are solely payments of principal and interest. However, if cross-selling clauses impose significant increases in interest rates or penalties if the customer does not purchase other products, then judgement is required to decide whether contractual cash flows could be introduced that would be inconsistent with a basic lending arrangement. [*IFRS 9.4.1.3, B4.1.7A*]

7.4.260   *Inflation-linked bonds*

7.4.260.10   A bond with a stated maturity and payments of principal and interest that are linked to an unleveraged inflation index of the currency in which the instrument is issued and for which the principal amount is protected may meet the SPPI criterion because:
- linking payments of principal and interest on the principal amount outstanding to the unleveraged inflation index resets the time value of money to the current level; and
- the interest cash flows on the bond reflect 'real' interest – i.e. the interest amounts are consideration for the time value of money on the principal amount outstanding. [*IFRS 9.B4.1.13*]

7.4.260.20   It appears that the SPPI criterion would be met even when there is no principal protection clause – i.e. the principal amount repayable is reduced in line with any cumulative reduction in the inflation index – because this would merely indicate that a component of the time value of money associated with the period during which the instrument is outstanding could be negative.

7.4.260.30   A bond may have euro-denominated payments of principal and interest that are linked to an unleveraged inflation index of one of the eurozone countries rather than of the eurozone as a whole. In this case, it appears that the bond meets the SPPI criterion. This is because it is consistent with the principle in 7.4.260.10 and IFRS 9 refers to an inflation index of the currency in which the instrument is issued. There is no requirement for the inflation index to cover the entire currency zone.

7.4.260.40   A country (or currency union) may publish a number of inflation indices (e.g. consumer price index, retail price index) and we believe that linking payments of principal and interest to any of these indices may be acceptable as long as they represent changes in price levels across a broad range of goods and services in all or part of a country (or currency union).

7.4.260.50   It also appears that the country of domicile and/or functional currency of the issuer does not affect the assessment of the SPPI criterion. This is because the country of domicile and functional currency of the issuer do not affect contractual cash flows. We believe that only a linkage between the inflation index used and the currency in which the instrument is denominated should be considered.

EXAMPLE 20A – UNLEVERAGED INFLATION-LINKED BOND – SPPI CRITERION IS MET (1)

7.4.260.60   Company D holds a euro-denominated bond with a stated maturity issued by Company E. The payments of principal and interest are linked to an unleveraged inflation index of Eurozone Country X. E is located in Country X and its functional currency is the euro.

7.4.260.70   In this example, we believe that the bond meets the SPPI criterion because the interest amounts are consideration for the time value of money on the principal amount outstanding.

EXAMPLE 20B – UNLEVERAGED INFLATION-LINKED BOND – SPPI CRITERION IS MET (2)

7.4.260.80   Modifying Example 20A, Company E is located in Canada and its functional currency is the Canadian dollar. Therefore, the issuing company, E, operates in an economic environment different from the eurozone.

7.4.260.90   We believe that the country of domicile and/or functional currency of the issuer does not affect the assessment of the SPPI criterion. Therefore, in this example, the bond meets the SPPI criterion.

EXAMPLE 20C – UNLEVERAGED INFLATION-LINKED BOND – SPPI CRITERION IS NOT MET

7.4.260.100   Company F holds a euro-denominated bond with a fixed maturity issued by Company G. The interest on the bond is linked to the inflation index of the US. G is located in the US and its functional currency is the US dollar.

7.4.260.110   In this example, the bond does not meet the SPPI criterion. This is because the interest payments are not linked to an inflation index of the currency in which the instrument is issued.

7.4.260.120   With inflation-linked instruments, there is usually a time lag between:
- the period over which the change in the relevant inflation index is measured; and
- the period during which the instrument is outstanding and over which coupon payments and changes in principal amounts contractually accrue.

7.4.260.130   This time lag usually results from a delay between the date of measuring the inflation index and the date of publication. It may also result from difficulties associated with accrual or payment dates on the instrument that do not coincide with dates for which the index is published. In this case, the time value of money element would be modified and an appropriate assessment needs to be made (see 7.4.180).

7.4.270   *Mutual agreement or unilateral choice*

7.4.270.10   Sometimes a contract may include a clause that provides for the parties to mutually agree to make possible changes to the terms of the contract at some point in the future. In our view, if a possible change of terms is subject to the future free and unconstrained mutual agreement of both parties, then it is not a cash flow characteristic that is included in the initial SPPI assessment.

EXAMPLE 21A – OTHER CHANGES IN CONTRACTUAL TERMS – FREE AND UNCONSTRAINED MUTUAL AGREEMENT

7.4.270.20   A loan agreement allows a borrower to propose at a future date a change in the interest-rate basis, currency or maturity of the loan; however, the lender has a free and unconditional choice whether to accept or reject the change.

7.4.270.30   In this example, the possible future change would not be included in the initial SPPI assessment.

7.4.270.40   The parties to a contract are generally able to agree to modify the terms at a later date. If the parties do subsequently agree to change the terms, then the entity would need to consider whether the existing financial asset should be derecognised and replaced with a new financial asset that is classified based on the modified contractual terms and the objective of the business model at that time. For a discussion of a modification of a financial asset, see 7.6.95.

7.4.270.50   In contrast, a change in cash flows may be a unilateral choice of one party; or one party may be able to propose a change and the other party may not have the free and unconditional choice to reject it. We believe that this is a characteristic that should be included in the SPPI assessment. For example, if the borrower could propose a change in the interest rate basis and the lender could not unconditionally withhold its consent, then the potential change in cash flows should be included in the SPPI assessment. For a discussion of assessing SPPI when a lending bank can adjust interest rates, see 7.4.280–285.

EXAMPLE 21B – OTHER CHANGES IN CONTRACTUAL TERMS – LOBO

7.4.270.60   Governmental body G issues a fixed rate instrument at par that includes both a lender's option and a borrower's option to amend its terms (LOBO) with a maturity of 50 years to secure its long-term funding. From year 11 onwards, the lender has the option to propose to revise the interest rate at periodic reset dates. The lender's reset rights are limited to the market rate at the time of revision. The borrower has the option either to:

- accept the lender's proposed revision to the interest rate; or
- redeem the instrument at par without any penalty.

7.4.270.70   In this example, we believe that the lender's option to reset the interest rate to the market rate at the reset date satisfies the SPPI criterion. This is because the option varies the interest rate in a way that is consideration for the time value of money, credit risk, other basic lending risks (e.g. liquidity risk) and costs (e.g. administrative costs) associated with the principal amount outstanding.

7.4.270.80   We believe that the borrower's option either to accept the lender's proposed revision to the interest rate or to redeem the instrument at par without any penalty also satisfies the SPPI criterion. This is because:

- the instrument was issued at par – for a discussion of the exception for certain prepayment features at par, see 7.4.220;
- the prepayment amount substantially represents unpaid principal and interest on the principal amount outstanding; and
- the exercise of the prepayment option is conditional only on the lender exercising its option.

7.4.280   *Ability of a lending bank to adjust interest rates*

7.4.280.10   Banks in many jurisdictions have a variety of published rates for retail loans – these could include base, prime or benchmark rates that are applied across a range of existing contracts and are also offered in the marketplace as a basis for pricing new loans of the same type. Actual loans to customers generally include a positive spread above these published rates to take into account, for example, the maturity of the loan, the credit quality of the borrower and the value of collateralised property.

7.4.280.20   In other cases, a specific loan agreement may give the lending bank the right to adjust the interest rate charged to the borrower. This right may come into effect only if certain events or circumstances occur or it may be exercised unilaterally depending on the bank's business policy. It is common for the borrower to have a prepayment option if the bank has the discretion to adjust the interest rate charged.

7.4.280.30   In our experience, in assessing whether various loans that give a lending bank discretion in setting or adjusting interest rates meet the SPPI criterion, the main considerations are likely to be similar.

7.4.280.40   Three possible types of scenarios that are likely to be common in practice and the constraints that the lending bank may be subject to are summarised in the table below. For a further discussion of relevant considerations that should be part of the assessment, see 7.4.285.

SCENARIO	CONSTRAINTS FOR THE LENDING BANK
Scenario 1: Bank's published rates apply across a range of retail products and contracts	
Although banks are able to change the base rate that they offer, they generally follow a market convention in setting their base rates. These rates are generally based on a funding rate, such as a central bank rate or LIBOR. Banks monitor the movements in the funding rate and there is often a correlation between the changes in the funding rate and the changes in the base rate. However, the correlation between the changes in the funding rate and the base rate is not always one-to-one and there may be some time lag. For example, a bank that is seeking to increase its market share may delay increasing its published rate in response to a change in the central bank rate or accept a reduction in its margin in order to attract new business. A bank also generally adds a spread to its funding rate to determine its base rate. This spread is at the discretion of the bank and may vary over time. Therefore, changes in the base rate or other similar published rates do not always represent solely changes in the time value of money and it is necessary to consider whether possible changes represent other permissible elements of the return – in particular, a profit margin that is consistent with a basic lending arrangement.	• *Prepayment option:* Borrowers are able to prepay loans without significant penalties and rates offered in the marketplace can easily be compared. Therefore, borrowers are able to refinance at a more favourable rate if the rate offered by their existing lender is not competitive. • *Market competition:* Except for timing differences, market competition often ensures that base rates are consistent between lending banks in a particular market. • *Regulation or statute:* Base rates are often part of a general market framework within which basic lending arrangements are made in a specific country or jurisdiction. Such a framework is often supported by consumer protection regulation, requiring banks to treat customers fairly. Together with competition between banks for lending business, the market framework provides a level of protection for the borrower that constrains the lender in setting its base rate.
Scenario 2: Variations in rates on specific loans dependent on specified contingent events	
Based on the terms of the lending arrangement, a bank can unilaterally change the interest rate charged to a customer but only for specified reasons or in certain contingent circumstances. Examples of these reasons or circumstances include changes in applicable law, directive or regulation or compliance by the lender with any direction given or requirement set by any governmental, fiscal, monetary or other authority.	As in Scenario 1, the bank's ability to change the rate may be constrained by the ability of the borrower to prepay the loan, by market competition and by consumer protection regulation. In Scenario 2, the bank's discretion is further constrained by the requirement for a specified contingent event to occur before the rate can be changed. The contract or applicable regulation may also require that the change be a reasonable or proportionate response to the contingent event – e.g. to take into account, in a proportionate manner, any change in costs reasonably incurred in operating the bank's mortgage business. For a discussion of the impact of a lender's funding costs, see 7.4.240.

SCENARIO	CONSTRAINTS FOR THE LENDING BANK
Scenario 2: Variations in rates on specific loans dependent on specified contingent events (continued)	
	However, unlike in Scenario 1, the ability to amend the rate is specific to each contract and published rates are not available. It is therefore not easy for borrowers to compare rates offered in the market and to easily switch between them.
Scenario 3: Bank has full discretion to increase the rate on specific loans to borrowers	
This scenario deals with bank loans to clients with the following terms and conditions. • The bank reserves the right during the term of the credit agreement to adjust the interest rate in accordance with its own business policy. • There is no explicit limitation on the amount of any adjustment. • If the borrower disagrees with an adjustment, then it has the right to terminate the contract and prepay the loan at principal plus accrued interest.	As in Scenarios 1 and 2, the bank's ability to change the rate is constrained by the borrower's ability to prepay and by competition in the lending market. The contract may be subject to more general statutory or legal requirements prohibiting unfair behaviour or requiring exercise of good faith. These loans typically have long maturities and the borrower's ability to refinance will also depend on the willingness of other lenders to offer long-term financing.

7.4.285   Relevant considerations for the assessment

7.4.285.10   IFRS 9's approach to assessing SPPI focuses on an overall assessment of what the entity is being compensated for and whether there is a basic lending arrangement, rather than on how much the entity receives for a particular element. [*IFRS 9.BC4.182(b)*]

7.4.285.20   In each of the three scenarios discussed in 7.4.280.40, the lending bank's ability to amend the contractual cash flows is constrained by some or all of the following factors:
• the borrower's ability to prepay and refinance the loan with another lender;
• competition in the particular lending market;
• a statutory or regulatory framework providing protection against unfair lending practices; and
• contractual restrictions requiring a specified contingent event to take place before the rate can be changed.

7.4.285.30   It appears that judgement is required in assessing whether constraints on the bank's ability to change the rate are sufficient to ensure that the contractual cash flows remain consistent with those of a basic lending arrangement – i.e. providing compensation only for the time value of money, credit risk, other lending costs and risks and a lender's profit margin. An entity should consider the particular facts and circumstances, including features of the particular lending market, when making the assessment of whether the SPPI criterion is met.

7.4.285.40 We believe that in some cases, the general market framework constrains the lender in such a way that it may be possible to conclude that the SPPI criterion is generally met without the need for significant judgement. That would be the case in Scenario 1 in 7.4.280.40 in many jurisdictions where competition between banks for new business ensures that it is not reasonably possible for changes to the rate to result in compensation for the bank that is inconsistent with a basic lending arrangement. In addition, IFRS 9 acknowledges that a lender's various published interest rates might be consistent with the SPPI criterion. [*IFRS 9.B4.1.13*]

7.4.285.50 In Scenario 2 in 7.4.280.40, we believe that it is necessary to consider the nature of the contingent events that could result in a change in contractual cash flows and the nature of that resulting change. If the nature of those events is such that they could result in an increase in basic lending risks and costs associated with the arrangement and the resulting adjustment to the contractual cash flows represents only compensation to the bank for those increases, then this contingent feature would be consistent with the SPPI criterion. However, a contract-by-contract analysis may be required.

7.4.285.60 Similarly, in Scenario 3 in 7.4.280.40 the assessment is likely to require a contract-by-contract analysis to determine whether there is any realistic possibility that the contractual cash flows would be changed in a way that is inconsistent with a basic lending arrangement. If the contract permits the bank to link the rate to a variable that would be inconsistent with a basic lending arrangement – e.g. equity prices – or if the bank intended to use its discretion to establish such a link, then the SPPI criterion would not be met. In other cases, the contractual terms may simply give the bank discretion to increase the interest rate and it may not be clear how the bank intends to use its discretion. We believe that in these cases, the assessment should take into account the competitive forces in the market in which the bank operates and how these can limit the bank's discretion in practice. Judgement may be necessary in many cases to determine whether the contractual terms are consistent with those in a basic lending arrangement. The fact that particular lending arrangements are common market practice does not support a presumption that they automatically qualify as basic lending arrangements.

7.4.290 *Convertible debt instruments*

7.4.290.10 Debt instruments that are convertible into a fixed number of equity instruments of the issuer do not meet the SPPI criterion because the return on the debt instrument is inconsistent with a basic lending arrangement and reflects the value of the issuer's equity (see 7.4.420.50). [*IFRS 9.B4.1.14*]

7.4.290.20 However, some debt instruments permit or require conversion into a variable number of shares of the issuer, designed with the intention that the value of the shares on the date of conversion will be equal to the amount of principal and interest outstanding. In these instances, the lender may be required to accept settlement in a variable number of shares instead of cash and has no right to demand settlement in cash. In this case, the issuer effectively uses its shares as currency and further analysis is required.

7.4.290.30 It appears that the instrument cannot meet the SPPI criterion unless the holder is not exposed to equity price risk and receiving the shares is substantially equivalent to receiving an amount of cash equal to the principal plus interest outstanding. This is because the guidance in

IFRS 9 specifically requires the contractual terms of the financial asset to give rise on specified dates to cash flows that are solely payments of principal and interest on the principal amount outstanding. IFRS 9 also states that contractual terms that introduce exposure to risks or volatility in the contractual cash flows that is unrelated to a basic lending arrangement – e.g. exposure to changes in equity prices– do not give rise to contractual cash flows that meet the SPPI criterion. [*IFRS 9.4.1.2(b), 4.1.2A(b), B4.1.7A*]

7.4.290.40   In practice, a number of provisions could result in the holder of an instrument either being exposed to equity price risk or receiving a share settlement that is not substantially equivalent to receiving an amount of cash equal to the principal plus interest outstanding. For example:

- the number of shares to be issued in settlement may be subject to a cap or a floor;
- the exercise price may either be at a discount to the market price of the shares or be based on the average market price over a fixed period before the conversion date, rather than the share price at the conversion date; and
- share settlement may involve an extended settlement or delivery period.

7.4.290.50   The holder of an instrument would also be receiving shares that are not substantially equivalent to receiving an amount of cash equal to the principal plus interest outstanding if the shares are not liquid – i.e. not traded in an active market or readily convertible into cash – or if there is a restriction on selling the shares. For example, debt convertible into a variable number of the issuer's shares if the regulator announces that the issuer is, or is about to become, non-viable would not meet the SPPI criterion because in non-viability scenarios, share values will probably be very volatile and/ or illiquid.

7.4.290.60   Therefore, an entity needs to apply judgement, based on the specific facts and circumstances, to assess whether it is exposed to equity price risk or would receive shares that are not substantially equivalent to receiving an amount of cash equal to the principal plus interest outstanding.

7.4.300   **De minimis or non-genuine features**

7.4.300.10   A contractual cash flow characteristic does not affect the classification of a financial asset if it could have only a de minimis effect on the financial asset's contractual cash flows. To make this determination, an entity considers the possible effect of the contractual cash flow characteristic in each reporting period and cumulatively over the life of the financial asset. [*IFRS 9.B4.1.18*]

7.4.300.20   Additionally, if a contractual cash flow characteristic could have an effect on the contractual cash flows that is more than de minimis (either in a single reporting period or cumulatively), but that cash flow characteristic is not genuine, then it does not affect the classification of a financial asset. A cash flow characteristic is not 'genuine' if it affects the instrument's contractual cash flows only on the occurrence of an event that would be extremely rare, highly abnormal and very unlikely to occur. [*IFRS 9.B4.1.18*]

7.4.300.30   In our experience, it may be difficult to demonstrate that a term is not genuine, because it would be unusual for parties to an agreement to negotiate a term that they considered to be of no significance. For example, a term may fail the SPPI criterion if it gives rise to cash flows in circumstances that are rare (but not extremely rare) or unlikely (but not very unlikely) to occur.

7.4.310   Non-recourse and limited-recourse assets

7.4.320   *Factors to consider in assessing the SPPI criterion*

7.4.320.10   A financial asset may have contractual cash flows that are described as principal and interest but that do not represent the payment of principal and interest on the principal amount outstanding. [*IFRS 9.B4.1.15*]

7.4.320.20   This may be the case if the instrument represents an investment in particular assets or cash flows. For example, if the contractual terms stipulate that the financial asset's cash flows increase as more cars use a particular toll road, then such terms are inconsistent with a basic lending arrangement. [*IFRS 9.B4.1.16*]

7.4.320.30   This may also be the case when a creditor's claim is limited to specified assets of the debtor or to the cash flows from specified assets – e.g. a non-recourse loan. However, the fact that a financial asset is non-recourse does not necessarily prevent it from meeting the SPPI criterion. The holder is required to assess ('look through to') the underlying assets or cash flows. If the terms of the financial asset being evaluated give rise to cash flows other than principal and interest on the principal amount outstanding, or if they limit the cash flows in a manner that is inconsistent with them representing principal and interest, then the SPPI criterion is not met. Whether the underlying assets are financial assets or non-financial assets does not in itself affect this assessment. [*IFRS 9.B4.1.16–B4.1.17*]

7.4.320.40   Non- or limited-recourse characteristics may arise from explicit contractual limitations on recourse, or may be achieved, for example, through isolating a single asset or specified assets in a structured entity and granting what is nominally a full-recourse loan to that entity. In the latter case, the loan is in substance non-recourse and judgement may also be required to determine whether the specific lending arrangement meets the SPPI criterion.

7.4.320.50   Judgement is required in assessing whether a non-recourse asset meets the SPPI criterion. In our view, the underlying purpose of the assessment is to identify cases in which the financial asset is intended to provide the holder with a return based on the performance of specific assets or another variable that does not represent exposure to and compensation for a basic lending arrangement and therefore fails the SPPI criterion – as opposed to cases in which the borrower's obligation to pay cash represents specified amounts of principal and interest but the obligation in default is limited in a way that is in substance consistent with the exposure to credit risk of a basic lending arrangement.

7.4.320.60   It may be difficult to draw the line between 'credit risk' and 'asset performance risk'. Even when a loan is made with full recourse to all assets of the borrower, the credit risk to which the lender is exposed includes the risk of adverse changes in the value of all those assets, together with the borrower's willingness and ability to repay the loan from its future earnings. Accordingly, in most cases, credit risk includes some indirect element of asset price risk. A non-recourse loan may limit recourse to one or some of the borrower's assets but this may not present a substantially different risk profile from a full-recourse loan.

7.4.320.70   It appears that in applying judgement the lender should evaluate the nature of the arrangement to determine whether the risk that it has taken on is appropriately characterised as credit risk for which it is compensated or, alternatively, whether it represents in part exposure to and payments for investing in and assuming the performance risk of specified assets of the borrower. We believe that factors that a lender could consider in making this evaluation may include the following:

- whether the contractual arrangement specifically defines the amounts and dates of the cash payments of the loan;
- the fair value of the collateral relative to the amount of the secured financial asset;
- the ability and willingness of the borrower to continue to make contractual payments on the secured financial asset, notwithstanding a decline in the value of the collateral;
- whether the borrower is an individual or a substantive operating entity or is a special-purpose entity;
- the risk of loss on the secured limited financial asset relative to a full-recourse loan to the debtor;
- whether another party has contributed sufficient equity to absorb expected losses before affecting the ability of the borrower to make payments on the loan;
- the manner in which the lender evaluates and manages the risks and benefits of secured financial assets of the same type as part of its business model;
- whether the spread is reasonable and similar to other loans that are full-recourse basic lending arrangements;
- whether the lender will benefit from any upside from the underlying asset(s); and
- the extent to which the collateral represents all or a substantial portion of the borrower's assets.

7.4.320.80   In cases of substantial over-collateralisation (i.e. when the fair value of the collateral is substantially greater than the amount of the loan), it may be relatively easy to conclude that the cash flows of the financial asset are not limited in a manner inconsistent with them being payments of solely principal and interest. In other cases, it may be apparent with minimal analysis that the non-recourse feature limits the cash flows to an extent that the payments are something other than principal and interest (e.g. a non-recourse loan to a non-consolidated structured entity whose only asset is an equity investment and whose only funding is the non-recourse loan).

7.4.320.90   In our view, if the contractual payments due under a financial asset are determined contractually by the cash flows received on specified assets, then the financial asset cannot generally meet the SPPI criterion. For example, the SPPI criterion is not met for a loan to a property developer on which interest is payable only if specified rental income is received. However, in our view a financial asset that represents a full or a pro rata share in the contractual cash flows of an underlying financial asset that meets the SPPI criterion could itself meet the SPPI criterion.

7.4.320.100   If a financial asset has specified cash flows that (without looking through to the underlying items) represent solely payments of principal and interest but the financial asset represents a senior share in the contractual cash flows of an underlying financial asset that meets the SPPI criterion, then we believe that the financial asset could also meet the SPPI criterion because such an arrangement does not introduce exposure to risk that is inconsistent with a basic lending arrangement and in particular the senior share does not involve exposure to any leveraging of credit or other risks. In these cases, we further believe that the underlying financial asset does not have to be in the scope of IFRS 9 for this to be possible – e.g. a finance lease receivable may have cash flows that represent principal and interest on the principal amount outstanding. However, if a financial asset represents an investment in a contractually linked instrument as described in 7.4.340, then the specific guidance on contractually linked instruments – rather than the guidance on non-recourse financial assets – applies.

7.4.320.110   An instrument would not fail to meet the SPPI criterion simply because it is ranked as being subordinate to other instruments issued by the same entity. An instrument that is subordinated to other instruments may meet the SPPI criterion if the debtor's non-payment is a breach of contract and the holder has a contractual right to unpaid amounts of principal and interest, even in the event of the debtor's bankruptcy. [*IFRS 9.B4.1.19*]

EXAMPLE 22 – RESIDENTIAL MORTGAGE LOANS

7.4.320.120   Bank B operates in Country X, where it is customary for residential household mortgage loans to be non-recourse to other assets of the borrower. B originates mortgages on standard market terms that include an interest rate linked to the central bank base rate and uses underwriting criteria similar to its competitors that include:

- a maximum loan-to-value ratio of 80%;
- an undertaking that the collateral represents the borrower's primary residence; and
- an evaluation of the borrower's:
  - credit history;
  - credit score;
  - employment history; and
  - current income.

7.4.320.130   B concludes that the SPPI criterion is met because, considering the underwriting criteria, payments under a standard mortgage comprise solely exposure to and compensation for basic lending risks.

EXAMPLE 23 – LOAN TO STRUCTURED ENTITY HOLDING AN AIRCRAFT

7.4.320.140   Bank C finances a non-consolidated structured entity holding an aircraft that is leased to an airline with a strong credit rating. The contractual payments on the loan include only stated principal and interest. In case of default, C's recourse is limited to cash flows from the aircraft lease and the aircraft. Receipt of the minimum lease payments would be adequate to enable the structured entity to make all payments of principal and interest on the loan.

7.4.320.150   Looking through to the underlying assets, C concludes that the cash flows are consistent with payments representing principal and interest on the principal amount outstanding.

7.4.320.160   If the minimum lease payments were not adequate to service the loan or if the lease were to another structured entity, then further analysis would be required. Judgement needs to be applied to the particular facts and circumstances. The assessment may lead to the conclusion that the SPPI criterion is not met if the underlying asset gives rise to other cash flows that are inconsistent with payments representing principal and interest on the principal amount outstanding.

EXAMPLE 24 – INFRASTRUCTURE LOANS

7.4.320.170   An investor sets up a Newco to receive a concession from the local government for the construction and operation of a water purification plant. Newco will be financed in the following manner:

- 10% provided by the investor in the form of equity and subordinated loans from shareholders; and
- 90% provided by senior loans from several financial institutions, which:
  – will be repaid over 20 years after construction ends – i.e. the period during which Newco will receive cash flows from its customers for the services it will provide;
  – bear fixed interest; and
  – have to be repaid before the shareholder loans and before any dividend can be paid.

7.4.320.180   The local government will pay Newco for a certain amount of shortfalls if the demand for Newco's services is lower than a specified threshold. These support levels are expected to ensure that Newco has sufficient funds to service the senior loans in full.

7.4.320.190   The financial institution investors conclude that their senior loans meet the SPPI criterion because payments comprise solely exposure to and compensation for basic lending risks. The financial institutions are seeking compensation for lending funds and do not have an exposure to the residual risks and rewards of the project.

EXAMPLE 25A – LOAN TO ACQUIRE CONTROLLING STAKE IN PUBLIC ENTITY – LOAN-TO-VALUE RATIO OF 50%

7.4.320.200   Investor M sets up a Newco to acquire the controlling stake in a public entity. Newco is financed 50% by M in the form of equity and a shareholder loan and 50% by Bank D in the form of a loan. D's loan:

- has a loan-to-value ratio of 50%;
- bears fixed interest; and
- will be repaid from dividends that are expected to be received from the public entity.

7.4.320.210   Receipt of dividends from the public entity's shares is expected to be adequate to enable Newco to make all payments of principal and interest on D's loan.

7.4.320.220   D's loan is senior to M's loan and secured by the public entity's shares. Newco can pay dividends from future profits only if certain financial covenants

> are met, mainly relating to the loan-to-value ratio of the bank loan and available cash flows.
>
> 7.4.320.230   D concludes that the cash flows on the loan are consistent with payments representing principal and interest on the principal amount outstanding. D receives compensation for lending funds and will not benefit from any upside from the underlying investment in the public entity's shares.
>
> 7.4.320.240   If the dividends were not expected to be adequate to service the loan, then further analysis would be required.

EXAMPLE 25B – LOAN TO ACQUIRE CONTROLLING STAKE IN PUBLIC ENTITY – LOAN-TO-VALUE RATIO OF 100%

> 7.4.320.250   Modifying Example 25A, under the terms of D's loan the par amount approximates the value of the public entity's shares on initial recognition (i.e. 100% loan-to-value ratio) and on maturity of the loan Newco can choose to repay the loan by giving up the shares instead of repaying unpaid principal and interest. In this example, the loan does not meet the SPPI criterion. This is because the cash flows on the loan are:
> - based on the performance of the underlying shares (i.e. if the shares are worth less than the outstanding amount on the loan, then the borrower would give up the shares); and
> - limited in a manner inconsistent with a basic lending arrangement.

7.4.330   *Credit-linked note issued by a structured entity*

7.4.330.10   A 'credit-linked note' is a debt instrument that transfers exposure to the credit risk of an entity, which is not the issuer of the instrument, to an investor.

7.4.330.20   In some cases, a structured entity writes a CDS and issues a single tranche of credit-linked notes to investors. Redemption of the full principal amount on the stated maturity of each credit-linked note is made only if no credit event has occurred on the reference asset that is underlying the CDS and not held by the structured entity. If there is a credit event on the reference asset, then the credit-linked note is prepaid at an amount that reflects the terms of the CDS (e.g. based on an auction price for the reference asset).

7.4.330.30   In this case, it appears that an investment in the credit-linked note would not meet the SPPI criterion. This is because the embedded credit linkage introduces exposure to risks or variability in the contractual cash flows that are inconsistent with a basic lending arrangement because:
- in the structure of the credit-linked note, the credit risk of another entity has been artificially introduced through the CDS; and
- if a credit event under the CDS occurs, then the prepayment amount reflects the terms of the CDS – i.e. the prepayment amount would not represent unpaid principal and interest (see 7.4.190.20).

7.4.330.40   In other cases, a structured entity may purchase and be required to hold a specified asset and issue a single tranche of notes to investors that have cash flows linked to the cash flows of that specified asset. It appears that an investment in a note may meet the SPPI criterion if the investment represents, in substance, a fully proportionate share in the contractual cash flows of an underlying financial asset that meets the SPPI criterion (see 7.4.320.90). If the structured entity issues multiple tranches of notes with different subordination rankings, then the guidance on contractually linked instruments in 7.4.340 applies.

EXAMPLE 26 – CREDIT-LINKED NOTE

7.4.330.50   Bank B sets up Structured Entity SE. SE issues a credit-linked note to Investor M for a par value of 100. The following facts are relevant for this example.

- M's claim is limited to specified assets of SE and the credit-linked note includes no recourse to other assets.
- SE deposits the cash with B and receives interest at three-month LIBOR on the deposit.
- SE writes a CDS to B to transfer the credit risk on a reference entity (Company C) to SE in exchange for a premium of 100 basis points.
- The coupon on the credit-linked note is three-month LIBOR plus 100 basis points, which synthetically replicates a credit spread for C.
- If a credit event occurs before maturity, then M receives the par value of 100 minus the loss on the CDS determined by a CDS auction. If there is no credit event, then the credit-linked note is redeemed at its par value of 100.

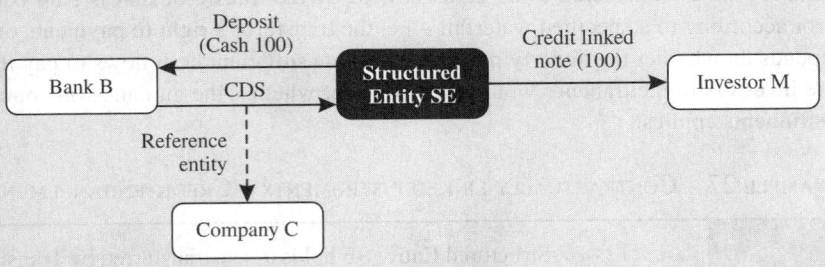

7.4.330.60   In this example, the SPPI criterion for the investment in the credit-linked note is not met because the pay-out is based on the fair value of C's debt at the time of default and the credit risk of C has been artificially introduced into the structure through the CDS.

7.4.340   Contractually linked instruments

7.4.340.10   Sometimes, an entity prioritises payments to holders of multiple contractually linked instruments that create concentrations of credit risk – i.e. tranches. Each tranche has a subordination ranking that specifies the order in which any cash flows generated by the issuer are allocated to the tranche (commonly referred to as 'the waterfall'). IFRS 9 provides specific guidance for such circumstances. The right to payments of principal and interest on the principal amount outstanding on more junior tranches – i.e. those exposed to more credit risk – depends on whether the issuer generates sufficient cash flows to pay more senior tranches. Generally, a contractually linked instrument only requires payment to the extent that there is sufficient cash available from the underlying pool – i.e. the issuer is not in default under this contract if the underlying pool does not generate sufficient cash. A look-through approach is required to determine whether the SPPI criterion is met (see 7.4.340.60). [*IFRS 9.B4.1.20–B4.1.26*]

7.4.340.15   The guidance on contractually linked instruments applies to transactions with multiple tranches as described in 7.4.340.10. Therefore, it does not apply if an entity issues only a single tranche. It also does not apply to a liquidity facility that is intended to cover a mismatch between interest payment dates (rather than to provide protection against credit losses) and under which failure to pay interest or principal on the liquidity facility is a default event. This would be the case if the liquidity facility is provided to an entity that issues contractually linked notes to third parties and it enables that entity to pay principal and interest to note holders if there is a delay in the cash flows from the underlying assets. In this case, the guidance on non-recourse loans may need to be considered for the liquidity facility because the liquidity facility is not regarded as a tranche (see 7.4.310) even though the guidance on contractually linked instruments is applied by the third parties for their investments in the contractually linked notes. [*IFRS 9.B4.1.20–B4.1.21*]

7.4.340.20   In some securitisation structures, the issuer may issue only one type of note but the transferor of the assets may provide some credit enhancement. It appears that credit enhancement in the form of excess spread or excess collateral constitutes a tranche when assessing whether the guidance on contractually linked instruments applies to a structure. This is because the credit enhancement is considered to be an asset held by the transferor that is paid back to the transferor according to a specified waterfall – i.e. the transferor's right to payments on its investment depends on whether the underlying assets generate sufficient cash flows to pay the note holders. The investors in the tranches would then consider whether the guidance on contractually linked instruments applies.

EXAMPLE 27 – CONTRACTUALLY LINKED INSTRUMENTS – CREDIT ENHANCEMENT

7.4.340.25   Structured Entity SE holds assets transferred by Transferor T and issues only one type of note. In accordance with a specified waterfall, any cash flows collected on the transferred assets are passed to the note holders or T. T provides credit enhancement in one of the following forms.

- *Excess spread:* This is the difference between the interest received on the underlying assets transferred to SE and the interest paid to the note holders. This excess spread is initially deposited into a reserve account held by SE and serves as a first line of protection for the note holders against losses. Accumulated excess spread that is not paid to note holders is ultimately paid to T.
- *Excess collateral:* This arises when the principal of the underlying assets is greater than the principal amount of the issued notes. The cash flows related to this excess collateral are paid to T using a schedule predefined in the waterfall.

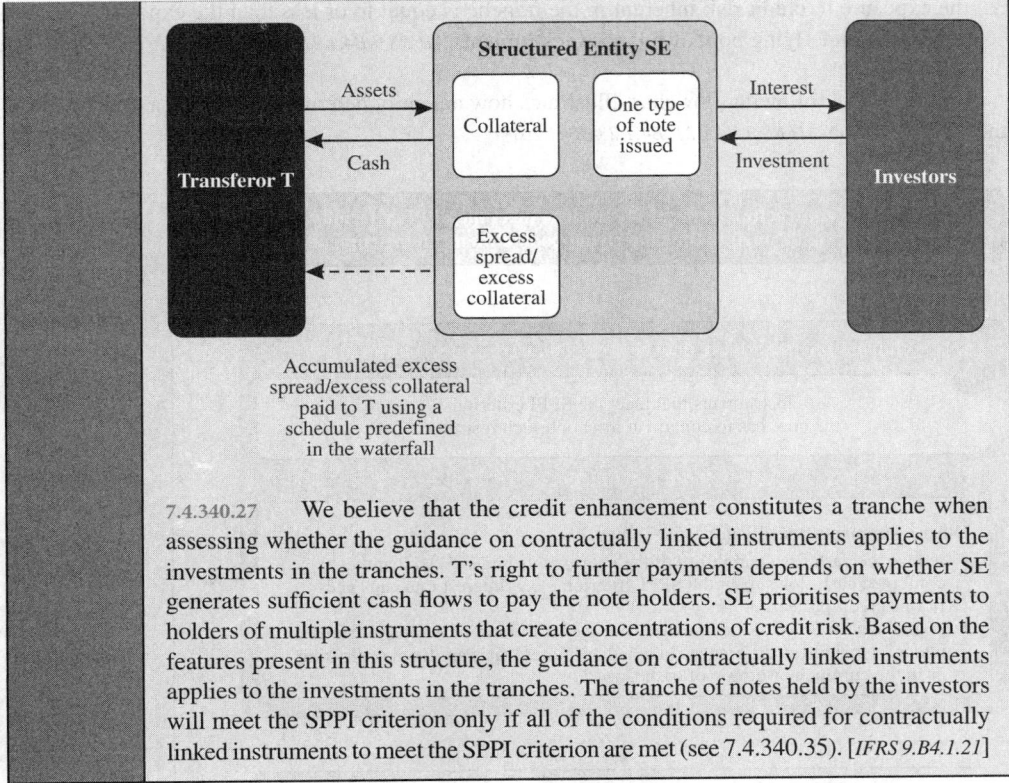

Accumulated excess
spread/excess collateral
paid to T using a
schedule predefined
in the waterfall

7.4.340.27   We believe that the credit enhancement constitutes a tranche when assessing whether the guidance on contractually linked instruments applies to the investments in the tranches. T's right to further payments depends on whether SE generates sufficient cash flows to pay the note holders. SE prioritises payments to holders of multiple instruments that create concentrations of credit risk. Based on the features present in this structure, the guidance on contractually linked instruments applies to the investments in the tranches. The tranche of notes held by the investors will meet the SPPI criterion only if all of the conditions required for contractually linked instruments to meet the SPPI criterion are met (see 7.4.340.35). [*IFRS 9.B4.1.21*]

7.4.340.30   The scope of the guidance on contractually linked instruments is based on the nature of the instruments issued and not on the nature of the instruments in the underlying pool (see 7.4.340.10). Therefore, the guidance on contractually linked instruments may also apply even if the underlying pool contains only non-financial assets that do not meet the SPPI criterion.

7.4.340.35   A tranche meets the SPPI criterion only if all of the following conditions are met:
1. the contractual terms of the tranche itself – without looking through to the underlying pool of financial instruments – give rise to cash flows that are solely payments of principal and interest on the principal amount outstanding;
2. the underlying pool of financial instruments:
    i.   contains one or more instruments that give rise to cash flows that are solely payments of principal and interest on the principal amount outstanding; and
    ii. may also contain instruments, such as derivatives, that:
        –   reduce the cash flow variability of the instruments under (i) and the combined cash flows (of the instruments under (i) and (ii)) give rise to cash flows that are solely payments of principal and interest on the principal amount outstanding – e.g. interest rate caps and floors, credit protection; or
        –   align the cash flows of the tranches with the cash flows of the pool of underlying instruments under (i) arising as a result of differences in whether interest rates are fixed or floating or the currency or timing of cash flows; and

3. the exposure to credit risk inherent in the tranche is equal to or less than the exposure to credit risk of the underlying pool of financial instruments. [*IFRS 9.B4.1.21, B4.1.23–B4.1.25*]

7.4.340.40   The following flowchart illustrates how an entity determines whether a tranche meets the SPPI criterion. [*IFRS 9.B4.1.21, B4.1.23–B4.1.26*]

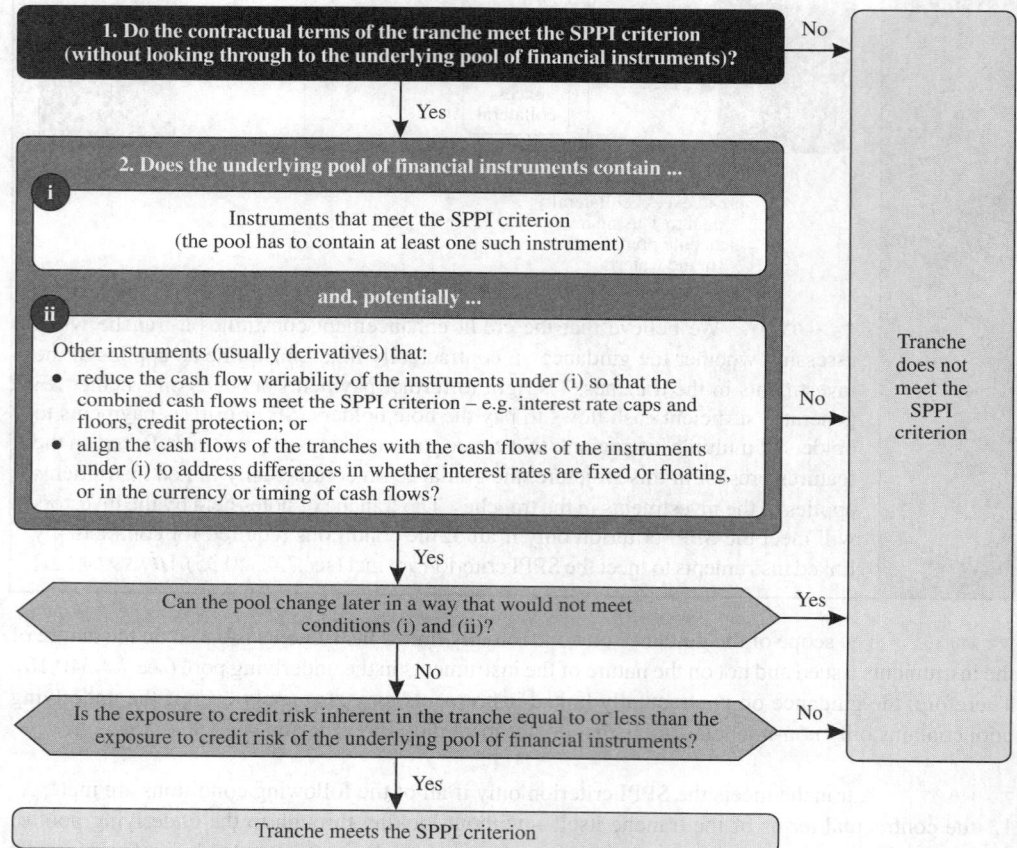

7.4.340.45   For the investment in the tranche to meet the SPPI criterion, the contractual terms of the tranche itself – i.e. without looking through to the underlying pool of assets – need to meet the SPPI criterion. For example, if the interest rate on the tranche is linked to a commodity index, then the investment in the tranche would fail the SPPI criterion because the exposure to commodity price risk is inconsistent with a basic lending arrangement. Similarly, if interest is not accrued on deferred interest payments, then the tranche's contractual cash flows would fail the SPPI criterion. In this case, interest amounts are not consideration for the time value of money on the principal amount outstanding. [*IFRS 9.B4.1.7A, B4.1.14, B4.1.21(a)*]

7.4.340.50   In performing the assessment of financial instruments in the underlying pool, a detailed instrument-by-instrument analysis of the pool may not be necessary. However, an entity has to use judgement and perform sufficient analysis to determine whether the SPPI criterion is met. In performing the analysis, an entity also considers the IFRS 9 guidance on de minimis or non-genuine features (see 7.4.300). [*IFRS 9.B4.1.25*]

7.4.340.60   The look-through approach drills down to the underlying pool of instruments that create, rather than pass through, the cash flows.

EXAMPLE 27A – CONTRACTUALLY LINKED INSTRUMENTS – LOOK THROUGH TO LPV 2 ASSETS

7.4.340.70   Company V invests in contractually linked notes issued by a limited-purpose vehicle (LPV 1), whose only asset is an investment in contractually linked notes issued by another such vehicle (LPV 2). In this example, V looks through to the assets of LPV 2 in performing the assessment. [*IFRS 9.B4.1.22*]

EXAMPLE 27B – CONTRACTUALLY LINKED INSTRUMENTS – LOOK THROUGH TO LPV 1 ASSETS

7.4.340.75   Company W invests in contractually linked notes issued by a limited-purpose vehicle (LPV 1), whose only asset is an investment in a non-recourse loan. The non-recourse loan is issued by another limited-purpose vehicle (LPV 2), whose only asset is a real estate property. In this example, W determines that the non-recourse loan meets the SPPI criterion – i.e. it does not give rise to any other cash flows or limit the cash flows in a manner inconsistent with payments representing principal and interest. Because the non-recourse loan meets the SPPI criterion, W regards the non-recourse loan as the underlying pool of instruments that create the cash flows. The fact that the non-recourse loan meets the SPPI criterion means that it is not simply passing through the original cash flows from the property held by LPV 2. If the non-recourse loan did not meet the SPPI criterion, then W's investment would not meet the SPPI criterion either. [*IFRS 9.B4.1.17, 22*]

7.4.340.80   The underlying pool must contain one or more financial instruments that have contractual cash flows that are solely payments of principal and interest on the principal amount outstanding. There is no requirement for the underlying financial instruments to be in the scope of IFRS 9. It therefore appears that the underlying pool may contain lease receivables and that this requirement can still be met if the lease receivables meet the definition of financial instruments and have contractual cash flows that are solely payments of principal and interest on the principal amount outstanding. However, if the lease receivable gives rise to other cash flows – e.g. cash flows based on asset price risk – then this would not be consistent with a basic lending arrangement. This is the case if the residual value risk on the assets being leased is retained by the holder of the lease receivables at the end of the lease. [*IFRS 9.B4.1.23*]

7.4.340.90   If an entity is not able to make an assessment based on the criteria in 7.4.340.35, then it measures its investment in the tranche at FVTPL. If the underlying pool of instruments can change after initial recognition in a way that the pool would not meet conditions (1) and (2) in the above flowchart (see also 7.4.340.35) – e.g. if the prospectus includes a clause that allows the entity to reinvest a certain percentage of the underlying pool into synthetic exposures at a later date – then the tranche does not meet the SPPI criterion. However, if the underlying pool includes instrument that are collateralised by assets that do not meet conditions (1) and (2) in the above flowchart, then the ability to take possession of such assets is disregarded for the assessment of the SPPI criterion. [*IFRS 9.B4.1.26*]

7.4.350 *Derivatives*

7.4.350.10   A pool may include derivative instruments that align the cash flows of a tranche with the cash flows of the underlying instruments or that reduce cash flow variability. In our view, when determining whether the exposure to credit risk inherent in the tranche is equal to or less than the exposure to credit risk of the underlying pool of financial instruments under condition (3) in 7.4.340.35, an entity should include only relevant credit-related gains and losses arising from the derivative instruments. These include:

- the effect of recoveries arising from derivatives, such as credit-default swaps, to the extent that they provide protection against credit losses on other underlying instruments in the pool; and
- credit losses arising from the non-performance risk of a counterparty to a derivative instrument.

7.4.350.20   The allocation of other gains and losses that arise from market risk on derivative instruments may be relevant in determining whether the contractual terms of a tranche itself give rise to cash flows that meet the SPPI criterion under condition (1) in 7.4.340.35. For example, if the cash flows from an interest rate swap included in the pool were allocated to a tranche to provide investors in the tranche with a return based on twice LIBOR, then the tranche would not meet the SPPI criterion.

7.4.350.30   When a pool includes more than one derivative, in our view an entity is able to combine derivatives when performing the assessment described in condition (2) in 7.4.340.35 if the combined derivative would give the same result as if a single derivative had been included in the portfolio.

EXAMPLE 28 – MORE THAN ONE DERIVATIVE IN POOL

7.4.350.40   Limited-purpose vehicle LPV has a portfolio of variable interest rate financial assets denominated in euro. It issues fixed rate contractually linked notes denominated in US dollars. LPV enters into two derivatives: (1) a pay variable euro, receive variable US dollar swap; and (2) a pay variable US dollar, receive fixed US dollar swap.

7.4.350.50   In this example, the combination of these two swaps is equivalent to one cross-currency interest rate swap to pay variable euro and receive fixed US dollars. Therefore, the holder of an investment in the notes could combine the two derivatives and assess them in combination, rather than performing an individual assessment for each derivative.

7.4.350.60   The pool of underlying instruments and their cash flows may change as a result of prepayments or credit losses, and of any permitted extinguishments or transfers. In our view, for the SPPI criterion to be met (see 7.4.340.35), the terms of the contractually linked structure should include a mechanism that is designed to ensure that the amount of any derivatives is reduced in response to any such events so that the derivatives do not fail to meet the cash flow variability or alignment tests. For example, an interest rate swap may contain a clause under which the notional amount is automatically reduced to match any declines in the principal amount of performing assets within an underlying pool.

7.4.360   *Exposure to credit risk*

7.4.360.10   For the SPPI criterion to be met, the exposure to credit risk inherent in the tranche needs to be equal to or less than the exposure to credit risk of the underlying pool of financial instruments. This would be the case, for example, if the credit rating of the tranche being assessed for classification is equal to or higher than the credit rating that would apply to a single tranche that funded the underlying pool of financial instruments. The term 'credit risk' is defined in IFRS 7 as 'the risk that one party to a financial instrument will cause a financial loss for the other party by failing to discharge an obligation' (see 7.10.520.10). [*IFRS 9.B4.1.21(c)*]

7.4.360.20   In a tranched structure, the issuer is usually obliged to make payments to an investor only if, and to the extent that, the underlying pool of assets generates sufficient cash flows. Therefore, shortfalls in cash flows and associated losses for investors arising from defaults in the underlying pool of assets result in a reduction in the issuer's obligations, rather than the issuer failing to discharge its obligations. In our view, in assessing the exposure to credit risk in the underlying pool of financial assets inherent in a tranche, an entity should consider both:
- losses that may result from contractual adjustments to the cash flows on the tranche arising from credit losses in the underlying pool of assets; and
- losses that may result from the issuer failing to discharge its obligations because of credit losses in the underlying pool of assets. [*IFRS 7.A, 9.A*]

7.4.360.30   Consistent with this analysis, the presence of such adjustment features does not imply a failure of condition (1) in 7.4.340.35. In other words, the contractual terms of the tranche itself could still give rise to cash flows that are solely payments of principal and interest on the principal amount outstanding.

7.4.360.40   The condition in 7.4.360.10 would be met if the range of expected losses on the issued instrument is equal to or lower than the weighted-average range of expected losses on the underlying pool of financial instruments. [*IFRS 9.B4.1.21(c), BC4.35(f)*]

EXAMPLE 29A – EXPOSURE TO CREDIT RISK INHERENT IN A TRANCHE

7.4.360.50   Company W, a limited-purpose entity, has issued two tranches of debt that are contractually linked. The Class I tranche has a carrying amount of 15 and the Class II tranche has a carrying amount of 10. Class II is subordinate to Class I, and receives distributions only after payments have been made to the holders of Class I. W's assets are a fixed pool of loans with a carrying amount of 25, all of which meet the SPPI criterion.

7.4.360.60   Investor X has invested in the Class I tranche. X determines that, without looking through the underlying pool, the contractual terms of the tranche give rise only to payments of principal and interest.

7.4.360.70   As the next step, X looks through to the underlying pool of investments of W. Because W has invested in loans that meet the SPPI criterion, the pool contains at least one instrument with cash flows that are solely principal and interest. W has no other financial instruments, and is not permitted to acquire any other financial instruments. Therefore, the underlying pool of financial instruments held by W does not have features that would prohibit the tranche from meeting the SPPI criterion.

7.4.360.80   The last step in the analysis is for X to assess whether the exposure to credit risk inherent in the tranche is equal to or lower than the exposure to credit risk of the underlying pool of financial instruments. Because the Class I tranche is the most senior tranche, the credit rating of the tranche is higher than the weighted-average credit rating of the underlying pool of loans. Accordingly, X concludes that Class I meets the SPPI criterion.

7.4.360.90   Investor Y has invested in the Class II tranche. This tranche is the most junior tranche and does not meet the credit risk criterion (see 7.4.360.10). Therefore, Y measures its investment in Class II at FVTPL. [*IFRS 9.BC4.35(f)*]

7.4.360.100   The standard does not mandate a single method to determine whether the credit risk condition is satisfied. In our view, it is not necessary to demonstrate that the weighted-average range test in 7.4.360.40 is passed in all circumstances to conclude that the credit risk condition is satisfied. We believe that an alternative approach may also be appropriate.

7.4.360.110   If the credit risk condition is not satisfied, then the investment in the tranche is measured at fair value. [*IFRS 9.BC4.35(f)*]

7.4.360.120   In some cases, a qualitative analysis of the tranche structure may lead to an answer for some tranches without detailed scenario modelling. This is consistent with Example 29A. In other cases, more detailed analysis may be required.

EXAMPLE 29B – EXPOSURE TO CREDIT RISK INHERENT IN A TRANCHE – MORE DETAILED ANALYSIS REQUIRED

7.4.360.130   An underlying pool consists of financial assets of 100. Credit losses are allocated to three tranches of contractually linked notes in the following order.

CREDIT LOSSES	TRANCHE ALLOCATED TO
Up to 10	C
10–20	B
20–100	A

7.4.360.140   In this example, it is apparent that Tranche C would fail the credit risk condition, whereas Tranche A would pass. However, further analysis would be

> required for Tranche B. If, for example, the weighted-average range of expected losses in the underlying pool did not exceed 10, then Tranche B would also pass the credit risk condition. However, if that range did exceed 10, then completing the assessment would require more detailed modelling.

7.4.360.150   As with other elements of the classification assessment, an entity assesses whether the credit risk condition is met on initial recognition of the contractually linked instrument. The assessment therefore reflects the circumstances and expectations at that date. This might result in a different conclusion from the one reached if the test had been based on the circumstances and expectations at the date on which the contractually linked instruments were created. [*IFRS 9.3.1.1*]

7.4.360.160   It appears that an entity should not reclassify the contractually linked instrument based on a reassessment of the exposure to credit risk inherent in the tranche on a subsequent date. This is because there is no guidance to allow an entity to reclassify financial assets based on a reassessment of the SPPI criterion after initial recognition (see 7.4.450.60). [*IFRS 9.4.4.1*]

EXAMPLE 29C – EXPOSURE TO CREDIT RISK INHERENT IN A TRANCHE – CHANGES IN ASSESSMENT OVER TIME

7.4.360.170   A structure is established that includes a most junior Tranche C. Tranche C provides credit protection to Tranche B (next most junior) and Tranche A (most senior). When the structure is established, an original investor in Tranche B concludes that the protection provided by Tranche C relative to the level of ECLs is sufficient to pass the credit risk test and that its investment may be classified as measured at amortised cost.

7.4.360.180   However, over time, credit losses are greater than expected and the credit protection provided by Tranche C is exhausted. Therefore, a subsequent investor in Tranche B concludes that the credit risk condition is failed. However, we believe that it is not appropriate for the original investor to reclassify its investment based on the change in circumstances.

7.4.370   *Collateralised debt obligation*

7.4.370.10   A CDO is a debt instrument that is a securitised interest in a pool of financial assets. It offers investors various maturities and credit risk characteristics using a multiple tranche structure. In assessing whether the contractual cash flows meet the SPPI criterion, it is important to distinguish between a cash and a synthetic CDO. Cash CDOs expose investors to credit risk through the CDO vehicle holding the reference assets. The debt obligation is collateralised through an actual pool of mortgages or loans (cash instruments). A synthetic CDO represents a pool of credit derivatives together with government bonds. In other words, rather than the debt obligation being collateralised through an actual pool of mortgages or loans (cash instruments), it is backed by government bonds together with a pool of credit derivatives, including CDSs and credit default options that synthetically generate credit risk.

7.4.370.20   An investment in a tranche of a cash CDO may meet the SPPI criterion if the underlying pool of assets meets the SPPI criterion and all other conditions of contractually linked instruments are met (see 7.4.340).

7.4.370.30   However, an investment in a tranche of a synthetic CDO would not meet the SPPI criterion. This is because the credit default swaps neither reduce the cash flow variability of the pool of assets nor align the cash flows of the tranches with the cash flows of the underlying pool of assets (see 7.4.340.35).

7.4.370.40   Similarly, if the underlying pool of financial instruments contains issued financial guarantee contracts, then an investment in a tranche would not meet the SPPI criterion. This is because the issued financial guarantee contracts neither reduce the cash flow variability of the pool of assets nor align the cash flows of the tranches with the cash flows of the underlying pool of assets.

7.4.380   Application of the SPPI criterion

7.4.380.10   The following are examples of instruments for which the SPPI criterion may be met. [*IFRS 9.B4.1.13*]

DESCRIPTION OF INSTRUMENT	RATIONALE
An instrument with a stated maturity and variable interest rate for which the borrower can choose a market interest rate that corresponds to the reset period on an ongoing basis.	The fact that the interest rate is reset during the life of the instrument does not disqualify the instrument from meeting the SPPI criterion. However, for example, if the borrower were able to choose to pay the one-month LIBOR rate for a three-month term without reset each month, then the time value of money element would be modified. In this case, an appropriate assessment would have to be made (see 7.4.180).
A bond with variable interest and an interest cap.	The instrument is like a combination of a fixed and a floating rate bond, because the cap reduces the variability of cash flows. No further analysis is needed of whether the cap is in or out of the money.
A full recourse loan secured by collateral.	The fact that a full recourse loan is secured by collateral does not affect the analysis.
A perpetual bond with mandatory interest payments that are required to be paid in perpetuity. Interest accrues on overdue unpaid interest.	The fact that an instrument is perpetual does not in itself mean that its contractual cash flows are not payments of principal and interest on the principal amount outstanding.

DESCRIPTION OF INSTRUMENT	RATIONALE
A fixed interest rate bond, all of whose contractual cash flows are non-discretionary, but whose issuer is subject to legislation that permits or requires a national resolving authority to impose losses on holders of particular instruments (including this instrument) in particular circumstances – e.g. if the issuer is having severe financial difficulties or additional regulatory capital is required.	The holder analyses the contractual terms of the instrument to determine whether it meets the SPPI criterion. This analysis does not consider the payments that result from the national resolving authority's power to impose losses on the holders of the instrument, because these powers, and the resulting payments, are not contractual terms of the financial instrument.
	Accordingly, these powers do not impact the analysis of whether the asset meets the SPPI criterion.
	However, a contractual feature that specifies that all or some of the principal and interest have to or may be written off if a specified event occurs – e.g. if the issuer has insufficient regulatory capital or is at a point of non-viability – would be relevant to the SPPI assessment; accordingly, a contractual bail-in feature could cause an instrument to fail to meet the SPPI criterion.

7.4.380.20   The following are examples of instruments for which the SPPI criterion is not met. [*IFRS 9.B4.1.14*]

DESCRIPTION OF INSTRUMENT	RATIONALE
An inverse floating interest rate loan – e.g. the interest rate on the loan increases if an interest rate index decreases.	The SPPI criterion is not met, because interest has an inverse relationship to market rates and so does not represent consideration for the time value of money on the principal amount outstanding.
A perpetual instrument that is callable at any time by the issuer at par plus accrued interest. Interest is payable only if the issuer remains solvent after payment. Any deferred interest does not accrue additional interest.	The SPPI criterion is not met, because the issuer may defer payments, and additional interest does not accrue on the amounts deferred. As a result, the holder is not entitled to consideration for the time value of money on the principal amount outstanding.

7.4.390   **OPTION TO DESIGNATE FINANCIAL ASSETS AS AT FVTPL**

7.4.390.10   On initial recognition, an entity may choose to designate a financial asset that would otherwise qualify for amortised cost or FVOCI classification as at FVTPL. This optional designation is permitted only if it eliminates or significantly reduces a measurement or recognition inconsistency (an 'accounting mismatch') that would otherwise arise from measuring financial assets or financial liabilities, or recognising gains or losses on them, on different bases. For a discussion of reducing accounting mismatch, see 7.5.50. [*IFRS 9.4.1.5*]

7.4.390.20   The designation of an instrument as at FVTPL on this basis may be used only on initial recognition and is not reversible. This is different to the designation of certain credit exposures (see 7.4.400) which may be made on initial recognition or subsequently. Therefore, this alternative to hedge accounting cannot be used if an entity buys an instrument and later decides to put in place a hedge. [*IFRS 9.4.1.5*]

7.4.390.30   There is no requirement for consistency in the use of the FVTPL designation, meaning that an entity can choose which, if any, of its financial assets are designated into this category. [*IFRS 9.B4.1.28*]

7.4.400   OPTION TO DESIGNATE CREDIT EXPOSURE AS AT FVTPL

7.4.400.10   Certain credit exposures can also be designated as at FVTPL if a credit derivative that is measured at FVTPL is used to manage the credit risk of all, or a part, of the exposures. This is conditional on the entity having elected to apply the hedge accounting requirements in chapter 6 of IFRS 9 (see 7.11.20.50). For a discussion of managing credit risk using credit derivatives, see 7.9.110. [*IFRS 9.6.7.1, 7.2.21*]

7.4.410   INVESTMENTS IN EQUITY INSTRUMENTS

7.4.420   Designation exception for investments in equity instruments

7.4.420.10   On initial recognition only, an entity may elect to present in OCI changes in the fair value of an investment in an equity instrument if it is not held for trading (see 7.4.140.20–80) and is not contingent consideration recognised by an acquirer in a business combination (see 2.6.280). The election is irrevocable and can be made on an instrument-by-instrument basis. [*IFRS 9.5.7.5, B5.7.1*]

7.4.420.20   Equity instruments are defined in the same way as in IAS 32. This means that a holder of an investment assesses whether the instrument meets the definition of equity from the perspective of the issuer. IAS 32 both defines an equity instrument and provides guidance on what other instruments are classified as equity (see chapter 7.3). However, the option to present the changes in fair value in OCI refers only to equity instruments defined as such by IAS 32; it does not apply to instruments defined as financial liabilities but classified as equity by the issuer – e.g. puttable instruments classified as equity by the issuer. [*IFRS 9.BC5.21, IAS 32.11, 16A–16D, IU 09-17*]

7.4.420.30   An entity may invest in a derivative that meets the definition of an equity instrument of the issuer because it satisfies the fixed-for-fixed criterion in IAS 32 (see 7.3.230.10). However, the entity could not elect to present the changes in the fair value of such an investment in OCI. This is because derivative instruments are within the definition of held for trading in IFRS 9, and the election applies only to investments that are not held for trading under the standard. For a discussion of the definition of held for trading, see 7.4.140.20–90 and 7.5.30. [*IAS 32.11, IFRS 9.A*]

7.4.420.40   In some cases, it may not be possible for a holder to determine whether the particular instrument that it holds meets the definition of an equity instrument of the issuer. For example, an entity may hold an investment in members' shares of a co-operative entity. The co-operative may be obliged to redeem members' shares subject to a right to refuse redemptions in excess of a certain amount. This means that it might treat a proportion of the total shares in issue as equity and the remaining proportion as financial liabilities. In this case, the holder would not be able to determine that the instruments that it holds meet the definition of an equity instrument. Therefore, in our view it would be precluded from applying the election to present the changes in fair value in OCI to its investment. [*IFRIC 2.9*]

7.4.420.45   It appears that a holder of a compound instrument cannot use the option to present the changes in fair value in OCI. This is because the instrument is not an equity instrument of the issuer in its entirety – i.e. it is made up of different components (a liability and an equity component of the issuer). This would be the case irrespective of the value of the liability component as long as the liability feature was genuine. For example, an investment in a convertible bond that is mandatorily convertible into a fixed number of the issuer's equity instruments but bears fixed interest payments would not be eligible for the option to present changes in fair value in OCI. However, if there were no interest payments and the bond was classified as equity in its entirety by the issuer, then the holder could elect to present changes in the instrument's fair value in OCI if the instrument is not held for trading.

7.4.420.50   In our view, if an entity exercises a conversion feature in a convertible bond and converts the bond to equity instruments of the issuer, then the equity instruments should be accounted for as new assets. The entity may, on initial recognition, elect to present changes in fair value of these new assets in OCI at the time of their initial recognition if they are not held for trading.

7.4.420.60   When an entity loses significant influence over an associate but retains an investment in an equity instrument that is in the scope of IFRS 9, the entity measures the retained interest at fair value. The fair value of the retained interest is regarded as its fair value on initial recognition as a financial asset under IFRS 9. It appears that an entity may elect to present the changes in the fair value of the investment in OCI, assuming that the conditions in 7.4.420.10 are met. This is because, in substance, the retained interest can be seen as a new financial asset that was not previously accounted for under IFRS 9. [*IAS 28.22*]

7.4.430   Associates and joint ventures

7.4.430.10   IAS 28 allows investments in associates and joint ventures held by, or held indirectly through, an entity that is a venture capital organisation, mutual fund, unit trust or similar entity, including an investment-linked insurance fund, to be measured at FVTPL in accordance with IFRS 9 (see 3.5.100).

7.4.440   Investment entities

7.4.440.10   Investment entities, as defined in IFRS 10, are required to account for their investments in most subsidiaries as at FVTPL in accordance with IFRS 9 (see chapter 5.6). In addition, one of the criteria for qualifying as an investment entity is that investments in associates and joint ventures are accounted for at FVTPL in accordance with IFRS 9. [*IFRS 10.31, A, BC250, IAS 27.11A*]

7.4.440.20   For venture capital organisations and similar entities that in any event do not qualify as investment entities, the exemption from equity accounting (see 7.4.430.10 and 3.5.100.10) remains elective.

7.4.450   RECLASSIFICATIONS

7.4.450.10   The reclassification of financial assets is required if, and only if, the objective of the entity's business model for managing those financial assets changes. [*IFRS 9.4.4.1, BCE.70*]

7.4.450.20   Such changes are expected to be very infrequent, and are determined by the entity's senior management as a result of external or internal changes. These changes have to be significant to the entity's operations and demonstrable to external parties. Accordingly, a change in the objective of an entity's business model will occur only when an entity either begins or ceases to carry out an activity that is significant to its operations – e.g. when the entity has acquired, disposed of or terminated a business line. [*IFRS 9.B4.4.1, BC4.115–BC4.116*]

7.4.450.30   The following are examples of a change in business model.
- An entity holds a portfolio of commercial loans for sale. Subsequently, it acquires an entity whose business model is to hold similar loans in order to collect contractual cash flows. The commercial loans originally held for sale are transferred to the acquired entity to be managed together with the entity's other loans.
- An entity decides to shut down one of its businesses. That business no longer accepts new business and the entity is actively marketing the portfolio of assets in that business for sale. [*IFRS 9.B4.4.1*]

7.4.450.40   The following do not represent a change in business model:
- a change in intention related to particular financial assets, even in circumstances of significant changes in market conditions;
- a temporary disappearance of a particular market for financial assets; or
- a transfer of financial assets between parts of the entity with different business models. [*IFRS 9.B4.4.3*]

7.4.450.50   The classification of financial assets depends on the way in which they are managed within a business model, and not solely on the objective of the business model itself (see 7.4.70). Changes in the way that assets are managed within the business model – e.g. an increased frequency of sales – will not result in the reclassification of existing assets, but may result in newly acquired assets being classified differently. Such changes may occur more frequently than changes in the objective of the business model itself. [*IFRS 9.B4.4.1*]

7.4.450.60   IFRS 9 does not contain any guidance requiring or allowing an entity to reclassify assets based on a reassessment of the SPPI criterion after initial recognition.

7.4.460   Lapse of a contractual term

7.4.460.10   Financial assets may contain a feature that is significant in determining the classification of a financial asset but this feature may expire before maturity of the financial asset. In our view, an entity should not reclassify the financial asset on expiry of the feature.

EXAMPLE 30 – RECLASSIFICATION – LAPSE OF CONTRACTUAL TERM

7.4.460.20   A bond convertible into a fixed number of equity instruments of the issuer does not meet the SPPI criterion (see 7.4.290.10). Therefore, the entire instrument is classified as at FVTPL.

7.4.460.30   However, assume that the bond has a 10-year maturity but the conversion feature is exercisable only for the first five years. If, at the end of five years, the conversion feature has not been exercised, then we believe that the bond should remain classified as at FVTPL until its maturity.

7.4.470   Timing of reclassification of financial assets

7.4.470.10   If an entity determines that its business model has changed in a way that is significant to its operations, then all affected assets are reclassified from the first day of the next reporting period (the reclassification date). The change in business model has to be effected before the reclassification date. In order for reclassification to be appropriate, the entity cannot engage in activities consistent with its former business model after the date of change in business model. Prior periods are not restated. [*IFRS 9.5.6.1, B4.4.2*]

7.4.470.20   IFRS 9 does not define the term 'reporting period'. In our view, the reclassification date is dependent on the frequency of the entity's reporting – i.e. quarterly, semi-annually etc. For example, if an entity with an annual reporting date of 31 December that reports quarterly determines that its business model has changed on 15 March, then we believe that its reclassification date is 1 April.

7.4.470.30   In some cases, there may be a long time period between the change in an entity's business model and the reclassification date. During this period, the financial assets existing at the date of change in business model continue to be accounted for as if the business model had not changed – even though this no longer reflects the actual business model in operation. However, in our view an entity should classify any new assets initially recognised after the date of change in business model based on the new business model in effect at the date of their initial recognition. [*IFRS 9.BC4.119*]

7.4.480   Internal transfers of financial instruments

7.4.480.10   Although internal transactions are eliminated on consolidation, an internal transfer between entities in the group might be an indication that there has been a change in the group's intent for holding the portfolios concerned. However, a transfer of financial assets between parts of an entity with different business models does not represent a change in the business model. [*IFRS 9.B4.4.3*]

7.4.480.20   In some circumstances, an entity's trading desk may be responsible for the acquisition of financial assets for the investment purposes of other divisions within the entity. In our view, when the trading desk clearly acts on behalf of the investing division – such that an investment is acquired and passed directly to that division – such an investment may be consistent with a held-to-collect business model or a held to collect and for sale business model. This applies even if – for operational reasons only – the investment is initially recognised in the trading book. However, should the trading desk have an existing portfolio of financial assets that were classified for accounting purposes as held-for-trading, such assets would retain their classification even if an investing division of the entity subsequently acquired some of the assets for its investment purposes.

7.5 Classification of financial liabilities

7.5 Classification of financial liabilities

CURRENTLY EFFECTIVE REQUIREMENTS

This publication reflects IFRS in issue at 1 August 2018, and the currently effective requirements cover annual periods beginning on 1 January 2018.

The requirements related to this topic are mainly derived from the following.

STANDARD	TITLE
IFRS 9	Financial Instruments

FORTHCOMING REQUIREMENTS AND FUTURE DEVELOPMENTS

For this topic, there are no forthcoming requirements or future developments.

7.5.10   OVERVIEW

7.5.10.10   The following flowchart provides an overview of the requirements for the classification and measurement of financial liabilities. It does not cover the following instruments:

- financial liabilities that arise when a transfer of a financial asset does not qualify for derecognition, or when the continuing involvement approach applies;
- financial guarantee contracts;
- commitments to provide a loan at a below-market interest rate; and
- contingent consideration issued in a business combination.

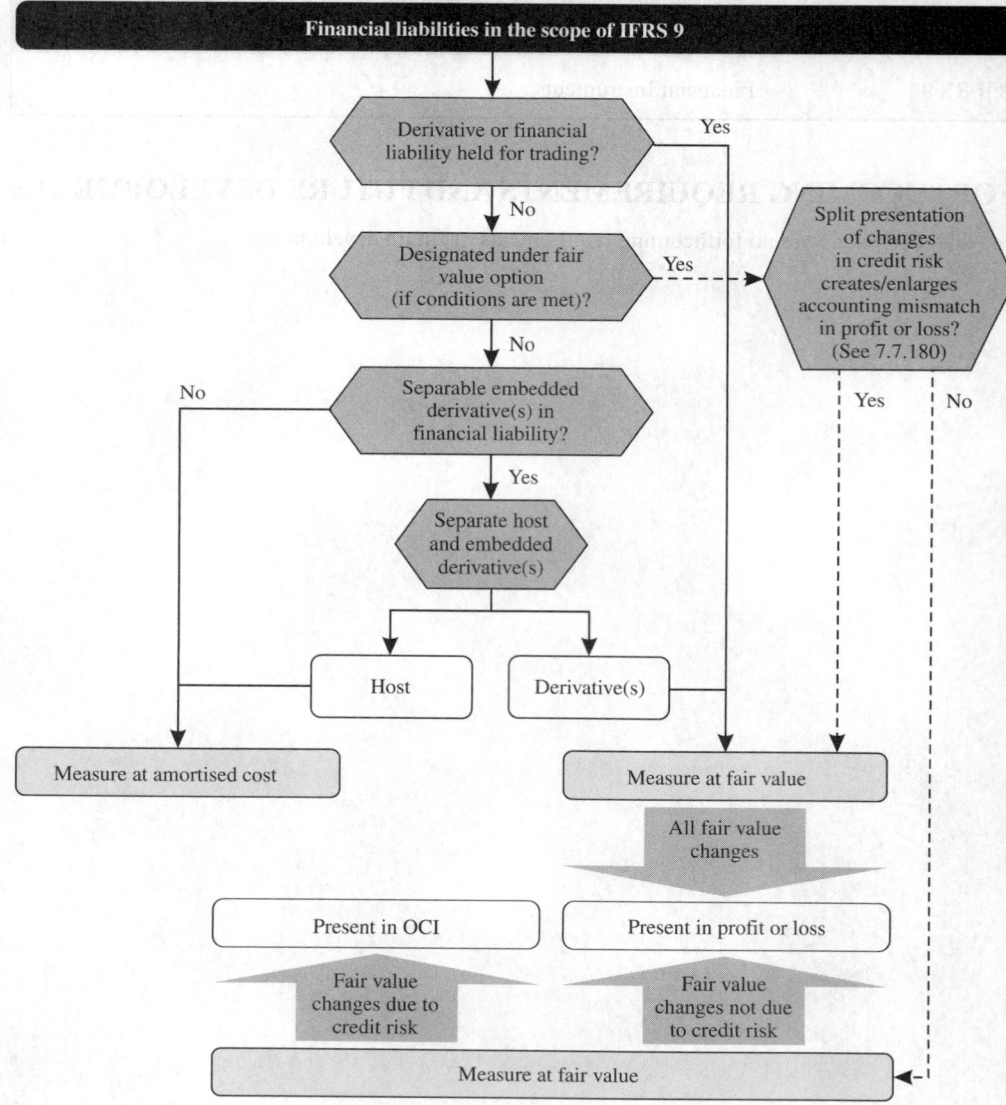

7.5.20   **BASIC PRINCIPLES**

7.5.20.10   On initial recognition, financial liabilities are classified as subsequently measured at amortised cost, except for the following instruments:
1. financial liabilities at FVTPL;
2. financial liabilities that arise when a transfer of a financial asset does not qualify for derecognition or when the continuing involvement approach applies;
3. financial guarantee contracts;
4. commitments to provide a loan at a below-market interest rate; and
5. contingent consideration recognised by an acquirer in a business combination. [*IFRS 9.4.2.1*]

7.5.20.20   The instruments under (1) and (5) are subsequently measured at fair value. The instruments under (2), (3) and (4) are measured under specific guidance. For a discussion of transfers of financial assets not qualifying for derecognition, see 7.6.240. For a discussion of financial guarantee contracts, see 7.1.120. For a discussion of loan commitments, see 7.1.245.

7.5.20.30   Financial liabilities at FVTPL can be divided into the following sub-categories:
●   financial liabilities that are held for trading (including derivatives); and
●   financial liabilities that on initial recognition are designated as at FVTPL.

7.5.30   **Financial liabilities held for trading**

7.5.30.10   A financial liability is held for trading if it is:
●   incurred principally for the purpose of repurchasing it in the near term;
●   on initial recognition, part of a portfolio of identified financial instruments that are managed together and for which there is evidence of a recent actual pattern of short-term profit taking; or
●   a derivative, except for a derivative that is a designated and effective hedging instrument. [*IFRS 9.A*]

7.5.30.20   Financial liabilities held for trading include derivatives with a negative fair value – except those that are hedging instruments – and obligations to deliver financial assets borrowed by a short seller. This category further includes financial liabilities that are incurred with an intention of repurchasing them in the near term and those that are part of a portfolio of financial liabilities for which there is evidence of a recent pattern of short-term profit taking. [*IFRS 9.BA.7*]

7.5.30.30   A financial liability cannot be considered as held for trading simply because it funds trading activities. However, financial liabilities that fund trading activities can be designated as at FVTPL if the criteria for designation are met (see 7.5.40). [*IFRS 9.BA.8*]

7.5.40   **OPTION TO DESIGNATE FINANCIAL LIABILITIES AS AT FVTPL**

7.5.40.10   IFRS 9 contains an option to designate irrevocably on initial recognition a financial liability as measured at FVTPL. However, certain eligibility conditions need to be met.
●   When doing so results in more relevant information because either:
    –   the designation eliminates or significantly reduces a measurement or recognition inconsistency that would otherwise arise from measuring assets or liabilities, or from recognising the gains and losses on them, using different bases (an 'accounting mismatch'); or

- a group of financial liabilities, or financial assets and financial liabilities, is managed and its performance is evaluated on a fair value basis, in accordance with a documented risk management or investment strategy. Information about the group is provided internally on that basis to the entity's key management personnel.
- If a contract contains one or more embedded derivatives and the host is not an asset in the scope of IFRS 9, then an entity may designate the entire hybrid (combined) contract as at FVTPL. However, this does not apply if the embedded derivative does not significantly modify the cash flows that would otherwise be required by the contract, or if it is obvious that separation of the embedded derivative would be prohibited (see 7.5.70.20). [*IFRS 9.4.2.2, 4.3.5*]

7.5.40.20   There is no requirement for consistency in the use of the FVTPL designation, meaning that an entity can choose which, if any, of its financial liabilities are designated into this category except for financial liabilities managed on a fair value basis (see 7.5.60.20). [*IFRS 9.B4.1.28*]

7.5.50   Reducing accounting mismatch

7.5.50.10   Determining whether the fair value option eliminates or significantly reduces an accounting mismatch requires judgement. In our view, an accounting mismatch may arise from other financial instruments or from items that are not financial instruments.

EXAMPLE 1A – REDUCING ACCOUNTING MISMATCH (1)

7.5.50.20   Company X has financial assets and financial liabilities that share a particular risk, such that their fair values change in opposite directions, tending to offset each other. However:
- only some of the instruments are measured at FVTPL, notably derivatives and those that are held for trading;
- hedge accounting cannot be applied because:
  - the hedge criteria (e.g. the effectiveness requirements) are not met; or
  - none of the instruments is a derivative or a non-derivative financial instrument measured at FVTPL; or
- even though hedge accounting is applicable, hedge documentation or effectiveness testing, for example, is too onerous.

7.5.50.30   X concludes that the accounting mismatch arises from the above circumstances and, therefore, these financial assets and financial liabilities qualify for designation as at FVTPL. [*IFRS 9.B4.1.30*]

EXAMPLE 1B – REDUCING ACCOUNTING MISMATCH (2)

7.5.50.40   Company Y has issued financial liabilities whose cash flows are linked to both (1) the cash flows received from investment property measured at fair value under IAS 40 (see 3.4.140) and (2) the fair value of that property. Y determines that the contractual linkage does not constitute an embedded derivative and, without designation, the financial liabilities would be accounted for at amortised cost.

> 7.5.50.50   Y concludes that the accounting mismatch arises from the above circumstances and, therefore, these financial liabilities qualify for designation as at FVTPL.

7.5.50.60   There may be a delay between acquiring a financial asset or incurring a financial liability and the related transaction that would create an accounting mismatch. In the event of a reasonable delay, designation of the financial asset or financial liability as at FVTPL is not precluded provided that the designation is made on initial recognition and, at the time when the first of the instruments is so designated, the acquisition or incurrence of the other is expected in the very near future in accordance with a documented strategy. [*IFRS 9.B4.1.31*]

7.5.50.70   One of the main benefits of this category is that it may allow an entity to avoid the cost and complexity of meeting the criteria for hedge accounting in some cases. For example, an entity that issues a fixed rate bond and immediately enters into an interest rate swap to convert the interest to a floating rate might, instead of applying hedge accounting, designate the bond as at FVTPL. Because both the bond and the swap would be measured at FVTPL, the offsetting effects of changes in market interest rates on the fair value of each instrument would be recognised in profit or loss without the need for hedge accounting. [*IFRS 9.BCZ4.60*]

7.5.50.80   However, the fair value changes of an item designated into this category will be affected by more than one risk, such that using this designation may not achieve the exact results that hedge accounting for a particular risk would. Continuing the example in 7.5.50.70, when applying hedge accounting for interest rate risk, the fixed rate bond would be adjusted for changes in its fair value attributable to interest rate risk only. However, designating the bond as at FVTPL means that it would be remeasured to fair value in respect of all risks, including the entity's own credit risk. This may result in a greater difference between the fair value gains and losses on the interest rate swap and those on the bond than when hedge accounting is applied.

7.5.60   Financial liabilities managed on fair value basis

7.5.60.10   An entity could be considered to be managing and evaluating the performance of a group of financial liabilities, or financial assets and financial liabilities on a fair value basis, such that those financial liabilities may qualify for designation as at FVTPL. For example, the entity has financial assets and financial liabilities that share one or more risks, which are managed and evaluated on a fair value basis according to a documented asset and liability management policy, such as a portfolio of issued structured products that contain multiple embedded derivatives and that are managed on a fair value basis using a mixture of derivatives and non-derivatives. [*IFRS 9.B4.1.34*]

7.5.60.20   This FVTPL designation relies on the way the entity manages and evaluates the performance of the group of financial instruments. Therefore, an entity that designates financial liabilities as at FVTPL on the basis of this condition has to designate all eligible financial liabilities that are managed and evaluated together. [*IFRS 9.B4.1.35*]

7.5.60.30   Documentation of an entity's strategy is required in order to meet this condition for designation as at FVTPL. The documentation need not be extensive but does need to be sufficient to meet the condition in 7.5.40.10. This documentation is not required for each individual item, but may be on a portfolio basis – e.g. if the performance management system for a department (approved by the entity's key management personnel) clearly demonstrates that its performance is evaluated on this basis, then no further documentation is required. [*IFRS 9.B4.1.36*]

7.5.70 Financial liabilities containing embedded derivatives

7.5.70.10   If a contract contains one or more embedded derivatives and the host is not an asset in the scope of IFRS 9, then an entity may designate the entire combined contract as at FVTPL unless the embedded derivative does not significantly modify the cash flows or it is clear that separation of the embedded derivative is prohibited (see 7.2.120.50). [*IFRS 9.4.3.5*]

7.5.70.20   An example of an embedded derivative for which it is clear that separation would be prohibited, and therefore designation of the entire hybrid contract as at FVTPL is not possible, is a mortgage loan issued that is prepayable at an amount approximating its amortised cost (see 7.2.240.10). Another example is an instrument containing a non-leveraged cap that is out of the money at inception. [*IFRS 9.B4.3.5, B4.3.8*]

7.5.70.30   An entity can apply the FVTPL designation to contractual agreements that contain one or more embedded derivatives only when the host contract is not an asset in the scope of IFRS 9. [*IFRS 9.4.3.5*]

7.5.70.40   If an entity does not apply the designation in 7.5.70.10 and the embedded derivative is required to be separated but its fair value cannot be measured reliably, then the entire combined contract is designated as at FVTPL. If the fair value of the embedded derivative cannot be measured reliably directly, then it is necessary to consider whether it can be measured reliably indirectly by deducting the fair value of the host contract from the fair value of the entire hybrid instrument. In our experience, circumstances in which the embedded derivative cannot be measured reliably (either directly or indirectly) are encountered rarely. However, in those rare circumstances the entire contract is designated as at FVTPL. [*IFRS 9.4.3.6–4.3.7*]

7.5.80 RECLASSIFICATIONS

7.5.80.10   Classification of financial liabilities is determined on initial recognition (see 7.5.20.10). Subsequent reclassification is prohibited. [*IFRS 9.4.2.1, 4.4.2*]

7.6   Recognition and derecognition

7.6   Recognition and derecognition

CURRENTLY EFFECTIVE REQUIREMENTS

This publication reflects IFRS in issue at 1 August 2018, and the currently effective requirements cover annual periods beginning on 1 January 2018.

The requirements related to this topic are mainly derived from the following.

STANDARD	TITLE
IFRS 9	Financial Instruments
IFRIC 19	Extinguishing Financial Liabilities with Equity Instruments

FORTHCOMING REQUIREMENTS

The current effective requirements are affected by the following forthcoming requirements. They are highlighted with a # and the impact is explained in the accompanying boxed text at the references indicated.

In May 2017, the IASB issued IFRS 17 *Insurance Contracts*, which is effective for annual periods beginning on or after 1 January 2021. See 7.6.365. IFRS 17 is the subject of chapter 8.1A.

FUTURE DEVELOPMENTS

The currently effective requirements that may be affected by future developments are highlighted with a * and are briefly discussed in 7.6.500.

7.6.10   INITIAL RECOGNITION

7.6.10.10   An instrument is recognised in the statement of financial position when the entity becomes party to a contract that is a financial instrument. [*IFRS 9.3.1.1*]

7.6.10.20   Situations in which an entity has become a party to the contractual provisions include committing to a purchase of securities or agreeing to enter into a derivative. In contrast, planned but not committed future transactions, no matter how likely, are not financial assets or financial liabilities because they do not represent situations in which the entity becomes a party to a contract requiring the future receipt or delivery of assets. For example, an entity's expected but uncommitted issue of commercial paper does not qualify as a financial liability. [*IFRS 9.B3.1.2*]

7.6.10.30   Similarly, if an entity makes an offer to enter into a contract to buy or sell a financial instrument, then the entity has not become party to a contract requiring the future receipt or delivery of a financial instrument. In our view, the entity should not account for such an offer until the counterparty accepts the offer and the entity becomes a party to a contractual arrangement. [*IFRS 9.B3.1.2*]

7.6.10.40   If a transfer of a financial asset does not qualify for derecognition, then the transferee does not recognise the transferred asset as its asset in its statement of financial position, but derecognises the cash or other consideration paid and recognises a receivable from the transferor. For further discussion on the accounting by the transferee in those cases, see 7.6.260.10. [*IFRS 9.B3.2.15*]

7.6.20   Trade and settlement date accounting

7.6.20.10   Applying the general recognition principle in IFRS 9 would result in all transactions that happen in regulated markets being accounted for on the trade date, which is when an entity becomes party to the contract. However, the standard recognises that many financial institutions and other entities use settlement date accounting for financial assets and that it would be cumbersome to account for such transactions as derivatives between the trade and settlement dates. [*IFRS 9.3.1.1–3.1.2, B3.1.3, B3.1.5–B3.1.6*]

7.6.20.20   Because of the short time between the trade date and the settlement date in these types of regulated market situations, such 'regular-way' contracts are not recognised as derivative contracts under IFRS 9. [*IFRS 9.BA.4*]

7.6.20.30   The purchase or sale of a non-derivative financial asset that will be delivered within the timeframe generally established by regulation or convention in the market concerned – e.g. a regular-way transaction (see 7.2.70) – may be recognised either on the date on which the entity commits to the transaction (the trade date) or on the date on which the instrument is actually transferred (the settlement date). [*IFRS 9.B3.1.3, B3.1.5–B3.1.6*]

7.6.20.40   An entity needs to choose a method to be applied consistently to all purchases and all sales of financial assets that are classified in the same way. [*IFRS 9.B3.1.3*]

7.6.20.50   A contract that requires or permits net settlement of the change in its value is not a regular-way contract and therefore trade date or settlement date accounting is not applied to the contract. Instead, such a contract is accounted for as a derivative in the period between the trade date and the settlement date. [*IFRS 9.B3.1.4*]

7.6.20.60   There are no specific requirements for trade date and settlement date accounting for financial liabilities and therefore financial liabilities are recognised on the date on which the entity becomes a party to the contractual provisions of the instrument – i.e. the trade date. Such contracts are not generally recognised unless one of the parties has performed under the agreement or the contract is a derivative contract not exempt from the scope of IFRS 9. [*IFRS 9.IG.B.32*]

7.6.20.70   The IFRS Interpretations Committee discussed whether the regular-way exemption (see 7.6.20.20) applies to short sales of a security. The Committee noted that requiring entities to account for short positions as derivatives might create considerable practical problems for their accounting systems and controls with little, if any, improvement to the quality of the financial information presented. Therefore, a liability arising from a short trading position is not accounted for as a derivative because it represents a transaction in a financial asset for which either trade date or settlement date accounting may be applied in line with the entity's policy choice. [*IU 01-07*]

7.6.20.80   If an entity that buys a financial asset applies settlement date accounting, then it accounts for changes in the fair value of that asset between the trade and settlement dates in the same way as it accounts for fair value changes that happen after recognition of the asset. This is in line with the logic that these changes in fair value between the trade date and the settlement date are attributable to the buyer rather than the seller because the seller's right to changes in the fair value ceases on the trade date (see 7.6.20.120). [*IFRS 9.B3.1.6, IG.D.2.2*]

7.6.20.90   Therefore, if the acquired asset is measured at fair value, then the buyer recognises changes in the asset's fair value between the trade date and the settlement date, regardless of whether trade date accounting or settlement date accounting is applied. Under settlement date accounting, although the underlying asset is not recognised until settlement date, changes in the fair value of the underlying asset are recognised. Therefore, the fair value adjustment is shown as a receivable or payable until settlement date, at which date the receivable or payable adjusts the amount initially recognised for the asset. This results in the asset being initially measured at its fair value on the settlement date. Fair value changes between trade date and settlement date are recognised in profit or loss for financial assets classified as at FVTPL, or in OCI for financial assets classified as at FVOCI and for investments in equity instruments designated as at FVOCI. [*IFRS 9.B3.1.5–B3.1.6, IG.D.2.2*]

7.6.20.100   If the item bought is measured at amortised cost, then any change in the fair value of the asset between trade date and settlement date is not recognised.

7.6.20.110   The trade date is considered to be the date of initial recognition for the purpose of applying the impairment requirements. For a discussion of the application of the impairment requirements when settlement date accounting is applied, see 7.8.70.30.

7.6.20.120   The difference between trade date and settlement date accounting for a sale of financial assets is in the timing of derecognition of the transferred assets and of recognition of any profit or loss on disposal. As explained in 7.6.20.80, the seller's right to changes in the fair value of an asset ceases on the trade date. Therefore, if the instrument is carried at fair value, then the seller stops recognising changes in value from the trade date regardless of whether trade date accounting or settlement date accounting is applied. [*IFRS 9.IG.D.2.2*]

7.6.20.130   If trade date accounting is applied, then the asset is derecognised and the profit or loss on disposal and a receivable for the sales proceeds are recognised on the trade date. [*IFRS 9.B3.1.5*]

7.6.20.140   If settlement date accounting is applied, then the asset continues to be recognised until settlement date, although no changes in its fair value after the trade date are recognised. On settlement date, the asset is derecognised and a profit or loss on the disposal is recognised. The proceeds are the contract amount; the carrying amount of the asset sold does not reflect gains and losses between the trade and settlement dates. [*IFRS 9.B3.1.6, IG.D.2.2*]

7.6.20.150   Because trade date accounting and settlement date accounting for regular-way purchases or sales of financial assets are specific practices that an entity may apply in preparing and presenting its financial statements and because an entity has a choice between them, a change from settlement date to trade date accounting (or vice versa) is a voluntary change in accounting policy (see 2.8.70). [*IFRS 9.3.1.2, IAS 8.5*]

7.6.20.160   A loan commitment is a firm commitment to provide credit under pre-specified terms and conditions. A loan commitment that is excluded from the scope of IFRS 9 (although subject to the application of its impairment requirements) is in our view also excluded from the requirements on trade date and settlement date accounting. For a discussion of the accounting implications of a loan commitment, see 7.1.250 and 7.7.30. [*IFRS 9.BCZ2.2*]

7.6.30   **Normal purchases and sales**

7.6.30.10   'Normal purchases and sales' are contracts for purchases and sales of non-financial instruments that are entered into and continue to be held for the receipt or delivery of the non-financial item in accordance with the entity's expected purchase, sale or usage requirements. Normal purchases and sales – even if they can be settled net in cash or another financial instrument or by exchanging financial instruments – are outside the scope of IFRS 9 unless they are designated at inception as at FVTPL (see 7.1.200). Therefore, IFRS 9 does not impact the timing of recognition of these contracts. [*IAS 37.66, IFRS 9.B3.1.2(b), 15.31*]

7.6.40   **Linked transactions**

7.6.40.10   Generally, the terms of each contract determine the appropriate accounting and two financial instruments, even if they are entered into simultaneously, are accounted for separately. However, in our view the following indicators should be considered in determining whether two financial instruments should be accounted for as a single combined instrument:
- whether they are entered into at the same time and in contemplation of each other;
- whether they have the same counterparty;
- whether they relate to the same risk; and
- whether there is an economic need or substantive business purpose for structuring the transactions separately that could not also have been accomplished in a single transaction. [*IFRS 9.IG.B.6*]

7.6.40.20   The IFRS Interpretations Committee discussed the aggregation of separate transactions as a single derivative and noted that the indicators listed in 7.6.40.10 may help an entity to determine the substance of the transaction, but that the presence or absence of any single specific indicator alone may not be conclusive. [*IFRS 9.IG.B.6, IU 03-14*]

7.6.40.30   In our view, structuring transactions separately may be regarded as a substantive business purpose when separate transactions are necessary to achieve a direct tax benefit. However, if such a tax benefit is derived primarily from an accounting result – e.g. when the purpose of structuring transactions separately is to achieve an accounting result that produces a tax advantage – then we believe that the substantive business purpose requirement is not met. Similarly, if an entity structures transactions separately to achieve an accounting result that produces a regulatory advantage, then in our view the substantive business purpose requirement is not met. [*IFRS 9.IG.B.6*]

7.6.50   Agency relationships

7.6.50.10   When an entity enters into what might be described as an 'agency relationship', an analysis is required of whether the entity is acting as an agent or as a principal in any transaction entered into as a result of that relationship. Determining whether an entity is acting as a principal or as an agent and whether as a result it becomes party to the contractual provisions of one or more financial instruments that it should recognise requires assessment of the substance of the contractual arrangements and consideration of all relevant facts and circumstances. This may require the application of judgement.

7.6.50.15   The IFRS Interpretations Committee discussed the principal versus agent accounting for centrally cleared client derivative contracts from the perspective of the clearing member and noted that:
- an entity first assesses whether the transaction(s) results in a contract (or contracts) that is (or are) in the scope of IFRS 9 and if it does then the entity applies the requirements of IFRS 9; and
- if a transaction is not in the scope of IFRS 9 and another standard does not specifically apply, then an entity applies the hierarchy principles (see 2.8.20) to determine an appropriate accounting policy. [*IAS 8.10–12, IU 06-17*]

EXAMPLE 1 – BROKER ACTING FOR CLIENT

7.6.50.20   Company S operates as a securities and derivatives broker at a stock exchange. S acts on behalf of one party, entering the customer's order (buy or sell) into the stock exchange's system. The order will be executed on the stock exchange when/if there is a corresponding counterparty offer available. All offers at the stock exchange are given by authorised brokers acting at the exchange. It is possible that the counterparty of the deal executed at the stock exchange is the same broker party – i.e. S acting on behalf of another customer.

7.6.50.30   The settlement term in the market in which S is the broker is trade date plus three days. After this term, the broker is obliged to settle the open deal if the buyer or the seller does not fulfil its part of the trade. On settlement date, the money will be paid by the broker acting on behalf of the buyer through the central depository and the broker acting on behalf of the seller will receive the money through the central depository. The only party known to the stock exchange is the broker.

> 7.6.50.40   In our view, despite the fact that the broker is acting on behalf of a client, the broker is entering into two separate transactions: one with the stock exchange and one with the client. Each transaction results in a financial instrument and therefore S recognises each one separately in its statement of financial position, unless net presentation is required (see 7.10.110).

7.6.60   **DERECOGNITION OF FINANCIAL ASSETS**

7.6.60.10   IFRS 9 contains specific provisions for the derecognition of financial assets. [*IFRS 9.3.2.1–3.2.23*]

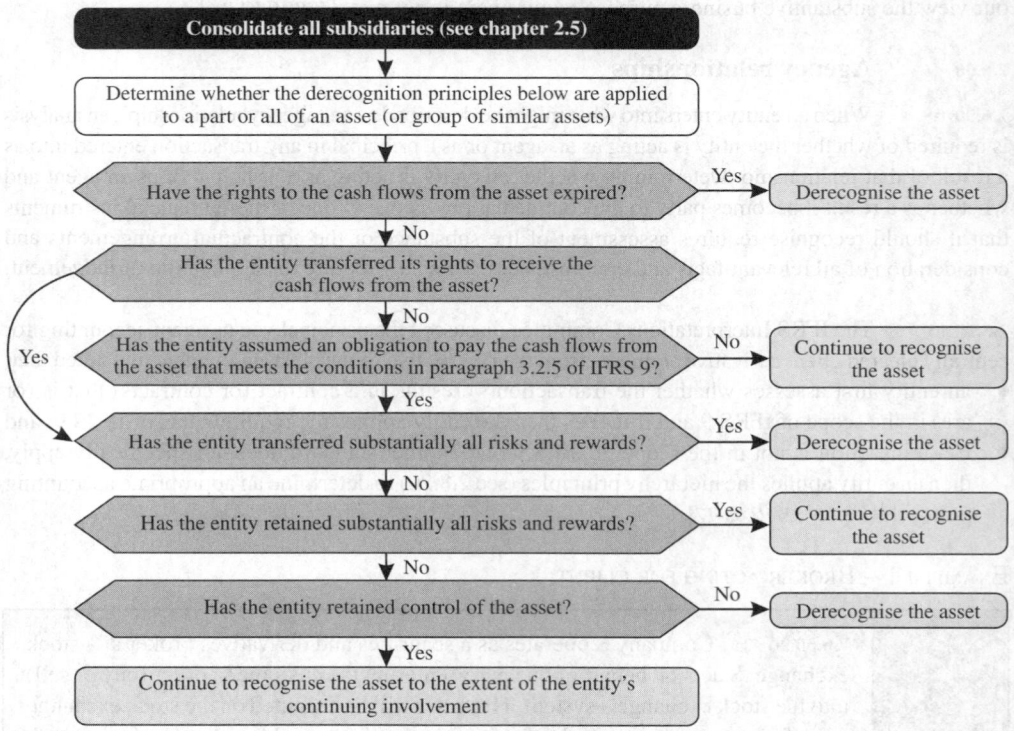

7.6.60.20   In consolidated financial statements, the derecognition criteria are applied at a consolidated level. This avoids the unnecessary consideration of transactions between individual entities in a group, the effect of which is eliminated on consolidation. Therefore, if financial instruments are transferred within a group, then the consolidated financial statements will not reflect derecognition for intra-group transfers, even if those transfers qualify for derecognition in the individual financial statements of the entity that is the transferor. [*IFRS 9.3.2.1*]

7.6.60.30   Accordingly, when derecognition is assessed at the consolidated level, the issue of whether the transferring entity (the transferor) consolidates the receiving entity (the transferee) has a significant impact on the accounting.

EXAMPLE 2 – DERECOGNITION ASSESSMENT IN CONSOLIDATED FINANCIAL STATEMENTS

7.6.60.40   Company T transfers financial assets to Structured Entity X, which it consolidates. In T's consolidated financial statements, the transaction considered in applying the derecognition requirements is that between the group (including X) and any external beneficial holders in X. [*IFRS 9.3.2.1*]

7.6.60.50   However, if X were not consolidated by T, then the transaction considered by T would be the transfer between T and X. [*IFRS 9.3.2.1*]

7.6.60.60   The assessment is different if the derecognition provisions are applied to separate financial statements of T (see 2.1.120). In that case, only the transactions between T and X are analysed.

7.6.70   **Derecognition criteria**

7.6.80   *Determining the financial asset subject to derecognition*

7.6.80.10   The derecognition criteria apply to all financial assets and are therefore used when assessing the derecognition of both debt *and* equity instruments issued by another entity. A financial asset or a group of similar financial assets can be broken down into various parts that can be segregated – e.g. the principal and interest cash flows of a debt instrument – and potentially transferred separately to other parties. Consequently, in applying the derecognition provisions the first step is to determine the financial asset(s) that is (are) subject to possible derecognition. This could be the following cash flows from a financial asset or a group of similar financial assets:

- specifically identified;
- fully proportionate share; or
- fully proportionate share of specifically identified cash flows. [*IFRS 9.3.2.2*]

7.6.80.20   If an entity transfers its rights to all of the cash flows of a financial asset or a group of similar financial assets, then the derecognition provisions apply to the entire financial asset or group. However, if an entity transfers its rights to only certain cash flows of a financial asset – e.g. the interest cash flows in a debt instrument – or to only certain cash flows of a group of similar financial assets, then it is important to determine the financial asset or assets to which the derecognition provisions apply. [*IFRS 9.3.2.2*]

7.6.80.30   In the case of a transfer (or expiry – see 7.6.90) of specifically identified cash flows arising from a financial asset (or a group of similar financial assets), the derecognition provisions apply only to those specifically identified cash flows. For example, if an entity issues an interest-only strip whereby it transfers the interest cash flows arising from a debt instrument and not the principal cash flows, then the derecognition provisions apply only to the cash flows arising from interest payments. [*IFRS 9.3.2.2(a)*]

7.6.80.40   In our view, when rights to some but not all of the cash flows of a financial asset are transferred, judgement may be required to determine whether the cash flows transferred are considered specifically identified. We believe that this judgement should include an assessment of whether the rights to the instalments transferred contain risks and rewards related to the rights to instalments retained. [*IFRS 9.BCZ3.13*]

7.6.80.50   In our view, in order to determine whether the cash flows transferred are specifically identified, the entity should examine the original contract and the transfer agreement to assess whether the cash flows transferred are in substance separate cash flows that are distinct from other cash flows in the original contract, including considering how cash receipts are allocated between the interests of the transferor and transferee.

7.6.80.60   In our view, in order to be considered specifically identified, the cash flows should be identified as substantively separate cash flows in the terms of the contract between the debtor and the creditor; by contrast, a portion of cash flows that is not specified in the terms of the financial asset and is created in the transfer agreement – e.g. for the purpose of providing a credit enhancement or subordination – does not constitute specifically identified cash flows. For example, if a loan agreement contains a single repayment of obligation of 100, then the right to the first 60 of repayment is not considered specifically identified because the loan agreement does not specify this amount of the first 60 as a separate cash flow. [*IFRS 9.3.2.2(b)*]

7.6.80.70   If loans and receivables are repayable in separate instalments, then an entity may need to choose an accounting policy, to be applied consistently, for analysing transfers of rights to instalments (see Example 3A).

EXAMPLE 3A – DERECOGNITION ASSESSMENT FOR SPECIFICALLY IDENTIFIED CASH FLOWS

7.6.80.80   Bank B has a loan of 100 and the contract requires the borrower to make repayment in five separate annual instalments of 20 and that each cash flow received, irrespective of when it is received, will be allocated first to settling the earliest outstanding instalment. B transfers the right to the first three instalments.

7.6.80.90   In our view, B may choose either of the following approaches.
- *Approach 1:* View each annual instalment as a separately identified cash flow because it is specified in the contract and the risks and rewards related to one instalment are unaffected by agreeing to transfer another instalment.
- *Approach 2:* View the rights to the first three instalments as a priority share in the total cash flows and therefore conclude that these instalments are not specifically identified.

7.6.80.100   Under Approach 1, even though the transferred cash flows are considered specifically identified cash flows, B needs to consider whether the transfer contract creates a dependency between the cash flows transferred and the cash flows retained that is not present in the original contract. This dependency may represent a credit enhancement that results in some (and possibly substantially all) of the risks and rewards in the transferred rights being retained by the transferor (see 7.6.140). [*IFRS 9.B3.2.17*]

7.6.80.110   Modifying the example, if the original loan agreement allocated cash receipts against overdue instalments on a pro rata basis but the transfer agreement required allocation of cash receipts against the earliest outstanding instalment, then this would represent a form of credit enhancement that is considered in the risks and rewards analysis. [*IFRS 9.B3.2.17*]

7.6.80.120   An entity applies the derecognition provisions only to a fully proportionate share if it transfers the following (or if the following are subject to expiry – see 7.6.90):
● only a fully proportionate share of the cash flows of a financial asset (or of a group of similar financial assets); or
● only a fully proportionate share of specifically identified cash flows as described in 7.6.80.30.

7.6.80.130   The derecognition provisions do not require there to be only one counterparty to whom such cash flows are transferred or that each counterparty obtains a proportionate right to the cash flows being transferred. However, in order to consider only the part(s) transferred for derecognition as a fully proportionate share, it is important to ensure that the transferring entity also retains only a fully proportionate share of the cash flows.

EXAMPLE 3B – DERECOGNITION ASSESSMENT FOR FULLY PROPORTIONATE SHARE OF CASH FLOWS

7.6.80.140   Company U transfers 80% of the interest cash flows on an existing investment to various counterparties; each counterparty takes up a different portion of the 80%, with the interests of some counterparties subordinated to those of others.

7.6.80.150   In this example, U still subjects the 80% to a derecognition assessment because it retains a fully proportionate share (20%) of the interest cash flows for itself. This is irrespective of the actual distribution of the 80% among the various counterparties. [*IFRS 9.3.2.2(a)*]

7.6.80.160   Except as described in 7.6.80.30–150, the derecognition assessment applies to a financial asset (or to a group of similar financial assets) in its entirety. For example, if an entity transfers the rights to the first or last 80 percent of cash receipts on a debt instrument, or 80 percent of the cash collections on a group of similar receivables but provides a guarantee to compensate the buyer for any credit losses up to 9 percent of the principal amount of the receivables, then the derecognition assessment is applied to the financial asset, or to the group of similar financial assets respectively, in its entirety and not only to the part that the entity has transferred. This is because the entity has not transferred a fully proportionate share of the cash flows, but rather a portion of the cash flows. [*IFRS 9.3.2.2(b)*]

7.6.80.170   IFRS 9 indicates that the derecognition assessment may be applied either to an individual financial asset or to a portfolio of similar financial assets. However, the standard does not specify the circumstances in which a portfolio assessment is appropriate. [*IFRS 9.3.2.2*]

7.6.80.180   In our view, if in a transfer there are contractual terms that have an effect on the risks and rewards of a group of financial assets, then the group of financial assets rather than each individual financial asset should be assessed for derecognition. Generally, the existence of such contractual terms is evidence that the financial assets are similar and share similar risks and rewards. For example, a financial guarantee issued by the transferor covering a percentage of credit losses in a portfolio of financial assets links the risks and rewards associated with the individual financial assets in that portfolio. Consequently, the financial asset that is considered is the group rather than individual financial assets. However, the financial guarantee itself is not considered to be part of the group that is transferred. Such a situation is often encountered in securitisations for which credit enhancement is provided by the transferor over a portfolio of financial assets in the form of financial guarantees, subordinated loans and reserve funds.

7.6.80.190   In our view, it is not appropriate to consider a group of debt and equity instruments as a group of similar financial assets.

7.6.80.200   All subsequent references to 'the financial asset' in this section (derecognition) refer to a financial asset, a part of a financial asset, a portfolio of financial assets or a part of a portfolio of financial assets, determined in accordance with 7.6.80.

7.6.90   *Evaluating whether contractual rights to cash flows have expired*

7.6.90.10   When the contractual rights to cash flows from the asset have expired, that asset is derecognised and no further analysis is required. [*IFRS 9.3.2.3*]

7.6.95   *Modification of terms*

7.6.95.05   IFRS 9 requires that a financial asset is derecognised when the contractual rights to its cash flows expire. However, there is no comprehensive guidance on how this criterion should be applied to modifications of financial assets. IFRS 9 states that in some circumstances the renegotiation or modification of the contractual cash flows of a financial asset can lead to its derecognition. The standard also:
- refers to 'a substantial modification' of a distressed asset as an example of a modification that results in derecognition; and
- includes an example of a modification that does not result in derecognition, in which the gross carrying amount of the modified asset is 30 percent lower than that of the original loan. [*IFRS 9.B5.5.25–26, IE66–IE73*]

7.6.95.10   The IASB and the IFRS Interpretations Committee have declined a number of requests to provide guidance on when a modification of a financial asset results in its derecognition. In May 2016, the Committee discussed the topic and acknowledged that, in its experience, the circumstances in which an entity should derecognise financial assets that have been modified or exchanged is an issue that arises in practice. However, because of the broad nature of the issue the Committee could not resolve it in an efficient manner and therefore decided not to add it to its agenda. [*IU 05-16*]

7.6.95.20   In our view, the holder of the financial asset should perform a quantitative and qualitative evaluation of whether the modification is substantial – i.e. whether the cash flows of the original financial asset and the modified or replacement financial asset are substantially different. If the cash flows are substantially different, then we believe that the contractual rights to cash flows from the original financial asset should be deemed to have expired. In our view, in making this evaluation an entity needs to develop its own policies and methods. In doing so it may, but is not required to, analogise to the guidance on the derecognition of financial liabilities (see 7.6.360).

7.6.95.25   A financial asset may be modified or replaced when a borrower is in financial difficulties. For example, the borrower and its creditors may negotiate a restructuring of some or all of the borrower's obligations to allow the borrower sufficient capacity to service the debt or refinance the contract, either entirely or partially. This is often referred to as 'forbearance'. Examples of forbearance practices include reducing interest rates, delaying the payment of principal and amending covenants. If a financial asset is modified as part of forbearance, then it may be more challenging to conclude that the original financial asset should be derecognised in its entirety. This is because in such a case the objective and nature of the modification is usually to maximise recovery of the original contractual cash flows rather than to originate a new asset on market terms.

7.6.95.30   If an entity plans to modify a financial asset in a way that would result in forgiveness of part of the existing contractual cash flows, then it considers whether a portion of the asset should be written off before the modification takes place (see 7.8.130.40 and 430). If the forgiven contractual cash flows are written off before the modification, then it is likely that the remaining contractual cash flows that are still recognised as the original financial asset at the point of modification will be similar to the new modified contractual cash flows. This approach will impact the result of the quantitative evaluation of whether derecognition of the financial asset is appropriate.

7.6.95.40   An entity needs to consider how to perform the quantitative evaluation for financial assets, particularly if analogising to the guidance on the derecognition of financial liabilities (see 7.6.360). Because of the interaction between the derecognition and impairment requirements, it may not be appropriate to apply the same '10 percent test' or threshold, particularly in cases of forbearance. Therefore, an entity needs to develop an accounting policy on how it performs the quantitative evaluation and the policy may encompass different criteria depending on the nature of the modification (e.g. forbearance cases vs other cases).

EXAMPLE 4 – WRITE-OFF BEFORE MODIFICATION

7.6.95.50   Bank B has a loan asset with a gross carrying amount of 1,000 and a loss allowance of 320. The borrower is in significant financial difficulty and B agrees to modify the loan by reducing its nominal amount to 700. B believes that the borrower will be able to meet the modified terms. No other terms of the loan are modified. B does not incur fees or costs and does not charge the borrower a fee as part of the modification.

7.6.95.60   Immediately before the modification, B determines that it has no realistic prospect of recovering 300 and, accordingly, writes it off against the gross carrying amount of the loan.

7.6.95.70   As part of determining whether the modification is substantial, B performs a quantitative evaluation by comparing:
- the gross carrying amount of the loan before the modification (adjusted by the write-off to 700); with
- the recalculated gross carrying amount, being the net present value of the modified contractual cash flows discounted using the original effective interest rate of the loan (which is also 700).

7.6.95.80   Because both amounts are the same and no other contractual terms of the original loan have been modified, B concludes that the modification is not substantial and, accordingly, the modification does not result in derecognition of the existing loan.

EXAMPLE 5 – MODIFICATION – QUALITATIVE ANALYSIS

7.6.95.90   Bank C holds a bond issued by Company X. X has five bonds in issue with maturities between one and five years. X experiences significant financial difficulties and agrees a bond exchange with its bondholders. Under the terms of the bond exchange:

- 10% of the principal amount of all bonds is forgiven;
- the remaining principal amount of each bond is exchanged for 10 new bonds with maturities between 8 and 12 years and different rates of interest;
- X arranges for a new guarantee for the bonds from an AA-rated bank; and
- the governing law for the new bonds is changed to the laws of another country with a materially different legal framework.

7.6.95.100   C performs a qualitative assessment and concludes that the change in the governing law, adding a high quality financial guarantee and the change from one existing bond to 10 new bonds constitute a substantial modification. Accordingly, C concludes that derecognition is appropriate on the basis of its qualitative analysis and no additional quantitative analysis is required. C derecognises the existing bond held and recognises 10 new bonds.

7.6.95.110   Modification of a financial asset may result in the modified cash flows not meeting the SPPI criterion (see 7.4.150) even though the original cash flows did so, or vice versa. A question then arises whether this change in the assessment of the SPPI criterion is a qualitative factor to consider in determining whether the modification of the financial asset is substantial. IFRS 9 does not require reassessment of the SPPI criterion following initial recognition of a financial asset and does not require or allow an entity to reclassify financial assets based on a reassessment of the SPPI criterion after initial recognition (see 7.4.450.60). However, the fact that a financial asset would be classified on a different basis if the SPPI criterion were reassessed may be a relevant factor to consider when performing the derecognition assessment. Therefore, it appears that an entity should choose an accounting policy, to be applied consistently, to either consider or not consider a reassessment of the SPPI criterion on modification as part of the qualitative assessment to determine whether the modification is substantial.

EXAMPLE 6 – ASSESSING IF CASH FLOWS OF A MODIFIED FINANCIAL ASSET ARE SUBSTANTIALLY DIFFERENT – SPPI CRITERION CONSIDERED

7.6.95.120   Company H holds a financial asset measured at amortised cost. H modifies the terms of the contract for the financial asset. H's accounting policy is to consider the SPPI criterion in determining whether the modification is substantial.

7.6.95.130   H performs a quantitative assessment and concludes that the net present value of the cash flows under the new terms, including any fees paid net of any fees received, are not substantially different from the present value of the remaining cash flows under the original terms.

7.6.95.140   H then performs a qualitative assessment and determines that the modified cash flows would not meet the SPPI criterion on the basis of reassessing at modification based on the fair value of the modified asset at that time and the modified contractual cash flows and par amount. H concludes that the modification is substantial because the modified contractual cash flows would not meet the SPPI criterion. Accordingly, H derecognises the old asset and recognises the new modified asset and – because the modified asset does not meet the SPPI criterion – classifies it at FVTPL.

7.6.95.150   Modifying the fact pattern, if H had an accounting policy of not considering the SPPI criterion in determining whether the modification is substantial, then, in the absence of any other qualitative factors to consider, H would not derecognise the financial asset. The asset would continue to be measured at amortised cost unless criteria for reclassification have been met (see 7.4.450).

7.6.100   *Evaluating whether there is a transfer*

7.6.100.10   A financial asset qualifies for derecognition under IFRS 9 either if the contractual rights to the cash flows from that financial asset expire or if an entity transfers a financial asset in a transfer that meets the criteria for derecognition specified in the standard. An entity transfers a financial asset if, and only if, it transfers the contractual rights to receive the cash flows of the financial asset (see 7.6.110) or it enters into a qualifying pass-through arrangement (see 7.6.120). [*IFRS 9.3.2.4*]

7.6.110   *Transfer of contractual rights*

7.6.110.10   In our view, to be considered a transfer of the contractual rights to receive the cash flows of the financial asset, the transfer of legal title should result in a transfer of all existing rights associated with the financial asset without any additional restrictions being imposed as a result of the transfer. A right to demand payment or to obtain legal title that is conditional on the transferor defaulting under a servicing agreement does not constitute a transfer of contractual rights. In this case, whether there is a transfer is evaluated using the pass-through requirements (see 7.6.120). [*IFRS 9.3.2.4*]

7.6.110.20   A transferor may continue to administer or provide servicing for assets that it has previously transferred to another entity. For example, a transferor may transfer all rights to receivables but then continue to collect the cash flows of those receivables as a servicer in the capacity of an agent of the transferee. The IFRS Interpretations Committee discussed a related issue and noted that the determination of whether the contractual rights to cash flows have been transferred is not affected by the transferor retaining the role of agent to collect the cash flows of the receivables in this case. Therefore, retention of the servicing rights by the entity transferring the financial asset does not in itself cause the transfer to fail the requirements of paragraph 3.2.4(a) of IFRS 9. [*IU 11-05*]

7.6.110.30   However, depending on the legal environment in which an entity operates and the contractually agreed terms, there may be circumstances in which it is not clear whether the contractual rights to receive the cash flows of the financial asset have been transferred. For example, the beneficial interests in a receivable could be sold without legal title to the financial asset being transferred; the seller avoids having to notify the debtor of the sale, thereby retaining its relationship with the debtor, and the debtor continues to make payments directly to the seller. In the event of breach, the buyer has the right to 'perfect' the sale by acquiring legal title to the receivables. In such circumstances, whether a transfer has taken place is a question of fact, viewed together with the legal environment in which the entity operates, and requires the use of judgement.

7.6.110.40   In our view, for a transfer of contractual rights to take place, the transferee should have an unconditional right to demand payment from the original debtor in the case of default by the original debtor (see 7.6.110.10). A right that is conditional on the transferor failing to pass on payments under a servicing contract is not enough. Consequently, in the example in 7.6.110.30, the fact that the buyer is able to perfect a sale only in the event of default means that there is no transfer of contractual rights. Therefore, the transaction would need to be assessed under the pass-through requirements (see 7.6.120).

7.6.110.50   In addition, because of the transfer requirements discussed in 7.6.110.10–40, we believe that it is not possible to achieve derecognition of a financial asset by synthetic means.

EXAMPLE 7 – SYNTHETIC STRUCTURE THROUGH WHICH CONTRACTUAL RIGHTS ARE NOT TRANSFERRED

7.6.110.60   Bank B has a portfolio of customer loans, which yield various fixed rate returns. B enters into a synthetic securitisation structure, comprising the following underlying transactions.

Credit default swap

7.6.110.70   B enters into a CDS with Limited-purpose Vehicle L, under which it transfers to L the default risk on a referenced portfolio of loans (originated customer loans) in exchange for a fixed premium.

Deposit

7.6.110.80   L provides a cash deposit to B, equal to the principal amount of the reference portfolio of loans, which serves as cash collateral against L's obligation under the CDS. B pays interest at LIBOR on the deposit.

7.6.110.90   The combination of the CDS premium and LIBOR interest on the deposit effectively provides L with a return equal to that earned by B on the referenced financial assets.

Notes

7.6.110.100   L issues credit-linked notes to external parties to fund its ability to take exposure to credit risk in the referenced financial assets. These notes pay interest at LIBOR plus a fixed margin, which is the margin earned by L on the written CDS less any amount needed by L to cover its operating costs. The principal on the notes equals the notional amount on the CDS and the deposit with B, which in turn is equal to the principal amount of the referenced financial assets. Any defaults on the referenced financial assets result in an equivalent reduction in the principal of the notes and the deposit with B.

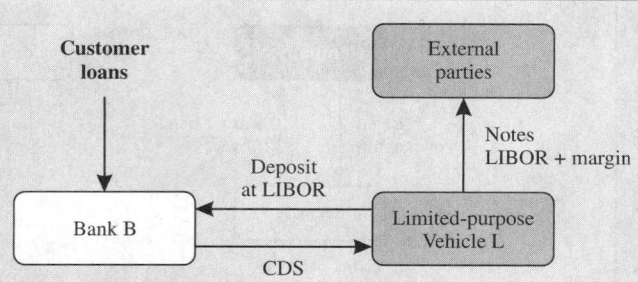

Analysis

7.6.110.110   Assuming that L is consolidated by B (see chapter 2.5), the transaction subject to the derecognition assessment in B's consolidated financial statements is the one that takes place between L and the credit-linked note holders.

7.6.110.120   Although the cash flows in the structure – related to the CDS, deposit and notes – are determined based on the portfolio of referenced financial assets, in our view the combined effect of these three instruments is not enough to conclude that the consolidated entity has transferred the referenced financial assets to the note holders. This is because the entity has not transferred the contractual cash flows arising from the referenced assets. [*IFRS 9.3.2.3–3.2.4*]

7.6.120   *Pass-through arrangements*

7.6.120.10   If an entity retains the contractual right to the cash flows of a financial asset, but also assumes a contractual obligation to pay the cash flows to the transferee (sometimes called a 'pass-through arrangement'), then the transaction is considered a transfer if and only if:

- the entity has no obligation to pay amounts to the transferee unless the entity collects equivalent amounts from the original financial asset;
- the entity is prohibited from selling or pledging the original financial asset under the terms of the pass-through arrangement; and
- the entity is obliged to remit all of the cash flows that it collects without material delay. [*IFRS 9.3.2.5*]

EXAMPLE 8 – QUALIFYING PASS-THROUGH ARRANGEMENT

7.6.120.20   Company N enters into an agreement with Company B in respect of a debt security that it owns.

- Physical custody of and legal title to the security are retained by N, but N agrees to pass any cash flows generated by the security to B immediately.
- There is no obligation for N to pay any amount to B other than the cash that it receives on the security – i.e. neither the principal nor any interest in the case of late payment.
- The agreement prohibits N from selling or pledging the security.

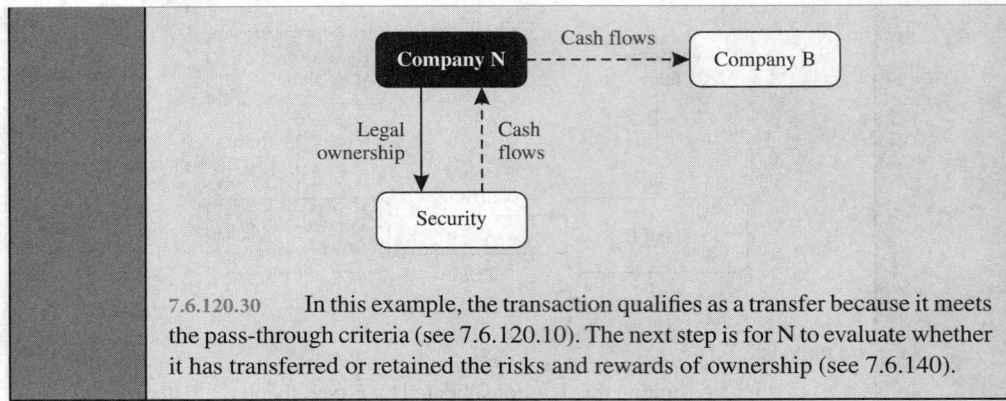

7.6.120.30   In this example, the transaction qualifies as a transfer because it meets the pass-through criteria (see 7.6.120.10). The next step is for N to evaluate whether it has transferred or retained the risks and rewards of ownership (see 7.6.140).

7.6.120.40   A typical situation in which a pass-through arrangement may exist is in a securitisation involving structured entities. For a further discussion of practical issues, see 7.6.280. [*IFRS 9.B3.2.2*]

7.6.120.50   Some transfer agreements include a general right of either party (transferor or transferee) to set off amounts payable by the transferor under the pass-through obligation against other amounts from other contracts owed by the transferee to the transferor. As a result, the transferor might not physically pay to the transferee any or all of the cash collected from the transferred assets, but instead set off the amount of cash collected against other amounts due from the transferee and pay to (or receive from) the transferee only the net amount.

7.6.120.60   If the 'other amounts' and 'other contracts' are not a reinvestment of cash flows collected from the financial assets on behalf of the transferee (see 7.6.320) and are not otherwise connected with the pass-through arrangement, then in our view a right to set off should not impact the pass-through analysis. This is because the transferor settles its obligation to remit the cash flows to the transferee by setting it off against a right to receive cash from the transferee under another contract. The manner of settlement does not negate the fact that the transferor has an obligation to pay amounts due to the transferee and settles that obligation.

7.6.130   Pass-through arrangements involving total return swaps on equity instruments

7.6.130.10   A holder of an equity instrument issued by another entity may enter into a total return swap under which the holder remits all of the cash flows – i.e. dividends – from the equity instrument and receives a stream of fixed or floating rate cash flows. If the terms of the total return swap or any other arrangements that are part of the transfer require the equity instrument to be transferred at the expiry of the total return swap, then in our view such a transfer may meet the pass-through require-ments in IFRS 9.

EXAMPLE 9 – TOTAL RETURN SWAP ON EQUITY INVESTMENT

7.6.130.20   On 1 July 2018, Company S enters into a forward contract to sell an equity instrument issued by another entity to Company T, with physical delivery to T on 30 June 2019.

7.6.130.30   On the same date, S and T enter into a total return swap that expires on 30 June 2018, under which S remits all of the cash flows – i.e. dividends – from that equity instrument without material delay and receives a stream of floating rate cash flows. Under the terms of the arrangement, S cannot pledge or sell the equity instrument and has no obligation to pay any dividends to T unless it receives an equivalent amount as dividends from the equity instrument.

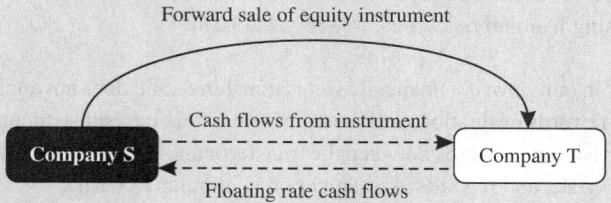

7.6.130.40   S concludes that the transaction meets the pass-through conditions. The next step is for S to evaluate whether it has transferred or retained the risks and rewards of ownership (see 7.6.140).

7.6.130.50   Conversely, if a total return swap or the transfer arrangement does not require the equity instrument to be transferred at expiry but requires only the transfer of all dividends during the period of the total return swap, then in our view the holder of the equity instrument has transferred a dividend strip only until the expiry of the total return swap. Because the dividend strip constitutes separately identifiable cash flows, it can be considered separately for derecognition. In our view, the dividend strip, until the expiry of the total return swap, meets the pass-through conditions if:

- the entity cannot separately pledge or sell the dividend strip arising from the equity instrument;
- the entity has no obligation to pay any dividends under the arrangement unless it receives an equivalent amount from the equity instrument; and
- the agreement provides for remittance of the cash flows without any material delay.

7.6.130.60   Consequently, assuming that the entity has transferred substantially all of the risks and rewards (see 7.6.140), the dividend strip until expiry of the total return swap should be derecognised and the remaining part of the equity instrument should continue to be recognised.

7.6.140   *Risks and rewards evaluation*

7.6.140.10   For all transactions that meet the transfer requirements, the entity next evaluates whether it has transferred or retained the risks and rewards of ownership of the financial asset. An entity derecognises a transferred financial asset if it has transferred substantially all of the risks and rewards of ownership of that asset. Conversely, it continues to recognise a transferred financial asset if it has retained substantially all of the risks and rewards of ownership of that asset. However, if an entity has neither transferred nor retained substantially all of the risks and rewards of ownership of a transferred asset, then it determines whether it has retained control of that asset to assess whether derecognition is appropriate (see 7.6.190). [*IFRS 9.3.2.6*]

7.6.140.20   The risks and rewards analysis is performed by comparing the entity's exposure, before and after the transfer, to the variability in the present value of the future net cash flows from the financial asset. This evaluation can be done either separately for each type of risk that the financial asset is exposed to or for all of the risks arising from the financial asset. Therefore, for each type of risk or for all of the risks transferred and retained, an entity determines its exposure to the variability in the amounts and timing of the net cash flows of the transferred asset arising from that type of risk or from all of the risks. Even if individual risk types are considered separately, the evaluation of whether an entity has transferred or retained substantially all of the risks and rewards is based on the aggregate exposure arising from all risk types. [*IFRS 9.3.2.7–3.2.8*]

7.6.140.30   In our view, if a financial asset is transferred and does not qualify for derecognition under the risks and rewards evaluation, and the transferor enters into subsequent transactions that affect the allocation of risks and rewards between the transferor and the transferee(s), then the transferor should reperform the risks and rewards assessment on a cumulative basis.

EXAMPLE 10 – RISKS AND REWARDS EVALUATION ON A CUMULATIVE BASIS

7.6.140.40   Company M enters into two separate transactions.
- It transfers financial assets to unconsolidated Structured Entity SE. The consideration for the transfer includes a note that represents an interest in the transferred assets.
- Subsequently, M sells the note unconditionally to an unrelated third party (Company X) and retains no further involvement with the transferred financial assets or SE.

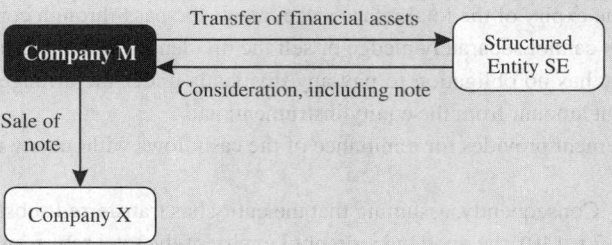

7.6.140.50   M evaluates the risks and rewards of its interests in the financial assets on a cumulative basis as follows.
- At the date of the transaction with SE, M concludes that it has retained substantially all of the risks and rewards of ownership of the transferred assets because M obtains the note that represents an interest in the transferred assets (see 7.6.180). Accordingly, M does not derecognise the transferred financial assets at this time.
- At the date of the transaction with X, M considers the subsequent sale and concludes that it has transferred substantially all of the risks and rewards of ownership of the financial assets and derecognises them.

7.6.150 *Risk types*

7.6.150.10   Different types of risk can be briefly summarised as follows.

- Price risk, which is an inherent risk in equity instruments.
- Risks inherent in debt instruments:
  - credit risk, also called 'risk of default';
  - interest rate risk, comprising fair value interest rate risk and cash flow interest rate risk;
  - prepayment risk – i.e. the risk that the principal is repaid earlier than expected; and
  - late-payment risk – i.e. the risk that payments received from the underlying financial assets are made later than expected, sometimes called 'slow-payment risk'.
- Risks inherent in both equity and debt instruments:
  - currency risk; and
  - other risks – this category covers any risks that may exist in practice in a particular fact pattern that is not explicitly covered by the above risk categories – e.g. dispute and legal risks (see 7.6.160) and structural and other liquidity risks (see 7.6.170).

7.6.160 *Dispute and legal risks*

7.6.160.10   'Dispute risk' (also known as 'warranty' or 'dilution risk') is the risk of a dispute over a financial asset – e.g. a receivable – because of a claim from the customer that the quality of goods delivered or services performed varied from what was agreed contractually. The risk is that the debtor may not be legally obliged to pay the stated amount of the receivable. Consequently, the originator may have sold a financial asset that does not legally exist or that does not exist to the extent of its stated amount.

7.6.160.20   Typically, the transferee will not accept liability for any such dispute risk – i.e. the transferor remains liable for any deductions arising from disputes and has to reimburse the transferee for losses incurred, or the transferee has a right to put the disputed financial asset(s) back to the transferor. Because there is no (legally existing) financial asset, there is no risk that could be transferred unless the transferee accepts this risk without the possibility of recourse; in our experience, the chance of this is remote.

7.6.160.30   In our view, dispute risk should not be included in the risks and rewards analysis, because it relates to the existence of a financial asset rather than to the risks and rewards inherent in an existing financial asset.

7.6.160.40   Similar considerations apply to other legal risks – i.e. we believe that they should not normally be included in the risks and rewards analysis because they relate to the existence of a financial asset rather than to the risks and rewards inherent in a financial asset. In addition, the transferee will not usually accept these risks without a right of recourse.

7.6.170 *Structural and other liquidity risks*

7.6.170.10   Structural liquidity risk arises primarily in securitisations when there is a mismatch between the cash inflows from financial assets and cash outflows on financial liabilities. It is important to differentiate structural liquidity risk from late-payment and default risk. For example, in a securitisation structural liquidity risk may arise because of variability in the timing of defaults on the assets whereby the structured entity that has issued securities to investors does not have enough cash to meet its obligations. This variability can arise without altering the cumulative expectation of defaults on the portfolio. In our view, this risk is not inherent in the financial asset transferred, but arises as a result of the structure of the transaction. Consequently, we believe that this risk should not be included in the risks and rewards analysis.

7.6.170.20   In certain structures, a transferor also provides a liquidity facility to the most senior debt component in the structure. In these circumstances, the provision of the liquidity facility does not generally impact the analysis of risks and rewards for derecognition purposes. However, if such a facility does not represent the most senior debt component in the structure, then it is possible that the transferor is absorbing credit risk through the provision of the facility. In these circumstances, the granting of such a liquidity facility will have an impact on the risks and rewards analysis because it makes the transferor absorb credit risk. Consequently, the terms of any liquidity facility need careful evaluation to determine whether it plays a part in the risks and rewards analysis.

7.6.180   *Substantially all risks and rewards*

7.6.180.10   No specific quantitative guidance is provided on what constitutes 'substantially all' of the risks and rewards of a financial asset. In our view, the analysis should be based on all of the facts and circumstances, considering all of the risks (except for dispute and legal risks) associated with the financial asset on a probability-weighted basis. If substantially all of the total variability in the present value of the future cash flows associated with the financial asset is retained, then we believe that the entity would be considered to have retained substantially all of the risks and rewards. [*IFRS 9.3.2.7*]

7.6.180.20   Assessing whether and to what extent exposure to variability in the present value of cash flows has been retained requires consideration of all relevant facts and circumstances.

7.6.180.30   If the transferee is a limited-purpose vehicle, then the consideration for the transfer often includes securities issued by, or other interests in, the limited-purpose vehicle. Usually, the limited-purpose vehicle is established for the purpose of holding similar transferred assets and paying the cash flows from such assets to the various interest holders in the limited-purpose vehicle in line with the terms of those interests and its governing arrangements. Accordingly, these interests represent a repackaging of some or all of the cash flows of the transferred assets.

7.6.180.40   The transferor may already have a pre-existing interest in the limited-purpose vehicle, such as subordinated debt or an equity-like interest, and this pre-existing interest may also represent an exposure to variability in the cash flows of newly transferred assets that is relevant to the analysis.

7.6.180.50   In other cases, the assets may be transferred to a substantive operating entity that carries on its own business activities and that holds many assets in addition to the financial assets transferred to it by the transferor. In our view, in these cases the analysis should focus on comparing the variability of the cash flows of the transferred assets with the variability of the cash flows of the instruments received as consideration for the transfer. This assessment should include consideration of any agreements such as a guarantee or put or call options related to the transferred assets and need not consider ordinary equity interests that the transferor already held in the transferee.

EXAMPLE 11 – UNCONDITIONAL SALE OF FINANCIAL ASSETS TO OPERATING SUBSIDIARY

> 7.6.180.60   A parent company enters into an unconditional sale of financial assets to a wholly owned subsidiary that carries on banking operations. We do not believe that derecognition of the assets in the separate financial statements of the parent is precluded merely as a result of its 100% ownership interest in the transferee (see 7.6.180.50).

7.6.180.70   If financial assets are transferred to a substantive operating entity in exchange for new equity interests in the transferee, then the transferor evaluates the nature of the variability to which those new interests expose it. If the transferee has substantive other operations, then the variability in discretionary dividends and changes in fair value arising from the new equity interests would usually be significantly different from an exposure to the transferred assets. In some cases, this may require consideration of the transferee's future plans – e.g. if the transferee is a start-up company. The smaller the transferred assets are in relation to the total operations of the substantive operating entity and the smaller the new equity interests are in relation to the total ownership interests in the substantive operating entity, the more likely it is that substantially all of the risks and rewards of ownership may be considered to have been transferred.

EXAMPLE 12 – EXCHANGE OF FINANCIAL ASSETS WITH SIGNIFICANTLY DIFFERENT CASH FLOWS

> 7.6.180.80   Company X holds an equity investment in Company W, an unlisted company. X had elected on initial recognition of the investment in W to present changes in its fair value in OCI. W's parent company is listed. X has agreed to exchange its shares in W for shares in W's parent. W is merged into its parent and X receives new shares in the merged entity.

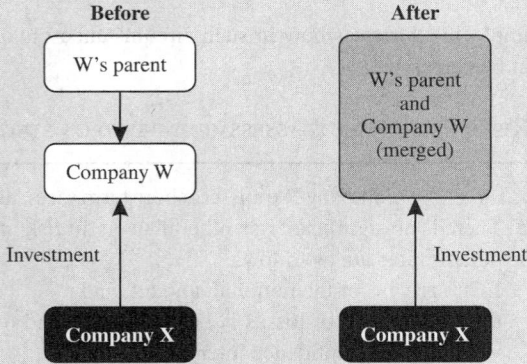

> 7.6.180.90   X no longer owns the shares in W. Instead, X has received new shares in the parent as consideration. In our view, the derecognition criteria are met in this example because, subsequent to the transfer, the equity instruments received by X

have cash flows that are significantly different from the cash flows of the original equity instrument – i.e. X has received new financial assets and not the existing assets only with a repackaging.

7.6.180.100   Consequently, X should derecognise the original assets (equity investment in W) and recognise the new financial assets at fair value (equity investment in the merged entity). Because the shares in W were designated as at FVOCI, any gain or loss on their derecognition is included in OCI. And because the new shares in the parent are not considered merely a repackaging of the shares in W, X may elect on initial recognition of those new shares whether to designate them at FVOCI or to account for them at FVTPL (see 7.4.60).

7.6.180.110   In our view, the fact that a transferor may have a reimbursement right from another entity – e.g. an insurance company – and thereby economically hedges its risk exposure arising from the transferred financial assets, is irrelevant in an analysis of risks and rewards. Only the risks and rewards between the transferor and the transferee are included in the analysis. Therefore, the analysis of risks and rewards does not consider whether and how the transferor has entered into other contracts with third parties that reimburse the transferor for losses incurred in connection with the transferred assets.

7.6.180.120   In our view, it is not generally necessary to use cash flow and/or similar models in performing a risks and rewards analysis. In most cases, evaluating the terms and conditions of the transaction should be enough to determine whether, and to what extent, an entity's exposure to variability in the amounts and timing of the net cash flows has changed as a result of the transfer.

7.6.180.130   However, under certain circumstances a degree of statistical analysis might be required. For example, in transactions in which the transferor and the transferee share the exposure to the variability in cash flows arising from credit risk, it might be difficult to determine whether substantially all of the risks and rewards have been transferred.

7.6.180.140   Example 13 illustrates how in such circumstances an analysis of the transfer of risks and rewards might be performed.

EXAMPLE 13 – RISKS AND REWARDS ASSESSMENT BASED ON STATISTICAL ANALYSIS

7.6.180.150   Company R transfers short-term receivables of 100 to Company S for 95. There is no significant risk other than credit risk inherent in the receivables and the default rates are as follows:
- ECLs are 5% of the notional amount; and
- the likely range of losses is between 4.5% and 6.5% of the notional amount, with a 99.9% confidence interval.

7.6.180.160   R provides a guarantee to reimburse S for losses exceeding 6.5%. The risk is that actual credit losses may exceed the ECLs of 5%. The rewards, which remain with S, are that actual credit losses may be less than the ECLs of 5%.

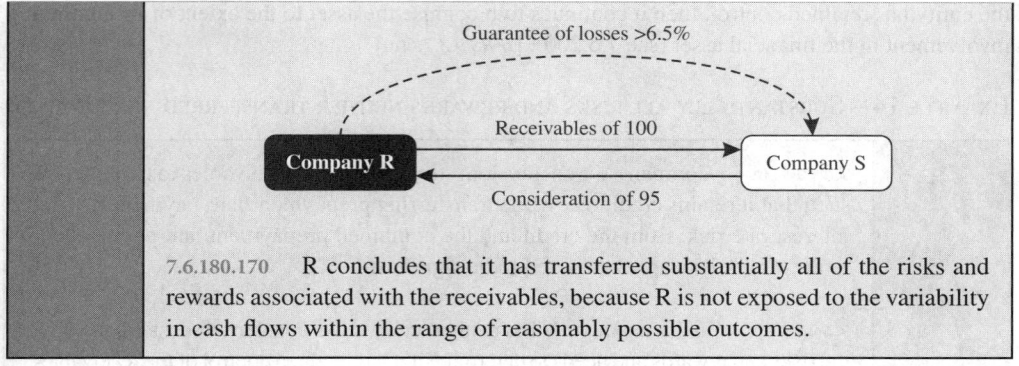

7.6.180.170   R concludes that it has transferred substantially all of the risks and rewards associated with the receivables, because R is not exposed to the variability in cash flows within the range of reasonably possible outcomes.

7.6.180.175   In evaluating risks and rewards it is important that the entity not only transfers substantial rewards but also that it transfers its exposure to a significant loss arising from a substantial risk. A risk of loss could be determined to be 'significant', for example, if it is based on historical loss experience for the type of financial asset transferred. For example, if a transfer of credit risk, which is generally considered to be a substantial risk of the financial assets transferred, will happen only in a catastrophe or similar situation because historical losses are covered through a guarantee by the transferor, then this is considered to be outside the range of likely loss outcomes. This would not be considered a transfer of a significant exposure to loss from credit risk.

7.6.180.180   In some cases, it is possible that a third party instead of the transferor provides credit enhancement. In our view, if the transferor is the beneficiary of the credit enhancement contract, but agrees to compensate the transferee for credit losses, then this is an indication that the transferor has retained the credit risk. In this case, the credit enhancement contract should be disregarded in evaluating whether the financial assets qualify for derecognition and it should be assumed that the transferor continues to bear the credit risk. To transfer the credit risk inherent in the financial assets, in our view the transferee needs to be the beneficiary under the credit enhancement contract and not the transferor.

7.6.180.190   If the transferor assigns the benefit of a financial guarantee contract to the transferee as beneficiary, and the financial guarantee is not in the scope of IFRS 9 from the holder's perspective, then in our view it is appropriate for the transferor to apply by analogy the derecognition criteria for financial assets to any prepayment asset relating to the financial guarantee (see 7.1.137.70). [*IAS 8.10–11*]

7.6.180.200   For financial assets with relatively short maturities, such as most trade receivables, the only substantial risk is generally credit risk. Accordingly, if an entity sells short-term receivables and guarantees to compensate the transferee for credit losses that are likely to occur, then it has retained substantially all of the risks and rewards of ownership. [*IFRS 9.B3.2.5(e)*]

7.6.190   *Control evaluation*

7.6.190.10   If an entity neither transfers nor retains substantially all of the risks and rewards of ownership of a financial asset, then it evaluates whether it has retained control of the financial asset. If the entity has not retained control of the asset, then it derecognises that asset. Conversely, if the entity has retained control, then it continues to recognise the asset to the extent of its continuing involvement in the financial asset (see 7.6.200). [*IFRS 9.3.2.6(c)*]

EXAMPLE 14 – SUBSTANTIALLY ALL RISKS AND REWARDS NEITHER TRANSFERRED NOR RETAINED

7.6.190.20   Company V transfers long-term mortgage receivables to Company W such that it retains credit risk while transferring prepayment/late-payment risk and interest rate risk. Both the credit and the combined prepayment/late-payment and interest rate risks are considered to be significant.

7.6.190.30   In this example, V has neither retained nor transferred substantially all of the risks and rewards and needs to determine if it has retained control of the receivables.

7.6.190.40   An entity is considered to have lost control if the transferee has the practical ability unilaterally to sell the transferred financial asset in its entirety to an unrelated third party without needing to impose additional restrictions on the sale. If there is an active market for the financial asset, then the transferee often has the practical ability to sell the financial asset, even if the contractual arrangements between the transferor and the transferee could require the transferee to return the financial asset to the transferor – e.g. if the financial asset is subject to an option that allows the transferor to repurchase it but the financial asset is readily obtainable in the market. [*IFRS 9.3.2.9, B3.2.7*]

7.6.190.50   Conversely, the transferee does not usually have the practical ability to sell the financial asset if there is no market for the financial asset, even if the contractual arrangements between the transferor and transferee permit such a sale. [*IFRS 9.3.2.9, B3.2.8(a)*]

7.6.190.55   In our view, determining whether there is a market for the financial asset and whether the transferee has the practical ability to sell in that market is a matter of judgement based on consideration of the facts and circumstances. It is not necessary in all cases to demonstrate that the market for the financial asset is active or organised. We believe that a market may be considered to exist if there are willing buyers for an asset and a sale to a market participant could be effected within a reasonable timescale and at a reasonable cost. The transferee does not have the practical ability to sell if a call option or a guarantee prevents the transferee from selling the financial asset – e.g. if the financial asset is subject to an option that allows the transferor to repurchase it and a replacement is not readily obtainable. As a result, the transferor would not be considered to have lost control. [*IFRS 9.3.2.9, B3.2.8–B3.2.9*]

7.6.190.60   In Example 14, if Company V attaches conditions to the transfer that prevent Company W from selling the mortgage receivables to a third party – e.g. to maintain customer relationships – then V has retained control over the transferred financial assets.

EXAMPLE 15A – CONTROL RETAINED THROUGH PURCHASED CALL OPTION (1)

7.6.190.70   Company P sells a portfolio of corporate loans to Company B. P simultaneously enters into a call option with B under which it has the right to repurchase the financial assets after five years.

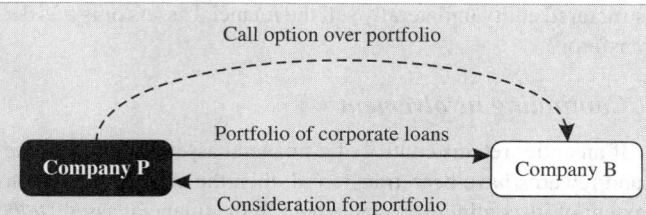

Call option over portfolio

Portfolio of corporate loans

Company P → Company B

Consideration for portfolio

7.6.190.80   Although B has the legal right to sell the financial assets, it does not have the practical ability to do so because it could be required to return them to P at the end of five years. If B attempts to sell the financial assets to another party, then it would have to attach a similar call option to be able to repurchase the financial assets in the event of P exercising its option.

7.6.190.90   It is also unlikely that there is an active market for such financial assets that would allow B to sell the financial assets and then repurchase them later without attaching the aforementioned call option to them.

7.6.190.100   Consequently, because of the call option held by P, it has retained control over the financial assets and will have to consider accounting under continuing involvement. [*IFRS 9.B3.2.7*]

EXAMPLE 15B – CONTROL RETAINED THROUGH PURCHASED CALL OPTION (2)

7.6.190.110   Company Q transfers trade receivables with an option that allows Q to reacquire overdue receivables at face value. Although the option has no stand-alone economic value, Q has retained control to be able to protect its customer relationships.

7.6.190.120   In our view, no distinction should be made in the separate financial statements between a derecognition transaction between a parent entity and one of its operating subsidiaries and one with an independent third party. Therefore, a parent entity should not normally include indirect control through the ownership of an operating subsidiary in the evaluation of control, because this control is not related to the financial asset.

7.6.190.130   When the transferee is a limited-purpose vehicle or other structured entity that is not consolidated (i.e. because it is not a subsidiary or because the derecognition analysis is carried out for the purposes of the transferor's separate financial statements), an evaluation of whether control of the transferred assets has been passed by the transferor raises certain practical considerations. In our view, the following questions should be addressed to assess whether control has been transferred.
- Is there any contractual restriction preventing the structured entity from selling or pledging the financial assets? It is common practice to have such restrictions in place, because when a structured entity is set up for a securitisation transaction the financial assets are also used as collateral. In our view, to meet the criterion that the entity has not retained control of the transferred assets, the structured entity cannot be prevented from selling the financial assets by means of any predetermined autopilot rules or pre-agreements.

- Can the structured entity unilaterally sell the financial assets or is this decision controlled directly by the transferor?

7.6.200   ***Continuing involvement***

7.6.200.10   If an entity retains control of a financial asset for which some but not substantially all of the risks and rewards have been transferred, then the entity continues to recognise the financial asset to the extent of its continuing involvement in the financial asset. [*IFRS 9.3.2.6(c)(ii)*]

7.6.200.20   If an entity's continuing involvement in a transferred asset takes the form of a guarantee, then the extent of the entity's continuing involvement is the lower of: (1) the carrying amount of the asset; and (2) the maximum amount of the consideration received that the entity could be required to repay. [*IFRS 9.3.2.16 (a)*]

EXAMPLE 16 – CONTINUED RECOGNITION BASED ON CONTINUING INVOLVEMENT

7.6.200.30   Company P transfers short-term receivables of 100 to Company Q. P provides a credit loss guarantee of 2. ECLs are 4 and have historically varied between 1 and 5. Q is not permitted to sell or pledge the receivables and there is no market for them.

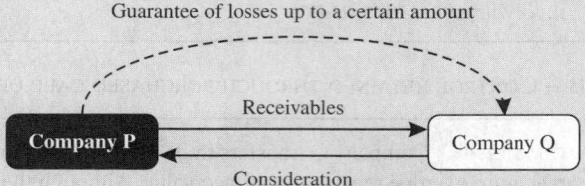

7.6.200.40   In our view, P has retained some, but not substantially all, of the risks and rewards of ownership associated with the receivables. In addition, because Q is not permitted to sell or pledge the receivables and there is no market for such receivables, P has not given up control and continues to recognise the receivables to the extent of its continuing involvement.

7.6.200.50   The maximum extent of P's continuing involvement is 2 (the amount of the guarantee). Therefore, P concludes that it should derecognise 98 and continue to recognise 2, which is the lower of: (1) the carrying amount of the financial asset; and (2) the maximum amount received in the transfer that P could be required to repay. [*IFRS 9.3.2.16(a), B3.2.13*]

7.6.200.60   A question arises about which exchange rate to use to determine the extent of the entity's continuing involvement when it guarantees an amount of credit losses on a transferred asset denominated in a foreign currency. In our view, in determining the extent of the entity's continuing involvement in this case, the guarantee amount should be calculated by applying the spot exchange rate at the reporting date to the maximum amount of the consideration received that the entity could be required to repay in the foreign currency – i.e. without considering potential future changes in the foreign currency exchange rate. This is because the maximum amount of the consideration received that could be repaid is a fixed monetary amount denominated in the foreign currency that meets the definition of a monetary item in IAS 21. Monetary items are translated into their functional currency at the spot exchange rate at the reporting date (see 2.7.110.10). [*IFRS 9.3.2.16(a), IAS 21.16*]

7.6.200.70   Generally, a measurement based on continuing involvement requires the net carrying amount of the financial asset and the associated financial liability to reflect, depending on the measurement basis of the financial asset, either the amortised cost or the fair value of the rights and obligations retained by the entity. However, notwithstanding the requirement to arrive at a particular net carrying amount, the financial asset and associated financial liability might not qualify for offsetting. [*IFRS 9.B3.2.13*]

7.6.200.80   To qualify for offsetting, an entity has to demonstrate that it currently has a legally enforceable right to set off – i.e. a cash flow received on the transferred financial asset would have to result in the elimination of a proportion of the financial liability of the transferor to the transferee. This would imply that the risks associated with the transferred financial asset lie with the transferee, which in turn would imply that derecognition should have taken place; a conclusion that is contrary to that reached in the derecognition analysis. Consequently, when a transaction does not result in derecognition, it is not generally possible to meet the offsetting criteria. Similarly, an entity is prohibited from offsetting any income arising on the transferred financial asset against expenses arising on the associated financial liability, which follows from the more general prohibition on offsetting in IAS 1 (see 7.10.110). [*IAS 32.42, IFRS 9.3.2.22*]

7.6.210   *Assessment of derecognition in separate financial statements*

7.6.210.10   The derecognition requirements in IFRS 9, other than the requirement to start by consolidating all subsidiaries, apply equally to separate financial statements (see 7.6.60). [*IFRS 9.3.2.1*]

7.6.210.20   However, the transfer that needs evaluation in the separate financial statements may be different from that at the consolidated level. Consequently, depending on the fact pattern, it is possible to achieve derecognition in separate financial statements while failing to do so in consolidated financial statements. In our experience, this situation may arise with transactions involving structured entities that are consolidated in the consolidated financial statements.

7.6.220   Accounting for a sale

7.6.230   *Transfers that qualify for derecognition*

7.6.230.10   Sometimes only part of a financial asset qualifies for derecognition – e.g. if an interest-only strip is retained. In these cases, the carrying amount of the entire financial asset before the transfer is allocated between the sold and retained portions based on their relative fair values on the date of the transfer. For this purpose, a retained servicing asset is treated as part of the original asset that continues to be recognised. [*IFRS 9.3.2.13*]

7.6.230.20   Sometimes new financial assets or financial liabilities are created in the transfer – e.g. a credit guarantee. New financial assets, financial liabilities or servicing liabilities created as a result of a transfer that qualifies for derecognition are recognised separately and measured at fair value. [*IFRS 9.3.2.10–3.2.11*]

7.6.230.30   On derecognition of a financial asset, a gain or loss is recognised based on the difference between: (1) the carrying amount of the financial asset (or part of the financial asset) derecognised; and (2) the consideration received (including any new asset obtained less any new liability assumed). If a debt financial asset classified at FVOCI (see 7.4.40.10) is derecognised, then the cumulative gain or loss previously recognised in OCI in respect of the derecognised financial asset is reclassified from equity to profit or loss as a reclassification adjustment – i.e. the overall gain or loss recognised in profit or loss on derecognition is the same as the amount that would have been recognised if the debt financial asset had been measured at amortised cost. It appears that if a part of a debt financial asset classified at FVOCI is derecognised, then a part of the cumulative gain or loss previously recognised in OCI is reclassified to profit or loss in accordance with this principle. This principle does not apply to investments in equity instruments that are designated as at FVOCI because there is no reclassification of any fair value gains or losses to profit or loss on disposal of those investments in equity instruments (see 7.4.60). [*IFRS 9.3.2.12–3.2.13, 9.5.7.10–5.7.11*]

7.6.230.40   If financial assets are exchanged in a transaction that meets the criteria for derecognition, then the financial assets received are measured at fair value and the profit or loss on disposal is calculated based on the fair value of the financial assets received. [*IFRS 9.3.1.1, 3.2.12*]

7.6.230.50   IFRS is silent on how to determine the cost or amortised cost of financial assets derecognised when they are part of a portfolio of identical assets. Therefore, an entity needs to apply the hierarchy for selecting accounting policies (see 2.8.20). It appears that the guidance on the measurement of inventories in IAS 2 should be applied (see 3.8.280). Accordingly, we believe that an entity should choose an accounting policy, to be applied consistently, to use a reasonable cost allocation method. This may include:

- cost formula – e.g. FIFO; or
- specific identification if the entity is able to identify the specific items sold and their costs. For example, a specific security may be identified as sold by linking the date, amount and cost of securities bought with the sale transaction, provided that there is no other evidence suggesting that the actual security sold was not the one identified under this method.

7.6.230.60   However, it appears that the use of a weighted-average cost formula is not appropriate to identify the cost of a financial asset derecognised if the asset is subject to the impairment requirements of IFRS 9. This is because for impairment purposes an assessment is required of whether the credit risk of the financial asset has increased significantly since initial recognition (see 7.8.30.10) and the fair value of a financial asset on the date of its initial recognition reflects its credit risk on that date. Accordingly we believe that each asset that is part of a portfolio of identical assets should be identified with a specific purchase date and price.

7.6.230.70   In some cases, entities may be able to use a pro rata allocation method to achieve a result similar to the weighted-average cost formula.

EXAMPLE 17 – DETERMINING THE COST OF DERECOGNISED FINANCIAL ASSETS – PRO RATA ALLOCATION METHOD

7.6.230.80   Company D buys 300 units of identical securities in two transactions:
- 100 units on 1 February; and
- 200 units on 1 September.

7.6.230.90   On 25 October, D sells 25% of the total position. D is able to identify the items sold as 25% of the first batch of 100 and 25% of the second batch of 200. The resulting carrying amount of the retained portion is the same as calculated using a weighted-average cost formula.

7.6.230.100   However, the method illustrated in Example 17 would be acceptable only if there are enough units purchased on each date to allow for the allocation. For example, if in Example 17 Company D purchased only one unit on each date, then it could not be concluded that a quarter of that unit was sold.

EXAMPLE 18 – DETERMINING THE COST OF DERECOGNISED FINANCIAL ASSETS THAT ARE PART OF A PORTFOLIO OF IDENTICAL ITEMS

7.6.230.110   Company C has made the following purchases of identical Bond B.
● On 1 December 2018: 1,000 units were purchased for 1,500.
● On 1 February 2019: 1,000 units were purchased for 2,000.

7.6.230.120   On 1 May 2019, C derecognises 1,000 units of Bond B.

7.6.230.130   Examples of acceptable accounting policies that C could select to determine the amortised cost of the derecognised bonds include the following.

COST ALLOCATION METHOD	RESULTING COST OF BONDS SOLD
FIFO	1,500
Pro rata allocation across all purchases	Because 50% of the whole portfolio was sold, this would mean that the cost of bonds sold is 50% of each purchase. The cost of bonds sold is calculated as follows. 1,750 = 1,500 x 50% + 2,000 x 50%.
Specific identification (if the criteria in 7.6.230.50 are met)	This could be 1,500, 2,000 or any combination of the costs of individual bonds, depending on which bonds were actually sold. For example, if the sold bonds comprised 100 bonds purchased on 1 December 2018 and 900 bonds purchased on 1 February 2019, then the cost of bonds sold would be: 1,950 = 150 + 1,800.

7.6.230.140 We believe that the accounting policies described in 7.6.230.130 should be applied consistently when assessing impairment and accounting for the resulting impairment losses.

EXAMPLE 19 – ASSESSING A SIGNIFICANT INCREASE IN CREDIT RISK WHEN USING THE PRO-RATA ALLOCATION METHOD

> **7.6.230.150** Continuing Example 18 if Company C used the pro rata allocation method, then the assessment of whether credit risk on the remaining 1,000 bonds has increased significantly would be made with reference to credit risk as follows:
> - as at 1 December 2018 for 500 bonds; and
> - as at 1 February 2019 for 500 bonds.

7.6.230.160 The guidance in 7.6.230.50–150 is relevant for financial assets that are debt instruments measured at amortised cost or FVOCI (see 7.4.20). It is not relevant for financial assets measured at FVTPL because the carrying amounts of such assets are the same (i.e. their fair value) and the impairment requirements do not apply.

7.6.240 *Transfers that do not qualify for derecognition*

7.6.250 *Accounting by transferor*

7.6.250.10 If a transfer does not qualify for derecognition, then the financial asset, or the retained portion of the financial asset, remains in the statement of financial position and a corresponding financial liability is recognised for any consideration received. [*IFRS 9.3.2.15, B3.2.12*]

7.6.250.20 If contractual rights and obligations – e.g. derivatives – related to a transfer prevent the transferor from derecognising the financial assets, then these rights and obligations are not accounted for separately. For example, a call option retained by the transferor may prevent the derecognition of certain financial assets, but recognising the financial assets as well as the call option would result in the entity double counting its rights to those financial assets. [*IFRS 9.B3.2.14*]

EXAMPLE 20A – RIGHTS THAT PREVENT DERECOGNITION THAT ARE NOT ACCOUNTED FOR SEPARATELY

> **7.6.250.30** Company X transfers receivables of 100 to Company Y in exchange for a note amounting to 100 that represents a beneficial interest in the transferred assets – i.e. payments on the note will be made only out of cash collected from the receivables.
>
>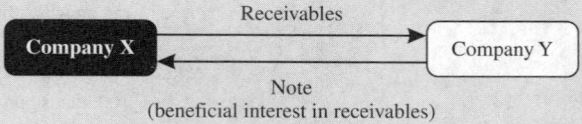
>
> **7.6.250.40** X does not derecognise the receivables because the note effectively passes substantially all of the risks and rewards of ownership of the receivables back to X (see 7.6.180).

7.6.250.50   In addition, X does not recognise a new asset for the right to receive cash flows from the note, because doing so would result in double counting the rights to the transferred receivables. Except for this retained interest in the transferred receivables, which are already recognised in X's statement of financial position, X has retained no consideration for the transfer. Because no new asset is recognised, neither is any corresponding financial liability.

7.6.250.60   It is important to contrast the situation in 7.6.250.20 with one in which the derivative requires separate recognition.

EXAMPLE 20B – RIGHTS AND OBLIGATIONS THAT DO NOT PREVENT DERECOGNITION THAT ARE ACCOUNTED FOR SEPARATELY

7.6.250.70   Company F transfers fixed rate financial assets to Company B. F simultaneously enters into an interest rate swap with B under which it receives fixed rate interest (equal to the rate on the transferred financial assets) and pays floating rate interest (equal to the rate on the notes issued by B to fund the acquisition of the financial assets); the payments are based on a notional amount equal to the principal amount of the transferred financial assets, but are not conditional on B receiving any cash flows from the underlying financial assets.

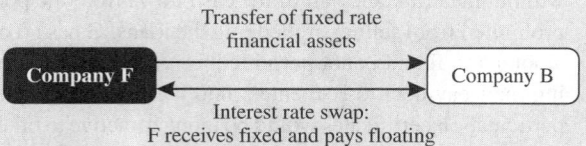

Transfer of fixed rate
financial assets

Company F   Company B

Interest rate swap:
F receives fixed and pays floating

7.6.250.80   In this example, the interest rate swap does not prevent the transaction from derecognising the financial assets, because the payments on the swap are not conditional on payments being made on the transferred assets. Therefore, F separately recognises the interest rate swap and subsequently accounts for it as a derivative (see 7.6.250.20). [*IFRS 9.B3.2.16(p)*]

7.6.260   *Accounting by transferee*

7.6.260.10   If a transfer of a financial asset does not qualify for derecognition, then the transferee does not recognise the transferred asset as its asset in its statement of financial position. Instead, the transferee derecognises the cash or other consideration paid and recognises a receivable from the transferor. [*IFRS 9.B3.2.15*]

7.6.260.20   IFRS 9 is silent on the accounting by the transferee for transactions that do not qualify for derecognition by the transferor when the transferee does not pay cash or other assets but instead issues a new debt instrument as consideration for the assets transferred (see Example 20A).

7.6.260.30   In our view, the transferee should usually recognise both a receivable from the transferor as a financial asset and the debt instrument as a financial liability in such cases. This is because the terms of each instrument generally determine the appropriate accounting and two financial instruments, even if they are entered into simultaneously, are accounted for separately (see 7.6.40). Therefore, unless these instruments should be accounted for as a single combined instrument based on the criteria in 7.6.40, we believe that the only case in which the transferee should not recognise a separate financial asset and a financial liability is when the debt instrument issued by the transferee serves only to pass the cash flows from the transferred asset back from the transferee to the transferor and the pass-through criteria (see 7.6.120) are met from the transferee's perspective in respect of the transferred asset legally owned by the transferee. In addition, the transferee does not offset the financial asset and the financial liability unless the criteria in IAS 32 are met (see 7.10.110). [*IAS 1.32, 32.42*]

EXAMPLE 21A – TRANSFEREE DOES NOT RECOGNISE SEPARATE ASSET AND LIABILITY

7.6.260.40   Company F transfers legal title to a portfolio of loans to Company G, which is not controlled by F, in exchange for participation certificates issued by G.

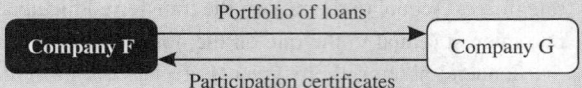

7.6.260.50   Under the terms of the participation certificates, G agrees to pay without material delay all of the cash flows from the portfolio of loans to F and is prohibited from selling or pledging the loans. G has no obligation to pay any other amounts to F and is not permitted to reinvest cash receipts from the loans pending their payment to F. F enters into the transaction because it considers that the participation certificates would be more attractive to other investors or as collateral for borrowings.

7.6.260.60   F does not derecognise the loans because it has retained substantially all of the risks and rewards of the loans. In our view, G should not recognise a financial asset or a financial liability at the time of the transfer because G has simultaneously obtained the contractual rights to the cash flows from the portfolio of loans and assumed a contractual obligation to pay those cash flows to F in a manner that meets the criteria for derecognition of those loans – i.e. the pass-through criteria (see 7.6.120) are met from G's perspective and G does not assume the risks and rewards of ownership of the loans.

EXAMPLE 21B – TRANSFEREE RECOGNISES SEPARATE ASSET AND LIABILITY

7.6.260.70   Modifying Example 21A, the participation certificate includes a guarantee that Company G will pay at least 90% of the contractual cash flows of the transferred loans to Company F in the event that a lesser amount is actually received from the loans. The ECLs on the loans are 3%.

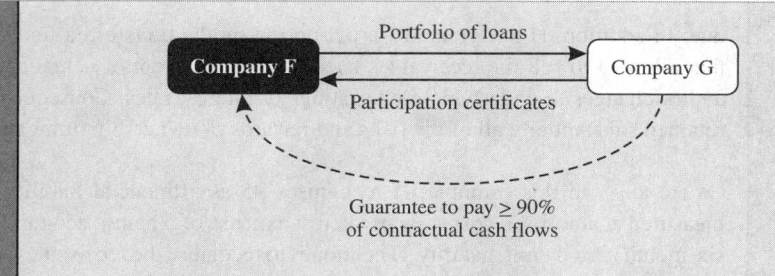

7.6.260.80   Because the guarantee is expected to be triggered only in remote circumstances, F has retained substantially all of the risks and rewards of the loans and does not derecognise them.

7.6.260.90   From G's perspective, the participation certificates no longer meet the pass-through criteria because G has an obligation to pay amounts to the holder in excess of the amounts collected from the loans if collections fall below the 90% level. In addition, the transfer has a business purpose as explained in Example 21A. Therefore, G recognises the participation certificates as a financial liability and a receivable from F.

7.6.270   *Receivables sold with full recourse*

7.6.270.10   Receivables sold with full recourse do not generally qualify for derecognition. Instead, the transaction is generally accounted for as a collateralised borrowing (see 7.6.250.10).

EXAMPLE 22 – RECEIVABLES TRANSFERRED WITH FULL RECOURSE

7.6.270.20   Company H sells trade receivables due in six months with a carrying amount of 100 for a cash payment of 95 to Company J, subject to full recourse. Under the right of recourse, H is obliged to compensate J for the failure of any debtor to pay when payment is due. In addition to the recourse, J is entitled to sell the receivables back to the transferor in the event of unfavourable changes in interest rates or credit ratings of the underlying debtors.

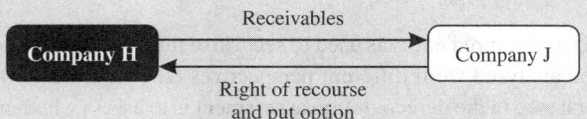

7.6.270.30   The transaction is accounted for by H as a collateralised borrowing because it does not qualify for derecognition. Even assuming that the contractual rights to all of the cash flows on the receivables have been transferred as a matter of law, this transaction still fails the derecognition requirements because H has retained substantially all of the risks and rewards associated with the financial assets. H is obliged to compensate J for the failure of the debtors to pay when payments are due. In addition, H has granted J a put option on the transferred financial assets that allows J to sell the receivables back to H in the event of actual credit losses and/or changes in underlying credit ratings or interest rates. Consequently, H has retained substantially all of the risks and rewards of ownership of the receivables.

7.6.270.40   In this example, H recognises 95 as a financial liability, which is measured at amortised cost with an interest expense of 5 being recognised over the six-month period until maturity. H continues to recognise the receivables as financial assets. Cash received on the receivables by either H or J reduces the receivables and, if it is received by or paid to J, the financial liability. If uncollected receivables are returned to H for cash, then the financial liability is reduced.

7.6.280   **SECURITISATIONS**

7.6.280.10   Entities commonly use securitisations to monetise financial assets – such as homogeneous consumer loans, credit card receivables, trade receivables or mortgage loans – by selling newly created securities collateralised by these financial assets to investors. Such securitisation transactions are often executed using structured entities that have limited activities. The purpose of the structured entities is to hold the interests in the securitised financial assets and to pass through cash flows earned on these financial assets to the investors in the notes issued by the structured entities. In a typical securitisation, the transferring entity assigns financial assets to the structured entity in return for cash proceeds. The transfer of financial assets, issue of notes to investors and payment of proceeds to the transferor usually take place simultaneously.

7.6.280.20   If financial assets are securitised using a structured entity, then determining whether those financial assets should be derecognised may be a complex issue. In many securitisation transactions involving structured entities, the pass-through requirements will be difficult to achieve or will not be met. In addition, because the purpose of a securitisation is often to raise highly rated, low-cost finance, the transferor typically provides some form of credit enhancement to the structured entity. For example, the transferor may provide additional collateral to the structured entity in the form of loans or cash, or may provide a guarantee to the investors in the notes issued by the structured entity. For further discussion of specific practical application issues, see 7.6.290–330.

7.6.280.30   If a structured entity is used to securitise financial assets, then the derecognition criteria may need to be analysed from different perspectives (see 7.6.60.20–30) depending on the circumstances. The first step in the derecognition assessment is to assess whether the structured entity should be consolidated under IFRS 10 (see chapter 2.5 and, in particular, 2.5.170).

7.6.280.40   If the structured entity is consolidated, then the transferor evaluates at the group level whether there has been a transfer of financial assets by the group, including the structured entity, to the investors in the securities issued by the structured entity. If there has been a transfer of financial assets by the group, then the transferor evaluates to what extent the group, including the structured entity, has transferred or retained the risks and rewards of (and, if necessary, whether it has retained control over) the financial assets.

7.6.280.50   If, however, the structured entity is not consolidated under IFRS 10, then the transferor evaluates at the group level whether there has been a transfer of financial assets by the group, excluding the structured entity, to the structured entity. If there has been, then the transferor evaluates to what extent the group, excluding the structured entity, has transferred or retained the risks and rewards of (and, if necessary, whether it has retained control over) the financial assets.

7.6.280.60   If the transferor is preparing separate financial statements, then for this purpose the transferor evaluates whether there has been a transfer of financial assets by it, as a separate entity, to the structured entity. If there has been, then it evaluates to what extent it, as a separate entity, has transferred or retained the risks and rewards of (and, if necessary, whether it has retained control over) the financial assets. [*IFRS 9.3.2.1*]

7.6.280.70   Securitisations usually involve portfolios of financial assets and include detailed terms setting out the allocation of cash flows between the various parties. Therefore, it is often challenging to determine:
- whether the derecognition guidance should be applied to a part of the portfolio of financial assets or to the portfolio in its entirety (see 7.6.80);
- whether there has been a transfer of the contractual rights to the cash flows of the financial assets or there is a qualifying pass-through arrangement (see 7.6.100, 290–300);
- the extent to which the transferor has transferred or retained the risks and rewards of any financial assets that have been transferred (see 7.6.140); and
- whether the transferor has retained control of any financial assets that have been transferred (see 7.6.190).

7.6.290   Evaluating pass-through criteria: Structured entity not consolidated (S)

7.6.290.10   If the structured entity is not consolidated as part of the transferor's consolidated financial statements in accordance with IFRS 10 or the transferor is preparing separate financial statements, and the transferor does not transfer the contractual rights to receive the cash flows to the structured entity, then the terms of a credit enhancement or other arrangement provided in connection with the transferred financial assets may affect the conclusion about whether the pass-through criteria are met.

7.6.290.20   If a credit enhancement can require the transferor to make additional future payments to the structured entity (or its investors) – e.g. an unfunded financial guarantee or other non-funded credit enhancement – then in our view the transfer would fail the pass-through requirements. This is because the transferor could be obliged to pay amounts to the structured entity even if it does not collect the equivalent amounts from the original assets. [*IFRS 9.3.2.5(a)*]

7.6.290.30   However, if a credit enhancement provided by the transferor could never require the transferor to make additional future payments to the structured entity or investors in the structured entity, then in our view the credit enhancement would not violate the pass-through requirement that the transferor has no obligation to pay amounts unless it collects equivalent amounts from the original financial assets. For example, credit enhancement could be provided by means of a pre-funded financial guarantee under which cash collateral is paid to the structured entity at or before the time of transfer, a subordinated loan that is made at or before the time of transfer, or a reserve fund that is built up from the cash collected from the underlying loans and that is retained by the structured entity.

This is because, following the transfer, the transferor would not be obliged to pay to the structured entity any amounts in excess of those that it collects from the original financial assets.

EXAMPLE 23 – GUARANTEE COLLATERALISED BY CASH HELD BY UNCONSOLIDATED STRUCTURED ENTITY

7.6.290.40   Company T agrees to pay the cash flows collected from a portfolio of financial assets to Structured Entity SE, which T does not consolidate. SE issues, for cash of 100, notes to third party investors that are collateralised by its right to receive the collected cash flows from T.

7.6.290.50   SE pays 95 of the cash and issues a subordinated note with a nominal value of 5 to T. The remaining 5 cash is held by SE and will be used to compensate the investors for up to 5 of cash shortfalls arising from defaults in the portfolio of financial assets.

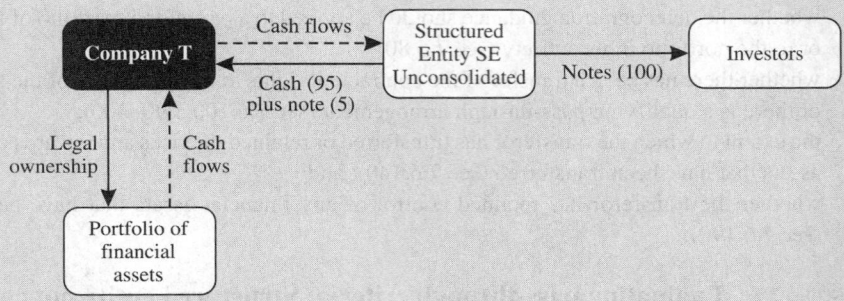

7.6.290.60   In evaluating whether the portfolio of financial assets is derecognised in T's consolidated financial statements, the arrangement does not violate the re-quirement that the transferor in a pass-through arrangement may be obliged to pay amounts to the eventual recipients only if it collects equivalent amounts from the original financial assets. That is because:

- T is only obliged to pay amounts that it collects from the portfolio; and
- SE, not T, has the obligation to pay the initial cash retention to the note holders if there are defaults, and SE is not consolidated by T.

7.6.290.70   The impact of higher-than-expected credit losses is that T receives less from the subordinated note issued by SE when the arrangement comes to an end, rather than T being required to pay additional amounts to SE to cover those losses. Although this variability in cash flows that T will receive is relevant to as-sessing the extent to which T has retained or transferred the risks and rewards of the financial assets, it does not violate the pass-through criteria.

7.6.300   **Evaluating pass-through criteria: Structured entity consolidated**

7.6.300.10   If the structured entity is consolidated, then the contractual arrangements between the consolidated group and the investors in the notes issued by the structured entity are analysed to determine whether the requirements for a qualifying pass-through arrangement are met (see 7.6.60.20–30). This is because the structured entity, and therefore the transferor's consolidated group, will not typically transfer the contractual rights to the cash flows on the underlying financial assets to the investors in the notes issued by the structured entity. However, the terms of the notes may provide for payments to be made to the holders based on cash received on the underlying financial assets in such a manner that the structured entity's only role is acting as an agent on behalf of the note holders. Therefore, it is possible that such a transaction could meet the pass-through conditions listed in 7.6.120.10.

7.6.300.20   For the purpose of evaluating whether there is an obligation to pay amounts in excess of those collected from the original financial assets, the transferor analyses obligations to pay amounts from the consolidated group, including the consolidated structured entity, to other holders of interests in the structured entity; cash flows between the transferor entity and the structured entity are not generally relevant for this purpose, because they are internal to the group. If the nature of credit enhancements is such that additional amounts will be paid to the investors in the notes issued by a structured entity in the event of default – i.e. the consolidated group will make additional payments in excess of the amounts collected from the original financial assets – then in our view the credit enhancements provided by the transferor will violate the pass-through requirements. This applies even if the guarantee or credit enhancement is supported by paying cash into the structured entity at the time of transfer.

EXAMPLE 24 – GUARANTEE COLLATERALISED BY CASH HELD BY CONSOLIDATED STRUCTURED ENTITY

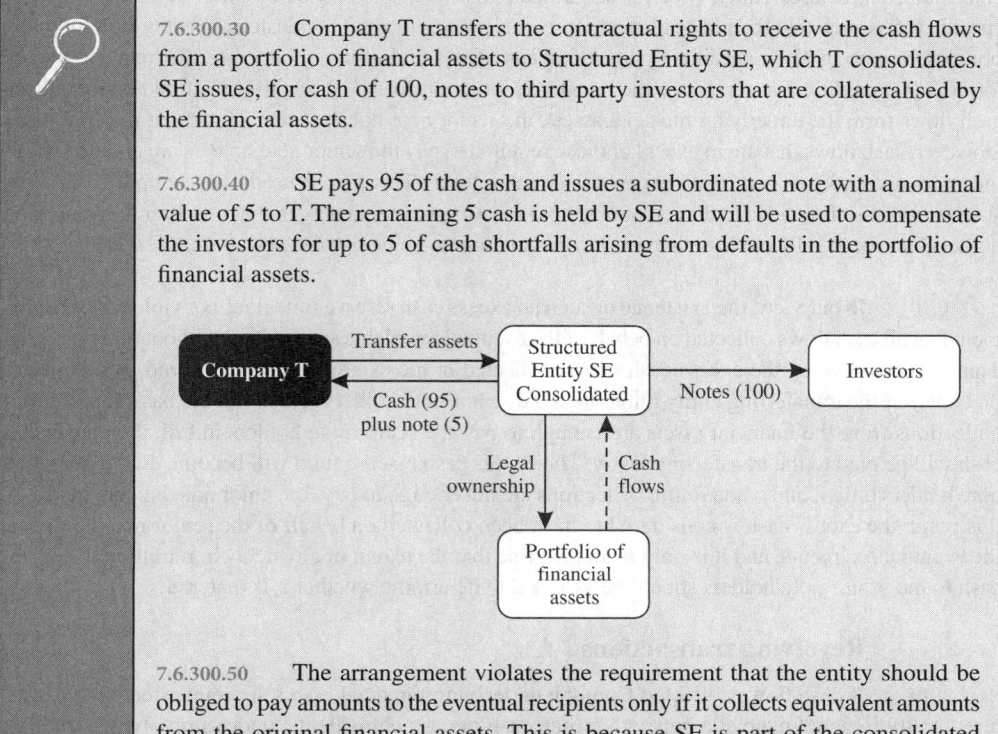

7.6.300.30   Company T transfers the contractual rights to receive the cash flows from a portfolio of financial assets to Structured Entity SE, which T consolidates. SE issues, for cash of 100, notes to third party investors that are collateralised by the financial assets.

7.6.300.40   SE pays 95 of the cash and issues a subordinated note with a nominal value of 5 to T. The remaining 5 cash is held by SE and will be used to compensate the investors for up to 5 of cash shortfalls arising from defaults in the portfolio of financial assets.

7.6.300.50   The arrangement violates the requirement that the entity should be obliged to pay amounts to the eventual recipients only if it collects equivalent amounts from the original financial assets. This is because SE is part of the consolidated

group and therefore the consolidated group is obliged to pay up to 5 of cash to the third party investors in excess of collections from the portfolio of financial assets.

7.6.300.60   Our views on some other specific application issues for determining whether a securitisation involving a structured entity qualifies as a pass-through arrangement are included in 7.6.310–320.

7.6.310   Without material delay

7.6.310.10   To meet the pass-through conditions, an entity is required to remit all cash flows that it collects on behalf of the eventual recipients without material delay. In our view, the entity can invest the cash flows for periods of up to three months without violating this requirement provided that:
- the investments are only in cash and cash equivalents (see 2.3.10); and
- all cash flows – both amounts collected and any income earned on investments in cash or cash equivalents – are remitted to the bond holders on the next payment date. [*IFRS 9.3.2.5(c)*]

7.6.310.20   Conversely, we believe that refinancing terms exceeding three months will not meet this criterion; neither will investments in cash and cash equivalents on a revolving basis over periods exceeding three months.

7.6.310.30   In some securitisation structures, the transferring entity holds a junior interest issued by a consolidated structured entity, which is subordinate to senior notes issued by the structured entity, with specific terms such that the junior interest represents a retention by the transferring entity of a fully pro-portionate share of all or specifically identified cash flows and a subordination of that retained interest to provide a credit enhancement to the transferee for credit losses. When the structured entity collects cash flows from the underlying financial assets, the senior note holders are paid without material delay. However, cash flows that are in excess of those required to pay the senior note holders are retained within the structured entity as part of an 'excess cash reserve fund'. This fund is used to make up for any future shortfalls in cash flows due to the senior note holders. Amounts remaining in the fund after the senior note holders have been fully paid are then paid to the junior note holder. [*IFRS 9.B3.2.17, BCZ3.21–BCZ3.23*]

7.6.310.40   In our view, the existence of such an excess cash reserve fund does not violate the requirement that all cash flows collected on behalf of the eventual recipients are remitted without material delay. This is because when the excess cash is first collected in the excess cash reserve fund, it is collected on behalf of the transferring entity rather than the senior note holders. This is on the basis that if future collections from the financial assets are enough to pay the senior note holders in full, then the excess cash will be paid to the transferring entity. The excess cash reserve fund will become due to the senior note holders only if and when future collections are not enough to pay the senior note holders in full. At this point, the excess cash is considered to have been collected on behalf of the senior note holders as the eventual recipients, and it is only from this time that the extent of any delay in remitting the excess cash to the senior note holders should be assessed to determine whether it is material.

7.6.320   Revolving transactions

7.6.320.10   If cash flows collected from the underlying financial assets are reinvested by the structured entity in new financial assets, other than cash or cash equivalents, under a revolving structure, then problems may be encountered in meeting the condition that all cash flows should be remitted to the eventual recipients without material delay. Further analysis of the terms and conditions governing this reinvestment is required to determine whether the conditions for a qualifying pass-through arrangement are met. [*IFRS 9.3.2.5*]

7.6.320.20   In our experience, there are four general scenarios that may be encountered, each having an effect on the pass-through requirement.

SCENARIOS	EFFECTS
The structured entity automatically reinvests the cash flows to buy additional receivables in accordance with predetermined contractual arrangements embedded in the structure.	In our view, the pass-through requirements are violated because the investments are not in cash or cash equivalents and therefore derecognition is precluded.
The structured entity remits the cash flows to the note holders without material delay, at which time the note holders may decide whether to reinvest the cash flows with the structured entity for the purpose of acquiring further financial assets.	In our view, this does not violate the pass-through requirements and the transaction should be considered further for derecognition.
The structured entity automatically reinvests the cash flows to buy additional financial assets, unless the note holders indicate at that stage that they do not want to reinvest in the structured entity – i.e. the cash flows are remitted to the note holders only if they decide not to reinvest.	In our view, the pass-through requirements are not violated because the structured entity is obliged to remit the cash flows to the note holders if it is so notified. The lack of a physical flow of cash from the structured entity to the note holder and back to the structured entity does not impact the derecognition analysis and the transaction should be considered further for derecognition.
The structured entity remits the cash flows to the note holders, but the note holders have an up-front contractual agreement that all cash flows will be reinvested immediately by the structured entity.	In our view, despite the physical flow of cash, the pass-through requirements are violated because the note holders are contractually obliged to reinvest the cash flows immediately in order for the structured entity to acquire additional financial assets. Therefore, derecognition is precluded.

7.6.330   Continuing involvement

7.6.330.10   If the pass-through requirements are met and it is concluded that some but not substantially all of the risks and rewards of the financial assets are transferred to the note holders, then it is likely that the transferor will have retained control of the transferred financial assets. This is because in a typical structure the structured entity is consolidated and will maintain legal title to the financial assets, whereas the note holders will have no rights to sell the underlying financial assets. Also, even if the structured entity is not consolidated, the transferor may retain control because the structured entity may not itself have the practical ability to sell the transferred assets. In such circumstances, partial derecognition may be appropriate under continuing involvement accounting (see 7.6.200). [*IFRS 9.B3.2.13*]

7.6.340 REPURCHASE AGREEMENTS AND SECURITIES LENDING

7.6.340.10   If a sale of a financial asset is subject to a repurchase agreement at a fixed price, or at the initial selling price plus interest, or if the asset is lent to a third party that agrees to return it, then the seller retains substantially all of the risks and rewards of ownership of the asset. Therefore, the seller does not derecognise the financial asset. If the transferee obtains the right to sell or pledge the financial asset that does not qualify for derecognition, then the seller reclassifies the financial asset in its statement of financial position – e.g. as a loaned financial asset or repurchase receivable. [*IFRS 9.B3.2.16(a)*]

7.6.340.20   This treatment also applies when:
- the financial asset subject to the agreement is of a type readily obtainable in the market, such that the transferee could sell the transferred financial asset and repurchase an identical financial asset in the market to meet its return obligation to the seller; or
- the agreement permits the transferee to return financial assets that are the same or substantially the same as the originally transferred asset or financial assets that are similar and of equal fair value. [*IFRS 9.B3.2.16(b)–(c)*]

7.6.340.30   Similarly, the transferee does not recognise the financial asset received under a repurchase or securities lending arrangement. If the transferee sells the financial asset, then it recognises a financial liability to return the financial asset based on its fair value. [*IFRS 9.B3.2.15*]

7.6.340.40   If there is an event of default by the seller and it is no longer entitled to reclaim the transferred financial asset, then the seller derecognises the financial asset and the transferee recognises the financial asset at fair value or, if it has sold the financial asset already, derecognises the financial liability to return the financial asset. [*IFRS 9.3.2.23(c)*]

7.6.350 WRITE-OFFS

7.6.350.10   For a discussion of write-offs of financial assets, see 7.8.430.

7.6.360 DERECOGNITION OF FINANCIAL LIABILITIES#

7.6.360.10   A financial liability is derecognised when it is extinguished – i.e. it is discharged or cancelled or expires. This may happen when:
- payment is made to the lender – e.g. when the issuer of a debt instrument redeems the instrument;
- the borrower is legally released from primary responsibility for the financial liability – this condition can be satisfied even if the borrower has given a guarantee, as long as the borrower is released from primary responsibility; or
- there is an exchange between an existing lender and borrower of debt instruments with substantially different terms or a substantial modification of the terms of an existing debt instrument (together referred to as 'modification of terms' in this chapter). [*IFRS 9.3.3.1–3.3.2, B3.3.1, B3.3.3*]

7.6.360.20   The derecognition conditions are also satisfied and a financial liability is derecognised when an entity repurchases its own debt instruments previously issued, irrespective of whether the entity intends to resell those instruments to other parties in the near term or is itself a market maker in those instruments. This is consistent with the treatment of own equity instruments acquired by an entity, except that in the case of an extinguishment of a financial liability a gain or loss may be recognised in profit or loss. [*IFRS 9.B3.3.2*]

7.6.360.30   It is not possible for an entity to extinguish a financial liability through an in-substance defeasance of its debt. An 'in-substance defeasance' arises when an entity transfers financial assets covering its obligations to a third party – typically into a trust or similar vehicle – that then makes payments to the lender from principal and interest on the transferred financial assets, without the third party having legally assumed the responsibility for the financial liability and without the lender being part of the contractual arrangements related to the third party. The entity is not legally released from the obligation and therefore derecognition of the financial liability is inappropriate. [*IFRS 9.B3.3.2–B3.3.3*]

7.6.360.40   An entity may arrange for a third party to assume primary responsibility for the obligation for a fee while continuing to make the contractual payments on behalf of the third party. To be able to derecognise the financial liability, the entity needs to have obtained legal release from the creditor whereby the creditor agrees to accept the third party as the new primary obligor. [*IFRS 9.B3.3.3–B3.3.4*]

7.6.360.50   As for a financial asset, when transferring a financial liability, parts of the financial liability could be retained and new financial instruments (either financial assets or financial liabilities) could be created. The accounting is similar to the accounting for the derecognition of parts of financial assets with the creation of new instruments. [*IFRS 9.3.3.3, 4.1.1*]

7.6.360.60   A gain or loss calculated as the difference between the carrying amount of a financial liability (or part of a financial liability) extinguished or transferred and the consideration paid is recognised in profit or loss. The consideration paid includes any non-cash assets transferred and new liabilities assumed. [*IFRS 9.3.3.3*]

7.6.365   FORTHCOMING REQUIREMENTS

7.6.365.10   Some entities operate an investment fund that provides investors with benefits determined by units in the fund or issue groups of insurance contracts with direct participation features and hold the underlying items. Such funds or underlying items may include the entity's financial liabilities.

7.6.365.20   Under consequential amendments to IFRS 9 introduced by IFRS 17 an entity may elect not to derecognise its financial liability included in such a fund or an underlying item when the entity repurchases it – i.e. the entity may continue to account for that instrument as a financial liability and to account for the repurchased instrument as if it were a financial asset measured at FVTPL. This election is irrevocable and is made on an instrument-by-instrument basis. [*IFRS 9.3.3.5*]

7.6.370   Modification of terms

7.6.370.10   Issues often arise over whether it is appropriate to derecognise a financial liability when its terms are renegotiated, including an exchange between an existing borrower and a lender of debt instruments, and including a renegotiation in exchange for an immediate cash payment or receipt. For a discussion of transactions involving the issue of equity instruments in exchange for the extinguishment of all or part of a liability, see 7.6.450.

7.6.370.20   When a debt instrument is restructured or refinanced and the terms have been substantially modified, the transaction is accounted for as an extinguishment of the old debt instrument, with a gain or loss (see 7.7.370). The new debt instrument is recognised at fair value (see 7.7.10). In our view, it is not appropriate to simply assume that the nominal amount of the new loan is the fair value. In the absence of an available quoted price in an active market for the new debt instrument, fair value is established using another valuation technique. In our view, if the valuation technique does not use only data from observable markets, then this does not preclude the recognition of a gain or loss because the estimate of fair value is used as the estimate of the transaction price. [*IFRS 9.3.3.2, B5.1.1, B5.1.2A*]

7.6.370.30   In our view, the requirements on modifications and exchanges of debt instruments do not extend to the usual repayment of a loan at maturity and its replacement by a new loan on arm's length terms, even if the new loan is with the same lender, because the original loan is not modified or exchanged but is settled in accordance with its original terms. Also, we believe that they do not apply to changes in the amounts or timing of payments required under a loan that arise from existing features included in the original debt agreement – e.g. interest rate step-ups or the acceleration of maturity contingent on a credit downgrade – because these are not modifications of terms. However, changes in estimated cash flows attributable to such features may result in the recognition of a gain or loss (see 7.7.330).

7.6.380   *Loan transfers*

7.6.380.10   An existing individual lender may transfer its right to the future cash flows of a loan without any involvement of the borrower. For a discussion of the accounting from the lender's perspective, see 7.6.100. Such a transfer may be performed under the existing loan agreement without any modifications to the terms of the loan agreement. In this case, the borrower is not legally released from its primary responsibility to repay the loan, and it continues to recognise the existing loan. However, in other cases an existing loan agreement may be cancelled and extinguished, and replaced by a new agreement with substantially different terms between the borrower and the new lender (see 7.6.360.10). In this case, the old loan is derecognised. For a discussion of the replacement of a loan agreement, see 7.6.400.20. [*IFRS 9.3.3.1–3.3.2, B3.3.1, B3.3.6*]

7.6.390   *Unit of assessment*

7.6.390.10   In our view, the derecognition assessment should generally be performed on an instrument-by-instrument basis, and not by grouping together similar financial liabilities. For example, an entity may have issued 100 individual bonds that are held by different parties, of which it intends to replace 60 with new debt instruments and redeem the other 40 bonds. The bonds should be considered individually for derecognition – i.e. the unit of account is each bond. Therefore, the assessment should be made for each of the 60 bonds replaced and not for all of the outstanding bonds in total. In this way, the entity would derecognise 40 of the bonds that are redeemed, and the remaining 60 bonds may or may not qualify for derecognition, depending on the extent to which the terms of the original and new instruments differ.

7.6.390.20   However, if an entity has issued one bond with a nominal amount of 100 held by a single party and intends to pay an amount of 40 and replace the bond with a debt instrument with modified terms and a nominal amount of 60, then the assessment is made for the bond as a whole. In our view, the agreement to make a payment of 40 is an element of the modification and accordingly that payment should be taken into account in the quantitative assessment (see 7.6.410) in calculating the present value of cash flows under the new arrangement.

7.6.390.30   In contrast, in some cases an entity may amend or settle a proportion of a single instrument, which is a fully pro rata share in the cash flows of the instrument, while there is no amendment to the remaining proportion or to any other instrument entered into with the creditor. In this case, in our view the unit of account is the part amended or settled because this is the only part whose terms are modified.

7.6.390.40   In our view, if an entity has issued multiple instruments held by a single party and the different instruments are modified together in what is in substance a single agreement, then the entity should assess the impact of the modification with reference to the group of instruments that together is the subject of the single modification agreement. In determining whether the modification of the different instruments is in substance a single agreement, an entity should consider the indicators discussed in 7.6.40.

7.6.400   *Loan syndications and loan participations*

7.6.400.10   In our experience, large borrowing arrangements are often funded by multiple investors. The process of involving several different investors in providing loan funding is often referred to as 'loan syndication' or 'loan participation'. In some cases, the borrowing arrangement represents a single loan between the borrower and a single lender, often referred to as the 'lead lender'. In such cases, the other investors are not direct creditors of the borrower; instead, their participation in the loan is established by a participation agreement with the lead lender. However, in other cases a borrowing arrangement that is funded by multiple investors represents multiple separate loans between the borrower and each of the respective lenders – i.e. the members of a syndicate. Whether a borrowing arrangement represents a single loan with the lead lender or multiple separate loans with each individual investor may be relevant in determining the application of the derecognition requirements for financial liabilities when there are changes to the borrowing arrangement or investor group.

7.6.400.20   For example, an investor that co-funded a borrowing arrangement may be replaced by another investor. If the overall borrowing arrangement represents multiple separate loans from each individual investor, then the borrower evaluates whether the replacement should be accounted for as an extinguishment of the separate loan from that specific individual lender (see 7.6.380.10). However, for a borrower that borrowed under a single loan, replacement of one of the investors that co-funded the loan is irrelevant to the borrower's accounting if the lead lender is not replaced. Also, any other amendments to the agreement between the lead lender and any of the other investors are irrelevant to the borrower's accounting as long as the loan agreement between the borrower and the lead lender is not modified. This is because the lead lender is the borrower's creditor and because the other investors' participation in the loan is set up in an agreement with the lead lender to which the borrower is not a party. [*IFRS 9.3.3.1–3.3.2, B3.3.1, B3.3.6*]

7.6.400.30   IFRS does not provide specific guidance to evaluate whether a borrowing arrangement funded by multiple investors represents a single loan or multiple separate loans. Therefore, in our view a borrower should determine whether the arrangement represents a single loan from a single lender or multiple separate loans from each individual investor based on an evaluation of the legal terms and substantive conditions of the arrangement. Factors that may indicate individually or in combination that an entity has obtained separate loans from each individual lender include the following:

- the terms of the arrangement differ between various investors;
- the borrower can selectively repay amounts to specific investors because repayments are not automatically allocated among investors on a pro rata basis;

- the borrower can selectively renegotiate portions of the total arrangement with individual investors or subsets of investors; and
- individual investors can negotiate their loan directly with the borrower without the approval of other investors.

7.6.405   *Exchange or modification through an intermediary*

7.6.405.10   Sometimes an intermediary (e.g. a bank) may be involved in restructuring or refinancing existing debt securities of an entity. For example, the intermediary arranges for the acquisition of existing debt securities held by third party investors and their exchange for new debt securities that will be held by new third party investors. In these situations, it is important to identify the role of an intermediary – i.e. whether it is acting as a principal (i.e. as the existing lender or investor in the debt securities) or is acting as an agent of the issuer. [*IFRS 9.3.3.2, B3.3.6*]

7.6.405.20   Whether an intermediary is acting as a principal in these situations depends on the terms of the arrangements and whether it is exposed to any risks. In our experience, this assessment includes consideration of whether an intermediary:
- independently initiates an exchange or modification of debt securities;
- commits its own funds for acquiring and placing debt securities and is subject to the risk of loss of those funds;
- is responsible for placing the modified debt securities of the issuer with new investors on a firmly committed basis (i.e. the intermediary is required to hold any debt securities that it is unable to sell to others) or on a best-efforts basis (i.e. the intermediary agrees to buy only those securities that it is able to sell to others);
- exposes itself to the risk of loss from acquiring, exchanging and selling debt securities; and
- receives only a pre-established fee or may derive variable gains based on the value of the securities issued by the issuer.

7.6.405.30   If the intermediary is acting as a principal, then for the purposes of the derecognition assessment the transaction between the issuer and the intermediary is considered a debt exchange between an existing borrower and lender. In this case, if the debt securities exchanged are not substantially modified, then they are not derecognised. If there is a substantial modification of the existing debt securities, then they are derecognised (see 7.6.360.10). [*IFRS 9.3.3.2, B3.3.6*]

7.6.405.40   If the intermediary is acting as an agent, then the derecognition assessment for the modified debt is performed assuming that the intermediary does not exist. If an issuer repurchases existing debt securities from their existing holders and issues new debt securities to new (i.e. different) holders, then the existing debt securities are derecognised (see 7.6.360.10). However, if the issuer agrees with an existing holder to repurchase existing debt securities in exchange for issuing new debt securities to that same holder, then the exchange is a debt exchange between an existing borrower and lender and the same principles as in 7.6.405.30 apply.

7.6.410   *Quantitative assessment**

7.6.410.10   Terms are considered to have been substantially modified when the net present value of the cash flows under the new terms, including any fees paid net of any fees received and discounted using the original effective interest rate – i.e. of the original debt instrument – differs by at least

10 percent from the present value of the remaining cash flows under the original terms (the so-called '10 percent test' or 'quantitative assessment'). [*IFRS 9.B3.3.6*]

7.6.410.20   IFRS 9 does not define the term 'fees' in this context. In our view, fees paid include amounts paid by the borrower to or on behalf of the lender, and fees received include amounts paid by the lender to or on behalf of the borrower, whether or not they are described as a fee, as part of the exchange or modification. Fees do not include any payments made by the borrower or lender to its own advisers or agents, or other transaction costs incurred by the borrower or lender.

EXAMPLE 25 – FEES INCLUDED IN 10% TEST

7.6.410.30   Company Z has a loan from Bank B. Z negotiates with B a modification to the terms of the loan, and Z incurs the following costs.

COST	AMOUNT
Modification fees payable to B	30,000
External adviser assisting Z with the terms of the modification transaction	15,000
Z's internal treasury staff based on time spent and an average hourly rate	12,000
External lawyer assisting B in drafting the contract; lawyer's fees paid by Z directly to the lawyer	8,000
Total costs	65,000

7.6.410.40   In this example, we believe that only 38,000, comprising the modification fees payable to B (30,000) and the amount paid to B's lawyer (8,000), should be considered to be 'fees' for the 10% test calculation. This is because only these amounts are paid by Z to or on behalf of B.

7.6.410.50   IFRS 9 does not contain any further guidance on how to determine the cash flows for the 10 percent test if the terms of a debt instrument are modified and the cash flows under the new or original terms of the instruments are not fixed. In our view, if either the original or the new terms include an early prepayment, call or put feature or a term extension feature that is not separately accounted for as a derivative, then the effect of the feature should be included in determining the cash flows under the quantitative assessment. In our view, any of the following approaches would be a reasonable application of this principle.

• Calculate probability-weighted cash flows taking into account different scenarios, including the exercise or non-exercise of the features, and use these cash flows as the basis for the 10 percent test.
• Calculate the present value for each of the different scenarios – i.e. exercise and non-exercise. The cash flow scenario that results in the smaller difference between the present values of the cash flows under the original terms and the cash flows under the revised terms would be the basis for the 10 percent test.
• Use the outcome of the most likely scenario to determine cash flows.

7.6.410.60   In our view, an entity should use judgement in determining the appropriate cash flows to be included in performing the 10 percent test if the original terms of the debt instrument provide for:

- a higher rate of interest in the event of default;
- the acceleration of maturity in the event of default;
- a higher credit spread in the event of credit deterioration; or
- other contingent payment terms or unusual interest terms.

7.6.410.70   We believe that similar judgement would apply in determining the cash flows under the new terms for the 10 percent test. This might be reflected by using the most likely scenario or probability-weighted outcomes in performing the 10 percent test.

7.6.410.80   For a floating rate instrument, there is no explicit guidance in IFRS 9 on how to determine the cash flows under the new terms or the remaining cash flows under the original terms of the debt instrument. In our view, any of the following approaches may be acceptable, provided that it is applied consistently, for determining the variable benchmark components of the cash flows under the new terms and of the remaining cash flows under the original terms to ensure a like-for-like comparison for the 10 percent test.

- Use the relevant benchmark interest rate determined for the current interest accrual period according to the original terms of the debt instrument.
- Use the relevant benchmark interest rate at the date of modification, except for any remaining coupons of the original liability for which the interest rate has been determined, in which case the contractual rate should be used.
- Use the relevant benchmark interest rates for the original remaining term based on the relevant forward interest rate curve – except for any remaining coupons of the original liability for which the interest rate has been determined, in which case the contractual rate should be used – and the relevant benchmark interest rates for the new term of the instrument based on the relevant forward interest rate curve.

EXAMPLE 26 – APPROACHES TO DETERMINE FLOATING RATE CASH FLOWS IN 10% TEST

7.6.410.90   On 30 June 2019, Company S modifies the terms of a bond that was paying interest based on six-month LIBOR that resets on 1 April and 1 October.

7.6.410.100   The following facts are also relevant for this example:
- on 1 April 2019, six-month LIBOR is reset to 3.5%;
- on 30 June 2019, six-month LIBOR is 4%; and
- under the modified terms, the bond will bear interest at a fixed rate of 4.5%.

7.6.410.110   We believe that, for the 10% test, S may determine the remaining future interest cash flows under the original terms of the bond by using:
- the six-month LIBOR applicable to the current reset period (3.5%);
- the six-month LIBOR on the date of modification (4%); however, S should use 3.5% for the period to 30 September 2019 because the interest rate for this period has already been fixed; or
- interest rates from the six-month LIBOR forward curve; however, S should use 3.5% for the period to 30 September 2019 because the interest rate for this period has already been fixed.

7.6.410.120   The original effective interest rate to be applied to discount the cash flows is the effective interest rate of the original unmodified instrument that is being used to calculate its amortised cost and interest expense under IFRS 9. However, in our view the original effective interest rate excludes adjustments made to the effective interest rate of a debt instrument as a result of having applied fair value hedge accounting because these adjustments do not reflect changes in the amount or timing of cash flows payable on the hedged debt instrument. [*IFRS 9.B3.3.6*]

7.6.410.130   For floating rate liabilities, in our view the original effective interest rate is the current effective interest rate that reflects movements in market rates of interest (see 7.6.410.80), determined according to the unmodified terms of the contract. Such an effective yield might be a variable benchmark interest rate plus/minus a fixed margin – e.g. three-month LIBOR plus 40 basis points. In this case, the original effective interest rate should consider adjustments to the benchmark interest rate, but the original credit risk spread should be held constant and not adjusted to reflect changes in credit risk spread.

7.6.410.140   The circumstances under which a modification of the terms of a financial liability is negotiated – e.g. because of financial difficulties of the borrower – are not relevant in determining whether the modification is an extinguishment of debt (see 7.6.420.60).

7.6.420   *Qualitative assessment*

7.6.420.10   In our view, if the difference in the present value of the cash flows under the quantitative assessment is at least 10 percent, then a modification should be accounted for as an extinguishment in all cases. However, if the difference in the present values of the cash flows is less than 10 percent, then an entity should perform a qualitative assessment to determine whether the terms of the two instruments are substantially different.

7.6.420.20   In our view, the purpose of a qualitative assessment is to identify substantial differences in terms that by their nature are not captured by a quantitative assessment. Accordingly, we believe that modifications whose effect is included in the quantitative assessment, and that are not considered substantial based on that assessment, cannot generally be considered substantial on their own from a qualitative perspective. Such modifications may include changes in principal amounts, maturities, interest rates, prepayment options and other contingent payment terms. However, if a financial liability has an effective interest rate of nil, then we believe that a change in the timing of cash flows will have no effect on the quantitative assessment. In this case, the change in timing of cash flows should be incorporated into the qualitative assessment to ensure that its impact is considered. A combination of cash flow changes captured by the quantitative test, but not on their own considered substantial, and other changes not captured by the quantitative test may together be considered a substantial modification. Performing the qualitative assessment may require a high degree of judgement based on the facts and circumstances of each individual case.

EXAMPLE 27 – CHANGE IN TERMS DOES NOT AFFECT QUANTITATIVE ASSESSMENT

7.6.420.23   Company T has a loan due to its parent that is payable on demand. The loan has an effective interest rate of zero. T renegotiates the terms so that the loan becomes payable in two years, rather than on demand. The other terms remain unchanged.

> **7.6.420.25** T carries out a quantitative assessment by calculating the present value of the current and modified cash flows using the original effective interest rate of zero. The discount rate of zero results in the present value of cash flows repayable on demand being the same as the present value of cash flows repayable in two years' time. The extension of maturity is not captured by the quantitative assessment, because the effective interest rate of the loan is zero.
>
> **7.6.420.27** We believe that in this case T should additionally consider whether the term extension is a substantial modification as part of its qualitative assessment because it has had no impact on the quantitative assessment.

7.6.420.30 In our view, the following types of changes in terms are of a formal or incidental nature rather than related to the substance of the liability and accordingly we believe that they carry no weight in the assessment of whether the modification of terms is substantial:

- legal form of the instrument;
- tax treatment; and
- whether the instrument is listed.

7.6.420.40 In our view, a substantial change in the currency of a debt instrument, or a deletion or addition of a substantial equity conversion feature to a debt instrument, is a substantial modification of the terms. A change in currency is considered substantial unless the exchange rate between the old and new currencies is pegged or managed within narrow bounds by law or relevant monetary authorities. For example, a debt instrument might be modified such that the new instrument is in a different currency – for which the exchange rate is not pegged to the old currency or is not managed within narrow bounds with that currency – and has a different maturity from the existing financial liability. We believe that the terms of the new debt instrument in this case would be substantially different even if the present values of the cash flows were almost identical using the quantitative test. Other modifications may require a higher degree of judgement about whether they represent a substantial change in terms – e.g. a change in the seniority or subordination of a financial liability.

7.6.420.50 In our view, an equity conversion option is substantial unless it is not reasonably possible that it will be exercised over its term – e.g. a call option that is deeply out of the money and expected to remain so. When an equity conversion option included in the original liability is modified as part of a restructuring of the debt, judgement should be applied in assessing whether the modification of the conversion option is substantial. This might include considering the change in fair value of the conversion option and its likelihood of exercise. If debt with detachable equity options is exchanged for convertible debt that includes non-detachable equity conversion options, then we believe that the exchange should be considered a modification of an equity conversion feature rather than its addition or deletion.

7.6.420.60 There are no special requirements for troubled debt restructurings under IFRS. The guidance on modifications of financial liabilities applies whether or not the borrower is experiencing financial difficulties. For further discussion, see 7.6.410.140.

7.6.430   *Accounting for a substantial modification of terms*

7.6.430.10   For a discussion of the accounting for a substantial modification of the terms of a debt instrument that meets the derecognition conditions in IFRS 9, see 7.7.370.

7.6.440   *Accounting for non-substantial modification of terms*

7.6.440.10   For a discussion of the accounting for non-substantial modification of the terms of a debt instrument that does not meet the derecognition conditions in IFRS 9, see 7.7.370.

7.6.450   *Extinguishment of liabilities with equity instruments*

7.6.450.10   IFRIC 19 addresses the accounting for a renegotiation of the terms of a financial liability that results in an entity issuing equity instruments to a creditor to extinguish all or part of the financial liability. [*IFRIC 19.2–3*]

7.6.450.20   IFRIC 19 does not apply if:
- the creditor is acting in its capacity as existing direct or indirect shareholder (see 1.2.190 and 7.7.375.40);
- the creditor and the entity are controlled by the same party or parties before and after the transaction and the substance of the transaction includes an equity distribution from, or contribution to, the entity (see 1.2.190 and 7.7.375.40); and
- the extinguishment is in accordance with the original terms of the financial liability (see 7.6.450.20). [*IFRIC 19.3*]

7.6.450.30   If equity instruments are issued to a creditor to extinguish all or part of a financial liability in a debt-for-equity swap, then the equity instruments are consideration paid. The equity instruments are measured at fair value, unless their fair value cannot be measured reliably, in which case the equity instruments are measured with reference to the fair value of the financial liability extinguished. In measuring the fair value of a financial liability extinguished that includes a demand feature, paragraph 47 of IFRS 13 is not applied – i.e. the requirement that the fair value of a financial liability with a demand feature is not less than the amount payable on demand, discounted from the first date on which the amount could be required to be paid, is not applied. The equity instruments are initially measured when the financial liability (or part of that liability) is extinguished. A gain or loss on extinguishment is recognised in accordance with 7.6.360.60. [*IFRS 9.3.3.3, IFRIC 19.5–7, 9*]

7.6.450.40   If only part of the financial liability is extinguished by the issue of equity instruments, then an assessment is made of whether some of the consideration paid relates to a modification of the part of the liability that remains outstanding. If it does, then the consideration paid is allocated between the part of the liability extinguished and the part of the liability that remains outstanding. The consideration allocated to the part that remains outstanding forms part of the assessment of whether there has been a substantial modification of the terms of that remaining liability (see 7.6.370). An entity considers all relevant facts and circumstances in making this allocation. In our view, judgement is required to determine both:
- the allocation of the consideration between the part of the liability extinguished and the modified part that remains outstanding; and

- the part of the liability that is extinguished and the part that remains outstanding and is modified. [*IFRIC 19.8, 10*]

7.6.450.50 Judgement is required because the cash flows of the remaining loan will not usually represent solely a fully proportionate share of the cash flows of the original loan and, in some cases, a simple allocation method based on the change in the nominal amount of the debt instrument may lead to unreasonable results, particularly if the effective interest payable on the remaining nominal amount is increased (see Example 28B).

EXAMPLE 28A – PARTIAL EXTINGUISHMENT BY EQUITY – ALLOCATION OF CONSIDERATION (1)

7.6.450.60 Company X has an existing loan from Bank B. On 31 December 2019, X renegotiates the loan and enters into a debt-for-equity swap with B whereby, in exchange for X issuing equity instruments to B:
- the nominal amount of the loan is reduced by 50%; and
- the terms of the remaining portion are amended by extending the maturity date and reducing the interest rate payable.

7.6.450.70 There are no fees or transaction costs. The following facts are also relevant for this example.

	OLD LOAN	NEW INSTRUMENTS	
		MODIFIED LOAN (50%)	EQUITY INSTRUMENTS
Nominal amount	1,000,000	500,000	
Carrying amount	1,000,000		
Fair value at 31 December 2019	910,000	350,000	560,000

7.6.450.80 X analyses the transaction as an extinguishment of a 50% proportionate share of the old loan, reflecting the reduction in nominal amount, and a modification of the other 50% proportionate share of the old loan. Based on this, X allocates the consideration paid by issuing equity instruments between the extinguishment of part of the old loan and the modification of the remaining loan based on the changes in fair value of the loan as a result of the renegotiation, as follows:
- the extinguishment of 50% of the loan at fair value – 455,000 (910,000 x 50%); and
- the modification of the remaining 50% of the loan – 105,000 (455,000 - 350,000 or alternatively 560,000 - 455,000).

7.6.450.90 Accordingly, X derecognises the 50% proportion of the loan that is extinguished and recognises a gain on this proportion of 45,000 (1,000,000 x 50% - 455,000). X considers the allocation of 105,000 of consideration to the modification of the remaining 50% of the loan in determining whether that remaining 50% proportion is substantially modified. If the remaining 50% of the loan is considered substantially modified, then that remaining 50% is also derecognised – leading to initial recognition of the new loan at its fair value of 350,000 and a further gain of 45,000 (1,000,000 x 50% - 105,000 - 350,000). [*IFRS 9.3.3.4, B3.3.6*]

7.6.450.100   As an alternative approach, X may instead first determine the allocation of the carrying amount of the old loan between the part that has been extinguished and the remaining part that has been modified based on the ratio of the decrease in the fair value of the loan to the fair value of the remaining part of the loan, as shown in the following table. [*IFRS 9.3.3.4*]

	FAIR VALUE	FAIR VALUE RATIO	ALLOCATED CARRYING AMOUNT
Old loan	910,000	-	1,000,000
Modified loan	350,000	38.5%	385,000
Extinguished loan	560,000[(1)]	61.5%	615,000

Note
1.   Calculated as 910,000 - 350,000.

7.6.450.110   Under this approach, in determining the allocation of the consideration paid by issuing equity instruments between the partial extinguishment of the loan and the modification of the remaining loan as required by IFRIC 19 (see 7.6.450.40), X concludes that the entire consideration of 560,000 is allocated to the extinguishment of part of the old loan. This is consistent with the approach used to determine the part of the old loan that is extinguished.

7.6.450.120   Accordingly, X derecognises the 61.5% proportion of the old loan that is extinguished and recognises a gain on this proportion of 55,000 (1,000,000 x 61.5% - 560,000). In determining whether the remaining 38.5% of the loan is substantially modified, X compares 38.5% of the present value of the cash flows of the old loan with the present value of the cash flows of the amended loan, discounted in each case using the original effective interest rate of the old loan (see 7.6.410.10). If the remaining 38.5% of the loan is considered substantially modified, then that remaining 38.5% is also derecognised – leading to initial recognition of the new loan at its fair value of 350,000 and a further gain of 35,000 (385,000 - 350,000). [*IFRS 9.3.3.4, B3.3.6*]

EXAMPLE 28B – PARTIAL EXTINGUISHMENT BY EQUITY – ALLOCATION OF CONSIDERATION (2)

7.6.450.130   Modifying Example 28A, the terms of the renegotiation are as follows:
- the nominal amount of the loan is reduced by 10%; and
- the terms of the remaining loan are amended by increasing the interest rate payable.

7.6.450.140   The following facts are also relevant for this example.

	OLD LOAN	NEW INSTRUMENTS	
		MODIFIED LOAN (90%)	EQUITY INSTRUMENTS
Nominal amount	1,000,000	900,000	
Carrying amount	1,000,000		
Fair value at 31 December 2018	1,000,000	960,000	40,000

7.6.450.150 If X were to allocate the carrying amount of the old loan between the amount that has been extinguished and the amount that has been modified based only on the reduction in the nominal amount of the loan, then it would compare:
- 10% of the carrying amount of the loan extinguished – i.e. 100,000 (1,000,000 x 10%); and
- the fair value of the consideration paid – i.e. 40,000.

7.6.450.160 This would lead to the recognition of a gain of 60,000 on derecognition of 100,000 of the old loan.

7.6.450.170 However, X considers all relevant facts and circumstances, including the following:
- the rate of interest payable on the remaining loan has been increased such that the fair value of the modified loan is 60,000 greater than would be implied by a 10% pro rata extinguishment; and
- the carrying amount of the old loan is equal to the fair value of the equity instruments plus the fair value of the modified loan.

7.6.450.180 Therefore, X concludes that the approach discussed in 7.6.450.80 would not be appropriate and that the fair value of the equity shares of 40,000 should be allocated against an extinguishment of only 40,000 of the original liability.

7.6.450.190 Accordingly, X derecognises 40,000 of the loan that is extinguished and recognises the consideration paid of 40,000 in equity.

7.6.460   *Amendment of contractual terms of financial liability resulting in change in classification to equity*

7.6.460.10   If the terms of a financial liability are amended such that the financial liability subsequent to the amendment of the terms meets the definition of an equity instrument, then in our view the transaction should be accounted for as an extinguishment of a financial liability in accordance with 7.6.450.30. For example, a company issues preference shares that meet the definition of a financial liability. Subsequently, the entity and the holders of the preference shares agree to amend the terms of the preference shares so that they meet the criteria for equity classification (see 7.3.20). We believe that such a transaction involves two steps: an extinguishment of a financial liability and the issue of new equity instruments at fair value. For further discussion, see 7.3.480.60.

7.6.465   **Trade payables and reverse factoring**

7.6.465.10   Under a reverse factoring arrangement (see 7.10.35–50), a factor agrees to pay amounts to a supplier in respect of invoices owed by the supplier's customer and receives settlement from that customer at a later date.

7.6.465.20   Typically, when an invoice is made subject to the reverse factoring arrangement and/ or when the factor pays the supplier, the customer does not discharge its financial liability to the supplier (see 7.6.360.10). However, the customer assesses whether it is legally released from the primary responsibility for the original financial liability under the invoice and this is replaced by a new financial liability to the factor. This assessment may require the assistance of a legal expert.

7.6.465.30   If there is no such legal release, then the customer assesses whether the financial liability has been substantially modified as a result of the reverse factoring arrangement (see 7.6.370). This is because a substantial modification of the terms of an existing financial liability (or a part of it) is also accounted for as an extinguishment of the original financial liability and the recognition of a new financial liability.

7.6.465.40   For a further discussion of reverse factoring, see 2.3.75.10–50, 7.10.35, 315 and 655.

7.6.470   # DERECOGNITION OF DERIVATIVES

7.6.470.10   Many derivatives – e.g. forward contracts and interest rate swaps – do or can involve two-way payments between the parties. These derivatives might change from being an asset to a liability or vice versa. Such derivatives are derecognised only when they meet both the derecognition criteria for financial assets (see 7.6.60) and the derecognition criteria for financial liabilities (see 7.6.360). [*IFRS 9.BC6.333*]

7.6.480   **Novation of derivatives to central counterparty**

7.6.480.10   An example of a transaction that results in the derecognition of a derivative is the novation of a derivative to a central counterparty. For example, assume that Company X and Company Y have entered into an over-the-counter derivative contract. Novation to a central counterparty involves cancelling the original derivative contract between X and Y and replacing it with two new derivative contracts – i.e. a new contract between X and the central counterparty, and a new contract between Y and the central counterparty.

7.6.480.20   A novation of a derivative to a central counterparty results in the derecognition of the derivative because, through the novation, each party to the original derivative has new contractual rights (or obligations) to cash flows from a new derivative with the central counterparty, and this new contract replaces the original contract with the original counterparty. Accordingly, the original derivative with the counterparty has expired and therefore the derecognition criteria for financial assets are met (see 7.6.90). In addition, the novation to the central counterparty releases the party from the responsibility to make payment to the original counterparty and therefore the derecognition criteria for financial liabilities are also met (see 7.6.360.10). [*IFRS 9.3.2.3(a), B3.3.1(b), BC334–BC336*]

7.6.480.30   For a discussion about the effect of a novation of a derivative on hedge accounting, see 7.9.970.

7.6.490   Variation margin payments and receipts

7.6.490.10   Many derivatives involve variation margin payments and receipts. Many of these transactions are cleared through clearing houses – e.g. futures contracts – and involve periodic (normally daily or intra-day) payments or receipts of variation margin that is required by the clearing house and reflects changes in the value of the related derivative.

7.6.490.20   Variation margin may take the form of cash, securities or other specified assets, typically liquid assets. An entity needs to determine based on the recognition and derecognition criteria for financial assets and financial liabilities (see 7.6.60 and 360) whether making variation margin payments and receipts represents:

- a partial settlement of contractual rights to receive or obligations to pay cash under the relevant derivative contracts, which means that derecognition of the variation margin payments or receipts and the corresponding carrying amount of the relevant derivative contracts is required at the time of payment; or
- the establishment or settlement of an accumulated variation margin balance that is a separate financial asset or financial liability.

7.6.490.25   If the payment or receipt of variation margin is not a settlement of the derivative contract, then the accumulated balance is usually a financial asset or financial liability – e.g. the balance may be required to be repaid in the future or may be used to settle the derivative contract at its maturity.

7.6.490.30   Whether the payment or receipt of variation margin represents a settlement of a derivative contract is assessed with reference to the concepts of extinguishment – i.e. the obligation specified in the contract is discharged or cancelled or expires – and of expiry of contractual rights to cash flows (see 7.6.90 and 360.10). Whether these derecognition criteria are met will depend on the specific contractual terms considered in conjunction with other relevant documentation and applicable law. [*IFRS 9.3.2.3(a), 3.3.1*]

EXAMPLE 29 – PAYMENT OF VARIATION MARGIN REPRESENTS SETTLEMENT ON FUTURE CONTRACTS – COLLATERALISED-TO-MARKET MODEL

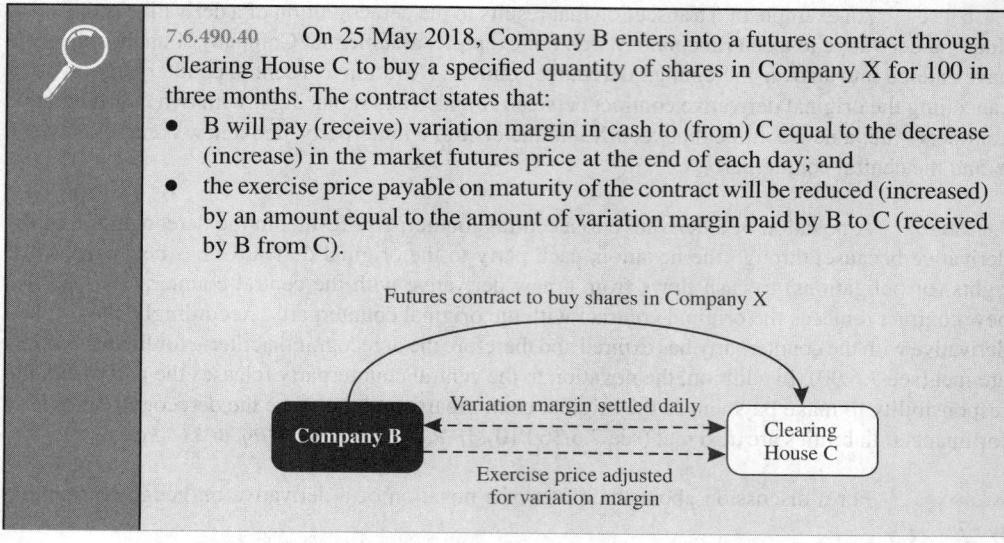

7.6.490.40   On 25 May 2018, Company B enters into a futures contract through Clearing House C to buy a specified quantity of shares in Company X for 100 in three months. The contract states that:

- B will pay (receive) variation margin in cash to (from) C equal to the decrease (increase) in the market futures price at the end of each day; and
- the exercise price payable on maturity of the contract will be reduced (increased) by an amount equal to the amount of variation margin paid by B to C (received by B from C).

Futures contract to buy shares in Company X

Variation margin settled daily

Company B   Clearing House C

Exercise price adjusted for variation margin

7.6.490.50   The contract does not allow for the variation margin to be repaid and no interest is payable on variation margin.

7.6.490.60   On 26 May 2018, the market futures price declines to 98. At the end of that day, B pays variation margin of 2 to C and the exercise price is reset to 98.

7.6.490.70   B concludes that the payment of variation margin represents a settlement of the futures contract because it extinguishes a specified part of its obligation to pay the exercise price on maturity.

7.6.490.80   Immediately before payment of variation margin on 26 May 2018, the futures contract is a derivative liability of 2. The payment of variation margin represents a derecognition of the derivative liability and, following the payment of 2, the fair value of the futures contract is zero because it has an exercise price equal to the current market price.

EXAMPLE 30 – PAYMENT OF VARIATION MARGIN REPRESENTS SEPARATE ASSET – COLLATERALISED-TO-MARKET MODEL

7.6.490.90   Company X enters into a 10-year interest rate swap derivative with Clearing House C under a 'collateralised-to-market' framework. The derivative requires net payments of coupons on each anniversary of the transaction through to maturity. X has other interest rate swaps outstanding with C. The rules of C state that:

- X will pay (receive) variation margin in cash to (from) C at the end of each day, such that the net accumulated balance of the variation margin is equal and opposite to the estimated fair value of all outstanding swap contracts between X and C;
- interest at a market rate is payable on the accumulated balance of variation margin;
- a party is entitled to set off the net balance of variation margin that it has paid (or received, as the case may be) against the obligation to make any payment (or right to receive any payment, respectively) of coupons on the swap contract on the date on which those coupons fall due for settlement; and
- on maturity or termination of all swap transactions between X and C and following settlement of all payments due under such swap contracts, any remaining balance of the variation margin is returned to the party that paid it.

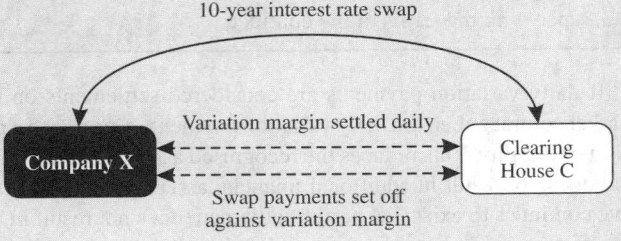

10-year interest rate swap

Variation margin settled daily

Company X

Clearing House C

Swap payments set off against variation margin

7.6.490.100   X concludes that the payment of variation margin does not represent a settlement of rights or obligations under the derivative. This is because these amounts will continue to become due and payable in the future in accordance with the terms of the derivative and are not reduced or increased by any amount of variation margin received or paid.

7.6.490.110   The accumulated variation margin balance represents a separate financial asset or financial liability because:
- the accumulated balance will either be used in the future to settle payments on this or other swaps or be returned to the payer; and
- interest is payable on the accumulated balance.

EXAMPLE 31 – PAYMENT OF VARIATION MARGIN REPRESENTS SETTLEMENT – SETTLED-TO-MARKET MODEL

7.6.490.120   Company X enters into a 10-year interest rate swap derivative with Clearing House D under a 'settled-to-market' framework. The terms of the contract are:
- X will pay to (receive from) D an amount in cash at the end of each day equal to the net of:
  - coupons due for settlement on the swap that day;
  - variation margin equal to the decrease (increase) in the net present value (NPV) of expected future coupons receivable on the swap, calculated based on current market rates; and
  - price alignment adjustment (PAA).
- PAA is calculated as a current market interest rate on the net cumulative amount of variation margin paid or received to date. However, there is no right or obligation to the return of variation margin and the contract states that payment of variation margin is a partial settlement of the outstanding derivative position and does not constitute collateral.
- The PAA is included as an extra cash flow within the derivative contract and is similar to the interest that would have been paid or received on cash collateral had a similar contract been transacted under a collateralised-to-market contract (as in Example 30 above).

7.6.490.130   X concludes that the daily net cash payments, including variation margin, should be accounted for as partial settlements of the derivative in accordance with the terms of the contract.

7.6.490.140   If daily variation payments are considered settlements on the underlying trade for a settled-to-market contract, then the daily variation payments give rise to a partial derecognition of the derivative asset or liability. This reduces the recognised asset or liability arising from the derivative's fair value and does not result in additional financial assets or financial liabilities being recognised. The derivative continues to exist (i.e. partial settlement does not result in termination) but has a current fair value of zero (or close to zero) immediately following the daily settlement payment.

7.6.490.150   If payments and receipts of variation margin are not a settlement of the related derivatives, then the entity needs to consider whether the variation margin balance and the related derivatives
should be offset in the statement of financial position (see 7.10.110). Conversely, for derivative
transactions in which daily variation payments represent settlements and not collateral, no offsetting
takes place between cumulative variation payment amounts and the underlying derivative because
they are a single unit of account.

7.6.500   FUTURE DEVELOPMENTS

7.6.500.10   The IFRS Interpretations Committee discussed a request to clarify which fees and costs
are included in a quantitative '10 percent test' for assessing whether to derecognise a financial liability (see 7.6.410). The Committee recommended and the IASB agreed to amend IFRS 9 as part of
the next *Annual Improvements to IFRSs Cycle* to specify that only fees paid or received between the
entity and the lender, including fees paid or received by either the entity or the lender on the other's
behalf, are considered in the '10 percent test'.

7.7 Measurement

7.7   Measurement

CURRENTLY EFFECTIVE REQUIREMENTS

This publication reflects IFRS in issue at 1 August 2018, and the currently effective requirements cover annual periods beginning on or after 1 January 2018.

The requirements related to this topic are mainly derived from the following.

STANDARD	TITLE
IFRS 9	Financial Instruments
IFRS 13	Fair Value Measurement
IFRS 15	Revenue from Contracts with Customers
IAS 21	The Effects of Changes in Foreign Exchange Rates

FORTHCOMING REQUIREMENTS AND FUTURE DEVELOPMENTS

For this topic, there are no forthcoming requirements or future developments.

7.7.10   MEASUREMENT ON INITIAL RECOGNITION

7.7.10.10   On initial recognition, a financial asset or financial liability is measured at fair value plus or minus directly attributable transaction costs, unless:

- the instrument is classified as at FVTPL, in which case transaction costs are not included; or
- the instrument is a trade receivable that is initially measured at the transaction price as defined in IFRS 15 (see 7.7.20). [*IFRS 9.5.1.1, 5.1.3, 15.60–65*]

7.7.10.20   Normally, the fair value on initial recognition is the transaction price as described in IFRS 9 – i.e. the fair value of the consideration given or received for the financial instrument. For a discussion of situations in which the fair value on initial recognition may differ from the transaction price, see 7.7.40 and 2.4.320. [*IFRS 9.5.1.1A, B5.1.2A*]

7.7.10.30   If part of the consideration given or received is for something in addition to the financial instrument, then the entity separately measures the fair value of the financial instrument in accordance with IFRS 13 (see chapter 2.4). Any additional element is accounted for separately. For example, in the case of a long-term loan that carries no interest, the fair value of the loan can be measured as the present value of all cash receipts discounted using the current market interest rate for a similar financial instrument. Any additional amount lent is an expense or a reduction of income unless it qualifies for recognition as an asset (see 7.7.80–90 and 110). [*IFRS 9.B5.1.1*]

7.7.20   Trade receivables

7.7.20.10   Trade receivables that do not have a significant financing component (determined in accordance with IFRS 15) are measured on initial recognition at their transaction price as defined in IFRS 15 – i.e. the amount of consideration to which the entity expects to be entitled for transferring the promised goods or services to the customer (see 4.2.90). [*IFRS 9.5.1.3, 15.60–65, A*]

7.7.20.20   For a discussion of factors considered in determining whether a contract contains a significant financing component, see 4.2.130.30.

7.7.20.30   Trade receivables with a significant financing component are not exempt from being measured at fair value on initial recognition, unless 7.7.20.40 applies. Therefore, differences may arise between the initial amount of revenue recognised in accordance with IFRS 15 – which is measured at the transaction price as defined in IFRS 15 – and the fair value of the trade receivable recognised at the date of initial recognition. Any difference between the measurement of the receivable in accordance with IFRS 9 and the corresponding amount of revenue recognised in accordance with IFRS 15 is presented as an expense. [*IFRS 15.108*]

7.7.20.40   If an entity expects, at contract inception, that the period between the entity transferring a promised good or service to the customer and the customer paying for that good or service will be one year or less, then as a practical expedient, the entity can choose not to adjust the promised amount of consideration for the effects of a significant financing component. If the entity applies this practical expedient, then the trade receivable is measured on initial recognition at the transaction price as defined in IFRS 15, in the same way as trade receivables that do not have a significant financing component. [*IFRS 9.5.1.3, 15.63*]

7.7.30   Settlement of contracts to acquire assets and loan commitments

7.7.30.10   A contract to acquire a financial asset is itself generally a financial instrument (see 7.1.30). The financial asset to be acquired is not generally recognised until the acquisition contract is settled because this is usually when the acquirer becomes a party to the contract that is the financial asset. In this case, the acquired financial asset is initially recognised based on its fair value on settlement date. If the contract to acquire the financial asset is accounted for as a derivative, then it is measured at FVTPL. Changes in the fair value of the derivative contract between the date of entering into the derivative contract and its settlement date are recognised in profit or loss as they arise. The fair value of this derivative contract immediately before settlement usually equals the difference between the fair value of the acquired asset at settlement and the purchase price payable at settlement, meaning that no additional gain or loss arises on settlement.

7.7.30.20   However, if the contract to acquire the financial asset is a regular-way contract, then it is not accounted for as a derivative. In this case, either trade date or settlement date accounting may apply to the acquired asset and this determines when the acquired asset is initially recognised and, for settlement date accounting, the treatment of changes in the fair value of the acquired asset between the trade date and settlement date (see 7.6.20). [*IFRS 9.3.1.1–3.1.2, B3.1.3–B3.1.6*]

7.7.33   *Loan commitments wholly or partly outside the scope of IFRS 9 – Loans measured at amortised cost*

7.7.33.10   As opposed to settlement of a contract to acquire an existing financial asset, a loan may be originated as a result of a drawdown under a loan commitment. To simplify the accounting for holders and issuers of loan commitments, many loan commitments are generally excluded from the scope of IFRS 9 (except as regards applicable impairment and derecognition requirements – see 7.1.250.20) so that an entity does not recognise changes in their fair value that result from changes in market interest rates or credit spreads, consistent with the amortised cost measurement model for certain financial assets and financial liabilities. [*IFRS 9.2.1(g), 5.5.1, BCZ2.2–BCZ2.8, BC5.128*]

7.7.33.20   Accordingly, in our view when a loan that will be measured at amortised cost is drawn down under an arm's length loan commitment that is outside the scope of IFRS 9 (except as regards applicable impairment and derecognition requirements – see 7.1.250.20), the resulting loan asset or liability may be viewed as a continuation of the loan commitment. Under this approach, the fair value measurement of the loan on initial recognition would be based on circumstances on the commitment date. Therefore, the fair value of the loan on initial recognition would usually be considered to be the amount advanced, adjusted for facility or commitment fees paid or received (see 7.7.50, 70 and 530), being the transaction price agreed on the commitment date (see 7.7.10.20) – i.e. no day one gain or loss would usually be recognised on the loan origination date.

7.7.33.30   For a loan asset that, subsequent to initial recognition, will be measured at amortised cost, this approach would be consistent with the impairment requirements because, for the purpose of applying those requirements, a financial asset resulting from a loan commitment is treated as a continuation of the loan commitment (see 7.8.70.20) – i.e. whether there has been a significant increase in credit risk since initial recognition is assessed with reference to the credit risk at the date the commitment is entered into and the discount rate used to measure ECLs on the loan commitment is the same as the effective interest rate of the resulting loan. [*IFRS 9.B5.5.47*]

EXAMPLE 1 – INITIAL MEASUREMENT OF A LOAN RESULTING FROM A LOAN COMMITMENT

7.7.33.40   On 1 April 2018, Bank B enters into a commitment to make a loan of 100 to borrower C on arm's length terms and at an interest rate of 5% a year; fees and costs are insignificant. On 31 May 2018, C draws down the loan. The fair value of the loan is 100 on 1 April and 98 on 31 May.

7.7.33.50   Applying the approach in 7.7.33.20, B initially recognises the gross carrying amount of the loan on 31 May using the fair value on 1 April of 100.

7.7.33.60   An alternative acceptable approach would be to view the loan that is drawn down as a separate financial instrument for the purposes of initial measurement, with the amount initially recognised for the loan on the draw-down date being based on an analysis of the circumstances at that time, including the entity's determination of the transaction price – i.e. the fair value of the consideration given for the loan – and the fair value of the loan at that time.

7.7.33.70   Accordingly, under this alternative acceptable approach, on initial recognition the carrying amount of a loan subsequently measured at amortised cost would be based on:
- the transaction price, if it is the best evidence of fair value on the draw-down date or if the entity's alternative estimate of fair value does not satisfy the observability condition in paragraph B5.1.2A(a) of IFRS 9 (see 7.7.40.50); or
- the entity's alternative estimate of fair value on the draw-down date if this alternative estimate satisfies the observability condition in paragraph B5.1.2A(a) of IFRS 9 (see 7.7.40.40).

7.7.35   ***Loan commitments wholly or partly outside the scope of IFRS 9 – Loans measured at FVTPL***

7.7.35.10   A loan drawn down under a loan commitment that is generally outside the scope of IFRS 9 (except as regards applicable impairment and derecognition requirements – see 7.1.250.20) may be mandatorily measured at FVTPL following initial recognition. For example, this may be the case if the contractual terms of the loan do not meet the SPPI criterion (see 7.4.150). A question arises about how the loan should be measured on initial recognition.

7.7.35.20   It appears that the rationale outlined in 7.7.33.20–70 for loans measured at amortised cost should not apply in this case. This is because the objective outlined in 7.7.33.10 is not relevant or achievable if the resulting loan is mandatorily remeasured at FVTPL at each reporting date. If the loan commitment had been measured at fair value, then gains and losses would already have been recognised before drawdown and irrespective of whether the fair value of the loan commitment (or resulting loan) is or was fully observable. In that case, the fair value of the loan commitment would be rolled into the initial fair value measurement of the loan with no day one gain or loss recognised on the loan. However, even if the loan commitment is not measured at FVTPL, it appears that the gain or loss that arises at the time of draw-down should still be considered to relate to settlement of the loan commitment rather than to represent a day one gain or loss on the loan.

7.7.35.30   Accordingly, we believe that a loan mandatorily measured at FVTPL should be initially recognised at fair value at the date of draw-down – i.e. the amount of cash advanced plus/minus the fair value of the loan commitment. Any gain or loss that arises relates to settlement of the loan commitment, rather than representing a day one gain or loss on the loan.

7.7.37 *Loans drawn down under loan commitment measured at FVTPL*

7.7.37.10   For loans drawn down under loan commitments that are measured at FVTPL, the analysis is similar to that discussed in 7.7.30.10 for derivative contracts to acquire a financial asset. In this case, the loan is initially measured at fair value at the time of drawdown. [*IFRS 9.BCZ2.3*]

7.7.40 Immediate gain or loss

7.7.40.10   Sometimes an entity acquires a financial instrument in one market and intends to sell it or to issue an offsetting instrument in a different market. There is an issue about whether the instrument may be initially measured at its fair value in the selling market and therefore whether a gain may be recognised on initial recognition ('day one gain').

7.7.40.20   Similarly, an entity may believe that the initial fair value of an instrument exceeds the consideration paid or received, because of the entity's repackaging of the instrument or a built-in 'fee'. There is an issue about whether this fee may be recognised immediately (similar to a day one gain).

7.7.40.30   Under IFRS 13, the transaction price – i.e. the fair value of the consideration given or received for the financial instrument – is normally the best evidence of the fair value of a financial instrument on initial recognition. However, there may be cases in which it is appropriate for an entity to conclude that the fair value on initial recognition is different from the transaction price – e.g. when the principal market is different from the market in which the instrument was acquired. For other examples of conditions that can result in a difference between the fair value on initial recognition and the transaction price, see 2.4.320. [*IFRS 9.B5.1.1, B5.1.2A, IFRS 13.57–60*]

7.7.40.40   If the entity's fair value measurement is evidenced by a quoted price in an active market for an identical asset or liability or is based on another valuation technique that uses only data from observable markets, then the entity immediately recognises a gain or loss. This gain or loss is equal to the difference between the fair value on initial recognition and the transaction price. [*IFRS 9.5.1.1A, B5.1.2A*]

7.7.40.50   If the entity determines that the fair value on initial recognition differs from the transaction price, but this fair value measurement is not evidenced by a valuation technique that uses only data from observable markets, then the carrying amount of the financial instrument on initial recognition is adjusted to defer the difference between the fair value measurement and the transaction price. This deferred difference is subsequently recognised as a gain or loss only to the extent that it arises from a change in a factor (including time) that market participants would consider in setting a price. [*IFRS 9.5.1.1A, B5.1.2A*]

7.7.40.60   However, in our experience some banks recognise losses equal to the difference between the fair value on initial recognition and the transaction price immediately, even if the valuation technique is not based wholly on observable market data. Additionally, in our experience banks may consider the recognition of day one gains if any unobservable inputs used in the valuation technique that forms the basis for determining the instrument's fair value on initial recognition are judged to be insignificant in relation to measuring the day one gain.

7.7.40.70   The following table illustrates the application of the day one gain or loss guidance on initial recognition if:

- a difference arises between the transaction price (say, 100) and management's alternative estimate of fair value (say, 99); and
- the observability condition is not satisfied (see 7.7.40.50). [*IFRS 9.B5.1.2A, B5.2.2A*]

APPLICATION OF DAY ONE GAIN AND LOSS GUIDANCE IF OBSERVABILITY CONDITION IS NOT MET	
Fair value:	Management's estimate of exit price 99
Initial measurement (ignoring transaction costs):	Fair value 99 *plus* difference between transaction price and fair value 1 (100 - 99) = 100

EXAMPLE 2 – INITIAL RECOGNITION AT TRANSACTION PRICE (FAIR VALUE OF CONSIDERATION)

7.7.40.80   Company D acquires a portfolio of credit-impaired loans for 30 from Company E. The carrying amount of the loans in E's books is 29 (a face value of 100 less impairment losses of 71). D has superior cash-collection processes in place and expects to recover 50 of the principal amount of the loans. Based on a discounted cash flow analysis, D values the loans at 36.

7.7.40.90   In our view, it would not be appropriate to conclude that the transaction price of 30 does not represent the fair value of the loans acquired. The valuation technique used to arrive at the value of 36 takes into account D's specific cash-collection processes. This is not an assumption that a market participant would use when pricing a loan in the portfolio because D's superior cash-collection processes are a characteristic specific to D.

7.7.40.100   Consequently, D should initially recognise the loans acquired at the transaction price. D's estimates of the amounts and timing of cash flows should instead be used to determine the credit-adjusted effective interest rate of the loans, which should be used in subsequent periods to measure their amortised cost.

7.7.50   Transaction costs

7.7.50.10   Transaction costs are included in the initial measurement of financial assets and financial liabilities, except for those measured at FVTPL and trade receivables initially measured at the transaction price as defined in IFRS 15 (see 7.7.20). [*IFRS 9.5.1.1*]

7.7.50.20   Transaction costs include only those costs that are directly attributable to the acquisition or origination of a financial asset or issue of a financial liability. They are incremental costs that would not have been incurred if the instrument had not been acquired, originated or issued – e.g. fees and commission paid to agents (including employees acting as selling agents), advisers, brokers and dealers, levies by regulatory agencies and securities exchanges, transfer taxes and duties, credit assessment fees, registration charges and similar costs. In our experience, few internal costs are likely to meet this requirement (see 7.7.60). The requirement is applied on an instrument-by-instrument basis. Transaction costs do not include the internal costs associated with developing a new investment product. [*IFRS 9.5.1.1, A, B5.4.8*]

7.7.50.30   For financial assets, transaction costs are added to the amount initially recognised, whereas for financial liabilities transaction costs are deducted from the amount initially recognised. Transaction costs on financial instruments measured at FVTPL are not included in the amount at which the instrument is initially measured; instead, they are immediately recognised in profit or loss. [*IFRS 9.5.1.1*]

EXAMPLE 3 – TRANSACTION COSTS

7.7.50.40   Company F issues debt of 1,000 at par and incurs direct incremental issue costs of 50. The debt will be redeemed at par. Ignoring interest, there is a difference of 50 between the carrying amount at inception of 950 and the redemption amount of 1,000.

7.7.50.50   This difference represents the transaction costs, and is recognised by F as an expense over the period during which the debt is outstanding under the effective interest method.

7.7.50.60   In our view, transaction costs that are directly related to the probable issue of a security that will be classified as a financial liability measured at amortised cost should be recognised as a prepayment (asset) in the statement of financial position. Such transaction costs should be deducted from the amount of the financial liability when it is initially recognised, or recognised in profit or loss when the issue is no longer expected to be completed.

7.7.50.70   Transaction costs that relate to the issue of a compound instrument are allocated to the liability and equity components of the instrument in proportion to the allocation of proceeds. [*IAS 32.38*]

7.7.50.80   In our view, an entity should choose an accounting policy, to be applied consistently, to allocate transaction costs that relate to a hybrid (combined) instrument that includes a non-derivative host contract that is not accounted for at FVTPL and an embedded derivative that is accounted for at FVTPL. The following are examples of approaches.

- Allocate the transaction costs to the non-derivative host contract and embedded derivative components of the instrument in proportion to the allocation of the total transaction price (e.g. proceeds), by analogy to the allocation of transaction costs that relate to a compound instrument (see 7.7.50.70). Under this approach, the amount of transaction costs allocated to the embedded derivative is charged immediately to profit or loss (see 7.7.50.30). However, if the embedded derivative is a non-option feature embedded with a host debt instrument, then an amount of zero is usually allocated to the embedded derivative (see 7.2.370.40).
- Measure the embedded derivative at fair value on initial recognition. The carrying amount of the non-derivative host contract on initial recognition is the difference between the fair value minus transaction costs of the hybrid instrument and the fair value of the embedded derivative (see 7.2.370.30). Under this approach, all of the transaction costs are always allocated to and deducted from the carrying amount of the non-derivative host contract on initial recognition. [*IAS 32.38*]

7.7.50.90   Any transaction costs that do not qualify for inclusion in the initial measurement of an instrument are expensed as they are incurred. [*IFRS 9.5.1.1*]

7.7.50.100   Transaction costs do not include debt premiums or discounts, financing costs or internal administrative or holding costs. In our view, service fees are not directly attributable to the acquisition of an asset or liability and should be expensed as they are incurred. Similarly, we believe that the costs of researching or developing an instrument or assessing alternatives with a number of parties should be expensed as the costs are incurred. [*IFRS 9.B5.4.8*]

7.7.50.110   Transaction costs incurred on initial recognition of an equity investment for which the irrevocable election is made to present changes in fair value in OCI are effectively recognised in OCI. This is because the investment is initially measured at fair value plus those transaction costs, but subsequently at fair value. However, in our view transaction costs incurred on disposal of an equity investment for which the irrevocable election is made to present changes in fair value in OCI should be recognised in profit or loss, because presentation in OCI is not specifically permitted or required by the standard. [*IFRS 9.B5.2.2, IAS 1.88*]

7.7.50.120   Transaction costs are generally included in the initial measurement of instruments on an individual basis. This means that the transaction costs should be identifiable with the acquisition or origination of each individual instrument. However, in our view it may be appropriate to accumulate the incremental costs attributable to the acquisition or origination of individual instruments within a portfolio and then allocate these costs to items in the portfolio using a method that produces results that are not materially different from those achieved if the amounts are identified with individual items. It is necessary to make such an allocation to individual balances in order for unamortised transaction costs to be associated correctly with items that are repaid early, are sold or become credit-impaired. This approach would be appropriate only when the portfolio comprises homogeneous items. [*IFRS 9.A*]

7.7.60   *Internal costs*

7.7.60.10   In our view, the only internal transaction costs allowed to be included in the initial measurement of a financial instrument are commissions, bonuses and other payments that are made to employees only on completion of each individual transaction. We believe that internal semi-variable costs – e.g. the costs of marketing a new product or of employing additional staff to deal with an increase in the volume of transactions – do not qualify as transaction costs. [*IFRS 9.B5.4.8*]

7.7.70   *Facility or commitment fees paid*

7.7.70.10   An issue that often arises is how to treat facility fees paid – i.e. initial fees paid to cover the negotiation and arrangement of a facility and periodic fees to compensate the bank for keeping funds available.

7.7.70.20   In our view, if it is probable that a facility will be drawn down, then an initial facility fee is typically, in substance, an adjustment to the interest cost; therefore, the fee should be deferred and treated as an adjustment to the instrument's effective interest rate and recognised as an expense over the instrument's estimated life. However, in our view if it is not probable that a facility will be drawn down, then the fee should be considered a service fee and recognised as an expense on a straight-line basis over the commitment period. [*IFRS 9.B5.4.1–B5.4.3*]

7.7.70.30   For a discussion of fee income received (i.e. accounting by a lender), see 7.7.530.

7.7.80   Low-interest and interest-free loans

7.7.80.10   In most cases, the fair value of a financial instrument on initial recognition is the transaction price (see 7.7.10.20). However, sometimes interest-free or low-interest loans are given – e.g. by a shareholder or government or as a means of attracting or supporting customers for other goods and services (see 2.4.320). [*IFRS 9.B5.1.1–B5.1.2*]

7.7.80.20   In our view, in assessing whether the interest charged on a loan is at a below-market rate, an entity should consider the terms and conditions of the loan, local industry practice and local market circumstances. Evidence that a loan is at market rates might include the interest rates currently charged by the entity or by other market participants for loans with similar remaining maturities, cash flow patterns, currency, credit risk, collateral and interest basis. For example, very low interest rates on current accounts would be viewed as market rates if they are commonly given in arm's length transactions between market participants in the relevant market (see 7.7.300.70).

7.7.90   *Determining fair value*

7.7.90.10   The fair value of financial instruments is determined in accordance with IFRS 13, which is the subject of chapter 2.4. The fair value of below-market loans can be measured, for example, as the present value of the expected future cash flows, discounted using a market-related rate. [*IFRS 9.B5.1.1*]

7.7.90.20   The fair value of a financial liability with a demand feature – e.g. a demand deposit – is not less than the amount payable on demand, discounted from the first date on which the entity could be required to repay the amount (see 2.4.420). Accordingly, the fair value of an interest-free loan liability of which the lender can demand repayment of the face value at any time – i.e. a loan repayable on demand – is not less than its face value. In our view, similar considerations should also apply to the lender's measurement of the fair value of an interest-free loan repayable on demand to the extent that a market participant acting in its best interest that acquires the loan asset would be assumed to maximise value by achieving immediate repayment. [*IFRS 13.47*]

7.7.90.30   If a loan has no fixed maturity date and is available in perpetuity, then in our view in measuring its fair value, discounting should reflect these terms because a market participant acting in its best interest would not assume repayment of the loan. In our view, the fair value of loans that have no specified repayment dates and that are not repayable on demand should reflect a market participant's assumptions about the timing of the future cash flows (see 2.4.90).

7.7.100   *Short-term receivables and payables*

7.7.100.10   The fair value of a financial instrument reflects the effect of discounting expected future cash flows. However, an entity is permitted to initially measure short-term receivables and payables with no stated interest rate at their invoiced amounts without discounting, if the effect of discounting is immaterial. Therefore, in our view receivables and payables with maturities of up to six months are not generally required to be discounted. However, in high-interest environments the impact of discounting may be significant even for maturities of less than six months. Notwithstanding the above, trade receivables resulting from contracts with customers in the scope of IFRS 15 are required or permitted to be measured initially at the transaction price as defined in IFRS 15 (rather than at fair value) if certain criteria are met (see 7.7.20). [*IFRS 9.5.1.3, 13.BC138A*]

7.7.110 **Accounting for differences between fair value and consideration given or received**

7.7.110.10   Any difference between the amount lent and the fair value of the instrument on initial recognition is recognised as a gain or a loss unless it qualifies for recognition as an asset or a liability (see 7.7.10.30). [*IFRS 9.B5.1.1*]

7.7.110.20   If a low-interest loan is given in anticipation of a right to receive goods or services at favourable prices, then the right may be recognised as an asset if it qualifies for recognition as an intangible asset (see 3.3.30 and 90) or other asset – e.g. prepaid expenses.

7.7.110.30   If the loan is from a government, then the credit is treated as a government grant (see 4.3.100). [*IAS 20.10A*]

7.7.110.40   In our view, if the loan is from a shareholder acting in the capacity of a shareholder, then the resulting credit should normally be reflected in equity because the substance of the favourable terms is typically a contribution by a shareholder (see 7.3.450).

EXAMPLE 4 – INTEREST-FREE LOAN FROM SHAREHOLDERS

7.7.110.50   The shareholders of Company G provide G with financing in the form of interest-free loan notes to enable it to acquire investments in subsidiaries. The loan notes will be redeemed solely out of dividends received from these subsidiaries and become redeemable only when G has sufficient funds to do so. In this context, 'sufficient funds' refers only to dividend receipts from subsidiaries. Therefore, G could not be forced to obtain additional external financing or to liquidate its investments to redeem the shareholder loans. Consequently, the loans could not be considered payable on demand.

7.7.110.60   G initially measures the loan notes at their fair value (minus transaction costs), being the present value of the expected future cash flows, discounted using a market-related rate. The amount and timing of the expected future cash flows are determined on the basis of the expected dividend flow from the subsidiaries.

7.7.110.70   Given that the loan notes are interest-free, there will be a difference between the nominal value of the loan notes – i.e. the cash amount received – and their fair value on initial recognition. Because the financing is provided by shareholders, acting in the capacity of shareholders, we believe that the resulting credit should be reflected in equity as a shareholder contribution in G's statement of financial position.

Ⓢ 7.7.120   **Intra-group low-interest and interest-free loans**

7.7.120.10   When low-interest or interest-free loans are granted to consolidated subsidiaries, the effect of discounting is eliminated on consolidation. Therefore, the discounting will be reflected only in the financial statements of the subsidiary (see 7.7.110.40) and any separate financial statements of the parent. In our view, in the separate financial statements of the parent the discount should be recognised as an additional investment in the subsidiary. [*IFRS 10.B86(c)*]

7.7.120.20   Similar principles apply to low-interest or interest-free loans to associates or joint ventures, except that if the equity method is applied, then the discounting effect on profit or loss may be eliminated only to the extent of the investor's interest in the investee (see 3.5.430). This may also be the case for subsidiaries accounted for by the parent in the parent's separate financial statements using the equity method.

7.7.120.30   In the case of loans between entities in a group, in addition to the possibility of these being granted on an interest-free basis, there may be no stated terms of repayment. This complicates the measurement of the loan if it is not clear when repayments will take place, what the value of such repayments will be and what the maturity of the loan is. In such cases, in our view consideration should first be given to whether:
- classification as a liability is appropriate;
- there is no agreed means of repayment, either directly in the agreement or via a side agreement; and
- it is possible to estimate when the loan repayments will take place (see 7.7.90.30).

7.7.120.40   In our view, having considered these factors and concluded that no alternative treatment is available, such a loan may be considered to be payable on demand. This means that it should be measured at its face value.

7.7.130   *Related party transactions*

7.7.130.10   In our view, the requirement to initially recognise all financial assets and financial liabilities at fair value applies to all low-interest or interest-free loans, including those to or from related parties. In addition, related party disclosures will be required if the counterparty is a related party (see chapter 5.5). [*IFRS 9.5.1.1*]

7.7.140   SUBSEQUENT MEASUREMENT

7.7.150   General considerations

7.7.150.10   Subsequent to initial recognition, financial assets and financial liabilities are generally measured at amortised cost or fair value. For a discussion of the subsequent measurement of financial assets, see 7.7.160; for a discussion of the subsequent measurement of financial liabilities, see 7.7.170.

7.7.150.20   If an entity continues to recognise a transferred asset to the extent of its continuing involvement in the asset, then the asset and the associated liability are measured on a basis that reflects the rights and obligations retained by the entity (see 7.6.200). [*IFRS 9.3.2.17*]

7.7.150.30   Financial assets and financial liabilities that are designated as hedged items may require further adjustment in accordance with the hedge accounting requirements (see 7.9.170). Furthermore, for financial assets and financial liabilities, including derivatives, designated as hedging instruments, the following gains and losses are presented in OCI:
- for fair value hedges of investments in equity instruments designated as at FVOCI, all gains and losses (see 7.9.170.20);
- for cash flow and net investment hedges, the effective portion of gains and losses; and
- in certain cases, the change in the fair value of the time value of an option, the forward element of a forward contract or a foreign currency basis spread to the extent it relates to the hedged item (see 7.9.200, 230 and 690). [*IFRS 9.5.2.3–5.3.2, 6.5.8–6.5.16*]

7.7.160   **Financial assets**

7.7.160.10   After initial recognition, financial assets are generally subsequently measured at amortised cost, FVOCI or FVTPL (see 7.4.10.10). The recognition and presentation of gains and losses for each measurement category are as follows. [*IFRS 9.5.2, 5.4, 5.7.5, 5.7.10–5.7.11*]

MEASUREMENT CATEGORY	RECOGNITION AND PRESENTATION OF GAINS AND LOSSES
Amortised cost	The following items are recognised in profit or loss: • interest revenue using the effective interest method (see 7.7.410); • ECLs and reversals (see chapter 7.8); and • foreign exchange gains and losses (see 2.7.140). When the financial asset is derecognised, the gain or loss is recognised in profit or loss.
FVOCI	Gains and losses are recognised in OCI, except for the following items, which are recognised in profit or loss in the same manner as for financial assets measured at amortised cost: • interest revenue using the effective interest method (see 7.7.410); • ECLs and reversals (see chapter 7.8); and • foreign exchange gains and losses (see 2.7.140). When the financial asset is derecognised, the cumulative gain or loss previously recognised in OCI is reclassified from equity to profit or loss.
Equity investments – presentation of gains or losses in OCI	Gains and losses are recognised in OCI. However, dividends are recognised in profit or loss unless they clearly represent a repayment of part of the cost of the investment. The amounts recognised in OCI are not reclassified to profit or loss under any circumstances.
FVTPL	Gains and losses, both on subsequent measurement and derecognition, are recognised in profit or loss.

7.7.160.20   If an entity designates a financial asset as the hedged item in a fair value hedge, or designates it as a hedging instrument, then it applies the hedge accounting requirements of IFRS 9, unless it continues to apply the hedge accounting requirements of IAS 39 (see chapter 7.9). [*IFRS 9.5.7.3*]

7.7.170   **Financial liabilities**

7.7.170.10   Subsequent to initial recognition, financial liabilities are measured at amortised cost calculated under the effective interest method (see 7.7.260) except for liabilities:
• measured at FVTPL;

- that arise when a transfer of a financial asset does not qualify for derecognition or is accounted for using the continuing involvement approach (see 7.6.200 and 240);
- that are commitments to provide a loan at a below-market interest rate and not measured at FVTPL (see 7.1.250.110); and
- that are financial guarantee contracts (see 7.1.120). [*IFRS 9.4.2.1*]

7.7.170.20   Gains or losses on financial liabilities measured at fair value that are not part of a hedging relationship are generally recognised in profit or loss. The only exception is for gains and losses on certain financial liabilities designated as at FVTPL when the entity is required to present the effects of changes in the liability's credit risk in OCI (see 7.7.180). [*IFRS 9.5.7.1*]

7.7.170.30   Gains or losses on financial liabilities measured at amortised cost that are not part of a hedging relationship are recognised in profit or loss:
- when the financial liability is derecognised; and
- through amortisation under the effective interest method. [*IFRS 9.5.7.2*]

7.7.170.40   If an entity designates a financial liability as the hedged item in a fair value hedge, or designates it as a hedging instrument, then it applies the hedge accounting requirements of IFRS 9, unless it continues to apply the hedge accounting requirements of IAS 39 (see chapter 7.9). [*IFRS 9.5.7.3*]

7.7.180   *Financial liabilities designated as at FVTPL*

7.7.190   *Presentation*

7.7.190.10   Gains or losses on a financial liability designated as at FVTPL are generally split and presented as follows:
- the amount of change in the fair value of the financial liability that is attributable to changes in the credit risk of that financial liability is presented in OCI; and
- the remaining amount of change in the fair value of the financial liability is presented in profit or loss (see 7.10.210.50). [*IFRS 9.5.7.7*]

7.7.190.20   There are two exceptions to this split presentation. In both cases, all gains and losses are presented in profit or loss.
- *Exception 1:* If split presentation would create or enlarge an accounting mismatch in profit or loss (see 7.7.200).
- *Exception 2:* Loan commitments and financial guarantee contracts issued that are designated as at FVTPL. [*IFRS 9.5.7.7–5.7.9, B5.7.8*]

7.7.190.30   Amounts presented in OCI under the split presentation are never reclassified to profit or loss. This prohibition applies even if a gain or loss related to a change in the financial liability's credit risk is realised by settling or repurchasing the financial liability at fair value. Although reclassification to profit or loss is prohibited, an entity may transfer the cumulative gain or loss within equity. [*IFRS 9.B5.7.9*]

7.7.200   *Accounting mismatch in profit or loss*

7.7.200.10   To determine when split presentation would create or enlarge an accounting mismatch in profit or loss, an entity assesses whether it expects the effects of changes in the financial liability's credit risk to be offset in profit or loss by a change in the fair value of another financial instrument measured at FVTPL. Such an expectation is required to be based on an economic relationship between the characteristics of the financial liability and the characteristics of the other financial instrument. IFRS 9 refers to 'another financial instrument' rather than only to a financial asset. Therefore, it could, for example, relate to a derivative, which might be a financial asset or a financial liability that is linked to a financial liability of the reporting entity that has been designated as at FVTPL. [*IFRS 9.B5.7.6*]

7.7.200.20   An accounting mismatch in profit or loss is not caused solely by the measurement method that an entity uses to determine the effects of changes in a financial liability's credit risk (see 7.7.210). For example, a method that does not isolate changes in a financial liability's credit risk from changes in liquidity risk would not create or enlarge an accounting mismatch. [*IFRS 9.B5.7.12*]

7.7.200.30   An accounting mismatch to which the split presentation exception applies may arise from a contractual linkage. It may also occur in the absence of a contractual linkage – e.g. it may arise from an economic relationship between the characteristics of the two instruments. However, such an economic relationship does not arise by coincidence. [*IFRS 9.B5.7.10–B5.7.11, BC5.40*]

EXAMPLE 5 – ACCOUNTING MISMATCH EXCEPTION TO SPLIT PRESENTATION

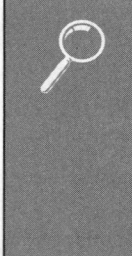

7.7.200.40   A financial asset held by Lender L can be prepaid contractually by Company D (the debtor) by delivering a corresponding debt instrument that was originally issued by L to fund its origination of the asset.

7.7.200.50   In this case, the change in the fair value of the asset reflects D's right to prepay by transferring the financial liability of L to L and therefore reflects changes in the credit risk of the financial liability. Accordingly, in L's financial statements the effects of changes in the credit risk of L's financial liability will be offset in profit or loss by a corresponding change in the fair value of the financial asset. Therefore, split presentation in respect of the financial liability is not permitted.

7.7.200.60   The circumstances in which the exception would apply are expected to be rare. Sometimes an entity may have used a financial liability designated as at FVTPL to fund financial assets whose values also happen to be exposed to changes in the general price of credit. This fact alone does not appear to justify an argument that the exception would apply. [*IFRS 9.BC5.39*]

EXAMPLE 6 – ACCOUNTING MISMATCH EXCEPTION – STRUCTURED NOTES

7.7.200.63   Bank T issues structured notes to its clients. The structured notes contain embedded derivatives and, on initial recognition, T designates the structured notes as at FVTPL. T aims to hedge the effect of changes in its own credit risk on the fair value of the structured notes by purchasing bonds of banks with a credit rating similar to its own. T designates the purchased bonds as at FVTPL. There is no contractual link between the structured notes and the purchased bonds.

7.7.200.65   In this case, although there may be a correlation between credit-related fair value changes on the structured notes and those on the purchased bonds, it

> results from movements in the general price of credit, rather than from an economic relationship between the characteristics of the structured notes and the purchased bonds (e.g. the fair values of the purchased bonds will not move in response to changes in the credit risk of the structured notes). Accordingly, the exception to split presentation does not apply and T presents changes in the fair value of the structured notes attributable to changes in credit risk in OCI.

7.7.200.70   An entity determines on initial recognition whether an accounting mismatch in profit or loss would be created by split presentation. This is not reassessed. However, the entity need not enter into all of the financial instruments giving rise to an accounting mismatch at exactly the same time. A reasonable delay is allowed, provided that any remaining transactions are expected to occur. [*IFRS 9.B5.7.7*]

7.7.200.80   An entity's methodology for determining whether split presentation creates or enlarges an accounting mismatch in profit or loss is applied consistently. However, if there are different economic relationships between the characteristics of the financial liabilities designated under the fair value option and the characteristics of the other financial instruments, then different methodologies may be used. [*IFRS 9.B5.7.7*]

7.7.200.90   The fair value option is permitted to be applied only to whole financial assets or financial liabilities and not to components or proportions. In our view, this indicates that the assessment of whether split presentation would create or enlarge an accounting mismatch in profit or loss should also be determined with reference to the entirety of the financial liability designated under the fair value option.

7.7.210   *Measuring changes in credit risk*

7.7.220   The meaning of credit risk

7.7.220.10   'Credit risk' is the risk that one party to a financial instrument will cause a financial loss for the other party by failing to discharge an obligation. There is a difference between:
- the risk that the issuer will fail to perform on the particular financial liability; and
- the general creditworthiness of the issuer. [*IFRS 7.A, 9.B5.7.13*]

7.7.220.20   For the purpose of applying the fair value option for financial liabilities, IFRS 9 focuses on the issuer's failure to perform on the particular financial liability. For example, the credit risk of a collateralised financial liability of an issuer will be less than the credit risk of an otherwise identical uncollateralised financial liability. [*IFRS 9.B5.7.13*]

7.7.220.30   However, there is a difference between credit risk of the liability and asset-specific performance risk related to the liability. Asset-specific performance risk is not related to the risk that the issuer of a financial liability will fail to perform; rather, it is related to the risk that one or more assets will perform poorly (or not at all). The standard provides two examples of asset-specific performance risk. The first is a financial liability with a unit-linking feature. Under the contractual terms of the financial liability, the amount due to investors is determined on the basis of the performance of specified assets. The second example refers to a financial liability issued by a structured entity with the following characteristics:
- the entity is legally isolated such that its assets are ring-fenced solely for the benefit of investors, even in the event of bankruptcy;
- the entity enters into no other transactions and its assets cannot be hypothecated; and

2067

- amounts are due to the entity's investors only if the ring-fenced assets generate cash flows. [*IFRS 9.B5.7.14–B5.7.15*]

7.7.220.40   In both examples, the effect of the assets on the fair value of the financial liability is asset-specific performance risk, not credit risk.

7.7.230   Measuring the effects of changes in credit risk

7.7.230.10   An entity determines the amount of the fair value change of a financial liability designated under the fair value option that is attributable to changes in its credit risk either:
- as the amount of change in its fair value that is not attributable to changes in market conditions that give rise to market risk – these conditions may include a benchmark interest rate, the price of another entity's financial instrument, a commodity price, a foreign exchange rate or an index of prices or rates; or
- using an alternative method that the entity believes more faithfully represents the amount of change in the financial liability's fair value that is attributable to changes in its credit risk. [*IFRS 9.B5.7.16–B5.7.17*]

7.7.230.20   The method for measuring changes in credit risk has to make maximum use of relevant observable inputs and minimum use of unobservable inputs. [*IFRS 9.B5.7.20*]

7.7.230.30   If the only significant relevant changes in market conditions for a financial liability are changes in an observed (benchmark) interest rate, then the amount of fair value changes that is attributable to changes in credit risk may be estimated under the so-called default method, which follows three steps.
- *Step 1:* Calculate the financial liability's internal rate of return (IRR) at the start of the period using the financial liability's fair value and contractual cash flows at that date. Deduct from this internal rate of return the observed (benchmark) interest rate at the start of the period. This gives an instrument-specific component of the internal rate of return.
- *Step 2:* Compute the present value of the cash flows of the financial liability at the reporting date using the financial liability's contractual cash flows at that date, and a discount rate equal to the sum of:
  - the observed (benchmark) interest rate at that date; and
  - the instrument-specific component of the internal rate of return determined in Step 1.
- *Step 3:* Deduct the present value calculated in Step 2 from the fair value of the financial liability at the reporting date. The resulting difference is the change in fair value that is not attributable to changes in the observed (benchmark) interest rate. This difference is presented in OCI. [*IFRS 9.B5.7.18–B5.7.19, IE1–IE5*]

7.7.230.40   The default method does not include a definition of 'benchmark' interest rate. In our experience, it is commonly understood to include inter-bank rates such as LIBOR for US dollar or sterling liabilities, or Euribor for euro liabilities. The default method treats a benchmark interest rate as akin to a risk-free rate; it excludes all changes in the benchmark rate as unrelated to, and not part of, changes in the financial liability's credit risk. However, many consider that inter-bank rates generally include a premium above the highest-quality government bond rates for the same term and currency, and that this premium may vary with market perceptions of changes in the credit risk of banks. The standard does not preclude either:
- using the risk-free rate as a benchmark rate; or
- using an alternative method that isolates a credit component of an inter-bank rate and includes it in the determination of changes in credit risk if the entity believes that it is a more faithful representation.

7.7.230.50   The default method is appropriate only if the only significant relevant changes in market conditions for a financial liability are changes in an observed (benchmark) interest rate. When other factors are significant, an entity uses an alternative measure that more faithfully measures the effects of changes in the financial liability's credit risk. For example, if the financial liability contains an embedded derivative, then the change in fair value of the derivative that is not attributable to changes in credit risk is excluded in calculating the amount to be included in OCI. [*IFRS 9.B5.7.18–B5.7.19, BC5.64*]

7.7.230.60   The basis for conclusions to IFRS 9 notes that if an entity repays the contractual amount of a financial liability, then the cumulative effect of changes in the financial liability's credit risk will net to zero. This is because its fair value will equal the contractual amount. However, if the wording of the guidance on the default method as set out in 7.7.230.30 were applied literally to all periods in a scenario covering more than one period, then it would usually lead to a result in which the fair value changes accumulated in OCI do not accumulate to a net amount of zero on repayment of the financial liability at its contractual maturity. Under the default method described in 7.7.230.30, the calculation of the credit risk component of the change in fair value is calculated separately for each period, and without reference to the cumulative position since inception. [*IFRS 9.BC5.53*]

EXAMPLE 7 – DETERMINING EFFECTS OF CHANGES IN CREDIT RISK – DEFAULT METHOD

7.7.230.70   Company H issues a financial liability for consideration of 100. It has an initial fair value and contractual repayment amount of 100, and a two-year maturity; it pays a coupon of 10% at the end of each year.

7.7.230.80   The benchmark interest rate throughout the two years remains at 7%. H uses the default method to estimate the amount of fair value changes that is attributable to changes in credit risk.

7.7.230.90   As the first step, the instrument-specific component of the internal rate of return is calculated as 3%. At the end of year 1, H discounts the future cash flows at 10% – i.e. 7% unchanged benchmark interest rate plus 3% risk component. The present value at the end of year 1 under Step 2 of the default method (see 7.7.230.30) is therefore 100 after payment of the interest. However, assume that the market spread on H's debt over the benchmark rate has increased, and that the fair value at the end of year 1 has decreased to 98. Therefore – in line with Step 3 under the default method – H recognises a gain of 2 in OCI.

7.7.230.100   At the end of year 2, both the present value of the cash flows calculated under Step 2 of the default method and the fair value of the financial liability are 110 immediately before repayment and zero immediately after repayment. Applying the wording of the guidance on the default method literally to the second year, the amount included in OCI for year 2 is calculated as zero. This means that there is no reversal of the gain of 2 recognised in OCI in year 1.

7.7.230.110   This example is summarised in the following table.

Steps under default method		Inception	Year 1	Year 2	
				Before repayment	After repayment
Step 1	Instrument-specific component of the internal rate of return	3%	N/A	N/A	N/A
Fair value of the financial liability		100	98	110	-
Step 2	Present value of the cash flows discounted at current benchmark rate plus instrument-specific component	100	100	110	-
Step 3	Amount recognised in OCI for the period	N/A	2	-	-
Cumulative amount recognised in OCI		N/A	2	2	2

7.7.230.120　An entity is not required to apply the default method as described in 7.7.230.30. It may modify its application of the default method so as to:
- compute the cumulative change in fair value attributable to changes in credit risk since inception; and
- allow the amount recognised in OCI to revert to zero at maturity.

7.7.230.130　The modification described in 7.7.230.120:
- replaces 'at the start of the period' in Step 1 of the default method (see 7.7.230.30) with 'at inception'; and
- treats the difference derived in Step 3 of the default method as the cumulative amount of fair value changes attributable to changes in credit risk for the life to date of the financial liability. This is instead of treating the difference as the amount of change for the current period.

7.7.230.140　Using the modified description in 7.7.230.130, the amount presented in OCI for the current period is the difference between:
- the cumulative amount calculated under Step 3 at the end of the current period; and
- the cumulative amount calculated under Step 3 at the end of the previous period. [*IFRS 9.B5.7.16*]

7.7.240　**FAIR VALUE**

7.7.240.10　Fair value is measured in accordance with IFRS 13, which is the subject of chapter 2.4.

7.7.250　**Investments in equity instruments**

7.7.250.10　All investments in equity instruments and contracts on those instruments are measured at fair value. [*IFRS 9.B5.2.3*]

7.7.250.20   For a discussion of the fair value measurement of unquoted equity instruments, including the circumstances in which cost may be an approximation of fair value, see 2.4.860.

7.7.260   AMORTISED COST

7.7.260.10   Amortised cost measurement can apply to both financial assets and financial liabilities. 'Amortised cost' is the amount at which a financial asset or a financial liability is measured on initial recognition, minus the principal repayments, plus or minus the cumulative amortisation using the effective interest method (see 7.7.270) of any difference between that initial amount and the maturity amount and, for financial assets, adjusted for any loss allowance. [*IFRS 9.A*]

7.7.260.20   When applying the effective interest method, interest is recognised in profit or loss in the period to which it relates, regardless of when it is to be paid. Therefore, interest is recognised in the period in which it accrues, even if payment is deferred. [*IFRS 9.B5.4.1–B5.4.7*]

7.7.260.30   The factors that an entity needs to consider in calculating the amortised cost of a financial asset or financial liability and recognising interest revenue and expense based on the effective interest method are as follows.

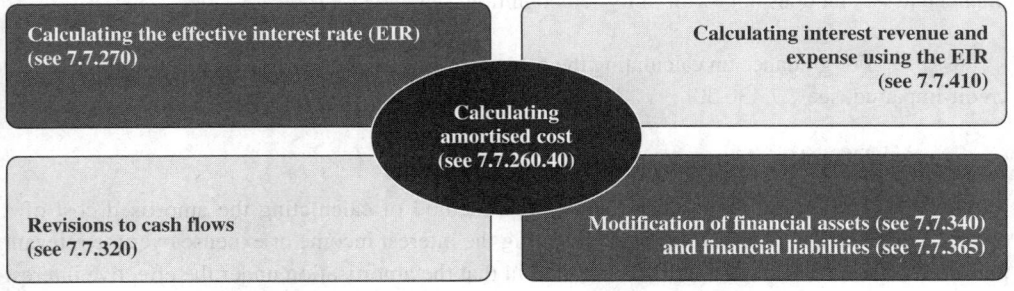

7.7.260.40   The elements of amortised cost are as follows. [*IFRS 9.A*]

	Financial assets	Financial liabilities
	Amount initially recognised (see 7.7.10)	
minus	Principal repayments	
plus or minus	Cumulative amortisation, using the EIR (see 7.7.270), of any difference between the initial amount and the maturity amount	
equals	Gross carrying amount (see 7.7.265)	
minus	Loss allowance (see chapter 7.8)	
equals	Amortised cost	Amortised cost (no adjustment for loss allowance)

7.7.265   Gross carrying amount

7.7.265.10   The gross carrying amount of a financial asset is its amortised cost before adjusting for impairment. It is calculated using the effective interest method (see 7.7.270). [*IFRS 9.A, IG.B.26*]

7.7.265.20   If a financial instrument measured at amortised cost is a hedged item in a fair value hedge, then its carrying amount is adjusted for the hedging gain or loss and the adjustment is amortised to profit or loss based on a recalculated effective interest rate. The amortisation (and so recalculation of the effective interest rate) may begin as soon as an adjustment is made, and begins no later than when the hedged item ceases to be adjusted for hedging gains or losses (see 7.7.390). Amortisation is based on a recalculated effective interest rate at the date on which amortisation begins. It appears that the unamortised adjustment for the hedging gain or loss amends the gross carrying amount of the financial asset. This is because the gross carrying amount is calculated using the effective interest method and, accordingly, is equal to the contractual cash flows discounted at what is (or would be) the recalculated effective interest rate. [*IFRS 9.6.5.10*]

7.7.265.30   For guidance on recalculating the gross carrying amount following a modification of a financial asset that does not result in its derecognition, see 7.7.350. [*IFRS 9.5.4.3*]

7.7.265.40   For guidance on calculating the gross carrying amount when a financial asset becomes credit-impaired, see 7.7.430.30.

7.7.270   Effective interest rate calculation

7.7.270.10   The 'effective interest method' is a method of calculating the amortised cost of a financial asset or financial liability and allocating the interest income or expense over the relevant period. It differs from the straight-line method in that the amortisation under the effective interest method reflects a constant periodic return on the carrying amount of the asset or liability. [*IFRS 9.A, B5.4.4*]

7.7.280   *General approach*

7.7.280.10   The effective interest rate is calculated on initial recognition of a financial asset or a financial liability. It is the rate that exactly discounts estimated future cash payments or receipts through the expected life of the financial instrument to:
- the gross carrying amount of the financial asset; or
- the amortised cost of the financial liability. [*IFRS 9.A*]

7.7.280.20   On initial recognition, the gross carrying amount of a financial asset, or the amortised cost of a financial liability, is generally equal to the fair value of the instrument, adjusted for transaction costs (see 7.7.10). [*IFRS 9.A*]

7.7.280.30   The estimate of expected cash flows considers all contractual terms (e.g. prepayment, call and similar options) but does not consider ECLs (i.e. the contractual cash flows are not reduced by ECLs). [*IFRS 9.A*]

7.7.280.40   The effective interest rate is revised as a result of:

- periodic re-estimation of cash flows of floating rate instruments to reflect movements in market rates of interest (see 7.7.330, 350 and 370);
- fair value hedge adjustments at the date on which an entity begins to amortise them (see 7.7.390 and 7.9.170); and
- it appears, costs and fees arising as part of modifications that do not result in derecognition (see 7.7.350.260, 280 and 370.30). [*IFRS 9.5.4.3, B3.3.6, B5.4.5–B5.4.6*]

7.7.280.45   To calculate interest income or expense in each relevant period, the effective interest rate is applied to the gross carrying amount of the asset (or amortised cost of credit-impaired assets (see 7.7.310)) or the amortised cost of the liability. [*IFRS 9.5.4.1*]

7.7.280.50   The difference between the effective interest for a given period and the instrument's coupon is the amortisation (or accretion) during that period of the difference between the initial measurement of the instrument and the maturity amount.

EXAMPLE 8 – EFFECTIVE INTEREST CALCULATION

7.7.280.60   Company K grants a five-year loan of 50,000 to Company L on 1 January 2018. There is an annual coupon of 10% paid on the last day of each year. L pays an up-front fee of 1,000 and the net loan proceeds are 49,000. The annual effective interest rate is calculated by solving for x in the following equation.

$$49,000 = \frac{5,000}{(1+x)} + \frac{5,000}{(1+x)^2} + \frac{5,000}{(1+x)^3} + \frac{5,000}{(1+x)^4} + \frac{55,000}{(1+x)^5}$$

7.7.280.70   Therefore, the effective interest rate is 10.53482% a year. The interest and the gross carrying amount are as follows.

DATE	INTEREST (10.53482%)	CASH FLOWS	GROSS CARRYING AMOUNT
1 January 2018	-	-	49,000
31 December 2018	5,162	5,000	49,162
31 December 2019	5,179	5,000	49,341
31 December 2020	5,198	5,000	49,539
31 December 2021	5,219	5,000	49,758
31 December 2022	5,242	55,000	-
Total	26,000	75,000	

7.7.290   *Contractual or estimated cash flows*

7.7.290.10   In determining the effective interest rate, an entity considers all of the contractual terms of an instrument, including any embedded derivatives – e.g. prepayment, call and similar options – that are not subject to separation (see 7.2.110), but without including ECLs. In our view, when an instrument gives either the issuer or the holder the option to require the instrument to be redeemed or cancelled early, and the terms are such that it is not certain whether the option will be exercised, then the probability of the option being exercised should be assessed in determining the estimated cash flows. [*IFRS 9.A*]

7.7.290.20   However, for financial liabilities with a demand feature – e.g. a demand deposit – the fair value is not less than the amount payable on demand, discounted from the first date on which the amount could be required to be paid (see 2.4.420). Therefore, for example, a non-interest-bearing or low-interest financial liability for which the holder can demand immediate repayment is not discounted on initial recognition, even if the issuer does not expect repayment of the liability in the near future (see 7.7.90.20). The impact of this requirement is that interest expense would be recognised at the coupon rate for a low-interest financial liability with an immediate demand feature. [*IFRS 13.47*]

7.7.290.30   The calculation of the effective interest rate includes:
- all fees and points paid or received between parties to the contract that are an integral part of the effective interest rate (see 7.7.530);
- transaction costs (see 7.7.50); and
- all other premiums or discounts (see 7.7.400). [*IFRS 9.A*]

7.7.290.40   ECLs are not taken into account in calculating the effective interest rate because under IFRS 9 the recognition of interest revenue reflects contractual terms and is separate from ECLs. However, for POCI assets, ECLs are included in the estimated cash flows when computing the credit-adjusted effective interest rate (see 7.7.310). [*IFRS 9.A, B5.4.1–B5.4.7, BC5.72*]

7.7.290.50   There is a presumption that future cash flows and the expected life can be estimated reliably for most financial instruments. In the rare case in which it is not possible to estimate the timing or amount of future cash flows reliably, the entity uses the contractual cash flows over the full contractual term of the financial instrument. [*IFRS 9.A*]

7.7.300   *Stepped interest*

7.7.300.10   Sometimes entities buy or issue debt instruments with a predetermined rate of interest that increases or decreases progressively (stepped interest) over the term of the debt instrument. In this case, the entity uses the effective interest method to allocate the interest income or expense over the term of the debt instrument to achieve a level yield to maturity that is a constant interest rate on the carrying amount of the instrument in each period. [*IFRS 9.A, IG.B.27*]

EXAMPLE 9A – EFFECTIVE INTEREST CALCULATION – STEPPED INTEREST

7.7.300.20   On 1 January 2018, Bank N takes a five-year deposit from a customer with the following rates of interest specified in the agreement.

YEAR	RATE
2018	2.0%
2019	2.1%
2020	2.2%
2021	2.4%
2022	3.0%

7.7.300.30   The effective interest rate for this instrument is 2.33% (rounded). Therefore, interest is accrued using the 2.33% rate.

EXAMPLE 9B – EFFECTIVE INTEREST CALCULATION – STEPPED INTEREST WITH EARLY WITHDRAWAL OPTION

7.7.300.40   Assume the same fact pattern as in Example 9A, except that the customer has an option to withdraw the deposit after four years without penalty. This option is considered to be closely related to the deposit contract (see 7.2.190).

7.7.300.50   If Bank N expects the deposit to be withdrawn after four years without penalty, then this expectation would be taken into account when calculating the instrument's effective interest rate. In this circumstance, the resulting effective interest rate would be approximately 2.17%. This rate would be used to accrue interest expense over the deposit's expected life.

7.7.300.60   A similar approach is adopted from the perspective of the holder of a financial instrument – i.e. the holder takes into consideration all contractual terms and the probability of any prepayment and call and similar options being exercised.

7.7.300.70   In respect of mortgage loans and credit cards that are issued with a low initial rate of interest to attract new customers, an issue similar to stepped interest arises. After the initial period, the interest rate typically returns to a standard market rate so that the lender is able to recover the discount over the remaining estimated life of the instrument. Normally, any initial discount that is widely offered to market participants should be recognised as part of the effective yield over the estimated life of the instrument. Alternatively, in our view the fair value of such an initial discount might be considered as a cost of attracting new business and recognised immediately as an expense. In our view, any discount that is not offered widely and is therefore in excess of that offered to all market participants should be recognised immediately as an expense (see 7.7.80).

7.7.310   *Credit-adjusted effective interest rate*

7.7.310.10   The effective interest rate for POCI financial assets (see 7.8.350) is calculated differently, and therefore does not follow the general approach (see 7.7.280). For POCI assets, the effective interest rate is calculated using expected cash flows inclusive of initial lifetime ECLs – i.e. the estimated contractual cash flows are reduced by lifetime ECLs. [*IFRS 9.A, B5.4.7*]

7.7.310.20   The resulting effective interest rate is defined as the credit-adjusted effective interest rate. [*IFRS 9.A*]

7.7.310.30   A credit-adjusted effective interest rate is not applied solely because the financial asset has high credit risk on initial recognition. [*IFRS 9.B5.4.7*]

7.7.320   Revisions to cash flows

7.7.320.10   If there is a change in the timing or amount of estimated cash flows (other than because of changes in estimates of ECLs), then the gross carrying amount of the financial asset or the amortised cost of the financial liability (or group of financial instruments) is adjusted in the period of change to reflect the revised actual and estimated cash flows, with a corresponding income or expense being recognised in profit or loss. The revised gross carrying amount of the financial asset (or amortised cost of the financial liability) is recalculated by discounting the revised estimated future cash flows at the instrument's original effective interest rate (or credit-adjusted effective interest rate for POCI assets) or, when applicable, the revised effective interest rate (see 7.7.280.40). This approach also applies to changes in contractual cash flows that result from a modification of a financial asset or financial liability that does not result in its derecognition (see 7.7.350 and 370). [*IFRS 9.5.4.3, A, B5.4.6, BC4.253*]

7.7.330   *Floating rate financial instruments*

7.7.330.10   The periodic re-estimation of cash flows to reflect movements in market rates of interest will change the effective interest rate of a floating rate financial asset or financial liability. [*IFRS 9.B5.4.5*]

7.7.330.20   IFRS 9 does not contain any further description or definition of 'floating rate' or guidance on how the term 'market rates of interest' should be interpreted in this context. Therefore, judgement may be required in applying these terms to different circumstances – e.g. when the contractual interest rate is calculated in accordance with a formula or is a discretionary rate. In many cases, a floating rate instrument may have a contractual interest rate that comprises more than one component such as a published benchmark rate or other published interest rate index (e.g. LIBOR) and a specified spread (e.g. a predetermined percentage spread above LIBOR). In some circumstances, although changes in the benchmark rate would be considered a change to which 7.7.330.10 would apply (leading to a change in the effective interest rate), the spread might be fixed (i.e. not subject to change) or any changes in the specified spread might not be considered to reflect movements in market rates of interest and would not lead to a change in the effective interest rate.

7.7.330.30   The periodic re-estimation of cash flows to reflect movements in market rates of interest refers to changing the rate of interest for a particular period or periods during which the instrument is outstanding and in relation to the amount outstanding during that period(s). It does not encompass changes in estimates of prepayment penalties even if the amount of the penalty is indexed to changes in market interest rates. [*IFRS 9.BC4.226*]

7.7.330.40   IFRS 9 does not specify how to calculate the effective interest rate for floating rate financial instruments. Therefore, in our view an entity may follow one of these two approaches for calculating the effective interest rate, which are illustrated in Example 10.

- *Approach 1:* Based on the actual benchmark interest rate that was set for the relevant period.
- *Approach 2:* Taking into account expectations of future benchmark interest rates and changes in these expectations.

EXAMPLE 10 – CALCULATING THE EFFECTIVE INTEREST RATE FOR FINANCIAL INSTRUMENTS WITH FLOATING BENCHMARK INTEREST

7.7.330.50   Company M issues at par a financial liability with:
- principal of 100;
- a contractual interest rate of 12-month LIBOR plus 2% (payable annually); and
- a maturity of three years.

12-month LIBOR on initial recognition of the liability is 2% and is used to set the first annual coupon. 12-month LIBOR is expected to be 3% in year 2 and 4% in year 3.

APPROACH	CALCULATION OF INITIAL EFFECTIVE INTEREST RATE
Approach 1	The initial effective interest rate is calculated as 4% per annum – i.e. 12-month LIBOR on initial recognition plus the margin of 2%.
Approach 2	The initial effective interest rate is calculated as approximately 5% per annum – i.e. the IRR of the following cash flows: <ul><li>expected coupons of 4, 5 and 6; and</li><li>principal repayable at maturity of 100.</li></ul>

7.7.330.60   We believe that an entity may apply the same approaches when the contractual terms of a financial instrument provide for the interest rate to be fixed for an initial period and then revert to a floating market rate of interest. An example is a 25-year mortgage loan that has an initial fixed rate of 4% for five years and then changes to the published standard variable rate (SVR) of the lender for the remaining 20 years. If the loan is measured at par on initial recognition, then:
- under Approach 1, the effective interest rate for the first five years would be 4% and then it would change to the actual SVR; and
- under Approach 2, the calculation of the effective interest rate would consider the initial fixed 4%, expectations of future levels of the SVR and changes in these expectations.

7.7.330.70   If the floating rate financial asset or financial liability is initially recognised at an amount equal to the principal receivable or payable on maturity, then periodic re-estimation of future interest payments would not normally have a significant effect on the carrying amount of the asset or liability. [*IFRS 9.B5.4.5*]

7.7.330.80   Under Approach 1, for a floating rate financial asset or financial liability that is initially recognised at a discount or premium, the interest income or expense is recognised based on the current market rate plus or minus amortisation or accretion of the discount or premium (see 7.7.400.20). [*IFRS 9.B5.4.4–B5.4.5*]

7.7.330.90   In our view, this approach could also be applied for a floating rate instrument that includes embedded derivatives that are not separated – e.g. an instrument on which the interest rate is subject to market indices such as inflation.

7.7.330.100   IFRS 9 does not prescribe any specific methodology for how transaction costs should be incorporated into the effective interest rate of a floating rate loan, except as discussed in 7.7.400. In our view, any consistent methodology that would establish a reasonable basis for the amortisation of the transaction costs may be used. For example, it would be reasonable to determine an amortisation schedule of the transaction costs based on the contractual interest rate in effect at inception.

7.7.340   **Modifications of financial assets**

7.7.350   *Modifications that do not result in derecognition*

7.7.350.10   If the modification of a financial asset does not result in its derecognition, then the gross carrying amount of the financial asset is recalculated and the resulting gain or loss is recognised as described in 7.7.320.10. [*IFRS 9.5.4.3, BC5.231–BC5.235*]

7.7.350.20   The principles for accounting for changes in cash flows on the modification of financial instruments that does not result in derecognition are similar to those for accounting for re-estimation of cash flows under the existing contract. Consequently, it appears that an entity may choose an accounting policy, to be applied consistently, to apply the guidance on floating rate financial instruments in 7.7.330 to changes in cash flows resulting from the modification of a floating rate component under the original contractual terms to a new rate of interest (whether floating or fixed) that reflects current market terms. We believe that under such a policy, the original effective interest rate of the financial asset should be revised, based on the new terms, to reflect changes in cash flows that reflect periodic changes in market rates. The revised effective interest rate would then be used to discount the modified contractual cash flows for calculation of the modification gain or loss (see 7.7.320.10) and, subject to the guidance on modification costs and fees in 7.7.350.260–280, for subsequent calculation of amortised cost. For a discussion of possible subsequent revisions to the effective interest rate after the date of the modification, see 7.7.350.60. [*IFRS 9.5.4.3, B5.4.5–B5.4.6, BC4.253*]

7.7.350.30   The original contractual terms may facilitate a repricing of an otherwise fixed interest rate (or an otherwise fixed component of an interest rate) to reflect a change in periodic market rates of interest, either because the lender has a right to demand immediate repayment without significant penalty, or because the borrower has an option to prepay without significant penalty (combined with its ability to obtain alternative financing at market rates from other possible lenders). In these cases, it appears that the entity may choose an accounting policy, to be applied consistently, to apply the approach in 7.7.350.20 to a revision of such an interest rate (or a component of an interest rate) to a new current market rate of interest. [*IFRS 9.B5.4.5*]

7.7.350.40   We believe that the policy described in 7.7.350.20 cannot be applied if the pricing of the modified loan reflects the granting of a concession to the borrower or similar forbearance activity. This is because the modified interest rate would not be a current market rate and would reflect the forbearance rather than changes in market rates of interest.

7.7.350.50   Application of the accounting policies described in 7.7.350.20–30 impacts the effective interest rate used in accounting for the modification and, subject to the guidance on modification costs and fees in 7.7.350.260–280, in measuring the financial instrument from that date onwards. If neither policy is elected or is available, then a renegotiation of a financial instrument that does not result in derecognition does not lead to a change in the original effective interest rate at the date of modification (subject to 7.7.350.260–280).

7.7.350.60   However, whether the effective interest rate is revised subsequently depends on the nature of the modified contractual terms. For example, if a floating component of an interest rate is modified to a fixed rate, then for periods following the modification the entity does not subsequently revise the post-modification effective interest rate in accordance with 7.7.330.10 because the modified cash flows are at a fixed rate and so do not change to reflect movements in market rates of interest after the date of modification. Conversely, if a fixed interest rate (or a fixed component of a floating rate) is modified to a floating rate, then for periods following the modification the entity subsequently revises the post-modification effective interest rate in accordance with 7.7.330.10 to reflect changes in the modified cash flows that reflect movements in market rates of interest after the date of modification. [*IFRS 9.B5.4.5*]

EXAMPLE 11A – MODIFICATION OF FIXED INTEREST RATE LOAN (1)

7.7.350.70   Bank O has a loan asset with a fixed annual coupon of 4%. The effective interest rate is also 4%. The borrower does not have a right to prepay the loan before its stated maturity and, similarly, O does not have a right to demand early repayment. The borrower, whose credit quality has improved, approaches O to reduce the coupons to a current market rate of 3%, payable semi-annually, and to reduce the term of the loan by one year. O agrees in order to preserve the relationship. No modification costs or fees are incurred.

7.7.350.80   O makes an assessment of whether the modification of the loan results in derecognition based on its accounting policy (see 7.6.95) and concludes that it does not. O calculates the modification loss as the difference between the net present values of:
- the pre-modification cash flows (based on 4% coupons) discounted at the effective interest rate of 4% – i.e. the pre-modification gross carrying amount; and
- the modified cash flows (based on the reduced 3% coupons) discounted at the original effective interest rate of 4% – i.e. the post-modification gross carrying amount.

7.7.350.90   O continues to use 4% as the effective interest rate for the subsequent calculation of amortised cost.

EXAMPLE 11B – MODIFICATION OF FIXED INTEREST RATE LOAN (2)

7.7.350.100   Bank P has a five-year loan asset with a fixed coupon of 3%. The effective interest rate is also 3%. The borrower does not have a right to prepay the loan before its maturity and, similarly, P does not have a right to demand early repayment. One year before the original maturity of the loan, P agrees to extend the maturity for two years to meet the customer's business needs and increases the interest rate to a market rate of 3.5%. No modification costs or fees are incurred.

7.7.350.110   P makes an assessment of whether the modification of the loan results in derecognition based on its accounting policy (see 7.6.95) and concludes that it does not. P calculates the modification gain as the difference between the net present values of:
- the pre-modification cash flows (based on 3% coupons) discounted at the effective interest rate of 3% – i.e. the pre-modification gross carrying amount; and
- the modified cash flows (based on the modified 3.5% coupons and longer maturity) discounted at the original effective interest rate of 3% – i.e. the post-modification gross carrying amount.

7.7.350.120   P continues to use 3% as the effective interest rate for the subsequent calculation of amortised cost.

EXAMPLE 11C – MODIFICATION OF FIXED INTEREST RATE TO FLOATING RATE

7.7.350.130   Bank T has a loan asset with a fixed coupon of 7%. The effective interest rate is also 7%. The borrower does not have a right to prepay the loan before its maturity and, similarly, T does not have a right to demand early repayment. Following changes in its interest rate risk management objectives, the borrower approaches T to change the interest rate to a current market floating rate of LIBOR plus 2% and T agrees. LIBOR at the date of modification is 5.2%, and the LIBOR curve to maturity of the loan is flat. No modification costs or fees are incurred.

7.7.350.140   T makes an assessment of whether the modification of the loan results in derecognition based on its accounting policy (see 7.6.95) and concludes that it does not. T calculates a modification gain as the difference between the net present values of:
- the pre-modification cash flows (based on 7% coupons) discounted at the effective interest rate of 7% – i.e. the pre-modification gross carrying amount; and
- the modified cash flows (based on the modified 7.2% (LIBOR 5.2% plus 2%) coupons) discounted at the original effective interest rate of 7% – i.e. the post-modification gross carrying amount.

7.7.350.150   T uses the original effective interest rate of 7% to calculate the gross carrying amount at the date of modification. However, because the modified contractual rate is a floating rate (LIBOR plus 2%), the effective interest rate is subsequently revised to reflect changes in LIBOR (see 7.7.350.60).

EXAMPLE 11D – REVISION TO FIXED SPREAD OF FLOATING RATE LOAN

7.7.350.160   Bank Q has a loan bearing interest of LIBOR plus 2%. The effective interest rate is also LIBOR plus 2%. The borrower has a right to prepay the loan before its maturity without significant penalty. Following an improvement in its creditworthiness, the borrower approaches Q with a view to negotiating a reduction in the spread. Q agrees to revise the fixed spread of 2% to a new lower spread of 1% that reflects current market rates for similar loans so that the borrower does not prepay the loan and refinance with another lender. No costs or fees are incurred at the time of the revision.

7.7.350.170   Q has adopted the accounting policy in 7.7.350.30, and therefore it revises the original effective interest rate to LIBOR plus 1%. It re-estimates the cash flows based on the revised terms (see 7.7.320.10) and recognises a gain or loss of approximately zero, as the difference between the net present values of:

- the pre-revision cash flows (based on LIBOR plus 2% coupons) discounted at the effective interest rate of LIBOR plus 2% – i.e. the pre-revision gross carrying amount; and
- the revised cash flows (based on the revised LIBOR plus 1% coupons) discounted at the revised original effective interest rate of LIBOR plus 1% – i.e. the post-revision gross carrying amount.

7.7.350.180   Under this approach, Q uses the revised original effective interest rate of LIBOR plus 1% for the subsequent calculation of amortised cost.

7.7.350.190   Alternatively, if Q had not adopted the accounting policy in 7.7.350.30, then it would have recognised a loss by discounting the revised cash flows using the pre-revision effective interest rate of LIBOR plus 2% because the spread is a fixed component. It would also have continued using an effective interest rate of LIBOR plus 2% for subsequent calculation of amortised cost.

EXAMPLE 11E – MODIFICATION OF OVERALL FLOATING INTEREST RATE

7.7.350.200   Bank R has a mortgage loan to a retail customer bearing interest at R's published SVR for mortgages. The effective interest rate also equals SVR. SVR is a discretionary rate determined periodically by R with reference to general levels of market interest rates, including rates offered by competitors for similar products, in the jurisdiction in which R operates. R and the borrower agree to modify the interest rate of the loan from SVR to a fixed rate of interest of 5%, which reflects current market conditions (e.g. fixed rates offered to similar borrowers for similar maturities). No modification costs or fees are incurred.

7.7.350.210   R makes an assessment of whether the modification of the loan results in derecognition based on its accounting policy (see 7.6.95) and concludes that it does not. R has adopted the accounting policy in 7.7.350.20, and therefore it revises the original effective interest rate to 5%. It calculates a modification gain or loss of approximately zero, as the difference between the net present values of:

- the pre-modification cash flows (based on SVR coupons) discounted at the effective interest rate that equals SVR – i.e. the pre-modification gross carrying amount; and
- the modified cash flows (based on the modified 5% coupons) discounted at the revised original effective interest rate of 5% – i.e. the post-modification gross carrying amount.

7.7.350.220   R uses the new fixed rate of 5% as the effective interest rate for the subsequent calculation of amortised cost without revising it in later periods. This is because although the original interest rate was a floating rate, the modified cash flows are fixed – i.e. they do not change to reflect movements in market rates of interest (see 7.7.350.60).

EXAMPLE 11F – REVISION TO FIXED RATE OF PREPAYABLE LOAN

7.7.350.230   Bank S has a loan asset bearing a stated interest rate of 4%. The effective interest rate is also 4%. The borrower has a right to prepay the loan before its maturity without significant penalty. Following a general fall in market interest rates, the borrower approaches S with a view to negotiating a reduction in the interest rate of the loan. S agrees to revise the stated rate of interest of 4% to a new lower stated rate of interest of 3% that reflects current market rates for similar loans so that the borrower does not prepay the loan and refinance with another lender. No costs or fees are incurred at the time of the revision.

7.7.350.240   S has adopted the accounting policy in 7.7.350.30, and therefore it revises the original effective interest rate to 3%. It re-estimates the cash flows based on the revised terms (see 7.7.320.10) and recognises a gain or loss of approximately zero, as the difference between the net present values of:

- the pre-revision cash flows (based on 4% coupons) discounted at the effective interest rate of 4% – i.e. the pre-revision gross carrying amount; and
- the revised cash flows (based on the revised 3% coupons) discounted at the revised original effective interest rate of 3% – i.e. the post-revision gross carrying amount.

7.7.350.250   S uses the new fixed rate of 3% as the effective interest rate for the subsequent calculation of amortised cost.

7.7.350.260   Any costs or fees incurred as part of the modification adjust the gross carrying amount of the modified financial asset and are amortised over the remaining term of the modified financial asset. However, there is no specific guidance on the basis of this amortisation. Because these costs or fees adjust the carrying amount of the asset as part of the amortised cost remeasurement, it appears that the effective interest rate should be adjusted following the modification. [*IFRS 9.5.4.3*]

7.7.350.270   IFRS 9 is not clear about whether fees received by the lender from the borrower as part of a modification adjust the gross carrying amount of the modified financial asset or are included in the modification gain or loss. It appears that one of the following approaches may be applied.

- *Approach 1*: Include the fees received in the calculation of the modification gain or loss. This is because the explicit requirement in IFRS 9 is to adjust the carrying amount for fees and costs incurred, and some argue that a fee that is received cannot be regarded as falling within the meaning of 'incurred'.
- *Approach 2*: Adjust the gross carrying amount for the fees received. This is because the language in paragraph 5.4.3 of IFRS 9, which sets out the requirements for financial assets, has been copied across from similar requirements for financial liabilities under which fees paid by the borrower to the lender are capitalised by the borrower (see 7.7.370.30).
- *Approach 3:* Adjust the gross carrying amount only for the fees received that have been charged by the lender to recover costs or fees incurred and recognise any excess as a modification gain or loss. This is because these receipts represent a reduction in the net costs or fees incurred. [*IFRS 9.5.4.3, B3.3.6*]

7.7.350.280   If an entity applies Approach 2 or Approach 3 in 7.7.350.270 – i.e. it includes some or all fees received in the gross carrying amount of the modified financial asset – then we believe that the effective interest rate should be adjusted to reflect the adjustment to the gross carrying amount as set out in 7.7.350.260.

7.7.350.290   The descriptions in contractual or other transaction documentation of amounts payable or receivable by the lender or the borrower in connection with the modification are not determinative of how they are accounted for. An entity considers the substance of the contractual arrangements to evaluate the nature of amounts paid or received. Judgement may be required to determine whether these amounts represent:

- a modification fee accounted for as described in 7.7.350.260–280 – e.g. a fee that compensates the lender for administrative efforts related to the modification;
- part of the modified or renegotiated contractual cash flows – e.g. a partial prepayment, such as a buy-down or prepayment of future interest payments to the lender when the amount paid represents consideration for the difference between the original and modified future contractual interest payments; or
- a combination of the two.

7.7.350.300   Excluding fees and costs, modifications of a financial asset that do not result in derecognition may impact profit or loss in two ways:

- by recognising a modification gain or loss that is equal to the change in the gross carrying amount of the modified financial asset; and
- by changing the amount of ECLs recognised as an impairment allowance (see 7.8.160). For example, if modification resulted in a reduction in contractual cash flows, then the expected cash shortfalls would also be likely to reduce.

7.7.350.310   In some cases, these impacts may be offsetting – e.g. when a modification results in a reduction in the contractual amount of a debt that reflects the debtor's assessed inability to pay the previous full contractual amount. In such cases, an entity may also have to assess whether the gross carrying amount of the financial asset should be partially written off before the modification, thereby reducing the gross modification gain or loss at the time of modification (see 7.8.430).

7.7.350.320   There is no guidance in IFRS 9 on the line item in the statement of profit or loss and OCI in which gains or losses on the modification of financial assets should be presented. A modification gain or loss may not necessarily relate to impairment (see chapter 7.8), because not all modifications are performed for credit risk reasons. Accordingly, an entity exercises judgement to determine an appropriate presentation for the gain or loss. It appears that if the modification is not related to financial difficulties of the borrower, then an entity may present the gain or loss from the modification in interest revenue. This is because the calculation of the modification gain or loss can be considered to be part of the application of the effective interest method.

7.7.360   *Modifications that result in derecognition*

7.7.360.10   When modification results in derecognition, the modified asset is recognised as a new financial asset and initially measured at its fair value plus eligible transaction costs (see 7.7.10 and 360.30). Ignoring any other fees and costs, derecognition effectively results in an overall gain or loss equal to the difference between:
- the amortised cost of the old asset; and
- the fair value of the new asset minus the amount of ECLs recognised as an impairment allowance on the new asset. [*IFRS 9.B5.5.25–B5.5.26*]

7.7.360.20   IFRS 9 is not explicit about the accounting for modification costs and fees incurred when the new financial asset is not classified as at FVTPL – i.e. whether they are:
- eligible for capitalisation as incremental transaction costs that are directly attributable to the acquisition of the new asset; or
- expensed immediately as relating to the derecognition of the old asset.

7.7.360.30   Consequently, it appears that an entity should apply judgement in developing its accounting policy for determining whether and which transaction costs are eligible for capitalisation. In some cases, it may be difficult to establish whether costs relate to the extinguishment of the old financial asset or acquisition of the new financial asset. In this case, we believe that an entity may analogise to the guidance for modification of financial liabilities – i.e. to include costs in the initial measurement of the new financial asset only if it can be incontrovertibly demonstrated that they relate solely to the new asset (see 7.7.375.20). Alternatively, it may be possible for an entity to distinguish between costs relating to the old financial asset and costs relating to the new one, or to allocate costs on a reasonable basis between the two. In this case, we believe that the entity may adopt an accounting policy, to be applied consistently, to capitalise incremental costs that are determined to relate directly to the acquisition of the new financial asset. Any costs not eligible for inclusion in the initial measurement of the new asset should be expensed immediately. [*IFRS 9.3.2.12, 5.1.1, A, B3.3.6*]

7.7.360.40   Similarly, IFRS 9 is not explicit about the accounting for modification fees received by the lender from the borrower. It appears that judgement may be required to determine what fees are included in the initial measurement of the new asset. We believe that the following fees should be included in the initial measurement of the new asset:
- fees that are considered in determining the fair value of the new asset and effectively represent adjustments between the carrying amount of the original asset and the fair value of the new asset (e.g. a fee charged to compensate the lender for agreeing to a below-market interest rate); and
- fees that represent reimbursement of transaction costs eligible to be included in the initial measurement of the new asset (see 7.7.360.30) and therefore reduce the net amount of capitalised transaction costs. [*IFRS 9.3.2.12, B5.1.2, B5.4.1*]

7.7.360.50   Any fees received for the modification that are not an adjustment to the initial measurement of the modified asset are included in profit or loss as part of the gain or loss on derecognition. [*IFRS 9.3.2.12*]

7.7.365   Modification of financial liabilities

7.7.370   *Modifications that do not result in derecognition*

7.7.370.10   If the exchange or modification is not accounted for as an extinguishment, then the amortised cost of the liability is recalculated and the resulting gains or losses are recognised as described in 7.7.320.10. [*IFRS 9.B5.4.6, BC4.253*]

7.7.370.20   The requirements for measuring the amortised cost of a financial liability are consistent with the requirements for measuring the gross carrying amount of a financial asset. Therefore, if a modification does not result in derecognition, then an entity applies the guidance in 7.7.350.20–240 to determine whether the effective interest rate of a modified financial liability may be revised. [*IFRS 9.BC4.253*]

7.7.370.30   Any costs and fees incurred are recognised as an adjustment to the carrying amount of the liability and amortised over the remaining term of the modified instrument. However, there is no specific guidance on the basis of this amortisation. Because these costs or fees adjust the carrying amount of the liability as part of the amortised cost measurement, it appears that the effective interest rate should be adjusted following the modification. [*IFRS 9.B3.3.6*]

7.7.370.40   An entity considers the substance of the contractual arrangements to evaluate whether amounts payable to or by the lender or the borrower represent a modification fee accounted for as described in 7.7.370.30 or part of the modified or renegotiated contractual cash flows. The guidance in 7.7.350.280 applies similarly to the borrower.

EXAMPLE 12 – COSTS INCURRED – NON-SUBSTANTIAL MODIFICATION OF TERMS

7.7.370.50   Company Z has a loan from Bank B. Z negotiates with B a modification of the terms of the loan and incurs the following costs.

COST	AMOUNT
Modification fees payable to B	30,000
External adviser assisting Z with the terms of the modification transaction	15,000
Z's internal treasury staff, based on time spent and an average hourly rate	12,000
External lawyer assisting B in drafting the contract; lawyer's fees paid by Z directly to the lawyer	8,000
Total costs	65,000

7.7.370.60   In this example, the modification transaction is not accounted for as an extinguishment. Therefore, the carrying amount of Z's loan is adjusted for costs of 53,000, comprising the fees for the modification payable to Bank B (30,000), the cost of Z's external adviser (15,000) and the amount paid to B's lawyer (8,000).

> However, the costs of Z's internal treasury department are recognised in profit or loss because they are not directly attributable incremental transaction costs (see 7.7.50).

7.7.375 *Modifications that result in derecognition*

7.7.375.10 If a modification of the terms of a debt instrument meets the derecognition conditions in IFRS 9 (see 7.6.370), then any difference between the carrying amount of the original liability and the consideration paid is recognised in profit or loss. The consideration paid includes non-financial assets transferred and the assumption of liabilities, including the new modified financial liability. Any new financial liability recognised is initially measured at fair value. [*IFRS 9.3.3.3*]

7.7.375.20 The effective interest rate of the new financial liability is calculated based on the revised terms of the financial liability at the date of the modification. In this case, any costs or fees incurred are recognised as part of the gain or loss on extinguishment and do not adjust the carrying amount of the new liability. Accordingly, in our view no transaction costs should be included in the initial measurement of the new liability unless it can be incontrovertibly demonstrated that they relate solely to the new liability instrument and in no way to the modification of the old liability. This would not usually be possible but might apply to taxes and registration fees payable on execution of the new liability instrument. [*IFRS 9.B3.3.6*]

EXAMPLE 13 – COSTS INCURRED – SUBSTANTIAL MODIFICATION OF TERMS

> **7.7.375.30** Modifying Example 12, if the modification transaction is accounted for as an extinguishment, then all of the costs incurred by Z as part of the modification transaction with B – i.e. 65,000 – are recognised in profit or loss.

7.7.375.40 In our view, the accounting treatment by the borrower for forgiveness of debt should be based on an analysis of the nature of the transaction.
- If a shareholder forgives the debt, then it is likely that the shareholder is acting in the capacity of a shareholder and that the forgiveness of debt should be treated as a capital transaction. The outstanding financial liability should be reclassified to equity and no gain or loss should be recognised (see 7.3.450.50). For a discussion of other debt-for-equity swaps, see 7.6.450.
- If there is clear evidence that the shareholder is acting as a lender – i.e. in the same way as an unrelated lender – then a gain or loss should be recognised in profit or loss (with accompanying related party disclosures – see chapter 5.5).
- If a government forgives a loan, then the forgiveness should be treated as a government grant (see chapter 4.3) unless the government is also a shareholder and is acting in that capacity.

7.7.375.50 IFRS does not specify where in the statement of profit or loss and OCI a gain or loss on the extinguishment of debt should be presented. In our view, it should be included in finance income or finance costs (see 7.10.70).

7.7.380 **Instruments acquired in a business combination**

7.7.380.10 All financial instruments that are acquired as part of a business combination are initially measured by the acquirer at their fair value at the date of acquisition (see 2.4.1000). [*IFRS 3.18*]

7.7.380.20   At the date of acquisition, the fair value of the instrument and the total cash flows expected over the remaining term of the instrument are used by the acquirer to calculate a new original effective interest rate for the instrument. The new original effective interest rate is used to determine the interest income or expense in the acquirer's consolidated financial statements but has no impact on the accounting in the acquiree's financial statements. [*IFRS 9.A*]

7.7.380.30   Because assets of the acquiree are measured in the acquirer's consolidated accounts at fair value at the date of acquisition and the effects of uncertainty about future cash flows are included in the fair value measurement, the acquirer does not recognise a separate valuation allowance to reflect any ECLs in the initial measurement at that date. For a discussion of recognising a loss allowance in such circumstances, see 7.8.20.50. [*IFRS 3.B41*]

7.7.380.40   In our view, an instrument that is credit-impaired at the date of acquisition should be treated by the acquirer as a POCI asset (see 7.8.340). Therefore, the estimated cash flows should be determined on the basis of the expected receipts as reduced by the initial ECLs, rather than on the basis of the cash flows that would arise if the borrower complied with the contractual terms. [*IFRS 3.B41, 9.B5.4.7*]

7.7.380.50   If the expected cash flows from that asset are subsequently revised upwards because of an improvement in the debtor's credit quality, then an entity recognises an impairment gain (see 7.8.370.20). [*IFRS 9.5.5.14*]

7.7.390   Hedged item in fair value hedge

7.7.390.10   An interest-bearing instrument that is the hedged item in a fair value hedge is remeasured based on changes in fair value in respect of the risk being hedged during the period of the hedging relationship (see 7.9.170). [*IFRS 9.6.5.8(b)*]

7.7.390.20   When hedge accounting is discontinued, or earlier, the carrying amount of the instrument and the total payments to be made over the remaining term of the instrument are used to calculate a revised effective interest rate for the instrument. The revised effective interest rate is used to determine interest income or expense in subsequent periods (see 7.9.170.90). [*IFRS 9.6.5.10*]

7.7.400   Discounts, premiums and pre-acquisition interest

7.7.400.10   The straight-line amortisation of discounts or premiums is not permitted. Instead, discounts and premiums – including fees, points paid or received and transaction costs – are generally recognised over the expected life of the related instrument using the effective interest rate at the date of initial recognition of the instrument. However, in some cases a shorter period is used if this is the period to which such discounts and premiums relate – e.g. when the variable is repriced to market rates before the expected maturity of the instrument. [*IFRS 9.B5.4.4*]

7.7.400.20   If a discount or premium arises on the acquisition of a floating rate instrument, then it is important to identify the reason for that discount or premium. For example, if a premium or discount on a floating rate instrument reflects *changes in market rates* since the floating-interest instrument was last repriced, then it will be amortised to the next repricing date. Alternatively, if the premium or discount results from a change in the credit spread over the floating rate specified in the instrument as a result of a *change in credit risk*, then it is amortised over the expected life of the instrument. [*IFRS 9.B5.4.4*]

7.7.400.30   For a group of prepayable mortgage loans, any discount, transaction costs and related fees may be required to be amortised over a period that is shorter than the contractual maturity. Historical prepayment patterns would be used to estimate expected lives and subsequent revisions to prepayment estimates will give rise to gains and losses that are recognised in profit or loss. [*IFRS 9.B5.4.4, B5.4.6*]

7.7.400.40   When an interest-bearing instrument is acquired between interest payment dates, the buyer normally has an obligation to pay the accrued interest to the seller when it is received or pays a higher price for the instrument to reimburse the seller for the accrued interest that will be paid to the buyer. Accordingly, interest that has accrued on an interest-bearing investment before it is acquired is not recognised as income. If there is an obligation to pay the accrued interest to the seller, then a receivable and a corresponding payable are recognised in respect of the accrued interest.

7.7.400.50   The amortisation of discounts or premiums is included in interest income or expense and is not required to be disclosed separately.

7.7.410   **Interest revenue and expense**

7.7.420   *General approach*

7.7.420.10   The effective interest rate is used to allocate interest revenue or expense over the expected life of the financial instrument as follows. [*IFRS 9.5.4.1, A, B5.4.1, B5.4.4*]

Financial assets	Apply the effective interest rate to the gross carrying amount.
Financial liabilities	Apply the effective interest rate to the amortised cost.

EXAMPLE 14 – INTEREST REVENUE CALCULATION

7.7.420.20   Continuing Example 8, on 1 January 2019 Company K revises its estimate of cash flows. It now expects that 40% of the contractual par amount will be prepaid at the end of 2019 and the remaining 60% on 31 December 2022.

7.7.420.30   As a result, the gross carrying amount of the instrument is adjusted. It is recalculated by discounting the amount that K expects to receive in 2019 and subsequent years using the original effective interest rate of 10.53482%. This results in the new gross carrying amount on 1 January 2019 of 49,400.

$$49,400 = \frac{(20,000 + 5,000)}{(1 + 0.1053482)} + \frac{3,000}{(1 + 0.1053482)^2} + \frac{3,000}{(1 + 0.1053482)^3} + \frac{(30,000 + 3,000)}{(1 + 0.1053482)^4}$$

7.7.420.40   The adjustment of 238 (49,400 - 49,162) (see 7.7.280.70) is recorded in profit or loss in 2019. The following table provides information about gross carrying amount, interest revenue and cash flows as they would be adjusted taking into account the change in estimate.

DATE	INTEREST (10.53482%)	CASH FLOWS	CHANGE IN ESTIMATE	GROSS CARRYING AMOUNT
1 January 2018	-	-	-	49,000
31 December 2018	5,162	5,000	238	49,400
31 December 2019	5,205	20,000 + 5,000	-	29,605
31 December 2020	3,119	3,000	-	29,724
31 December 2021	3,131	3,000	-	29,855
31 December 2022	3,145	30,000 + 3,000	-	-

7.7.430 *Approach for credit-impaired financial assets*

7.7.430.10   For credit-impaired financial assets (see 7.8.350.10), interest revenue is calculated by applying the effective interest rate (or credit-adjusted effective interest rate if the asset was credit-impaired on initial recognition) to the amortised cost of the asset. An asset is credit-impaired if:
● it was credit-impaired on initial recognition (a POCI asset); or
● it became credit-impaired after initial recognition. [*IFRS 9.5.4.1*]

7.7.430.20   For an asset that became credit-impaired after initial recognition, interest revenue is calculated by applying the effective interest rate to the amortised cost of the asset in reporting periods subsequent to the asset becoming credit-impaired. The calculation of interest revenue reverts to the gross basis in subsequent reporting periods if the asset is no longer credit-impaired. However, for POCI assets, the calculation of interest revenue can never revert to a gross basis, even if the credit risk of the asset improves. [*IFRS 9.5.4.1–5.4.2*]

7.7.430.25   In the basis for conclusions to IFRS 9, the IASB noted that, conceptually, an entity would assess whether financial assets have become credit-impaired on an ongoing basis and reflect this assessment in the presentation of interest revenue. However, because this approach would be unduly onerous, an entity is only required to make the assessment of whether a financial asset is credit-impaired at each reporting date and change the interest calculation from the beginning of the following reporting period. It appears that an entity is not precluded from adjusting the interest calculation more frequently if it assesses impairment more frequently, because more frequent adjustment would be more consistent with what the IASB regards as the conceptual objective. We believe that if an entity assesses impairment more frequently than at each reporting date, then it should choose an accounting policy, to be applied consistently, either to:
● change the interest income recognition from the beginning of the reporting period following the identification of an asset as credit-impaired or no longer credit-impaired; or
● align the process for changes to interest income recognition with the process for assessing and recognising impairment for internal or regulatory reporting. [*IFRS 9.5.5.3, BC5.78*]

7.7.430.30   IFRS 9 does not contain specific guidance on how to measure the gross carrying amount (see 7.7.260.40) when a financial asset becomes credit-impaired (see 7.8.350.10) after initial recognition. Therefore, it appears that the gross carrying amount and the ECL allowance (see 7.8.160) should be measured using the general definitions in the same way as for financial assets that are not credit-impaired, even though interest revenue is calculated on a net basis by applying the effective interest rate to the amortised cost of the asset (subject to the gross carrying amount and related ECL allowance being reduced to the extent that there is no reasonable expectation of recovering the contractual cash flows – see 7.8.430). Accordingly, we believe that the calculation of interest on a net basis only affects the recognition of income in profit or loss, but does not affect the measurement of the gross carrying amount or the ECL allowance in the statement of financial position and in related disclosures. This approach results in consistent application of the concepts of gross carrying amount and loss allowance across all financial assets (except for POCI assets – see 7.8.340). [*IFRS 9.A, BC5.75*]

EXAMPLE 15 – CALCULATION OF GROSS CARRYING AMOUNT OF A CREDIT-IMPAIRED ASSET

7.7.430.40   Company T has a zero coupon loan asset with the following terms:
- a nominal amount of 1,000 is repayable on maturity;
- the maturity date is 31 December 2021; and
- the effective interest rate is 10% per annum.

7.7.430.50   On 31 December 2019, the loan becomes credit-impaired and the cash flows expected from the loan at maturity amount to 400. The table below sets out calculations of the gross carrying amount, loss allowance (see 7.8.195) and amortised cost of the loan at that date.

ITEM	HOW TO CALCULATE	CALCULATION	AMOUNT
Gross carrying amount	Present value of the contractual cash flows that are due to T under the contract – i.e. the amount repayable at maturity – discounted at the effective interest rate	$1{,}000 / 1.1^2$	826
Loss allowance	Difference between the gross carrying amount and the present value of the cash flows that T expects to receive (see 7.8.195)	$826 - 400 / 1.1^2$	496
Amortised cost of the loan	Difference between the gross carrying amount and the ECL allowance	$826 - 496$	330

7.7.430.60   Assuming there is no change in the cash flows that T expects to receive, T records the following entry in respect of the loan on 31 December 2020.

	DEBIT	CREDIT
Gross carrying amount	83[1]	
Interest income (profit or loss)		33[2]
ECL allowance		50[3]

Notes
1. Calculated as the difference between the present value of the contractual amount repayable at maturity determined at 31 December and 1 January 2020 – i.e. 1,000 / 1.1 - 826.
2. Calculated by applying the effective interest rate of 10% per annum to the amortised cost at 1 January 2020 – i.e. 330 x 0.1.
3. This brings the balance of the ECL allowance at 31 December 2020 to 546, which is equal to the difference between the updated gross carrying amount of 909 (1,000 / 1.1) and the present value of the cash flows that T expects to receive of 363 (400 / 1.1). The amount of 363 is the updated amortised cost.

7.7.430.70   The following table shows the reconciliation of the loan's gross carrying amount, amortised cost and loss allowance during 2020.

	GROSS CARRYING AMOUNT	LOSS ALLOWANCE	AMORTISED COST
Balance at 1 January 2020	826	(496)	330
Interest income	33	-	33
Unwinding of discount on present value of ECLs	50	(50)	-
Balance at 31 December 2020	909	(546)	363

7.7.440   FINANCIAL INSTRUMENTS MEASURED IN FOREIGN CURRENCY

7.7.450   General considerations

7.7.450.10   Entities may have exposure to foreign currency risk, either from transactions in foreign currencies or from investments in foreign operations. The principles for foreign currency transactions explained in chapter 2.7 apply equally to financial instruments. The application of these principles to various foreign currency financial instruments is explained below.

7.7.450.20   'Monetary items' are units of currency held and assets and liabilities to be received or paid, in a fixed or determinable number of units of currency. This definition is narrower than the definition of a financial instrument, which means that not all financial instruments are monetary. Consequently, contractual rights or obligations to receive or pay cash when the amount of money is neither fixed nor determinable are non-monetary financial instruments. This is the case, for example, with equity securities and other instruments if the holder has no right to a determinable amount of money (see 2.7.120.10–20). [*IAS 21.8*]

7.7.450.30 Derivative contracts are settled at amounts that are determinable at the settlement date in accordance with the terms of the contract and the price of the underlying. Derivatives that are settled in cash are monetary items, even if the underlying is a non-monetary item. [*IFRS 9.B5.7.2, IAS 21.16*]

7.7.450.40 In our view, the liability component of a convertible bond should be considered to be a monetary item because it is an obligation to pay a fixed or determinable amount of currency units.

7.7.460 Monetary items measured at amortised cost

7.7.460.10 Monetary items denominated in a foreign currency and carried at amortised cost are measured as follows.
- The functional currency carrying amount at the beginning of the reporting period – i.e. the amount reported in the functional currency of the entity at the previous reporting date – is the starting point.
- The interest income to be recognised in the period is the amount calculated in the foreign currency under the effective interest method, multiplied by the appropriate average spot exchange rate for the period. This accrual adjusts the functional currency amortised cost at the beginning of the reporting period. For a financial asset, any impairment allowance or write-off is similarly first calculated as an adjustment to the amortised cost in the foreign currency and then translated into the functional currency at the appropriate rate as an adjustment to the functional currency amortised cost.
- Then the foreign currency amortised cost of the monetary item is calculated as at the reporting date.
- The functional currency carrying amount at the reporting date is the foreign currency amortised cost at the reporting date multiplied by the spot exchange rate at the reporting date.
- Then the functional currency carrying amount at the reporting date as calculated above is compared with the functional currency carrying amount at the beginning of the reporting period, adjusted for the interest accrual and any payments or impairment charges during the period. Any difference between these two amounts is an exchange gain or loss, which is recognised in profit or loss. [*IFRS 9.B5.7.2, IG.E.3.4, IAS 21.23(a), 28*]

7.7.470 Monetary financial assets measured at FVOCI

7.7.470.10 For the purpose of recognising foreign exchange differences, assets classified as measured at FVOCI are treated as monetary items and as if they were measured at amortised cost in the foreign currency. Accordingly, the foreign exchange differences arising from changes in amortised cost are recognised in profit or loss and not in OCI. [*IFRS 9.5.7.10, B5.7.2A, IG.E.3.2, IG.E.3.4, IAS 21.23(a)*]

7.7.470.20 The foreign currency differences on these instruments are measured as follows.
- The functional currency amortised cost at the beginning of the reporting period – i.e. the amount calculated (but not reported) in the functional currency of the entity at the previous reporting date – is the starting point.
- The interest income to be recognised in the period is the amount calculated in the foreign currency under the effective interest method, multiplied by the average spot exchange rate for the period. This accrual adjusts the functional currency amortised cost at the beginning of the reporting period. For monetary financial assets measured at FVOCI, interest calculated under the effective interest

method is required to be recognised in profit or loss. Any impairment allowance or write-off is similarly first calculated as an adjustment to the amortised cost in the foreign currency and then translated into the functional currency at the appropriate rate.

- Then the foreign currency amortised cost of the monetary item is calculated as at the reporting date.
- The functional currency amortised cost at the reporting date is the foreign currency amortised cost at the reporting date multiplied by the spot exchange rate at the reporting date.
- Then the functional currency amortised cost at the reporting date is compared with the functional currency amortised cost at the beginning of the reporting period adjusted for the interest accrual and any payments or impairment charges during the period. Any difference between these two amounts is an exchange gain or loss, which is recognised in profit or loss. [*IFRS 9.IG.E.3.2*]

7.7.470.30   The reported carrying amount of FVOCI monetary items is calculated as follows.

- The fair value of the monetary item at the reporting date is calculated in the foreign currency.
- The functional currency carrying amount at the reporting date is determined by multiplying the fair value in the foreign currency by the spot exchange rate at the reporting date.
- The difference between the functional currency carrying amount at the reporting date – i.e. fair value – and the functional currency amortised cost at the reporting date, adjusted for impairment loss, is the cumulative gain or loss to be recognised in OCI at the reporting date. [*IFRS 9.IG.E.3.2*]

EXAMPLE 16 – ACCOUNTING FOR MONETARY ASSET MEASURED AT FVOCI

7.7.470.40   On 31 December 2017, Company P, which has the euro as its functional currency, buys a bond denominated in US dollars. The following facts are also relevant for this example.

	31 DEC 2017	31 DEC 2018
Fair value of the bond	USD 1,000	USD 1,060
Remaining years to maturity	5	4
Fixed coupon on principal of USD 1,250	4.7% or USD 59	
Annual effective interest rate	10%	
Loss allowance	USD 20	USD 50

7.7.470.50   Exchange rates at 31 December 2017 and 31 December 2018 and the average exchange rate during 2018 are as follows.

	USD	EUR
Exchange rate at 31 December 2017	1.0	1.5
Average exchange rate during 2018	1.0	1.75
Exchange rate at 31 December 2018	1.0	2.0

7.7.470.60   P classifies the bond as measured at FVOCI and consequently recognises fair value gains and losses in OCI. At 31 December 2017, P recognises the bond as follows.

	DEBIT (EUR)	CREDIT (EUR)
Bond	1,500[1]	
Cash		1,500
To recognise initial acquisition of bond		
Impairment loss (profit or loss)	30[2]	
Other comprehensive income		30
To recognise ECLs		

Notes
1.   Calculated as EUR 1,500 = USD 1,000 x 1.5.
2.   Calculated as EUR 30 = USD 20 x 1.5.

7.7.470.70   P determines:
- the amortised cost of the bond at 31 December 2017;
- the interest income for 2018 under the effective interest method;
- the coupon received on 31 December 2018;
- the impairment loss allowance at 31 December 2018; and
- the amortised cost of the bond at 31 December 2018.

	USD	RATE	EUR
Amortised cost of bond at 31 December 2017	980	1.5	1,470
Interest income	100[1]	1.75	175
Coupon received	(59)	2	(118)
Impairment loss	(30)[2]	2[3]	(60)
Amortised cost of bond at 31 December 2018	991	2	1,982
Exchange difference			515[4]

Notes
1.   Calculated as USD 1,000 x 10%.
2.   Calculated as USD 30 = USD 50 - USD 20.
3.   The journal entry for recognising ECLs is made by M at the reporting date.
4.   Calculated as EUR 1,982 + EUR 118 + EUR 60 - EUR 175 - EUR 1,470.

7.7.470.80   The exchange difference represents:
- a gain of EUR 490 (980 x (2 - 1.5)) arising on the initial amortised cost; and
- a gain of EUR 25 (100 x (2 - 1.75)) arising on the interest income. [*IFRS 9.IG.E.3.2*]

7.7.470.90   P determines the cumulative gain or loss to be recognised in OCI as follows.

31 DECEMBER 2018	USD	RATE	EUR
Fair value of the bond	1,060	2	2,120
Amortised cost of the bond	(991)	2	(1,982)
Cumulative fair value changes in OCI (gain)	69	2	138

7.7.470.100   P records the following entry on 31 December 2018.

	DEBIT (EUR)	CREDIT (EUR)
Bond	620	
Cash	118	
Impairment loss	60	
Interest income		175
Exchange gain		515
Fair value change in OCI		108[1]
To recognise changes in fair value, interest income and repayment, impairment and foreign exchange on bond		

Note
1.   EUR 108 = EUR 138 (cumulative fair value changes in OCI) - EUR 30 (impairment loss already recognised in the prior period).

7.7.480   Non-monetary items measured at fair value

7.7.480.10   Non-monetary financial instruments, such as investments in equity securities, measured at fair value are reported using the exchange rates that existed when the fair values were determined. Therefore, the fair value is first determined in the foreign currency, which is translated into the functional currency. Foreign exchange gains and losses are not separated from the total fair value changes. Therefore, for FVOCI equity investments the entire change in fair value, including any related foreign exchange component, is recognised in OCI. If the non-monetary item is measured at FVTPL, then the entire fair value change is recognised in profit or loss. [*IAS 21.23(c), 30, IFRS 9.B5.7.3*]

7.7.490   Dual-currency loan liabilities

7.7.490.10   A dual-currency loan is an instrument with the principal and interest denominated in different currencies. A dual-currency loan liability with principal denominated in the functional currency and interest payments denominated in a foreign currency contains an embedded foreign currency derivative. However, the embedded derivative is not separated from the host financial liability because changes in the spot rate on the foreign currency-denominated element (the accrued interest or the principal) are measured under IAS 21 at the closing rate, with any resulting foreign exchange gains or losses recognised in profit or loss. However, IAS 21 does not provide guidance on how to account for a dual-currency loan. [*IFRS 9.B4.3.8(c)*]

EXAMPLE 17 – MEASUREMENT OF DUAL-CURRENCY LOANS

7.7.490.20   Company R issues a bond with the principal denominated in euro and the interest denominated in US dollars. The functional currency of R is sterling. In our view, to reflect the foreign currency exposure R should treat the dual-currency bond as consisting of two components for measurement purposes:
- a zero-coupon bond liability denominated in euro; and
- an instalment bond liability with annual payments denominated in US dollars.

7.7.490.30   On initial recognition, the two components are recognised at fair value. Subsequently, assuming that the instrument is not classified as at FVTPL, R measures each component separately at amortised cost under the effective interest method. The interest expense related to each component is calculated separately in the relevant foreign currency – i.e. in euro for the zero-coupon bond and in US dollars for the instalment bond – and translated into sterling at the average rate for the period. The carrying amount of both elements is translated into sterling at each reporting date using the closing exchange rate, with movements recognised in profit or loss (see 2.7.140.10).

7.7.500   **DIVIDEND INCOME**

7.7.510   **Recognition of dividend income**

7.7.510.10   IFRS 9 defines dividends as distributions of profits to holders of equity investments in proportion to their holdings of a particular class of capital. Dividend income is recognised in profit or loss only when:
- the entity's right to receive payment is established;
- it is probable that the economic benefits associated with the dividend will flow to the entity; and
- the amount of the dividend can be measured reliably (see also 7.3.680). [*IFRS 9.5.7.1A, A*]

7.7.510.20   In our view, the shareholder's right to receive payment of dividends on *quoted* investments is normally established on the date on which the security trades ex-dividend. At this date, the fair value of the security decreases by approximately the dividend amount. Therefore, recognising a dividend on the ex-dividend date avoids double counting, which would happen if the dividend were included both as income and in the measurement of the fair value of the investment. The 'ex-dividend date' is the first date on which a sale of the instrument would not settle before the record date. The 'record date' is the date on which shareholders have to be included in the register of shareholders to receive the dividend. Calculation of the ex-dividend date will depend on local trading and settlement practices.

7.7.510.30   In our view, for dividends on *unquoted* investments, a shareholder's right to receive payment is normally established when the shareholders have approved the dividends. However, if the relevant law provides that a board decision or announcement requires no further approval *and* is binding on the declaring entity, then the dividend would be recognised on a board decision or announcement (see also 7.3.680.20–30). When determining the fair value of such investments, care should be taken to avoid double counting dividends both as receivables and as part of the fair value estimate.

EXAMPLE 18 – DIVIDEND INCOME – TIMING OF RECOGNITION

> 7.7.510.40 Company S's directors declare a dividend on 10 March. The dividend is approved by shareholders on 25 March and will be paid to shareholders of record – i.e. in the shareholders' register – on 31 March.
>
> 7.7.510.50 If S's shares are listed in a market that has three-day settlement, then the shares would trade ex-dividend from 28 March (assuming that all are business days). Therefore, we believe that dividend income should be recognised on 28 March. If S's shares are not listed and the right to receive dividends is established when the shareholders have approved it, then we believe that the dividends should be recognised when they are approved – i.e. on 25 March. Thereafter, the dividends should be excluded when estimating the fair value of the shares.

7.7.510.60 If an entity makes an irrevocable election to present subsequent changes in the fair value of an investment in an equity instrument in OCI, then it recognises dividends from that investment in profit or loss in accordance with 7.7.510.10–30, unless the dividends clearly represent a recovery of part of the cost of the investment. In the latter case, the recognition of the right to the dividend as a separate asset and the corresponding decrease in the fair value of the investment would have no net effect on OCI. In our view, a dividend has to meet the definition of dividend income under IFRS 9 to be recognised in profit or loss (see 7.7.510.10). [*IFRS 9.5.7.6, A, B5.7.1*]

7.7.520   Share dividends

7.7.520.10 In some cases, shareholders may receive or choose to receive dividends in the form of additional shares rather than cash. These may be referred to as 'scrip', 'stock' or 'share dividends'. In our view, the accounting treatment of share dividends depends on whether the investor has a cash alternative – i.e. a right to demand a cash payment representing the fair value of the shares.

7.7.520.20 In our view, the substance of share dividends with a cash alternative is the payment of a cash dividend, with reinvestment of the cash in additional shares. Therefore, we believe that dividend income should be recognised for the amount of the cash dividend alternative. The corresponding debit should be treated as an additional investment.

7.7.520.30 In other cases, an entity may receive bonus shares or other equity instruments on a pro rata basis with other ordinary shareholders with no cash alternative. Share investments are categorised as financial assets measured at FVOCI or at FVTPL and measured at fair value (see 7.4.20). If all ordinary shareholders receive bonus shares or other equity instruments in proportion to their shareholdings, then the fair value of each shareholder's interest should be unaffected by the bonus issue. In our view, in such circumstances dividends should not be recognised as revenue because it is not probable that there is an economic benefit associated with the transaction that will flow to the investor. [*IFRS 9.5.7.1A, IU 01-10*]

7.7.520.40   If only certain shareholders are granted additional shares, then the fair value of the interests of those shareholders will increase. In this case, in our view it is most appropriate to measure the shares received at their fair value and recognise a corresponding amount of finance income.

7.7.530   FEE INCOME

7.7.530.10   The recognition of revenue for fees depends on the nature of the fees and the basis of accounting for any associated financial instrument. Fees that are an integral part of the effective interest rate of a financial instrument and fees on an instrument measured at FVTPL are in the scope of IFRS 9. Other fees are in the scope of the revenue recognition requirements of IFRS 15 (see 4.2.10). [*IFRS 15.5, BC28*]

7.7.530.20   In most instances, fees earned in relation to the recognition of a financial asset result in an adjustment of the effective interest rate. Examples of such fees include:
- origination or commitment fees – when it is probable that an entity will enter into a specific lending agreement;
- compensation from the borrower for transaction costs (see 7.7.50) incurred by the lender; and
- appraisal fees for evaluating collateral – e.g. for mortgage loans. [*IFRS 9.B5.4.2*]

7.7.530.30   However, if the financial instrument is measured at FVTPL, then the fees are recognised as revenue on initial recognition of the instrument. [*IFRS 9.B5.4.1*]

7.7.530.40   Examples of financial service fees that are not an integral part of the effective yield of an associated financial instrument and are therefore recognised in accordance with IFRS 15 include:
- fees charged for servicing a loan;
- commitment fees to originate loans when it is unlikely that a specific lending arrangement will be entered into and the loan commitment is not measured at FVTPL;
- loan syndication fees received by an entity that arranges a loan and retains no part of the loan package for itself (or retains a part at the same effective interest rate for comparable risk as other participants);
- a commission earned on the allotment of shares to a client;
- placement fees for arranging a loan; and
- investment management fees. [*IFRS 9.B5.4.3*]

7.7.530.50   A contract with a customer that results in a recognised financial instrument in an entity's financial statements may be partially in the scope of IFRS 9 and partially in the scope of IFRS 15. If this is the case, then the entity first applies IFRS 9 to separate and measure the part of the contract that is in the scope of IFRS 9 and then applies IFRS 15 to the residual. [*IFRS 15.7*]

7.7.530.60   In some cases, it may be difficult to determine whether an amount charged to a customer at inception of a loan represents a fee for structuring a loan or part of the transaction price for the financial asset – i.e. whether it is in the scope of IFRS 9 or IFRS 15.

7.7.530.70   For example, a bank may structure a transaction, using its expertise and experience ('intellectual capital') for a particular customer and facilitate the initial steps required – e.g. consultations with experts, valuations, registration and drafting legal documentation. The customer is charged a fee up front for the structuring service.

7.7.530.80   An entity first applies IFRS 9 to the transaction. If the fee is regarded as part of the transaction price for the loan, then the transaction price, net of the fee, would normally represent the best evidence of the fair value of the loan on initial recognition and IFRS 9 would preclude recognition of revenue unless the entity determines that:
- the fair value of the loan on initial recognition differs from the transaction price; and
- the fair value is determined by applying a valuation technique that uses only data from observable markets (see 7.7.40). [*IFRS 9.B5.1.2A*]

7.7.530.90   It appears that an entity should recognise all or part of a structuring fee as revenue under IFRS 15 only if the fair value of the loan is determined using data from observable markets and if it can be demonstrated that the amount of revenue recognised is consistent with the effort and expertise provided for the structuring service – i.e. that it approximates fair value for the service provided.

EXAMPLE 19 – STRUCTURING FEE

7.7.530.100   Bank B advances 50,000 as a loan to Customer C. B uses its expertise and experience in structuring the loan and charges C a structuring fee of 1,000. Therefore, the net amount advanced to C is 49,000. The fair value of the loan cannot be determined by applying a valuation technique that uses only data from observable markets.

7.7.530.110   First, B applies IFRS 9 to separate and measure the part of the contract that is in the scope of IFRS 9. Because the fair value of the loan cannot be determined by applying a valuation technique that uses only data from observable markets, we believe that B should recognise the loan at its transaction price of 49,000. This results in no residual amount to which IFRS 15 is applied.

7.7.530.120   Modifying the fact pattern, the fair value of the loan is 50,000 and it is determined by applying a valuation technique that uses only data from observable markets. In this case, we believe that B should recognises the loan at its fair value and the residual amount of 1,000 should be accounted for under IFRS 15.

7.7.540   RECLASSIFICATIONS

7.7.540.10   If an entity reclassifies financial assets (see 7.4.450), then it applies the reclassifications prospectively from the reclassification date. It does not restate any previously recognised gains (including impairment gains), losses (including impairment losses) or interest. [*IFRS 9.5.6.1*]

7.7.540.20   The measurement requirements on the reclassification of financial assets are as follows. [*IFRS 9.5.6, B5.6.1–B5.6.2, IE103–IE114*]

		Reclassification to		
		FVTPL	**FVOCI**	**Amortised cost**
Reclassification from	**FVTPL**	N/A	Fair value on reclassification date = new gross carrying amount. Calculate effective interest rate based on new gross carrying amount. Recognise subsequent changes in fair value in OCI.	Fair value on reclassification date = new gross carrying amount. Calculate effective interest rate based on new gross carrying amount.
	FVOCI	Reclassify accumulated OCI balance to profit or loss on reclassification date.	N/A	Reclassify financial asset at fair value. Remove cumulative balance from OCI and use it to adjust the reclassified fair value. Adjusted amount = amortised cost. Effective interest rate determined on initial recognition and gross carrying amount are not adjusted as a result of reclassification.
	Amortised cost	Fair value on reclassification date = new carrying amount. Recognise difference between amortised cost and fair value in profit or loss.	Fair value on reclassification date = new carrying amount. Recognise difference between amortised cost and fair value in OCI. Effective interest rate determined on initial recognition is not adjusted as a result of reclassification.	N/A

7.8   Impairment

7.8   Impairment

CURRENTLY EFFECTIVE REQUIREMENTS

This publication reflects IFRS in issue at 1 August 2018, and the currently effective requirements cover annual periods beginning on 1 January 2018.

The requirements related to this topic are mainly derived from the following.

STANDARD	TITLE
IFRS 3	Business Combinations
IFRS 9	Financial Instruments
IFRS 15	Revenue from Contracts with Customers

FORTHCOMING REQUIREMENTS

The requirements in this chapter are affected by the following forthcoming requirements. They are highlighted with a # and the impact is explained in the accompanying boxed text at the references indicated.

In January 2016, the IASB issued IFRS 16 *Leases*, which is effective for annual periods beginning on or after 1 January 2019. See 7.8.415. IFRS 16 is the subject of chapter 5.1A.

FUTURE DEVELOPMENTS

For this topic, there are no future developments.

7.8.10   SCOPE

7.8.10.10   The following table sets out instruments that are in and out of the scope of the impairment requirements of IFRS 9. [*IFRS 9.2*]

IN SCOPE	OUT OF SCOPE
• Financial assets that are debt instruments measured at amortised cost or FVOCI (see 7.4.10.10). These include loans, trade receivables and debt securities • Loan commitments issued that are not measured at FVTPL (see 7.1.245) • Financial guarantee contracts issued that are in the scope of IFRS 9 and are not measured at FVTPL (see 7.1.60) • Lease receivables in the scope of IAS 17 • Contract assets in the scope of IFRS 15	• Investments in equity instruments (see 7.8.10.20) • Financial instruments measured at FVTPL

7.8.10.20   Investments in equity instruments are outside the scope of the impairment requirements, because they are accounted for either:
- at FVTPL; or
- at FVOCI, with no reclassification of any fair value gains or losses to profit or loss (see 7.4.60 and 7.7.160).

7.8.20   THE ECL CONCEPT

7.8.20.10   The impairment model in IFRS 9 is an expected loss model, which means that it is not necessary for a loss event to occur before an impairment loss is recognised. As a result, all financial assets generally carry a loss allowance; for the exceptions from recognising a loss allowance, see 7.8.340. [*IFRS 9.5.5.1, 5.5.13*]

7.8.20.20   ECLs are a probability-weighted estimate of credit losses – i.e. the present value of cash shortfalls – over the expected life of the financial instrument (see 7.8.210). The definition of 'cash shortfalls' and the measurement of ECLs are discussed in 7.8.160. For a financial asset that is credit-impaired (see 7.8.340), the ECLs are the difference between the asset's gross carrying amount and the present value of estimated future cash flows. [*IFRS 9.A, B5.5.28, B5.5.33*]

7.8.20.30   The following practices related to impairment are not acceptable under IFRS 9.
- Recognising a provision for losses based on a set percentage of receivable balances, unless the resulting estimates are consistent with the impairment requirements in IFRS 9.
- Recognising a loss for the gross expected shortfalls on non-performing assets and suspending interest accruals. This is sometimes referred to as putting a loan on 'non-accrual status'.
- Recognising an impairment loss in excess of the impairment requirements of IFRS 9, even if local regulations require a specific amount to be set aside ('general risk provisions'). In our view, if an entity wishes to identify reserves in addition to the loss allowance calculated under IFRS, then it may do so by transferring amounts from retained earnings to a separate category of equity – e.g. a loan loss reserve (see 7.3.630.20). It is not acceptable to recognise any amounts in profit or

loss or to reduce the carrying amount of the assets by more than the loss allowance determined in accordance with the impairment requirements in IFRS 9. [*IFRS 9.5.5.1*]

7.8.20.40   Entities are generally required to recognise an allowance for ECLs for all financial assets – even those that are newly originated or acquired. Although an entity is not required to recognise the loss allowance on initial recognition of the new financial asset, but rather at the next reporting date, the effect is akin to recognising a day one loss. [*IFRS 9.BC5.198*]

7.8.20.45   An entity remeasures a loss allowance immediately before derecognition of a financial instrument so that it can calculate the gain or loss arising on derecognition. [*IAS 1.82(aa), 82(ba), IFRS 9.3.2.12*]

7.8.20.50   Under IFRS 3, a financial asset acquired as part of a business combination does not attract a loss allowance at its date of acquisition. It appears that this guidance is provided specifically for the purpose of calculating goodwill, because any reduction in fair value by the loss allowance would have resulted in an overstatement of goodwill. Accordingly, it appears that under IFRS 9 an asset acquired in a business combination would attract a loss allowance at the first reporting date after it is recognised, even if that date is the date on which the business combination has taken place. This effectively means that, for the recognition of impairment, such assets are treated in the same way as other financial assets (see 7.7.380). [*IFRS 3.B41*]

7.8.20.60   The assessment of ECLs is based on reasonable and supportable information – that is, information reasonably available without undue cost or effort at the reporting date. However, in our view this does not imply that a full loan review in accordance with the entity's normal operating procedures should be carried out at the reporting date as long as the entity has procedures, processes and systems that provide the relevant information required for such an assessment for the purposes of financial reporting. [*IFRS 9.B5.5.49*]

7.8.20.70   Impairment is measured at an amount equal to 12-month ECLs, lifetime ECLs or changes in lifetime ECLs. The following flowchart provides an overview of when each measurement basis applies.

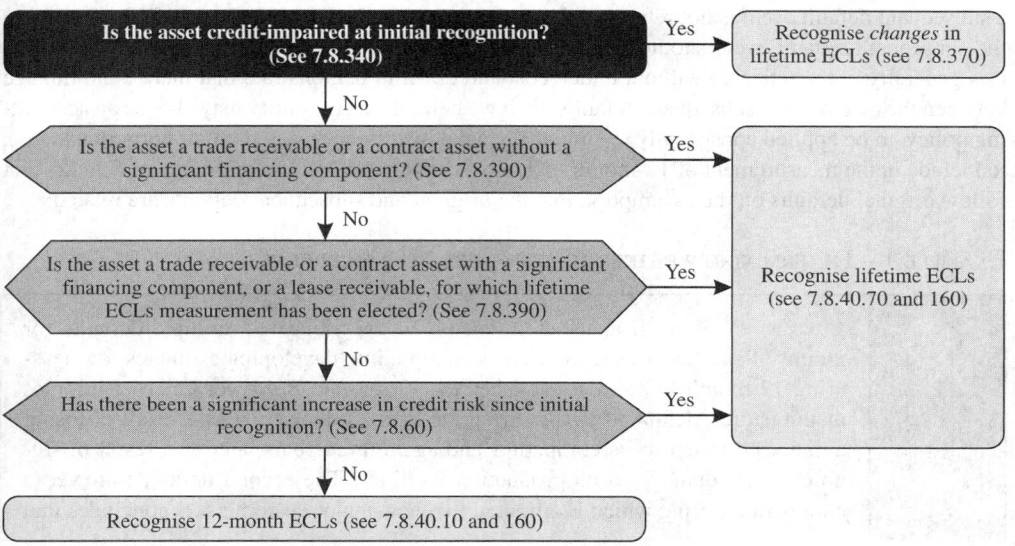

7.8.30   **GENERAL APPROACH**

7.8.30.10   Under the general approach, impairment is measured as either 12-month ECLs or lifetime ECLs, depending on whether there has been a significant increase in credit risk since initial recognition. If a significant increase in credit risk of an instrument has occurred since initial recognition, then impairment is measured as lifetime ECLs. [*IFRS 9.5.5.3, 5.5.5*]

7.8.40   **12-month ECLs and lifetime ECLs**

7.8.40.10   '12-month ECLs' are defined as the portion of lifetime ECLs that represents the ECLs resulting from default events on the financial instrument that are possible within 12 months after the reporting date. This means that 12-month ECLs represent the lifetime cash shortfalls (see 7.8.170) that will result from a default occurring in the 12 months after the reporting date (or a shorter period if the expected life of a financial instrument is less than 12 months) weighted by the probability of that default occurring. [*IFRS 9.A, B5.5.43*]

7.8.40.20   A financial instrument may be subject to the risk of multiple default events during its life, some occurring within 12 months after the reporting date (original defaults) and some occurring more than 12 months after the reporting date (subsequent defaults). In between the original and subsequent default(s), the borrower may revert to performing in accordance with the contractual terms. A question arises about whether ECLs associated with subsequent defaults that follow original defaults should be taken into account in measuring 12-month ECLs. If a subsequent default occurs before the expiry of an appropriate cure or probation period (see 7.8.50.50), then the subsequent default event is regarded as a continuation of the original default event, rather than as a separate default, and so is included in measuring 12-month ECLs.

7.8.40.30   In other cases, it appears that ECLs resulting from a subsequent default should be considered to result from the original default and be taken into account in measuring 12-month ECLs if the subsequent default event relates to the original default (e.g. it is considered to have a causal connection with the original default). Conversely, if reasonable and supportable evidence shows that a subsequent default event is not related to the original default, then we believe that ECLs following the subsequent default event should not be included in 12-month ECLs. If an entity believes that it is generally not practicable without undue cost and effort to demonstrate that there is no linkage between the original and subsequent defaults, then we believe that the entity may choose an accounting policy, to be applied consistently to similar financial instruments (e.g. retail or corporate loans), to include in the measurement of 12-month ECLs losses associated with all subsequent defaults that follow original defaults on the assumption that the original and subsequent defaults are related.

EXAMPLE 1 – DETERMINING WHETHER MULTIPLE DEFAULTS ARE RELATED

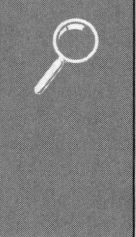

7.8.40.40   Bank B analyses its historical experience of multiple defaults for groups of similar loans to be used as an input into developing estimates for measuring 12-month ECLs. B establishes that Corporate Borrower C, an electronics manufacturer, defaulted twice during the life of a loan: first as a result of losing a major customer to its competitor and again three years later as a result of significant fire damage to its production facilities. The second default followed a cure period during which B attracted two new major customers. B concludes that the first and second defaults are not related. B therefore excludes losses associated with the second default when developing an estimate of loss given default (LGD) associated with the first default to be used in developing estimates for measuring 12-month ECLs.

7.8.40.50   B establishes that Corporate Borrower D, a commodity producer, also defaulted twice. The first default resulted from a 30% fall in commodity prices. After that, the loan was restructured. In addition, commodity prices increased by 5% and D started making full contractual payments in line with the restructured agreement. However, D defaulted again 18 months after the original default because of continuing low commodity prices and increased production costs. B concludes that the first and second defaults were related and therefore includes losses following the second default event when developing an estimate of LGD associated with the first default to be used in developing estimates for measuring 12-month ECLs.

7.8.40.60   B also establishes that for retail credit card borrowers who defaulted twice or more on their credit card facility, it is impracticable to demonstrate that there is no linkage between default events due to the absence of detailed information about the reasons for defaults. Consequently, B chooses an accounting policy for credit card retail facilities to include losses associated with subsequent defaults that follow original defaults when developing estimates for measuring 12-month ECLs on the assumption that the defaults are related.

7.8.40.70   'Lifetime ECLs' are defined as the ECLs that result from all possible default events over the expected life of the financial instrument. [*IFRS 9.A*]

7.8.40.80   A loss allowance equal to 12-month ECLs is recognised unless:
- the credit risk on a financial instrument has increased significantly since initial recognition (see 7.8.60); or
- special measurement requirements apply (see 7.8.340 and 390). [*IFRS 9.5.5.3, 5.5.5*]

7.8.40.90   If the credit risk on financial instruments, for which lifetime ECLs have been recognised, subsequently improves so that the requirement for recognising lifetime ECLs is no longer met, then the loss allowance is measured at an amount equal to 12-month ECLs, as illustrated below. [*IFRS 9.5.5.7*]

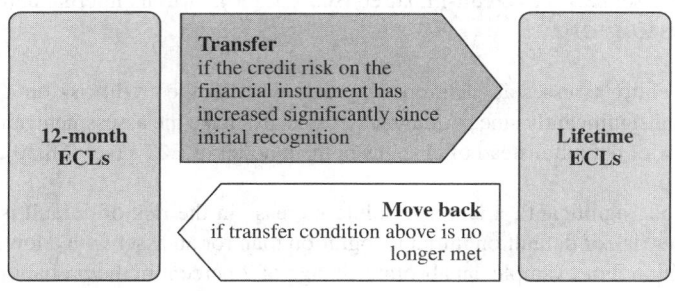

7.8.50   **Definition of default**

7.8.50.10   IFRS 9 does not define the term 'default', but instead requires each entity to do so. The definition has to be consistent with that used for internal credit risk management purposes for the relevant financial instrument, and has to consider qualitative indicators – e.g. breaches of covenants – when appropriate. The definition of default is applied consistently, unless information that becomes available indicates that another default definition is more appropriate for a particular financial instrument. [*IFRS 9.B5.5.37*]

7.8.50.20   An entity can use a regulatory definition of default if it is consistent with the entity's credit risk management practices and considers qualitative indicators. [*IFRS 9.B5.5.37, BC5.248*]

7.8.50.30   An entity defines the term 'default' in the context of its specific types of assets. In some cases, it may be appropriate to consider an asset to be in default if a contractual payment is not made when it is due. In other cases, default may occur earlier – e.g. when a borrower breaches loan covenants or when there are indicators that the borrower is unlikely to pay. [*IFRS 9.B5.5.37, BC5.252*]

7.8.50.40   There is a rebuttable presumption that default does not occur later than when a financial asset is 90 days past due unless an entity has reasonable and supportable information to corroborate a more lagging default criterion. [*IFRS 9.B5.5.37*]

7.8.50.50   The definition of default may consider a cure or probation period – i.e. if a financial asset has previously entered default, a period necessary for the borrower to demonstrate that concerns about it meeting all of its contractual obligations have reduced significantly before the financial asset exits default. For example, even if a borrower ceases to be 90 days past due in accordance with the existing or modified contractual terms of a loan, it may not be appropriate for the lender to immediately assume that the loan is no longer in default. This is because to reach such a conclusion the lender may need to collect supporting evidence, such as good payment behaviour over a period of time. For example, a history of missed or incomplete payments would not typically be erased by simply making one payment on time. An entity determines a policy for setting cure or probation periods that is monitored for continuous relevance and applied consistently. [*IFRS 9.B5.5.27*]

7.8.60   **Significant increase in credit risk**

7.8.60.10   The term 'significant increase in credit risk' is not defined in IFRS 9. An entity decides how to define it in the context of its specific types of instruments.

7.8.60.20   An entity cannot align the timing of its recognition of lifetime ECLs to the date on which a financial asset becomes credit-impaired (see 7.7.430), or to its internal definition of default (see 7.8.50). [*IFRS 9.B5.5.21*]

7.8.60.30   An entity assesses at each reporting date whether the credit risk on a financial instrument has increased significantly since initial recognition. To make the assessment, an entity considers changes in the risk of default instead of changes in the amount of ECLs (see 7.8.50). [*IFRS 9.5.5.9*]

7.8.60.40   To be 'significant', a larger absolute increase in the risk of default is required for an asset with a higher risk of default on initial recognition than for an asset with a lower risk of default on initial recognition. For example, an absolute change of 2 percent in the probability of default occurring (PD) is more significant for an asset with an initial PD of 5 percent than for an asset with an initial PD of 20 percent. In addition, to be significant, a larger absolute increase in the risk of default is required for a longer-term financial asset than for a short-term financial asset (all other factors being equal). [*IFRS 9.B5.5.9–10, BC5.173–BC5.174*]

EXAMPLE 2 – SIGNIFICANT INCREASE IN CREDIT RISK – A RELATIVE CONCEPT

7.8.60.50   Bank B uses an internal credit rating system of 1 to 10, with 1 denoting the lowest credit risk and 10 denoting the highest credit risk. B considers an increase of two rating grades to represent a significant increase in credit risk. It considers Grades 3 and lower to be 'low credit risk' (see 7.8.150).

7.8.60.60   At the reporting date, B has the following two loans to Company C outstanding.

	GRADE ON INITIAL RECOGNITION	GRADE AT REPORTING DATE
Loan A	2	5
Loan B	4	5

7.8.60.70   B assesses whether there has been a significant increase in credit risk in respect of the loans and reaches the following conclusions.

	SIGNIFICANT CREDIT RISK INCREASE?	RECOGNISE ALLOWANCE EQUAL TO …
Loan A	Yes	Lifetime ECLs
Loan B	No	12-month ECLs

7.8.60.80   The measurement basis for the loss allowance is different irrespective of the fact that both loans have the same grade at the reporting date. This is because only the credit risk of Loan A has increased significantly since initial recognition.

7.8.60.90   It may be that there is an actual contractual default – e.g. a missed interest payment – without there being a significant increase in credit risk. For example, this could be the case when a payment is more than 30 days past due and the 30-day presumption is rebutted (see 7.8.120).

7.8.60.100   The assessment of whether credit risk has increased significantly is relevant even for a financial instrument with a maturity of less than 12 months. Although in this case lifetime ECLs and 12-month ECLs are the same amount, the disclosure requirements in IFRS 7 differentiate between assets in respect of which credit risk has increased significantly and those for which it has not (see 7.10.280.10 and 610.20).

7.8.60.110   If there is evidence that there is no longer a significant increase in credit risk relative to initial recognition, then the loss allowance on an instrument returns to being measured as 12-month

ECL. Some qualitative indicators of an increase in credit risk (e.g. delinquency or forbearance) may be indicative of an increased risk of default that persists after the indicator itself has ceased to exist. In these cases, it may be necessary for the entity to determine a probation period during which the financial asset is required to demonstrate good behaviour to provide evidence that its credit risk has declined sufficiently. For example, when the contractual terms of a loan have been modified, evidence that the criteria for recognising lifetime ECL are no longer met may include a history of up-to-date payment performance against the modified contractual terms. When appropriate, an entity determines a policy for setting probation periods that is monitored to reflect changes in how qualitative indicators impact credit risk and is applied consistently. [*IFRS 9 B5.5.27*]

7.8.70   *Date of initial recognition*

7.8.70.10   The assessment of whether there has been a significant increase in credit risk is made relative to expectations on initial recognition, irrespective of whether a financial instrument has been repriced to reflect an increase in credit risk after initial recognition. For example, certain debt instruments include features under which the credit spread resets when their credit rating changes. In assessing whether there has been a significant increase in credit risk in respect of these instruments, an entity considers the relative increase in credit risk since initial recognition, rather than from the date of credit spread reset. [*IFRS 9.B5.5.7*]

7.8.70.20   The assessment of a significant increase in credit risk requires an entity to identify the date on which it initially recognised a financial instrument. For loan commitments and financial guarantee contracts, the date of initial recognition is the date on which the entity becomes a party to the irrevocable commitment. For the purpose of applying the impairment requirements, a financial asset that is recognised as a result of the draw-down of a loan commitment is treated as a continuation of the loan commitment. It appears that this means that, for loans drawn down under loan commitments – e.g. revolving credit facilities – the assessment is made relative to the credit risk when the commitment contract was signed, rather than the credit risk when each balance was drawn. If a loan commitment contract is modified and the modification results in the derecognition of the original commitment and the recognition of the modified commitment as a new instrument (see 7.8.130), then the date of recognition of the modified commitment is treated as the date of initial recognition for the purpose of assessing whether credit risk has increased significantly. [*IFRS 9.5.5.6, B5.5.47*]

7.8.70.30   An entity has an accounting policy choice to recognise the purchase or sale of a non-derivative financial asset that will be delivered within the timeframe generally established by regulation or convention in the market concerned – on the trade date or the settlement date. When applying settlement date accounting (see 7.6.20) an entity considers the trade date to be the date of initial recognition for the purpose of applying the impairment requirements. It appears that this means that an entity should recognise ECLs from that date as if the asset had already been recognised in the statement of financial position. [*IFRS 9.5.7.4*]

7.8.80   *Approaches to be used in assessment*

7.8.80.10   An entity may apply various approaches in assessing whether there has been a significant increase in credit risk – including using different approaches for different financial instruments. An approach that does not include an explicit PD as an input, such as a credit loss rate approach, can be used provided that the entity is able to separate the changes in the risk of default occurring from other changes in ECLs – e.g. due to collateral. Any approach used considers:

- the change in the risk of default occurring since initial recognition;
- the expected life of the financial instrument; and
- reasonable and supportable information that is available without undue cost or effort that may affect credit risk. [*IFRS 9.B5.5.12*]

7.8.80.20   Generally, the assessment of whether there has been a significant increase in credit risk is made for a specific instrument rather than for a counterparty, because:
- the magnitude of changes in credit risk may be different for different instruments transacted with the same party; and
- different instruments issued by the same counterparty may have had a different credit risk on initial recognition – e.g. they may have been acquired at different points in time. [*IFRS 9.BC5.166–BC5.168*]

7.8.80.30   However, assessing credit risk on a basis that considers a counterparty's credit risk more holistically may be consistent with the impairment requirements – e.g. making an initial assessment of whether credit risk has increased significantly as part of an overall assessment – as long as this assessment satisfies the requirements on when to recognise lifetime ECLs (see 7.8.30), and the outcome would not be different from the outcome if the financial instruments had been assessed individually. [*IFRS 9.IE43–IE47, BC5.166–BC5.168*]

7.8.80.40   To identify a significant increase in credit risk, an entity uses a method that considers the characteristics of the financial instrument and historical default patterns for comparable financial instruments. In assessing whether credit risk has increased significantly, an entity uses the change in the risk of default occurring over the expected life of the financial instrument. [*IFRS 9.5.5.9, B5.5.13*]

7.8.80.45   For financial instruments whose default patterns are not concentrated at a specific point during their expected life, changes in the 12-month risk of default may be a reasonable approximation of changes in the lifetime risk of default, unless circumstances indicate that a lifetime assessment is necessary. Therefore, if an entity plans to use changes in the 12-month risk of a default occurring for the assessment, it appears that this should be based on a robust analysis to support a conclusion that changes in the 12-month risk of a default occurring are a reasonable approximation for the assessment of changes in the lifetime risk of default occurring. The level of initial analysis required would depend on the circumstances; a quantitative analysis may be necessary and it may be appropriate to segregate portfolios (e.g. by maturity) in order to facilitate the analysis for groups of similar financial instruments. We believe that an entity should also carry out ongoing monitoring or reviews to assess whether such a conclusion remains appropriate. For example, an entity might:
- identify the key factors that affect the appropriateness of using changes in the 12-month risk of default occurring;
- monitor those factors; and
- consider whether any changes in those factors indicate that the use of changes in the 12-month risk of default occurring is no longer an appropriate proxy for changes in the lifetime risk of default occurring. [*IFRS 9.B5.5.13–B5.5.14*]

7.8.80.50   The following are examples of situations in which using changes in the 12-month risk of default is not appropriate:
- for loans whose significant payment obligations are only after the next 12 months – e.g. bullet loans or financial instruments that are non-amortising in the first few years;

- when changes in macro-economic or other credit-related factors occur that are not adequately reflected in the 12-month risk of default; or
- when changes in credit-related factors have an impact on the credit risk of the financial instrument that is more pronounced beyond 12 months. [*IFRS 9.B5.5.14*]

7.8.80.60   The change in credit risk cannot be assessed simply by comparing the change in the absolute risk of default over time, because of the relationship between the remaining life and the risk of default. For example, the risk of default over the remaining life of a loan will tend to reduce over time, as the remaining life becomes shorter. Therefore, if the actual risk of default of a particular loan has not reduced over time, then this may indicate an increase in the credit risk of that loan. However, this may not be the case for financial instruments that have significant payment obligations only close to maturity. In such cases, an entity also considers other qualitative factors to determine whether there has been a significant increase in credit risk. [*IFRS 9.B5.5.11, BC5.174*]

7.8.80.70   Most banks calculate PD measures for regulatory purposes. These regulatory PD measures may often be used as a starting point for calculating PDs that are suitable for IFRS 9 purposes. Examples of adjustments that may be required include:
- replacing a 'through-the-cycle' approach with a 'point-in-time' methodology;
- removing any floors in the regulatory measure that would result in conservative bias;
- extending the period over which PD is measured from 12 months to lifetime, where appropriate; and
- including the impact of information about current conditions and forecasts of future economic conditions. [*IFRS 9.BC5.282–BC5.286*]

7.8.85   *Financial instruments subject to a guarantee*

7.8.85.10   When making an assessment of whether credit risk has increased significantly, an entity uses the change in the risk of default occurring instead of the change in the amount of ECLs (see 7.8.60.30). For example, if a financial asset is subject to a financial guarantee contract that is integral to the terms of the asset (see 7.1.130), then the ability of the lender to recover cash flows from the guarantee is excluded from the assessment of whether credit risk on the guaranteed asset has increased significantly since initial recognition. The existence of a financial guarantee may be relevant to assessing changes in credit risk, but only to the extent that it affects the likelihood of the borrower defaulting on the instrument. For example, this could be the case if a parent guarantees the debt of a subsidiary, because it may be in the parent's interest to provide funds to the subsidiary enabling it to make payments on the debt, rather than let the subsidiary default and make a payment under the guarantee. [*IFRS 9.5.5.9, B5.5.17(j)–B5.5.17(l)*]

7.8.90   *Individual vs collective basis of assessment*

7.8.90.10   IFRS 9 does not specify when the assessment of whether there has been a significant increase in credit risk is made on an individual or collective basis. The objective of the impairment requirements in IFRS 9 is to recognise lifetime ECLs for all financial instruments for which there has been a significant increase in credit risk since initial recognition – whether assessed on an individual or a collective basis. For some instruments, an entity may be able to identify the key drivers behind changes in credit risk on an individual instrument basis. For these instruments, individual assessment of increase in credit risk may be sufficient. However, for some other instruments a significant increase in credit risk may not be evident on an individual instrument basis before the financial instrument becomes past due. For example, this could be the case when there is little or no updated information that is routinely obtained and monitored on an individual instrument until a customer breaches the contractual terms – e.g. for many retail loans. In these cases, an assessment of whether there has been a significant increase in credit risk on an individual basis would not faithfully represent changes in credit risk since initial recognition. Accordingly, if more forward-looking information (see 7.8.110) is available on a collective basis, then an entity makes the assessment on a collective basis. [*IFRS 9.5.5.4, 5.5.11, B5.5.3*]

7.8.90.15   To decide whether individual or collective assessment is required, an entity identifies the key drivers behind changes in credit risk and may approach the analysis as follows:
- if the key drivers can be monitored on an individual instrument basis, then the entity so monitors them and no further collective assessment may be required;
- if the key drivers cannot be monitored on an individual instrument basis but can be monitored for a segment of a portfolio, then the entity performs a collective assessment for that segment; and
- if the key drivers cannot be monitored either on an individual instrument basis or for a segment of a portfolio, then the entity performs a collective assessment for a proportion of the portfolio. [*IFRS 9.B5.5.6*]

7.8.90.20   For the purpose of assessing significant increases in credit risk on a collective basis, financial instruments are grouped on the basis of shared credit risk characteristics. For example:
- instrument type;
- credit risk ratings;
- collateral type;
- date of initial recognition;
- remaining term to maturity;
- industry;
- geographic location of the borrower; and
- the value of collateral relative to the financial asset if it has an impact on the PD – e.g. loan-to-value ratios for non-recourse loans in some jurisdictions. [*IFRS 9.B5.5.5*]

7.8.90.25   A collective assessment should not obscure significant increases in credit risk at an individual financial instrument level. Therefore, an entity needs to ensure that sub-portfolios are not defined too widely.

7.8.90.30   Forborne exposures may display different credit risk characteristics from non-forborne exposures. Similarly, loans that were in arrears and have returned to current status may have different risk characteristics from loans that have never been in arrears.

7.8.90.40   The aggregation of financial instruments may change over time as new information becomes available. [*IFRS 9.B5.5.6*]

EXAMPLE 3A – SIGNIFICANT INCREASE IN CREDIT RISK FOR A SEGMENT OF A PORTFOLIO

7.8.90.50   Bank D has a portfolio of mortgages that were provided to finance residential real estate in a specific region. This region includes a mining community that is largely dependent on the export of coal and related products. D becomes aware of a significant decline in coal exports and anticipates the closure of several coal mines. D anticipates an increase in the unemployment rate in this community and determines that the credit risk and the risk of default of borrowers in the region who rely on the coal mines have increased significantly, even if those borrowers are not past due at the reporting date.

7.8.90.60   Accordingly, D segments its mortgage portfolio on the basis of industries – i.e. a shared credit risk characteristic – to identify borrowers that rely on the coal mines. For these mortgages, D recognises a loss allowance equal to lifetime ECLs.

7.8.90.70   However, D continues to recognise a loss allowance equal to 12-month ECLs for newly originated loans to borrowers who rely on the coal mines, because these have not experienced a significant increase in credit risk since initial recognition. [*IFRS 9.IE38*]

7.8.90.80   If a collective assessment is required but an entity is not able to perform one for a segment of the portfolio, then it performs a collective assessment for a proportion of the portfolio. [*IFRS 9.B5.5.6*]

EXAMPLE 3B – SIGNIFICANT INCREASE IN CREDIT RISK FOR A PROPORTION OF A PORTFOLIO

7.8.90.90   Bank E originates a homogeneous portfolio of 100 variable interest rate mortgage loans. Historically, an increase in interest rates has been a lead indicator of future defaults on similar mortgages. E does not have information on individual mortgages (except for past-due information) that would indicate a significant increase in credit risk, and is not able to group them on the basis of shared risk characteristics for this purpose.

7.8.90.100   As a result, E assesses whether there is a significant increase in the credit risk of mortgages in the portfolio on a collective basis using information on expected increases in interest rates during the expected life of the mortgages. Based on historical information, E estimates that an increase in interest rates of 1% will cause a significant increase in credit risk on 10% of the portfolio. None of the mortgage loans is past due and E has not identified a significant increase in credit risk on any loan on an individual basis.

7.8.90.110   Therefore, as a result of an anticipated increase in interest rates of 1%, E determines that there has been a significant increase in credit risk on 10% of the portfolio. Accordingly, E recognises lifetime ECLs on 10% of the portfolio. E recognises 12-month ECLs on the remaining portfolio. [*IFRS 9.IE39*]

7.8.100   *Comparison with the maximum initial credit risk*

7.8.100.10   The assessment of significant increases in credit risk can be implemented more simply for some groups of financial instruments by:

- determining the maximum credit risk for the particular portfolio on initial recognition; and then
- comparing that maximum credit risk to the credit risk of financial instruments in that portfolio at the reporting date. [*IFRS 9.BC5.161*]

7.8.100.20   However, this approach is possible only if all of the financial instruments in the portfolio have a similar credit risk on initial recognition – e.g. a credit rating within a relatively narrow band. If this is not the case, then it will not be possible to identify a single credit rating that reflects a significant increase in credit risk for all financial instruments in the portfolio. [*IFRS 9.BC5.161*]

EXAMPLE 4 – ASSESSMENT BY COMPARISON WITH THE MAXIMUM INITIAL CREDIT RISK

7.8.100.30   Bank F has a portfolio of automobile loans. On origination, F assigns an internal credit risk rating from 1 to 10 to each loan, with 1 denoting the lowest credit risk and 10 denoting the highest credit risk. The risk of default occurring increases exponentially – meaning that the difference between Grades 1 and 2 is smaller than that between Grades 2 and 3 etc.

7.8.100.40   Loans in the portfolio are offered only to existing customers with an internal credit rating of Grade 3 or 4 on initial recognition. Therefore, 4 is the maximum internal credit rating grade that F will accept for this portfolio of loans. F determines that all loans in the portfolio have a similar initial credit risk on initial recognition because they are graded either 3 or 4.

7.8.100.50   F deems that a change from Grade 3 to Grade 4 does not represent a significant increase in credit risk, but a change from Grade 4 to Grade 5 does represent a significant increase in credit risk. Therefore, a significant increase in credit risk occurs for each loan in the portfolio when its internal credit rating deteriorates beyond Grade 4 after initial recognition.

7.8.100.60   This means that F does not have to know the initial credit risk rating of each loan in the portfolio to assess the change in credit risk since initial recognition, but needs only to determine whether, at the reporting date, the credit risk rating of each loan in the portfolio is worse than Grade 4.

7.8.100.70   However, F could not apply this approach to another portfolio in which loans are originated with an initial credit risk rating between Grade 4 and Grade 7, because this range of initial credit risk ratings is too wide. [*IFRS 9.IE40–IE42*]

7.8.110   *Information to be used in assessment*

7.8.110.10   To assess whether there has been a significant increase in credit risk, an entity considers reasonable and supportable information that is available without undue cost or effort, and is relevant for the particular financial instrument being assessed. The information used includes factors that are specific to the borrower and general economic conditions. Possible data sources include internal loss experience and ratings, and external ratings, reports and statistics. [*IFRS 9.5.5.4, B5.5.2, B5.5.51*]

7.8.110.20   Credit risk analysis is a multi-factor and holistic analysis. Whether a specific factor is relevant, and its weighting compared with other factors, depends on:
- the type of financial instrument;
- the characteristics of the financial instrument and the borrower; and
- the geographic region. [*IFRS 9.B5.5.16*]

7.8.110.30   If factors or indicators are not identifiable at an individual financial instrument level, then they are assessed for appropriate portfolios, groups of portfolios or portions of portfolios (see 7.8.90). [*IFRS 9.B5.5.16*]

7.8.110.40   In some cases, the qualitative and non-statistical quantitative information available may be sufficient for the assessment. In other cases, a statistical model or credit ratings process may be used. In some cases, an entity may base the assessment on both of the following types of information if both are relevant:
- a specific internal rating category; and
- qualitative factors that are not captured through the internal credit ratings process. [*IFRS 9.B5.5.18*]

7.8.110.50   Care needs to be taken before determining that the acquisition or development of apparently relevant information may require undue cost or effort. In particular, if a bank already collects and uses relevant data for regulatory, financial reporting or risk management purposes, then it would be expected to use that data for IFRS 9 purposes. [*IFRS 9.B5.5.49*]

7.8.110.60   The assessment is forward-looking and therefore considers reasonable and supportable information about the effects of multiple potential future economic scenarios and the likelihood of their occurrence. For a discussion of how to incorporate forward-looking information into the measurement of ECLs, see 7.8.238.

7.8.113   *Credit grading system*

7.8.113.10   The appropriateness of how a credit grading system is used in the assessment will depend on the specific facts and circumstances, including the range of factors taken into account in determining individual credit grades, how the credit grading system operates and how grades relate to the risk of a default occurring. Credit risk grading systems used by entities are usually designed for internal risk management purposes and therefore it cannot be assumed that they will always be an appropriate means of identifying significant increases in credit risk. For example, an entity needs to consider whether credit grades:
- are reviewed with sufficient frequency;
- include all reasonable and supportable information, including information that is forward-looking; and
- reflect the risk of default over the expected life of the financial instrument.

7.8.113.20   Information obtained from credit risk grading system may need to be supplemented by additional data to form an appropriate basis for identifying significant increases in credit risk. For example, credit risk grading systems may not fully incorporate forward-looking information and, if so, its impact would have to be assessed separately. [*IFRS 9.5.5.17*]

7.8.115   *Behavioural data*

7.8.115.10   Entities may collect behavioural data on how customers use the facilities offered to them. Such data may be relevant in identifying significant increases in credit risk. However, many behavioural indicators (e.g. failure of the borrower to make a specified number of minimum monthly repayments or failure to make payment on a borrowing from another lender) often lag increases in credit risk and consequently they need to be considered in conjunction with other, more forward-looking information. If an entity uses behavioural data as inputs for identifying significant increases in credit risk, then it:

- focuses on identifying pre-delinquency behavioural indicators – e.g. increased utilisation rates or increased cash drawings;
- uses indicators that are relevant to the risk of default occurring;
- establishes a link between the behavioural indicators of credit risk and changes in the risk of default occurring since initial recognition of a financial instrument;
- needs to be mindful that although behavioural indicators are often predictive of defaults in the short term, they may often be less predictive of defaults in the longer term; and
- considers whether the use of behavioural indicators is appropriate for the type of financial instrument being assessed – e.g. if a loan has only back-ended payments, then behavioural indicators based on timeliness of payment will not be appropriate. [*IFRS 9.B5.5.17(n)*]

7.8.117 *Internal price indicators*

7.8.117.10   A significant change in internal price indicators of credit risk – e.g. credit spread that would result if a similar financial instrument with the same terms and the same counterparty were newly originated at the reporting date – could be relevant information in assessing changes in credit risk. However, some financial instruments with standard terms and pricing are granted to any customer who meets certain minimum criteria which means that the same terms might be granted to customers with significantly different credit risks on initial recognition. Therefore, an entity could not conclude only on the basis of the absence of a change in factors such as pricing and contractual terms that there has not been a significant increase in credit risk. Credit risk analysis is a multi-factor and holistic analysis, and entities consider all reasonable and supportable information that is available without undue cost or effort and that is relevant to the estimate of ECLs. [*IFRS 9.B5.5.16, B5.5.17(a)*]

7.8.120 *Rebuttable presumption of 30 days past due*

7.8.120.10   There is a rebuttable presumption that credit risk on a financial instrument has increased significantly when payments are more than 30 days past due. However, delinquency is a lagging indicator, and a significant increase in credit risk typically occurs before an asset is past due. Therefore, when information that is more forward-looking than data about past-due payments is available without undue cost or effort, it is considered in determining whether there has been a significant increase in credit risk, and the entity does not rely solely on past-due data. For example, this information could be available at a portfolio level (see 7.8.90) or may include behavioural data (see 7.8.115). [*IFRS 9.5.5.11, B5.5.2*]

7.8.120.20   The presumption in 7.8.120.10 is not an absolute indicator, but is presumed to be the latest point at which lifetime ECLs should be recognised, even when using forward-looking information. [*IFRS 9.B5.5.19*]

7.8.120.30   The presumption in 7.8.120.10 can be rebutted only if an entity has reasonable and supportable information demonstrating that even if contractual payments are more than 30 days past due, this does not represent a significant increase in credit risk. For example, this might be the case if:

- non-payment was an administrative oversight instead of resulting from the borrower's financial difficulty; or

- historical evidence demonstrates that there is no correlation between a significant increase in the risk of default on financial assets and payments on them being more than 30 days past due, but there is such a correlation for financial assets on which payments are more than 60 days past due. [*IFRS 9.5.5.11, B5.5.20*]

7.8.130   *Modified financial assets*

7.8.130.10   If the contractual cash flows of a financial asset are modified, then the entity is required to distinguish between:
- a modification that results in derecognition of the original financial asset; and
- a modification that does not result in such derecognition (see 7.7.340). [*IFRS 9.5.5.12*]

7.8.130.15   For modifications that do not result in derecognition of the original financial asset:
- the gross carrying amount of the asset is recalculated and a modification gain or loss is recognised (see 7.7.350); and
- the impairment requirements are applied to the modified asset in the same way as they would for other unmodified financial instruments, taking into account the revised contractual terms. The ECL allowance on the modified asset cannot be assumed to be nil, because an entity is required to consider the possibility that a credit loss occurs, even if the likelihood of that credit loss occurring is very low. [*IFRS 9.5.4.3, 5.5.18*]

7.8.130.20   If the modification does not result in derecognition of the original financial asset, then the subsequent assessment of whether there is a significant increase in credit risk is made by comparing:
- the risk of default at the reporting date based on the modified contractual terms of the financial asset; with
- the risk of default on initial recognition based on the original, unmodified contractual terms of the financial asset. [*IFRS 9.5.5.12*]

7.8.130.30   If the modification of a financial asset does not result in derecognition of the asset, then the modified asset is not considered automatically to have a lower credit risk merely because its cash flows have been modified. In our experience, if the modification of a financial asset amounts to granting forbearance, then this is generally regarded as evidence of a significant increase in credit risk and may also represent evidence that the financial asset is credit-impaired. For an asset that is modified while having an allowance equal to lifetime ECLs, an example of evidence that the criteria for recognising lifetime ECLs are no longer met includes a history of up-to-date and timely payment performance against the modified contractual terms. Typically, a borrower would need to demonstrate consistently good payment behaviour over a period of time before the credit risk is considered to be improved – e.g. a history of missed or incomplete payments are not typically ignored if the customer makes one payment on time following the modification. [*IFRS 9.B5.5.17(m), B5.5.27*]

7.8.130.40   If an entity plans to modify a financial asset in a way that would result in forgiveness of part of the existing contractual cash flows, then the entity considers whether any portion of the asset has to be written off before the modification takes place. This is because an impending forgiveness of certain cash flows may mean that the entity has no reasonable prospect of recovery of those cash flows (see 7.8.430). [*IFRS 9.5.4.4*]

EXAMPLE 5 – MODIFICATION OF A FINANCIAL ASSET THAT DOES NOT RESULT IN DERECOGNITION

7.8.130.50   Bank B has a loan asset with:
- a gross carrying amount of 1,000;
- a loss allowance of 240; and
- an amortised cost of 760.

7.8.130.60   B determines that the loan has suffered a significant increase in credit risk and consequently recognises lifetime ECLs. Shortly after, B decides to modify the loan by reducing its nominal amount to provide relief to the borrower to reflect the borrower's reduced payment capacity and negotiates with the borrower towards cancelling part of the borrower's obligation. A modification is agreed and the gross carrying amount of the new modified loan is 760. B believes that the borrower will be able to meet the new modified terms. The modification does not result in derecognition of the existing loan.

7.8.130.70   Before the modification, B writes off 240 (1,000 - 760) because in view of the expected restructuring that involves forgiveness of 240, B considers that it has no reasonable expectation of recovering this amount. At the next reporting date, B calculates the loss allowance for the modified loan in the same way as it would for other unmodified financial instruments, taking into account the revised contractual terms.

7.8.130.80   If the modification of a financial asset results in derecognition, then the modified asset is considered to be a new asset. Accordingly, the date of modification is treated as the date of initial recognition for the purposes of the impairment requirements. [*IFRS 9.B5.5.25–B5.5.26*]

7.8.130.90   Following a modification that results in derecognition of the original financial asset, there could be evidence that the modified financial asset is credit-impaired on initial recognition. This might occur, for example, in a situation in which a substantial modification relates to a distressed asset. For a further discussion of such assets, see 7.8.340. [*IFRS 9.B5.5.26*]

7.8.140   *Financial assets that have been reclassified*

7.8.140.10   If a financial asset has been reclassified out of the FVTPL measurement category into the amortised cost or FVOCI measurement category (see 7.7.540), then, for the purpose of assessing whether there has been a significant increase in credit risk, the reclassification date is treated as the date of initial recognition. Therefore, to determine whether there has been a significant increase in credit risk, only changes in the asset's credit risk following the reclassification date are considered. [*IFRS 9.B5.6.2*]

7.8.140.20   However, when a financial asset is reclassified between the amortised cost and FVOCI measurement categories (in either direction), then the credit risk at the asset's original date of initial recognition (rather than the reclassification date) continues to be used for assessing changes in credit risk. This is because both categories are subject to the same impairment requirements (see 7.8.420.10). [*IFRS 9.B5.6.1(b)*]

7.8.140.30   If a financial asset is reclassified from the amortised cost or FVOCI measurement category into the FVTPL measurement category, then an impairment assessment is no longer required. [*IFRS 9.B5.6.2*]

7.8.150   FINANCIAL INSTRUMENTS WITH LOW CREDIT RISK

7.8.150.10   As an exception to the general requirements, an entity may assume that the credit risk has not increased significantly since initial recognition if the credit risk on the financial instrument is low at the reporting date. An entity can choose to apply this simplification on an instrument-by-instrument basis. [*IFRS 9.5.5.10, BC5.183–BC5.184*]

7.8.150.20   The credit risk of a financial instrument is low if:
- the instrument has a low risk of default;
- the borrower has a strong capacity to meet its contractual cash flow obligations in the near term; and
- adverse changes in economic and business conditions in the longer term may, but will not necessarily, reduce the borrower's ability to fulfil its obligations. [*IFRS 9.B5.5.22*]

7.8.150.30   A financial instrument with an external rating of 'investment grade' is an example of an instrument that may be considered to have a low credit risk. However, a financial instrument does not have to be externally rated for the exception to apply. When an internal grade is used to determine whether the credit risk of an instrument is low, the internal assessment of low credit risk is required to be consistent with a globally understood definition of low credit risk for the type of financial instrument being assessed. The assessment is required to consider the perspective of a market participant, and to take into account all of the terms and conditions of the financial instruments. [*IFRS 9.B5.5.23*]

7.8.150.40   To conclude that an instrument with an external rating equivalent to 'investment grade' has low credit risk, the entity needs to consider whether the external rating is determined using methodologies that are consistent with a globally understood definition of low credit risk and whether there is evidence of an increase in credit risk that is not yet reflected in the rating. [*IFRS 9.IE27*]

7.8.150.50   A financial instrument is not considered to have a low credit risk simply because:
- the value of collateral results in a low risk of loss – this is because collateral usually affects the magnitude of the loss rather than the risk of default;
- it has a lower risk of default than the entity's other financial instruments; or
- it has a lower risk of default relative to the credit risk of the jurisdiction in which the entity operates – e.g. it is a government exposure that has a lower risk of default than exposures to private sector borrowers in the same country. [*IFRS 9.B5.5.22*]

7.8.150.55   In our experience, entities are unable to apply the low credit risk exception to retail exposures. This is because it is unlikely that the entity would be able to perform an individual credit assessment demonstrating that the borrower has the required degree of resilience or alignment with a market participant perspective of a globally understood definition of low credit risk, such as investment-grade status, even if the PD at the reporting date is believed to be low.

7.8.150.60   The low credit risk exception does not mean that there is a bright line threshold for the recognition of lifetime ECLs when an instrument's credit risk ceases to be low. Instead, when an instrument no longer has a low credit risk, the general requirements for assessing whether there has been a significant increase in credit risk apply (see 7.8.60). [*IFRS 9.B5.5.24*]

7.8.160   MEASUREMENT OF ECLs

7.8.160.10   ECLs are a probability-weighted estimate of credit losses over the expected life of the financial instrument (see 7.8.200). Credit losses are the present value of expected cash shortfalls (see 7.8.170). [*IFRS 9.A, B5.5.28*]

7.8.160.20   The measurement of ECLs reflects:
- an unbiased and probability-weighted amount (see 7.8.210);
- the time value of money (see 7.8.220); and
- reasonable and supportable information that is available without undue cost or effort (see 7.8.230). [*IFRS 9.5.5.17*]

7.8.160.30   IFRS 9 does not prescribe a single method to measure ECLs. The methods used to measure ECLs may vary based on the type of financial asset and the information available. [*IFRS 9.B5.5.12*]

7.8.160.40   IFRS 9 allows entities to use practical expedients when estimating ECLs, provided that they are consistent with the principles in 7.8.160.10. It gives an example of such an expedient: a provision matrix to measure ECLs for trade receivables (see 7.8.400). [*IFRS 9.B5.5.35*]

7.8.160.50   The impairment loss (or reversal) recognised in profit or loss is the amount required to adjust the loss allowance to the appropriate amount at the reporting date. [*IFRS 9.5.5.8*]

7.8.170   Cash shortfalls

7.8.170.10   A cash shortfall is the difference between:
- the cash flows due to the entity in accordance with the contract; and
- the cash flows that the entity expects to receive. [*IFRS 9.B5.5.28*]

7.8.170.20   Because the estimation of credit losses considers the amount and timing of payments, a cash shortfall arises even if the entity expects to be paid in full but later than the date on which payment is contractually due. This delay gives rise to an ECL, except to the extent that the entity expects to receive additional interest in respect of the late payment that compensates it for the delay at a rate at least equal to the effective interest rate. [*IFRS 9.B5.5.28*]

7.8.170.30   Cash shortfalls are identified as follows.
- *For 12-month ECLs:* Cash shortfalls resulting from default events that are possible in the next 12 months (or a shorter period if the expected life is less than 12 months) – i.e. not just the cash shortfalls that are expected over the next 12 months.
- *For lifetime ECLs:* Cash shortfalls resulting from default events that are possible over the expected life of the financial instrument. [*IFRS 9.A, B5.5.43*]

7.8.170.40   The term 'cash shortfalls' refers to overall shortfalls against contractual terms, and not just shortfalls on particular dates when cash is received or due. Therefore, cash shortfalls consider later recoveries of missed payments. [*IFRS 9.B5.5.28*]

EXAMPLE 6 – DEFINITION OF 'CASH SHORTFALLS'

7.8.170.50 On 31 January 2018, Company G originates a two-year loan with a principal of 100 and a 5% coupon payable annually. On 31 December 2018, G estimates that there has been a significant increase in credit risk on the loan and that, if the borrower were to default, then the estimated future cash flows would be as follows.

	CONTRACTUAL CASH FLOWS	EXPECTED CASH FLOWS	SHORTFALL
31 January 2019	5	3	2
15 February 2019	-	2	(2)
31 January 2020	105	70	35
31 March 2020	-	20	(20)

7.8.170.60 All shortfalls – i.e. both positive and negative amounts – are included in the measurement of the ECLs for the loan.

7.8.170.70 A question may arise about how to apply the definition of cash shortfalls to contractually linked instruments (CLIs) (see 7.4.340) that are subject to the impairment requirements. For example, a CLI meets the SPPI criterion and has stated cash flows that are solely payments of principal and interest (without looking through to the underlying pool of financial instruments), but the issuer is not contractually obliged to make those payments to the extent that it does not receive sufficient cash from the underlying pool. Because 'cash shortfall' is defined as the difference between the contractual cash flows that are due to the entity under the contract and the cash flows that the entity expects to receive, it might be argued that for such a CLI this difference is generally zero. However, restricting cash flows due under a CLI to the extent that there is cash available from the underlying pool of assets is a means for passing credit losses on assets in the pool through to the holder of the CLI. Therefore, it appears that the calculation of cash shortfalls on a CLI for the purposes of impairment should be consistent with the rationale for concluding that a CLI meets the SPPI criterion and cash shortfalls on a CLI should be calculated with reference to the difference between:

- the stated contractual cash flows (i.e. principal and interest) without reduction for credit losses in the underlying pool; and
- the cash flows expected to be received after allocation of credit losses in the underlying pool. [*IFRS 9.A, B4.1.21, B5.5.28*]

7.8.175 *Proceeds from sale of defaulted asset*

7.8.175.10 An entity's risk management policies and practices may include, in some circumstances, selling defaulted assets to third parties. IFRS 9 does not limit the cash flows that the entity can expect to receive only to contractual cash flows that are collected from the borrower. Further, it states that credit risk management activities that are aimed at minimising potential credit losses, such as sales, are integral to a held-to-collect business model (see 7.4.100). Accordingly, it appears that cash flows that are expected to be recovered from sale of a defaulted asset (net of selling costs) – rather than expected cash flows that the new owner of the defaulted asset would recover – should be included in the measurement of ECLs if:

- selling the asset is one of the recovery methods that the entity expects to pursue in a default scenario;
- the entity is neither legally nor practically prevented from selling the asset; and
- the entity has reasonable and supportable information on which to base its expectations and assumptions. [*IFRS 9.A*]

7.8.175.20 We believe that the inclusion of such expected post-default sale proceeds in the measurement of ECLs would be appropriate for financial instruments in all stages – i.e. those subject to 12-month ECLs and those subject to lifetime ECLs (both credit-impaired and not credit-impaired). This is because, when measuring ECLs in all stages, entities consider possible default scenarios. However, we believe that it would not be appropriate for an entity to include expected proceeds from sales of non-defaulted assets even if such a sale is expected. This is because it could not be argued that the sale represents a means of recovering contractual cash flows of the asset following default and ECLs relate to default scenarios. [*IFRS 9.5.5.17(a), 5.5.18, B5.5.28, B5.5.43*]

7.8.180 *Loan commitments*

7.8.180.10 For undrawn loan commitments, a cash shortfall is the difference between:

- the contractual cash flows that are due to an entity if the holder of the loan commitment draws down the loan; and
- the cash flows that the entity expects to receive if the loan is drawn down. [*IFRS 9.B5.5.30*]

7.8.180.20 When estimating the draw-downs, the relevant amounts are as follows.

- *12-month ECLs:* the expected portion of the loan commitment that will be drawn down within 12 months of the reporting date.
- *Lifetime ECLs:* the expected portion of the loan commitment that will be drawn down during the expected life of the loan commitment. [*IFRS 9.B5.5.31*]

7.8.190 *Financial guarantee contracts*

7.8.190.10 For financial guarantee contracts, a cash shortfall is the difference between:

- the expected payments to reimburse the holder for a credit loss that it incurs; and
- any amount that an entity expects to receive from the holder, the debtor or any other party. [*IFRS 9.B5.5.32*]

7.8.190.20 If the asset is fully guaranteed, then the estimation of cash shortfalls for a financial guarantee contract is consistent with the estimation of cash shortfalls for the asset subject to the guarantee. [*IFRS 9.B5.5.32*]

7.8.190.30 If an entity issues a financial guarantee contract and receives premiums from the holder of the guarantee over the life of the contract, rather than up-front, then it appears that the expected cash flows from premiums receivable under the guarantee should not be included in the measurement of the ECLs on the financial guarantee contract. This is because the cash outflows under the guarantee should be considered separately from the future premiums receivable and from the risk of any failure to collect them owing to the credit risk of the premium payer.

7.8.195 *Credit-impaired financial assets*

7.8.195.10   For a financial asset that is credit-impaired at the reporting date, but that was not credit-impaired when it was purchased or originated, an entity measures the ECLs as the difference between:
- the gross carrying amount (see 7.7.265); and
- the present value of estimated future cash flows discounted at the asset's original effective interest rate. [*IFRS 9.B5.5.33*]

7.8.195.20   For a discussion of the gross carrying amount of credit-impaired financial assets, see 7.7.430.

7.8.200   **The period over which to estimate ECLs**

7.8.200.10   The maximum period over which ECLs are measured is the contractual period – including any extension options – over which there is exposure to credit risk on the financial instrument. This is the case even if a longer period is consistent with business practice. For loan commitments and financial guarantee contracts, this period is the maximum contractual period over which an entity has a present contractual obligation to extend credit. [*IFRS 9.5.5.19, B5.5.38*]

7.8.200.15   When an entity sells a financial asset and the sale results in the asset's derecognition, it remeasures a loss allowance immediately before derecognition so that it can calculate the gain or loss arising on derecognition (see 7.8.20.45). In remeasuring the loss allowance of a non-defaulted asset (see 7.8.175), it appears that the entity should estimate the period of exposure considering the contractual terms of the instrument – i.e. it should not reduce the contractual period of exposure to the date of sale. For guidance on remeasuring the loss allowance of a defaulted asset that is expected to be sold, see 7.8.175. [*IFRS 9.3.2.12, B5.5.38*]

7.8.200.20   The extension options referred to in 7.8.200.10 include a borrower's option but not a lender's option. This is because IFRS 9 requires ECLs to be estimated over the maximum contractual period over which the entity is exposed to credit risk. If extension is within the control of the lender, then the lender cannot be forced to continue extending credit and therefore such an option cannot be considered as lengthening the maximum period of exposure to credit risk. Similarly, the maximum contractual period is determined taking account of the lender's ability to demand repayment or cancellation. [*IFRS 9.5.5.19*]

7.8.200.30   It appears that the maximum contractual period over which the entity is exposed to credit risk should be determined in accordance with the substantive contractual terms of the financial instrument. For example, if a lender is legally prevented from exercising a contractual right to terminate an exposure, then such a right is not substantive. However, for the purpose of determining the maximum contractual period, we believe that a situation in which a lender is legally prevented from exercising a contractual right is distinct from a situation in which a lender expects to choose not to exercise a contractual right for practical or operational reasons. This is because in the latter case the lender is under no legal or contractual commitment that would extend the period of exposure to credit risk until such time as the non-exercise occurs.

EXAMPLE 7 – MAXIMUM PERIOD TO CONSIDER WHEN MEASURING ECLs

7.8.200.40   Bank J issues variable interest rate mortgage loans to its retail customers with the following terms.
- Stated contractual maturity of six months.
- Interest rate is fixed for each six-month period at the beginning of the period.
- At maturity, if neither the borrower nor J terminates the loan, then it is automatically rolled over for another six months.

7.8.200.50   On the basis of historical evidence, such loans may extend many times and can last up to 30 years. J does not complete regular credit file reviews for individual loans and as a result does not usually cancel a loan unless it receives information about an adverse credit event in respect of a particular borrower.

7.8.200.60   The maximum period that J considers when measuring ECLs is six months because this is the maximum contractual period over which it is exposed to credit risk (see 7.8.200.10). It does not apply the requirements of 7.8.205.10 relating to certain financial instruments that contain both a loan and an undrawn commitment because this paragraph applies to financial instruments with a drawn and undrawn component where the borrower has flexibility in how frequently they make draw-downs on the facility. However, in this example the facility is not of a revolving nature and the borrower does not have flexibility regarding draw-downs.
[*IFRS 9.5.5.19–20, BC5.254–BC5.256*]

7.8.200.70   In the fact pattern illustrated in Example 7, difficulty may arise in practice in estimating the risk of default if, historically, loans generally roll over every six months and the borrower rarely makes repayment at the contractual maturity date. In these circumstances, a lender will have little if any historical data on the risk of default that may occur at maturity. IFRS 9 requires the risk of default to be estimated over the maximum contractual period over which the entity is exposed to credit risk. This means that the risk of default is based on the entity's expectations of actual default in that period. An entity does not adjust this expectation by making an assumption that it will require repayment at the contractual maturity date if it is not its intention to do so. Nor can an entity assume that default is not possible within the contractual maturity period on the basis that it plans to allow the loan to roll over. An entity will need to consider developing appropriate qualitative indicators of default such as unlikeliness or inability to pay to assess changes in the risk of default occurring during the maximum contractual period – in particular, IFRS 9 does not limit the definition of default to only a continuing failure to make payment when due over an extended period (see 7.8.50). [*IFRS 9.B5.5.37*]

7.8.200.80   Similar considerations apply in the separate financial statements of a parent when it has made a loan to a subsidiary that is contractually repayable on demand (assuming that the loan is not in the scope of the exception in 7.8.205.10). Even if the parent does not expect to demand repayment of the loan in the near term, the maximum period over which it measures ECLs is close to nil. In estimating the risk of default, the parent does not assume that it will call the loan immediately, if it is not its intention to do so, and does not automatically assume that the risk of default is 100 percent simply because the subsidiary may not be able to immediately repay the full amount of the loan. In measuring ECLs, the parent considers qualitative indicators of default (in addition to actual failure to pay), which may include:

- ability of the subsidiary to refinance the loan with a third party;
- adverse changes in the subsidiary's initial business plans since granting the loan; and
- the overall viability of the subsidiary's operations.

7.8.203 *Financial guarantee contracts*

7.8.203.10   If premiums in respect of a financial guarantee contract are receivable over the life of the contract and the contract lapses if premiums are not received when they are due, then the impact of this contingent cancellation has to be considered in estimating the expected period of exposure in respect of the financial guarantee contract.

7.8.205 *Revolving credit facilities*

7.8.205.10   Certain financial instruments include both a loan and an undrawn commitment component, and the entity's contractual ability to demand repayment and cancel the undrawn commitment does not limit its exposure to credit losses to the contractual notice period. For such instruments (and only for such instruments), an entity measures ECLs over the period for which it is exposed to credit risk – and for which ECLs would not be mitigated by credit risk management actions – even if that period extends beyond the maximum contractual period. This exception is intended to apply to a narrow set of circumstances and is relevant for instruments with an inter-relationship between the drawn and undrawn amounts that are not distinguished for risk management purposes but rather treated as a single set of cash flows. [*IFRS 9.5.5.20, BC5.260–BC5.261*]

7.8.205.20   An example of an instrument in 7.8.205.10 is a revolving credit facility – e.g. certain credit cards or overdraft facilities. These facilities can be contractually withdrawn by the lender with short notice (e.g. one day); however, in practice lenders continue to extend credit for a longer period and may only withdraw the facility when they become aware of adverse changes in the credit risk of the borrower, which could be too late to prevent some or all of the ECLs. These financial instruments generally have the following characteristics:

- they do not have a fixed term or repayment structure, and usually have a short contractual cancellation period – e.g. one day;
- the contractual ability to cancel the contract is not enforced in the entity's normal day-to-day management activities, but only when the entity becomes aware of an increase in the credit risk at the facility level; and
- they are managed on a collective basis. [*IFRS 9.B5.5.39*]

EXAMPLE 8 – MEASUREMENT OF ECLs FOR A PERIOD LONGER THAN MAXIMUM CONTRACTUAL COMMITMENT PERIOD

7.8.205.30   Bank H provides credit cards to its customers. H manages the portfolio on a collective basis, and for credit risk management purposes H does not distinguish between the drawn and undrawn balances. The credit cards have a one-day notice period, after which H has a contractual right to cancel the credit card; however, H does not enforce this right in its day-to-day management activities, but cancels facilities only when it becomes aware of an increase in credit risk and starts to monitor customers on an individual basis. Therefore, H does not consider its exposure to credit losses to be limited to the contractual notice period.

7.8.205.40   On the basis of historical information and experience with similar portfolios, H determines that the expected period over which it is exposed to credit losses is 30 months.

7.8.205.50   At the reporting date, the outstanding balance on the credit card portfolio is 60, and the available undrawn balance is 40. In measuring the ECLs, H considers its expectations about future draw-downs over the expected life of the portfolio – or over the next 12 months if there has not been a significant increase in credit risk – using its credit risk models.

7.8.205.60   H measures the ECLs on the credit card portfolio based on its estimates of outstanding balances. H determines that the expected outstanding balances at the time of default would be 55 (comprising the drawn balance of 50 and an additional 5 from the available undrawn balance) for credit cards for which 12-month ECLs are required to be recognised, and 15 (comprising the drawn balance of 10 and an additional 5 from the available undrawn balance) for credit cards for which lifetime ECLs are required to be recognised. [*IFRS 9.IE58–IE64*]

7.8.205.70   Paragraph 7.8.205.20 describes the general characteristics of financial instruments referred to in 7.8.205.10. These characteristics, although they are not determinative, are consistent with and reinforce the features set out in 7.8.205.10. If one or more of the characteristics described in 7.8.205.20 is not present, then the entity needs to consider carefully whether an instrument could still fall in the scope of the exception in 7.8.205.10. For example, if an instrument is not managed on a collective basis, then a question arises whether the entity's contractual ability to demand repayment and cancel the undrawn commitment really would not limit the entity's exposure to credit losses to the contractual notice period. The features required for a financial instrument to fall in the scope of this exception are:
- the financial instrument must be of a type that has the ability to have both a loan and an undrawn commitment component;
- the entity must have the contractual ability to demand repayment of the loan component and to cancel the undrawn commitment component; and
- the entity's exposure to credit losses is not limited to the contractual notice period. [*IFRS 9.5.5.20*]

7.8.205.72   Although retail credit cards and overdrafts issued to individuals are often given as examples of instruments falling in the scope of the exception in 7.8.205.10, such instruments may be granted to a corporate borrower as well. An entity assesses whether an instrument is in the scope of the requirements set out in 7.8.205.10–20 based on the specific facts and circumstances, irrespective of whether the borrower is an individual or a corporate entity.

7.8.205.74   Often, the critical factor in the analysis will be how the entity manages the credit risk of the exposure. The exception described in 7.8.205.10 is intended to address products for which the lender's exposure to credit loss is not limited to the contractual notice period because the lender does not have enough information to take credit risk management actions soon enough to avoid credit losses. This contrasts with more intensive individual day-to-day management of facilities that would allow an entity to detect and act on potential credit problems on individual facilities on an ongoing basis. Judgement may be required to determine whether a facility is in the scope of the exception in 7.8.205.10. For some portfolios, the entity may have more information than for others and so be able to take action earlier. In practice, it will probably vary with the type and size of customer. However, a corporate facility with a one-day cancellation period will rarely, if ever, be monitored every single day so that the entity is always able to take action before an increase in credit risk; such an unrealistic threshold is not what is required to determine that the exception in 7.8.205.10 does not apply.

EXAMPLE 9A – CORPORATE FACILITY – EXCEPTION DOES NOT APPLY

7.8.205.76   Bank L has granted a revolving facility to a listed corporate customer, Company C, which has an investment-grade credit rating. The facility has a one-day contractual cancellation period. The facility is managed on an individual basis by a credit risk officer whose primary role is to manage the credit risk of C and 10 other corporate customers of L. In line with L's credit risk management policy, the credit risk officer reviews monthly covenant status reporting and management accounts received from C, has frequent meetings with C's management and monitors regulatory announcements and press and credit agency reports on C on a daily basis.

7.8.205.78   L concludes that the facility granted to C is not in the scope of the exception in 7.8.205.10 – i.e. the maximum period over which L measures ECLs is the one-day contractual exposure period.

EXAMPLE 9B – CORPORATE FACILITY – EXCEPTION APPLIES

7.8.205.80   Bank M has a portfolio of 100 similar revolving facilities granted to small and medium-sized corporate customers. The facilities have a one-day contractual cancellation period. The credit risk of the portfolio is managed by one credit risk officer. In line with M's credit risk management policy, the credit risk of the facilities is managed predominantly by system-generated exception reports based on behavioural data, including utilisation of the facilities and overdue status.

7.8.205.82   M concludes that facilities in this portfolio are in the scope of the exception in 7.8.205.10 – i.e. the maximum period over which M measures ECLs is not limited to one day.

7.8.205.85   One of the conditions for applying the requirement in 7.8.205.10 is that the financial instrument has to have both a drawn component and an undrawn component. It appears that it is not necessary for the financial instrument to have both a drawn and an undrawn component at all times, and it is possible for it to have only a drawn or only an undrawn component at a particular reporting date if the financial instrument is of a type that has the ability to have both a drawn and an undrawn commitment component. Examples of such instruments are revolving facilities, such as credit cards.

The nature of these facilities is that the drawn and undrawn amounts are subject to change as new advances are drawn and existing advances are repaid.

7.8.205.90   It appears that a facility is not precluded from being in the scope of the exception in 7.8.205.10 solely because it has a stated fixed term if it is immediately revocable at the option of the issuer.

EXAMPLE 10A – REVOLVING FACILITY WITH FIXED TERM

7.8.205.100   Bank B issues a revolving facility to Borrower A. The facility has a stated maturity of five years from the date of signing but is immediately revocable, without cause, at the discretion of B.

7.8.205.110   We believe that the stated fixed maturity of the facility would not by itself prevent the instrument from being in the scope of the exception in 7.8.205.10 because the fixed-term feature does not negate B's contractual right to cancel the undrawn component at any time.

EXAMPLE 10B – FIXED-TERM LOAN DRAWN UNDER REVOLVING FACILITY

7.8.205.120   Bank C issues a facility with no fixed term and which is immediately revocable at C's discretion but drawing under the facility can be made in the form of a loan with a five-year maturity and C cannot demand repayment of a drawn loan before its maturity.

7.8.205.130   We believe that drawing in the form of a loan with a five-year maturity where C cannot demand repayment before maturity would prevent the instrument from falling in the scope of the exception in 7.8.205.10 because it would negate the lender's contractual right to immediately revoke the facility. Consequently, for the drawn portion of the facility, the maximum period to consider when measuring ECLs would be five years, subject to any prepayment features.

7.8.205.140   In this scenario, it may also be necessary to consider the unit of account to which the requirements of IFRS 9 are applied, because one contract may relate to more than one financial instrument. In particular, a multi-purpose facility might be capable of being drawn down in a number of different ways (e.g. as a revolving overdraft or as a loan with or without a fixed term). Also, if the fixed-term feature was for a shorter period, then judgement would be required to determine whether the feature would prevent a particular financial instrument from falling in the scope of the exception in 7.8.205.10.

7.8.205.150   When determining the period over which to estimate ECLs for the instruments described in 7.8.205.10, but for which ECLs would not be mitigated by the entity's normal credit risk management actions, an entity considers factors such as historical information and experience about:
● the period over which the entity was exposed to credit risk on similar financial instruments;

- the length of time for related defaults to occur on similar financial instruments following a significant increase in credit risk; and
- the credit risk management actions that the entity expects to take once the credit risk on the financial instrument has increased – e.g. the reduction or removal of undrawn limits. [*IFRS 9.B5.5.40*]

7.8.205.160   It appears that the credit risk management actions referred to in 7.8.205.150 are those that:

- an entity expects to take – rather than *all* credit risk management actions that it is legally and operationally able to take;
- serve to mitigate credit risk – consequently, actions that do not mitigate credit risk, such as the reinstatement of previously curtailed credit limits, should not be considered; and
- serve to either terminate or limit the credit risk exposure.

7.8.205.170   In determining which credit risk management actions an entity expects to take, an entity considers its normal credit risk mitigation process, past practice and future intentions.

EXAMPLE 11A – DETERMINING THE PERIOD OF EXPOSURE – TYPE OF CREDIT RISK MANAGEMENT ACTIONS TO INCORPORATE

7.8.205.180   Bank H issues credit cards to its retail customers with the following terms.
- Customers in good standing can charge up to a predefined contractual credit limit.
- H has the contractual ability to cancel the card account at its discretion even if the customer pays on time and the card account is not in default.
- The card agreement has no stated maturity date but drawn balances are subject to minimum repayment schedules.

7.8.205.190   In addition, H has the following policies.
- H rarely cancels the accounts of customers that have not been and are not delinquent.
- H determines that a significant increase in credit risk has occurred no later than when contractual payments are 30 days past due.
- When contractual payments are 60 days past due, the ability of the customer to draw is put on hold. If the customer then makes all past due payments and is no longer delinquent, then H may reinstate the customer's ability to draw.
- When contractual payments reach 90 days past due, the exposure is considered to be in default and the account is considered to be credit-impaired. At that time, the commitment is cancelled.

7.8.205.200   In applying the conditions in 7.8.205.160 for the purpose of determining the period of exposure and future draw-downs for the instruments described in 7.8.205.10, we believe that H should consider its expected practice of mitigating credit risk by putting accounts on hold after 60 days past due, but should not consider any subsequent expected reinstatement of those accounts.

EXAMPLE 11B – DETERMINING THE PERIOD OF EXPOSURE – INCORPORATING CREDIT RISK
MANAGEMENT ACTIONS

7.8.205.203   At 31 December 2018, Bank K has a portfolio of 100 credit card
facilities that on initial recognition shared similar credit risk characteristics. K
carries out substantive annual credit reviews of these facilities using behavioural
score cards. If a review identifies an increase in credit risk beyond K's credit risk
appetite, then K removes the undrawn amount of the facility. K estimates that at
the next review date the credit risk of the portfolio will be as follows.

- *Portfolio segment A:* The credit risk of 30 facilities will increase, but the increase
  will exceed K's risk appetite for only 15 of those facilities. Accordingly, K
  expects to carry out credit risk-mitigating action in respect of these 15 facilities.
- *Portfolio segment B:* The credit risk of the remaining 70 facilities will stay the
  same or reduce.

PORTFOLIO SEGMENT	NUMBER OF FACILITIES	INCREASE IN CREDIT RISK	CREDIT RISK-MITIGATING ACTION TAKEN
A	30	Yes	Only for 15 of the facilities
B	70	No	No

7.8.205.205   At 31 December 2018, K determines the period of exposure for the
facilities as follows.

- For the 15 facilities for which credit risk has increased beyond K's risk appetite, the period of exposure will be limited by the next substantial annual
  credit review date.
- For the remaining 85 facilities, the period of exposure will not be limited by the
  next substantive annual credit review. The period of exposure for these facilities
  will be determined based on historical experience with similar financial instruments and may be limited by subsequent annual credit reviews.

7.8.205.207   If K's credit risk management policy was to reduce the undrawn
limits, rather than remove them entirely, then it would not be appropriate to limit
the period of exposure with reference to the next substantial annual review date
for the entire commitment, but only for the portion expected to be removed.

7.8.205.210   The exception in 7.8.205.10 applies to instruments in which both drawn and undrawn
components are managed together as a single exposure. However, for the purpose of estimating the
period of exposure and the amount of exposure at default, drawn and undrawn components have a
different impact. This is because the credit risk associated with the undrawn element is immediately
eliminated if an entity cancels the undrawn element, but the exposure on the drawn component remains
until the balance has been recovered (or written off).

7.8.205.220   For certain revolving facilities – such as certain credit cards or overdrafts – in practice, contractual credit limits are often exceeded when the customer is in default. A question arises

whether expected draw-downs in excess of contractual credit limits need to be considered when estimating exposure at default for the purpose of measuring ECLs. The cash shortfalls are defined as the difference between contractual cash flows that are due to the entity and cash flows that the entity expects to receive (see 7.8.170). Accordingly, when measuring ECLs, it appears that any expected draw-downs in excess of the contractually agreed limit at the reporting date should be excluded from the calculations. This is the case even if an entity has a history of allowing customers to exceed their contractual limits. This is because the impairment model is based on the contractual terms of the financial instrument at the reporting date and the specific exception in 7.8.205.10 relates only to the period of exposure and cannot be extended by analogy. [*IFRS 9.B5.5.30, A*]

7.8.205.230   Some revolving facilities are issued with no absolute credit limits. In these cases, a careful analysis of the contractual terms is required to determine the impact on measuring ECLs.

EXAMPLE 12 – MEASURING ECLs FOR A CHARGE CARD

7.8.205.240   Bank L issues charge cards with the following features.
- There is no absolute credit limit.
- L approves each transaction dynamically at the point of sale based on the customer's perceived creditworthiness estimated using statistical models and inputs, such as spending history and known income.
- L can suspend or cancel the card at its discretion even if the customer pays on time and the card is not in default. L has done so in practice.

7.8.205.250   In this example:
- the contractual credit limits are zero and so future draw-downs would not be taken into account; and
- the facility is outside the scope of the exception in 7.8.205.10 because there is no undrawn element – i.e. there is no firm commitment to extend credit.

7.8.210   Probability-weighted outcome

7.8.210.10   The estimate of ECLs reflects an unbiased and probability-weighted amount, determined by evaluating a range of possible outcomes rather than based on a best- or worst-case scenario. An entity is not required to identify every possible scenario, but the estimate always reflects at least two scenarios:
- the probability that a credit loss occurs, even if this probability is very low; and
- the probability that no credit loss occurs. [*IFRS 9.5.5.17(a), 5.5.18, B5.5.41*]

7.8.210.20   In practice, the requirement to consider at least two scenarios may not necessitate a complex analysis. In some cases, relatively simple modelling is sufficient, without the need for a large number of detailed simulations of scenarios. For example, for a large group of financial instruments with shared risk characteristics, the average credit losses may be a reasonable estimate of the probability-weighted amount. However, if there are significant asymmetries or non-linear impacts from different scenarios, then more detailed modelling may be required (see also 7.8.238). [*IFRS 9.B5.5.42*]

7.8.210.30   The requirement in 7.8.210.10 applies to all exposures, including exposures to a government, irrespective of how unlikely a default is.

7.8.220   **Time value of money**

7.8.220.10   The estimate of ECLs reflects the time value of money, using the following discount rates. [*IFRS 9.5.5.17(b), B5.5.44–B5.5.48*]

TYPE OF INSTRUMENT	DISCOUNT RATE
Financial assets other than POCI financial assets and lease receivables	The effective interest rate determined on initial recognition or an approximation thereof (the current effective interest rate for floating rate financial assets – see 7.7.330) or, when applicable, a revised rate (see 7.8.220.40–50). [*IFRS 9.B5.5.44*]
POCI assets	The credit-adjusted effective interest rate determined on initial recognition (see 7.7.310 and 7.8.340). [*IFRS 9.B5.5.45*]
Lease receivables	The discount rate used in measuring the lease receivable in accordance with IAS 17. [*IFRS 9.B5.5.46*]
Undrawn loan commitments	The effective interest rate, or an approximation thereof, that will be applied to the financial asset resulting from the loan commitment. [*IFRS 9.B5.5.47*]
Undrawn loan commitments for which the effective interest rate cannot be determined, and financial guarantee contracts	The discount rate that reflects the current market assessment of the time value of money and the risks that are specific to the cash flows; but only if, and to the extent that, the risks are taken into account by adjusting the discount rate instead of adjusting the cash shortfalls being discounted (see 7.8.220.60). [*IFRS 9.B5.5.48*]

7.8.220.15   If a financial instrument has a variable interest rate, then ECLs are discounted using the current effective interest rate. It appears that the term 'current' can be interpreted as either the actual rate current at the reporting date or the projected interest rate derived from the current yield curve. We believe that there should be consistency between the rate used to recognise interest income and project future cash flows (including cash shortfalls) and the rate used to discount those cash flows (see 7.7.320 and 330). [*IFRS 9.B5.5.44*]

7.8.220.20   ECLs are discounted to the reporting date, not to the expected default date or another date. [*IFRS 9.B5.5.44*]

7.8.220.30   To calculate the effective interest rate that will apply to the financial asset resulting from a loan commitment, an entity needs to determine what the gross carrying amount of the asset will be on initial recognition (see 7.7.30).

7.8.220.40   If a financial instrument is a hedged item in a fair value hedge, then its carrying amount is adjusted for the hedging gain or loss and the adjustment is amortised to profit or loss based on a recalculated effective interest rate. The amortisation may begin as soon as the adjustment is made, but no later than when the hedged item ceases to be adjusted for the hedging gain or loss. It appears that when an entity revises the effective interest rate to reflect the hedge adjustment, this revised effective interest rate should be used in measuring ECLs (see 7.7.390 and 7.9.170.90). [*IFRS 9.6.5.10*]

7.8.220.50   If an entity revises the effective interest rate of a financial asset to reflect costs and fees arising as part of a modification that does not result in derecognition (see 7.7.280.40), then it appears that this revised effective interest rate should be used in measuring ECLs. [*IFRS 9.5.4.3*]

7.8.220.60   It appears that when determining the discount rate used for measuring ECLs for undrawn loan commitments for which the effective interest rate cannot be determined or for financial guarantee contracts, any adjustment made to the discount rate for risks that are specific to the cash flows should be negative – i.e. it should reduce the discount rate that reflects the current market assessment of the time value of money. This is because the reduction should increase the present value of the obligation, reflecting additional compensation that an issuer would demand to accept a more risky obligation.

7.8.230   Information to be used in measurement

7.8.230.10   The estimates of ECLs are required to reflect reasonable and supportable information that is available without undue cost or effort – including information about past events and current conditions, and forecasts of future economic conditions. Information that is available for financial reporting purposes is considered to be available without undue cost or effort. [*IFRS 9.5.5.17, B5.5.49*]

7.8.230.20   The degree of judgement required to estimate cash shortfalls depends on the availability of detailed information. As the forecast horizon increases – i.e. as the period for which an entity needs to make its estimate becomes longer – the availability of detailed information decreases, and the judgement required to estimate ECLs increases. An entity is not required to prepare detailed estimates for periods that are far in the future. For such periods, an entity could develop projections by extrapolating the information that is available for earlier periods. [*IFRS 9.B5.5.50*]

7.8.230.30   An entity is not required to undertake an exhaustive search for information but is required to consider all reasonable and supportable information that is available without undue cost or effort that is relevant for the estimation. The information used includes:
- factors that are specific to the borrower; and
- general economic conditions, including assessment of both the current conditions and the forecast direction of the change of conditions. [*IFRS 9.B5.5.51*]

7.8.230.40   The following are examples of potential data sources:
- internal historical credit loss experience;
- internal and external credit ratings;
- the credit loss experience of other entities; and
- external reports and statistics. [*IFRS 9.B5.5.51*]

7.8.230.50   An entity reviews the methodology and assumptions used for estimating ECLs regularly, to reduce any differences between estimates and actual credit losses. [*IFRS 9.B5.5.52*]

7.8.233   *Historical data*

7.8.233.10   Historical information is an important base from which to measure ECLs. It is adjusted on the basis of current observable data to reflect current conditions and an entity's forecast of future conditions during the life of the instrument. However, in some cases the best reasonable and supportable information could be the unadjusted historical information, depending on the nature of the information and when it was calculated, compared with circumstances at the reporting date. [*IFRS 9.B5.5.52*]

7.8.233.20   If ECLs are estimated using historical credit loss experience, then information about historical loss rates is applied to groups that are defined in a manner that is consistent with the groups for which the historical loss rates were observed. [*IFRS 9.B5.5.53*]

7.8.233.30   Estimates of changes in ECLs reflect, and are directionally consistent with, changes in related observable data from period to period. Examples of such observable data are:
- unemployment rates;
- property prices;
- commodity prices; and
- payment status. [*IFRS 9.B5.5.52*]

EXAMPLE 13 – ADJUSTING HISTORICAL DATA TO CURRENT ECONOMIC CONDITIONS

7.8.233.40   Company K has a portfolio of similar loans. Data about unemployment in K's region is a key factor in estimating ECLs for these loans. Except for certain specific past-due exposures, K has measured impairment in the portfolio as 12-month ECLs.

7.8.233.50   At the reporting date, the unemployment rate in the region is 8%. However, consensus estimates available to K at the reporting date are that the unemployment rate will increase to 11% in the next 12 months. Accordingly, K uses the 11% unemployment forecast in estimating ECLs for these loans. (Similarly, if consensus estimates were that the unemployment rate would reduce to 6%, then K would use this data, which might cause a reduction in the loss allowance.)

7.8.233.60   In addition, K considers whether, as a result of this forecast, the risk of default has increased such that a lifetime ECLs measurement is required for all, or a portion, of the portfolio (see 7.8.60).

7.8.235   *Entity's own expected actions and expectations*

7.8.235.10   Estimates of future cash flows may depend on an entity's approach to managing impaired loans – e.g. collection policies, workout strategies, forbearance practices, anticipated debt restructurings and foreclosure practices. Therefore, changes in the entity's approach to managing impaired loans may lead to changes in these estimates and in the amounts of recognised impairment. If changes in the entity's approach occur, then the entity discloses the changes along with any material effect on financial performance (see also 7.8.175 and 205.150–207). [*IFRS 7.7, 33, IAS 8.39*]

7.8.235.20   Although actual or contemplated changes in collection plans and strategies may have a significant effect on estimates of cash shortfalls, it is unlikely that possible changes in collection plans and strategies that are not yet contemplated by management would have a significant effect on current estimates of cash shortfalls, unless management's current plans and strategies are unrealistic. However, an entity considers whether the expected continuation of plans and strategies is an assumption about the future or other source of estimation uncertainty at the reporting date that should be disclosed in accordance with paragraph 125 of IAS 1 – i.e. one that has a significant risk of resulting in a material adjustment to the carrying amounts of assets and liabilities within the next reporting period (see 2.8.120.10). [*IAS 1.125*]

7.8.235.30   ECLs reflect an entity's own expectations of credit losses. However, an entity also considers observable market information about the credit risk of the particular financial instrument or similar financial instruments. However, when considering market information, market prices and credit spreads on financial assets do not directly yield an estimate of expected cash flows, because they include other elements – e.g. liquidity spreads or a premium for bearing the risk that credit losses may be greater than expected – and are not always observable. Therefore, using such information in the measurement of ECLs may be challenging and requires judgement. [*IFRS 9.B5.5.54*]

7.8.235.40   Entities that have no, or insufficient, sources of entity-specific data are permitted to use peer group experience for comparable financial instruments (or groups of financial instruments). [*IFRS 9.B5.5.51*]

7.8.237   *Information available after initial modelling*

7.8.237.10   ECLs are measured at each reporting date considering all reasonable and supportable information available at that date without undue cost and effort (see 7.8.230.10). For operational reasons, entities often perform the initial modelling of ECLs before the reporting date. In such a case, the entity has to consider whether its initial modelling of ECLs has to be adjusted to reflect information that becomes available after the initial modelling has been carried out but before the reporting date. [*IFRS 9.5.5.17*]

7.8.237.20   New information may also become available between the reporting date and the date on which the financial statements are authorised for issue. ECLs are a probability-weighted estimate of credit losses at the reporting date. Such an estimate needs to take into account relevant possible future scenarios based on a range of expectations at the reporting date, using information available at that date. Based on information available at the reporting date, probabilities are assigned to events – e.g. a change of interest rate or an outcome of a public vote – that may occur after the reporting date. Therefore, no adjustment for events occurring after the reporting date would usually be appropriate unless information received after the reporting date indicates that there was a failure to consider appropriately all information that was reasonably available at the reporting date (see also chapter 2.9). [*IFRS 9.5.5.17*]

7.8.238   *Incorporating forward-looking information*

7.8.238.10   Forward-looking information used for the measurement of ECLs needs to be relevant for the particular financial instrument or group of financial instruments to which the impairment requirements are applied. Different factors may be relevant to different financial instruments and therefore the relevance of a particular piece of information may vary between financial instruments, depending on the specific drivers of credit risk. For example, expectations about future levels of unemployment in a specific industry or region may be relevant only to loans granted to borrowers who work in that industry or region. If different financial instruments or portfolios assessed share some similar risk characteristics, then relevant forward-looking information needs to be considered in a comparable and consistent manner to reflect those characteristics. [*IFRS 9.IE29–IE39*]

7.8.238.20   The measurement of ECLs reflects the entity's own expectations. However, in arriving at the estimate of ECLs, an entity uses all reasonable and supportable information that is available without undue cost and effort, including relevant external forward-looking information. For example, an entity may need to consider forward-looking information from a variety of sources to ensure that the information used is reasonable and supportable. [*IFRS 9.5.5.17(c), B5.5.51, B5.5.54*]

7.8.238.30   Judgement is applied to determine what constitutes reasonable and supportable forward-looking information. At any point in time, there will be a spectrum of forward-looking information available, some of which will be reasonable and supportable and some of which will have little or no supportable basis. The judgement may be particularly challenging and difficult for information about emerging issues and uncertain future events that are not included in an entity's planning and forecasting process and/or those whose economic consequences are particularly challenging to determine. For example, although it may be possible to assess the likelihood of a particular event occurring, it may be more difficult to determine the effect of the event on the risk of default occurring and/or the credit losses that would be associated with that event. Information about an event and its consequences may not be reasonable and supportable if, despite an effort in good faith, the entity has an insufficient basis on which to form a reasonable estimate of its impact. However, an entity cannot assert that there is an absence of reasonable and supportable information about a matter simply because modelling its effects appears difficult, or merely because it would involve a wider than usual range of possible results.

7.8.238.35   As the period over which ECLs are measured increases, the availability of detailed information decreases and the degree of judgement required to estimate ECLs increases. For periods that are far in the future, an entity may extrapolate its projections from available detailed information. Judgement is required, in the context of the overall estimate, about how to use the data that is available to develop projections over a longer horizon. Any extrapolation has to be consistent with the general principle that an entity estimates ECLs using reasonable and supportable information that is available without undue cost and effort to arrive at an unbiased probability-weighted measurement. Historical data is an important base from which to measure ECLs but measurements of ECLs reflect differences from historical circumstances and changes in observable data. An entity will need to estimate whether and how economic and loss parameters will continue to diverge from or revert to historical information and over what period any reversion may occur. The entity will need to determine that the projections are reasonable in the circumstances and cannot simply apply methods that are arbitrary or otherwise unsupported. For example, in some circumstances it may not be appropriate to assume that parameters will immediately revert to long-term historical averages at the end of a detailed forecast period or that they will continue at the same levels as included in the detailed forecasts for the entire remaining period over which ECLs are measured. [*IFRS 9.B5.5.50, B5.5.52*]

7.8.238.40   Because the objective in measuring ECLs is to determine a probability-weighted estimate (see 7.8.210), a possible event or outcome is not ignored solely because it is considered to be remote or uncertain. Reasonable and supportable information includes information about future events that are unlikely to occur. However, because ECLs are probability-weighted, the likelihood of an event happening affects the magnitude of its impact on estimates of ECLs, and the materiality of any potential impact may be a relevant factor to consider. [*IFRS 9.B5.5.42, B5.5.51*]

7.8.238.50   The measurement of ECLs reflects an unbiased and probability-weighted amount that is determined by evaluating a range of possible outcomes. Accordingly, if there is a non-linear relationship between the different forward-looking scenarios and their associated credit losses, then basing the estimate of ECLs on the result of only one scenario (that reflects the probabilities of different outcomes) would not achieve this objective. Instead, more than one forward-looking scenario needs to be incorporated into the measurement of ECLs. [*IFRS 9.5.5.17(a)*]

EXAMPLE 14 – MEASURING ECLs – NON-LINEAR IMPACT OF FORWARD-LOOKING SCENARIOS

7.8.238.60   Company E measures ECLs on a portfolio of loans and formulates the following forward-looking scenarios.

	UNEMPLOYMENT RATE	ECLs FOR EACH SCENARIO	LIKELIHOOD OF OCCURRING	PROBABILITY-WEIGHTED ECLs
Scenario 1	4%	30	20%	6
Scenario 2	5%	70	50%	35
Scenario 3	6%	170	30%	51
ECLs recognised				92

7.8.238.70   In measuring ECLs, E applies the probability of each scenario occurring to the amount of ECLs estimated under each scenario. The ECL that E recognises is 92.

7.8.238.80   It would not be appropriate for E to use:
- a single central economic scenario based on the most likely outcome (i.e. ECL of 70) because this would not reflect an unbiased probability-weighted amount that is determined by evaluating a range of possible outcomes; or
- a single scenario based on a weighted-average unemployment estimate of 5.1% (4% x 20% + 5% x 50% + 6% x 30%) because there is a non-linear relationship between the different forward-looking scenarios and their associated credit losses.

7.8.238.90   The considerations discussed in 7.8.238.10–50 also apply to incorporating forward-looking information into the assessment of whether credit risk on a financial instrument has increased significantly since initial recognition. To the extent relevant, forward-looking information used for the measurement of ECLs needs to be consistent with that used for the assessment of a significant increase in credit risk. However, in some cases, information might have an impact on the measurement of ECLs but not on the assessment of a significant increase in credit risk, and vice versa. For example, if a loan is collateralised, then the value of collateral would only be relevant to the measurement of ECLs, unless the collateral has an impact on the probability of the default occurring (see 7.8.110.60). [*IFRS 9.B5.5.17(j)*]

7.8.238.100   Example 15 illustrates one possible approach to incorporating forward-looking information into determining whether credit risk on an instrument has increased significantly.

EXAMPLE 15 – MULTIPLE ECONOMIC SCENARIOS – ASSESSMENT OF SIGNIFICANT INCREASE IN CREDIT RISK

7.8.238.110   Bank G measures ECLs on a loan and formulates the following forward-looking scenarios at the reporting date.

	LIFETIME PD	LIKELIHOOD OF SCENARIO OCCURRING	PROBABILITY-WEIGHTED 12-MONTH ECL	PROBABILITY-WEIGHTED LIFETIME ECL
Scenario 1	1%	20%	5	10
Scenario 2	4%	50%	15	40
Scenario 3	8%	30%	30	150
Total			50	200

7.8.238.120   G determines that a lifetime PD in excess of 5% represents a significant increase in credit risk, considering the PD on initial recognition of the loan. It calculates the probability-weighted lifetime PD at the reporting date as 4.6% (20% x 1% + 50% x 4% + 30% x 8%). Because the PD at the reporting date of 4.6% is less than 5%, G determines that no significant increase in credit risk of the loan has occurred since its initial recognition.

7.8.238.130   G recognises ECLs of 50 (5 + 15 + 30) in respect of the loan. It would not be appropriate for G to recognise ECLs of 170 (5 + 15 + 150), being the sum of 12-month ECL under Scenarios 1 and 2 (because the PDs for those scenarios indicate no significant increase in credit risk) and lifetime ECL under Scenario 3 (because the PD for this scenario indicates a significant increase in credit risk). This is because an assessment of whether credit risk has increased significantly is made for an asset as a whole, so the whole asset is either subject to a 12-month or a lifetime measurement of ECL.

7.8.240   Collateral

7.8.240.10   The estimate of ECLs reflects the cash flows expected from collateral and other credit enhancements that are part of the contractual terms of the financial instrument and are not recognised separately from the financial instrument being assessed for impairment. The collateral and other credit enhancements included in the measurement of ECLs are those integral to the contractual terms of the financial instrument. It appears that collateral or other credit enhancements included in the measurement of ECLs are not limited to those that are explicitly part of the contractual terms of a financial instrument (see 7.1.130). [*IFRS 9.A, B5.5.55*]

7.8.240.20   Irrespective of whether foreclosure is probable, the estimate of expected cash shortfalls on a collateralised financial asset reflects:
- the amount and timing of cash flows that are expected from foreclosure (including cash flows that are expected beyond the asset's contractual maturity); less
- costs for obtaining and selling the collateral. [*IFRS 9.B5.5.55*]

EXAMPLE 16 – MEASUREMENT OF LIFETIME ECLs OF A COLLATERALISED LOAN

7.8.240.30   Bank L holds a collateralised loan. L determines that the credit risk of the loan has increased significantly since initial recognition – i.e. the risk of

default has increased significantly. However, because the value of the collateral is significantly higher than the amount due from the loan, the LGD is very small.

7.8.240.40   Although L does not believe that it is probable that it will suffer a credit loss if a default occurs, it recognises lifetime ECLs for the asset. This is because a significant increase in credit risk is assessed with reference to the risk of default rather than to the LGD. However, the amount of the ECL would be very small, because the asset is expected to be fully recoverable through the collateral held under almost all possible scenarios. [*IFRS 9.IE18–IE23*]

7.8.240.50   The amount of cash flows that are expected from foreclosure are cash flows that the entity actually expects to receive in the future. Because expected cash flows are a probability-weighted estimate, they include possible scenarios in which the cash flows recoverable from collateral decrease (or, where relevant, increase).

7.8.240.60   In some cases, observable quoted forward prices for collateral may exist, especially for financial collateral. However, forward prices for financial collateral would generally reflect a premium or discount to the current market price – i.e. a spot price – with the premium or discount reflecting benchmark interest rates that would often be below the asset's original effective interest rate. Therefore, for the purpose of estimating the cash flows from the collateral, such prices that do not include a risk premium would not support the inflation of estimated future values based on a projected rate of return for the collateral that includes a risk premium.

7.8.240.70   In our experience, lenders often realise collateral at a discount to appraised values and this expected discount is reflected in the measurement of impairment.

7.8.240.80   When measuring an impairment loss on a financial asset denominated in the entity's functional currency but collateralised by an asset denominated in a foreign currency, in our view the estimated foreign currency future cash flows resulting from the foreclosure of the collateral should be translated into the functional currency of the reporting entity using the appropriate forward rates and then included in the calculation of cash shortfalls.

7.8.240.90   When an entity is calculating the impairment loss for a collateralised financial asset, in our view a gain should not be recognised, even if the collateral is expected to have a higher value than the gross carrying amount of the loan, if any surplus will be returned to the borrower.

7.8.240.100   Any collateral obtained as a result of foreclosure is not recognised as a separate asset unless it meets the recognition criteria in IFRS for the relevant asset. If the recognition criteria are met, then in our view any collateral received should be initially measured based on the carrying amount of the defaulted loan. Thereafter, it should be accounted for under the relevant standard and classified as held-for-sale if appropriate (see 5.4.20). [*IFRS 9.B5.5.55*]

7.8.240.110   In our view, the accounting treatment of collateral after foreclosure is dependent on the legal environment in which the entity operates and the terms on which the collateral is provided. For example, in the case of a mortgage loan collateralised by a property, two distinct sets of circumstances could apply.

- The bank (lender) could repossess the property as a result of the borrower's default with the intention of recovering the amounts owing on the understanding that any amounts received in excess of the mortgage balance would be refunded to the borrower; and any shortfall would remain the obligation of the borrower. The bank may continue to charge interest on the outstanding balance. The bank would remain exposed to interest rate risk on the mortgage and would not be exposed directly to property price risk. We believe that repossession is used only to reinforce the bank's contractual right to cash flows from the loan and consequently the bank should continue to recognise the loan and should not recognise the property.
- The bank could repossess the property, which in terms of the contract comprises the full and final settlement of the mortgage – i.e. the bank would retain any excess proceeds over the outstanding balance on the mortgage and the borrower would be released from its obligation in the event of a shortfall. Therefore, the bank would be directly exposed to property price risk rather than to interest rate risk on the loan and we believe that the bank should derecognise the loan and recognise the property.

7.8.250   Individual vs collective basis of measurement

7.8.250.10   IFRS 9 does not provide general guidance on when ECLs should be measured on an individual or collective basis. However, it states that if an entity does not have reasonable and supportable information that is available without undue cost or effort to measure lifetime ECLs on an individual basis, then it recognises lifetime ECLs on a collective basis, by considering comprehensive credit risk information. In addition to using past-due information, this measurement incorporates all relevant credit information – including forward-looking macro-economic information. [*IFRS 9.B5.5.4*]

7.8.250.20   To measure ECLs on a collective basis, financial assets are grouped on the basis of shared credit risk characteristics. For examples of shared credit risk characteristics, see 7.8.90.20. [*IFRS 9.B5.5.5*]

7.8.250.30   An asset might be evaluated for a significant increase in credit risk on an individual basis, but its ECLs are measured on a collective basis. For example, when an individual retail loan is more than 30 days past due (see 7.8.120), it may be considered that the credit risk on it has increased significantly and that the lifetime ECLs measurement basis therefore applies. However, ECLs may be measured on a collective basis as part of a portfolio using information on portfolio default rates. In practice, the measurement of ECLs on many financial instruments is likely to involve both collective and individual elements. [*IFRS 9.B5.5.4–B5.5.6*]

7.8.260   Modified financial assets

7.8.260.10   If the terms of a financial asset are renegotiated or modified and this does not result in the derecognition of the financial asset, then an entity recalculates the gross carrying amount of the financial asset and recognises a modification gain or loss in profit or loss (see 7.7.350). If modification results in derecognition, then a new financial asset is recognised (see 7.7.360). [*IFRS 9.5.4.3, IE68–IE70*]

7.8.260.20   It appears that these principles are also relevant to measuring the impairment of a financial asset to the extent that it is expected that a modification relating to the debtor's financial difficulty will be effected.

- If the expected modification will not result in the derecognition of the existing asset, then the expected cash flows arising from the modified financial asset are included in calculating the cash shortfalls from the existing asset.

- If the expected modification will result in the derecognition of the existing asset, then the expected fair value of the new asset is treated as the final cash flow from the existing financial asset at the time of its derecognition. This amount is included in calculating the cash shortfalls from the existing financial asset that are discounted from the expected date of derecognition to the reporting date using the original effective interest rate of the existing financial asset. [*IFRS 9.5.4.3, A, B5.5.25*]

EXAMPLE 17 – IMPAIRMENT LOSS – EXPECTED RESTRUCTURING RESULTS IN DERECOGNITION

7.8.260.30   At 31 December 2018, Company M has a loan asset with an amortised cost of 1,000 and an effective interest rate of 10% a year. The borrower is in financial difficulties.

7.8.260.40   M expects that it will participate in a debt restructuring in six months' time that will involve a substantial modification to the cash flows receivable under the loan agreement, including a 50% reduction in the principal amount, a reduction in the contractual interest rate and a substantial extension of maturity. The restructuring will lead to the derecognition of the existing loan asset and recognition of a new loan. M has evaluated a range of possible outcomes and, as a result, expects the fair value of the new loan at the time of the restructuring to be 300.

7.8.260.50   As a result, the amortised cost of the existing financial asset at 31 December 2018 is approximately 286 (i.e. $300 / (1 + 10\%)^{6/12}$). If the restructuring proceeds in the manner expected on 30 June 2019, then any difference between the actual fair value of the new loan and the previous estimate of 300 would give rise to an additional impairment loss or a reversal of impairment loss in 2019.

7.8.260.60   A question arises about whether expected modifications of financial assets that are not related to the borrower's financial difficulties may be considered in calculating ECLs. It appears that in such cases an entity may consider them (and as a result shorten the exposure period) only if all of the following conditions are met:
- the modification is expected to result in derecognition of the financial asset;
- the original loan is contractually prepayable; and
- the modification is expected to be performed on market terms. [*IFRS 9.A, B5.5.51*]

7.8.260.70   This is because in calculating ECLs, an entity estimates cash flows considering all contractual terms of the instrument, including prepayment options. The modification described in 7.8.260.60 may be viewed as the borrower exercising its prepayment option and then obtaining a new loan at market terms. [*IFRS 9.A, B5.5.51*]

7.8.270   Financial assets that have been reclassified

7.8.270.10   At the reclassification date, the fair value of a financial asset reclassified from FVTPL into the amortised cost or FVOCI measurement category becomes its new gross carrying amount (see 7.7.540.20). Following the reclassification date, an impairment loss is initially recognised for the asset. Therefore, similar to the origination or acquisition of a new financial asset that is initially classified as measured at amortised cost or FVOCI, a day one loss will result from this type of reclassification if the asset is not credit-impaired at the reclassification date (see 7.8.20.40 and 360). [*IFRS 9.5.6.3, 5.6.6, B5.6.2*]

7.8.270.20   If a financial asset is reclassified from amortised cost or FVOCI to FVTPL, the fair value at the reclassification date becomes the new carrying amount, but an impairment allowance is no longer necessary (see 7.7.540.20). Therefore, a credit to profit or loss arises that relates to the reversal of the loss allowance previously associated with the reclassified asset. [*IFRS 9.5.6.2, 5.6.7*]

EXAMPLE 18 – RECLASSIFICATIONS OUT OF FVTPL AND INTO AMORTISED COST MEASUREMENT CATEGORY

7.8.270.30   Company N purchases a portfolio of bonds for 500 and classifies them as measured at FVTPL. In the next reporting period, N changes its business model such that the bonds are held to collect the contractual cash flows; accordingly, N reclassifies the portfolio into the amortised cost measurement category.

7.8.270.40   The following information at the reclassification date is also relevant for this example:
- the fair value of the bonds is 490;
- the 12-month ECLs of the portfolio are estimated to be 4; and
- the bonds are not credit-impaired.

7.8.270.50   N records the following entries at the reclassification date.

	DEBIT	CREDIT
Bonds (at amortised cost) – gross carrying amount	490	
Bonds (at FVTPL)		490
To recognise reclassification of bonds from FVTPL to amortised cost measurement category		
Impairment expense (profit or loss)	4	
Bonds (at amortised cost) – loss allowance		4
To initially recognise impairment		

7.8.270.60   If the reporting date of N is on the reclassification date, then the day one loss on the reclassification date is equal to the amount of 12-month ECLs at that date. [*IFRS 9.IE104–IE107, IE110*]

7.8.280   Interaction with other measurement requirements

7.8.290   *Financial guarantee contracts*

7.8.290.10   IFRS 9 requires liabilities that result from financial guarantee contracts in its scope (see 7.1.60) to be measured, after initial recognition, at the higher of:
- the amount of the provision for ECLs; and
- the amount initially recognised (see 7.7.10), less the cumulative amount of income recognised in accordance with the principles of IFRS 15 (see 7.1.120). [*IFRS 9.4.2.1(c)*]

7.8.290.20   When an arm's length fee or premium for a financial guarantee is paid to the issuer in full at inception of the contract, the measurement basis in 7.8.290.10 is likely to result in no ECLs recognised in respect of the guarantee – either on initial recognition or subsequently – unless there are adverse developments. This is because:

- the amount initially recognised – i.e. the fair value of the financial guarantee – reflects lifetime ECLs at that time; and
- ECLs on a good-quality instrument will usually decrease over time, so ECL provisions may generally be less than the amounts initially recognised, less the cumulative amount of income recognised under IFRS 15.

7.8.300   *Loan commitments*

7.8.300.10   Similar to the accounting for financial guarantee contracts, the liabilities that result from commitments to provide a loan at a below-market interest rate are measured after initial recognition at the higher of:

- the amount of the provision for ECLs; and
- the amount initially recognised, less the cumulative amount of income recognised in accordance with the principles of IFRS 15 (see 7.1.250.110). [*IFRS 9.4.2.1(d)*]

7.8.300.20   Whether a provision for ECLs is recognised on a loan commitment may depend on whether the commitment is to provide a loan at or below a market interest rate (see 7.1.250). This is illustrated in Example 19.

EXAMPLE 19 – MEASUREMENT OF ECLs FOR LOAN COMMITMENTS

Scenario 1: Below-market rate loan commitment

7.8.300.30   On 31 December 2018, Company P issues a commitment to provide a loan at a below-market interest rate. Its fair value on initial recognition (which is also P's reporting date) is 10. P measures ECLs for the loan commitment at an amount equal to 12-month ECLs and estimates these to be 2.

7.8.300.40   On 31 December 2018, P records the loan commitment at 10, which is the higher of:

- the provision for ECLs of 2; and
- the amount initially recognised (fair value of 10) less the cumulative amount of income recognised under IFRS 15 (zero, because the loan commitment has just been issued).

7.8.300.50   No ECLs are recognised, because the fair value of the loan commitment is higher than the 12-month ECLs.

Scenario 2: At-market rate loan commitment

7.8.300.60   Company P issues a loan commitment with an at-market interest rate for its fair value of 5, with the remaining facts unchanged from Scenario 1. P records the fee received of 5 as a liability (see 7.7.530) and recognises a provision for ECLs of 2. This is because the specific measurement requirements for loan commitments

 issued with a below-market interest rate, summarised in 7.8.300.10, do not apply to other loan commitments issued.

7.8.310 *Hedged assets*

7.8.310.10   The principles for hedge accounting do not override the accounting for impairment of the hedged item. Therefore, impairment of the hedged item is recognised even if hedge accounting is being applied. However, the hedge accounting principles may require a gain on a hedging instrument to be recognised in profit or loss and offset (partly) against the recognised impairment. [*IFRS 9.5.5.1, 6.5.8, 6.5.11*]

7.8.310.20   If an entity has elected to apply the hedge accounting requirements of IFRS 9 and uses a credit derivative that is measured at FVTPL to manage the credit risk of a financial instrument, then it may designate that financial instrument, or a portion of it, as at FVTPL in certain circumstances (see 7.9.110). The designation can be made on, or subsequent to, initial recognition of a financial instrument or while the financial instrument is unrecognised. Any instrument designated as at FVTPL under this option will stop attracting an impairment allowance from the date of designation. Conversely, if an entity revokes the designation (see 7.9.130.20–45), then the impairment requirements in IFRS 9 will start to apply (see 7.8.270). [*IFRS 9.6.7.1*]

7.8.320 *Financial assets denominated in foreign currency*

7.8.320.10   Monetary financial assets denominated in a foreign currency are treated as assets measured at amortised cost in the foreign currency. This means that ECL is first determined in the foreign currency and then translated into the functional currency using the exchange rate at the date on which the ECL is recognised (see 7.7.440). [*IFRS 9.B5.7.2, 9.B5.7.2A*]

7.8.320.20   Foreign exchange gains and losses on an impaired monetary financial asset measured at amortised cost continue to be recognised in profit or loss. If, through a subsequent improvement in circumstances, an entity is able to reverse the impairment loss, then it appears that the reversal should be recognised at the spot exchange rate at the date on which the reversal is recognised. [*IFRS 9.5.5.8*]

7.8.325 *Portfolio of identical assets*

7.8.325.10   When an entity derecognises some, but not all, financial assets from a portfolio of identical assets held, an issue arises about how to identify the assets derecognised. This is relevant for the measurement of impairment – i.e. if the financial assets in the portfolio were acquired at different dates, then the assessment of whether credit risk has increased significantly is made with reference to those different dates.

7.8.325.20   IFRS is silent on how an entity identifies financial assets derecognised when they are part of a portfolio of identical assets. The discussion of this topic in the context of guidance on accounting for a sale is included in 7.6.230.50–150. The same considerations are relevant for the measurement of ECLs.

<h2>7.8.330   Measurement of ECLs – Worked example</h2>

7.8.330.10   Example 20 demonstrates the principles underlying measurement of 12-month ECLs and lifetime ECLs.

EXAMPLE 20 – MEASUREMENT OF 12-MONTH ECLs AND LIFETIME ECLs

7.8.330.20   Company R originates a 10-year loan for 1,000,000. The interest is paid annually. The loan's coupon and effective interest rate are 5%.

Scenario 1: Recognition of 12-month ECLs is appropriate

7.8.330.30   R concludes that the recognition of 12-month ECLs is appropriate. Using the most relevant information available, R makes the following estimates:
- the loan has a 12-month PD of 0.5%; and
- the LGD – which is an estimate of the amount of loss if the loan were to default (see 7.8.40.10) – is 25%, and would occur in 12 months' time if the loan were to default.

7.8.330.40   The loss allowance for 12-month ECLs is 1,250, which is calculated by multiplying the amount of cash flows receivable (1,050,000[1]) by the PD (0.5%) and by the LGD (25%), and discounting the resulting amount using the effective interest rate for one year (5%).

Scenario 2: Recognition of lifetime ECLs is appropriate

7.8.330.50   R concludes that the recognition of lifetime ECLs is appropriate. Using the most relevant information available, R makes the following estimates:
- the loan has a lifetime PD of 20%; and
- the LGD is 25% and would occur on average in 24 months' time if the loan were to default.

7.8.330.60   The loss allowance for lifetime ECLs is 47,619, which is calculated as $(1,050,000^{[2]} / 1.05^2) \times 20\% \times 25\%$.

Summary

7.8.330.70   The difference between calculating 12-month ECLs and lifetime ECLs in this example comprises:
- the different PD applied – either the 12-month PD or the lifetime PD; and
- the timing of the losses occurring.

7.8.330.80   Other potential sources of differences include:
- different LGDs; and
- different exposures at default. [*IFRS 9.IE49–IE50*]

Notes
1.   Includes the amount of principal and interest receivable in 12 months' time.
2.   Includes the amount of principal and interest receivable in 24 months' time, assuming that the interest for year 1 would be paid fully.

7.8.340 ASSETS THAT ARE CREDIT-IMPAIRED ON INITIAL RECOGNITION

7.8.350 Definition

7.8.350.10 POCI assets are assets that are credit-impaired on initial recognition. An asset is credit-impaired if one or more events have occurred that have a detrimental impact on the estimated future cash flows of the asset. The following are examples of such events:

- significant financial difficulty of the issuer or the borrower;
- a breach of contract – e.g. a default or past-due event;
- a lender having granted a concession to the borrower – for economic or contractual reasons relating to the borrower's financial difficulty – that the lender would not otherwise consider;
- it becoming probable that the borrower will enter bankruptcy or other financial reorganisation;
- the disappearance of an active market for that financial asset because of financial difficulties; or
- the purchase of a financial asset at a deep discount that reflects the incurred credit losses. [*IFRS 9.A*]

7.8.350.20 It may not be possible to identify a single discrete event that caused the asset to be credit-impaired. Instead, the combined effect of several events may cause financial assets to become credit-impaired. [*IFRS 9.A*]

7.8.360 Measurement on initial recognition

7.8.360.10 On initial recognition, POCI assets do not carry an impairment allowance. Instead, lifetime ECLs are incorporated into the calculation of the effective interest rate (see 7.7.310). [*IFRS 9.5.5.13, A, B5.4.7*]

EXAMPLE 21A – INITIAL RECOGNITION OF POCI ASSETS

7.8.360.20 Company S buys a portfolio of amortising credit-impaired loans with a remaining life of four years for 800, which is the fair value at that date. The remaining contractual cash flows at the time of purchase are 1,000 and the expected cash flows are as follows. Assume that all cash flows are expected to be paid at the year end.

YEAR	1	2	3	4
Expected cash flows	220	220	220	220

7.8.360.30 The effective interest rate of 3.925% p.a. is calculated as the internal rate of return of the initial purchase price – i.e. 800 – and the cash flows expected to be collected.

7.8.360.40 S records the following entry on initial recognition.

	DEBIT	CREDIT
Loan asset	800	
Cash		800
To recognise loans on initial recognition		

7.8.370 Subsequent measurement

7.8.370.10 The ECLs for POCI assets are always measured at an amount equal to lifetime ECLs. However, the amount recognised as a loss allowance for these assets is not the total amount of lifetime ECLs, but instead the changes in lifetime ECLs since initial recognition of the asset. [*IFRS 9.5.5.13–5.5.14*]

7.8.370.20 Favourable changes in lifetime ECLs are recognised as an impairment gain, even if the favourable changes are more than the amount, if any, previously recognised in profit or loss as impairment losses. [*IFRS 9.5.5.14*]

EXAMPLE 21B – SUBSEQUENT MEASUREMENT OF POCI ASSETS – NO CHANGES IN EXPECTATIONS

7.8.370.30 Continuing Example 21A, Company S's expectation about future cash flows from the portfolio at the end of year 1 has not changed since initial recognition.

7.8.370.40 At the end of year 1, S calculates interest income of 31 by applying the effective interest rate – i.e. 3.925% p.a. – to the amortised cost of the loan of 800. In addition, S receives a cash payment of 220.

7.8.370.50 S records the following entries in year 1.

	DEBIT	CREDIT
Loan assets	31	
Interest income		31
To recognise interest income in year 1		
Cash	220	
Loan assets		220
To recognise receipt of cash in year 1		

7.8.370.60 At the end of year 1, the loan portfolio is recognised in the statement of financial position at 611, which is its gross carrying amount and amortised cost (being 800 plus interest of 31 less cash received of 220).

7.8.370.70 This example illustrates that no impairment expense or allowance is recognised if, in subsequent periods, experience and expectations about the collectability of cash flows are unchanged from expectations on initial recognition.

EXAMPLE 21C – SUBSEQUENT MEASUREMENT OF POCI ASSETS – POSITIVE CHANGES IN EXPECTATIONS

7.8.370.80 Continuing Example 21A, the creditworthiness of the borrowers in the portfolio has improved, and at the end of year 1 Company S expects the following cash flows to be collected.

YEAR	1	2	3
Expected cash flows	250	250	250

7.8.370.90   At the end of year 1, S calculates interest income of 31 by applying the effective interest rate – i.e. 3.925% p.a. – to the amortised cost of the loan of 800, and records the same entries as in Example 21B to recognise interest income and cash received.

	DEBIT	CREDIT
Loan assets	31	
Interest income		31
To recognise interest income in year 1		
Cash	220	
Loan assets		220
To recognise receipt of cash in year 1		

7.8.370.100   In addition, the revised expected cash flows are discounted using the original effective interest rate, and the resulting favourable change in lifetime ECLs of 83[1] is recognised as an impairment gain at the end of year 1, as follows.

	DEBIT	CREDIT
Loss allowance	83	
Impairment gain		83
To recognise impairment gain for year 1		

7.8.370.110   At the end of year 1, the loan portfolio is recognised in the statement of financial position at its amortised cost of 694, being:
- a gross carrying amount of 611 (being 800 plus interest of 31 less cash received of 220); plus
- a loss allowance, being a debit balance of 83.

7.8.370.120   The loss allowance at the end of year 1 is a debit balance because there has been a cumulative decrease in ECLs since initial recognition and for POCI assets the loss allowance reflects only changes in lifetime ECLs since initial recognition. This is in contrast to non-POCI assets, for which the loss allowance reflects the full 12-month or lifetime ECLs. [*IFRS 9.5.5.13*]

Note
1.   Calculated as $(30 / 1.03925) + (30 / 1.03925^2) + (30 / 1.03925^3)$.

7.8.380   **Modifications**

7.8.380.10   When the contractual cash flows of a POCI asset are modified and the modification does not result in derecognition, the calculation of the modification gain or loss is the difference between:

- the gross carrying amount of the asset before the modification; and
- the recalculated gross carrying amount. [*IFRS 9.5.4.3*]

7.8.380.20   The recalculated gross carrying amount is the present value of the estimated future cash payments or receipts through the expected life of the modified financial asset discounted using the credit-adjusted effective interest rate before the modification. [*IFRS 9.5.4.3, A*]

7.8.390   TRADE AND LEASE RECEIVABLES AND CONTRACT ASSETS

7.8.390.10   A loss allowance on trade receivables or contract assets that result from transactions in the scope of IFRS 15, or on lease receivables that result from transactions in the scope of IAS 17, may be measured using a simplified approach, as set out below. [*IFRS 9.5.5.15–5.5.16*]

Type of financial asset	Measurement of loss allowance
Trade receivables[1] and contract assets[1], [2] that do not have a significant financing component	Lifetime ECLs.
Trade receivables[1] and contract assets[1], [2] that have a significant financing component, and lease receivables	Accounting policy election to measure the loss allowance either: • in accordance with the general approach (see 7.8.30); or • as lifetime ECLs. An entity may apply the policy election for trade receivables, contract assets and lease receivables independently of each other. In addition, the policy election may be applied separately for finance and operating lease receivables.

Notes
1.   For the determination of whether a trade receivable or a contract asset has a 'significant financing component', see 7.7.20.
2.   For the definition of contract asset, see 4.270.20.

7.8.390.15   A question arises about whether the simplified approach described in 7.8.390.10 for trade receivables can be applied by an entity (i.e. a factor) that has not supplied goods or services to the customer but has instead acquired receivables from the original supplier and recognised those receivables in its statement of financial position (i.e. the original supplier has derecognised the receivables). It appears that the factor should not apply the simplified approach described in 7.8.390.10 for measuring impairment of those receivables. This is because the simplified approach is limited to trade receivables that result from transactions that are in the scope of IFRS 15 from the perspective of the reporting entity. The transaction that led to the factor recognising the receivables was not a contract in the scope of IFRS 15, but a contract in the scope of IFRS 9. [*IFRS 9.5.5.15*]

7.8.400   Trade receivables

7.8.400.10   Generally, trade receivables that do not contain a significant financing component have a short duration – typically less than 12 months – which means that measuring the loss allowance as lifetime ECLs generally does not differ from measuring it as 12-month ECLs. [*IFRS 9.BC5.222*]

7.8.400.20   Trade receivables without a significant financing component are measured on initial recognition at the transaction price determined in accordance with IFRS 15 (see chapter 4.2), and do not have a contractual interest rate. This implies that the effective interest rate for these receivables is zero. Accordingly, the discounting of cash shortfalls to reflect the time value of money when measuring ECLs is not generally required.

7.8.400.30   However, further analysis and judgement may be required if a trade receivable is not paid when it is due and is modified so as to effectively incorporate a significant financing component, and so using an effective interest rate of zero may no longer be appropriate (see 7.6.95 and 7.7.360).

7.8.400.40   IFRS 9 allows the use of practical expedients when measuring ECLs, and gives an example of a provision matrix for trade receivables. An entity that applies a provision matrix might, for example:
- consider whether it is appropriate to segment trade receivables – e.g. because its historical credit loss experience shows significantly different loss patterns for different customer segments; these segments could be based on geographic region, product type, customer rating, collateral or trade credit insurance, or type of customer, such as wholesale or retail; and
- use historical loss experience on its trade receivables, and adjust historical loss rates to reflect:
  - information about current conditions; and
  - reasonable and supportable forecasts of future economic conditions. [*IFRS 9.B5.5.35*]

EXAMPLE 22 – USING A PROVISION MATRIX FOR SHORT-TERM TRADE RECEIVABLES

7.8.400.50   Company T has a portfolio of trade receivables of 30,000 at the reporting date. None of the receivables includes a significant financing component. T operates only in one geographic region and has a large number of small clients.

7.8.400.60   T uses a provision matrix to determine the lifetime ECLs for the portfolio. It is based on T's historical observed loss rates, and is adjusted by a forward-looking estimate that includes the probability of a worsening economic environment within the next year. At each reporting date, T updates the observed loss history and forward-looking estimates. [*IFRS 9.IE74–IE77*]

7.8.400.70   On this basis, T uses the following provision matrix.

	ECL RATE	TRADE RECEIVABLES	IMPAIRMENT ALLOWANCE
Current	0.3%	15,000	45
1–30 days past due	1.6%	7,500	120
31–60 days past due	3.6%	4,000	144
61–90 days past due	6.6%	2,500	165
Over 90 days past due	10.6%	1,000	106
Total		30,000	580

7.8.410   Lease receivables#

7.8.410.10   When measuring ECLs on lease receivables, an entity uses:
- cash flows that are consistent with the cash flows used in measuring the lease receivable under IAS 17; and
- the discount rate used in measuring the lease receivable under IAS 17. [*IFRS 9.B5.5.34, B5.5.46*]

7.8.410.20   Under IAS 17 the lessor initially recognises a finance lease receivable at the amount of its net investment, which comprises the present value of the minimum lease payments and any unguaranteed residual value (URV) accruing to the lessor (see 5.1.330). The lessor reviews the estimated URV on a regular basis. If there is a reduction in the estimated URV, then the lessor revises the income allocation over the lease term and immediately recognises in profit or loss any reduction in respect of the amount accrued. A question arises about how this guidance in IAS 17 interacts with the impairment requirements of IFRS 9. [*IAS 17.41, IFRS 9.2.1(b)(i)*]

7.8.410.30   It appears that the impairment requirements of IFRS 9 should be applied only to the minimum lease payments – i.e. the carrying amount of the URV should be excluded from the impairment assessment. This is because IAS 17 has specific guidance on the recognition of reductions in the URV that are reflected in the net investment in a finance lease. However, we believe that when measuring impairment of minimum lease payments under IFRS 9, any excess of the recoverable value of the leased asset over the carrying amount of the URV should be considered as recoveries from collateral when calculating cash shortfalls (see 5.1.430.40 and 7.8.170). [*IAS 17.41*]

EXAMPLE 23 – IMPACT OF UNGUARANTEED RESIDUAL VALUE ON ECLs

7.8.410.40   Lessor M leases an asset under a five-year finance lease at an implicit interest rate of 10%. At inception of the lease, the estimated URV at the end of year 5 is 1,000.

7.8.410.50   At the end of year 1, M calculates ECLs. The following table illustrates the amount of the leased asset that is included as collateral for calculating ECLs, when evaluating the possibility of a default occurring at the end of year 4, based on three alternative scenarios.
- *Scenario A:* No change in the estimated URV since initial recognition.
- *Scenario B:* A downward change in the estimated URV since initial recognition.
- *Scenario C:* An upward change in the estimated URV since initial recognition.

SCENARIO	ESTIMATED URV AT END OF YEAR 5	PRESENT VALUE OF URV AT THE END OF YEAR 4	ESTIMATED RECOVERABLE VALUE OF THE LEASED ASSET AT THE END OF YEAR 4	COLLATERAL RECOVERIES TO BE INCLUDED IN CALCULATION OF ECLs
	(A)	(B)	(C)	(D) = (C) - (B)
A	1,000	909[(1)]	1,500	591
B	800	727[(2)]	1,200	473
C	1,200	909[(1)]	2,000	1,091

> **Notes**
> 1. Calculated as 1,000 / 1.1 (i.e. 1,000 discounted for one year). The increase in the estimated unguaranteed residual value under Scenario C is excluded from the carrying amount of the finance lease receivable because under IAS 17 only reductions are reflected in the carrying amount of the finance lease.
> 2. Calculated as 800 / 1.1 (i.e. 800 discounted for one year).

7.8.415   FORTHCOMING REQUIREMENTS

7.8.415.10   IFRS 16 substantially carries forward the lessor accounting requirements in IAS 17 (see 5.1A.410).

7.8.420   DEBT INSTRUMENTS MEASURED AT FVOCI

7.8.420.10   The loss allowance for debt instruments at FVOCI is measured on the same basis as for amortised cost assets, but no loss allowance is recognised in the statement of financial position, because the carrying amount of these assets is their fair value. However, an entity is required to provide disclosures about the loss allowance amount (see 7.10.270). [*IFRS 9.5.5.2, 7.16A*]

EXAMPLE 24 – RECOGNITION OF IMPAIRMENT LOSSES ON DEBT INSTRUMENTS MEASURED AT FVOCI

7.8.420.20   On its reporting date of 31 December 2018, Company V purchases a debt instrument with a par amount and fair value of 1,000 and classifies it as measured at FVOCI. The instrument is not credit-impaired. The effective interest rate equals the annual coupon rate payable on each following 31 December. V estimates 12-month ECLs for the instrument of 10.

7.8.420.30   On 31 December 2018, V recognises an impairment of 10 in profit or loss with the corresponding entry in OCI.

	DEBIT	CREDIT
Debt securities	1,000	
Cash		1,000
To recognise debt instrument		
Impairment loss (profit or loss)	10	
OCI		10
To recognise impairment loss		

7.8.420.40   At the end of the next reporting period, the fair value of the debt instrument decreases to 950. V concludes that there has not been a significant increase in credit risk since initial recognition and that the impairment gain in respect of 12-month ECLs on 31 December 2019 is 4 (i.e. 12-month ECLs have decreased from 10 to 6). Accordingly, V records the following entry at that date (after recording the interest income and coupon receipt).

	DEBIT	**CREDIT**
Debt securities		50[(1)]
Impairment loss (profit or loss)		4[(2)]
OCI	54[(3)]	
To recognise the change in fair value and impairment gain		

Notes
1. Calculated as 1,000 - 950, being the amount needed to state the debt security at fair value as at the reporting date.
2. Calculated as 10 - 6, being the change in ECLs since initial recognition.
3. Balancing amount.

7.8.420.50   V also provides disclosures about the accumulated impairment of 6 (see 7.10.270). [*IFRS 9.IE78–IE80*]

7.8.430   WRITE-OFFS

7.8.430.10   The gross carrying amount of a financial asset is reduced when there is no reasonable expectation of recovery. A write-off constitutes a derecognition event. Write-offs can relate to a financial asset in its entirety, or to a portion of it. [*IFRS 9.5.4.4, B3.2.16(r), B5.4.9*]

7.8.430.15   IFRS 9 does not define the term 'no reasonable expectation' and the assessment may require judgement. Clearly, if there is zero probability of an amount being recovered (e.g. following the conclusion of the borrower's liquidation), then there is no reasonable expectation of recovering the amount. However, the assessment may be more challenging in other cases.

7.8.430.20   In principle, write-offs do not have an impact on profit or loss, because the amounts written off are reflected in the loss allowance. However, when there is some possibility of making future recoveries, there is a tension between the probability-weighted measurement of ECLs – which reflects a range of possible credit losses, including the possibility that no credit loss occurs – and making a write-off that leads to derecognition and a result that attributes a zero value to the possibility of any future recoveries. It would not be consistent with either the guidance on measurement of ECLs or the guidance on write-offs to write off an amount in respect of which significant recoveries are expected because there is a reasonable expectation of making those recoveries. Therefore, it appears that a write-off is appropriate only to the extent that no significant recoveries are expected in respect of the amount to be written off.

7.8.430.25   Accordingly, an entity may need to apply judgement to develop criteria to be applied in practice for making write-offs. This may include identifying a confidence level or probability threshold that is determined to represent 'no reasonable expectation' of recovery for particular types of financial assets. If significant recoveries of previously written off amounts arise in practice, then we believe that an entity should recalibrate its write-off criteria. For example, writing off all similar exposures when they are 180 days past due is appropriate only if it is supported by evidence that there is no reasonable expectation of recovery, including consideration of historical experience of recoveries on similar assets.

7.8.430.27   It appears that the determination of whether a write-off is required is performed for an individual financial asset (including a part of the asset), rather than for a portfolio of financial assets. This is because the standard discusses writing off individual financial assets or parts of financial assets. However, we believe that entities may use portfolio-level data and expectations, where appropriate, to estimate the amount of write-off that is required (see 7.8.250.20).

EXAMPLE 25 – WRITE-OFF PORTION OF ASSET

7.8.430.30   Company W holds a collateralised financial asset measured at amortised cost.

7.8.430.35   As a result of the borrower experiencing significant financial difficulties, at 31 December 2018 W determines that the loan is credit-impaired. On a probability-weighted basis, W estimates that the present value of future cash flows amounts to 60% of the gross carrying amount of the financial asset. Accordingly, W recognises a loss allowance equal to 40% of its gross carrying amount. In addition, W determines that it still has some reasonable expectation of recovering the full gross carrying amount. Accordingly, W does not write off any portion of the asset.

7.8.430.40   On 31 December 2019, W revises its estimates. On a probability-weighted basis, W estimates that the present value of future cash flows amounts to 25% of the gross carrying amount of the financial asset. These future cash flows are expected to be recovered solely from repossession and sale of the collateral in the near term. W's cash flow estimates are based on probability-weighting a range of possible outcomes. The most favourable scenario assumes recoveries of 30%. Accordingly, W first recognises a loss allowance for the asset equal to 75% of the gross carrying amount. Also, W concludes that it has no reasonable expectation of recovering more than 30% and therefore writes off 70% of the gross carrying amount of the financial asset and reduces the loss allowance by the same amount.

7.8.430.50   An entity may have no reasonable expectation of receiving an amount when it is contractually due but have a reasonable expectation of receiving that same amount later. If the entity has a contractual right to receive interest for the period of delay but has no reasonable expectation of receiving it, then the entity writes off a portion of the gross carrying amount equal to the net present value of this additional contractual interest to reflect the fact that it has no reasonable expectation of receiving it. However, IFRS 9 does not state whether a write-off is also required if an entity has no contractual right to receive interest for the period of delay. It appears that in this scenario, an entity should choose an accounting policy, to be applied consistently, to either:
- write off a portion of the gross carrying amount immediately in order to faithfully represent the present value of contractual cash flows (the amount of the write-off will reduce the gross carrying amount to the highest amount in the range of present values for which the entity has some reasonable expectation of recovery); or
- not write off a portion of the gross carrying amount immediately because it still has some reasonable expectation of recovering the nominal amount of contractual cash flows in full. However, in this case a write-off will be required later, as illustrated in Example 26B. [*IFRS 9.5.4.4, B3.2.16(r), B5.4.9, BC5.81*]

EXAMPLE 26A – DELAY OF CASH FLOWS – IMMEDIATE WRITE-OFF

7.8.430.60   Bank N has an accounting policy to write off a portion of a loan if it has no reasonable expectation of receiving a contractual amount when it is due and has no right to interest on the late amount. N has a loan asset with the following terms:
- a nominal amount of 1,000 repayable at maturity on 31 December 2018; and
- an effective interest rate of 5% per annum (equal to the contractual rate).

7.8.430.70   On 31 December 2018, N determines that it does not have a reasonable expectation of receiving 1,000 on that date but instead has a reasonable expectation of receiving it three years later. N does not have a legal right to additional interest to compensate for the delay. The accrued contractual interest has been paid as at 31 December 2018, so the gross carrying amount of the loan is 1,000. N writes off at 31 December 2018 the difference between the gross carrying amount of 1,000 and the present value of 1,000 discounted for three years – i.e. 136 $(1,000 - 1,000 / 1.05^3)$.

7.8.430.80   N records the following entry in respect of the write-off of a portion of the loan on 31 December 2018.

	DEBIT	CREDIT
Loss allowance	136	
Gross carrying amount		136

7.8.430.90   Assuming that there is no change in expected cash flows at 31 December 2019, the following is a reconciliation of the loan's gross carrying amount, loss allowance and amortised cost during 2019.

	GROSS CARRYING AMOUNT	LOSS ALLOWANCE[1]	AMORTISED COST
Balance at 1 January 2019	864	-	864
Interest income	43[2]	-	43
Balance at 31 December 2019	907	-	907

Notes
1. For simplicity, it is assumed that the loss allowance is zero after write-off – i.e. the total loss allowance before write-off equals the loss allowance written off.
2. Because the loan is credit-impaired, interest is calculated by applying the effective interest rate of 5% per annum to the amortised cost at 1 January 2019 – i.e. 864 x 0.05.

EXAMPLE 26B – DELAY OF CASH FLOWS – NO IMMEDIATE WRITE-OFF

7.8.430.100   Modifying Example 26A, Bank N has an accounting policy not to write off a portion of a loan if it has no reasonable expectation of receiving a contractual amount when it is due.

7.8.430.110   Assuming that there is no change in expected cash flows at 31 December 2019, the following is a reconciliation of the loan's gross carrying amount, loss allowance and amortised cost during 2019.

	GROSS CARRYING AMOUNT	LOSS ALLOWANCE[1]	AMORTISED COST
Balance at 1 January 2019	1,000	(136)	864
Interest income	43[2]	-	43
Interest write-off[3]	(43)	43	-
Balance at 31 December 2019	1,000	(93)	907

Notes

1. For simplicity, it is assumed that the total loss allowance relates only to the delay of cash flows.
2. Because the loan is credit-impaired, interest is calculated by applying the effective interest rate of 5% per annum to the amortised cost at 1 January 2019 – i.e. 864 x 0.05. It is initially recognised on the gross carrying amount.
3. Because there is no legal right to receive additional interest, the interest accrued in 2019 on the gross carrying amount is written off at the end of the year.

7.8.430.120   IFRS 9 does not provide guidance on the timing of recognising recoveries of amounts previously written off. Because a write-off constitutes a derecognition event, it appears that a threshold higher than symmetry with the criterion for writing off is required in order to recognise an expected recovery of an amount previously written off – i.e. an entity may not write back amounts written off merely because the write-off criterion is no longer met. We believe that an entity may use one of the following approaches to recognition of recoveries:

- when cash is received;
- when recovery is virtually certain; or
- an alternative probability-based approach.

7.8.430.130   Similarly, there is no guidance in IFRS 9 on the presentation of recoveries of amounts previously written off in a specific line item in the statement of profit or loss and OCI. It appears that an entity may (but is not required to) present such recoveries in the line item 'impairment losses, including reversals of impairment losses or impairment gains, determined in accordance with IFRS 9' (see 7.10.60). This is because these recoveries are similar in nature to reversals of impairment losses. When such amounts are material, we believe that they should be disclosed separately. [*IAS 1.82(ba), 97*]

7.8.440   INTERACTION BETWEEN ECLs AND INTEREST INCOME

7.8.440.10   There is a relationship between the guidance on the recognition of ECLs and the guidance on the recognition of interest income (see 7.7.410). The following diagram illustrates this interaction.

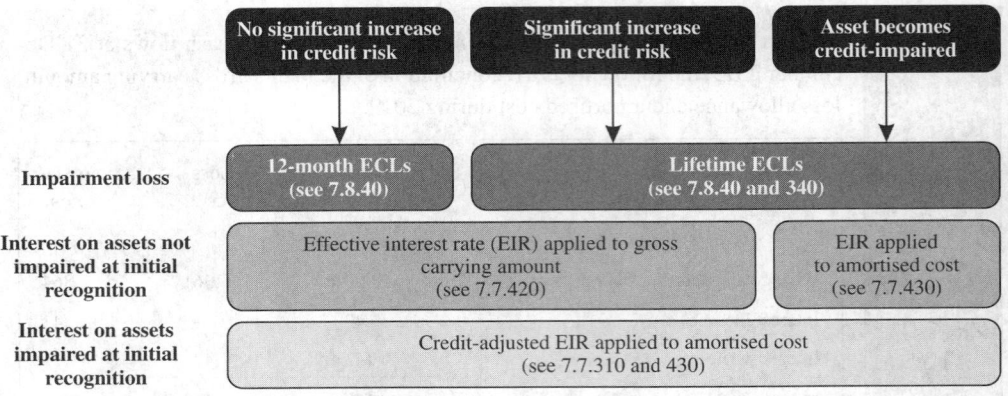

7.8.440.20   If there are significant improvements in expected recoveries on a credit-impaired financial asset, then the amount of the reversal of impairment may be more than the cumulative impairment loss recognised in profit or loss for the asset. This excess represents the reversal of all or some of the additional impairment allowance previously recognised in the statement of financial position as a result of the difference between the interest income recognised in profit or loss by applying the effective interest rate to the amortised cost and the increase in the gross carrying amount arising from applying the effective interest rate to the gross carrying amount while the asset is credit-impaired (see 7.7.430.30–70). In this case, it appears that all of the impairment reversal should be recognised in the impairment line in profit or loss – i.e. no amounts should be recognised in interest income. This is because the impairment gain or loss recognised in profit or loss is the amount of the ECLs (or reversal) that is required to adjust the loss allowance at the reporting date to the amount that is required to be recognised under IFRS 9 (see 7.8.160.50). [*IFRS 9.5.5.8, B5.4.6*]

EXAMPLE 27 – IMPAIRMENT REVERSAL

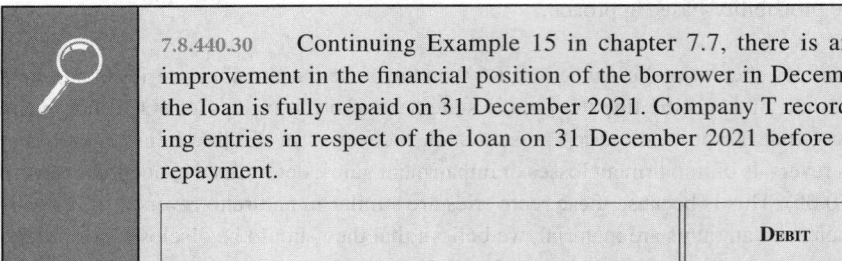

7.8.440.30   Continuing Example 15 in chapter 7.7, there is an unexpected improvement in the financial position of the borrower in December 2021 and the loan is fully repaid on 31 December 2021. Company T records the following entries in respect of the loan on 31 December 2021 before recording the repayment.

	DEBIT	CREDIT
Gross carrying amount	91[(1)]	
Interest income (profit or loss)		36[(2)]
ECL allowance		55[(3)]
To recognise interest income and the update of the gross carrying amount before reversing impairment		

	DEBIT	CREDIT
ECL allowance	601[4]	
Impairment reversal (profit or loss)		601
To recognise impairment reversal		

Notes

1. Calculated as the difference between the contractual amount repayable at 31 December 2021 and the gross carrying amount on 1 January 2021 – i.e. 1,000 - 909.
2. Calculated by applying the effective interest rate of 10% per annum to the amortised cost at 1 January 2021 – i.e. 363 x 10%.
3. Unwinding of discount on present value of ECLs.
4. Cumulative loss allowance at 31 December 2021 before impairment reversal.

7.8.440.40 The following table shows the reconciliation of the loan's gross carrying amount, amortised cost and loss allowance during 2021 before recording the repayment.

	GROSS CARRYING AMOUNT	LOSS ALLOWANCE	AMORTISED COST
Balance at 1 January 2021	909	(546)	363
Interest income	36	-	36
Unwinding of discount on present value of ECLs	55	(55)	-
Impairment reversal	-	601	601
Balance at 31 December 2021	1,000	-	1,000

7.9 Hedge accounting

7.9 Hedge accounting

CURRENTLY EFFECTIVE REQUIREMENTS

This publication reflects IFRS in issue at 1 August 2018, and the currently effective requirements cover annual periods beginning on or after 1 January 2018.

The requirements related to this topic are mainly derived from the following.

STANDARD	TITLE
IFRS 9	Financial Instruments
IAS 39	Financial Instruments: Recognition and Measurement
IFRIC 16	Hedges of a Net Investment in a Foreign Operation

FORTHCOMING REQUIREMENTS

For this topic, there are no forthcoming requirements.

FUTURE DEVELOPMENTS

This topic is subject to future developments that may affect aspects of macro hedge accounting. See 7.9.1260.

7.9.10   INTRODUCTION

7.9.10.10   The objective of hedge accounting is to represent, in the financial statements, the effect of an entity's risk management activities that use financial instruments to manage exposures arising from particular risks that could affect profit or loss or, in limited circumstances, OCI. [*IFRS 9.6.1.1*]

7.9.10.20   Entities enter into different transactions as part of their business activities, which expose them to different business risks. Although entities assume some of these risks as a part of their normal business activities, there are certain risks that they might want to eliminate or reduce to an acceptable level as part of their risk management activities.

7.9.10.30   Without hedge accounting, an entity that hedges economic exposures as part of its risk management activities might potentially record the hedging instrument and the hedged item on different bases. For example, under the model in IFRS 9 certain financial assets or financial liabilities are measured at amortised cost whereas derivatives, even if they hedge the risks arising from these financial assets or financial liabilities, are measured at FVTPL (see 7.7.140). This results in an accounting mismatch in profit or loss, which results in volatility in reported results.

7.9.10.40   Similarly, other standards require or permit assets and liabilities to be measured on bases other than FVTPL and certain contracts are recognised in financial statements only to the extent of performance (see 1.2.55). When an entity offsets the risks arising from these recognised assets and liabilities or unrecognised contracts by entering into derivatives, there is a resulting accounting mismatch in profit or loss. A similar issue arises when an entity seeks to manage risks relating to future transactions with derivatives.

7.9.10.50   Hedge accounting provides an accounting solution to the above issue. Accordingly, if an entity, as a part of its risk management activities, uses financial instruments to manage exposures arising from particular risks that could affect profit or loss or, in limited circumstances, OCI, then it may apply hedge accounting provided that all of the qualifying criteria in IFRS 9 are met. [*IFRS 9.6.1.1, BC6.82*]

7.9.10.60   If an entity applies hedge accounting, then it can measure its assets, liabilities and firm commitments on a different basis from that stipulated under other requirements of IFRS, or can defer the recognition in profit or loss of gains or losses on derivatives.

7.9.10.70   Three hedge accounting models are available, and the type of model applied depends on whether the hedged exposure is a fair value exposure, a cash flow exposure or a foreign currency exposure on a net investment in a foreign operation; these models are discussed in 7.9.140.

7.9.10.80   Although the objective of hedge accounting is to represent the effect of an entity's risk management activities in its financial statements, hedge accounting is voluntary. Consequently, an entity is not forced to align its accounting with its risk management activities if it does not wish to apply hedge accounting.

7.9.10.90   If an entity wishes to apply hedge accounting, then the accounting may be applied on a transaction-by-transaction basis or for a group of similar transactions. If an economic hedge does not qualify for hedge accounting, then any derivative used is measured at fair value with all changes in fair value recognised in profit or loss. These changes may not be offset by gains or losses on the hedged item when the hedged item is not also measured at FVTPL or the hedged item relates to future cash flow variability. In our view, an entity's risk management disclosures should contain appropriate explanation of economic hedges that do not qualify for hedge accounting (see 7.10.380.60). [*IFRS 7.31*]

7.9.20   Aligning hedge accounting with an entity's risk management objectives

7.9.20.10   IFRS 9 requires an entity's hedge accounting to be closely aligned with its actual risk management objectives. The hedge ratio is the quantity of the hedged item that the entity actually hedges vs the quantity of the hedging instrument that the entity actually uses to hedge that quantity of hedged item. In addition, an entity needs to rebalance its hedging relationships to maintain alignment with risk management. The entity is also prohibited from voluntarily de-designating a hedge accounting relationship that remains consistent with its risk management objectives (see 7.9.910 and 940.10). [*IFRS 9.6.1.1, 6.4.1, B6.5.15, B6.5.24*]

7.9.20.20   Judgement is involved in assessing how closely a hedge accounting designation needs to align with an entity's risk management objectives to be able to qualify for hedge accounting – e.g. IFRS 9 clarifies that some 'proxy hedging' strategies are permitted even if they do not exactly represent the actual risk management approach (see 7.9.30). [*IFRS 9.BCE.204*]

7.9.20.30   IFRS 9 distinguishes between an entity's risk management strategy and its risk management objectives. [*IFRS 9.B6.5.24*]

7.9.20.40   A 'risk management strategy' is established at the highest level at which an entity determines how it manages risk. It typically identifies the risks to which the entity is exposed and sets out how the entity responds to them. A risk management strategy is usually long-term in nature and may include flexibility to react to changes in circumstances – e.g. as interest rate or commodity price levels change over time, an entity may change its desired extent of hedging. Risk management strategies normally cascade down an entity through policies containing more specific guidelines. [*IFRS 9.B6.5.24*]

7.9.20.50   A 'risk management objective' applies at the hedging relationship level. A risk management strategy can involve many different hedging relationships (each with its own risk management objective) that contribute to executing the overall risk management strategy. [*IFRS 9.B6.5.24*]

7.9.30   Proxy hedging

7.9.30.10   'Proxy hedging' refers to using designations that do not exactly represent the actual risk management approach. For example:

- using a gross designation when risks are actually managed on a net position basis; or
- using designations of variable rate debt instruments when risk management is actually based on the interest rate risk of fixed rate debt instruments.

7.9.30.20   Under IFRS 9, it appears that it is acceptable in certain situations for the designation for hedge accounting purposes to differ from the entity's risk management view. In many situations, it is not possible to designate an exact 'one-to-one copy' of the actual risk management perspective, but it appears that hedge accounting may be permitted if the hedging designation reflects the same type of risk that is being managed and the instruments used for that purpose. For example, it appears that an entity is permitted to designate a hedge of interest rate risk on a gross basis, even though the risk is actually managed on a net basis. [*IFRS 9.BC6.96–BC6.101*]

7.9.30.30   The IFRS Interpretations Committee discussed whether an entity can continue to designate as a hedge the entire non-financial item on transition to IFRS 9 if its risk management objective is to hedge only a component of the non-financial item (see 7.11.225.30–70). [*IU 01-16*]

7.9.40   SCOPE AND ALTERNATIVES TO HEDGE ACCOUNTING

7.9.50   General hedge accounting

7.9.50.10   IFRS 9 includes requirements for general hedge accounting. 'General hedge accounting' refers to the accounting for hedging relationships that include a single hedged item or a closed portfolio of a group of items that constitute a gross or net position. A 'closed portfolio' is a portfolio to or from which items cannot be added, removed or substituted without treating each change as the transition to a new portfolio or a new layer. [*IFRS 9.IN10, BC6.84*]

7.9.50.20   However, an entity's risk management strategies often assess risk exposures on a continuous basis and at a portfolio level. Over time, new exposures are added to the hedged portfolios and other exposures are removed from them, which is why they are often referred to as 'open portfolios'. When an open portfolio is hedged as part of a risk management strategy, the general hedge accounting model can be applied by treating the open portfolio as a series of discrete closed portfolios, which exist for a shorter period than the overall risk management strategy's time horizon. That is, the hedging relationship will be periodically discontinued and a new relationship will be designated for the revised closed portfolio of items. [*IFRS 9.BC6.85–BC6.86*]

7.9.50.30   Although treating open portfolios as a series of discrete closed portfolios for accounting purposes is possible under IFRS 9, it gives rise to several complexities – e.g. tracking the individual hedging relationships, amortising the hedge adjustments and reclassifying gains or losses deferred in a separate component of equity. [*IFRS 9.BC6.86*]

7.9.50.40   Sometimes, it may be impracticable to fully align the accounting treatment with the way in which exposures are viewed from a risk management perspective, because the open portfolios actually hedged may be adjusted too frequently. [*IFRS 9.BC6.86*]

7.9.50.50   Applying risk management to open portfolios is often referred to as 'macro hedging'. Recognising that the new general hedge accounting model does not always work well when macro hedging is applied to open portfolios, the IASB has taken steps to further accommodate macro hedging strategies within IFRS (see 7.9.60 and 1260).

7.9.50.60   Although the general hedge accounting model in IFRS 9 is focused on hedging closed portfolios, it incorporates the following concepts that have an element of an open portfolio:
- applying hedge accounting to:
  - layers of cash flows;
  - net positions; and

–   nil net positions; and
●   rebalancing a hedging relationship's hedging instruments and hedged items.

7.9.60   Macro hedge accounting

7.9.60.10   As noted in 7.9.50.50, the IASB has a separate active project to address macro hedge accounting (see 7.9.1260). In the meantime, IFRS 9 carries forward specific requirements from IAS 39 for portfolio fair value hedges of interest rate risk and discusses so-called 'macro cash flow hedging strategies'.

7.9.70   *Portfolio fair value hedges of interest rate risk*

7.9.70.10   IAS 39 contains a separate hedge accounting model for fair value hedges of the interest rate exposure of open portfolios of financial assets or financial liabilities. This is sometimes described as 'portfolio fair value hedges of interest rate risk' (see 7.9.500). [*IAS 39.81A, 89A, AG114–AG132, BC173–BC174*]

7.9.70.20   An entity using the guidance for portfolio fair value hedges of interest rate risk applies all applicable hedge accounting requirements in IAS 39, including paragraphs 81A, 89A and AG114–AG132 (see 7.9.500). Those hedging relationships may continue unchanged on adoption of IFRS 9. [*IFRS 9.6.1.3, BC6.88, BC6.91, BC6.92(c)*]

7.9.70.30   Although IFRS 9 permits entities to continue to designate portfolio fair value hedges of interest rate risk under IAS 39, these hedging strategies are subject to new expanded disclosure requirements (see 7.10.380). [*IFRS 9.6.1.3, C11*]

7.9.70.40   Under IAS 39, some entities may have analogised to the guidance for portfolio fair value hedges of interest rate risk and designated portfolio fair value hedges of other risks – e.g. foreign exchange risk. However, IFRS 9 expressly limits the continued use of that guidance to portfolio fair value hedges of interest rate risk. [*IFRS 9.6.1.3*]

7.9.80   Option to continue to apply hedge accounting under IAS 39

7.9.80.10   It appears that the IASB's clarifications have removed several of the potential hurdles to designating macro cash flow hedging relationships under IFRS 9. However, in response to the remaining concerns of some constituents, IFRS 9 allows an entity to choose as its accounting policy to defer application of the new general hedging model and continue to apply the hedge accounting requirements of IAS 39 in their entirety until the standard resulting from the IASB's project on macro hedge accounting is effective (see 7.11.220). [*IFRS 9.7.2.21, BC6.102–BC6.104*]

7.9.90   Option to designate financial assets and financial liabilities as at FVTPL

7.9.90.10   When entering into a derivative transaction to eliminate or reduce a fair value risk exposure, an entity may find it easier to designate a potential hedged item that is a non-derivative financial asset or liability at FVTPL, rather than applying hedge accounting. Such a designation does not require the entity to perform an assessment of effectiveness; nor does it require rigorous documentation. However, the entity needs to comply with the conditions for applying the fair value option, which is irrevocable (see 7.4.390 and 7.5.40).

7.9.100 **Option to designate contracts to buy or sell non-financial items as at FVTPL**

7.9.100.10 To mitigate accounting mismatches and provide meaningful information in line with an entity's risk management approach, IFRS 9 allows an entity to irrevocably designate a contract to buy or sell a non-financial item that meets the own-use exception (see 7.1.200) – at inception of the contract – as measured at FVTPL. An entity may make the designation only if it eliminates or significantly reduces an accounting mismatch that would otherwise arise if the contract were accounted for as an unrecognised executory contract (see 7.1.200). [*IFRS 9.2.5*]

7.9.110 **Managing credit risk using credit derivatives**

7.9.120 *Option to designate credit exposure as at FVTPL*

7.9.120.10 Many financial institutions use credit derivatives to manage credit risk exposures arising from their lending activities, but they often do not meet the hedge accounting requirements. This is because it is often very difficult or impossible to isolate credit risk in a way that allows the change in fair value that is attributable solely to credit risk to be separately identifiable. [*IFRS 9.BC6.469–BC6.470, BC6.500–BC6.504*]

7.9.120.20 To accommodate the management of credit risk, IFRS 9 introduces a new option to designate certain credit exposures as at FVTPL as a substitute for hedge accounting. Under this option, if an entity uses a credit derivative that is measured at FVTPL to manage the credit risk of all (or a part) of a credit exposure, then it may designate that credit exposure (or a proportion of it) as at FVTPL. If only part of the credit risk of a credit exposure is managed using a credit derivative that is measured at FVTPL, then the credit exposure is measured at FVTPL only to the extent that it is managed using a credit derivative. [*IFRS 9.6.7.1, BC6.543–BC6.544*]

7.9.120.30 A credit exposure may be a financial instrument in or outside the scope of IFRS 9 that is managed for credit risk – e.g. a loan commitment. The designation can be made only if:
- the name of the credit exposure – e.g. the borrower or the holder of a loan commitment – matches the reference entity of the credit derivative ('name matching'); and
- the seniority of the financial instrument matches that of the instruments that can be delivered in accordance with the credit derivative. [*IFRS 9.6.7.1*]

7.9.120.40 An entity may make the designation on initial recognition or subsequently, or while the financial instrument is unrecognised – e.g. an unrecognised loan commitment. The entity is required to document the designation concurrently, although the level of detail for this documentation is not specified. [*IFRS 9.6.7.1*]

EXAMPLE 1 – DESIGNATING PROPORTION OF LOAN COMMITMENT AS AT FVTPL

7.9.120.50 Bank B extends a fixed rate loan commitment of 900 to a customer. The loan commitment does not net settle, and B does not have a past practice of selling the loans resulting from similar commitments. B's risk management strategy is to mitigate the credit risk exposure of any individual loan commitment to the extent that it exceeds 500. Therefore, B enters into a CDS of 400 related to the potential borrower.

7.9.120.60   B accounts for the CDS of 400 at FVTPL, as it would for any other derivative. Although B does not recognise the loan commitment (see 7.1.250) it can elect to designate the proportion of the loan commitment that exceeds 500, provided that certain conditions are met. If B elects to do so, then it accounts for the 400 / 900 proportion of the loan commitment at FVTPL, and thereby is able to offset the changes in fair value of the CDS.

EXAMPLE 2 – DESIGNATING DEBT INVESTMENT AFTER INITIAL RECOGNITION AS AT FVTPL

7.9.120.70   Company X invests in the debt of Company Z and measures it at amortised cost. One year after making this investment, X decides to mitigate Z's credit risk with a CDS.

7.9.120.80   X accounts for the CDS at FVTPL, as it would for any other derivative. If certain conditions are met, then X can elect to designate the debt investment as at FVTPL after its initial recognition – thereby providing an offset in profit or loss to the future changes in fair value of the CDS. However, any difference between the carrying amount of the debt and its fair value at the election date is recognised in profit or loss, which does not have a corresponding profit or loss offset (see 7.9.130).

7.9.120.90   In Examples 1 and 2, the profit or loss offset available under IFRS 9 is not perfect, because risks other than credit risk – e.g. interest rates – affect the fair value of the item that has been designated as at FVTPL differently from their effect on the CDS.

7.9.130   *Accounting for credit exposures designated as at FVTPL*

7.9.130.10   If a financial instrument is designated as at FVTPL after its initial recognition, or was not previously recognised, then any difference between the carrying amount – e.g. zero if the financial instrument was previously unrecognised – and the fair value at the time of designation is recognised immediately in profit or loss. [*IFRS 9.6.7.2*]

7.9.130.20   An entity discontinues measuring the financial instrument that gave rise to the credit risk, or a proportion of that financial instrument, at FVTPL if:
- the conditions described in 7.9.120.30 (i.e. name matching and seniority) are no longer met – for example:
  - the credit derivative expires or is sold, terminated or settled; or
  - the credit risk of the financial instrument is no longer managed using credit derivatives – e.g. because of improvements in the credit quality of the borrower or the loan commitment holder or changes to capital requirements imposed on an entity; and
- the financial instrument that gives rise to the credit risk is not otherwise required to be measured at FVTPL – i.e. the entity's business model has not changed in the meantime in such a way that reclassification to FVTPL is required. [*IFRS 9.6.7.3*]

7.9.130.30   When the discontinuation criteria are met (see 7.9.130.20), discontinuation of the fair value designation is mandatory. This ensures alignment with the way in which the exposure is managed. [*IFRS 9.BC6.478*]

7.9.130.40   On discontinuation, the fair value of the financial instrument at the date of discontinuation becomes its new carrying amount. Subsequently, the same measurement basis that was used before designating the financial instrument at FVTPL is applied, including amortisation that results from the new carrying amount. For example, a financial asset that had originally been classified as measured at amortised cost reverts to that measurement and its effective interest rate is recalculated based on its new gross carrying amount on the date of discontinuation (7.7.390). Similarly, a loan commitment or a financial guarantee contract that is not designated as at FVTPL is measured at the higher of:

- the amount determined in accordance with the impairment requirements of IFRS 9 (see chapter 7.8); and
- the new carrying amount at the date of discontinuation less the cumulative amount of income recognised in accordance with IFRS 15 (see chapter 4.2). [*IFRS 9.6.7.4*]

7.9.130.45   IFRS 9 specifies the cases in which revocation of designation is required and does not include any permission for voluntarily de-designation. In our view, the designation of a credit exposure as at FVTPL cannot be voluntarily revoked. This option is included in IFRS 9 as an alternative to hedge accounting because credit risk of a financial item is not a risk component that meets the eligibility criteria for hedged items. [*IFRS 9.BC6.470*]

7.9.130.50   Because an entity may make the fair value designation for a credit exposure after its initial recognition, some time after discontinuation an entity may make a new fair value designation if it meets the qualifying criteria again (see 7.9.120.40). [*IFRS 9.BC6.481*]

EXAMPLE 3 – ELECTING FVTPL TO REFLECT RISK MANAGEMENT STRATEGY

7.9.130.60   Company R uses a credit derivative to manage the deteriorating credit quality of a loan receivable. The following facts are relevant for this example.

- On 15 June 2018, the qualifying criteria are met and R designates the loan as at FVTPL.
- On 30 October 2018:
  - the credit risk of the loan improves and R sells the credit derivative; and
  - the fair value of the loan becomes the new gross carrying amount, and the loan is subsequently measured at amortised cost.
- On 15 November 2018:
  - the credit risk of the loan deteriorates again and R buys a new credit derivative to protect its exposure; and
  - R designates the loan at FVTPL (again). The difference between the amortised cost and fair value of the loan at the date of designation is recognised in profit or loss, thereby creating potential profit or loss volatility.

7.9.130.70   This accounting outcome reflects R's risk management strategy of using credit derivatives to protect against the exposures when the credit quality of the loans drops below a certain level.

7.9.140   HEDGE ACCOUNTING MODELS

7.9.140.10   There are three types of hedging relationships:
- fair value hedge;

- cash flow hedge; and
- net investment hedge. [*IFRS 9.6.5.2*]

7.9.140.20   In addition, IFRS 9 permits an entity to designate portfolio fair value hedges of interest rate risk (see 7.9.500). [*IFRS 9.6.1.3*]

7.9.150   Fair value hedges

7.9.160   *Definition*

7.9.160.10   A 'fair value hedge' is a hedge of the exposure to changes in fair value of a recognised asset or liability or an unrecognised firm commitment, or a component of any such item, that is attributable to a particular risk and could affect:

- profit or loss; or
- OCI, if the hedged item is an equity investment for which the entity has elected to present changes in fair value in OCI (see 7.4.420). [*IFRS 9.6.5.2(a), 6.5.3*]

7.9.160.20   The following are examples of fair value hedges:

- using an interest rate swap to hedge the interest rate risk of a fixed rate interest-bearing asset or liability; and
- using a forward contract to hedge the commodity price risk or foreign exchange risk of a firm commitment to purchase an asset or to incur a liability. [*IFRS 9.6.3.1, B6.5.1, B6.5.3*]

7.9.160.30   A hedge of the foreign currency risk of a firm commitment may be accounted for as either a fair value hedge or a cash flow hedge, although in our experience cash flow hedging is applied more commonly. Fair value hedge accounting can be applied only if there is a firm commitment. Consequently, if a highly probable forecast transaction exists before an entity enters into a firm commitment, then the hedge is accounted for as a cash flow hedge until the entity enters into a firm commitment, from which time it can be accounted for as a fair value hedge. Generally, it is simpler to implement a single model for hedge accounting purposes, rather than having to switch models during the life of the hedge. [*IFRS 9.6.5.4, B6.5.3*]

7.9.170   *Accounting*

7.9.170.10   The hedging instrument is measured at fair value with changes in fair value recognised in profit or loss, or in OCI if the hedging instrument hedges an equity investment for which the entity has elected to present changes in fair value in OCI (see 7.4.420). As an exception, if the hedging instrument is the foreign currency risk component of a non-derivative financial asset or a non-derivative financial liability designated in a hedge of foreign currency risk, then the hedging instrument is measured for foreign currency risk at the spot rate in accordance with IAS 21 (see 2.7.80) with the gain or loss recognised in profit or loss or OCI, as appropriate. [*IFRS 9.6.2.2, 6.5.8(a), B6.2.3*]

7.9.170.20   The hedged item is remeasured to fair value in respect of the hedged risk during the period of the hedging relationship using the guidance in IFRS 13 (see chapter 2.4), even if it is normally measured at amortised cost – e.g. a fixed rate borrowing. Any resulting adjustment to the carrying amount of the hedged item related to the hedged risk is recognised in profit or loss, even if this change would normally be recognised in OCI – e.g. for a financial asset measured at FVOCI (see 7.10.330). However, if the hedged item is an equity investment for which the entity has elected to present changes in fair value in OCI (see 7.4.420), then those amounts remain in OCI. In our view, the categorisation of the fair value hedge adjustment as either a monetary or a non-monetary item should be consistent with the categorisation of the hedged item under IAS 21 (see 2.7.120). [*IFRS 9.6.5.3, 6.5.8(b)*]

7.9.170.30   On entering into a firm commitment, an entity would not typically recognise the commitment in the statement of financial position. However, for a hedge of a firm commitment (or a component thereof), fair value hedge accounting results in the change in the fair value of the firm commitment attributable to the hedged risk during the period of the hedging relationship being recognised as an asset or a liability in the statement of financial position, with a corresponding gain or loss recognised in profit or loss. [*IFRS 9.6.5.8(b)*]

7.9.170.40   When a hedged item in a fair value hedge is a firm commitment (or a component thereof) to acquire an asset or assume a liability, the initial carrying amount of the asset or liability that results from the entity meeting the commitment is adjusted to include the cumulative change in the fair value of the hedged item that was recognised in the statement of financial position. [*IFRS 9.6.5.9*]

7.9.170.50   The adjustment to the carrying amount of the hedged item in a fair value hedge often results in the item being measured neither at cost nor at fair value. This is because the adjustment:
- is made only for changes attributable to the risk being hedged – i.e. not for all risks;
- occurs only during the period in which hedge accounting is applied; and
- is limited to the extent to which the item is hedged. [*IFRS 9.6.3.7, 6.5.8(b)*]

EXAMPLE 4 – HEDGED ITEM MEASURED NEITHER AT COST NOR AT FAIR VALUE

7.9.170.60   Company Z has a fixed interest liability denominated in its functional currency and measured at amortised cost. Z enters into a pay-LIBOR receive-fixed interest rate swap to hedge half of the notional amount of the liability in respect of its benchmark interest exposure. The swap qualifies for hedge accounting.

7.9.170.70   Half of the liability – i.e. the proportion that is hedged – will be remeasured by Z with respect to changes in fair value arising from changes in benchmark interest rates from the beginning of the hedging relationship. Z does not remeasure the liability for any changes in fair value arising from changes in credit spread, liquidity spread or other factors.

7.9.170.80   In a fair value hedge, any ineffectiveness is automatically recognised in profit or loss – or in OCI, if the hedging instrument hedges an equity investment for which the entity has elected to present changes in fair value in OCI – because changes in the measurement of both the hedging instrument and the hedged item are reported through profit or loss (or OCI). This is different from a cash flow hedge, in which the ineffectiveness is calculated and recognised separately (see 7.9.200). [*IFRS 9.6.5.8, 6.5.11*]

7.9.170.90   Any adjustment arising from 7.9.170.20 and 40 is amortised to profit or loss if the hedged item is a financial instrument (or a component thereof) measured at amortised cost. If the hedged item is a financial asset, other than an equity investment, that is measured at FVOCI, then the amount amortised is the cumulative gain or loss previously recognised in profit or loss in accordance with 7.9.170.20. Amortisation may begin as soon as an adjustment exists, and begins no later than when the hedged item ceases to be adjusted for hedging gains and losses. Amortisation is based on a recalculated effective interest rate at the date on which amortisation begins. [*IFRS 9.6.5.10*]

EXAMPLE 5 – AMORTISATION OF FAIR VALUE HEDGE ADJUSTMENT TO FINANCIAL ASSET MEASURED AT FVOCI

7.9.170.100   Company Y, which has the Canadian dollar as its functional currency, invests in a newly issued 5% CAD 1,000 bond on 1 January 2018, which matures on 31 December 2020. Y measures the bond at FVOCI. On the same date, Y also enters into a one-year forward to hedge the notional amount of the bond in respect of changes in the market yield on the bond. The forward qualifies for hedge accounting.

7.9.170.110   On 31 December 2018, the market yield on the bond increases by 1%. Therefore, Y recognises CAD 18 (CAD 1,000 notional at inception minus the present value of remaining cash flows discounted at the market yield of 6%) as the fair value change of the bond that resulted from changes in the market yield. Y amortises CAD 18 in 2019 and 2020 (CAD 9 over each year).

7.9.170.120   For a discussion of the accounting when an entity discontinues hedge accounting for a fair value hedge, see 7.9.930.

7.9.180   Cash flow hedges

7.9.190   *Definition*

7.9.190.10   A 'cash flow hedge' is a hedge of the exposure to variability in cash flows that is attributable to a particular risk associated with all of, or a component of, a recognised asset or liability (such as all or some future interest payments on variable rate debt) or a highly probable forecast transaction, and could affect profit or loss. [*IFRS 9.6.5.2(b)*]

7.9.190.20   The following are examples of cash flow hedges:
- using an interest rate swap to hedge the interest rate risk of a floating rate interest-bearing asset or liability;
- using a forward contract to hedge the foreign currency risk of foreign currency denominated future operating lease or payroll payments; and
- using a forward contract to hedge the commodity price risk of highly probable forecast purchase or sale transactions. [*IFRS 9.B6.5.2–B6.5.3*]

7.9.200   *Accounting*

7.9.200.10   If the hedging instrument is a derivative or a non-derivative financial asset or non-derivative financial liability measured at FVTPL, then the effective portion of changes in fair value of the hedging instrument is recognised in OCI. The ineffective portion of the gain or loss on the hedging instrument is recognised immediately in profit or loss. [*IFRS 9.6.2.2, 6.5.11*]

7.9.200.20   If the hedging instrument is the foreign currency risk component of a non-derivative financial asset or non-derivative financial liability designated in a hedge of foreign currency risk, then the effective portion of gains and losses on the foreign currency risk component of the hedging instrument determined in accordance with IAS 21 (see 2.7.80) is recognised in OCI. The ineffective portion of the gain or loss is recognised immediately in profit or loss. [*IFRS 9.6.2.2, 6.5.11, B6.2.3*]

7.9.200.30   The separate component of equity associated with the hedged item – i.e. the cash flow hedge reserve – is adjusted to the lower of the following (in absolute amounts):
- the cumulative gain or loss on the hedging instrument from inception of the hedging relationship. This is the cumulative change in fair value or, if the hedging instrument is a non-derivative financial asset or a non-derivative financial liability designated in a hedge of foreign currency risk, the cumulative remeasurement for foreign currency risk at the spot rate in accordance with IAS 21 (see 2.7.80); and
- the cumulative change in fair value (present value) of the hedged item from inception of the hedging relationship. This is the present value of the cumulative change in the hedged expected future cash flows. [*IFRS 9.6.5.11(a)(i)–(ii)*]

7.9.200.40   The portion of the gain or loss on the hedging instrument that is determined to be an effective hedge – i.e. the portion that is offset by the change in the cash flow hedge reserve calculated in accordance with 7.9.200.10 – is recognised in OCI. [*IFRS 9.6.5.11(b)*]

7.9.200.50   Any remaining gain or loss on the hedging instrument – or any gain or loss required to balance the change in the cash flow hedge reserve calculated in accordance with 7.9.200.10 – is hedge ineffectiveness that is recognised in profit or loss. [*IFRS 9.6.5.11(c)*]

7.9.200.60   The amount that has been accumulated in the cash flow hedge reserve in accordance with 7.9.200.10 is accounted for as explained in 7.9.200.70–90.

7.9.200.70   If a hedged forecast transaction subsequently results in the recognition of a non-financial asset or non-financial liability, or a hedged forecast transaction for a non-financial asset or non-financial liability becomes a firm commitment for which fair value hedge accounting is applied, then the entity removes the accumulated amount from the cash flow hedge reserve and includes it directly in the initial cost or other carrying amount of the asset or liability. This is not a reclassification adjustment and therefore it does not affect OCI. [*IFRS 9.6.5.11(d)(i)*]

7.9.200.80   For cash flow hedges other than those covered in 7.9.200.70, the accumulated amount is reclassified from the cash flow hedge reserve to profit or loss as a reclassification adjustment (see 4.1.240.70) in the period or periods during which the hedged expected future cash flows affect profit or loss – e.g. in the periods during which interest income or interest expense is recognised or when a forecast sale occurs. [*IFRS 9.6.5.11(d)(ii)*]

7.9.200.90   The standard is not explicit about the manner in which gains or losses should be reclassified from the cash flow hedge reserve when the forecast transaction impacts multiple periods or when there are multiple forecast transactions that impact multiple periods. Therefore, in our view an entity should develop a systematic and rational method based on its risk management objective for determining the amounts to be reclassified in each reporting period if the hedged cash flows affect profit or loss in multiple reporting periods. [*IFRS 9.6.5.11(d)(ii)*]

EXAMPLE 6 – RECLASSIFYING GAINS AND LOSSES ON A CASH FLOW HEDGE

7.9.200.100 On 31 December 2018, Company D issues a floating rate bond that bears interest based on a benchmark rate payable annually and matures on 31 December 2022. The bond is issued at par of 1,000. In accordance with its risk management strategy, D enters into a four-year pay-fixed 3% receive-benchmark interest rate swap on 31 December 2018. On the same date, D designates the swap as a cash flow hedge of the variability of future interest payments on the bond attributable to changes in the benchmark rate. The timing of the swap's cash flows matches those of the bond. The fair value of the swap at inception is zero.

7.9.200.110 The effects of credit risk are insignificant to the effectiveness of the hedging relationship and there are no sources of ineffectiveness during the hedging period. Therefore, all gains and losses on remeasurement of the swap to fair value are included in OCI.

7.9.200.120 Considering its risk management objective and how the effective interest method is applied to a floating rate liability, D determines that it will reclassify an amount from OCI to profit or loss during each period reflecting the time-based accrual of the net coupon payable or receivable on the swap. Therefore, in each year it reclassifies amounts equal to the net settlements on the swap.

7.9.200.130 However, if the accumulated amount is a loss and the entity expects that all or a portion of that loss will not be recovered in one or more future periods, then it immediately reclassifies the amount that is not expected to be recovered into profit or loss as a reclassification adjustment (see 4.1.240.70). [*IFRS 9.6.5.11(d)(iii)*]

7.9.200.140 For a discussion of the accounting when an entity discontinues hedge accounting for a cash flow hedge, see 7.9.960.30.

7.9.210 **Net investment hedges**

7.9.210.10 IFRS 9 does not override the principles of IAS 21 (see chapter 2.7), but it does provide a model for hedging an entity's foreign currency exposure arising from net investments in foreign operations.

7.9.220 *Definition*

7.9.220.10 A 'net investment hedge' is a hedge of a net investment in a foreign operation as defined in IAS 21 (see 2.7.170) for the foreign currency exposure arising when the net assets of that foreign operation are included in the financial statements. [*IFRS 9.6.5.2(c)*]

7.9.220.20 The hedged risk is the foreign currency exposure arising from a net investment in a foreign operation when the net assets of that foreign operation are included in the financial statements (see 7.9.1030).

7.9.220.30   Often the exposure to changes in the value of a net investment arising from movements in foreign exchange rates is hedged through borrowings denominated in the foreign operation's functional currency or, in more limited circumstances, derivative currency contracts.

7.9.230   *Accounting*

7.9.230.10   A net investment hedge, including a hedge of a monetary item that is accounted for as part of the net investment (see 2.7.150.10), is accounted for similarly to a cash flow hedge:
- the portion of the gain or loss on the hedging instrument that is determined to be an effective hedge is recognised in OCI; and
- the ineffective portion is recognised in profit or loss. [*IFRS 9.6.5.13(a)–(b)*]

7.9.230.15   The IFRS Interpretations Committee observed that, when accounting for a net investment hedge, an entity should apply the 'lower of' test in determining the effective portion of the gains or losses arising from the hedging instrument (see 7.9.200.30) and that this avoids the recycling of exchange differences arising from the hedged item before the disposal of the foreign operation. [*IU 03-16, IFRS 9.6.5.13(a)*]

7.9.230.20   If the hedging instrument in a net investment hedge is a derivative, then it is measured at fair value. The effective portion of the change in its fair value – computed with reference to the functional currency of the parent entity against whose functional currency the hedged risk is measured – is recognised in OCI and presented within equity in the foreign currency translation reserve (see 2.7.260). The ineffective portion of the gain or loss on the hedging instrument is recognised immediately in profit or loss. [*IFRS 9.6.5.13, IFRIC 16.3, 15*]

7.9.230.30   If the hedging instrument is a non-derivative – e.g. a foreign currency borrowing – then the effective portion of the foreign exchange gain or loss arising on translation of the hedging instrument under IAS 21 into the functional currency of the hedging entity is recognised in OCI and presented within equity in the foreign currency translation reserve (see 2.7.260). The effective portion is computed with reference to the functional currency of the parent entity against whose functional currency the hedged risk is measured. [*IFRS 9.6.5.13, B6.2.3, B6.5.4, IFRIC 16.15*]

7.9.230.40   On disposal of a net investment in a foreign operation, the cumulative foreign exchange differences arising on translation of the foreign operation, and the effective portion of the gain or loss on the hedging instrument presented within equity in the foreign currency translation reserve (the 'cumulative amounts'), are treated as follows.
- On disposal of the entire interest in a foreign operation or disposal of part of an ownership interest that results in the entity losing control over the entity that includes the foreign operation (see 2.7.340), or on the cessation of equity accounting, the cumulative amounts previously recognised in OCI are reclassified to profit or loss and no amount of the reclassification is allocated to NCI (see 2.5.760.40). As an exception, when a parent loses control of a subsidiary by contributing it to an associate or joint venture and elects to eliminate the part of the gain or loss in respect of the continuing interest in the assets and liabilities contributed, then in our view only a proportionate share of the cumulative amounts previously recognised in OCI should be reclassified to profit or loss (see 3.5.470).

- When an entity partially disposes of a subsidiary that includes a foreign operation, but retains control, the entity re-attributes a proportionate share of the cumulative amounts previously recognised in OCI to NCI (see 2.7.340.140).
- In any other partial disposal of a foreign operation, the entity reclassifies to profit or loss only a proportionate share of the cumulative amounts previously recognised in OCI (see 2.7.340.150). [*IAS 21.48–49, IFRS 9.6.5.14, IFRIC 16.6, 16–17*]

7.9.230.50   Therefore, it is necessary for an entity to keep track of the amount recognised in OCI separately in respect of each foreign operation, to identify the amounts to be reclassified to profit or loss on disposal or partial disposal.

7.9.230.60   The method of consolidation – i.e. the step-by-step or the direct method – may affect the amount that is included in the foreign currency translation reserve for an individual foreign operation. When the step-by-step method of consolidation is applied, it may lead to the reclassification to profit or loss of an amount that is different from the amount used to assess hedge effectiveness. An entity may eliminate this difference by retrospectively determining the amount that would have resulted from using the direct method of consolidation. The amount so determined would then be reclassified from equity to profit or loss on disposal or partial disposal, as discussed in 7.9.230.40. This adjustment is not required by IAS 21. However, an entity needs to choose an accounting policy, to be applied consistently, for all net investments (see 2.7.340.20). [*IFRIC 16.17*]

7.9.230.70   For a discussion of the accounting when an entity discontinues hedge accounting for a net investment hedge, see 7.9.940.90.

7.9.240   Hedge accounting criteria

7.9.240.10   A hedging relationship qualifies for hedge accounting only if all of the following criteria are met:
- the hedging relationship consists only of eligible hedging instruments (see 7.9.560) and eligible hedged items (see 7.9.290);
- at inception of the hedging relationship, there is formal designation and documentation of the hedging relationship and the entity's risk management objective and strategy for undertaking the hedge. This documentation should include:
  - the identification of the hedging instrument;
  - the identification of the hedged item;
  - the nature of the risk being hedged; and
  - how the entity will assess whether the hedging relationship meets the hedge effectiveness requirements (see 7.9.790), including its analysis of the sources of hedge ineffectiveness and how it determines the hedge ratio; and
- the hedging relationship meets all of the hedge effectiveness requirements discussed in 7.9.790. [*IFRS 9.6.4.1*]

7.9.240.20   IFRS 9 does not mandate a specific format for the documentation, and in our experience hedge documentation may vary in terms of layout, methodology and processes used. Various formats are acceptable as long as the documentation includes the content listed in 7.9.240.10.

7.9.250   **Flexibility in type of hedge accounting**

7.9.250.10   In some cases, a hedge can be designated either as a cash flow hedge or as a fair value hedge. The following examples demonstrate this.

- A hedge of the foreign currency risk of a firm commitment may be designated as a fair value hedge or as a cash flow hedge.
- A forward contract to buy foreign currency may be designated as the hedging instrument in a fair value hedge of a foreign currency financial liability, or alternatively in a cash flow hedge of the forecast settlement of that liability.
- A receive-fixed pay-floating interest rate swap may be designated as a fair value hedge of a fixed interest liability or as a cash flow hedge of a variable interest asset. However, the interest rate swap cannot be designated as a cash flow hedge of a fixed interest liability because it converts known (fixed) interest cash outflows, for which there is no exposure to variability in cash flows, into unknown (variable) interest cash outflows. Similarly, the swap cannot be designated as a fair value hedge of a variable interest asset because a variable interest instrument is not exposed to changes in fair value arising from changes in market interest rates.
- A purchased put option on a commodity may be designated as the hedging instrument in a fair value hedge of the commodity inventory or, alternatively, in a cash flow hedge of a forecast sale of the commodity inventory when such a sale is highly probable to occur. [*IFRS 9.6.5.2, 6.5.4*]

7.9.250.20   The designation is determined at inception of the hedge. [*IFRS 9.6.4.1*]

7.9.250.30   Although the net profit or loss effect of a hedging relationship will ultimately be the same regardless of the type of hedge accounting applied, the timing of recognition in the statement of financial position and in profit or loss and the nature of the accounting adjustments made will differ. Therefore, it is important to choose the model at inception of the hedge and to designate and document the hedge accordingly.

7.9.250.40   The decision regarding which hedge accounting model to use may also be influenced by an entity's information systems. The entity assesses whether its existing information systems are best set up to manage and track the information required under a fair value hedge model or a cash flow hedge model. This decision may also depend on the characteristics of the hedged items and whether the hedge accounting criteria can be met.

7.9.250.50   Under a fair value hedge model, an asset or liability designated as a hedged item is re-measured for fair value changes attributable to the hedged risk. For exposure to an interest-sensitive rate (assets and liabilities), the original effective interest rate is modified through the amortisation of this 'hedge adjustment'. This usually requires a system that is able to track changes in the hedged risk and that can calculate associated changes in the fair value of the hedged item. Also, the system should be able to recompute the effective yield of the hedged item and amortise the changes to profit or loss over the remaining life of the hedged item.

7.9.250.60   Under a cash flow hedge model, the ineffective portion is calculated separately and recognised in profit or loss. However, the effective portion of the fair value changes of the hedging instrument is recognised in OCI and is reclassified to profit or loss only when the hedged expected cash flows affect profit or loss (see 7.9.200), or the amount is a loss and the entity expects that all or a portion of that loss will not be recovered in one or more future periods. In addition, it is necessary to demonstrate that forecast transactions are highly probable. This requires a system that enables an entity to track the timing of the cash flows of the hedged item, as well as the timing of the reclassification of the hedging gains and losses from equity. Although this may prove a challenge, for many entities this information can be based on the cash flow information already captured in their risk management systems. [*IFRS 9.6.5.11*]

7.9.260 When hedge accounting is not necessary

7.9.260.10   In some cases, there is no accounting mismatch and therefore hedge accounting is not necessary. Examples include:
- hedges of recognised foreign currency monetary items with offsetting monetary items – the remeasurement of both items with respect to changes in foreign exchange rates is required to be recognised in profit or loss; and
- hedges of changes in the fair value of instruments measured at FVTPL – both the hedged item and derivative hedging instruments are remeasured to FVTPL.

7.9.270 Income taxes

7.9.270.10   For transactions recognised directly in equity or in OCI, all current and deferred taxes are also recognised in equity or in OCI (see 3.13.530). In respect of hedge accounting, this means that current and deferred taxes on gains or losses on hedging instruments recognised in OCI in a cash flow or net investment hedge are also recognised in OCI until such time as the gain or loss is reclassified to profit or loss. [*IAS 12.61A*]

7.9.280 HEDGED RISKS AND ITEMS

7.9.290 Qualifying hedged items

7.9.290.10   The hedged item is the item that is exposed to the specific risk(s) that an entity has chosen to hedge based on its risk management activities. To qualify for hedge accounting, the hedged item needs to be reliably measurable. A 'hedged item' can be:
- a single recognised asset or liability, unrecognised firm commitment, highly probable forecast transaction or net investment in a foreign operation;
- a group of recognised assets or liabilities, unrecognised firm commitments, highly probable forecast transactions or net investments in a foreign operation, if they meet certain conditions (see 7.9.400); or
- aggregated exposures – i.e. a combination of a non-derivative exposure and a derivative exposure (see 7.9.420). [*IFRS 9.6.1.3, 6.3.1–6.3.4*]

7.9.290.20   For a fair value hedge of the interest rate exposure of a portfolio of financial assets or financial liabilities, the hedged item can be a portion that is a currency amount (see 7.9.500).

7.9.290.30   To qualify as hedged items, assets, liabilities, firm commitments and highly probable ⑤ forecast transactions need to involve a party external to the entity. Hedge accounting can be applied to transactions between entities in the same group only in the individual or separate financial statements of those entities and not in the consolidated financial statements of the group. However, as an exception, the foreign currency risk of an intra-group monetary item – e.g. a foreign currency-denominated payable or receivable between two subsidiaries – may qualify as a hedged item in the consolidated financial statements if it results in an exposure to foreign exchange rate gains or losses that are not fully eliminated on consolidation (see 7.9.1170). [*IFRS 9.6.3.5–6.3.6*]

7.9.300   Designating hedged items

7.9.300.10   An entity can designate an item as a hedged item for the purposes of hedge accounting if it meets the eligibility criteria (see 7.9.290). [*IFRS 9.6.3.1, 6.3.7*]

7.9.300.20   An entity can designate an item in its entirety or a component of an item as the hedged item. However, only the following types of components, or any combination thereof, may be designated:
- risk components that are separately identifiable and reliably measureable (see 7.9.310);
- one or more selected contractual cash flows – e.g. hedging the coupon payments on financial liabilities for all risks (see 7.9.360); and/or
- components of nominal amounts (see 7.9.370). [*IFRS 9.6.3.7*]

7.9.300.30   To qualify for hedge accounting, the hedged risk should ultimately be capable of affecting either profit or loss or OCI, if the hedged item is an equity investment for which the entity has elected to present changes in fair value in OCI (see 7.4.420). [*IFRS 9.6.3.6, 6.5.2–6.5.3*]

7.9.300.40   The designation of a hedging instrument for only a portion of the time that it remains outstanding is specifically prohibited (see 7.9.580). However, an entity may designate a financial instrument as the hedged item for only a portion of its period to maturity. It is possible to designate a hedging relationship after initial recognition of the hedged item, hedging instrument or both. [*IFRS 9.6.2.4, B6.3.3, B6.5.29(b)*]

7.9.300.50   An entity's own equity instruments under IAS 32 may not be designated as the hedged item in either a fair value or a cash flow hedge, because changes in fair value or cash flows arising from these instruments do not affect profit or loss (see 7.9.530). [*IFRS 9.6.5.2*]

7.9.300.60   Equity investments for which an entity has elected to present changes in fair value in OCI may qualify as hedged items in a fair value hedge (see 7.9.490). [*IFRS 9.6.5.2–6.5.3*]

7.9.300.70   A forecast purchase of an equity instrument that, once acquired, will be accounted for at FVTPL or at FVOCI cannot be designated as a hedged item in a cash flow hedge (see 7.9.520). In our view, a highly probable purchase of additional foreign currency-denominated shares in a subsidiary – i.e. buying additional shares in a controlled entity – may qualify as the hedged item because the acquisition of additional shares will impact profit or loss when the shares are disposed of. Also, a net investment in a foreign operation in the consolidated financial statements may qualify as the hedged item for foreign exchange risk (see 7.9.470). [*IFRS 9.B6.5.2*]

7.9.310   Risk components

7.9.310.10   Risk components include the changes in the cash flows or fair value of an item attributable to a specific risk or risks. To be eligible for designation as a hedged item, a risk component needs to meet the following criteria:

- it is a separately identifiable component of the financial or non-financial item; and
- the changes in the cash flows or fair value of the item attributable to changes in that risk component are reliably measurable. [*IFRS 9.6.3.7(a), B6.3.8*]

7.9.310.20   When determining if a risk component is eligible for designation as a hedged item, an entity assesses the component in the context of the particular market structure to which the risk relates and in which the hedging activity takes place. This is true for both contractually specified and non-contractually specified risks, as well as for risks related to both financial and non-financial items. [*IFRS 9.6.3.7(a), B6.3.9*]

7.9.310.30   The following are examples of a specific risk of a financial item being designated as the hedged risk:
- the foreign exchange risk on the principal amount of a foreign currency borrowing;
- the interest rate risk on a five-year fixed rate bond investment;
- the inflation risk on an inflation-linked financial liability; and
- hedging the foreign currency risk on interest cash flows – but not the foreign currency risk – on the principal cash flows of a foreign currency borrowing.

7.9.310.40   The following are examples of a specific risk of a non-financial item being designated as the hedged risk:
- the benchmark crude oil price risk component of future jet fuel purchases;
- the contractually specified oil gas price risk component of natural gas; and
- the benchmark quality coffee price risk component of a specialised coffee product that requires additional processing of the benchmark quality coffee.

7.9.310.50   The evaluation of whether a risk component is separately identifiable and reliably measurable may require judgement. If a component is explicitly specified in a contract – e.g. a pricing formula that uses a reference to a benchmark commodity price – then concluding that it is separately identifiable may be straightforward. If the component is not contractually specified, then the entity will need to consider whether the risk is separately considered in pricing the hedged item in the related market– e.g. crude oil prices may be a price component of jet fuel prices. Whether sufficient observable forward transactions for the component exist may be a factor to consider in concluding whether a component is reliably measurable. [*IFRS 9.B6.3.8–B6.3.10*]

7.9.310.60   Knowledge of the relevant market structure is also critical. There is no requirement that the component be the main or largest component, or that the movement of the fair value of the component be in the same direction as the value of the entire item. Also, the fact that a non-financial item contains a physical component does not in itself mean that the component is eligible to be designated as a hedged risk. For example, steel is a physical component of cars, but this does not mean that an entity can automatically designate steel as a risk component in a hedge of the forecast sale of cars. This is because the price of the cars may be related only indirectly to the price of steel. In general, the greater the degree of subsequent transformation and value added in the production of a non-financial item, the more difficult it is to identify a distinguishable effect of a physical component on the price of that non-financial item. [*IFRS 9.B6.3.8–B6.3.10*]

7.9.310.70   The following flowchart summarises a possible approach to evaluating whether a risk is separately identifiable and reliably measurable.

Evaluating whether a risk is separately identifiable

Is there a contract? — No → Is the risk separately considered in pricing the hedged item based on an analysis of the related market structure? — No → Risk is not separately identifiable (not a permitted hedged risk)

Yes ↓

Does the contract specify how the risk is priced into the contract? — No → (to "Is the risk separately considered...")

Yes ↓ / Yes ↓

Risk is separately identifiable (permitted hedged risk if also 'reliably measurable')

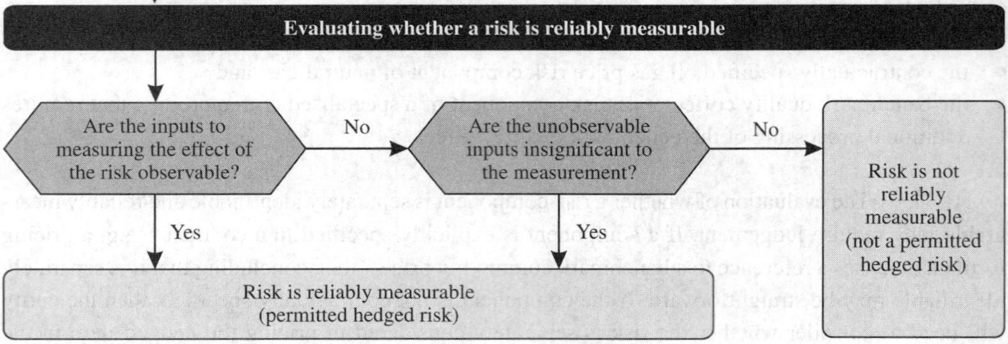

Evaluating whether a risk is reliably measurable

Are the inputs to measuring the effect of the risk observable? — No → Are the unobservable inputs insignificant to the measurement? — No → Risk is not reliably measurable (not a permitted hedged risk)

Yes ↓ / Yes ↓

Risk is reliably measurable (permitted hedged risk)

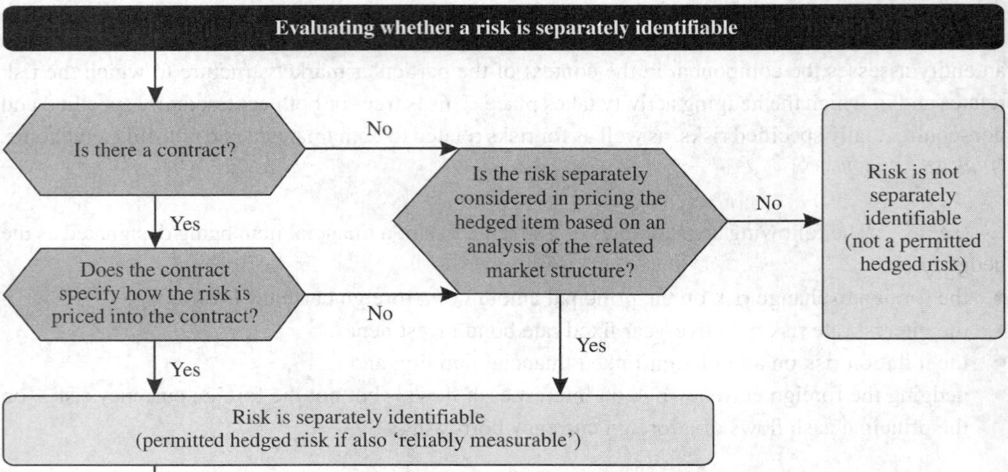

EXAMPLE 7 – CONTRACTUALLY SPECIFIED RISK COMPONENT

7.9.310.80   Company B has a long-term contract to buy natural gas. The contract is priced using a contractually specified formula that references gas oil, fuel oil and transportation charges. B's risk management strategy is to hedge 100% of its exposure to gas oil price risk, and B enters into a gas oil forward contract to hedge this price risk. The contract explicitly specifies how the gas oil component is determined. In addition, there is a market for gas oil forward instruments that extends to the maturity of the natural gas contract.

7.9.310.90   On the basis of the above factors, B determines that the gas oil price exposure is separately identifiable and reliably measurable. Therefore, the gas oil price exposure is an eligible risk component for designation as a hedged item. [*IFRS 9.B6.3.10*]

EXAMPLE 8 – NON-CONTRACTUALLY SPECIFIED RISK COMPONENT

7.9.310.100   Company C has a long-term contract to buy jet fuel. C's risk management strategy is to hedge a portion of its exposure to jet fuel price risk based on expected consumption up to 24 months before delivery. C then increases the coverage volume as delivery gets nearer. C uses the following derivatives as hedging instruments based on the liquidity of the respective derivative markets and the time remaining until the forecast purchase:

- 12 to 24 months: crude oil contracts;
- 6 to 12 months: gas oil contracts; and
- under 6 months: jet fuel contracts.

7.9.310.110   Crude oil and gas oil are not contractually specified components of jet fuel prices. Therefore, C has to determine whether crude oil and gas oil are separately considered in pricing jet fuel. C analyses the market structure for oil and oil products and determines that there is a relationship between crude oil and gas oil prices, and jet fuel prices. C determines that the relationship results from different refining margins (also known as 'cracking spreads') that allow the price of jet fuel to be made up of building blocks. Therefore, C is exposed to these two risk components, even though they are not specified contractually: crude oil and gas oil prices.

7.9.310.120   If C determines that the two risk components are separately identifiable and reliably measurable, then it may designate crude oil or gas oil as risk components of the forecast jet fuel purchases. [*IFRS 9.B6.3.10*]

7.9.320   *One-sided risks*

7.9.320.10   An entity may designate all changes in the cash flows or fair value of a hedged item in a hedging relationship. It may also designate only changes in the cash flows or fair value of a hedged item above or below a specified price or other variable – i.e. a one-sided risk. The intrinsic value of a purchased option hedging instrument (assuming that it has the same principal terms as the designated risk), but not its time value, reflects a one-sided risk in a hedged item (see 7.9.660). [*IFRS 9.B6.3.12*]

EXAMPLE 9 – EXCLUDING TIME VALUE OF PURCHASED OPTION

7.9.320.20   Company B forecasts a future purchase of a commodity and purchases a commodity call option to hedge against future increases in commodity prices above the strike price specified in the purchased option. B designates as the hedged item the variability of future cash flow outcomes arising from the forecast commodity purchase as a result of a price increase above the strike price.

7.9.320.30   In this example, only increases in cash outflows that result from an increase in the price above the specified level are designated. The hedged risk does not include the time value of a purchased option because the time value is not a component of the forecast transaction that affects profit or loss.

7.9.330   *Inflation risk*

7.9.330.10   A contractually specified inflation risk component of the cash flows of a recognised inflation-linked bond is separately identifiable and reliably measurable, as long as other cash flows of the instrument are not affected by the inflation risk component. [*IFRS 9.B6.3.15*]

7.9.330.20   There is a rebuttable presumption that, unless inflation is contractually specified, it is not separately identifiable and reliably measurable and, therefore, it is not an eligible risk component of a financial instrument. However, in limited cases it is possible to designate non-contractually specified inflation as a risk component of a financial instrument because of the particular circumstances of the inflation environment and the relevant debt market. [*IFRS 9.B6.3.13–B6.3.15*]

7.9.330.30   If an entity wishes to hedge non-contractually specified inflation as a risk component of a financial instrument, then it has to rebut the presumption that non-contractually specified inflation is not separately identifiable and reliably measurable. To do that, the entity needs to determine whether it is capable of constructing a forward inflation curve based on observable real interest rates from a liquid market for the hedge period. This may be challenging in some environments. [*IFRS 9.B6.3.14*]

7.9.330.40   The existence of a government-sponsored price index for a country – e.g. a CPI or producer price index – is not sufficient to construct an inflation curve using real interest rates for the hedge period. This is because price indexes are generally developed using historical and current prices, whereas a forward inflation curve represents expectations of future prices. [*IFRS 9.B6.3.14*]

7.9.340   *Foreign currency exposures*

7.9.340.10   In our view, hedge accounting is not permitted for hedges that convert one foreign currency exposure into another foreign currency exposure, unless the entity has a corresponding position in the second foreign currency or that second foreign currency is closely correlated to the entity's functional currency.

EXAMPLE 10 – CONVERTING ONE CURRENCY EXPOSURE INTO ANOTHER

7.9.340.20   Company S's functional currency is the rand. S has issued a yen-denominated bond and has a US dollar receivable; both instruments have the equivalent notional amount and the same maturity. To hedge both the US dollar and the yen exposures, S enters into a forward contract to convert yen into US dollars. This relationship between the bond and the receivable (the hedged items) and the yen-to-US dollar forward (the hedging instrument) qualifies for hedge accounting.

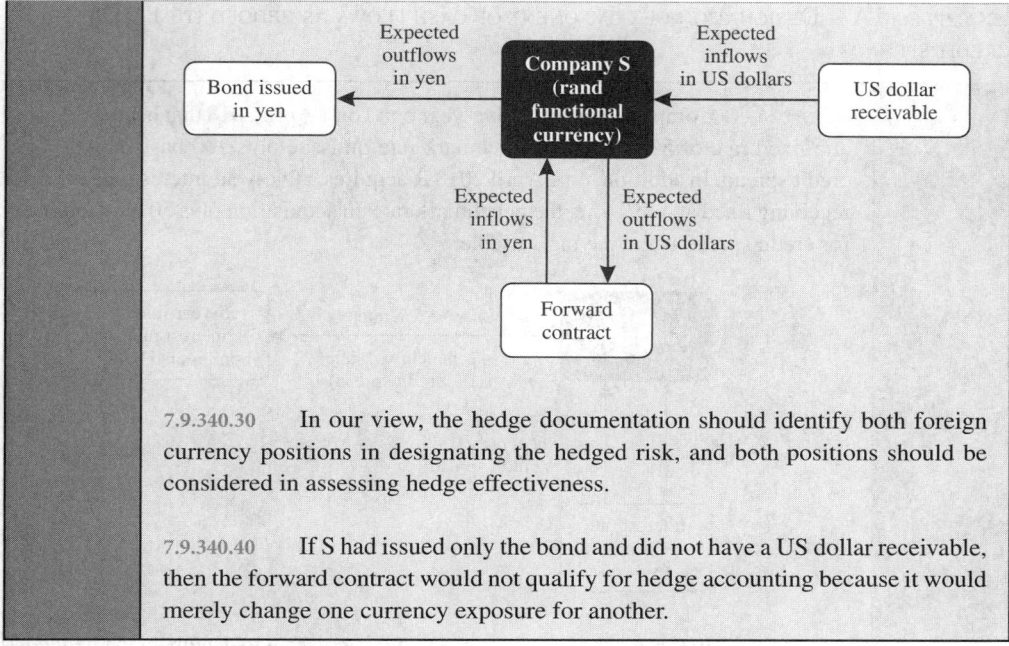

7.9.340.30   In our view, the hedge documentation should identify both foreign currency positions in designating the hedged risk, and both positions should be considered in assessing hedge effectiveness.

7.9.340.40   If S had issued only the bond and did not have a US dollar receivable, then the forward contract would not qualify for hedge accounting because it would merely change one currency exposure for another.

7.9.340.50   Non-financial items themselves – e.g. property, plant and equipment and intangible assets – generally have no separately measurable foreign currency risk. However, one situation in which the foreign currency risk on non-financial items will affect profit or loss is if the owner has a forecast sale that will be denominated in a foreign currency. In our view, the risk that the sales proceeds in the entity's functional currency will change because of changes in foreign exchange rates qualifies to be hedged in a cash flow hedge if the forecast sale is highly probable.

7.9.340.60   A firm commitment to acquire a business in a business combination can qualify as the hedged item only in a hedge of foreign currency risk. In our view, the same applies to a forecast business combination, assuming that the transaction is highly probable and meets the other hedge accounting criteria (see 7.9.470). [*IFRS 9.B6.3.1*]

7.9.350   *General business risks*

7.9.350.10   To qualify for hedge accounting, the hedged risk needs to be specific and identifiable. A hedge against general business risks, such as physical damage of an asset, an increase in the price payable in a business combination or the risk that a transaction will not occur, does not qualify for hedge accounting. [*IFRS 9.B6.3.1, B6.3.8–B6.3.15*]

7.9.360   **Contractual cash flow components**

7.9.360.10   If an entity designates one or more selected contractual cash flows of an item as a hedged item, then the remaining cash flows of that item are not considered for assessment of hedge effectiveness and measurement of hedge ineffectiveness. [*IFRS 9.6.3.7, 6.4.1*]

EXAMPLE 11A – DESIGNATION OF COMPONENT OF CASH FLOWS AS HEDGED ITEM – DIFFERENT CREDIT SPREADS

7.9.360.20   Company R issues a five-year bond on 1 April 2018 that bears interest at a fixed rate of 5% – i.e. the benchmark rate on issue plus 100 basis points for credit spread. In addition, on 1 April 2018 R acquires a five-year interest rate swap, receiving fixed at 4.5% – i.e. the benchmark rate on acquisition plus 50 basis points for credit spread – and paying variable.

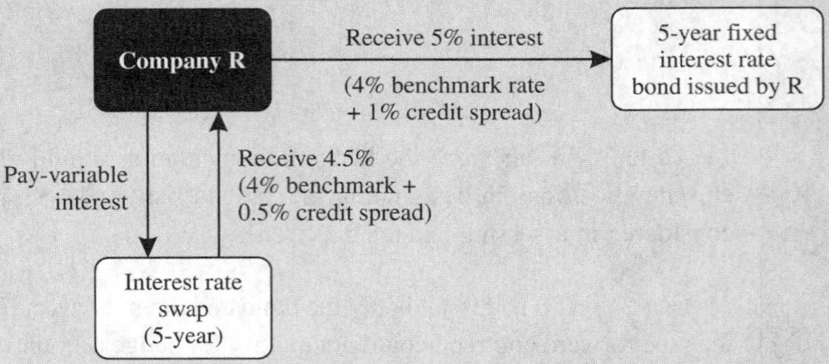

```
                              Receive 5% interest         ┌──────────────────┐
        ┌──────────────┐     ───────────────────────>     │   5-year fixed   │
        │  Company R   │                                   │   interest rate  │
        └──────────────┘      (4% benchmark rate           │ bond issued by R │
            │    ▲             + 1% credit spread)          └──────────────────┘
            │    │
            │    │          Receive 4.5%
  Pay-variable  │          (4% benchmark +
   interest     │          0.5% credit spread)
            │    │
            ▼    │
        ┌──────────────┐
        │ Interest rate│
        │     swap     │
        │   (5-year)   │
        └──────────────┘
```

7.9.360.30   In this example, we believe that it is possible to designate the hedged item as the principal cash flow plus a component of the interest coupons – i.e. 4.5% of the 5% contractual interest cash flows. This will reduce hedge ineffectiveness compared with when the entire 5% interest cash flows are designated as a hedged item.

EXAMPLE 11B – DESIGNATION OF COMPONENT OF CASH FLOWS AS HEDGED ITEM – SUBSEQUENT CHANGE IN BENCHMARK RATES

7.9.360.40   Company S issued a five-year bond in 2016 that bears interest at a fixed rate of 5%. In 2018, S acquires a three-year interest rate swap, receiving fixed at 3% and paying variable. Apart from the interest rates, the other terms of the hedged item and hedging instrument match. The mismatch between the interest rate on the bond and the interest rate on the fixed leg of the swap arises from a decrease in benchmark rates over the two-year period.

7.9.360.50   In this example, we believe that it is possible to designate the hedged item as the principal cash flow plus a component of the interest coupons – i.e. 3% of the 5% contractual interest cash flows. This will reduce hedge ineffectiveness compared with when the entire 5% interest cash flows are designated as a hedged item.

7.9.360.60   In our view, it is possible for an entity to designate selected contractual cash flows of the variable interest payments or receipts on a financial asset or financial liability as the hedged item if, in addition to the conditions outlined in 7.9.240, 290 and 300, the following conditions are met:

- the actual interest payments or receipts on the hedged item are expected, based on historical evidence, to exceed the hedged cash flows during the entire hedging relationship; and
- there is a reasonable economic relationship between the selected contractual cash flows designated as the hedged item and the variable rate on which the contractual cash flows are based.

7.9.360.70   In our view, an entity may designate the changes in the cash flows of a financial asset or financial liability that relate to only a component of its term – i.e. a 'partial term' cash flow hedge.

EXAMPLE 12 – PARTIAL TERM CASH FLOW HEDGE

7.9.360.80   Company R has a highly probable forecast issue of fixed rate debt expected to occur on 31 December 2018. R wants to hedge the variability in the proceeds received from the debt issue arising from changes in the benchmark interest rate that occur from 1 October 2018 to 31 October 2018. On 1 October 2018, R designates a cash flow hedge using a forward starting interest rate swap with a swap component that starts on 31 October 2018, and has the same maturity as that of the fixed rate debt, as the hedging instrument to hedge that risk. When the swap component starts on 31 October 2018, R will de-designate the derivative.

7.9.360.90   For the purposes of hedge ineffectiveness, R measures the change in the theoretical proceeds cash flow up to 31 October 2018 and discounts that change assuming that the cash settlement of that amount occurs on 31 December 2018 (when the forecast issuance is actually expected to occur). Therefore, ineffectiveness will result from the time value of money from 31 October 2018 to 31 December 2018.

7.9.370   Components of nominal amounts

7.9.370.10   An entity may designate a specified part of the amount of an item as the hedged item. It designates the component for accounting purposes consistently with its risk management objective. [*IFRS 9.6.3.7(c), B6.3.16*]

7.9.370.20   Two types of components of nominal amounts can be designated as the hedged item in a hedging relationship:
- a component that is a proportion of an entire item; or
- a layer component. [*IFRS 9.6.3.7(c), B6.3.16*]

7.9.370.30   The term 'proportion' indicates a certain percentage of an item. An example of a component that is a proportion of an entire item is designating 50 percent of the contractual cash flows of a fixed rate bond as the hedged item in a fair value hedging relationship. [*IFRS 9.B6.3.17*]

7.9.370.40   A 'layer component' may be specified from:
- a defined, but open, population; or
- a defined nominal amount. [*IFRS 9.B6.3.18*]

7.9.370.50   Examples of layer components include:

- part of a monetary transaction volume – e.g. the next USD 10,000 of cash flows from sales denominated in a foreign currency after the first USD 20,000 in November 2018;
- part of a physical volume – e.g. the bottom layer, measuring five million cubic metres, of the natural gas stored in Location Z;
- part of a physical or other transaction volume – e.g. the first 100 barrels of oil purchases or the first 100 MWh of electricity sales in November 2018; and
- a layer from the nominal amount of the hedged item – e.g. the last 80 of a 100 firm commitment, the bottom layer of 20 of a fixed rate bond of 100 or the top layer of 30 from a total amount of 100 of fixed rate debt that can be prepaid at fair value (the defined nominal amount is 100). [*IFRS 9.B6.3.18*]

7.9.370.60   The layer component may be designated as the hedged item in a fair value hedging relationship, in which case the entity is required to specify it from a defined nominal amount. [*IFRS 9.B6.3.19*]

7.9.370.70   To comply with the requirements for qualifying fair value hedges, an entity is required to remeasure the hedged item for fair value changes attributable to the hedged risk. The fair value hedge adjustment is recognised in profit or loss no later than when the item is derecognised. Consequently, it is necessary to track the item to which the fair value hedge adjustment relates. For a layer component in a fair value hedge, this requires an entity to track the nominal amount from which it is defined – e.g. for a fixed rate bond of 100, the total defined nominal amount of 100 will need to be tracked in order to track a bottom layer of 20 or a top layer of 30. [*IFRS 9.B6.3.19*]

7.9.370.80   A layer component of a contract that includes a prepayment option whose fair value is affected by changes in the hedged risk will be eligible as a hedged item in a fair value hedge only if the effect of the option is included in determining the change in fair value of the hedged item. [*IFRS 9.B6.3.20*]

7.9.370.90   Designating a layer or proportion component of a nominal amount as the hedged item can give rise to different accounting outcomes. For example, assume that a prepayable debt instrument with a nominal amount of 100 and maturity of five years repays 20 per year.

- If the hedged component is designated as 20 percent of the debt instrument – i.e. a proportion component – then the determination of the gain or loss on the hedged component arising from the hedged risk would consider 20 percent of all cash flows of the instrument over its entire life.
- Alternatively, if the hedged component is designated as the last 20 of principal of the debt instrument – i.e. the bottom layer – then the determination of the gain or loss on the hedged component would consider only the last payment of 20. This may result in a more effective hedging relationship.

EXAMPLE 13 – HEDGING A LAYER COMPONENT THAT INCLUDES A PREPAYMENT OPTION

7.9.370.100   Company X has the Japanese yen as its functional currency. It invests in US dollar-denominated prepayable floating rate loans of USD 200. The loans are classified as at FVOCI. X's risk management strategy is to hedge the foreign exchange risk of the loans.

7.9.370.110   On the same date, X enters into a floating-for-floating USD-JPY cross-currency interest rate swap (CCIRS) with a nominal amount of USD 100. X designates a fair value hedge as follows:

- hedged item: the bottom layer of USD 100 of the loans;
- hedging instrument: CCIRS (excluding foreign currency basis spread, which will be accounted for as a cost of hedging); and
- hedged risk: spot USD-JPY foreign exchange risk.

7.9.370.120   The benefit of this hedging relationship is that the foreign currency basis spreads will be amortised over the period of the hedge as a cost of hedging.

7.9.370.130   In this case, changes in the hedged risk (i.e. USD-JPY spot exchange risk) affect the fair value of the US dollar-denominated prepayment option because X is hedging changes in the fair value of the US dollar loans measured in Japanese yen. Therefore, X is required to include the effect of the prepayment option when it determines the change in the fair value of the bottom layer of the loans.

7.9.370.140   X may measure gains or losses on the hedged item by applying the spot foreign exchange rate to the amortised cost of the USD 100 bottom layer of the loans. This is because:

- the amortised cost of the hedged item reflects the present value of the expected cash flows and these already consider the effect of prepayment options. Therefore, the amortised cost measurement includes the effects of any changes in prepayment expectations caused by movement in foreign exchange rates;
- the loans bear a floating rate of interest and so the fair value of the prepayment option is not additionally affected by movements in market interest rates (except for movements in interest rates between the interest reset dates); and
- as discussed in 7.9.853.70, we believe that for fair value hedges of spot foreign currency risk, changes in the fair value of the hedged item can be measured by applying the changes in the spot foreign exchange rate to its amortised cost.

7.9.380   'Sub-benchmark' prohibition

7.9.380.10   If a component of the cash flows of a financial or a non-financial item is designated as the hedged item, then that component needs to be less than or equal to the total cash flows of the entire item. However, all of the cash flows of the entire item may be designated as the hedged item and hedged for only one particular risk. [*IFRS 9.B6.3.21*]

7.9.380.20   For example, in the case of a financial liability that has an effective interest rate below LIBOR, an entity cannot designate both:

- a component of the liability equal to interest at LIBOR (plus the principal amount in the case of a fair value hedge); and
- a negative residual component. [*IFRS 9.B6.3.21–B6.3.22*]

7.9.380.30   However, in the case of a fixed rate financial liability whose effective interest rate is below the benchmark rate (e.g. 100 basis points below LIBOR), for example, an entity may designate as the hedged item the change in the value of the entire liability – i.e. principal plus interest at LIBOR minus 100 basis points – that is attributable to the changes in LIBOR. [*IFRS 9.B6.3.23*]

7.9.380.40   In addition, if a fixed rate financial instrument is hedged some time after its origination, and interest rates have changed in the meantime, then an entity can designate a risk component equal to a benchmark rate that is higher than the contractual rate paid on the item. The entity can do this provided that the benchmark rate is less than the effective interest rate calculated on the assumption that the entity had purchased the instrument on the day on which it first designated the hedged item. [*IFRS 9.B6.3.23*]

EXAMPLE 14 – SUB-BENCHMARK ISSUE IN NON-FINANCIAL CONTEXT

7.9.380.50   Company X has forecast sales of a specific type of crude oil from a particular oil field that are priced using Brent crude oil. X sells that crude oil under a contract using a contractual pricing formula that sets the price per barrel at Brent minus 10 with a floor of 15. In this case, X can designate as the hedged item the entire cash flow variability under the sales contract that is attributable to the change in the benchmark crude oil price. [*IFRS 9.B6.3.25*]

7.9.380.60   However, X cannot designate a component that is equal to the full change in Brent. Therefore, as long as the forward price (for each delivery) does not fall below 25, the hedged item has the same cash flow variability as a crude oil sale at Brent (or with a positive spread). However, if the forward price for any delivery falls below 25, then the hedged item has a lower cash flow variability than a crude oil sale at Brent (or with a positive spread). [*IFRS 9.B6.3.25*]

7.9.390   **Hedging a group of items**

7.9.400   *Eligibility of a group of items as hedged items*

7.9.400.10   A group of items, which can be a gross or net position, has to meet the following conditions to be an eligible hedged item for fair value and cash flow hedges:
- the position consists of items (including components of items), that individually would be eligible hedged items; and
- the items in the group are managed together on a group basis for risk management purposes. [*IFRS 9.6.6.1(a)–(b)*]

7.9.400.20   In addition to these two conditions, there are further requirements for a cash flow hedge of a group of items for which an offsetting position arises because the variability in cash flows of items in the group is not expected to be approximately proportional to the group's overall variability in cash flows. These are that:
- it is a hedge of foreign currency risk; and
- the designation specifies the reporting period in which the forecast transactions are expected to affect profit or loss, as well as their nature and volume. [*IFRS 9.6.6.1(c), B6.6.7–B6.6.8*]

7.9.400.30   The following flowchart summarises the requirements for groups of items to be eligible as the hedged item.

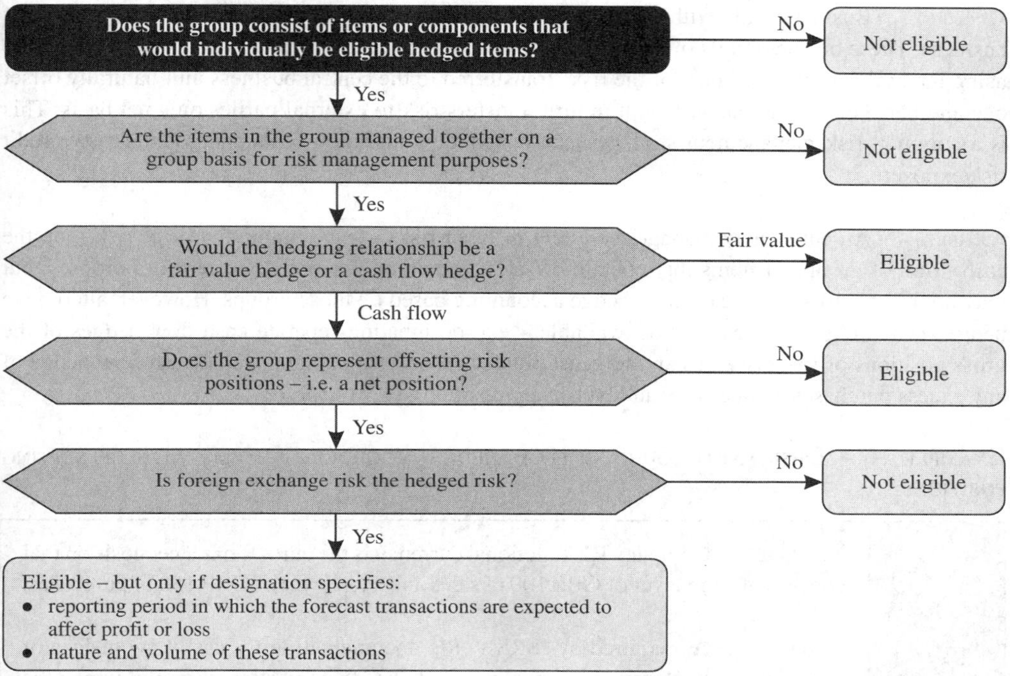

Does the group consist of items or components that would individually be eligible hedged items?	No →	Not eligible

↓ Yes

Are the items in the group managed together on a group basis for risk management purposes?	No →	Not eligible

↓ Yes

Would the hedging relationship be a fair value hedge or a cash flow hedge?	Fair value →	Eligible

↓ Cash flow

Does the group represent offsetting risk positions – i.e. a net position?	No →	Eligible

↓ Yes

Is foreign exchange risk the hedged risk?	No →	Not eligible

↓ Yes

Eligible – but only if designation specifies:
- reporting period in which the forecast transactions are expected to affect profit or loss
- nature and volume of these transactions

EXAMPLE 15 – DESIGNATION OF A GROUP OF ITEMS THAT IS NOT A NET POSITION UNDER A CASH FLOW HEDGE

7.9.400.32   Company R has a group of investments in floating rate corporate bonds denominated in the same currency and subject to the same benchmark floating rate. R plans to designate an interest rate swap contract as a hedging instrument in a cash flow hedge in order to hedge changes in the floating interest rate.

7.9.400.34   In this case, the group of floating rate corporate bonds does not result in a 'net' position because it consists of financial assets without offsetting risk positions (i.e. long only strategy). As a result, the group of assets may be hedged. The fact that the hedge does not relate to foreign currency risk is not relevant for the analysis. [*IFRS 9.6.6.1*]

7.9.400.40   Foreign exchange risk is the only risk permitted to be designated in a cash flow hedge of a group of items that contains offsetting risk positions. For example:
- a group comprises both forecast purchases and forecast sales; and
- the effect of the hedged foreign exchange risk on the forecast purchases serves to offset the effect of the hedged foreign exchange risk on the forecast sales. [*IFRS 9.6.6.1(c)*]

7.9.400.50   Together, the forecast sales and forecast purchases create a net position with respect to foreign exchange risk – e.g. a top layer of foreign currency-denominated forecast sales of GBP 100 and a top layer of foreign currency-denominated forecast purchases of GBP 150. [*IFRS 9.6.6.1(c)*]

7.9.400.60   Business units within an entity are exposed to various risks in the normal course of business. These business units often transfer the risks to one central business unit within the entity, using internal derivatives. Many of the risks transferred to the central business unit naturally offset one another. The central business unit in turn transfers risk to external parties on a net basis. This is a common risk management strategy used to reduce transaction costs and counterparty credit risk exposure.

7.9.400.70   An entity may manage the effect of other risks – e.g. commodity price risk – on the cash flows of groups of items that contain offsetting positions for risk management purposes, but may not be able to achieve cash flow hedge accounting based on those groups. However, alternative hedge accounting strategies may be available – e.g. designating separate cash flow hedges of the gross positions of forecast sales and forecast purchases, or designating a single cash flow hedge of any excess purchases or sales (i.e. an 'over-hang' position). [*IFRS 9.6.6.1(c)*]

EXAMPLE 16 – DESIGNATION OF CASH FLOW HEDGE OF GROUP OF ITEMS WITH OFFSETTING POSITIONS

7.9.400.80   Company R's functional currency is the euro. R has a net position that consists of a top layer of GBP 100 of sales and a top layer of GBP 150 of purchases.

7.9.400.90   As required by IFRS 9, R's documentation for cash flow hedges of net positions for foreign currency risk specifies the reporting period in which the forecast transactions are expected to affect profit or loss, as well as their nature and volume. [*IFRS 9.6.6.1(c), B6.6.8*]

7.9.400.100   To sufficiently specify the designation of the hedged net position, R specifies in its original documentation of the hedging relationship that sales can be of Product A or Product B and that purchases can be of Machinery Type A, Machinery Type B or Raw Material A.

7.9.400.110   R also specifies the volumes of the transaction by each nature, as follows.

SALES	PURCHASES
R documents that the top layer of sales (GBP 100) is made up of a forecast sales volume of the first GBP 70 of Product A and the first GBP 30 of Product B.	R documents that the top layer of purchases (GBP 150) is made up of purchases of the first GBP 60 of Machinery Type A, the first GBP 40 of Machinery Type B and the first GBP 50 of Raw Material A.
If those sales volumes are expected to affect profit or loss in different reporting periods, then R includes that in its documentation. For example:	If those purchase volumes are expected to affect profit or loss in different reporting periods, then R includes in the documentation a disaggregation of the purchase volumes

SALES	PURCHASES
• the first GBP 70 from sales of Product A that are expected to affect profit or loss in the first reporting period; and • the first GBP 30 from sales of Product B that are expected to affect profit or loss in the second reporting period.	by the reporting periods in which they are expected to affect profit or loss. For example: • the first GBP 60 of purchases of Machinery Type A that are expected to affect profit or loss from the third reporting period over the next 10 reporting periods; • the first GBP 40 of purchases of Machinery Type B that are expected to affect profit or loss from the fourth reporting period over the next 20 reporting periods; and • the first GBP 50 of purchases of Raw Material A that are expected to be received in the third reporting period and sold – i.e. affect profit or loss – in that and the following reporting period.

7.9.400.120   Specifying the nature of the forecast transaction volumes includes aspects such as the depreciation pattern for items of property, plant and equipment of the same kind, if the nature of those items is such that the depreciation pattern could vary depending on how the entity uses those items. [*IFRS 9.6.6.1(c), B6.6.8*]

7.9.400.130   For example, in the context of Example 16, if R uses items of Machinery Type A in two different production processes that result in straight-line depreciation over 10 reporting periods and the units-of-production method, respectively, then its documentation of the forecast purchase volume for Machinery Type A disaggregates that volume into those depreciation patterns.

7.9.400.140   A net position is eligible as a hedged item in a fair value or a cash flow hedge only if the entity hedges the exposure on a net basis for risk management purposes. Whether an entity hedges on a net basis is a matter of fact and is not based solely on assertion or documentation. [*IFRS 9.B6.6.1*]

7.9.400.150   If an entity applies hedge accounting to a net position, then it is required to designate the overall group of items that includes the items that make up the net position. [*IFRS 9.B6.6.4*]

EXAMPLE 17 – OVERALL GROUP OF ITEMS DESIGNATED WHEN APPLYING HEDGE ACCOUNTING TO NET POSITION

7.9.400.160   Company S's functional currency is the euro. S has a group of firm sale commitments in nine months' time for GBP 100. It also has a group of firm purchase commitments in 18 months' time for GBP 120.

> 7.9.400.170   In this example, when S designates the group that constitutes a net position as the hedged item, it cannot designate an abstract amount of a net position up to GBP 20 – i.e. an over-hang position. Instead, it designates a gross amount of purchases and a gross amount of sales that together give rise to the hedged net position in a cash flow hedge. [*IFRS 9.B6.6.4*]

7.9.400.180   To determine whether a hedge of a net position is effective, an entity considers the changes in the fair value or cash flows of the items in the net position that have a similar effect to the hedging instrument in conjunction with the fair value change on the hedging instrument. For further discussion of assessing effectiveness, see 7.9.790. [*IFRS 9.B6.6.5*]

EXAMPLE 18 – DETERMINING WHETHER HEDGE OF NET POSITION IS EFFECTIVE

> 7.9.400.190   Continuing Example 17, Company S hedges the foreign currency risk of the group that constitutes the net short position of GBP 20 using a forward exchange contract for GBP 20. When determining whether the hedge effectiveness requirements are met, S considers the relationship between:
> - the:
>   - foreign currency risk-related changes in value of the group of GBP 100 firm sale commitments; and
>   - fair value changes of the hedging instrument contract for GBP 20; and
> - the foreign currency risk-related changes in the value of the group of GBP 120 firm purchase commitments. [*IFRS 9.B6.6.5, B6.6.9*]
>
> 7.9.400.200   Similarly, when determining the amounts that are recognised in the cash flow hedge reserve, S compares:
> - the fair value change on the forward exchange contract together with the foreign currency risk-related changes in the value of the sales transactions; with
> - the foreign currency risk-related changes in the value of the purchase transactions. [*IFRS 9.B6.6.5, B6.6.9*]
>
> 7.9.400.210   During the period from hedge inception to recognition of the sales transaction, S recognises in OCI only amounts related to the forward exchange contract. When the sales transactions are recognised in the financial statements, S recognises gains or losses on these transactions as a reclassification adjustment from OCI to profit or loss – i.e. the change in the value attributable to the change in the foreign exchange rate between designation of the hedging relationship and the recognition of revenue. [*IFRS 9.B6.6.5, B6.6.9*]

7.9.400.220   An otherwise eligible group that is a nil net position – i.e. the hedged items among themselves fully offset the risk that is managed on a group basis – is eligible to be designated as the hedged item in a hedging relationship that does not include a hedging instrument if:
- the hedge is part of a rolling net risk hedge strategy for a hedged position that changes in size over time;
- over the life of the rolling net risk hedge strategy, eligible hedging instruments will be used to hedge the net risk when the net position is not nil;

- hedge accounting is normally applied by the entity to such net positions when the net position is not nil, and they are hedged with eligible hedging instruments; and
- not applying hedge accounting to the nil net position would give rise to inconsistent accounting outcomes, because the accounting would not recognise the offsetting risk positions that would otherwise be recognised in a hedge of a net position. [*IFRS 9.6.6.6*]

7.9.400.230   A group that is a nil net position is most likely coincidental and therefore is expected to be rare in practice. [*IFRS 9.BC6.467*]

EXAMPLE 19 – DETERMINING WHETHER HEDGE OF NET NIL POSITION IS EFFECTIVE

7.9.400.240   Modifying Examples 17 and 18, Company S has the following nil net position:
- a top layer of GBP 100 of sales;
- a top layer of GBP 100 of purchases; and
- no separate foreign exchange forward contract.

7.9.400.250   In this example, S considers the relationship between the following to determine whether the hedging relationship is effective:
- the foreign currency risk-related changes in the value of the group of firm foreign currency-denominated sale commitments; and
- the foreign currency risk-related changes in the value of the group of firm foreign currency-denominated purchase commitments. [*IFRS 9.B6.6.6, B6.6.10*]

7.9.400.260   When determining the amounts that are recognised in the cash flow hedge reserve, S compares:
- the foreign currency risk-related changes in the value of the sales transactions; and
- the foreign currency risk-related changes in the value of the purchase transactions. [*IFRS 9.B6.6.6, B6.6.10*]

7.9.400.270   However, those amounts are recognised only once the related transactions are recognised in the financial statements. [*IFRS 9.B6.6.6, B6.6.10*]

EXAMPLE 20 – RECLASSIFICATION FROM CASH FLOW HEDGE RESERVE TO PROFIT OR LOSS IN CASH FLOW HEDGE OF NET POSITION

7.9.400.280   Company M's functional currency is the Canadian dollar. On 1 April 2018, M entered into a group of firm US dollar-denominated sale commitments in three months' time for USD 100 and a group of firm US dollar-denominated commitments to pay expenses in six months' time for USD 80. It hedged the foreign currency risk of the group that constitutes the net position of USD 20 using a forward exchange contract to sell USD 20 after three months.

7.9.400.290   The following facts are also relevant for this example.

DATE	SPOT RATE[1] CAD 1 = USD	FORWARD RATE[1] CAD 1 = USD	FAIR VALUE OF FORWARD CAD
1 April 2018	1	1	-
30 June 2018	0.5	0.5	(20)
30 September 2018	0.4	-	-

Note
1. In this example, the spot rate and the forward rate are the same for simplicity.

7.9.400.300   M records the following entries (amounts in Canadian dollars).

	DEBIT	CREDIT
1 April 2018 No entries		
30 June 2018 Cash Sales *To recognise sales of USD 100 at spot rate: USD 100 / 0.5*	200	200
Hedging reserve (OCI) Forward contract *To recognise change in fair value of forward*	20	20
Foreign exchange gain or loss (profit or loss) Hedging reserve (OCI) *To recognise hedge adjustment for sale transaction*	100[1]	100
Forward contract Cash *To record settlement of forward contract*	20	20
30 September 2018 Expenses Cash *To record payment of expenses of USD 80 at spot rate: USD 80 / 0.4*	200	200
Hedging reserve (OCI) Foreign exchange gain or loss (profit or loss) *To recognise hedge adjustment for expense transaction*	80	80[2]

> **Notes**
> 1.   Comprises CAD 20 of losses on the foreign exchange forward contract and CAD 80 of foreign exchange losses on the expenses that will occur in three months. The result of the accounting is to reflect that the hedge fixed the sales price in CAD terms at CAD 100.
> 2.   The amount remaining in the cash flow hedge reserve is reclassified to profit or loss. The result of the accounting is to reflect that the net position made up of the sales and the expenses was hedged for foreign exchange risk with the forward contract for three months – i.e. from 1 April to 30 June.

7.9.400.310   In summary, the increase in expenses (in Canadian dollar terms) caused by foreign exchange movements – which would not normally be recognised until 30 September 2018 – and the loss on the foreign exchange forward contract offset the increase in sales (in Canadian dollar terms) caused by foreign currency movements at 30 June 2018 – i.e. the net position was hedged for foreign exchange risk for the three months ended 30 June 2018. The profit or loss for the three months ended 30 September 2018 is adjusted to reflect the fact that CAD 80 of the increase in expenses (in Canadian dollar terms) caused by foreign exchange movements was already recognised in the period ended 30 June 2018 – i.e. its recognition was accelerated to effect the hedge accounting for the net position. [*IFRS 9.B6.6.15*]

7.9.410   *Designating component of nominal amount of group of items*

7.9.410.10   An entity may designate a proportion of an eligible group of items as a hedged item if doing so is consistent with its risk management objective. An entity may also designate a layer component of an eligible group of items – e.g. the bottom layer – if the following requirements are met:

- the layer is separately identifiable and reliably measurable;
- the risk management objective is to hedge a layer component;
- the items in the overall group from which the layer is identified are exposed to the same hedged risk;
- for hedges of existing items, an entity can identify and track the overall group of items from which the hedged layer is defined; and
- the change in fair value of the hedged layer in a fair value hedge considers the effect of any prepayment options of individual items within the group if the fair value of the prepayment option is affected by the hedged risk. [*IFRS 9.6.6.2–6.6.3*]

7.9.410.20   A hedging relationship may include layers from multiple different groups of items. For example, assume a net position hedge of a group of highly probable forecast sales and a group of highly probable forecast purchases: the hedging relationship can comprise, in combination, a layer component of the group of sales and a layer component of the group of purchases. [*IFRS 9.B6.6.8, B6.6.12*]

7.9.420   **Aggregated exposures**

7.9.420.10   An aggregated exposure consists of a non-derivative exposure that can qualify as a hedged item and a derivative. Such a combination may create a different exposure that is managed as a single exposure for a particular risk or risks. An entity may designate such an aggregated exposure as the hedged item. The components that make up the aggregated exposure do not need to be designated in a separate hedging relationship. [*IFRS 9.6.3.4, B6.3.3*]

7.9.420.20   The following diagram illustrates the effectiveness assessment and ineffectiveness measurement of a hedge of an aggregated exposure.

Hedging relationship

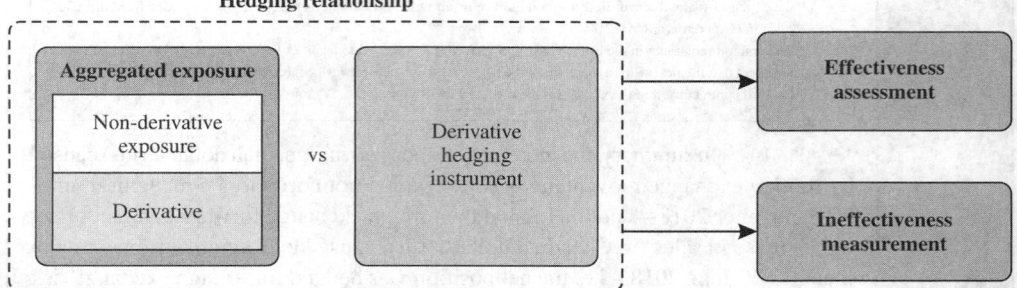

If the aggregated exposure is designated as a hedged item in a hedging relationship, then assessment and measurement would also be performed at that level

EXAMPLE 21 – AGGREGATED EXPOSURE – CASH FLOW HEDGE/CASH FLOW HEDGE

7.9.420.30   Company X's functional currency is the euro. X hedges its US dollar-denominated 1,000 tonne forecast purchase of steel using a US dollar-denominated steel forward contract.

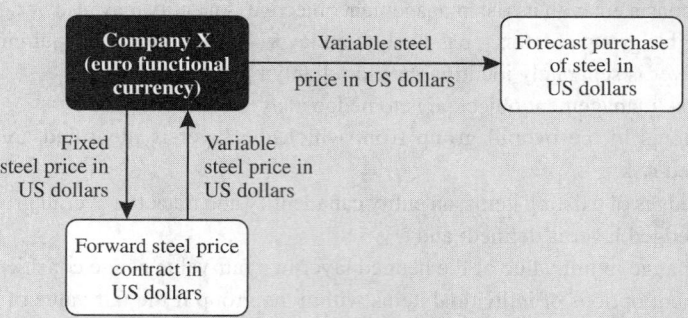

7.9.420.40   The forward contract has a delivery date that matches the expected delivery of the forecast purchase. X documents this as a cash flow hedge and designates:

- the forecast steel purchase as the hedged item;
- the variability in US dollar cash flows from the forecast purchase due to steel prices as the hedged risk; and
- the forward steel contract as the hedging instrument.

7.9.420.50   One month later, X enters into a foreign currency forward contract to hedge the foreign exchange risk between the euro and the US dollar arising from both the US dollar-denominated forecast steel purchase and the US dollar-denominated forward contract, because it views the two collectively as a US dollar aggregated exposure.

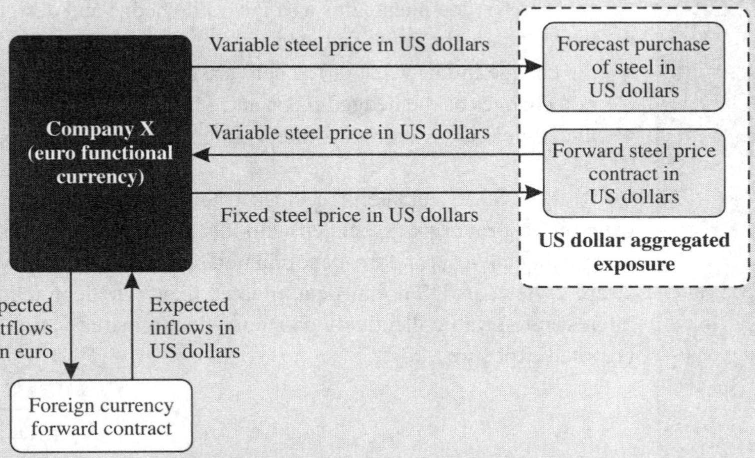

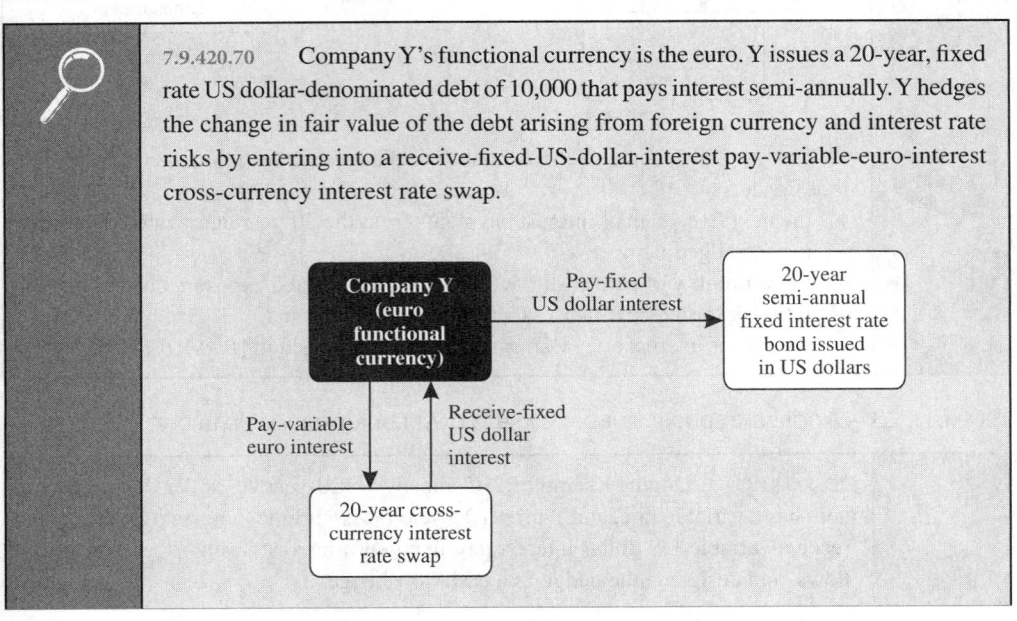

7.9.420.60   X documents this second-level hedge as a cash flow hedge in which it designates:

- the aggregated US dollar fixed price exposure as the hedged item;
- the variability in euro cash flows related to the euro/US dollar foreign exchange risk as the hedged risk; and
- the foreign currency forward contract as the hedging instrument. [*IFRS 9.IE116–IE127*]

EXAMPLE 22 – AGGREGATED EXPOSURE – FAIR VALUE HEDGE/CASH FLOW HEDGE

7.9.420.70   Company Y's functional currency is the euro. Y issues a 20-year, fixed rate US dollar-denominated debt of 10,000 that pays interest semi-annually. Y hedges the change in fair value of the debt arising from foreign currency and interest rate risks by entering into a receive-fixed-US-dollar-interest pay-variable-euro-interest cross-currency interest rate swap.

7.9.420.80   Y documents this as a fair value hedge and designates:

- the 20-year debt as the hedged item;
- the change in fair value of the debt arising from foreign currency and interest rate changes as the hedged risks; and
- the 20-year cross-currency interest rate swap as the hedging instrument.

7.9.420.90   One year later, Y decides to hedge the variability of cash flows arising from interest rate risk associated with this aggregated exposure for the next five years using a five-year euro-denominated receive-variable pay-fixed interest rate swap. Y views its US dollar-denominated fixed rate debt and the cross-currency interest rate swap collectively as a euro-denominated variable rate 20-year aggregated exposure.

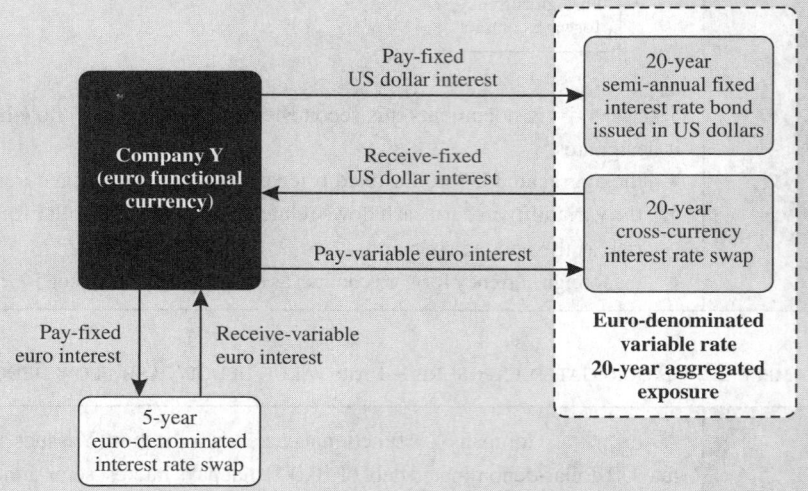

7.9.420.100   Y documents this second-level hedge as a cash flow hedge in which it designates:

- the next five years of interest payments from the 20-year aggregated exposure as the hedged item;
- the variability of euro cash flows from this aggregated exposure due to interest rate risk for the next five years as the hedged risk; and
- the 5-year interest rate swap as the hedging instrument. [*IFRS 9.IE128–IE137*]

EXAMPLE 23 – AGGREGATED EXPOSURE – CASH FLOW HEDGE/FAIR VALUE HEDGE

7.9.420.110   Changing Example 22, Company Y's 20-year US dollar-denominated debt has a variable rate, and Y uses a 20-year cross-currency interest rate swap – a receive-variable-US dollar interest pay-fixed-euro interest swap – to fix the cash flows, and designate the hedge as a cash flow hedge.

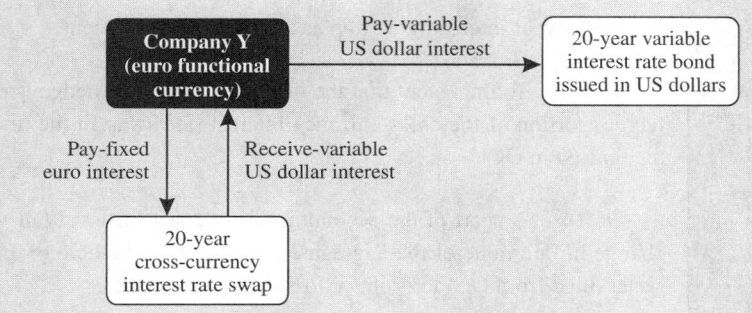

7.9.420.120 Y documents this as a cash flow hedge and designates:
- the 20-year debt as the hedged item;
- the variability in US dollar interest payments resulting from foreign currency changes and variability in interest rates as the hedged risks; and
- the 20-year cross-currency interest rate swap as the hedging instrument.

7.9.420.130 Five years later, Y decides to hedge the change in the fair value of the aggregated exposure using a 15-year euro-denominated pay-variable receive-fixed interest rate swap. The aggregated fixed rate euro exposure of the debt and the receive-variable-US dollar interest pay-fixed-euro interest swap is then the hedged item in a fair value hedge.

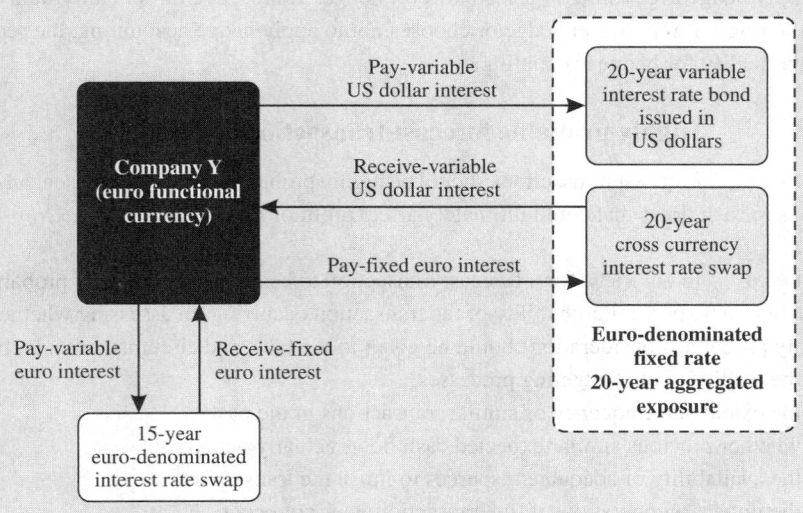

7.9.420.140 Y documents this second-level hedge as a fair value hedge in which it designates:
- the 20-year aggregated exposure as the hedged item;
- the change in the fair value of this aggregated exposure arising from interest rate risk for the next 15 years as the hedged risk; and

> • the 15-year interest rate swap as the hedging instrument.
>
> 7.9.420.150   To the extent that the first-level cash flow hedge is effective, the effective portion of the cross-currency interest rate swap in the first-level hedge is recognised in OCI.
>
> 7.9.420.160   As part of the accounting for the second-level fair value hedge, the change in fair value of the aggregated exposure attributable to the hedged risk is reclassified from OCI to profit or loss. [*IFRS 9.IE138–IE147*]

7.9.420.170   There is no need to de-designate and redesignate the first-level hedge when establishing the second-level hedge. This avoids complexity and increased ineffectiveness, because the derivative in the first hedge would probably have a fair value other than zero at that time. [*IFRS 9.B6.3.3*]

7.9.420.180   Additional complexity arises if there is basis risk in the first-level hedging relationship – i.e. the terms of the hedging instrument and the hedged item in the first-level hedge do not exactly match. Ineffectiveness caused by basis risk present in the first-level hedge would also result in ineffectiveness in the second-level hedge.

7.9.420.190   Furthermore, IFRS 9 does not require hedge accounting to be applied at the first level to apply hedge accounting to a second-level hedge. That is, even if an entity fails to achieve hedge accounting for a first-level hedge or chooses not to apply hedge accounting, the second-level hedge might qualify for hedge accounting.

7.9.430   Highly probable forecast transactions

7.9.430.10   Forecast transactions should be highly probable and should present an exposure to variations in cash flows that could ultimately affect profit or loss. [*IFRS 9.6.3.3, 6.5.2(b)*]

7.9.430.20   In our view, for a forecast transaction to be considered 'highly probable', there should be at least a 90 percent probability of the transaction occurring. In assessing whether a transaction is highly probable, consideration should be given to the facts and circumstances, including:
• the quality of the budgeting processes;
• the extent and frequency of similar transactions in the past;
• whether previous similar expected cash flows actually occurred;
• the availability of adequate resources to finish the transaction;
• the impact on operations if the transaction does not occur;
• the possibility of different transactions being used to achieve the same purpose;
• how far into the future the transaction is expected to occur; and
• the quantity of anticipated transactions. [*IFRS 9.6.3.3*]

7.9.430.30   It is normally possible to meet the highly probable criterion if significant similar transactions are expected and hedge accounting is limited to a percentage of these expected transactions.

For example, the hedged item may be designated as the first 80 of anticipated sales of approximately 100 expected in September 2018, because it is highly probable that 80 percent of the anticipated sales will be made. However, if the hedged item is designated as 100 of anticipated sales of 100 in September 2018, then it is unlikely that the highly probable criterion will be met.

7.9.430.40   In our view, the highly probable criterion might not be met when an entity purchases an option as a hedge of a particular foreign currency because it has made a bid for a large contract in that foreign currency. For example, if it is not highly probable that the entity will win the bid for the contract, then the foreign currency cash flows would not be highly probable because they are dependent on the probability of the entity winning the bid for the contract.

7.9.430.50   In our view, it is more likely that a large number of homogenous forecast transactions will meet the highly probable criterion than a single forecast transaction. When determining whether a single forecast transaction meets this criterion, an entity considers the facts and circumstances that influence the probability of occurrence of the transaction. Indicators that may suggest that a forecast transaction is not highly probable may be an illiquid market in which the forecast transaction takes place, a low number of transactions, no past experience of the entity with such transactions or historical experience that such transactions do not occur often.

EXAMPLE 24 – HIGHLY PROBABLE HOMOGENEOUS FORECAST TRANSACTIONS

7.9.430.60   Bank B entered into mortgage loan commitments with potential customers. These commitments give the customer 90 days to lock in a mortgage at a discounted variable rate. To reduce the interest rate risk inherent in the anticipated mortgage transactions, B enters into forward-starting interest rate swaps based on the expected acceptances.

7.9.430.70   When evaluating the probability of acceptance by only a single customer, a high probability would be difficult to demonstrate. However, when evaluating the probability of a group of commitments, it is possible that B can estimate with high probability the amount of mortgages that will eventually be closed. Therefore, B could use cash flow hedge accounting for the hedge of interest rate risk on the amount of mortgages that are highly probable of being closed.

7.9.430.80   Similarly, when designating assets or liabilities with prepayment risk in a cash flow hedge, assessing the probability of interest cash flows arising from the entire portfolio rather than for a single instrument could result in identifying a bottom layer of interest cash flows that could then be considered highly probable (see 7.9.460).

7.9.430.90   An entity should be careful in its designation of forecast transactions as hedged items, because a history of such forecast transactions not occurring when expected could jeopardise its ability to continue to designate these types of hedges in the future. [*IFRS 9.B6.5.27*]

7.9.440   *Defining period in which forecast transaction expected to occur*

7.9.440.10   IFRS 9 does not specify a timeframe in which the forecast transaction should occur. However, for it to be an eligible hedged item, the forecast transaction must be highly probable. Further, the hedge has to relate to a specifically identified and designated risk, and the hedged item must be reliably measurable. If the forecast transaction is not expected to occur within a reasonably specific and narrow range of time, then it would be difficult to measure the item reliably. Therefore, in our view a highly probable forecast transaction should be the one that is expected to occur within a reasonably specific and narrow range of time. We believe that the forecast transaction should be identified and documented with sufficient specificity so that when the transaction occurs it is clear whether it is the hedged transaction. An entity is not required to predict and document the exact date on which a forecast transaction is expected to occur, but the documentation should identify a time period in which the forecast transaction is expected to occur within a reasonably specific and narrow range, as a basis for assessing hedge effectiveness. [*IFRS 9.6.3.2–6.3.3, B6.3.1*]

7.9.440.20   In determining appropriate time periods for hedge accounting purposes, an entity may look to the following.
- *Forecasts and budgets:* An entity would not generally identify longer time periods for hedge accounting purposes than those used for forecasting and budgeting.
- *The nature of the business or industry:* The forecasting and budgeting periods used by an entity are influenced by its ability to reliably forecast the timing of its transactions. Generally, the forecast periods for manufacturers of ships or aircraft will be longer than those for retail stores. Usually, retailers sell smaller items in large quantities and can more easily forecast the timing of sales over shorter periods of time.

7.9.440.30   Although the factors in 7.9.440.20 provide an indication of the appropriate time period in which the transaction is expected to occur, the actual time period is always determined on a case-by-case basis and will involve some degree of judgement. Generally, the sooner that the anticipated transaction is expected to occur, the easier it will be to demonstrate that the highly probable criterion is met.

7.9.440.40   In our view, some delay in the occurrence of a highly probable forecast transaction is acceptable as long as the transaction is considered to be the *same* forecast transaction – i.e. the transaction that subsequently happens is clearly identifiable as the original forecast transaction. Therefore, the subsequent transaction should have the same specifications as the originally forecast transaction.

7.9.440.50   We believe that it would not be appropriate, for example, for a retailer to designate as the hedged item the first 50 of foreign currency sales in January and when this does not happen to argue that it is highly probable that there will be 50 of additional foreign currency sales in February to replace the lost sales in January. In such a case, there would be a forecast error regarding the 50 sales in January – i.e. these sales would be considered 'no longer expected to occur' – which means that hedge accounting would be terminated (see 7.9.930). However, if a shipbuilder has a highly probable forecast sale of a specified ship to a particular customer but the expected delivery date moves from January to February, then it may be required to continue hedge accounting because of the specific nature of the hedged forecast cash flow (see 7.9.980).

7.9.440.60   If the hedged item is a series of forecast transactions, then the hedged item is identified and documented with sufficient specificity so that when the transaction occurs it is clear that it is the hedged transaction. For this reason, the documentation should specify that the hedged item is an identifiable portion of a series of transactions that will occur in a specified period. It is not acceptable to designate a set percentage of transactions in a period, or the last in a series of transactions, as the hedged item because these cannot be identified specifically when they occur. For example, the hedged item may be designated as the first 20,000 of anticipated foreign currency sales in September 2018, but not as 20,000 of anticipated foreign currency sales in September 2018. As another example, the hedged item is not permitted to be designated as 20 percent of anticipated foreign currency sales over the 2018 financial year. [*IFRS 9.6.2.3, 6.3.2, 6.4.1(b)*]

7.9.450   *Expected interest cash flows*

7.9.450.10   To meet the hedge accounting criteria, a forecast debt issue needs to be highly probable. This could be the case once the entity enters into an agreement to issue the debt, but may be evidenced at an earlier stage when management decides on a debt issue as part of its funding strategy.

7.9.450.20   An entity may apply cash flow hedge accounting to an anticipated debt issue because changes in interest rates between the date of deciding on the debt issue and the actual issue date will influence the rate at which the debt will be issued or the discount or premium that will apply to the proceeds. For example, if the long-term interest rate were to increase, then the debt would be issued at a higher rate or for lower proceeds than anticipated originally.

7.9.450.30   Normally, a gain or loss on an appropriate hedging instrument will offset the higher/lower interest rate or the decrease/increase in proceeds. Using the cash flow hedge model, the effective portion of the gains or losses resulting from the hedging instrument until the debt is issued will be recognised in OCI. On issuance of the debt, such gains and losses will remain in equity and be reclassified to profit or loss in the periods in which the hedged forecast cash flows affect profit or loss – i.e. when the interest expense is recognised. This will require the entity to track the amount of gains or losses recognised in OCI to ensure that the correct amounts are reclassified to profit or loss at the correct times.

EXAMPLE 25A – HEDGE OF FORECAST INTEREST PAYMENTS

7.9.450.40   Company K is in the process of issuing a bond. K wishes to hedge the risk of changes in interest rates between the date on which it decides to issue the bond and the date of issue. This can be done using an interest future or other derivative instruments.

7.9.450.50   To the extent that the hedge is effective, the gain or loss on the derivative will be recognised in OCI. This gain or loss will remain in equity and will be reclassified to profit or loss as interest payments on the bond affect profit or loss and will effectively adjust the interest expense recognised on the bond.

EXAMPLE 25B – HEDGE OF FORECAST INTEREST PAYMENTS – MULTIPLE TRANCHES

> **7.9.450.60**   Company M plans to issue two tranches of floating rate notes, each with a maturity of three years. M intends to issue the second tranche on maturity of the first. M decides to enter into a six-year swap to hedge the variability in expected interest cash flows on both note issues.
>
> **7.9.450.70**   For hedge accounting purposes, M decides that the hedge will be designated as a hedge of the expected interest payments in different periods, including interest payments arising from the forecast refinancing of the debt. To qualify for hedge accounting, at the inception of the hedge the criteria for hedge accounting needs to be met, including the criteria that:
> - the hedge effectiveness requirements are met; and
> - the second issue after three years must be highly probable.

7.9.450.80   In our view, in order for a forecast issue of debt to qualify for hedge accounting, all of its critical terms should be highly probable. For example, an entity with a euro functional currency may have a highly probable bond issue, but the currency of issue may not have been determined. If the entity issues the bond in US dollars, then it will enter into a currency swap to convert the cash flows to euro. However, regardless of the currency in which the bond is issued, the entity wishes to hedge its euro interest rate exposure using an interest rate swap. We believe that, because the currency denomination of the forecast bond is not highly probable, the forecast bond issue cannot qualify for hedge accounting.

7.9.450.90   Similarly, it will not be possible to achieve hedge accounting for forecast issues of commercial paper unless the currency and maturity (including rollovers) of the future issues can be determined reliably. However, IFRS 9 allows the designation of aggregated exposures (see 7.9.420). Therefore, a forecast synthetic exposure (e.g. a forecast issue of a bond with unknown currency and a forecast currency swap with an offsetting unknown currency leg) can qualify for hedge accounting of the interest rate risk as long as the aggregated exposure is highly probable and, once it has occurred, is eligible as a hedged item. In this case, if the entity concludes that it is highly probable that it will either issue US dollar bonds and enter into a receive-USD pay-floating euro cross-currency interest rate swap or issue a euro floating rate bond, then we believe that the euro floating interest rate exposure can qualify for hedge accounting because it is highly probable that this interest rate risk will arise in a specified period of time and the aggregated exposure will also be an eligible item once the transactions have been entered into.

7.9.460   *Prepayment risk*

7.9.460.10   Prepayment risk may also affect whether a forecast transaction designated in a cash flow hedge is considered highly probable to occur. However, when the hedged item is designated as the first cash flows of a portfolio occurring in a given period, the effect of a prepayment is less likely to cause the hedged forecast transactions not to be highly probable as long as there are sufficient cash flows in the period. This can be demonstrated by the entity preparing a cash flow maturity schedule that shows sufficient levels of expected cash flows in each period to support a highly probable assertion. For example, a bank may be able to determine accurately what levels of prepayments are expected for a particular class of its originated loans. The bank might hedge only a portion of the contractual cash flows from that portfolio of loans because it expects a number of borrowers to repay their loans early.

7.9.470   Cash flow hedges and business combinations

7.9.470.10   A firm commitment to acquire a business in a business combination can be a hedged item only for foreign exchange risk because other risks cannot be specifically identified and measured. In our view, an entity may also hedge the foreign exchange risk of a highly probable forecast business combination. In our view, in the consolidated financial statements a cash flow hedge of the foreign exchange risk of a firm commitment to acquire a business or a forecast business combination relates to the foreign currency equivalent of the consideration paid. [*IFRS 9.B6.3.1*]

7.9.470.20   In a cash flow hedge designation, the effective portion of the gain or loss arising from the hedging instrument is recognised in OCI. However, an issue arises about when and how this amount accumulated in equity is reclassified to profit or loss. The answer depends on whether the hedge represents a hedge of a non-financial item or a financial item. [*IFRS 9.6.5.11*]

7.9.470.30   In our view, because a hedge of a firm commitment to acquire a business or forecast business combination relates to the foreign currency equivalent of the consideration paid, the acquisition of an equity interest in the entity may be viewed as either a hedge of the purchase of shares of an entity or a hedge of the purchase of a business. A hedge of the purchase of shares represents a hedge of a financial item, whereas a hedge of the purchase of a business represents a hedge of a non-financial item. Therefore, we believe that an entity should choose an accounting policy, to be applied consistently, on whether such hedges are considered hedges of a financial item or non-financial item.

7.9.470.40   For hedges of a financial item, the accounting for the reclassification from equity to profit or loss is complicated by the fact that the shares acquired are not recognised in the consolidated financial statements and therefore will never directly impact profit or loss. However, for hedges of financial and non-financial items, the effective portion of the gain or loss arising from the hedging instrument relates to the foreign currency equivalent of the consideration paid. Therefore, recognition of the effective portion of the gain or loss arising from the hedging instrument in profit or loss occurs when the residual (i.e. goodwill) arising from the business combination affects profit or loss.

7.9.470.50   In our view, if the hedge is a hedge of a financial item, then the entity should retain the gain or loss from the hedging instrument recognised in OCI as a separate component of equity until the goodwill from the hedged business combination in part or in full affects profit or loss – e.g. through transactions such as impairment of goodwill or sale of the business acquired. When the goodwill from the hedged business combination affects profit or loss, all or a portion of the gain or loss recognised in OCI should be reclassified to profit or loss.

7.9.470.60   In our view, if the hedge is a hedge of a non-financial item, then the entity should recognise the gain or loss from the hedging instrument recognised in OCI as an adjustment to goodwill when the business combination occurs.

7.9.470.70   In our view, a hedge of a firm commitment to acquire a business or a forecast business combination that will be effected through the acquisition of the assets and liabilities that comprise the business – rather than the acquisition of an equity interest in the entity – should be accounted for as a hedge of a non-financial item because the legal form of the transaction does not involve the acquisition of a financial asset.

7.9.480   **All-in-one cash flow hedges**

7.9.480.10   An entity may enter into a contract to purchase or sell a non-financial item or a financial asset and the contract may be required to be accounted for as a derivative. For example, a fixed price contract to purchase a commodity would not be eligible for the own-use scope exemption when the entity has a past practice of taking delivery of the underlying and selling it within a short period after delivery for trading purposes (see 7.1.210). In such a scenario, if the derivative will be settled gross, then the entity may designate this derivative as the hedging instrument in a cash flow hedge of the variability of the consideration to be paid or received in the future transaction that will occur on gross settlement of the derivative contract itself – i.e. a hedge of the forecast transaction that is implicit in the derivative itself – assuming that the other cash flow hedging criteria are met. [*IFRS 9.6.2.1, 6.3.1*]

7.9.480.20   This hedging strategy is referred to as an 'all-in-one cash flow hedge' and applies to all fixed price contracts that are accounted for as derivatives. By designating an all-in-one cash flow hedge, the entity avoids recognising in profit or loss the changes in the fair value of the purchase/sale contract that would otherwise be recognised in profit or loss because the contract is accounted for as a derivative.

7.9.480.30   An all-in-one hedge may also be designated in a forecast purchase or sale involving a financial asset. For example, a financial institution manages the price risk associated with forecast purchases of loans by entering into forward agreements to purchase mortgage loans at a fixed price. This forward contract to purchase loans meets the definition of a derivative and is required to be accounted for at FVTPL. However, the forward loan purchase agreement may be designated as a cash flow hedge of the forecast purchase of loans – i.e. as an all-in-one hedge of price risk – provided that the contract will be settled gross.

7.9.490   **Equity investments for which the fair value changes are present in OCI**

7.9.490.10   An entity may, on initial recognition, make an irrevocable election to present subsequent changes in the fair value of an investment in equity instruments in OCI if the investment is not held for trading. Such an investment is an eligible hedged item in a fair value hedge. If such investments are designated in a fair value hedge, then the changes in the fair value of derivative hedging instruments and hedged items are reflected in OCI; therefore, any hedge ineffectiveness will be recognised in OCI. These amounts accumulated in OCI are never reclassified to profit or loss (see 7.9.170). [*IFRS 9.5.7.5, BC6.105–BC6.116*]

7.9.500   **Portfolio fair value hedges of interest rate risk**

7.9.500.10   IFRS 9 permits entities to designate portfolio fair value hedges of interest rate risk using the guidance in IAS 39. [*IFRS 9.6.1.3*]

7.9.500.20   Entities (banks in particular) often manage interest rate risk on a portfolio basis – e.g. for a portfolio of mortgage loans or vehicle financing arrangements. Such hedging practices, whereby an entity hedges its net exposures, do not generally qualify for hedge accounting. However, an entity is permitted to designate the interest rate exposure of a portfolio of financial assets or financial liabilities as the hedged item in a portfolio fair value hedge. The hedged item is designated in terms of an amount of currency rather than as individual assets or liabilities. Although the portfolio may – for risk management purposes – include only assets, only liabilities or both assets and liabilities, the amount designated is an amount of assets or an amount of liabilities. Designation of a net amount – comprising both assets and liabilities – is not permitted. The entity may hedge a portion of the interest rate risk associated with the designated amount. [*IAS 39.78, 81A, AG114(c), AG116, AG118*]

7.9.500.30   The portfolio fair value hedge model accommodates prepayment risk more readily than the normal fair value hedge model for individual assets or liabilities. However, the model can be applied only for hedges of interest rate risk and cannot be used for other risk types – e.g. foreign currency risk. Under the portfolio fair value hedge model, prepayable items are scheduled into repricing time periods based on expected, rather than contractual, repricing dates. This captures the effect of prepayments and consequently there is no need to assess separately the impact of prepayment risk on the fair value of the portfolio. [*IAS 39.81A, AG114(b)*]

7.9.500.40   Because under this hedging model the hedged item is designated as an amount of currency, all of the assets or liabilities from which the hedged item is derived should be items whose fair value changes in response to changes in the interest rate being hedged and items that could have qualified for fair value hedge accounting if they had been designated as hedged items individually. In particular, because the fair value of a financial liability with a demand feature (such as demand deposits and some types of time deposits) is not less than the amount payable on demand, discounted from the first date on which the amount could be required to be paid (see 2.4.420), such an item cannot qualify for hedge accounting for any time period beyond the shortest period in which the holder can demand payment. For example, because the fair value of a liability that is repayable immediately on demand is usually equal to the amount payable on demand, there is no fair value exposure to hedge because the fair value of such a deposit is unaffected by interest rates and does not change when interest rates change. [*IFRS 13.47, AG118(b), BC187(d)*]

7.9.500.50   IAS 39 provides specific guidance on the measurement of effectiveness for such a hedging relationship, as well as the presentation of the fair value adjustment and its subsequent amortisation to profit or loss. However, because a single method for assessing hedge effectiveness is not specified (see 7.9.790), in our view such specific guidance does not preclude the use of regression analysis for testing the effectiveness (see 7.9.830.60) of such macro fair value hedges. [*IAS 39.AG126–AG127*]

7.9.500.60   In the event that the hedged prepayable items are subject to a prepayment penalty that represents the difference between the fair value of the hedged item and its carrying amount, in our view it is acceptable to schedule the hedged items based on contractual repricing dates. The penalty has the effect of eliminating all fair value exposures arising from prepayment risk.

7.9.500.70   For a fair value hedge of the interest rate exposure arising from a portion of a portfolio of financial assets or financial liabilities, the gain or loss attributable to the hedged item may be presented as a single separate line item within assets or liabilities depending on whether the hedged item is an asset or a liability for that particular repricing time period. If amortising this gain or loss using a recalculated effective interest rate is impracticable, then it is amortised using the straight-line method (see 7.9.170.90). [*IAS 39.89A*]

7.9.510   ITEMS THAT DO NOT QUALIFY AS HEDGED ITEMS

7.9.510.10   There are a number of items that for different reasons do not qualify for hedge accounting. In these cases, the normal recognition and measurement principles of IFRS are applied.

7.9.520   Forecast purchase of equity investments that will be measured at fair value

7.9.520.10   A forecast purchase of an equity instrument that, once acquired, will be accounted for at FVTPL or at FVOCI cannot be the hedged item in a cash flow hedge. This is because any gain or loss on the hedging instrument that would be deferred could not be appropriately reclassified to profit or loss during a period in which it would achieve offset. [*IFRS 9.B6.5.2*]

7.9.530   Own equity instruments

7.9.530.10   An entity's own equity instruments cannot be the hedged item because there is no risk exposure that affects profit or loss because transactions in own shares are recognised directly in equity. Likewise, forecast transactions in an entity's own equity cannot be a hedged item and neither can distributions to holders of the entity's equity instruments. However, a dividend that has been declared but not yet paid and is recognised as a financial liability may qualify as a hedged item – e.g. for foreign currency risk if it is denominated in a foreign currency. [*IFRS 9.6.5.2*]

7.9.540   Dividends

7.9.540.10   Entities might also wish to hedge anticipated dividends from foreign operations. However, expected dividends do not give rise to an exposure that will be recognised in profit or loss in the consolidated financial statements and do not form part of the net investment in a foreign operation. Therefore, these cannot be hedged in a cash flow hedge or a net investment hedge in the consolidated financial statements. It is only once dividends are declared and become a receivable that hedge accounting may be applied in the consolidated financial statements. For example, dividends declared and receivable from a foreign subsidiary may be hedged for foreign currency risk because changes in foreign exchange rates would affect consolidated profit or loss. [*IFRS 9.6.3.5, 6.5.2*]

7.9.550   Exposures within an associate or joint venture

7.9.550.10   In our view, an investor in an associate or joint venture cannot hedge an exposure that exists within the associate or joint venture. This is because the potential hedged item is not a forecast transaction or recognised asset or liability of the investor. The investor's equity ownership represents shared ownership of the associate or joint venture's net assets and liabilities, and the investor cannot look through to the associate or joint venture's individual assets or liabilities and designate one of them as the hedged item.

EXAMPLE 26 – EQUITY-ACCOUNTED INVESTEES

7.9.550.20   Company R is an investor in Joint Venture J. J issues LIBOR-based variable rate debt. R cannot designate a cash flow hedge of J's variable rate debt because the potential hedged item is not a forecast transaction or recognised asset or liability of R from R's point of view because R does not have any direct exposure

> to J's variable rate debt. Similarly, the impact of the debt interest payments is indirect on R's profit or loss because the impact is netted with the other results of J through R's application of the equity method. [*IFRS 9.6.5.2*]

7.9.560   HEDGING INSTRUMENTS

7.9.560.10   The following contracts with a party external to the reporting entity – i.e. external to the group or individual entity that is being reported on – may qualify as hedging instruments.
- All derivatives measured at FVTPL, except:
  - written options not designated as offsets to purchased options (see 7.9.610); and
  - derivatives embedded in hybrid contracts that are not accounted for separately.
- Certain non-derivative financial assets or non-derivative financial liabilities (see 7.9.590).
  [*IFRS 9.6.2.1–6.2.3, B6.2.4*]

7.9.560.20   A qualifying hedging instrument may be designated in its entirety in a hedging relationship or, alternatively, a proportion of the entire hedging instrument may be designated in the hedging relationship – e.g. 50 percent of the nominal amount. However, a hedging instrument may not be designated for a part of its change in fair value that results from only a portion of the time period during which the hedging instrument remains outstanding. [*IFRS 9.6.2.4(c)*]

7.9.560.30   An entity may view in combination, and jointly designate as the hedging instrument, any combination of the following; this includes those circumstances in which the risk or risks arising from some hedging instruments offset those arising from others:
- derivatives or a proportion of them; and
- non-derivatives or a proportion of them. [*IFRS 9.6.2.5*]

7.9.560.40   An entity may exclude from the designation of a hedging instrument:
- the time value of purchased options;
- the forward element of forward contracts; and
- foreign currency basis spreads (see 7.9.650). [*IFRS 9.6.2.4*]

7.9.560.50   An entity is required to account for the excluded time value of purchased options as a 'cost of hedging'. It may also account for the excluded forward element of forward contracts and excluded foreign currency basis spreads as a cost of hedging. For a further discussion of the accounting for excluded costs of hedging, see 7.9.690. [*IFRS 9.6.5.15–6.5.16*]

7.9.560.60   The following uses of hedging instruments are permitted:
- designating a derivative as a hedging instrument subsequent to its initial recognition;
- designating two or more derivatives in combination as the hedging instrument, as long as the combination does not result in a net written option (see 7.9.560.30 and 610);
- designating two or more non-derivatives, or a combination of derivatives and non-derivatives (see 7.9.560.30);
- replacing or rolling over a hedging instrument at its maturity, if the replacement or rollover is part of the risk management activities of an entity and is documented at inception of the hedging relationship;

- designating a derivative with an external party that offsets an internal derivative as a hedging instrument (see 7.9.1150);
- applying hedge accounting in the consolidated financial statements to a derivative entered into by a group entity other than the one that has the risk exposure (see 7.9.1140); and
- applying hedge accounting to a derivative even though that derivative is fully offset by another derivative with equal but opposite terms, as long as the second instrument was not entered into in contemplation of the first or there is a substantive business purpose for entering into both instruments in separate transactions (see 7.9.1160.40). [*IFRS 9.6.2.1–6.2.3, IG.B.6, IG.C.6*]

7.9.570   Hedging more than one risk type

7.9.570.10   A hedging instrument, or a proportion thereof, is designated in its entirety, because there is normally a single fair value measure for a hedging instrument and the factors (risk components) that cause changes in fair value are co-dependent. Using an entire instrument or a proportion of an instrument is acceptable for hedge accounting, but using only a portion – e.g. a single risk component – is not generally allowed. For example, a cross-currency interest rate swap is designated with respect to all changes in its fair value, including those arising from foreign currency risk and interest rate risk. [*IFRS 9.6.2.4*]

7.9.570.20   However, it is possible to designate a single hedging instrument – e.g. a cross-currency swap – as a hedge of more than one risk type if the following conditions are met:
- the risks being hedged are separately identifiable and reliably measurable;
- the effectiveness requirements are met; and
- there is specific designation of the hedging instrument and the different risk positions. [*IFRS 9.B6.2.6, B6.3.8–B6.3.15*]

7.9.570.30   Consequently, part of a derivative hedging instrument may be designated for a particular risk of the hedged item, provided that the other parts of the hedging instrument are designated as hedging other risks of other hedged items (or the same hedged item) and all other hedge accounting criteria are met. However, practical difficulties in separating fair values between inter-related risks could present difficulties in meeting the conditions under which such a designation is permissible.

EXAMPLE 27 – HEDGING MORE THAN ONE RISK TYPE

7.9.570.40   Company W has the euro as its functional currency and issues a floating rate sterling-denominated bond. W also has a fixed rate US dollar financial asset with the same maturity and payment dates as the bond. To offset the currency and interest rate risk on the financial asset and financial liability, W enters into a pay-US dollar fixed receive-sterling floating interest rate swap.

7.9.570.50   The swap may be designated as a hedging instrument of the US dollar financial asset against the fair value exposure arising from changes in US interest rates and the foreign currency risk between the US dollar and sterling. Alternatively, it could be designated as a cash flow hedge of the cash flow exposure arising from the variable cash outflows of the sterling bond and the foreign currency risk arising from movements in the US dollar/sterling exchange rate.

7.9.570.60   Both of these designations would be permissible even though the hedge does not convert the foreign currency exposure into W's functional currency (euro). In our view, this type of hedge is appropriate only if W has foreign currency exposures to both US dollar and sterling and is not creating a new foreign currency position, but rather is decreasing its risk exposure compared with its functional currency. Both foreign currency exposures should be referred to in the hedge documentation (see 7.9.240.10). It should be clear in the documentation that the relationship between the swap and the US dollar financial asset qualifies for hedge accounting only because of the existence of both a US dollar financial asset and a sterling financial liability. [*IFRS 9.6.3.7(a), B6.2.6*]

7.9.580   Designation for entire period

7.9.580.10   Derivatives and non-derivatives are designated as hedging instruments for the entire period for which they are outstanding because the entire fair value of the hedging instrument is considered when assessing the effectiveness of the hedge. For example, a pay-fixed receive-floating interest rate swap with a maturity of 10 years cannot be designated as a hedging instrument of a floating rate bond for just the first eight years by using the eight-year yield curve to measure the changes in the fair value of the swap when assessing hedge effectiveness. Such a method would allow an entity to exclude part of the hedging instrument's fair value, which is not allowed. Hedge designation would, however, be permitted in this case if the derivative were designated as the hedging instrument in its entirety – i.e. the changes in the fair value of the swap are computed using all of its cash flows based on the 10-year yield curve when assessing hedge effectiveness. However, such a strategy would lead to ineffectiveness and may also result in hedge accounting being precluded if the hedging relationship does not meet hedge effectiveness requirements. [*IFRS 9.6.2.4(c)*]

7.9.580.20   It is possible to designate a derivative or non-derivative as the hedging instrument subsequent to initial recognition provided that the fair value for the entire remaining period for which the derivative or non-derivative remains outstanding is included when assessing hedge effectiveness. For example, if a derivative is designated as a hedging instrument at inception – but hedge accounting ceases because the hedge criteria are not met or the designation is revoked at a later date – then it is possible to designate the derivative as the hedging instrument in another hedging relationship at a later stage, as long as the designation and assessment of hedge effectiveness include the fair value for the entire period for which the derivative remains outstanding. [*IFRS 9.6.2.4(c)*]

7.9.580.30   A derivative may be designated as the hedging instrument in a hedge of a highly probable forecast transaction that has a maturity shorter than the remaining maturity of the hedging derivative. Because the derivative is required to be designated for its entire remaining term to maturity, in such a hedge there will be some ineffectiveness because of the differences in maturity dates of the hedged item and hedging derivative. Also, the ineffectiveness might sometimes be so significant that it precludes application of hedge accounting altogether if the economic relationship criterion is not met.

7.9.590   Non-derivative financial assets and financial liabilities

7.9.590.10   Non-derivative financial assets or non-derivative financial liabilities measured at FVTPL may be designated as hedging instruments in hedging relationships, except for financial liabilities designated as at FVTPL for which the amount of changes in fair value attributable to changes in credit risk is presented in OCI. These eligible instruments may be designated as a hedge of any risk – not only foreign currency risk. [*IFRS 9.6.2.2*]

7.9.590.20   For hedges of foreign currency risk, an entity may designate the foreign currency risk component of a non-derivative financial asset or a non-derivative financial liability as the hedging instrument. This is permitted only if the financial instrument is not an investment in an equity instrument for which the entity has elected to present changes in fair value in OCI. [*IFRS 9.6.2.2*]

EXAMPLE 28 – NON-DERIVATIVE HEDGE OF FOREIGN CURRENCY RISK

7.9.590.30   Company J has the yen as its functional currency and has a fixed interest rate US dollar borrowing. J accounts for the borrowing as at amortised cost.

7.9.590.40   J may designate the US dollar borrowing as a hedge of the foreign exchange exposure on a net investment in a US dollar foreign operation or a US dollar sales commitment. However, J cannot designate the US dollar borrowing as a hedge of the interest and foreign currency exposure on a fixed rate US dollar debt security or the entire fair value exposure on a US dollar sales commitment. This is because non-derivatives, other than equity investment for which an entity has elected to present changes in fair value in OCI, measured at amortised cost or at FVOCI qualify as hedging instruments for hedges of foreign currency risk only. [*IFRS 9.6.2.2*]

7.9.590.50   A firm commitment or forecast transaction does not qualify as a hedging instrument if it is neither a derivative nor a non-derivative financial asset or non-derivative financial liability. If an embedded derivative is separated from a firm commitment and accounted for as a derivative measured at FVTPL, then it could qualify as a hedging instrument. [*IFRS 9.6.2.1–6.2.2*]

7.9.590.60   Whether a non-derivative financial instrument accounted for at FVTPL as a result of electing the fair value option may be used as a hedging instrument depends on the relevant facts and circumstances. Designation as a hedging instrument should not contradict the entity's election of the fair value option – i.e. it should not recreate an accounting mismatch that the fair value option addressed. [*IFRS 9.BC6.136–BC6.139*]

EXAMPLE 29 – NON-DERIVATIVE FINANCIAL ASSET MEASURED AT FVTPL DESIGNATED AS HEDGING INSTRUMENT

7.9.590.70   Company R has a highly probable forecast purchase of a commodity that it wants to hedge. However, it is not cost-effective for R to enter into a derivative to hedge the commodity price risk of its forecast purchase because the amount of the purchase is less than the standard notional size of the relevant commodity derivative contract offered in the marketplace.

7.9.590.80   Instead, R purchases shares in an investment fund that holds commodity-linked instruments with the objective of hedging its commodity price risk exposure from the forecast purchase. R purchases the number of shares that correspond to the notional exposure to the commodity risk.

7.9.590.90   The shares in the commodity investment fund are measured at FVTPL, so they are eligible for designation as the hedging instrument in a cash flow hedge of the forecast commodity purchase.

7.9.600   *Lease payments and receipts*

7.9.600.10   In our view, whether cash flows payable or receivable under a lease arrangement should be financial instruments or non-financial instruments with respect to their designation as a hedging instrument depends on whether the lease is classified as a finance lease or an operating lease.

7.9.600.20   We believe that a recognised finance lease payable or receivable can qualify as a hedging instrument of foreign currency risk even though it is not generally in the scope of IFRS 9, provided that all hedge accounting requirements are met (see 7.9.240). [*IAS 32.AG9*]

7.9.600.30   Conversely, we believe that an operating lease cannot be designated as a hedging instrument. This is because payments due or receivable under an operating lease are not recognised financial liabilities or financial assets that could qualify as a hedging instrument. However, individual payments currently due and payable with respect to the elapsed period of the lease term for which performance has occurred are financial instruments. [*IAS 32.AG9*]

7.9.610   **Written options**

7.9.610.10   A derivative instrument that combines a written option and a purchased option – e.g. an interest rate collar – cannot qualify as a hedging instrument if it is, in effect, a net written option at the date of designation. Factors considered in determining whether a combination of derivatives is in effect a net written option include:

* whether any net premium is received either at inception or over the life of the combined instrument;
* whether the written option component and the purchased option component have similar critical terms and conditions and, with the exception of strike prices, the same underlying variable(s), currency, denomination and maturity; and
* whether the notional amount of the written option component is greater than the notional amount of the purchased option component. [*IFRS 9.6.2.6, B6.2.4, BC6.153*]

7.9.610.20   An entity may also designate two or more instruments (or proportions of them) as a hedging instrument only if, in combination, they are not, in effect, a net written option at the date of designation. [*IFRS 9.6.2.6, B6.2.4*]

7.9.610.30   In our view, an entity should assess at the date of hedge designation the fair value of a collar (or a combined purchased and written option) that is designated as a hedging instrument (or instruments) to determine whether any net premium is received. This is because the assessment of whether an instrument is a net written option is performed at the date of designation and a negative fair value is indicative of the receipt of a net premium that is compensation for written optionality that presents a risk of greater potential loss. [*IFRS 9.6.2.6, B6.2.4, BC6.153*]

EXAMPLE 30 – NET WRITTEN OPTION TEST

7.9.610.40   On 1 January 2018, Company Z forecasts the purchase of goods in October 2018. Z's risk management policy requires it to hedge price increases on the forecast purchases while minimising the cost of the hedge. On 1 January, Z decides that it wishes to use a combination of options that would effectively lock the unit price of the forecast purchases between 6 and 10.

7.9.610.50   Accordingly, on 1 January, Z purchases a call option with a unit strike price of 10 and pays a premium of 9,000. However, Z is not able to write a put option on the same day. Z writes a put option on 15 January with a unit strike price of 6 and receives a premium of 10,000. On that date, the fair value of the purchased call option has increased to 12,000.

7.9.610.60   The hedging relationship is designated on 15 January. To determine whether the combination of the purchased call option and written put option qualifies as a hedging instrument on 15 January, Z performs the following analysis.
- *Fair value:* The fair value of the combined instruments is determined to be 2,000 (implying a net purchased option) on 15 January.
- *Critical terms:* Except for the strike price, all of the terms (including the quantities of underlying goods) of the purchased call option and the written put options match.

7.9.610.70   Based on this analysis, Z determines that the combination of the purchased option and the written option is not a net written option. Therefore, it qualifies as a hedging instrument.

7.9.610.80   However, an instrument or combination of instruments that in effect is a net written option qualifies as a hedging instrument only if it is designated as an offset to a purchased option, including one that is embedded in another financial instrument – e.g. a written call option used to hedge a callable liability. [*IFRS 9.6.2.6, B6.2.4*]

7.9.620   Basis swaps

7.9.620.10   An entity may swap one floating rate exposure into another using basis swaps. Basis swaps are interest rate swaps that exchange one base rate for another. For example, an entity that issues a bond paying 12-month Euribor enters into a basis swap whereby it receives 12-month Euribor and pays three-month Euribor, with the notional and maturity of the swap matching those of the bond. A question arises about whether such a basis swap can be designated as a hedge of the floating rate bond.

7.9.620.20   Although swapping one base rate for another with a different repricing period may eliminate some of the cash flow variation or some of the fair value variation, there is no model that explicitly allows for hedge accounting when one floating rate is swapped into another. Because the bond in 7.9.620.10 has a floating rate of interest, it may be eligible for cash flow hedge accounting.

However, because the interest rate swap exchanges one floating cash flow stream into another, some variability in cash flows remains.

7.9.620.30   Therefore, in our view a basis swap does not generally qualify as a hedging instrument in a cash flow hedge except in the very specific circumstances discussed in 7.9.620.40.

7.9.620.40   If an entity has both an asset and a liability on which it receives interest at a rate indexed to the base rate on the pay leg (e.g. LIBOR) of the basis swap, and pays interest at a rate equal to the base rate on the receive leg (e.g. Euribor) of the basis swap, then in our view hedge accounting is appropriate provided that the other hedge criteria are satisfied. Both the existing asset and the liability are designated as hedged items in the same hedging relationship and both positions are considered in effectiveness assessment. If the hedge fails to meet the hedge effectiveness requirements for either of the positions, then hedge accounting is terminated for the entire hedging relationship. In this case, the combined variability in cash flows resulting from movements in base rates arising from both the asset and the liability is eliminated by the basis swap. Consequently, we believe that it is possible to designate the basis swap in a cash flow hedging relationship in this limited circumstance. [*IFRS 9.6.3.7(a), B6.2.6*]

7.9.630   **Constant maturity interest rate swaps**

7.9.630.10   An entity may issue instruments that have a floating rate of interest that resets periodically according to the fixed-maturity market rate based on an instrument that has a duration extending beyond that of the reset period (a 'constant maturity' interest rate) – e.g. a 10-year bond on which the interest rate resets semi-annually to the current weighted-average yield on treasury bonds with a 10-year maturity. The effect of this feature is that the interest rate is always equal to the market return on an instrument with 10 years left to maturity, even as the instrument paying the coupon itself nears maturity. To hedge its exposure to the constant maturity interest rate, an entity may enter into an interest rate swap that pays LIBOR or a similar rate and receives the constant maturity rate.

7.9.630.20   A question arises about whether such an interest rate swap can be designated as the hedging instrument in a hedge of the liability – i.e. the issued floating rate instrument. It is necessary to consider whether the constant maturity feature in the liability comprises a separable embedded derivative. Only after this analysis can the appropriateness of hedge accounting for the proposed transaction be considered.

7.9.630.30   In our view, the constant maturity feature comprises an embedded derivative (a 'constant maturity' swap). This embedded derivative is not closely related to the host financial liability because it could potentially double the holder's initial rate of return and could result in a rate of return that is at least twice what the market return would be for a contract with the same terms as the host contract, unless it has a cap at an appropriate level to prevent the doubling effect (see 7.2.250.10). [*IFRS 9.B4.3.8*]

7.9.630.40   In the absence of an appropriate cap, the entity separately accounts for a fixed rate host financial liability and a constant maturity swap. Because the constant maturity swap is a non-option embedded derivative, its terms have to be determined so as to result in a fair value of zero at inception (see 7.2.370.40). Both the embedded derivative and the interest rate swap will be measured at fair value, with gains and losses recognised in profit or loss. Hedge accounting is not necessary in these circumstances, because both the interest rate swap and the separately accounted for embedded derivative would be accounted for at FVTPL. [*IFRS 9.A*]

7.9.630.50   However, if the terms of the liability include an appropriate cap, then the embedded derivative is not accounted for separately and an issue arises over whether such a financial liability can be hedged with an interest rate basis swap that pays LIBOR and receives the same constant maturity rate. Although the bond issued is a variable rate bond, the variable rate that it pays is a constant maturity rate. Consequently, the bond has a fair value exposure arising from the difference between the discounting rate used to value the bond (the repricing basis) and the 10-year constant maturity rate (the interest-rate basis). For a 'plain vanilla' floating rate bond, there is no such difference and consequently no fair value exposure arising from interest rate changes. Similarly, the basis swap in this example, being a basis swap that has a repricing basis different from its interest rate basis, also has a fair value exposure for its entire life.

7.9.630.60   Consequently, in our view the constant maturity bond with an appropriate interest rate cap in 7.9.630.50 can be designated as the hedged item in a fair value hedge of interest rate risk with the hedging instrument being a constant maturity basis swap that also has a matching interest rate cap, assuming that the other hedge accounting criteria are met. In such a hedging relationship, the hedge is of the fair value exposure for the life of the hedged item and hedging instrument, rather than of an exposure that exists only between repricing dates. Conversely, in our view it is not possible to designate a plain vanilla floating rate bond in a fair value hedging relationship using a plain vanilla basis swap as the hedging instrument, because neither the bond nor the swap has a fair value exposure over its entire life. This designation is possible only when a fair value exposure exists for the entire life of the hedged item and the instrument.

7.9.640   Derivatives with knock-in or knock-out features

7.9.640.10   Except for some written options, the use of derivatives as hedging instruments is not prohibited if the other requirements for hedge accounting are met (see 7.9.240). Therefore, if an entity intends to designate a derivative with a knock-in or knock-out feature as a hedging instrument, then in our view the entity should assess whether the feature indicates that the instrument is a net written option for which hedge accounting is precluded (see 7.9.610). In our view, knock-in or knock-out features should be considered a net written option if a net premium is received by the entity in the form of a favourable rate or other term in exchange for these features. [*IFRS 9.B6.2.4*]

EXAMPLE 31 – DERIVATIVES WITH KNOCK-IN OR KNOCK-OUT FEATURES

7.9.640.20   Company N enters into an arm's length pay-6% receive-LIBOR interest rate swap under which the rights and obligations of both N and the counterparty are extinguished if a contingent event occurs. If N had entered into an otherwise identical interest rate swap without the knock-out feature, then the swap would have been priced at pay-8% receive-LIBOR.

7.9.640.30   Unless the hedged item contains an offsetting and closely related embedded net purchased option, N is not permitted to designate the swap as a hedging instrument because the favourable difference between the fixed payment legs represents a net premium that N receives over the life of the instrument in return for writing the option (see 7.9.610).

7.9.640.40   Even if a derivative with a knock-in or a knock-out feature is not considered a net written option and therefore is not precluded from being designated as a hedging instrument, the entity will have to consider whether it meets the hedge effectiveness requirements. Even when the hedge effectiveness requirements are met, significant ineffectiveness can arise if the hedged item does not contain a similar offsetting knock-in or knock-out feature. [*IFRS 9.B6.5.5*]

7.9.650   Elements that may be excluded from designated hedging instrument

7.9.660   *Time value of purchased options*

7.9.660.10   Purchased options may be used as hedging instruments provided that the hedge accounting criteria are met. Options, in contrast to forward and futures contracts, contain both an intrinsic value and a time value. [*IFRS 9.6.2.1, 6.2.4*]

7.9.660.20   The cash flows of forecast transactions do not generally include a time value component but options do – e.g. a forecast transaction in a foreign currency that is hedged with an option. If the option is designated in its entirety (including time value), then the hedge ineffectiveness is measured by comparing the full fair value change of the option and the present value of the change in cash flows of the forecast transaction (see 7.9.853). The change in fair value of the option and the change in the present value of the cash flows of the forecast transaction will not be the same because the change in the time value element of the option is not offset by an equal and opposite change in the cash flows of the forecast transaction. [*IFRS 9.B6.3.12*]

7.9.660.30   An entity may separate the intrinsic value and the time value of a purchased option contract and designate only the change in intrinsic value as the hedging instrument. In this case, the hedge ineffectiveness is measured based on changes in intrinsic value alone. Designating only the changes in the intrinsic value of an option as a hedging instrument in the hedge of a one-sided risk (see 7.9.320) in a hedged item may achieve perfect hedge effectiveness if the principal terms of the hedged item (i.e. amount, maturity etc) and the hedging instrument are the same. [*IFRS 9.6.2.4, B6.3.12*]

7.9.660.40   In our view, either the spot or the forward price/rate can be used in determining the intrinsic value of an option. However, the approach should be consistent with the risk management objective of an entity, specified as part of the hedge documentation and applied consistently during the term of the hedge. Furthermore, if the forward rate is used for determining the fair value of an American-style option, then the rate should be determined using the option's maturity date.

7.9.660.50   The time value of a purchased option represents the premium that the purchaser pays over the option's intrinsic value. The time value may be considered to be a cost of obtaining protection against unfavourable changes of prices, while retaining participation in any favourable changes. This is similar to an insurance premium, which compensates the insurer for assuming the downside risk of a particular item without its related upside potential. [*IFRS 9.BC6.389–BC6.390*]

7.9.660.60   The time value of an option is subject to 'time decay'. This means that it loses its value over time as the option approaches expiry, which occurs at an increasingly rapid rate. At expiry, the option's time value reaches zero. However, the time value of an option does not decay in a linear fashion. [*IFRS 9.BC6.390*]

7.9.660.70   If an entity excludes the time value of a purchased option from the designation of a hedging instrument, then the time value is accounted for separately as a cost of hedging (see 7.9.690). [*IFRS 9.6.5.15*]

7.9.670   *Forward element of forward contracts*

7.9.670.10   An entity may separate the forward element and the spot element of a forward contract and designate only the change in the spot element as the hedging instrument. [*IFRS 9.6.2.4(b)*]

7.9.670.20   The forward element of a forward contract represents the difference between the forward price and the current spot price of the underlying. The characteristics of forward elements depend on the underlying item – for example:
- for foreign exchange rate risk, the forward element represents the interest differential between the two currencies;
- for interest rate risk, the forward element reflects the term structure of interest rates; and
- for commodity risk, the forward element represents what is called the 'cost of carry' – e.g. storage costs. [*IFRS 9.BC6.416*]

7.9.670.30   Some entities may have more funding in their functional currency than they could invest in financial assets in their functional currency. To generate an economic return on their surplus funds, these entities exchange these funds into a foreign currency and invest in assets denominated in that foreign currency. To manage their exposure to foreign exchange risk (and to stabilise their interest margin), these entities commonly enter into foreign exchange derivatives – e.g. foreign currency forwards. Usually, such transactions simultaneously involve the following components:
- swapping the functional currency surplus funds into a foreign currency;
- investing the foreign currency funds in a foreign currency-denominated financial asset for a period of time; and
- entering into a foreign currency forward to convert the foreign currency funds back into the functional currency at the end of the investment period. This amount typically covers the principal plus interest at maturity. [*IFRS 9.BC6.423*]

7.9.670.40   The combination of these three components effectively allows the entity to 'lock in' a net interest margin and generate a fixed economic return over the investment period.

7.9.670.50   IFRS 9 permits the forward element of the forward contract that exist at inception of the hedging relationship to be recognised in profit or loss over time on a systematic and rational basis and to accumulate subsequent fair value changes through OCI. [*IFRS 9.BC6.424*]

7.9.670.60   If an entity excludes the forward element of a forward contract from the designation of a hedging instrument, then the forward element may be separately accounted for as a cost of hedging (see 7.9.690). [*IFRS 9.6.5.16*]

7.9.680   *Foreign currency basis spreads*

7.9.680.10   An entity may separate the foreign currency basis spread of a financial instrument and exclude it from the designated hedging instrument. [*IFRS 9.6.2.4(b)*]

7.9.680.20   Foreign currency basis spreads are commonly found in cross-currency swaps, but they may also be found in other financial instruments that involve exchanges of cash flows that are denominated in different currencies. [*IFRS 9.BC6.295–BC6.296*]

7.9.680.30   A foreign currency basis spread can be considered to be a charge to convert one currency into another. Foreign currency basis spreads are an economic phenomenon that would not exist in a perfect market because the existence of such a spread creates opportunities for economic arbitrage that would result in its reduction to zero. However, in actual markets for cross-currency swaps the foreign currency basis spread is not zero because of factors that prevent perfect arbitrage – for example:

- the credit risk embedded in the underlying reference rates of the currencies;
- the supply and demand for the particular cross-currency swap; and
- the interaction between the spot and the forward foreign exchange markets. [*IFRS 9.BC6.295–BC6.296*]

7.9.680.40   If an entity excludes the foreign currency basis spread of a financial instrument from the designation of a hedging instrument, then the foreign currency basis spread may be separately accounted for as a cost of hedging (see 7.9.690 and Example 53). [*IFRS 9.6.5.16*]

7.9.690   Accounting for excluded costs of hedging

7.9.690.10   If the time value of a purchased option (see 7.9.660) is separated and excluded from the designated hedging instrument, then the excluded portion is separately accounted for as a cost of hedging. [*IFRS 9.6.5.15*]

7.9.690.20   If the forward element of a forward contract (see 7.9.670), or the foreign currency basis spread of a financial instrument (see 7.9.680), is separated and excluded from the designated hedging instrument, then the change in fair value of the excluded portion may be accounted for as a cost of hedging. [*IFRS 9.6.5.16*]

7.9.690.30   Although accounting for a purchased option's time value as a cost of hedging is required if the time value is excluded from the hedging instrument, it is optional for the forward element of a forward contract and the foreign currency basis spread of a financial instrument if those elements are excluded from the hedging instrument. [*IFRS 9.6.2.4, 6.5.15–6.5.16*]

7.9.690.40   Therefore, for purchased options there is only one decision to make: whether to exclude the time value from the designation of the hedging instrument and account for it separately. However, for forward contracts and financial instruments with foreign currency basis spreads, there are two decisions to make:

- whether to exclude the forward element or foreign currency basis spread from the designation of the hedging instrument; and
- whether to account for any excluded element at FVTPL or as a cost of hedging. [*IFRS 9.6.2.4, 6.5.15–6.5.16*]

7.9.690.50   If an entity excludes a portion from the designated hedging instrument in accordance with 7.9.650 and accounts for it as a cost of hedging (see 7.9.690.10–20), then the change in fair value of the excluded portion is recognised in OCI and accumulated in a separate component of equity to the extent that it relates to the hedged item. This results in less profit or loss volatility, but more volatility in OCI. The method used to account for the amount accumulated in the separate component of equity is determined by whether the hedged item is transaction-related or time period-related.

7.9.700   *Transaction-related vs time period-related hedged item*

7.9.700.10   The accounting for the excluded portion of a designated hedging instrument as a cost of hedging depends on whether the hedged item is a transaction-related or a time period-related hedged item. An entity assesses the type of hedged item based on the nature of the hedged item, including how and when it affects profit or loss. This is required regardless of whether the hedging relationship is a cash flow hedge or a fair value hedge. [*IFRS 9.6.5.15, B6.5.29, B6.5.34, B6.5.39*]

7.9.700.20   The excluded portion of the designated hedging instrument is a *transaction-related* hedged item if the nature of the hedged item is a transaction for which the time value has the character of costs of the transaction. [*IFRS 9.6.5.15, B6.5.29(a), B6.5.34(a), B6.5.39*]

7.9.700.30   Examples of transaction-related hedged items include:
- a hedge of the future purchase of a commodity against commodity price risk, in which the transaction costs are included in the initial measurement of the inventory; and
- a hedge of an inventory purchase denominated in a foreign currency against foreign currency risk, in which the transaction costs are included in the initial measurement of the inventory. [*IFRS 9.6.5.15, B6.5.29(a), B6.5.34(a), B6.5.39*]

7.9.700.40   The excluded portion of the designated hedging instrument is a *time period-related* hedged item if the nature of the hedged item is such that:
- the excluded portion of the designated hedging instrument has the character of the cost of obtaining protection against a risk over a particular period of time; but
- the hedged item does not result in a transaction that involves the notion of a transaction cost (see 7.9.700). [*IFRS 9.6.5.15, B6.5.29(b), B6.5.34(b), B6.5.39*]

7.9.700.50   Examples of time period-related hedged items include:
- a hedge of commodity inventory against fair value changes for six months using a commodity option or forward contract with a corresponding life;
- a hedge of a net investment in a foreign operation for 18 months using a foreign exchange option, forward contract or cross-currency swap; and
- a hedge of changes in interest expense related to a floating rate bond. [*IFRS 9.6.5.15, B6.5.29(b), B6.5.30, B6.5.34(b), B6.5.39*]

7.9.710   *Accounting for excluded portion of designated hedging instrument*

7.9.720   *Transaction-related hedged items*

7.9.720.10   The change in fair value of the excluded portion of a designated hedging instrument that is accounted for as a cost of hedging and that hedges a transaction-related hedged item is recognised in OCI to the extent that it relates to the hedged item. The cumulative change in fair value is presented in a separate component of equity. [*IFRS 9.6.5.15(b), 6.5.16, B6.5.29(a), B6.5.34(a), B6.5.39*]

7.9.720.20   The hedged item may subsequently result in the recognition of a non-financial asset or non-financial liability, or a firm commitment for which fair value hedge accounting is applied.

In such cases, the entity removes the amount from the separate component of equity and includes it directly in the initial cost or other carrying amount of the item. This is not a reclassification adjustment (see 4.1.240.70) and therefore does not affect OCI. In other cases, the entity will reclassify the amount from the separate component of equity to profit or loss as a reclassification adjustment in the period or periods during which the hedged expected future cash flows affect profit or loss. [*IFRS 9.6.5.15(b), 6.5.16, B6.5.29(a), B6.5.34(a), B6.5.39*]

7.9.720.30   If all or part of the excluded portion of a designated hedging instrument recognised in OCI is not expected to be recovered in future periods, then the amount not expected to be recovered is immediately reclassified into profit or loss as a reclassification adjustment. It appears that an entity should interpret the phrase 'expected to be recovered' in relation to an excluded portion in the same manner as it assesses recoverability of losses accumulated in the cash flow hedge reserve (see 7.9.200.90). The nature of amounts accumulated in the cost of hedging reserve is similar to amounts accumulated in the cash flow hedge reserve because both reserves retain portions of the gain or loss on the hedging instrument that relate to the hedged item. We believe that recoverability of gains or losses on the hedging instrument accumulated in OCI for a single hedging relationship may be assessed in aggregate. If losses accumulated in the cash flow hedge reserve and the costs of hedging reserve are not all expected to be recovered, then the entity needs to develop an accounting policy to determine the amounts to be reclassified from each reserve into profit or loss as a reclassification adjustment. [*IFRS 9.6.5.15(b), 6.5.16, B6.5.29(a), B6.5.34(a), B6.5.39*]

7.9.730   *Time period-related hedged items*

7.9.730.10   The change in fair value of the excluded portion of a designated hedging instrument that is accounted for as a cost of hedging and that hedges a time period-related hedged item is recognised in OCI to the extent that it relates to the hedged item and is accumulated in a separate component of equity. [*IFRS 9.6.5.15(c), 6.5.16, B6.5.29(b), B6.5.30, B6.5.34(b), B6.5.39*]

7.9.730.20   The excluded portion of the designated hedging instrument at the date of designation, to the extent that it relates to the hedged item, is amortised on a systematic and rational basis over the period during which the hedge adjustment for the designated hedging instrument could affect profit or loss, or OCI if the hedged item is an equity instrument for which the entity has elected to present changes in fair value in OCI. This period is also likely to be the hedged period. In each reporting period, the amortisation amount is reclassified from the separate component of equity to profit or loss as a reclassification adjustment (see Example 32). [*IFRS 9.6.5.15(c), 6.5.16, B6.5.29(b), B6.5.30, B6.5.34(b), B6.5.39*]

7.9.730.30   However, if the hedging relationship is discontinued, then the net amount that has been accumulated in the separate component of equity, inclusive of cumulative amortisation, is reclassified immediately into profit or loss as a reclassification adjustment. [*IFRS 9.6.5.15(c), 6.5.16, B6.5.29(b), B6.5.34(b), B6.5.39*]

7.9.730.40   The characteristics of the hedged item (including how and when the hedged item affects profit or loss) also affect the period over which the forward element of a forward contract that hedges a time period-related hedged item is amortised – i.e. over the period to which the forward element relates. For example, if a forward contract hedges the exposure to variability in three-month interest rates for a three-month period that starts in six months' time, then the forward element is amortised during the period that spans months seven to nine. [*IFRS 9.B6.5.35*]

EXAMPLE 32 – PURCHASED OPTION THAT HEDGES TIME PERIOD-RELATED HEDGED ITEM – PERIOD
TO AMORTISE TIME VALUE

7.9.730.50   Company X buys an interest rate option (a cap) to protect against increases in the interest expense on a five-year floating rate bond. X designates the changes in the intrinsic value of the interest rate cap as the hedging instrument and excludes the changes in the time value of the cap from the designated hedging instrument.

7.9.730.60   The time value paid for the cap is amortised to profit or loss over the same period over which any intrinsic value of the cap would affect profit or loss – i.e. the hedged period. [*IFRS 9.B6.5.30*]

Scenario 1: Cap commences when bond issued

7.9.730.70   The cap commences on the day on which the bond is issued, and expires in three years; it therefore hedges against increases in interest rates for the first three years of the five-year floating rate bond. In this scenario, the time value paid for the cap is amortised over the first three years because that is the period over which any intrinsic value of the cap would affect profit or loss.

Scenario 2: Cap is a forward start option

7.9.730.80   The cap is a forward start option that commences on the first anniversary and expires on the third anniversary of the bond issuance; it therefore hedges against increases in interest rates in the second and third years of the life of the five-year floating rate bond. In this scenario, the time value paid for the cap is amortised during these second and third years because this is the period over which any intrinsic value of the cap would affect profit or loss.

7.9.730.90   Under both scenarios, assume that X changes its risk management objective and terminates the cap early. In this case, the cumulative change in the time value of the cap, net of amortisation, previously recognised in OCI would be immediately reclassified to profit or loss even though the floating rate interest payments on the bond are still expected to occur (see 7.9.730.30). However, changes in the intrinsic value of the cap before its termination would remain in OCI until the related interest expense is recognised (see 7.9.960.30). [*IFRS 9.6.5.12*]

7.9.730.100   Although IFRS 9 does not require the costs of hedging to be separately presented in the statement of profit or loss and OCI, they still need to be separately accounted for when they are excluded from the hedging instrument, as illustrated in Example 32. This is because IFRS 7 requires disclosure of a reconciliation of each component of equity and an analysis of OCI. Specifically, disclosures are required about:

- the effective portion of the gain or loss on the hedging instrument when it is initially recognised in OCI and when it is subsequently removed from OCI; and

- amounts relating to elements excluded from a designated hedging instrument, showing separately the amounts that relate to transaction-related hedged items and the amounts that relate to time period-related hedged items (see 7.10.167.10). [*IFRS 7.24E(a)–(c)*]

7.9.740 *Hedged item that is both transaction-related and time period-related*

7.9.740.10   Many entities use purchased options or forward contracts to hedge the variability in functional currency cash flows arising from sales transactions denominated in a foreign currency. In this case, the hedged risk can be designated as the variability in cash flows arising from both a sale that takes place in one reporting period, and the receivable created by that sale that is collected in a subsequent reporting period. The hedged item therefore relates to both a transaction (i.e. the sale) and a time period (i.e. the time period between the receivable's initial recognition and its collection).

7.9.740.20   IFRS 9 does not provide guidance on hedged items that can be considered both transaction-related and time period-related. In such cases, it appears that there is a single hedged item that changes from transaction-related to time-period related without de-designating the hedging relationship. We believe that the accounting for the excluded portion of the designated hedging instrument should follow that of a transaction-related hedged item during the period until the sale is made (see 7.9.720) and subsequently that of a time period related-hedged item (see 7.9.730). The excluded portion of the designated hedging instrument should be allocated between a transaction-related portion and a time period-related portion. Although we believe that a rateable allocation based on time would be appropriate, alternative rational and systematic methods of allocation may also be appropriate (see Example 52).

7.9.750 *Zero-cost collars*

7.9.750.10   The accounting for the excluded time value of purchased options described in 7.9.690 also applies to a combination of a purchased and a written option (one being a put option and one being a call option) that, at the date of designation as a hedging instrument, has a net zero time value – i.e. a 'zero-cost collar'. In this case, an entity recognises any changes in time value in OCI, even though the cumulative change in time value over the total period of the hedging relationship is zero. [*IFRS 9.B6.5.31*]

7.9.750.20   Therefore, if the time value of the collar relates to:
- a transaction-related hedged item, then the amount of time value that adjusts the hedged item or is reclassified to profit or loss at the end of the hedging relationship is zero; and
- a time period-related hedged item, then the total amortisation expense for the time value is zero; this is because the amortisation expense is based on the time value at the date of designation as the hedging instrument, which is zero. [*IFRS 9.B6.5.31*]

7.9.750.30   A zero-cost collar has no time value at inception; however, its time value fluctuates during the life of the hedge. Time value is subject to time decay, and the time value of both the purchased and the written option will decline over time as the collar approaches expiry. If changes in the time value were not included in OCI, then they would affect profit or loss each period. For hedged items that do not contain a corresponding written option, recognising the time value of zero-cost collars in OCI reduces volatility in profit or loss, but increases volatility in OCI. [*IFRS 9.BC6.412*]

7.9.760   *Forward contracts with forward element of zero*

7.9.760.10   The accounting for the excluded forward element of a forward contract described in 7.9.690 also applies if, at the date on which the forward contract is designated as a hedging instrument, the forward element is zero. In this case, an entity recognises any changes in the fair value of the forward element in OCI – even though the cumulative change in the forward element over the total period of the hedging relationship is zero. [*IFRS 9.B6.5.36*]

7.9.760.20   Therefore, if the forward element of a forward contract relates to:

- a transaction-related hedged item, then the amount of forward element that adjusts the hedged item or is reclassified to profit or loss at the end of the hedging relationship is zero; and
- a time period-related hedged item, then the total amortisation expense for the forward element is zero; this is because the amortisation expense is based on the value of the forward element at the date of designation as the hedging instrument, which is zero. [*IFRS 9.B6.5.36*]

7.9.770   **Aligned excluded portion vs actual excluded portion**

7.9.770.10   The accounting for the excluded portion of a designated hedging instrument as a cost of hedging (see 7.9.690) applies only to the extent that the excluded portion relates to the hedged item. This is referred to as the 'aligned' portion – e.g. the aligned time value, the aligned forward element or the aligned foreign currency basis spread. An entity determines the aligned portion using the valuation of the instrument – i.e. purchased option, forward contract or cross-currency swap – that would have critical terms perfectly matching the hedged item. [*IFRS 9.B6.5.32, B6.5.37–B6.5.39*]

7.9.770.20   The aligned portion is the time value of a purchased option, forward element of a forward contract or foreign currency basis spread of a financial instrument, as applicable, with critical terms that perfectly match the hedged item. An entity needs to determine which features of the financial instrument it considers to be critical. For example, for an option, the entity needs to determine what type of option is appropriate – e.g. American, European, Bermudan etc. This will require the entity to use its judgement, which should be applied consistently.

7.9.770.30   The actual excluded portion may differ from the aligned excluded portion. In this case, the entity uses the method described in 7.9.770.40–50 to account for the difference during the hedging relationship. [*IFRS 9.B6.5.33*]

7.9.770.40   If, at inception of the hedging relationship, the actual excluded portion is *higher* than the aligned excluded portion, then the entity:

- determines the amount that is accumulated in a separate component of equity on the basis of the aligned excluded portion; and
- recognises in profit or loss the differences in fair value changes between the actual excluded portion and the aligned excluded portion. [*IFRS 9.B6.5.33*]

7.9.770.50   However, if at inception of the hedging relationship the actual excluded portion is *lower* than the aligned excluded portion, then the entity:

- determines the amount that is accumulated in a separate component of equity with reference to the lower of the cumulative change in fair value of the actual excluded portion and the aligned excluded portion; and

- recognises in profit or loss any remainder of the change in fair value of the actual excluded portion. [*IFRS 9.B6.5.33*]

7.9.770.60   The following flowchart summarises the accounting for differences between the actual excluded portion and the aligned excluded portion when the time value is excluded from the designation of a purchased option.

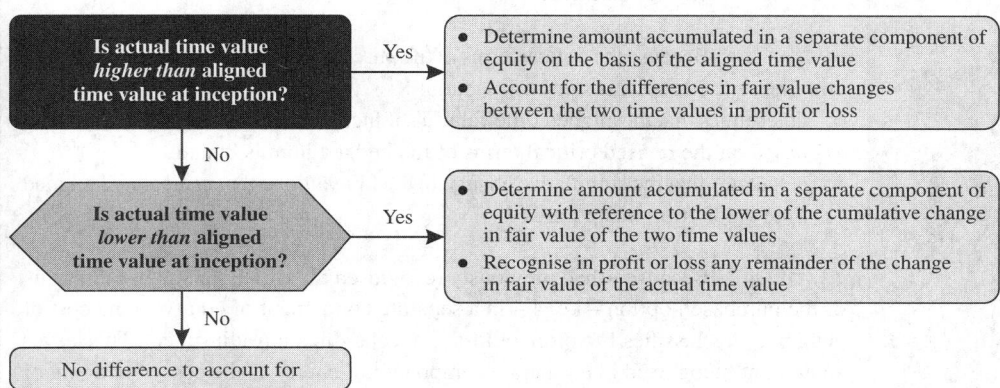

7.9.770.70   The critical terms of the hedged item may change during the course of the hedge accounting relationship – e.g. the timing of the hedged forecast transaction may change. When the time value of a purchased option, the forward element of a forward contract or the foreign currency basis spread of a financial instrument is excluded from the designation of the hedging instrument and accounted for as a cost of hedging, an issue arises about how to account for the change. If the change does not result in the discontinuation of hedge accounting (see 7.9.930), then it appears that the entity should:

- recalculate the aligned excluded portion as of inception of the hedging relationship based on the revised critical terms of the hedged item; and
- determine the cumulative change in the fair value of the recalculated aligned excluded portion from inception to determine the amount that is accumulated in a separate component of equity as the cost of hedging.

7.9.770.80   We believe that any adjustment to the change in the fair value of the actual excluded portion that had previously been accumulated in a separate component of equity as a cost of hedging should be recognised as a reclassification adjustment through profit or loss.

EXAMPLE 33 – CHANGE IN CRITICAL TERMS OF HEDGED ITEM

7.9.770.90   On 1 June 2018, Company R purchases an at-the-money option for a premium of 10 and designates its intrinsic value in a cash flow hedge of a highly probable forecast sales transaction that is expected to occur on 15 May 2019. At inception of the hedging relationship, all of the critical terms of the hedged item and the hedging instrument match – the aligned time value is determined to be equal to the actual time value of 10. R determines that the highly probable forecast sale is a transaction-related hedged item.

7.9.770.100   On 15 October 2018, R changes its estimate of the timing of the forecast sales transaction. The hedged forecast sales transaction is now expected to occur on 15 April 2019. In addition, the option is out of the money – i.e. it has no intrinsic value – and has a fair value of 6. R assesses the documentation of the hedged forecast transaction and determines that the hedging relationship still qualifies – i.e. it is not discontinued.

7.9.770.110   Because the critical terms of the purchased option are no longer aligned with the revised forecast sales transaction, R:
- determines that the aligned time value as of inception of the hedging relationship based on the revised critical terms of the hedged item is 8; and
- calculates that the cumulative change in the fair value of the recalculated aligned time value from inception is 3.

7.9.770.120   Because R had previously recognised the entire change in time value of the purchased option – i.e. 4 – in a separate component of equity as the cost of hedging, R reclassifies 1 to profit or loss as a reclassification adjustment. This leaves an amount recognised in a separate component of equity as the cost of hedging of 3, which equals the cumulative change in the fair value of the recalculated aligned time value from inception.

EXAMPLE 34 – ALIGNED TIME VALUE VS ACTUAL TIME VALUE

7.9.770.130   Company E uses a purchased option to hedge its forecast commodity purchase. In doing so, it designates the option's intrinsic value as a hedging instrument.

7.9.770.140   In this example, the time value of the purchased option relates to a transaction-related hedged item, because the transaction costs will include in the initial measurement of the inventory when the forecast commodity purchase occurs.

7.9.770.150   The accounting for the time value of such an option depends on whether its time value at inception of the hedging relationship is higher or lower than the aligned time value.

Scenario 1: Actual time value higher than aligned time value

7.9.770.160   E pays an up-front premium of 13 for a purchased option with an intrinsic value of zero. On that day, it determines that the aligned time value is 10, which is less than the actual time value because the forecast commodity purchase is expected to occur before the maturity of the purchased option.

7.9.770.170   E accounts for the time value of the option as follows.

	ACTUAL	ALIGNED				
Term (periods)	5	5[1]				
Time value	13	10[2]				
Period (end)	t_0	t_1	t_2	t_3	t_4	t_5
Fair value of actual time value	13	11	13	9	7	-
Fair value of aligned time value	10	7	11	8	6	-
Statement of financial position						
Financial asset (option)[3]	13	11	13	9	7	-
Retained earnings	-	(1)	1	2	2	3[5]
Equity reserve – Cost of hedging[4]	-	3	(1)	2	4	10[5]
	13	13	13	13	13	13

Statement of profit or loss and OCI							t_5 (CUMULATIVE)
Profit or loss							
Period-to-period movement in fair value of actual time value that does not relate to the hedged item	(gain)/loss		(1)	2	1	-	1	**3**
OCI							
Period-to-period movement in fair value of aligned time value	(gain)/loss		3	(4)	3	2	6	**10**
Total comprehensive income			2	(2)	4	2	7	**13**

Notes
1. Rounded up.
2. The aligned time value is determined using the valuation of an option that would have critical terms that perfectly match the hedged item.
3. Time value only; excludes intrinsic value to simplify example.
4. Cumulative changes in fair value of aligned time value.
5. The amount that is accumulated in OCI is determined only on the basis of the aligned time value; the excess of the actual time value over the aligned time value of 3 (13 - 10) is accounted for as a derivative with cumulative fair value changes recognised in profit or loss.

Scenario 2: Actual time value lower than aligned time value

7.9.770.180   E pays an up-front premium of 10 for a purchased option with an intrinsic value of zero. On that day, it determines that the aligned time value is 12, which is more than the actual time value because the forecast commodity purchase is expected to occur after the maturity of the purchased option.

7.9.770.190   E accounts for the time value of the option as follows.

	ACTUAL	ALIGNED				
Term (periods)	5[(1)]	5				
Time value	10	12[(2)]				
Period (end)	t_0	t_1	t_2	t_3	t_4	t_5
Fair value of actual time value	10	12	9	8	5	-
Fair value of aligned time value	12	15	11	11	7	-
Cumulative change of actual time value		2	(1)	(2)	(5)	(10)
Cumulative change of aligned time value		3	(1)	(1)	(5)	(12)
Lower of cumulative change[(3)]		2	(1)	(1)	(5)	(10)
Statement of financial position						
Financial asset (option)[(4)]	10	12	9	8	5	-
Retained earnings	-	-	-	1	-	-[(6)]
Equity reserve – Cost of hedging[(5)]	-	(2)	1	1	5	10[(6)]
	10	10	10	10	10	10

						t_5 (CUMULATIVE)
Statement of profit or loss and OCI						
Profit or loss						
Period-to-period movement of remainder of change in fair value of actual time value (gain)/ loss		-	-	1	(1)	-	-
OCI						
Period-to-period movement of the lower of cumulative change (gain)/ loss		(2)	3	-	4	5	10
Total comprehensive income		(2)	3	1	3	5	10

Notes
1. Rounded up.
2. The aligned time value is determined using the valuation of an option that would have critical terms that perfectly match the hedged item.
3. Because the actual time value is lower than the aligned time value, a 'lower of' test is needed that compares the cumulative changes in fair value of the actual and aligned time values. This avoids accounting for more time value of an option than was actually paid for.
4. Time value only; excludes intrinsic value to simplify example.
5. Lower of cumulative change.
6. The amount that is accumulated in OCI is determined with reference to the lower of the cumulative fair value change of the actual time value and the aligned time value – i.e. 10. The cumulative fair value change of the excess of the aligned time value over the actual time value of 2 (12 - 10) is not recognised in profit or loss. This avoids accounting for more time value than was actually paid for.

7.9.780   HEDGE EFFECTIVENESS AND INEFFECTIVENESS

7.9.790   Hedge effectiveness

7.9.790.10   'Hedge effectiveness' is the extent to which changes in the fair value or cash flows of the hedging instrument offset changes in the fair value or cash flows of the hedged item for the hedged risk(s). 'Hedge ineffectiveness', however, is the extent to which the changes in the fair value or cash flows of the hedging instrument are greater or less than those on the hedged item for the hedged risk(s). [*IFRS 9.B6.4.1*]

7.9.790.20   When designating a hedging relationship, and on an ongoing basis, an entity analyses the sources of hedge ineffectiveness that are expected to affect the hedging relationship during its term. This analysis serves as the basis for the entity's assessment of whether the hedge meets the effectiveness requirements. [*IFRS 9.B6.4.2*]

7.9.790.30   A hedging relationship meets the hedge effectiveness requirements if:
● there is an economic relationship between the hedged item and the hedging instrument;
● the effect of credit risk does not dominate the value changes that result from the economic relationship; and
● the hedge ratio of the hedging relationship:
– is the same as that resulting from the quantities of:
● the hedged item that the entity actually hedges; and
● the hedging instrument that the entity actually uses to hedge that quantity of hedged item; and
– is not achieved by intentionally weighting the hedged item and the hedging instrument to create hedge ineffectiveness – whether or not it is recognised – to achieve an accounting outcome that would be inconsistent with the purpose of hedge accounting. [*IFRS 9.6.4.1(c)*]

7.9.800   *Economic relationship between hedged item and hedging instrument*

7.9.800.10   Having an 'economic relationship' means that the hedging instrument and the hedged item have values that generally move in the opposite direction because of the same risk – i.e. the hedged risk. In other words, an expectation is required that the value of the hedging instrument and the value of the hedged item will systematically change in response to movements in either:

- the same underlying; or
- underlyings that are economically related in such a way that they respond in a similar way to the risk that is being hedged – e.g. Brent and West Texas Intermediate crude oil. [*IFRS 9.B6.4.4*]

7.9.800.20   The underlyings may not be the same, but have to be economically related. In this case, there can be situations in which the values of the hedging instrument and the hedged item move in the same direction. For example, the price differential between two related underlyings may change while the underlyings themselves do not move significantly. Such situations still meet the economic relationship test if the values of the hedging instrument and the hedged item are still typically expected to move in the opposite direction when the underlyings move. [*IFRS 9.B6.4.5*]

7.9.800.30   An entity analyses the possible behaviour of the hedging relationship during its term, to ascertain whether the relationship can be expected to meet its risk management objective. The mere existence of a statistical correlation between two variables does not, by itself, demonstrate that an economic relationship exists. [*IFRS 9.B6.4.6*]

7.9.810   *Effect of credit risk*

7.9.810.10   Entities consider the effect of both changes in counterparty credit risk and own credit risk on the assessment of hedge effectiveness and the measurement of hedge ineffectiveness (see 2.4.460.30). [*IFRS 9.B6.4.7*]

7.9.810.20   The hedge accounting model is based on a general notion of offset between gains and losses on the hedging instrument and the hedged item. Therefore, the effect of credit risk on the value of both the hedging instrument and the hedged item impacts hedge effectiveness. [*IFRS 9.B6.4.7*]

7.9.810.30   The effect of credit risk means that even if there is an economic relationship between the hedging instrument and the hedged item, the level of offset might become erratic. This can result from a change in the credit risk of either the hedging instrument or the hedged item that is so great that the credit risk dominates the value changes that result from the economic relationship. That is, the loss (or gain) from credit risk frustrates the effect of changes in the underlyings on the value of the hedging instrument or the hedged item – even if those changes were significant. [*IFRS 9.B6.4.7*]

7.9.810.40   Conversely, if during a particular period there is little change in the underlyings, then even small credit risk-related changes in the value of the hedging instrument or hedged item might affect the value more than the underlyings. However, this does not create credit risk dominance on the hedging relationship. [*IFRS 9.B6.4.7*]

7.9.810.50   An example where credit risk could dominate a hedging relationship is when an entity hedges an exposure to commodity price risk using an uncollateralised derivative. If the counterparty to that derivative experiences a severe deterioration in its credit standing, then the effect of changes in the counterparty's credit standing might start to outweigh the effect of changes in the commodity price on the fair value of the hedging instrument, whereas the changes in the value of the hedged item will continue to depend largely on the commodity price changes. [*IFRS 9.B6.4.8*]

7.9.810.60   In many cases, depending on the extent and nature of collateralisation and the credit standing of the counterparty, an entity may be able to determine that the effect of credit risk of a derivative does not dominate the value changes on a qualitative basis.

7.9.810.70   If hedge effectiveness is assessed using a quantitative model (see 7.9.830), then the fair value changes of a derivative used in that model reflect the present value effect of its credit risk on the value of the economic relationship. This is because the effect of the credit risk of a derivative is reflected in its fair value (see 2.4.460). However, hedge effectiveness is assessed prospectively and more analysis and judgement may be needed to determine whether the effect of credit risk dominates the value changes that result from the economic relationship in the future.

7.9.810.80   Whether the effect of credit risk on the value of the hedged item could cause hedge ineffectiveness also depends on whether credit risk is part of the designated hedged risks. If an entity designates overall changes in the fair value of the hedged item as the hedged risk and credit risk is part of that designated risk, then in our view changes in the credit risk of the hedged item would not fail the hedge effectiveness assessment, provided that they are effectively offset by the changes in the value of the hedging instrument.

7.9.810.90   An entity also considers the nature of the hedged item in determining whether the hedged item has any credit risk. For example, in a fair value hedge of inventory there is no credit risk on the hedged item. Conversely, credit risk may exist in a cash flow hedge of a forecast sale of inventory.

7.9.810.100   In a cash flow hedge, the credit risk on the hedged item may also affect the assessment of whether the forecast transaction is highly probable (see 7.9.980).

7.9.815 *Effect of credit risk – Interaction with IFRS 9 impairment requirements for hedges of financial assets*

7.9.815.10   Financial institutions usually monitor and determine credit risk on loan assets for regulatory and reporting purposes, including impairment testing under IFRS 9. Some of that information may be used in assessing the effect of credit risk on the effectiveness of hedges of loan assets.

7.9.815.20   When applying the impairment requirements under IFRS 9, an entity needs to assess whether there has been a significant increase in the credit risk of a financial asset and whether the financial asset is credit-impaired. However, under the hedge accounting model the hedge effectiveness is determined by the economic relationship between the hedging instrument and the hedged item considering the effect of credit risk on the value of both. [*IFRS 9.B.6.4.7*]

7.9.815.30   If a hedged financial asset is considered to have low credit risk (see 7.8.150) or its credit risk has not increased significantly, then the entity may qualitatively determine that the effect of the credit risk on the value of the hedged item does not dominate the value changes that result from the economic relationship. Therefore, in these cases the credit risk of the hedged item would not give rise to a failure to meet the hedge effectiveness requirements and would not lead to ineffectiveness in a hedge of interest rate risk.

7.9.815.40   However, further analysis and judgement may be required when a significant increase in the credit risk of a financial item is identified under the IFRS 9 impairment requirements. Generally, a significant increase in credit risk (see 7.8.60) may be an important indicator to consider in assessing hedge effectiveness, but it does not necessarily mean that credit risk dominates the economic relationship. This is because the assessment of a significant increase in credit risk is a relative assessment, rather than an absolute one. In other words, the assessment of significant increase in credit risk under the impairment requirements in IFRS 9 is done by comparing the asset's risk of default on initial recognition and at the reporting date (see 7.8.60). Conversely, the assessment of the effect of credit risk on hedge effectiveness is based on considering value changes.

7.9.815.50   In our experience, credit risk on a credit-impaired financial asset is likely to dominate the value changes that result from the economic relationship. Therefore, if an asset is credit-impaired, then hedge accounting would not be permissible, unless credit risk is part of the designated hedged risk (see 7.9.810.80).

7.9.815.60   Similarly, it appears that in many circumstances, if a hedged asset becomes credit-impaired, then the current hedge accounting relationship should be discontinued. This is because when there is a change in estimated cash flows of the hedged asset, the hedge is no longer expected to be effective in achieving offsetting changes in fair value or cash flows attributable to the hedged risk that is consistent with the originally documented risk management strategy for the particular hedging relationship. For example, in the case of a hedge of benchmark interest rate risk, there cannot be interest rate sensitivity on cash flows that will not be recovered.

7.9.820   *Hedge ratio*

7.9.820.10   An entity uses the same hedge ratio for the hedging relationship as the one that results from the actual quantities of:
- the hedged items; and
- the hedging instruments used. [*IFRS 9.B6.4.9*]

7.9.820.20   For example, an entity hedges 85 percent of the exposure on an item. The hedging relationship is designated using a hedge ratio resulting from:
- 85 percent of the exposure; and
- the quantity of the hedging instrument that the entity actually uses to hedge that 85 percent.

7.9.820.30   Similarly, if an entity hedges an exposure using a nominal amount of 40 units of a financial instrument, then it designates the hedging relationship using a hedge ratio that is the same as that resulting from:
- that quantity of 40 units (and not based on a higher or lower quantity); and
- the quantity of the hedged item that it actually hedges with those 40 units.

7.9.820.40   The hedged item and hedging instrument should not be intentionally weighted to reflect an imbalance that would create hedge ineffectiveness – whether or not it is recognised – that could result in an accounting outcome that would be inconsistent with the purpose of hedge accounting. An entity adjusts the hedge ratio if doing so is necessary to avoid such an imbalance. [*IFRS 9.B6.4.10*]

7.9.820.50   Establishing an appropriate hedge ratio is primarily a risk management decision. In other words, an entity analyses the possible behaviour of the hedging relationship during its term to ascertain whether it can be expected to meet the risk management objective.

7.9.820.60   Entities are responsible for clearly defining and consistently applying their effectiveness assessment policies. Management information (or analysis) used for decision-making purposes can be used as a basis to assess whether a hedging relationship meets the hedge effectiveness requirements. [*IFRS 9.B6.4.18*]

7.9.820.70   An entity cannot, under the guise of risk management, use a hedge ratio that results in a deliberate mismatch that creates ineffectiveness to achieve an accounting outcome that is inconsistent with the purpose of hedge accounting. In assessing whether an accounting outcome is inconsistent with the purpose of hedge accounting, an entity considers:

- whether the intended hedge ratio is established:
  - to avoid recognising hedge ineffectiveness for cash flow hedges; or
  - to achieve fair value hedge adjustments for more hedged items, with the aim of increasing the use of fair value accounting, but without offsetting fair value changes of the hedging instrument; and
- whether there is a commercial reason for the particular weightings of the hedged item and the hedging instrument, even though it creates hedge ineffectiveness. [*IFRS 9.B6.4.11*]

EXAMPLE 35 – COMMERCIAL REASON FOR PARTICULAR WEIGHTINGS OF HEDGED ITEM AND HEDGING INSTRUMENT

7.9.820.80   Company X hedges 100 tonnes of highly probable future coffee purchases using standard coffee futures contracts that have a contract size of 37,500 pounds (1 tonne = 2,204.6 pounds). Because the standard volume of the hedging instrument does not allow X to enter into exactly 100 tonnes of hedging instrument (a 'lot size issue'), X can only use either five or six contracts (equivalent to 85.0 and 102.1 tonnes respectively) to hedge the purchase volume of 100 tonnes – i.e. it is not possible to achieve the theoretical best hedge. [*IFRS 9.B6.4.11(b)*]

7.9.820.90   X actually uses six contracts; therefore, it designates the hedging relationship using the hedge ratio that results from the number of coffee futures contracts that it actually uses – the hedged item is 100 tonnes of future coffee purchases and the hedging instrument is six coffee futures contracts equivalent to 102.1 tonnes. This is because the hedge ineffectiveness resulting from the mismatch in the weightings of the hedged item and the hedging instrument would not result in an accounting outcome that is inconsistent with the purpose of hedge accounting. [*IFRS 9.B6.4.11(b)*]

7.9.830   *Frequency and methods for assessing hedge effectiveness*

7.9.830.10   An entity assesses hedge effectiveness:
- at inception of the hedging relationship; and
- on an ongoing basis – at a minimum, at each reporting date or on a significant change in the circumstances affecting the hedge effectiveness requirements, whichever comes first. [*IFRS 9.B6.4.12*]

7.9.830.20   The assessment relates to expectations about hedge effectiveness; therefore, the test is only forward-looking or prospective. [*IFRS 9.B6.4.12*]

7.9.830.30   The methods, either quantitative or qualitative, for assessing whether a hedging relationship meets the hedge effectiveness requirements are not prescribed. However, an entity uses a method that captures the relevant characteristics of the hedging relationship, including the sources of hedge ineffectiveness. [*IFRS 9.B6.4.13*]

7.9.830.40   An entity's hedge documentation specifies how it will assess whether the hedging relationship meets the hedge effectiveness requirements, including the method or methods used. [*IFRS 9.6.4.1(b), B6.4.19*]

7.9.830.50   The method that will be used to assess effectiveness is determined on a hedge-by-hedge basis. There is no requirement to adopt a consistent method for all hedging relationships. However, in our view an entity should adopt a method for assessing hedge effectiveness that is applied consistently for similar types of hedges unless different methods are justified. For example, an entity should use the same methods for assessing effectiveness for forecast sales to the same export market undertaken on a regular basis. [*IFRS 9.6.4.1(b)*]

7.9.830.60   Regression analysis is an example of a quantitative method that can be used to analyse the possible behaviour of the hedging relationship during its term to ascertain whether it can be expected to meet the risk management objective. Entities might use linear regression techniques for determining *whether* and *by how much* a change in one variable will result in a change in another variable. However, the mere existence of a statistical correlation between two variables does not, by itself, support a valid conclusion that an economic relationship exists between the hedged item and the hedging instrument. [*IFRS 9.6.4.1(b), B6.4.6*]

7.9.830.70   If the critical terms of the hedging instrument and the hedged item – e.g. the nominal amount, maturity and underlying – match or are closely aligned, then it may be possible to use a qualitative methodology to determine whether an economic relationship exists between the hedged item and the hedging instrument. In other cases, a quantitative assessment may be more appropriate. The terms 'critical terms' and 'closely aligned' are not defined. An entity uses its judgement in developing accounting policies to identify which terms it considers critical and what it considers to be closely aligned. [*IFRS 9.B6.4.14*]

7.9.830.80   Examples of situations in which the critical terms match or are closely aligned include:
- a hedge of a foreign currency sales commitment with a futures contract to sell the same amount of the same foreign currency on the same date;
- a hedge of benchmark interest rate risk associated with a recognised asset or liability using a swap with the same notional amount and with the same key terms as the asset or liability;
- a hedge of a forecast commodity sale with a forward contract to purchase the same quantity of the same commodity on the same date and either:
  - the change in the discount or premium on the forward contract is excluded from the assessment of effectiveness and recognised directly in profit or loss; or
  - the change in expected cash flows on the forecast transaction is based on the forward price of the commodity; and
- a hedge of a specific bond held with a forward contract to sell an equivalent bond with the same notional amount, currency and maturity.

7.9.830.90   The fact that a derivative is in or out of the money when it is designated as a hedging instrument does not in itself mean that a qualitative assessment is inappropriate. The appropriateness depends on the circumstances and whether hedge ineffectiveness arising from that fact could be of such a magnitude that a qualitative assessment would not adequately consider it. [*IFRS 9.B6.4.15*]

7.9.830.100   Conversely, if the critical terms are not closely aligned, then there will be increased uncertainty about the extent of offset. Therefore, an entity may sometimes need to use a quantitative effectiveness assessment methodology to support its conclusion that an economic relationship exists between the hedged item and the hedging instrument. Similarly, the entity might also need a quantitative assessment of whether the hedge ratio used for designating the hedging relationship meets the hedge effectiveness requirements. [*IFRS 9.B6.4.16*]

7.9.830.110   Under a qualitative approach, besides assessing other hedge effectiveness criteria, an entity assesses at inception and in subsequent periods whether the critical terms have changed. If any of the critical terms changes in subsequent periods, then an entity assesses the impact of such changes on the economic relationship between the hedged item and the hedging instrument. [*IFRS 9.6.4.1, B6.4.12–B6.4.14*]

7.9.830.120   An entity would have to consider the need to change assessment methodologies if there were changes in circumstances that affected hedge effectiveness. This is to ensure that all relevant characteristics of the hedging relationship, including sources of hedge ineffectiveness, are still captured. [*IFRS 9.B6.4.17*]

7.9.830.130   The hedge effectiveness assessment is forward-looking only and there is no prescribed bright line effectiveness range. Judgement has to be applied to determine whether the entity's hedge accounting documentation provides sufficient evidence that the hedging relationship meets the hedge effectiveness requirements. [*IFRS 9.B6.4.12*]

7.9.840   Hedge ineffectiveness

7.9.850   *Measuring hedge ineffectiveness*

7.9.850.10   Hedge ineffectiveness is measured based on the actual performance of the hedging instrument and the hedged item, by comparing the changes in their values in currency unit amounts. [*IFRS 9.BC6.278–BC6.279*]

7.9.850.20   The gain or loss on the hedged item is measured independently from that on the hedging instrument – i.e. it cannot be assumed that the change in fair value or cash flows of the hedged item in respect of the hedged risk equals the fair value change of the hedging instrument. The reason for this is that any ineffectiveness of the hedging instrument needs to be recognised in profit or loss. [*IFRS 9.6.5.8, 6.5.11*]

7.9.850.30   A fair value measurement, determined in accordance with IFRS 13, assumes that the transaction to sell or purchase the asset or transfer the liability takes place in the principal market or, in the absence of a principal market, in the most advantageous market. In some cases, the hedged item can be a non-financial item whose location is a characteristic that is relevant in determining its fair value (see 2.4.70). If the market in which the fair value of the hedged item is priced is different from the market in which the fair value of the hedging instruments is priced (see 2.4.100), then this difference may cause ineffectiveness in the hedging relationship. [*IFRS 13.16*]

7.9.850.40   For all hedges, changes in both counterparty credit risk and own credit risk impact the measurement of changes in the fair value of a derivative hedging instrument. These changes will probably have no offsetting effect on the measurement of the changes in the value of the hedged item attributable to the hedged risk. Such differences in measurement resulting from changes in counterparty and own credit risk may impact assessments of effectiveness. If these changes dominate the value changes resulting from the economic relationship, then the hedging relationship does not qualify for hedge accounting (see 7.9.810). Even when it is concluded that the hedge effectiveness requirements are met, these differences will result in ineffectiveness being recognised in profit or loss for fair value hedges. Such differences would also require the recognition of ineffectiveness in profit or loss for cash flow hedges if the cumulative gain or loss on the hedging instrument is greater than the cumulative change in fair or present value of the expected future cash flows on the hedged item. Similarly, for net investment hedges in which the hedging instrument is a derivative, ineffectiveness is recognised in profit or loss if the gain or loss on the hedging instrument exceeds the foreign exchange differences arising on the designated net investment. [*IFRS 9.6.4.1, B6.5.22*]

7.9.850.50   Imagine that an entity has a group of derivative assets and liabilities with a particular counterparty and the entity meets the criteria for applying the portfolio measurement exception to that counterparty's credit risk. In this case, the effect of the entity's net exposure to the credit risk of that counterparty or the counterparty's net exposure to the credit risk of the entity may result in a portfolio-level credit risk adjustment (see 2.4.430). However, for recognising ineffectiveness an entity needs to determine the individual credit risk adjustments to arrive at the fair values of the individual hedging derivatives or the appropriate credit adjustment for a group of derivatives that have been designated together as the hedging instrument in a single hedging relationship. In our view, the entity should adopt a reasonable and consistently applied methodology for allocating credit risk adjustments determined at a portfolio level to individual derivative instruments for the purpose of measuring the fair values of individual hedging instruments that are used in measuring hedge ineffectiveness.

7.9.850.60   When measuring hedge ineffectiveness, an entity is required to consider the time value of money and so it determines the value of the hedged item on a present value basis. [*IFRS 9.B6.5.4*]

7.9.853   *Hedges of foreign currency risk*

7.9.853.10   If an entity designates a monetary asset or liability denominated in a foreign currency as the hedged item in a fair value or cash flow hedge of foreign currency risk, then it appears that the entity may measure the attributable gain or loss on the hedged item by applying the change in the spot foreign exchange rate to the amortised cost of the monetary item. This is because amortised cost is a present value measurement and this method is consistent with the requirement in IFRS 9 that, for hedges of foreign currency risk, the foreign currency risk component of a non-derivative financial instrument designated as a hedging instrument is determined in accordance with IAS 21 (see 7.9.1080.10). [*IFRS 9.B6.2.3, B6.5.4, BC6.281*]

EXAMPLE 36 – MEASURING SPOT FOREIGN CURRENCY RISK – ON-BALANCE SHEET HEDGED ITEM

7.9.853.20   Company T, whose functional currency is sterling, recognises a euro-denominated receivable for a EUR 100,000 sale of goods at 1 January 2018. The receivable is expected to settle on 30 June 2018. To hedge its exposure

to the euro, T executes a forward contract on 1 January 2018 and immediately designates the forward contract as a cash flow hedge of variations attributable to changes in the spot euro/sterling exchange rate. The forward element is separately accounted for as a cost of hedging. The nature of the hedged item is time period-related and there is perfect alignment between the hedged item and forward element.

7.9.853.30   During the period in which the receivable is outstanding, the spot exchange rates and forward exchange rates are as follows.

REPORTING DATE	EUR/GBP SPOT EXCHANGE RATE	EUR/GBP FORWARD RATE FOR 30 JUNE 2018
1 January 2018	0.60	0.6240
31 March 2018	0.75	0.7723
30 June 2018	0.65	0.6500

7.9.853.40   The forward element associated with the forward contract is 2,400 ((0.6240 - 0.60) x 100,000), which represents the difference between the current euro/sterling spot exchange rate and euro/sterling forward rate on a EUR 100,000 notional. The forward element will be reclassified from the cost of hedging reserve over the hedging period because the hedged item is time period-related.

7.9.853.50   The change in fair value of the forward contract is as follows (amounts in sterling).

REPORTING DATE	TOTAL CHANGE IN FAIR VALUE DURING QUARTER	CHANGE IN FAIR VALUE ATTRIBUTABLE TO SPOT EXCHANGE RATE RISK DURING QUARTER	CHANGE IN FAIR VALUE ATTRIBUTABLE TO FORWARD ELEMENT DURING QUARTER
31 March 2018	(14,258)	(15,000)	742
30 June 2018	11,658	10,000	1,658

7.9.853.60   T records the following entries (amounts in sterling).

	DEBIT	CREDIT
31 March 2018		
Hedging reserve (OCI)	15,000	
Cost of hedging (OCI)		742
Derivative (liability)		14,258
To recognise change in fair value of forward		

	Debit	Credit
Accounts receivable	15,000	
Foreign exchange gain or loss (profit or loss)		15,000
To recognise foreign exchange gain on accounts receivable		
Foreign exchange gain or loss (profit or loss)	15,000	
Hedging reserve (OCI)		15,000
To reclassify effective portion of change in fair value of forward contract attributable to spot exchange rate risk		
Cost of hedging (OCI)	1,200	
Cost of hedging (profit or loss)		1,200
To reclassify cost of hedging for forward element attributable to the period in which the receivable is recognised		
30 June 2018		
Derivative (liability)	11,658	
Cost of hedging (OCI)		1,658
Hedge reserve (OCI)		10,000
To recognise change in fair value of forward		
Foreign exchange gain or loss (profit or loss)	10,000	
Accounts receivable		10,000
To recognise foreign exchange loss on accounts receivable		
Hedging reserve (OCI)	10,000	
Foreign exchange gain or loss (profit or loss)		10,000
To reclassify effective portion of change in fair value of forward contract attributable to spot exchange rate risk		
Cost of hedging (OCI)	1,200	
Cost of hedging (profit or loss)		1,200
To reclassify cost of hedging for forward element attributable to the period of recognised receivable		
Derivative asset	2,600	
Cash		2,600
To settle derivative at expiry of the forward		
Cash	65,000	
Accounts receivable		65,000
To record settlement of foreign currency-denominated receivable at spot rate		

7.9.853.70   A question arises about how to consider the time value of money in the measurement of the present value of a forecast transaction (other than the settlement of an already recognised monetary asset or liability) designated in a cash flow hedge of spot foreign currency risk. It appears that the calculation of the gain or loss on the hedged transaction should explicitly include discounting to arrive at a present value calculation in order to satisfy the requirements for measuring hedge ineffectiveness in 7.9.850.60. [*IFRS 9.B6.5.4, BC6.281*]

EXAMPLE 37 – MEASURING SPOT FOREIGN CURRENCY RISK – FORECAST HEDGED ITEM

7.9.853.80   Company W, whose functional currency is sterling, forecasts a cash sale of goods for EUR 100,000 on 30 June 2018. To hedge its exposure to the euro, W executes a forward contract on 1 January 2018 that settles on 30 June 2018. W immediately designates the forward contract as a cash flow hedge of variations attributable to changes in the euro/sterling spot exchange rate. The forward element will be separately accounted for as a cost of hedging. The nature of the hedged item is transaction-related and there is perfect alignment between the hedged item and forward element.

7.9.853.90   The spot exchange rates and forward exchange rates are as follows.

BALANCE SHEET DATE	EUR/GBP SPOT EXCHANGE RATE	EUR/GBP FORWARD RATE FOR 30 JUNE 2018
1 January 2018	0.60	0.6240
31 March 2018	0.75	0.7723
30 June 2018	0.65	0.6500

7.9.853.100   The risk-free rates for each currency used to discount the cash flows are as follows.

REPORTING DATE	CHANGE IN FAIR VALUE ATTRIBUTABLE TO SPOT EXCHANGE RATE RISK DURING QUARTER	CHANGE IN FAIR VALUE ATTRIBUTABLE TO FORWARD ELEMENT DURING QUARTER
1 January 2018	1.0%	3.0%
31 March 2018	1.0%	4.0%

7.9.853.110   The forward element associated with the forward contract is GBP 2,262[(1)]. This amount represents the difference at inception between the euro/sterling spot exchange rate and the contracted forward rate applied to the EUR 100,000 notional, discounted from the settlement date.

7.9.853.120 W measures ineffectiveness by applying the hypothetical derivative method. The critical terms (including maturity) of the hedged item perfectly match the critical terms of the forward contract. Consequently, the time value of money that is included in determining the change in fair value of the forward contract attributable to spot exchange risk will be the same as for the hypothetical derivative. Therefore, there are no known sources of hedge ineffectiveness. The change in fair value of the forward contract is as follows (amounts in sterling).

REPORTING DATE	TOTAL CHANGE IN FAIR VALUE DURING QUARTER	DISCOUNTED CHANGE IN FAIR VALUE ATTRIBUTABLE TO SPOT EXCHANGE RATE RISK DURING QUARTER	CHANGE IN FAIR VALUE ATTRIBUTABLE TO FORWARD ELEMENT DURING QUARTER
31 March 2018	(14,258)	(14,378)	120
30 June 2018	11,657	9,515	2,142

7.9.853.130 W records the following entries at 31 March 2018 to recognise the change in fair value of the derivative (amounts in sterling). The change in fair value of the forward contract attributable to the spot exchange rate of 14,378 represents the difference between the fair value of the spot component of the forward contract at inception in an asset position of 2,262[1] and at 31 March 2018 in a liability position of 12,116[2].

	DEBIT	CREDIT
31 March 2018		
Hedging reserve (OCI)	14,378	
Cost of hedging (OCI)		120
Derivative (liability)		14,258
To recognise change in fair value of forward		

7.9.853.140 W records the following entries when the forward contract settles on 30 June 2018 and the forecast transaction occurs (amounts in sterling). W reclassifies all amounts included in the cost of hedging reserve into profit or loss on 30 June 2018 because the hedged item represents a transaction-related hedged item. As a result of the effective cash flow hedge, the overall impact on W's statement of profit or loss is 62,400[3], which represents the euro/sterling forward rate applied to the notional of the hedged item at the time the forward contract is executed.

	DEBIT	CREDIT
30 June 2018		
Derivative (liability)	11,657	
Cost of hedging (OCI)		2,142
Hedge reserve (OCI)		9,515
To recognise change in fair value of forward		
Accounts receivable	65,000	
Revenue from a contract with a customer		65,000
To record sale at spot rate		
Other revenue	4,862	
Hedging reserve (OCI)		4,862
To reclassify effective portion of change in fair value of forward contract attributable to spot exchange rate risk		
Cost of hedging (OCI)	2,262	
Cost of hedging (profit or loss)		2,262
To reclassify cost of hedging for forward element attributable to the sale		
Derivative asset	2,600	
Cash		2,600
To settle derivative at expiry of the forward		
Notes		
1. Calculated as ((0.6240 - 0.6000) x 100,000) x (1 / (1 + 0.03)2).		
2. Calculated as ((0.7500 - 0.6240) x 100,000) x (1 / (1 + 0.04)).		
3. Calculated as 65,000 - 4,862 + 2,262. For a discussion of cost of hedging presentation, see 7.10.167.		

7.9.853.150   When an entity designates a hedge of a net investment in a foreign operation, it may designate the hedged risk as either forward exchange rate risk or spot exchange rate risk. Foreign currency gains and losses on the translation of the carrying amount of a foreign operation's net assets are recognised in accordance with IAS 21 by measuring the net investment at the relevant spot exchange rate. Therefore, if an entity designates spot exchange rate risk as the hedged risk, then it appears that it may measure the gain or loss on the hedged item by applying the change in the spot foreign exchange rate to the designated carrying amount of the net investment. For a further discussion of the designation and measurement of the effective portion of net investment hedges, see 7.9.230. [*IAS 21.39, IFRS 9.B6.5.4, BC6.281, IU 03-16*]

7.9.855   *Use of hypothetical derivative method*

7.9.855.10   To calculate the change in the fair value of the hedged item for the purpose of measuring hedge ineffectiveness, an entity may use a derivative that would have terms that match the critical terms of the hedged item. This is commonly referred to as a 'hypothetical derivative'. Using a hypothetical derivative is not a method in its own right, but is one possible way of calculating the change in the fair value of the hedged item. The hypothetical derivative replicates the hedged item and therefore results in the same outcome as if that change in fair value were determined using a different approach. Therefore, using a hypothetical derivative is a mathematical expedient. Consequently, a hypothetical derivative cannot be used to include features in the fair value of the hedged item that exist only in the hedging instrument, and not in the hedged item. An entity may also assess whether a hedging relationship meets the hedge effectiveness requirements by using a hypothetical derivative. [*IFRS 9.B6.5.5*]

7.9.855.20   Therefore, when using a hypothetical derivative to calculate the present value of the cumulative change in cash flows, an entity cannot simply impute a foreign currency basis spread in the hypothetical derivative, even though actual derivatives under which different currencies are exchanged might include such a charge – e.g. cross-currency interest rate swaps. [*IFRS 9.B6.5.5*]

7.9.855.30   In a hedge of the foreign currency risk of a recognised monetary asset or liability using a cross-currency interest rate swap, the fair value of the swap will be affected by any foreign currency basis spread, but the fair value of the recognised monetary asset or liability will not be affected by foreign currency basis spreads because it does not involve an exchange of one currency for another. Therefore, if a hypothetical derivative is used to measure hedge ineffectiveness, then the hypothetical derivative does not include the foreign currency basis spread element. [*IFRS 9.B6.5.5*]

7.9.855.40   However, the change in fair value of the hedged item caused by changes in foreign exchange rates can be measured using a hypothetical derivative that is created by exchanges of cash flows in different currencies – e.g. a cross-currency interest rate swap – as long as foreign currency basis spreads are not included in the measurement of the hypothetical derivative. This is because the only way to measure a change in fair value arising from changes in exchange rates is to measure it in terms of another currency. [*IFRS 9.B6.5.5*]

7.9.855.50   If an entity wants to prevent foreign currency basis spreads from affecting measurements of hedge ineffectiveness, then it needs to consider excluding the foreign currency basis spread of the hedging financial instrument from the designation of the hedging relationship (see 7.9.680). [*IFRS 9.B6.5.5*]

7.9.855.60   The measurement of the change in fair value of the hedged item caused by the hedged risk is the same regardless of whether a hypothetical derivative is used. [*IFRS 9.B6.5.5*]

7.9.860   **Accounting for hedge ineffectiveness**

7.9.860.10   In a cash flow hedge or a net investment hedge, the hedge ineffectiveness recognised in profit or loss is calculated under the offset method on a cumulative basis to ensure that all ineffectiveness is recognised in profit or loss immediately. [*IFRS 9.6.5.11, 6.5.13*]

7.9.860.20   In a cash flow hedge or a net investment hedge, if the cumulative gain or loss on the hedging instrument is more than the cumulative change in the fair value of the expected future cash flows on the hedged item attributable to the hedged risk, then the difference is recognised in profit or loss as ineffectiveness. However, if the reverse is true, then the full cumulative gain or loss on the hedging instrument is recognised in OCI. Consequently, the ineffectiveness is recognised in profit or loss only when the cumulative change in fair value of the hedging instrument is greater than the cumulative change in fair value of the expected future cash flows on the hedged item attributable to the hedged risk. [*IFRS 9.6.5.11, 6.5.13*]

7.9.860.30   In a fair value hedge, ineffectiveness is recognised automatically in profit or loss as a result of separately remeasuring the hedging instrument and the hedged item. No separate calculation is required of the amount of ineffectiveness to be recognised in profit or loss. [*IFRS 9.6.5.8*]

7.9.870   Time value, forward element and foreign currency basis spreads

7.9.870.10   Depending on an entity's risk management objective and whether it is appropriately documented at inception of the hedging relationship, an entity can exclude the time value of an option, the forward element of a forward contract or the foreign currency basis spread of a financial instrument from the designation of a hedging derivative (see 7.9.650). [*IFRS 9.6.2.4*]

7.9.870.20   The excluded portions – the time value of an option, the forward element of a forward contract and the foreign currency basis spread of a financial instrument – of hedging instruments are not considered for measuring hedge ineffectiveness. However, an entity is not permitted to exclude the credit risk (or any other risk) associated with a derivative from the measurement of hedge ineffectiveness. [*IFRS 9.6.2.4*]

7.9.870.30   The choice for separating the forward element from a forward contract and foreign currency basis spreads of a financial instrument is available on a hedge-by-hedge basis and there is no requirement to have a consistently applied policy. [*IFRS 9.6.2.4*]

7.9.870.40   If the time value, the forward element or the foreign currency basis spreads are not excluded from the designated hedging instrument, then the full fair value of the hedging instrument is used in measuring ineffectiveness. [*IFRS 9.6.2.4*]

7.9.880   Interest rate risk

7.9.880.10   It is quite common for financial instruments with an exposure to interest rate risk also to be exposed to prepayment risk. For a prepayable asset or liability, changes in interest rates have an effect on the fair value of the asset or liability by changing the expectations about the timing of future cash flows. This has an impact on the effectiveness assessment and ineffectiveness measurement.

7.9.880.20   Prepayment risk affects the timing as well as the amount of cash flows. Consequently, this may impact the effectiveness of fair value hedges as well as the highly probable requirement for forecast cash flows. A prepayable hedged item will generally experience smaller fair value changes when interest rates fall than a non-prepayable hedged item, whereas fair value changes as interest rates rise will be closer to those of a non-prepayable item.

7.9.880.30   Therefore, the risk of prepayment or changes to the timing of future cash flows is considered when an entity designates its hedging relationships. In our view, prepayment is not a risk that is capable of separate designation; instead, it is a component of interest rate risk and is designated as such. This is because it is difficult to measure and isolate the change in fair value arising from a change in prepayments separately from the overall change arising from a change in interest rates.

7.9.880.40   In a portfolio fair value hedge of interest rate risk (see 7.9.500), the assessment of hedge effectiveness can be performed using a maturity schedule. Such a schedule usually determines the net position for each maturity period by aggregating assets and liabilities maturing or repricing in that maturity period. However, the net exposure should be associated with a specific asset, liability or cash inflow or outflow to apply hedge accounting, such that the correlation of the changes of the hedging instrument and the designated hedged item can be assessed.

7.9.885   *Financial instruments with a benchmark rate component floored at zero*

7.9.885.10   A debt instrument on which the interest rate is linked to a benchmark rate but with the benchmark component floored at zero may be a hedged item in a cash flow hedge of the variability of interest payments or receipts due to changes in the benchmark rate. In this case, the hedging instrument and the hedged item have values that move in opposite directions because of the same risk (i.e. the same benchmark rate). If the benchmark rate becomes negative, then a question arises about whether the designated hedged risk continues to exist because interest cash flows on the debt instrument are not variable during the period in which the benchmark rate is negative. In our view, in these situations the designated hedged risk continues to exist and remains eligible for hedge accounting because the benchmark rate may turn positive in future periods and therefore there is still exposure to variability in future interest cash flows. In many cases, it is possible that an economic relationship can be demonstrated and it is possible that the expected value of the hedging instrument and the value of the hedged item will change in response to movements in the same benchmark rate (see 7.9.800). [*IFRS 9.6.5.2(b)*]

7.9.885.20   Another question that arises if an entity hedges benchmark-based interest cash flows floored at zero is whether the hedged benchmark-based cash flows can be regarded as highly probable if the benchmark rate becomes negative. Again, in our view the analysis is not changed merely by the benchmark rate becoming negative. This is because there may still be an economic relationship between the hedging instrument and the hedged item, and the hedged forecast transactions are the receipts or payments of interest and these transactions are still forecast to occur, although the benchmark-based component may be zero.

7.9.885.30   Under IFRS 9, an entity cannot de-designate a hedging relationship that still meets the risk management objective and continues to meet all other qualifying criteria (after taking into account any rebalancing of the hedging relationship). However, if there is an embedded floor in the hedged item but no equal and opposite floor on the benchmark-based cash flows in the hedging instrument, then the embedded floor in the hedged item means that the negative benchmark rate will cause the hedge not to be fully effective. Therefore, assuming that the economic relationship test is met (see 7.9.800), hedge ineffectiveness may arise because changes in the benchmark rate will not have an equal and opposite effect on the hedging instrument and the hedged item (see 7.9.885.80).

7.9.885.40   Rebalancing may allow the continuation of the hedging relationship in situations in which the relationship between the hedging instrument and the hedged item changes in a way that can be compensated for by adjusting the hedge ratio. Also, the entity has to determine whether – considering this mismatch between the variability of the cash flows of the hedging instrument and the hedged item – the hedge still meets the risk management objective on the basis of which it qualified for hedge accounting and continues to meet all other qualifying criteria. [*IFRS 9.6.4.1(b), B6.5.9, B6.5.23*]

EXAMPLE 38 – CASH FLOW HEDGES OF FLOATING INTEREST RATES – NEGATIVE INTEREST RATE ENVIRONMENT

7.9.885.50   Company R has a loan receivable in which the interest rate is linked to LIBOR. The loan is not prepayable and credit risk is not significant.

7.9.885.60   R's strategy is to hedge the variability in LIBOR cash flows receivable from the loan by applying cash flow hedging using an interest rate swap. The derivative has the same notional and maturity as the hedged item and is designated in the hedging relationship from inception. R considers alternative hedging relationships depending on whether there is a floor on the LIBOR rate in the swap and/or in the loan in a negative interest rate environment.

Scenario 1: Hedged item and hedging instrument do not contain floors

7.9.885.70   R can designate a vanilla interest rate swap as a hedging instrument in a cash flow hedge of the variability in LIBOR cash flows receivable from the loan. As a consequence, an economic relationship with little ineffectiveness is expected to be achieved because all critical terms are matched.

Scenario 2: Only the hedged item has a floor

7.9.885.80   In this scenario, the LIBOR cash flows on the loan are floored at zero and the proposed hedging instrument is a vanilla interest rate swap that pays LIBOR and receives a fixed rate. As noted in 7.9.885.10, a loan in which the interest rate is linked to LIBOR but floored at zero may be a hedged item in a cash flow hedge of the variability of interest payments or receipts due to changes in LIBOR. R must firstly make an assessment of whether an economic relationship exists (see 7.9.885.10–20). However, assuming that an economic relationship can be demonstrated, hedge ineffectiveness may arise because changes in LIBOR will not have an equal and opposite effect on the hedging instrument and the hedged item (see 7.9.885.30). Rebalancing may allow the continuation of the hedging relationship by adjusting the designated quantities of the hedged item or of the hedging instrument of the existing hedging relationship. This is done for the purpose of maintaining a hedge ratio that complies with the hedge effectiveness requirements and is consistent with the risk management objective (see 7.9.885.10–40). [*IFRS 9.B6.5.7*]

Scenario 3: Only the hedging instrument has a floor

7.9.885.90   In this scenario, R considers an interest rate swap that pays LIBOR floored at zero and receives a fixed rate. With this instrument, R would pay the greater of LIBOR and zero. This swap is in effect a net written option and so does not qualify as a hedging instrument. As noted in 7.9.610.30, an instrument or combination of instruments that in effect is a net written option qualifies as a hedging instrument only if it is designated as an offset to a purchased option. [*IFRS 9.6.2.6, B6.2.4*]

Scenario 4: Both the hedged item and the hedging instrument have a floor

7.9.885.100   R designates, as the hedging instrument, an interest rate swap that pays LIBOR floored at zero and receives a fixed rate. The hedged item is the variability in LIBOR cash flows receivable from a loan that also contains a floor on the LIBOR component at zero.

7.9.885.110   Similar to Scenario 3, the hedging instrument is in effect a net written option and the fair value is zero at the date of designation. However, the LIBOR cash flows on the loan are also floored at zero and this is considered a purchased option. A written option may be designated as a hedging instrument if it is designated as an offset to a purchased option (see 7.9.610.30). As a consequence, considering that all other critical terms are matched, the presence of floors in both the hedged item and the hedging instrument results in an economic relationship with little ineffectiveness.

7.9.885.120   An additional question arises when considering the designation of a hedged item with embedded optionality in a cash flow hedge. That is, should the time value of the embedded option be included within the change in value of the hedged item for effectiveness purposes? IFRS 9 permits the exclusion of the time value of an option contract from the hedging relationship. This results in accounting for the time value of the option (see 7.9.560.50). That is, the change in fair value of the time value of the option is recognised in OCI to the extent that it relates to the hedged item and is accumulated in a separate component of equity. However, the standard does not address a situation in which the hedged item and the hedging instrument both contain time value. [*IFRS 9.6.2.4(a), 6.5.15*]

7.9.885.130   In our view, if the hedged item contains embedded optionality, matched by optionality within the hedging instrument, then the inclusion of time value from both the hedged item and the hedging instrument within the hedging relationship would provide high effectiveness.

EXAMPLE 39 – INCLUSION OF TIME VALUE WITHIN HEDGED ITEM IN CASH FLOW HEDGING RELATIONSHIP

7.9.885.140   Company X has a variability in LIBOR cash flows receivable from a loan. The loan also contains a floor on the LIBOR component at zero. X wants to hedge the variability in LIBOR cash flows, considering the following hedging relationship.

- Hedged item: variability in LIBOR cash flows (i.e. the hedged item will receive the greater of LIBOR and zero).
- Hedging instrument: interest rate swap that pays LIBOR and receives a fixed rate. LIBOR cash flows under the swap are floored at zero (i.e. the interest rate swap pays the greater of LIBOR and zero).
- The maturity of the hedged item and the hedging instrument are the same (i.e. two years).
- The hedged item and the hedging instrument are of the same notional amount. The loan is not prepayable and the credit risk is not significant.
- The hedging instrument (including the interest rate swap and the embedded floor) has nil fair value at inception and the change in the fair value goes through OCI after inception.

7.9.885.150   In this case, if LIBOR is above 0%, then X will receive LIBOR interest from the loan and will pay LIBOR interest on the floating leg of the swap. Conversely, if LIBOR is below 0%, then X will receive 0% from the loan and will pay 0% on the floating leg of the swap. In both scenarios, the time between inception and maturity is two years and this period of time will be reflected in the calculation for measurement of hedge ineffectiveness.

7.9.885.160   For the calculation of the variability in the hedged item, the embedded premium (including the intrinsic value and the time value) is considered within the hedged item cash flows and so forms part of the calculation at inception. Accordingly, the inclusion of time value from both the hedged item and the hedging instrument within the hedging relationship results in high effectiveness.

7.9.885.170   In our view, the methods outlined in 7.9.890–900 are some of the methods that could be used for measuring hedge ineffectiveness in a cash flow hedge or a fair value hedge of interest rate risk using an interest rate swap.

7.9.890   *Change in fair value method*

7.9.890.10   Ineffectiveness is measured by considering movements in the present value of the cumulative expected/contractual future interest cash flows that are designated as the hedged item and the cumulative change in the fair value of the designated hedging instrument – e.g. a pay-fixed receive-floating interest rate swap.

7.9.900   *Hypothetical derivative method*

7.9.900.10   Ineffectiveness is measured by comparing the change in the fair value of the actual derivative designated as the hedging instrument and the change in the fair value of a hypothetical derivative representing the hedged item. The hypothetical derivative is defined so that it matches the critical terms of the hedged item – e.g. notional, repricing dates, index on which the asset's or liability's variable rate is based, mirror image caps and floors etc – and if it is calibrated using the hedged price (or rate) level. For example, if the hedge is for a two-side risk at the current market interest rate level, then the hypothetical derivative would represent a market interest rate swap that is calibrated to a value of zero at the time of designation of hedging relationship. The hypothetical derivative would be expected to perfectly offset the hedged cash flows, and the change in fair value of the hypothetical derivative is regarded as a proxy for the present value of the cumulative change in the expected future cash flows on the hedged item. [*IFRS 9.B6.5.5*]

7.9.900.20   A hypothetical derivative replicates the hedged item. As such, it cannot be used to include features in the value of the hedged item that exist only in the hedging instrument (but not in the hedged item). Therefore, features of the derivative instrument – e.g. the credit risk of the derivative counterparty or the currency basis spread in a CCIRS – that are not part of the hedged item cannot be included in the hypothetical derivative. [*IFRS 9.B6.5.5*]

7.9.900.30   In our view, the valuation methodology for determining the change in fair value of the hypothetical derivative should use market valuation conventions – e.g. the discount rate – to measure a derivative. If there is a change in market valuation conventions, then it is appropriate for an entity to adjust the inputs when determining the change in fair value of the hypothetical derivative. For example, assume that an entity has previously used six-month LIBOR as the discount rate when determining the change in fair value of a pay-fixed receive-floating interest rate swap. Because of changes in market valuation conventions, the entity now determines that an overnight index swap (OIS) discount rate is the appropriate discount rate for determining the change in fair value. We believe that it is appropriate for the entity to adjust the discount rate from six-month LIBOR to OIS when determining the change in fair value of both the actual instrument and the hypothetical derivative. Such an adjustment should not be considered a de-designation/redesignation event.

7.9.900.40   If an interest rate swap is used to hedge the interest rate risk of a debt instrument, and if the swap and the debt instrument are transacted at the same date and have same principal terms (e.g. notional, repricing dates, basis etc), then designating the hedge at the transaction date of these instruments could minimise hedge ineffectiveness. However, if the hedge is designated subsequent to entering into the hedging swap, then it is unlikely that the fixed leg of the hedging swap will be equal to the fixed rate on the perfectly effective hypothetical derivative and therefore it may lead to hedge ineffectiveness.

7.9.910   REBALANCING

7.9.910.10   A hedging relationship may subsequently fail to meet the hedge effectiveness requirement regarding the hedge ratio – e.g. the hedge ratio may no longer represent what is actually used for risk management purposes; however, the entity's risk management objective for that designated hedging relationship may remain the same. In this case, the entity adjusts the hedge ratio so that it meets the qualifying criteria again. If the risk management objective for the designated hedging relationship has changed, then rebalancing does not apply. Instead, hedge accounting is discontinued. [*IFRS 9.6.5.5, B6.5.15*]

7.9.910.20   The following flowchart summarises the rebalancing requirements for a change in the extent of offset of the hedging relationship.

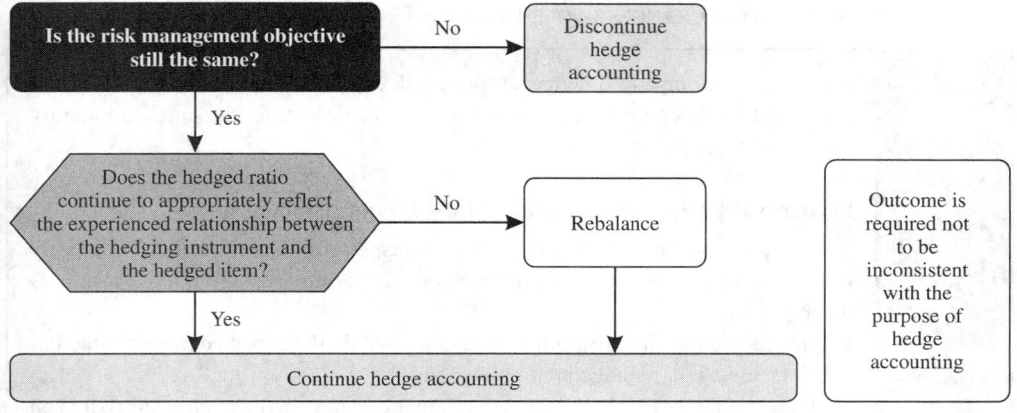

7.9.910.30   Rebalancing a hedging relationship allows hedge accounting to continue when the change in the relationship of the hedging instrument and the hedged item can be compensated for by adjusting the hedge ratio. That is, rebalancing is relevant only when basis risk exists between the hedged item and the hedging instrument. Any hedge ineffectiveness to date is recognised in profit or loss – or in OCI if the hedged item is an equity investment for which an entity has elected to present changes in fair value in OCI – immediately before rebalancing the hedging relationship. [*IFRS 9.B6.5.8*]

7.9.910.40   By adjusting the hedge ratio, an entity compensates for changes in the relationship between the hedging instrument and the hedged item arising from the underlyings or risk variables. This adjustment allows an entity to continue the hedging relationship when the relationship between the hedging instrument and the hedged item changes in a way that can be compensated for by adjusting the hedge ratio. [*IFRS 9.B6.5.9*]

7.9.910.50   If the hedge ratio is adjusted through rebalancing, then it has to satisfy the criteria that are required to qualify for hedge accounting at inception of the hedge – i.e. the hedge ratio:
* should typically reflect the quantities of the hedging instrument and the hedged item that the entity actually uses; but
* should not result in an accounting outcome that is inconsistent with the purpose of hedge accounting (see 7.9.820). [*IFRS 9.6.4.1(c), B6.5.14*]

7.9.910.60   Therefore, the qualifying criteria for hedge accounting prohibit inappropriate hedge ratios resulting from an inappropriate initial designation or from not adjusting a hedge ratio that has become inappropriate.

7.9.910.70   Not every change in the extent of offset constitutes a change in the relationship between the hedging instrument and hedged item. An entity determines whether the changes in offset are:
* fluctuations around a hedge ratio that remains valid; or
* an indication that the hedge ratio no longer appropriately reflects the relationship between the hedging instrument and the hedged item. [*IFRS 9.B6.5.11*]

EXAMPLE 40 – EVALUATING CHANGES IN OFFSET

7.9.910.80   Company B hedges its price risk exposure to a forecast purchase of a commodity in Location C with exchange-traded contracts for the same commodity but of a different grade in Location D.

Scenario 1: Hedge ratio remains valid – Do not rebalance

7.9.910.90   Because of fluctuations in transportation costs of the commodity in Location C, B recognises some ineffectiveness on the hedging relationship. B determines that:

- the fluctuations in transportation costs are within the expected range of fluctuations in its risk management policy; and
- there has not been a long-term or systematic change in the relationship between the price of the commodity in Location C and the price of the exchange-traded contracts for the commodity in Location D. [*IFRS 9.B6.5.10–B6.5.11*]

7.9.910.100   The amounts of the hedged item and the hedging instruments have not changed for risk management purposes; therefore, there is an expectation that the hedging relationship will remain within the expected range. The change in the extent of offset is therefore a matter of measuring and recognising hedge ineffectiveness, but not of adjusting the hedge ratio. [*IFRS 9.B6.5.10–B6.5.11*]

Scenario 2: Hedge ratio is no longer appropriate – Rebalance

7.9.910.110   There is a change in the relationship between the two commodities, and the correlation between the price of the commodity in Location C and the price of the exchange-traded commodity contracts in Location D is altered as a result. In this scenario, rebalancing the hedge ratio to reflect the new correlation ensures that the hedging relationship maintains a hedge ratio that complies with the hedge effectiveness requirements. An example of such a change might be a new use for one of the commodities, such that demand for it has been increased for the foreseeable future. [*IFRS 9.B6.5.10–B6.5.11*]

Scenario 3: Hedge ratio is no longer appropriate – Discontinue hedge accounting

7.9.910.120   If there was a default by the counterparty of the derivative commodity contract, then changing the hedge ratio would not ensure that the hedging relationship meets the hedge effectiveness requirements. Therefore, rebalancing would not enable B to continue a hedging relationship when the relationship between the hedging instrument and the hedged item changes in a way that cannot be compensated for by adjusting the hedge ratio. [*IFRS 9.B6.5.10–B6.5.11*]

7.9.910.130   If an entity rebalances a hedging relationship, then it updates its hedge documentation. This includes analysing the sources of hedge ineffectiveness that are expected to affect the hedging relationship during its remaining term. [*IFRS 9.B6.5.21*]

7.9.920   **Mechanics**

7.9.920.10   A rebalancing adjustment of the hedging relationship can be effected as follows:
- an entity can increase the weighting of the hedged item either by increasing the volume of the hedged item or by decreasing the volume of the hedging instrument; or
- it can increase the weighting of the hedging instrument either by increasing the volume of the hedging instrument or by decreasing the volume of the hedged item. [*IFRS 9.B6.5.16*]

7.9.920.20   The changes in volume refer to the quantities that are part of the hedging relationship. Decreases in volume do not necessarily mean that the items or transactions no longer exist, or are no longer expected to occur; instead, they mean that the items or transactions are not part of the hedging relationship. A rebalancing that results in a decrease in the volume of the hedged item is treated as a partial discontinuation of that part of the hedging relationship (see 7.9.950).

7.9.920.30   The following diagram summarises the mechanics of rebalancing.

Adjustment	Measurement of fair value changes	
	Hedged item	**Hedging instrument**
Increase volume of hedged item	Previously designated volume is unchanged; additional volume is included from date of rebalancing	Unchanged
Decrease volume of hedged item	Reduced volume is unchanged; decrease in volume is discontinued from date of rebalancing	Unchanged
Increase volume of hedging instrument	Unchanged	Previously designated volume is unchanged; additional volume is included from date of rebalancing
Decrease volume of hedging instrument	Unchanged	Reduced volume is unchanged; decrease in volume is measured at FVTPL from date of rebalancing

7.9.920.40   Rebalancing a fair value hedging relationship may involve decreasing the volume of a hedged item that is a financial instrument. In this case, the entity may need to begin amortising the amount related to the volume that is no longer part of the hedging relationship (see 7.9.170.90 and 960.20). This means that entities will have to keep track of the accumulated gains or losses for the risk being hedged at the level of the individual hedged items.

7.9.920.50   Adjusting the hedge ratio by increasing the volume of the hedging instrument does not affect the measurement of the hedged item or the measurement of the previously designated hedging instrument. However, increasing the volume of the hedging instrument affects subsequent changes in the value of the instrument in two ways:

- subsequent changes in the value of the hedging instrument will reflect the increase in the volume of the hedging instrument; and
- it is likely that the original hedging instrument and the additional hedging instrument have different terms, because they were entered into at different times; therefore, subsequent changes in the value of the hedging instrument will be different, reflecting the difference in terms.

7.9.920.60   A similar effect occurs when an entity adjusts the hedge ratio by increasing the volume of the hedged item – e.g. increasing the size of a forecast transaction.

7.9.930   DISCONTINUATION

7.9.940   Discontinuation of entire hedging relationship

7.9.940.10   A hedging relationship is discontinued in its entirety when as a whole it ceases to meet the qualifying criteria after considering the rebalancing of the hedging relationship (if applicable). Voluntary discontinuation when the qualifying criteria are met is prohibited. The following are examples of when discontinuation is required:
- the risk management objective of an entity for the hedging relationship has changed – i.e. continuing to apply hedge accounting would no longer reflect its risk management objective;
- the hedging instrument expires or is sold, terminated or exercised; this excludes scenarios in which the expiry or termination is a replacement or rollover of a hedging instrument into another that is part of, and consistent with, the entity's documented risk management objective – discontinuation would not be required in these scenarios;
- there is no longer an economic relationship between the hedged item and hedging instrument; and
- the effect of credit risk starts dominating the value changes that result from the economic relationship. [*IFRS 9.6.5.6, B6.5.26*]

EXAMPLE 41 – ROLLOVER HEDGE STRATEGY

7.9.940.20   Company X forecasts a highly probable purchase of a commodity in one year. As part of its risk management strategy, X wants to fix the cash flow variability that would arise from changes in market prices of the commodity from now until the date of purchase. However, the market to which X has access does not offer commodity future contracts for a duration longer than three months. Therefore, X decides to hedge its exposure to changes in commodity prices by entering into four successive commodity futures.

7.9.940.30   If X documents this hedging strategy, including the expected rollovers of the hedging futures, at inception of the hedge, then the expiry of one future contract and its replacement with a successive future contract with the same characteristics would not be deemed to be a termination of the hedge.

7.9.940.40   If there is no longer an economic relationship between the hedged item and the hedging instrument or the effect of credit risk starts dominating the value changes that result from the economic relationship, then no amount of rebalancing can enable the relationship to continue to qualify for hedge accounting. This is why discontinuation of the hedging relationship is required in those circumstances. [*IFRS 9.6.5.6*]

7.9.940.50   Hedge accounting is also discontinued if the recognised asset, liability, firm commitment or forecast transaction is no longer eligible for designation as a hedged item. This occurs, for example, when an entity acquires, or otherwise begins to consolidate, the counterparty to a hedged forecast transaction or firm commitment, resulting in that transaction no longer involving a party external to the reporting entity. Another example is when an entity sells, or is otherwise required to deconsolidate, a subsidiary (see 2.5.760), resulting in a hedged item of that subsidiary becoming derecognised. Also, when there is a change in the functional currency of an entity, foreign currency exposures denominated in the new functional currency no longer qualify for hedge accounting for foreign currency risk.

7.9.940.60   A hedging relationship is discontinued when the hedging instrument is sold or terminated. In our experience, certain events of default, such as a filing for bankruptcy by the counterparty, would – under the standard International Swaps and Derivatives Association (ISDA) terms for some derivatives – either result automatically in termination of the derivative or permit the entity to terminate the derivative in exchange for a net cash settlement and to replace it with another instrument having similar terms with another counterparty. Whether this is the case is likely to depend on the legal and contractual arrangements in each country. In our view, unless it is a replacement of a hedging instrument as part of the entity's existing documented hedging strategy, the termination of a hedging derivative and its replacement by another derivative with another counterparty would result in the termination of the existing hedging relationship and, if it is appropriately designated, the establishment of a new one.

7.9.940.70   If an entity discontinues a hedging relationship, then it can designate a new hedging relationship that involves the hedging instrument or the hedged item. However, that designation constitutes the start of a new hedging relationship, not the continuation of the old one. [*IFRS 9.B6.5.28*]

7.9.940.80   Beginning a new hedging relationship with an existing hedging instrument that has a fair value other than zero may result in hedge ineffectiveness. This is because the initial fair value of the instrument is itself subject to change with market changes. Unless an offsetting fair value effect is also present in the hedged item, hedge ineffectiveness may result.

7.9.950   Partial discontinuation of hedging relationship

7.9.950.10   A part of a hedging relationship is discontinued when only part of the hedging relationship ceases to meet the qualifying criteria. This may be as a result of rebalancing (see 7.9.910) or when some of the volume of the hedged item that is a forecast transaction is no longer highly probable to occur. When partial discontinuation applies, hedge accounting continues for the remainder of the hedging relationship. [*IFRS 9.6.5.6, B6.5.27*]

7.9.950.20   For example, an entity fails to predict the volume of hedged highly probable forecast transactions accurately. As a result, the expected volume is lower than the originally designated volume. In this case, partial discontinuation is appropriate. [*IFRS 9.B6.5.27*]

7.9.950.30   If some of the volume of the hedged item in a forecast transaction is no longer highly probable, then the hedging relationship can continue for the portion of the hedged item that is still highly probable. In cases of equivalent changes to only a portion of the hedged item and hedging instrument, this suggests that the risk management objective of the entity has not changed for the remaining portions of the hedged item and hedging instrument. For example, a portion related to the notional amount of the hedging instrument can be cancelled to align with the remaining reduced quantity of hedged item and maintain the hedge ratio in a hedging relationship. Accordingly, the existing hedging relationship continues for the remaining part of the hedged item. Another example may be a change in risk management objective that leads to de-designation of part of a hedging instrument and a similar part of the hedged item. [*IFRS 9.B6.5.24–B6.5.27*]

EXAMPLE 42A – PARTIAL DISCONTINUATION – CHANGE IN AN ENTITY'S RISK MANAGEMENT OBJECTIVE

7.9.950.40   Bank X's risk management objective is to hedge the foreign currency exposure from its financial assets in a range between 50% and 75% of the exposure. The level of hedging depends on market conditions. X has designated a cash flow hedge covering 70% of the foreign currency exposure from its financial assets. The hedging instruments include several forward foreign exchange contracts.

7.9.950.50   Following changes in market conditions, X modifies its risk management objective to hedge only 60% of the foreign currency exposure from its financial assets (the exposure size remains the same). As a result, X transfers some forward contracts offsetting 10% of the foreign currency exposure from the financial assets to its trading books.

7.9.950.60   X discontinues part of the hedging relationship by de-designating these forward contracts while the hedging relationship for the remaining forward contracts continues.

7.9.950.70   A single hedging instrument can be designated as a hedging instrument of different hedged risk positions in different hedging relationships (see 7.9.570). It appears that if one of these hedging relationships is specifically discontinued, then all the other hedging relationships are discontinued unless the part of the hedging instrument that relates to the specifically discontinued hedging relationship is immediately redesignated into a new hedging relationship, in which case the other hedging relationships continue. This is because a qualifying hedging instrument is generally required to be designated in its entirety. [*IFRS 9.B6.2.6*]

EXAMPLE 42B – PARTIAL DISCONTINUATION – DE-DESIGNATION AND REDESIGNATION OF PART OF HEDGING INSTRUMENT

7.9.950.80   Company B's functional currency is sterling. B has a five-year debt liability denominated in euro. B also has Subsidiary X whose functional currency is the US dollar. To hedge the foreign exchange rate risk on its net investment in X and on the debt liability, B enters into a five-year receive-euro pay-US dollar forward contract. B designates the forward contract in two hedging relationships as a hedge of:

- US dollar/sterling risk on the net investment in X; and
- sterling/euro risk on the cash flows of the debt liability.

7.9.950.90   Three years later, B sells its net investment in X. Accordingly, B de-designates the net investment hedge for X. On the same date, B simultaneously designates the USD-GBP portion of the forward contract as a hedge of its net investment in Subsidiary Y, whose functional currency is also the US dollar. The euro liability is unaffected and B's risk management objective has not changed for the cash flow hedge.

7.9.950.100   B continues hedge accounting for the unaffected cash flow hedge. This is because the cash flow hedge continues to meet all of the qualifying criteria for hedge accounting, including the requirement that a qualifying instrument be designated in its entirety. Given the simultaneous de-designation and redesignation of the net investment hedges, the forward contract is designated in its entirety at all times (see 7.9.560.20).

7.9.960   Accounting for discontinuation of hedging relationship

7.9.960.10   Hedge accounting is discontinued prospectively from the date of discontinuation of a hedging relationship. [*IFRS 9.B6.5.22*]

7.9.960.20   If an entity discontinues hedge accounting for a fair value hedge, then it ceases to adjust the carrying amount of the hedged item for the change in fair value arising from the hedged risk from the date of discontinuation. The carrying amount of the hedged item continues to reflect the hedge accounting adjustments that were made before discontinuation. [*IFRS 9.6.5.6, 6.5.8*]

7.9.960.30   If an entity discontinues hedge accounting for a cash flow hedge, then it accounts for the amount that has been accumulated in the cash flow hedge reserve as follows.
- A hedged future cash flow that is no longer highly probable to occur may still be expected to occur. If the hedged future cash flows are still expected to occur, then that amount remains in the cash flow hedge reserve until the future cash flows occur. However, if the amount is a loss and the entity expects that all or a portion of that loss will not be recovered in one or more future periods, then it immediately reclassifies the amount that is not expected to be recovered into profit or loss as a reclassification adjustment (see 4.1.240.70 and 7.9.200.130). When the future cash flows occur, the accounting described in 7.9.200.70–90 applies.
- If the hedged future cash flows are no longer expected to occur, then that amount is immediately reclassified from the cash flow hedge reserve to profit or loss as a reclassification adjustment (see 4.1.240.70). [*IFRS 9.6.5.12*]

EXAMPLE 43 – DISCONTINUATION – RECLASSIFYING GAINS AND LOSSES – HEDGED FUTURE CASH FLOWS EXPECTED TO OCCUR

7.9.960.40   On 31 December 2018, Company D issues a floating rate bond that bears interest based on a benchmark rate payable annually and matures on 31 December 2022. The bond is issued at par of 1,000. In accordance with its risk

management strategy, D enters into a four-year pay-fixed 3% receive-benchmark interest rate swap on 31 December 2018. On the same date, D designates the swap as a cash flow hedge of the variability of future interest payments on the bond attributable to changes in the benchmark rate. The timing of the swap's cash flows matches those of the bond. The fair value of the swap at inception is zero.
- US dollar/sterling risk on the net investment in X; and
- sterling/euro risk on the cash flows of the debt liability.

7.9.960.50   The effects of credit risk are insignificant to the effectiveness of the hedging relationship and there are no sources of ineffectiveness during the hedging period. Therefore, during 2019 and 2020 all gains and losses on remeasurement of the swap to fair value are included in OCI.

7.9.960.60   On 31 December 2020, D changes its risk management strategy and it no longer wishes to hedge its exposure to variable interest payments. Therefore, on that date D terminates the interest rate swap by receiving its current fair value of 28 from the counterparty and discontinues hedge accounting. Interest payments on the bond are still expected to occur through to maturity on 31 December 2022.

7.9.960.70   At 31 December 2020, the market one-year benchmark rate is 4% and the one-year benchmark forward rate for fixing on 31 December 2021 and settling on 31 December 2022 is 5%.

7.9.960.80   We believe that D may apply the following approaches to reclassify the accumulated balance of 28 recognised in OCI at 31 December 2020 to profit or loss during 2021 and 2022 (see 7.9.200.90).
- *Approach 1:* Using the information on the yield curve, D analyses the fair value of the swap of 28 as representing the present value of expected net receipts of 10 on 31 December 2021 and 18 on 31 December 2022 – i.e. the expected present values of the cash flows that would have occurred under the swap if it had not been terminated. Based on this analysis, D reclassifies 10 during 2021 and 18 during 2022.
- *Approach 2:* D amortises the total balance of 28 on a straight-line basis over the two-year period – i.e. 14 in each year.

7.9.960.90   If an entity discontinues hedge accounting for a net investment hedge, then it ceases to defer any foreign exchange gains or losses on the designated hedging instruments in OCI as part of the foreign currency translation reserve from the date of discontinuation. Any cumulative gain or loss on the hedging instrument relating to the effective portion of the hedge that has been accumulated in the foreign currency translation reserve remains there and is reclassified from equity to profit or loss as a reclassification adjustment on the disposal or partial disposal of the foreign operation (see 2.7.340).

7.9.960.100   Any subsequent changes in value of the hedging instrument – a derivative or a non-derivative financial asset – measured at FVTPL are recognised in profit or loss. For the subsequent accounting for any excluded portion of the hedging instrument that was accounted as a cost of hedging before the discontinuation of hedge accounting, see 7.9.690. [*IFRS 9.6.5.6–6.5.7*]

7.9.970   Clearing derivatives with central counterparties

7.9.970.10   There is relief from discontinuing an existing hedging relationship if a novation that was not contemplated in the original hedging documentation meets the following criteria:
- the novation is made as a consequence of laws or regulations, or the introduction of laws or regulations;
- the novation results in one or more clearing counterparties becoming the new counterparty to each of the parties to the novated derivative; and
- any changes to the terms of the novated derivative are limited to those necessary to effect such a replacement of the counterparty, but only if those changes are consistent with the terms that would be expected if the novated derivative were originally cleared with the clearing counterparty. These changes include:
    - changes in the contractual collateral requirements of the novated derivative;
    - rights to set off receivables and payables balances with the clearing counterparty; and
    - charges levied by the clearing counterparty. [*IFRS 9.6.5.6*]

7.9.970.20   The following flowchart summarises how to apply the criteria.

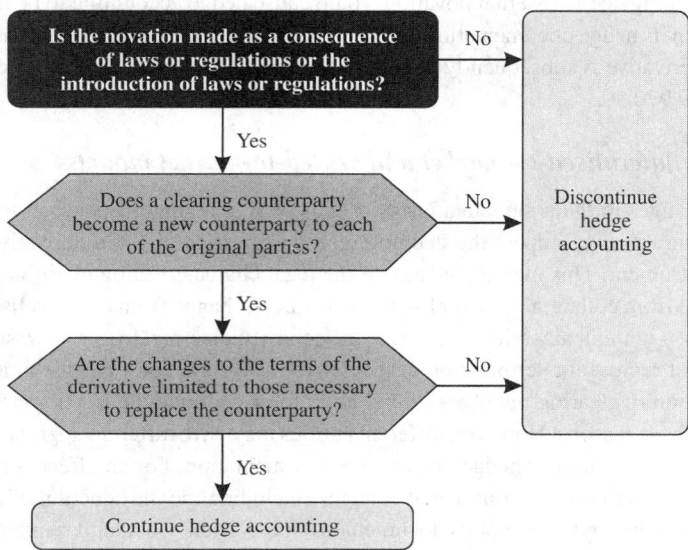

7.9.970.30   A 'clearing counterparty' is a central counterparty (sometimes referred to as a 'clearing organisation' or a 'clearing agency'), or an entity or entities – e.g. a clearing member of a clearing organisation or a client of a clearing member of a clearing organisation – that are acting as counterparty to effect clearing by a central counterparty. [*IFRS 9.6.5.6*]

7.9.970.40   If the parties to the hedging instrument replace their original counterparties with different counterparties, then the relief is available only if each of those parties effects clearing with the same central counterparty. [*IFRS 9.6.5.6*]

7.9.970.50   For hedging relationships that continue after the hedging instrument is novated to a clearing counterparty, IFRS 9 is still applied as usual to account for the derivative and the hedging relationship. For example, any changes in the credit quality of the counterparty, or in the contractual collateral requirements, are reflected in the fair value of the novated derivative and in the measurement of hedge ineffectiveness. [*IFRS 9.6.5.6*]

7.9.970.60   In some jurisdictions, a novation of a derivative to a clearing counterparty may not be required by laws and regulations, but an entity may voluntarily novate a derivative as a consequence of laws and regulations. In these cases, to continue hedge accounting the voluntary novation needs to be associated with laws or regulations that are relevant to the central clearing of derivatives. The mere possibility of laws or regulations being introduced is not a sufficient basis for the continuation of hedge accounting. [*IFRS 9.BC6.347*]

7.9.970.70   There may be other situations in which a derivative is novated but the criteria to continue hedge accounting are not met – e.g. an entity agrees to a counterparty novating an over-the-counter derivative to a third party as a consequence of laws or regulations, and no clearing counterparty is introduced.

7.9.970.80   To mitigate the risk that novation would cause hedge accounting to be discontinued, an entity may state in its hedge documentation that its intention is for the hedging relationship to continue if the hedging derivative is subsequently novated in circumstances other than those contemplated in the criteria in 7.9.970.10.

7.9.975   *Collateralised-to-market and settled-to-market models*

7.9.975.10   Changes to the contractual terms of the clearing arrangements used for the execution of derivative contracts may impact the hedging relationship if an affected derivative is designated as a hedging instrument. This may be the case if the legal characterisation of variation margin payments is changed from collateral to partial settlement – i.e. a change from collateralised-to-market to settled-to-market – without any other changes to the contractual terms. In our view, such a change on its own would not represent a termination of the derivative contract or a change in its critical terms and would not require clearing members or end users to discontinue the existing hedge accounting relationship for those reasons. However, different entities may have different approaches to assessing effectiveness, as set out in their hedge accounting documentation. For an affected hedge, an entity would need to consider how the contractual changes (including the introduction of price alignment adjustment) impact the application of its documented approach and whether it remains fit for purpose (see 7.6.490).

7.9.980   *Effect of delays and other changes in forecast transaction*

7.9.980.10   The notion of a highly probable forecast transaction implies a higher degree of probability than one that is merely expected to occur. If a forecast transaction is no longer highly probable but is still expected to occur, then this means that the criteria for hedge accounting are no longer met and, prospectively, the entity ceases applying hedge accounting. However, the net cumulative gain or loss that was recognised in OCI during the effective period of the hedge remains in equity until the expected transaction actually occurs. The same treatment applies in any other case when hedge accounting is terminated because the hedging criteria are no longer met (see 7.9.940.10 and 950.10). [*IFRS 9.6.5.12*]

7.9.980.20   If a hedged forecast transaction is no longer expected to occur within the original time period or a relatively short period thereafter, then hedge accounting is terminated. The related cumulative gain or loss on the hedging instrument that was recognised in OCI is immediately reclassified to profit or loss. An entity cannot continue to defer the cumulative gain or loss in equity on the basis that the original hedged transaction has been replaced by a new forecast transaction that has features similar to those of the original hedged transaction. In our view, if the extension of the time period is relatively short, then the hedge may still qualify for hedge accounting if the effectiveness criteria continue to be met (see 7.9.240). [*IFRS 9.6.5.12(b)*]

7.9.980.30   In determining the appropriate accounting treatment for delayed transactions, it is important to distinguish between hedged cash flows related to:
- a firm commitment;
- a highly probable forecast transaction with an identified counterparty; and
- forecast transactions with unidentified counterparties.

7.9.990   *Firm commitments and forecast transactions with identified counterparties*

7.9.990.10   When the timing of delivery or payments or other terms under a firm commitment are changed, an entity evaluates whether the original firm commitment still exists or whether a new firm commitment has been created. The latter situation would result in the original hedging relationship being terminated and hedge accounting being discontinued prospectively (see 7.9.930). [*IFRS 9.6.5.6, 6.5.7(b), 6.5.12*]

7.9.990.20   If a firm commitment is delayed but will still occur, then it is important to determine the cause and extent of the delay. In our view, when delays occur in the cash flows associated with a firm commitment, hedge accounting may be continued under the following circumstances:
- the firm commitment can still be uniquely identified; and
- a binding agreement still exists and the cash flows are still expected to occur within a relatively short period of time after the original delivery/payment date.

7.9.990.30   The contract supporting a firm commitment should specify a date or range of dates within which the cash flows are expected to occur. If a date, such as a delivery or completion date, is not specified, then the transaction is unlikely to meet the definition of a firm commitment; rather, it can be hedged only as a forecast transaction with an identified counterparty.

7.9.990.40   For a highly probable forecast transaction with an identified counterparty, there may be a little more flexibility in what could be regarded as a relatively short period of time if a delivery date has not yet been established.

7.9.990.50   The key issue, when taking into account all of the facts and circumstances surrounding the delay, is whether the entity can demonstrate that the delayed transaction is the *same transaction* as the one that was originally hedged.

7.9.990.60   When the timing of a firm commitment or a highly probable forecast transaction is delayed, some degree of ineffectiveness is likely to occur if the timing of the hedged item and the timing of the hedging instrument are no longer the same (see 7.9.840). When the hedging instrument originally had a duration longer than the original expected timeframe for the firm commitment or forecast transaction, then the ineffectiveness could, in fact, reduce as a result of the delay in the hedged transaction. In other cases, the hedged cash flow may arise earlier than originally expected. Because the hedging instrument will expire later than the hedged cash flows, some ineffectiveness is likely to occur in this situation as well. However, the hedging instrument cannot be redesignated for a shorter period. [*IFRS 9.6.2.4(c)*]

7.9.1000   *Forecast transactions with unidentified counterparties*

7.9.1000.10   An example of a forecast transaction with an unidentified counterparty is the sale of mobile handsets. Typically, the hedged cash flow would be the first x amount of sales revenue to be received on the sale of handsets in a particular month or quarter (see 7.9.370). Exactly which retailer or end user will purchase the handsets is not specified in the hedge documentation.

7.9.1000.20   Cash flows from forecast transactions with unidentified counterparties are generally designated with reference to the time period in which the transactions are expected to occur (see 7.9.440).

7.9.1000.30   When forecast cash flows in a particular period do not occur, it is possible that such a shortfall will be offset by increased cash flows in a later period. For example, assume that an entity initially forecasts sales of summer clothing of 100 in each of the first two quarters of the coming year. Subsequently, the entity revises its forecast to sales of 75 in the first quarter and 125 in the second quarter. The total amount of sales in the two quarters remains unchanged at 200.

7.9.1000.40   For hedge accounting to be continued, the original forecast transaction still needs to exist and be highly probable. If the hedged item is a forecast transaction (e.g. forecast sales) with unidentified counterparties within a certain time period, then it is unlikely that the entity will be able to demonstrate that sales in later periods replace a shortfall in an earlier period. Consequently, hedge accounting is discontinued. [*IFRS 9.6.3.3, 6.5.22*]

7.9.1000.50   In our view, the transactions should be grouped into relatively narrow bands of time within which the forecast transactions are expected to occur. In determining the length of the period, the industry and environment in which the entity operates should be considered. In our view, for forecast transactions with unidentified counterparties, this narrow range of time should be interpreted more strictly (i.e. a shorter time period used) than for forecast transactions with identified counterparties.

7.9.1010   *History of forecast transactions failing to occur*

7.9.1010.10   If an entity has a history of designating forecast transactions as hedged items and subsequently determining that the forecast transactions are no longer expected to occur, then this may call into question:

- the entity's ability to predict forecast transactions accurately; and
- whether similar forecast transactions would be highly probable and therefore eligible as hedged items. [*IFRS 9.B6.5.27*]

7.9.1020 NET INVESTMENT HEDGE

7.9.1030 Net assets of foreign operation

7.9.1030.10   The hedged item in a net investment hedge is the foreign currency exposure on the carrying amount of the net assets of the foreign operation, but only if they are included in the financial statements. This includes consolidated subsidiaries in consolidated financial statements and also includes financial statements that include associates and joint ventures, as well as financial statements that include a foreign branch or a joint operation. Therefore, if an entity has an investment in an associate or joint venture, or a foreign operation that is conducted through a branch or joint operation, then the investment would qualify as the hedged item in a net investment hedge in the individual financial statements (see 2.1.110). [*IFRIC 16.2, 7*]

7.9.1030.20   In a hedge of a net investment in a foreign operation, a derivative, a non-derivative financial instrument or a combination of both may be used as the hedging instrument. The hedging instrument can be held by any entity within the group. [*IFRIC 16.14*]

7.9.1030.30   The hedged risk is the foreign currency exposure arising from the functional currency of the foreign operation and the functional currency of any parent – i.e. immediate, intermediate or ultimate parent of the foreign operation. The method of translating the foreign currency financial statements of the foreign operation as described in IAS 21 (see 2.7.230) does not change, whichever hedging strategy is used. The foreign exchange differences arising between the functional currency of the foreign operation and the presentation currency of any parent cannot be designated as the hedged risk (see 7.9.1060). The foreign currency risk arising from the net investment in the consolidated financial statements can be hedged only once. [*IFRIC 16.10, 12–13, AG2, BC14*]

EXAMPLE 44 – NET INVESTMENT HEDGES

7.9.1030.40   Parent P, whose functional currency is sterling, has the following net investments in each of its subsidiaries.
- Subsidiary S1's functional currency is the euro. P directly owns S1 and has a EUR 500 net investment in the subsidiary.
- Subsidiary S2's functional currency is the US dollar. P directly owns S2 and has a USD 300 net investment in the subsidiary.
- Subsidiary S3's functional currency is the Australian dollar. S2 directly owns S3 and has an AUD 100 net investment in S3. Therefore, assuming an Australian dollar/US dollar exchange rate of 1.25, P's total USD 300 net investment in S2 includes USD 80 in respect of S2's AUD 100 net investment in S3. In other words, S2's net assets other than its investment in S3 are USD 220. [*IFRIC 16.AG2, AG9*]

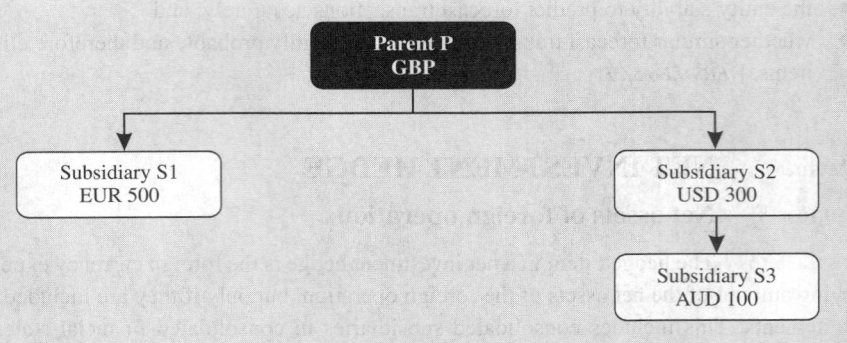

7.9.1030.50   In this situation, the following are examples of alternative net investment hedge designations that may be possible in the consolidated financial statements of P.

- P can hedge its net investment in each of subsidiaries S1, S2 and S3 for the foreign exchange risk between their respective functional currencies and sterling. The maximum amounts that can be designated as effective hedges in P's consolidated financial statements are:
  - EUR 500 net investment in S1 for sterling/euro risk;
  - USD 220 net investment in S2 for sterling/US dollar risk; and
  - AUD 100 net investment in S3 for sterling/Australian dollar risk.
- P can hedge its net investment in only S1 and S2 for the foreign exchange risk between their respective functional currencies and sterling. In this case, up to the full USD 300 investment in S2 can be designated. However, P cannot designate both the full USD 300 of its net investment in S2 with respect to the sterling/US dollar risk and its AUD 100 net investment in S3 with respect to the sterling/Australian dollar risk because this would involve hedging the net investment in S3 with respect to the sterling twice.
- P can hedge, in its consolidated financial statements, its AUD 100 net investment in S3 for the US dollar/Australian dollar risk between the functional currencies of S2 and S3, and also designate a hedge of the entire USD 300 of its net investment in S2 with respect to sterling/US dollar risk, because the designation of the US dollar/Australian dollar risk between S2 and S3 does not include any sterling/US dollar risk.

7.9.1030.60   The hedged risk cannot be designated as the fair value of the underlying shares, or the foreign currency exposure on the fair value of the shares, because the consolidation process recognises the subsidiary's profit or loss, rather than changes in the investment's fair value. The same is true of a net investment in an associate or joint venture, because equity accounting recognises the investor's share of the associate's profit or loss (see 3.5.180). [*IFRS 9.B6.3.2*]

7.9.1030.70   Groups with foreign operations may wish to hedge the foreign currency exposure arising from the expected profits from the foreign operations by using derivatives or other financial instruments. In our view, a forecast transaction in the foreign operation's own functional currency does not create an exposure to variability in cash flows that could affect profit or loss at the consolidated level. Therefore, hedge accounting cannot be applied at the consolidated level. From a foreign operation's own perspective, cash flows generated from its operations are in its own functional currency and therefore do not give rise to a foreign currency risk exposure; such cash flows therefore cannot be hedged. However, a foreign operation may hedge its foreign currency exposure in respect of transactions denominated in currencies other than its functional currency.

7.9.1030.80   Hedging an amount of net assets equal to or less than the carrying amount of the net assets of a foreign operation is permitted. In this case, ineffectiveness is measured based on the amount of the net assets hedged. [*IFRS 9.6.3.1, 6.3.7*]

7.9.1030.90   In assessing hedge effectiveness, the change in value of the hedging instrument is determined with reference to the functional currency of the parent against which the hedged risk is measured. Depending on where the hedging instrument is held, in the absence of hedge accounting the total change in value of the hedging instrument may be recognised in profit or loss, OCI or both. However, the assessment of hedge effectiveness is not affected by whether the change in value of the hedging instrument is recognised in profit or loss or OCI. The assessment of hedge effectiveness is also not affected by the method of consolidation – i.e. the direct or step-by-step method (see 2.7.60.10) – or whether the hedging instrument is a derivative or non-derivative instrument. [*IFRIC 16.15*]

EXAMPLE 45 – DESIGNATION OF A FINANCIAL INSTRUMENT AS A HEDGED ITEM IN A FAIR VALUE HEDGE AND AS A HEDGING INSTRUMENT IN A NET INVESTMENT HEDGE

7.9.1030.100   Company X, whose functional currency is South Korean won, issues a fixed interest rate bond denominated in US dollars (Bond A) to acquire a foreign subsidiary (Company Y). The notional amount of Bond A and the investment in Y are each USD 1,000.

7.9.1030.110   X has the following hedging relationship.
- Hedged item: Bond A (fixed interest rate risk).
- Hedging instrument: interest rate swap that pays LIBOR and receives a fixed interest rate.
- The notional amount of the interest rate swap is USD 1,000.
- The swap is a qualifying hedging instrument for a fair value hedge and Bond A is the hedged item.

7.9.1030.120   It is possible for X also to designate the foreign currency risk component of Bond A as the hedging instrument in a hedge of the net investment in Y provided that the fair value hedge adjustment is expected to be immaterial compared with the hedged net investment amount. If this is the case, then the ratio between Bond A and the net investment in Y may result in ineffectiveness, but not in hedge failure.

7.9.1040   Expected net profit or loss of net investment in foreign operation

7.9.1040.10   The hedged item may be an amount of net assets that is equal to or less than the carrying amount of the net assets of the foreign operation at the beginning of any given period. [*IFRS 9.6.3.1, 6.3.7, IFRIC 16.2, 11, AG3–AG6*]

7.9.1040.20   Consequently, the expected profits from the foreign operation in that period cannot be designated as the hedged item in a net investment hedge. Translation risk arises once the net profit is recognised as an increase in net assets of the foreign operation. The additional net assets can be designated as a hedged item in a net investment hedge as they arise, although in our experience most groups will revisit their net investment hedges only quarterly or semi-annually. [*IFRS 9.6.3.1, 6.3.7, IFRIC 16.2, 11*]

7.9.1040.30   Expected net profits from a foreign operation expose a group to potential volatility in consolidated profit or loss because transactions in the foreign operation are translated into the group's presentation currency at spot rates at the transaction dates, or at appropriate average rates (see 2.7.240). However, because expected net profits in future reporting periods do not constitute recognised assets, liabilities or forecast transactions that will ultimately affect profit or loss at the consolidated level, they cannot be designated in a hedging relationship under either a fair value or a cash flow hedge model. [*IAS 21.39–40*]

7.9.1040.40   Expected net losses in a foreign operation will reduce the net investment balance, which could result in an over-hedged position. Therefore, if a group expects its foreign operation to make losses, then it may decide to hedge less than the full carrying amount of the net assets. Otherwise it could result in hedge ineffectiveness. In our view, an entity should take into account expected losses in a foreign operation when assessing hedge effectiveness if they are highly probable.

7.9.1050   Monetary items

7.9.1050.10   An investor's net investment may also include monetary items that are receivable from or payable to the foreign operation, settlement of which is neither planned nor likely to occur in the foreseeable future. Loans provided by a subsidiary to a fellow subsidiary may form part of the group's net investment in a foreign operation, even when the loan is in neither the parent's nor the borrowing subsidiary's functional currency. Consequently, the net investment may include an intra-group loan in any currency when settlement is neither planned nor likely to occur in the foreseeable future.

EXAMPLE 46 – NET INVESTMENT HEDGE WITH INTRA-GROUP LOAN

7.9.1050.20   In 2016, Company P, whose functional currency is the euro, bought Company S for GBP 100. The carrying amount of S's net assets was GBP 60, and P recognised fair value adjustments to specific assets and liabilities of GBP 30 and goodwill of GBP 10. During 2016, P extended a loan to S of GBP 20.

7.9.1050.30   In 2018, the carrying amount (excluding fair value adjustments from the acquisition) of S's assets and liabilities is GBP 70. The remaining fair value adjustments are GBP 25 and goodwill remains at GBP 10. The loan has not been repaid, nor is it intended to be repaid.

> 7.9.1050.40   The carrying amount of the net investment that P may designate as the hedged item is equal to the amount of P's net investment in S, including goodwill: GBP 125 (70 + 25 + 10 + 20).

7.9.1060   Presentation currency

7.9.1060.10   The group's presentation currency is not relevant to net investment hedging. Translation of the financial statements of an entity into the group presentation currency under IAS 21 is an accounting exercise that does not create an exposure to foreign exchange risk; therefore, hedge accounting for such translation risk is not permitted. An economic exchange risk arises only from an exposure between two or more functional currencies, not from translation into a presentation currency. [*IFRIC 16.BC13–BC14*]

7.9.1060.20   When a group's presentation currency differs from the parent's functional currency, then the appropriate hedged risk to be designated in a net investment hedge is still the exposure to changes in the exchange rate between the foreign operation's functional currency and the parent's functional currency. Therefore, net investment hedging may be applied only to hedge the exchange rate risk that exists between the functional currency of a parent entity and the functional currency of the foreign operation.

7.9.1070   Hedging instruments used in net investment hedge

7.9.1070.10   The designated hedging instrument in a net investment hedge may be a derivative and/or the foreign currency risk component of a non-derivative financial liability (see 7.9.310). [*IFRS 9.6.2.2*]

7.9.1080   *Non-derivative financial instruments*

7.9.1080.10   When the hedging instrument is a non-derivative financial instrument, IFRIC 16 suggests designating the spot foreign exchange risk as the hedged risk in a net investment hedge. The foreign currency risk component of a non-derivative financial instrument designated as a hedging instrument is determined in accordance with IAS 21. [*IFRS 9.B6.2.3, IFRIC 16*]

7.9.1090   *Forward contracts*

7.9.1090.10   When the hedging instrument is a forward contract, the entity may hedge the spot foreign exchange rate or the forward rate. If exposure to changes in the forward rate is designated as the hedged risk, then the forward element included in the forward rate is part of the hedged foreign currency risk. Therefore, total changes in the fair value of the hedging derivative contract, including the forward element – i.e. the spot-forward premium or forward points – are recognised in OCI and accumulated in a separate component of equity. [*IFRIC 16.AG2, IFRS 9.6.2.4*]

7.9.1090.20   When an entity uses a forward contract to hedge the spot foreign exchange rate risk of a net investment in foreign operations, then the changes in the fair value of the hedging derivative that are attributable to changes in spot foreign exchange differences are recognised in OCI. The accounting for the changes in the forward element of the forward contract – the excluded portion of the hedging instrument – is recognised immediately in profit or loss, unless the entity elects to account for the forward element as costs of hedging, in which case the forward element of the forward contract is accounted for as a cost of hedging (see 7.9.690). [*IFRS 9.6.2.4(b), 6.5.16*]

7.9.1100 **Cross-currency interest rate swaps**

7.9.1100.10   Net investments in foreign operations are commonly hedged with forward contracts or non-derivative financial items such as foreign currency loans. Some entities may want to use, as hedging instruments, cross-currency interest rate swaps (CCIRSs) or a synthetic borrowing that is a combination of a borrowing and an interest rate swap and/or a CCIRS. In our view, although they are more complex, these hedging strategies may qualify for hedge accounting if particular care is taken in identifying and designating the hedging instrument and the hedged item.

7.9.1110   *Fixed-for-fixed cross-currency interest rate swap*

7.9.1110.10   Economically, a foreign currency forward contract and a fixed-for-fixed CCIRS are similar; the primary difference is that the interest component of the fixed-for-fixed CCIRS is explicitly identified through an exchange of coupons instead of being implicit as in the case of the forward points component in a foreign currency forward contract. Therefore, the coupon exchanges in a fixed-for-fixed CCIRS are equivalent to the forward points in a foreign currency forward contract.

7.9.1110.20   In our view, a fixed-for-fixed CCIRS can be designated as the hedging instrument in a hedge of the net investment in a foreign operation. The amount of the hedged item would be the notional amount of the CCIRS, excluding its coupon exchanges. As is the case for a hedge using a forward contract (see 7.9.670), we believe that there are two possible approaches that can be applied in designating the hedged risk: an approach based on changes in the forward exchange rate and an approach based on changes in the spot exchange rate.

7.9.1110.30   Under the first approach, the entity designates the hedge based on changes in forward rates. In our view, the hypothetical derivative method may be used to assess hedge effectiveness requirements and to measure hedge ineffectiveness. The perfectly effective hypothetical derivative would have the same relevant critical terms – e.g. notional, underlying, maturity etc – as the hedged item. In many cases, the perfectly effective hypothetical derivative could be constructed as a CCIRS with terms identical to the hedging instrument, if the actual CCIRS's critical terms are the same as those of the hedged item and if the foreign currency basis spread of the actual CCIRS is excluded from the designated hedging instrument. In this case, the hedging relationship might achieve near perfect hedge effectiveness. Under this approach, if an entity elects to exclude the foreign currency basis spread of the actual CCIRS, then from the designated hedging instrument, then it may account for the foreign currency basis spread as cost of hedging (see 7.9.690).

7.9.1110.40   Under the first approach, the effective portion of the fair value gains and losses, including any interest accruals, on the hedging instrument would be recognised in OCI and presented in the foreign currency translation reserve. The actual payment or receipt of interest on the hedging instrument represents partial settlement of the hedging instrument's carrying amount and does not lead to any reclassification from OCI to profit or loss.

7.9.1110.50   Under the second approach, the entity designates the hedge based on changes in spot rates. Changes in the fair value of the notional amount of the CCIRS that arise from changes in spot exchange rates would be effective in offsetting changes in the designated amount of the hedged net investment. Such changes would be recognised in OCI and presented in the foreign currency translation reserve. The remaining fair value changes in the CCIRS, which are equivalent to the forward points in a forward contract plus the foreign currency basis spread on the CCIRS, would be excluded from the hedging relationship. The entity may account for these excluded portions of the CCIRS as a cost of hedging (see 7.9.690).

7.9.1120 *Floating-for-floating cross-currency interest rate swap*

7.9.1120.10   In our view, a floating-for-floating CCIRS with initial and final exchanges of notional amounts could potentially be designated as a hedging instrument in a net investment hedge. Provided that the hedge criteria are met, this hedging strategy should qualify for hedge accounting. When designating the floating-for-floating CCIRS as a hedging instrument, an entity may elect to exclude foreign currency basis spread from the designated hedging instrument and account for it as cost of hedging (see 7.9.690).

7.9.1120.20   When using a floating-for-floating CCIRS, a net investment hedge can be designated as a hedged item for the forward exchange rate risk. However, in our view the perfectly effective hypothetical cannot be constructed as a CCIRS with terms identical to the actual floating-for-floating CCIRS, because floating interest rate cash flows do not exist in the hedged item. Instead, the perfectly effective hypothetical derivative may be constructed as either a fixed-for-fixed CCIRS or a forward contract. In either case, the floating interest payments on the CCIRS will give rise to some ineffectiveness because of movements in interest rate curves between repricing dates.

7.9.1120.30   In our experience, if the notional amount of a floating-for-floating CCIRS does not exceed the amount of a net investment, then designating the notional amount of the CCIRS as a hedging instrument in a hedge based on changes in spot rates is more likely to result in lower ineffectiveness. This is because the floating interest rate cash flows and principal amounts of the CCIRS would be discounted at market in the respective currencies, resulting in amounts that approximate the notional amount of the hedged item, and are converted at the spot rate – thereby following the changes in the value of the hedge item, which is also converted using the spot rate.

7.9.1130 *Fixed-for-floating cross-currency interest rate swap*

7.9.1130.10   A fixed-for-floating CCIRS is exposed to both interest rate risk and foreign currency risk. In our view, a fixed-for-floating CCIRS cannot generally be designated as a hedging instrument in a net investment hedge because the interest rate risk inherent in the instrument gives rises to ineffectiveness that precludes hedge accounting.

7.9.1130.20   Depending on the risk management objective of the entity, it may be possible to designate such an instrument in its entirety in more than one hedging relationship simultaneously. For example, a pay-fixed US dollar receive-floating euro CCIRS can be viewed as comprising a pay-fixed US dollar receive-fixed euro CCIRS and a pay-fixed euro receive-floating euro interest rate swap. The pay-fixed US dollar receive-fixed euro CCIRS can be designated as a hedging instrument of a US dollar net investment, whereas the pay-fixed euro receive-floating euro interest rate swap can be designated as either a fair value hedge of a fixed rate asset or a cash flow hedge of a floating rate liability. When such an approach is adopted, the hedge documentation should clearly identify the various hedged items for which the CCIRS is designated as the hedging instrument.

HEDGING ON A GROUP BASIS

7.9.1140.10   For a foreign currency hedge transacted on a group basis, it is important for the foreign currency exposure of the hedging instrument and the hedged transaction to be the same.

EXAMPLE 47 – FOREIGN CURRENCY HEDGE TRANSACTED ON GROUP BASIS

7.9.1140.20   Company P has the euro as its functional currency and Company S, a subsidiary of P, has the Swiss franc as its functional currency. S has a foreign currency exposure arising from a highly probable forecast transaction denominated in US dollars.

7.9.1140.30   If P hedges this exposure through its central treasury by entering into a Swiss franc-to-US dollar forward contract, then the transaction may qualify for hedge accounting in P's consolidated financial statements.

7.9.1140.40   However, if P enters into a euro-to-US dollar forward contract, then the contract does not qualify as a hedging instrument because the currency of the forward contract does not match the underlying exposure that the entity wishes to hedge unless it can be demonstrated that the euro and the Swiss franc are highly correlated.

7.9.1150   ## Internal derivatives

7.9.1150.10   One of the key issues that arise in applying hedge accounting at the group level is the need to eliminate internal derivatives for the purposes of consolidation.

7.9.1150.20   An entity may use internal derivatives to transfer risk from individual operations within the group to a centralised treasury. Derivatives between entities within the same reporting group can also be used to control and monitor risks through the central treasury function to benefit from pricing advantages and to offset equal and opposite exposures arising from different parts of the group. However, all such internal derivatives eliminate on consolidation and therefore are not eligible for hedge accounting in the consolidated financial statements, even if at a group level the overall net position is hedged externally. Therefore, only derivatives involving external third parties can be designated as hedging instruments in consolidated financial statements. [*IFRS 9.6.2.3*]

7.9.1150.30   However, it is possible for the centralised treasury to enter into one or more derivatives with external counterparties to offset the internal derivatives. These external derivatives may qualify as hedging instruments in the consolidated financial statements provided that they are legally separate contracts and serve a valid business purpose – e.g. laying off risk exposures on a gross basis. In our view, a relationship should exist between the internal transactions and one or multiple related external transactions, and this relationship should be documented at inception of the hedging relationship.

7.9.1160   ## Externalisation and round-tripping

7.9.1160.10   In consolidated financial statements, hedge accounting may be applied to an external hedge even if the group entity that is subject to the risk being hedged is not a direct party to the hedging instrument. [*IFRS 9.6.2.3*]

EXAMPLE 48 – EXTERNALISATION AND ROUND-TRIPPING

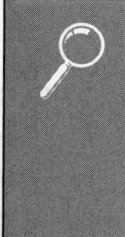

7.9.1160.20   Subsidiary B has a financial asset (with a counterparty outside the group) on which it receives a fixed rate of interest. For the purpose of hedging its individual exposure to the fixed interest rate, B enters into a pay-fixed receive-floating interest rate swap with the group's central treasury. The swap is an internal derivative, which does not qualify as a hedging instrument in the consolidated financial statements.

7.9.1160.30   To achieve hedge accounting at the group level, the central treasury enters into a matching pay-fixed receive-floating interest rate swap with an external counterparty and documents this link. The fixed interest financial asset and the external derivative can then be designated in a hedging relationship that qualifies for hedge accounting in the consolidated financial statements.

7.9.1160.40   By entering into an external derivative, the group 'externalises' the transaction to achieve hedge accounting in the consolidated financial statements. However, there may be circumstances in which the entity would concurrently enter into two offsetting external derivatives. The first would be designated as the hedging instrument in the consolidated financial statements, whereas the offsetting swap would be included in the entity's trading book. Normally, the reason for the offsetting transaction is to 'create' an external hedging instrument for hedge accounting purposes without changing the risk position of the central treasury. At the same time as entering into an external derivative that would qualify as a hedging instrument as described in Example 48, the central treasury would enter into an exactly offsetting swap with the same counterparty. This is known as 'round-tripping'.

7.9.1160.50   It is clear that when offsetting derivatives are entered into concurrently, an entity is prohibited from viewing the derivatives separately and therefore designating one of them in a hedging relationship, unless the derivatives were not entered into in contemplation of one another or there is a substantive business purpose for structuring the transactions separately. Therefore, to qualify for hedge accounting when following the round-tripping approach, it is necessary for an entity to demonstrate compliance with one of these two conditions (see 7.6.40). [*IFRS 9.IG.B.6, IG.C.6*]

7.9.1160.60   In our view, a substantive business purpose generally exists in the following circumstances.
- When group risk management is undertaken by a central treasury function, which gives separate consideration to whether and how much of an offsetting position is required. Because the cheapest form of risk mitigation is usually entering into offsetting transactions with the same derivative counterparty, it is plausible that a facility may exist to enter into an offsetting transaction. However, such an offset should not automatically be put in place by an entity, but should be based on an evaluation of whether such an offsetting position is required.
- When an entity's internal derivatives are novated to a central clearing party and then subjected to trade compression with otherwise unrelated derivatives originally entered into with third parties and also novated to the central clearing party. If the inter-company derivatives had not been novated to a central clearing party, then the inter-company derivatives would have been eliminated on consolidation and would not have externalised any risk. Similarly, there would have been no externalisation of market risk if the derivatives were novated to the central clearing party but left otherwise unchanged (e.g. there would be only equal and opposite trades between the group and

the central clearing party). However, in some cases novation followed by trade compression may externalise risk that otherwise would have been eliminated on consolidation.

Example 49 – Hedges transacted on group basis

7.9.1160.70 Consider the following two situations.

- Company H performs a day-end review of its risk exposures, documents this review and enters into offsetting derivatives as part of its risk balancing procedures.
- Company B immediately enters into an offsetting derivative for each transaction and undertakes no further formal risk management procedures.

7.9.1160.80 H is likely to be able to prove that it has a substantive business purpose for entering into offsetting derivatives. B, however, has a practice of automatically entering into offsetting derivatives, without giving further consideration to its actual risk exposures. Accordingly, B would have difficulty in meeting the substantive business purpose condition.

7.9.1160.90 In addition, in our view entering into a derivative with a non-substantive counterparty does not validate an internal hedge. For example, a limited-purpose vehicle established to act as a dedicated counterparty to validate internal hedges might not be regarded as a substantive third party counterparty even if consolidation of the limited-purpose vehicle is not required.

7.9.1160.100 An entity may designate a hedging relationship at the consolidated level that differs from the hedging relationship designated at the level of an individual entity within the group, provided that the hedge criteria are met. [*IFRS 9.6.1.1, 6.4.1*]

7.9.1170 Intra-group balances or transactions as hedged item

7.9.1170.10 Intra-group balances and transactions are generally eliminated on consolidation and therefore are not permitted to be designated as hedged items at the group level. However, foreign currency exposures on intra-group monetary items give rise to foreign exchange gains and losses that do not eliminate in the consolidated financial statements (see 2.7.130). Intra-group monetary items lead to an exposure that affects group profit or loss if items have been transacted between group entities with different functional currencies. [*IFRS 9.6.3.6*]

7.9.1170.20 For example, an intra-group payable/receivable between a parent with the euro as its functional currency and its foreign subsidiary denominated in US dollars (the subsidiary's functional currency) creates such a foreign currency exposure at the group level. Consequently, the foreign currency risk on recognised intra-group monetary items qualifies for hedge accounting in the consolidated financial statements.

7.9.1170.30 In our view, it is not possible to extend this rationale to the designation of intra-group monetary items as hedging instruments in a hedge of foreign currency risk. This is because IFRS 9 explicitly requires that only instruments involving external parties be designated as hedging instruments. Therefore, intra-group monetary items cannot be designated as hedging instruments in the consolidated financial statements. [*IFRS 9.6.2.3*]

7.9.1170.40 The foreign currency risk of a highly probable forecast intra-group transaction may qualify as the hedged item in the consolidated financial statements provided that the transaction is denominated in a currency other than the currency of the entity entering into the transaction, and the foreign currency risk will affect consolidated profit or loss. Examples of forecast intra-group transactions that will affect consolidated profit or loss include:

- forecast purchases or sales of inventory between group members, provided that there is an onward sale to a party outside the group; and
- a forecast sale of equipment by one group entity to another, because the depreciation charge recognised on the equipment will differ if the transaction is denominated in a currency other than the buying entity's functional currency. [*IFRS 9.B6.3.5*]

7.9.1170.50 However, royalties, head office charges and similar items do not affect profit or loss in the consolidated financial statements because these transactions are eliminated completely. Therefore, such items do not usually qualify as hedged items unless there is a related external transaction. [*IFRS 9.B6.3.5*]

7.9.1180   WORKED EXAMPLES

7.9.1180.10 The following examples demonstrate a number of the issues that have been discussed in this chapter.

7.9.1190   Example 50 – Cash flow hedge of variable rate liability

7.9.1190.10 On 1 January 2018, Company P issues non-callable five-year floating rate bonds of 100 million denominated in its functional currency. The floating interest of six-month LIBOR plus 50 basis points (0.5%) is payable semi-annually. The bonds are issued at par.

7.9.1190.20 As part of P's risk management policy, it determines that it does not wish to expose itself to cash flow fluctuations from changes in market interest rates. After the issue of the bonds, P immediately enters into a five-year interest rate swap with a notional of 100 million. Under the terms of the swap, P pays 6% fixed and receives floating cash flows based on six-month LIBOR (set at 5.7% for the period from 1 January to 30 June 2018). The timing of the swap's cash flows matches those of the bond. The fair value of the swap at inception is zero.

7.9.1190.30 The swap is designated and documented as the hedging instrument in a cash flow hedge of the variability of future interest payments on the bond attributable to movements in the benchmark interest rate – i.e. six-month LIBOR only – excluding the credit spread on the bond of 50 basis points. The hedging relationship meets the hedge effectiveness requirements.

7.9.1190.40 P indicates in its hedge documentation that it will use the hypothetical derivative method for assessing the effectiveness of the hedging relationship.

P identifies a hypothetical swap in the bond under which it receives 6% fixed – i.e. the fixed market rate of interest at the time of issuing the bond – and pays six-month LIBOR. Although the interest rate on the bond is LIBOR plus 50 basis points, P has designated as the hedged risk only the benchmark interest component of the total interest rate risk exposure of the bond. Therefore, the hypothetical swap has a floating leg equal to LIBOR, rather than LIBOR plus 50 basis points.

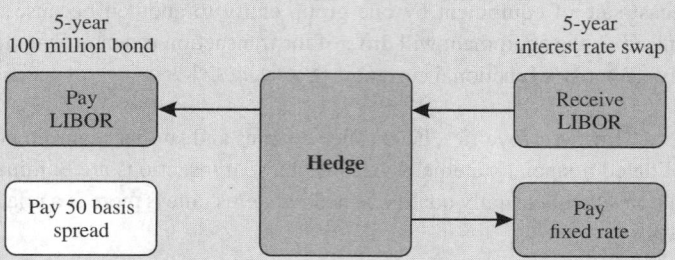

7.9.1190.50 Considering the combined effect of the bond and the swap, the interest that is effectively payable is fixed at 6.5% (6% fixed on the swap plus the additional actual 0.5% on the bond). P records the following entries.

	DEBIT	CREDIT
1 January 2018		
Cash	100,000,000	
Bonds payable		100,000,000
To recognise proceeds from bond issue		

7.9.1190.60 No entry is necessary for the swap because its fair value is zero at inception.

7.9.1190.70 At 30 June 2018, six-month LIBOR increases to 6.7%. The fair value of the swap is determined to be 3,803,843 after the settlement of interest due on 30 June 2018. The fair value of the hypothetical swap is also 3,803,843 at this date. Therefore, the hedge is considered to be 100% effective. The full change in the fair value of the swap is recognised in OCI.

	DEBIT	CREDIT
30 June 2018		
Interest expense	3,100,000	
Cash		3,100,000
To recognise payment of 6.2% floating interest (LIBOR of 5.7% plus premium of 0.5%)		

	DEBIT	CREDIT
Interest expense	150,000	
Cash		150,000
To recognise net settlement of swap from 1 January to 30 June 2018 (pay 6% fixed 3,000,000; receive 5.7% floating 2,850,000)		
Swap (asset)	3,803,843	
Hedging reserve (OCI)		3,803,843
To recognise change in fair value of swap after settlement of interest		

7.9.1190.80   At 31 December 2018, interest rates have not changed. However, the credit risk associated with the counterparty to the swap has worsened and is now higher than the general market rate. The increased credit risk of the counterparty results in a specific credit spread of 0.4%. Consequently, the rate used to determine the fair value of the swap is 0.4% higher than that used to value the hypothetical swap, because the hypothetical swap is not affected by counterparty credit risk (see 7.9.900.20).

7.9.1190.90   The fair value of the swap is 3,414,177 at 31 December 2018. The fair value of the hypothetical swap is 3,436,978 at the same date. The change in the fair value of the swap and the change in the fair value of the hypothetical swap offset (99% offset). However, no ineffectiveness is recognised and the difference of 22,801 is recognised in OCI because the hedging reserve is adjusted to the lesser of the cumulative gain or loss on the hedging instrument and the cumulative change in fair value of the expected future cash flows on the hedged item attributable to the hedged risk, both from inception of the hedge (see 7.9.860).

	DEBIT	CREDIT
31 December 2018		
Interest expense	3,600,000	
Cash		3,600,000
To recognise payment of 7.2% floating interest (LIBOR of 6.7% plus premium of 0.5%)		
Cash	350,000	
Interest income		350,000
To recognise net settlement of swap from 1 July to 31 December 2018 (pay 6% fixed 3,000,000; receive 6.7% floating 3,350,000)		

	DEBIT	CREDIT
Hedging reserve (OCI)	389,666	
Swap (asset)		389,666
To recognise change in fair value of swap		

7.9.1190.100 The statement of financial position at 31 December 2018 is as follows.

ASSETS		LIABILITIES AND EQUITY	
Cash	93,500,000	Retained earnings	(6,500,000)
Swap	3,414,177	Hedging reserve	3,414,177
		Bonds payable	100,000,000
	96,914,177		96,914,177

7.9.1200

Example 51 – Cash flow hedge using interest rate cap

7.9.1200.10 On 1 January 2018, Company R obtains a three-year loan of 10 million. The interest rate on the loan is variable at LIBOR plus 2%. R is concerned that interest rates may rise during the three years, but wants to retain the ability to benefit from LIBOR rates below 8%. To hedge itself, R purchases for 300,000 an out-of-the-money interest rate cap from a bank. Under the cap, when LIBOR exceeds 8% for a particular year R receives from the bank an amount calculated as 10 million x (LIBOR - 8%).

7.9.1200.20 The combination of the cap and the loan results in R paying interest at a variable rate (LIBOR plus 2%) not exceeding 10%. On both the variable rate loan and the interest rate cap, rates are reset on 1 January and interest is settled on 31 December.

7.9.1200.30 R designates and documents the intrinsic value of the purchased interest rate cap as the hedging instrument in a cash flow hedge of the interest rate risk attributable to the future interest payments on the loan for changes in LIBOR above 8%.

7.9.1200.40 The critical terms of the cap are identical to those of the loan and R concludes that, both at inception of the hedge and on an ongoing basis, the cash flows on the hedging instrument are expected to offset cash flows attributable to changes in LIBOR when LIBOR is greater than 8%. Therefore, the economic relationship criterion is met. Because the cap is being used to purchase one-way protection against any increase in LIBOR, R does not need to assess effectiveness in instances when LIBOR is less than 8%. The cumulative gains or losses on the interest rate cap – adjusted to remove time value gains and losses – can reasonably be expected to equal the present value of the cumulative change in expected future cash flows on the debt obligation when LIBOR is greater than 8%.

7.9.1200.50   During the three-year period, LIBOR rates and related amounts are as follows.

DATE	RATE	RECEIVABLE UNDER CAP	INTEREST PAYABLE ON LOAN	NET INTEREST PAYABLE	NET INTEREST PAYABLE
2018	7%	-	900,000	900,000	9%
2019	9%	(100,000)	1,100,000	1,000,000	10%
2020	10%	(200,000)	1,200,000	1,000,000	10%

7.9.1200.60   The fair value, intrinsic value and time value of the interest rate cap and changes therein at the end of each accounting period, but before the settlement of interest, are as follows.

DATE	FAIR VALUE	INTRINSIC VALUE	TIME VALUE	CHANGE IN FAIR VALUE GAIN/(LOSS)	CHANGE IN TIME VALUE GAIN/(LOSS)
1 January 2018	300,000	-	300,000	-	-
31 December 2018	280,000	-	280,000	(20,000)	(20,000)
31 December 2019	350,000	200,000	150,000	70,000	(130,000)
31 December 2020	300,000	300,000	-	(50,000)	(150,000)

7.9.1200.70   In this example, the intrinsic value of the cap is calculated based on simplified assumptions. Alternatively, and more precisely, the intrinsic value of the cap (in the case of a long position) can be calculated for each single period by subtracting the cap rate from the forward LIBOR of the respective period, multiplying the result with the notional amount of the cap contract and then discounting the result to the date under consideration. The sum of the discounted values yields the intrinsic value of the cap.

7.9.1200.80   Given that the option hedges the interest rate risk over the three-year period, R determines that the time value of the option relates to a time period-related hedged item. Accordingly, R accounts for the fair value changes of the time value in OCI and amortises the time value at the date of designation of 300,000 over the three years through a reclassification to profit or loss as a cost of hedging.

7.9.1200.90 Assuming that all criteria for hedge accounting have been met, R records the following entries.

	DEBIT	CREDIT
1 January 2018		
Cash	10,000,000	
Loan payable		10,000,000
To recognise proceeds from loan		
Interest rate cap (asset)	300,000	
Cash		300,000
To recognise purchase of interest rate cap		
31 December 2018		
Interest expense	900,000	
Cash		900,000
To recognise interest expense on loan (LIBOR + 2%)		
Costs of hedging (OCI)	20,000	
Interest rate cap (asset)		20,000
To recognise change in fair value of cap (time value change)		
Costs of hedging (profit or loss)	100,000	
Costs of hedging (OCI)		100,000
To amortise the time value at the date of designation as a cost of hedging		
31 December 2019		
Interest expense	1,100,000	
Cash		1,100,000
To recognise interest expense on loan (LIBOR + 2%)		
Costs of hedging (OCI)	130,000	
Interest rate cap (asset)	70,000	
Hedging reserve (OCI)		200,000
To recognise change in fair value of cap (130,000 represents the change in time value; 200,000 represents increase in interest rate cap's intrinsic value)		
Costs of hedging (profit or loss)	100,000	
Costs of hedging (OCI)		100,000
To amortise the time value at the date of designation as a cost of hedging		

	DEBIT	CREDIT
Hedging reserve (OCI)	100,000	
Hedge income/interest income (profit or loss)		100,000
To reclassify proportion of increase in intrinsic value of cap related to realised cash flow to profit or loss		
Cash	100,000	
Interest rate cap (asset)		100,000
To recognise cash received on settlement of interest rate cap		
31 December 2020		
Interest expense (profit or loss)	1,200,000	
Cash		1,200,000
To recognise interest expense on loan (LIBOR + 2%)		
Costs of hedging (OCI)	150,000	
Interest rate cap (asset)		50,000
Hedging reserve (OCI)		100,000
To recognise change in fair value of cap (150,000 represents change in time value; 100,000 represents increase in the interest rate cap's intrinsic value)		
Costs of hedging (profit or loss)	100,000	
Costs of hedging (OCI)		100,000
To amortise the time value at the date of designation as a cost of hedging		
Hedging reserve (OCI)	200,000	
Hedge income/interest income (profit or loss)		200,000
To reclassify proportion of increased intrinsic value of cap related to realised cash flow to profit or loss		
Cash	200,000	
Interest rate cap (asset)		200,000
To recognise cash received on final settlement of interest rate cap		

7.9.1200.100 As a result of the hedge, R has effectively capped its interest expense on the three-year loan at 10%, with an additional 1% expense incurred as costs of hedging. Specifically, during those periods when the contractual terms of this loan would result in an interest expense greater than 10% or 1 million – i.e. in instances when LIBOR exceeds 8% – the payments received from the interest rate cap effectively reduce interest expense to 10% as illustrated below.

7.9.1200.110 However, R paid 300,000 for the interest rate cap to protect against an increase in interest rates. Therefore, 300,000 is accounted for as a cost of hedging and amortised over the three-year period over which the hedge adjustment could affect the profit or loss.

	2018	**2019**	**2020**
Interest on LIBOR plus 2% debt	900,000	1,100,000	1,200,000
Reclassified from OCI (effect of cap)	-	(100,000)	(200,000)
Costs of hedging	100,000	100,000	100,000
Total expense	1,000,000	1,100,000	1,100,000

7.9.1210

Example 52 – Hedged item both transaction-related and time period-related

7.9.1210.10 Company R, whose functional currency is the yen, forecasts a sale of inventory for USD 200,000 on 31 May 2018. To hedge its exposure to the US dollar, R purchases a European put option to sell USD 200,000 on 31 July 2018, which is the settlement date of the receivable.

7.9.1210.20 The following terms of the purchased put option are also relevant for this example.

Date purchased	28 February 2018
Contract amount	USD 200,000
Expiry/exercise date	31 July 2018
Strike price	USD 1 = JPY 100 (JPY 20,000,000)
Premium	JPY 78,250[1]

Note
1.   Solely time value because option is purchased at the money.

7.9.1210.30 R designates the intrinsic value of the option as a cash flow hedge of its foreign currency exposure related to the forecast sale expected to occur on 31 May 2018 as well as the settlement of the resultant receivable expected to settle on 31 July 2018. R's risk management objective is to preserve its functional currency equivalent cash flows at USD 1 = JPY 100. Assume that all hedge criteria are met on 28 February 2018.

7.9.1210.40   The spot exchange rates and fair value of the option, including fair value changes in intrinsic value and time value are as follows (amounts in yen).

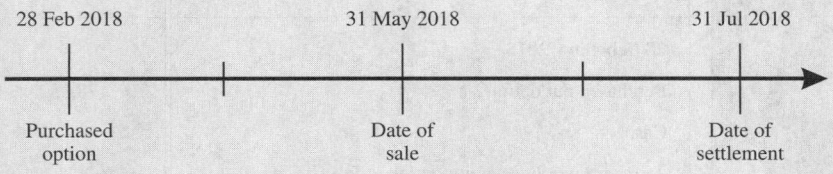

	SPOT RATE	FAIR VALUE	INTRINSIC VALUE	TIME VALUE
28 February 2018	110.00	78,250	-	78,250
31 March 2018	105.00	257,345	-	257,345[1]
30 April 2018	100.00	244,504	-	244,504
31 May 2018	99.00	484,063	200,000	284,063
30 June 2018	93.00	1,409,505	1,400,000	9,505
31 July 2018	90.00	2,000,000	2,000,000	-

Note
1.   The time value of the option on 31 March 2018 increases because of high market volatility.

7.9.1210.50   In this example, it appears that there is one hedged item whose nature changes from transaction-related to time period-related. R elects to allocate the amount of the initial time value to the transaction-related and time period-related portions rateably based on the number of days between inception of the hedging relationship and the sale, and the number of days between the sale and settlement of the receivable. The date of the hedge inception is 28 February 2018, and the hedging relationship lasts for 153 days. The sale occurs 92 days after hedge inception, and the receivable settles 61 days after the sale occurs.

7.9.1210.60   It appears that the accounting for the option's time value that relates to the transaction-related portion of the hedged item should follow the guidance for the time value of an option related to a transaction-related hedged item – i.e. an amount should be transferred out of the separate component of equity when the sale occurs. This amount should be determined rateably (92 / 153 x the original time value). The accounting for the time value of the option that relates to the time period-related portion of the hedged item should follow the guidance for the time value of an option related to a time period-related hedged item – i.e. the remaining original time value is amortised until the date on which the receivable is settled (61 / 153 x the original time value). However, the amounts accounted for in both periods are the change in the original time value allocated as noted above consistent with the risk management objective, not the changes in each period.

7.9.1210.70   R records the following entries (amounts in yen).

	DEBIT	CREDIT
28 February 2018		
Purchased put option	78,250	
Cash		78,250
To record purchase of put option at fair value		
31 March 2018		
Purchased put option	179,095	
Costs of hedging (OCI)		179,095
To recognise change in fair value of put option		
30 April 2018		
Costs of hedging (OCI)	12,841	
Purchased put option		12,841
To recognise change in fair value of put option		
31 May 2018		
Purchased put option	239,559	
Hedging reserve (OCI)		200,000
Costs of hedging (OCI)		39,559
To recognise change in fair value of put option		
Accounts receivable	19,800,000	
Revenue		19,800,000
To record sale at spot rate		
Hedging reserve (OCI)	200,000[(1)]	
Revenue		200,000
To reclassify effective portion of change in fair value of put option		
Costs of hedging (profit or loss)	47,052	
Costs of hedging (OCI)		47,052
To reclassify option premium attributable to forecast period: 92 / 153 days x 78,250		

	DEBIT	CREDIT
30 June 2018		
Purchased put option	925,442	
Costs of hedging (OCI)	274,558	
Hedging reserve (OCI)		1,200,000
To recognise change in fair value of put option		
Foreign exchange gain or loss	1,200,000	
Accounts receivable		1,200,000
To recognise foreign exchange loss on accounts receivable		
Hedging reserve (OCI)	1,200,000	
Foreign exchange gain or loss		1,200,000
To reclassify effective portion of change in fair value of put option: JPY 93 x 200,000 - JPY 99 x 200,000		
Costs of hedging (profit or loss)	15,343	
Costs of hedging (OCI)		15,343
To reclassify option premium attributable to period of recognised receivable hedge: 30 / 153 days x 78,250		
31 July 2018		
Purchased put option	590,495	
Costs of hedging (OCI)	9,505	
Hedging reserve (OCI)		600,000
To recognise change in fair value of put option		
Foreign exchange gain or loss	600,000	
Accounts receivable		600,000
To recognise foreign exchange loss on accounts receivable		
Hedging reserve (OCI)	600,000	
Foreign exchange gain or loss		600,000
To reclassify effective portion of change in fair value of put option: JPY 90 x 200,000 - JPY 93 x 200,000		
Cash	18,000,000	
Accounts receivable		18,000,000
To record settlement of foreign currency-denominated receivable at spot rate		

	DEBIT	CREDIT
Cash	2,000,000	
Purchased put option		2,000,000
To record settlement of put option		
Costs of hedging (profit or loss)	15,855	
Costs of hedging (OCI)		15,855
To reclassify option premium attributable to period of recognised receivable hedge: 31 / 153 days x 78,250		

Note

1. This amount is limited to the defined hedged exchange rate of USD 1 = JPY 100 – i.e. within the positive intrinsic value: JPY 99 x 200,000 - JPY 100 x 200,000.

7.9.1210.80   The resulting impact of entries on the statement of profit or loss and OCI is summarised as follows (amounts in yen).

PROFIT OR LOSS	2018
Revenue	20,000,000
Foreign exchange gain or loss	-
Costs of hedging	(78,250)
Net profit or loss	19,921,750
OCI	**2018**
Hedging reserve	-
Costs of hedging	-

7.9.1220   **Example 53 – Hedge of issued foreign currency debt using cross-currency interest rate swap**

7.9.1220.10   On 1 January 2018, Company R, whose functional currency is the yen, enters into the following transactions.

- *Borrowing:* USD 100 million for two years with a floating rate at 12 months' LIBOR.
- *CCIRS:* Two-year floating-to-fixed with the following terms:
    - *floating receive leg:* floating USD at 12 months' LIBOR on USD 100 million;
    - *fixed pay leg:* fixed JPY at 2.5% – representing 2.0% plus currency basis spread at 1 January 2018 of 0.5% – on JPY 8,000 million; and
    - *principal exchange:* a final exchange of principal amounts on maturity of the contract.

7.9.1220.20   Both the borrowing and the CCIRS pay interest annually at the end of the period.

7.9.1220.30   R designates the cross-currency interest rate swap as a cash flow hedge for changes in both LIBOR and foreign exchange rates and elects to separate and exclude the foreign currency basis spread of the CCIRS from the designation of the hedging instrument and account for that component as a cost of hedging. R measures ineffectiveness using the hypothetical derivative method. In this example, the hedged item is considered to be a time period-related hedged item.

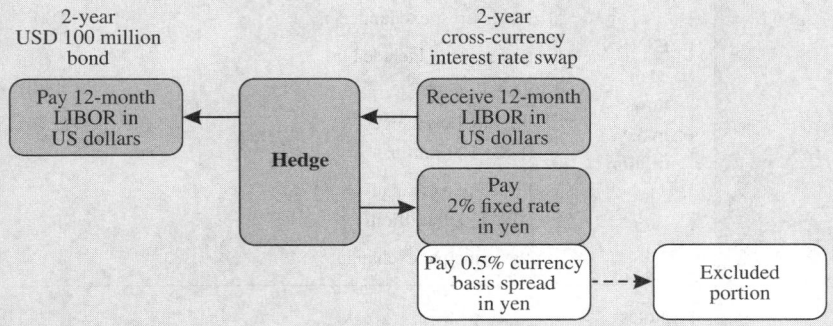

7.9.1220.40   The following facts are also relevant for this example.

		1 JAN 2018	**31 DEC 2018**	**31 DEC 2019**
Market rates	Foreign exchange rates – closing (JPY/USD)	80	100	90
	Foreign exchange rates – average for year then ended[1] (JPY/USD)		100	90
	Currency basis spread in the CCIRS market (JPY)	0.5%	0.4%	
	Benchmark interest rate curve (USD) at 1 January 2018	4.0%	5.0%	
	Benchmark interest rate curve (USD) at 31 December 2018		5.0%	
	Benchmark interest rate curve (JPY) at 1 January 2018	2.0%	2.0%	
	Benchmark interest rate curve (JPY) at 31 December 2018		2.2%	

		1 JAN 2018	**31 DEC 2018**	**31 DEC 2019**
Borrowing cash flows in JPY million	Principal (USD 100 million)	8,000		(9,000)
	Interest expense		(400)[2]	(450)[3]
CCIRS cash flows in JPY million	Floating receive leg		400	450
	Fixed pay leg		(200)[4]	(200)[4]
	Net interest exchange		200	250
	Basis spread included in fixed pay leg		(40)[5]	(40)[5]
	Principal exchange (USD 100 million)			9,000
	Principal exchange (JPY 8,000 million)			(8,000)
	Net principal exchange			1,000

Notes
1. Foreign exchange average rates are assumed to be the same as the closing rate.
2. Calculated as USD 100 x 4.0% x 100 (USD/JPY average rate).
3. Calculated as USD 100 x 5.0% x 90 (USD/JPY average rate).
4. Calculated as JPY 8,000 x 2.5%.
5. Calculated as JPY 8,000 x 0.5%.

7.9.1220.50   The fair values of the cross-currency swap before and after interest exchange are as follows.

	1 JAN 2018 **JPY MILLION**	**31 DEC 2018** **JPY MILLION**	**31 DEC 2019** **JPY MILLION**
Fair value of cross-currency swap (before exchange of interest or principal)	0	2,208	1,250
Fair value of cross-currency swap (after exchange of interest or principal)	0	2,008	0

7.9.1220.60   R determines that the hypothetical derivative is a CCIRS. Because the critical terms of the actual cross-currency swap that has been designated as the hedging instrument and the hedged US dollar-denominated borrowing exactly match, the hypothetical derivative has the same terms as those of the actual CCIRS but excluding the foreign currency basis spread. Therefore, the fair value of the fixed leg of the hypothetical derivative is calculated as: fixed JPY leg excluding the foreign currency basis spread (i.e. 2.0%) discounted by the benchmark interest rates – i.e. those rates do not include currency basis spreads. The fair values are as follows.

	1 Jan 2018 JPY million	31 Dec 2018 JPY million	31 Dec 2019 JPY million
Fair value of hypothetical derivative (before exchange of interest or principal)	0	2,256	1,290
Fair value of hypothetical derivative (after exchange of interest or principal)	0	2,016	0

7.9.1220.70   R records the following entries.

In millions	Debit (JPY)	Credit (JPY)
31 December 2018		
Interest expense on borrowing (profit or loss)	400	
Cash		400
To recognise interest expense on floating rate borrowing		
Foreign exchange loss on borrowing (profit or loss)	2,000	
Borrowing (statement of financial position)		2,000
To recognise foreign exchange loss on borrowing: *USD 100 million x (100 - 80)*		
CCIRS (statement of financial position)	2,208	
Hedging reserve (OCI)		2,256[1]
Costs of hedging (OCI)	48[2]	
To recognise change in fair value of CCIRS: *JPY 2,208 - JPY 0*		
Cash	200	
CCIRS (statement of financial position)		200
To recognise net settlement of CCIRS interest exchange		
Costs of hedging (profit or loss)	40[3]	
Costs of hedging (OCI)		40
To amortise costs of hedging in profit or loss over hedge *period as reclassification adjustment*		
Hedging reserve (OCI)	240[4]	
Interest expense (profit or loss)		240[4]
To reclassify deferred hedge results to reflect that interest *expense has been fixed*		

In millions	DEBIT (JPY)	CREDIT (JPY)
Hedging reserve (OCI)	2,000	
Foreign exchange gain (profit or loss)		2,000
To reclassify deferred hedge results to offset spot remeasurement adjustment to borrowing		
31 December 2019		
Interest expense on borrowing (profit or loss)	450	
Cash		450
To recognise interest expense on floating rate borrowing		
Borrowing (statement of financial position)	1,000	
Foreign exchange gain on borrowing (profit or loss)		1,000
To recognise foreign exchange gain on borrowing: USD 100 million x (90 - 100)		
Hedging reserve (OCI)	726[5]	
Costs of hedging (OCI)	32[6]	
CCIRS (statement of financial position)		758
To recognise change in fair value of CCIRS: JPY 2,008 - JPY 1,250		
Cash	250	
CCIRS (statement of financial position)		250
To recognise net settlement of CCIRS interest exchange		
Borrowing (statement of financial position)	9,000	
Cash		9,000
To record repayment of borrowing		
Cash	1,000	
CCIRS (statement of financial position)		1,000
To record net settlement of CCIRS principal exchange		
Costs of hedging (profit or loss)	40[3]	
Costs of hedging (OCI)		40
To amortise costs of hedging in profit or loss over hedge period as reclassification adjustment		

In millions	DEBIT (JPY)	CREDIT (JPY)
Hedging reserve (OCI)	290[7]	
Interest expense (profit or loss)		290
To reclassify deferred hedged results to reflect that interest expense has been fixed		
Foreign exchange loss (profit or loss)	1,000	
Hedging reserve (OCI)		1,000
To reclassify deferred hedged results to offset spot remeasurement adjustment to borrowing		

Notes
1. The effective portion of the change in fair value of the hedging instrument (not the actual CCIRS) – represented by the change in fair value of the hypothetical derivative (JPY 2,256 million - JPY 0) – is recognised in OCI.
2. No ineffectiveness is recorded because the fair value of the hedging instrument, which excludes the foreign currency basis spread, equals the fair value of the hypothetical derivative (constructed to also exclude the foreign currency basis spread). Because no ineffectiveness arises, the remaining difference, the change in foreign currency basis spread element, is recorded in OCI as a cost of hedging.
3. Calculated as the total costs of hedging cash flows within the CCIRS that is excluded from the designated hedging instrument of JPY 80 million (JPY 8,000 million x 0.5% x 2) amortised on a straight-line basis over two years.
4. Because the designated hedging instrument does not include the foreign currency basis spread element, the fixed interest rate that is the result of the hedge excludes the foreign currency basis spread element. The reclassification adjustment is calculated as follows.
   A: receive USD 100 million x 4% x 100 = JPY 400 million
   B: less: pay JPY 8,000 million x 2.0% = JPY 160 million
   A – B: JPY 400 million - JPY 160 million = JPY 240 million.
5. The effective portion of the change in fair value of the hedging instrument (not the actual CCIRS) – represented by the change in fair value of the hypothetical derivative (JPY 2,016 million - JPY 1,290 million) – is recorded in OCI.
6. No ineffectiveness is recorded because fair value of the hedging instrument, which excludes the foreign currency basis spread, equals the fair value of the hypothetical derivative (constructed to also exclude the foreign currency basis spread). Because no ineffectiveness arises, the remaining difference – the change in foreign currency basis spread element – is recorded in OCI as a cost of hedging.
7. Because the designated hedging instrument does not include the foreign currency basis spread element, the fixed interest rate that is the result of the hedge excludes the currency basis spread element. The reclassification adjustment is calculated as follows.
   A: receive USD 100 million x 5% x 90 = JPY 450 million
   B: less: pay JPY 8,000 million x 2.0% = JPY 160 million
   A – B: JPY 450 million - JPY 160 million = JPY 290 million.

7.9.1220.80   The resulting impact of entries on the statement of financial position and the statement of profit or loss and OCI is summarised as follows (amounts in millions of yen).

	31 DEC 2018	31 DEC 2018	TOTAL
Statement of financial position			
Borrowing	(10,000)	-	
CCIRS	2,008	-	
Hedging reserve (equity)	(16)	-	
Costs of hedging (equity)	8	-	

	31 Dec 2018	31 Dec 2018	Total
Profit or loss – year ended			
Interest expense[1]	160	160	320
Costs of hedging[1]	40	40	80
Foreign exchange gain or loss	-	-	-
Hedge ineffectiveness	-	-	-
Net profit or loss	200	200	400
OCI – year ended			
Effective portion of cash flow hedge:			
– Recognised in OCI	(2,256)	726	(1,530)
– Reclassified to profit or loss	2,240	(710)	1,530
Total	(16)	16	-
Costs of hedging:			
– Recognised in OCI	48	32	80
– Reclassified to profit or loss	(40)	(40)	(80)
Total	8	(8)	-

Note

1. Interest expense at 2% on JPY 8,000 million. The effects from the foreign currency basis spread are recognised in profit or loss in cost of hedging and represent the excluded 0.5% currency basis spread on JPY 8,000 million.

7.9.1230 **Example 54 – Fair value hedge of foreign currency risk on equities for which entity has elected to present changes in fair value in OCI**

7.9.1230.10   Company S operates in Singapore and has the Singapore dollar as its functional currency. On 1 April 2018, S buys a portfolio of equity shares of Company T on the London Stock Exchange in which transactions are denominated in sterling and dividends on T's shares are paid in sterling. T's shares are traded only on the London Stock Exchange and T operates only in the UK. T's shares are acquired for GBP 30 million. S elects to present changes in the fair value of T's shares in OCI.

7.9.1230.20   Although a steady growth in the value of the shares is expected in the medium to long term, it creates an increased foreign currency exposure. Therefore, S decides to hedge only the foreign exchange exposure on a portion of the market value of the portfolio in foreign currency. This is because of the uncertainty about the short-term development in the market value and, therefore, the exposure. S enters into a foreign currency forward contract to sell GBP 25.5 million and receive Singapore dollars on 15 October 2018. This contract will then be rolled for as long as the position is outstanding (see 7.9.940.10).

7.9.1230.30   The forward contract is designated as a fair value hedge of the foreign currency risk associated with the GBP 25.5 million portion of the fair value of the shares. The forward element of the forward contract is excluded from the designated hedging instrument. The hedge meets the hedge effectiveness requirements and hedge ineffectiveness will be measured by comparing the changes in the fair value of the GBP 25.5 million portion of shares arising from changes in spot exchange rates with the changes in the value of the forward contract also arising from changes in spot rates – because the forward element is excluded from the hedging relationship. S does not account for the forward element as costs of hedging.

7.9.1230.40   The terms of the forward contract are as follows:
- sell GBP 25,500,000;
- buy SGD 64,359,915; and
- maturity of 15 October 2018.

7.9.1230.50   The terms imply a forward rate of 2.5239.

7.9.1230.60   During the period of the hedge, the value of the forward is as follows (amounts in SGD).

DATE	SPOT RATE GBP 1 = SGD	VALUE OF CONTRACT FORWARD	VALUE CHANGE GAIN/(LOSS)	SPOT ELEMENT GAIN/(LOSS)	FORWARD ELEMENT GAIN/(LOSS)
1 April 2018	2.55	-	-	-	-
30 June 2018	2.41	3,031,769	3,031,769	3,570,000	(538,231)
30 September 2018	2.39	3,406,748	374,979	510,000	(135,021)
15 October 2018	2.45	1,884,915	(1,521,833)	(1,530,000)	8,167
			1,884,915	2,550,000	(665,085)

7.9.1230.70   The value of the foreign equity portfolio changes as follows, as a result of changes in equity prices and changes in the exchange rate.

DATE	VALUE (GBP)	VALUE (SGD)	VALUE CHANGE (SGD)
1 April 2018	30,000,000	76,500,000	-
30 June 2018	35,000,000	84,350,000	7,850,000
30 September 2018	28,000,000	66,920,000	(17,430,000)
15 October 2018	32,000,000	78,400,000	11,480,000

7.9.1230.80   Assuming that all of the criteria for hedge accounting have been met, S records the following entries.

	DEBIT (SGD)	CREDIT (SGD)
1 April 2018 *No entries in profit or loss or statement of financial position required for the forward contract, because fair value of forward contract is zero*		
Equity investments Cash *To recognise purchase of securities;* *GBP 30 million at 2.55*	76,500,000	76,500,000
30 June 2018 Equity investments Equity investments revaluation reserve (OCI) *To recognise change in fair value of securities*	7,850,000	7,850,000
Derivatives (assets) Derivative revaluation loss (profit or loss) Derivative revaluation gain (OCI) *To recognise change in fair value of forward contract* *[Derivative revaluation gain (OCI): GBP 25.5 million* *x (2.41 - 2.55)]*	3,031,769 538,231	3,570,000
30 September 2018 Equity investments revaluation reserve (OCI) Equity investments *To recognise change in fair value of securities*	17,430,000	17,430,000

	DEBIT (SGD)	CREDIT (SGD)
Derivatives (assets)	374,979	
Derivative revaluation loss (profit or loss)	135,021	
Derivative revaluation gain (OCI)		510,000
To recognise change in fair value of forward contract [Derivative revaluation gain (OCI): GBP 25.5 million x (2.39 - 2.41)]		
15 October 2018		
Equity investments	11,480,000	
Equity investments revaluation reserve (OCI)		11,480,000
To recognise change in fair value of securities		
Derivative revaluation loss (OCI)	1,530,000	
Derivative revaluation gain (profit or loss)		8,167
Derivatives (assets)		1,521,833
To recognise change in fair value of forward contract [Derivative revaluation loss (OCI): GBP 25.5 million x (2.45 - 2.39)]		
Cash	1,884,915	
Derivatives (assets)		1,884,915
To recognise settlement of forward		

7.9.1230.90   The hedge stays effective for the full period because changes in the fair value of the forward contract, resulting from changes in spot rates, perfectly offset changes in the value of GBP 25.5 million of the equity portfolio due to the same spot exchange rates.

7.9.1230.100   Variability in the fair value of the shares in foreign currency would not affect the assessment of hedge effectiveness unless the fair value of the shares in foreign currency declined below GBP 25.5 million.

7.9.1240   **Example 55 – Hedge of net investment in foreign operation**

7.9.1240.10   Company G, whose functional currency is the euro, has a net investment in a foreign subsidiary of GBP 50 million. On 1 October 2018, G enters into a foreign exchange forward contract to sell GBP 50 million and receive euro on 1 April 2019. G will review the net investment balance on a quarterly basis and adjust the hedge to the value of the net investment. The forward element of the forward contract is excluded from the designated hedging instrument. G does not account for the forward element as costs of hedging.

7.9.1240.20 The exchange rate and fair value of the forward contract move as follows.

DATE	SPOT RATE GBP 1 = EUR	FORWARD RATE GBP 1 = EUR	FAIR VALUE OF FORWARD CONTRACT EUR
1 October 2018	1.71	1.70	-
31 December 2018	1.64	1.63	3,430,000
31 March 2019	1.60	N/A	5,000,000

7.9.1240.30 Assuming that all criteria for hedge accounting have been met, G records the following entries.

	DEBIT (EUR)	CREDIT (EUR)
1 October 2018		
No entries in profit or loss or statement of financial position required; fair value of forward contract is zero		
31 December 2018		
Derivatives (asset)	3,430,000	
Foreign exchange losses (profit or loss)	70,000	
Foreign currency translation reserve (OCI)		3,500,000
To recognise change in fair value of forward		
Foreign currency translation reserve (OCI)	3,500,000	
Net investment in subsidiary (asset)		3,500,000
To recognise foreign exchange loss on net investment in subsidiary (adjustment to net investment is derived by translating subsidiary's statement of financial position at spot rate at each reporting date)		
31 March 2019		
Derivatives (asset)	1,570,000	
Foreign exchange losses (profit or loss)	430,000	
Foreign currency translation reserve (OCI)		2,000,000
To recognise change in fair value of forward		
Foreign currency translation reserve (OCI)	2,000,000	
Net investment in subsidiary (asset)		2,000,000
To recognise change in foreign exchange losses on net investment		

	DEBIT (EUR)	CREDIT (EUR)
Cash	5,000,000	
Derivatives (assets)		5,000,000
To recognise settlement of forward		

7.9.1240.40 The gain on the hedging transaction will remain in equity until the subsidiary is disposed of (see 7.9.230.40).

7.9.1250

Example 56 – Hedging other market price risks

7.9.1250.10 Company X owns equity securities in an entity listed on a domestic stock exchange. X has elected to present changes in fair value of the equity securities in OCI. At 1 January 2018, the fair value of the securities is 120 million; the fair value on initial recognition was 115 million. The revaluation gain of 5 million is recognised in OCI.

7.9.1250.20 At 30 June 2018, the value of the securities has increased from 120 million to 130 million. The securities are remeasured at fair value with the cumulative change of 15 million recognised in OCI.

7.9.1250.30 At 30 June 2018, because of volatility in the price risk of the securities and to comply with internal risk management policies, management decides to purchase a European put option on the securities with a strike price equal to the current market price of 130 million and a maturity date of 30 June 2019. The option premium paid is 12 million.

7.9.1250.40 Management has documented the hedging relationship, designated the purchased option (including the time value of the option) as a hedging instrument and assessed that the purchased put option is an effective hedge in offsetting decreases in the fair value of the equity securities below 130 million. The fair value of the securities and the put option during the period are as follows.

DATE	VALUE OF SECURITIES	TOTAL OPTION VALUE
1 January 2018	120,000,000	-
30 June 2018	130,000,000	12,000,000
30 September 2018	136,000,000	7,000,000
31 December 2018	118,000,000	17,000,000

7.9.1250.50 X makes the following entries to record the remeasurement of the securities and the payment of the option premium.

	DEBIT	CREDIT
30 June 2018		
Equity securities	10,000,000	
Equity securities revaluation reserve (OCI)		10,000,000
To recognise remeasurement gain on equity securities		
Hedging derivatives (assets)	12,000,000	
Cash		12,000,000
To recognise payment of option premium		
30 September 2018		
Equity securities	6,000,000	
Equity securities revaluation reserve (OCI)		6,000,000
To recognise remeasurement gain on equity securities		
Equity securities revaluation reserve (OCI)	5,000,000	
Hedging derivatives (assets)		5,000,000
To recognise remeasurement loss on option		

7.9.1250.60   The option is still expected to be effective as a hedge of decreases in the fair value of the equity securities below the strike price of the option.

7.9.1250.70   At 31 December 2018, the value of the hedged securities decreases to 118 million. The value of the put option increases to 17 million. As such, the following entries are made to recognise the change in the fair value of the equity securities and the changes in the fair value of the option.

	DEBIT	CREDIT
31 December 2018		
Equity securities revaluation reserve (OCI)	18,000,000	
Equity securities		18,000,000
To recognise decrease in fair value of securities		
Hedging derivatives (assets)	10,000,000	
Equity securities revaluation reserve (OCI)		10,000,000
To recognise remeasurement gain on the option		

7.9.1250.80   At 31 December 2018, the equity securities are recognised at a fair value of 118 million compared with an original cost of 115 million. However, a net cumulative gain of 8 million (including the gain of 5 million on the purchased option) has been included in the equity securities revaluation reserve from 1 January 2018 to 31 December 2018.

7.9.1260   **FUTURE DEVELOPMENTS**

7.9.1270   **Discussion Paper – Accounting for dynamic risk management**

7.9.1270.10   Although IAS 39 and IFRS 9 provide models for macro hedge accounting, these contain restrictions that limit entities' ability to reflect some common dynamic risk management (DRM) activities; moreover, some of these models deal specifically with interest rate risk management rather than other types of risk. Without an accounting model that reflects the broader use of DRM activities, some have asserted that it can be difficult to faithfully represent these activities in financial statements.

7.9.1270.20   In response to these issues, in April 2014 the IASB published Discussion Paper *Accounting for Dynamic Risk Management – a Portfolio Revaluation Approach to Macro Hedging* as the first due process document for the project. Because the project involves fundamental accounting questions and is not simply a modification to current hedge accounting models, the IASB did not proceed straight to issuing an exposure draft.

7.9.1280   *Portfolio revaluation approach*

7.9.1280.10   The discussion paper put forward an outline of one possible approach to macro hedge accounting – the portfolio revaluation approach (PRA) – under which entities' managed exposures would be identified and revalued for changes in the managed risk.
- *Managed exposures:* These would be identified and remeasured for changes in the managed risk, with the gain or loss recognised in profit or loss. The remeasurement would be based on a present value technique.
- *Hedging instruments:* Risk management derivatives – i.e. hedging instruments – would continue to be measured at FVTPL.
- *Result of hedge accounting:* The performance of an entity's DRM activities would be captured by the net effect of the above measurements in profit or loss.
- *Other risks:* Risks that are not managed would not be included in this approach – i.e. PRA is not a full fair value model.

7.9.1280.20   The IASB believes that the PRA would be operationally easier to apply than the current hedge accounting models for open portfolios, because it would reduce the complexities associated with one-to-one designations requirements.

7.9.1290   *Managed exposures*

7.9.1290.10   A key question in applying the PRA would be the extent to which DRM activities should be reflected in the accounting. The discussion paper explored a number of areas that would broaden the scope of the PRA as compared with the existing requirements. The discussion paper considered whether, for example, the following items should be eligible for inclusion:
- pipeline transactions – i.e. forecast volumes of draw-downs of fixed interest rate products at advertised rates;
- the equity model book – i.e. entities managing own equity to earn a minimum target return similar to interest; and
- behaviouralised expected cash flows related to core demand deposit liabilities, prepayment risk and changes in expected customer behaviour.

7.9.1300   ***Two scope alternatives***

7.9.1300.10   The discussion paper presented two possible ways of applying the PRA.

- *Focus on DRM:* Under this approach, the PRA would apply to all dynamically managed exposures regardless of whether they have been hedged.
- *Focus on risk mitigation:* The PRA would apply only when entities have undertaken risk mitigation activities through hedging.

7.9.1310   **Current status and next steps**

7.9.1310.10   Based on the feedback received from respondents on the discussion paper, the IASB tentatively decided to:

- first consider how the information needs of constituents concerning dynamic risk management activities could be addressed through disclosures before considering those areas that need to be addressed through recognition and measurement;
- prioritise the consideration of interest rate risk and consider other risks at a later stage in the project; and
- establish an Expert Advisory Panel at a later stage in the project. [*IASBU 05-15*]

7.9.1310.20   KPMG's periodic *IFRS Newsletter: Financial Instruments* features the IASB's discussions and progress on this project. This publication, and other KPMG resources on financial instruments, are available at kpmg.com/ifrs.

7.10   Presentation and disclosures

7.10 Presentation and disclosures

CURRENTLY EFFECTIVE REQUIREMENTS

This publication reflects IFRS in issue at 1 August 2018, and the currently effective requirements cover annual periods beginning on or after 1 January 2018.

The requirements related to this topic are mainly derived from the following.

STANDARD	TITLE
IFRS 7	Financial Instruments: Disclosures
IFRS 9	Financial Instruments
IFRS 13	Fair Value Measurement
IAS 1	Presentation of Financial Statements
IAS 32	Financial Instruments: Presentation

Specific requirements for insurers that apply the overlay approach are not included in this chapter, but are discussed in 8.1.160.

FORTHCOMING REQUIREMENTS

The currently effective requirements are affected by the following forthcoming requirements. They are highlighted with a # and the impact is explained in the accompanying boxed text at the references indicated.

- In January 2016, the IASB issued IFRS 16 *Leases*, which is effective for annual periods beginning on or after 1 January 2019. See 7.10.465. IFRS 16 is the subject of chapter 5.1A.
- In May 2017, the IASB issued IFRS 17 *Insurance Contracts*, which is effective for annual periods beginning on or after 1 January 2021. See 7.10.15, 205 and 467. IFRS 17 is the subject of chapter 8.1A.

FUTURE DEVELOPMENTS

The forthcoming requirements that may be affected by future developments are highlighted with a * and are briefly discussed in 7.10.760.

7.10.10 SCOPE#

7.10.10.10   IFRS 7 sets out the disclosure requirements for all financial instruments. The objective of the disclosures is to enhance financial statement users' understanding of:

- the significance of financial instruments to an entity's overall financial position and performance;
- the risk exposures resulting from such financial instruments; and
- how the entity manages those risks. [*IFRS 7.1*]

7.10.10.20   IFRS 7 applies to all entities and to all types of recognised and unrecognised financial instruments – e.g. loan commitments. The standard also applies to contracts to buy or sell a non-financial item that are in the scope of IFRS 9 (see 7.1.200). For financial instruments that are excluded from the scope of IFRS 7, see 7.1.40. The credit risk disclosure requirements (see 7.10.520) also apply, with certain exceptions, to contract assets and lease receivables (see 7.10.620). [*IFRS 7.3–5A, 35A*]

7.10.10.30   As can be seen from the table in 7.1.40, interests in subsidiaries, associates and joint ventures accounted for in accordance with IFRS 10, IAS 27 or IAS 28 are excluded from the disclosure requirements in IFRS 7. However, when such interests are accounted for in accordance with IFRS 9 (see 7.1.160), they are subject to the disclosure requirements of IFRS 7, and those in IAS 27 and IFRS 12. [*IFRS 7.3(a)*]

7.10.10.40   Also, as can be seen from the table in 7.1.40, insurance contracts as defined in IFRS 4 are excluded from the scope of IFRS 7 (see 7.1.50). However, certain derivatives embedded in those contracts, and financial guarantee contracts to which IFRS 9 is applied (see 7.1.60), are subject to the disclosure requirements of IFRS 7. [*IFRS 7.3(d)*]

7.10.15 FORTHCOMING REQUIREMENTS

7.10.15.10   Consequential amendments introduced by IFRS 17 specify that investment components that are required to be separated from insurance contracts in the scope of IFRS 17 are subject to the disclosure and presentation requirements of IFRS 7 and IAS 32, as well as the measurement requirements of IFRS 9. [*IFRS 7.3(d), 9.2.1(e), IAS 32.4(d)*]

7.10.15.20   Financial instruments that an entity issues with a discretionary participation feature are scoped out of the measurement requirements of IFRS 9, but they are subject to the disclosure requirements of IFRS 7 and some of the presentation requirements of IAS 32 (see 7.1.40). By contrast, investment contracts with discretionary participation features in the scope of IFRS 17 are excluded from the scope of the disclosure requirements of IFRS 7 and all of the presentation requirements of IAS 32, as well as the measurement requirements of IFRS 9. [*IFRS 7.3(d), 9.2.1(e), IAS 32.4(d)*]

7.10.20 PRESENTATION: GENERAL CONSIDERATIONS

7.10.30 Statement of financial position

7.10.30.10   As a minimum, financial assets are presented in the statement of financial position, with separate presentation of cash and cash equivalents, trade and other receivables, and investments accounted for under the equity method (see chapter 3.5). Financial liabilities are presented in the statement of financial position, with separate presentation of trade and other payables. Additional line items may be presented. [*IAS 1.54*]

7.10.30.20   Using different measurement bases for different classes of assets suggests that their nature or function differs; therefore, instruments that are measured at amortised cost, and those that are measured at fair value, are generally presented as separate line items. However, in our view in certain cases instruments with different measurement bases may be included in the same line item – e.g. a host financial liability that is carried at amortised cost and a separated embedded derivative (see 7.2.110), or an instrument carried at amortised cost that is the hedged item in a fair value hedge and other similar instruments that are not hedged. In these cases, the notes to the financial statements should disclose the carrying amount of each category of financial instruments that are combined in a single line item in the statement of financial position. [*IFRS 7.8, IAS 1.59*]

7.10.35   *Trade payables and reverse factoring*

7.10.35.10   Amounts owed to a supplier of goods or services are generally presented as trade payables – i.e. liabilities to pay for goods or services that have been received and have been invoiced or formally agreed with the supplier. [*IAS 1.54(k), 37.11(a)*]

7.10.35.20   In a traditional factoring arrangement, a supplier of goods or services obtains cash from a bank or other financial institution (i.e. the factor) against receivables due from its customers. The arrangement might take different legal forms – e.g. the receivables might be sold outright to the factor or pledged as security for a loan from the factor and the factor may or may not have recourse to the supplier in the event that the customer does not settle. A traditional factoring arrangement is initiated by the supplier and the factor, rather than the customer. In some cases, the customer might be unaware of the arrangement. In our experience, in such an arrangement, the customer generally continues to classify the amounts payable as trade payables, even if it is aware of the factoring arrangement.

7.10.35.30   In contrast, reverse factoring is initiated by the customer and the factor. The terms of reverse factoring arrangements vary but are usually three-party agreements involving the customer, the factor and the supplier. Under a reverse factoring arrangement, the factor agrees to pay amounts to the supplier in respect of invoices owed by the customer, receiving settlement from that customer at a later date.

7.10.35.40   A reverse factoring arrangement may provide liquidity to the customer if it allows deferral of payment to the factor beyond the original maturity of the supplier's invoice or if the arrangement enables the customer to negotiate extended payment terms with its supplier. Depending on the terms of the arrangement, and similar to traditional factoring, the reverse factoring arrangement may also provide to the supplier:
● liquidity by enabling it to receive cash before the invoice due date; and
● access to funding at a lower interest rate based on the customer's credit rating.

7.10.35.50   Similarly, the reverse factoring arrangement may allow the customer to take advantage of an early payment discount offered by the supplier. The reverse factoring arrangement may also allow the supplier and the customer to make administrative savings through more streamlined collection and payment procedures.

7.10.35.60   In some cases, a reverse factoring arrangement may result in the derecognition of the original trade payable and the recognition of a new financial liability (see 7.6.360); in other cases, there will be no derecognition of the original trade payable to which the reverse factoring arrangement applies.

7.10.35.70   In our view, regardless of whether the original trade payable is derecognised, an entity should consider the appropriate presentation of amounts related to reverse factoring arrangements in the statement of financial position (see 3.1.10.30), including whether the headings and line items should be adapted to suit the particular circumstances – for example:
- reclassifying amounts to a different line – e.g. within 'other financial liabilities'; or
- presenting an additional line item – e.g. supplier factoring facility – either on the face of the statement of financial position or by disaggregation of amounts that have a different nature or function in the notes [*IAS 1.29–30, 55*]

7.10.35.80   An entity needs to apply judgement in determining whether the reverse factoring arrangement indicates that separate presentation (on the face of the statement of financial position or in the notes) of the amounts due is appropriate – e.g. reclassification of the trade payable to bank borrowing. We believe that the following are examples of features that may indicate that the nature or function of the financial liability is sufficiently different from a trade payable and therefore separate presentation may be appropriate:
- the principal business purpose of the reverse factoring arrangement is to provide funding to the customer, rather than to provide funding to the supplier or to facilitate efficient payment processing;
- the factor is a bank or similar financial institution; and
- the arrangement:
  - significantly extends payment terms beyond the normal terms agreed with other suppliers;
  - adds a requirement for the customer to pay interest or to pay interest at a higher rate;
  - requires additional collateral or a guarantee; or
  - changes the terms defining default and cancellation.

7.10.35.90   None of the features in 7.10.35.80 is necessarily a determinative indicator on its own. We believe that an entity should weigh those features to determine whether separate presentation (on the face of the statement of financial position or in the notes) is appropriate.

7.10.35.100   For a further discussion of reverse factoring, see 2.3.75, 7.6.465, 7.10.315 and 655.

7.10.40   *Classes vs categories of financial instruments*

7.10.40.10   Some of the IFRS 7 disclosure requirements mandate disclosure by category of financial instruments, as specified in IFRS 9, whereas others are by class of financial instruments. Examples of 'categories of financial instruments' are:
- financial assets measured at FVTPL (see 7.4.50), which include:
  - financial assets that are mandatorily measured at FVTPL; and
  - financial assets designated as at FVTPL on initial recognition or designated subsequently, when an entity uses a credit derivative that is measured at FVTPL to manage the credit exposure arising from such financial assets (see 7.4.390–400 and 7.9.120);
- financial assets measured at amortised cost (see 7.4.30);
- financial assets measured at FVOCI, which include:

- financial assets mandatorily measured at FVOCI (see 7.4.40); and
- investments in equity instruments designated as at FVOCI on initial recognition (see 7.4.60);
- financial liabilities measured at FVTPL, which include:
  - financial liabilities that meet the definition of held for trading (see 7.5.30); and
  - financial liabilities designated as at FVTPL on initial recognition (or designated subsequently, when an entity uses a credit derivative that is measured at FVTPL to manage the credit exposure arising from such liabilities) (see 7.5.40 and 7.9.120); and
- financial liabilities measured at amortised cost (see 7.5.20.10). [*IFRS 7.8, 9.4.1–4.2*]

7.10.40.20   There is no specific guidance on what comprises a 'class' except that financial instruments are grouped into classes that:
- are appropriate to the nature of the disclosure; and
- take into account the characteristics of those financial instruments. [*IFRS 7.6, B1*]

7.10.40.30   Examples of classes of financial instruments include cash and cash equivalents, unsecured bank facilities and convertible notes (liability). In determining classes, the entity, as a minimum:
- distinguishes instruments measured at amortised cost from those measured at fair value; and
- treats financial instruments outside the scope of IFRS 7 as a separate class or classes. [*IFRS 7.6, B2*]

7.10.40.40   In deciding how much detail to include and how to aggregate the information, an entity has to strike a balance between too much and too little detail. It also needs to ensure that the information is sufficient to allow a reconciliation to the line items presented in the statement of financial position. [*IFRS 7.6, B3*]

7.10.40.50   In our view, derivative assets and liabilities should be presented in separate line items in the statement of financial position if they are significant. If derivative instruments are not significant, then they may be included in other financial assets and other financial liabilities, respectively. Additional details should be disclosed in the notes to the financial statements.

7.10.50   *Current vs non-current classification of financial instruments**

7.10.50.10   If an entity makes a distinction between current and non-current assets and liabilities in the statement of financial position (classified statement of financial position – see 3.1.10.10), then instruments within the financial instrument classes are classified as current or non-current in accordance with their expected recovery (financial assets) or contractual settlement date (financial liabilities). The amounts classified as current and non-current reflect the carrying amounts of the financial assets and financial liabilities. For financial assets measured at amortised cost, this means that the current and non-current classification would reflect the carrying amounts net of the allowance for ECLs. [*IFRS 9.A, IAS 1.60, 66, 69*]

7.10.50.20   In particular, an asset is classified as current when it:
- is expected to be realised in or is held for sale in the entity's normal operating cycle;
- is held primarily for trading purposes;
- is expected to be realised within 12 months of the reporting date; or
- is cash or a cash equivalent that is not restricted from being exchanged or used to settle a liability for at least 12 months after the reporting date (see 2.3.10). [*IAS 1.66, 68*]

7.10.50.30   A liability is classified as current when it:
- is expected to be settled in the entity's normal operating cycle;
- is held primarily for trading purposes;
- is due to be settled within 12 months of the reporting date; or
- is not subject to an unconditional right of the entity at the reporting date to defer settlement of the liability for at least 12 months after the reporting date. [*IAS 1.69*]

7.10.50.40   However, a liability is not classified as current only because the counterparty has an option to require settlement within 12 months in equity instruments issued by the entity. [*IAS 1.69*]

7.10.50.50   Derivatives not held primarily for trading purposes are classified as current or non-current based on their outstanding maturities. For example, derivatives with maturities exceeding 12 months that the entity intends to hold for more than 12 months from the reporting date are classified as non-current assets or liabilities. [*IAS 1.BC38J*]

7.10.50.60   In addition to derivatives (see 3.1.30.45 and 7.10.50.50), the FVTPL category (see 7.4.50 and 7.5.20.30) also includes:
- assets and liabilities held primarily for the purpose of being traded – e.g. certain financial assets that meet the definition of held-for-trading – which are classified as current; and
- assets and liabilities of longer duration – e.g. those that were designated on initial recognition into this category. [*IFRS 9.A*]

7.10.50.70   In our view, such assets and liabilities of longer duration should be presented as non-current to the extent that they are not expected to be realised, or are not due to be settled, within 12 months of the reporting date or within the entity's normal operating cycle. In our view, this also applies to financial assets measured at FVOCI. [*IAS 1.68*]

7.10.60   Statement of profit or loss and OCI

7.10.60.10   Line items presenting the following amounts are required to be included in profit or loss to the extent they are material:
- revenue, presenting separately interest revenue calculated using the effective interest method;
- gains or losses arising from the derecognition of financial assets measured at amortised cost;
- finance costs;
- impairment losses, including reversals of impairment losses or impairment gains, determined in accordance with IFRS 9;
- gains or losses arising on the reclassification of a financial asset from the amortised cost measurement category to FVTPL measurement; and
- gains or losses arising on the reclassification of a financial asset from the FVOCI measurement category to FVTPL measurement. [*IAS 1.82*]

7.10.60.20   The IFRS Interpretations Committee discussed the application of the requirement to present separately a line item for interest revenue calculated using the effective interest method and noted that it applies only to financial assets that are subsequently measured at amortised cost or FVOCI (subject to the effect of any qualifying hedging relationship applying the hedge accounting requirements). [*IAS 1.82(a), IU 03-18*]

7.10.60.30   However, the Committee did not consider whether an entity could present other interest amounts in the statement of profit or loss and OCI. It appears that an entity may present interest income from other financial assets in another revenue line item if it arises in the course of the entity's ordinary activities (see 4.1.15).

7.10.60.40   Although there is a specific requirement to present gains and losses arising from the derecognition of financial assets measured at amortised cost as a separate line item (see 7.10.60.10), there is no similar specific requirement to present gains and losses included in profit or loss arising from the derecognition of financial assets at FVOCI as a separate line item. [*IAS 1.82(aa)*]

7.10.60.50   Except as set out in 7.10.60.10, there is no specific guidance on presenting gains and losses on financial instruments in profit or loss (see also 4.1.130). In all other cases, in our view, gains and losses on financial instruments should be reported in the most appropriate line item according to their nature.

7.10.60.60   For example, an entity may present foreign currency gains and losses on financial assets and financial liabilities that arise from operating activities – e.g. payables arising on the purchase of goods – as part of income and expenses before finance costs, and foreign currency gains and losses related to financing activities as part of finance income and finance costs (see 2.7.160.20 and 7.10.70). [*IAS 21.28, IFRS 9.5.7.2, B5.7.2*]

7.10.60.70   If hedge accounting is not applied to a derivative instrument that is entered into as an economic hedge, then in our view derivative gains and losses may be shown in profit or loss as either operating or financing items depending on the nature of the item being economically hedged.

7.10.60.80   For financial assets and financial liabilities at FVTPL, there is no need to distinguish between the fair value changes and interest and dividend income or expense (see 7.10.65, 330.20 and 370.10). The net fair value changes – i.e. gains and losses – on each financial asset or financial liability are usually classified as finance income or finance costs (see 7.10.70). However, fair value changes (net gains or net losses) on these instruments are presented separately, if they are material. [*IAS 1.35, 97*]

7.10.65   *Split presentation of gains and losses on financial instruments measured at FVTPL*

7.10.65.10   For non-derivatives measured at FVTPL, an entity may present either:
- foreign exchange gains and losses and/or interest income and expense separately from other fair value changes; or
- the entire fair value change on a net basis as a single amount.

7.10.65.20   There are no specific requirements in IFRS addressing the presentation of gains and losses on derivatives except for hedging derivative gains and losses. For guidance on presenting hedging derivative gains and losses, see 7.10.160.

7.10.65.30   Whichever method is adopted, if an entity elects to disclose the results of operating activities (or a similar line item) in profit or loss, then it presents any amounts that it normally regards as being of an operating nature as part of operating activities (see also 4.1.120.10–30, 7.10.70.20 and 70). [*IAS 1.BC56*]

7.10.65.40 If interest on non-derivative instruments measured at FVTPL is presented separately, then it is measured on using the effective interest method or a similar basis, excluding transaction costs. Because transaction costs directly attributable to the acquisition of a financial instrument classified as at FVTPL are not included in its initial measurement but are instead expensed as they are incurred, they are not included in calculating an effective interest rate for the instrument (see 7.7.50.10 and 90). [*IFRS 7.BC34, 9.5.1.1, A*]

7.10.65.50 If a non-derivative financial asset measured at FVTPL does not meet the SPPI criterion (see 7.4.150), then it appears that judgement is required to determine whether separate presentation of interest and the method for calculating it are appropriate in the context of the economic character-istics of the instrument. We believe that interest cannot be presented for instruments that are entirely equity instruments (see chapter 7.3). We also believe that an entity may be able to apply one of the following approaches to calculate interest on a debt instrument.

- *Approach 1:* Apply the calculation in 7.10.65.40 to the cash flows of the whole instrument. In determining for which instruments it is appropriate to calculate and present interest under this approach, the entity should consider the expected frequency and significance of re-estimation adjustments due to non-SPPI features throughout the life of the asset.
- *Approach 2:* Use the embedded derivative separation guidance for financial liabilities (see 7.2.110) to define a host financial asset and apply the calculation in 7.10.65.40 to the cash flows of the host financial asset only.

7.10.65.60 Any interest income that is calculated for a financial instrument measured at FVTPL cannot be presented in the line item for interest revenue calculated using the effective interest method, unless the instrument is designated as a hedging instrument with respect to that revenue (see 7.10.60.10–20).

7.10.70 *Finance income and finance costs*

7.10.70.10 A separate line item is required in profit or loss for finance costs. There is no requirement to present a separate 'finance income' line item in profit or loss unless such presentation is relevant to an understanding of the entity's financial performance. However, an entity is required to present in profit or loss interest revenue calculated using the effective interest method (see 7.10.60.10). In addition, significant categories of revenue other than interest revenue – e.g. dividends – are disclosed in the financial statements. [*IAS 1.82(b), 85, 97*]

7.10.70.20 There is no guidance in IFRS on what should be included in finance income and fi-nance costs. Non-financial sector entities usually include the following items in finance income and finance costs, unless they are included in another line item under 7.10.60.10:

- interest income and expense (see 7.7.270);
- dividend income;
- foreign exchange gains and losses arising from investing and financing activities – e.g. exchange gains and losses on financial investments or exchange gains and losses on foreign currency bor-rowings (see 2.7.160.20);
- gains and losses on derivatives related to investing and financing activities – e.g. gains and losses on interest rate swaps, or gains and losses on foreign currency forward contracts that hedge foreign currency borrowings (see 7.9.170);
- gains and losses on the derecognition of financial investments (see 4.1.130), except for those arising from investments in equity instruments designated as at FVOCI (see 7.10.90.10);

- gains and losses on trading activities involving financial instruments;
- gains and losses on financial instruments designated as at FVTPL;
- the unwinding of discounts on non-financial assets and non-financial liabilities; and
- gains and losses on the derecognition of financial liabilities (see 7.6.430.10 and 450.30, and 7.10.65 and 70.70).

7.10.70.30   The IFRS Interpretations Committee discussed the accounting implications of the economic phenomenon of negative effective interest rates on the presentation of income and expenses in profit or loss. The Committee noted that interest resulting from a negative effective interest rate on a financial asset reflects a gross outflow (instead of a gross inflow) of economic benefits; consequently, it did not meet the definition of interest revenue under IFRS at that time and should not be presented as such. Instead, it noted that negative interest arising from financial assets should be presented in an appropriate expense classification, accompanied by additional information as required by IAS 1. IFRS 9 does not define revenue or income. However, income continues to be defined in the Conceptual Framework and IFRS 15, and negative interest arising from financial assets does not meet those definitions because it represents a decrease (instead of an increase) in assets that results in a decrease in equity. [*IU 01-15, IFRS 15.A, IAS 1.85, 112(c), CF 4.68–69*]

7.10.70.40   Interest income and expense on items that are not financial instruments includes interest that is recognised in respect of an asset or liability that is measured at a discounted amount – for example:
- the interest expense that arises on a provision that is initially measured at a discounted amount (see 3.12.120);
- the interest on a contract asset or a contract liability recognised for a contract with a customer that contains a significant financing component (see 4.2.130); or
- the interest that is imputed on the cost of inventories when payment for the inventories is deferred beyond normal credit terms (see 3.8.150).

7.10.70.50   Dividend income is presented as a separate line item in profit or loss when such presentation is relevant to an understanding of the entity's financial performance. [*IAS 1.85*]

7.10.70.60   In our view, finance income and finance costs should not be presented on a net basis (e.g. as 'net finance costs') in profit or loss without presenting an analysis of finance income and finance costs. However, this does not preclude presentation of finance income immediately followed by finance costs and a subtotal – e.g. 'net finance costs' – in profit or loss. [*IAS 1.32, 82, 85–85B*]

7.10.70.70   If an entity elects to disclose the results of operating activities (or a similar line item), then it presents foreign exchange gains and losses and gains and losses on derivatives that it normally regarded as being of an operating nature as part of operating activities (see also 2.7.160.20, 4.1.120.10–30, and 7.10.65 and 70.20). [*IAS 1.BC56, 21.52*]

7.10.70.80   In our view, expenses related to shares that are classified as a liability – e.g. dividends on redeemable preference shares – may be included with interest on other liabilities or presented separately within finance costs.

7.10.70.90   The profit or loss of banks and similar financial institutions comprises mainly interest revenue (see 7.10.70.10) and interest expense and other finance income and finance costs. The presentation and disclosure for financial institutions is illustrated in KPMG's *Guides to financial statements* series.

7.10.70.100   For further discussion of specific presentation issues arising from the application of IFRS 7, see 7.10.320.

7.10.80   *Impairment losses*

7.10.80.10   Impairment losses, including reversals of impairment losses and impairment gains, determined in accordance with IFRS 9 are presented as a separate line item in the profit or loss section of the statement of comprehensive income or in the statement of profit or loss (see 7.10.60.10). [*IAS 1.82(ba)*]

7.10.80.20   For a discussion of the presentation of reimbursements under a separate financial guarantee contract, see 7.1.143.

7.10.80.30   For a discussion of the presentation of recoveries of amounts that were previously written off, see 7.8.430.130.

7.10.90   *Other comprehensive income*

7.10.90.10   For financial assets mandatorily measured at FVOCI, the cumulative gain or loss previously recognised in OCI is reclassified from equity to profit or loss when the asset is derecognised. However, if an entity makes an irrevocable election to present in OCI changes in the fair value of an investment in an equity instrument, gains and losses that are recognised in OCI are not transferred to profit or loss on disposal of the investment or in any other circumstances. Such gains and losses may, however, be reclassified within equity. [*IFRS 9.5.7.5, 5.7.10, B5.7.1*]

7.10.90.20   Each component of OCI classified by nature is presented as a separate line item in the statement of profit or loss and OCI. This includes:
- the amount of change in the fair value on equity instruments measured at FVOCI;
- the amount of change in the fair value of financial assets mandatorily measured at FVOCI;
- the amount of change in the fair value of financial liabilities measured at FVTPL that is attributable to changes in credit risk;
- the effective portion of the net gain or loss on hedges of net investments in foreign operations;
- the amount of change in the fair value of the hedging instrument in a fair value hedge if it hedges an equity instrument that an entity has elected to measure at FVOCI;
- the amount of change in value of the time value of options when separating the intrinsic value and time value of an option and designating as the hedging instrument only changes in the intrinsic value (see 7.9.660);
- the amount of change in the value of the forward elements of forward contracts when separating the forward element and spot element of a forward contract and designating as a hedging instrument only the changes in the spot element (see 7.9.670);
- the amount of changes in the value of the foreign currency basis spread of a financial instrument when excluding it on designation of the instrument as the hedging instrument (see 7.9.680); and
- the effective portion of changes in fair value in respect of hedging instruments in cash flow hedges.

7.10.90.30   An entity groups these line items into those that may be subsequently reclassified to profit or loss (when specific conditions are met) and those that will not. [*IAS 1.7, 82A(a)*]

7.10.90.35   IFRS 9 specifies whether and when amounts previously recognised in OCI are reclassified to profit or loss. However, in some circumstances it may be unclear at the time when a gain or loss is recognised in OCI whether it will subsequently be reclassified to profit or loss. For example, if an entity hedges a future purchase of a non-financial item, then the related hedging gains and losses will subsequently be included in the initial cost of the non-financial item and affect profit or loss when the non-financial item is disposed of or written down. Conversely, if the future hedged cash flows are no longer expected to occur or if a loss is no longer expected to be recoverable, then the hedging gains or losses will be reclassified to profit or loss (see 7.9.960.30). Accordingly, in our view gains or losses on cash flow hedges and costs of hedging relating to the future recognition of a non-financial asset or liability should be presented in OCI as items that may be subsequently reclassified to profit or loss when specific conditions are met. [*IFRS 9.6.5.11, 6.5.15, IAS 1.82A(a)*]

7.10.90.40   Separate components of OCI are created in accordance with the requirements of IFRS 9. Reclassification adjustments are included with the related component of OCI in the period during which the adjustment is reclassified to profit or loss. They may be presented in the statement of profit or loss and OCI or in the notes to the financial statements. At any point in time, the cumulative amounts previously recognised in these separate components of OCI represent a cumulative gain or loss that may be reclassified to profit or loss at some future date – except for amounts that relate to the change in the fair value of equity instruments elected to be measured at FVOCI and those attributable to the changes in the credit risk of financial liabilities designated to be measured at FVTPL that are presented in OCI. In our view, it would not be appropriate for an entity to reduce or increase components of OCI for any reasons other than those allowed under IFRS 9 – except for related tax effects under IAS 12 (see 3.13.570). [*IAS 1.92–94*]

7.10.100   *Net gains and losses on financial assets or financial liabilities measured at FVTPL*

7.10.100.10   The net fair value changes (i.e. gains and losses) on each financial asset or financial liability measured at FVTPL are usually classified as finance income or finance costs (see 7.10.70 and 60.80) – unless it is a financial liability designated as at FVTPL and the effects of changes in that liability's credit risk are required to be presented in OCI. Fair value changes are presented separately if they are material. [*IAS 1.35, 97*]

7.10.110   **Offsetting**

7.10.110.10   Financial assets and financial liabilities are offset and a net amount is presented in the statement of financial position only if both of the following conditions are met:
- the entity currently has a legally enforceable right to set off the recognised amounts – i.e. a legal right to settle or eliminate all or a portion of an amount due to a creditor by applying against that amount an amount due from the creditor; and
- the entity has the intention to:
  - settle on a net basis; or
  - realise the asset and settle the liability simultaneously. [*IAS 32.42, 45*]

7.10.112   *Multiple financial instruments*

7.10.112.10   The offsetting criteria relate only to determining whether two or more separate financial instruments should be offset and presented net in the statement of financial position. They are not relevant in determining how a single financial instrument should be measured and presented. For example, an interest rate swap comprises an obligation to pay and receive interest cash flows over time – i.e. payments and receipts might be made on a gross basis at different points in time or, even if each individual periodic cash flow is determined as a single net payment or receipt for that period, it might be expected that net amounts will be received in some periods and net amounts paid in other periods. However, the swap is a single derivative financial instrument that is measured at its fair value, which reflects the net value of the expected cash inflows and outflows even though those cash inflows and outflows will not be settled on a net basis.

EXAMPLE 1A – CASH POOLING ARRANGEMENT – MULTIPLE GROUP ENTITIES

7.10.112.20 For cash management purposes, Company B and its subsidiaries enter into a cash pooling arrangement, whereby debit and credit balances in the same currency with Bank C are pooled to optimise the interest earned and paid on the aggregated balance.

7.10.112.30 Before considering the offsetting requirements in IAS 32, B needs to assess whether the arrangement between the B group and C involves either:
- a single financial instrument; or
- multiple financial instruments.

7.10.112.40 If this cash pooling arrangement results in a single omnibus account that B holds with C, and the aggregate balance represents a single amount payable or receivable between B and C, then any accumulated 'memorandum balances' on constituent 'sub-accounts' that record transactions initiated by subsidiaries of B do not represent amounts payable or receivable between those subsidiaries and C, but rather reflect intra-group amounts payable or receivable between those subsidiaries and B. In this case, B presents the aggregated balance on the single omnibus account as a financial asset or financial liability in its consolidated statement of financial position. Therefore, the offsetting requirements are irrelevant.

7.10.112.50 Alternatively, assume that B and each of its subsidiaries have accounts with C in their own names and the balance on each of these accounts represents an amount payable or receivable between that individual member of the B group and C. In that case, for the purposes of B's consolidated financial statements, each account is a separate financial asset or financial liability and B should consider the offsetting criteria to determine whether they should be presented separately or offset.

7.10.112.60 Judgement may be required in determining whether an arrangement involves a single or multiple financial instruments. Generally, rights and obligations arising under different contracts give rise to separate financial instruments. Furthermore, a single legal contract may give rise to more than one financial instrument, such as separate derivatives, loans and deposits or trade receivables and payables. However, in some cases, it may be necessary to aggregate different financial instruments and account for them as a single combined financial instrument (see 7.6.40.10). To determine whether multiple balances or transactions arising from a single legal contract between two entities represent a single or multiple financial instruments, an entity may consider whether:

- each transaction results in separate performance rights and obligations that may be transferred or settled separately;
- transactions are intended to be performed concurrently or consecutively with other transactions;
- transactions relate to the same risks or may be exposed to different risks;
- the pricing of individual transactions is independent; and
- transactions are negotiated as separate trades and/or have different commercial objectives.

EXAMPLE 1B – DERIVATIVE MASTER AGREEMENT

7.10.112.70   Company X enters into a derivative master agreement with Bank B. The agreement states that:

- the parties may agree in the future to enter into a variety of swap, forward, option or other derivative transactions and to terminate such transactions;
- the terms of each transaction or termination, including pricing, will be subject to negotiation based on market conditions at the time;
- any such transactions will form part of the master agreement, which constitutes the only contract at law between the parties;
- collateral is paid or received in accordance with the detailed terms of a credit support annex;
- either party may demand net settlement of amounts due and payable on the same day in the same currency; and
- in the event of either party's default, the other party may demand that all outstanding transactions are terminated at their market values and that a single net settlement of all such amounts is made.

7.10.112.80   Based on the factors in 7.10.112.70, X concludes that each derivative transaction entered into under the master agreement represents a separate financial asset or financial liability.

EXAMPLE 1C – CASH POOLING ARRANGEMENT – MULTIPLE-CURRENCY FACILITY

7.10.112.90   Company T enters into a cash pooling agreement with Bank X. Under the terms of the agreement, all of which are contained in a single document, T has several current accounts in different currencies with the following conditions.

- All accounts are held by T at X in Country Y.
- T is generally free to make drawings from and deposits into each account and the individual accounts can be in a positive or negative position subject to an overall credit limit on T's net drawn balances. T could not withdraw the positive balance on one of the accounts, unless the net balance on all accounts following withdrawal would still be within the overall credit limit.
- The credit limit is stated in a single reference currency. It is applied and monitored by X using current market rates of exchange.
- If foreign exchange rates change and the credit limit is breached, then X may require T to bring the aggregated balances back within the credit limit.

- Interest is calculated on each account on a gross basis at a predetermined fixed or variable rate for the respective currency.
- The agreement has a stated maturity date that applies to all accounts and to the credit limit. At the maturity date, unless T and X agree to extend the agreement, all accounts are closed and the remaining balances are settled on a net basis in the reference currency.
- In the event of default of either party, the non-defaulting party may demand that balances on all accounts are translated into the reference currency and settled net. The same would apply in the event of either party's bankruptcy.
- There is no regular transfer of balances into a sweep account and there is no intention to settle any amounts net or simultaneously, except for any balances that remain at maturity.
- T receives quarterly statements showing the individual gross balances for each account and a subtotal of all of those in debit/credit positions in the single reference currency.

7.10.112.100   The fact that the various accounts arise from a single contractual agreement does not mean that there is a single financial instrument. Similarly, stating a common maturity date does not necessarily mean that there is a single financial instrument. Although there is an overall credit limit and requirements for set off in certain circumstances, each current account is denominated in a different currency and gives rise to performance rights and obligations in that currency. Performance rights and obligations in relation to one currency account are different from those of other accounts and balances on different accounts may be individually settled. Accordingly, T and X conclude that in this example each current account is a separate financial instrument.

7.10.115   *Unit of account*

7.10.115.10   IAS 32 does not specify whether the unit of account when considering the offsetting requirements in IAS 32 should be:

- *entire financial assets and financial liabilities:* in this case, the entity considers whether all – and not just some – of the cash flows from one instrument satisfy the offsetting criteria with respect to another instrument. If they all do, then the instrument is offset in its entirety; otherwise, no offsetting is applied (Approach 1); or
- *individual identifiable cash flows from financial assets and financial liabilities:* in this case, an entity considers whether each individual cash flow of a financial instrument satisfies the offsetting criteria with respect to the cash flows of another instrument. If it does, then the portion of the individual instrument that represents those cash flows is offset (Approach 2). [*IAS 32.BC105–BC106*]

7.10.115.20   In our experience, the approach that is adopted by an entity depends on industry practice, the entity's operational capabilities and the complexity and volume of transactions subject to set off. For example, energy producers and traders generally apply the offsetting criteria to identifiable cash flows, whereas financial institutions generally apply the offsetting criteria to entire financial assets and financial liabilities. An approach of applying to individual cash flows may lead to more offsetting but may be more burdensome to apply. Offsetting is mandatory when the offsetting criteria are satisfied, and therefore an entity may find it impracticable to apply an approach based on individual cash flows. In our view, an entity should choose an accounting policy, to be applied consistently to similar assets and liabilities, to apply either Approach 1 or 2 in 7.10.115.10. [*IAS 32.BC111*]

7.10.120 *Current legally enforceable right to set off*

7.10.120.10   An entity currently has a legally enforceable right to set off if the right is:
- not contingent on a future event; and
- enforceable both in the normal course of business and in the event of default, insolvency or bankruptcy of the entity and all of the counterparties. [*IAS 32.AG38B*]

EXAMPLE 2A – OFFSETTING – LEGAL ENFORCEABILITY FOR ALL COUNTERPARTIES

7.10.120.20   Company B enters into an agreement with Company C that gives B a right to set off.

7.10.120.30   To determine whether its right is legally enforceable in the normal course of business and in the event of default, insolvency or bankruptcy of the entity and all of the counterparties, B evaluates whether it can enforce its right in the normal course of business as well as in the case of its own default, insolvency or bankruptcy, and in the case of C's default, insolvency or bankruptcy.

7.10.120.40   In doing so, B considers whether C has any rights that do or might prevent B from enforcing its right to set off. For example, if, in the event of C's bankruptcy, C could insist on separate settlement of any amounts due to and from B, then B's right to set off would not be enforceable in those circumstances and it would not satisfy the offsetting criteria. [*IAS 32.42(a), AG38B, AG38D, BC80*]

7.10.120.50   Rights to set off may arise on the termination of a contract. In many cases, the termination of a contract may be contingent on an event that is outside the entity's control – e.g. the counterparty's default or bankruptcy. In such cases, the right to set off is clearly conditional and could not qualify for offsetting. However, in some cases the termination of a contract may be a free choice of the entity and is therefore within the entity's control – e.g. the exercise of an early repayment option in a loan. IAS 32 does not discuss whether events that are within the entity's control should be considered contingent on the occurrence of a future event. Therefore, it is not clear whether such rights could be considered currently legally enforceable. However, even if a right to set off arising on termination of a contract could be considered not to be contingent on a future event, such a right on its own would not qualify for offsetting, unless termination would arise in the normal course of business and the entity intends to settle net. [*IAS 32.AG38B, BC82*]

7.10.120.60   To qualify for offsetting, a right to set off needs to be exercisable when the amounts are due and payable. In addition, the passage of time and uncertainties in the amounts to be settled are not considered contingencies. [*IAS 32.BC82–BC84*]

EXAMPLE 2B – OFFSETTING – AMOUNT OR TIMING OF PAYMENT UNCERTAIN

7.10.120.70   Company D has a loan receivable of 100 from Company E that is due and payable on 30 June 2019. D has also written a net-cash-settled put option to E.

7.10.120.80   The following facts are also relevant for this example.
- Under the option, D is obliged to pay E the amount (if any) by which the market price of commodity X exceeds 10 on the exercise date.
- If the market price of commodity X is below 10 on the exercise date, then no payment is required.
- The option matures on 30 June 2019.
- The fair value of the option liability on 31 December 2018 is 30.
- The two transactions – i.e. the loan and the put option – are subject to a right to set off that requires net settlement of amounts due and payable on the same date in all circumstances.
- There are no collateral or margin arrangements.

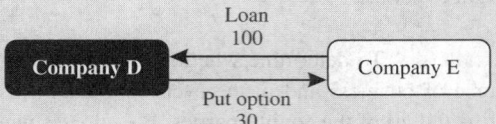

7.10.120.90   Whether D is required to present the loan receivable from E and the derivative liability owed to E net in the statement of financial position will depend on whether the option is a European option (exercisable only on 30 June 2019) or an American option (exercisable at any time up to 30 June 2019).

Scenario 1: European option

7.10.120.100   If the option written by D is a European option – i.e. exercisable only on 30 June 2019 – then both the loan and the written option fall due for settlement on 30 June 2019 and the right to set off ensures that settlement will be on a net basis.

7.10.120.110   It is uncertain whether any amount will actually be due in respect of the option; however, if an amount does arise, then it will certainly be set off. The passage of time and uncertainties in the amounts to be paid do not preclude D from currently having a legally enforceable right to set off. The fact that payments subject to the right will arise only at a future date is not itself a contingency or condition that precludes offsetting.

7.10.120.120   Therefore, in this scenario D presents the loan receivable from E and the derivative liability owed to E net in the statement of financial position.

Scenario 2: American option

7.10.120.130   If the option written by D is an American option – i.e. exercisable at any time up to and including 30 June 2019 – then E can choose to exercise its option before 30 June 2019. If E does exercise early, then D does not have the right to set off, and the two transactions will be settled separately.

7.10.120.140   Therefore, in this scenario D presents the loan receivable from E and the derivative liability due to E separately in the statement of financial position. [*IAS 32.BC83–BC84*]

7.10.120.150   The following do not meet the offsetting criteria in IAS 32:
- rights to set off that can be enforced only in the normal course of business; or
- rights to set off that cannot be enforced in the event of the entity's own default, insolvency or bankruptcy. [*IAS 32.BC81, BC92*]

7.10.120.160   An entity would typically consider the following in determining whether it has a legally enforceable right to set off:
- the counterparties to the contract;
- the terms of the contract; and
- laws in the relevant jurisdictions, including the respective bankruptcy regimes and laws. This would typically include the entity's own jurisdiction, the jurisdiction of other counterparties to the contract and the specific laws governing the contract.

EXAMPLE 2C – CASH POOLING ARRANGEMENT – CURRENT LEGALLY ENFORCEABLE RIGHT TO SET OFF

7.10.120.170   Continuing Example 1, assume that the cash pooling arrangement with Bank C involves separate bank accounts and borrowings in each of the group entities' names – i.e. there are multiple financial instruments between the B group and Bank C. Determining whether the reporting entity has a currently enforceable right to set off requires consideration of the terms of the contract(s). For example, the terms of the contract may permit each individual entity within the B group that has more than one account with C to set off debit and credit balances on those accounts that the individual entity has with C, but may not permit the B group or its members to require set off between accounts held by different members of the B group with C. C would have to perform a similar analysis for the purposes of its financial statements. However, C would not be able to demonstrate that it has a current legally enforceable right to set off if members of the B group are free to withdraw funds from accounts that are in credit and C cannot require those funds instead to be set off against accounts that are overdrawn.

7.10.130   *Intention to settle on net basis or realise asset and settle liability simultaneously*

7.10.130.10   To meet the intention criterion (see 7.10.110.10), an entity must intend either to:
- settle the financial asset and the financial liability on a net basis; or
- realise the financial asset and settle the financial liability simultaneously (see 7.10.130.20). [*IAS 32.42(b), AG38E*]

7.10.130.20   When assessing whether there is an intention to settle net, an entity considers normal business practices, the requirements of the financial markets and other circumstances that may limit its ability to settle net. [*IAS 32.47*]

EXAMPLE 3 – CASH POOLING ARRANGEMENT – INTENTION TO SETTLE NET

7.10.130.30   Continuing Examples 1 and 2C, assume that the B group determines that:
- there are multiple financial instruments involved in the arrangement; and
- there is a current legally enforceable right to set off debit and credit balances held by group members with Bank C.

7.10.130.40   To determine whether it has the intention to settle net, B considers the nature of the set off arrangement.

7.10.130.50   There are two main types of cash management schemes involving multiple financial instruments:
- *zero balancing/cash sweep:* Balances on the separate accounts falling under the arrangement are set off and physically transferred to a single account on a regular basis; and
- *notional pooling:* Balances on the separate accounts falling under the arrangement are not physically transferred and the bank calculates the synthetic (net) balance on a number of designated accounts with interest being earned and paid on the net amount.

7.10.130.60   If the balances on the accounts are physically transferred into a single account, then B needs to assess the frequency of set off to determine whether the intention criterion is met. If the cash balances are physically moved into a single netting account on a daily basis, then this would mean that at the end of each day (including the reporting date) the amounts in the bank accounts involved in the cash management arrangement will be physically settled and aggregated in one bank account. Other than the single balance in the main account, all other bank balances will be zero, making the IAS 32 balance sheet offsetting considerations irrelevant (i.e. the position at the end of each day will approximate that described under Approach 1 in 7.10.115.10 because there will be only one account between the B group and C with a non-zero balance).

7.10.130.70   However, if the sweep does not take place on a daily basis, then B assesses whether the frequency of sweeping supports the intention to settle net requirement in paragraph 42(b) of IAS 32. This requires an evaluation of whether balances outstanding at the reporting date will be settled through netting at the next sweep date (or by net settlement before then – e.g. if B intends its group members to make transfers from accounts that are in credit to those that are overdrawn) or whether they will be settled through normal day-to-day business before the next sweep.

7.10.130.80   In the case in 7.10.130.70, if C has a current legally enforceable right to set off, then it will have to make a similar analysis. However, it will usually be difficult for C to demonstrate that it intends to settle net in the normal course of business because entities in the B group may choose to withdraw funds from accounts that are in credit or may pay down overdrawn balances using funds obtained from other sources.

7.10.130.90   If the balances on the accounts are not physically transferred into a single account or otherwise intended to be settled on a net basis, then an entity would fail the intention to settle net requirement, because the arrangement does not result in the balances being settled net. Consequently, net balance sheet presentation would not be allowed.

7.10.130.100   The IFRS Interpretations Committee discussed a scenario that is similar to that in 7.10.130.70 and noted that a group needs to assess whether, at the reporting date, there is an intention to settle its subsidiaries' bank account balances on a net basis or whether the intention is for its subsidiaries to use those individual bank account balances for other purposes before the next net settlement date.

7.10.130.110   The Committee observed that in the scenario that it considered, the group expects cash movements to take place on individual bank accounts before the next net settlement date because the group expects its subsidiaries to use those bank accounts in their normal course of business. Consequently, the Committee noted that, to the extent to which the group did not expect to settle its subsidiaries' period-end account balances on a net basis, it would not be appropriate for the group to assert that it had the intention to settle the entire period-end balances on a net basis at the reporting date. This is because presenting these balances net would not appropriately reflect the amounts and timings of the expected future cash flows, taking into account the group's and its subsidiaries' normal business practices.

7.10.130.120   However, the Committee also observed that in other cash pooling arrangements a group's expectations regarding how subsidiaries will use their bank accounts before the next net settlement date may be different. Consequently, it was noted that, in those circumstances, the group would be required to apply judgement in determining whether there was an intention to settle on a net basis at the reporting date. [*IU 03-16*]

7.10.130.130   If an entity will settle amounts in a manner such that the outcome is, in effect, equivalent to net settlement, then it meets the intention criterion in IAS 32. A gross settlement system is equivalent to net settlement if, and only if, it has features that:
- eliminate or result in insignificant credit and liquidity risk; and
- will process receivables and payables in a single settlement process or cycle. [*IAS 32.AG38F*]

7.10.130.140   IAS 32 identifies an example of a gross settlement system that would be equivalent to net settlement. It has all of the following features.
a. Financial assets and financial liabilities are submitted for processing at the same point in time.
b. The parties are committed to fulfilling the settlement obligation once the financial assets and financial liabilities are submitted for processing.

c. Once they have been submitted, there is no potential for the cash flows arising from the financial assets and financial liabilities to change (unless processing fails – see (d)).
d. Assets and liabilities that are collateralised with securities are settled on a system in which the processing of the receivable or payable fails if the transfer of the related securities fails (and vice versa).
e. Failed transactions are re-entered for processing until they are settled.
f. The same settlement institution carries out the settlement.
g. There is an intra-day credit facility that:
    –   will provide sufficient overdraft amounts to each party at the settlement date; and
    –   is virtually certain to be honoured if it is called on. [*IAS 32.AG38F*]

7.10.140   *Applying the offsetting requirements*

7.10.140.10   The offsetting requirements may apply to instruments such as receivables and payables with the same counterparty if a legal right to set off is agreed to between the parties. Generally, it would not be appropriate to offset assets and liabilities that the entity has with different counterparties. To qualify for offsetting, there would have to be an agreement in place between all parties, which would be unusual. Also, it may be difficult in practice to demonstrate the intention to settle net or simultaneously with all parties to the arrangement. Consequently, it is unlikely that either of the conditions for offsetting will be met. [*IAS 32.45*]

7.10.140.20   Individual instruments that, when viewed together, would form a synthetic instrument do not usually qualify for offsetting. For example, in the case of a fixed rate liability and a fixed-to-floating interest rate swap that together form a synthetic floating rate liability, there is generally no legal right to set off the swap's cash flows and the interest payments on the liability. Also, the settlement of the liability and the realisation of the swap may not occur simultaneously. [*IAS 32.49(a)*]

7.10.140.30   When a transfer of financial assets does not qualify for derecognition (see 7.6.60), the associated liability and the corresponding assets are not offset. [*IAS 32.42*]

7.10.140.40   In addition, offsetting is usually not appropriate when:
●   financial assets are set aside in a trust by a debtor for the purpose of discharging an obligation without those assets having been accepted by the creditor in settlement of the obligation; or
●   an entity incurs an obligation as a result of certain loss events, which it expects to recover through a claim made under an insurance contract. [*IAS 32.49(d)–(e)*]

7.10.140.50   An entity may be required to provide (receive) cash or non-cash collateral in connection with certain types of transactions. The offsetting requirements do not give special consideration to items referred to as 'collateral'. Accordingly, collateral that is represented by a recognised financial instrument is presented net against the related financial asset or financial liability if, and only if, it meets the offsetting criteria in IAS 32. If an entity can be required to return or receive back collateral, then it does not currently have a legally enforceable right to set off in all of the following circumstances:
●   in the normal course of business;
●   in the event of default; and
●   on the insolvency or bankruptcy of one of the counterparties. [*IAS 32.49(c), BC103*]

7.10.140.60   Generally, the offsetting criteria in IAS 32 (see 7.10.110.10) are not satisfied, and therefore offsetting is not appropriate, when an entity pledges financial or other assets as collateral for recourse or non-recourse financial liabilities. In addition, in arrangements involving collateral, the offsetting criteria are not satisfied and presenting the respective financial asset and financial liability net is not permissible when the legal right to set off is enforceable only in the case of default. [*IAS 32.42(a), AG38B*]

7.10.140.70 Derivative assets and liabilities are usually presented on a gross basis as separate line items in the statement of financial position, because they do not generally meet the offsetting criteria. This is because they are usually entered into with different counterparties, and therefore there is no right to set off the recognised amounts. Even if they are entered into with (or novated to) the same counterparty, derivative assets and liabilities often have different settlement dates or cash flow structures. Therefore, it is normally difficult to identify matching cash flows that could be offset at a specific date, even if this was allowed by the contractual relationships. In addition, a legal right to set off may often be conditional on a specified future event, in which case there is no current legally enforceable right to set off.

EXAMPLE 4A – OFFSETTING – LEGAL ENFORCEABILITY AND NET SETTLEMENT IN SPECIFIC CIRCUMSTANCES ONLY

7.10.140.80 Bank F enters into a master netting arrangement with Counterparty G because they undertake a number of financial instruments transactions together. The agreement provides for a single net settlement of all financial instruments covered by the agreement in the event of default on any one contract.

7.10.140.90 The master netting arrangement creates a right to set off that becomes enforceable and affects the realisation or settlement of individual financial assets and financial liabilities only following a specified event of default. Therefore, it does not provide a basis for offsetting. A master netting arrangement does not provide a basis for offsetting unless both of the offsetting criteria are met – i.e. the entity has a current legally enforceable right and an intention to settle net or simultaneously. [*IAS 32.50*]

EXAMPLE 4B – OFFSETTING – LEGAL ENFORCEABILITY AND NET SETTLEMENT IN ALL CIRCUMSTANCES – PASSAGE OF TIME OR UNCERTAINTIES IN AMOUNTS DO NOT PRECLUDE OFFSETTING

7.10.140.100 Bank H is a member of a clearing house. Transactions entered into with other members of the clearing house are novated such that the clearing house is the legal counterparty to H for all such transactions. The contractual terms are as follows:

- cash margins are payable or receivable between H and the clearing house based on the fair value of outstanding transactions;
- the payment (receipt) of a cash margin does not itself extinguish or settle any obligation (right) to make (receive) future cash flows under the outstanding transactions; rather, it creates a distinct receivable (payable) that may be set off against those obligations (rights) when they mature (see 7.6.490);
- only one net cash payment or receipt, which covers final settlement of maturing transactions, periodic payments on existing transactions and net payment or receipt of cash margin, occurs each day between H and the clearing house; and

- in the event of default, insolvency or bankruptcy of any of the parties in the arrangement, the outstanding amounts will be set off.

7.10.140.110   In our view, the cash flows arising from each daily settlement are, in effect, net settlements. Accordingly, offsetting is appropriate in these circumstances. This is because, despite uncertainties about the amounts and timing, payments that will arise in the future will be set off. The passage of time or uncertainties in amounts to be paid will not preclude H from currently having a legally enforceable right to set off. Therefore, because H has the current legally enforceable right to set off and the intention to settle net or simultaneously, it satisfies the offsetting criteria in IAS 32. [*IAS 32.42, 48*]

7.10.150   Hedging

7.10.160   *Gains and losses*

7.10.160.10   IFRS 9 does not specify which line items in profit or loss the gains and losses related to a hedging transaction (including those reclassified from the cash flow hedge reserve) should be presented in, except for hedges of groups of items (see 7.10.170).

7.10.160.20   However, an entity is required to disclose which line items in profit or loss:
- have been affected because of a reclassification from a cash flow hedge reserve or foreign currency translation reserve; and
- include hedge ineffectiveness (see 7.10.410). [*IFRS 7.24C*]

7.10.160.30   For some types of fair value hedges, the objective of the hedge is not primarily to offset the fair value changes of the hedged item but instead to transform the cash flows of the hedged item. For example, an entity may be hedging the fair value interest rate risk of a fixed rate debt instrument using an interest rate swap. The entity's hedge objective is to transform the fixed interest cash flows into floating interest cash flows. This objective is reflected in the accounting for the hedging relationship by accruing the net interest accrual on the interest rate swap into profit or loss, generally through interest income or expense. The net interest accrual may be presented in the line item for interest revenue calculated using the effective interest method if the instrument is designated as a hedging instrument with respect to a financial asset for which interest income is included in that line item (see 7.10.60.20 and 65.60). [*IFRS 9.B6.6.16*]

7.10.167   *Costs of hedging*

7.10.167.10   Although IFRS 9 does not require the costs of hedging to be separately presented in profit or loss, costs of hedging still need to be separately accounted for when they are excluded from the hedging instrument (see 7.9.690). [*IFRS 7.24E*]

7.10.167.20   When an entity hedges a sale, whether in a forecast transaction or a firm commitment, the costs of hedging related to that sale are reclassified to profit or loss as part of the cost related to that sale in the same period as the revenue from the hedged sale is recognised. It appears that when these costs of hedging are reclassified to profit or loss, an entity may choose an accounting policy, to be applied consistently, to present them:

- as revenue – because they relate to a hedge of revenue. However, they should not be presented or disclosed as revenue from contracts with customers in the scope of IFRS 15 because they are not (see 4.1.15); or
- in another appropriate line item of income or expense – because the term 'cost related to that sale' could be interpreted as precluding presentation as revenue. [*IFRS 9.B6.5.29(a)*]

7.10.170 *Hedged groups*

7.10.170.10   For assets and liabilities that are hedged together as a group in a fair value hedge, the gain or loss in the statement of financial position on the individual assets and liabilities is recognised as an adjustment to the respective individual items comprising the group. [*IFRS 9.6.6.5*]

7.10.170.20   For cash flow hedges or fair value hedges of a group of items that does not have any offsetting risk positions, the hedging instrument gains or losses (reclassified to profit or loss for cash flow hedges) are apportioned to the line items in profit or loss that are affected by the hedged items on a systematic and rational basis. The net gains or losses arising from a single hedging instrument are not grossed up. [*IFRS 9.B6.6.14*]

7.10.170.30   If a group of items in a fair value or cash flow hedge has offsetting risk positions affecting different line items in profit or loss, then any hedging instrument gains or losses in profit or loss (reclassified to profit or loss for cash flow hedges) are presented in a separate line from those affected by the hedged items. Therefore, in profit or loss, the amount in the line item that relates to the hedged item itself – e.g. revenue or cost of sales – remains unaffected. The requirement to present the hedging instrument's net gains and losses in a separate line item avoids grossing up a single hedging instrument's net gains or losses into offsetting gross amounts and recognising them in different line items in profit or loss. [*IFRS 9.6.6.4, B6.6.15*]

7.10.170.40   In the case of a hedge of a net position – e.g. a net position of a fixed rate asset and a fixed rate liability – the net interest accrual is required to be presented in a separate line item in profit or loss. This is to avoid grossing up a single instrument's net gains or losses into offsetting gross amounts and recognising them in different line items – e.g. this avoids grossing up net interest receipt on a single interest rate swap into gross interest revenue and gross interest expense. [*IFRS 9.B6.6.16*]

7.10.180 SIGNIFICANCE OF FINANCIAL INSTRUMENTS FOR FINANCIAL POSITION AND PERFORMANCE

7.10.180.10   An entity provides sufficient disclosures to enable users of the financial statements to evaluate the significance of financial instruments to the entity's financial position and performance. To help satisfy this principle, IFRS 7 lists specific disclosure requirements (see 7.10.190–470). [*IFRS 7.7*]

7.10.190 Statement of financial position

7.10.200 *Carrying amount#*

7.10.200.10   The carrying amounts of the following categories of financial assets and financial liabilities are disclosed, either in the statement of financial position or in the notes:
- financial assets measured at FVTPL (see 7.10.200.20);
- financial assets measured at amortised cost;

- financial assets measured at FVOCI (see 7.10.200.30);
- financial liabilities measured at FVTPL (see 7.10.200.40); and
- financial liabilities measured at amortised cost. [*IFRS 7.8*]

7.10.200.20   The carrying amounts of financial assets that are mandatorily measured at FVTPL (see 7.4.50) are disclosed separately from the carrying amounts of those designated as such on initial recognition (or designated subsequently, when an entity uses a credit derivative that is measured at FVTPL to manage the credit exposure arising from such financial assets – see 7.9.110). IFRS 7 does not specifically require separate disclosures of the carrying amounts of financial assets meeting the definition of held for trading and the carrying amounts of other financial assets mandatorily measured at FVTPL. However, an entity may consider additional disclosure if it helps users to evaluate the significance of financial instruments for the entity's financial position and performance. [*IFRS 7.1, 7–8(a), B3, IG5–IG6*]

7.10.200.30   The carrying amounts of financial assets mandatorily measured at FVOCI (see 7.4.40) are disclosed separately from the carrying amounts of investments in equity instruments designated as such on initial recognition (see 7.4.60). [*IFRS 7.8(h)*]

7.10.200.40   The carrying amounts of financial liabilities measured at FVTPL by virtue of meeting the definition of held for trading (see 7.5.30) are disclosed separately from the carrying amounts of those designated as such on initial recognition (or designated subsequently, when an entity uses a credit derivative that is measured at FVTPL to manage the credit exposure arising from such liabilities – see 7.9.110). [*IFRS 7.8(e)*]

7.10.205   **FORTHCOMING REQUIREMENTS**

7.10.205.10 Under consequential amendments to IFRS 7 introduced by IFRS 17, if an entity chooses the accounting policy for its treasury shares discussed in 7.3.515 or the accounting policy for its financial liabilities discussed in 7.6.365, then it discloses the carrying amounts of the resulting financial assets separately. [*IFRS 7.8(a), 9.3.3.5, IAS 32.33A*]

7.10.210   *Financial assets or financial liabilities designated as at FVTPL*

7.10.210.10   As noted in 7.4.50 and 7.5.40, entities may designate financial assets and financial liabilities into the financial assets or financial liabilities at FVTPL category.

7.10.210.20   If an entity designates a contract that meets the own-use scope exception as at FVTPL (see 7.1.200.40), then the contract is generally subject to the IFRS 7 disclosure requirements, except for those in 7.10.210.30–80 that apply to a financial instrument designated as at FVTPL under different requirements of IFRS 9.

7.10.210.30   If an entity has designated as at FVTPL a financial asset that would otherwise be measured at FVOCI or amortised cost, then it discloses:
- the maximum exposure to credit risk of that financial asset at the reporting date;
- the amount by which this risk is mitigated by credit derivatives or similar instruments;
- the amount of change in the fair value of the financial asset that is attributable to changes in credit risk, both for the period and cumulatively; and

- the amount of change in the fair value of any related credit derivative or similar instrument, both for the period and cumulatively since the financial asset was designated. [*IFRS 7.9*]

7.10.210.40   If the entity has designated a financial liability as at FVTPL (see 7.5.40) and is required to present all changes in the fair value of that liability in profit or loss – i.e. including the effects of changes in credit risk (see 7.7.190) – then it discloses:
- the amount of change in the fair value of the financial liability that is attributable to changes in credit risk, both for the period and cumulatively; and
- the difference between the carrying amount of the financial liability and the amount that the entity will be contractually required to pay at maturity. [*IFRS 7.10A*]

7.10.210.50   For financial liabilities designated as at FVTPL for which an entity is required to present the effects of changes in that liability's credit risk in OCI, an entity is required to disclose:
- the amount of change, cumulatively, in the fair value of the financial liability that is attributable to changes in credit risk;
- the difference between the carrying amount of the financial liability and the amount that the entity will be contractually required to pay at maturity;
- any transfers of the cumulative gain or loss within equity during the period, including the reason for the transfers; and
- the amount presented in OCI that was realised on the derecognition of liabilities during the period. [*IFRS 7.10*]

7.10.210.60   In our view, the amount that the entity is 'contractually required to pay at maturity' should be the undiscounted amount payable at maturity. Furthermore, when the amount payable at maturity is not fixed – e.g. in the case of a liability containing an embedded derivative that modifies the principal amount payable at maturity – the amount disclosed should be based on conditions existing at the reporting date.

7.10.210.70   The change in the instrument's fair value attributable to changes in credit risk is determined either:
1. as the amount of the change in its fair value not attributable to changes in market conditions; or
2. using an alternative method that represents more faithfully the amount of the change in fair value attributable to credit risk (see 7.7.230). [*IFRS 7.9–10A, 9.B5.7.13–B5.7.20*]

7.10.210.80   In the case of both a financial asset and a financial liability designated as at FVTPL, when the change in the instrument's fair value attributable to changes in credit risk is determined as set out in 7.10.210.70, an entity discloses:
- a detailed description of the methods used to determine the change in fair value attributable to changes in credit risk, including an explanation of why the method is appropriate;
- if the entity does not believe that the information provided to comply with the standard faithfully represents the change in the instrument's fair value attributable to credit risk, then the reasons for reaching this conclusion and the factors that the entity considers relevant;
- a detailed description of the methodologies to determine whether presenting the effects of changes in a liability's credit risk in OCI would create or enlarge an accounting mismatch in profit or loss; and
- the economic relationship described in 7.7.200.10, when an entity is required to present the effects of changes in a liability's credit risk in profit or loss. [*IFRS 7.9(c), 10(a), 10A(a), 11*]

7.10.220   *Credit exposures designated as at FVTPL*

7.10.220.10   An entity is permitted to designate certain credit exposures as at FVTPL, if it uses credit derivatives that are measured at FVTPL to manage the credit risk of all, or a part of, such credit exposures (see 7.9.130). If an entity so designates a financial instrument, then that financial instrument is subject to the disclosure requirements in 7.10.210.30 and 80. [*IFRS 7.9, 11*]

7.10.220.20   In addition, the following disclosure requirements also apply:
- a reconciliation of each of the nominal amount and the fair value at the beginning and end of the period of the credit derivatives that have been used to manage the credit risk;
- the gain or loss recognised in profit or loss on designation of a financial instrument (or a proportion of it) as measured at FVTPL; and
- if the designation is discontinued, the financial instrument's fair value that has become its new carrying amount and the related nominal or principal amount (except for providing comparative information in accordance with IAS 1, an entity does not need to continue this disclosure in subsequent periods). [*IFRS 7.24G*]

7.10.230   *Equity instruments elected to be measured at FVOCI*

7.10.230.10   An entity can elect to present changes in the fair value of an investment in certain equity instruments in OCI (see 7.4.420).

7.10.230.20   If an entity has made such an election, then it discloses:
- which investments in equity instruments have been so designated;
- the reasons for the designation;
- the fair value of each investment at the reporting date;
- dividends recognised during the period, separately for investments derecognised during the reporting period and those held at the reporting date; and
- any transfers of the cumulative gain or loss within equity during the period and the reason for those transfers. [*IFRS 7.11A*]

7.10.230.25   When disclosing which investments in equity instruments have been designated as at FVOCI, it appears that an entity should apply judgement in determining what disclosures would provide the most useful information for financial statement users. We believe that in most cases, disclosing the names of individual investees would be appropriate – e.g. if an entity has a small number of individually significant investments, particularly if this disclosure enables users to access additional information about those investees from other sources. However, in some cases disclosure at a higher level of aggregation and disclosures other than the names of investees may provide more useful information. For example, if an entity has a large number of individually insignificant investments in a few industries, then disclosure by industry may be appropriate. Similarly, if an entity holds investments for which no public information is available, then disclosure about the nature and purpose of those investments may be relevant.

7.10.230.30   If an entity derecognised investments in equity instruments measured at FVOCI during the reporting period, then it discloses:
- the reasons for disposing of the investments;

- the fair value of the investments at the date of derecognition; and
- the cumulative gain or loss on disposal. [*IFRS 7.11B*]

7.10.240   **Reclassifications**

7.10.240.10   If an entity has reclassified financial assets (see 7.4.450), then the following disclosure requirements apply. [*IFRS 7.12B–12D*]

TYPE OF RECLASSIFICATION	PERIODS DURING WHICH DISCLOSURES ARE REQUIRED	DISCLOSURES REQUIRED
All reclassifications in the current or previous reporting period	Period of reclassification and the periods following reclassification	• Date of reclassification • Detailed explanation of the change in business model and a qualitative description of its effect on the entity's financial statements • Amount reclassified into and out of each category
Reclassifications from FVTPL to amortised cost or FVOCI	Each reporting period following reclassification until derecognition	• Effective interest rate determined on the date of reclassification • Interest revenue recognised
Reclassifications from FVOCI to amortised cost, or from FVTPL to amortised cost or FVOCI	Current reporting period	• Fair value of the financial assets at the reporting date • Fair value gain or loss that would have been recognised in profit or loss or OCI during the reporting period if the financial assets had not been reclassified

7.10.250   **Offsetting disclosures**

7.10.250.10   An entity discloses information to enable users of its financial statements to evaluate the effect or potential effect of netting arrangements on its financial position. The disclosures are required for financial assets and financial liabilities that are:
- offset in the statement of financial position in accordance with IAS 32 (see 7.10.110.10); and
- subject to an enforceable master netting arrangement or similar agreement that covers similar financial instruments and transactions, irrespective of whether the financial assets and financial liabilities meet the offsetting criteria in IAS 32 (see 7.10.140.80–90). [*IFRS 7.13A–13B, B40*]

7.10.250.20   To apply the disclosure requirements, an entity follows these steps:
- identify which instruments are in the scope;
- determine how to (dis)aggregate the quantitative disclosures;
- calculate the amounts to be disclosed;
- describe the types and nature of rights to set off that do not meet the offsetting criteria in IAS 32; and
- determine whether additional disclosures are required.

7.10.250.30   Neither IAS 32 nor IFRS 7 defines 'master netting arrangements or similar agreements'. Therefore, an entity may need to use judgement in identifying them. IAS 32 notes the following as characteristics of master netting arrangements:

- they provide for net settlement of financial instruments covered by the agreement in the event of default on, or termination of, any contact;
- they provide protection against losses when a counterparty is unable to meet its obligations; and
- they commonly create a right to set off that may be enforced only following a specified event of default, or in other circumstances that are not expected to arise in the normal course of business. [*IAS 32.50*]

7.10.250.40   Financial assets and financial liabilities subject to similar agreements that cover similar financial instruments and transactions are in the scope of the disclosure requirements of IFRS 7. 'Similar agreements' and 'similar financial instruments and transactions' are explained in IFRS 7 as follows.

TERM	INCLUDES
Similar agreements	• Derivative clearing agreements • Global master repurchase agreements • Global master securities lending agreements • Any related rights to financial collateral
Similar financial instruments and transactions	• Derivatives • (Reverse) Sale-and-repurchase agreements • Securities borrowing and lending agreements

7.10.250.50   Financial instruments that are outside the scope of the disclosure requirements – unless they are offset in the statement of financial position in accordance with IAS 32 – include:

- loans and customer deposits at the same institution; and
- instruments subject only to a collateral agreement. [*IFRS 7.B41*]

7.10.250.60   An entity discloses the following quantitative information separately for recognised financial assets and recognised financial liabilities in a tabular format unless another format is more appropriate:

a. the gross amounts;
b. the amounts offset in accordance with the offsetting criteria in IAS 32;
c. the net amounts presented in the statement of financial position – i.e. the difference between (a) and (b). These amounts are reconciled to the line item amounts presented in the statement of financial position;
d. the amounts subject to enforceable master netting arrangements or similar agreements that do not meet the offsetting criteria in IAS 32, including:
   - amounts related to recognised financial assets and financial liabilities that do not meet the offsetting criteria in IAS 32; and
   - amounts related to financial collateral; and
e. the net amounts after deducting the amounts in (d) from those in (c). [*IFRS 7.13C*]

7.10.250.70 The disclosure requirements in 7.10.250.60 may be grouped by type of financial instrument or transaction. Alternatively, an entity may present disclosures (a)–(c) in 7.10.250.60 by type of financial instrument, and disclosures (c)–(e) by counterparty. [*IFRS 7.B51–B52*]

7.10.250.80 To satisfy the minimum disclosure requirements described in 7.10.250.60, an entity calculates the amounts as follows. [*IFRS 7.13A, 13C, B43–B49*]

ITEM (SEE 7.10.250.60)	WHAT IT INCLUDES
a. **Gross amounts**	The carrying amounts of recognised financial assets and financial liabilities that are in the scope of the disclosure requirements (see 7.10.250.10). However, the gross amounts disclosed exclude any amounts recognised as a result of a right to financial collateral that does not meet the offsetting criteria in IAS 32. Such collateral is included under (d) below.
b. **Amounts offset**	The amounts included in (a) that have been offset in the statement of financial position in accordance with IAS 32.
c. **Net amounts presented in the statement of financial position**	The difference between (a) and (b) above.
d. **Amounts subject to enforceable master netting or similar agreements that are not included in (b)**	• For recognised assets and liabilities that do not meet the offsetting criteria in IAS 32, the amount disclosed is the carrying amount to which the right to set off applies. • For financial collateral received or pledged that is not offset in the statement of financial position in accordance with IAS 32, the amount disclosed is the fair value of the collateral actually pledged or received. However, in each case the entity limits the amounts disclosed to eliminate the effect of over-collateralisation. This adjustment is calculated at the level of the financial asset or the financial liability (or group of financial assets/liabilities) to which the right to collateral relates.
e. **Net amounts**	The difference between (c) and (d) above.

7.10.250.90 An entity discloses recognised financial assets and financial liabilities based on their carrying amounts. Different measurement requirements may apply to the various financial assets or financial liabilities within an individual line item in the statement of financial position. Therefore, offsetting may result in a presentation that includes measurement differences. For example, within a line item, a financial asset that is measured at fair value may be offset against a liability that is measured at amortised cost. An entity is required to describe any such measurement differences. [*IFRS 7.B42*]

7.10.250.100 An entity is required to reconcile the disclosed net amounts included in the statement of financial position, (c) in 7.10.250.60, to the individual line item amounts presented in the statement of financial position. The scope of the disclosures does not extend to all financial assets and financial liabilities; it is possible that only some of the instruments within a particular line item might be captured, while others are not. Therefore, the net amounts disclosed under item (c) in 7.10.250.60 may represent subsets of amounts presented in individual line items. [*IFRS 7.B46*]

7.10.250.110   An entity describes the nature and the types of rights to set off that do not meet the criteria for offsetting in IAS 32. For example, it describes:
- conditional rights;
- the reasons why rights to set off that are not contingent do not meet the offsetting criteria in IAS 32; and
- the terms of the related rights to financial collateral. [*IFRS 7.13E, B50*]

7.10.250.120   The disclosure requirements described in 7.10.250.60 are minimum requirements. An entity supplements them with additional qualitative disclosures if necessary for financial statement users to evaluate the actual or potential effect of netting arrangements on its financial position. When disclosing quantitative information by counterparty, an entity considers qualitative disclosure about the types of counterparties. [*IFRS 7.B52–B53*]

7.10.260   *Collateral*

7.10.260.10   An entity that has pledged financial assets as collateral for liabilities and contingent liabilities discloses:
- the carrying amount of these assets pledged as collateral; and
- the terms and conditions related to the pledge. [*IFRS 7.14*]

7.10.260.20   When an entity has accepted collateral that it is entitled to sell or repledge in the absence of default by the owner, it discloses:
- the fair value of the collateral held (financial and non-financial assets);
- the fair value of such collateral sold or repledged, and whether the entity has an obligation to return it; and
- any terms and conditions associated with its use of this collateral. [*IFRS 7.15*]

7.10.270   *Loss allowance for ECLs*

7.10.270.10   An entity recognises a loss allowance for ECLs in the statement of financial position if it relates to a financial asset measured at amortised cost, a lease receivable or a contract asset. The amortised cost of the assets in the statement of financial position is stated net of the loss allowance. Neither IFRS 9 nor IFRS 7 contains any specific requirements on the presentation of the loss allowance on the face of the statement of financial position and IAS 1 does not list the loss allowance as an amount that is required to be presented as a separate line item in the statement of financial position. [*IFRS 9.5.5.1, A, IAS 1.54*]

7.10.270.20   No loss allowance is recognised in the statement of financial position in respect of debt instruments that are measured at FVOCI, because the carrying amount of these assets is their fair value. However, an entity discloses the loss allowance in the notes to the financial statements. [*IFRS 7.16A, 9.5.5.2*]

7.10.270.30   An entity recognises the loss allowance for ECLs as a provision if they relate to a loan commitment or a financial guarantee contract. However, if a financial instrument includes both a drawn component (i.e. a financial asset) and an undrawn loan commitment component, and the entity cannot identify the ECLs on the loan commitment component separately from those on the financial asset component (i.e. the drawn amount), then it recognises the ECLs on the undrawn balance of the loan commitment together with the ECLs on the drawn amount. In doing so, to the extent that the combined amount of ECLs exceeds the gross carrying amount of the financial asset, the remaining balance is presented as a provision. [*IFRS 7.B8E, BC48V, 9.A*]

7.10.270.40   The acquirer in a business combination does not recognise a separate valuation allowance as at the date of acquisition for assets acquired in a business combination that are measured at their acquisition date fair values; this is because the uncertainty about future cash flows is included in the fair value measurement. It appears that an asset acquired in a business combination would attract a loss allowance at the first reporting date after it is recognised (see 2.6.610.10 and 7.8.20.50). [*IFRS 3.B41*]

7.10.280   *Reconciliations of amounts arising from ECLs*

7.10.280.10   An entity is required to provide, by class of financial instrument, reconciliations from the opening balance to the closing balance of the impairment loss allowance. The reconciliation is given separately for loss allowances against assets and for provisions (unless they are presented together – see 7.10.270.30), and shows the changes during the period for:
- instruments for which 12-month ECLs are measured;
- instruments for which lifetime ECLs are measured, separately for:
  - financial instruments that are not credit-impaired;
  - financial assets that are credit-impaired at the reporting date, but are not POCI assets; and
  - trade receivables, contract assets or lease receivables for which the loss allowances are always measured as lifetime ECLs; and
- POCI assets. [*IFRS 7.35A, 35H, B8E*]

7.10.280.20   An entity also provides a narrative explanation of the changes in the loss allowances disclosed in the reconciliation. [*IFRS 7.B8D*]

7.10.280.30   The reconciliation in 7.10.280.10 is supplemented by an explanation of how significant changes in the respective gross carrying amounts of financial instruments during the period contributed to the changes in the loss allowances. This explanation has to include relevant qualitative and quantitative information. Examples of such changes may include:
- originations or acquisitions of financial instruments;
- modifications of contractual cash flows that do not result in derecognition (see 7.7.340);
- derecognitions (including write-offs); and
- movements between the 12-month and lifetime ECLs measurement categories (and vice versa). [*IFRS 7.35I*]

7.10.280.40   For the purposes of the disclosure requirements in 7.10.280.10–30, it appears that the amount of the loss allowance for financial guarantee contracts and loan commitments should be the amount of the loss allowance for ECLs determined in accordance with IFRS 9 (see chapter 7.8), even if the instrument is actually measured at a higher amount equal to its initial carrying amount less the cumulative amount of income recognised in accordance with IFRS 15 (see 7.1.120.10 and 250.110). Therefore, we believe that the amount disclosed may not necessarily be the same as the carrying amount of these instruments. [*IFRS 7.35A, 35H, 35I*]

7.10.290   *Compound financial instruments with multiple embedded derivatives*

7.10.290.10   An entity may issue a compound financial instrument that contains multiple embedded derivative features whose values are interdependent. In this case, it discloses the existence of these features. For example, a callable convertible debt instrument has more than one embedded derivative feature; the value of the call option depends on both interest rates and equity prices. The interdependency between interest rates and equity prices is disclosed. [*IFRS 7.17, BC29–BC31*]

7.10.300   *Defaults and breaches*

7.10.300.10   If the entity has defaulted during the period on the principal, interest, sinking fund or redemption provisions of a loan payable – i.e. a financial liability, other than a short-term trade payable on normal credit terms – recognised in the statement of financial position, then it discloses:
- details of the default or breach;
- the amount recognised at the reporting date in respect of the loan payable on which the default or breach occurred; and
- with respect to the above amounts, whether the default or breach was remedied or the terms of the loan payable renegotiated before the financial statements were authorised for issue. [*IFRS 7.18*]

7.10.300.20   An entity also discloses the items listed in 7.10.300.10 if during the period there were other breaches of loan agreement terms and those breaches were not remedied or the terms were not renegotiated before the reporting date such that the lender could demand accelerated repayment. [*IFRS 7.19*]

7.10.310   *Embedded derivatives*

7.10.310.10   There is no specific guidance on the presentation of embedded derivatives and the related host contracts (see 7.2.380). [*IFRS 9.4.3.3–4.3.4*]

7.10.310.20   In our view, when an embedded derivative is not required to be accounted for separately (see 7.2.110), it should be presented in the same line item as the host contract.

7.10.310.30   When an embedded derivative is accounted for separately, an issue arises about whether it should be:
- included in the same line item as the host contract, on the basis that the two instruments are subject to the same contract; or
- presented separately, together with other derivative instruments.

7.10.310.40   IFRS does not address whether an embedded derivative should be presented separately in the statement of financial position. Therefore, the general presentation rules in IAS 1 and IAS 32 apply (see chapter 3.1). In our view, if the host contract is a financial liability and the offsetting criteria are met for the host and the embedded derivative, then a separable embedded derivative and the host contract should be presented on a net basis (see 7.10.110). [*IFRS 9.4.3.4*]

7.10.315   *Reverse factoring arrangements*

7.10.315.10   In addition to appropriate presentation and disaggregation of relevant balances, an entity that is the customer in a reverse factoring arrangement (see 7.10.35) is required to disclose information about those arrangements that is relevant to an understanding of its financial position and performance. This disclosure might include an explanation of the nature of the arrangements and how they are reflected in the financial statements. Relevant IFRS disclosure requirements include:

- disclosure of significant accounting policies; and
- disclosure of significant judgements that management has made in the process of applying the accounting policies and that have the most significant effect on the amounts recognised in the financial statements. [*IAS 1.117–122*]

7.10.315.20   For a further discussion of reverse factoring, see 2.3.75, 7.6.465, 7.10.35 and 655.

7.10.320   Statement of profit or loss and OCI

7.10.330   *Items of income, expense, gains or losses*

7.10.330.10   Net gains or losses on the following are disclosed either in the statement of profit or loss and OCI or in the notes to the financial statements:

- financial assets or financial liabilities measured at FVTPL, separately for:
  - those that are designated as such on initial recognition or subsequently, when an entity uses a credit derivative that is measured at FVTPL to manage the credit exposure arising from such financial instruments – with gains and losses on financial liabilities that are recognised in OCI shown separately from those recognised in profit or loss; and
  - those mandatorily measured at FVTPL;
- financial liabilities measured at amortised cost;
- investments in equity instruments irrevocably elected to be measured at FVOCI; and
- financial assets mandatorily measured at FVOCI – with gains and losses recognised during the period in OCI shown separately from those reclassified to profit or loss on derecognition. [*IFRS 7.20(a)*]

7.10.330.20   An entity discloses within its accounting policies whether it has separated interest income and expense on items measured at FVTPL (see 7.10.60.80 and 370.10). [*IFRS 7.B5(e)*]

7.10.330.30   Total interest revenue calculated using the effective interest method is required to be separately presented in profit or loss (see 7.10.60.10). Total interest revenue and total interest expense for financial assets measured at amortised cost and those mandatorily measured at FVOCI (showing these amounts separately) or financial liabilities that are not measured at FVTPL (calculated under the effective interest method) are disclosed either in profit or loss or in the notes to the financial statements. The total interest expense disclosed forms part of finance costs, which are required by paragraph 82(b) of IAS 1 to be presented separately in profit or loss. [*IFRS 7.20(b), IG13*]

7.10.330.40   If interest income or expense includes both amounts from instruments measured at FVTPL and amounts from instruments not measured at FVTPL, then an entity is required to disclose total interest income and total interest expense for financial assets and financial liabilities that are not measured at FVTPL. In doing so, an entity is required to show separately total interest revenue on financial assets that are measured at amortised cost and total interest revenue on financial assets mandatorily measured at FVOCI. [*IFRS 7.20(b)*]

7.10.330.50   An entity is required to disclose an analysis of the gain or loss (showing gains and losses separately) recognised in profit or loss arising from the derecognition of financial assets measured at amortised cost, including disclosure of the reasons for the derecognition. [*IFRS 7.20A*]

7.10.340   *Fee income and expense*

7.10.340.10   An entity discloses fee income and expense arising from financial assets and financial liabilities that are not measured at FVTPL, and from trust or other fiduciary activities. The amounts disclosed exclude amounts included in calculating the effective interest rate. [*IFRS 7.20(c)*]

7.10.350   *Derecognition*

7.10.350.10   If the terms of a financial liability are modified substantially, resulting in an extinguishment of the old financial liability, then the old liability is derecognised and the restructured financial instrument is treated as a new financial liability (see 7.6.370). In our view, any gains or losses arising as a result of the derecognition of the old financial liability (including any unamortised discount or premium) should be presented as a separate line item within the disclosure of finance income or expense, respectively.

7.10.360   **Other disclosures**

7.10.370   *Accounting policies*

7.10.370.10   The summary of accounting policies includes disclosure of the measurement basis (or bases) used in preparing the financial statements. An entity also discloses any other accounting policies that are relevant to understanding the financial statements. For example, the disclosure may include:
- for financial assets designated as at FVTPL:
  - their nature; and
  - how the entity satisfied the criteria for designation at FVTPL (see 7.4.390);
- for financial liabilities designated as at FVTPL:
  - their nature;
  - the criteria for designating on initial recognition; and
  - how the entity satisfied the conditions for designation of financial liabilities as at FVTPL (see 7.2.160 and 7.5.40);
- whether regular-way transactions are accounted for using trade or settlement date accounting (see 7.2.70); and
- for each category of financial instruments, how the net gains and losses are determined – e.g. for items measured at FVTPL whether the entity includes interest or dividend income (see 7.10.60.80 and 330.20). [*IFRS 7.21, B5, IAS 1.117*]

7.10.380   *Hedge accounting*

7.10.380.10   When an entity adopts IFRS 9, it may choose as its accounting policy to defer the application of the IFRS 9 general hedge accounting model until the standard resulting from the IASB's project on accounting for dynamic risk management (see 7.9.80) is effective. However, the disclosure requirements set out in 7.10.380.20–450 may not be deferred once IFRS 9 is adopted. [*IFRS 7.44Z, 9.BC6.104*]

7.10.380.20   For those risk exposures that an entity hedges, and for which it elects to apply hedge accounting, an entity discloses:

- its risk management strategy and how it applies that strategy to manage risk;
- how its hedging activities may affect the amount, timing and uncertainty of its future cash flows; and
- the effect that hedge accounting has had on its financial position and performance. [*IFRS 7.21A*]

7.10.380.30   An entity presents the required disclosures in a single note or separate section in its financial statements. However, it does not need to duplicate information that is already presented elsewhere – e.g. management commentary or risk report – provided that this information is incorporated by cross-reference and is available to users of the financial statements on the same terms as the financial statements and at the same time. [*IFRS 7.21B*]

7.10.380.40   For those disclosures that require an entity to separate the information disclosed by risk category, each category of risk is determined on the basis of the risk exposures that the entity decides to hedge and for which hedge accounting is applied. This determination is made consistently for all hedge accounting disclosures. [*IFRS 7.21C*]

7.10.380.50   Although an entity is permitted to determine the extent of aggregation or disaggregation of the disclosures, it is required to consider the level of aggregation that it uses for other disclosure requirements in IFRS 7 and IFRS 13. [*IFRS 7.21D*]

7.10.380.60   In our view, when hedge accounting is not applied, either because an entity chooses not to apply hedge accounting or because the criteria for hedge accounting are not met, information should be provided to explain the relationship between the derivatives and the transactions for which there are economic hedges. We believe that this should be done to enable users of the financial statements to understand the extent to which risk is mitigated through the use of the derivatives.

7.10.390   *Risk management strategy*

7.10.390.10   An entity is required to explain its risk management strategy for each risk category of risk exposures that it decides to hedge and for which hedge accounting is applied. The explanation should enable users of financial statements to evaluate, for example:
- how each risk arises;
- how the entity manages each risk, including whether the entity hedges an item in its entirety for all risks or hedges a risk component(s) of an item and why; and
- the extent of risk exposures that the entity manages. [*IFRS 7.22A*]

7.10.390.20   Minimum disclosures to meet the above requirements include a description of:
- the hedging instruments and how they are used to hedge risk exposures;
- how the entity determines the economic relationship between the hedged item and the hedging instrument for the purpose of assessing hedge effectiveness; and
- how the entity establishes the hedge ratio and what the sources of hedge ineffectiveness are. [*IFRS 7.22B*]

7.10.390.30   When an entity designates a specific risk component as a hedged item, it discloses additional qualitative or quantitative information about:
- how it determined the risk component that is designated as the hedged item, including a description of the nature of the relationship between the risk component and the item as a whole; and

- how the risk component relates to the item in its entirety – for example, the designated risk component historically covered on average 80 percent of the changes in fair value of the item as a whole. [*IFRS 7.22C*]

7.10.400   *Amount, timing and uncertainty of future cash flows*

7.10.400.10   An entity discloses, by risk category, quantitative information to enable users of its financial statements to evaluate:
- the terms and conditions of hedging instruments; and
- how they affect the amount, timing and uncertainty of the entity's future cash flows. [*IFRS 7.23A*]

7.10.400.20   The following breakdown is required to meet the above requirement:
- a profile of the timing of the nominal amount of the hedging instrument; and
- if applicable, the average price or rate – e.g. strike or forward prices – of the hedging instrument. [*IFRS 7.23B*]

7.10.400.30   There may be situations in which an entity frequently resets (i.e. discontinues and restarts) hedging relationships because both the hedging instrument and the hedged item frequently change – i.e. the entity uses a dynamic process in which both the exposure and the hedging instruments used to manage that exposure do not remain the same for long. In this case, the entity is exempted from providing the quantitative disclosures described in 7.10.400.10–20. Instead, it discloses:
- information about what the ultimate risk management strategy is in relation to those hedging relationships;
- a description of how it reflects its risk management strategy by using hedge accounting and designating those particular hedging relationships; and
- an indication of how frequently the hedging relationships are discontinued and restarted as part of the entity's process in relation to those hedging relationships. [*IFRS 7.23C*]

7.10.400.40   When the volume of hedging relationships to which the exemption in 7.10.400.30 applies is unrepresentative of normal volumes during the period – i.e. the volume at the reporting date does not reflect the volumes during the period – an entity discloses that fact and the reason that it believes the volumes are unrepresentative. [*IFRS 7.24D*]

7.10.400.50   For each risk category, an entity discloses a description of the sources of hedge ineffectiveness that are expected to affect the hedging relationship during its term. If other sources of hedge ineffectiveness emerge in the hedging relationship, then an entity:
- discloses those sources; and
- explains the resulting hedge ineffectiveness. [*IFRS 7.23D–23E*]

7.10.400.60   For cash flow hedges, an entity discloses a description of any forecast transaction for which hedge accounting was used in the previous period but that is no longer expected to occur. [*IFRS 7.23F*]

7.10.410   *Effects of hedge accounting on financial position and performance*

7.10.420   Hedging instrument

7.10.420.10   An entity discloses, in a tabular format, the following amounts related to items designated as hedging instruments, separately by risk category for each type of hedge:

- the carrying amount of the hedging instruments, separating financial assets from financial liabilities;
- the location of the hedging instrument in the statement of financial position;
- the change in fair value of the hedging instrument used as the basis for recognising hedge ineffectiveness for the period; and
- the nominal amounts (including quantities such as tonnes or cubic metres) of the hedging instruments. [*IFRS 7.24A, IG13C*]

7.10.430   Hedged item

7.10.430.10   An entity discloses, in a tabular format, the following amounts related to hedged items separately by risk category for each type of hedge.

Fair value hedges	• The carrying amount of the hedged item recognised in the statement of financial position, separating assets from liabilities. • The accumulated amount of fair value hedge adjustments on the hedged item included in the above carrying amount. • The location of the hedged item in the statement of financial position. • The change in value of the hedged item used as the basis for recognising hedge ineffectiveness for the period. • The balance of fair value hedge adjustments remaining in the statement of financial position for any hedged items that have ceased to be adjusted for hedging gains and losses. [*IFRS 7.24B(a), IG13D*]
Cash flow hedges and hedges of a net investment in a foreign operation	• The change in value of the hedged item used as the basis for recognising hedge ineffectiveness for the period. • The balances in the cash flow hedge reserve and the foreign currency translation reserve for continuing hedges. • The balances remaining in the cash flow hedge reserve and the foreign currency translation reserve from any hedging relationships for which hedge accounting is no longer applied. [*IFRS 7.24B(b), IG13D*]

7.10.440   Hedge ineffectiveness and hedging gains and losses

7.10.440.10   An entity discloses, in a tabular format, the following amounts separately by risk category for each type of hedge.

Fair value hedges	• Hedge ineffectiveness – i.e. the difference between the hedging gains or losses on the hedging instrument and the hedged item – recognised in profit or loss (or OCI for hedges of an equity instrument for which an entity has elected to present changes in fair value in OCI). • The location of the recognised hedge ineffectiveness in the statement of profit or loss and OCI. [*IFRS 7.24C(a), IG13E*]
Cash flow hedges and hedges of a net investment in a foreign operation	• Hedging gains or losses of the reporting period that were recognised in OCI. • Hedge ineffectiveness recognised in profit or loss. • The location of the recognised hedge ineffectiveness in profit or loss.

Cash flow hedges and hedges of a net investment in a foreign operation (continued)	• The amount reclassified from the cash flow hedge reserve or the foreign currency translation reserve into profit or loss as a reclassification adjustment (see 4.1.250.70), differentiating between:
	  – amounts for which hedge accounting has previously been used but for which the hedged future cash flows are no longer expected to occur; and
	  – amounts that have been transferred because the hedged item has affected profit or loss.
	• The location of the reclassification adjustment (see 4.1.250.70) in the statement of profit or loss and OCI.
	• For hedges of net positions, the hedging gains or losses recognised in a separate line item in the statement of profit or loss and OCI. [*IFRS 7.24C(b), IG13D, IAS 1.7, 92*]

7.10.440.20   Entities are required to disclose the change in fair value of the hedging instrument and the change in value of the hedged items on the basis that is used to calculate the hedge ineffectiveness that is recognised in the statement of profit or loss and OCI. [*IFRS 7.BC35LL*]

7.10.440.30   The difference between these amounts in the tabular disclosure for the hedging instrument (see 7.10.420) and in the tabular disclosure for the hedged item (see 7.10.430) will be equal to the amounts disclosed in the table for hedge ineffectiveness recognised in the statement of profit or loss and OCI (see 7.10.440.10). [*IFRS 7.BC35LL*]

7.10.450   Reconciliations

7.10.450.10   An entity provides a reconciliation of each component of accumulated OCI and an analysis of OCI in accordance with IAS 1. The information is provided separately by risk category. This disaggregation by risk may be provided in the notes to the financial statements. The reconciliation is required to have the same level of detail as the information that identifies the effects of hedge accounting on the statement of profit or loss and OCI. Therefore, the reconciliation should differentiate, at a minimum, between:

• hedging gains or losses of the reporting period that were recognised in OCI in respect of cash flow hedges and hedges of a net investment in a foreign operation;
• the amount reclassified from the cash flow hedge reserve or the foreign currency translation reserve into profit or loss as a reclassification adjustment (differentiating between amounts for which hedge accounting was previously used but for which the hedged future cash flows are no longer expected to occur, and amounts that have been transferred because the hedged item has affected profit or loss);
• the amount removed from the cash flow hedge reserve and included directly in the initial cost or other carrying amount of:
  – a non-financial asset or a non-financial liability that is recognised subsequent to a hedged forecast transaction; or
  – a firm commitment that results from a hedged forecast transaction for a non-financial asset or non-financial liability for which fair value hedge accounting is applied;
• the amount reclassified from the cash flow hedge reserve into profit or loss as a reclassification adjustment in relation to a loss (or a portion of it) that the entity does not expect to recover in one or more future periods;
• the amounts associated with the time value of purchased options that hedge transaction-related hedged items and amounts associated with the time value of purchased options that hedge time

period-related hedged items (when an entity designates as the hedging instrument only the change in intrinsic value of the option); and
- the amounts associated with the forward elements of forward contracts and the foreign currency basis spreads of financial instruments that hedge transaction-related hedged items and amounts associated with the forward elements of forward contracts and the foreign currency basis spreads of financial instruments that hedge time period-related hedged items (when an entity designates as the hedging instrument only the change in the value of the spot element of the forward contract or excludes the foreign currency basis spread). [*IFRS 7.24E–24F, BC35EE*]

7.10.460   *Fair value#*

7.10.460.10   For each class of financial assets and financial liabilities, an entity discloses the fair value in a manner that allows users of financial statements to compare it with its carrying amount. However, this disclosure is not required:
- if the carrying amount is a reasonable approximation of fair value; and
- for a contract containing a discretionary participation feature when the fair value of the feature cannot be measured reliably. [*IFRS 7.25, 29*]

7.10.460.20   The carrying amounts of short-term receivables and payables are likely to approximate their fair values in a low-interest rate environment in which the effect of discounting is not material. In such cases, it is not necessary to disclose these instruments' fair values. However, the fair values of long-term liabilities and receivables carried at amortised cost are disclosed because the effect of discounting is expected to be material. [*IFRS 7.29(a), 13.BC138A*]

7.10.460.30   Disclosures of fair values are not required for contracts containing discretionary participation features for which a reliable fair value cannot be obtained. [*IFRS 7.29(c)*]

7.10.460.40   In this case, the entity discloses:
- the fact that the fair value of these instruments cannot be measured reliably;
- a description of the financial instruments;
- the carrying amount;
- an explanation of why fair value cannot be measured reliably;
- information about the market for the instruments;
- information about whether and how the entity intends to dispose of the instruments; and
- if an instrument is derecognised:
  - the fact that the fair value could not be measured reliably;
  - the carrying amount at the time of derecognition; and
  - the amount of the gain or loss recognised. [*IFRS 7.29–30*]

7.10.460.50   An entity such as a mutual fund or a co-operative, whose share capital is classified as financial liabilities, may present its share capital as net assets attributable to shareholders in its statement of financial position. If the carrying amounts of the issued shares classified as financial liabilities are not a reasonable approximation of their fair values, then in our view the entity should disclose the fair values of the shares even if this presentation option is elected (see 7.3.50.50 and 2.4.980.20–30). [*IFRS 7.25, 29, IAS 32.IE32*]

7.10.460.60   The fair value disclosures are based on financial asset and financial liability classes. They are offset only to the extent that their carrying amounts are offset in the statement of financial position (see 7.10.110). [*IFRS 7.26*]

7.10.460.70   IFRS 13 provides guidance on fair value measurement and the related disclosure requirements, which are the subject of chapter 2.4 (see 2.4.490).

7.10.463   FORTHCOMING REQUIREMENTS

7.10.465   LEASES

7.10.465.10   IFRS 16 introduces an exception from disclosure of fair value for lease liabilities. [*IFRS 7.29(d)*]

7.10.467   INSURANCE CONTRACTS

7.10.467.10   IFRS 17 both limits the scope of IFRS 7 with respect to investment contracts with discretionary participation features (see 7.10.15.10) and removes the exception from disclosure of fair value for contracts containing a discretionary participation feature for which a reliable fair value cannot be obtained (see 7.10.460.30–40). If the contract is in the scope of IFRS 17, then it is excluded from the scope of IFRS 7 and therefore is subject to the disclosure requirements of IFRS 17, not IFRS 7. However, if the contract is in the scope of IFRS 7, then the contract is subject to the fair value disclosure requirements in IFRS 7 without any such exception. [*IFRS 7.3(d), 29*]

7.10.470   *Day one gain or loss*

7.10.470.10   In some cases, the fair value of a financial asset or a financial liability on initial recognition may differ from the transaction price. If an entity does not recognise a gain or loss on initial recognition because fair value is neither evidenced by a quoted price in an active market for an identical asset or liability nor based on a valuation technique that uses only data from observable markets, then it discloses the following for each class of financial asset and financial liability:

- the accounting policy for subsequently recognising the difference in profit or loss;
- the aggregate difference yet to be recognised in profit or loss at the beginning and end of the period, and a reconciliation of changes in this difference during the period; and
- the reason why the transaction price is not the best evidence of the fair value, including a description of the evidence that supports the fair value (see 7.7.40.50). [*IFRS 7.28*]

7.10.480   NATURE AND EXTENT OF RISKS ARISING FROM FINANCIAL INSTRUMENTS

7.10.480.10   The general disclosure principle in IFRS 7 requires an entity to make qualitative and quantitative disclosures that enable users of its financial statements to evaluate the nature and the extent of risks arising from financial instruments to which the entity is exposed at the reporting date, and how the entity has managed them. The extent of disclosure depends on the extent of the entity's exposure to risks arising from financial instruments. The types of risks covered by the disclosures include, but are not limited to, credit risk, liquidity risk and market risk. [*IFRS 7.31*]

7.10.480.20   The disclosures are included either in the financial statements or in another statement, such as a management commentary or risk report. The location of the disclosures may be limited by local laws. If the disclosures are made outside the financial statements, then the financial statements are cross-referenced to this information (see 5.8.10.90). The disclosures are made available to users on the same terms and timing as the financial statements. [*IFRS 7.B6*]

7.10.480.30   IFRS 7 addresses risks arising from financial instruments and contracts to buy or sell a non-financial item that are in the scope of IFRS 9. Consequently, the following are excluded from the scope of IFRS 7, even though they may give rise to financial risk for the entity:
• exposures from commodity contracts that meet the own-use exemption and have not been designated as at FVTPL (see 7.1.200.20);
• purchase and sale contracts for non-financial items that are to be settled in a foreign currency unless they are scoped into IFRS 9; and
• highly probable forecast transactions (see 7.9.430). [*IFRS 7.5, 31*]

7.10.480.40   An entity may manage its financial risk based on its total exposure – i.e. including risk arising from those items not included in the scope of IFRS 7 – and these exposures may be included in reports to key management personnel. In this case, in our view IFRS 7 does not prohibit an entity from providing additional disclosures about its total financial risk exposure rather than just the risk arising from financial instruments. However, we believe that all such additional disclosures should be clearly separated from those required by IFRS 7.

7.10.490   Qualitative disclosures

7.10.490.10   An entity discloses the following, for each type of risk arising from financial instruments:
• the exposure to the risk and how it arises;
• the entity's objectives, policies and processes for managing the risk; and
• the methods used to measure the risk. [*IFRS 7.33(a)–(b)*]

7.10.490.20   If there are any changes to the factors described in 7.10.490.10 from the previous period, then an entity discloses the reason for the changes. The changes may arise from changes in exposures themselves or the way in which the entity manages them. [*IFRS 7.33(c)*]

7.10.500   Quantitative disclosures

7.10.500.10   An entity discloses summary quantitative data about its exposure to each risk arising from its financial instruments at the reporting date. The disclosure is based on information that is provided internally to key management personnel of the entity – e.g. the board of directors or the CEO. If an entity uses several methods to manage risk, then it bases the disclosure on the method that provides the most relevant and reliable information. The quantitative disclosures described in 7.10.510–680 are required, if they are not already provided as part of the summary quantitative data based on information that is provided internally to key management personnel. [*IFRS 7.34*]

7.10.500.20   The quantitative data disclosed at the reporting date may not be representative of the risk exposure over the course of the reporting period. In this case, the entity provides additional disclosure that is representative. [*IFRS 7.35*]

7.10.510 **Concentrations of risk**

7.10.510.10   An entity discloses concentrations of risk. [*IFRS 7.34(c)*]

7.10.510.20   Concentrations of risk arise from financial instruments that:
- have similar characteristics; and
- are affected in a similar manner when there are changes in economic or other conditions. [*IFRS 7.B8*]

7.10.510.30   For example, a concentration of credit risk exists when a number of counterparties are located in a geographic region or are engaged in similar activities and have similar economic characteristics that would cause their ability to meet contractual obligations to be similarly affected by changes in economic or other conditions.

7.10.510.40   Identifying concentrations of risk is a matter of judgement and therefore an entity discloses:
- a description of how management determines concentrations;
- a description of the shared characteristics that identify each concentration – e.g. counterparty, geographic area, currency or market; and
- the amount of the risk exposure associated with financial instruments sharing that characteristic. [*IFRS 7.B8*]

7.10.520 *Credit risk*

7.10.520.10   'Credit risk' is the risk that one party to a financial instrument will cause a financial loss for the other party by failing to discharge an obligation. In our view, the credit risk disclosures are not required for investments in equity instruments, because these do not impose an obligation on the issuer to make any payments to the holder and, consequently, the holder is not exposed to the risk of the issuer failing to discharge an obligation. [*IFRS 7.A*]

7.10.530 *Financial instruments to which impairment requirements in IFRS 9 apply*

7.10.530.10   For financial instruments to which the impairment requirements in IFRS 9 apply, an entity is required to present disclosures about credit risk as set out in 7.10.540–610. These disclosures should be sufficient to enable users of the financial statements to understand the effect of credit risk on the amount, timing and uncertainty of future cash flows. [*IFRS 7.35B*]

7.10.530.20   To achieve this objective, credit risk disclosures provide:
- information about an entity's credit risk management practices and how they relate to the recognition and measurement of ECLs – including the methods, assumptions and information used to measure ECLs;
- quantitative and qualitative information to evaluate the amounts in the financial statements arising from ECLs – including changes and the reasons for those changes in the amount of ECLs; and
- information about an entity's credit risk exposure – including significant credit risk concentrations. [*IFRS 7.35B*]

7.10.530.30   To meet the objectives in 7.10.530.10 an entity is required to consider:

- how much detail to disclose;
- how much emphasis to place on each of the requirements;
- the appropriate level of aggregation or disaggregation; and
- whether users of financial statements need additional explanations to evaluate the quantitative information disclosed. [*IFRS 7.35D*]

7.10.530.40   If disclosures provided in accordance with 7.10.540–610 are insufficient to meet the disclosure objectives set out in 7.10.530.20, then an entity discloses additional information necessary to meet the objective. [*IFRS 7.35E*]

7.10.530.50   The disclosures required by the standard may be given either in:
- the financial statements; or
- another statement that is available on the same terms and at the same time as the financial statements (with a cross-reference from the financial statements). [*IFRS 7.35C*]

7.10.540   Credit risk management practices

7.10.540.10   An entity is required to explain its credit risk management practices and how they relate to the recognition and measurement of ECLs. To meet this objective, an entity discloses information that enables users of the financial statements to understand and evaluate:
- how it determines whether the credit risk of financial instruments has increased significantly since initial recognition, including whether and how:
  - financial instruments are considered to have low credit risk (see 7.8.150), including the classes of financial instruments to which the low credit risk exception has been applied; and
  - the presumption that financial assets with contractual payments more than 30 days past due have a significant increase in credit risk (see 7.8.120) has been rebutted;
- its definitions of default for different financial instruments, including the reasons for selecting those definitions;
- how instruments are grouped if ECLs are measured on a collective basis (see 7.8.250);
- how it determines that financial assets are credit-impaired (see 7.8.350);
- its write-off policy, including the indicators that there is no reasonable expectation of recovery; and
- how the modification requirements (see 7.8.130) have been applied, including how the entity:
  - determines whether the credit risk of a financial asset that has been modified while subject to a lifetime ECL allowance has improved to the extent that the loss allowance reverts to being measured at an amount equal to 12-month ECLs; and
  - monitors the extent to which the loss allowance on those assets subsequently reverts to being measured at an amount equal to lifetime ECLs. [*IFRS 7.35F, B8A–B8B*]

7.10.550   *ECL calculation*

7.10.550.10   An entity is required to explain the inputs, assumptions and estimation techniques used when:
- estimating 12-month and lifetime ECLs;
- determining whether the credit risk of financial instruments has increased significantly since initial recognition; and
- determining whether financial assets are credit-impaired. [*IFRS 7.35G, B8C*]

7.10.550.20   This includes explaining:
- the basis of inputs and assumptions;
- how forward-looking information has been incorporated into the determination of ECLs, including the use of macro-economic information; and
- changes in estimation techniques or significant assumptions made during the reporting period and the reasons for those changes. [*IFRS 7.35G, B8C*]

7.10.560   Amounts arising from ECLs

7.10.570   *Modifications and forbearance*

7.10.570.10   The following disclosures are required in respect of a financial asset that has been modified while subject to a lifetime ECL allowance, but whose modification does not result in derecognition. [*IFRS 7.35J*]

DISCLOSURES REQUIRED IN PERIOD OF MODIFICATION	DISCLOSURES REQUIRED UNTIL DERECOGNITION
• Amortised cost before the modification • Net modification gain or loss	• Gross carrying amount at the reporting date of financial assets whose loss allowance changed to 12-month ECLs during the reporting period

7.10.570.20   Except as set out in 7.10.570.10, IFRS does not contain specific disclosure requirements relating to forbearance activities (see 7.6.95.10). However, an entity is required to disclose significant accounting policies and judgements related to impairment, including the criteria for identifying significant increases in credit risk and observable data that financial assets are credit-impaired and its definition of default. Furthermore, an entity discloses the assumptions made about the future and other sources of estimation uncertainty that have a significant risk of a material adjustment to the carrying amounts of assets and liabilities. For example, loans subject to forbearance may be subject to management processes separate from other credit exposures, may have different risk characteristics and may be subject to different inputs and assumptions in impairment loss calculations. [*IAS 1.122, 125, IFRS 7.21*]

7.10.570.30   Qualitative disclosures in respect of the nature and extent of forbearance practices may include narrative information about:
- types of forbearance activities and programmes, and of the exposures subject to them;
- objectives, policies and processes for managing risk and the methods used to measure risk; and
- changes from the previous period. [*IFRS 7.33*]

7.10.570.40   Quantitative disclosures in respect of forbearance practices may include:
- the carrying amounts of assets subject to forbearance – analysed, for example, by type of forbearance measure, business or geographic area, as appropriate;
- forbearance activities during the period, including a reconciliation of opening and closing balances;
- related impairment allowances;
- newly recognised assets (see 7.6.95.30);
- interest income; and
- an analysis of credit quality. [*IFRS 7.34(a), 35H*]

7.10.580 *Collateral*

7.10.580.10 The objective of the disclosure requirements for collateral and other credit enhancements is to enable users of the financial statements to understand their effect on the amounts arising from ECLs. These disclosures are required by class of financial instrument and include:

- the amount that best represents the entity's maximum exposure to credit risk at the reporting date, without taking account of any collateral held or other credit enhancements;
- except for lease receivables, a narrative description of collateral held as security and other credit enhancements, including:
  - a discussion of the nature and quality of the collateral held;
  - an explanation of any significant changes in quality as a result of a deterioration or changes in the entity's collateral policies during the reporting period; and
  - information about financial instruments for which the entity has not recognised a loss allowance because of the collateral; and
- quantitative information about the collateral held as security and other credit enhancements – e.g. quantification of the extent to which collateral and other credit enhancements mitigate credit risk – for financial assets that are credit-impaired at the reporting date. [*IFRS 7.35A, 35K*]

7.10.580.20 An entity is not required to disclose information about the fair value of the collateral and other credit enhancements, or to quantify the exact value of the collateral that was included in the calculation of ECLs. [*IFRS 7.B8F*]

7.10.580.30 A narrative description of collateral and its effect on ECLs might include information about:

- the main types of collateral held as security and other credit enhancements – e.g. guarantees, credit derivatives and other agreements;
- the volume of collateral held and other credit enhancements, and their significance in terms of the loss allowance;
- the policies and process for valuing and managing collateral and other credit enhancements;
- the main types of counterparties to collateral and other credit enhancements, and their credit-worthiness; and
- information about risk concentrations within the collateral and other credit enhancements. [*IFRS 7.B8G*]

7.10.590 *POCI assets*

7.10.590.10 For POCI assets, in addition to the reconciliations as set out in 7.10.280, an entity discloses the total amount of undiscounted ECLs on initial recognition for financial assets initially recognised during the reporting period. [*IFRS 7.35H(c)*]

7.10.600 *Written-off assets*

7.10.600.10 A write-off of a financial asset is a derecognition event (see 7.8.430). At each reporting date, an entity discloses the contractual amount outstanding of financial assets that were written off during the reporting period and are still subject to enforcement activity. [*IFRS 7.35L*]

7.10.610   Credit risk exposure

7.10.610.10   To enable users of the financial statements to assess an entity's credit risk exposure, and to understand its significant credit risk concentrations, an entity is required to disclose, by credit risk rating grade (or by past-due status if the entity uses only past-due information to assess significant increases in credit risk – see 7.8.120):
- the gross carrying amount of financial assets; and
- the exposure to credit risk on loan commitments and financial guarantee contracts. [*IFRS 7.35M, B8I*]

7.10.610.20   This information is disclosed separately for:
- financial assets that are subject to a 12-month ECL allowance;
- financial assets that are subject to a lifetime ECL allowance but are not credit-impaired;
- financial assets that are credit-impaired at the reporting date but are not POCI assets;
- POCI assets; and
- trade receivables, contract assets and lease receivables for which lifetime ECLs are always recognised. [*IFRS 7.35M*]

7.10.610.30   The number of credit risk rating grades used for the disclosure has to be consistent with the number that the entity reports to key management personnel for credit risk management purposes. [*IFRS 7.B8I*]

7.10.610.40   When ECLs are measured on a collective basis (see 7.8.250), an entity may not be able to allocate the gross carrying amounts (or exposures) to the credit risk rating grades for which lifetime ECLs are recognised. In these cases, the entity:
- provides the disclosures in 7.10.610.10 for those financial instruments that can be directly allocated to a credit risk rating grade; and
- discloses separately the gross carrying amount of financial instruments for which lifetime ECLs are measured on a collective basis. [*IFRS 7.B8J*]

7.10.620   Trade receivables, contract assets and lease receivables

7.10.620.10   The disclosure requirements in 7.10.540–610 apply to trade receivables, contract assets and lease receivables. However, reduced disclosures apply to trade receivables, contract assets and lease receivables for which the loss allowance is always equal to lifetime ECLs, as follows:
- the disclosure requirements in 7.10.570.10 apply to trade receivables, contract assets and lease receivables on which lifetime ECLs are always recognised only if they are modified while more than 30 days past due; and
- some disclosure requirements in 7.10.580.10 (as indicated in that paragraph) do not apply to lease receivables. [*IFRS 7.35A*]

7.10.620.20   In addition, an entity is permitted to use a provision matrix for complying with the disclosure requirements on credit risk exposure (see 7.10.610) for trade receivables, contract assets and lease receivables for which lifetime ECLs are always recognised. [*IFRS 7.35N*]

7.10.620.30   IFRS 15 requires an entity to disclose, separately from other impairment losses, impairment losses recognised on trade receivables or contract assets arising from the entity's contracts with customers. [*IFRS 15.113(b)*]

7.10.630 *Financial instruments to which impairment requirements in IFRS 9 do not apply*

7.10.630.10 For all financial instruments in the scope of IFRS 7, but to which the impairment provisions of IFRS 9 do not apply, an entity discloses, by class of financial instrument, the amount that best represents the entity's maximum exposure to credit risk, unless this exposure is best represented by the carrying amount. The amount does not take into account any collateral held or other credit enhancements, unless the IAS 32 offsetting criteria are met (see 7.10.110). [*IFRS 7.36(a), B9, B10(c)*]

7.10.630.20 In addition, the entity discloses a description of any collateral held as security and other credit enhancements and their financial effect in respect of the amount that best represents the maximum exposure to credit risk. [*IFRS 7.36(b)*]

7.10.630.30 IFRS 7 does not specify how an entity should apply the term 'financial effect' in practice. Providing quantitative disclosure of the financial effect of collateral may be appropriate in some cases. However, in other cases it may be impracticable to obtain quantitative information; or, if it is available, the information may not be determined to be relevant, meaningful or reliable.

7.10.630.40 If quantitative disclosure is deemed appropriate, then some possible quantitative approaches may include a quantification of:
- the current value of collateral – e.g. fair value or net realisable value of collateral or other credit enhancements – for each class of assets adjusted for the effect of over-collateralisation; or
- the effect that collateral or other credit enhancements have on the measurement of the related financial instruments – i.e. an estimate of the difference between the entity's actual measurement and what it might have been without the collateral or other credit enhancements.

7.10.630.50 As part of its determination of whether quantitative disclosure of the current value of collateral is appropriate, an entity may, for example, consider whether:
- the collateral is specifically identifiable and therefore measurable – e.g. a fixed charge over specified assets vs a floating charge that has not yet attached to any specific assets; and
- the entity is able to access the collateral at its full value and is not restricted by a higher-ranking or pari passu charge of another creditor.

EXAMPLE 5A – APPROPRIATENESS OF QUANTITATIVE DISCLOSURE OF FINANCIAL EFFECT OF COLLATERAL (1)

7.10.630.60 Bank K holds a portfolio of loans classified as at FVTPL secured on residential properties. The security is in the form of the first charge over each property. Historically, in the event of default K has enforced this type of collateral and was able to dispose of it in an established market. K updates the value of the collateral regularly and monitors the loan to value ratios internally for risk management purposes.

7.10.630.70 Therefore, K determines that disclosure of the current value of the collateral is appropriate and provides relevant information on the extent to which the collateral mitigates the credit risk on its portfolio of loans.

EXAMPLE 5B – APPROPRIATENESS OF QUANTITATIVE DISCLOSURE OF FINANCIAL EFFECT OF COLLATERAL (2)

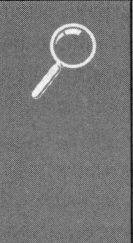

7.10.630.80   Company L holds a portfolio of second-lien residential mortgage loans classified as measured at FVTPL. In this case, disclosing the fair value of the collateral held may be inappropriate if historically, in the case of default, its right to collateral has been worthless.

7.10.630.90   Therefore, it may be more appropriate for L to disclose the fact that its right to collateral may be worthless in default and that the fair value of the collateral may be irrelevant in those circumstances.

7.10.630.100   If quantitative disclosure of the financial effect of certain types of collateral or other credit enhancements is not considered appropriate, then an entity is still required to disclose sufficient qualitative information for a financial statement user to understand:
- how the entity considers and incorporates collateral or other credit enhancements into its credit risk management; and
- how this incorporation of collateral or other credit enhancements in its credit risk management relates to its quantitative disclosures of its maximum exposure to credit risk. [*IFRS 7.32A, 33(b), 36(b)*]

7.10.640   *Collateral and other credit enhancements obtained*

7.10.640.10   An entity may obtain financial or non-financial assets under collateral and credit enhancement arrangements. If those assets meet the recognition criteria in IFRS, then it discloses the nature and the carrying amount of the assets held. In addition, when the assets are not readily convertible into cash, the entity discloses its policies for using the assets in its operations or disposing of them. These requirements apply only to assets held at the reporting date. [*IFRS 7.38*]

7.10.650   **Liquidity risk**

7.10.650.10   'Liquidity risk' is the risk that an entity will encounter difficulty in meeting the obligations associated with its financial liabilities that are settled by delivering cash or another financial asset. [*IFRS 7.A*]

7.10.650.20   An entity discloses a maturity analysis for:
- non-derivative financial liabilities, including issued financial guarantee contracts, that shows their remaining contractual maturities; and
- derivative financial liabilities, including the remaining contractual maturities for those derivative financial liabilities for which contractual maturities are essential for an understanding of the timing of the cash flows – e.g. loan commitments and interest rate swaps designated in a cash flow hedging relationship. [*IFRS 7.39(a)–(b), B11B*]

7.10.650.30   In our view, the maturity analysis should include all derivative financial liabilities, but contractual maturities only are required for those essential for an understanding of the timing of the cash flows.

7.10.650.40 In determining what is 'essential' for an understanding of the cash flows, we believe that an entity should apply judgement over what is appropriate based on management's liquidity risk management strategy and the facts and circumstances. For example, most non-trading derivatives that are held for risk management purposes might be expected to be held to maturity. Also, most hedging strategies will not involve closing out a derivative before maturity. However, some 'trading' derivatives – e.g. interest rate swaps that a bank executes with corporate counterparties – might be expected to be held until maturity, and some hedging strategies may involve closing out a derivative before maturity.

7.10.650.50 An entity explains how it manages the liquidity risk inherent in the maturity analyses described in 7.10.650.20. This includes a maturity analysis for financial assets that it holds as part of managing liquidity risk – e.g. financial assets that are expected to generate cash inflows to meet cash outflows on financial liabilities – if this information is necessary to enable financial statement users to evaluate the nature and extent of liquidity risk. In addition, disclosure of financial assets pledged as collateral – e.g. cash collateral and securities under repurchase transactions – may be considered necessary in this context if this information is provided internally to key management personnel. [*IFRS 7.39(c), B11E*]

7.10.650.60 In disclosing the maturity analyses described in 7.10.650.20, an entity does not separate an embedded derivative from a hybrid (combined) financial instrument. For such an instrument, the entity applies the disclosure requirements for non-derivative financial liabilities – i.e. it discloses the remaining contractual maturities. [*IFRS 7.B11A*]

7.10.650.70 IFRS 7 does not define contractual maturities. Therefore, it leaves open to interpretation the amounts that need to be included in the maturity analysis for certain types of financial liabilities, such as derivatives and perpetual instruments. In our view, both the interest and principal cash flows should be included in the analysis because this best represents the liquidity risk being faced by the entity. The principal amount of a perpetual instrument represents the present value of the payments of the interest stream. As a minimum, for such an instrument, the principal amount should be disclosed and sufficient appropriate narrative disclosures should be provided to present a meaningful picture of the entity's liquidity exposures.

7.10.650.80 IFRS 7 does not mandate the number of time bands to be used in the analysis. Instead, it requires the entity to use its judgement to determine an appropriate number of time bands. [*IFRS 7.B11*]

7.10.650.90 When the creditor can choose when an amount is paid, the liability is included in the time band that represents the earliest date on which the entity could be required to pay. This disclosure shows the worst-case scenario from the perspective of the entity. For example, a demand deposit would be included in the earliest time band. [*IFRS 7.B11C(a), BC57*]

7.10.650.100 The amounts disclosed are the contractual undiscounted cash flows. In our view, the amounts disclosed should generally be gross unless the liabilities will be settled net. These amounts will differ from the amounts included in the statement of financial position, because those amounts are based on discounted cash flows. [*IFRS 7.B11D*]

7.10.650.110 When the amount payable is not fixed, the amount to be disclosed is determined with reference to conditions existing at the reporting date. For example, for a floating rate bond with interest payments indexed to three-month Euribor, in our view the amount to be disclosed should be based on forward rates rather than spot rates prevailing at the reporting date because the spot interest rates do not represent the level of the index based on which the cash flows will be payable. The forward interest rates better describe the level of the index in accordance with the conditions existing at the reporting date. [*IFRS 7.B11D*]

7.10.650.120   When an issued guarantee meets the definition of a financial guarantee contract under IFRS 9 (see 7.1.70), the maximum amount of the guarantee is disclosed in the earliest period in which the guarantee could be called. [*IFRS 7.B11C(c)*]

7.10.650.130   In disclosing summary quantitative data about exposure to liquidity risk on the basis of information provided internally to key management, an entity explains how this data is determined. If the outflows included in the data could occur either significantly earlier or at significantly different amounts, then the entity discloses that fact and provides further quantitative information to enable users to evaluate the extent of this risk, unless this information is included in the contractual maturity analysis required by IFRS 7. The amounts disclosed need to be explained so that it is clear whether they are compiled on a contractual or another basis. [*IFRS 7.34(a), B10A*]

7.10.650.140   An entity may have liabilities that are subject to accelerated repayment before their stated maturities in certain circumstances. For example, a term loan may become repayable on demand if the entity fails to comply with covenants on its financial condition or performance, or if its credit rating is downgraded. Depending on the circumstances, information about such terms and their effect may be necessary to allow users to evaluate the nature and extent of liquidity risk. Additional disclosure may be appropriate – e.g. on concentrations of liquidity risk arising from such terms or how the entity manages the associated liquidity risk. [*IFRS 7.31, 34(c), B10A, B11F(f)*]

7.10.655   *Reverse factoring arrangements*

7.10.655.10   Reverse factoring arrangements (see 7.10.35) may impact the customer's exposure to – and be part of its management of – liquidity risk from financial instruments. An entity that is the customer in a reverse factoring arrangement is required to disclose information that enables users of financial statements to evaluate the nature and extent of these risks. The disclosure requirements that may be particularly relevant to such arrangements include:
- qualitative disclosures about the entity's exposure to liquidity risk:
    - the exposure to risk and how it arises;
    - the entity's objectives, policies and processes for managing the risk and the method used to measure the risk; and
    - any changes in the above from the previous period; and
- quantitative information relating to liquidity risk, including concentrations of it. [*IFRS 7.31, 33–34*]

7.10.655.20   For a further discussion of reverse factoring, see 2.3.75, 7.6.465, 7.10.35 and 315.

7.10.660   *Market risk*

7.10.660.10   'Market risk' is the risk that the fair value or future cash flows of a financial instrument will fluctuate because of changes in market prices. Market risk comprises three types of risk: currency risk, interest rate risk and other price risk. [*IFRS 7.A, IG32*]

7.10.660.20   An entity presents a sensitivity analysis for each type of market risk that it is exposed to as at the reporting date, including the methods and assumptions used in preparing the analysis. If the methods and assumptions change from one period to another, then the entity discloses such changes together with the reasons for them. [*IFRS 7.40*]

7.10.660.30   An entity may hold an investment in an equity instrument quoted in a foreign currency. In our view, the entity is not required to split the currency risk from other price risk for an equity instrument. However, for a debt instrument, as a minimum, the split between currency risk and interest rate risk is presented. [*IFRS 7.B23*]

7.10.660.40   The sensitivity analysis reflects the impact, on profit or loss and equity, of changes in the relevant risk variables that are reasonably possible at the reporting date. The 'reasonably possible' change does not include remote or worst-case scenarios or stress tests. The sensitivity calculation assumes that the reasonably possible change had occurred at the reporting date and had been applied to the risk exposures at that date. For example, if an entity has a floating rate liability at the reporting date, then it would disclose the effect on profit or loss (e.g. interest expense) for the current year if interest rates had varied by reasonably possible amounts. [*IFRS 7.40(a), B18–B19*]

7.10.660.50   The sensitivity analysis described in 7.10.660.20 is not required if the entity already prepares an analysis that reflects interdependencies between risk variables – e.g. a value at risk (VAR) approach – and uses it to manage its financial risk. If the entity uses this analysis to fulfil its disclosure requirements, then it explains the method used in preparing the analysis. This includes the main parameters and assumptions underlying the data. Furthermore, the entity explains the objective of the method used and any limitations that may result in the method not fully capturing the risk exposure arising from the underlying assets and liabilities. If the entity applies VAR to only a part of its financial instruments portfolio, then it provides a separate sensitivity analysis described in 7.10.660.20 for those financial instruments not included in the VAR analysis. [*IFRS 7.41, B20*]

7.10.660.60   In our view, the sensitivity analysis should include financial assets and financial liabilities measured at amortised cost as well as those financial instruments measured at fair value.

7.10.660.70   An entity provides a sensitivity analysis for the whole of its business – e.g. in the case of a bank, this will include both its trading and its non-trading books. The entity may also provide different types of analysis for different classes of financial instruments. [*IFRS 7.B21*]

7.10.660.80   In our view, 'translation risk', arising from translating the financial statements of a foreign operation into the presentation currency of the group, does not meet the definition of currency risk as defined in IFRS 7. Consequently, in our view translation risk should not be included in the sensitivity analysis on a consolidated basis. In our view, in consolidated financial statements the sensitivity analysis should address each currency to which an entity in the group has significant exposure based on each entity's functional currency.

7.10.660.90   When the functional currency of an entity is different from that of its foreign operation, the resulting economic exposure can usually be hedged (see 7.9.1020). Therefore, in our view an entity may include net investments in foreign operations in the sensitivity analysis in consolidated financial statements if, and only if, that net investment has been hedged, and only to the extent that it has been hedged.

7.10.670   *Other market risk disclosures*

7.10.670.10   If an entity believes that the sensitivity analysis is not representative of a risk inherent in a financial instrument, then it discloses this fact and the reason why it believes that the sensitivity analysis is unrepresentative. This may be the case, for example, when the year-end risk exposure is not representative of the risk exposure during the year. [*IFRS 7.42*]

7.10.670.20   Financial instruments that are classified as equity of the entity do not impact profit or loss or equity, because they are not remeasured. Therefore, no sensitivity analysis is required. [*IFRS 7.B28*]

7.10.675   *Application by investment entities*

7.10.675.10   Investment entities are required to measure certain subsidiaries at FVTPL, rather than consolidating them (see chapter 5.6). This includes circumstances in which an investment entity is required to measure at fair value its investments in a subsidiary that is itself an investment entity (see 5.6.200). [*IFRS 10.31*]

7.10.675.20   An investment in a subsidiary that is measured at fair value is in the scope of IFRS 7 and may represent a significant concentration of risk. Furthermore, the parent may be directly or indirectly exposed to risks arising from the subsidiary's financial instruments; also, key management of the parent and the subsidiary may be the same persons and use the same information for managing the risks of both entities. [*IFRS 7.3(a)*]

7.10.675.30   An investment entity parent considers what information should be disclosed to comply with the disclosure objective of IFRS 7. Depending on the facts and circumstances, the risk disclosures of the investment entity parent may include information about risks arising from financial instruments held by an investment entity subsidiary and be based on corresponding disclosures of the investment entity subsidiary – for example:
- analysis of credit quality;
- concentration of risk;
- summarised interest rate gap analysis; and
- foreign currency risk.

EXAMPLE 6 – RISK DISCLOSURES OF THE FEEDER FUND

7.10.675.40   Feeder Fund F, an open-ended investment fund, invests substantially all of its assets in Master fund M, another open-ended investment fund that has the same investment objectives as F. As at 31 December 2018, F owns 100% of M (2017: 100%).

7.10.675.50   M is primarily involved in investing in a highly diversified portfolio of equity securities issued by companies listed on major stock exchanges, unlisted companies, unlisted investment funds, investment-grade debt securities and derivatives, with the objective of providing investors in F with above-average returns over the medium to long term.

7.10.675.60   F is managed together with M as an integrated structure. Managing the funds together also helps to ensure that cash flows from the underlying assets of M match the redemption obligations of M – and ultimately of F. The pricing of the shares in M held by F is based on M's net asset value.

7.10.675.70   F's management decides that the objectives of IFRS 7 are met by providing disclosures on:
- the amount and terms of its investment in – and the nature of its relationship with – M;
- credit risk, interest rate risk, currency risk and other price risk of the underlying investments held by M; and
- the liquidity risk of both M and F.

7.10.680 TRANSFERS OF FINANCIAL ASSETS

7.10.680.10   An entity discloses information on:
- transferred financial assets that are not derecognised in their entirety; and
- transferred financial assets that are derecognised in their entirety in which the entity retains continuing involvement. [*IFRS 7.42A*]

7.10.690 Disclosures for transfers of financial assets

7.10.690.10   The following disclosures are required for each class of transferred assets that are not derecognised in their entirety:
- the nature of the transferred assets;
- the nature of the risks and rewards associated with those assets to which the entity is exposed; and
- the nature of the relationship between the transferred assets and the associated liabilities and the restrictions on the entity's use of those assets. [*IFRS 7.42D(a)–(c)*]

7.10.690.20   The following additional disclosures are required for each class of transferred assets that are not derecognised in their entirety in specific circumstances:
- when the counterparty to the associated liabilities has recourse only to the transferred assets:
  - the fair value of the transferred assets;
  - the fair value of the associated liabilities; and
  - the net position – i.e. the difference between the fair value of the transferred assets and the associated liabilities;
- when the entity continues to recognise all of the transferred assets, the carrying amounts of the transferred assets and associated liabilities; and
- when the entity continues to recognise the assets to the extent of its continuing involvement:
  - the total carrying amount of the original assets before the transfer;
  - the carrying amount of the assets that the entity continues to recognise; and
  - the carrying amount of associated liabilities. [*IFRS 7.42D(d)–(f)*]

7.10.690.30   The following disclosures are required for each type of continuing involvement in transferred assets that are derecognised in their entirety:
- the carrying amounts and fair values of the assets and liabilities representing the entity's continuing involvement;
- the entity's maximum exposure to loss from its continuing involvement;
- a maturity analysis of the undiscounted cash flows that may be payable to the transferee in respect of those assets;

- the gain or loss on transfer and income and expense arising from the entity's continuing involvement; and
- qualitative disclosures to explain and support the quantitative disclosures. [*IFRS 7.42E, 42G(a)–(b)*]

7.10.690.40 In addition, if the total amount of proceeds from transfer activity is not evenly distributed throughout the reporting period, then the following disclosures are required for each type of continuing involvement in transferred assets that are derecognised in their entirety:
- the part within the reporting period to which the greatest transfer activity is attributable;
- the amount – e.g. related gains or losses – recognised from transfer activity in that part of the reporting period; and
- the total amount of proceeds from transfer activity in that part of the reporting period. [*IFRS 7.42G(c)*]

7.10.700   Scope of disclosure requirements on transfers of financial assets

7.10.700.10 Entities often transfer financial assets to structured entities (see 7.6.280). If financial assets have been transferred to an unconsolidated structured entity, then disclosures required by IFRS 12 may be appropriate in addition to disclosures of transfers of financial assets required by IFRS 7. For further discussion of disclosures about structured entities, see 5.10.230–270.

7.10.700.20 To assess what information on which financial assets needs to be disclosed, an entity determines:
- which financial assets have been transferred;
- whether it has derecognised a transferred financial asset in its entirety; and
- whether it has continuing involvement in a transferred financial asset that it derecognised in its entirety. [*IFRS 7.42A, 42C, 9.3.2.3–3.2.6*]

7.10.700.30 This is illustrated in the following flowchart.

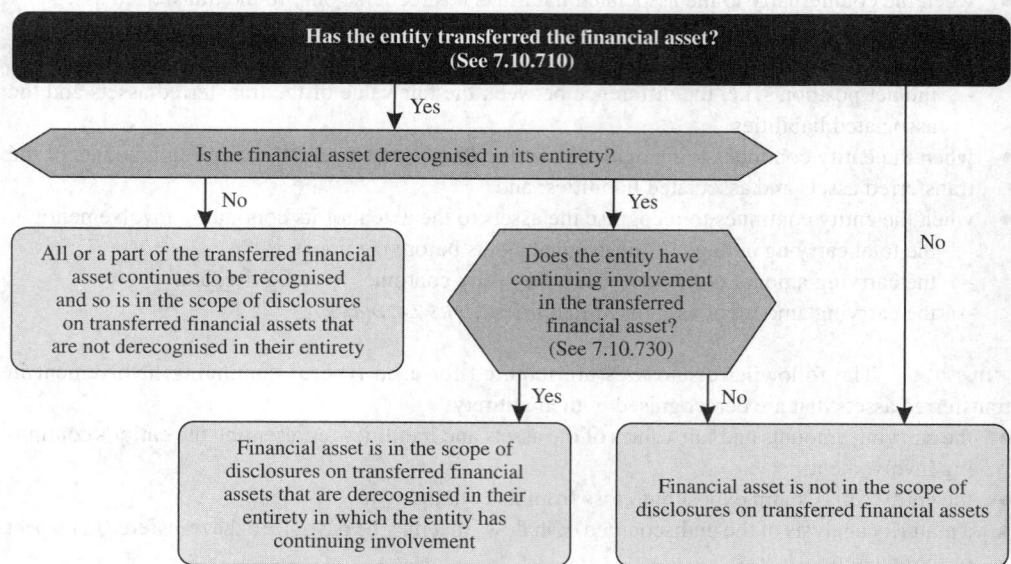

7.10.700.40   The definition of 'transfer' and the concept of 'continuing involvement' for the purposes of these disclosures are different from those in IFRS 9 for the purpose of determining whether a financial asset is derecognised (see 7.6.60). [*IFRS 7.42A, 42C, BC65S, 9.3.2.3–3.2.6*]

7.10.710   *Definition of a 'transfer'*

7.10.710.10   For the purposes of these disclosures, an entity transfers all or a part of a financial asset if it:
- transfers the contractual rights to receive the cash flows of that asset; or
- retains the contractual rights to receive cash flows and assumes a contractual obligation to pay these cash flows to one or more recipients. Such an arrangement is a transfer for the purposes of the disclosure requirements even if it does not comply with the pass-through requirements of IFRS 9 and would not therefore be considered a transfer under IFRS 9 (see 7.6.120). [*IFRS 7.42A*]

7.10.720   *Identifying contractual obligation to pay cash flows of asset*

7.10.720.10   A transfer is subject to the disclosure requirements in IFRS 7 for transfers of financial assets if the entity retains the contractual rights to receive the cash flows of a financial asset but assumes a contractual obligation to pay the cash flows to one or more recipients in an arrangement. The purpose of these disclosure requirements is to provide users of financial statements with a better understanding of the relationship between the transferred financial assets and the associated liabilities. Therefore, in our view there should be a direct (explicit or implicit) link between the cash receipts on specified financial assets that the entity owns and the obligation to remit the cash receipts to another party, in order for the arrangement to be considered a transfer subject to these disclosure requirements. [*IFRS 7.BC65E*]

7.10.720.20   In arrangements that do not involve structured entities (see 5.10.190), the legal documentation may directly identify the assets and cash receipts that are being referenced and explicitly set out the requirements for directly passing through cash flows when an amount is received on the specified financial asset. This may make the analysis of such transactions relatively straightforward.

7.10.720.30   In some cases, an arrangement may require the entity to make payments based on the performance of an underlying financial asset, whereby there is no link between the cash receipts on specified financial assets that the entity owns and the obligation to pay cash. We do not believe that such an arrangement is subject to the disclosure requirements on transfers of financial assets. Examples of arrangements that we believe are not subject to the disclosure requirements in IFRS 7 include:
- credit-linked notes in which payments are referenced to the default of specified assets that an entity is not required to own; and
- equity-linked notes and total return swaps in which payments are referenced to the fair value of – but not receipts from – underlying financial assets.

7.10.720.40   In our view, all of the terms of an arrangement should be considered in determining whether it is subject to the disclosure requirements on transfers of financial assets. Arrangements involving consolidated structured entities may be more complex. Notes issued by these entities might not themselves directly reference specific cash receipts or financial assets. However, the governing terms of the overall arrangement may indicate that the structured entity owns specified financial assets and that, as a result of a 'waterfall' or a similar arrangement, notes issued to third parties represent an obligation to pass on cash receipts from those assets to the note holders.

7.10.720.50   To qualify as a pass-through arrangement under IFRS 9 (see 7.6.120), cash receipts need to be remitted to the eventual recipients without material delay and may only be reinvested in cash and cash equivalents before being paid on. In our view, these strict criteria do not apply in determining whether an arrangement is a transfer subject to the disclosure requirements in IFRS 7. Accordingly, an arrangement that does not meet the strict criteria in IFRS 9 may be subject to the disclosure requirements on transfers of financial assets.

7.10.720.60   Judgement may be involved in distinguishing between:
- an obligation to pass on cash flows from specified financial assets that is subject to the transfer of financial assets disclosure requirements; and
- interests in or linked to investment funds issued by the reporting entity that are not subject to these disclosure requirements.

7.10.720.70   In typical mutual or unit-linked fund structures, investors hold instruments that are redeemable based on the value of assets in the fund. In these cases, cash flows are collected from existing assets. Assets may also be sold to generate cash proceeds. An entity is not required to pay these amounts to investors but instead cash received by the fund is reinvested in different assets. Cash payments are made to investors in accordance with the entity's dividend policies and when investors redeem their investment in the fund. In our view, in these circumstances, the nature of the arrangement results in a financial liability that is indexed to the value of a moving pool of assets that the entity manages, rather than in an obligation to pass on the cash flows of specified financial assets when they are received. Consequently, we believe that the arrangement is not subject to the disclosure requirements on transfers of financial assets.

7.10.720.80   Similarly, in our view, in certain arrangements – e.g. complex arrangements involving consolidated structured entities, other entities in the consolidated group and external holders of instruments issued by the structured entity – judgement may be required to determine whether the arrangement results in:
- an obligation to pass on cash flows from specified financial assets held within the structured entity that is subject to the transfer of financial assets disclosure requirements; or
- a general obligation for which assets held within the structured entity act only as a form of collateral. In this case, the collateral is subject to the collateral disclosure requirements (see 7.10.260), but we believe that the disclosure requirements in respect of transfers of financial assets do not apply to the arrangement.

7.10.720.90   In our view, factors that may affect this judgement include the following:
- the purpose and design of the structured entity;
- the extent of recourse to the transferor's wider group;
- the nature and extent of differences between the cash flow profile of beneficial interests issued by the structured entity and the cash flow profile of financial assets held in the structured entity; and
- rights to substitute financial assets held within the structured entity.

7.10.730   *Continuing involvement*

7.10.730.10   For the purposes of the disclosures, an entity has continuing involvement in a transferred financial asset if, as part of the transfer, it retains any of the contractual rights or obligations relating to the transferred financial assets or obtains any new contractual rights or obligations relating to those assets. Continuing involvement may result from contractual provisions in the transfer agreement or in a separate agreement entered into with the transferee or another party in connection with the transfer. Normal representations and warranties, contracts to reacquire the transferred financial asset at fair value, and a qualifying pass-through arrangement under IFRS 9 do not constitute continuing involvement. [*IFRS 9.3.2.5, 7.42C, B31*]

7.10.730.20   An entity does not have continuing involvement for disclosure purposes in a transferred financial asset if it has neither an interest in the future performance of the transferred financial asset nor a responsibility under any circumstances to make payments in respect of the transferred financial asset in the future, other than paying on cash flows of the transferred financial asset that an entity collects and is required to transfer to the transferee. [*IFRS 7.B30*]

7.10.730.30   In many cases, entities retain the right or obligation to service, for a fee, transferred financial assets that qualify for derecognition in their entirety. These servicing arrangements represent continuing involvement for the purposes of the disclosures on transfers of financial assets, if the conditions in 7.10.730.10–20 are met. A servicer has continuing involvement in a transferred asset (for the purposes of the disclosure requirements) if it has an interest in the future performance of the transferred assets – e.g. if the servicing fee is dependent on the amount or timing of the cash flows from the transferred assets, or a fixed servicing fee would not be paid in full if the transferred assets do not perform. [*IFRS 7.42C, B30–B30A*]

7.10.740   Interactions between derecognition requirements in IFRS 9 and disclosure requirements in IFRS 7

7.10.740.10   Some of the interactions between the application of the IFRS 9 derecognition requirements and the IFRS 7 disclosure requirements are illustrated in the table below.
- The first column relates to the financial asset that is being considered for derecognition – it could be either the entire financial asset or an eligible part.
- The second column relates to whether the financial asset is derecognised under IFRS 9.
- The third and fourth columns indicate whether IFRS 7's disclosure requirements for either:
  - transferred financial assets that are not derecognised in their entirety; or
  - transferred financial assets that are derecognised in their entirety
  apply in the circumstances described. [*IFRS 7.42A, 42C, 9.3.2.3—3.2.6*]

FACT PATTERN	DERECOGNITION IN LINE WITH IFRS 9?	IN SCOPE OF IFRS 7 DISCLOSURE REQUIREMENTS FOR TRANSFERRED FINANCIAL ASSETS THAT ARE	
		NOT DERECOGNISED IN THEIR ENTIRETY?	DERECOGNISED IN THEIR ENTIRETY?
Entity retains the contractual rights to receive the cash flows of the financial asset, but assumes a contractual obligation to pay these cash flows to a third party in a way that does not comply with the pass-through requirements of IFRS 9.	No; the entity continues to recognise the financial asset in its entirety.	Yes	No

2359

FACT PATTERN	DERECOGNITION IN LINE WITH IFRS 9?	IN SCOPE OF IFRS 7 DISCLOSURE REQUIREMENTS FOR TRANSFERRED FINANCIAL ASSETS THAT ARE	
		NOT DERECOGNISED IN THEIR ENTIRETY?	DERECOGNISED IN THEIR ENTIRETY?
Entity transfers the financial asset in a way that meets the definition of transfer in IFRS 9 but retains substantially all the risks and rewards of the transferred financial asset.	No; the entity continues to recognise the financial asset in its entirety.	Yes	No
Entity transfers the financial asset in a way that meets the definition of transfer in IFRS 9 but neither transfers nor retains substantially all the risks and rewards of the transferred financial asset and does not retain control of the asset.	Yes; the financial asset is derecognised in its entirety.	No	Yes; it retains continuing involvement in the transferred financial asset because the entity neither transfers nor retains substantially all of the risks and rewards of the transferred financial asset.
Entity transfers the financial asset in a way that meets the definition of transfer in IFRS 9 but neither transfers nor retains substantially all the risks and rewards of the transferred financial asset and retains control of the asset.	The financial asset continues to be recognised to the extent of the entity's continuing involvement in the asset.	Yes	No
Entity transfers the financial asset in a way that meets the definition of transfer in IFRS 9 and transfers substantially all of the risks and rewards the transferred financial asset but retains an insignificant portion of the risks and rewards.	Yes; the financial asset is derecognised in its entirety.	No	Yes, it retains continuing involvement because it retains an insignificant portion of the risks and rewards.

7.10.750   Transferred financial asset

7.10.750.10   When applying the disclosure requirements, the term 'transferred financial asset' refers to all or a part of a financial asset. Therefore, when an entity transfers a part of a financial asset, its evaluation of whether and which disclosures are required depends on:

- whether that part is derecognised in its entirety; and

- whether the entity retains continuing involvement in that part. [*IFRS 7.42A, 42D–42E*]

EXAMPLE 7A – APPLICATION OF DISCLOSURES TO PROPORTION OF FINANCIAL ASSET (1)

7.10.750.20 An entity transfers the contractual rights to only a fully proportionate share of 40% of the cash flows of a financial asset – i.e. the derecognition guidance in IFRS 9 is applied to that part of the financial asset. This fully proportionate 40% share is not derecognised in its entirety because the transfer does not meet the IFRS 9 requirements for full derecognition of that part. In this case, the fully proportionate 40% share is subject to the disclosure requirements for transferred financial assets that are not derecognised in their entirety.

EXAMPLE 7B – APPLICATION OF DISCLOSURES TO PROPORTION OF FINANCIAL ASSET (2)

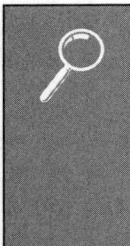

7.10.750.30 Conversely, if this fully proportionate 40% share of a financial asset met the derecognition criteria in IFRS 9 and the entity retained continuing involvement in that derecognised part, then the fully proportionate 40% share would be subject to the disclosure requirements for transferred financial assets that are derecognised in their entirety but for which the entity retains continuing involvement.

7.10.750.40 In both Examples 7A and 7B, the fully proportionate 60% share that has not been transferred is not in the scope of the disclosure requirements because it has not been transferred. [*IFRS 7.42A, 42E*]

7.10.750.50 A more complex question relates to transfers of some, but not all, of the cash flows of a financial asset when these transferred cash flows are not a part that meets the criteria for separate derecognition analysis in paragraph 3.2.2(a) of IFRS 9 (see 7.6.80.30–150). Although paragraph 3.2.2 of IFRS 9 requires the derecognition guidance in IFRS 9 to be applied to a part only if that part meets specified criteria, it does not define a 'part' of a financial asset for the purposes of the IFRS 7 transfer disclosures. Therefore, in our view an obligation to pay some of the cash flows from a financial asset should be considered a transfer for the purposes of these disclosures even if the cash flows passed on do not meet the criteria in paragraph 3.2.2(a) of IFRS 9.

7.10.750.60 If the part of a financial asset that is transferred does not meet the criteria in paragraph 3.2.2(a) of IFRS 9, then in our view an entity can satisfy the disclosure requirements in respect of the carrying amounts of transferred assets (see 7.10.690.20) by disclosing the carrying amount of the entire asset or by applying a reasonable allocation methodology, together with such additional explanation as may be appropriate in the circumstances.

7.10.760 FUTURE DEVELOPMENTS

7.10.760.10 The IASB is working on a maintenance project to address the classification of liabilities. In February 2015, the IASB published Exposure Draft *Classification of Liabilities – Proposed amendments to IAS 1*. The proposals were aimed at clarifying the criteria for classifying a liability as current or non-current by making it explicit that only rights in existence at the reporting date should affect the classification of a liability. Under the proposals, an entity would need to have a right – rather than an *unconditional right* – at the reporting date to defer settlement for at least 12 months in order to classify a liability as non-current, assuming that the other criteria are met (see 3.1.40). The Board will decide on the direction of the project in Q3 2018.

7.11   Transition to IFRS 9

7.11   Transition to IFRS 9

CURRENTLY EFFECTIVE REQUIREMENTS

This publication reflects IFRS in issue at 1 August 2018, and the currently effective requirements cover annual periods beginning on 1 January 2018.

The requirements related to this topic are mainly derived from the following.

Standard	Title
IFRS 4*	Insurance Contracts
IFRS 7	Financial Instruments: Disclosures
IFRS 9	Financial Instruments
IAS 8	Accounting Policies, Changes in Accounting Estimates and Errors
IAS 39	Financial Instruments: Recognition and Measurement

*   These include requirements arising from *Applying IFRS 9 Financial Instruments with IFRS 4 Insurance Contracts – Amendments to IFRS 4*.

FORTHCOMING REQUIREMENTS

The currently effective requirements are affected by the following forthcoming requirements. They are highlighted with a # and the impact is explained in the accompanying boxed text at the references indicated.

In October 2017, the IASB issued *Prepayment Features with Negative Compensation – Amendments to IFRS 9*, which are effective for annual periods beginning on or after 1 January 2019. See 7.11.95.

7.11.10   OVERVIEW OF TRANSITION

7.11.10.10   IFRS 9 was published in stages and a number of versions were in existence. IFRS 9 (2014) superseded IFRS 9 (2009), IFRS 9 (2010) and IFRS 9 (2013). There was a limited period of time in which entities could elect to adopt these earlier versions of IFRS 9 (see 7.11.20.40). [*IFRS 9.7.1.1, 7.3.1–7.3.2*]

7.11.10.20   The following is an overview of the transition requirements under IFRS 9 (2014). There are exceptions from these general principles, which are further explained in this chapter. [*IFRS 9.7.1.1, 7.2.1, 7.2.15, 7.2.22*]

EFFECTIVE DATE:	Annual periods beginning on or after 1 January 2018. However, insurance entities meeting certain criteria are permitted to defer the adoption of IFRS 9 until 1 January 2021 (see 8.1.160).
TRANSITION FOR CLASSIFICATION AND MEASUREMENT (INCLUDING IMPAIRMENT):	Generally retrospective, but with significant exemptions.
TRANSITION FOR HEDGE ACCOUNTING:	Generally prospective, but with limited exceptions.
COMPARATIVES:	No requirement to restate except in limited circumstances related to hedge accounting.

7.11.20   Date of initial application

7.11.20.10   A key term in the transition to IFRS 9 is 'the date of initial application', which is the date on which an entity first applies IFRS 9. This date is the beginning of the reporting period in which an entity adopts IFRS 9, and not the beginning of the comparative period. [*IFRS 9.7.2.2*]

7.11.20.20   The date of initial application is relevant to several assessments necessary to apply IFRS 9. Examples include:
- assessing whether a financial asset is held within a business model:
  - whose objective is to hold assets to collect contractual cash flows; or
  - in which assets are managed to achieve a particular objective by both collecting contractual cash flows and selling financial assets (see 7.11.80);
- for an investment in an equity instrument that is not held for trading, electing to present changes in fair value in OCI (see 7.11.100);
- designating, or revoking designations of, financial assets or financial liabilities as at FVTPL (see 7.11.110);
- designating own-use contracts as at FVTPL (see 7.11.130);
- assessing whether presenting the effects of changes in a financial liability's credit risk in OCI would create or enlarge an accounting mismatch in profit or loss (see 7.11.150);
- as part of the assessment of impairment, determining whether there has been a significant increase in credit risk since initial recognition or whether that determination would require significant cost or effort (see 7.11.210); and

● assessing compliance with qualifying hedge accounting criteria (see 7.11.220.50). [*IFRS 9.7.2.3–7.2.5, 7.2.8–7.2.10, 7.2.18, 7.2.20, 7.2.23*]

EXAMPLE 1 – ADOPTION IN 2018

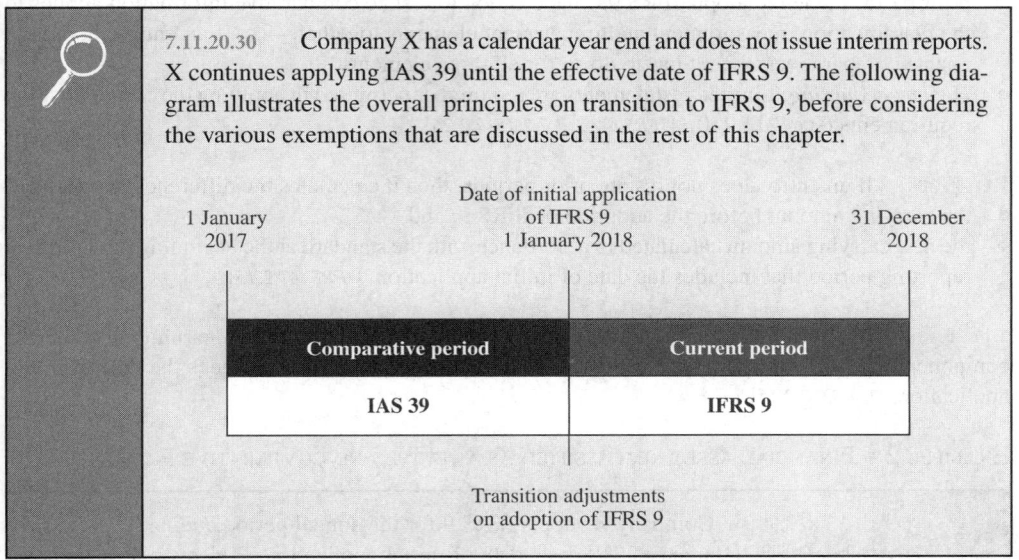

7.11.20.30   Company X has a calendar year end and does not issue interim reports. X continues applying IAS 39 until the effective date of IFRS 9. The following diagram illustrates the overall principles on transition to IFRS 9, before considering the various exemptions that are discussed in the rest of this chapter.

	Date of initial application of IFRS 9	
1 January 2017	1 January 2018	31 December 2018
Comparative period	**Current period**	
IAS 39	IFRS 9	

Transition adjustments
on adoption of IFRS 9

7.11.20.40   Only if the entity's relevant date of initial application was before 1 February 2015 could it have elected to adopt earlier versions of IFRS 9 for annual periods beginning before 1 January 2018. If an entity initially applied a previous version of IFRS 9 on or before 31 January 2015, then it was permitted to continue to apply that version until IFRS 9's mandatory effective date. This chapter generally considers the transition requirements in IFRS 9 (2014) from the perspective of an entity that has not previously adopted an earlier version of IFRS 9. The sequential adoption of different versions of IFRS 9 is discussed in 7.11.260. [*IFRS 9.7.3.2*]

7.11.20.50   When an entity first applies IFRS 9, it may elect to continue to apply the hedge accounting requirements of IAS 39 instead of IFRS 9 until the IASB's project on accounting for dynamic risk management is completed (see 7.9.80). [*IFRS 9.7.2.21*]

7.11.30   Retrospective application and comparative information

7.11.30.10   The basic principle in IFRS 9 is retrospective application in accordance with IAS 8 (see chapter 2.8) unless IFRS 9 contains more specific provisions for a particular aspect of the transition. However, IFRS 9 contains significant exemptions from retrospective application. The specific transition requirements of IFRS 9 together with their exemptions are discussed in the context of the different elements of IFRS 9: classification (see 7.11.70), measurement (see 7.11.140), impairment (see 7.11.210) and hedge accounting (see 7.11.215). [*IFRS 9.7.2.1, IAS 8.19, 22*]

7.11.30.20   Subject to an overriding condition that restatement is not permitted if it requires the use of hindsight, the following applies to comparative information on transition.

- *Financial assets and financial liabilities already derecognised on initial application (see 7.11.60):* An entity is not permitted to restate even if comparatives are restated voluntarily in respect of classification and measurement generally.
- *Classification, measurement and impairment:* An entity is permitted but not required to restate prior periods when it adopts IFRS 9. This election to restate comparative information applies to the classification, measurement and impairment elements together – i.e. if an entity chooses to restate comparatives, then it has to do so for all three elements.
- *Hedge accounting:* Limited restatements are required or permitted in applying the cost of hedging requirements (see 7.11.220). [*IFRS 9.7.2.1, 7.2.15, 7.2.26*]

7.11.30.30   If an entity does not restate prior periods, then it calculates the difference between:
- the carrying amount before the adoption of IFRS 9; and
- the new carrying amount calculated in accordance with the standard at the beginning of the annual reporting period that includes the date of initial application. [*IFRS 9.7.2.15*]

7.11.30.40   If a difference exists, then it is recognised in opening retained earnings (or another component of equity, if appropriate) of the annual reporting period that includes the date of initial application. [*IFRS 9.7.2.15*]

EXAMPLE 2 – FINANCIAL ASSET RECLASSIFIED AS AT FVTPL AND COMPARATIVE INFORMATION

7.11.30.50   Company E adopts IFRS 9 for the annual period ending 31 December 2018; 1 January 2018 is its date of initial application. E elects not to restate comparative information. Therefore, the comparatives are unchanged and reflect the previous accounting for financial assets and financial liabilities under IAS 39. The impact of retrospective application of IFRS 9 is recognised in opening equity as at 1 January 2018.

7.11.30.60   E has an investment in a financial asset that was measured at amortised cost under IAS 39. E has determined that under IFRS 9 the asset will be measured at FVTPL. The carrying amounts and fair values of the asset at the respective year ends were as follows.

DATE	CARRYING AMOUNT	FAIR VALUE
31 December 2016	350	355
31 December 2017	368	370

7.11.30.70   E presents one year of comparative information without restatement. E recognises 2 in opening retained earnings as at 1 January 2018. This is the difference between the fair value at 31 December 2017 of 370 and the carrying amount at that date of 368. The comparative figures for 2017 remain unchanged – i.e. an asset of 368 is recognised in the statement of financial position as at 31 December 2017.

7.11.30.80   If E elects to restate comparative information, then, under the general rules of retrospective application of IAS 8, in the 2018 financial statements the difference between the fair value and the previous carrying amount at the beginning of the earliest period presented would be recognised in opening retained earnings as at 1 January 2017.

7.11.30.90   This would mean that 5, being the difference between the fair value at 31 December 2016 of 355 and the previous carrying amount at that date of 350, would be recognised as a credit adjustment to opening retained earnings at 1 January 2017. The change in fair value between 31 December 2016 of 355 and 31 December 2017 of 370, a gain of 15, would be recognised in profit or loss for the year ended 31 December 2017 (i.e. in the comparatives).

7.11.30.100   Regardless of whether an entity chooses to restate prior periods, transitional disclosures are required. For a discussion of these transitional disclosure requirements, see 7.11.230–250. [*IFRS 9.7.2.15*]

7.11.40   Interim reporting

7.11.40.10   If an entity prepares interim financial statements in accordance with IAS 34, then it does not need to apply the requirements of IFRS 9 to interim periods before the date of initial application if doing so is impracticable as defined by IAS 8. [*IFRS 9.7.2.16*]

7.11.50   Elections for insurers applying IFRS 4

7.11.50.10   An insurer electing the temporary exemption from IFRS 9 may continue to apply IAS 39 rather than IFRS 9 for annual periods beginning before 1 January 2021 if it does not early adopt IFRS 17 (see 8.1.180). If this is the case, then the insurer is required to provide disclosures to enable users of financial statements to compare entities that apply the temporary exemption from IFRS 9 with those that do not (see 8.1.270). For the purposes of these disclosures, the insurer uses the applicable transitional provisions in IFRS 9 to the extent necessary (see 8.1.280.10). [*IFRS 4.47*]

7.11.50.20   Under the temporary exemption from IFRS 9, an insurer may apply IFRS 9's presentation and disclosure requirements for gains and losses on financial liabilities designated as at FVTPL while continuing otherwise to apply IAS 39. If an insurer elects to do so, then it applies the relevant transitional requirements of IFRS 9 (see 7.11.30.10–20, 110 and 150). The insurer is permitted but not required to restate prior periods when it adopts the requirements. [*IFRS 4.20C, 7.2.15*]

7.11.50.30   When an insurer transitions to IFRS 9, it may apply the overlay approach to certain financial assets until it adopts IFRS 17. The insurer applies the overlay approach retrospectively. The insurer restates comparative information under the overlay approach if, and only if, it restates comparative information when applying IFRS 9 (see 7.11.30.20 and 8.1.280.20–90). [*IFRS 4.35C, 49*]

7.11.60   FINANCIAL ASSETS OR FINANCIAL LIABILITIES ALREADY DERECOGNISED ON INITIAL APPLICATION

7.11.60.10   IFRS 9 is not applied to items that have already been derecognised at the date of initial application. Accordingly, even when an entity restates comparative information to reflect the adoption of IFRS 9, information related to financial assets and financial liabilities derecognised before the date of initial application continues to be reported in accordance with IAS 39 (for a discussion of comparative information, see 7.11.30). This means that the comparative information could contain a mixture of IAS 39 accounting (for items that are derecognised in periods before the date of initial application) and IFRS 9 accounting (for financial instruments that continue to be recognised at the date of initial application). [*IFRS 9.7.2.1*]

EXAMPLE 3A – FINANCIAL ASSETS OR FINANCIAL LIABILITIES DERECOGNISED BEFORE DATE OF INITIAL APPLICATION

7.11.60.20   Company C adopts IFRS 9 for its annual period ending 31 December 2018. Its date of initial application is 1 January 2018. On 1 November 2017, C sold an investment in a debt security that was classified as available-for-sale under IAS 39.

7.11.60.30   IFRS 9 does not apply to financial assets that are derecognised before the date of initial application. Therefore, even if C elects to restate comparative information the debt security continues to be presented in accordance with the requirements of IAS 39 for available-for-sale assets in the comparative information included in C's 2018 financial statements.

7.11.60.40   The following diagram illustrates the accounting for the investment on transition to IFRS 9.

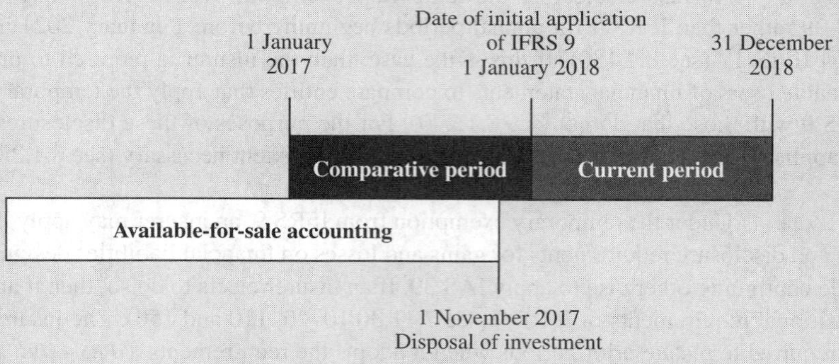

| | Date of initial application | |
| 1 January 2017 | of IFRS 9 1 January 2018 | 31 December 2018 |

Comparative period · Current period

Available-for-sale accounting

1 November 2017
Disposal of investment

EXAMPLE 3B – FINANCIAL ASSETS OR FINANCIAL LIABILITIES NOT DERECOGNISED BEFORE DATE OF INITIAL APPLICATION

7.11.60.50   Company K adopts IFRS 9 for its annual period ending 31 December 2018. Its date of initial application is 1 January 2018. On 1 September 2018, K sells an investment in a debt security that was classified as available-for-sale under IAS 39.

7.11.60.60   In this example, the exemption does not apply because the asset was not derecognised before the date of initial application. Accordingly, the debt security is accounted for in accordance with the requirements of IFRS 9:

- throughout the year ending 31 December 2018 (to the date of sale); and
- in any comparative period for which K elects to restate comparative information.

7.11.60.70   The following diagram illustrates the accounting for the investment on transition to IFRS 9 assuming that K does not restate comparatives.

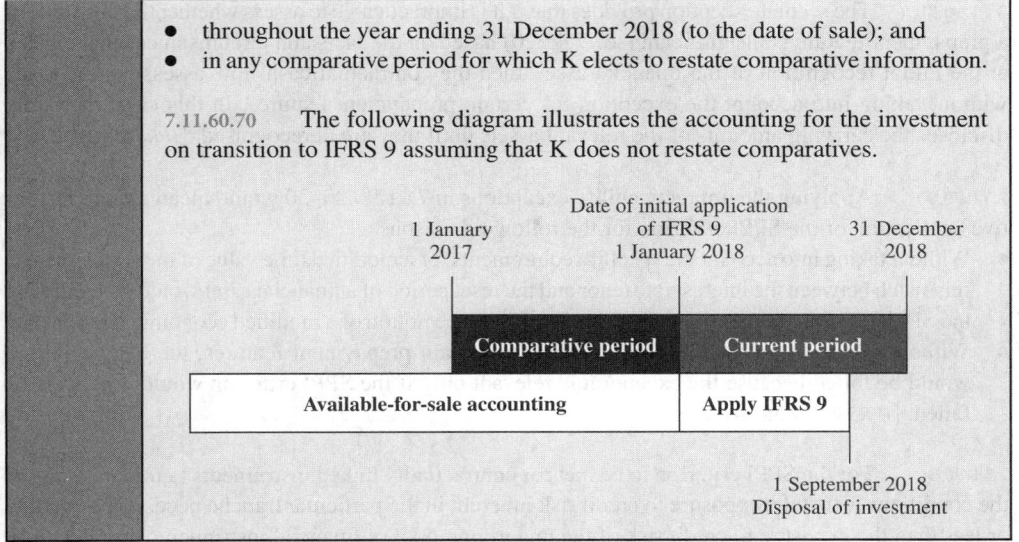

CLASSIFICATION

7.11.70

7.11.70.10   On adopting IFRS 9, an entity determines which of its financial assets meet the criteria to be measured at amortised cost or FVOCI.

Business model

7.11.80

7.11.80.10   As an exception to retrospective application, the assessment of whether the objective of an entity's business is:
- to hold an asset to collect the contractual cash flows; or
- to achieve a particular objective by both collecting contractual cash flows and selling,

is based on facts and circumstances at the date of initial application. [*IFRS 9.7.2.3*]

7.11.80.20   An entity is not required to consider business models that may have applied in previous periods. The resulting classification is applied retrospectively, irrespective of the entity's business model in prior reporting periods. [*IFRS 9.7.2.3*]

SPPI criterion#

7.11.90

7.11.90.10   There are no specific transition requirements for the date at which an entity needs to assess whether the SPPI criterion is met. Therefore, the general requirements apply – i.e. an entity makes this assessment on the basis of facts and circumstances existing at the time of initial recognition of the financial asset. There are two exceptions related to this requirement.

7.11.90.20   The first exception provides that if it is impracticable to assess a modified time value of money element (see 7.4.180) based on the facts and circumstances that existed at the initial recognition of the financial asset, then the contractual cash flow assessment is made without taking into account the specific requirements for the modification of the time value of money element. In this case, the entity discloses the carrying amounts of the relevant assets until they are derecognised. [*IFRS 9.7.2.4, 7.42R*]

7.11.90.30   The second exception provides that if it is impracticable to assess whether the fair value of a prepayment feature is insignificant (see 7.4.220) based on the facts and circumstances that existed at the initial recognition of the financial asset, then the contractual cash flow assessment is made without taking into account the exception for certain prepayment features. In this case, the entity discloses the carrying amounts of the relevant assets until they are derecognised. [*IFRS 9.7.2.5, 7.42S*]

7.11.90.40   Applying the impracticability exceptions in 7.11.90.20–30 would mean a more restrictive application of the SPPI criterion for the following reasons.
● Without taking into account the specific requirements for a modified time value of money element, a mismatch between the interest rate tenor and the reset period of a financial asset would generally fail the SPPI criterion if the assessment is made without the notion of a modified economic relationship.
● Without taking into account the exception for certain prepayment features, the SPPI criterion would be failed because the exception is relevant only if the SPPI criterion would otherwise be failed. [*IFRS 9.BC7.55–BC7.56*]

7.11.90.50   For the SPPI criterion to be met for contractually linked instruments (a tranche), one of the conditions is that the exposure to credit risk inherent in the particular tranche needs to be equal to or less than the exposure to credit risk of the underlying pool of financial instruments (see 7.4.340). It appears that this assessment should be based on the facts and circumstances that existed when the entity initially recognised its investment in the instrument, and not at the date of initial application.

7.11.95   FORTHCOMING REQUIREMENTS

7.11.95.10   *Prepayment Features with Negative Compensation – Amendments to IFRS 9* allow financial assets with prepayment features that may result in negative compensation to be measured at amortised cost or at FVOCI if they meet the other relevant requirements of IFRS 9 (see 7.4.225).

7.11.95.20   The amendments are effective for annual periods beginning on or after 1 January 2019 and are applied retrospectively in accordance with IAS 8 subject to the following modifications.

7.11.95.30   If an entity first applies these amendments at the same time as it first applies IFRS 9 – i.e. before the amendments are effective – then there are no specific transition requirements for the amendments. The entity discloses the fact that the amendments have been adopted early.

7.11.95.40   However, if an entity first applies the amendments after it first applies IFRS 9, then the following transition requirements are applied. An entity:
● may designate a financial asset or financial liability as at FVTPL if that designation would not previously have satisfied the accounting mismatch condition but it is now satisfied as a result of applying the amendments. The designation is made on the basis of the facts and circumstances that exist at the date of initial application of the amendments;
● revokes its previous designation of a financial asset or financial liability as at FVTPL if that designation was previously made in accordance with the accounting mismatch condition but the condition is no longer satisfied as a result of applying the amendments. The revocation is made on the basis of the facts and circumstances that exist at the date of initial application of the amendments;

- is not required to restate prior periods to reflect the amendments. The restatement of prior periods is allowed only if it is possible without the use of hindsight; and
- is required to disclose certain information for each class of financial assets and financial liabilities that were affected by the amendments.

The other transition requirements discussed in this chapter are also applied if doing so is necessary to apply the amendments, in which case reference to the 'date of initial application' is read to mean the beginning of the reporting period in which an entity first applies the amendments. [*IFRS 9.7.2.29–7.2.34*]

7.11.100   Investments in equity instruments

7.11.100.10   At the date of initial application, an entity may elect to present changes in the fair value of an investment in an equity instrument that is not held for trading in OCI. [*IFRS 9.7.2.8(b)*]

7.11.100.20   As an exception to retrospective application, an entity makes this election by determining whether an asset is held for trading as if it had acquired the asset on the date of initial application. Therefore, it appears that it is possible to elect to present changes in fair value through OCI for an investment in an equity instrument that was classified as held-for-trading at the original date of acquisition but does not meet the held-for-trading definition at the date of initial application. [*IFRS 9.5.7.5, B7.2.1*]

7.11.110   Financial assets or financial liabilities designated as at FVTPL

7.11.110.10   The fair value option for financial assets and financial liabilities is re-opened based on the facts and circumstances at the date of initial application. At this date, an entity:
- may choose to designate any financial asset or financial liability as at FVTPL if the accounting mismatch criterion in the standard is met. However, new designations on the basis that financial liabilities are managed on a fair value basis or contain an embedded derivative are not possible;
- revokes an existing designation of a financial asset if the accounting mismatch criterion is not met;
- revokes an existing designation of a financial liability if it was originally designated on the basis of the accounting mismatch criterion but that criterion is no longer met;
- may choose to revoke any existing designation of a financial asset even if the accounting mismatch criterion is met; and
- may choose to revoke any existing designation of a financial liability – but only if the liability was originally designated on the basis of the accounting mismatch criterion – even if the accounting mismatch criterion continues to be met. Therefore, if liabilities were originally designated because they were managed on a fair value basis or contained an embedded derivative, then an entity is not permitted to revoke the previous designation on transition to IFRS 9. [*IFRS 9.7.2.8–7.2.10*]

EXAMPLE 4 – FINANCIAL LIABILITIES DESIGNATED AS AT FVTPL

7.11.110.20   Company D has a financial asset that was accounted for as a loan and receivable under IAS 39 and that is required to be reclassified as at FVTPL on transition to IFRS 9. D manages the asset in conjunction with an existing financial liability that has been accounted for at amortised cost.

> 7.11.110.30   At the date of initial application, D determines that designating the financial liability as at FVTPL would reduce an accounting mismatch that would otherwise arise from measuring the financial liability at amortised cost and the financial asset as at FVTPL.
>
> 7.11.110.40   As a result, in this example, D chooses to designate the financial liability as at FVTPL at the date of initial application.

7.11.120   Timing of elective designations or revocations on transition

7.11.120.10   Certain elective designations and revocations that may be made at the date of initial application are discussed in 7.11.100–110. In those cases, an entity makes the designation or revocation on the basis of the facts and circumstances that exist at the date of initial application. The revised classification is applied retrospectively.

7.11.120.20   It appears that such elective designations and revocations at the date of initial application do not require an act of designation or revocation to be performed at the date of initial application. We believe that the physical act of designation or revocation at the date of initial application should be made as soon as is practicable but may be made at any time during the course of preparing the financial statements – through to their authorisation for issue – in which the standard is adopted for the first time. However, if acts of designation or revocation are performed after the date of initial application, then it may be difficult to demonstrate that the designations were made solely using information available on that date.

7.11.120.30   In all cases the designation or revocation is based on the facts and circumstances at the date of initial application, and not on subsequent changes in facts and circumstances. These facts and circumstances include, if relevant:
- whether a financial asset is held within a business model:
  - whose objective is to hold assets to collect contractual cash flows; or
  - in which assets are managed to achieve a particular objective by both collecting contractual cash flows and selling financial assets (see 7.11.80);
- whether designation as at FVTPL would reduce or eliminate an accounting mismatch – this includes consideration of the classification and measurement of other assets and liabilities at the date of initial application in accordance with IFRS 9 (see 7.11.110); and
- whether an equity investment is held for trading (see 7.11.100). [*IFRS 9.7.2.3, 7.2.8–7.2.10*]

7.11.130   Contracts that meet own-use scope exception designated as at FVTPL

7.11.130.10   IFRS 9 introduces a new option to designate a contract to buy or sell a non-financial item that meets the own-use scope exception as at FVTPL if doing so eliminates or significantly reduces a recognition inconsistency that would otherwise arise from not recognising the contract because of its exclusion from the scope of IFRS 9 (see 7.9.100).

7.11.130.20   This option is generally available only at inception of the contract. However, at the date of initial application, an entity is allowed to make this designation for an existing contract but only if it designates all similar contracts. The change in net assets resulting from the designation is

2374

recognised in retained earnings at the date of initial application. It appears that restatement of comparatives is not permitted. Because entities would not have been required to measure the fair values of these contracts at previous reporting dates, restatement of comparatives would typically involve hindsight. [*IFRS 9.7.2.14A, BCZ2.38*]

7.11.140   MEASUREMENT

7.11.150   Assessment of accounting mismatch for own credit risk

7.11.150.10   An entity assesses whether presenting the effects of changes in a financial liability's credit risk in OCI would create or enlarge an accounting mismatch in profit or loss on the basis of the facts and circumstances that exist at the date of initial application of IFRS 9 (see 7.7.200). The accounting treatment is applied retrospectively on this basis. [*IFRS 9.7.2.14*]

7.11.160   Hybrid instruments

7.11.160.10   If under IFRS 9 a hybrid instrument is required to be measured at fair value in its entirety, but its fair value has not been determined in previous periods, then the sum of the fair values of the components at the end of each comparative period is deemed to be the fair value of the entire instrument at those dates if an entity restates prior periods. These circumstances might arise when a hybrid instrument was required to be separated into a non-derivative host contract and an embedded derivative under IAS 39. At the date of initial application, an entity recognises any difference between the fair value of the entire hybrid contract and the sum of the fair values of the components of the hybrid contract in opening retained earnings [*IFRS 9.7.2.6–7.2.7*]

7.11.160.20   This transition requirement applies when an entity has not, in previous periods, determined the fair value of the hybrid instrument in its entirety. An entity will not have the necessary information to determine fair value retrospectively without using hindsight. However, it would have been required to measure both the embedded derivative and host separately at fair value to apply the disclosure requirements in IFRS 7. The fair value of the entire hybrid contract is determined at the date of initial application and compared with the sum of the fair values of the components of the hybrid contract to determine the amount to be recognised in the opening retained earnings of the reporting period that includes the date of initial application. [*IFRS 9.BC.7.16*]

EXAMPLE 5 – TRANSITION ADJUSTMENTS – HYBRID INSTRUMENTS

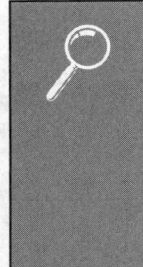

7.11.160.30   Company C has a calendar year end. C adopts IFRS 9 in its 31 December 2018 annual financial statements and its date of initial application is 1 January 2018. C elects to restate its comparatives on transition to IFRS 9.

7.11.160.40   C has a hybrid instrument with a financial asset host. Under IAS 39, the host was accounted for at amortised cost, and the embedded derivative was separated and accounted for at FVTPL. In accordance with IFRS 7, C previously disclosed the fair value of the host at each reporting date. C determines that under IFRS 9 the entire hybrid instrument will be accounted for at FVTPL. C had not, in previous periods, determined the fair value of the hybrid instrument in its entirety.

7.11.160.50   The following facts about the hybrid instrument are also relevant for this example.

DATE	FAIR VALUE: EMBEDDED DERIVATIVE	FAIR VALUE: HOST CONTRACT	FAIR VALUE: HYBRID INSTRUMENT
1 January 2017	5	87	N/A
31 December 2017/1 January 2018	8	90	96
31 December 2018	N/A	N/A	94

7.11.160.60   The amortised cost of the host contract at 1 January 2017 was 88. The fair value of the embedded derivative that was separated from the host contract at 1 January 2017 was 5.

7.11.160.70   C recognises the following amounts in its statement of financial position under IFRS 9.

DATE	AMOUNT RECOGNISED FOR THE HYBRID CONTRACT	
1 January 2017	(5 + 87)	92
31 December 2017	(8 + 90)	98
31 December 2018		94

7.11.160.80   C recognises the following amounts in profit or loss under IFRS 9.

PERIOD	AMOUNT RECOGNISED IN PROFIT OR LOSS	
1 January 2017 – 31 December 2017	(98 - 92)	gain of 6
1 January 2018 – 31 December 2018	(94 - 96)	loss of 2

7.11.160.90   C records a transition adjustment in opening retained earnings as at 1 January 2017 of 1 (debit). This is the difference between the amortised cost of the host of 88 and its fair value of 87. The difference between the sum of the fair values of the host and the embedded derivative at 1 January 2018 and the fair value of the hybrid instrument at that date of 2 ((90 + 8) - 96) is included as a transition adjustment of 2 (debit) in opening retained earnings at 1 January 2018, and not in profit or loss for either period.

7.11.160.100   Under IAS 39, the economic characteristics and risks of an embedded derivative in a financial asset may have been considered closely related to those of the host contract and therefore the embedded derivative may not have been separated from the host contract. In this scenario, the fair value of the hybrid instrument in its entirety would have been determined in previous annual periods – either because the entire instrument would have been measured at fair value under IAS 39, or for the purposes of disclosure under IFRS 7. In this case, the specific transition requirement outlined in 7.11.160.10 would not apply.

7.11.170 Effective interest method

7.11.170.10   It may be impracticable to retrospectively apply the effective interest method – e.g. for financial instruments reclassified to the amortised cost or FVOCI categories (see 2.8.90). In this case, if comparatives are restated on transition to IFRS 9, then the fair value of the financial instrument at the end of each comparative period presented is treated as the gross carrying amount of the financial asset or the amortised cost of the financial liability. The fair value of the financial instrument at the date of initial application is treated as the new gross carrying amount of the financial asset or the new amortised cost of the financial liability at that date. [*IFRS 9.7.2.11, IAS 8.5*]

7.11.170.20   Because the fair value at the end of each comparative period is treated as the gross carrying amount, it appears that all changes in fair value – other than principal advances and repayments – should be recognised as interest in profit or loss in the restated comparative information presented.

7.11.180 Previously reclassified financial assets

7.11.180.10   Under IAS 39, an entity may have previously reclassified a financial asset from the held-for-trading or available-for-sale categories, measured at fair value, to loans and receivables, measured at amortised cost. Under IAS 39, the entity would have reclassified the financial asset at its fair value; this fair value would have become the new amortised cost.

7.11.180.20   On transition to IFRS 9, entities are generally required to apply the classification and measurement requirements retrospectively, as if the new classification under IFRS 9 had always been applied (see 7.11.30.10). Therefore, it appears that if such a previously reclassified financial asset is classified as measured at amortised cost or FVOCI under IFRS 9, then the gross carrying amount should be recalculated as if the asset had always been measured at amortised cost or FVOCI (subject to the impracticability exemption in 7.11.170), rather than by carrying forward any measurements under IAS 39.

7.11.190 Unquoted equity investments measured at cost

7.11.190.10   As an exception to retrospective application, if unquoted equity investments or related derivatives were previously measured at cost, then they are measured at fair value at the date of initial application. The difference between the fair value and the previous carrying amount of the instrument at the date of initial application is recorded as an adjustment to the opening retained earnings (or another component of equity, as appropriate) of the reporting period of initial application. Therefore, only fair value changes after the date of initial application are recognised in profit or loss or OCI. For the purpose of reporting in the comparative period, these instruments are reported at cost. [*IFRS 9.7.2.12–7.2.13*]

EXAMPLE 6 – TRANSITION ADJUSTMENTS – UNQUOTED EQUITY INVESTMENTS MEASURED AT COST

7.11.190.20   Continuing Example 3A, assume that Company C has an equity investment that was measured at cost less impairment under IAS 39. The carrying amount of the investment is 450. Under IFRS 9, C determines that the fair value of the investment at the date of initial application of 1 January 2018 is 630.

> 7.11.190.30   C recognises the difference between the carrying amount of 450 and the fair value on the date of initial application of 630 in opening retained earnings at 1 January 2018. For the year ended 31 December 2017, C presents the equity investments at 450.
>
> 7.11.190.40   Any fair value changes that arise between 1 January 2018 and 31 December 2018 are recognised in profit or loss – unless C elects at 1 January 2018 to present the changes in fair value of the investment in OCI.

7.11.200   Modifications of financial assets

7.11.200.10   IFRS 9 introduces new guidance on measuring financial assets that are renegotiated or otherwise modified and the renegotiation or modification does not result in derecognition (see 7.7.350). Under this guidance, the gross carrying amount of the financial asset is recalculated as the present value of the renegotiated or modified contractual cash flows discounted at the financial asset's original effective interest rate. The difference between this recalculated amount and the existing gross carrying amount is recognised as a modification gain or loss in profit or loss. [*IFRS 9.5.4.3*]

7.11.200.20   Except for modifications because of financial difficulties of the borrower, IAS 39 was silent on how to account for modifications of financial assets that do not result in derecognition. In our experience, the common approach adopted when impairment was not applicable was to recognise the difference in contractual cash flows arising from the modification over the remaining life of the financial asset by adjusting the effective interest rate prospectively, rather than adjusting the carrying amount and recognising the difference immediately in profit or loss.

7.11.200.30   There are no specific transition requirements in this respect. Because IFRS 9 requires retrospective application, it appears that entities that previously adjusted the effective interest rate prospectively should assess what the gross carrying amount would have been had the modification been accounted for in accordance with the IFRS 9 requirements. If comparative information for prior periods is not restated, then we believe that the difference in the gross carrying amount at the date of initial application should be taken to opening retained earnings of the annual period that includes the date of initial application.

EXAMPLE 7 – TRANSITION ADJUSTMENTS – MODIFICATIONS OF FINANCIAL ASSETS

> 7.11.200.40   On 1 January 2017, Bank D agrees to modify the terms of a fixed rate loan to a borrower, whose credit quality has improved, by reducing the interest rate charged. Under IAS 39 and IFRS 9, the modification does not result in derecognition of the original loan which is measured at amortised cost. Under IAS 39, D recognises the difference in contractual cash flows arising from the modification over the remaining life of the loan by adjusting the effective interest rate prospectively.
>
> 7.11.200.50   D initially applies IFRS 9 on 1 January 2018. D assesses what the gross carrying amount would have been had the modification been accounted for in accordance with IFRS 9. D recognises the difference in the gross carrying amount at 1 January 2018 in opening retained earnings at 1 January 2018.

7.11.205 Modifications and exchanges of financial liabilities

7.11.205.10 In the basis for conclusions to *Prepayment Features with Negative Compensation – Amendments to IFRS 9*, the IASB confirmed that the requirements for recalculating the amortised cost of a modified financial liability under IFRS 9 (2014) are consistent with the requirements for recalculating the gross carrying amount of a modified financial asset when its modification or exchange does not result in derecognition – i.e. the amortised cost of the financial liability is recalculated by discounting the modified contractual cash flows using the original effective interest rate. An entity recognises any adjustment to the amortised cost of the financial liability in profit or loss as income or expense at the date of the modification or exchange (see 7.7.350 and 370). [*IFRS 9.BC4.252–BC4.253*]

7.11.205.20 IAS 39 did not provide guidance on accounting for the difference in present value. In our view, under IAS 39 any difference in present value arising as a result of the modification of a financial liability that did not result in derecognition should have been recognised as an adjustment to the effective interest rate and amortised over the remaining life of the modified financial liability (see 7I.5.400.10–20).

7.11.205.30 As in the case of modifications of financial assets (see 7.11.200.30), there are no specific transition requirements for this change in accounting treatment. Therefore, it appears that entities that previously adjusted the effective interest rate prospectively as described in 7.11.205.20 should assess what the amortised cost and effective interest rate would have been had the modification been accounted for in accordance with 7.7.370. If comparative information for prior periods is not restated (see 7.11.30.20), then we believe that the difference in the amortised cost at the date of initial application should be taken to opening retained earnings of the annual period that includes the date of initial application of IFRS 9 (2014).

7.11.210 IMPAIRMENT

7.11.210.10 The impairment requirements of IFRS 9 are applied retrospectively in accordance with IAS 8, subject to the exemption described in 7.11.210.60 below. [*IFRS 9.7.2.17*]

7.11.210.20 At the date of initial application, an entity determines the credit risk at the date on which the financial instrument was initially recognised and compares it with the credit risk at the date of initial application to assess whether there has been a significant increase in credit risk since initial recognition. [*IFRS 9.7.2.18*]

7.11.210.30 In making this assessment, an entity may apply:
- the low credit risk exception (see 7.8.150); and
- the rebuttable presumption for contractual payments that are more than 30 days past due (see 7.8.120), if the entity will identify significant increases in credit risk based on past-due information. [*IFRS 9.7.2.19*]

7.11.210.40 An entity is not required to undertake an exhaustive search for information for determining, at the date of initial application, whether there has been a significant increase in credit risk since initial recognition of a financial asset. Instead, the entity approximates the credit risk on initial recognition by considering all reasonable and supportable information that is available without undue cost or effort. This information comprises all internal and external information, including portfolio information. [*IFRS 9.B7.2.2–B7.2.3*]

7.11.210.50   An entity with little historical information can use the following sources of information:
- information from internal reports and statistics – e.g. that may have been generated when deciding whether to launch a new product;
- information about similar products; and
- peer group experience for comparable financial instruments. [*IFRS 9.B7.2.4*]

7.11.210.60   If, at the date of initial application, determining whether there has been a significant increase in credit risk since the initial recognition of a financial instrument would require undue cost or effort, then the loss allowance is measured as lifetime ECLs (see 7.8.40) at each reporting date until the financial instrument is derecognised, unless an entity applies the low credit risk exception (see 7.11.210.30) and the credit risk of the financial instrument is low. If the credit risk of a financial instrument is low at a reporting date, then an entity may assume that the credit risk on that asset has not increased significantly since initial recognition, and may recognise a loss allowance equal to 12 months' ECLs (see 7.8.40). [*IFRS 9.7.2.20*]

7.11.210.70   If the entity previously recognised a loss allowance measured as lifetime ECLs at the date of initial application through opening retained earnings (or another component of equity, as appropriate) and subsequently recognises a loss allowance equal to 12 months' ECLs, then this would cause a reversal of impairment losses that is recognised in profit or loss. [*IFRS 9.7.2.15*]

7.11.215   HEDGE ACCOUNTING

7.11.220   General transitional requirements

7.11.220.10   When an entity adopts IFRS 9, it may choose as its accounting policy to defer application of the new general hedging model until the standard resulting from the IASB's project on accounting for dynamic risk management is completed. In this case, the entity continues to apply the hedge accounting requirements in IAS 39 in their entirety to all of its hedging relationships. An entity that chooses that policy also applies IFRIC 16 without the IFRS 9 consequential amendments. However, the new disclosure requirements may not be deferred (see 7.10.380). [*IFRS 9.7.2.21, BC6.104*]

7.11.220.20   Because this is an accounting policy choice, it appears that an entity may subsequently change its accounting policy in accordance with IAS 8 and cease to apply the IAS 39 hedge accounting requirements. An entity that does so will begin to apply the IFRS 9 hedge accounting requirements at the beginning of that reporting period, in which case it will apply the relevant transition requirements of IFRS 9. [*IFRS 9.BC6.104*]

7.11.220.30   The hedge accounting requirements of IFRS 9 are applied prospectively subject to the following exceptions.
- Retrospective application of the accounting for the time value of purchased options as a cost of hedging is required for all hedging relationships previously designated and qualifying as a hedging relationship under IAS 39 in which the hedging instrument is designated as the intrinsic value of an option.

- Retrospective application of the accounting for the forward element of forward contracts as a cost of hedging is permitted for hedging relationships previously designated and qualifying as a hedging relationship under IAS 39 in which the hedging instrument is designated as the spot element of a forward contract, provided that this election is applied consistently. If an entity elects retrospective application of this accounting, then it is required to apply it to all hedging relationships that qualify for this election.
- Retrospective application of the accounting for foreign currency basis spreads as a cost of hedging is permitted.
- Retrospective application of the derivative novation requirements is compulsory. These state that there is no expiry or termination of the hedging instrument if:
  - as a result of laws or regulations, the parties to the hedging instrument agree that one or more clearing counterparties replace their original counterparty to become the new counterparty to each of the parties; and
  - other changes to the hedging instrument are limited to those that are necessary to effect such a counterparty replacement. [*IFRS 9.7.2.22, 7.2.26*]

7.11.220.40   Retrospective application of the cost of hedging requirements (whether permitted or required) does not apply to hedging relationships that were terminated before the beginning of the earliest comparative period. [*IFRS 9.7.2.26*]

7.11.220.42   The general transition requirements include a statement that IFRS 9 is not applied to items that have already been derecognised at the date of initial application (see 7.11.60.10). It is not clear whether this statement applies to the specific provisions of IFRS 9 on retrospective application of the hedge accounting requirements set out in 7.11.220.30–40. Also, a question arises about how the term 'items that have already been derecognised' should be interpreted in the context of transition to the hedge accounting requirements. 'Items that have already been derecognised' could be interpreted as referring to the hedged item, the hedging instrument, the hedging relationship and/or any amounts accumulated in the OCI reserve. For example, if the hedging instrument in a cash flow hedge is terminated before the date of initial application and the hedged future cash flows have not occurred but are still expected to occur, then the amount accumulated in OCI remains in the cash flow hedge reserve until the future cash flows occur (see 7.9.960.30) – i.e. the hedging instrument has been derecognised but the cash flow hedge reserve has not. Therefore, it appears that an entity may choose an accounting policy (or policies), to be applied consistently, in relation to:

- whether the statement that IFRS 9 should not be applied to 'items that have already been derecognised at the date of initial application' applies to hedge accounting transition requirements; and
- if it does apply, then how to interpret this statement. [*IFRS 9.7.2.1*]

7.11.220.45   A related question arises if an entity had previously designated a cash flow hedge of a forecast transaction that resulted in the recognition of a non-financial asset or liability but the hedging relationship has been discontinued before the date of initial application because the hedged transaction occurred and the non-financial asset or liability was recognised. If the entity's policy for such hedges under IAS 39 was to reclassify gains and losses from the cash flow hedge reserve to profit or loss only when the hedged transaction impacted profit or loss, then it will be required on adopting IFRS 9's hedge accounting chapter to change its accounting policy prospectively to remove the relevant amounts from the cash flow hedge reserve and include them in the initial cost or carrying amount of the asset or liability (see 7.9.200.70). In this case, it is unclear both how the notion of 'items that have already been derecognised' is applied and whether prospective application applies if the non-financial item was initially recognised before the date of initial application of the new policy. Therefore, on initial application of the IFRS 9 hedge accounting requirements, it appears that in such a case the entity should choose an accounting policy, to be applied consistently, in relation to the gain or loss recognised in OCI and still accumulated in the cash flow hedge reserve at the date of initial application – i.e. to:

- reclassify it to profit or loss as a reclassification adjustment when the non-financial item affects profit or loss; or
- include it in the cost or carrying amount of the non-financial item at the date of initial application. [*IFRS 9.6.5.11(d)(i)*]

7.11.220.50   All qualifying criteria are required to be met as at the date of initial application of the new hedge accounting requirements to apply hedge accounting from that date. Retrospective designation of hedging relationships is not permitted and, therefore, a hedge has to have actually been designated and documented in a manner consistent with the requirements of IFRS 9 at or before the date of initial application to qualify for hedge accounting from that date. On initial application of the IFRS 9 hedge accounting requirements, an entity may start applying those requirements from the same point in time as it stops applying the IAS 39 hedge accounting requirements. [*IFRS 9.7.2.23, 7.2.25(a)*]

7.11.220.60   Hedging relationships that qualify for hedge accounting in accordance with IAS 39 that also qualify under IFRS 9, after taking into account any rebalancing on transition, are regarded as continuing hedging relationships. When applicable, an entity is required to use the hedge ratio in accordance with IAS 39 as the starting point for rebalancing the hedge ratio of a continuing hedging relationship. Any gain or loss from such a rebalancing is recognised in profit or loss. [*IFRS 9.7.2.24, 7.2.25(b)*]

7.11.220.70   If fair value hedge accounting was applied to an asset that was measured at amortised cost or at FVOCI (i.e. available-for-sale) under IAS 39, but is measured at FVTPL under IFRS 9, then in our experience hedge accounting will generally be discontinued. The hedged item will then be subject to full fair value measurement through profit or loss, rather than remeasurement only in respect of the risk being hedged. Even if the entity elects to restate comparative information, it is not required to make any adjustment in respect of the derivative hedging instrument for periods before the date of initial application. This is because gains and losses would already have been reflected in profit or loss.

7.11.225   Changing the hedge designation

7.11.225.10   IFRS 9 permits forward points of a forward contract to be excluded from the designation of a hedging instrument. The excluded forward points may then be accounted for as costs of hedging (see 7.9.690). Under IAS 39, when hedging a recognised foreign currency monetary financial asset or financial liability for foreign currency risk, some entities may have designated the hedged risk as changes in the forward rate (as opposed to hedging changes in the spot rate and therefore excluding the forward points from the hedging relationship). Some entities may also have designated the hedged risk as changes in the forward rate when hedging a highly probable forecast sale or purchase of a non-financial item through to the transaction's cash settlement date. IFRS 9 clarifies that because recognised foreign currency monetary financial assets and financial liabilities are translated into the entity's functional currency using the spot rate under IAS 21 (see 2.7.110.10), the forward rate method is not appropriate under IFRS 9. [*IFRS 9.BC6.414–BC6.426*]

7.11.225.20   An entity may achieve a similar accounting outcome as under the forward rate method by designating the spot rate as the hedged risk, excluding the forward element from the hedging instrument, and recognising the forward element as a cost of hedging. Accordingly, it appears that entities that previously applied the forward rate method to hedges of financial assets or financial liabilities or highly probable forecast future cash flows will need to change their hedge designations by the date of initial application of IFRS 9. However, we believe that, on transition to hedge accounting under IFRS 9, entities may continue to apply hedge accounting for such existing hedging relationships under the costs of hedging accounting permitted by IFRS 9.

7.11.225.30   IAS 39 does not permit the designation of a component of a non-financial item as a hedged item, unless it is a foreign exchange risk component. Conversely, IFRS 9 does permit the designation of the risk component of a non-financial item as a hedged item if the identified risk component is separately identifiable and reliably measurable. The question arises whether an entity can treat a hedging relationship that was previously designated under IAS 39 as a hedge of the entire non-financial item as a continuing hedging relationship under IFRS 9 if the entity changes the hedged item to a component of the non-financial item to align with its risk management objective.

7.11.225.40   The IFRS Interpretations Committee discussed this issue and noted that when an entity changes the hedged item in a hedging relationship from an entire non-financial item to a component of the non-financial item on transition to IFRS 9, it is required to do so on a prospective basis. It also noted that changing the hedged item while continuing the original hedging relationship would be equivalent to retrospective application of the hedge accounting requirements in IFRS 9, which is prohibited except in the limited circumstances described in 7.11.220.30. Therefore, the original hedging relationship cannot be treated as a continuing hedging relationship on transition to IFRS 9. [*IU 01-16*]

Example 8 – Continuing hedging relationship on transition

> **7.11.225.42**   On 1 January 2017, Company X forecast a purchase of jet fuel on 31 December 2018. On the same date, in accordance with its risk management policies, X entered into a forward contract with a maturity date of 31 December 2018 indexed to a crude oil benchmark to hedge the crude oil component of the forecast purchase of jet fuel. Because IAS 39 does not permit the designation of a risk component of a non-financial item (other than foreign currency risk), X designated the hedging relationship for the purposes of IAS 39 with the entire forecast purchase of jet fuel as the hedged item and the derivative as the hedging instrument.
>
> **7.11.225.44**   On 1 January 2018, X adopts IFRS 9, including the general hedge accounting requirements. On transition to IFRS 9, if X changes the hedged item to the crude oil component of the forecast jet fuel purchase, then the hedging relationship cannot be treated as a continuing hedging relationship.

7.11.225.50   A related question that arises is whether an entity can continue with its original hedge designation of the entire non-financial item on transition to IFRS 9 when the entity's risk management objective is to hedge only a component of the non-financial item.

7.11.225.60   The Committee also discussed this issue and observed that:

- the basis for conclusions to IFRS 9 supports the use of hedge designations that are not exact copies of actual risk management ('proxy hedging') if they reflect risk management – i.e. they relate to the same type of risk that is being managed and the same type of instruments that are being used for that purpose (see 7.9.30); and
- the use of proxy hedging in cases in which it reflects the entity's risk management (i.e. it relates to the same type of risk that is being managed and the same type of instruments that are being used for that purpose) did not appear to be restricted to instances in which IFRS 9 had prohibited an entity from designating hedged items in accordance with its actual risk management. [*IFRS 9.BC6.97–BC98, BC6.100*]

7.11.225.70 As a result, the Committee noted that hedge designations of an entire non-financial item could continue on transition to IFRS 9 if they meet the qualifying criteria in IFRS 9. [*IU 01-16*]

7.11.227 Option to designate credit exposures as at FVTPL

7.11.227.10 The hedge accounting chapter of IFRS 9 introduces a new option to designate certain credit exposures as at FVTPL as a substitute for hedge accounting if certain criteria are met (see 7.9.120). An entity may make the designation on initial recognition or subsequently, or while the financial instrument is unrecognised – e.g. an unrecognised loan commitment. The designation is required to be documented concurrently. The accounting treatment is not applied retrospectively. [*IFRS 9.6.7.1*]

7.11.227.20 There are no specific transition requirements in this respect. Because a credit exposure can be designated subsequent to initial recognition, it appears that entities can designate credit exposures existing at the date of initial application of the hedge accounting chapter of IFRS 9 as at FVTPL if certain criteria are met. Therefore, if the option is applied from the date of initial application, then the designation should be documented at this date.

7.11.227.30 If an entity continues to apply the general hedge accounting requirements of IAS 39 (see 7.11.220.10), then it appears that the entity cannot apply the option to designate a credit exposure as at FVTPL. This is because the option to designate a credit exposure as at FVTPL is contained in the hedge accounting chapter of IFRS 9. [*IFRS 9.7.2.21*]

7.11.230 DISCLOSURES

7.11.230.10 In the period of initial adoption of IFRS 9, an entity needs to provide the disclosures specified in IAS 8 (see 2.8.60). This includes, to the extent practicable, the effect of adopting IFRS 9 on each financial statement line item and on basic and diluted EPS, for the current period and each prior period presented. However, in the period of initial adoption an entity is not required to disclose the line item amounts that would have been reported in accordance with the classification and measurement requirements (which include requirements for amortised cost and impairment) of:

- IFRS 9 for prior periods; and
- IAS 39 for the current period. [*IAS 8.28, IFRS 7.42Q*]

7.11.230.20 The following disclosures are required in tabular format (unless another format is more appropriate) for each class of financial assets and financial liabilities at the date of initial application:

- the original measurement category and carrying amount under IAS 39;

- the new measurement category and carrying amount under IFRS 9; and
- the amount of any financial assets and financial liabilities that were previously designated as at FVTPL, but for which the designation has been revoked; the entity distinguishes between mandatory and elective de-designations. [*IFRS 7.42I*]

7.11.230.30　Entities also need to provide qualitative disclosures to enable users to understand:
- how the entity applied the classification requirements of IFRS 9 to those financial assets whose classification has changed as a result of applying IFRS 9; and
- the reasons for any designation or de-designation of financial assets or financial liabilities as measured at FVTPL at the date of initial application. [*IFRS 7.42J*]

7.11.240　Classification and measurement

7.11.240.10　In the reporting period in which an entity initially applies the classification and measurement requirements of IFRS 9 for financial assets (i.e. when the entity makes the transition from IAS 39 to IFRS 9 for financial assets), it is required to provide the disclosures in 7.11.240.20–70. [*IFRS 9.7.2.15, 7.42K*]

7.11.240.20　At the date of initial application of IFRS 9, an entity discloses changes in the classification of financial assets and financial liabilities, showing separately:
- changes in the carrying amounts on the basis of their measurement categories in accordance with IAS 39 that are not the result of a change in measurement attribute on transition to IFRS 9; and
- changes in the carrying amounts arising from a change in measurement attribute on transition to IFRS 9 – e.g. a reclassification from amortised cost to FVTPL. [*IFRS 7.42L*]

7.11.240.30　In the reporting period in which IFRS 9 is initially applied, an entity discloses the following for financial assets and financial liabilities that have been reclassified so that they are measured at amortised cost, and for financial assets that have been reclassified out of FVTPL so that they are measured at FVOCI as a result of the transition to IFRS 9:
- the fair value of the financial assets or financial liabilities at the reporting date; and
- the fair value gain or loss that would have been recognised in profit or loss or OCI during the reporting period if the financial assets or financial liabilities had not been reclassified. [*IFRS 7.42M*]

7.11.240.40　The disclosures in 7.11.240.20–30 are required only in the annual reporting period in which IFRS 9 is initially applied. [*IFRS 7.42L*]

7.11.240.50　In the reporting period in which IFRS 9 is initially applied, an entity discloses the following for financial assets and financial liabilities that have been reclassified out of the FVTPL category as a result of the transition to IFRS 9:
- the effective interest rate determined on the date of initial application; and
- the interest income or expense recognised. [*IFRS 7.42N*]

7.11.240.60　If an entity treats the fair value as the new gross carrying amount of a financial asset or the new amortised cost for a financial liability at the date of initial application (see 7.11.170.10), then the disclosures in 7.11.240.50 are made for each reporting period following reclassification until derecognition. Otherwise, the disclosures in 7.11.240.50 are required only in the annual reporting period containing the date of initial application. [*IFRS 7.42N*]

7.11.240.70   The disclosures set out in 7.11.240.10–60, together with those required by paragraph 25 of IFRS 7 on fair value (see 7.10.460), need to be such that they permit reconciliation at the date of initial application between:

- the measurement categories presented in accordance with IAS 39 and IFRS 9; and
- the classes of financial instrument. [*IFRS 7.42O*]

7.11.240.80   When it is impracticable at the date of initial application for an entity to assess a modified time value of money element based on the facts and circumstances that existed at the initial recognition of the financial asset and the exception in 7.11.90.20 is applied, an entity discloses the carrying amount at the reporting date of those financial assets until they are derecognised. [*IFRS 7.42R*]

7.11.240.90   When it is impracticable at the date of initial application for an entity to assess whether the fair value of a prepayment feature was insignificant based on the facts and circumstances that existed at the initial recognition of the financial asset and the exception in 7.11.90.30 is applied, an entity discloses the carrying amount at the reporting date of those financial assets until they are derecognised. [*IFRS 7.42S*]

7.11.250   **Impairment**

7.11.250.10   On the date of initial application of the impairment requirements of IFRS 9, an entity discloses reconciliations between:

- the closing balances for impairment allowances under IAS 39 and provisions under IAS 37; and
- the opening balances for loss allowances under IFRS 9. [*IFRS 7.42P*]

7.11.250.20   For financial assets, an entity provides this disclosure by measurement category in accordance with IAS 39 and IFRS 9, showing separately the effect of changes in measurement category on the loss allowance at the date of initial application. [*IFRS 7.42P*]

7.11.260   **SEQUENTIAL APPLICATION OF IFRS 9**

7.11.260.10   If an entity adopts IFRS 9 (2014) in its entirety without having first adopted IFRS 9 (2009), IFRS 9 (2010) or IFRS 9 (2013), then it has a single date of initial application for IFRS 9 (2014) in its entirety. [*IFRS 9.7.2.2, 7.2.15*]

7.11.260.15   Only if the entity's relevant date of initial application was before 1 February 2015 could it have elected to adopt earlier versions of IFRS 9 for annual periods beginning before 1 January 2018. If an entity initially applied a previous version of IFRS 9 on or before 31 January 2015, then it was allowed to continue to apply that version until IFRS 9's mandatory effective date. The guidance in this section therefore generally applies only to an entity that has already adopted an earlier version of IFRS 9.

7.11.260.20   Depending on the date of initial application and the reporting date, application of the following versions of IFRS 9 were possible:

- IAS 39 with adoption in isolation of the requirements in IFRS 9 for presenting the effects of changes in a financial liability's credit risk in OCI;
- IFRS 9 (2009) – with or without adoption of the requirements for presenting the effects of changes in a financial liability's credit risk in OCI;

- IFRS 9 (2010);
- IFRS 9 (2013) – with or without an election to continue to apply IAS 39's hedge accounting requirements; or
- IFRS 9 (2014) – with or without an election to continue to apply IAS 39's hedge accounting requirements and with or without application of the overlay approach (see 8.1.160).

7.11.260.30   If an entity early adopted IFRS 9 (2009), IFRS 9 (2010) or IFRS 9 (2013), and later adopts IFRS 9 (2014) (e.g. when IFRS 9 becomes mandatorily effective), then the guidance in IFRS 9 (2014) on sequential application indicates that the entity has a different date of initial application with respect to each version of IFRS 9 that it has adopted. For example, if an entity adopted IFRS 9 (2009) and then IFRS 9 (2014), the date of initial application related to IFRS 9 (2009) is determined when the entity adopted IFRS 9 (2009) and applied its transition requirements, whereas the date of initial application related to IFRS 9 (2014) is determined when the entity adopts IFRS 9 (2014). The date of initial application of the later version of IFRS 9 does not generally impact the previous adoption or transition requirements and reliefs of an earlier version. Instead, this date is used in applying the incremental transition requirements and reliefs of the subsequently adopted version of IFRS 9. [*IFRS 9.7.2.15, 7.2.27*]

7.11.260.40   If an entity adopted the requirements of IFRS 9 (2009) on the classification and measurement of financial assets, then it applied the transition requirements of IFRS 9 (2009) at the date of initial application of IFRS 9 (2009). On transition from IFRS 9 (2009) to IFRS 9 (2010), the following were incremental transition reliefs that related to the classification and measurement of financial liabilities.
- The requirements of IFRS 9 (2010) are not applied to financial liabilities that have been derecognised at the date of initial application of IFRS 9 (2010) (see 7.11.60).
- An entity assesses whether presenting the effects of changes in a financial liability's credit risk in OCI would create or enlarge an accounting mismatch in profit or loss, on the basis of facts and circumstances that exist at the date of initial application of IFRS 9 (2010) (see 7.11.150.10).
- Derivative liabilities linked to unquoted equity instruments that were previously accounted for at cost are measured at fair value at the date of initial application of IFRS 9 (2010). This is consistent with the requirements for financial assets. Any difference between the previous carrying amount and fair value is recognised in the opening retained earnings of the reporting period that includes the date of initial application (see 7.11.190).

7.11.260.50   The same principle would apply if the entity transitioned directly from IFRS 9 (2009) to IFRS 9 (2013) or IFRS 9 (2014), such that the above reliefs would be applied at the date of initial application of IFRS 9 (2013) or IFRS 9 (2014).

7.11.260.60   On transition from IFRS 9 (2010) to IFRS 9 (2013) or IFRS 9 (2014), there are incremental transition reliefs that relate to hedge accounting that are applied at the date of initial application of IFRS 9 (2013) or IFRS 9 (2014) (see 7.11.220.30). [*IFRS 9.7.2.21–7.2.26*]

7.11.260.70   On transition from IFRS 9 (2013) to IFRS 9 (2014), there are incremental transition reliefs that relate to classification and measurement (which includes amortised cost and impairment) that are applied at the date of initial application of IFRS 9 (2014) (see 7.11.80.10, 90 and 210). [*IFRS 9.7.2.4–5, 7.2.17–20*]

7.11.260.80   An entity is not generally permitted to apply the transition reliefs of IFRS 9 more than once. This means that an entity cannot apply any of those transition provisions again if they have already been applied at an earlier date. [*IFRS 9.7.2.27*]

7.11.260.90   However, an entity is permitted but not required to claim exemption from restating prior periods when it adopts the classification and measurement requirements (which includes amortised cost and impairment) of IFRS 9 more than once. If the entity previously elected not to restate comparative information on adoption of IFRS 9 (2009) but did elect to restate comparative information on adoption of the classification and measurement requirements of IFRS 9 (2010), IFRS 9 (2013) or IFRS 9 (2014), then the restated comparative information would reflect all of the requirements in IFRS 9 (2010), IFRS 9 (2013) or IFRS 9 (2014) respectively. [*IFRS 9.7.2.15, 7.2.27*]

7.11.260.95   It appears that an entity should reassess its business model when it initially adopts IFRS 9 (2014) based on the guidance in that standard. This is because IFRS 9 (2014) introduced additional FVOCI classification requirements and additional application guidance on the business model assessment. For example, if an entity has previously concluded under IFRS 9 (2009) that its business model for certain financial assets was not held-to-collect and classified the financial assets at FVTPL, then we believe that it should reconsider its business model when it initially applies IFRS 9 (2014). Because the additional classification requirements for financial assets were only introduced in IFRS 9 (2014), the transition relief in 7.11.80.10 could not have been previously applied.

7.11.260.100   Also, on transition from IFRS 9 (2009), IFRS 9 (2010), or IFRS 9 (2013) to IFRS 9 (2014), the fair value option for financial assets and financial liabilities is re-opened based on the facts and circumstances at the date of initial application of IFRS 9 (2014). This classification is applied retrospectively. At the date of initial application, an entity:

- revokes an existing designation of a financial asset as at FVTPL if it was originally designated on the basis of the accounting mismatch criterion but that criterion is no longer met;
- may choose to designate a financial asset or financial liability as at FVTPL if the accounting mismatch criterion in IFRS 9 would not previously have been satisfied but is met as a result of the application of IFRS 9 (2014); and
- revokes an existing designation of a financial liability as at FVTPL if it was originally designated on the basis of the accounting mismatch criterion but that criterion is no longer met. [*IFRS 9.7.2.28*]

7I. FINANCIAL INSTRUMENTS: IAS 39

7I.1 Scope and definitions

7I. FINANCIAL INSTRUMENTS: IAS 39

7I.1   Scope and definitions

REQUIREMENTS FOR INSURERS THAT APPLY IFRS 4

In July 2014, the IASB issued IFRS 9 *Financial Instruments*, which is effective for annual periods beginning on or after 1 January 2018. However, an insurer may defer the application of IFRS 9 if it meets certain criteria (see 8.1.180).

This chapter reflects the requirement of IAS 39 *Financial Instruments: Recognition and Measurement* and the related standards, excluding any amendments introduced by IFRS 9. These requirements are relevant to insurers that apply the temporary exemption from IFRS 9 or the overlay approach to designated financial assets (see 8.1.160) and cover annual periods beginning on 1 January 2018. For further discussion, see Introduction to Sections 7 and 7I.

The requirements related to this topic are mainly derived from the following.

STANDARD	TITLE
IFRS 7	Financial Instruments: Disclosures
IFRS 15	Revenue from Contracts with Customers
IAS 32	Financial Instruments: Presentation
IAS 39	Financial Instruments: Recognition and Measurement

FORTHCOMING REQUIREMENTS

The requirements in this chapter are affected by the following forthcoming requirements. They are highlighted with a # and the impact is explained in the accompanying boxed text at the references indicated.
- In January 2016, the IASB issued IFRS 16 *Leases*, which is effective for annual periods beginning on or after 1 January 2019. See 7I.1.105. IFRS 16 is the subject of chapter 5.1A.
- In October 2017, the IASB issued *Long-term Interests in Associates and Joint Ventures – Amendments to IAS 28*, which are effective for annual periods beginning on or after 1 January 2019. See 7I.1.115.

FUTURE DEVELOPMENTS

For this topic, there are no future developments.

71.1.10   **OVERVIEW OF FINANCIAL INSTRUMENTS STANDARDS**

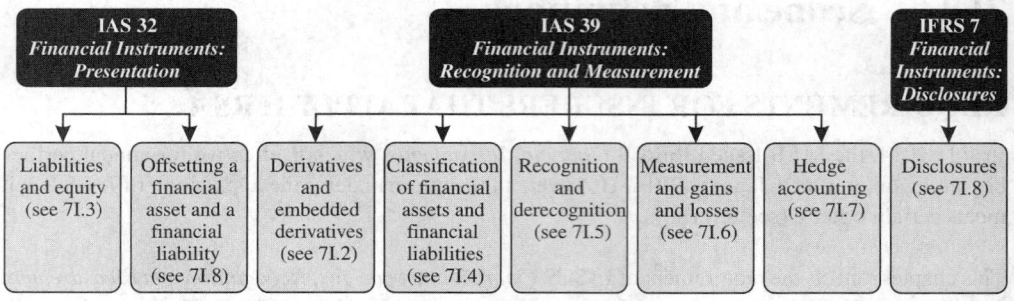

71.1.20   **SCOPE**

71.1.20.10   The reporting of financial instruments is primarily addressed by three specific standards: IAS 32, IAS 39 and IFRS 7. In addition, the measurement of fair value of financial instruments and disclosures about fair value are addressed by IFRS 13 (see chapter 2.4).

71.1.20.20   IAS 32 provides a definition of the term 'financial instrument'. It also defines the related concepts of financial assets, financial liabilities and equity instruments. IAS 32 provides guidance on whether a financial instrument is considered a financial asset, a financial liability or an equity instrument or whether it is a compound instrument that includes both liability and equity components. This guidance is focused largely on determining whether a financial instrument that an entity has issued is classified as a financial liability or as equity (see chapter 71.3). IAS 32 does not generally address recognition or measurement issues, but does contain accounting principles for derivatives on own equity instruments and for initial measurement, modification and conversion of compound instruments (see chapter 71.3). IAS 32 also addresses the presentation of interest and dividends (see chapter 71.3) and the offsetting of financial assets and financial liabilities (see chapter 71.8). [*IAS 32.4–10*]

71.1.20.30   IAS 39 provides recognition and measurement requirements for financial assets and financial liabilities. This includes both primary financial instruments (e.g. cash, receivables, debt and shares in another entity) and derivative financial instruments (e.g. options, forwards, futures, interest rate swaps and currency swaps). [*IAS 39.2–7*]

71.1.20.40   IFRS 7 requires entities to provide disclosures that enable users of their financial statements to evaluate the significance of financial instruments for the entity's financial position and performance, and the nature and extent of risks arising from financial instruments to which the entity is exposed and how the entity manages those risks. [*IFRS 7.3–5*]

71.1.20.50   The scopes of the above three standards are not identical and are subject to different exclusions that are described in more detail in this chapter. Consequently, a scope exclusion in one standard cannot be assumed to apply equally in the context of the other standards. In broad outline, IAS 32 generally applies to all financial instruments, including equity issued, whereas IAS 39 applies only to financial assets and financial liabilities. IFRS 7 also generally applies to all financial instruments, although most of its disclosure requirements relate to financial assets and financial liabilities. However, certain financial assets and financial liabilities that are excluded from the scope of IAS 39 are included in the scope of IFRS 7. In addition, IAS 32 and IAS 39 require certain contracts to buy or sell non-financial items to be accounted for as if they were financial instruments (see 7I.1.150). Derivatives embedded in non-financial contracts may also be accounted for in accordance with the financial instruments standards (see 7I.1.190).

7I.1.25 **DEFINITIONS**

7I.1.25.10   A 'financial instrument' is any contract that gives rise to both a financial asset of one entity and a financial liability or equity instrument of another entity. [*IAS 32.11*]

7I.1.25.20   Deferred revenue and prepaid expenses are not financial instruments because they are settled by the delivery or receipt of goods or services. [*IAS 32.AG11*]

7I.1.25.30   A 'financial asset' is any asset that is:
- cash;
- a contractual right:
  - to receive cash or another financial asset; or
  - to exchange financial assets or financial liabilities under potentially favourable conditions; or
- an equity instrument of another entity; or
- a contract that will or may be settled in the entity's own equity instruments and is:
  - a non-derivative for which the entity is or may be obliged to receive a variable number of the entity's own equity instruments; or
  - a derivative that will or may be settled other than by the exchange of a fixed amount of cash or another financial asset for a fixed number of the entity's own equity instruments. For this purpose, the entity's own equity instruments do not include: puttable financial instruments or instruments that impose on the entity an obligation to deliver to another party only on liquidation a pro rata share of the net assets of the entity that do not meet the definition of equity instruments even if they are classified as equity instruments (see 7I.3.60); or instruments that are contracts for the future receipt or delivery of the entity's own equity instruments. [*IAS 32.11*]

7I.1.25.40   Gold bullion is a commodity and not a financial asset; therefore, it is not in the scope of IAS 32 or IAS 39. Physical holdings of other commodities are also outside the scope of the financial instruments standards. However, contracts to buy or sell commodities or non-financial assets in the future are accounted for as derivatives if certain criteria are met (see 7I.1.150). [*IAS 39.IG.B.1*]

7I.1.25.50   A 'financial liability' is defined as:
- a contractual obligation:
  - to deliver cash or another financial asset to another entity; or
  - to exchange financial instruments under potentially unfavourable conditions; or
- a contract that will or may be settled in the entity's own equity instruments and is:
  - a non-derivative for which the entity is or may be obliged to deliver a variable number of its own equity instruments; or
  - a derivative that will or may be settled other than by the exchange of a fixed amount of cash or another financial asset for a fixed number of the entity's own equity instruments. For this purpose, rights, options or warrants to acquire a fixed number of the entity's own equity

instruments for a fixed amount of any currency are equity instruments if the entity offers rights, options or warrants pro rata to all of its existing owners of the same class of its own non-derivative equity instruments. Also, for this purpose, the entity's own equity instruments are limited as described in 7I.1.25.30. [*IAS 32.11*]

7I.1.25.60   An 'equity instrument' is any contract that evidences a residual interest in the assets of an entity after deducting all of its liabilities (see chapter 7I.3). [*IAS 32.11*]

7I.1.25.70   The following two categories of financial instruments issued by an entity are exempt from liability classification even if they contain an obligation for the entity to deliver cash or another financial asset:
- puttable financial instruments that meet certain conditions; and
- an instrument, or a component of an instrument, that contains an obligation for the issuing entity to deliver to the holder a pro rata share of the net assets of the issuing entity only on its liquidation. [*IAS 32.16–16D*]

7I.1.25.80   These instruments are classified as equity instruments provided that both the financial instrument and the issuing entity meet certain conditions (see 7I.3.60).

7I.1.25.90   IAS 32 provides a framework on the accounting for transactions in an entity's own equity instruments, including derivatives whose underlying is an entity's own equity instruments. IAS 32 also addresses the accounting treatment of treasury shares. For further discussion of these issues, see chapter 7I.3. [*IAS 32.21–24, 33, AG27, AG36*]

7I.1.25.100   The terms 'contract' and 'contractual' used in the definitions in 7I.1.25.30 and 50 refer to an agreement between two or more parties that has clear economic consequences and that the parties have little, if any, discretion to avoid, usually because the agreement is enforceable by law. Contracts defining financial instruments may take a variety of forms and do not need to be in writing. An example of an item not meeting the definition of a financial instrument is a tax liability, because it is not based on a contract between two or more parties; instead, it arises as a result of tax law. [*IAS 32.13, AG12*]

7I.1.30   SPECIFIC EXEMPTIONS FROM FINANCIAL INSTRUMENTS STANDARDS

	IAS 32	IAS 39	IFRS 7	APPLICABLE STANDARD
Interests in subsidiaries[1]	✘	✘	✘	IFRS 10 IAS 27
Interests in associates and joint ventures[1]	✘	✘	✘	IAS 28 IAS 27
Employers' rights and obligations under employee benefit plans	✘	✘	✘	IAS 19
Financial instruments, contracts and obligations under share-based payment transactions	✘	✘	✘	IFRS 2

	IAS 32	IAS 39	IFRS 7	APPLICABLE STANDARD
Rights and obligations under insurance contracts (except embedded derivatives and certain financial guarantees)	✘	✘	✘	IFRS 4[(2)]
Financial instruments with a discretionary participation feature (except embedded derivatives)	✘[(3)]	✘	-	IFRS 4
Rights and obligations under leases	-	✘	-	IAS 17[(4)]
Equity instruments issued by the entity, including warrants and options that meet the definition of an equity instrument (for the issuer)	-	✘	-	IAS 32
Financial instruments issued by the entity that are classified as equity instruments in accordance with paragraphs 16A and 16B or paragraphs 16C and 16D of IAS 32 (for the issuer)	-	✘	✘	IAS 32
Forward contracts between an acquirer and a selling shareholder for the sale/acquisition of an acquiree that will result in a business combination at a future date of acquisition	-	✘	-	IFRS 3
Loan commitments that cannot be settled net in cash or another financial instrument that are not designated as at FVTPL and are not commitments to provide loans at below-market interest	-	✘	-	IAS 37
Rights to reimbursement payments in relation to provisions	-	✘	-	IAS 37
Financial instruments that are rights and obligations in the scope of IFRS 15, except for those that IFRS 15 specifies are accounted for in accordance with IAS 39 – e.g. receivables (see 4.2.470.60 and 7I.6.400.05)	-	✘	-	IFRS 15

'✘' indicates a specific exclusion from the standard.

Notes
1. However, in some cases IFRS 10, IAS 27 or IAS 28 requires or permits an entity to account for an interest in a subsidiary, associate or joint venture in accordance with some or all of the requirements of IAS 39 (see chapters 3.5 and 5.6), in which case the requirements of IAS 32, IAS 39 and IFRS 7 apply. An entity applies IAS 32 to derivatives linked to interests in subsidiaries, associates or joint ventures. An entity also applies IAS 39 and IFRS 7 to such derivatives, unless the derivative meets the definition of an equity instrument in IAS 32 (see 7I.1.110 and 130).
2. IAS 39 applies to an insurance contract that is an issued financial guarantee not accounted for under IFRS 4. IAS 39 applies to a financial guarantee that arises when a transfer of a financial asset does not qualify for derecognition or when continuing involvement applies. Financial guarantee contracts held are not in the scope of IAS 39. For a discussion of the accounting for financial guarantee contracts from the perspective of the holder, see 7I.1.80. [*IAS 39.47(b)*]
3. The issuer of such instruments is exempt from applying the financial liability/equity classification principles to the discretionary participation feature (see 8.1.110).
4. However, the following are subject to the specified provisions of IAS 39 and to the requirements of IFRS 7: (1) lease receivables recognised by a lessor – derecognition and impairment provisions; (2) finance lease payables recognised by a lessee – derecognition provisions; and (3) derivatives embedded in leases – embedded derivative provisions (see 7I.1.100).

71.1.40 **Insurance contracts**

71.1.40.10 There is a dividing line in IFRS between financial risk and insurance risk that is especially relevant for counterparty risk because it determines the nature of the contract as either an insurance contract to which IFRS 4 may apply or a financial instrument in respect of which IAS 32 and IAS 39 apply.

71.1.40.20 An 'insurance contract' is a contract under which the insurer accepts significant insurance risk from the policyholder by agreeing to compensate the policyholder if a specified uncertain future event adversely affects the policyholder (see 8.1.20). [*IFRS 4.A*]

71.1.40.30 Although IAS 32 and IAS 39 do not address the accounting for insurance contracts, they do not scope out insurance entities. Insurance entities apply IAS 32 and IAS 39 to all financial instruments other than those that meet the definition of an insurance contract or a contract with a discretionary participation feature. Therefore, financial instruments that meet the definition of an insurance contract and that are in the scope of IFRS 4 are not subject to IAS 39. However, IAS 39 applies to a derivative that is embedded in a contract in the scope of IFRS 4, unless the derivative itself is also in the scope of IFRS 4 (see 8.1.30). [*IAS 39.2(e)*]

71.1.50 **Financial guarantee contracts**

71.1.50.10 Financial guarantee contracts issued by an entity fall in the scope of IAS 39 from the issuer's perspective except as discussed in 71.1.70.10. In our view, a financial guarantee contract held by an entity that is not an integral element of another financial instrument is not in the scope of IAS 39 (see 71.1.80.50). [*IAS 39.2(e)*]

71.1.60 ***Definition***

71.1.60.10 A 'financial guarantee contract' is a contract that requires the issuer to make specified payments to reimburse the holder for a loss that it incurs because a specified debtor fails to make payment when it is due in accordance with the original or modified terms of a debt instrument. [*IAS 39.9*]

71.1.60.13 To be classified as a financial guarantee contract, a contract needs to comply with all of the following conditions.
- The reference obligation is a debt instrument (see 71.1.62).
- The holder is compensated only for a loss that it incurs (see 71.1.64).
- The contract does not compensate the holder for more than the actual loss that it incurs (see 71.1.66). [*IAS 39.9*]

71.1.60.15 Financial guarantee contracts can have various legal forms, including certain letters of credit, credit default contracts and insurance contracts. However, the legal form of such contracts does not affect their accounting treatment. [*IAS 39.AG4*]

EXAMPLE 1 – FINANCIAL GUARANTEE CONTRACT – LETTER OF CREDIT

71.1.60.16 Bank B issues a letter of credit in the amount of up to 10,000 on behalf of its Customer C, identifying a foreign Supplier S as the beneficiary. Under the letter of credit, B promises to reimburse S for actual losses that S incurs if C fails

> to make the payments when due for its future specified purchases of 10,000 from S. The terms of the arrangement also require any subsequent recovery of reimbursed amounts from C to be returned to B.
>
> 7I.1.60.18   The arrangement meets the definition of a financial guarantee contract. This is because under the terms of the letter of credit B is required to reimburse S for a loss incurred if C – i.e. the specified debtor – fails to make a payment when it is due in accordance with the original debt instrument – i.e. the trade receivable.

7I.1.60.20   Credit-related contracts that require payment in circumstances other than those mentioned in 7I.1.60.10 – e.g. if there is no failure by a specified debtor to make payment when it is due or if the holder would not incur a loss – are generally credit derivatives that are measured at fair value under IAS 39. For the definition of derivatives, see 7I.2.20. [*IFRS 4.IG2.1.12, IAS 39.9, AG4(b)*]

7I.1.62   *Reference obligation is a debt instrument*

7I.1.62.10   The first condition in the definition of a financial guarantee contract is that the contract should compensate the holder only for losses that it incurs on debt instruments – i.e. the 'reference obligation' in a financial guarantee contract should be a debt instrument. However, in our view this does not preclude a contract that contains a revolving portfolio as the reference obligation from being classified as a financial guarantee contract under IAS 39. [*IAS 39.9*]

7I.1.62.20   IAS 39 requires that a financial guarantee contract compensate the holder for losses that it incurs because of failure by 'specified debtors' to make payment when it is due. Consequently, in our view such a revolving portfolio structure does not violate the requirements of a financial guarantee contract if the following criteria are met.
- The portfolio of debt instruments is specified – i.e. the contract includes a list of debtors included in the reference portfolio at all times.
- All replacements to the portfolio are documented and contain restrictions, so that the replacement mechanism does not indirectly compensate the holder for any form of fair value loss on the reference portfolio. [*IAS 39.9*]

7I.1.62.30   The standard does not state what is meant by the term 'debt instrument' in the context of the definition of a financial guarantee contract. In our view, alternative approaches to the application of the definition are possible.

7I.1.62.40   Based on a narrow reading, an entity may consider that the phrase is restricted to certain non-derivative debt instruments that do not include separable embedded derivatives – e.g. instruments that meet the definition of loans and receivables or would meet that definition if they were not quoted in an active market. Under this approach, the inclusion of a derivative instrument in the reference portfolio in 7I.1.62.20 would violate the requirement that a financial guarantee contract compensate the holder only for losses that it incurs on debt instruments.

7I.1.62.50   Alternatively, we believe that an entity may adopt a policy of applying the term to encompass derivatives and hybrid instruments that do or may give rise to an obligation of the debtor to make specified payments when they are due and that compensate the holder of the financial guarantee contract for the debtor's failure to make timely payment of those specified amounts.

7I.1.62.60   However, whatever the entity's policy, the definition of a financial guarantee contract is still met only if the contract compensates the holder solely for losses arising from the debtor's failure to make payment when it is due and not for losses arising from market risk.

EXAMPLE 2A – FINANCIAL GUARANTEE CONTRACT – HYBRID INSTRUMENTS

7I.1.62.70   Investor Z buys structured notes that provide a return based on the movement in an equity index. Z also obtains a guarantee from a bank that, if the issuer of the notes fails to make payment of the full amount due on maturity of the notes, then the bank will pay the shortfall to Z. Such a contract may qualify as a financial guarantee contract depending on Z's accounting policy (see 7I.1.62.50).

7I.1.62.80   However, if the bank guaranteed to Z that it would pay any losses that Z incurred under the terms of the note because of a decrease in the equity index, then the contract would be a derivative and not a financial guarantee contract.

7I.1.64   *Holder compensated only for a loss that it incurs*

7I.1.64.10   The second condition that has to be met for a contract to be classified as a financial guarantee contract under IAS 39 is that it should compensate the holder only for a loss that it incurs on the debt instrument. In our view, such a loss cannot be an opportunity loss or a fair value loss on a debt instrument but should be an actual loss that the entity incurs as a result of failure by a specified debtor to make payment when it is due. Consequently, contracts compensating the holder for losses arising from the restructuring of an entity do not lead automatically to a loss for the holder of the debt instrument other than a fair value loss, and it is possible that the holder will recover from the restructuring event. Therefore, we do not believe that a contract that compensates the holder for such losses meets the definition of a financial guarantee contract. [*IAS 39.9*]

7I.1.64.20   However, IAS 39 is silent on when the cash flows should occur for compensation of a loss that an entity incurs. In our view, a contract may still meet the definition of a financial guarantee contract if the issuer makes payment to the holder for a past due amount provided that the contract requires any subsequent recovery of that amount from the specified debtor to be reimbursed to the issuer of the financial guarantee (see 7I.1.66).

7I.1.64.30   The definition of a financial guarantee contract does not require the holder of the guarantee also to hold the underlying debt instrument(s) as an asset, as long as the contract compensates the holder only for its losses arising from the debtor's failure to make payment when it is due on those debt instruments.

EXAMPLE 2B – FINANCIAL GUARANTEE CONTRACT – CREDIT-LINKED NOTES

7I.1.64.40 Limited-purpose Vehicle L issues to investors 1,000 credit-linked notes with a stated 1,000 principal and 10% interest rate. Cash collected on an underlying pool of specified debt instruments held by L is used to fund distributions to investors. L has no other assets or operations and is prohibited from selling the debt instruments. Contractually, L is required to pay investors only to the extent that cash is collected from the underlying assets. A bank issues a guarantee to investors that they will receive the full 1,000 of principal and 10% interest from L. This is effected by the bank making payment of any shortfalls to an investor within 90 days, subject to the investor being required to reimburse any subsequent recoveries of such shortfalls to the bank.

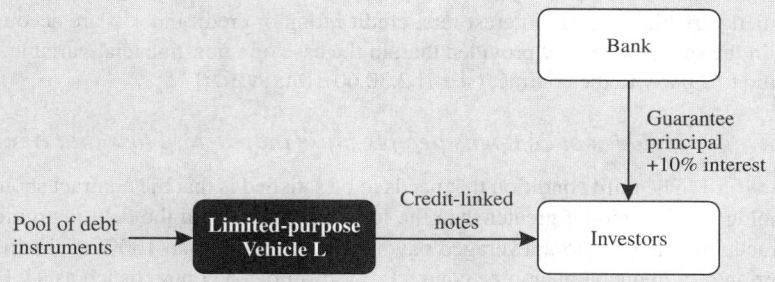

7I.1.64.50 In this example, L's only exposure to risk that could lead to its failure to pay the stated return on the notes is the credit risk of the underlying pool of debt instruments. The investor would also suffer a loss if L were to fail to make payments when they were due in accordance with the terms of the notes even when L has obtained sufficient cash from its assets.

7I.1.64.60 In our view, the guarantee agreement is a financial guarantee contract because the bank compensates the investor only for the loss that the investor would incur from a failure by specified debtors (either by the specified debtors in the underlying pool of debt instruments in L or by L itself) to make payment when it is due.

7I.1.64.65 However, if the investor could fail to obtain the full 10% contractual return because of other risks – e.g. interest rate risk as a result of the portfolio containing floating rate loans – and the bank provided a guarantee covering shortfalls arising from those other risks, then the guarantee would not meet the definition of a financial guarantee contract.

7I.1.64.70 Generally, a contract does not qualify as a financial guarantee contract if it provides for payments by the issuer in respect of amounts that are not past due. However, in many debt agreements non-payment of an amount that is due contractually would be an event of default that would trigger the entire remaining amount (principal and accrued interest) on the debt instrument to fall due.

7I.1.64.80   For example, a contract between a guarantor and the holder of a loan with a maturity of five years allows for physical settlement – i.e. the guarantor is required to buy the entire outstanding debt amount at par plus accrued interest in the event of any non-payment by the debtor (e.g. a missed interest payment) that persists for 30 days beyond its due date. Under the terms of the loan, such a non-payment is an event of default. In our view, the contract would meet the definition of a financial guarantee contract if the non-payment condition that requires settlement of the guarantee also causes the entire outstanding debt amount to become immediately repayable. The issue of whether immediate repayment of the full amount of the debt instrument actually is requested by the creditor following the default does not affect the analysis.

7I.1.64.90   Guarantee contracts that require payments to be made in response to changes in another specified variable – e.g. an interest rate, credit rating or credit index – are accounted for as derivatives in the scope of IAS 39 provided that, in the case of a non-financial variable, the variable is not specific to a party to the contract (see 7I.2.30.60). [IAS 39.AG4]

7I.1.66   *Holder not compensated for more than actual loss that it incurs*

7I.1.66.10   The third condition that needs to be satisfied is that the contract should not compensate the holder for an amount greater than the loss that it incurs on the debt instrument. Consequently, contracts that give rise to a leveraged payout that is greater than 100% of the loss do not meet the definition of a financial guarantee contract. For example, a contract such as a CDS that pays out to the protection buyer even if the holder does not have any exposure to the specified debt instrument does not meet the definition and is accounted for as a derivative. [IFRS 4.IG2.1.12, IAS 39.9]

7I.1.68   *Examples*

EXAMPLE 3A – FINANCIAL GUARANTEE CONTRACT – MEETING THE THREE CONDITIONS

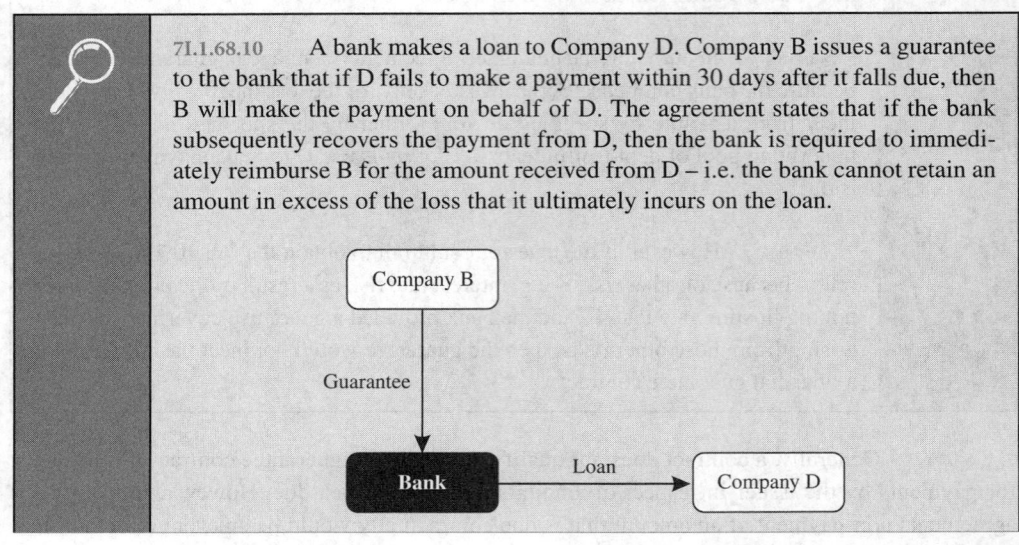

7I.1.68.10   A bank makes a loan to Company D. Company B issues a guarantee to the bank that if D fails to make a payment within 30 days after it falls due, then B will make the payment on behalf of D. The agreement states that if the bank subsequently recovers the payment from D, then the bank is required to immediately reimburse B for the amount received from D – i.e. the bank cannot retain an amount in excess of the loss that it ultimately incurs on the loan.

Company B

Guarantee

Bank ————Loan————▶ Company D

7I.1.68.15   In this example, the contract meets the definition of a financial guarantee contract and is accounted for as such in B's financial statements. This is because the three conditions for classification as a financial guarantee contract have been met.

- The reference obligation is a debt instrument.
- The holder of the financial guarantee contract is compensated only for a loss that it incurs as a result of the debtor's failure to make a payment when it is due. In the example, the bank actually may or may not have incurred a loss when payment was not made within 30 days of the due date (because the debtor may make an appropriate payment later). However, as described in 7I.1.64.10–20, if payment is made by the issuer before a loss is actually incurred by the holder, then the instrument can still qualify as a financial guarantee contract if the contract includes a provision that any subsequent recoveries of the overdue amount be repaid to the guarantor. This is because the inclusion of this provision ensures that the holder of the financial guarantee can be compensated only for its actual losses incurred.
- The financial guarantee contract does not compensate the holder for more than its actual losses incurred. In the example, this is achieved by the inclusion of the provision that any subsequent repayments of the overdue amount be repaid to the guarantor.

EXAMPLE 3B – FINANCIAL GUARANTEE CONTRACT – FAILING THE CONDITIONS

7I.1.68.20   Modifying Example 3A, assume the same arrangement except that Company B will make payments to the bank based on changes in the credit rating of Company D.

7I.1.68.25   In this example, the contract does not meet the definition of a financial guarantee contract, because B is required to make payments to the bank even if there is no failure by D to make payment when due and the bank does not incur a loss. Therefore, both B and the bank account for the contract as a derivative in their financial statements.

7I.1.70   *Accounting by the issuer*

7I.1.70.10   Although financial guarantee contracts issued meet the definition of an insurance contract if the risk transferred is significant, they are generally outside the scope of IFRS 4 and are accounted for under IAS 39. However, if an entity issuing financial guarantee contracts has previously asserted explicitly that it regards them as insurance contracts and has accounted for them as such, then the issuer may make an election on a contract-by-contract basis to apply either IAS 39 or IFRS 4 to each contract. The election for each contract is irrevocable. [*IFRS 4.4(d), B18(g), IAS 39.2(e), AG4(a), BC23A*]

7I.1.70.20   If the issuer applies IAS 39 to a financial guarantee contract, then it measures the contract:

- initially at fair value. If the financial guarantee contract was issued in a stand-alone arm's length transaction to an unrelated party, then its fair value at inception is likely to equal the premium received unless there is evidence to the contrary; and
- subsequently at the higher of:
  - the amount determined in accordance with IAS 37 (see chapter 3.12); and
  - the amount recognised initially less, when appropriate, the cumulative amount of income recognised in accordance with the principles of IFRS 15 (see chapter 4.2). [*IAS 39.47(c), AG4(a)*]

Ⓢ 7I.1.70.30   In the case of a guarantee provided by a parent over the liability of a subsidiary, even if no consideration is or will be received by the parent, the parent is required to recognise a liability in its separate financial statements for the fair value of the guarantee. In our view, if no payments from the subsidiary to the parent are agreed for such a guarantee, then the parent has provided the guarantee in its capacity as a shareholder and accounts for the issuance of the guarantee as a capital contribution to the subsidiary.

7I.1.70.40   An exception to the general measurement principles is provided for financial guarantee contracts that arise when a transfer of financial assets does not qualify for derecognition or results in continuing involvement. Such contracts are measured in accordance with specific provisions in IAS 39 (see 7I.5.290). [*IAS 39.29–31, 47(b)*]

7I.1.70.50   As stated in 7I.1.70.10, if the issuer has previously explicitly asserted that it regards such contracts as insurance contracts and has used the accounting applicable to insurance contracts, then the issuer may apply either IAS 39 or IFRS 4 to such contracts on a contract-by-contract basis (see 8.1.10.30). [*IAS 39.2(e)*]

7I.1.70.60   For an entity whose business includes writing financial guarantee contracts, it will generally be clear from contract documentation, previously published financial statements and the entity's communications with customers, regulators or others whether it regards, and has previously accounted for, such contracts as insurance contracts. [*IAS 39.AG4A*]

7I.1.70.70   In other cases it may be less clear. For example, an entity might provide financial guarantees from time to time that are incidental to its main business, perhaps to support borrowings of its subsidiaries or major customers. In such cases, in our view judgement is required in determining whether previous assertions in financial statements or elsewhere are sufficiently explicit to continue to apply insurance accounting.

7I.1.80   *Accounting by the holder*

7I.1.80.10   In our view, the criteria for identifying a contract as a financial guarantee contract are the same for both the holder and the issuer.

7I.1.80.20   An entity may buy a debt instrument whose terms include, or that is accompanied by, a guarantee of payments on the debt instrument, which is issued by a party other than the issuer of the debt instrument and which has the features of a financial guarantee contract. In our view, in determining its accounting for such a guarantee, the holder should determine whether the guarantee is an integral element of the debt instrument that is accounted for as a component of that instrument or is a contract that is accounted for separately. If the holder determines that the guarantee is an integral element of the debt instrument, then in our view the guarantee should not be accounted for separately. Instead, the holder should consider the effect of the protection when measuring the fair value of the debt instrument, when estimating the expected cash receipts from the debt instrument and when assessing impairment of the debt instrument.

EXAMPLE 4A – FINANCIAL GUARANTEE – INTEGRAL ELEMENT OF DEBT INSTRUMENT

7I.1.80.30   Company B bought a bond issued by Company D that is quoted in an active market. The terms of the bond include an inseparable financial guarantee from D's parent.

7I.1.80.35   In this example, B concludes that the financial guarantee is an integral part of the bond because the bond was acquired with the benefit of the financial guarantee contract that is included in the terms of the bond and reflected in the quoted price of the bond.

EXAMPLE 4B – FINANCIAL GUARANTEE – NOT INTEGRAL ELEMENT OF DEBT INSTRUMENT

7I.1.80.40   Continuing Example 4A, Company B bought a bond issued by Company E that is quoted in an active market. Nine months later, B bought a financial guarantee contract on the bond from an unrelated third party bank.

7I.1.80.45   In this example, B concludes that the financial guarantee bought from the bank is not an integral part of the bond because the financial guarantee was acquired from an unrelated third party (the bank) after B's initial recognition of the bond and the financial guarantee is neither included in the terms of the bond nor reflected in the quoted price of the bond.

7I.1.80.50   In our view, a financial guarantee contract held by an entity that is not an integral part of another financial instrument is not in the scope of IAS 39. In our view, the holder should account for such a financial guarantee contract as a prepayment measured at an amount equal to the guarantee premium and a compensation right accounted for by analogy to the guidance for reimbursements in IAS 37 (see 7I.1.83–87). However, in our view an entity may also choose an accounting policy, to be applied consistently, to measure a non-integral financial guarantee contract that it holds at FVTPL if the contract:

- is held for trading, by analogy to the requirements for financial assets held for trading under IAS 39; or
- guarantees a debt instrument that is measured at FVTPL, to reduce any accounting mismatch that would otherwise arise.

7I.1.80.60   In our view, the holder may apply by analogy the derecognition criteria for financial assets to any prepayment asset relating to a financial guarantee that is accounted for by analogy to IAS 37.

7I.1.83   **Compensation rights**

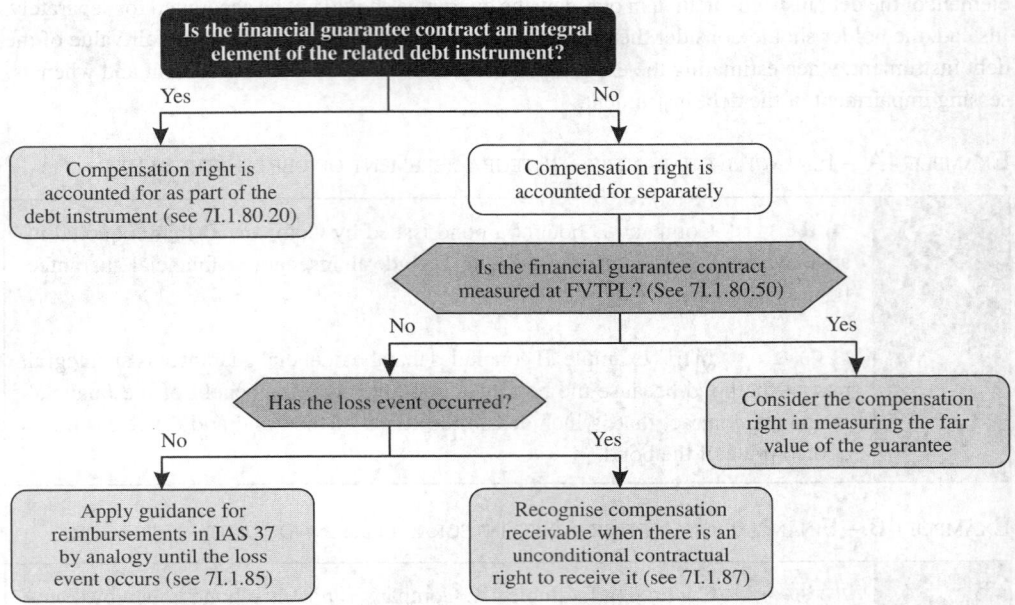

7I.1.83.10   If the holder accounts for a non-integral financial guarantee contract by analogy to the guidance for reimbursements in IAS 37 (see 7I.1.80.50), then in our view the accounting for any compensation right under the contract would depend on whether the loss event that creates a right for the holder to assert a claim has occurred at the reporting date.

7I.1.85   Compensation rights: Loss event has not occurred

7I.1.85.10   In our view, a recognised impairment loss for which there is not yet a contractual right to assert a claim is similar in nature to a provision as defined in IAS 37. A provision is a liability that is a present obligation arising from a past event, of uncertain timing or amount; an impairment loss recognised before the event that allows an entity to assert a claim is an insured loss related to a past event, but there may be uncertainty about the timing or amount of the ultimate actual loss that will be incurred. In the case of a financial guarantee contract, there is usually a timing difference between the recognition of the impairment loss and the related loss event – e.g. when the impairment is estimated on a collective basis for a portfolio of contracts, whereas the loss event that creates a right for the entity to assert a claim specifically identified in the financial guarantee contract as being the delinquency or bankruptcy of a specific debtor.

7I.1.85.20   If the loss event that creates a right for the entity to assert a claim at the reporting date has not occurred, but an impairment loss has been recognised under IAS 39, then we believe that the compensation right should be accounted for by analogy to the guidance for reimbursements in IAS 37 because that is the guidance in IFRS dealing with the most similar issue (see 2.8.10). [*IAS 8.11, 37.53*]

7I.1.85.30   We believe that no net gain should be accrued when there is no current right to assert a claim under the financial guarantee contract. During the period between the initial recognition of the compensation right and the occurrence of the loss event that creates a right for the entity to assert a claim, the amount of the compensation right recognised should be limited to the difference between the impaired carrying amount of the asset and the amount that the carrying amount of the asset would have been had the impairment not been recognised. [*IAS 37.53*]

7I.1.85.40   In our view, if the impairment loss recognised includes items not covered by the financial guarantee contract, then the asset recognised for the compensation should be limited to the impairment loss covered by the financial guarantee contract. For example, an impairment loss recognised on an available-for-sale financial asset (see 7I.6.470) may include not only a credit loss covered by a financial guarantee contract, but also other fair value changes that have occurred. We believe that only the credit portion of the impairment loss covered by the financial guarantee contract should be considered when recognising and measuring the asset for the compensation right.

EXAMPLE 4C – FINANCIAL GUARANTEE – COMPENSATION RIGHT WHEN INSURED LOSS EVENT HAS NOT YET OCCURRED

7I.1.85.50   On 1 January 2016, Bank N bought a five-year zero-coupon bond issued by Company B. The bond matures on 31 December 2020 and on this date B is due to pay N 100. The bond is classified as a loan and receivable in N's financial statements.

7I.1.85.60   On 1 January 2017, in line with its new risk management policy, N entered into a financial guarantee contract with Insurer C, a third party. The terms of the financial guarantee contract are as follows.
- C will pay N up to 100 if B has not paid the full 100 to N by 31 January 2021.
- If B pays N less than the 100 owed, then C will pay N the difference between 100 and the amount received from B.
- If, after any payment from C to N, B subsequently repays any amount to N, then N is required to pay this amount to C – i.e. C will not compensate N for an amount greater than the loss incurred.

7I.1.85.70   N determines that the financial guarantee contract is not integral to the bond and accounts for it by analogy to the guidance for reimbursements in IAS 37 (see 7I.1.80.50).

7I.1.85.80   In December 2018, B's credit rating declines, reflecting recently disclosed operating losses and liquidity shortfalls. N concludes that there is objective evidence of impairment in respect of the bond. The following facts at 31 December 2018 are also relevant to this example.
- The amortised cost of the bond before impairment is 83.
- The original effective interest rate on the bond is 10%.
- The appropriate discount rate for C is 5%.
- N estimates that B will repay only 70 out of the 100 on maturity.

7I.1.85.90   N performs the following calculations at 31 December 2018.

	AMOUNT
Amortised cost of the bond before impairment	83
Present value of estimated future cash flow from the bond	58[1]
Impairment loss	(25)[2]
Present value of the compensation right	(27)[3]
Present value of the compensation right limited to the amount of impairment	25

Notes
1. Calculated as the expected amount to be repaid by B discounted at the original effective interest rate on the bond of 10% – i.e. $70 / (1 + 10\%)^2$.
2. Calculated as 83 - 58.
3. Calculated as the expected shortfall in the amount receivable from B discounted at C's discount rate of 5% – i.e. $(100 - 70) / (1 + 5\%)^2$. For simplicity, the compensation from C is discounted for two years rather than two years and one month.

7I.1.85.100   N records the following entries[1] in the year ending 31 December 2018.

	DEBIT	CREDIT
Impairment loss (profit or loss)	25	
Allowance for credit losses (statement of financial position)		25
To recognise impairment loss on bond (see 7I.6.470.20)		
Compensation right (statement of financial position)	25	
Compensation right (profit or loss[2])		25
To recognise compensation right		

Notes
1. This example does not illustrate N's accounting for the premiums paid to C. For a discussion of the accounting for premiums, see 7I.1.80.50.
2. In the statement of profit or loss and OCI, the amount related to the compensation right may be presented in the same line item as the impairment loss that triggers the compensation.

7I.1.85.110   Continuing with the example, N performs the following calculations for the year ending 31 December 2019.

	AMOUNT
Amortised cost of the bond on 31 December 2019	64[1]
Interest income on the bond for 2019	6[2]
Amortised cost of the bond on 31 December 2019 if it had not been impaired	91[3]
Present value of the compensation right on 31 December 2019 (limited)	27[4]
Remeasurement of the compensation right	2[5]

Notes

1. Calculated as the expected amount to be repaid by B, which remains unchanged in 2019, discounted at the original effective interest rate on the bond of 10% – i.e. 70 / (1 + 10%).
2. Calculated as 58 x 10%.
3. Calculated as the amortised cost of the bond before impairment on 31 December 2018 plus accretion of the interest for 2019 at the original effective interest rate on the bond of 10% – i.e. 83 + 8.
4. Calculated as the amortised cost of the bond on 31 December 2019 if it had not been impaired less its actual amortised cost on 31 December 2019 – i.e. 91 - 64. In the absence of the imposed limit, the compensation right would have been 29 (27 x 1.05) or (30 / 1.05).
5. Calculated as 27 - 25.

7I.1.85.120 N records the following entries in the year ending 31 December 2019.

	DEBIT	CREDIT
Allowance for credit losses (statement of financial position)	6	
Interest income (profit or loss)		6
To accrete interest on bond for 2019		
Compensation right (statement of financial position)	2	
Compensation right (profit or loss)		2
To remeasure compensation right		

7I.1.87 Compensation rights: Loss event has occurred

7I.1.87.10 If the loss event that creates a right for the entity to assert a claim has occurred, then in our view the entity should recognise a receivable for the compensation when it has an unconditional contractual right to receive the compensation. The compensation receivable should be measured based on the amount and timing of the expected cash flows discounted at a rate that reflects the credit risk of the issuer of the financial guarantee contract. We believe that an entity would have an unconditional contractual right to receive compensation if:

- the entity has a contract under which it can make a claim for compensation; and
- the loss event that creates a right for the entity to assert a claim at the reporting date has occurred and the claim is not disputed by the issuer.

7I.1.87.20 Any difference between the carrying amount of the previously recognised compensation right and the compensation receivable is recognised in profit or loss.

7I.1.90 **Share-based payments**

7I.1.90.10 A separate standard provides guidance on the accounting for share-based payments. Accordingly, the initial classification and measurement, and subsequent measurement, of financial instruments arising from share-based payment transactions in the scope of IFRS 2 are subject to the requirements of that standard (see 4.5.2030). Without this scope exclusion, financial instruments arising from these transactions would generally fall in the scope of IAS 32 and IAS 39. [*IAS 32.4(f), 39.2(i)*]

7I.1.100   Lease rights and obligations#

7I.1.100.10   Rights and obligations under leases are recognised and measured under IAS 17 (see chapter 5.1) and consequently are not subject to the general recognition and measurement requirements of IAS 39. However, lease receivables recognised by a lessor are subject to the derecognition and impairment requirements of IAS 39. Also, finance lease payables recognised by a lessee are subject to the derecognition principles of IAS 39. [*IAS 39.2(b)*]

7I.1.100.20   Derivatives embedded in leases (both finance and operating leases) are subject to IAS 39's embedded derivative requirements (see 7I.2.130.30). [*IAS 39.2(b)*]

7I.1.100.30   A finance lease is a financial instrument. IFRS 7 applies to all financial instruments, and rights and obligations under leases are not specifically excluded from its scope. Consequently, recognised financial assets and financial liabilities arising from finance leases are subject to the financial instrument disclosure requirements (see chapter 7I.8). [*IAS 32.AG9*]

7I.1.105   FORTHCOMING REQUIREMENTS

7I.1.105.10   IFRS 16 introduces changes to the accounting by lessees and substantially carries forward the existing accounting requirements for lessors in IAS 17. For lessees, IFRS 16 introduces a single, on-balance sheet lease accounting model and eliminates the distinction between operating and finance leases (see chapter 5.1A). Lease liabilities recognised by a lessee are scoped out of IAS 39, except that they are subject to the derecognition principles of IAS 39. [*IAS 39.2(b)*]

7I.1.110   Investments in subsidiaries, associates and joint ventures#

7I.1.110.10   Investments in subsidiaries, associates and joint ventures that are consolidated or equity accounted in the consolidated financial statements (see chapters 2.5, 3.5 and 3.6) are excluded from the scope of IAS 32 and IAS 39. [*IAS 32.4(a), 39.2(a)*]

(S) 7I.1.110.20   However, IAS 39 applies to such investments in the separate financial statements of the parent or investor if it elects to account for those instruments in accordance with IAS 39. In addition, IAS 39 applies when an investment entity is required by IFRS 10 to measure its subsidiaries at FVTPL (see chapter 5.6). [*IAS 27.10(b), IFRS 10.31*]

7I.1.110.30   IAS 39 applies to derivatives on an interest in a subsidiary, associate or joint venture unless the derivative meets the definition of an equity instrument of the entity in IAS 32 (see 7I.1.30 and 7I.3.20.40). Such derivatives qualify for exemption from the scope of IAS 39 when they may be settled only by the entity exchanging a fixed amount of cash or another financial asset for a fixed number of its own equity instruments (see 7I.3.187.10). [*IAS 32.4(a), 39.2(a)*]

7I.1.110.40   However, IAS 39 does not apply to derivatives containing potential voting rights that in substance currently give access to the economic benefits associated with ownership interests in a subsidiary, associate or joint venture that are accounted for in accordance with 7I.1.110.10. In this case, the derivatives are taken into account in determining the reporting entity's interest in the investee (see 2.5.140, 470 and 690). In our view, IAS 39 also does not apply to derivatives to acquire

NCI in a subsidiary that are accounted for under the anticipated-acquisition method (see 2.5.700). [*IFRS 10.B90–B91, IAS 39.2(a)*]

7I.1.110.50   Even if a derivative over shares in a subsidiary is not accounted for as a derivative under IAS 39 (see 7I.1.110.30–40), an entity is required to recognise a financial liability in its consolidated financial statements for an obligation to acquire equity instruments of the consolidated group (see 7I.3.190) – e.g. a written put option or forward purchase contract over equity shares of a consolidated subsidiary.

7I.1.110.60   A parent may invest in a convertible instrument issued by a subsidiary. In our view, if (S) the convertible instrument is classified as equity by the subsidiary – e.g. because it is mandatorily convertible into a fixed number of ordinary shares (see 7I.3.183) – then in the separate financial statements of the parent its investment in the convertible instrument should be considered to be an investment in a subsidiary and therefore would be excluded from the scope of IAS 39 unless the parent has elected otherwise (see 7I.1.110.20).

7I.1.110.70   However, IFRS does not otherwise mandate symmetrical accounting between the holder and the issuer of an instrument. This is especially the case if a subsidiary classifies a financial instrument issued to its parent as a financial liability only because the subsidiary has a fixed life – i.e. all other conditions for equity classification are met. In our view, the parent should classify the acquired financial instrument based on its characteristics, including whether the instrument represents a residual interest in the subsidiary, and in this instance no symmetry in classification is required between the subsidiary and the parent (see 7I.3.10).

7I.1.115   FORTHCOMING REQUIREMENTS

7I.1.115.10   *Long-term Interests in Associates and Joint Ventures – Amendments to IAS 28* clarify that an entity applies IAS 39 to long-term interests in an associate or joint venture that form part of the net investment in the associate or joint venture but to which the equity method is not applied (see 3.5.425). [*IAS 28.14A, 46*]

7I.1.120   Forward contracts between acquirer and selling shareholder in business combination

7I.1.120.10   IAS 39 excludes from its scope forward contracts between an acquirer and a selling shareholder to buy or sell an acquiree that will result in a business combination at a future date of acquisition. The term of such a forward contract should not exceed a reasonable period normally necessary to obtain any required approvals and to complete the transaction. The scope exclusion applies from the perspectives of both the acquirer and a selling shareholder. [*IAS 39.2(g)*]

7I.1.120.20   To qualify for the scope exclusion, completion of the business combination should not be dependent on further actions of either party. Accordingly, the scope exclusion does not apply to option contracts, whether or not they are currently exercisable, that on exercise would result in a business combination; for a discussion of business combinations effected through derivatives, see 2.6.320. Option contracts allow one party to the contract discretion over whether a business combination occurs and therefore are not covered by the scope exemption. Similarly, in our view the scope exclusion does not apply to a combination of put and call options, often described as a 'synthetic forward'. [*IAS 39.BC24B–BC24C*]

7I.1.120.30   The completion of a business combination may be conditional on approval by the share-holders of either party or by a regulator or other governmental body. The purpose of the exclusion is to prevent particular contracts from being accounted for as derivatives while necessary regulatory and legal processes, including any required approvals, are completed. Therefore, in our view applica-tion of the scope exclusion is not usually precluded by the business combination being dependent on obtaining shareholder or regulatory approvals within a reasonable timeframe. We believe that this principle would extend to a contractual requirement for shareholder approval that has been included in the contract in the interests of good corporate governance, even though such an approval would not otherwise be required by law. [*IAS 39.2(g), BC24A–BC24C*]

7I.1.120.40   However, in some cases judgement may be required to determine whether contractual arrangements relating to approval have been designed so as to provide management of either party with an option over whether completion will happen or to allow deferral of completion beyond a reasonably necessary period such that application of the scope exclusion would not be appropriate. For example, this might be the case if completion of an agreement is permissible under law only if the seller obtains a specific regulatory approval but the agreement does not require the seller to make any effort to seek that approval but allows the seller instead to cancel the contract without penalty rather than applying for the approval.

7I.1.120.50   The scope exemption does not apply by analogy to contracts to acquire investments in associates and similar transactions, such as investments in joint ventures (see 3.5.260). [*IAS 39.BC24D*]

7I.1.130   Venture capital, mutual funds and similar entities

7I.1.130.10   Venture capitalists, mutual funds, unit trusts and similar entities that do not qualify as investment entities under IFRS 10 (see chapter 5.6) may choose to account for investments in associ-ates and joint ventures at fair value under IAS 39, with all changes in fair value recognised in profit or loss, rather than applying the equity method. However, there is no exemption for these entities from the requirement to consolidate all entities that they control (see 3.5.100.10). [*IAS 28.18, 39.AG3, IFRS 10.31–32*]

7I.1.130.20   In our view, an entity that has substantive and separately managed venture capital op-erations may use the exemption from applying the equity method, even if the entity also has other operations. However, this exemption may be applied only to the investments held as part of the venture capital portion of the entity's operations.

7I.1.130.30   For a discussion of whether an investor qualifies as a venture capital organisation and the accounting implications, see 3.5.100.

7I.1.130.40   If a venture capital organisation meets the exemption in IAS 28 and accounts for an investment at FVTPL, then it would not ordinarily be able to reclassify that investment out of FVTPL. In our view, a very limited exemption does exist if an investment has been transferred from a venture capital division within a group and the following conditions have been met.
- The group has different activities and one of the activities is a venture capital activity that is clearly ring-fenced from the business activity of the rest of the group. For this condition to be met, the venture capital division should have its own strategy, objectives and management reporting system.

- The investment has been transferred from the venture capital division to another business in the group.
- After the transfer, the investment is no longer managed as part of the venture capital division. [*IAS 39.50*]

7I.1.130.50   If the conditions in 7I.1.130.40 are met, then the investment may be reclassified out of FVTPL.

7I.1.140   Reimbursements

7I.1.140.10   Rights to reimbursement for expenditure that an entity is required to make to settle a liability recognised as a provision are outside the scope of IAS 39. They are recognised and measured in accordance with IAS 37 (see 3.12.190). [*IAS 39.2(j)*]

7I.1.150   Purchases and sales of non-financial items

7I.1.150.10   A contract to buy or sell a non-financial item may be required to be accounted for as a derivative, even though the non-financial item itself falls outside the scope of the financial instruments standards. Non-financial items include commodities such as gold, oil, wheat and soya beans, as well as motor vehicles, aircraft and real estate. If contracts to buy or sell non-financial items can be settled net in cash or another financial instrument, including if the non-financial item is readily convertible into cash, then they are included in the scope of the financial instruments standards. [*IAS 32.8, 39.5*]

7I.1.150.20   There is an exception to this scope inclusion for contracts that are entered into and continue to be held for the receipt or delivery of a non-financial item in accordance with the entity's expected purchase, sale or usage requirements (the 'normal sales and purchases' or 'own-use' exemption). [*IAS 32.8, 39.5*]

7I.1.150.30   The accounting for a contract to buy non-financial items – e.g. commodities, property, plant and equipment, intangible assets and investment properties – differs depending on whether the purchase contract is regarded as a derivative. If the purchase contract is considered to be a derivative, then the purchase contract and the initial recognition of the non-financial item on settlement of the derivative are treated as separate transactions. The derivative is measured at FVTPL under IAS 39 (see 7I.6.140) and the consideration paid for the non-financial item is the cash paid plus the fair value of the derivative on settlement. If the purchase contract is not regarded as a derivative, then it is treated as an executory contract (see 1.2.60). Under this approach there is only one transaction, being the purchase of a non-financial item under the contract, and the consideration paid for that non-financial item is the agreed price under the purchase contract.

EXAMPLE 5 – CONTRACT TO BUY NON-FINANCIAL ITEMS

7I.1.150.40   Company J enters into a contract to buy 100 tonnes of cocoa beans at 1,000 per tonne for delivery in 12 months. On the settlement date, the market price for cocoa beans is 1,500 per tonne. If the contract cannot be settled net in cash, or if the own-use exemption applies, then the contract is considered to be an executory contract outside the scope of IAS 39.

> **71.1.150.50**   Under IFRS, only one transaction is recognised, being the purchase of inventory under IAS 2 (see chapter 3.8), and the consideration paid is 100,000.
>
> **71.1.150.60**   However, if the contract can be settled net in cash and the own-use exemption does not apply, then two transactions are recognised. The purchase contract is accounted for as a derivative under IAS 39. The purchase of inventory is a separate transaction and the consideration paid under IAS 2 is cash of 100,000 plus the fair value of the derivative on settlement of 50,000, bringing the total cost of inventory to 150,000.
>
> **71.1.150.70**   For a discussion of the hedging of non-financial items, see 71.7.440.

71.1.160   *Settlement net in cash*

71.1.160.10   A commitment to buy or sell a non-financial item is considered settled net in cash if:

- the terms of the contract permit either party to settle net in cash or another financial instrument or by exchanging financial instruments – e.g. a written option that permits cash settlement;
- the entity has a past practice of settling similar contracts net in cash or other financial instruments or by exchanging financial instruments;
- the entity has a past practice of taking delivery of the underlying and selling it within a short period after delivery for trading purposes; or
- the non-financial item that is subject to the contract is readily convertible into cash. [*IAS 32.9, 39.6*]

71.1.160.20   A contract that can be settled net in cash or one with the underlying item readily convertible into cash may qualify as a contract entered into and held in accordance with the entity's expected purchase, sale or usage requirements as long as the entity has no past practice of settling similar contracts net or trading the underlying. [*IAS 32.8–9, 39.5*]

71.1.160.30   However, a contract cannot be considered entered into in accordance with the entity's expected purchase, sale or usage requirements if the entity has a past practice of settling similar contracts net in cash or other financial instruments or by exchanging financial instruments, or taking delivery of the underlying and selling it within a short period after delivery for trading purposes. Such contracts are in the scope of IAS 39. [*IAS 32.9, 39.6*]

71.1.160.40   In our view, 'past practice' should be interpreted narrowly. Infrequent historical incidences of net settlement in response to events that could not have been foreseen at inception of a contract would not taint an entity's ability to apply the own-use exemption to other contracts. An example is an unplanned and unforeseeable breakdown (outage) in a power plant. However, any regular or foreseeable events leading to net settlements or closing out of contracts would taint the ability to apply the own-use exemption to similar contracts.

71.1.160.50   In our view, the concept of 'similar contracts' includes all contracts held for a similar purpose.

EXAMPLE 6A – CONTRACT HELD FOR SIMILAR PURPOSES

7I.1.160.60 Power-generating Company P has sales contracts for electricity, each of which is held for one of the following purposes:
1. held for trading – i.e. P has entered or intends to enter into offsetting purchase contracts;
2. may result in delivery of the underlying power (commodity) but is available to be closed out from time to time as required – i.e. net cash settlement with the counterparty before or on the delivery date;
3. intended to be settled by delivery of the underlying power but may be closed out only in the case of *force majeure* or other similar unforeseen events; or
4. will always be settled by delivery of the underlying power.

7I.1.160.64 Only contracts of types (3) and (4) qualify as own-use. However, in our view P should designate contract types (3) and (4) into an own-use category at inception in order to qualify for the exemption. Transfers out of these categories – e.g. closing out a contract other than because of an unforeseen one-off event – would taint P's ability to use the own-use exemption in the future.

7I.1.160.67 Furthermore, P should be able to distinguish between contracts that qualify for the own-use exemption and other contracts. The designation need not refer specifically to the accounting treatment under IFRS, but it should be sufficient to ensure that the different purposes of each type of contract are clearly distinguished. For example, if an entity has two distinct business models for managing contracts to buy and sell commodities, each with different risk management policies, it may be sufficient if the entity clearly indicates at inception of each contract to which business model the contract relates.

EXAMPLE 6B – PHYSICAL AND DERIVATIVE CONTRACTS MANAGED TOGETHER

7I.1.160.70 Company C is a chocolate manufacturer. C enters into a combination of physical contracts for the purchase of cocoa beans and cash-settled futures contracts. The physical contracts and the derivatives are managed together to hedge fixed-price sales contracts from an economic point of view.

7I.1.160.75 In our view, the physical contracts and the derivatives would be regarded as similar in purpose and therefore the physical contracts would not qualify for the own-use exemption.

7I.1.160.80 A contract for differences is a contract wherein two parties agree to pay or receive in cash the difference between the spot price and the fixed price on an underlying item, without actual delivery or receipt of that underlying item.

7I.1.160.90 Sometimes the market structure in some countries or industries may preclude a supplier and customer from entering into a direct transaction for the purchase/sale of a non-financial item.

In such situations, the supplier may enter into a contract with a market intermediary to sell the non-financial item at the spot price and the customer may enter separately into a contract with a market intermediary (possibly the same intermediary as that for the supplier) to buy the non-financial item at the spot price. Depending on the structure of the market, the market intermediary may act as a principal in its separate contracts with the customer and the supplier or, alternatively, it may act as an agent on behalf of the customer and the supplier. To fix the price for the non-financial item, the supplier and the customer may enter separately into a direct contract for differences between themselves and agree to pay/receive the difference between the spot price and a fixed price for that non-financial item.

7I.1.160.100   If the market intermediary is acting as a principal in its separate contracts with the customer and the supplier, although the customer and supplier may be permitted to apply the own-use exemption to their respective contracts with the market intermediary to buy or sell the non-financial item, then in our view the own-use exemption cannot be applied to the separate contract for differences between the customer and the supplier, because the contract for differences is not a contract to buy or sell a non-financial item that will be settled by the delivery or receipt of that non-financial item. [*IU 08-05*]

EXAMPLE 7A – CONTRACT FOR DIFFERENCES

7I.1.160.110   Market regulations in the electricity market established by law may preclude an electricity generator and a customer (retailer) from contracting directly for the delivery and purchase of electricity – i.e. the generator has to deliver electricity to, and a customer can buy electricity only from, a central 'grid', whereby the grid acts as a principal in its separate contracts with the customer and the generator.

7I.1.160.115   The generator and the customer manage their exposure to the risk of fluctuations in electricity spot prices by entering into a bilateral contractual arrangement (a contract for differences) that is settled outside the spot market, whereby the two parties – i.e. the generator and the customer – agree to exchange in cash the difference between the contractually agreed fixed price and the variable spot price that the customer pays in the market. The notional volume in such a contract for differences is generally determined either by the physical energy flow under the customer's contract with the grid to buy electricity or the generator's contract with the grid to deliver electricity.

7I.1.160.120   In our view, the transactions comprising the customer's contract with the grid to buy electricity and the customer's contract for differences with the generator, or the generator's contract with the grid to deliver electricity and the generator's contract for differences with the customer, do not form a single arrangement because:
- these transactions have two distinct, separate purposes; and
- each contract is with different parties.

7I.1.160.130   The structure is not considered to be a single accounting unit, and therefore the contract for differences and the customer's contract to buy electricity (or the generator's contract to deliver electricity) are analysed separately under IAS 39. Because the contract for differences is settled in cash, it is precluded from qualifying for the own-use exemption, despite the linkage of the notional volume of the contract for differences to the physical energy flow under the customer's contract with the grid to buy electricity (or the generator's contract with the grid to deliver electricity). However, the customer's contract with the grid to buy electricity or the generator's contract with the grid to deliver electricity may qualify for the own-use exemption.

7I.1.160.140 The customer/generator would, however, be able to designate a contract-for-differences derivative in a hedge of the variability in cash flows arising from the forecast purchases/sales of electricity at the spot rate if it satisfies the hedge designation and effectiveness criteria in IAS 39 (see 7I.7.120).

EXAMPLE 7B – INTERMEDIARY IN A WHOLESALE MARKET

7I.1.160.150 Company B is an intermediary in a wholesale market. B enters into fixed-price contracts to buy aluminium in the market and sells it in the same condition to customers, who use it in their manufacturing processes. The market for aluminium is liquid. All contracts are intended to be settled physically. The specific purpose of these contracts is to generate stable profits from the margin between the purchase and sale prices. Open positions are kept to a minimum.

7I.1.160.160 B aims to buy aluminium as cheaply as possible for its customers and it does not provide the customers with any additional services. The contracts are not and do not contain written options.

7I.1.160.170 B concludes that the contracts are entered into and held for the purpose of generating profit from a dealer's margin, rather than for the purposes of the receipt or delivery of a non-financial item in accordance with its expected purchase, sale or use requirements. Accordingly, the contracts are in the scope of IAS 39 and are measured at FVTPL.

7I.1.160.180 Modifying the scenario, the conclusion may be different if B provided significant services to its customers – e.g. shipping, distribution or repackaging of the commodity into small retail units. Significant services are typically provided if the entity buys and sells in different markets (e.g. buys wholesale and sells retail). If additional services are provided, then determining whether a contract is entered into and held for the purposes of the receipt or delivery of a non-financial item in accordance with its expected purchase, sale or use requirements may involve significant judgement.

7I.1.160.190 For a related discussion of the definition of a broker-dealer, see 3.8.70.25.

7I.1.170   *Readily convertible into cash*

7I.1.170.10   In our view, the following indicators are useful in determining whether a non-financial item is readily convertible into cash.

- There is an active market for the non-financial item. This refers to the spot market rather than the forward market. The relevant 'spot market' is the market where the entity sells its products based on its business model. An entity assesses whether this specific market is active, according to the guidance provided in IFRS 13 (see 2.4.280). It is important that buyers and sellers are present at any time. This is indicated, for example, by daily trading frequency (traded contracts) and daily trading volumes. Other indicators that might be considered are:
  - binding prices for the item are readily obtainable;
  - transfers of the item involve standardised documentation;
  - individual contract sales do not require significant negotiation or unique structuring;
  - the period required until the contract is finally closed is not extensive because of the need to permit legal consultation and document review; and
  - the difference between the transaction price and the entity's assessment of the value of the contract is insignificant (because a significant difference may indicate low liquidity).
- The non-financial item is fungible.
- Transaction costs, including commission, distribution and transport costs, are insignificant compared with gross sale proceeds. [*IFRS 13.A*]

7I.1.180   *Written options*

7I.1.180.10   A written option to buy or sell a non-financial asset that can be settled net in cash or another financial instrument – including when the non-financial item subject to the contract is readily convertible into cash – can never qualify for the own-use exemption because the entity cannot control whether the purchase or sale will take place. Therefore, such a contract cannot be entered into to meet an entity's expected purchase, sale or usage requirements. However, written options for commodities that cannot be settled net in cash (see 7I.1.160) are not in the scope of IAS 39. [*IAS 32.10, 39.7*]

7I.1.180.20   Sometimes forward contracts, which may qualify for the own-use exemption, are combined with written options in one contract. For example, an agreement to sell a fixed amount of a product at a fixed price may be combined with a written option under which a customer may buy additional amounts. In our view, in such cases the contract may be split so that the forward element may qualify as own-use even though the written option component will not.

7I.1.180.30   In the energy sector, it is common for a power company to provide 'whole of meter' contracts, under which the customer pays a fixed price per unit for the number of units of power it uses in a particular period. In our view, such contracts are not generally written options because the customer does not have the right to buy more or less of the product depending on the market price, nor does the customer have the ability to settle such contracts net in cash. In the case of electricity, the product cannot be stored or resold by customers and therefore from the perspective of the customer the power obtained under such contracts is not readily convertible into cash.

7I.1.190   *Embedded derivatives*

7I.1.190.10   A contract to buy or sell a non-financial item may be required to be treated as a derivative and measured at FVTPL in the period between the trade date and the settlement date (see 7I.5.20.45). [*IAS 39.AG54*]

7I.1.190.20   If a contract to buy or sell a non-financial item is not a derivative but contains an embedded derivative, then an entity determines whether the embedded derivative should be separated from the host contract and accounted for separately (see 7I.2.110). If the embedded derivative is accounted for separately, then in our view the host contract might still qualify for the own-use exemption.

7I.1.190.30   For contracts to buy or sell non-financial items that are not treated as derivatives, the underlying purchase or sale transaction is accounted for in accordance with the relevant standard. Such contracts are generally executory contracts (see 1.2.60) to buy or sell the underlying non-financial item. However, if such contracts contain a 'price adjustment' clause, then an assessment is made about whether such a clause is an embedded derivative that requires separation under IAS 39 (see 7I.2.110). In our view, whether a contract to buy or sell a non-financial item has an embedded derivative that requires separation – e.g. in the form of a price adjustment clause – does not affect the conclusion about whether the host contract meets the own-use exemption under IAS 39 (see 7I.1.150.20). [*IAS 39.5, 10, AG35(b)*]

7I.1.190.40   For a discussion of derivatives embedded in contracts in the scope of IFRS 15, see 7I.1.210.10.

7I.1.200   Loan commitments

7I.1.200.10   A loan commitment may be an arrangement under which:
- both the lender and the borrower are committed to a future loan transaction – i.e. a forward contract to grant/receive a loan; or
- the lender is obliged contractually to grant a loan, but the borrower is not required to take the loan – i.e. lender's written option.

7I.1.200.20   Generally, loan commitments, both issued and held, are excluded from the scope of IAS 39 but are subject to the derecognition provisions of the standard. However, a loan commitment falls entirely in the scope of IAS 39 when:
- the entity designates the loan commitment as a financial liability at FVTPL;
- the entity has a past practice of selling the assets resulting from its loan commitments shortly after their origination, in which case IAS 39 applies to all loan commitments in the same class and they are treated as derivatives;
- the loan commitment can be settled net in cash or by delivering or issuing another financial instrument – i.e. such a loan commitment is a derivative; or
- the commitment is to provide a loan at a below-market interest rate. [*IAS 39.2(h), 4*]

7I.1.200.30   A loan commitment that can be settled net in cash or by delivering or issuing another financial instrument is a derivative in the scope of IAS 39 (see 7I.1.200.20) – i.e. a loan commitment is excluded from the scope of IAS 39 only if it cannot be settled net. Paying a loan out in instalments is not regarded as net settlement of a loan commitment. [*IAS 39.4(b), BC18*]

EXAMPLE 8 – NET SETTLEMENT OF LOAN COMMITMENT

7I.1.200.40   Bank B and Company L enter into an agreement that in two years B will lend to L and L will borrow from B 100 for 10 years at a fixed interest rate.

7I.1.200.50   B cannot terminate the loan commitment. However, the contract gives L an option to terminate the commitment on payment of a termination fee. The termination fee is calculated as the difference, if positive, between:

- the present value of the loan's contractual cash flows discounted at the risk-free market interest rate at the date of termination plus the original credit spread determined at the date the contract was signed; and
- the present value of the loan's contractual cash flows discounted at the fixed interest rate of the loan.

7I.1.200.60   Because the loan commitment can be settled by L making a net cash payment based on the effect of changes in interest rates on the value of the loan commitment, B and L conclude that the loan commitment is a derivative in the scope of IAS 39.

7I.1.200.70   A loan commitment that is a hedged item in a fair value or cash flow hedge is accounted for as a hedged item under IAS 39. Generally, only loan commitments that are scoped out of IAS 39 could qualify as a hedged item; loan commitments in the scope of IAS 39 are generally accounted for as derivatives and therefore do not qualify as hedged items. [*IAS 39.4, IG.F.2.1*]

7I.1.200.80   IAS 39 includes specific requirements for the measurement of a loan commitment to provide a loan at a below-market interest rate when the loan commitment is not measured at FVTPL. Such a loan commitment is measured initially at fair value and subsequently at the higher of (1) the amount recognised under IAS 37 (see chapter 3.12); and (2) the amount initially recognised less the cumulative amount of income recognised in accordance with the principles of IFRS 15 (see chapter 4.2). Loan commitments that are not in the scope of IAS 39 are accounted for under IAS 37. However, all loan commitments are subject to the derecognition provisions of IAS 39. [*IAS 39.2(h), 4(c), 47(d)*]

7I.1.200.90   In our view, under IAS 37 it is likely that a provision for a loan commitment would be recognised either if an entity is committed to making a loan that would be considered to be impaired or otherwise only when the contract becomes onerous.

7I.1.210   Rights and obligations in the scope of IFRS 15

7I.1.210.10   IAS 39 excludes from its scope rights and obligations that are in the scope of IFRS 15, except for those that IFRS 15 specifies are accounted for in accordance with IAS 39 – e.g. trade receivables. At the same time, IFRS 15 excludes from its scope financial instruments and other contractual rights and obligations that are in the scope of IAS 39. IFRS 15 also states that a contract may be partially in its scope and partially in the scope of another standard, such as IAS 39. In such cases, IFRS 15 states that if the other standard specifies how to separate and/or initially measure one or more parts of the contract, then an entity first applies the separation and/or measurement requirements of that other standard. For example, if a contract contains a financial instrument in the scope of IAS 39, then the entity separates and measures that financial instrument using the guidance in IAS 39 and excludes from the transaction price under IFRS 15 the amount initially measured in accordance with IAS 39. Accordingly, the entity first considers whether the contract contains an embedded derivative that is in the scope of IAS 39, and whether IAS 39 requires it to be accounted for separately (see 7I.2.110). [*IFRS 15.5(c), 7, 108, C9, IAS 39.2(k)*]

7I.1.210.20   The impairment requirements of IAS 39 apply to contract assets in the scope of IFRS 15 (see 4.2.470 and 7I.6.400.05). [*IFRS 15.107, C9, IAS 39.2A*]

7I.2 Derivatives and embedded derivatives

7I.2 Derivatives and embedded derivatives

REQUIREMENTS FOR INSURERS THAT APPLY IFRS 4

In July 2014, the IASB issued IFRS 9 *Financial Instruments*, which is effective for annual periods beginning on or after 1 January 2018. However, an insurer may defer the application of IFRS 9 if it meets certain criteria (see 8.1.180).

This chapter reflects the requirement of IAS 39 *Financial Instruments: Recognition and Measurement* and the related standards, excluding any amendments introduced by IFRS 9. These requirements are relevant to insurers that apply the temporary exemption from IFRS 9 or the overlay approach to designated financial assets (see 8.1.160) and cover annual periods beginning on 1 January 2018. For further discussion, see Introduction to Sections 7 and 7I.

The requirements related to this topic are mainly derived from the following.

STANDARD	TITLE
IAS 39	Financial Instruments: Recognition and Measurement
IFRIC 9	Reassessment of Embedded Derivatives

FORTHCOMING REQUIREMENTS

The requirements in this chapter are affected by the following forthcoming requirements. They are highlighted with a # and the impact is explained in the accompanying boxed text at the reference indicated.

In January 2016, the IASB issued IFRS 16 *Leases*, which is effective for annual periods beginning on or after 1 January 2019. See 7I.2.267. IFRS 16 is the subject of chapter 5.1A.

FUTURE DEVELOPMENTS

For this topic, there are no future developments.

71.2.10   **DERIVATIVES**

71.2.20   **Definition**

71.2.20.10   A 'derivative' is a financial instrument or other contract in the scope of IAS 39 that has all of the following features:

- its value changes in response to one or more underlying variables – e.g. an interest rate (see 71.2.30);
- it has an initial net investment smaller than would be required for other instruments that have a similar response to the variable (see 71.2.40); and
- it will be settled at a future date (see 71.2.50). [*IAS 39.9*]

71.2.20.20   The definition of a derivative does not require specific settlement features. As such, a contract that allows either net or gross settlement may be a derivative. [*IAS 39.IG.B.3*]

71.2.20.30   The definition of a derivative is relevant in considering the treatment of both stand-alone contracts and features that are embedded in hybrid contracts (see 71.2.110). In our view, a stand-alone derivative should not be split into its component parts. For example, an interest rate collar should not be separated into an interest rate cap and an interest rate floor that are accounted for separately.

71.2.30   *Change in value based on an 'underlying'*

71.2.30.10   A derivative is a financial instrument that provides the holder (or writer) with the right (or obligation) to receive (or pay) cash or another financial instrument in amounts determined with reference to price changes in an underlying price or index, or changes in foreign exchange or interest rates, at a future date. A derivative may have more than one underlying variable. [*IAS 39.IG.B.8*]

71.2.30.20   A derivative usually has a notional amount, which can be an amount of currency, a number of shares, a number of units of weight or volume or other units specified in the contract. However, in our view contracts without notional amounts or with variable notional amounts may also meet the definition of a derivative. The holder or writer is not required to invest in or receive the notional amount at inception of the contract. [*IAS 39.AG9*]

71.2.30.30   A contract to pay or receive a fixed amount on the occurrence or non-occurrence of a future event meets the definition of a derivative, provided that this future event depends on a financial variable or a non-financial variable not specific to a party to the contract. For example, an entity may enter into a contract under which it will receive a fixed payment of 100 if a specified index increases by a determined number of points in the next month. The settlement amount is not based on and does not need to change proportionately with an underlying. [*IAS 39.AG9*]

71.2.30.40   The underlying variable on which the fair value of a derivative instrument is based may be that of:

- the price of a financial instrument – e.g. a bond or equity security;
- the price of a commodity – e.g. gold, oil or wheat;
- a rate – e.g. an interest rate or a foreign exchange rate;
- an index of prices – e.g. a stock exchange index; or
- some other variable that has a measurable value – e.g. a climatic, geological or other physical variable. [*IAS 39.IG.B.2*]

71.2.30.50   An option, forward or swap that is exercisable at the fair value of the underlying item always has a fair value of zero. Therefore, it does not meet the definition of a derivative because its value does not depend on an underlying variable. [*IAS 39.9*]

71.2.30.60   The definition of a derivative excludes instruments with a non-financial underlying variable that is specific to a party to the contract. However, IFRS does not provide guidance on how to determine whether a non-financial variable is specific to a party to the contract. In our view, the analysis comprises two questions:
1. Is the variable non-financial or financial?
2. Is it specific to a party to the contract?

71.2.30.70   In our view, this exclusion is primarily intended to exclude insurance contracts. For example, a residual value guarantee on a motor vehicle, in which the holder is compensated not only for a decline in the market value of the vehicle but also for the condition of the vehicle, does not meet the definition of a derivative.

71.2.30.80   However, in our view items such as EBITDA, profit, sales volume, revenue or cash flows of one counterparty may be considered to be non-financial variables that are specific to a party to the contract even though the contract, or the embedded feature being considered, does not meet the definition of an insurance contract (see 8.1.20). In addition, we believe that the gross domestic product of a counterparty that is a government or the non-viability of the issuer of a debt instrument – e.g. the issuer's regulatory capital ratio falling below a specified minimum threshold – may be considered to be a non-financial variable that is specific to a party to the contract. In our view, an entity should choose an accounting policy, to be applied consistently, on whether such items are considered to be non-financial variables that are specific to a party to the contract.

71.2.30.90   If an instrument has more than one underlying variable – i.e. it is dual-indexed – with one underlying being a non-financial variable specific to one of the parties, then judgement is required in determining whether the instrument is a derivative. The assessment depends, in our view, on the predominant characteristics of the instrument. We believe that a dual-indexed instrument is normally a derivative if it behaves in a manner that is highly correlated with the behaviour of the financial underlying variables (or other variables that are not specific to a party to the contract).

71.2.30.100   The implementation guidance accompanying IAS 39 identifies the following examples of a derivative.
*   A contract to exchange an amount of foreign currency determined by the sales volume of the entity at a fixed exchange rate at a future date.
*   An 'equity kicker' feature under which the lender of a subordinated loan is entitled to receive shares of the borrower free of charge, if the shares are listed. [*IAS 39.IG.B.8, IG.C.4*]

71.2.30.110   Consistent with the equity kicker example described above, in our view a contractual feature in a debt instrument that converts the instrument into equity shares of the issuer on occurrence of a specified 'non-viability event' (e.g. the issuer's regulatory capital falling below a specified level) is a derivative component (see Examples 10A and 10B).

71.2.40   *No or 'smaller' initial net investment*

71.2.40.10   There is no quantified guidance on how much smaller the initial net investment should be, compared with the investment required for other contracts that would be expected to have a similar response to changes in market factors, for the contract to meet the definition of a derivative. The standard requires the initial net investment to be less than the investment needed to acquire the underlying non-derivative financial instrument. However, 'less than' does not necessarily mean 'insignificant' in relation to the overall investment and needs to be interpreted on a relative basis. [*IAS 39.AG11*]

71.2.40.20   Debt and equity securities are generally not derivatives, although their fair values respond to changes in the underlying – e.g. interest rates or a share price – in similar ways to derivatives on these instruments. This is because it is not possible to identify another instrument that would require a greater initial net investment and have a similar response to changes in the relevant market factors.

71.2.40.30   Many derivatives, such as at-market forward contracts, do not have any initial net investment.

71.2.40.40   Purchased options normally require the payment of an up-front premium, but the amount paid is normally small in relation to the amount that would be paid to acquire the underlying instrument. However, certain call options may have a very low exercise price so that the amount paid to acquire the option is likely to be equivalent to the amount that would be paid to acquire the underlying asset outright at inception of the option. In our view, such options should be treated as a purchase of the underlying asset and not as derivatives. In other words, if an option is so deep in the money, at the date of issue or acquisition, that the cost of the option is almost equal to the value of the underlying asset at that date, then it should be accounted for as an investment in the underlying asset and not as a derivative. [*IAS 39.IG.B.9*]

71.2.40.50   A cross-currency swap meets the definition of a derivative, even though there is an exchange of currencies at inception of the contract, because there is zero initial *net* investment. [*IAS 39.AG11*]

71.2.40.60   Any required deposits or minimum balance requirement held in margin accounts as security for derivatives are not considered part of the initial investment. For example, the initial margin required in respect of exchange-traded futures comprises cash collateral rather than being part of the initial investment in the underlying commodity. [*IAS 39.IG.B.10*]

71.2.40.70   Sometimes one leg of a derivative is prepaid. Whether the remaining part still constitutes a derivative depends on whether all of the criteria in the definition are still met. [*IAS 39.IG.B.4–IG.B.5*]

71.2.40.80   If a party to an interest rate swap prepays its pay-fixed obligation at inception but will continue to receive the floating-rate leg over the life of the swap, then the floating-rate leg of the swap is still a derivative instrument. This is because all of the criteria for a derivative are met: the initial net investment – i.e. the amount prepaid by the entity – is less than investing in a similar primary financial instrument that responds equally to changes in the underlying interest rate; the instrument's fair value changes in response to changes in interest rates; and the instrument is settled at a future date. If the party prepays the pay-fixed obligation at a subsequent date, then this would be regarded as a termination of the old swap and an origination of a new instrument that is evaluated under IAS 39. [*IAS 39.IG.B.4*]

7I.2.40.90   In the reverse situation, if a party to an interest rate swap prepays its pay-variable obligation at inception using current market rates, then the swap is no longer a derivative because the prepaid amount now provides a return that is the same as that of a fixed-payment annuity or an amortising fixed rate debt instrument in the amount of the prepayment. Therefore, the initial net investment equals that of other financial instruments with fixed annuities. [*IAS 39.IG.B.5*]

7I.2.50   *Settlement at a future date*

7I.2.50.10   Derivatives require settlement at a future date. A forward contract is settled on a specified future date, an option has a future exercise date and interest rate swaps have multiple dates on which interest is settled. An option is considered settled on exercise or at its maturity. Therefore, even though the option may not be expected to be exercised when it is out of the money, it still meets the criterion of settlement at a future date. Any contract in which there is a delay between the trade date and settlement date is a derivative if the other criteria are also met. [*IAS 39.IG.B.7*]

7I.2.50.20   Settlement of a derivative, such as an interest rate swap, may be either a gross or a net exchange of cash or other financial instruments. [*IAS 39.IG.B.3*]

7I.2.50.30   A key element for a contract to buy or sell a non-financial item to be treated as a derivative in the scope of IAS 39 is that the transaction should allow for net settlement in the form of cash or the right to another financial instrument (see 7I.1.150). [*IAS 39.AG10, IG.A.1–IG.A.2*]

7I.2.60   Exemptions from derivative treatment

7I.2.70   *Regular-way contracts*

7I.2.70.10   'Regular-way contracts' are contracts to buy or sell financial assets that will be settled within the timeframe established by regulation or convention in the market concerned, not necessarily an organised market. Regular-way contracts are not treated as derivatives between the trade date and settlement date. [*IAS 39.9, 38, AG53–AG56*]

EXAMPLE 1 – REGULAR-WAY CONTRACT

7I.2.70.20   Company X purchases a security in a market in which three days is the normal settlement period for this type of transaction. X's commitment to settle the security in three days is not treated as a derivative because three days is the normal settlement period for this type of transaction in the environment in which the transaction takes place.

7I.2.70.30   However, in a market with three-day settlement, if a contract entered into by X specifies that settlement will take place only in three months, then the exception would not apply and X would need to treat the contract as a derivative between the trade date and the settlement date.

7I.2.70.40   IFRS does not offer any specific guidance on how to treat a delay in the settlement of a regular-way contract. In our view, a delay would not preclude the use of the regular-way exemption if the contract requires delivery within the timeframe established by the convention in the market and the delay is caused by a factor that is outside the control of the entity.

7I.2.80   **Derivatives on own equity**

7I.2.80.10   Derivatives on own equity are excluded from the scope of IAS 39 if they meet the definition of an equity instrument (see 7I.3.20.40, 50 and 120). [*IAS 39.2(d)*]

7I.2.90   *Gaming contracts*

7I.2.90.10   A gaming institution may enter into different types of transactions with its customers. The following are examples.

- Transactions in which the gaming institution administers a scheme among its customers and receives a commission based on the amount wagered – e.g. parimutuel betting. In these transactions, the gaming institution will receive its commission regardless of the outcome of the wager.
- Transactions in which the gaming institution takes a position against its customers. In these transactions, the value of the individual contract is contingent on the outcome of a specified event and the gaming institution is not, therefore, normally guaranteed a specific commission or return – e.g. a bookmaker that lays fixed odds on the outcome of a sporting event.

7I.2.90.20   In our view, the first type of transaction in 7I.2.90.10 does not meet the definition of a derivative, because the value of such contracts does not fluctuate based on an underlying variable. We believe that these transactions should be accounted for under IFRS 15 (see chapter 4.2). Conversely, the second type of transactions in 7I.2.90.10 will normally meet the definition of a derivative, because the value of such contracts varies depending on the likelihood of the occurrence of a specified event. In this case, such transactions will be accounted for under IAS 39.

7I.2.100   *Rights and obligations arising on transfer of financial asset*

7I.2.100.10   Rights and obligations arising on a transfer of a financial asset that does not qualify for derecognition are not treated as derivatives under IAS 39, if recognising the derivative would result in recognising the same rights or obligations twice (see 7I.5.300.20). [*IAS 39.AG49*]

7I.2.110   **EMBEDDED DERIVATIVES**

7I.2.120   **Definition and outline**

7I.2.120.10   A hybrid (combined) contract is a contract that includes both a non-derivative host contract and one or more embedded derivatives. [*IAS 39.10, AG33A*]

7I.2.120.20   IAS 39 requires an embedded derivative to be separated from the host contract and accounted for as a stand-alone derivative if the following conditions are met:

- the economic characteristics and risks of the embedded derivative are not closely related to those of the host contract (see 7I.2.200);
- a separate instrument with the same terms as the embedded derivative would meet the definition of a derivative (see 7I.2.20); and
- the hybrid instrument is not measured at FVTPL (see 7I.2.150). [*IAS 39.11*]

7I.2.120.30   The following flowchart illustrates how to apply the requirements for separating an embedded derivative from a hybrid instrument.

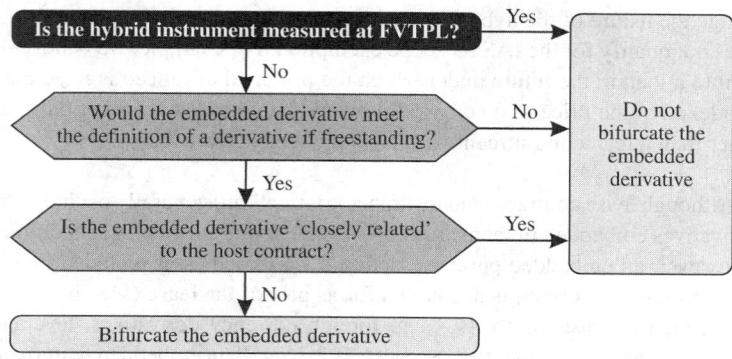

7I.2.120.40   A derivative contract attached to a host contract that is transferable separately from the host contract, or that is added by a third party, is a stand-alone derivative and not an embedded derivative. For example, a finance lease or loan may have an associated interest rate swap. If the swap can be sold separately, then it is a stand-alone derivative and not an embedded derivative, even if both the derivative and the host contract have the same counterparty. [*IAS 39.10*]

7I.2.120.50   Each component of a 'synthetic instrument' is accounted for separately, unless there is a requirement to account for the separate instruments as a single combined instrument (see 7I.5.40). A synthetic instrument is a combination of separate instruments that, viewed together, 'create' a different instrument.

EXAMPLE 2 – ACCOUNTING FOR COMPONENTS OF SYNTHETIC INSTRUMENT

7I.2.120.60   Company D holds a five-year floating-rate debt instrument and a five-year pay-floating, receive-fixed interest rate swap; together these two instruments create, for D, a synthetic five-year fixed rate investment. The individual components of the synthetic instrument are not embedded derivatives; instead, they are stand-alone instruments, which are accounted for separately. [*IAS 39.IG.C.6*]

7I.2.130   Scope exclusions

7I.2.130.10   In our view, if an item that is otherwise excluded from the scope of IAS 39 contains an embedded derivative, then the entity should evaluate whether the particular IFRS that addresses the accounting for the scoped-out item also addresses the accounting for the embedded derivative. If that IFRS addresses the accounting for the embedded derivative, then we believe that the entire hybrid instrument should be accounted for in accordance with that particular IFRS. If the IFRS does not address the accounting for the embedded derivative, then we believe that the principles in IAS 39 should be used to evaluate whether the embedded derivative should be separated. If the embedded derivative is required to be separated, then the host contract is accounted for under the relevant IFRS and the embedded derivative is accounted for under IAS 39.

7I.2.130.20   In our view, before considering whether an embedded derivative should be separated from a host contract, an entity should evaluate whether the economic characteristics of the embedded derivative change the nature of the hybrid instrument to such an extent that the hybrid instrument in its entirety does not qualify for the IAS 39 scope exemption. For example, we believe that a commitment to enter into a loan in the future under which the principal advanced is fixed but the principal repayable is indexed to the price of a commodity would be regarded at inception as a freestanding derivative rather than a loan commitment with an embedded derivative.

7I.2.130.30   Although lease contracts and insurance contracts are generally excluded from the scope of IAS 39, derivatives embedded in them are subject to the requirements for separation of embedded derivatives. However, an embedded purchase option for a leased asset included in a lease contract is not separated because the option is accounted for as part of the lease (see chapter 5.1). All other derivatives embedded in lease contracts – e.g. foreign currency derivatives, leveraged escalation clauses etc – are considered for separation (see also 7I.2.267). If an embedded feature in an insurance contract itself transfers significant insurance risk, then the feature meets the definition of an insurance contract and therefore is not required to be separated under the embedded derivative guidance (see 8.1.30.50–70) [*IAS 39.2(b), (e), AG33(f), IFRS 4.7, B11*]

7I.2.130.40   If an embedded derivative is separated, then the host contract is accounted for under IAS 39 if it is itself a financial instrument in the scope of IAS 39, or otherwise in accordance with other appropriate standards if it is not a financial instrument (see 7I.2.130.10). [*IAS 39.11*]

7I.2.140   Multiple embedded derivatives

7I.2.140.10   If a single hybrid contract has more than one embedded derivative with different underlying risk exposures and those embedded derivatives are readily separable and are independent of each other, then they are accounted for separately from each other. For example, a debt instrument may contain options to choose the interest rate index on which interest is determined and the currency in which the principal is repaid. These are two distinct embedded derivative features with different underlying risk exposures, which are accounted for separately from each other. [*IAS 39.AG29*]

7I.2.140.20   Multiple embedded derivatives in a single hybrid contract that relate to the same risk exposure, or that are not readily separable and independent of each other, are treated as a single compound embedded derivative (see 7I.2.210). [*IAS 39.AG29*]

EXAMPLE 3 – ACCOUNTING FOR HOST CONTRACT

7I.2.140.30   Company X issues a debt instrument that includes two embedded derivative features.
- *Feature 1:* Varies the interest rate on the debt instrument.
- *Feature 2:* Allows the holder of the debt instrument to put it back to the issuer.

7I.2.140.40   X treats these two features as a single compound embedded derivative because they both relate to interest rate risk.

7I.2.150   Hybrid instruments measured at FVTPL

7I.2.150.10   If the hybrid (combined) instrument – i.e. the host contract plus the embedded derivative – is measured at FVTPL, then separate accounting is not permitted. [*IAS 39.11*]

7I.2.150.20   If a contract is a financial instrument and contains one or more embedded derivatives, then an entity may designate the entire combined contract as a financial asset or financial liability at FVTPL unless:

- the embedded derivative does not significantly modify the cash flows that would otherwise arise on the contract; or
- it is clear with little or no analysis when a similar hybrid instrument is first considered that separation would be prohibited. [*IAS 39.11A*]

7I.2.150.25   The designation discussed in 7I.2.150.20 is used only when:

- it reduces the complexities associated with separating embedded derivatives; or
- measuring the entire instrument at FVTPL is more reliable than measuring the fair value of the embedded derivative. [*IAS 39.AG33A–AG33B*]

EXAMPLE 4A – DESIGNATING ENTIRE COMBINED CONTRACT AT FVTPL (1)

7I.2.150.30   Company B has an investment in convertible bonds. If B classifies the investment as an available-for-sale asset, then changes in the fair value of the hybrid instrument would be recognised in OCI, and B would be required to account for and measure the embedded derivative (equity conversion option) separately at FVTPL. However, it may be simpler for B to designate the entire investment as at FVTPL and thereby avoid the need to separately measure and account for the embedded conversion option.

EXAMPLE 4B – DESIGNATING ENTIRE COMBINED CONTRACT AT FVTPL (2)

7I.2.150.40   Company B also has a complex investment product that comprises a host bond contract and a number of embedded derivatives based on interest rates, equity prices etc. Again, it may be simpler for B to determine a fair value for the instrument as a whole than to account separately for the embedded derivative components.

7I.2.160   Inability to measure reliably

7I.2.160.10   If the fair value of an embedded derivative cannot be measured reliably, although the characteristics are such that separation is required, then the entire combined contract – i.e. host contract and embedded derivative – is designated as at FVTPL. In our experience, this situation will be encountered only in rare circumstances (see 7I.4.70.40). [*IAS 39.12*]

7I.2.170   Separation not voluntary

7I.2.170.10   If an embedded derivative is not required to be separated, then IAS 39 does not permit an entity to separate it from the hybrid instrument – i.e. separation is not optional. [*IAS 39.11*]

7I.2.180   Existence of a contractual commitment

7I.2.180.10   For an embedded derivative to exist, the contract needs to represent a contractual commitment. For example, forecast but uncommitted sales in a foreign currency, no matter how likely, cannot contain an embedded derivative.

7I.2.190   **When to separate**

7I.2.200   *Closely related criterion*

7I.2.200.10   Determining whether an embedded derivative is closely related to the host contract requires consideration of the nature – i.e. the economic characteristics and risks – of the host contract and the nature of the underlying of the derivative. If the natures of both the underlying and the host contract are similar, then they are generally closely related. [*IAS 39.11, AG30–AG33*]

7I.2.200.20   In our view, a derivative with economic characteristics and risk types that are broadly similar to those of the host contract is not necessarily closely related to the host contract. This is, for example, the case in the following situations.
- An equity host contract and an embedded equity index-linked derivative are not closely related unless they are both exposed to the equity characteristics of the same entity.
- The derivative embedded in an inflation-indexed lease contract is closely related to the lease only if the inflation index relates to the same economic environment as the lease contract. [*IAS 39.AG27, AG33(f)*]

7I.2.200.25   A leverage feature that is not insignificant usually causes an embedded derivative feature not to be closely related; an exception is discussed in 7I.2.250. 'Leverage' in this context (for contracts other than options) means that the feature increases the variability of the contractual cash flows of the hybrid instrument at a greater rate than would be inferred from the host instrument's economic relationship with the relevant underlying. [*IAS 39.AG30, AG33*]

7I.2.200.30   Evaluating whether an embedded derivative is closely related to its host contract requires identifying the nature of the host contract. The nature of a host financial instrument – i.e. debt or equity – is not always obvious. A debt host contract is usually characterised by a fixed or determinable maturity and fixed or determinable payments, whereas an equity host contract has no stated or predetermined maturity and gives the holder a residual interest in the net assets of an entity. [*IAS 39.AG27*]

EXAMPLE 5 – HOST CONTRACT FOR STATED MATURITY INSTRUMENT LINKED TO SHARE PRICE

7I.2.200.40   A five-year instrument has a principal of 100 that will be redeemed on a specified date at an amount equal to the principal plus the change in the fair value of 10 shares in a listed company over the term of the instrument.

7I.2.200.50   Even though the redemption amount is linked to a listed company's share price, the instrument has a stated maturity and the host contract has the nature of a debt instrument. [*IAS 39.AG27, IG.C.5*]

7I.2.210   *Multiple embedded derivatives*

7I.2.210.10   As discussed in 7I.2.140.20, in many cases multiple embedded derivatives are treated as a single compound embedded derivative. In our view, if there is specific guidance in IAS 39 on whether one or more components of a compound embedded derivative are closely related to the host contract, then this guidance should be applied in assessing whether the compound embedded derivative should be separated. We believe that if the guidance requires a component of the compound derivative to be separated, then usually the compound derivative as a whole should be separated. [*IAS 39.AG30–AG33*]

EXAMPLE 6 – SEPARATING MULTIPLE EMBEDDED DERIVATIVES

7I.2.210.20   Company Y issues a 10-year debt instrument at 100 (par). The following are key terms of the debt instrument.

- *Interest rate:* The debt pays interest at a floating rate of three-month LIBOR plus a fixed margin.
- *Interest rate floor (embedded derivative 1):* The floating interest rate will not be lower than 5% for any period. The interest rate floor is not in the money on issuing the debt and is not leveraged.
- *Prepayment option (embedded derivative 2):* Y may at any time voluntarily prepay principal and related accrued interest outstanding in whole or in part plus a penalty of 20% of the outstanding amount.

7I.2.210.30   Both embedded derivatives relate to the same risk – i.e. interest rate risk. They are also not readily separable and independent of each other, because the incentive to prepay increases as the floor becomes in the money when interest rates fall, and prepaying extinguishes the floor.

7I.2.210.40   In this example, a component of the compound embedded derivative, the prepayment option, is not closely related to the host contract based on the specific guidance in IAS 39, because the prepayment amount is not approximately equal to the amortised cost of the host instrument. Therefore, Y concludes that the compound instrument as a whole is not closely related to the host contract and separates it. [*IAS 39.AG33(b)*]

7I.2.220   *Reassessment of embedded derivatives*

7I.2.220.10   The assessment of whether an embedded derivative is required to be separated from the host contract and accounted for as a derivative is made at inception of the contract – i.e. when the entity first becomes a party to the contract. Subsequent reassessment is prohibited unless there is a change in the terms of the contract that significantly modifies the cash flows that would otherwise be required under the contract, in which case reassessment is required. [*IFRIC 9.7*]

EXAMPLE 7 – REASSESSMENT OF EMBEDDED DERIVATIVES

7I.2.220.20   Company X has not separated a foreign currency derivative embedded in a host sales contract because the feature is not leveraged, it does not contain an option and the payments are denominated in the functional currency of the customer.

7I.2.220.30   The functional currency of the customer changes three months after inception of the contract. X does not reassess whether to separate the derivative embedded in the contract. This is because there have been no changes to the terms of the contract that significantly modify the cash flows that would otherwise be required under the contract.

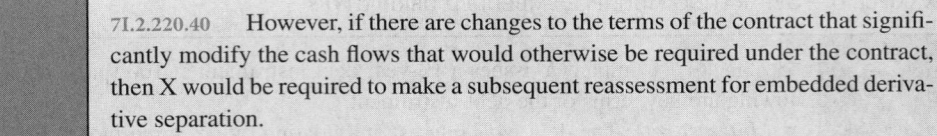

71.2.220.40   However, if there are changes to the terms of the contract that significantly modify the cash flows that would otherwise be required under the contract, then X would be required to make a subsequent reassessment for embedded derivative separation.

71.2.220.50   In addition, when an entity reclassifies a hybrid financial asset out of the FVTPL category (see 71.4.220.20), it is also required to assess whether an embedded derivative is required to be separated from the host contract. The assessment is made on the basis of the circumstances that existed at the later of:

- when the entity first became a party to the contract; and
- when there was a change in the terms of the contract that significantly modified the cash flows that would otherwise have been required under the contract. [*IFRIC 9.7, 7A*]

71.2.220.60   If an entity is unable to separately measure the fair value of an embedded derivative that would have to be separated on reclassification out of the FVTPL category, then reclassification is prohibited and the entire hybrid financial asset remains in the FVTPL category (see 71.2.160.10). [*IAS 39.13*]

EXAMPLE 8 – ASSESSMENT OF EMBEDDED DERIVATIVES ON RECLASSIFICATION

71.2.220.70   On 1 January 2018, Company X buys a 10-year debt instrument for 100 (par), which is redeemable at any time at the issuer's option for 100. X classifies the debt instrument as held-for-trading and it is accounted for at fair value with changes in fair value recognised in profit or loss.

71.2.220.80   On 1 October 2018, the conditions for reclassification from the FVTPL category to 'loans and receivables' are met and X reclassifies the debt instrument to loans and receivables (see 71.4.220.20). At this date, the fair value of the debt instrument is 70 and this becomes the new amortised cost of the debt instrument (see 71.4.220.60).

71.2.220.90   On reclassification, X evaluates the embedded call option to determine whether it is an embedded derivative that requires separation from the host debt instrument. Because there have been no changes in the terms of the host debt instrument between the date of purchase and the date of reclassification, X performs the embedded derivatives assessment based on the circumstances that existed on the date of purchase – i.e. 1 January 2018 (see 71.2.220.50).

71.2.220.100   On 1 January 2018, given the amortised cost of the debt instrument of approximately 100, X would probably have concluded that the embedded call option was closely related to the host debt instrument (see 71.2.240). This is because the exercise price of the call option would be approximately equal to the amortised cost of the host debt instrument at each exercise date. Therefore, X does not separate the embedded call option on reclassification.

 7I.2.220.110   In contrast, if there had been a significant change in the terms of the contract, then the embedded derivative assessment would be based on circumstances that existed on the modification date.

7I.2.230   *Extension features*

7I.2.230.10   An option or automatic provision to extend the remaining term to maturity of a debt instrument is not closely related to the host debt instrument unless there is a concurrent adjustment to the approximate current market rate of interest at the time of the extension. However, depending on its terms, an entity may consider an extension feature in a debt host contract to be equivalent to a loan commitment that would not be in the scope of IAS 39 and consequently would not be accounted for as a derivative if it were a separate instrument (see 7I.1.200). In our view, when an entity adopts this approach it should not separate such an extension feature as an embedded derivative from the host debt contract. [*IAS 39.11, AG30(c)*]

7I.2.240   *Calls, puts or prepayment options*

7I.2.240.10   A call, put or prepayment option embedded in a host debt contract or host insurance contract is closely related to the host contract in either of the following scenarios.
- The exercise price of the option is approximately equal on each exercise date to the amortised cost of the host debt instrument or the carrying amount of the host insurance contract.
- The exercise price of the prepayment option reimburses the lender for an amount up to the approximate present value of lost interest for the remaining term of the host contract. 'Lost interest' is the product of the principal amount prepaid, multiplied by the interest rate differential. The 'interest rate differential' is the excess of the effective interest rate of the host contract over the effective interest rate that the entity would receive at the prepayment date if it reinvested the principal amount prepaid in a similar contract for the remaining term of the host contract. This exception is conditional on the exercise price compensating the lender for loss of interest by reducing the economic loss from reinvestment risk. [*IAS 39.11, AG30(g)*]

7I.2.240.15   If a convertible debt instrument (see 7I.3.230) contains a call or put option, then the assessment of whether the call or put option is closely related to the host debt contract is made before separating the equity element of the convertible debt instrument. [*IAS 39.AG30(g)*]

7I.2.240.20   It is generally presumed that a call, put or prepayment option is closely related to the host contract if the exercise price is approximately equal to the amortised cost of the host contract at each exercise date. However, in our view, to evaluate whether a contingent call, put or prepayment option should be bifurcated, an entity should also consider the nature of the contingency. Accordingly, we believe that a contingent call, put or prepayment option with an exercise price approximately equal to the amortised cost of the host debt contract at each exercise date should not be bifurcated from the host contract if and only if the underlying contingent event that triggers exercisability of the option:
- is a non-financial variable that is specific to a party to the contract; or
- has economic characteristics and risks that are closely related to those of the host debt contract
  – e.g. based on the interest rate or credit risk of the host debt contract.

7I.2.240.30   Examples of contingent events that would be a non-financial variable specific to a party to the contract or closely related might include a change in control of the issuer, a change in relevant taxation or law that specifically affects the instrument, the occurrence or non-occurrence of an IPO of the issuer or a change in the credit rating of the instrument.

EXAMPLE 9A – ISSUER REDEMPTION OPTION WITH SHARE PRICE BEING UNDERLYING RISK EXPOSURE

7I.2.240.40   Company X issues a five-year bond containing an early-redemption option. The option allows X to redeem the bond at any time after the second anniversary of the issue date, subject to a 30-day notice period, if the volume-weighted-average price of X's shares, for at least 20 consecutive trading days, equals or exceeds 125% of X's share price at the issue date of the bond.

7I.2.240.50   Because the redemption option's underlying risk exposure is X's share price, rather than the interest rate or credit risk of the host contract, X concludes that the call option should be separated from the host contract and measured at FVTPL (see 7I.6.140).

EXAMPLE 9B – ISSUER REDEMPTION OPTION IN CONVERTIBLE BOND

7I.2.240.60   Modifying Example 9A, the instrument is a convertible bond that the holder has the right to convert into a fixed number of shares any time after the second anniversary of the issue date. X determines that the conversion feature is an equity component (see 7I.3.187). If X exercises its option to redeem the bond, then the holder has the opportunity to convert within the 30-day notice period.

7I.2.240.70   The economic effect of the call option is to incentivise the holder to convert, thereby limiting the value of the conversion feature from the holder's perspective.

7I.2.240.80   X makes an assessment of whether the call option is closely related to the host contract before separating the equity element (see 7I.2.240.15). X therefore considers the convertible bond including the equity conversion option in assessing whether the redemption feature has economic characteristics and risks that are closely related to those of the host contract.

7I.2.240.90   Because both the host contract (including the conversion option) and the embedded call option include economic characteristics related to X's share price, it is possible that the call option would not be separated in the financial statements of X. This would depend on whether it can be demonstrated that the call option's exercise price is approximately equal on each exercise date to the amortised cost of the host contract (including the conversion option). [*IAS 39.AG30(g)*]

EXAMPLE 10A – DUAL-INDEXED EMBEDDED FEATURE – DERIVATIVE SEPARATED

7I.2.240.100   Bank X issues a 20-year, fixed rate bond of 1,000 at par. The bond includes a contractual conversion feature that requires conversion of the bond into a variable number of equity shares of X if X's Common Equity Tier 1 ratio (as determined in accordance with applicable banking regulations) drops below 7.5% (the contingent event or the non-viability event). Under the conversion mechanism, the number of shares to be issued would be determined so as to have a fair value equal to the bond's par amount plus accrued interest but subject to a fixed cap on the number of shares to be issued. X does not classify the bond as measured at FVTPL.

7I.2.240.110   X determines that the fair value of the conversion feature is mainly dependent on:
- *the probability of the contingent event occurring:* This is a non-financial variable specific to X, which is a party to the contract;
- *the fair value of the host bond:* The conversion feature would result in X issuing shares with a fair value equal to par plus accrued interest (subject to the cap), which may be different from the fair value of the bond received in exchange; and
- *the fair value of X's equity shares:* The cap on the number of shares to be issued means that if the share price is below a particular price level on the conversion date, then the number of shares to be issued would be capped and, consequently, the total fair value of the shares to be issued may be less than the bond's par amount plus accrued interest.

7I.2.240.120   X has made an accounting policy choice to treat the contingent event as a non-financial variable that is specific to a party to the contract (see 7I.2.30.80). However, X determines that the conversion feature meets the definition of a derivative (see 7I.2.30.110). In this case, because the value of the conversion feature is dependent on changes in the fair value of X's equity shares, X concludes that the economic characteristics and risks of the conversion feature are not closely related to the host debt instrument. Therefore, X separates the conversion feature from the bond and accounts for the conversion feature at FVTPL (see 7I.2.380).

EXAMPLE 10B – DUAL-INDEXED EMBEDDED FEATURE – DERIVATIVE NOT SEPARATED

7I.2.240.130   Changing Example 10A, assume that the conversion feature does not include any cap on the number of shares to be issued. Therefore, changes in the fair value of X's equity shares no longer affect the value of the conversion feature. In this case, X determines that the fair value of the conversion feature is mainly dependent only on:
- the probability of the contingent event occurring; and
- the fair value of the host bond.

7I.2.240.140   X does not separately account for the conversion feature as a derivative because the conversion feature is closely related to the host bond – i.e. the exercise

> price of the conversion feature at the time of conversion will be approximately equal
> at all times to the amortised cost of the host – and the exercise of the conversion
> feature is triggered only by the contingent event, which is a non-financial variable
> that is specific to a party to the contract (see 7I.2.240.20).

7I.2.240.150 Under IFRS 4, an insurer is not required to separate a policyholder's option to surrender an insurance contract for a fixed amount (or for an amount based on a fixed amount and an interest rate). [*IFRS 4.8*]

7I.2.250 *Interest rate features in host debt contracts and insurance contracts*

7I.2.250.10 An exception to the requirement that all derivatives with leverage be separated is provided for embedded interest rate derivatives in which the underlying is an interest rate or index that can change the amount of interest that would otherwise be paid or received on an interest-bearing host debt contract or insurance contract. For a hybrid instrument with such an embedded derivative, leverage does not automatically result in separation unless:

- the embedded interest rate feature could prevent the holder of the hybrid instrument from recovering substantially all of its investment at settlement date; or
- the embedded interest rate feature could result in the holder receiving a rate of return on the hybrid instrument that is at least double its initial rate of return on the host instrument and could result in a rate of return that is at least twice the market return of an instrument with the same terms as the host instrument ('double-double test'). [*IAS 39.AG33(a)*]

7I.2.250.20 In our view, this analysis should not be based on the likelihood of these limits being exceeded in practice, but rather on whether the contractual terms make it *possible* that the limits will be exceeded.

7I.2.255 *Embedded interest rate caps and floors*

7I.2.255.10 An embedded floor or cap on the interest rate on a debt contract or insurance contract is closely related to the host contract, provided that the cap is at or above the market rate of interest and the floor is at or below the market rate of interest when the contract is issued and the cap or floor is not leveraged in relation to the host contract. [*IAS 39.AG33(b)*]

7I.2.255.20 The IFRS Interpretations Committee has discussed when an interest rate floor should be separated from a floating rate host contract and accounted for as a derivative. The Committee stated that:

- an entity should compare the overall interest rate floor (i.e. the benchmark interest rate referenced in the contract plus contractual spreads and if applicable any premiums, discounts or other elements that would be relevant to the calculation of the effective interest rate) for the contract to the market rate of interest for a similar contract without the interest rate floor (i.e. the host contract);
- in order to determine the appropriate market rate of interest for the host contract, an entity is required to consider the specific terms of the host contract and the relevant spreads (including credit spreads) appropriate for the transaction; and

- the term 'market rate of interest' is linked to the concept of fair value as defined in IFRS 13 and is described as the rate of interest 'for a similar instrument (similar as to currency, term, type of interest rate and other factors) with a similar credit rating' (see 7I.6.20.30 and 60.20). [*IU 01-16, IAS 39.AG64*]

7I.2.255.30   The Committee also noted that the requirements in paragraph AG33(b) of IAS 39 (see 7I.2.255.10–20) should be applied to an interest rate floor in a negative interest rate environment in the same way as they would be applied in a positive interest rate environment because paragraph AG33(b) of IAS 39 does not distinguish between positive and negative interest rates. [*IU 01-16*]

7I.2.255.40   In determining the unit of account for the purposes of the assessment in 7I.2.255.10, in our view an entity should choose an accounting policy, to be applied consistently, to evaluate the cap or floor as one instrument or as a series of separate caplets or floorlets, one for each payment date.

7I.2.255.50   If the cap or floor is assessed as one instrument, then we believe that the market rate of interest with which each cap or floor is compared could be the swap rate plus relevant spreads (including credit spreads). If the swap rate (i.e. the currently quoted rate for the fixed leg of an interest rate swap against a floating benchmark rate as determined by its particular market) is used, then it should be for the same period as the cap or floor. This is because the guidance in IAS 39 in relation to 'market rate of interest' requires consideration of the rate of interest for a similar instrument with a similar term. Therefore, we believe that it would be inappropriate to use the spot rate for the first reset period as a proxy for the whole period of the cap or floor. If an entity determines, based on the assessment, that the embedded cap or floor is not closely related to the host contract, then in our view the entire cap or floor should be separated and not only those embedded caplets or floorlets that are in the money. This is consistent with the unit of account assessment. [*IAS 39.AG64*]

7I.2.255.60   If the unit of account for the purposes of the assessment is a series of separate caplets or floorlets, then we believe that the market rate of interest with which each caplet or floorlet is compared should be the forward rate for the period of that particular caplet or floorlet plus relevant spreads (including credit spreads). If an entity determines, based on the assessment, that one or more – but not necessarily all – of the embedded caplets or floorlets are not closely related to the host contract, then in our view all caplets or floorlets should be separated and not only those embedded caplets or floorlets that are in the money. This is consistent with the guidance on multiple embedded derivatives (see 7I.2.140 and 210).

7I.2.260   Foreign currency derivatives embedded in non-financial or insurance contracts

7I.2.260.10   A host contract that is an insurance contract or a non-financial instrument may be denominated in a foreign currency – e.g. the premiums on an insurance contract or the price of non-financial items in a purchase-or-sale transaction. In these circumstances, the foreign currency embedded derivative is not accounted for separately from the host contract, provided that it is not leveraged, does not contain an option feature and the payments required under the contract are denominated in one of the following currencies:

- the functional currency of one of the substantial parties to the contract;
- the currency in which the price of the related goods or services being delivered under the contract is routinely denominated in commercial transactions around the world; or
- the currency that is commonly used in contracts to buy or sell non-financial items in the economic environment in which the transaction takes place. [*IAS 39.AG33(d)*]

7I.2.260.20   In our view, if the conditions in 7I.2.260.10 are not met, then a foreign currency embedded derivative should be separated from the host contract. This is because those conditions are explicit requirements that should be satisfied in order for the host contract and the derivative to be considered 'closely related'.

EXAMPLE 11 – SEPARABLE FOREIGN CURRENCY DERIVATIVE EMBEDDED IN NON-FINANCIAL CONTRACT

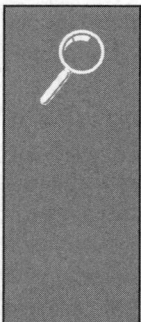

7I.2.260.25   Company E enters into a contract to provide goods and services to Company B. E and B have the same functional currency. The settlement of the host contract is to be made in that currency. However, certain of the goods and services that E will buy from unrelated third parties to fulfil its obligations will be denominated in a foreign currency. Accordingly, E and B agree that the final contract settlement price will be adjusted based on the movement in the foreign currency. Because the embedded derivative is a foreign currency embedded derivative and does not meet the conditions in 7I.2.260.10, both parties conclude that it should be separated from the host contract even though it may have some economic relationship to the cost and value of the goods and services supplied.

7I.2.260.30   IAS 39 does not provide guidance on how to identify 'substantial parties to the contract'. In our view, the legal parties to a contract are not necessarily also the substantial parties to it. When determining who is a substantial party to a contract, an entity needs to consider all of the facts and circumstances related to the contract, including whether a legally contracting party possesses the requisite knowledge, resources and technology to fulfil the contract without relying on related parties. To make this assessment, an entity needs to look through the legal form of the contract to evaluate the substance of the underlying relationships. In our view, only one entity within a consolidated group can be deemed a substantial party with respect to a particular contract with an entity outside the group.

7I.2.260.35   In our view, an entity that will provide the majority of the resources required under a contract is the substantial party to that contract. Identifying this entity is a subjective assessment and should be based on an analysis of both quantitative and qualitative factors. Certain resources – e.g. employees and material costs specifically used to fulfil the contract – can be quantified. Qualitative factors that may not be easily measured include developed technology, knowledge, experience and infrastructure.

7I.2.260.40   'Routinely denominated', as noted in the second bullet in 7I.2.260.10, should in our view be interpreted narrowly. Transactions qualifying for this exemption that may be considered to be routinely denominated in US dollars in commercial transactions around the world include:

- oil transactions;
- transactions related to large passenger aircraft; and
- transactions in certain precious metals – such as gold and silver – and diamonds. [*IAS 39.IG.C.9*]

7I.2.260.50   To qualify, the currency would have to be used in similar transactions around the world, and not just in one local area. For example, if cross-border transactions in natural gas are denominated in US dollars in North America and in euro in Europe, then neither the US dollar nor the euro is the currency in which natural gas is routinely denominated. [*IAS 39.IG.C.9*]

7I.2.260.60   In our view, 'routinely denominated in commercial transactions around the world' means that a large majority of transactions in international commerce around the world are traded in that currency. This implies that with respect to any particular commodity, transactions cannot be considered routinely denominated in more than one currency.

7I.2.260.70   In our view, if transactions on a local or regional exchange are denominated in a local currency but are priced using the international price – e.g. US dollars per barrel of oil – at the spot exchange rate, then those transactions are, in effect, denominated in the international currency.

7I.2.260.80   In addition, we believe that the existence of a relatively small proportion of transactions denominated in a local currency in one or two markets, or particular jurisdictions, does not preclude a commodity from meeting the definition of 'routinely denominated in commercial transactions around the world'.

7I.2.260.90   The third exemption noted in 7I.2.260.10 for a currency that is commonly used in the economic environment in which non-financial items are bought and sold may apply when a country's local currency is not stable, causing businesses in that environment to adopt a more stable and liquid currency for internal and cross-border trade. In our view, the application of this exemption is not limited to countries with a local currency that is not stable, and it may be applied in other countries as long as the 'commonly used currency' criterion is met. Accordingly, we believe that the exemption may also apply when the local currency is stable, but business practice has developed to commonly use a more liquid foreign currency such as the US dollar or the euro in either internal or cross-border trade. Before concluding that a currency, other than the local currency of a country, is commonly used in contracts to buy or sell non-financial items in that country, careful consideration needs to be given to business practices in that country.

7I.2.260.95   In our view, the assessment of 'commonly used currency' in a specified environment requires judgement and should be evaluated in the context of the particular facts and circumstances in the jurisdiction, but not in the context of a specific industry. That judgement should be supported by an analysis of the specific economic environment in which the transaction takes place. We believe that the following parameters can provide evidence about whether a currency is commonly used in a particular jurisdiction:
- for a cross-border transaction, analysing the level of foreign trade transactions in that currency;
- for a domestic transaction, analysing the level of domestic commercial transactions in that currency; or
- as an alternative, for cross-border transactions and/or domestic transactions, analysing the level of all transactions – i.e. both foreign trade transactions and domestic commercial transactions – in that currency.

7I.2.260.100   In our view, for the analysis in 7I.2.260.95, an entity should establish criteria, to be applied consistently, to determine the extent to which transactions with entities whose functional currency is the currency being evaluated are considered. The following are possible approaches.

- *Exclude all of these transactions from the analysis:* Under this approach, to conclude that the euro is a currency that is commonly used in Country X (a non-eurozone country), for example, the transactions that require consideration are those entered into by entities in X with other entities that do not have the euro as their functional currency; this would exclude the majority of cross-border transactions with entities in the eurozone.

- *Include these transactions in the analysis:* Under this approach, to conclude that the euro is a currency commonly used in Country X, cross-border transactions with entities in the eurozone would be included in the analysis. However, we believe that it would be inappropriate to conclude that the exemption should apply based solely on the level of transactions with entities whose functional currency is the currency being evaluated. There should also be evidence that the currency is used in the relevant economic environment for other reasons, such as liquidity or convenience. For example, to conclude that the euro is a currency commonly used in X, there should be evidence that the euro is commonly used for other reasons linked to business practice in X and not only because of transactions with euro functional currency counterparties.

7I.2.260.110   Furthermore, in our view the analysis of a commonly used currency should be performed on a country-by-country basis and not with reference to specific goods and services. For example, it is not appropriate to conclude that a particular currency is commonly used for cross-border leasing transactions and therefore that the foreign exchange embedded derivatives in all cross-border leases denominated in that currency do not require separation.

(S) 7I.2.260.120   In our view, if a group entity has a separable foreign currency derivative, then the derivative is separable both in its separate financial statements and in the consolidated financial statements even if the transaction is denominated in the functional currency of the parent, which may be chosen as the presentation currency of the consolidated financial statements (see 2.7.30–40). The consolidated entity does not have a functional currency and as such cannot be viewed as having a definable foreign currency exposure that would remove the need for separation on consolidation.

7I.2.265   Foreign currency derivatives embedded in host debt instruments#

7I.2.265.10   A host contract that is a debt instrument may contain a stream of principal or interest payments that are denominated in a foreign currency – e.g. a dual-currency bond. In these circumstances, the embedded foreign currency derivative is closely related to the host debt instrument. Such a derivative is not separated from the host contract because IAS 21 requires foreign currency gains and losses on monetary items to be recognised in profit or loss. [*IAS 39.AG33(c), 21.28*]

7I.2.267   FORTHCOMING REQUIREMENTS

7I.2.267.10   IFRS 16 introduces a single, on-balance sheet lease accounting model for lessees and eliminates the distinction between operating and finance leases. Unless a lessee elects the recognition exemptions for short-term leases and/or leases of low value assets (see 5.1A.140), it recognises a lease liability for its obligation to make lease payments (see 5.1A.270.10). If the lease rentals are denominated in a foreign currency (without any leveraged or optional foreign currency features), then they will impact the lessee's embedded derivative assessment because the obligation to pay future rentals is a monetary liability in the foreign currency subject to retranslation under IAS 21 (see 7I.2.265), rather than an embedded derivative in a non-financial contract. [*IAS 32.AG9, IFRS 16.22*]

7I.2.267.20 If a lessee separated a foreign currency embedded derivative from a lease contract before the adoption of IFRS 16 and that derivative would no longer qualify for separation, then applying a modified retrospective approach under IFRS 16 (see 5.1A.670) would require it to account for the change in accounting policy on the date of initial application of IFRS 16 as follows.

- Eliminate the previously separated derivative through retained earnings.
- Recognise a lease liability and a right-of-use asset in accordance with IFRS 16 – i.e. the lease liability is recognised as a monetary item denominated in a foreign currency.
- Consider whether there is a different embedded derivative (e.g. foreign currency option-type derivative) that should be separated from the IFRS 16 lease liability.

7I.2.267.30 If in a similar case, a lessee instead applies the full retrospective approach under IFRS 16, then the adjustments are required to be applied and measured retrospectively in accordance with IAS 8. In this case, the comparatives are restated and retained earnings are adjusted at the beginning of the comparative period.

7I.2.270 Inflation-indexed embedded derivatives

7I.2.270.10 Inflation-indexed lease payments are considered to be closely related to the host lease contract provided that there is no leverage feature (e.g. a multiple that would be applied to the inflation rate such that the lease payments would increase by x times inflation) and the index relates to inflation in the entity's economic environment (e.g. the consumer price index of the country in which the leased asset is operated). If the index is based on inflation rates in a different economic environment, then the embedded derivative is not closely related. [*IAS 39.AG33(f)*]

EXAMPLE 12 – SEPARABLE INFLATION-INDEXED DERIVATIVE EMBEDDED IN LEASE CONTRACT

7I.2.270.15 Company L leases a building in Canada, with rental payments denominated in Canadian dollars. The rent is changed each year by multiplying the percentage change in the Canadian consumer price index by a factor of 1.5. Because the adjustments to the rents are higher than the actual inflation rate (i.e. there is a multiplier above 1 that has more than an insignificant effect), L concludes that the embedded derivative is leveraged and should be separated from the host lease contract.

7I.2.270.20 In our view, inflation-indexed embedded derivatives in loans are considered to be closely related to the host debt instrument if the inflation index is one commonly used for this purpose in the economic environment of the currency in which the debt is denominated and it is not leveraged.

7I.2.280 Specific hybrid financial instruments

7I.2.280.10 Specific hybrid financial instruments that may be encountered in practice, particularly in the financial services sector, are discussed in 7I.2.290–360. The names of these instruments may vary from one country to another, but their accounting treatment is similar.

7I.2.290 *Bonds with a constant-maturity yield*

7I.2.290.10 Bonds with a constant-maturity yield have a floating interest rate that resets periodically on the basis of a market rate that has a duration extending beyond that of the reset period. For example, the interest rate on a 10-year bond resets semi-annually to the then-current weighted-average yield on identified treasury bonds with a 10-year maturity. The effect of this feature is that the interest rate is always equivalent to the market return on an instrument with 10 years' remaining maturity, even when the instrument itself has a maturity of less than 10 years.

7I.2.290.20   In our view, such a constant-maturity feature comprises an embedded derivative – i.e. a constant-maturity swap. The embedded derivative is not closely related to the host debt instrument because it could potentially double the holder's initial rate of return and result in a rate of return that is at least twice what the market return would be for a contract with the same terms as the host contract, unless it has a cap at an appropriate level to prevent the doubling effect. In this example, after seven years the bond would still be yielding a return that is the same as that for an instrument with a 10-year maturity. It is possible that this would be twice the market rate on an instrument similar to the host contract without the constant-maturity feature and with three years left to maturity. However, if the bond also contained a cap that was not leveraged and was above the market rate of interest when the bond was issued, and which prevented the amount of interest increasing so as to double the holder's initial rate of return, then in our view the combined constant-maturity-and-cap feature would be considered closely related. In our view, when assessing whether separation of the embedded derivative is required, the host debt instrument can be assumed to be either a fixed rate or a variable rate instrument. [*IAS 39.AG33(a)–(b)*]

7I.2.300   *Cash or share bonds*

7I.2.300.10   In a cash or share bond, the principal is determined with reference to movements in fair value of a single equity instrument or an equity index. If the fair value of the equity index or share price falls below a certain level, then it is the fair value of this equity index or share price that will be the basis for repayment – rather than the nominal value of the bond itself – or the bond will be settled by delivering the underlying shares. Therefore, the holder of the instrument might not recover substantially all of its initial investment. The bond will pay a higher coupon to compensate the holder for this increased level of risk.

7I.2.300.20   The holder of such a bond has in effect written a put option. In the example in 7I.2.300.10, the underlying of the written option is either the single equity instrument or the equity index. The option premium is embedded in the interest rate of the bond, which will therefore exceed the current market rate at the date of issuing the bond. This derivative embedded in the bond is not closely related to the host contract and is therefore separated. [*IAS 39.AG30(d)*]

7I.2.310   *Bonds with interest payments linked to equity index*

7I.2.310.10   If the interest payment on a bond is linked to movements in an equity index, then the fixed interest on the debt instrument is swapped against a variable return based on the movement in the equity index. The interest payments are not dependent on interest rate risk but on equity risk. Therefore, this swap is not closely related to the host contract and is separated. [*IAS 39.AG30(d), IG.B.13–IG.B.14*]

7I.2.310.20   An equity index would typically comprise a number of equity instruments of different entities and therefore its movements would arise from the changes in the fair value of numerous underlying equity instruments. To be considered closely related to the host contract, the embedded derivative would have to possess equity characteristics related to the issuer of the bond (host contract). Consequently, even if the host contract (bond) were to meet the definition of an equity instrument, it is unlikely that the embedded derivative could be considered closely related and therefore it is separated. [*IAS 39.11(a), AG27*]

71.2.320 *Step-down bonds*

71.2.320.10   Step-down bonds contain an interest feature such that the fixed interest rate declines over the life of the bond. For example, the first coupon is fixed at 10 percent whereas the last coupon is fixed at 5 percent.

71.2.320.20   The interest step-down feature alone would not be an embedded derivative that needs to be separated from the host contract. Instead, the step-down feature is taken into account in determining the amortised cost and the effective interest rate on the bond. Therefore, at inception part of the interest received is deferred and released when the interest rate coupon falls below the effective interest rate of the bond. [*IAS 39.IG.B.27*]

71.2.330 *Reverse (inverse) floating notes*

71.2.330.10   Reverse (inverse) floating notes are bonds that have a coupon that varies inversely with changes in specified general interest rate levels or indexes – e.g. Euribor. For such bonds, coupon payments are typically made according to a pre-set formula such as the following.

X% - (Y x three-month Euribor on a specified date)
where X = a fixed interest rate and Y = a leverage factor

71.2.330.20   Such instruments can be viewed as a combination of a fixed rate debt instrument with a fixed-for-floating interest rate swap that is referenced to an interest rate index. Therefore, the instrument contains an embedded derivative. The embedded derivative is not closely related to the host contract and needs to be separated if it could:

- prevent the investor from recovering substantially all of its initial recorded net investment in the bond (if the inverse floater contains no floor to prevent erosion of principal resulting from negative coupons); or
- increase the investor's rate of return on the bond to an amount that is at least twice the initial rate of return on the host contract and could result in a rate of return that is at least twice what the market rate would be for an instrument similar to the host contract. [*IAS 39.AG33(a)*]

71.2.330.30   If such an instrument is capped at less than twice the market rate at the date of issue and floored at zero, then the embedded interest rate swap is considered closely related and is not separated. [*IAS 39.AG33(a)*]

EXAMPLE 13A – INVERSE RATE FEATURE – NOT CLOSELY RELATED

71.2.330.40   Company X issues a bond at par, which pays coupons linked to LIBOR. The bond includes a binary interest rate feature, whereby the bond pays:
- 9% coupon, if LIBOR is below 3%; and
- 1% coupon, if LIBOR is 3% or above.

7I.2.330.50   X needs to determine whether the binary interest rate feature is closely related to the host bond. To do so, X needs to identify the terms of the host contract. In this case, X identifies the host contract's terms as:

- excluding the binary interest rate feature; and
- issued at par and paying coupons of LIBOR plus a fixed spread of 0.5%. The spread is determined based on market data and results in an overall market rate of interest on the host contract that reflects its terms and its credit and liquidity risk. At the time of issuing the bond, LIBOR is 4% and therefore the initial rate of return on the host contract is 4.5%.

7I.2.330.60   X now needs to compare possible rates of return on the hybrid bond containing the binary interest rate feature with those of the host instrument.

STEP	DETAIL	RESULT
Step 1	Calculate whether the binary interest rate feature could at least double the holder's initial rate of return on the host contract.	If LIBOR remains at or above 3%, the holder's rate of return on the hybrid contract would remain at 1% which is less than the initial rate of return on the host contract of 4.5%. However, if LIBOR declines below 3%, the return on the hybrid bond would increase to 9% which is double the initial rate of return on the host contract of 4.5%.
Step 2	For scenarios in which Step 1 is satisfied, calculate whether the binary interest rate feature could result in a rate of return that is at least twice the market return for a contract with the same terms as the host contract.	When LIBOR is below 3%, a contract with the same terms as the host contact would provide a market return of no more than 3.5% (i.e. LIBOR of 3% plus a fixed margin of 0.5%). Therefore, when LIBOR is below 3%, the hybrid bond would result in a rate of return of 9% that is more than twice what the market return would be on a contract with the same terms as the host contract.

7I.2.330.70   Based on the analysis, X determines that the binary interest rate feature is not closely related to the host bond.

EXAMPLE 13B – INVERSE RATE FEATURE – CLOSELY RELATED

7I.2.330.80   Modifying Example 13A, assume that the bond pays 7% coupon (instead of 9%) when LIBOR goes below 3% and all other information remains the same.

7I.2.330.90   If LIBOR goes to below 3%, then the bond's coupon of 7%:
- would be at least double the market return on a contract with the same terms as the host contract (i.e. LIBOR of less than 3% plus a fixed margin of 0.5%); but
- could never double the initial rate of return on host contract of 4.5%.

7I.2.330.100   Further, because the bond pays a minimum of 1% (when LIBOR goes above 3%), the binary interest rate feature would not prevent the holder of the bond from recovering substantially all of its recognised investment in the bond – i.e. the bond's par issuance amount. Accordingly, unlike in Example 13A, the binary interest rate feature in this example is considered closely related to the host bond.

7I.2.340   *Callable zero-coupon bonds*

7I.2.340.10   Callable zero-coupon bonds typically have long maturities – e.g. 30 years. The issuer has the right to redeem the bond at predetermined dates before the contractual maturity at the accreted amount. In this case, the embedded derivative (call option) is closely related to the host contract if the bond is callable at an amount that is approximately equal to the amortised cost of the host debt instrument at each predetermined date, and is not separated (see 7I.2.240.10–20). [*IAS 39.AG30(g)*]

7I.2.340.20   In our view, if the embedded call, put or prepayment option has other underlying financial risks (or non-financial risks that are not specific to a party to the contract) that are not closely related to those of the host contract – e.g. equity price risk – then the economic characteristics and risks of the embedded call, put or prepayment option are not closely related to the host contract and should be separated (see 7I.2.240). [*IAS 39.11, AG30(g)*]

7I.2.350   *Perpetual reset bonds*

7I.2.350.10   Perpetual reset bonds do not have a stated maturity, although the issuer may have the right to redeem the bonds at a specified date. If the issuer does not exercise this right, then the interest rate on the bonds will be reset to a new level (based on a predetermined formula) on this date.

7I.2.350.20   In our view, it is a matter of judgement, based on all relevant facts and circumstances, whether the issuer should analyse such a perpetual reset bond as:
- a host perpetual debt instrument with an embedded call option and an embedded interest rate reset feature; or
- a host debt instrument with a fixed maturity (based on the reset date) and an embedded term-extension feature. [*IAS 39.AG28, IG.C.1*]

7I.2.350.30   We believe that factors to consider when making this judgement, which is done on initial recognition, should include:
- the nature of the interest rate reset feature; and
- whether the probability of the entity calling the bond is determined to substantially exceed the probability of not exercising the call option, or vice versa.

7I.2.350.40   If the host debt instrument is considered to have a fixed maturity, then the embedded feature, which is an automatic provision to extend the term of the debt, is not closely related to the host contract unless there is a concurrent adjustment to the market rate of interest at the date of the extension. Because the resetting of the interest rate is based on a predetermined formula, this may or may not reflect current market rates, and consequently such a feature is not generally considered to be closely related and is separated as an embedded derivative unless it is considered to be equivalent to a loan commitment that would not be in the scope of IAS 39 (see 7I.2.230). [*IAS 39.2(h), 4, AG30(c)*]

7I.2.360   *Credit-linked notes and cash collateralised debt obligations*

7I.2.360.10   Credit-linked notes are debt instruments that are bundled with an embedded credit derivative or a financial guarantee. In exchange for a higher yield on the note, investors accept exposure to a specified credit risk that is not the credit risk of the issuer of the note. Coupon payments and/or repayment of the principal are made only if no default occurs in the specified debt portfolio, which may or may not be held by the issuer.

7I.2.360.20   One form of credit-linked notes is collateralised debt obligations (CDOs), which are securitised interests in pools of financial assets. The assets usually comprise loans or debt instruments. Multiple tranches of securities are normally issued by the CDO vehicle, offering investors various maturities and credit risk characteristics. Senior and mezzanine tranches are typically rated, with the ratings reflecting both the credit quality of underlying collateral and how much protection a given tranche is afforded by the more junior tranches.

7I.2.360.30   In evaluating whether the holder of an investment in a CDO needs to separate an embedded derivative, it is important to distinguish between cash and synthetic CDOs. Cash CDOs expose investors to credit risk through the CDO vehicle holding the reference assets.

7I.2.360.40   In our view, the holder of an investment in a credit-linked note is generally required to separate the embedded credit default swap (CDS) because the credit risk inherent in the embedded derivative is not closely related to the credit risk of the issuer. However, we believe that the holder of an investment in a cash CDO is not required to separate an embedded credit derivative if the exposure is structured such that the embedded credit feature meets the definition of a financial guarantee and not a derivative. The terms of the cash CDO need to be evaluated to determine whether the embedded feature meets the definition of a financial guarantee contract (see 7I.1.50).

7I.2.360.50   A synthetic CDO represents a pool of credit derivatives together with government bonds. In other words, rather than the debt obligation being collateralised through an actual pool of mortgages or loans (cash instruments), it is backed by government bonds together with a pool of credit derivatives including CDSs and credit default options. In such structures, the issuer of the synthetic CDO is the protection buyer, and the holders of the synthetic CDO are the protection sellers, because the credit risk inherent in the credit derivatives is passed to the holder. These synthetic CDOs have all the characteristics of normal debt obligations – i.e. fixed or determinable payments and a fixed maturity. However, holders of such instruments share a credit risk inherent in the pool of credit derivatives that is different from the credit risk of the issuing entity.

7I.2.360.60   In our view, the credit derivative embedded in such a synthetic CDO should be accounted for separately by the holder. This embedded derivative should be valued with reference to the credit risk inherent in the pool of credit derivatives that back the obligation. In some cases, the underlying credit derivatives may be packaged into a limited-purpose vehicle, which in turn issues the obligation. The credit risk of the embedded derivative is still the credit risk of the underlying pool of credit derivatives, and not the credit risk of the limited-purpose vehicle. The fact that junior and senior tranches are issued does not change the fact that each tranche contains a separate embedded derivative, although the value of the embedded derivatives in senior tranches may be small. [*IAS 39.AG30(h)*]

7I.2.360.70   Distinguishing between cash and synthetic CDOs can become complex when, for example, an entity invests in a CDO whose reference portfolio includes CDOs issued by another entity (generally termed 'CDO squared' or 'CDO^2'). In our view, the holder of a CDO^2 should account for it based on the reference portfolio of the first CDO (a 'look-through' approach). In this circumstance, the accounting treatment reflects the true risks of the investment – i.e. the holder's risk exposure in the referenced portfolio is impacted by the underlying risks of the CDOs contained within the portfolio. [*IAS 39.AG30(h)*]

7I.2.370   Specific hybrid non-financial contracts

7I.2.370.10   Embedded derivatives are often associated with financial instruments. However, they may arise in non-financial contracts – e.g. contracts for the delivery of goods and services. These embedded derivatives are also subjected to the analysis described in 7I.2.120–270 and accounted for separately, when it is appropriate. In such cases, the host contract will not be a financial instrument, but will be accounted for under other appropriate standards. Examples 11 and 14 illustrate circumstances in which embedded derivatives exist in non-financial contracts. [*IAS 39.10–11*]

EXAMPLE 14 – PRICE-INDEXATION OF A NON-FINANCIAL ITEM

7I.2.370.20   Company X is a manufacturing company. It enters into a contract for the purchase of three specialised machines that will be delivered and installed at the end of 2018, 2019 and 2020 respectively. The price of each machine is determined with reference to a formula that uses the market price of such a machine at the end of 2017 as the base price. This base price is adjusted for twice the change in an employment cost index, as well as an index that reflects cost increases associated with the industry.

7I.2.370.30   The indexation incorporates leverage into the pricing mechanism. Therefore, X considers this embedded derivative for separate accounting.

7I.2.370.40   However, if X is able to demonstrate that the market prices of similar machines ordinarily move in tandem with the indexation – i.e. there is a high degree of correlation between the two – then separation would not be required.

EXAMPLE 15 – MAINTENANCE COST GUARANTEE

7I.2.370.50   Company Y is a logistics company. Y buys its entire fleet of delivery vehicles from one vehicle manufacturer. The vehicle manufacturer provides a guarantee to Y under which it agrees to reimburse the logistics company for vehicle maintenance costs in excess of a specified level.

> 7I.2.370.60   Whether this arrangement contains an embedded derivative within the purchase contract depends on the terms of the guarantee. If the fair value of an instrument changes in response to the change in a specified non-financial variable that is not specific to a party to the contract, then such an instrument meets the definition of a derivative under IAS 39.
>
> 7I.2.370.70   In our view, the variation in maintenance charges comprises a non-financial variable. Furthermore, this non-financial variable is specific to the fleet held by the logistics company because it is dependent on the condition of the company's own vehicles. Consequently, this feature of the contract does not meet the definition of a derivative and does not require separate accounting under IAS 39.

7I.2.370.80   When an obligation to deliver goods or services under a non-financial contract is settled, the parties usually will initially recognise a new financial instrument in respect of the contractual right to receive or obligation to pay the purchase price. It may therefore be necessary for the parties to consider whether any embedded derivative is required to be separated from this new financial instrument.

EXAMPLE 16 – PROVISIONAL PRICING OF COMMODITY CONTRACT

> 7I.2.370.90   On 31 December 2017, Company R, a commodity producer, enters into an executory contract with Company B, a commodity processor, to deliver a specified amount of unrefined commodity X on 31 January 2018. The final purchase price is payable on 31 March 2018 and is determined with reference to the quoted spot market price for commodity X on that date (i.e. the purchase price is 'provisional' until that date). The parties have agreed that the purchase price is not determined until 31 March 2018 because it is expected that it will take B approximately two months to process the commodity for sale to its customers. The commodity contract is subject to the own-use exemption (see 7I.1.150).
>
> 7I.2.370.100   On 31 December 2017, R and B each consider whether the provisional pricing feature should be separated from the commodity contract and separately accounted for as an embedded derivative. They each conclude that the provisional pricing feature is closely related to the economic characteristics and risks of the host contact because:
> - the final price is indexed to the spot market price of the commodity that is delivered under the host contract; and
> - the timing lag between the delivery date and the price fixing date relates to the estimated time to process the commodity that is delivered under the host contract.
>
> 7I.2.370.110   On 31 January 2018, R settles its contractual obligation to deliver the commodity and, as a result, R and B recognise a new financial asset and a new financial liability respectively in relation to the purchase price that is payable on 31 March 2018. The host contract is now a debt financial instrument. R and B each

conclude that the provisional pricing feature needs to be separately accounted for as a derivative because payments indexed to a commodity price are not closely related to a host debt instrument because the risks inherent in the host and the embedded derivative are dissimilar. [*IAS 39.AG30(e)*]

7I.2.380 **Accounting for separable embedded derivatives**

7I.2.380.10   Separable embedded derivatives are required to be measured at fair value, with all changes in fair value recognised in profit or loss unless they form part of a qualifying cash flow or net investment hedging relationship. [*IAS 39.46, 55*]

7I.2.380.20   The initial bifurcation of a separable embedded derivative does not result in any gain or loss being recognised. [*IAS 39.AG28, IG.C.1–IG.C.2*]

7I.2.380.30   Because the embedded derivative component is measured at fair value on initial recognition, the carrying amount of the host contract on initial recognition is the difference between the carrying amount of the hybrid instrument and the fair value of the embedded derivative. If the fair values of the hybrid instrument and host contract are more reliably measurable than that of the derivative component – e.g. because of the availability of quoted market prices – then it may be acceptable to use those values to determine the fair value of the derivative on initial recognition indirectly – i.e. as a residual amount. [*IAS 32.31, 39.13, AG28*]

7I.2.380.40   When separating an embedded derivative that is a forward contract, the forward price is set such that the fair value of the embedded forward contract is zero at inception. The same applies if the embedded derivative is a swap. Consequently, the forward price needs to be at market on initial recognition. When separating an embedded derivative that is an option, the separation is based on the stated terms of the option feature documented in the hybrid instrument. As a result, the embedded derivative would have a fair value of other than zero on initial recognition of the hybrid instrument. However, the embedded derivative is valued based on terms that are clearly present in the hybrid instrument. [*IAS 39.AG28, IG.C.1–IG.C.2*]

EXAMPLE 17 – ACCOUNTING FOR SEPARABLE EMBEDDED FORWARD CONTRACT

7I.2.380.50   Company G, whose functional currency is sterling, enters into a contract on 1 March 2018 to buy goods from Company B, whose functional currency is the euro. The purchase contract stipulates payment in US dollars and requires G to pay USD 380 on delivery of the goods in six months' time. The applicable exchange rates on 1 March 2018 are:
- spot rate: USD 1 = GBP 0.556; and
- six-month forward rate: USD 1 = GBP 0.526.

7I.2.380.60   The contract between G and B contains a foreign currency derivative that requires separation under IAS 39 because it does not fall under any of the exemptions for non-separation of embedded foreign currency derivatives (see 7I.2.260).

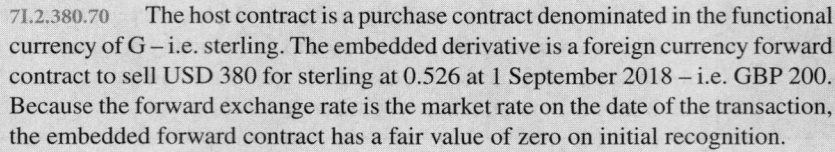

7I.2.380.70   The host contract is a purchase contract denominated in the functional currency of G – i.e. sterling. The embedded derivative is a foreign currency forward contract to sell USD 380 for sterling at 0.526 at 1 September 2018 – i.e. GBP 200. Because the forward exchange rate is the market rate on the date of the transaction, the embedded forward contract has a fair value of zero on initial recognition.

7I.2.380.80   The embedded foreign currency forward contract is accounted for as if it were a freestanding derivative (see 7I.6.140), and the host instrument as an executory contract (see 1.2.130).

7I.2.380.90   If an executory contract to purchase goods or services with an embedded separable derivative related to variability in the price payable contains different delivery and payment dates, then a question arises about the maturity of the embedded derivative. In our view, an entity should choose an accounting policy, to be applied consistently, to determine the maturity of the embedded derivative as the delivery date or the payment date. We believe that, regardless of the accounting policy chosen, the terms of the embedded derivative and its valuation should reflect the actual terms of the hybrid instrument and not presume cash flows on the delivery date if cash flows only occur after the delivery date. When the goods or services are delivered, a financial instrument should be recognised for the amount payable under the contract – i.e. the nature of the contract changes from an executory contract to a financial instrument contract. The separable embedded derivative may be a payment denominated in a third currency (see Example 17) or an embedded foreign currency option under which an entity can choose between different settlement currencies at the payment date based on an exchange rate fixed at inception of the executory contract. The accounting policy choice may have an impact on whether an embedded derivative continues to be separated subsequent to recognition of the financial instrument on the delivery date.

EXAMPLE 18 – EXECUTORY CONTRACT WITH SEPARABLE EMBEDDED DERIVATIVE

7I.2.380.100   Modifying Example 17, delivery of the goods occurs on 1 June 2018, three months after entering into the purchase contract and settlement in USD occurs on 1 September 2018, six months after entering into the contract. G considers the maturity of the embedded derivative to be at the delivery date.

7I.2.380.110   At inception, the contract between G and B contains a foreign currency derivative that requires separation under IAS 39 because it does not fall under any of the exemptions for non-separation of embedded foreign currency derivatives (see 7I.2.260). G measures the fair value of the embedded derivative using the six month forward rate reflecting the substantive terms of the hybrid contract. Because the forward exchange rate is the market rate on the date of the transaction, the embedded forward contract has a fair value of zero on initial recognition.

7I.2.380.120   When B settles its contractual obligation to deliver the goods, B and G recognise a new financial asset and a new financial liability, respectively, in relation to the foreign currency purchase price that is payable in three months. The contract is now a debt financial instrument.

7I.2.380.130   The separated embedded derivative is derecognised and included in the carrying amount of the debt instrument. B and G no longer separate an embedded derivative because they each have a foreign currency-denominated debt instrument. B and G will each recognise foreign currency gains and losses on this monetary item in profit or loss.

7I.2.380.140   Conversely, if G considers the maturity of the embedded derivative to be at the payment date, then the embedded derivative that was already separated at inception of the executory contract remains separated once delivery has taken place. In this case, G has a debt financial instrument that represents an obligation to pay the purchase price under the host contract denominated in sterling of GBP 200. [*IAS 39.AG33(c)–(d)*]

7I.2.380.150   Embedded derivatives accounted for separately may be designated as hedging instruments. The normal hedge accounting criteria outlined in 7I.7.120 apply to embedded derivatives used as hedging instruments. [*IAS 39.72*]

7I.2.390   Presentation and disclosures

7I.2.390.10   IAS 39 does not require separate presentation of separated embedded derivatives in the statement of financial position. In our view, under certain circumstances embedded derivatives that are separated from a host financial instrument should be presented together with the host contract (see 7I.8.200). However, an entity is required to disclose separately financial instruments carried at amortised cost and those carried at fair value. Therefore, embedded derivatives that are separated from financial instruments but not presented separately in the statement of financial position should be disclosed in the notes. [*IAS 39.11, IFRS 7.8, B2(a)*]

7I.3 Equity and financial liabilities

7I.3   Equity and financial liabilities

REQUIREMENTS FOR INSURERS THAT APPLY IFRS 4

In July 2014, the IASB issued IFRS 9 *Financial Instruments*, which is effective for annual periods beginning on or after 1 January 2018. However, an insurer may defer the application of IFRS 9 if it meets certain criteria (see 8.1.180).

This chapter reflects the requirement of IAS 39 *Financial Instruments: Recognition and Measurement* and the related standards, excluding any amendments introduced by IFRS 9. These requirements are relevant to insurers that apply the temporary exemption from IFRS 9 or the overlay approach to designated financial assets (see 8.1.160) and cover annual periods beginning on 1 January 2018. For further discussion, see Introduction to Sections 7 and 7I.

The requirements related to this topic are mainly derived from the following.

STANDARD	TITLE
IAS 1	Presentation of Financial Statements
IAS 12	Income Taxes
IAS 32	Financial Instruments: Presentation
IAS 39	Financial Instruments: Recognition and Measurement
IFRIC 2	Members' Shares in Co-operative Entities and Similar Instruments
IFRIC 17	Distributions of Non-cash Assets to Owners
IFRIC 19	Extinguishing Financial Liabilities with Equity Instruments

FORTHCOMING REQUIREMENTS AND FUTURE DEVELOPMENTS

For this topic, there are no forthcoming requirements or future developments.

7I.3.10	**CLASSIFICATION**
7I.3.20	**Basic principles**

7I.3.20.10   An instrument, or its components, is classified on initial recognition as a financial liability, a financial asset or an equity instrument in accordance with the substance of the contractual arrangement and the definitions of a financial liability, a financial asset and an equity instrument. [*IAS 32.15*]

7I.3.20.20   An instrument is classified as a financial liability if it is:
- a contractual obligation:
  - to deliver cash or other financial assets; or
  - to exchange financial assets or financial liabilities with another entity under potentially unfavourable conditions (for the issuer of the instrument); or
- a contract that will or may be settled in the entity's own equity instruments and is:
  - a non-derivative that comprises an obligation for the entity to deliver a variable number of its own equity instruments; or
  - a derivative that will or may be settled other than by the entity exchanging a fixed amount of cash or other financial assets for a fixed number of its own equity instruments. [*IAS 32.11*]

7I.3.20.30   An obligation to transfer cash may arise from a requirement to repay the principal or to pay interest or dividends.

7I.3.20.40   In general, an 'equity instrument' is any contract that evidences a residual interest in the assets of an entity after deducting all of its liabilities. It meets both of the following conditions.
- There is no contractual obligation:
  - to deliver cash or another financial asset to another party; or
  - to exchange financial assets or financial liabilities with another party under potentially unfavourable conditions (for the issuer of the instrument).
- If the instrument will or may be settled in the issuer's own equity instruments, then it is either:
  - a non-derivative that comprises an obligation for the issuer to deliver a fixed number of its own equity instruments; or
  - a derivative that will be settled only by the issuer exchanging a fixed amount of cash or other financial assets for a fixed number of its own equity instruments. [*IAS 32.11, 16*]

7I.3.20.50   As an exception to the general principles, the following are classified as equity instruments if certain conditions (discussed in more detail in 7I.3.70–80) are met:
- puttable instruments; and
- instruments, or components of instruments, that impose on the entity an obligation to deliver to another party a pro rata share of the net assets of the entity only on liquidation. [*IAS 32.16A, 16C*]

7I.3.20.60   Any financial instrument that an issuer could be obliged to settle in cash, or by delivering other financial assets, is a financial liability regardless of the financial ability of the issuer to settle the contractual obligation or the probability of settlement. The IFRS Interpretations Committee discussed this issue and noted that such a contractual obligation could be established explicitly or indirectly, but it needs to be established through the terms and conditions of the instrument. [*IAS 32.19–20, IU 11-06*]

EXAMPLE 1 – CLASSIFICATION AS LIABILITY OR EQUITY – LINKED INSTRUMENTS

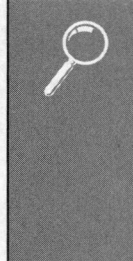

7I.3.20.70   Company K issues a non-redeemable financial instrument (the 'base' instrument) with dividends payable if interest is paid on another instrument (the 'linked' instrument). K is required to pay the interest on the linked instrument.

7I.3.20.75   In this example, the linkage to the linked instrument, on which interest is contractually payable, creates a contractual obligation to pay dividends on the base instrument. Therefore, K concludes that this obligation should be classified as a liability.

7I.3.20.80   When determining whether to classify a financial instrument as a financial liability or as equity, an entity assesses the substance of a contractual arrangement rather than its legal form. In assessing the substance of a contractual arrangement, the entity needs to consider all of the terms and conditions of the financial instrument, including relevant local laws, regulations and the entity's governing charter in effect at the date of classification (see 7I.3.30.130). Therefore, it is possible for instruments that qualify as equity for legal or regulatory purposes to be classified as liabilities for the purposes of financial reporting. [*IAS 32.15, 18*]

7I.3.20.90   The IFRS Interpretations Committee discussed the classification of a financial instrument as a liability or as equity and noted that in assessing the substance of a contractual arrangement, an entity needs to exclude a contractual term that lacks substance. The Committee also noted that IAS 32 does not require or permit factors not within the contractual arrangement to be taken into consideration in classifying a financial instrument as a liability or as equity. For example, economic compulsion should not be used as the basis for classification. This is because a contractual obligation could be established explicitly or indirectly, but it has to be established through the terms and conditions of the instrument (see 7I.3.20.60). Therefore, by itself, economic compulsion does not result in a financial instrument being classified as a liability. [*IAS 32.20, IU 11-06, 01-14*]

7I.3.20.100   Judgement is required to determine whether a contractual right – e.g. to avoid delivering cash, another financial asset or a variable number of the entity's own equity instruments – is substantive and therefore needs to be considered in determining the classification of an instrument as a financial liability or equity (see 7I.3.30.40 and 183.100–140). [*IAS 32.15, 20, IU 01-14*]

7I.3.20.110   Instruments commonly affected by these requirements include:
- preference shares;
- classes of shares that have special terms and conditions;
- subordinated instruments; and
- convertible and perpetual instruments.

7I.3.20.120   Equity instruments include shares, options and warrants, and any other instrument that evidences a residual interest in an entity and meets the relevant conditions in 7I.3.20.40–100.

7I.3.20.130   The classification of an instrument as either liability or equity determines whether any interest, dividends, losses and gains related to that instrument are recognised as income or expense in profit or loss. [*IAS 32.36*]

7I.3.20.140   If an instrument is classified as a liability, then coupon payments and any amortisation of discounts or premiums on the instrument are recognised as part of finance costs in profit or loss, under the effective interest method. Sometimes all of the fair value of the consideration received on issuing an instrument that includes a discretionary dividend feature is allocated to and recognised as a financial liability. For further discussion of the classification of discretionary dividends in such cases, see 7I.3.220. [*IAS 32.35–36, AG37*]

7I.3.20.150   If, however, some or all of an instrument is classified as equity, then discretionary distributions are accounted for directly in equity. See also 7I.3.220 and 600. [*IAS 32.35–36, AG37*]

7I.3.20.160   The classification of an instrument, or its component parts, as either financial liability or equity is made on initial recognition. It is not generally revised as a result of subsequent changes in circumstances – with the exception of puttable instruments and instruments that impose on the entity an obligation only on liquidation (see 7I.3.170). However, a reclassification between financial liability and equity or vice versa may be required in certain circumstances (see 7I.3.390). [*IAS 32.15*]

Ⓢ **7I.3.20.170**   The classification of financial instruments as equity or financial liabilities in the consolidated financial statements may differ from their classification in any separate or individual financial statements of entities within a group (see 7I.3.190.20). [*IAS 32.AG29*]

Ⓢ EXAMPLE 2 – CLASSIFICATION IN CONSOLIDATED AND SEPARATE FINANCIAL STATEMENTS

7I.3.20.180   Company P has two subsidiaries, Companies B and G. G issues non-redeemable preference shares to a party outside the group. B writes a put option on the preference shares issued by G. The put option, if it is exercised, will require B to purchase the preference shares from the holder for cash.

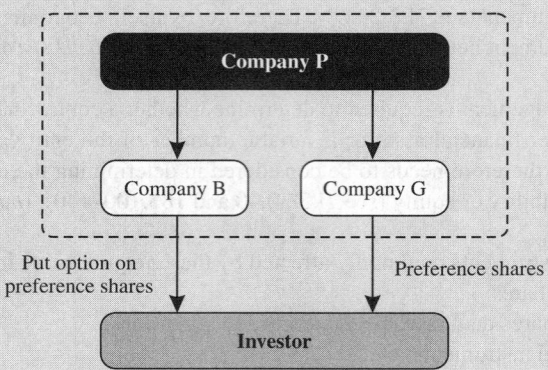

7I.3.20.190   In its separate financial statements, G classifies the preference shares as equity because it does not have a contractual obligation to redeem the shares or to pay dividends. However, in the consolidated financial statements, the group as a whole has a contractual obligation to redeem the preference shares (through the put option written by B). P therefore classifies the preference shares as a financial liability in the consolidated financial statements.

7I.3.30   Contractual obligation to deliver cash or another financial asset

7I.3.30.10   The primary factor determining classification is whether the instrument establishes a contractual obligation for the issuer to make payments (principal, interest/dividends or both). A right on the part of the holder does not necessarily translate to a contractual obligation on the part of the issuer. [*IAS 32.17*]

7I.3.30.15   The holder of an equity instrument might have the *right* to receive dividends if they are paid; however, the issuer does not have a *contractual obligation* to make payments until the dividend is appropriately authorised and is no longer at the discretion of the entity. The holder has a financial asset, whereas the issuer has an equity instrument rather than a financial liability. [*IAS 32.17*]

7I.3.30.20   IAS 32 further clarifies that an instrument that creates an obligation is a financial liability if the entity does not have the unconditional right to avoid delivering cash or another financial asset in settlement of that obligation. A contractual obligation is not negated merely because of a lack of funds, statutory restrictions or insufficient profits or reserves. [*IAS 32.19, AG25*]

EXAMPLE 3A – LIABILITY FOR PREPAID CARD

7I.3.30.21   Company C issues a prepaid card with the following features in exchange for cash:

- there are no expiry date or back-end fees;
- the balance on the card does not reduce unless it is spent by the cardholder;
- the balance on the card is non-refundable and cannot be exchanged for cash;
- the balance on the card is redeemable only for goods or services to a specified monetary amount at specified third party merchants; and
- when the cardholder purchases goods or services and redeems the balance at a merchant, C delivers cash to the merchant. [*IU 03-16*]

7I.3.30.22   The liability for the prepaid card meets the definition of a financial liability because C:

- has a contractual obligation to deliver cash to the merchants on behalf of the cardholder when the cardholder uses the prepaid card to purchase goods or services; and
- does not have an unconditional right to avoid delivering cash to settle this contractual obligation. [*IU 03-16*]

EXAMPLE 3B – CONTRACTUAL OBLIGATION CONTINGENT ON COVENANTS IMPOSED BY LOCAL LAW

7I.3.30.23   Company B has issued a loan, the terms of which stipulate that it is repayable only if its repayment does not violate certain covenants imposed by local law.

7I.3.30.24   In this example, B does not have the unconditional right to avoid making payments; also, the breach of covenants that prevents repayment at a specific point in time defers, rather than negates, the obligation. Consequently, B classifies the loan as a financial liability.

7I.3.30.27   An obligation that will be settled only if a holder exercises its right to redeem is a financial liability, irrespective of how likely or unlikely it is that the holder will actually exercise its right. [*IAS 32.19*]

7I.3.30.30   When the terms of a financial instrument provide for cash settlement at the option of the holder, entities may obtain a letter of undertaking from the holder indicating that this option will not be called on. In our view, such an undertaking, unless it is legally enforceable and irrevocable, is not sufficient to warrant classification of the instrument as equity rather than as a financial liability. For example, assume that the holder of such an instrument has signed such a letter of undertaking but is able to sell the instrument. Furthermore, assume that the purchaser would not be restricted by the letter of undertaking that was signed by the seller. In this scenario, the instrument would be classified as a financial liability.

7I.3.30.40   In most cases, the terms and conditions of an instrument establish a contractual obligation explicitly. However, such an obligation may also arise implicitly. For example, an instrument may include a non-financial obligation that is required to be settled if the entity fails to make distributions or redeem the instrument; this is a financial liability, because the entity can avoid payment only by settling the non-financial obligation. In another example, an instrument may provide that on settlement an entity delivers either cash or another financial asset, or its own shares whose value substantially exceeds the value of the cash or other financial asset; this is also a financial liability, because the value of the share settlement alternative is such that the entity will settle in cash. Therefore, the holder has in substance been guaranteed receipt of an amount that is at least equal to the cash settlement option. [*IAS 32.20, BC9*]

EXAMPLE 4 – NON-FINANCIAL OBLIGATION

> 7I.3.30.43   Company G issues an instrument that includes a term under which G is required to deliver a property in settlement if the instrument is not redeemed after 10 years. The instrument is a financial liability because G can avoid settling the financial obligation only by settling the non-financial obligation.

EXAMPLE 5 – SHARE SETTLEMENT OPTION

> 7I.3.30.46   Company B issues an instrument that is required to be settled either in cash or in a fixed number of B's own shares, the value of which will substantially exceed the amount of cash. The instrument is a financial liability because, although B does not have an explicit contractual obligation to settle in cash, the value of the share settlement option is so high that B will always settle in cash.

7I.3.30.50   Instruments containing features that are classified as financial liabilities generally include the following:
- instruments that are redeemable at the option of the holder – e.g. redeemable preference shares;
- non-redeemable preference shares with dividends that are not discretionary (see 7I.3.220);
- instruments that become redeemable on the occurrence of an uncertain future event that is beyond the control of both the holder and the issuer of the instrument (see 7I.3.40); and
- subordinated liabilities.

7I.3.30.60　　As an exception to the general principles, some instruments that are redeemable, either at the option of the holder or on liquidation – which is either certain to occur and outside the control of the entity, or uncertain to occur but at the option of the instrument holder – are classified as equity instruments of the entity if certain conditions are met (see 7I.3.70–80). [*IAS 32.16A, 16C*]

7I.3.30.70　　An entity also needs to distinguish between:
- a contractual obligation to deliver cash or another financial asset, which gives rise to a financial liability; and
- a statutory obligation, which does not necessarily result in a financial liability. [*IAS 32.AG12*]

7I.3.30.80　　For example, local law might require an entity to pay a minimum specified amount as dividends in each period for a particular instrument. In our view, such an obligation does not represent a contractual obligation and consequently the obligation is not classified as a financial liability under IAS 32. However, when an entity voluntarily incorporates a minimum specified amount of dividends into the terms of an instrument – e.g. to achieve a desired tax outcome or to achieve a certain regulatory status – in our view the payment of such dividends represents a contractual obligation of the entity and consequently the obligation is classified as a financial liability. [*IAS 32.AG12*]

EXAMPLE 6A – CONTRACTUAL OBLIGATIONS TO MAINTAIN TAX STATUS

7I.3.30.90　　Company S is a real estate investment trust (REIT). Under a contractual agreement with its shareholders, S is required to maintain its REIT tax status. To do so, under local tax law S needs to pay out a specified percentage of its taxable income as dividends each year. There is no legal obligation, outside the contractual terms in the shareholder agreement, for S to comply with those specific provisions of the local tax law. Instead, the decision to be taxed as a REIT is voluntary.

7I.3.30.100　　In this example, a contractual obligation to pay dividends is created indirectly (see 7I.3.20.90) – i.e. it is a combination of the contractual requirement in the shareholder agreement to maintain the REIT tax status and the requirement in the local tax law to pay dividends in order to maintain that status. The tax law itself does not oblige S to make dividend payments because it is a voluntary election available to those that meet certain criteria. However, when viewed in combination with the contractual agreement with its shareholders, S has an obligation to make dividend payments. The clause under which S needs to comply with the REIT dividend requirements is a contractual obligation and not a statutory obligation. Therefore, this obligation is classified as a financial liability.

EXAMPLE 6B – NO CONTRACTUAL OBLIGATIONS TO MAINTAIN TAX STATUS

7I.3.30.110　　In contrast to Example 6A, the contractual terms of the shareholder agreement for Company T, another REIT, do not require the entity to maintain REIT tax status. Instead, the agreement provides the management of Company T with full

discretion over the declaration of dividends even though a failure to declare and pay dividends may jeopardise its tax status. In this scenario, the legal requirement to pay dividends in order to maintain REIT tax status would not impact the classification of Company T's shares.

7I.3.30.120   Some debt instruments issued by banks may be subject to a statutory provision requiring them to be converted into equity or written down when a supervisory authority determines that such an action is required. These instruments are commonly referred to as 'statutory bail-in instruments'. Bail-in occurs before a bank becomes insolvent – i.e. at the 'point of non-viability'. Statutory bail-in requirements do not impact the issuer's classification as financial liabilities or equity on initial recognition. However, bail-in features that are contractual terms of the instruments are considered in classification by the issuer.

7I.3.30.130   Although only contractual obligations give rise to financial liability classification, in certain circumstances terms and conditions existing outside the contract can affect the classification of an instrument by giving the issuer an unconditional right to avoid payment. For example, the contractual right of the holder of a share issued by an entity to request redemption does not, in itself, require that financial instrument to be classified as a financial liability. Rather, the issuer is required to consider all of the terms and conditions of the instrument in determining its classification as a financial liability or equity. Those terms and conditions include relevant local laws, regulations and the entity's governing charter in effect at the date of classification. If a local law, regulation or the entity's governing charter gives the issuer of the instrument an unconditional right to avoid redemption, then the instrument is classified as equity. [*IFRIC 2.5–8*]

7I.3.30.140   The overall context of IFRIC 2 is the classification of instruments, issued by co-operatives and similar entities, that are puttable instruments – defined in IAS 32 as financial liabilities but with equity classification required if certain criteria are met. Its focus is the interaction of contractual obligations to redeem an instrument and terms outside the contract that can affect the exercise of those contractual obligations. Accordingly, in our view IFRIC 2 should be interpreted such that restrictions on redemption outside the contract itself may negate the existence of a contractual obligation and lead to equity classification. However, we believe that it should not be interpreted to mean that a non-contractual obligation to make payments on an instrument that does not contain a contractual obligation will lead to financial liability classification of that instrument. For a discussion of members' shares in co-operative entities and similar instruments, see 7I.3.55.

7I.3.40   Contingent settlement provisions

7I.3.40.10   An instrument may contain a contractual obligation to deliver cash or another financial asset depending on the outcome of an uncertain future event that is beyond the control of both the issuer and the holder of the instrument. Examples of such uncertain events are changes in:
- a stock market index;
- interest rate;
- taxation requirements; and
- the issuer's future revenues or debt-to-equity ratio. [*IAS 32.25*]

7I.3.40.20   When an instrument contains such contingent settlement provisions, the issuer does not have the unconditional right to avoid making payments. Therefore, the instrument is a financial liability, unless one of the following applies:

- the part of the contingent settlement provision that could require settlement in cash or another financial asset is not genuine; or
- the issuer can be required to settle in cash or another financial asset only in the event of its own liquidation (as long as liquidation is neither predetermined nor at the option of the holder – see 7I.3.40.90).

7I.3.40.25   If the instrument containing such contingent settlement provisions is a puttable instrument, then it may qualify for classification as equity if it meets all of the relevant criteria (see 7I.3.70). [*IAS 32.16A–16B*]

EXAMPLE 7A – CONTRACTUAL OBLIGATION IF IPO DOES NOT TAKE PLACE

7I.3.40.30   Company Y issues a bond that is convertible automatically into a fixed number of ordinary shares when an IPO takes place. The offering is planned for two years' time, but is subject to the approval of a regulator. The bond is redeemable in cash only if the IPO does not take place.

7I.3.40.35   In this example, Y cannot avoid the obligation, because it cannot ensure that regulatory approval will be received; nor can it ensure that the IPO will actually occur. In this scenario, the bond is potentially redeemable in cash and the contingency is beyond the control of both Y and the holder of the bond. The bond therefore contains a liability, regardless of the likelihood of cash settlement.

7I.3.40.37   The contingent conversion feature qualifies as an equity instrument because the bond can convert only into a fixed number of equity shares (see 7I.3.187 and 200.20). Therefore, the bond is accounted for as a compound instrument with liability and equity components (see 7I.3.230). [*IAS 32.16(b)(ii), 28*]

EXAMPLE 7B – CONTRACTUAL OBLIGATION IF IPO TAKES PLACE

7I.3.40.40   If the bond in Example 6A were redeemable in cash only if the IPO took place, then the instrument would be classified as equity. In this situation, the issuer would have the unconditional ability to avoid the obligation if it can decide whether to launch an IPO.

7I.3.40.50   If an entity issues an instrument that becomes immediately redeemable in cash on the occurrence of a change in control of that entity, such as when a majority of the entity's shareholders choose to sell their shares to an acquiring party in a takeover, then in our view this feature should be classified as a financial liability. This is because we believe that such a change-in-control event is an uncertain future event that is not within the control of the entity; therefore, the entity does not have an unconditional right to avoid delivering cash. This would generally apply even if such a takeover required formal approval by a majority of shareholders at a general meeting, because it is reasonable to assume in this case that shareholders would be acting in their capacity as individual investors rather than as a body as part of the entity's internal corporate governance processes (see 7I.3.40.60–70).

7I.3.40.60   In our view, careful analysis of the specific facts and circumstances and judgement are required to assess whether the shareholders of an entity are acting as a body under the entity's governing charter – i.e. as issuer (part of the entity), or as individual investors (not as part of the entity).

7I.3.40.63   When shareholders participate in the normal governance process, and in a routine manner related to the decision involved, they are generally acting as part of the entity. For example, assume that an entity has perpetual bonds with interest payments linked to dividends on ordinary shares, which need to be approved by the shareholders. These are classified as equity if the payment of dividends is at the discretion of the entity. The following may indicate that the entity's shareholders are acting as a body on behalf of the entity when approving or disapproving the payment of dividends on ordinary shares:

- dividend approvals are a recurring item on the agenda of the annual general meeting; and
- the dividend approval process is carried out consistently over the years as a matter of routine.

7I.3.40.65   In such cases, we believe that the approval of dividends is within the control of the entity, that paragraph 25 of IAS 32 does not apply and that the term 'issuer' incorporates both the entity and its shareholders.

7I.3.40.67   However, shareholders are not acting as a body under the entity's governing charter when they are acting as individual investors. For example, shareholders are generally considered to be acting outside the normal governance process when they are voting to dispose of their individual shareholding.

7I.3.40.70   In such cases, we believe that a change in shareholding is not within the control of the entity, that paragraph 25 of IAS 32 applies and that the term 'issuer' does not incorporate both the entity and its shareholders.

7I.3.40.73   As an exception, a contractual provision requiring settlement in cash or another financial asset that is considered non-genuine does not result in financial liability classification for that instrument. In our view, only in extremely rare, highly abnormal and very unlikely circumstances will a contingent settlement feature be considered 'non-genuine'. We believe that a contingent settlement feature should be considered non-genuine only if:

- it has no economic substance; and
- it could be removed by the parties to the contract without any compensation, either in the form of payment or by altering the other terms and conditions of the contract.

7I.3.40.75   In our view, in all other cases such provisions should be considered genuine and therefore should affect classification. For example, an instrument may provide for cash settlement in the event of a change in tax law because the terms of the instrument were structured so that the holder and/or issuer could enjoy a specific tax benefit. However remote the chances of the tax law changing, such an instrument should be classified as a financial liability. A contingent settlement event – such as a tax change or a takeover of the issuer – would always be regarded as genuine unless it was inserted into the contract only to achieve financial liability classification. [*IAS 32.AG28*]

7I.3.40.80   In our view, subsequent changes in circumstances that lead to a genuine contingent settlement feature becoming extremely rare, highly abnormal and very unlikely to occur – i.e. a change in probability – do not change the initial assessment that the contingent settlement feature is considered genuine and therefore do not result in reclassification of the instrument from financial liability to equity. Likewise, subsequent changes in circumstances that lead to a non-genuine contingent settlement feature becoming likely to occur do not result in a reclassification of an instrument from equity to financial liability. However, appropriate disclosure may be required (see 7I.8.10.10).

7I.3.40.90   As an exception, a contractual provision that requires settlement of a financial instrument only in the event of liquidation of the issuer does not result in financial liability classification for that instrument. However, the entity's liquidation date may be predetermined; alternatively, the holder of such an instrument may have the right to liquidate the issuer of the instrument. In those cases, the exception does not generally apply and financial liability classification may be required (see 7I.3.80). [*IAS 32.16C, 25(b)*]

7I.3.40.93   Unless the conditions for classification as equity under the exceptions to the general principles described in 7I.3.80 are met, in our view the following liquidation rights should also result in financial liability classification:
*   a liquidation right held by the instrument holder that becomes exercisable on the occurrence of an event that is not within the control of the entity – e.g. a change in control (see 7I.3.40.50). This is because the entity cannot prevent the holder from obtaining the liquidation right if the uncertain event occurs. For example, if the liquidation right becomes exercisable on a change in control – e.g. when the majority of the issuer's shareholders choose to sell their shares in a takeover – then the contingent event is not the liquidation itself but the change in control, which is not within the discretion of the entity; and
*   liquidation rights held by the instrument holders as a class rather than included in the individual instrument – e.g. the majority of preference shareholders have a contractual right to force the liquidation of the issuer. This is because the entity cannot avoid its potential obligation to deliver cash or another financial asset if the instrument holders make a decision to liquidate the entity.

7I.3.40.97   However, we believe that financial liability classification is not generally appropriate when ordinary shareholders collectively have the right to force the liquidation of the entity. This is because the ordinary shareholders' right to liquidate the entity at a general meeting would generally be considered part of the normal or ordinary governance processes of the entity (see 7I.3.40.63). Therefore, the ordinary shareholders acting through the general meeting would be considered to be acting as part of the entity.

7I.3.40.100   A contract that would otherwise be settled by delivery of a fixed number of the entity's own equity instruments in exchange for a fixed amount of cash may provide for net cash settlement in the event of the counterparty's involuntary liquidation or bankruptcy. In our view, the existence of such a clause does not preclude the entity from classifying the contract as equity.

7I.3.50   Obligation to acquire own equity instruments

7I.3.50.10   Financial instruments that give the holder the right to 'put' them back to the issuer for cash or other financial assets ('puttable instruments') are financial liabilities of the issuer. However, if certain conditions are met, then they are classified as equity (see 7I.3.70). The put option creates a contractual obligation that the issuer does not have the unconditional ability to avoid. In our view, the fact that the instrument may not be puttable immediately does not affect its classification as a financial liability, although that fact may affect its measurement (see 7I.3.190) in addition to its classification as a current or non-current liability. [*IAS 32.16A, 18(b)*]

7I.3.50.20   This principle applies even when:
- the amount of cash or other financial assets is determined on the basis of an index or other variable that has the potential to increase or decrease – e.g. a share index; or
- the legal form of the puttable instrument gives the holder a right to a residual interest in the assets of the issuer. [*IAS 32.18(b)*]

7I.3.50.30   The amount payable to the holder of a puttable instrument might vary in response to an index or another variable whose economic characteristics are not closely related to those of the host contract. In this case, the instrument may contain an embedded derivative that requires separation (see 7I.2.110). As a result, either:
- the entire puttable instrument (hybrid) is measured at FVTPL; or
- the embedded derivative is separated and accounted for at FVTPL (see 7I.6.120).

7I.3.50.40   Investors in many mutual funds, unit trusts and similar entities have the right to redeem their interests in exchange for cash that is equivalent to their share of the net asset value of the entity. This gives the issuer (the fund) a contractual obligation and therefore these instruments are classified as financial liabilities, unless they meet the conditions to be classified as equity (see 7I.3.70–80). These instruments are financial liabilities independent of considerations such as when the right is exercisable, how the amount payable on exercise is determined and whether the instrument has a fixed maturity. However, these considerations may affect whether the instruments qualify for equity classification under the exceptions in 7I.3.70–80. [*IAS 32.18(b)*]

7I.3.50.50   The requirement addressed in 7I.3.50.40 means that some entities do not present any equity. However, IAS 32 does not preclude such instruments from being included in the statement of financial position within a 'total members' interests' subtotal. [*IAS 32.IE32*]

7I.3.55   *Members' shares in co-operative entities and similar instruments*

7I.3.55.10   The principles in 7I.3.50.40 apply equally to shares issued to members of a co-operative entity that give the holder the right to request redemption. Members' shares and similar instruments that would be classified as equity if they did not give the holder the right to request redemption are classified as equity only if:
- the entity has an unconditional right to refuse redemption; or

• redemption is unconditionally prohibited by local law, regulation or the entity's governing charter (see also 7I.3.30.90). [*IFRIC 2.2, 6–8*]

7I.3.55.20   A distinction is made between unconditional and conditional prohibitions on redemption. Only an unconditional prohibition on redemption can lead to the classification of members' shares and similar instruments as equity.

7I.3.55.30   An unconditional prohibition prevents an entity from incurring a liability for redemption, regardless of whether the entity will be able to satisfy the obligation. However, a conditional prohibition prevents *payments* from being made unless certain conditions are met – e.g. liquidity constraints. A conditional prohibition may only defer payment of a liability that has already been incurred. For example, members' shares can be redeemed as soon as the local liquidity or reserve requirements are met. [*IFRIC 2.BC14*]

7I.3.55.40   An unconditional prohibition may be partial, in that it allows redemption but requires a stated minimum amount of members' shares or paid-in capital to be maintained at all times. In this case, the proportion of members' shares subject to the unconditional prohibition on redemption is classified as equity – even though each individual instrument may be redeemed. [*IFRIC 2.9*]

EXAMPLE 8 – PARTIAL UNCONDITIONAL PROHIBITION ON REDEEMING SHARES

7I.3.55.50   Local law prohibits a co-operative from redeeming members' shares if that would cause the amount of paid-in capital from members' shares to fall below 75% of its highest ever reported amount. If the highest amount of paid-in capital from members' shares ever reported was 100, then 75 would always be classified as equity – even though each member could, individually, request redemption of their share.

7I.3.55.60   An unconditional prohibition may be based on a factor that can change over a period of time. [*IFRIC 2.9*]

EXAMPLE 9 – PARTIAL UNCONDITIONAL PROHIBITION ON REDEEMING SHARES THAT CHANGES OVER TIME

7I.3.55.70   The governing charter of Co-operative C states that 25% of the highest number of members' shares ever in issue should be maintained as equity. C decides to amend its governing charter by reducing this percentage to 20%. Assuming that all other factors remain the same, then the number of members' shares subject to the unconditional prohibition would reduce.

7I.3.55.80   Consequently, C would increase its financial liability to redeem members' shares, while simultaneously decreasing the amount of members' shares classified as equity. This, and other such changes to the amount of members' shares or paid-in capital subject to an unconditional prohibition on redemption, are treated as transfers between financial liabilities and equity. [*IFRIC 2.9*]

7I.3.55.90   For a discussion of changes in the effective terms of an instrument, see 7I.3.410. [*IFRIC 2.9*]

7I.3.55.100   In our view, an unconditional prohibition may also result in equity classification when it prohibits a contingent event from taking place. For a discussion of contingent events, see 7I.3.40.

EXAMPLE 10 – CONTINGENT EVENT UNCONDITIONALLY PROHIBITED BY LAW

7I.3.55.110   Company C has issued a put option on specified equity instruments that is exercisable if there is change in control of C. C is controlled by the government; for public interest reasons, the law unconditionally prohibits a change in control.

7I.3.55.115   In this example, C concludes that no liability should be recognised for the potential obligation to redeem the equity instruments unless there is a change in the law to remove the prohibition.

7I.3.55.120   On initial recognition, an entity measures its financial liability at fair value. In the case of members' shares with a redemption feature, the entity measures the fair value of the financial liability for redemption at no less than the discounted maximum amount payable under the redemption provisions of its governing charter or applicable law. The discount runs from the first date on which the amount could be required to be paid. [*IFRIC 2.10*]

7I.3.60   **Puttable instruments and obligations arising on liquidation classified as equity by exception**

7I.3.60.10   As exceptions to the general principles for liability and equity classification, a puttable instrument or an instrument (or a component of an instrument) that imposes on the entity an obligation only on liquidation is classified as equity if the conditions discussed in 7I.3.70 or 80 are met.

7I.3.60.20   Puttable instruments, and instruments that impose an obligation on the entity only on liquidation, are classified as equity in the separate or individual financial statements of the issuing entity (see 2.5.720.30). However, in the consolidated financial statements of the group, if the instrument is issued by a subsidiary and is not held by another member of the group, it is classified as a financial liability because the exception is not extended to classification as NCI in the consolidated financial statements. [*IAS 32.AG29A, BC68*]

7I.3.70   *Puttable instruments*

7I.3.70.10   A puttable instrument is a financial instrument that:
- gives the holder the right to put the instrument back to the issuer for cash or another financial asset; or
- is automatically put back to the issuer on the occurrence of an uncertain future event or the death or retirement of the instrument holder.

7I.3.70.20   Even though a puttable instrument contains an obligation for the entity to deliver cash or another financial asset, it is classified as equity if all of the conditions in the following flowchart are met. [*IAS 32.16A–16B*]

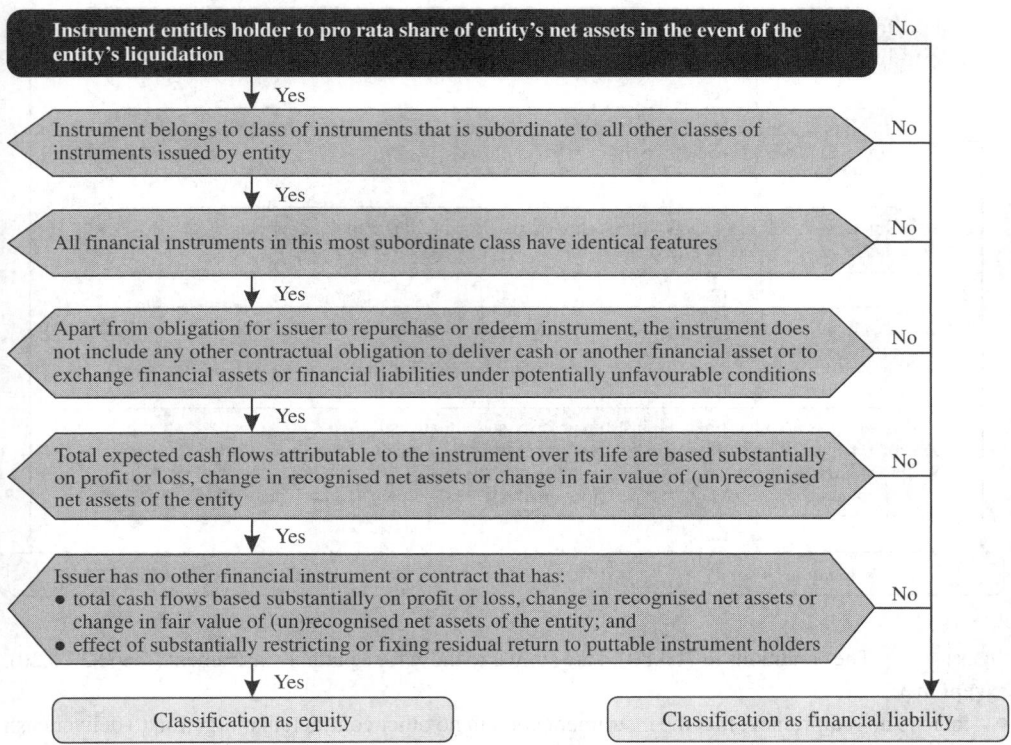

7I.3.70.30 The issuer of a puttable instrument first evaluates the terms of the instrument to determine whether it is a financial liability or equity instrument in its entirety, or is a compound instrument that contains both a liability and an equity component, in accordance with the general definitions of liabilities and equity in IAS 32. If the puttable instrument is initially determined to be a financial liability, or to contain a financial liability component, then the whole instrument is tested for equity classification under the exception in 7I.3.60.10. If the instrument meets all of the conditions for equity classification under the exception, then the whole instrument is classified as equity. If the whole instrument does not meet the conditions for equity classification under the exception, then it is classified wholly as a liability or is split into its liability and equity components in accordance with the general requirements on financial liability and equity classification in IAS 32. [*IAS 32.11, 16A, 28*]

7I.3.80 *Instruments that oblige the entity on liquidation*

7I.3.80.10 An entity may issue instruments that contain a contractual obligation for the entity to deliver to the holder a pro rata share of its net assets only on liquidation. In this case, the obligation arises if liquidation is either:

- certain to occur and is outside the control of the entity – e.g. a limited-life entity; or
- uncertain to occur but is at the option of the instrument holder – e.g. some partnership interests.

7I.3.80.15 For such an instrument (or component) to qualify for equity classification by exception, all of the conditions in the following flowchart need to be met. [*IAS 32.16C–16D*]

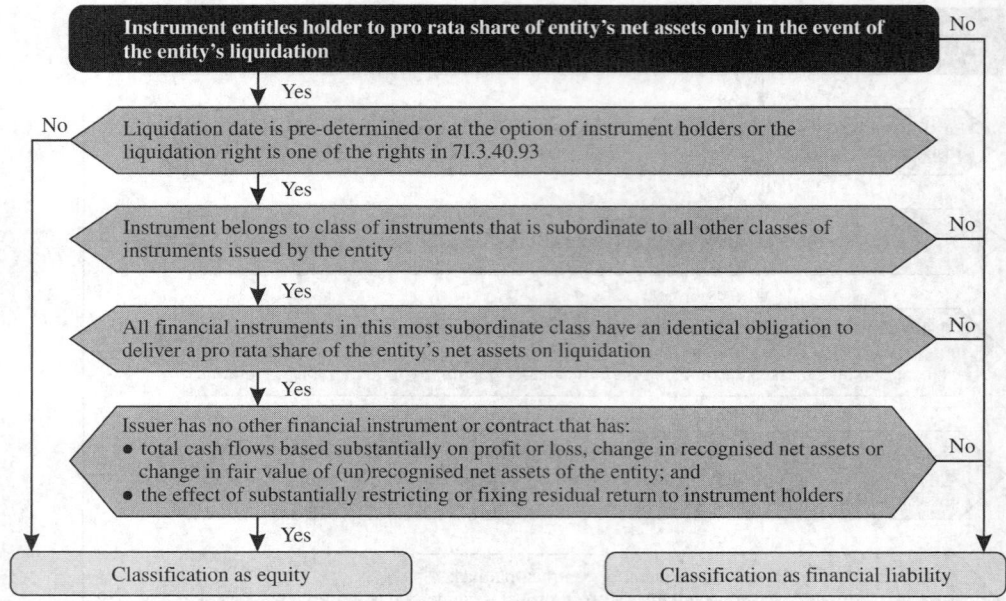

7I.3.80.20   The conditions in 7I.3.80.15 are similar to those for a puttable instrument (see 7I.3.70.20), except that:

- there is no requirement that the instrument contain no other contractual obligation to deliver cash or other financial assets;
- there is no requirement to consider the total expected cash flows over the life of the instrument; and
- there is only one feature that needs to be identical among the instruments in the most subordinate class: this is the obligation for the issuing entity to deliver to the holder a pro rata share of its net assets on liquidation.

7I.3.80.30   The reason for this distinction between a puttable instrument and an instrument that imposes on the entity an obligation only on liquidation is the difference in the timing of settlement of the obligations. A puttable instrument can be exercised before liquidation of the entity. Therefore, it is important to identify all contractual obligations that exist throughout its entire life to ensure that it always represents the most residual interest. However, for an instrument that imposes on the entity an obligation only on liquidation of the entity, it is appropriate to focus only on the obligations that exist at liquidation. [*IAS 32.BC67*]

7I.3.90   *Components of instruments*

7I.3.90.10   The exception in 7I.3.80 applies to 'components of instruments that impose on the entity an obligation to deliver to another party a pro rata share of the net assets of the entity only on liquidation'. Therefore, if the instrument contains other contractual obligations, then those other obligations may need to be accounted for separately as financial liabilities in accordance with IAS 32.

7I.3.90.20   An example of such an instrument is a unit holder's interest in a limited-life entity that:
- is not puttable; and
- includes only a right to:
  – fixed non-discretionary dividends each period; and
  – a pro rata share of the entity's net assets on its liquidation.

7I.3.90.25   The obligation to pay fixed non-discretionary dividends represents a contractual obligation that is classified as a financial liability; the obligation to deliver a pro rata share of the entity's net assets on its liquidation is classified as equity, provided that all other criteria are met. However, if there is no mandatory dividend requirement, and dividends are entirely at the discretion of the entity, then the units are classified wholly as equity provided that all other criteria are met.

7I.3.90.30   In our view, in applying the last condition set out in 7I.3.80.15 when evaluating a component of an instrument for equity classification, an entity should choose an accounting policy, to be applied consistently, on whether the term 'other financial instrument' encompasses other components of that same financial instrument or only financial instruments other than the one that contains the component being evaluated.

7I.3.94   Analysis not restricted to instruments other than the instrument under evaluation

7I.3.94.10   An instrument may include an obligation to distribute mandatory dividends based on profits of the entity, and an obligation to distribute a pro rata share of the net assets on a fixed liquidation date. Assume that the entity applies the last condition in 7I.3.80.15 to the component of the instrument that comprises the obligation arising only on liquidation; and that, to do this, its policy is to treat the mandatory dividend feature like another financial instrument. In this case, equity classification of the obligation arising only on liquidation would be precluded. This is because the mandatory dividends are based on profits and therefore the condition in paragraph 16D of IAS 32 is not met.

7I.3.97   Analysis restricted to instruments other than the instrument under evaluation

7I.3.97.10   However, assume that the entity's policy is to restrict the analysis under 7I.3.80.15 to consider only financial instruments other than the one that contains the obligation arising on liquidation. In this case, the mandatory dividend feature in itself would not preclude equity classification of the obligation arising on liquidation. This is because the feature is part of the same instrument, and the condition for equity treatment in paragraph 16D of IAS 32 could be met. For further discussion of this condition for equity treatment, see 7I.3.150.

EXAMPLE 11 – MANDATORY DIVIDEND FEATURE BASED ON PROFITS

7I.3.97.20   Company C, which has a limited life, issues non-redeemable Instrument X that requires payment of a dividend equalling 90% of its profits. The holders of Instrument X will also participate in the liquidation of C on a pro rata basis.

7I.3.97.30   The instrument is issued for its fair value of 1,000. The fair value of the mandatory dividend feature is 800 on issuance; this component of the instrument is classified as a financial liability.

Scenario 1: Analysis not restricted to instruments other than Instrument X

7I.3.97.40   C's policy is to regard the mandatory dividend feature as another financial instrument for the purpose of applying the condition in 7I.3.80.15 to the component that provides a pro rata participation in liquidation.

7I.3.97.50   In this scenario, equity classification of the component that provides a pro rata participation in liquidation is precluded. This is because the mandatory dividends are substantially based on profits; therefore, the condition in paragraph 16D of IAS 32 is not met.

Scenario 2: Analysis restricted to instruments other than Instrument X

7I.3.97.60   C's policy is to restrict the analysis under 7I.3.80.15 to consider only financial instruments other than Instrument X.

7I.3.97.70   In this scenario, the mandatory dividend feature of Instrument X in itself does not preclude equity classification of the component that provides a pro rata participation in liquidation. This is because the feature is part of the same financial instrument, and the condition for equity treatment in paragraph 16D of IAS 32 could be met.

7I.3.100   *Pro rata share of entity's net assets on liquidation*

7I.3.100.10   A pro rata share of the entity's net assets on liquidation is determined by:
- dividing the entity's net assets on liquidation into units of equal amount; and
- multiplying that amount by the number of units held by the financial instrument holder. [*IAS 32.16A(a), 16C(a)*]

7I.3.100.20   In our view, the requirement in 7I.3.100.10 means that each instrument holder has an entitlement to an identical monetary amount per unit on liquidation. For example, an instrument that entitles the holder to a fixed dividend on liquidation, in addition to a share of the entity's net assets, would not qualify under this requirement. Similarly, if payments to instrument holders on liquidation are subject to fees that are not computed on an identical per-unit basis – e.g. a fixed fee per holder rather than per unit – then the instrument would not satisfy this criterion. Furthermore, instruments that entitled the holder to a pro rata share of only a specific portion or component of the net assets of an entity would not satisfy this criterion.

7I.3.110   *Class of instruments subordinate to all other classes*

7I.3.110.10   In determining whether an instrument is in the most subordinate class, an entity evaluates the instrument's claim on liquidation as if it were to liquidate on the date on which it classifies the instrument. [*IAS 32.AG14B*]

7I.3.110.20   IAS 32 does not preclude the existence of several types or classes of equity. The IFRS Interpretations Committee discussed the classification of puttable instruments that are subordinate to all other classes of instruments when an entity also has perpetual instruments that are classified as equity. The Committee noted that a financial instrument is first classified as a liability or equity instrument in accordance with the general requirements of IAS 32. As a second step, the entity considers the exceptions in paragraphs 16A and 16B, or 16C and 16D of IAS 32 (see 7I.3.70–80), to determine whether a financial instrument should be classified as equity. It would do so if the financial instrument meets the definition of a financial liability because either:

- it is puttable to the issuer; or
- it imposes on the issuer an obligation on liquidation because liquidation is either:
  - certain to occur and outside the control of the entity; or
  - uncertain to occur but is at the option of the instrument holder. [*IU 03-09*]

EXAMPLE 12 – LEVEL OF SUBORDINATION

7I.3.110.30   Company X issues two types of instruments. Instrument A is a perpetual instrument with no put rights; Instrument B is a puttable instrument. Both could qualify as equity, provided that all applicable criteria in IAS 32 are met. The existence of the puttable feature in Instrument B does not in itself imply that the instrument is less subordinate than Instrument A, because the level of an instrument's subordination is determined by its priority in liquidation.

7I.3.110.33   If Instrument A and Instrument B are equally subordinate, then together they form the most subordinate class for the purposes of the 'identical features' test discussed in 7I.3.120. However, in this case Instrument B would fail equity classification because of the existence of the put feature, which does not exist in Instrument A.

7I.3.110.37   If Instrument B is more subordinate than Instrument A – e.g. if Instrument A is entitled to a fixed claim on liquidation and Instrument B is entitled to the residual net assets – then Instrument B may qualify for equity classification, provided that all other conditions in the exceptions are met.

7I.3.110.40   Many investment funds have a nominal amount of founder shares that are issued to the fund manager. These shares are typically non-redeemable and have no entitlements to dividends. In our view, even a small amount of founder shares would disqualify investors' shares that are puttable from equity classification if the founder shares are subordinate to the puttable investors' shares. This is because the puttable investors' shares are not the most subordinate class of instruments.

7I.3.110.50   If an investment fund issues redeemable participating shares and founder shares that rank pari passu in respect of their respective nominal amounts in liquidation and the founder shares have no further payment rights, then in our view the founder shares and participating shares together form the most subordinate class. However, because the redeemable participating shares have other rights, we believe that the participating shares would be classified as liabilities, because they do not have identical features to those of the founder shares (see 7I.3.120).

7I.3.120   *Identical features test*

7I.3.120.10   In respect of puttable instruments, all financial instruments in the most subordinated class are required to have identical features to qualify for equity classification. No instrument holder in the most subordinate class of instruments can have preferential terms or conditions. In our view, this should be interpreted strictly to mean identical contractual terms and conditions. This includes non-financial features, such as governance rights, related to the holders of the instruments in their roles as owners of the entity. Differences in cash flows and contractual terms and conditions of an instrument attributable to an instrument holder in its role as non-owner are therefore not considered to violate the identical features test – provided that the transaction is on similar terms to an equivalent transaction that might occur between a non-instrument holder and the issuing entity. [*IAS 32.AG14C, AG14F–AG14G, AG14I*]

EXAMPLE 13 – GUARANTEE OF GENERAL PARTNERS IN LIMITED PARTNERSHIP

7I.3.120.20   A general partner in Limited Partnership P provides a guarantee to P and is remunerated for providing that guarantee. If the guarantee and the associated cash flows relate to the general partner in its role as guarantor, and not in its role as owner of P, then P disregards the guarantee and the associated cash flows when assessing whether the contractual terms of the limited partnership instruments held by the general partner and limited partners are identical.

EXAMPLE 14 – ADDITIONAL INFORMATION RIGHTS

7I.3.120.30   A fund manager that holds units in an investment fund may have access to certain information rights that are not granted to other unit holders. If these information rights are granted to the fund manager in its role as manager of the fund, then they are not considered to violate the identical features test.

(S) 7I.3.120.40   As discussed in 7I.3.160, in our experience units issued by sub-funds within umbrella investment funds fail equity classification in the financial statements of the umbrella fund (when the umbrella fund and sub-funds form a single legal entity). In our view, contractual features that would violate the identical features test include:
- different rates of management fees;
- a choice *on issuance* by holders whether to receive income or additional units as distributions (such that the distributive or accumulative feature differs for each instrument after they are issued);
- different lock-up periods;
- different reference assets on which the pro rata share of net assets is calculated; or
- different currencies in which payments are denominated.

7I.3.120.50   However, in our view the following features do not violate the identical features test, because there are no inherent differences in the features of each instrument within the most subordinate class:
- administrative charges based on the volume of units redeemed before liquidation, as long as all unit holders in the most subordinate class are subject to the same fee structure;
- different subscription fees payable on initial subscription, as long as all other features become identical once the subscription fees are paid;
- choice by holders *on each distribution date* to receive income or additional units as distributions, as long as the same ability to choose distributions or reinvestment is afforded to all of the unit

holders in the most subordinate class – i.e. the choice is an identical feature for all of the instruments in this most subordinate class; and

- a term contained in identical instruments that carry equal voting rights that caps the maximum amount of voting rights that any individual holder may exercise.

7I.3.130 *No other contractual obligation to deliver cash or another financial asset*

7I.3.130.10   In respect of puttable instruments, one of the conditions for equity classification is that the instrument does not include any other contractual obligation to deliver cash other than the put feature. [*IAS 32.16A(d)*]

EXAMPLE 15 – ADDITIONAL CONTRACTUAL OBLIGATION TO DELIVER CASH

7I.3.130.20   Unlisted unit trust T issues instruments that enable the holder to put the instrument back to T at any time. T is contractually required to distribute its net accounting profit on an annual basis.

7I.3.130.30   In this example, T concludes that the requirement to distribute the net accounting profit annually is an additional obligation to deliver cash. Therefore, these instruments do not qualify for equity classification.

7I.3.140 *Total expected cash flows attributable to instrument over its life*

7I.3.140.10   In respect of puttable instruments, one of the conditions for equity classification is that the total expected cash flows attributable to the instrument over its life are based substantially on the profit or loss, the change in the recognised net assets, or the change in the fair value of the recognised and unrecognised net assets of the entity. In this context, profit or loss, and the change in recognised net assets, are measured in line with relevant IFRSs. [*IAS 32.16A(e), AG14E*]

7I.3.140.20   In some cases, an instrument may be puttable at a pro rata share of the entity's recog- nised net assets, as calculated in its *separate* financial statements. IFRS does not discuss whether such instruments could qualify for equity classification if the issuer is a parent entity required to present consolidated financial statements – i.e. in which it consolidates its investments in subsidiaries. IFRS includes no requirement for puttable instruments issued by a parent to be classified differently in the parent's separate financial statements and consolidated financial statements – provided that no additional arrangements exist between the holder of an instrument and subsidiaries of the issuer. Therefore, in our view when the entity is a parent, its profit or loss, change in recognised net assets or change in the fair value of the recognised and unrecognised net assets may be measured either on a separate or on a consolidated basis. For example, consider an instrument that is puttable at a pro rata share of a parent's recognised net assets as presented in its separate IFRS financial statements. This may qualify for classification as equity in both the separate and consolidated IFRS financial statements, provided that all other conditions in the exceptions are also met.

7I.3.140.30   Instruments that are puttable at a pro rata share of recognised net assets determined in accordance with a different basis of accounting – e.g. local GAAP – may still satisfy the condition in 7I.3.140.10, depending on the circumstances. For example, it may be possible to argue that the effect of differences between local GAAP and IFRS is immaterial when applied to the entity; or it might be argued that the effect is temporary and expected to converge over the life of the instrument, such that the total 'expected' cash flows are 'based substantially' on IFRS profit or loss or change in recognised net assets. In our view, the use of the terms 'expected' and 'based substantially' indicates that judgement should be exercised in determining whether the requirement is met in the individual circumstances of each specific situation, including consideration of how local GAAP and IFRS apply to the reporting entity's business and the terms of the instrument.

7I.3.140.40   When the redemption amount of a puttable instrument is based on the change in fair value of the recognised and unrecognised net assets of the entity, judgement should still be applied to determine whether the total expected cash flows test is met but, in our experience, it will often be straightforward to determine.

7I.3.150   *Other financial instruments or contracts*

7I.3.150.10   An issuer may need to assess whether it has any other financial instrument or contract that precludes equity classification. In doing so, the entity does not consider a non-financial contract with the holder of the puttable instrument or the holder of the instrument that imposes an obligation only on liquidation. If there were such a contract, then the entity would have to determine that the non-financial contract has terms and conditions that are similar to those of an equivalent contract that might occur with a non-instrument holder. [*IAS 32.16B, 16D, AG14J*]

7I.3.160   *Instruments issued by umbrella fund*

7I.3.160.10   In certain jurisdictions, a collective investment scheme may be structured as an umbrella fund that operates one or more sub-funds, whereby investors purchase instruments that entitle the holder to a share of the net assets of a particular sub-fund. The umbrella fund and sub-funds together form a legal entity, although the assets and the obligations of individual funds are fully or partially segregated.

7I.3.160.20   If the umbrella fund presents financial statements that include the assets and liabilities of the sub-funds, which together with the umbrella fund form a single legal entity, then the sub-fund instruments are assessed for equity classification in those financial statements from the perspective of the umbrella fund as a whole. Therefore, these instruments cannot qualify for equity classification under the conditions in 7I.3.70 or 80. This is because they could not meet the 'pro rata share of the entity's net assets on liquidation' test (see 7I.3.100) and, if they are puttable instruments, the identical features test (see 7I.3.120).

7I.3.160.30   In an alternative umbrella fund structure, the sub-funds may be subsidiaries of the umbrella fund. The umbrella fund may present consolidated financial statements in line with IFRS 10 that consolidate the sub-funds as subsidiaries. The exceptions to the general principles described in 7I.3.70–80 are not extended to the classification of NCI in consolidated financial statements. Therefore, instruments issued by such sub-funds are classified as liabilities in the consolidated financial statements if they:
- qualified for equity classification under the conditions in 7I.3.70 or 80 in the separate financial statements of each sub-fund; and
- represent NCI. [*IAS 32.AG29A*]

7I.3.160.40   If the sub-funds are subsidiaries of the umbrella fund, but the umbrella fund qualifies as an investment entity, then the investments in the sub-funds are generally measured at FVTPL (see 5.6.10.10). The umbrella fund does not present consolidated financial statements and therefore no NCI arises in the umbrella fund's financial statements in respect of the investments in the sub-funds that are measured at FVTPL.

7I.3.160.50   The umbrella fund may present combined financial statements. In this case, to the extent that they are expressed as being prepared in accordance with IFRS, in our view puttable sub-fund instruments would not qualify for equity classification in the combined financial statements for the reasons described in 7I.3.160.20–30.

7I.3.170   *Reclassification*

7I.3.170.10   A puttable instrument or an instrument that imposes on the entity an obligation only on liquidation is reclassified as equity from the date on which it has all of the features and meets the conditions set out in 7I.3.70.20 and 80.15. An instrument is reclassified from equity to financial liabilities from the date on which it ceases to have all of the features or meet all of the conditions for equity classification. [*IAS 32.16E*]

7I.3.170.20   This indicates a continuous assessment model under which an entity reassesses its classification of instruments:
- whenever there are changes to the capital structure of the entity – e.g. when new classes of shares are issued or when existing shares are redeemed; or
- when there is a change in expectations over:
  - total expected cash flows; and
  - the evaluation of whether they are based substantially on IFRS profit or loss or change in recognised net assets.

7I.3.170.30   When a puttable instrument, or an instrument that imposes on the entity an obligation only on liquidation, is reclassified from equity to financial liabilities, the liability is measured initially at the instrument's fair value at the date of reclassification. Any difference between the carrying amount of the equity instrument and the fair value of the financial liability at the date of reclassification is recognised in equity. [*IAS 32.16F(a)*]

7I.3.170.40   When a puttable instrument, or an instrument that imposes on the entity an obligation only on liquidation, is reclassified from financial liabilities to equity, the equity instrument is measured at the carrying amount of the financial liability at the date of reclassification. [*IAS 32.16F(b)*]

7I.3.170.50   In either case, there is no pre-tax profit or loss impact arising from the reclassification. Any potential income tax accounting implications under IAS 12 (see 3.13.520) resulting from the reclassification need to be considered.

7I.3.180   Instruments to be settled in own equity

7I.3.180.10   A contract that will be settled by the entity issuing its own equity instruments does not create an obligation on the part of the entity to deliver cash or another financial asset. However, IAS 32 imposes additional requirements that have to be met in order to classify such instruments as equity. [*IAS 32.21*]

7I.3.183   *Non-derivative contracts*

7I.3.183.10   If a non-derivative contract will or may be settled in the issuer's own equity instruments, then it is a financial liability – provided that it includes a contractual obligation for the issuer to deliver a *variable number* of its own equity instruments. It is classified as a liability because the holder does not have a direct equity exposure, as would be the case if the issuer were obliged to deliver a fixed number of shares. [*IAS 32.11, 16(b)(i), 21, AG27(d)*]

7I.3.183.20   Also, if a contract may be settled either in the issuer's own equity instruments (whether fixed or variable in number) or in cash or other financial assets, at the option of the *holder*, then the instrument is a financial liability or contains a liability component – e.g. a bond convertible into shares at the holder's option. [*IAS 32.11, 16(b)*]

7I.3.183.30   The IFRS Interpretations Committee discussed the classification of a financial instrument as a liability or as equity and noted that if the *issuer* of a financial instrument has the contractual right to choose to settle the instrument either in cash or in a fixed number of its own shares, then the instrument meets the definition of an equity instrument provided that the instrument does not establish an obligation to deliver cash indirectly through its terms and conditions (see 7I.3.20). This is because the issuer does not have a contractual obligation to deliver cash or to deliver a variable number of its own shares. [*IAS 32.16, AG25, IU 09-13*]

7I.3.183.40   A contract is a financial liability if an entity has an obligation to deliver a number of its own equity instruments that varies so that the total fair value of the equity instruments delivered is equal to the amount of the contractual obligation. The amount of that contractual obligation could be fixed, or it could vary in response to changes in another market variable that is unrelated to the market value of the entity's equity instruments – e.g. the gold price. In these circumstances, the holder is not exposed to any gain or loss arising from movements in the fair value of the equity instruments. Consequently, in such instances the entity is using its equity instruments as currency. Such contracts are financial liabilities of the entity. [*IAS 32.21*]

7I.3.183.50   The IFRS Interpretations Committee noted that a single obligation to deliver a variable number of an entity's own equity instruments is a non-derivative obligation that meets the definition of a financial liability and cannot be subdivided into components for the purpose of evaluating whether the instrument contains a component that meets the definition of equity. [*IAS 32.11, IU 05-14*]

EXAMPLE 16 – OBLIGATION TO DELIVER VARIABLE NUMBER OF SHARES SUBJECT TO CAP AND FLOOR

7I.3.183.60   Company M has issued a financial instrument for 8,000. The instrument has a stated maturity date. At maturity, M must deliver a variable number of its own equity shares, as follows:
- if the share price is below 80, then M issues 100 shares (cap);
- if the share price is above 100, then M issues 80 shares (floor); and
- if the share price is between 80 and 100, then M issues a variable number of shares with a market value of 8,000.

71.3.183.70 The IFRS Interpretations Committee discussed a similar scenario and noted that the instrument in such an example is a financial liability because it comprises an obligation to deliver a variable number of shares. Although the variability is limited by a cap and a floor, the overall number of equity instruments that the issuer is obliged to deliver is not fixed and therefore the entire obligation meets the definition of a financial liability. It would not be appropriate to divide the instrument into components – e.g. the minimum number of shares to deliver under the floor – for the purpose of evaluating whether the instrument contains a component that meets the definition of equity. [*IU 05-14*]

71.3.183.80 The Committee also noted that such cap and floor features are embedded derivatives that need to be separated from the host liability – which in this example represents an obligation to deliver a variable number of shares with a fixed value of 8,000 – and to be measured at fair value, with all changes in fair value recognised in profit or loss, assuming that the instrument has not been designated in its entirety as at FVTPL (see 71.2.110 and 71.4.40). [*IU 05-14*]

71.3.183.90 This is because:
- the 'fixed-for-fixed' requirement is not met in respect of these features because the cap and floor are net settled derivatives which do not result in the exchange of a fixed amount of cash for a single fixed number of equity shares (see 71.3.187.10); and
- their values change in response to the price of the issuer's equity shares and therefore they are not closely related to the host debt contract. [*IU 05-14*]

71.3.183.100 An instrument may establish a contractual obligation to deliver a variable number of shares indirectly through its terms and conditions, even if the issuer has a contractual right to settle the instrument by delivering a fixed number of shares. This is illustrated in Example 17.

EXAMPLE 17 – CLASSIFICATION AS LIABILITY OR EQUITY – IS A CONTRACTUAL RIGHT SUBSTANTIVE?

71.3.183.110 Company Z issues a financial instrument that matures after five years.
- On maturity, the instrument is settled by delivering a variable number of Z's own equity instruments with a market value equal to a fixed cash amount, subject to a cap and a floor, similar to Example 16 – i.e. there are both a minimum and a maximum number of equity instruments that could be delivered if the price of a single equity instrument is higher or lower than certain amounts.
- Z also has a contractual right to settle the instrument at any time before maturity by delivering the maximum number of equity instruments specified in the contract – i.e. the cap amount.

7I.3.183.120   In discussing a similar scenario, the IFRS Interpretations Committee noted that an entity cannot automatically assume that the financial instrument meets the definition of an equity instrument because it has a contractual right to settle early by delivering a fixed number of its own equity instruments. This is because this contractual right might not be substantive – because the issuer may have to deliver significantly more shares to settle early than it may otherwise be obliged to deliver at maturity – and therefore would not be considered in determining the classification of the instrument (see 7I.3.20). [*IAS 32.15, 20, IU 01-14*]

7I.3.183.130   Judgement is required to determine whether the early settlement option is substantive and therefore should be taken into account in classifying the instrument. In particular, Z needs to consider whether there are actual economic or other business reasons for it to exercise that option. [*IU 01-14*]

7I.3.183.140   In making this assessment, Z considers the following factors:
- whether the instrument would have been priced differently if its early settlement option had not been included within the contractual terms;
- the width of the range between the cap and the floor; and
- Z's share price and its volatility. [*IU 01-14*]

7I.3.187   ***Derivative contracts***

7I.3.187.10   A derivative contract is an equity instrument if it can be settled only by the entity receiving or delivering a fixed number of its own equity instruments for a fixed amount of cash or another financial asset (the so-called 'fixed-for-fixed' requirement). For example, an issued share option that gives the holder the right to buy a fixed number of the entity's shares for a fixed amount of cash or for a fixed stated principal amount of a bond is an equity instrument. IAS 32 also goes on to state that changes in the fair value of an instrument as a result of changes in market interest rates that do not affect the amount of cash or other financial assets to be received or paid, or the number of equity instruments to be received or delivered, do not impact classification as an equity instrument. A contract that is settled by an entity issuing a variable number of own shares for a fixed amount of cash, or a fixed number of own shares for a variable amount of cash, is a financial asset or financial liability of the entity. [*IAS 32.11, 16(b)(ii), 22*]

7I.3.187.20   IAS 32 does not address an exchange of a fixed number of the entity's own equity instruments. In our view, a contract to exchange a fixed number of one class of non-derivative own equity instruments for a fixed number of a different class of non-derivative own equity instruments should be classified as an equity instrument. For example, an issued share option that gives the non-controlling shareholder of an entity's subsidiary the right to exchange a fixed number of shares in that subsidiary for a fixed number of shares in the parent entity is an equity instrument in the consolidated financial statements of the parent entity. [*IAS 32.16*]

7I.3.187.30   For convertible bonds where the holder has the ability to convert into a fixed percentage of the issuer's outstanding shares, an issue arises over whether the conversion option meets the fixed-for-fixed requirement.

EXAMPLE 18 – BOND CONVERTIBLE INTO A FIXED PERCENTAGE OF AN ENTITY'S OUTSTANDING SHARES

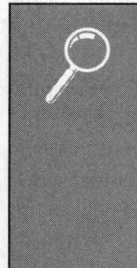

7I.3.187.40   Company S issued a convertible bond for a principal amount of 5 million that matures in 10 years. The holder of the instrument has the option to convert the bond into ordinary shares of S. S may issue or redeem additional ordinary shares at any time. The number of ordinary shares to be received on conversion will represent a fixed percentage (i.e. 5%) of the issued and outstanding shares of S.

7I.3.187.50   The conversion option does not meet the fixed-for-fixed requirement because the number of ordinary shares to be received upon conversion will vary when there are changes in the number of outstanding shares of S.

7I.3.187.60   An obligation in a foreign currency represents a variable amount of cash. Consequently, contracts (both freestanding and embedded) are classified as financial assets or financial liabilities if they will be settled by an entity delivering a fixed number of its own equity instruments in exchange for a fixed amount of foreign currency. However, there is an exception for rights, options or warrants to acquire a fixed number of the entity's own equity instruments for a fixed amount of any currency. This exception requires that the entity offers the rights, options or warrants pro rata to all of its existing owners of the same class of its own non-derivative equity instruments. Under the exception, these rights, options or warrants are equity instruments. The exception does not extend to other instruments that grant the holder the right to purchase the entity's own equity instruments for a fixed amount denominated in a foreign currency (such as the conversion feature in bonds). For further discussion of foreign currency convertible bonds, see 7I.3.270. [*IAS 32.11(b)(ii), 16(b)(ii), BC4F, BC4K*]

7I.3.187.70   In our view, the requirement that a contract be settled by delivering a fixed number of its own shares for a fixed amount of cash, in order to be classified as equity, can also be met if the number of shares to be delivered or the amount of cash to be received changes over the life of the contract but the change is predetermined at inception of the contract.

EXAMPLE 19 – BERMUDAN OPTION

7I.3.187.80   Company B issues an option, which the parties can exercise at predetermined dates (a Bermudan option). At each date, the option can be settled by B delivering a fixed number of its own shares for a fixed amount of cash. However, the number of shares and the amount of cash depend on the date of exercise of the option; the exact terms of the exchange at each exercise date were determined when B entered into the contract – i.e. the number of shares to be delivered is fixed for each date at inception.

7I.3.187.90   Such a contract is in fact a series of European-style option contracts that would each be settled by B delivering a fixed amount of its own shares for a fixed amount of cash. Consequently, B concludes that the contract, assuming that it meets the other requirements, should be classified as an equity instrument.

71.3.187.100   Similarly, in our view adjustment clauses that alter the conversion ratio only to prevent dilution (anti-dilution) do not violate the fixed-for-fixed requirement and therefore do not result in the instrument being classified as a financial liability. 'Anti-dilution' refers to the adjustment of the conversion ratio to compensate holders of the instrument for changes in the number of equity instruments outstanding that relate to share issuances or redemptions not made at fair value – e.g. arising from rights issues or bonus issues. Anti-dilution can also include the adjustment of the conversion ratio to compensate holders of the instrument for dividend payments to existing shareholders that were not taken into account when the conversion ratio was initially set. Anti-dilution does not comprise any other form of compensation to the instrument holder for fair value losses – e.g. when compensation by adjusting the conversion ratio is given if the share price falls below a certain level or if new shares are issued at a then-current market price that is below the conversion price.

71.3.187.110   Many convertible bonds include takeover clauses that either allow or require the holder to exercise its conversion option at an enhanced conversion ratio if control of the issuer changes. A takeover may negatively affect bond holders relative to shareholders in a number of ways – e.g. if current shareholders are bought out by an acquirer, and the issuer's business is transferred to a new entity or the underlying shares are de-listed. The bond holder might suffer the loss of its conversion option (if conversion is required) or the loss of an option to convert into publicly traded shares (if the issuer's shares are no longer publicly traded). In the absence of compensation to the bond holder, the shareholders would benefit from the relative loss of value suffered by the bond holders. In our view, if a takeover clause provides an enhanced conversion ratio that is designed to compensate bond holders for this loss of optionality that arises on a takeover and is intended to preserve the relative economic interests of bond holders and shareholders, then it does not violate the fixed-for-fixed requirement.

71.3.187.120   Except as described in 71.3.187.100–110, in our view the requirement that a contract be settled by delivering a fixed number of the entity's own shares for a fixed amount of cash cannot be met when the right to the number of shares to be delivered is contingent on *both* the exercise date of the instrument *and* equity prices or any other index.

EXAMPLE 20 – PATH-DEPENDENT OPTION

71.3.187.130   Company G issues a convertible bond containing a right for the holder to convert the bond into shares of the issuer. The number of shares received at each exercise date is dependent on the average share prices prevailing three months before the exercise date – i.e. a path-dependent option.

71.3.187.135   G concludes that the instrument does not meet the fixed-for-fixed requirement, because there is not only variability in the date of exercise but also variability in the actual number of shares that will be issued at each exercise date. In Example 19, even though there was variability in the date of exercise, such a contract represents a series of European-style option contracts that will each be settled by delivering a fixed amount of own shares for a fixed amount of cash.

71.3.187.140   Any consideration received or paid for an instrument that is classified as an equity instrument – e.g. the option premium – is added to or deducted from equity. [*IAS 32.22*]

7I.3.190   Obligation to purchase own equity instruments

7I.3.190.10   An instrument that creates an obligation or potential obligation for an entity to purchase its own equity instruments for cash or another financial asset (see 7I.3.50) gives rise to a financial liability. The amount of the liability is measured at the present value of the redemption amount. This is the case whether the exercise price is variable – e.g. based on a multiple of EBITDA – or fixed. A liability is recognised even if the contract itself is an equity instrument. Consequently, even if a contract entered into to purchase an entity's own equity instruments is classified as equity – i.e. a fixed amount of cash for a fixed number of equity instruments – an accounting entry is required to recognise a liability. The liability is accounted for at the present value of the redemption amount with a corresponding debit to equity. In effect, a reclassification is made from equity to reflect the obligation to repurchase the equity instruments in the future. If the contract expires without the obligation being settled – e.g. if a written put option expires unexercised – then the carrying amount of the liability at that time is reclassified to equity. For further discussion, see 7I.3.410. [*IAS 32.23*]

7I.3.190.20   This applies equally from a consolidated financial statements perspective to an (potential) obligation to purchase *a subsidiary's* equity instruments held by non-controlling shareholders because a subsidiary's equity constitutes the group's own equity in its consolidated financial statements. For a discussion of the subsequent accounting for changes in the carrying amount of liabilities resulting from forwards and put options over NCI, see 2.5.720. [*IAS 32.23, IFRS 10.22, IU 11-06*]

7I.3.190.30   However, in our view an obligation or potential obligation – either in the form of forward or option contracts – to purchase an associate's or a joint venture's equity instruments should be classified as a derivative in the separate, individual and/or consolidated financial statements of the investor. This is because associates and joint ventures are not part of the group (see 3.5.280).

7I.3.193   *Written put option to be settled in shares of parent*

7I.3.193.10   The discussion in this section considers three different scenarios in which non-controlling shareholders have a right to put the subsidiary's equity shares to the parent in exchange for equity shares of the parent.

7I.3.193.20   In Scenario 1, a subsidiary issues equity shares to non-controlling shareholders and a parent writes put options that give the non-controlling shareholders a right to put their equity shares in the subsidiary to the parent in exchange for a *fixed* number of the parent's equity shares. In this case, in the parent's consolidated financial statements, the option gives non-controlling shareholders a right to exchange a fixed number of one class of non-derivative own equity instruments for a fixed number of a different class of non-derivative own equity instruments. In our view, such a contract should be classified as equity (see 7I.3.187.20).

7I.3.193.30   In Scenario 2, a subsidiary issues equity shares to non-controlling shareholders and a parent writes put options that give the non-controlling shareholders the right to put their equity shares in the subsidiary to the parent in exchange for a *variable* number of the parent's equity shares. In this case, IAS 32 is not clear about how such instruments held by non-controlling shareholders should be classified in the parent's consolidated financial statements.

7I.3.193.40   In our view, an entity should choose one of the following accounting policies, to be applied consistently, to account for such instruments.

- *Approach 1:* Classify the subsidiary's shares held by non-controlling shareholders together with the put options as financial liabilities. Under this approach, in accordance with paragraph AG29 of IAS 32, taking into account all of the terms and conditions agreed between members of the group and the holders of the instrument, the subsidiary's shares are effectively considered to be non-derivative contracts – i.e. a contractual obligation for the parent to deliver a variable number of its own equity shares – and there is no separate accounting for the put options (see 7I.3.20.20 and 183.10).
- *Approach 2:* Account for the written put options separately as derivative liabilities. The basis of this approach is that the put option is a separate instrument and there is no obligation to deliver cash or another financial asset. Accordingly, the subsidiary's shares that are held by non-controlling interest holders are presented as equity reflecting existing ownership interests in the subsidiary and the put option is accounted for at FVTPL in accordance with IAS 39 (see 7I.3.187.10).

7I.3.193.45   The put options in Scenario 2 in 7I.3.193.30 may be written either together with the issuance of the shares to the non-controlling shareholders or subsequent to the issuance of these shares. When the put option is written subsequent to the issuance of the shares, under Approach 1 in 7I.3.193.40, a reclassification would be required such that a financial liability is recognised and measured at fair value at that date. Under Approach 2 in 7I.3.193.40, the put options are recognised as derivative liabilities regardless of the timing of their issuance.

7I.3.193.50   Modifying Scenario 2, assume that the parent also has an option to settle by paying cash rather than delivering its own equity shares when the non-controlling shareholders exercise the options and deliver their shares in the subsidiary to the parent. If the parent's accounting policy is to consider the combination of the shares and the written put options as financial liabilities (Approach 1 in 7I.3.193.40), then the existence of the parent's right to settle in cash does not affect its accounting treatment because the combination still represents a financial liability. However, if the parent's accounting policy is to account for the written put options separately (Approach 2 in 7I.3.193.40), then in our view the parent should also choose one of the following accounting policies, to be applied consistently, in respect of the written put options.

- *Recognise a financial liability for the present value of the exercise price:* Under this approach, the written put option is a separate instrument that gives rise to a financial liability for the present value of the exercise price in accordance with paragraph 23 of IAS 32. The put option represents an obligation to purchase own shares in the group for cash. In this case, there is an issue of how to account for the debit side of the transaction because NCI are initially recognised separately from the written put option. For further discussion of the accounting for the shares in the subsidiary held by the non-controlling shareholders, see 2.5.690.
- *Account for the written put options as derivative liabilities at FVTPL:* Under this approach, the shares held by the non-controlling shareholders are classified as equity. The related put options are accounted for as derivative liabilities under IAS 39 – i.e. at fair value with changes therein recognised in profit or loss. [*IAS 32.23, 26–27*]

7I.3.193.60   We believe that the accounting policy choice in 7I.3.193.50 arises because IAS 32 is not clear about the issuer's accounting for a written put option on its own equity instruments if it can avoid delivering cash or another financial asset (see 7I.3.210.40). [*IU 11-16*]

7I.3.193.70   To summarise the principles set out in 7I.3.193.10–60, the following table contains the various scenarios and the respective classifications in the parent's consolidated financial statements.

SCENARIO	CLASSIFICATION
Subsidiary issues equity shares to non-controlling shareholders. Parent writes put options that give the non-controlling shareholders a right to put their equity shares in the subsidiary to the parent in exchange for a *fixed* number of the parent's equity shares.	Classify the subsidiary's shares held by non-controlling shareholders together with the put options as equity.
Subsidiary issues equity shares to non-controlling shareholders. Parent writes put options that give the non-controlling shareholders the right to put their equity shares in the subsidiary to the parent in exchange for a *variable* number of the parent's equity shares.	*Approach 1:* Classify the subsidiary's shares held by non-controlling shareholders together with the put options as financial liabilities. *Approach 2:* Classify the subsidiary's shares held by non-controlling shareholders as equity. Account for the written put options separately as derivative liabilities.
Subsidiary issues equity shares to non-controlling shareholders. Parent writes put options that give the non-controlling shareholders the right to put their equity shares in the subsidiary to the parent in exchange for a *variable* number of the parent's equity shares. Parent also has an option to settle by paying cash rather than delivering its own equity shares.	*Approach 1:* Classify the subsidiary's shares held by non-controlling shareholders together with the put options as financial liabilities. *Approach 2a:* Recognise a financial liability for the present value of the exercise price. For further discussion of the accounting for the shares in the subsidiary held by the non-controlling shareholders, see 2.5.690. *Approach 2b:* Classify the subsidiary's shares held by non-controlling shareholders as equity. Account for the written put options separately as derivative liabilities.

7I.3.195   *Written put option to be settled in shares of another subsidiary*

7I.3.195.10   A put option granted to the non-controlling shareholders might give them a right to put their equity shares in a subsidiary to the parent in exchange for a *variable* number of equity shares of another subsidiary of the same parent. Assuming that settlement of the option does not lead to deconsolidation of the other subsidiary, in our view in its consolidated financial statements, the parent should choose an accounting policy, to be applied consistently, from the alternatives set out in 7I.3.193.40 – i.e. either to classify the subsidiary's shares together with the put options as financial liabilities or to account for the written put options as derivative liabilities.

7I.3.195.20   However, if a put option granted to the non-controlling shareholders gives them a right to put their equity shares in the subsidiary to the parent in exchange for a *fixed* number of equity shares of another subsidiary of the same parent, then in the parent's consolidated financial statements the option gives the non-controlling shareholders a right to exchange a fixed number of one class of non-derivative own equity instruments for a fixed number of a different class of non-derivative own equity instruments. In our view, such a contract should be classified as equity (see 7I.3.187.20).

7I.3.200   Contingent consideration in business combination

7I.3.200.10   Contingent consideration may be included in the consideration transferred in a business combination (see 2.6.280). IFRS 3 requires an obligation to pay contingent consideration to be classified as a liability or equity on the basis of the definitions of a financial liability and an equity instrument in paragraph 11 of IAS 32. That means that the obligation has to be to deliver a fixed number of shares in order for consideration that is settled in own equity instruments to be classified as equity. The subsequent accounting for the contingent consideration is dependent on this classification (see 2.6.1120). [*IFRS 3.40*]

7I.3.200.20   In our view, the existence of any contingency regarding whether a fixed number of own shares will be delivered does not necessarily disqualify the contingent consideration from equity classification. We believe that if one of the possible outcomes in respect of the contingency is the delivery of neither shares nor other consideration, then this does not in itself preclude equity classification. This is because the delivery of no consideration does not constitute a 'settlement'. For example, if the arrangement involved issuing either zero or a single fixed amount of equity shares, then the fixed-for-fixed criterion would be met. This is because the only way that settlement could take place would be by delivering a single fixed amount of shares.

7I.3.200.30   Also, in our view the classification analysis should be performed for an obligation to pay contingent consideration as referred to in IFRS 3 rather than for the entire contract. An entire-contract approach is not generally feasible, given that a contingent consideration arrangement is usually just one element of an overall sale-and-purchase agreement that governs all aspects of the business combination. We believe that a single business combination may involve more than one obligation to pay contingent consideration and that each obligation should be analysed separately for whether it is equity or liability. [*IFRS 3.40*]

7I.3.200.40   In our view, an entity should choose an accounting policy, to be applied consistently, to analyse such relationships under one of two approaches.
*   *Approach 1:* Obligations are separate when there is no necessary relationship between their outcomes or settlement (see 7I.3.200.43).
*   *Approach 2:* Obligations are separate only if there is no underlying causal relationship or significant correlation between their outcomes or settlement (see 7I.3.200.45).

7I.3.200.43   Under the first approach, one obligation is seen as separate from another obligation if there is no necessary relationship between the outcome or settlement of the obligations. For example, non-cumulative obligations to deliver shares based on different profit targets for different years may be seen as independent and therefore separate. This is because there is no necessary link between meeting the target for one year and meeting the target for another year. However, if there were an overlap between the periods, then the targets would not be independent.

7I.3.200.45   Under the second approach, an obligation is seen as separate from another obligation only if there is no underlying causal relationship or significant correlation between the outcome or settlement of the obligations. Therefore, if this policy is chosen, non-cumulative requirements to deliver shares based on different profit targets for different years are seen as a single obligation. This is because the underlying operational and economic factors that influence performance in one year will tend to influence performance in another year. For example, an entity's performance across a number of years may be influenced by the successful development of, or failure to develop, a new product line.

EXAMPLE 21 – CONTINGENT CONSIDERATION IN BUSINESS COMBINATION

7I.3.200.50   To illustrate the principles set out in 7I.3.200.40–45, the following table contains several scenarios and the respective classification assessments.

SCENARIO	CLASSIFICATION
The vendor receives shares in the acquirer to the value of 50 if the acquiree's cumulative profits over a three-year period are at least 20.	Liability, because there is a single obligation to deliver a variable number of shares.
The vendor receives 50 shares in the acquirer if the acquiree's cumulative profits over a three-year period are at least 20.	Equity, because there is a single obligation to deliver a fixed number of shares.
The vendor receives 50 shares in the acquirer if the acquiree's cumulative profits over a three-year period are at least 20, and 100 shares if profits are at least 40.	Liability, because the arrangement involves settling with either 50 or 100 shares – i.e. a variable rather than a fixed number. The profit targets relate to the same period, and therefore they are not independent.
The vendor will receive one share in the acquirer for every 1 of profit in excess of 10.	Liability; the analysis is similar to the preceding scenario except that the number of shares is more obviously variable.
Share-settled contingent consideration is payable in three tranches: 1,000 shares if an earnings target is achieved for year 1; 1,000 shares if an earnings target is achieved for year 2; and 1,000 shares if an earnings target is achieved for year 3. Each target relates to annual earnings of the acquiree and is non-cumulative.	The classification depends on the policy adopted as described in 7I.3.200.40–45. This may be considered three separate obligations to deliver a fixed 1,000 shares each (equity) or a single obligation to deliver 1,000, 2,000 or 3,000 shares (liability).

7I.3.210   **Settlement options in derivative instruments**

7I.3.210.10   A choice of the manner in which derivative financial instruments are settled – e.g. when the issuer or the holder could opt to settle net or gross – could determine their classification. IAS 32 states that a derivative financial instrument with settlement options is a financial asset or financial liability unless *all* of the settlement alternatives result in equity classification. Consequently, settlement options, even those that are at the discretion of the entity, could result in instruments being classified as financial assets or financial liabilities. [*IAS 32.26–27*]

EXAMPLE 22 – HOLDER SETTLEMENT OPTION

> **7I.3.210.15** Company K issues a warrant that gives the holder the right to acquire a fixed number of the issuer's own equity instruments for a fixed amount of cash. If the warrant expires unexercised, then the issuer will pay to the holder a fixed cancellation fee. K classifies the warrant as a financial liability because the holder may choose to receive cash or shares.

7I.3.210.17 The provisions in IAS 32 regarding settlement options apply only to derivative financial instruments. Therefore, if an instrument does not meet the definition of a derivative, then its classification as a liability or as equity depends on whether the entity has a contractual obligation to deliver cash or other financial assets, or to deliver a variable number of its own equity instruments (see 7I.3.20). [*IAS 32.11*]

EXAMPLE 23 – ISSUER SETTLEMENT OPTION

> **7I.3.210.18** Company H issues preference shares at par that are redeemable in five years and do not carry the right to receive dividends. At the end of five years H has the option to redeem the shares, either in a fixed number of its own shares or in cash at an amount that is equal to the fair value of the shares.
>
> **7I.3.210.20** Under the terms of the instrument, H does not have an obligation to transfer cash or another financial asset, or to deliver a variable number of its own shares (see 7I.3.183.30); nor does the entire instrument meet the definition of a derivative, because it fails the initial net investment criterion (see 7I.2.40). Therefore, the provisions regarding settlement options do not apply, and H classifies the instrument as equity.
>
> **7I.3.210.25** For a discussion of whether the issuer's option to settle in cash should be separated as an embedded derivative, see 7I.3.225.

7I.3.210.30 Additionally, settlement options could determine the manner in which certain derivative instruments are accounted for. An entity is required to recognise a liability for the present value of the redemption amount if the contract contains an obligation to purchase its own equity instruments for cash or another financial asset. When the contract allows the counterparty discretion to require gross physical settlement, a gross liability for the present value of the redemption amount is recorded. The option is at the counterparty's discretion and therefore the entity cannot avoid gross physical settlement – i.e. the obligation to purchase its own equity instrument for cash or another financial asset (see 7I.3.190). [*IAS 32.23, 26–27, IE6, IE31*]

7I.3.210.40 However, IAS 32 is not clear on the effect of settlement options in a derivative instrument allowing the issuer discretion to choose gross or net settlement of a contract to purchase its own equity instruments for cash or another financial asset – e.g. a forward to purchase or a written put option. Therefore, in our view an entity should choose an accounting policy, to be applied consistently, from the following alternatives.

- *Recognise a liability for the present value of the redemption amount:* According to the illustrative examples that accompany the standard, an entity should recognise a liability for the present value of the redemption amount if one of the settlement alternatives is to exchange cash for shares (gross physical settlement).
- *Apply derivative liability accounting in accordance with IAS 39:* Because the entity can choose net rather than gross settlement, it can avoid the obligation to purchase its own equity instruments for cash or another financial asset (see 7I.3.190). [*IAS 32.23, 26–27, IE6, IE31*]

7I.3.220   Discretionary payments – Dividends and other payments

7I.3.220.10   A contractual requirement to pay dividends is an obligation to deliver cash; therefore, it gives rise to a financial liability. This does not change, even if the agreement to pay is conditional on the entity earning sufficient distributable profits; a restriction on the ability of an entity to satisfy a contractual obligation does not negate this obligation (see 7I.3.30). [*IAS 32.19(a), 25, AG25*]

7I.3.220.20   Dividends or other payments may be discretionary – i.e. there is no obligation to pay. For example, in many jurisdictions dividends on ordinary shares vary depending on the level of profitability; the entity can decide whether to pay dividends, and how much to pay. Although there may be an expectation that dividends will be paid if a certain level of profitability is achieved, this expectation is not a contractual obligation. Therefore, the entity is able to avoid the transfer of cash or another financial asset. [*IAS 32.19*]

7I.3.220.30   Generally, when preference shares are non-redeemable, the appropriate classification is determined by the other rights that attach to them – in particular, distributions to holders. If the dividends are cumulative, then this suggests that the issuer may delay but cannot avoid the payment of dividends. However, if the issuer can choose to avoid the payment of dividends under all circumstances until liquidation of the entity, then the dividends are discretionary and do not give rise to an obligation. For example, if a non-redeemable preference share has a cumulative dividend, but payment is discretionary until liquidation and there are no other features that would lead to liability classification, then the instrument is classified as equity (see 7I.3.310.10). [*IAS 32.AG26*]

7I.3.220.40   If preference shares are redeemable and dividends are discretionary, then the issuer considers whether unpaid dividends are added to the redemption amount of the preference shares. If any unpaid dividends are added to the redemption amount and the entity does not have the unconditional ability to avoid redemption before liquidation, then the dividends are not in substance discretionary and the entire instrument including the discretionary dividend feature is a financial liability. Furthermore, if an entity is or may be obliged to redeem the instrument at fair value, then in our view unpaid dividends are implicitly added to the redemption amount if the payment of dividends decreases the fair value of the instrument being redeemed. Similarly, if an issuer of a puttable instrument is or may be obliged to repurchase the instrument at any time at an amount equal to a pro rata share of net assets, then we believe that unpaid dividends are implicitly added to the redemption amount if the payment of dividends decreases the amount of the entity's net assets and the amount that the entity is obliged to pay increases as a result of non-payment of dividends. [*IAS 32.AG37*]

7I.3.220.50   There is an issue about whether to present discretionary dividends in profit or loss or equity if all of the fair value of the consideration received on issuing instruments with a discretionary dividend feature is allocated to and recognised as a financial liability. In principle, discretionary dividends may always be considered an equity feature, because an entity does not have a contractual obligation to deliver cash or another financial asset. However, when all of the fair value of the consideration received on issuing instruments is allocated to and recognised as a financial liability, IAS 32 is not clear about whether:

- discretionary dividends are presented in equity because, in principle, discretionary dividends are always an equity feature irrespective of whether any amount is allocated to equity; or
- discretionary dividends are presented in profit or loss because dividend payments on an instrument wholly recognised as a liability are recognised as an expense (see 7I.3.20.140). [*IAS 32.36, AG37*]

7I.3.220.60 Based on the reasoning in 7I.3.220.50 and subject to the guidance in 7I.3.220.40, in our view an entity should choose an accounting policy, to be applied consistently, to present the discretionary dividends in profit or loss or equity if none (or no more than a trivial amount) of the fair value of the consideration received on issuing instruments with a discretionary dividend feature is allocated to and recognised as equity.

7I.3.220.70 The following flowchart shows the assessment required to determine whether discretionary dividends should be presented in profit or loss or equity.

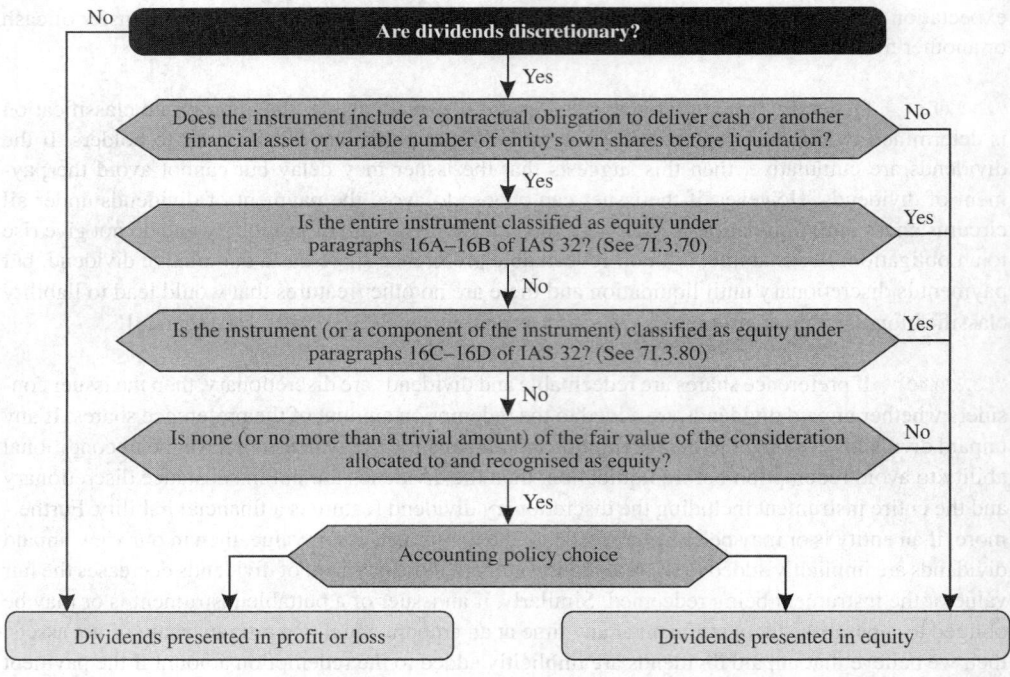

7I.3.220.80 In our view, a similar assessment to that described in 7I.3.220.50–70 applies to the assessment of the presentation of discretionary dividends on NCI shares subject to a put option written by the entity. If an entity chooses to apply the anticipated-acquisition method to account for NCI subject to a put option written by the entity, then the NCI are accounted for as if the put option had already been exercised. In this case, the NCI are derecognised and a financial liability is recognised for the present value of the redemption amount in the consolidated financial statements (see 2.5.700). Subject to the guidance in 7I.3.220.40, we believe that an entity should choose an accounting policy from the alternatives described in 7I.3.220.50–60, to be applied consistently to the presentation of discretionary dividends on NCI shares subject to a put option written by the entity. We believe that these accounting policy choices are available only if the subsequent changes in NCI put liabilities are recognised in profit or loss (see 2.5.700.40).

7I.3.220.90   The following flowchart shows the assessment required to determine whether discretionary dividends on NCI shares subject to a put option written by the entity should be presented in profit or loss or equity.

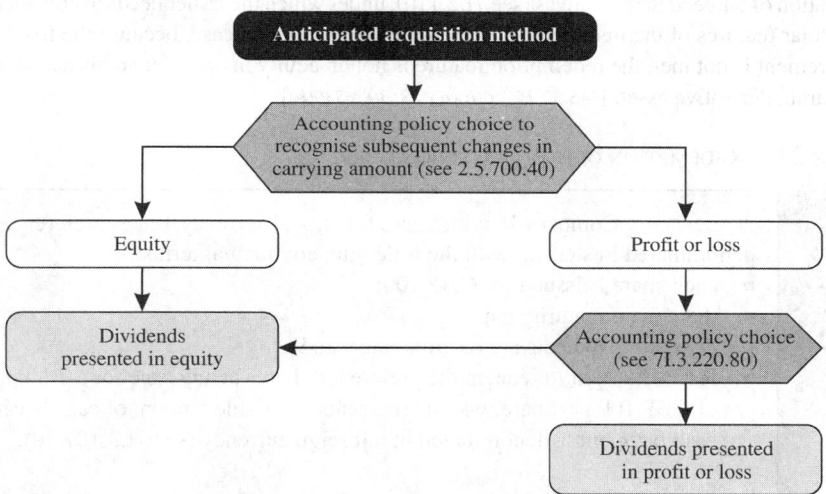

7I.3.220.100   We believe that the accounting policy choice described in 7I.3.220.80 is not available if the present-access method is applied to account for NCI, because the NCI continues to be recognised as equity when the put option is written. Discretionary dividends are paid on the NCI recognised as equity in the consolidated financial statements (see 2.5.710.10–20).

7I.3.225   Issuer's option to settle in cash

7I.3.225.10   An issuer's option to redeem a non-derivative equity instrument by delivering cash does not cause the instrument to be classified as a financial liability because the issuer does not have a contractual obligation to deliver cash or to deliver a variable number of its own shares under the instrument (see 7I.3.183.30). [*IAS 32.16, AG25, IU 09-13*]

7I.3.225.20   However, if the issuer of such an equity instrument has an option to redeem it by delivering a variable amount of cash, and therefore the fixed-for-fixed requirement is not met for this feature (see 7I.3.187.10), then a question arises about whether the whole instrument should be considered as an equity instrument or whether the issuer's option to redeem the instrument is an embedded derivative that should be separated.

7I.3.225.25   In our view, an entity should choose one of the following accounting policies, to be applied consistently, to account for such redemption options.

- *Account for the whole instrument as an equity instrument without separating the redemption option:* Under this approach, such a redemption option is not accounted for as an embedded derivative, but is considered part of the equity instrument. This is because the redemption option is already considered in determining that the entire instrument is a non-derivative equity instrument. In addition, discretionary payment features – such as discretionary dividends – are not usually separated from a non-derivative equity instrument but instead are considered an integral component of the instrument.
- *Separate the redemption option as an embedded derivative asset:* This approach is based on the guidance on compound financial instruments (see 7I.3.230) and the guidance in IAS 39 on the separation of embedded derivatives (see 7I.2.110), under which the issuer needs to consider whether particular features of the instrument should be separated. In this case, because the fixed-for-fixed requirement is not met, the redemption feature is not an equity instrument and is accounted for as a separate derivative asset. [*IAS 32.15, 16(b)(ii), 28, 39.AG30(b)*]

EXAMPLE 24 – REDEMPTION OPTION IN FOREIGN CURRENCY

7I.3.225.30   Company R, with a euro functional currency, issues preference shares denominated in sterling with the following contractual terms:

- each share is issued for GBP 100;
- there is no maturity date;
- dividend payments are discretionary; and
- R has the right to redeem the preference shares at any time for a cash payment of GBP 100 per share, which represents a variable amount of cash because the cash payment is denominated in a foreign currency (see 7I.3.187.30).

7I.3.225.40   The preference shares meet the definition of an equity instrument because R does not have a contractual obligation to deliver cash or to deliver a variable number of its own shares. For the cash redemption option, we believe that R should choose an accounting policy, to be applied consistently, from the approaches discussed in 7I.3.225.20–25 to either:

- account for the preference shares in their entirety as equity; or
- separate its option to redeem the shares in cash as an embedded derivative because the redemption amount is in a foreign currency and therefore the option does not meet the fixed-for-fixed requirement (see 7I.3.187.30 and 270). Therefore, R recognises the amount of the consideration equal to the fair value of the redemption option on initial recognition as a derivative asset. Subsequently, R measures the derivative at fair value with changes therein included in profit or loss.

7I.3.230   Compound instruments

7I.3.230.10   An instrument may contain both a financial liability (e.g. an obligation to make interest and/or scheduled principal payments) and an equity component (e.g. a conversion feature in a convertible bond). Such an instrument is a compound instrument. [*IAS 32.29, AG31*]

7I.3.230.20   The issuer of non-derivative compound instruments classifies the liability and equity components of the instrument separately as a financial liability and equity ('split accounting'). Components of compound instruments are analysed and classified in accordance with the basic classification principles in 7I.3.20. [*IAS 32.28*]

7I.3.230.30   A typical form of a compound instrument is a convertible bond, in which the holder is entitled to convert the instrument into equity instruments of the entity. Another form of compound instrument is one in which the equity characteristics lie in the dividend or interest stream rather than in the convertibility of the principal amount. For example, consider a non-cumulative mandatorily redeemable preference share, on which dividends are payable at the discretion of the issuer. In this case, the present value of the redemption amount represents the financial liability, with any remaining proceeds being attributed to equity. [*IAS 32.AG31*]

7I.3.230.40   The same split accounting applies to share purchase warrants attached to debt instruments, irrespective of whether they are formally detachable from the debt instruments. The share purchase warrants are split and accounted for as an equity component by the issuer if the warrants meet the definition of an equity instrument. In this case, the amount allocable to the debt instrument is determined first, with any remaining proceeds being attributed to the warrants. [*IAS 32.31*]

7I.3.230.50   Subject to 7I.3.20.160, the initial classification of a convertible instrument into its liability and equity components is not revised subsequent to initial recognition – even if the likelihood of the conversion option being exercised changes over time. However, a reclassification may be required in certain circumstances (see 7I.3.290 and 390). [*IAS 32.30*]

7I.3.230.60   For a discussion of the measurement of the financial liability and equity components of a compound financial instrument, see 7I.3.330.

7I.3.240   *Accounting for early redemption*

7I.3.240.10   On early redemption of a convertible instrument, the redemption payment is allocated to the liability and equity components. The method used is consistent with that used initially to allocate the instrument between its debt and equity components (see 7I.3.330). The fair value of the liability component at the redemption date is compared with its carrying amount, giving rise to a gain or loss on redemption that is recognised in profit or loss. The remainder of the redemption payment is recognised in equity. [*IAS 32.AG33*]

7I.3.250   *Accounting for conversion*

7I.3.250.10   On conversion of a convertible instrument that is a compound instrument at maturity, the entity derecognises the liability component that is extinguished when the conversion feature is exercised and recognises the same amount as equity. The original equity component remains as equity, although it may be transferred within equity (see 7I.3.550). No gain or loss is recognised in profit or loss. [*IAS 32.AG32*]

7I.3.250.20   If the conversion feature is an American-style option that can be exercised before the redemption date, then a question arises about whether to derecognise the liability component based on its carrying amount (e.g. amortised cost based on the stated maturity ignoring the conversion option) at the time of early conversion, or to derecognise the liability component after remeasuring it to the redemption amount at conversion.

7I.3.250.22 Under the first approach, the carrying amount of the liability on conversion (e.g. amortised cost based on the stated maturity ignoring the conversion option) is reclassified to equity and no gain or loss is recognised on conversion (see 7I.3.250.10). Under the second approach, the liability is remeasured to the redemption amount at conversion, with additional interest expense being recognised in profit or loss under paragraph AG8 of IAS 39, because it is considered a prepayment of the liability component (see 7I.6.260.10).

7I.3.250.24 In our view, the first approach is appropriate because this conversion in effect represents a conversion at maturity, because of the way the American-style option operates. The financial liability component should be accounted for as a non-prepayable liability, and an American-style equity option recognised in equity. Consequently, we believe that there is no prepayment feature in the liability that leads to the recognition of a gain or loss arising from the revision of cash flow estimates (see 7I.6.260.10).

7I.3.250.26 However, a gain or loss may arise when convertible instruments contain embedded derivatives (see also 7I.3.280.50). If a convertible bond contains a prepayment feature that enables the issuer to call the bond and the prepayment feature has not been separately accounted for as a derivative, then in our view when the issuer announces its intention to exercise the call option it should recognise a catch-up adjustment to the amortised cost accounting for the financial liability under paragraph AG8 of IAS 39 (see 7I.6.260.10).

7I.3.250.28 We believe that the requirements for early redemption (see 7I.3.240) do not apply because they address situations in which convertible debt is bought back not under the terms inherent in the instrument (call option) but instead through agreement between the issuer and holder to buy back at fair value without using any options embedded in the instrument – e.g. tender offers.

EXAMPLE 25A – CONVERTIBLE BOND WITH AMERICAN-STYLE OPTION

7I.3.250.30 Company B issues a 10-year convertible bond that is convertible at any time after five years at the option of the holder (an American-style option). If the bond is not converted, then the par amount is repayable on maturity after 10 years. The conversion feature is classified at inception as equity, because it meets the fixed-for-fixed requirement (see 7I.3.187.10). The host debt instrument is measured at amortised cost.

7I.3.250.40 A question arises about whether to derecognise the liability component based on its amortised cost carrying amount at the time of early conversion, or to derecognise the liability component after remeasuring it to the par amount at conversion.

7I.3.250.50 We believe that such conversion in effect represents a conversion at maturity. This is because the bond does not have a fixed maturity of 10 years, because of the way the American-style option operates. Consequently, we believe that there is no prepayment feature in the liability that leads to the recognition of a gain or loss arising from the revision of cash flow estimates.

> 7I.3.250.60   The conversion arises from the exercise of the equity conversion option, which is an American-style option recognised in equity and not remeasured through profit or loss under IAS 32. Therefore, we believe that no gain or loss should be recognised in profit or loss on conversion of the bond.

EXAMPLE 25B – CONVERTIBLE BOND WITH AMERICAN-STYLE OPTION AND ISSUER PREPAYMENT OPTION

> 7I.3.250.70   Modifying Example 25A, the convertible bond contains a prepayment feature that enables the issuer to call the bond at any time after five years at par. However, the holder still has the option to exercise its conversion right during a short period following the announcement of the issuer to call the bond. The prepayment option is not accounted for separately if it is closely related to the host liability contract (see 7I.2.240).
>
> 7I.3.250.75   We believe that when the issuer announces its intention to exercise the call option it should recognise a catch-up adjustment to the amortised cost accounting under paragraph AG8 of IAS 39 (see 7I.6.260.10). This is because, in contrast to Example 25A, the issuer's call option is separate from the holder's conversion option. If the holder does not exercise the conversion option, then the conversion option is extinguished.
>
> 7I.3.250.77   If the holder exercises the conversion option, then the liability component should be converted to equity. No gain or loss should be recognised in profit or loss on conversion or redemption because the carrying amount of the liability component has already been adjusted to the par amount before conversion or redemption.

7I.3.250.80   In both Examples 25A and 25B, the carrying amount of the liability component at conversion is reclassified to equity on exercise of the conversion option. However, in Example 25A the carrying amount of the liability component is less than the par amount at the conversion date; in Example 25B, the carrying amount of the liability component is adjusted to par under paragraph AG8 of IAS 39 before conversion, with an impact on profit or loss.

7I.3.260   *Amendment to induce early conversion*

7I.3.260.10   An entity may amend the terms of a convertible instrument to induce early conversion – e.g. by offering a more favourable conversion ratio in the event of conversion before a specified date. When the terms are amended, the issuer recognises in profit or loss the difference between:

- the fair value of the consideration that the holder receives on conversion of the instrument under the revised terms; and
- the fair value of the consideration that the holder would have received under the original terms.
[*IAS 32.AG35*]

7I.3.270   **Foreign currency convertible bond**

7I.3.270.10   If a convertible bond is denominated in a currency other than the functional currency of the entity, then an issue arises regarding the classification of the conversion option.

7I.3.270.15   As discussed in 7I.3.187.60, an obligation denominated in a foreign currency represents a variable amount of cash. Contracts, both freestanding and embedded, that will be settled by an entity delivering a fixed number of its own equity instruments in exchange for a fixed amount of foreign currency are classified as financial assets or financial liabilities. [*IAS 32.BC4K*]

EXAMPLE 26 – FOREIGN CURRENCY CONVERTIBLE BOND

7I.3.270.20   Company G with a euro functional currency issues a convertible bond denominated in US dollars. The bond carries a fixed rate of interest and is convertible at the end of 10 years, at the holder's option, into a fixed number of euro-denominated shares of G. No settlement alternative is provided to the issuer.

7I.3.270.25   The conversion option is an obligation for G to issue a fixed number of shares in exchange for a variable amount of cash. The cash is fixed in US dollar terms but variable in functional currency terms. Therefore, G classifies the conversion feature in the convertible bond as a derivative liability.

7I.3.270.30   A related issue arises if a convertible bond denominated in a foreign currency is issued by a subsidiary that has a functional currency different from that of its parent, and that bond is convertible into the shares of the parent. The IFRS Interpretations Committee discussed a similar issue and noted that a group does not have a functional currency (see 2.7.70.20). In our view, two approaches are possible in the consolidated financial statements. We believe that an entity should choose an accounting policy, to be applied consistently, to base the classification in the consolidated financial statements on the functional currency of either the parent or the subsidiary. [*IU 11-06*]

7I.3.270.40   In addition, in our view:
- if the bond is denominated in a currency other than the functional currency of either the parent or the subsidiary, then the conversion feature is a (derivative) liability;
- the currency in which the shares are denominated is not relevant to the analysis: the only requirement is that the number of shares is fixed; and
- the presentation currency or currencies of the group's consolidated financial statements (see 2.7.40) has no impact on the analysis.

7I.3.270.50   Another issue arises in cases of inflation indexation. For example, an entity issues a convertible bond denominated in its functional currency. Both principal and interest payments of the instrument are indexed to changes in the CPI inflation of the economic environment of the entity. In our view, such indexation creates variability in the amount of cash being exchanged for a fixed number of shares and therefore the conversion feature should be classified as a financial liability. This principle applies even if the functional currency of the entity is the currency of a hyperinflationary economy (see chapter 2.10).

7I.3.280   Cash settlement option in convertible bond

7I.3.280.10   Many convertible bonds include a cash settlement option for the issuer if the holder exercises its right to convert the bonds into ordinary shares. For example, an entity with a euro functional currency issues euro-denominated fixed rate bonds with a 20-year maturity; the holder has the option to convert these into a fixed number of the issuer's ordinary shares at any time during the life of the bond. If the holder exercises its conversion option, then the issuer has the right to settle either:

- by delivering a fixed number of shares; or
- in cash at an amount equal to the market value of the shares to be issued.

7I.3.280.20   Generally, a convertible bond is a compound instrument – i.e. having characteristics of both equity and a liability. In the example in 7I.3.280.10 the convertible bond comprises the following features, which are clearly characteristics associated with a financial liability:

- an obligation to make fixed interest payments; and
- an obligation to deliver cash to the holder on redemption of the bond in the event of the holder not exercising its conversion option.

7I.3.280.30   In addition, the instrument contains a conversion feature whereby there may be an exchange of a fixed number of shares for a fixed amount of cash. The issuer can settle the conversion option either by paying the holder the market value of the shares in cash, or by exchanging its own shares for cash – i.e. physical delivery. Consequently, the conversion option can be settled other than by the issuer exchanging a fixed number of shares for a fixed amount of cash. [*IAS 32.26*]

7I.3.280.40   Because the conversion option is a derivative, the settlement option causes it to be classified as a financial liability instead of as an equity instrument. Therefore, in this case the convertible bond is not a compound instrument under IAS 32. Rather, it is a hybrid instrument comprising a host liability for the interest and principal amount plus an embedded derivative instrument for the conversion option (see also 7I.3.210). The host liability is measured at amortised cost and the derivative, not being closely related to the host, is measured at FVTPL; alternatively, the entire instrument is measured at FVTPL (see 7I.4.70). For a discussion of the accounting for embedded derivatives, see 7I.2.110.

7I.3.280.50   In our view, in contrast to the accounting for conversion of a compound instrument (see 7I.3.250.10), an entity should choose an accounting policy, to be applied consistently to all reclassifications from financial liability to equity because of a change in the effective terms when the contractual terms of the instrument have not changed, including for example the conversion of a hybrid instrument that is classified entirely as a financial liability. For a description of the acceptable accounting policies, see 7I.3.410.40.

7I.3.290   Restructuring a convertible bond

7I.3.290.10   Continuing the example in 7I.3.280.10–40, the issuer might restructure the convertible bond by removing the cash settlement alternative in the conversion option. As a result, the issuer would have a contract that requires it to physically deliver a fixed number of shares in exchange for a fixed amount of the bond on exercise by the holder. Such a contract meets the definition of an equity instrument, and so the conversion option is classified as such. However, the restructuring would not fall in the scope of IFRIC 19, because the entity does not issue equity instruments to extinguish the derivative component (see 7I.3.380 and 7I.5.410).

7I.3.290.20   However, concluding that the restructured conversion option should be presented as equity is only the first step in accounting for the restructuring.

7I.3.290.30   An entity also needs to consider whether the restructuring is deemed a significant modification of the terms of the bond, resulting in it being accounted for as a debt extinguishment (see 7I.5.380).

7I.3.290.40   IAS 39 provides specific guidance when there is a modification in the cash flows of a debt instrument (see 7I.5.380). However, when the terms of the conversion option are revised, there is no such cash flow effect. In such circumstances, in our view the impact of the modification from the holder's perspective should be considered.

7I.3.290.45   Consider a convertible bond with a cash settlement option for the issuer if the holder exercises its right to convert the bonds into ordinary shares. If the holder exercises its conversion option, then the issuer has the right to settle either:
- by delivering a fixed number of shares; or
- in cash at an amount equal to the market value of the shares to be issued.

7I.3.290.48   The holder might receive cash directly from the issuer at an amount equal to the market value of the shares, instead of receiving the shares and converting them into cash. The amount of cash accruing to the holder with or without the cash settlement option is almost the same. Consequently, removal of the cash settlement option does not in our view represent a substantial modification of the bond. As a result, the restructuring does not lead to the derecognition or extinguishment of the 'original' convertible bond and the recognition of a 'new' convertible bond. [*IAS 39.AG62*]

7I.3.290.50   However, the restructuring does result in the extinguishment of the derivative component, because it is exchanged for an equity component (see 7I.3.400.20). From the holder's perspective, this is an exchange of financial assets. However, because there is no cash transfer in the transaction, the consideration paid will usually be the fair value of the instrument received – i.e. the new conversion option without a cash settlement feature. Because the fair value of the 'old' conversion option is almost identical at the date of the restructuring to the fair value of the 'new' conversion option (see 7I.3.290.60), no significant gain or loss arises.

7I.3.290.60   From the issuer's perspective, the 'old' conversion option would have been measured at FVTPL until the restructuring of the convertible bond. At the date of restructuring, the derivative component is derecognised and a new instrument is recognised in equity at fair value – assuming that the fair value of both options is the same.

7I.3.300   Perpetual instruments

7I.3.300.10   Perpetual debt instruments normally provide the holder with a contractual right to receive an indefinite stream of interest payments at a market rate of interest, with no redemption of principal. Even though the holder will not receive repayment of the principal, such instruments are a liability of the issuer because there is a contractual obligation to make a stream of future interest payments to the holder. Assuming that the terms of the instrument are at the market rate, the face value or the carrying amount of the instrument reflects the present value of the holder's right to receive these interest payments in perpetuity. [*IAS 32.AG6*]

7I.3.310 Preference shares

7I.3.310.10 Preference shares that provide for redemption at the option of the holder give rise to a contractual obligation and are therefore classified as financial liabilities. If preference shares are not redeemable at the option of the holder, then the appropriate classification depends on the other terms and conditions associated with such shares – in particular, the attached dividend rights. If dividends are discretionary, then this fact supports the classification of the preference shares as equity instruments. If dividends are not discretionary, then they represent a contractual obligation, and the instrument is classified as a financial liability of the issuer (see also 7I.3.220.30). [*IAS 32.AG25–AG26*]

7I.3.310.20 A typical example of a cumulative perpetual preference share is one with the following characteristics:
- the issuer has an obligation to pay dividends on preference shares only if it pays dividends on its ordinary shares; and
- the preference dividends are cumulative.

7I.3.310.30 The fact that dividends are payable only if ordinary dividends, which are discretionary, are paid ('dividend stopper feature') does not create an obligation. However, because of the cumulative feature, the instrument is classified as equity only if:
- the accumulated dividends can be deferred indefinitely – i.e. until liquidation of the entity; and
- there is no other feature of the instrument that would lead to financial liability classification (see also 7I.3.40.90–93). [*IAS 32.25*]

7I.3.310.40 The terms of certain preference shares provide for the accrual of interest on cumulative discretionary dividends even before such dividends are declared. In other words, interest accrues from the point in time at which the dividend *might* have been declared, such that if the dividend is declared, then an amount of interest becomes payable automatically. In our view, the accrual of interest alone does not cause such dividends to give rise to a contractual obligation to deliver cash or another financial asset as long as the dividends remain discretionary – i.e. the entity can avoid the payment of both dividends and interest on unpaid dividends until liquidation of the entity.

7I.3.310.50 A preference dividend in which payment is contingent on the availability of future distributable profits differs from a discretionary dividend. With a discretionary dividend, the issuer is able to avoid the payment of dividends indefinitely. However, the payment of a contingent dividend cannot be avoided indefinitely (see also 7I.3.40). The fact that the issuer might currently be unable to pay the dividend has no bearing on its classification. Consequently, contingent dividends are classified as a liability. [*IAS 32.25*]

EXAMPLE 27A – PREFERENCE SHARES – SEPARATE FINANCIAL STATEMENTS

7I.3.310.60 Company K issues preference shares with the following contractual terms:
- the shares are redeemable at the option of the issuer, at a fixed redemption price of 100 per share plus any accrued unpaid dividends;

- there is no fixed redemption date – i.e. the holder has no right to demand repayment at a certain date; and
- the payment of dividends is at the discretion of the issuer. However, K is required to pay dividends if its parent pays dividends on its ordinary shares.

7I.3.310.63 Therefore, in this example the payment of dividends is contingent on the occurrence of an uncertain future event that is beyond the control of both the issuer and the holder of the instrument.

7I.3.310.65 Consequently, K recognises a financial liability. In substance, this instrument is a perpetual instrument with variable contingent dividend payments. Therefore, the amount of the initial investment represents the expected value of the variable contingent dividend payments, which are classified as a liability.

EXAMPLE 27B – PREFERENCE SHARES – CONSOLIDATED FINANCIAL STATEMENTS

7I.3.310.70 The classification of the instrument in Example 27A would be different in the consolidated financial statements of the parent if the payment of dividends at the consolidated level were at the discretion of the parent (see 7I.3.20.170).

7I.3.320 RECOGNITION AND MEASUREMENT

7I.3.320.10 IFRS does not have any specific measurement rules related to equity, other than in respect of:
- splitting compound instruments (see 7I.3.330.10);
- the cost of equity transactions (see 7I.3.490); and
- own equity instruments acquired and reissued or cancelled (see 7I.3.430.10).

7I.3.320.15 In part this is because the financial instruments standards do not generally apply to own equity. [*IAS 39.2(d)*]

7I.3.320.20 As a general principle, the definitions of income and expenses exclude transactions with holders of equity instruments. Therefore, no gains or losses are reported in profit or loss on transactions in equity instruments. All of the effects of transactions with owners are recognised directly in equity. However, certain derivatives on own equity, when they do not meet the definition of equity, will be treated as derivative assets or liabilities and will result in gains and losses recognised in profit or loss (see 7I.6.120).

7I.3.320.30 The recognition and measurement requirements for equity instruments that are issued in share-based payment transactions are specified by IFRS 2 (see chapter 4.5).

7I.3.330 Compound instruments

7I.3.330.10 When allocating the initial carrying amount of a compound instrument to the underlying financial liability and equity components, an entity first determines the fair value of the liability component. This includes any embedded derivatives – whether or not they have to be accounted for separately. The fair value of the liability component is determined with reference to the fair value of a similar stand-alone debt instrument (including any embedded non-equity derivatives). The amount allocated to the equity component is the residual amount after deducting the fair value of the financial liability component from the fair value of the entire compound instrument. For a discussion of the recognition of deferred tax liabilities on compound financial instruments, see 3.13.250. [*IAS 32.31–32*]

EXAMPLE 28 – ALLOCATING PROCEEDS OF ISSUED BOND TO COMPONENTS

7I.3.330.20   Company Y issues 2,000 convertible bonds at the start of year 1. The bonds have a three-year term and are issued at par with a face value of 1,000 per bond, giving total proceeds of 2,000,000. The bonds have the following contractual terms:
- interest is payable annually in arrears at a nominal annual interest rate of 6%; and
- each bond is convertible at any time until maturity into 250 ordinary shares.

7I.3.330.25   When the bonds are issued, the prevailing market interest rate for a similar liability without a conversion option is 9%.

7I.3.330.30   The present value of the financial liability component is calculated using a discount rate of 9% (the market interest rate for similar bonds having no conversion rights).

Present value of the principal – 2,000,000 payable at the end of three years	1,544,367
Present value of the interest – 120,000 (2,000,000 x 6%) payable annually in arrears for three years	303,755
Total liability component	1,848,122
Equity component (balancing figure)	151,878
Proceeds of the bond issue	2,000,000

7I.3.330.40   Coupon accruals and the unwinding of the discount are accounted for as interest expense. However, when dividends are declared post-conversion of the bonds, these relate to the equity component and are presented in equity as a distribution of profits.

7I.3.340   **Share splits and bonus issues**

7I.3.340.10   In the case of a simple split of shares or a bonus issue, IFRS does not require any adjustment to total equity or to individual components of equity presented in the financial statements, although they may affect basic and diluted EPS (see 5.3.530). However, the laws of the country of incorporation may require a reallocation of capital within equity.

7I.3.340.20   There is no guidance in IFRS on whether a share dividend should be treated as a share split or bonus issue. For a discussion of the treatment of share dividends, see 7I.3.600.90 and 7I.6.720.

_{7I.3.350} **Prepaid capital contributions**

_{7I.3.350.10} Shareholders may pay for shares before they are issued. An issue then arises about whether the prepayment should be recognised directly in equity or shown as a liability.

_{7I.3.350.20} If there is any possibility that the entity may be required to repay the amount received – e.g. if the share issue is conditional on uncertain future events – then in our view the amount received should be shown as a liability. However, if there is no possibility of the prepayment being refunded, so that the entity's obligation is to deliver only a fixed number of shares, then in our view the amount should be credited to a separate category of equity – e.g. a prepaid share reserve. The notes to the financial statements should disclose the prepayment and the terms of the shares to be issued.

_{7I.3.360} **Receivables in respect of equity contributions**

_{7I.3.360.10} An entity may be owed an amount:
- in respect of a contribution for new equity shares that have already been issued; or
- as an equity contribution for which no new shares will be issued (see 7I.3.370).

_{7I.3.360.15} In this case, an issue arises about when the equity should be recognised.

_{7I.3.360.20} In our view, the equity and a corresponding receivable should be recognised if the receivable meets the definition of a financial asset. This requires the entity to have a contractual right to receive the amount at the reporting date. A 'contractual right' is more than an informal agreement or a non-contractual commitment.

_{7I.3.360.30} If the shareholder is not committed contractually to making the contribution at the reporting date, then no receivable is recorded in respect of the transaction.

_{7I.3.360.40} If a receivable is recognised but payment is not expected in the short term, then the amount is discounted and recorded, in both equity and receivables, at the present value of the amount to be received; unwinding of the discount on the receivable is accounted for as interest income (see 7I.6.230).

_{7I.3.360.50} An entity might decide to increase its share capital through a shareholders' resolution to issue new shares. However, in certain jurisdictions this does not establish a contractual right for the entity to receive cash or another financial asset; nor does it contractually bind the shareholders. In our view, unless and until there is a contractual right and the new shares are issued or outstanding, no receivable or outstanding shares should be recognised with respect to the transaction.

_{7I.3.370} **Non-reciprocal capital contributions**

_{7I.3.370.10} Sometimes an entity receives amounts from shareholders in the form of capital contributions, being either cash or other non-monetary assets, which are non-reciprocal – i.e. no financial or non-financial obligation exists. This may happen, for example, when an entity requires additional financing or is in financial difficulty. Amounts might be received from all shareholders or only certain shareholders. For a discussion in the context of NCI, see 2.5.520.

_{7I.3.370.20} IFRS does not contain any specific guidance on transactions with shareholders. However, in applying the definitions of financial liabilities and equity, in our view the amount received should be accounted for in accordance with its substance.

- If there is any possibility of having to repay the amount received, then a liability should be recognised for the advance.
- If there is no requirement to repay the amount under any circumstances and any repayment would be entirely at the discretion of the entity that receives the contribution, then the economic substance will normally be an equity contribution and not income; this is because the shareholder is generally acting in its capacity as a shareholder in such cases. In our experience, it is highly unlikely that an entity would receive a non-reciprocal capital contribution from an unrelated third party.

7I.3.370.30   If the amount is classified as equity, then the sub-classification within equity will be determined by the legal framework in which the entity operates. The legal framework may require or permit classification as additional paid-in capital, share premium and/or as a separate reserve – e.g. 'contributed assets'.

7I.3.370.40   The recognition criteria for receivables in respect of equity transactions (see 7I.3.360) should be applied in determining when a non-reciprocal capital contribution is recognised.

7I.3.370.50   If a shareholder forgives debt, then it is likely that:
- the shareholder is acting in its capacity as a shareholder; and
- the forgiveness of debt should be treated as a capital transaction (see 7I.5.390.20).

7I.3.380   Extinguishing financial liabilities with equity instruments

7I.3.380.10   A debtor and a creditor may renegotiate the terms of a financial liability with the result that the debtor extinguishes the liability fully or partially by issuing equity instruments to the creditor – i.e. a debt-for-equity swap. IFRIC 19 addresses the accounting by the debtor in a debt-for-equity swap transaction (see 7I.5.410). [*IFRIC 19.1*]

7I.3.390   RECLASSIFICATION OF INSTRUMENTS BETWEEN LIABILITY AND EQUITY

7I.3.390.10   The following discussion of reclassification (see 7I.3.390–410) applies to reclassifications of an instrument or its component parts between financial liability and equity and vice versa, with the exception of:
- puttable instruments (see 7I.3.170);
- instruments that impose on the entity an obligation to deliver to another party a pro rata share of the net assets of the entity only on liquidation (see 7I.3.170); and
- compound instruments on conversion at maturity (see 7I.3.250).

7I.3.390.20   As discussed in 7I.3.20.160, the classification of an instrument, or its component parts, as either a financial liability or equity is made on initial recognition and is not generally revised as a result of subsequent changes in circumstances. However, a reclassification between financial liability and equity or vice versa may be required if:
- an entity amends the contractual terms of an instrument;
- the effective terms of an instrument change without any amendment of the contractual terms; or
- there is a relevant change in the composition of the reporting entity.

7I.3.400   Reclassification due to amendment of contractual terms

7I.3.400.10   An entity may amend the contractual terms of an instrument such that the classification of the instrument changes from a financial liability to equity or vice versa.

EXAMPLE 29 – RECLASSIFICATION FROM EQUITY TO FINANCIAL LIABILITY

> 7I.3.400.12   Company J has perpetual preference shares, which it has classified as equity instruments. They were issued for 1,000, and carry the right to receive a discretionary dividend of 10%.
>
> 7I.3.400.13   J later amends the terms of the instrument such that:
> - redemption is required in the event of a change in control of the entity; and
> - dividends are payable if interest is paid on another instrument on which the issuer is required to pay interest.
>
> 7I.3.400.14   J no longer has the unconditional ability to avoid redemption, because a change in control is not within the control of the entity (see 7I.3.40). Furthermore, a contractual obligation to pay dividends has been created (see 7I.3.20.70–75). For these reasons, J reclassifies the instrument from equity to a financial liability.

7I.3.400.15   In its discussions, the IFRS Interpretations Committee noted that a financial liability is initially recognised at the date of reclassification and it is initially measured at its fair value minus, in the case of a financial liability not at FVTPL, transaction costs that are directly attributable to the issue of the financial liability (see 7I.6.20.10). Additionally, the original equity instrument is derecognised at the reclassification date and no gain or loss is recognised (see 7I.3.430.10). If, in Example 29, the fair value of the financial liability on initial recognition amounts to 1,200, then an adjustment of 200 needs to be recognised in equity on derecognition of the equity instrument. [*IAS 32.33, 39.43, IU 11-06*]

7I.3.400.20   However, when the classification of an instrument changes from a financial liability to equity due to an amendment of the contractual terms, in our view this represents the extinguishment of a financial liability and the issue of equity instruments. In this case, the resulting gain or loss on the extinguishment of the liability should be recognised in profit or loss (see 7I.5.370.50 and 380) or, when appropriate, as an equity contribution (see 7I.3.370.50). This view is in line with IFRIC 19 (see 7I.3.380 and 7I.5.410–420). For a discussion of the restructuring of convertible bonds, see 7I.3.290.

7I.3.410   Reclassification due to change of effective terms without amendment of contractual terms

7I.3.410.10   In our view, the effective terms of an instrument are considered to have changed if relevant contractual provisions of an instrument become effective or cease to be effective as a result of:
- the passage of time;
- the action of a party; or
- other contingent events that are anticipated in the contractual terms of the instrument.

7I.3.410.12   A change in the composition of the reporting entity may arise in consolidated financial statements from acquisitions or disposals of subsidiaries. In our view, such a change in group structure may trigger a reassessment of the terms and conditions agreed between members of the group and the holder of an instrument and reassessment of whether the group as a whole has an obligation to pay cash or other financial assets to the instrument holder.

7I.3.410.13   The following are examples of changes in the effective terms of instruments.

EXAMPLE 30A – RECLASSIFICATION – FIXED EXERCISE PRICE AS RESULT OF PASSAGE OF TIME

7I.3.410.14   Company X issues convertible debt with the conversion ratio based on the lower of a fixed amount and an amount indexed to the entity's share price one year after the date of issuance. At the end of that year, the conversion ratio would become fixed and therefore reclassification of the conversion option as equity would be appropriate. The exercise price of the derivative that is settled in the entity's own equity instruments therefore becomes fixed as a result of the passage of time.

EXAMPLE 30B – RECLASSIFICATION – EXPIRED PUT OPTION

7I.3.410.15   Company Y issues a put option in an instrument that allows the holder to put the instrument back to Y for a fixed amount of cash during only the first three years of the instrument's life. If the put option expires unexercised at the end of the three years, then reclassification as equity would be appropriate.

EXAMPLE 30C – RECLASSIFICATION – REDEMPTION OF LINKED INSTRUMENT

7I.3.410.16   Company Z issues a non-redeemable financial instrument (the 'base' instrument) with dividends payable if interest is paid on another instrument (the 'linked' instrument). Z is required to pay the interest on the linked instrument. When the linked instrument is redeemed, without any other changes in terms and conditions, the effective terms of the base instrument have changed. This is because it no longer contains a contractual obligation to make payments and therefore re-classification as equity is appropriate.

EXAMPLE 30D – RECLASSIFICATION – CHANGE IN COMPOSITION OF REPORTING ENTITY

7I.3.410.17   Company Z writes a call option under which it has an obligation to deliver a fixed amount of equity shares in an unrelated party, Company X, in exchange for a fixed amount of cash.

7I.3.410.18   Because equity shares in X are financial assets from the perspective of Z, Z classifies the option as a financial liability on initial recognition. However, if Z subsequently obtains control over and consolidates X, then Z would reclassify the option from financial liability to equity in its consolidated financial statements. This is because the option would now represent an obligation to deliver a fixed number of equity instruments in Z's group in exchange for a fixed amount of cash.

7I.3.410.20   In our view, there is no difference between the accounting for reclassifications from equity to liability due to an amendment of the contractual terms (see 7I.3.400.15) and such reclassifications due to a change in the effective terms. Therefore, we believe that a financial liability should be initially recognised at the date of reclassification. We believe that it should be initially measured at its fair value minus, in the case of a financial liability not at FVTPL, transaction costs that are directly attributable to the issue of the financial liability (see 7I.6.20.10). Additionally, the original equity instrument should be derecognised at the reclassification date and no gain or loss should be recognised (see 7I.3.430.10).

7I.3.410.30   IAS 32 does not contain explicit general guidance on accounting for reclassifications from financial liability to equity because of a change in effective terms; and neither IAS 32 nor IAS 39 provides comprehensive guidance on the measurement of an equity instrument on initial recognition. [*IAS 32.16F(b), 96B, AG33*]

7I.3.410.40   Therefore, it is not clear whether it is appropriate to recognise a gain or loss in profit or loss on reclassification from financial liability to equity because of a change in the effective terms without any amendment of the contractual terms. In our view, an entity should choose an accounting policy, to be applied consistently, from the following alternatives.
- *By analogy to the conversion for compound instruments at maturity:* The equity instrument is measured at the carrying amount of the liability (component) and no gain or loss is recognised on reclassification (see 7I.3.250).
- *By analogy to IFRIC 19:* The equity instrument is measured at its fair value and any difference between this fair value and the carrying amount of the liability is recognised in profit or loss (see 7I.3.380 and 7I.5.410).

7I.3.420   TREASURY SHARES

7I.3.430   Recognition and measurement

7I.3.430.10   Generally, any amounts paid by an entity to acquire its own equity instruments are debited directly to equity. This applies whether the equity instruments are cancelled immediately or held for resale – i.e. treasury shares. Amounts received on the sale of treasury shares are credited directly to equity. No gains or losses are recognised in profit or loss on any purchase, sale, issue or cancellation of own equity instruments, or in respect of any changes in the value of treasury shares. [*IAS 32.33*]

7I.3.430.20   Own equity instruments held in connection with an equity compensation plan are presented as treasury shares (see 4.5.2280.10). [*IAS 32.4(f), 33–34*]

7I.3.430.30   Assets held in respect of employee benefit plans other than equity compensation plans may include the employer's own shares. For a discussion of the treatment of these shares, see 4.4.620.20.

7I.3.440   Treasury shares held for trading purposes

7I.3.440.10   Some entities hold their own equity instruments for trading purposes; for example, they may be part of a portfolio of investments held for trading purposes.

7I.3.440.20 There are no exemptions for treasury shares held for trading purposes. Such instruments are not recognised as assets or measured at fair value with gains and losses recognised in profit or loss, which is the treatment for other trading investments (see 7I.6.120). [*IAS 32.33, AG36*]

7I.3.450   Treasury shares held for hedging purposes

7I.3.450.10 Treasury shares may be held for economic hedging purposes – e.g. to hedge an exposure to an issued index-linked structured note when the index includes the entity's own share price, or to hedge against the cost of a share-based payment arrangement. Holding treasury shares as an economic hedge is not sufficient to override the treasury share accounting requirements – even though this may give rise to a profit or loss mismatch. In this situation, the index derivative feature in the issued structured notes is measured at fair value with all changes therein recognised in profit or loss (see 7I.6.120). Any own equity instruments held to hedge the index are accounted for as treasury shares, and changes in their value are not recognised.

7I.3.450.20 In our view, the hedge accounting principles explained in chapter 7I.7 do not apply to treasury shares. Treasury shares cannot be designated as a hedging instrument. The only non-derivatives that qualify as hedging instruments are financial assets or financial liabilities (for foreign exchange risk only) and own equity is not considered to be a financial asset or financial liability. Also, treasury shares cannot be designated as the hedged item; the hedged risk should be one that could affect reported income whereas gains and losses on treasury shares are not recognised in profit or loss. [*IAS 39.72, AG97*]

7I.3.460   Treasury shares held by subsidiaries

7I.3.460.10 In consolidated financial statements, treasury share accounting applies to own equity instruments that are held by a consolidated subsidiary. [*IAS 32.33*]

EXAMPLE 31A – TREASURY SHARES HELD BY SUBSIDIARIES

7I.3.460.20   Company S is a subsidiary of Parent P. S has a 2% investment in P and S classifies its investment as available-for-sale in its separate financial statements. The following facts are also relevant for this example:
- the investment was acquired at a cost of 72; and
- the current fair value of the investment is 87.

7I.3.460.25   P records the following entry in respect of the treasury shares on consolidation.

	DEBIT	CREDIT
Available-for-sale revaluation reserve	15	
Treasury shares (equity)	72	
Available-for-sale investments		87
To eliminate available-for-sale investment on consolidation and to recognise treasury shares		

EXAMPLE 31B – TREASURY SHARES HELD BY SUBSIDIARIES – SALE

7I.3.460.30   Continuing Example 31A, in the next period S sells its investment in P for its fair value of 90. S will have recorded the investment in P at 90 (revalued to the date of sale) and accumulated 18 in its available-for-sale revaluation reserve.

7I.3.460.35   S recognises a profit of 18 in profit or loss on the sale of the investment in its separate financial statements, which represents the recycling of the amount accumulated in the available-for-sale revaluation reserve. On consolidation, P records the following entry to eliminate the profit recognised by S.

	DEBIT	CREDIT
Profit on disposal (profit or loss)	18	
Equity		18
To eliminate profit recognised by S on the sale of the treasury shares		

7I.3.460.40   For further discussion of the presentation of any surplus or deficit on the sale of treasury shares, see 7I.3.480. Any current or deferred tax on the transactions is also recognised in equity (see 3.13.590).

7I.3.470   **Treasury shares held by associates and joint ventures**

7I.3.470.10   An associate or joint venture may have an investment in its investor. The carrying amount of the investee under the equity method will include the investor's share of the investee's investment in the investor's own shares. [*IAS 32.33*]

7I.3.470.20   In our view, the investor should not make any adjustment in respect of treasury shares held by an associate or joint venture. We do not believe that the investor should reclassify this portion of the carrying amount of the investment in the associate or joint venture as a deduction from equity. Similarly, if dividends are declared on these equity instruments, then no adjustment should be made to the entity's share of the associate's or joint venture's profit during the year. We believe that the lack of control over an associate or joint venture, and the definition of a group – i.e. a parent and all of its subsidiaries (see 2.1.100.10) – distinguish these from cases in which treasury shares are held by a subsidiary. Information about own equity instruments held by associates or joint ventures should be disclosed in the notes to the financial statements. [*IAS 1.79, 32.33, IFRS 10.A*]

7I.3.480   **Presentation**

7I.3.480.10   IFRS does not mandate a specific method of presenting treasury shares within equity. However, local laws may prescribe the allocation method. Therefore, an entity needs to take into account its legal environment when choosing how to present its own shares within equity. An entity needs to choose a presentation format, to be applied consistently to all treasury shares. Possible presentation options are explained below, although other methods may also be used.

	PRESENTATION OF TREASURY SHARES	**OUTCOMES**
7I.3.480.20	**Total cost of treasury shares as a separate category of equity**	• The cost of treasury shares purchased is debited to a separate category of equity. • When treasury shares are sold or reissued, the amount received for the instruments is credited to this category. • Any surplus or deficit on the sale of treasury shares is shown as an adjustment to share premium or reserves, including retained earnings, or a combination thereof. This method is illustrated in KPMG's *Guides to financial statements* series.
7I.3.480.30	**Par value of treasury shares as a separate category of equity**	• The par value of treasury shares purchased is debited to a separate category of equity. • When treasury shares are sold or reissued, the par value of the instruments is credited to this category. • Any premium or discount to par value is shown as an adjustment to share premium or reserves, including retained earnings, or a combination thereof.
7I.3.480.40	**Par value of treasury shares as a deduction from share capital**	• The par value of treasury shares purchased is debited to share capital. • When treasury shares are sold or reissued, the par value of the instruments is credited to share capital. • Any premium or discount to par value is shown as an adjustment to share premium or reserves, including retained earnings, or a combination thereof.

7I.3.490   COSTS OF AN EQUITY TRANSACTION

7I.3.490.10   Qualifying costs attributable to an equity transaction – e.g. issuing or buying back own shares – are debited directly to equity. In our view, this includes qualifying costs attributable to the distribution of a dividend because equity transactions include dividends to equity participants. Income tax relating to the transaction costs of an equity transaction are accounted for in accordance with IAS 12 (see 3.13.590). [*IAS 32.35–35A, 37*]

7I.3.490.20   Issuing shares in a private placement for cash consideration is an equity transaction and, therefore, in our view the costs directly related to issuing equity instruments in a private placement should be recognised directly in equity.

7I.3.490.30   Listing transactions often involve both listing existing shares and issuing new ones. In our view, the costs directly attributable to issuing new shares should be recognised directly in equity and any costs attributable to listing existing shares should be expensed as they are incurred.

7I.3.490.40   In our view, similar to a listing of existing shares, secondary offerings – i.e. where existing shares are offered by the entity to new shareholders – and share splits do not result in new equity instruments being issued, so any costs associated with these transactions should be expensed as they are incurred. [*IAS 32.35–36*]

EXAMPLE 32 – LISTING OF SHARES ISSUED BY NEWCO – TRANSACTION IS NOT A BUSINESS COMBINATION

7I.3.490.43   A Newco (see 5.13.180) is set up as the new parent of an existing Company C, whose shares are unlisted, to provide the existing shareholders in C with shares that are listed. Newco will issue shares to C's existing shareholders in exchange for their shares in C. Newco's shares are listed and Newco incurs costs for issuing them. No additional cash is invested by the shareholders.

7I.3.490.45   Because only one business is placed under Newco in this transaction, the transaction is not a business combination and so Newco applies book value (carry-over basis) accounting (see 5.13.60 and 190). Under this accounting, Newco's consolidated financial statements are considered a continuation of those of C and therefore no equity transaction is reported. Therefore, we believe that the costs incurred by Newco in issuing the shares to the existing shareholders of C should be expensed in Newco's consolidated financial statements as they are incurred because those costs are in effect the costs of listing the existing shares of the continuing entity (via a restructuring), rather than costs of issuing new shares.

7I.3.490.47   The requirement to record in equity all costs attributable to an equity transaction also applies to costs incurred on the issue of equity instruments in relation to a business combination (see 2.6.530). [*IFRS 3.53*]

7I.3.490.50   Qualifying costs that relate to both existing shares and new shares are allocated on a rational and consistent basis – e.g. based on the number of shares. [*IAS 32.38*]

EXAMPLE 33 – ALLOCATION OF TRANSACTION COSTS BETWEEN EXISTING AND NEW SHARES

7I.3.490.55   Company G issues 160 new shares and lists 80 existing shares in an IPO. The total costs related to both existing and new shares are 300. G allocates the cost between the listing of existing shares and the issue of new shares based on the number of shares. Therefore, the cost allocated to the new shares is 200 (300 x 160 / 240), which is recognised directly in equity. The cost allocated to listing the existing shares is 100 (300 x 80 / 240), which is recognised in profit or loss.

7I.3.490.60   Only costs that relate to both listing existing shares and issuing new shares are allocated as explained in 7I.3.490.50. We believe that costs that are directly attributable only to the listing itself should be recognised in profit or loss as they are incurred (see 7I.3.490.30). The IFRS Interpretations Committee discussed this issue and noted that judgement may be required to determine which costs relate solely to activities other than equity transactions – e.g. listing existing shares – and which costs relate jointly to equity transactions and other activities. [*IU 09-08*]

7I.3.500   Qualifying costs

7I.3.500.10   Only incremental costs that are attributable directly to equity transactions such as issuing or buying back own equity instruments or distributing dividends are recognised in equity. These costs may be internal or external, but need to be incremental. Other costs are recognised in profit or loss even if they relate to newly issued shares. For further discussion of incremental internal transaction costs, see 7I.6.30–40. [*IAS 32.37*]

7I.3.500.20   Assume that an entity is issuing new shares and simultaneously listing them. The following are examples of costs related to the transaction that we believe should be recognised in equity, if they are incremental costs:

- fees for legal and tax advice related to the share issue;
- the cost of preparing and printing the prospectus;
- fees incurred in respect of valuing the shares;
- fees incurred in respect of valuing other assets – e.g. property – if the valuation is required to be disclosed in the prospectus;
- underwriting fees;
- fees and commissions paid to employees acting as selling agents that relate to the share issue;
- costs incurred in holding press conferences related to the share issue; and
- the cost of handling share applications.

7I.3.500.30   In our view, few internal costs will meet the incremental test in practice because we believe that this will be difficult to demonstrate.

7I.3.500.40   In our view, costs that relate to the listing itself and that are not directly attributable to the new share issue should be expensed. For example, stock exchange registration costs do not relate to the issue of shares but rather to the listing of the issued shares; accordingly, they should be expensed as they are incurred.

7I.3.500.50   In our view, the costs of advertising a share issue should be recognised directly in equity if the advertising relates directly to the share issue and is not general advertising aimed at enhancing the entity's brand. An example may include incremental costs related to a road show in which the entity is specifically targeting potential investors. If only a part of the advertising relates to the share issue, then an apportionment of the costs may be appropriate.

7I.3.510   Costs of anticipated equity transactions

7I.3.510.10   Equity transaction costs may be incurred before the equity instrument is issued or bought back or before the dividend is distributed. IFRS is silent on how to treat costs incurred before the equity transaction has been recorded.

7I.3.510.20   In our view, costs that are related directly to a probable future equity transaction should be recognised as a prepayment (asset) in the statement of financial position. The costs should be transferred to equity when the equity transaction is recognised, or recognised in profit or loss if the issue or buy-back is no longer expected to be completed or the dividend is no longer expected to be distributed.

7I.3.520   Costs of issuing compound instruments

7I.3.520.10   In the case of compound instruments, transaction costs are allocated to the individual components in proportion to the allocation of the proceeds. The costs related to the liability component are dealt with in accordance with the requirements for transaction costs associated with financial liabilities (see 7I.6.30). However, the costs related to the equity component are reported as a deduction from equity. [*IAS 32.37–38*]

7I.3.530   Related tax benefits

7I.3.530.10   The tax effects of any transaction costs that are recognised in equity are generally also recognised directly in equity. [*IAS 32.35A, 12.61A(b)*]

7I.3.530.20   If the tax benefits associated with the transaction costs are not probable, then the deferred tax asset is not recognised. In these cases, the gross transaction costs are deducted from equity. If in a subsequent period the tax benefits related to the transaction costs qualify for recognition, then the corresponding credit will generally be recognised directly in equity. For further discussion, see 3.13.590.

7I.3.540   Presentation in equity

7I.3.540.10   IFRS does not specify which component of equity the transaction costs recognised in equity should be charged against. In our view, an entity should choose an accounting policy, to be applied consistently, on the component of equity against which the transaction costs are recognised.

7I.3.540.20   For a discussion about presenting income tax effects within equity, see 3.13.530.60.

7I.3.540.30   If shares have a par value, then regulatory issues may prevent the amount from being deducted from share capital. In this case, the transaction costs may be presented as a deduction from share premium, other paid-in capital or retained earnings; or they might be shown as a separate reserve. If the transaction costs are presented as a deduction from share capital, then in our view the entity should disclose the impact.

EXAMPLE 34 – IMPACT OF TRANSACTION COSTS PRESENTED AS DEDUCTION FROM SHARE CAPITAL

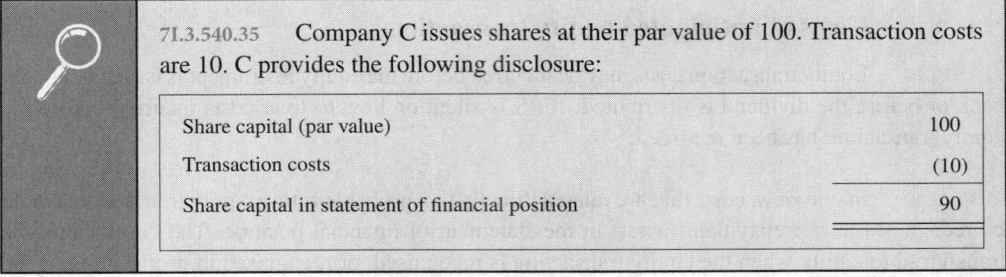

7I.3.540.35   Company C issues shares at their par value of 100. Transaction costs are 10. C provides the following disclosure:

Share capital (par value)	100
Transaction costs	(10)
Share capital in statement of financial position	90

7I.3.540.40   Example 35 illustrates the combined application effect of the approaches explained in 7I.3.530 and 540.30.

EXAMPLE 35 – RECOGNITION OF SHARE ISSUANCE, RELATED COSTS AND TAX

7I.3.540.45   In year 1, Company Q issues additional shares for proceeds of 6,000. The total par value of these shares is 600. The costs of the transaction are 1,200. Under the local tax law, transaction costs are deducted only in year 2. Because it is probable that Q will earn sufficient taxable profit in year 2, Q recognises a deferred tax asset related to the transaction costs. The tax rate is 30%.

7I.3.540.50   Q records the following entries in its financial statements.

	DEBIT	CREDIT
Cash	6,000	
Share capital		600
Share premium		5,400
To recognise share issuance		
Deferred tax asset (1,200 x 30%)	360	
Share premium	840	
Cash		1,200
To recognise transaction costs and related tax impact		

7I.3.550   EQUITY PRESENTATION

7I.3.550.10   There are no specific requirements in IFRS on how to present the individual components of equity. Therefore, in our view net accumulated losses may be deducted, on a decision by the shareholders or application of the articles of association, from another component of equity – e.g. additional paid-in capital – if this is permitted by applicable laws.

7I.3.550.20   Laws in some countries require reserves to be established for specific purposes. For example, banks may be required to set aside amounts for general banking risks or losses on loans. Some entities also establish reserves if national tax laws grant exemptions from, or reductions in, tax liabilities when transfers to such reserves are made. IFRS neither requires nor prohibits the creation of such reserves, which are merely allocations and designations of components of equity. If such reserves are created, then in our view they should be classified as a separate component of equity and created by an appropriation from another category of equity – e.g. retained earnings. Transfers to these reserves and their related tax effects should be recognised directly within equity, and should not be recognised in profit or loss. Also, these reserves may not be recognised as liabilities in the statement of financial position. Disclosure of the nature and purpose of each reserve within equity is required. [*IAS 1.79(b)*]

7I.3.560   **Income tax**

7I.3.560.10   Income tax relating to distributions to holders of an equity instrument and to transaction costs of an equity transaction is accounted for in accordance with IAS 12. Current tax and deferred tax that relate to items that are recognised directly in equity are generally recognised directly in equity. For a further discussion of income taxes related to payment of dividends, see 3.13.740.

7I.3.560.15   The amount of current and deferred tax recognised directly in equity is disclosed separately. There is no requirement to present the tax impact of items recognised in equity separately in the statement of changes in equity. In our experience, these tax effects are often disclosed in the notes to the financial statements (see 2.2.10). [*IAS 12.52B, 61A(b), 81(a), 32.35A*]

7I.3.560.20   In our experience, the tax effects of equity transactions are generally presented in the same category of equity as the underlying transaction, as opposed to creating a separate category of equity for taxes (see 3.13.530.60).

7I.3.570   **Non-controlling interests**

7I.3.570.10   NCI are presented in the consolidated statement of financial position within equity, separately from the parent's shareholders' equity (see 2.5.330). Therefore, a statement of changes in equity includes an analysis of the amounts attributable to NCI. [*IAS 1.54(q), 106, IFRS 10.22*]

7I.3.580   **CAPITAL DISCLOSURES**

7I.3.580.10   An entity discloses information that enables users of its financial statements to evaluate the entity's objectives, policies and processes for managing capital. It discloses the following.
● Qualitative information, including a description of:
  – what it manages as capital;
  – when the entity is subject to externally imposed capital requirements:
    ● the nature of those requirements; and
    ● how those requirements are incorporated into the management of capital; and
  – how it is meeting its objectives for managing capital.
● Summary quantitative data about what it manages as capital. Some entities regard some financial liabilities – e.g. some forms of subordinated debt – as part of capital. Other entities regard capital as excluding some components of equity – e.g. components arising from cash flow hedges.
● Any changes in qualitative information and quantitative data from the previous period.
● Whether during the period it complied with any externally imposed capital requirements to which it is subject.
● When the entity has not complied with such externally imposed capital requirements, the consequences of such non-compliance. [*IAS 1.134–135*]

7I.3.590   **CAPITAL MAINTENANCE**

7I.3.590.10   IFRS does not establish requirements about what assets or net assets should be retained and what may be distributed. This is a legal issue that will depend on the regulatory environment in which an entity operates.

7I.3.590.20   If there is a legal prohibition on the distribution of certain reserves, and an entity wishes to indicate these restrictions in the statement of changes in equity, then in our view the entity should transfer the restricted amounts to a separate component of equity – e.g. a non-distributable reserve or a capital reserve – if the applicable law permits. Any such transfer would be made through the statement of changes in equity (see chapter 2.2 and 7I.3.550.20). In any case, the restrictions on distribution are disclosed in the notes to the financial statements. [*IAS 1.79(b)*]

7I.3.600   DIVIDENDS

7I.3.600.10   Dividends and other distributions to holders of equity instruments are recognised directly in equity (see also 7I.3.20.150).

7I.3.600.20   A liability for a dividend payable is not recognised until an entity has an obligation to pay dividends. In the case of discretionary dividends, a liability for a dividend payable is not recognised until the dividend is both appropriately authorised *and* no longer at the entity's discretion – i.e. when the entity has an obligation to pay. In our view, it is not appropriate to recognise a liability based only on a constructive obligation. This is consistent with the basis for conclusions to IAS 10 and the definition of a financial liability in IAS 32 (see 7I.3.20). Therefore, a constructive obligation cannot arise in connection with a dividend. [*IAS 10.12, BC4*]

7I.3.600.30   In the case of discretionary dividends, the legal requirements of the particular jurisdiction are important in determining the point in time at which a liability is recognised. For example, suppose that the relevant law stated that a board decision or announcement required no further approval and was binding on the entity – e.g. the board has no discretion to withdraw its decision or announcement and no legal discretion to avoid making payment. In this case, the dividend liability is recognised on the board decision or announcement. However, suppose that the entity can choose to avoid payment until it is approved by the shareholders, or can withdraw its decision or announcement of the dividend (see 7I.3.220). In this case, it would not be appropriate to recognise a liability at the time of the board decision or announcement.

7I.3.600.40   In our view, an obligation to pay an interim dividend should be recognised when the entity has an obligation to make the payment and the amount to be paid can be determined reliably – i.e. the shareholders do not have an obligation to pay back the interim dividend.

7I.3.600.50   Sometimes, in addition to the declaration or the approval process required as a condition for the payment of the dividends, additional conditions – e.g. the fulfilment/waiver of all conditions precedent for completion of a proposed business combination and the holder of the equity instruments continues to hold the securities until the record date on which the fulfilment/waiver of those conditions is announced – may determine the timing or amount of the dividend to be recognised. In this case, the liability is recognised when the obligation exists and for the amount that the entity has an obligation to pay.

7I.3.600.60   Dividends on shares that are classified as liabilities are presented in profit or loss as a finance cost unless the dividends are discretionary. Even if the legal form of the payment is a dividend, it is not recognised directly in equity. For further discussion of the classification of discretionary dividends, see 7I.3.220. Financing costs on shares classified as liabilities are determined under the effective interest method.

7I.3.600.70   IFRS does not provide any guidance on accounting for share dividends – i.e. the issue of additional shares to shareholders characterised as a dividend.

7I.3.600.80   Sometimes shares with a value equal to the cash dividend amount are offered as an alternative to the cash dividend. When the shares are issued, the liability is settled and a credit to equity is recognised as the proceeds of the issue. In our view, this practice is acceptable. Any reallocation of capital within equity needs to be in accordance with the applicable law.

7I.3.600.90   In our view, a share dividend that is not an alternative to a cash dividend should be treated in the same way as a share split or a bonus issue – i.e. no entries are required (see 7I.3.340).

7I.3.610   Distributions of non-cash assets to owners

7I.3.610.10   IFRIC 17 addresses specific forms of distributions. The interpretation deals with measurement and presentation issues in this respect.

7I.3.610.20   A 'distribution' is a non-reciprocal transfer of assets from an entity to its owners, commonly referred to as a 'dividend'. There is no restriction placed on the term 'distribution' other than that it is non-reciprocal. Neither the reason for the transfer of assets nor its legal characterisation is a factor in determining whether it falls in the scope of the interpretation. Therefore, for example, a distribution that is in effect a return of capital is in the scope of the interpretation. [*IFRIC 17.2–3, BC4–BC5*]

7I.3.610.30   IFRIC 17 addresses how an entity making distributions of non-cash assets to owners acting in their capacity as owners accounts for those distributions in its financial statements (separate, individual and/or consolidated). IFRIC 17 also applies to distributions in which each owner may elect to receive either their share of the non-cash asset or a cash alternative. Perhaps the most significant transactions included in the scope of the interpretation are demergers or spin-offs, in which an entity distributes its ownership interests in one or more subsidiaries to existing shareholders. [*IFRIC 17.3*]

7I.3.610.40   IFRIC 17 does not apply to:
- common control transactions (see 5.13.90);
- distributions of part of the ownership interests in a subsidiary when control is retained; and
- distributions in which owners of the same class of equity instruments are not treated equally. [*IFRIC 17.4–7*]

7I.3.610.50   IFRIC 17 also does not apply to the financial statements of the recipient of the distribution; recipients apply the requirements of IAS 39 and IAS 27 to the receipt of dividends (see 7I.6.690). [*IAS 39.55A, 27.12, IFRIC 17.8*]

7I.3.610.60   A liability for the distribution is recognised when the distribution is authorised and is no longer at the entity's discretion. This timing will vary depending on the legal requirements of individual jurisdictions (see 7I.3.600.20). [*IFRIC 17.10*]

7I.3.610.70   The liability for the distribution is measured, initially and until the settlement date, at the fair value of the assets to be distributed. Any changes in the measurement of the liability are recognised in equity; this is consistent with the accounting for the liability at the time of initial recognition. For distributions in which the owners may elect to receive either non-cash assets or a cash alternative, the entity considers the fair value of each alternative and their associated probabilities when measuring the liability. [*IFRIC 17.11–13*]

7I.3.610.80   Unless it is required by other standards – e.g. financial assets classified as at FVTPL or as available-for sale under IAS 39 – the assets to be distributed are not remeasured to fair value when the liability is recognised. Instead, assets to be distributed that are in the measurement scope of IFRS 5 are measured in accordance with that standard (see 5.4.40). Assets to be distributed that are not in the measurement scope of IFRS 5 (e.g. deferred tax assets) continue to be measured in accordance with other standards (e.g. IAS 12).

7I.3.610.90   At the date on which the distribution occurs – i.e. settlement date – the following takes place.
- The liability is remeasured based on the fair value of the assets to be distributed, with any change therein recognised in equity.
- The liability and the assets distributed are derecognised.
- Any difference between the fair value of the assets distributed and their carrying amount in the financial statements is recognised as a separate line item in profit or loss; this has a consequential effect on EPS.
- Any amounts recognised in OCI in relation to the assets distributed – e.g. fair value revaluation reserves – are reclassified to profit or loss or they may be transferred within equity depending on the derecognition requirements in other standards, on the same basis as would be required if the non-cash assets had been disposed of. [*IFRIC 17.13–15, BC38*]

7I.3.610.100   In our experience, the amount recognised in profit or loss at the settlement date is not generally a loss. This is because, if the fair value of the assets had been lower than their carrying amount, an impairment loss would have been recognised before settlement. [*IFRIC 17.BC39*]

EXAMPLE 36 – DISTRIBUTION OF NON-CASH ASSETS TO OWNERS

7I.3.610.110   Company P distributes items of property, plant and equipment as dividends to all of its owners acting in their capacity as owners. The carrying amount of the property, plant and equipment is 100 and the fair value is 130 at the date on which the distribution is authorised.

7I.3.610.120   At the date of settlement of the distribution, the carrying amount of the property, plant and equipment is 95 and the fair value is 125.

7I.3.610.130   Company P records the following entries in its financial statements.

	DEBIT	CREDIT
Equity	130	
Liability for distribution		130
To recognise liability at fair value of assets to be distributed		

	DEBIT	CREDIT
Liability for distribution	5	
Equity		5
To recognise change in carrying amount of liability up to settlement date		
Liability for distribution	125	
Property, plant and equipment		95
Profit or loss		30
To derecognise liability and assets distributed		

7I.4 Classification of financial assets and financial liabilities

71.4   Classification of financial assets and financial liabilities

7I.4 Classification of financial assets and financial liabilities

REQUIREMENTS FOR INSURERS THAT APPLY IFRS 4

In July 2014, the IASB issued IFRS 9 *Financial Instruments*, which is effective for annual periods beginning on or after 1 January 2018. However, an insurer may defer the application of IFRS 9 if it meets certain criteria (see 8.1.180).

This chapter reflects the requirement of IAS 39 *Financial Instruments: Recognition and Measurement* and the related standards, excluding any amendments introduced by IFRS 9. These requirements are relevant to insurers that apply the temporary exemption from IFRS 9 or the overlay approach to designated financial assets (see 8.1.160) and cover annual periods beginning on 1 January 2018. For further discussion, see Introduction to Sections 7 and 7I.

The requirements related to this topic are mainly derived from the following.

STANDARD	TITLE
IAS 39	Financial Instruments: Recognition and Measurement

FORTHCOMING REQUIREMENTS AND FUTURE DEVELOPMENTS

For this topic, there are no forthcoming requirements or future developments.

7I.4.10   **CLASSIFICATION**

7I.4.10.10   IAS 39 establishes specific categories into which all financial assets and financial liabilities are classified. The classification of financial instruments dictates how these financial assets and financial liabilities are measured subsequently in the financial statements of an entity. There are four categories of financial assets:
- financial assets at FVTPL;
- held-to-maturity investments;
- loans and receivables; and
- available-for-sale financial assets. [*IAS 39.9, 45*]

7I.4.10.15   Categories of financial liabilities include:
- financial liabilities at FVTPL; and
- other financial liabilities. [*IAS 39.9, 47*]

7I.4.10.20   In our view, if an entity acquires financial instruments as part of a business combination (see 2.6.560), then the entity should classify the acquired financial instruments at the date of acquisition applying the normal classification rules, without regard to how the instruments were classified by the acquiree before the acquisition. If these classifications differ from the classifications made by the acquiree, then the reclassifications are not treated as transfers between portfolios in the consolidated financial statements of the acquirer – i.e. they would not raise issues of 'tainting' with respect to items classified as held-to-maturity.

7I.4.10.30   The classification rules for each of the categories are discussed below.

7I.4.20   **Financial assets or financial liabilities at FVTPL, including derivatives**

7I.4.20.10   This category includes:
- financial assets or financial liabilities held for trading – i.e. any financial asset or financial liability acquired or incurred to generate short-term profits or that is part of a portfolio of financial instruments that are managed together for that purpose;
- all derivatives other than hedging instruments (see 7I.7.310);
- contingent consideration as defined in IFRS 3 classified as a financial liability that is in the scope of IAS 39; and
- financial assets or financial liabilities that are designated by the entity at the time of initial recognition as measured at FVTPL (see 7I.4.40). [*IFRS 3.58, IAS 39.9*]

7I.4.20.20   Investment entities, as defined in IFRS 10, are required to account for their investments in most subsidiaries at FVTPL in accordance with IAS 39 (see chapter 5.6). In addition, one of the criteria for qualifying as an investment entity is that investments in associates and joint ventures are accounted for at FVTPL in accordance with IAS 39. [*IFRS 10.31, A, BC250*]

7I.4.30   *Financial assets and financial liabilities held for trading*

7I.4.30.10   A financial asset or financial liability is classified as held-for-trading if it is:
- acquired or incurred principally for the purpose of selling or repurchasing it in the near term;
- on initial recognition, part of a portfolio of identified financial instruments that are managed together and for which there is evidence of a recent actual pattern of short-term profit taking; or

- a derivative, except for a derivative that is a designated and effective hedging instrument. [*IAS 39.9*]

7I.4.30.20   'Trading' generally refers to the active and frequent buying and selling of an item. Financial assets and financial liabilities classified as held-for-trading are generally held with the objective of generating a profit from short-term fluctuations in price or dealer's margin. However, in our view these general characteristics are not a prerequisite for all financial instruments that the standard requires to be classified as held-for-trading. [*IAS 39.AG14*]

EXAMPLE 1 – FINANCIAL ASSETS HELD FOR TRADING

> 7I.4.30.30   Bank B originates a loan with the intention of syndication but fails to find sufficient commitments from other participants. B intends to sell all or part of the loan in the near term rather than hold it for the foreseeable future.
>
> 7I.4.30.35   The definition of 'loans and receivables' in IAS 39 requires a loan or a portion of a loan that is intended to be sold immediately or in the near term to be classified as held-for-trading on initial recognition. In our view – notwithstanding the general characteristics of trading activity (see 7I.4.30.20) – the loan or the portion that B intends to sell in the near term should be classified as held-for-trading in accordance with the specific guidance in the standard. [*IAS 39.9*]
>
> 7I.4.30.37   If subsequent to initial recognition B changes its intention with respect to the loan and demonstrates the intention and ability to hold the loan for the foreseeable future or until maturity, then B may, at such a subsequent date, reclassify the loan from the FVTPL category to either loans and receivables or the available-for-sale category (see 7I.4.220.20–40). [*IAS 39.50(c)*]

7I.4.30.40   The definition of 'held for trading' includes an asset or liability being part of a portfolio of financial instruments. Although IAS 39 does not define 'portfolio' explicitly, in this context it is possible to consider a portfolio to be a collection of financial assets or financial liabilities that are managed as part of the same group. For example, the takings and placings of a money market desk may be viewed as comprising one portfolio that qualifies for classification as held-for-trading. [*IAS 39.9, IG.B.11*]

7I.4.30.50   The intention to profit from short-term fluctuations in price or dealer's margin need not be stated explicitly by the entity. Other evidence may indicate that a financial asset is being held for trading purposes. Evidence of trading may be inferred, based on the turnover and the average holding period of financial assets included in the portfolio. For example, an entity may buy and sell shares for a specific portfolio, based on movements in those entities' share prices. If this is done on a frequent basis, then the entity has established a pattern of trading for the purpose of generating profits from short-term fluctuations in price. Additional purchases of shares into this portfolio would also be designated as held-for-trading. [*IAS 39.9, IG.B.11*]

7I.4.30.60   In our view, if an entity makes an investment in a fund that is managed independently by a third party, then whether the entity should classify its investment in that fund as trading is not influenced by the fact that the underlying assets within the fund are traded actively. Therefore, the entity's investment in that fund would not meet the definition of an asset held for trading unless the entity actively trades in the investments it holds in such funds. This situation may be contrasted with one in which an entity holds a portfolio of investments that are managed by a portfolio manager on the entity's behalf. In such cases, the entity determines the investment policies and procedures and, consequently, if the portfolio manager actively buys and sells instruments within the portfolio to generate short-term profits, then the instruments in the portfolio are considered held for trading and are classified as at FVTPL. [*IAS 39.9, IG.B.12*]

7I.4.30.70   Alternatively, a manager of an investment portfolio might buy and sell investments to rebalance the portfolio in line with an investment mandate. This activity would generally not result in the investments being classified as held-for-trading because the activity may not be aimed at generating profits from short-term fluctuations in prices. Furthermore, if an entity acquires a non-derivative financial asset with the intention of holding it for a period irrespective of short-term fluctuations in price, then such an instrument cannot be classified as held-for-trading. [*IAS 39.IG.B.12*]

7I.4.30.80   Financial liabilities held for trading include derivatives with a negative fair value – except those that are hedging instruments – and obligations to deliver financial assets borrowed by a short seller. This category further includes financial liabilities that are incurred with an intention of repurchasing them in the near term and those that are part of a portfolio of financial liabilities for which there is evidence of a recent pattern of short-term profit taking. [*IAS 39.AG15*]

7I.4.30.90   A financial liability cannot be considered as held for trading simply because it funds trading activities. However, financial liabilities that fund trading activities can be designated as at FVTPL if the criteria for designation are met (see 7I.4.40). [*IAS 39.AG15*]

7I.4.30.100   The standard does not define 'near term'. In our view, an entity should adopt a definition and apply a consistent approach to the definition used. If there is the intention of generating a profit from short-term fluctuations in price or dealer's margin, then the financial asset is classified appropriately as held-for-trading, even if the asset is not subsequently sold within a short period of time.

7I.4.30.110   To generate short-term profits, traders may actively trade an asset's risks rather than the asset itself. For example, a bank may invest in a 30-day money market instrument for the purpose of generating profit from short-term fluctuations in the interest rate. When the favourable movement in the interest rate occurs, instead of selling the instrument the bank may issue an offsetting liability instrument. The 30-day money market instrument is classified as held-for-trading despite the fact that there is no intention to sell the instrument physically. The offsetting liability instrument is also classified as held-for-trading because it was issued for trading purposes and will be managed together with the related asset. [*IAS 39.AG15*]

7I.4.40   *Financial assets and financial liabilities designated as at FVTPL*

7I.4.40.10   In addition to financial assets and financial liabilities held for trading, financial assets and financial liabilities are classified in the FVTPL category when an entity chooses, on initial recognition, to designate such instruments as at FVTPL using the fair value option. An entity may use this designation only in either of the following circumstances.

- When doing so results in more relevant information because either:
  – it eliminates or significantly reduces a measurement or recognition inconsistency that would result from measuring assets or liabilities or recognising gains or losses on them on different bases (an 'accounting mismatch'); or
  – a group of financial assets or financial liabilities (or both) is managed and its performance is evaluated on a fair value basis in accordance with the entity's documented risk management or investment strategy and information is provided to key management personnel on this basis.
- In respect of an entire hybrid contract, when the contract contains one or more embedded derivatives, unless those embedded derivatives either:
  – do not significantly modify the cash flows that would otherwise be required by the contract; or
  – are ones for which it is clear with little or no analysis when first considering a similar hybrid instrument that separation is prohibited (see 7I.4.70.20). [*IAS 39.9, 11A*]

7I.4.40.20   Investments in equity securities that do not have a quoted market price in an active market, and whose fair value cannot be measured reliably, cannot be designated as at FVTPL. [*IAS 39.9*]

7I.4.40.30   The designation of an instrument as at FVTPL may be used only on initial recognition and is not reversible. Therefore, this alternative to hedge accounting cannot be used if an entity buys or issues an instrument and later wishes to put a hedge in place.

7I.4.40.40   There is no requirement for consistency in the use of the FVTPL designation, meaning that an entity can choose which, if any, of its financial assets and financial liabilities are designated into this category. [*IAS 39.AG4C*]

7I.4.50   *Reducing accounting mismatch*

7I.4.50.10   Determining whether the fair value option eliminates or significantly reduces an accounting mismatch requires judgement. In our view, an accounting mismatch may arise from other financial instruments or from items that are not financial instruments. The following examples illustrate circumstances in which an accounting mismatch may cause the relevant financial assets and financial liabilities to qualify for designation as at FVTPL.

- An entity has liabilities whose cash flows are linked contractually to the performance of certain assets that would otherwise have been classified as available-for-sale – e.g. liabilities with a discretionary participation feature that pay benefits based on realised investment returns of a specified pool of the insurer's assets.
- An entity has liabilities under insurance contracts that are measured using current information as allowed under IFRS 4, and related financial assets that otherwise would be classified as available-for-sale or measured at amortised cost.
- An entity has financial assets and financial liabilities that share a particular risk, such that their fair values change in opposite directions, tending to offset each other. However:
  – only some of the instruments are measured at FVTPL, notably derivatives and those that are held for trading;
  – hedge accounting cannot be applied because:
    - the hedge criteria (e.g. the effectiveness requirements) are not met; or

- none of the instruments is a derivative and without hedge accounting there is a significant inconsistency in the recognition of gains or losses; or
  - even though hedge accounting is applicable, hedge documentation or effectiveness testing, for example, is too onerous.
- An entity has issued financial liabilities whose cash flows are linked to both (1) the cash flows received from investment property measured at fair value under IAS 40 (see 3.4.140), and (2) the fair value of that property. The entity determines that the contractual linkage does not constitute an embedded derivative and, without designation, the financial liabilities would be accounted for at amortised cost. [*IAS 39.AG4E*]

7I.4.50.20   There may be a delay between acquiring a financial asset or incurring a financial liability and the related transaction that would create an accounting mismatch. In the event of a reasonable delay, designation of the respective financial asset and financial liability as at FVTPL is not precluded provided that the designation is made on initial recognition and, at the time that the first of the instruments is so designated, the acquisition or incurrence of the other is expected in the very near future in accordance with a documented strategy. [*IAS 39.AG4F*]

7I.4.50.30   One of the main benefits of this category is that it may allow an entity to avoid the cost and complexity of meeting the criteria for hedge accounting in some cases. For example, an entity that purchases (or issues) a fixed rate bond and immediately enters into an interest rate swap to convert the interest to a floating rate might, instead of claiming hedge accounting, designate the bond as at FVTPL. Because both the bond and the swap will be measured at FVTPL, the offsetting effects of changes in market interest rates on the fair value of each instrument will be recognised in profit or loss without the need for hedge accounting. [*IAS 39.BC74A*]

7I.4.50.40   However, the fair value changes of an item designated into this category will be affected by more than one risk such that using this designation may not achieve the exact results that hedge accounting for a particular risk would. Continuing the example in 7I.4.50.30, when applying hedge accounting for interest rate risk, the fixed rate bond would be adjusted for changes in its fair value attributable to interest rate risk only. However, designating the bond as at FVTPL means that it will be remeasured to fair value in respect of all risks, including the entity's own credit risk (for a bond issued by the entity) or the counterparty's credit risk (for a bond purchased by the entity). This may result in a greater difference between the fair value gains and losses on the interest rate swap and those on the bond than when hedge accounting is applied.

7I.4.60   *Assets and liabilities managed on fair value basis*

7I.4.60.10   The following examples illustrate circumstances in which an entity could be considered to be managing and evaluating the performance of a group of financial assets, financial liabilities or both on a fair value basis, such that those financial assets and financial liabilities may qualify for designation as at FVTPL.
- The entity is a venture capital organisation, mutual fund, unit trust or similar entity that invests in financial assets with the objective of profiting from their total return in the form of interest or dividends and changes in fair value.
- The entity has financial assets and financial liabilities that share one or more risks, which are managed and evaluated on a fair value basis according to a documented asset and liability manage-

ment policy – e.g. a portfolio of structured products that contain multiple embedded derivatives and that are managed on a fair value basis using a mixture of derivatives and non-derivatives.

- The entity is an insurer that holds a portfolio of financial assets and manages that portfolio to maximise its total return from interest or dividends and changes in fair value, and evaluates its performance on that basis. [*IAS 39.AG4I*]

7I.4.70 *Assets and liabilities containing embedded derivatives*

7I.4.70.10   If a contract contains one or more embedded derivatives, then an entity may designate the entire combined contract as at FVTPL unless the embedded derivative does not significantly modify the cash flows or it is clear that separation of the embedded derivative is prohibited. [*IAS 39.11A*]

7I.4.70.20   An example of an embedded derivative for which it is clear that separation would be prohibited, and therefore designation of the entire hybrid contract as at FVTPL is not possible, is a mortgage loan that is prepayable at an amount approximating its amortised cost (see 7I.2.240.10). Another example would be an instrument containing a non-leveraged cap that is out of the money at inception.

7I.4.70.30   An entity can apply the fair value option to contractual arrangements that contain one or more embedded derivatives only when the host contract meets the definition of a financial instrument under IAS 39. [*IAS 39.11A*]

7I.4.70.40   If an entity does not apply the designation in 7I.4.70.10 and the embedded derivative is required to be separated but its fair value cannot be measured reliably, then the entire combined contract is designated as at FVTPL. If the fair value of the embedded derivative cannot be measured reliably directly, then it is necessary to consider whether it can be measured reliably indirectly by deducting the fair value of the host contract from the fair value of the entire hybrid instrument. In our experience, circumstances in which the embedded derivative cannot be measured reliably (either directly or indirectly) are encountered rarely. However, in those rare circumstances the entire contract is designated as at FVTPL. [*IAS 39.12–13*]

7I.4.80   **Held-to-maturity investments**

7I.4.80.10   Held-to-maturity investments are non-derivative financial assets with fixed or determinable payments and a fixed maturity that an entity has the positive intention and ability to hold to maturity, other than those that:

- the entity designates on initial recognition as at FVTPL;
- the entity designates as available-for-sale; and
- meet the definition of loans and receivables. [*IAS 39.9*]

7I.4.80.20   Types of instruments that may meet the held-to-maturity definition include:

- a fixed-maturity debt security that bears interest at a fixed or variable rate;
- a fixed-maturity debt security even if there is a high risk of non-payment, provided that the security's contractual payments are fixed or determinable and the other criteria for classification are met;
- a debt instrument that is callable by the issuer, as long as substantially all of the carrying amount would be recovered if the call were exercised; and

- shares with a fixed maturity that are classified as liabilities by the issuer (see chapter 7I.3). [*IAS 39.9, AG17–AG18*]

7I.4.80.30   The following instruments cannot be classified as held-to-maturity:
- equity securities;
- an investment that the investor intends to hold for an undefined period or that does not have fixed or determinable payments;
- an investment that the investor stands ready to sell in response to changes in market conditions;
- a perpetual debt instrument that will pay interest in perpetuity;
- an instrument that is redeemable at the option of the issuer at an amount significantly below amortised cost;
- an instrument that is puttable by the holder, because paying for the put feature is inconsistent with an intention to hold the instrument to maturity – i.e. it is questionable whether the holder has the intent to hold the instrument to its maturity if the holder simultaneously acquires the right to require the issuer to redeem the instrument before its maturity date;
- an asset for which the entity does not have adequate resources to hold to maturity; and
- an asset that is subject to legal constraints that mean that the entity may be unable to hold it to maturity. [*IAS 39.9, AG16–AG19, AG23*]

7I.4.80.40   The effect of using the held-to-maturity classification is that the investments will be measured at amortised cost. The category is generally used for fixed interest debt instruments quoted in an active market that are exposed to significant fair value risk. Debt instruments that are not quoted in an active market meet the definition of loans and receivables and would not be classified as held-to-maturity.

7I.4.80.50   An entity is not permitted to classify any investments as held-to-maturity if the entity has – during the current annual reporting period or during the two preceding annual reporting periods – sold or reclassified more than an insignificant amount in relation to the total amount of held-to-maturity investments before maturity, other than sales or reclassifications that:
- are so close to maturity or the investment's call date – e.g. less than three months before maturity – that changes in the market rate of interest would not have a significant effect on the fair value;
- occur after the entity has collected substantially all of the investments' original principal through scheduled payments or prepayments; or
- are attributable to an isolated event that is beyond the entity's control, is non-recurring and could not have been reasonably anticipated by the entity. [*IAS 39.9*]

7I.4.80.60   A prerequisite for the classification of an investment as held-to-maturity is the entity's intent and ability to actually hold that investment until maturity. An entity assesses its intent and ability to hold its held-to-maturity investments not only at initial acquisition, but again at each reporting date. [*IAS 39.AG25*]

7I.4.80.70   Circumstances may arise in which the entity disposes of a significant amount of its held-to-maturity investments after the reporting date, but before the financial statements are authorised for issue. In our view, this calls into question the entity's intent and ability at the reporting date to hold those investments to maturity and may require the classification of these investments to be revised at the reporting date. If a reclassification is required, then this would result in tainting the entire held-to-maturity portfolio. Such a case requires further consideration of the other evidence available at the reporting date to support the entity's intent and ability.

71.4.80.80   There is no requirement to use the held-to-maturity classification. An instrument with fixed and determinable payments may be designated as available-for-sale even if the entity might hold the instrument until its maturity. In our view, this applies even if there are legal restrictions that require an instrument to be held until its maturity.

71.4.80.90   Hedge accounting is not allowed for hedges of the interest rate risk or prepayment risk on held-to-maturity investments (see 71.7.170.80). [*IAS 39.79*]

71.4.90   *Fixed maturity and determinable payments*

71.4.90.10   Investments classified as held-to-maturity should have a fixed maturity and fixed or determinable payments, meaning a contractual arrangement that defines both the amounts and dates of payments to the holder, such as interest and principal payments on debt. A significant risk of non-payment does not preclude an investment from being classified as held-to-maturity automatically. [*IAS 39.9, AG17*]

71.4.90.20   Because held-to-maturity investments should have a fixed maturity, mainly debt contracts are classified as held-to-maturity. Nevertheless, even certain debt instruments have an unlimited or unspecified maturity. For example, perpetual bonds that provide for interest payments for an indefinite period would not qualify as held-to-maturity investments. [*IAS 39.AG17*]

71.4.90.30   In our view, investments that have an equity nature because payments are dependent on residual cash flows – e.g. subordinated notes for which the amount of interest or principal paid to the holder will be determined based on the residual remaining after interest and principal amounts in respect of other creditors are paid – should not be classified as held-to-maturity investments.

71.4.90.40   Similarly, in our view investments in funds for which the amount to be paid out as distributions or on liquidation is not fixed or determinable because it is based on the performance of the fund should not generally be classified as held-to-maturity, even if the fund has a final liquidation date – e.g. 10 years after the fund closes to additional investments.

71.4.90.50   However, the host contract in a hybrid financial asset may be designated as held-to-maturity if it meets the relevant criteria.

EXAMPLE 2 – FINANCIAL ASSETS HELD TO MATURITY

> 71.4.90.60   Bank Q has the positive intent and ability to hold a bond issued by an oil company to maturity. The interest on the bond is indexed to the price of oil. The fact that the return is dependent on the price of oil means that the bond includes an embedded derivative that is not closely related to the host contract (see 71.2.200). The embedded derivative and host contract are separated, resulting in an embedded commodity contract to be measured at FVTPL and a host debt instrument.
>
> 71.4.90.70   Because Q has the positive intent and ability to hold the host contract to maturity, it classifies the host contract as held-to-maturity. [*IAS 39.IG.B.13–IG.B.14*]

7I.4.100   ***Intent to hold to maturity***

7I.4.100.10   If an entity has the intent to hold an investment only for some period, but has not actually defined that period to be to maturity, then the positive intent to hold to maturity does not exist. Likewise, if the issuer has the right to settle the investment at an amount that is significantly below the carrying amount, and therefore is expected to exercise that right, then the entity cannot demonstrate a positive intent to hold the investment until maturity. Also, an embedded option that may shorten the stated maturity of a debt instrument casts doubt on an entity's intent to hold an investment until maturity. Therefore, the purchase of an instrument with a put feature is inconsistent with the positive intent to hold the asset until maturity, except for some put options described in 7I.4.150.40. However, if the issuer may call the instrument at or above its carrying amount, then this does not affect the investor's intent to hold the instrument until maturity. The issuer's call option, if it is exercised, simply accelerates the instrument's maturity. [*IAS 39.AG16, AG18–AG19*]

7I.4.100.20   The demonstration of positive intent to hold an investment to maturity would not be negated by a highly unusual and unlikely occurrence, such as a run on a bank, that could not be anticipated by the entity when deciding whether it has the positive intent (and ability) to hold an investment until maturity. [*IAS 39.AG21*]

7I.4.100.30   A debt instrument that is convertible at the option of the holder cannot generally be classified as held-to-maturity. This applies in particular when there is no specified date for exercising the conversion option. Paying for an early conversion right is inconsistent with an intention to hold the investment to its maturity. However, in our view an investment that is convertible at the option of the holder at the maturity date may be classified as held-to-maturity.

7I.4.100.40   Also, the risk profile of a particular financial investment may raise similar questions about the entity's intention. For example, the high risk and volatility of a mortgage-backed interest-only certificate make active management of such strips more likely than holding them to maturity. The same reasoning may apply to debt instruments with high credit risk – e.g. high-yield (junk) bonds and subordinated bonds. A significant risk of non-payment of interest and principal on a bond is not in itself a consideration in qualifying for the held-to-maturity category as long as there is an intent and ability to hold the bond until maturity. However, an entity would taint its held-to-maturity portfolio if it subsequently sold such a bond as a result of a rating downgrade that could have been foreseen. [*IAS 39.AG17, IG.B.15*]

7I.4.110   ***Ability to hold to maturity***

7I.4.110.10   An entity cannot demonstrate an ability to hold an investment to maturity if:
- financial resources are not available to the entity to finance the investment to maturity – e.g. if it is expected or likely that an entity will acquire another business and will need all of its funding for this investment, then the resources may not be available to continue to hold certain debt instruments; or
- legal or other constraints could frustrate the intention of the entity to hold the investment to maturity – e.g. there might be an expectation that a regulator will exercise its right in certain industries, such as the banking and insurance industries, to force an entity to sell certain investments in the event of a credit risk change of the entity. [*IAS 39.AG23*]

7I.4.120   ***Tainting of held-to-maturity portfolio***

7I.4.120.10   If an entity sells or transfers more than an insignificant amount of the portfolio of held-to-maturity investments, then it may not classify any investment as held-to-maturity for the remainder of the current annual reporting period plus two annual reporting periods after the annual reporting period in which the event occurred. [*IAS 39.9*]

7I.4.120.20   Although 'more than an insignificant amount' is interpreted in relation to the total amount of held-to-maturity investments, the standard does not provide more detailed guidance; rather, this is assessed by an entity based on the facts and circumstances when a potential tainting situation arises. It is also important to consider the reasons for an entity's actions when determining if the portfolio has been tainted. [*IAS 39.9*]

EXAMPLE 3 – TAINTING OF HELD-TO-MATURITY PORTFOLIO

7I.4.120.30   Company T sells 1,000 bonds from its held-to-maturity portfolio during the reporting period because the fair value of the bonds had appreciated significantly over the carrying amount and management decided that T should realise the gains through a sale.

7I.4.120.35   In these circumstances, selling investments from the held-to-maturity portfolio taints the entire portfolio, and all remaining investments in that category are reclassified. T will be prohibited from classifying any investments as held-to-maturity for the remainder of the current annual reporting period plus two full annual reporting periods.

7I.4.120.40   The tainting rules are intended to bring some discipline to an entity's assertion that it intends and is able to hold an investment until maturity. Tainting requires a reclassification of the total remaining held-to-maturity portfolio in the financial statements into the available-for-sale category. [*IAS 39.IG.B.19–IG.B.21*]

7I.4.120.50   The tainting requirements apply group-wide, so that a subsidiary that sells more than an insignificant amount of investments classified as held-to-maturity in the consolidated financial statements can preclude the entire group from using the held-to-maturity category in its consolidated financial statements. If an entity has various portfolios of held-to-maturity investments – e.g. by industry or by country of issue – then the sale or transfer of more than an insignificant amount of instruments from one of the portfolios taints all the other held-to-maturity portfolios of the entity. [*IAS 39.IG.B.20–IG.B.21*]

7I.4.120.60   Selling securities classified as held-to-maturity under repurchase agreements does not constrain the entity's intent and ability to hold those investments until maturity, unless the entity does not expect to be able to maintain or recover access to those investments. For example, if an entity is expected to receive back other comparable securities, but not the securities lent, then classification as held-to-maturity is not appropriate. [*IAS 39.IG.B.18*]

7I.4.130   *Exceptions to tainting*

7I.4.130.10   There are a limited number of exceptions to the tainting rules. First, the tainting rules do not apply if only an insignificant amount of held-to-maturity investments is sold or reclassified. Any sale or reclassification should be a one-off event. If an entity sells or transfers insignificant portions periodically, then this may cast doubt on the entity's intent and ability with regard to its held-to-maturity portfolio. If the sales are not isolated, then the amount sold or reclassified is assessed on a cumulative basis in assessing whether the sales are insignificant. [*IAS 39.9*]

71.4.130.20   Another exception is when almost the entire principal has been collected through scheduled payments or through prepayments. The remaining part would not be affected materially by changes in the interest rate and therefore the sale would not result in a significant gain or loss. IAS 39 does not define the phrase 'substantially all' of the principal investment; however, in our view the main question is whether the remaining fair value exposure is significant. [*IAS 39.9*]

71.4.130.30   Circumstances may arise that the entity could not reasonably have foreseen or anticipated. If, in such a situation, an entity sells or reclassifies held-to-maturity investments, then the remaining portfolio is not tainted if the event leading to the sale or reclassification of investments is isolated and non-recurring. If the event is not isolated or is potentially recurring, and the entity anticipates further sales or reclassification of held-to-maturity investments, then this inevitably casts doubt on its ability to hold the remaining portfolio until maturity. Also, if the event could reasonably have been anticipated at the date on which the held-to-maturity classification was made, then the investment would not have been classified as such initially. If an entity has control over or initiated the isolated or non-recurring event – e.g. sales made after a change in senior management – then this also calls into question the entity's intent to hold the remaining portfolio until maturity. [*IAS 39.9, IG.B.16*]

71.4.130.40   Situations that may not have been anticipated when investments were included in the held-to-maturity category and would not call into question the entity's intent and ability to hold investments to maturity may result, for example, from any of the following:

- a significant deterioration in the creditworthiness of the issuer of the investment that could not have been anticipated when the investment was acquired;
- significant changes in tax laws, affecting specific investments in the portfolio;
- major business combinations or disposals with consequences for the interest rate risk position and credit risk policies of an entity; and
- significant changes in statutory or regulatory requirements. [*IAS 39.AG22, IG.B.15, IG.B.17*]

71.4.140   *Deterioration in creditworthiness*

71.4.140.10   Although IAS 39 does not provide a definition of a significant deterioration in an issuer's creditworthiness, an example of this would be a significant downgrade by a credit rating agency. Downgrades as reflected in an entity's proprietary internal credit rating system may also support the demonstration of significant deterioration. An external credit rating may be a lagging indicator of creditworthiness. [*IAS 39.AG22, IG.B.15*]

71.4.140.15   An entity might assess that a significant deterioration in the issuer's creditworthiness has occurred based on its own current analysis of the issuer's creditworthiness supported by evidence available from market prices – e.g. a significant increase in bond yields and credit default swap spreads could imply a higher probability of risk of default and therefore could be an indicator of significant deterioration in the issuer's creditworthiness. If the deterioration could reasonably have been foreseen, then the investment did not qualify to be classified as held-to-maturity. A credit downgrade of a notch within a class or from one rating class to an immediately lower rating class could often be considered reasonably anticipated. Therefore, a sale or reclassification triggered by such a minor downgrading would result in tainting. [*IAS 39.AG22, IG.B.15*]

71.4.140.20   In our view, in order for a sale or reclassification to be considered attributable to a significant deterioration in creditworthiness, the entity's change of intent with respect to the investment – i.e. a decision that it may sell the investment – and the sale or reclassification should generally follow within a reasonably short period after it identified the significant deterioration. Determining what is an appropriate period is a matter of judgement that depends on the particular facts and circumstances, including the entity's policies and procedures for making such decisions. Sales or reclassifications should usually take place before the end of the reporting period in which the significant credit deterioration occurred to avoid tainting, given that an entity is required to reassert its intent and ability to hold held-to-maturity investments to maturity at each reporting date. However, sales or reclassifications shortly after the reporting date may be acceptable, because of the time required for an entity to complete its evaluation of the issuer's creditworthiness and finalise its response.

7I.4.140.25   If, after completing its evaluation and relevant decision-making processes, an entity concludes that significant credit deterioration has occurred and that, notwithstanding that identified deterioration, it re-asserts its intent to hold to maturity, then we believe that it is unlikely that the entity would be able to demonstrate that a subsequent sale or reclassification is attributable to that deterioration. However, if there is a further subsequent significant deterioration in creditworthiness, then a sale or reclassification shortly following that further significant deterioration might not trigger tainting.

EXAMPLE 4 – EXCEPTION TO TAINTING

> 7I.4.140.27   Company H classifies an AAA-rated bond as held-to-maturity. The bond is downgraded to A and H reasserts its intent to hold it to maturity. Subsequently, the bond is further downgraded from A to CCC and considered impaired, then H sells the bond. In this example, the sale shortly after that further significant deterioration does not trigger tainting.

7I.4.140.30   An entity might hold a number of held-to-maturity investments issued by a single issuer that have all suffered a significant deterioration in creditworthiness. Also, it might hold a number of investments issued by different issuers that are affected by a similar significant deterioration in creditworthiness. If the entity decides to sell or reclassify some of these investments because of the significant deterioration in creditworthiness, then it is not required to reclassify the other investments that have also suffered a significant deterioration in creditworthiness if it continues to have the intent and ability to hold those other investments to maturity. However, it would be necessary to consider whether the circumstances surrounding the entity's explicit decision to sell or reclassify some investments called into question its intent and ability to hold the other investments to maturity, given they have all suffered a similar significant deterioration in creditworthiness. For example, if an entity's policies require management to sell any investment that is downgraded below a certain rating, then it would be expected that all investments that are downgraded below this threshold would be reclassified.

7I.4.150   *Changes in tax laws*

7I.4.150.10   A significant change in tax laws – such as the elimination or the significant reduction of the tax-exempt status of an investment – might not cast doubt on the intention or ability of the entity with respect to the held-to-maturity category. [*IAS 39.AG22*]

7I.4.150.20   For example, an entity has a captive finance company in a tax haven and, because of changes in tax laws that affect the whole group, needs to relocate its treasury activities and in that process liquidate the held-to-maturity portfolio in the finance company. In our view, the classification as held-to-maturity in other group entities would not be violated, because the entity could not have foreseen the change in tax laws.

71.4.150.30   However, in our view a change in the applicable marginal tax rate for interest income is not sufficient justification for sales of held-to-maturity investments without tainting, because this change impacts all debt instruments held by the entity. [*IAS 39.AG22(b)*]

71.4.150.40   In our view, if an entity holds a put option that it intends to use only in the event of a change in laws, then a voluntary exercise of that option by the entity would nevertheless result in tainting. However, if the exercise of an option is conditional on a change in laws, or the option comes into existence only as a result of a change in laws, then a sale through the exercise of such an option would not give rise to tainting.

71.4.160   *Major business combination or disposition*

71.4.160.10   Although a major business combination or the sale of a significant segment of the entity is a controllable event, it may have consequences for the entity's interest rate risk and credit risk positions. In such situations, sales that are necessary to maintain the entity's existing risk positions and that support proper risk management do not taint the held-to-maturity portfolio. [*IAS 39.AG22*]

71.4.160.20   Although sales subsequent to business combinations and segment disposals might not taint the held-to-maturity portfolio, sales of held-to-maturity investments before a business combination or disposal, or in response to an unsolicited tender offer, will cast doubt on the entity's intent to hold its remaining investments until maturity. [*IAS 39.IG.B.19*]

71.4.160.30   In our view, if investments acquired in a business combination were classified as held-to-maturity by the acquiree, but the acquirer does not have the intent or ability to hold these securities until maturity, then in the consolidated financial statements the instruments should not be classified as held-to-maturity. However, transferring investments held by the acquirer before the acquisition from the held-to-maturity portfolio would result in tainting.

71.4.160.40   In our view, a sale following a group reorganisation (including a common control transaction) that is not a major business combination or disposition would result in tainting. We do not believe that a sale of a held-to-maturity asset between group entities would result in tainting in the consolidated financial statements, as long as the investment remains classified as held-to-maturity in the consolidated financial statements.

(S) 71.4.160.50   However, in the separate financial statements of the individual entities within the group, such intra-group transactions may give rise to tainting.

71.4.170   *Changes in statutory or regulatory requirements*

71.4.170.10   Examples of changes in statutory or regulatory requirements that do not have tainting implications for the held-to-maturity portfolio are:
- changes either in the applicable laws or in regulations affecting the entity that modify what constitutes a permissible investment or the maximum level of certain types of investments, as a result of which the entity has to sell (part of) these investments; and

- significant increases in the industry's capital requirements or in the risk weightings of held-to-maturity investments used for risk-based capital purposes, as a result of which the size of the held-to-maturity portfolio has to be decreased. [*IAS 39.AG22*]

7I.4.170.20   The exceptions are intended to shield entities operating in regulated industries from potential tainting situations resulting from actions taken by the industry's regulator. These are actions applicable to the industry as a whole and not to a specific entity. However, sales could occur in response to an entity-specific increase in capital requirements set by the industry's regulator. In that case, it will be difficult to demonstrate that the regulator's action could not reasonably have been anticipated by the entity, unless the increase in entity-specific capital requirements represents a significant change in the regulator's policy for setting entity-specific capital requirements. [*IAS 39.IG.B.17*]

7I.4.180   Loans and receivables

7I.4.180.10   Loans and receivables are non-derivative financial assets with fixed or determinable payments that are not quoted in an active market, other than those:
- that the entity intends to sell immediately or in the near term, which are classified as held-for-trading, and those that the entity designates on initial recognition as at FVTPL;
- that the entity designates on initial recognition as available-for-sale; or
- for which the holder may not recover substantially all of its initial investment, other than because of credit deterioration, which are classified as available-for-sale. [*IAS 39.9*]

7I.4.180.20   An interest acquired in a pool of assets that are not loans and receivables – e.g. an interest in a mutual fund or similar fund – is not a loan or receivable. Cash collateralised debt obligations (CDOs) (see 7I.2.360) are securitised interests in a pool of financial assets that expose investors to credit risk on reference assets through the vehicle holding the reference assets. In our view, the holder of a cash CDO may be able to classify the financial asset as loans and receivables if the reference assets in the pool meet the criteria in 7I.4.180.10.

7I.4.180.30   In our view, 'fixed or determinable payments' generally means that the cash flows are either fixed or determined by a formula.

7I.4.180.40   The main requirement for a financial asset to be classified as a loan or receivable is that it has fixed or determinable payments and is not a derivative. However, the definition also excludes any instrument that is quoted in an active market. This means that a listed debt security that is actively traded in a market cannot be classified within loans and receivables, even if it is acquired at the date of its original issue by providing funds directly to the issuer. [*IAS 39.AG26*]

7I.4.180.45   An entity is prohibited from classifying a financial asset as a loan or receivable if it may not recover substantially all of its initial investment, other than because of credit deterioration (see 7I.4.180.10). [*IAS 39.9*]

7I.4.180.46   In our view, a financial asset bearing a negative interest rate or yield may, depending on the circumstances, be eligible for classification as loans and receivables. We believe that a negative interest rate or yield would not preclude eligibility if the instrument contractually requires the borrower to repay amounts that on a present value basis (considering market rates of interest) would result in the holder recovering substantially all of its recorded investment, thus satisfying the condition in 7I.4.180.45. For example, a floating-rate loan that is indexed to a benchmark interest rate that might become negative could be eligible for classification as loans and receivables. [*IAS 39.BC29*]

EXAMPLE 5 – FINANCIAL ASSETS WITH LOSS PARTICIPATION FEATURE

7I.4.180.47 Company S holds a debt instrument issued by Company P, a widget manufacturer, which carries a right to annual interest at the rate of 7% subject to the following contractual loss participation features:

- no interest in years when P's performance results in an accounting loss;
- any such loss suffered by P is allocated against the principal amount of the instrument on a proportionate basis and is recovered in subsequent periods if and to the extent that P makes an accounting profit; and
- any losses absorbed by the instrument at the time of redemption are not recovered.

7I.4.180.48 S concludes that the loss participation feature is not a derivative in the scope of IAS 39, because it considers the dependency on P's accounting profits to be a non-financial variable specific to P (see 7I.2.30.60–80).

7I.4.180.49 P may suffer a loss that is not linked to credit deterioration. Consequently, the loss participation feature may lead to S not recovering substantially all of its initial investment in the instrument due to a reason other than credit deterioration. Therefore, S cannot classify its investment in the debt instrument as loans and receivables.

7I.4.180.50 Both originated loans and purchased loans are included in this category. This ensures, as far as possible, a consistent accounting treatment across all loan portfolios. Also, because many entities manage purchased loans and originated loans together, this prevents system problems arising from having to separate purchased loans from originated loans purely for financial reporting purposes. [*IAS 39.BC28*]

7I.4.180.60 In addition, an entity has a free choice to classify any loan or receivable as available-for-sale on initial recognition.

7I.4.180.70 Reclassifications and sales of loans and receivables are possible without any of the tainting issues applicable to the held-to-maturity category (see 7I.4.120). However, in our view if financial assets classified as loans and receivables are subsequently sold within a short period after origination or purchase, then this may cast doubt on whether other assets classified as loans and receivables are not held for the purpose of selling in the near term.

7I.4.190 Available-for-sale financial assets

7I.4.190.10 Available-for-sale financial assets are non-derivative financial assets that are designated as available-for-sale or that are not classified as:

- loans and receivables;
- held-to-maturity investments; or
- financial assets at FVTPL. [*IAS 39.9*]

7I.4.190.20　A financial asset that the entity intends to hold to maturity, or a loan and receivable, may also be designated as available-for-sale on initial recognition. This category normally includes all debt securities quoted in an active market other than those classified as held-to-maturity and all equity securities that are not classified as at FVTPL. [*IAS 39.9*]

7I.4.190.30　Any financial asset that does not fall into any of the three categories in 7I.4.190.10 is classified as available-for-sale.

7I.4.200　Other financial liabilities

7I.4.200.10　Other financial liabilities constitute the residual category similar to the available-for-sale category of financial assets. All financial liabilities other than trading liabilities, financial liabilities designated as at FVTPL and derivatives that are hedging instruments fall automatically into this category. Common examples are an entity's trade payables, borrowings and customer deposit accounts.

7I.4.210　RECLASSIFICATION OF FINANCIAL ASSETS

7I.4.210.10　An entity may wish or need to reclassify a financial asset from one category to another subsequent to its initial recognition. However, reclassifications are permitted/required only if certain criteria are met and may not be allowed at all without tainting implications. In our view, a financial asset is required to meet the definition of the category of a financial asset into which it is proposed to be reclassified at the time of reclassification in order for the reclassification to be permissible. [*IAS 39.9, 50–54*]

7I.4.210.20　The following table summarises the possible reclassifications of financial assets. The criteria for reclassification and the circumstances under which reclassification is permitted or required are discussed in further detail below. [*IAS 39.9, 50–54*]

FROM: / To:	FVTPL	AVAILABLE-FOR-SALE	HELD-TO-MATURITY	LOANS AND RECEIVABLES	MEASURED AT COST
FVTPL (non-derivatives held for trading)	N/A	P	P	P	R
FVTPL (derivatives or designated)	N/A	✗	✗	✗	R
Available-for-sale	✗	N/A	P	P	R
Held-to-maturity	✗	R	N/A	✗	✗
Loans and receivables	✗	P	✗	N/A	✗
Measured at cost	R	R	✗	✗	N/A

P – permitted in certain circumstances
R – required in certain circumstances
✗ – not allowed

71.4.220 **To or from FVTPL category**

71.4.220.10   An entity may not reclassify any financial asset into the FVTPL category after initial recognition. An entity may not reclassify out of the FVTPL category any derivative financial asset or any financial asset designated as at FVTPL on initial recognition. When a financial asset is held for trading, it is included in this category based on the objective for which it was acquired initially, which was for trading purposes. Reclassifying such an asset out of this category would generally be inconsistent with this initial objective. [*IAS 39.50(a)–(c)*]

71.4.220.20   However, an entity may be permitted to reclassify a non-derivative financial asset out of the held-for-trading category if it is no longer held for the purpose of being sold or repurchased in the near term. There are different criteria for reclassifications of loans and receivables, and of other qualifying assets.
- If the financial asset would have met the definition of loans and receivables (see 71.4.180) if it had not been required to be classified as held-for-trading on initial recognition, then it may be reclassified if the entity has the intention and ability to hold the financial asset for the foreseeable future or until maturity.
- If the financial asset is not of the type described in the previous bullet, then it may be reclassified only in rare circumstances. IAS 39 does not provide a definition of 'rare circumstances' but rare circumstances arise from a single event that is unusual and highly unlikely to recur in the near term. In our view, it is not a necessary feature of rare circumstances that the market for the asset has ceased to be active or become highly illiquid. [*IAS 39.50(c), 50B, 50D, BC104D*]

71.4.220.30   The reclassification criteria do not refer directly to financial assets that are classified as held-for-trading because they are or were part of a portfolio of financial instruments that are managed together and for which there is evidence of a recent pattern of short-term profit taking. In our view, if a financial asset was classified as held-for-trading because previously it was managed as part of such a portfolio but it is no longer managed as part of such a portfolio, then it may be eligible for reclassification out of trading, provided that at the date of reclassification the entity did not hold the financial asset for the purpose of selling it in the near term. However, if the financial asset continues to be managed as part of a portfolio for which there is evidence of a recent pattern of short-term profit taking, then it is unlikely that the entity would be able to assert credibly that the asset is no longer held for the purpose of selling it in the short term. If the entity is not able to demonstrate this intent, then the financial asset would not be eligible to be reclassified.

71.4.220.40   To be eligible for reclassification, the financial asset should meet the definition of loans and receivables, except for it having been classified as held-for-trading. In our view, a financial asset would meet this criterion if it would have met the definition of loans and receivables immediately before, and at the time of, reclassification, except for it previously having been classified as held-for-trading, and it is not necessary for the financial asset to have met the definition of loans and receivables on initial recognition. Furthermore, notwithstanding that the financial asset meets the definition of loans and receivables at the time of reclassification, it is not precluded from being reclassified to the available-for-sale category.

71.4.220.50   Financial assets previously classified as at FVTPL, which are reclassified out of this category, may contain embedded derivatives. Before the reclassification, the embedded derivative would not have been accounted for separately as a derivative because the entire instrument was classified as at FVTPL (see 7I.2.150.10). If a financial asset is classified out of trading and is no longer accounted for at FVTPL, then on reclassification an entity assesses whether the financial asset contains an embedded derivative that requires separate accounting (see 7I.2.220.50). If an entity is unable to separately measure the fair value of an embedded derivative that would have to be separated on reclassification out of the FVTPL category, then reclassification is prohibited and the entire hybrid financial instrument remains in the FVTPL category. [*IAS 39.13*]

7I.4.220.60   If an entity reclassifies a financial asset out of the FVTPL category, then the financial asset is reclassified at its fair value on the date of reclassification and this fair value becomes the new cost or amortised cost, as applicable. Any gain or loss previously recognised in profit or loss is not reversed. On the same date, a new original effective interest rate is calculated based on the expected future cash flows as at the reclassification date. [*IAS 39.50C, 50F*]

7I.4.220.70   A reclassification from the held-for-trading category takes effect prospectively from the date it is made and cannot be applied retrospectively. A reclassification may not be effected before the date on which the entity has met all of the criteria for reclassification, including as applicable a change in management intent and:
● the occurrence of a rare circumstance; or
● meeting the definition of loans and receivables. [*IAS 39.50(c), 50B, 50D, 103H*]

7I.4.220.80   If an entity reclassifies a financial asset out of the held-for-trading category on the basis that it is no longer held for the purpose of selling it in the near term, or that the entity has the intention and ability to hold the asset for the foreseeable future or until maturity, then there is no automatic consequence of subsequent sales of such assets similar to the tainting rules for sales of held-to-maturity assets. However, in our view if reclassified financial assets are sold subsequently, then this may cast doubt on whether the entity has the intention and ability to hold those or other reclassified financial assets for the foreseeable future or until maturity or, more generally, whether other assets are not held for the purpose of selling in the near term.

7I.4.220.90   Entities within the same group may undertake transactions in instruments classified in the FVTPL category. From the perspective of the consolidated financial statements, unless the instruments were financial assets held for trading and the criteria for reclassification out of the held-for-trading category were met (see 7I.4.220.20), such instruments may not be reclassified out of the FVTPL category purely as a result of intra-group transactions even if the instruments are not classified into this category by the acquiring group entity in its own financial statements.

EXAMPLE 6 – INTRA-GROUP TRANSACTION

 7I.4.220.95   Subsidiary X sells a debt instrument that it designated on initial recognition as at FVTPL to Subsidiary Y. However, Y classifies that instrument as available-for-sale. The consolidated financial statements should continue to reflect that debt instrument as at FVTPL.

7I.4.220.100   In some circumstances, an entity's trading desk may be responsible for the acquisition of financial assets for the investment purposes of other divisions within the entity. In our view, when the trading desk clearly acts on behalf of the investing division – such that an investment is acquired and passed directly to that division – the entity is not precluded from classifying the investment into the available-for-sale or held-to-maturity category on initial recognition. This applies even if – for operational reasons only – the investment is recognised initially in the trading book. However, should the trading desk have an existing portfolio of financial assets which were classified for accounting purposes as held-for-trading, such assets would retain their classification even if an investing division of the entity subsequently acquired some of the assets for its investment purposes, unless the criteria for reclassification out of the held-for-trading category were met (see 7I.4.220.20).

7I.4.220.110   Movements of derivatives out of or into the FVTPL category when they become designated and effective hedging instruments in cash flow or net investment hedges or when they no longer qualify as designated and effective hedging instruments in such hedges are not 'reclassifications'.

7I.4.230   **From held-to-maturity to available-for-sale**

7I.4.230.10   An investment is reclassified from held-to-maturity to available-for-sale if and when the entity no longer has the positive intent or ability to hold the investment to maturity. All held-to-maturity investments are required to be reclassified to the available-for-sale category if there is tainting of the held-to-maturity portfolio (see 7I.4.120). [*IAS 39.51–52*]

7I.4.230.20   A reclassification of an instrument out of the held-to-maturity category will generally trigger the tainting rules (see 7I.4.120). [*IAS 39.9, 52*]

7I.4.230.30   Adjustments on remeasurement from amortised cost to fair value on the date of the reclassification are generally recognised in OCI. However, if the reclassified asset is impaired at the date of the reclassification, then any impairment loss based on the asset's fair value – i.e. the difference between its carrying amount (amortised cost) and its fair value – is recognised in profit or loss. [*IAS 39.55(b)*]

7I.4.240   **From available-for-sale category to measurement at amortised cost**

7I.4.250   *From available-for-sale to loans and receivables*

7I.4.250.10   A financial asset that is classified as available-for-sale that would have met the definition of loans and receivables (see 7I.4.180) if it had not been designated as available-for-sale may be reclassified out of the available-for-sale category to loans and receivables if the entity has the intention and ability to hold the financial asset for the foreseeable future or until maturity. In our view, such an asset should meet the definition of loans and receivables at the date of reclassification to qualify for reclassification into that category, but it is not necessary for the financial asset to have met the definition on initial recognition. For a discussion of the consequences of subsequent sales of such assets, see 7I.4.220.80. [*IAS 39.50E*]

7I.4.250.20   If an entity reclassifies a financial asset from the available-for-sale category to loans and receivables, then the financial asset is reclassified at its fair value on the date of reclassification and this fair value becomes its new cost or amortised cost, as applicable. Any gain or loss previously recognised in OCI is accounted for in accordance with 7I.4.260.30. On the same date, a new original effective interest rate is calculated based on the expected future cash flows as at the reclassification date. [*IAS 39.50F, IU 07-10*]

7I.4.250.30   A reclassification from the available-for-sale category to loans and receivables takes effect prospectively from the date it is made and cannot be applied retrospectively. A reclassification cannot be effected before the date on which the entity met all of the criteria for reclassification – i.e. management has the intent and ability to hold the financial asset for the foreseeable future or until maturity and the financial asset would have met the definition of loans and receivables. [*IAS 39.50E, 103H*]

7I.4.250.40   If an available-for-sale asset is impaired, then it may still be reclassified provided it meets the definition of loans and receivables and the entity has the intention and ability to hold the asset for the foreseeable future or until maturity.

7I.4.260   *From available-for-sale to held-to-maturity*

7I.4.260.10   A reclassification from the available-for-sale category to the held-to-maturity category is permitted once any tainting period has lapsed or if there is a change in intent or ability. [*IAS 39.54*]

EXAMPLE 7 – CHANGE IN INTENT

7I.4.260.15   Company Y has a loan portfolio and classifies the instruments as available-for-sale. Y subsequently decides to document its investment policy to hold the loan portfolio to maturity. Y concludes that the act of formalising the investment policy is a change in intent. Therefore, Y is allowed to reclassify the loan portfolio from available-for-sale to held-to-maturity if it has an ability to hold it to maturity.

7I.4.260.20   The fair value immediately before the reclassification to the held-to-maturity category becomes the new amortised cost. [*IAS 39.54*]

7I.4.260.30   Following reclassification of a financial asset with a fixed maturity, any gain or loss previously recognised in OCI and the difference between the newly established amortised cost and the maturity amount are both amortised over the remaining term of the financial asset under the effective interest method (see 7I.6.240). However, any gain or loss previously recognised in OCI is immediately reclassified from equity to profit or loss if the asset is subsequently impaired. For a financial asset with no stated maturity, any gain or loss previously recognised in OCI is reclassified from equity to profit or loss when the financial asset is disposed of or impaired. [*IAS 39.54*]

7I.4.270   To or from financial instruments measured at cost

7I.4.270.10   For certain unquoted equity instruments and derivatives linked to such instruments (see 7I.6.210), a reclassification to measure a financial instrument at cost that was measured previously at fair value is required but only in the rare case that a reliable measure of the fair value is no longer available. The reason for any such reclassifications is disclosed. [*IAS 39.54*]

7I.4.270.20   If a reliable measure becomes available for a financial instrument for which a reliable measure was previously not available, and the financial instrument is required to be measured at fair value if a reliable measure is available, then the financial instrument is remeasured at fair value. The difference between the carrying amount and fair value at the date of such remeasurement is recognised in profit or loss if the financial instrument is classified as held-for-trading or is recognised in OCI if the financial instrument is classified as available-for-sale. [*IAS 39.53*]

7I.4.280   From loans and receivables to at FVTPL

7I.4.280.10   Financial assets that would otherwise meet the definition of loans and receivables are classified as at FVTPL on initial recognition if the intent is to sell such loans immediately or in the short term, or if they are part of a portfolio of loans for which there is an actual pattern of short-term profit taking (see 7I.4.30). An entity may further decide to designate specific loans and receivables into the FVTPL category on initial recognition. A subsequent reclassification from loans and receivables to the FVTPL category is prohibited. [*IAS 39.9, 50*]

7I.4.290   From loans and receivables to available-for-sale

7I.4.290.10   The definition of loans and receivables excludes financial assets that are quoted in an active market. If a market subsequently becomes active, then in our view that would generally not permit a reclassification from loans and receivables to the available-for-sale category unless the market is expected to remain active for the foreseeable future. [*IAS 39.9*]

7I.4.300   Internal transfers of financial instruments

7I.4.300.10   Although internal transactions are eliminated on consolidation, an internal transfer might be an indication that there has been a change in the group's intent for holding the portfolios concerned.

7I.4.310   RECLASSIFICATION OF FINANCIAL LIABILITIES

7I.4.310.10   IAS 39 prohibits reclassifications of financial liabilities out of or into the FVTPL category after initial recognition.

7I.4.320   Loan commitments

7I.4.320.10   Loan commitments measured at FVTPL on the basis that they were so designated on initial recognition or because they are derivatives may not be reclassified. However, in our view if the loan commitment is drawn down and a financial asset representing the advance is recognised, then that financial asset would be eligible for reclassification if it satisfied all eligibility criteria (see 7I.4.210).

7I.5   Recognition and derecognition

7I.5 Recognition and derecognition

REQUIREMENTS FOR INSURERS THAT APPLY IFRS 4

In July 2014, the IASB issued IFRS 9 *Financial Instruments*, which is effective for annual periods beginning on or after 1 January 2018. However, an insurer may defer the application of IFRS 9 if it meets certain criteria (see 8.1.180).

This chapter reflects the requirement of IAS 39 *Financial Instruments: Recognition and Measurement* and the related standards, excluding any amendments introduced by IFRS 9. These requirements are relevant to insurers that apply the temporary exemption from IFRS 9 or the overlay approach to designated financial assets (see 8.1.160) and cover annual periods beginning on 1 January 2018. For further discussion, see Introduction to Sections 7 and 7I.

The requirements related to this topic are mainly derived from the following.

Standard	Title
IAS 39	Financial Instruments: Recognition and Measurement
IFRIC 19	Extinguishing Financial Liabilities with Equity Instruments

FORTHCOMING REQUIREMENTS AND FUTURE DEVELOPMENTS

For this topic, there are no forthcoming requirements or future developments.

7I.5.10   INITIAL RECOGNITION

7I.5.10.10   An instrument is recognised in the statement of financial position when the entity becomes party to a contract that is a financial instrument. [*IAS 39.14*]

7I.5.10.20   Situations in which an entity has become a party to the contractual provisions include committing to a purchase of securities or agreeing to enter into a derivative. In contrast, planned but not committed future transactions, no matter how likely, are not financial assets or financial liabilities because they do not represent situations in which the entity becomes a party to a contract requiring the future receipt or delivery of assets. For example, an entity's expected but uncommitted issue of commercial paper does not qualify as a financial liability. [*IAS 39.AG35*]

7I.5.10.30   Similarly, if an entity makes an offer to enter into a contract to buy or sell a financial instrument, then the entity has not become party to a contract requiring the future receipt or delivery of a financial instrument. In our view, the entity should not account for such an offer until the counterparty accepts the offer and the entity becomes a party to a contractual arrangement. [*IAS 39.AG35*]

7I.5.10.40   If a transfer of a financial asset does not qualify for derecognition, then the transferee does not recognise the transferred asset as its asset in its statement of financial position, but derecognises the cash or other consideration paid and recognises a receivable from the transferor. For further discussion on the accounting by the transferee in those cases, see 7I.5.305. [*IAS 39.AG50*]

7I.5.20   Trade and settlement date accounting

7I.5.20.10   Applying the general recognition principle in IAS 39 would result in all transactions that happen in regulated markets being accounted for on trade date, which is when an entity becomes party to the contract. However, the standard recognises that many financial institutions and other entities use settlement date accounting for financial assets and that it would be cumbersome to account for such transactions as derivatives between the trade and settlement dates. [*IAS 39.14, 38, AG53, AG55–AG56*]

7I.5.20.20   Because of the short time between the trade date and the settlement date in these types of regulated market situations, such 'regular-way' contracts are not recognised as derivative contracts under IAS 39. [*IAS 39.AG12*]

7I.5.20.30   The purchase or sale of a non-derivative financial asset that will be delivered within the timeframe generally established by regulation or convention in the market concerned – e.g. a regular-way transaction (see 7I.2.70) – may be recognised either on the date on which the entity commits to the transaction (the trade date) or on the date on which the instrument is actually transferred (the settlement date). [*IAS 39.AG53, AG55–AG56*]

7I.5.20.40   An entity needs to choose a method to be applied consistently to all purchases and all sales of financial assets that are classified in the same category. [*IAS 39.AG53*]

7I.5.20.45   A contract that requires or permits net settlement of the change in its value is not a regular-way contract and therefore trade date or settlement date accounting is not applied to the contract. Instead, such a contract is accounted for as a derivative in the period between the trade date and the settlement date (see 7I.1.190.10). [*IAS 39.AG54*]

7I.5.20.50   There are no specific requirements for trade date or settlement date accounting for financial liabilities and therefore financial liabilities are recognised on the date on which the entity becomes a party to the contractual provisions of the instrument – i.e. the trade date. Such contracts are not generally recognised unless one of the parties has performed under the agreement or the contract is a derivative contract not exempt from the scope of IAS 39. [*IAS 39.IG.B.32*]

7I.5.20.55   The IFRS Interpretations Committee discussed whether the regular-way exemption (see 7I.5.20.20) applies to short sales of a security. The Committee noted that requiring entities to account for short positions as derivatives might create considerable practical problems for their accounting systems and controls with little, if any, improvement to the quality of the financial information presented. Therefore, a liability arising from a short trading position is not accounted for as a derivative because it represents a transaction in a financial asset for which either trade date or settlement date accounting may be applied in line with the entity's policy choice. [*IU 01-07*]

7I.5.20.60   If an entity that buys a financial asset applies settlement date accounting, then it accounts for changes in the fair value of that asset between the trade and settlement dates in the same way as it accounts for fair value changes that happen after recognition of the asset. This is in line with the logic that these changes in fair value between the trade date and settlement date are attributable to the buyer rather than the seller because the seller's right to changes in the fair value ceases on the trade date (see also 7I.5.20.80). [*IAS 39.AG56, IG.D.2.2*]

7I.5.20.65   Therefore, if the acquired asset is measured at fair value, then the buyer recognises changes in the asset's fair value between the trade date and settlement date, regardless of whether trade date accounting or settlement date accounting is applied. Under settlement date accounting, although the underlying asset is not recognised until settlement date, changes in the fair value of the underlying asset are recognised. Therefore, the fair value adjustment is shown as a receivable or payable until settlement date, at which date the receivable or payable adjusts the amount initially recognised for the asset. This results in the asset being initially measured at its fair value on the settlement date. Fair value changes between trade date and settlement date are recognised in profit or loss for financial assets classified as at FVTPL, or in OCI for financial assets classified as available-for-sale. [*IAS 39.AG55–AG56, IG.D.2.2*]

7I.5.20.70   If the item bought is measured at cost or amortised cost, then any change in the fair value of the asset between trade date and settlement date is not recognised. [*IAS 39.AG56, IG.B.32*]

7I.5.20.80   The difference between trade date and settlement date accounting for a sale of financial assets is in the timing of derecognition of the transferred assets and of recognition of any profit or loss on disposal. As explained in 7I.5.20.60, the seller's right to changes in the fair value of an asset ceases on the trade date. Therefore, if the instrument is carried at fair value, then the seller stops recognising changes in value from the trade date regardless of whether trade date accounting or settlement date accounting is applied. [*IAS 39.IG.D.2.2*]

7I.5.20.90   If trade date accounting is applied, then the asset is derecognised and the profit or loss on disposal and a receivable for the sales proceeds are recognised on the trade date. [*IAS 39.AG55*]

7I.5.20.100   If settlement date accounting is applied, then the asset continues to be recognised until settlement date, although no changes in its fair value after the trade date are recognised. On settlement date, the asset is derecognised and a profit or loss on the disposal is recognised. The proceeds are the contract amount; the carrying amount of the asset sold does not reflect gains and losses between the trade and settlement dates. [*IAS 39.AG56, IG.D.2.2*]

7I.5.20.110   Because trade date accounting and settlement date accounting for regular-way purchases or sales of financial assets are specific practices that an entity may apply in preparing and presenting its financial statements and because an entity has a choice between them, a change from settlement date to trade date accounting (or vice versa) is a voluntary change in accounting policy (see 2.8.70). [*IAS 39.38, 8.5*]

7I.5.20.120   A loan commitment is a firm commitment to provide credit under pre-specified terms and conditions. A loan commitment that is excluded from the scope of IAS 39 is in our view also excluded from the requirements on trade date and settlement date accounting. For a discussion of the accounting implications of a loan commitment, see 7I.1.200 and 7I.6.23. [*IAS 39.BC15*]

7I.5.30   Normal purchases and sales

7I.5.30.10   'Normal purchases and sales' are contracts for purchases and sales of non-financial in-struments that are entered into and continue to be held for the receipt or delivery of the non-financial item in accordance with the entity's expected purchase, sale or usage requirements. Normal purchases and sales – even if they can be settled net in cash or another financial instrument or by exchanging financial instruments – are outside the scope of IAS 39. Therefore, IAS 39 does not impact the timing of recognition of these contracts. For example, under IFRS 15 an entity does not recognise a liability for a binding purchase order until it obtains control over the underlying goods (see 3.8.90), unless the contract is onerous (see 3.12.630). [*IAS 37.66, 39.AG35(b)*]

7I.5.40   Linked transactions

7I.5.40.10   Generally, the terms of each contract determine the appropriate accounting and two financial instruments, even if they are entered into simultaneously, are accounted for separately. However, in our view the following indicators should be considered in determining whether two financial instruments should be accounted for as a single combined instrument:
- whether they are entered into at the same time and in contemplation of each other;
- whether they have the same counterparty;
- whether they relate to the same risk; and
- whether there is an economic need or substantive business purpose for structuring the transac-tions separately that could not also have been accomplished in a single transaction. [*IAS 39.IG.B.6*]

7I.5.40.15   The IFRS Interpretations Committee discussed the aggregation of separate transactions as a single derivative and noted that the indicators listed in 7I.5.40.10 may help an entity to determine the substance of the transaction, but that the presence or absence of any single specific indicator alone may not be conclusive. [*IAS 39.IG.B.6, IU 03-14*]

7I.5.40.20   In our view, structuring transactions separately may be regarded as a substantive business purpose when separate transactions are necessary to achieve a direct tax benefit. However, if such a tax benefit is derived primarily from an accounting result – e.g. when the purpose of structuring transactions separately is to achieve an accounting result that produces a tax advantage – then we believe that the substantive business purpose requirement is not met. Similarly, if an entity structures transactions separately to achieve an accounting result that produces a regulatory advantage, then in our view the substantive business purpose requirement is not met. [*IAS 39.IG.B.6*]

7I.5.50   **Agency relationships**

7I.5.50.10   When an entity enters into what might be described as an 'agency relationship', an analysis is required of whether the entity is acting as an agent or as a principal in any transaction entered into as a result of that relationship. Determining whether an entity is acting as a principal or as an agent, and whether as a result it becomes party to the contractual provisions of one or more financial instruments that it should recognise requires assessment of the substance of the contractual arrangements and consideration of all relevant facts and circumstances. This may require the application of judgement.

7I.5.50.15   The IFRS Interpretations Committee discussed the principal versus agent accounting for centrally cleared client derivative contracts from the perspective of the clearing member and noted that:
- an entity first assesses whether the transaction(s) results in a contract (or contracts) that is (or are) in the scope of IAS 39 and if it does then the entity applies the requirements of IAS 39; and
- if a transaction is not in the scope of IAS 39 and another standard does not specifically apply, then an entity applies the hierarchy principles (see 2.8.20) to determine an appropriate accounting policy. [*IAS 8.10–12, IU 06-17*]

EXAMPLE 1 – BROKER ACTING FOR CLIENT

7I.5.50.20   Company S operates as a securities and derivatives broker at a stock exchange. S acts on behalf of one party, entering the customer's order (buy or sell) into the stock exchange's system. The order will be executed on the stock exchange when/if there is a corresponding counterparty offer available. All offers at the stock exchange are given by authorised brokers acting at the exchange. It is possible that the counterparty of the deal executed at the stock exchange is the same broker party – i.e. S acting on behalf of another customer.

7I.5.50.30   The settlement term in the market in which S is the broker is trade date plus three days. After this term, the broker is obliged to settle the open deal if the buyer or the seller does not fulfil its part of the trade. On settlement date, the money will be paid by the broker acting on behalf of the buyer through the central depository and the broker acting on behalf of the seller will receive the money through the central depository. The only party known to the stock exchange is the broker.

7I.5.50.40   In our view, despite the fact that the broker is acting on behalf of a client, the broker is entering into two separate transactions: one with the stock exchange and one with the client. Each transaction results in a financial instrument and therefore S recognises each one separately in its statement of financial position, unless net presentation is required (see 7I.8.90).

7I.5.60   DERECOGNITION OF FINANCIAL ASSETS

7I.5.60.10   IAS 39 contains specific provisions for the derecognition of financial assets. [*IAS 39.15–37*]

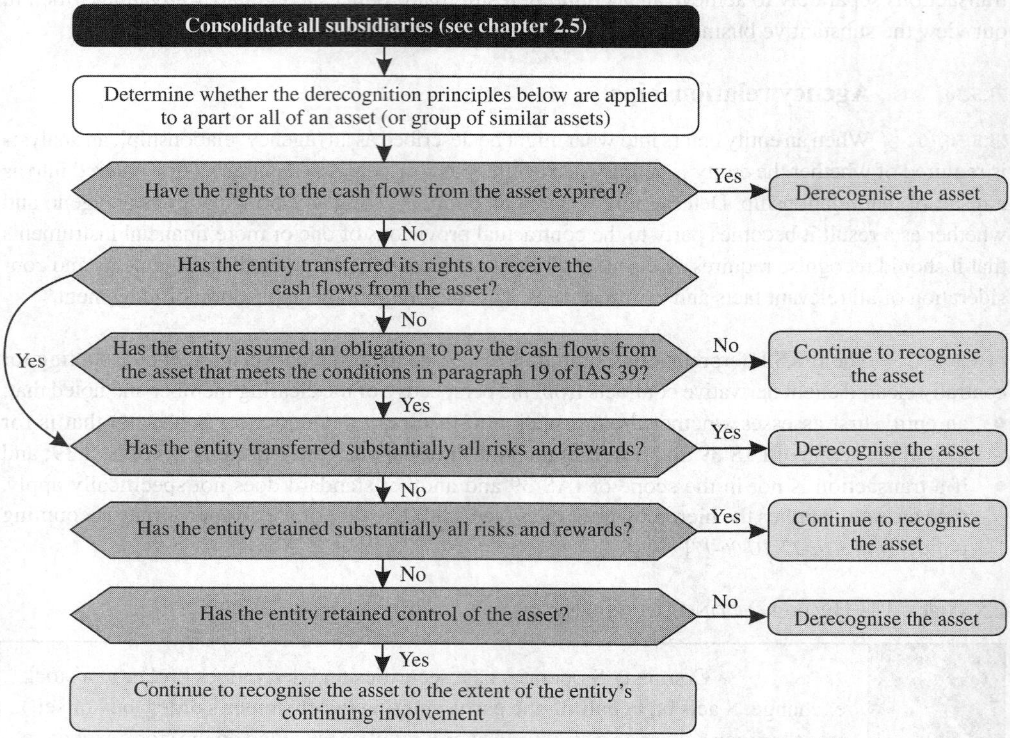

```
┌─────────────────────────────────────────────────────────────┐
│         Consolidate all subsidiaries (see chapter 2.5)        │
└─────────────────────────────────────────────────────────────┘
                              │
┌─────────────────────────────────────────────────────────────┐
│ Determine whether the derecognition principles below are      │
│ applied to a part or all of an asset (or group of similar     │
│ assets)                                                       │
└─────────────────────────────────────────────────────────────┘
                              │
        Have the rights to the cash flows from the      Yes → Derecognise the asset
        asset expired?
                              │ No
        Has the entity transferred its rights to receive the
        cash flows from the asset?
                              │ No
        Has the entity assumed an obligation to pay      No → Continue to recognise
        the cash flows from the asset that meets the          the asset
        conditions in paragraph 19 of IAS 39?
                              │ Yes
   Yes →  Has the entity transferred substantially all   Yes → Derecognise the asset
          risks and rewards?
                              │ No
        Has the entity retained substantially all        Yes → Continue to recognise
        risks and rewards?                                     the asset
                              │ No
        Has the entity retained control of the asset?    No → Derecognise the asset
                              │ Yes
        Continue to recognise the asset to the extent of the entity's
        continuing involvement
```

7I.5.60.20   In consolidated financial statements, the derecognition criteria are applied at a consolidated level. This avoids the unnecessary consideration of transactions between individual entities in a group, the effect of which is eliminated on consolidation. Therefore, if financial instruments are transferred within a group, then the consolidated financial statements will not reflect derecognition for intra-group transfers, even if those transfers qualify for derecognition in the individual financial statements of the entity that is the transferor. [*IAS 39.15*]

7I.5.60.30   Accordingly, when derecognition is assessed at the consolidated level, the issue of whether the transferring entity (the transferor) consolidates the receiving entity (the transferee) has a significant impact on the accounting.

EXAMPLE 2 – DERECOGNITION ASSESSMENT IN CONSOLIDATED FINANCIAL STATEMENTS

7I.5.60.40   Company T transfers financial assets to Structured Entity X, which it consolidates. In T's consolidated financial statements, the transaction considered in applying the derecognition requirements is that between the group (including X) and any external beneficial holders in X. [*IAS 39.15*]

> 7I.5.60.50   However, if X were not consolidated by T, then the transaction considered by T would be the transfer between T and X. [*IAS 39.15*]
>
> 7I.5.60.60   The assessment is different if the derecognition provisions are applied to separate financial statements of T (see 2.1.120). In that case, only the transactions between T and X are analysed.

7I.5.70   **Derecognition criteria**

7I.5.80   *Determining the financial asset subject to derecognition*

7I.5.80.10   The derecognition criteria apply to all financial assets and are therefore used when assessing the derecognition of both debt *and* equity instruments issued by another entity. A financial asset or a group of similar financial assets can be broken down into various parts that can be segregated – e.g. the principal and interest cash flows of a debt instrument – and potentially transferred separately to other parties. Consequently, in applying the derecognition provisions the first step is to determine the financial asset(s) that is (are) subject to possible derecognition. This could be the following cash flows from a financial asset or a group of similar financial assets:

- specifically identified;
- fully proportionate share; or
- fully proportionate share of specifically identified cash flows. [*IAS 39.16*]

7I.5.80.20   If an entity transfers its rights to all of the cash flows of a financial asset or a group of similar financial assets, then the derecognition provisions apply to the entire financial asset or group. However, if an entity transfers its rights to only certain cash flows of a financial asset – e.g. the interest cash flows in a debt instrument – or to only certain cash flows of a group of similar financial assets, then it is important to determine the financial asset or assets to which the derecognition provisions apply. [*IAS 39.16*]

7I.5.80.30   In the case of a transfer (or expiry – see 7I.5.90) of specifically identified cash flows arising from a financial asset (or a group of similar financial assets), the derecognition provisions apply only to those specifically identified cash flows. For example, if an entity issues an interest-only strip whereby it transfers the interest cash flows arising from a debt instrument and not the principal cash flows, then the derecognition provisions apply only to the cash flows arising from interest payments. [*IAS 39.16(a)*]

7I.5.80.40   In our view, when rights to some but not all of the cash flows of a financial asset are transferred, judgement may be required to determine whether the cash flows transferred are considered specifically identified. We believe that this judgement should include an assessment of whether the rights to the instalments transferred contain risks and rewards related to the rights to instalments retained. [*IAS 39.BC53*]

7I.5.80.50   In our view, in order to determine whether the cash flows transferred are specifically identified, the entity should examine the original contract and the transfer agreement to assess whether the cash flows transferred are in substance separate cash flows that are distinct from other cash flows in the original contract, including considering how cash receipts are allocated between the interests of the transferor and transferee.

7I.5.80.60   In our view, in order to be considered specifically identified, the cash flows should be identified as substantively separate cash flows in the terms of the contract between the debtor and the creditor;

by contrast, a portion of cash flows that is not specified in the terms of the financial asset and is created in the transfer agreement – e.g. for the purpose of providing a credit enhancement or subordination – does not constitute specifically identified cash flows. For example, if a loan agreement contains a single repayment of obligation of 100, then the right to the first 60 of repayment is not considered specifically identified because the loan agreement does not specify this amount of 60 as a separate cash flow. [*IAS 39.16(b)*]

7I.5.80.70   If loans and receivables are repayable in separate instalments, then an entity may need to choose an accounting policy, to be applied consistently, for analysing transfers of rights to instalments (see Example 3A).

EXAMPLE 3A – DERECOGNITION ASSESSMENT FOR SPECIFICALLY IDENTIFIED CASH FLOWS

7I.5.80.80   Bank B has a loan of 100 and the contract requires the borrower to make repayment in five separate annual instalments of 20 and that each cash flow received, irrespective of when it is received, will be allocated first to settling the earliest outstanding instalment. B transfers the right to the first three instalments.

7I.5.80.90   In our view, B may choose either of the following approaches.
- *Approach 1:* View each annual instalment as a separately identified cash flow because it is specified in the contract and the risks and rewards related to one instalment are unaffected by agreeing to transfer another instalment.
- *Approach 2:* View the rights to the first three instalments as a priority share in the total cash flows and therefore conclude that these instalments are not specifically identified.

7I.5.80.100   Under Approach 1, even though the transferred cash flows are considered specifically identified cash flows, B needs to consider whether the transfer contract creates a dependency between the cash flows transferred and the cash flows retained that is not present in the original contract. This dependency may represent a credit enhancement that results in some (and possibly substantially all) of the risks and rewards in the transferred rights being retained by the transferor (see 7I.5.190). [*IAS 39.AG52*]

7I.5.80.110   Modifying the example, if the original loan agreement allocated cash receipts against overdue instalments on a pro rata basis but the transfer agreement required allocation of cash receipts against the earliest outstanding instalment, then this would represent a form of credit enhancement that is considered in the risks and rewards analysis. [*IAS 39.AG52*]

7I.5.80.120   An entity applies the derecognition provisions only to a fully proportionate share if it transfers the following (or if the following are subject to expiry – see 7I.5.90):
- only a fully proportionate share of the cash flows of a financial asset (or of a group of similar financial assets); or
- only a fully proportionate share of specifically identified cash flows as described in 7I.5.80.120.

7I.5.80.130   The derecognition provisions do not require there to be only one counterparty to whom such cash flows are transferred or that each counterparty obtains a proportionate right to the cash flows being transferred. However, in order to consider only the part(s) transferred for derecognition as a fully proportionate share, it is important to ensure that the transferring entity also retains only a fully proportionate share of the cash flows.

EXAMPLE 3B – DERECOGNITION ASSESSMENT FOR FULLY PROPORTIONATE SHARE OF CASH FLOWS

7I.5.80.140   Company U transfers 80% of the interest cash flows on an existing investment to various counterparties; each counterparty takes up a different portion of the 80%, with the interests of some counterparties subordinated to those of others.

7I.5.80.150   In this example, U still subjects the 80% to a derecognition assessment because it retains a fully proportionate share (20%) of the interest cash flows for itself. This is irrespective of the actual distribution of the 80% among the various counterparties. [*IAS 39.16(a)*]

7I.5.80.160   Except as described in 7I.5.80.30–150, the derecognition assessment applies to a financial asset (or to a group of similar financial assets) in its entirety. For example, if an entity transfers the rights to the first or last 80 percent of cash receipts on a debt instrument, or 80 percent of the cash collections on a group of similar receivables but provides a guarantee to compensate the buyer for any credit losses up to 9 percent of the principal amount of the receivables, then the derecognition assessment is applied to the financial asset, or to the group of similar financial assets respectively, in its entirety and not only to the part that the entity has transferred. This is because the entity has not transferred a fully proportionate share of the cash flows, but rather a portion of the cash flows. [*IAS 39.16(b)*]

7I.5.80.170   IAS 39 indicates that the derecognition assessment may be applied either to an individual financial asset or to a portfolio of similar financial assets. However, the standard does not specify the circumstances in which a portfolio assessment is appropriate. [*IAS 39.16*]

7I.5.80.180   In our view, if in a transfer there are contractual terms that have an effect on the risks and rewards of a group of financial assets, then the group of financial assets rather than each individual financial asset should be assessed for derecognition. Generally, the existence of such contractual terms is evidence that the financial assets are similar and share similar risks and rewards. For example, a financial guarantee issued by the transferor covering a percentage of credit losses in a portfolio of financial assets links the risks and rewards associated with the individual financial assets in that portfolio. Consequently, the financial asset that is considered is the group rather than individual financial assets. However, the financial guarantee itself is not considered to be part of the group that is transferred. Such a situation is often encountered in securitisations for which credit enhancement is provided by the transferor over a portfolio of financial assets in the form of financial guarantees, subordinated loans and reserve funds.

7I.5.80.190   In our view, it is not appropriate to consider a group of debt and equity instruments as a group of similar financial assets.

7I.5.80.200   All subsequent references to 'the financial asset' in this section (derecognition) refer to a financial asset, a part of a financial asset, a portfolio of financial assets or a part of a portfolio of financial assets, determined in accordance with 7I.5.80.

7I.5.90   **Evaluating whether contractual rights to cash flows have expired**

7I.5.90.10   When the contractual rights to cash flows from the asset have expired, that asset is derecognised and no further analysis is required. [*IAS 39.17*]

7I.5.95   *Modification of terms*

7I.5.95.10   A financial asset may be modified or replaced as part of a transaction with the same counterparty. For example, when a borrower is in financial difficulties, the borrower and its creditors may negotiate a restructuring of some or all of the borrower's obligations to allow the borrower sufficient capacity to service the debt or refinance the contract, either entirely or partially. Such circumstances are often referred to as 'forbearance'. Examples of forbearance practices include reducing interest rates, delaying the payment of principal and amending covenants. If a financial asset is modified as part of forbearance, then it may be more challenging to conclude that the original financial asset should be derecognised in its entirety. This is because in such a case the objective and nature of the modification is usually to maximise recovery of the original contractual cash flows rather than to originate a new asset on market terms.

7I.5.95.20   In our view the holder of the financial asset should perform a quantitative and qualitative evaluation of whether the cash flows of the original financial asset and the modified or replacement financial asset are substantially different. If the cash flows are substantially different, then we believe that the contractual rights to cash flows from the original financial asset should be deemed to have expired. In our view, in making this evaluation, an entity may analogise to the guidance on the derecognition of financial liabilities (see 7I.5.370).

7I.5.95.30   If the terms of a financial asset carried at amortised cost are renegotiated or otherwise modified because of financial difficulties of the borrower or issuer, then any impairment is measured using the effective interest rate of the financial asset before the modification of terms. In other words, even if the asset is derecognised, an impairment assessment is made and an impairment loss is recognised if necessary, before derecognising the asset. In our view, this requirement to assess impairment applies irrespective of whether the modification of the existing asset leads to its derecognition. For a discussion of how to measure impairment in such a case, see 7I.6.490.30–50. For a discussion on the interaction between forbearance activities and impairment, see 7I.6.490. [*IAS 39.17, AG84*]

7I.5.100   *Evaluating whether there is a transfer*

7I.5.100.10   A financial asset qualifies for derecognition under IAS 39, either if the contractual rights to the cash flows from that financial asset expire or if an entity transfers a financial asset in a transfer that meets the criteria for derecognition specified in the standard. An entity transfers a financial asset if, and only if, it transfers the contractual rights to receive the cash flows of the financial asset (see 7I.5.110) or it enters into a qualifying pass-through arrangement (see 7I.5.160). [*IAS 39.17–18*]

7I.5.110   *Transfer of contractual rights*

7I.5.110.10   In our view, to be considered a transfer of the contractual rights to receive the cash flows of the financial asset, the transfer of legal title should result in a transfer of all existing rights associated with the financial asset without any additional restrictions being imposed as a result of the transfer. A right to demand payment or to obtain legal title that is conditional on the transferor defaulting under a servicing agreement does not constitute a transfer of contractual rights. In this case, whether there is a transfer is evaluated using the pass-through requirements (see 7I.5.160). [*IAS 39.18*]

7I.5.110.20   A transferor may continue to administer or provide servicing for assets that it has previously transferred to another entity. For example, a transferor may transfer all rights to receivables but then continue to collect the cash flows of those receivables as a servicer in the capacity of an agent of the transferee. The IFRS Interpretations Committee discussed a related issue and noted that the determination of whether the contractual rights to cash flows have been transferred is not affected by the transferor retaining the role of agent to collect the cash flows of the receivables in this case. Therefore, retention of the servicing rights by the entity transferring the financial asset does not in itself cause the transfer to fail the requirements of paragraph 18(a) of IAS 39. [*IU 11-05*]

7I.5.110.30   However, depending on the legal environment in which an entity operates and the contractually agreed terms, there may be circumstances in which it is not clear whether the contractual rights to receive the cash flows of the financial asset have been transferred. For example, the beneficial interests in a receivable could be sold without legal title to the financial asset being transferred; the seller avoids having to notify the debtor of the sale, thereby retaining its relationship with the debtor, and the debtor continues to make payments directly to the seller. In the event of breach, the buyer has the right to 'perfect' the sale by acquiring legal title to the receivables. In such circumstances, whether a transfer has taken place is a question of fact, viewed together with the legal environment in which the entity operates, and requires the use of judgement.

7I.5.110.40   In our view, for a transfer of contractual rights to take place, the transferee should have an unconditional right to demand payment from the original debtor in the case of default by the original debtor (see 7I.5.110.10). A right that is conditional on the transferor failing to pass on payments under a servicing contract is not enough. Consequently, in the example in 7I.5.110.30, the fact that the buyer is able to perfect a sale only in the event of default means that there is no transfer of contractual rights. Therefore, the transaction would need to be assessed under the pass-through requirements (see 7I.5.160).

7I.5.110.50   In addition, because of the transfer requirements discussed in 7I.5.110.10–40, we believe that it is not possible to achieve derecognition of a financial asset by synthetic means.

EXAMPLE 4 – SYNTHETIC STRUCTURE THROUGH WHICH CONTRACTUAL RIGHTS ARE NOT TRANSFERRED

7I.5.110.60   Bank B has a portfolio of customer loans, which yield various fixed rate returns. B enters into a synthetic securitisation structure, comprising the following underlying transactions.

7I.5.120   Credit default swap

7I.5.120.10   B enters into a CDS with Limited-purpose Vehicle L, under which it transfers to L the default risk on a referenced portfolio of loans (originated customer loans) in exchange for a fixed premium.

7I.5.130   Deposit

7I.5.130.10   L provides a cash deposit to B equal to the principal amount of the reference portfolio of loans, which serves as cash collateral against L's obligation under the CDS. B pays interest at LIBOR on the deposit.

7I.5.130.20   The combination of the CDS premium and LIBOR interest on the deposit effectively provides L with a return equal to that earned by B on the referenced financial assets.

7I.5.140   Notes

7I.5.140.10   L issues credit-linked notes to external parties to fund its ability to take exposure to credit risk in the referenced financial assets. These notes pay interest at LIBOR plus a fixed margin, which is the margin earned by L on the written CDS less any amount needed by L to cover its operating costs. The principal on the notes equals the notional amount on the CDS and the deposit with B, which in turn is equal to the principal amount of the referenced financial assets. Any defaults on the referenced financial assets result in an equivalent reduction in the principal of the notes and the deposit with B.

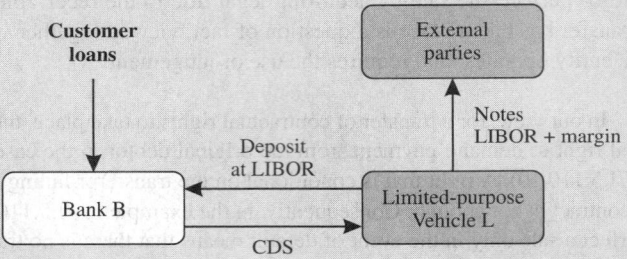

7I.5.150   Analysis

7I.5.150.10   Assuming that L is consolidated by B (see chapter 2.5), the transaction subject to the derecognition assessment in the B's consolidated financial statements is the one that takes place between L and the credit-linked note holders.

7I.5.150.20   Although the cash flows in the structure – related to the CDS, deposit and notes – are determined based on the portfolio of referenced financial assets, we believe that the combined effect of these three instruments is not enough to conclude that the consolidated entity has transferred the referenced financial assets to the note holders. This is because the entity has not transferred the contractual cash flows arising from the referenced assets. [*IAS 39.17–18*]

7I.5.160   *Pass-through arrangements*

7I.5.160.10   If an entity retains the contractual right to the cash flows of a financial asset, but also assumes a contractual obligation to pay the cash flows to the transferee (sometimes called a 'pass-through arrangement'), then the transaction is considered a transfer if and only if:

- the entity has no obligation to pay amounts to the transferee unless the entity collects equivalent amounts from the original financial asset;
- the entity is prohibited from selling or pledging the original financial asset under the terms of the pass-through arrangement; and

- the entity is obliged to remit all of the cash flows that it collects without material delay. [*IAS 39.19*]

EXAMPLE 5 – QUALIFYING PASS-THROUGH ARRANGEMENT

7I.5.160.20   Company N enters into an agreement with Company B in respect of a debt security that it owns.
- Physical custody of and legal title to the security are retained by N, but N agrees to pass any cash flows generated by the security to B immediately.
- There is no obligation for N to pay any amount to B other than the cash that it receives on the security – i.e. neither the principal nor any interest in the case of late payment.
- The agreement prohibits N from selling or pledging the security.

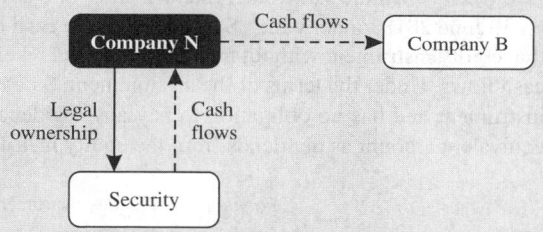

7I.5.160.30   In this example, the transaction qualifies as a transfer because it meets the pass-through criteria (see 7I.5.160.10). The next step is for N to evaluate whether it has transferred or retained the risks and rewards of ownership (see 7I.5.190).

7I.5.160.40   Some transfer agreements include a general right of either party (transferor or transferee) to set off amounts payable by the transferor under the pass-through obligation against other amounts from other contracts owed by the transferee to the transferor. As a result, the transferor might not physically pay to the transferee any or all of the cash collected from the transferred assets, but instead set off the amount of cash collected against other amounts due from the transferee and pay to (or receive from) the transferee only the net amount.

7I.5.160.50   If the 'other amounts' and 'other contracts' are not a reinvestment of cash flows collected from the financial assets on behalf of the transferee (see 7I.5.350) and are not otherwise connected with the pass-through arrangement, then in our view a right to set off should not impact the pass-through analysis. This is because the transferor settles its obligation to remit the cash flows to the transferee by setting it off against a right to receive cash from the transferee under another contract. The manner of settlement does not negate the fact that the transferor has satisfied its obligation to pass amounts due to the transferee.

7I.5.170   Pass-through arrangements involving structured entities

7I.5.170.10   A typical situation in which a pass-through arrangement may exist is in a securitisation involving structured entities. For a further discussion of practical issues, see 7I.5.320. [*IAS 39.AG37*]

7I.5.180   Pass-through arrangements involving total return swaps on equity instruments

7I.5.180.10   A holder of an equity instrument issued by another entity may enter into a total return swap under which the holder remits all of the cash flows – i.e. dividends – from the equity instrument and receives a stream of fixed or floating rate cash flows. If the terms of the total return swap or any other arrangements that are part of the transfer require the equity instrument to be transferred at the expiry of the total return swap, then in our view such a transfer may meet the pass-through requirements in IAS 39.

EXAMPLE 6 – TOTAL RETURN SWAP ON EQUITY INVESTMENT

7I.5.180.13   On 1 July 2017, Company S enters into a forward contract to sell an equity instrument issued by another entity to Company T, with physical delivery to T on 30 June 2018.

7I.5.180.15   On the same date, S and T enter into a total return swap that expires on 30 June 2018, under which S remits all of the cash flows – i.e. dividends – from that equity instrument without material delay and receives a stream of floating rate cash flows. Under the terms of the arrangement, S cannot pledge or sell the equity instrument and has no obligation to pay any dividends to T unless it receives an equivalent amount as dividends from the equity instrument.

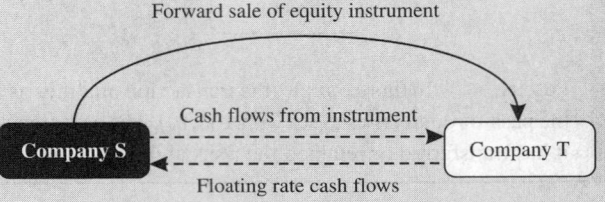

Forward sale of equity instrument

Cash flows from instrument

Company S ← → Company T

Floating rate cash flows

7I.5.180.17   S concludes that the transaction meets the pass-through conditions. The next step is for S to evaluate whether it has transferred or retained the risks and rewards of ownership (see 7I.5.190).

7I.5.180.20   Conversely, if a total return swap or the transfer arrangement does not require the equity instrument to be transferred at expiry but requires only the transfer of all dividends during the period of the total return swap, then in our view the holder of the equity instrument has transferred a dividend strip only until the expiry of the total return swap. Because the dividend strip constitutes separately identifiable cash flows, it can be considered separately for derecognition. In our view, the dividend strip, until the expiry of the total return swap, meets the pass-through conditions if:

- the entity cannot separately pledge or sell the dividend strip arising from the equity instrument;
- the entity has no obligation to pay any dividends under the arrangement unless it receives an equivalent amount from the equity instrument; and
- the agreement provides for remittance of the cash flows without any material delay.

7I.5.180.30   Consequently, assuming that the entity has transferred substantially all of the risks and rewards (see 7I.5.190), the dividend strip until expiry of the total return swap should be derecognised and the remaining part of the equity instrument should continue to be recognised.

7I.5.190 *Risks and rewards evaluation*

7I.5.190.10 For all transactions that meet the transfer requirements, the entity next evaluates whether it has transferred or retained the risks and rewards of ownership of the financial asset. An entity derecognises a transferred financial asset if it has transferred substantially all of the risks and rewards of ownership of that asset. Conversely, it continues to recognise a transferred financial asset if it has retained substantially all of the risks and rewards of ownership of that asset. However, if an entity has neither transferred nor retained substantially all of the risks and rewards of ownership of a transferred asset, then it determines whether it has retained control of that asset to assess whether derecognition is appropriate (see 7I.5.240). [*IAS 39.20*]

7I.5.190.20 The risks and rewards analysis is performed by comparing the entity's exposure, before and after the transfer, to the variability in the present value of the future net cash flows from the financial asset. This evaluation can be done either separately for each type of risk that the financial asset is exposed to or for all of the risks arising from the financial asset. Therefore, for each type of risk or for all of the risks transferred and retained, an entity determines its exposure to the variability in the amounts and timing of the net cash flows of the transferred asset arising from that type of risk or from all of the risks. Even if individual risk types are considered separately, the evaluation of whether an entity has transferred or retained substantially all of the risks and rewards is based on the aggregate exposure arising from all risk types. [*IAS 39.21–22*]

7I.5.190.30 In our view, if a financial asset is transferred and does not qualify for derecognition under the risks and rewards evaluation, and the transferor enters into subsequent transactions that affect the allocation of risks and rewards between the transferor and the transferee(s), then the transferor should reperform the risks and rewards assessment on a cumulative basis.

EXAMPLE 7 – RISKS AND REWARDS EVALUATION ON A CUMULATIVE BASIS

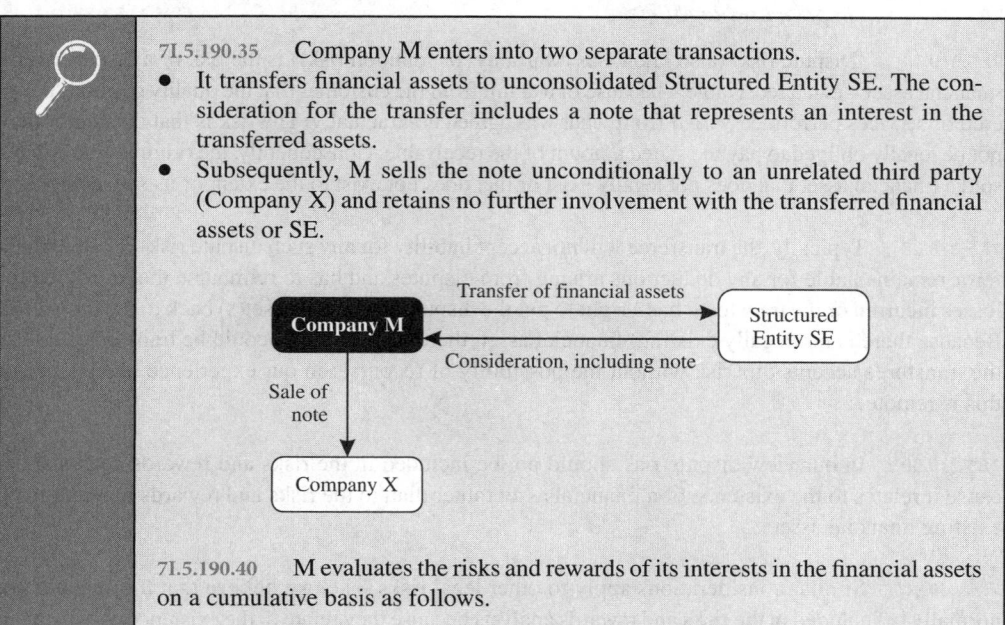

7I.5.190.35 Company M enters into two separate transactions.
- It transfers financial assets to unconsolidated Structured Entity SE. The consideration for the transfer includes a note that represents an interest in the transferred assets.
- Subsequently, M sells the note unconditionally to an unrelated third party (Company X) and retains no further involvement with the transferred financial assets or SE.

Transfer of financial assets

Company M → Structured Entity SE

Consideration, including note

Sale of note

Company X

7I.5.190.40 M evaluates the risks and rewards of its interests in the financial assets on a cumulative basis as follows.

- At the date of the transaction with SE, M concludes that it has retained substantially all of the risks and rewards of ownership of the transferred assets because it obtains the note that represents an interest in the transferred assets (see 7I.5.230). Accordingly, M does not derecognise the transferred financial assets at this time.
- At the date of the transaction with X, M considers the subsequent sale and concludes that it has transferred substantially all of the risks and rewards of ownership of the financial assets and derecognises them.

7I.5.200 *Risk types*

7I.5.200.10   Different types of risk can be briefly summarised as follows.
- Price risk, which is an inherent risk in equity instruments.
- Risks inherent in debt instruments:
  - credit risk, also called 'risk of default';
  - interest rate risk, comprising fair value interest rate risk and cash flow interest rate risk;
  - prepayment risk – i.e. the risk that the principal is repaid earlier than expected; and
  - late-payment risk – i.e. the risk that payments received from the underlying financial assets are made later than expected, sometimes called 'slow-payment risk'.
- Risks inherent in both equity and debt instruments:
  - currency risk; and
  - other risks – this category covers any risks that may exist in practice in a particular fact pattern that is not explicitly covered by the above risk categories: e.g. dispute and legal risks (see 7I.5.210), and structural and other liquidity risks (see 7I.5.220).

7I.5.210 *Dispute and legal risks*

7I.5.210.10   'Dispute risk' (also known as 'warranty' or 'dilution risk') is the risk of a dispute over a financial asset – e.g. a receivable – because of a claim from the customer that the quality of goods delivered or services performed varied from what was agreed contractually. The risk is that the debtor may not be legally obliged to pay the stated amount of the receivable. Consequently, the originator may have sold a financial asset that does not legally exist or that does not exist to the extent of its stated amount.

7I.5.210.20   Typically, the transferee will not accept liability for any such dispute risk – i.e. the transferor remains liable for any deductions arising from disputes and has to reimburse the transferee for losses incurred or the transferee has a right to put the disputed financial asset(s) back to the transferor. Because there is no (legally existing) financial asset, there is no risk that could be transferred unless the transferee accepts this risk without the possibility of recourse; in our experience, the chance of this is remote.

7I.5.210.30   In our view dispute risk should not be included in the risks and rewards analysis, because it relates to the existence of a financial asset rather than to the risks and rewards inherent in an existing financial asset.

7I.5.210.40   Similar considerations apply to other legal risks – i.e. we believe that they should not normally be included in the risks and rewards analysis because they relate to the existence of a financial asset rather than to the risks and rewards inherent in a financial asset. In addition, the transferee will not usually accept these risks without a right of recourse.

71.5.220   *Structural and other liquidity risks*

71.5.220.10   Structural liquidity risk arises primarily in securitisations when there is a mismatch between the cash inflows from financial assets and cash outflows on financial liabilities. It is important to differentiate structural liquidity risk from late-payment and default risk. For example, in a securitisation structural liquidity risk may arise because of variability in the timing of defaults on the assets whereby the structured entity that has issued securities to investors does not have enough cash to meet its obligations. This variability can arise without altering the cumulative expectation of defaults on the portfolio. In our view, this risk is not inherent in the financial asset transferred, but arises as a result of the structure of the transaction. Consequently, we believe that this risk should not be included in the risks and rewards analysis.

71.5.220.20   In certain structures, a transferor also provides a liquidity facility to the most senior debt component in the structure. In these circumstances, the provision of the liquidity facility does not generally impact the analysis of risks and rewards for derecognition purposes. However, if such a facility does not represent the most senior debt component in the structure, then it is possible that the transferor is absorbing credit risk through the provision of the facility. In these circumstances, the granting of such a liquidity facility will have an impact on the risks and rewards analysis because it makes the transferor absorb credit risk. Consequently, the terms of any liquidity facility need careful evaluation to determine whether it plays a part in the risks-and-rewards analysis.

71.5.230   *Substantially all risks and rewards*

71.5.230.10   No specific quantitative guidance is provided on what constitutes 'substantially all' of the risks and rewards of a financial asset. In our view, the analysis should be based on all of the facts and circumstances, considering all of the risks (except for dispute and legal risks) associated with the financial asset on a probability-weighted basis. If substantially all of the total variability in the present value of the future cash flows associated with the financial asset is retained, then we believe that the entity would be considered to have retained substantially all of the risks and rewards. [*IAS 39.21*]

71.5.230.20   Assessing whether and to what extent exposure to variability in the present value of cash flows has been retained requires consideration of all relevant facts and circumstances.

71.5.230.30   If the transferee is a limited-purpose vehicle, then the consideration for the transfer often includes securities issued by, or other interests in, the limited-purpose vehicle. Usually, the limited-purpose vehicle is established for the purpose of holding similar transferred assets and paying the cash flows from such assets to the various interest holders in the limited-purpose vehicle in line with the terms of those interests and its governing arrangements. Accordingly, these interests represent a repackaging of some or all of the cash flows of the transferred assets.

71.5.230.40   The transferor may already have a pre-existing interest in the limited-purpose vehicle, such as subordinated debt or an equity-like interest, and this pre-existing interest may also represent an exposure to variability in the cash flows of newly transferred assets that is relevant to the analysis.

7I.5.230.50   In other cases, the assets may be transferred to a substantive operating entity that carries on its own business activities and that holds many assets in addition to the financial assets transferred to it by the transferor. In our view, in these cases the analysis should focus on comparing the variability of the cash flows of the transferred assets with the variability of the cash flows of the instruments received as consideration for the transfer. This assessment should include consideration of any agreements such as a guarantee or put or call options related to the transferred assets and need not consider ordinary equity interests that the transferor already held in the transferee.

(S) EXAMPLE 8 – UNCONDITIONAL SALE OF FINANCIAL ASSETS TO OPERATING SUBSIDIARY

> 7I.5.230.60   A parent company enters into an unconditional sale of financial assets to a wholly owned subsidiary that carries on banking operations. We do not believe that derecognition of the assets in the separate financial statements of the parent is precluded merely as a result of its 100% ownership interest in the transferee (see 7I.5.230.50).

7I.5.230.70   If financial assets are transferred to a substantive operating entity in exchange for new equity interests in the transferee, then the transferor evaluates the nature of the variability to which those new interests expose it. If the transferee has substantive other operations, then the variability in discretionary dividends and changes in fair value arising from the new equity interests would usually be significantly different from an exposure to the transferred assets. In some cases, this may require consideration of the transferee's future plans – e.g. if the transferee is a start-up company. The smaller the transferred assets are in relation to the total operations of the substantive operating entity and the smaller the new equity interests are in relation to the total ownership interests in the substantive operating entity, the more likely it is that substantially all of the risks and rewards of ownership may be considered to have been transferred.

EXAMPLE 9 – EXCHANGE OF FINANCIAL ASSETS WITH SIGNIFICANTLY DIFFERENT CASH FLOWS

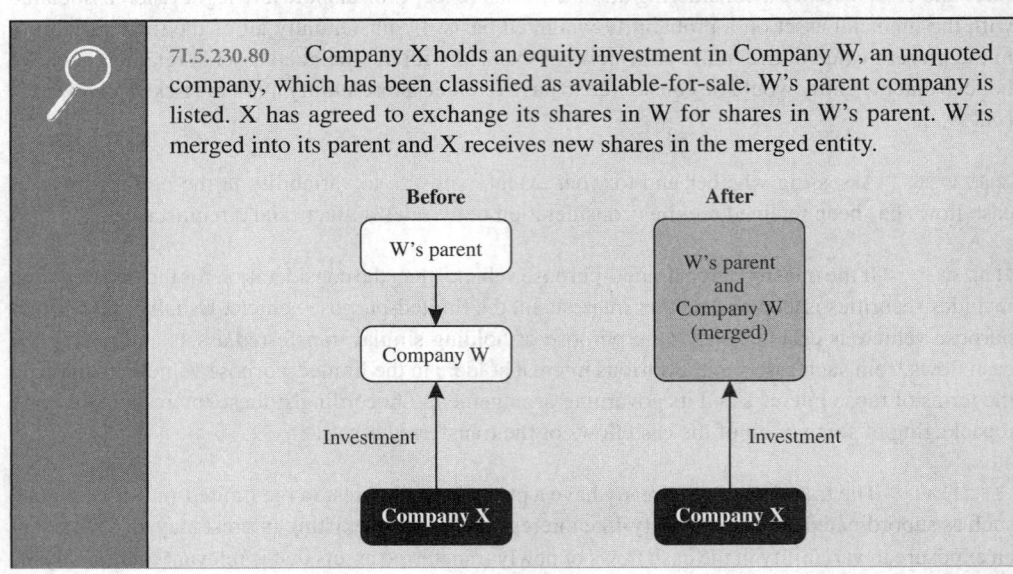

> 7I.5.230.80   Company X holds an equity investment in Company W, an unquoted company, which has been classified as available-for-sale. W's parent company is listed. X has agreed to exchange its shares in W for shares in W's parent. W is merged into its parent and X receives new shares in the merged entity.

> 71.5.230.85   X no longer owns the shares in W. Instead, X has received new shares in the parent as consideration. In our view, the derecognition criteria are met in this example because, subsequent to the transfer, the equity instruments received by X have cash flows that are significantly different from the cash flows of the original equity instrument – i.e. X has received new financial assets and not the existing assets only with a repackaging. Consequently, X should derecognise the original assets (equity investment in W) and recognise the new financial assets (equity investment in the merged entity) at fair value.

71.5.230.90   In our view, the fact that a transferor may have a reimbursement right from another entity – e.g. an insurance company – and thereby economically hedges its risk exposure arising from the transferred financial assets, is irrelevant in an analysis of risks and rewards. Only the risks and rewards between the transferor and the transferee are included in the analysis. Therefore, the analysis of risks and rewards does not consider whether and how the transferor has entered into other contracts with third parties that reimburse the transferor for losses incurred in connection with the transferred assets.

71.5.230.100   In our view, it is not generally necessary to use cash flow and/or similar models in performing a risks and rewards analysis. In most cases, evaluating the terms and conditions of the transaction should be enough to determine whether, and to what extent, an entity's exposure to variability in the amounts and timing of the net cash flows has changed as a result of the transfer.

71.5.230.110   However, under certain circumstances a degree of statistical analysis might be required. For example, in transactions in which the transferor and the transferee share the exposure to the variability in cash flows arising from credit risk, it might be difficult to determine whether substantially all of the risks and rewards have been transferred.

71.5.230.120   Example 10 illustrates how in such circumstances an analysis of the transfer of risks and rewards might be performed.

EXAMPLE 10 – RISKS AND REWARDS ASSESSMENT BASED ON STATISTICAL ANALYSIS

> 71.5.230.130   Company R transfers short-term receivables of 100 to Company S for 95. There is no significant risk other than credit risk inherent in the receivables and the default rates are as follows:
> - expected credit losses are 5% of the notional amount; and
> - the likely range of losses is between 4.5% and 6.5% of the notional amount, with a 99.9% confidence interval.
>
> 71.5.230.140   R provides a guarantee to reimburse S for losses exceeding 6.5%. The risk is that actual credit losses may exceed the expected credit losses of 5%. The rewards, which remain with S, are that actual credit losses may be less than the expected credit losses of 5%.

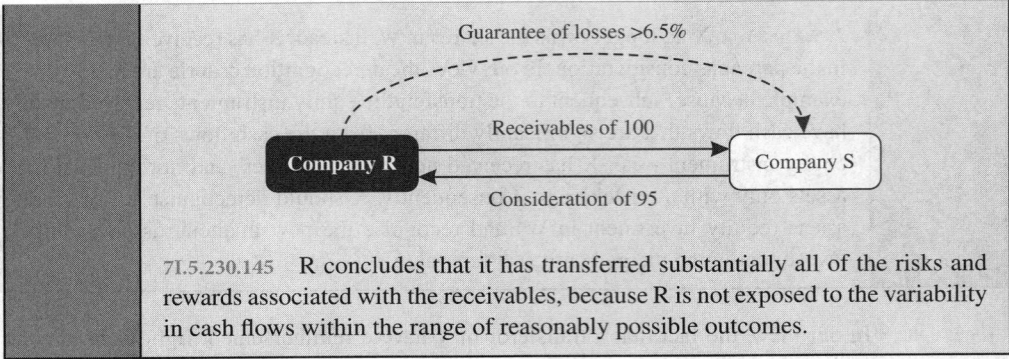

Guarantee of losses >6.5%

Receivables of 100

Company R   Company S

Consideration of 95

7I.5.230.145 R concludes that it has transferred substantially all of the risks and rewards associated with the receivables, because R is not exposed to the variability in cash flows within the range of reasonably possible outcomes.

7I.5.230.147 In evaluating risks and rewards it is important that the entity not only transfers substantial rewards but also that it transfers its exposure to a significant loss arising from a substantial risk. A risk of loss could be considered 'significant', for example, if it is based on historical loss experience for the type of financial asset transferred. For example, if a transfer of credit risk, which is generally considered to be a substantial risk of the financial assets transferred, will happen only in a catastrophe or similar situation because historical losses are covered through a guarantee by the transferor, then this is considered to be outside the range of likely loss outcomes. This would not be considered a transfer of a significant exposure to loss from credit risk.

7I.5.230.150 In some cases, it is possible that a third party instead of the transferor provides credit enhancement. In our view, if the transferor is the beneficiary of the credit enhancement contract, but agrees to compensate the transferee for credit losses, then this is an indication that the transferor has retained the credit risk. In this case, the credit enhancement contract should be disregarded in evaluating whether the financial assets qualify for derecognition and it should be assumed that the transferor continues to bear the credit risk. To transfer the credit risk inherent in the financial assets, in our view the transferee needs to be the beneficiary under the credit enhancement contract and not the transferor.

7I.5.230.155 If the transferor assigns the benefit of a financial guarantee contract to the transferee as beneficiary, and the financial guarantee is not in the scope of IAS 39 from the holder's perspective, then in our view it is appropriate for the transferor to apply by analogy the derecognition criteria for financial assets to any prepayment asset relating to the financial guarantee (see 7I.1.80.10). [*IAS 8.10–11*]

7I.5.230.160 For financial assets with relatively short maturities, such as most trade receivables, the only substantial risk is generally credit risk. Accordingly, if an entity sells short-term receivables and guarantees to compensate the transferee for credit losses that are likely to occur, then it has retained substantially all of the risks and rewards of ownership. [*IAS 39.AG40(e)*]

7I.5.240 *Control evaluation*

7I.5.240.10 If an entity neither transfers nor retains substantially all of the risks and rewards of ownership of a financial asset, then it evaluates whether it has retained control of the financial asset. If the entity has not retained control of the asset, then it derecognises that asset. Conversely, if the entity has retained control, then it continues to recognise the asset to the extent of its continuing involvement in the financial asset (see 7I.5.250). [*IAS 39.20(c)*]

EXAMPLE 11 – SUBSTANTIALLY ALL RISKS AND REWARDS NEITHER TRANSFERRED NOR RETAINED

7I.5.240.20   Company V transfers long-term mortgage receivables to Company W such that it retains the credit risk while transferring the prepayment/late-payment risk and interest rate risk. Both the credit and the combined prepayment/late-payment and interest rate risks are considered to be significant.

7I.5.240.25   In this example, V has neither retained nor transferred substantially all of the risks and rewards and needs to determine if it has retained control of the receivables.

7I.5.240.30   An entity is considered to have lost control if the transferee has the practical ability uni-laterally to sell the transferred financial asset in its entirety to an unrelated third party without needing to impose additional restrictions on the sale. If there is an active market for the financial asset, then the transferee often has the practical ability to sell the financial asset, even if the contractual arrange-ments between the transferor and the transferee could require the transferee to return the financial asset to the transferor – e.g. if the financial asset is subject to an option that allows the transferor to repurchase it but the financial asset is readily obtainable in the market. [*IAS 39.23, AG42*]

7I.5.240.40   Conversely, the transferee does not usually have the practical ability to sell the financial asset if there is no market for the financial asset, even if the contractual arrangements between the transferor and transferee permit such a sale. [*IAS 39.23, AG43(a)*]

7I.5.240.43   In our view, determining whether there is a market for the financial asset and whether the transferee has the practical ability to sell in that market is a matter of judgement based on consid-eration of the facts and circumstances. It is not necessary in all cases to demonstrate that the market for the financial asset is active or organised. We believe that a market may be considered to exist if there are willing buyers for an asset and a sale to a market participant could be effected within a reasonable timescale and at a reasonable cost. The transferee does not have the practical ability to sell if a call option or a guarantee prevents the transferee from selling the financial asset – e.g. if the financial asset is subject to an option that allows the transferor to repurchase it and a replacement is not readily obtainable. As a result, the transferor would not be considered to have lost control. [*IAS 39.23, AG43–AG44*]

7I.5.240.45   In Example 11, if Company V attaches conditions to the transfer that prevent Company W from selling the mortgage receivables to a third party – e.g. to maintain customer relationships – then V has retained control over the transferred financial assets. [*IAS 39.23, AG43–AG44*]

EXAMPLE 12A – CONTROL RETAINED THROUGH PURCHASED CALL OPTION (1)

7I.5.240.50   Company P sells a portfolio of corporate loans to Company B. P simultaneously enters into a call option with B under which it has the right to repurchase the financial assets after five years.

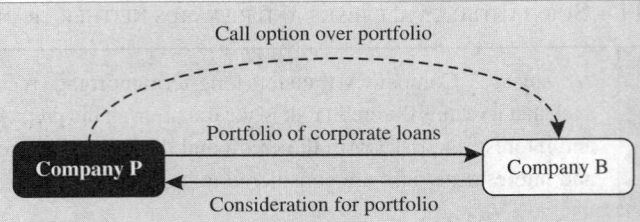

Call option over portfolio

Portfolio of corporate loans

Company P → Company B

Consideration for portfolio

7I.5.240.55   Although B has the legal right to sell the financial assets, it does not have the practical ability to do so because it could be required to return them to P at the end of five years. If B attempts to sell the financial assets to another party, then it would have to attach a similar call option to be able to repurchase the financial assets in the event of P exercising its option.

7I.5.240.56   It is also unlikely that there is an active market for such financial assets that would allow B to sell the financial assets without attaching the aforementioned call option to them.

7I.5.240.57   Consequently, because of the call option held by P, it has retained control over the financial assets and will have to consider accounting under continuing involvement. [*IAS 39.AG42*]

EXAMPLE 12B – CONTROL RETAINED THROUGH PURCHASED CALL OPTION (2)

7I.5.240.60   Company Q transfers trade receivables with an option that allows Q to reacquire overdue receivables at face value. Although the option has no stand-alone economic value, Q has retained control to be able to protect its customer relationships.

(S) 7I.5.240.70   In our view, no distinction should be made in the separate financial statements between a derecognition transaction between a parent entity and one of its operating subsidiaries and one with an independent third party. Therefore, a parent entity should not normally include indirect control through the ownership of an operating subsidiary in the evaluation of control, because this control is not related to the financial asset.

(S) 7I.5.240.80   When the transferee is a limited-purpose vehicle or other structured entity that is not consolidated (i.e. because it is not a subsidiary or because the derecognition analysis is carried out for the purposes of the transferor's separate financial statements), an evaluation of whether control of the transferred assets has been passed by the transferor raises certain practical considerations. In our view, the following questions should be addressed to assess whether control has been transferred.
- Is there any contractual restriction preventing the structured entity from selling or pledging the financial assets? It is common practice to have such restrictions in place, because when a structured entity is set up for a securitisation transaction the financial assets are also used as collateral. In our view, to meet the criterion that the entity has not retained control of the transferred assets, the structured entity cannot be prevented from selling the financial assets by means of any pre-determined autopilot rules or pre-agreements.

- Can the structured entity unilaterally sell the financial assets or is this decision controlled directly by the transferor?

7I.5.250   *Continuing involvement*

7I.5.250.10   If an entity retains control of a financial asset for which some but not substantially all of the risks and rewards have been transferred, then the entity continues to recognise the financial asset to the extent of its continuing involvement in the financial asset. [*IAS 39.20(c)(ii)*]

7I.5.250.15   If an entity's continuing involvement in a transferred asset takes the form of a guarantee, then the extent of the entity's continuing involvement is the lower of: (1) the carrying amount of the asset; and (2) the maximum amount of the consideration received that the entity could be required to repay. [*IAS 39.30(a)*]

EXAMPLE 13 – CONTINUED RECOGNITION BASED ON CONTINUING INVOLVEMENT

7I.5.250.20   Company P transfers short-term receivables of 100 to Company Q. P provides a credit loss guarantee of 2. ECLs are 4 and historically have varied between 1 and 5. Q is not permitted to sell or pledge the receivables and there is no market for them.

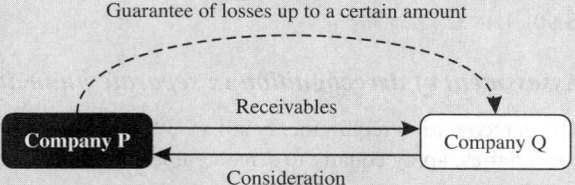

7I.5.250.25   In our view, P has retained some, but not substantially all, of the risks and rewards of ownership associated with the receivables. In addition, because Q is not permitted to sell or pledge the receivables and there is no market for such receivables, P has not given up control and continues to recognise the receivables to the extent of its continuing involvement.

7I.5.250.27   The maximum extent of P's continuing involvement is 2 (the amount of the guarantee). Therefore, we believe that P should derecognise 98 and continue to recognise 2, which is the lower of (1) the carrying amount of the financial asset; and (2) the maximum amount received in the transfer that P could be required to repay. [*IAS 39.30(a), AG48*]

7I.5.250.28   A question arises about how to determine the extent of the entity's continuing involvement when it guarantees an amount of credit losses on a transferred asset denominated in a foreign currency. In our view, in determining the extent of the entity's continuing involvement in this case, the guarantee amount should be calculated by applying the spot exchange rate at the reporting date to the maximum amount of the consideration received that the entity could be required to repay in the foreign currency – i.e. without considering potential future changes in the foreign currency exchange rate. This is because the maximum amount of the consideration received that could be repaid is a fixed monetary amount denominated in the foreign currency that meets the definition of a monetary item in IAS 21. Monetary items are translated into their functional currency at the spot exchange rate at the reporting date (see 2.7.110.10). *[IAS 39.30(a), 21.16]*

71.5.250.30   Generally, a measurement based on continuing involvement requires the net carrying amount of the financial asset and the associated financial liability to reflect, depending on the measurement basis of the financial asset, either the amortised cost or the fair value of the rights and obligations retained by the entity. However, notwithstanding the requirement to arrive at a particular net carrying amount, the financial asset and associated financial liability might not qualify for offsetting. *[IAS 39.AG48]*

71.5.250.40   To qualify for offsetting, an entity has to demonstrate that it currently has a legally enforceable right to set off – i.e. a cash flow received on the transferred financial asset would have to result in the elimination of a proportion of the financial liability of the transferor to the transferee. This would imply that the risks associated with the transferred financial asset lie with the transferee, which in turn would imply that derecognition should have taken place; a conclusion that is contrary to that reached in the derecognition analysis. Consequently, when a transaction does not result in derecognition, it is not generally possible to meet the offsetting criteria. Similarly, an entity is prohibited from offsetting any income arising on the transferred financial asset against expenses arising on the associated financial liability, which follows from the more general prohibition on offsetting in IAS 1 (see 71.8.90). *[IAS 32.42, 39.36]*

Ⓢ 71.5.260   *Assessment of derecognition in separate financial statements*

71.5.260.10   The derecognition requirements in IAS 39, other than the requirement to start by consolidating all subsidiaries, apply equally to separate financial statements (see 71.5.60). *[IAS 39.15]*

71.5.260.20   However, the transfer that needs evaluation in the separate financial statements may be different from that at the consolidated level. Consequently, depending on the fact pattern, it is possible to achieve derecognition in separate financial statements while failing to do so in consolidated financial statements. In our experience, this situation may arise with transactions involving structured entities that are consolidated in the consolidated financial statements.

71.5.270   **Accounting for a sale**

71.5.280   *Transfers that qualify for derecognition*

71.5.280.10   Sometimes only part of a financial asset qualifies for derecognition – e.g. if an interest-only strip is retained. In these cases, the carrying amount of the entire financial asset before the transfer is allocated between the sold and retained portions based on their relative fair values on the date of the transfer. For this purpose, a retained servicing asset is treated as part of the original asset that continues to be recognised. *[IAS 39.27]*

71.5.280.20   Sometimes new financial assets or financial liabilities are created in the transfer – e.g. a credit guarantee. New financial assets, financial liabilities or servicing liabilities created as a result of a transfer that qualifies for derecognition are recognised separately and measured at fair value. *[IAS 39.24–25]*

71.5.280.30   On derecognition of a financial asset, a gain or loss is recognised based on the difference between (1) the carrying amount of the financial asset (or part of the financial asset) derecognised; and (2) the consideration received (including any new asset obtained less any new liability assumed), and the cumulative gain or loss previously recognised in OCI in respect of the derecognised financial asset or the part of the derecognised financial asset. [*IAS 39.26–27*]

71.5.280.40   If financial assets are exchanged in a transaction that meets the criteria for derecognition, then the financial assets received are measured at fair value and the profit or loss on disposal is calculated based on the fair value of the financial assets received. [*IAS 39.14, 26*]

71.5.280.50   IFRS is silent on how to determine the cost of financial assets sold when they are part of a homogeneous portfolio. Therefore, the application of the hierarchy for the selection of accounting policies (see 2.8.20) is applied. In our view, the guidance on cost formulas for inventories should be applied (see 3.8.280). Therefore, any reasonable cost allocation method – e.g. average cost or first-in, first-out – may be used. However, the use of specific identification is not precluded if the entity is able to identify the specific items sold and their costs. For example, a specific security may be identified as sold by linking the date, amount and cost of securities bought with the sale transaction, provided that there is no other evidence suggesting that the actual security sold was not the one identified under this method.

71.5.280.60   We believe that an entity should choose a reasonable cost allocation method, to be applied consistently, to determine the cost of financial assets sold when the financial assets are part of a homogeneous portfolio. In addition, in our view the approach used to determine the cost of financial assets sold should be applied consistently when assessing impairment and accounting for the resulting impairment losses (see 71.6.450).

71.5.290   *Transfers that do not qualify for derecognition*

71.5.300   *Accounting by transferor*

71.5.300.10   If a transfer does not qualify for derecognition, then the financial asset, or the retained portion of the financial asset, remains in the statement of financial position and a corresponding financial liability is recognised for any consideration received. [*IAS 39.29, AG47*]

71.5.300.20   If contractual rights and obligations – e.g. derivatives – related to a transfer prevent the transferor from derecognising the financial assets, then these rights and obligations are not accounted for separately. For example, a call option retained by the transferor may prevent the derecognition of certain financial assets, but recognising the financial assets as well as the call option would result in the entity double counting its rights to those financial assets. [*IAS 39.AG49*]

EXAMPLE 14A – RIGHTS THAT PREVENT DERECOGNITION THAT ARE NOT ACCOUNTED FOR SEPARATELY

71.5.300.30   Company X transfers receivables of 100 to Company Y in exchange for a note amounting to 100 that represents a beneficial interest in the transferred assets – i.e. payments on the note will be made only out of cash collected from the receivables.

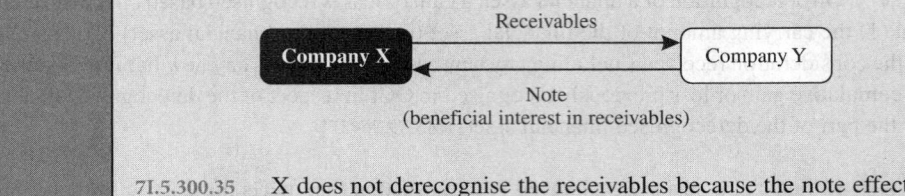

Receivables

Company X ⟶ Company Y

Note
(beneficial interest in receivables)

7I.5.300.35   X does not derecognise the receivables because the note effectively passes substantially all of the risks and rewards of ownership of the receivables back to X (see 7I.5.230).

7I.5.300.40   In addition, X does not recognise a new asset for the right to receive cash flows from the note, because doing so would result in double counting the rights to the transferred receivables. Except for this retained interest in the transferred receivables, which are already recognised in X's statement of financial position, X has retained no consideration for the transfer. Because no new asset is recognised, neither is any corresponding financial liability.

7I.5.300.50   It is important to contrast the situation in 7I.5.300.20 with one in which the derivative requires separate recognition.

EXAMPLE 14B – RIGHTS AND OBLIGATIONS THAT DO NOT PREVENT DERECOGNITION THAT ARE ACCOUNTED FOR SEPARATELY

7I.5.300.60   Company F transfers fixed rate financial assets to Company B. F simultaneously enters into an interest rate swap with B under which it receives fixed rate interest (equal to the rate on the transferred financial assets) and pays floating rate interest (equal to the rate on the notes issued by B to fund the acquisition of the financial assets); the payments are based on a notional amount equal to the principal amount of the transferred financial assets, but are not conditional on B receiving any cash flows from the underlying financial assets.

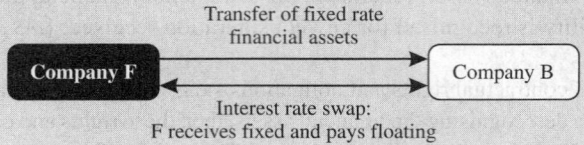

Transfer of fixed rate
financial assets

Company F ⟷ Company B

Interest rate swap:
F receives fixed and pays floating

7I.5.300.70   In this example, the interest rate swap does not prevent F from derecognising the financial assets, because the payments on the swap are not conditional on payments being made on the transferred assets. Therefore, F recognises the interest rate swap separately and subsequently accounts for it as a derivative (see 7I.5.300.20). [*IAS 39.AG51(p)*]

7I.5.305   *Accounting by transferee*

7I.5.305.10   If a transfer of a financial asset does not qualify for derecognition, then the transferee does not recognise the transferred asset as its asset in its statement of financial position. Instead, the transferee derecognises the cash or other consideration paid and recognises a receivable from the transferor. [*IAS 39.AG50*]

7I.5.305.20   IAS 39 is silent on the accounting by the transferee for transactions that do not qualify for derecognition by the transferor when the transferee does not pay cash or other assets but instead issues a new debt instrument as consideration for the assets transferred (see Example 14A).

7I.5.305.30   In our view, the transferee should usually recognise both a receivable from the transferor as a financial asset and the debt instrument as a financial liability in such cases. This is because the terms of each instrument generally determine the appropriate accounting and two financial instruments, even if they are entered into simultaneously, are accounted for separately (see 7I.5.40). Therefore, unless these instruments should be accounted for as a single combined instrument based on the criteria in 7I.5.40, we believe that the only case in which the transferee should not recognise a separate financial asset and a financial liability is when the debt instrument issued by the transferee serves only to pass the cash flows from the transferred asset back from the transferee to the transferor and the pass-through criteria (see 7I.5.160) are met from the transferee's perspective in respect of the transferred asset legally owned by the transferee. In addition, the transferee does not offset the financial asset and the financial liability unless the criteria in IAS 32 are met (see 7I.8.90). [*IAS 1.32*]

EXAMPLE 15A – TRANSFEREE DOES NOT RECOGNISE SEPARATE ASSET AND LIABILITY

7I.5.305.40   Company F transfers legal title to a portfolio of loans to Company G, which is not controlled by F, in exchange for participation certificates issued by G.

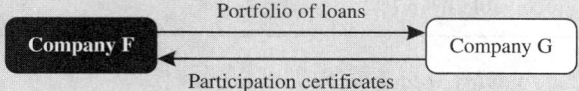

Portfolio of loans

Company F → Company G

Participation certificates

7I.5.305.45   Under the terms of the participation certificates, G agrees to pay without material delay all of the cash flows from the portfolio of loans to F and is prohibited from selling or pledging the loans. G has no obligation to pay any other amounts to F and is not permitted to reinvest cash receipts from the loans pending their payment to F. F enters into the transaction because it considers that the participation certificates would be more attractive to other investors or as collateral for borrowings.

7I.5.305.50   F does not derecognise the loans because it has retained substantially all of the risks and rewards of the loans. In our view, G should not recognise a financial asset or a financial liability at the time of the transfer because G has simultaneously obtained the contractual rights to the cash flows from the portfolio of loans and assumed a contractual obligation to pay those cash flows to F in a manner that meets the criteria for derecognition of those loans – i.e. the pass-through criteria (see 7I.5.160) are met from G's perspective and G does not assume the risks and rewards of ownership of the loans.

EXAMPLE 15B – TRANSFEREE RECOGNISES SEPARATE ASSET AND LIABILITY

7I.5.305.60　Modifying Example 15A, the participation certificate includes a guarantee that Company G will pay at least 90% of the contractual cash flows of the transferred loans to Company F in the event that a lesser amount is actually received from the loans. The ECLs on the loans are 3%.

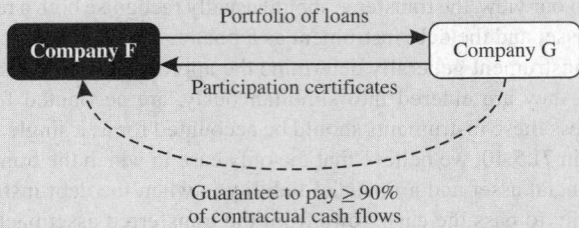

7I.5.305.70　Because the guarantee is expected to be triggered only in remote circumstances, F has retained substantially all of the risks and rewards of the loans and does not derecognise them.

7I.5.305.80　From G's perspective, the participation certificates no longer meet the pass-through criteria because G has an obligation to pay amounts to the holder in excess of the amounts collected from the loans if collections fall below the 90% level. In addition, the transfer has a business purpose as explained in Example 15A. Therefore, G recognises the participation certificates as a financial liability and a receivable from F.

7I.5.310　*Receivables sold with full recourse*

7I.5.310.10　Receivables sold with full recourse do not generally qualify for derecognition. Instead, the transaction is generally accounted for by the transferor as a collateralised borrowing (see 7I.5.300.10).

EXAMPLE 16 – RECEIVABLES TRANSFERRED WITH FULL RECOURSE

7I.5.310.20　Company H sells trade receivables due in six months with a carrying amount of 100 for a cash payment of 95 to Company J, subject to full recourse. Under the right of recourse, H is obliged to compensate J for the failure of any debtor to pay when payment is due. In addition to the recourse, J is entitled to sell the receivables back to the transferor in the event of unfavourable changes in interest rates or credit ratings of the underlying debtors.

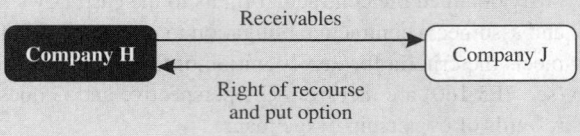

71.5.310.30   The transaction is accounted for by H as a collateralised borrowing because it does not qualify for derecognition. Even assuming that the contractual rights to all of the cash flows on the receivables have been transferred as a matter of law, this transaction still fails the derecognition requirements because H has retained substantially all of the risks and rewards associated with the financial assets. H is obliged to compensate J for the failure of the debtors to pay when payments are due. In addition, H has granted J a put option on the transferred financial assets that allows J to sell the receivables back to H in the event of actual credit losses and/or changes in underlying credit ratings or interest rates. Consequently, H has retained substantially all of the risks and rewards of ownership of the receivables.

71.5.310.40   In this example, H recognises 95 as a financial liability, which is measured at amortised cost with an interest expense of 5 being recognised over the six-month period until maturity. H continues to recognise the receivables as financial assets. Cash received on the receivables by either H or J reduces the receivables and, if it is received by or paid to J, the financial liability. If uncollected receivables are returned to H for cash, then the financial liability is reduced.

71.5.320   **SECURITISATIONS**

71.5.320.10   Entities commonly use securitisations to monetise financial assets, such as homogeneous consumer loans, credit card receivables, trade receivables or mortgage loans, by selling newly created securities collateralised by these financial assets to investors. Such securitisation transactions are often executed using structured entities that have limited activities. The purpose of the structured entities is to hold the interests in the securitised financial assets and to pass through cash flows earned on these financial assets to the investors in the notes issued by the structured entities. In a typical securitisation, the transferring entity assigns financial assets to the structured entity in return for cash proceeds. The transfer of financial assets, issue of notes to investors and payment of proceeds to the transferor usually take place simultaneously.

71.5.320.20   If financial assets are securitised using a structured entity, then determining whether those financial assets should be derecognised may be a complex issue. In many securitisation transactions involving structured entities, the pass-through requirements will be difficult to achieve or will not be met. In addition, because the purpose of a securitisation is often to raise highly rated, low-cost finance, the transferor typically provides some form of credit enhancement to the structured entity. For example, the transferor may provide additional collateral to the structured entity in the form of loans or cash, or may provide a guarantee to the investors in the notes issued by the structured entity. For further discussion of specific practical application issues, see 7I.5.330–355.

71.5.320.30   If a structured entity is used to securitise financial assets, then the derecognition criteria may need to be analysed from different perspectives (see also 7I.5.60.20–30) depending on the circumstances. The first step in the derecognition assessment is to assess whether the structured entity should be consolidated under IFRS 10 (see chapter 2.5 and, in particular, 2.5.20).

7I.5.320.40   If the structured entity is consolidated, then the transferor evaluates at the group level whether there has been a transfer of financial assets by the group, including the structured entity, to the investors in the securities issued by the structured entity. If there has been a transfer of financial assets by the group, then the transferor evaluates to what extent the group, including the structured entity, has transferred or retained the risks and rewards of (and, if necessary, whether it has retained control over) the financial assets.

7I.5.320.50   If, however, the structured entity is not consolidated under IFRS 10, then the transferor evaluates at the group level whether there has been a transfer of financial assets by the group, excluding the structured entity, to the structured entity. If there has been, then the transferor evaluates to what extent the group, excluding the structured entity, has transferred or retained the risks and rewards of (and, if necessary, whether it has retained control over) the financial assets.

Ⓢ **7I.5.320.60**   If the transferor is preparing separate financial statements, then for this purpose the transferor evaluates whether there has been a transfer of financial assets by it, as a separate entity, to the structured entity. If there has been, then it evaluates to what extent it, as a separate entity, has transferred or retained the risks and rewards of (and, if necessary, whether it has retained control over) the financial assets. [*IAS 39.15*]

7I.5.320.70   Securitisations usually involve portfolios of financial assets and include detailed terms setting out the allocation of cash flows between the various parties. Therefore, it is often challenging to determine:

- whether the derecognition guidance should be applied to a part of the portfolio of financial assets or to the portfolio in its entirety (see 7I.5.80);
- whether there has been a transfer of the contractual rights to the cash flows of the financial assets or there is a qualifying pass-through arrangement (see 7I.5.100, 330–340);
- the extent to which the transferor has transferred or retained the risks and rewards of any financial assets that have been transferred (see 7I.5.190); and
- whether the transferor has retained control of any financial assets that have been transferred (see 7I.5.240).

Ⓢ **7I.5.330**   **Evaluating pass-through criteria: Structured entity not consolidated**

7I.5.330.10   If the structured entity is not consolidated – i.e. it is not consolidated as part of the transferor's consolidated financial statements in accordance with IFRS 10 or the transferor is preparing separate financial statements – and the transferor does not transfer the contractual rights to receive the cash flows to the structured entity, then the terms of a credit enhancement or other arrangement provided in connection with the transferred financial assets may affect the conclusion about whether the pass-through criteria are met.

7I.5.330.20   If a credit enhancement can require the transferor to make additional future payments to the structured entity (or its investors) – e.g. an unfunded financial guarantee or other non-funded credit enhancement – then in our view the transfer would fail the pass-through requirements. This is because the transferor could be obliged to pay amounts to the structured entity even if it does not collect the equivalent amounts from the original assets. [*IAS 39.19(a)*]

7I.5.330.30   However, if a credit enhancement provided by the transferor could never require the transferor to make additional future payments to the structured entity or investors in the structured entity, then in our view the credit enhancement would not violate the pass-through requirement that the transferor has no obligation to pay amounts unless it collects equivalent amounts from the original financial assets. For example, credit enhancement could be provided by means of a pre-funded financial guarantee under which cash collateral is paid to the structured entity at or before the time of transfer, a subordinated loan that is made at or before the time of transfer, or a reserve fund that is built up from the cash collected from the underlying loans and that is retained by the structured entity. This is because, following the transfer, the transferor would not be obliged to pay to the structured entity any amounts in excess of those that it collects from the original financial assets.

EXAMPLE 17 – GUARANTEE COLLATERALISED BY CASH HELD BY UNCONSOLIDATED STRUCTURED ENTITY

7I.5.330.40   Company T agrees to pay the cash flows collected from a portfolio of financial assets to Structured Entity SE, which T does not consolidate. SE issues, for cash of 100, notes to third party investors that are collateralised by its right to receive the collected cash flows from T.

7I.5.330.50   SE pays 95 of the cash and issues a subordinated note with a nominal value of 5 to T. The remaining 5 cash is held by SE and will be used to compensate the investors for up to 5 of cash shortfalls arising from defaults in the portfolio of financial assets.

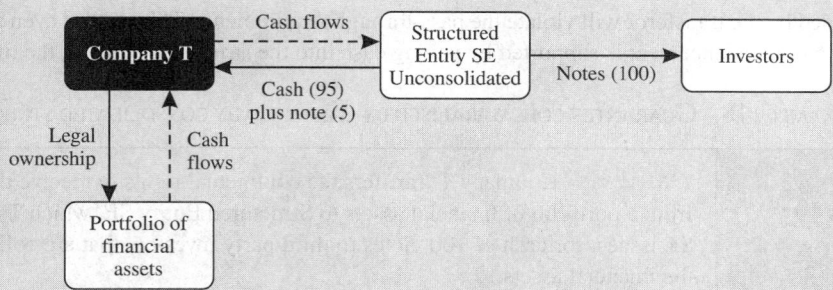

7I.5.330.60   In evaluating whether the portfolio of financial assets is derecognised in T's consolidated financial statements, the arrangement does not violate the requirement that the transferor in a pass-through arrangement may be obliged to pay amounts to the eventual recipients only if it collects equivalent amounts from the original financial assets. That is because:
- T is only obliged to pay amounts that it collects from the portfolio; and
- SE, not T, has the obligation to pay the initial cash retention to the note holders if there are defaults, and SE is not consolidated by T.

7I.5.330.70   The impact of higher-than-expected credit losses is that T receives less from the subordinated note issued by SE when the arrangement comes to an end rather than T being required to pay additional amounts to SE to cover those losses. Although this variability in cash flows that T will receive is relevant to assessing the extent to which T has retained or transferred the risks and rewards of the financial assets, it does not violate the pass-through criteria.

7I.5.340   **Evaluating pass-through criteria: Structured entity consolidated**

7I.5.340.10   If the structured entity is consolidated, then the contractual arrangements between the consolidated group and the investors in the notes issued by the structured entity are analysed to determine whether the requirements for a qualifying pass-through arrangement are met (see 7I.5.60.20–30). This is because the structured entity, and therefore the transferor's consolidated group, will not typically transfer the contractual rights to the cash flows on the underlying financial assets to the investors in the notes issued by the structured entity. However, the terms of the notes may provide for payments to be made to the holders based on cash received on the underlying financial assets in such a manner that the structured entity's only role is acting as an agent on behalf of the note holders. Therefore, it is possible that such a transaction could meet the pass-through conditions listed in 7I.5.160.10.

7I.5.340.20   For the purpose of evaluating whether there is an obligation to pay amounts in excess of those collected from the original financial assets, the transferor analyses obligations to pay amounts from the consolidated group, including the consolidated structured entity, to other holders of interests in the structured entity; cash flows between the transferor entity and the structured entity are not generally relevant for this purpose, because they are internal to the group. If the nature of credit enhancements is such that additional amounts will be paid to the investors in the notes issued by a structured entity in the event of default – i.e. the consolidated group will make additional payments in excess of the amounts collected from the original financial assets – then in our view the credit enhancements provided by the transferor will violate the pass-through requirements. This applies even if the guarantee or credit enhancement is supported by paying cash into the structured entity at the time of transfer.

EXAMPLE 18 – GUARANTEE COLLATERALISED BY CASH HELD BY CONSOLIDATED STRUCTURED ENTITY

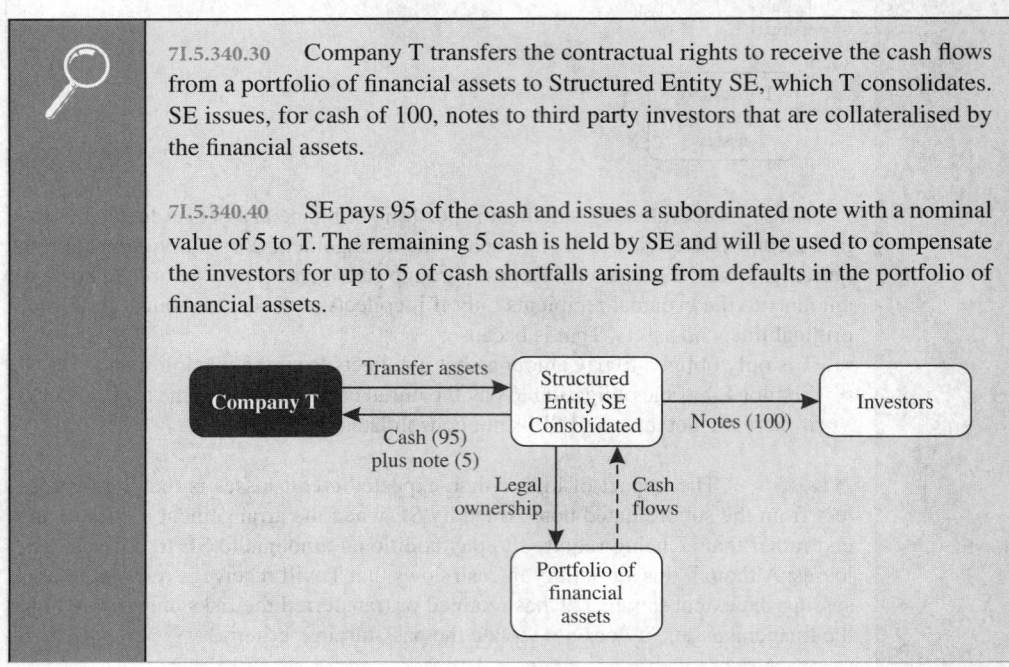

7I.5.340.30   Company T transfers the contractual rights to receive the cash flows from a portfolio of financial assets to Structured Entity SE, which T consolidates. SE issues, for cash of 100, notes to third party investors that are collateralised by the financial assets.

7I.5.340.40   SE pays 95 of the cash and issues a subordinated note with a nominal value of 5 to T. The remaining 5 cash is held by SE and will be used to compensate the investors for up to 5 of cash shortfalls arising from defaults in the portfolio of financial assets.

7I.5.340.50 The arrangement violates the requirement that the entity should be obliged to pay amounts to the eventual recipients only if it collects equivalent amounts from the original financial assets. This is because SE is part of the consolidated group and therefore the consolidated group is obliged to pay up to 5 of cash to the third party investors in excess of collections from the portfolio of financial assets.

7I.5.340.60 Our views on some other specific application issues for determining whether a securitisation involving a structured entity qualifies as a pass-through arrangement are included in 7I.5.345–355.

7I.5.345 **Without material delay**

7I.5.345.10 To meet the pass-through conditions, an entity is required to remit all cash flows that it collects on behalf of the eventual recipients without material delay. In our view, the entity can invest the cash flows for periods of up to three months without violating this requirement provided that:
- the investments are only in cash and cash equivalents (see 2.3.10); and
- all cash flows, both amounts collected and any income earned on investments in cash or cash equivalents, are remitted to the bond holders on the next payment date. [*IAS 39.19(c)*]

7I.5.345.20 Conversely, we believe that refinancing terms exceeding three months will not meet this criterion; neither will investments in cash and cash equivalents on a revolving basis over periods exceeding three months.

7I.5.345.30 In some securitisation structures, the transferring entity holds a junior interest issued by a consolidated structured entity, which is subordinate to senior notes issued by the structured entity, with specific terms such that the junior interest represents a retention by the transferring entity of a fully proportionate share of all or specifically identified cash flows and a subordination of that retained interest to provide a credit enhancement to the transferee for credit losses. When the structured entity collects cash flows from the underlying financial assets, the senior note holders are paid without material delay. However, cash flows that are in excess of those required to pay the senior note holders are retained within the structured entity as part of an 'excess cash reserve fund'. This fund is used to make up for any future shortfalls in cash flows due to the senior note holders. Amounts remaining in the fund after the senior note holders have been fully paid are then paid to the junior note holder. [*IAS 39.AG52, BC61–BC63*]

7I.5.345.40 In our view, the existence of such an excess cash reserve fund does not violate the requirement that all cash flows collected on behalf of the eventual recipients are remitted without material delay. This is because when the excess cash is first collected in the excess cash reserve fund, it is collected on behalf of the transferring entity rather than the senior note holders. This is on the basis that if future collections from the financial assets are enough to pay the senior note holders in full, then the excess cash will be paid to the transferring entity. The excess cash reserve fund will become due to the senior note holders only if and when future collections are not enough to pay the senior note holders in full. At this point, the excess cash is considered to have been collected on behalf of the senior note holders as the eventual recipients, and it is only from this time that the extent of any delay in remitting the excess cash to the senior note holders should be assessed to determine whether it is material.

7I.5.350   **Revolving transactions**

7I.5.350.10   If cash flows collected from the underlying financial assets are reinvested by the structured entity in new financial assets, other than cash or cash equivalents, under a revolving structure, then problems may be encountered in meeting the condition that all cash flows should be remitted to the eventual recipients without material delay. Further analysis of the terms and conditions governing this reinvestment is required to determine whether the conditions for a qualifying pass-through arrangement are met. [*IAS 39.19*]

7I.5.350.20   In our experience, there are four general scenarios that may be encountered, each having an effect on the pass-through requirements.

Scenarios	Effects
The structured entity automatically reinvests the cash flows to buy additional receivables in accordance with predetermined contractual arrangements embedded in the structure.	In our view, the pass-through requirements are violated because the investments are not in cash or cash equivalents and therefore derecognition is precluded.
The structured entity remits the cash flows to the note holders without material delay, at which time the note holders may decide whether to reinvest the cash flows with the structured entity for the purpose of acquiring further financial assets.	In our view, this does not violate the pass-through requirements and the transaction should be considered further for derecognition.
The structured entity automatically reinvests the cash flows to buy additional financial assets, unless the note holders indicate at that stage that they do not want to reinvest in the structured entity – i.e. the cash flows are remitted to the note holders only if they decide not to reinvest.	In our view, the pass-through requirements are not violated because the structured entity is obliged to remit the cash flows to the note holders if it is so notified. The lack of a physical flow of cash from the structured entity to the note holder and back to the structured entity does not impact the derecognition analysis and the transaction should be considered further for derecognition.
The structured entity remits the cash flows to the note holders, but the note holders have an up-front contractual agreement that all cash flows will be reinvested immediately by the structured entity.	In our view, despite the physical flow of cash, the pass-through requirements are violated because the note holders are contractually obliged to reinvest the cash flows immediately in order for the structured entity to acquire additional financial assets. Therefore, derecognition is precluded.

7I.5.355   **Continuing involvement**

7I.5.355.10   If the pass-through requirements are met and it is concluded that some but not substantially all of the risks and rewards of the financial assets are transferred to the note holders, then it is likely that the transferor will have retained control of the transferred financial assets. This is because in a typical structure the structured entity is consolidated and will maintain legal title to the financial assets whereas the note holders will have no rights to sell the underlying financial assets. Also, even if the structured entity is not consolidated, the transferor may retain control because the structured entity may not itself have the practical ability to sell the transferred assets. In such circumstances, partial derecognition may be appropriate under continuing involvement accounting (see 7I.5.250). [*IAS 39.AG43*]

7I.5.360 REPURCHASE AGREEMENTS AND SECURITIES LENDING

7I.5.360.10   If a sale of a financial asset is subject to a repurchase agreement at a fixed price, or at the initial selling price plus interest, or if the asset is lent to a third party that agrees to return it, then the seller retains substantially all of the risks and rewards of ownership of the asset. Therefore, the seller does not derecognise the financial asset. If the transferee obtains the right to sell or pledge the financial asset that does not qualify for derecognition, then the seller reclassifies the financial asset in its statement of financial position – e.g. as a loaned financial asset or repurchase receivable. [*IAS 39.AG51(a)*]

7I.5.360.20   This treatment also applies when:
- the financial asset subject to the agreement is of a type readily obtainable in the market, such that the transferee could sell the transferred financial asset and repurchase an identical financial asset in the market to meet its return obligation to the seller; or
- the agreement permits the transferee to return financial assets that are the same or substantially the same as the originally transferred asset or financial assets that are similar and of equal fair value. [*IAS 39.AG51(b)–(c)*]

7I.5.360.30   Similarly, the transferee does not recognise the financial asset received under a repurchase or securities lending arrangement. If the transferee sells the financial asset, then it recognises a financial liability to return the financial asset based on its fair value. [*IAS 39.AG50*]

7I.5.360.40   If there is an event of default by the seller and it is no longer entitled to reclaim the transferred financial asset, then the seller derecognises the financial asset and the transferee recognises the financial asset at fair value or, if it has sold the financial asset already, derecognises the financial liability to return the financial asset. [*IAS 39.37(c)*]

7I.5.370 DERECOGNITION OF FINANCIAL LIABILITIES

7I.5.370.10   A financial liability is derecognised when it is extinguished – i.e. it is discharged or cancelled or expires. This may happen when:
- payment is made to the lender – e.g. when the issuer of a debt instrument redeems the instrument;
- the borrower is legally released from primary responsibility for the financial liability – this condition can be satisfied even if the borrower has given a guarantee, as long as the borrower is released from primary responsibility; or
- there is an exchange between an existing lender and borrower of debt instruments with substantially different terms or a substantial modification of the terms of an existing debt instrument (together referred to as 'modification of terms' in this chapter). [*IAS 39.39–40, AG57, AG62*]

7I.5.370.20   The derecognition conditions are also satisfied and a financial liability is derecognised when an entity repurchases its own debt instruments previously issued, irrespective of whether the entity intends to resell those instruments to other parties in the near term or is itself a market maker in those instruments. This is consistent with the treatment of own equity instruments acquired by an entity, except that in the case of an extinguishment of a financial liability a gain or loss may be recognised in profit or loss. [*IAS 39.AG58*]

7I.5.370.30   It is not possible for an entity to extinguish a financial liability through an in-substance defeasance of its debt. An 'in-substance defeasance' arises when an entity transfers financial assets covering its obligations to a third party – typically into a trust or similar vehicle – that then makes payments to the lender from principal and interest on the transferred financial assets, without the third party having legally assumed the responsibility for the financial liability and without the lender being part of the contractual arrangements related to the third party. The entity is not legally released from the obligation and therefore derecognition of the financial liability is inappropriate. [*IAS 39.AG58–AG59*]

7I.5.370.35   An entity may arrange for a third party to assume primary responsibility for the obligation for a fee while continuing to make the contractual payments on behalf of the third party. To be able to derecognise the financial liability, the entity needs to have obtained legal release from the creditor whereby the creditor agrees to accept the third party as the new primary obligor. [*IAS 39.AG59–AG60*]

7I.5.370.40   As for a financial asset, when transferring a financial liability, parts of the financial liability could be retained and new financial instruments (either financial assets or financial liabilities) could be created. The accounting is similar to the accounting for the derecognition of parts of financial assets with the creation of new instruments. [*IAS 39.41, 43*]

7I.5.370.50   A gain or loss calculated as the difference between the carrying amount of a financial liability (or part of a financial liability) extinguished or transferred and the consideration paid is recognised in profit or loss. The consideration paid includes any non-cash assets transferred and new liabilities assumed. [*IAS 39.41*]

7I.5.380   Modification of terms

7I.5.380.10   Issues often arise over whether it is appropriate to derecognise a financial liability when its terms are renegotiated, including an exchange between an existing borrower and a lender of debt instruments, and including a renegotiation in exchange for an immediate cash payment or receipt. For a discussion of transactions involving the issue of equity instruments in exchange for the extinguishment of all or part of a liability, see 7I.5.410.

7I.5.380.20   When a debt instrument is restructured or refinanced and the terms have been substantially modified, the transaction is accounted for as an extinguishment of the old debt instrument, with a gain or loss (see 7I.5.390). The new debt instrument is recognised at fair value (see 7I.6.20). In our view, it is not appropriate to simply assume that the nominal amount of the new loan is the fair value. In the absence of an available quoted price in an active market for the new debt instrument, fair value is established using another valuation technique. In our view, if the valuation technique does not use only data from observable markets, then this does not preclude the recognition of a gain or loss because the estimate of fair value is used as the estimate of the transaction price. [*IAS 39.40, AG64, AG76*]

7I.5.380.30   In our view, the requirements on modifications and exchanges of debt instruments do not extend to the usual repayment of a loan at maturity and its replacement by a new loan on arm's length terms, even if the new loan is with the same lender, because the original loan is not modified or exchanged but is settled in accordance with its original terms. Also, we believe that they do not apply to changes in the amounts or timing of payments required under a loan that arise from existing features included in the original debt agreement – e.g. interest rate step-ups or the acceleration of maturity contingent on a credit downgrade – because these are not modifications of terms. However, changes in estimated cash flows attributable to such features may result in the recognition of a gain or loss (see 7I.6.260).

7I.5.381 *Loan transfers*

7I.5.381.10 An existing individual lender may transfer its right to the future cash flows of a loan without any involvement of the borrower. For a discussion of the accounting from the lender's perspective, see 7I.5.100. Such a transfer may be performed under the existing loan agreement without any modifications to the terms of the loan agreement. In this case, the borrower is not legally released from its primary responsibility to repay the loan and it continues to recognise the existing loan. However, in other cases an existing loan agreement may be cancelled and extinguished, and replaced by a new agreement with substantially different terms between the borrower and the new lender (see 7I.5.370.10). In this case, the old loan is derecognised. For a discussion of the replacement of a loan agreement, see 7I.5.383.20. [*IAS 39.39–40, AG57, AG62*]

7I.5.382 *Unit of assessment*

7I.5.382.10 In our view, the derecognition assessment should generally be performed on an instrument-by-instrument basis, and not by grouping together similar financial liabilities. For example, an entity may have issued 100 individual bonds that are held by different parties, of which it intends to replace 60 with new debt instruments and redeem the other 40 bonds. The bonds should be considered individually for derecognition – i.e. the unit of account is each bond. Therefore, the assessment should be made for each of the 60 bonds replaced and not for all of the outstanding bonds in total. In this way, the entity would derecognise 40 of the bonds that are redeemed, and the remaining 60 bonds may or may not qualify for derecognition, depending on the extent to which the terms of the original and new instruments differ.

7I.5.382.20 However, if an entity has issued one bond with a nominal amount of 100 held by a single party and intends to pay an amount of 40 and replace the bond with a debt instrument with modified terms and a nominal amount of 60, then the assessment is made for the bond as a whole. In our view, the agreement to make a payment of 40 is an element of the modification and accordingly that payment should be taken into account in the quantitative assessment (see 7I.5.385) in calculating the present value of cash flows under the new arrangement.

7I.5.382.30 In contrast, in some cases an entity may amend or settle a proportion of a single instrument, which is a fully pro rata share in the cash flows of the instrument, while there is no amendment to the remaining proportion or to any other instrument entered into with the creditor. In this case, in our view the unit of account is the part amended or settled because this is the only part whose terms are modified.

7I.5.382.40 In our view, if an entity has issued multiple instruments held by a single party and the different instruments are modified together in what is in substance a single agreement, then the entity should assess the impact of the modification with reference to the group of instruments that together is the subject of the single modification agreement. In determining whether the modification of the different instruments is in substance a single agreement, an entity should consider the indicators discussed in 7I.5.40.

7I.5.383   *Loan syndications and loan participations*

7I.5.383.10   In our experience, large borrowing arrangements are often funded by multiple investors. The process of involving several different investors in providing loan funding is often referred to as 'loan syndication' or 'loan participation'. In some cases, the borrowing arrangement represents a single loan between the borrower and a single lender, often referred to as the 'lead lender'. In such cases, the other investors are not direct creditors of the borrower; instead, their participation in the loan is established by a participation agreement with the lead lender. However, in other cases a borrowing arrangement that is funded by multiple investors represents multiple separate loans between the borrower and each of the respective lenders – i.e. the members of a syndicate. Whether a borrowing arrangement represents a single loan with the lead lender or multiple separate loans with each individual investor may be relevant in determining the application of the derecognition requirements for financial liabilities when there are changes to the borrowing arrangement or investor group.

7I.5.383.20   For example, an investor that co-funded a borrowing arrangement may be replaced by another investor. If the overall borrowing arrangement represents multiple separate loans from each individual investor, then the borrower evaluates whether the replacement should be accounted for as an extinguishment of the separate loan from that specific individual lender (see 7I.5.381.10). However, for a borrower that borrowed under a single loan, replacement of one of the investors that co-funded the loan is irrelevant to the borrower's accounting if the lead lender is not replaced. Also, any other amendments to the agreement between the lead lender and any of the other investors are irrelevant to the borrower's accounting as long as the loan agreement between the borrower and the lead lender is not modified. This is because the lead lender is the borrower's creditor and because the other investors' participation in the loan is set up in an agreement with the lead lender to which the borrower is not a party. [*IAS 39.39–40, AG57, AG62*]

7I.5.383.30   IFRS does not provide specific guidance to evaluate whether a borrowing arrangement funded by multiple investors represents a single loan or multiple separate loans. Therefore, in our view a borrower should determine whether the arrangement represents a single loan from a single lender or multiple separate loans from each individual investor based on an evaluation of the legal terms and substantive conditions of the arrangement. Factors that may indicate individually or in combination that an entity has obtained separate loans from each individual lender include the following:

- the terms of the arrangement differ between various investors;
- the borrower can selectively repay amounts to specific investors because repayments are not automatically allocated among investors on a pro rata basis;
- the borrower can selectively renegotiate portions of the total arrangement with individual investors or subsets of investors; and
- individual investors can negotiate their loan directly with the borrower without the approval of other investors.

7I.5.384   *Exchange or modification through an intermediary*

7I.5.384.10   Sometimes an intermediary (e.g. a bank) may be involved in restructuring or refinancing existing debt securities of an entity. For example, the intermediary arranges for the acquisition of existing debt securities held by third party investors and their exchange for new debt securities that will be held by new third party investors. In these situations, it is important to identify the role of an intermediary – i.e. whether it is acting as a principal (i.e. as the existing lender or investor in the debt securities) or is acting as an agent of the issuer. [*IAS 39.40, AG62*]

7I.5.384.20   Whether an intermediary is acting as a principal in these situations depends on the terms of the arrangements and whether it is exposed to any risks. In our experience, this assessment includes consideration of whether an intermediary:

● independently initiates an exchange or modification of debt securities;
● commits its own funds for acquiring and placing debt securities and is subject to the risk of loss of those funds;
● is responsible for placing the modified debt securities of the issuer with new investors on a firmly committed basis (i.e. the intermediary is required to hold any debt securities that it is unable to sell to others) or on a best-efforts basis (i.e. the intermediary agrees to buy only those securities that it is able to sell to others);
● exposes itself to the risk of loss from acquiring, exchanging and selling debt securities; and
● receives only a pre-established fee or may derive variable gains based on the value of the securities issued by the issuer.

7I.5.384.30   If the intermediary is acting as a principal, then for the purposes of the derecognition assessment the transaction between the issuer and the intermediary is considered a debt exchange between an existing borrower and lender. In this case, if the debt securities exchanged are not substantially modified, then they are not derecognised. If there is a substantial modification of the existing debt securities, then they are derecognised (see 7I.5.370.10). [*IAS 39.40, AG62*]

7I.5.384.40   If the intermediary is acting as an agent, then the derecognition assessment for the modified debt is performed assuming that the intermediary does not exist. If an issuer repurchases existing debt securities from their existing holders and issues new debt securities to new (i.e. different) holders, then the existing debt securities are derecognised (see 7I.5.370.10). However, if the issuer agrees with an existing holder to repurchase existing debt securities in exchange for issuing new debt securities to that same holder, then the exchange is a debt exchange between an existing borrower and lender and the same principles as in 7I.5.384.30 apply.

7I.5.385   *Quantitative assessment*

7I.5.385.10   Terms are considered to have been substantially modified when the net present value of the cash flows under the new terms, including any fees paid net of any fees received and discounted using the original effective interest rate – i.e. of the original debt instrument – differs by at least 10 percent from the present value of the remaining cash flows under the original terms (the so-called '10 percent test' or 'quantitative assessment'). [*IAS 39.AG62*]

7I.5.385.20   IAS 39 does not define the term 'fees' in this context. In our view, fees paid include amounts paid by the borrower to or on behalf of the lender, and fees received include amounts paid by the lender to or on behalf of the borrower, whether or not they are described as a fee, as part of the exchange or modification. Fees do not include any payments made by the borrower or lender to its own advisers or agents, or other transaction costs incurred by the borrower or lender.

EXAMPLE 19 – FEES INCLUDED IN 10% TEST

7I.5.385.23   Company Z has a loan from Bank B. Z negotiates with B a modification to the terms of the loan, and Z incurs the following costs.

COST	AMOUNT
Modification fees payable to B	30,000
External adviser assisting Z with the terms of the modification transaction	15,000
Z's internal treasury staff based on time spent and an average hourly rate	12,000
External lawyer assisting B in drafting the contract; lawyer's fees paid by Z directly to the lawyer	8,000
Total costs	65,000

7I.5.385.27   In this example, we believe that only 38,000, comprising the modification fees payable to B (30,000) and the amount paid to B's lawyer (8,000), should be considered to be 'fees' for the 10% test calculation. This is because only these amounts are paid by Z to or on behalf of B.

7I.5.385.30   IAS 39 does not contain any further guidance on how to determine the cash flows for the 10 percent test if the terms of a debt instrument are modified and the cash flows under the new or original terms of the instruments are not fixed. In our view, if either the original or the new terms include an early prepayment, call or put feature or a term extension feature that is not separately accounted for as a derivative, then the effect of the feature should be included in determining the cash flows under the quantitative assessment. In our view, any of the following approaches would be a reasonable application of this principle.

- Calculate probability-weighted cash flows taking into account different scenarios, including the exercise or non-exercise of the features, and use these cash flows as the basis for the 10 percent test.
- Calculate the present value for each of the different scenarios – i.e. exercise and non-exercise. The cash flow scenario that results in the smaller difference between the present values of the cash flows under the original terms and the cash flows under the revised terms would be the basis for the 10 percent test.
- Use the outcome of the most likely scenario to determine cash flows.

7I.5.385.40   In our view, an entity should use judgement in determining the appropriate cash flows to be included in performing the 10 percent test if the original terms of the debt instrument provide for:

- a higher rate of interest in the event of default;
- the acceleration of maturity in the event of default;
- a higher credit spread in the event of credit deterioration; or
- other contingent payment terms or unusual interest terms.

7I.5.385.50   We believe that similar judgement would apply in determining the cash flows under the new terms for the 10 percent test. This might be reflected by using the most likely scenario or probability-weighted outcomes in performing the 10 percent test.

7I.5.385.60   For a floating rate instrument, there is no explicit guidance in IAS 39 on how to determine the cash flows under the new terms or the remaining cash flows under the original terms of the debt instrument. In our view, any of the following approaches may be acceptable, as long as it is applied consistently, for determining the variable benchmark components of the cash flows under the new terms and of the remaining cash flows under the original terms to ensure a like-for-like comparison for the 10 percent test.

- Use the relevant benchmark interest rate determined for the current interest accrual period according to the original terms of the debt instrument.
- Use the relevant benchmark interest rate at the date of modification, except for any remaining coupons of the original liability for which the interest rate has been determined, in which case the contractual rate should be used.
- Use the relevant benchmark interest rates for the original remaining term based on the relevant forward interest rate curve – except for any remaining coupons of the original liability for which the interest rate has been determined, in which case the contractual rate should be used – and the relevant benchmark interest rates for the new term of the instrument based on the relevant forward interest rate curve.

EXAMPLE 20 – APPROACHES TO DETERMINE FLOATING RATE CASH FLOWS IN 10% TEST

7I.5.385.70   On 30 June 2018, Company S modifies the terms of a bond that was paying interest based on six-month LIBOR that resets on 1 April and 1 October.

7I.5.385.72   The following facts are also relevant for this example:
- on 1 April 2018, six-month LIBOR is reset to 3.5%;
- on 30 June 2018, six-month LIBOR is 4%; and
- under the modified terms, the bond will bear interest at a fixed rate of 4.5%.

7I.5.385.75   We believe that, for the 10% test, S may determine the remaining future interest cash flows under the original terms of the bond by using:
- the six-month LIBOR applicable to the current reset period (3.5%);
- the six-month LIBOR on the date of modification (4%); however, S should use 3.5% for the period to 30 September 2018 because the interest rate for this period has already been fixed; or
- interest rates from the six-month LIBOR forward curve; however, S should use 3.5% for the period to 30 September 2018 because the interest rate for this period has already been fixed.

7I.5.385.80   The original effective interest rate to be applied to discount the cash flows is the effective interest rate of the original unmodified instrument that is being used to calculate its amortised cost and interest expense under IAS 39. However, in our view the original effective interest rate excludes adjustments made to the effective interest rate of a debt instrument as a result of having applied fair value hedge accounting because these adjustments do not reflect changes in the amount or timing of cash flows payable on the hedged debt instrument. [*IAS 39.AG62*]

7I.5.385.90   For floating rate liabilities, in our view the original effective interest rate is the current effective interest rate that reflects movements in market rates of interest (see also 7I.5.385.60), determined according to the unmodified terms of the contract. Such an effective yield might be a variable benchmark interest rate plus/minus a margin – e.g. three-month LIBOR plus 40 basis points. In other words, the original effective interest rate should consider adjustments to the benchmark interest rate, but the original credit risk spread should be held constant and not adjusted to reflect changes in credit risk spread.

7I.5.385.100   The circumstances under which a modification of the terms of a financial liability is negotiated – e.g. because of financial difficulties of the borrower – are not relevant in determining whether the modification is an extinguishment of debt (see also 7I.5.387.60).

7I.5.387   *Qualitative assessment*

7I.5.387.10   In our view, if the difference in the present value of the cash flows under the quantitative assessment is at least 10 percent, then a modification should be accounted for as an extinguishment in all cases. However, if the difference in the present values of the cash flows is less than 10 percent – then an entity should perform a qualitative assessment to determine whether the terms of the two instruments are substantially different.

7I.5.387.20   In our view, the purpose of a qualitative assessment is to identify substantial differences in terms that by their nature are not captured by a quantitative assessment. Accordingly, we believe that modifications whose effect is included in the quantitative assessment, and that are not considered substantial based on that assessment, cannot generally be considered substantial on their own from a qualitative perspective. Such modifications may include changes in principal amounts, maturities, interest rates, prepayment options and other contingent payment terms. However, if a financial liability has an effective interest rate of nil, then we believe that a change in the timing of cash flows will have no effect on the quantitative assessment. In this case, the change in timing of cash flows should be incorporated into the qualitative assessment to ensure that its impact is considered. A combination of cash flow changes captured by the quantitative test, but not on their own considered substantial, and other changes not captured by the quantitative test may together be considered a substantial modification. Performing the qualitative assessment may require a high degree of judgement based on the facts and circumstances of each individual case.

EXAMPLE 21 – CHANGE IN TERMS DOES NOT AFFECT QUANTITATIVE ASSESSMENT

7I.5.387.23   Company T has a loan due to its parent that is payable on demand. The loan has an effective interest rate of zero. T renegotiates the terms of the loan so that it becomes payable in two years, rather than on demand. Other terms remain unchanged.

7I.5.387.25   T carries out a quantitative assessment by calculating the present value of the current and modified cash flows using the original effective interest rate of zero. The discount rate of zero results in the present value of cash flows repayable on demand being the same as the present value of cash flows repayable in two years' time. The extension of maturity is not captured by the quantitative assessment, because the effective interest rate of the loan is zero.

 7I.5.387.27   We believe that in this case T should additionally consider whether the term extension is a substantial modification as part of its qualitative assessment because it has had no impact on the quantitative assessment.

7I.5.387.30   In our view, the following types of changes in terms are of a formal or incidental nature rather than related to the substance of the liability and accordingly we believe that they carry no weight in the assessment of whether the modification of terms is substantial:

- legal form of the instrument;
- tax treatment; and
- whether the instrument is listed.

7I.5.387.40   In our view, a substantial change in the currency of a debt instrument, or a deletion or addition of a substantial equity conversion feature to a debt instrument, is a substantial modification of the terms. A change in currency is considered substantial unless the exchange rate between the old and new currencies is pegged or managed within narrow bounds by law or relevant monetary authorities. For example, a debt instrument might be modified such that the new instrument is in a different currency – for which the exchange rate is not pegged to the old currency or is not managed within narrow bounds with that currency – and has a different maturity from the existing financial liability. We believe that the terms of the new debt instrument in this case would be substantially different even if the present values of the cash flows were almost identical using the quantitative test. Other modifications may require a higher degree of judgement about whether they represent a substantial change in terms – e.g. a change in the seniority or subordination of a financial liability.

7I.5.387.50   In our view, an equity conversion option is substantial unless it is not reasonably possible that it will be exercised over its term – e.g. a call option that is deeply out of the money and expected to remain so. When an equity conversion option included in the original liability is modified as part of a restructuring of the debt, judgement should be applied in assessing whether the modification of the conversion option is substantial. This might include considering the change in fair value of the conversion option and its likelihood of exercise. If debt with detachable equity options is exchanged for convertible debt that includes non-detachable equity conversion options, then we believe that the exchange should be considered a modification of an equity conversion feature rather than its addition or deletion.

7I.5.387.60   There are no special requirements for troubled debt restructurings under IFRS. The guidance on modifications of financial liabilities applies whether or not the borrower is experiencing financial difficulties. For further discussion, see 7I.5.385.100.

7I.5.390   *Accounting for substantial modification of terms*

7I.5.390.10   If a modification of the terms of a debt instrument meets the derecognition conditions in IAS 39, then any difference between the carrying amount of the original liability and the consideration paid is recognised in profit or loss. The consideration paid includes non-financial assets transferred and the assumption of liabilities, including the new modified financial liability. Any new financial liability recognised is initially measured at fair value. If a modification of terms is accounted for as an extinguishment, then any costs or fees incurred are recognised as part of the gain or loss on extinguishment and do not adjust the carrying amount of the new liability. Accordingly, in our view no transaction costs should be included in the initial measurement of the new liability unless it can be demonstrated incontrovertibly that they relate solely to the new liability instrument and in no way to the modification of the old liability. This would not usually be possible but might apply to taxes and registration fees payable on execution of the new liability instrument. [*IAS 39.41*]

EXAMPLE 22 – COSTS INCURRED ON SUBSTANTIAL MODIFICATION OF TERMS

> 7I.5.390.15   Continuing Example 19, if the modification transaction is accounted for as an extinguishment, then all of the costs incurred by Company Z as part of the modification transaction with B – i.e. 65,000 – should be recognised in profit or loss.

7I.5.390.20   In our view, the accounting treatment for forgiveness of debt should be based on an analysis of the nature of the transaction.

- If a shareholder forgives the debt, then it is likely that the shareholder is acting in the capacity of a shareholder and that the forgiveness of debt should be treated as a capital transaction. The outstanding financial liability should be reclassified to equity and no gain or loss should be recognised (see 7I.3.370.50). For a discussion of other debt-for-equity swaps, see 7I.5.410.
- If there is clear evidence that the shareholder is acting as a lender – i.e. in the same way as an unrelated lender – then a gain or loss should be recognised in profit or loss (with accompanying related party disclosures – see chapter 5.5).
- If a government forgives a loan, then the forgiveness should be treated as a government grant (see chapter 4.3) unless the government is also a shareholder and is acting in that capacity.

7I.5.390.30   IFRS does not specify where in the statement of profit or loss and OCI a gain or loss on the extinguishment of debt should be presented. In our view, it should be included in finance income or finance costs (see 7I.8.80).

7I.5.400   *Accounting for non-substantial modification of terms*

7I.5.400.10   IAS 39 does not provide guidance on the accounting treatment for the difference in the present value arising as a result of a modification in terms of a debt instrument that does not result in derecognition – i.e. because the terms are not substantially different.

7I.5.400.20   A gain or loss can be recognised only when a debt instrument is derecognised. Consequently, if there has been a modification in the terms of a debt instrument that does not meet the derecognition conditions, then the carrying amount of the liability is adjusted for fees and transaction costs incurred and no gain or loss is recognised. In our view, any difference in present value arising as a result of the modification should be recognised as an adjustment to the effective interest rate and amortised over the remaining life of the modified financial liability. We believe that the guidance in paragraph AG8 of IAS 39 does not apply to a renegotiation of the contractual terms of an instrument because that guidance is for changes in estimates within the existing contractual terms (see 7I.6.260.10). [*IAS 39.40–41, AG8, AG62*]

EXAMPLE 23 – COSTS INCURRED ON NON-SUBSTANTIAL MODIFICATION OF TERMS

7I.5.400.30   Continuing Example 19, if the modification transaction is not accounted for as an extinguishment, then the carrying amount of Company Z's loan is adjusted for costs of 53,000, comprising the fees for the modification payable to B (30,000), the cost of Z's external adviser (15,000) and the amount paid to B's lawyer (8,000). However, the costs of Z's internal treasury department are recognised in profit or loss because they are not directly attributable incremental transaction costs (see 7I.6.30).

7I.5.410   *Extinguishment of liabilities with equity instruments*

7I.5.410.10   IFRIC 19 addresses the accounting for a renegotiation of the terms of a financial liability that results in an entity issuing equity instruments to a creditor to extinguish all or part of the financial liability. [*IFRIC 19.2–3*]

7I.5.410.20   IFRIC 19 does not apply if:

- the creditor is acting in its capacity as existing direct or indirect shareholder (see 1.2.190 and 7I.5.390.20);
- the creditor and the entity are controlled by the same party or parties before and after the transaction and the substance of the transaction includes an equity distribution from, or contribution to, the entity (see 1.2.80 and 7I.5.390.20); and
- the extinguishment is in accordance with the original terms of the financial liability (see 7I.3.390). [*IFRIC 19.3*]

7I.5.410.30   If equity instruments are issued to a creditor to extinguish all or part of a financial liability in a debt-for-equity swap, then the equity instruments are consideration paid. The equity instruments are measured at fair value, unless their fair value cannot be measured reliably, in which case the equity instruments are measured with reference to the fair value of the financial liability extinguished. In measuring the fair value of a financial liability extinguished that includes a demand feature, paragraph 47 of IFRS 13 is not applied – i.e. the requirement that the fair value of a financial liability with a demand feature is not less than the amount payable on demand, discounted from the first date on which the amount could be required to be paid, is not applied. The equity instruments are initially measured when the financial liability (or part of that liability) is extinguished. A gain or loss on extinguishment is recognised in accordance with 7I.5.370.50. [*IAS 39.41, IFRIC 19.5–7, 9*]

7I.5.410.40   If only part of the financial liability is extinguished by the issue of equity instruments, then an assessment is made of whether some of the consideration paid relates to a modification of the part of the liability that remains outstanding. If it does, then the consideration paid is allocated between the part of the liability extinguished and the part of the liability that remains outstanding. The consideration allocated to the part that remains outstanding forms part of the assessment of whether there has been a substantial modification of the terms of that remaining liability (see 7I.5.380). An entity considers all relevant facts and circumstances in making this allocation. In our view, judgement is required to determine both:

- the allocation of the consideration between the part of the liability extinguished and the modified part that remains outstanding; and

- the part of the liability that is extinguished and the part that remains outstanding and is modified.
  [*IFRIC 19.8, 10*]

7I.5.410.50   Judgement is required because the cash flows of the remaining loan will not usually represent solely a fully proportionate share of the cash flows of the original loan and, in some cases, a simple allocation method based on the change in the nominal amount of the debt instrument may lead to unreasonable results, particularly if the effective interest payable on the remaining nominal amount is increased (see Example 24B).

EXAMPLE 24A – PARTIAL EXTINGUISHMENT BY EQUITY – ALLOCATION OF CONSIDERATION (1)

7I.5.410.60   Company X has an existing loan from Bank B. On 31 December 2018, X renegotiates the loan and enters into a debt-for-equity swap with B whereby, in exchange for X issuing equity instruments to B:
- the nominal amount of the loan is reduced by 50%; and
- the terms of the remaining portion are amended by extending the maturity date and reducing the interest rate payable.

7I.5.410.70   There are no fees or transaction costs. The following facts are also relevant for this example.

| | | NEW INSTRUMENTS | |
	OLD LOAN	MODIFIED LOAN (50%)	EQUITY INSTRUMENTS
Nominal amount	1,000,000	500,000	
Carrying amount	1,000,000		
Fair value at 31 December 2017	910,000	350,000	560,000

7I.5.410.80   X analyses the transaction as an extinguishment of a 50% proportionate share of the old loan, reflecting the reduction in nominal amount, and a modification of the other 50% proportionate share of the old loan. Based on this, X allocates the consideration paid by issuing equity instruments between the extinguishment of part of the old loan and the modification of the remaining loan based on the changes in fair value of the loan as a result of the renegotiation, as follows:
- the extinguishment of 50% of the loan at fair value – 455,000 (910,000 x 50%); and
- the modification of the remaining 50% of the loan – 105,000 (455,000 - 350,000 or alternatively 560,000 - 455,000).

7I.5.410.90   Accordingly, X derecognises the 50% proportion of the loan that is extinguished and recognises a gain on this proportion of 45,000 (1,000,000 x 50% - 455,000). X considers the allocation of 105,000 of consideration to the modification of the remaining 50% of the loan in determining whether that remaining 50% proportion is substantially modified.

- If the remaining 50% of the loan is considered substantially modified, then that remaining 50% is also derecognised – leading to initial recognition of the new loan at its fair value of 350,000 and a further gain of 45,000 (1,000,000 x 50% - 105,000 - 350,000).
- If the remaining 50% of the loan is not considered to be substantially modified, then its carrying amount is reduced by the consideration paid of 105,000 to 395,000 and a new effective interest rate is calculated based on the modified terms. [*IAS 39.42, AG62*]

7I.5.410.100   As an alternative approach, X may instead first determine the allocation of the carrying amount of the old loan between the part that has been extinguished and the remaining part that has been modified based on the ratio of the decrease in the fair value of the loan to the fair value of the remaining part of the loan, as shown in the following table. [*IAS 39.42*]

	FAIR VALUE	FAIR VALUE RATIO	ALLOCATED CARRYING AMOUNT
Old loan	910,000	-	1,000,000
Modified loan	350,000	38.5%	385,000
Extinguished loan	560,000[1]	61.5%	615,000

Note
1. Calculated as 910,000 - 350,000.

7I.5.410.110   Under this approach, in determining the allocation of the consideration paid by issuing equity instruments between the partial extinguishment of the loan and the modification of the remaining loan as required by IFRIC 19 (see 7I.5.410.40), X concludes that the entire consideration of 560,000 is allocated to extinguishment of part of the old loan. This is consistent with the approach used to determine the part of the old loan that is extinguished.

7I.5.410.120   Accordingly, X derecognises the 61.5% proportion of the old loan that is extinguished and recognises a gain on this proportion of 55,000 (1,000,000 x 61.5% - 560,000). In determining whether the remaining 38.5% of the loan is substantially modified, X compares 38.5% of the present value of the cash flows of the old loan with the present value of the cash flows of the amended loan, discounted in each case using the original effective interest rate of the old loan (see 7I.5.385.10).
- If the remaining 38.5% of the loan is considered substantially modified, then that remaining 38.5% is also derecognised – leading to initial recognition of the new loan at its fair value of 350,000 and a further gain of 35,000 (385,000 - 350,000).
- If the remaining 38.5% of the loan is not considered to be substantially modified, then its carrying amount of 385,000 is not adjusted and a new effective interest rate is calculated based on the modified terms. [*IAS 39.42, AG62*]

EXAMPLE 24B – PARTIAL EXTINGUISHMENT BY EQUITY – ALLOCATION OF CONSIDERATION (2)

7I.5.410.130 Modifying Example 24A such that the terms of the renegotiation are as follows:
- the nominal amount of the loan is reduced by 10%; and
- the terms of the remaining loan are amended by increasing the interest rate payable.

7I.5.410.140 The following facts are also relevant for this example.

		NEW INSTRUMENTS	
	OLD LOAN	MODIFIED LOAN (90%)	EQUITY INSTRUMENTS
Nominal amount	1,000,000	900,000	
Carrying amount	1,000,000		
Fair value at 31 December 2017	1,000,000	960,000	40,000

7I.5.410.150 If X were to allocate the carrying amount of the old loan between the amount that has been extinguished and the amount that has been modified based only on the reduction in the nominal amount of the loan, then it would compare:
- 10% of the carrying amount of the loan extinguished – i.e. 100,000 (1,000,000 x 10%); and
- the fair value of the consideration paid – i.e. 40,000.

7I.5.410.160 This would lead to the recognition of a gain of 60,000 on derecognition of 100,000 of the old loan.

7I.5.410.170 However, X considers all relevant facts and circumstances, including the following:
- the rate of interest payable on the remaining loan has been increased such that the fair value of the modified loan is 60,000 greater than would be implied by a 10% pro rata extinguishment; and
- the carrying amount of the old loan is equal to the fair value of the equity instruments plus the fair value of the modified loan.

7I.5.410.180 Therefore, X concludes that the approach discussed in 7I.5.410.80 would not be appropriate and that the fair value of the equity shares of 40,000 should be allocated against an extinguishment of only 40,000 of the original liability.

7I.5.410.190 Accordingly, X derecognises 40,000 of the loan that is extinguished and recognises the consideration paid of 40,000 in equity. No gain or loss is recognised from the transaction and a new effective interest rate is calculated based on the modified terms – assuming that the modification of the remaining part of the loan was not considered substantial.

7I.5.420   *Amendment of contractual terms of financial liability resulting in change in classification to equity*

7I.5.420.10   If the terms of a financial liability are amended such that the financial liability subsequent to the amendment of the terms meets the definition of an equity instrument, then in our view the transaction should be accounted for as an extinguishment of a financial liability in accordance with 7I.5.410.30. For example, a company issues preference shares that meet the definition of a financial liability. Subsequently, the entity and the holders of the preference shares agree to amend the terms of the preference shares so that they meet the criteria for equity classification (see 7I.3.20). We believe that such a transaction involves two steps: an extinguishment of a financial liability and the issue of new equity instruments at fair value. For further discussion, see 7I.3.400.20.

7I.5.425   **Trade payables and reverse factoring**

7I.5.425.10   Under a reverse factoring arrangement (see 7I.8.45), a factor agrees to pay amounts to a supplier in respect of invoices owed by the supplier's customer and receives settlement from that customer at a later date.

7I.5.425.20   Typically, when an invoice is made subject to the reverse factoring arrangement and/ or when the factor pays the supplier, the customer does not discharge its financial liability to the supplier (see 7I.5.370.10). However, the customer assesses whether it is legally released from the primary responsibility for the original financial liability under the invoice and this is replaced by a new financial liability to the factor. This assessment may require the assistance of a legal expert.

7I.5.425.30   If there is no such legal release, then the customer assesses whether the financial liability has been substantially modified as a result of the reverse factoring arrangement (see 7I.5.380). This is because a substantial modification of the terms of an existing financial liability (or a part of it) is also accounted for as an extinguishment of the original financial liability and the recognition of a new financial liability.

7I.5.425.40   For a further discussion of reverse factoring, see 2.3.75 and 7I.8.45, 205 and 375.

7I.5.430   **DERECOGNITION OF DERIVATIVES**

7I.5.430.10   Many derivatives – e.g. forward contracts and interest rate swaps – do or can involve two-way payments between the parties. These derivatives might change from being an asset to a liability or vice versa. Such derivatives are derecognised only when they meet both the derecognition criteria for financial assets (see 7I.5.60) and the derecognition criteria for financial liabilities (see 7I.5.370). [*IAS 39.BC220B*]

7I.5.440   **Novation of derivatives to central counterparty**

7I.5.440.10   An example of a transaction that results in the derecognition of a derivative is the novation of a derivative to a central counterparty. For example, assume that Company X and Company Y have entered into an over-the-counter derivative contract. Novation to a central counterparty involves cancelling the original derivative contract between X and Y and replacing it with two new derivative contracts – i.e. a new contract between X and the central counterparty, and a new contract between Y and the central counterparty.

7I.5.440.20   A novation of a derivative to a central counterparty results in the derecognition of the derivative because, through the novation, each party to the original derivative has new contractual rights (or obligations) to cash flows from a new derivative with the central counterparty, and this new contract replaces the original contract with the original counterparty. Accordingly, the original derivative with the counterparty has expired and therefore the derecognition criteria for financial assets are met (see 7I.5.90). In addition, the novation to the central counterparty releases the party from the responsibility to make payment to the original counterparty and therefore the derecognition criteria for financial liabilities are also met (see 7I.5.370.10). [*IAS 39.17(a), AG57(b), BC220C–BC220E*]

7I.5.440.30   For a discussion about the effect of a novation of a derivative on hedge accounting, see 7I.7.685.

7I.5.450   Variation margin payments and receipts

7I.5.450.10   Many derivatives involve variation margin payments and receipts. Many of these transactions are cleared through clearing houses – e.g. futures contracts – and involve periodic (normally daily or intra-day) payments or receipts of variation margin that is required by the clearing house and reflects changes in the value of the related derivative.

7I.5.450.20   Variation margin may take the form of cash, securities or other specified assets, typically liquid assets. An entity needs to determine based on the recognition and derecognition criteria for financial assets and financial liabilities (see 7I.5.60 and 370) whether making variation margin payments and receipts represents:

- a partial settlement of contractual rights to receive or obligations to pay cash under the relevant derivative contracts, which means that derecognition of the variation margin payments or receipts and the corresponding carrying amount of the relevant derivative contracts is required at the time of payment; or
- the establishment or settlement of an accumulated variation margin balance that is a separate financial asset or financial liability.

7I.5.450.25   If the payment or receipt of variation margin is not a settlement of the derivative contract, then the accumulated balance is usually a financial asset or financial liability – e.g. the balance may be required to be repaid in the future or may be used to settle the derivative contract at its maturity.

7I.5.450.30   Whether the payment or receipt of variation margin represents a settlement of a derivative contract is assessed with reference to the concepts of extinguishment – i.e. the obligation specified in the contract is discharged or cancelled or expires – and of expiry of contractual rights to cash flows (see 7I.5.90 and 370.10). Whether these derecognition criteria are met will depend on the specific contractual terms considered in conjunction with other relevant documentation and applicable law. [*IAS 39.17(a), 39*]

EXAMPLE 25 – PAYMENT OF VARIATION MARGIN REPRESENTS SETTLEMENT ON FUTURE CONTRACTS – COLLATERALISED-TO-MARKET MODEL

7I.5.450.40   On 25 May 2018, Company B enters into a futures contract through Clearing House C to buy a specified quantity of shares in Company X for 100 in three months. The contract states that:

- B will pay (receive) variation margin in cash to (from) C equal to the decrease (increase) in the market futures price at the end of each day; and
- the exercise price payable on maturity of the contract will be reduced (increased) by an amount equal to the amount of variation margin paid by B to C (received by B from C).

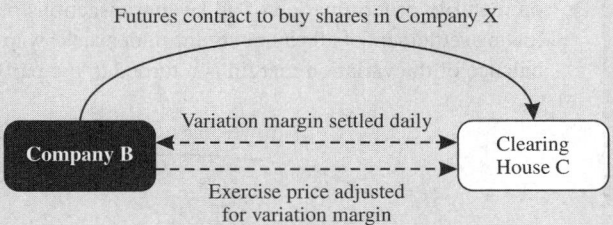

Futures contract to buy shares in Company X

Variation margin settled daily

Company B

Clearing House C

Exercise price adjusted for variation margin

7I.5.450.50 The contract does not allow for the variation margin to be repaid and no interest is payable on variation margin.

7I.5.450.60 On 26 May 2018, the market futures price declines to 98. At the end of that day, B pays variation margin of 2 to C and the exercise price is reset to 98.

7I.5.450.70 B concludes that the payment of variation margin represents a settlement of the futures contract because it extinguishes a specified part of its obligation to pay the exercise price on maturity.

7I.5.450.80 Immediately before payment of variation margin on 26 May 2018, the futures contract is a derivative liability of 2. The payment of the variation margin represents a derecognition of the derivative liability and, following the payment of 2, the fair value of the futures contract is zero because it has an exercise price equal to the current market price.

EXAMPLE 26 – PAYMENT OF VARIATION MARGIN REPRESENTS SEPARATE ASSET– COLLATERALISED-TO-MARKET MODEL

7I.5.450.90 Company X enters into a 10-year interest rate swap derivative with Clearing House C under a 'collateralised-to-market' framework. The derivative requires net payments of coupons on each anniversary of the transaction through to maturity. Company X has other interest rate swaps outstanding with Clearing House C. The rules of C state that:

- X will pay (receive) variation margin in cash to (from) C at the end of each day, such that the net accumulated balance of the variation margin is equal and opposite to the estimated fair value of all outstanding swap contracts between X and C;

- interest at a market rate is payable on the accumulated balance of variation margin;
- a party is entitled to set off the net balance of variation margin that it has paid (or received, as the case may be) against the obligation to make any payment (or right to receive any payment, respectively) of coupons on the swap contract on the date on which those coupons fall due for settlement; and
- on maturity or termination of all swap transactions between X and C and following settlement of all payments due under such swap contracts, any remaining balance of the variation margin is returned to the party that paid it.

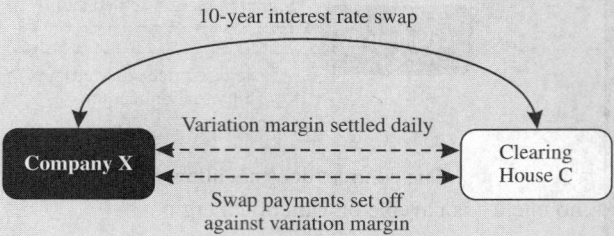

7I.5.450.100   X concludes that the payment of variation margin does not represent a settlement of rights or obligations under the derivative. This is because these amounts will continue to become due and payable in the future in accordance with the terms of the derivative and are not reduced or increased by any amount of variation margin received or paid.

7I.5.450.110   The accumulated variation margin balance represents a separate financial asset or financial liability because:

- the accumulated balance will either be used in the future to settle payments on this or other swaps or be returned to the payer; and
- interest is payable on the accumulated balance.

EXAMPLE 27 – PAYMENT OF VARIATION MARGIN REPRESENTS SETTLEMENT – SETTLED-TO-MARKET MODEL

7I.5.450.120   Company X enters into a 10-year interest rate swap derivative with Clearing House D under a 'settled-to-market' framework. The terms of the contract are:

- X will pay to (receive from) D an amount in cash at the end of each day equal to the net of:
  - coupons due for settlement on the swap that day;
  - variation margin equal to the decrease (increase) in the net present value (NPV) of expected future coupons receivable on the swap, calculated based on current market rates; and
  - price alignment adjustment (PAA).

- PAA is calculated as a current market interest rate on the net cumulative amount of variation margin paid or received to date. However, there is no right or obligation to the return of variation margin and the contract states that payment of variation margin is a partial settlement of the outstanding derivative position and does not constitute collateral.
- The PAA is included as an extra cash flow within the derivative contract and is similar to the interest that would have been paid or received on cash collateral had a similar contract been transacted under a collateralised-to-market contract (as in Example 26 above).

7I.5.450.130   X concludes that the daily net cash payments, including variation margin, should be accounted for as partial settlements of the derivative in accordance with the terms of the contract.

7I.5.450.140   If daily variation payments are considered settlements on the underlying trade for a settled-to-market contract, then the daily variation payments give rise to a partial derecognition of the derivative asset or liability. This reduces the recognised asset or liability arising from the derivative's fair value and does not result in additional financial assets or financial liabilities being recognised. The derivative continues to exist (i.e. partial settlement does not result in termination) but has a current fair value of zero (or close to zero) immediately following the daily settlement payment.

7I.5.450.150   If payments and receipts of variation margin are not a settlement of the related derivatives, then the entity needs to consider whether the variation margin balance and the related derivatives should be offset in the statement of financial position (see 7I.8.90). Conversely, for derivative transactions in which daily variation payments represent settlements and not collateral, no offsetting takes place between cumulative variation payment amounts and the underlying derivative because they are a single unit of account.

7I.6   Measurement and gains and losses

7I.6 Measurement and gains and losses

REQUIREMENTS FOR INSURERS THAT APPLY IFRS 4

In July 2014, the IASB issued IFRS 9 *Financial Instruments*, which is effective for annual periods beginning on or after 1 January 2018. However, an insurer may defer the application of IFRS 9 if it meets certain criteria (see 8.1.180).

This chapter reflects the requirement of IAS 39 *Financial Instruments: Recognition and Measurement* and the related standards, excluding any amendments introduced by IFRS 9. These requirements are relevant to insurers that apply the temporary exemption from IFRS 9 or the overlay approach to designated financial assets (see 8.1.160) and cover annual periods beginning on 1 January 2018. For further discussion, see Introduction to Sections 7 and 7I.

The requirements related to this topic are mainly derived from the following.

STANDARD	TITLE
IFRS 13	Fair Value Measurement
IFRS 15	Revenue from Contracts with Customers
IAS 21	The Effects of Changes in Foreign Exchange Rates
IAS 39	Financial Instruments: Recognition and Measurement

The requirements in this chapter include newly effective requirements arising from IFRS 15 *Revenue from Contracts with Customers*, which are effective for annual periods beginning on or after 1 January 2018. The new requirements may be applied using the retrospective method or the cumulative effect method (see 4.2.510). The impact of the new requirements on the initial measurement of trade receivables, scope of impairment requirements and fee income under IAS 39 is reflected in 7I.6.20.10, 22.10–40, 30.10, 400.05 and 730.10–120.

FORTHCOMING REQUIREMENTS AND FUTURE DEVELOPMENTS

For this topic, there are no forthcoming requirements or future developments.

INTRODUCTION

7I.6.10.10   This chapter provides guidance on the measurement of financial assets and financial liabilities, including financial instruments denominated in foreign currency, and addresses certain issues related to revenue arising from financial instruments.

7I.6.20   **MEASUREMENT ON INITIAL RECOGNITION**

7I.6.20.10   On initial recognition, a financial asset or financial liability is measured at fair value plus directly attributable transaction costs, unless:

- the instrument is classified as at FVTPL, in which case transaction costs are not included; or
- the instrument is a trade receivable that is initially measured at the transaction price as defined in IFRS 15 (see 7I.6.22). [*IAS 39.43, 44A, IFRS 15.60–65*]

7I.6.20.20   Normally, the fair value on initial recognition is the transaction price – i.e. the fair value of the consideration given or received for the financial instrument. For a discussion of situations in which the fair value on initial recognition may differ from the transaction price, see 7I.6.25 and 2.4.320. [*IAS 39.43A, AG64*]

7I.6.20.30   If part of the consideration given or received is for something in addition to the financial instrument, then the entity separately measures the fair value of the financial instrument in accordance with IFRS 13 (see chapter 2.4). Any additional element is accounted for separately. For example, in the case of a long-term loan that carries no interest, the fair value of the loan can be measured as the present value of all cash receipts discounted using the current market interest rate for a similar financial instrument. Any additional amount lent is an expense or a reduction of income unless it qualifies for recognition as an asset (see 7I.6.60–70 and 90). [*IAS 39.AG64*]

7I.6.22   **Trade receivables**

7I.6.22.10   Trade receivables that do not have a significant financing component (determined in accordance with IFRS 15) are measured on initial recognition at their transaction price as defined in IFRS 15 – i.e. the amount of consideration to which the entity expects to be entitled for transferring the promised goods or services to the customer (see 4.2.90). [*IAS 39.44A, IFRS 15.60–65, A*]

7I.6.22.20   For a discussion of factors considered in determining whether a contract contains a significant financing component, see 4.2.130.30.

7I.6.22.30   Trade receivables with a significant financing component are not exempt from being measured at fair value on initial recognition, unless 7I.6.22.40 applies. Therefore, differences may arise between the initial amount of revenue recognised in accordance with IFRS 15 – which is measured at the transaction price as defined in IFRS 15 – and the fair value of the trade receivable recognised at the date of initial recognition. Any difference between the measurement of the receivable in accordance with IAS 39 and the corresponding amount of revenue recognised in accordance with IFRS 15 is presented as an expense. [*IFRS 15.108, C9*]

7I.6.22.40   If an entity expects, at contract inception, that the period between the entity transferring a promised good or service to the customer and the customer paying for that good or service will be one year or less, then as a practical expedient, the entity can choose not to adjust the promised amount of consideration for the effects of a significant financing component. If the entity applies this practical expedient, then the trade receivable is measured on initial recognition at the transaction price as defined in IFRS 15, in the same way as trade receivables that do not have a significant financing component. [*IAS 39.44A, IFRS 15.63*]

7I.6.23   Settlement of contracts to acquire assets and loan commitments

7I.6.23.10   A contract to acquire a financial asset generally is itself a financial instrument (see 7I.1.25). The financial asset to be acquired is not generally recognised until the acquisition contract is settled because this is usually when the acquirer becomes a party to the contract that is the financial asset. In this case, the acquired financial asset is initially recognised based on its fair value on the settlement date. If the contract to acquire the financial asset is accounted for as a derivative, then it is measured at FVTPL. Changes in the fair value of the derivative contract between the date of entering into the derivative contract and its settlement date are recognised in profit or loss as they arise. The fair value of this derivative contract immediately before settlement usually equals the difference between the fair value of the acquired asset at settlement and the purchase price payable at settlement, meaning that no additional gain or loss arises on settlement.

7I.6.23.20   However, if the contract to acquire the financial asset is a regular-way contract, then it is not accounted for as a derivative. In this case, either trade date or settlement date accounting may be applicable to the acquired asset and this would determine when the acquired asset is initially recognised and, for settlement date accounting, the treatment of changes in the fair value of the acquired asset between the trade date and the settlement date (see 7I.5.20). [*IAS 39.14, 38, AG53–AG56*]

7I.6.23.30   As opposed to settlement of a contract to acquire an existing financial asset, a loan may be originated as a result of a drawdown under a loan commitment. To simplify the accounting for holders and issuers of loan commitments, many loan commitments are excluded from the scope of IAS 39 so that an entity does not recognise changes in their fair value that result from changes in market interest rates or credit spreads, consistent with the amortised cost measurement model for loans and receivables.

7I.6.23.40   Accordingly, in our view, when a loan that will be measured at amortised cost is drawn down under an arm's length loan commitment that is outside the scope of IAS 39 and that is not onerous, the resulting loan asset or liability may be viewed as a continuation of the loan commitment. Under this approach, the fair value measurement of the loan on initial recognition is based on circumstances on the commitment date. Therefore, the fair value of the loan on initial recognition would usually be considered to be the amount advanced, adjusted for facility or commitment fees paid or received (see 7I.6.30, 50 and 730), being the transaction price agreed on the commitment date (see 7I.6.20.20) – i.e. no day one gain or loss would usually be recognised on the loan origination date.

EXAMPLE 1 – INITIAL MEASUREMENT OF A LOAN RESULTING FROM A LOAN COMMITMENT

7I.6.23.45   On 1 April 2018, Bank B enters into a commitment to make a loan of 100 to Borrower C on arm's length terms and at an interest rate of 5% a year (assume that any fees and costs are insignificant). On 31 May 2018, C draws down the loan. The fair value of the loan is 100 on 1 April and 98 on 31 May.

> 7I.6.23.47   Applying the approach in 7I.6.23.40, B initially recognises the loan on 31 May using the fair value on 1 April of 100.

7I.6.23.50   An alternative acceptable approach is to view the loan that is drawn down as a separate financial instrument for the purposes of initial measurement, with the amount initially recognised for the loan on the draw-down date being based on an analysis of the circumstances at that time, including the entity's determination of the transaction price for the loan – i.e. the fair value of the consideration given for the loan – and the fair value of the loan at that time. Accordingly, the carrying amount under this alternative acceptable approach would be:

- based on the transaction price if that is the best evidence of fair value on the draw-down date or if the entity's alternative estimate of fair value does not satisfy the observability condition in paragraph AG76(a) of IAS 39 (see 7I.6.25.50); or
- the entity's alternative estimate of fair value on the draw-down date if this alternative estimate satisfies the observability condition in paragraph AG76(a) of IAS 39 (see 7I.6.25.40).

7I.6.23.60   For loans drawn down under loan commitments that are measured at FVTPL, the analysis is similar to that discussed in 7I.6.23.10 for derivative contracts to acquire a financial asset. In this case, the loan is initially measured at fair value at the time of drawdown. [*IAS 39.BC16*]

7I.6.25   **Immediate gain or loss**

7I.6.25.10   Sometimes an entity acquires a financial instrument in one market and intends to sell it or to issue an offsetting instrument in a different market. There is an issue about whether the instrument may be initially measured at its fair value in the selling market and therefore whether a gain may be recognised on initial recognition ('day one gain').

7I.6.25.20   Similarly, an entity may believe that the initial fair value of an instrument exceeds the consideration paid or received, because of the entity's repackaging of the instrument or a built-in 'fee'. There is an issue about whether this fee may be recognised immediately (similar to a day one gain).

7I.6.25.30   Under IFRS 13, the transaction price – i.e. the fair value of the consideration given or received for the financial instrument – is normally the best evidence of the fair value of a financial instrument on initial recognition. However, there may be cases in which it is appropriate for an entity to conclude that the fair value on initial recognition is different from the transaction price – e.g. when the principal market is different from the market in which the instrument was acquired. For other examples of conditions that can result in a difference between the fair value on initial recognition and the transaction price, see 2.4.320. [*IAS 39.AG64, AG76, IFRS 13.57–60*]

7I.6.25.40   If the entity's fair value measurement is evidenced by a quoted price in an active market for an identical asset or liability or is based on another valuation technique that uses only data from observable markets, then the entity immediately recognises a gain or loss. This gain or loss is equal to the difference between the fair value on initial recognition and the transaction price. [*IAS 39.43A, AG76*]

7I.6.25.50   If the entity determines that the fair value on initial recognition differs from the transaction price, but this fair value measurement is not evidenced by a valuation technique that uses only data from observable markets, then the carrying amount of the financial instrument on initial recognition is adjusted to defer the difference between the fair value measurement and the transaction price. This deferred difference is subsequently recognised as a gain or loss only to the extent that it arises from a change in a factor (including time) that market participants would consider in setting a price. [*IAS 39.43A, AG76–AG76A*]

7I.6.25.60   However, in our experience some banks recognise losses equal to the difference between the fair value on initial recognition and the transaction price immediately, even if the valuation technique is not based wholly on observable market data. Additionally, in our experience banks may consider the recognition of day one gains if any unobservable inputs used in the valuation technique that forms the basis for determining the instrument's fair value on initial recognition are judged to be insignificant in relation to measuring the day one gain.

7I.6.25.70   The table below illustrates the application of the day one gain or loss guidance on initial recognition if:
- a difference arises between the transaction price (say, 100) and management's alternative estimate of fair value (say, 99); and
- the observability condition is not satisfied (see 7I.6.25.50). [*IAS 39.AG76–AG76A*]

APPLICATION OF DAY ONE GAIN AND LOSS GUIDANCE IF OBSERVABILITY CONDITION IS NOT MET	
Fair value:	Management's estimate of exit price 99
Initial measurement (ignoring transaction costs):	Fair value 99 *plus* difference between transaction price and fair value 1 (100 - 99) = 100

EXAMPLE 2 – INITIAL RECOGNITION AT TRANSACTION PRICE (FAIR VALUE OF CONSIDERATION)

7I.6.25.80   Company D acquires a portfolio of impaired loans for 30 from Company E. The carrying amount of the loans in E's books is 29 (a face value of 100 less impairment losses of 71). D has superior cash-collection processes in place and expects to recover 50 of the principal amount of the loans. Based on a discounted cash flow analysis, D values the loans at 36.

7I.6.25.90   In our view, it would not be appropriate to conclude that the transaction price of 30 does not represent the fair value of the loans acquired. The valuation technique used to arrive at the value of 36 takes into account D's specific cash-collection processes. This is not an assumption that a market participant would use when pricing a loan in the portfolio because D's superior cash-collection processes are a characteristic specific to D.

7I.6.25.100   Consequently, D should initially recognise the loans acquired at the transaction price. D's estimates of the amounts and timing of cash flows should instead be used to determine the effective interest rate of the loans, which should be used in subsequent periods to measure their amortised cost.

7I.6.30   **Transaction costs**

7I.6.30.10   Transaction costs are included in the initial measurement of financial assets and financial liabilities, except for those classified as at FVTPL and trade receivables initially measured at the transaction price (see 7I.6.22). [*IAS 39.43, 44A*]

7I.6.30.15   Transaction costs include only those costs that are directly attributable to the acquisition or origination of a financial asset or issue of a financial liability. They are incremental costs that would not have been incurred if the instrument had not been acquired, originated or issued – e.g. fees and commission paid to agents (including employees acting as selling agents), advisers, brokers and dealers, levies by regulatory agencies and securities exchanges, transfer taxes and duties, credit assessment fees, registration charges and similar costs. In our experience, few internal costs are likely to meet this requirement (see 7I.6.40). The requirement is applied on an instrument-by-instrument basis. Transaction costs do not include the internal costs associated with developing a new investment product. [*IAS 39.9, 43, AG13*]

7I.6.30.20   For financial assets, transaction costs are added to the amount initially recognised, whereas for financial liabilities transaction costs are deducted from the amount initially recognised. Transaction costs on financial instruments at FVTPL are not included in the amount at which the instrument is initially measured; instead, they are immediately recognised in profit or loss. [*IAS 39.IG.E.1.1*]

EXAMPLE 3 – TRANSACTION COSTS

> 7I.6.30.30   Company F issues debt of 1,000 at par and incurs direct incremental issue costs of 50. The debt will be redeemed at par. Ignoring interest, there is a difference of 50 between the carrying amount at inception of 950 and the redemption amount of 1,000.
>
> 7I.6.30.35   This difference represents the transaction costs and is recognised by F as an expense over the period that the debt is outstanding under the effective interest method.

7I.6.30.40   In our view, transaction costs that are directly related to the probable issue of a security that will be classified as a financial liability measured at amortised cost should be recognised as a prepayment (asset) in the statement of financial position. Such transaction costs should be deducted from the amount of the financial liability when it is initially recognised, or recognised in profit or loss when the issue is no longer expected to be completed.

7I.6.30.50   Transaction costs that relate to the issue of a compound instrument are allocated to the liability and equity components of the instrument in proportion to the allocation of proceeds. [*IAS 32.38*]

7I.6.30.60   In our view, an entity should choose an accounting policy, to be applied consistently, to allocate transaction costs that relate to a hybrid (combined) instrument that includes a non-derivative host contract that is not accounted for at FVTPL and an embedded derivative that is accounted for at FVTPL. The following are examples of approaches.
• Allocate the transaction costs to the non-derivative host contract and embedded derivative components of the instrument in proportion to the allocation of the total transaction price (e.g. pro-

ceeds), by analogy to the allocation of transaction costs that relate to a compound instrument (see 7I.6.30.50). Under this approach, the amount of transaction costs allocated to the embedded derivative will be charged immediately to profit or loss (see 7I.6.30.20). However, if the embedded derivative is a non-option feature embedded with a host debt instrument, then an amount of zero would usually be allocated to the embedded derivative (see 7I.2.380.40).

- Measure the embedded derivative at fair value on initial recognition. The carrying amount of the non-derivative host contract on initial recognition is the difference between the fair value plus or minus transaction costs of the hybrid instrument and the fair value of the embedded derivative (see 7I.2.380.30). Under this approach, all of the transaction costs will always be allocated to and included in or deducted from the carrying amount of the non-derivative host contract on initial recognition. [*IAS 32.38*]

7I.6.30.70   Any transaction costs that do not qualify for inclusion in the initial measurement of an instrument are expensed as they are incurred. These costs are normally included in the finance costs line item. [*IAS 39.43*]

7I.6.30.80   Transaction costs do not include debt premiums or discounts, financing costs or internal administrative or holding costs. In our view, service fees are not directly attributable to the acquisition of an asset or liability and should be expensed as they are incurred. Similarly, we believe that the costs of researching or developing an instrument or assessing alternatives with a number of parties should be expensed as the costs are incurred. [*IAS 39.9, AG13*]

7I.6.30.90   Transaction costs are generally included in the initial measurement of instruments on an individual basis. This means that the transaction costs should be identifiable with the acquisition or origination of each individual instrument. However, in our view it may be appropriate to accumulate the incremental costs attributable to the acquisition or origination of individual instruments within a portfolio and then allocate these costs to items in the portfolio using a method that produces results that are not materially different from those achieved if the amounts are identified with individual items. It is necessary to make such an allocation to individual balances in order for unamortised transaction costs to be associated correctly with items that are repaid early, are sold or become impaired. This approach would be appropriate only when the portfolio comprises homogeneous items. [*IAS 39.9*]

7I.6.40   *Internal costs*

7I.6.40.10   In our view, the only internal transaction costs allowed to be included in the initial measurement of a financial instrument are commissions, bonuses and other payments that are made to employees only on completion of each individual transaction. We believe that internal semi-variable costs – e.g. the costs of marketing a new product or of employing additional staff to deal with an increase in the volume of transactions – do not qualify as transaction costs. [*IAS 39.AG13*]

7I.6.50   *Facility or commitment fees paid*

7I.6.50.10   An issue that often arises is how to treat facility fees – i.e. initial fees to cover negotiation and arrangement of a facility and periodic fees to compensate the bank for keeping funds available.

7I.6.50.20   In our view, if it is probable that a facility will be drawn down, then an initial facility fee is typically, in substance, an adjustment to the interest cost; therefore, the fee should be deferred and treated as an adjustment to the instrument's effective interest rate and recognised as an expense over the instrument's estimated life. However, if it is not probable that a facility will be drawn down, then the fee is considered a service fee and recognised as an expense on a straight-line basis over the commitment period.

7I.6.50.30   For a discussion of fee income received (i.e. accounting by a lender), see 7I.6.730.

7I.6.60   Low-interest and interest-free loans

7I.6.60.10   In most cases, the fair value of a financial instrument on initial recognition will be equal to its transaction price. However, sometimes interest-free or low-interest loans are given – e.g. by a shareholder or government or as a means of attracting or supporting customers for other goods and services (see 2.4.320). [*IAS 39.AG64–AG65*]

7I.6.60.20   In our view, in assessing whether the interest charged on a loan is at a below-market rate, an entity should consider the terms and conditions of the loan, local industry practice and local market circumstances. Evidence that a loan is at market rates might include the interest rates currently charged by the entity or by other market participants for loans with similar remaining maturities, cash flow patterns, currency, credit risk, collateral and interest basis. For example, very low interest rates on current accounts would be viewed as market rates if they are commonly given in arm's length transactions between market participants in the relevant market (see also 7I.6.280.70).

7I.6.70   *Determining fair value*

7I.6.70.10   The fair value of financial instruments is determined in accordance with IFRS 13, which is the subject of chapter 2.4. The fair value of below-market loans can be measured, for example, as the present value of the expected future cash flows, discounted using a market-related rate. [*IAS 39.AG64*]

7I.6.70.20   The fair value of a financial liability with a demand feature – e.g. a demand deposit – is not less than the amount payable on demand, discounted from the first date on which the entity could be required to repay the amount (see 2.4.420). Accordingly, the fair value of an interest-free loan liability of which the lender can demand repayment of the face value at any time – i.e. a loan repayable on demand – is not less than its face value. In our view, similar considerations would also apply to the lender's measurement of fair value of an interest-free loan repayable on demand to the extent that a market participant acting in its best interest that acquires the loan asset would be assumed to maximise value by achieving immediate repayment. [*IFRS 13.47*]

7I.6.70.30   If a loan has no fixed maturity date and is available in perpetuity, then in our view in measuring its fair value, discounting should reflect these terms because a market participant acting in its best interest would not assume repayment of the loan. In our view, the fair value of loans that have no specified repayment dates and that are not repayable on demand should reflect a market participant's assumptions about the timing of the future cash flows (see 2.4.90).

7I.6.80   *Short-term receivables and payables*

7I.6.80.10   The fair value of a financial instrument reflects the effect of discounting expected future cash flows. However, an entity is permitted to initially measure short-term receivables and payables with no stated interest rate at their invoiced amounts without discounting, if the effect of discounting is immaterial. Therefore, in our view receivables and payables with maturities of up to six months are generally not required to be discounted. However, in high-interest environments, the impact of discounting may be significant even for maturities of less than six months. Notwithstanding the above, trade receivables resulting from contracts with customers in the scope of IFRS 15 are required or permitted to be measured initially at the transaction price as defined in IFRS 15 (rather than at fair value) if certain criteria are met (see 7I.6.22). [*IFRS 13.BC138A, IAS 39.44A*]

7I.6.90 *Accounting for differences between fair value and consideration given or received*

7I.6.90.10   Any difference between the amount lent and the fair value of the instrument on initial recognition is recognised as a gain or a loss unless it qualifies for recognition as an asset or a liability (see 7I.6.20.30). [*IAS 39.AG64*]

7I.6.90.20   If a low-interest loan is given in anticipation of a right to receive goods or services at favourable prices, then the right may be recognised as an asset if it qualifies for recognition as an intangible asset (see 3.3.30 and 90) or other asset – e.g. prepaid expenses.

7I.6.90.30   If the loan is from a government, then the credit is treated as a government grant (see 4.3.100). [*IAS 20.10A*]

7I.6.90.40   In our view, if the loan is from a shareholder acting in the capacity of a shareholder, then the resulting credit should normally be reflected in equity because the substance of the favourable terms is typically a contribution by a shareholder (see 7I.3.370).

EXAMPLE 4 – INTEREST-FREE LOAN FROM SHAREHOLDERS

7I.6.90.50   The shareholders of Company G provide G with financing in the form of interest-free loan notes to enable it to acquire investments in subsidiaries. The loan notes will be redeemed solely out of dividends received from these subsidiaries and become redeemable only when G has sufficient funds to do so. In this context, 'sufficient funds' refers only to dividend receipts from subsidiaries. Therefore, G could not be forced to obtain additional external financing or to liquidate its investments to redeem the shareholder loans. Consequently, the loans could not be considered payable on demand.

7I.6.90.60   G initially measures the loan notes at their fair value (minus transaction costs), being the present value of the expected future cash flows, discounted using a market-related rate. The amount and timing of the expected future cash flows are determined on the basis of the expected dividend flow from the subsidiaries.

7I.6.90.70   Given that the loan notes are interest-free, there will be a difference between the nominal value of the loan notes – i.e. the cash amount received – and their fair value on initial recognition. Because the financing is provided by shareholders, acting in the capacity of shareholders, we believe that the resulting credit should be reflected in equity as a shareholder contribution in G's statement of financial position.

7I.6.100 *Intra-group low-interest and interest-free loans*

7I.6.100.10   When low-interest or interest-free loans are granted to consolidated subsidiaries, the effect of discounting is eliminated on consolidation. Therefore, the discounting will be reflected only in the financial statements of the subsidiary (see 7I.6.90.40) and any separate financial statements of the parent. In our view, in the separate financial statements of the parent the discount should be recognised as an additional investment in the subsidiary. [*IFRS 10.B86(c)*]

71.6.100.20   Similar principles apply to low-interest or interest-free loans to associates or joint ventures, except that if the equity method is applied, then the discounting effect on profit or loss may be eliminated only to the extent of the investor's interest in the investee (see 3.5.430). This may also be the case for subsidiaries accounted for by the parent in the parent's separate financial statements using the equity method.

71.6.100.30   In the case of loans between entities in a group, in addition to the possibility of these being granted on an interest-free basis, there may be no stated terms of repayment. This complicates the measurement of the loan if it is not clear when repayments will take place, what the value of such repayments will be and what the term of the loan is. In such cases, in our view consideration should first be given to whether:

- classification as a liability is appropriate;
- there is no agreed means of repayment, either directly in the agreement or via a side agreement; and
- it is possible to estimate when the loan repayments will take place (see 7I.6.70.30).

71.6.100.40   In our view, having considered these factors and concluded that no alternative treatment is available, such a loan may be considered to be payable on demand. This means that it should be measured at its face value.

71.6.110   *Related party transactions*

71.6.110.10   In our view, the requirement to initially recognise all financial assets and financial liabilities at fair value applies to all low-interest or interest-free loans, including those to or from related parties. In addition, related party disclosures will be required if the counterparty is a related party (see chapter 5.5). [*IAS 39.43*]

71.6.120   SUBSEQUENT MEASUREMENT

71.6.130   General considerations

71.6.130.10   Subsequent to initial measurement:
- derivatives (including separated embedded derivatives) are measured at fair value with changes therein included in profit or loss;
- other financial assets at FVTPL and available-for-sale financial assets are measured at fair value with changes therein included in profit or loss or, for available-for-sale financial assets, in OCI;
- loans and receivables and held-to-maturity investments are measured at amortised cost;
- financial liabilities at FVTPL are measured at fair value with changes therein included in profit or loss; and
- other financial liabilities are generally measured at amortised cost (see 7I.6.180). [*IAS 39.46–47*]

71.6.130.20   If an entity continues to recognise a transferred asset to the extent of its continuing involvement in the asset, then the asset and the associated liability are measured on a basis that reflects the rights and obligations retained by the entity (see 7I.5.250). [*IAS 39.31*]

7I.6.130.30   Financial assets and financial liabilities that are designated as hedged items may require further adjustment in accordance with the hedge accounting requirements (see 7I.7.50). Furthermore, the effective portion of gains and losses on financial assets and financial liabilities, including derivatives, designated as hedging instruments in cash flow or net investment hedges is presented in OCI (see 7I.7.80 and 110). [*IAS 39.46–47*]

7I.6.140   **Derivatives**

7I.6.140.10   Derivatives are measured at fair value except for those contracts that are linked to and must be settled using unquoted equity instruments whose fair value cannot be measured reliably. Such derivatives are measured at cost. In our view, this exemption cannot be extended to cover other underlying variables with no available market data (see 7I.6.210). [*IAS 39.46(c), 47(a), AG80–AG81*]

7I.6.150   **Held-to-maturity investments**

7I.6.150.10   Held-to-maturity investments – e.g. quoted bonds with a fixed maturity – are measured at amortised cost under the effective interest method (see 7I.6.220). [*IAS 39.46(b)*]

7I.6.160   **Loans and receivables**

7I.6.160.10   Loans and receivables are measured at amortised cost under the effective interest method. [*IAS 39.46(a)*]

7I.6.160.20   Loans and receivables that are perpetual and that have either a fixed or a market-based variable rate of interest are measured at cost. For example, in the case of perpetual loans with no repayments of principal and for which fixed or market-based interest payments are due to be paid in perpetuity, the amortised cost at each point in time will equal the fair value of the proceeds given, plus transaction costs and accrued interest. Consequently, there is no amortisation of a difference between the initial amount and a maturity amount. [*IAS 39.IG.B.24*]

7I.6.160.30   Short-duration receivables with no stated interest rate may be measured at their original invoice amount unless the effect of imputing interest would be significant – e.g. in high-inflation countries (see 7I.6.80.10). [*IFRS 13.BC138A*]

7I.6.170   **Available-for-sale financial assets**

7I.6.170.10   Available-for-sale financial assets are measured at fair value. However, there is an exemption for available-for-sale financial assets whose fair value cannot be measured reliably. This exemption applies only to unquoted equity instruments when there is significant variability in the range of reasonable fair value estimates and the probabilities of the various estimates within the range cannot be assessed reasonably. IAS 39 assumes that it is normally possible to estimate the fair value of a financial asset that has been acquired from a third party. Consequently, in our view the exemption would apply mainly to start-up entities (see 7I.6.210). [*IAS 39.46(c), AG80–AG81*]

7I.6.170.15   In rare cases, even though it may be possible to measure the fair value on initial recognition reliably, it may become more difficult over time to measure the fair value of an available-for-sale instrument reliably. In our view, in such cases the financial asset should be subsequently measured at its cost, subject to impairment testing, based on the carrying amount determined at the last date on which the fair value could be determined reliably. [*IAS 39.46, AG80–AG81*]

7I.6.170.20   Fair value changes are recognised in OCI. When the relevant asset is derecognised, on sale or other disposal, or is impaired, the cumulative fair value changes recognised in OCI are reclassified from equity to profit or loss as a reclassification adjustment. For a partial disposal, a proportionate share of the fair value gains and losses previously recognised in OCI is reclassified from equity to profit or loss. Such gains and losses include all fair value changes until the date of disposal (see 7I.5.280.50). [*IAS 39.26–27, 55(b), 67*]

7I.6.170.30   In our view, when financial assets classified as available-for-sale are distributed as dividends in kind to shareholders, the accumulated gains or losses in OCI should be reclassified from equity to profit or loss on derecognition of the financial assets, even if the transaction with shareholders is accounted for in equity.

7I.6.170.40   Interest income is recognised under the effective interest method, with the effective interest rate being calculated on the instrument's initial recognition. Therefore, even though a debt instrument is measured at fair value, the holder applies the effective interest method and calculates the amortised cost of the instrument to determine interest income. Impairment losses and foreign exchange gains and losses on available-for-sale debt instruments are excluded from the fair value gains and losses recognised in OCI. Instead, they are recognised in profit or loss as they arise. [*IAS 39.55(b)*]

7I.6.180   Liabilities

7I.6.180.10   Subsequent to initial recognition, financial liabilities are measured at amortised cost calculated under the effective interest method except for liabilities:
- measured at FVTPL (see 7I.4.20);
- that arise when a transfer of a financial asset does not qualify for derecognition or is accounted for using the continuing involvement approach (see 7I.5.250 and 290);
- that are commitments to provide a loan at a below-market interest rate and not measured at FVTPL (see 7I.1.200.80); and
- that are financial guarantee contracts (see 7I.1.70). [*IAS 39.2, 47*]

7I.6.190   FAIR VALUE

7I.6.200   General

7I.6.200.10   Fair value is measured in accordance with IFRS 13, which is the subject of chapter 2.4.

7I.6.210   Equity instruments: Fair value exemption

7I.6.210.10   It is presumed that the fair value of all financial instruments is reliably measurable. This presumption can be overcome only for an investment in an equity instrument that does not have a quoted price in an active market and whose fair value cannot be reliably measured, and for derivatives that are linked to and are settled by the delivery of such instruments. This exemption applies both to instruments classified as trading and to those classified as available-for-sale. [*IAS 39.46*]

7I.6.210.15   The fair value of investments in equity instruments that do not have a quoted price in an active market and of related derivatives is reliably measurable if:
- the variability in the range of reasonable fair value estimates is not significant for that instrument; or

- the probabilities of various estimates within the range can be reasonably assessed. [*IAS 39.AG80–AG81*]

7I.6.210.20   This exemption is very limited. It is unlikely that an investment would be bought if its fair value could not be estimated. In particular, venture capitalists and other entities that undertake significant investing activities use some form of valuation technique to evaluate investment decisions. In our view, in these circumstances – i.e. assuming that another valuation technique cannot be appropriately applied – the same techniques used to make investment decisions should be used subsequently to determine the fair value of an investment. The exemption may be used only in rare cases when it can be demonstrated that the valuation technique generates a wide range of possible fair values and when the probability of the various outcomes cannot be estimated. For a discussion of this in the context of investments in investment funds, see 2.4.930.20–30.

7I.6.210.30   When determining the fair value of these instruments, an entity uses a supportable methodology for identifying the point within a range of reasonable estimates that is most representative of the fair value rather than simply choosing a fair value from the range (see 2.4.130.50). [*IFRS 13.63*]

7I.6.210.40   If an embedded derivative that is required to be separated cannot be measured reliably because it will be settled using an unquoted equity instrument whose fair value cannot be reliably measured, then the entire combined contract is designated as a financial instrument at FVTPL. The entity might conclude, however, that the equity component of the combined instrument may be significant enough to preclude it from obtaining a reliable estimate of fair value for the entire instrument. In that case, the combined instrument is measured at cost less impairment. [*IAS 39.13*]

7I.6.220   AMORTISED COST

7I.6.220.10   Amortised cost applies to both financial assets and financial liabilities. The effective interest method is used for amortising premiums, discounts and transaction costs for both financial assets and financial liabilities. [*IAS 39.9*]

7I.6.220.20   When applying the effective interest method, interest is recognised in profit or loss in the period to which it relates, regardless of when it is to be paid. Therefore, interest is recognised in the period in which it accrues, even if payment is deferred. [*IAS 39.9, AG5–AG8C*]

7I.6.230   Effective interest rate calculation

7I.6.240   *Effective interest method*

7I.6.240.10   The 'effective interest method' is a method of calculating the amortised cost of a financial asset or financial liability and allocating the interest income or expense over the relevant period. It differs from the straight-line method in that the amortisation under the effective interest method reflects a constant periodic return on the carrying amount of the asset or liability. [*IAS 39.9*]

7I.6.240.20   The 'effective interest rate' is the rate that exactly discounts the estimated stream of future cash payments or receipts, without consideration of future credit losses, over the expected life of the financial instrument or through to the next market-based repricing date, to the net carrying amount of the financial asset or financial liability on initial recognition. [*IAS 39.9, AG5–AG8*]

71.6.240.30 The effective interest rate is calculated on initial recognition of an instrument. For floating rate financial instruments, periodic re-estimation of cash flows to reflect movements in market rates of interest alters the effective interest rate. To calculate the effective interest in each relevant period, the effective interest rate is applied to the amortised cost of the asset or liability at the previous reporting date. [*IAS 39.AG7*]

71.6.240.40 The difference between the calculated effective interest for a given period and the instrument's coupon is the amortisation (or accretion) during that period of the difference between the initial measurement of the instrument and the maturity amount.

EXAMPLE 5 – EFFECTIVE INTEREST CALCULATION

71.6.240.50 Company K grants a five-year loan of 50,000 to Company L on 1 January 2018. There is an annual coupon of 10% paid on the last day of each year. L pays an up-front fee of 1,000 and the net loan proceeds are 49,000. The annual effective interest rate is calculated by solving for x in the following equation.

$$49,000 = \frac{5,000}{(1+x)} + \frac{5,000}{(1+x)^2} + \frac{5,000}{(1+x)^3} + \frac{5,000}{(1+x)^4} + \frac{55,000}{(1+x)^5}$$

71.6.240.60 Therefore, the effective interest rate is 10.53482% a year. The interest and amortised cost are as follows.

DATE	INTEREST (10.53482%)	CASH FLOWS	AMORTISED COST
1 January 2018	-	-	49,000
31 December 2018	5,162	5,000	49,162
31 December 2019	5,179	5,000	49,341
31 December 2020	5,198	5,000	49,539
31 December 2021	5,219	5,000	49,758
31 December 2022	5,242	55,000	-
Total	26,000	75,000	

71.6.250 **Contractual or estimated cash flows**

71.6.250.10 In determining the effective interest rate, an entity considers all of the contractual terms of an instrument, including any embedded derivatives – e.g. prepayment, call and similar options – that are not subject to separation, but without inclusion of future credit losses (see 71.2.110). In our view, when an instrument gives either the issuer or the holder the option to require the instrument to be redeemed or cancelled early, and the terms of the instrument are such that it is not certain whether the option will be exercised, then the probability of the option being exercised should be assessed in determining the estimated cash flows. [*IAS 39.9*]

7I.6.250.20   However, for financial liabilities with a demand feature – e.g. a demand deposit – the fair value is not less than the amount payable on demand, discounted from the first date on which the amount could be required to be paid (see 2.4.420). Therefore, for example, a non-interest-bearing or low-interest financial liability for which the holder can demand immediate repayment is not discounted on initial recognition, even if the issuer does not expect repayment of the liability in the near future (see 7I.6.70.20). The impact of this requirement is that interest expense would be recognised at the coupon rate for a low-interest financial liability with an immediate demand feature. [*IFRS 13.47*]

7I.6.250.30   The calculation of the effective interest rate includes:
- all fees and points paid or received between parties to the contract that are an integral part of the effective interest rate (see 7I.6.730);
- transaction costs (see 7I.6.30); and
- all other premiums or discounts. [*IAS 39.9*]

7I.6.250.40   Future credit losses are not taken into account because doing so would be a departure from the incurred-loss model for impairment (see 7I.6.400). In some cases – e.g. when a financial asset is acquired at a deep discount – credit losses have already occurred and are reflected in the purchase price (see 7I.8.170.20). Such credit losses are included in the estimated cash flows when computing the effective interest rate. Any adjustments arising from revisions to estimated cash flows subsequent to initial recognition are recognised as part of the carrying amount of the financial asset, with a corresponding amount recognised in profit or loss. [*IAS 39.9, AG5–AG8*]

7I.6.250.50   The IFRS Interpretations Committee discussed the requirement to include incurred credit losses that are reflected in the asset's price on initial recognition in the estimated cash flows used to determine the effective interest rate and noted that this requirement applies to both purchased and originated assets. Even though origination of a debt instrument with an incurred loss is unusual, there may be situations in which such transactions occur. For example, debt instruments can be originated outside the normal underwriting process as part of a restructuring when the debtor is in significant financial difficulty. This could include situations in which modifications of debt instruments result in derecognition of the original financial asset and the recognition of a new financial asset (see 7I.6.490). These cases are not limited to those in which debt instruments are effectively forced upon existing lenders, but could also arise in other transactions. [*IAS 39.AG5, IU 11-12*]

7I.6.250.60   There is a presumption that future cash flows and the expected life can be estimated reliably for most financial instruments. In the rare case in which it is not possible to estimate the timing or amount of future cash flows reliably, the entity uses the contractual cash flows over the full contractual term of the financial instrument. [*IAS 39.9*]

7I.6.260   *Changes in timing or amount of estimated cash flows*

7I.6.260.10   If there is a change in the timing or amount of estimated future cash flows (other than because of impairment), then the carrying amount of the instrument (or group of financial instruments) is adjusted in the period of change to reflect the actual and/or revised estimated cash flows, with a corresponding gain or loss being recognised in profit or loss. The revised carrying amount is recalculated by discounting the revised estimated future cash flows at the instrument's original effective interest rate or, when applicable, the revised effective interest rate calculated in accordance with paragraph 92 of

IAS 39 in relation to the amortisation of the fair value hedge adjustment for fair value hedges. In our view, this approach to changes in estimated cash flows should apply to changing prepayment expectations and other estimates of cash flows under the current terms of the financial instrument but not to a renegotiation of the contractual terms of an instrument (see 7I.5.95, 380, 7I.6.290 and 490). [*IAS 39.AG8*]

7I.6.260.20   An entity may reclassify certain financial assets out of the FVTPL category and/or the available-for-sale category in certain circumstances (see 7I.4.210). If a financial asset is so reclassified and the entity subsequently increases its estimates of future cash receipts as a result of increased estimates of recoverability of those cash receipts, then the effect of that increase is recognised as an adjustment to the effective interest rate from the date of the change in estimate rather than as an adjustment to the carrying amount of the asset at the date of the change in estimate – i.e. any increase in estimated future cash receipts is not recognised immediately as a gain in profit or loss. [*IAS 39.AG8*]

7I.6.260.30   The use of estimated cash flows specifically excludes the effect of expected future credit losses. Therefore, the amortised cost calculation cannot be used to remove credit spread from interest income to cover future losses. [*IAS 39.9*]

7I.6.260.40   The contractual terms of some financial instruments may be linked to the performance of other assets, as illustrated in Example 6.

EXAMPLE 6 – ESTIMATING CASH FLOWS FOR COLLATERALISED NOTES

7I.6.260.43   Limited-purpose Vehicle L holds a portfolio of loans and receivables and has issued to investors notes collateralised by those loans.

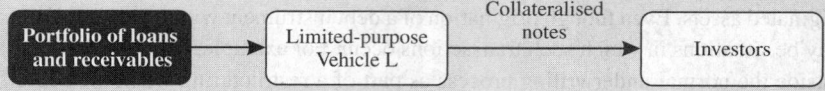

7I.6.260.47   The contractual terms of the notes are such that L has an obligation to pay cash on its notes only to the extent that it receives cash from its loans and receivables. Also assume that the notes do not contain embedded derivatives requiring separation (see 7I.2.360) and, at the measurement date, the portfolio of loans and receivables held by L includes:

- actual defaults by the debtors of 10;
- incurred losses calculated in accordance with IAS 39 of 15; and
- expected losses of 20 (including 15 of incurred losses).

7I.6.260.50   In our view, there are two acceptable approaches for the issuer to estimate cash flows on the notes.

- *Incurred-loss method:* This is based on the theory that taking into account losses incurred on the underlying loan assets is consistent with the requirements that an entity should estimate cash flows considering all contractual terms of an instrument but not future credit losses. Therefore, expected cash flows would be reduced by 15.

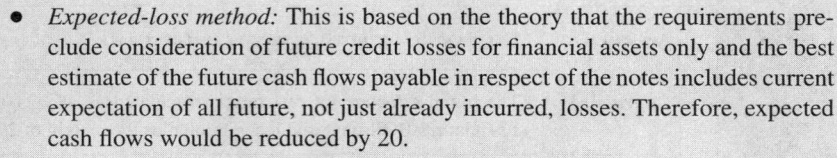

- *Expected-loss method:* This is based on the theory that the requirements preclude consideration of future credit losses for financial assets only and the best estimate of the future cash flows payable in respect of the notes includes current expectation of all future, not just already incurred, losses. Therefore, expected cash flows would be reduced by 20.

7I.6.260.60   We believe that estimating cash flows for the notes taking into account only actual defaults by the debtors is not consistent with the requirements of the standard.

7I.6.270   Floating rate financial assets and financial liabilities

7I.6.270.10   The periodic re-estimation of cash flows to reflect movements in market rates of interest will change the effective interest rate of a floating rate financial asset or liability. [*IAS 39.AG7*]

7I.6.270.20   IAS 39 does not contain any further description or definition of 'floating rate' or guidance on how the term 'market rates of interest' should be interpreted in this context. Therefore, judgement may be required in applying these terms to different circumstances – e.g. when the contractual interest rate is calculated in accordance with a formula or is a discretionary rate. In many cases, a floating rate instrument may have a contractual interest rate that comprises more than one component such as a published benchmark rate or other published interest rate index (e.g. LIBOR) and a specified spread (e.g. a predetermined percentage spread above LIBOR). In some circumstances, although changes in the benchmark rate would be considered a change to which the guidance in 7I.6.270.10 would be applied (leading to a change in the effective interest rate), the spread might be fixed (i.e. not subject to change) or any changes in the specified spread might not be considered to reflect movements in market rates of interest and would not lead to a change in the effective interest rate.

7I.6.270.30   IAS 39 does not specify how to calculate the effective interest rate for floating rate financial instruments. Therefore, in our view an entity is allowed to follow one of these two approaches for calculating the effective interest rate, which are illustrated in Example 7.
- *Approach 1:* Based on the actual benchmark interest rate that was set for the relevant period.
- *Approach 2:* Taking into account expectations of future interest rates, and changes in these expectations.

EXAMPLE 7 – CALCULATING THE EFFECTIVE INTEREST RATE FOR FLOATING RATE FINANCIAL INSTRUMENTS

7I.6.270.40   Company M issues at par a financial liability with:
- principal of 100;
- a contractual interest rate of 12-month LIBOR plus 2% (payable annually); and
- a maturity of three years.

7I.6.270.50   12-month LIBOR on initial recognition of the liability is 2% and is used to set the first annual coupon. 12-month LIBOR is expected to be 3% in year 2 and 4% in year 3.

Approach	Calculation of initial effective interest rate
Approach 1	The initial effective interest rate is calculated as 4% per annum – i.e. 12-month LIBOR on initial recognition plus the margin of 2%.
Approach 2	The initial effective interest rate is calculated as approximately 5% per annum – i.e. the internal rate of return of the following cash flows: • expected coupons of 4, 5 and 6; and • principal repayable at maturity of 100.

7I.6.270.60   We believe that an entity may apply the same approaches when the contractual terms of a financial instrument provide for the interest rate to be fixed for an initial period and then revert to a floating market rate of interest. An example is a 25-year mortgage loan that has an initial fixed rate of 4% for five years and then changes to the published standard variable rate (SVR) of the lender for the remaining 20 years. If the loan is measured at par on initial recognition, then:
- under Approach 1, the effective interest rate for the first five years would be 4% and then it would change to the actual SVR; and
- under Approach 2, the calculation of the effective interest rate would consider the initial fixed 4%, expectations of future levels of the SVR and changes in these expectations.

7I.6.270.70   If the floating rate financial asset or financial liability is initially recognised at an amount equal to the principal receivable or payable on maturity, then periodic re-estimation of future interest payments would not normally have a significant effect on the carrying amount of the asset or liability. [*IAS 39.AG7*]

7I.6.270.80   Under Approach 1, for a floating rate financial asset or financial liability that is initially recognised at a discount or premium, the interest income or expense is recognised based on the current market rate plus or minus amortisation or accretion of the discount or premium (see 7I.6.320.30). [*IAS 39.AG6–AG7*]

7I.6.270.90   In our view, this approach could also be applied for a floating rate instrument that includes embedded derivatives that are not separated – e.g. an instrument on which the interest rate is subject to market indices such as inflation.

7I.6.270.100   IAS 39 does not prescribe any specific methodology for how transaction costs should be amortised for a floating rate loan, except as discussed in 7I.6.320. In our view, any consistent methodology that would establish a reasonable basis for amortisation of the transaction costs may be used. For example, it would be reasonable to determine an amortisation schedule of the transaction costs based on the interest rate in effect at inception.

7I.6.280   **Stepped interest**

7I.6.280.10   Sometimes entities buy or issue debt instruments with a predetermined rate of interest that increases or decreases progressively (stepped interest) over the term of the debt instrument. In this case, the entity uses the effective interest method to allocate the interest in-come or expense over the term of the debt instrument to achieve a level yield to maturity that is a constant interest rate on the carrying amount of the instrument in each period. [*IAS 39.9, IG.B.27*]

EXAMPLE 8A – EFFECTIVE INTEREST CALCULATION – STEPPED INTEREST

7I.6.280.20   On 1 January 2018, Bank N takes a five-year deposit from a customer with the following rates of interest specified in the agreement.

YEAR	RATE
2018	2.0%
2019	2.1%
2020	2.2%
2021	2.4%
2022	3.0%

7I.6.280.30   The effective interest rate for this instrument is 2.33% (rounded). Therefore, interest is accrued using the 2.33% rate.

EXAMPLE 8B – EFFECTIVE INTEREST CALCULATION – STEPPED INTEREST WITH EARLY WITHDRAWAL OPTION

7I.6.280.40   Assume the same fact pattern as in Example 8A, except that the customer has an option to withdraw the deposit after four years without penalty. This option is considered to be closely related to the deposit contract (see 7I.2.190).

7I.6.280.50   If Bank N expects the deposit to be withdrawn after four years without penalty, then this expectation would be taken into account when calculating the instrument's effective interest rate. In this circumstance, the resulting effective interest rate would be approximately 2.17%. This rate would be used to accrue interest expense over the deposit's expected life.

7I.6.280.60   A similar approach is adopted from the perspective of the holder of a financial instrument – i.e. the holder takes into consideration all contractual terms and the probability of any prepayment and call and similar options being exercised.

7I.6.280.70   In respect of mortgage loans and credit cards that are issued with a low initial rate of interest to attract new customers, an issue similar to stepped interest arises. After the initial period, the interest rate typically returns to a standard market rate so that the lender is able to recover the discount over the remaining estimated life of the instrument. Normally, any initial discount that is widely offered to market participants is recognised as part of the effective yield over the estimated life of the instrument. Alternatively, in our view the fair value of such an initial discount might be considered as a cost of attracting new business and recognised immediately as an expense. In our view, any discount that is not offered widely and is therefore in excess of that offered to all market participants should be recognised immediately as an expense (see 7I.6.60).

7I.6.290 **Modification of financial liabilities**

7I.6.290.10   If the terms of a financial liability are modified substantially, resulting in an extinguishment of the old financial liability, then the old liability is derecognised and the restructured financial instrument is treated as a new financial liability (see 7I.5.390). [*IAS 39.39–40*]

7I.6.290.20   If a modification of a financial liability results in derecognition of the financial liability, then the effective interest rate of the new financial liability is calculated based on the revised terms of the financial liability at the date of the modification. In this case, any costs or fees incurred are recognised as part of the gain or loss on extinguishment and do not adjust the carrying amount of the new liability. Accordingly, in our view no transaction costs should be included in the initial measurement of the new liability unless it can be incontrovertibly demonstrated that they relate solely to the new liability instrument and in no way to the modification of the old liability. This would not usually be possible but might apply to taxes and registration fees payable on execution of the new liability instrument. [*IAS 39.41, AG62*]

7I.6.290.30   If the exchange or modification is not accounted for as an extinguishment, then any costs and fees incurred are recognised as an adjustment to the carrying amount of the liability and amortised over the remaining term of the modified instrument by recomputing the effective interest rate on the instrument (see 7I.5.400). [*IAS 39.AG62*]

7I.6.300 **Instruments acquired in business combination**

7I.6.300.10   All financial instruments that are acquired as part of a business combination are initially measured by the acquirer at their fair value at the date of acquisition (see 2.4.1000). [*IFRS 3.18*]

7I.6.300.20   At the date of acquisition, the fair value of the instrument and the total cash flows expected over the remaining term of the instrument are used by the acquirer to calculate a new original effective interest rate for the instrument. The new original effective interest rate is used to determine the interest income or expense in the acquirer's consolidated financial statements but has no impact on the accounting in the acquiree's financial statements. [*IAS 39.9*]

7I.6.300.30   Because assets of the acquiree are measured in the acquirer's consolidated accounts at fair value at the date of acquisition, the acquirer does not recognise a separate valuation allowance to reflect any credit losses incurred at that date. In our view, for an instrument that has incurred credit losses at the date of acquisition (see 7I.6.250.40 and 400), the estimated cash flows should be determined on the basis of the expected receipts as reduced by those incurred credit losses, rather than on the basis of the cash flows that would arise if the borrower complied with the contractual terms. Generally, the expected cash flows should exclude any future credit losses. In our experience, it may be difficult to make a distinction between incurred and future losses if it is considered that the borrower will not be able to meet the contractual terms in full. However, to the extent that the distinction can be made, future losses should be excluded from the estimates. [*IFRS 3.B41, IAS 39.AG5*]

7I.6.300.40   Continuing the example above, if the expected cash flows from that asset are subsequently revised upwards because of an improvement in the debtor's credit quality, then in our view the upward revision is recognised in profit or loss but should not be presented as a recovery of impairment. This is because no impairment loss had been recognised in the acquirer's consolidated financial statements on the asset subsequent to initial recognition and therefore there is no impairment to reverse. [*IAS 39.AG8*]

7I.6.310   Hedged item in fair value hedge

7I.6.310.10   An interest-bearing instrument that is the hedged item in a fair value hedge is remeasured based on changes in fair value in respect of the risk being hedged during the period of the hedging relationship (see 7I.7.50), even if the item is normally measured at amortised cost. [*IAS 39.89(b)*]

7I.6.310.20   When hedge accounting is discontinued or earlier, the carrying amount of the instrument and the total payments to be made over the remaining term of the instrument are used to calculate a revised effective interest rate for the instrument. The revised effective interest rate is used to determine interest income or expense in subsequent periods (see 7I.7.680.100). [*IAS 39.92*]

7I.6.320   Discounts, premiums and pre-acquisition interest

7I.6.320.10   The straight-line amortisation of discounts or premiums is not permitted. Instead, discounts and premiums – including fees, points paid or received and transaction costs – are generally recognised over the expected life of the related instrument using the effective interest rate at the date of initial recognition of the instrument. However, in some cases a shorter period is used if this is the period to which such discounts and premiums relate – e.g. when the variable is repriced to market rates before the expected maturity of the instrument. [*IAS 39.AG6*]

7I.6.320.20   Therefore, for a group of prepayable mortgage loans, any discount, transaction costs and related fees may be required to be amortised over a period shorter than the contractual maturity. Historical prepayment patterns would be used to estimate expected lives and subsequent revisions to prepayment estimates will give rise to gains and losses that are recognised in profit or loss. [*IAS 39.AG6, AG8*]

7I.6.320.30   If a discount or premium arises on the acquisition of a floating rate instrument, then it is important to identify the reason for that discount or premium. For example, if a premium or discount on a floating rate instrument reflects *changes in market rates* since the floating-interest instrument was last repriced, then it will be amortised to the next repricing date. Alternatively, if the premium or discount results from a change in the credit spread over the floating rate specified in the instrument as a result of a *change in credit risk*, then it is amortised over the expected life of the instrument. [*IAS 39.AG6*]

7I.6.320.40   When an interest-bearing instrument is acquired between interest payment dates, the buyer normally has an obligation to pay the accrued interest to the seller when it is received or pays a higher price for the instrument to reimburse the seller for the accrued interest that will be paid to the buyer. Accordingly, interest that has accrued on an interest-bearing investment before it is acquired is not recognised as income. If there is an obligation to pay the accrued interest to the seller, then a receivable and a corresponding payable are recognised in respect of the accrued interest.

7I.6.320.50   The amortisation of discounts or premiums is included in interest income or expense and is not required to be disclosed separately.

7I.6.330   Interest income after impairment recognition

7I.6.330.10   If a financial asset or a group of similar financial assets has been written down as a result of an impairment loss, then interest income is thereafter recognised using the rate of interest used to discount the future cash flows for the purpose of measuring the impairment loss. For assets measured at amortised cost, this interest rate would be the original effective interest rate (see 7I.6.480.10). In our view, for an available-for-sale financial asset, an entity may use a new effective interest rate computed based on the fair value at the date of impairment. [*IAS 39.AG93*]

7I.6.330.20   It is inappropriate simply to suspend interest recognition on a non-performing interest-bearing instrument, such as a loan and receivable. Future interest receipts are taken into account when the entity estimates the future cash flows of the instrument. If no contractual interest payments will be collected, then the only interest income recognised is the unwinding of the discount on those cash flows expected to be received. [*IAS 39.AG93*]

7I.6.330.30   For a detailed discussion of the impairment of financial instruments, see 7I.6.400.

7I.6.340   FINANCIAL INSTRUMENTS MEASURED IN FOREIGN CURRENCY

7I.6.350   General considerations

7I.6.350.10   Entities may have exposure to foreign currency risk, either from transactions in foreign currencies or from investments in foreign operations. The principles for foreign currency transactions explained in chapter 2.7 apply equally to financial instruments. The application of these principles to various foreign currency financial instruments is explained below.

7I.6.350.20   'Monetary items' are units of currency held and assets and liabilities to be received or paid, in a fixed or determinable number of units of currency. This definition is narrower than the definition of a financial instrument, which means that not all financial instruments are monetary. Consequently, contractual rights or obligations to receive or pay cash when the amount of money is neither fixed nor determinable are non-monetary financial instruments. This is the case, for example, with equity securities and other instruments if the holder has no right to a determinable amount of money. [*IAS 21.8*]

7I.6.350.30   Derivative contracts are settled at amounts that are determinable at the settlement date in accordance with the terms of the contract and the price of the underlying. Derivatives that are settled in cash are monetary items, even if the underlying is a non-monetary item. [*IAS 21.16, 39.AG83*]

7I.6.350.40   In our view, the liability component of a convertible bond should be considered to be a monetary item because it is an obligation to pay a fixed or determinable amount of currency units.

7I.6.360   Monetary items carried at amortised cost

7I.6.360.10   Monetary items denominated in a foreign currency and carried at amortised cost – i.e. loans and receivables, held-to-maturity investments and other liabilities – are measured as follows.
- The functional currency carrying amount at the beginning of the reporting period – i.e. the amount reported in the functional currency of the entity at the previous reporting date – is the starting point.
- The interest income to be recognised in the period is the amount calculated in the foreign currency under the effective interest method, multiplied by the average spot exchange rate for the period. This accrual adjusts the functional currency amortised cost at the beginning of the reporting period.

- Then the foreign currency amortised cost of the monetary item is calculated as at the reporting date.
- The functional currency carrying amount at the reporting date is the foreign currency amortised cost at the reporting date multiplied by the spot exchange rate at the reporting date.
- Then the functional currency carrying amount at the reporting date as calculated above is compared with the functional currency carrying amount at the beginning of the reporting period adjusted for the interest accrual and any payments during the period. Any difference between these two amounts is an exchange gain or loss, which is recognised in profit or loss. [*IAS 21.23(a), 28, 39.AG83, IG.E.3.4*]

7I.6.370   Available-for-sale monetary items

7I.6.370.10   For the purpose of recognising foreign exchange differences, available-for-sale monetary items (such as debt securities) are treated as if they were measured at amortised cost in the foreign currency. Accordingly, the foreign exchange differences arising from changes in amortised cost are recognised in profit or loss and not in OCI. [*IAS 21.23(a), 28, 39.AG83, IG.E.3.2, IG.E.3.4*]

7I.6.370.20   The foreign currency differences on these instruments are measured as follows.
- The functional currency amortised cost at the beginning of the reporting period – i.e. the amount calculated (but not reported) in the functional currency of the entity at the previous reporting date – is the starting point.
- The interest income to be recognised in the period is the amount calculated in the foreign currency under the effective interest method, multiplied by the average spot exchange rate for the period. This accrual adjusts the functional currency amortised cost at the beginning of the reporting period. For available-for-sale monetary items, interest calculated under the effective interest method is required to be recognised in profit or loss (see 7I.6.170.40).
- Then the foreign currency amortised cost of the monetary item is calculated as at the reporting date.
- The functional currency amortised cost at the reporting date is the foreign currency amortised cost at the reporting date multiplied by the spot exchange rate at the reporting date.
- Then the functional currency amortised cost at the reporting date is compared with the functional currency amortised cost at the beginning of the reporting period adjusted for the interest accrual and any payments during the period. Any difference between these two amounts is an exchange gain or loss, which is recognised in profit or loss. [*IAS 39.IG.E.3.2*]

7I.6.370.30   The reported carrying amount of such available-for-sale monetary items is calculated as follows.
- The fair value of the monetary item at the reporting date is calculated in the foreign currency.
- The functional currency carrying amount at the reporting date is determined by multiplying the fair value in the foreign currency by the spot exchange rate at the reporting date.
- The difference between the functional currency carrying amount at the reporting date – i.e. fair value – and the functional currency amortised cost at the reporting date is the cumulative gain or loss to be recognised in OCI at the reporting date. [*IAS 39.IG.E.3.2*]

EXAMPLE 9 – ACCOUNTING FOR AVAILABLE-FOR-SALE MONETARY ITEM

7I.6.370.40   On 31 December 2017, Company P, which has the euro as its functional currency, buys a bond denominated in US dollars. The following facts are also relevant for this example.

	31 Dec 2017	**31 Dec 2018**
Fair value of the bond	USD 1,000	USD 1,060
Remaining years to maturity	5	4
Fixed annual coupon on principal of USD 1,250	4.7% or USD 59	
Annual effective interest rate	10%	

7I.6.370.50 Exchange rates at 31 December 2017 and 31 December 2018 and the average exchange rate during 2018 were as follows.

	USD	EUR
Exchange rate at 31 December 2017	1.0	1.5
Average exchange rate during 2018	1.0	1.75
Exchange rate at 31 December 2018	1.0	2.0

7I.6.370.60 P classifies the bond as available-for-sale. P initially recognises the bond as follows.

	DEBIT (EUR)	CREDIT (EUR)
Bond	1,500	
Cash		1,500
To recognise initial acquisition of bond		

7I.6.370.70 P determines:
- the amortised cost of the bond at 31 December 2017;
- the interest income for 2018 under the effective interest method;
- the coupon received on 31 December 2018;
- the amortised cost of the bond at 31 December 2018; and
- the exchange difference on the bond for 2018.

	USD	RATE	EUR
Amortised cost of bond at 31 December 2017	1,000	1.5	1,500
Interest income	100[1]	1.75	175
Coupon received	(59)	2	(118)
Amortised cost of bond at 31 December 2018	1,041	2	2,082
Exchange difference			525[2]

Notes
1. Calculated as USD 1,000 x 10%.
2. Calculated as EUR 2,082 + EUR 118 - EUR 175 - EUR 1,500.

71.6.370.80   The exchange difference represents:

- a gain of EUR 500 (1,000 x (2 - 1.5)) arising on the initial amortised cost; and
- a gain of EUR 25 (100 x (2 - 1.75)) arising on the interest income. [*IAS 39.IG.E.3.2*]

71.6.370.90   P determines the cumulative gain or loss to be recognised in OCI as follows.

31 December 2018	USD	RATE	EUR
Fair value of the bond	1,060	2	2,120
Amortised cost of the bond	(1,041)	2	(2,082)
Cumulative fair value changes in OCI (gain)	(19)	2	(38)[(1)]

Note
1.   The balance of the cumulative gain or loss in OCI related to the bond at 31 December 2017 is zero, and therefore the amount of gain or loss to be recognised in OCI in the statement of profit or loss and OCI for 2018 equals the balance of cumulative gain or loss to be recognised in OCI at 31 December 2018.

71.6.370.100   P records the following entry on 31 December 2018.

	DEBIT (EUR)	CREDIT (EUR)
Bond	620[(1)]	
Cash	118	
Interest income		175
Exchange gain		525
Fair value change in OCI		38
To recognise changes in fair value, interest income and repayment, and foreign exchange on bond		

Note
1.   Calculated as EUR 2,120 - EUR 1,500.

71.6.380   **Non-monetary items measured at fair value**

71.6.380.10   Non-monetary items measured at cost are not translated subsequent to initial recognition. However, some non-monetary financial instruments, such as investments in equity securities, are measured at fair value. Such instruments are reported using the exchange rates that existed when the fair values were determined. Therefore, the fair value is first determined in the foreign currency, which is translated into the functional currency. Foreign exchange gains and losses are not separated from the total fair value changes. Therefore, for available-for-sale equity investments, the entire change in fair value, including any related foreign exchange component, is recognised in OCI. If the non-monetary item is classified as at FVTPL, then the entire fair value change is recognised in profit or loss. [*IAS 21.23, 30, 39.AG83*]

71.6.390 **Dual-currency loans**

71.6.390.10 A dual-currency loan is an instrument with the principal and interest denominated in different currencies. A dual-currency loan with principal denominated in the functional currency and interest payments denominated in a foreign currency contains an embedded foreign currency derivative. However, the embedded derivative is not separated because changes in the spot rate on the foreign currency denominated element (the accrued interest or the principal) are measured under IAS 21 at the closing rate, with any resulting foreign exchange gains or losses recognised in profit or loss. However, IAS 21 does not provide guidance on how to account for a dual-currency instrument. [*IAS 39.AG33(c)*]

EXAMPLE 10 – MEASUREMENT OF DUAL-CURRENCY LOANS

71.6.390.20 Company Q issues a bond with the principal denominated in euro and the interest denominated in US dollars. The functional currency of Q is sterling. In our view, to reflect the foreign currency exposure Q should treat the dual-currency bond as consisting of two components for measurement purposes:
- a zero-coupon bond denominated in euro; and
- an instalment bond with annual payments denominated in US dollars.

71.6.390.30 On initial recognition, the two components are recognised at fair value. Subsequently, assuming that the instrument is not classified as at FVTPL, Q measures each component separately at amortised cost under the effective interest method. The interest expense related to each component is calculated separately in the relevant foreign currency – i.e. in euro for the zero-coupon bond and in US dollars for the instalment bond – and translated into sterling at the average rate for the period. The carrying amount of both elements is translated to sterling at each reporting date using the closing exchange rate, with movements recognised in profit or loss (see 2.7.140.10).

71.6.400 **IMPAIRMENT OF FINANCIAL ASSETS**

71.6.400.05 The following table sets out instruments that are in and out of the scope of the impairment requirements of IAS 39. [*IFRS 15.107, C9, IAS 39.2, 2A*]

IN SCOPE	OUT OF SCOPE
• Loans and receivables and held-to-maturity investments, i.e. assets measured at amortised cost	• Financial instruments measured at FVTPL
• Available-for-sale financial assets	• Financial guarantee contracts issued (see 7I.1.50)
• Assets measured at cost because fair value is not reliably measurable	• Loan commitments issued (see 7I.1.200)
• Lease receivables in the scope of IAS 17	
• Contract assets in the scope of IFRS 15	

71.6.400.10 Addressing the impairment of financial assets is a two-step process. First, the entity assesses whether there is objective evidence that impairment exists for a financial asset or a group of financial assets. This assessment is done at least at each reporting date. If there is no objective evidence of impairment, then no impairment loss is recognised at that time for that financial asset or group of financial assets. However, if there is objective evidence of impairment, then the entity calculates the amount of any impairment loss and recognises it during that reporting period. [*IAS 39.46, 58–59*]

7I.6.400.20   The assessment of whether there is objective evidence of an incurred impairment loss on a financial asset is based on all available information at the reporting date. However, in our view this does not imply that a full loan review in accordance with the entity's normal operating procedures should be carried out at the reporting date as long as the entity has procedures, processes and systems that provide the relevant information required for such an assessment for the purposes of financial reporting. [*IAS 39.58*]

7I.6.400.30   As is discussed in 7I.6.410, there is different guidance on the impairment of investments in equity instruments from that for investments in debt instruments. IFRS does not define a debt instrument or an equity instrument from the holder's perspective. In our view, determining whether the holder has an investment in a debt instrument or in an equity instrument requires the use of judgement and consideration of the specific facts and circumstances. A debt instrument is usually characterised by a fixed or determinable maturity and fixed or determinable payments, whereas an equity instrument gives the holder a residual interest in the net assets of the entity.

7I.6.400.35   The nature of the investment may impact the identification of objective evidence of impairment and recording of reversals of impairment losses. Once it has been determined, the nature of the holder's investment is interpreted in a consistent way for the purposes of other requirements of the standard that distinguish between debt and equity instruments, such as identification of the host contract for assessing embedded derivatives and the reference asset for financial guarantee contracts.

7I.6.410   Objective evidence of impairment

7I.6.410.10   A financial asset or a group of financial assets is considered to be impaired only if objective evidence indicates that one or more events ('loss events'), happening after its initial recognition, have an effect on the estimated future cash flows of that asset. It may not be possible to pinpoint one specific event that caused the impairment because it may have been caused by the combined effects of a number of events. When a loss event is identified, an impairment loss is recognised if that loss event has an impact on the cash flows of the financial asset that can be estimated reliably – i.e. if a loss event is identified, then an entity is required to consider the impact on the estimated cash flows to determine whether an impairment loss should be recognised. [*IAS 39.59*]

7I.6.410.20   Indicators that a financial asset or a group of financial assets may be impaired include:
- significant financial difficulty of the borrower or the issuer;
- breach of contract, such as default or delinquency in interest or principal payments (payment defaults);
- it becoming probable that the borrower or issuer will enter bankruptcy or other financial reorganisation;
- renegotiation of the terms of an asset because of financial difficulty of the borrower or issuer, including granting a concession to the borrower or issuer;
- disappearance of an active market for a financial asset because of financial difficulties; and

- observable data indicating a measurable decrease in the estimated future cash flows from a group of financial assets since their initial recognition, although the decrease cannot yet be identified with the individual assets in the group. [*IAS 39.59*]

7I.6.410.30   For example, for loans to investment property vehicles or property developers, repayment of principal or interest may be dependent on the income from or value of real estate – e.g. rental income may be used to pay interest, and the repayment of principal may be dependent on the sale or refinancing of the property. Adverse changes in property markets and property-specific factors – e.g. loss or bankruptcy of tenants, development delays or cost overruns – may represent an impairment trigger for property-based lending.

7I.6.410.40   Loss events arising from significant financial difficulty of the borrower or the issuer often occur before any actual payment default on the financial asset.

7I.6.410.50   For the purpose of identifying loss events, IAS 39 does not limit the description of breach of contract or default or delinquency to only 90 or 180 days past due. These terms – i.e. breach of contract or default or delinquency – may encompass other breaches of contract (e.g. covenants), including any failure of the debtor to pay when due.

7I.6.410.60   A change in credit rating is not of itself evidence of impairment. However, it may be evidence of impairment when it is considered with other available information, such as one of the indicators noted in 7I.6.410.20. In addition, when evaluating evidence of impairment an entity takes into account:
- information about the debtor's/issuer's liquidity and solvency;
- trends for similar financial assets; and
- local economic trends and conditions. [*IAS 39.60, IG.E.4.1*]

7I.6.410.70   Similarly, in our view a commitment to sell a financial asset measured at amortised cost at an amount below its amortised cost is not of itself evidence of impairment, but may be evidence of impairment when it is considered with other available information. We believe that whether such an asset is impaired and the measurement of impairment should be based on the general impairment guidance discussed in this section, focusing on the cash flows that the asset will generate. It would not be appropriate to simply write the asset down to the expected selling price or to recognise a gain or loss on sale before derecognition of the asset. In addition, an entity should assess whether a contractual agreement to sell a financial asset at a future date is a regular-way sale (see 7I.2.70) or whether it should be accounted for as a derivative in the scope of IAS 39 (see 7I.2.10).

7I.6.410.80   Although a loan measured at amortised cost is not in the scope of the measurement requirements of IFRS 5, it may be in the scope of its presentation requirements if it meets the criteria for classification as held-for-sale at the reporting date (see 5.4.20.20). [*IFRS 5.2, 5*]

7I.6.420   *Debt instruments*

7I.6.420.10   A debt instrument is impaired if there is an indication that a loss event that has happened since initial recognition has an impact on the estimated future cash flows. A decline in the fair value of a debt instrument because of changes in market interest rates is not in itself an indication of impairment. For example, the fair value of a fixed rate debt security would decrease if market interest rates increased. This is not evidence of impairment if the future contractual cash flows associated with the debt security are still expected to be received. [*IAS 39.59–60*]

7I.6.420.20   A debt instrument may be acquired at a deep discount that reflects incurred credit losses (see also 7I.8.170.20). If the carrying amount of the debt instrument is subsequently adjusted upwards because of improved recoverability, and then adjusted downwards again because of reduced recoverability, then there is an issue about whether the downwards adjustment is an impairment loss (see 7I.6.260).

EXAMPLE 11 – IMPAIRMENT LOSS – DEBT INSTRUMENTS

7I.6.420.30   An impaired debt instrument with a nominal principal of 100 was initially recognised by Company R at its fair value of 70 on acquisition. Its carrying amount (amortised cost) was subsequently increased to 80 under the effective interest method to reflect revised estimated cash flows arising from increased recoverability. The carrying amount of the debt instrument was subsequently reduced to 75 because of further revisions to estimated cash flows as a result of reduced recoverability.

7I.6.420.40   In our view, two approaches to the presentation of this downward adjustment are possible.
- Recognise an adjustment of 5 to interest or other income (see 7I.6.260) on the basis that the reduced recoverability was not below that expected on initial recognition of the debt instrument; therefore, it can be argued that such a decline does not represent a loss event that has happened since initial recognition. This analysis is based on the premise that for a loss event to happen subsequent to initial recognition, it has to reduce the expected cash flows below those expected on initial recognition.
- Recognise an impairment loss of 5 on the basis that a loss event has happened in the period since the initial recognition of the debt instrument. [*IAS 39.AG8*]

7I.6.430   *Equity instruments*

7I.6.430.10   For equity instruments, impairment cannot be identified based only on analysing cash flows considering the indicators in 7I.6.410. Additionally, if there has been a significant or prolonged decline in the fair value of an equity instrument below its cost, then this is considered objective evidence of impairment. In our view, there is no basis for overriding this evidence in the light of qualitative factors. [*IAS 39.61, IG.E.4.10, IU 07-09*]

7I.6.430.20   For an equity instrument denominated in a foreign currency, the assessment of significant or prolonged decline in fair value is made in the functional currency of the holder of the instrument because this is consistent with how any impairment loss is determined. [*IU 07-09*]

7I.6.430.30   In our view, in evaluating whether a decline in fair value is significant in periods after an impairment loss has been recognised, the extent of the decline should be evaluated in relation to the cost of the instrument, not its carrying amount at the date on which the last impairment loss was recognised. Similarly, in our view in evaluating whether the period of a subsequent decline in the fair value of equity instruments is prolonged, the period of the decline is the entire period for which fair value has been below cost and not just the period since the last impairment loss was recognised. Therefore, we believe that once a decline in fair value below cost has been recognised as an impairment, any subsequent further decline below the carrying amount at the date on which that impairment loss was recognised is also an impairment, even if the fair value had recovered since the original decline and regardless of whether the 'new' decline is significant or prolonged. [*IAS 39.61, IG.E.4.9*]

7I.6.430.35   However, in our view, for assessing whether a decline in fair value of an available-for-sale equity instrument that is or was a hedged item in a fair value hedging relationship is significant or prolonged, its cost should be adjusted for the effects of fair value hedge accounting – i.e. it should include the fair value gains and losses already recognised in profit or loss as a result of hedge accounting (see 7I.7.50). This is because we believe that adjustments to the carrying amount that are recognised in profit or loss (except for impairment losses) change the cost basis. This is consistent with the treatment of inventories and monetary amounts that have been fair value hedged. We believe that the adjusted cost should also be used for measuring the impairment loss (see 7I.6.530.50–80). [*IAS 39.89(b), IG.F.3.6*]

7I.6.430.40   In our view, an entity should establish criteria that it applies consistently to determine whether a decline in a quoted market price is significant or prolonged. IFRS does not contain any specific quantitative thresholds for 'significant' or 'prolonged'. In our view, for equity securities that are quoted in an active market, the general concepts of significance and materiality should apply. We believe that:
- a decline in excess of 20 percent should generally be regarded as significant; and
- a decline in a quoted market price that persists for nine months should generally be considered to be prolonged. However, it may be appropriate to consider a shorter period.

7I.6.430.50   In our view, apart from significant or prolonged thresholds, an entity can establish additional events triggering impairment. These can include, among other things, a combination of significant and prolonged thresholds based on the particular circumstances and nature of that entity's portfolio. For example, a decline in the fair value in excess of 15 percent persisting for six months could be determined by an entity to be an impairment trigger.

7I.6.430.60   However, in our view the combination of thresholds applied should result in a decline that is either significant or prolonged, under the guidance set out in 7I.6.430.40, being recognised as impairment.

7I.6.430.70   In our view, if a decline in fair value is significant or prolonged, then there is objective evidence of impairment and an impairment loss should be recognised, regardless of how long management intends to hold the investment. Therefore, if there has been a significant or prolonged decline in the market price at the reporting date, then an impairment loss should be recognised, even if the prospects of recovery are good.

7I.6.430.80   A significant or prolonged decline in the fair value of an equity instrument below its cost that is in line with the overall level of decline in the relevant market does not mean that an entity can conclude the equity instrument is not impaired. [*IU 07-09*]

7I.6.430.90   Once it has been concluded that there has been a significant or prolonged decline, an impairment may not be reversed. A subsequent change in market value normally reflects circumstances that have arisen subsequently.

7I.6.430.100   In the case of shares in an investment fund, it is likely that a decrease in the fair value of an investment fund arises from an impairment of at least some of the underlying assets held by the fund. However, in our view an interest in an investment fund should be evaluated based on the fair value of the investment fund itself rather than on the underlying investments held by the fund, because there are some risks that can be evaluated only by considering the investment fund as a whole.

7I.6.430.110   Even if a decline in fair value is neither significant nor prolonged, it is still necessary to consider other objective evidence that may indicate impairment. This requires an assessment of the indicators described in 7I.6.430.50, as well as significant adverse changes in the technological, market, economic or legal environment in which the issuer operates that indicate that the cost of the investment may not be recovered. In our experience, additional indicators of impairment of equity securities may include:

- a decline in the fair value of the equity instrument that seems to be related to issuer conditions rather than to general market or industry conditions;
- market and industry conditions, to the extent that they influence the recoverable amount of the financial asset – e.g. if the fair value at the date of acquisition had been extremely high because of a market level that is unlikely to be recovered in the future, then this may be an impairment indicator arising from pure market and/or industry conditions;
- a declining relationship of market price per share to net asset value per share at the date of evaluation compared with the relationship at acquisition;
- a declining price/earnings ratio at the time of evaluation compared with that at the date of acquisition;
- financial conditions and near-term prospects of the issuer, including any specific adverse events that may influence the issuer's operations;
- recent losses of the issuer;
- a qualified independent auditor's report on the issuer's most recent financial statements;
- negative changes in the dividend policy of the issuer, such as a decision to suspend or decrease dividend payments; and
- realisation of a loss on subsequent disposal of the investment. [*IAS 39.61*]

7I.6.430.120   In our view, this assessment should be performed for all equity securities whose fair value is below cost, but for which the decline in fair value is not considered significant or prolonged. In our view, the higher or longer the entity's thresholds for determining whether a decline is significant or prolonged, the more comprehensive the qualitative evaluation needs to be. [*IAS 39.61*]

7I.6.430.130   Generally, we would expect an equity security to become impaired earlier than a debt security issued by the same counterparty because of the nature of each instrument and the rights each conveys to its holder.

7I.6.440   *Portfolios of assets*

7I.6.450   *Determining cost*

7I.6.450.10   IFRS is silent on how to determine the cost of financial assets when they are part of a homogeneous portfolio. Therefore, an entity should develop an accounting policy applying the hierarchy for selecting accounting policies (see 2.8.20). In our view, the guidance on cost formulas for inventories should be applied (see 3.8.280). Therefore, any reasonable cost allocation method – i.e. average cost or first-in, first-out – may be used and applied consistently. However, an entity is not precluded from using specific identification if it is able to identify the costs of the specific assets.

7I.6.450.20   In our view, the entity should apply the same cost allocation accounting policy both for assessing and measuring impairment losses and for determining the cost of the financial assets sold (see 7I.5.280.60).

71.6.460   *Evidence of decrease in estimated cash flows*

71.6.460.10   A decrease in the estimated future cash flows from a group of financial assets usually indicates impairment of that group of assets. Evidence of a decrease in estimated cash flows from a group of assets includes:

- an adverse change in the payment status of borrowers in the group – e.g. an increased number of customers exceeding their credit limit or not making payments on time; or
- a change in national or local economic conditions that is likely to cause higher defaults on payments. [*IAS 39.59(f)*]

71.6.470   **Impairment loss calculations**

71.6.470.10   If there is objective evidence that a financial asset is impaired, then the entity determines the amount of any impairment loss. The measurement of the impairment loss differs for assets carried at amortised cost or cost, and available-for-sale financial assets. For assets carried at amortised cost, impairment is measured based on incurred credit losses using the instrument's original effective interest rate (see 71.6.480.10). However, for available-for-sale financial assets an impairment loss is calculated based on fair value, which reflects market interest rates and market expectations of expected future, as well as incurred, credit losses. [*IAS 39.63, 67–68, IG.E4.2*]

71.6.470.20   For assets carried at amortised cost, an impairment loss may be recognised by writing down the asset or recording an allowance to be deducted from the carrying amount of the asset. [*IAS 39.63*]

71.6.480   *Loans and receivables and held-to-maturity investments*

71.6.480.10   In calculating an impairment loss for a financial asset (or a group of financial assets) carried at amortised cost, an entity uses the financial asset's *original* effective interest rate to discount the estimated future cash flows. In determining the original effective interest rate, an entity takes into account the following.

- For a variable rate financial asset, the discount rate used is the current effective interest rate(s) determined under one of the approaches in 71.6.270.30. This rate might comprise a variable benchmark interest rate plus/minus a fixed margin – e.g. three-month LIBOR plus 40 basis points. In other words, the appropriate current effective interest rate considers changes of the variable benchmark interest rate, but the original credit risk spread is held constant.
- When a financial asset has been reclassified out of the available-for-sale category to loans and receivables (see 71.4.250.20) or out of the FVTPL category (see 71.4.220.60), a new original effective interest rate is calculated based on the expected future cash flows as at the reclassification date. This effective interest rate would be adjusted if the entity, subsequent to reclassification, increases its estimates of future cash receipts as a result of increased recoverability of those cash receipts (see 71.6.260.20).
- When the financial asset is the hedged item in a fair value hedge, the original effective interest rate is adjusted to take account of recognised changes in fair value attributable to the hedged risk (see 71.6.530.40).
- If the terms of a loan, receivable or held-to-maturity investment are renegotiated or modified because of financial difficulties of the borrower or issuer, then impairment is measured using the original effective interest rate before the modification of the terms. [*IAS 39.AG84, IU 07-10*]

7I.6.480.20   An impairment loss for financial assets measured at amortised cost is the difference between the asset's carrying amount and the present value of the estimated future cash flows discounted at the asset's original effective interest rate (see 7I.6.480.10). The estimated future cash flows include only those credit losses that have been incurred at the time of the impairment loss calculation – i.e. it is an 'incurred-loss model'. Losses expected as a result of future events, no matter how likely, are not taken into account. This is particularly relevant when financial assets are assessed for impairment collectively. [*IAS 39.59, 63*]

7I.6.480.30   The asset's original effective interest rate (see 7I.6.480.10) is used in calculating the impairment loss because discounting at the current market rate of interest would, in effect, impose fair value measurement on the financial asset. This would not be appropriate because such assets are measured at amortised cost. The aim of this requirement is to recognise losses arising from changes in expected cash flows as a result of loss events happening after initial recognition, not to reflect changes in the value of the asset because of changes in credit spreads or market interest rates. However, as a practical expedient, a creditor may measure impairments on the basis of an instrument's fair value using an observable market price. [*IAS 39.63, AG84*]

7I.6.480.40   The process for estimating the amount of an impairment loss may result in a single amount or in a range of possible amounts. In the latter case, an entity recognises an impairment loss equal to the best estimate within the range taking into account all relevant information available before the financial statements are authorised for issue about conditions existing at the reporting date. [*IAS 39.AG86*]

7I.6.480.50   Estimates of future cash flows may depend on an entity's approach to managing impaired loans – e.g. collection policies, workout strategies, forbearance practices, anticipated debt restructurings and foreclosure practices. Therefore, changes in the entity's approach to managing impaired loans may lead to changes in these estimates and in the amounts of recognised impairment. If changes in the entity's approach occur, then an entity discloses such changes along with any material effect on financial performance. [*IFRS 7.7, 33, IAS 8.39*]

7I.6.480.60   Although actual or contemplated changes in collection plans and strategies may have a significant effect on best estimates of impairment, it is unlikely that possible changes in collection plans and strategies that are not yet contemplated by management would have a significant effect on current best estimates of impairment, unless management's current plans and strategies are unrealistic. However, an entity considers whether the expected continuation of plans and strategies is an assumption about the future or other source of estimation uncertainty at the reporting date that should be disclosed in accordance with paragraph 125 of IAS 1 – i.e. one that has a significant risk of resulting in a material adjustment to the carrying amounts of assets and liabilities within the next reporting period (see 2.8.120.10). [*IAS 1.125*]

7I.6.490   *Actual or expected restructuring of impaired assets*

7I.6.490.10   When a debtor is in financial difficulties, the debtor and its creditors may negotiate a restructuring of some or all of the debtor's obligations to allow the debtor sufficient capacity to service the debt or refinance the contract, either entirely or partially. Such circumstances are often referred to as 'forbearance'. Examples of forbearance practices include reducing interest rates, delaying payment of principal and amending covenants. As discussed in 7I.6.410.20, renegotiation of the terms of a financial asset because of financial difficulty of the debtor is an indicator that the asset may be impaired. For assessing and measuring impairment, the lender considers the impact of the modified terms on the estimated future cash flows of the financial asset.

7I.6.490.13   It cannot simply be assumed without appropriate evidence that a forborne exposure will perform in accordance with the modified terms. This may be unlikely if the borrower is in financial difficulties and there is no reduction in the present value of the contractual cash flows. [*IAS 39.IG.E.4.3*]

7I.6.490.15   Also, forborne exposures may display different credit risk characteristics from non-forborne exposures – e.g. increased propensity to future default – that would indicate that they need to be segregated for impairment purposes.

7I.6.490.20   As noted in 7I.6.480.10, if the terms of a financial asset measured at amortised cost are renegotiated or modified because of financial difficulties of the borrower or issuer, then impairment is measured using the original effective interest rate before the modification. However, in our view if an existing financial asset is replaced with a new financial asset and the cash flows of the two instruments are substantially different, then the contractual rights to cash flows from the original financial asset should be deemed to have expired; in this case, the original financial asset is derecognised and the new financial asset is recognised and initially measured at fair value (see 7I.5.95). We believe that the same analysis is applicable regardless of whether the legal form of the transaction is the cancellation of the existing debt instrument in exchange for a new debt instrument of the debtor or the modification of the terms of the existing debt instrument. Accordingly, if a renegotiation or modification of terms of an existing financial asset is such that the cash flows of the modified asset are substantially different from those of the original unmodified asset, then the original financial asset is derecognised and the modified financial asset is recognised as a new financial asset and initially measured at fair value. [*IAS 39.17, AG84*]

7I.6.490.30   In our view, these principles also impact the measurement of impairment of a financial asset carried at amortised cost if it is expected that a restructuring relating to the debtor's financial difficulty will be effected.
- If the expected restructuring will not result in derecognition of the existing asset, then the estimated cash flows arising from the modified financial asset are included in the measurement of the existing asset based on their expected timing and amounts discounted at the original effective interest rate of the existing financial asset.
- If the expected restructuring will result in derecognition of the existing asset, then the expected fair value of the new asset is treated as the final cash flow from the existing financial asset at the time of its derecognition. This amount is discounted from the expected date of derecognition to the reporting date using the original effective interest rate of the existing financial asset. [*IAS 39.17, AG84*]

EXAMPLE 12 – IMPAIRMENT LOSS – EXPECTED RESTRUCTURING RESULTS IN DERECOGNITION

7I.6.490.40   At 31 December 2018, Company S has a loan asset with an amortised cost of 1,000 and an effective interest rate of 10% a year. The borrower is in financial difficulties. S expects that it will participate in a debt restructuring in six months' time that will involve a substantial modification to the cash flows receivable under the loan agreement, including a 50% reduction in the principal amount, a reduction in the contractual interest rate and a substantial extension of maturity. S expects that the fair value of the new loan at the time of the restructuring will be 300.

71.6.490.50   As a result, S measures the existing financial asset at approximately 286 (i.e. 300 / (1 + 10%)$^{6/12}$) at 31 December 2018. If the restructuring proceeds in the manner expected on 30 June 2019, then any difference between the actual fair value of the new loan and the previous estimate of 300 would give rise to an additional impairment loss or a reversal of the impairment loss in 2019.

71.6.500   *Available-for-sale financial assets*

71.6.500.10   For financial assets measured at fair value, impairment is relevant only for those classified as available-for-sale because changes in fair value are generally recognised in OCI rather than in profit or loss. For such assets, when there is objective evidence of impairment, the cumulative loss that had been recognised in OCI is reclassified from equity to profit or loss. Furthermore, once an investment in equity instruments has been impaired, all subsequent losses are recognised in profit or loss until the asset is derecognised. [*IAS 39.67, IG.E.4.9*]

71.6.500.20   In the case of an equity instrument included in the available-for-sale category, the cumulative loss referred to in 71.6.500.10 is the difference between the acquisition cost (see 71.6.450.10 and 530) and the current fair value of the instrument, less any impairment loss on that equity instrument previously recognised in profit or loss. In the case of a debt instrument included in the available-for-sale category, the cumulative loss is the difference between the amortised cost – i.e. the acquisition cost net of principal repayments and amortisation – and the current fair value of the instrument, less any impairment loss on that debt instrument previously recognised in profit or loss. [*IAS 39.68*]

71.6.500.30   Any previous net upward revaluation recognised in OCI for the asset is reversed first. Any additional write-down below the initial amount recognised for the asset is recorded as an impairment loss in profit or loss. [*IAS 39.68*]

71.6.500.40   If the asset was previously revalued through OCI to an amount below the carrying amount on initial recognition, then the cumulative loss that had been recognised in OCI for that asset is reclassified from equity and recognised as an impairment loss in profit or loss. The entire amount of the revaluation below acquisition cost is recognised as an impairment loss even if the estimated cash flows indicate that some of that decline is reversible. [*IAS 39.68*]

71.6.500.50   The implementation guidance to IAS 39 acknowledges that the available-for-sale revaluation reserve in equity may become negative. This may happen through the remeasurement to fair value of available-for-sale assets and is not necessarily an indication that the available-for-sale asset is impaired and that the cumulative net loss that has been recognised in OCI should be reclassified to profit or loss. IAS 39 contains detailed guidance on indicators of impairment and assessing a decline in the fair value as evidence of impairment. [*IAS 39.59–61, IG.E.4.10*]

71.6.510   *Subsequent impairment of available-for-sale debt instruments*

71.6.510.10   IAS 39 does not explicitly address the accounting treatment of a subsequent further decline in the fair value of an impaired available-for-sale debt instrument when there is no objective evidence of any further credit-related loss event. In our view, an entity should choose an accounting policy, to be applied consistently, to recognise such further declines either in OCI or in profit or loss. For a discussion of the possible inter-relationship with the entity's accounting policy for reversals of impairment losses on available-for-sale debt instruments, see 7I.6.660.50. Before applying an accounting policy to recognise such a further decline in OCI, an entity should first consider all available evidence to determine whether the further decline in fair value is objective evidence of a further credit-related loss event, including consideration of the magnitude and duration of the subsequent loss. If there is objective evidence of a further credit-related loss event, then the further decline in fair value is recognised in profit or loss.

7I.6.520 *Assets measured at cost because fair value not reliably measurable*

7I.6.520.10   For financial assets measured at cost because their fair value is not reliably measurable – i.e. certain unquoted equity instruments and derivatives linked to such instruments (see 7I.6.210) – the impairment loss is measured as the difference between the carrying amount and the present value of estimated future cash flows discounted at the current market rate of return for a similar financial asset. [*IAS 39.66*]

7I.6.530 *Hedged assets*

7I.6.530.10   The principles for hedge accounting do not override the accounting treatment under IAS 36 or IAS 39 if there is impairment of the hedged item. Therefore, if a hedged item is impaired, then this impairment is recognised even if the risk that causes the impairment is being hedged and hedge accounting is being applied. However, the hedge accounting principles may require a gain on a hedging instrument used to hedge the risk that gave rise to the impairment to be recognised simultaneously in profit or loss and offset (partly) against the recognised impairment. In a fair value hedge, in our view, the cost basis of the hedged item used for measuring the impairment loss should be adjusted for the effects of the hedge accounting – i.e. it should include the fair value gains and losses already recognised in profit or loss as a result of hedge accounting (see 7I.6.530.40–50). [*IAS 39.58*]

EXAMPLE 13 – IMPAIRMENT LOSS – CASH FLOW HEDGE OF EXPECTED SALE OF ASSETS

7I.6.530.20   Company T holds a portfolio of securities that are classified as available-for-sale. The cost of the portfolio is 300. T has an option to put the securities to a third party for a fixed price of 250. T may apply hedge accounting to this transaction provided that the hedging relationship meets the relevant criteria (see 7I.7.120). T designates the option as a hedge of the cash flows from an expected future sale of the securities, with the hedged risk being the elimination of the variability in cash flows arising from the price of the securities going below 250.

7I.6.530.25   The fair value of the portfolio subsequently decreases by 120 and there is objective evidence of impairment. The amount of the impairment, which is recognised in profit or loss, is the difference between the cost of the securities (300) and the fair value (180), irrespective of whether T has hedged the downside risk on the cash flows from an expected sale using an option. However, because at this point the impairment on the hedged item affects profit or loss, the related gain on the put option would also be recognised in profit or loss. This means that a gain of 70 (250 - 180), ignoring time value, will be recognised in profit or loss and will partly offset the impairment loss on the securities. [*IAS 39.100*]

71.6.530.30   For cash flow hedges of highly probable acquisitions of financial and non-financial assets, amounts previously recognised in OCI may be reclassified from equity to profit or loss when the asset affects profit or loss. For non-financial assets, this is possible only if the accounting policy is not to apply a basis adjustment for such items. If such an asset is impaired, then an appropriate amount of the gain or loss previously recognised in OCI is reclassified from equity to profit or loss. [*IAS 39.97–98*]

71.6.530.40   In a fair value hedge of a debt instrument, both the original effective interest rate (see 71.6.480.10) and the amortised cost of the hedged item are adjusted to take account of recognised changes in fair value attributable to the hedged risk. The adjusted effective interest rate is calculated using the adjusted carrying amount of the debt instrument. The impairment loss is the difference between the carrying amount of the asset after any adjustments as a result of applying hedge accounting, and the estimated future cash flows of the hedged item discounted at the adjusted effective interest rate. [*IAS 39.IG.E.4.4*]

71.6.530.50   In a fair value hedge of an available-for-sale equity instrument, we believe that for measuring the impairment loss, the cost of the asset should be adjusted for the effects of the fair value hedge accounting (see 71.6.430.35).

EXAMPLE 14 – IMPAIRMENT LOSS – AVAILABLE-FOR-SALE EQUITY INSTRUMENT THAT IS A HEDGED ITEM IN FAIR VALUE HEDGE

71.6.530.60   At 1 January 2017, Company U purchased a foreign currency available-for-sale equity instrument for 100 in U's functional currency. The foreign currency risk is hedged in a fair value hedge using a derivative instrument. At 31 December 2017, the fair value of the equity instrument was 200. The entire increase in the fair value of the equity instrument of 100 was a result of the change in the exchange rate. There were no changes to the instrument's quoted market price in the foreign currency. The fair value of the hedging instrument was a liability of 100. Therefore, U recognised a gain of 100 for the equity instrument, and an offsetting loss of 100 for the derivative, both in profit or loss.

71.6.530.70   At 31 December 2018, the fair value of the equity instrument is 120. The entire decrease in the fair value of the equity instrument of 80 is a result of a decline in the instrument's quoted market price in the foreign currency by 40%. There are no changes in the exchange rate during 2018 and there is no change in the fair value of the hedging instrument at 31 December 2018.

71.6.530.80   In our view, for assessing and measuring impairment at 31 December 2018, U should compare the acquisition cost adjusted for the effect of the fair value hedge (i.e. 200) with the current fair value of 120. Therefore, F recognises an

impairment loss of 80 at 31 December 2018, as a result of the significant decline in the fair value of the investment below its cost.

7I.6.540 *Collateral*

7I.6.540.10   If the entity holds collateral for a financial asset, and the collateral does not qualify for recognition as a separate asset under other standards, then the collateral is not recognised as an asset separate from the impaired financial asset before foreclosure because this would result in double counting. [*IAS 39.AG84, IG.E.4.8*]

7I.6.540.20   In our view, the accounting treatment of collateral after foreclosure is dependent on the legal environment in which the entity operates and the terms on which the collateral is provided. For example, in the case of a mortgage loan collateralised by a property, two distinct sets of circumstances could apply.

- The bank (lender) could repossess the property as a result of the borrower's default with the intention of recovering the amounts owing on the understanding that: any amounts received in excess of the mortgage balance will be refunded to the borrower; and any shortfall remains the obligation of the borrower. The bank may continue to charge interest on the outstanding balance. The bank remains exposed to interest rate risk on the mortgage and is not exposed directly to property price risk. We believe that repossession is used only to reinforce the bank's contractual right to cash flows from the loan and consequently the bank should continue to recognise the loan and should not recognise the property.
- The bank could repossess the property, which in terms of the contract comprises the full and final settlement of the mortgage – i.e. the bank retains any excess proceeds over the outstanding balance on the mortgage and the borrower is released from its obligation in the event of a shortfall. Therefore, the bank is directly exposed to property price risk rather than to interest rate risk on the loan and we believe that the bank should derecognise the loan and recognise the property.

7I.6.540.30   If a financial asset carried at amortised cost is secured by collateral that is not accounted for separately from that financial asset, then in calculating the impairment loss for that financial asset an entity could choose to use either of the following approaches, whether or not foreclosure is probable.

- *Approach 1:* Use the fair value of the collateral at the reporting date less costs for obtaining and selling the collateral.
- *Approach 2:* Use the cash flows that may result from foreclosure less the costs for obtaining and selling the collateral. [*IAS 39.AG84, IG.E.4.8*]

7I.6.540.40   Under Approach 1 in 7I.6.540.30, in determining the cash flows from the collateral an entity uses the current fair value of the collateral at the reporting date, assuming that this current fair value will be realised in the future, and then discounts this current fair value back from the expected future date of realisation to the reporting date using the financial asset's original effective interest rate (see 7I.6.480.10). Under Approach 2 in 7I.6.540.30, in determining the cash flows from the collateral an entity estimates the fair value of the collateral at the expected future date of realisation of the collateral and then discounts this value back to the reporting date using the financial asset's original effective interest rate (see 7I.6.480.10).

7I.6.540.41   Applying either Approach 1 or Approach 2 in measuring impairment is conditional on the entity having the legal ability to enforce the collateral and obtain the proceeds of its realisation in the event of the debtor's default. Also, the entity needs to consider the nature and length of any enforcement procedures required under applicable laws and regulations in determining the expected future date of realisation.

7I.6.540.43   In some cases, observable quoted forward prices for collateral may exist, especially for financial collateral. However, forward prices for financial collateral would generally reflect a premium or discount to the current market price – i.e. a spot price – with the premium or discount reflecting benchmark interest rates that would often be below the asset's original effective interest rate. Therefore, for the purpose of estimating the cash flows from the collateral – i.e. Approach 2 in 7I.6.540.30 – such prices that do not include a risk premium would not support inflation of estimated future values based on a projected rate of return for the collateral that includes a risk premium.

7I.6.540.45   In our experience, lenders often realise collateral at a discount to appraised values and expected discounts on the realisation of collateral are reflected in the measurement of impairment.

EXAMPLE 15 – IMPAIRMENT LOSS – USE OF CURRENT FAIR VALUE OF COLLATERAL

7I.6.540.50   Bank V issued a mortgage loan of 1,000, which is collateralised by the financed residential property. At the reporting date, V identified objective evidence of impairment and estimated that the only cash flows to be received will arise from the foreclosure of the collateral. The current fair value of the collateral is estimated at 1,000. It will take V two years to foreclose the collateral and during this period no other cash flows are expected.

7I.6.540.55   In our view, if V elects to use the current fair value of the collateral in determining cash flows from the collateral for computing the impairment loss, then V should discount the current fair value of the collateral (i.e. 1,000) from the expected future date of realisation back to the reporting date using the loan's original effective interest rate (see 7I.6.480.10). The impairment loss recognised would be the difference between the loan's carrying amount and the net present value of the estimated future cash flows.

7I.6.540.60   When measuring an impairment loss incurred on a financial asset denominated in the entity's functional currency but collateralised by an asset denominated in a foreign currency, in our view the estimated foreign currency future cash flows resulting from the foreclosure of the collateral should be translated into the functional currency of the reporting entity using the appropriate forward rates and then discounted together with the estimated cash flows in the functional currency, if there are any, using the instrument's original effective interest rate (see 7I.6.480.10).

7I.6.540.70   When an entity is calculating the impairment loss for a collateralised financial asset, in our view a gain should not be recognised, even if the collateral is expected to have a higher value than the carrying amount of the loan, if any surplus will be returned to the borrower.

7I.6.540.80   On the date of foreclosure, in our view any collateral received should be initially measured based on the carrying amount of the defaulted loan. Thereafter, it should be accounted for under the relevant standard and classified as held-for-sale if appropriate (see 5.4.20).

7I.6.550   *Measuring impairment of financial assets denominated in foreign currency*

7I.6.550.10   For monetary financial assets denominated in a foreign currency, there is no specific guidance on how to measure impairment losses. In our view, the present value of estimated future cash flows or fair value of the asset should be first determined in the foreign currency. This amount should be translated into the functional currency using the exchange rate at the date on which the impairment is recognised. The difference between the translated amount and the carrying amount in the functional currency should be recognised in profit or loss. In certain circumstances, this may lead to an impairment loss determined in the foreign currency and a foreign exchange gain on translation of the carrying amount of the financial asset into the functional currency.

7I.6.550.20   Foreign exchange gains and losses on an impaired monetary financial asset measured at amortised cost continue to be recognised in profit or loss. If, through a subsequent improvement in circumstances, an entity is able to reverse the impairment loss, in part or entirely, then in our view the reversal should be recognised at the spot exchange rate at the date on which the reversal is recognised. [*IAS 39.65*]

7I.6.550.30   For non-monetary financial assets classified as available-for-sale, the amount of loss to be removed from equity and included in profit or loss is the cumulative net difference between the asset's acquisition cost and current fair value in the functional currency. This will include all foreign currency changes on the asset that had been recognised in OCI, but not foreign currency changes that had been recognised in profit or loss as a result of applying fair value hedge accounting (see 7I.6.530.50). [*IAS 21.23, 39.68, IG.E.4.9*]

7I.6.550.40   In our view, an entity may record any subsequent reversal of impairment of a debt instrument classified as available-for-sale at the spot rate in effect on the date on which the reversal is recognised. Any subsequent reversal is limited to the amount of loss, denominated in foreign currency, previously recognised. In our view, until the previously recognised loss denominated in foreign currency is fully reversed, the related exchange differences should be recognised in profit or loss. As a minimum, the accounting treatment applied should be disclosed along with the nature and the amount of any impairment loss or reversal. [*IAS 39.70*]

7I.6.550.50   Generally, changes in foreign exchange rates would not trigger impairment for an investment in a debt instrument. However, there may be situations in which the fair value of an asset in its currency of denomination is affected by exchange rates. This may happen if there is a sudden and severe devaluation of a foreign currency. The devaluation of the currency may influence the credit risk and country risk associated with entities operating in that environment. In our view, an entity that has foreign currency loans or receivables or that holds debt securities denominated in a foreign currency that becomes devalued should consider whether the decline should be treated as an impairment loss rather than as a normal foreign exchange translation loss.

Impairment examples

EXAMPLE 16A – IMPAIRMENT LOSS CALCULATION – LOANS AND RECEIVABLES

7I.6.560.10   Bank W granted a loan (classified as loans and receivables) on 31 December 2015 to Company X. The interest rate on the loan was 10% and the loan was issued at 98% of its face value. The maturity date is 31 December 2020. The effective interest rate at the date of origination was 10.53%.

7I.6.560.20   At 31 December 2018, it becomes clear that X is experiencing severe financial difficulties and W determines that this represents objective evidence that the loan is impaired. At that date, the carrying amount of the loan at amortised cost is 4,954.

7I.6.560.30   W expects that it will receive the contractual interest payment of 10% due at 31 December 2019. However, on maturity of the loan, W expects to recover only 2,500 of the 5,000 principal due and does not expect to receive the interest payment due at 31 December 2020.

7I.6.560.40   The impairment loss is measured as the difference between the carrying amount of the loan and the present value of the estimated future cash flows on the loan, using as a discount rate the original effective interest rate of 10.53%. Given that only 2,500 of the principal and the 31 December 2019 interest payment are expected to be received, the present value at 31 December 2018 using the original effective interest rate is 2,499. In this example, accrued interest is paid at 31 December 2018 and therefore is not included in the calculation. The discounted remaining cash flows are calculated as follows.

$$2{,}499 \;=\; \frac{500}{1.1053} \;+\; \frac{2{,}500}{(1.1053)^2}$$

7I.6.560.50   An impairment loss of 2,455 (4,954 - 2,499) is recognised in profit or loss at 31 December 2018. W reassesses the impairment loss at each reporting date.

EXAMPLE 16B – IMPAIRMENT LOSS CALCULATION – AVAILABLE-FOR-SALE FINANCIAL ASSETS

7I.6.560.60   If the loan in Example 16A had been classified as available-for-sale, then the amount of the impairment loss would be measured as the difference between the acquisition cost of the loan, net of principal repayments and amortisation, and the current fair value of the loan.

7I.6.560.70   W calculates the fair value of the loan by obtaining the current market interest rate for loans similar to the loan under consideration and uses this to discount the estimated future cash flows of the loan. Assume that an effective interest rate of 12.5% would apply for loans to entities with similar credit risk profiles to X's and that have terms and structures similar to X's loan. W uses this rate to determine the fair value of the loan as follows.

$$2,420 \;=\; \frac{500}{1.125} \;+\; \frac{2,500}{(1.125)^2}$$

7I.6.560.80   The calculated fair value of 2,420 results in an impairment loss of 2,534 (4,954 - 2,420). This is the amount that is reclassified from equity to profit or loss. It is adjusted for any amount previously reclassified from equity to profit or loss.

EXAMPLE 16C – IMPAIRMENT LOSS CALCULATION – AVAILABLE-FOR-SALE FINANCIAL ASSETS COLLATERALISED BY LIQUID SECURITIES

7I.6.560.90   Assume the same information as in Examples 16A and 16B, except that the loan (classified as available-for-sale) is collateralised by liquid securities. W expects that it will be able to recover the amount owed on the loan only by taking legal possession of the securities.

7I.6.560.100   The fair value of the loan would not exceed the fair value of the securities less any costs expected to obtain and sell the securities (see 7I.6.540.30). The cumulative loss to be reclassified from equity to profit or loss is calculated as the difference between the loan's acquisition cost, net of principal repayments and amortisation, and the fair value calculated with reference to the collateral. However, the collateral itself is not recognised in W's statement of financial position until the securities meet the recognition criteria for financial assets.

7I.6.570   **Collective impairment assessment**

7I.6.580   *Determining whether individual or collective assessment is appropriate*

7I.6.580.10   For financial assets that are individually significant, the assessment is performed on an individual basis. For financial assets that are not individually significant, the assessment can be performed on an individual or collective (portfolio) basis. If an asset is assessed individually for impairment and found to be impaired, then it is not included in a collective assessment for impairment. [*IAS 39.64, AG88, IG.E.4.7*]

7I.6.580.20   IAS 39 does not provide specific guidance on determining whether a loan is individually significant. Instead, the standard indicates that the assessment of significance differs from one entity to another such that identical exposures will be evaluated on different bases, individually or collectively, depending on their significance to the entity holding them. In our view, an entity may use its normal loan review policies and procedures in determining what is considered a significant exposure. [*IAS 39.BC114*]

7I.6.580.30   A collective evaluation of impairment is performed for:

- assets that have not been assessed individually for impairment; and
- assets that are tested individually but for which no impairment is identified. [*IAS 39.64*]

7I.6.580.40   In our view, a collective evaluation of impairment for available-for-sale financial assets is not required.

7I.6.580.50   Impairment losses recognised on a collective basis represent an interim step pending the identification of impairment losses on individual assets in the group of financial assets that are collectively assessed for impairment. As soon as information is available that specifically identifies losses on individually impaired assets in a group, those assets are no longer included in the collective evaluation for impairment. [*IAS 39.AG88*]

7I.6.580.60   In the case of assets tested individually but not impaired, an entity might conclude that no collective provision is required, either because no portfolio of similar items can be identified (see 7I.6.580.80) or because all possible risks have been considered in the individual impairment tests.

7I.6.580.70   Loss probabilities and other loss statistics differ at a group level between assets that have been evaluated individually for impairment and found not to be impaired and assets that have not been assessed individually for impairment, with the result that a different amount of impairment loss may be required. [*IAS 39.64, AG87*]

7I.6.580.75   Therefore, in our view financial assets that have been assessed individually for impairment and found not to be impaired should generally be treated as one or more separate portfolios for the purposes of the collective assessment of impairment, based on the principle that financial assets should be grouped into homogeneous portfolios – i.e. based on similar credit risk characteristics. For example, if the underlying reason for not recording an impairment loss is sufficient collateral for some of those financial assets, and a change in the expected cash flow structure for the other financial assets, then those financial assets are not normally homogeneous because they do not share the same credit risk characteristics and therefore they should be treated as two separate portfolios. [*IAS 39.64, AG87, IG.E.4.7*]

7I.6.580.80   Assets are grouped for collective assessment for impairment only if they share similar credit risk characteristics. This may be identified based on:
- credit risk grades;
- types of loan;
- geographic location of the borrower;
- type of collateral;
- type of counterparty;
- aging profile; and
- maturity. [*IAS 39.AG87*]

7I.6.580.85   Loans that have been in arrears and returned to current status may have different risk characteristics – e.g. higher probability of subsequent default – than loans that have never been in arrears. This needs to be considered in the determination of collective impairment.

7I.6.580.90   In our view, a portfolio approach to impairment is not appropriate for individual equity instruments because equity instruments of different issuers do not have similar risk characteristics and therefore their equity price risk differs.

7I.6.590 *Impairment of reclassified assets*

7I.6.590.10   An entity may reclassify a financial asset from the available-for-sale category to loans and receivables (see 7I.4.250). If such a financial asset is subsequently impaired, then the gain or loss that was previously recognised in OCI is reclassified to profit or loss (see 7I.4.250.20). In our view, this requires the entity to assess whether each individual reclassified financial asset is impaired at each reporting date following reclassification. [*IU 07-10*]

7I.6.590.20   If an individual assessment does not result in the identification of impairment, then the entity includes that reclassified asset in a collective assessment of impairment if it is appropriate to do so (see 7I.6.580.60–70). If the entity identifies impairment on a collective basis, then in our view it is not necessary for the entity to reclassify from equity to profit or loss the full amount of loss recognised in OCI for the asset before reclassification.

7I.6.600 *Recognition of impairment losses incurred but not reported*

7I.6.600.10   IAS 39 requires the recognition of impairment for losses that have been 'incurred but not reported'. The objective of the collective assessment for impairment is to identify losses that have been incurred, but not yet identified, on an individual basis. [*IAS 39.AG89–AG90*]

7I.6.600.20   Of particular relevance to a collective assessment of impairment is the example of deaths of cardholders in a credit card portfolio, which is identified as the major cause of defaults. This example assumes that although the death rate may not change from year to year, it is reasonable to assume that some deaths have occurred and therefore that the portfolio contains assets that are impaired even if the impaired loans have not been identified individually. It is clear from IAS 39 that an unchanged death rate represents observable data supporting the estimate that one or more borrowers have died and that, based on experience, this will result in the loss of one or more cash flows. Because observable data includes unchanged data, there will normally be observable data that, through the passage of time, can be used to support estimates based on historical loss experience. [*IAS 39.AG90*]

7I.6.600.30   For a portfolio of loans, it may be more appropriate to refer to 'risk conditions' being in place as indicators of impairment, rather than 'impairment triggers', because triggers may not be specifically or individually identified or captured. Risk conditions represent a set of market and economic events or variables that are associated, based on historical evidence, with the impairment of financial assets.

7I.6.600.40   In our view, considering risk conditions rather than impairment triggers is consistent with the requirements in IAS 39 as long as each risk condition is associated with a combination of observable data that is relevant to losses in that portfolio and that has been observed in practice. In our view, it is not necessary to establish statistical cause-and-effect relationships between a change in a risk condition and an estimate of incurred losses. However, we believe that the number of risk conditions identified should be enough to make it possible to find a set of historical data that closely approximates the actual data that is observed at the reporting date. Over time, an entity should develop its database of observed risk conditions to improve and update its ability to match risk conditions with an estimate of incurred losses. [*IAS 39.AG89*]

7I.6.600.50   Future cash flows are estimated on the basis of historical loss experience for assets with similar credit risk characteristics. Not having its own specific historical data is not a sufficient rationale for an entity not to perform the collective impairment assessment. Relevant and reliable information available in the market should be obtained to perform the assessment. Entities that have no or insufficient entity-specific loss experience should use peer group experience for comparable groups of financial assets. Therefore, the historical data used, whether internal or external, should be consistent with the characteristics of the group of financial assets being tested. [*IAS 39.AG89, AG91*]

7I.6.600.60   We believe that the historical data used in the analysis should support the assessment of losses incurred but not reported and should:

- reflect the relationship between a change in the factor and impairment loss. These may be social drivers or economic factors; and
- be updated to reflect current economic conditions resulting in impairment losses recognised being directionally consistent with changes in related observable data from period to period.

7I.6.600.70   In our view, the practical implementation of the requirement to recognise impairment losses incurred but not reported on loans and receivables can be based on the analysis of historical loss data, together with the analysis of the underlying factors causing loss, and the emergence periods.

7I.6.610   *Emergence period*

7I.6.610.10   One of the possible methodologies for quantifying the collective allowance, or component thereof, is the 'emergence period' approach. This approach recognises that there will be a period between the occurrence of a specific impairment event and objective evidence of impairment becoming apparent on an individual basis. In other words, it is the time that it takes an entity to identify that the loss event actually happened or a time period that lapses between the date on which the loss event happened and the date on which an entity identified that it had happened. This period is referred to as the 'emergence period'.

7I.6.610.20   In our view, an emergence period should be established individually for each entity, each portfolio and/or possibly for each risk condition or combination thereof. Emergence periods may vary across entities and portfolios and according to the risk conditions.

7I.6.610.30   As a result, entities can use historical loss experience as an indicator of impairment provided that it can be linked to the factors (risk conditions) causing impairment loss – e.g. interest rates, unemployment rates, gross domestic product growth rate etc. Consequently, we believe that entities should recognise an impairment loss subsequent to the loan origination date if historical loss experience indicates that X percent of loans have become impaired as a result of the risk conditions in place and it takes an entity Y months (the emergence period) to identify which individual exposures became impaired. In our view, the emergence period should generally be relatively short, but this will depend on the entity's credit risk management policies and procedures, the nature of the portfolio being considered – e.g. consumer or commercial loans, credit card balances or mortgage loans – and the relevant risk conditions. We believe that it is unlikely that an emergence period will exceed 12 months.

7I.6.610.40   In the retail business, the emergence period might be the time period between the occurrence of a loss event and the default date (breach of contract), because the actual default of customers may be the only or most reliable way to identify a loss event.

7I.6.610.50   In our view, entities should justify and support their assessment of the emergence periods by back-testing them. However, this back-testing does not need to identify an exact time period elapsing between a loss event happening and a loss event being identified because this would require individual (specific) identification of loss events, which is impracticable in many circumstances. Instead, back-testing should test the reasonableness of the estimate made by management based on the identified loss factors. This should be reassessed when there is evidence that the loss events or customer behaviour or the entity's processes have changed. In our view, emergence periods should remain relatively stable, subject to the changes mentioned above, and any changes should be justified and disclosed.

7I.6.620   *Measuring collective impairment*

7I.6.620.10   The estimated future cash flows determined for assets carried at amortised cost assessed for impairment on a collective basis are discounted at a rate that approximates the original effective interest rate (see 7I.6.480.10). For portfolios of similar assets, these assets will have a range of interest rates and therefore judgement is necessary to determine a discounting methodology appropriate to that portfolio, which may result in using the average effective yield if it is a homogeneous portfolio. [*IAS 39.63, AG92*]

7I.6.620.20   The methodology used may include a 'risk migration' approach. Entities may use their historical risk migration data together with observable market data to support their assessment of losses incurred but not reported. However, a downgrade of an entity's credit rating is not in itself evidence of impairment, although it may be evidence of impairment when it is considered with other available information. Therefore, if a risk migration methodology is used, then in our view it should distinguish between migration data that evidences incurred losses and data that evidences expected future losses. [*IAS 39.60*]

7I.6.620.30   Although impairment losses can be determined using a portfolio methodology for groups of similar assets, this does not mean that an entity is allowed to take an immediate write-down on recognising a new financial asset. [*IAS 39.59, AG92, IG.E.4.2*]

7I.6.630   *Bad debts and loan losses*

7I.6.630.10   The following practices related to bad debt losses are not acceptable under IFRS.
- Recognising a provision for losses based on a set percentage of receivable balances having certain characteristics – e.g. according to the number of days overdue – rather than actual incurred losses, unless these percentages are validated using historical data.
- Recognising a loss for the gross expected shortfall on non-performing assets and suspending interest accruals. This is sometimes referred to as putting a loan on 'non-accrual status'.
- Recognising an impairment loss in excess of incurred losses calculated based on estimated cash flows, even if local regulations require a specific amount to be set aside ('general risk provisions'). In our view, if an entity wishes to identify reserves in addition to the impairment losses calculated under IFRS, then it may do so by transferring amounts from retained earnings to a separate category of equity – e.g. a loan loss reserve (see 7I.3.550.20). It is not acceptable to recognise any amounts in profit or loss or to reduce the carrying amount of the assets by more than the estimated actual loss. [*IAS 39.63, AG90–AG93, IG.E.4.2, IG.E.4.5–IG.E.4.6*]

71.6.640   **Reversals of impairment losses**

71.6.650   *Loans and receivables and held-to-maturity investments*

71.6.650.10   If in a subsequent period the amount of any impairment loss of a loan or receivable or held-to-maturity investment decreases because of an event happening subsequent to the write-down, then the previously recognised impairment loss is reversed through profit or loss, with a corresponding increase in the carrying amount of the underlying asset. The reversal is limited to an amount that does not state the asset at more than what its amortised cost would have been in the absence of impairment. [*IAS 39.65*]

71.6.660   *Available-for-sale financial assets*

71.6.660.10   Impairment losses on an available-for-sale equity instrument may not be reversed through profit or loss. Any increase in the fair value of such an instrument after an impairment loss has been recognised is treated as a revaluation and is recognised in OCI. [*IAS 39.69*]

71.6.660.20   If, in a subsequent period, the fair value of an available-for-sale debt instrument increases and the increase can be objectively related to an event happening after the impairment loss was recognised, then the impairment loss is reversed, with the amount of the reversal recognised in profit or loss. IAS 39 does not further describe the nature of an 'event' that gives rise to reversal of an impairment loss through profit or loss, nor does it discuss situations in which there continues to be some objective evidence of impairment but in which the amount of the impairment may be reduced. This raises two questions: what types of events trigger reversal; and how to measure the amount of any reversal? [*IAS 39.70*]

71.6.660.30   In our view, entities should choose an accounting policy, to be applied consistently, with regard to the nature of an event that would trigger reversal, as follows.
- An entity may limit reversals to reversals of credit events that gave rise to the impairment and that have a positive impact on the estimated future cash flows of the asset (Option 1).
- An entity may interpret reversal events as also including subsequent improvements in the credit standing of the issuer that do not affect the estimate of expected future cash flows from the asset, and then should specify criteria for identifying such events (Option 2).
- Alternatively, an entity may interpret reversal events also to include any event that reverses an amount that was included in the measurement of the original impairment (see 71.6.470.10). For example, to the extent that the original impairment loss included a decline in the fair value of the asset related to an increase in benchmark interest rates, a subsequent increase in the fair value related to a subsequent decline in benchmark interest rates would represent a reversal event (Option 3).

71.6.660.40   In developing their accounting policies, entities should also consider how to measure the amount of the impairment loss that is reversed through profit or loss when there is an increase in fair value and a reversal event has been identified.
- In our view, if there is no longer objective evidence that the asset is impaired at the reporting date, then, depending on its accounting policy under 71.6.660.30, the entity should reverse through profit or loss either (1) the full original impairment loss previously recognised in profit or loss; or (2) the lesser of the full original impairment loss previously recognised in profit or loss and the subsequent increase in fair value.

- In our view, if there continues to be objective evidence of impairment at the reporting date but the amount of the original impairment loss was reduced, then the cumulative loss that continues to be recognised in profit or loss should not be less than any excess of the original cost over the current fair value of the asset. When Option 3 as described in 7I.6.660.30 is applied and there is no improvement in the credit standing of the issuer, the amount of reversal is limited to the portion of the original impairment loss that actually has been reversed as a result of a subsequent decrease in benchmark interest rates (or another relevant factor).
- In our view, for the purpose of measuring the amount of impairment loss to be reversed, the original impairment loss as well as the subsequent increase in fair value should be reduced for any increase in the amortised cost of the debt instrument arising from interest accretion recognised in profit or loss subsequent to recognition of original impairment.

7I.6.660.50   The scenarios in the following example illustrate the application of these principles.

EXAMPLE 17 – IMPAIRMENT LOSS REVERSAL – AVAILABLE-FOR-SALE DEBT INSTRUMENTS

Scenario 1: Reversal when there is no longer any objective evidence of impairment

7I.6.660.60   Company Y buys an available-for-sale debt instrument for 100. The fair value of the instrument decreases to 70 and an impairment loss of 30 is recognised in profit or loss. Subsequently, the fair value of the instrument increases to 95, the amortised cost is 74 and Y determines that there is no longer any objective evidence of impairment.

7I.6.660.70   Depending on its chosen accounting policy, Y would either:
- recognise in profit or loss the reversal of 26, comprising the full amount of the original impairment loss of 30 less the subsequent increase of 4 in the amortised cost of the instrument, and record the current cumulative loss (the amount by which fair value is below original cost) of 5 in OCI; or
- recognise in profit or loss only 21 as a reversal of original impairment, being the subsequent increase in fair value of 25 less the subsequent increase of 4 in the amortised cost of the instrument.

Scenario 2: Reversal when there is a change in the liquidity/risk premium but no change in the estimated cash flows

7I.6.660.80   Company Z buys an available-for-sale debt instrument for 100. The fair value of the instrument decreases to 70 and an impairment loss of 30 is recognised in profit or loss. Z determines that this loss comprises the effect of a credit-related decrease in estimated future cash flows of 20 and the effect of an increase in the liquidity/risk premium of 10. Subsequently, the fair value of the instrument increases to 75 and the amortised cost to 72; there is no change in the estimated future cash flows and Z determines that the entire subsequent net increase in the fair value of 3, net of interest accretion of 2 recognised in profit or loss, relates to a subsequent reduction in the liquidity/risk premium.

71.6.660.90   Under Option 1 as described in 71.6.660.30, Z would recognise the subsequent net increase in fair value of 3 in OCI because there is no credit-related increase in expected future cash flows. Under Option 3, Z would recognise the net increase in fair value of 3 in profit or loss because there was a partial reversal of the increase in liquidity/risk premium that was included in the measurement of the original impairment loss. Under Option 2, the answer would depend on Company Z's policy for identifying improvements in the credit standing of the issuer.

Scenario 3: Reversal when there is only a change in the risk-free interest rate

71.6.660.100   Company B buys an available-for-sale debt instrument for 100. The fair value of the instrument decreases to 70 and an impairment loss of 30 is recognised in profit or loss. B determines that this loss comprises the effect of a credit-related decrease in future cash flows of 20 and the effect of an increase in the risk-free interest rate of 10. Subsequently, the fair value of the instrument increases to 85; there is no change in the estimated future cash flows and B determines that the entire subsequent increase in the fair value of 15 relates to a reduction in the risk-free interest rate. Assume that there is no interest accretion in the intervening period.

71.6.660.110   Under Options 1 and 2 as described in 71.6.660.30, B would record the subsequent increase in fair value in OCI because there is no credit-related increase in future cash flows and no other improvement in the credit standing of the issuer.

71.6.660.120   Under Option 3, B would record 10 of the increase in fair value in profit or loss because there was a reversal of the increase in the risk-free interest rate that was one of the events that was incorporated in the original impairment loss. B would not record the entire fair value increase of 15 related to the reduction in the risk-free rate in profit or loss because the amount of reversal is limited to the portion of the original impairment loss that actually has been reversed as a result of the subsequent decrease in the risk-free rate.

71.6.660.130   In our view, the accounting policy choices adopted for reversals of impairments do not necessitate the selection of particular accounting policies for subsequent impairments or vice versa. However, IAS 8 requires management to use its judgement in developing accounting policies that result in information that is, inter alia, neutral and prudent. Accordingly, entities should consider whether selection of policies that would lead to both (1) subsequent declines (losses) in the fair value of an impaired debt instrument arising from changes in interest rates and risk premiums being recognised in OCI; and (2) subsequent increases (gains) arising from the same cause, without any improvement in expected cash recoveries, being recognised in profit or loss would be consistent with these criteria.

71.6.670   *Assets carried at cost because fair value not reliably measurable*

71.6.670.10   For an investment in unquoted equity instruments and a derivative asset that is linked to and must be settled by delivery of such an instrument, both of which are carried at cost because their fair value cannot be measured reliably, impairment losses may not be reversed. [*IAS 39.66*]

Interim financial statements

7I.6.680.10   Under IFRS, an entity is prohibited from reversing an impairment loss, recognised in a previous interim period, for an available-for-sale equity instrument or a financial instrument carried at cost (not amortised cost). [*IFRIC 10.8*]

7I.6.690   **DIVIDEND INCOME**

7I.6.700   **Recognition of dividend income**

7I.6.700.10   IAS 39 defines dividends as distributions of profits to holders of equity investments in proportion to their holdings of a particular class of capital. Dividend income is recognised in profit or loss only when:

- the entity's right to receive payment is established;
- it is probable that the economic benefits associated with the dividend will flow to the entity; and
- the amount of the dividend can be measured reliably (see also 7I.3.600). [*IAS 39.9, 55A*]

7I.6.700.20   In our view, the shareholder's right to receive payment of dividends on *quoted* investments is normally established on the date on which the security trades ex-dividend. At this date, the fair value of the security decreases by approximately the dividend amount. Therefore, recognising a dividend on the ex-dividend date avoids double counting, which would happen if the dividend were included both as income and in the measurement of the fair value of the investment. The 'ex-dividend date' is the first date on which a sale of the instrument would not settle before the record date. The 'record date' is the date on which shareholders have to be included in the register of shareholders to receive the dividend. Calculation of the ex-dividend date will depend on local trading and settlement practices.

7I.6.700.30   In our view, for dividends on *unquoted* investments, a shareholder's right to receive payment is normally established when the shareholders have approved the dividends. However, if the relevant law provides that a board decision or announcement requires no further approval *and* is binding on the declaring entity, then the dividend would be recognised on a board decision or announcement (see 7I.3.600.20–30). When determining the fair value of such investments, care should be taken to avoid double counting dividends both as receivables and as part of the fair value estimate.

EXAMPLE 18 – DIVIDEND INCOME – TIMING OF RECOGNITION

7I.6.700.40   Company C's directors declare a dividend on 10 March. The dividend is approved by shareholders on 25 March and will be paid to shareholders of record – i.e. in the shareholders' register – on 31 March.

7I.6.700.50   If C's shares are listed in a market that has three-day settlement, then the shares would trade ex-dividend from 28 March (assuming that all are business days). Therefore, we believe that dividend income should be recognised on 28 March. If C's shares are not listed and the right to receive dividends is established when the shareholders have approved it, then we believe that the dividends should be recognised when they are approved – i.e. on 25 March. Thereafter, the dividends should be excluded when estimating the fair value of the shares.

71.6.710   Dividends from subsidiaries, associates and joint ventures

71.6.710.10   An entity recognises a dividend from a subsidiary, an associate or a joint venture in profit or loss in its separate financial statements when its right to receive the dividend is established. [*IAS 27.12*]

71.6.710.20   A subsidiary, associate or joint venture may make distributions to its shareholders in excess of its retained profits. A distribution that does not represent a distribution of profits would not meet the definition of dividends in IAS 39. However, in our view, even if the investment is accounted for as available-for-sale under IAS 39, an entity may choose an accounting policy, to be applied consistently, to recognise such distributions as dividend income in profit or loss (see 3.5.640.60) in its separate financial statements.

71.6.710.30   The receipt of such a distribution may be an indicator of impairment of the investment in the subsidiary, associate or joint venture (see 3.10.600.30).

71.6.720   Share dividends

71.6.720.10   In some cases, shareholders may receive or choose to receive dividends in the form of additional shares rather than cash. These may be referred to as 'scrip', 'stock' or 'share dividends'. In our view, the accounting treatment of share dividends depends on whether the investor has a cash alternative – i.e. a right to demand a cash payment representing the fair value of the shares.

71.6.720.20   In our view, the substance of share dividends with a cash alternative is the payment of a cash dividend, with reinvestment of the cash in additional shares. Therefore, we believe that dividend income should be recognised for the amount of the cash dividend alternative. The corresponding debit should be treated as an additional investment.

71.6.720.30   In other cases, an entity may receive bonus shares or other equity instruments on a pro rata basis with other ordinary shareholders with no cash alternative. Share investments are generally categorised as available-for-sale financial assets or as at FVTPL and measured at fair value (see 71.4.10). If all ordinary shareholders receive bonus shares or other equity instruments in proportion to their shareholdings, then the fair value of each shareholder's interest should be unaffected by the bonus issue. In our view, in such circumstances, dividends should not be recognised as revenue because it is not probable that there is an economic benefit associated with the transaction that will flow to the investor. [*IAS 39.55A, IU 01-10*]

71.6.720.40   If only certain shareholders are granted additional shares, then the fair value of the interests of those shareholders will increase. In this case, in our view it is most appropriate to measure the shares received at their fair value and recognise a corresponding amount of finance income.

71.6.730   FEE INCOME

71.6.730.10   The recognition of revenue for fees depends on the nature of the fees and the basis of accounting for any associated financial instrument. Fees that are an integral part of the effective interest rate of a financial instrument and fees on an instrument measured at FVTPL are in the scope of IAS 39. Other fees are in the scope of the revenue recognition requirements of IFRS 15 (see 4.2.10). [*IFRS 15.5, C9, BC28*]

7I.6.730.20   In most instances fees earned in relation to the recognition of a financial asset result in an adjustment of the effective interest rate. Examples of such fees include:
- origination or commitment fees – when it is probable that an entity will enter into a specific lending agreement;
- compensation from the borrower for transaction costs (see 7I.6.30) incurred by the lender; and
- appraisal fees for evaluating collateral – e.g. for mortgage loans. [*IAS 39.AG8B*]

7I.6.730.30   However, if the financial instrument is measured at FVTPL, then the fees are recognised as revenue on initial recognition of the instrument. [*IAS 39.AG8A*]

7I.6.730.40   Examples of financial service fees that are not an integral part of the effective yield of an associated financial instrument and are therefore recognised in accordance with IFRS 15 include:
- fees charged for servicing a loan;
- commitment fees to originate loans when it is unlikely that a specific lending arrangement will be entered into and the loan commitment is not measured at FVTPL;
- loan syndication fees received by an entity that arranges a loan and retains no part of the loan package for itself (or retains a part at the same effective interest rate for comparable risk as other participants);
- a commission earned on the allotment of shares to a client;
- placement fees for arranging a loan; and
- investment management fees. [*IAS 39.AG8C*]

7I.6.730.50   A contract with a customer that results in a recognised financial instrument in an entity's financial statements may be partially in the scope of IAS 39 and partially in the scope of IFRS 15. If this is the case, then the entity first applies IAS 39 to separate and measure the part of the contract that is in the scope of IAS 39 and then applies IFRS 15 to the residual. [*IFRS 15.7, C9*]

7I.6.730.60   In some cases, it may be difficult to determine whether an amount charged to a customer at inception of a loan represents a fee for structuring the loan or part of the transaction price for the financial asset – i.e. whether it is in the scope of IAS 39 or IFRS 15.

7I.6.730.70   For example, a bank may structure a transaction, using its expertise and experience ('intellectual capital') for a particular customer and facilitate the initial steps required – e.g. consultations with experts, valuations, registration and drafting legal documentation. The customer is charged a fee up front for the structuring service.

7I.6.730.80   An entity first applies IAS 39 to the transaction. If the fee is regarded as part of the transaction price for the loan, then the transaction price, net of the fee, would normally represent the best evidence of the fair value of the loan on initial recognition and IAS 39 would preclude recognition of revenue unless the entity determines that:
- the fair value of the loan on initial recognition differs from the transaction price; and
- the fair value is determined applying a valuation technique that uses only data from observable markets (see 7I.6.25). [*IAS 39.AG76*]

7I.6.730.90   In our view, an entity should recognise all or part of a structuring fee as revenue under IFRS 15 only if the fair value of the loan is determined using data from observable markets and if it can be demonstrated that the amount of revenue recognised is consistent with the effort and expertise provided for the structuring service – i.e. that it approximates fair value for the service provided.

EXAMPLE 19 – STRUCTURING FEE

7I.6.730.100   Bank B advances 50,000 as a loan to Customer C. B uses its expertise and experience in structuring the loan and charges C a structuring fee of 1,000. Therefore, the net amount advanced to C is 49,000. The fair value of the loan cannot be determined by applying a valuation technique that uses only data from observable markets.

7I.6.730.110   First, B applies IAS 39 to separate and measure the part of the contract that is in the scope of IAS 39. Because the fair value of the loan cannot be determined by applying a valuation technique that uses only data from observable markets, we believe that B should recognise the loan at its transaction price of 49,000. This results in no residual amount to which IFRS 15 is applied.

7I.6.730.120   Modifying the fact pattern, the fair value of the loan is 50,000 and it is determined by applying a valuation technique that uses only data from observable markets. In this case, we believe that B should recognise the loan at its fair value and the residual amount of 1,000 should be accounted for under IFRS 15.

7I.6.730.130   IFRS 7 requires the disclosure of fee income or expense arising from financial instruments that are not at FVTPL, and from trust or other fiduciary activities, other than for amounts included in the effective interest (see 7I.8.230). [*IFRS 7.20(c)*]

7I.7 Hedge accounting

7I.7 Hedge accounting

CURRENTLY EFFECTIVE REQUIREMENTS

In July 2014, the IASB issued IFRS 9 *Financial Instruments*, which is effective for annual periods beginning on or after 1 January 2018. However:

- on initial application of IFRS 9, an entity may choose an accounting policy to continue to apply the hedge accounting requirements in IAS 39 in their entirety instead of those in chapter 6 of IFRS 9 until a new standard resulting from the IASB's ongoing project on accounting for dynamic risk management becomes effective (see 7.9.80) or apply the hedge accounting requirements in IAS 39 for a fair value hedge of the interest rate exposure of a portfolio of financial assets or financial liabilities (see 7.9.70); and
- an insurer may defer the application of IFRS 9 if it meets certain criteria (see 8.1.180).

This chapter reflects the requirement of IAS 39 *Financial Instruments: Recognition and Measurement* and the related standards, excluding any amendments introduced by IFRS 9. These requirements are relevant for annual periods beginning on 1 January 2018. For further discussion, see Introduction to Sections 7 and 7I.

The requirements related to this topic are mainly derived from the following.

STANDARD	TITLE
IAS 39	Financial Instruments: Recognition and Measurement
IFRIC 16	Hedges of a Net Investment in a Foreign Operation

FORTHCOMING REQUIREMENTS

The requirements in this chapter are affected by the following forthcoming requirements. They are highlighted with a # and the impact is explained in the accompanying boxed text at the references indicated.

In January 2016, the IASB issued IFRS 16 *Leases*, which is effective for annual periods beginning on or after 1 January 2019. See 7I.7.435. IFRS 16 is the subject of chapter 5.1A.

FUTURE DEVELOPMENTS

This topic is subject to future developments that may affect aspects of macro hedge accounting. See 7I.7.1000.

7I.7.10   INTRODUCTION

7I.7.10.10   IAS 39 uses a mixed measurement model that requires the measurement of financial assets and financial liabilities on different bases. For example, certain financial assets and financial liabilities are measured at amortised cost whereas, in principle, all derivatives are measured at FVTPL (see 7I.6.120). This results in an accounting mismatch in profit or loss, which results in volatility in reported results.

7I.7.10.20   Similarly, other standards require or permit assets and liabilities to be measured on bases other than FVTPL and certain contracts are recognised in financial statements only to the extent of performance (see 1.2.55). When an entity offsets the risks arising from these recognised assets and liabilities or unrecognised contracts by entering into hedging instruments, there is a resulting accounting mismatch in profit or loss.

7I.7.10.30   Consequently, under hedge accounting, an entity could selectively measure assets, liabilities and firm commitments on a basis different from that stipulated under other requirements of IFRS, or could defer the recognition in profit or loss of gains or losses on derivatives. Because hedge accounting results in an entity deviating from the normal measurement or presentation requirements under IFRS, it is permitted only when strict documentation and effectiveness testing requirements are met.

7I.7.10.40   There are three hedge accounting models and the type of model applied depends on whether the hedged exposure is a fair value exposure, a cash flow exposure or a foreign currency exposure on a net investment in a foreign operation.

7I.7.10.50   Hedge accounting is voluntary and the decision to apply hedge accounting is made on a transaction-by-transaction basis or for a group of similar transactions. If an economic hedge does not qualify for hedge accounting, then any derivative used is measured at fair value with all changes in fair value recognised in profit or loss. These changes will not be offset by gains or losses on the hedged item when the hedged item is not also measured at FVTPL. In our view, an entity's risk management disclosures should contain appropriate explanation of economic hedges that do not qualify for hedge accounting (see 7I.8.270.40). [*IFRS 7.31*]

7I.7.10.60   When entering into a derivative transaction to reduce or eliminate a fair value risk exposure, an entity may find it easier to designate a potential hedged item that is a non-derivative financial asset or liability as at FVTPL, rather than applying hedge accounting. Such a designation does not require the entity to perform an assessment of effectiveness; nor does it require rigorous documentation. However, the entity needs to comply with the conditions for applying the fair value option, which is irrevocable (see 7I.4.40).

7I.7.20   HEDGE ACCOUNTING MODELS

7I.7.30   Fair value hedges

7I.7.40   *Definition*

7I.7.40.10   A 'fair value hedge' is a hedge of changes in the fair value of a recognised asset or liability, an unrecognised firm commitment, or an identified portion of such an asset, liability or firm commitment, that is attributable to a particular risk and could affect profit or loss. [*IAS 39.86(a)*]

7I.7.40.20   The following are examples of fair value hedges:

- a hedge of interest rate risk associated with a fixed rate interest-bearing asset or liability – e.g. converting a fixed rate instrument to a floating rate instrument using an interest rate swap;
- a hedge of a firm commitment to purchase an asset or to incur a liability; or
- a hedge of interest rate risk on a portfolio basis (a portfolio fair value hedge (see 7I.7.210)). [*IAS 39.78, AG102*]

7I.7.40.30   A hedge of the foreign currency risk of a firm commitment may be accounted for as either a fair value hedge or a cash flow hedge, although in our experience cash flow hedging is applied more commonly. Fair value hedge accounting can be applied only if there is a firm commitment. Consequently, if a highly probable forecast transaction exists before an entity enters into a firm commitment, then the hedge would have to be accounted for as a cash flow hedge until the entity enters into a firm commitment – from which time it could be accounted for as a fair value hedge. Generally, it is simpler to implement a single model for hedge accounting purposes, rather than having to switch models during the life of the hedge. [*IAS 39.87*]

7I.7.50   *Accounting*

7I.7.50.10   If the hedging instrument is a derivative, then it is measured at fair value, with changes in fair value recognised in profit or loss. The hedged item is remeasured for changes in fair value attributable to the hedged risk during the period of the hedging relationship using the guidance in IFRS 13 (see chapter 2.4), even if it is normally measured at amortised cost – e.g. a fixed rate borrowing. Any resulting adjustment to the carrying amount of the hedged item related to the hedged risk is recognised in profit or loss, even if such a change would normally be recognised in OCI – e.g. for an available-for-sale financial asset (see 7I.8.220). In our view, the categorisation of the fair value hedge adjustment as either a monetary or a non-monetary item, under IAS 21, should be consistent with the categorisation of the hedged item under IAS 21 (see 2.7.120). [*IAS 39.89*]

7I.7.50.15   In accordance with IFRS 13, a fair value measurement assumes that the transaction to sell the asset or transfer the liability takes place in the principal market, or in the absence of a principal market, in the most advantageous market. In some cases, the hedged item in a fair value hedge can be of a non-financial nature and its location is a characteristic that is relevant in determining its fair value (see 2.4.70). If the market in which the fair value of the hedged item is priced is different from the market in which the fair value of the hedging instruments is priced (see 2.4.100), then this difference may cause ineffectiveness in the hedging relationship and affect the assessment of hedge effectiveness in a fair value hedging relationship. [*IFRS 13.16*]

7I.7.50.20   On entering into a firm commitment, an entity would not typically recognise the firm commitment in the statement of financial position. However, for a hedge of a firm commitment, fair value hedge accounting results in the change in the fair value of the firm commitment attributable to the hedged risk during the period of the hedging relationship being recognised as an asset or a liability in the statement of financial position. When the firm commitment is settled, the amount previously recognised in the statement of financial position in respect of the fair value of the firm commitment is transferred to adjust the initial measurement of the asset or liability recognised. [*IAS 39.93–94*]

7I.7.50.30   The adjustment to the carrying amount of the hedged item in a fair value hedge often results in the item being measured neither at cost nor at fair value. This is because the adjustment:

- is made only for changes attributable to the risk being hedged – not for all risks;
- occurs only during the period in which hedge accounting is applied; and
- is limited to the extent that the item is hedged. [*IAS 39.90*]

EXAMPLE 1 – HEDGED ITEM MEASURED NEITHER AT COST NOR AT FAIR VALUE

7I.7.50.40   Company Z has a fixed interest liability denominated in its functional currency and measured at amortised cost. Z enters into a pay-LIBOR receive-fixed interest rate swap to hedge half of the notional amount of the liability in respect of its benchmark interest exposure. The swap qualifies for hedge accounting. Half of the liability – i.e. the proportion that is hedged – will be remeasured with respect to changes in fair value arising from changes in benchmark interest rates from the beginning of the hedging relationship. The liability will not be remeasured for any changes in its fair value arising from changes in credit spread, liquidity spread or other factors.

7I.7.50.50   In a fair value hedge any ineffectiveness is automatically reported in profit or loss because changes in the measurement of both the hedging instrument and the hedged item are reported through profit or loss, unlike in a cash flow hedge, in which the ineffectiveness has to be calculated and recognised separately.

7I.7.60   Cash flow hedges

7I.7.70   *Definition*

7I.7.70.10   A 'cash flow hedge' is a hedge of the exposure to variability in cash flows associated with a recognised asset or liability or a highly probable forecast transaction that is attributable to a particular risk and could affect profit or loss. [*IAS 39.86(b)*]

7I.7.70.20   Examples of cash flow hedges are:
- hedges of floating rate interest-bearing instruments using an interest rate swap, cap, floor or collar;
- hedges of the foreign currency exposure on foreign currency denominated future operating lease or payroll payments; and
- hedges of highly probable forecast purchase or sale transactions. [*IAS 39.AG103*]

7I.7.80   *Accounting*

7I.7.80.10   If the hedging instrument is a derivative, then the hedging instrument is measured at fair value, with the effective portion of changes in its fair value recognised in OCI and presented within equity, normally in a hedging reserve. The ineffective portion of the gain or loss on the hedging instrument is recognised immediately in profit or loss. [*IAS 39.95*]

7I.7.80.20   If the hedging instrument is a non-derivative financial asset or non-derivative financial liability, which is permitted only for hedges of foreign currency risk, then the effective portion of the foreign exchange gains and losses on the hedging instrument is recognised in OCI.

71.7.80.30   The change in fair value of the hedging instrument that is recognised in OCI is reclassified to profit or loss when the hedged item affects profit or loss. Consequently, if the impact of the hedged risk on profit or loss arising from the hedged item is deferred, then the amount recognised in the cash flow hedge reserve may remain in equity until the hedged item affects profit or loss. The standard is not explicit about the manner in which gains or losses should be reclassified from the cash flow hedge reserve when the forecasted transaction impacts multiple periods or when there are multiple forecasted transactions that impact multiple periods. Therefore, in our view an entity should develop a systematic and rational method based on its risk management objective for determining the amounts to be reclassified in each reporting period if the hedged cash flows affect profit or loss in multiple reporting periods. [*IAS 39.97–100*]

EXAMPLE 2 – RECLASSIFYING GAINS AND LOSSES ON A CASH FLOW HEDGE

71.7.80.40   On 31 December 2018, Company D issues a floating rate bond that bears interest based on a benchmark rate payable annually and matures on 31 December 2022. The bond is issued at par of 1,000. In accordance with its risk management strategy, D enters into a four-year pay-fixed 3% receive-benchmark interest rate swap on 31 December 2018. On the same date, D designates the swap as a cash flow hedge of the variability of future interest payments on the bond attributable to changes in the benchmark rate. The timing of the swap's cash flows matches those of the bond. The fair value of the swap at inception is zero.

71.7.80.50   The effects of credit risk are insignificant to the effectiveness of the hedging relationship and there are no sources of ineffectiveness during the hedging period. Therefore, all gains and losses on remeasurement of the swap to fair value are included in OCI.

71.7.80.60   Considering its risk management objective and how the effective interest method is applied to a floating rate liability, D determines that it will reclassify an amount from OCI to profit or loss during each period reflecting the time-based accrual of the net coupon payable or receivable on the swap. Therefore, in each year it reclassifies amounts equal to the net settlements on the swap.

71.7.80.70   An entity has some flexibility in the accounting for such reclassifications.
- If the future transaction results in the recognition of a non-financial asset or a non-financial liability, then an entity may either include the cumulative amount in equity in the initial carrying amount of that asset or liability (basis adjustment) or retain the amount in equity and reclassify it to profit or loss in the same period(s) during which the asset or liability affects profit or loss – e.g. when the asset is sold or as it is depreciated. The same choice applies to a forecast transaction of a non-financial asset or a non-financial liability that becomes a firm commitment for which fair value hedge accounting subsequently is applied. An entity chooses an accounting policy, to be applied consistently to all cash flow hedges of transactions that lead to the recognition of non-financial assets or liabilities.
- If the future transaction results in the acquisition of a financial instrument, then the cumulative amount remains in equity and is reclassified to profit or loss in the period(s) during which the

financial instrument's hedged forecast cash flows affect profit or loss – e.g. as it is amortised or when it is impaired or sold. For example, an entity has a highly probable forecast purchase of a listed equity security that it designates as the hedged item in a cash flow hedge. On 30 November 2018, the entity purchases the equity security and classifies it as available-for-sale. Subsequently, changes in the fair value of the equity instrument are recognised in OCI until either an impairment event or a disposal occurs. In our view, the gain or loss on the hedging instrument should remain in equity until the equity instrument is either impaired or sold.

- If an entity expects that all or a portion of a loss recognised in OCI will not be recovered in one or more future periods, then it reclassifies from equity to profit or loss as a reclassification adjustment the amount that is not expected to be recovered.

7I.7.80.80   The accounting in 7I.7.80.70 also applies when cash flow hedge accounting is used to hedge the exposure to the foreign currency risk of firm commitments. For hedges of foreign currency risk of firm commitments to acquire a business and forecast business combinations, see 7I.7.265.

7I.7.90   **Net investment hedges**

7I.7.90.10   IAS 39 does not override the principles of IAS 21 (see chapter 2.7), but it does provide the hedge accounting model for hedging an entity's foreign exchange exposure arising from net investments in foreign operations.

7I.7.100   *Definition*

7I.7.100.10   A 'net investment hedge' is a hedge of the foreign currency exposure arising from a net investment in a foreign operation using a derivative and/or a non-derivative financial item as the hedging instrument. [*IAS 39.86(c)*]

7I.7.100.20   The hedged risk is the foreign currency exposure arising from a net investment in a foreign operation when the net assets of that foreign operation are included in the financial statements (see 7I.7.750.10).

7I.7.100.30   Often the exposure to changes in the value of a net investment arising from movements in foreign exchange rates is hedged through borrowings denominated in the foreign operation's functional currency or, in more limited circumstances, derivative currency contracts.

7I.7.110   *Accounting*

7I.7.110.10   If the hedging instrument in a net investment hedge is a derivative, then it is measured at fair value. The effective portion of the change in fair value of the hedging instrument – computed with reference to the functional currency of the parent entity against whose functional currency the hedged risk is measured – is recognised in OCI and presented within equity in the foreign currency translation reserve (see 2.7.260). The ineffective portion of the gain or loss on the hedging instrument is immediately recognised in profit or loss. [*IAS 39.102, IFRIC 16.3, 15*]

7I.7.110.20   If the hedging instrument is a non-derivative – e.g. a foreign currency borrowing – then the effective portion of the foreign exchange gain or loss arising on translation of the hedging instrument under IAS 21 into the functional currency of the hedging entity is recognised in OCI. The effective portion is computed with reference to the functional currency of the parent entity against whose functional currency the hedged risk is measured. [*IFRIC 16.15*]

7I.7.110.30   On disposal of a net investment in a foreign operation, the cumulative foreign exchange differences arising on translation of the foreign operation, and the effective portion of the gain or loss on the hedging instrument presented within equity in the foreign currency translation reserve (the 'cumulative amounts'), are treated as follows.

- On disposal of the entire interest in a foreign operation and disposal of part of an ownership interest that results in the entity losing control over the other entity that includes the foreign operation (see 2.7.340.100) or on the cessation of equity accounting, the cumulative amounts previously recognised in OCI are reclassified to profit or loss and no amount of the reclassification is allocated to NCI (see 2.5.760.40). As an exception, when a parent loses control of a subsidiary by contributing it to an associate or joint venture and elects to eliminate the part of the gain or loss in respect of the continuing interest in the assets and liabilities contributed, then in our view only a proportionate share of the cumulative amounts previously recognised in OCI should be reclassified to profit or loss (see 3.5.470).
- When an entity partially disposes of a subsidiary that includes a foreign operation, but retains control, the entity re-attributes a proportionate share of the cumulative amounts previously recognised in OCI to NCI (see 2.7.340.140).
- In any other partial disposal of a foreign operation, the entity reclassifies to profit or loss only a proportionate share of the cumulative amounts previously recognised in OCI (see 2.7.340.150). [*IAS 21.48–49, 39.102, IFRIC 16.6, 16–17*]

7I.7.110.40   Therefore, it is necessary for an entity to keep track of the amount recognised in OCI separately in respect of each foreign operation, to identify the amounts to be reclassified to profit or loss on disposal or partial disposal.

7I.7.110.50   The method of consolidation – i.e. the step-by-step or the direct method – may affect the amount that is included in the foreign currency translation reserve for an individual foreign operation. When the step-by-step method of consolidation is applied, it may lead to the reclassification to profit or loss of an amount that is different from the amount used to assess hedge effectiveness. An entity may eliminate this difference by retrospectively determining the amount that would have resulted from using the direct method of consolidation. The amount so determined would then be reclassified from equity to profit or loss on disposal or partial disposal, as discussed in 7I.7.110.30. This adjustment is not required by IAS 21. However, an entity needs to choose an accounting policy, to be applied consistently, for all net investments (see 2.7.340.20). [*IFRIC 16.17*]

7I.7.120   Hedge accounting criteria

7I.7.120.10   Hedge accounting is permitted only if all of the following conditions are met.
- There is formal designation and written documentation at the inception of the hedge (see 7I.7.120.30).
- The effectiveness of the hedging relationship can be measured reliably. This requires the fair value of the hedging instrument, and the fair value (or cash flows) of the hedged item with respect to the risk being hedged, to be reliably measurable.
- The hedge is expected to be highly effective in achieving fair value or cash flow offsets in accordance with the original documented risk management strategy.

- The hedge is assessed and determined to be highly effective on an ongoing basis throughout the hedging relationship. A hedge is highly effective if changes in the fair value of the hedging instrument, and changes in the fair value or expected cash flows of the hedged item attributable to the hedged risk, offset within the range of 80–125 percent.
- For a cash flow hedge of a forecast transaction, the transaction is highly probable and creates an exposure to variability in cash flows that could ultimately affect profit or loss. [*IAS 39.88*]

7I.7.120.20   In our experience, the key challenges in implementing hedge accounting are identifying a specific asset or liability, or portfolio of similar assets or liabilities, to designate as the hedged item and demonstrating that the hedge is highly effective (both prospectively and retrospectively).

7I.7.120.30   At inception of the hedge, an entity establishes formal documentation of the hedging relationship. The hedge documentation prepared at inception includes a description of the following:
- the entity's risk management objective and strategy for undertaking the hedge;
- the nature of the risk being hedged;
- clear identification of the hedged item – the asset, liability, firm commitment or cash flows arising from a forecast transaction – and the hedging instrument; and
- how hedge effectiveness will be assessed both prospectively and retrospectively. The entity describes the method and procedures in sufficient detail to establish a firm and consistent basis for measurement in subsequent periods for the particular hedge. [*IAS 39.88*]

7I.7.120.40   IAS 39 does not mandate a specific format for the documentation and, in our experience, hedge documentation may vary in terms of layout, methodology and processes used. Various formats are acceptable as long as the documentation includes the content listed in 7I.7.120.30.

7I.7.130   **Risk reduction**

7I.7.130.10   Risk exposure is assessed on a transaction basis and entity-wide risk reduction is not a condition for hedge accounting. For example, an entity may have fixed rate assets and liabilities that provide a natural economic hedge that leaves the entity with no exposure to interest rate risk. The entity may decide to enter into a pay-fixed receive-floating swap and to designate this as a hedge of the fixed rate assets. Although this would increase the entity's overall exposure to interest rate risk, hedge accounting may be applied to this transaction provided that the relevant hedge accounting criteria are met. [*IAS 39.IG.F.2.6*]

7I.7.140   **Flexibility in type of hedge accounting**

7I.7.140.10   In some cases, a hedge can be designated either as a cash flow hedge or as a fair value hedge. The following examples demonstrate this.
- A hedge of the foreign currency risk of a firm commitment may be designated as a fair value hedge or as a cash flow hedge.
- A forward contract to buy foreign currency may be designated as the hedging instrument in a fair value hedge of a foreign currency financial liability or alternatively in a cash flow hedge of the forecast settlement of that liability.
- A receive-fixed pay-floating interest rate swap may be designated as a fair value hedge of a fixed interest liability or as a cash flow hedge of a variable interest asset. However, the interest rate

swap cannot be designated as a cash flow hedge of a fixed interest liability because it converts known (fixed) interest cash outflows, for which there is no exposure to variability in cash flows, into unknown (variable) interest cash outflows. Similarly, the swap cannot be designated as a fair value hedge of a variable interest asset because a variable interest instrument is not exposed to changes in fair value arising from changes in market interest rates.

- A purchased put option on a commodity may be designated as the hedging instrument in a fair value hedge of the commodity inventory or, alternatively, in a cash flow hedge of a forecast sale of the commodity inventory when such a sale is highly probable to occur. [*IAS 39.87, IG.F.3.3, IG.F.3.6*]

7I.7.140.20   The designation is done at inception of the hedge. [*IAS 39.88*]

7I.7.140.30   Although the net profit or loss effect of a hedging relationship will ultimately be the same regardless of the type of hedge accounting applied, the timing of recognition in the statement of financial position and in profit or loss, effectiveness testing and the nature of the accounting adjustments made will differ. Therefore, it is important to choose the model and the method of effectiveness testing at inception of the hedge and to designate and document the hedge accordingly.

7I.7.140.40   The decision regarding which hedge accounting model to use may also be influenced by the entity's information systems. The entity assesses whether its existing information systems are best set up to manage and track the information required under a fair value hedge model or a cash flow hedge model. This decision may also depend on the characteristics of the hedged items and whether hedge accounting criteria can be met.

7I.7.140.50   Under a fair value hedge model, an asset or liability designated as a hedged item is re-measured for fair value changes attributable to the hedged risk. For exposure to an interest-sensitive rate (assets and liabilities), the original effective yield is modified through the amortisation of this 'hedge adjustment'. Usually, this requires a system that is able to track changes in the hedged risk and that can calculate associated changes in the fair value of the hedged item. Also, the system should be able to recompute the effective yield of the hedged item and amortise the changes to profit or loss over the remaining life of the hedged item. [*IAS 39.IG.F.6.2*]

7I.7.140.60   Under a cash flow hedge model, the ineffective portion is calculated separately and recognised in profit or loss. However, the effective portion of the fair value changes of the hedging instrument is recognised in OCI and is reclassified to profit or loss only when the hedged expected cash flows affect profit or loss (see 7I.7.80.30), or the amount is a loss and the entity expects that all or a portion of that loss will not be recovered in one or more future periods. In addition, it is necessary to demonstrate that forecast transactions are highly probable. This requires a system that enables an entity to track the timing of the cash flows of the hedged item, as well as the timing of the reclassification of the hedging gains and losses from equity. Although this may prove a challenge, for many entities such information can be based on the cash flow information already captured in their risk management systems. [*IAS 39.95–100*]

7I.7.140.70   In our experience, for hedges of interest rate risk, it is generally easier to meet the hedge criteria and to apply hedge accounting if the cash flow hedge model is used. This is because complex systems are necessary to make partial fair value adjustments to the carrying amount of interest-bearing hedged items and it is often difficult to demonstrate hedge effectiveness, particularly if there is a risk of prepayments (see 7I.7.260).

7I.7.150   Situations in which hedge accounting is not necessary

7I.7.150.10   In some cases, there is no accounting mismatch and therefore hedge accounting is not necessary. Examples of situations in which hedge accounting is not necessary are:

- hedges of recognised foreign currency monetary items with offsetting monetary items – the remeasurement of both items with respect to changes in foreign exchange rates is required to be recognised in profit or loss; and
- hedges of changes in the fair value of instruments measured at FVTPL – both the hedged item and derivative hedging instruments are remeasured to FVTPL. [*IAS 39.IG.F.1.1*]

7I.7.160   Income taxes

7I.7.160.10   For transactions recognised directly in equity or in OCI, all current and deferred taxes are also recognised in equity or in OCI (see 3.13.530). In respect of hedge accounting, this means that current and deferred taxes on gains or losses on hedging instruments recognised in OCI in a cash flow or net investment hedge are also recognised in OCI until such time as the gain or loss is reclassified to profit or loss. [*IAS 12.61A*]

7I.7.170   QUALIFYING HEDGED ITEMS

7I.7.170.10   The hedged item is the item that is exposed to the specific risk(s) that an entity has chosen to hedge.

7I.7.170.20   The hedged item can be:

- a single recognised asset or liability, unrecognised firm commitment, highly probable forecast transaction or net investment in a foreign operation;
- a group of recognised assets or liabilities, unrecognised firm commitments, highly probable forecast transactions or net investments in foreign operations, if they share the same hedged risk; or
- in a portfolio hedge of interest rate risk, a portion – i.e. an amount of currency – of a portfolio of financial assets or financial liabilities that share the risk being hedged. [*IAS 39.78*]

(S) 7I.7.170.30   To qualify for hedge accounting, the hedged item should involve a party external to the entity. Hedge accounting can be applied to transactions between entities in the same group only in the individual or separate financial statements of those entities and not in the consolidated financial statements of the group. However, as an exception, the foreign currency risk of an intra-group monetary item – e.g. a foreign currency denominated payable or receivable between two subsidiaries – may qualify as a hedged item in the consolidated financial statements if it results in an exposure to foreign exchange rate gains or losses that are not fully eliminated on consolidation (see 7I.7.870). [*IAS 39.80*]

7I.7.170.40   In our view, a synthetic instrument that combines non-derivative and derivative instruments cannot qualify as a hedged item, because a derivative instrument normally cannot be designated as the hedged item (see 7I.7.280.10). [*IAS 39.78, IG.F.2.1*]

71.7.170.50   Because hedge accounting is assessed on a transaction-by-transaction basis, in our view a non-derivative hedging instrument in one hedging relationship can be designated as a hedged item in a different hedging relationship. [*IAS 39.IG.F.2.6*]

EXAMPLE 3 – NON-DERIVATIVE INSTRUMENT USED AS BOTH HEDGING INSTRUMENT AND HEDGED ITEM

71.7.170.60   Company B's functional currency is sterling. B has two hedges in place. The first hedge is a net investment hedge of yen net assets of a foreign operation whereby the hedging instrument is a yen-denominated floating rate bond issued by B. The second hedge is a cash flow hedge of the variability in the interest cash flows on the yen-denominated floating rate bond arising from changes in benchmark interest rates whereby the hedging instrument is a yen pay-fixed receive-floating interest rate swap. In this example, the issued bond is the hedging instrument of foreign currency risk while it is simultaneously designated as the hedged item in a cash flow hedge of interest rate risk.

71.7.170.70   To qualify for hedge accounting, the hedged risk should ultimately be capable of affecting profit or loss. [*IAS 39.80, 86*]

71.7.170.80   An exception is that a held-to-maturity investment may never be the hedged item in a hedge of interest rate or prepayment risk. The designation of an investment as held-to-maturity requires an intention to hold the investment until maturity without regard to changes in the fair value or cash flows of the investment because of changes in interest rates. In addition, because prepayment risk on interest-bearing instruments is primarily a function of interest rates, this risk is like interest rate risk and therefore cannot also be the hedged risk when the hedged item is a held-to-maturity investment. This is an important factor to consider before classifying an investment as held-to-maturity (see 71.4.80). [*IAS 39.79*]

71.7.170.90   Although a held-to-maturity investment may not be hedged for interest rate risk, the reinvestment of cash flows generated by such an asset may be hedged. Additionally, a held-to-maturity investment can be hedged with respect to credit risk and/or foreign currency risk. Also, the forecast purchase of an asset to be classified as held-to-maturity may be hedged for the period until the asset is recognised in the statement of financial position. [*IAS 39.79, IG.F.2.10–IG.F.2.11*]

71.7.170.100   The designation of a hedging instrument for only a portion of the time that it remains outstanding is specifically prohibited (see 71.7.370.10). However, an entity may designate a financial instrument as hedged for only a portion of its period to maturity (see 71.7.180.20 and 190). It is possible to designate a hedging relationship after initial recognition of the hedged item, hedging instrument or both. [*IAS 39.IG.F.2.17*]

71.7.170.110   If the hedged item is a non-financial asset or non-financial liability, then the item is designated as a hedged item for foreign currency risks or in its entirety for all risks. However, in our view an entity may hedge, in a fair value hedging relationship, a recognised non-financial item for a specified period. A recognised non-financial item such as inventory does not have a fixed tenure and therefore can be hedged up to a specific date as long as the item is hedged for all changes in fair value and the other conditions for hedge accounting are met. [*IAS 39.82*]

7I.7.170.120   An entity's own equity instruments under IAS 32 may not be designated as the hedged item in either a fair value or a cash flow hedge, because changes in fair value or cash flows arising from such an instrument do not affect profit or loss (see 7I.7.290.10). [*IAS 39.86, IG.F.2.7*]

7I.7.170.130   A non-monetary item, such as an investment in equity securities quoted on an exchange (or other recognised marketplace) in which trades are denominated in a foreign currency and classified as available-for-sale, may also be the hedged item. [*IAS 39.IG.F.2.19*]

EXAMPLE 4 – NON-MONETARY ITEM USED AS HEDGED ITEM

7I.7.170.140   Company Q acquires equity securities in Company B on a foreign stock exchange in which trades are denominated in a foreign currency. Q classifies its investment as available-for-sale. To hedge against foreign currency risk, Q enters into a forward currency contract to sell foreign currency. The forward contract may be designated as a hedging instrument for the fair value changes of the securities related to foreign currency risk provided that:

- the acquired securities are not traded on a stock exchange on which trades are denominated in the same currency as Q's functional currency. This might be the case if B's equity securities are dual-listed and one of the listings is on an exchange where trades are denominated in Q's functional currency; and
- dividends to Q are not denominated in Q's functional currency.

7I.7.170.150   If an equity security is traded in multiple currencies and one of those currencies is the functional currency of the investor, then designation of the foreign exchange risk of the equity security is not permitted. However, in our view a forecast sale or purchase of a foreign currency-denominated equity security may qualify for cash flow hedge accounting. In our view, a highly probable purchase of additional foreign currency denominated shares in a subsidiary – i.e. buying additional shares in a controlled entity – may qualify as the hedged item as the acquisition of additional shares will impact profit or loss when the shares are disposed of. Also, a net investment in a foreign operation in the consolidated financial statements may qualify as the hedged item for foreign exchange risk. [*IAS 39.IG.F.2.19*]

7I.7.180   Hedging a portion

7I.7.180.10   In addition to hedging all changes in the fair value or cash flows of a financial instrument, an entity may designate the following as the hedged item:
- all of the cash flows of the financial instrument for cash flow or fair value changes attributable to some, but not all, risks; or
- some, but not all, of the cash flows of the financial instrument for cash flow or fair value changes attributable to all or certain risks – i.e. a portion of the cash flows of the financial instrument may be designated for changes attributable to all or certain risks. [*IAS 39.81, AG99E*]

7I.7.180.20   For example, an entity may be permitted to designate the following portions of a financial item as the hedged item.
- Hedging all cash flows for a specific risk – e.g. hedging only the foreign exchange risk on the principal and interest cash flows on a foreign currency borrowing.

- Hedging specifically identified cash flows for all risks – e.g. hedging the coupon payments on financial liabilities for all risks.
- Hedging a portion of specifically identified cash flows for a specific risk – e.g. hedging the interest rate risk for the first five years of a 10-year fixed rate bond with a five-year pay-fixed receive-floating interest rate swap. In this situation, the bond is hedged for less than its full term. However, the hedging instrument is designated for its entire term to maturity.
- Hedging a portion of specifically identified cash flows for a specific risk – e.g. hedging the interest rate risk on only the risk-free component of coupon payments on financial liabilities – excluding the credit risk premium.
- Hedging specifically identified cash flows for a specific risk – e.g. hedging the foreign currency risk on interest cash flows – but not the foreign currency risk on the principal cash flows of a foreign currency borrowing. [*IAS 39.81*]

7I.7.180.30   In addition, it is possible to designate a portion of a net investment as the hedged item (see 7I.7.760.10).

7I.7.180.40   As described in 7I.7.180.20, there are numerous options available when identifying portions of cash flows as the hedged item in relation to the specific risk(s) being hedged. An entity may hedge a portion of cash flows due to all risks or specifically identifiable risks inherent in the hedged item, or it may hedge all or a portion of cash flows due to specific risks inherent in the hedged item. However, to be eligible for hedge accounting, the designated risks and portions should be separately identifiable components of the financial instrument and changes in the cash flows or fair value of the entire financial instrument arising from changes in the designated risks and portions should be reliably measurable. For example, when designating a fixed rate bond for fair value changes arising from changes in the risk-free or benchmark interest rate, the risk-free or benchmark interest rate normally is regarded as being both a separately identifiable component and reliably measurable. [*IAS 39.AG99F*]

7I.7.180.50   If a portion of the cash flows of a financial asset or liability is designated, then that portion should be less than the total cash flows of the asset or liability. However, the entity may designate all of the cash flows of the entire financial asset or financial liability as the hedged item and hedge them for only one particular risk. For example, a financial liability bearing interest at LIBOR less 100 basis points could be hedged in its entirety – i.e. principal plus interest at LIBOR less 100 basis points – for the change in its cash flows attributable to changes in LIBOR, but could not be hedged for changes in value of the LIBOR component of the total cash flows. [*IAS 39.AG99C*]

7I.7.180.60   The entity may choose a hedge ratio other than one-to-one to improve the effectiveness of the hedge. This generally involves identifying whether there is a statistical relationship between the hedging instrument and the hedged item and, if there is such a relationship, then using the correlation between the items as the hedge ratio.

7I.7.180.70   In our view, it is possible for an entity to designate a portion of the variable interest payments or receipts on a financial asset or liability as the hedged item if, in addition to the conditions outlined in 7I.7.120.10 and 180.40, the following conditions are met.
- The actual interest payments or receipts on the hedged item are expected, based on historical evidence, to exceed the hedged cash flows during the entire hedging relationship.

- There is a reasonable economic relationship between the component of cash flows designated as the hedged item and the variable rate on which the contractual cash flows are based.

EXAMPLE 5 – DESIGNATION OF PORTION OF VARIABLE INTEREST PAYMENTS OR RECEIPTS AS HEDGED ITEM

7I.7.180.80   Company X will issue two variable rate notes (liabilities) with a notional of 1,000 each, which reset on the basis of the following rates:
- 90-day LIBOR; and
- 90-day LIBOR plus 100 basis points.

7I.7.180.90   X simultaneously enters into two swaps with the same notional as the notes, receiving LIBOR and paying fixed, to hedge its exposure to variability in interest rates.

7I.7.180.100   In this case, the margin above LIBOR is fixed and consequently any change in the cash flows of the swaps will perfectly offset the change in cash flows of the liabilities. Therefore, in our view it is not necessary to designate a portion of cash flows as the hedged item when the margin above the benchmark rate is fixed.

7I.7.180.110   However, in certain instances the margin above the benchmark rate may not be fixed. For example, consider a bank that raises 90-day deposits at three-month Euribor plus 50 basis points. On maturity it is highly probable that customers will roll over the deposits and the interest rate on the deposits will be reset to market, which may not be based on three-month Euribor plus 50 basis points. In accordance with its hedging strategy, the bank enters into a swap paying fixed and receiving three-month Euribor flat.

7I.7.180.120   We believe that in this specific scenario it is not possible to designate a Euribor portion of the variable cash flows as the hedged item because there is not a reasonable economic relationship between the rate on which the contractual cash flows are based and the benchmark rate identified as the hedged item. Therefore, the Euribor portion is not separately identifiable. The entire cash flow variability should be taken into consideration in designating the hedging relationship.

7I.7.180.130   In our view, it is possible to reduce ineffectiveness in certain circumstances by designating a portion of the cash flows as the hedged item, as long as the conditions in 7I.7.120.10 and 180.40 are met.

EXAMPLE 6A – DESIGNATION OF PORTION OF CASH FLOWS AS HEDGED ITEM – DIFFERENT CREDIT SPREADS

7I.7.180.133   Company R issues a five-year bond on 1 January 2018 that bears interest at a fixed rate of 5% – i.e. the benchmark rate on issue plus 100 basis points for credit spread. In addition, on 1 January 2018 R acquires a five-year interest rate swap, receiving fixed at 4.5% – i.e. the benchmark rate on acquisition plus 50 basis points for credit spread – and paying variable.

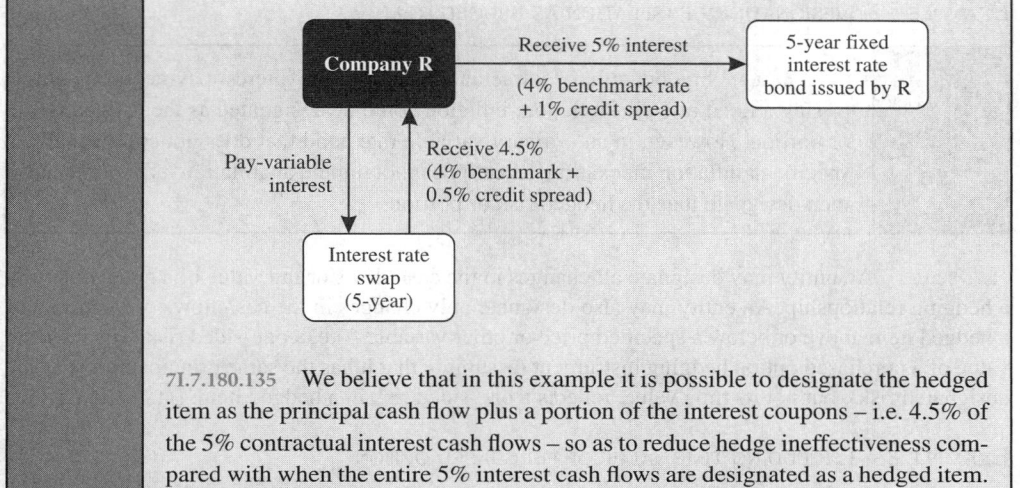

7I.7.180.135 We believe that in this example it is possible to designate the hedged item as the principal cash flow plus a portion of the interest coupons – i.e. 4.5% of the 5% contractual interest cash flows – so as to reduce hedge ineffectiveness compared with when the entire 5% interest cash flows are designated as a hedged item. We believe that the hedged item is a separately identifiable and reliably measurable portion of the bond's cash flows – i.e. the principal cash flow plus the 4.5% portion of the 5% coupon cash flows. Therefore, the portion of the bond's cash flows can be designated as a valid hedged item.

EXAMPLE 6B – DESIGNATION OF PORTION OF CASH FLOWS AS HEDGED ITEM – SUBSEQUENT CHANGE IN BENCHMARK RATES

7I.7.180.137 Company S issues a five-year bond in 2015 that bears interest at a fixed rate of 5%. In 2018, S acquires a three-year interest rate swap, receiving fixed at 3% and paying variable. Apart from the interest rates, the other terms of the hedged item and hedging instrument match. The mismatch between the interest rate on the bond and the interest rate on the fixed leg of the swap arises from a decrease in benchmark rates over the two-year period.

7I.7.180.140 We believe that in this example it is possible to designate the hedged item as the principal cash flow plus a portion of the interest coupons – i.e. 3% of the 5% contractual interest cash flows – so as to minimise hedge ineffectiveness. We believe that the hedged item is a separately identifiable and reliably measurable portion of the bond's cash flows – i.e. the principal cash flow plus the 3% portion of the 5% coupon cash flows. Therefore, the portion of the bond's cash flows can be designated as a valid hedged item.

7I.7.180.150 Inflation cannot be designated as a risk or a portion of a financial instrument because it is not separately identifiable or reliably measurable, unless:

- it is a contractually specified portion of the cash flows of a recognised inflation-linked bond (assuming there is no embedded derivative required to be separately accounted); and
- the other cash flows of the instrument are not affected by the inflation portion. [*IAS 39.AG99F*]

EXAMPLE 7 – DESIGNATION OF INFLATION AS HEDGED ITEM

71.7.180.160   In a bond that contractually specifies the interest payments as comprising a fixed rate plus inflation, inflation could be designated as the hedged risk or portion. However, in an ordinary variable rate bond that does not contractually specify an inflation indexation, an entity cannot impute an inflation indexation and then designate it as the hedged risk or portion.

71.7.180.170   An entity may designate all changes in the cash flows or fair value of a hedged item in a hedging relationship. An entity may also designate only changes in the cash flows or fair value of a hedged item above or below a specified price or other variable – i.e. a one-sided risk. The intrinsic value of a purchased option hedging instrument (assuming that it has the same principal terms as the designated risk), but not its time value, reflects a one-sided risk in a hedged item. [*IAS 39.AG99BA*]

EXAMPLE 8 – EXCLUDING TIME VALUE OF PURCHASED OPTION

71.7.180.180   Company B forecasts a future purchase of a commodity and it purchases a commodity call option to hedge against future increases in commodity prices above the strike price specified in the purchased option. B designates the variability of future cash flow outcomes arising from the forecast commodity purchase as a result of a price increase above the strike price. In such a situation, only cash flow losses that result from an increase in the price above the specified level are designated. The hedged risk does not include the time value of a purchased option because the time value is not a component of the forecast transaction that affects profit or loss.

71.7.180.190   In our view, an entity may designate the changes in the cash flows of a financial asset or financial liability that relate to only a portion of its term – i.e. a 'partial term' cash flow hedge. [*IAS 39.IG.F.2.17*]

EXAMPLE 9 – PARTIAL TERM CASH FLOW HEDGE

71.7.180.200   Company R has a highly probable forecast issue of fixed rate debt expected to occur on 31 December 2018. R desires to hedge the variability in the proceeds received from the debt issue arising from changes in the benchmark interest rate that occur from 1 October 2018 up to 31 October 2018. On 1 October 2018, R designates a cash flow hedge using a forward starting interest rate swap with a swap component that starts on 31 October 2018 as the hedging instrument to hedge that risk. When the swap component starts on 31 October 2018, R will de-designate the derivative.

71.7.180.210   To assess effectiveness, R measures the change in the theoretical proceeds cash flow up to 31 October 2018 and discounts that change assuming the cash settlement of that amount occurs on 31 December 2018 (when the forecast issuance is actually expected to occur). Therefore, ineffectiveness will result from the time value of money from 31 October 2018 to 31 December 2018.

7I.7.190   **Hedging a proportion**

7I.7.190.10   The term 'portion' (see 7I.7.180.10) should be distinguished from the term 'proportion', the latter being used to indicate a certain percentage only.

7I.7.190.20   It is possible to designate a proportion of the cash flows, fair value or net investment as a hedged item – e.g. 85 percent of the exposure. However, once a partial designation is made, hedge effectiveness is measured on the basis of the hedged exposure. Considering effectiveness on the basis of changes in the fair value or cash flows associated with the full underlying, or a proportion different from that designated as the hedged item – to maximise effectiveness – is not permitted. [*IAS 39.81, AG107A*]

7I.7.190.30   If a proportion of the cash flows or fair value of a financial asset or financial liability is designated as the hedged item, then that designated proportion should be less than the total cash flows of the asset or liability. [*IAS 39.AG99C*]

7I.7.200   **Hedging a group of items**

7I.7.200.10   The hedged item can be a portfolio of similar assets, liabilities, highly probable forecast transactions or net investments in foreign operations. Only 'similar' items may be grouped together in a portfolio. Items are considered to be similar if:
- they share the hedged risk; and
- the change in fair value attributable to the hedged risk for each individual item is expected to be approximately proportional to the overall change in the fair value of the portfolio attributable to the hedged risk. [*IAS 39.83, BC176*]

7I.7.200.20   However, it is not necessary that each item in the portfolio share all of the same risks and be correlated with respect to all risks, as long as the hedged risk is a common risk characteristic. For example, in our view a portfolio of interest-bearing receivables may be hedged for benchmark interest rate exposure because, although each receivable in the portfolio has a different credit risk exposure, the receivables all carry a similar exposure to benchmark interest rates. [*IAS 39.83, IG.F.6.2*]

7I.7.200.30   An entity can group more than one net investment in foreign operations together as the hedged item, provided that such investments are denominated in the same currency.

7I.7.200.40   An example of a portfolio that would not qualify as a hedged item is a portfolio of different securities that replicates a particular share index. An entity may hold such a portfolio and economically hedge it with a put option on the share index. However, in this scenario the fair value changes of individual items in the portfolio would not be approximately proportional to the fair value change of the entire group. Therefore, the portfolio does *not* qualify for hedge accounting. However, as an alternative to hedge accounting, the financial instruments comprising the portfolio could be designated as at FVTPL (see 7I.4.40). [*IAS 39.IG.F.2.20*]

7I.7.200.50   Generally, when items are grouped together and designated as a portfolio in a hedging relationship, the portfolio in its entirety comprises the hedged item – i.e. all of the financial assets or financial liabilities included in the portfolio are included in the hedging relationship in their entirety for the risk being hedged. However, in the case of a portfolio hedge of interest rate risk, the hedged item may comprise a portion of the portfolio of financial assets or financial liabilities that share the risk being hedged (see 7I.7.210). [*IAS 39.78, 81A*]

7I.7.200.60   The following are examples of items that may be designated as a portfolio for hedge accounting.

- A portfolio of short-term non-callable corporate bonds may be hedged as one portfolio with respect to a shared risk-free interest rate. To achieve the required correlation, the bonds would need to have the same or very similar maturity or repricing date and exposure to the same underlying interest rate.
- A group of expected future sales may be hedged as one portfolio with respect to foreign currency risk. Usually, such a designation requires the individual sales to be denominated in the same currency and be expected to take place in the same time period (see 7I.7.710.50).

7I.7.200.70   To identify a group of transactions, an entity is required to identify the hedged transactions with sufficient specificity so that it is possible to determine which transactions are the hedged transactions when they occur. This can be done either by specifying the number of units expected to be purchased/sold – e.g. the first 500 units out of expected purchases/sales of 800 units – or by specifying the monetary value of the purchases or sales – e.g. the first 25 of foreign currency sales in March 2018 (see 7I.7.720). It is not permitted to designate the first 50 percent of sales as the hedged item because this designation would not lead to an identifiable amount being hedged – i.e. the first 50 percent of sales would depend on the total amount of sales in the period – which is not known until after the fact.

7I.7.210   Portfolio fair value hedges of interest rate risk

7I.7.210.10   Entities, banks in particular, often manage interest rate risk on a portfolio basis – e.g. for a portfolio of mortgage loans or vehicle financing arrangements. Such hedging practices, whereby an entity hedges its net exposures, do not generally qualify for hedge accounting. However, an entity is permitted to designate the *interest rate* exposure of a portfolio of financial assets or financial liabilities as the hedged item in a portfolio fair value hedge. The hedged item is designated in terms of an amount of currency rather than as individual assets or liabilities. Although the portfolio may – for risk management purposes – include only assets, only liabilities or both assets and liabilities, the amount designated is an amount of assets or an amount of liabilities. Designation of a net amount – comprising both assets and liabilities – is not permitted. The entity may hedge a portion of the interest rate risk associated with the designated amount. [IAS 39.78, 81A, AG114(c), AG116, AG118]

7I.7.210.20   The portfolio fair value hedge model accommodates prepayment risk more readily than the normal fair value hedge model for individual assets or liabilities. However, the model can be applied only for hedges of interest rate risk and cannot be used for other risk types – e.g. foreign currency risk. Under the portfolio fair value hedge model, prepayable items are scheduled into repricing time periods based on expected, rather than contractual, repricing dates. This captures the effect of prepayments and consequently there is no need to assess separately the impact of prepayment risk on the fair value of the portfolio. [IAS 39.81A, AG114(b)]

7I.7.210.30   Because under this hedging model the hedged item is designated as an amount of currency, all the assets or liabilities from which the hedged item is derived should be items whose fair value changes in response to changes in the interest rate being hedged and items that could have qualified for fair value hedge accounting if they had been designated as hedged items individually.

In particular, because the fair value of a financial liability with a demand feature (such as demand deposits and some types of time deposits) is not less than the amount payable on demand, discounted from the first date on which the amount could be required to be paid (see 2.4.420), such an item cannot qualify for hedge accounting for any time period beyond the shortest period in which the holder can demand payment. For example, because the fair value of a liability that is repayable immediately on demand is usually equal to the amount payable on demand, there is no fair value exposure to hedge because the fair value of such a deposit is unaffected by interest rates and does not change when interest rates change. [*IFRS 13.47, AG118(b), BC187(d)*]

7I.7.210.40   The standard provides specific guidance on the measurement of effectiveness for such a hedging relationship, as well as the presentation of the fair value adjustment and its subsequent amortisation to profit or loss. However, because a single method for assessing hedge effectiveness is not specified (see 7I.7.530), in our view such specific guidance does not preclude the use of regression analysis for testing the effectiveness (see 7I.7.560) of such macro fair value hedges. [*IAS 39.AG126–AG127*]

7I.7.210.50   In the event that the hedged prepayable items are subject to a prepayment penalty that represents the difference between the fair value of the hedged item and its carrying amount, in our view it is acceptable to schedule the hedged items based on contractual repricing dates. The penalty has the effect of eliminating all fair value exposures arising from prepayment risk.

7I.7.210.60   For a fair value hedge of the interest rate exposure arising from a portion of a portfolio of financial assets or financial liabilities, the gain or loss attributable to the hedged item may be presented as a single separate line item within assets or liabilities depending on whether the hedged item is an asset or a liability for that particular repricing time period. If amortising this gain or loss using a recalculated effective interest rate is impracticable, then it is amortised using a straight-line method (see 7I.7.680.100). [*IAS 39.89A*]

7I.7.220   Net positions

7I.7.220.10   Many entities use net position hedging strategies under which a centralised treasury function accumulates risk originated in the operational subsidiaries or divisions. The treasury function hedges the net exposure in accordance with the group's risk policies by entering into a hedging transaction with a party external to the group.

7I.7.220.20   Net position hedging does not by itself qualify for hedge accounting treatment because of the inability to:

- associate hedging gains and losses with a specific item being hedged when measuring effectiveness; and
- determine the period in which such gains and losses should be recognised in profit or loss. [*IAS 39.84*]

7I.7.220.30   However, an entity is not necessarily precluded from hedge accounting by hedging net positions. That is, an entity may choose to manage and (economically) hedge risk on a net basis, but for hedge accounting purposes designate a specific item within the net position as the hedged item.

For example, if an entity has 100 assets and 90 liabilities with risks and terms of a similar nature, it can designate 10 of the assets as the hedged item. [*IAS 39.AG101*]

Highly probable forecast transactions

7I.7.230.10   Forecast transactions should be highly probable and should present an exposure to variations in cash flows that could ultimately affect profit or loss. [*IAS 39.88(c)*]

7I.7.230.20   In our view, for a forecast transaction to be considered highly probable, there should be at least a 90 percent probability of the transaction occurring. In assessing whether a transaction is highly probable, consideration should be given to:
- the quality of the budgeting processes;
- the extent and frequency of similar transactions in the past;
- whether previous similar expected cash flows actually occurred;
- the availability of adequate resources to finish the transaction;
- the impact on operations if the transaction does not occur;
- the possibility of different transactions being used to achieve the same purpose;
- how far into the future the transaction is expected to occur; and
- the quantity of anticipated transactions. [*IAS 39.88(c), IG.F.2.4, IG.F.3.7*]

7I.7.230.30   Normally it is possible to meet the highly probable criterion if significant similar transactions are expected and hedge accounting is limited to a percentage of these forecast transactions. For example, the hedged item may be designated as the first 80 of anticipated sales of approximately 100 expected in March 2018, because it is highly probable that 80 percent of the anticipated sales will be made. However, if the hedged item is designated as 100 of anticipated sales of 100 in March 2018, then it is unlikely that the highly probable criterion will be met. [*IAS 39.IG.F.3.7*]

7I.7.230.40   In our view, the highly probable criterion might not be met when an entity purchases an option as a hedge of a particular foreign currency because it has made a bid for a large contract in that foreign currency. For example, if it is not highly probable that the entity will win the bid for the contract, then the foreign currency cash flows would not be highly probable because they are dependent on the probability of the entity winning the bid for the contract.

7I.7.230.50   In our view, it is more likely that a large number of homogenous forecast transactions will meet the highly probable criterion than a single forecast transaction. When determining whether a single forecast transaction meets this criterion, an entity considers the facts and circumstances that influence the probability of occurrence of the transaction. Indicators that may suggest that a forecast transaction is not highly probable may be an illiquid market in which the forecast transaction takes place, a low number of transactions, no past experience of the entity with such transactions or historical experience that such transactions do not occur often.

EXAMPLE 10 – HIGHLY PROBABLE HOMOGENEOUS FORECAST TRANSACTIONS

7I.7.230.60   Bank B enters into fixed rate mortgage loan commitments with potential customers. Such commitments give the customer 90 days to lock in a mortgage at a discounted variable rate. To reduce the interest rate risk inherent in

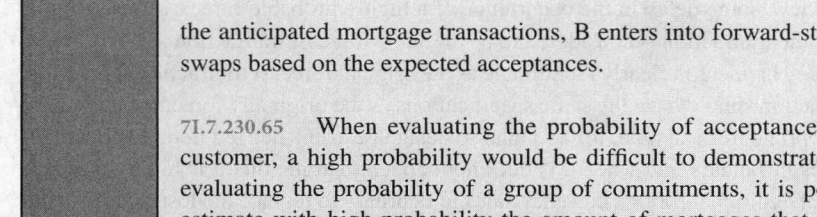

the anticipated mortgage transactions, B enters into forward-starting interest rate swaps based on the expected acceptances.

7I.7.230.65   When evaluating the probability of acceptance by only a single customer, a high probability would be difficult to demonstrate. However, when evaluating the probability of a group of commitments, it is possible that B can estimate with high probability the amount of mortgages that eventually will be closed. Therefore, B could use cash flow hedge accounting for the hedge of interest rate risk on the amount of mortgages that are highly probable of being closed.

7I.7.230.70   Similarly, when designating assets or liabilities with prepayment risk in a cash flow hedge, assessing the probability of interest cash flows arising from the entire portfolio rather than for a single instrument could result in identifying a bottom layer of interest cash flows that then could be considered as highly probable.

7I.7.230.80   An entity should be careful in its designation of forecast transactions as hedged items, because a history of such forecast transactions not occurring when expected could jeopardise its ability to continue to designate these types of hedges in the future. [*IAS 39.IG.F.3.7*]

7I.7.240   *Defining period in which forecast transaction expected to occur*

7I.7.240.10   The standard does not specify a timeframe in which the forecast transaction should occur, although it should be expected to occur within a 'reasonable, specific and generally narrow range of time'. The forecast transaction should be identified and documented with sufficient specificity so that when the transaction occurs it is clear whether the transaction is the hedged transaction. An entity is not required to predict and document the exact date on which a forecast transaction is expected to occur, but the documentation should identify a time period in which the forecast transaction is expected to occur within a reasonably specific and narrow range, as a basis for assessing hedge effectiveness. [*IAS 39.IG.F.3.11*]

7I.7.240.20   In determining appropriate time periods for hedge accounting purposes an entity may look to the following.
- *Forecasts and budgets:* An entity would not generally identify longer time periods for hedge accounting purposes than those used for forecasting and budgeting.
- *The nature of the business or industry:* The forecasting and budgeting periods used by an entity are influenced by its ability to reliably forecast the timing of its transactions. Generally, the forecast periods for manufacturers of ships or aircraft would be longer than those of retail stores. Usually, retailers sell smaller items in large quantities and can forecast more easily the timing of sales over shorter periods of time.

7I.7.240.30   Although the factors in 7I.7.240.20 provide an indication of what may be the appropriate time period in which the transaction is expected to occur, the actual time period is always determined on a case-by-case basis and will involve some degree of judgement. Generally, the sooner that the anticipated transaction is expected to occur, the easier it will be to demonstrate that the highly probable criterion is met. [*IAS 39.IG.F.3.7*]

7I.7.240.40   In our view, some delay in the occurrence of a highly probable forecast transaction is acceptable as long as the transaction is considered to be the *same* forecast transaction – i.e. the transaction that subsequently happens is clearly identifiable as the original forecast transaction. Therefore, the subsequent transaction should have the same specifications as the originally forecast transaction. It would not be appropriate, for example, for a retailer to designate as the hedged item the first 50 of foreign currency sales in January and when this does not happen to argue that it is highly probable that there will be 50 of additional foreign currency sales in February to replace the lost sales in January. In such a case, there would be a forecast error regarding the 50 sales in January – i.e. these sales would be considered 'no longer expected to occur' – which means that hedge accounting would be terminated (see 7I.7.680). However, if a shipbuilder has a highly probable forecast sale of a specified ship to a particular customer but the expected delivery date moves from January to February, then it may be possible to continue hedge accounting because of the specific nature of the hedged forecast cash flow (see 7I.7.690).

7I.7.240.50   If the hedged item is a series of forecast transactions, then the hedged item is identified and documented with sufficient specificity so that when the transaction occurs it is clear that it is the hedged transaction. For this reason, the documentation should specify that the hedged item is an identifiable portion of a series of transactions that will occur in a specified period. It is not acceptable to designate a set percentage of transactions in a period, or the last in a series of transactions, as the hedged item because these cannot be identified specifically when they occur. For example, the hedged item may be designated as the *first* 20,000 of anticipated foreign currency sales in March 2018, but not as 20,000 of anticipated foreign currency sales in March 2018. As another example, the hedged item is not permitted to be designated as 20 percent of anticipated foreign currency sales over the 2018 financial year. [*IAS 39.IG.F.3.10*]

7I.7.250   *Expected interest cash flows*

7I.7.250.10   To meet the hedge accounting criteria, a forecast debt issue should be highly probable. This could be the case once the entity enters into an agreement to issue the debt, but may be evidenced at an earlier stage when management decides on a debt issue as part of its funding strategy.

7I.7.250.20   An entity may apply cash flow hedge accounting to an anticipated debt issue because changes in interest rates between the date of deciding on the debt issue and the actual issue date will influence the rate at which the debt will be issued or the discount or premium that will apply to the proceeds. For example, if the long-term interest rate were to increase, then the debt would be issued at a higher rate or for lower proceeds than anticipated originally.

7I.7.250.30   Normally a gain or loss on an appropriate hedging instrument will offset the higher/lower interest rate or the decrease/increase in proceeds. Using the cash flow hedge model, the effective portion of the gains or losses resulting from the hedging instrument until the debt is issued will be recognised in OCI. On issuance of the debt, such gains and losses will remain in equity and be reclassified to profit or loss in the same periods in which the hedged forecast cash flows affect profit or loss – i.e. when the interest expense is recognised. This will require the entity to track the amount of gains or losses recognised in OCI to ensure that the correct amounts are reclassified to profit or loss at the correct times.

EXAMPLE 11A – HEDGE OF FORECAST INTEREST PAYMENTS

> 7I.7.250.40   Company K is in the process of issuing a bond. K wishes to hedge the risk of changes in interest rates between the time it decides to issue the bond and the date of issue. This could be done using an interest future or other derivative instruments. To the extent that the hedge is effective, the gain or loss on the derivative will be recognised in OCI. This gain or loss will remain in equity and will be reclassified to profit or loss as interest payments on the bond affect profit or loss and will effectively adjust the interest expense recognised on the bond.

EXAMPLE 11B – HEDGE OF FORECAST INTEREST PAYMENTS – MULTIPLE TRANCHES

> 7I.7.250.50   Company M plans to issue two tranches of floating rate notes, each with a maturity of three years. M intends to issue the second tranche on maturity of the first. In this situation, M may enter into a six-year swap to hedge the variability in expected interest cash flows on both note issues. For hedge accounting purposes, the hedge could be designated as a hedge of the expected interest payments in different periods, including interest payments arising from the forecast refinancing of the debt. To qualify for hedge accounting, at inception of the hedge the criteria for hedge accounting need to be met, including the criteria that:
> - the hedge will be highly effective; and
> - the second issue after three years is highly probable.

7I.7.250.60   In our view, in order for a forecast issue of debt to qualify for hedge accounting, all of its critical terms should be highly probable. For example, an entity with a euro functional currency may have a highly probable bond issue, but the currency of issue may not have been determined. If the entity issues the bond in US dollars, then it will enter into a currency swap to convert the cash flows to euro. However, regardless of the currency in which the bond is issued, the entity wishes to hedge its euro interest rate exposure using an interest rate swap. In our view, because the currency denomination of the forecast bond is not highly probable, the forecast bond issue cannot qualify for hedge accounting. Similarly, it will not be possible to achieve hedge accounting for forecast issues of commercial paper unless the currency and maturity (including rollovers) of the future issues can be determined reliably.

7I.7.260   *Prepayment risk*

7I.7.260.10   Prepayment risk may also affect whether a forecast transaction designated in a cash flow hedge is considered highly probable to occur. However, when the hedged item is designated as the first cash flows of a portfolio occurring in a given period, the effect of a prepayment is less likely to cause the hedged forecast transactions not to be highly probable as long as there are sufficient cash flows in the period. This could be demonstrated by the entity preparing a cash flow maturity schedule that shows sufficient levels of expected cash flows in each period to support a highly probable assertion. For example, a bank may be able to determine accurately what levels of prepayments are expected for a particular class of its originated loans. The bank might hedge only a portion of the contractual cash flows from that portfolio of loans because it expects a number of borrowers to repay their loans early.

7I.7.265   **Cash flow hedges of firm commitments to acquire a business and forecast business combinations**

7I.7.265.10   A firm commitment to acquire a business in a business combination can be a hedged item only for foreign exchange risk because other risks cannot be specifically identified and measured. In our view, an entity may also hedge the foreign exchange risk of a highly probable forecast business combination. In our view, in the consolidated financial statements, a cash flow hedge of the foreign exchange risk of a firm commitment to acquire a business or a forecast business combination relates to the foreign currency equivalent of the consideration paid. [*IAS 39.AG98*]

7I.7.265.20   In a cash flow hedge designation, the effective portion of the gain or loss arising from the hedging instrument is recognised in OCI. However, an issue arises about when and how this amount accumulated in equity is reclassified to profit or loss. The answer depends on whether the hedge represents a hedge of a non-financial item or a financial item.

7I.7.265.30   In our view, a hedge of a firm commitment to acquire a business or a forecast business combination that will be effected through the acquisition of the assets and liabilities – that comprise the business rather than the acquisition of an equity interest in the entity – should be accounted for as a hedge of a non-financial item because the legal form of the transaction does not involve the acquisition of a financial asset.

7I.7.265.40   In our view, because a hedge of a firm commitment to acquire a business or forecast business combination relates to the foreign currency equivalent of the consideration paid, the acquisition of an equity interest in the entity may be viewed as either a hedge of the purchase of shares of an entity or a hedge of the purchase of a business. A hedge of the purchase of shares represents a hedge of a financial item, whereas a hedge of the purchase of a business represents a hedge of a non-financial item. Therefore, we believe that an entity should choose an accounting policy, to be applied consistently, on whether such hedges are considered hedges of a financial item or non-financial item.

7I.7.265.50   For hedges of a financial item, the accounting for the reclassification from equity to profit or loss is complicated by the fact that the shares acquired are not recognised in the consolidated financial statements and therefore will never directly impact profit or loss. However, for hedges of financial and non-financial items, the effective portion of the gain or loss arising from the hedging instrument relates to the foreign currency equivalent of the consideration paid. Therefore, reclassification of the effective portion of the gain or loss arising from the hedging instrument from equity to profit or loss occurs when the residual (i.e. goodwill) arising from the business combination affects profit or loss.

7I.7.265.60   In our view, if the hedge is a hedge of a financial item, then the entity should retain the gain or loss from the hedging instrument recognised in OCI as a separate component of equity until the goodwill from the hedged business combination in part or in full affects profit or loss – e.g. through transactions such as impairment of goodwill or sale of the business acquired. When the goodwill from the hedged business combination affects profit or loss, all or a portion of the gain or loss recognised in OCI should be reclassified to profit or loss.

7I.7.265.70   In our view, if the hedge is a hedge of a non-financial item, then the entity should choose an accounting policy, to be applied consistently, to apply a basis adjustment (see 7I.7.80.70) in respect of a transaction that results in the acquisition of a non-financial item. Therefore, the entity may either apply the principles outlined in 7I.7.265.60 similar to the accounting for a financial item or recognise the gain or loss from the hedging instrument recognised in OCI as an adjustment to goodwill when the business combination occurs.

7I.7.270   ITEMS THAT DO NOT QUALIFY AS HEDGED ITEMS

7I.7.270.10   There are a number of items that for different reasons do not qualify for hedge account-ing. In these cases, the normal recognition and measurement principles of IFRS are applied.

7I.7.280   Derivatives

7I.7.280.10   Derivatives are generally precluded from being the hedged item. Therefore, derivatives can generally serve only as hedging instruments. An exception to this is a purchased option that is embedded in another financial instrument and that is closely related to the host contract (see 7I.2.200) such that it is not separately accounted for as a derivative. In this case, it is possible to designate the embedded derivative as the hedged item in a fair value hedge, with a written option as the hedging instrument. [*IAS 39.AG94, IG.F.2.1*]

7I.7.290   Own equity instruments

7I.7.290.10   An entity's own equity instruments cannot be the hedged item because there is no risk exposure that affects profit or loss because transactions in own shares are recognised directly in equity. Likewise, forecast transactions in an entity's own equity cannot be a hedged item and neither can distributions to holders of the entity's equity instruments. However, a dividend that has been declared but not yet paid and is recognised as a financial liability may qualify as a hedged item – e.g. for foreign currency risk if it is denominated in a foreign currency. [*IAS 39.86, IG.F.2.7*]

7I.7.300   Dividends

7I.7.300.10   Entities might also wish to hedge anticipated dividends from foreign operations. However, expected dividends do not give rise to an exposure that will be recognised in profit or loss in the consolidated financial statements. Therefore, these cannot be hedged in a cash flow hedge or a net investment hedge in the consolidated financial statements. It is only once dividends are declared and become a receivable that hedge accounting may be applied in the consolidated financial statements. For example, dividends declared and receivable from a foreign subsidiary may be hedged for foreign currency risk because changes in foreign exchange rates would affect consolidated profit or loss.

7I.7.305   Exposures within associate or joint venture

7I.7.305.10   In our view, an investor in an associate or a joint venture cannot hedge an exposure that exists within the associate or joint venture. That is because the potential hedged item is not a forecast transaction or recognised asset or liability of the investor. The investor's equity ownership represents shared ownership of the associate or joint venture's net assets and liabilities, and the investor cannot look through to the associate or joint venture's individual assets or liabilities and designate one of them as the hedged item.

EXAMPLE 12 – EQUITY-ACCOUNTED INVESTEES

7I.7.305.20 Company R is an investor in Joint Venture J. J issues LIBOR-based variable rate debt. R cannot designate a cash flow hedge of J's variable rate debt because the potential hedged item is not a forecast transaction or a recognised asset or liability of R. R does not have any direct exposure to J's variable rate debt. Similarly, the impact of the debt interest payments is indirect on R's profit or loss because the impact is netted with the other results of J through R's application of the equity method. [*IAS 39.86*]

7I.7.310 QUALIFYING HEDGING INSTRUMENTS

7I.7.310.10 All derivatives, including separable embedded derivatives, can qualify as hedging instruments, with the following limitations.
- Written options may be designated as hedging instruments only for hedges of purchased options (see 7I.7.340).
- A derivative may not be designated as a hedging instrument for only a portion of its remaining period to maturity.
- Derivatives are generally designated as hedging instruments in their entirety. Except as noted in 7I.7.310.20, it is not permitted to designate only certain components of a derivative as a hedging instrument. For example, the foreign currency component of a cross-currency swap may not be designated as the hedging instrument without the interest rate component of the swap also being designated in the same or another qualifying hedging relationship. However, a *proportion* of the entire hedging instrument may be designated as the hedging instrument (see 7I.7.360). [*IAS 39.72, 74–75, AG94*]

7I.7.310.20 There are two exceptions from the requirement not to split the components of derivative hedging instruments:
- separating the intrinsic value and time value of an option; and
- separating the interest element and the spot price element in a forward. [*IAS 39.74*]

7I.7.310.30 The following uses of hedging instruments are permitted:
- designating a derivative as a hedging instrument subsequent to its initial recognition;
- designating two or more derivatives in combination as the hedging instrument, as long as none of the derivatives is a written option (see 7I.7.340.40);
- designating two or more non-derivatives, or a combination of derivatives and non-derivatives (see 7I.7.830.40), as a hedge of foreign currency risk;
- replacing or rolling over a hedging instrument at its maturity, if the replacement or rollover is planned and documented at inception of the hedging relationship;
- designating a derivative with an external party that offsets an internal derivative as a hedging instrument (see 7I.7.850);
- applying hedge accounting in the consolidated financial statements to a derivative entered into by a group entity different from the one that has the risk exposure (see 7I.7.840); and
- applying hedge accounting to a derivative even though that derivative is fully offset by another derivative with equal but opposite terms, as long as the second instrument was not entered into in

contemplation of the first or there is a substantive business purpose for entering into both instruments in separate transactions (see 7I.7.860.40). [*IAS 39.74–77, IG.F.1.12–IG.F.1.14, IG.F.3.9*]

7I.7.310.40   Non-derivatives may be designated as hedging instruments for hedges of foreign currency risk only. [*IAS 39.72*]

7I.7.320   **Purchased options**

7I.7.320.10   Purchased options may be used as hedging instruments provided that the hedge accounting criteria are met. Options, in contrast to forward and futures contracts, contain both an intrinsic value and a time value. [*IAS 39.AG94*]

7I.7.320.20   The cash flows of forecast transactions do not generally include a time value component but options do – e.g. a forecast transaction in a foreign currency that is hedged with an option. If the option is designated in its entirety (including time value), then effectiveness testing is based on comparing the full fair value change of the option and the present value of the change in cash flows of the forecast transaction (see 7I.7.600). The change in fair value of the option and the change in the present value of the cash flows of the forecast transaction will not be the same because the change in the time value element of the option is not offset by an equal and opposite change in the cash flows of the forecast transaction. [*IAS 39.AG99BA*]

7I.7.320.30   The time value of an option may be excluded from the hedging relationship. In this case, the option is more likely to be an effective hedge if the hedging relationship excludes time value and effectiveness is measured based on changes in intrinsic value alone. Designating only the changes in the intrinsic value of an option as a hedging instrument in the hedge of a one-sided risk in a hedged item may achieve perfect hedge effectiveness if the principal terms of the hedged item (i.e. amount, maturity etc) and the hedging instrument are the same. However, this results in changes in the time value of the option being recognised directly in profit or loss regardless of the hedging model used (see 7I.7.600.20). [*IAS 39.74, AG99BA*]

7I.7.320.40   In our view, either the spot or the forward price/rate can be used in determining the intrinsic value of an option. However, the approach should be specified as part of the hedge documentation and applied consistently during the term of the hedge. Furthermore, if the forward rate is used for determining the fair value of an American-style option, then the rate should be determined using the option's maturity date.

7I.7.330   **Dynamic hedging strategies**

7I.7.330.10   An entity may apply 'delta-neutral' hedging strategies and other dynamic strategies under which the quantity of the hedging instrument is constantly adjusted to maintain a desired hedge ratio. This may include a dynamic hedging strategy that assesses both the intrinsic value and the time value of an option contract. To qualify for hedge accounting, the entity documents how it will monitor and update the hedge and measure hedge effectiveness, properly track all terminations and redesignations of the hedging instruments and demonstrate that all other hedge accounting criteria are met (see 7I.7.120), including the requirement that the hedging instruments are designated for the whole time period that they remain outstanding. An entity is also required to be able to demonstrate an expectation that the hedge will be highly effective for a specified short period of time during which the hedge is not expected to be adjusted. Accordingly, an entity documents that under such dynamic strategies both prospective and retrospective effectiveness are assessed over these short periods as if each of these short periods were a separate hedging relationship. In our view, when the quantity of the hedging instrument is adjusted, such as a change in the proportion of the derivative instrument designated as the hedging instrument or the addition of or deletion from a group of hedging derivatives (other than documented rollovers and replacements (see 71.7.680.90–95)), then the existing hedging relationship should generally be discontinued prospectively. [*IAS 39.74–75, 91(a), 101(a), IG.F.1.9*]

71.7.330.20   In our view, an entity is not precluded from designating a dynamic hedging strategy under which, to maintain a desired hedge ratio, the quantity of the designated hedged item rather than the quantity of the hedging instruments is adjusted. For example, an entity has designated a forecast foreign currency transaction as the hedged item in a cash flow hedging relationship. The hedged risk is the variability in the cash flows arising from movements in the spot foreign exchange rate and the hedging instrument is a foreign currency option. The entity designates a dynamic hedging relationship under which the designated amount of the hedged item is adjusted each week based on weekly changes in the delta of the foreign currency option. Each time the hedged item is adjusted, the existing hedging relationship is generally terminated and a new hedging relationship is designated. Under this approach, effectiveness is assessed separately for each weekly period and ineffectiveness is recognised to the extent that the change in the fair value of the option over this period is greater than the change in present value of the hedged cash flows. The present value of the hedged cash flows is based on their expected settlement dates.

71.7.340   Written options

71.7.340.10   The potential loss on an option that an entity writes could be significantly greater than the potential gain in the fair value of the related hedged item. In other words, a written option is not effective in reducing the profit or loss exposure of a hedged item and therefore does not qualify as a hedging instrument unless it is designated as an offset of a closely related purchased option that is embedded in, and not separated from, a host contract. If the embedded purchased option is separated, then hedge accounting would be unnecessary because both the separated purchased option and the written option would be measured at FVTPL. [*IAS 39.AG94*]

71.7.340.20   In our view, a combined hedging instrument that is created in a single transaction with the same counterparty and that is made up of a number of components that are not separately transferable may be designated as a hedging instrument, even if one of the components is a written option – e.g. a zero-cost collar created in a single transaction with the same counterparty – as long as the combination of derivative components does not result in a net written option. [*IAS 39.77, IG.F.1.3*]

71.7.340.30   Consequently, an interest rate collar or other single derivative instrument that includes a written option component and a purchased option component can be designated as a hedging instrument as long as the instrument is a net purchased option or zero-cost collar, as opposed to a net written option. The following are considered in determining whether a combination of derivatives constitutes a net written option.

- No net premium is received either at inception or over the life of the combination. If a premium is received, then it would be evidence that the instrument is a net written option because it serves to compensate the writer of the option for the risk incurred.

- The option components have similar critical terms and conditions and, with the exception of strike prices, the same underlying variable or variables, currency, denomination and maturity.
- The notional amount of the written option component is not greater than the notional amount of the purchased option component. [*IAS 39.IG.F.1.3*]

7I.7.340.40   An entity is not permitted to designate as the hedging instrument a combination of derivatives, concluded in *separate transactions*, that includes a written option or a net written option even if the result of such a grouping is economically equivalent to entering into a net purchased option or a zero-cost collar. For example, a zero-cost collar that is created synthetically by entering into a cap in one transaction and a floor in a separate transaction would not qualify as a hedging instrument. [*IAS 39.77*]

7I.7.350   Non-derivatives

7I.7.350.10   Only for foreign currency hedges, the hedging instrument may be:
- a loan or receivable;
- a held-to-maturity investment;
- an available-for-sale monetary asset; or
- a financial liability or a cash balance. [*IAS 39.72, AG95*]

7I.7.350.15   However, a foreign currency firm commitment or forecast transaction does not qualify as a hedging instrument because it is neither a derivative nor a non-derivative financial asset or liability. [*IAS 39.IG.F.1.2*]

EXAMPLE 13 – NON-DERIVATIVES CAN ONLY HEDGE FOREIGN CURRENCY RISK

> 7I.7.350.20   Company J has the yen as its functional currency and has a fixed interest rate US dollar borrowing. The borrowing may be designated as a hedge of the foreign exchange exposure on a net investment in a US dollar foreign operation or a US dollar sales commitment. However, the US dollar borrowing may not be designated as a hedge of the interest and foreign currency exposure on a fixed rate US dollar debt security or the entire fair value exposure on a US dollar sales commitment. This is because non-derivatives qualify as hedges of foreign currency risk only. [*IAS 39.IG.F.1.1–IG.F.1.2*]

7I.7.350.30   In a foreign currency hedge, the currency of the hedging instrument and the currency of the hedged item should be the same or it should be possible to demonstrate a high degree of correlation between the two currencies. Therefore, extending Example 13, the US dollar borrowing may not be designated as a hedge of a euro sales commitment unless a very strong correlation between the US dollar and the euro can be demonstrated.

7I.7.350.40   A combination of derivatives and non-derivatives, or proportions thereof, may be used as the hedging instrument in a hedge of foreign currency risk (see 7I.7.830.40). [*IAS 39.77*]

7I.7.350.50   In our view, an operating lease cannot be designated as a hedging instrument for a hedge of foreign currency risk. This is because payments due or receivable under an operating lease are not recognised financial liabilities or assets that could qualify as a hedging instrument for a hedge of foreign currency risk. However, if the operating lease payments are denominated in a foreign currency, then the foreign exchange exposure of these lease payments could qualify as a hedged item (rather than as a hedging instrument) in a cash flow hedge (see 7I.7.430.30–50).

7I.7.350.60   Conversely, in our view a recognised finance lease receivable can qualify as a hedging instrument of foreign currency risk even though finance lease receivables otherwise are outside the scope of IAS 39, provided that all hedge accounting requirements are met (see 7I.7.430.10).

7I.7.350.70   In our view, a financial liability arising from an entity's obligation to repurchase its own equity instruments does not qualify as a hedging instrument. The ability to use non-derivative items as hedging instruments is restricted to cash instruments. In this case, even though the repurchase obligation is measured at amortised cost as if it were a non-derivative financial liability, the instrument is in fact a derivative instrument and not a cash instrument. [*IAS 39.72, BC144–BC145*]

7I.7.360   Proportion of an instrument

7I.7.360.10   A proportion of a financial instrument may be designated as the hedging instrument. For example, 50 percent of the notional amount of a forward contract may be designated as the hedging instrument in a cash flow hedge of a highly probable forecast sale. Gains or losses on the proportion of the derivative financial instrument not designated as the hedging instrument are recognised immediately in profit or loss. [*IAS 39.75*]

7I.7.370   Designation for entire period

7I.7.370.10   Derivatives and non-derivatives are designated as hedging instruments for the entire period for which they are outstanding because the entire fair value of the hedging instrument is considered when assessing the effectiveness of the hedge. For example, a pay-fixed receive-floating interest rate swap with a maturity of 10 years cannot be designated as a hedging instrument of a floating rate bond for just the first eight years by using the eight-year yield curve to measure the changes in the fair value of the swap when assessing hedge effectiveness. Such a method would allow an entity to exclude part of the hedging instrument's fair value, which is not allowed. Hedge designation would, however, be permitted in this case if the derivative were designated as the hedging instrument in its entirety – i.e. the changes in the fair value of the swap are computed using all of its cash flows based on the 10-year yield curve when assessing hedge effectiveness. However, such a strategy would lead to ineffectiveness and may also result in hedge accounting being precluded if the hedging relationship is not expected to be highly effective. [*IAS 39.74–75*]

7I.7.370.20   It is possible to designate a derivative or non-derivative as the hedging instrument subsequent to initial recognition provided that the fair value for the entire remaining period for which the derivative or non-derivative remains outstanding is included when assessing hedge effectiveness. For example, if a derivative is designated as a hedging instrument at inception – but hedge accounting ceases because the hedge criteria are no longer met or the designation is revoked at a later date – then it is possible to designate the derivative as the hedging instrument in another hedging relationship at a later stage as long as the designation and assessment of hedge effectiveness include the fair value for the entire period for which the derivative remains outstanding.

7I.7.370.30   A derivative may be designated as the hedging instrument in a hedge of a forecast transaction that has a maturity shorter than the remaining maturity of the hedging derivative. Because the derivative is required to be designated for its entire remaining term to maturity, in such a hedge there will be some ineffectiveness because of the differences in maturity dates of the hedged item and hedging derivative. Also, the ineffectiveness may sometimes be significant so as to preclude application of hedge accounting altogether if the hedge is assessed as not being highly effective.

7I.7.380   **Basis swaps**

7I.7.380.10   An entity may swap one floating rate exposure into another using basis swaps. Basis swaps are interest rate swaps that exchange one base rate for another. For example, an entity that issues a bond paying 12-month Euribor enters into a basis swap whereby it receives 12-month Euribor and pays three-month Euribor, with the notional and maturity of the swap matching those of the bond. The question arises about whether such a basis swap can be designated as a hedge of the floating rate bond.

7I.7.380.20   Although swapping one base rate for another with a different repricing period may eliminate some of the cash flow variation or some of the fair value variation, there is no model that explicitly allows for hedge accounting when one floating rate is swapped into another. Because the bond in 7I.7.380.10 has a floating rate of interest, it may be eligible for cash flow hedge accounting. However, because the interest rate swap exchanges one floating cash flow stream into another, some variability in cash flows remains.

7I.7.380.30   Therefore, in our view a basis swap does not generally qualify as a hedging instrument in a cash flow hedge except in the very specific circumstances discussed in 7I.7.380.40.

7I.7.380.40   If an entity has both an asset and a liability on which it receives interest at a rate indexed to the base rate on the pay leg (e.g. LIBOR) of the basis swap, and pays interest at a rate equal to the base rate on the receive leg (e.g. Euribor) of the basis swap, then in our view hedge accounting would be appropriate assuming that the other hedge criteria are satisfied. Both the existing asset and the liability are designated as hedged items in the same hedging relationship and both positions are considered in effectiveness testing. If the hedge fails to be highly effective in offsetting the exposure to variability in cash flows in response to changes in the designated interest rates on either or both of the designated asset or liability, then hedge accounting is terminated for the entire relationship. In this case, the combined variability in cash flows arising from movements in base rates arising from both the asset and the liability is eliminated by the basis swap. Consequently, we believe that it is possible to designate the basis swap in a cash flow hedging relationship in this limited circumstance. [*IAS 39.IG.F.2.18*]

7I.7.390   **Liability bearing constant maturity interest rate**

7I.7.390.10   An entity may issue instruments that have a floating rate of interest that resets periodically according to the fixed-maturity market rate based on an instrument that has a duration extending beyond that of the reset period (a 'constant maturity' interest rate) – e.g. a 10-year bond on which the interest rate resets semi-annually to the current weighted-average yield on treasury bonds with a 10-year maturity. The effect of this feature is that the interest rate always is equal to the market return on an instrument with 10 years left to maturity, even as the instrument paying the coupon itself nears maturity. To hedge its exposure to the constant maturity interest rate, an entity may enter into an interest rate swap that pays LIBOR or a similar rate and receives the constant maturity rate.

7I.7.390.20   A question arises over whether such an interest rate swap can be designated as the hedging instrument in a hedge of the liability – i.e. the issued floating rate instrument. First, it is necessary to consider whether the constant maturity feature in the liability comprises a separable embedded derivative. Only after this analysis can the appropriateness of hedge accounting for the proposed transaction be considered.

7I.7.390.30   In our view, the constant maturity feature comprises an embedded derivative (a 'constant maturity' swap). This embedded derivative is not closely related to the host debt instrument because it could potentially double the holder's initial rate of return and could result in a rate of return that is at least twice what the market return would be for a contract with the same terms as the host contract, unless it has a cap at an appropriate level to prevent the doubling effect (see 7I.2.250).

7I.7.390.40   In the absence of an appropriate cap, the entity separately accounts for a fixed rate host debt instrument and a constant maturity swap. Because the constant maturity swap is a non-option embedded derivative, its terms would have to be determined so as to result in a fair value of zero at inception (see 7I.2.380.40). Both the embedded derivative and the interest rate swap will be measured at fair value, with gains and losses recognised in profit or loss. Hedge accounting would not be permitted in these circumstances because the interest rate swap would have to be designated as the hedging instrument in a hedge of the separately accounted-for embedded derivative, which is not permitted. [*IAS 39.IG.F.2.1*]

7I.7.390.50   However, if the terms of the liability include an appropriate cap, then the embedded derivative is not accounted for separately and an issue arises over whether such a loan can be hedged with an interest rate basis swap that pays LIBOR and receives the same constant maturity rate. Although the bond issued is a variable rate bond, the variable rate it pays is a constant maturity rate. Consequently, the bond has a fair value exposure arising from the difference between the discounting rate used to value the bond (the repricing basis) and the 10-year constant maturity rate (the interest-rate basis). For a 'plain vanilla' floating rate bond, there is no such difference and consequently no fair value exposure arising from interest rate changes. Similarly, the basis swap in this example, being a basis swap that has a repricing basis different from its interest rate basis, also has a fair value exposure for its entire life.

7I.7.390.60   Consequently, in our view the constant maturity bond with an appropriate interest rate cap in 7I.7.390.50 can be designated as the hedged item in a fair value hedge of interest rate risk with the hedging instrument being a constant maturity basis swap that also has a matching interest rate cap, assuming that the other hedge accounting criteria are met. In such a hedging relationship, the hedge is of the fair value exposure for the life of the hedged item and hedging instrument, rather than of an exposure that exists only between repricing dates. Conversely, in our view it is not possible to designate a plain vanilla floating rate bond in a fair value hedging relationship using a plain vanilla basis swap as the hedging instrument, because neither the bond nor the swap has a fair value exposure over its entire life. This designation is possible only when a fair value exposure exists for the entire life of the hedged item and the instrument.

7I.7.400   Hedging zero-coupon bond with plain vanilla interest rate swap

7I.7.400.10   Zero-coupon debt instruments in the form of bonds, bills of exchange and commercial paper are exposed to, among other risks, fair value interest rate risk. Entities may seek to hedge this risk using plain vanilla interest rate swaps. In our view, to achieve hedge accounting in these circumstances, an entity would need to adopt a dynamic hedging strategy.

EXAMPLE 14 – HEDGING ZERO-COUPON BOND WITH PLAIN VANILLA INTEREST RATE SWAP

7I.7.400.20   Company V acquires a one-year zero-coupon bond at 95 with a face value (redemption amount) of 100. At the same date, V enters into a one-year interest rate swap. The swap reprices on a quarterly basis and the interest rate on the fixed leg of the swap is equal to the bond's yield. Swap settlements are made quarterly. V wishes to designate the interest rate swap as the hedging instrument in a fair value hedge of interest rate risk arising from the bond.

7I.7.400.30   Such a designation is unlikely to be effective because there are significant differences between the instruments and the way in which their fair values respond to changes in market interest rates. In particular, there are only two cash flows on the bond (an acquisition outflow of 95 and a redemption inflow of 100), whereas there are four cash flows on the interest rate swap because interest coupons are exchanged on a quarterly basis. Therefore, the hedge is unlikely to meet the prospective effectiveness requirements; at any time after the first period, the fair value change of a single cash flow of 100 at the bond's redemption date will not correspond to the fair value change of the three remaining interest cash flows on the swap.

7I.7.400.40   To achieve hedge accounting in these circumstances, an entity would need to adopt a dynamic hedging strategy. At each payment date of the swap, it would need to adjust the hedging instrument – e.g. by designating an additional swap into the hedging relationship. Using this strategy, the entity would need to prove that the hedge remains effective for the period until the hedging instrument is next adjusted. This hedging strategy would have to be documented clearly at inception of the hedging relationship. [*IAS 39.AG107*]

7I.7.410   **Derivatives with knock-in or knock-out features**

7I.7.410.10   Except for some written options, the use of derivatives as hedging instruments is not prohibited if the other requirements for hedge accounting are met (see 7I.7.120). Therefore, if an entity intends to designate a derivative with a knock-in or knock-out feature as a hedging instrument, then in our view the entity should assess whether the knock-in or knock-out feature indicates that the instrument is a net written option for which hedge accounting is precluded (see 7I.7.340). In our view, knock-in or knock-out features should be considered a net written option if a net premium is received by the entity in the form of a favourable rate or other term in exchange for these features. [*IAS 39.72*]

EXAMPLE 15 – DERIVATIVES WITH KNOCK-IN OR KNOCK-OUT FEATURES

7I.7.410.20   Company N enters into an arm's length pay-6% receive-LIBOR interest rate swap under which the rights and obligations of both N and the counterparty are extinguished if a contingent event occurs. If N had entered into an otherwise identical interest rate swap without the knock-out feature, then the swap would have been priced at pay-8% receive-LIBOR. Unless the hedged item contains an offsetting and closely related embedded net purchased option, N is not permitted to designate the swap as a hedging instrument because the favourable difference between the fixed payment legs represents a net premium that N receives over the life of the instrument in return for writing the option (see 7I.7.340).

71.7.410.30   Even if a derivative with a knock-in or a knock-out feature is not considered a net written option and therefore not precluded from being designated as a hedging instrument, it is unlikely that such an instrument will be highly effective in offsetting changes in the fair value or the cash flows arising from the hedged risk unless the hedged item contains a similar offsetting knock-in or knock-out feature. [*IAS 39.88, IG.F.5.5*]

71.7.420   QUALIFYING HEDGED RISKS

71.7.420.10   The hedged risk is the specific financial risk of the qualifying hedged item (see 7I.7.170) that the entity is exposed to and has chosen to hedge.

71.7.420.20   The hedged risk should be one that could affect profit or loss. For example, a hedge of the purchase price of treasury shares could not qualify for hedge accounting because all treasury share transactions are recognised in equity (see 7I.3.430). [*IAS 39.86, AG110*]

71.7.420.30   A financial asset or liability can be hedged against exposure to any one or more of its individual risk types that is identifiable and measurable, including market prices, interest rates or a component of interest rates, foreign currency rates and credit risk. Conversely, a non-financial item may be hedged with respect to either all of its risks or foreign currency risk only (see 7I.7.440). [*IAS 39.81–82, IG.F.3.5*]

71.7.430   Lease payments and receipts#

71.7.430.10   In our view, whether cash flows payable or receivable under a lease arrangement should be financial items or non-financial items with respect to their designation as a hedged item depends on whether the lease is classified as a finance lease or an operating lease. In our view, a recognised finance lease payable or receivable is a financial item even though such an item is not generally in the scope of IAS 39 (see 7I.7.100). [*IAS 32.AG9*]

71.7.430.20   However, an operating lease arrangement is an executory contract. Under an operating lease arrangement the lessor performs when, and only when, the asset is made available for the lessee in the agreed time period – i.e. the lessor does not fully perform under the contract by initially providing the lessee with the access to the leased asset. Accordingly, in our view an operating lease should not be regarded as a financial item, although individual payments currently due and payable with respect to the elapsed period of the lease term for which performance has occurred are financial items.

EXAMPLE 16 – HEDGE OF FUTURE CASH FLOWS IN OPERATING LEASE

71.7.430.30   A lessor or lessee may wish to designate the future cash flows in an operating lease arrangement as the hedged item in a hedge of the variability in cash flows arising from movements in a benchmark interest rate or the inflation rate, when rentals are indexed to such a rate.

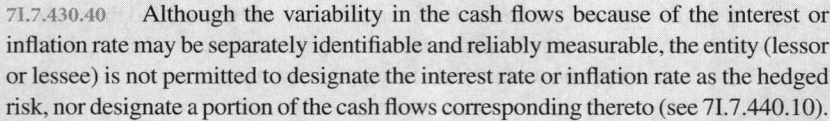

7I.7.430.40   Although the variability in the cash flows because of the interest or inflation rate may be separately identifiable and reliably measurable, the entity (lessor or lessee) is not permitted to designate the interest rate or inflation rate as the hedged risk, nor designate a portion of the cash flows corresponding thereto (see 7I.7.440.10).

7I.7.430.50   However, the entity (lessor or lessee) may be able to designate the entire variability in cash flows arising from the operating lease arrangement if it can demonstrate high effectiveness. If operating lease rentals are denominated in a foreign currency, then the entity (lessor or lessee) may be able to designate the variability in those cash flows arising from foreign currency risk as the hedged risk (see 7I.7.450).

7I.7.435   **FORTHCOMING REQUIREMENTS**

7I.7.435.10   IFRS 16 introduces a single, on-balance sheet lease accounting model for lessees and eliminates the distinction between operating and finance leases. Unless a lessee elects the recognition exemptions for short-term leases and/or leases of low value assets (see 5.1A.140), it recognises a right-of-use asset representing its right to use the underlying asset and a lease liability for the present value of its obligation to make future lease payments.

7I.7.435.20   The lease liability is similar to blended payments of principal and interest under a loan. The treatment of the lease liability is similar to how a lessor recognises a finance lease receivable. Accordingly, it appears that the lease liability recognised by a lessee for future lease payments under IFRS 16 is a financial item even though the liability is not generally in the scope of IAS 39 (see 7.1.100). Therefore, if a lessee applies IFRS 16 while applying the hedging requirements in IAS 39, then it may designate the future cash flows in a lease arrangement as the hedged item in their entirety or, unlike in Example 16, for a specific risk component (see 7I.7.180.40) – e.g. for variability in cash flows arising from a benchmark interest rate or the inflation rate, when rentals are indexed to such a rate. [*IAS 32.AG9*]

7I.7.440   **Non-financial items**

7I.7.440.10   A non-financial item is hedged with respect to either all of its risks or foreign currency risk only. This is because foreign currency risk is the only risk associated with a non-financial item that is considered to be separately measurable. Consequently, even if an entity is able to isolate and measure the appropriate portion of the cash flows or fair value changes attributable to a specific risk component, it is not allowed to designate these cash flows or fair value changes as the hedged item. This is an outright prohibition in IAS 39. [*IAS 39.82, AG100*]

EXAMPLE 17 – HEDGING NON-FINANCIAL ITEMS FOR RISKS OTHER THAN FOREIGN CURRENCY RISK

7I.7.440.20   Company C is a producer of chocolate bars. C wishes to hedge the fair value of its inventory in respect of changes in the sugar price by taking out a sugar forward in the commodity market. It would not be permissible in this situation to

designate as the hedged risk the price risk only related to the price of sugar because the hedged item is a non-financial item and the risk of changes in sugar prices is a risk component other than foreign currency risk.

7I.7.440.25   As an alternative, C may designate the sugar forward as a hedge of all fair value changes of the entire chocolate bar inventory. However, it is not generally possible to predict or reliably measure the effect that a change in the price of an ingredient or component will have on the price of an entire non-financial asset or liability. Consequently, it is unlikely that a direct and consistent relationship exists between changes in the sugar price and changes in the fair value of C's chocolate bar inventory. Because chocolate bars consist of ingredients other than sugar (cocoa, milk etc), the hedge is unlikely to be highly effective and in that case hedge accounting would not be possible unless the other ingredients are also hedged.

7I.7.440.27   However, it may be possible to achieve hedge accounting if all of the main ingredients are hedged and the ineffectiveness arising from changes in fair value of the unhedged ingredients is not significant.

7I.7.440.30   However, in our view it is acceptable to hedge a non-financial item with respect to all of its risks *other than* foreign currency risk.

EXAMPLE 18 – HEDGING NON-FINANCIAL ITEM FOR ALL RISKS OTHER THAN FOREIGN CURRENCY RISK

7I.7.440.35   Company G has the euro as its functional currency. G wishes to hedge its forecast purchases of jet oil. The forecast purchase exposes G to two risks, both of which are reliably measurable: price risk of jet oil denominated in US dollars, and foreign exchange risk of US dollars against the euro. G would be able to designate the foreign currency component of jet oil purchases as the hedged item. Moreover, we believe that because the price risk of the jet oil denominated in US dollars represents the risk of the underlying purchases in their entirety, except for retranslation to euro, it is also acceptable to designate this as the hedged risk.

7I.7.440.40   Certain commodity exchange-traded derivatives are based on a standard quality or grade. Examples of commodities that are traded in a standardised form are wheat, corn, coffee beans and metals. Entities often enter into derivatives for a standard commodity before determining the actual quality of product that they require for production. When a commodity exchange-traded derivative is used to hedge a non-financial item, an entity is still limited to designating the hedged risk as either all of its risks or foreign currency risk only.

EXAMPLE 19 – HEDGING FUTURE SALES USING COMMODITY FUTURES

7I.7.440.50   Company C is a producer of commodities. C uses traded commodity futures to hedge committed future sales of commodities. The contract price for the physical sale of the commodities is split into two components, which are specified

in the contract terms: the standard commodity price based on the index underlying the futures contract; and a discount or premium for the specific quality, delivery location, timing and payment terms for the specific delivery. This clearly enables the separation of the appropriate portion of the cash flows of the physical contract attributable to changes in the price of the standard commodity. However, given the outright prohibition in IAS 39, C would not be allowed to designate as the hedged item only the portion of cash flows under the sales contract that are linked to the standard commodity price or designate all the cash flows in the contract but for the risk of the changes in standard commodity price only.

7I.7.440.60   Instead, the actual selling price is designated as the hedged item. However, because of the difference between the hedging instrument (futures contract based on the standard commodity) and the hedged item (actual fair value/price of the product to be sold), hedge ineffectiveness may arise. Additionally, it may be difficult to demonstrate on a prospective basis that the hedging relationship is expected to be highly effective in achieving offsetting changes in fair value or cash flows attributable to the hedged risk throughout the hedging period.

7I.7.440.70   The problem of ineffectiveness can be addressed partly by designating the hedging instrument and hedged item in a relationship using a hedge ratio of other than one. Although the futures contract based on a standard commodity and the actual purchase or sale differ in some respects, it may be possible to identify a correlation between the price of the standardised commodity and the actual commodity. This may be done using statistical models such as regression analysis. The slope of the resulting regression line can be used to establish a hedge ratio that maximises hedge effectiveness.

7I.7.440.75   For example, C might hedge its future purchase of Brazilian coffee with a commodity future whose underlying is the price of Colombian coffee. Assuming that there is a valid statistical relationship between the two prices, and a regression analysis identifies a slope of 1.02 for the regression line, a derivative with a notional amount of 1.02 tonnes of Colombian coffee could be designated as a hedge of the purchase of one tonne of Brazilian coffee. Although some ineffectiveness will inevitably result, using a hedge ratio of other than one may help to keep this within an acceptable range such that hedge accounting can be continued. [*IAS 39.AG100*]

7I.7.440.80   A similar issue arises when an entity hedges an ingredient of a non-financial item.

EXAMPLE 20 – HEDGING INGREDIENT OF NON-FINANCIAL ITEM

7I.7.440.82   Company N hedges the purchase of jet fuel. N may want to hedge its entire jet fuel price exposure or a component of this price exposure. The price of jet fuel is derived from the prices of the various components that make up jet fuel. Each of the components is traded independently, with market prices available for each component. Although the quantity of each of the components in a metric tonne of jet fuel always is fixed, the relative value of each of the components differs because the prices of these components change more or less independently.

7I.7.440.84   Various strategies are possible when hedging a transaction such as jet fuel purchases. However, not all would qualify for hedge accounting.
- *Hedge the components of jet fuel price:* N may choose to hedge its price exposure to only certain components of jet fuel (e.g. brent or gas oil) and to retain its price exposure to the other components. This may be because of:
    - the relatively more liquid nature of these components;
    - the fact that these components represent the most significant components of jet fuel prices; or
    - the independent nature of the pricing of the various components.

7I.7.440.86   For example, brent and gas oil swaps could be economic hedges of the corresponding brent or gas oil components of jet fuel purchases. This may result in perfect effectiveness for these components because the critical terms of the derivative and the component match, their prices move in tandem and the notional amount of the derivative equals the quantity of the component in the jet fuel that will be purchased. However, as noted in 7I.7.440.10, hedge accounting for components of risk for non-financial items such as jet fuel is prohibited.

7I.7.440.88   Therefore, in order for this hedging strategy to qualify for hedge accounting, the entire price risk of the jet fuel purchase is designated as the hedged item and a high degree of correlation should be demonstrated between the price of the hedged ingredient and the jet fuel price. Alternatively, if there is some degree of correlation, then N may use a hedge ratio of other than one to maximise hedge effectiveness. However, if the prices of the individual components move more or less independently, then it may not be possible to demonstrate any correlation. This would also make it difficult to demonstrate on a prospective basis that the hedging relationship is expected to be highly effective throughout the hedging period even within the prescribed range of 80–125% (see 7I.7.510).
- *Hedge the entire price of jet fuel:* To meet the requirements regarding the hedging of commodity price risk, N may use a jet fuel derivative to hedge the entire price risk exposure arising from the purchase of jet fuel. This hedging strategy would qualify for hedge accounting, assuming that all other criteria have been met.

7I.7.440.90   Commodity price exposure on inventory qualifies as a hedged risk even if the inventory is measured at cost; the profit or loss impact arises when the inventory is sold. However, as noted in 7I.7.440.86, the hedged item is the entire change in the fair value of the inventory and not just a component of the fair value changes. For example, it is not possible to hedge only the rubber component in an inventory of tyres. [*IAS 39.IG.F.3.6*]

Foreign currency exposures

7I.7.450.10   In our view, hedge accounting is not permitted for hedges that convert one foreign currency exposure into another foreign currency exposure, unless the entity has a corresponding position in the second foreign currency or that second foreign currency is closely correlated to the entity's functional currency.

EXAMPLE 21 – CONVERTING ONE CURRENCY EXPOSURE TO ANOTHER CURRENCY EXPOSURE

7I.7.450.20   Company S has the rand as its functional currency. S has issued a yen-denominated bond and has a US dollar receivable; both instruments have the equivalent notional amount and the same maturity. To hedge both the US dollar and the yen exposures, S enters into a forward contract to convert yen to US dollars. This relationship between the bond and the receivable (the hedged items) and the yen-to-US dollar forward (the hedging instrument) would qualify for hedge accounting.

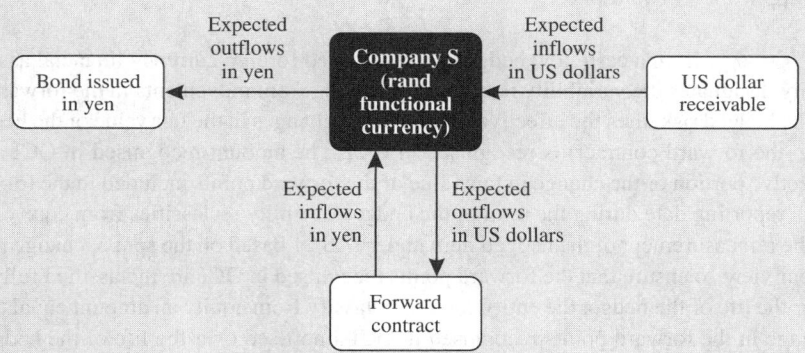

7I.7.450.30   In our view, the hedge documentation should identify both foreign currency positions in designating the hedged risk, and in measuring effectiveness both positions should be considered. If the hedge fails to be highly effective in offsetting the exposure to changes in the designated foreign currency exposures on either or both of the designated US dollar receivable or the yen-denominated bond, then hedge accounting is terminated for the entire relationship. However, if S had issued only the bond and did not have a US dollar receivable, then the forward contract would not qualify for hedge accounting because it merely changes one currency exposure for another. [*IAS 39.IG.F.2.18*]

7I.7.450.40   Non-financial items themselves – e.g. property, plant and equipment and intangible assets – generally have no separately measurable foreign currency risk. One situation in which the foreign currency risk on non-financial items will affect profit or loss is if the owner has a forecast sale that will be denominated in a foreign currency. In our view, the risk that the sales proceeds in the entity's functional currency would change because of changes in foreign exchange rates qualifies to be hedged in a cash flow hedge if the forecast sale is highly probable. [*IAS 39.IG.F.3.6, IG.F.5.6, IG.F.6.5*]

7I.7.450.50   In addition, in our view when the transaction date – i.e. delivery date of the non-financial asset – precedes the cash settlement date of the related receivable or payable in a highly probable forecast sale or purchase, the variability in cash flows arising from movements in the foreign exchange rates may be hedged until the transaction date or the cash settlement date. For example, an entity forecasts a highly probable future sale denominated in a foreign currency to occur on 30 September 2018, in respect of which the cash settlement is expected to occur on 31 October 2018. In our view, the entity may hedge the forecast sale in respect of the risk of changes in foreign exchange rates either to 30 September 2018 or to 31 October 2018. In the former case, a cash inflow from the sale and a simultaneous cash outflow for the financing of the sale would be deemed to occur on 30 September 2018. Financing the sale is a different transaction from the forecast sale transaction, and therefore the timing of the settlement of the financing does not result in ineffectiveness for the hedging relationship.

7I.7.450.60   In our view, an entity may designate its exposure to changes in either the spot or the forward rate as the hedged risk. If exposure to changes in the forward rate is designated as the hedged risk, then the interest component included in the forward rate is part of the hedged foreign currency risk. Changes in the fair value or cash flows of the hedged item are measured based on changes in the applicable forward rate.

7I.7.450.70   If, in a cash flow hedge of a recognised foreign currency financial asset or liability, an entity designates the variability in cash flows arising from movements in the forward exchange rates as the hedged risk, then the effective portion of the changes in the fair value of the hedging instrument (e.g. the forward contract) is recognised in OCI. The amount recognised in OCI also includes the effective portion of the change in fair value of the forward points included in the forward contract. At each reporting date during the term of the hedge, the entity reclassifies from equity an amount equal to the remeasurement of the hedged item under IAS 21 based on the spot exchange rates. In addition, in our view, to ensure that the forward points recognised in OCI are reclassified fully to profit or loss over the life of the hedge, the entity should reclassify from equity an amount equal to the cumulative change in the forward points recognised in OCI amortised over the life of the hedging relationship using the interest rate implicit in the forward contract.

7I.7.450.80   If, in a cash flow hedge of a highly probable forecast sale or purchase of a non-financial item, an entity uses a forward contract to hedge the forward exchange rate through to the transaction's cash settlement date, then in our view cash flow hedge accounting may be applied as described below.

- The effective portion of the gain or loss on the hedging instrument computed with reference to the hedged forward rate is recognised in OCI during the period before the occurrence of the forecast purchase or sale.
- The functional currency interest rate implicit in the hedging relationship as a result of entering into the forward contract (i.e. forward points) is used to determine the amount of cost or income to be ascribed to each period of the hedging relationship. The period of the hedging relationship in this case includes the period from the date of the hedge designation to the date of cash settlement of the forecast transaction.
- For a highly probable forecast sale, the amount of cost or income ascribed to the forecast period until the date the sale occurs is reclassified from equity to profit or loss on that date. For a highly probable forecast purchase, the amount of cost or income ascribed to the forecast period until the date of purchase is either reclassified from equity as a basis adjustment to the initial cost or other carrying amount of the purchased non-financial item on the date of purchase, or reclassi-

fied from equity to profit or loss in the same period or periods during which the item acquired affects profit or loss.

- On occurrence of the forecast sale – i.e. the transaction date – the difference between the spot foreign exchange rates at the inception of the hedge and on the transaction date is reclassified from equity to profit or loss. In a hedge of a forecast purchase, a similar amount may be reclassified from equity as a basis adjustment to the initial cost or other carrying amount of the purchased non-financial item on the date of purchase. Alternatively, the entity may choose not to adjust the cost or the carrying amount of the purchased non-financial item and instead reclassify the deferred gain or loss from equity to profit or loss in the same period or periods during which the item acquired affects profit or loss.
- At each reporting date during the life of the recognised foreign currency receivable or payable, the entity reclassifies from equity to profit or loss an amount equal to the remeasurement of the receivable or payable under IAS 21 based on the spot exchange rates.
- The cost or income ascribed to each period during the life of the recognised foreign currency receivable or payable is reclassified from equity to profit or loss at each reporting date.

7I.7.450.90   As an alternative to the cash flow hedge accounting described in 7I.7.450.80, an entity may apply cash flow hedge accounting as follows.
- The effective portion of the gain or loss on the hedging instrument computed with reference to the hedged forward exchange rate is recognised in OCI during the period before the occurrence of the forecast purchase or sale.
- For a highly probable forecast sale, this cumulative amount recognised in OCI for the effective portion of the gain or loss on the hedging instrument is reclassified from equity to profit or loss on the date the sale occurs. For a highly probable forecast purchase, this cumulative amount is either reclassified from equity as a basis adjustment to the initial cost or other carrying amount of the purchased non-financial item on the date of purchase or reclassified from equity to profit or loss in the same period or periods during which the item acquired affects profit or loss.
- At each reporting date during the life of the recognised foreign currency receivable or payable, the effective portion of the gain or loss on the hedging instrument – computed with respect to the forward exchange rate and recognised in OCI – is reclassified to profit or loss. [*IAS 39.IG.F.5.6*]

7I.7.450.100   A firm commitment to acquire a business in a business combination can qualify as the hedged item only in a hedge of foreign currency risk. In our view, the same applies to a forecast business combination, assuming that the transaction is highly probable and meets the other hedge accounting criteria (see 7I.7.265). In addition, for the purpose of the investor's separate financial statements, in our view a hedge of the cash flow variability associated with a forecast purchase or sale of an investment in a subsidiary (e.g. an investment in equity shares) can qualify as a hedged item. This is because the investment is or will be recognised as a separate asset (carried at cost or available-for-sale) in those separate financial statements and its disposal or impairment could affect profit or loss in those separate financial statements. [*IAS 39.88(c), AG98*]

7I.7.460   General business risks

7I.7.460.10   To qualify for hedge accounting, the hedged risk should be specific and identifiable. A hedge against general business risks, such as physical damage of an asset, an increase in the price payable in a business combination or the risk that a transaction will not occur, does not qualify for hedge accounting. [*IAS 39.AG98, AG110, IG.F.2.8*]

7I.7.470   Hedges of more than one risk type

7I.7.470.10   A hedging instrument, or a proportion thereof, is designated in its entirety, because there is normally a single fair value measure for a hedging instrument and the factors (risk components) that cause changes in fair value are co-dependent. Using an entire instrument or a proportion of an instrument is acceptable for hedge accounting, but using only a portion – e.g. a single risk component – is not generally allowed. For example, a cross-currency interest rate swap is designated with respect to all changes in its fair value, including those arising from foreign currency risk and interest rate risk. [*IAS 39.74–75*]

7I.7.470.20   However, it is possible to designate a single derivative – e.g. a cross-currency swap – as a hedge of more than one risk type if the following conditions are met:
- the risks being hedged can be identified clearly;
- the effectiveness of the hedge can be demonstrated; and
- it is possible to ensure that there is specific designation of the hedging instrument and the different risk positions. [*IAS 39.76*]

7I.7.470.30   Consequently, part of a derivative hedging instrument may be designated for a particular risk of a hedged item provided that the other parts of the hedging instrument are designated as hedging other risks of other hedged items (or the same hedged item) and all other hedge accounting criteria are met. However, practical difficulties in separating fair values between inter-related risks could present difficulties in meeting the conditions under which such a designation is permissible.

EXAMPLE 22 – HEDGE OF MORE THAN ONE RISK TYPE

7I.7.470.40   Company W with the euro as its functional currency issues a floating rate sterling-denominated bond. W also has a fixed rate US dollar financial asset with the same maturity and payment dates as the bond. To offset the currency and interest rate risk on the financial asset and financial liability, W enters into a pay-US dollar fixed receive-sterling floating interest rate swap.

7I.7.470.50   The swap may be designated as a hedging instrument of the US dollar financial asset against the fair value exposure arising from changes in US interest rates and the foreign currency risk between US dollar and sterling. Alternatively, it could be designated as a cash flow hedge of the cash flow exposure arising from the variable cash outflows of the sterling bond and the foreign currency risk arising from movements in the US dollar/sterling exchange rate.

7I.7.470.60   Both of these designations would be permissible even though the hedge does not convert the foreign currency exposure into W's functional currency of the euro. In our view, this type of hedge is appropriate only as long as W has foreign currency exposures to both US dollar and sterling and is not creating a new foreign currency position but rather is decreasing its risk exposure compared with its functional currency (see 7I.7.450). Both foreign currency exposures should be referred to in the hedge documentation, and the hedge is a single hedging relationship (see 7I.7.120.30). It should be clear in the documentation that the relationship between the swap and the US dollar financial asset qualifies for hedge accounting

only because of the existence of both a US dollar financial asset and a sterling financial liability – i.e. both are hedged items in a single hedging relationship. [*IAS 39.IG.F.2.18*]

7I.7.480   Hedging other market price risks

7I.7.480.10   Entities that hold equity securities as investments are exposed to market price risk. Hedge accounting for the price risk of such securities is relevant only for securities classified as available-for-sale because fair value changes are recognised as a component of equity. For financial assets and financial liabilities measured at FVTPL, gains and losses are recognised directly in profit or loss, making hedge accounting unnecessary. The issues related to hedge accounting for equity price risk are similar to those for commodity price risk (see 7I.7.440).

7I.7.490   Hedging credit risk

7I.7.490.10   IAS 39 indicates that a financial item may be hedged with respect to credit risk. In order for a hedging relationship to be eligible for hedge accounting, the designated risk should be separately identifiable and changes in the cash flows or fair value of the entire hedged item arising from changes in the designated risk should be reliably measurable such that effectiveness can be measured. This provides a practical barrier to hedging credit risk to the extent that it may not be possible to measure changes in the fair value of a hedged debt instrument arising from changes in credit risk separately from those arising from changes in liquidity risk. [*IAS 39.81*]

7I.7.490.20   A credit default swap (CDS) is a derivative financial instrument that provides protection against the risk of default by an obligor with respect to a reference debt instrument of the obligor. Under a typical CDS, if a specified credit event occurs, then the seller of protection would either purchase the reference debt instrument from the buyer of protection for a fixed amount, usually par or par plus accrued interest, or pay the difference between that fixed amount and the fair value of the reference debt instrument at that time. The buyer of protection would pay fixed periodic premiums to the seller until the end of the term of the CDS or a credit event occurs. A holder of a debt instrument may purchase a CDS referenced to that debt instrument, or a similar debt instrument of the same obligor, to provide protection against the risk of a fair value loss arising on the occurrence of a credit event as specified in the CDS contract. In our view, an entity may designate this risk as the hedged risk in a hedging relationship provided that the entity can reliably measure changes in the fair value of the debt instrument attributable to this risk and can demonstrate high effectiveness. This approach may be acceptable in the following circumstances, assuming that the relevant testing demonstrated high effectiveness:

- the hedging CDS is referenced to the hedged asset and there is an active market (see 2.4.280.10) for such CDSs, in which case there is likely to be high effectiveness; or
- the hedging CDS is referenced to a similar but not identical obligation issued by the same issuer as the hedged asset and there is an active market for both: CDSs of the same type as the hedging CDS and CDSs referenced to the hedged asset.

7I.7.500   All-in-one cash flow hedges

7I.7.500.10   An entity may enter into a contract to purchase or sell a non-financial item or a financial asset and the contract may be required to be accounted for as a derivative. For example, a fixed price contract to purchase a commodity would not be eligible for the own-use scope exemption when the entity has a past practice of taking delivery of the underlying and selling it within a short period after delivery for trading purposes (see 7I.1.160.10). In such a scenario, if the derivative will be settled gross, then the entity may designate this derivative as the hedging instrument in a cash flow hedge of the variability of the consideration to be paid or received in the future transaction that will occur on gross settlement of the derivative contract itself – i.e. a hedge of the forecast transaction that is implicit in the derivative itself – assuming that the other cash flow hedging criteria are met. [*IAS 39.IG.F.2.5*]

7I.7.500.20   This hedging strategy is referred to as an 'all-in-one cash flow hedge' and applies to all fixed price contracts that are accounted for as derivatives. By designating an all-in-one cash flow hedge, the entity avoids recognising in profit or loss the changes in the fair value of the purchase/sale contract that would otherwise be recognised in profit or loss because the contract is accounted for as a derivative.

7I.7.500.30   An all-in-one hedge may also be designated in a forecast purchase or sale involving a financial asset. For example, a financial institution manages the price risk associated with forecast sales of loans that it originates by entering into forward loan sale agreements to sell mortgage loans at a fixed price. This forward contract to sell loans meets the definition of a derivative and is required to be accounted for at FVTPL. However, the forward loan sale agreement may be designated as a cash flow hedge of the forecast sale of loans – i.e. as an all-in-one hedge of price risk – provided that the contract will be settled gross.

7I.7.510   EFFECTIVENESS TESTING

7I.7.510.10   To qualify for hedge accounting, a hedge should be 'expected to be' (prospectively) and 'actually have been' (retrospectively) highly effective. In other words, a hedge is regarded at inception and at subsequent assessment dates as highly effective only if the following conditions are met:
- the hedge is expected to be highly effective in achieving offsetting changes in fair value or cash flows attributable to the hedged risk during the period for which the hedge is designated or for the period until the amount of the hedging instrument next is adjusted (see 7I.7.530.10) (prospective effectiveness); and
- the actual results of the hedge are within the range of 80–125 percent (retrospective effectiveness). [*IAS 39.88(b), AG105*]

7I.7.510.20   If either one of these tests fails, then hedge accounting may not be applied at all. Even when a hedging relationship is expected to be highly effective and meets the retrospective effectiveness criterion – i.e. actual effectiveness is in the range of 80–125 percent – ineffectiveness still may arise from the relationship. Such ineffectiveness is recognised immediately in profit or loss even if it is within the 80–125 percent range. [*IAS 39.95(b), 102(b)*]

7I.7.520   Frequency of effectiveness tests

7I.7.520.10   At a minimum, effectiveness is measured at each reporting date, including interim reporting dates. [*IAS 39.AG106*]

7I.7.520.20   If a hedge no longer is effective, then hedge accounting is discontinued prospectively from the last date on which the hedge was proven to be effective (see 7I.7.680). Therefore, the more frequently that effectiveness is tested, the sooner the entity will identify the opportunity to rebalance its hedges to minimise the impact of ineffectiveness. This provides an incentive to perform hedge effectiveness testing frequently for hedges that may fail the effectiveness tests. [*IAS 39.AG113*]

7I.7.530   Methods for measuring effectiveness

7I.7.530.10   The methods that are used in measuring effectiveness are not prescribed. The method an entity adopts depends on its risk management strategy and hedge accounting systems and practices. For example, if the entity's risk management strategy is to adjust the amount of the hedging instrument periodically to reflect changes in the hedged position, then the entity needs to demonstrate that the hedge is expected to be highly effective only for the period until the amount of the hedging instrument next is adjusted. [*IAS 39.88(a), AG107*]

7I.7.530.20   The method that will be used in measuring hedge effectiveness is specified in the hedge documentation. [*IAS 39.88(a)*]

7I.7.530.30   An entity is not required to use a single method for prospective and retrospective assessments of effectiveness, and the method applied may be different for different types of hedges. In our experience, the periodic measurement of hedge effectiveness usually involves a method that compares the actual change in fair value of the hedged asset or liability or in cash flows with respect to the hedged risk with the change in the fair value of the hedging instrument (an offset method). When assessing both prospective and retrospective effectiveness and when measuring actual effectiveness, the creditworthiness of the counterparty to the hedging instrument and of the entity itself and the likelihood of default are considered (see 7I.7.580 and 2.4.460.30). For example, the value of a swap could be affected by changes in the credit rating of the swap counterparty or in the entity's credit rating. [*IAS 39.AG107, IG.F.4.3, IG.F.5.2, IFRS 13.42–44*]

7I.7.530.40   Also, the method that will be used to measure effectiveness is determined on a hedge-by-hedge basis. There is no requirement to adopt a consistent method for all hedging relationships. However, in our view an entity should adopt a method for assessing hedge effectiveness that is applied consistently for similar types of hedges unless different methods are explicitly justified. For example, an entity should use the same methods for assessing effectiveness prospectively, as well as the same methods for measuring actual hedge effectiveness, for forecast sales to the same export market undertaken on a regular basis. [*IAS 39.88(a)*]

7I.7.530.50   An entity may decide to designate less than 100 percent of the exposure on an item – e.g. the changes in fair value attributable to interest rate risk on 85 percent of the notional amount of a fixed rate debt instrument. In such circumstances, the hedged item comprises the actual percentage being hedged – 85 percent in this case – and ineffectiveness is measured and effectiveness is assessed based on the change in the fair value of that exposure. [*IAS 39.AG107A*]

7I.7.530.60   Effectiveness calculations may be done on a pre-tax or post-tax basis. Whichever method is used, the basis of calculating the change in fair value or cash flows of the hedged item and the change in fair value of the hedging instrument should be consistent. [*IAS 39.IG.F.4.1*]

71.7.540   *Prospective effectiveness*

71.7.540.10   Prospective effectiveness may be demonstrated in several ways – e.g. by:
- demonstrating a high statistical correlation between the fair value or cash flows of the hedged item and those of the hedging instrument using, for example, a statistical model such as regression analysis to analyse this correlation for a given period;
- comparing past changes in the fair value or cash flows of the hedged item that are attributable to the hedged risk with past changes in the fair value or cash flows of the hedging instrument (offset method); or
- demonstrating that a 'critical terms match' (see 71.7.590) exists at inception and in subsequent periods. [*IAS 39.AG105, IG.F.4.4*]

71.7.540.20   There is no specific guidance on what is meant by 'highly effective in achieving offsetting changes' in the context of prospective effectiveness. In our view, this should be interpreted as a statistical relationship within a range of 80–125 percent, in line with the requirement for retrospective effectiveness testing.

71.7.540.30   A prospective effectiveness test that is based on an 80–125 percent range provides some latitude for hedging non-financial assets and non-financial liabilities. For example, transactions for the sale or purchase of commodities that practically can be hedged only using exchange-traded commodity contracts that refer to standardised quantities and grades of the particular quantity (see 71.7.440.40). The primary concern is that such hedging relationships will not qualify for hedge accounting as a result of ineffectiveness that arises because of the terms of the hedging instrument being different from those of the hedged item. However, if the fair values or cash flows of the hedging instrument and hedged item respectively are expected to generate an 80–125 percent offset, then there is a chance that such a hedging relationship will qualify for hedge accounting.

71.7.540.40   Also, such a prospective effectiveness test would accommodate interest rate hedges using swaps when, for example, ineffectiveness arises because of differences between the fixed rate in the swap and that on the hedged item, or in the timing of cash flows on the hedged item and those on the swap. Although ineffectiveness will be recognised in profit or loss, the hedging relationship will not necessarily fail to qualify for hedge accounting on the basis of there not being an almost perfect offset of fair values or cash flows at inception.

71.7.540.50   An effectiveness assessment approach that considers only the cash flows generated by a derivative hedging instrument as they are paid or received is prohibited. The expectations of cash flows in subsequent periods and any resulting ineffectiveness are taken into account in assessing effectiveness. [*IAS 39.IG.F.5.5*]

71.7.540.60   It is common for entities to hedge their exposure to interest rate variability by entering into a pay-fixed receive-variable interest rate swap. If such a hedge is designated in a cash flow hedging relationship, then it would be inappropriate for the entity to measure retrospective effectiveness by comparing the actual cash flows on the swap with the actual cash flows on the hedged item. Such an effectiveness test would ignore the impact of past interest rate movements on the future cash flows of both the hedged item and the hedging instrument – i.e. it would ignore the impact of the movements in past rates on forward rates. Although the actual cash flows on the hedged item and hedging instrument may offset perfectly, the future cash flows may not. Such a situation may arise when the cash flows on the hedged item and hedging instrument are based on different yield curves or when the maturities of the hedged item and hedging instrument are different. [*IAS 39.IG.F.5.5*]

7I.7.540.70   When the critical terms of the hedged item and the hedging instruments are not exactly the same, prospective hedge effectiveness is assessed and documented other than by a 'critical terms match' (see 7I.7.590). When a statistical model is used, the hedge documentation should specify how the results of the analysis are to be interpreted. [*IAS 39.AG108, IG.F.4.4*]

7I.7.550   *Retrospective or ongoing assessment of effectiveness*

7I.7.550.10   Effectiveness is measured on an ongoing basis and the hedging relationship should be shown actually to have been highly effective throughout the reporting period. [*IAS 39.88(e)*]

7I.7.550.20   The gain or loss on the hedged item is measured independently from that on the hedging instrument – i.e. it cannot be assumed that the change in fair value or cash flows of the hedged item in respect of the hedged risk equals the fair value change of the hedging instrument. The reason for this is that any ineffectiveness of the hedging instrument is recognised in profit or loss. [*IAS 39.89, 95(b)*]

7I.7.550.30   Retrospective effectiveness may be measured on a cumulative or period-by-period basis. Normally it is advantageous to measure effectiveness on a cumulative basis. For example, if the hedging instrument is an interest rate swap that resets at different times to the interest rate on the underlying, then the hedge is more likely to meet the effectiveness tests if effectiveness is measured on a cumulative basis. [*IAS 39.IG.F.4.2*]

7I.7.550.40   No particular method for retrospective effectiveness testing is required under IAS 39. An entity may use the offset method for hedge effectiveness testing. The offset method expresses the degree of offset between changes in the fair value of the hedging instrument and changes in the fair value or cash flows of the hedged item, as a percentage. [*IAS 39.AG105, IG.F.5.5*]

7I.7.550.50   In our view, when statistical methods such as regression analysis are used to demonstrate the effectiveness of a hedging relationship, it is permitted to use data originated before the date on which the hedging relationship was designated to demonstrate retrospective effectiveness.

EXAMPLE 23 – USE OF REGRESSION TO ASSESS HEDGE EFFECTIVENESS

7I.7.550.60   Company T is assessing retrospective hedge effectiveness during the first reporting period after inception of a fair value hedge – e.g. one quarter after inception – and the changes in the fair value of the hedging instrument did not offset the changes in the fair value of the hedged item attributable to the hedged risk as anticipated.

7I.7.550.70   If T had chosen initially to use an offset approach, which is based only on the hedge period, then it would conclude that the retrospective hedge effectiveness test is failed.

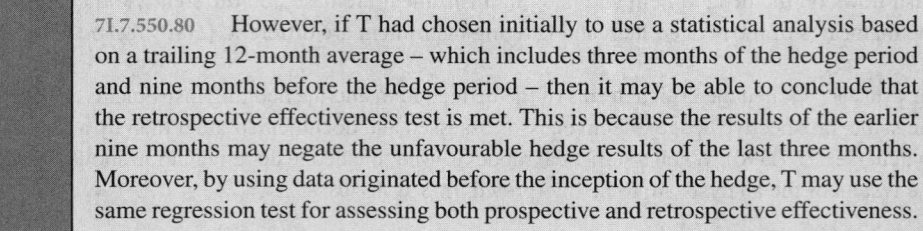

71.7.550.80   However, if T had chosen initially to use a statistical analysis based on a trailing 12-month average – which includes three months of the hedge period and nine months before the hedge period – then it may be able to conclude that the retrospective effectiveness test is met. This is because the results of the earlier nine months may negate the unfavourable hedge results of the last three months. Moreover, by using data originated before the inception of the hedge, T may use the same regression test for assessing both prospective and retrospective effectiveness.

71.7.550.90   In our view, the use of a statistical method such as regression analysis requires the quality of the output from the statistical method to be evaluated on an ongoing basis to ensure that the results are statistically valid. If a statistical method does not provide valid results, then it cannot be used to demonstrate hedge effectiveness. For example, an entity concludes that a hedge is effective using regression analysis because it meets the 80–125 percent requirement (see 71.7.510.10). However, had the offset method been applied then the hedge would have consistently failed the 80–125 percent requirement. In our view, the fact that the hedging relationship, on a consistent basis, would not have been highly effective had the offset method been applied indicates that the data used for the regression analysis may not be statistically valid.

71.7.550.100   For a further discussion of a cash flow hedge of interest rate risk using interest rate swaps, see 71.7.610.

71.7.560   *Regression analysis*

71.7.560.10   Linear regression techniques are used for determining *whether* and *by how much* a change in one variable will result in a change in another variable. Consequently, through the use of regression analysis, it is possible to demonstrate the effectiveness of a hedging relationship by determining how much of the change in the fair value or cash flows of the dependent variable is caused by a change in the fair value or cash flows of the independent variable. In our view, the hedging instrument or the hedged item may be assigned as the dependent variable and likewise either can be assigned as the independent variable.

71.7.560.20   In reviewing the regression model, in our view as a minimum the following parameters should be assessed.
- R squared (co-efficient of determination), which measures the proportion of the variability in the dependent variable that can be explained by the variation in the independent variable.
- Slope of the regression line, which indicates the change in the dependent variable for every change in the independent variable. The slope should be within a 0.8–1.25 range, which indicates that the hedging relationship is within the 80–125 percent effectiveness requirement.
- Confidence interval of the slope being within the 80–125 percentage range; in our view, a minimum 95 percent confidence level should be used when assessing the effectiveness of the hedging relationship.

71.7.570   Actual ineffectiveness

71.7.570.10   In a cash flow hedge, regardless of the methods that are used to assess prospective and retrospective effectiveness, the actual ineffectiveness recognised in profit or loss is calculated under the offset method on a cumulative basis to ensure that all ineffectiveness is recognised in profit or loss immediately. [*IAS 39.IG.F.5.5*]

7I.7.570.20   In a cash flow hedge, if the cumulative gain or loss on the hedging instrument is more than the cumulative change in the fair value of the expected future cash flows on the hedged item attributable to the hedged risk, then the difference is recognised in profit or loss as ineffectiveness. However, if the reverse is true, then the full cumulative gain or loss on the hedging instrument is recognised in OCI. Consequently, in a cash flow hedge ineffectiveness is recognised in profit or loss only when the cumulative change in fair value of the hedging instrument is greater than the cumulative change in fair value of the expected future cash flows on the hedged item attributable to the hedged risk. [*IAS 39.95–96*]

7I.7.570.30   In other words, ineffectiveness arising from over-hedging is recognised in profit or loss, but ineffectiveness arising from under-hedging is not recognised because the hedged item is not recognised.

7I.7.570.40   In a fair value hedge, ineffectiveness is recognised automatically in profit or loss as a result of separately remeasuring the hedging instrument and the hedged item. No separate calculation is required of the amount of ineffectiveness to be recognised in profit or loss.

7I.7.580   **Effect of credit risk on effectiveness testing and ineffectiveness measurement**

7I.7.580.10   Entities consider the effect of both changes in counterparty credit risk and own credit risk on the assessment of hedge effectiveness and the measurement of hedge ineffectiveness (see 2.4.460.30). [*IAS 39.AG109, IG.F.4.3, IFRS 13.42–44*]

7I.7.580.20   For all hedges, an entity considers the risk that the counterparty to the hedging instrument will default by failing to make any contractual payments to the entity. For cash flow hedges, if it becomes probable that a counterparty will default by failing to make any contractual payments to the entity, then the entity will be unable to conclude that the hedging relationship will be highly effective. [*IAS 39.IG.F.4.3*]

7I.7.580.30   For all hedges, changes in both counterparty credit risk and own credit risk impact the measurement of changes in the fair value of a derivative hedging instrument. These changes will likely have no offsetting effect on the measurement of the changes in the value of the hedged item attributable to the hedged risk. Such differences in measurement resulting from changes in counterparty and own credit risk will impact assessments of effectiveness and may lead to a conclusion that the hedging relationship has not been and/or is not expected to be highly effective (see 7I.7.680). Even when it is concluded that a hedge has been highly effective, such differences will result in ineffectiveness being recognised in profit or loss for fair value hedges. Such differences would also require the recognition of ineffectiveness in profit or loss for cash flow hedges if the cumulative gain or loss on the hedging instrument is greater than the cumulative change in fair or present value of the expected future cash flows on the hedged item. Similarly, for net investment hedges in which the hedging instrument is a derivative, ineffectiveness is recognised in profit or loss if the gain or loss on the hedging instrument exceeds the foreign exchange differences arising on the designated net investment. [*IAS 39.AG107, IG.F.5.2*]

7I.7.580.40   An entity may have a group of derivative assets and liabilities with a particular counterparty and meet the criteria for applying the portfolio measurement exception related to that counterparty's credit risk (see 2.4.430). In that case, the effect of the entity's net exposure to the credit risk of that counterparty or the counterparty's net exposure to the credit risk of the entity may result in a portfolio-level credit risk adjustment. However, for assessing hedge effectiveness and recognising ineffectiveness, an entity needs to determine the individual credit risk adjustments to arrive at the fair values of the individual hedging derivatives or the appropriate credit adjustment for a group of derivatives that have been designated together as the hedging instrument in a single hedging relationship. In our view, the entity should adopt a reasonable and consistently applied methodology for allocating credit risk adjustments determined at a portfolio level to individual derivative instruments for the purpose of measuring the fair values of individual hedging instruments that are used in assessing effectiveness and measuring hedge ineffectiveness.

7I.7.590 Matching critical terms

7I.7.590.10   If the critical terms of the hedging instrument and the hedged item exactly match, then this may demonstrate prospective effectiveness – a qualitative approach for assessing prospective effectiveness. However, an entity is still required to assess hedge effectiveness retrospectively based on the actual results of the hedge (see 7I.7.510.10 and 540.10). [*IAS 39.AG108, IG.F.4.7*]

7I.7.590.20   In our view, an entity can apply a qualitative approach for assessing prospective effectiveness only when:
- all critical terms exactly match, which as a minimum includes notional, maturity, repricing dates and underlying – e.g. the index on which the asset or liability's variable rate is based; and
- the hedging instrument has a fair value that is zero or approximates zero at inception and any difference between the transaction price of zero and the fair value at inception of the hedge is attributable solely to differing prices within the bid-ask spread between the actual entry transaction and a hypothetical exit transaction.

7I.7.590.30   If the fair value of the hedging instrument is other than zero at inception, then the difference between the transaction price of zero and the fair value may be attributable to the bid-ask spread and/or to other factors – e.g. the terms of the derivative do not reflect current market pricing when the hedge is designated. If the initial non-zero fair value of the hedging instrument is attributable to other factors, then the initial non-zero fair value reflects a source of potential future ineffectiveness (see 7I.7.670). This is not consistent with the assumption of high prospective effectiveness underlying the critical terms match approach.

7I.7.590.40   Applying a qualitative approach does not mean applying the 'shortcut method' as allowed under US GAAP, whereby an entity compares the critical terms of the hedging instrument and the hedged item at inception and is not required to perform any reassessment in subsequent periods. This is not permitted under IFRS. A qualitative approach requires all critical terms to be reviewed and compared at inception and in subsequent periods. If it is concluded that there is no change in any critical term, then such a test would be sufficient to satisfy the prospective effectiveness testing requirements. However, the effect of credit risk is considered (see 7I.7.580). Also, retrospective effectiveness can never be assumed and is always measured numerically.

71.7.590.50   Examples of situations in which the critical terms exactly match are:
- a hedge of a foreign currency sales commitment with a futures contract to sell the same amount of the same foreign currency on the same date, if the fair value of the future at inception of the hedge is zero;
- a hedge of benchmark interest rate risk associated with a recognised asset or liability using a swap with a zero fair value at inception of the hedge and the same notional amount as the asset or liability and with the same key terms;
- a hedge of a forecast commodity sale with a forward contract to purchase the same quantity of the same commodity on the same date, if the fair value of the forward at inception of the hedge is zero, and either the change in the discount or premium on the forward contract is excluded from the assessment of effectiveness and recognised directly in profit or loss, or the change in expected cash flows on the forecast transaction is based on the forward price of the commodity; and
- a hedge of a specific bond held with a forward contract to sell an equivalent bond with the same notional amount, currency and maturity, if the forward contract has at the designation date a fair value of zero. [*IAS 39.AG108, IG.F.4.7*]

71.7.600   Time value and interest element

71.7.600.10   If it is appropriately documented at inception of the hedging relationship, then the time value of an option may be excluded from the effectiveness tests and effectiveness may be tested based solely on the intrinsic value of the option. Similarly, the interest element of a forward contract may be excluded and effectiveness may be measured based solely on the spot component of the forward contract. This choice is available on a hedge-by-hedge basis, and there is no requirement to have a consistently applied policy. However, an entity is not permitted to exclude the credit risk (or any other risk) associated with a derivative from the measurement of hedge effectiveness. [*IAS 39.74*]

71.7.600.20   Changes in the fair value of components of the hedging instrument that are excluded from effectiveness measurement – i.e. the time value or interest component – are recognised immediately in profit or loss. [*IAS 39.96(c)*]

71.7.600.30   If the hedging instrument is an option, then measuring effectiveness based only on the intrinsic value of the option may improve the effectiveness of the hedging relationship. This is because the hedged transaction is unlikely to have an equivalent time value effect; therefore, if the time value component of the option is included, then it will give rise to ineffectiveness. When intrinsic value designation is used and the option remains out of the money during the period for which effectiveness is being assessed – on a period-by-period basis or cumulative basis depending on the method used by the entity (see 71.7.550.30) – then quantitative retrospective effectiveness assessment is not necessary. However, prospective assessment is still required.

71.7.600.40   If the time value or the interest element is included in the measurement of hedge effectiveness, then the full fair value of the option or forward contract, respectively, is used in the effectiveness calculation.

71.7.600.50   Whichever method is used to deal with the time value or interest elements of hedged items and hedging instruments, the basis of calculating the change in fair value or cash flows of the hedged item and the change in fair value of the hedging instrument is consistent. For example, if the interest element is excluded from the measurement of changes in the fair value of the hedging instrument, then the change in the cash flows or fair value of the hedged item attributable to the hedged risk is measured based on spot rates. However, if the interest element is included in the effectiveness measurement, then the change in fair value or cash flows of the hedged item attributable to the hedged risk is based on forward rates. [*IAS 39.IG.F.5.5*]

7I.7.600.60   It is possible to apply a dynamic hedging strategy, including both the intrinsic and time values of an option, although there is little guidance about how this should be performed. A delta-neutral hedging strategy, whereby the hedging instrument is adjusted constantly to maintain a desired hedge ratio, may qualify for hedge accounting if the other hedge accounting criteria are met (see 7I.7.330).

7I.7.610   Interest rate risk

7I.7.610.10   To maximise effectiveness, when hedging interest rate risk, the hedged risk is normally designated as the benchmark interest rate only and the credit risk spread on the hedged item is excluded from the hedged risk. This is because credit risk normally will not affect the fair value or cash flows of the hedged item and the hedging instrument in the same way.

7I.7.610.20   Similarly, if the interest exposure on an interest-bearing instrument is hedged for only a portion of the instrument's remaining period to maturity, then it is easier to meet the effectiveness rules if the hedged risk is documented as being based on the same yield curve as the derivative. For example, an entity hedges the interest rate risk on a 10-year bond for the first five years using a five-year interest rate swap. Effectiveness could be maximised by designating the swap as a hedge of the fair value of the interest payments on the bond for the first five years, and of the change in the value of the principal amount of the bond arising from changes in the yield curve related to the five years of the swap. If the hedged risk is simply designated as the change in fair value of the bond, then the hedge is likely to be ineffective because the value of the bond will be affected by changes in the 10-year yield curve whereas the value of the derivative will be affected by changes in the five-year yield curve. [*IAS 39.IG.F.2.17*]

7I.7.610.30   It is quite common for financial instruments having an exposure to interest rate risk also to be exposed to prepayment risk. For a prepayable asset or liability, changes in interest rates will have an effect on the fair value of the asset or liability by changing the expectations about the timing of future cash flows. This has an impact on effectiveness assessment and measurement.

7I.7.610.40   Prepayment risk affects the timing as well as the amount of cash flows. Consequently, this may impact the effectiveness of fair value hedges as well as the highly probable requirement for forecast cash flows. A prepayable hedged item will generally experience smaller fair value changes when interest rates fall than a non-prepayable hedged item, while fair value changes as interest rates rise will be closer to those of a non-prepayable item. When hedging a portfolio of such instruments, effectiveness is likely to be more difficult to demonstrate for a fair value hedge than for a cash flow hedge. In a static fair value hedge, it may be difficult to group a portfolio of fixed rate assets subject to prepayment risk, because it may be difficult to prove that the changes in fair value of the individual assets are approximately proportional to the overall change in fair value of the portfolio, unless each item contains identical prepayment options. As a result, fixed rate assets subject to prepayment risk may have to be hedged on a one-to-one basis. In this case, ineffectiveness will arise unless the hedging instrument also contains a prepayment option.

7I.7.610.50 Therefore, the risk of prepayment or changes to the timing of future cash flows is considered when an entity designates its hedging relationships. In our view, prepayment is not a risk that is capable of separate designation; rather, it is a component of interest rate risk and is designated as such. This is because it is difficult to measure and isolate the change in fair value arising from a change in prepayments separately from the overall change arising from a change in interest rates.

7I.7.610.60 In a portfolio fair value hedge of interest rate risk the assessment of hedge effectiveness can be performed using a maturity schedule. Such a schedule usually determines the net position for each maturity period by aggregating assets and liabilities maturing or repricing in that maturity period. However, the net exposure should be associated with a specific asset, liability or cash inflow or outflow to apply hedge accounting, such that the correlation of the changes of the hedging instrument and the designated hedged item can be assessed.

7I.7.615 *Financial instruments with a benchmark rate component floored at zero*

7I.7.615.10 A debt instrument on which the interest rate is linked to a benchmark rate but with the benchmark component floored at zero may be a hedged item in a cash flow hedge of the variability of interest payments or receipts due to changes in the benchmark rate. If the benchmark rate becomes negative, then a question arises about whether the designated hedged risk continues to exist because interest cash flows on the debt instrument are not variable during the period in which the benchmark rate is negative. In our view, in these situations the designated hedged risk continues to exist and remains eligible for hedge accounting because the benchmark rate may turn positive in future periods and therefore there is still exposure to variability in future interest cash flows. [*IAS 39.86(b)*]

7I.7.615.20 Another question that arises if an entity hedges benchmark-based interest cash flows floored at zero is whether the hedged benchmark-based cash flows can be regarded as highly probable if the benchmark rate becomes negative. Again, in our view the analysis is not changed merely by the benchmark rate becoming negative. This is because the hedged forecast transactions are the receipts or payments of interest and these transactions are still forecast to occur, although the benchmark-based component may be zero.

7I.7.615.30 However, if there is an embedded floor in the hedged item but no equal and opposite floor on the benchmark-based cash flows in the hedging instrument, then the embedded floor in the hedged item means that the negative benchmark rate will cause the hedge not to be fully effective. Therefore, hedge ineffectiveness may arise because changes in the benchmark rate will not have an equal and opposite effect on the hedging instrument and the hedged item.

7I.7.615.40 Also, the entity has to determine whether – considering this mismatch between the variability of the cash flows of the hedging instrument and the hedged item – the hedge is expected to be highly effective on a prospective basis. [*IAS 39.88(c)*]

EXAMPLE 24 – CASH FLOW HEDGES OF FLOATING INTEREST RATES – NEGATIVE INTEREST RATE ENVIRONMENT

7I.7.615.50 Company R has a loan receivable in which the interest rate is linked to LIBOR. The loan is not prepayable and credit risk is not significant.

7I.7.615.60   R's strategy is to hedge the variability in LIBOR cash flows receivable from the loan by applying cash flow hedging using an interest rate swap. The derivative has the same notional and maturity as the hedged item and is designated in the hedging relationship from inception. R considers alternative hedging relationships depending on whether there is a floor on the LIBOR rate in the swap and/or in the loan in a negative interest rate environment.

Scenario 1: Hedged item and hedging instrument do not contain floors

7I.7.615.70   R can designate a vanilla interest rate swap as a hedging instrument in a cash flow hedge of the variability in LIBOR cash flows receivable from the loan. As a consequence, hedge effectiveness is expected to be achieved because all critical terms are matched.

Scenario 2: Only the hedged item has a floor

7I.7.615.80   In this scenario, the LIBOR cash flows on the loan are floored at zero and the proposed hedging instrument is a vanilla interest rate swap that pays LIBOR and receives a fixed rate. As noted in 7I.7.615.10, a loan in which the interest rate is linked to LIBOR but floored at zero may be a hedged item in a cash flow hedge of the variability of interest payments or receipts due to changes in LIBOR. First R must make a prospective test in order to assess the effectiveness of the hedging relationship at inception. However, assuming that the hedging relationship is expected to be highly effective at inception (see 7I.7.510), hedge ineffectiveness may arise in future periods because changes in LIBOR will not have an equal and opposite effect on the hedging instrument and the hedged item (see 7I.7.615.10–40).

Scenario 3: Only the hedging instrument has a floor

7I.7.615.90   In this scenario, R considers an interest rate swap that pays LIBOR floored at zero and receives a fixed rate. With this instrument, R would pay the greater of LIBOR and zero. This swap is in effect a net written option and so does not qualify as a hedging instrument. As noted in 7I.7.340, an instrument or combination of instruments that in effect is a net written option qualifies as a hedging instrument only if it is designated as an offset to a purchased option. [*IAS 39.AG94*]

Scenario 4: Both the hedged item and the hedging instrument have a floor

7I.7.615.100   R designates, as the hedging instrument, an interest rate swap that pays LIBOR floored at zero and receives a fixed rate. The hedged item is the variability in LIBOR cash flows receivable from a loan that also contains a floor on the LIBOR component at zero.

7I.7.615.110   Similar to Scenario 3, the hedging instrument is in effect a net written option and the fair value is zero at the date of designation. However, the LIBOR cash flows on the loan are also floored at zero and this is considered a purchased option.

A written option may be designated as a hedging instrument if it is designated as an offset to a purchased option (see 7I.7.310.10). As a consequence, considering that all other critical terms are matched, the presence of floors in both the hedged item and the hedging instrument results in high effectiveness.

7I.7.615.120 An additional question arises when considering the designation of a hedged item with embedded optionality in a cash flow hedge. That is, should the time value of the embedded option be included within the change in value of the hedged item for effectiveness purposes? IAS 39 permits the exclusion of the time value of an option contract from the hedging relationship. This results in the immediate recognition of the change in the time value of the hedging option through earnings and can be helpful in cases where equivalent time value does not exist in the hedged item. However, the standard does not address a situation in which the hedged item and the hedging instrument both contain time value. [*IAS 39.74(a)*]

7I.7.615.130 In our view, if the hedged item contains embedded optionality matched by optionality within the hedging instrument, then the inclusion of time value from both the hedged item and the hedging instrument within the hedging relationship would provide high effectiveness.

EXAMPLE 25 – INCLUSION OF TIME VALUE WITHIN HEDGED ITEM IN CASH FLOW HEDGING RELATIONSHIP

7I.7.615.140 Company X has a variability in LIBOR cash flows receivable from a loan. The loan also contains a floor on the LIBOR component at zero. X wants to hedge the variability in LIBOR cash flows considering the following hedging relationship.

- Hedged item: variability in LIBOR cash flows (i.e. the hedged item will receive the greater of LIBOR and zero).
- Hedging instrument: interest rate swap that pays LIBOR and receives a fixed rate. LIBOR cash flows under the swap are floored at zero (i.e. the interest rate swap pays the greater of LIBOR and zero).
- The maturity of the hedged item and the hedging instrument are the same (i.e. two years).
- The hedged item and the hedging instrument are of the same notional amount. The loan is not prepayable and the credit risk is not significant.
- The hedging instrument (including the interest rate swap and the embedded floor) has nil fair value at inception and the change in the fair value goes through OCI after inception.

7I.7.615.150 In this case, if LIBOR is above 0%, then X will receive LIBOR interest from the loan and will pay LIBOR interest on the floating leg of the swap. Conversely, if LIBOR is below 0%, then X will receive 0% from the loan and will pay 0% on the floating leg of the swap. In both scenarios, the time between inception and maturity is two years and this period of time will be reflected in the calculation for measurement of hedge ineffectiveness.

71.7.615.160   For the calculation of the variability in the hedged item, the embedded premium (including the intrinsic value and the time value) is considered within the hedged item cash flows and so forms part of the calculation at inception. Accordingly, the inclusion of time value from both the hedged item and the hedging instrument within the hedging relationship results in high effectiveness.

71.7.615.170   In our view, the following are some of the methods that could be used for measuring hedge ineffectiveness in a cash flow hedge of interest rate risk using an interest rate swap.

71.7.620   *Change in fair value method*

71.7.620.10   Ineffectiveness is measured by considering movements in the present value of the cumulative expected/contractual future interest cash flows that are designated as the hedged item and the cumulative change in the fair value of the designated hedging instrument – e.g. a pay-fixed receive-floating interest rate swap. Although this approach is permitted and simple to apply, it will lead to ineffectiveness. This is because the overall change in the fair value of the hedging instrument will be influenced by the change in value of the pay-fixed leg of the interest rate swap as this pay-fixed leg does not reprice to the current fixed market rate at each testing date. As a result, ineffectiveness arises because there is no such change in the present value of the hedged item because it does not include a fixed leg.

71.7.630   *Hypothetical derivative method*

71.7.630.10   Ineffectiveness is measured by comparing the change in the fair value of the actual derivative designated as the hedging instrument and the change in the fair value of a hypothetical derivative representing the hedged item. The hypothetical derivative is defined so that it matches the critical terms of the hedged item – e.g. notional, repricing dates, index on which the asset or liability's variable rate is based, mirror image caps and floors etc. The hypothetical derivative should have a zero fair value at inception of the hedge. The hypothetical derivative would be expected to offset perfectly the hedged cash flows, and the change in fair value of the hypothetical derivative is regarded as a proxy for the present value of the cumulative change in the expected future cash flows on the hedged item.

71.7.630.20   The hypothetical derivative method is likely to be more difficult to apply in our experience because a separate hypothetical derivative needs to be identified for each hedging relationship. However, this method does result in lower ineffectiveness in most instances compared with the change in fair value method. Typically, only one hypothetical derivative is identified for each hedged item based on the terms of the hedged item. Without such a restriction entities could design a perfect hypothetical derivative to match exactly the terms of the hedging instrument, thereby reporting no ineffectiveness.

71.7.630.30   In our view, the valuation methodology for determining the change in fair value of the hypothetical derivative should utilise market valuation conventions – e.g. the discount rate – to measure a derivative. If there is a change in market valuation conventions, then it is appropriate for an entity to adjust the inputs when determining the change in fair value of the hypothetical derivative. For example, an entity has previously used six-month LIBOR as the discount rate when determining the change in fair value of a pay-fixed receive-floating interest rate swap. Because of changes in market valuation conventions, the entity now determines that three-month LIBOR is the appropriate discount rate for determining the change in fair value. We believe that it is appropriate for the entity to adjust the discount rate from six-month LIBOR to three-month LIBOR when determining the change in fair value of both the actual instrument and the hypothetical derivative. Such an adjustment would not be considered a de-designation/redesignation event.

7I.7.630.40   In our view, a related issue arises when an entity's hedge documentation is silent on whether the hypothetical derivative instrument is collateralised and the resulting impact on determining the change in its fair value. For example, an entity had previously designated a collateralised interest rate swap as the hedging instrument in a cash flow hedge of a variable rate debt instrument. The hedge documentation is silent because it relates to whether the hypothetical derivative instrument is collateralised. The entity has determined that because of changes in market valuation conventions, it is appropriate to use an overnight index swap rate (OIS) discount rate to determine the change in fair value of similar collateralised interest rate swaps. Although the entity had previously used six-month LIBOR as the discount rate to determine the fair value of the hypothetical derivative, we believe that it is appropriate for the entity to adjust the discount rate from six-month LIBOR to OIS without de-designating and redesignating the hedging relationship. Such an adjustment is allowed only as a one-time refinement of the methodology for assessing hedge effectiveness. [*IAS 39.88*]

7I.7.630.50   In our view, the hypothetical derivative method is not available in a fair value hedging relationship, and therefore ineffectiveness may arise when there is a change in market valuation conventions that affect the discount rate that would be used to determine the fair value of a hedging instrument. For example, an entity has designated a collateralised pay-fixed receive-floating interest rate swap in a fair value hedge for changes in six-month LIBOR of a fixed rate bond. A shift in market valuation convention from using six-month LIBOR to an OIS discount rate in determining the change in fair value of the interest rate swap would not allow the entity to start using an OIS discount rate when determining the change in fair value of the bond for changes in six-month LIBOR.

7I.7.640   *Measuring hedge ineffectiveness*

7I.7.640.10   In most circumstances, the effectiveness of both the variable and the fixed legs of the swap needs to be considered when using one of the methods described in 7I.7.620–630. Considering only the change in fair value of the floating leg of the swap would in our view be appropriate for effectiveness testing purposes when using the hypothetical derivative only when the fixed rate on the swap is equal to the fixed rate that would have been obtained on the hedged item at its designation date – i.e. when the fixed leg of the hedging swap equals the fixed leg on a hypothetical derivative that, had such hypothetical derivative been created on the hedge designation date, would perfectly offset the hedged cash flows. In other words, if the fixed leg of the swap is the market rate at inception of the hedging relationship such that the swap has a fair value of zero or close to zero, and there are no differences in the principal terms (notional, repricing dates, basis) and credit risk (or credit risk is not designated in the hedging relationship), then such a method for testing effectiveness may be appropriate. In such circumstances, the changes in fair value arising on the fixed leg of the hedging instrument and on the fixed leg of the perfectly effective hypothetical derivative offset each other perfectly and consequently do not contribute to any ineffectiveness in the relationship.

7I.7.640.20   If the hedge is designated subsequent to entering into the hedging swap, then it is unlikely that the fixed leg of the hedging swap will be equal to the fixed rate on the perfectly effective hypothetical derivative. Therefore, a method that compares only the changes in the fair values of the floating legs of the hedging swap and the hedged item is not appropriate to use in this case.

7I.7.640.30   In our view, IFRS does not permit what has been termed as 'terminal value' hedging under US GAAP. Additionally, it is not appropriate to identify and designate as the hedged item a portion containing a risk exposure similar to that of a written option – e.g. designating a written option as the hypothetical derivative in highly probable forecast cash flows. For example, if an entity purchases an option to hedge the downside foreign currency risk in a highly probable foreign currency revenue stream, then it is not appropriate to designate as the hedged item a portion of the forecast cash flows such that it represents an exposure to losses in a way that this portion is a written option, including time value, that then perfectly offsets the purchased option.

7I.7.640.40   It is not possible, in the absence of actual optionality in the hedged item, to designate the hedged risk in a manner such that it has a time value component. Therefore, in most cases hedge effectiveness can be achieved only by excluding the time value from the hedging relationship (see 7I.7.600).

7I.7.640.50   Forecast transactions create a cash flow exposure to interest rate changes because interest payments will be based on the actual market rate when the transaction occurs. In these circumstances, hedge effectiveness is based on the highly probable expected interest payments calculated using the forward interest rate based on the applicable yield curve. For forecast transactions such as anticipated debt issues, it is not possible to determine what the actual market interest rate will be for the debt issue. In these situations, retrospective hedge effectiveness may be measured based on changes in the interest rates that have occurred between the designation of the hedge and the date on which effectiveness testing is performed. The forward interest rates that should be used are those that correspond with the term of the expected transaction at inception and at the date of the effectiveness testing. The implementation guidance to IAS 39 provides an example of how hedge effectiveness may be measured for a forecast transaction in a debt instrument. [IAS 39.IG.F.5.5]

7I.7.650   *Clean vs dirty prices*

7I.7.650.10   In hedging interest rate risk arising from fixed rate financial assets or financial liabilities using interest rate swaps, a highly effective hedging relationship can usually be achieved by ensuring that the principal terms of the hedged item and hedging instrument match. However, when the interest rate on the swap reprices at a date other than the reporting date (at which date effectiveness is assessed), ineffectiveness may arise from the variable leg of the swap because of interest rate movements between these two dates. For example, an interest rate swap reprices every three months and the last repricing date is 30 November, which is before the reporting date. On 30 November, the interest on the variable leg of the swap is fixed for the next three months. Consequently, changes in market interest rates between this date and the reporting date of 31 December will cause the fair value of the floating leg of the swap to change, giving rise to ineffectiveness – this is reflected in the 'dirty' price of the swap. During initial periods and periods near the end of a hedging relationship, this ineffectiveness may be substantial enough, in relative terms, to preclude hedge accounting.

7I.7.650.20   In our view, an entity could indicate that in assessing hedge effectiveness it will disregard the accrued interest on the hedging instrument and the hedged item – this is referred to as the 'clean' price of the swap. In this case, it may be possible to prove that the relationship was effective on a retrospective basis – i.e. within the 80–125 percent range – and therefore to continue hedge accounting, assuming that the other conditions continue to be met. Disregarding accrued interest implies that the entity will, for the purpose of assessing hedge effectiveness only, determine the fair value of the swap as the clean price. By considering clean prices, while the entire ineffectiveness from the floating leg of the swap would not be eliminated, the resulting ineffectiveness would then be limited to fair value changes on the unaccrued portion of the interest coupon to the next swap settlement date.

7I.7.650.30   In our view, such a methodology should improve both the retrospective and the prospective effectiveness of the hedging relationship. However, this does not mean that there will be no ineffectiveness. The entity is still required to calculate the extent to which the hedge was ineffective and this amount should be recognised in profit or loss. So although the continuation of hedge accounting should be possible, the actual ineffectiveness should be recognised in profit or loss under the offset method (see 7I.7.570).

7I.7.660   *Ineffectiveness in fair value hedge arising from different fixed rates*

7I.7.660.10   Entities may designate fixed rate financial assets or financial liabilities as hedged items in a fair value hedge, with the hedged risk being changes in fair value arising from changes in interest rates. The hedged cash flows in this case would include all coupons and principal payments arising from the instruments. In such a hedging relationship, issues may arise in respect of effectiveness because of mismatches between the fixed rate on the hedged item and the fixed interest rate on the hedging instrument. Such a mismatch could arise in the following circumstances.

- The hedged financial asset or financial liability bears interest at a fixed rate calculated as the benchmark rate on issue plus a certain number of basis points for credit spread, whereas the fixed leg of the hedging instrument is based on the benchmark interest rate at inception plus a different number of basis points for credit spread.
- The interest rate on the hedged financial asset or financial liability is based on the benchmark interest rate at the date of issue, whereas the fixed leg of the hedging instrument is based on the benchmark interest rate at a later date. This difference is arising from movements in the benchmark rate between these two dates.

7I.7.660.20   For both cases in 7I.7.660.10, in our view it may be possible to designate a portion of the cash flows of the fixed rate financial asset or financial liability as the hedged item to achieve high effectiveness. For further discussion, see 7I.7.180.130–140.

7I.7.670   *Assessing hedge effectiveness when hedging with off-market derivative*

7I.7.670.10   In certain scenarios, an entity may enter into a hedging relationship in which the designated hedging instrument is a non-option derivative with the initial non-zero fair value that is attributable to factors other than the bid-ask spread – e.g. when an entity has to de-designate a hedging relationship and then redesignates the derivative in another hedging relationship (see 7I.7.590.30).

7I.7.670.20   In our view, the ineffectiveness that is caused by the hedging instrument having a non-zero fair value at the designation date of the hedging relationship may be reduced by excluding the following two elements when computing, for hedge effectiveness testing purposes only, the change in the hedging instrument's fair value, as well as the related effects on the hedged item:
- the interest accretion due to passage of time alone; and

- the realisation/settlement of the off-market element. This can be analogised to the receipts of principal on a debt security that are not fair value gains or losses, but are a return of capital.

7I.7.670.30 In our view, it is appropriate to exclude the interest accretion because it is not attributable to changes in any risk factor between two successive effectiveness assessment dates, and it arises only because of the passage of time, similar to accrued interest (see 7I.7.650). Also, it is appropriate to exclude the realisation/settlement of the off-market element because it is a return/payment of the amount invested in the derivative at the designation date of the hedging relationship.

EXAMPLE 26 – EXCLUSION OF INTEREST ACCRETION AND REALISATION/SETTLEMENT OF OFF-MARKET ELEMENT FROM EFFECTIVENESS ASSESSMENT

7I.7.670.40 On 1 October 2017, Company X entered into a three-year interest rate swap at current market terms – i.e. zero fair value at inception – with a notional amount of 10,000. Under the terms of the swap, X receives 6% and pays LIBOR. On 1 October 2018, X designates the swap as the hedging instrument in a fair value hedge of a financial liability with the same notional, maturity and contractual interest payments of 6%. On the hedge designation date, the interest rate swap has a fair value of 400 (an asset), because the swap curve has moved since 1 October 2017, and the fixed leg of the swap if priced on 1 October 2018 would be 4%.

7I.7.670.50 For hedge effectiveness testing purposes, we believe that X could exclude the following from the fair value change of the interest rate swap.
- The interest accretion due to passage of time of the interest rate swap from the fair value of 400, which represents the discounted excess 2% cash flows to be received over the remaining life of the swap, to the undiscounted amount of the excess 2% cash flows as the swap moves closer to maturity – e.g. 408.
- The realisation of the off-market element of the interest rate swap, which would be a portion of each net interest payment – e.g. approximately 204 each year until maturity.

7I.7.670.60 Although the interest accretion and realisation/settlement of the off-market element may be excluded for hedge effectiveness testing purposes, they impact the change in the fair value of the derivative. However, the related changes in fair value are immediately recognised in profit or loss similar to the time value of an option or the interest element of a forward contract (see 7I.7.600).

7I.7.680 DISCONTINUING HEDGE ACCOUNTING

7I.7.680.10 Hedge accounting is discontinued prospectively if:
- the hedged transaction no longer is highly probable;
- the hedging instrument expires or is sold, terminated or exercised;
- the hedged item is sold, settled or otherwise disposed of;
- the hedge no longer is highly effective; or
- the entity revokes the designation.

7I.7.680.15   If an entity does not meet all hedge effectiveness criteria, then hedge accounting is terminated as at the date on which the hedge was last proved effective, which may be the previous interim or annual reporting date, or from the date on which the hedged item or hedging instrument is derecognised. For this reason, testing hedge effectiveness more frequently is a way of reducing the impact of the unexpected termination of a hedging relationship. If the entity can identify the event or change in circumstances that caused the hedge to fail the effectiveness criteria, and can prove that the hedge was effective before the date on which this occurred, then the entity can cease hedge accounting from the date of such event or change in circumstances. If there is a retrospective hedge effectiveness test failure, then even if prospective effectiveness can be demonstrated for the existing hedging relationship, hedge accounting based on the previous designation is discontinued, although it may be possible to designate prospectively a new hedging relationship. Also, because the retrospective effectiveness criterion is not met, hedge accounting cannot be applied for the period just ended. In contrast, if a hedging relationship is demonstrated to be highly effective for the period just ended, but the prospective effectiveness criterion is not met, then hedge accounting is discontinued prospectively from the date of such assessment. Also, in this case it is necessary to report any ineffectiveness in profit or loss on the date on which hedge accounting is discontinued. [*IAS 39.91, 101, AG113, IG.F.6.2(i)*]

7I.7.680.20   Hedge accounting would also be discontinued if the recognised asset, liability, firm commitment or forecast transaction is no longer eligible for designation as a hedged item. This would occur, for example, when an entity acquires, or otherwise begins to consolidate, the counterparty to a hedged forecast transaction or firm commitment, resulting in that transaction no longer involving a party external to the reporting entity. Another example is when an entity sells, or otherwise is required to deconsolidate, a subsidiary (see 2.5.760), resulting in a hedged item of that subsidiary becoming derecognised. Also, when there is a change in the functional currency of an entity, foreign currency exposures denominated in the new functional currency will no longer qualify for hedge accounting for foreign currency risk.

7I.7.680.30   When an entity voluntarily terminates a hedging relationship in between two regular effectiveness assessment dates, then in our view the hedging relationship should be assessed for effectiveness on the date of voluntary termination to determine whether it was retrospectively effective. If the hedge is determined to be retrospectively effective, then hedge accounting should be applied up to the date of voluntary termination, including recognising any ineffectiveness up to that date in profit or loss. If, however, the retrospective test is failed, then hedge accounting cannot be applied after the last date on which the effectiveness criteria were met.

7I.7.680.40   A hedging relationship is discontinued when the hedging instrument is sold or terminated. In our experience, certain events of default, such as a filing for bankruptcy by the counterparty, would – under the standard International Swaps and Derivatives Association (ISDA) terms for some derivatives – either result automatically in termination of the derivative or permit the entity to terminate the derivative in exchange for a net cash settlement and to replace it with another instrument having similar terms with another counterparty. Whether this is the case is likely to depend on the legal and contractual arrangements in each country. In our view, unless it is a replacement of a hedging instrument as part of the entity's existing documented hedging strategy, the termination of a hedging derivative and its replacement by another derivative with another counterparty would result in the termination of the existing hedging relationship and, if it is appropriately designated, the establishment of a new one.

7I.7.680.50   Beginning a new replacement hedging relationship using a derivative that has a fair value other than zero may result in hedge ineffectiveness in the future (see 7I.7.670). This is because the initial fair value of the derivative is itself subject to change with changes in market interest rates. Unless an offsetting fair value effect is also present in the hedged item, ineffectiveness may result.

7I.7.680.60   If the hedged item is partially repaid (determination depends on how the hedged item has been defined in the hedge designation) before its expected repayment date, then this will cause the entity to be over-hedged because the notional amount of the hedging instrument may be more than the remaining outstanding amount of the hedged item. In this case, the entity would be required to terminate the existing hedging relationship unless the existing hedging relationship continues to be highly effective with the reduced hedged item – i.e. if the originally designated hedging instrument continues to be highly effective in offsetting the changes in fair value or cash flows of the now-reduced hedged item. If, as a result of the partial repayment of the hedged item, the over-hedge is such that the 80–125 percent effectiveness test is no longer met, then the original hedging relationship is discontinued in its entirety. The entity may redesignate the remaining hedged item in a new hedging relationship, which may include a proportion of the original hedging instrument, if all the criteria for hedge accounting are met. The adverse effect of a partial repayment of the hedged item on continuity of the entire hedging relationship may be mitigated by use of a layering hedge strategy as discussed in 7I.7.720.

7I.7.680.70   If a hedging instrument ceases to be part of a hedging relationship, then it may be redesignated in a new hedging relationship, as long as the redesignation is for the entire remaining term of the instrument. For example, a forward contract of 100 that was initially designated as the hedging instrument to hedge forecast transactions of 100 would no longer be expected to be highly effective if revisions to forecasts subsequent to the hedge designation date indicate that only 70 of the forecast transactions are now highly probable. In this situation, the original hedge designation would be discontinued because it would no longer meet the highly effective criteria. A new hedging relationship under which a proportion (e.g. 70 percent) of the original forward is designated to hedge the highly probable forecast transactions of 70 is permissible. The new hedging relationship may not be fully effective because the forward contract would normally have a fair value other than zero at the date of redesignation (see 7I.7.670). Changes in fair value of the remaining proportion of the forward (i.e. 30 percent), if not designated in another hedging relationship, would be recognised in profit or loss. [*IAS 39.75*]

7I.7.680.72   An entity may seek to alter an existing hedging relationship by introducing a new hedging instrument, changing the hedged risk or changing the ratio between the quantity of hedging instruments and hedged items. Subject to 7I.7.680.80, in our view the introduction of a new hedging instrument, changing the hedged risk and adjustment of the hedge ratio represent fundamental changes to the hedge designation that require the entire existing hedging relationship to be de-designated and, if appropriate, permit a new hedging relationship to be redesignated.

7I.7.680.74   An entity may designate a single derivative in a hedge of more than one risk type (see 7I.7.470). We believe that the principle contained in 7I.7.680.72 would also apply in its entirety to a hedge of more than one risk type if there is such a change with respect to one of the hedged risks – i.e. the existing hedging relationship relating to all risk types would be de-designated in its entirety. This is because the existing hedging relationship is a single hedging relationship even though it relates to more than one hedged risk. [*IAS 39.76*]

EXAMPLE 27 – REDESIGNATION IN A NEW CASH FLOW HEDGE

71.7.680.76   Company C, whose functional currency is sterling, issues a 20-year fixed-rate debt liability denominated in US dollars in year 0. C's risk management strategy is to hedge currency risk and interest rate risk. C plans to convert the first 10 years of interest and foreign currency exposure to a fixed interest rate denominated in sterling. For the last 10 years of the debt instrument, C plans to convert the exposure to a floating interest rate in sterling. This strategy will be achieved by the following.

- *Year 0*: Enter into a 20-year cross-currency interest rate swap to receive a fixed interest rate and principal in US dollars and pay a variable interest rate and principal in sterling (Swap 1).
- *Year 0*: Enter into a 10-year interest rate swap to receive a variable rate in sterling and pay a fixed rate in sterling (Swap 2).
- *Year 10*: On maturity of Swap 2, plan to enter into a new 10-year interest rate swap to receive a variable rate in sterling and pay a fixed rate in sterling (Swap 3). The variable interest receipts in sterling on Swap 3 will offset the variable interest payments in sterling on Swap 1 until the maturity date of this transaction.

71.7.680.77   At inception of the hedging relationship in year 0, C anticipates that it will enter into Swap 3 in year 10 and reflects this in its hedge documentation. Swaps 1 and 2 are combined and designated as the hedging instrument in a cash flow hedge of currency risk for years 0 to 10 and a fair value hedge of currency and interest rate risk for years 11 to 20. C expects that, in year 10, the remainder of Swap 1 and Swap 3 will be jointly designated as a cash flow hedge of currency risk for years 11 to 20.

71.7.680.78   On initial designation in year 0, the cash flows in years 11 to 20 are hedged for both currency and interest rate risk. When Swap 3 is designated in year 10, then the risk being hedged in years 11 to 20 will be only currency risk. Under IAS 39 the replacement or rollover of a hedging instrument into another hedging instrument is not an expiration or termination if such replacement or rollover is part of the entity's documented hedging strategy. However, the introduction of a new hedging instrument with a different risk profile to the existing hedging instrument represents a fundamental change to the hedge designation (see 71.7.680.72). Therefore, C needs to de-designate the entire hedging relationship and, if it wishes to continue hedge accounting, designate a new cash flow hedge that includes the remainder of Swap 1 and Swap 3. If so, the terms of any hypothetical derivative used to demonstrate the effectiveness of the new hedging relationship would be established on the date of designation. [*IAS 39.101 (a)*]

71.7.680.80   A replacement or rollover of a hedging instrument is not deemed to be a termination if the new instrument has the same characteristics as the instrument being replaced, it continues to meet the hedge criteria and the rollover strategy was documented properly at inception of the initial hedge.

In our view, using a rollover hedge strategy, the entity may continue to perform hedge effectiveness testing on a cumulative basis from the beginning of the period in which the first hedging instrument was rolled over. The amortisation of any fair value adjustment made to the hedged item under a fair value hedge may continue to be deferred until the rollover hedge strategy is discontinued. [*IAS 39.91*]

EXAMPLE 28 – ROLLOVER HEDGE STRATEGY

7I.7.680.90   Company X forecasts a highly probable purchase of a commodity in one year. As part of its risk management strategy, X wants to fix the cash flow variability that would arise from changes in market prices of the commodity from now until the date of purchase. However, the market to which X has access does not offer commodity future contracts for a duration longer than three months. Therefore, X decides to hedge its exposure to changes in commodity prices by entering into four successive commodity futures.

7I.7.680.95   If X documents this hedging strategy, including the expected rollovers of the hedging futures, at inception of the hedge, then the expiry of one future contract and its replacement with a successive future contract with the same characteristics would not be deemed to be a termination of the hedge.

7I.7.680.100   When an effective hedging relationship no longer exists, the accounting for the hedging instrument and the hedged item revert to accounting under the usual principles of IAS 39 and other applicable standards. All derivatives in the scope of IAS 39 are accounted for at fair value, with changes in fair value recognised in profit or loss. When fair value hedge accounting is discontinued prospectively, any hedging adjustment made previously to a hedged financial instrument for which the effective interest method is used is amortised to profit or loss by adjusting the effective interest rate of the hedged item from the date on which amortisation begins. Amortisation may begin as soon as an adjustment exists – i.e. while the hedging relationship still exists – but cannot begin later than the date on which the hedged item ceases to be adjusted for changes in fair value attributable to the hedged risk. If, in the case of a portfolio hedge of interest rate risk, amortising using a recalculated effective interest rate is impracticable, then the adjustment is amortised using a straight-line method. The adjustment is amortised fully by the maturity of the financial instrument or, in the case of a portfolio hedge of interest rate risk, by the expiry of the relevant repricing time period. In the event that the hedged item is derecognised, the adjustment is recognised immediately in profit or loss when the item is derecognised. [*IAS 39.92*]

7I.7.680.110   For a hedge of a net investment in a foreign operation, the cumulative amount previously recognised in OCI remains in the foreign currency translation reserve until there is a disposal or partial disposal of the investment (see 7I.7.110.30–40). A partial disposal of a net investment in a foreign operation may require the existing hedge to be terminated if the hedging instrument is no longer highly effective in offsetting the foreign currency risk on the reduced net investment. [*IAS 39.102*]

7I.7.685   **Clearing derivatives with central counterparties**

7I.7.685.10   There is relief from discontinuing an existing hedging relationship if a novation that was not contemplated in the original hedging documentation meets the following criteria:

- the novation is made as a consequence of laws or regulations, or the introduction of laws or regulations;
- the novation results in one or more clearing counterparties becoming the new counterparty to each of the parties to the novated derivative; and
- any changes to the terms of the novated derivative are limited to those necessary to effect such a replacement of the counterparty but only if those changes are consistent with the terms that would be expected if the novated derivative were originally cleared with the clearing counterparty; these changes include:
  - changes in the contractual collateral requirements of the novated derivative;
  - rights to set off receivables and payables balances with the clearing counterparty; and
  - charges levied by the clearing counterparty. [*IAS 39.91*]

7I.7.685.20 The following flowchart summarises how to apply the criteria.

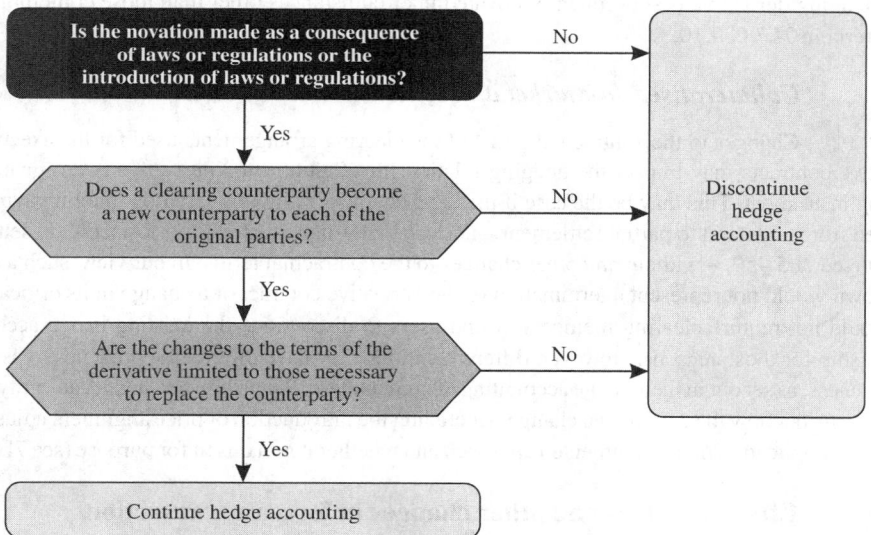

7I.7.685.30 A 'clearing counterparty' is a central counterparty (sometimes referred to as a 'clearing organisation' or a 'clearing agency'), or an entity or entities – e.g. a clearing member of a clearing organisation or a client of a clearing member of a clearing organisation – that are acting as counterparty to effect clearing by a central counterparty. [*IAS 39.91*]

7I.7.685.40 If the parties to the hedging instrument replace their original counterparties with different counterparties, then the relief is available only if each of those parties effects clearing with the same central counterparty. [*IAS 39.91*]

7I.7.685.50 For hedging relationships that continue after the hedging instrument is novated to a clearing counterparty, IAS 39 is still applied as usual to account for the derivative and the hedging relationship. For example, any changes in the credit quality of the counterparty, or in the contractual collateral requirements, are reflected in the fair value of the novated derivative and in the measurement of hedge ineffectiveness. [*IAS 39.AG113A*]

7I.7.685.60   In some jurisdictions, a novation of a derivative to a clearing counterparty may not be required by laws and regulations, but an entity may voluntarily novate a derivative as a consequence of laws and regulations. In such cases, to continue hedge accounting the voluntary novation should be associated with laws or regulations that are relevant to the central clearing of derivatives. The mere possibility of laws or regulations being introduced is not a sufficient basis for the continuation of hedge accounting. [*IAS 39.BC220Q*]

7I.7.685.70   There may be other situations in which a derivative is novated but the criteria to continue hedge accounting are not met – e.g. an entity agrees to a counterparty novating an over-the-counter derivative to a third party as a consequence of laws or regulations, and no clearing counterparty is introduced.

7I.7.685.80   To mitigate the risk that novation would cause hedge accounting to be discontinued, an entity may state in its hedge documentation that its intention is for the hedging relationship to continue if the hedging derivative is subsequently novated in circumstances other than those contemplated in the criteria in 7I.7.685.10.

7I.7.687   *Collateralised-to-market and settled-to-market models*

7I.7.687.10   Changes to the contractual terms of the clearing arrangements used for the execution of derivative contracts may impact the hedging relationship if an affected derivative is designated as a hedging instrument. This may be the case if the legal characterisation of variation margin payments is changed from collateral to partial settlement – i.e. a change from collateralised-to-market to settled-to-market (see 7I.5.450) – without any other changes to the contractual terms. In our view, such a change on its own would not represent a termination of the derivative contract or a change in its critical terms and would not require clearing members or end users to discontinue the existing hedge accounting relationship for those reasons. However, different entities may have different approaches to assessing effectiveness, as set out in their hedge accounting documentation. For an affected hedge, an entity would need to consider how the contractual changes (including the introduction of price alignment adjustment) impact the application of its documented approach and whether it remains fit for purpose (see 7I.5.450).

7I.7.690   **Effect of delays and other changes in forecast transaction**

7I.7.690.10   The notion of a highly probable forecast transaction implies a higher degree of probability than one that is merely expected to occur. If a forecast transaction is no longer highly probable but is still expected to occur, then this means that the criteria for hedge accounting are no longer met and, prospectively, the entity ceases applying hedge accounting. However, the net cumulative gain or loss that was recognised in OCI during the effective period of the hedge remains in equity until the expected transaction actually occurs. The same treatment applies in any other case when hedge accounting is terminated because the hedging criteria are no longer met. [*IAS 39.101(b)*]

EXAMPLE 29 – DISCONTINUATION – RECLASSIFYING GAINS AND LOSSES – HEDGED FUTURE CASH FLOWS EXPECTED TO OCCUR

7I.7.690.20   On 31 December 2018, Company D issues a floating rate bond that bears interest based on a benchmark rate payable annually and matures on 31 December 2022. The bond is issued at par of 1,000. In accordance with its risk

management strategy, D enters into a four-year pay-fixed 3% receive-benchmark interest rate swap on 31 December 2018. On the same date, D designates the swap as a cash flow hedge of the variability of future interest payments on the bond attributable to changes in the benchmark rate. The timing of the swap's cash flows matches those of the bond. The fair value of the swap at inception is zero.

7I.7.690.30   The effects of credit risk are insignificant to the effectiveness of the hedging relationship and there are no sources of ineffectiveness during the hedging period. Therefore, during 2019 and 2020 all gains and losses on remeasurement of the swap to fair value are included in OCI.

7I.7.690.40   On 31 December 2020, D changes its risk management strategy and it no longer wishes to hedge its exposure to variable interest payments. Therefore, on that date D terminates the interest rate swap by receiving its current fair value of 28 from the counterparty and discontinues hedge accounting. Interest payments on the bond are still expected to occur through to maturity on 31 December 2022.

7I.7.690.50   At 31 December 2020, the market one-year benchmark rate is 4% and the one-year benchmark forward rate for fixing on 31 December 2021 and settling on 31 December 2022 is 5%.

7I.7.690.60   We believe that D may apply the following approaches to reclassify the accumulated balance of 28 recognised in OCI at 31 December 2020 to profit or loss during 2021 and 2022 (see 7I.7.80.30).
- *Approach 1:* Using the information on the yield curve, D analyses the fair value of the swap of 28 as representing the present value of expected net receipts of 10 on 31 December 2021 and 18 on 31 December 2022 – i.e. the expected present values of the cash flows that would have occurred under the swap if it had not been terminated. Based on this analysis, D reclassifies 10 during 2021 and 18 during 2022.
- *Approach 2:* D amortises the total balance of 28 on a straight-line basis over the two-year period – i.e. 14 in each year.

7I.7.690.70   If a hedged forecast transaction is no longer expected to occur within the original time period or a relatively short period thereafter, then hedge accounting is terminated. The related cumulative gain or loss on the hedging instrument that was recognised in OCI is immediately reclassified to profit or loss. An entity cannot continue to defer the cumulative gain or loss in equity on the basis that the original hedged transaction has been replaced by a new forecast transaction that has features similar to those of the original hedged transaction. In our view, if the extension of the time period is relatively short, then the hedge still may qualify for hedge accounting if the effectiveness criteria continue to be met (see 7I.7.510). [*IAS 39.101*]

7I.7.690.80   In determining the appropriate accounting treatment for delayed transactions, it is important to distinguish between hedged cash flows related to:

- a firm commitment;
- a highly probable forecast transaction with an identified counterparty; and
- forecast transactions with unidentified counterparties.

7I.7.700   *Firm commitments and forecast transactions with identified counterparties*

7I.7.700.10   When the timing of delivery or payments or other terms under a firm commitment are changed, an entity evaluates whether the original firm commitment still exists or whether a new firm commitment has been created. The latter situation would result in the original hedging relationship being terminated and hedge accounting being discontinued prospectively (see 7I.7.680). [*IAS 39.91, 101*]

7I.7.700.20   If a firm commitment is delayed but will still occur, then it is important to determine the cause and extent of the delay. In our view, when delays occur in the cash flows associated with a firm commitment, hedge accounting may be continued under the following circumstances:

- the firm commitment can still be uniquely identified; and
- a binding agreement still exists and the cash flows are still expected to occur within a *relatively short period of time* after the original delivery/payment date.

7I.7.700.30   The contract supporting a firm commitment should specify a date or range of dates within which the cash flows are expected to occur. If a date, such as a delivery or completion date, is not specified, then the transaction is unlikely to meet the definition of a firm commitment; rather, it can be hedged only as a forecast transaction with an identified counterparty.

7I.7.700.40   For a highly probable forecast transaction with an identified counterparty, there may be a little more flexibility in what could be regarded as a relatively short period of time if a delivery date has not yet been established. [*IAS 39.IG.F.3.11*]

7I.7.700.50   The key issue, when taking into account all facts and circumstances surrounding the delay, is whether the entity can demonstrate that the delayed transaction is the *same transaction* as the one that originally was hedged.

7I.7.700.60   When the timing of a firm commitment or a highly probable forecast transaction is delayed, some degree of ineffectiveness is likely to occur, if the timing of the hedged item and the timing of the hedging instrument no longer are the same. When the hedging instrument originally had a duration longer than the original expected timeframe for the firm commitment or forecast transaction, then the effectiveness could, in fact, improve as a result of the delay in the hedged transaction. In other cases, the hedged cash flow may arise earlier than originally expected. Because the hedging instrument will expire later than the hedged cash flows, some ineffectiveness is likely to occur in this situation as well. However, the hedging instrument may not be redesignated for a shorter period. [*IAS 39.IG.F.5.4*]

7I.7.710   *Forecast transactions with unidentified counterparties*

7I.7.710.10   An example of a forecast transaction with an unidentified counterparty is the sale of mobile handsets. Typically, the hedged cash flow would be the first x amount of sales revenue to be received on the sale of handsets in a particular month or quarter (see 7I.7.720). Exactly which retailer or end user will purchase the handsets is not specified in the hedge documentation.

7I.7.710.20   Cash flows from forecast transactions with unidentified counterparties are designated with reference to the time period in which the transactions are expected to occur. [*IAS 39.IG.F.3.7*]

7I.7.710.30   When forecast cash flows in a particular period do not occur, it is possible that such a shortfall will be offset by increased cash flows in a later period. For example, an entity initially forecasts sales of summer clothing of 100 in each of the first two quarters of the coming year. Subsequently, the entity revises its forecast to sales of 75 in the first quarter and 125 in the second quarter. The total amount of sales in the two quarters remains unchanged at 200.

7I.7.710.40   For hedge accounting to be continued, the original forecast transaction should still exist and be highly probable. If the hedged item is a forecast transaction (e.g. forecast sales) with unidentified counterparties within a certain time period, then it is unlikely that an entity will be able to demonstrate that sales in later periods replace a shortfall in an earlier period. Consequently, hedge accounting is discontinued. In addition, a history of designating hedges of forecast transactions and then determining that they are no longer expected to occur may call into question the entity's ability to predict forecast transactions accurately, as well as the appropriateness of using hedge accounting in the future for similar transactions. [*IAS 39.88, 101*]

7I.7.710.50   In our view, the transactions should be grouped into relatively narrow bands of time within which the forecast transactions are expected to occur. In determining the length of such a period, the industry and environment in which the entity operates should be considered. In our view, for forecast transactions with unidentified counterparties, this narrow range of time should be interpreted more strictly (i.e. a shorter time period used) than for forecast transactions with identified counterparties.

7I.7.720   *Use of layering with 'first payments received (paid)' approach*

7I.7.720.10   In hedging groups of forecast transactions in a cash flow hedge using a first payments received (paid) approach (see 7I.7.200.70), an entity may choose to enter into multiple derivative contracts and layer these contracts such that each derivative will be designated in a separate hedging relationship.

EXAMPLE 30 – USE OF LAYERING APPROACH

7I.7.720.15   On 1 January 2018, Company J, whose functional currency is sterling, forecasts EUR 1,000 sales to occur during the month of June 2018. On the same date, it enters into four separate forward contracts, each to sell EUR 250, that expire in June 2018. Instead of combining the four forward contracts and designating them as the hedging instrument in a single hedge (see 7I.7.310.30), J may designate four separate cash flow hedging relationships in which the first forward contract hedges the cash flows from the first EUR 250 of forecast sales, the second forward hedges the next EUR 250 of sales that have not been identified as hedged forecast sales in a previously designated hedging relationship etc.

7I.7.720.20   Using this layering approach meets the requirements to identify, for each of the individual hedging relationships, the hedged forecast transactions with sufficient specificity for J to determine which transactions are the hedged transactions when they occur. The layering approach provides J with the flexibility to add additional hedging relationships (i.e. add layers) and to remove existing relationships (i.e. delete layers) without affecting the other hedging relationships via termination and redesignation because no change is required to the identification of the hedged forecast transactions associated with those other relationships.

7I.7.720.25   This approach is possible because the designation of each relationship will always identify the hedged forecast transactions as the first payments received after (1) those cash flows that already have been identified as hedged forecast transactions in a previously designated hedging relationship that continues to be active and (2) those cash flows that were previously identified in a hedging relationship that has been terminated (i.e. is inactive) but still are at least expected to occur such that some portion of the gain or loss on the terminated hedging relationship remains in OCI.

7I.7.720.30   If subsequent to designation J revises its sales forecasts and determines that only EUR 725 of future sales remain highly probable to occur, then under the layered hedge designation:
- the first two hedging relationships in respect of the first EUR 500 of forecast sales will continue unaffected;
- the third hedging relationship will be likely to continue, albeit with higher ineffectiveness, if the third EUR 250 forward contract remains highly effective in offsetting the foreign currency risk on future cash flows of EUR 225; and
- the fourth hedging relationship will be terminated.

7I.7.720.40   In contrast, if J had designated all four forward contracts as the combined hedging instrument in a single hedging relationship, then hedge accounting would be required to be terminated for all forecast sales because the combined hedging instrument to sell EUR 1,000 would not be effective in offsetting the foreign currency risk arising from only EUR 725 of highly probable sales.

7I.7.720.50   Adding a derivative to the existing layers will put that relationship at the end of the priority chain, such that it will be designated as hedging the first forecast transactions occurring after (1) and (2), as discussed in 7I.7.720.25, without impacting the designation of those earlier relationships. Furthermore, if a derivative matures such that a relationship early in the priority chain terminates, then the identification of the forecast transactions for the relationships later in the priority chain is not impacted because they will continue to hedge the first payments received after (1) those that already are hedged in active hedging relationships and (2) those that were previously identified in a hedging relationship that has been terminated (i.e. is inactive) for which amounts remain in equity.

7I.7.720.55   If no amounts remain in equity related to the derivative that matured, the forecast transactions that are identified with the active relationships and those inactive relationships that continue to have amounts in equity are the forecast transactions occurring earlier in the priority chain than before. This is because those relationships will have moved up in priority because of the disappearance of the earlier layer as a result of the derivative's maturity and the reclassification of its related amounts from equity to profit or loss. When a relationship moves up in the priority chain, then the perfectly effective hypothetical derivative – assuming that the entity employs the hypothetical derivative method discussed in 7I.7.630 – associated with that relationship will be adjusted to reflect the most recent best estimate of the forecast transactions that are identified with that relationship. The terms of the adjusted perfectly effective hypothetical derivative would be so determined that if constructed at hedge inception it would have a fair value of zero.

7I.7.720.60   We believe that the layering approach is a simple and effective methodology for identifying the hedged forecast transactions for many hedging programmes. However, entities cannot lose sight of the fact that each hedging relationship stands on its own; that is, entities cannot apply a hedge documentation approach that ignores the priority chain designation of forecast transactions. Therefore, complexities arise and the level of documentation may be higher in certain hedging programmes, particularly those in which an entity is actively managing groups of existing hedging relationships – e.g. terminating or de-designating derivatives before maturity – and is experiencing shortfalls of forecast transactions.

7I.7.730   Impairment of hedged item

7I.7.730.10   An entity discontinues fair value hedge accounting when the hedge no longer meets the criteria for hedge accounting (see 7I.7.120). [*IAS 39.91*]

7I.7.730.20   In our view, in many circumstances when a hedged asset has been impaired, the current hedge accounting relationship should be discontinued. This is because when there is a change in estimated cash flows of the hedged asset, the hedge is no longer expected to be highly effective in achieving offsetting changes in fair value or cash flows attributable to the hedged risk that is consistent with the originally documented risk management strategy for the particular hedging relationship. For example, in the case of a hedge of benchmark interest rate risk, there cannot be interest rate sensitivity on cash flows that are not expected to be recovered.

7I.7.730.30   An entity discontinues hedge accounting from the last date on which compliance with the hedge effectiveness criteria was demonstrated. However, if the entity can identify the event or change in circumstances that caused the hedging relationship to fail the effectiveness criteria, and demonstrates that the hedge was effective before the event or change in circumstances occurred, then the entity discontinues hedge accounting from the date of the event or change in circumstances. [*IAS 39.AG113*]

7I.7.730.40   There may be circumstances in which an entity may determine that continuation of the current hedging relationship is still appropriate – e.g. the impairment is for a small amount, and the entity can conclude that effectiveness based on the original hedging relationship will remain within 80–125 percent. Judgement should be applied based on the specific facts and circumstances of a particular situation.

7I.7.730.50   If the existing hedging relationship is discontinued, then it may be possible to designate a new hedging relationship based on the revised estimated recoverable cash flows. Whether this is possible is a matter of judgement that depends on the entity's ability to reliably estimate the recoverable cash flows and separately identify the effect of changes in the benchmark interest rate on the item's fair value, as well as the availability of a hedging instrument that would be effective in relation to the revised recoverable cash flow profile.

7I.7.740 **NET INVESTMENT HEDGE**

7I.7.750 **Net assets of foreign operation**

7I.7.750.10 The hedged item in a net investment hedge is the foreign currency exposure on the carrying amount of the net assets of the foreign operation, but only if they are included in the financial statements. This includes consolidated subsidiaries in consolidated financial statements and also includes financial statements that include associates and joint ventures, as well as financial statements that include a foreign branch or a joint operation. Therefore, if an entity has an investment in an associate or joint venture, or a foreign operation that is conducted through a branch or a joint operation, then such an investment would qualify as the hedged item in a net investment hedge in the individual financial statements (see 2.1.110). [*IFRIC 16.2, 7*]

7I.7.750.20 In a hedge of a net investment in a foreign operation, a derivative instrument, a non-derivative instrument or a combination of both (see 7I.7.830.40) may be used as the hedging instrument. The hedging instrument can be held by any entity within the group. [*IFRIC 16.14*]

7I.7.750.30 The 'hedged risk' is the foreign currency exposure arising from the functional currency of the foreign operation and the functional currency of any parent – i.e. immediate, intermediate or ultimate parent of the foreign operation. The foreign exchange differences arising between the functional currency of the foreign operation and the presentation currency of any parent cannot be designated as the hedged risk (see 7I.7.780). The foreign currency risk arising from the net investment in the consolidated financial statements can be hedged only once. [*IFRIC 16.10, 12–13, AG2, BC14*]

7I.7.750.40 When the hedging instrument is a forward contract, the entity may hedge the spot foreign exchange rate or the forward rate. If exposure to changes in the forward rate is designated as the hedged risk, then the interest component included in the forward rate is part of the hedged foreign currency risk. Therefore, total changes in the fair value of the hedging derivative contract, including the interest element – i.e. the spot-forward premium or forward points – are recognised in OCI and accumulated in a separate component of equity. However, when the entity hedges the spot foreign exchange rate, then the change in the interest element of the hedging derivative contract is recognised immediately in profit or loss and only the changes in the fair value of the hedging derivative that are attributable to changes in spot foreign exchange differences are recognised in OCI. When the hedging instrument is a non-derivative financial instrument, IFRIC 16 suggests designating the spot foreign exchange risk as the hedged risk. The method of translating the foreign currency financial statements of the foreign operation as described in IAS 21 (see 2.7.230) does not change, whichever hedging strategy is used.

EXAMPLE 31 – NET INVESTMENT HEDGES

7I.7.750.50 Parent P, whose functional currency is sterling, has the following net investments in each of its subsidiaries.
- Subsidiary S1's functional currency is the euro. P directly owns S1 and has a EUR 500 net investment in the subsidiary.

- Subsidiary S2's functional currency is the US dollar. P directly owns S2 and has a USD 300 net investment in the subsidiary.
- Subsidiary S3's functional currency is the Australian dollar. S2 directly owns S3 and has an AUD 100 net investment in the subsidiary. Therefore, assuming an Australian dollar/US dollar exchange rate of 1.25, P's total USD 300 net investment in S2 includes USD 80 in respect of S2's AUD 100 net investment in S3. In other words, S2's net assets other than its investment in S3 are USD 220. [*IFRIC 16.AG2, AG9*]

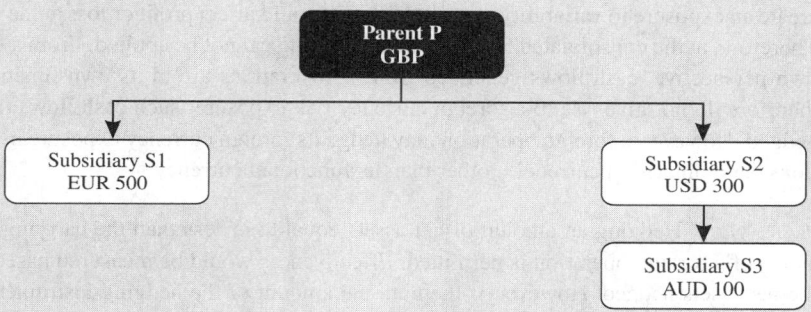

71.7.750.60   In this situation, the following are examples of alternative net investment hedge designations that may be possible in the consolidated financial statements of P.

- P can hedge its net investment in each of subsidiaries S1, S2 and S3 for the foreign exchange risk between their respective functional currencies and sterling. The maximum amounts that can be designated as effective hedges in P's consolidated financial statements are:
  - EUR 500 net investment in S1 for sterling/euro risk;
  - USD 220 net investment in S2 for sterling/US dollar risk; and
  - AUD 100 net investment in S3 for sterling/Australian dollar risk.
- P can hedge its net investment in only S1 and S2 for the foreign exchange risk between their respective functional currencies and sterling. In this case, up to the full USD 300 investment in S2 could be designated. Note, however, that P could not designate both the full USD 300 of its net investment in S2 with respect to the sterling/US dollar risk and its AUD 100 net investment in S3 with respect to the sterling/Australian dollar risk because this would involve hedging the net investment in S3 with respect to the sterling twice.
- P can hedge, in its consolidated financial statements, its AUD 100 net investment in S3 for the US dollar/Australian dollar risk between the functional currencies of S2 and S3, and also designate a hedge of the entire USD 300 of its net investment in S2 with respect to sterling/US dollar risk, because the designation of the US dollar/Australian dollar risk between S2 and S3 does not include any sterling/US dollar risk.

71.7.750.70   The hedged risk cannot be designated as the fair value of the underlying shares, or the foreign currency exposure on the fair value of the shares, because the

> consolidation process recognises the subsidiary's profit or loss, rather than changes in the investment's fair value. The same is true of a net investment in an associate or joint venture, because equity accounting recognises the investor's share of the associate's profit or loss (see 3.5.180). [*IAS 39.AG99*]

7I.7.750.80   Groups with foreign operations may wish to hedge the foreign currency exposure arising from the expected profits from the foreign operations by using derivatives or other financial instruments. In our view, a forecast transaction in the foreign operation's own functional currency does not create an exposure to variability in cash flows that could affect profit or loss at the consolidated level. Therefore, at the consolidated level, hedge accounting cannot be applied. From a foreign operation's own perspective, cash flows generated from its operations are in its own functional currency and therefore do not give rise to a foreign currency risk exposure; such cash flows therefore cannot be hedged. However, a foreign operation may hedge its foreign currency exposure in respect of transactions denominated in currencies other than its functional currency.

7I.7.750.90   Hedging an amount of net assets equal to or less than the carrying amount of the net assets of a foreign operation is permitted. Effectiveness would be measured based on the amount of the net assets hedged. However, if the notional amount of the hedging instrument exceeds the carrying amount of the underlying net assets – e.g. because of losses incurred by the foreign operation that reduce its net assets – then changes in fair value on the excess portion of the hedging instrument are recognised in profit or loss immediately. [*IAS 39.102*]

7I.7.750.100   In testing hedge effectiveness, the change in value of the hedging instrument is determined with reference to the functional currency of the parent against which the hedged risk is measured. Depending on where the hedging instrument is held, in the absence of hedge accounting the total change in value of the hedging instrument may be recognised in profit or loss, OCI or both. However, the assessment of hedge effectiveness is not affected by whether the change in value of the hedging instrument is recognised in profit or loss or OCI. The assessment of hedge effectiveness is also not affected by the method of consolidation – i.e. the direct or step-by-step method – or whether the hedging instrument is a derivative or non-derivative instrument. [*IFRIC 16.15*]

EXAMPLE 32 – DESIGNATION OF A FINANCIAL INSTRUMENT AS A HEDGED ITEM IN A FAIR VALUE HEDGE AND AS A HEDGING INSTRUMENT IN A NET INVESTMENT HEDGE

7I.7.750.110   Company X, whose functional currency is South Korean won, issues a fixed interest rate bond denominated in US dollars (Bond A) to acquire a foreign subsidiary (Company Y). The notional amount of Bond A and the investment in Y are each USD 1,000.

7I.7.750.115   X has the following hedging relationship.
- Hedged item: Bond A (fixed interest rate risk).
- Hedging instrument: interest rate swap that pays LIBOR and receives a fixed interest rate.
- The notional amount of the interest rate swap is USD 1,000.

- The swap is a qualifying hedging instrument for a fair value hedge and Bond A is the hedged item.

7I.7.750.120 It is possible for X also to designate the foreign currency risk component of Bond A as the hedging instrument in a hedge of the net investment in Y provided that the fair value hedge adjustment is expected to be immaterial compared with the hedged net investment amount. If this is the case, then the ratio between Bond A and the net investment in Y may result in ineffectiveness, but not in hedge failure.

7I.7.760   Expected net profit or loss of net investment in foreign operation

7I.7.760.10   The hedged item may be an amount of net assets equal to or less than the carrying amount of the net assets of the foreign operation at the beginning of any given period. [*IAS 39.81, IFRIC 16.2, 11, AG3–AG6*]

7I.7.760.20   Consequently, the expected profits from the foreign operation in that period cannot be designated as the hedged item in a net investment hedge. Translation risk arises once the net profit is recognised as an increase in net assets of the foreign operation. The additional net assets can be designated as a hedged item in a net investment hedge as they arise, although in our experience most groups will revisit their net investment hedges only quarterly or semi-annually. [*IAS 39.81, IFRIC 16.2, 11*]

7I.7.760.30   Expected net profits from a foreign operation expose a group to potential volatility in consolidated profit or loss because transactions in the foreign operation are translated into the group's presentation currency at spot rates at the transaction dates, or at appropriate average rates (see 2.7.240). However, because expected net profits in future reporting periods do not constitute recognised assets, liabilities or forecast transactions that will ultimately affect profit or loss at the consolidated level, they cannot be designated in a hedging relationship under either a fair value or a cash flow hedge model. [*IAS 21.39–40*]

7I.7.760.40   Expected net losses in a foreign operation will reduce the net investment balance, which could result in an over-hedged position. Therefore, if a group expects its foreign operation to make losses, then it may decide to hedge less than the full carrying amount of the net assets. Otherwise it will not be able to satisfy the hedge accounting criterion that the hedging relationship is expected to be highly effective on an ongoing basis. In our view, an entity should take into account expected losses in a foreign operation when assessing hedge effectiveness if they are highly probable.

7I.7.770   Monetary items

7I.7.770.10   An investor's net investment may also include monetary items that are receivable from or payable to the foreign operation, settlement of which is neither planned nor likely to occur in the foreseeable future. Loans provided by a subsidiary to a fellow subsidiary may form part of the group's net investment in a foreign operation, even when the loan is in neither the parent's nor the borrowing subsidiary's functional currency. Consequently, the net investment may include an intra-group loan in any currency when settlement is neither planned nor likely to occur in the foreseeable future.

EXAMPLE 33 – NET INVESTMENT HEDGE WITH INTRA-GROUP LOAN

7I.7.770.20   In 2015, Company T, whose functional currency is the euro, bought Company B for GBP 100. The carrying amount of B's net assets was GBP 60, and T recognised fair value adjustments to specific assets and liabilities of GBP 30 and goodwill of GBP 10. During 2015, T extended a loan to B of GBP 20.

7I.7.770.30   In 2018, the carrying amount (excluding fair value adjustments from the acquisition) of B's assets and liabilities is GBP 70. The remaining fair value adjustments are GBP 25 and goodwill remains at GBP 10. The loan has not been repaid nor is it intended to be repaid. The carrying amount of the net investment that T may designate as the hedged item is equal to the amount of T's net investment in B, including goodwill. This amount would be GBP 125 (70 + 25 + 10 + 20).

7I.7.780   Presentation currency

7I.7.780.10   The group's presentation currency is not relevant to net investment hedging. Translation of the financial statements of an entity into the group presentation currency under IAS 21 is an accounting exercise that does not create an exposure to foreign exchange risk; therefore, hedge accounting for such translation risk is not permitted. An economic exchange risk arises only from an exposure between two or more functional currencies, not from translation into a presentation currency. [*IFRIC 16.BC13–BC14*]

EXAMPLE 34 – PRESENTATION CURRENCY DIFFERS FROM FUNCTIONAL CURRENCY

7I.7.780.20   When a group's presentation currency differs from the parent's functional currency, then the appropriate hedged risk to be designated in a net investment hedge is still the exposure to changes in the exchange rate between the foreign operation's functional currency and the parent's functional currency. Therefore, net investment hedging may be applied only to hedge the exchange rate risk that exists between the functional currency of a parent entity and the functional currency of the foreign operation.

7I.7.790   Cross-currency interest rate swaps

7I.7.790.10   Net investments in foreign operations are commonly hedged with forward contracts or non-derivative financial items such as foreign currency loans. Some entities may want to use, as hedging instruments, cross-currency interest rate swaps (CCIRSs) or a synthetic borrowing that is a combination of a borrowing and an interest rate swap and/or a CCIRS (see 7I.7.830). In our view, although they are more complex, these hedging strategies may qualify for hedge accounting if particular care is taken in identifying and designating the hedging instrument and the hedged item.

7I.7.800   *Fixed-for-fixed cross-currency interest rate swap*

7I.7.800.10   Economically, a foreign currency forward contract and a fixed-for-fixed CCIRS are similar; the primary difference between the two is that the interest component of the fixed-for-fixed

CCIRS is explicitly identified through an exchange of coupons instead of being implicit as in the case of the forward points component in a foreign currency forward contract. Therefore, the coupon exchanges in a fixed-for-fixed CCIRS are equivalent to the forward points in a foreign currency forward contract. In our view, a fixed-for-fixed CCIRS can be designated as the hedging instrument in a hedge of the net investment in a foreign operation. The amount of the hedged item would be the notional amount of the CCIRS, excluding its coupon exchanges. As is the case of a hedge using a forward contract, we believe that there are two possible approaches that can be applied in designating the hedged risk: an approach based on changes in the forward exchange rate and an approach based on changes in the spot exchange rate.

7I.7.800.20   Under the first approach, the entity designates the hedge based on changes in forward rates. In our view, the hypothetical derivative method may be used to assess effectiveness. The perfectly effective hypothetical derivative would have the same relevant critical terms – e.g. notional, underlying etc – as the hedged item and the same maturity as the hedging instrument. In many cases, the perfectly effective hypothetical derivative could be constructed as a CCIRS with identical terms as the actual CCIRS, if the actual CCIRS' critical terms are the same as those of the hedged item. In this case, the hedging relationship might achieve near perfect hedge effectiveness.

7I.7.800.30   Under the first approach, the effective portion of the fair value gains and losses, including any interest accruals, on the hedging instrument would be recognised in OCI and presented in the foreign currency translation reserve. The actual payment or receipt of interest on the hedging instrument represents partial settlement of the hedging instrument's carrying amount and does not lead to any reclassification from OCI to profit or loss.

7I.7.800.40   Under the second approach, the entity designates the hedge based on changes in spot rates. Changes in the fair value of the notional amount of the CCIRS that arise from changes in spot exchange rates would be effective in offsetting changes in the designated amount of the hedged net investment. Such changes would be recognised in OCI and presented in the foreign currency translation reserve. The remaining fair value changes in the CCIRS, which are equivalent to the forward points in a forward contract, would be excluded from the hedging relationship and measured at FVTPL.

7I.7.810   *Floating-for-floating cross-currency interest rate swap*

7I.7.810.10   In our view, a floating-for-floating CCIRS with initial and final exchanges of notional amounts potentially could be designated as a hedging instrument in a net investment hedge. Provided that the hedge is expected to be highly effective throughout the hedging relationship and the other hedge criteria are met, this hedging strategy should qualify for hedge accounting.

7I.7.810.20   When using floating-for-floating CCIRS, a net investment hedge can be designated as a hedged item for the forward exchange rate risk. However, in our view the perfectly effective hypothetical cannot be constructed as a CCIRS with terms identical to the actual floating-for-floating CCIRS, because floating interest rate cash flows do not exist in the hedged item. Instead, the perfectly effective hypothetical derivative may be constructed as either a fixed-for-fixed CCIRS or a forward contract. In either case, the floating interest payments will give rise to some ineffectiveness because of movements in interest rate curves between repricing dates.

71.7.810.30   In our experience, if the notional amount of a floating-for-floating CCIRS does not exceed the amount of a net investment, then designating the notional amount of the CCIRS as a hedging instrument in a hedge based on changes in spot rates is more likely to result in lower ineffectiveness. This is because the floating interest rate cash flows and principal amounts of the CCIRS would be discounted at market in the respective currencies, resulting in amounts that approximate the notional amount of the hedged item, and are converted at the spot rate – thereby following the changes in the value of the hedge item, which is also converted using the spot rate.

71.7.820   *Fixed-for-floating cross-currency interest rate swap*

71.7.820.10   A fixed-for-floating CCIRS is exposed to both interest rate risk and foreign currency risk. In our view, a fixed-for-floating CCIRS cannot generally be designated as a hedging instrument in a net investment hedge because the interest rate risk inherent in the instrument gives rises to ineffectiveness that precludes hedge accounting.

71.7.820.20   However, it may be possible to designate such an instrument in its entirety in more than one hedging relationship simultaneously and achieve hedge accounting. For example, a pay-fixed US dollar receive-floating euro CCIRS can be viewed as comprising a pay-fixed US dollar receive-fixed euro CCIRS and a pay-fixed euro receive-floating euro interest rate swap. The pay-fixed US dollar receive-fixed euro CCIRS can be designated as a hedging instrument of a US dollar net investment, while the pay-fixed euro receive-floating euro interest rate swap can be designated as either a fair value hedge of a fixed rate asset or a cash flow hedge of a floating rate liability.

71.7.820.30   When such an approach is adopted, the hedge documentation should clearly identify the various hedged items for which the CCIRS is designated as the hedging instrument. Only in measuring effectiveness is the CCIRS separated into a fixed-for-fixed CCIRS and a fixed-for-floating interest rate swap. In the event that any of the hedges becomes ineffective, in our view hedge accounting would be terminated for all the hedging relationships in which the CCIRS is the designated hedging instrument.

71.7.830   *Synthetic borrowing*

71.7.830.10   A synthetic borrowing is created through the combination of a borrowing in one currency with a CCIRS that effectively changes the interest and principal payments of the original borrowing into a different currency. For example, Company T has a euro functional currency. T has a net investment in a sterling functional currency subsidiary and a bond in issue that is denominated in US dollars. T wishes to enter into a pay-floating sterling receive-fixed US dollar CCIRS and to designate the bond and the CCIRS together as the hedging instrument in a hedge of a net investment.

71.7.830.20   The combination of a borrowing and a CCIRS may seem to be similar to a plain vanilla borrowing, but there are significant differences between the synthetic position and the plain vanilla position.

71.7.830.30   For a plain vanilla borrowing, only the foreign currency translation gains or losses on the amortised cost arising from foreign currency spot risk are recognised in accordance with IAS 21. The effective portion of these translation gains or losses will offset the corresponding IAS 21 translation gains or losses on the net investment and both are recognised in OCI. However, for a synthetic borrowing the bond and the CCIRS are not measured on a consistent basis. The carrying amount of the US dollar bond is translated into euro under IAS 21, but is not remeasured to fair value for changes in interest rates, whereas the CCIRS is measured at fair value with respect to both currency and interest rate risk.

7I.7.830.40   A combination of derivatives and non-derivatives can be used as the hedging instrument only in respect of foreign currency risk. Because the synthetic borrowing – i.e. the plain vanilla bond combined with the CCIRS – has an exposure to both interest rate and foreign currency risk, in our view such a combined designation would not generally be appropriate because the interest rate exposure on the hedging instrument would likely cause the hedge not to be highly effective. One solution that would reduce volatility in profit or loss would be to measure both the bond and the CCIRS at fair value. However, in our view there is no possibility under IFRS to measure the bond at fair value and then to include these fair value changes in a net investment hedging relationship. [*IAS 39.77*]

7I.7.840   HEDGING ON A GROUP BASIS

7I.7.840.10   For a foreign currency hedge transacted on a group basis, it is important that the foreign currency exposure of the hedging instrument and the hedged transaction is the same.

EXAMPLE 35 – FOREIGN CURRENCY HEDGE TRANSACTED ON GROUP BASIS

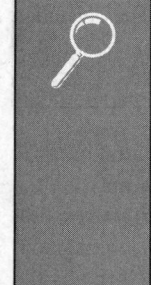

7I.7.840.20   Company E has the euro as its functional currency and Company F, a subsidiary of E, has the Swiss franc as its functional currency. F has a foreign currency exposure arising from a highly probable forecast transaction denominated in US dollars. If E hedges this exposure through its central treasury by entering into a Swiss franc-to-US dollar forward contract, then the transaction may qualify for hedge accounting in E's consolidated financial statements. However, if E enters into a euro-to-US dollar forward contract, then the contract does not qualify as a hedging instrument because the currency of the forward contract does not match the underlying exposure that the entity wishes to hedge unless it can be demonstrated that the euro and the Swiss franc are highly correlated.

7I.7.850   Internal derivatives

7I.7.850.10   One of the key issues that arise in applying hedge accounting at the group level is the need to eliminate internal derivatives for the purposes of consolidation.

7I.7.850.20   An entity may use internal derivatives to transfer risk from individual operations within the group to a centralised treasury. Derivatives between entities within the same reporting group can also be used to control and monitor risks through the central treasury function to benefit from pricing advantages and to offset equal and opposite exposures arising from different parts of the group. However, all such internal derivatives eliminate on consolidation and therefore are not eligible for hedge accounting in the consolidated financial statements, even if at a group level the overall net position is hedged externally. Therefore, only derivatives involving external third parties can be designated as hedging instruments in consolidated financial statements. However, it is possible for the centralised treasury to enter into one or more derivatives with external counterparties to offset the internal derivatives. Such external derivatives may qualify as hedging instruments in the consolidated financial statements provided that they are legally separate contracts and serve a valid business purpose – e.g. laying off risk exposures on a gross basis. In our view, a relationship should exist between the internal transactions and one or multiple related external transactions, and this relationship should be documented at inception of the hedging relationship. [*IAS 39.73, IG.F.1.4*]

71.7.860 Externalisation and round-tripping

71.7.860.10 In consolidated financial statements, hedge accounting may be applied to an external hedge even if the group entity that is subject to the risk being hedged is not a direct party to the hedging instrument. [*IAS 39.IG.F.1.4, IG.F.2.14*]

EXAMPLE 36 – EXTERNALISATION AND ROUND-TRIPPING

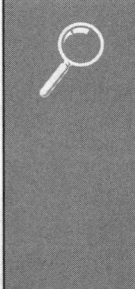

71.7.860.20 Subsidiary B has a financial asset (with a counterparty outside the group) on which it receives a fixed rate of interest. For the purposes of hedging its individual exposure to the fixed interest rate, B enters into a pay-fixed receive-floating interest rate swap with the group's central treasury. The swap is an internal derivative, which does not qualify as a hedging instrument in the consolidated financial statements. To achieve hedge accounting at the group level, the central treasury enters into a matching pay-fixed receive-floating interest rate swap with an external counterparty and documents this link. The fixed interest financial asset and the external derivative then can be designated in a hedging relationship that qualifies for hedge accounting in the consolidated financial statements. [*IAS 39.IG.F.1.4*]

71.7.860.30 By entering into an external derivative the group 'externalises' the transaction in order to achieve hedge accounting in the consolidated financial statements. However, there may be circumstances in which the entity concurrently would enter into two offsetting external derivatives. The first of these derivatives would be designated as the hedging instrument in the consolidated financial statements, whereas the offsetting swap would be included in the entity's trading book. Normally the reason for the offsetting transaction is to 'create' an external hedging instrument for hedge accounting purposes without changing the risk position of the central treasury. At the same time as entering into an external derivative that would qualify as a hedging instrument as described in Example 36, the central treasury would enter into an exactly offsetting swap with the same counterparty. This is known as 'round-tripping'.

71.7.860.40 It is clear that when offsetting derivatives are entered into concurrently, an entity is prohibited from viewing the derivatives separately and therefore designating one of them in a hedging relationship, unless the derivatives were not entered into in contemplation of one another or there is a substantive business purpose for structuring the transactions separately. Therefore, to qualify for hedge accounting when following the round-tripping approach, it is necessary for an entity to demonstrate compliance with one of these two conditions. [*IAS 39.IG.F.1.14*]

71.7.860.50 In our view, a substantive business purpose generally exists in the following circumstances:
- when group risk management is undertaken by a central treasury function, which gives separate consideration to whether and how much of an offsetting position is required. Because the cheapest form of risk mitigation is usually entering into offsetting transactions with the same derivative

counterparty, it is plausible that a facility may exist to enter into an offsetting transaction. However, such an offset should not automatically be put in place by an entity, but should be based on an evaluation of whether such an offsetting position is required; and

- when an entity's internal derivatives are novated to a central clearing party and then subjected to trade compression with otherwise unrelated derivatives originally entered into with third parties and also novated to the central clearing party. If the inter-company derivatives had not been novated to a central clearing party, then the inter-company derivatives would have been eliminated on consolidation and would not have externalised any risk. Similarly, there would have been no externalisation of market risk if the derivatives were novated to the central clearing party but left otherwise unchanged (e.g. there would be only equal and opposite trades between the group and the central clearing party). However, in some cases novation followed by trade compression may externalise risk that otherwise would have been eliminated on consolidation.

EXAMPLE 37 – HEDGES TRANSACTED ON GROUP BASIS

7I.7.860.55   Consider the following two situations.
- Company H performs a day-end review of its risk exposures, documents this review and enters into offsetting derivatives as part of its risk balancing procedures.
- Company B immediately enters into an offsetting derivative for each transaction and undertakes no further formal risk management procedures.

7I.7.860.60   H is likely to be able to prove that it has a substantive business purpose for entering into offsetting derivatives. B, however, has a practice of automatically entering into offsetting derivatives, without giving further consideration to its actual risk exposures. Accordingly, B would have difficulty in meeting the 'substantive business purpose' condition.

7I.7.860.70   In addition, in our view entering into a derivative with a non-substantive counterparty does not validate an internal hedge. For example, a limited-purpose vehicle established to act as a dedicated counterparty to validate internal hedges might not be regarded as a substantive third party counterparty even if consolidation of the limited-purpose vehicle is not required. [*IAS 39.IG.F.1.4, IG.F.2.16*]

7I.7.860.80   An entity may designate a hedging relationship at the consolidated level that differs from the hedging relationship designated as at the level of an individual entity within the group, provided that the hedge criteria are met.

7I.7.870   Intra-group balances or transactions as hedged item

7I.7.870.10   Intra-group balances and transactions eliminate on consolidation and therefore are not permitted to be designated as hedged items at the group level. However, foreign currency exposures on intra-group monetary items give rise to foreign exchange gains and losses that do not eliminate in the consolidated financial statements (see 2.7.130). Intra-group monetary items lead to an exposure that affects group profit or loss in the following instances:
- items have been transacted between group entities with different functional currencies; and

- the items are denominated in a currency other than the functional currency of the entity entering into the transaction. [*IAS 39.80*]

EXAMPLE 38 – INTRA-GROUP BALANCES OR TRANSACTIONS AS HEDGED ITEM

7I.7.870.20   An intra-group payable/receivable between a parent with a euro functional currency and its foreign subsidiary denominated in US dollars (the subsidiary's functional currency) creates such a foreign currency exposure at the group level. Consequently, the foreign currency risk on recognised intra-group monetary items qualifies for hedge accounting in the consolidated financial statements.

7I.7.870.30   In our view, it is not possible to extend this rationale to the designation of intra-group monetary items as hedging instruments in a hedge of foreign currency risk. This is because IAS 39 explicitly requires that only instruments involving external parties be designated as hedging instruments. Therefore, intra-group monetary items cannot be designated as hedging instruments in the consolidated financial statements. [*IAS 39.73*]

7I.7.870.40   The foreign currency risk of a highly probable forecast intra-group transaction may qualify as the hedged item in the consolidated financial statements provided that the transaction is denominated in a currency other than the currency of the entity entering into the transaction, and the foreign currency risk will affect consolidated profit or loss. Examples of forecast intra-group transactions that will affect consolidated profit or loss include:

- forecast purchases or sales of inventory between group members, provided that there is an onward sale to a party outside the group; and
- a forecast sale of equipment by one group entity to another because the depreciation charge recognised on the equipment will differ if the transaction is denominated in a currency other than the buying entity's functional currency. [*IAS 39.AG99A*]

7I.7.870.50   However, royalties, head office charges and similar items would not affect profit or loss in the consolidated financial statements because these transactions are eliminated completely. Therefore, such items do not usually qualify as hedged items unless there is a related external transaction. [*IAS 39.AG99A*]

7I.7.880   **WORKED EXAMPLES**

7I.7.880.10   The following examples demonstrate a number of the issues that have been discussed in this chapter.

7I.7.890   **Example 39 – Cash flow hedge of variable rate liability**

7I.7.890.10   On 1 January 2018, Company P issues non-callable five-year floating rate bonds of 100 million denominated in its functional currency. The floating interest of six-month LIBOR plus 50 basis points (0.5%) is payable semi-annually. The bonds are issued at par.

7I.7.890.20 As part of P's risk management policy, it determines that it does not wish to expose itself to cash flow fluctuations from changes in market interest rates. After the issue of the bonds, P immediately enters into a five-year interest rate swap with a notional of 100 million. Under the terms of the swap, P pays 6% fixed and receives floating cash flows based on six-month LIBOR (set at 5.7% for the period from 1 January to 30 June 2018). The timing of the swap's cash flows matches those of the bond. The fair value of the swap at inception is zero.

7I.7.890.30 The swap is designated and documented as the hedging instrument in a cash flow hedge of the variability of future interest payments on the bond attributable to movements in the benchmark interest rate – i.e. six-month LIBOR only – excluding the credit spread on the bond of 50 basis points. The hedging relationship is expected to be highly effective.

7I.7.890.40 P indicates in its hedge documentation that it will use the hypothetical derivative method for assessing the effectiveness of the hedging relationship. P identifies a hypothetical swap in the bond under which it receives 6% fixed – i.e. the fixed market rate of interest at the time of issuing the bond – and pays six-month LIBOR. Although the interest rate on the bond is LIBOR plus 50 basis points, P has designated as the hedged risk only the benchmark interest component of the total interest rate risk exposure of the bond. Therefore, the hypothetical swap has a floating leg equal to LIBOR, rather than LIBOR plus 50 basis points.

7I.7.890.50 Considering the combined effect of the bond and the swap, the interest that effectively is payable is fixed at 6.5% (6% fixed on the swap plus the additional actual 0.5% on the bond). P records the following entries.

	DEBIT	CREDIT
1 January 2018		
Cash	100,000,000	
Bonds payable		100,000,000
To recognise proceeds from bond issue		

7I.7.890.60 No entry is necessary for the swap because its fair value is zero at inception.

7I.7.890.70 At 30 June 2018, six-month LIBOR increases to 6.7%. The fair value of the swap is determined to be 3,803,843 after the settlement of interest due on 30 June 2018. The fair value of the hypothetical swap is also 3,803,843 at this date. Therefore, the hedge is considered to be 100% effective. The full change in the fair value of the swap is recognised in OCI.

	DEBIT	CREDIT
30 June 2018		
Interest expense	3,100,000	
Cash		3,100,000
To recognise payment of 6.2% floating interest (LIBOR of 5.7% plus premium of 0.5%)		
Interest expense	150,000	
Cash		150,000
To recognise net settlement of swap from 1 January to 30 June 2018 (pay 6% fixed 3,000,000; receive 5.7% floating 2,850,000)		
Swap (asset)	3,803,843	
Hedging reserve (OCI)		3,803,843
To recognise change in fair value of swap after settlement of interest		

71.7.890.80   At 31 December 2018, interest rates have not changed. However, the credit risk associated with the counterparty to the swap has worsened and is now higher than the general market rate. The increased credit risk of the counterparty results in a specific credit spread of 0.4%. Consequently, the rate used to determine the fair value of the swap will be 0.4% higher than that used to value the hypothetical swap, because the hypothetical swap is not affected by counterparty credit risk (see 71.7.580.40).

71.7.890.90   The fair value of the swap is 3,414,177 at 31 December 2018. The fair value of the hypothetical swap is 3,436,978 at the same date. Based on the offsetting of the change in the fair value of the swap and the change in the fair value of the hypothetical swap (99% offset), the hedge is still effective within the acceptable range of 80–125%. The difference of 22,801 is recognised in OCI because the hedging reserve is adjusted to the lesser of the cumulative gain or loss on the hedging instrument and the cumulative change in fair value of the expected future cash flows on the hedged item attributable to the hedged risk, both from inception of the hedge (see 71.7.570.20).

	DEBIT	CREDIT
31 December 2018		
Interest expense	3,600,000	
Cash		3,600,000
To recognise payment of 7.2% floating interest (LIBOR of 6.7% plus premium of 0.5%)		

	DEBIT	CREDIT
Cash	350,000	
Interest income		350,000
To recognise net settlement of swap from 1 July to 31 December 2018 (pay 6% fixed 3,000,000; receive 6.7% floating 3,350,000)		
Hedging reserve (OCI)	389,666	
Swap (asset)		389,666
To recognise change in fair value of swap		

7I.7.890.100   The statement of financial position at 31 December 2018 will be as follows.

ASSETS		LIABILITIES AND EQUITY	
Cash	93,500,000	Retained earnings	(6,500,000)
Swap	3,414,177	Hedging reserve	3,414,177
		Bonds payable	100,000,000
	96,914,177		96,914,177

7I.7.900   **Example 40 – Cash flow hedge using interest rate cap**

7I.7.900.10   On 1 January 2018, Company R obtains a three-year loan of 10 million. The interest rate on the loan is variable at LIBOR plus 2%. R is concerned that interest rates may rise during the three years, but wants to retain the ability to benefit from LIBOR rates below 8%. To hedge itself, R purchases for 300,000 an out-of-the-money interest rate cap from a bank. Under the cap, when LIBOR exceeds 8% for a particular year R receives from the bank an amount calculated as 10 million x (LIBOR - 8%).

7I.7.900.20   The combination of the cap and the loan results in R paying interest at a variable rate (LIBOR plus 2%) not exceeding 10%. On both the variable rate loan and the interest rate cap, rates are reset on 1 January and interest is settled on 31 December.

7I.7.900.30   R designates and documents the intrinsic value of the purchased interest rate cap as the hedging instrument in a cash flow hedge of the interest rate risk attributable to the future interest payments on the loan for changes in LIBOR above 8%. Changes in the time value of the option are excluded from the assessment of hedge effectiveness and are recognised in profit or loss as they arise.

71.7.900.40   The critical terms of the cap are identical to those of the loan and R concludes that, both at inception of the hedge and on an ongoing basis, the hedging relationship is expected to be highly effective in achieving offsetting cash flows attributable to changes in LIBOR when LIBOR is greater than 8%. Because the cap is being used to purchase one-way protection against any increase in LIBOR, R does not need to assess effectiveness in instances when LIBOR is less than 8%. The cumulative gains or losses on the interest rate cap – adjusted to remove time value gains and losses – can reasonably be expected to equal the present value of the cumulative change in expected future cash flows on the debt obligation when LIBOR is greater than 8%. This is reassessed at each reporting date.

71.7.900.50   During the three-year period LIBOR rates and related amounts are as follows.

Date	Rate	Receivable under cap	Interest payable on loan	Net interest payable	Net interest payable
2018	7%	–	900,000	900,000	9%
2019	9%	(100,000)	1,100,000	1,000,000	10%
2020	10%	(200,000)	1,200,000	1,000,000	10%

71.7.900.60   The fair value, intrinsic value and time value of the interest rate cap and changes therein at the end of each accounting period, but before the settlement of interest, are as follows.

Date	Fair value	Intrinsic value	Time value	Change in fair value gain/(loss)	Change in time value gain/(loss)
1 January 2018	300,000	–	300,000	–	–
31 December 2018	280,000	–	280,000	(20,000)	(20,000)
31 December 2019	350,000	200,000	150,000	70,000	(130,000)
31 December 2020	300,000	300,000	–	(50,000)	(150,000)

71.7.900.70   IAS 39 does not specify how to compute the intrinsic value of a cap option when the option involves a series of payments. In this example, the intrinsic value of the cap is calculated based on simplified assumptions. Alternatively, and more precisely, the intrinsic value of the cap (in the case of a long position) can be calculated for each single period by subtracting the cap rate from the forward LIBOR of the respective period, multiplying the result by the notional amount of the cap contract and then discounting the result to the date under consideration. The sum of the discounted values yields the intrinsic value of the cap.

7I.7.900.80 Assuming that all criteria for hedge accounting have been met, R records the following entries.

	DEBIT	CREDIT
1 January 2018 Cash Loan payable *To recognise proceeds from loan*	10,000,000	10,000,000
Interest rate cap (asset) Cash *To recognise purchase of interest rate cap*	300,000	300,000
31 December 2018 Interest expense Cash *To recognise interest expense on loan (LIBOR + 2%)*	900,000	900,000
Hedge expense (profit or loss) Interest rate cap (asset) *To recognise change in fair value of cap (time value change)*	20,000	20,000
31 December 2019 Interest expense Cash *To recognise interest expense on loan (LIBOR + 2%)*	1,100,000	1,100,000
Hedge expense (profit or loss) Interest rate cap (asset) Hedging reserve (OCI) *To recognise change in fair value of cap (130,000 represents the change in time value, which is excluded from assessment of hedge effectiveness; 200,000 represents increase in interest rate cap's intrinsic value)*	130,000 70,000	200,000
Hedging reserve (OCI) Hedge income/interest income (profit or loss) *To reclassify proportion of increase in intrinsic value of cap related to realised cash flow to profit or loss*	100,000	100,000
Cash Interest rate cap (asset) *To recognise cash received on settlement of interest rate cap*	100,000	100,000
31 December 2020 Interest expense (profit or loss) Cash *To recognise interest expense on loan (LIBOR + 2%)*	1,200,000	1,200,000

	DEBIT	CREDIT
Hedge expense (profit or loss)	150,000	
Interest rate cap (asset)		50,000
Hedging reserve (OCI)		100,000
To recognise change in fair value of cap (150,000 represents change in time value, which is excluded from assessment of hedge effectiveness; 100,000 represents increase in the interest rate cap's intrinsic value)		
Hedging reserve (OCI)	200,000	
Hedge income/interest income (profit or loss)		200,000
To reclassify proportion of increased intrinsic value of cap related to realised cash flow to profit or loss		
Cash	200,000	
Interest rate cap (asset)		200,000
To recognise cash received on final settlement of interest rate cap		

7I.7.900.90   As a result of the hedge, effectively R has capped its interest expense on the three-year loan at 10%. Specifically, during those periods when the contractual terms of this loan would result in an interest expense greater than 10% or 1 million – i.e. in instances when LIBOR exceeded 8% – the payments received from the interest rate cap effectively reduce interest expense to 10% as illustrated below. However, the recognition in profit or loss of changes in the fair value of the cap arising from changes in time value results in variability of total interest expense.

	2018	2019	2020
Interest on LIBOR plus 2% debt	900,000	1,100,000	1,200,000
Reclassified from OCI (effect of cap)	-	(100,000)	(200,000)
Interest expense adjusted by effect of hedge	900,000	1,000,000	1,000,000
Change in time value of cap	20,000	130,000	150,000
Total expense	920,000	1,130,000	1,150,000

7I.7.910   **Example 41 – Cash flow hedge of foreign currency sales transactions**

7I.7.910.10   Company M produces components that are sold to domestic (UK) and foreign customers (US). Company M's functional currency is sterling. Export sales to customers in the US are denominated in the customers' functional currency (US dollars). To reduce the foreign currency risk from the export sales, M has the following hedging policy.
- A transaction is committed when the pricing, quantity and timing are fixed.
- Committed transactions are hedged 100%.

- Anticipated transactions that are highly probable are hedged 50%.
- Only transactions anticipated to occur within six months are hedged.

7I.7.910.20   For export sales, cash payment falls due one month after the invoice date. M projects sales to its foreign customers during April 2018 of 100,000 units, amounting to sales revenue of USD 10 million.

7I.7.910.30   At 28 February 2018, all of the USD 10,000,000 of sales in April 2018 are still anticipated but uncommitted. Therefore, only 50% of the total anticipated sales are hedged. The hedge is transacted by entering into a foreign currency forward contract (forward 1) to sell USD 5 million and receive sterling at 0.6829 on 15 May 2018 and is documented as a cash flow hedge of the cash receipts pertaining to the first USD 5 million of forecast sales. The hedge is expected to be highly effective. Hedge effectiveness will be assessed by comparing the changes in the discounted cash flows of the incoming amounts of US dollars to the changes in the fair value of the forward contract. M includes the interest element of the foreign currency forward contract when measuring hedge effectiveness. This is expected to result in a highly effective cash flow hedge because the fair value of the sales transactions during the period of the hedge will be affected by US dollar interest rates as well as by the spot exchange rates.

7I.7.910.40   A review of the sales order book at 31 March 2018 shows that all of the anticipated sale contracts for invoicing in April are now signed. In accordance with the hedging policy, a further foreign currency forward contract (forward 2) is entered into to sell USD 5 million and receive sterling at 0.7100 on 15 May 2018 in order to hedge the cash receipts pertaining to the next USD 5 million of forecast sales.

7I.7.910.50   The spot and forward exchange rates and the fair value of the forward contracts are as follows.

DATE	SPOT RATE USD 1 = GBP	FORWARD RATE USD 1 = GBP	FAIR VALUE OF FORWARD SALE OF USD 5,000,000 (FORWARD 1) GBP	FAIR VALUE OF FORWARD SALE OF USD 5,000,000 (FORWARD 2) GBP
28 February 2018	0.6860	0.6829	-	N/A
31 March 2018	0.7120	0.7100	(134,491)	-
30 April 2018	0.7117	0.7108	(139,152)	(3,990)
15 May 2018	0.7208	N/A	(189,500)	(54,000)

7I.7.910.60   The fair value of the foreign currency forward contracts at each measurement date is computed as the present value of the expected settlement amount, which is the difference between the contractually set forward rate and the actual forward rate on the date of measurement multiplied by the notional foreign currency amount. The discount rate used is 6%.

71.7.910.70   During April 2018, export sales of USD 10 million are invoiced and recognised in profit or loss. The deferred gain or loss on the hedging forward contracts that was recognised in OCI up to the date of sale is reclassified from equity to profit or loss. The cash flows being hedged are recognised in the statement of financial position as receivables of USD 10 million. M determines that hedge accounting no longer is necessary because foreign currency gains and losses on the amounts receivable are recognised in profit or loss and will mostly be offset by the revaluation gains and losses on the forwards.

71.7.910.80   Assuming that all criteria for hedge accounting have been met, M records the following entries.

	DEBIT (GBP)	CREDIT (GBP)
28 February 2018 *No entries in profit or loss or statement of financial position required; fair value of forward contract is zero*		
31 March 2018 Hedging reserve (OCI) Derivatives (liabilities) *To recognise change in fair value of forward 1*	134,491	134,491
1 to 30 April 2018 Trade receivables Export sales *To recognise USD 10,000,000 sales transactions at exchange rates on dates of transactions (on average assumed to be 0.7115)*	7,115,000	7,115,000
30 April 2018 Trade receivables Foreign exchange gain on trade receivables (profit or loss) *To remeasure trade receivables at closing spot rate: USD 10,000,000 x (0.7117 - 0.7115)*	2,000	2,000
Hedging reserve (OCI) Derivatives (liabilities) *To recognise change in fair value of forward 1 for period*	4,661	4,661

	Debit (GBP)	Credit (GBP)
Hedging reserve (OCI)	3,990	
Derivatives (liabilities)		3,990
To recognise change in fair value of forward 2 for period		
Export sales (profit or loss)	143,142	
Hedging reserve (OCI)		143,142
To reclassify deferred hedge results on recording sales (GBP 139,152 + GBP 3,990)		
1 to 15 May 2018		
Cash	3,575,000	
Trade receivables		3,575,000
To recognise receipts from receivables from first USD 5,000,000 of sales at spot rate at date of payment (on average 0.7150)		
Trade receivables	16,500	
Foreign exchange gain on trade receivables (profit or loss)		16,500
To recognise gain on trade receivables: USD 5,000,000 x (0.7150 - 0.7117)		
15 May 2018		
Cash	29,000	
Foreign exchange gain on cash (profit or loss)		29,000
To remeasure bank balance at spot rate: USD 5,000,000 x (0.7208 - 0.7150)		
Trade receivables	45,500	
Foreign exchange gain on trade receivables (profit or loss)		45,500
To recognise foreign exchange gain on trade receivables: USD 5,000,000 x (0.7208 - 0.7117)		
Foreign exchange loss on forward (profit or loss)	50,348	
Derivatives (liabilities)		50,348
To recognise change in fair value of forward 1 for period		
Foreign exchange loss on forward (profit or loss)	50,010	
Derivatives (liabilities)		50,010
To recognise change in fair value of forward 2 for period		

	DEBIT (GBP)	CREDIT (GBP)
Derivatives (liabilities)	189,500	
Cash		189,500
To recognise settlement of forward 1		
Derivatives (liabilities)	54,000	
Cash		54,000
To recognise settlement of forward 2		
15 to 31 May 2018		
Cash	3,655,000	
Trade receivables		3,655,000
To recognise payments of receivables at spot rate at date of payment (on average 0.7310)		
Foreign exchange loss on cash (profit or loss)	51,000	
Cash		51,000
To recognise foreign exchange loss on forwards settled before all receivables settled (US dollars bank account was overdrawn for a period): USD 5,000,000 x (0.7310 - 0.7208)		
Trade receivables	51,000	
Foreign exchange gain on trade receivables (profit or loss)		51,000
To recognise foreign exchange gain on settlement of receivables: USD 5,000,000 x (0.7310 - 0.7208)		

7I.7.910.90   After all transactions have been settled, the statement of financial position, including the profit or loss impact, is as follows (amounts in sterling).

ASSETS		EQUITY	
Cash	6,964,500	Export sales (retained earnings)	6,971,858
		Foreign exchange loss (retained earnings)	(7,358)
Total assets	6,964,500	Total equity	6,964,500

7I.7.910.100   The bank balance reflects the settlement of the two forward contracts (amounts in sterling).

Forward 1: USD 5,000,000 at 0.6829	3,414,500
Forward 2: USD 5,000,000 at 0.7100	3,550,000
Total	6,964,500

7I.7.910.110   The foreign exchange loss in this example has two causes.

- Timing mismatches – receivables and sales are recognised at the spot exchange rate at the date of the transaction (on average 0.7115) during April 2018, whereas the release from the hedging reserve is recognised at the end of April 2018 (for practical reasons), when the rate was 0.7117. Furthermore, receivables are collected during the month of May 2018 and recognised at the relevant spot rates, whereas the forward contracts are settled on 15 May 2018.
- Interest element on the forward contracts for the period in which hedge accounting is not applied (1 to 15 May 2018) – from 30 April 2018 the cash flow hedge is de-designated, but the forward contracts remain as an economic hedge of the receivables to be collected during May 2018. The foreign exchange results on the receivables are recognised in profit or loss, as are changes in the fair value of the forward contracts. However, a perfect offset is not achieved because of the interest element included in the changes in fair value of the forward contracts.

7I.7.910.120   As an alternative to the cash flow hedge accounting described in this example, M could have applied the approach suggested in 7I.7.450.80, with the following results.

- On occurrence of the forecast sales – i.e. the transaction date – the difference between the spot foreign exchange rates at the inception of each of the two hedges and spot foreign exchange rates on the sale dates would have been reclassified from equity to profit or loss.
- The forward points (interest cost in this case) in each hedging relationship that are ascribed to the period until sale would have been recognised in profit or loss on sale. For example, in the hedge of the cash receipts pertaining to the first USD 5 million of forecast sales using the first forward contract, the forward points of GBP 15,500 (USD 5,000,000 x (0.6860 - 0.6829)) would be allocated to sales in the ratio of the period from hedge inception to date of sale and period from date of sale until estimated date of cash collection.
- The net effect of these steps would be that the sales under each of the two hedging relationships would be recognised in sterling in profit or loss at the respective spot exchange rates at hedge inception, less an allocation of the interest cost represented by the forward point ascribed to the sale under each hedge.
- Subsequent to recognition of the receivables arising from the US dollar sales, the entire change in the fair value of the hedging forward contracts would be recognised in OCI and the forward points – other than those allocated to the period up to sale as discussed above – would be amortised and reclassified from equity to profit or loss. If there was a reporting date between the dates when the receivables are recognised and when they are collected, then M would reclassify from equity to profit or loss an amount equal to the remeasurement of the receivable or payable under IAS 21 based on the spot exchange rates.

7I.7.920 ## Example 42 – Termination of hedge accounting

7I.7.920.10   Modifying Example 41, assume that on 31 March 2018 the committed transactions actually are only USD 3 million and that no more transactions for April 2018 are anticipated. It is now unlikely that the original forward contract to sell USD 5 million would be highly effective in hedging the cash flows pertaining to the now expected future sales of USD 3 million. Therefore, the original hedging relationship is discontinued. However, M may designate the remaining USD 3 million of committed sales as the hedged item in a new hedging relationship.

7I.7.920.20   The unrealised foreign exchange loss deferred in equity related to the forecast sales of USD 2 million that are no longer expected to occur are immediately recognised in profit or loss because the cash flow is no longer expected to occur. The unrealised foreign exchange loss related to the USD 3 million of sales that still are expected to occur remains in equity.

7I.7.920.30   M records the following entry.

	DEBIT (GBP)	CREDIT (GBP)
31 March 2018		
Foreign exchange losses (profit or loss)	53,796	
Hedging reserve (OCI)		53,796
To reclassify portion of deferred losses that reflects cash flows no longer expected to occur (134,491 x 2 / 5)		

7I.7.930 ## Example 43 – Fair value hedge of foreign currency risk on available-for-sale equities

7I.7.930.10   Company S is a large pension fund set up for the employees of a brewery. In recent years the pension fund assets have grown and management is finding it increasingly difficult to achieve sufficient diversification in the domestic equity market. Also, management believes that it is possible to earn a higher return on equity shares in certain foreign markets. Consequently, management decides to invest in a large foreign equity market. However, all of S's pension obligations are denominated in Singapore dollars, its functional currency, and as part of the investment strategy S seeks to hedge all significant exposure to foreign currency risk beyond certain limits.

7I.7.930.20   On 1 April 2018, S buys a portfolio of equity shares of Company T on the London Stock Exchange in which transactions are denominated in sterling and dividends on T's shares are paid only in sterling. T's shares are traded only on the London Stock Exchange and T operates only in the UK. T's shares are acquired for GBP 30 million and are classified as available-for-sale financial assets.

7I.7.930.30   Although a steady growth in the value of the shares is expected in the medium to long term, creating an increased foreign currency exposure, S decides to hedge only the foreign exchange exposure on a portion of the market value of the portfolio in foreign currency. This is because of the uncertainty about the short-term development in the market value and, therefore, the exposure. S enters into a foreign currency forward contract to sell GBP 25.5 million and receive Singapore dollars on 15 October 2018. This contract will then be rolled for as long as the position is outstanding (see 7I.7.680.80).

7I.7.930.40   The forward contract is designated as a fair value hedge of the foreign currency risk associated with the GBP 25.5 million portion of the fair value of the shares. The time value of the forward contract is excluded from the assessment of hedge effectiveness. The hedge is expected to be highly effective and hedge effectiveness will be assessed by comparing the changes in the fair value of the GBP 25.5 million portion of shares arising from changes in spot exchange rates with the changes in the value of the forward contract also arising from changes in spot rates – because the time value is excluded from the hedging relationship.

7I.7.930.50   The terms of the forward contract are as follows:
* sell GBP 25,500,000;
* buy SGD 64,359,915; and
* maturity of 15 October 2018.

7I.7.930.60   The terms imply a forward rate of 2.5239.

7I.7.930.70   During the period of the hedge, the value of the forward is as follows (amounts in SGD).

Date	Spot rate (GBP 1 = SGD)	Value of contract forward	Value change Gain/(loss)	Spot element Gain/(loss)	Forward element Gain/(loss)
1 April 2018	2.55	-	-	-	-
30 June 2018	2.41	3,031,769	3,031,769	3,570,000	(538,231)
30 September 2018	2.39	3,406,748	374,979	510,000	(135,021)
15 October 2018	2.45	1,884,915	(1,521,833)	(1,530,000)	8,167
			1,884,915	2,550,000	(665,085)

7I.7.930.80 The value of the foreign equity portfolio changes as follows, as a result of changes in equity prices and changes in the exchange rate.

DATE	VALUE (GBP)	VALUE (SGD)	VALUE CHANGE (SGD)
1 April 2018	30,000,000	76,500,000	-
30 June 2018	35,000,000	84,350,000	7,850,000
30 September 2018	28,000,000	66,920,000	(17,430,000)
15 October 2018	32,000,000	78,400,000	11,480,000

7I.7.930.90 Assuming that all the criteria for hedge accounting have been met, S records the following entries.

	DEBIT (SGD)	CREDIT (SGD)
1 April 2018 *No entries in profit or loss or statement of financial position required; fair value of forward contract is zero*		
Available-for-sale financial assets Cash *To recognise purchase of securities; GBP 30 million at 2.55*	76,500,000	76,500,000
30 June 2018 Available-for-sale financial assets Available-for-sale revaluation reserve (OCI) *To recognise change in fair value of securities*	7,850,000	7,850,000
Derivatives (assets) Derivative revaluation gain (profit or loss) *To recognise change in fair value of forward*	3,031,769	3,031,769
Hedge revaluation loss (profit or loss) Available-for-sale revaluation reserve (OCI) *To reclassify fair value change of securities in respect of hedged risk to profit or loss; GBP 25.5 million x (2.41 - 2.55)*	3,570,000	3,570,000

	DEBIT (SGD)	CREDIT (SGD)
30 September 2018		
Available-for-sale revaluation reserve (OCI)	17,430,000	
Available-for-sale financial assets		17,430,000
To recognise change in fair value of securities		
Derivatives (assets)	374,979	
Derivative revaluation gain (profit or loss)		374,979
To recognise change in fair value of forward		
Hedge revaluation loss (profit or loss)	510,000	
Available-for-sale revaluation reserve (OCI)		510,000
To reclassify fair value change of securities in respect of hedged risk to profit or loss; GBP 25.5 million x (2.39 - 2.41)		
15 October 2018		
Available-for-sale financial assets	11,480,000	
Available-for-sale revaluation reserve (OCI)		11,480,000
To recognise change in fair value of securities		
Derivative revaluation loss (profit or loss)	1,521,833	
Derivatives (assets)		1,521,833
To recognise change in fair value of forward		
Available-for-sale revaluation reserve (OCI)	1,530,000	
Hedge revaluation gain (profit or loss)		1,530,000
To reclassify fair value change of securities in respect of hedged risk to profit or loss: GBP 25.5 million x (2.45 - 2.39)		
Cash	1,884,915	
Derivatives (assets)		1,884,915
To recognise settlement of forward		

71.7.930.100   The hedge stays effective for the full period because changes in the fair value of the forward contract, arising from changes in spot rates, perfectly offset changes in the value of GBP 25.5 million of the equity portfolio arising from the same spot exchange rates.

7I.7.930.110   Variability in the fair value of the shares in foreign currency would not affect the assessment of hedge effectiveness unless the fair value of the shares in foreign currency declined below GBP 25.5 million.

7I.7.930.120   In order for fair value hedge accounting to be applied, the portfolio of shares that was designated as the hedged item at 1 April 2018 should continue to be the hedged item for the entire period of the hedge. This means that active management of the portfolio may preclude fair value hedge accounting.

7I.7.930.130   As an alternative approach, management may designate the hedge as a hedge of the anticipated disposal of the shares, providing that the timing of such disposal is highly probable, and apply cash flow hedge accounting. Cash flow hedge accounting requires specifying the size and timing of the cash flow being hedged. The model that is more appropriate may also depend on the entity's ability to collect the relevant information required under each model.

7I.7.940

Example 44 – Cash flow hedge of foreign currency risk of recognised financial liability

7I.7.940.10   On 1 January 2018, Company G issues a non-callable three-year 5.5% fixed rate bond of USD 15 million at par. G's functional currency is sterling.

7I.7.940.20   As part of its risk management policy, G decides to eliminate the exposure arising from movements in the US dollar/sterling exchange rates on the principal amount of the bond for three years. G enters into a foreign currency forward contract to buy USD 15 million and sell GBP 9,835,389 at 31 December 2020.

7I.7.940.30   G designates and documents the forward contract as the hedging instrument in a cash flow hedge of the variability in cash flows arising from the repayment of the principal amount of the bond because of movements in forward US dollar/sterling exchange rates.

7I.7.940.40   G states in its hedge documentation (see 7I.7.120.30) that it will use the hypothetical derivative method to assess hedge effectiveness. G identifies the hypothetical derivative as a forward contract under which it sells USD 15 million and purchases GBP 9,835,389 at 31 December 2020 (the repayment date of the bond). The hypothetical foreign currency forward contract has a fair value of zero at 1 January 2018.

7I.7.940.50   The spot and the forward exchange rates and the fair value of the foreign currency forward contract are as follows.

Date	Spot rate USD 1 = GBP	Forward rate USD 1 = GBP	Fair value of forward contract GBP
1 January 2018	0.6213	0.6557	-
31 December 2018	0.5585	0.5858	(957,205)
31 December 2019	0.5209	0.5280	(1,833,457)
31 December 2020	0.5825	0.5825	(1,097,889)

7I.7.940.60   For the purposes of this example, it is assumed that the average exchange rates approximate the exchange rates at the ends of the respective years.

7I.7.940.70   The hedge remains effective for the entire period, with changes in the fair value of the hypothetical forward contract and the hedging instrument being perfectly offset. Because G has designated the variability in cash flows arising from movements in the forward rates as the hedged risk, the entire change in the fair value of the forward contract is recognised in OCI. At each reporting date, G reclassifies from equity an amount equal to the movement in the spot rate on the principal amount of the bond. In addition, to ensure that the forward points recognised in OCI are reclassified fully to profit or loss over the life of the hedge, G reclassifies from equity an amount equal to the cumulative change in the forward points recognised in OCI amortised over the life of the hedging relationship using the interest rate implicit in the forward contract.

7I.7.940.80   Assuming that all criteria for hedge accounting have been met, G records the following entries.

	Debit (GBP)	Credit (GBP)
1 January 2018 *No entries in profit or loss or statement of financial position required; fair value of forward contract is zero*		
Cash	9,319,500	
Bond (financial liability)		9,319,500
To recognise issue of bond: USD 15 million at 0.6213		
31 December 2018 Hedging reserve (OCI)	957,205	
Derivative (liability)		957,205
To recognise change in fair value of forward contract (100% effective)		

	Debit (GBP)	Credit (GBP)
Bond (financial liability)	942,000	
Foreign currency translation (profit or loss)		942,000
To recognise foreign exchange gain on issued bond		
Foreign currency translation (profit or loss)	942,000	
Hedging reserve (OCI)		942,000
To reclassify movement in spot rate		
Foreign currency translation (profit or loss)	168,884	
Hedging reserve (OCI)		168,884
To reclassify forward points using interest rate implicit in forward contract		
Interest expense (profit or loss)	460,763	
Cash		460,763
Interest: 5.5% of USD 15 million at 0.5585		
31 December 2019		
Hedging reserve (OCI)	876,252	
Derivative (liability)		876,252
To recognise change in fair value of forward contract (100% effective)		
Bond (financial liability)	564,000	
Foreign currency translation (profit or loss)		564,000
To recognise foreign exchange gain on issued bond		
Foreign currency translation (profit or loss)	564,000	
Hedging reserve (OCI)		564,000
To reclassify movement in spot rate		
Foreign currency translation (profit or loss)	171,945	
Hedging reserve (OCI)		171,945
To reclassify forward points using interest rate implicit in forward contract		

	Debit (GBP)	Credit (GBP)
Interest expense (profit or loss)	429,743	
Cash		429,743
To recognise interest: *5.5% of USD 15 million at 0.5209*		
31 December 2020		
Derivative (liability)	735,568	
Hedging reserve (OCI)		735,568
To recognise change in fair value of forward contract (100% effective)		
Foreign currency translation (profit or loss)	924,000	
Bond (financial liability)		924,000
To recognise foreign exchange loss on issued bond		
Hedging reserve (OCI)	924,000	
Foreign currency translation (profit or loss)		924,000
To reclassify movement in spot rate		
Foreign currency translation (profit or loss)	175,060	
Hedging reserve (OCI)		175,060
To reclassify forward points using interest rate implicit in forward contract		
Bond (financial liability)	8,737,500	
Cash		8,737,500
To recognise settlement of bond: *USD 15 million at 0.5825*		
Derivative (liability)	1,097,889	
Cash		1,097,889
To recognise settlement of forward contract		
Interest expense (profit or loss)	480,563	
Cash		480,563
To recognise interest: *5.5% of USD 15 million at 0.5825*		

Example 45 – Hedging on group basis – Foreign currency risk

7I.7.950.10   A group consists of a parent entity (including a corporate treasury) and its subsidiaries, Subsidiary J and Subsidiary B, all of which have a euro functional currency. J has highly probable cash inflows from future revenues of USD 200 that it expects to receive in 60 days. To hedge this exposure, J enters into a forward contract with the corporate treasury to pay USD 200 in 60 days.

7I.7.950.20   B has highly probable forecast purchases of US dollar 500 that it expects to pay in 60 days. B hedges this exposure by entering into a forward contract with the corporate treasury to receive US dollar 500 in 60 days.

7I.7.950.30   The parent entity itself has no expected exposure to that foreign currency during this period.

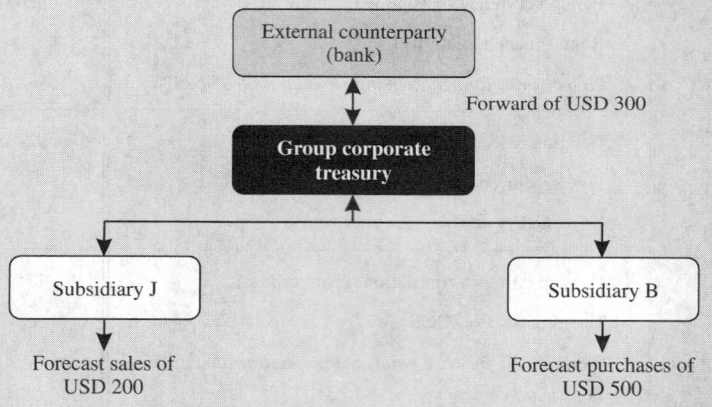

7I.7.950.40   The effect of the internal derivatives with the subsidiaries is to transfer the foreign currency risk to the corporate treasury. The net foreign currency exposure from US dollars in the next time period is a USD 300 outflow. The corporate treasury hedges this exposure by entering into a forward contract with an external third party.

7I.7.950.50   To apply hedge accounting to this transaction, the group designates the external forward contract as a hedge of a gross exposure in one of the subsidiaries rather than the net exposure. The group does this by designating the first USD 300 of cash outflows from purchases in B as the hedged item and the external forward contract as the hedging instrument. Whether adjustments are required on consolidation to the hedge accounting entries made by J and B depends on whether the forecast transactions of J and B are recognised in profit or loss at the same time. Two possibilities are considered in 7I.7.960 and 970.

7I.7.960   *Transactions recognised concurrently in income*

7I.7.960.10   The forecast sales and forecast purchases of J and B respectively are recognised in profit or loss at the same time and both subsidiaries applied cash flow hedge accounting for their respective internal derivatives. On consolidation the internal transactions offset, leaving only the external derivative and its associated gain or loss to be accounted for. The group can apply hedge accounting to the relationship between this external derivative and the first USD 300 of outflows representing B's purchases without making any adjustments to the hedge accounting entries made at the subsidiary level. The internal derivatives are used as an indicator of the external transaction that qualifies for hedge accounting.

7I.7.970   *Transactions recognised in different periods*

7I.7.970.10   The forecast sales of J are recognised in profit or loss in July, whereas B's purchases are recognised in June. Both subsidiaries applied cash flow hedge accounting for their respective internal derivatives. On consolidation as at 30 June, the internal transactions will not offset completely because they are recognised in profit or loss in different periods. Consequently, the group cannot automatically apply hedge accounting to the relationship between the external derivative and the first USD 300 of outflows representing B's purchases; some adjustments will have to be made to the subsidiaries' accounting. In this case, the internal derivatives cannot be used as an indicator of the external transaction that qualifies for hedge accounting. An alternative approach would be to:

- enter into external derivatives to hedge aggregate long positions and short positions in each currency and each time period separately – i.e. by aggregating and not netting internal derivatives at corporate treasury – and then designating the external derivatives as hedging instruments at the group level; and
- put in place additional documentation at the group level to link each external derivative to its associated group of internal derivatives such that the chain of hedge documentation is complete, via the internal contracts, between each hedged cash flow within the group and a portion of the related external derivative.

7I.7.980   Example 46 – Hedge of net investment in foreign operation

7I.7.980.10   Company G, whose functional currency is the euro, has a net investment in a foreign subsidiary of GBP 50 million. On 1 October 2018, G enters into a foreign exchange forward contract to sell GBP 50 million and receive euro on 1 April 2019. G will review the net investment balance on a quarterly basis and adjust the hedge to the value of the net investment. The time value of the forward contract is excluded from the assessment of hedge effectiveness.

7I.7.980.20   The exchange rate and fair value of the forward contract move as follows.

Date	Spot rate GBP 1 = Eur	Forward rate GBP 1 = Eur	Fair value of forward contract Eur
1 October 2018	1.71	1.70	-
31 December 2018	1.64	1.63	3,430,000
31 March 2019	1.60	N/A	5,000,000

7I.7.980.30   Assuming that all criteria for hedge accounting have been met, G records the following entries.

	Debit (Eur)	Credit (Eur)
1 October 2018		
No entries in profit or loss or statement of financial position required; fair value of forward contract is zero		
31 December 2018		
Derivatives (asset)	3,430,000	
Foreign exchange losses (profit or loss)	70,000	
Foreign currency translation reserve (OCI)		3,500,000
To recognise change in fair value of forward		
Foreign currency translation reserve (OCI)	3,500,000	
Net investment in subsidiary (asset)		3,500,000
To recognise foreign exchange loss on net investment in subsidiary (adjustment to net investment would be derived by translating subsidiary's statement of financial position at spot rate at each reporting date)		
31 March 2019		
Derivatives (asset)	1,570,000	
Foreign exchange losses (profit or loss)	430,000	
Foreign currency translation reserve (OCI)		2,000,000
To recognise change in fair value of forward		
Foreign currency translation reserve (OCI)	2,000,000	
Net investment in subsidiary (asset)		2,000,000
To recognise change in foreign exchange losses on net investment		

	DEBIT (EUR)	CREDIT (EUR)
Cash	5,000,000	
Derivatives (assets)		5,000,000
To recognise settlement of forward		

7I.7.980.40   The gain on the hedging transaction will remain in equity until the subsidiary is disposed of (see 7I.7.110.30–40).

7I.7.990   **Example 47 – Hedging other market price risks**

7I.7.990.10   Company X owns equity securities in an entity listed on a domestic stock exchange. The securities are classified as available-for-sale. At 1 January 2018, the fair value of the securities is 120 million; the fair value on initial recognition was 115 million. The revaluation gain of 5 million is recognised in OCI.

7I.7.990.20   At 30 June 2018, the value of the securities has increased from 120 million to 130 million. The securities are remeasured at fair value with the cumulative change of 15 million recognised in OCI.

7I.7.990.30   At 30 June 2018, because of volatility in the price risk of the securities and to comply with internal risk management policies, management decides to purchase a European put option on the securities with a strike price equal to the current market price of 130 million and a maturity date of 30 June 2019. The option premium paid is 12 million.

7I.7.990.40   Management has documented the hedging relationship and assessed that the purchased put option is an effective hedge in offsetting decreases in the fair value of the equity securities below 130 million. The time value component will not be included in determining the effectiveness of the hedge. The fair value of the securities and the put option during the period are as follows.

DATE	VALUE OF SECURITIES	TOTAL OPTION VALUE	INTRINSIC VALUE	TIME VALUE
1 January 2018	120,000,000	-	-	-
30 June 2018	130,000,000	12,000,000	-	12,000,000
30 September 2018	136,000,000	7,000,000	-	7,000,000
31 December 2018	126,000,000	9,000,000	4,000,000	5,000,000

7I.7.990.50   The following entries are made to record the remeasurement of the securities and the payment of the option premium.

	DEBIT	CREDIT
30 June 2018		
Available-for-sale securities	10,000,000	
Available-for-sale revaluation reserve (OCI)		10,000,000
To recognise remeasurement gain on available-for-sale securities		
Hedging derivatives (assets)	12,000,000	
Cash		12,000,000
To recognise payment of option premium		
30 September 2018		
Available-for-sale securities	6,000,000	
Available-for-sale revaluation reserve (OCI)		6,000,000
To recognise remeasurement gain on available-for-sale securities		
Hedging costs (profit or loss)	5,000,000	
Hedging derivatives (assets)		5,000,000
To recognise remeasurement loss on option because of change in time value (not part of hedging relationship)		

7I.7.990.60   The option is still expected to be effective as a hedge of decreases in the fair value of the available-for-sale securities below the strike price of the option.

7I.7.990.70   At 31 December 2017, the value of the hedged securities decreases to 126 million. The value of the put option increases to 9 million; of that amount, 4 million represents intrinsic value and 5 million represents time value. As such, the following entries are made to recognise the change in the fair value of the available-for-sale securities and the changes in the fair value of the option.

7I.7.990.80   For illustrative purposes, these entries have been separated into two parts to demonstrate the accounting for the changes in the value of the securities that are not being hedged (decrease to 130 million) and the changes in value that are being hedged (decrease below 130 million). Likewise, changes in the fair value of the option are separated to demonstrate changes in the time value, which have been excluded from the hedging relationship, and changes in the option's intrinsic value.

	DEBIT	CREDIT
31 December 2018		
Available-for-sale revaluation reserve (OCI)	6,000,000	
Available-for-sale securities		6,000,000
To recognise unhedged decrease in fair value of securities (from 136 million to 130 million)		
Hedge results (profit or loss)	4,000,000	
Available-for-sale securities		4,000,000
To recognise hedged decrease in fair value of securities (from 130 million to 126 million)		
Hedging costs (profit or loss)	2,000,000	
Hedging derivatives (assets)		2,000,000
To recognise changes in time value of option (excluded from hedging relationship)		
Hedging derivatives (assets)	4,000,000	
Hedge results (profit or loss)		4,000,000
To recognise change in intrinsic value of option (effective part of hedge)		

7I.7.990.90   At 31 December 2018, the equity securities are recognised at a fair value of 126 million compared with an original cost of 115 million. As a result of the hedging strategy designated by X in 7I.7.990.40 using a European put option with a strike price of 130 million, a gain of 15 million has been included in the available-for-sale revaluation reserve, while a loss of 4 million – i.e. the decline in the value from 130 million to 126 million – has been included in profit or loss.

7I.7.1000   FUTURE DEVELOPMENTS

7I.7.1010   Discussion Paper – Accounting for dynamic risk management

7I.7.1010.10   Although IAS 39 and IFRS 9 provide models for macro hedge accounting, these contain restrictions that limit entities' ability to reflect some common dynamic risk management (DRM) activities; moreover, some of these models deal specifically with interest rate risk management rather than other types of risk. Without an accounting model that reflects the broader use of DRM activities, some have asserted that it can be difficult to faithfully represent these activities in financial statements.

7I.7.1010.20   In response to these issues, in April 2014 the IASB published Discussion Paper *Accounting for Dynamic Risk Management – a Portfolio Revaluation Approach to Macro Hedging* as the first due process document for the project. Because the project involves fundamental accounting questions and is not simply a modification to current hedge accounting models, the IASB did not proceed straight to issuing an exposure draft.

7I.7.1020 *Portfolio revaluation approach*

7I.7.1020.10   The discussion paper put forward an outline of one possible approach to macro hedge accounting – the portfolio revaluation approach (PRA) – under which entities' managed exposures would be identified and revalued for changes in the managed risk.

- *Managed exposures:* These would be identified and remeasured for changes in the managed risk, with the gain or loss recognised in profit or loss. The remeasurement would be based on a present value technique.
- *Hedging instruments:* Risk management derivatives – i.e. hedging instruments – would continue to be measured at FVTPL.
- *Result of hedge accounting:* The performance of an entity's DRM activities would be captured by the net effect of the above measurements in profit or loss.
- *Other risks:* Risks that are not managed would not be included in this approach – i.e. PRA is not a full fair value model.

7I.7.1020.20   The IASB believes that the PRA would be operationally easier to apply than the current hedge accounting models for open portfolios, because it would reduce the complexities associated with one-to-one designations requirements.

7I.7.1030 *Managed exposures*

7I.7.1030.10   A key question in applying the PRA would be the extent to which DRM activities should be reflected in the accounting. The discussion paper explored a number of areas that would broaden the scope of the PRA as compared with the existing requirements. The discussion paper considered whether, for example, the following items should be eligible for inclusion:

- pipeline transactions – i.e. forecast volumes of draw-downs of fixed interest rate products at advertised rates;
- the equity model book – i.e. entities managing own equity to earn a minimum target return similar to interest; and
- behaviouralised expected cash flows related to core demand deposit liabilities, prepayment risk and changes in expected customer behaviour.

7I.7.1040 *Two scope alternatives*

7I.7.1040.10   The discussion paper presented two possible ways of applying the PRA.

- *Focus on DRM:* Under this approach, the PRA would apply to all dynamically managed exposures regardless of whether they have been hedged.
- *Focus on risk mitigation:* The PRA would apply only when entities have undertaken risk mitigation activities through hedging.

7I.7.1050 **Current status and next steps**

7I.7.1050.10   Based on the feedback received from respondents on the discussion paper, the IASB tentatively decided to:

- first consider how the information needs of constituents concerning dynamic risk management activities could be addressed through disclosures before considering those areas that need to be addressed through recognition and measurement;
- prioritise the consideration of interest rate risk and consider other risks at a later stage in the project; and
- establish an Expert Advisory Panel at a later stage in the project. [*IASBU 05-15*]

7I.7.1050.20   KPMG's periodic *IFRS Newsletter: Financial Instruments* features the IASB's discussions and progress on this project. This publication, and other KPMG resources on financial instruments, are available at kpmg.com/ifrs.

7I.8 Presentation and disclosures

7I.8   Presentation and disclosures

REQUIREMENTS FOR INSURERS THAT APPLY IFRS 4

In July 2014, the IASB issued IFRS 9 *Financial Instruments*, which is effective for annual periods beginning on or after 1 January 2018. However, an insurer may defer the application of IFRS 9 if it meets certain criteria (see 8.1.180).

This chapter reflects the requirement of IAS 39 *Financial Instruments: Recognition and Measurement* and the related standards, excluding any amendments introduced by IFRS 9. These requirements are relevant to insurers that apply the temporary exemption from IFRS 9 or the overlay approach to designated financial assets (see 8.1.160) and cover annual periods beginning on 1 January 2018. For further discussion, see Introduction to Sections 7 and 7I.

The requirements related to this topic are mainly derived from the following.

STANDARD	TITLE
IFRS 7	Financial Instruments: Disclosures
IFRS 13	Fair Value Measurement
IAS 1	Presentation of Financial Statements
IAS 32	Financial Instruments: Presentation

FORTHCOMING REQUIREMENTS

The requirements in this chapter are affected by the following forthcoming requirements. They are highlighted with a # and the impact is explained in the accompanying boxed text at the reference indicated.

In January 2016, the IASB issued IFRS 16 *Leases*, which is effective for annual periods beginning on or after 1 January 2019. See 7I.8.285. IFRS 16 is the subject of chapter 5.1A.

FUTURE DEVELOPMENTS

For this topic, there are no future developments.

7I.8.10   **OVERVIEW**

7I.8.10.10   IFRS 7 sets out the disclosure requirements for all financial instruments. The objective of the disclosures is to enhance financial statement users' understanding of:
- the significance of financial instruments to an entity's overall financial position and performance;
- the risk exposures resulting from such financial instruments; and
- how the entity manages those risks. [*IFRS 7.1*]

7I.8.20   **SCOPE**

7I.8.20.10   IFRS 7 applies to all entities and to all types of recognised and unrecognised financial instruments – e.g. loan commitments. The standard also applies to contracts to buy or sell a non-financial item that are in the scope of IAS 39 (see 7I.1.150). For financial instruments that are excluded from IFRS 7, see 7I.1.30. [*IFRS 7.3–5*]

7I.8.20.20   As can be seen from the table in 7I.1.30, interests in subsidiaries, associates and joint ventures accounted for in accordance with IFRS 10, IAS 27 or IAS 28 are excluded from the disclosure requirements in IFRS 7. However, when such interests are accounted for in accordance with IAS 39 (see 7I.1.110), they are subject to the disclosure requirements of IFRS 7, and those in IAS 27 and IFRS 12. [*IFRS 7.3(a)*]

7I.8.20.30   Also, as can be seen from the table in 7I.1.30, insurance contracts as defined in IFRS 4 are excluded from the scope of IFRS 7 (see 7I.1.40). However, certain derivatives embedded in those contracts, and financial guarantee contracts to which IAS 39 is applied (see 7I.1.50), are subject to the disclosure requirements of IFRS 7. [*IFRS 7.3(d)*]

7I.8.30   **PRESENTATION: GENERAL CONSIDERATIONS**

7I.8.40   **Statement of financial position**

7I.8.40.10   As a minimum, financial assets are presented in the statement of financial position, with separate presentation of cash and cash equivalents, trade and other receivables, and investments accounted for under the equity method (see chapter 3.5). Financial liabilities are presented in the statement of financial position, with separate presentation of trade and other payables. Additional line items may be presented. [*IAS 1.54*]

7I.8.40.20   Using different measurement bases for different classes of assets suggests that their nature or function differs; therefore, instruments that are measured at cost or amortised cost, and those that are measured at fair value, are generally presented as separate line items. However, in our view in certain cases instruments with different measurement bases may be included in the same line item – e.g. a host financial instrument that is carried at amortised cost and a separable embedded derivative (see 7I.2.110), or an instrument carried at amortised cost that is the hedged item in a fair value hedge and other similar instruments that are not hedged. In these cases, the notes to the financial statements should disclose the carrying amount of each category of financial instruments that are combined in a single line item in the statement of financial position. [*IFRS 7.8, IAS 1.59*]

7I.8.45   *Trade payables and reverse factoring*

7I.8.45.10   Amounts owed to a supplier of goods or services are generally presented as trade payables – i.e. liabilities to pay for goods or services that have been received and have been invoiced or formally agreed with the supplier. [*IAS 1.54(k), 37.11(a)*]

7I.8.45.20   In a traditional factoring arrangement, a supplier of goods or services obtains cash from a bank or other financial institution (i.e. the factor) against receivables due from its customers. The arrangement might take different legal forms – e.g. the receivables might be sold outright to the factor or pledged as security for a loan from the factor and the factor may or may not have recourse to the supplier in the event that the customer does not settle. A traditional factoring arrangement is initiated by the supplier and the factor, rather than the customer. In some cases, the customer might be unaware of the arrangement. In our experience, in such an arrangement, the customer generally continues to classify the amounts payable as trade payables, even if it is aware of the factoring arrangement.

7I.8.45.30   In contrast, reverse factoring is initiated by the customer and the factor. The terms of reverse factoring arrangements vary but are usually three-party agreements involving the customer, the factor and the supplier. Under a reverse factoring arrangement, the factor agrees to pay amounts to the supplier in respect of invoices owed by the customer, receiving settlement from that customer at a later date.

7I.8.45.40   A reverse factoring arrangement may provide liquidity to the customer if it allows deferral of payment to the factor beyond the original maturity of the supplier's invoice or if the arrangement enables the customer to negotiate extended payment terms with its supplier. Depending on the terms of the arrangement, and similar to traditional factoring, the reverse factoring arrangement may also provide to the supplier:

- liquidity by enabling it to receive cash before the invoice due date; and
- access to funding at a lower interest rate based on the customer's credit rating.

7I.8.45.50   Similarly, the reverse factoring arrangement may allow the customer to take advantage of an early payment discount offered by the supplier. The reverse factoring arrangement may also allow the supplier and the customer to make administrative savings through more streamlined collection and payment procedures.

7I.8.45.60   In some cases, a reverse factoring arrangement may result in the derecognition of the original trade payable and the recognition of a new financial liability (see 7I.5.370); in other cases, there will be no derecognition of the original trade payable to which the reverse factoring arrangement applies.

7I.8.45.70   In our view, regardless of whether the original trade payable is derecognised, an entity should consider the appropriate presentation of amounts related to reverse factoring arrangements in the statement of financial position (see 3.1.10.30), including whether the headings and line items should be adapted to suit the particular circumstances – for example:

- reclassifying amounts to a different line – e.g. within 'other financial liabilities'; or
- presenting an additional line item – e.g. supplier factoring facility – either on the face of the statement of financial position or by disaggregation of amounts that have a different nature or function in the notes. [*IAS 1.29–30, 55*]

7I.8.45.80   An entity needs to apply judgement in determining whether the reverse factoring arrangement indicates that separate presentation (on the face of the statement of financial position or in the notes) of the amounts due is appropriate – e.g. reclassification of the trade payable to bank borrowing. We believe that the following are examples of features that may indicate that the nature or function of the financial liability is sufficiently different from a trade payable and therefore separate presentation may be appropriate:

- the principal business purpose of the reverse factoring arrangement is to provide funding to the customer, rather than to provide funding to the supplier or to facilitate efficient payment processing;
- the factor is a bank or similar financial institution; and
- the arrangement:
  - significantly extends payment terms beyond the normal terms agreed with other suppliers;
  - adds a requirement for the customer to pay interest or to pay interest at a higher rate;
  - requires additional collateral or a guarantee; or
  - changes the terms defining default and cancellation.

7I.8.45.90   None of the features in 7I.8.45.80 is necessarily a determinative indicator on its own. We believe that an entity should weigh those features to determine whether separate presentation (on the face of the statement of financial position or in the notes) is appropriate.

7I.8.45.100   For a further discussion of reverse factoring, see 2.3.75, 7I.5.425, 7I.8.205 and 375.

7I.8.50   *Classes vs categories of financial instruments*

7I.8.50.10   Some of the IFRS 7 disclosure requirements mandate disclosure by *category* of financial instruments, whereas others are by *class* of financial instruments. 'Categories of financial instruments' are:

- financial assets or financial liabilities at FVTPL;
- held-to-maturity investments;
- loans and receivables;
- available-for-sale financial assets; and
- other liabilities (see 7I.4.10.10–15). [*IFRS 7.8, IAS 39.9*]

7I.8.50.20   There is no specific guidance on what comprises a *class* except that financial instruments are grouped into classes that:

- are appropriate to the nature of the disclosure; and
- take into account the characteristics of those financial instruments. [*IFRS 7.6, B1*]

7I.8.50.30   Examples of classes of financial instruments include cash and cash equivalents, unsecured bank facilities and convertible notes (liability). In determining classes, the entity, as a minimum:

- distinguishes instruments measured at amortised cost from those measured at fair value; and
- treats financial instruments outside the scope of IFRS 7 as a separate class or classes. [*IFRS 7.6, B2*]

7I.8.50.40   In deciding how much detail to include and how to aggregate the information, an entity has to strike a balance between too much and too little detail. It also needs to ensure that the information is sufficient to allow a reconciliation to the line items presented in the statement of financial position. [*IFRS 7.6, B3*]

7I.8.50.50   In our view, derivative assets and liabilities should be presented in separate line items in the statement of financial position if they are significant. If derivative instruments are not significant, then they may be included in other financial assets and other financial liabilities, respectively. Additional details should be disclosed in the notes to the financial statements.

7I.8.60   *Current vs non-current classification of financial instruments*

7I.8.60.10   If an entity makes a distinction between current and non-current assets and liabilities in the statement of financial position (classified statement of financial position – see 3.1.10.10), then instruments within the financial instrument classes are classified as current or non-current in accordance with their expected recovery (financial assets) or contractual settlement date (financial liabilities). [*IAS 1.60*]

7I.8.60.20   In particular, an asset is classified as current when it:
- is expected to be realised in or is held for sale in the entity's normal operating cycle;
- is held primarily for trading purposes;
- is expected to be realised within 12 months of the reporting date; or
- is cash or a cash equivalent that is not restricted from being exchanged or used to settle a liability for at least 12 months after the reporting date (see 2.3.10). [*IAS 1.66, 68*]

7I.8.60.30   A liability is classified as current when it:
- is expected to be settled in the entity's normal operating cycle;
- is held primarily for trading purposes;
- is due to be settled within 12 months of the reporting date; or
- is not subject to an unconditional right of the entity at the reporting date to defer settlement of the liability for at least 12 months after the reporting date. [*IAS 1.69*]

7I.8.60.35   However, a liability is not classified as current only because the counterparty has an option to require settlement within 12 months in equity instruments issued by the entity. [*IAS 1.69*]

7I.8.60.40   Derivatives not held primarily for trading purposes are classified as current or non-current based on their outstanding maturities. For example, derivatives with maturities exceeding 12 months that the entity intends to hold for more than 12 months from the reporting date are classified as non-current assets or liabilities. [*IAS 1.BC38J*]

7I.8.60.50   In addition to derivatives (see 3.1.30.45 and 7I.8.60.40), the FVTPL category also includes:
- assets and liabilities held primarily for the purpose of being traded – e.g. certain financial assets classified as held-for-trading – which are classified as current; and
- assets and liabilities of longer duration – e.g. those that were designated on initial recognition into this category.

7I.8.60.60   In our view, such assets and liabilities of longer duration should be presented as non-current to the extent that they are not expected to be realised, or are not due to be settled, within 12 months of the reporting date or within the entity's normal operating cycle. In our view, this also applies to available-for-sale financial assets. [*IAS 1.68*]

7I.8.65 **Statement of profit or loss and OCI**

7I.8.70 *Profit or loss*

7I.8.70.10 Other than as set out below, there is currently no specific guidance on presenting gains and losses on financial instruments in profit or loss (see also 4.1.130). In our view, gains and losses on financial instruments should be reported in the most appropriate line item according to their nature. [*IAS 1.86, 39.56*]

7I.8.70.20 For example, an entity may present foreign currency gains and losses on financial assets and financial liabilities that arise from operating activities – e.g. payables arising on the purchase of goods – as part of income and expenses before finance costs, and foreign currency gains and losses related to financing activities as part of finance income and finance costs (see 2.7.160.20 and 7I.8.80). [*IAS 21.28, 39.55–56, AG83*]

7I.8.70.30 There is also no specific guidance on the presentation of gains and losses on derivatives (see 7I.8.225.10). However, if an entity elects to disclose the results of operating activities (or a similar line item), then it presents foreign exchange gains and losses and gains and losses on derivatives that it normally regards as being of an operating nature as part of operating activities. See also 2.7.160.20, 4.1.120.10–30, 7I.8.70.50–60 and 80.20. [*IAS 1.BC56, 21.52*]

7I.8.70.40 For financial assets and financial liabilities at FVTPL, there is no need to distinguish between the fair value changes and interest and dividend income or expense (see 7I.8.220.20). The net fair value changes – i.e. gains and losses – on each financial asset or financial liability are usually classified as finance income or finance costs (see 7I.8.80). However, fair value changes (net gains or net losses) on these instruments are presented separately, if they are material. [*IAS 1.35, 97*]

7I.8.70.50 For non-derivatives measured at FVTPL, an entity may present either:
- foreign exchange gains and losses and/or interest income and expense separately from other fair value changes; or
- the entire fair value change on a net basis as a single amount.

7I.8.70.60 Whichever method is adopted, if an entity elects to disclose the results of operating activities (or a similar line item) in profit or loss, then it presents any amounts that it normally regards as being of an operating nature as part of operating activities. In addition, if interest on non-derivative instruments measured at FVTPL is presented separately, then it is measured using the effective interest method or a similar basis, excluding transaction costs, and presented as interest income or expense. Because transaction costs directly attributable to the acquisition of a financial instrument classified as at FVTPL are not included in its initial measurement, but are instead expensed as they are incurred, they are not included in calculating an effective interest rate for the instrument (see 7I.6.30.10 and 70). See also 4.1.120.10–30, 7I.8.70.30 and 80.20. [*IFRS 7.BC34, IAS 39.43A*]

7I.8.70.70 If hedge accounting is not applied to a derivative instrument that is entered into as an economic hedge, then in our view derivative gains and losses may be shown in profit or loss as either operating or financing items, depending on the nature of the item being economically hedged.

7I.8.80   **Finance income and finance costs**

7I.8.80.10   A separate line item is required in profit or loss for finance costs. There is no requirement to present a separate 'finance income' line item in profit or loss unless such presentation is relevant to an understanding of the entity's financial performance. Significant categories of revenue, including interest and dividends, are disclosed in the financial statements. [*IAS 1.82(b), 85, 97*]

7I.8.80.20   There is no guidance in IFRS on what should be included in finance income and finance costs. Non-financial sector entities usually include the following items in finance income and finance costs:
- interest income and expense (see 7I.6.230);
- dividend income;
- foreign exchange gains and losses arising from investing and financing activities – e.g. exchange gains and losses on financial investments or exchange gains and losses on foreign currency borrowings (see 2.7.160.20);
- gains and losses on derivatives related to investing and financing activities – e.g. gains and losses on interest rate swaps, or gains and losses on foreign currency forward contracts that hedge foreign currency borrowings (see 7I.7.50);
- gains and losses on the derecognition of financial investments (see 4.1.130);
- gains and losses on trading activities involving financial instruments;
- gains and losses on financial instruments designated as at FVTPL;
- impairment losses and reversals of impairment losses on financial investments;
- the unwinding of discounts on non-financial assets and non-financial liabilities; and
- gains and losses on the derecognition of financial liabilities (see 7I.5.390.30, 410.30, 7I.8.70.30 and 50–60).

7I.8.80.25   The IFRS Interpretations Committee discussed the accounting implications of the economic phenomenon of negative effective interest rates on the presentation of income and expenses in profit or loss. The Committee noted that interest resulting from a negative effective interest rate on a financial asset reflects a gross outflow (instead of a gross inflow) of economic benefits; consequently, it did not meet the definition of interest revenue under IFRS at that time and should not be presented as such. Instead, it noted that negative interest arising from financial assets should be presented in an appropriate expense classification, accompanied by additional information as required by IAS 1. IAS 39 does not define revenue or income. However, income continues to be defined in the Conceptual Framework and IFRS 15, and negative interest arising from financial assets does not meet those definitions because it represents a decrease (instead of an increase) in assets that results in a decrease in equity. [*IU 01-15, IFRS 15.A, IAS 1.85, 112(c), CF 4.68–69*]

7I.8.80.30   Interest income and expense includes interest that is recognised in respect of an asset or liability that is measured at a discounted amount – for example:
- the interest expense that arises on a provision that is initially measured at a discounted amount (see 3.12.120);
- the interest on a contract asset or a contract liability recognised for a contract with a customer that contains a significant financing component (see 4.2.130); or
- the interest that is imputed on the cost of inventories when payment for the inventories is deferred beyond normal credit terms (see 3.8.150).

7I.8.80.40   Dividend income is presented as a separate line item in profit or loss when such presentation is relevant to an understanding of the entity's financial performance. [*IAS 1.85*]

7I.8.80.50   In our view, finance income and finance costs should not be presented on a net basis (e.g. as 'net finance costs') in profit or loss without presenting an analysis of finance income and finance costs. However, this does not preclude presentation of finance income immediately followed by finance costs and a subtotal – e.g. 'net finance costs' – in profit or loss. [*IAS 1.32, 82, 85–85B*]

7I.8.80.60   In our view, expenses related to shares that are classified as a liability – e.g. dividends on redeemable preference shares – may be included with interest on other liabilities or presented separately within finance costs.

7I.8.80.70   The profit or loss of banks and similar financial institutions comprises mainly finance income and finance costs. The presentation and disclosure for financial institutions is illustrated in KPMG's *Guides to financial statements* series.

7I.8.80.80   For further discussion of specific presentation issues arising from the application of IFRS 7, see 7I.8.210.

7I.8.85   *Other comprehensive income*

7I.8.85.10   Each component of OCI classified by nature is presented as a separate line item in the statement of profit or loss and OCI. This includes:
- the net change in fair value on available-for-sale financial assets;
- the effective portion of the net gain or loss on hedges of net investments in foreign operations; and
- the effective portion of changes in fair value in respect of hedging instruments in cash flow hedges. [*IAS 1.82A(a)*]

7I.8.85.20   Separate components of OCI are created in accordance with the requirements of IAS 39, which also determine how and when amounts previously recognised in these components are reclassified to profit or loss. Reclassification adjustments are included with the related component of OCI in the period during which the adjustment is reclassified to profit or loss. They may be presented in the statement of profit or loss and OCI or in the notes to the financial statements. At any point in time, the cumulative amounts previously recognised in these separate components of OCI represent a cumulative gain or loss that will be reclassified to profit or loss at some future date. In our view, it would not be appropriate for an entity to reduce or increase components of OCI for any reasons other than those allowed under IAS 39 – except for related tax effects under IAS 12 (see 3.13.570). [*IAS 1.92–94*]

7I.8.90   **Offsetting**

7I.8.90.10   Financial assets and financial liabilities are offset and a net amount is presented in the statement of financial position only if both of the following conditions are met:
- the entity currently has a legally enforceable right to set off the recognised amounts – i.e. a legal right to settle or eliminate all or a portion of an amount due to a creditor by applying against that amount an amount due from the creditor; and
- the entity has the intention to:
  - settle on a net basis; or
  - realise the asset and settle the liability simultaneously. [*IAS 32.42, 45*]

7I.8.91   *Multiple financial instruments*

7I.8.91.10   The offsetting criteria relate only to determining whether two or more separate financial instruments should be offset and presented net in the statement of financial position. They are not relevant in determining how a single financial instrument should be measured and presented. For example, an interest rate swap comprises an obligation to pay and receive interest cash flows over time – i.e. payments and receipts might be made on a gross basis at different points in time or, even if each individual periodic cash flow is determined as a single net payment or receipt for that period, it might be expected that net amounts will be received in some periods and net amounts paid in other periods. However, the swap is a single derivative financial instrument that is measured at its fair value, which reflects the net value of the expected cash inflows and outflows even though those cash inflows and outflows will not be settled on a net basis.

EXAMPLE 1A – CASH POOLING ARRANGEMENT – MULTIPLE GROUP ENTITIES

7I.8.91.20   For cash management purposes, Company B and its subsidiaries enter into a cash pooling arrangement, whereby debit and credit balances in the same currency with Bank C are pooled to optimise the interest earned and paid on the aggregated balance.

7I.8.91.30   Before considering the offsetting requirements in IAS 32, B needs to assess whether the arrangement between the B group and C involves either:
● a single financial instrument; or
● multiple financial instruments.

7I.8.91.40   If this cash pooling arrangement results in a single omnibus account that B holds with C, and the aggregate balance represents a single amount payable or receivable between B and C, then any accumulated 'memorandum balances' on constituent 'sub-accounts' that record transactions initiated by subsidiaries of B do not represent amounts payable or receivable between those subsidiaries and C, but rather reflect intra-group amounts payable or receivable between those subsidiaries and B. In this case, B presents the aggregated balance on the single omnibus account as a financial asset or financial liability in its consolidated statement of financial position. Therefore, the offsetting requirements are irrelevant.

7I.8.91.50   Alternatively, assume that B and each of its subsidiaries have accounts with C in their own names and the balance on each of these accounts represents an amount payable or receivable between that individual member of the B group and C. In that case, for the purposes of B's consolidated financial statements, each account is a separate financial asset or financial liability and B should consider the offsetting criteria to determine whether they should be presented separately or offset.

7I.8.91.60   Judgement may be required in determining whether an arrangement involves a single or multiple financial instruments. Generally, rights and obligations arising under different contracts give rise to separate financial instruments. Furthermore, a single legal contract may give rise to more than one financial instrument, such as separate derivatives, loans and deposits or trade receivables and payables. However, in some cases, it may be necessary to aggregate different financial instruments and account for them as a single combined financial instrument (see 7I.5.40.10). To determine whether multiple balances or transactions arising from a single legal contract between two entities represent a single or multiple financial instruments, an entity may consider whether:

- each transaction results in separate performance rights and obligations that may be transferred or settled separately;
- transactions are intended to be performed concurrently or consecutively with other transactions;
- transactions relate to the same risks or may be exposed to different risks;
- the pricing of individual transactions is independent; and
- transactions are negotiated as separate trades and/or have different commercial objectives.

EXAMPLE 1B – DERIVATIVE MASTER AGREEMENT

7I.8.91.70   Company X enters into a derivative master agreement with Bank B. The agreement states that:

- the parties may agree in the future to enter into a variety of swap, forward, option or other derivative transactions and to terminate such transactions;
- the terms of each transaction or termination, including pricing, will be subject to negotiation based on market conditions at the time;
- any such transactions will form part of the master agreement, which constitutes the only contract at law between the parties;
- collateral is paid or received in accordance with the detailed terms of a credit support annex;
- either party may demand net settlement of amounts due and payable on the same day in the same currency; and
- in the event of either party's default, the other party may demand that all outstanding transactions are terminated at their market values and that a single net settlement of all such amounts is made.

7I.8.91.80   Based on the factors in 7I.8.91.70, X concludes that each derivative transaction entered into under the master agreement represents a separate financial asset or financial liability.

EXAMPLE 1C – CASH POOLING ARRANGEMENT – MULTIPLE-CURRENCY FACILITY

7I.8.91.90   Company T enters into a cash pooling agreement with Bank X. Under the terms of the agreement, all of which are contained in a single document, T has several current accounts in different currencies with the following conditions.

- All accounts are held by T at X in Country Y.
- T is generally free to make drawings from and deposits into each account, and the individual accounts can be in a positive or negative position subject to an overall credit limit on T's net drawn balances. T could not withdraw the positive balance on one of the accounts, unless the net balance on all accounts following withdrawal would still be within the overall credit limit.

- The credit limit is stated in a single reference currency. It is applied and monitored by X using current market rates of exchange.
- If foreign exchange rates change and the credit limit is breached, then X may require T to bring the aggregated balances back within the credit limit.
- Interest is calculated on each account on a gross basis at a predetermined fixed or variable rate for the respective currency.
- The agreement has a stated maturity date that applies to all accounts and to the credit limit. At the maturity date, unless T and X agree to extend the agreement, all accounts are closed and the remaining balances are settled on a net basis in the reference currency.
- In the event of default of either party, the non-defaulting party may demand that balances on all accounts are translated into the reference currency and settled net. The same would apply in the event of either party's bankruptcy.
- There is no regular transfer of balances into a sweep account and there is no intention to settle any amounts net or simultaneously, except for any balances that remain at maturity.
- T receives quarterly statements showing the individual gross balances for each account and a subtotal of all of those in debit/credit positions in the single reference currency.

7I.8.91.100   The fact that the various accounts arise from a single contractual agreement does not mean that there is a single financial instrument. Similarly, stating a common maturity date does not necessarily mean that there is a single financial instrument. Although there is an overall credit limit and requirements for set off in certain circumstances, each current account is denominated in a different currency and gives rise to performance rights and obligations in that currency. Performance rights and obligations in relation to one currency account are different from those of other accounts and balances on different accounts may be individually settled. Accordingly, T and X conclude that in this example each current account is a separate financial instrument.

7I.8.92   *Unit of account*

7I.8.92.10   IAS 32 does not specify whether the unit of account when considering the offsetting requirements in IAS 32 should be:
- *entire financial assets and financial liabilities:* In this case, the entity considers whether all – and not just some – of the cash flows from one instrument satisfy the offsetting criteria with respect to another instrument. If they all do, then the instrument is offset in its entirety; otherwise, no offsetting is applied (Approach 1); or
- *individual identifiable cash flows from financial assets and financial liabilities:* In this case, an entity considers whether each individual cash flow of a financial instrument satisfies the offsetting criteria with respect to the cash flows of another instrument. If it does, then the portion of the individual instrument that represents those cash flows is offset (Approach 2). [*IAS 32.BC105–BC106*]

7I.8.92.20   In our experience, the approach that is adopted by an entity depends on industry practice, the entity's operational capabilities and the complexity and volume of transactions subject to set off. For example, energy producers and traders generally apply the offsetting criteria to identifiable cash flows, whereas financial institutions generally apply the offsetting criteria to entire financial assets and financial liabilities. An approach of applying to individual cash flows may lead to more offsetting but may be more burdensome to apply. Offsetting is mandatory when the offsetting criteria are satisfied, and therefore an entity may find it impracticable to apply an approach based on individual cash flows. In our view, an entity should choose an accounting policy, to be applied consistently to similar assets and liabilities, to apply either Approach 1 or 2 in 71.8.91.10. [*IAS 32.BC111*]

71.8.93 *Current legally enforceable right to set off*

71.8.93.10   An entity currently has a legally enforceable right to set off if the right is:
- not contingent on a future event; and
- enforceable both in the normal course of business and in the event of default, insolvency or bankruptcy of the entity and all of the counterparties. [*IAS 32.AG38B*]

EXAMPLE 2A – OFFSETTING – LEGAL ENFORCEABILITY FOR ALL COUNTERPARTIES

71.8.93.20   Company B enters into an agreement with Company C that gives B a right to set off.

71.8.93.30   To determine whether its right is legally enforceable in the normal course of business and in the event of default, insolvency or bankruptcy of the entity and all of the counterparties, B evaluates whether it can enforce its right in the normal course of business as well as in the case of its own default, insolvency or bankruptcy, and in the case of C's default, insolvency or bankruptcy.

71.8.93.40   In doing so, B considers whether C has any rights that do or might prevent B from enforcing its right to set off. For example, if, in the event of C's bankruptcy, C could insist on separate settlement of any amounts due to and from B, then B's right to set off would not be enforceable in those circumstances and it would not satisfy the offsetting criteria. [*IAS 32.42(a), AG38B, AG38D, BC80*]

71.8.93.50   Rights to set off may arise on the termination of a contract. In many cases, the termination of a contract may be contingent on an event that is outside the entity's control – e.g. the counterparty's default or bankruptcy. In such cases, the right to set off is clearly conditional and could not qualify for offsetting. However, in some cases the termination of a contract may be a free choice of the entity and is therefore within the entity's control – e.g. the exercise of an early repayment option in a loan. IAS 32 does not discuss whether events that are within the entity's control should be considered contingent on the occurrence of a future event. Therefore, it is not clear whether such rights could be considered currently legally enforceable. However, even if a right to set off arising on termination of a contract could be considered not to be contingent on a future event, such a right on its own would not qualify for offsetting, unless termination would arise in the normal course of business and the entity intends to settle net. [*IAS 32.AG38B, BC82*]

71.8.93.60   To qualify for offsetting, a right to set off needs to be exercisable when the amounts are due and payable. In addition, the passage of time and uncertainties in the amounts to be settled are not considered contingencies. [*IAS 32.BC82–BC84*]

EXAMPLE 2B – OFFSETTING – AMOUNT OR TIMING OF PAYMENT UNCERTAIN

7I.8.93.70   Company B has a loan receivable of 100 from Company C that is due and payable on 30 June 2019. B has also written a net-cash-settled put option to C.

7I.8.93.80   The following facts are also relevant for this example.
- Under the option, B is obliged to pay C the amount (if any) by which the market price of commodity X exceeds 10 on the exercise date.
- If the market price of commodity X is below 10 on the exercise date, then no payment is required.
- The option matures on 30 June 2019.
- The fair value of the option liability on 31 December 2018 is 30.
- The two transactions – i.e. the loan and the put option – are subject to a right to set off that requires net settlement of amounts due and payable on the same date in all circumstances.
- There are no collateral or margin arrangements.

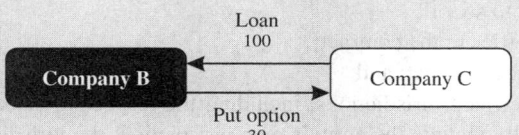

7I.8.93.90   Whether B is required to present the loan receivable from C and the derivative liability owed to C net in the statement of financial position will depend on whether the option is a European option (exercisable only on 30 June 2019) or an American option (exercisable at any time up to 30 June 2019).

Scenario 1 – European option

7I.8.93.100   If the option written by B is a European option – i.e. exercisable only on 30 June 2019 – then both the loan and the written option fall due for settlement on 30 June 2019 and the right to set off ensures that settlement will be on a net basis.

7I.8.93.110   It is uncertain whether any amount will actually be due in respect of the option; however, if an amount does arise, then it will certainly be set off. The passage of time and uncertainties in the amounts to be paid do not preclude B from currently having a legally enforceable right to set off. The fact that payments subject to the right will arise only at a future date is not itself a contingency or condition that precludes offsetting.

7I.8.93.120   Therefore, in this scenario B presents the loan receivable from C and the derivative liability owed to C net in the statement of financial position.

Scenario 2 – American option

71.8.93.130   If the option written by B is an American option – i.e. exercisable at any time up to and including 30 June 2019 – then C could choose to exercise its option before 30 June 2019. If C does exercise early, then B does not have the right to set off, and the two transactions will be settled separately.

71.8.93.140   Therefore, in this scenario B presents the loan receivable from C and the derivative liability due to C separately in the statement of financial position. [*IAS 32.BC83–BC84*]

71.8.93.150   The following do not meet the offsetting criteria in IAS 32:
- rights to set off that can be enforced only in the normal course of business; or
- rights to set off that cannot be enforced in the event of the entity's own default, insolvency or bankruptcy. [*IAS 32.BC81, BC92*]

71.8.93.160   An entity would typically consider the following in determining whether it has a legally enforceable right to set off:
- the counterparties to the contract;
- the terms of the contract; and
- laws in the relevant jurisdictions, including the respective bankruptcy regimes and laws. This would typically include the entity's own jurisdiction, the jurisdiction of other counterparties to the contract and the specific laws governing the contract.

EXAMPLE 2C – CASH POOLING ARRANGEMENT – CURRENT LEGALLY ENFORCEABLE RIGHT TO SET OFF

71.8.93.170   Continuing Example 1, assume that the cash pooling arrangement with Bank C involves separate bank accounts and borrowings in each of the group entities' names – i.e. there are multiple financial instruments between the B group and C. Determining whether the reporting entity has a currently enforceable right to set off requires consideration of the terms of the contract(s). For example, the terms of the contract may permit each individual entity within the B group that has more than one account with C to set off debit and credit balances on those accounts that the individual entity has with C, but may not permit the B group or its members to require set off between accounts held by different members of the B group with C. C would have to perform a similar analysis for the purposes of its financial statements. However, C would not be able to demonstrate that it has a current legally enforceable right to set off if members of the B group are free to withdraw funds from accounts that are in credit and C cannot require those funds instead to be set off against accounts that are overdrawn.

71.8.95   *Intention to settle on net basis or realise asset and settle liability simultaneously*

71.8.95.10   To meet the intention criterion (see 71.8.90.10), an entity must intend either to:
- settle the financial asset and the financial liability on a net basis; or

- realise the financial asset and settle the financial liability simultaneously (see 7I.8.95.20). [*IAS 32.42(b), AG38E*]

7I.8.95.20   When assessing whether there is an intention to settle net, an entity considers normal business practices, the requirements of the financial markets and other circumstances that may limit its ability to settle net. [*IAS 32.47*]

EXAMPLE 3 – CASH POOLING ARRANGEMENT – INTENTION TO SETTLE NET

7I.8.95.30   Continuing Examples 1 and 2C, assume that the B group determines that:
- there are multiple financial instruments involved in the arrangement; and
- there is a current legally enforceable right to set off debit and credit balances held by group members with Bank C.

7I.8.95.40   To determine whether it has the intention to settle net, B considers the nature of the set off arrangement.

7I.8.95.50   There are two main types of cash management schemes involving multiple financial instruments:
- *zero balancing/cash sweep:* Balances on the separate accounts falling under the arrangement are set off and physically transferred to a single account on a regular basis; and
- *notional pooling:* Balances on the separate accounts falling under the arrangement are not physically transferred and the bank calculates the synthetic (net) balance on a number of designated accounts with interest being earned and paid on the net amount.

7I.8.95.60   If the balances on the accounts are physically transferred into a single account, then B needs to assess the frequency of set off to determine whether the intention criterion is met. If the cash balances are physically moved into a single netting account on a daily basis, then this would mean that at the end of each day (including the reporting date) the amounts in the bank accounts involved in the cash management arrangement will be physically settled and aggregated in one bank account. Other than the single balance in the main account, all other bank balances will be zero, making the IAS 32 balance sheet offsetting considerations irrelevant (i.e. the position at the end of each day will approximate that described under Approach 1 in 7I.8.92.10 because there will be only one account between the B group and C with a non-zero balance).

7I.8.95.70   However, if the sweep does not take place on a daily basis, then B assesses whether the frequency of sweeping supports the intention to settle net requirement in paragraph 42(b) of IAS 32. This requires an evaluation of whether balances outstanding at the reporting date will be settled through netting at the next sweep date (or by net settlement before then – e.g. if B intends its group members to make transfers from accounts that are in credit to those that are overdrawn) or whether they will be settled through normal day-to-day business before the next sweep.

7I.8.95.80   In the case in 7I.8.95.70, if C has a current legally enforceable right to set off, then it will have to make a similar analysis. However, it will usually be difficult for C to demonstrate that it intends to settle net in the normal course of business because entities in the B group may choose to withdraw funds from accounts that are in credit or may pay down overdrawn balances using funds obtained from other sources.

7I.8.95.90   If the balances on the accounts are not physically transferred into a single account or otherwise intended to be settled on a net basis, then an entity would fail the intention to settle net requirement, because the arrangement does not result in the balances being settled net. Consequently, net balance sheet presentation would not be allowed.

7I.8.95.100   The IFRS Interpretations Committee discussed a scenario that is similar to that in 7I.8.95.70 and noted that a group needs to assess whether, at the reporting date, there is an intention to settle its subsidiaries' bank account balances on a net basis or whether the intention is for its subsidiaries to use those individual bank account balances for other purposes before the next net settlement date.

7I.8.95.110   The Committee observed that in the scenario that it considered, the group expects cash movements to take place on individual bank accounts before the next net settlement date because the group expects its subsidiaries to use those bank accounts in their normal course of business. Consequently, the Committee noted that, to the extent to which the group did not expect to settle its subsidiaries' period-end account balances on a net basis, it would not be appropriate for the group to assert that it had the intention to settle the entire period-end balances on a net basis at the reporting date. This is because presenting these balances net would not appropriately reflect the amounts and timings of the expected future cash flows, taking into account the group's and its subsidiaries' normal business practices.

7I.8.95.120   However, the Committee also observed that in other cash pooling arrangements a group's expectations regarding how subsidiaries will use their bank accounts before the next net settlement date may be different. Consequently, it was noted that, in those circumstances, the group would be required to apply judgement in determining whether there was an intention to settle on a net basis at the reporting date. [*IU 03-16*]

7I.8.95.130   If an entity will settle amounts in a manner such that the outcome is, in effect, equivalent to net settlement, then it meets the intention criterion in IAS 32. A gross settlement system is equivalent to net settlement if, and only if, it has features that:
- eliminate or result in insignificant credit and liquidity risk; and
- will process receivables and payables in a single settlement process or cycle. [*IAS 32.AG38F*]

7I.8.95.140   IAS 32 identifies an example of a gross settlement system that would be equivalent to net settlement. It has all of the following features.

a. Financial assets and financial liabilities are submitted for processing at the same point in time.
b. The parties are committed to fulfilling the settlement obligation once the financial assets and financial liabilities are submitted for processing.
c. Once they have been submitted, there is no potential for the cash flows arising from the financial assets and financial liabilities to change (unless processing fails – see (d)).
d. Assets and liabilities that are collateralised with securities are settled on a system in which the processing of the receivable or payable fails if the transfer of the related securities fails (and vice versa).
e. Failed transactions are re-entered for processing until they are settled.
f. The same settlement institution carries out the settlement.
g. There is an intra-day credit facility that:
   – will provide sufficient overdraft amounts to each party at the settlement date; and
   – is virtually certain to be honoured if it is called on. [*IAS 32.AG38F*]

7I.8.97 *Applying the offsetting requirements*

7I.8.97.10   The offsetting requirements may apply to instruments such as receivables and payables with the same counterparty if a legal right to set off is agreed to between the parties. Generally, it would not be appropriate to offset assets and liabilities that the entity has with different counterparties. To qualify for offsetting, there would have to be an agreement in place between all parties, which would be unusual. Also, it may be difficult in practice to demonstrate the intention to settle net or simultaneously with all parties to the arrangement. Consequently, it is unlikely that either of the conditions for offsetting will be met. [*IAS 32.45*]

7I.8.97.20   Individual instruments that, when viewed together, would form a synthetic instrument do not usually qualify for offsetting. For example, in the case of a fixed rate liability and a fixed-to-floating interest rate swap that together form a synthetic floating rate liability, there is generally no legal right to set off the swap's cash flows and the interest payments on the liability. Also, the settlement of the liability and the realisation of the swap may not occur simultaneously. [*IAS 32.49(a)*]

7I.8.97.30   When a transfer of financial assets does not qualify for derecognition (see 7I.5.60), the associated liability and the corresponding assets are not offset. [*IAS 32.42*]

7I.8.97.40   In addition, offsetting is usually not appropriate when:
- financial assets are set aside in a trust by a debtor for the purpose of discharging an obligation without those assets having been accepted by the creditor in settlement of the obligation; or
- an entity incurs an obligation as a result of certain loss events, which it expects to recover through a claim made under an insurance contract. [*IAS 32.49(d)–(e)*]

7I.8.97.50   An entity may be required to provide (receive) cash or non-cash collateral in connection with certain types of transactions. The offsetting requirements do not give special consideration to items referred to as 'collateral'. Accordingly, collateral that is represented by a recognised financial instrument is presented net against the related financial asset or financial liability if, and only if, it meets the offsetting criteria in IAS 32. If an entity can be required to return or receive back collateral, then it does not currently have a legally enforceable right to set off in all of the following circumstances:
- in the normal course of business;
- in the event of default; and

- on the insolvency or bankruptcy of one of the counterparties. [*IAS 32.49(c), BC103*]

7I.8.97.60   Generally, the offsetting criteria in IAS 32 (see 7I.8.90.10) are not satisfied, and therefore offsetting is not appropriate, when an entity pledges financial or other assets as collateral for recourse or non-recourse financial liabilities. In addition, in arrangements involving collateral, the offsetting criteria are not satisfied and presenting the respective financial asset and financial liability net is not permissible when the legal right to set off is enforceable only in the case of default. [*IAS 32.42(a), AG38B*]

7I.8.97.70   Derivative assets and liabilities are usually presented on a gross basis as separate line items in the statement of financial position, because they do not generally meet the offsetting criteria. This is because they are usually entered into with different counterparties, and therefore there is no right to set off the recognised amounts. Even if they are entered into with (or novated to) the same counterparty, derivative assets and liabilities often have different settlement dates or cash flow structures. Therefore, it is normally difficult to identify matching cash flows that could be offset at a specific date, even if this was allowed by the contractual relationships. In addition, a legal right to set off may often be conditional on a specified future event, in which case there is no *current* legally enforceable right to set off.

EXAMPLE 4A – OFFSETTING – LEGAL ENFORCEABILITY AND NET SETTLEMENT IN SPECIFIC CIRCUMSTANCES ONLY

> **7I.8.97.80**   Bank B enters into a master netting arrangement with Counterparty C because they undertake a number of financial instruments transactions together. The agreement provides for a single net settlement of all financial instruments covered by the agreement in the event of default on any one contract.
>
> **7I.8.97.85**   The master netting arrangement creates a right to set off that becomes enforceable and affects the realisation or settlement of individual financial assets and financial liabilities only following a specified event of default. Therefore, it does not provide a basis for offsetting. A master netting arrangement does not provide a basis for offsetting unless both of the offsetting criteria are met – i.e. the entity has a current legally enforceable right *and* an intention to settle net or simultaneously. [*IAS 32.50*]

EXAMPLE 4B – OFFSETTING – LEGAL ENFORCEABILITY AND NET SETTLEMENT IN ALL CIRCUMSTANCES – PASSAGE OF TIME OR UNCERTAINTIES IN AMOUNTS DO NOT PRECLUDE OFFSETTING

> **7I.8.97.90**   Bank K is a member of a clearing house. Transactions entered into with other members of the clearing house are novated such that the clearing house is the legal counterparty to K for all such transactions. The contractual terms are as follows:
> - cash margins are payable or receivable between K and the clearing house based on the fair value of outstanding transactions;
> - the payment (receipt) of a cash margin does not itself extinguish or settle any obligation (right) to make (receive) future cash flows under the outstanding transactions; rather, it creates a distinct receivable (payable) that may be set off against those obligations (rights) when they mature (see 7I.5.450);

- only one net cash payment or receipt, which covers final settlement of maturing transactions, periodic payments on existing transactions and net payment or receipt of cash margin, occurs each day between K and the clearing house; and
- in the event of default, insolvency or bankruptcy of any of the parties in the arrangement, the outstanding amounts will be set off.

7I.8.97.100   In our view, the cash flows arising from each daily settlement are, in effect, net settlements. Accordingly, offsetting is appropriate in these circumstances. This is because, despite uncertainties about the amounts and timing, payments that will arise in the future will be set off. The passage of time or uncertainties in amounts to be paid will not preclude K from currently having a legally enforceable right to set off. Therefore, because K has the current legally enforceable right to set off and the intention to settle net or simultaneously, it satisfies the offsetting criteria in IAS 32. [*IAS 32.42, 48*]

7I.8.100   SIGNIFICANCE OF FINANCIAL INSTRUMENTS FOR FINANCIAL POSITION AND PERFORMANCE

7I.8.100.10   An entity provides sufficient disclosures to enable users of the financial statements to evaluate the significance of financial instruments to the entity's financial position and performance. To help satisfy this principle, IFRS 7 lists specific disclosure requirements (see 7I.8.110–290). [*IFRS 7.7*]

7I.8.110   Statement of financial position

7I.8.120   *Carrying amount*

7I.8.120.10   The carrying amounts of the following categories of financial assets and financial liabilities are disclosed, either in the statement of financial position or in the notes:
- financial assets measured at FVTPL;
- held-to-maturity investments;
- loans and receivables;
- available-for-sale financial assets;
- financial liabilities at FVTPL; and
- financial liabilities measured at amortised cost. [*IFRS 7.8*]

7I.8.120.20   The carrying amounts of instruments that are designated as at FVTPL are disclosed separately from the carrying amounts of instruments held for trading purposes. [*IFRS 7.8*]

7I.8.130   *Financial assets or financial liabilities designated as at FVTPL*

7I.8.130.10   As noted in 7I.4.40, entities may designate financial assets and financial liabilities into the financial assets or financial liabilities at FVTPL category.

7I.8.130.20   An entity may have designated a loan or receivable as at FVTPL. In this case, it discloses:
- the maximum exposure to credit risk of that loan or receivable at the reporting date;
- the amount by which this risk is mitigated by credit derivatives or similar instruments;

- the amount of change in the fair value of the loan or receivable that is attributable to changes in credit risk, both for the period and cumulatively; and
- the amount of change in the fair value of any related credit derivative or similar instrument, both for the period and cumulatively since the loan or receivable was designated. [*IFRS 7.9*]

7I.8.130.30   If the entity has designated a financial liability as at FVTPL, then it discloses:
- the amount of change in the fair value of the financial liability that is attributable to changes in credit risk, both for the period and cumulatively; and
- the difference between the carrying amount of the financial liability and the amount that the entity will be contractually required to pay at maturity. [*IFRS 7.10*]

7I.8.130.40   In our view, the amount that the entity is 'contractually required to pay at maturity' should be the undiscounted amount payable at maturity. Furthermore, when the amount payable at maturity is not fixed – e.g. in the case of a liability containing an embedded derivative that modifies the principal amount payable at maturity – the amount disclosed should be based on conditions existing at the reporting date.

7I.8.130.50   In the case of both a loan or receivable and a financial liability, the change in the instrument's fair value attributable to changes in credit risk is determined either: (1) as the amount of the change in its fair value not attributable to changes in market conditions; or (2) using an alternative method that represents more faithfully the amount of the change in fair value attributable to credit risk. In this regard, an entity discloses:
- the methods used to determine the change in fair value attributable to changes in credit risk; and
- if the entity does not believe that the information provided in order to comply with the standard faithfully represents the change in the instrument's fair value attributable to credit risk, then the reasons for reaching this conclusion and the factors that the entity considers relevant. [*IFRS 7.9(c), 10(a), 11*]

7I.8.140   *Reclassification*

7I.8.140.10   If an entity reclassifies a financial asset into or out of either the cost or amortised cost category or the fair value category, with the exception of those reclassifications permitted by paragraph 50B (rare circumstances) or 50D or 50E (assets that would have met the definition of loans and receivables and are intended to be held for the foreseeable future or to maturity) of IAS 39 (see 7I.4.220.20 and 250.10), then the amount reclassified and the reason for the reclassification are disclosed. This would be relevant for held-to-maturity investments being reclassified from the available-for-sale category because the two-year tainting period has expired (see 7I.4.120 and 260); it would also apply in exceptional circumstances in which a fair value measure for a financial asset no longer is available. [*IFRS 7.12*]

7I.8.140.20   If an entity reclassifies a financial asset out of FVTPL or available-for-sale as permitted by paragraph 50B, 50D or 50E of IAS 39 (see 7I.4.220.20 and 250.10), then it discloses:
- the amount reclassified into and out of each category;
- for each reporting period until derecognition of the reclassified financial assets, the carrying amounts and fair values of all financial assets that have been reclassified in the current and previous reporting periods;

- if the financial asset was reclassified because of rare circumstances, then the facts and circumstances indicating that the situation was rare;
- for the reporting period in which the financial asset was reclassified, the fair value gain or loss on the financial asset recognised in profit or loss or OCI in both the current and previous reporting period;
- for each reporting period following the reclassification, including the reporting period in which the financial asset was reclassified, until derecognition of the financial asset:
  - the fair value gain or loss that would have been recognised in profit or loss or OCI if the financial asset had not been reclassified; and
  - the gain, loss, income and expense recognised in profit or loss; and
- the effective interest rate and the estimated amounts of cash flows that the entity expects to recover, as at the date of reclassification of the financial asset. [*IFRS 7.12A*]

7I.8.145   *Derecognition*

7I.8.145.10   If the terms of a financial liability are modified substantially, resulting in an extinguishment of the old financial liability, then the old liability is derecognised and the restructured financial instrument is treated as a new financial liability (see 7I.5.380). In our view, any gains or losses arising as a result of the derecognition of the old financial liability (including any unamortised discount or premium) should be presented as a separate line item within the disclosure of finance income or expense, respectively.

7I.8.150   *Offsetting disclosures*

7I.8.150.10   An entity discloses information to enable users of its financial statements to evaluate the effect or potential effect of netting arrangements on its financial position. The disclosures are required for financial assets and financial liabilities that are:
- offset in the statement of financial position in accordance with IAS 32 (see 7I.8.90.10); and
- subject to an enforceable master netting arrangement or similar agreement that covers similar financial instruments and transactions, irrespective of whether the financial assets and financial liabilities meet the offsetting criteria in IAS 32 (see 7I.8.97.80–85). [*IFRS 7.13A–13B, B40*]

7I.8.150.20   To apply the disclosure requirements, an entity follows these steps:
- identify which instruments are in the scope;
- determine how to (dis)aggregate the quantitative disclosures;
- calculate the amounts to be disclosed;
- describe the types and nature of rights to set off that do not meet the offsetting criteria in IAS 32; and
- determine whether additional disclosures are required.

7I.8.150.30   Neither IAS 32 nor IFRS 7 defines 'master netting arrangements or similar agreements'. Therefore, an entity may need to use judgement in identifying them. IAS 32 notes the following as characteristics of master netting arrangements:
- they provide for net settlement of financial instruments covered by the agreement in the event of default on, or termination of, any contact;
- they provide protection against losses when a counterparty is unable to meet its obligations; and

- they commonly create a right to set off that may be enforced only following a specified event of default, or in other circumstances that are not expected to arise in the normal course of business. [*IAS 32.50*]

71.8.150.40   Financial assets and financial liabilities subject to similar agreements that cover similar financial instruments and transactions are in the scope of the disclosure requirements of IFRS 7. 'Similar agreements' and 'similar financial instruments and transactions' are explained in IFRS 7 as follows.

TERM	INCLUDES
Similar agreements	<ul><li>Derivative clearing agreements</li><li>Global master repurchase agreements</li><li>Global master securities lending agreements</li><li>Any related rights to financial collateral</li></ul>
Similar financial instruments and transactions	<ul><li>Derivatives</li><li>(Reverse) Sale-and-repurchase agreements</li><li>Securities borrowing and lending agreements</li></ul>

71.8.150.50   Financial instruments that are outside the scope of the disclosure requirements – unless they are offset in the statement of financial position in accordance with IAS 32 – include:
- loans and customer deposits at the same institution; and
- instruments subject only to a collateral agreement. [*IFRS 7.B41*]

71.8.150.60   An entity discloses the following quantitative information separately for recognised financial assets and recognised financial liabilities in a tabular format unless another format is more appropriate:
a.   the gross amounts;
b.   the amounts offset in accordance with the offsetting criteria in IAS 32;
c.   the net amounts presented in the statement of financial position – i.e. the difference between (a) and (b). These amounts are reconciled to the line item amounts presented in the statement of financial position;
d.   the amounts subject to enforceable master netting arrangements or similar agreements that do not meet the offsetting criteria in IAS 32, including:
   –   amounts related to recognised financial assets and financial liabilities that do not meet the offsetting criteria in IAS 32; and
   –   amounts related to financial collateral; and
e.   the net amounts after deducting the amounts in (d) from those in (c). [*IFRS 7.13C*]

71.8.150.65   The disclosure requirements in 71.8.150.60 may be grouped by type of financial instrument or transaction. Alternatively, an entity may present disclosures (a)–(c) in 71.8.150.60 by type of financial instrument, and disclosures (c)–(e) by counterparty. [*IFRS 7.B51–B52*]

71.8.150.70   To satisfy the minimum disclosure requirements described in 71.8.150.60, an entity calculates the amounts as follows. [*IFRS 7.13A, 13C, B43–B49*]

ITEM (SEE 7I.8.150.60)	WHAT IT INCLUDES
a. Gross amounts	The carrying amounts of recognised financial assets and financial liabilities that are in the scope of the disclosure requirements (see 7I.8.150.10). However, the gross amounts disclosed exclude any amounts recognised as a result of a right to financial collateral that does not meet the offsetting criteria in IAS 32. Such collateral is included under (d) below.
b. Amounts offset	The amounts included in (a) that have been offset in the statement of financial position in accordance with IAS 32.
c. Net amounts presented in the statement of financial position	The difference between (a) and (b) above.
d. Amounts subject to enforceable master netting or similar agreements that are not included in (b)	• For recognised assets and liabilities that do not meet the offsetting criteria in IAS 32, the amount disclosed is the carrying amount to which the right to set off applies. • For financial collateral received or pledged that is not offset in the statement of financial position in accordance with IAS 32, the amount disclosed is the fair value of the collateral actually pledged or received. However, in each case the entity limits the amounts disclosed to eliminate the effect of over-collateralisation. This adjustment is calculated at the level of the financial asset or the financial liability (or group of financial assets/liabilities) to which the right to collateral relates.
e. Net amounts	The difference between items (c) and (d) above.

7I.8.150.80   An entity discloses recognised financial assets and financial liabilities based on their carrying amounts. Different measurement requirements may apply to the various financial assets or financial liabilities within an individual line item in the statement of financial position. Therefore, offsetting may result in a presentation that includes measurement differences. For example, within a line item, a financial asset that is measured at fair value may be offset against a liability that is measured at amortised cost. An entity is required to describe any such measurement differences. [*IFRS 7.B42*]

7I.8.150.90   An entity is required to reconcile the disclosed net amounts included in the statement of financial position, (c) in 7I.8.150.60, to the individual line item amounts presented in the statement of financial position. The scope of the disclosures does not extend to all financial assets and financial liabilities; it is possible that only some of the instruments within a particular line item might be captured, while others are not. Therefore, the net amounts disclosed under item (c) in 7I.8.150.60 may represent subsets of amounts presented in individual line items. [*IFRS 7.B46*]

7I.8.150.100   An entity describes the nature and the types of rights to set off that do not meet the criteria for offsetting in IAS 32. For example, it describes:

- conditional rights;
- the reasons why rights to set off that are not contingent do not meet the offsetting criteria in IAS 32; and
- the terms of the related rights to financial collateral. [*IFRS 7.13E, B50*]

7I.8.150.110   The disclosure requirements described in 7I.8.150.60 are minimum requirements. An entity supplements them with additional qualitative disclosures if necessary for financial statement users to evaluate the actual or potential effect of netting arrangements on its financial position. When disclosing quantitative information by counterparty, an entity considers qualitative disclosure about the types of counterparties. [*IFRS 7.B52–B53*]

7I.8.160   *Collateral*

7I.8.160.10   An entity that has pledged financial assets as collateral for liabilities and contingent liabilities discloses:
- the carrying amount of these assets pledged as collateral; and
- the terms and conditions related to the pledge. [*IFRS 7.14*]

7I.8.160.20   When an entity has accepted collateral that it is entitled to sell or repledge in the absence of default by the owner, it discloses:
- the fair value of the collateral held (financial and non-financial assets);
- the fair value of such collateral sold or repledged, and whether the entity has an obligation to return it; and
- any terms and conditions associated with its use of this collateral. [*IFRS 7.15*]

7I.8.170   *Allowance account for credit losses*

7I.8.170.10   If an entity recognises an impairment of financial assets resulting from credit losses in a separate account, then it discloses a reconciliation of changes in that account during the period for each class of financial asset. In the rare circumstances that an entity does not use such an account, then there is no requirement to produce equivalent information. [*IFRS 7.16, BC27*]

7I.8.170.20   In our view, it is not appropriate to set up an impairment allowance account on the initial recognition of a financial asset. Financial instruments are measured on initial recognition at fair value, plus transaction costs if appropriate. The impairment of a financial asset is recognised only if there is objective evidence of impairment as a result of events that occur after the initial recognition of an asset (see 7I.6.410.10 and 420). In addition, IFRS 3 provides specific guidance related to business combinations. Under this guidance, the acquirer in a business combination does not recognise a separate valuation allowance as at the date of acquisition for assets acquired in a business combination that are measured at their acquisition date fair values; this is because the uncertainty about future cash flows is included in the fair value measurement (see 2.6.610.10). [*IFRS 3.B41, IAS 39.43*]

7I.8.180   *Compound financial instruments with multiple embedded derivatives*

7I.8.180.10   An entity may issue a compound financial instrument that contains multiple embedded derivative features whose values are interdependent. In this case, it discloses the existence of these features. For example, a callable convertible debt instrument has more than one embedded derivative feature; the value of the call option depends on both interest rates and equity prices. The interdependency between interest rates and equity prices is disclosed. [*IFRS 7.17, BC29–BC31*]

7I.8.190   *Defaults and breaches*

7I.8.190.10   If the entity has defaulted during the period on the principal, interest, sinking fund or redemption provisions of a loan payable – i.e. a financial liability, other than a short-term trade payable on normal credit terms – recognised in the statement of financial position, then it discloses:

- details of the default or breach;
- the amount recognised at the reporting date in respect of the loan payable on which the default or breach occurred; and
- with respect to the above amounts, whether the default or breach was remedied or the terms of the loan payable renegotiated before the financial statements were authorised for issue. [*IFRS 7.18*]

7I.8.190.20   An entity also discloses the items listed in 7I.8.190.10 if during the period there were other breaches of loan agreement terms, and those breaches were not remedied or the terms were not renegotiated before the reporting date such that the lender could demand accelerated repayment. [*IFRS 7.19*]

7I.8.200   *Embedded derivatives*

7I.8.200.10   There is no specific guidance on the presentation of embedded derivatives and the related host contracts (see 7I.2.390.10). [*IAS 39.11*]

7I.8.200.20   In our view, when an embedded derivative is not required to be accounted for separately (see 7I.2.110), it should be presented in the same line item as the host contract.

7I.8.200.30   When an embedded derivative is accounted for separately, an issue arises about whether it should be:

- included in the same line item as the host contract, on the basis that the two instruments are subject to the same contract; or
- presented separately, together with other derivative instruments.

7I.8.200.40   IFRS does not address whether an embedded derivative should be presented separately in the statement of financial position. Therefore, the general presentation rules in IAS 1 and IAS 32 apply (see chapter 3.1). In our view, if the host contract is a financial instrument and the offsetting criteria are met for the host and the embedded derivative, then a separable embedded derivative and the host contract should be presented on a net basis (see 7I.8.90). [*IAS 39.11*]

7I.8.205   *Reverse factoring arrangements*

7I.8.205.10   In addition to appropriate presentation and disaggregation of relevant balances, an entity that is the customer in a reverse factoring arrangement (see 7I.8.45) is required to disclose information about those arrangements that is relevant to an understanding of its financial position and performance. This disclosure might include an explanation of the nature of the arrangements and how they are reflected in the financial statements. Relevant IFRS disclosure requirements include:

- disclosure of significant accounting policies; and

- disclosure of significant judgements that management has made in the process of applying the accounting policies and that have the most significant effect on the amounts recognised in the financial statements. [*IAS 1.117–122*]

7I.8.205.20   For a further discussion of reverse factoring, see 2.3.75, 7I.5.425, 7I.8.45 and 375.

7I.8.210   Statement of profit or loss and OCI

7I.8.220   *Items of income, expense, gains or losses*

7I.8.220.10   Net gains or losses on the following are disclosed either in the statement of profit or loss and OCI or in the notes to the financial statements:
- financial assets or financial liabilities measured at FVTPL, separately for:
  - those that are designated as such on initial recognition; and
  - those classified as held-for-trading;
- available-for-sale financial assets, showing separately:
  - the amount of gain or loss recognised in OCI during the period; and
  - the amount reclassified from equity to profit or loss for the period;
- held-to-maturity investments;
- loans and receivables; and
- financial liabilities measured at amortised cost. [*IFRS 7.20(a)*]

7I.8.220.20   An entity discloses within its accounting policies whether it has separated interest income and expense on items measured at FVTPL (see 7I.8.70.40). [*IFRS 7.B5(e)*]

7I.8.220.30   Total interest income and total interest expense for financial assets or financial liabilities that are not at FVTPL (calculated under the effective interest method) are disclosed either in the statement of profit or loss and OCI or in the notes. Total interest expense disclosed forms part of finance costs, which are required by paragraph 82(b) of IAS 1 to be presented separately in the statement of profit or loss and OCI (see 7I.8.80). [*IFRS 7.20(b), IG13*]

7I.8.220.40   If interest income or expense includes both amounts from instruments at FVTPL and amounts from instruments not at FVTPL, then an entity is required to disclose total interest income and total interest expense for financial assets and financial liabilities that are not at FVTPL. [*IFRS 7.20(b)*]

7I.8.225   *Split presentation of gains and losses on derivatives*

7I.8.225.10   There are no specific requirements in IFRS addressing the presentation of gains and losses on derivatives. However, in our view it would be inappropriate to separate and present gains and losses on derivatives using a method different from one of those described in 7I.8.225.20–50.

7I.8.225.20   If an entity designates derivatives as hedging instruments for accounting purposes, or applies the fair value option to an economically hedged non-derivative as an alternative to hedge accounting (see 7I.4.40), then in our view gains or losses on both the non-derivative, being the item that is economically hedged or subject to hedge accounting, and the derivative may be split for presentation purposes in order to reflect best the impact on profit or loss of the economics of the relationship. For example, if a bank applies the fair value option to a portfolio of fixed rate loans that are hedged economically using a portfolio of interest rate swaps, then we believe that it is appropriate to separate accrued interest, measured on an effective interest basis, from other fair value changes on both the loans and the swaps and to present the accrued amounts in interest income.

7I.8.225.30   Gains and losses on derivatives designated in a hedging relationship as hedging instruments have three possible elements:
1. the effective portion;
2. the ineffective portion; and
3. the portion excluded from the assessment of effectiveness.

7I.8.225.40   There are several options to consider when presenting such gains and losses. The following options relate to a fair value hedge.
*   Present the entire change in fair value of the derivative hedging instrument in the same line item(s) as gains and losses from the hedged item.
*   Present the effective and ineffective portions of the derivative hedging instrument in the same line item(s) as gains and losses from the hedged item. Present the portion excluded from the assessment of hedge effectiveness in the same line item(s) as gains or losses on non-hedging derivative instruments.
*   Present only the effective portion of the derivative hedging instrument in the same line item(s) as gains and losses from the hedged item. Present the ineffective portion and the excluded portion in the same line item(s) as gains or losses on non-hedging derivative instruments.

7I.8.225.50   Of the options noted in 7I.8.225.40, we prefer the third method. This is because only the effective portion of the hedging derivative matches the opposite gains or losses on the hedged item.

7I.8.225.60   The same options exist for a cash flow hedge. However, the timing of recognition in profit or loss of the effective portion of the hedging instrument would be different.

7I.8.225.70   In our view, the options for the presentation in the statement of profit or loss and OCI also apply to the presentation in the statement of cash flows (see 2.3.60).

7I.8.230   *Fee income and expense*

7I.8.230.10   An entity discloses fee income and expense arising from financial assets and financial liabilities that are not measured at FVTPL, and from trust or other fiduciary activities. The amounts disclosed exclude amounts included in calculating the effective interest rate. [*IFRS 7.20(c)*]

7I.8.240   *Interest income*

7I.8.240.10   An entity discloses interest income on impaired financial assets. In our view, when impairment testing is carried out on a portfolio basis (see 7I.6.460) and the portfolio is found to be impaired, the interest income disclosure should be consistent with the portfolio approach used for impairment testing. [*IFRS 7.20(d)*]

7I.8.240.20   For each class of financial asset, the amount of any impairment loss is disclosed. In addition, IFRS 15 requires an entity to disclose, separately from other impairment losses, impairment losses recognised on trade receivables or contract assets arising from the entity's contracts with customers. [*IFRS 7.20(e), 15.113(b), C9*]

7I.8.250 Other disclosures

7I.8.260 *Accounting policies*

7I.8.260.10 The summary of accounting policies includes disclosure of the measurement basis (or bases) used in preparing the financial statements. An entity also discloses any other accounting policies that are relevant to understanding the financial statements. As an example, the disclosure may include:

- the nature of financial assets and financial liabilities designated as at FVTPL;
- the criteria for designating financial assets and financial liabilities as at FVTPL;
- how the entity satisfied the criteria for designating financial assets and financial liabilities as at FVTPL (see 7I.4.40 and 7I.2.160);
- the criteria for designating financial assets as available-for-sale;
- whether regular-way transactions are accounted for using trade or settlement date accounting (see 7I.2.70);
- when an impairment allowance account for credit losses is used, the criteria for determining when this account is used in place of directly reducing the carrying amount of the impaired asset;
- when an impairment allowance account for credit losses is used, the criteria for writing off amounts charged to the allowance account against the carrying amount of the impaired financial asset;
- for each category of financial instruments, how the net gains and losses are determined – e.g. for items measured at FVTPL whether the entity includes interest or dividend income;
- the criteria for determining that there is objective evidence that an impairment loss has occurred; and
- when terms of the financial assets that otherwise would be past due or impaired have been renegotiated, the accounting policies for financial assets that are subject to the renegotiated terms. [*IFRS 7.21, B5, IAS 1.117*]

7I.8.270 *Hedge accounting*

7I.8.270.10 An entity is required to make specific disclosures about its outstanding hedge accounting relationships. The following disclosures are made separately for fair value hedges, cash flow hedges and hedges of net investments in foreign operations:

- a description of each type of hedge;
- a description of the financial instruments designated as hedging instruments for the hedge and their fair values at the reporting date;
- the nature of the risks being hedged;
- gains or losses on the hedging instrument and the hedged item attributable to the hedged risk in a fair value hedge;
- ineffectiveness recognised in profit or loss arising from cash flow hedges; and
- ineffectiveness recognised in profit or loss arising from hedges of net investments in foreign operations. [*IFRS 7.22, 24*]

7I.8.270.20 In addition, for a cash flow hedge the entity discloses:

- the periods in which the transactions are expected to occur, and when they are expected to affect profit or loss;

- a description of any forecast transactions that were hedged, but are no longer expected to occur;
- the amount recognised in OCI during the period;
- the amount reclassified from equity to profit or loss during the period, showing the amount included in each line item in the statement of profit or loss and OCI; and
- the amount removed from equity and added to the initial measurement of a non-financial asset or non-financial liability during the period. [*IFRS 7.23*]

7I.8.270.30   For a discussion on presenting gains and losses on derivatives designated in a hedging relationship, see 7I.8.225.

7I.8.270.40   In our view, when hedge accounting is not applied, either because an entity chooses not to apply hedge accounting or because the criteria for hedge accounting are not met, information should be provided to explain the relationship between the derivatives and the transactions for which there are economic hedges. We believe that this should be done to enable users of the financial statements to understand the extent to which risk is mitigated through the use of the derivatives.

7I.8.280   *Fair value#*

7I.8.280.10   For each class of financial assets and financial liabilities, an entity discloses the fair value in a manner that allows users of financial statements to compare it with its carrying amount. However, this disclosure is not required:
- if the carrying amount is a reasonable approximation of fair value;
- for an investment in equity instruments that do not have a quoted market price in an active market – and for derivatives linked to such equity instruments – that are measured at cost because fair value cannot be determined reliably; and
- for a contract containing a discretionary participation feature when the fair value of the feature cannot be measured reliably. [*IFRS 7.25, 29*]

7I.8.280.20   The carrying amounts of short-term receivables and payables are likely to approximate their fair values in a low-interest rate environment in which the effect of discounting is not material. In such cases, it is not necessary to disclose these instruments' fair values. However, the fair values of long-term liabilities and receivables carried at amortised cost are disclosed because the effect of discounting is expected to be material. [*IFRS 7.29(a), 13.BC138A*]

7I.8.280.30   As described in 7I.6.210.20, IAS 39 presumes that a reliable fair value can be determined for almost all financial instruments. The only exceptions to this are:
- certain unquoted equity instruments or derivatives linked to and to be settled by delivery of such equity instruments; and
- contracts containing discretionary participation features for which a reliable fair value cannot be obtained. [*IAS 39.46, AG81*]

7I.8.280.40   If any of the instruments described in 7I.8.280.30 are not stated at fair value, then the entity discloses:
- the fact that the fair value of these instruments cannot be measured reliably;
- a description of the financial instruments;
- the carrying amount;

- an explanation of why fair value cannot be measured reliably;
- information about the market for the instruments;
- information about whether and how the entity intends to dispose of the instruments; and
- if an instrument is derecognised:
  - the fact that the fair value could not be measured reliably;
  - the carrying amount at the time of derecognition; and
  - the amount of the gain or loss recognised. [*IFRS 7.29–30*]

7I.8.280.50   An entity, such as a mutual fund or a co-operative, whose share capital is classified as financial liabilities may present its share capital as net assets attributable to shareholders in its statement of financial position. If the carrying amounts of the issued shares classified as financial liabilities are not a reasonable approximation of their fair values, then in our view the entity should disclose the fair values of the shares even if this presentation option is elected (see 7I.3.50.50 and 2.4.980.20–30). [*IFRS 7.25, 29, IAS 32.IE32*]

7I.8.280.60   The fair value disclosures are based on financial asset and financial liability classes. They are offset only to the extent that their carrying amounts are offset in the statement of financial position (see 7I.8.90). [*IFRS 7.26*]

7I.8.280.70   IFRS 13 provides guidance on fair value measurement and the related disclosure requirements, which are the subject of chapter 2.4 (see 2.4.490).

7I.8.285   **FORTHCOMING REQUIREMENTS**

7I.8.285.10   IFRS 16 introduces an exception from disclosure of fair value for lease liabilities. [*IFRS 7.29(d)*]

7I.8.290   *Day one gain or loss*

7I.8.290.10   In some cases, the fair value of a financial asset or a financial liability on initial recognition may differ from the transaction price. If an entity does not recognise a gain or loss on initial recognition because fair value is neither evidenced by a quoted price in an active market for an identical asset or liability nor based on a valuation technique that uses only data from observable markets, then it discloses the following for each class of financial asset and financial liability:

- the accounting policy for subsequently recognising the difference in profit or loss;
- the aggregate difference yet to be recognised in profit or loss at the beginning and end of the period, and a reconciliation of changes in this difference during the period; and
- the reason why the transaction price is not the best evidence of the fair value, including a description of the evidence that supports the fair value (see 7I.6.25.50). [*IFRS 7.28*]

7I.8.300   **NATURE AND EXTENT OF RISKS ARISING FROM FINANCIAL INSTRUMENTS**

7I.8.300.10   The general disclosure principle in IFRS 7 requires an entity to make qualitative and quantitative disclosures that enable users of its financial statements to evaluate the nature and the extent of risks arising from financial instruments to which the entity is exposed at the reporting date, and how the entity has managed them. The extent of disclosure depends on the extent of the entity's exposure to risks arising from financial instruments. The types of risks covered by the disclosures include, but are not limited to, credit risk, liquidity risk and market risk. [*IFRS 7.31*]

7I.8.300.20   The disclosures are included either in the financial statements or in another statement, such as a management commentary or risk report. The location of the disclosures may be limited by local laws. If the disclosures are made outside the financial statements, then the financial statements are cross-referenced to this information (see 5.8.10.90). The disclosures are made available to users on the same terms and timing as the financial statements. [*IFRS 7.B6*]

7I.8.300.30   IFRS 7 addresses risks arising from financial instruments and contracts to buy or sell a non-financial item that are in the scope of IAS 39. Consequently, the following are excluded from the scope of IFRS 7, even though they may give rise to financial risk for the entity:

- exposures from commodity contracts that meet the own-use exemption (see 7I.1.150.20);
- purchase and sale contracts for non-financial items that are to be settled in a foreign currency unless they are scoped into IAS 39; and
- highly probable forecast transactions (see 7I.7.230). [*IFRS 7.5, 31*]

7I.8.300.40   An entity may manage its financial risk based on its total exposure – i.e. including risk arising from those items not included in the scope of IFRS 7 – and these exposures may be included in reports to key management personnel. In this case, in our view IFRS 7 does not prohibit an entity from providing additional disclosures about its total financial risk exposure rather than just the risk arising from financial instruments. However, we believe that all such additional disclosures should be clearly separated from those required by IFRS 7.

7I.8.310   Qualitative disclosures

7I.8.310.10   An entity discloses the following, for each type of risk arising from financial instruments:

- the exposure to the risk and how it arises;
- the entity's objectives, policies and processes for managing the risk; and
- the methods used to measure the risk. [*IFRS 7.33(a)–(b)*]

7I.8.310.20   If there are any changes to the factors described in 7I.8.310.10 from the previous period, then an entity discloses the reason for the changes. The changes may result from changes in exposures themselves, or the way in which the entity manages them. [*IFRS 7.33(c)*]

7I.8.320   Quantitative disclosures

7I.8.320.10   An entity discloses summary quantitative data about its exposure to each risk arising from its financial instruments at the reporting date. The disclosure is based on information that is provided internally to key management personnel of the entity – e.g. the board of directors or the CEO. If an entity uses several methods to manage risk, then it bases the disclosure on the method that provides the most relevant and reliable information. The quantitative disclosures described in 7I.8.330–390 are required, if they are not already provided as part of the summary quantitative data based on information that is provided internally to key management personnel. [*IFRS 7.34*]

71.8.320.20   The quantitative data disclosed at the reporting date may not be representative of the risk exposure over the course of the reporting period. In this case, the entity provides additional disclosure that is representative. [*IFRS 7.35*]

71.8.330   *Concentrations of risk*

71.8.330.10   An entity discloses concentrations of risk. [*IFRS 7.34(c)*]

71.8.330.20   Concentrations of risk arise from financial instruments that:
● have similar characteristics; and
● are affected in a similar manner when there are changes in economic or other conditions. [*IFRS 7.B8*]

71.8.330.30   Identifying concentrations of risk is a matter of judgement and therefore an entity discloses:
● a description of how management determines concentrations;
● a description of the shared characteristics that identify each concentration – e.g. counterparty, geographic area, currency or market; and
● the amount of the risk exposure associated with financial instruments sharing that characteristic. [*IFRS 7.B8*]

71.8.340   *Credit risk*

71.8.340.10   'Credit risk' is the risk that one party to a financial instrument will cause a financial loss for the other party by failing to discharge an obligation. In our view, the credit risk disclosures are not required for investments in equity instruments, because these do not impose an obligation on the issuer to make any payments to the holder and, consequently, the holder is not exposed to the risk of the issuer failing to discharge an obligation. [*IFRS 7.A*]

71.8.340.20   An entity discloses, by class of financial instrument, the amount that best represents the entity's maximum exposure to credit risk, unless this exposure is best represented by the carrying amount. The amount does not take into account any collateral held or other credit enhancements, unless the IAS 32 offsetting criteria are met. For example, the amount for a financial asset would typically be the gross carrying amount less any required offset (in accordance with IAS 32) and any impairment losses recognised. This disclosure is not required for financial instruments whose carrying amount best represents the maximum exposure to credit risk. [*IFRS 7.36(a), B9, B10(c)*]

71.8.340.30   An entity discloses information about the credit quality of financial assets (by class) that are neither past due nor impaired. [*IFRS 7.36(c)*]

71.8.350   *Collateral and other credit enhancements held*

71.8.350.10   The entity discloses a description of any collateral held as security and other credit enhancements and their financial effect in respect of the amount that best represents the maximum exposure to credit risk. [*IFRS 7.36(b)*]

71.8.350.20   IFRS 7 does not specify how an entity should apply the term 'financial effect' in practice. Providing quantitative disclosure of the financial effect of collateral may be appropriate in some cases.

However, in other cases it may be impractical to obtain quantitative information; or, if it is available, the information may not be determined to be relevant, meaningful or reliable.

7I.8.350.30   If quantitative disclosure is deemed appropriate, some possible quantitative approaches may include a quantification of:

- the current value of collateral – e.g. fair value or net realisable value of collateral or other credit enhancements – for each class of assets adjusted for the effect of over-collateralisation; or
- the effect that collateral or other credit enhancements have on the entity's impairment losses – i.e. an estimate of the difference between the entity's actual impairment losses and what they might have been without the collateral or other credit enhancements.

7I.8.350.40   As part of its determination of whether quantitative disclosure of the current value of collateral is appropriate, an entity may, for example, consider whether:

- the collateral is specifically identifiable and therefore measurable – e.g. a fixed charge over specified assets vs a floating charge that has not yet attached to any specific assets; and
- the entity is able to access the collateral at its full value and is not restricted by a higher-ranking or pari passu charge of another creditor.

EXAMPLE 5A – APPROPRIATENESS OF QUANTITATIVE DISCLOSURE OF FINANCIAL EFFECT OF COLLATERAL (1)

7I.8.350.50   Bank X holds a portfolio of loans secured on residential properties. The security is in the form of the first charge over each property. Historically, in the event of default X has enforced this type of collateral and was able to dispose of it in an established market. X updates the value of the collateral regularly and monitors internally for risk management purposes the loan to value ratios. Therefore, X determines that disclosure of the current value of the collateral is appropriate and provides relevant information on the extent to which the collateral mitigates the credit risk on its portfolio of loans.

EXAMPLE 5B – APPROPRIATENESS OF QUANTITATIVE DISCLOSURE OF FINANCIAL EFFECT OF COLLATERAL (2)

7I.8.350.60   Company Y holds a portfolio of second-lien residential mortgage loans. In this case, disclosing the fair value of the collateral held may be inappropriate if historically, in the case of default, its right to collateral has been worthless. Therefore, it may be more appropriate for Y to disclose the fact that its right to collateral may be worthless in default and that the fair value of the collateral may be irrelevant in those circumstances.

7I.8.350.70   If quantitative disclosure of the financial effect of certain types of collateral or other credit enhancements is not considered appropriate, then an entity would still be required to disclose sufficient qualitative information for a financial statement user to understand:

- how the entity considers and incorporates collateral or other credit enhancements into its credit risk management; and
- how such incorporation of collateral or other credit enhancements in its credit risk management relates to its quantitative disclosures of its maximum exposure to credit risk, possibly including its effect in relation to disclosures of credit quality. [*IFRS 7.32A, 33(b), 36(b)*]

7I.8.350.80   An entity may obtain financial or non-financial assets under collateral and credit enhancement arrangements. If those assets meet the recognition criteria in IFRS, then it discloses the nature and the carrying amount of the assets held. In addition, when such assets are not readily convertible into cash, the entity discloses its policies for using the assets in its operations or disposing of them. These requirements apply only to assets held at the reporting date. [*IFRS 7.38*]

7I.8.360   *Financial assets either past due or impaired*

7I.8.360.10   For each class of financial asset, an entity discloses an ageing analysis of financial assets that are past due but not impaired as at the reporting date. [*IFRS 7.37(a)*]

7I.8.360.20   An entity discloses an analysis of:
- financial assets that are individually determined to be impaired as at the reporting date; and
- the factors considered by the entity in determining that the financial asset was impaired. [*IFRS 7.37(b)*]

7I.8.365   *Forbearance*

7I.8.365.10   IFRS does not contain specific disclosure requirements relating to forbearance activities (see 7I.5.95.10). However, an entity is required to disclose significant measurement bases related to impairment, including the criteria that it uses for identifying objective evidence of impairment and its accounting policy for financial assets that are subject to renegotiated terms if the financial asset would have been otherwise past due or impaired. Furthermore, an entity discloses the assumptions made about the future and other sources of estimation uncertainty that have a significant risk of a material adjustment to the carrying amounts of assets and liabilities. For example, loans subject to forbearance may be subject to management processes separate from other credit exposures, may have different risk characteristics and may be subject to different inputs and assumptions in impairment loss calculations. [*IAS 1.125, IFRS 7.21, B5(g)*]

7I.8.365.15   To meet the disclosure objectives in IFRS 7 (see 7I.8.10.10), an entity determines the level of detail and aggregation of information (see 7I.8.50.40) for disclosures in respect of forborne loans based on the level of forbearance activities, potential exposure to losses related to these activities and their impact on the entity's performance. [*IFRS 7.6, B3*]

7I.8.365.20   Qualitative disclosures in respect of the nature and extent of forbearance practices may include narrative information about:
- types of forbearance activities and programmes, and of the exposures subject to them;
- objectives, policies and processes for managing risk and the methods used to measure risk; and
- changes from the previous period. [*IFRS 7.33*]

7I.8.365.30   Quantitative disclosures in respect of forbearance practices may include:

- carrying amounts of assets subject to forbearance – analysed, for example, by type of forbearance measure or business or geographic area, as appropriate;
- forbearance activities during the period, including a reconciliation of opening and closing balances;
- related impairment allowances;
- newly recognised assets (see 7I.5.95.20);
- interest income; and
- analysis of credit quality. [*IFRS 7.16, 20, 34(a), 36(c)*]

7I.8.370   ## *Liquidity risk*

7I.8.370.10   'Liquidity risk' is the risk that an entity will encounter difficulty in meeting the obligations associated with its financial liabilities that are settled by delivering cash or another financial asset. [*IFRS 7.A*]

7I.8.370.20   An entity discloses a maturity analysis for:
- non-derivative financial liabilities, including issued financial guarantee contracts that shows their remaining contractual maturities; and
- derivative financial liabilities, including the remaining contractual maturities for those derivative financial liabilities for which contractual maturities are essential for an understanding of the timing of the cash flows – e.g. loan commitments and interest rate swaps designated in a cash flow hedging relationship. [*IFRS 7.39(a)–(b), B11B*]

7I.8.370.30   In our view, the maturity analysis should include *all* derivative financial liabilities, but contractual maturities only are required for those essential for an understanding of the timing of the cash flows.

7I.8.370.40   In determining what is essential for an understanding of the cash flows, we believe that an entity should apply judgement over what is appropriate based on management's liquidity risk management strategy and the facts and circumstances. For example, most non-trading derivatives that are held for risk management purposes might be expected to be held to maturity. Also, most hedging strategies will not involve closing out a derivative before maturity. However, some 'trading' derivatives – e.g. interest rate swaps that a bank executes with corporate counterparties – might be expected to be held until maturity, and some hedging strategies may involve closing out a derivative before maturity.

7I.8.370.50   An entity explains how it manages the liquidity risk inherent in the maturity analyses described in 7I.8.370.20. This includes a maturity analysis for financial assets it holds as part of managing liquidity risk – e.g. financial assets that are expected to generate cash inflows to meet cash outflows on financial liabilities – if this information is necessary to enable financial statement users to evaluate the nature and extent of liquidity risk. In addition, disclosure of financial assets pledged as collateral – e.g. cash collateral and securities under repurchase transactions – may be considered necessary in this context if this information is provided internally to key management personnel. [*IFRS 7.39(c), B11E*]

7I.8.370.60   In disclosing the maturity analyses described in 7I.8.370.20, an entity does not separate an embedded derivative from a hybrid (combined) financial instrument. For such an instrument, the entity applies the disclosure requirements for non-derivative financial liabilities – i.e. it discloses the remaining contractual maturities. [*IFRS 7.B11A*]

7I.8.370.70   IFRS 7 does not define contractual maturities. Therefore, it leaves open to interpretation the amounts that need to be included in the maturity analysis for certain types of financial liabilities, such as derivatives and perpetual instruments. In our view, both the interest and principal cash flows should be included in the analysis because this best represents the liquidity risk being faced by the entity. The principal amount of a perpetual instrument represents the present value of the payments of the interest stream. As a minimum, for such an instrument, the principal amount should be disclosed and sufficient appropriate narrative disclosures should be provided, to present a meaningful picture of the entity's liquidity exposures.

7I.8.370.80   IFRS 7 does not mandate the number of time bands to be used in the analysis. Rather, it requires the entity to use its judgement to determine an appropriate number of time bands. [*IFRS 7.B11*]

7I.8.370.90   When the creditor can choose when an amount is paid, the liability is included in the time band that represents the earliest date on which the entity could be required to pay. This disclosure shows the worst case scenario from the perspective of the entity. For example, a demand deposit would be included in the earliest time band. [*IFRS 7.B11C(a), BC57*]

7I.8.370.100   The amounts disclosed are the contractual undiscounted cash flows. In our view, the amounts disclosed should generally be gross unless the liabilities will be settled net. These amounts will differ from the amounts included in the statement of financial position, because those amounts are based on discounted cash flows. [*IFRS 7.B11D*]

7I.8.370.110   When the amount payable is not fixed, the amount to be disclosed is determined with reference to conditions existing at the reporting date. For example, for a floating rate bond with interest payments indexed to three-month Euribor, in our view the amount to be disclosed should be based on forward rates rather than spot rates prevailing at the reporting date because the spot interest rates do not represent the level of the index based on which the cash flows will be payable. The forward interest rates better describe the level of the index in accordance with the conditions existing at the reporting date. [*IFRS 7.B11D*]

7I.8.370.120   When an issued guarantee meets the definition of a financial guarantee contract under IAS 39 (see 7I.1.50), the maximum amount of the guarantee is disclosed in the earliest period in which the guarantee could be called. [*IFRS 7.B11C(c)*]

7I.8.370.130   In disclosing summary quantitative data about exposure to liquidity risk on the basis of information provided internally to key management, an entity explains how this data is determined. If the outflows included in the data could occur either significantly earlier or at significantly different amounts, then the entity discloses that fact and provides further quantitative information to enable users to evaluate the extent of this risk, unless this information is included in the contractual maturity analysis required by IFRS 7. The amounts disclosed need to be explained so that it is clear whether they are compiled on a contractual or another basis. [*IFRS 7.34(a), B10A*]

7I.8.370.140   An entity may have liabilities that are subject to accelerated repayment before their stated maturities in certain circumstances. For example, a term loan may become repayable on demand if the entity fails to comply with covenants on its financial condition or performance, or if its credit rating is downgraded. Depending on the circumstances, information about such terms and their effect may be necessary to allow users to evaluate the nature and extent of liquidity risk. Additional disclosure may be appropriate – e.g. on concentrations of liquidity risk arising from such terms or how the entity manages the associated liquidity risk. [*IFRS 7.31, 34(c), B10A, B11F(f)*]

7I.8.375 *Reverse factoring arrangements*

7I.8.375.10   Reverse factoring arrangements (see 7I.8.45) may impact the customer's exposure to – and be part of its management of – liquidity risk from financial instruments. An entity that is the customer in a reverse factoring arrangement is required to disclose information that enables users of financial statements to evaluate the nature and extent of these risks. The disclosure requirements that may be particularly relevant to such arrangements include:

- qualitative disclosures about the entity's exposure to liquidity risk:
  - the exposure to risk and how it arises;
  - the entity's objectives, policies and processes for managing the risk and the method used to measure the risk; and
  - any changes in the above from the previous period; and
- quantitative information relating to liquidity risk, including concentrations of it. [*IFRS 7.31, 33–34*]

7I.8.375.20   For a further discussion of reverse factoring, see 2.3.75, 7I.5.425, 7I.8.45 and 205.

7I.8.380   *Market risk*

7I.8.380.10   'Market risk' is the risk that the fair value or future cash flows of a financial instrument will fluctuate because of changes in market prices. Market risk comprises three types of risk: currency risk, interest rate risk and other price risk. [*IFRS 7.A, IG32*]

7I.8.380.20   An entity presents a sensitivity analysis for each type of market risk that it is exposed to as at the reporting date, including the methods and assumptions used in preparing the analysis. If the methods and assumptions change from one period to another, then the entity discloses such changes together with the reasons for them. [*IFRS 7.40*]

7I.8.380.30   An entity may hold an investment in an equity instrument quoted in a foreign currency. In our view, the entity is not required to split the currency risk from other price risk for an equity instrument. However, for a debt instrument, as a minimum, the split between currency risk and interest rate risk is presented. [*IFRS 7.B23*]

7I.8.380.40   The sensitivity analysis reflects the impact, on profit or loss and equity, of changes in the relevant risk variables that are reasonably possible at the reporting date. The 'reasonably possible' change does not include remote or worst case scenarios or stress tests. The sensitivity calculation assumes that the reasonably possible change had occurred at the reporting date and had been applied to the risk exposures at that date. For example, if an entity has a floating rate liability at the reporting date, then it would disclose the effect on profit or loss (e.g. interest expense) for the current year if interest rates had varied by reasonably possible amounts. [*IFRS 7.40(a), B18–B19*]

7I.8.380.50   The sensitivity analysis described in 7I.8.380.20 is not required if the entity already prepares an analysis that reflects interdependencies between risk variables – e.g. a value at risk (VAR) approach – and uses it to manage its financial risk. If the entity uses this analysis to fulfil its disclosure requirements, then it explains the method used in preparing the analysis. This includes the main parameters and assumptions underlying the data. Furthermore, the entity explains the objective of the method used and any limitations that may result in the method not fully capturing the risk exposure arising from the underlying assets and liabilities. If the entity applies VAR to only a part of its financial instruments portfolio, then it provides a separate sensitivity analysis described in 7I.8.380.20 for those financial instruments not included in the VAR analysis. [*IFRS 7.41, B20*]

7I.8.380.60   In our view, the sensitivity analysis should include financial assets and financial liabilities measured at amortised cost as well as those financial instruments measured at fair value.

7I.8.380.70   An entity provides a sensitivity analysis for the whole of its business – e.g. in the case of a bank, this will include both its trading and its non-trading books. The entity may also provide different types of analysis for different classes of financial instruments. [*IFRS 7.B21*]

7I.8.380.80   In our view, 'translation risk', arising from translating the financial statements of a foreign operation into the presentation currency of the group, does not meet the definition of currency risk as defined in IFRS 7. Consequently, in our view translation risk should not be included in the sensitivity analysis on a consolidated basis. In our view, in consolidated financial statements the sensitivity analysis should address each currency to which an entity in the group has significant exposure based on each entity's functional currency.

7I.8.380.90   When the functional currency of an entity is different from that of its foreign operation, the resulting economic exposure can usually be hedged (see 7I.7.740). Therefore, in our view an entity may include net investments in foreign operations in the sensitivity analysis in consolidated financial statements if, and only if, that net investment has been hedged, and only to the extent that it has been hedged.

7I.8.390   *Other market risk disclosures*

7I.8.390.10   If an entity believes that the sensitivity analysis is not representative of a risk inherent in a financial instrument, then it discloses this fact and the reason why it believes that the sensitivity analysis is unrepresentative. This may be the case, for example, when the year-end risk exposure is not representative of the risk exposure during the year. [*IFRS 7.42*]

7I.8.390.20   Financial instruments that are classified as equity of the entity do not impact profit or loss or equity, because they are not remeasured. Therefore, no sensitivity analysis is required. [*IFRS 7.B28*]

7I.8.395   *Application by investment entities*

7I.8.395.10   Investment entities are required to measure certain subsidiaries at FVTPL, rather than consolidating them (see chapter 5.6). This includes circumstances in which an investment entity is required to measure at fair value its investments in a subsidiary that is itself an investment entity (see 5.6.200). An investment in a subsidiary that is measured at fair value is in the scope of IFRS 7 and may represent a significant concentration of risk. Furthermore, the parent may be directly or indirectly exposed to risks arising from the subsidiary's financial instruments; also, key management of the parent and the subsidiary may be the same persons and use the same information for managing the risks of both entities. An investment entity parent considers what information should be disclosed to comply with the disclosure objective of IFRS 7. Depending on the facts and circumstances, the risk disclosures of the investment entity parent may include information about risks arising from financial instruments held by an investment entity subsidiary and be based on corresponding disclosures of the investment entity subsidiary – for example:

- analysis of credit quality;
- concentration of risk;
- summarised interest rate gap analysis; and
- foreign currency risk. [*IFRS 7.3(a), 10.31*]

EXAMPLE 6 – RISK DISCLOSURES OF THE FEEDER FUND

7I.8.395.20   Feeder Fund F, an open-ended investment fund, invests substantially all of its assets in Master fund M, another open-ended investment fund and which has the same investment objectives as F. As at 31 December 2018, F owns 100% of M (2017: 100%).

7I.8.395.30   M is primarily involved in investing in a highly diversified portfolio of equity securities issued by companies listed on major stock exchanges, unlisted companies, unlisted investment funds, investment-grade debt securities and derivatives, with the objective of providing investors in F with above-average returns over the medium to long term.

7I.8.395.40   F is managed together with M as an integrated structure. Managing the funds together also helps to ensure that cash flows from the underlying assets of M match the redemption obligations of M – and ultimately of F. The pricing of the shares in M held by F is based on M's net asset value.

7I.8.395.50   F's management decides that the objectives of IFRS 7 are met by providing disclosures on:
- the amount and terms of its investment in – and the nature of its relationship with – M;
- credit risk, interest rate risk, currency risk and other price risk of the underlying investments held by M; and
- the liquidity risk of both M and F.

7I.8.400   TRANSFERS OF FINANCIAL ASSETS

7I.8.400.10   An entity discloses information on:
- transferred financial assets that are not derecognised in their entirety; and
- transferred financial assets that are derecognised in their entirety, in which the entity retains continuing involvement. [*IFRS 7.42A*]

7I.8.410   Disclosures for transfers of financial assets

7I.8.410.10   The following disclosures are required for each class of transferred assets that are not derecognised in their entirety:

- the nature of the transferred assets;
- the nature of the risks and rewards associated with those assets to which the entity is exposed; and
- the nature of the relationship between the transferred assets and the associated liabilities and the restrictions on the entity's use of those assets. [*IFRS 7.42D(a)–(c)*]

7I.8.410.20   The following additional disclosures are required for each class of transferred assets that are not derecognised in their entirety in specific circumstances:
- when the counterparty to the associated liabilities has recourse only to the transferred assets:
  - the fair value of the transferred assets;
  - the fair value of the associated liabilities; and
  - the net position – i.e. the difference between the fair value of the transferred assets and the associated liabilities;
- when the entity continues to recognise all of the transferred assets, the carrying amounts of the transferred assets and associated liabilities; and
- when the entity continues to recognise the assets to the extent of its continuing involvement:
  - the total carrying amount of the original assets before the transfer;
  - the carrying amount of the assets that the entity continues to recognise; and
  - the carrying amount of associated liabilities. [*IFRS 7.42D(d)–(f)*]

7I.8.410.30   The following disclosures are required for each type of continuing involvement in transferred assets that are derecognised in their entirety:
- the carrying amounts and fair values of the assets and liabilities representing the entity's continuing involvement;
- the entity's maximum exposure to loss from its continuing involvement;
- a maturity analysis of the undiscounted cash flows that may be payable to the transferee in respect of those assets;
- the gain or loss on transfer and income and expense arising from the entity's continuing involvement; and
- qualitative disclosures to explain and support the quantitative disclosures. [*IFRS 7.42E, 42G(a)–(b)*]

7I.8.410.40   In addition, if the total amount of proceeds from transfer activity is not evenly distributed throughout the reporting period, then the following disclosures are required for each type of continuing involvement in transferred assets that are derecognised in their entirety:
- the part within the reporting period to which the greatest transfer activity is attributable;
- the amount – e.g. related gains or losses – recognised from transfer activity in that part of the reporting period; and
- the total amount of proceeds from transfer activity in that part of the reporting period. [*IFRS 7.42G(c)*]

7I.8.415   Scope of disclosure requirements on transfers of financial assets

7I.8.415.10   Entities often transfer financial assets to structured entities (see 7I.5.320). If financial assets have been transferred to an unconsolidated structured entity, then disclosures required by IFRS 12 may be appropriate in addition to disclosures of transfers of financial assets required by IFRS 7. For further discussion of disclosures about structured entities, see 5.10.230–270.

7I.8.415.20   To assess what information on which financial assets needs to be disclosed, an entity determines:
- which financial assets have been transferred;

- whether it has derecognised a transferred financial asset in its entirety; and
- whether it has continuing involvement in a transferred financial asset that it derecognised in its entirety. [*IFRS 7.42A, 42C, IAS 39.17–20*]

7I.8.415.30   This is illustrated in the following flowchart.

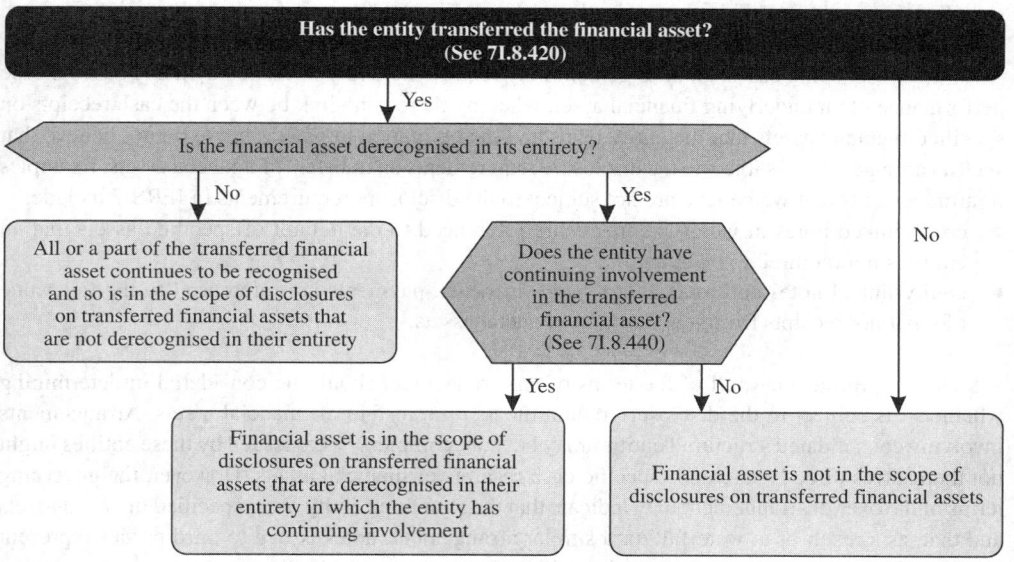

7I.8.415.40   The definition of 'transfer' and the concept of 'continuing involvement' for the purposes of these disclosures are different from those in IAS 39 for the purpose of determining whether a financial asset is derecognised (see 7I.5.60). [*IFRS 7.42A, 42C, BC65S, IAS 39.17–20*]

7I.8.420   *Definition of a 'transfer'*

7I.8.420.10   For the purposes of the disclosures, an entity transfers all or a part of a financial asset if it:
- transfers the contractual rights to receive the cash flows of that asset; or
- retains the contractual rights to receive cash flows and assumes a contractual obligation to pay these cash flows to one or more recipients. Such an arrangement is a transfer for the purposes of the disclosure requirements even if it does not comply with the pass-through requirements of IAS 39 and would not therefore be considered a transfer under IAS 39 (see 7I.5.160). [*IFRS 7.42A*]

7I.8.430   *Identifying contractual obligation to pay cash flows of asset*

7I.8.430.10   A transfer is subject to the disclosure requirements in IFRS 7 for transfers of financial assets if the entity retains the contractual rights to receive the cash flows of a financial asset but assumes a contractual obligation to pay the cash flows to one or more recipients in an arrangement. The purpose of these disclosure requirements is to provide users of financial statements with a better understanding of the relationship between the transferred financial assets and the associated liabilities. Therefore, in our view there should be a direct (explicit or implicit) link between the cash receipts on specified financial assets that the entity owns and the obligation to remit the cash receipts to another party, in order for the arrangement to be considered a transfer subject to these disclosure requirements. [*IFRS 7.BC65E*]

7I.8.430.20   In arrangements that do not involve structured entities (see 5.10.190), the legal documentation may directly identify the assets and cash receipts that are being referenced and explicitly set out the requirements for directly passing through cash flows when an amount is received on the specified financial asset. This may make the analysis of such transactions relatively straightforward.

7I.8.430.30   In some cases, an arrangement may require the entity to make payments based on the performance of an underlying financial asset, whereby there is no link between the cash receipts on specified financial assets that the entity owns and the obligation to pay cash. We do not believe that such an arrangement is subject to the disclosure requirements on transfers of financial assets. Examples of arrangements that we believe are not subject to the disclosure requirements in IFRS 7 include:

- credit-linked notes in which payments are referenced to the default of specified assets that an entity is not required to own; and
- equity-linked notes and total return swaps in which payments are referenced to the fair value of – but not receipts from – underlying financial assets.

7I.8.430.40   In our view, all of the terms of an arrangement should be considered in determining whether it is subject to the disclosure requirements on transfers of financial assets. Arrangements involving consolidated structured entities may be more complex. Notes issued by these entities might not themselves directly reference specific cash receipts or financial assets. However, the governing terms of the overall arrangement may indicate that the structured entity owns specified financial assets and that, as a result of a 'waterfall' or a similar arrangement, notes issued to third parties represent an obligation to pass on cash receipts from those assets to the note holders.

7I.8.430.50   To qualify as a pass-through arrangement under IAS 39 (see 7I.5.160), cash receipts need to be remitted to the eventual recipients without material delay and may only be reinvested in cash and cash equivalents before being paid on. In our view, these strict criteria do not apply in determining whether an arrangement is a transfer subject to the disclosure requirements in IFRS 7. Accordingly, an arrangement that does not meet the strict criteria in IAS 39 may be subject to the disclosure requirements on transfers of financial assets.

7I.8.430.60   Judgement may be involved in distinguishing between:

- an obligation to pass on cash flows from specified financial assets that is subject to the transfer of financial assets disclosure requirements; and
- interests in or linked to investment funds issued by the reporting entity that are not subject to these disclosure requirements.

7I.8.430.70   In typical mutual or unit-linked fund structures, investors hold instruments that are redeemable based on the value of assets in the fund. In these cases, cash flows are collected from existing assets. Assets may also be sold to generate cash proceeds. An entity is not required to pay these amounts to investors but instead cash received by the fund is reinvested in different assets. Cash payments are made to investors in accordance with the entity's dividend policies and when investors redeem their investment in the fund. In our view, in these circumstances, the nature of the arrangement results in a financial liability that is indexed to the value of a moving pool of assets that the entity manages, rather than in an obligation to pass on the cash flows of specified financial assets when they are received. Consequently, we believe that the arrangement is not subject to the disclosure requirements on transfers of financial assets.

7I.8.430.80   Similarly, in our view, in certain arrangements – e.g. complex arrangements involving consolidated structured entities, other entities in the consolidated group and external holders of instruments issued by the structured entity – judgement may be required to determine whether the arrangement results in:

- an obligation to pass on cash flows from specified financial assets held within the structured entity that is subject to the transfer of financial assets disclosure requirements; or
- a general obligation for which assets held within the structured entity act only as a form of collateral. In this case, the collateral is subject to the collateral disclosure requirements (see 7I.8.160); but we believe that the disclosure requirements in respect of transfers of financial assets do not apply to the arrangement.

7I.8.430.90   In our view, factors that may affect this judgement include the following:

- the purpose and design of the structured entity;
- the extent of recourse to the transferor's wider group;
- the nature and extent of differences between the cash flow profile of beneficial interests issued by the structured entity and the cash flow profile of financial assets held in the structured entity; and
- rights to substitute financial assets held within the structured entity.

7I.8.440   *Continuing involvement*

7I.8.440.10   For the purposes of the disclosures, an entity has continuing involvement in a transferred financial asset if, as part of the transfer, it retains any of the contractual rights or obligations relating to the transferred financial assets or obtains any new contractual rights or obligations relating to those assets. Continuing involvement may result from contractual provisions in the transfer agreement or in a separate agreement entered into with the transferee or another party in connection with the transfer. Normal representations and warranties, contracts to reacquire the transferred financial asset at fair value, and a qualifying pass-through arrangement under IAS 39 do not constitute continuing involvement. [*IAS 39.19, IFRS 7.42C, B31*]

7I.8.440.20   An entity does not have continuing involvement for disclosure purposes in a transferred financial asset if it has neither an interest in the future performance of the transferred financial asset nor a responsibility under any circumstances to make payments in respect of the transferred financial asset in the future, other than paying on cash flows of the transferred asset that an entity collects and is required to transfer to the transferee. [*IFRS 7.B30*]

7I.8.440.30   In many cases, entities (especially financial institutions) retain the right or obligation to service, for a fee, transferred financial assets that qualify for derecognition in their entirety. These servicing arrangements represent continuing involvement for the purposes of the disclosures on transfers of financial assets if the conditions in 7I.8.440.10–20 are met. A servicer has continuing involvement in a transferred asset (for the purposes of the disclosure requirements) if it has an interest in the future performance of the transferred assets – e.g. if the servicing fee is dependent on the amount or timing of the cash flows from the transferred assets, or a fixed servicing fee would not be paid in full if the transferred assets do not perform. [*IFRS 7.42C, B30–B30A*]

<table>
<tr><td>71.8.450</td><td>Interactions between derecognition requirements in IAS 39 and disclosure requirements in IFRS 7</td></tr>
</table>

71.8.450.10   Some of the interactions between the application of the IAS 39 derecognition requirements and the IFRS 7 disclosure requirements are illustrated in the table below.

- The first column relates to the financial asset that is being considered for derecognition – it could be either the entire financial asset or an eligible part.
- The second column relates to whether the financial asset is derecognised under IAS 39.
- The third and fourth columns indicate whether IFRS 7's disclosure requirements for either:
  - transferred financial assets that are not derecognised in their entirety; or
  - transferred financial assets that are derecognised in their entirety apply in the circumstances described. [*IFRS 7.42A, 42C, IAS 39.17–20*]

FACT PATTERN	DERECOGNITION IN LINE WITH IAS 39?	IN SCOPE OF IFRS 7 DISCLOSURE REQUIREMENTS FOR TRANSFERRED FINANCIAL ASSETS THAT ARE	
		NOT DERECOGNISED IN THEIR ENTIRETY?	DERECOGNISED IN THEIR ENTIRETY?
Entity retains the contractual rights to receive the cash flows of the financial asset, but assumes a contractual obligation to pay these cash flows to a third party in a way that does not comply with the pass-through requirements of IAS 39.	No; the entity continues to recognise the financial asset in its entirety.	Yes	No
Entity transfers the financial asset in a way that meets the definition of transfer in IAS 39 but retains substantially all the risks and rewards of the transferred financial asset.	No; the entity continues to recognise the financial asset in its entirety.	Yes	No
Entity transfers the financial asset in a way that meets the definition of transfer in IAS 39 but neither transfers nor retains substantially all the risks and rewards of the transferred financial asset and does not retain control of the asset.	Yes; the financial asset is derecognised in its entirety.	No	Yes; it retains continuing involvement in the transferred financial asset because the entity neither transfers nor retains substantially all the risks and rewards of the transferred financial asset.

Fact pattern	Derecognition in line with IAS 39?	In scope of IFRS 7 disclosure requirements for transferred financial assets that are	
		Not derecognised in their entirety?	Derecognised in their entirety?
Entity transfers the financial asset in a way that meets the definition of transfer in IAS 39 but neither transfers nor retains substantially all the risks and rewards of the transferred financial asset and retains control of the asset.	The financial asset continues to be recognised to the extent of the entity's continuing involvement in the asset.	Yes	No
Entity transfers the financial asset in a way that meets the definition of transfer in IAS 39 and transfers substantially all the risks and rewards of the transferred financial asset but retains an insignificant portion of the risks and rewards.	Yes; the financial asset is derecognised in its entirety.	No	Yes; it retains continuing involvement because it retains an insignificant portion of the risks and rewards.

7I.8.460   Transferred financial asset

7I.8.460.10   When applying the disclosure requirements, the term 'transferred financial asset' refers to all or a part of a financial asset. Therefore, when an entity transfers a part of a financial asset, its evaluation of whether and which disclosures are required depends on:
- whether that part is derecognised in its entirety; and
- whether the entity retains continuing involvement in that part. [*IFRS 7.42A, 42D–42E*]

EXAMPLE 7A – APPLICATION OF DISCLOSURES TO PROPORTION OF FINANCIAL ASSET (1)

7I.8.460.20   An entity transfers the contractual rights to only a fully proportionate share of 40% of the cash flows of a financial asset – i.e. the derecognition guidance in IAS 39 is applied to that part of the financial asset. This fully proportionate 40% share is not derecognised in its entirety because the transfer does not meet the IAS 39 requirements for full derecognition of that part. In this case, the fully proportionate 40% share is subject to the disclosure requirements for transferred financial assets that are not derecognised in their entirety.

EXAMPLE 7B – APPLICATION OF DISCLOSURES TO PROPORTION OF FINANCIAL ASSET (2)

7I.8.460.30   Conversely, if this fully proportionate 40% share of a financial asset met the derecognition criteria in IAS 39 and the entity retained continuing involvement in that derecognised part, then the fully proportionate 40% share would be subject

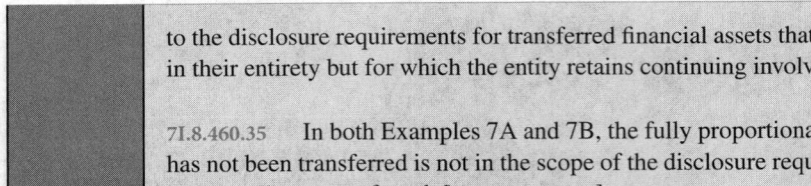

to the disclosure requirements for transferred financial assets that are derecognised in their entirety but for which the entity retains continuing involvement.

7I.8.460.35   In both Examples 7A and 7B, the fully proportionate 60% share that has not been transferred is not in the scope of the disclosure requirements because it has not been transferred. [*IFRS 7.42A, 42E*]

7I.8.460.40   A more complex question relates to transfers of some, but not all, of the cash flows of a financial asset, when these transferred cash flows are not a part that meets the criteria for separate derecognition analysis in paragraph 16(a) of IAS 39 (see 7I.5.80.30–150). Although paragraph 16 of IAS 39 requires the derecognition guidance in IAS 39 to be applied to a part only if that part meets specified criteria, it does not define a 'part' of a financial asset for the purposes of the IFRS 7 transfer disclosures. Therefore, in our view an obligation to pay some of the cash flows from a financial asset should be considered a transfer for the purposes of these disclosures even if the cash flows passed on do not meet the criteria in paragraph 16(a) of IAS 39.

7I.8.460.50   If the part of a financial asset that is transferred does not meet the criteria in paragraph 16(a) of IAS 39, then in our view an entity can satisfy the disclosure requirements in respect of the carrying amounts of transferred assets (see 7I.8.410.20) by disclosing the carrying amount of the entire asset or by applying a reasonable allocation methodology, together with such additional explanation as may be appropriate in the circumstances.

8. INSURANCE

8.1 Insurance contracts

8.   INSURANCE

8.1   Insurance contracts

CURRENTLY EFFECTIVE REQUIREMENTS

This publication reflects IFRS in issue at 1 August 2018, and the currently effective requirements cover annual periods beginning on 1 January 2018.

The requirements related to this topic are mainly derived from the following.

REFERENCE	TITLE
IFRS 4	Insurance Contracts

The currently effective requirements include newly effective requirements arising from the following.

- IFRS 15 *Revenue from Contracts with Customers,* which is effective for annual periods beginning on or after 1 January 2018. The new requirements may be applied using the retrospective method or the cumulative effect method (see 4.2.510). The impact of the new requirements on the accounting for insurance contracts is reflected in 8.1.10.
- IFRS 9 *Financial Instruments*, which is effective for annual periods beginning on or after 1 January 2018. Transition requirements for IFRS 9 are the subject of chapter 7.11. The impact of the new requirements on insurance contracts is reflected throughout this chapter. However, because the temporary exemption from IFRS 9 permits an insurer that meets certain requirements to apply IAS 39 rather than IFRS 9 (see 8.1.160):
  - this chapter refers to the requirements of both IFRS 9 and IAS 39; and
  - section 7I provides guidance on the application of IAS 39.

An insurer that applies the temporary exemption from IFRS 9 (see 8.1.160) should read this chapter focusing on the references to IAS 39 and refer to the guidance on financial instruments in section 7I.

FORTHCOMING REQUIREMENTS

In May 2017, the IASB issued IFRS 17 *Insurance Contracts*, which is effective for annual periods beginning on or after 1 January 2021. IFRS 17 is the subject of section 8.1A.

FUTURE DEVELOPMENTS

For this topic, there are no future developments.

8.1.10   SCOPE

8.1.10.10   IFRS 4 applies to insurance contracts (including reinsurance contracts) that an entity issues and reinsurance contracts that it holds (i.e. to the contractual rights and obligations arising from these contracts). In addition, the scope of IFRS 4 also includes financial instruments with a discretionary participation feature (DPF) that an entity issues (see 8.1.110). It does not address other aspects of accounting by insurers – e.g. accounting for financial instruments that are in the scope of IFRS 9 (see chapter 7.1) or IAS 39 (see chapter 7I.1), except when applying the amendments to IFRS 4 as discussed in 8.1.160, or other assets and liabilities of insurance entities. It does not address accounting for insurance contracts by policyholders, other than holders of reinsurance contracts. [*IFRS 4.2–4, 6*]

8.1.10.20   IFRS 4 focuses on types of contracts rather than types of entities. Therefore, it applies to both entities regulated as insurance entities and all other entities. Insurers are subject to the requirements of other applicable IFRSs in respect of products or components of products that are not insurance contracts. For example, IFRS 15 applies to fees and related costs on investment management contracts (see 4.2.10.40 and 370) and IAS 37 may apply when an insurer is sued over an insurance policy or a claim (see 3.12.20.30).

8.1.10.25   In addition, some contracts that may meet the definition of insurance contracts are excluded from the scope of the standard, such as product warranties issued directly by a manufacturer or retailer, employers' assets and liabilities under employee benefit plans, some financial guarantees and contingent consideration payable or receivable in a business combination. Rights and obligations excluded from IFRS 4 may be dealt with specifically in another standard – e.g. assets and liabilities under employee benefit plans are covered by IAS 19 (see chapter 4.4); financial instruments, including certain financial guarantees, are covered by IFRS 9 (see chapter 7.1) or IAS 39 (see chapter 7I.1); and provisions, contingent liabilities and contingent assets are covered by IAS 37 (see chapter 3.12). [*IFRS 4.4, B18–B19*]

8.1.10.30   Although financial guarantee contracts meet the definition of an insurance contract, they are generally outside the scope of IFRS 4 and are accounted for under IFRS 9 (see 7.1.60) or IAS 39 (see 7I.1.50). However, if an entity issuing such contracts has previously asserted explicitly that it regards financial guarantee contracts as insurance contracts and has accounted for them as such, then it may apply IFRS 4 to such contracts. For an insurer, it is likely to be clear from previous practices, contract documents etc whether issued financial guarantee contracts have been regarded as and accounted for as insurance contracts. For entities that write financial guarantee contracts that are incidental to their main business – e.g. to support borrowings of subsidiaries or of customers – it may be less clear whether the entity has made such an explicit assertion. For such entities, in our view it is not necessary that insurance contract terminology be used in documenting its financial guarantee contracts. The explicit assertion may be apparent from information in previous financial statements and other published information. [*IFRS 4.4, B18*]

8.1.20   Definition of insurance contract

8.1.20.10   An 'insurance contract' is a contract under which the insurer accepts significant insurance risk from the policyholder by agreeing to compensate the policyholder if a specified uncertain future event adversely affects the policyholder. This specified uncertain future event is known as the 'insured event'. [*IFRS 4.A*]

8.1.20.20   Some guidance is provided to clarify the definition in 8.1.20.10. One of the central characteristics of an insurance contract is the specified uncertain future event. Uncertainty (or risk) is the essence of an insurance contract. Therefore, uncertainty is required at the inception of an insurance contract regarding:

- whether an insured event will occur;
- when it will occur; or
- how much the insurer will need to pay if it occurs. [*IFRS 4.B2*]

8.1.20.30   The specified uncertain future event that is covered by an insurance contract creates 'insurance risk'. 'Insurance risk' is any risk, other than financial risk, transferred from the holder to the issuer of a contract. 'Financial risk' is the risk of a possible future change in a specified interest rate, financial instrument price, commodity price, foreign exchange rate, index of prices or rates, credit rating or credit index or other variable, provided, in the case of a non-financial variable, that it is not specific to a party to the contract. Risks to the holder such as death, illness, disability, loss of property resulting from damage, theft etc are each an insurance risk because they are specific to a party to the contract. [*IFRS 4.A–B*]

8.1.20.40   If a contract refers to a variable that determines significant cash flows under that contract, and that variable is non-financial and specific to a party to the contract, then that variable is considered to give rise to insurance risk, assuming it is a *transferred* risk, rather than to financial risk.

EXAMPLE 1 – RESIDUAL VALUE GUARANTEES

8.1.20.43   If a contract written by a manufacturer or dealer guarantees the residual value of a vehicle owned by the holder of the contract, and the amount payable under the guarantee will vary significantly depending on the specific condition of the vehicle at the date of sale, then the contract is an insurance contract.

8.1.20.50   Conversely, if the owner is required to restore the vehicle to a specified condition before disposal in the marketplace, such that the guarantee is of a market value that is not dependent on the condition of the vehicle, then in our view the contract is not an insurance contract. [*IFRS 4.B8–B9*]

8.1.20.60   Lapse or persistency risk (i.e. the risk that the counterparty will cancel the contract earlier or later than the issuer had expected in pricing the contract) or expense risk (i.e. the risk of unexpected increases in the administrative costs associated with servicing a contract, rather than in costs associated with insured events) are not insurance risks because they are not risks that are transferred by the counterparty to the contract issuer and they do not adversely affect the counterparty. However, if the issuer of a contract exposed to lapse, persistency or expense risk (but not, from the perspective of the issuer, insurance risk) mitigates those risks by using a second contract to transfer all or part of those risks to another party, then the second contract exposes that other party to significant insurance risk and is therefore an insurance contract from the perspective of that other party (issuer). However, the holder (transferor of insurance risk) is the policyholder of that second contract and therefore does not apply IFRS 4 to that contract. [*IFRS 4.B12, B15–B16*]

8.1.20.70   A contract that exposes the issuer to financial risk without significant insurance risk is not an insurance contract and therefore the contract is accounted for as a financial instrument under IFRS 9 (see chapter 7.1) or IAS 39 (see chapter 7I.1). Insurance risk is significant when there is at least one scenario that has commercial substance in which the insurer would suffer a significant loss as a result of an insured event taking place. A loss event has commercial substance if it has a discernible effect on the economics of the transaction, so that the insurer would be required to pay additional significant benefits to the policyholder beyond those that would be paid if the insured event does not occur. It does not matter that the insured event is extremely unlikely or that the expected present value of contingent cash flows is a small proportion of the expected present value of all of the remaining contractual cash flows. [*IFRS 4.B22–B28*]

8.1.20.73   The additional benefits referred to above can include a requirement to pay a benefit earlier than if the policyholder survives for a longer period and the payment is not adjusted for the time value of money. [*IFRS 4.B27*]

EXAMPLE 2A – SIGNIFICANT INSURANCE RISK – ADDITIONAL BENEFITS

> 8.1.20.77   An investment contract that pays a fixed amount at maturity, but also pays the same amount in the case of death during the term of the contract, is an insurance contract as long as the death benefit, in present value terms, could significantly exceed the present value of the amount payable at maturity. [*IFRS 4.B26*]

8.1.20.80   Insurance risk is assessed in relation to the individual contract and without considering portfolio effects. Therefore, the insurance risk on an individual contract may be significant even if material losses are not expected in a portfolio of contracts (i.e. gains on some contracts in a portfolio offset the losses on other contracts in the portfolio). However, if a relatively homogeneous book of small contracts is known to consist of contracts that all transfer insurance risk, then an insurer need not examine each contract within this book to identify a few non-derivative contracts that transfer insignificant insurance risk. For example, the significance of insurance risk in endowment contracts typically depends on the age of the policyholder at the outset of the contract or on the contract duration. When insurance risk is known generally to be significant based on these factors, the few contracts with an unusually low entry age or unusually short duration, forming part of a portfolio of endowment contracts, need not be considered separately. [*IFRS 4.B25, IG2.1.5*]

8.1.20.90   Some contracts do not transfer any insurance risk to the issuer at inception, although they do transfer insurance risk at a later time. In these cases, the contract is not considered an insurance contract until the risk transfer happens. [*IFRS 4.B29*]

EXAMPLE 2B – SIGNIFICANT INSURANCE RISK – CHANGES IN LEVEL OF INSURANCE RISK

> 8.1.20.93   A contract may provide a specified investment return and specify that the policyholder will receive, or can elect to receive, a life-contingent annuity at current annuity rates determined by the insurer when the annuity begins. Such a

contract is not an insurance contract at the outset. For such a contract to be an insurance contract at the outset, it is necessary for the annuity rate or the determination basis to be fixed at that time. [*IFRS 4.B29, IG2.1.7*]

8.1.20.95   Once a contract has qualified as an insurance contract, it remains an insurance contract until all rights and obligations are extinguished or expired. Therefore, an insurance contract is not reclassified as an investment contract during its life, even if insurance risk becomes insignificant or non-existent. [*IFRS 4.B30*]

8.1.20.100   Because of the requirements for 'significant insurance risk' under IFRS 4, it may be the case that a contract accounted for as a financial instrument under previous GAAP is an insurance contract under IFRS. In our view, the previous accounting for that contract should continue under IFRS unless a change in accounting policy can be justified as an improvement (see 8.1.90). It would not be appropriate to change previous GAAP accounting for the contract (e.g. to apply previous GAAP insurance accounting) simply because the definition of an insurance contract under IFRS is met. The additional requirements of IFRS 4 with respect to the liability adequacy test, unbundling and embedded derivatives would also apply.

8.1.20.110   Conversely, if a contract is not an insurance contract under IFRS 4 but did qualify for insurance accounting under previous GAAP, then for IFRS accounting purposes the contract is not an insurance contract and is accounted for under the applicable financial instruments standard or other relevant standards. The continuation of previous GAAP is prohibited for a contract that does not qualify as an insurance contract under IFRS 4. [*IFRS 4.2–3*]

8.1.20.120   A loan or bond is an insurance contract if it provides for forgiveness of, or a significant reduction in, principal or interest payments on the occurrence of a specified uncertain event that adversely affects the debtor as a result of a pre-existing risk, other than financial risk. Examples are a loan for which the full balance is forgiven on the death of the debtor, or a catastrophe bond under which payments are reduced significantly if the specified triggering event includes a condition that the issuer of the bond suffers a loss. In this case, the creditor is the issuer of the insurance contract and the debtor is the policyholder. [*IFRS 4.A, IG2.1.19–IG2.1.20, IG2.1.23–IG2.1.24*]

8.1.20.130   A financial instrument is not an insurance contract if the modification to the contractual cash flows does not transfer a pre-existing risk (e.g. waiver of only a termination fee that would otherwise be due under the terms of the loan) or the triggering event does not include a condition that the debtor suffer a loss (e.g. a debtor can choose to settle the amount outstanding on a loan by surrendering the collateral). In our view, a non-recourse feature in a secured loan that, in the event of the debtor's default, limits the remedies of the creditor to seizure of the collateral or its proceeds does not make the loan an insurance contract. This is the case even if the collateral is a non-financial asset and the debtor has a pre-existing exposure to the value of the collateral – e.g. the non-financial collateral was owned by the debtor before receiving the loan and was not purchased using the proceeds of the loan. This is because the feature is not an agreement by the creditor to compensate the debtor in the event of a decline in the value of the collateral. [*IFRS 4.A, IG2.1.19– IG2.1.20, IG2.1.23–IG2.1.24*]

8.1.30   **Deposit components and embedded derivatives in insurance contracts**

8.1.30.10   Some insurance contracts contain a deposit component, which is a component that would, if it were a stand-alone instrument, be a financial instrument. The deposit component is required to be 'unbundled' and accounted for as a financial instrument if the rights or obligations under that component otherwise would not be recognised under the insurer's accounting policies and the component can be measured separately. If, for example, an insurer's liability adequacy test is sufficient to ensure that the full obligation under a deposit component, including any guaranteed amounts, is recognised, then unbundling is not required. [*IFRS 4.10, 12*]

8.1.30.20   Nevertheless, an insurer may choose to unbundle a deposit component, provided the deposit component can be measured separately from the insurance component. For example, certain reinsurance contracts specify that any compensation received from the reinsurer for losses will be reimbursed to the reinsurer by increases in future reinsurance premiums. Because the repayment is not contingent, the obligation arises from a deposit component and the deposit obligation is required to be unbundled and accounted for separately as a financial liability, provided that it can be measured separately, unless the accounting policies of the holder of the reinsurance contract would require recognition of the repayment obligation. [*IFRS 4.10*]

8.1.30.30   Components of insurance contracts that meet the definition of a derivative are in the scope of IFRS 9 (see chapter 7.1) or IAS 39 (see chapter 7I.1) and are therefore subject to the general requirements for embedded derivatives, with two exceptions as noted in 8.1.30.50. [*IFRS 4.IG4*]

8.1.30.40   IFRS 9 (see 7.2.120.50) and IAS 39 (see 7I.2.120.20) require an embedded derivative to be separated from the host contract and accounted for as a stand-alone derivative if the following conditions are met:
- the economic characteristics and risks of the embedded derivative are not closely related to those of the host contract;
- a separate instrument with the same terms as the embedded derivative would meet the definition of a derivative; and
- the hybrid instrument is not measured at fair value with changes in fair value recognised in profit or loss. [*IFRS 9.4.3.2–3, IAS 39.11*]

8.1.30.50   IFRS 4 provides two significant exemptions to the general requirements for the separation of embedded derivatives. These exemptions apply to:
- components that meet the definition of an insurance contract – e.g. they have significant insurance risk; and
- surrender options with fixed terms. [*IFRS 4.7–9*]

8.1.30.60   Because insurance contracts are not in the scope of IFRS 9 or IAS 39, the requirements in that standard to separate embedded derivatives (see 7.2.110 or 7I.2.110, respectively) are not applicable to insurance contracts embedded in a host contract. A component meeting the definition of an insurance contract does not need to be separated from its host contract. For example, an option to take a life-contingent annuity contract would not be separated from a host insurance contract.

8.1.30.70   An insurer is not required to separate a fixed-price surrender option from a host insurance liability, or a surrender option based on a fixed amount and an interest rate. Even though the surrender value may be viewed as a deposit component, IFRS 4 does not require unbundling of a contract if all obligations arising under the deposit component are recognised.

8.1.30.80   Because liabilities under unit-linked contracts are generally measured at their current unit values, there is no need to separate a host deposit contract and an embedded derivative for such contracts. [*IFRS 9.B.4.3.8(g), IAS 39.AG33(g)*]

8.1.40   Contracts containing guaranteed minimum death and/or survival benefits

8.1.40.10   Some unit-linked savings contracts include a guaranteed minimum benefit that is payable, *either* on the death of the policyholder *or* on maturity of the contract, if the guaranteed minimum benefit is higher than the bid value of the units (the unit value) at the time when a claim is made. If the contract is surrendered, then the policyholder receives cash for the value of the units surrendered (less surrender penalties). Therefore, the benefit payable on death or maturity may exceed the benefit paid on surrender of the contract. If the guaranteed minimum benefits are larger, in present value terms, than the unit value payable on surrender (before consideration of surrender penalties), then these contracts transfer insurance risk because additional amounts are payable if the insured event (either death or survival, depending on the terms of the contract) occurs. For these types of contracts, the issuer determines whether insurance risk is significant, taking into account both the probability of the insured event taking place and, if the insured event takes place, the probability of the unit value being significantly below the guaranteed amount at that time. If this insurance risk is significant, then the contract is classified as an insurance contract. [*IFRS 4.B22*]

8.1.40.20   In the scenario described in 8.1.40.10, there are two triggers needed to cause a significant additional benefit:
- the bid value of the units has to fall below the guaranteed minimum benefit (financial risk); and
- the insured event has to happen (insurance risk).

8.1.40.25   The first trigger is a pre-condition for the existence of insurance risk in the contract. Insurance risk exists only if financial risk has already resulted in losses when the insured event takes place.

8.1.40.30   The classification of a savings contract containing guarantees of this type should be determined on its own merits by considering the level of the guaranteed minimum payments and the likelihood that the bid price of the units will fall below that level. For this financial risk to be significant, as a precursor for the existence of insurance risk, in our view it should be *reasonably possible*, based on historical and expected volatility in similar investments, that unit values could fall significantly below the guaranteed amount during the term of the contract.

8.1.40.40   In many cases with investments of high volatility and a guarantee close to the initial investment, an insurance contract classification will be appropriate. However, if the term of the contract is relatively short, the volatility of the units is relatively low or the level of the guaranteed minimum benefit is relatively low compared with the initial investment, then it might be more difficult for an insurer to justify an insurance contract classification.

8.1.40.50   If the guarantee applies to *both* a death benefit *and* survival benefit, then in our view the amount subject to insurance risk is the difference between the amount payable on death and the amount payable on survival, in present value terms, considering the time value of money and any premium payable in future for continuing the rights under the contract. We believe that the lower surrender value is not relevant in this case because unless the policyholder elects to surrender the policy, which is not an insurable event, either death or survival to maturity is certain.

8.1.50   RECOGNITION AND MEASUREMENT

8.1.60   Accounting policies for insurance contracts

8.1.60.10   To allow an insurer to continue using its existing accounting practices for insurance contracts as far as possible, entities are exempted from applying certain portions of the hierarchy for selecting accounting policies (see 2.8.20) to insurance contracts. Specifically, in developing accounting policies under IFRS for insurance contracts written and reinsurance contracts held, an insurer is not generally required to consider whether the resulting information would be relevant and reliable using the qualitative characteristics in the Conceptual Framework; nor is it required to consider the requirements of other standards by analogy. It is this exemption that largely permits an insurer to continue its existing practices for insurance contracts. Without this exemption, an insurer adopting standards would have needed to assess whether its accounting policies for insurance contracts complied with the hierarchy requirements, especially the Conceptual Framework, and all other IFRSs, including IAS 37 (see chapter 3.12). [*IFRS 4.13*]

8.1.60.20   Although the continuation of many existing practices is permitted, the introduction of some practices as changes in accounting policies is prohibited. For example, an entity is not required to eliminate excessive prudence in accounting for insurance contracts nor is it required, on consolidation, to apply consistent accounting policies to insurance contracts held by each entity within a group. There is also no requirement to use discounting in the measurement of insurance liabilities. However, these policies may not be adopted if they were not used before adopting IFRS 4. For example, an entity that did not use excessive prudence may not adopt a policy of doing so on or after adopting IFRS 4. [*IFRS 4.25–26*]

8.1.60.30   Nevertheless, the impact of the exemption from portions of the hierarchy is limited by five specific requirements. An insurer *does not*:
- recognise as a liability any provisions for possible future claims under insurance contracts if those contracts are not in existence at the reporting date, such as catastrophe and equalisation provisions; or
- offset reinsurance assets against the related insurance liabilities or offset reinsurance income and expenses against expenses or income from the related insurance contracts. [*IFRS 4.14*]

8.1.60.40   An insurer:
- derecognises an insurance liability only when the obligation specified in the contract is discharged, cancelled or expires;
- considers whether its reinsurance assets are impaired; and
- carries out a liability adequacy test. [*IFRS 4.14–15, 20, B30*]

8.1.60.50   With the exception of insurance assets (e.g. salvage and subrogation, premium receivables), deferred acquisition costs related to insurance contracts, present value of future profits (PVFP) (see 8.1.100) and reinsurance assets, an insurer's accounting for its assets will follow other applicable IFRS. For a discussion of the accounting for costs to obtain an investment management contract, see 4.2.260.

8.1.70 Liability adequacy test

8.1.70.10   An insurer assesses at the reporting date whether its recognised insurance liabilities (less related deferred acquisition costs and related intangible assets) are adequate, using current estimates of future cash flows under the insurance contracts. Any shortfall is recognised in profit or loss. [*IFRS 4.15*]

8.1.70.20   At a minimum, the assessment of the adequacy of the liability considers current estimates of all contractual cash flows and of related cash flows, such as claim handling costs, as well as cash flows resulting from embedded options and guarantees. IFRS 4 does not specify whether, in performing the liability adequacy test, cash flows should be discounted or, if discounting is applied, what discount rate should be used. However, if the assessment shows that the liability is inadequate, then the shortfall is recognised in profit or loss. If an insurer's existing accounting policies include an assessment that meets this requirement, then no further test is required. If they do not, then IAS 37 (see chapter 3.12) is applied to determine whether the recognised liabilities are adequate. [*IFRS 4.16–18*]

8.1.70.30   In our view, if an insurer's liability adequacy test takes into account amounts recoverable under reinsurance contracts, then that practice may be continued under IFRS 4. However, the resulting net liability should be presented gross in the statement of financial position by separating the amount recognised for the reinsurance asset from the insurance liability. In our view, such a change in presentation would not be a change in accounting policy. In our view, in performing such a liability adequacy test it would not be appropriate, however, to include estimated reinsurance recoveries from contracts that are not in force at the reporting date.

8.1.80 Reinsurance

8.1.80.10   IFRS 4 applies to all insurance contracts (including reinsurance contracts) that an entity issues and to reinsurance contracts that an entity holds. Reinsurance contracts that an entity holds are an exception to the general scope of IFRS 4, which otherwise excludes accounting by policyholders. Therefore, there are separate requirements for the cedant's reinsurance assets as set out in 8.1.80.20–50. [*IFRS 4.2, 4(f)*]

8.1.80.20   The general requirements of IFRS prohibit the offsetting of assets and liabilities as well as income and expenses except in certain defined circumstances in IFRS 9 and IAS 39 (see 7.10.110 and 7I.8.90, respectively). An entity is prohibited from offsetting reinsurance assets against the related insurance liabilities and income or expenses from reinsurance contracts against expenses or income from the related insurance contracts. Even if offsetting is permitted or required under existing accounting policies, an entity changes its policies in these respects. [*IFRS 4.14(d), BC106*]

8.1.80.30   The cedant considers at the reporting date whether its reinsurance assets are impaired. In our view, for entities that account for their financial instruments under IAS 39 the impairment test to be applied is based on the impairment test applied to financial assets and the guidance in IAS 39 should therefore be followed (see 7I.6.400). The focus of the test is credit risk, which arises from the risk of default by the reinsurer and from disputes over coverage, and not on matters arising from the measurement of the underlying direct insurance liabilities. [*IFRS 4.14(e), 20, BC107–BC108*]

8.1.80.35   If an entity accounts for its financial instruments under IFRS 9, then we believe that it can continue to apply the guidance in IAS 39 for the purposes of this impairment test. This is because reinsurance assets are not in the scope of IAS 39 or IFRS 9. Instead, the guidance in IAS 39 is used as an accounting policy for assessing the impairment of reinsurance assets under IFRS 4.

8.1.80.40   A reinsurance asset is considered impaired if:
- there is objective evidence that the cedant may not receive all amounts due to it under the terms of the contract, as a result of an event that occurred after initial recognition of the reinsurance asset; and
- that event has a reliably measurable impact on the amounts that the cedant will receive from the reinsurer. [*IFRS 4.20*]

8.1.80.50   An impairment may not be recognised for estimates of credit losses expected to arise from future events. In our view, it is unlikely that an insurer's reinsurance assets would be sufficiently similar in terms of nature and risk such that a portfolio-based impairment test could be applied. Therefore, we believe that any impairment is likely to be based on specific credit events related to each individual reinsurer.

8.1.90   Changes in accounting policies

8.1.90.10   An entity is permitted to make changes in its accounting policies for insurance contracts as long as the change improves either the relevance or the reliability of its financial statements without reducing either. [*IFRS 4.22*]

8.1.90.20   The assessment of relevance and reliability is judged by the criteria in the hierarchy for selecting accounting policies (see 2.8.20) without the need to achieve full compliance with those criteria. This limit on voluntary changes in accounting policies applies both to changes made by an insurer that already applies IFRS and to a first-time adopter of IFRS (see chapter 6.1). [*IFRS 4.21, 23*]

8.1.90.30   An insurer is permitted, for example, to change a policy in order to do the following.
- Remeasure some insurance liabilities (but not necessarily all of them) to reflect changes in current market interest rates; at that time, measurement can be changed to reflect other current estimates and assumptions as well.
- Switch to a comprehensive, widely used, investor-oriented model for insurance policy liabilities, even if this means a move towards recognising future investment margins. However, such margins can be included only if this change is made as part of an overall switch to an investor-oriented model and not as an isolated change.
- Apply 'shadow accounting' to remeasure insurance liabilities to reflect recognised but unrealised gains and losses on related financial assets measured at FVOCI under IFRS 9 (see 7.4.40) or classified as available-for-sale under IAS 39 (see 7I.4.190), in the same way that realised gains or losses are reflected. Under shadow accounting, the effect of unrealised losses and gains on an insurance liability is recognised in OCI, consistent with the recognition of those unrealised gains

and losses on the related financial assets. Shadow accounting may also be applied to insurance liabilities with payments that are linked contractually to the carrying amount of owner-occupied properties. Shadow accounting may also be applied to deferred acquisition costs and certain intangible assets related to these insurance liabilities. [*IFRS 4.24, 27–28, 30, BC180*]

8.1.90.33   In applying IFRS 9, an entity may elect to present gains or losses on some equity investments in OCI (see 7.4.60, 420). On disposal of these investments, the gains or losses are not reclassified from equity to profit or loss. In our view, IFRS 4 allows the use of shadow accounting through OCI for the remeasurement of liabilities to reflect gains or losses that are not recognised in profit or loss on disposal of the related assets. The relevant criterion in IFRS 4 is that unrealised gains or losses on the investment are recognised in OCI. The standard does not specify where realised gains or losses should be recognised. In our view, if shadow accounting is applied, then remeasurement of the liabilities reflecting gains or losses on these assets should be recognised in OCI as unrealised gains or losses are recognised on the investment and should not be reclassified to profit or loss on derecognition of the investment.

8.1.90.35   When an entity applies its existing accounting policies to insurance contracts under IFRS 4, it applies the policies based on GAAP existing at the date on which the entity adopts IFRS 4. In our view, if after IFRS 4 is adopted changes occur to the previous GAAP on which an insurer's existing policies were based, then the entity may amend its policies in line with those previous GAAP changes only if the entity can demonstrate that the changes fulfil the criteria specified in 8.1.90.10–20. That is, in our view the entity is not required to adopt changes in the previous GAAP, and indeed can do so only when it demonstrates that the criteria in 8.1.90.10–20 are met. Accordingly, in some circumstances the entity may not be able to do so and will be required to apply the 'frozen' previous GAAP.

8.1.90.40   In our view, an entity that is intending to move from its existing regulatory-based approach towards US GAAP for its insurance contract liabilities would satisfy the requirements for accounting policy selection with respect to a comprehensive, widely used, investor-oriented model for insurance contracts. However, entities applying US GAAP may do so only for their insurance contracts, as defined under IFRS, and cannot also apply other specialised industry accounting practices for items covered by other IFRS.

8.1.90.50   An entity may wish to change its accounting policy for the measurement of insurance liabilities by moving from a contract-by-contract assessment to a portfolio-based measurement of the liability. Because IAS 37 would apply in the absence of a liability adequacy test that meets the minimum requirements, in our view a change in accounting policy that moves towards the requirements of IAS 37 would generally be considered to increase the relevance of the financial information presented. In our view, such a change would not meet the requirement to increase relevance without impairing the reliability of the resulting information if it results in offsetting gains and losses on dissimilar contracts. However, the requirement could be met to the extent, for example, that the previous contract-by-contract measurement resulted in excessive prudence.

8.1.90.60   When an entity applies the IAS 37 model with respect to a liability adequacy test, IFRS 4 requires the test to be applied at the level of a portfolio of contracts that are subject to broadly similar risks. In deliberating IFRS 4, the IASB noted that there is no conceptual justification for offsetting a loss on one contract against a gain on another contract. Therefore, in our view a change to a portfolio-based approach would not be appropriate if it results in the offsetting of gains and losses from dissimilar contracts – e.g. if expected losses on contracts with a 5 percent guaranteed return were offset against potential gains arising on contracts with a 2 percent guaranteed return. To increase the relevance of the resulting information, we believe that a change to a portfolio-based measurement should define portfolios sufficiently narrowly that such offsetting effects are eliminated. [*IFRS 4.18, BC100*]

8.1.90.70   To avoid artificial accounting mismatches when an insurer changes its accounting policies for insurance liabilities, such as remeasuring the insurance liabilities to reflect current market interest rates and recognising the changes in insurance liabilities in profit or loss, an insurer is permitted to reclassify some or all of its financial assets as at FVTPL. This reclassification is treated as a change in accounting policy (see 2.8.50). [*IFRS 4.45*]

8.1.100   INSURANCE CONTRACTS ACQUIRED IN BUSINESS COMBINATION

8.1.100.10   When an entity acquires another entity in a business combination, the acquirer measures, at the date of exchange, the identifiable assets acquired, the liabilities and contingent liabilities assumed, and equity instruments issued at fair value (see 2.6.600). [*IFRS 3.18*]

8.1.100.20   Therefore, at the date of acquisition, an insurer measures at fair value the assets and liabilities arising under insurance contracts acquired in a business combination. An insurer is permitted, but not required, to use an expanded presentation that splits the fair value of acquired insurance contracts into two components:

- a liability measured in accordance with the insurer's existing accounting policies, which would generally be larger than the fair value of the acquired contracts; and
- an intangible asset, representing the difference between the fair value of the acquired insurance contracts and the larger reported amount under the first component. [*IFRS 4.31*]

8.1.100.30   This intangible asset is often described as the present value of in-force business, PVFP or value of business acquired. For a non-life insurance business, a similar presentation may be used – e.g. if acquired claim liabilities are not discounted. [*IFRS 4.BC147(b)*]

8.1.100.40   The recognised acquired intangible asset is excluded from the scope of the general standard on intangibles (see chapter 3.3). This was done to permit insurers to continue to use their existing method of amortisation. The subsequent measurement of this intangible asset is required to be consistent with the measurement of the related insurance liability. In our view, this means that, unlike goodwill, this intangible asset should generally be amortised over the estimated life of the contracts or a run-off period of insurance contract provisions. Because these intangible assets related to insurance liabilities are covered by the liability adequacy test (as to insurance liabilities-related intangible assets), these assets are also excluded from the scope of the general standard on impairment (see chapter 3.10). [*IFRS 4.33, BC149*]

8.1.100.50   An insurer acquiring a portfolio of insurance contracts (portfolio transfer), outside a business combination, may also use the expanded presentation described in 8.1.100.20. [*IFRS 4.32*]

8.1.100.60   However, IAS 36 and IAS 38 apply to intangible assets such as customer lists and customer relationships because such assets do not represent contractual insurance rights and contractual insurance obligations that existed at the date of a business combination (value of future business). [*IFRS 4.33, BC150*]

8.1.100.70   An illustrative example published with IFRS 3 deals with customer relationships acquired together with a portfolio of one-year motor contracts that are cancellable by policyholders. Because an insurer establishes its relationships with policyholders through insurance contracts, the customer relationship with policyholders meets the contractual-legal criterion for identification as an intangible asset and is recognised separately from goodwill. [*IFRS 3.IE30(d)*]

8.1.110   CONTRACTS WITH DPFs

8.1.110.10   A DPF is a contractual right of the investor or policyholder to receive additional benefits, as a supplement to guaranteed benefits. In our view, both the DPF and the guaranteed benefits should be present at the inception of the contract to fall into the scope of IFRS 4 because there has to be a guaranteed benefit to the holder for the definition of a DPF to be met. The amount or timing of the additional benefits received by the policyholder contractually is at the discretion of the issuer. These additional benefits are generally based on the performance of a specified pool of contracts, on the realised and/or unrealised investment returns on a designated pool of assets or on the profit or loss of the entity. If a contract stipulates that unrealised gains become payable to the policyholder when they are realised, then in our view the policyholder's right to these gains meets the definition of a DPF if the timing of realisation of the gains is at the discretion of the insurer. To fall within the definition of a DPF, the additional benefits should be a significant portion of the total contractual benefits. Such contracts may be insurance contracts or investment contracts and are often described as 'participating' or 'with-profits' contracts. [*IFRS 4.A, IU 01-10*]

8.1.110.20   In our view, the amount of a DPF is limited to the amount of discretionary benefit that is referred to either in the contract or in related law. If a contract establishes a minimum share of a surplus (up to 100 percent of the surplus) that will, subject to discretion over timing, be paid under the DPF, then in our view the entire surplus is part of the DPF because the timing of any payments is discretionary with respect to the whole surplus. However, if a contract establishes a right to share in a specified amount of the surplus, subject to discretion over timing and with no further rights beyond the specified amounts, then we believe that only the specified amount meets the definition of a DPF – i.e. any additional amounts that are paid voluntarily by the insurer do not meet the definition.

8.1.110.25   If a contract establishes a right to share in surplus but specifies neither a minimum nor a specified share in a surplus, then in our view the entire surplus is part of the DPF. However, if a contract, including any applicable law, contains no mention whatsoever of additional amounts that may be payable beyond a specified amount, so that any additional amount paid by the insurer is paid despite the lack of a contractual right of the policyholder, then we believe that such an additional amount that is paid is not part of a DPF. The classification is also valid regardless of the amounts paid in practice – e.g. paid because of competitive considerations. However, in certain cases application of the liability adequacy test considering all the expected cash flows under the contract may result in the measurement of the liability exceeding the amount that meets the definition of a DPF.

8.1.110.30   Any guaranteed amount to which the policyholder has an unconditional right is classified as a liability by the entity issuing the policy. The amount payable under the DPF, if it is measured separately from the guaranteed amount, may be classified as a liability or as a separate component of equity. It may not be classified in an intermediate (mezzanine) category that is neither liability nor equity. The standard does not specify how the classification should be determined. However, it does require the presentation adopted to be applied consistently. [*IFRS 4.34*]

8.1.110.40   If a contract that meets the definition of a financial instrument but not an insurance contract contains a DPF, then the contract falls into the scope of IFRS 4 and the guidance of IFRS 4 for insurance contracts also applies. If the entire DPF within the investment contract is classified as a liability, then the liability adequacy test is applied to the whole contract. If some or all of the DPF is classified as equity, then the liability amount includes, as a minimum, the amount that would be recognised for the guaranteed element under IFRS 9 or IAS 39. However, if the recognised liability is clearly higher, then the issuer does not need to determine the amount that would result from applying IFRS 9 or IAS 39 to the guaranteed element. [*IFRS 4.2, 35*]

8.1.110.43   If a DPF amount is classified as a liability, then it is considered in applying the liability adequacy test. In our view, amounts that the policyholder could enforce at the reporting date should also be included in applying the liability adequacy test even if that portion of the DPF is classified as equity. For example, amounts that would be required to be paid in the event that a surrender option is exercised should be included in applying the liability adequacy test.

8.1.110.45   In a contract that establishes the policyholder's right to receive a share of the surplus and the insurer classifies this DPF as a liability, the insurer may expect to pay an amount less than the entire difference between the guaranteed amount and the specified share of surplus. In our view, notwithstanding the insurer's expectation of paying a lower amount, the entire difference between the guaranteed amount and the specified share of accumulated surplus should be included in the measurement of the DPF liability.

8.1.110.47   In our view, if a DPF amount that is presented as equity is subject to a constructive obligation (see 3.12.60), then, as a minimum, the nature of the equity amount should be described, including the nature of the constraints over the entity's discretion.

8.1.110.50   Premiums received may be recognised as revenue for both insurance contracts and investment contracts containing a DPF. However, the portion of profit or loss attributable to the equity component is presented as an allocation of profit or loss (in a manner similar to the presentation of NCI), and not as expense or income. [*IFRS 4.34(c)*]

8.1.110.60   For a discussion of the disclosure of financial instruments with a DPF, see 8.1.150.

8.1.112   INVESTMENT CONTRACTS WITH AN OPTION TO SWITCH BETWEEN UNIT-LINKED FUNDS AND FUNDS WITH DPFs

8.1.112.10   Investment contracts often give an investor the option to invest in both a range of unit-linked funds and funds with DPFs. Investment contracts such as unit-linked products are accounted for under IFRS 9 or IAS 39, whereas investment contracts with DPFs are in the scope of IFRS 4. [*IFRS 4.2, 35*]

8.1.112.20   Investment contracts may provide the investor with the option of switching from one fund or product to another – e.g. from a unit-linked product to a product with a DPF. Switches may happen at any time during the term of a contract, with the ability to switch sometimes unrestricted and sometimes limited. Although investment contracts with the option to switch are usually financial instruments under IFRS 9 or IAS 39, IFRS 4 applies to financial instruments with a DPF and so the appropriate accounting treatment is not always immediately apparent.

8.1.114   Classification

8.1.114.10   A contract (or group of contracts) would be classified as DPF from its inception if, at inception, historical data suggests that it is likely that investors will switch a significant portion of their investments into DPF funds for a sufficiently long period during the life of the contract and that the investment return (surplus) arising on the DPF component is significant compared with the entire investment returns under the contract. In our view, the assessment of significance should consider both the amounts and timing of expected cash flows. If these requirements are not met, then a contract (or group of contracts) would not be classified as DPF even if investments are placed in a DPF fund at inception. In our view, whether the definition is met may be assessed based on portfolios of similar contracts.

8.1.116   Reclassification as a result of changes in investor behaviour

8.1.116.10   Because the definition of a contract is based on the probability of switching and the significance of DPF-type benefits over the life of the contract, the decision of an investor to switch between funds will not impact the classification of a contract. However, an entity would need to consider changing the classification of a contract, or a group of contracts, if there is a significant change in investor behaviour such that it either becomes less likely or more likely that investors will invest in DPF funds for significant periods during the life of the contract. In our view, the classification and accounting for such contracts should be changed prospectively from the date on which the expectations change.

8.1.118   Reclassification when DPF option no longer available

8.1.118.10   In some cases, the investor's option to switch between DPF and unit-linked funds may expire during the life of a contract. In our view, the expiry of an option to switch would not, on its own, lead to a reclassification, although changing expectations with regard to behaviour before the option expires may cause a change in classification.

8.1.118.20   We believe that a contract (or group of contracts) in which investments are held in unit-linked funds and for which the option to switch to DPF funds no longer exists should nevertheless be classified as DPF if the amount of historical DPF-type benefits is sufficient that it is still likely that DPF benefits will be a significant portion of total contractual benefits.

8.1.118.30   Similarly, we believe that a contract (or group of similar contracts) in which funds are invested in a DPF fund with no further option to switch into a unit-linked fund should be classified as DPF only if it is still expected that historical and future DPF-type benefits will be a significant portion of total contractual benefits.

8.1.120   PRESENTATION AND DISCLOSURES

8.1.130   Self-insurance/captive insurance

8.1.130.10   A number of entities within a group may insure certain risks with a third party insurer under an arrangement in which another entity within the group (a captive reinsurer) takes some or all of that risk back into the group. The question that then arises is whether and to what extent the amounts in the statement of profit or loss and OCI and the statement of financial position, in respect of the insurance and reinsurance contracts with the third party insurer, should be eliminated or offset in consolidated financial statements.

8.1.130.20   IFRS 4 notes that (for the purpose of assessing the significance of insurance risk) contracts entered into simultaneously with a single counterparty (or contracts that are otherwise interdependent) form a single contract. This approach is consistent with the requirements for financial instruments accounted for under IFRS 9 (see 7.6.40) or IAS 39 (see 7I.5.40) whereby two transactions would be considered as a single contract when they are entered into at the same time, in contemplation of each other, with the same counterparty and when there is no substantive business reason for undertaking the two transactions separately. [*IFRS 4.B25*]

8.1.130.30   In our view, the amounts in the statement of financial position in respect of premiums and claims payable to and receivable from the captive reinsurer should not be offset unless the strict offsetting requirements are met in IFRS 9 or IAS 39 (see 7.10.110 and 7I.8.90, respectively). In our view, it may be appropriate to offset premium and claims expenses and income in the statement of profit or loss and OCI, but only if the third party insurer is acting as a conduit for the captive reinsurer – in other words, if the contracts are interdependent. This would sometimes be the case if the captive reinsurer does not have the regulatory approval required to issue a direct insurance contract.

8.1.130.40   We believe that a primary indicator that the third party insurer is acting as a conduit rather than as a principal in the transaction would be that the insurer is not exposed to credit risk from the captive reinsurer. For example, the third party insurer may not be required to pay claims unless and until it has received payment from the captive reinsurer. If the third party is exposed to the credit risk of the captive, then in our view this would indicate that the transactions are not interdependent and no offsetting in the statement of profit or loss and OCI should be permitted.

8.1.140   Presentation of premium income as revenue

8.1.140.10   In some jurisdictions, general practice has been to present insurance premiums received as revenue, with a deduction for unearned premiums presented elsewhere in the statement of profit or loss and OCI. In our view, consistent with the definition of revenue in IFRS 15, revenue on insurance contracts represents premiums earned for insurance cover provided during the period. Therefore, we believe that premiums received should not be described as revenue. However, this does not preclude the presentation of premiums received as additional information in the statement of profit or loss and OCI as long as this amount is not described as revenue.

8.1.150   Disclosures

8.1.150.10   An entity provides disclosures that explain the amounts in the financial statements arising from insurance contracts. It also provides information that enables a user to evaluate the nature and extent of risks arising from insurance contracts. [*IFRS 4.36, 38*]

8.1.150.20   An insurer discloses:
- its accounting policies for insurance contracts;
- the amounts of the recognised assets, liabilities, income and expense arising from insurance contracts;
- how the most significant assumptions used to measure those amounts are determined (and, if practicable, the assumptions themselves); and
- information about the effect of changes in assumptions. [*IFRS 4.37*]

8.1.150.30   An insurer also discloses the reconciliations of changes in insurance liabilities, reinsurance assets and related deferred acquisition costs. [*IFRS 4.37*]

8.1.150.40   In addition to the disclosure requirements in 8.1.150.10–30, an insurer discloses:
- its risk management objectives and policies and methods for managing insurance risk;
- the sensitivity to insurance risk;
- concentrations of insurance risk – e.g. low-frequency, high-severity risks such as earthquakes, cyclical risks;
- claims development information, covering all periods for which material claims (for which uncertainty remains) are outstanding, but need not go back more than 10 years; and
- information about credit, liquidity and market risks of insurance contracts as if the insurance contracts were in the scope of IFRS 7. [*IFRS 4.39*]

8.1.150.50   The implementation guidance suggests extensive *possible* disclosures. However, an insurer decides in light of its circumstances how much detail has to be given to satisfy the disclosure requirements, how much emphasis it places on different aspects and how it aggregates information to portray the overall picture without combining information that has materially different characteristics. [*IFRS 4.IG11–IG71*]

8.1.150.60   Since financial instruments with a DPF are financial instruments, the disclosure requirements for financial instruments in IFRS 7 (see chapters 7.10 and 7I.8) also apply. However, there is some additional relief regarding the requirement to disclose fair values, if the fair value cannot be measured reliably. [*IFRS 4.2, 7.29(c)*]

8.1.160   APPLYING IFRS 9 WITH IFRS 4

8.1.160.10   *Applying IFRS 9 Financial Instruments with IFRS 4 Insurance Contracts – Amendments to IFRS 4* apply:
- for the temporary exemption from IFRS 9 – for annual periods beginning on or after 1 January 2018; and
- for the overlay approach – for annual periods beginning when an entity first applies IFRS 9.

8.1.160.20   KPMG's publication *First Impressions: Amendments to IFRS 4* provides a more in-depth discussion of the amendments than this section.

8.1.170   Overview

8.1.170.10   The following diagram illustrates how key elements of the requirements are explained throughout this section. The corresponding section numbers are in brackets.

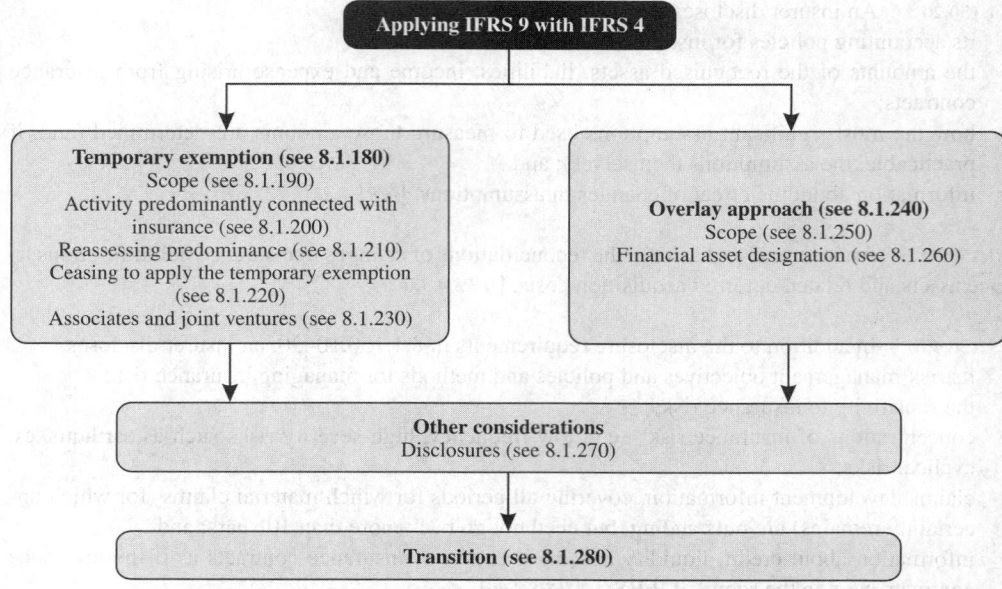

8.1.170.20   The amendments to IFRS 4 introduce two optional approaches for certain entities to address the differing effective dates of IFRS 9 and IFRS 17 (see chapter 8.1A):

- the temporary exemption from IFRS 9; and
- the overlay approach.

8.1.170.30   The temporary exemption from IFRS 9 permits an entity to apply IAS 39 rather than IFRS 9 for annual periods beginning before 1 January 2021 as long as IFRS 17 has not been early adopted. [*IFRS 4.20A, 35A*]

8.1.170.40   The overlay approach permits an entity, for designated financial assets, to adjust its profit or loss for the difference between the amount reported in profit or loss under IFRS 9 and the amount that would have been reported in profit or loss for those assets if the entity had applied IAS 39. [*IFRS 4.35A–35B*]

8.1.170.50   An entity is required to present the effect of the overlay adjustment:

- in profit or loss: as a separate line item (pre-tax); and
- in OCI: as a separate component – this item is grouped with other items that will be reclassified subsequently to profit or loss. [*IFRS 4.35D, BC244*]

8.1.180   Temporary exemption from IFRS 9

8.1.190   *Scope*

8.1.190.10   The temporary exemption from IFRS 9 applies for those entities whose activities are predominantly connected with insurance. Eligibility is assessed at the reporting entity level and is therefore applied at the reporting entity level – i.e. it applies to all financial assets and financial liabilities held by the reporting entity. [*IFRS 4.20B(b), BC252, BC260–BC263*]

8.1.190.20   An entity that has already applied any version of IFRS 9 is not permitted to stop applying it and revert to IAS 39. However, an entity that applies only the presentation requirements in IFRS 9 for gains and losses on financial liabilities designated as at FVTPL (see 7.7.180) can apply the temporary exemption from IFRS 9. Such an entity is permitted to subsequently apply only these specific presentation requirements and still apply the temporary exemption from the rest of IFRS 9. [*IFRS 4.20B–20C, 9.5.7.1(c), 5.7.7–5.7.9, 7.2.14, 7.1.2, B5.7.5–B5.7.20*]

8.1.200   *Activities predominantly connected with insurance*

8.1.200.10   An entity initially assesses whether its activities are predominantly connected with insurance on its annual reporting date immediately before 1 April 2016. [*IFRS 4.20B(b)*]

8.1.200.20   An entity's activities are considered predominantly connected with insurance if:
- the carrying amount of its liabilities arising from contracts that are in the scope of IFRS 4, including deposit components and embedded derivatives unbundled from insurance contracts in the scope of IFRS 4, is significant compared with the total carrying amount of all of its liabilities; and
- the ratio of the total carrying amount of its liabilities connected with insurance compared with the total carrying amount of all of its liabilities is:
  - greater than 90 percent; or
  - greater than 80 percent but less than or equal to 90 percent, and the entity does not engage in a significant activity unconnected with insurance. [*IFRS 4.20D, 35A*]

8.1.200.30   In determining the ratio of an entity's total carrying amount of its liabilities connected with insurance compared with the total carrying amount of all of its liabilities, the following types of liabilities are considered to be connected with insurance:
- those arising from contracts that are in the scope of IFRS 4, including deposit components and embedded derivatives unbundled from insurance contracts in the scope of IFRS 4;
- non-derivative investment contract liabilities measured at FVTPL under IAS 39, including those designated as at FVTPL; and
- other liabilities that arise because the insurer issues, or fulfils obligations arising from, the contracts above. [*IFRS 4.20E*]

8.1.200.40   Examples of these other liabilities include:
- derivatives used to mitigate risks arising from insurance contracts and the assets backing those contracts;
- tax, salaries and other employment benefit liabilities of the insurance activities; and
- debt issued that is included in the insurer's regulatory capital. [*IFRS 4.20E, BC255*]

EXAMPLE 3 – PERFORMING THE ASSESSMENT

8.1.200.50   Company D has an annual reporting date of 31 December 2015. This is its initial assessment date because it is the annual reporting date immediately before 1 April 2016.

8.1.200.60   D's total liabilities at 31 December 2015 consist of:
- 45% contracts in the scope of IFRS 4;

- 10% deposit components unbundled from insurance contracts;
- 25% investment contracts not in the scope of IFRS 4 that are measured at FVTPL;
- 12% other liabilities that arise because D issues and fulfils obligations arising from the contracts above; and
- 8% deposits from D's banking customers.

8.1.200.70   In this example, D concludes that the carrying amount of liabilities arising from contracts in the scope of IFRS 4 is significant compared with the total carrying amount of all of its liabilities because 55% of its total liabilities are in the scope of IFRS 4, including deposit components unbundled from insurance contracts. [*IFRS 4.BC258*]

8.1.200.80   D calculates that 92% of the carrying amount of its liabilities is connected with insurance, as the only liabilities not connected with insurance are the 8% deposits from banking customers.

8.1.200.90   Because D's predominance ratio is greater than 90%, it qualifies to apply the temporary exemption from IFRS 9 without having to consider whether it engages in a significant activity unconnected with insurance.

8.1.200.100   If the ratio of the total carrying amount of an entity's liabilities connected with insurance compared with the total carrying amount of all of its liabilities is greater than 80 percent but less than or equal to 90 percent, then an entity has to determine whether it engages in a significant activity unconnected with insurance. [*IFRS 4.20D*]

8.1.200.110   In performing this assessment, the entity considers:
- only those activities from which it may earn income and incur expenses; and
- qualitative and/or quantitative factors, including publicly available information about the industry classification that users of financial statements assign to it. [*IFRS 4.20F*]

8.1.210   *Reassessing predominance*

8.1.210.10   After the initial assessment, an entity may be required or permitted to complete an updated assessment. To determine whether it should or may perform a reassessment, an entity carries out the following analysis. [*IFRS 4.20G*]

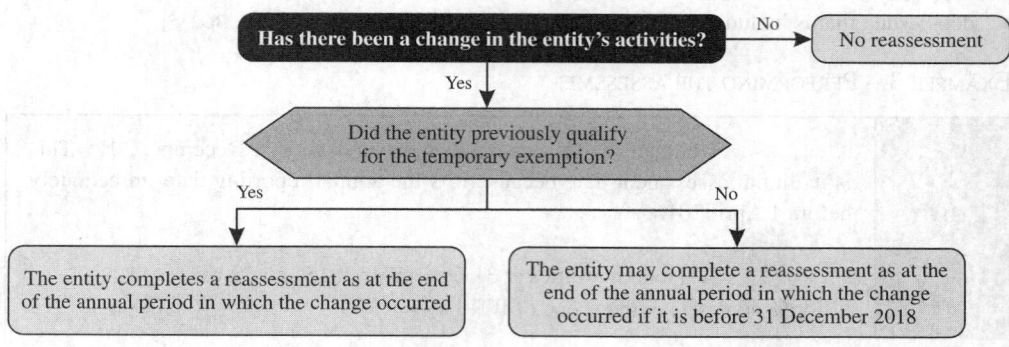

8.1.210.20   A change in an entity's activities that would result in a reassessment is one that is:
- determined by senior management as a result of external or internal changes;
- significant to the entity's operations; and
- demonstrable to external parties. [*IFRS 4.20H*]

8.1.210.30   Such a change occurs only when an entity begins or ceases to perform an activity that is significant to its operations, or if it significantly changes the magnitude of one of its activities. A change in funding structure that does not affect its activities would not result in a reassessment. A plan to sell a business line would not give rise to a reassessment; however, the actual sale of the business line could change the entity's activities and give rise to a reassessment. A change that results in a reassessment is expected to be very infrequent. [*IFRS 4.20H–20I*]

8.1.220   *Ceasing to apply the temporary exemption from IFRS 9*

8.1.220.10   If an entity is required to stop applying the temporary exemption from IFRS 9 sooner than its annual reporting period beginning before 1 January 2021 as a result of a reassessment, then it is permitted to continue to apply IAS 39 until the earlier of:
- the end of the annual period that begins immediately after the reassessment; and
- its last annual reporting period beginning before 1 January 2021. [*IFRS 4.20A, 20J*]

8.1.220.20   An entity that previously applied the temporary exemption from IFRS 9 is permitted to apply IFRS 9 at the beginning of any subsequent annual reporting period. [*IFRS 4.20A, 20K*]

8.1.230   *Entities that invest in associates and joint ventures*

8.1.230.10   If an entity accounts for an investment in an associate or joint venture under the equity method, then it may retain the relevant accounting policies applied by the associate or joint venture. This relief applies on an investment-by-investment basis. [*IFRS 4.20O, 20Q*]

8.1.230.20   If an investor applies IFRS 9 and an associate or joint venture applies the temporary exemption from IFRS 9 in its financial statements, then the investor is permitted to retain the IAS 39 accounting used by the associate or joint venture. [*IFRS 4.20O*]

8.1.230.30   If an investor applies the temporary exemption from IFRS 9 and an associate or joint venture applies IFRS 9 in its financial statements, then the investor is permitted to retain the IFRS 9 accounting used by the associate or joint venture. [*IFRS 4.20O*]

8.1.230.40   An entity may change the choice of which standard (i.e. IAS 39 or IFRS 9) is applied in the equity method accounting for a specific investment in an associate or joint venture in certain circumstances. If IFRS 9 was previously applied in the equity method accounting for a specific investment, then the investor continues to apply it to that investment. Conversely, if the temporary exemption from IFRS 9 was used in the equity method accounting for a specific investment, then IFRS 9 may subsequently be applied to it. [*IFRS 4.20P*]

8.1.240   Overlay approach

8.1.250   *Scope*

8.1.250.10   An insurer is permitted to apply the overlay approach to designated financial assets. The overlay approach may be elected only when an entity first applies IFRS 9, including:

- when it first applies IFRS 9 after applying the temporary exemption from IFRS 9; or
- after applying only the requirements in IFRS 9 relating to the presentation of gains and losses on financial liabilities designated as at FVTPL (see 7.7.180). [*IFRS 4.35B–35C, 9.5.7.1(c), 5.7.7–5.7.9, 7.2.14, 7.1.2, B5.7.5–B5.7.20*]

8.1.260 *Financial asset designation*

8.1.260.10   An entity is permitted to make this designation on an instrument-by-instrument basis. Financial assets are eligible for designation only if they:
- are not held in respect of an activity that is unconnected with contracts in the scope of IFRS 4;
- are measured at FVTPL under IFRS 9; and
- would not be measured at FVTPL in their entirety under IAS 39. [*IFRS 4.35E, 35G*]

8.1.260.20   Financial assets held by an entity to maintain insurance regulatory requirements or internal capital objectives may be eligible. Financial assets held in funds relating to investment contracts that are outside the scope of IFRS 4 are not eligible. [*IFRS 4.35E, BC240*]

8.1.260.30   After electing this approach, an entity:
- may designate financial assets for the overlay approach on their initial recognition;
- may designate a previously recognised financial asset for the overlay approach if it now meets the criteria in 8.1.260.10 but previously did not; and
- is required to de-designate a financial asset if it no longer meets those same criteria. [*IFRS 4.35F, 35I(a)*]

8.1.260.40   When an entity de-designates a financial asset, any balance in accumulated OCI associated with it is reclassified to profit or loss. [*IFRS 4.35J, IAS 1.7*]

8.1.260.50   Shadow accounting (see 8.1.90) may apply if an entity uses the overlay approach. [*IFRS 4.BC246*]

EXAMPLE 4 – OVERLAY APPROACH

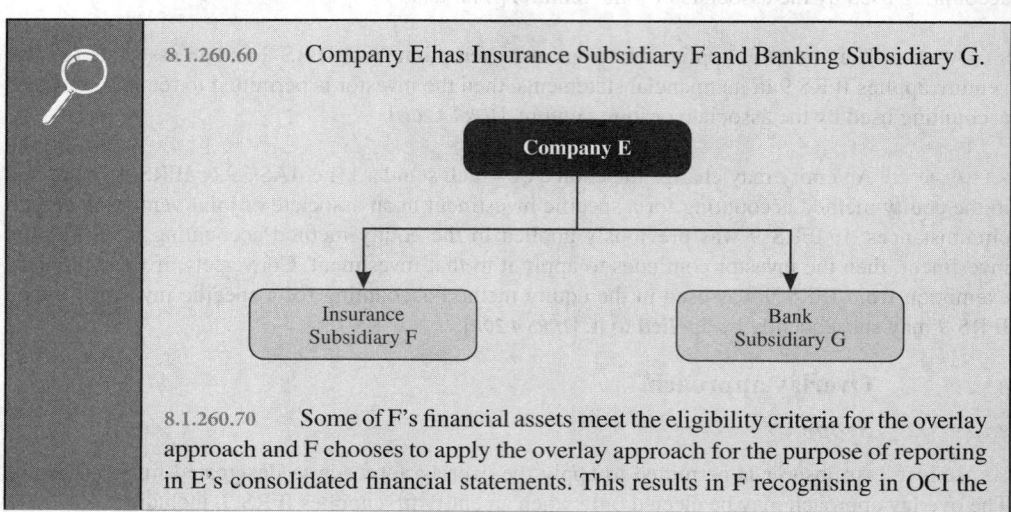

8.1.260.60   Company E has Insurance Subsidiary F and Banking Subsidiary G.

Company E

Insurance Subsidiary F

Bank Subsidiary G

8.1.260.70   Some of F's financial assets meet the eligibility criteria for the overlay approach and F chooses to apply the overlay approach for the purpose of reporting in E's consolidated financial statements. This results in F recognising in OCI the

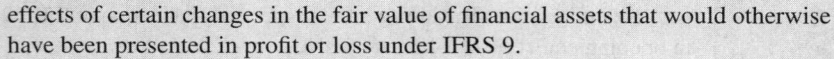

> effects of certain changes in the fair value of financial assets that would otherwise have been presented in profit or loss under IFRS 9.
>
> 8.1.260.80   If F subsequently transfers to G those financial assets to which F had previously applied the overlay approach and, following the transfer, the transferred assets are associated with G's banking activities – which are unconnected with contracts in the scope of IFRS 4 – then the cumulative effect of changes in the fair value of those financial assets, previously presented in OCI, would be immediately reclassified to profit or loss in E's financial statements.

8.1.270   Disclosures

8.1.270.10   If an entity applies the temporary exemption from IFRS 9, then it provides disclosures that enable users of financial statements to:
- understand how the entity qualified for the temporary exemption from IFRS 9; and
- compare entities that apply the temporary exemption from IFRS 9 with those that do not. [*IFRS 4.39B–39C*]

8.1.270.20   If an entity applies the overlay approach, then it provides disclosures that enable users of financial statements to understand how the total amount reclassified between profit or loss and OCI was calculated and how it affects the financial statements. [*IFRS 4.39K*]

8.1.270.30   Disclosures are required about how an entity determines the financial assets for which an overlay adjustment is made, an explanation of how the overlay adjustment was derived in the period and its impacts on each affected line item in profit or loss. [*IFRS 4.39L*]

8.1.280   Transition

8.1.280.10   Some disclosures required when applying the temporary exemption are provided based on groups, similar to the groups that would be separately disclosed under IFRS 9. When an entity starts applying the temporary exemption from IFRS 9, it uses the applicable transition provisions in IFRS 9 to the extent needed to provide the disclosures required. When it stops applying the approach, it also follows the transition provisions under IFRS 9. [*IFRS 4.20C, BC274*]

8.1.280.20   When an entity starts applying the overlay approach, it does so retrospectively to designated financial assets on transition to IFRS 9. For example, an entity recognises an adjustment to the opening balance of accumulated OCI for the difference between the fair value of a designated financial asset under IFRS 9 and its carrying amount under IAS 39. An entity restates comparative information under the overlay approach only if it restates comparative information when applying IFRS 9 (see 7.11.30.20). [*IFRS 4.49*]

EXAMPLE 5 – TRANSITION TO THE OVERLAY APPROACH

> 8.1.280.30   Company X adopts IFRS 9 for the annual period ending 31 December 2018; 1 January 2018 is its date of initial application. X elects not to restate com-

parative information. The impact of retrospective application of IFRS 9 is recognised in opening equity as at 1 January 2018.

8.1.280.40   X has a financial asset that was classified as available-for-sale under IAS 39. X has determined that under IFRS 9 the asset will be measured at FVTPL. It acquired the financial asset on 31 December 2016 for 75. At 31 December 2017, the fair value of the instrument is 90. Under IAS 39, the difference of 15 between cost and fair value was recognised in OCI.

8.1.280.50   On initial application of IFRS 9, X transfers 15 from accumulated OCI into opening retained earnings at 1 January 2018, reflecting the reclassification of the asset from available-for-sale to FVTPL.

8.1.280.60   On transition to IFRS 9, X elects to apply the overlay approach to the financial asset.

8.1.280.70   Therefore X transfers 15 back from retained earnings to accumulated OCI at 1 January 2018. This is the reinstatement of the accumulated OCI balance as an overlay adjustment.

8.1.280.80   On 31 December 2018, X sells the financial asset for its fair value at that date of 90.

8.1.280.90   Accordingly, on sale, X derecognises the asset of 90 under IFRS 9 and reclassifies from OCI to profit or loss an overlay adjustment of 15 that results in the profit or loss for the designated financial asset being the same as if the insurer had applied IAS 39.

8.1.280.100 An entity is permitted to stop applying the overlay approach at the beginning of any annual reporting period before it implements IFRS 17. If it does, then the change in accounting policy is accounted for retrospectively to the extent practicable (see 2.8.70). [*IFRS 4.35I(b), IAS 8.19–25*]

8.1A   Insurance contracts: IFRS 17

8.1A   Insurance contracts: IFRS 17

FORTHCOMING REQUIREMENTS

In May 2017, the IASB published IFRS 17 *Insurance Contracts*. IFRS 17 supersedes IFRS 4 *Insurance Contracts*.

IFRS 17 applies for annual periods beginning on or after 1 January 2021. Early adoption is permitted for entities that apply IFRS 9 *Financial Instruments* and IFRS 15 *Revenue from Contracts with Customers* on or before the date of the initial application of IFRS 17.

IFRS 4 includes a temporary exemption from IFRS 9 and the overlay approach (see 8.1.160). From the date of initial application of IFRS 17 – i.e. the beginning of the period in which an entity first applies IFRS 17 – these approaches are no longer available and IFRS 9 is applied, without delay or adjustment.

The requirements related to this topic are mainly derived from the following.

REFERENCE	TITLE
IFRS 17	Insurance Contracts

FUTURE DEVELOPMENTS

The IASB has formed a Transition Resource Group for IFRS 17, to provide a public forum for stakeholders to follow the discussion of implementation questions. These discussions will also help the Board determine what, if any, action will be needed to address those questions.

OVERVIEW

8.1A.10.10   The following diagram illustrates how key elements of the standard are explained throughout this chapter. The corresponding section numbers are in brackets.

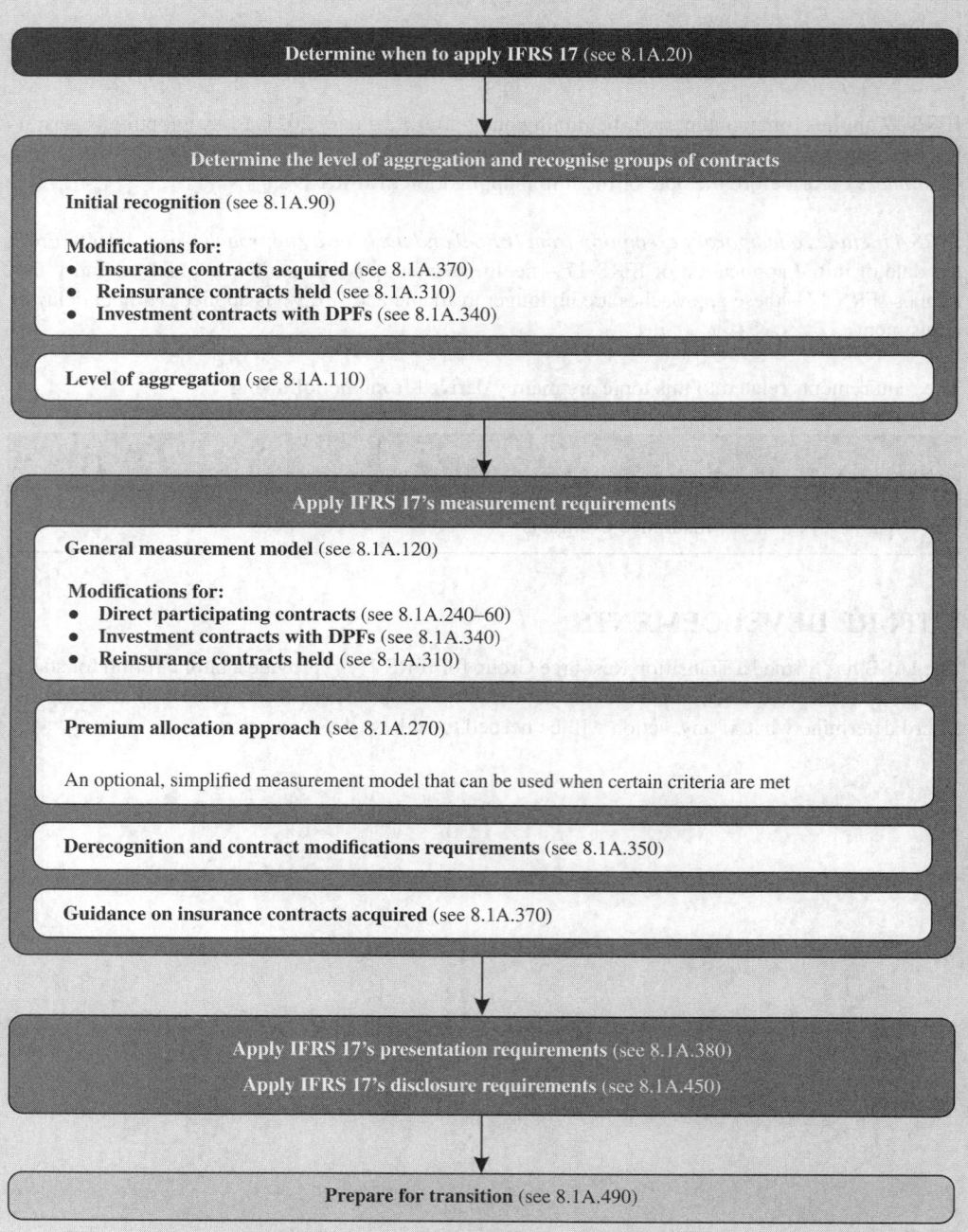

8.1A.20   SCOPE

8.1A.20.10   IFRS 17 focuses on types of contracts, rather than types of entities. Therefore, it applies to all entities, whether they are regulated as insurance entities or not. Insurers are subject to the requirements of other applicable standards for products (or components of products) that are not insurance contracts. For example, IFRS 15 applies to fees and related costs on investment management contracts.

8.1A.20.20   An entity applies IFRS 17 to contracts that meet the definition of an insurance contract, which generally include insurance or reinsurance contracts that it issues and reinsurance contracts that it holds. However, there are some exceptions to this general principle. [*IFRS 17.3*]

EXCEPTION	FURTHER DETAILS	REFERENCE
Investment contracts with DPF	Investment contracts issued with DPFs do not meet the definition of an insurance contract, but are accounted for under IFRS 17 if the entity also issues insurance contracts.	8.1A.40
Scope exemptions	There are some contracts that could meet the insurance contract definition but are not in the scope of IFRS 17 – e.g. product warranties or residual value guarantees issued by a manufacturer, dealer or retailer.	8.1A.50
Fixed-fee service contracts	Fixed-fee service contracts meet the definition of an insurance contract but may be accounted for under IFRS 15 in certain circumstances.	8.1A.60
Financial guarantee contracts	Some credit-related guarantees and credit insurance contracts meet the definition of an insurance contract but may be accounted for under the financial instruments standards.	8.1A.70

8.1A.20.30   An insurance contract is "a contract under which one party – the issuer – accepts 'significant insurance risk' from another party – the policyholder". If a "specified uncertain future event – the insured event – adversely affects the policyholder", then the policyholder has a right to obtain compensation from the issuer under the contract. [*IFRS 17.A*]

8.1A.20.40   'Insurance risk' is a risk, other than financial risk, that is transferred from the policyholder to the issuer of a contract. The issuer accepts a risk from the policyholder that the policyholder was already exposed to. The following table includes examples of insurance risk and financial risk. [*IFRS 17.A, B11*]

INSURANCE RISK	FINANCIAL RISK
Risks such as: • death or survival; • injury;	The risk of a possible future change in one or more of: • interest rates; • financial instrument prices;

INSURANCE RISK	FINANCIAL RISK
• illness; • disability; • loss of property due to damage or theft; • failure of a debtor to make a payment when it is due; or • a possible change in a non-financial variable that is specific to a party to the contract.	• commodity prices; • currency exchange rates; • indices of prices or rates; • credit rating or credit indices; or • any other variable, except for a non-financial variable that is specific to a party to the contract.

8.1A.20.50   A contract is not an insurance contract if it exposes the issuer only to financial risk but not to significant insurance risk. However, contracts that expose the issuer to both financial risk and significant insurance risk are insurance contracts. For example, a life insurance contract with a guaranteed minimum rate of return (financial risk) and a promised death benefit that may significantly exceed the policyholder's account balance (insurance risk) is an insurance contract. [*IFRS 17.B7, B9*]

8.1A.20.60   The risk of a possible future change in a non-financial variable is an insurance risk only if that variable is specific to a party of the contract. The occurrence (or non-occurrence) of a weather event or earthquake that damages or destroys an asset of the insured party is insurance risk. Therefore, contracts that cover these risks can meet the definition of an insurance contract. Insurance swaps and other contracts that trigger a payment depending on changes in climatic, geological or other physical variables that are specific to a party to the contract can also meet the definition. [*IFRS 17.B8, B26(j)–(k)*]

8.1A.20.70   Weather or catastrophe indices – e.g. an index of earthquake losses in a particular region – are not specific to a party to the contract, so they do not meet the definition of insurance risk. Contracts commonly referred to as 'catastrophe bonds', which provide for reduced payments of principal, interest or both – depending on climatic, geological or other physical variables whose effects are not specific to a party to the contract – are not insurance contracts. [*IFRS 17.B27(g)–(h)*]

8.1A.20.80   A loan or bond is an insurance contract if it provides for forgiveness of, or a significant reduction in, principal or interest payments when a specified uncertain event occurs that adversely affects the debtor as a result of a pre-existing non-financial risk. Examples are not limited to natural catastrophes and include:
• a loan for which the full balance is forgiven on the death of the debtor; or
• a catastrophe bond under which payments are reduced significantly if the specified triggering event includes a condition that the issuer of the bond suffers a loss. [*IFRS 17.B26(j)–(k)*]

8.1A.20.90   Contracts that cover the risk of changes in the fair value of a specific non-financial asset held by a party to the contract, reflecting changes in the condition of the asset and market prices, can meet the definition of an insurance contract. Those that cover only the risk of changes in market prices are not specific to the insured party and do not meet the definition. For the scope exemption for residual value guarantees provided by a manufacturer, dealer or retailer, and a lessee's residual value guarantee embedded in a finance lease, see 8.1A.50. [*IFRS 17.B8*]

EXAMPLE 1 – RESIDUAL VALUE GUARANTEES

8.1A.20.100   Insurer S (not a manufacturer, dealer or retailer) issues a contract that:
- guarantees the residual value of a vehicle owned by the holder of the contract; and
- pays an amount that will vary depending on the specific condition of the vehicle at the date of sale.

8.1A.20.110   This contract can meet the definition of an insurance contract.

8.1A.20.120   Modifying the scenario, if a similar contract requires the owner to restore the vehicle to a specified condition before disposal in the market place – such that the guarantee is of a market value that does not depend on the condition of the vehicle – then in our view the contract is not an insurance contract.

8.1A.20.130   Insurance risk is significant only if there is a scenario that has commercial substance in which, on a present value basis, there is a possibility that an issuer could suffer a loss caused by the insured event and pay significant additional amounts beyond what would be paid if the insured event had not occurred. To have commercial substance, it has to have a discernible effect on the economics of the transaction. [*IFRS 17.B18–B21*]

8.1A.20.140   For example, a life insurance contract in which the amount paid on death is higher than on surrender or maturity can meet the definition of an insurance contract, unless the amount contingent on death is insignificant in all scenarios. [*IFRS 17.B23*]

8.1A.20.150   The significance of insurance risk is assessed on a contract-by-contract basis. As a result, even if there is a minimal probability of significant losses for a portfolio or group of contracts, insurance risk can be significant for an individual contract. [*IFRS 17.B22*]

8.1A.20.160   In addition, insurance risk can be significant even if the insured event is extremely unlikely to occur, or if the expected probability-weighted present value of the contingent cash flows is a small proportion of the expected probability-weighted present value of all of the remaining contractual cash flows. [*IFRS 17.B18*]

8.1A.20.170   When determining whether significant additional amounts will be paid in any scenario, an entity needs to consider the impact of the time value of money. If a contract requires an entity to make payments earlier than expected on the occurrence of an insured event and the cash value of those payments is not adjusted to reflect the time value of money, then there may be scenarios in which additional amounts are payable on a present value basis. For similar reasons, a contract that delays timely reimbursement to the policyholder can eliminate significant insurance risk, because the delayed payments may have a lower present value. [*IFRS 17.B20*]

EXAMPLE 2 – FIXED DEATH BENEFIT

8.1A.20.180 Company X issues a whole-life insurance contract under which it will provide a fixed death benefit when the policyholder dies. There is no expiry date for the cover.

8.1A.20.190 Although it is certain that the policyholder will die, the date of death is uncertain. If an individual policyholder dies earlier than expected, then X has to make a payment earlier than was expected. Significant insurance risk could arise because the payment of the fixed death benefit is not adjusted for the time value of money. [*IFRS 17.B20*]

8.1A.20.200 Some unit-linked savings contracts contain a guaranteed minimum benefit that is payable on the death of the policyholder, if it is higher than the bid value of the units (the unit value) on death. If the contract is surrendered, then the policyholder receives cash for the value of the units surrendered (less any surrender penalties). Therefore, the benefit payable on death may exceed the benefit paid on surrender or maturity of the contract. If there is a possible scenario, in present value terms, in which the guaranteed minimum benefit is larger than the unit value payable on surrender (before consideration of surrender penalties or maturity), then the contract transfers insurance risk. This is because additional amounts are payable by the insurer, over and above the unit value. For these types of contracts, the issuer determines whether insurance risk is significant, taking into account both the possibility of the insured event occurring and the possibility of the unit value being significantly below the guaranteed amount when the insured event occurs. If this insurance risk is significant, then the contract is classified as an insurance contract. [*IFRS 17.B18, B21*]

8.1A.20.210 Factors to consider in this assessment include the term of the contract, the volatility of the unit value and the level of the guaranteed minimum benefit compared with the initial investment. It might be more difficult for the issuer to conclude that the contract is an insurance contract if the contract term is relatively short, the level of the guaranteed minimum benefit is relatively low compared with the initial investment or the volatility of the unit value is relatively low.

8.1A.20.220 Transfer of uncertainty (or risk) is the essence of an insurance contract. Therefore, for a contract to be an insurance contract, uncertainty is required at the contract's inception over at least one of the following:
- the probability that an insured event will occur;
- when it will occur; or
- how much the insurer will need to pay if it occurs. [*IFRS 17.B3*]

8.1A.20.230 Some insurance contracts cover events that have already occurred but for which the ultimate pay-out is still uncertain – e.g. insurance contracts that provide coverage against adverse development of existing claims. In these cases, the insured event determines the ultimate cost of the claim. [*IFRS 17.B5*]

8.1A.20.240 The definition of an insurance contract requires an adverse effect on the policyholder as a precondition for compensation. 'Lapse risk' or 'persistency risk' is the risk that the policyholder will cancel the contract at a time other than when the issuer expected when pricing the contract. This risk is not considered an insurance risk because the payment to the policyholder is not contingent on an uncertain future event that adversely affects the policyholder. The risk of unexpected increases in the administrative costs associated with servicing a contract is known as 'expense risk'. This risk does not include unexpected costs associated with the insured event and is not an insurance risk, because an unexpected change in these expenses does not adversely affect the policyholder. [*IFRS 17.B12–B15*]

8.1A.20.250   If the issuer of a contract is exposed to lapse, persistency or expense risk and mitigates those risks by using a second contract to transfer all or part of those risks to another entity, then the second contract exposes the other entity to insurance risk. Therefore, the second contract can meet the definition of an insurance contract from the perspective of the other entity. However, from the perspective of the entity that used this contract to transfer the risk to the other insurer, this second contract is a contract of direct insurance that it holds – i.e. the entity is a policyholder and it is not a reinsurance contract held – and therefore the entity does not apply IFRS 17 to it (see 8.1A.50). [*IFRS 17.7(g), B15*]

8.1A.20.260   Some contracts do not transfer any insurance risk to the issuer at inception, but do transfer it later. These contracts are not considered to be an insurance contract until the risk transfer occurs. For example, a contract may provide a specified investment return and also specify that the policyholder can elect to receive a life-contingent annuity at then-current annuity rates determined by the entity when the annuity option is exercised. This will not be an insurance contract until the election is made, because it does not transfer insurance risk until that point. For a similar contract to be an insurance contract at the outset, the annuity rate or the determination basis needs to be specified at the inception of the contract (unless the insurance risk is insignificant). [*IFRS 17.B24–B25*]

8.1A.20.270   A financial instrument is not an insurance contract if the modification to the contractual cash flows does not transfer a pre-existing risk (e.g. waiver of only a termination fee that would otherwise be due under the terms of the loan) or the triggering event does not include a condition that the debtor suffer a loss (e.g. a debtor can choose to settle the amount outstanding on a loan by surrendering the collateral). In our view, a non-recourse feature in a secured loan that, in the event of the debtor's default, limits the remedies of the creditor to seizure of the collateral or its proceeds does not make the loan an insurance contract. This is the case even if the collateral is a non-financial asset and the debtor has a pre-existing exposure to the value of the collateral – e.g. the non-financial collateral was owned by the debtor before receiving the loan and was not purchased using the proceeds of the loan. This is because the feature is not an agreement by the creditor to compensate the debtor in the event of a decline in the value of the collateral. [*IFRS 17.A*]

8.1A.20.280   A contract that meets the definition of an insurance contract remains an insurance contract until all rights and obligations expire (or it is derecognised because its terms are modified) (see 8.1A.360). [*IFRS 17.B25*]

8.1A.20.290   Reinsurance contracts are also insurance contracts that need to meet the definition of an insurance contract. However, even if a reinsurance contract does not expose the reinsurer to the possibility of a significant loss, it is still deemed to transfer significant insurance risk if it transfers substantially all of the insurance risk relating to the reinsured portions of the underlying insurance contracts to the reinsurer. [*IFRS 17.B19*]

8.1A.30   **Substance of insurance contracts**

8.1A.30.10   The relationship between an insurer and the policyholder is established by contract. A 'contract' is an agreement between two or more parties that creates enforceable rights and obligations. Enforceability is a matter of law. Contracts can be written, oral or implied by the entity's customary business practices. [*IFRS 17.2*]

8.1A.30.20   Contracts that have the legal form of insurance but pass all significant insurance risk back to the policyholder are not insurance contracts. For example, some financial reinsurance contracts pass all significant insurance risk back to the cedant by adjusting payments made by the cedant as a direct result of insured losses. Some group contracts also have similar features. These contracts are normally financial instruments or service arrangements and are accounted for under IFRS 9 or IFRS 15, as applicable. [*IFRS 17.B27(b)*]

8.1A.30.30   Insurance contracts that are issued by an entity to another entity in its group are insurance contracts in the individual or separate financial statements of the issuing entity. However, in the group's consolidated financial statements there is no insurance contract. [*IFRS 17.B27(c)*]

8.1A.30.40   Mutual insurance entities generally accept significant insurance risk from individual policyholders and then pool these risks. Although policyholders of contracts issued by mutual entities bear the pooled risks of the contracts in their role as owners, the mutual entity is considered to be a separate entity that has accepted insurance risk. [*IFRS 17.B16*]

8.1A.30.50   A set or series of insurance contracts may have the same or related counterparties and achieve or be designed to achieve an overall commercial effect. In this situation, it might be necessary to treat the set or series as a whole, in order to report the substance of the contracts. This could be the case, for example, if one contract completely negates the rights and obligations arising from another contract entered into at the same time and with the same counterparty. [*IFRS 17.9*]

8.1A.40   **Investment contracts with DPFs**

8.1A.40.10   An investment contract with DPFs is a financial instrument that provides an investor with a contractual right to receive, as a supplement to an amount not subject to the discretion of the issuer, additional amounts that are:
- expected to be a significant portion of the total contractual benefits;
- contractually paid at the discretion of the issuer (regarding timing or amount); and
- contractually based on returns from a specified pool of contracts or a type of contract, realised and/or unrealised investment returns on a specified pool of assets held by the issuer, or the profit or loss of the entity or fund that issues the contract. [*IFRS 17.3, 71, B27(a)*]

8.1A.40.20   Because these contracts do not transfer insurance risk, they do not meet the definition of an insurance contract. However, they are in the scope of IFRS 17 if they are issued by an entity that also issues insurance contracts. [*IFRS 17.71*]

8.1A.40.30   In our view, both the right to receive the amount subject to the issuer's discretion and the right to receive the amount that is not subject to the issuer's discretion (i.e. guaranteed amount) should be present at inception of the contract for it to fall in the scope of IFRS 17. If a contract stipulates that unrealised gains become payable to the policyholder when they are realised, then in our view the contract could meet the definition of an investment contract with a DPF if the timing of realisation of the gains is at the discretion of the insurer.

8.1A.40.40   Investment contracts may provide the investor with the option of switching from one fund or product to another – e.g. from an investment contract to an investment contract with a DPF. Switches may happen at any time during the term of a contract, with the ability to switch sometimes unrestricted and sometimes limited. IFRS 9 applies to investment contracts but IFRS 17 applies to investment contracts with a DPF, provided the entity also issues insurance contracts, and so the appropriate accounting treatment is not always immediately apparent.

8.1A.40.50   Such a contract is classified as an investment contract with a DPF from its inception if, at inception, the amounts that are subject to the discretion of the entity are expected to be a significant portion of the total contractual benefit, considering the option to switch funds. This may be the case when historical data suggests that it is expected that investors will switch a significant portion of their investments into DPF funds for a sufficiently long period during the life of the contract and that the investment return (surplus) arising on the DPF funds is significant compared with the total contractual benefits under the contract. In our view, the assessment of significance should consider both the amounts and timing of expected cash flows. If these requirements are not met, then a contract would not be classified under IFRS 17 as an investment contract with a DPF even if investments are placed in a DPF fund at inception.

8.1A.50   Scope exemptions

8.1A.50.10   IFRS 17 does not apply to the following contracts. The issuer accounts for these contracts under the accounting standard(s) listed. [*IFRS 17.71*]

NOT IN SCOPE	APPLICABLE ACCOUNTING STANDARDS AND ADDITIONAL EXPLANATION/EXAMPLES
Warranties issued directly by a manufacturer, dealer or retailer in connection with a sale of its goods or services to a customer [*IFRS 17.7(a), B26(g), BC89–BC90*]	IFRS 15 and IAS 37 Warranties issued directly by a manufacturer, dealer or retailer to cover any defects that were undetected in manufacturing a product, or provide coverage for the customer for faults that arise after the product is transferred to them, are not in the scope of IFRS 17 even though they may meet the insurance contract definition. Warranties issued by a third party for goods sold by a manufacturer, dealer or retailer are in the scope of IFRS 17 – e.g. extended car warranty cover issued by an entity that is not a manufacturer, dealer or retailer. However, if such a contract is considered a fixed-fee service contract, then it may instead be accounted for under IFRS 15.

NOT IN SCOPE	APPLICABLE ACCOUNTING STANDARDS AND ADDITIONAL EXPLANATION/EXAMPLES
Employers' assets and liabilities under employee benefit plans [*IFRS 17.7(b)*]	IAS 19 and IFRS 2
Retirement benefit obligations reported by defined benefit retirement plans [*IFRS 17.7(b)*]	IAS 26
Contractual rights or contractual obligations that are contingent on the future use of, or right to use, a non-financial item [*IFRS 17.7(c)*]	IFRS 15, IFRS 16 and IAS 38 Examples include some licence fees, royalties, variable lease payments and similar items.
Residual value guarantees provided by a manufacturer, dealer or retailer, and a lessee's residual value guarantee embedded in a lease [*IFRS 17.7(d)*]	IFRS 15 and IFRS 16
Financial guarantee contracts – unless the issuer met certain requirements and made an irrevocable election to apply IFRS 17 to the contract [*IFRS 17.7(e)*]	IAS 32, IFRS 7 and IFRS 9
Contingent consideration payable or receivable in a business combination [*IFRS 17.7(f)*]	IFRS 3
Insurance contracts in which the entity is the policy-holder, unless these contracts are reinsurance contracts held by the entity [*IFRS 17.7(g)*]	IAS 37 addresses the accounting for reimbursement rights arising from insurance contracts for expenditure required to settle a provision. IAS 16 addresses some aspects of reimbursement under an insurance contract for the impairment or loss of property, plant and equipment.

8.1A.60   Fixed-fee service contracts

8.1A.60.10   A 'fixed-fee service contract' is a contract under which the level of service depends on an uncertain event. These contracts meet the definition of an insurance contract. The fact that the issuer provides goods or services to the policyholder instead of cash to settle its obligation to compensate the policyholder for insured events does not preclude a contract from being an insurance contract. [*IFRS 17.B6, BC95*]

8.1A.60.20   IFRS 17 permits, but does not require, an entity to apply IFRS 15 to fixed-fee service contracts if the contracts' primary purpose is the provision of a service. This choice is available for contracts that meet the following conditions.

- The contract price set by the entity does not reflect an assessment of the risk associated with an individual customer.
- The contract compensates customers by providing a service, rather than by making cash payments.
- The insurance risk that is transferred by the contract arises primarily from uncertainty about the frequency of the customer's use of the service, rather than about its cost. [*IFRS 17.8*]

8.1A.60.30   If a fixed-fee service contract has the characteristics specified in (see 8.1A.60.20), then an entity may exclude it from the scope of IFRS 17 and account for it like other service contracts with customers. This choice is made on a contract-by-contract basis and is irrevocable for each contract. [*IFRS 17.8*]

8.1A.60.40   An example of such a contract is a fixed-fee maintenance contract in which the service provider agrees to repair specified equipment after a malfunction for a fixed fee. This is because the malfunction of the equipment adversely affects its owner and it is uncertain whether a particular machine will break down within the coverage period. Another example is a fixed-fee contract for car breakdown services in which the service provider agrees to provide roadside assistance to repair or tow the car. For a discussion of IFRS 15 (see chapter 4.2). [*IFRS 17.BC95*]

8.1A.70   Financial guarantee contracts

8.1A.70.10   A financial guarantee contract grants the policyholder the right to be reimbursed by the issuer for a loss that it incurs when a specified debtor fails to make payment when it is due under the terms of a debt instrument. These types of financial guarantees usually meet the definition of an insurance contract. [*IFRS 9.A, 17.B29*]

8.1A.70.20   Conversely, a credit-related contract that is structured to pay the holder even if the holder has not incurred a loss on an underlying debt does not meet the definition of an insurance contract because it does not transfer significant insurance risk. [*IFRS 17.B27(f), B29–B30*]

8.1A.70.30   An entity is not required to apply IFRS 17 to financial guarantee contracts that meet the definition of an insurance contract. However, IFRS 17 permits the issuer of these contracts to account for them under IFRS 17 if it has previously asserted explicitly that it regards such contracts as insurance contracts and accounted for them on that basis. This election may be made on a contract-by-contract basis, but the election for each contract is irrevocable. In all other cases, an issuer accounts for a financial guarantee contract in accordance with the financial instruments standards (see 7.1.60). [*IFRS 17.7(e), B29*]

8.1A.70.40   For an insurer, it is likely to be clear from previous practices, contract documents etc whether issued financial guarantee contracts have been regarded as and accounted for as insurance contracts. For entities that write financial guarantee contracts that are incidental to their main business – e.g. to support borrowings of subsidiaries or of customers – it may be less clear whether the entity has made such an explicit assertion. For these entities, in our view it is not necessary that insurance contract terminology be used in documenting its financial guarantee contracts. The explicit assertion may be apparent from information in previous financial statements and other published information.

SEPARATING COMPONENTS FROM AN INSURANCE CONTRACT

8.1A.80.10   Insurance contracts create a bundle of rights and obligations that work together to generate a package of cash flows. Some types of insurance contracts provide only insurance coverage – e.g. most short-term non-life contracts. However, many– e.g. unit-linked and other participating contracts – contain one or more components that would be in the scope of another standard if the entity accounted for them separately. For example, some insurance contracts contain:

- investment components – e.g. pure deposits, such as financial instruments whereby an entity receives a specified sum and undertakes to repay that sum with interest;
- good and service components – e.g. non-insurance services, such as pension administration, risk management services, asset management or custody services; and
- embedded derivatives – e.g. financial derivatives, such as interest rate options or options linked to an equity index. [*IFRS 17.10, BC98*]

8.1A.80.20   Investment components and goods and services components have to be separated from an insurance contract if they are distinct. An entity is prohibited from applying IFRS 15 or IFRS 9 to components of an insurance contract when separation is not required. [*IFRS 17.11–12, BC114*]

8.1A.80.30   An 'investment component' represents the amounts that an insurance contract requires the entity to repay to a policyholder even if an insured event does not occur. It is separated from the host insurance contract and accounted for in accordance with IFRS 9 if it and the insurance component are not 'highly inter-related' and a contract with equivalent terms is sold or could be sold separately in the same market or jurisdiction. There is no need to undertake an exhaustive search to identify whether an investment component is sold separately; however, all information that is reasonably available needs to be considered. [*IFRS 17.A, 11(b), B31–B32*]

8.1A.80.40   Investment and insurance components are 'highly inter-related' if:

- a policyholder cannot benefit from one component without the other being present – e.g. the lapse or maturity of one component causes the lapse or maturity of the other; or
- the entity cannot measure one component without considering the other – e.g. when the value of one component varies according to the value of the other. [*IFRS 17.B32*]

8.1A.80.50   For example, in some unit-linked contracts the death benefit is the difference between a fixed amount and the value of a deposit component – therefore, the components could not be measured independently.

8.1A.80.60   Investment components that are not distinct from the insurance contract are not separated from the insurance contract, but are accounted for together with the insurance component. However, receipts and payments from these investment components are excluded from insurance contract revenue and insurance service expenses presented in profit or loss. [*IFRS 17.85*]

8.1A.80.70   A promise to provide goods or non-insurance services is distinct, and is separated from the insurance contract, if the policyholder can benefit from the goods or services either on their own or with other resources that are readily available to the policyholder. However, goods or services are not distinct if the cash flows and risks associated with the good or service are highly inter-related with the cash flows and risk of the insurance component and the entity provides a significant service of integrating the good or service with the insurance components. Activities that the entity has to undertake to fulfil the contract are not considered for separation if the entity does not transfer a good or a service to the policyholder as those activities occur. [*IFRS 17.12, B33–B35*]

8.1A.80.80   Embedded derivatives can meet the definition of an insurance contract in certain circumstances. For example, when the related payment that is affected by the derivative is made when the insured event takes place (e.g. a life-contingent annuity in which the insurance risk is the policyholder's survival) and the amount paid is linked to a cost of living index (the embedded derivative). In this case, the embedded derivative also transfers insurance risk, because the number of payments to which the index applies depends on the policyholder's survival – i.e. an uncertain future event. If the insurance risk being transferred is significant, then the embedded derivative is also an insurance contract and is not separated from the host contract. [*IFRS 17.B10*]

8.1A.80.90   If the embedded derivative does not meet the definition of an insurance contract, then an entity applies IFRS 9 to determine when an embedded derivative is separated from the host insurance contract and to account for the separated embedded derivative (see 7.2.120.50). Determining whether an embedded derivative is closely related to the host contract requires consideration of the nature – i.e. the economic characteristics and risks – of the host contract and the nature of the underlying of the derivative. If the natures of both the underlying and the host contract are similar, then they are generally closely related. An embedded derivative in an insurance contract is closely related to the host contract if it and the host insurance contract are so interdependent that an entity cannot measure the embedded derivative separately (see 7.2.110). [*IFRS 9.4.3.2–4.3.3, B4.3.5–B4.3.8*]

8.1A.80.100   An entity attributes cash flows to a distinct investment component or to a separated embedded derivative on a stand-alone basis – i.e. it measures the investment component or embedded derivative as if it had issued that item as a separate contract. After excluding the cash flows related to separate investment components and embedded derivatives, an entity applies IFRS 15 (see chapter 4.2) to separate promised goods or non-insurance services from the insurance component. In applying IFRS 15 to separate the promise, the entity applies the requirements of IFRS 17 and, on initial recognition, attributes:

- cash inflows between the insurance component and any promise to transfer distinct goods or non-insurance services – this is done based on the stand-alone selling price of the components (any discounts and cross-subsidies are allocated to components proportionately or on the basis of observable evidence);
- cash outflows based on whether they relate directly to the insurance component or the promised goods or services; and
- any remaining cash outflows between the insurance component and any promised goods or non-insurance services on a rational and systematic basis, reflecting the costs that the entity would expect to incur if it had issued that component as a separate contract. [*IFRS 17.12–13, BC111–BC113*]

8.1A.80.110   An entity then applies IFRS 17 to all remaining components of the host insurance contract. [*IFRS 17.13*]

EXAMPLE 3A – SEPARATING COMPONENTS FROM AN INSURANCE CONTRACT – INVESTMENT
COMPONENTS

8.1A.80.120   Company C issues a life insurance contract with an account balance. The policyholder pays a premium of 1,000 at contract inception. The account balance:
- increases if annual voluntary amounts are paid by the policyholder;
- is adjusted by investment returns from specified assets; and
- decreases when C charges fees.

8.1A.80.130   Another financial institution sells an investment product comparable to the account balance, but without the insurance coverage.

8.1A.80.140   The contract matures on the earlier of the policyholder's death or cancellation of the contract. On maturity, C pays:
- a death benefit of 5,000 and the account balance, if the policyholder has died; or
- the account balance, if the policy is cancelled.

8.1A.80.150   The fact that a comparable investment product is sold by another financial institution indicates that the investment component may be distinct. However, the insurance and investment components are highly inter-related because the right to death benefits provided by the insurance cover either lapses or matures at the same time as the account balance. As a result, the account balance is not considered distinct and is not separated from the insurance contract.

8.1A.80.160   The asset management activities are not distinct and are not separated from the insurance contract because they are part of the activities that C has to undertake to fulfil the contract, and it does not transfer a good or a service to the policyholder because it performs those activities. [*IFRS 17.IE42–IE50*]

8.1A.80.170   The lowest unit of account under IFRS 17 is the contract, including all insurance components and excluding any separated non-insurance components. Some insurance contracts may combine different types of insurance components into the legal form of a single contract. In our experience, a contract with the legal form of a single insurance contract generally reflects its substance as a single contract. However, there may be circumstances in which the substance of the contractual rights and obligations included in the form of a single legal contract is that of multiple insurance contracts. It appears that in these circumstances an entity should separate the legal contract into the different insurance components to reflect the substance of the contractual rights and obligations.

8.1A.80.180   We believe that assessing the substance of a contract and concluding that it differs from its legal form as a single contract involves significant judgement and careful consideration of all relevant facts and circumstances – i.e. it is not a matter of policy choice. Combining different types of products or coverages that have different risks into one legal insurance contract is not, in itself, sufficient to conclude that the legal form of the contract does not reflect the substance of its contractual rights and obligations. In addition, the fact that a reinsurance contract held provides cover for underlying contracts that are included in different groups is not, in itself, sufficient to conclude that accounting for the reinsurance contract held as a single contract does not reflect the substance of its contractual rights and obligations. Similarly, the availability of information to separate cash flows for different risks is not, in itself, sufficient to conclude that the contract does not reflect the substance of its contractual rights and obligations. Considerations that might be relevant in the assessment include:

- interdependency between the different risks covered;
- whether components lapse together;
- whether components are sold separately; and
- whether insurance components are bundled together solely for the administrative convenience of the policyholder.

EXAMPLE 3B – SEPARATING COMPONENTS FROM AN INSURANCE CONTRACT – INSURANCE COMPONENTS

8.1A.80.190   Company X issues a contract containing long-term life insurance coverage with annual renewable health riders. The health riders provide the policy-holder with insurance against long-term illness. At each annual renewal date, X can reassess the risks and set a price that fully reflects these risks only for the renewable health riders – i.e. it cannot reprice or cancel the life coverage of the contract. The policyholder may choose to cancel the entire contract or to cancel only the health rider and maintain the life coverage.

8.1A.80.200   X considers the following factors in determining that the substance of the contract reflects its form as a single contract:
- the renewable health riders are not sold separately;
- if the life coverage lapses or is cancelled, then the renewable health riders lapse or are cancelled at the same time; and
- based on past experience, the renewable health riders are rarely cancelled and most of them remain in force until the end of the life insurance component's coverage period.

8.1A.80.210   Based on its analyses, X concludes that the legal form of the contract reflects the substance of the insurer's contractual rights and obligations. As a result, X assesses the boundary of the contract in its entirety. Therefore, the cash flows within the contract's boundary include the cash flows related to the expected renewals of health riders beyond their annual repricing dates because X has a continuing substantive obligation to provide coverage under the contract (because the life coverage premiums are not subject to full repricing).

8.1A.90   RECOGNITION

8.1A.90.10   An entity recognises a group of insurance contracts that it issues from the earliest of:
- the beginning of the coverage period of the group of contracts;
- the date when the first payment from a policyholder in the group becomes due; and
- for a group of onerous contracts (see 8.1A.230), when the group becomes onerous, if facts and circumstances indicate there is such a group. [*IFRS 17.25–26*]

8.1A.90.20   If there is no due date specified in the contract, then it is considered to be the date when the first payment is received from the policyholder. A group of contracts initially recognised in a reporting period only includes contracts issued by the reporting date. New contracts are added to the group, in subsequent reporting periods in which any new contracts are issued, subject to the level of aggregation requirements (see 8.1A.110.20). [*IFRS 17.26, 28*]

EXAMPLE 4 – RECOGNITION OF AN INSURANCE CONTRACT

> 8.1A.90.30   Company X is bound by the terms of an insurance contract at 1 June 2018. The coverage period of the insurance contract starts on 1 January 2019, which is also the premium due date. This example assumes that the group comprises only this contract.
>
> 8.1A.90.40   On 1 June 2018 and at each reporting date between 1 June 2018 and 31 December 2018 – i.e. the pre-coverage period – X assesses whether any facts or circumstances indicate that the group is onerous. If it is, then X recognises the group on the date when it becomes onerous. If it is not, then X recognises the group on 1 January 2019.

8.1A.90.50   An entity recognises an asset or a liability for any insurance acquisition cash flows relating to a group of issued insurance contracts that it pays or receives before the group is recognised. It appears that this can include insurance acquisition cash flows relating to contracts that have not yet been issued. This is because the requirement is intended to distinguish a group of insurance contracts issued from a group of reinsurance contracts held. These assets and liabilities are derecognised when the group of insurance contracts to which the cash flows are allocated is recognised. [*IFRS 17.27*]

8.1A.100   MEASUREMENT

8.1A.100.10   The liability (or asset) recognised for a group of insurance contracts is measured, on initial recognition and subsequently, as the sum of:
- the fulfilment cash flows, which are a risk-adjusted, explicit, unbiased and probability-weighted estimate of the present value of future cash flows that will arise as the entity fulfils the contracts; and
- the contractual service margin (CSM), which is the amount that represents the unearned profit that the entity will recognise as services are provided and so results in no gain arising from the initial recognition of the group. [*IFRS 17.IN6(d), A, 44(d), 45(d), B119*]

8.1A.100.20   The fulfilment cash flows consist of the following components (see diagram at 8.1A.190):
- estimates of future cash flows that will arise as the insurer fulfils the contracts (see 8.1A.130);
- an adjustment to reflect the time value of money (i.e. discounting) and the financial risks related to the future cash flows (to the extent that they are not already included in the estimates of future cash flows) (see 8.1A.170); and
- an explicit risk adjustment for non-financial risk (see 8.1A.180). [*IFRS 17.32, 37*]

8.1A.100.30   Subsequent to initial recognition, the total liability of a group of insurance contracts comprises the liability for remaining coverage and the liability for incurred claims. The liability for remaining coverage is the entity's obligation for insured events related to the unexpired portion of the coverage period and is measured as the fulfilment cash flows that relate to service that will be provided under the contract in future periods, plus the remaining CSM. The liability for incurred claims is the entity's obligation to investigate and pay valid claims for insured events that have already occurred, including events that have occurred but have not been reported. It is measured as the fulfilment cash flows for claims and expenses already incurred but not yet paid. [*IFRS 17.IN7, 40, A, BC25*]

8.1A.100.40   This measurement model applies to all groups of insurance contracts in the scope of IFRS 17. However, simplifications or modifications apply to groups of:
- insurance contracts measured using the premium allocation approach (PAA) (see 8.1A.270);
- investment contracts with DPFs (see 8.1A.340); and
- reinsurance contracts held (see 8.1A.310). [*IFRS 17.29*]

8.1A.100.50   The way in which this model is applied to direct participating contracts, referred to as the 'variable fee approach', is explained in more detail in 8.1A.240–60.

8.1A.110   Level of aggregation

8.1A.110.10   In determining the level of aggregation, an entity identifies portfolios of insurance contracts. An entity divides each portfolio into a minimum of:
- a group of contracts that are onerous on initial recognition (see 8.1A.230), if there are any;
- a group of contracts that on initial recognition have no significant possibility of becoming onerous subsequently, if there are any; and
- a group of any remaining contracts in the portfolio. [*IFRS 17.14, 16*]

8.1A.110.20   An entity cannot include contracts issued more than one year apart in the same group. Therefore, each portfolio will be disaggregated into annual cohorts, or cohorts consisting of periods of less than one year. It is possible for a group to comprise only one contract. [*IFRS 17.22–23*]

8.1A.110.30   The aggregation of contracts into groups is required for all contracts in the scope of IFRS 17. The groups of a portfolio are established on initial recognition and are not reassessed subsequently. [*IFRS 17.24*]

8.1A.110.40   Insurance contracts that are subject to similar risks and managed together are included within a portfolio, as defined under IFRS 17. Generally, contracts in the same product line would be included within the same portfolio if they are managed together, and contracts in different product lines would have dissimilar risks and therefore be included in different portfolios. For example, a set of single-premium fixed annuities is likely to be in a different portfolio from a set of term life contracts. [*IFRS 17.14, A*]

8.1A.110.50   An entity may measure whether contracts are onerous on initial recognition for sets of contracts (i.e. higher than the individual contract level) if it has reasonable and supportable information to conclude that a set of contracts will all be in the same group. If it cannot support such a conclusion, then the entity determines the group by considering individual contracts. [*IFRS 17.17, BC129*]

8.1A.110.60   Consistent with the assessment of how to identify whether contracts are onerous on initial recognition, an entity may assess whether contracts have no significant possibility of becoming onerous subsequently for sets of contracts (i.e. higher than the individual contract level) if it has reasonable and supportable information to conclude that a set of contracts will all be in the same group. If it cannot support such a conclusion, then the entity determines the group by assessing individual contracts. [*IFRS 17.17, BC129*]

8.1A.110.70   An entity determines which contracts have no significant possibility of becoming onerous using information about estimates provided by the entity's internal reporting and based on the likelihood of changes in assumptions that, if they occurred, would result in the contracts becoming onerous. An entity does not disregard information provided by that reporting about the effects of changes in assumptions on different contracts and the possibility of them becoming onerous. However, it is not required to gather additional information beyond its internal reporting about the effects of changes in assumptions on different contracts. [*IFRS 17.19, BC130*]

8.1A.110.80   If applying these level of aggregation requirements would result in contracts within a portfolio falling into different groups only because law or regulation specifically constrains the entity's practical ability to set a different price or level of benefits for policyholders with different characteristics, then the entity may include those contracts in the same group. This exemption applies only when there is a specific constraint imposed by a law or regulation. It is not available when an entity sets a price for contracts without distinguishing characteristics because:
- it thinks that using that characteristic may result in a law or regulation prohibiting the use of it in the future or because not considering it is likely to fulfil a public policy objective (sometimes referred to as 'self-regulation');
- law or regulation in a neighbouring jurisdiction explicitly prohibits differentiation based on that specific characteristic; or
- differentiating based on that characteristic may have a negative effect on the entity's brand and reputation. [*IFRS 17.20, BC133–BC134*]

8.1A.110.90   This exemption cannot be applied by analogy to any other items. [*IFRS 17.20*]

8.1A.110.100   An entity is permitted to disaggregate its portfolios of insurance contracts into more than the three groups described in 8.1A.110.10. For example, it can divide a portfolio into more groups of contracts that are:
- onerous on initial recognition, if the entity's internal reporting provides information at a more detailed level about the extent to which the contracts are onerous; and
- not onerous on initial recognition, if its internal reporting provides information that distinguishes between different levels of profitability or different possibilities of contracts becoming onerous after initial recognition. [*IFRS 17.21*]

8.1A.110.110   The requirement for groups to be limited to periods covering one year or less is based on the amounts to be reported, not necessarily the methodology used to arrive at those amounts. Therefore, it could be possible that an entity need not restrict groups in this way to achieve the same accounting outcome in some circumstances. For example, for contracts in groups that fully share risks with contracts in another group, the groups together will give the same results as a single, combined risk-sharing portfolio. [*IFRS 17.22, BC138*]

EXAMPLE 5 – LEVEL OF AGGREGATION

8.1A.110.120 Company H identifies its universal life insurance line of business as a portfolio of insurance contracts under IFRS 17. This portfolio is made up of two types of contracts.

- *Single-premium universal single life:* A life insurance contract that covers one individual policyholder and pays out a death benefit if they die during the coverage period.
- *Single-premium universal joint life:* A life insurance contract that covers two individual policyholders and pays out a death benefit if one of them dies during the coverage period, after which the policy ends.

8.1A.110.130 For internal reporting, the data and information obtained about this portfolio are segregated by the different types of contracts. Therefore, the information is provided – and available to be monitored and analysed – separately for each type of product.

8.1A.110.140 The availability and use of product-specific data for internal management purposes results in H identifying which contracts are onerous on initial recognition, and their likelihood of becoming onerous after initial recognition. Given that this data is readily available, H decides to perform its grouping assessment at a product level, instead of at a portfolio level.

8.1A.110.150 When an entity recognises a group of contracts in a reporting period, an entity includes only those contracts that have been issued by the reporting date. However, it may issue more contracts in a group after the reporting date, as long as the group is limited to contracts issued no more than a year apart. For the determination of the discount rate on initial recognition, entities are permitted to use weighted-average discount rates over the period during which contracts in the group are issued. [*IFRS 17.22, 28, B73*]

8.1A.110.160 When an entity adds contracts to an existing group in a new reporting period, this may result in a change in the discount rates determined on initial recognition. In this case, the entity applies a revised weighted-average discount rate from the start of the reporting period in which the new contracts are added to the group. If the entity prepares interim reports, then it cannot change the treatment of accounting estimates made in previous interim financial statements when applying this standard in subsequent interim financial statements, or in the annual financial statements. [*IFRS 17.28, B127, BC236*]

8.1A.120 **Applying the general measurement model**

8.1A.130 *Estimating future cash flows*

8.1A.130.10 IFRS 17 requires estimates of future cash flows of a group of insurance contracts to:
- incorporate all reasonable and supportable information that is available without undue cost or effort about the amount, timing and uncertainty of those future cash flows in an unbiased way;
- include all of the future cash flows within the boundary of each contract in the group;

- reflect the perspective of the entity, provided that, when relevant, the estimates are consistent with observable market prices for those variables; and
- be current and explicit. [*IFRS 17.33*]

8.1A.130.20   When measuring groups of contracts, an entity may estimate the fulfilment cash flows at a higher level of aggregation than a group or portfolio as long as it is able to include the appropriate fulfilment cash flows in the group that it is measuring by allocating these estimates to its groups of contracts. [*IFRS 17.24*]

8.1A.140   *Contract boundary*

8.1A.140.10   The measurement of a group of insurance contracts includes all of the future cash flows within the boundary of each contract in the group. The contract boundary distinguishes the future cash flows that relate to existing insurance contracts from those that relate to future insurance contracts. It is reassessed at each reporting date and, therefore, may change over time. When determining the contract boundary, an entity considers its substantive rights and obligations – whether they arise from contract, law or regulation – and disregards terms that have no commercial substance. [*IFRS 17.2, 33, B61, BC164*]

8.1A.140.20   Cash flows are within the contract boundary if they arise from substantive rights and obligations that exist during the reporting period in which the entity can compel the policyholder to pay the premium, or has a substantive obligation to provide the policyholder with services. This substantive obligation ends when:
- the entity has the 'practical ability' to reassess the risks of the particular policyholder and can set a price or level of benefits that fully reflects these reassessed risks; or
- both of the following conditions are met:
  – the entity has the 'practical ability' to reassess the risk of the portfolio of insurance contracts that contains the contract and can set a price or level of benefits that fully reflects the risk of that portfolio; and
  – the pricing of the premiums for coverage up to the reassessment date does not take into account the risks that relate to periods after the reassessment date. [*IFRS 17.34*]

8.1A.140.30   An entity has the 'practical ability' to set a price at the renewal date, which fully reflects the risks in the contract from that date, when it is not restricted from:
- setting the same price as it would for a new contract issued on that date with the same characteristics as the existing contract;
- amending the benefits to be consistent with the price that it will charge; or
- setting a price for an individual contract that reflects overall changes in the risks in a portfolio of insurance contracts, even if the price set for each individual policyholder does not reflect the change in risk for that specific policyholder. [*IFRS 17.B64*]

8.1A.140.40   It appears that the assessment of the criteria in 8.1A.140.20 relates to the risks of the policyholder (i.e. policyholder risks). This is because the portfolio assessment is considered an extension of the risk assessment from the individual to the portfolio level. Therefore, the assessment should not be extended to all types of risks and pricing considerations applied by an entity when pricing a contract.

8.1A.140.50   It appears that policyholder risks include risks transferred from the policyholder to the entity. We believe that this can include both insurance and financial risks but excludes lapse risk and expense risk that are created by the contract (see 8.1A.20.240).

8.1A.140.60   When determining whether it can set a price or level of benefits that fully reflects the reassessed risks of a portfolio, an entity needs to consider whether it has the practical ability to reassess the risks of the portfolio and, as a result, set a price or level of benefits that fully reflects those risks.

EXAMPLE 6A – CONTRACT BOUNDARY FOR ANNUALLY REPRICING CONTRACTS – PORTFOLIO

8.1A.140.70   Company X issues a health insurance contract with the following terms.
- The contract covers health risk and has an annual term that is guaranteed to be renewable each year.
- The annual premium charged for each year reflects X's expectation of its exposure to risk for that year of coverage.
- When the contract is initially issued, the individual policyholder's risks are assessed by a health examination, which could impact the premium charged to the policyholder – e.g. if the health examination uncovers an adverse health condition, then a premium adjustment may be added to the policy to cover the additional risk exposure.
- When the contract is renewed for an additional year, X does not have the ability to reassess the individual policyholder's health. However, at each anniversary date it can reprice the premium to reflect the reassessed risks for the next year based on its overall health insurance contracts portfolio's claims experience and expectations.

8.1A.140.80   The cash flows related to future renewals (i.e. the guaranteed renewable term) of the contract are outside the contract boundary for the following reasons:
- X has the practical ability to reassess the risks of the health insurance contracts portfolio and, as a result, can set a price that fully reflects these reassessed risks; and
- the pricing of premiums for coverage up to the reassessment date does not take into account the risks that relate to periods after the reassessment date because the premium for each year reflects the risks for each year of coverage.

EXAMPLE 6B – CONTRACT BOUNDARY FOR ANNUALLY REPRICING CONTRACTS – NOT PORTFOLIO

8.1A.140.90   Company Y issues a life insurance contract with the following terms.
- The contract has a stated term of 10 years. The policyholder has a right to cancel the contract at each anniversary date.
- The initial schedule of premiums chargeable for each year reflects Y's expectations of its exposure to risk for that year of coverage.

- When the contract is initially issued, the individual policyholder's risks are assessed by a health examination, which could impact the premium charged to the policyholder – e.g. if the health examination uncovers an adverse health condition, then a premium adjustment may be added to the policy to cover the insurer's additional risk exposure. The individual policyholder's health is not reassessed after this date.
- At each anniversary date, Y can adjust the premiums to reflect a reassessment of risks for the next year based only on changes to regional mortality tables that reflect death rates across the general population analysed by age – i.e. the risks are reassessed only at a general level.

8.1A.140.100 The contract boundary includes the expected cash flows related to the full term of the contract – i.e. 10 years – because Y does not have the practical ability to reassess the risks at an individual or portfolio of insurance contracts level and to price the contract to reflect such reassessed risks. Rather, Y only has the ability to set a price that reflects changes in mortality experience across the general population at a regional level.

8.1A.140.110 When an entity has the practical ability to reassess the risks of an existing insurance contract but is restricted from repricing the contract to reflect this reassessment, the contract still binds the entity and its related cash flows lie within the existing contract's boundary. However, if the restriction has no commercial substance, then the contract does not bind the entity. Therefore, the substance of the restriction should be analysed to determine whether the contract binds the entity. [*IFRS 17.BC161, BC164*]

8.1A.140.120 Cash flows within the boundary of an insurance contract are those that relate directly to the fulfilment of the contract, and include those over which the entity has discretion, including the following. [*IFRS 17.B65, BC168*]

CASH FLOWS WITHIN THE BOUNDARY INCLUDE:	EXAMPLES
Premiums and any other costs specifically chargeable to the policyholder	<ul><li>Premium adjustments</li><li>Instalment premiums</li><li>Any additional cash flows that result from those premiums</li></ul>
Payments to, or on behalf of, a policyholder	<ul><li>Incurred claims that have not yet been paid</li><li>Incurred claims that have not yet been reported</li><li>Future claims</li><li>Payments that vary depending on returns on underlying items</li></ul>
Costs of providing benefits in kind	<ul><li>Replacement of stolen articles</li></ul>
Payments in a fiduciary capacity to meet the policyholder's tax obligations	<ul><li>Payment of death duties or inheritance tax</li></ul>

CASH FLOWS WITHIN THE BOUNDARY INCLUDE:	EXAMPLES
Potential cash inflows from recoveries on future claims, as long as they have not been recognised as a separate asset	• Salvage and subrogation
Transaction-based taxes and levies that arise directly from existing insurance contracts or are attributable to them	• Premium taxes • Value-added taxes and goods and services taxes • Fire service levies • Guarantee fund assessments
Payment to, or on behalf of, a policyholder resulting from derivatives that are not separated from the contract	• Options and guarantees embedded in the contract
Insurance acquisition cash flows	• See 8.1A.150
Claim handling costs – investigating, processing and resolving claims	• Legal and loss adjusters' fees • Internal costs of investigating claims and processing claims payments
Policy administration and maintenance costs	• Costs of billing premiums • Costs of handling policy changes – e.g. conversions • Recurring commissions expected to be paid to intermediaries if the policyholder continues paying premiums within the boundary of the insurance contract
Allocation of fixed and variable overheads directly attributable to fulfilling insurance contracts	Those that are allocated to contracts or groups using methods that are systematic, rational and consistently applied to all costs with similar characteristics are within the contract boundary. These include: • Accounting • Human resources • IT and support • Building depreciation • Rent • Maintenance • Utilities

8.1A.140.130 The following cash flows are not included in the estimates of future cash flows:
- Cash flows related to the following items (because they are accounted for separately):
  - investment returns;
  - components separated from the insurance contract;
  - reinsurance contracts held; and
  - income tax payments or receipts that the entity does not pay or receive in a fiduciary capacity.
- Cash flows relating to costs that are not directly attributed to the portfolio of insurance contracts – e.g. some product development and training costs.

- Cash flows arising from abnormal amounts of wasted labour or other resources used to fulfil the contract.
- Cash flows between different components of the reporting entity that do not change the amount that will be paid to policyholders – e.g. policyholder funds and shareholder funds.
- Cash flows that may arise from future insurance contracts – e.g. those outside the boundary of existing insurance contracts. [*IFRS 17.B66*]

8.1A.150   *Insurance acquisition cash flows*

8.1A.150.10   Insurance acquisition cash flows arise from selling, underwriting and starting a group of insurance contracts. These cash flows need to be directly attributable to a portfolio of insurance contracts to which the group belongs. Cash flows that are not directly attributable to the groups or individual insurance contracts within the portfolio can be included. [*IFRS 17.A, B65(e)*]

8.1A.150.20   Insurance acquisition cash flows:
- can arise internally (e.g. in the sales department) or externally (e.g. by using external sales agents);
- include not only the incremental costs of originating insurance contracts, but also other direct costs and a proportion of the indirect costs that are incurred in originating insurance contracts; and
- include cash flows related to both successful and unsuccessful acquisition efforts. [*IFRS 17.BC182–BC183*]

8.1A.150.30   The insurance acquisition cash flows included in the measurement of a group are those arising from the costs of selling, underwriting and starting the group of insurance contracts that are directly attributable to the portfolio of insurance contracts to which the group belongs. These cash flows include those that are not directly attributable to groups or to individual contracts within the portfolio (see 8.1A.150.10). When allocating insurance acquisition cash flows to groups of insurance contracts, entities need to consider, in an unbiased way, all reasonable and supportable information that is available without undue cost or effort (see 8.1A.130.10). It appears that an entity should apply the following approach to include insurance acquisition cash flows in the measurement of groups:
- if they are directly attributable to an *individual contract*, then it should include them only in the measurement of the group to which that individual contract belongs;
- if they are directly attributable to a *group of contracts*, then it should include them only in the measurement of that group; and
- if they are directly attributable to a *portfolio of contracts*, then they should be allocated to groups within the portfolio in an appropriate manner using reasonable and supportable information.

8.1A.150.40   Accordingly, if a commission is paid unconditionally on issuance of an individual insurance contract (i.e. it is not refundable), then the specified commission should be included in the measurement of the group to which the initially issued contract belongs and it should not be allocated to any future or other group. This may result in the initial contract being onerous on initial recognition if the insurance acquisition cash outflows, including the specified commission, are greater than the net cash inflows included within the contract boundary.

EXAMPLE 7 – INSURANCE ACQUISITION CASH FLOWS THAT MAY BE ASSOCIATED WITH FUTURE CONTRACT RENEWALS

8.1A.150.50   A sales agent sells an insurance contract on behalf of Company H. The contract has an initial term of one year but the customer may choose to renew the contract in future years at a revised premium level set by H. H pays the sales agent at issuance of the contract an unconditional sales commission for initially writing the contract. Therefore, the sales agent commission is directly attributable to the individual contract. We believe that it should be included in the measurement of the group of contracts containing the contract that it relates to.

8.1A.150.60   Modifying the fact pattern, H includes a claw-back condition in the sales agreement under which part of the commission paid to the sales agent is recovered if the policyholder does not renew the contract – i.e. the sales commission paid to the sales agent is not unconditional. It appears that, due to the claw-back condition, the initial sales agent commission is partly associated with future renewals of the initial contract. If the contract boundary of the initial contract does not extend beyond the initial term, then we believe that the recoverable portion of the initial sales agent commission associated with a future renewal should be recognised as an asset until that renewal occurs or the portion is recovered.

8.1A.160   *Information used to make estimates*

8.1A.160.10   An entity estimates the probabilities and amounts of future payments under existing contracts on the basis of:
- information about the known or estimated characteristics of the contracts;
- information about reported claims and historical data about the entity's own experience supplemented by data from other sources, if necessary; and
- current price information, if it is available. [*IFRS 17.B41*]

8.1A.160.20   An entity adjusts its historical information to reflect current conditions when, for example:
- the characteristics of the insured population differ from those of the population on which the historical information is based;
- trends are expected to change – e.g. historical trends will not continue or new trends will emerge; or
- other changes occur that might affect the relevance of historical information – e.g. changes in underwriting and claims management procedures. [*IFRS 17.B41(c)*]

8.1A.160.30   Current price information might be available to use as a basis for estimating future cash flows. For example, prices of:
- reinsurance transactions;
- financial instruments that cover similar risks – e.g. catastrophe bonds or weather derivatives; and
- portfolio transfers. [*IFRS 17.B41(d)*]

8.1A.160.40   Careful consideration is needed to adjust these prices to arrive at the cash flows that would arise from fulfilling the insurance contract. [*IFRS 17.B41(d)*]

8.1A.160.50   Estimates of future cash flows reflect the perspective of the entity provided that any estimates of relevant market variables are consistent with the observable market prices for those variables. Market variables generally give rise to financial risk and non-market variables generally give rise to non-financial risk. However, instances will exist in which this does not hold true – e.g. interest rates that cannot be observed in, or directly derived from, markets. [*IFRS 17.33(b), B42–B43*]

8.1A.160.60   Market and non-market variables consist of the following. [*IFRS 17.B42*]

Market variables	Non-market variables
Can be observed in, or derived directly from, markets. For example: • interest rates; and • equity prices of publicly traded securities.	Consists of all variables, other than market variables. For example: • historical data on costs – including frequency and severity of claims, and mortality; and • views on future trends in the above.

8.1A.160.70   Estimates of market variables are as consistent as possible with observable market prices at the reporting date. An entity is required to maximise the use of this information rather than substitute its own estimates. Where variables need to be derived – e.g. because there is a lack of observable market variables – they are required to be as consistent as possible with observable market variables. [*IFRS 17.B44*]

8.1A.160.80   A replicating asset (or portfolio of assets) is one whose cash flows exactly match, in all scenarios, some of the contractual cash flows that arise from a group of insurance contracts in amount, timing and uncertainty. When such an asset (or portfolio of assets) does exist, the entity may use the replicating asset technique. Under this technique, the entity uses the fair value of the asset(s) to represent the relevant fulfilment cash flows instead of explicitly estimating the cash flows and discount rate. [*IFRS 17.B46*]

8.1A.160.90   If a replicating asset (or portfolio of assets) exists for some of the cash flows of an insurance contract, and the entity chooses not to use the replicating asset technique in determining the fulfilment cash flows, then the entity needs to satisfy itself that the replicating asset technique would be unlikely to lead to a materially different measurement of those cash flows. This might be the case when there are significant interdependencies between cash flows that vary based on returns on assets and other cash flows, and stochastic modelling may be more robust, or easier to implement, than using the replicating asset technique. [*IFRS 17.B47–B48*]

EXAMPLE 8 – INFORMATION USED TO MAKE ESTIMATES – APPLYING THE REPLICATING ASSET TECHNIQUE

8.1A.160.100   Company X issues an insurance contract that contains an insurance feature that generates cash flows equal to the cash flows from a put option on a basket of traded assets. There is publicly available price information on the relevant put option.

> 8.1A.160.110 Because the replicating asset (in this case, the put option) has cash flows that exactly match the cash flows for certain cash flows relating to one feature of the insurance contract, X may use the publicly available price information (i.e. the fair value of the put option) to determine the relevant fulfilment cash flows resulting from that feature.

8.1A.160.120 Estimates of non-market variables reflect all reasonable and supportable information – external and internal – that is available without undue cost or effort, and give greater weight to the more persuasive information. [*IFRS 17.B49–B50*]

8.1A.160.130 Estimated probabilities for non-market variables are required not to contradict observable market variables. For example, estimated probabilities for future inflation rate scenarios are required to be as consistent as possible with the probabilities implied by market interest rates. Market variables can vary independently or be correlated with non-market variables. For example, lapse rates (a non-market variable) could be correlated with interest rates (a market variable). When they are correlated, the probabilities for scenarios and the risk adjustments for non-financial risk that relate to the market variables are required to be consistent with the observed market prices that depend on those market variables. [*IFRS 17.B51–B53*]

8.1A.160.140 Mortality statistics can be available from both internal and external resources. An entity gives greater weight to the more persuasive information. For example, internal mortality statistics may be more persuasive (if they are available) than external mortality statistics – e.g. national statistics – that relate to a population with different demographic characteristics from those of the insured population of an entity. Conversely, if the internal mortality information is derived from a small population and external mortality information is current and believed to represent the insured population, then the external information might be given greater weight. [*IFRS 17.B50*]

8.1A.160.150 As the portfolio of products and the related experience changes, this assessment might result in different results over time for the same product in the same entity.

EXAMPLE 9A – INFORMATION USED TO MAKE ESTIMATES – INTERNAL VS EXTERNAL INFORMATION ABOUT NON-MARKET VARIABLES (1)

> 8.1A.160.160 Company E plans to launch a new insurance product with a new type of insurance risk that it has not previously issued – e.g. adding identity theft coverage to traditional property insurance contracts.
>
> 8.1A.160.170 Because E lacks internal information to produce its future cash flow estimates, it might place more weight on information found in international research performed by the reinsurance industry, or in the cost of reinsuring that element of the risk, to estimate the new risk.
>
> 8.1A.160.180 As E continues issuing the products and gathers information over time in the specific environment that it is operating in, it might place more weight on its internal information.

EXAMPLE 9B – INFORMATION USED TO MAKE ESTIMATES – INTERNAL VS EXTERNAL INFORMATION ABOUT NON-MARKET VARIABLES (2)

8.1A.160.190   Company H issues a life insurance contract with an investment component, under which the policyholder has an option on retirement to either:
- receive a lump sum settlement; or
- annuitise the contract value and receive annuity payments until death.

8.1A.160.200   H might lack internal information about policyholder behaviour at the current life cycle of the contract – e.g. if the contracts are still within the early years of the coverage period, then the policyholders will not yet have reached retirement age. Therefore, it may need to rely on external information to develop estimates of expected policyholder behaviour – e.g. external statistics based on products with similar features.

8.1A.160.210   The requirement that estimates incorporate all reasonable and supportable information available without undue cost or effort about the amount, timing and uncertainty of future cash flows is achieved by estimating the expected value of the full range of possible outcomes – i.e. the probability-weighted mean. [*IFRS 17.33, BC150*]

8.1A.160.220   The expected present value of future cash flows is determined by:
- developing a range of scenarios that reflects the full range of possible outcomes, in which each scenario specifies:
  - the amount and timing of the cash flows for a particular outcome; and
  - the estimated probability of the outcome; and
- applying to each scenario:
  - a discount factor to determine the present value; and
  - a weighting based on the estimated probability of the outcome. [*IFRS 17.B38*]

8.1A.160.230   The objective is not to develop a most likely outcome or a more-likely-than-not outcome for future cash flows. [*IFRS 17.B38*]

8.1A.160.240   The scenarios developed exclude possible claims under possible future contracts and include unbiased estimates of the probability of catastrophic losses under existing contracts. [*IFRS 17.33, B40, BC150*]

8.1A.160.250   When considering the full range of possible outcomes, the objective is to incorporate all reasonable and supportable information available without undue cost or effort in an unbiased way, rather than to identify every possible scenario. It is not necessary in practice to generate explicit scenarios when determining the mean, if the resulting estimate is consistent with this objective. [*IFRS 17.B39*]

8.1A.160.260   Therefore, it could be appropriate to use a small number of parameters, or relatively simple modelling, when the measurement result is within an acceptable range of precision. However, more sophisticated, stochastic modelling is likely to be needed when the cash flows and their probabilities are driven by complex underlying factors – e.g. for cash flows generated by options inter-related with the insurance coverage. [*IFRS 17.B39*]

8.1A.160.270 Information that is available from an entity's own information system is considered to be available without undue cost or effort. [*IFRS 17.B37*]

8.1A.160.280 At the reporting date, an entity reviews and updates its previous estimates while considering whether:
- the updated estimates faithfully represent the conditions that exist at that date; and
- the changes in estimates faithfully represent the changes in conditions during that period. [*IFRS 17.33(c), B54*]

8.1A.160.290 When updating estimates, an entity considers the evidence that supported its previous estimates and all of the new available evidence, and gives greater weight to the more persuasive evidence. [*IFRS 17.33(c), B54*]

8.1A.160.300 An entity takes into account current expectations of future events that might affect the cash flows, but not current expectations of future changes in legislation that would change or discharge the present obligation or create a new obligation under the existing contract. Such changes in legislation impact the future cash flows only when they are substantively enacted. [*IFRS 17.60, BC156*]

8.1A.160.310 Estimates of future cash flows are 'explicit'. This means that the adjustment for non-financial risk is estimated separately from the other estimates. The adjustments for the time value of money and financial risk are also estimated separately from the cash flow estimates, unless the most appropriate measurement technique combines those estimates. [*IFRS 17.33(d)*]

8.1A.160.320 Some contracts require the policyholder to share the returns of a specified pool of underlying items with policyholders of other contracts. Additionally, these contracts require that either:
- the policyholder bears a reduction in its share of returns on the underlying items as a result of required payments to those other policyholders that share in that pool; or
- the other policyholders bear a reduction in their share of returns on the underlying items as a result of a required payment to the policyholder. [*IFRS 17.B67*]

8.1A.160.330 When these contracts are in different groups, the cash flows for each group reflect the effects on the entity. So, the fulfilment cash flows for a group:
- include payments arising from the terms of existing contracts to policyholders of contracts in other groups; and
- exclude payments to policyholders in the group that have been included in the fulfilment cash flows of another group. [*IFRS 17.B68–B69*]

8.1A.160.340 To determine the fulfilment cash flows of groups that affect or are affected by contracts in other groups, different practical approaches can be used. If it is possible to identify the change in the underlying items and resulting change in cash flows only at a higher level than the group, then the effects of the change in the underlying items are allocated to each group on a systematic and rational basis. [*IFRS 17.B70*]

8.1A.160.350   After all of the coverage has been provided to the contracts in a group, the fulfilment cash flows may still include payments expected to be made to current policyholders in other groups or to future policyholders. In these cases, an entity can recognise and measure a liability for the fulfilment cash flows arising from all groups. Therefore, it does not have to continue to allocate these fulfilment cash flows to specific groups. [*IFRS 17.B71*]

8.1A.170   *Adjusting estimates of future cash flows for the time value of money*

8.1A.170.10   Discounting adjusts the estimates of expected future cash flows to reflect the time value of money and the financial risks associated with those cash flows (to the extent that the financial risks are not already included in the cash flow estimates). The discount rates applied to the estimates of expected future cash flows reflect the time value of money, the characteristics of the cash flows and the liquidity characteristics of the insurance contracts. They are consistent with observable current market prices and exclude the effects of factors that affect observable market prices used in determining the discount rate but do not affect the expected future cash flows of the insurance contract. [*IFRS 17.36, B86*]

8.1A.170.20   Discount rates are determined on a basis consistent with other estimates that are used to measure the insurance contracts. For example:

- cash flows that do not vary based on the returns on underlying items are discounted at a rate that does not reflect any such variability – i.e. based on a risk-free rate;
- cash flows that do vary based on the returns on any financial underlying items are discounted using rates that reflect that variability (or adjusted for the effect of that variability and discounted using a rate that reflects the adjustment made);
- nominal cash flows are discounted at a rate that includes the effect of inflation; and
- real cash flows are discounted at a rate that excludes the effect of inflation. [*IFRS 17.B74*]

8.1A.170.30   Cash flows that vary based on the return on underlying items are discounted or adjusted to reflect that variability, regardless of whether:

- the variability arises from contractual terms or discretion of the issuer; or
- the entity holds the underlying items. [*IFRS 17.B75*]

8.1A.170.40   When some of the cash flows vary based on the return on underlying items and some do not, an entity can either:

- divide the cash flows and apply the relevant discount rates for each stream of cash flows; or
- apply discount rates appropriate for the estimated cash flows as a whole – e.g. using stochastic modelling techniques or risk-neutral measurement techniques. [*IFRS 17.B77*]

8.1A.170.50   The discount rate does not contradict any available and relevant market information, and reflects current market conditions from the perspective of a market participant. An entity determines the discount rate based on an estimation technique if:

- observable market prices with the same characteristics – e.g. timing, currency and liquidity – are not available; or
- similar instruments are available but do not separately identify factors of the financial instrument that differentiate it from the insurance contract. [*IFRS 17.B78*]

8.1A.170.60   In applying an estimation technique, an entity:

- maximises the use of observable inputs;
- reflects all reasonable and supportable information on non-market variables available without undue cost or effort;
- does not contradict observable market variables when using non-market variables; and
- exercises judgement to assess the level of similarity between the features of the insurance contract and those of the instrument for which observable market prices are available, adjusting for any differences. [*IFRS 17.B44, 13.69, 83, 89*]

8.1A.170.70   An estimation technique to derive discount rates is not prescribed by IFRS 17. However, the standard does specify that a 'top-down' or 'bottom-up' approach may be used. In theory, for insurance contracts with cash flows that do not vary based on the performance of the underlying items, both approaches should result in the same discount rate, although differences may arise in practice. The example below illustrates these approaches for an insurance contract with cash flows that do not vary based on the performance of the underlying items. [*IFRS 17.B80–B81, B84*]

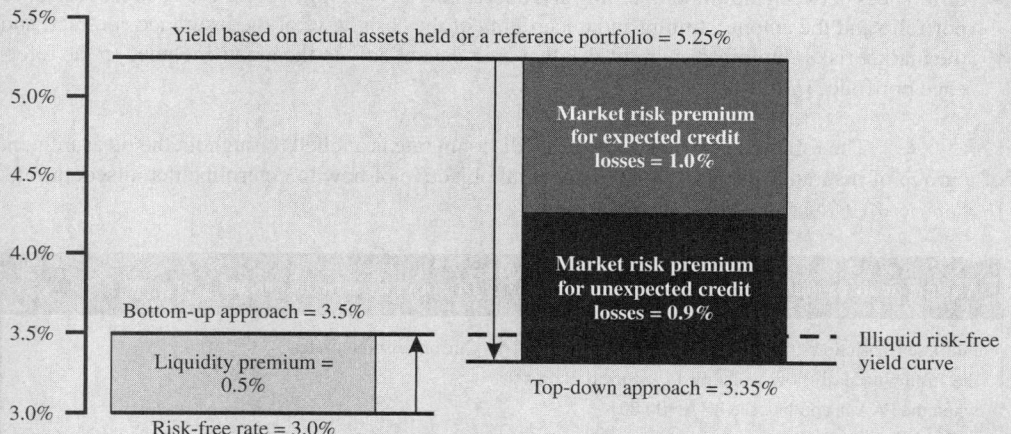

8.1A.170.80   For cash flows that do not vary based on the returns on underlying items, an entity may determine the discount rate based on a liquid risk-free yield curve. This is adjusted to eliminate differences between the liquidity characteristics of the financial instruments that underlie the chosen curve and those of the insurance contract. For example, risk-free rates are often derived from the prices of highly liquid traded bonds with no or negligible credit risk (used as a proxy for risk-free rates), which can often be sold in the market at short notice without incurring significant costs. By contrast, insurance contract liabilities cannot generally be liquidated by policyholders without incurring significant cost before contractual maturity, if at all. [*IFRS 17.B79–B80*]

8.1A.170.90   An entity may determine the discount rates based on a yield curve that reflects the current market rates of return implicit in a fair value measurement of a reference portfolio of assets. The yield curve is adjusted to eliminate any factors that are not relevant to the insurance contracts. However, an entity is not required to adjust the yield curve for differences in liquidity characteristics of the insurance contracts and the reference portfolio. There are no specific requirements on how to choose the reference portfolio that forms the starting point for this approach. However, if it has assets with characteristics similar to the insurance contracts, then fewer adjustments would be needed to arrive at the relevant discount rate for the insurance contracts. [*IFRS 17.B81, B85*]

8.1A.170.100 Once the reference portfolio of assets has been identified, a yield curve is estimated as follows:

- using observable market prices in active markets for the assets in the reference portfolio;
- if a market is not active for the assets in the reference portfolio, then observable market prices for similar assets are adjusted to make them comparable to the assets in the reference portfolio; and
- if there is no market for the assets in the reference portfolio, then an estimation technique is used in a manner consistent with the definition of fair value under IFRS 13. [*IFRS 17.B82*]

8.1A.170.110 After the yield curve has been identified, adjustments are made as necessary to arrive at the relevant discount rate for the insurance contracts. If an insurance contract's cash flows do not vary based on the cash flows of the assets in the reference portfolio, then the yield curve is adjusted for:

- differences between the amount, timing and uncertainty of cash flows of the assets in the reference portfolio and the amount, timing and uncertainty of the cash flows of the insurance contract; and
- the market risk premiums for credit risk that are relevant only to the assets included in the reference portfolio. [*IFRS 17.B83*]

8.1A.170.120 The following table shows when a discount rate is applied throughout the measurement of a group of insurance contracts, and the general objective of how to determine that discount rate. [*IFRS 17.36–37, 44(b), 56, 59(b), B72, B96, B113*]

ASPECTS OF MEASUREMENT	DISCOUNT RATES TO BE APPLIED
Fulfilment cash flows (for a discussion of how to adjust the fulfilment cash flows relating to incurred claims when the PAA is applied, see 8.1A.300.20)	Current discount rates
CSM interest accretion for contracts without direct participation features (including insurance contracts issued and reinsurance contracts held)	Discount rates determined on initial recognition of the group
Adjustments to the CSM for changes in the fulfilment cash flows for contracts without direct participation features	Discount rates determined on initial recognition of the group
Adjustments to the CSM for changes in the fulfilment cash flows for direct participating contracts that do not vary based on the returns on underlying items (excluding the change in the effect of the time value of money and financial risks not arising from underlying items)	Current discount rates
For groups applying the PAA (see 8.1A.270), liability for remaining coverage adjustment for the time value of money	Discount rates determined on initial recognition of the group

8.1A.180   *Determining the risk adjustment for non-financial risk*

8.1A.180.10   The risk adjustment for non-financial risk reflects the compensation that an entity requires for bearing the uncertainty about the amount and timing of cash flows that arises from non-financial risk. It measures the compensation that the entity would require to make it indifferent between fulfilling a liability that has a range of possible outcomes arising from non-financial risk and fulfilling a liability that will generate fixed cash flows with the same expected present value as the insurance contract. [*IFRS 17.A, B87*]

8.1A.180.20   The risk adjustment for non-financial risk is explicit and considers risks arising from an insurance contract other than financial risk. This includes insurance risk and other non-financial risks – e.g. lapse and expense risk. Risks that do not arise from the insurance contract – e.g. general operational risk are not included. [*IFRS 17.B86, B89–B90*]

EXAMPLE 10 – DETERMINING THE RISK ADJUSTMENT FOR NON-FINANCIAL RISK

8.1A.180.30   Company N issues two insurance contracts with the following expected cash outflows at the end of the coverage period.

	OUTCOME A (50% PROBABILITY)	OUTCOME B (50% PROBABILITY)	PROBABILITY-WEIGHTED RESULT
Contract 1	Pay 100	Pay 0	Pay 50
Contract 2	Pay 60	Pay 40	Pay 50

8.1A.180.40   To determine the risk adjustment, N measures the compensation that it would require to make it indifferent between fulfilling a liability from each contract, and a contract with a liability that is fixed at 50.

8.1A.180.50   Given the uncertainty in the amount of cash outflows, N would generally require additional compensation for both Contracts 1 and 2. However, given the higher level of variability in the amount of cash outflows in Contract 1, it would generally require greater compensation for Contract 1 than for Contract 2.

8.1A.180.60   The risk adjustment for non-financial risk reflects the degree of diversification benefit that the entity includes when determining the compensation that it requires for bearing that risk and the entity's degree of risk aversion, reflected by both favourable and unfavourable outcomes.

8.1A.180.70   The objective of the risk adjustment for non-financial risk is to reflect the entity's perception of the economic burden of the non-financial risk that it bears. Therefore, the entity specifies a level of aggregation for determining the risk adjustment for non-financial risk that is consistent with its perception of its non-financial risk burden. [*IFRS 17.BC213(b)*]

8.1A.180.80   The risk adjustment for non-financial risk reflects an entity's own perception of its degree of risk aversion; it is not measured from a market participant's point of view. Determining the risk adjustment for non-financial risk based on the amount required by market participants requires a measurement based on an exit price – e.g. fair value – rather than a fulfilment value. [*IFRS 17.BC209, BC215*]

8.1A.180.90   IFRS 17 does not prescribe methods for determining the risk adjustment for non-financial risk. Therefore, management's judgement is necessary to determine an appropriate risk adjustment technique to use. In determining which technique to use, an entity considers whether the technique provides concise and informative disclosures that allow users of its financial statements to benchmark its performance against that of its peers. The following characteristics are considered as part of this determination. [*IFRS 17.B91–B92*]

LOWER RISK ADJUSTMENT	HIGHER RISK ADJUSTMENT
• High-frequency and low-severity • Short-duration contracts • Narrow probability distributions • More-known-about trends and current estimates • Emerging claims experience that reduces uncertainty about estimates	• Low-frequency and high-severity (e.g. catastrophe risk) • Long-duration contracts • Wide probability distributions • Little-known-about trends and current estimates • Emerging claims experience that increases uncertainty about estimates

8.1A.180.100   Given that some non-market variables – e.g. lapse rates – can be correlated with market variables – e.g. interest rates – when determining the risk adjustment for non-financial risk an entity needs to ensure that any non-financial risks that depend on market variables are consistent with observable market prices that depend on those market variables. [*IFRS 17.B53*]

8.1A.190 *Initial recognition of the CSM*

8.1A.190.10   On initial recognition of a profitable group of insurance contracts, the CSM is the equal and opposite amount of the net inflow that arises as the sum of the total of the fulfilment cash flows, the derecognition of any asset or liability recognised for insurance acquisition cash flows and any cash flows arising from the contracts in the group at that date. [*IFRS 17.32, 38*]

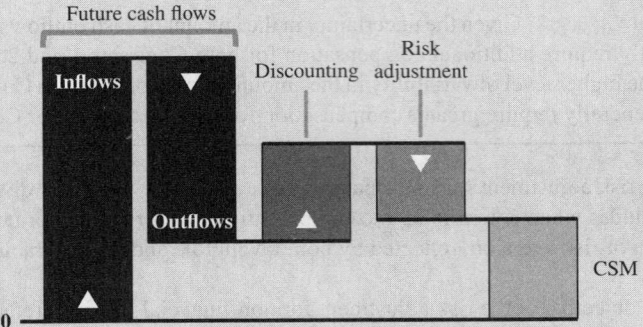

Note: Depending on the facts and circumstances, the size and direction of the components could vary.

8.1A.190.20   For groups of onerous contracts, the total of the fulfilment cash flows, the derecognition of any asset or liability recognised for insurance acquisition cash flows and any cash flows arising from the contracts in the group at that date is a net cash outflow. A loss is recognised immediately in profit or loss for the entire net cash outflow. This results in the carrying amount of the insurance liability for the group being equal to the fulfilment cash flows and the CSM of the group being zero. A loss component is created for this net cash flow, which determines the amounts that are subsequently presented in profit or loss as reversals on onerous groups. These amounts are not included in insurance revenue. [*IFRS 17.47–48*]

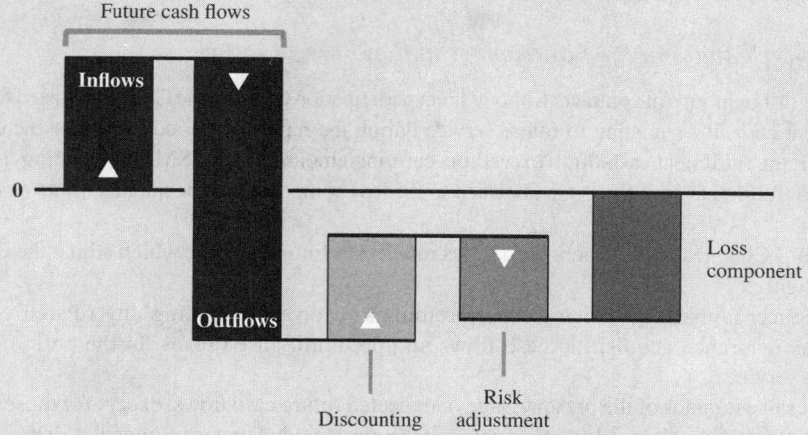

Note: Depending on the facts and circumstances, the size and direction of the components could vary.

8.1A.200 *Subsequent measurement of the CSM*

8.1A.200.10 The fulfilment cash flows are remeasured at each reporting date to reflect estimates based on current assumptions, applying the same requirements that apply on initial measurement (see 8.1A.190). Changes in estimates of the fulfilment cash flows are reflected in either profit or loss or OCI – or, in some cases, they adjust the CSM – depending on their nature. The CSM is also updated to reflect the unwinding of discount rates for the time value of money. The balance is allocated to profit or loss each period to reflect the provision of services in the period. The CSM at each reporting date represents the profit in the group of contracts that has not yet been recognised in profit or loss because it relates to future service to be provided. [*IFRS 17.43–44, BC22–BC24*]

8.1A.200.20 Accordingly, the CSM at the reporting date equals:
- the CSM at the previous reporting date; plus
- the effect of new contracts added to the group; plus
- interest accreted on the CSM during the period (see 8.1A.200.40); plus/minus
- changes in fulfilment cash flows relating to future service (see 8.1A.210); plus/minus
- effects of currency exchange differences on the CSM (see 8.1A.200.50); minus
- the amount of the CSM recognised in profit or loss because of the transfer of services during the period (see 8.1A.220). [*IFRS 17.44*]

8.1A.200.30 The sum of the updated fulfilment cash flows and the updated CSM represents the carrying amount of the group of insurance contracts at each reporting date.

8.1A.200.40 For contracts without direct participation features, interest is accreted on the carrying amount of the CSM during the reporting period using the discount rate applied on initial recognition to reflect the time value of money. The discount rate is the one applicable to nominal cash flows that do not vary based on returns on any underlying items. [*IFRS 17.44(b), B72(b)*]

8.1A.200.50   If a group of insurance contracts generates cash flows in a foreign currency, then the group is considered a monetary item for the purpose of applying IAS 21 (see 2.7.120.20). This means that the CSM is also a monetary item and therefore it is adjusted for the effect of any currency exchange differences. This also applies under the PAA (see 8.1A.270). [*IFRS 17.30, 44(d), BC278*]

8.1A.210   *Changes in the fulfilment cash flows*

8.1A.210.10   For groups of contracts without direct participation features, the CSM is adjusted for changes in fulfilment cash flows relating to future service during the reporting period, except to the extent that increases in the fulfilment cash flows exceed the carrying amount of the CSM (i.e. resulting in a loss) or decreases in fulfilment cash flows are allocated to the loss component of the liability. [*IFRS 17.44(c)*]

8.1A.210.20   Changes in fulfilment cash flows relating to future service, which adjust the CSM, may arise through:
- experience adjustments arising from premiums received, including any related cash flows such as insurance acquisition cash flows and premium-based taxes, in the period related to future service;
- changes in estimates of the present value of expected future cash flows, except for those that relate to the effect of the time value of money and the effect and changes in financial risk;
- changes in the risk adjustment for non-financial risk that relate to future service; and
- differences between the investment component expected to become payable in the period and the actual investment component that becomes payable in the period. [*IFRS 17.B96*]

8.1A.210.30   Experience adjustments arise from differences between the estimates at the beginning of the period of the amounts expected:
- *for premium receipts:* in the period and the actual cash flows in the period; or
- *for insurance service expenses:* to be incurred in the period and the actual amounts incurred in the period. [*IFRS 17.A*]

8.1A.210.40   In general, for the liability for remaining coverage, experience adjustments relate to past or current service and therefore do not adjust the CSM. However, experience adjustments arising from premiums received in the period that relate to future service are an exception to this general rule – i.e. they do adjust the CSM. [*IFRS 17.B97(b), BC233*]

8.1A.210.50   Investment components are the amounts that an insurance contract requires the entity to repay to a policyholder even if an insured event does not occur. IFRS 17 requires any unexpected repayment of an investment component to adjust the CSM. However, it is also adjusted for changes in future estimates of cash flows, which include reductions in future repayments of investment components. Therefore, the net effect on the CSM comprises only the effect of a change in the timing of the repayment of the investment component. An entity is not required to determine the amount of an investment component until a claim is incurred. [*IFRS 17.A, BC235*]

8.1A.210.60   Changes in estimates of fulfilment cash flows in the liability for incurred claims relate to current or past services. Accordingly, they do not adjust the CSM. [*IFRS 17.B97*]

8.1A.210.70   The following chart illustrates the general principle for adjusting the insurance liability for changes in fulfilment cash flows.

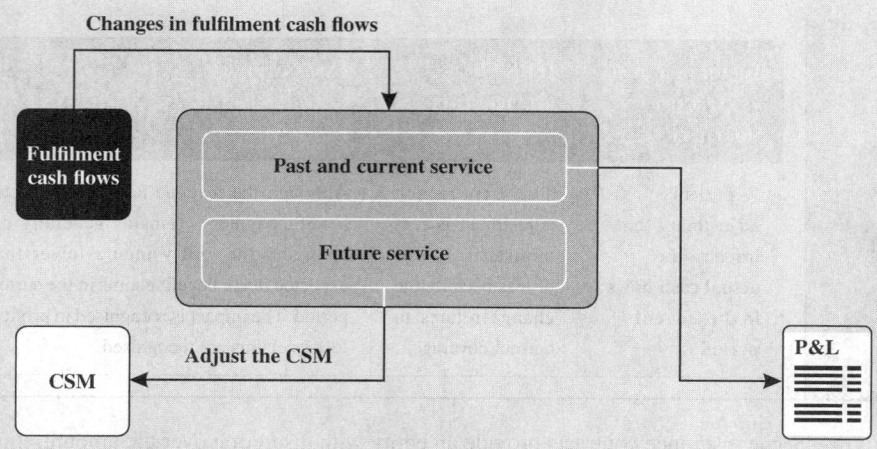

8.1A.210.80 Changes in fulfilment cash flows that relate to future services adjust the CSM, rather than being recognised immediately in the statement of profit or loss and OCI. In some cases, experience adjustments result in changes in the fulfilment cash flows that adjust the CSM as well. [*IFRS 17.BC233–BC234*]

EXAMPLE 11 – CHANGES IN FULFILMENT CASH FLOWS

8.1A.210.90 Company M issues a group of life insurance contracts for which premiums are received up-front. In the first reporting period after initial recognition, actual mortality is 80% of what was expected – i.e. more policyholders than expected survive until the end of the period. The following table explains how M reflects this in the subsequent measurement of the insurance contract liability.

IMPACT OF ACTUAL VS EXPECTED MORTALITY	IFRS 17 REQUIREMENTS	EXPLANATION
Impact on fulfilment cash flows	This change adjusts the CSM because the change relates to future coverage.	The future cash flows change to reflect the ongoing obligation to provide future services for more contracts than was previously estimated, because more contracts are in force for future periods than was expected at the beginning of the period. This impact on the statement of profit or loss and OCI is partially offset by the fact that the CSM released in the current period is calculated after adjusting for changes in the CSM during the period.

IMPACT OF ACTUAL VS EXPECTED MORTALITY	IFRS 17 REQUIREMENTS	EXPLANATION
Experience adjustment that impacts the actual cash flows in the current period	The experience adjustment is recognised in profit or loss because the change relates to current coverage.	Although the revenue based on expected benefit payments remains generally unchanged, the entity incurs lower than expected death benefit claims in the current period. The impact is recognised in profit or loss as claims are recognised.

8.1A.210.100 Some insurance contracts provide an entity with discretion over the amount, timing or nature of cash flows to be paid to policyholders. A change in the discretionary cash flows is regarded as relating to future service and therefore adjusts the CSM. To identify these changes, at inception of the contract an entity specifies the basis on which it expects to determine its commitment under the contract – e.g. based on a fixed interest rate or on returns that vary based on specified asset returns. [*IFRS 17.B98–B100*]

8.1A.210.110 The basis specified at inception of the contract is used to distinguish between the effect of changes in assumptions related to financial risk on that commitment and those that relate to discretionary changes to that commitment. Subsequent discretionary changes to these cash flows that are based on the entity's commitment, relate to future service and adjust the CSM. Conversely, subsequent changes to that commitment resulting from financial risk assumptions do not adjust the CSM. [*IFRS 17.B99*]

8.1A.210.120 At contract inception, if an entity cannot specify the basis on which it expects to determine its commitment under the contract, then its commitment is the return implicit in the estimate of fulfilment cash flows, updated to reflect current assumptions that relate to financial risk. [*IFRS 17.B100*]

EXAMPLE 12 – CHANGES IN FULFILMENT CASH FLOWS – SPECIFYING DISCRETION

8.1A.210.130 Company E issues an insurance contract (without a direct participation feature) with a five-year coverage period under which, in the event of the death of the policyholder, the beneficiary receives the greater of:
- a fixed death benefit; and
- the account balance.

8.1A.210.140 If the policyholder survives at the end of the coverage period, then it receives the account balance. The account balance receives a minimum interest return guarantee of 2%. Any additional return is at E's discretion.

8.1A.210.150 At inception, E expects the return from an internally specified pool of assets to be 5%, and specifies that it expects to provide a return to the policyholder that will leave E with a 0.5% spread after meeting the guarantee. This is the initial commitment specified by E when identifying changes to the commitment that would adjust the CSM.

8.1A.210.160 An actual return in the first subsequent period of 6% does not impact the CSM, because E has not changed the commitment mechanism, even though it will provide the policyholder with a higher return than expected. Rather, the effect of the financial risk will be recognised in profit or loss or OCI as part of insurance finance income or expense.

8.1A.210.170 A change in the commitment in subsequent periods that results in E retaining a lower or higher spread would adjust the CSM, because it would change its commitment relating to future services to be provided.

8.1A.220 *Release of the CSM*

8.1A.220.10 The CSM is adjusted in each reporting period for an amount recognised in profit or loss to reflect the service provided under the group of insurance contracts in that period. This amount is determined by:

- identifying the coverage units in the group;
- allocating the CSM at the reporting date (i.e. the end of the period) – before recognising any release to profit or loss to reflect the services provided – equally to coverage units actually provided in the current period and expected at this date to be provided in the future; and
- recognising in profit or loss the amount allocated to coverage units provided in the period. [*IFRS 17.30, 43, 44(e), B119*]

8.1A.220.20 The number of coverage units in a group is the quantity of coverage provided by the contracts in the group, determined by considering for each contract the quantity of benefits provided under a contract and its expected coverage duration. [*IFRS 17.B119*]

8.1A.220.30 An entity recognises the CSM in profit or loss over the period for which it promised coverage under the contract, rather than the period over which the liability is expected to be settled. The margin that the entity recognises for bearing risk – i.e. the risk adjustment for non-financial risk – is recognised in profit or loss as the entity is released from risk in both the coverage period and the settlement period. [*IFRS 17.BC283*]

8.1A.230 *Determining a loss component for the liability for remaining coverage*

8.1A.230.10 On initial recognition of a group of insurance contracts, the sum of the fulfilment cash flows, any derecognised assets or liabilities for insurance acquisition cash flows allocated to the group of insurance contracts and any cash flows arising from contracts in the group at that date is a net cash outflow. This amount is considered the loss component of the liability for remaining coverage. [*IFRS 17.47, 49*]

8.1A.230.20 A group of contracts that has a CSM at inception can become onerous (or more onerous) in subsequent periods, if unfavourable changes in the fulfilment cash flows arising from changes in estimates of future cash flows relating to future service exceed the carrying amount of the CSM. The excess is considered the loss component of the liability for remaining coverage and is recognised in profit or loss when it is first measured. This determines the amounts that are subsequently presented in profit or loss as reversals of losses on onerous groups and are consequently excluded from the determination of insurance revenue (see 8.1A.410). [*IFRS 17.48(a), 49*]

8.1A.230.30   Once a group of contracts has a loss component as part of its liability for remaining coverage, certain subsequent changes in the fulfilment cash flows of that liability are allocated on a systematic basis between the loss component of the liability for remaining coverage and the liability for remaining coverage, excluding the loss component. The systematic allocation results in the total amounts allocated to the loss component being zero by the end of the coverage period of the group of contracts. [*IFRS 17.44(c), 50, 52*]

8.1A.230.40   These subsequent changes are those estimates of the present value of future cash flows for claims and expenses released from the liability for remaining coverage because of:
- incurred insurance service expenses;
- changes in the risk adjustment for non-financial risk recognised in profit or loss as a result of the release from risk; and
- insurance finance income or expense. [*IFRS 17.51*]

8.1A.230.50   Subsequent decreases in fulfilment cash flows arising from changes in estimates of future cash flows relating to future service are solely allocated to the loss component, until it is reduced to zero. After it has reached zero, a CSM is created for the excess of the decrease over the amount allocated to the loss component. [*IFRS 17.44, 50–52*]

8.1A.240   *Modifications to subsequent measurement of the CSM for direct participating contracts*

8.1A.240.10   Direct participating contracts, create an obligation to pay the policyholder an amount equal to the fair value of the underlying items, less a variable fee for future service. The variable fee comprises the entity's share in the fair value of the underlying items less fulfilment cash flows (e.g. amounts payable to the policyholder) that do not vary based on the underlying items. [*IFRS 17.B104, BC243*]

8.1A.240.20   An entity assesses whether a contract is considered a direct participating contract based on its expectations at inception of the contract, and this is not reassessed subsequently unless the contract is modified (see 8.1A.360). An insurance contract is considered a direct participating contract when:
- the contractual terms (see 8.1A.240.30) specify that the policyholder participates in a share of a clearly identified pool of underlying items (see 8.1A.240.40);
- the entity expects to pay the policyholder an amount equal to a substantial share of the fair value returns on the underlying items; and
- the entity expects a substantial proportion of any change in the amounts to be paid to the policyholder to vary with the change in the fair value of the underlying items. [*IFRS 17.B101–B102*]

8.1A.240.30   The contractual terms have to specify that the policyholder participates in a share of a clearly identified pool of underlying items. This does not preclude the existence of the entity's discretion to vary the amounts paid to the policyholder. However, the link to the underlying items has to be enforceable, and enforceability is a matter of law. [*IFRS 17.B105*]

8.1A.240.40   The contractual terms have to specify a determinable fee which can be expressed as a percentage of portfolio returns or portfolio asset values. This is done by the contract specifying that the policyholder participates in a share of a clearly identified pool of underlying items. The pool of underlying items can comprise any items as long as they are clearly identified by the contract. For example, the pool of underlying items may include reference to a portfolio of assets, the net assets of the entity or a subsidiary within the group that is the reporting entity, or a specified subset of net assets of the entity. An entity is not required to hold the identified pool of underlying items. [*IFRS 17.B101, BC245*]

8.1A.240.50   A clearly identified pool of underlying items does not exist when:
- an entity can change the underlying items that determine the amount of the entity's obligation with retrospective effect; or
- there are no underlying items identified, even if the policyholder could be provided with a return that generally reflects the entity's overall performance and expectations, or the performance expectations of a subset of assets that the entity holds. [*IFRS 17.B106*]

EXAMPLE 13 – LINK TO CLEARLY IDENTIFIED POOL OF UNDERLYING ITEMS

8.1A.240.60   Company B issues two different types of life insurance contracts that provide death benefits for the whole life of the policyholder. The death benefit is determined as the higher of a guaranteed amount and the account balance.
- *Contract X:* The contract specifies that the policyholder account balance is credited a fixed 3% annual rate. B has discretion to change the crediting rate.
- *Contract Y:* The contract specifies that the policyholder's account balance is credited with an annual rate that would leave B with a margin of 0.5% of the return from assets in a defined portfolio, Portfolio Z. B has discretion to change the crediting rate.

8.1A.240.70   B holds assets in Portfolio Z to cover both types of contracts and the expected annual return of the portfolio is 3.5%.

8.1A.240.80   Although both contracts initially credit a 3% return on the policyholder account balance, only Contract Y creates a link between the policyholder's return and a clearly identified pool of underlying items. Contract Y identifies a link to the assets in Portfolio Z and therefore could meet the definition of a direct participating contract.

8.1A.240.90   Although the obligation to the policyholder under Contract X reflects a crediting rate set by B that generally reflects B's expectations of the performance of the underlying assets that support the contract, it does not reflect clearly identified underlying items and therefore is not considered a direct participating contract. [*IFRS 17.B106*]

8.1A.240.100 An entity considers the term 'substantial', as discussed in 8.1A.240.20, in the context of the objective of direct participating contracts, which is to provide investment management services and to be compensated for those services by a fee that is determined with reference to the underlying items. The variability in these amounts is considered over the duration of the group of insurance contracts and on a present value probability-weighted average basis. Therefore, a contract in which the policyholder participates in a substantial share of a clearly identified pool of underlying items, but in which the annual returns are measured on a basis other than fair value, can still be considered a direct participating contract if the entity expects to pay a substantial share of the fair value returns on the underlying items over the duration of the group. [*IFRS 17.B101, B107–B108, BC245*]

EXAMPLE 14 – POLICYHOLDER PARTICIPATION BASED ON A MEASURE OTHER THAN FAIR VALUE

8.1A.240.110 Company L issues a life insurance policy under which Policyholder P participates in 90% of the returns of a clearly identified pool of underlying items. The clearly identified pool of underlying items is made up of stated rate coupon quoted bonds measured at amortised cost. P's account value is credited on an annual basis with 90% of the returns of the underlying items (including all returns from sale if they are not held until maturity by the insurer) associated with the contract, measured on an effective interest basis.

8.1A.240.120 This contract would be classified as a direct participating contract if L expects, over the duration of the group:
- to pay P an amount equal to a substantial share of the fair value returns from the underlying items associated with the contract; and
- a substantial portion of any change in the amounts to be paid to P to vary with the change in the fair value of the underlying items associated with the contract. [*IFRS 17.B101(b)–(c), B107*]

8.1A.240.130 Although P only receives an equivalent return of 90% of the underlying items associated with the contract on an accrual basis annually, P still participates in any gains/losses that arise from the disposal or maturity of the underlying items over the duration of the group. Therefore, this contract is not precluded from being a direct participating contract.

8.1A.250 Measuring direct participating contracts

8.1A.250.10 The general measurement model is applied on initial recognition of direct participating contracts in the same way as it is applied for contracts without direct participation features. As for subsequent measurement, differences arise within the treatment of the CSM, which includes specific modifications that reflect the specific nature of direct participating contracts.

8.1A.250.20 The modifications to the general measurement model on subsequent measurement reflect the notion that the entity substantially provides investment-related services and is compensated for the services by a fee that is determined with reference to the underlying items. Therefore, under the modified model the CSM at the reporting date equals:
- the CSM at the previous reporting date; plus

- the effect of any new contracts added to the group; plus/minus
- the entity's share of the change in the fair value of the underlying items (see 8.1A.250.40); plus/minus
- changes in the fulfilment cash flows relating to future service (see 8.1A.250.50); plus/minus
- the effect of any currency exchange differences arising on the CSM (see 8.1A.200.50); minus
- the amount of the CSM recognised as insurance revenue because of the transfer of services in the period (see 8.1A.220). [*IFRS 17.45, B101, B107(b)*]

8.1A.250.30   Entities need not identify the adjustments to the CSM for the changes in the entity's share of the fair value of the underlying items separately from those related to changes in the fulfilment cash flows relating to future service. Therefore, a combined amount may be determined for some or all of the adjustments. [*IFRS 17.45, B114*]

8.1A.250.40   Changes in the obligation to pay the policyholder an amount equal to the fair value of the underlying items are recognised in profit or loss or OCI. However, changes related to the entity's share of the fair value of the underlying items – i.e. the variable fee – relate to future service and, accordingly, adjust the CSM, except to the extent that:
- the entity's share of a decrease in the fair value of the underlying items exceeds the carrying amount of the CSM (i.e. resulting in a loss recognised as part of the insurance service result);
- the entity's share of an increase in the fair value of the underlying items reverses losses previously recognised; or
- the entity meets the conditions for the risk mitigation option and chooses not to reflect in the CSM some or all of the changes in the effect of financial risk on its share of the underlying items (see 8.1A.250.70). [*IFRS 17.45(b), B111–B112, B115, BC243, BC247*]

8.1A.250.50   The CSM is adjusted for changes in fulfilment cash flows relating to future service. These include changes in estimates of the fulfilment cash flows, consistent with those for contracts without direct participation features (see 8.1A.210), and changes in the effect of the time value of money and financial risks not arising from the underlying items – e.g. financial guarantees. [*IFRS 17.B113*]

8.1A.250.60   These changes do not adjust the CSM to the extent that:
- increases in the fulfilment cash flows exceed the carrying amount of the CSM (i.e. resulting in a loss);
- decreases in fulfilment cash flows are allocated to the loss component of the liability; or
- the entity meets the conditions for the risk mitigation option and chooses not to reflect in the CSM some or all of the changes in the effect of the time value of money and financial risks not arising from the underlying items (see 8.1A.250.70). [*IFRS 17.45(c), B115*]

8.1A.250.70   An entity may choose to exclude from the CSM some or all of the effect of financial risk on the entity's share of the underlying items or changes in the effect of the time value of money and financial risks not arising from the underlying items if the following criteria are met:
- it uses a derivative to mitigate financial risks arising from the insurance contracts – e.g. the effect of financial guarantees;
- it applies a previously documented risk management objective and strategy for using derivatives to mitigate financial risk arising from the insurance contracts;
- an economic offset exists between the insurance contracts and the derivative; and
- credit risk does not dominate the economic offset. [*IFRS 17.B113–B118*]

8.1A.250.80 The fulfilment cash flows in a group to which this exception applies are determined in a consistent way at each reporting date. If an entity chooses not to adjust the CSM for some changes in the fulfilment cash flows, then it discloses the effect of that choice on the adjustment to the CSM that would otherwise have been made in the current period. [*IFRS 17.B112, B117*]

8.1A.250.90 If the entity no longer meets the conditions for using the option – e.g. an economic offset ceases to exist – then it:

- ceases to apply the option from that date; and
- does not make any adjustment for changes previously recognised in profit or loss. [*IFRS 17.B118*]

8.1A.260 Measuring certain underlying items

8.1A.260.10 Some standards currently provide for fair value measurement of assets that are underlying items for different types of participating arrangements. These standards are amended by IFRS 17 to allow for more options to reduce mismatches between the measurements used for the assets held by the entity and the measurement of the liability that is supported by those assets. The following table describes the options and related guidance available in certain instances, including when accounting for direct participating contracts. [*IAS 32.33A, 16.29A–29B, 28.18–19, 40.32A–32B*]

ASSET TYPE	WHEN DOES THE FAIR VALUE OPTION APPLY?	OTHER RELEVANT REQUIREMENTS
Investment properties	An entity may apply the fair value model or the cost model for all investment properties backing liabilities that pay a return linked directly to the fair value of, or returns from, specified assets including those investment properties – e.g. investment funds, direct participating contracts.	For investment properties that are held by a fund or as underlying items, the entity is not permitted to measure them partly at cost and partly at fair value.
Investments in associates and joint ventures	An entity may apply IFRS 9 FVTPL measurement for investments in an associate or a joint venture that are held by, or indirectly held through, an entity that is a venture capital organisation, a mutual fund, a unit trust or a similar entity, including investment-linked insurance funds – e.g. a fund held by an entity as the underlying items for a group of direct participating contracts.	These options are applied separately for each investment on initial recognition. Specific guidance is provided for circumstances in which only part of the investment is held in this way.
Owner-occupied property	An entity may apply the fair value model of IAS 40 to owner-occupied property held by an investment fund or as underlying items of direct participating contracts.	Owner-occupied property measured using the fair value model of IAS 40 is treated as a separate class of property, plant and equipment.

8.1A.260.20 IFRS 17 also amends IFRS 9 and IAS 32 to address cases in which own financial liabilities and shares are held in investment funds operated by the entity and which provide their investors with benefits determined by the fund's units, or held as underlying items of a group of direct participating insurance contracts. [*IFRS 9.3.3.5, 7.8(a), IAS 32.33A*]

8.1A.260.30   If an entity holds its own financial liabilities – e.g. issued corporate bonds – as underlying items for a group of direct participating contracts that it issues or investment funds that it operates, then it may elect to continue to account for the instruments as financial liabilities and to account for the repurchased instruments as if they were financial assets, and measure them at FVTPL, instead of derecognising the liabilities. [*IFRS 9.3.3.5*]

8.1A.260.40   If an entity holds its own treasury shares as underlying items for a group of direct participating contracts or such investment funds, then it may elect to continue to account for them as equity and to account for the reacquired instruments as if they were financial assets, and measure them at FVTPL. [*IAS 32.33A*]

8.1A.260.50   The choices in 8.1A.260.30–40 are made when the repurchase of each instrument is made and are irrevocable. An entity discloses separately the fair values of the financial assets. [*IFRS 9.3.3.5, 7.8(a), IAS 32.33A*]

8.1A.270   Premium allocation approach

8.1A.270.10   An entity is permitted to apply the PAA to measure a group of insurance contracts if, at inception of the group, the coverage period of each contract in the group of insurance contracts is one year or less or the entity reasonably expects the PAA would produce a measurement of the liability for remaining coverage for the group of insurance contracts that would not differ materially from the measurement that would be achieved by applying the general measurement requirements (see 8.1A.120). When comparing the possible different liability for remaining coverage measurements, an entity should consider the impact of the liability release patterns to profit or loss and the impact of the time value of money. [*IFRS 17.53*]

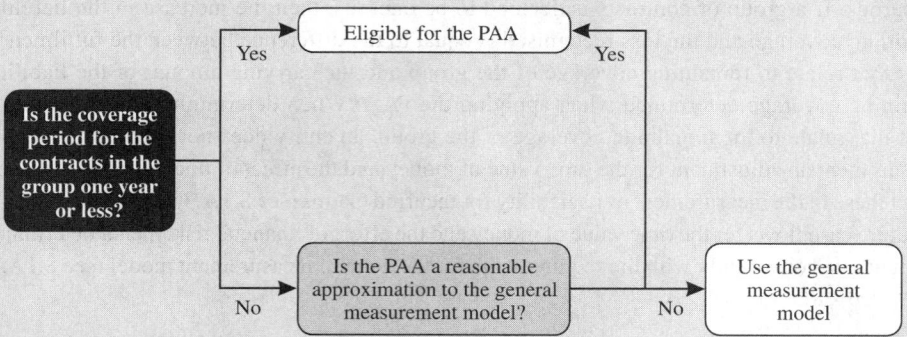

8.1A.270.20   If, at inception of the group, an entity expects significant variability in the fulfilment cash flows during the period before a claim is incurred, then an entity cannot reasonably expect the PAA to produce a measurement of the liability for remaining coverage for a group of insurance contracts that would not differ materially from the one that would be produced by applying the general measurement requirements. Variability in the fulfilment cash flows increases, for example, with the extent of future cash flows relating to any embedded derivatives that exist in the contracts and the length of the coverage period. [*IFRS 17.54*]

8.1A.270.30   The aggregation requirements that apply to contracts under the PAA are consistent with those under the general measurement model (see 8.1A.110). However, for contracts that apply the PAA it is assumed that no contracts in the portfolio are onerous on initial recognition, unless facts and circumstances indicate otherwise and the assessment of whether contracts have no significant possibility of becoming onerous subsequently is performed by assessing the likelihood of changes in applicable facts and circumstances. [*IFRS 17.14–24*]

8.1A.280   *Initial measurement applying the PAA*

8.1A.280.10   On initial recognition, the liability for remaining coverage is equal to the premiums received less any insurance acquisition cash flows at that date (unless the entity chooses to recognise certain insurance acquisition cash flows as expenses when they are incurred, see 8.1A.280.40). The amount of premiums received does not include premiums due or expected. [*IFRS 17.55(a)*]

8.1A.280.20   The initial measurement does not explicitly identify the present value of future cash flows, the effects of risk and the time value of money. Consequently, the subsequent measurement does not involve an analysis of the variations in those components before a claim is incurred because the rationale for applying the PAA is that there are unlikely to be significant changes in them. However, when facts and circumstances indicate that a group of contracts is onerous, the entity calculates the liability for remaining coverage using the general measurement model's fulfilment cash flow requirements (see 8.1A.210), with certain simplifications if certain conditions are met (see 8.1A.280.30). [*IFRS 17.57, BC289*]

8.1A.280.30   An entity recognises a loss and an increase in the liability for remaining coverage if facts and circumstances indicate, at any time during the coverage period, that a group of contracts is onerous. If a group of contracts is deemed to be onerous, then the increase in the liability for remaining coverage and the loss recognised is equal to the difference between the fulfilment cash flows that relate to remaining coverage of the group and the carrying amount of the liability for remaining coverage determined when applying the PAA. When determining the fulfilment cash flows that relate to the remaining coverage of the group, an entity does not need to include in the measurement an adjustment for the time value of money and the effect of financial risk if it does not reflect these in the measurement of its liability for incurred claims (see 8.1A.300). If the entity adjusts the future cash flows for the time value of money and the effect of financial risk, then it determines the discount rate consistently with the requirements for the general measurement model (see 8.1A.170). [*IFRS 17.57–58*]

8.1A.280.40   Acquisition cash flows are deferred (by reducing the liability recognised on initial recognition) and are recognised as an expense over time in a systematic way. However, if the coverage period of each contract in the group on initial recognition is one year or less, then an entity may choose to recognise insurance acquisition cash flows as an expense when they are incurred. [*IFRS 17.55(a), 59(a), B125*]

8.1A.290 *Subsequent measurement applying the PAA*

8.1A.290.10   At each subsequent reporting date, the liability for remaining coverage equals:
- the previous carrying amount; plus
- the premiums received in the period; minus
- insurance acquisition cash flows, adjusted for the amortisation of them (unless the entity chooses to recognise the insurance acquisition cash flows as an expense when they are incurred, when applicable), see 8.1A.280.40; plus
- adjustments to a financing component (unless this adjustment is not applied), see 8.1A.290.20; minus
- insurance revenue recognised, see 8.1A.290.30; minus
- investment components paid or transferred to the liability for incurred claims.

8.1A.290.20   If insurance contracts in a group have a significant financing component, then the carrying amount of the liability for the remaining coverage is adjusted to reflect the time value of money using a discount rate determined on initial recognition and the effect of financial risk. However, if on initial recognition the entity expects the time between providing each part of the coverage and the related premium due date to be one year or less, then the entity may elect not to adjust the liability for the time value of money and the effect of financial risk. [*IFRS 17.56*]

8.1A.290.30   Insurance contract revenue for the period is the amount of expected premium receipts allocated to the period (excluding investment components and adjusted to reflect the time value of money and the effect of financial risk, if applicable). The allocation to each period of coverage is based on the passage of time. However, if the pattern of the release of risk during the coverage period differs significantly from the passage of time, then the expected premium receipts are allocated to periods of coverage on the basis of the expected timing of incurred insurance service expenses. The basis of allocation is changed if facts and circumstances change over the coverage period. [*IFRS 17.B126–B127*]

EXAMPLE 15 – REVENUE RECOGNITION UNDER THE PAA

8.1A.290.40   Company E issues insurance contracts on 30 June 2021 with the following terms:
- coverage period of 12 months;
- premiums of 1,200 – all received at inception;
- the applicable discount rate on initial recognition is 5%; and
- the expected pattern of release of risk is not significantly different from the passage of time. [*IFRS 17.IE13*]

8.1A.290.50   E's accounting policy is to adjust the liability for remaining coverage for the effect of the time value of money.

8.1A.290.60   E's annual reporting date is 31 December, at which time there are no incurred claims.

8.1A.290.70 The insurance acquisition cash flows are insignificant.

At inception

8.1A.290.80 The liability for remaining coverage is the premiums received of 1,200.

31 December 2021

8.1A.290.90 The effect of the time value of money increases the liability for remaining coverage as follows (in this example, a simple interest calculation is applied to the opening balance of the liability).

$$1,200 \times (1+ (0.05 \times 6 / 12)) = \mathbf{1,230}$$

8.1A.290.100 The insurance contract revenue is the amount of expected premium receipts, adjusted to reflect the time value of money, allocated to the period.

$$1,230 \times 6 / 12 = \mathbf{615}$$

8.1A.290.110 The liability for remaining coverage is the sum of the previous carrying amount plus the adjustment for the time value of money less the amount recognised as insurance contract revenue during the period.

$$1,230 - 615 = \mathbf{615}$$

Statement of profit or loss and OCI for the six months ended 31 December 2021

Insurance contract revenue	615
Insurance finance expense	(30)
Profit	585

Facts and circumstances change

8.1A.290.120 At 31 December 2021, facts and circumstances indicate that the group of contracts is onerous. E calculates the fulfilment cash flows under the general measurement model as 800.

8.1A.290.130 As a result, E recognises a loss and an increase in the liability for remaining coverage as the difference between the liability for remaining coverage of 615 and the fulfilment cash flows of 800.

8.1A.290.140 This results in a liability of 800 and a loss of 185 that is recognised in profit or loss on 31 December 2021.

8.1A.300 *Liability for incurred claims applying the PAA*

8.1A.300.10 The liability for incurred claims is measured for contracts under the PAA at the amount of the fulfilment cash flows relating to incurred claims, in accordance with the requirements of the general measurement model (see 8.1A.120). However, if the future cash flows are expected to be paid or received within one year or less from when they are incurred, then an entity may choose not to adjust the future cash flows for the time value of money. [*IFRS 17.59(b)*]

8.1A.300.20 If an entity discounts the liability for incurred claims (by requirement or choice) and chooses to apply the disaggregation policy choice (see 8.1A.440.20), then the interest rate used to recognise the insurance finance income or expense in profit or loss is a rate that applies to nominal cash flows that do not vary based on the returns on any underlying items, at the date of the incurred claim. [*IFRS 17.B72(e)(iii), B133*]

EXAMPLE 16 – APPLYING THE PAA AT INCEPTION AND SUBSEQUENTLY

8.1A.300.30 Company E issues a group of insurance contracts with the following terms:

- coverage period of 12 months (the contract does not lapse after a claim is made);
- premiums of 1,200 – all received at inception;
- insurance acquisition cash flows of 24 – all paid at inception;
- actual claims after one month of 60; and
- a risk adjustment for non-financial risk on the incurred claims of 10.

8.1A.300.40 In this example, the insurance acquisition cash flows are deferred, and the discounting of future cash flows and accretion of interest are ignored.

8.1A.300.50 Also, in this example insurance services are provided and the insurance acquisition cash flows are expensed evenly over the coverage period.

At inception

8.1A.300.60 The liability for remaining coverage is the sum of the premium received less payments related to insurance acquisition cash flows.

1,200 - 24 = **1,176**

After one month

8.1A.300.70 The amortisation of the insurance acquisition cash flows is as follows.

24 / 12 = **2**

8.1A.300.80 The insurance contract revenue is the amount of expected premium receipts allocated to the period.

$$1{,}200 / 12 = \mathbf{100}$$

8.1A.300.90   The liability for remaining coverage is the sum of the previous carrying amount plus the amount of direct insurance acquisition cash flow amortisation for the period less the amount recognised as insurance contract revenue during the period.

$$1{,}176 + 2 - 100 = \mathbf{1{,}078}$$

8.1A.300.100   The liability for incurred claims is the actual claims for the period including the risk adjustment for non-financial risk on incurred claims.

$$60 + 10 = \mathbf{70}$$

Profit or loss

Insurance contract revenue	100
Amortisation of insurance acquisition cash flows	(2)
Claims incurred	(70)
Impact on profit or loss	28

8.1A.310   Reinsurance contracts held

8.1A.310.10   A 'reinsurance contract' is a type of insurance contract that is issued by an entity (the reinsurer) to compensate another entity (the cedant) for claims arising from insurance contract(s) issued by the cedant. [*IFRS 17.A, BC296*]

8.1A.310.20   The cedant accounts for a group of reinsurance contracts held separately from the underlying contract(s) that it relates to because the cedant does not normally have a right to reduce the amounts that it owes to the underlying policyholder. The cedant's contractual obligations to the underlying policyholder(s) are not extinguished because the underlying contract(s) is reinsured. [*IFRS 17.BC298*]

8.1A.310.30   An insurer also needs to identify cash flows within the contract boundary (see 8.1A.140) for any reinsurance contracts held. It appears that cash flows are within the boundary of a reinsurance contract held if they arise from substantive rights and obligations of the entity—i.e. the holder of the contract. For reinsurance contracts held:
- a 'substantive right' is a right to receive services from the reinsurer; and
- a 'substantive obligation' is an obligation to pay amounts to the reinsurer (i.e. the reinsurer can compel the entity to pay reinsurance premiums).

8.1A.310.40   Therefore, cash flows are within the contract boundary of a reinsurance contract held if they arise from substantive rights and obligations that exist during the reporting period in which the cedant is compelled to pay amounts to the reinsurer or has a substantive right to receive services from the reinsurer.

8.1A.310.50   The cedant measures and accounts for groups of reinsurance contracts that it holds based on the recognition and measurement requirements for issued insurance contracts, modified to reflect the following facts.

- Reinsurance contracts held are generally assets, rather than liabilities. They are separate from the underlying insurance contracts; however, they correspond with them.
- For reinsurance contracts held, the cedant pays a premium to a reinsurer and receives a reimbursement from the reinsurer if it pays valid claims arising from the underlying contracts. Generally, insurers do not make profits from reinsurance contracts held. Rather, they pay a margin to the reinsurer as an implicit part of the premium. The cedant has a net cost or a net gain on purchasing the reinsurance – i.e. a CSM that can be positive or negative. [*IFRS 17.29(b), 60–68, BC302*]

8.1A.310.60   Reinsurance contracts issued or held cannot be direct participating contracts. An entity may use the PAA to simplify the measurement of the liability for remaining coverage of a group of reinsurance contracts held if on initial recognition of the group it meets the eligibility criteria, adapted to reflect the features of reinsurance contracts held (see 8.1A.270.10). Because the PAA eligibility assessment is performed separately for the underlying insurance contracts and the reinsurance contracts held, it might result in different outcomes. [*IFRS 17.29(b), 69–70, B109, BC301*]

8.1A.310.70   An entity applies the aggregation requirements to divide portfolios of reinsurance contracts into groups, adapted to reflect the features of reinsurance contracts held. Applying these requirements could result in groups that comprise a single contract. [*IFRS 17.61*]

8.1A.310.80   If a group of reinsurance contracts held provide proportionate coverage, an entity recognises the group of contracts at the later of the beginning of the coverage period of the group or the initial recognition of any underlying contract. In all other cases, it recognises the group of contracts from the beginning of the coverage period of the group. [*IFRS 17.62*]

8.1A.310.90   In some cases, the reinsurance contract covers the losses of individual underlying contracts on a proportionate basis, and in others it covers the aggregated losses from a group of underlying contracts that exceed a specified amount. [*IFRS 17.BC304*]

8.1A.310.100   If the group of reinsurance contracts held covers the loss of a group of contracts on a proportionate basis, then the treatment described in 8.1A.310.80 means that the entity does not recognise the group of reinsurance contracts held until it has recognised at least one of the underlying contracts. [*IFRS 17.BC305(a)*]

8.1A.310.110   If the group of reinsurance contracts held covers the aggregated losses from a group of underlying contracts that exceed a specified amount, then the entity benefits from coverage – in case the underlying losses exceed the threshold – from the beginning of the coverage period of the group of reinsurance contracts held as these losses accumulate throughout the coverage period. Therefore, a group of these reinsurance contracts held is recognised when its coverage period begins. [*IFRS 17.BC305(b)*]

8.1A.310.120   An entity uses consistent assumptions to measure the estimates of the present value of the future cash flows for the group of reinsurance contracts held and the estimates of the present value of the future cash flows for the group(s) of underlying insurance contracts. As a result, the cash flows used to measure the group of reinsurance contracts held reflect the extent to which those cash flows depend on cash flows of the contracts that they cover. [*IFRS 17.63, BC300*]

8.1A.310.130   The effect of any risk of non-performance by the reinsurer, including the effects of collateral and losses from disputes, is considered when determining the estimates of the present value of future cash flows for the group of reinsurance contracts held. Therefore, estimates of amounts and timing of cash flows related to this risk are based on probability-weighted outcomes after calculating the effect of non-performance risk. Changes in the fulfilment cash flows that result from changes in the risk of non-performance of the reinsurer do not relate to future service and are recognised immediately in profit or loss. [*IFRS 17.63, 67, BC307–BC309*]

8.1A.310.140   The risk adjustment for non-financial risk for a group of reinsurance contracts held represents the amount of risk being transferred by the cedant to the reinsurer. [*IFRS 17.64*]

8.1A.320   *Initial recognition of the CSM*

8.1A.320.10   The CSM on initial recognition for a group of reinsurance contracts represents a net cost or net gain from purchasing reinsurance. On initial recognition, if the coverage of the group of reinsurance contracts relates to events that occurred before the purchase of the group (e.g. coverage against an adverse development of claims incurred), then any net cost of purchasing reinsurance coverage is recognised immediately in profit or loss as an expense. In all other cases, the CSM equals the inverse amount of the sum of the fulfilment cash flows, the amount derecognised for assets or liabilities previously recognised for related cash flows and any cash flows arising from the contracts in the group at the date of initial recognition of the group. [*IFRS 17.65*]

8.1A.320.20   The amount paid by a cedant typically exceeds the expected risk-adjusted present value of the cash flows generated by the reinsurance contracts held. Therefore, a debit CSM that represents a net cost of purchasing reinsurance (i.e. the net cash outflows) is typically recognised on initial recognition of a group of reinsurance contracts held. However, a credit CSM that represents a net gain on purchasing reinsurance (i.e. the net cash inflows) can also occur, albeit in rare circumstances. This net gain, which represents a reduction in the cost of purchasing reinsurance, is not immediately recognised in profit or loss on initial recognition of the group, but is deferred. In these circumstances, entities review the measurement of the underlying insurance contracts to evaluate if they are overstated. [*IFRS 17.BC310–BC311*]

EXAMPLE 17A – REINSURANCE CONTRACTS HELD – MEASUREMENT ON INITIAL RECOGNITION (1)

8.1A.320.30   Company X issues a group of insurance contracts, all of which are issued on the same date, with a coverage period of five years. It expects to receive total premiums of 1,000 on initial recognition and to pay claims of 900, on a present value basis, over the coverage period. The risk adjustment for non-financial risk is 60. [*IFRS 17.IE124–IE129*]

8.1A.320.40 At the same time, X enters into a reinsurance contract that covers 30% of each claim arising from the underlying contracts. The risk adjustment for non-financial risk is expected to be 18 for the reinsurance contract held and the risk of non-performance of the reinsurer is negligible.

8.1A.320.50 X identifies a group comprising the single reinsurance contract held and recognises this group at the date on which the underlying group of contracts is initially recognised.

8.1A.320.60 The following table describes the measurement of the group of underlying insurance contracts and the measurement of the reinsurance contract held, under two scenarios. In scenario one, the single reinsurance premium paid on initial recognition is 300 and in the second, it is 260.

	GROUP OF INSURANCE CONTRACTS ISSUED	REINSURANCE CONTRACT HELD – SCENARIO 1	REINSURANCE CONTRACT HELD – SCENARIO 2
Estimates of present value of cash inflows	(1,000)	(270)	(270)
	Premium	*Claims recovery*	*Claims recovery*
Estimates of present value of cash outflows	900	300	260
	Claims	*Premiums*	*Premiums*
Risk adjustment for non-financial risk	60	(18)	(18)
Fulfilment cash flows	(40)	12	(28)
CSM	40	(12)	28

8.1A.320.70 X recognises a CSM for the reinsurance contract held under both scenarios. In Scenario 1, the CSM reflects a net cost of purchasing reinsurance, and in Scenario 2 the CSM reflects a net gain. Both are recognised over the reinsurance coverage period.

EXAMPLE 17B – REINSURANCE CONTRACTS HELD – MEASUREMENT ON INITIAL RECOGNITION (2)

8.1A.320.80 Modifying Example 17A, Company X charges and expects to receive total premiums of 850 on initial recognition for the underlying group of insurance contracts.

8.1A.320.90 The following table describes the measurement of the group of underlying insurance contracts and the measurement of the reinsurance contract held, under both scenarios.

	GROUP OF INSURANCE CONTRACTS ISSUED	REINSURANCE CONTRACT HELD – SCENARIO 1	REINSURANCE CONTRACT HELD – SCENARIO 2
Estimates of present value of cash inflows	(850)	(270)	(270)
Estimates of present value of cash outflows	900	300	260
Risk adjustment for non-financial risk	60	(18)	(18)
Fulfilment cash flows	**110**	**12**	**(28)**
CSM	-	**(12)**	**28**
Loss recognised on initial recognition	**110**	**-**	**-**

8.1A.320.100 Now, the group of insurance contracts issued is onerous on initial recognition. Therefore, X recognises a loss for its onerous group of underlying contracts. The group of insurance contracts issued being considered onerous does not affect the amounts of the CSM recognised for the reinsurance contract held under both scenarios.

8.1A.330 *Subsequent measurement of the CSM*

8.1A.330.10 The CSM at each reporting date is determined consistent with the requirements for general measurement model (see 8.1A.120). The amount of the CSM recognised in profit or loss because of services received in the period is determined by allocation of the CSM remaining at the reporting date (before any allocation) over the current and remaining coverage periods of the group of reinsurance contracts held. [*IFRS 17.66*]

8.1A.330.20 When a change in the fulfilment cash flows allocated to a group of underlying contracts that relate to future service does not adjust the CSM for the group of underlying contracts (i.e. losses on onerous groups recognised after initial recognition in profit or loss), the corresponding changes in the fulfilment cash flows relating to future service of the reinsurance contracts held are also recognised in profit or loss. [*IFRS 17.66(c)(ii), BC315, IE138*]

8.1A.340 **Investment contracts with DPFs**

8.1A.340.10 For investment contracts with DPFs (see 8.1A.40), the following modifications are applied to the recognition and measurement requirements of the general measurement model. [*IFRS 17.3(c), 71*]

AREA	MODIFICATION FOR INVESTMENT CONTRACTS WITH DPFS
Recognition	The date of initial recognition is specified as that on which the entity becomes party to the contract.

AREA	MODIFICATION FOR INVESTMENT CONTRACTS WITH DPFS
Contract boundary	Cash flows are within the contract boundary if they result from a substantive obligation of the entity to deliver cash at a present or future date. The entity has no substantive obligation to deliver cash if it has the practical ability to set a price for the promise to deliver cash that fully reflects the amount of cash promised and related risks.
Allocation of the CSM	The CSM is recognised over the duration of the group of contracts in a systematic way that reflects the transfer of investment services under the contract – i.e. the pattern of provision of investment related services.

8.1A.340.20   All other requirements of the standard apply, unmodified, to investment contracts with DPFs.

8.1A.350   DERECOGNITION

8.1A.350.10   An entity derecognises an insurance contract when it is extinguished – i.e. when the specified obligation in the contract expires or is discharged or cancelled. This is the point when an entity is no longer at risk nor required to transfer economic resources to satisfy the contract. An entity that purchases reinsurance – i.e. the cedant – derecognises the underlying (direct) insurance contracts only if they are extinguished by the reinsurance contract. Insurance contracts are also derecognised when they are modified if certain criteria are met (see 8.1A.360). [*IFRS 17.74–75, BC306*]

8.1A.350.20   Typically, entities do not derecognise insurance contracts when purchasing reinsurance contracts because the reinsurance contracts protect the entity from the losses on the underlying insurance contracts, but do not eliminate the entity's responsibility to fulfil its obligations under those contracts. [*IFRS 17.75, BC306*]

8.1A.350.30   The derecognition criteria are consistent with those for financial liabilities under IFRS 9. An entity derecognises an insurance contract from within a group of insurance contracts by adjusting the group's:
- fulfilment cash flows to eliminate those that relate to the rights and obligations that have been derecognised from the group;
- CSM for the change in those fulfilment cash flows to the extent applicable (see 8.1A.210); and
- number of coverage units for the expected remaining coverage to reflect the coverage units derecognised from the group (see 8.1A.220). [*IFRS 9.3.3.1, 17.76, BC321*]

8.1A.350.40   The accounting treatment differs when derecognition of an insurance contract is the result of the contract being transferred to a third party. In this case – to the extent applicable – the CSM of the respective group is adjusted for the difference between the adjustment to the fulfilment cash flows and the premium charged by the third party. [*IFRS 17.77(a)*]

8.1A.360   **Contract modifications**

8.1A.360.10   Contract modification could be a result of an agreement between the parties to a contract or a change in regulation. The exercise of a right included in the contract is not a modification. If the terms of a contract are modified in a way that would have significantly changed the accounting for the contract had the new terms always existed, then the modification triggers derecognition of the original contract and recognition of a new contract. All other contract modifications are accounted for as changes in estimates of fulfilment cash flows. [*IFRS 17.72–73, BC317*]

8.1A.360.20   An entity derecognises an existing insurance contract and recognises the modified contract as a new contract if its terms are modified as follows.
- If the modified terms would have had any of the following effects, had they been included at contract inception:
  - the contract would have been excluded from the scope of IFRS 17;
  - the entity would have separated different components from the host insurance contract, resulting in a different insurance contract to which the standard applies;
  - the modified contract would have had a substantially different contract boundary; or
  - the modified contract would have been included in a different group of contracts.
- If the original contract is a direct participating contract (see 8.1A.240), but the modified contract no longer is (or vice versa).
- If the entity applied the PAA to the original contract, but the modified contract no longer meets the eligibility criteria for it (see 8.1A.270). [*IFRS 17.72*]

8.1A.360.30   An entity derecognises an insurance contract from within a group of insurance contracts as a result of contract modification by adjusting:
- the fulfilment cash flows allocated to the group to eliminate those that relate to the rights and obligations of the contract derecognised from the group;
- the CSM of the group, to the extent applicable (see 8.1A.210), for the difference between the adjustment to those fulfilment cash flows and the premium that the entity would have charged had it entered into a contract with the new terms at the date of contract modification, less any additional premium charged for the modification; and
- the number of coverage units for the expected remaining coverage to reflect the coverage units derecognised from the group (see 8.1A.220). [*IFRS 17.76–77(a)*]

8.1A.360.40   An entity measures the new insurance contract assuming that it has received, at the date of modification, the premium used to measure the CSM adjustment discussed in 8.1A.360.30. [*IFRS 17.77(b)*]

8.1A.370   **INSURANCE CONTRACTS ACQUIRED**

8.1A.370.10   Insurance contracts issued and reinsurance contracts held that are acquired in a business combination or a transfer of insurance contracts are treated as if they had been issued by the acquirer at the date of the transaction. The entity identifies the groups of contracts acquired based on the level of aggregation requirements and determines the CSM for insurance contracts issued and reinsurance contracts held (unless the PAA applies) as if it had entered into the contracts at the date of the transaction. [*IFRS 17.39, B93–B95*]

8.1A.370.20   For measurement purposes, the consideration received or paid for the contracts is treated as a proxy for the premiums received. The consideration for the contracts excludes any consideration for other assets and liabilities acquired in the same transaction. [*IFRS 17.B94*]

8.1A.370.30   For contracts acquired in a business combination, this consideration is deemed to be the contracts' fair value at the transaction date. This fair value is determined using the requirements in IFRS 13, except for the requirement that the fair value of a financial liability with a demand feature cannot be less than the amount payable on demand. [*IFRS 17.B94, BC166, 13.47*]

8.1A.370.40   If the contracts acquired are onerous, then the difference between the consideration received or paid and the fulfilment cash flows is treated differently depending on whether the transaction is a business combination or a transfer of insurance contracts. [*IFRS 17.B95*]

TYPE OF TRANSACTION	ONEROUS CONTRACTS
Business combination	Recognise the difference as a part of the goodwill or gain on a bargain purchase.
Transfer of insurance contracts	Recognise the difference as a loss immediately in profit or loss, and establish a loss component of the liability for remaining coverage.

8.1A.370.50   Once the newly acquired contracts have been initially recognised, an entity applies all of the other requirements of IFRS 17 in the same way as for any other insurance contract.

EXAMPLE 18 – INSURANCE CONTRACTS ACQUIRED IN A BUSINESS COMBINATION – MEASUREMENT

8.1A.370.60   On 31 December 2021, Company C completes a business combination transaction and acquires, among other assets and liabilities, insurance contracts that have been in force for 10 years. The fair value of the liability for these contracts at the transaction date is 30. On the date of acquisition:
- under Scenario A, C estimates that the fulfilment cash flows are 20; and
- under Scenario B, C estimates that the fulfilment cash flows are 45. [*IFRS 17.BC326–BC327, IE139–IE151*]

8.1A.370.70   Although the contracts have been in force for 10 years, C initially recognises and measures them as if they had been issued on 31 December 2021.

8.1A.370.80   On initial recognition, C measures the insurance contract liability as follows.

	SCENARIO A	SCENARIO B
Fulfilment cash flows	20	45
CSM	10	-
Insurance contract liability on initial recognition	30	45

Scenario A

8.1A.370.90   The fair value exceeds the fulfilment cash flows. Therefore, the difference of 10 represents the CSM on initial recognition. C initially measures the contracts acquired at their fair value of 30.

Scenario B

8.1A.370.100   Because the fulfilment cash flows exceed the fair value, there is no CSM. Therefore, the portfolio is initially measured at the fulfilment cash flows of 45.

8.1A.370.110   The excess of the fulfilment cash flows over the contract's fair value – i.e. 45 - 30 = 15 – effectively increases the goodwill to be recognised. This might be the case if the acquirer agrees to receive a lower price (or pay more) because of other synergies that the contracts provide.

8.1A.370.120   Had this transaction been a transfer of insurance contracts that was not a business combination – in which the consideration received was 30 and no goodwill was recognised – the difference of 15 would have been recognised in the statement of profit or loss as a loss on initial recognition and a loss component for the liability for remaining coverage would be established for the same amount.

8.1A.370.130   Contracts acquired in their claims settlement period – e.g. after the end of the coverage period originally agreed between the transferor and the customer – as a result of a transfer of insurance contracts or a business combination are treated as new contracts written by the acquiring entity on the date of acquisition. The coverage period for contracts issued by the entity usually relates to the period over which a loss event occurs. However, for similar contracts acquired after that period has passed, the discovery of a loss, or an adverse development of claims, is deemed to be the insured event and the coverage period for these contracts is estimated on that basis. [*IFRS 17.B3–B5*]

EXAMPLE 19 – INSURANCE CONTRACTS ACQUIRED – CONTRACTS ACQUIRED IN THEIR SETTLEMENT PERIOD

8.1A.370.140   Company J holds the following groups of insurance contracts:
- a group of one-year-coverage motor insurance contracts that it issued five years ago with long-tail claims; and
- an acquired group of similar contracts that were issued five years ago.

8.1A.370.150   The coverage period for the contracts issued by J is one year. The coverage period for the contracts acquired is determined based on the claims development period starting from the date of acquisition.

8.1A.370.160   This means that although the revenue related to the contracts issued by J has been recognised in the past, the revenue related to the acquired contracts is recognised over an extended period as insurance revenue, unless it contains an investment component. Consequently, changes in estimates related to claims development will be recognised in profit or loss for the contracts issued by J, but may adjust future profitability via changes in the CSM for the contracts acquired by J.

8.1A.370.170   The different manner in which the coverage period is determined for contracts issued by J and those acquired by J could also impact the model applied for these contracts. In this case, J could apply the PAA to the contracts that it issued, because their coverage period is one year. However, considering the long coverage period of the acquired contracts, it is possible that the PAA might not apply.

8.1A.380   PRESENTATION

8.1A.390   Statement of financial position

8.1A.390.10   Groups of insurance contracts issued that are assets and those that are liabilities, and groups of reinsurance contracts held that are assets and those that are liabilities, are presented separately in the statement of financial position. These carrying amounts include any assets or liabilities for insurance acquisition cash flows paid or received before the group is recognised. [*IFRS 17.27, 78–79, IAS 1.54*]

8.1A.400   Statement of profit or loss and OCI

8.1A.400.10   Amounts recognised in the statement of profit or loss and OCI are disaggregated into an insurance service result comprising insurance revenue (see 8.1A.410) and insurance service expenses (see 8.1A.420), and insurance finance income or expense (see 8.1A.440). [*IFRS 17.80, IAS 1.82*]

8.1A.400.20   Insurance revenue and insurance service expenses presented in profit or loss exclude any investment components – i.e. even though premiums charged may contain investment components, these investment components do not represent consideration for providing services and are not included in the insurance revenue. In addition, an entity is prohibited from presenting premium information that is not considered insurance revenue in other line items in profit or loss. [*IFRS 17.85, BC357*]

8.1A.400.30   Income or expense from reinsurance contracts held is presented separately from expense or income from insurance contracts issued. Amounts recognised in the statement(s) of profit or loss and OCI are disaggregated between the insurance service result and insurance finance income or expense. Income or expense from a group of reinsurance contracts held, other than insurance finance income or expense, may be presented either as a single net amount or as separate amounts (i.e. recovered from the reinsurer and an allocation of the premiums paid). In particular:

- cash flows that are contingent on the claims or benefit experience of the underlying contracts – e.g. profit commissions – are included as part of the expected claim reimbursement (unless they are considered an investment component); and
- any amounts that the entity expects to receive from the reinsurer that are not contingent on the claims experience of the underlying contracts – e.g. some types of ceding commissions – are treated as a reduction in the premiums to be paid to the reinsurer. [*IFRS 17.82, 86, BC346*]

8.1A.410 *Insurance revenue*

8.1A.410.10   Insurance revenue depicts the provision of coverage and other services arising from the group of insurance contracts at an amount that reflects the consideration to which an entity expects to be entitled in exchange for those services. The total consideration for a group of insurance contracts covers amounts expected to arise over the group's duration. These amounts comprise amounts related to the provision of services and insurance acquisition cash flows. [*IFRS 17.83, B120–B121*]

8.1A.410.20   As an entity provides services during the period, the liability for remaining coverage decreases and is released in the form of revenue. However, the liability for remaining coverage includes components that do not relate to services expected to be covered by the total consideration received. The changes in these components are not included in the insurance revenue recognised.

8.1A.410.30   Two approaches can be used to arrive at the insurance revenue for the provision of services for a period.
- *Direct approach:* The insurance revenue related to the provision of services is the sum of the changes in the liability for remaining coverage in the period that relates to services for which an entity expects to receive consideration. These changes comprise:
  - insurance service expenses incurred in the period, based on the amounts expected at the beginning of the period, excluding:
    - amounts allocated to the loss component of the liability for remaining coverage;
    - repayments of investment components;
    - transaction-based taxes collected on behalf of third parties; and
    - the amortisation of insurance acquisition cash flows;
  - the change in the risk adjustment for non-financial risk relating to past and current services, excluding amounts allocated to the loss component of the liability for remaining coverage or included as insurance finance income or expense; and
  - the amount of the CSM recognised in profit or loss in the period.
- *Indirect approach:* The insurance revenue related to the provision of services is the sum of all changes in the liability for remaining coverage minus the sum of the changes in the liability for remaining coverage that do not relate to services for which the entity expects to receive consideration. These changes comprise:
  - changes that do not relate to services provided in the period:
    - cash inflows from premiums received (including those from investment components);
    - repayments of investment components;
    - transaction-based taxes collected on behalf of third parties;
    - insurance finance income or expense;

- insurance acquisition cash flows; and
- derecognition of liabilities transferred to a third party; and
– changes that relate to services, but for which the entity does not expect consideration – i.e. changes in the loss component of the liability for remaining coverage. [*IFRS 17.B121(a), B123, B124*]

8.1A.410.40   IFRS 17 requires insurance acquisition cash flows to be included in the fulfilment cash flows. This approach reduces the CSM on initial recognition, and the insurance acquisition cash flows eventually affect profit or loss through the CSM release process – i.e. as a reduction in insurance revenue. To reflect the fact that the insurance contracts are generally priced to recover these acquisition cash flows, an entity is required to add back the part of the premium that is intended to compensate for the acquisition cash flows to insurance revenue over the coverage period and to recognise an equal amount as an insurance service expense over the same period. The amount of revenue related to recovering insurance acquisition cash flows is determined by allocating the portion of the premium that relates to recovering those cash flows to each reporting period in a systematic way based on the passage of time, with the same amount recognised as an insurance service expense. [*IFRS 17.B121(b), B125, BC179*]

8.1A.420   *Insurance service expenses*

8.1A.420.10   Insurance service expenses arising from groups of insurance contracts issued are recognised in profit or loss as they are incurred. They exclude amounts that are allocated to repayments of investment components. [*IFRS 17.84–85*]

8.1A.430   *Worked examples*

8.1A.430.10   The following examples illustrate the mechanics of revenue recognition that have been discussed in 8.1A.410–20.

8.1A.430.20   The following worked example illustrates the mechanics of revenue recognition under the general measurement model.

EXAMPLE 20 – REVENUE RECOGNITION – GENERAL MEASUREMENT MODEL

8.1A.430.30   Company E issues a group of insurance contracts with a coverage period of four years. The contracts have no participation features or investment components. At inception, the total premiums from the group of 1,500 are received and insurance acquisition cash flows of 100 are paid. [*IFRS 17.IE4–IE29, IE81–IE98*]

8.1A.430.40   E expects claims and expenses of 800 to be incurred evenly over the coverage period, and no contracts to lapse. The risk adjustment for non-financial risk on initial recognition is 80. For simplicity, this example assumes that it is released evenly over the coverage period and that the discount rate is negligible.

8.1A.430.50   Over the coverage period, all events happen as expected and E does not change any assumptions related to future periods. E measures the insurance contract liability on initial recognition and at the end of each year as follows.

	INITIAL RECOGNITION	YEAR 1	YEAR 2	YEAR 3	YEAR 4
Estimates of the present value of cash inflows	1,500	-	-	-	-
Estimates of the present value of cash outflows, including acquisition cash flows	(900)	(600)	(400)	(200)	-
Risk adjustment	(80)	(60)	(40)	(20)	-
Fulfilment cash flows	520	(660)	(440)	(220)	-
CSM	(520)	(390)[(1)]	(260)	(130)	-
Insurance contract liability	-	(1,050)	(700)	(350)	-

Note

1. 520 - 520 / 4 = 390. An amount of the CSM for a group of contracts is recognised in profit or loss in each period to reflect the services provided under the group of contracts in that period. The amount is determined by identifying the coverage units in the group, reflecting the quantity of benefits provided under each contract in the group and its expected coverage duration. In this example, the service provided in each period is the same because all of the contracts are expected to provide the same amount of benefits for all four years of coverage.

8.1A.430.60 The following table includes the change in the liability for remaining coverage for each period.

	YEAR 1	YEAR 2	YEAR 3	YEAR 4
Opening balance	-	(1,050)	(700)	(350)
Premiums received	(1,500)	-	-	-
Acquisition cash flows	100	-	-	-
Expected claims	200	200	200	200
Risk adjustment recognised	20	20	20	20
CSM allocation	130	130	130	130
Closing balance	(1,050)	(700)	(350)	-

8.1A.430.70   The following table describes the insurance revenue calculated by using the approach as described in 8.1A.410 and the expense for each year.

	YEAR 1	YEAR 2	YEAR 3	YEAR 4
Expected claims	200	200	200	200
Risk adjustment recognised	20	20	20	20
CSM allocation	130	130	130	130
Revenue for services provided	350[1]	350	350	350
Revenue to cover acquisition cash flows	25	25	25	25
Insurance revenue	**375**	**375**	**375**	**375**
Service expenses	200	200[2]	200	200
Insurance acquisition expenses	25[3]	25	25	25
Insurance service expenses	**225**	**225**	**225**	**225**
Insurance service result	150	150	150	150

Notes

1.   The insurance revenue for services provided is the total change in the liability for remaining coverage of 1,050 minus the premiums received of 1,500 plus the acquisition cash flows of 100.

2.   If the actual claim in year 2 had been 250 instead of 200, then E would recognise an incurred claim of 250 as an insurance service expense, reflecting an experience adjustment of 50. The revenue for the period is determined based on the claims expectations at the beginning of the period.

3.   100 / 4 = 25. The revenue related to insurance acquisition cash flows is recognised in a systematic way based on the passage of time. Additionally, the same amount is recognised as an expense.

Changes in assumptions related to future coverage that create an onerous group of contracts

8.1A.430.80   If at the end of year 3, the expected claims for year 4 are estimated to be 550, then this is considered to be a change in assumptions that relate to future service.

8.1A.430.90   The table in 8.1A.430.100 shows how the estimations for years 3 and 4 would be changed in this case. For simplicity, it is assumed that the risk adjustment for non-financial risk is not impacted by this change.

8.1A.430.100   The following table includes the insurance contract liability on initial recognition and at the end of each year.

	INITIAL RECOGNITION	YEAR 1	YEAR 2	YEAR 3	YEAR 4
Estimates of the present value of cash inflows	1,500	-	-	-	-
Estimates of the present value of cash outflows	(900)	(600)	(400)	(550)	-
Risk adjustment	(80)	(60)	(40)	(20)	-
Fulfilment cash flows	520	(660)	(440)	(570)	-
CSM	(520)	(390)	(260)	-(1)	-
Insurance contract liability	-	(1,050)	(700)	(570)	-

Note
1. Because the increase in the fulfilment cash flows (550 - 200) exceeds the CSM balance (260), the CSM is reduced to zero and the excess (90 = (550 - 200) - 260) is immediately recognised as a loss in profit or loss and is included in the liability for remaining coverage as a loss component.

8.1A.430.110 The following table includes the change in the liability for remaining coverage for each period.

	YEAR 1	YEAR 2	YEAR 3	YEAR 4
Opening balance	-	(1,050)	(700)	(570)
Premiums received	(1,500)	-	-	-
Acquisition cash flows	100	-	-	-
Expected claims not allocated to loss component	200	200	200	463(2)
Risk adjustment recognised not allocated to loss component	20	20	20	17(2)
CSM allocation	130	130	-	-
Loss component	-	-	(90)	90
Closing balance	(1,050)	(700)	(570)(1)	-

Notes
1. This balance includes a loss component of 90. The loss component determines the amounts that are presented in profit or loss as reversals of losses on onerous groups (a reduction in insurance service expenses) and are consequently excluded from revenue.

2. E allocates the subsequent changes in the fulfilment cash flows of the liability for remaining coverage on a systematic basis between the loss component for the liability for remaining coverage and the liability for remaining coverage, excluding the loss component (see 8.1A.230.30). In this example, E has based its method on the ratio of the opening balance of the loss component (90) compared with the opening balance of the total future cash outflows and the risk adjustment for non-financial risk (570). For the period, 16% (90 / 570) of subsequent changes in the fulfilment cash flows are allocated to the loss component.

Therefore, this ratio is applied to the incurred insurance claim to determine its allocation between the loss component of the liability for remaining coverage and the liability for remaining coverage, excluding the loss component (87 = 550 x 16%). Similarly, the ratio is applied to the release of the risk adjustment for non-financial risk (3 = 20 x 16%). The remaining 463 of the claims (550 - 87) and 17 of the risk adjustment for non-financial risk (20 - 3) are recognised as revenue.

8.1A.430.120 The following table analyses the insurance revenue and expense for each period.

	YEAR 1	YEAR 2	YEAR 3	YEAR 4
Expected claims not allocated to loss component	200	200	200	463
Risk adjustment recognised not allocated to loss component	20	20	20	17
CSM allocation	130	130	-	-
Revenue for services provided	350	350	220	480
Revenue to cover acquisition cash flows	25	25	25	25
Insurance revenue	**375**	**375**	**245**	**505**
Incurred claims	200	200	200	550
Loss on onerous groups of contracts	-	-	90	(90)
Insurance acquisition expenses	25	25	25	25
Insurance service expenses	**225**	**225**	**315**	**485**
Insurance service result	150	150	(70)	20[1]

Note

1. This is effectively the risk adjustment released (17 recognised as insurance revenue and 3 recognised as a reduction in insurance service expenses).

8.1A.430.130 The following worked example illustrates the mechanics of revenue recognition for groups of direct participating contracts.

EXAMPLE 21 – REVENUE RECOGNITION – VARIABLE FEE APPROACH

8.1A.430.140 Company X issues a group of unit-linked insurance contracts with a coverage period of three years that provides the policyholder with either:

- on survival at the end of the coverage period, the account balance; or
- on death during the coverage period, the higher of a guaranteed death benefit of 170 or the account balance. [*IFRS 17.IE99–IE112*]

8.1A.430.150 The group consists of 100 contracts with an equal premium of 150 each, all of which was received immediately after initial recognition. On initial recognition, X expects that one policyholder will die at the end of each year.

8.1A.430.160 The account balance is based on the premium paid and increases by the investment returns from a specified and clearly identified pool of assets. The account balance is reduced annually by 2% for a services charge at the end of each year. X expects the underlying fund to return 10% each year, has determined the risk-free interest rate to be 6% and has estimated a risk adjustment for non-financial risk of 25 (of which 12 is expected to be recognised in profit or loss in the first year).

8.1A.430.170 The contracts meet the definition of direct participating contracts and X chooses to include all insurance finance income or expense for the period in profit or loss – i.e. it does not apply the disaggregation policy choice. X purchases and holds the underlying items, and measures them at FVTPL.

8.1A.430.180 X measures the group of insurance contracts on initial recognition as follows.

	INITIAL RECOGNITION
Estimates of present value of cash inflows	15,000
Estimates of present value of cash outflows	(14,180)[1]
Risk adjustment	(25)
Fulfilment cash flows	795
CSM	(795)
Insurance contract liability	-

Note
1. The estimates of the present value of cash outflows reflect the use of current discount rates in discounting the future cash outflows and include an estimate of the time value of the guarantee (TVOG) inherent in providing a minimum death benefit, measured consistently with observable market prices for the guarantee. The TVOG is a calculation that requires actuarial input.

8.1A.430.190 At the end of year 1, X determines the fair value of the underlying items as follows.

	YEAR 1
Opening balance	-
Premiums received	15,000
Investment return	1,500[1]
Annual charge	(330)[2]
Payments for death	(162)[3]
Closing balance	16,008

Notes
1. The investment return is calculated as the beginning balance multiplied by the investment return in the period – i.e. (15,000 x 0.10).
2. The annual charge is derived as the net account balance after adjusting for the change in the investment return multiplied by the annual service charge of 2% – i.e. ((15,000 + 1,500) x 0.02).
3. The payment for death relates to the death claim paid out of the underlying items of the group based on the deaths in this period, after adjusting the current account balance for adjustments in the period – i.e. ((15,000 + 1,500 - 330) x (1 / 100)).

8.1A.430.200 At the end of year 1, the movement of the liability is as follows.

	ESTIMATES OF PRESENT VALUE OF FUTURE CASH FLOWS	RISK ADJUSTMENT FOR NON-FINANCIAL RISK	CSM	TOTAL LIABILITY
Opening balance	820	(25)	(795)	-
Premiums received	(15,000)	-	-	(15,000)
Death benefits paid	170[1]	-	-	170
Change in the fair value of underlying items	-	-	(1,500)[2]	(1,500)
The effect of and changes in the time value of money and financial risks	(1,403)[3]	-	1,403[2]	-
Release to the statement of profit or loss and OCI	-	12	300[4]	312
Closing balance	(15,413)	(13)	(592)	(16,018)

Notes
1. During the period, X incurred a claim of 170 on the death of one policyholder. Given that the account balance per policyholder of 162 is less than the minimum guaranteed death benefit of 170, the claim incurred is 170. The payment of the claim includes 162 paid from the policyholder's account balance (investment component) and 8 paid from X's account.
2. X adjusts the CSM for the net of changes in its share of the fair value of the underlying items and the fulfilment cash flows that do not vary based on the returns on the underlying items related to future service, plus the effect of and changes in the time value of money and financial risks. X does not need to identify these adjustments separately. Given that in this example, there are no changes in the fulfilment cash flows that do not vary based on returns on underlying items, X adjusts the CSM for the net of changes in the fair value of the underlying items and changes in fulfilment cash flows that relate to the effect of and changes in the time value of money and financial risks.
3. The effect of and changes in the time value of money and financial risks include the changes in the time value of the guarantee and the effect of any changes in the obligation to the policyholder.
4. The CSM is recognised in profit or loss each period to reflect the services provided in that period. This release pattern is based on an allocation of the CSM at the reporting date (before recognising any amounts in profit or loss) equally to each coverage unit. In year 1, the CSM immediately before recognition of the CSM in profit or loss is 892 (795 + 30 + 67). During year 1, X provided 100 units of coverage (the death during the year occurred at the end of year 1). X expects to provide coverage for 99 and 98 contracts in years 2 and 3, respectively. So, the percentage of service provided in year 1 is 34% (100 / (100 + 99 + 98)). Applying this percentage of services provided in the period to the CSM immediately before recognition results in 300 (892 x 0.34) of the CSM being recognised in profit or loss during the period.

8.1A.430.210 The following table analyses the insurance revenue and expense for year 1, calculated using the direct approach.

	YEAR 1
Expected claims and other expenses	8
Changes to the risk adjustment for non-financial risk	12
CSM allocation during the period	300
Insurance revenue	320[1]
Insurance service expenses	8[2]
Insurance service result	312
Investment income	1,500
Insurance finance expenses	(1,500)[3]
Finance result	-
Profit	312

Notes
1. Under the indirect approach, the insurance revenue provided is derived from the total change in the liability for remaining coverage of 16,018, excluding premiums received of 15,000, insurance finance expenses of 1,500 and the investment component – i.e. the payment for death from the policyholder's account balance – of 162.
   Alternatively, under the direct approach the insurance revenue is derived as the sum of the change in the risk adjustment for non-financial risk (12), the CSM recognised in profit or loss during the period as services are provided (300) and the expected insurance claims, excluding the investment components (8 = 170 – 162).
2. Insurance service expenses includes the amounts payable to the policyholder (170) less the investment component paid from the policyholder's account balance (162).
3. The changes in the obligation to pay the policyholder an amount equal to the fair value of the underlying items do not relate to future service and, therefore, do not adjust the CSM. These changes are therefore recognised in insurance finance income or expense.

8.1A.440   *Insurance finance income or expense*

8.1A.440.10   Insurance finance income or expense comprises the change in carrying amount of the group of insurance contracts arising from the effect of and changes in the time value of money and financial risk. However, for direct participating contracts the entity's share of the change in the fair value of the underlying items and the changes in fulfilment cash flows relating to future service that are allocated to the loss component of the liability for remaining coverage (and not the CSM) are recognised in profit or loss as part of insurance service expenses, rather than insurance finance income or expense. This is because these amounts are considered part of the variable fee for service, even though they are or may be driven by changes in financial risk assumptions. [*IFRS 17.87, 87(c), BC246–BC247*]

8.1A.440.20   An entity can choose as its accounting policy, to be applied consistently at the level of a portfolio of insurance contracts, to present the insurance finance income or expense in profit or loss or disaggregated between profit or loss and OCI (the disaggregation policy choice). Similarly, the insurance finance income or expense of reinsurance contracts held may be presented in profit or loss in its entirety, or disaggregated between profit or loss and OCI. The amount included in OCI is the difference between the total insurance finance income or expense and the amount included in profit or loss. Under IAS 8, an entity selects and applies consistent accounting policies for similar portfolios of insurance contracts. In assessing whether portfolios of insurance contracts are similar, the entity considers for each portfolio the assets that it holds and how it accounts for them. [*IFRS 17.88–90, B129, IAS 8.13*]

8.1A.440.30   When an entity applies the disaggregation policy choice, the insurance finance income or expense that is recognised in profit or loss is determined depending on whether the group is a group of direct participating contracts for which the entity holds the underlying items and, if not, whether changes in financial risk assumptions would have a substantial effect on the amounts paid to policyholders. The following diagram illustrates how an entity determines the amount of insurance finance income or expense that is presented in profit or loss. [*IFRS 17.88–90*]

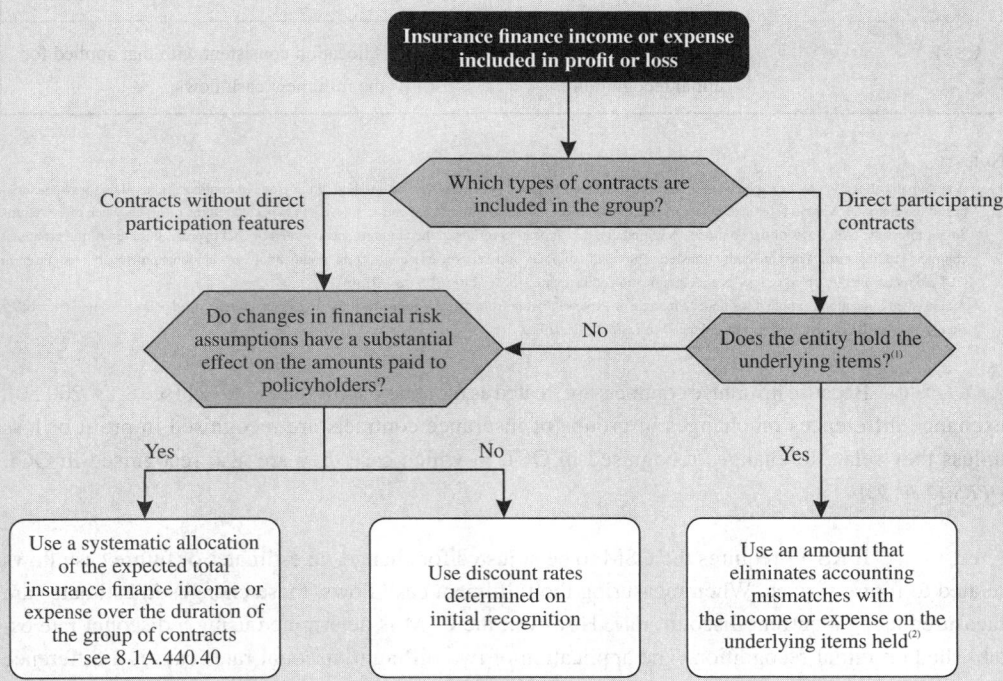

Notes
1.   Whether an entity holds the underlying items (either by choice or requirement) may change over time. If there is a change, then the accounting policy choice available to the entity may change and the entity may be required to change the way that it determines the amount of insurance finance income or expense included in profit or loss. In this case, the entity applies the old disaggregation policy choice up to the date of the change, reclassifies the amount accumulated in OCI to profit or loss as a reclassification adjustment, and then applies the new disaggregation policy choice prospectively without restating prior-period comparatives. [*IFRS 17.B135–B136*]
2.   The insurance finance income or expense included in profit or loss is the amount that exactly matches the expenses or income included in profit or loss for the underlying items. When the entity transfers a group of contracts or derecognises a contract on modification, any amounts previously recognised in OCI are not reclassified to profit or loss. [*IFRS 17.91(b), B134*]

8.1A.440.40 A systematic allocation[(1)] of the expected total insurance finance income or expense is applied as follows.

SYSTEMATIC ALLOCATION OF FINANCE INCOME AND EXPENSE ARISING FROM:	CONTRACTS WITHOUT DIRECT PARTICIPATION FEATURES	DIRECT PARTICIPATING CONTRACTS
Fulfilment cash flows[(2)]	Use a rate that allocates the remaining revised expected finance income or expense over the remaining duration of the group of contracts at a constant rate (the effective yield approach). For contracts that use a crediting rate to determine amounts due to policyholders, use an allocation that is based on the amounts credited in the period and expected to be credited in future periods to the policyholders (the projected crediting rate approach).	
CSM	Use discount rate determined on initial recognition.	Allocation consistent with that applied for the fulfilment cash flows.

Notes

1. A systematic allocation of the expected total insurance finance income or expenses over the duration of the group of contracts is based on the characteristics of the contracts without reference to factors that do not affect the cash flows of the contracts – e.g. the expected returns on assets when those returns do not affect the cash flows of the contracts. Additionally, this allocation results in the amounts accumulated in OCI over the duration of the groups of contracts totaling zero. When the entity transfers a group of contracts or derecognises a contract on modification, any amounts previously recognised in OCI are reclassified to profit or loss as a reclassification adjustment. *[IFRS 17.88(b), 91(a), B130]*

2. A consistent allocation is applied for finance income or expense arising from the risk adjustment for non-financial risk, if it is disaggregated from other changes in the risk adjustment for non-financial risk. *[IFRS 17.B132(b)]*

8.1A.440.50 Because insurance contracts are treated as monetary items under IAS 21 (see 8.1A.200.50), exchange differences on changes in groups of insurance contracts are recognised in profit or loss unless they relate to changes recognised in OCI, in which case they are also recognised in OCI. *[IFRS 17.30, 92]*

8.1A.440.60 IFRS 17 requires the CSM to be adjusted for changes in estimates of future cash flows related to future service. When measuring the fulfilment cash flows, these changes in estimates are measured using a current discount rate. However, the CSM is determined using a discount rate established on initial recognition. The application of two different discount rates causes a difference between the change in the fulfilment cash flows and the adjustment to the CSM (related to the change in the fulfilment cash flows). This difference gives rise to a gain or loss that is recognised as part of insurance finance income or expense, and therefore is subject to the disaggregation policy choice. *[IFRS 17.BC275]*

8.1A.440.70 Generally, insurance revenue recognised in a reporting period includes the changes in liability for remaining coverage that result from changes in the risk adjustment for non-financial risk, excluding:

- changes that adjust the CSM because they relate to future service; and
- amounts allocated to the loss component of the liability for remaining coverage. [*IFRS 17.B124(b)*]

8.1A.440.80   The risk adjustment for non-financial risk might include a financial risk component – e.g. the effect of a change in discount rate on the risk adjustment. However, entities are not required to disaggregate it between the insurance service result and insurance finance income or expense. If an entity does not disaggregate the change in the risk adjustment for non-financial risk between these two, then the entire change in the risk adjustment for non-financial risk is included in the insurance service result. [*IFRS 17.81*]

8.1A.440.90   If an entity decides to disaggregate the changes in the risk adjustment for non-financial risk between the insurance service result and insurance finance income or expense, then insurance revenue excludes the finance income or expense related to the change in the risk adjustment for non-financial risk. [*IFRS 17.B124(b)(i)*]

EXAMPLE 22 – DISAGGREGATING INSURANCE FINANCE INCOME OR EXPENSE – THE MECHANICS

8.1A.440.100   Company E issues a group of insurance contracts with a coverage period of four years. The contracts have no participation features or investment components. At inception, E receives total premiums of 1,000 from the group.

8.1A.440.110   E expects claims and expenses of 800 to be incurred at the end of the fourth year of coverage. It does not expect any lapses.

8.1A.440.120   For simplicity, in this example the risk adjustment for non-financial risk is negligible. There are no insurance acquisition cash flows that are directly attributable to the portfolio of insurance contracts that this group is a part of.

8.1A.440.130   Over the coverage period, all events happen as expected and E does not change any assumptions relating to future periods.

8.1A.440.140   The discount rate determined for measuring the fulfilment cash flows on initial recognition is 5%. At the end of year 1, that discount rate is 5% and at the end of years 2, 3 and 4 it is 3%.

8.1A.440.150   Changes in financial risk assumptions do not have a substantial effect on the amounts paid to policyholders. E decides to disaggregate insurance finance income or expense and includes in profit or loss an amount determined by a systematic allocation of the expected total insurance finance income or expense over the duration of the group of contracts, using the discount rate determined on initial recognition.

8.1A.440.160   E measures the insurance contract liability on initial recognition and at the end of each year as follows.

	INITIAL RECOGNITION	YEAR 1	YEAR 2	YEAR 3	YEAR 4
Estimates of present value of cash inflows	1,000	-	-		-
Estimates of present value of cash outflows	(658)[1]	(691)	(754)[2]	(777)	-
Fulfilment cash flows	342	(691)	(754)	(777)	-
CSM	(342)	(269)	(188)	(98)	-
Insurance contract liability	-	(960)	(942)	(875)	-

Notes
1. $800 / 1.05^4 = 658$.
2. $800 / 1.03^2 = 754$.

8.1A.440.170 On initial recognition, E estimates that the CSM will be released to profit or loss at each subsequent reporting date, as follows.

	YEAR 1	YEAR 2	YEAR 3	YEAR 4
Opening balance	342	269	188	98
Interest accretion	17[1]	13	9	5
Release to profit or loss	(90)[2]	(94)	(99)	(103)
Closing balance	269	188	98	-

Notes
1. $342 \times 0.05 = 17$. The same interest rate is used for the subsequent periods.
2. $(342 + 17) / 4 = 90$.

8.1A.440.180 The following table includes the change in the liability for remaining coverage for each period.

	YEAR 1	YEAR 2	YEAR 3	YEAR 4
Opening balance	-	(960)	(942)	(875)
Premiums received	(1,000)	-	-	-
Insurance finance income/ (expense) in profit or loss	(50)[1]	(48)[2]	(46)[4]	(43)
Insurance finance income/ (expense) in OCI	-	(28)[3]	14[5]	15
Expected claims	-	-	-	800
CSM allocation	90	94	99	103
Closing balance	(960)	(942)	(875)	-

> **Notes**
> 1. An expense of 50 comprises the time value of money for the fulfilment cash flows of (658 x 0.05) and for the CSM of 17.
> 2. An expense of 48 comprises the time value of money for the fulfilment cash flows of (691 x 0.05) and for the CSM of 13.
> 3. The amount recognised in OCI of 28 is the difference between the total insurance finance income or expense of 76 and the amount recognised in profit or loss of 48. The total insurance finance income or expense of 76 is the difference between the estimates of present value of future cash flows (754) and the corresponding amount at the end of year 1 (691), plus interest on the CSM (13).
> 4. An expense of 46 comprises the time value of money for the fulfilment cash flows of (800 / 1.052 x 0.05) and for the CSM of 9.
> 5. The amount recognised in OCI of 14 is the difference between the total insurance finance expense of 32 (777 - 754 + 9) and the amount recognised in profit or loss of 46.

Changes in assumptions

8.1A.440.190 Modifying the fact pattern, at the end of year 3 E changes its assumptions so that it now expects insurance claims of only 450 at the end of year 4. As a result, the fulfilment cash flows decrease by 340, being the change of 350 discounted at the current rate of 3%. This change increases the CSM by 333, being the change of 350 discounted using the original discount rate of 5%. The difference of 7, which represents a reduction in the carrying amount of the group of contracts due to discount rate changes, is recognised as insurance finance income in OCI.

8.1A.450   DISCLOSURES

8.1A.450.10 The general disclosure objective is for an entity to disclose information that, together with information presented in the primary financial statements, provides a basis for users of its financial statements to assess the effects that insurance contracts have on its financial position, financial performance and cash flows. IFRS 17 contains specific disclosure requirements to achieve this objective, which focus on information about amounts recognised in the financial statements, significant judgements and changes in those judgements and the nature and extent of risks that arise from insurance contracts. If these specific disclosures are insufficient to meet this objective, then an entity discloses additional information that is necessary to meet the objective. [*IFRS 17.93–94*]

8.1A.450.20 An entity is required to consider the level of detail that is necessary to satisfy the general disclosure objective and how much emphasis to place on each of the disclosure requirements. The usefulness of the information cannot be obscured by either the inclusion of a large amount of insignificant detail or the aggregation of items that have different characteristics. Examples of aggregation bases that may be appropriate for disclosure purposes include the type of contract (e.g. major product lines), geographic areas (e.g. country or region), and reportable segments (e.g. as defined in IFRS 8 – see 5.2.20). [*IFRS 17.94–96*]

8.1A.450.30 The presentation and disclosures for insurance companies are illustrated in KPMG's *Guides to financial statements* series.

8.1A.460   Disclosures about recognised amounts

8.1A.460.10   Separate reconciliations are disclosed for insurance contracts issued and reinsurance contracts held. In each reconciliation, the opening and closing net carrying amounts are disclosed and disaggregated into a total for groups of contracts that are assets and those that are liabilities. An entity discloses reconciliations that depict how the net carrying amounts of insurance contracts changed during the period because of cash flows and amounts recognised in the statement of profit or loss and OCI. These reconciliations explain how the amounts in the statements of financial position and profit or loss and OCI are linked and provide different types of information about the insurance service result. [*IFRS 17.98–99, 102, BC350–BC353*]

8.1A.460.20   An entity discloses the following reconciliations from the opening to the closing balances in tabular format. [*IFRS 17.99–101, 103–105*]

TABULAR INFORMATION	WHAT IS SEPARATELY INCLUDED IN THE RECONCILIATION?
AMOUNTS RELATED TO INSURANCE SERVICES	
Based on the components comprising the total asset or liability, which are: • the net liability (or asset) for remaining coverage, excluding any loss component; • any loss component; and • the liability for incurred claims[(1)].	These amounts include: • insurance revenue; • insurance service expenses; • incurred claims and other expenses; • amortisation of insurance acquisition cash flows; • changes that relate to past service – i.e. changes in fulfilment cash flows relating to the liability for incurred claims; • changes that relate to future service – i.e. losses on onerous groups of contracts and reversals of such losses; and • investment components excluded from insurance revenue and insurance service expenses.
Based on the general measurement model components comprising the total asset or liability[(1)], which are: • the estimates of the present value of the future cash flows; • the risk adjustment for non-financial risk; and • the CSM.	These amounts include changes related to: • future service, including the effects of contracts initially recognised; • current service; and • past service.
AMOUNTS NOT RELATED TO INSURANCE SERVICES	
On either basis.	These amounts include: • cash flows in the period; • the effects of changes in the risk of non-performance by the reinsurer;

Tabular information	What is separately included in the reconciliation?
	• insurance finance income or expenses; and • additional information that may be needed to understand the change in the net carrying amount.

Note
1. For groups of contracts measured under the PAA, an entity is required to disclose separate reconciliations for the estimates of the present value of the future cash flows and the risk adjustment for non-financial risk that comprise the liability for incurred claims.

8.1A.460.30   An entity also discloses the following, except for groups of contracts to which the PAA has been applied:
• an analysis of the insurance revenue recognised in the period;
• an analysis of the effect on the statement of financial position for contracts that are initially recognised in the period – based on the components of the general measurement model; and
• an explanation of when the entity expects to recognise the remaining CSM at the reporting period date in profit or loss – this disclosure may be made quantitatively or qualitatively. [*IFRS 17.106–109*]

8.1A.460.40   For groups of contracts to which the PAA has been applied, an entity discloses:
• how it has satisfied the eligibility requirements for applying the PAA; and
• the accounting policy choices that it has made about whether:
  – to adjust the liability for remaining coverage and the loss component for the time value of money and the effect of financial risk; and
  – to recognise insurance acquisition cash flows as expenses when they are incurred. [*IFRS 17.97*]

8.1A.460.50   An entity also provides disclosures to enable users of its financial statements to evaluate the sources of finance income or expenses recognised in profit or loss and OCI. It does this by explaining the total amount of insurance finance income or expense in the period and the relationship between these amounts and the investment return on its assets. Additional disclosures are required for direct participating contracts – e.g. an entity describes the composition of the underlying items and their fair value. [*IFRS 17.110–113*]

8.1A.470   Disclosures about significant judgements

8.1A.470.10   An entity discloses information about the significant judgements that it makes and changes in those judgements. These include the methods used to measure insurance contracts and the processes for estimating the inputs into those methods. Information about the inputs includes quantitative information, unless this is impracticable. An entity also discloses any changes in the methods and processes for estimating inputs used to measure those contracts, the reason for each change and the type of contracts affected. For example, an entity discloses the approaches used to:
• distinguish changes in estimates of future cash flows arising from the exercise of discretion from other changes in estimates of future cash flows for contracts without direct participation features;

- determine the risk adjustment for a non-financial risk, including whether it disaggregates changes in that risk into an insurance finance component and a service component;
- determine discount rates; and
- determine investment components. [*IFRS 17.117*]

8.1A.470.20   If the entity applies the disaggregation policy choice (see 8.1A.440.20), then it also explains how it determines the insurance finance income or expense recognised in profit or loss. [*IFRS 17.118*]

8.1A.470.30   An entity discloses the confidence level used to determine the risk adjustment for non-financial risk. If it uses a technique other than the confidence level technique, then it discloses the technique used and the confidence level that corresponds to the results of that technique. [*IFRS 17.119, B92*]

8.1A.470.40   An entity also discloses the yield curve (or range of yield curves) used to discount cash flows that do not vary based on the returns on underlying items. If an entity provides this information in aggregate for a number of groups of contracts, then it provides the disclosures in the form of weighted averages or relatively narrow ranges. [*IFRS 17.120*]

8.1A.480   Disclosures about risks

8.1A.480.10   An entity discloses information that focuses on the insurance and financial risks (typically including credit risk, liquidity risk and market risk) that arise from insurance contracts and how they have been managed. The objective of disclosing this information is to enable users of its financial statements to evaluate the nature, amount, timing and uncertainty of future cash flows that arise from contracts under IFRS 17. For each type of risk, an entity discloses:
- the exposure to risks, how they arise and changes in these from previous period;
- the entity's objective, policies and processes for measuring and managing risk, and changes in these from previous period; and
- summary quantitative information about the exposure to the risk at the reporting date. This is based on information provided internally to key management personnel or, if it is not provided as such, based on specific disclosure requirements. [*IFRS 17.121–125*]

8.1A.480.20   The specific disclosure requirements about exposure to risk at the reporting date include:
- information about risk concentration;
- sensitivity analyses to change in risk variables arising from insurance contracts (i.e. insurance and market risks);
- claims development – i.e. actual claims compared with previous estimates;
- maximum exposure to credit risk, and information about the credit quality of reinsurance contracts held that are assets; and
- information about liquidity risk. [*IFRS 17.127–132*]

8.1A.480.30   Specific disclosures for liquidity risks include separate maturity analyses based on the estimated timing of cash flows for both groups of insurance contracts issued and groups of reinsurance contracts held that are liabilities, which show the net cash flows for each of the first five years after the reporting date and, in aggregate, for periods beyond that point. However, an entity is not required to include liabilities for remaining coverage measured using the PAA in these analyses. An entity also discloses any amounts payable on demand separately. [*IFRS 17.132*]

8.1A.480.40   The disclosures also include information about the effect of the regulatory frameworks in which the entity operates – e.g. minimum capital requirements or required interest rate guarantees. [*IFRS 17.126*]

8.1A.490   TRANSITION

8.1A.490.10   IFRS 17 is applied retrospectively unless this is impracticable. However, if an entity uses a derivative to mitigate financial risk arising from a group of direct participating insurance contracts, then the option to exclude all or some of the effect of the changes in the financial risk arising from the group of insurance contracts from the CSM is applied prospectively from the start of the annual reporting period in which an entity first applies IFRS 17 – i.e. the date of initial application. For further discussion of this policy choice, see 8.1A.250.70. [*IFRS 17.C2–C4, BC375–BC378*]

8.1A.490.20   At the date of transition – i.e. the beginning of the period immediately preceding the date of initial application, with corresponding differences recognised in equity, an entity recognises and measures each group of insurance contracts as if IFRS 17 had always been applied and derecognises any existing balances that would not exist if IFRS 17 had always been applied. Only when it is impracticable for an entity to complete a full retrospective application for a group of contracts can an entity choose between applying a modified retrospective approach (see 8.1A.500) and the fair value approach (see 8.1A.540). This choice is relevant for a group of contracts only if reasonable and supportable information can be obtained to apply the modified retrospective approach; otherwise, the fair value approach is applied. [*IFRS 17.C4–C6*]

8.1A.490.30   The use of hindsight might result in retrospective application being impracticable (see 2.8.90). [*IAS 8.5*]

8.1A.500   Modified retrospective approach

8.1A.500.10   The objective of the modified retrospective approach is to use reasonable and supportable information that is available without undue cost or effort to achieve the closest possible outcome to full retrospective application. However, if an entity cannot obtain reasonable and supportable information to apply the modified retrospective approach, then it applies the fair value approach (see 8.1A.540). [*IFRS 17.C6*]

8.1A.500.20   When applying the modified retrospective approach, an entity maximises the use of information that is available without undue cost or effort that would have been used to apply a full retrospective approach. Therefore, an entity uses each of the permitted modifications discussed in 8.1A.510 only to the extent that it does not have reasonable and supportable information to apply a full retrospective approach. [*IFRS 17.C6, C8*]

8.1A.500.30   To the extent that an entity is not able to identify groups of contracts and the contract's classification based on information available at inception or initial recognition, an entity determines, using information available at the date of transition (permitted modification):

- how to identify groups of insurance contracts: when completing this assessment, an entity may group contracts issued more than one year apart, if necessary;
- whether a contract is considered a direct participating contract; and
- how to identify discretionary cash flows for contracts without direct participation features. [*IFRS 17.C9–C10*]

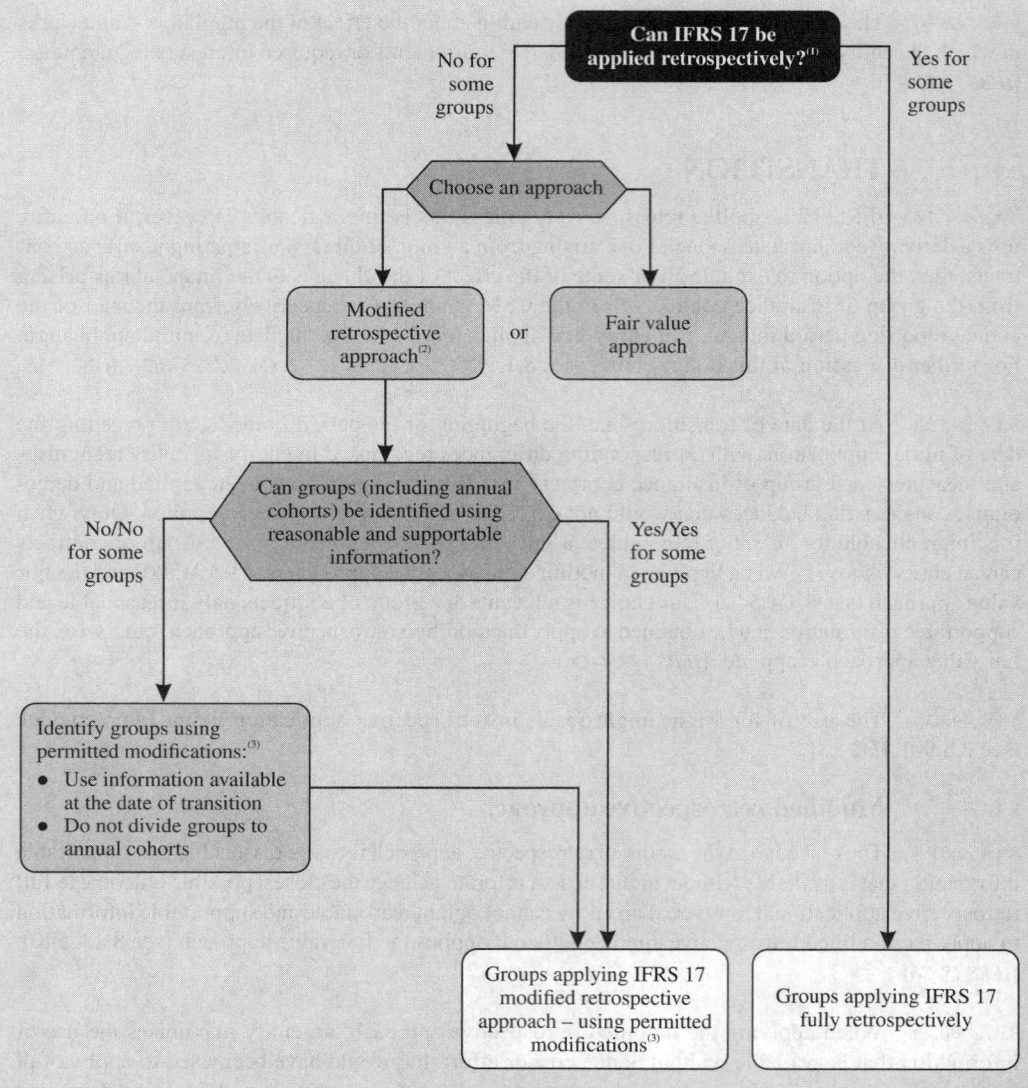

Notes
1. Retrospective application of IFRS 17 is required, unless impracticable.
2. If an entity cannot obtain reasonable and supportable information to apply the modified retrospective approach, then it applies the fair value approach.
3. Using permitted modifications only to the extent reasonable and supportable information is not available to apply a retrospective approach.

8.1A.510 *Determining the CSM or loss component for groups of contracts without direct participation features*

8.1A.510.10   The permitted modifications for the measurement of groups of insurance contracts without direct participation features focus on determining the CSM or loss component at transition, by estimating the CSM or loss component on initial recognition and rolling it forward to determine the liability for remaining coverage at the date of transition. [*IFRS 17.C9–C16*]

Amount to be determined for a group of contracts	Timing	Permitted modification
Future cash flows	Initial recognition	Estimated as the amount of the future cash flows at the date of transition, adjusted for the cash flows that are known to have occurred between the date of initial recognition of the group and the date of transition.
		If the amount of the future cash flows can be determined retrospectively for an earlier date than the date of transition, then that amount is used instead.
		The cash flows that are known to have occurred include cash flows resulting from contracts that ceased to exist before the date of transition.
Discount rates	Initial recognition or subsequently	Estimated using an observable yield curve that approximates the yield curve determined under IFRS 17 (see 8.1A.170) for at least three years before the date of transition.
		If such an observable yield curve does not exist, then the entity applies a spread (averaged over at least three years before the date of transition) to an observable yield curve. The spread adjusts the observable yield curve to approximate a yield curve determined under the standard.
Risk adjustment for non-financial risk	Initial recognition or subsequently	Determined as the risk adjustment for non-financial risk at the date of transition adjusted for the expected release of risk before that date. The expected release of the risk adjustment is determined with reference to the release of risk for similar insurance contracts that the entity issues at the date of transition.
CSM	Initial recognition and the date of transition	The permitted modifications as described above are applied as necessary to determine the CSM on initial recognition.
		The amount of CSM at the date of initial recognition is adjusted to: • accrete interest based on the discount rates that were determined to apply on initial recognition; and • reflect the transfer of services before the date of transition by determining the amount recognised in profit or loss, by comparing the remaining coverage units with the coverage units provided under the group of contracts before the date of transition.
Loss component	Initial recognition and date of transition	The same requirements and permitted modifications are applied to determine any loss component on initial recognition and amounts subsequently allocated to it.

8.1A.510.20 The carrying amount of the liability for remaining coverage of a group of insurance contracts at the date of transition is the sum of the fulfilment cash flows and the CSM at this date. For onerous groups of contracts, a loss component at the date of transition is identified. These amounts form the basis for revenue recognition in subsequent periods. [*IFRS 17.C9–C16*]

EXAMPLE 23 – TRANSITION – MEASURING A GROUP OF CONTRACTS WITHOUT DIRECT PARTICIPATION FEATURES

8.1A.510.30 Company E has an annual reporting date of 31 December and initially applies IFRS 17 on 1 January 2021 – i.e. the date of initial application. The beginning of the earliest period presented is 1 January 2020 – i.e. the date of transition. [*IFRS 17.IE186–IE171*]

8.1A.510.40 E has a portfolio of non-participating term life contracts. It concludes that it can apply the full retrospective approach at the date of transition to some groups of contracts in the portfolio.

8.1A.510.50 However, it is impracticable to apply the full retrospective approach at the date of transition for the other groups of contracts included in the portfolio. For these groups, E chooses to apply the modified retrospective approach using reasonable and supportable information that is available.

8.1A.510.60 Applying the permitted modifications to these groups, E identifies several groups of insurance contracts within the portfolio, based on information that is available on the date of transition. E has reasonable and supportable information to include contracts that were issued no more than one year apart in each group, and therefore identifies the groups on this basis. One of these groups is Group A.

8.1A.510.70 The estimates of fulfilment cash flows for Group A at the date of transition are as follows.

Expected cash flows (outflows)	770
Discounting effect	(150)
Risk adjustment	100
Fulfilment cash flows estimated at transition (outflows)	720

Analysis

8.1A.510.80 Under the modified retrospective approach, E estimates the CSM of Group A on initial recognition based on the following.

PERMITTED MODIFICATIONS APPLIED	ESTIMATES ON INITIAL RECOGNITION
Net expected cash inflows	(30)
The expected cash outflows at transition of 770 are adjusted for the cash inflows that are known to have occurred between initial recognition and the date of transition of 800.	
Time value of money	(200)
Adjusted by 50 for the effect of discounting on initial recognition applying an observable yield curve that approximates the yield curve determined under IFRS 17 for at least three years before the date of transition, to the expected cash flows above.	
Risk adjustment for non-financial risk	120
The estimated risk adjustment for non-financial risk at transition is grossed up by 20 for the release of non-financial risk between initial recognition and the date of transition with reference to release patterns for similar contracts issued at the date of transition.	
Fulfilment cash flows on initial recognition	(110)
CSM on initial recognition	110

8.1A.510.90   To determine the CSM at transition, E adjusts the CSM on initial recognition of 110 for the estimate of the CSM that would have been recognised in profit or loss before the date of transition of 90, and arrives at a CSM of 20.

8.1A.510.100   As a result, the carrying amount of the insurance contract liability of Group A at the date of transition is as follows.

Fulfilment cash flows	720
CSM	20
Insurance contract liability at date of transition	740

8.1A.520   ***Determining the CSM or loss component for groups of direct participating contracts***

8.1A.520.10   The CSM or loss component for a group of direct participating contracts at the date of transition equals:
- the fair value of the underlying items at the date of transition; minus
- the fulfilment cash flows at the date of transition; adjusted for:
  - amounts charged to policyholders before the date of transition;
  - amounts paid before the date of transition that would not have varied based on the underlying items;

— the change in the risk adjustment for non-financial risk caused by the release from risk before the date of transition; minus

• the CSM that relates to services provided before the date of transition. [*IFRS 17.C17*]

8.1A.520.20   The CSM that relates to services provided before the date of transition is based on the ratio of the remaining coverage units at the date of transition and the coverage units provided under the groups of contracts before the date of transition. If this results in a loss component, then the loss component is adjusted to zero, with a corresponding increase in the liability for remaining coverage, excluding the loss component. [*IFRS 17.C17*]

EXAMPLE 24 – TRANSITION – MEASURING A GROUP OF CONTRACTS WITH DIRECT PARTICIPATION FEATURES

8.1A.520.30   Company E has an annual reporting date of 31 December and initially applies IFRS 17 on 1 January 2021 – i.e. the date of initial application. The beginning of the earliest period presented is 1 January 2020 – i.e. the date of transition. [*IFRS 17.IE192–IE199*]

8.1A.520.40   E has a portfolio of participating contracts. It determines that it is impracticable to apply the full retrospective approach at the date of transition for the groups of contracts included in this portfolio and, applying the modified retrospective approach, it identifies Group B as a group of direct participating contracts.

8.1A.520.50   E determines the total fair value of the underlying items at the date of transition for Group B as follows.

Premium received at inception	1,000
Changes in fair value of underlying items before the date of transition	219
Charges deducted from underlying items	(55)
Deduction for death benefits and other expenses	(216)
E paid an additional amount of 23 that does not vary based on the returns on underlying items according to a minimum death benefit – i.e. it was not deducted from the account balance.	
Fair value of the underlying items at date of transition	948

8.1A.520.60   E estimates the fulfilment cash flows at the date of transition to be 922, and the changes in the risk adjustment for non-financial risk caused by the release from risk before the date of transition at 14. It also determines that 60% of the total coverage units have been provided before that date.

8.1A.520.70   E estimates the CSM at the date of transition as follows.

Fair value of underlying items at date of transition	948
Fulfilment cash flows at date of transition	(922)
Charges deducted from underlying items	55
Amounts paid that do not vary based on returns on underlying items	(23)
Change in risk adjustment for non-financial risk	(14)
Subtotal of CSM before allocation to periods	44
Allocation of CSM to past periods	(26)
CSM at date of transition	18

8.1A.530 *Determining insurance finance income or expense*

8.1A.530.10   To determine insurance finance income or expense for periods subsequent to the date of transition, an entity determines the discount rate on initial recognition, based on the following. [*IFRS 17.C18–C19*]

DO THE GROUPS OF INSURANCE CON-TRACTS INCLUDE CONTRACTS ISSUED MORE THAN ONE YEAR APART?	DISCOUNT RATES THAT AN ENTITY DETERMINES
Yes	Discount rates at the date of transition.
No	The rate that was determined to apply on initial recognition – i.e. retrospectively identified or determined using the permitted modification for discount rates.

8.1A.530.20   Applying the disaggregation policy choice for insurance finance income or expense, the amount accumulated in OCI impacts insurance finance income or expense for periods subsequent to the date of transition. Therefore, the amounts accumulated in OCI on the date of transition are determined as follows.

CHARACTERISTICS OF THE GROUPS OF INSURANCE CONTRACTS	AMOUNTS ACCUMULATED IN OCI
Groups of direct participating contracts for which the entity holds the underlying items	The amount accumulated in OCI for the underlying items.
Groups of other contracts for which changes in financial assumptions have a substantial effect on the amounts paid to policyholders	Zero.

Characteristics of the groups of insurance contracts	Amounts accumulated in OCI
All other groups	The amount calculated using the discount rate that was used to arrive at the CSM on initial recognition – i.e. retrospectively identified or determined using the permitted modification for discount rates. For such groups of contracts that include contracts issued more than one year apart, the accumulated amount in OCI may be determined at zero.

8.1A.530.30   To determine the insurance finance income or expense recognised in profit or loss for periods subsequent to the date of transition for groups of insurance contracts that apply the PAA and apply the disaggregation policy choice for insurance finance income or expense, an entity determines the following.

Do the groups of insurance contracts include contracts issued more than one year apart?	An entity determines...
Yes	The amount accumulated in OCI – it may be: • calculated using discount rates determined to apply at the date of incurred claims – i.e. retrospectively identified or determined using the permitted modification for discount rates; or • zero.
No	The amount accumulated in OCI – it is calculated using discount rates determined to apply at the date of incurred claims – i.e. retrospectively identified or determined using the permitted modification for discount rates.

8.1A.540   Fair value approach

8.1A.540.10   Using this approach, an entity determines the CSM or loss component at the date of transition for a group of contracts based on the difference between the fair value of the group and the fulfilment cash flows of the group at that date. This fair value is determined using the requirements in IFRS 13, except for the requirement that the fair value of a financial liability with a demand feature cannot be less than the amount payable on demand. [*IFRS 17.C20*]

8.1A.540.20   When this approach is applied, an entity uses reasonable and supportable information for what it would have determined given the terms of the contract and the market conditions at the date of inception or initial recognition, as appropriate or reasonable and supportable information that is available at the date of transition, to determine:
• how to identify groups of insurance contracts;
• whether a contract meets the definition of an insurance contract with a direct participation feature; and

- how to identify discretionary cash flows for insurance contracts without direct participation features. [*IFRS 17.C21–C23*]

8.1A.540.30 When identifying groups of insurance contracts, an entity may group contracts issued more than one year apart. However, it may divide groups into those issued within a year if it has reasonable and supportable information to make the division (see 8.1A.110.20). [*IFRS 17.C23*]

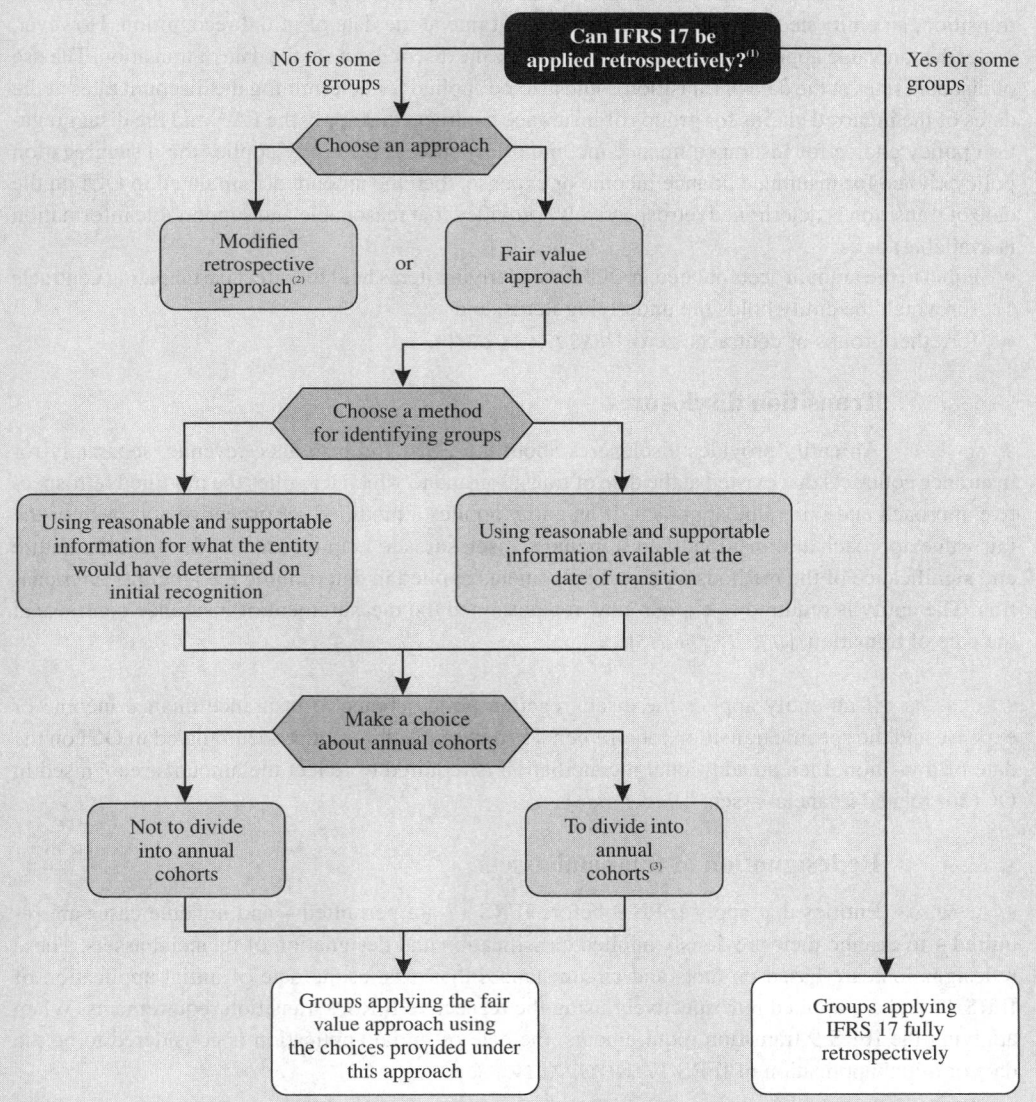

Notes

1. Retrospective application of IFRS 17 is required, unless impracticable.
2. If an entity cannot obtain reasonable and supportable information to apply the modified retrospective approach, then it applies the fair value approach.
3. Only if reasonable and supportable information is available to do so.

8.1A.540.40   It appears that when applying the fair value approach on transition an entity is not permitted to include in the measurement of the fulfilment cash flows any insurance acquisition cash flows occurring before the date of transition. Because these cash flows are not included in the measurement at the date of transition, we believe that they cannot be included in the presentation of insurance revenue and expenses for reporting periods subsequent to the date of transition.

8.1A.540.50   To determine insurance finance income or expense for periods subsequent to the date of transition, an entity needs to determine the discount rate at the date of initial recognition. However, under the fair value approach it can instead determine the discount rate at the date of transition. The use of discount rates at the date of transition could also be applied for determining the discount rates at the dates of the incurred claims for groups of insurance contracts that apply the PAA and the disaggregation policy choice for insurance finance income or expense. If the entity applies the disaggregation policy choice for insurance finance income or expense, then the amount accumulated in OCI on the date of transition is determined retrospectively (provided that reasonable and supportable information is available) or as:

- equal to the amount accumulated in OCI for underlying items held for direct participating contracts for which the entity holds the underlying items; and
- for other groups of contracts, zero. [*IFRS 17.C23–C24*]

8.1A.550   Transition disclosures

8.1A.550.10   An entity provides disclosures about the CSM and insurance revenue, separately for insurance contracts that existed at the date of transition and to which it applies the modified retrospective approach and fair value approach. If an entity applies a modified retrospective approach or the fair value approach at transition, then it includes disclosures to help its users understand the nature and significance of the methods used and judgements applied in determining the amounts on transition. The entity is required to explain how it determined the measurement of insurance contracts at the date of transition. [*IFRS 17.114–115*]

8.1A.550.20   If an entity applies the disaggregation policy choice to insurance finance income or expense and the specific transition requirements to determine the amount accumulated in OCI on the date of transition, then an additional reconciliation is required to reflect the amounts recognised in OCI for related financial assets. [*IFRS 17.116*]

8.1A.560   Redesignation of financial assets

8.1A.560.10   Entities that apply IFRS 9 before IFRS 17 are permitted – and in some cases are required – to change their previously applied classification and designation of financial assets. These redesignations are based on facts and circumstances that exist at the date of initial application of IFRS 17 and are applied retrospectively using the respective IFRS 9 transition requirements. When applying the IFRS 9 transition requirements, the date of initial application is considered to be the date of initial application of IFRS 17. [*IFRS 17.C29–C30*]

8.1A.560.20   An entity may reassess whether a financial asset is held within a business model whose objective is to hold financial assets in order to collect contractual cash flows, or within a business model whose objective is achieved by both collecting contractual cash flows and selling financial assets. This reassessment is relevant only to assets that are not held in respect of an activity that is unconnected with contracts in the scope of IFRS 17. For example, financial assets held in funds relating to investment contracts that are outside the scope of IFRS 17 are not eligible for reassessment and reclassification. [*IFRS 17.C29–C30*]

8.1A.560.30   An entity may newly designate financial assets under the fair value option as measured at FVTPL if this would eliminate or significantly reduce an accounting mismatch. An entity is required to revoke previous designations of financial assets as measured at FVTPL (see 7A.4.390) if the designation no longer eliminates or significantly reduces any accounting mismatch as a result of applying IFRS 17. An entity may newly elect to present in OCI any changes in the fair value of an investment in an equity instrument that is not held for trading and revoke previous elections to that effect (see 7A.4.420). [*IFRS 17.C29–C30*]

8.1A.560.40   If an entity applies these redesignation permissions and requirements, then it provides certain qualitative disclosures and, in some cases, quantitative disclosures. [*IFRS 17.C32–C33*]

8.1A.570   Comparative financial information

8.1A.570.10   An entity is required to present comparative financial information applying IFRS 17 for the annual period immediately preceding the date of initial application of IFRS 17. It may also present adjusted comparative information for any earlier periods and, in this case, the date of transition is the beginning of that adjusted comparative period. If an entity presents unadjusted comparative information for earlier periods, then it is required to clearly identify the information as not having been adjusted, stating that it has been prepared on a different basis, and explain that basis. [*IFRS 17.C25–C27*]

8.1A.570.20   Entities are not required to disclose previously unpublished information about claims development that occurred earlier than five years before the end of the annual reporting period in which IFRS 17 is applied for the first time. Entities not disclosing this information disclose this fact. [*IFRS 17.C28*]

8.1A.570.30   An entity that applied IFRS 9 before IFRS 17 and applies any of the transition requirements and choices for the reclassification or redesignation of financial assets is permitted to restate comparative information about these financial assets, but only if doing so is possible without the use of hindsight. If an entity does not restate prior periods, then the difference between the carrying amounts previously reported and at the date of initial application is recognised in the opening balance of retained earnings or another component of equity. However, if previous periods are restated, then all relevant IFRS 9 requirements apply. [*IFRS 17.C31*]

REPRODUCED CHAPTER

2.4   Fair value measurement

2.4   Fair value measurement

CURRENTLY EFFECTIVE REQUIREMENTS

This publication reflects IFRS in issue at 1 August 2018, and the currently effective requirements cover annual periods beginning on 1 January 2018.

The requirements related to this topic are mainly derived from the following.

Standard	Title
IFRS 13	Fair Value Measurement

KPMG's publication *Fair Value Measurement: Questions and Answers* is an additional resource that provides guidance on fair value measurement under both US GAAP and IFRS.

FORTHCOMING REQUIREMENTS

The currently effective requirements are affected by the following forthcoming requirements. They are highlighted with a # and the impact is explained in the accompanying boxed text at the references indicated.

In May 2017, the IASB issued IFRS 17 *Insurance Contracts*, which is effective for annual periods beginning on or after 1 January 2021. See 2.4.423. IFRS 17 is the subject of chapter 8.1A.

FUTURE DEVELOPMENTS

The currently effective requirements that may be affected by future developments are highlighted with a * and are briefly discussed in 2.4.1090.

2.4.10   INTRODUCTION TO FAIR VALUE MEASUREMENT

2.4.10.10   This section provides a brief introduction to some of the key terms used in fair value measurement, as well as a diagram that shows the flow of this chapter in relation to the process of measuring fair value and determining the appropriate disclosures.

2.4.20   Overview

2.4.20.10   The key term that drives the measurement process is 'fair value': the price that would be received to sell an asset or paid to transfer a liability in an orderly transaction between market participants at the measurement date. Fair value is an 'exit price' – e.g. the price to sell an asset rather than the price to buy that asset. An exit price embodies expectations about the future cash inflows and cash outflows associated with an asset or liability from the perspective of a 'market participant' – i.e. based on buyers and sellers who have certain characteristics, such as being independent and knowledgeable about the asset or liability.

2.4.20.20   Fair value is a market-based measurement, rather than an entity-specific measurement, and is measured using assumptions that market participants would use in pricing the asset or liability, including assumptions about risk. As a result, an entity's intention to hold an asset or to settle or otherwise fulfil a liability is not relevant in measuring fair value.

2.4.20.30   Fair value is measured assuming a transaction in the 'principal market' for the asset or liability – i.e. the market with the highest volume and level of activity. In the absence of a principal market, it is assumed that the transaction would occur in the 'most advantageous market'. This is the market that would maximise the amount that would be received to sell an asset or minimise the amount that would be paid to transfer a liability, taking into account transaction and transport costs. In either case, the entity needs to have access to that market, although it does not necessarily have to be able to transact in that market on the measurement date.

2.4.20.40   A fair value measurement is made up of one or more 'inputs', which are the assumptions that market participants would make in valuing the asset or liability. The most reliable evidence of fair value is a quoted price in an active market. When this is not available, entities use another valuation technique to measure fair value, maximising the use of relevant observable inputs and minimising the use of unobservable inputs.

2.4.20.50   These inputs also form the basis of the 'fair value hierarchy', which is used to categorise a fair value measurement (in its entirety) into one of three levels. This categorisation is relevant for disclosure purposes. The disclosures about fair value measurements are extensive, with more disclosures being required for measurements in the lowest category (Level 3) in the hierarchy.

2.4.30   Steps in fair value measurement

2.4.30.10   The following flowchart sets out key points in applying IFRS 13, with references to the relevant sections in this chapter.

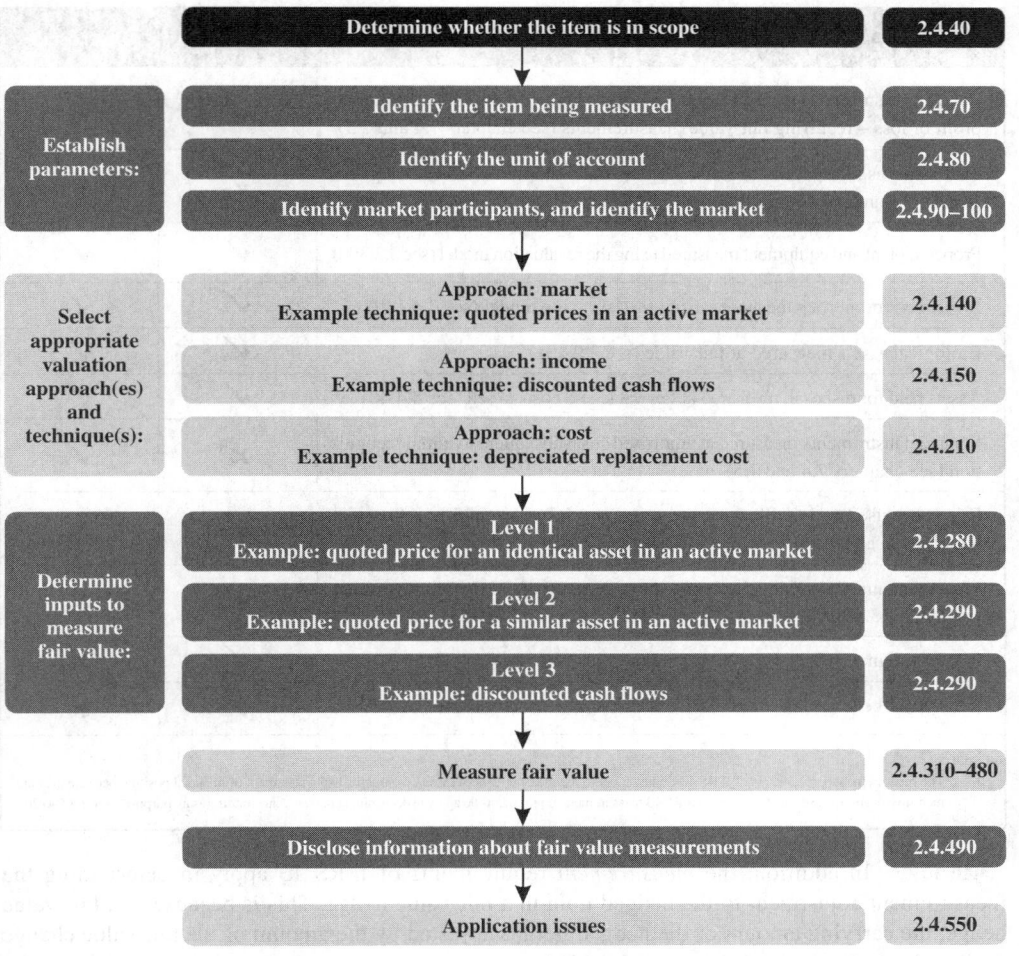

	Determine whether the item is in scope	2.4.40
Establish parameters:	**Identify the item being measured**	2.4.70
	Identify the unit of account	2.4.80
	Identify market participants, and identify the market	2.4.90–100
Select appropriate valuation approach(es) and technique(s):	**Approach: market** **Example technique: quoted prices in an active market**	2.4.140
	Approach: income **Example technique: discounted cash flows**	2.4.150
	Approach: cost **Example technique: depreciated replacement cost**	2.4.210
Determine inputs to measure fair value:	**Level 1** **Example: quoted price for an identical asset in an active market**	2.4.280
	Level 2 **Example: quoted price for a similar asset in an active market**	2.4.290
	Level 3 **Example: discounted cash flows**	2.4.290
	Measure fair value	2.4.310–480
	Disclose information about fair value measurements	2.4.490
	Application issues	2.4.550

2.4.40   SCOPE

2.4.40.10   Subject to certain exceptions (see 2.4.50), IFRS 13 applies to the following:

- fair value measurements (both initial and subsequent) that are required or permitted by other standards;
- fair value measurements that are required or permitted to be disclosed by other standards, but which are not included in the statement of financial position; and
- measurements that are based on fair value, or disclosures of such measurements. [*IFRS 13.5–8, BC25*]

2.4.40.20   The following are some examples of assets and liabilities that fall in the scope of IFRS 13 for the purposes of measurement and/or disclosure. For a more in-depth discussion of the scope of the disclosure requirements, including the distinction between recurring and non-recurring fair value measurements, see 2.4.490. [*IFRS 13.5, 7*]

Topic	Measurement	Disclosure
Financial instruments measured at fair value through OCI or fair value through profit or loss – recurring fair value measurements (see chapters 7.4 and 7.5)	✓	✓
Fair value used as deemed cost by a first-time adopter of IFRS – e.g. for property, plant and equipment (see 6.1.300)	✓	✓
Property, plant and equipment measured using the revaluation model (see 3.2.300)	✓	✓
Investment properties measured using the fair value model (see 3.4.140)	✓	✓
Biological assets measured at fair value (see 3.9.40)	✓	✓
Assets held for disposal, measured at fair value less costs to sell (see 5.4.40)	✓	✓
Financial instruments measured at amortised cost subsequent to initial recognition (see chapters 7.4 and 7.5)	✗ [1]	✓
Fair value used to initially measure non-financial assets and non-financial liabilities in a business combination (see 2.4.510.10 and 2.6.600)	✓	✗
Measurements of the fair value less costs of disposal of CGUs for impairment testing (see 3.10.190)	✓	✗
Plan assets in a defined benefit scheme (see 4.4.620)	✓	✗
Retirement benefit plan investments measured at fair value under IAS 26	✓	✗

Note
1. The measurement requirements of IFRS 13 do not apply to the measurement of these investments in the statement of financial position because they are measured at amortised cost. However, the IFRS 13 measurement requirements do apply in determining the fair value for disclosure purposes (see 2.4.540.20).

2.4.40.30   In addition, the *measurement* requirements of IFRS 13 apply in determining the measurement adjustment to the hedged item in a fair value hedge. This is because in a fair value hedge, the carrying amount of the hedged item is adjusted by the amount of the fair value change attributable to the hedged risks (see 7.9.170).

2.4.40.40   However, the *disclosure* requirements of IFRS 13 relating to assets and liabilities that are measured at fair value only apply to the measurement of the hedged item in a fair value hedge if the measurement basis in the statement of financial position is or is based on fair value, independent of hedge accounting – e.g. the hedged item is a financial asset measured at fair value through OCI. In other cases, if the hedged item in a fair value hedge is measured neither at cost nor at fair value (see 7.9.170.50), then only the disclosures in paragraph 97 of IFRS 13 are required (see 2.4.540). [*IFRS 13.97*]

EXAMPLE 1 – SCOPE – HEDGING

2.4.40.50   Company B has a fixed interest liability denominated in its functional currency and measured at amortised cost. B enters into a pay-LIBOR receive-fixed interest rate swap to hedge 50% of the notional amount of the liability in respect of its benchmark interest rate exposure. The swap qualifies for hedge accounting (see 7.9.370.20–30).

2.4.40.60   Half of the liability – i.e. the proportion that is hedged – will be remeasured by B with respect to changes in fair value arising from changes in the benchmark interest rate from the beginning of the hedging relationship (see 7.9.170). B does not remeasure the liability for any changes in fair value arising from changes in credit spread, liquidity spread or other factors.

2.4.40.70   The fair value related to changes in the benchmark interest rate is measured in accordance with IFRS 13. However, the fair value disclosures for assets and liabilities measured at fair value do not apply because the hedged item, the liability, is measured on a hybrid basis (adjusted amortised cost) that is not fair value or based on fair value. Therefore, B provides only the disclosures required by paragraph 97 of IFRS 13 (see 2.4.540).

2.4.50   Not in scope

2.4.50.10   IFRS 13 does not apply to the following:
- share-based payment transactions in the scope of IFRS 2 (see chapter 4.5);
- leasing transactions in the scope of IAS 17 (see chapter 5.1); or
- measurements that are similar to fair value but that are not fair value – e.g. net realisable value in IAS 2 (see chapter 3.8), or value in use in IAS 36 (see chapter 3.10). [*IFRS 13.6*]

2.4.50.20   In addition, provisions measured at the best estimate of the expenditure required to settle the present obligation under IAS 37 are outside the scope of IFRS 13 (see 3.12.110).

2.4.60   FAIR VALUE PRINCIPLES

2.4.60.10   'Fair value' is the price that would be received to sell an asset or paid to transfer a liability in an orderly transaction between market participants at the measurement date. [*IFRS 13.9, A*]

2.4.60.20   Fair value is an exit price – e.g. the price to sell the asset rather than to buy the asset. An exit price embodies expectations about the future cash inflows and outflows associated with the asset or liability from the perspective of a market participant (see 2.4.90) that holds the asset or owes the liability at the measurement date. [*IFRS 13.A, BC39*]

2.4.60.30   Fair value is a market-based measurement, rather than an entity-specific measurement, and is measured using assumptions that market participants (see 2.4.90) would use in pricing the asset or liability, including assumptions about risk. As a result, an entity's intention to hold an asset or to settle or otherwise fulfil a liability is not relevant in measuring fair value, which is always the exit price. For example, the fact that an entity asserts that prices in orderly transactions are too low relative to its own value expectations, and accordingly that it would be unwilling to sell at such prices, is not relevant. [*IFRS 13.2–3*]

2.4.60.40   An 'orderly' transaction assumes that sufficient time to market the asset or liability in the usual and customary manner has occurred before the measurement date. For certain types of assets, such as liquid financial instruments (e.g. actively traded stock), the usual and customary market exposure may be short. In other situations (e.g. real estate assets), a longer market exposure would be required to generate interest, contact potential buyers, conduct negotiations, complete due diligence and complete legal agreements. [*IFRS 13.A, B43(a)*]

2.4.70   The item being measured

2.4.70.10   An entity takes into account characteristics of the asset or liability that market participants would take into account in a transaction for the asset or liability at the measurement date. In the case of an asset, these characteristics may include, for example:
- the condition and location of the asset (see 2.4.110); and
- restrictions, if any, on the sale or use of the asset. [*IFRS 13.11*]

2.4.70.20   It is important to distinguish a characteristic of an asset or liability from a characteristic arising from an entity's holding of the asset or liability, which is an entity-specific characteristic.

2.4.70.30   Factors used to evaluate whether a restriction on an asset is a characteristic of the asset or entity-specific may include whether the restriction is:
- transferred to a (potential) buyer;
- imposed on a holder by regulations;
- part of the contractual terms of the asset; or
- attached to the asset through a purchase contract or another commitment.

EXAMPLE 2 – RESTRICTIONS ON USE OF AN ASSET

2.4.70.40   Company B acquired a plot of land currently used as storage space for its factory in a business combination. As a condition of the acquisition, B is not allowed to change the use of the land for five years. However, the area in which the property is located has recently been re-zoned, and other land nearby has been redeveloped as residential property.

2.4.70.50   B has received legal advice that although it is restricted under the terms of the acquisition from changing the current use of the land, the land could be sold to a third party who would not be bound by the restriction. For this reason, B concludes that the restriction is a characteristic of the current holder rather than of the asset itself, and would not be considered in measuring the fair value of the land.

2.4.70.60   In measuring the fair value of a security held as an asset with a restriction on its sale or transfer, judgement is required to determine whether and in what amount an adjustment is required to the price of a similar unrestricted security to reflect the restriction.
- For security-specific restrictions – i.e. the restriction is an attribute of the instrument – the price used in the fair value measurement reflects the effect of the restriction if this would be considered by a market participant in pricing the security; this may require an adjustment to the quoted price of otherwise similar but unrestricted securities. For additional guidance, see 2.4.245.

- For entity-specific restrictions – i.e. the restriction is an attribute of the holder – the price used in the fair value measurement is not adjusted to reflect the restriction because it would not be considered by a market participant in pricing the security. [*IFRS 13.11, IE28*]

2.4.70.70   Securities that are subject to an entity-specific restriction are considered identical to those that are not subject to entity-specific restrictions. Consequently, a quoted price in an active market is a Level 1 input for a security that is subject to an entity-specific restriction (see 2.4.245.10). This is the case even if the entity is not able to sell the particular security on the measurement date because of an entity-specific restriction; an entity needs to be able to access the market but it does not need to be able to transact in the market at the measurement date to be able to measure the fair value on the basis of the price in that market (see 2.4.100). [*IFRS 13.19–20, 76*]

EXAMPLE 3 – SECURITIES SUBJECT TO LOCK-UP PROVISION

2.4.70.80   Company D offers securities in a public offering and enters into an underwriting agreement with Company E. The underwriting agreement between D and E contains a lock-up provision that prohibits D and its founders, directors and executive officers from selling their securities for a period of 180 days.

2.4.70.90   In this example, the lock-up provision arises from the underwriting agreement – i.e. a contract separate from the security – and applies only to D and its affiliates. Therefore, the restriction is entity-specific and is not considered in measuring the fair value of the securities.

2.4.70.100   In some borrowing arrangements, securities held by an investor are pledged as collateral supporting debt, or other commitments, of the investor. In these situations, the investor is restricted from selling the securities pledged during the period that the debt or other commitment is outstanding. Restrictions on securities resulting from the securities being pledged as collateral represent entity-specific restrictions that are not considered in measuring the fair value of the securities.

EXAMPLE 4 – SECURITIES SOLD UNDER REPURCHASE AGREEMENT

2.4.70.110   Bank F enters into a sale-and-repurchase agreement with Bank B in which F sells a security to B and agrees to repurchase an identical security at a future date at a fixed price. Under IFRS 9, F does not derecognise the security, and the agreement is accounted for as a secured borrowing (see 7.6.340). During the term of the sale-and-repurchase agreement, F does not own the security and so is unable to sell it or otherwise use it.

2.4.70.120   In this example, the restriction on F's ability to sell or use the security represents an entity-specific restriction. Therefore, the restriction is not considered in measuring the fair value of the security.

2.4.70.130   For a discussion of security-specific restrictions when the fair value of a liability or own equity instrument is measured with reference to the identical instrument held as an asset by a market participant, see 2.4.410.

2.4.80   **Unit of account**

2.4.80.10   The 'unit of account' is the level at which an asset or a liability is aggregated or disaggregated in an IFRS for recognition purposes. It also drives the level at which an asset or a liability is aggregated or disaggregated for the purpose of measuring fair value, although in practice the term 'unit of valuation' may be used especially when the unit of account for recognition and measurement are different. In this chapter, we refer to the unit of account in the context of both recognition and measurement. [*IFRS 13.14, A*]

2.4.80.20   IFRS 13 does not specify the unit of account; instead, it depends on the relevant standard that establishes the recognition of the item. For example, the unit of account under IAS 36 is typically the CGU and the unit of account under IFRS 9 is typically the individual financial instrument (e.g. a share). [*IFRS 13.14, BC47*]

2.4.80.30   Although the unit of account is usually key to determining the level at which fair value is measured, it is not a concept that has been used explicitly in IFRS, and there is uncertainty regarding the unit of account for investments in subsidiaries, associates and joint ventures. The unit of account for such investments is not clear because the investment held by the entity comprises a number of individual shares. The following are examples of situations in which the unit of account for such an investment needs to be determined in order to measure fair value.

(S) • An investment in a subsidiary, associate or joint venture accounted for in accordance with IFRS 9 in separate financial statements (see 2.1.120).
  • An investment in a subsidiary, associate or joint venture held by an investment entity (see chapter 5.6).
  • Investments in associates and joint ventures that are accounted for in accordance with IFRS 9 by a venture capital or similar organisation (see 3.5.100).
  • Shares in a subsidiary, associate or joint venture distributed to owners (see 7.3.690).
  • A previously held equity interest in an acquiree in accounting for a business combination achieved in stages (see 2.6.1140).
  • A retained interest following a loss of control, joint control or significant influence (see 2.5.760 and 3.5.560).

2.4.80.40   In our view, an entity may choose an accounting policy, to be applied consistently, to identify the unit of account of an investment in a subsidiary, associate or joint venture as:
  • the investment as a whole; or
  • the individual share making up the investment.

2.4.80.50   In applying a consistent accounting policy in accordance with IAS 8 (see 2.8.30), an entity should choose the same policy for similar items. The choice of accounting policy is important, because the value of an aggregate holding may be different from the sum of the values of the components measured on an individual basis.

2.4.80.60   In certain circumstances, when measuring fair value based on the unit of account, an entity may use a valuation technique that determines the fair value by considering the fair values of the component parts of the unit of account. This may be appropriate if market participants would consider these separate fair values when pricing the item in its entirety. [*IFRS 13.22*]

EXAMPLE 5 – MEASURING FAIR VALUE BASED ON COMPONENT PARTS OF THE UNIT OF ACCOUNT

2.4.80.70   Investment Fund D holds an investment in Company B that is accounted for at fair value. B is a private holding company with two subsidiaries operating each in a different line of business. Both subsidiaries have issued public debt and publish their financial statements.

2.4.80.80   D values its investment in B by valuing the two subsidiaries separately and includes any potential holding company value effects. Because the subsidiaries have different characteristics – i.e. growth prospects, risk profiles, investment requirements etc – this approach allows separate consideration of each of the subsidiaries' facts and circumstances and is consistent with the approach that a market participant would consider in valuing an investment in B.

2.4.80.90   For further discussion of the unit of account in the context of premiums and discounts, see 2.4.240, and for a discussion of how the unit of account interacts with the portfolio measurement exception, see 2.4.430.

2.4.90   Market participants

2.4.90.10   'Market participants' are buyers and sellers in the principal or most advantageous market (see 2.4.100) for the asset or liability that have all the following characteristics.

- They are independent of each other – i.e. they are not related parties as defined in IAS 24 (see chapter 5.5), although the price in a related party transaction may be used as an input to a fair value measurement (see 2.4.220) if the entity has evidence that the transaction was entered into on market terms.
- They are knowledgeable, having a reasonable understanding about the asset or liability and the transaction using all available information, including information that might be obtained through due diligence efforts that are usual and customary.
- They are able to enter into a transaction for the asset or liability.
- They are willing to enter into a transaction for the asset or liability – i.e. they are motivated but not forced or otherwise compelled to do so. [*IFRS 13.A*]

2.4.90.20   An entity considers the perspective of market participants and measures fair value based on the assumptions that would be made by market participants acting in their economic best interests. An entity does not need to identify specific market participants; instead, it identifies the characteristics that distinguish market participants, considering:

- the asset or liability;
- the principal (or most advantageous) market for the asset or liability; and
- market participants with whom the entity would enter into a transaction in that market. [*IFRS 13.22–23*]

2.4.90.30   Market participants are assumed to be knowledgeable about the asset or liability, using all available information, including information that would be expected to become available in customary and usual due diligence. To the extent that additional uncertainty exists, it is factored into the fair value measurement. [*IFRS 13.A, BC58–BC59*]

2.4.100 **Principal and most advantageous markets**

2.4.100.10   The 'principal market' is the market with the greatest volume and level of activity for the asset or liability. A fair value measurement assumes that the transaction to sell the asset or to transfer the liability takes place in the principal market for the asset or liability. [*IFRS 13.16, A*]

2.4.100.20   In the absence of a principal market, the transaction is assumed to take place in the most advantageous market for the asset or liability. This is the market that either maximises the amount that would be received to sell the asset or minimises the amount that would be paid to transfer the liability, after taking into account transaction costs and transport costs (see 2.4.110). [*IFRS 13.16, A*]

2.4.100.30   In many cases, the principal market and the most advantageous market will be the same. [*IFRS 13.BC48*]

2.4.100.40   For a market to be considered the principal or most advantageous market, the entity needs to be able to access that market at the measurement date. However, the identification of a principal market is not limited to those markets in which the entity would actually sell the asset or transfer the liability. Furthermore, although the entity has to be able to access the market, the entity does not need to be able to buy or sell the particular asset (or transfer the particular liability) on the measurement date in that market. [*IFRS 13.19–20*]

2.4.100.50   Because the entity has to have access to the principal (or most advantageous) market in order to use a price from that market, the identification of the relevant market is considered from the perspective of the entity. This may give rise to different principal or most advantageous markets for entities with different activities and for different businesses within an entity. For example, if a swap transaction takes place between an investment bank and a commercial entity, then the former may have access to wholesale and retail markets whereas the latter may only have access to retail markets. See also Example 13. [*IFRS 13.19, IE24–IE26*]

2.4.100.60   In addition, in some cases different entities within a consolidated group (and businesses within those entities) may have different principal markets for the same asset or liability. For example, a parent company may trade a particular asset in its principal market for that asset. However, because of regulatory restrictions, its overseas subsidiary is prohibited from transacting in that market. As a result, the overseas subsidiary has a different principal market for the same asset. [*IFRS 13.19*]

2.4.100.70   An entity is not required to undertake an exhaustive search of all possible markets to identify the principal market, or in the absence of a principal market, the most advantageous market; however, it takes account of all information that is reasonably available. For example, if reliable information about volumes transacted is available in trade magazines, then it may be appropriate to consider this information in determining the principal market. [*IFRS 13.17, BC53*]

2.4.100.80   In the absence of evidence to the contrary, the principal (or most advantageous) market is presumed to be the market in which an entity normally enters into transactions to sell the asset or transfer the liability. IFRS 13 contains this practical expedient because the IASB concluded that entities normally enter into transactions in the principal market for the asset or liability – i.e. the most liquid market that the entity can access. [*IFRS 13.17, BC53*]

2.4.100.90 IFRS 13 does not provide detailed guidance on:
- how an entity should identify the principal market;
- over what period the entity should analyse transactions in the asset or liability to make the determination; or
- how often the entity should update its analysis.

2.4.100.100 In our view, an entity should update its analysis to the extent that events have occurred or activities have changed in a manner that could change the entity's determination of the principal (or most advantageous) market for the asset or liability.

2.4.100.110 The concept of a market does not mean that there needs to be a structured, formal or organised market – e.g. a dealer network or an organised exchange. If such a market does not exist, then an entity needs to focus on identifying market participants to which it would sell the asset or transfer the liability in a hypothetical transaction. It also needs to consider the assumptions that those market participants would use in pricing the asset or liability, assuming that they act in their economic best interest. [*IFRS 13.22–23*]

2.4.110 *Transaction and transport costs*

2.4.110.10 'Transaction costs' are directly attributable costs that an entity would incur in selling an asset or transferring a liability. [*IFRS 13.A*]

2.4.110.20 'Transport costs' are not included in transaction costs. They are the costs that an entity would incur to transport an asset from its current location to the principal or most advantageous market. [*IFRS 13.A, 26*]

2.4.110.30 Whether transaction and transport costs are taken into account in identifying the principal and most advantageous market, and in measuring fair value, can be summarised as follows.

	TRANSACTION COSTS	TRANSPORT COSTS
Identifying the principal market	✘	✘
Identifying the most advantageous market	✓	✓
Measuring fair value	✘	✓

2.4.110.40 Transaction and transport costs are not considered in identifying the principal market, because such a market is identified based only on the volume and level of activity. However, such costs are considered in identifying the most advantageous market, because such a market is identified based on the net proceeds from the assumed transaction. [*IFRS 13.A, 25–26, BC62*]

2.4.110.50 Once the market for the transaction has been identified, the measurement of fair value is an independent, different calculation.

2.4 Fair value measurement

- Fair value is not adjusted for transaction costs; instead, they are accounted for in accordance with other applicable standards. This is because transaction costs are a characteristic of the transaction, and not a characteristic of the asset or liability.
- Fair value is adjusted for transport costs, if location is a characteristic of the asset. For example, the fair value of crude oil held in the Arctic Circle would be adjusted for the cost of transporting the oil from the Arctic Circle to the appropriate market. [*IFRS 13.25–26*]

2.4.110.60   An identified basis differential cannot generally be used as a proxy for transport costs. This is because an identified basis differential between the price at the location of the asset and at the principal (or most advantageous) market generally also includes other factors besides location. Basis differentials reflect multiple factors, such as timing, quality and location, and can be volatile because they capture the passage of time (a financing element), changes in the relative value of different qualities or grades of commodities, and changes in the attractiveness of locations from the central pricing hub relative to each other factor. Supply and demand is a critical factor in influencing the changes in basis because of quality and location. A basis differential is therefore not a simple fixed transport charge, but rather a complex and volatile variable in and of itself. [*IFRS 13.A, 26*]

EXAMPLE 6 – PRINCIPAL AND MOST ADVANTAGEOUS MARKETS

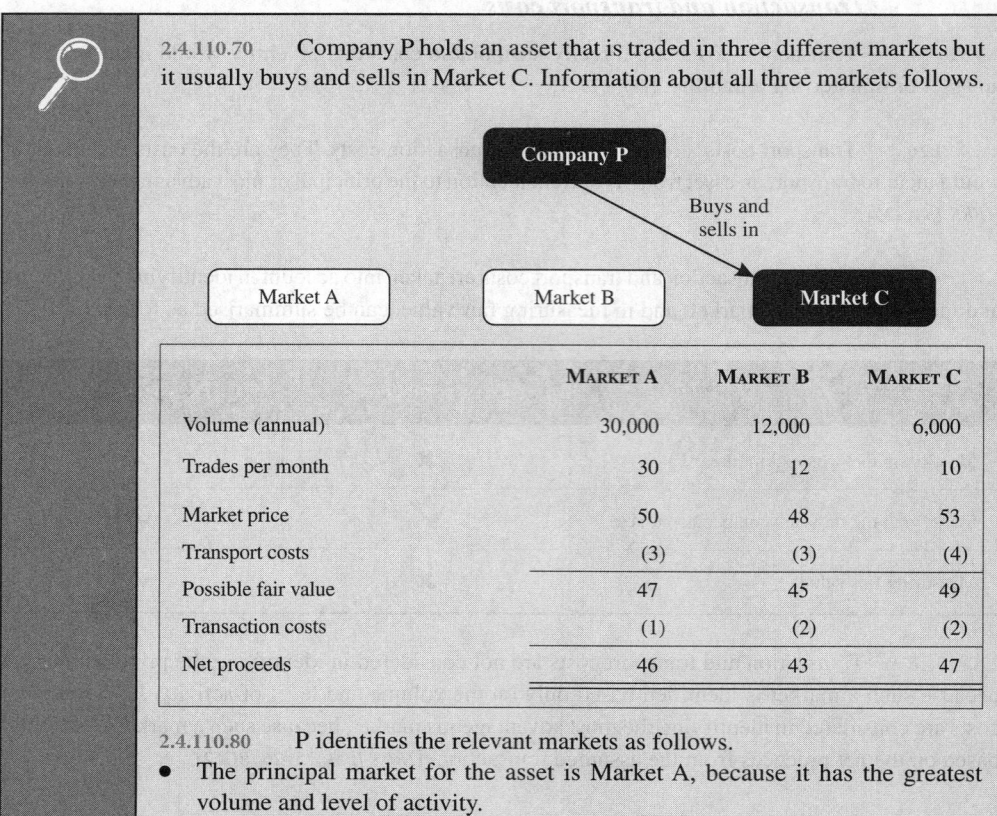

2.4.110.70   Company P holds an asset that is traded in three different markets but it usually buys and sells in Market C. Information about all three markets follows.

	MARKET A	MARKET B	MARKET C
Volume (annual)	30,000	12,000	6,000
Trades per month	30	12	10
Market price	50	48	53
Transport costs	(3)	(3)	(4)
Possible fair value	47	45	49
Transaction costs	(1)	(2)	(2)
Net proceeds	46	43	47

2.4.110.80   P identifies the relevant markets as follows.
- The principal market for the asset is Market A, because it has the greatest volume and level of activity.
- The most advantageous market is Market C, because it has the highest net proceeds.

R82

2.4.110.90   P bases its measurement of fair value on prices in Market A, even though it does not normally transact in that market and it is not the most advantageous market. Therefore, fair value is 47, considering transport costs but not transaction costs, even though P normally transacts in Market C and could maximise its net proceeds in that market.

2.4.110.100   If P is unable to access Markets A and B, then it would use Market C as the most advantageous market. In that case, fair value would be 49 (market price less transport costs).

2.4.110.110   Example 6 highlights that it is not always appropriate to assume that the principal market is the market in which the entity usually transacts. In that example, P has information about Market A that it cannot ignore, which results in P identifying Market A as the principal market.

2.4.110.120   In sourcing market prices to value an asset or liability, spot prices on the measurement date rather than forward prices are used. A spot price is a price for almost immediate delivery on the measurement date, whereas a forward or futures price is a price to exchange the item at a future date.

2.4.110.130   In our view, an asset for which location is a characteristic, and that is not located in the principal market, should not be valued using the forward or futures price. This is because we believe that the asset should be assumed to be available in the principal market at the measurement date. The price in the principal market is adjusted for transport costs to that market from where the asset is located to measure the fair value (see 2.4.110.50).

EXAMPLE 7 – SPOT VS FORWARD PRICE TO VALUE INVENTORY

2.4.110.140   Company X is a commodity broker that measures physical inventory at fair value less costs to sell (see 3.8.70). At the measurement date (31 December 2018), X has physical inventory located in India and it would take two months to deliver the inventory from India to the principal market in New York.

2.4.110.150   In measuring the fair value of the inventory, X uses the spot price in New York on 31 December 2018, adjusted for appropriate transport costs. It does not use the two-month forward price that is quoted on 31 December 2018.

2.4.110.160   In addition, we believe that the fair value of the inventory on 31 December 2018, which is based on the spot price, should also be discounted to reflect:
- the fact that it would take two months to deliver the inventory to the principal market and so it cannot be converted to cash immediately; and
- other risks involved in such a transfer – e.g. damage to the inventory during shipment.

2.4.110.170   As noted in 2.4.110.50, transaction costs are not subtracted from a fair value measurement because they are a characteristic of the transaction and not of the asset or liability. However, it may be appropriate for future transaction costs – i.e. in subsequent sales transactions – to be deducted in a discounted cash flow analysis. For example, if discounted cash flows are used to determine the fair value of real estate, and the analysis includes an assumption that a market participant would sell the property in the future, then it may be appropriate to subtract transaction costs – e.g. selling costs – expected to be incurred at the time of that future disposition (see Example 26). [*IFRS 13.25*]

2.4.110.180   In contrast, it would not generally be appropriate to consider future transaction costs in a discounted cash flow analysis when valuing a business enterprise; this is because it is assumed that a market participant would maximise economic benefit by continuing to operate the business indefinitely. In our experience, market participants entering into a transaction for a business would not generally consider transaction costs associated with a sale in the future. A terminal value within a discounted cash flow analysis generally reflects the value of future cash flows at the end of a discrete cash flow period but does not imply that a market participant would sell the business at that point in time. For further discussion of a discounted cash flow analysis, see 2.4.160.

2.4.120   VALUATION APPROACHES AND TECHNIQUES

2.4.130   General principles

2.4.130.10   In measuring the fair value of an asset or a liability, an entity selects those valuation approaches and techniques that are appropriate in the circumstances and for which sufficient data is available to measure fair value. The technique chosen should maximise the use of relevant observable inputs and minimise the use of unobservable inputs (see 2.4.220). [*IFRS 13.61*]

2.4.130.20   IFRS 13 refers to a 'valuation approach' as a broad category of techniques, whereas a 'valuation technique' refers to a specific technique such as a particular option pricing model. Valuation techniques used to measure fair value fall under three approaches:
- market approach (see 2.4.140);
- income approach (see 2.4.150); and
- cost approach (see 2.4.210). [*IFRS 13.62*]

2.4.130.30   With one exception related to quoted prices in an active market for an identical asset or liability (see 2.4.280), IFRS 13 does not establish requirements for specific valuation technique(s) to be used. In some cases, only a single valuation technique will be appropriate; in other cases, however, using more than one valuation technique will be more appropriate. [*IFRS 13.63*]

2.4.130.40   Any, or a combination, of the three approaches could be used to measure fair value if the techniques are appropriate in the circumstances. Judgement is required in selecting the valuation technique(s), including consideration of the information available. For example, an investor in unquoted equity instruments is likely to place more emphasis on the market approach if there are sufficiently comparable entity peers. However, the investor is likely to place more emphasis on the income approach based on a present value technique if, for example, there are no close comparable entities and reliable cash flows estimates can be made. [*IFRS 13.EM.02-13.13*]

2.4.130.50   If multiple valuation techniques are used in measuring fair value, then the entity evaluates the results and weighs them based on the reasonableness of the range of values indicated by those results. The objective is to find the point within the range that is most representative of fair value in the circumstances. [*IFRS 13.63*]

2.4.130.60   This determination is a matter of judgement; it is not appropriate to simply average the outcomes of the various valuation techniques. An entity considers, among other things, the reliability of the valuation techniques and the inputs that are used in those techniques. If a particular valuation technique falling under the market approach relies on higher-level inputs (e.g. observable market prices) than a valuation technique falling under the income approach that relies heavily on projections of income, then the entity may conclude that it is appropriate to apply greater weight to the measurement of fair value generated by the valuation technique falling under the market approach, because it relies on higher-level inputs. Higher-level inputs (e.g. Level 1 or Level 2 inputs) that are available and relevant cannot be ignored. [*IFRS 13.61, BC142*]

2.4.130.70   In some cases, a secondary method is used only to corroborate the reasonableness of the most appropriate valuation technique.

2.4.140   Market approach

2.4.140.10   Valuation techniques that fall under the market approach often derive market multiples from a set of comparable assets. A market multiple expresses the value of a business or other asset in terms of its ratio to a financial, operating or physical metric. For example, a price to earnings ratio expresses an entity's per-share value in terms of its earnings per share. The multiple can then be applied to the metric of an entity with similar characteristics but different scale, subject to adjustment for differences between the entity and the selected comparable. [*IFRS 13.B5–B6*]

2.4.140.20   If multiples are derived from a number of comparable entities, then there will typically be a range of multiples calculated. Selection within the range is based on market participants' expectations. For example, in estimating the fair value of a CGU in impairment testing (see chapter 3.10), the point in the range of multiples that is selected considers differences between the CGU and comparable entities in terms of size, growth, profitability, risk, investment requirements etc. [*IFRS 13.B5–B6*]

2.4.140.30   In using quoted prices for similar assets or liabilities, adjustments are often necessary for differences between the subject asset and the comparable assets. If there is a high degree of subjectivity in estimating the adjustment – e.g. because the asset differs in important respects from the closest comparable assets – then the resulting value indication may be less reliable than when the range of possible adjustments is narrower, because the subject asset is very similar to the comparable assets.

2.4.140.40   Matrix pricing is a valuation technique that falls under the market approach. Matrix pricing is a mathematical technique mainly used to value debt securities without relying exclusively on quoted prices for the specific securities, but rather by relying on the securities' relationship to other benchmark quoted securities. Therefore, matrix prices are based on quoted prices for securities with similar coupons, ratings and maturities, rather than on actual prices for the asset being measured. For a discussion of the use of matrix pricing if an entity holds a large number of similar assets or liabilities that are measured at fair value, for which quoted prices in active markets are available but not readily accessible, see 2.4.280.100. [*IFRS 13.B7*]

2.4.150 **Income approach**

2.4.150.10   The valuation techniques that fall under the income approach convert future amounts such as cash flows or income streams to a current amount on the measurement date. The fair value measurement reflects current market expectations about those future amounts, discounted to their present value. The concept behind the income approach is that an asset is worth what it is expected to earn, discounted for the time value of money and associated risks. [*IFRS 13.B10*]

2.4.150.20   Common valuation techniques falling under the income approach include:
- present value techniques (see 2.4.160);
- option pricing models (see 2.4.190); and
- the multi-period excess earnings method (see 2.4.200.10). [*IFRS 13.B11*]

2.4.160 *Present value techniques*

2.4.160.10   The application guidance in IFRS 13 describes two approaches to applying a present value technique:
- the discount rate adjustment technique; and
- the expected present value technique. [*IFRS 13.B12*]

2.4.160.20   IFRS 13 does not prescribe a specific method; instead, the present value technique used to measure fair value depends on facts and circumstances specific to the asset or liability being measured and the availability of sufficient data – e.g. cash flow estimates, risk premiums, discount rates – and other factors that would be considered by market participants. [*IFRS 13.B12*]

2.4.160.30   Present value techniques differ in how they capture these elements; however, there are some commonalities in determining the inputs into the valuation techniques. [*IFRS 13.B14*]

2.4.160.40   The assumptions used for the cash flows and discount rates reflect market participants' views. In addition, the assumptions consider only the factors attributable to the asset or the liability being measured. [*IFRS 13.B14*]

2.4.160.50   The fair value of a financial instrument reflects the effect of discounting expected future cash flows. However, an entity is permitted to initially measure short-term receivables and payables with no stated interest rate at their invoiced amounts without discounting, if the effect of discounting is immaterial. Therefore, in our view receivables and payables with maturities of up to six months are not generally required to be discounted. However, in high-interest environments the impact of discounting may be significant even for maturities of less than six months. Notwithstanding the above, trade receivables resulting from contracts with customers in the scope of IFRS 15 are required or permitted to be measured initially at the transaction price as defined in IFRS 15 (rather than at fair value) if certain criteria are met – see 7.7.20. [*IFRS 9.5.1.3, 13.BC138A*]

2.4.170 *Risk and uncertainty*

2.4.170.10   A valuation using present value techniques is based on assumptions that are inherently uncertain, because they reflect estimates of the future rather than known amounts. Even contractual cash flows that may appear certain at first glance contain risk because of uncertainty about the ability of the counterparty to meet its contractual obligations. For example, contractual cash flows on a loan are subject to a risk of default. A risk premium is therefore included in the fair value measurement to reflect the amount that risk-averse market participants would demand to be compensated for the uncertainty of the cash flows. [*IFRS 13.B15–B16, BC144*]

2.4.170.20   Different options are available for making adjustments for risk in present value techniques. The discount rate adjustment technique uses a single estimate of cash flows – contractual, promised or most likely cash flows – and adjusts for risk in the discount rate. In addition, IFRS 13 notes two possible methods to incorporate risk in an expected present value technique, which is based on probability-weighted cash flows.
● Method 1 adjusts for risk in the expected cash flows, which are then discounted at the risk-free rate.
● Method 2 uses a risk-adjusted discount rate with expected cash flows. [*IFRS 13.B17*]

2.4.170.30   There is no preferred method for making adjustments for risk in a present value technique; it depends on facts and circumstances specific to the asset or liability being measured. The risk adjustment may need to be considered in both cash flows and the discount rate. However, rates used to discount cash flows do not reflect risks for which the estimated cash flows have been adjusted (and vice versa) because otherwise the effect would be double counted. [*IFRS 13.B14*]

2.4.170.40   To use a risk-free rate in valuing an asset (Method 1 in 2.4.170.20), the expected cash flows need to be adjusted to represent certainty-equivalent cash flows. This means that a market participant would be indifferent between investing in the risky asset and investing in a risk-free investment that generated those cash flows. In our experience, although it is theoretically possible that expected cash flows from an asset could be adjusted to incorporate all relevant risks so that the investor was indifferent, the practical application of this approach is very difficult outside of option pricing and certain derivative modelling. This is because expected cash flows include both positive as well as negative possible outcomes; therefore, before risk adjustment, they represent only the probability-weighted-average outcome. [*IFRS 13.B17, B25*]

2.4.180   *Discount rates*

2.4.180.10   Discount rates reflect assumptions that are consistent with those inherent in the cash flows to avoid double counting or omitting the effects of certain risk factors. [*IFRS 13.B14*]

2.4.180.20   Assumptions about cash flows and discount rates should be internally consistent. For example, if the cash flows include the effect of expected inflation, then the discount rate also incorporates inflation expectations. [*IFRS 13.B14*]

2.4.180.30   In our experience, for some assets and liabilities it is rare that a discount rate can be observed directly from the market. For example, the cost of equity of a business, which is often used as an input into a weighted-average cost of capital calculation in valuing a CGU based on discounted cash flows, cannot be observed. In such circumstances, it will generally be necessary to build up a market participant discount rate that appropriately reflects the risks associated with the cash flows of the asset or liability being measured at fair value. Other standards that deal with discount rates, such as IAS 36, refer to an entity's weighted-average cost of capital as the starting point in determining a possible appropriate discount rate (see 3.10.300).

2.4.190   **Option pricing models**

2.4.190.10   Option pricing models such as the Black-Scholes-Merton formula or a binomial model can be used to calculate the fair value of options. Option valuation models implicitly or explicitly use mathematical techniques such as closed-form solutions or numerical methods to identify a range of future scenarios. From these possible scenarios, the payoff of an option can be calculated. These intrinsic values at future exercise are then probability-weighted and discounted to their present value to estimate the fair value of the option at the measurement date. [*IFRS 13.B11(b)*]

2.4.200   *Other techniques*

2.4.200.10   The multi-period excess earnings method is commonly used to measure the fair value of intangible assets, such as customer relationships and technology assets, acquired in a business combination. The method is based on a discounted cash flow analysis that measures the fair value of an asset by taking into account not only operating costs but also charges for contributory assets; this isolates the value related to the asset to be measured and excludes any value related to contributory assets. [*IFRS 13.B11(c)*]

2.4.200.20   The with-versus-without method is useful for measuring the fair value of acquired intangible assets that market participants would be expected to use defensively (see Example 11). It measures the incremental cash flows that would be achieved by market participants arising from their ownership of an existing intangible asset by locking up the competing acquired intangible asset. Fair value is measured as the difference between the fair value of the group of assets of the market participant:
- assuming that the acquired intangible asset were to be actively used by others in the market; and
- assuming that the acquired intangible asset was withdrawn from the market.

2.4.200.30   The relief-from-royalty method measures the fair value of intangible assets using assumptions about what it would cost a market participant to use the acquired intangible asset if another entity owned it. This technique is appropriate only if the highest and best use of the asset (see 2.4.330) is to use it actively in the market. As a result of owning the asset, a market participant is relieved from making royalty payments that might otherwise be required. This method includes assumptions about the stream of payments that would be required, usually in the form of royalties, to another party for the right to use the asset. The fair value of the intangible asset is measured as the discounted stream of payments from which the acquiring entity is relieved because it owns the asset.

2.4.210   Cost approach

2.4.210.10   The cost approach comprises valuation techniques that reflect the amount that would be required to replace the service capacity of an asset. The concept behind the cost approach is that an investor will pay no more for an asset than the cost to buy or construct a substitute asset of comparable utility, adjusted for obsolescence. [*IFRS 13.B8–B9*]

2.4.210.20   The primary method used to measure fair value under the cost approach is the depreciated replacement cost (DRC) method. This method is sometimes used to measure the fair value of plant and equipment. A DRC valuation considers how much it would cost to reproduce an asset of equivalent utility taking into account physical, functional and economic obsolescence. It estimates the replacement cost of the required capacity rather than the actual asset. Because the cost approach is based on service capacity, it is not relevant for measuring the fair value of financial assets.

2.4.210.30   For further discussion about the DRC method in the context of valuing plant and equipment, see 2.4.600.

2.4.220 INPUTS TO VALUATION TECHNIQUES

2.4.230 General principles

2.4.230.10   Inputs to valuation techniques are the assumptions that market participants would use in pricing the asset or liability. These inputs include assumptions about risk, such as the risk inherent in a particular valuation technique used to measure fair value and the risk inherent in the inputs to the valuation technique. [*IFRS 13.A*]

2.4.230.20   An entity selects the valuation techniques:
- that are appropriate in the circumstances;
- for which sufficient data is available; and
- that maximise the use of relevant observable inputs and minimise the use of unobservable inputs. [*IFRS 13.61*]

2.4.230.30   Exchange markets, dealer markets, brokered markets and principal-to-principal markets are examples of markets that might provide observable inputs for valuation techniques. [*IFRS 13.68*]

2.4.230.40   In some cases, an entity may need to adjust the available observable inputs significantly, because of the different characteristics of the asset or liability being measured or market conditions at the measurement date. Unobservable inputs are a part of a fair value measurement if they are required inputs in order to arrive at a fair value measurement and if they relate to factors that market participants would consider.

2.4.230.50   For example, the fair value of an unquoted security held as an asset may be based primarily on observable market multiples. However, to the extent that market participants would be expected to apply a discount because the shares valued are not publicly traded, a discount for lack of marketability needs to be considered, even though this is not directly observable. For further discussion of unquoted equity instruments, see 2.4.860.

2.4.230.60   It would not be appropriate to adjust the results of a valuation technique for entity-specific factors such as the entity's perspective on uncertainty in estimated cash flows and administration costs that it expects to incur. Such factors are incorporated into a valuation technique based on the amounts that market participants would consider in setting a price. [*IFRS 13.22, 89*]

2.4.240 Premiums, discounts and blockage factors

2.4.240.10   An entity selects inputs that are consistent with the characteristics of the asset or liability that market participants would take into account in pricing the asset or liability. In some cases, an initial value indication may not reflect a characteristic of the asset or liability that market participants would take into account. As a result, it may be appropriate to make an adjustment – e.g. a control premium, a marketability or liquidity discount or a non-controlling interest discount – to a preliminary value indication in measuring fair value. [*IFRS 13.69*]

2.4.240.20   An entity does not apply a premium or discount if:
- it is inconsistent with the item's unit of account (see 2.4.240.30);

- it reflects size as a characteristic of the entity's holding – e.g. a blockage factor (see 2.4.240.40–70);
- the characteristic is already reflected in the preliminary value indication (see 2.4.240.110); or
- there is a quoted price in an active market for an identical asset or liability – i.e. a Level 1 input (see 2.4.280). [*IFRS 13.69*]

2.4.240.25   A liquidity adjustment may be appropriate in measuring fair value if:
- the instrument being valued is categorised in Level 2 or Level 3 of the fair value hierarchy;
- the other inputs in the valuation have not factored in the liquidity of the instrument; and
- market participants would include an adjustment when buying or selling the instrument. [*IFRS 13.69, 79–80*]

2.4.240.30   The unit of account determines the extent to which an asset or liability is aggregated or disaggregated for the purpose of measuring fair value. For example, if the unit of account is an individual financial instrument (e.g. a share), then it would not be appropriate to include a premium based on holding multiple units in measuring fair value. For a discussion of the unit of account, see 2.4.80.

2.4.240.40   As noted in 2.4.80.30–50, the unit of account in respect of investments in subsidiaries, associates and joint ventures is unclear, and in our view an entity may choose an accounting policy, to be applied consistently, in identifying the unit of account. For example, if the unit of account is the investment as a whole, then it may be appropriate to include a control premium in measuring the fair value of investments in subsidiaries even if Level 1 prices exist for an individual share (see 2.4.840).

2.4.240.50   An entity may hold a large number of identical financial instruments, but the market for the instrument does not have sufficient trading volume to absorb the quantity held by the entity without affecting the price. A 'blockage factor' is a discount that adjusts the quoted price of an asset or a liability because the market's normal trading volume is not sufficient to absorb the quantity held by the entity. IFRS 13 clarifies that a blockage factor is not a characteristic of an asset or a liability but a characteristic of the size of the entity's holding. As a result, the standard expressly prohibits application of a blockage factor. [*IFRS 13.69, 80, BC156*]

2.4.240.60   However, size may in some cases be a characteristic of an asset or liability (see 2.4.70). In these cases, adjustments may be required because of the size of the asset or liability. [*IFRS 13.11, BC156*]

2.4.240.70   Therefore, in our view if it is appropriate to make a liquidity adjustment (see 2.4.240.25), then the amount of the adjustment should be determined based on the liquidity of the specific asset's or liability's unit of account in the entity's principal (or most advantageous) market and not on the size of the entity's holding relative to the market's daily trading volume.

EXAMPLE 8 – OPTION TO BUY CONTROLLING INTERESTS

2.4.240.80   Company T purchases an option to buy 51% of the shares in Company S, a listed company, which if exercised would result in T owning a controlling interest in S. A Level 1 price is available for the underlying shares of S, but not for the option to buy 51%, which is the unit of account under IFRS 9.

> 2.4.240.90   The fair value of the option would therefore take into account adjustments to the share price if they are necessary to reflect the value of the option, such as including a control premium.

2.4.240.100   For a discussion of the implications of the guidance in 2.4.240.40–90 on specific items, see 2.4.550.

2.4.240.110   If a characteristic of an asset or a liability is not reflected in a preliminary value indication, then a separate adjustment may be required to measure the fair value of the asset or liability. If the assets being measured are non-controlling shares in a private entity and the preliminary value indication was arrived at using market multiples derived from the share prices of comparable public entities, then the resulting preliminary value indication is on a marketable, minority interest basis, because the publicly traded shares are marketable and represent the price of non-controlling holdings. To use such multiples to measure the fair values of non-marketable, non-controlling shares in a private entity, an adjustment would not generally be required to reflect the fact that the shares are non-controlling, because this is already reflected in the comparable entity share prices used to calculate the market multiples. However, an adjustment would generally be required to reflect the non-marketable nature of the assets relative to the publicly traded shares.

2.4.245   Restrictions on the sale of a security

2.4.245.10   If an entity measures the fair value of an asset such as a security that is subject to a restriction on its sale or transfer, then it determines whether it is appropriate to apply an adjustment to the price of a similar unrestricted security to reflect the restriction. To make that determination, the entity first analyses whether the restriction is security-specific or entity-specific. For entity-specific restrictions, the price used in the fair value measurement is not adjusted to reflect the restriction (see 2.4.70.70). Although an entity may not be able to sell a particular security on the measurement date because of an entity-specific restriction, it is still considered to have access to the market.

2.4.245.20   For security-specific restrictions, the price used in the fair value measurement reflects the effect of the restriction if it would be considered by a market participant in pricing the security. This may require an adjustment to the quoted price of otherwise identical but unrestricted securities. In determining the appropriate discount, an entity needs to evaluate all of the relevant drivers of the discount. These include the length of the restriction, the risk of the underlying security (e.g. volatility), expected dividends, the float and market capitalisation of the issuer, the liquidity of the market and other qualitative and quantitative factors specific to the security. [*IFRS 13.11, IE28*]

2.4.245.30   Generally, it is not appropriate to apply a discount that is a fixed percentage of the unrestricted price over the entire life of the restriction period in measuring fair value. For example, if at the measurement date the period of the security-specific restriction is two years and the discount is estimated to be 10 percent, then assuming no changes other than the passage of time the following year's discount would be less than 10 percent because the restriction period is reduced to one year.

2.4.245.40   In our experience, measuring the discount is often based on quantitative approaches (e.g. an option pricing model) that explicitly incorporate the duration of the restriction and the characteristics of the underlying security – e.g. risk, dividends, rights and preferences etc. When using these models to derive the discount, an entity needs to consider the ability of the model to appropriately quantify the liquidity adjustment under the specific facts and circumstances. For example, some option pricing models may not appropriately measure the discount that a market participant would apply. [*IFRS 13.IE28, EM.02-13.67*]

2.4.250   Inputs based on bid and ask prices

2.4.250.10   If assets or liabilities have a bid and an ask price, then an entity uses the price within the bid-ask spread that is most representative of fair value in the circumstances. Although it is not required, the use of bid prices for long positions, and ask prices for short positions, is permitted. [*IFRS 13.70*]

2.4.250.20   The bid-ask spread includes transaction costs, and may include other components. The price in the principal or most advantageous market is not adjusted for transaction costs (see 2.4.110). Therefore, an entity makes an assessment of what the bid-ask spread represents in determining the price that is most representative of fair value within the bid-ask spread in the circumstances. [*IFRS 13.BC164*]

2.4.250.30   The standard does not prohibit using mid-market prices or other pricing conventions generally used by market participants as a practical expedient for fair value measurements within a bid-ask spread. However, in our view the use of mid-market prices is subject to the condition that the mid-market price provides a reasonable approximation of an exit price. We believe that use of the practical expedient does not override the general fair value measurement guidance, and should not be used if it leads to a measurement that is not representative of fair value. Therefore, an entity should not ignore available evidence that a mid-market price does not result in a price that is representative of fair value. For example, if the bid-ask spread is particularly wide, or if the applicable bid-ask spread has widened significantly for a specific asset or liability, then a mid-market price may not be representative of fair value. [*IFRS 13.71*]

2.4.260   FAIR VALUE HIERARCHY

2.4.260.10   To increase consistency and comparability, IFRS 13 establishes a fair value hierarchy based on the inputs to valuation techniques used to measure fair value. The inputs are categorised into three levels – the highest priority is given to unadjusted quoted prices in active markets for identical assets or liabilities, and the lowest priority is given to unobservable inputs. [*IFRS 13.72*]

2.4.260.20   The fair value hierarchy is made up of three levels, with Level 1 being the highest level.
- *Level 1 inputs:* Unadjusted quoted prices in active markets for identical assets or liabilities that the entity can access at the measurement date.
- *Level 2 inputs:* Inputs other than quoted prices included within Level 1 that are observable for the asset or liability, either directly (i.e. as prices) or indirectly (i.e. derived from prices).
- *Level 3 inputs:* Unobservable inputs for the asset or liability. [*IFRS 13.76, 81, 86, A*]

2.4.270   Categorisation of fair value measurements

2.4.270.10   Fair value measurements are categorised in their entirety based on the lowest level input that is significant to the entire measurement; this is outlined in the flowchart below. [*IFRS 13.73*]

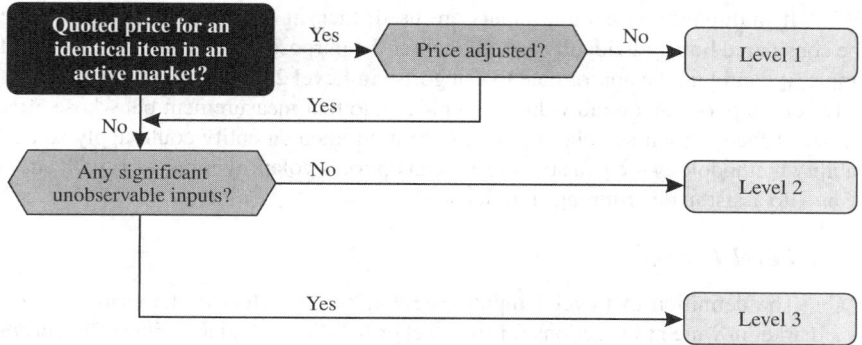

2.4.270.20   The level into which a fair value measurement is categorised in its entirety is determined with reference to the observability and significance of the inputs used in the valuation technique. Categorisation into Level 1 can only be achieved through the market approach using quoted prices in an active market for an identical asset or liability, without adjustments (see 2.4.140 and 280). [*IFRS 13.73–74, 76, 81, 86, A, IU 01-15*]

2.4.270.25   In our view, a valuation technique that uses only unadjusted quoted prices in an active market at the measurement date for an identical instrument may be categorised in its entirety within Level 1 if it uses more than one Level 1 input and the valuation technique does not include adjustments to those Level 1 inputs. This is because there could be more than one Level 1 price for an identical instrument – even in the same market and at the same time – e.g. a bid price and an ask price (see 2.4.250). Therefore, we believe that a fair value measurement that is based on a valuation technique that uses a simple average of current Level 1 prices at the measurement date to produce a value from those inputs may be considered a Level 1 measurement – e.g. a mid-market price that is an average of a Level 1 bid price and a Level 1 ask price. Similarly, we believe that the price within the bid-ask spread that is most representative of fair value may also be classified as Level 1, if the bid and ask prices are Level 1 prices.

2.4.270.27   However, we believe that a fair value measurement that is based on a model that uses complex algorithms or quoted prices in an active market from different points in time before the measurement date cannot be considered a Level 1 measurement. Similarly, a fair value measurement that is based on a model that uses only quoted prices in an active market as inputs, but not all of those inputs relate to the identical instrument being measured cannot be considered a Level 1 measurement. For further discussion on dealing with pricing services and broker quotes, see 2.4.300.

2.4.270.30   Valuation techniques often incorporate both observable and unobservable inputs. If fair value is measured using inputs from multiple levels of the fair value hierarchy, then the inclusion of a lower-level input (Level 3 is lower than Level 2) in an entity's measurement may indicate that the input is significant. This is because the entity's decision to include the lower-level input provides evidence that the entity considers the input to be significant to the overall fair value measurement. However, the final determination of whether inputs are significant is a matter of judgement that requires an entity to consider:
- factors specific to the asset or liability; and
- the effect of the input on the overall fair value measurement, including possible alternative assumptions for the input. [*IFRS 13.73–74*]

2.4.270.40   If multiple unobservable inputs are used, then in our view the unobservable inputs should be considered both individually and in total for the purpose of determining their significance. For example, it would not be appropriate to categorise in Level 2 a fair value measurement that has multiple Level 3 inputs that are individually significant to that measurement but whose effects happen to offset. If factors such as volatility inputs are used, then an entity could apply some form of comparability methodology – e.g. a stress test on an option's volatility input or a 'with and without' comparison – to assist in determining significance.

2.4.280   *Level 1 inputs*

2.4.280.10   The definition of Level 1 inputs (see 2.4.260.20) refers to the term 'active market', which is a market in which transactions for the asset or liability take place with sufficient frequency and volume for pricing information to be provided on an ongoing basis. [*IFRS 13.76, A*]

2.4.280.20   Whether transactions take place with sufficient frequency and volume is a matter of judgement, and depends on the specific facts and circumstances of the market for the asset or liability. Even if a market is considered inactive – i.e. the price for the asset or liability is not a Level 1 input – it may still provide relevant pricing information (see 2.4.290 and 480). [*IFRS 13.B44*]

2.4.280.30   In our view, it is not necessary for there to be a large number of dealers or brokers in order for an active market to exist. In some cases, information about pricing and volumes traded may be available from only one independent source – e.g. a broker. In determining whether that one source is providing an active market in the instrument, in our view an entity should take into account its past experience, knowledge of the local market and professional judgement.

2.4.280.40   In our view, the determination of whether a market is active should not be based on the size of the entity's holding. For example, a market that trades 100,000 shares of Company X ordinary shares per day may be considered active, even if the entity holds 20,000,000 shares of X.

2.4.280.50   Even if the volume or level of activity for an asset or a liability has significantly decreased, the market for that asset or liability may still be active. In such circumstances, the quoted price for the asset or liability in that market would still be categorised within Level 1. For a discussion of measuring fair value if the volume or level of activity has significantly decreased, see 2.4.480.

2.4.280.60   To be categorised as Level 1, the measurement needs to be the quoted price of an identical instrument. It is not a measurement based on a quoted rate or index to be used as an input into a valuation model to calculate the fair value of the instrument. For example, over-the-counter derivative contracts are individual agreements between specific counterparties. Therefore, they are not usually categorised as a Level 1 measurement, because there is unlikely to be an active market for an identical instrument. [*IFRS 13.76*]

2.4.280.65   In our view, certain types of executable prices – e.g. third party quotes that represent binding offers – can be considered 'quoted' prices even though they do not represent the price of an actual transaction. For example, in many markets – in particular when market makers or similar intermediaries are involved – the market price is determined on the basis of bid and ask prices (see 2.4.250), which are binding offers but do not represent the price of an actual transaction unless and until the offer is accepted and a trade occurs. We believe that these prices may represent quoted prices in the market and therefore be considered Level 1 prices when the market is active. This is because current quoted bid and ask prices (or similar binding offers to trade) from market makers or exchanges may be more representative of the price at which a market participant could sell an asset at the measurement date than the prices of actual transactions that occurred at an earlier point in time. If such a price is considered a 'quoted' price but the market is not active, then the price will be categorised in Level 2 (see 2.4.290.30).

2.4.280.67 We believe that determining whether a binding offer is considered a 'quoted' price in the market and whether a market that is subject to the binding offer is considered 'active' requires judgement and depends on the specific facts and circumstances. In particular, it would be unusual for binding offers to be available at widely different price levels if the market is active. Similarly, a wide bid-ask spread may be associated with a market not being active.

2.4.280.70 Generally, an entity is not allowed to adjust Level 1 prices. However, in the following limited circumstances, which are explained below, an adjustment may be appropriate:
- as a practical expedient;
- the quoted price in an active market does not represent fair value at the measurement date; or
- the fair value of a liability or own equity instruments is measured using the quoted price of an identical instrument traded as an asset. [*IFRS 13.77, 79*]

2.4.280.80 As a practical expedient, an entity may measure the fair value of certain assets and liabilities under an alternative method that does not rely exclusively on quoted prices. Such a practical expedient is appropriate only if:
- the entity holds a large number of similar assets or liabilities that are measured at fair value; and
- a quoted price in an active market is available but not readily accessible for each of these assets or liabilities individually. [*IFRS 13.79(a)*]

2.4.280.90 In our view, the use of such an alternative method as a practical expedient is also subject to the condition that it results in a price that is representative of fair value. We believe that application of a practical expedient is not appropriate if it would lead to a measurement that is not representative of an exit price at the measurement date.

2.4.280.100 An example of an alternative pricing method as described in 2.4.280.80–90 is matrix pricing. This pricing method involves using a selection of data points (usually quoted prices) or yield curves to calculate prices for separate financial instruments that share characteristics similar to the data points. Matrix pricing using observable market-based data points will usually result in a Level 2 fair value measurement. [*IFRS 13.79(a)*]

2.4.280.110 In practice, an entity generally uses the closing price from the principal (or most advantageous) market on its reporting date. Some entities use prices that reflect after-hours trading, which in practice is most common for instruments that trade in foreign markets that close before similar markets in other time zones. Consideration should be given to the circumstances in which adjustments to Level 1 prices may be appropriate. [*IFRS 13.B34(a)*]

2.4.280.120 If the closing price is used, then the entity considers whether that price represents the fair value at the measurement date. In an exchange market, closing prices are both readily available and generally representative of fair value. However, the definition of a closing price may represent different things on different exchanges for different types of financial instruments. For example, a closing price may range from the last transaction price for the day to a price derived from a complicated calculation or process. If an asset or a liability is subject to a bid-ask spread (see 2.4.250), then an entity needs to assess the nature of the closing price. [*IFRS 13.B34(a)*]

2.4.280.130   In some cases, the quoted price in an active market may not represent fair value at the measurement date – e.g. if a significant event takes place after the close of a market but before the measurement date, such as the announcement of a business combination. In that case, an entity chooses an accounting policy, to be applied consistently, for identifying those events that may affect fair value measurements. This exception is limited to situations in which the significant event takes place after the close of the market but before the measurement date. It does not apply to situations in which the event takes place after the measurement date. [*IFRS 13.79(b)*]

EXAMPLE 9 – ADJUSTMENT TO LEVEL 1 INPUTS – AFTERMARKET TRANSACTIONS

2.4.280.140   Company P invests in shares of Company T that are listed on the London Stock Exchange (LSE). On the reporting date, P obtains the closing price of the shares from the LSE. After the closing time of the LSE but still on the reporting date, T makes a public announcement that affects the fair value of its shares; this is evidenced by prices for a small number of aftermarket transactions in depository receipts on the shares of T that are traded on the New York Stock Exchange.

2.4.280.150   In this example, P uses the aftermarket prices to make appropriate adjustments to the closing price from the LSE, in order to measure the fair value of the shares at the measurement date. Because the adjustment is derived from observed market prices, the resulting fair value measurement is a Level 2 measurement.

2.4.280.160   In our experience, pricing data from aftermarket trades or trades for identical or similar assets or liabilities in another market may be useful to determine the existence of a significant event that affects the fair value measurement of an asset or liability. Pricing data may also be used to determine the amount of the adjustment to be made to the last quoted price sourced from the entity's principal (or most advantageous) market.

2.4.280.170   If an entity uses pricing data from aftermarket trades or trades for identical or similar assets or liabilities in another market to determine the amount of the adjustment, then it should support that adjustment through an analysis of how the pricing data or their underlying factors affect the fair value of the asset or liability.

2.4.280.180   This analysis may be based on quantitative and qualitative factors to assess whether the pricing data is relevant to the fair value measurement of the asset or liability being measured. For example, if an entity uses a statistical method in its analysis, then to the extent that the analysis supports a correlation coefficient that is other than 1:1, that factor may need to be applied to pricing data from aftermarket trades or trades for identical or similar assets or liabilities in another market to develop the adjustment to be applied to the last quoted price in the entity's principal (or most advantageous) market.

2.4.280.190   This analysis may also include a comparison between the pricing data from aftermarket trades or trades for identical or similar assets or liabilities in another market and the subsequent price in the entity's principal (or most advantageous) market. To the extent that a difference is found through this analysis, an adjustment to the last quoted price from the entity's principal (or most advantageous) market may need to reflect this difference.

EXAMPLE 10 – ADJUSTMENT TO LEVEL 1 INPUTS – OIL FUTURES CONTRACTS

2.4.280.200   Company G holds oil futures contracts at the New York Mercantile Exchange (NYMEX). On the reporting date, G obtains the closing price of the oil futures from NYMEX. On the reporting date, but subsequent to the closing time of NYMEX, there is a public announcement that affects oil prices and related financial instruments. This is evidenced by prices of oil forward contracts transacted in the over-the-counter market on the reporting date.

2.4.280.210   G needs to evaluate the futures prices with forward contracts to factor how correlated the futures and forward markets are. If this analysis supports a correlation, and the correlation coefficient is other than 1:1, then that factor may need to be applied to the aftermarket forward prices to determine the appropriate adjustments to the price quoted on NYMEX.

2.4.280.220   Because of the adjustment to the price obtained from the principal market, the resulting fair value measurement would generally be expected to be a Level 2 measurement. However, if an adjustment using unobservable inputs is significant, then a Level 3 designation would be appropriate. [*IFRS 13.75*]

2.4.280.230   An entity may measure the fair value of a liability or its own equity instruments using the quoted price of an identical instrument traded as an asset. However, there may be specific differences between the item being measured and the asset. This may happen, for example, if the identical instrument traded as an asset includes a credit enhancement that is excluded from the liability's unit of account (see 2.4.80 and 380). [*IFRS 13.39(b), 79(c)*]

2.4.280.240   Any adjustment to a quoted price in an active market will result in the fair value measurement being categorised into a lower level of the fair value hierarchy. Although a price that is adjusted based on one of the limited circumstances in 2.4.280.70 is no longer a Level 1 measurement, in our view an entity should not make other adjustments to that measurement (e.g. for market or other risks), except if the criteria to make one of the other adjustments to Level 1 prices in 2.4.280.70 are met. We believe that the circumstances that allow an entity to exceptionally adjust Level 1 inputs only allow for adjustments related to those circumstances. [*IFRS 13.79*]

2.4.280.250   Positions in a single asset or liability (including a group of identical assets or liabilities) that are traded in an active market are measured at fair value within Level 1 as the product of the quoted price for the individual asset or liability and the quantity held. This is the case even if:
- the market's normal daily trading volume is insufficient to absorb the quantity held; or
- placing orders to sell the position in a single transaction might affect the quoted price (see 2.4.240).
  [*IFRS 13.80*]

2.4.290   *Level 2 and Level 3 inputs*

2.4.290.10   The determination of whether a fair value measurement is categorised into Level 2 or Level 3 depends on:

- the observability of the inputs that are used in the valuation technique(s); and
- the significance of the inputs to the fair value measurement. [*IFRS 13.73, 81, 84, 86, A*]

2.4.290.20   'Observable inputs' are inputs that are developed using market data, such as publicly available information about actual events or transactions and that reflect the assumptions that market participants would use in pricing the asset or liability. [*IFRS 13.A*]

2.4.290.30   Level 2 inputs include:
- quoted prices (see also 2.4.280.65–67) for similar assets or liabilities in active markets;
- quoted prices for identical or similar assets and liabilities in markets that are not active; and
- other inputs that are observable for the asset or liability – e.g. interest rates, implied volatilities, credit spreads or yield curves that are observed in the market. [*IFRS 13.82*]

2.4.290.40   'Market-corroborated inputs' that are derived principally from or corroborated by observable market data (by correlation or other means) are also Level 2 inputs. For example, the variable leg of an interest rate swap is based on a specific bank's prime rate. If the bank's prime rate is derived through extrapolation and the extrapolated values are corroborated by observable market data through correlation with an interest rate that is observable over substantially the full term of the swap, then the bank's prime rate is a market-corroborated input that is categorised as a Level 2 input. [*IFRS 13.82(d), A, B35(c)*]

2.4.290.50   Correlation is a statistical concept, indicating the strength and direction of a linear relationship between two variables. In our view, for an input to be considered a Level 2 input by using correlation, the correlation between the input and relevant observable market data should be high. In using correlation or other statistical means to support Level 2 inputs, an entity may apply similar statistical considerations that are used to analyse the possible behaviour of a hedging relationship during its term to ascertain whether it can be expected to meet the risk management objective (see 7.9.830.60).

2.4.290.60   In establishing the level in the hierarchy of an input corroborated using correlation analyses, an entity considers factors including the R-squared confidence level of the statistical analysis and the number of data points.

2.4.290.70   An input to a fair value measurement of an asset or a liability with a specified term is a Level 2 input only if it is observable for substantially the full term of the asset or liability. If this is not the case, then the input is a Level 3 input. Whether the resulting fair value measurement would be categorised as Level 2 or Level 3 depends on the significance of that input to the measurement in its entirety. [*IFRS 13.73, 82, A*]

EXAMPLE 11 – LEVEL 2 INPUT NOT AVAILABLE FOR SUBSTANTIALLY THE FULL TERM

2.4.290.80   Company E has an over-the-counter contract to buy natural gas every month for the next 30 months. E accounts for the contract as a derivative instrument, measured at fair value in the statement of financial position. Natural gas prices that are quoted in an active market are available for 24 months after the reporting date. For the remaining 6 months of the term, E uses internally developed estimates of future natural gas prices. Therefore, in this example, market prices are not available for substantially the entire term of the contract, and the impact of the unobservable inputs is significant.

> 2.4.290.90   As a result, E categorises the fair value measurement of this contract as a Level 3 measurement. In the following year, if quoted natural gas prices continue to be available for the following 24 months, then the fair value measurement might be categorised as a Level 2 measurement.

2.4.290.100   As noted in 2.4.130.10 and 230.20, an entity minimises the use of unobservable inputs in measuring fair value. However, situations may occur in which relevant inputs are not observable. In such situations, unobservable inputs are used based on the best information available about the assumptions that market participants would make in pricing the asset or liability, including assumptions about risk. Adjustments to Level 2 inputs based on unobservable inputs may be necessary depending on the characteristics of the asset or liability being measured. In that case, an entity assesses whether the effects of these adjustments are significant to the entire measurement (see 2.4.270). If so, then the fair value measurement is categorised as Level 3. [*IFRS 13.61, 75, 83–84, 86–87, 89*]

2.4.290.110   Examples of unobservable inputs include:
- foreign currency interest rates that:
  - are not observable; and
  - cannot be corroborated by observable market data for the term of the financial instrument being valued;
- volatility for a share option derived from the share's historical prices, because it does not generally represent market participants' current expectations about future volatility;
- a current estimate using the entity's own data about the future cash outflow to be paid to fulfil a decommissioning obligation assumed in a business combination; and
- a financial forecast of cash flows or profit or loss developed using the entity's own data and used as an input to measure the fair value of a CGU. [*IFRS 13.B36*]

2.4.290.120   Instruments may be transferred into or out of Level 3 for a number of reasons – for example:
- changes in the inputs used in a valuation;
- refinements in modelling techniques;
- the initiation or cessation of market transactions in similar instruments; or
- the passage of time (see Example 11).

2.4.290.130   In developing unobservable inputs because of the unavailability of relevant observable inputs, an entity is not precluded from using its own data. However, an entity adjusts its own data if reasonably available information indicates that other market participants would use different information. An example of a possible adjustment would be buyer-specific synergies – i.e. synergies available to a specific acquirer in a business combination that would not be available to market participants and therefore are excluded from the valuation. [*IFRS 13.89*]

2.4.300   Pricing services and broker quotes

2.4.300.10   Using a pricing service does not change the way that inputs are categorised in the fair value hierarchy. Prices obtained from a pricing service are not considered observable simply because they were obtained from a third party.

2.4.300.20   The IFRS Interpretations Committee discussed the classification of prices provided by third parties within the fair value hierarchy. The Committee noted that when assets or liabilities are measured on the basis of prices provided by third parties, the classification of those measurements within the fair value hierarchy depends on the evaluation of the inputs used by the third party to derive those prices; it is not based on the pricing methodology used. Therefore, the Committee noted that a fair value measurement that is based on prices provided by third parties may be categorised within Level 1 only if the measurement relies solely on unadjusted quoted prices in an active market for an identical instrument that the entity can access at the measurement date (see 2.4.270). [*IU 01-15*]

2.4.300.30   An entity using a pricing service needs to understand the source of the inputs used by the pricing service in order to properly categorise any fair value measurements based on those inputs. For example, if a pricing service provides an unadjusted quoted price from an active market for an identical instrument, then a fair value measurement based only on that price would be a Level 1 measurement. Alternatively, if the pricing service provides prices based on in-house models, then any resulting fair value measurement would be a Level 2 or Level 3 measurement, depending on the observability and significance of the inputs used in the model for the measurement and for adjusting other inputs. [*IFRS 13.73, 75–76, A*]

EXAMPLE 12 – PRICE PROVIDED BY A THIRD PARTY PRICING SERVICE – FAIR VALUE HIERARCHY

2.4.300.40   Company H is a party to an interest rate swap transaction in an over-the-counter (OTC) market. There are no quoted prices in the OTC market for interest rate swaps that are identical to H's swap. H obtains rates from Company R, which provides pricing services, to use in the measurement of the fair value of the swap. To provide H with the rates, R uses transaction rates for similar swaps in the OTC market.

2.4.300.50   Although similar swaps may have been transacted in the OTC market, these swaps have different counterparties as well as different fixed coupons and residual maturities, and therefore are not identical to H's interest rate swap. The price at which H would be able to sell its interest rate swap would result from a negotiated transaction taking into account the credit ratings of the two parties to the swap and the terms of the specific swap.

2.4.300.60   Because H's swap is not identical to similar swaps for which there are transactions in the OTC market, the price cannot be categorised as a Level 1 measurement, but as Level 2 or Level 3 depending on whether significant unobservable inputs are used to produce the price.

2.4.300.70   In some cases, pricing services may provide Level 2 inputs determined using a matrix pricing methodology, even though Level 1 inputs are available to both the entity and the pricing service (see 2.4.280.100). Using Level 2 inputs in these situations is not appropriate unless the entity meets the criteria in 2.4.280.70–90. If these criteria are not met, then the entity obtains quoted prices in active markets (Level 1 inputs) either from the pricing service or from other sources. [*IFRS 13.79(a)*]

2.4.300.80   Consensus pricing services obtain information from multiple subscribers who each submit prices to the pricing service. The pricing service returns consensus prices to each subscriber based on the data received. In assessing consensus data, it is important to understand what the prices submitted represent. If the estimates provided to the service do not represent executable quotes or are not based on observable prices, then a fair value measurement derived from the consensus price will be a Level 3 measurement. However, if the inputs to the price received from the pricing service are Level 1 or Level 2 inputs, then the use of those prices will generally result in a Level 2 measurement. [*IFRS 13.73*]

2.4.300.90   Similar considerations apply to prices obtained from brokers. A broker quote is not generally a binding offer. Even if it is, it may not represent the price at which an orderly transaction would take place between market participants. If a broker quote reflects actual current market transactions in an identical instrument, then it may be a Level 1 or Level 2 input. However, if a broker quote is an indicative price based on the broker's valuation models, then it is a Level 2 or Level 3 input, depending on the significance and observability of the inputs to the model – i.e. as with a price from a pricing service, an indicative price from a broker is not automatically considered to be an observable input merely because it has been obtained from a third party. See also 2.4.480.110. [*IFRS 13.73, A, B34(c)*]

2.4.300.100   In the case of centrally cleared derivatives, the central clearing organisation provides a daily value mark that is used to calculate the variation margin – i.e. the daily amount that is paid by or to a clearing member reflecting the change in the value of the collateral (for collateralised-to-market derivatives) or the daily settlement amount (for settled-to-market derivatives). For a discussion of the recognition and derecognition of variation margin payments and receipts, see 7.6.490.

2.4.300.110   The valuation technique used by the central clearing organisation for both collateralised and settled-to-market derivatives might not be consistent with IFRS 13. This is because each clearing organisation may calculate variation margins differently and the margin may reflect assumptions specific to the clearing organisation rather than being consistent with those that a market participant would make. The daily settlement amount is not a quoted transaction price or an exit price in an active market. This amount may not represent a price at which an entity would be able to sell or assign its derivative exposure to another market participant. Although for derivative contracts cleared under a settled-to-market model, the value provided by a central clearing organisation may be used for daily settlements, the marking of a daily settlement payment does not extinguish the transaction and future payments and receipts will arise in accordance with its terms and conditions. For these reasons, an entity cannot generally rely solely on the central clearing organisation's value when measuring the fair value of the derivative. [*IFRS 13.22*]

2.4.300.120   Although the clearing organisation is not a market maker, the inputs to its calculation of value for variation margin purposes will generally reflect a selection of market data and may be close to but not necessarily the same as a fair value calculated by market participants. Therefore, the value mark may be a meaningful data point and may serve as a starting point for measuring fair value. An entity using a central clearing organisation needs to understand the source of the information used by the clearing organisation in order to properly categorise any fair value measurements based on those inputs.

2.4.300.130   When the daily variation payments on a settled-to-market derivative are considered settlements on the underlying trade (and therefore give rise to a partial derecognition of the derivative asset or liability), the derivative continues to exist but generally has a current fair value of zero (or close to zero) immediately following the daily settlement payment (see 7.6.490.120–140).

MEASURING FAIR VALUE
2.4.310

Fair value on initial recognition
2.4.320

2.4.320.10   If an asset is acquired (or a liability assumed), then the transaction price paid for the asset (or received to assume the liability) normally reflects an entry price. However, IFRS 13 requires fair value measurements to be based on an exit price (see 2.4.60). Although conceptually different, in many cases the exit and entry price are equal and therefore fair value on initial recognition generally equals the transaction price. [*IFRS 13.57–58*]

2.4.320.20   However, entities are required to take into account factors specific to the transaction and the asset or liability that might indicate that the transaction price and initial fair value measurement may differ. These may include:
- the transaction being between related parties;
- the transaction taking place under duress – e.g. if the seller is experiencing financial difficulty;
- the unit of account represented by the transaction price differing from the unit of account of the asset or liability measured at fair value – e.g. if the transaction price represents the purchase of multiple items;
- the transaction price (i.e. entry or purchase price) is not the price within the bid-offer spread that is most representative of fair value (i.e. an exit or selling price) – this may apply when an entity uses bid prices for asset positions and ask prices for liabilities; and/or
- the market in which the transaction takes place being different from the principal (or most advantageous) market. [*IFRS 13.70, B4*]

2.4.320.30   The presence of one or more of these factors does not automatically result in a fair value measurement that differs from the transaction price. For example, the price in a related party transaction may be used as an input into a fair value measurement if the entity has evidence that the transaction was entered into on market terms. [*IFRS 13.B4(a)*]

EXAMPLE 13 – DIFFERENCE BETWEEN TRANSACTION PRICE AND FAIR VALUE ON INITIAL RECOGNITION

2.4.320.40   Company R, a retail counterparty, enters into an interest rate swap in a retail market with Company D, a dealer, for no initial consideration – i.e. the transaction price is zero.
- D can access both the retail market (i.e. with retail counterparties) and the dealer market (i.e. with dealer counterparties).
- R can only access the retail market.

2.4.320.50   From the perspective of D, the dealer market is the principal market for the swap, which is different from the market in which it initially entered into the swap transaction (the retail market). Therefore, for D the transaction price of zero may not necessarily represent the fair value of the swap on initial recognition.

2.4.320.60   Conversely, R cannot access the dealer market, and the retail market is the principal market from its perspective. If R were to transfer its rights and obligations under the swap, then it would do so with a dealer counterparty in that retail market. Therefore, the transaction price of zero represents the fair value of the swap to R on initial recognition (ignoring the potential effect of the bid-ask spread). [*IFRS 13.IE24–IE26*]

2.4.320.70   In another example, it may be appropriate to measure the fair value of a hybrid instrument based on the separate fair value measurements of its individual components – i.e. the host contract and one or more embedded derivatives – if that is how market participants would price the instrument in the principal (or most advantageous) market for the hybrid instrument. If the resulting measurement on initial recognition is different from the transaction price, then the entity considers these factors in order to conclude whether it is an appropriate measure of fair value.

2.4.320.80   A day one gain or loss arises if the transaction price for an asset and/or liability differs from the fair value used to measure it on initial recognition. IFRS 13 requires day one gains or losses to be recognised in profit or loss, unless the IFRS that requires or permits fair value measurement specifies otherwise. For a discussion of this issue in the context of financial instruments, see 7.7.40. [*IFRS 13.60, BC135*]

2.4.320.90   Because transaction costs are not a component of a fair value measurement, they do not represent a difference between an exit price and an entry price (see 2.4.110). [*IFRS 13.BC33*]

EXAMPLE 14 – EFFECT OF TRANSACTION COSTS

2.4.320.100   In the following chart, a seller sells an asset in an orderly transaction at a price of 100. The seller pays broker commission of 5% out of the proceeds of the sale, and the buyer incurs transaction costs of 2.

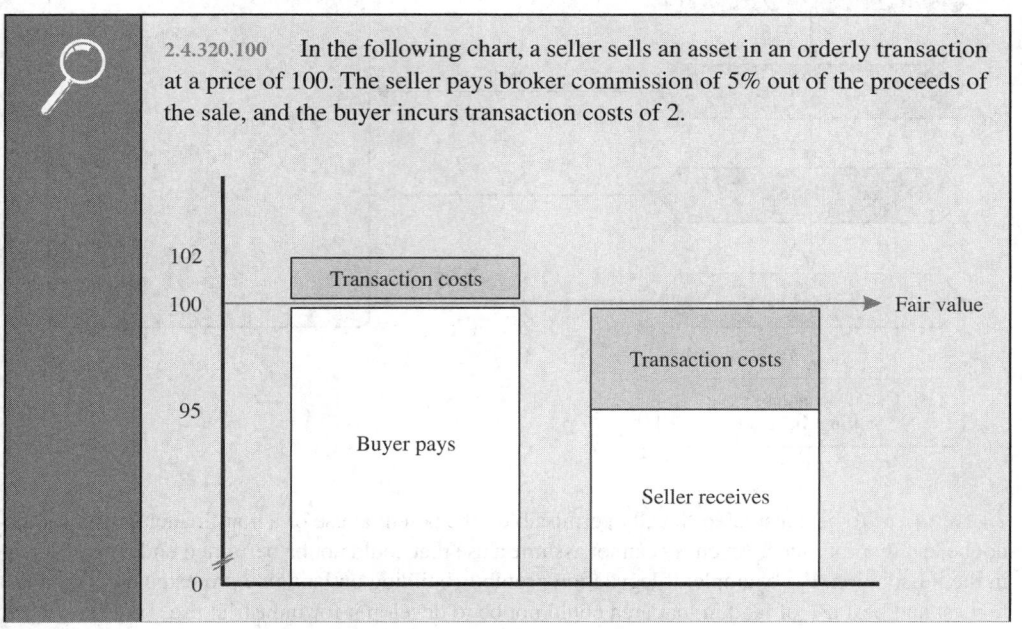

> 2.4.320.110   In this example, fair value is 100 and not 95 (100 exit price less 5 transaction costs). From the buyer's perspective, the fair value is the same – i.e. 100. The buyer's transaction costs of 2 are also not part of the fair value measurement.

2.4.320.120   Bid-ask spreads may represent a difference between an entry and exit price in markets for financial instruments, or if an intermediary is needed to bring together a buyer and a seller (see 2.4.250). [*IFRS 13.BC165*]

2.4.330   Highest and best use

2.4.340   *General principles*

2.4.340.10   'Highest and best use' is a valuation concept that represents the use of a non-financial asset by market participants that would maximise the value of the asset or the group of assets and liabilities (e.g. a business) within which the asset would be used. This concept does not apply to financial assets or liabilities or own equity instruments because they do not have alternative uses. [*IFRS 13.A, BC63, BC65*]

2.4.340.20   A fair value measurement of a non-financial asset considers a market participant's ability to generate economic benefits by using the asset at its highest and best use or by selling it to another market participant who would use the asset in its highest and best use; it is most often relevant in measuring the fair value of real estate. The following flowchart illustrates the factors to be considered in identifying the highest and best use. [*IFRS 13.27–28*]

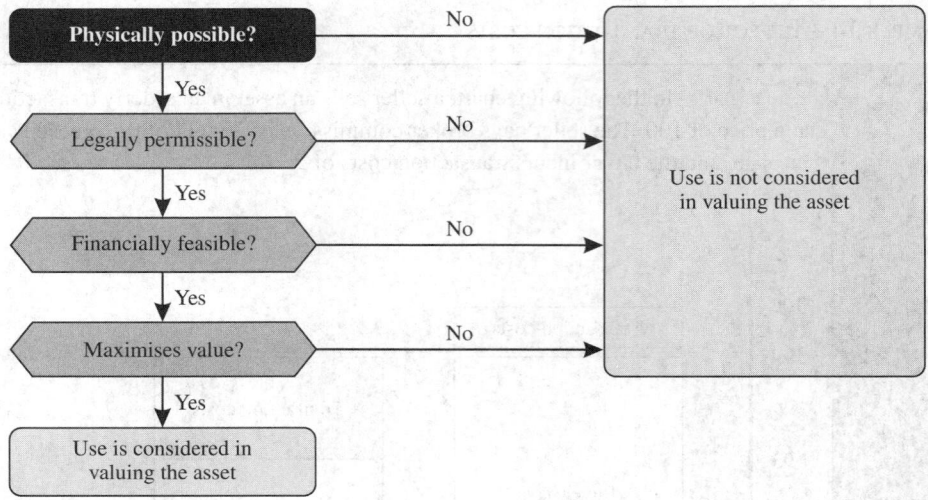

2.4.340.30   To be considered 'legally permissible', the potential use of a non-financial asset should not be legally prohibited. An entity cannot assume a use that could not be permitted under current law in the jurisdiction. For example, if legislation prohibits building on land in a protected area, then the highest and best use of land in that area could not be to develop it for industrial use. However, a use of an asset does not need to be legal at the measurement date. For example, a fair value measurement of land and buildings assumes zoning different from the current zoning if market participants would assume such a change in zoning. In such circumstances, the fair value measurement would incorporate the cost to convert the asset and obtain a different zoning permission, including the risk and uncertainty that such permission would not be granted. [*IFRS 13.BC69*]

EXAMPLE 15 – HIGHEST AND BEST USE – VALUE OF LAND

2.4.340.40   Company X acquired a brewery that is located in an area that has recently been re-zoned to allow both residential and industrial use. X determines that market participants would take into account the potential to develop the brewery site for residential use in pricing the land on which the brewery is currently located.

2.4.340.50   Therefore, X measures the fair value of the land based on the higher of:
- the value of the land as currently developed as a brewery; and
- the value of the land as a vacant site for residential use, taking into account the costs of demolishing the brewery and other costs necessary to convert the land to a vacant site. [*IFRS 13.IE7–IE8*]

2.4.340.60   In the absence of evidence to the contrary, the entity's current use of an asset is assumed to be its highest and best use. This means that an entity is not required to engage in exhaustive efforts to identify other potential highest and best uses. However, if readily available market information or other factors suggest that a different use by a market participant would maximise the value of the asset, then such information should not be ignored. The basis for conclusions to IFRS 13 notes the IASB's expectation that, after considering the cost to convert an asset to an alternative use, the entity's current use would generally be its highest and best use. [*IFRS 13.29, BC71*]

2.4.340.70   An entity may not intend to actively use a non-financial asset for reasons such as:
- the existence of an overlap with existing assets; or
- an intention to protect its competitive position. [*IFRS 13.30*]

2.4.340.80   Notwithstanding its actual use by an entity, the fair value of a non-financial asset is measured assuming that it is used by market participants in its highest and best use. This use will depend on the characteristics of market participants (see 2.4.90). [*IFRS 13.30*]

2.4.340.90   In evaluating the highest and best use to market participants, the possible perspectives of financial and strategic buyers may be considered to determine the asset's highest and best use. In general, the key difference between the two categories of potential market participants is that strategic buyers have existing operations and may have complementary assets with which an intangible asset, for example, may be used either actively or defensively, whereas financial buyers do not. There are exceptions, such as when financial buyers have existing investments in a specific market with which acquired assets may be used or when financial buyers may be pursuing a roll-up strategy. [*IFRS 13.27, 29–30*]

2.4.340.100   The highest and best use of an intangible asset to market participants may be to actively use the intangible asset with other assets, including potentially other assets already owned by the market participants. This use could apply to both financial and strategic buyers. Alternatively, the highest and best use may be to use the intangible asset defensively in a manner that results in a highest and best use of a group of complementary assets. This may be the highest and best use for strategic buyers, but would be less likely to apply to financial buyers who are more likely to use the intangible asset actively. [*IFRS 13.27, 29–31*]

EXAMPLE 16 – HIGHEST AND BEST USE – VALUE OF A BRAND

2.4.340.110   Company B acquires a brand in a business combination. B decides not to use the brand on the assumption that its removal from the market will generate greater incremental value as a result of increased revenues from its existing brands. However, a market participant would choose to continue to use the brand, because it would not hold the other brands that B does.

2.4.340.120   In this example, the fair value of the brand would be based on its continued use, because a market participant would choose to continue actively using the brand. This is despite the fact that B's decision not to use the brand results in higher benefits to B.

2.4.350   ***In combination vs stand-alone***

2.4.350.10   A fair value measurement of a non-financial asset is based on its use either:
- in combination with other assets as a group or in combination with other assets and liabilities; or
- on a stand-alone basis. [*IFRS 13.31*]

2.4.350.20   The valuation premise depends on the use that is consistent with the perspective of market participants of the non-financial asset's highest and best use. [*IFRS 13.31*]

2.4.350.30   If the highest and best use would be to use a non-financial asset in combination with other assets, then it is assumed that the other assets would also be available to market participants, and that this would be considered in pricing the asset. However, the fair value measurement assumes that the asset is sold consistent with the unit of account specified in other standards (see 2.4.80). [*IFRS 13.31(a)(i), 32*]

2.4.350.40   If the highest and best use is to use the asset in combination with other assets, then the same valuation premise is used for the other non-financial assets with which it would be used. [*IFRS 13.31(a)(iii)*]

EXAMPLE 17 – CUSTOMER RELATIONSHIP

2.4.350.50   Company B acquired contractual customer relationships and technology assets as part of a business combination. B considers the following in determining whether the highest and best use of the customer relationships would be on a stand-alone basis or in combination with complementary assets.

- The relationships with customers arose in the context of the sale of a product incorporating the technology. A market participant without complementary technology would probably realise lower value from the customer relationships, because of the probability of lower expected sales.
- However, a market participant with access to complementary technology would probably realise higher sales and profits than on a stand-alone basis and would consider this in valuing the customer relationships.

2.4.350.60   In this example, the valuation premise for the customer relationships would therefore be in combination with the technology – i.e. an in-combination valuation premise. Similarly, the same analysis would apply to the technology – i.e. the technology would be more valuable as a result of its use with customer relationships.

2.4.360   **Liabilities and own equity instruments**

2.4.360.10   IFRS 13 contains specific requirements for applying the fair value measurement framework to liabilities (including financial liabilities) and an entity's own equity instruments. The following flowchart illustrates the process that an entity uses in measuring the fair value of such items. [*IFRS 13.37–41, 79(c)*]

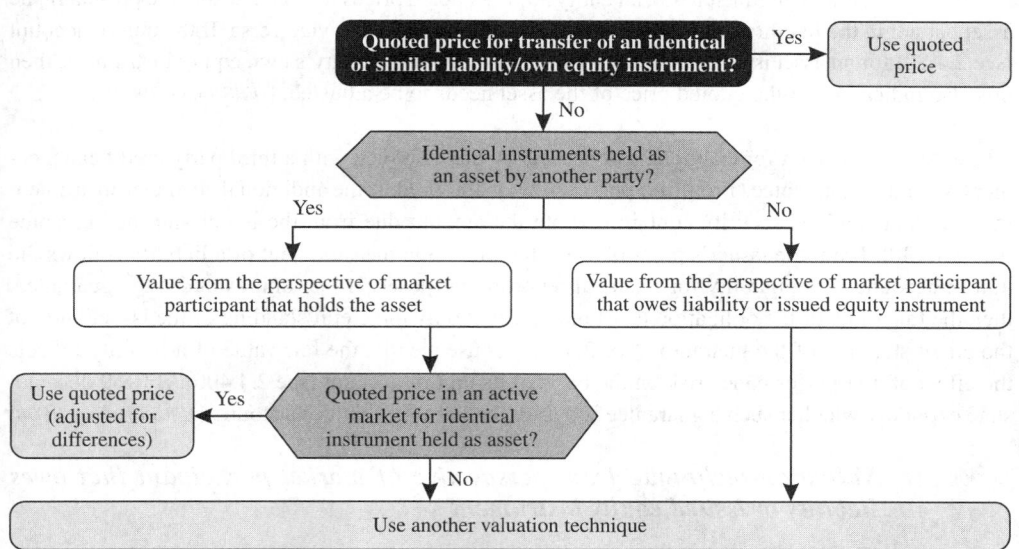

2.4.370   *Quoted price for transfer of liability or own equity instrument*

2.4.370.10   In measuring the fair value of a liability or an entity's own equity instrument, it is assumed that the item is transferred to a market participant at the measurement date – e.g. the liability remains outstanding and the market participant transferee would be required to fulfil it. It is also assumed that the non-performance risk related to a liability is the same before and after the transfer. For a discussion of non-performance risk, see 2.4.400. [*IFRS 13.34, 42*]

2.4.370.20   The transfer notion is conceptually consistent with the exit price concept (see 2.4.60). In our experience, there are many cases in which there is no observable market to provide pricing information about the transfer of a liability or an entity's own equity instruments. Also, in many cases an entity may not be able to transfer its liability to a third party. However, there may be an observable market for such items if they are held by other parties as assets. Therefore, the fair values of most financial liabilities and own equity instruments are measured from the perspective of a market participant that holds the identical instrument as an asset (see 2.4.380). [*IFRS 13.35, 37, BC81*]

2.4.370.30   Furthermore, the transfer notion reflects the fact that fair value is a market-based and not an entity-specific measurement. For example, the expected costs to an entity to fulfil an obligation may be lower than the price to transfer it to a market participant, because the entity has advantages relative to the market. However, even in such cases an entity is required to measure fair value based on the price that would be paid to transfer the liability. [*IFRS 13.BC81*]

2.4.380   *Measurement from perspective of market participant that holds identical asset*

2.4.380.10   If there is no quoted price for the transfer of an identical or a similar liability or an entity's own equity instruments, and another market participant holds the identical item as an asset, then the entity measures the item's fair value from the perspective of such a market participant. [*IFRS 13.37*]

2.4.380.20   In these circumstances, an entity adjusts quoted prices for features that are present in the asset but not in the liability or the entity's own equity instrument, or vice versa. If the unit of account (see 2.4.80) for an asset is not the same as for the liability or the entity's own equity instrument, then this also indicates that the quoted price of the asset needs to be adjusted. [*IFRS 13.39, 79(c)*]

2.4.380.30   Consider, for example, a debt security that is issued with a third party credit enhancement such as a guarantee. From the perspective of the holder, the individual financial instrument may be the combined security containing both the amount due from the issuer and the guarantee (see 7.1.130). From the issuer's point of view, the fair value measurement of a liability follows the unit of account of the liability for financial reporting purposes. If that unit excludes the guarantee, then the fair value of the obligation takes into account only the credit standing of the issuer and not the credit standing of the guarantor (see 2.4.80). Consequently, the fair value of a liability reflects the effect of non-performance risk on the basis of its unit of account (see 2.4.400). IFRS 9 does not state explicitly whether such a guarantee is part of the liability's unit of account. [*IFRS 13.39(b), BC98*]

2.4.390   *Valuation technique from perspective of market participant that owes liability or issued equity instrument*

2.4.390.10   There may be liabilities or an entity's own equity instruments that are not held by another party as an asset and for which there is no quoted price for the transfer of an identical or similar liability or own equity instrument – e.g. for some decommissioning liabilities assumed in a business combination. In such cases, an entity uses a valuation technique to measure the fair value of the item from the perspective of a market participant that owes the liability or that issued the equity instrument. In using a present value technique, an entity estimates the future cash outflows that market participants would expect to incur in fulfilling the obligation. This would include any compensation for risk and the profit margin that a market participant would require to undertake the activity. [*IFRS 13.40–41(a), B31–B33*]

2.4.390.20   The risk adjustment is often the most difficult factor to quantify in a fair value measurement of a non-financial liability. Estimating the risk adjustment, as well as other inputs, may be especially difficult if an entity has an obligation with a unique or unusual risk – as opposed to situations in which there are several obligations with similar risks. In the latter case, the entity may have experience from previous outcomes that enables it to estimate the range of possible results. Also, the price that a market participant might require to assume an obligation may reflect possible portfolio diversification effects. For example, if outcomes are not perfectly correlated, then negative outcomes may be (partially) offset by positive outcomes. In that case, a market participant may demand a lower risk premium. A greater risk adjustment would be likely if the inputs to a fair value measurement were more uncertain.

2.4.390.30   An entity may estimate future cash outflows that market participants would expect to incur in fulfilling the obligation by taking the following steps:
- estimate the cash flows that the entity would incur in fulfilling the obligation;
- exclude the cash flows that other market participants would not incur;
- include the cash flows that other market participants would incur but that the entity would not incur; and
- estimate the profit margin that a market participant would require to assume the obligation. [*IFRS 13.41(a), B31*]

2.4.400   *Non-performance risk, including credit risk*

2.4.400.10   The fair value of a liability reflects the effect of 'non-performance risk', which is the risk that an entity will not fulfil an obligation. Non-performance risk is assumed to be the same before and after the transfer of the liability. Non-performance risk includes, but may not be limited to, an entity's own credit risk. 'Credit risk' is defined as the risk that one party to a financial instrument will cause a financial loss for the other party by failing to discharge an obligation. See also 2.4.460 and 7.10.520. [*IFRS 13.42, A, 7.A*]

2.4.400.20   The effect of non-performance risk may differ depending on:
- the nature of the liability – e.g. whether the liability is an obligation to deliver cash (a financial liability) or an obligation to deliver goods or services (a non-financial liability); and
- the terms of credit enhancements related to the liability, if there are any – e.g. a pledge of assets against default. [*IFRS 13.43*]

2.4.400.30   The fair value of a liability reflects the effect of non-performance risk on the basis of its unit of account. Therefore, the issuer of a liability that is issued with an inseparable third party credit enhancement does not include the effect of that credit enhancement in the liability's fair value measurement if it accounts separately for the liability and the credit enhancement. Consequently, if the liability is a separate unit of account from the perspective of the issuing entity, then the fair value of that liability reflects the issuer's own non-performance risk and not that of the guarantor. See also 2.4.80 and 380.20–30. [*IFRS 13.43–44*]

2.4.400.35   Generally, an expected present value technique is used to measure the fair value of a decommissioning liability. An entity is not precluded from using a discount rate adjustment technique or a technique based on a market approach. However, applying these techniques is rare because observable market prices, including market interest rates for decommissioning liabilities, generally do not exist. [*IFRS 13.B31–B33*]

EXAMPLE 18 – FAIR VALUE OF A STAND-ALONE DECOMMISSIONING LIABILITY

2.4.400.40   On 1 November 2018, Company B assumes a decommissioning liability in a business combination and is therefore required to measure the liability at fair value in the acquisition accounting. B is legally required to remediate a mine pit at the end of its useful life, which is estimated to be in 10 years. B uses a present value technique to measure the fair value of the decommissioning liability.

2.4.400.50   If B were allowed to transfer its decommissioning liability to a market participant, then B concludes that a market participant would use all of the following inputs in estimating the price.

Labour costs	100
Allocated overhead and equipment costs – 60% of labour costs	60
Third party contractor margin of 20%, based on margins that contractors in the industry generally receive for similar activities – 160 x 20%	32
Annual inflation rate of 4%, based on market data for the applicable jurisdiction – 192 x 4% compounded for 10 years	92
5% risk adjustment that reflects the compensation that an external party would require in order to accept the risk that the cash flows might differ from those expected given the uncertainty in locking in today's price for a project that will not occur for 10 years – 284 x 5%	14
A risk-free rate based on 10-year government bonds in the applicable jurisdiction	5%
An adjustment to the discount rate to reflect B's non-performance risk, including its credit risk	3%

2.4.400.60   The following chart shows the make-up of these costs to give a fair value of the decommissioning liability of 138: present value at 8% of 298 (100 + 60 + 32 + 92 + 14) in 10 years.

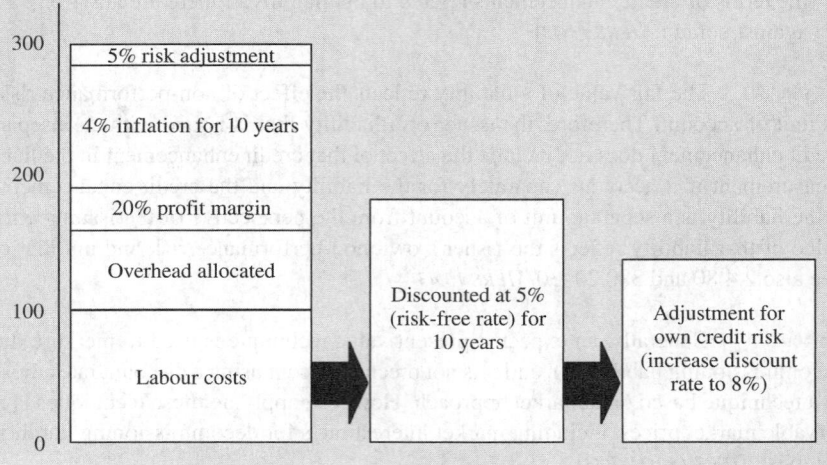

> 2.4.400.70   The adjustment for the time value of money is shown separately from the credit risk adjustment, to illustrate the direction of the adjustment. However, in our experience only one discount rate calculation would be undertaken. [*IFRS 13.IE35–IE39*]

2.4.400.80   As Example 18 shows, the adjustment for the entity's own non-performance risk has reduced the fair value of the liability – just as higher credit risk reduces the fair value of a financial asset.

2.4.410   *Restrictions on transfer of liabilities or own equity instruments, or on sale of related asset*

2.4.410.10   Separate inputs to reflect restrictions on the transfer of a liability or an entity's own equity instruments are not included in the fair value of a liability or an entity's own equity instruments. Such a restriction is assumed to be reflected implicitly or explicitly in the other inputs used by market participants to price such instruments. Therefore, if the effect of a restriction is already included in the other inputs, then an additional input or adjustment to reflect a restriction on transferability results in double counting. [*IFRS 13.45–46, BC99*]

2.4.410.20   Consequently, in measuring a liability or an entity's own equity instruments from the perspective of a market participant that holds the item as an asset, an entity ensures that the price of the asset does not reflect the effect of a restriction preventing the sale of that asset. It is assumed that restrictions on the sale of an asset relate to the marketability of that asset, whereas restrictions on the corresponding liability relate to performance of the obligation (see 2.4.70 and 240). [*IFRS 13.39, BC100*]

2.4.420   *Financial liabilities with demand feature#*

2.4.420.10   The fair value of a financial liability with a demand feature cannot be less than the amount payable on demand, discounted from the first date on which the amount could be required to be paid. [*IFRS 13.47*]

EXAMPLE 19 – FINANCIAL LIABILITY WITH DEMAND FEATURE

2.4.420.20   Bank B offers a fixed rate savings deposit product whereby individuals deposit an amount of 1,000 on 1 January 2018 for a period of two years. This product provides a fixed return of 5% per annum, giving a return of 103 after two years. The individuals are able to withdraw their money after one year, but in this case the total amount paid would only be 1,040. Assume that the market interest rate is 8% one year after inception of the deposit.

2.4.420.30   In this example, B calculates the present value of its liability at 31 December 2018, considering the remainder of the original period of two years, at an amount of 1,021 (1,103 discounted for one year by 8%). However, the fair value of the financial liability at 31 December 2018 is not less than the amount payable on demand, which is 1,040. Therefore, the fair value of the liability is measured at 1,040.

2.4.425   *Fair value less costs of disposal of a CGU containing a decommissioning liability*

2.4.425.10   Under IAS 36, recognised liabilities are considered in determining the recoverable amount of a CGU when the disposal of the CGU would require the buyer to assume the liability. For example, a decommissioning liability is generally considered in determining the recoverable amount of a CGU that is tested for impairment (see 3.10.240.120). In this case, the fair value less costs of disposal (or the estimated cash flow from ultimate disposal) is the price to sell the assets of the CGU together with the decommissioning liability. [*IAS 36.78*]

2.4.425.20   When the fair value less costs of disposal of a CGU containing a decommissioning liability is calculated using discounted cash flows, a question arises about how the liability should be factored into the fair value measurement. The approach used needs to be consistent with how a market participant would determine fair value. The approach to measuring the decommissioning liability, including the discount rate applied, may vary over the life of a project. In our experience, there are two approaches used in practice.
- *Approach 1:* The CGU's assets and the decommissioning liability are treated as one unit of valuation.
- *Approach 2:* The CGU's assets and the decommissioning liability are treated as two separate units of valuation.

2.4.425.30   In our experience, Approach 1 in 2.4.425.20 is the more commonly used approach when decommissioning is expected to occur very far in the future. Under this approach, a market participant considers the risk and return profile of the assets and the liability of the CGU as one unit of valuation and considers the liability's cash flows as part of the overall project's cash flows, rather than valuing the liability on a stand-alone basis. Therefore, an entity applies a single discount rate – such as the weighted-average cost of capital (WACC) – to all cash flows, including the cash outflows for a decommissioning liability. When developing the cost of equity as an input into the determination of the WACC, the selected beta is often derived from comparable publicly traded businesses that have decommissioning liabilities.

2.4.425.40   Later in a CGU's life, the cash inflows from the CGU's assets may become insignificant compared with the cash outflows to cover the liability. As a result, a market participant is more likely to apply Approach 2 in 2.4.425.20, which allows separate consideration of the remaining cash inflows and the decommissioning outflows. Under this approach, an entity measures the fair value of the CGU excluding the decommissioning liability and then deducts from it the stand-alone fair value of the liability. The underlying assumption in this approach is that a market participant would consider the risk and return profile of the assets of the CGU and the related decommissioning liability separately as two units of valuation. In such cases, the fair value of the CGU excluding the decommissioning liability is determined using a relevant market participant rate specific to the assets only and the fair value of the decommissioning liability is determined as the amount that would be paid to a third party to assume the liability (see 2.4.400.35–70).

2.4.425.50   The discount rate applied to the cash flows generated by the CGU in Approach 1 differs from that applied to the cash flows excluding the liability in Approach 2. This is because excluding the decommissioning liability under Approach 2 changes the riskiness of the cash flows.

2.4.430   Portfolio measurement

2.4.430.10   An entity that holds a group of financial assets and financial liabilities is exposed to market risks – i.e. interest rate risk, currency risk and other price risk – and to the credit risk of each of the counterparties. If certain conditions are met, then IFRS 13 permits an entity to measure the fair value of a group of financial assets and financial liabilities with offsetting risk positions on the basis of its net exposure. [*IFRS 13.48*]

2.4.430.20   Under the exception, the fair value of the group is measured on the basis of the price that would be received to sell a net long position (or paid to transfer a net short position) for a particular risk exposure in an orderly transaction between market participants at the measurement date. Therefore, application of the portfolio measurement exception is considered to be consistent with the way in which market participants would price the net risk position at the measurement date. [*IFRS 13.BC119*]

2.4.430.30   In our view, application of the portfolio measurement exception changes the unit of account from the individual financial asset or financial liability to the net position for a particular risk exposure (see 2.4.80). Accordingly, we believe that the size of the net risk exposure is a characteristic to be considered in measuring the fair value of the net risk exposure (see 2.4.240). [*IFRS 13.14, 48, 53, 56, 69*]

2.4.430.40   An entity is permitted to apply the portfolio measurement exception to a group of financial assets, financial liabilities and other contracts that are in the scope of IFRS 9 – i.e. the portfolio may include contracts to buy or sell a non-financial item that are accounted for in accordance with IFRS 9 (see 7.1.200) – if the answer to all of the questions in the following flowchart is 'yes'. [*IFRS 13.48–49, 52, BC47(b), BC119A–BC119B*]

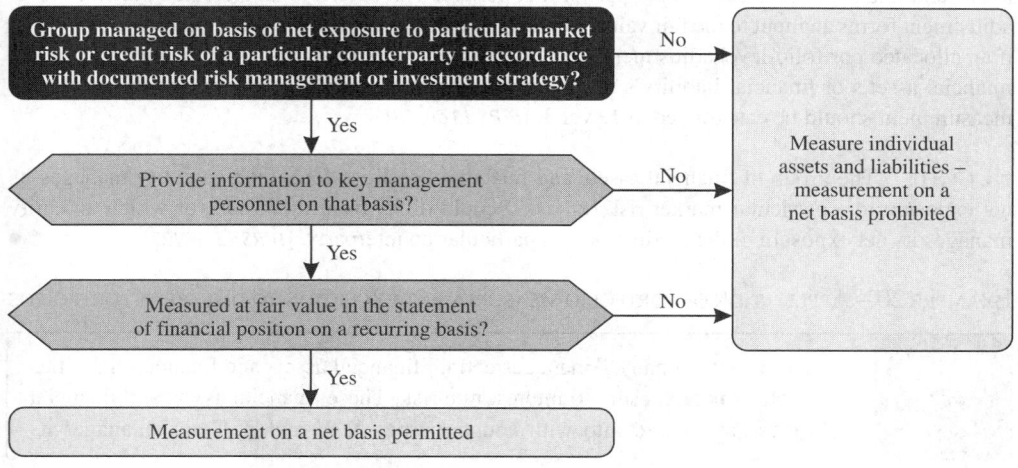

2.4.430.50   Judgement may be required to evaluate whether, based on the specific facts and circumstances, it is appropriate to apply the exception.

2.4.430.60   If the entity is permitted to use the exception, then it chooses an accounting policy, to be applied consistently, for a particular portfolio. However, an entity is not required to maintain a static portfolio. [*IFRS 13.51, BC121*]

2.4.430.70   The exception does not apply to financial statement presentation. Therefore, if an entity applies the exception, then the basis of measurement of a group of financial instruments might differ from the basis of presentation. For example, a portfolio of derivative financial instruments might be measured based on the price of the entity's net exposure to a particular market risk (or the credit risk of a particular counterparty). If the entity presents those derivative assets and derivative liabilities separately in its statement of financial position (see 7.10.110), then the portfolio-level adjustments – e.g. bid-ask adjustment or credit risk adjustments – are allocated to the individual assets and liabilities on a reasonable and consistent basis. [*IFRS 13.50*]

2.4.430.80   The exception also does not apply to hedge accounting. Therefore, for assessing hedge effectiveness and measuring ineffectiveness, an entity needs to determine the individual risk adjustments (in particular, credit risk adjustments) to arrive at the fair values of the individual hedging derivatives or the appropriate credit risk adjustment for a group of derivatives that have been designated together as the hedging instrument in a single hedging relationship. In our view, the entity should adopt a reasonable and consistently applied methodology for allocating credit risk adjustments determined at a portfolio level to individual derivative instruments for the purpose of measuring the fair values of individual hedging instruments that are used in assessing effectiveness and measuring hedge ineffectiveness (see 7.9.850.50). [*IFRS 13.50*]

2.4.430.90   For a discussion of potential bases of allocating portfolio-level adjustments related to credit risk, see 2.4.450.20–40.

2.4.430.100   If an entity applies the exception, then the portfolio-level adjustments are considered in categorising, in the fair value hierarchy, the fair value measurements of the individual financial assets and financial liabilities that are part of that portfolio. In our view, an allocated portfolio-level adjustment forms an input to the fair value measurement of the individual asset or liability. Therefore, if an allocated portfolio-level adjustment is an unobservable input and has a significant effect on the financial asset's or financial liability's fair value measurement, then we believe that this fair value measurement should be categorised as Level 3. [*IFRS 13.50, 73*]

2.4.430.110   The group of financial assets and financial liabilities for which an entity manages its net exposure to a particular market risk (or risks) could differ from the group for which an entity manages its net exposure to the credit risk of a particular counterparty. [*IFRS 13.BC127*]

EXAMPLE 20 – APPLICATION OF PORTFOLIO MEASUREMENT EXCEPTION TO DIFFERENT PORTFOLIOS

2.4.430.120   Company T manages certain financial assets and financial liabilities based on its net exposure to interest rate risk. These financial assets and financial liabilities are entered into with counterparties X, Y and Z. T also manages its

financial assets and financial liabilities with counterparty X, regardless of market risk exposure, based on the net exposure to X's credit risk.

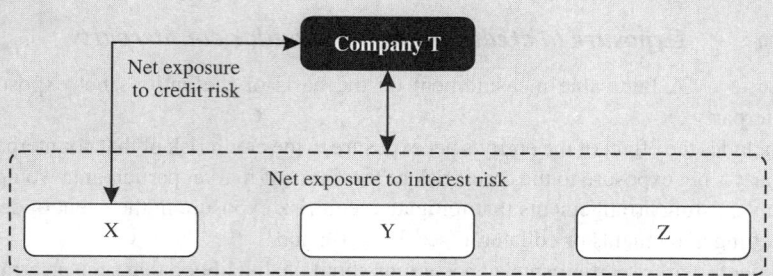

2.4.430.130   Therefore, assuming that all other criteria are met, a financial asset or a financial liability of T that is subject to interest rate risk and that is entered into with counterparty X, is both part of one group that may be measured based on the price for the net exposure to interest rate risk and of another group that may be measured based on the price for the net exposure to X's credit risk.

2.4.440   *Exposure to market risk*

2.4.440.10   An entity that measures fair value on the basis of its net exposure to a particular market risk (or risks):

- applies the price within the bid-ask spread that is most representative of fair value (see 2.4.250); and
- ensures that the nature and duration of the risk(s) to which the exception is applied are substantially the same. [*IFRS 13.53–55*]

2.4.440.20   Any basis risk resulting from market risk parameters that are not identical is reflected in the fair value of the net position. For example, if an entity manages its interest rate risk on a net portfolio basis, then it may include financial instruments with different interest rate bases in one portfolio. However, any difference in the interest rate bases – e.g. GBP LIBOR vs UK treasury yields – is reflected in the fair value measurement. [*IFRS 13.54, BC123*]

EXAMPLE 21A – NATURE OF MARKET RISKS

2.4.440.30   Company B cannot combine interest rate risk associated with a financial asset with the commodity price risk associated with a financial liability. The nature of these risks is not substantially the same; therefore, based on these risks, these financial instruments do not qualify for the portfolio measurement exception. [*IFRS 13.54, BC123*]

EXAMPLE 21B – DURATION OF MARKET RISKS

2.4.440.40   Company C has a 12-month futures contract to offset 12 months' worth of interest rate risk exposure on a five-year financial instrument. C may be allowed to measure the exposure to 12-month interest rate risk on a net basis. However,

> it measures the interest rate risk exposure from year 2 to year 5 on a gross basis.
> [*IFRS 13.55, BC123*]

2.4.450 *Exposure to credit risk of a particular counterparty*

2.4.450.10   A fair value measurement on the basis of the entity's net exposure to a particular counterparty:
- includes the effect of the entity's net exposure to the credit risk of that counterparty or the counterparty's net exposure to the credit risk of the entity, if market participants would take into account any existing arrangements that mitigate credit risk exposure in the event of default – e.g. master netting agreements or collateral (see 2.4.470); and
- reflects market participants' expectations about the likelihood that such an arrangement would be legally enforceable in the event of default. [*IFRS 13.56*]

2.4.450.20   As discussed in 2.4.430.70–80, when an entity applies the portfolio measurement exception to measure the fair value of a group of financial assets and financial liabilities entered into with a particular counterparty, it may need to allocate the portfolio-level credit risk adjustment to the individual instruments within the portfolio. This allocation is required to be done on a reasonable and consistent basis, although there are no specific examples in IFRS 13. [*IFRS 13.50*]

2.4.450.30   In our experience, the following allocation methods are generally used for allocating credit risk adjustments.
- *Relative fair value approach:* Under this approach, the portfolio-level credit risk adjustment is allocated to the individual instruments in the portfolio based on their relative fair values. There are two methods that are used in practice:
  - allocate the adjustment to all instruments in the portfolio based on their relative fair values; or
  - allocate the adjustment only to those instruments that are in the same position (asset or liability) as the net position with the counterparty, based on their relative fair values; if for example the net position is an asset, then the portfolio-level credit risk adjustment is allocated only to the financial *assets* in the portfolio based on their relative fair values.
- *Relative credit adjustment approach:* Under this approach, the portfolio-level credit risk adjustment is allocated to the individual instruments in the portfolio based on their relative stand-alone credit risk adjustment. The application of this approach requires the entity to calculate the credit risk adjustment both on a gross basis – assuming that the portfolio measurement exception is not applied – and on a net basis.

2.4.450.40   If an entity applies the portfolio measurement exception and the portfolio includes multiple counterparties (see Example 20), then the credit risk adjustment will be considered separately for each individual counterparty. Therefore, the allocation will need to be performed separately for the individual financial assets and financial liabilities with each counterparty.

2.4.460 **Derivatives: Own and counterparty credit risk**

2.4.460.10   A fair value measurement for a liability is based on the price at which it would be transferred to a market participant – assuming that the non-performance risk, including the effect of the entity's own credit risk, remains the same before and after the transfer (see 2.4.370 and 400).

In addition, in the absence of a quoted market price for the transfer of a liability, the liability's fair value is measured from the perspective of a market participant that holds the liability as an asset (see 2.4.380). This would imply consistency between the calculation of own credit risk adjustments and counterparty credit risk adjustments in measuring derivative assets and liabilities. In principle, and assuming no differences in the unit of account, the credit risk adjustments made in the fair value measurement by both counterparties to the financial instrument should be the same. [*IFRS 13.9, 34, 37*]

2.4.460.20   Some derivatives might change from being an asset to a liability or vice versa – e.g. an interest rate swap or a forward contract – because:

- there may be a mixture of expected net cash inflows and expected net cash outflows for different settlement dates; and
- the amounts and direction of cash flows may change as a result of changes in market underlyings.

2.4.460.30   For such derivatives, an entity considers both its own and the counterparty's credit risk if market participants would do so in measuring the fair value of these instruments. Therefore, an entity should design and implement a method for appropriately considering credit risk adjustments in valuing these derivatives. If market participants would consider both counterparty and the entity's own credit risk, but the entity calculates the credit risk adjustment based on a method that considers only the current classification of the derivative (as either an asset or liability), then the entity determines whether additional credit risk adjustments are necessary based on all the expected cash flows of the derivative and the potential for the other classification. [*IFRS 13.11, 42*]

2.4.460.40   In practice, entities often determine an explicit credit valuation adjustment (CVA) to incorporate counterparty credit risk and an explicit debit valuation adjustment (DVA) to incorporate own non-performance risk, as necessary, into the fair value measurement of derivatives. Determining CVAs/DVAs can be complex. In our experience, multiple approaches are used in practice and tailored to an entity's particular facts and circumstances.

2.4.460.50   A CVA adjusts a derivative valuation to reflect the expected losses due to counterparty credit risk. Expected losses are affected by the probability of default, the credit exposure at the time of default and the loss given default. A DVA adjusts a derivative valuation to reflect the counterparty's expected losses due to the entity's own credit risk. A DVA can be thought of as a CVA from the counterparty's perspective.

2.4.460.60   First, an entity assesses whether a CVA/DVA is necessary for measuring the fair value of a derivative. For some derivatives that are valued using a market approach (e.g. exchange-traded futures contracts), the market value already incorporates non-performance risk so determining a separate CVA/DVA is not necessary. In our experience, centrally cleared OTC derivatives (e.g. centrally cleared interest rate swaps) frequently do not have significant CVA/DVA because the margin requirements of the exchange or clearing house minimise the credit risk of those contracts. However, for non-centrally cleared OTC derivatives incorporation of CVA/DVA is often significant (see 2.4.465). [*IFRS 13.42, BC92*]

2.4.460.70   The inclusion of counterparty credit risk and the entity's own credit risk in the fair value measurements of derivative instruments may affect hedging relationships. A change in the fair value of the hedging derivative instrument arising from the counterparty or the entity's own credit risk may affect the hedge effectiveness assessment and hedge ineffectiveness measurement (see 7.9.810 and 850.40).

2.4.465   Uncollateralised and partially collateralised derivatives: Discount rate

2.4.465.10   In our experience, there is no consensus over the most appropriate discount rate to apply in a valuation model used for measuring the fair value of uncollateralised derivatives. Recently, more banks have moved to incorporating funding valuation adjustments (FVA) in their valuations to reflect the cost (or benefit) of funding hedges of these transactions. In our experience, the biggest international over-the-counter derivatives dealers now include FVA, and for this type of business, while methodologies continue to evolve, including this type of adjustment is market practice for these participants.

2.4.465.20   However, considerable debate remains regarding the nature of inputs used to determine and calibrate FVA and therefore there is diversity in practice in how entities calculate FVA when it is incorporated in their valuations. Particular complexities include transactions that are partially collateralised, including those subject to one-way collateral requirements (i.e. only one counterparty is required to post collateral) or to collateral thresholds (i.e. collateral amounts are adjusted only when the net exposure exceeds a specified amount), and restrictions on the rehypothecation of collateral.

2.4.465.30   In our experience, in determining whether an adjustment for FVA is needed, and if so how to calculate it, an entity considers the pricing practices that would be used by market participants if derivatives were sold at the measurement date. In doing so, an entity considers the funding cost and benefit that market participants would take into account in pricing the instrument, which may differ from the entity's estimate of its own funding cost or benefit (see 2.4.90).

2.4.465.40   One challenge for calculating FVA is the potential for overlap in a valuation model between an adjustment for a funding rate that a market participant would consider and the adjustments for the counterparty's credit risk and the entity's own credit risk (see 2.4.460) – i.e. an overlap of FVA with a CVA and a DVA. This potential overlap occurs because funding cost discounting techniques usually incorporate both liquidity and credit components, and they may be difficult to separate.

2.4.465.50   Therefore, when incorporating FVA in the fair value measurement, an entity needs to ensure that the valuation appropriately eliminates any overlap of FVA with DVA and CVA, and that a symmetrical approach is applied to the measurement of derivative assets and liabilities. A symmetrical approach to measurement is consistent with the requirement for the measurement of a liability with no quoted price for the transfer of an identical or a similar liability to be made from the perspective of a market participant that holds the identical item as an asset (see 2.4.380).

2.4.470   Collateral, master netting and credit support agreements

2.4.470.10   The effect of a requirement to provide collateral that is part of the contractual terms of an individual financial instrument is a characteristic of the financial instrument. Therefore, this effect is included in the fair value measurement of that financial instrument – e.g. a typical residential mortgage. In this case, the requirement to provide collateral may affect the discount rate or any other credit risk adjustments that are used in measuring fair value. [*IFRS 13.11, 69, B19*]

2.4.470.15   In our experience, in valuing fully collateralised derivatives, the majority of derivative market participants agree that the estimated cash flows should be discounted at the rate agreed for cash collateral posted under the derivative's credit support annex (CSA), which is typically an overnight benchmark rate in the respective currency (e.g. sterling overnight index average (SONIA), euro overnight index average (EONIA) or federal funds rate). The overnight index swap (OIS) market reflects assumptions by market participants about the overnight rate. For a discussion of issues potentially relevant to partially collateralised derivatives and more complex collateral arrangements, see 2.4.465.

2.4.470.20   If the unit of account is the individual financial instrument, then a separate arrangement that mitigates credit risk exposure in the event of default – e.g. a master netting agreement or a credit support agreement that requires the exchange of collateral on the basis of each party's net exposure to the credit risk of a group of financial instruments – is not reflected in the fair value of the individual financial instrument. [*IFRS 13.14*]

2.4.470.30   However, if an entity applies the portfolio measurement exception to a group of financial assets and financial liabilities entered into with a particular counterparty, then the effect of such an agreement would be included in measuring the fair value of the group of financial assets and financial liabilities if market participants would do so (see 2.4.450). [*IFRS 13.56, 69*]

2.4.470.40   In our experience, for individual instruments that are actively traded on an exchange, the actual counterparty to the trade transaction is, in many instances, the exchange entity – e.g. the clearing house for the exchange. For these exchange transactions, we understand that even when there is no master netting agreement between the exchange and the entity, credit risk is usually deemed to be minimal because the operating procedures of the exchanges require the daily posting of collateral, which is, in effect, an arrangement that mitigates credit risk exposure in the event of default.

2.4.475   Assets subject to executory contracts

2.4.475.10   Some assets recorded in an entity's financial statements are the subject of executory contracts that directly affect the use of, and cash flows from, those assets. For example, a leasing company might have several aircraft recorded as property, plant and equipment that are leased to third parties under operating leases.

2.4.475.20   If the unit of account is the underlying asset on a stand-alone basis (see 2.4.80), then the effects of executory contracts, including any contractual cash flows, are not included in measuring the fair value of the underlying asset. This is because in these cases the executory contracts are entity-specific (see 2.4.70). In these cases, the fair value of the asset is measured using the price that would be received from a market participant to sell the asset at the measurement date. Alternatively, if the unit of account is determined to be an aggregation of the contract with the underlying asset, then the effects of the executory contract would be considered. [*IFRS 13.14, 31*]

2.4.475.30   If the unit of account is determined to be the underlying asset on a stand-alone basis but the entity has evidence that suggests that a market participant would sell both the executory contract and the underlying asset as a group, then it may be appropriate to measure the fair value of the entire group. The group fair value would then be allocated to the assets in the group, although IFRS 13 does not provide any guidance in this regard. [*IFRS 13.31*]

2.4.480   MEASURING FAIR VALUE IF VOLUME OR LEVEL OF ACTIVITY SIGNIFICANTLY DECREASED

2.4.480.10   A fair value measurement may be affected if there has been a significant decrease in the volume or level of activity for that item compared with normal market activity for that item. Judgement may be required in determining whether, based on the evidence available, there has been such a significant decrease. An entity assesses the significance and relevance of all facts and circumstances. [*IFRS 13.B37, B42*]

2.4.480.20   Factors that might be taken into account include the following.
- There are few recent transactions.
- Price quotations are not based on current information.
- Price quotations vary substantially over time or between market makers.
- Indices that were highly correlated with the fair value of the item at previous measurement dates are demonstrably uncorrelated with recent indications of fair value for that item.
- There is a significant increase in implied liquidity risk premiums, yields or performance indicators for transactions observed in the market or quoted prices compared with the entity's estimate of expected cash flows.
- There is a wide or significantly increased bid-ask spread.
- There is a significant decline in primary market activity for similar assets or liabilities.
- Little information is publicly available. [*IFRS 13.B37*]

2.4.480.30   If an entity concludes that the volume or level of activity for an asset or liability has significantly decreased, then further analysis of the transactions or quoted prices is required. A decrease in the volume or level of activity on its own might not indicate that a transaction or a quoted price is not representative of fair value, or that a transaction in that market is not orderly. It is not appropriate to conclude that all transactions in a market in which there has been a decrease in the volume or level of activity are not orderly. [*IFRS 13.B38, B43*]

2.4.480.40   However, determining whether a transaction is orderly is more difficult if there has been a significant decrease in the volume or level of activity in relation to normal market activity for the asset or liability (or similar assets or liabilities). To evaluate the circumstances, and to determine whether a transaction is orderly, judgement may be required. If an entity determines that a transaction or quoted price does not represent fair value, then an adjustment to that price is necessary if it is used as a basis for determining fair value. [*IFRS 13.B38, B43*]

2.4.480.50   If the volume or level of activity has significantly decreased and the entity concludes that the market for that asset or liability is not active, then it may be appropriate for an entity to change the valuation technique used or to use multiple valuation techniques to measure the fair value of an item. If multiple valuation techniques are used, then the entity considers the reasonableness of the range of the different fair value indications. The objective of the weighting process is to determine the point within the range that is most representative of fair value under current market conditions. A wide range of fair value estimates may be an indication that further analysis is needed. [*IFRS 13.B40*]

2.4.480.60   A fair value measurement reflects an orderly transaction between market participants (see 2.4.60.40). Therefore, regardless of the valuation techniques used, a fair value measurement includes appropriate risk adjustments that are reflective of an orderly transaction between market participants under current market conditions; this includes a risk premium reflecting the amount that market participants would demand as compensation for the uncertainty inherent in the future cash flows of an asset or liability. [*IFRS 13.9, B39*]

2.4.480.70 It is generally reasonable to assume that the transaction in which an asset or liability was exchanged between market participants is an orderly transaction. However, there are circumstances in which an entity needs to assess whether a transaction is orderly. Circumstances that may indicate that a transaction is not orderly include the following.

- There was inadequate exposure to the market to allow usual and customary marketing activities.
- The seller marketed the asset or liability to a single market participant.
- The seller is in distress.
- The seller was forced to sell to meet regulatory or legal requirements.
- The transaction price is an outlier compared with other recent transactions for identical or similar items. [*IFRS 13.B43*]

2.4.480.80 However, even if the seller was forced to sell, this would not necessarily indicate that the transaction is not orderly. For example, if an entity sells assets to market participants to meet regulatory requirements but the regulator does not establish the transaction price and the entity has a reasonable amount of time to market the assets, then the transaction price provides evidence of fair value.

2.4.480.90 If the evidence indicates that a transaction was not orderly, then the entity places little (if any) weight on the transaction price in measuring fair value. However, if the evidence indicates that the transaction was orderly, then the entity considers the transaction price in estimating the fair value of the asset or liability. The weight placed on that transaction price depends on the circumstances – such as the volume and timing of the transaction and the comparability of the transaction to the asset or liability being measured. If an entity does not have sufficient information to conclude whether a transaction was orderly, then it takes the transaction price into account, but places less weight on it compared with transactions that are known to be orderly. [*IFRS 13.B44*]

2.4.480.100 Although an entity need not undertake exhaustive efforts to determine whether a transaction is orderly, it does not ignore information that is reasonably available. If an entity is party to a transaction, then it is presumed to have sufficient information to conclude whether the transaction is orderly. [*IFRS 13.B44*]

2.4.480.110 An entity is allowed to use quoted prices that are provided by third parties (such as brokers or pricing services) if these quoted prices are determined in accordance with the fair value measurement requirements. If there has been a significant decrease in the volume or level of activity for an item, then an entity evaluates whether third party prices are developed using current market information that reflects orderly transactions and market participant assumptions. If an entity obtains prices from a third party pricing service or broker as inputs to a fair value measurement, then it places less weight on quotes that do not reflect the result of such transactions. Furthermore, the entity takes into account the nature of the quotes and gives a higher weight to quotes representing binding offers than to those representing indicative bids. Whether third party prices represent observable or unobservable inputs depends on their nature and source (see 2.4.300). [*IFRS 13.B45–B47*]

2.4.490 DISCLOSURES

2.4.490.10 The disclosures required by IFRS 13 are split into two categories.

- Disclosures for assets and liabilities measured at fair value in the statement of financial position after initial recognition (see 2.4.500). These disclosures are more extensive.

- Disclosures in relation to fair value measurements that are required or permitted to be disclosed by other IFRSs, but which are *not* included in the statement of financial position (see 2.4.540).

2.4.490.20   For a discussion of items to which the measurement requirements of IFRS 13 apply, but to which the disclosure requirements do not apply because of an exemption in IFRS 13, see 2.4.40.20–70.

2.4.490.30   In addition, the IFRS 13 disclosures do not apply to revenue that is measured at fair value in the case of non-cash consideration (see 4.2.150). This is because revenue is not an asset or liability recognised in the statement of financial position.

2.4.500   Assets and liabilities measured at fair value

2.4.500.10   IFRS 13 contains a comprehensive disclosure framework that combines the fair value measurement disclosures previously required by other standards and certain additional disclosures. The objectives of the disclosures for assets and liabilities that are measured at fair value are:
- to provide information that enables users of financial statements to assess the methods and inputs used to develop those measurements; and
- to assess the effect of the measurements on profit or loss or OCI of recurring fair value measurements that are based on significant unobservable inputs – i.e. recurring Level 3 measurements. [*IFRS 13.91*]

2.4.500.20   To determine whether the disclosures provided meet the disclosure objectives of the standard, an entity considers the following factors:
- the level of detail necessary to satisfy the disclosure requirements;
- how much emphasis to place on each of the various requirements;
- how much aggregation or disaggregation to undertake; and
- whether additional information to evaluate the quantitative information disclosed is needed. [*IFRS 13.92*]

2.4.500.30   These disclosures also apply to assets and liabilities measured at a value based on fair value and in the scope of IFRS 13 – e.g. biological assets measured at fair value less costs to sell (see 3.9.40). [*IFRS 13.93*]

2.4.510   *Classes of assets and liabilities*

2.4.510.10   The disclosure requirements are based on 'classes' of assets and liabilities, but do not apply to classes of assets and liabilities that are measured at fair value only on initial recognition. For example, the disclosure requirements do not apply to the fair values of assets acquired in a business combination and subsequently measured under the cost model. [*IFRS 13.93, BC184*]

2.4.510.15   Determining the appropriate classes of assets and liabilities requires judgement. A class of assets and liabilities could be more disaggregated than a single line item in the statement of financial position, and an entity needs to provide information sufficient to allow reconciliation to the statement of financial position. However, if a particular standard specifies the class for an asset or a liability – e.g. IAS 16 for property, plant and equipment (see 3.2.320) – then an entity may use that class in providing the disclosures if it meets the criteria in 2.4.510.20. [*IFRS 13.93–94*]

2.4.510.20   A class of assets or liabilities is determined based on:
- the nature, characteristics and risks of the asset or liability (e.g. shared activities or business sectors, vintage, geographic concentration, credit quality or other economic characteristics); and
- the level into which it is categorised in the fair value hierarchy. [*IFRS 13.94*]

2.4.510.25   In our view, other relevant factors to consider include:
- the extent of homogeneous or shared risks within the class of assets or liabilities;
- differences in valuation inputs and techniques used to determine the fair value measurements;
- the ranges in values of significant unobservable inputs. For example, if the range of values for an unobservable input used in measuring the fair value of a class of assets is very wide, then this may indicate that the information is not sufficiently disaggregated;
- the sensitivity of measurements to changes in unobservable inputs;
- whether other disclosures in the financial statements provide sufficient information about the classes of assets and liabilities (e.g. a schedule of investments for investment companies); and
- the significance of the class of assets or liabilities relative to the context of a particular disclosure.

2.4.510.30   The number of classes for assets and liabilities categorised as Level 3 of the fair value hierarchy may need to be greater than those categorised within other levels, given the greater degree of uncertainty and subjectivity of fair value measurements within Level 3. [*IFRS 13.94*]

2.4.520   *Recurring vs non-recurring measurements*

2.4.520.10   There are different disclosure requirements depending on whether a fair value measurement in the statement of financial position after initial recognition is recurring or non-recurring.
- Recurring fair value measurements arise from assets and liabilities that are measured on a fair value basis at each reporting date – e.g. biological assets under IAS 41. Assets accounted for under a revaluation model – e.g. a class of property, plant and equipment under IAS 16 – are also recurring fair value measurements, even though a revaluation is not necessarily performed at each reporting date (see 3.2.300).
- Non-recurring fair value measurements are fair value measurements that are triggered by particular circumstances – e.g. an asset classified as held-for-sale under IFRS 5. [*IFRS 13.93(a)*]

2.4.530   *Summary of disclosures*

2.4.530.10   The disclosure requirements, which are most extensive for recurring Level 3 measurements, are summarised in the following table.

IFRS 13.93:	REQUIREMENT	FAIR VALUE MEASUREMENT						FAIR VALUE ONLY DISCLOSED		
		RECURRING			NON-RECURRING					
		L1	L2	L3	L1	L2	L3	L1	L2	L3
(a)	Fair value at the reporting date									
(a)	Reasons for the measurement									
(b)	Level within hierarchy									

IFRS 13.93:	REQUIREMENT	FAIR VALUE MEASUREMENT						FAIR VALUE ONLY DISCLOSED		
		RECURRING			NON-RECURRING					
		L1	L2	L3	L1	L2	L3	L1	L2	L3
(c)	Transfers within hierarchy, including the policy for the timing of transfers	■	■	■						
(d)	Description of valuation technique and inputs used		■	■		■	■		■	■
(d)	Any changes to valuation technique and the reasons why		■	■		■	■		■	■
(d)	Quantitative information about significant unobservable inputs			■			■			■
(e)	Reconciliation of opening and closing balances (including information on transfers in or out)			■						
(f)	Unrealised gains/losses from remeasurement			■						
(g)	Description of valuation processes and policies			■			■			■
(h)(i)	Narrative sensitivity to changes in unobservable inputs			■			■			
(h)(ii)	Quantitative sensitivity to changes in unobservable inputs (for financial assets and financial liabilities only)			■						
(i)	If highest and best use differs from actual, then the reasons why	■	■	■	■	■	■			
IFRS 13.98	For a liability measured at fair value, the existence of an inseparable third party credit enhancement	■	■	■	■	■	■			

■ Disclosure required – in tabular format unless another format is more appropriate. [*IFRS 13.99*]

This table does not refer to disclosures in relation to fair value measurements that are required or permitted to be disclosed by other standards (e.g. IFRS 7 for financial instruments).

2.4.530.20   In our view, the fair value measurement disclosures (for both recurring and non-recurring fair value measurements) should be based on the fair value at which the item is measured at the reporting date, even if that fair value was determined as of an earlier date. For example, if a class of property, plant and equipment is revalued at 31 October and the entity's year end is 31 December, then the disclosures apply to the fair value determined at 31 October.

2.4.530.30   An entity discloses its accounting policy choices in relation to:

- the timing of transfers between levels in the hierarchy – e.g. the date of the event or the change in circumstances that caused the transfer, the beginning of the reporting period, or the reporting date for items (c) and (e) in the table in 2.4.530.10; and
- a decision to apply the portfolio measurement exception (see 2.4.430). [*IFRS 13.95–96*]

2.4.530.40   In relation to the requirement to provide quantitative information about the significant unobservable inputs used in the fair value measurement – included in item (d) in the table in 2.4.530.10 – the extent and level of aggregation of these disclosures will depend on the specific facts and circumstances. For example, if the range of values for an unobservable input used for measuring the fair value for a class of assets or liabilities is very wide, then this may indicate that the information is not sufficiently disaggregated to meet the disclosure objectives (see 2.4.500). [*IFRS 13.91–92, 93(d)*]

2.4.530.50   The standard does not specify how to summarise this information for each class of assets or liabilities – e.g. whether to include information about the range of values or a weighted average for each unobservable input used for each class. An entity considers the level of detail that is necessary to meet the disclosure objectives. For example, if the range of values for an unobservable input that the entity uses is wide, then this may indicate that the entity should disclose both the range and the weighted average of the values. This is because disclosing information about a range without an average provides no information about how the inputs are distributed within that range or whether or to what extent inputs within that range have actually been used. Similarly, disclosing information about a weighted average without a range provides no information about the dispersion of the inputs used around that average. [*IFRS 13.91–92, 93(d), IE63*]

EXAMPLE 22 – DISCLOSURE OF SENSITIVITY TO CHANGES IN UNOBSERVABLE INPUTS FOR FINANCIAL ASSETS

2.4.530.60   Company Z discloses quantitative information about unobservable volatility inputs used to measure the fair values of a class of equity derivatives. This class includes 100 derivatives, 90 of which are valued using a volatility of 20% per annum and the remaining 10 are valued using a volatility of 50% per annum.

2.4.530.70   Z considers whether this difference means that its disclosure of unobservable inputs should be disaggregated to a level of two smaller classes, one with 90 derivatives and one with 10. If Z determines that disclosure at the level of the class that includes all 100 derivatives is appropriate and it proposes to disclose the range of values of the volatilities used (i.e. 20–50%), then it should also consider disclosing the weighted average of the inputs (assumed to be 23%); otherwise, its disclosures would not indicate that the significant majority of the inputs used are at the low end of the range and therefore the disclosure objectives of the standard may not be met.

2.4.530.75   Disclosure of quantitative information about significant unobservable inputs is not required if the inputs to the valuation were not developed by the entity itself but were externally developed (e.g. when an entity uses prices from prior transactions or broker quotes without adjustment). However, an entity cannot ignore other quantitative information that is reasonably available. For example, if an entity develops an adjustment to a broker quote that is significant to the measurement in its entirety, then the inputs used to determine the adjustment are included in the quantitative input disclosures, even if the entity excludes the unadjusted portion of the broker quote from the disclosure.

2.4.530.77   In some circumstances, an entity might use a third party valuation specialist to measure the fair values of certain assets or liabilities. In this case, management of the entity might provide the specialist with inputs and assumptions that are significant to the valuation (e.g. projected financial information prepared by an investee). Significant unobservable valuation inputs provided to third party valuation specialists by the entity cannot be omitted from the quantitative disclosures. [*IFRS 13.93(d), BC195*]

2.4.530.80   Meeting the requirement to disclose the amount of the unrealised gains or losses included in profit or loss for the period relating to those assets and liabilities held at the reporting date – item (f) in the table in 2.4.530.10 – may be straightforward for some types of instruments; however, identifying the change in unrealised gains or losses included in profit or loss for the period may be difficult for those instruments that are subject to periodic cash settlements. In many situations, periodic cash settlements constitute both a realisation of gains or losses arising in prior periods – i.e. settlement of the initial carrying amount – and a realisation of gains or losses arising in the current period. [*IFRS 13.93(f)*]

2.4.530.85   In our view, an entity may define the change in unrealised gains or losses as those gains or losses included in profit or loss for the current period relating to assets and liabilities held at the reporting date *exclusive* of settlements received or paid in the current period for movements in fair value that occurred in the period. In that case, an entity will need to develop a reasonable method to allocate cash settlements received or paid during the period to:
- the unrealised gain or loss as of the beginning of the period or the initial carrying amount, which would not affect the realised gains or losses in the period; and
- the change in fair value during the period, which would constitute realisation of gains or losses in the period.

2.4.530.90   In relation to item (h)(ii) in the table in 2.4.530.10 for financial assets and financial liabilities, if changing one or more of the unobservable inputs to reflect reasonably possible alternative assumptions would significantly affect fair value, then an entity discloses the effect on fair value, including how the effect was calculated. For this purpose, significance is judged with respect to profit or loss, total assets or total liabilities or, if changes in fair value are recognised in OCI, then total equity. [*IFRS 13.93(h)(ii)*]

2.4.530.100   In our view, 'reasonably possible alternative' assumptions are assumptions that could reasonably have been included in the valuation model at the reporting date based on the circumstances at that date. A quantitative sensitivity analysis for financial instruments provides information about the sensitivity of the fair value measurement to changes to reasonably possible alternative unobservable inputs at the measurement date. Therefore, we do not believe that this disclosure is intended to be a forward-looking sensitivity analysis about an entity's exposure to future changes in market variables. [*IFRS 13.BC209*]

2.4.530.110   For a liability measured at fair value and issued with an inseparable third party credit enhancement (see 2.4.380.30), an entity discloses:
- the existence of the credit enhancement; and
- whether that credit enhancement is reflected in the fair value measurement of the liability. [*IFRS 13.98*]

2.4.533   *Application by investment entities*

2.4.533.10   An investment entity parent that measures an investment in an investment entity subsidiary at fair value through profit or loss needs to consider which disclosures in its financial statements are required to meet the disclosure objectives of IFRS 13 and of IFRS 7. These objectives are to enable users of the parent's financial statements to understand the valuation techniques and inputs used to develop fair value measurements in those financial statements and to evaluate the significance of the financial instruments held by the parent and the nature and extent of the related risks. This might include providing some or all of the disclosures in IFRS 13 for the subsidiary's investments. This may apply particularly for a feeder fund that invests in a master fund. See also 5.10.290.50 and 7.10.675. [*IFRS 7.7, 31, 13.91–92*]

2.4.533.20   For example, a feeder fund might disclose the categorisation of the underlying investments of the master fund in the fair value hierarchy and a description of the valuation techniques and inputs used to measure the fair values of those underlying investments. This may be particularly relevant if:
- the fair values of the master fund's investments are an input into the fair value measurement of the feeder fund's investment in the master fund (e.g. the investment in the master fund is valued based on the master fund's net asset value); or
- the feeder fund's financial statements otherwise disclose the fair values of the master fund's investments or related risk information. [*IFRS 7.7, 31, 13.91–92*]

2.4.535   *Additional information*

2.4.535.10   Entities may disclose additional information if they consider it helpful to users of the financial statements (see 2.4.500). For example, an entity may:
- separate the Level 3 fair value gains and losses into amounts arising from changes in observable inputs and amounts arising from changes in unobservable inputs; or
- for a Level 3 instrument that is economically hedged by an instrument with a fair value measurement in Level 1 or Level 2, disclose the extent to which the fair value movements offset or correlate.

2.4.540   **Assets and liabilities not measured at fair value but fair value disclosed**

2.4.540.10   The disclosure requirements in relation to fair value measurements that are required or permitted to be disclosed by other standards, but which are *not* included in the statement of financial position, are limited to items (b), (d) and (i) in the table in 2.4.530.10. In respect of item (d), disclosure of quantitative information about significant unobservable inputs is not required. [*IFRS 13.97*]

2.4.540.20   For example, the IFRS 13 disclosures apply to financial instruments that are not measured at fair value in the statement of financial position but for which fair value is disclosed in accordance with IFRS 7 – e.g. financial assets and financial liabilities measured at amortised cost (see 2.4.40.20). However, IFRS 13 disclosures are not required for such an instrument if an entity does not disclose the fair value of that instrument because it applies one of the fair value disclosure exceptions in IFRS 7 – e.g. when the carrying amount is a reasonable approximation of fair value (see 7.10.460.10). [*IFRS 7.25, 29*]

2.4.550	**APPLICATION TO SPECIFIC ITEMS**
2.4.560	**Property, plant and equipment**

2.4.560.10   IAS 16 deals with the accounting for property, plant and equipment and is the subject of chapter 3.2. However, the principles in IFRS 13 provide general guidance in measuring the fair value of any class of property, plant and equipment that is accounted for using the revaluation model. In measuring fair value, the general guidance in 2.4.10–540 applies. This section discusses specific points of interest in relation to property, plant and equipment.

2.4.570	*The item being measured*

2.4.570.10   In some cases, an item of property, plant and equipment will provide maximum value to market participants through its use in combination with other assets or with other assets and liabilities (see 2.4.350). In that case, if the asset requires installation in a particular location before it can be used, then such installation costs are generally considered an attribute of the asset in measuring fair value. Therefore, all costs (excluding transaction costs) that are necessary to transport and install an asset for future use are included in the measurement of fair value. [*IFRS 13.B3, IE11–IE12*]

2.4.570.20   Examples include delivery and other costs necessary to install an asset for its intended use. For an asset which is already installed and configured for use, installation costs are added to the estimated uninstalled value indication (e.g. replacement cost) for the asset, which results in measurement of fair value on an installed basis. [*IFRS 13.B3, IE12*]

2.4.570.30   The fair value measurements of many assets that require installation will use Level 3 inputs other than installation costs. However, for some common machinery that is traded in industrial markets, Level 2 inputs may be available. In this situation, the inclusion of installation costs in the measurement of fair value may result in a Level 3 categorisation of the measurement if those costs are significant (see 2.4.270). [*IFRS 13.73, 81, 86*]

2.4.580	*Unit of account*

2.4.580.10   The unit of account (discussed generally in 2.4.80) of property, plant and equipment is determined under IAS 16, although the standard itself is unclear. As discussed in 3.2.10.25, in our view an item that is separately identifiable and individually significant will generally constitute a unit of account under IAS 16.

2.4.580.20   A market may only exist for a group of assets as a whole, even though the component parts (e.g. land and building) are separate units of account. In that case, it will be necessary to measure the fair value of the group as a whole and then to allocate the valuation to the individual components. IFRS 13 does not provide any guidance on the appropriate method of allocation.

2.4.590	*Valuation approaches and techniques*

2.4.590.10   The fair value of property, plant and equipment is typically measured using techniques that fall under the market approach. However, the cost approach is also used for specialised plant and equipment, and this section discusses specific points of interest in respect of applying the DRC method. For a general discussion of valuation approaches and techniques, including the use of multiple approaches/techniques, see 2.4.120.

2.4.600 *DRC method*

2.4.600.10   As noted in 2.4.210.20, a DRC valuation considers how much it would cost to reproduce an asset of equivalent utility and includes an optimisation adjustment to take into account physical, functional and economic obsolescence. It estimates the cost to replace the required capacity of the asset rather than the actual asset.

2.4.600.20   In a DRC valuation, the adjustment for depreciation takes into account the age of the asset in relation to its useful life and its residual value. The adjustment for optimisation takes into account situations in which the asset is obsolete, over-engineered or has capacity greater than that required by a market participant.

EXAMPLE 23A – PROPERTY, PLANT AND EQUIPMENT – DRC ADJUSTMENT FOR OPTIMISATION

2.4.600.30   Company T operates a network of water pipes. The diameter of the pipes is greater than that required currently – and greater than is expected to be required – even for necessary stand-by or safety purposes. Therefore, the DRC valuation is optimised to eliminate the cost of replacing the surplus capacity in T's network.

2.4.600.40   If an asset has surplus capacity, then in our view the optimisation adjustment for the DRC valuation should consider whether the surplus capacity has an alternative use. If there is no alternative use, then no replacement cost should be included for this surplus capacity. However, if there is an alternative use that is physically possible and financially feasible, then in our view the surplus capacity should be included in the valuation. However, surplus capacity is unlikely to have an alternative use unless it is physically and operationally separable from the required capacity.

EXAMPLE 23B – PROPERTY, PLANT AND EQUIPMENT – DRC METHOD AND SURPLUS CAPACITY

2.4.600.50   Continuing Example 23A, in addition to the surplus diameter of the pipes, Company T's network includes an additional discrete segment of pipes that is surplus to requirements, but which could be closed off and used for other purposes such as a liquid storage facility. Although the surplus diameter would be excluded (as explained in Example 23A), we believe that the surplus segment should be included in the valuation.

2.4.600.60   If an asset is obsolete, then the DRC valuation is optimised by reducing the replacement cost of the entity's specific asset so that it is not greater than the cost of a modern equivalent asset that provides an equivalent standard of performance or service capacity.

2.4.600.70   A DRC valuation, before application of appropriate adjustments for economic obsolescence, provides an estimate of the costs to re-create an asset, but a market participant would not pay that amount for an asset if it would generate a below-market return. As a result, the determination of economic obsolescence may involve taking into account future cash flow projections – i.e. the use of techniques associated more frequently with an income approach (see 2.4.150). A measure of DRC that does not consider economic obsolescence, if applicable, would be incomplete.

2.4.610 **Investment property**

2.4.610.10   IAS 40 deals with the accounting for investment property and is the subject of chapter 3.4. However, the principles in IFRS 13 provide general guidance, supplemented by aspects of IAS 40, in measuring the fair value of investment property – either if the fair value model is applied or if fair value is disclosed. In measuring fair value, the general guidance in 2.4.10–540 applies. This section discusses specific points of interest in relation to investment property.

2.4.620   *The item being measured*

2.4.620.10   In measuring fair value, an entity takes into account characteristics of the investment property that market participants would take into account in a transaction at the measurement date. For investment property, key characteristics include the condition and location of the asset (see 2.4.70.10) and any restrictions on the sale or use of the asset. For further discussion of the item being measured, see 2.4.70 and Example 2, which deals with a restriction on the sale of land.

2.4.630   *Unit of account*

2.4.630.10   The unit of account (discussed generally in 2.4.80) of investment property is determined under IAS 40, and is discussed in 3.4.20–30. For example, the unit of account could comprise land, a building or part of a building, or both. If investment property is leased on a furnished basis, then the unit of account generally includes the related movable furniture.

2.4.630.20   The valuation of investment property will typically include all related assets and liabilities – e.g. prepaid rentals. In that case, the entity chooses an accounting policy, to be applied consistently, about how any related assets and liabilities are presented in the statement of financial position (see 2.4.720). [*IAS 40.50(b)*]

2.4.640   *Market participant assumptions*

2.4.640.10   As explained in 2.4.90, an entity considers the perspective of market participants and measures fair value based on the assumptions that would be made by market participants acting in their economic best interests. Therefore, in measuring the fair value of investment property, an entity takes into consideration future cash flows arising from planned improvements to the extent that they reflect the assumptions of market participants.

EXAMPLE 24 – INVESTMENT PROPERTY – MARKET PARTICIPANT ASSUMPTIONS

2.4.640.20   Company D acquires land for which planning permission is granted for the development of a large commercial and residential complex. The principal reason that a market participant would acquire the land is to undertake this development project. Therefore, D takes into account the expected cash inflows and outflows arising from the project in measuring the fair value of the land using an income approach.

2.4.650   *Transaction costs*

2.4.650.10   The initial measurement of an investment property is at cost. The cost of investment property includes transaction costs and other directly attributable expenditure for preparing the asset for its intended use (see 3.4.120.20).

2.4.650.20　　An entity does not consider transaction costs in subsequently measuring fair value (see 2.4.110). This means that if the property market remains flat or declines between the date of acquisition and the date of revaluation, then the capitalised transaction costs included in the initial carrying amount of a property measured at fair value will be recognised as a loss in profit or loss.

EXAMPLE 25 – INVESTMENT PROPERTY – TRANSACTION COSTS

2.4.650.30　　Company R acquires an investment property for 300 and incurs transaction costs of 5. Therefore, the initial carrying amount of the property is 305.

2.4.650.40　　R elects to measure its investment property using the fair value model. At the reporting date, there has been no movement in the market and the fair value of the property is 300. The loss of 5, which is equivalent to the transaction costs on acquisition, is recognised in profit or loss.

2.4.650.50　　Conversely, if the fair value of the property at the reporting date is 310, then the gain recognised in profit or loss is 5 – i.e. the difference between the initial carrying amount of 305 and the fair value.

2.4.660　*Valuation approaches and techniques*

2.4.660.10　　The fair value of investment property is typically measured using techniques that fall under the market approach and/or the income approach; this section discusses specific points of interest in respect of measuring the fair value of investment property. For a general discussion of valuation approaches and techniques, including the use of multiple approaches/techniques, see 2.4.120.

2.4.660.20　　Under the market approach, fair value is generally measured as a product of metrics, such as price per square foot or per square metre, and the area of the investment property. The two commonly used valuation techniques under the income approach are the yield method and the discounted cash flow technique.

2.4.660.30　　The fair value of an investment property takes into account, among other things, future income from current lease contracts even if the rental payments under the contracts are above or below current market terms. [*IAS 40.40*]

2.4.670　*Income approach: Yield method*

2.4.670.10　　Under the yield method, the yield on a property is generally calculated as the current or market rental income on a property divided by the property's value. This method is most relevant if:
- there are sufficient market transactions from which yield information may be identified;
- sufficient information is available to identify and adjust for differences between the property being valued and comparable properties; and
- the pattern and risk of the subject and comparable properties' cash flows are similar.

2.4.670.20　　The yield method is less reliable if comparable transactions cannot be readily identified. This might be the case if there are reduced transaction volumes or if significant subjective adjustments to yields are required because of differences between the subject property and comparable properties in terms of physical characteristics, age, location, leases in place etc. In addition, if the cash flows on the subject property are expected to change in the future at a rate that is different from the rate of change of the cash flows of comparable properties, then the yield method may not be appropriate.

2.4.670.30   If properties have complex arrangements or changing income flows, then a discounted cash flow method may be more appropriate (see 2.4.680).

2.4.680   *Income approach: Discounted cash flow method*

2.4.680.10   Using the present value technique, fair value is measured by discounting expected cash inflows and outflows arising from the investment property at the rate of return that investors (market participants) in the property would require.

2.4.680.20   In our experience, the forecasted cash flows may be based on an evaluation of the property on a lease-by-lease basis or on a more aggregated basis. In general, a lease-by-lease analysis allows a comprehensive incorporation of the specific facts and circumstances of individual leases; these include actual rental rates, rent-free periods, the dates of lease renewals, vacancy rates, future rental rates and leasehold improvement costs.

2.4.680.30   An estimate of future market rents is required for periods not covered by current contractual agreements or for scenarios that incorporate the probability of contractual rents not continuing into the future – e.g. because the tenant fails to pay.

2.4.680.40   Estimates of future rental income consider both the level of rents and estimates of void and rent-free periods; the latter factors are especially important in difficult market conditions. Some entities may use current rents as a proxy for future market trends. Others look to recent trends in rent levels to estimate how rents may change in the future. Care is required in any approach that assumes a simple extrapolation of recent trends. Consideration is also given to the potential for rents to go back to the mean level – e.g. if recent rents are very high relative to historical levels, then consideration is given to a potential cyclical change in rent levels.

2.4.680.50   All cash flows are discounted in a discounted cash flow analysis. This includes owner costs such as the costs of exterior maintenance, insurance, taxes, technical replacements and property management costs.

2.4.680.60   Physically similar investment properties can have significantly different values because of leases in place; differences in location are also a reason for value differences. For example, a fully let building with above-market rents and financially strong tenants will have a significantly higher value than a building that is similar in physical respects but that is vacant.

2.4.680.70   In evaluating the sustainability of a rental cash flow, the credit quality of a tenant is considered. The credit quality of an existing tenant is especially important if the remaining term of a lease is longer, or if a lease renewal is expected. Credit risk may be less of an issue if rental rates under the lease are 'at-market'. In such circumstances, if the lessee does not continue to pay under the lease, then the lessor should theoretically be able to secure a new tenant at the same lease rate. However, the lessor in such circumstances might be expected to incur costs to remove a defaulting tenant, or to experience a period with no lease revenue because of vacancy as well as potentially incurring marketing, incentive and leasehold improvement costs.

2.4.680.80   Particular care is required in evaluating the reasonableness of assumptions used in relation to vacant (void) periods and incentive costs such as rent-free periods or landlord-borne fit-out costs. The longer the period that a property is expected to be unlet and the higher the incentive costs required to secure new tenants, the lower the property's value.

2.4.690   *Discounted cash flow method: Transaction costs*

2.4.690.10   As noted in 2.4.110.170, it may be appropriate for future transaction costs – i.e. in subsequent sales transactions – to be deducted in a discounted cash flow analysis. For example, if discounted cash flows are used to determine the fair value of real estate, and the analysis includes an assumption that a market participant would sell the property in the future, then it may be appropriate to subtract transaction costs (e.g. selling costs) expected to be incurred at the time of that future disposition.

EXAMPLE 26 – INVESTMENT PROPERTY – FUTURE TRANSACTION COSTS

2.4.690.20   Company E measures the fair value of its investment real estate. A discounted cash flow analysis resulting in an estimated value of 100 for the real estate at the measurement date includes a cash inflow (discounted) of 80 for future sale proceeds and a cash outflow (discounted) of 5 for selling costs associated with the future sale at the end of an assumed five-year holding period. The remaining cash flows (discounted) of 25 are from net operating cash inflows during the five-year holding period. If the real estate were sold at the measurement date, then selling costs of 4 would be incurred by the existing investor.

2.4.690.30   E measures the fair value at 100 – i.e. including the assumed cash outflow for transaction costs at the end of the five-year holding period – on the basis that the discounted cash flow analysis is prepared from the perspective of a market participant buyer who would consider future transaction costs in determining the price that it would be willing to pay for the asset.

2.4.690.40   However, it would not be appropriate for E to measure the asset at a value of 96 – i.e. estimated value of 100 less transaction costs of 4 that would be incurred if the asset were sold at the measurement date – because market participants would transact at 100 on the measurement date. [*IFRS 13.25*]

2.4.700   *Investment property under construction*

2.4.700.10   In our experience, valuers typically measure the fair value of investment property under construction by estimating the fair value of the completed investment property and then deducting from that amount the estimated costs to complete construction, financing costs and a reasonable profit margin.

2.4.700.20   Although the cumulative cost of construction may be an appropriate input to consider in measuring the fair value of investment property under construction, particularly in very early stages of development, it would generally not be expected to equal the property's fair value. In the absence of observable and comparable transactions, in our experience the property's fair value is generally based on a discounted cash flow method where cash inflows and outflows are discounted at a risk-adjusted rate of return required by market participants.

2.4.700.30   In practice, as development progresses, the probability of completion increases and certain risks associated with the asset decrease, thereby increasing the fair value. Those risks include failure to secure necessary planning and other permissions on a timely basis, construction cost over-runs, changes in market conditions during construction that could lead to delays in leasing/sales and/or reduced lease rates or selling prices, and higher than projected operating expenses. In addition, there is an element of developer's profit that would be expected to increase the fair value of the property.

2.4.700.40   In our view, market participant assumptions used in a discounted cash flow method should include estimates of cash outflows needed to complete the project – which should consider the developer's profit for the remaining work to be completed – as well as cash inflows and outflows from operating the property and ultimately selling it at some point in the future. We believe that a market participant would also be expected to consider the likelihood of achieving those estimated cash inflows based on the risks associated with completion of development and ultimate operations of the property.

2.4.700.50   If a situation arises in which it is determined that the cumulative cost of construction is a reasonable proxy for fair value – e.g. in the very early stages of development – then it would not be appropriate to include third party costs associated with the acquisition of an investment in the determination of cost. Such costs typically relate to direct incremental costs incurred for due diligence and closing the transaction and would be excluded from a fair value measurement following the general principle that the fair value of an asset or liability is not adjusted for transaction costs (see 2.4.110).

2.4.700.60   The change in the carrying amount of investment property under construction in any given period will include additions recognised at cost as well as changes in the property's fair value. Generally, the amount recorded in profit or loss is the change in carrying amount after accounting for additions at cost.

EXAMPLE 27 – INVESTMENT PROPERTY UNDER CONSTRUCTION

2.4.700.70   Company D is constructing a property for future use as investment property. D uses the fair value model and capitalises attributable borrowing costs (see chapter 4.6). The following information is relevant for this example.

Carrying amount of property at 1 March 2018 (fair value)	1,000
During the period ended 30 June 2018:	
• Construction costs capitalised	400
• Borrowing costs capitalised	100
Fair value of property at 30 June 2018	1,700

2.4.700.80   In this example, D records a fair value gain of 200 in profit or loss (1,700 - 1,000 - 400 - 100).

2.4.710   *Use of independent valuer*

2.4.710.10   An entity is encouraged, but is not required, to have valuations carried out by an independent valuer who holds a recognised and relevant professional qualification and who has recent experience in the location and category of investment property being valued. In our experience, entities take into account the following factors in deciding whether to engage an independent valuer:

- the materiality of the assets to the statement of financial position;
- the degree of fluctuation in the market;
- the ease with which a non-expert can make a reasonable estimate of fair value from publicly available information – e.g. information on recent transactions involving comparable properties; and
- whether the entity has its own staff with relevant qualifications. [*IAS 40.32*]

2.4.710.20   If the property market is reasonably stable and there are frequent transactions in comparable properties for which information is readily available, then an entity may, for example, adopt a practice of engaging independent property experts only every three years and estimating changes in fair value by other methods in the intervening periods. Such an approach is not, in itself, an accounting policy but rather an estimation method. If, for example, the market has been unusually volatile in the past accounting period, or has become less active, then the estimation method may not be appropriate and it may be necessary to obtain additional valuation information from professional valuers.

2.4.720   *Presentation of separate assets and liabilities*

2.4.720.10   Once the fair value of investment property has been measured, an entity ensures that it does not double count assets or liabilities that are recognised separately. [*IAS 40.50*]

2.4.720.20   In our view, an entity should choose an accounting policy, to be applied consistently, to present investment property and any related assets or liabilities included in the valuation as follows in the statement of financial position.

- *Investment property only:* Under this approach, only investment property is presented, measured at the amount determined in the valuation.
- *Separate assets and liabilities:* Under this approach, investment property and the related assets and liabilities are each presented separately; investment property is recognised at the amount determined in the valuation minus (plus) amounts allocated to other assets (liabilities).

EXAMPLE 28 – INVESTMENT PROPERTY – MULTIPLE ASSETS INCLUDED IN VALUATION

2.4.720.30   Company S owns an investment property that it is leasing to Company B for five years under an operating lease. No rent is payable in year 1 and the rent for years 2 to 5 equals 100 per annum.

2.4.720.40   At the end of year 1, S has accrued rental income of 80 (see 5.1.310.110) and the fair value of the investment property is 1,000. The future cash flows of 400 from the lease are included in measuring fair value.

2.4.720.50   To avoid double counting, S decides to present two assets in its statement of financial position:
- accrued rental income of 80 ((100 x 4) / 5); and
- investment property of 920 (1,000 - 80).

2.4.720.60   For a discussion of investment property measured at fair value for which a government grant has been received, see 4.3.70.

Biological assets

2.4.730.10   IAS 41 deals with the accounting for biological assets and is the subject of chapter 3.9. However, the principles in IFRS 13 provide general guidance in measuring the fair value element of fair value less costs to sell of both biological assets and agricultural produce at the point of harvest, supported by aspects of IAS 41. In measuring fair value, the general guidance in 2.4.10–540 applies. This section discusses specific points of interest in relation to biological assets, which in general will also apply to agricultural produce.

2.4.740   *The item being measured*

2.4.740.10   In measuring fair value, an entity takes into account characteristics of the biological assets that market participants would take into account in a transaction at the measurement date. For biological assets, key characteristics include the age, weight, condition and location of the assets. For a general discussion of the item being measured, see 2.4.70.

2.4.750   *Unit of account*

2.4.750.10   The unit of account (discussed generally in 2.4.80) for biological assets could be either a single asset or a group of assets. For assets that are unique – e.g. horses held for breeding – each asset will be a separate unit of account.

2.4.750.20   IAS 41 allows assets to be grouped according to their significant attributes. For example, livestock or fish may be grouped according to age or weight, crops may be grouped according to quality, and trees in a forest may be grouped according to age and type. [*IAS 41.15*]

2.4.750.30   Agricultural produce (e.g. fruit) growing on a bearer plant (e.g. a fruit tree) is a biological asset in the scope of IAS 41. Bearer plants, however, are in the scope of IAS 16. Therefore, the bearer plant and the produce growing on it are two separate units of account. [*IAS 41.1, 2(b), 5C*]

2.4.750.40   In many cases, biological assets are physically attached to the land, and an active market only exists for the combined package of the biological assets, land and land improvements. In that case, it may be necessary to measure the fair value of the combined package and then to deduce the fair value of the biological assets – e.g. by deducting the fair value of just the land and the land improvements (see Example 29). [*IAS 41.25*]

2.4.760   *Principal (or most advantageous) market*

2.4.760.10   As explained in 2.4.100, fair value is measured with reference to the principal (or most advantageous) market to which the entity has access. This means that an entity cannot simply assume that its local market is the appropriate reference market for the purpose of applying IFRS 13. An entity is required to consider all information that is reasonably available in determining the principal (or most advantageous) market to which it has access at the measurement date.

2.4.760.20   Owners of biological assets may enter into contracts to sell forward the assets or related produce. These contracts may not provide evidence of current fair value, because fair value should reflect the current market in which a willing buyer and seller would enter into a spot transaction to sell the assets. If there is such a contract, then the asset to be sold is still measured at fair value less costs to sell (see 2.4.110–140 and 475.20). However, the forward contract itself may be relevant for the accounting under other standards – e.g. the contract might need to be recognised as an asset or a liability under IFRS 9 (see 7.1.200), or an onerous contract provision might be required under IAS 37 (see 3.12.630). [*IAS 41.16*]

2.4.770 *Valuation approaches and techniques*

2.4.770.10   The fair value of biological assets is typically measured using techniques that fall under the market approach and/or the income approach; this section discusses specific points of interest in respect of measuring the fair value of biological assets. For a general discussion of valuation approaches and techniques, including the use of multiple approaches/techniques, see 2.4.120.

2.4.780 *Market approach*

2.4.780.10   If there is no active market, then an entity could measure fair value using techniques such as prices of recent market transactions, market prices for similar assets or sector benchmarks etc. In using such prices, an entity makes adjustments to reflect differences in characteristics and/or stages of growth of the assets. These methods would be appropriate if there are recent transactions or if markets exist for similar assets.

EXAMPLE 29 – BIOLOGICAL ASSETS – RECENT MARKET TRANSACTIONS

2.4.780.20   Company V owns a timber plantation in the northern region of the country. There have been no recent transactions for plantations in that part of the country. However, a similar timber plantation was recently sold in another region.

2.4.780.30   In measuring fair value, V uses the price of the transaction, adjusted for significant differences in the characteristics of the timber plantations. The price of the transaction is also allocated between the biological asset (the trees) and any other assets (e.g. land, irrigation equipment etc) to measure the fair value of the biological asset itself.

2.4.790 *Income approach**

2.4.790.10   The fair value of a biological asset is likely to include not only the asset's harvest value, but also a value for potential additional biological transformation that a market participant would include in the valuation. This requires a number of factors to be considered, such as:
- risks associated with the asset – e.g. weather and disease;
- estimated yields; and
- estimated costs of bringing the asset to its intended condition.

2.4.790.20   These risks address the uncertainty related to future cash flows – i.e. the possibility of variations in cash flows – and are reflected in either the discount rate and/or the estimate of expected cash flows.

2.4.790.30   In estimating future selling prices for the purpose of discounting expected net cash flows, the assumptions used should be consistent with those of market participants. These will depend on the characteristics of the biological assets, including their stage of development, the markets in which they are sold and the sources of possible pricing information. The assumptions that market participants would make about future selling prices will depend on a number of factors, including the following.

- The expected time to sell the asset – i.e. the time to the asset's maturity or harvest. For example, some biological assets such as poultry have a short period to maturity whereas others such as timber have a long growing cycle.
- Possible events or changes in circumstances between the measurement date and the expected date of sale. For example, expected regulatory changes may affect the demand for or supply of a biological asset and its price. The longer the period from the measurement date to the assumed sale date, the greater the number and magnitude of possible events and changes in circumstances that may occur. To some extent, possible future events or changes in circumstances may already be reflected in current prices.
- The effects of seasonal changes in pricing. For example, prices may be lower at principal harvest times when supply is greatest.

2.4.790.40   Considering these factors and depending on the specific facts and circumstances, an entity could estimate the future selling price using:
- current prices, especially if the time from the measurement date to the assumed sale date is short;
- prices in futures markets, which may be correlated with expected future selling prices;
- reliable statistical models used to forecast expected future selling prices; or
- prices for future periods or annual price increases established in regulated markets.

2.4.790.50   If an entity uses present value techniques to measure fair value, then the calculations generally include a contributory asset charge for assets that are owned by the entity and used in agricultural activity. For example, if an entity owns the land on which its agricultural activities are carried out, then in measuring the fair value of its biological assets, the entity deducts an amount (contributory asset charge) that reflects a charge for use of the land in the agricultural activities. This charge may be consistent with the rent on land without the biological asset.

2.4.790.60   IAS 41 continues to include a general caveat that the fair value measurement does not include cash flows related to financing the assets, taxation, or re-establishing biological assets after harvest – e.g. replanting trees. [*IAS 41.22*]

2.4.800   *Cost as an approximation of fair value*

2.4.800.10   IAS 41 acknowledges that in some cases cost may approximate fair value, and provides the following examples:
- little biological transformation has taken place since initial recognition – e.g. spruce seedlings planted just before the measurement date; or
- the impact of biological transformation is not material – e.g. the initial growth in a 30-year pine plantation production cycle. [*IAS 41.24*]

2.4.800.20   Whether cost does approximate fair value will depend on the specific facts and circumstances of the biological assets being valued.

2.4.810   *Use of independent valuer*

2.4.810.10   In measuring fair value, there is no requirement under IAS 41 to involve an independent valuer. [*IAS 41.B33*]

2.4.820   **Impairment of non-financial assets**

2.4.820.10   IAS 36 provides guidance on the impairment testing of non-financial assets and is the subject of chapter 3.10. However, the principles in IFRS 13 provide general guidance in measuring the fair value element of fair value less costs of disposal for the purposes of impairment testing. In measuring fair value, the general guidance in 2.4.10–540 applies.

2.4.820.20   The unit of account (discussed generally in 2.4.80) of non-financial assets subject to impairment testing is determined under IAS 36, and depends on the level at which assets are tested for impairment. The unit of account could comprise a single asset, a CGU or a group of CGUs (see 3.10.40).

2.4.820.30   For a CGU that corresponds to an investment in a subsidiary, associate or joint venture, see 2.4.830 for a discussion of determining the unit of account for fair value measurement.

2.4.830   **Investments in subsidiaries, associates and joint ventures**

2.4.830.10   As discussed in 2.4.80, the unit of account may be an investment in a subsidiary, associate or joint venture. In that case, in our view an entity may choose an accounting policy, to be applied consistently, to identify the unit of account of an investment in a subsidiary, associate or joint venture as:
- the investment as a whole; or
- each individual share making up the investment.

2.4.830.20   If the unit of account is each individual share making up the investment, then a premium related to the whole investment cannot be added in measuring the fair value of the investment. However, if the unit of account is the investment as a whole, then it may be appropriate to add such a premium in measuring the fair value of the investment – even if Level 1 prices exist for individual shares.

2.4.830.30   For a discussion of the valuation of unquoted equity securities, see 2.4.860.

2.4.840   *Control premiums*

2.4.840.10   In respect of an investment in a subsidiary, an acquirer (market participant) may be willing to pay a price that reflects a control premium, if it believes that it can create value by increasing cash flows and/or reducing risk. There are three broad ways in which this may be achieved.
- An acquirer may believe that it can change the stand-alone cash flows of the business through better management. In our experience, it is uncommon to assert that a new owner would be able to better manage the stand-alone operations of the business.
- An acquirer may believe that as a controlling shareholder it would have a lower risk, and therefore a lower required rate of return, than a minority shareholder in a public company. In our experience, this is likely to be less important in markets with strong corporate governance and minority shareholder protections.

- An acquirer may expect to create synergies through combining the acquired business with existing operations to increase the aggregate cash flow of the combining units. In our experience, this is typically the most significant factor contributing to the existence of a control premium.

2.4.840.20   The amount of a control premium is best corroborated by specific, comparable and current transactions in the investee's industry. The factors giving rise to such premiums in industry transactions are considered, and their potential existence in a hypothetical acquisition is assessed. For example, control premiums in industry transactions may reflect specific synergies that were expected to be available to the combining entities. Such synergies may arise from the nature of the entities' operations, including the degree of overlap therein, anticipated tax benefits from the transaction etc. These benefits might not be available to a market participant acquirer of the investee, and therefore would not be included in measuring fair value.

2.4.840.30   If there is no (or limited) current market activity to support the amount of the control premium, then historical transactions may need to be considered. However, a control premium based on arbitrary 'rule of thumb' percentages, or on an amount selected to avoid an impairment loss, for example, are not appropriate. Changes in control premiums from prior periods should be supported by objective evidence.

2.4.850   *Premiums other than control premiums*

2.4.850.10   An analysis of whether a shareholding that conveys joint control or significant influence might be valued in excess of its pro rata share of an entity's market capitalisation would consider similar factors to those outlined in 2.4.840.10 – i.e. based on an evaluation of the potential of such a shareholder to increase cash flows or reduce risk. However, a non-controlling influential shareholder generally receives the same pro rata cash flows as other minority shareholders. Therefore, in our experience it may be difficult to support a fair value significantly in excess of the quoted share price.

2.4.860   Unquoted equity securities

2.4.860.05   Investments in unquoted equity securities (and contracts on those instruments) are required to be measured at fair value. Cost may be an appropriate estimate of fair value in limited circumstances (see 2.4.920). [*IFRS 9.B5.2.3, BC5.13*]

2.4.860.10   There are a number of sources of guidance that entities can refer to in valuing unquoted equity securities, including the IASB's educational material (referenced in this section), a practice aid issued by the American Institute of Certified Public Accountants, and valuation guidelines issued by the International Private Equity and Venture Capital Association. Although such guidance may be useful, care is required because such guidance is not necessarily consistent with IFRS 13.

2.4.860.20   Under IFRS 9, investments in equity securities are measured at fair value with changes in fair value recognised either in profit or loss or in OCI (see chapter 7.7). In measuring fair value, the general guidance in 2.4.10–540 applies. This section discusses specific points of interest in respect of the valuation approaches and techniques used to measure the fair value of unquoted equity securities.

2.4.860.30   As noted in 2.4.130.10, in measuring the fair value of an asset or a liability, an entity selects those valuation approaches and techniques that are appropriate in the circumstances and for which sufficient data is available to measure fair value. The technique chosen should maximise the

use of relevant observable inputs and minimise the use of unobservable inputs. Factors relevant to measuring the fair value of unquoted equity securities include the following:
- the information that is reasonably available to an investor;
- market conditions;
- the investment horizon and investment type;
- the stage in the investee's life cycle;
- the nature of an investee's business – e.g. volatile or cyclical business; and
- the industry in which an investee operates. [*IFRS 13.EM.02-13.18*]

2.4.860.40   It is likely that greater weight will be placed on market multiples based on comparable entities (a technique under the market approach – see 2.4.870) if there are sufficiently comparable peers or if a significant amount of information is available regarding recent observed transactions involving similar entities. Similarly, it is likely that greater weight will be placed on a discounted cash flows method (a technique under the income approach – see 2.4.880) if the investee has unique characteristics that cause its cash flow profile to differ significantly from those of otherwise comparable businesses. [*IFRS 13.EM.02-13.13*]

2.4.870   *Market approach*

2.4.870.10   The following inputs are most commonly used in applying valuation techniques under the market approach:
- transaction prices paid for an identical or a similar instrument of the investee; and
- comparable entity valuation multiples derived from quoted prices in exchange markets or from prices paid in transactions. [*IFRS 13.EM.02-13.26–27*]

2.4.870.20   The transaction price of an investment in an unquoted equity instrument, which is identical to the investment being valued and made close to the measurement date, might be a reasonable starting point for measuring fair value at the measurement date. However, all information about the performance and operations of the investee and the pricing of comparable entities from the transaction date up to the measurement date is taken into account. [*IFRS 13.EM.02-13.28*]

2.4.870.30   Similarly, the transaction price of an investment in an equity instrument of an investee which is similar, rather than identical, to the investment being valued, and made close to the measurement date might be a reasonable starting point for measuring the fair value of the investment. Examples of such transactions include:
- the issue of new classes of shares to other investors; and
- transactions in such shares between other investors. [*IFRS 13.EM.02-13.32*]

2.4.870.40   In such cases, as noted in 2.4.140.30, valuation techniques are usually applied to determine the value of the subject asset (e.g. an ordinary share) taking into account the value of the comparable asset (e.g. preferred share). For example, in the case of an investee that had issued ordinary shares and preferred shares, a recent round of equity financing relating to Series C preferred shares is considered in measuring the fair value of an investment in ordinary shares, which have different liquidation preferences. It may be difficult to estimate the value effect of such differences on a per-share basis and an overall enterprise value analysis may be necessary. An equity value allocation method, such as an option pricing method, could be applied to reflect such differences. Alternatively, the recent price may be an input to a valuation technique – e.g. calibrating the valuation model to value the instrument using the recent price of a similar instrument. For a discussion of multiple valuation techniques, see 2.4.130. [*IFRS 13.EM.02-13.33*]

2.4.870.45   The following factors need to be considered when determining the nature and level of the adjustment:

- the rights and preferences associated with the instruments issued in the recent investment round (e.g. liquidation preferences, conversion ratios, dividends and anti-dilution provisions) compared with those of the instrument that is being valued;
- the proximity of the transaction to the measurement date and any events occurring between the recent investment round and the measurement date;
- the size of the recent investment round; and
- whether the recent investment round was made up of existing investors participating pro-rata. [*IFRS 13.B44(b), EM.02-13.33*]

2.4.870.50   In measuring fair value using market multiples derived from transactions, the investor considers whether the associated transactions represent the sale of a controlling interest. Any control premium is excluded in measuring the fair value of unquoted equity securities that represent a non-controlling interest or if the unit of account is the individual equity instrument (see 2.4.80 and 240). However, in using market multiples derived from quoted prices of public entities, such a non-controlling interest discount is not generally necessary because those multiples usually reflect non-controlling interest transactions. [*IFRS 13.EM.02-13.36–37*]

2.4.870.60   An investor also considers the non-marketable nature of the unquoted equity instruments being measured and the effect on fair value, as compared with equity instruments of comparable entity peers that are publicly traded and, therefore, likely to be more liquid. An adjustment to reflect the non-marketable nature of the investment might be required in those cases (see 2.4.240). [*IFRS 13.EM.02-13.64*]

2.4.870.70   Even when an IPO is a likely event for a private entity, the expected IPO price is not generally representative of the fair value of the entity's shares at the measurement date. This is because the ultimate IPO price is not finalised until the registration date and the market price will not be determinable until trading takes place. Furthermore, the expected IPO price reflects the value of the entity's shares under the assumption that they are publicly traded (i.e. a liquid instrument), whereas they are not in fact publicly traded at the measurement date. Nonetheless, the expected IPO price is a meaningful data point that needs to be considered in measuring the fair value of the entity's shares. In our experience, it is usual for management to obtain an understanding of differences between the expected IPO price and the measurement of fair value. This review can help support the reasonableness of assumptions underpinning the valuation.

2.4.880   *Income approach*

2.4.880.10   A common technique under the income approach that is used to measure the fair value of unquoted equity securities is the discounted cash flow method (see 2.4.890). Other methods used under this approach are:

- the dividend discount model (see 2.4.900.10);

- the constant-growth dividend discount model (see 2.4.900.20–30 and 50); and
- the capitalisation model (see 2.4.900.40–50). [*IFRS 13.EM.02-13.70*]

2.4.890   *Discounted cash flow method*

2.4.890.10   Under the discounted cash flow method, fair value is measured by discounting the estimated future cash flows of an investee using a rate of return that comprises the time value of money and the risks of the investment (see 2.4.160). [*IFRS 13.B13–B30, EM.02-13.71–72*]

2.4.890.20   If an investee is expected to have an indefinite life, then for practical reasons most models estimate cash flows for a discrete period and then either:
- use a constant growth model – e.g. the Gordon growth model;
- apply a capitalisation rate to the cash flows immediately following the end of the discrete period; or
- use an exit multiple to estimate a terminal value. [*IFRS 13.EM.02-13.71*]

2.4.890.30   Generally, there are two possible ways to value equity instruments using the discounted cash flow method: using either equity value or enterprise value.

2.4.890.40   Under the equity value approach, the fair value of the equity of the investee is measured directly. The cash flows used for the calculation are the cash flows available for distribution to all equity capital providers, which are the cash flows from the assets after debt payments and after making reinvestments that are needed for future growth. Accordingly, the discount rate used for the equity value reflects only the cost of equity. [*IFRS 13.EM.02-13.73*]

2.4.890.50   Under the enterprise value approach, the fair value of the equity of the investee is measured indirectly by measuring the enterprise value (which comprises the fair value of both the equity and the debt instruments of the investee) and then subtracting the value of the investee's debt. The cash flows used for the calculation are the cash flows available to all capital providers (equity and debt holders), which are the cash flows from the assets before any debt payments but after making reinvestments that are needed for future growth. Accordingly, the discount rate used for the enterprise value reflects the cost of debt and equity finance, in proportion to their use – i.e. the WACC; for further discussion of the weighted-average cost of capital, see 3.10.300. [*IFRS 13.EM.02-13.73*]

2.4.890.60   Regardless of the approach used, the assumptions about cash flows and discount rates need to be consistent. For example, post-tax (pre-tax) cash flows are discounted using a post-tax (pre-tax) discount rate. Similarly, the currency of the cash flows and the discount rate need to be the same. [*IFRS 13.EM.02-13.74*]

2.4.890.70   In measuring fair value using the discounted cash flow method, an investor considers any necessary adjustments (e.g. non-controlling or marketability discount) that market participants would incorporate in pricing the equity instruments at the measurement date and which are consistent with the investment's unit of account (see 2.4.80 and 240). [*IFRS 13.EM.02-13.76*]

2.4.900   *Other income approach methods*

2.4.900.10   Under the dividend discount model, the fair value of an equity instrument is measured as the present value of all of its expected future dividends in perpetuity. This model is often used in measuring the fair value of equity instruments for which the investee consistently pays dividends. [*IFRS 13.EM.02-13.115–116*]

2.4.900.20   The constant-growth dividend discount model is used as a simplified shortcut to the dividend discount model, which requires the estimation of dividend payments for every period into the indefinite future. [*IFRS 13.EM.02-13.117*]

2.4.900.30   The constant-growth dividend discount model assumes that dividends grow at a constant growth rate. Therefore, this model might be used for entities growing at a rate equal to, or lower than, the nominal growth in the economy with well-established dividend payment policies that they intend to continue into the future. Under this model, fair value is measured by discounting the initial dividend payment (after one period) using a rate that is calculated by deducting the constant percentage of growth from the discount rate. [*IFRS 13.EM.02-13.117–121*]

2.4.900.40   The capitalisation model assumes that the annual income stream is constant in perpetuity or that it grows at a constant annualised rate of growth (or decline). Accordingly under this model, similar to the constant-growth dividend discount model, fair value is measured by discounting the annual income using the capitalisation rate, which is calculated by deducting the constant percentage of growth from the discount rate. [*IFRS 13.EM.02-13.122–124*]

2.4.900.50   The assumptions associated with the capitalisation model and the constant-growth dividend discount model would generally not be met and therefore these models are generally not used as the primary source for fair value measurement. However, they might be used in some cases as cross-checking models. [*IFRS 13.EM.02-13.124*]

2.4.910   *Adjusted net asset method*

2.4.910.10   Under the adjusted net asset method (a technique generally considered to be under the cost approach), the fair value of unquoted equity securities is measured based on the fair value of the investee's assets and liabilities (both recognised in the statement of financial position and unrecognised). This method might be appropriate for an investee whose value is mainly derived from the holding of assets rather than from deploying those assets as part of a broader business. Examples of such investees are property-holding companies and investment entities; for a discussion of when it may be appropriate to use net asset value method for measuring the fair value of investment funds, see 2.4.970. [*IFRS 13.EM.02-13.125*]

2.4.910.20   In addition, this method might be appropriate for an investee that is not making an adequate return on assets or that is making only marginal levels of profits because it is in the very early stages of its development – e.g. an investee that has virtually no financial history or no developed product. [*IFRS 13.EM.02-13.126*]

2.4.910.30   The application of this method may require the use of many different valuation approaches and/or techniques simultaneously, to measure the fair value of the investee's assets and liabilities. [*IFRS 13.EM.02-13.20*]

2.4.910.40   If the investee has significant intangible assets (including goodwill), then it is generally not appropriate to use the adjusted net asset method for measuring fair value. This is because the measurement of the fair value of intangible assets that are significant to an investee or of a significant amount of goodwill is usually based on the same inputs that are used for measuring the fair value of the equity instruments of the investee in their entirety using an alternative valuation technique such as the discounted cash flow method. [*IFRS 13.EM.02-13.127*]

2.4.910.50   The adjusted net asset method measures a controlling interest. Therefore, the entity considers an adjustment for a non-controlling discount (see 2.4.80 and 240). In addition, in using this method, adjustments might be required under other conditions – for example:

- for a lack of liquidity or marketability – e.g. if the investee's associated assets and liabilities are publicly traded;
- for a significant time gap between the investee's reporting date and the measurement date – e.g. if the measurement of the fair values of the investee's associated assets and liabilities was made at the investee's reporting date and during the period until the investor's measurement date, the investee has made additional investments, incurred additional liabilities or the fair values of the associated assets and liabilities have changed; and
- for fund's fees or similar agreements that are not captured in the net asset valuation (see 2.4.940). [*IFRS 13.EM.02-13.128*]

2.4.920   *Cost as approximation of fair value*

2.4.920.10   All investments in equity instruments and contracts on those instruments are measured at fair value. For investments in *quoted* equity instruments, cost is never the best estimate of fair value. In limited circumstances, cost may be used as an approximation of fair value for:

- unquoted equity instruments; and
- contracts linked to them that are settled by delivery of such instruments. [*IFRS 9.B5.2.3, BC5.13–BC5.19*]

2.4.920.20   This may be the case if:

- the most recent available information is not sufficient to determine fair value; or
- there is a wide range of possible fair value measurements and cost represents the best estimate of fair value within that range. [*IFRS 9.B5.2.3*]

2.4.920.25   The basis for conclusions to IFRS 9 notes that the circumstances in 2.4.920.20 never apply to equity investments held by entities such as financial institutions and investment funds (see 2.4.930). [*IFRS 9.BC5.18*]

2.4.920.30   Examples of indicators of the circumstances in which cost may not be representative of fair value include:

- a significant change in the performance of the investee compared with budgets, plans or milestones;
- changes in expectation that the investee's technical product milestones will be achieved or the timing thereof;
- a significant change in the market for the investee's equity or its products or potential products;
- a significant change in the global economy or the economic environment in which the investee operates;
- a significant change in the performance of comparable entities, or in the valuations implied by the overall market;
- internal matters of the investee such as fraud, commercial disputes, litigation, changes in management or strategy; and

- evidence from external transactions in the investee's equity, either by the investee (such as a fresh issue of equity), or by transfers of equity instruments between third parties. [*IFRS 9.B5.2.4, 13.EM.02-13.28*]

2.4.920.40   The list of indicators in 2.4.920.30 is not exhaustive. An investor considers all information about the performance and operations of the investee that becomes available after the date of initial recognition, including whether the environment in which the investee operates is dynamic and whether there have been changes in market conditions and the passage of time. [*IFRS 9.B5.2.5, 13.EM.02-13.29*]

2.4.920.50   To determine if cost can be used as an approximation of fair value, the investor needs to carefully consider all facts and circumstances. In some cases – e.g. start-up companies – performance in accordance with original plans or the launch of a new product as expected, may lead to a significant increase in the fair value of the investment. This is because uncertainty over those events is removed. This may mean that even if there are no significant changes in performance against plans, cost may not be an appropriate estimate of fair value. In addition, all else being equal, an investment is usually expected to increase over time at a rate equal to the cost of equity less the dividend yield, before consideration of any changes associated with changes in the entity or markets.

2.4.920.60   In our experience, cost may be an appropriate estimate of fair value at the measurement date for a pre-revenue entity, when there is no catalyst for a change in fair value and the transaction date is relatively close to the measurement date.

2.4.925   *Fair value hierarchy*

2.4.925.10   Usually, there are no current observable prices for shares in private companies and accordingly the measurement of fair value is based on valuation techniques that use unobservable inputs. As a result, the fair value measurement is generally classified as Level 3 in the fair value hierarchy. [*IFRS 13.73*]

2.4.930   **Investment funds and similar investment vehicles**

2.4.930.10   In measuring fair value, the general guidance in 2.4.10–540 applies. This section discusses specific points of interest in relation to investments in investment funds and similar investment vehicles.

2.4.930.20   Although IFRS 9 includes guidance on circumstances in which cost might be representative of fair value (see 2.4.920 and 7.7.250), those circumstances would never apply to equity investments held by particular entities, such as financial institutions and investment funds. [*IFRS 9.BC5.18*]

2.4.930.30   In some cases, a fund invests in another fund. In our view, in this case the same principles apply. Therefore, if a fair value is not available for the investment in the fund directly, then an attempt should be made to value the underlying investments in the underlying fund.

2.4.940   *The item being measured*

2.4.940.10   Because the instrument held by the entity is an ownership interest in the fund and not an interest in the underlying assets of the fund, the measurement of fair value takes into account the rights and obligations inherent in that ownership interest – e.g. an obligation by the entity to meet future cash calls made by the fund. The entity considers any such obligations inherent in the ownership interest in its measurement of fair value.

2.4.940.20   This principle applies equally if fair value is measured with reference to net asset value (see 2.4.970). An entity considers any rights or obligations not reflected in the net asset value measurement for the fund (e.g. fees or similar agreements) and makes adjustments to arrive at fair value.

2.4.940.30   When an investment entity holds an investment through an intermediate entity that is accounted for at fair value through profit or loss, the direct investment in the intermediate entity represents the unit of account being measured at fair value. [*IFRS 13.14*]

EXAMPLE 30 – INVESTMENT HELD THROUGH AN INTERMEDIATE COMPANY

2.4.940.40   Company F, an investment entity, has a 100% direct investment in Company B, whose only purpose is investment in the ordinary shares of Public Company C. Therefore, F has an indirect equity investment in C. F accounts for its investment in B at fair value through profit or loss.

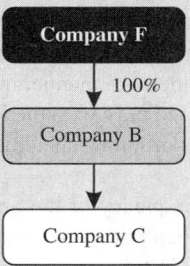

2.4.940.50   The direct investment in B represents the unit of account being measured at fair value by F. The indirect investment in the ordinary shares of C is not considered to be a separate unit of account by F. Although the market price of C's shares may be used as a valuation input in measuring the fair value of the investment in B, F considers whether there are other characteristics that a market participant would take into account (e.g. liquidity risk) when valuing its investment in B as the unit of account (see 2.4.910.50). For guidance on categorisation of the investment in B in the hierarchy level, see 2.4.990.70.

2.4.950   *Valuation approaches and techniques*

2.4.950.10   The fair value of an investment in a fund is often measured using the net asset value of the fund – either as fair value or as a key input. This section discusses specific points of interest in respect of measuring the fair value of an investment in a fund. For a general discussion of valuation approaches and techniques, including the use of multiple approaches/techniques, see 2.4.120.

2.4.960   *General considerations*

2.4.960.10   In our view, if the valuation reported by the fund – e.g. based on net asset value (see 2.4.970) – represents the amount at which an orderly transaction between market participants would occur at the measurement date, then this value should be used in measuring fair value.

2.4.960.20   If the valuation reported by the fund does not represent the amount at which an orderly transaction between market participants would occur at the measurement date, then the value of the investment in the fund is determined by applying another valuation technique, including consideration of the fund's underlying investments.

2.4.970   *Net asset value as representative of fair value*

2.4.970.05   If there is a quoted price in an active market (i.e. Level 1 price – see 2.4.280) for an investment in the fund, then the fair value of the investment is determined using the quoted price, whether or not it is equal to the net asset value. If there is no quoted price in an active market, then the entity needs to assess whether the net asset value is otherwise representative of the fair value of the investment in the fund. For a discussion of when the prices of units in a fund represent Level 1 prices, see 2.4.990.

2.4.970.10   If net asset value is used as an input in an entity's measurement of fair value (with or without further adjustments), then the entity needs to understand how net asset value is calculated, including the key inputs and valuation techniques used by the fund to value the underlying assets and liabilities.

2.4.970.20   To assess whether the net asset value or another price is representative of a quoted price in an active market, an entity considers the manner in which an investment in the fund is traded. Units in open-ended funds are often traded only with the fund or its agent at a published price – either net asset value, or net asset value plus or minus an adjustment.

2.4.970.30   Depending on the frequency of the updating of published unit prices and the trading volume at these prices, the published prices may represent a quoted price in an active market. However, in some circumstances, units in open-ended funds may be traded both with the fund at net asset value and in a secondary market – e.g. for exchange-traded funds. Also, in some circumstances, an open-ended fund may suspend redemptions, in which case the published net asset value would not represent a quoted price in an active market.

2.4.970.40   Units or shares in a fund may trade at a premium or discount to net asset value, because of supply and demand or other factors specific to the fund. For example, units or shares may trade at a discount because a market participant may consider an investment in the fund less attractive than a direct investment in the underlying assets of the fund because of the risk of future investment management changes and the loss of control over portfolio management decisions or because of a lack of liquidity or marketability of the investment. Conversely, market participants may be willing to pay a premium to invest in a fund managed by a specific investment manager.

2.4.970.50   Therefore, the existence of a discount between the net asset value reported by a fund and an entity's transaction price to sell or buy the investment does not, in and of itself, result in the transaction being considered not orderly. For example, if the transaction occurred with adequate exposure to the market, with a customary marketing period, and did not occur under duress, then it is likely that the transaction would be considered orderly. For a general discussion of this issue, see 2.4.480, which is written in the context of a significant decrease in the volume or level of activity in a market.

2.4.970.60   Although secondary market trading may not be sufficient to constitute an active market, it is still important to consider any secondary market transactions and transaction prices because, regardless of the level of market activity and trading volume, transaction prices that represent transactions that are orderly should not be ignored in measuring fair value. [*IFRS 13.B44(b)*]

2.4.970.70   To assess whether net asset value is otherwise representative of the fair value, an entity considers the following situations in which net asset value may not be representative of fair value.

- The net asset value is not dated as at the entity's measurement date.
- The net asset value is not calculated in a manner consistent with the fair value measurement principles of IFRS 13.
- The investment cannot currently be redeemed at net asset value – e.g. some open-ended funds may suspend redemptions.
- There is a significant decrease in the volume and level of activity of subscriptions or redemptions compared with normal market activity.
- The investment is traded in a secondary market at a significant discount or premium to net asset value.
- There are other uncertainties that increase the risk of the investment (e.g. deteriorated financial condition of the investment manager, allegations of fraud or non-compliance with laws and regulations).
- There are other terms attached to the investment – e.g. a commitment to make future investments.

2.4.970.80   If an open-ended redeemable fund does not allow daily redemptions at net asset value but allows, and actually has, periodic subscriptions and redemptions at net asset value, then their existence may provide evidence that net asset value approximates fair value.

2.4.970.90   In our experience, net asset value would usually be representative of the fair value of investments in open-ended investment funds that are open to new investors and allow redemptions at net asset value.

2.4.970.100   In addition, new subscriptions to a fund at its reported net asset value on or near the measurement date may provide evidence that market participants are not currently requiring a discount to net asset value or paying a premium above net asset value. Similarly, redemptions from the fund at its reported net asset value on or near the measurement date may provide evidence that market participants are currently not demanding a premium over net asset value or selling at a discount to net asset value. If both subscriptions and redemptions have occurred at net asset value near the entity's measurement date for its investment in the fund, then evidence may exist that net asset value approximates fair value.

2.4.970.110   In determining whether net asset value approximates fair value, the weight placed on the evidence provided by transactions with the fund (i.e. subscriptions and redemptions) depends on:

- market changes since the transaction activity occurred;
- the volume of both redemptions and subscriptions;
- the extent to which subscriptions were received from new investors; and
- limitations or expected limitations on the entity's ability to redeem in the future.

2.4.970.120   However, if no subscriptions and redemptions have occurred close to the reporting date, then an assertion that fair value approximates net asset value may be more difficult to support.

2.4.980   *Effect of bid-ask spread on financial information reported by investment funds*

2.4.980.10   An entity may not depart from the requirements of IFRS 13 to comply with regulatory requirements. For example, some investment funds are required to report their net asset values to investors using mid-market prices; under IFRS 13, we believe that an entity may use mid-market pricing as a practical expedient only if it provides a reasonable approximation of an exit price (see 2.4.250). [*IFRS 13.70–71*]

2.4.980.20   Problems may arise in the reporting by investment funds that offer linked investment products – i.e. the fund's obligation to unit holders is linked to the value of the underlying investments. The investments held by the fund and the liability to unit holders are not necessarily valued using the same price within the bid-ask spread (e.g. mid-market price) because different prices within the bid-ask spread may represent the exit price for the assets and liabilities (see 2.4.250). Owing to differences in the valuation bases of the investments and the unit liability, a mismatch results in the statement of financial position.

2.4.980.30   This in turn causes a presentation issue. In our view, one solution may be to present the unit liability in a two-line format. The first line would be the amount of the net assets attributable to holders of redeemable shares measured in accordance with the prospectus, which reflects the actual redemption amount at which the redeemable shares would be redeemed at the reporting date; the next line would include an adjustment for the difference between this and the amount recognised in the statement of financial position. This reflects the fact that, for a fund with no equity, all recognised income and expense is attributed to unit holders, which also means that a dilution levy of such amount would be required if all units were redeemed.

2.4.980.40   The problem in 2.4.980.20 may also be encountered by other entities, such as insurance companies offering linked investment products. We believe that the approach discussed in 2.4.980.30 could also be applied in these circumstances.

2.4.990   **Fair value hierarchy**

2.4.990.10   For funds in which ownership interests in the fund are publicly traded in an active market, the fair value measurement is based on the quoted price – i.e. a Level 1 input.

2.4.990.20   An entity may hold units in an open-ended unlisted investment fund. The units in the fund are often bought and sold but only by or to the fund or fund manager – i.e. the units are not traded on a stock exchange and cannot be sold to third parties. Because the fund is not listed, the fund calculates the price of the units only at a specific time each day to enable units to be bought and sold. The transactions take place only at this time on each day, and at the price so determined by the fund manager. The fair value of the units is determined to be the price calculated by the fund manager. Whether this is a Level 1 measurement will depend on the number and frequency of trades that occur in the units (see 2.4.280).

2.4.990.30   Daily pricing is likely to constitute evidence that trades take place with sufficient frequency. If the number of trades occurring is sufficient for the market in these units to be considered an active market then, notwithstanding that the units are being bought and sold by the fund and are not being traded between unrelated third party market participants, a fair value measurement of the units using the unadjusted daily price for the reporting date would be a Level 1 measurement.

2.4.990.40   However, if there is a quoted price but the number of trades occurring is not sufficient for the market in these units to be considered active, then a fair value measurement of the units using the unadjusted price for the reporting date would not be categorised as Level 1 in the fair value hierarchy.

2.4.990.50   If net asset value does not represent a quoted price, then it may continue to be used as an appropriate input for fair value measurement purposes (see 2.4.220 and 970). The appropriate categorisation of the resulting fair value measurement within the fair value hierarchy will be as Level 2 or Level 3 (see 2.4.290) based on the observability and significance of:
- the fair values of the underlying investments; and
- any adjustments for rights and obligations inherent within the ownership interest held by the entity (see 2.4.940).

2.4.990.60   Because many of the net asset value adjustments mentioned above will be based on unobservable inputs, the resulting fair value measurements that are subject to such adjustments are generally Level 3 measurements, unless those inputs are not significant to the measurement as a whole.

2.4.990.70   If the sole purpose of an intermediate entity is to hold publicly traded equity investments, then the fair value of the investment in the intermediate entity may be determined by adjusting the fair value of the publicly traded equity investments for the effects of risks (e.g. liquidity risk) of the intermediate entity (see 2.4.940.40–50). The investment in the intermediate entity is not an identical asset to the publicly traded equity investments that it holds, regardless of whether adjustments were applied to the fair value of the publicly traded equity investments. Therefore, assuming that the intermediate entity is not listed and actively traded, it would not be appropriate to categorise the investment in Level 1 of the hierarchy level.

2.4.995   Loans to customers measured at amortised cost

2.4.995.10   Loans are classified following the requirements of IFRS 9 (see chapter 7.4) and are usually measured at amortised cost subsequent to initial recognition, with fair value being disclosed (see 7.4.30 and 7.10.460). As a result, the fair value of such loans needs to be measured for disclosure purposes. In measuring fair value, the general guidance in 2.4.10–540 applies. This section discusses specific points of interest in relation to loans to customers measured at amortised cost.

2.4.996   *Unit of account*

2.4.996.10   The unit of account for loans is generally the individual loan (see 2.4.80.20) unless the portfolio measurement exception applies (see 2.4.430). [*IFRS 13.48, BC47*]

2.4.996.20   In some cases, observed sales transactions may relate to portfolios of loans. Therefore, an entity needs to determine the relevance of the price for the sale of a portfolio of similar loans for the purpose of valuing an individual loan. In doing that, the entity needs to consider whether a different liquidity discount or similar adjustment is implied in the portfolio price compared with that which would apply to the sale of an individual loan – e.g. a sale of a large portfolio of loans may include a blockage factor (discount) that would not be applicable to a sale of a smaller individual loan. [*IFRS 13.69*]

2.4.997   *Valuation approaches and techniques*

2.4.997.10   Some loans might be valued using a market approach – e.g. if there are secondary market transactions and prices for identical or similar loans. In our experience, most loans are not traded in secondary markets and they are often valued using the income approach. This is because the valuation technique applied needs to maximise the use of relevant observable inputs and minimise the use of unobservable inputs; and when there is not a secondary market for the sale of a loan, in some cases more relevant inputs might be derived from rates or prices in the origination market. [*IFRS 13.61, 67*]

2.4.997.20   When loans are valued using origination rates or prices, the entity needs to consider whether a sale to a market participant would reflect a premium or discount from the price in the origination market. For example, the entity could calibrate its valuation models against prices for any actual sales of similar loans. If there is not a secondary market for loans but they are valued using inputs from markets for more liquid traded instruments, then the entity also needs to consider whether a liquidity adjustment is required.

2.4.997.30   Income approaches need to be consistent with the assumptions that market participants would make with respect to future cash flows and to discount rates. Estimates of future cash flows used might, depending on the circumstances, reflect either:
- contractual cash flows, gross of expected credit losses; or
- expected cash flows, net of expected credit losses (i.e. risk-adjusted cash flows).

2.4.997.40   The discount rates used in each case need to be consistent with the cash flow estimates used. In using contractual cash flows, the discount rate would include a premium representing compensation for expected and unexpected credit losses. In using expected cash flows, the discount rate would not include an adjustment for *expected* credit losses because this is already reflected in the expected cash flows. However, the discount rate would include a premium for *unexpected* credit losses – i.e. to reflect the cost of bearing the risk that credit losses will be different from expected.

2.4.997.50   Factors that impact the estimates of expected cash flows and discount rates include the following:
- the time value of money – i.e. the risk-free rate;
- the currency of the instrument;
- the credit risk of the instrument – i.e. the credit spread over the risk-free interest rate – considering both the credit standing of the issuer and the specific terms of the instrument, such as collateral and other credit risk enhancements, seniority, subordination or non-recourse features;
- prepayment risk;
- liquidity risk;
- legal concerns – e.g. deficiencies in the security documents between the borrower and lender or in title documents of the borrower to secured assets or legislative provisions that provide priority to other creditors, such as tax authorities or employees; and
- other risks and uncertainties inherent in the cash flows that relate to specific contractual terms of the loan (not including credit risk) – e.g. terms that link cash flows to inflation or to variables specific to the borrower such as revenues or EBITDA.

2.4.997.60   An entity needs to consider all available information and to use judgement to determine, for particular loans, whether any adjustments are required to reflect differences between the characteristics of instruments from which inputs are derived and the loans being valued. For example, adjustments may be required to reflect differences in liquidity, underwriting criteria, collateral, maturity, vintage, customer type, geographic location, prepayment options or rates or other differences in credit risk.

2.4.997.70   In some cases, the par amount of a loan may be a reasonable approximation of the fair value of a loan if the interest rate is set at the discretion of the lender and the borrower is able to prepay at any time without penalty. However, before reaching such a conclusion, the entity needs to consider whether there are any factors that indicate that a market participant would price the loan at an amount different from par – e.g. based on any recent secondary market transaction data or because the loan is impaired or the loan has otherwise elevated credit risk.

2.4.997.80   For other types of floating interest rate loans – e.g. where the lender does not have full discretion to change interest rates and only the benchmark component is floating – the factors leading to differences between par and fair value will generally be stronger because:
- of the effect of interest rate changes since the last reset date; and
- the contractual spread above the benchmark rate is not usually repriced to reflect changes in market participants' views of credit and liquidity risks to the measurement date.

2.4.997.90   An entity may sell its loans to market participants that securitise them. The securitisation market cannot be the principal market for the loans because what is being sold or transferred in the securitisation market are the securities issued by the vehicle that securitised the loans. [*IFRS 13.11, 16*]

2.4.997.100   However, in measuring the fair value of loans, it may be appropriate to consider prices for securities that would be issued by a market participant that securitises the loans as an input into the valuation technique if market participants would consider this pricing. This is because a valuation technique needs to maximise observable inputs and minimise unobservable inputs. This would be the case particularly if a reliable observable price for the loans is not available. If the valuation technique uses these inputs, then the fair value of the loans would generally be obtained by adjusting the securitisation prices (including the value of retained interests) for the costs that would be incurred and the estimated profit margin that would be required by a market participant to securitise the loans. [*IFRS 13.67*]

2.4.998   *Fair value hierarchy*

2.4.998.10   In our experience, loans to customers are mostly classified as Level 3 in the fair value hierarchy because of a lack of secondary market transactions. In particular, credit-impaired loans generally fall into Level 3 because the valuation is driven by estimates of expected cash flows, which are in most cases not observable. The same may be true for loans that are credit-impaired at acquisition or origination or for other loans with elevated credit risk, even if they are not credit-impaired under IFRS 9. However, in our experience loans to banks are less likely to be classified as Level 3 because more information about the pricing of debt instruments issued by the bank is usually available.

2.4.999   *Low-interest and interest-free loans*

2.4.999.10   Sometimes interest-free or low-interest loans are provided – e.g. by a shareholder or government – to attract customers or as a means of passing on tax benefits. For specific considerations regarding the measurement of fair value of such loans, see 7.7.80 and 120.

2.4.1000 **Business combinations**

2.4.1000.10   Fair value measurements are pervasive in applying acquisition accounting under IFRS 3, which is the subject of chapter 2.6. The following are examples of areas in which fair value measurements are applied in the context of acquisition accounting:

- measuring consideration transferred, including deferred consideration (see 2.6.270) and contingent consideration (see 2.6.280);
- measuring the gain or loss on the effective settlement of a non-contractual pre-existing relationship (see 2.6.360);
- measuring assets acquired and liabilities assumed (see 2.6.600);
- measuring 'ordinary' NCI that the acquirer chooses to measure at fair value (see 2.6.940) and 'other' NCI (see 2.6.950); and
- measuring the non-controlling equity interest in the acquiree before obtaining control in a business combination achieved in stages (see 2.6.1140).

2.4.1000.20   The principles in IFRS 13 provide general guidance in measuring fair values in the context of acquisition accounting. In measuring fair value, the general guidance in 2.4.10–540 applies, as well the specific application guidance in 2.4.550–995 to the extent relevant. This section discusses specific points of interest in relation to certain assets and liabilities.

2.4.1010   *Intangible assets*

2.4.1010.10   Given the specialised nature of most intangible assets, measuring fair value using the market approach may not always be possible. In our experience, intangible assets are usually measured using a technique that falls under the income approach – present value technique (see 2.4.160), the multi-period excess earnings method (see 2.4.200.10), the with-versus-without method (see 2.4.200.20), and/or the relief-from-royalty method (see 2.4.200.30).

2.4.1010.20   In our experience, the cost approach is rarely appropriate in practice for determining the fair value of intangible assets other than internal-use software.

2.4.1010.30   One of the most important aspects of valuing an intangible asset that will not be used actively to generate direct cash flows, but which is expected to be used defensively to increase the value of other assets, is determining the characteristics of market participants. The entity's decision not to actively use the asset is not determinative in concluding who the appropriate market participants are or the highest and best use of the intangible asset to market participants (see 2.4.340.70–120). [*IFRS 13.30*]

2.4.1010.40   As for other non-financial assets, the fair value of an intangible asset to be retired or whose active use will be discontinued should be based on its highest and best use by market participants (see 2.4.330). One common methodology is the with-versus-without method. This method is useful for intangible assets that market participants would be expected to use defensively. It measures the incremental cash flows that would be achieved by market participants arising from their ownership of an existing intangible asset by locking up the competing acquired intangible asset. Fair value is measured as the difference between the fair value of the group of assets – i.e. the acquired and the existing assets – of the market participant:

- assuming that the acquired intangible asset were to be actively used by others in the market; and
- assuming that the acquired intangible asset was withdrawn from the market. [*IFRS 13.27, 30*]

2.4.1020   *Inventories*

2.4.1020.10   In our experience, the technique used to measure the fair value of inventories acquired depends on the stage of development in the production cycle. The fair value of manufactured finished goods and work in progress is typically measured based on the estimated selling price, less certain costs (and a margin thereon), that would be realised by a market participant.

2.4.1020.20   In our experience, the fair value of finished goods inventory is most frequently estimated under the market approach or income approach – i.e. at the estimated selling price less the sum of the costs to sell and a reasonable profit allowance for the selling effort (selling profit), both of which are estimated from the perspective of a market participant.

2.4.1020.30   Judgement is required in determining a reasonable amount of profit attributable to the effort incurred by the acquiree pre-acquisition, and the profit attributable to the effort that is likely to be incurred post-acquisition. In our view, the analysis should take into account the current profitability of the product at the date of acquisition, even if conditions were different when the inventory was manufactured.

EXAMPLE 31 – BUSINESS COMBINATION – FAIR VALUE OF FINISHED GOODS

2.4.1020.40   The acquiree in a business combination has finished goods measured at a cost of 100; the expected selling price is 150. The inventory is specialised and there are very few potential customers; this inventory has already been earmarked for one of those customers. Distribution costs are estimated at 20.

2.4.1020.50   In the absence of any additional factors indicating that market participants would arrive at a different estimate of the fair value of the inventory, we believe that the fair value of the inventory would be close to 130 (150 - 20), because the selling effort to be incurred is minimal.

2.4.1020.60   In our experience, work in progress of the acquiree is typically valued in a similar manner as finished goods inventory, most frequently under the market approach or income approach – i.e. at the estimated selling price of the work in progress, as if it were finished, less the sum of costs to complete, costs to sell and a reasonable profit allowance for the completion and selling effort of the acquirer, all of which are estimated from the perspective of a market participant.

2.4.1020.70   In our experience, the valuation approach used for recognising the fair value of raw materials is usually a market approach using observable market prices (if any are available) or a cost approach, both of which are estimated from the perspective of a market participant.

2.4.1030   *Unquoted financial liabilities*

2.4.1030.10   When an unquoted financial liability is assumed in a business combination, the general valuation principles outlined in 2.4.360 apply. However, a specific question arises about whether the assumptions underlying the fair value measurement – in particular, credit risk – should take into account the position of the combined entity.

2.4.1030.20   Following general principles, the assumptions should be consistent with those that a market participant would make in valuing the financial liability at the time of the business combination.
● If as a result of the business combination the acquirer becomes a legal obligor of the liability – e.g. by providing a guarantee – then in our experience market participants would value the liability on that basis. For example, non-performance risk, including credit risk, would be based on the risk that the combined entity will not fulfil the obligation.
● If only the acquiree remains the legal obligor after the acquisition, then judgement is required in assessing whether a market participant's view of non-performance risk changes as a result of the acquisition. For example, an acquiree in financial difficulty may be acquired by a group with a good credit rating such that a market participant may consider that the acquirer might support the acquiree in fulfilling its obligations even though the acquirer may have no legal obligation to do so.

2.4.1040   Financial guarantee contracts

2.4.1040.10   Depending on the circumstances, IFRS 4 or IFRS 9 may deal with the accounting for a financial guarantee contract. For a further discussion of the accounting by the issuer and the holder of a financial guarantee contract, see 7.1.60–130. Under IFRS 9, an issued financial guarantee contract is usually measured initially at fair value. In measuring fair value, the general guidance in this chapter applies. This section discusses specific fair value considerations in relation to financial guarantee contracts. [*IFRS 9.B2.5(a)*]

2.4.1050   *Valuation approaches and techniques*

2.4.1050.10   If a financial guarantee contract is issued in a stand-alone arm's length transaction to an unrelated party, then its fair value at inception is likely to equal the premium received unless there is evidence to the contrary. If there is no up-front payment – i.e. premiums will be paid at a later date – then the fair value of a financial guarantee contract between unrelated parties at inception is likely to be zero under IFRS. For a further discussion, see 7.1.120. [*IFRS 13.58–59, B4*]

2.4.1050.20   The following are examples of valuation techniques used to determine the fair value of a financial guarantee contract in other cases:
● market prices of comparable instruments;
● discounted cash flow models; and
● interest rate differentials.

2.4.1060   *Market prices of comparable instruments*

2.4.1060.10   Under the market price of comparable instruments technique, the issuer identifies a market price for financial guarantees that are similar to those that either it or a member of the group has issued or received in exchange for consideration. It might also be possible to identify market prices for similar guarantees, credit default swaps or credit insurance products. These prices could be adjusted to estimate the fair value of the financial guarantee. In our experience, this may be the easiest technique to apply.

2.4.1070   *Discounted cash flow models*

2.4.1070.10   There are different discounted cash flow models that can be applied to estimate the fair value of a financial guarantee. One method is to use a probability-weighted discounted cash flow analysis that incorporates the expected default rate of the borrower and expected recoveries in the event of default. As a starting point, the default rate can be estimated, for example, using historical default and recovery rates among entities with the same credit rating as the borrower. An entity needs to consider whether the historical default and recovery rates should be adjusted to reflect current and forecasted economic conditions.

2.4.1080   *Interest rate differentials*

2.4.1080.10   Under the interest rate differentials technique, the fair value of a guarantee provided to a lender in connection with a loan made to another entity for no consideration is estimated at inception as the difference, in present value terms, between the interest charged on the guaranteed loan and the interest that would have been charged to the borrower had the loan not been guaranteed. This difference is presumed to reflect the price that the lender is willing to pay for the guarantee. This technique requires the issuer of the guarantee to estimate the interest rate that would have been charged to the borrower without the financial guarantee based on an evaluation of the borrower's credit standing on a stand-alone basis.

2.4.1090   FUTURE DEVELOPMENTS

2.4.1090.10   The IFRS Interpretations Committee discussed a request to remove the current requirement in IAS 41 to exclude taxation cash flows (i.e. use pre-tax cash flows) when measuring the fair value of biological assets using a present value technique. The Committee recommended and the IASB agreed to amend IAS 41 as part of the next *Annual Improvements to IFRSs Cycle*. The proposals would enable fair value measurement of biological assets on a post-tax basis.

APPENDICES AND INDEX

CURRENTLY EFFECTIVE REQUIREMENTS AND FORTHCOMING REQUIREMENTS

Below is a list of standards and interpretations, including the latest revisions or amendments to the standards and interpretations, in issue at 1 August 2018 that are effective for annual reporting periods beginning on 1 January 2018. This list notes the principal chapter(s) within which the requirements are discussed. It also notes forthcoming requirements in issue at 1 August 2018 that are effective for annual reporting periods beginning after 1 January 2018. This list does not include revisions or amendments to standards that became effective before 1 January 2018 or minor consequential amendments to standards or interpretations made as a result of a new or an amended IFRS.

STANDARD	RELATED CHAPTER(S)	LATEST EFFECTIVE AMENDMENTS OR REVISIONS	FORTHCOMING REQUIREMENTS
IFRS 1 *First-time Adoption of International Financial Reporting Standards*	6.1	IFRS 15 *Revenue from Contracts with Customers* Issued: May 2014 Effective: 1 January 2018	IFRS 16 *Leases* Issued: January 2016 Effective: 1 January 2019
		IFRS 9 *Financial Instruments* Issued: July 2014 Effective: 1 January 2018	IFRS 17 *Insurance Contracts* Issued: May 2017 Effective: 1 January 2021
		IFRIC 22 *Foreign Currency Transactions and Advance Consideration* Issued: December 2016 Effective: 1 January 2018	
		Applying IFRS 9 Financial Instruments with IFRS 4 Insurance Contracts – Amendments to IFRS 4 Issued: September 2016 Effective: 1 January 2018	

Standard	Related chapter(s)	Latest effective amendments or revisions	Forthcoming requirements
IFRS 1 *First-time Adoption of International Financial Reporting Standards* (continued)		*Annual Improvements to IFRSs 2014–2016 Cycle – Amendments to IFRS 1* Issued: December 2016 *Effective:* 1 January 2018	
IFRS 2 *Share-based Payment*	4.5	IFRS 9 *Financial Instruments* Issued: July 2014 *Effective:* 1 January 2018 *Classification and Measurement of Share-based Payment Transactions – Amendments to IFRS 2* Issued: June 2016 *Effective:* 1 January 2018	-
IFRS 3 *Business Combinations*	2.4, 2.6, 3.3, 5.13	IFRS 15 *Revenue from Contracts with Customers* Issued: May 2014 *Effective:* 1 January 2018	IFRS 16 *Leases* Issued: January 2016 *Effective:* 1 January 2019 IFRS 17 *Insurance Contracts* Issued: May 2017 *Effective:* 1 January 2021 *Annual Improvements to IFRSs 2015–2017 Cycle – Amendments to IFRS 3* Issued: December 2017 *Effective:* 1 January 2019
IFRS 4 *Insurance Contracts*	8.1	IFRS 15 *Revenue from Contracts with Customers* Issued: May 2014 *Effective:* 1 January 2018 IFRS 9 *Financial Instruments* Issued: July 2014 *Effective:* 1 January 2018	IFRS 17 *Insurance Contracts* Issued: May 2017 *Effective:* 1 January 2021

STANDARD	RELATED CHAPTER(S)	LATEST EFFECTIVE AMENDMENTS OR REVISIONS	FORTHCOMING REQUIREMENTS
IFRS 4 *Insurance Contracts* (continued)		*Applying IFRS 9 Financial Instruments with IFRS 4 Insurance Contracts – Amendments to IFRS 4* Issued: September 2016 *Effective:* 1 January 2018	
IFRS 5 *Non-current Assets Held for Sale and Discontinued Operations*	5.4	-	IFRS 16 *Leases* Issued: January 2016 *Effective:* 1 January 2019
IFRS 6 *Exploration for and Evaluation of Mineral Resources*	5.11	-	-
IFRS 7 *Financial Instruments: Disclosures*	7.1, 7.10, 7I.1, 7I.8	IFRS 9 *Financial Instruments* Issued: July 2014 *Effective:* 1 January 2018	IFRS 16 *Leases* Issued: January 2016 *Effective:* 1 January 2019 IFRS 17 *Insurance Contracts* Issued: May 2017 *Effective:* 1 January 2021
IFRS 8 *Operating Segments*	5.2	-	-
IFRS 9 *Financial Instruments*	7	Issued: July 2014 *Effective:* 1 January 2018 *Applying IFRS 9 Financial Instruments with IFRS 4 Insurance Contracts – Amendments to IFRS 4* Issued: September 2016 *Effective:* 1 January 2018	IFRS 16 *Leases* Issued: January 2016 *Effective:* 1 January 2019 IFRS 17 *Insurance Contracts* Issued: May 2017 *Effective:* 1 January 2021 *Long-term Interests in Associates and Joint Ventures – Amendments to IAS 28* Issued: October 2017 *Effective:* 1 January 2019

STANDARD	RELATED CHAPTER(S)	LATEST EFFECTIVE AMENDMENTS OR REVISIONS	FORTHCOMING REQUIREMENTS
IFRS 10 *Consolidated Financial Statements*	2.1, 2.5, 5.6, 5.13	*Annual Improvements to IFRSs 2014–2016 Cycle – Amendments to IAS 28* Issued: December 2016 *Effective:* 1 January 2018	IFRS 17 *Insurance Contracts* Issued: May 2017 *Effective:* 1 January 2021 *Sale or Contribution of Assets between an Investor and its Associate or Joint Venture – Amendments to IFRS 10 and IAS 28* Issued: September 2014 *Effective:* Deferred indefinitely
IFRS 11 *Joint Arrangements*	3.6	-	*Annual Improvements to IFRSs 2015–2017 Cycle – Amendments to IFRS 11* Issued: December 2017 *Effective:* 1 January 2019
IFRS 12 *Disclosure of Interests in Other Entities*	5.10	-	IFRS 17 *Insurance Contracts* Issued: May 2017 *Effective:* 1 January 2021
IFRS 13 *Fair Value Measurement*	2.4, 2.6, 3.2, 3.3, 3.4, 3.9, 3.10, 5.4, 5.6, 7.7, 7.10, 7I.6, 7I.8	IFRS 15 *Revenue from Contracts with Customers* Issued: May 2014 Effective: 1 January 2018 IFRS 9 *Financial Instruments* Issued: July 2014 *Effective:* 1 January 2018	IFRS 16 *Leases* Issued: January 2016 *Effective:* 1 January 2019 IFRS 17 *Insurance Contracts* Issued: May 2017 *Effective:* 1 January 2021
IFRS 14 *Regulatory Deferral Accounts*	6.2	-	-
IFRS 15 *Revenue from Contracts with Customers*	4.2, 5.7, 7I.6	*Issued:* May 2014 *Effective:* 1 January 2018	IFRS 16 *Leases* Issued: January 2016 *Effective:* 1 January 2019 IFRS 17 *Insurance Contracts* Issued: May 2017 *Effective:* 1 January 2021

STANDARD	RELATED CHAPTER(S)	LATEST EFFECTIVE AMENDMENTS OR REVISIONS	FORTHCOMING REQUIREMENTS
IFRS 16 *Leases*	5.1A	-	*Issued:* January 2016 *Effective:* 1 January 2019
IFRS 17 *Insurance Contracts*	8.1A	-	*Issued:* May 2017 *Effective:* 1 January 2021
IAS 1 *Presentation of Financial Statements*	1.1, 2.1, 2.2, 2.8, 2.9, 3.1, 4.1, 5.8, 7.10, 7I.8, 8.1A	IFRS 15 *Revenue from Contracts with Customers* *Issued:* May 2014 *Effective:* 1 January 2018 IFRS 9 *Financial Instruments* *Issued:* July 2014 *Effective:* 1 January 2018	IFRS 16 *Leases* *Issued:* January 2016 *Effective:* 1 January 2019 IFRS 17 *Insurance Contracts* *Issued:* May 2017 *Effective:* 1 January 2021 *Amendments to References to the Conceptual Framework in IFRS Standards* *Issued:* March 2018 *Effective:* 1 January 2020
IAS 2 *Inventories*	3.8	IFRS 15 *Revenue from Contracts with Customers* *Issued:* May 2014 *Effective:* 1 January 2018	IFRS 16 *Leases* *Issued:* January 2016 *Effective:* 1 January 2019
IAS 7 *Statement of Cash Flows*	2.3	-	-
IAS 8 *Accounting Policies, Changes in Accounting Estimates and Errors*	2.8	-	IFRS 17 *Insurance Contracts* *Issued:* May 2017 *Effective:* 1 January 2021 *Amendments to References to the Conceptual Framework in IFRS Standards* *Issued*: March 2018 *Effective*: 1 January 2020
IAS 10 *Events after the Reporting Period*	2.9	-	-

STANDARD	RELATED CHAPTER(S)	LATEST EFFECTIVE AMENDMENTS OR REVISIONS	FORTHCOMING REQUIREMENTS
IAS 12 *Income Taxes*	3.13	-	IFRIC 23 *Uncertainty over Income Tax Treatments* *Issued:* June 2017 *Effective:*1 January 2019 *Annual Improvements to IFRSs 2015–2017 Cycle – Amendments to IAS 12* *Issued:* December 2017 *Effective:* 1 January 2019
IAS 16 *Property, Plant and Equipment*	2.4, 3.2, 3.4, 5.7	IFRS 15 *Revenue from Contracts with Customers* *Issued:* May 2014 *Effective:* 1 January 2018	IFRS 16 *Leases* *Issued:* January 2016 *Effective:* 1 January 2019 IFRS 17 *Insurance Contracts* *Issued:* May 2017 *Effective:* 1 January 2021
IAS 17 *Leases*	3.4, 5.1	IFRS 15 *Revenue from Contracts with Customers* *Issued:* May 2014 *Effective:* 1 January 2018	IFRS 16 *Leases* *Issued:* January 2016 *Effective:* 1 January 2019 IFRS 17 *Insurance Contracts* *Issued:* May 2017 *Effective:* 1 January 2021
IAS 19 *Employee Benefits*	4.4	-	*Plan Amendment, Curtailment or Settlement – Amendments to IAS 19* *Issued:* February 2018 *Effective:* 1 January 2019
IAS 20 *Accounting for Government Grants and Disclosure of Government Assistance*	4.3	-	-
IAS 21 *The Effects of Changes in Foreign Exchange Rates*	2.7, 2.10, 7.7, 7I.6	IFRS 9 *Financial Instruments* *Issued:* July 2014 *Effective:* 1 January 2018	-

Standard	Related chapter(s)	Latest effective amendments or revisions	Forthcoming requirements
IAS 21 *The Effects of Changes in Foreign Exchange Rates* (continued)		IFRIC 22 *Foreign Currency Transactions and Advances Consideration* *Issued:* December 2016 *Effective:* 1 January 2018	
IAS 23 *Borrowing Costs*	4.6	-	IFRS 16 *Leases* *Issued:* January 2016 *Effective:* 1 January 2019 *Annual Improvements to IFRSs 2015–2017 Cycle – Amendments to IAS 23* *Issued:* December 2017 *Effective:* 1 January 2019
IAS 24 *Related Party Disclosures*	5.5	-	-
IAS 26 *Accounting and Reporting by Retirement Benefit Plans*	Not covered; see section *About this publication.*		
IAS 27 *Separate Financial Statements*	2.1, 5.13	-	-
IAS 28 *Investments in Associates and Joint Ventures*	2.1, 3.5	IFRS 9 *Financial Instruments* *Issued:* July 2014 *Effective:* 1 January 2018 *Annual Improvements to IFRSs 2014–2016 Cycle – Amendments to IAS 28* *Issued:* December 2016 *Effective:* 1 January 2018	*Sale or Contribution of Assets between an Investor and its Associate or Joint Venture – Amendments to IFRS 10 and IAS 28* *Issued:* September 2014 *Effective:* Deferred indefinitely IFRS 17 *Insurance Contracts* *Issued: May 2017* *Effective: 1 January 2021*

STANDARD	RELATED CHAPTER(S)	LATEST EFFECTIVE AMENDMENTS OR REVISIONS	FORTHCOMING REQUIREMENTS
IAS 28 *Investments in Associates and Joint Ventures* (continued)			*Long-term Interests in Associates and Joint Ventures – Amendments to IAS 28* Issued: October 2017 Effective: 1 January 2019
IAS 29 *Financial Reporting in Hyperinflationary Economies*	2.7, 2.10	-	-
IAS 32 *Financial Instruments: Presentation*	7.10, 7I.1, 7I.3, 7I.8	-	IFRS 16 *Leases* Issued: January 2016 Effective: 1 January 2019 IFRS 17 *Insurance Contracts* Issued: May 2017 Effective: 1 January 2021
IAS 33 *Earnings per Share*	5.3	-	-
IAS 34 *Interim Financial Reporting*	5.9	IFRS 15 *Revenue from Contracts with Customers* Issued: May 2014 Effective: 1 January 2018	-
IAS 36 *Impairment of Assets*	2.4, 3.10	IFRS 9 *Financial Instruments* Issued: July 2014 Effective: 1 January 2018	IFRS 16 *Leases* Issued: January 2016 Effective: 1 January 2019 IFRS 17 *Insurance Contracts* Issued: May 2017 Effective: 1 January 2021
IAS 37 *Provisions, Contingent Liabilities and Contingent Assets*	3.12	IFRS 15 *Revenue from Contracts with Customers* Issued: May 2014 Effective: 1 January 2018	IFRS 16 *Leases* Issued: January 2016 Effective: 1 January 2019 IFRIC 23 *Uncertainty over Income Tax Treatments* Issued: June 2017 Effective: 1 January 2019

STANDARD	RELATED CHAPTER(S)	LATEST EFFECTIVE AMENDMENTS OR REVISIONS	FORTHCOMING REQUIREMENTS
IAS 37 *Provisions, Contingent Liabilities and Contingent Assets* (continued)			IFRS 17 *Insurance Contracts* *Issued:* May 2017 *Effective:* 1 January 2021
IAS 38 *Intangible Assets*	2.4, 3.3, 5.7	IFRS 15 *Revenue from Contracts with Customers* *Issued:* May 2014 *Effective:* 1 January 2018	IFRS 16 *Leases* *Issued:* January 2016 *Effective:* 1 January 2019
IAS 39 *Financial Instruments: Recognition and Measurement*	7I.1–7I.7	IFRS 9 *Financial Instruments* *Issued:* July 2014 *Effective:* 1 January 2018	-
IAS 40 *Investment Property*	2.4, 3.4, 5.7	IFRS 15 *Revenue from Contracts with Customers* *Issued:* May 2014 *Effective:* 1 January 2018 *Transfers of Investment Property – Amendments to IAS 40* *Issued:* December 2016 *Effective:* 1 January 2018	IFRS 16 *Leases* *Issued:* January 2016 *Effective:* 1 January 2019 IFRS 17 *Insurance Contracts* *Issued:* May 2017 *Effective:* 1 January 2021
IAS 41 *Agriculture*	2.4, 3.9, 4.3	-	-
IFRIC 1 *Changes in Existing Decommissioning, Restoration and Similar Liabilities*	3.2, 3.12	-	-
IFRIC 2 *Members' Shares in Co-operative Entities and Similar Instruments*	7.3, 7I.3	-	IFRS 17 *Insurance Contracts* *Issued: May 2017* *Effective:* 1 January 2021
IFRIC 4 *Determining whether an Arrangement contains a Lease*	5.1	IFRS 15 *Revenue from Contracts with Customers* *Issued:* May 2014 *Effective:* 1 January 2018	IFRS 16 *Leases* *Issued:* January 2016 *Effective:* 1 January 2019

STANDARD	RELATED CHAPTER(S)	LATEST EFFECTIVE AMENDMENTS OR REVISIONS	FORTHCOMING REQUIREMENTS
IFRIC 5 *Rights to Interests arising from Decommissioning, Restoration and Environmental Rehabilitation Funds*	3.12	-	-
IFRIC 6 *Liabilities arising from Participating in a Specific Market – Waste Electrical and Electronic Equipment*	3.12	-	-
IFRIC 7 *Applying the Restatement Approach under IAS 29 Financial Reporting in Hyperinflationary Economies*	2.10	-	-
IFRIC 9 *Reassessment of Embedded Derivatives*	7I.2	IFRS 9 *Financial Instruments* Issued: July 2014 Effective: 1 January 2018	IFRS 16 *Leases* Issued: January 2016 Effective: 1 January 2019
IFRIC 10 *Interim Financial Reporting and Impairment*	3.10, 5.9	IFRS 9 *Financial Instruments* Issued: July 2014 Effective: 1 January 2018	IFRS 16 *Leases* Issued: January 2016 Effective: 1 January 2019 IFRS 17 *Insurance Contracts* Issued: May 2017 Effective: 1 January 2021
IFRIC 12 *Service Concession Arrangements*	3.3, 5.12	IFRS 15 *Revenue from Contracts with Customers* Issued: May 2014 Effective: 1 January 2018	IFRS 16 *Leases* Issued: January 2016 Effective: 1 January 2019
IFRIC 14 *IAS 19 – Limit on a Defined Benefit Asset, Minimum Funding Requirements and their Interaction*	4.4	-	-
IFRIC 16 *Hedges of a Net Investment in a Foreign Operation*	7I.7	-	-
IFRIC 17 *Distributions of Non-cash Assets to Owners*	5.4, 5.13, 7.3, 7I.3	-	-

STANDARD	RELATED CHAPTER(S)	LATEST EFFECTIVE AMENDMENTS OR REVISIONS	FORTHCOMING REQUIREMENTS
IFRIC 19 *Extinguishing Financial Liabilities with Equity Instruments*	7.3, 7I.3	-	-
IFRIC 20 *Stripping Costs in the Production Phase of a Surface Mine*	5.11	-	-
IFRIC 21 *Levies*	3.12	-	-
IFRIC 22 *Foreign Currency Transactions and Advance Consideration*	2.7, 6.1	*Issued:* December 2016 *Effective:* 1 January 2018	-
IFRIC 23 *Uncertainty over Income Tax Treatments*	3.12, 3.13	-	*Issued:* June 2017 *Effective:* 1 January 2019
SIC-7 *Introduction of the Euro*	None	-	-
SIC-10 *Government Assistance – No Specific Relation to Operating Activities*	4.3	-	-
SIC-15 *Operating Leases – Incentives*	5.1	IFRS 15 *Revenue from Contracts with Customers* *Issued:* May 2014 *Effective:* 1 January 2018	IFRS 16 *Leases* *Issued:* January 2016 *Effective:* 1 January 2019
SIC-25 *Income Taxes – Changes in the Tax Status of an Entity or its Shareholders*	3.13	-	-
SIC-27 *Evaluating the Substance of Transactions Involving the Legal Form of a Lease*	5.1	-	IFRS 16 *Leases* *Issued:* January 2016 *Effective:* 1 January 2019
SIC-29 *Service Concession Arrangements: Disclosures*	5.12	-	-
SIC-32 *Intangible Assets – Web Site Costs*	3.3	-	-

TABLE OF CONCORDANCE

This table primarily shows how guidance that was included in the fourteenth edition has moved. The table of concordance does not include changes to paragraph numbers made as a result of forthcoming requirements, changes in the format of examples or editorial amendments.

2017/18 Edition REFERENCE 14TH EDITION	CURRENT REFERENCE 15TH EDITION	2017/18 Edition REFERENCE 14TH EDITION	CURRENT REFERENCE 15TH EDITION
2.4.300.100	2.4.300.100–120	3.12.199.05–30	7.1.139.20–40, 7I.1.85.10–40
2.4.920.15	2.4.920.30		
2.4.920.20	2.4.920.40	3.12.199.50–120	7.1.139.50–110, 7I.1.85.50–120
2.4.920.40	2.4.920.50		
2.4.970.30	2.4.970.05	3.12.199.40	7.1.140.20, 7I.1.87.20
2.7.90.20	2.7.93.20	3.12.375	3.12.370
2.7.90.25–60	2.7.95.10–75	3.12.390–475	3.12.380–470
2.7.230.20	2.7.230.70	3.12.640.50–70	3.12.640.40–60
3.2.380.60	3.2.380.35	3.12.754.80	3.12.754.90
3.2.380.70	3.2.380.15	3.12.760.20	3.12.760.25
3.2.380.80–110	3.2.380.60–90	3.13.160.50	3.13.730.10
3.4.250.40	Deleted	3.13.660.100	3.13.660.70
3.5.540.20–50	3.5.530.30–60	3.13.665.40–50	3.13.665.80–90
3.5.560–690	3.5.540–670	3.13.730–780	3.13.760–810
3.8.100.10	3.8.100.20		
3.8.440.10–90	3.8.400.10–90	3.13.790–830	3.13.820–860
3.10.310–330	3.10.680–860	3.13.840–1090	3.13.870–1020
3.10.340–586	3.10.310–585	3.13.1100–1180	3.13.1130–1210
3.10.680	3.10.870	3.13.1190	3.13.1220
3.12.196	7.1.130.20, 7I.1.83	3.13.1200	3.13.1230
3.12.197.10	3.12.195.20, 7I.1.83.10	3.13.1205–1210	3.13.1240–1250

2017/18 EDITION REFERENCE 14TH EDITION	CURRENT REFERENCE 15TH EDITION	2017/18 EDITION REFERENCE 14TH EDITION	CURRENT REFERENCE 15TH EDITION
3.13.1210	3.13.1250	5.1A.80	5.1A.100
3.13.1220	3.13.1260	5.1A.90	5.1A.40
4.2A.190.32–38	4.2.190.50–80	5.1A.100.10–20	5.1A.90.10–20
4.2A.190.40	4.2.190.130	5.1A.100.50–130	5.1A.90.50–150
4.2A.190.50	4.2.190.140	5.1A.110.10–240.40	5.1A.140.10–255.40
4.2A.220.162–168	4.2.220.170–200	5.1A.240.50–270.20	5.1A.255.80–280.20
4.2A.220.170–180	4.2.220.290–300	5.1A.270.30	5.1A.280.10
4.2A.230.60–70	4.2.230.50–60	5.1A.270.40	5.1A.120.10, 130.10
4.2A.290.80	4.2.290.30	5.1A.280.10–310.10	5.1A.290.10–315.10
4.2A.290.90–140	4.2.290.80–130	5.1A.310.20–50	5.1A.320.20–50
4.2A.380.20	4.2.380.30	5.1A.320–520	5.1A.340–465
4.5.930.30–50	Deleted	5.1A.530–560.10	5.1A.475–490.10
4.5.930.60–70	4.5.930.40–50	5.1A.560.20–570.20	5.1A.490.30–495.20
4.5.960.10	Deleted	5.1A.580–640.10	5.1A.500–540.10
4.5.1350.20–80	Deleted	5.1A.650–750.120	5.1A.550–675.100
4.5.2160.10–20	Deleted	5.1A.760.10	5.1A.690.10
4.6.10.40	4.6.20.140	5.1A.760.20–800.10	5.1A.690.30–730.10
5.1A.40	5.1A.110	5.7.40.30–40	5.7.40.20–30
5.1A.50	5.1A.60	5.7.60–90	5.7.50–80
5.1A.60	5.1A.50	5.12.70.20	5.12.70.90
5.1A.70.20	5.1A.90.30	5.12.70.25	5.12.70.20
5.1A.70.30	5.1A.95.10	5.12.70.28	5.12.70.30
5.1A.70.40–70	5.1A.95.30–50	5.12.70.65–80	5.12.70.140–170
5.1A.70.80	5.1A.90.40	5.12.70.90	5.12.70.180
5.1A.70.90–120	5.1A.75.10–40	5.12.70.100–110	5.12.70.190–200
5.1A.70.130–140	5.1A.75.90–100	5.12.85	5.12.90
5.1A.75.10–20	5.1A.80.10–20	6.1.600.20	Deleted
5.1A.75.30–40	5.1A.80.40–50	6.1.610	Deleted
		6.1.620.10–20, 40–70	Deleted
		6.1.620.30	6.1.610.40

2017/18 Edition REFERENCE 14TH EDITION	CURRENT REFERENCE 15TH EDITION
6.1.640	Deleted
7A.1.120.20	7.1.120.170
7A.1.120.30	7.1.120.180
7A.1.130.20	7.1.134.10, 136.10
7A.1.130.30–40	7.1.132.40–50
7A.1.130.50–60	7.1.132.130–140
7A.1.130.70	7.1.136.10, 139.20
7A.1.130.80–140	7.1.137.10–70
7.4.340.20	7.4.340.35
7A.6.95.10	7.6.95.25
7A.7.250.20–40	Deleted
7A.7.310.10–60	7.7.300.10–60
7A.7.310.70	7.7.300.70
7A.7.320	7.7.310
7A.7.330.10	7.7.320.10
7A.7.300.10	7.7.330.10
7A.7.300.20	7.7.330.40
7A.7.300.30	7.7.330.50
7A.7.300.40–50	7.7.330.70–80
7A.7.300.60–70	7.7.330.90–100
7A.7.350.22–25	7.7.350.260–270
7A.7.350.30	7.7.350.70–90
7A.7.350.40	7.7.350.100–120
7A.7.350.50–60	7.7.350.300–310
7A.7.350.70	7.7.350.320
7A.7.360.10	7.7.360.10–20
7A.7.375.10	7.7.370.30
7A.7.375.20	7.7.370.50–60
7A.7.370.10	7.7.375.10

2017/18 Edition REFERENCE 14TH EDITION	CURRENT REFERENCE 15TH EDITION
7A.7.370.15	7.7.375.20
7A.7.370.20–30	7.7.375.30
7A.7.370.40–50	7.7.375.40–50
7A.7.550	Deleted
7A.9.450.80	7.9.450.90
7A.9.850.70	7.9.853.10
7A.9.850.80–130	7.9.855.10–60
7A.9.960.40–50	7.9.960.90–100
7A.10.60.50	7.10.65.10
7A.10.60.60	7.10.65.30–40
7A.10.160.40–50	7.10.167.10–20
7.11.20.50–60	Deleted
7.11.20.80	7.11.50.30
7.11.30.30	7.11.50.30
7.11.50	Deleted
7.11.120.40–60	Deleted
3.12.196.10	7I.1.80.20
7.1.80.10	7I.1.80.50–60
7.1.190.40–60	Deleted
7.6.270.12–40	7I.6.270.30–100
7.6.740.10–20	7I.6.730.20–30
7.6.750.10	7I.6.730.40
7.6.760.20–50	7I.6.730.60–90
7.6.760.60	7I.6.730.130
7.7.80.40–50	7I.7.80.70–80
7.7.690.20–30	7I.7.690.70–80
7.8.225.25	Deleted
8.1.20.50	Deleted
8.1A.20.60–120	8.1A.20.130–190

2017/18 Edition REFERENCE 14th Edition	Current REFERENCE 15th Edition
8.1A.20.130–150	8.1A.220–240
8.1A.20.160	8.1A.20.260
8.1A.20.170–180	8.1A.20.280–290
8.1A.30.30	8.1A.30.50
8.1A.60.10	8.1A.60.10, 20, 40
8.1A.70.10	8.1A.70.30
8.1A.80.10–20	8.1A.80.20–30
8.1A.80.30–50	8.1A.80.60–80
8.1A.80.60	8.1A.80.100
8.1A.80.70–110	8.1A.80.120–160
8.1A.110.20	Deleted
8.1A.110.30–90	8.1A.110.20–80
8.1A.110.110–150	8.1A.110.120–160
8.1A.140.40	8.1A.140.120
8.1A.160.20–80	8.1A.160.50–110
8.1A.160.90	8.1A.160.210, 240
8.1A.170.20–60	8.1A.170.50–90
8.1A.180.70	8.1A.180.90
8.1A.200.30–40	8.1A.20.40–50
8.1A.210.30	8.1A.210.40
8.1A.210.40	8.1A.210.60
8.1A.210.50	8.1A.210.100
8.1A.230.40	8.1A.230.50
8.1A.240.50–80	8.1A.240.60–90
8.1A.240.30–60	8.1A.240.40–70
8.1A.310.20	8.1A.310.20, 50
8.1A.310.30–50	8.1A.310.60–80
8.1A.310.60–80	8.1A.310.120–140
8.1A.370.30–40	8.1A.370.40–50

2017/18 Edition REFERENCE 14th Edition	Current REFERENCE 15th Edition
8.1A.410.30	8.1A.410.40
8.1A.430.10–110	8.1A.430.20–120
8.1A.460.20	8.1A.460.30
8.1A.540.40	8.1A.540.50

LIST OF EXAMPLES

2.5   Consolidation

2.6 Business combinations

2.7   Foreign currency translation

2.8 Accounting policies, errors and estimates

2.9 Events after the reporting date

2.10 Hyperinflation

3.6   Joint arrangements

3.8 Inventories

3.9 Biological assets

3.10 Impairment of non-financial assets

3.12 Provisions, contingent assets and liabilities

3.13   Income taxes

4.1 General

4.2 Revenue

4.3 Government grants

4.4 Employee benefits

4.5 Share-based payments

4.6   Borrowing costs

5.1   Leases

5.1A Leases: IFRS 16

5.2   Operating segments

5.3   Earnings per share

5.13   Common control transactions and Newco formations

6.1 First-time adoption of IFRS

6.2 Regulatory deferral accounts and first-time adoption of IFRS

7.1 Scope and definitions

7.2 Derivatives and embedded derivatives

7.3   Equity and financial liabilities

7.4   Classification of financial assets

7.5   Classification of financial liabilities

7.6   Recognition and derecognition

7.7 Measurement

7.10 Presentation and disclosures

7.11 Transition to IFRS 9

7I.1   Scope and definitions

7I.2   Derivatives and embedded derivatives

7I.3 Equity and financial liabilities

7I.4 Classification of financial assets and financial liabilities

7I.5 Recognition and derecognition

7I.8 Presentation and disclosures

8.1 Insurance contracts

8.1A Insurance contracts: IFRS 17

INDEX

A

Index

Index

Index

R

Notes

Notes

Notes

Notes

Notes

Notes

Notes